The New York Times
THE 20TH CENTURY

The Great Events
from the Victorian Age to the
Turn of the Millennium

GALAHAD BOOKS
NEW YORK

First Galahad Books edition published in 2001.

Galahad Books
A division of BBS Publishing Corporation
386 Park Avenue South
New York, NY 10016

Galahad Books is a registered trademark of BBS Publishing Corporation.

Published by arrangement with The New York Times Company.

Library of Congress Control Number:

ISBN: 1-57866-141-2

Printed in Spain by Bookprint, S.L., Barcelona

THE NEW YORK TIMES COMPANY
229 WEST 43 STREET
NEW YORK, N.Y. 10036

ARTHUR O. SULZBERGER, JR.

CHAIRMAN,
THE NEW YORK TIMES COMPANY

PUBLISHER,
The New York Times

At the dawn of the 21st century, we are proud to offer this look back on 100 years of New York Times reporting. Captured here by hundreds of correspondents and editors are the historic events of our time, even as they were happening.

Looking at these articles today, you can almost feel the impact of their time and place. Indeed, it is not hard to see why the dean of 20th century American journalism, James B. Reston, called this the century of the journalist. It has been an era of remarkable progress and change, and reporters like Scotty Reston made it an unforgettable part of our lives.

In this chronicle of the 20th century, we are presenting not only the front-page portion of the articles, but also the "jumps" – the inside page or pages on which the lead story and related articles appear. In this way, readers will find the coverage in depth, making each event both a first and lasting impression of this historical panorama.

This volume portrays a century of triumph and courage, unspeakable brutality and tragedy, human greatness and human failure. These events are the stepping stones to history yet to happen. Together, for good and bad, they point the way to our future.

THE 20TH CENTURY

January 23, 1901	Queen Victoria Dead at Osborne
September 7, 1901	President Shot at Buffalo Fair
January 23, 1905	Day of Terror in Czar's Capital
April 19, 1906	Over 500 Dead, $200,000,000 Lost in San Francisco Earthquake
June 26, 1906	Thaw Murders Stanford White
October 18, 1907	First Wireless Press Message across the Atlantic
September 10, 1908	Wright Flies Over an Hour
September 7, 1909	Peary Discovers North Pole after Eight Trials in 23 Years
March 26, 1911	141 Men and Girls Die in Waist Factory Fire
May 16, 1911	Standard Oil Company Must Dissolve in 6 Months
March 8, 1912	Amundsen Reaches the South Pole
April 16, 1912	Titanic Sinks Four Hours After Hitting Iceberg
February 11, 1913	Scott Finds South Pole; Then Perishes with Four Men in Antarctic Blizzard; Bodies Found After Eight Months
June 29, 1914	Heir to Austria's Throne is Slain with his Wife by a Bosnian Youth to Avenge Seizure of his Country
July 29, 1914	Austria Formally Declares War on Servia
August 2, 1914	Germany Declares War on Russia, First Shots Are Fired
May 8, 1915	Lusitania Sunk by a Submarine
April 30, 1916	Dublin Revolt is Near Collapse
March 16, 1917	Revolution in Russia; Czar Abdicates
May 19, 1917	President Calls the Nation to Arms; Draft Bill Signed
November 9, 1917	Revolutionists Seize Petrograd
November 11, 1918	Armistice Signed, End of the War! Berlin Seized by Revolutionists
January 22, 1919	Irish Assembly Proclaims the Irish Republic
January 26, 1919	League of Nations Plan is Adopted
June 29, 1919	Peace Signed, Ends the Great War
November 20, 1919	Senate Session Ends, Treaty is Defeated
August 27, 1920	Colby Proclaims Woman Suffrage
December 7, 1921	Ireland to Be a Free State Within British Empire
February 17, 1923	Tut-Ankh-Amen's Inner Tomb is Opened
July 22, 1925	Scopes Guilty, Fined $100, Scores Law
January 8, 1927	New York and London Talk Freely, Opening New Radiophone Service
April 8, 1927	Far-Off Speakers Seen as well as Heard Here in a Test of Television
May 22, 1927	Lindbergh Does It! To Paris in 33 ½ Hours; Flies 1,000 Miles Through Snow and Sleet; Cheering French Carry Him off Field
June 19, 1928	Amelia Earhart Flies Atlantic, First Woman to Do It
March 25, 1929	Fox in Talkies Only; Signs 200 Show Folk
October 30, 1929	Stocks Collapse in 16,410,030-Share Day, But Rally at Close Cheers Brokers
March 2, 1932	Lindbergh Baby Kidnapped from Home of Parents on Farm near Princeton
January 31, 1933	Hitler Made Chancellor of Germany But Coalition Cabinet Limits Power
December 6, 1933	Prohibition Repeal is Ratified
July 1, 1934	Hitler Crushes Revolt by Nazi Radicals
December 11, 1936	Edward VIII Renounces British Crown; York will Succeed Him as George VI
May 7, 1937	Hindenburg Burns in Lakehurst Crash
July 3, 1937	Miss Earhart Forced Down at Sea, Howland Isle Fears; Coast Guard Begins Search
March 12, 1938	Nazis Seize Austria After Hitler Ultimatum
November 10, 1938	Berlin Raids Reply to Death of Envoy *(Krystalnacht)*
September 1, 1939	German Army Attacks Poland
May 30, 1940	Allies Abandoning Flanders, Flood Yser Area; A Rescue Fleet at Dunkerque; Foe Pounds Port; One Force Cut Off from the Sea as Lille Falls
June 15, 1940	Germans Occupy Paris
December 8, 1941	Japan Wars on U.S. and Britain; Makes Sudden Attack on Hawaii; Heavy Fighting at Sea Reported
December 9, 1941	U.S. Declares War, Pacific Battle Widens
September 9, 1943	Italy Surrenders, Will Resist Germans
June 6, 1944	Allied Armies Land in France in the Havre-Cherbourg Area; Great Invasion is Under Way
November 8, 1944	Roosevelt Wins Fourth Term
April 13, 1945	President Roosevelt is Dead; Truman to Continue Policies
May 2, 1945	Hitler Dead in Chancellery, Nazis Say; Doenitz, Successor, Orders War to Go on; Berlin Almost Won; U.S. Armies Advance
May 8, 1945	The War in Europe is Ended! Surrender is Unconditional; V-E will be Proclaimed Today; Our Troops on Okinawa Gain
August 7, 1945	First Atomic Bomb Dropped on Japan; Missile is Equal to 20,000 Tons of TNT; Truman Warns Foe of a 'Rain of Ruin'
September 2, 1945	Japan Surrenders to Allies, Signs Rigid Terms on Warship; Truman Sets Today as V-J Day
January 11, 1946	UNO Opened; Attlee Asks World Unity
October 2, 1946	12 Nazi War Leaders Sentenced to Be Hanged
January 31, 1948	Gandhi is Killed by a Hindu; India Shaken, World Mourns
May 15, 1948	Zionists Proclaim New State of Israel; Truman Recognizes it and Hopes for Peace; Tel Aviv is Bombed, Egypt Orders Invasion
September 24, 1949	Atom Blast in Russia Disclosed
October 1, 1949	Mao Heads Peiping Regime; Program Supports Moscow
January 22, 1950	Hiss Guilty on Both Perjury Counts; Betrayal of U.S. Secrets is Affirmed
February 1, 1950	Truman Orders Hydrogen Bomb Built
June 28, 1950	Truman Orders U.S. Air, Navy Units to Fight in Aid of Korea

April 11, 1951	Truman Relieves M'Arthur of All His Posts; Finds Him Unable to Back U.S.-U.N. Policies
February 7, 1952	King George VI Dies in Sleep at Sandringham; Elizabeth, Queen at 25
March 6, 1953	Stalin Dies After 29-Year Rule
June 2, 1953	2 of British Team Conquer Everest; Queen Gets News as Coronation Gift
June 20, 1953	Rosenbergs Executed as Atom Spies
July 27, 1953	Truce is Signed, Ending the Fighting in Korea
March 2, 1954	Five Congressmen Shot in House by 3 PR Nationalists
May 18, 1954	High Court Bans School Segregation; 9-to-0 Decision Grants Time to Comply
December 3, 1954	Final Vote Condemns M'Carthy, 67-22, for Abusing Senate
April 13, 1955	Salk Polio Vaccine Proves Success; Millions Will Be Immunized Soon; City Schools Begin Shots April 25
September 20, 1955	Peron's Regime is Overthrown
July 26, 1956	Andrea Doria and Stockholm Collide
November 3, 1956	British and French Push Toward Landing; Israelis Capture Gaza
November 4, 1956	Soviets Attack Hungary, Seizes Nagy
September 25, 1957	President Sends Troops to Little Rock
October 5, 1957	Soviet Fires Earth Satellite into Space; it is Circling the Globe at 18,000 M.P.H.
August 9, 1958	Nautilus Sails Under the Pole and 1830 Miles of Arctic Icecap
January 9, 1959	Havana Welcomes Castro at End of Triumphal Trip
March 13, 1959	Hawaii is Voted into Union as 50th State
January 4, 1961	U.S. Breaks its Diplomatic Ties with Cuba
April 12, 1961	Soviet Orbits Man and Recovers Him; Space Pioneer Reports: 'I Feel Well'; Sent Messages While Circling Earth
April 18, 1961	Anti-Castro Units Land in Cuba
May 6, 1961	U.S. Hurls Man 115 Miles into Space; Shepard Works Controls in Capsule, Reports by Radio in 15-Minute Flight
February 21, 1962	Glenn Orbits Earth 3 Times Safely
October 2, 1962	3000 Troops Put Down Mississippi Rioting and Seize 200 as Negro Attends Classes
October 23, 1962	U.S. Imposes Arms Blockade on Cuba on Finding Offensive-Missile Sites; Kennedy Ready for Soviet Showdown
August 29, 1963	200,000 March for Civil Rights in Orderly Washington Rally
November 23, 1963	Kennedy is Killed by Sniper as He Rides in Car in Dallas; Johnson Sworn in on Plane
November 25, 1963	President's Assassin Shot to Death in Jail Corridor by a Dallas Citizen; Grieving Throngs View Kennedy Bier
January 12, 1964	Cigarettes Peril Health, U.S. Report Concludes; 'Remedial Action' Urged
February 17, 1964	4 Beatles and How They Grew
June 20, 1964	Civil Rights Bill Passed, 73–27; Johnson Urges All to Comply
August 5, 1964	U.S. Planes Attack North Vietnam Bases; President Orders 'Limited' Retaliation After Communists' PT Boats Renew Raids
June 9, 1967	Egypt and Syria Agree to U.N. Ceasefire
December 4, 1967	Heart Transplant Keeps Man Alive in South Africa
April 5, 1968	Martin Luther King is Slain in Memphis
April 6, 1968	Army Troops in Capital as Negroes Riot
June 6, 1968	Kennedy is Dead, Victim of Assassin
August 21, 1968	Czechoslovakia Invaded by Russians and Four Other Warsaw Pact Forces; They Open Fire on Crowds in Prague
August 29, 1968	Humphrey Nominated on the First Ballot After His Plank on Vietnam is Approved; Police Battle Demonstrators in Streets
July 21, 1969	Men Walk on Moon; Astronauts Land on Plain; Collect Rocks, Plant Flag
April 15, 1970	Crew of Crippled Apollo 13 Starts Back After Rounding Moon
May 5, 1970	4 Kent State Students Killed by Troops
July 1, 1971	Supreme Court, 6–3, Upholds Newspaper on Publication of the Pentagon Report
October 26, 1971	U.N. Seats Peking and Expels Taipei
May 16, 1972	Wallace is Shot; Condition Serious; A Suspect Seized
June 30, 1972	Supreme Court, 5-4, Bars Death Penalty
September 6, 1972	9 Israelis on Olympic Team Killed with 4 Arab Captors
January 23, 1973	High Court Rules Abortions Legal the First 3 Months
January 28, 1973	Vietnam Peace Pacts Signed; America's Longest War Halts
May 1, 1973	Nixon Accepts Onus for Watergate, But Says He Didn't Know About Plot
March 2, 1974	Federal Grand Jury Indicts 7 Nixon Aides on Conspiracy Charges on Watergate
August 9, 1974	Nixon Resigns; He Urges a Time of 'Healing'; Ford Will Take Office Today
August 10, 1974	Ford Sworn in as President; Asserts "Nightmare is Over"
September 9, 1974	Ford Gives Pardon to Nixon, Who Regrets "My Mistakes"
April 30, 1975	Minh Surrenders, Vietcong in Saigon; 1,000 Americans and 5,500 Vietnamese Evacuated by Copter to U.S. Carriers
July 5, 1976	Nation and Millions in City Joyously Hail Bicentennial
July 21, 1976	Viking Robot Sets Down Safely on Mars and Sends Back Pictures
April 19, 1978	Senate Votes to Give Up Panama Canal
June 29, 1978	High Court Backs Some Affirmative Action by Colleges, But Orders Bakke Admitted
July 27, 1978	Scientists Praise British Birth as Triumph
November 21, 1978	400 Are Found Dead in Mass Suicide by Cult
December 16, 1978	U.S. and China Opening Full Relations
January 17, 1979	Shah Leaves Iran for Indefinite Stay; Crowds Exult
March 27, 1979	Egypt and Israel Sign Formal Treaty, Ending a State of War After 30 Years
March 31, 1979	U.S. Aides See a Risk of Meltdown at Pennsylvania Nuclear Plant; More Radioactive as is Released
May 4, 1979	Conservatives Win British Vote; Margaret Thatcher First Woman to Head a European Government

January 21, 1981	Reagan Takes Oath as 40th President; Promises an 'Era of National Renewal'/Minutes Later, 52 Hostages in Iran Fly to Freedom after 444-Day Ordeal
March 31, 1981	Reagan Wounded in Chest by Gunman
April 15, 1981	Columbia Returns: Shuttle Era Opens
May 14, 1981	Pope is Shot in Car in Vatican Square
July 8, 1981	Reagan Nominating Woman to Serve on Supreme Court
October 7, 1981	Sadat Assassinated at Army Parade
December 14, 1981	Poland Restricts Civil and Union Rights; Solidarity Activists Urge General Strike
January 9, 1982	U.S. Settles Phone Suit, Drops IBM Case; AT&T to Split Up, Transforming Industry
June 7, 1982	Big Israeli Force Invades South Lebanon
June 15, 1982	Britain Announces Argentine Surrender to End 10-Week War on the Falklands
May 25, 1983	Health Chief Calls AIDS Battle 'No. 1 Priority'
June 19, 1983	Shuttle Rockets to Orbit with 5 Aboard (First U.S. Woman in Space)
October 24, 1983	Beirut Death Toll at 161 Americans; French Casualties Rise in Bombings
October 26, 1983	1,900 U.S. Troops, with Caribbean Allies, Invade Grenada
November 1, 1984	Gandhi, Slain, is Succeeded by Son
December 28, 1985	Airport Terrorists Kill 13 and Wound 113 at Israeli Counters in Rome and Vienna
January 29, 1986	The Shuttle Explodes; 6 in Crew and High-School Teacher are Killed
February 26, 1986	Marcos Flees and is Taken to Guam; U.S. Recognizes Aquino as President
April 30, 1986	Soviet, Reporting Atom Plant 'Disaster,' Seeks Help Abroad to Fight Reactor Fire
October 20, 1987	Stocks Plunge 508 Points, A Drop of 22.6%
March 17, 1988	North, Poindexter and 2 Others Indicted on Iran-Contra Fraud and Theft Charges
May 7, 1988	For Computers, the Year 2000 May Prove a Bit Traumatic
December 22, 1988	Jetliner Carrying 258 to U.S. Crashes in Scottish Town
June 4, 1989	Troops Attack and Crush Beijing Protest; Thousands Fight Back, Scores Are Killed
November 11, 1989	Joyous East Germans Pour Through Wall; Party Pledges Freedoms, and City Exults
February 12, 1990	Mandela Freed, Urges Step-Up in Pressure to End White Rule
May 13, 1990	Some Computer Conversation is Changing Human Contact
August 3, 1990	Invading Iraqis Seize Kuwait and its Oil
October 3, 1990	Two Germanys Unite After 45 Years with Jubilation and a Vow of Peace
January 17, 1991	U.S. and Allies Open Air War on Iraq; Bomb Baghdad and Kuwaiti Targets; 'No Choice' But Force, Bush Declares
February 28, 1991	Bush Halts Offensive Combat; Kuwait Freed, Iraqis Crushed
October 12, 1991	Thomas Accuser Tells Hearing of Obscene Talk and Advances
December 26, 1991	Gorbachev, Last Soviet Leader, Resigns; U.S. Recognizes Republics' Independence
May 1, 1992	23 Dead After 2nd Day of Los Angeles Riots
April 20, 1993	Scores Die as Cult Compound is Set Afire
September 14, 1993	Rabin and Arafat Seal their Accord as Clinton Applauds 'Brave Gamble'
January 18, 1994	Severe Earthquake Hits Los Angeles
May 11, 1994	South Africans Hail President Mandela; First Black Leader Pledges Racial Unity
April 20, 1995	At least 31 Are Dead, Scores are Missing After Car Bomb Attack in Oklahoma City Wrecks 9-Story Federal Office Building
October 4, 1995	Jury Clears Simpson in Double Murder; Spellbound Nation Divides on Verdict
November 5, 1995	Rabin Slain After Peace Rally in Tel Aviv
November 22, 1995	Accord Reached to End the War in Bosnia
February 23, 1997	Scientist Reports First Cloning Ever of Adult Mammal
June 3, 1997	McVeigh Guilty on All Counts in the Oklahoma City Bombing
July 1, 1997	China Resumes Control of Hong Kong, Concluding 156 Years of British Rule
August 31, 1997	Diana Killed in a Car Accident in Paris
May 24, 1998	Irish Voters, North and South, Give Resounding "Yes" to Peace
August 18, 1998	Clinton Admits Lewinsky Liaison to Jury; Tells Nation "It Was Wrong," But Private
September 28, 1998	McGwire's Grand Finale Makes it 70
December 20, 1998	Clinton Impeached; He Faces Senate Trial, 2d in History
January 1, 1999	11 Countries Tie Europe Together in One Currency
February 13, 1999	Clinton Acquitted Decisively: No Majority for Either Charge
March 25, 1999	NATO Opens Broad Barrage Against Serbs
April 22, 1999	15 Bodies Are Removed from School in Colorado
November 6, 1999	U.S. Judge Declares Microsoft is a Market-Stifling Monopoly
January 1, 2000	1/1/00, A Glittering Party for Times Square
April 23, 2000	Cuban Boy Seized by US Agents and Reunited with His Father
June 8, 2000	Microsoft Breakup is Ordered for Antitrust Law Violations
June 15, 2000	Koreas Reach Accord Seeking Reconciliation After 50 Years
June 27, 2000	Genetic Code of Human Life is Cracked by Scientists
October 1, 2000	Mideast Violence Continues to Rage; Death Toll Rises
October 6, 2000	Yugoslavs Claim Belgrade for a New Leader
November 8, 2000	Bush and Gore Vie for an Edge with Narrow Electoral Split; Hillary Clinton Goes to Senate
November 9, 2000	Bush Barely Ahead of Gore in Florida as Recount Holds Key to the Election
December 13, 2000	Bush Prevails: By Single Vote, Justices End Recount, Blocking Gore after 5-Week Struggle
December 14, 2000	Bush Pledges to Be President of 'One Nation' Not One Party; Gore, Conceding, Urges Unity

The New York Times

THE 20TH CENTURY

"All the News That's Fit to Print."

The New York Times.

THE WEATHER.

Fair; wind northeasterly, becoming southerly.

COPYRIGHT, 1901, BY THE NEW YORK TIMES COMPANY.

VOL. L...NO. 15,926. NEW YORK, WEDNESDAY, JANUARY 23, 1901.—SIXTEEN PAGES. ONE CENT In Greater New York, Jersey City, and Newark. Elsewhere, TWO CENTS.

QUEEN VICTORIA DEAD AT OSBORNE

Passed Away Quietly at 6:30 o'Clock Last Evening.

SCENE AT THE BEDSIDE

Family, with Bowed Heads, Listened to Bishop's Prayers.

QUEEN BADE THEM FAREWELL

Said to Have Spoken Words of Great Moment to Prince of Wales.

ALBERT EDWARD NOW KING

Privy Council and Parliament Will Meet in London To-day, and the Proclamation of the New Monarch's Succession Will Follow—Grief Over the Queen's Death and Admiration for Her Character Universal in the United Kingdom, the British Colonies, Europe, and America—Arrangements for the Funeral Not Yet Announced.

COWES, Isle of Wight, Jan. 23.—Queen Victoria is dead. The greatest event in the memory of this generation, almost the most stupendous change in existing conditions in England that could be imagined, has taken place quietly, almost gently, upon the anniversary of the death of Queen Victoria's father, the Duke of Kent.

The end of this splendid career came in a simply furnished room in Osborne House. This most respected of all women, living or dead, lay in a great four-posted bed. Around her were gathered the majority of her descendants. Well within view of her dying eyes there hung a portrait of the Prince Consort. It was he who designed the room and every part of the Castle. In scarcely audible words the white-haired Bishop of Winchester prayed beside her, as he had often before prayed with his sovereign, for he was her Chaplain at Windsor.

With bowed heads the imperious ruler of the German Empire, the man who is now King of England, the woman who has succeeded to the title of Queen, the Princes and Princesses, and those of less than royal designation listened to the Bishop's ceaseless prayer.

Naturally, the family, while recognizing the claim for public information, insist that some details of the events around the deathbed shall be sacred for the present, and have imposed the strictest secrecy on the whole household. The Queen is, however, said to have bidden farewell, in a feeble voice, to her family. She first recognized the Prince of Wales, to whom she spoke a few words of great moment; then Emperor William and the others present filed past and heard a whispered good-bye. All those in the bedroom were in tears.

Six o'clock passed. The Bishop continued his intercession. One of the younger children asked a question in a shrill, childish treble, and was immediately silenced. The women of the royal family sobbed faintly and the men shuffled uneasily.

THE END QUITE PEACEFUL.

At exactly 6:30 Sir James Reid held up his hand, and the people in the room knew that England had lost her Queen. The Bishop pronounced the benediction.

The Queen passed away quite peacefully. She suffered no pain. Those who were now mourners went to their rooms. A few minutes later the inevitable element of materialism stepped into this pathetic chapter of international history, for the Court ladies went busily to work ordering their mourning from London.

The wheels of the world were jarred when the announcement came; but in this palace at Osborne everything pursued the usual course. Down in the kitchen they were cooking a huge dinner for an assemblage the like of which has seldom been known in England, and the dinner preparations proceeded just as if nothing had happened.

An incident characteristic of the Queen's solicitude for others occurred two days ago, when, in one of the intervals of consciousness, she summoned strength to suggest to her dressers, who had been acting as nurses, that they take the opportunity of getting some fresh air.

QUEEN ASKS FOR HER DOG.

On Monday afternoon the Queen asked that her little Pomeranian be brought to her bedside.

It was feared that the Queen was dying at about 9 o'clock yesterday morning, and carriages were sent to Osborne cottage and the rectory to bring all the Princes and Princesses and the Bishop of Winchester to her bedside. It seemed then very near the end; but, when things looked the worst, the Queen, in one of the rallies due to her wonderful constitution, opened her eyes and recognized the Prince of Wales, the Princess, and Emperor William. She asked to see one of her faithful servants, a member of the household. He hastened to the room, but before he got there the Queen had passed into a fitful sleep.

Four o'clock marked the beginning of the end. Again the family were summoned, and this time the relapse was not followed by recovery.

The Prince of Wales was very much affected when the doctors at length informed him that his mother had breathed her last. Emperor William, himself deeply affected, did his best to minister comfort to his sorrow-stricken uncle, whose new dignity he was the first to acknowledge.

OUTSIDE OSBORNE HOUSE GATES.

No member of the royal family left Osborne House yesterday for the customary drives. A changing group of correspondents and townspeople loitered about the gates all day long, but never reached the proportions of the crowd of Monday.

It was a melancholy day. Occasional drizzles obscured the emerald hills beyond the castle. Greater simplicity or a more entire lack of any of that pomp traditionally attached to royalty could not be found in any country house in the kingdom than here, where the best-beloved monarch of centuries was dying and the ruler of another great nation waited by her bedside as grandson rather than as Emperor.

Two stalwart policemen guarding the gates against intruders were the sole reminders of officialdom. They were compelled in the morning to refuse admission to three dusky visitors from India who drove up arrayed in such gorgeous robes that the bystanders instinctively lifted their hats, mistaking them for potentates. The trio announced themselves as lecturers touring England in behalf of a foreign mission, and insisted upon an audience with the Prince of Wales to tender the sympathies of India.

Many of the country gentry and a few titled personages appeared at the lodge and registered their names in the visitors' book, the thrifty flunky who officiated doing a profitable business by selling the original copies of official bulletins to souvenir enthusiasts. Artists and photographers obtained pictures of the gates and grounds and any prominent persons who appeared.

THE LORD CHAMBERLAIN ARRIVES

Everybody feared that the Queen would never waken from the sleep which the noontime bulletin spoke of, and everybody was watching the flag on the castle tower, expecting it to sink to half mast. Lord Clarendon, the new Lord Chamberlain, with Prince Christian of Schleswig-Holstein and the Duke of Argyll, arrived at Osborne in the afternoon. The arrival of the Lord Chamberlain was an ominous sign, as he announces to a new monarch his accession to the throne.

When the 4 o'clock bulletin announced that the Queen was sinking, all the watchers at the gates of Osborne House made up their minds to remain to the end. The cold was intense, and a few favored ones sought shelter in the royal lodge, just inside, where they waited in absolute silence.

NEWS OF THE EVENT ANNOUNCED.

The telephone bell rang at 7:04 P. M., but before a royal servant had time to take the message the Chief of the Queen's Police emerged from the darkness, and, with bared head, said:

"Gentlemen, the Queen passed away at 6:30."

All present reverently uncovered, and then shrill whistles outside and the ringing of the bells of the bicycles in waiting were the signals for messengers to race to Cowes with the news. In a few moments the place was deserted. Simultaneously, mounted messengers, on white horses, dashed from Osborne. What happened within the royal residence is purely surmise.

On their arrival at Cowes the correspondents found the news had been known both at East and West Cowes fifteen minutes before it had been announced to those in waiting at the gates of Osborne House. The streets were already filled with sorrowful crowds discussing her Majesty's death.

Prince and Princess Louis of Battenberg arrived at Osborne just too late to see her Majesty alive.

From all parts of the world there are still pouring into Cowes messages of condolence. They come from crowned heads, millionaires, tradesmen, and paupers, and are variously addressed to the Prince of Wales and the King of England.

RESULT OF ROBERTS'S NEWS?

The record of the last days of the reign of Victoria is not yet fully known. The correspondent of The Associated Press was the only correspondent admitted to Osborne House, and his interview with Sir Arthur John Bigge, private secretary to the late Queen, was the only official statement that was given out.

For several weeks the Queen had been failing. On Monday week she summoned Lord Roberts and asked him some very searching questions regarding the war in South Africa. On Tuesday she went for a drive, but was visibly affected. On Wednesday she suffered a paralytic stroke, accompanied by intense physical weakness. It was her first illness in all her eighty-one years, and she would not admit she was sick. Then her condition grew so serious that, against her wishes, the family were summoned. When they arrived her reason had practically succumbed to paralysis and weakness.

The events of the last few days, described in the bulletins, are too fresh to need repetition.

THE LAST BULLETINS.

OSBORNE HOUSE GATES, Isle of Wight, Jan. 22.—An official bulletin issued at 8 o'clock said:

The Queen this morning shows signs of diminishing strength, and her Majesty's condition again assumes a more serious aspect.
JAMES REID,
R. DOUGLAS POWELL,
THOMAS BARLOW.

The bulletin issued at noon said there had been no change for the worse in the Queen's condition since the morning bulletin.

At 4 P. M. another bulletin was posted. It said the Queen was slowly sinking.

At 6:45 P. M. the end was announced as follows:

Her Majesty the Queen breathed her last at 6:30 P. M., surrounded by her children and grandchildren.
JAMES REID,
R. DOUGLAS POWELL,
THOMAS BARLOW.

THE QUEEN'S FUNERAL.

Will Probably Be at Frogmore—Many Royalties Expected.

COWES, Isle of Wight, Jan. 23.—The body of Queen Victoria is being embalmed to-night, and will probably be taken to Windsor on Saturday.

The coffin arrived last evening from London.

Emperor William's arrangements are not settled, but it is believed that he will not depart until after the funeral, which will probably be a ceremony never before equaled in this country.

LONDON, Jan. 23.—There is little doubt that the funeral of Queen Victoria will take place at Frogmore, Hertfordshire, though nothing in regard to this matter has yet been announced.

Her Majesty was so closely related to the European Courts, big and little, that the gathering of royalties at the obsequies will be unprecedented.

ATHENS, Jan. 22.—King George will start for London to-night.

PARIS, Jan. 23.—The French Government will be represented at the funeral of Queen Victoria by an extraordinary embassy.

The members have not yet been chosen, but the embassy will be headed by Vice Admiral de Lajaille, who on several occasions welcomed Queen Victoria at Cherbourg in the name of France.

TO-DAY'S CEREMONIES.

Privy Council and Parliament to Meet—The Proclamation of the King.

LONDON, Jan. 23.—The Privy Council will meet in London to-day, and the proclamation of the King will take place thereafter at all places required by custom.

The King will come to London to preside over the Council. The Ministers will attend, give up their seals of office, be resworn, receive the proclamation of the King, pass votes of condolence and congratulation, and adjourn.

After giving up their seals the Ministers receive them back from the new ruler. The Privy Councilors will also be sworn afresh.

Shortly before midnight yesterday an official announcement was issued calling Parliament to assemble at 4 o'clock this afternoon to enable members of the House of Lords and House of Commons to take the oath of allegiance to the King. Precedent orders that Parliament shall meet within twenty-four hours of the death of the ruler.

At the offices of the Lord Chamberlain and of the City Remembrancer, at the Guildhall and at the College of Heralds, the officials were busy yesterday preparing for the formalities which for the first time in a generation are to take place—the proclaiming of a new ruler of the United Kingdom. All the ancient gazettes, Court circulars, and other papers which describe the ceremonial of 1837 were taken from the libraries, that the officials might familiarize themselves with the ancient pageantry whereby a sovereign is proclaimed. The City Remembrancer said yesterday:

"It will depend on the pleasure of the new monarch to decide how far the ancient customs will be modified to suit modern methods; but, in a country where precedents are so firmly adhered to as England, it may be anticipated that we shall follow closely on the acts which prevailed when the Queen ascended the throne. The Privy Council, which is a very large body, will meet at once at St. James's Palace, where the form of proclamation declaring that 'we, etcetera, with one voice and consent of tongue and heart declare and proclaim the high mighty Prince Albert Edward, etcetera, who, by the death of the monarch, has become our only lawful and rightful liege, etcetera.'

"This proclamation will give the new title the King may assume, but this is not yet announced to us. The proclamation will then be sent to Heralds' College, and the following day the Earl Marshal, the Garter King at Arms, the Herald's Pursuivants, and other officials, with the college members and the Household troops, will proceed from the palace, clad in their splendid surcoats, and proceed to Trafalgar Square. There the King at Arms will halt, command silence, and read the proclamation. Proceeding down the Strand to Temple Bar, a halt will again be made, to demand an entrance into the City to proclaim the King. There the Lord Mayor and Sheriffs, in their state carriages, will form a great procession, and when the Earl Marshal's party comes just within the City boundary the proclamation will be read again, and the procession will pass down Ludgate Hill and Cheapside to the Royal Exchange, where similar ceremonies will close the spectacle."

DEEP GLOOM IN LONDON.

Places of Amusement All Closed—How the News Was Received.

LONDON, Jan. 23.—Silence, gloom, and darkness characterize London to-night. From Whitechapel to Mayfair streets usually gay with nightly festivity are dark, deserted, and desolate, and this depression of the public mind is likely to continue for many days to come.

Only a few hours ago the pleasure-seeking populace was hurrying to the theatres and music halls, only to find in every case the doors closed and big, black-bordered bills announcing that the performances had been suspended. The people, thus turned into the streets, gave for a short time an unusually thronged appearance to the West End. Many turned in the direction of Buckingham Palace and Marlborough House, where absolute silence reigned. Small bills, signed "Balfour," were posted outside, announcing the death of the monarch.

Everywhere, in vehicles and on the streets, the one topic of conversation was what would happen under the new reign, rather than the life and death of Victoria. Much interest was evinced in the way in which the enormous fortune of the dead Queen would be distributed, the general notion being that Osborne House would go to Princess Beatrice, and that she and Princess Christian would come into a considerable portion of Queen Victoria's wealth.

The probability that the King will take up a practically permanent residence in Buckingham Palace was much canvassed. This is a question that comes very much home to Londoners. Queen Victoria's preference for Balmoral Castle and Osborne House has been a complaint of long standing in the metropolis, and it is hoped that the new reign will see a change in this respect. The presence of the Court in London would give a brightness and gayety to the city which have long been absent.

Not until Queen Victoria has been laid to rest beside the Prince Consort at Frogmore will the theatres or music halls reopen. Moreover, business will come to a practical standstill. Music in all the hotels and public places ceased last evening. Fashionable resorts were empty, and very few of the nightly habitués were in evidence.

Americans who have passed through great National calamities may recall the crêpe-draped buildings and the National hush; but they can ill-conceive, since the death of Lincoln, any such expression of gloom as has already fallen on the United Kingdom. Marlborough House, so long the home of the new monarch; Buckingham Palace, where Queen Victoria made her last stay in London, and St. James's Palace, the residence of so many former monarchs, are to-night all black and deserted. Sentries in black overcoats keep silent vigil before the closed gates and bolted doors.

Early in the evening from St. Paul's, Westminster Abbey, and other churches bells were solemnly tolling or ringing muffled peals. In some cases the shops were already exhibiting signs of mourning. Beyond these things, however, and the boys crying extra editions in every direction, there was little that would outwardly indicate the passing of the country through an experience novel to almost the whole people.

SORROW IS UNIVERSAL.

Telegrams arriving from all parts of the country and the colonies re-echo the deep feeling of sorrow pervading all classes. These show that everywhere bells have been tolled and public performances and private functions suspended.

In Dublin the expressions of regret were universal. The bells of St. Patrick's Cathedral were tolled. Earl Cadogan, the Lord Lieutenant, was absent from Dublin yesterday, but it is expected that he will return immediately to preside at a meeting of the Irish Privy Council to proclaim the new King.

The news was received with the greatest sorrow at Balmoral, Windsor, and Eton, where Queen Victoria was regarded in an especially personal manner by the inhabitants.

Princess Beatrice telegraphed the tidings to ex-Empress Eugénie at Farnborough.

SCENES YESTERDAY AFTERNOON.

The gloomy faces of the crowds incessantly approaching the bulletin board at the Mansion House indicated yesterday how little the public hoped to receive better news of the condition of the Queen. Men of all ages and conditions, women and even children were content to spend a long time in awaiting their turn to get within reading distance of the board. As the throng moved slowly past the notice board, those who were unable to get there personally sent messenger boys with notebook and pencils to copy the text of everything posted. The grief of all was evident. Never were there so many black ties in the city before the actual arrival of a time of general mourning.

There was a remarkable scene outside the Mansion House early in the afternoon. On receipt of the alarming reports something resembling a groan was uttered by the hundreds of people assembled, and then some one started singing the national anthem. All heads were bared, and in a moment the crowds were singing "God Save the Queen" with a fervor proving how earnestly they wished for her Majesty's recovery. The passengers in passing carriages, cabs, and omnibuses joined in the singing, the drivers reverently doffing their hats.

At 4:35 P. M. the following was posted:

Osborne, 4 P. M.

My painful duty obliges me to inform you that the life of our beloved Queen is in the greatest danger. ALBERT EDWARD.

In reply the Lord Mayor, Frank Green, dispatched the following:

"I have received your Royal Highness's sad intimation with profound grief, which is shared by the citizens of London, who still pray that under Divine Providence the irreparable loss to her Majesty's devoted family and loyal subjects throughout the empire may still be averted. Will your Royal Highness be pleased to accept this heart-felt expression of my deep and sincere sympathy?"

THE FINAL ANNOUNCEMENT.

The latest bulletins previous to the announcement of the Queen's death, especially the message sent by the Prince of Wales, dispelled the last gleam of hope. The crowds silently dispersed from in front of the Mansion House, and only a few groups awaited the appearance of the inevitable announcement. This came at 7 o'clock in the form of a dispatch to the Lord Mayor from the new King as follows:

Osborne, 6:45 P. M.

My beloved mother has just passed away, surrounded by her children and grandchildren. ALBERT EDWARD.

The Lord Mayor immediately sent the following reply:

"Your Royal Highness's telegram announcing the nation's great loss I have received with profound distress and grief, and have communicated this most sad intimation to my fellow-citizens. Her Majesty's name and memory will forever live in the hearts of her people.

"May I respectfully convey to your Royal Highness and to all the members of the royal family the earnest sympathy and condolence of the City of London in your great sorrow?"

The scrap of paper a foot square, posted on the wall of the Mansion House, gave the first notice to London's homeward hurrying thousands of the death of the Queen. Excavations by which the street had been torn up made access to the bulletin difficult, but the bared heads of a silent group under a flickering gas jet told the crowds on the 'bus tops and sidewalks that the Queen was no more.

"BIG BEN" IS TOLLED.

A quarter of an hour later more than a thousand newsboys had invaded the streets with black-ruled newspapers, crying, "Death of the Queen," while through the dark streets boomed the deep-toned notes of "Big Ben," the big bell of St. Paul's Cathedral, the bells of the city re-echoing the news.

The shops closed as soon as the bells began to toll, and the blinds of the Mansion House were drawn down as soon as the message from the Prince of Wales was received by the Lord Mayor.

The bell tolled at St. Paul's Cathedral was the gift of William III., and is used only on occasions of the death of royal personages, Archbishops of Canterbury, Lord Mayors of London, and Bishops of London. The tolling continued for two hours at intervals of a minute and could be heard for miles in the direction of the wind.

Some hundreds of people stood in front of the cathedral around the spot where Queen Victoria prayed on the sixtieth anniversary of her accession to the throne.

LONDON PRESS COMMENTS.

Universal Grief Reflected in Editorials—Labouchere's Warm Eulogy.

LONDON, Jan. 23.—All the morning papers appear in heavy mourning borders, with editorials eulogistic of the dead Queen and recalling the leading events and characteristics of her reign. Very few political references as to the future are made. The Daily Mail says:

"We can but regret that the Queen was not permitted to see the end of the South African struggle. She has been taken from us in a dark hour which, we may hope, is a prelude to the dawn, and when we can ill spare her ripe experience and her vast knowledge of measures and men."

"Let us think of her this morning," says the Daily Chronicle, "by her highest title, not by her crown and sceptre, but by her own magnificent and splendid ideal of womanhood. This it is which touches the heart's core of a proud and imperial race. We have lost mother, wife, and Queen."

The Chronicle remarks that President McKinley was slightly premature in sending a communication to "His Majesty, the King," inasmuch as the Prince of Wales has not yet been proclaimed by the Privy Council.

The Daily Telegraph publishes two editorials under the captions "The Queen" and "The King." In the latter it says:

"Most happily for him, he has, with infinite credit to himself, passed through a period of probation in some ways more difficult and certainly more prolonged than that to which any successor to a throne in modern times has been subjected. He assumes the burden of his imperial task equipped with all the invaluable experience which the most painstaking discharge of great duties could secure him during the lifetime of his august mother. So accustomed have we become to his direct, personal patronage of every charity and every beneficial movement, many of which he initiated himself, that we are apt to forget the exhausting nature of the strain almost daily imposed upon his strength. He has won among the masses of the people a popularity that has been vouchsafed to few of his predecessors."

The Times says:

"The confidence inspired by her personal character enabled Queen Victoria on many occasions to use her intimate knowledge with effect in smoothing the rugged places of international relations or in modifying a policy which, through sheer inadequacy of information, would have led to undesirable friction. We have also to thank the Queen for influence of the most potent kind consistently and vigorously used to enforce high ideals of social and personal virtue, of religious faith and of Christian life."

Referring to the intellectual upheaval and the enormous social and economic progress which characterized the Victorian era, The Times expresses regret that the impetus has to some extent spent itself.

"At the close of Victoria's reign," continues The Times, "we find ourselves somewhat less secure of our position than we could desire, somewhat less abreast of the problems of the age than we ought to be, considering the initial advantages we secured."

"The great English-speaking Republic beyond the Atlantic has not failed to send us officially by the mouth of President McKinley, and unofficially by innumerable newspaper articles and other tokens of popular feeling, proof of how heartily and profoundly it shares in our grief. Need we say for ourselves and our colonies how dear to us in such an hour is the fellowship in woe which our American kinsmen so generously and warmly tender us?"

In another article The Times says:

"If anything can in some measure console the nation for the irreparable loss it has sustained, it is the well-founded conviction that the Queen has left behind her a worthy successor, who may be trusted to walk in her footsteps.

"In the whole range of English social and political life no position is more difficult to fill satisfactorily and without reproach than that of the heir apparent, and it may be justly said that the way this position has been filled has contributed to the remarkable increase in the devotion to the throne and the dynasty which has been one of the most striking characteristics of Victoria's reign.

"As Albert Edward has been a scrupulously constitutional Prince, we may confidently predict that he will be a scrupulously constitutional King. In the fulfillment of this onerous task he will have by his side a Queen who is already enthroned in the hearts of her loving subjects."

Henry Labouchère, M. P., in Truth has a remarkable tribute to Queen Victoria, a tribute all the more remarkable because of his democratic ideas and frank criticisms of royalty.

"Among all her millions of subjects," he says, "there are but few who will not mourn for her loss as for one of their own household. Nor will the mourners be found among her own subjects alone. It is not too much to say that never in the history of the world has a single death caused such universal grief. Alike in happiness and sorrow, she lived a life beyond reproach, without thought of self and unreservedly devoted to the duties of the hour. Although occupying perhaps the proudest position ever filled by a woman, and never wanting in a certain queenly dignity, her tastes, habits, demeanor, and even her dress were marked by the rarest simplicity.

"She has been indeed the mother of her people, and as a mother she will be mourned. In all the affairs of State she manifested the same wisdom that inspired her private life, nor did her own country alone enjoy the fruits of her experience and sagacity. Through her kindred and descendants abroad her influence for many years has been felt in Continental politics, always on the side of peace; and, in at least one crisis, she is known to have rendered service to the whole of Europe.

"Her sudden and lamentable breakdown was due entirely to worry and overwork. She had been greatly distressed by events in South Africa and by domestic griefs."

The Daily News says that Queen Victoria was always a peacemaker. It refers to the incident of her modifying in a pacific sense Lord Russell's dispatch in the Trent case.

The Standard, expressing regret that the Queen was not spared to see peace restored in South Africa, says: "The end for which she strove and prayed has yet to come, and the hope is perhaps visionary that the common grief of Britons and Afrikanders may abate those racial animosities which stand in the way of pacification."

Referring to the conspicuous success of Queen Victoria's reign, The Standard says:

"There was a time when republicanism was a serious phrase on English lips. To-day no whisper of discontent with the monarchical Constitution breaks the mourning of a loyal nation around the bier of the sovereign. It will be said of her in the annals of our land that she strengthened the Throne by loving the people, and that she was a great Queen and the mother of Kings because she was a good, noble, and true-hearted woman."

THE NATIONS' TRIBUTES.

Enmity for Great Britain Hushed and Only Sympathy Expressed.

PARIS, Jan. 23.—The news of the death of Queen Victoria was known in Paris at 8 o'clock last evening through special editions of the evening papers, which newsboys carried throughout the city. Great sympathy was expressed on all sides.

As soon as definite information reached Parliament the Presidents of the chambers announced that the next session would be adjourned as a sign of mourning.

When the news was known at the Ministry of Foreign Affairs, M. Delcassé, the Foreign Minister, went to the British Embassy to express to the Acting Ambassador the condolence of the French Government. President Loubet postponed his visit until the return of Sir Edmund Monson.

Not until then, moreover, will the arrangements relative to mourning be made. The British flag, draped with crape, will be placed over the entrance to the embassy to-day.

Last evening there was a steady stream of callers to inscribe their names in the register at the embassy.

Few and far between, indeed, are the Paris papers this morning which do not sound the note of regret at the passing of Victoria. In addition to long obituaries, special writers publish appreciations, reviewing the Queen's life work, noting in what respects it contributed to the greatness of the British nation, and speculating in some cases upon the reign about to open. Foremost of these special writers is M. Hanotaux, who, in Le Journal, refers to the extent of England's debt to Victoria.

"Her temperament and judgment, thanks to the precious lessons of Lord Melbourne," says M. Hanotaux, "were in complete accord with English Parliamentary institutions. Her success as a sovereign was due to her close attention to the affairs of State, her frequent journeys, her interviews with foreign statesmen, and above all, to the extraordinary position of being allied to several of the reigning sovereigns of Europe."

Le Gaulois says:

"Her action may be summed up in a brief phrase, little authority and much influence. The changes which are about to take place express better than blind and foolish flattery the place she occupied in Europe. That will be her true funeral oration, the final word of which will be that she, the possessor of most ordinary faculties, accomplished more than certain conquerors, and has left a greater gap than Catherine or Elizabeth."

Le Siecle says:

"Doubtless the Prince of Wales will follow the good example of his mother, whose death will mark no change of policy or opinion in Great Britain. He will peaceably enjoy the loyalty of the empire, accorded during the long reign of the Queen."

Le Temps, discussing the outlook, says:

"The sadness, alarm, anxieties, moral sufferings, and pecuniary cares arising out of the Transvaal war have created a new feeling in England. Queen Victoria has been like a mother of a family, a living link with the prosperity of the past, an anchor of security for the British people. With her disappearance will come the unknown, the groping into the dark future."

BERLIN, Jan. 22.—The news of the death of Queen Victoria had been hourly expected in Berlin, and on its arrival special editions of the newspapers sold like wildfire, the announcement being read with silent and respectful sympathy. The fact that Empress Augusta Victoria started to-day for Homburg to be near Dowager Empress Frederick added to the sad circumstances of the occasion.

Immediately after the receipt of the news Count von Eulenburg, the Chief Court Marshal, ordered the flags half masted on all public buildings. Although the hour of the evening was somewhat advanced, a number of the embassies and legations, including the United States Embassy, did the same.

Special mourning orders to the Schloss, the army, the Court, and the public departments were issued this evening. These will be published to-morrow and go immediately into effect.

The German nation fully shares in the feelings of the British people toward the venerable and illustrious sovereign who has just breathed her last.

Semi-official paragraphs in the press this evening rebut the idea, commonly held in Germany, that the new King will be inclined to be hostile toward Germany. On the contrary, they assert that he will act in the interests of Great Britain and the British people alone.

A sense of gratification is felt by all Germans that Emperor William was present at Osborne during the last hours of Queen Victoria's life and that the lofty feelings of filial piety which prompted his action have met with such full and unqualified recognition on the part of the British nation.

THE HAGUE, Jan. 22.—The Dutch press printed the news of the death of Queen Victoria with mourning borders.

The Court will go into mourning; but it is probable that there will be no change in the arrangements for the marriage of Queen Wilhelmina.

ROME, Jan. 22.—A most painful impression was produced by the receipt of the news of Queen Victoria's death.

King Victor Emmanuel, Queen Helena, the Pope, and members of the Government immediately telegraphed condolences.

GRIEF IN CANADA.

Flags at Half Mast Everywhere and Amusement Places Closed.

TORONTO, Ontario, Jan. 22.—To Torontonians no tidings fraught with greater sorrow ever flashed over the wires than those which recorded the death of the Queen. All classes of the community show their heartfelt grief. From early morning till the announcement of her Majesty's death, great crowds gathered and waited around the different newspaper offices, eagerly scanning each bulletin as it was posted up. When at last the dreaded news came, heads were reverently uncovered, and the crowds dispersed silently. For half an hour the bells kept tolling their mournful messages, while national flags, half-masted, swung from every pole.

The children in every school in the city this forenoon sang for the last time "God Save the Queen." The Mayor will proclaim a day of mourning.

MONTREAL, Jan. 22.—The bulletin officially announcing the death of her Majesty turned Montreal into a city of mourning. No sooner was the fact announced than the fire bells began to ring out at minute intervals, and mingled with them came the tolling of the big cathedral bells of both the English and Catholic churches. Flags appeared at half-mast everywhere, and the crowds in the streets and at the bulletin boards of the various papers, their heads in most cases bared, reverently read the announcement.

All entertainments of a social nature have been canceled, and even skating rinks, hockey rinks, and places of public amusement have been closed.

OTTAWA, Jan. 22.—The news of the Queen's death reached Ottawa at 2 P. M. The Secretary of State at once issued a proclamation continuing in office all who held positions under the Crown. This is merely formal.

All public buildings in the Dominion at once placed the union jack at half mast, and it will so remain until sundown on the day of the Queen's funeral.

ST. JOHN'S, N. F., Jan. 22.—The announcement of Queen Victoria's death has called forth expressions of the keenest regret in Newfoundland, the oldest colony of the British Empire. The Colonial Cabinet met this evening and adopted resolutions of condolence, which were cabled to London.

To-morrow will be observed as a day of mourning throughout the colony.

Arrangements are being made for the proclamation of the new sovereign upon receipt of an official intimation of his accession.

HALIFAX, N. S., Jan. 22.—Symbols of mourning for Queen Victoria are everywhere displayed. Flags fly half-mast on ships and from the frowning fortress, and the royal standard, for the first time in many years, is half-mast at the Citadel.

All performances have been canceled, and on the day of the Queen's funeral the tolling of half a hundred bells will mingle with the loud notes of minute guns for the departed sovereign.

A sketch of the life of Queen Victoria will be found on Pages 6 and 7 of this issue.

AMERICAN TRIBUTES TO QUEEN VICTORIA

President McKinley Cables Condolences to the New King.

WASHINGTON FLAGS LOWERED

Such a Mark of Respect Had Never Been Before Paid on the Death of a Monarch—Action by Congress.

WASHINGTON, Jan. 22.—Four days of anxiety, in a large measure, prepared official Washington for the news which was flashed across the cable this afternoon from England. So it happened that all things that could be decently done in anticipation of the death of Queen Victoria had been disposed of, and all was in readiness for the execution of the formalities which are indispensable to such occasions. The President and his advisers were in receipt from time to time of all news which came from Osborne House. When the end came it found appropriate measures of condolence framed, and even orders, ready for execution, looking to the half-masting of the flags over the executive departments and the carrying out of the usual formalities.

The half-masting of the National ensign was an unusual tribute. This has been done once or twice on the occasion of the funeral of some great ruler, but never before in the case of the death of a monarch. The adjournment of the House was also an unusual mark of respect.

THE PRESIDENT'S MESSAGE.

The news announcing the death of Queen Victoria was conveyed to President McKinley simultaneously with its receipt by the newspapers. Soon afterward the President sent the following message of condolence to the new King:

Washington, Jan. 22, 1901.

His Majesty the King, Osborne House, Isle of Wight:

I have received with profound sorrow the lamentable tidings of the death of her Majesty the Queen. Allow me, Sir, to offer my sincere sympathy and that of the American people in your personal bereavement and in the loss Great Britain has suffered in the death of its venerable and illustrious sovereign, whose noble life and beneficent influence have promoted the peace and won the affection of the world.

WILLIAM McKINLEY.

Secretary of State Hay cabled the following message to Ambassador Choate at London:

Department of State, Jan. 22, 1901.

Choate, Ambassador, London:

You will express to Lord Lansdowne the profound sorrow of the Government and people of the United States at the death of the Queen and the deep sympathy we feel with the people of the British Empire in their great affliction. JOHN HAY.

The actual dispatch of the message from the President to the new King of England and from Secretary Hay to Ambassador Choate was delayed only long enough to receive the physicians' statement announcing the demise of the Queen, and then they were sent forward at once and copies were furnished to the press.

The flag on the Executive Mansion was placed at half-mast at 3:30 o'clock.

THE SENATE'S RESOLUTION.

The Senate was in executive session when the news of Queen Victoria's death was announced, but the bulletin announcing her death was passed around by the doorkeepers. Expressions of regret and of admiration for the virtues of the dead sovereign were heard on all hands. Senators Allison and Morgan held a hurried consultation, as the result of which the latter drew up a resolution, which the former presented when the executive session closed. The resolution was as follows:

"That the death of her Royal and Imperial Majesty, Victoria, of noble virtues and great renown, is sincerely deplored by the Senate of the United States of America."

The resolution was adopted unanimously.

Afterward Mr. Allison offered the following resolution:

"That the President pro tem. of the Senate cause to be conveyed to the Prime Minister of Great Britain a suitably engrossed copy of the foregoing resolution."

This was agreed to.

Senator Lodge, evidently voicing the sentiment of most of his colleagues, said later:

"The Queen's death is to the people of the United States a real sorrow. Her reign, the longest in English history, has been a great and memorable one, but it has perhaps nothing greater or more memorable than her own ability and purity of character; her fidelity to her high duties, and her devotion to those ideals of conduct and domestic life which appeal most profoundly to all English-speaking people. The Queen has always been a steadfast friend to the United States, and during her long life has made that friendship traditional in her family. Americans can never forget that England was withheld from active interference in our own civil war largely, if not wholly, by the influence of the Queen and the wise counsels of Prince Albert."

THE HOUSE ADJOURNS.

The House received the news at about 2 o'clock, and for the time being it was the theme of universal discussion among the members. Speaker Henderson had shown deep interest in the Queen's condition, and the first bulletin announcing her death was taken to him in his private office and to Chairman Hitt of the Committee on Foreign Affairs. Mr. Hitt conferred with his colleagues as to the precedents in such cases, and then framed a brief and expressive resolution of sympathy and respect to be introduced in the House later. For a time it was feared that this might give rise to some expressions from Boer sympathizers, but, on the contrary, it was developed that the sentiment of respect for the departed sovereign was shared by all alike.

At the conclusion of the general debate on the District of Columbia Appropriation bill Mr. Hitt offered the resolution, which was as follows:

"Resolved, That the House of Representatives of the United States of America has learned with profound sorrow of the death of her Majesty Queen Victoria and sympathizes with her people in the loss of their beloved sovereign; that the President be requested to communicate this expression of the sentiment of the House to the Government of Great Britain; that, as a further mark of respect to the memory of Queen Victoria, the House do now adjourn."

The reading of the resolution was listened to with impressive silence. Mr. Hitt stated very briefly that this resolution followed the precedents in similar cases. It was, he said, copied almost literally from the resolution adopted upon the occasion of the death of the President of the French Republic, and followed the expression adopted upon the death of the Czar of Russia. He did not, he said, think that the occasion called for any extended remarks, and asked for a vote.

The resolution was unanimously adopted, and the House at 3:05 P. M. stood adjourned until noon to-morrow.

After the adjournment members gathered in knots and discussed the event, the tributes being to the womanly virtues and purity of home life of the Queen, no less than to her national service.

PRAISE FROM CABINET MINISTERS.

Secretary of State Hay, on being informed of the Queen's death, declined to make a statement for publication on the ground that, being under obligation to send an official message to the British Government on the subject, he did not feel called upon to make a further supplementary private statement.

Attorney General Griggs said:

"Hers has been a noble life. Whether she was greater as a Queen or as a woman is hard to say. Her good influence upon

INDEX TO DEPARTMENTS.

society and individual character is beyond estimate or calculation. It is rare that the personal worth of a royal personage equals in public estimation the reputation that attaches to the royal office, but, great as has been the glory of her political reign, her personal sway over the manners, the morals, and the hearts of men and women of all nations has given her a worldwide dominion, and brings at her death an extent of profound sorrow and mourning which comprehends the whole civilized world."

Secretary of the Treasury Gage said:

"The death of England's well-loved Queen closes the happiest period in all her country's existence. Victoria was, by force of character, conspicuous in molding the life and tendencies of the English people during her reign. She will be venerated by them because of her personal qualities, purity of mind, and integrity of character. She was endowed with a clear and independent judgment, which early won the profound respect of her official advisers and the love of her countrymen. This respect and love have increased as the years have gone by. A sovereign under the theory of 'divine right,' she was in reality the head of a highly democratic State. Her sympathies were toward the people. The people recognized the fact, and repaid her with a generous and loving confidence. To few on earth has it been given so to guide the unfolding destinies of a mighty nation. She will live in the hearts of the people wherever the English tongue is spoken as a good woman, a wise ruler, and a worthy exemplar for all who may be clothed with political responsibility, whether under democratic or aristocratic forms of government. The greatest laureate of her reign might well have had her in mind when he wrote:

'Tis only noble to be good.
Kind hearts are more than coronets.'"

Secretary of the Navy Long said:

"I feel the greatest respect for Queen Victoria, both as the sovereign of a mighty empire and as a woman who has borne herself with dignity through a long reign and set an example of a noble, devoted, pure, and useful life."

Secretary of the Interior Hitchcock expressed his sympathy as follows:

"The American people will deeply and sincerely sympathize with their kinsmen across the sea in their irreparable loss of a devoted sovereign, whose pure and gracious personality and illustrious reign have so abundantly blessed the people of her great dominion, and which have contributed so effectively to Christian civilization in every quarter of the world."

Postmaster General Smith expressed his sympathy in the following statement:

"She has been a model Queen and a model woman, and her death will be a source of sorrow throughout the world."

Secretary of Agriculture Wilson said:

"She has been a good, exemplary Christian woman, and one of the wisest rulers Great Britain has had."

AT THE BRITISH EMBASSY.

The announcement of the death of Queen Victoria was received with universal sorrow at the many embassies and legations in Washington, and nowhere was the sentiment of bereavement more poignantly felt than at the British Embassy. Lord Pauncefote had expected that the end could not be long deferred, and had been prepared for the sad intelligence that the Queen was no more. But it came to him almost as a personal affliction, for it was only a few months ago that he was the guest of the Queen at Osborne, when she elevated him to the Peerage. Aside from this, her Majesty had frequently shown most gracious consideration to the Ambassador and Lady Pauncefote, inviting them to Windsor and to Osborne for visits which were something more than brief official calls.

On the last occasion when Lord Pauncefote saw the Queen at Osborne, she was in excellent health, considering her years, her mental faculties keen and observant. She drove about the palace grounds and conversed freely and pleasantly with the circle of friends gathered about her, which included, besides Lord and Lady Pauncefote, Prince Christian, and a number of the members of the royal family.

The Foreign Office has kept the Embassy advised by cable of the Queen's condition, and from these dispatches it became evident some days ago that the Queen's death was near at hand. The Ambassador and the members of his family, as well as the large circle of officials about him, are keenly affected by the event, for to each one of them the Queen had been something more than a monarch, and had been regarded as a gentle superior and friend.

Official business proceeds as usual, for in the eye of the law the national existence is in no wise interrupted by the death of the Sovereign. But throughout the Embassy, and particularly in the private quarters of the Ambassador, a sense of deep gloom prevails. About the Embassy there are many personal mementoes of devotion to the Queen. At the head of the main staircase hangs a superb oil portrait showing her Majesty soon after her coronation, young, radiant, and beautiful. It is by Sir George Hayter, Court Painter during the early days of the Victorian reign, and is a counterpart of that in the Grand Corridor at Windsor Palace. In the Ambassador's library hangs another portrait of the Queen, showing her with the royal diadem on her brow.

The proprieties of the occasion forbid Lord Pauncefote to publicly speak at this time, but to his large circle of friends he has expressed his heartfelt sorrow. Among the British officials there is but one view as to the reign of Victoria. They look upon it as transcending in importance the Elizabethan or other eras, and as being more fraught with great achievements than any epoch in English history. But the personal character of the Queen attracts as much respect and tribute as the glories of her reign.

It is too early to say what official tribute the British Embassy will pay to the dead Sovereign. These formalities must await the determination of the new King and his Ministers. It is probable that the King will reissue to Lord Pauncefote the credentials of Ambassador to the United States, and the Foreign Office will announce what the period of mourning is to be. Whether there will be commemorative exercises, similar to those held in Washington after the death of the Empress of Austria and of the King of Italy, will depend upon the instructions issued from London. In any event, Lord Pauncefote and those about him are withdrawn for some time from participation in the social and official affairs at the capital.

The German Embassy shares in the universal sorrow, and there is an added sentiment of bereavement in the fact that Emperor William is the grandson of the dead Queen. The German Ambassador, Dr. von Holleben, gives expression to his deep grief, and pays a tribute of respect and admiration for the noble life and the illustrious reign of the departed Queen.

At the French Embassy, M. Cambon, the Ambassador, spoke of the exemplary qualities of the Queen and her service to her country. M. Cambon's brother, Paul Cambon, is the French Ambassador at London, and in this capacity has had frequent audiences with the Queen, and has had opportunity to learn the gentleness and dignity of her character.

Count Cassini, the Russian Ambassador, spoke in the same vein of the noble qualities of the Queen. Similar expressions were made by the Duke de Arcos, the Spanish Minister; Minister Wu of China, Minister Takahira of Japan, and others. Indeed, the sentiments of mingled grief and admiration were universal and sincere. All the Ambassadors, Ministers, and their suites took early occasion, after receiving word of the Queen's death, to call at the British Embassy and leave their cards. Lord Pauncefote saw only a few of his most intimate associates, and received from them personal expressions of condolence.

ACTION IN OTHER CITIES.

Flags at Half Mast — Arrangements for Memorial Services.

ALBANY, Jan. 22.—A special service in honor of the memory of Queen Victoria will be held at All Saints' Cathedral, in this city, the leading church of the Episcopal diocese of Albany. The Right Rev. William Croswell Doane, when he learned of the death of the Queen, made this announcement:

"Mindful of the many people of English descent living in Albany, and convinced of the universal sympathy of all our citizens in the great sorrow of the death of the Queen of England, the Dean and Chapter of the Cathedral of All Saints unite with the Bishop in appointing a solemn service of memorial in the cathedral, of which notice will be given when the day is determined. It is the intention of the authorities of the cathedral that the service shall be representative, so far as the clergy go, of all the religious bodies, of any societies specially affiliated with England, and of all citizens of Albany who desire to unite in the commemoration of a noble life."

CHICAGO, Jan. 22.—Elaborate memorial services in honor of Great Britain's dead Queen will be held in Chicago by former Britons. Representative Chicago Englishmen, Irishmen, and Scotchmen, together with Canadians and other former subjects of the late sovereign, met this afternoon and arranged for a mass meeting to-morrow, at which plans for the memorial services will be adopted. Local representatives of foreign Governments presented themselves at the British Consulate this afternoon and tendered formal expressions of sympathy.

BOSTON, Jan. 22.—When the news of the Queen's death was received this afternoon a number of business houses displayed flags at half mast. Many of the vessels in the harbor also displayed colors, running up their ensign, streamers, and bunting half way on their staffs, fore and aft.

Immediately on receiving word of the death of the Queen, Mayor Hart instructed the City Messenger to have the flag on City Hall placed at half mast.

When the House of Representatives was opened this afternoon Chaplain Waldron referred feelingly to the death of the Queen and prayed for the proper guidance of the English Nation.

CHARLESTON, S. C., Jan. 22.—When Charleston was stricken by the earthquake in 1886 Queen Victoria promptly cabled a message of sympathy, and an autograph copy of the message is now among the archives of the city. To-night the City Counsel authorized the Mayor to send a message of condolence to the King on the death of the Queen.

KANSAS CITY, Mo., Jan. 22.—Great sorrow was expressed among all classes here to-day at the death of the Queen. F. Stanley Young, the British Vice Consul in Kansas City, called for a meeting of British residents and others to arrange a memorial service.

SACRAMENTO, Cal., Jan. 22.—The Senate to-day adopted the following resolution:

"That when the Senate adjourns it do so out of respect to the memory of Victoria I., late Queen of Great Britain and Ireland, and Empress of India, and as a mark of sympathy with that sentiment, which in the presence of her death makes all the world kin."

OLYMPIA, Washington, Jan. 22.—The Washington Legislature to-day passed a concurrent resolution of respect to the memory of the Queen.

LITTLE ROCK, Ark., Jan. 22.—The House to-day adopted a motion to adjourn out of respect to the memory of Queen Victoria.

MR. HARRISON'S TRIBUTE.

INDIANAPOLIS, Ind., Jan. 22.—When notified of the Queen's death to-day, ex-President Harrison said:

"No other death could have excited so general a sorrow. There are persons in every nation, other than Great Britain, whose death would more profoundly move the people of that nation, but Queen Victoria's death will bring real sadness to the hearts of more men and women than any other. The drumbeat did not define her dominions; the union jack was not the symbol of her larger empire. More hearts pulsated with love for her, and more knees bowed before her queenly personality than before the Queen of Great Britain. 'God Save the Queen' had become well-nigh a universal anthem.

"Heredity does not stay our quest for the real man or woman upon whose head a crown has fallen. Indeed, that has come to be the way of the world. The sovereign whose life is not clean, noble, sympathetic, whose personal character is below the best thought of his people is not loved, and the powers of an unloved King or Queen are shorn, however the law may run. Queen Victoria's power was larger than the law.

"I do not care to speculate as to the effect of the Queen's death upon European politics further than to say that a mighty influence on the side of peace has been lost. The British people will find it hard to adjust their minds and hearts to a succession. There will be a disposition to make the pause unusually long after the first member of the proclamation 'The Queen is dead,' but the other member will follow, and 'Long live the King' will be spoken resolutely by Britons everywhere.

"The new sovereign will be loyally supported in his constitutional prerogatives, and will not be denied an opportunity to win that dominion over the hearts of his people which they yielded to his mother."

What W. J. Bryan Said.

Special to The New York Times.

LINCOLN, Neb., Jan. 22.—Among the many expressions of sympathy and regret heard here, occasioned by the death of Queen Victoria, is the following from W. J. Bryan, who said:

"The death of Queen Victoria will be regretted in all lands. Her personal virtues won for her the love of her subjects and the respect of the world. Her successor will find it difficult to fill her place in public esteem."

Cardinal Gibbons Sorrowful.

BALTIMORE, Jan. 22.—Cardinal Gibbons, upon being informed of the death of Queen Victoria, plainly showed in face and manner that the intelligence caused him profound sorrow. "The death of Queen Victoria," said his Eminence, after a brief pause, "will send a thrill of sorrow throughout the world, not only because of the almost universal diffusion of the British Empire, but still more because of the domestic virtues of the woman whose long and eventful reign will be ever memorable in the annals of England and whose character will command the love of her subjects and the admiration of the civilized world."

EDWARD VII. LOSES A SUBJECT.

Robert Dawson of Chicago Renounced Allegiance Yesterday.

Special to The New York Times.

CHICAGO, Jan. 22.—To Robert Dawson belongs the distinction of being the first man of Chicago to declare his intention of renouncing allegiance to King Edward VII. of England.

The news of Queen Victoria's death had hardly reached here when Dawson filed a declaration of his intention to become a citizen of the United States. He appeared in the office of the Clerk of the Cook County Circuit Court shortly after noon and inquired for the naturalization clerk. When asked to what Prince, King, or potentate he owed allegiance, he responded, emphatically, "The King of Great Britain."

STOPPED IN MIDDLE OF HIS OATH.

News of Queen's Death Prevented Naturalization of British Subject.

An unusual incident marked the proceedings yesterday in the Naturalization Bureau in the Court House. Henry Zimmer, a British subject, was in the act of forswearing his allegiance to the Queen of England before Chief Clerk Loos, when another clerk rushed in and announced the death of the Queen.

Clerk Loos had just reached the part of the oath in which the person being naturalized promises to forswear allegiance to all foreign powers and potentates, and especially to the Queen of England, when the announcement of the Queen's death was made.

The words making Mr. Zimmer an American citizen had not been pronounced. There was a hasty consultation among the officials of the Naturalization Bureau, the upshot of which was that Chief Clerk Loos decided that he would not naturalize any more British subjects until the news of the Queen's death had officially been confirmed and her successor to the throne of England named officially.

Mr. Zimmer was disappointed at the turn affairs had taken, but left the building with the promise to return as soon as the throne of England had been filled.

TRIBUTE OF NEW YORK SCOTS.

Queen's Death Casts Gloom Over Their Annual Burns Celebration.

The death of Queen Victoria cast a gloom over the thirteenth annual Burns celebration of the New York Scottish Society, which was held at Assembly Hall, 156 Fifth Avenue, last night. There were about 500 members of the society present. The event of the evening was the speech of the Rev. Donald Sage Mackay of the Collegiate Reformed Church, on the death of Queen Victoria. When the speaker finished there were not a few wet eyes in the hall. Dr. Mackay said:

"It cannot be out of place to say a few words in reference to that common sorrow which touches all our hearts to-night—the death of Queen Victoria in the fullness of her years and amid the love and devotion of her people and with the respect of the whole world.

"Queen Victoria leaves behind her a record of high duty nobly done. The dignity of her womanhood, more than the dignity of her position, has made the title of 'Queen' a title of respect wherever her name is spoken. The womanliness of the Queen made possible the queenliness of the woman. In that fierce light which beats upon a throne she has stood all these years as one whom no slander could touch and no calumny harm. To-night as we express here a common sympathy with her children and her children's children, we are glad to think of her as one who held the citadel of a pure womanhood sacred and inviolate. She is enthroned in the memory of her people, but because of her greatness in the empire of the State, but because of her greatness in the empire of the home."

The programme for the evening consisted of Scotch ballads and organ numbers, a sword dance and a Highland fling, and an oration on Robert Burns. Miss Jessie N. Maclachlan, the Scotch soprano, made her first appearance in this city and was enthusiastically received.

NEW YORK'S MOURNING FOR QUEEN VICTORIA

Trinity Bell Tolls and Flags Are Hung at Half Mast.

Messages of Condolence Sent to the Prince of Wales and Lord Salisbury —Societies to Take Action.

The tolling of the bell of Trinity Church and, the lowering to half mast of flags on many buildings apprised New Yorkers shortly after 1 o'clock yesterday afternoon that Queen Victoria had passed away.

The first announcement of the Queen's death was received here shortly before 1 o'clock, and was confirmed by additional dispatches. William C. Broughton, sexton of Trinity Church, received early a private cable from London and immediately began tolling the bell.

The news spread rapidly throughout the city. The newspaper extras were selling on the streets at 1:30, and the newsboys did a rushing trade. On every street corner groups formed discussing the tidings, and on all sides were heard expressions of sorrow and praise for the departed Queen. Large crowds gathered in front of the newspaper offices' bulletin boards until late in the evening.

Immediately upon receipt of the news from London the flag on the Commercial Cable building, opposite the City Hall, was lowered to half mast, and very soon the same was done on almost every building on Broadway.

At 2:40 P. M. a cable dispatch was received at the British Consulate, 17 State Street, confirming the report of the Queen's death. It was not official confirmation, which would come through the Embassy at Washington, but it was of such a nature as to remove all doubt in the mind of the Consul General, Sir Percy Sanderson, who at once ordered the British union jack hoisted at half mast, and the Consulate closed, and the following notice posted on the doors:

In consequence of the death of Her Most Gracious Majesty Queen Victoria this Consulate General is closed.

The British Consulate will remain closed except for important business. A book was opened yesterday for callers to inscribe their names.

The flag of the Russian Consulate, which is in the same building, was at once put at half-mast, and the National flags of Austria-Hungary, Mexico, France, Germany, Italy, Sweden, and many other countries were unfurled to the breezes at half-mast directly the news was heard at the respective Consulates.

The Earl of Drogheda, who is at the Cambridge Hotel, was much affected by the news. At other hotels where visiting Englishmen are guests the latter manifested great sorrow.

IN THE FINANCIAL DISTRICTS.

The news was received in Wall Street at 1:14 P. M. It was at once followed by a general display of flags at half-mast, until the street looked like a continuous line of waving bunting right down to the East River. In the insurance and underwriting districts where British interests are especially prominent almost every building displayed one or more English flags at half-mast.

A big royal standard was suspended from the windows of the Royal Insurance Company of London, and flags at half mast were also exhibited on the following buildings: North British and Mercantile, Commercial Union of London, Liverpool and London and Globe, Anglo-American, J. P. Morgan & Co., H. B. Hollins & Co., Manhattan Trust Company, Baring, Magoun & Co., Central National Bank, Hanover National Bank, Western National Bank, the United Bank, the Equitable Life Insurance Building, the Maritime Exchange, the Bowling Green Building, the Battery Park Building, the Chesebrough Building, and scores of other skyscrapers.

Some comment was heard because the flag on the City Hall was not placed at half staff. It had been reported that this was done in keeping with the Mayor's order, but this was denied. It was said, on the other hand, that no official notice of the death had been received until the time flags are usually taken in for the night, and that the flag would be placed at half mast to-day.

The news had no perceptible effect on the stock market quotations, other than a trifling halt.

It seemed to be the opinion of the more prominent financiers that the Queen's death would work very little if any change in the policy of the British Empire.

Cecil Baring, head of the banking house of Baring, Magoun & Co., and a member of the Baring family of London, said that in his opinion affairs in the British Empire would go along without the slightest hitch. He looked for no change of policy, thought that the present campaign in South Africa would be continued to a successful end, and that the value of good securities would be little affected.

Up town most of the well-known hotels had their flags at half-mast, and before dark a large number of the leading business places up town also had their flags at half-mast. Arnold, Constable & Co. and the Constable Building were among the first places to be so decorated. Aitken, Son & Co., at Eighteenth Street and Broadway, had a large British flag and half a dozen American flags all at half-mast. Among other buildings where the usual tribute of sorrow was paid were Tiffany's, Steinway's, and the University Building, in Washington Square.

Many of the vessels in the harbor, irrespective of nationality, also showed the sign of respect to the memory of the Queen by lowering their ensigns. For miles along the Brooklyn shore and along the New York side of the East River every English ship had her ensign at half-mast.

The big British steamship companies are making arrangements to drape their Broadway offices and piers, and yesterday orders were telephoned to lower the ensigns on several of the big liners. The Campania of the Cunard Line and the Vaderland and the Southwark of the Red Star Line each lowered its ensign, also the Manitou of the Atlantic Transport Line. The Patricia of the Holland-America Line and the cruising yacht of the Hamburg-American Line paid a similar tribute.

At a meeting of the Empire State Society of the Sons of the American Revolution, held at the rooms of the Aldine Association, the following was adopted and cabled to the American Ambassador at London:

The Empire State Society Sons of the American Revolution learns with sorrow the death of her gracious Majesty, Victoria, Queen of Great Britain and Empress of India. She has left a crown on earth for one more glorious in heaven. Her character remains an example to the world for all time.
EDWIN VAN D. GAZZAM, Secretary.

The Canadian Society of New York sent the following message to the Marquis of Salisbury:

Jan. 22, 1901.
To the Marquis of Salisbury, London, England:
The Canadian Society of New York sends loving sympathy to family of our late gracious Queen. BARTINDALE, President.

The New York branch of the Salvation Army sent a message of condolence to the Prince of Wales. It read:

Jan. 21, 1901.
His Royal Highness, the Prince of Wales, Osborne:
On behalf of American Salvationists we assure your Royal Highness and members of royal family of our profoundest sympathy and prayers.
FREDERICK AND EMMA BOOTH TUCKER.

The following reply was received:

Osborne Gov't, Jan. 22, 1901.
Frederick Booth Tucker, American Salvationists, 123 West Fourteenth Street, New York:
Prince of Wales thanks the American Salvationists for telegram of sympathy.

The Associated Press received the following telegram from Alfred Harmsworth, editor of The London Daily Mail:

ST. AUGUSTINE, Fla., Jan. 22.—May I be allowed to convey to the American newspapers my fraternal congratulations on the magnificent enterprise and broad spirit with which they have handled the passing of our lamented Queen.
ALFRED HARMSWORTH,
Editor London Daily Mail.

Sir Percy Sanderson, British Consul General, issued an announcement last night that all British subjects resident in the city are invited to attend a meeting to be held at the Down-Town Association, 60 Pine Street, to-morrow at 4 o'clock in the afternoon, to take suitable action on the death of the Queen.

Notices were sent out last night for a special meeting of the St. Andrew's Society, to take notice of the death of the Queen. Andrew Carnegie, the society's President, has offered the use of Carnegie Hall for the purpose, but it was thought that a larger attendance would be attracted if the meeting were held down town. The dinner given annually by the society in honor of the birthday of Robert Burns has been postponed. It had been arranged for Friday.

At the regular annual business meeting of the St. George's Society, to be held at Delmonico's to-night, appropriate action will be taken in relation to the passing of the Queen and the accession of the King. G. G. Ward, President, called yesterday afternoon upon the British Consul General and discussed plans for a union memorial meeting of all the local societies composed of British citizens. This meeting will probably be held in Trinity Church.

St. David's Society will also hold a special meeting to adopt resolutions on the Queen's death. The time and place of meeting will probably be announced to-day by Julien T. Davies, its President.

Dr. John A. Irwin, President of the British Schools and Universities Club, issued yesterday a call to members for a memorial service on Sunday. It will probably take place in the Church of the Heavenly Rest, the Rev. D. Parker Morgan, rector.

OPINIONS OF THE QUEEN.

Bishop Potter spoke on the Queen as follows:

"In my opinion, there has been no political bond that has bound together the British Empire with more power, if as much, as the bond of personal devotion to this beautiful character and personality. I was much struck, on my recent trip around the world, to observe the extent to which this extreme personal devotion was noticeable. People who had never seen the Queen, had never even been in England, and never expected to go there, appeared to feel the same personal devotion as Englishmen themselves. The attraction and cohesive force of this sentiment upon colonial life was very remarkable."

Bishop Hartzell said:

"The death of Queen Victoria removes from the midst of men a most exalted personality. Her influence for good, as wife, mother, and Queen, has been wonderful, and history will accord to her a first place as a leader and benefactor of the race."

Charles D. Pierce, Consul General of the Orange State and Treasurer of the Boer Relief Fund in this country, observed that the Queen, "who was possessed in the highest degree of those Christian sentiments that have underlain the whole course of her reign," was forced into the war "by the malign influences of a Chamberlain and a Milner, who, by systematic misrepresentation, kept the truth from her." Of the Boers he said: "They have always believed that the Queen was their friend."

NO INSURANCE ON QUEEN HERE.

Report that She Had Interests in New York Real Estate Discredited.

Insurance companies of this country are by many supposed to have carried large risks dependent on the life of Queen Victoria. According to officials of the three largest insurance companies in this city that supposition is wrong.

Richard A. McCurdy, President of the Mutual Life Insurance Company, said last night that his company carried no insurance risk dependent on the life of the Queen.

"Queen Victoria," said Mr. McCurdy, "has not been an insurable risk for many years on account of her age and the condition of her health. If there is any insurance on her life it must be of old standing and in British companies. At the time of the Queen's jubilee many policies were taken out by tradesmen and business men of England, who had an interest in the Queen's survival beyond that date because of the loss which her death before that time would have caused them. We took a large amount of these risks, but, fortunately for us, the Queen survived beyond the term of their expiration—they were only for a few months—and the money paid in was so much gain to us."

James H. Hyde, a Director in the Equitable Life Assurance Company, and that his company does not insure the lives of sovereigns on account of their liability of being assassinated.

John A. McCall, President of the New York Life Insurance Company, said that the Queen was not insured in his company, and that the company never received an application for such insurance from any one, here or abroad.

The report that the Queen had large interests in real estate in this city was discredited by all these officials. One of them said:

"The reasons, such as fear of revolutions, &c., which might prompt other monarchs to invest part of their money at least outside of their own country would not hold good in the case of England, with its great stability, largely due to its insular pride."

News Broken to Empress Frederick.

LONDON, Jan. 23.—"The news of her mother's death was tenderly broken to Dowager Empress Frederick late this evening," says a dispatch to The Daily Mail from Frankfort. "It was a terrible shock, but the Empress is bearing up bravely. The trials of the last few days, however, have exercised a most prejudicial effect upon her health, which causes serious anxiety."

CHILD HURT UNDER A CAR.

Uninjured by Wheels, She Was Burned by the Electric Fluid.

Special to The New York Times.

VICKSBURG, Miss., Jan. 22.—Emma Marshall, the pretty little daughter of Policeman Marshall, was fatally injured late this afternoon in a peculiar manner by an electric car, and the accident also came very near resulting in the death of Motorman Williams. The child was playing in the street, and ran in front of Williams's car. She was knocked down and the car passed half way over her before Williams succeeded in stopping it. He, thinking the girl had been crushed, started to reverse his controller to back the car off the body.

Spectators, who saw that the child was alive and safe so long as the car remained standing, yelled to Williams not to move, but he misunderstood them, evidently thinking they were about to attack him for killing the child, and turned on all the power. There was a flash, a tongue of blue flame came out from under the car, and the little girl was burned almost beyond recognition.

POWER FROM NIAGARA FALLS.

Its Use Will Be a Feature at the Pan-American Exposition.

Special to The New York Times.

NIAGARA FALLS, N. Y., Jan. 22.—In the central station of the Niagara Falls Power Company there are now ten huge dynamos in operation, each one of which generates 5,000 horse power, which is said to be the largest amount of electricity generated under a single roof in the world. Ground for this remarkable power plant was broken on Oct. 4, 1890.

When the plan of the Pan-American Exposition was conceived it was quickly recognized that the presence of Niagara electrical energy would be a wonderful factor in the success of the exposition, and as the plans of the exposition have been developed the value of the transmitted force from Niagara has become so pronounced in connection with the Pan-American Exposition that its application and use in various ways are expected to be a leading feature of the exposition.

GUGGENHEIMS IN THE TRUST.

Last of the Smelter Plants Will Be Transferred Soon.

Special to The New York Times.

DENVER, Col., Jan. 22.—Maurice Untermyer of New York, one of the attorneys of the American Smelting Company, said today that the Guggenheim family will in the future practically have charge of the Smelter Trust.

The Guggenheim plants remained independent for months after the trust was formed. When they came in it was on a basis of $20,000,000 for their different works at Perth Amboy, N. J.; Pueblo, and Monterey, Mexico, and with the understanding that the Guggenheim family was to be consulted in all the business and plans of the combine. Samuel Guggenheim was made Chairman of the Executive Board of the American Smelting Company, which virtually places him at the head of the concern.

Mr. Untermyer is on his way to Mexico to close up the transfer of the Monterey smelters to the trust.

PAPER MILLS IN THE WEST.

New Company Will Acquire Property of Denver Paper Company.

Special to The New York Times.

DENVER, Col., Jan. 22.—The Federal Court to-day discharged the receiver of the Denver Paper Company and authorized the transfer of the property to the Rocky Mountain Paper Company, capitalized at $1,350,000, which will be incorporated at once. The property includes the Denver Mill and the Platte River Mill, both near Denver. The capacity of the mills will be doubled.

Contracts have been made through the President of the new company, Thomas H. Savery, who is also Vice President of the Pusey & Jones Company of Wilmington, Del., manufacturers of paper machinery, to equip the consolidated mills with whatever may be required to make them equal to the most advanced and representative plants in the East. Three carloads of new machinery will be set up in the next two weeks.

KING OF GREAT BRITAIN

Personal Character of Victoria's Son and Successor.

Popular with All Classes, He Has Refrained from Politics—His Affability and Tact.

The new King of England comes to the throne of Great Britain and Ireland, its honors and responsibilities, in the third month of the sixtieth year of his rather uneventful and yet somewhat spectacular life. For forty years he has performed the public and spectacular duties of a sovereign. He steps to the throne rather with the reputation of a man of the world than that of a statesman and politician.

A tactful, courteous man, he takes up his sceptre with the reputation of a popular idol of the people, such as would not have been attached to him had he been called on to assume authority a score of years ago. A rather plentiful sowing of the wild oats that young noblemen think necessary had then aroused something of opposition to him. But that reputation he has, to a certain extent, lived down, and since the serious illness of 1871, that threatened his life, he has become, in fact, the first gentleman of England, if not of Europe.

Tactfulness may be called the chief characteristic of Great Britain's new sovereign. He has possessed it to such degree that even on his taking up the duties of his sovereignty it is very doubtful if the most intimate advisers of the late Queen know what is his politics, or if he has any, for that matter, so close-mouthed has he been. Never by any public pronouncement has he permitted his future subjects to know what were his views on the various political questions that agitated them. Yet he has managed to avoid offense to any of the factions in which the English nation is divided.

He has by the same policy avoided any complications in international politics, and, save for the marked preference he has shown for the society of Americans, his preferences in international affairs are hardly more than to be guessed at. Certainly there is no public record on which to base an assertion that he favors this or that policy. So he ascends the throne a man bound to no expressed policy, with hands unfettered, and free to act as he thinks best for the good of the great nation he is called on to rule. He is thus a unique personage.

There has been no Marlborough House clique, politically, and so, as far as is known publicly at least, he has no friends to reward or enemies to punish. Yet he is said to be a man of pronounced political views and with a well-defined policy that he has quietly outlined while patiently awaiting the event that has now called him to the throne.

Born at Buckingham Palace Nov. 9, 1841, the eldest son of Victoria and Albert started out in life burdened with fewer names than it is usually the fate of such royal personages to bear, as he was named only Albert Edward. Less than a month after his birth he was by patent created Prince of Wales and Earl of Chester. To these titles were afterward added a string of a score or so. Educated by private tutors on a plan outlined by his father, he later studied for a time at Edinburgh and later at Christ Church, Oxford, and at Cambridge as well.

Then followed a period of travel in Europe and the East, followed by the trip to Canada and America in 1860. This latter was undertaken under the guidance of the Duke of Newcastle at the instance of the Prince Consort, who did not altogether approve of the sort of life the heir to the throne was living, nor the companions he sought among the gilded youth of the time.

That tour was, in fact, a triumphant one for the lad. His receptions in Canada and this country alike were enthusiastic in the extreme. Chicago, Washington, Richmond, Philadelphia, New York, Boston, and Portland, Me., alike extended to him a most cordial welcome. He was constantly feasted and fêted. President Buchanan and his official family made him more than welcome. The like courtesies extended elsewhere laid the foundation for the liking he always entertained for Americans.

After this trip here he made a tour of Germany, Italy, and the Holy Land in 1862, with Dean Stanley as his mentor. A year later he was married to Alexandra, daughter of the Danish Prince, who some months later became King Christian IX. On her mother's side Alexandra was descended from George II. of England, so that she was related to him. The wedding ceremony was performed in St. George's Chapel, Windsor, March 10, 1863.

The year following his marriage the Prince visited Denmark, Sweden, and Russia. Still later there were trips to Egypt, Turkey, the Holy Land, Greece, and other Mediterranean countries. The culmination of his experiences as a traveler was the trip to India in 1875-6, for which Parliament voted a grant of £100,000. This was made on the warship Serapis, and is said to have cost the nation upward of £200,000 before all the bills were settled.

Six children were born to the Prince of Wales, four of whom are still living, the eldest, and heir to the throne of his father, being George Frederick Ernest Albert, Duke of York, and father of four children, three sons and a daughter. Other living children of the Prince are the Duchess of Fife; Maud, wife of Prince Charles of Denmark, and the unmarried Princess Victoria. His eldest son, the Duke of Clarence and Avondale, died shortly after his betrothal to Princess Mary of Teck, who later married the Duke of York. The youngest child of the Prince, also a son, died shortly after its birth. As royal marriages go, the marriage of the Prince was considered a happy one, and the royal pair have appeared in public as a satisfied pair, whatever their private life may have been.

Twice since he has been the apparent heir to the throne have fears been entertained that the Prince would not live to assume his sovereign rights. The first time was in 1871, when he had a severe attack of typhoid fever. The Prince was removed to his home, at Sandringham, and there, after a long illness, recovered his health and strength. In July, 1898, while on a visit to Baron Ferdinand Rothschild at Weddeston Manor, he slipped on the stairs and fell, breaking his knee-cap. Other complications ensuing, he was confined to his house for several weeks, and then England feared that he would not outlive his injuries.

It was as a lover of sports that the Prince came nearest to the hearts of the mass of his people. He has been a constant attendant at the sports of the colleges, a lover of cricket and boating, as well as of athletics. Shooting was ever his favorite sport, and amounted almost to a passion with him. For racing he had a penchant, and for years he has maintained a racing stable, having twice won the Derby. His yachting successes were mostly with the Britannia. As a young man he was a good rider, but increasing weight compelled him to abandon the saddle. He drives some, but is not an enthusiast.

Cards were, and probably are still, the favorite game of the new sovereign. Fondness for the pasteboards and playing for high stakes have made trouble for Albert Edward on many occasions. Chief of these, perhaps, was the Tranby Croft baccarat scandal, in which were involved Sir Gordon Cumming, Mrs. Wilson, and Lady Brooke—"the babbling Brooke" she was called after it. This brought the Prince into court and made no end of talk, both in England and here, in 1889. Only the shrewdness of the Duchess of Devonshire prevented an almost as bad scandal from being made public property as it was private chatter in the set in which the Prince and his friends moved.

In this George Russell, the private secretary of the Prince previous to the installation of Sir Francis Knollys, was implicated and later Russell's operations became so flagrant that he was obliged to leave England and was expelled from the clubs to which he belonged. It was his unwillingness to stop playing baccarat during Goodwood race week that led to a quarrel between the Prince and the Duke of Richmond, one of the most trusted advisers of the Queen. The Duke found the Prince and his party playing baccarat for high stakes, so he claimed, after the Prince had given him his word there should be no card playing in the house.

There was a violent scene, and only by the greatest of tact was a scandal prevented. Later the Prince refused an invitation to Welbeck Abbey, going instead to the house of Willie James, an Australian millionaire, with his party, while the Duke of York and his friends were entertained at Welbeck Abbey. This led to a social upheaval and gossip that lasted a whole season. It was also asserted that the Queen would not allow the Prince to occupy Windsor during Ascot Week because he insisted on baccarat while the races were the attraction there. So set was the Prince on his card games that he took a private cottage there for the week instead of occupying Windsor without the cards.

The income of the Prince has been set at £100,000 per annum, of which amount £40,000 came from the settlement made for him at the time of his marriage. The balance came from the Duchy of Cornwall, and aggregated a trifle more than £60,000 per annum.

Frank, loyal, and warm-hearted, and almost affectionate, his friends say, the Prince has ever been. Those who have had the pleasure of his association say the same of him. He was emphatically of the "good-fellow" sort—simple, courteous, but a stickler for the courtesy and deference his position as heir to the throne demanded. For one occupying the position he has for so many years, he was approachable, good-natured, and affable, so long as those who met him remembered his prerogatives, used Sir whenever they spoke to him, and remembered never to speak until spoken to or failed to make topics instead of allowing him to do the suggesting.

The Prince was an honorary officer of so many military corps in Europe that his uniforms alone constituted a formidable wardrobe. Yet he had so little liking for display in this direction that he never wore them except on occasions when it was absolutely necessary for him to do so. Taken all in all, an Englishman would sum him up as being "not at all a bad sort."

The new King is a habitual theatregoer, and, though the death of his brother Alfred, Duke of Edinburgh and Saxe-Coburg-Gotha, last Summer, and the enforced period of mourning in the Court, kept him away from the playhouses more than four months, some enterprising London chronicler estimates that he went to the theatre no fewer than forty-eight times in the year 1900.

As Prince of Wales, however, he never dabbled in theatricals and never became so closely allied with persons of the theatre as his illustrious predecessor who bore that title, and made it glitter at the beginning of the nineteenth century.

Albert Edward has presided at banquets of the Royal General Theatrical Fund and other formal theatrical gatherings, and has met all the leaders of the English stage in his time. In short, he has cared for the theatre, but he has not meddled with it or ever posed as its patron. He has shown only the Englishman's traditional liking for "the play" as an entertainment.

With his two nephews, William of Germany and Nicholas of Russia, he will now become one of a trio that will rule the greater part of Europe. How he will get on with them is the problem that the world will now patiently wait to see solved.

DOELGER'S LIVELY ENCOUNTER.

Claims Men Were Trying to Rob Him, but They Wait Until He Summons the Police.

A telephone message received by Sergt. Walsh of the East Fifty-first Street Station shortly after 11 o'clock last night informed him that burglars were in the building at 234 East Fifty-fifth Street.

Capt. Lantry was in the station at the time. He ordered the patrol wagon to be made ready, and with Detectives McLaughlin and Roach and several policemen started for the place. They found that the building was occupied as the office of Joseph Doelger & Sons, brewers. A bright light was burning in the front office.

The building was surrounded. Some of the policemen tried to enter by the front door, but found it locked. Capt. Lantry and Detective McLaughlin went to the rear of the building through a hallway and were making an entrance through a window, when Peter Stobel, a watchman, who was on the inside, opened the front door, allowing the policemen to enter. In the meantime Capt. Lantry and the detective had entered a rear office. Lying on the floor they saw two well-dressed men. Standing over them, holding a Cuban machete in his hands, ready to strike the men, was Joseph Doelger, Jr.

When Capt. Lantry and several of the policemen who had entered by the front entrance approached Doelger dropped the machete, and fell into a chair prostrate. The police took the men to the station, where they described themselves as William Miller, twenty-seven years old, clerk in a broker's office and living at 323 East Seventy-second Street, and William Brown, twenty-five years old, a clerk, living at 307 East Seventy-sixth Street.

Doelger told the police that he had met the men on the street and had invited them into the office. He fell asleep and awoke in time, he said, to see the men going through his pockets. Doelger alleges the men took between $4 and $6 from him.

The prisoners denied the charge, saying that Doelger had been out drinking with them, and that soon after entering the office he fell asleep. Without any cause, they assert, Doelger jumped to the telephone and told the police that he was being robbed. Miller and Brown were locked up, charged with larceny.

Newport News Coal Trimmers' Strike.

Special to The New York Times.

NORFOLK, Va., Jan. 22.—As a result of the strike of all the coal trimmers at Newport News to-day, vessels are arriving at Lambert's Point, in Norfolk Harbor, for cargoes. The price paid for trimming cargoes is the cause of the trouble. Failing in an effort to secure the rate desired by the Coal Trimmers' Union, all the men stopped work at Newport News this afternoon, and since then every ship arriving there has been ordered here.

"All the News That's Fit to Print."

The New York Times.

THE WEATHER.
Fair, with variable winds, mostly east to south.

VOL. L...NO. 16,121. NEW YORK, SATURDAY, SEPTEMBER 7, 1901.—SIXTEEN PAGES. ONE CENT In Greater New York, Jersey City, and Newark. } Elsewhere. TWO CENTS.

PRESIDENT SHOT AT BUFFALO FAIR

Wounded in the Breast and Abdomen.

HE IS RESTING EASILY

One Bullet Extracted, Other Cannot Be Found.

Assassin Is Leon Czolgosz of Cleveland, Who Says He Is an Anarchist and Follower of Emma Goldman.

BUFFALO, Sept. 6.—President McKinley, while holding a reception in the Temple of Music at the Pan-American Exposition at 4 o'clock this afternoon, was shot and twice wounded by Leon Czolgosz, an Anarchist, who lives in Cleveland.

One bullet entered the President's breast, struck the breast bone, glanced and was later easily extracted. The other bullet entered the abdomen, penetrated the stomach, and has not been found, although the wounds have been closed.

The physicians in attendance upon the President at 10:40 o'clock to-night issued the following bulletin:

"The President is rallying satisfactorily and is resting comfortably. 10:15 P. M., temperature, 100.4 degrees; pulse, 124; respiration, 24.

"P. M. RIXEY,
"M. B. MANN,
"R. E. PARKE,
"H. MYNTER,
"EUGENE WANBIN.

"Signed by George B. Cortelyou, Secretary to the President."

This condition was maintained until 1 o'clock A. M., when the physicians issued the following bulletin:

"The President is free from pain and resting well. Temperature, 100.2; pulse, 120; respiration, 24."

The assassin was immediately overpowered and taken to a police station on the Exposition grounds, but not before a number of the throng had tried to lynch him. Later he was taken to Police Headquarters.

The exact nature of the President's injuries is described in the following bulletin issued by Secretary Cortelyou for the physicians who were called:

"The President was shot about 4 o'clock. One bullet struck him on the upper portion of the breast bone, glancing and not penetrating; the second bullet penetrated the abdomen five inches below the left nipple and one and one-half inches to the left of the median line. The abdomen was opened through the line of the bullet wound. It was found that the bullet had penetrated the stomach.

"The opening in the front wall of the stomach was carefully closed with silk sutures; after which a search was made for a hole in the back wall of the stomach. This was found and also closed in the same way. The further course of the bullet could not be discovered, although careful search was made. The abdominal wound was closed without drainage. No injury to the intestines or other abdominal organs was discovered.

"The patient stood the operation well, pulse of good quality, rate of 130, and his condition at the conclusion of operation was gratifying. The result cannot be foretold. His condition at present justifies hope of recovery."

Leon Czolgosz, the assassin, has signed a confession, covering six pages of foolscap, in which he states that he is an Anarchist and that he became an enthusiastic member of that body through the influence of Emma Goldman, whose writings he had read and whose lectures he had listened to. He denies having any confederate, and says he decided on the act three days ago and bought the revolver with which the act was committed in Buffalo.

He has seven brothers and sisters in Cleveland, and the Cleveland Directory has the names of about that number living in Hosmer Street and Ackland Avenue, which adjoin. Some of them are butchers and others are in other trades.

Czolgosz is now detained at Police Headquarters, pending the result of the President's injuries. He does not appear in the least degree uneasy or penitent for his action. He says he was induced by his attention to Emma Goldman's lectures and writings to decide that the present form of government in this country was all wrong, and he thought the best way to end it was by the killing of the President. He shows no sign of insanity, but is very reticent about much of his career.

While acknowledging himself an Anarchist, he does not state to what branch of the organization he belongs.

HOW THE DEED WAS DONE.

Assassin Came with the Crowd to Greet the President and Shot When Two Feet from Him.

BUFFALO, Sept. 6.—Czolgoz's attempt on the life of the President was made at about 4 o'clock in the Temple of Music, where Mr. McKinley had gone to hold a reception at that hour. He had spent the day at Niagara with about 100 invited guests, and arrived at the exposition grounds at 3:30. Mrs. McKinley proceeded to the Mission Building and the President went directly to the Temple of Music.

A vast crowd had assembled long before the arrival of Mr. McKinley. The daily organ recital was nearing its end as the President entered and went to the slightly raised dais at one end of the hall.

The President, though well guarded by United States Secret Service detectives, was fully exposed to such an attack as occurred. He stood at the edge of the raised dais, and throngs of people crowded in at the various entrances to see their Chief Executive, perchance to clasp his hand, and then fight their way out in the good-natured mob that every minute swelled and multiplied at the points of ingress and egress to the building.

The President was in a cheerful mood and was enjoying the hearty evidences of good-will which everywhere met his gaze. Upon his right stood John G. Milburn of Buffalo, President of the Pan-American Exposition, chatting with the President, and introducing to him persons of note who approached. Upon the President's left stood Mr. Cortelyou.

THE ASSASSIN APPEARS.

It was shortly after 4 o'clock when one of the throng which surrounded the Presidential party, a medium-sized man of ordinary appearance and plainly dressed in black, approached as if to greet the President. Both Secretary Cortelyou and President Milburn noticed that the man's hand was swathed in a bandage or handkerchief. Reports of bystanders differ as to which hand. He worked his way with the stream of people up to the edge of the dais, until he was within two feet of the President.

President McKinley smiled, bowed, and extended his hand in that spirit of geniality the American people so well know, when suddenly the man raised his hand and two sharp reports of a revolver rang out loud and clear above the hum of voices and the shuffling of myriad feet. The assassin had fired through the handkerchief which concealed the revolver.

There was an instant of almost complete silence, like the hush that follows a clap of thunder. The President stood stock still, a look of hesitancy, almost of bewilderment, on his face. Then he retreated a step while a pallor began to steal over his features. The multitude seemed only partially aware that something serious had happened.

Then came a commotion. With the leap of a tiger three men threw themselves forward as with one impulse and sprang toward the would-be assassin. Two of them were United States Secret Service men, who were on the lookout and whose duty it was to guard against just such a calamity as had here befallen the President and the Nation. The third was a bystander, a negro, who had only an instant before grasped the hand of the President. In a twinkling the assassin was borne to the ground, his weapon was wrested from his grasp, and strong arms pinioned him down.

Then the vast multitude which thronged the edifice began to come to a realizing sense of the awfulness of the scene of which they had been witnesses. A murmur arose, spread, and swelled to a hum of confusion, then grew to a babel of sounds, and later to a pandemonium of noises.

The crowds that a moment before had stood mute and motionless in bewildered ignorance of the enormity of the deed, now with a single impulse surged forward, while a hoarse cry welled up from a thousand throats, and a thousand men charged forward to lay hands upon the perpetrator of the dastardly crime.

CONFUSION REIGNS.

For a moment the confusion was terrible. The crowd surged forward regardless of consequences. Men shouted and fought, women screamed and children cried. Some of those nearest the doors fled from the edifice in fear of a stampede, while hundreds of others from the outside struggled blindly forward in the effort to enter the crowded building and solve the mystery of excitement and panic which every moment grew and swelled within the congested interior of the palatial edifice.

Inside on the slightly raised dais was enacted within those few feverish moments a tragedy, so dramatic in character, so thrilling in its intensity, that few who looked on will ever be able to give a succinct account of what really did transpire. Even the actors who were playing the principal rôles came out of it with blanched faces, trembling limbs, and beating hearts, while their brains throbbed with a tumult of conflicting emotions which left behind only a chaotic jumble of impressions which could not be clarified into a lucid narrative of the events as they really transpired.

But of the multitude which witnessed or bore a part in the scene there was but one mind which seemed to retain it's equilibrium, one hand which remained steady, one eye which gazed with unflinching calmness, and one voice which retained its even tenor and faltered not at the most critical juncture.

They were the mind and the hand and the eye and the voice of President McKinley.

After the first shock of the assassin's shots, he retreated a step, then, as the detectives leaped upon his assailant, he turned, walked steadily to a chair and seated himself, at the same time removing his hat and bowing his head in his hands.

In an instant Secretary Cortelyou and President Milburn were at his side. His waistcoat was hurriedly opened, the President meanwhile admonishing those about him to remain calm and telling them not to be alarmed.

"But you are wounded," cried his secretary; "let me examine."

"No, I think not," answered the President. "I am not badly hurt, I assure you."

Nevertheless his outer garments were hastily loosened, and when a trickling stream of crimson was seen to wind its way down his breast spreading its stain over the white surface of the linen their worst fears were confirmed.

A force of Exposition guards were on the scene by this time, and an effort was made to clear the building. The crush was terrific. Spectators crowded down the stairways from the galleries, the crowd on the floor surged forward toward the rostrum, while despite the strenuous efforts of police and guards the throng without struggled madly to obtain admission.

IN THE HOSPITAL.

The President's assailant in the meantime had been hustled to the rear of the building by Exposition Guards McCauley and James, where he was held while the building was cleared, and later turned over to Superintendent Bull of the Buffalo Police Department, who took the prisoner to No. 13 Police Station, and later to Police Headquarters.

As soon as the crowd in the Temple of Music had been dispersed sufficiently the President was removed in the automobile ambulance and taken to the Exposition Hospital, where an examination was made.

The best medical skill was summoned and within a brief period several of Buffalo's best-known practitioners were at the patient's side. The President retained the full exercise of his faculties until placed on the operating table and subjected to an anaesthetic.

Upon the first examination it was ascertained that one bullet had taken effect in the right breast just below the nipple, causing a comparatively harmless wound. The other took effect in the abdomen, about five inches below the left nipple, two inches to the left of the navel, and about on a level with it.

Upon arriving at the Exposition Hospital the second bullet was probed for. The walls of the abdomen were opened, but teh ball was not located. The incision was hastily closed and after a hasty consultation it was decided to the remove the patient to the home of President Milburn. This was done, the automobile-ambulance being used for the purpose.

Arrived at the Milburn residence, all persons outside the medical attendants, nurses, and the officials immediately concerned were excluded and the task of probing for the bullet, which had lodged in the abdomen, was begun by Dr. Roswell Park.

When it was decided to remove the President from the Exposition Hospital to the Milburn residence, the news was broken to Mrs. McKinley as gently as might be, by the members of the Milburn family. She bore the shock remarkably well, and displayed the utmost fortitude.

CROWD READY TO LYNCH.

While the wounded President was being borne from the Exposition to the Milburn residence between rows of onlookers with bared heads, a far different spectacle was being witnessed along the route of his assailant's journey from the scene of his crime to Police Headquarters. The trip was made so quickly that the prisoner was safely landed within the wide portals of the police station and the doors closed before any one was aware of his presence.

The news of the attempted assassination had in the meanwhile been spread broadcast by the newspapers. Like wildfire it spread from mouth to mouth. Then bulletins began to appear on the boards along "Newspaper Row," and when the announcement was made that the prisoner had been taken to Police Headquarters, only two blocks distant from the newspaper section, the crowds surged down toward the terrace, eager for a glimpse of the prisoner. At Police Headquarters they were met by a strong cordon of police, drawn up across the pavement on Pearl Street, who denied admittance to any but officials authorized to take part in the examination of the prisoner.

In a few minutes the crowd had grown from tens to hundreds, and these in turn quickly swelled to thousands, until the street was completely blocked by a surging mass of eager humanity. It was at this juncture that some one raised the cry of "Lynch him!" Like a flash the cry was taken up, and the whole crowd re-echoed the cry, "Lynch him!" "Hang him!" Closer the crowd surged forward.

Denser the throng became as new arrivals each moment swelled the swaying multitude. The situation was becoming critical when suddenly the big doors were flung open and a squad of reserves advanced with solid front, drove the crowd back from the curb, then across the street, and gradually succeeded in dispersing them from about the entrance to the station.

By this time there were probably 30,000 people assembled in the vicinity of Pearl, Seneca, Erie Streets, and the Terrace. The crowd was so great that it became necessary to rope off the entire street in front of Police Headquarters, and at a late hour to-night the police were still patrolling in the streets in the neighborhood, in squads of three or four. Inside the station house were assembled District Attorney Penny, Superintendent of Police Bull, Capt. Reagan of the First Precinct, and other officials.

The prisoner at first proved quite communicative, so much so in fact, that little dependence could be placed on what he said. He first gave his name as Fred Nieman, said his home was in Detroit, and that he had been in Buffalo about a week. He said he had been boarding at a place in Broadway. Later this place was located as John Nowak's saloon, a Raines-law hotel, 1,078 Broadway. Here the prisoner occupied Room 8.

THE PRISONER'S STORY.

Nowak, the proprietor, said he knew very little about his guest. He came there, he declared, last Saturday, saying he had come to see the Pan-American, and that his home was in Toledo. He had been alone at all times about Nowak's place, and had had no visitors. In his room was found a small traveling bag of cheap make. It contained an empty cartridge box and a few articles of clothing.

With these facts in hand the police went at the prisoner with renewed vigor in the effort to obtain either a full confession or a straight account of his identity and movements prior to his arrival in Buffalo. He at first admitted that he was an Anarchist in sympathy at least, but denied strenuously that the attempt on the life of the President was a result of a preconcerted plot on the part of any Anarchist society.

At times he was defiant and again indifferent. But at no time did he betray the remotest sign of remorse. He declared the deed was not premeditated, but in the same breath refused to say why he perpetrated it. When charged by District Attorney Penny with being the instrument of an organized band of conspirators, he protested vehemently that he never even thought of perpetrating the crime until this morning.

After long and persistent questioning it was announced at Police Headquarters that the prisoner had made a confession, which he signed.

MRS. McKINLEY COURAGEOUS.

Bears Up Well When She Hears of the Attempt on Mr. McKinley's Life.

BUFFALO, N. Y., Sept. 6.—After the President was cared for at the Exposition grounds, Director General W. I. Buchanan started for the Milburn residence to forestall any information that might reach Mrs. McKinley there by telephone or otherwise. Very luckily, he was first to arrive with the information. The Niagara Falls trip had tired Mrs. McKinley, and on returning to the Milburn residence she went to her room to rest.

Mr. Buchanan broke the news as gently as possible to the nieces of Mr. and Mrs. McKinley, and consulted with them, and Mrs. Milburn as to the best course to pursue in breaking the news to Mrs. McKinley. It was finally decided that on her awaking, or shortly thereafter, Mr. Buchanan should break the news to her, if, in the meantime her physician, Dr. Rixey, had not yet arrived.

Mrs. McKinley awoke from her sleep at about 5:30 o'clock. She was feeling splendidly, she said, and at once took up her crocheting, which, as is well known, is one of her favorite diversions.

Immediately on Mr. Buchanan's arrival at the Milburn home he had telephonic communication therewith cut off, for already there had been several calls, and he decided on this as the wisest course to pursue lest Mrs. McKinley, hearing the continued ringing of the bells, might inquire what it meant.

While the light of day remained, Mrs. McKinley continued with her crocheting, keeping to her room. When the day began to wane and the President had not arrived, she began to feel anxious concerning him. "I wonder why he does not come?" she asked one of her nieces. There was no clock in Mrs. McKinley's room, and when it was 7 o'clock she had no idea it was so late, and this is when she began to feel anxious concerning her husband, for he was due to return to Mr. Milburn's house about 6 o'clock.

At 7 o'clock Dr. Rixey arrived at the Milburn residence. He had been driven hurriedly down Delaware Avenue in an open carriage, and at once entered the house. At 7:20 o'clock Dr. Rixey came out of the house accompanied by Col. Webb Hayes, a son of the late ex-President Hayes, who is a friend of President McKinley. They entered a carriage and returned to the Exposition hospital.

After Dr. Rixey had gone, Mr. Buchanan said that the doctor had broken the news in a most gentle way to Mrs. McKinley. He said she stood it bravely, though considerably affected. If it was possible to bring him to her, she wanted it done. Dr. Rixey assured her that the President could be brought with safety from the Exposition grounds, and when he left the Milburn house it was to complete all arrangements for the removal of the President.

A big force of regular patrolmen were assigned to the Milburn residence.

"CAUGHT THE ASSASSIN."

Capt. Wiser of Coast Artillery Says His Men Did So.

WASHINGTON, Sept. 6.—The War Department to-night received the following telegram from Capt. John B. Wiser, commanding the Seventy-third Company of Coast Artillery at Buffalo:

"BUFFALO, N. Y., Sept. 6, 1901.—Adjutant General, U. S. A., Washington: President shot at reception in Temple of Music about 4 P. M. Corporal Bertschey and detail of men of my company caught the assassin at once and held him down till the secret service men overpowered him and took the prisoner out of their hands, my men being unarmed. Condition of President not known. Revolver in my possession.

"WISER, Commanding."

OPINIONS OF SURGEONS.

Injury to Stomach Serious for a Man of the President's Age—Danger of Peritonitis.

According to well-known surgeons, there are in New York four or five persons each year who, through various causes, suffer from injuries similar to those received yesterday by President McKinley at Buffalo. Operations similar to those performed on the President have been successful and the patients have recovered. The prominent surgeons interviewed last evening said that the chances of recovery would be much greater if President McKinley were a younger man.

Dr. John B. Walker of 33 West Thirty-third Street said:

"Any injury to the stomach similar to that which has been inflicted on President McKinley is serious. There have been cases of stomach perforation where the patients have recovered. The diagnosis of any perforated wound of the stomach in an adult is very serious. The trouble is that inflammation following such an injury is more acute to an older person than to one more youthful. The fear is that the contents of the stomach will ooze into the intestines and peritonitis set in."

"Do you recall any recent cases similar to that of President McKinley," was asked.

"Dr. Bull performed an operation on a young man a short time ago. The intestines were perforated and an operation similar to that performed on President McKinley resulted in complete recovery. If President McKinley were a man between thirty-five and forty years of age the chances would be more in his favor. I cannot recall at this time a case of a man of the age of the President recovering from similar wounds. There is one advantage the President had, and that is the prompt assistance of a surgeon. Dr. Roswell Park is one of the most eminent surgeons in the United States."

"What other cases do you recall?"

"The case of the football player in Princeton who was shot by a negro is one of the latest. In that case the young man was of powerful physique. He did not receive the attention of a surgeon for twelve hours, and the result was that peritonitis set in and death occurred in a few days."

MR. ROOSEVELT EN ROUTE.

One Receipt of News the Vice President Leaves for Buffalo.

BURLINGTON, Vt., Sept. 6.—The first news of the attempted assassination of President McKinley reached Vice President Roosevelt at Isle La Motte at 5:30 o'clock this afternoon, when the Vice President was informed over the telephone that there was a rumor that the President had been shot. It was confirmed by another message a moment later.

The Vice President seemed stunned by the news, and put his hands to his head, then exclaimed, "My God!" Those around him were immediately informed of the tragedy, and it was decided to announce it to the company of a thousand persons who had gathered to hear Col. Roosevelt speak at the annual outing of the Vermont Fish and Game League. Senator Proctor made the announcement, and men, women, and children wept.

A later bulletin was received, stating that the President was resting quietly and that the chances were favorable for his recovery. "Good!" exclaimed the Vice President, and his face lighted up. He showed his pleasure by eagerly announcing the good news to the assembly.

The Vice President then left immediately on the yacht Elfrida, owned by W. Seward Webb, and came to this city as quickly as possible, having directed that all messages should be held for him here. The yacht was to have gone to Arrow Point, where a special train was waiting for the Vice President, but the train was sent on to Burlington, and was there when the yacht came into the harbor, at 8:15.

President Clement of the Rutland Railroad placed the train at the disposal of the Vice President, and made arrangements to take him on it to Buffalo. Col. Roosevelt was asked at the wharf for a statement for publication, and said:

"I am so inexpressibly grieved, shocked, and horrified that I can say nothing."

He boarded the train at once and left for Buffalo.

CABINET WILL ASSEMBLE.

Postmaster General Smith and Secretaries Root and Gage Off for Buffalo.

PHILADELPHIA, Sept. 6. — Postmaster General Charles Emory Smith was greatly affected by the news of the shooting of President McKinley, and expressed himself as shocked beyond measure. He immediately telegraphed to Washington and Buffalo, asking for further particulars than the early news dispatches contained. Mr. Smith said he hoped the President's injuries might not prove so serious as was at first intimated.

Mr. Smith left here on a late train to-night for Buffalo. He expects to be at the President's bedside by 9 o'clock to-morrow morning.

NEWBURY, N. H., Sept. 6.—A message containing information from Buffalo was received here early this evening and forwarded by messenger to the home of Secretary Hay. No reply came to it, and up to a late hour Secretary Hay could not be reached.

BUCKFIELD, Me., Sept. 6.—John D. Long, Secretary of the Navy, who has been passing his vacation at the Long homestead, two miles from this place, learned to-night of the shooting of President McKinley. He was deeply affected, and proceeded to his home at once, declaring that he was undecided about future plans. The Secretary positively refused to say anything for publication.

PITTSBURG, Sept. 6.—When informed of the shooting of President McKinley, Attorney General Knox said: "I cannot imagine how any living creature could harbor such a thought as to take the life of the President. I am so shocked at the awful news that I cannot talk further."

Mr. Knox left at 11 P. M. for Buffalo. Just before leaving he said:

"I can only express the common sentiment of horror at the cruelty of the dastardly blow inflicted upon the lovable and beloved man who has stood for all that is best for the people, who have so implicitly trusted him. His bodily wounds, grievous as they are, will cause him less pain than the thought that any human heart could have harbored against him the malice that inspired the deed."

DUBLIN, N. H., Sept. 6.—Secretary of the Interior Hitchcock, who has been at Mount Monadnock, when informed to-night of the tragic incident at Buffalo, said:

"I am too horrified to make any expression whatever." He immediately prepared to leave for Buffalo.

Secretary of War Elihu Root left the Grand Central Station at 11:10 last night for Buffalo in a special train. He was accompanied by a Dr. Dixon, a specialist, with whom he is hastening to the bedside of the President. The train was made up of a single coach and locomotive, and all possible speed will be made to reach Buffalo on record-breaking time

When Secretary Root was asked to express an opinion of the President's injury, he said:

"What is there to say? I do not know how seriously injured President McKinley is, but I hope his condition is not so serious as reported. I am almost overcome by the terrible news."

Secretary Root came up from Southampton, L. I., in a special train. With Dr. Dixon and a valet, he rode in a cab to the Grand Central Station. The special train had already been made up, and in less than three minutes after their arrival at the station they were speeding on their way to Buffalo.

Special to The New York Times.

CHICAGO, Sept. 6.—Secretary of the Treasury Gage, who was visiting his son, Eli Gage, in Evanston, seemed dazed by the news, and with bowed head walked slowly into the house. Preparations were made at once for the Secretary to go to Buffalo, accompanied by his son. Before he took the train for Buffalo, an hour later, Secretary Gage said:

"I am too shocked to speak. The news of such a happening is simply overwhelming to me. The President was always confident that no harm would ever come to him. He is a man who is honored by all. I received no official message that he had been assassinated. The first tidings were brought me by friends."

WASHINGTON STUNNED BY THE TRAGEDY

No Member of Cabinet Is at the Capital City.

MILITARY GUARD DETAILED

Under the Law Vice President Roosevelt Will Discharge the Purely Routine Duties of the President.

Special to The New York Times.

WASHINGTON, Sept. 6.—For the third time in thirty-seven years Washington has been stunned by the shooting of a President of the United States. Like lightning out of the fair September sky the report from Buffalo arrested attention here about 5 o'clock, and in a few moments anxious crowds were hurrying from all parts of the city to the offices of the newspapers seeking additional information. People stopped in their hurry to ask of every one met whether the President had been killed, and there was the utmost impatience because of the brevity and indefiniteness of the bulletins and the failure of assurance that the wounds inflicted upon Mr. McKinley were not fatal. To-night the street in front of the newspaper offices is crowded with women and men hungering with anxiety and waiting to catch the announcements that come at long intervals through a megaphone operated by a man in an upper window of a newspaper office.

Grief has not checked a torrent of indignation at the crime committed against humanity and a President who has always trusted himself implicity to the protection of his fellows, venturing from day to day to walk the streets without guard. The rage against the assassin was immediate and outspoken with men of all parties, for Mr. McKinley has no personal enemies here or elsewhere.

The disability of the President occurred at a moment when the Administration was entirely unrepresented at Washington by a Cabinet officer. When the information of the shooting reached the White House by a telephone message from Buffalo, Col. Montgomery and a few clerks were the only members of the President's official family present, Col. Pruden getting the news while he was dining at home. From the moment he heard the news, Col. Montgomery began making efforts to reach the members of the Cabinet, except Secretary of Agriculture Wilson, who is in Buffalo. There was a stream of visitors to the White House from the moment the news of the shooting was received until late to-night, but few of the visitors were persons high in official life.

HOW THE NEWS WAS RECEIVED.

The force at the White House since the President's departure has been in constant communication with him, and while he has conducted most of the business of his office at his home, in Canton, Ohio, the majority of the papers with which he has had to deal have been prepared in Washington and forwarded through the White House clerical force. All reports received from him by officials here were cheerful and high-spirited.

The work of the official day was done when the news of the calamity arrived here and the executive departments had generally emptied themselves of their workmen, and very few of the officials were to be found at their desks.

Mr. Adee, the acting head of the State Department, was met at the station as he was leaving for his country home near Laurel, Md., and returned at once to the State Department. He waited for official confirmation of the news, and it was not until he received a copy of the bulletin issued by the physicians through Secretary Cortelyou that he undertook to acquaint officially the Governments of all the nations of the world with the facts of the shooting. He then drew up a message, which will be sent to every United States Embassy, Legation, and Consulate throughout the civilized world directing them to acquaint the Governments to which they are accredited of the facts. With these he embodied a condensation of the physicians' bulletin with Mr. Cortelyou's statement.

In the Navy Department Mr. Hackett, the acting Secretary, who had also quitted the building, was speedily recalled by Capt. Cowles, the acting head of the Navigation Bureau, and he immediately put himself in readiness to take any official action that might be necessary to meet the emergency. At Buffalo in the Exposition grounds the navy had a splendid representation in the shape of the marine battalion under Capt. Leonard, and this force will be immediately available if it is decided by the persons about the President that a guard is necessary near his person.

At the War Department Gen. Gillespie, Chief Engineer of the army, was acting Secretary in the absence of Secretary Root, and Assistant Secretary Sanger, who is away on leave. He also had quitted the building, but he had not been gone half an hour before word reached him and he hastily returned to his desk. He immediately sent messages to the Secretary of war and to Gen. Brooke, commanding the Department of the East, giving such unofficial information as was available.

Gen. Gillespie finally got into communication with Secretary Root and Assistant Secretary Sanger, and as a result of the telephonic talk he proceeded to use some of the forces at his disposal. He telegraphed an order to Fort Foster, N. H., to have an officer, a physician, and a squad of men proceed immediately to the house where the President is lying to act as a guard.

PROVIDING FOR EMERGENCIES.

Steps were next taken to provide for the future of the Executive branch of the Government. It was realized that even under the most favorable conditions the President's injuries are of such a character as to make it almost certain that he cannot undertake for a long time to discharge the duties of Chief Executive, even in the most formal way. Every member of the Cabinet able to travel is expected to at once go to Buffalo, and there a Cabinet council will be held to decide upon the course to be followed by the Executive branch. Vice President Roosevelt is in readiness to do whatever is necessary and to meet the obligations imposed upon the Vice President by the Constitution of the United States. These are contained in Paragraph 6, Section 1, Article II., in the following words:

> 6. In case of the removal of the President from office, or of his death, resignation, or inability to discharge the powers and duties of the said office, the same shall devolve on the Vice President, &c.

Under the terms of this article, as soon as Mr. Roosevelt is assured by proper authority, probably in this case by the senior member of the Cabinet, Secretary Hay, who will doubtless be in Buffalo by to-morrow evening, he will undertake at once in a provisional way to discharge such duties as may devolve on him. Much will depend upon the report of the physicians on the character of the President's injuries as to the extent to which Mr. Roosevelt will discharge the Presidential duties, if he undertakes them at all, and it is almost certain that in the absence of great emergency in public affairs, even if called to assume these obligations, the Vice President will confine himself in the exercise of his powers to the discharge of the most routine and indispensable functions.

Such public men as were in the city called at the White House during the evening. They included Assistant Secretary Spaulding of the Treasury Department, Assistant Secretary Hackett of the Navy Department, ex-United States Senator H. W. Blair, Controller Dawes, and Register Lyons of the Treasury, and Capt. Towner, Assistant Commissioner of Indian Affairs. There were also calls from representatives of several foreign legations.

No official confirmation of the shooting came to the White House for three hours after its occurrence, when Col. Montgomery, the chief operator at the White House, was informed at 7:20 o'clock by Secretary Cortelyou at Buffalo that a surgical operation upon the President was in progress, and that "so far everything is favorable." Later he gave information of the completion of the operation, and followed that statement with other messages giving private information as to the President's condition and his removal to Mr. Milburn's residence.

STRONG MILITARY GUARD.

During the early evening a conference was held at the War Department of such of the prominent army officers as could be gathered at short notice by Gen. Gillespie. He informed them that he had communicated with Gen. Brooke at Governors Island and that the General had replied that he would start immediately for Buffalo, where he expected in the early morning to take personal charge of all arrangements made for the guarding of the President.

Meanwhile he had directed that the troops which had been placed as a guard around the hospital in the Exposition grounds be transferred to the Milburn home, where the President lies, to serve as a guard and keep back the public and preserve quiet. Gen. Brooke has at Buffalo at his disposal a company of coast artillery, stationed in the Exposition grounds; a company of the Fifteenth Infantry, also stationed at Fort Porter, within the limits of the Exposition preserves, and other troops at Fort Niagara.

The conference decided that there was little more that the War Department could undertake at this time. Surgeon General Van Reypen of the navy, who came down to the Navy Department, called at Gen. Gillespie's office, and, discussing the case from a medical point of view, took occasion to mention Dr. Nicholas Senn of Chicago as an expert of high grade in such cases of injury, and the suggestion was promptly telegraphed to Buffalo that his services be secured.

Assistant Secretary Ailes of the Treasury Department received a message to-night from Secretary Gage at Chicago stating that he was about to leave at once for Buffalo, where he will arrive to-morrow morning.

Admiral Dewey arrived in Washington early in the afternoon. He proceeded at once to his suburban home and was occupied with the details of the approaching Schley court of inquiry when the news reached him by the telephone. He at once sought all the particulars and placed himself in readiness for any service that might be required of him, informing Acting Secretary Hackett of that fact.

The Admiral found himself unable to express his feelings at the news, and all that could be extracted from him was that he was plunged in grief too deep for utterance at this time. He said that he could not now express an opinion as to the effect that the calamity might have on the court of inquiry, or even whether it would result in the postponement of the approaching sitting.

DIPLOMATS' CONDOLENCES.

Owing to the absence of many of the Diplomatic Corps at Buffalo and of many others at the various Summer resorts there were only two representatives of this body of rank in Washington to-day. Minister Wu was one of these, and when seen tonight he was a picture of distress. He said he realized keenly the tremendous indebtedness of China to President McKinley's kindly impulses in her great trials in the past year, and was shocked at the great calamity that had befallen him. He said he could not conceive of any sort of motive for such an inexcusable deed as that of Nieman's, and he was severe in his denunciation of Anarchists. He asked why they were permitted to hatch such plots as this in a Republic where the people could readily change their President if they were in the slightest degree dissatisfied with his official conduct or his private personality. In conclusion, he expressed the hope that the President would shortly recover.

Another diplomatic representative in Washington was Señor Herran, representing the Government of the United States of Colombia. He also was greatly distressed and he affirmed that his whole country would sympathize with the President in this moment of pain. He also could not understand, he said, why such a benevolent character as President McKinley should be thus assaulted by one of the people, and he declared it is time that the Anarchists should be suppressed.

It was somewhat gratifying to the officials here that the very first expression of official sympathy should come from the Island of Cuba, in the shape of the following telegram:

> Sept. 6, 1901.
> (Received at War Department, 7:45 P. M.
> Havana.
> Adjutant General, Washington:
> Mayor and City Council of Havana have called, expressing sorrow and solicitude for the President, and desire that his family be advised of these expressions.
> SCOTT, Adjutant General.

Mr. H. T. Scott of the Union Iron Works at San Francisco, at whose house the President staid while visiting that city, telegraphed the Navy Department as follows:

"So shocked with news, words fail to express our feelings."

Messages of sympathy and of inquiry already have begun to arrive at the State Department.

HOW THE NEWS WAS RECEIVED IN NEW YORK

People Awed and Grieved by Attempt on the President's Life.

SYMPATHY FOR HIS WIFE

Great Crowds Surrounded the Bulletin Boards and Snatched Papers from the Newsboys—Scenes in the Hotels, Theatres and Clubs.

Not since that memorable July 2 twenty years ago, when the news was received here of the shooting of President Garfield in a railway station in Washington, has New York been the scene of so much suppressed excitement and heartfelt mourning as were displayed throughout the city yesterday afternoon, when it became known that President McKinley was the third of the Nation's Chief Executives to receive an assassin's bullet.

It was shortly after 4 o'clock when the telegram bearing the message of such tremendous import reached the city from Buffalo. It was the very briefest message, and yet it told the story with remarkable correctness, stating that the President had been shot twice in the stomach in the Temple of Music in the Exposition grounds at Buffalo by a man whose identity was not known.

Within less than three minutes after the arrival of the message, which was received by all the local newspapers, it was duplicated on the bulletin board of THE NEW YORK TIMES, and a few moments later on the boards of every journal on Newspaper Row. The casual passer-by glanced at it, stopped, rubbed his or her eyes, and read again. After that, like the shifting grains of sand in an eddying stream, the crowd gathered along Park Row and waited hungrily, but half incredulously, for more news. It came by piecemeal, but the added scraps for some time added little to the first announcement, and many hundreds of pedestrians hurried off to tell it to their fellows without waiting to equip themselves with details.

A little later and the great down-town buildings began to empty their hordes of workers for the day, and then City Hall Square became a great sea of upturned faces, shifting and eddying in a struggle to get nearer the bulletin boards, where employes with brushes and crayons were working with might and main to keep up with the scraps of information received from the scene of the great tragedy.

It was the hour when half New York was going home, and because of this fact the news traveled through the city with lightning rapidity. Within a short time after the receipt of the first news of the shooting the evening papers had extras on the street, and the newsboys, scenting prosperity from afar, were out in countless swarms, their united voices as they cried their wares blending into one continuous ear-splitting screech.

DEMEANOR OF THE CROWDS.

The crowds resembled in appearance the gatherings on the streets on election nights. There was the same swirling, pushing, and shoving of a great mass of eager humanity, and there was the same mixture of men and women crowding for points of vantage, but the disposition of the crowds last night was far different. They were not the cheering masses that the New Yorker expects to see at such times. They were philosophical—stoical in their interest.

At one of the boards, when a bulletin announcing that the physicians at the President's bedside had held a consultation and believed that the sufferer would live the news was received in dead silence by the onlookers.

"What a commentary on the American people and their common sense," exclaimed a man standing on the outskirts of the crowd. "If it were President Loubet of France who lay stricken Paris would be a seething whirlpool of excitement."

The feeling displayed everywhere was primarily one of awe and grief. The general run of people in the streets were palpably feeling more than they had the power readily to express. As a consequence there was a noticeable dearth of the demonstrations which accompanied the receipt of the news that Garfield had been shot or the terrible outbreak of wrath and deep sorrow which was a feature of the assassination of President Lincoln. While there was much anxiety to know how the President was progressing, the feeling seemed to be such as to call for a lowering of the voice, and in the cases of the more impressionable, the brushing away of a tear from the eye, rather than any more visible demonstration for the stricken Chief Magistrate, or wrath toward his assailant. This was the keynote of the situation all through the evening. It was a dogged waiting for the good or ill tidings, without spectacular outbreak.

Although the extra editions of the newspapers were sold in enormous numbers, it was not by this means that the news of the great tragedy spread over the city with lightning like rapidity. The papers were grabbed by purchasers almost before they left the offices, and it was a long time before the presses could print sufficient to supply their up-town depots. As one edition after another came out they were sold to men who in their eagerness did not wait for the change for their nickels, but bought one edition after another in the hope of finally getting the connected story of the shooting.

The thousands on their way to their homes from the down-town districts spread the news on the ferryboats and on the trains as they scattered. Conductors, motormen, and passengers on the trolley cars as they sped up town shouted it to passers-by on the street corners where the cars halted. Elevated guards shouted it to station men as they went northward.

Once started, the message conveyed here in the first telegram from Buffalo spread like a prairie fire, and it is unnecessary to say that it was added to by the thousands of narrators until by 6 o'clock it is safe to say that every man, woman, and child on Manhattan Island at least knew of the shooting, and then came the myriads of questions which were long unanswered. Was the President killed? Who did the shooting? Did he escape? How did it happen? And to these the answers were varied according to the information of those questioned.

MANY RUMORS FLOATED.

Owing to the meagre news obtainable the rumor mongers got in their work with telling effect. One story was that the President had been stabbed to death. Another had it that the assassin had been torn limb from limb by the populace before the Buffalo police had time to rescue him. Many thousands of persons left their homes after the evening meal and journeyed out into the city in search of information.

Business was almost closed for the day when the first news of the shooting was received, but from that moment it ceased almost altogether. In clubs, in saloons, on the streets, wherever men are accustomed to congregate, there were eager crowds, all discussing the same subject. Many saloonkeepers in the uptown districts sent emissaries all the way down town to Newspaper Row to copy the bulletins, and these scraps of information were given second-hand on bulletins in the remote districts, where thousands congregated to discuss the tragedy. If there was any grim humor displayed in any of these gatherings it related to the bearing the shooting of the President had on the prospects of Vice President Roosevelt. The Vice President was referred to as "a child of destiny" many times.

It was in the clubs and hotels that the keenest interest was displayed during the after-dinner hours. The interest in the bulletin boards at the big up-town hostelries was intense during the early part of the evening. When it was reported that the President would probably recover, and there were no contradictory reports, the onlookers seemed to take it for granted that the event would not become a historical tragedy, and the question "What will happen to the stock market to-morrow?" became the word on every tongue.

All sorts of rumors were abroad. It was said that J. P. Morgan had corralled the chief bankers and capitalists on board his yacht and was holding a ways and means conference. It was wildly stated that the Presidents of all the big banks were in session at the Metropolitan Club. Men were offering odds that certain stocks would break for so much, and the bets were taken, not singly, but by the score. Knots of men gathered in the up-town cafés and restaurants, and their talk was all of the dollars that would be lost on the morrow.

The attitude of the politicians was different. In the corridors of the Fifth Avenue Hotel, the headquarters of the Republicans, genuine sorrow was depicted upon the faces of all. There were several men there who know William McKinley well, and some of these were deeply affected as they recited incidents in the career of the man which were not connected with the office of President of the United States.

In the Democratic Club and in the corridors of the Hoffman House, where were congregated the men whose political sympathies were not with the Chief Executive, politics were forgotten in the grief which was evident on purely personal grounds.

"I didn't believe," said an ex-Senator, "that the President had a private enemy in the world; at least, none so pronounced as to perpetrate such a dastardly deed. It is a terrible thing that has happened. I am overwhelmed at the enormity of it."

Men whose interests lay in politics were unanimous in their expressions in a similar vein, irrespective of party leanings.

SYMPATHY FOR MRS. McKINLEY.

In nearly every gathering place throughout the city many expressions of profound sympathy were expressed for Mrs. McKinley, together with the fear that the shock to her in her present delicate health will result disastrously. In fact, the conversations everywhere bore largely on the personal sorrow brought into the home of the President, and showed that the heart of the whole Nation has been touched by the devotion of the couple as displayed during the recent illness of Mrs. McKinley.

As has been said, there were fewer expressions of rage toward the would-be assassin than might have been expected. That the man is an Anarchist was accepted as a matter of course, and the attitude of the crowd toward him was pretty much that displayed toward a mad dog when it became known that he had been landed in jail. He was cast aside in the discussion as a blind, unreasonable animal that is sure to get his just deserts. One man from the South expressed himself in an up-town hotel to the effect that the fellow ought to be burned at the stake, but his opinion was not echoed.

As the hour grew late the crowds around the bulletin boards grew larger, and all the news of the President was eagerly read. All over the city it was noted that women were much in evidence. They seemed to take as much interest in the news as did the men, and many an earnest request for the latest word from Buffalo came from feminine lips, addressed to perfect strangers. It was not an uncommon sight to see women in tears as some scrap of information with a note of pathos in it was flashed on the bulletin boards or passed from lip to lip.

About the only class of people who were conspicuous by their absence last night were the few avowed anarchists of the city. Tere were grim inquiries made for them during the evening in a number of meeting places, but they were decidedly not in evidence. In fact, about the most violent utterances during the evening were heard in connection with the anarchists in general. This feeling seemed to be most violently expressed in Harlem. There were a number of impromptu mass meetings held in One Hundred and Twenty-fifth Street, where the sidewalk orators talked of burning out the anarchists of Paterson, N. J., like rats in a barn.

And thus the night wore on, the waiting crowds gradually thinning as the people concluded to wait until morning, hoping, yet dreading, to hear the full tidings from the bedside of the Nation's Chief.

AT THE THEATRES.

Bulletins Read Between the Acts and Preparations Made to Close—Crowds in the Tenderloin.

The news of the shooting of President McKinley caused much excitement in the Tenderloin. The newspapers, which deluged the district, were greedily bought at all sorts of prices and groups discussing the tragedy were to be seen far into the night. The gloom and expressions of sorrow which spread over the whole district were most marked. Everywhere was heard the exclamation, "It's terrible; it's horrible!"

The desks of the hotels and the different telegraph offices were besieged with crowds desiring accurate news. The early evening brought crowds, which filled Upper Broadway, hoping to hear favorable news of the President's condition. Last November the same crowd was in the Tenderloin shouting madly and rejoicing at the victory of President McKinley.

The effect on this part of the city where the amusement places abound was most apparent in the great falling off in the attendance of the theatres. Many of these places that had sold out their entire seating capacity were not half filled. This was notably the case at the Empire Theatre, the Criterion Theatre, and Wallack's, not to speak of nearly a score or more where the patronage was 50 per cent. below what it ordinarily would have been. At nearly every theatre in the city bulletins containing the news of the President's condition were read between the acts. They were received as the various reports came with applause or exclamations of sorrow.

Charles Frohman, through Al Hayman, his representative, gave orders shortly after receiving the information of the crime to close all his theatres in town in the event of the President's death. Similar action was contemplated by Messrs. Weber & Field.

"We will not ring down the curtain if the President dies," said Mr. Weber last night, "but we will at once announce it, and we do not expect that an American audience will remain after being told of that sorrowing fact. We will not ask our actors to work under the circumstances."

All along Broadway these sentiments of Mr. Weber were echoed. Not a manager of a theatre could be found but who said that even in the event of the news of the President's death coming in the middle of a performance they would immediately notify the audience and ring down the curtain.

Brooklyn Democracy's Sympathy.

Prior to the transaction of any formal business at an executive meeting of the Brooklyn Democracy held in the Arbuckle Building on Fulton Street last night, Chairman Rufus L. Scott called attention to the attempted assassination of President McKinley. A resolution was presented by Otto Kempner, embodying the sentiment expressed by Mr. Scott, and extending the deepest sympathy to the President and his wife. The resolution was unanimously adopted.

DEEP REGRET IN ENGLAND

Indignation at Czolgosz's Deed Is Unbounded.

TRIBUTES OF LONDON PAPERS

The Times Says President McKinley Is Now in the Plenitude of His Popularity.

LONDON TIMES—NEW YORK TIMES
Special Cablegram.

LONDON, Sept. 7.—The Times, referring editorially to-day to the attempt on the life of President McKinley, says it will be a relief to the feelings of the people of the United States that the criminal is not one of themselves. The editorial proceeds:

"At any rate they [the American people] may be assured of the complete and cordial sympathy of their British kinsfolk in their grief and anger. President McKinley's personal character is respected both in our own country and by foreign nations, and the fatuous wickedness of the attempt on his life will meet with universal reprobation.

"We will not contemplate the possibility of a fatal result, but in any case the Government of the United States will not be disturbed. Vice President Roosevelt is a man of ability and distinction, in whose hands there is no doubt the country's interests would be safe; but Mr. McKinley is stronger now than ever before, and it would be a cruel stroke of fortune were he to be cut off in the plenitude of his popularity, when his policy has been apparently vindicated by success at all points.

"The attempt on the President will awaken indignation and sympathy in every civilized country, and nowhere more than in these British Isles, where, despite occasional misunderstandings and jealousies, time strengthens the manifold ties of kinship which unite us to our American cousins."

The article goes on to refer to the President's speech at Buffalo on Thursday, which, it says, "gave indications of independence of thought and courageous initiative not previously apparent in Mr. McKinley's career." It concludes by asserting that it is unintelligible that the head of an Administration with such a record of prosperity, so personally popular, and so recently approved by the suffrages of his countrymen should be singled out for assassination except by a madman.

By The Associated Press.

LONDON, Sept. 7.—The news of the attempt upon the life of President McKinley spread slowly in London. The first ticker reports were discredited; then, with the confirmation and general dissemination of the news, arose a far-reaching feeling of sorrow and indignation, which, wherever Americans were gathered, almost gained the proportions of a panic, accompanied by feverish anxiety for further details. The thousands of Americans now in London were mostly at the theatres when the news arrived; and, returning to their hotels, found anxious groups of Englishmen and Americans discussing what, without distinction of race, is regarded as a national calamity.

London's telephones, usually silent at night, tingled with impatient inquiries addressed to newspapers and American correspondents in the hope of securing a denial of the report. The announcement of the attempted assassination was received too late for extra editions of the papers to announce the news to the mass of the English people, and they will not learn until they take up their morning papers of the attempt to kill the President.

The news was conveyed to J. W. Mackay, Col. Ochiltree, C. L. Pullman, and J. W. Gates, and many others, all of whom desired to express their unspeakable indignation at the cowardly act, the deepest sympathy with President McKinley, and hopes for his recovery. Added to this personal patriotic sentiment was the dread that whatever the outcome of the outrage upon the President, it would perhaps fatally react upon Mrs. McKinley.

Comparatively few Englishmen heard the news last night, but all these expressed horror and sympathy as genuine as if it had been the King instead of the President. The latter's kindly personality, his friendship for England, and his kindly message of condolence upon the occasion of Queen Victoria's death were all called up in voices as low and awe-stricken as those of any purely American gathering.

The Lord Mayor of London, when informed of the attempt upon the President's life, last night expressed the greatest grief and emotion. He said:

"I shall call a meeting of the Aldermen to-morrow formally to express to Mrs. McKinley and the American people the horror and grief felt at the attempt. Personally the news comes to me with the greatest possible shock, and I am sure that every citizen of London will join me in expressing feelings of horror at the terrible calamity."

Ex-Gov. Brown of Georgia, Mr. and Mrs. Nat C. Goodwin, and other Americans who were to have dined at the Carlton, canceled their engagement on hearing the news, and all the orchestras ceased playing. Crowds surrounded the bulletin boards.

All the newspapers this morning publish long accounts from Buffalo describing the attempt upon President McKinley's life; dispatches from abroad regarding the reception of the news, which excites renewed and anxious discussion of means to prevent Anarchist outrages, references to previous attempts, and the urgent need of the adoption of greater police precautions than ever in republics and the freest countries. The Daily Telegraph says editorially:

"It is with the profoundest regret that the world learns to-day that another distinguished name is added to the shamefully long list of rulers who have fallen victims to the insensate wickedness of the assassin.

"The most unfeigned and heartfelt sympathy will go forth from every family in Christendom to Mrs. McKinley in this hour of deepest sorrow and trial. Americans will acquit us of all suspicion of insincerity when we claim that the blow will be felt with almost equal severity in Great Britain as in the United States."

Referring to the sympathy displayed by America at the time of the death of Queen Victoria, The Daily Telegraph says:

"Sympathy can only be repaid by sympathy, though it is a mournful satisfaction that the debt we so gratefully discharged should have fallen due so soon."

The article concludes by dilating upon the inexplicability of the crime "committed in a free country at a time of its greatest well-being on a most popular ruler," and the need of still further protection against insensate Anarchists.

The Daily Mail thinks the motive underlying such crimes is notoriety, and that if such criminals could be dealt with on the spot one great inducement to the commission of such attempts would be removed. The Mail suggests that all rulers should be accompanied by armed men, instructed to shoot the assassins on the spot.

The Daily News says:

"This ghastly outrage, by which a brave, upright governor of men perishes as Lincoln and Garfield perished, in the execution of his duty, comes home to the hearts of Englishmen with inexpressible poignancy. We are proud of America, and an act like this, which plunges the Republic into bitter grief, reminds us as nothing else can do that we are members of the same house, 'bone of their bone, flesh of their flesh.' The death of no public man outside of this country could affect us like the death of the American President."

While denouncing in the strongest terms the madness of Anarchist criminals, The Daily News says it thinks the growth of the trust system is a perpetual danger to the American Commonwealth.

The same paper, in a short leading article, remarks upon the peculiarity of the provision of the United States Constitution that the murder of the President places the Vice President in the Presidential chair. It thinks a case conceivable in which an Anarchist might attempt to murder the President with this very motive, and that an obvious reform of the law suggests itself.

The Standard prints an editorial couched in similar terms of sorrow and indignation and says: "The prayers of Christendom will be given for the President's recovery." The Standard devotes the bulk of its article to a denunciation of Anarchists. It declares that it does not wonder that the crowd desired to lynch Nieman, and expresses an opinion identical with that of The Daily Mail, that the knowledge that immediate death awaited such attempts would prove an effectual deterrent.

The Daily Chronicle says:

"It is no protection to be called President; it is no special danger to be an autocrat. The eulogists of Mr. McKinley's courage in disregarding threatening letters would not be surprised if the outcome of the outrage was the revival of the agitation for a stricter exclusion of undesirable persons and the expulsion of suspects from the country."

The Chronicle thinks the closest possible alliance between the police of all nations, combined with the greatest vigilance, is the only effective weapon society has against the common enemies of mankind, and it declares that the death of President McKinley would be a grievous calamity on political grounds, no less than on the ground of human feeling.

"His name," says The Chronicle, "is linked with a new epoch in American history. He has made the United States an empire, but his work is not finished, and we trust he will be spared to finish it."

NEWS SENT TO KING EDWARD.

Assassin's Deed Will Result in Redoubling of Precautions to Insure Royalties' Safety.

BERLIN, Sept. 6.—King Edward was traveling from Frankfort to Hamburg when the news of the attempt upon President McKinley's life was received, and a telegram was immediately dispatched to meet him, acquainting him with the deed.

The Altona-Kiel Railway was strongly guarded by a large force of police, and it cannot be doubted that this latest Anarchistic attempt will result in the redoubling of police precautions upon the Continent in view of the various royal meetings now taking place.

If there had ever been any likelihood that the Czar would go to Paris, it may now be regarded as a certainty that he will not do so. He had already decided yesterday to return direct to Russia from France without returning to Denmark.

COPENHAGEN, Sept. 6.—The news of the attempt upon the life of President McKinley created a painful impression at Fredensborg. Emperor Nicholas, King Christian of Denmark, and King George of Greece dispatched telegraphic messages of sympathy for Mrs. McKinley.

SYMPATHY IN PARIS.

PARIS, Sept. 7.—The news of the attempt upon President McKinley's life reached Paris too late for publication in yesterday's evening papers, and consequently it was not known outside of newspaper circles, but there it created a feeling akin to consternation. Mr. McKinley was considered the last person in the world in danger of assassination. It can safely be predicted that the news will create a tremendous sensation in Paris to-day, and the United States is sure of receiving every mark of sympathy from Frenchmen of all shades of opinion, as the President has always been considered a friend of France.

Articles in the four leading organs of French opinion, The Figaro, The Matin, The Gaulois, and The Eclair breathe this sympathy.

The Gaulois says:

"We feel the necessity of expressing to the great people of the United Stats, to whom so many ties unite us, our sympathy with them and horror at the crime that has cast them into mourning, but the great faith of this grand people in God will enable them again to recover themselves and pursue the course of their destiny."

The Matin speaks with particularly kindly appreciation of Mr. McKinley's political modesty and the purity of his home life. It concludes its article as follows:

"Hazard is often cruel and unjust, but never more so than when it allows a criminal madman to kill, in the name of some abominable ideal of liberty, the most democratic chief of the freest people."

The Figaro pays a warm tribute to the personal honesty of Mr. McKinley, but sees in him a representative of the spirit of trust and protection, and asks whether the explanation of the crime is not to be found in the fact that Mr. McKinley personifies in the eyes of the crowd aristocracy and wealth.

"Nevertheless," says the Figaro, "France joins in the anguish and indignation of the American people, because, although Mr. McKinley was first responsible for the bills which restricted commercial relations between the two peoples, he afterward consented to mitigate this régime and renewed the current of trade between them. We remember the affectionate telegrams that Mr. McKinley sent to the President of France at the time of the peace negotiations between Spain and the United States, and the conciliatory and humane policy of America in China, while Mr. McKinley has been astonishing the world by his moderation and spirit of justice in the dispute between Colombia and Venezuela. We, therefore, express the sincerest wish that America may be spared mourning."

The Eclair declares that the attempt to assassinate the President will arouse as much indignation and condemnation in France as in the United States, and recalls the sympathy expressed by the American people at the time of the assassination of President Carnot.

SYMPATHY OF DIPLOMATS.

BUFFALO, Sept. 6.—Solemnity and sorrow were written on the faces of the Diplomatic Corps as they moved about the Niagara Hotel this evening. The news reached some of them on the Exposition grounds; others had gone to their hotels on their return with the President from the trip to the Falls, and did not learn of the calamity until late in the afternoon. Upon learning it each one hurried to the Milburn home to inquire as to the President's condition and to express sorrow over the misfortune that had befallen him.

Señor Don Manuel de Azpiroz, the Mexican Ambassador, and his Secretaries were among the first callers. Señor de Azpiroz is by virtue of seniority and rank the head of all the members of the Diplomatic Corps now in Buffalo. While at Mr. Milburn's house he conferred with the other Ministers and called a meeting of the Diplomatic Corps, to be held in the apartments at the Niagara Hotel at 9 o'clock. Only Ministers and Secretaries of Legation were admitted to the meeting, which was behind closed doors. Señor de Azpiroz, through his Secretary, expressed his sorrow.

"It grieves me much," he said, "and will grieve my Government. It is a sad blow not only to the people of the United States, but to all representatives of foreign Governments who have met President McKinley. I shall send individually to the State Department an expression of my sorrow and sympathy and my secretary has prepared a collective note of condolence to be signed by all members of the Diplomatic Corps here present."

Other members of the Corps expressed similar sentiments of sorrow and horror at the terrible crime.

The following is the message of condolence sent to the Government:

To the Secretary of State, Washington:

The Mexican Ambassador expresses to the Government of the United States his deep regrets for the atrocious attempt against the life of his Excellency President McKinley. The diplomatic representatives of Ecuador, Costa Rica, Spain, Japan, Peru, Colombia, Korea, Turkey, Russia, Venezuela, Brazil, and China, at present in this city, have requested the Ambassador to express in their names the same sentiments. M. DE AZPIROZ.

The members of the Diplomatic Corps intended to return to Washington to-night, but have decided to postpone their departure.

SENATOR HANNA'S GRIEF.

Close Friend of the President Hastens to the Latter's Bedside.

Special to The New York Times.

CLEVELAND, Sept. 6.—Senator M. A. Hanna, when informed that President McKinley had been shot, exclaimed: "I cannot believe anything like that!"

Later a telegram was handed to Senator Hanna and he then said: "I am forced to believe that the rumor is true. I cannot say anything about it. It seems too horrible to even contemplate that such a thing could have happened to so splendid a man as Mr. McKinley, and at this time and upon such an occasion. It is horrible, awful. Mr. McKinley never had any fear of danger from that source. Of course I never talked to him upon such a subject, but I know he never even dreamed of anything like this happening. I cannot be interviewed on this. It is too awful. I have sent a telegram to friends in Buffalo and have asked them to reply immediately. So far I have received no answer."

Shortly after 4 o'clock Senator Hanna left the Union Club and boarded a street car for his office on Superior Street. To a reporter who accompanied him he turned suddenly in the car and exclaimed: "What is this great country coming to when such men as Lincoln, Garfield, and McKinley fall by the bullet of assassins?"

"Oh, it is fearful, dreadful, horrible. I shall hurry to the bedside of the President as rapidly as the train will take me. I only hope that he is not seriously injured, but I am afraid that my hopes will be in vain. I do want to reach the President before he dies, if he is going to die. No one can be safe from the work of an insane man it seems. It is terrible."

BUFFALO, Sept. 6.—Senator Hanna arrived here from Cleveland to-night, and went directly to the home of Mr. Milburn, reaching there at 11:28 o'clock.

GRIEF AND ANGER STIR LEADING MEN

Clubmen and Politicians Express Their Feelings Freely.

Ex-Secretary Carlisle and Senator Platt Among Those Who Talk—Business Depression Would Follow the President's Death, Declares the Former.

The hotels and the political clubs were crowded last evening with members who were drawn together by the news of the attempt on President McKinley's life. At the Manhattan Club there were half a hundred members. At the Reform Club, the Union League, the Union Club, and the Democratic Club there were large gatherings of members. Among those who spoke are the following, with their views:

JOHN G. CARLISLE, ex-Secretary of the Treasury—It is an outrage that such a deed should have been perpetrated in a free country. Every citizen should feel heartfelt sorrow. If President McKinley should die there would be business depression all over the country. The depression would not be permanent and the business interests would finally revive after the shock. It is getting to be a serious matter when the fact is considered that this is the third President whose life has been sought by assassins.

Senator THOMAS C. PLATT—I was dazed when I heard the news. I could hardly realize it. It does not seem possible that a man could do such a thing. He was not crazy. There was too much method about the way he committed his crime. I think it wrong to attribute madness to all persons who try to kill people. I would advocate a drumhead court-martial and let the man be taken off at once. This is one of the instances where I think lynch law would be justified. It is appalling to think of it.

It is difficult for me to think what to say. My whole sympathy is with the President. There should be a special law to deal with Anarchists—he must have been an Anarchist—of the class that attempted the life of the President. If the latter lives, and all pray that he will, his assailant can only be sent to prison for ten years. Speedy and fit punishment should follow such crimes as this.

WILLIAM LINDSAY of Kentucky, ex-United States Senator—I am greatly shocked. The claim of insanity is advanced, but I am convinced the would-be assassin is a fit subject to be executed. What sort of reputation will we have as a free republic if crimes of this character are to occur at intervals? Everybody respects President McKinley and all will pray for his speedy recovery.

Ex-Gov. P. B. S. PINCHBECK of Louisiana—President McKinley is a lovable man, and I did not suppose he had an enemy in the world. All will repudiate the act of the would-be murderer and insist on fitting punishment. It is hard to tell what would be the effect of the death of the President. It is too horrible to contemplate.

Chief Justice SNODGRASS of Tennessee—The shooting of President McKinley is a public calamity. Let us hope he will recover. I believe he will. But if the worst comes I think Vice President Roosevelt will prove a safe man. All Vice Presidents ought to be regarded as safe. Mr. McKinley's death would plunge the country into mourning, and in no part of it would there be more sincere sorrow than in the South.

WILLIAM BROOKFIELD, ex-Chairman of the Republican State Committee—I pray Almighty God that our President will recover. It is a crime that he cannot go abroad among his own people without being in danger of his life. He is the third President shot down. It is a blot on the fair name of the country.

JACOB HESS, ex-Police Commissioner—It is a horrible crime, but I am hopeful of the President's recovery. There should be a special law for the punishment of criminals of this class. Burning at the stake would be none too severe.

ANTHONY N. BRADY, Financier.—In common with all Americans I deplore the attempt on the President's life. The latest dispatches encourage me in the belief that he will recover. Naturally his death would have an effect on the market, but that is as nothing compared with the personal loss of his friends and the great calamity that his demise would visit on the country.

GEORGE W. DUNN, Chairman of the Republican State Committee—I was in hope that the reports from Buffalo were untrue. I am deeply grieved, but am quite hopeful that Mr. McKinley will recover. He has proved a very careful Chief Executive, and the country felt a sense of safety under his Administration. Should he die, which God forbid, I believe Vice President Roosevelt would make no mistakes. No matter what people may say, Col. Roosevelt is in perfect accord with Senator Platt and has consulted him very recently. But this is no time to talk politics.

WILLIAM PITT KELLOGG, ex-Governor of Louisiana—The possibility of the death of President McKinley is awful to contemplate. It would be the calamity of the age. While I have great respect for Vice President Roosevelt, his assumption of the office of President at this time would be disastrous to both the financial and political world. Mr. Roosevelt himself might not do anything to snarl affairs, but the popular belief in his belligerency would cause it. I sincerely hope the President may be spared.

Consul SOLOMON BERLINER—The attempted assassination of President McKinley is horrible. Summary justice should be visited on the would-be assassin. Let us hope the President will recover.

VIRGIL P. KLINE of Cleveland, Ohio, Chief Counsel for the Standard Oil Company, and a Democrat—It is a public calamity. The death of Mr. McKinley would be a great blow to the country. Although a Democrat, I have voted for him twice. I know him to be a safe man and of strict integrity. He enjoys the confidence of all. In my opinion Roosevelt would not be a safe man as President. Naturally, the death of the President would have a bad effect on the market.

WILLIAM B. KIRK, ex-Mayor of Syracuse and ex-Treasurer of the Democratic State Committee—Mr. McKinley's death would upset everything. He has made an excellent President and just at this time the whole world is commenting favorably on his reciprocity speech. He has made a safe President. No punishment is too severe for the wretch who attempted his life. God spare us our President.

GEORGE W. WANAMAKER, Deputy Appraiser, Port of New York.—The attempt on the life of President McKinley is a severe shock not only to the people of the United States but to the civilized world. We are supposed to be a free people with very democratic ideas, but it is about time that additional safeguards were thrown about our Chief Magistrates. The freedom of handshaking affords Anarchists extra opportunities, and it should be stopped. The King of Italy and the Empress of Austria died at the hands of Anarchists, but the latter did not have the opportunities that can be utilized by Anarchists in America. All will pray for the speedy recovery of the President.

ABRAHAM GRUBER—An awful crime, for which swift retribution should follow. I am hopeful of the recovery of the President. His death would be a public calamity.

REUBEN L. FOX, Secretary of the Republican State Committee—I cannot believe that the President will die. Such a contingency is too awful to contemplate. He has proved a wise and safe ruler, and enjoys the confidence of the whole country, North, South, East, and West. Still his death would bring about no material change in political or economical conditions. But let us hope that that will not happen. Vice President Roosevelt enjoys the confidence of the persons prominent in the affairs of the State.

EDWARD COOPER, ex-Mayor—The attempt on the life of the President is a monstrous thing, and every decent man will condemn it. I most sincerely hope that President McKinley will recover.

F. B. THURBER—It is extraordinary that in this free country three such Presidents as Lincoln, Garfield, and McKinley should be shot down. These men have done so much for mankind that they are revered the world over.

Senator N. L. ELSBERG—In common with every American, I deplore the attempt on the life of the President. Mr. McKinley not only enjoys the confidence of our countrymen, but is respected abroad. His Administration has done much to gain the respect of other countries for the United States. His death, at this time, would be almost an irreparable loss.

EX-POSTMASTER CHARLES W. DAYTON.—There has been absolute gloom at the Manhattan Club this evening. Scenes have been witnessed here the like of which have not occurred since the assassination of President Garfield in 1881. The man who could have committed that act must have been a wild beast. No man can possibly conceive what his motive was, because President McKinley was such a gracious man and has made no enemies. He has injured no man, and the attempt on his life is a calamity to this country.

It seems dreadful that every twenty or so years an attempt is made on the life of a President of the United States. The acts of assassination are all the more alarming because they have occurred under a democratic form of government. It is enough to make a man tremble for the future of the country. I only hope that the man who committed the deed is a raving lunatic just out of the asylum. It would be better for the future of the country if this is the case.

EDWARD M. SHEPARD.—This is an unspeakably horrid crime. It is appalling that assassination should reach a ruler of a free democratic republic, twice chosen as President, as Mr. McKinley has been by a tremendous preponderance of his fellow-citizens. A man who is not only a statesman, but a man in his personal relations of great amiability and generosity and personally loved as few of his predecessors have been. This is malignant wickedness indeed. The American people will be at one in their affectionate sympathy with the President and those near him, especially his wife.

WILLIAM J. GAYNOR, Supreme Court Justice.—It is deplorable, but I hope he will recover. It is only a few days ago that I was saying that he was, in my judgment, one of the best Presidents we ever had. From the beginning of the Spanish war up to this time he went through all the troubles and complications of the war and those growing out of it making scarcely one mistake. I do not say this simply because I believe in the course he pursued. My belief in that course caused me to observe his conduct all the more closely because of what I deemed the unreasonable and sometimes mean criticism he was subjected to. He is a good and a very able man.

Col. HIBBERT B. MASTERS, President of the Brooklyn Union League Club—President McKinley is an honorary member of this club and is as close to the hearts of all the members as it is possible for a man to be who has pursued an honest and manly course, and the club regards him as one of the ablest Presidents we have had. There has been but one expression, and that is of the deepest sympathy. We are praying that the result will be favorable.

C. V. FORNES, long President of the Catholic Club—The universal sentiment of the members of this organization is one of profound sympathy for the President and his wife. Not only has Mr. McKinley endeared himself to the people by his personal characteristics, but he has been a capable and conscientious Executive. Under his Administration the country's honor has been more than safe and its welfare assured. In the very prime of his career his loss to the country could not be measured. The Catholic Club joins with the American people in hoping earnestly for his speedy recovery.

Gen. H. E. TREMAIN, President of the Republican Club—The entire country is of one mind. The death of President McKinley would be a calamity to the Nation as well as to the entire world. He has proved himself a friend of the plain people. His entire Administration has been one of prosperity. It is his ambition and untiring effort to advance the interests of his country.

Col. FRANKLIN BARTLETT.—The attempt on the President's life has shocked the civilized world. His death would be a National calamity. The heart of the whole people will go out to the President and his family.

CHARLES A. TOWNE, ex-United States Senator from Minnesota—I am shocked by the news of the attempt on the President's life, and with all Americans feel great grief. I know Mr. McKinley intimately and appreciate his lovely character. The event comes as a great sorrow to the Nation. I should regret exceedingly to hear of the death of Mr. McKinley from the fact that I do not feel that the country would be as safe under Col. Roosevelt as under the President.

CONTROLLER COLER—I feel as every one does over the news from Buffalo, and hope that the Almighty God will preserve to us our President. He has probably had no more earnest political opponent or more ardent personal friend and admirer than myself, and though many of us have differed with him in political views, yet no one will deny that the character of William McKinley is far better than that of most men who have sat in the President's chair.

GEN. W. H. JACKSON of Tennessee—A shocking crime. A sad commentary on the alleged civilization of the North. That would-be assassin would get short shrift in the South. I pray that Mr. McKinley will speedily recover. He is respected in all parts of the United States.

CHARLES STECKLER.—The affair takes the heart out of me. I cannot find words to express my horror. All good citizens hope the President's injuries will not prove fatal.

COL. CHINN of Kentucky—I am a Democrat, but I am an admirer of Mr. McKinley, as are all sensible people of all parties. He has proved himself one of the greatest of this country's Presidents. He is a President of the people, despite all the howlings of extremists to the contrary.

The attempt to assassinate him was an outrage, and if the thing could be done out of the public view, the assassin ought to be burned up inch by inch. No punishment would be too severe. There is no crime that could so seriously affect the country as a whole, could so demoralize our trade, and our Government, or could so disgust our good citizens.

"As for the effect on business in Kentucky, my own State, the result will not be disastrous, for Kentucky is primarily an agricultural State. The same remark applies to the rest of the South. However, no Southerner who is worthy of the name can fail to deplore this terrible occurrence. Outside of the horror of the deed itself and the sorrow that will be felt over any mishap to the respected President, there is another reason why the South will deplore it.

The South does not like Roosevelt, and the possibility of Mr. McKinley's death brings up the unpleasant suggestion that the unpopular Vice President may become President within a few days. Kentuckians are especially hostile to Roosevelt because of his remark that if Taylor, who was accused of assassinating Goebel, should come to the State of New York, he (Roosevelt) would not allow him to be extradited.

Since then the Rough Rider's prestige in the Blue Grass State has waned rapidly. A wall of disapproval would go up there and elsewhere in the South if Roosevelt should become the Nation's Chief Executive.

Dr. E. E. BEEMAN of Cleveland—It is outrageous. They ought to do away with the President's assailant as fast as they can. Without doubt the effect of this occurrence, especially if the President dies, will be serious in trade matters. Like all the rest who have stocks, I am anxious about them, for it seems as though everything will go down in a hurry to-morrow.

For my part, I think this attack was largely due to the steel strike and the wild Anarchistic talk that has accompanied it. A lot of workingmen, without any reason whatever, stopped work, although they had had good positions and were making a good living. They not only stopped, but their influence went out to arouse people against the supposed tyranny of the existing powers. Very probably all that talk about such non-existent oppression accounts for this young lunatic's attempt on the President's life.

"As to Roosevelt, I think he is a very good mountain lion catcher, but as for being President—well, it's another matter. However, there can be no one occurrence, not even the assassination of the President of the United States, that can totally demoralize business in the country, nor can even that calamity permanently affect the prosperity that the McKinley Administration has brought about."

EDWARD B. JORDAN, Collector of Internal Revenue, Brooklyn—It is a terrible occurrence, and has cast a gloom over the entire country. It will be the fervent prayer of every one that God may spare the life of one of the greatest Presidents the country ever had.

LUDWIG NISSEN, Prominent in the Citizens' Union in Brooklyn—It was a dastardly act, and we have come to a pretty pass when men in public office cannot please everybody, and are made objects of the assassin. It has reached a point where we will be unable to secure honorable men for high office if they are to be the victims of unreasoning hate and irresponsible Anarchists. I feel the greatest sorrow because I have the highest regard for President McKinley.

If he should be taken away it would be a great calamity to the business interests and to all the inhabitants of the country. It will be an especial blow to our new possessions, because Mr. McKinley has studied their needs and requirements as no one else has. He is a humane, just, and kindly man, and it seems incredible to think of any one attempting his life.

Postmaster FRANCIS H. WILSON—I was terribly shocked when the news of the dastardly attempt on the President's life first reached Brooklyn, and I am happy that his life has been spared. Expressions of sympathy are to be heard on all sides, and there is a general feeling that he is one of the greatest Presidents we have ever had, of a very high degree of statsmanship, and on a level with the great men of the world. It would have been a pity if the attempt had been successful. Everybody sincerely hopes that he will speedily recover.

Ex-Mayor THOMAS F. GILROY—I am so shocked that I hardly know what to say, but I think it is a sad commentary on our institutions that the elect of the people of this great and glorious country could not be protected from the knife or bullet of the assassin, whether he be insane or not. When it is remembered that of the last seven Presidents three have been assassinated if this fiend's work prove fatal, it seems to me that something could or should be done to throw absolute protection around the lives of our Chief Magistrates.

His death, I do not believe, would have any serious effect on business. The prosperity of this country is on too firm a basis to be affected by the death of any man. From a political standpoint it would be hard to speculate upon the President's death. I believe, however, that the affairs of the country would be safe in the hands of Vice President Roosevelt. He has made a safe Governor and would make a safe President.

ISAAC A. HOPPER, Tammany Leader of the Thirty-first Assembly District—This affair is a sad calamity, but the country has grown to such proportions that the demise of no one man could affect it materially. I look forward to nothing more than a day of National mourning should the shot prove fatal. I am a stanch Democrat, but I think that when we elect a President we should both protect and respect him. This affair is very unfortunate, for it shows us in a very bad light to the monarchical Governments of Europe, as it gives them the impression that there is great discontent here, and that we are not, after all, able to govern ourselves.

HENRY WHITE, Secretary of the Garment Workers of America—While most of us have differed from Mr. McKinley in politics, still he has always been known as a man of strong sympathies and a thorough humanitarian. As both Governor of Ohio and as a Congressman he favored unions in a number of notable instances. In his Presidential campaign he was influenced in behalf of capital, but naturally he is the friend of labor. Of course, every honest workman deplores the shooting and looks upon it as a great calamity. Mr. McKinley stood for settled policies, and if he be allowed to finish his term these policies will be put to the test.

EDWARD H. HEALY, President of the Union Republican Club—My opinion is, that this affair will bring together all good and honest men who desire good government in this country. It seems to me that something should be done to prevent foreigners from coming to this country and enjoying all its privileges, and then, if they see fit, take the life of the man who brings about this prosperity. There is one consolation in all this trouble, however, and that is, that the Government will not suffer, as it will be under good hands in any event.

RELATIVES HEAR THE NEWS.

The President's Sisters Bear Up Bravely—Abner McKinley Starts for Buffalo.

CANTON, Ohio, Sept. 6.—The news of the attempted assassination of President McKinley spread like wildfire throughout this city. The first news, the bulletin to The Repository, was given to Mrs. M. C. Barber, Mrs. McKinley's sister.

Not long after the first reports were received citizens began to gather in small groups in front of the McKinley residence, in North Market Street. Before many minutes elapsed a surging crowd of anxious persons had gathered, and many ventured up to the door of the McKinley home to ask the servants what was the latest news received.

Some of the President's neighbors, who reside in the vicinity, also called at the residence to ask what, if anything, had been heard from Buffalo. To all comers the maid who has charge of the household in the absence of the President replied that no word had been received.

CLEVELAND, Ohio, Sept. 6.—The news of the attempted assassination of the President was broken to his sisters, Mrs. A. J. Duncan and Miss Helen McKinley, both of whom live in this city, by a son of Mrs. Duncan, who hurried to the home of his mother, and as gently as possible told the two sisters of the President of the terrible happening. Both women bore up under the shock and showed much bravery. They had both feared an attempt upon the life of their brother, and their fears were at last realized.

DENVER, Sept. 6.—Abner McKinley, who, with his wife and two daughters, left here this morning for Bailey, in South Platte Cañon, in a special train over the Colorado and Southern Road, was notified late this afternoon of the shooting of the President. He at once started back for Denver. He reached here about 7:30 o'clock, and at 10 o'clock started for Chicago over the Burlington Road.

He will travel to Buffalo over the Lake Shore unless President McKinley dies before he reaches Chicago, in which event he will go direct to Washington.

THE ASSASSIN'S PRECEPTOR.

Emma Goldman, who is said to have inspired Czolgosz to shoot the President, is fond of being styled "the American Louise Michel," but she lacks the talent, the education, and the sincerity of the French original. She is the most radical of the "autonomist" group which denounces Most as too conservative. She was the friend of Alexander Bergmann, now serving a sentence of twenty-one years for shooting Henry C. Frick in Pittsburg during the Homestead troubles.

The noted Anarchist is said now to be about thirty years old. She is a Russian Jew, and the daughter of a tailor. Her parents were poor, and lived near Koova, Russia. She received little or no education, and in her youth heard nothing of Anarchism or its kindred theories. She has been in this country about nine years. She became Mrs. Gruenbaum when about twenty, and lived in Rochester, N. Y., for a year and a half after her marriage. Her husband is said to be there now. Subsequently she met Louis Bernstein, one of the best-read and most radical Anarchists in this State.

About five years ago she came to New York. She dropped her husband's name and called herself Goldman, her maiden name. She was the only woman member of the Jewish Pioneers of Liberty, and startled even Most's followers by the violence of her doctrines. One night at one of the meetings of the Jewish Pioneers she jumped upon a table and shouted:

"The day is near, brethren, when, instead of cooking coffee for you, your wives will be cooking dynamite."

It was at one of the meetings of this society that she met Alexander Bergmann. Bergmann's shooting of Frick split the Anarchists in this city, and Emma Goldman, who was disliked by the conservatives, joined the autonomists, who styled Most and his followers "milk and water" Anarchists.

Emma Goldman has been arrested a number of times in various cities for her fiery and incendiary speeches. In November, 1899, she sailed for England. At that time she expressed herself as dissatisfied with the American workman, and said he was bad and ungrateful. She returned to this country only recently, and went right on preaching what seemed to be the doctrine she preached before she went away.

Gen. Alger Shocked.

DETROIT, Mich., Sept. 6.—When Secretary Cortelyou's bulletin on President McKinley's condition was read to ex-Secretary of War R. A. Alger this evening he was rejoiced to hear that the President had passed through the operation so successfully. He said of the attempt on the Chief Executive's life:

"It was a profound and awful shock to both Mrs. Alger and myself. Words cannot express how deeply we feel for the President and his devoted wife. I have already telegraphed the sympathy of myself and Mrs. Alger to Secretary Cortelyou."

Mr. Dawes Goes to Buffalo.

WASHINGTON, Sept. 6.—Probably the closest friend of the President in Washington at the time of the shooting was Charles G. Dawes, the Controller of the Currency, whose relations with the President are of the most intimate character. Mr. Dawes immediately arranged to go to Buffalo so as to be near the Chief Executive and Mrs. McKinley, and left here on the 7:15 o'clock train accompanied by Elmer Dover the private secretary to Senator Hanna. John Barber, Mrs. McKinley's nephew, who has just passed the examination for Paymaster in the army, also was at the station with Mr. Dawes. At first he intended to go to Buffalo also, but later changed his mind and instead went to Canton, where his mother, Mrs. McKinley's sister, resides.

"All the News That's Fit to Print."

The New York Times.

THE WEATHER.
Fair; light to fresh north winds.

VOL. LIV...NO. 17,178. NEW YORK, MONDAY, JANUARY 23, 1905.—TWELVE PAGES. ONE CENT In Greater New York, Jersey City and Newark. Elsewhere, TWO CENTS.

CZAR'S SUBJECTS ARM FOR REVOLT

St. Petersburg Strike Leaders Decide to Fight.

WORKMEN WANT REVENGE

Rumors of Outbreaks in Finland and Elsewhere.

DOWAGER CZARINA FLEES

Joins Czar at Tsarskoe-Selo—Number Shot in Capital Placed as High as 5,000.

ST. PETERSBURG, Monday, Jan. 23.—Leaders of the strikers who came into conflict with the troops yesterday assembled last night and decided to continue the struggle with arms.

The strikers, goaded to desperation by the events yesterday, a day of violence, fury, and bloodshed, are in a state of open insurrection against the Government. It is rumored that 30,000 or 40,000 armed strikers from Kolpino, sixteen miles distant, are marching on St. Petersburg.

The workmen are now arming with every available weapon for a renewal of the struggle. They have few firearms, but are turning the implements of trade into improvised weapons.

There are rumors of trouble in Finland and disaffection on the part of the troops. Strike leaders say they are awaiting news from Moscow and other large cities, where the troops are not believed to be so loyal as the Guards regiments.

The Moscow Regiment yesterday refused to fire on the working people.

No one knows how many men, women, and children were killed and wounded yesterday by the volleys of the troops. Some estimates are as high as 5,000, but 500 is probably nearer the true number.

The Emperor is at Tsarskoe-Selo, whither the Empress Dowager has fled.

PEACEABLE MEN SHOT DOWN.

Petitioners Met by the Troops of Grand Duke Vladimir.

Special Cable to THE NEW YORK TIMES.

LONDON, Jan. 22.—St. Petersburg's streets were the theatre to-day of scenes unparalleled in the history of the world. A wholesale massacre of Russian strikers occurred, and the dead and wounded are numbered by thousands.

The strikers undertook to-day to present to the Czar a petition for the redress of their wrongs.

Instead of meeting the Czar they had to deal with Grand Duke Vladimir, and the morgues and hospitals are full of the victims of his cruelty. The correspondent of The Daily Mail, in telegraphing an account of the tragedy, says:

"This morning all was still and strangely quiet. It was bitterly cold, with a piercing wind and driving fine snow. People muffled in furs went to church as usual. A few strolled toward the Palace Square to see what was to be seen, and, finding nothing, started away again.

"There were no troops in front of the palace, and the bridges across the Neva were open to traffic.

"St. Petersburg under the freshly fallen snow was a white, fair city, from which the gilt minarets of the Admiralty, the cathedral, and the St. Peter and St. Paul fortress shot up tongues of flame in the growing sunshine.

"The church bells were calling. Swift sleighs with splendid horses were gliding by. It was impossible then to connect the scene with the pitiful tragedy that was so swiftly to follow.

"At 10 o'clock the troops began to move about, passing in different directions along the radiating suburban thoroughfares. Cavalry, infantry, and Cossacks in small detachments made no great military display, but infantry and some Guards marched away in regiments, their fixed bayonets glittering wickedly.

"The official programme was going to be literally carried out. Evidently no procession from any industrial suburb was to be allowed to approach the centre of the capital.

"An hour later a little tour in a fast sleigh showed that Central St. Petersburg was ringed with a triple cordon of defenses, terrible as those of Liao-Yang, as if to resist an invading army.

"Out on every main road, on the Ekaterinoffsky Prospect on the left bank of the river, at every strategic point where there were cross-roads, detachments of troops were placed on the further side. Every bridge crossing the Neva to Vassili Ostrov was strongly held, while from the inside of the great courtyards of the Winter Palace a mass of troops came out into the Palace Square.

"Most noticeable, as always, were the Preobrajensky Guards in their striking uniform, and the Pavlovsky Guards in high bronze helmets. There were also grenadier guards and the glittering cuirasses and eagle caps of the cuirassiers of guards, the Czarina's regiment, mounted all on black

"The cavalcade was a magnificent sight as it wheeled round in the great square.

"It was plain thus early that there would be no demonstration in front of the Palace. It only remained to see with how much consideration any attempt to hold one would be repressed.

"It was not long to wait before all uncertainty was removed. What followed it is impossible to describe, because it is impossible to know what occurred in many places widely apart.

"The narratives of eye-witnesses are as yet uncollected, but from many different directions people set out upon the projected pilgrimage, only to be shot down in masses by their uniformed brothers almost before their procession had started from the suburbs.

"The Putiloff strikers left their barrack homes about the factory according to their programme, bringing with them their wives and children, even their babies, as had been arranged. Father Gopon marched at their head, bearing a crucifix aloft above the great roll containing the precious petition.

"They marched down the Peterhoff Chaussée, where the works stand, down hill to where, at the Neva gate, the triumphal arch erected after the Turkish war stands at the junction with the main Baltic thoroughfare.

"There the Ismailovsky Guards, a regiment of which the Czar is honorary Colonel, were drawn up in waiting.

"As the head of the procession approached the acting Colonel called upon them to stop. Father Gopon, still holding the crucifix, advanced and demanded that the Colonel receive and forward the petition.

"This request was declined. Then, after a minute's hesitation and discussion, the procession continued to advance. A sharp order was given. The soldiers raised their rifles, and a volley rang out, but they had only used blank cartridges.

"Another order. This time ball cartridge, and men, women, and children fell in heaps.

"Father Gopon, still clutching the crucifix, stood among the dead and dying with the petition.

"Still another volley, and then the crowd no longer. The procession turned and fled, all but 300, who were lying dead, and 500 writhing wounded.

"Some who had revolvers fired as they fled. Others carried icepicks, some had stones, but practically they were unarmed.

"It was all over with the Putiloff strike procession, and at 11:41 o'clock the strikers were still in sight of their works. As they retreated the soldiers followed, and before a quarter of an hour most of them had fled to their homes, and there only remained the dead and wounded, who were removed with the usual Russian skill to be taken to hospital or home.

"What happened to the Putiloff contingent happened at other places. A procession starting its advance found its progress barred almost before it was begun, and as it attempted to continue it was mowed down by volleys.

"Twenty thousand people started from Kolpino, a manufacturing village twenty-five miles away. At the Moscow arch, on the confines of the town, they met with six volleys. A thousand fell dead and 1,500 were wounded.

"From up the river a great crowd marched to the Nevsky gate, where 500 fell dead and 700 were founded

"The Vassili Ostrov workers only lost 200 killed and 700 wounded."

TROOPS FIRE AT LODZ.

Many Demonstrators Shot Down—Rising in Finland Feared.

LONDON TIMES—NEW YORK TIMES Special Cablegram.

PARIS, Jan. 22.—A dispatch from St. Petersburg gives an account of a public demonstration at Lodz, a manufacturing town in Russian Poland, in which the crowd carried flags and raised cries of "Long Live Poland!"

Troops stationed in houses along the route of the procession fired upon it through the windows. Some persons were killed and several wounded.

Great excitement prevails.

Another St. Petersburg dispatch says very serious news has been received from Finland, where all the factory hands are on strike and a general rising is feared.

CIVIL WAR THREATENED.

Workmen Have Lost Faith in Czar, and Now Mean to Fight.

ST. PETERSBURG, Monday, Jan. 23.—A condition almost bordering on civil war exists in the terror-stricken Russian capital.

The city is under martial law, with Prince Vasilchikoff as commander of over 50,000 of the Emperor's crack guards. Troops are bivouacked in the streets and at various places on the Nevsky Prospect, the main thoroughfare of the city.

It is rumored that M. Witte will be appointed dictator to-day, but the report is not confirmed.

A member of the Emperor's household is quoted as saying that the conflict of yesterday will end the war with Japan, and that Russia will have a Constitution or Emperor Nicholas will lose his head.

The authorities, while they seem to realize the magnitude of the crisis with which the dynasty and the autocracy are confronted on account of yesterday's events, are apparently paralyzed for the moment.

An official statement was promised at midnight, at which hour it was announced that it had been postponed till to-morrow.

Intense indignation is bound to be aroused all over Russia. The workmen and revolutionists expect news from Moscow and other big centres, where the troops are not of the same class as the Guard regiments of St. Petersburg.

The Warsaw and Baltic Railroad is reported to have been torn up for a mile and a half, but the damage is said to have been repaired.

The blood which crimsoned the snow has fired the brains and passions of the strikers and turned women as well as men into wild beasts, and the cry of the infuriated populace is for vengeance.

The sympathy of the middle classes is with the workmen. Comment on the action of the troops and authorities is very bitter, and sarcastic remarks are made that officers are braver against the defenseless public than against the Japanese, and that "ammunition may be scarce in the Far East, but is too plentiful here."

If Father Gopon, the master mind of the movement, aimed at open revolution, he managed the affair like a genius, for he has done a great deal to break the faith of the people in the "Little Father," who, they were convinced and who Father Gopon had taught them to believe, would right their wrongs and redress their grievances.

Maxim Gorky the Russian novelist, expresses the opinion that yesterday's work will break the faith of the people in the Emperor. He said last evening:

"To-day inaugurated revolution in Russia. The Emperor's prestige will be irrevocably shattered by the shedding of innocent blood. He has alienated himself forever from this people.

"Gopon taught the workmen to believe that an appeal direct to the 'Little Father' would be heeded. They have been undeceived.

"Gopon is now convinced that peaceful means have failed and that the only remedy is force. It is now the people against the oppressors, and the battle will be fought to the bitter end."

At a big meeting last night the following message from M. Gorky was read:

"Beloved Associates: We have no Emperor. Innocent blood lies between him and the people. Now begins the people's struggle for freedom. May it prosper. My blessing upon you all. Would I might be with you to-night; but I have much to do."

A workman who was introduced to speak in Father Gopon's name made a fiery speech. He appealed to the Liberals to furnish arms. The meeting adopted a letter denouncing the officers and regiments that fired on the workmen and another letter extolling the Moscow regiment which refused to fire.

The following is the text of a letter addressed by Father Gopon to Emperor Nicholas on Saturday night:

"Sovereign: I fear your Ministers have not told you the full truth about the situation. The whole people, trusting in you, have resolved to appear at the Winter Palace at 2 P. M. in order to inform you of their needs. If, vacillating, you do not appear before the people, then the moral bonds between you and the people, who trust in you, will disappear, because innocent blood will flow between you and the people.

"Appear to-morrow before your people and receive our address of devotion in a courageous spirit. I and the representatives of labor and my brave workingmen and comrades guarantee the inviolability of your person."

With darkness it was feared that the mob might begin to loot and pillage, and even burn; but beyond the breaking of a few windows in the Nevsky Prospect and the pillaging of fruit shops, little disorder was reported. Some windows of the palace of Grand Duke Alexis were smashed.

Most of the theatres were closed, but at the People's Palace, which was open, two Liberals attempted to harangue the audience, proposing at the close of the performance that the audience testify to their sympathy with their fallen brothers. The orators were promptly arrested, but the audience walked out.

St. Petersburg is sleeping quietly at this hour, 4:45 A. M., worn out by the excitement of a long day. Laborers and spectators have long since left the streets, and the military and police have had little to do for hours beyond driving off occasional riotous bands of irresponsible rogues bent on window-breaking and marauding and dispersing groups of too demonstrative Socialists or Liberals returning from protracted meetings where their minds were filled with incendiary speeches.

Since midnight the Russian capital has been as peaceful as it was the preceding night; but in the Palace Square and in all the principal streets and open places throughout the town bivouac fires are gleaming and infantrymen sleeping near their stacked rifles or marching hither and thither.

Cavalrymen on wearied horses are patrolling the long thoroughfares. No further firing has been heard and no more reports of collisions have been received.

A renewal of rioting is not expected until late in the morning, if at all to-day, as the strikers, thoroughly wearied by yesterday's events, will be inclined to wait until the military precautions have somewhat relaxed.

Two hundred journalists and professional men met in this city on Saturday evening to discuss means to avoid bloodshed. A committee, consisting of the authors Kharsenieff, Gorky, Annensky, and Gesief, several professors, and the workmen's advocate Kedrim, was appointed to interview Minister of the Interior Sviatopolk-Mirsky.

They arrived at the Ministry of the Interior at 10 o'clock Saturday night, but were received coldly, the officials declaring that it was impossible for them to see the Minister that night. The committeemen announcing their intention to wait till the Minister would see them, they were persuaded to go away by Assistant Minister Rydzefsky, who, being told that their errand was to prevent bloodshed, resolutely refused to call Prince Sviatopolk-Mirsky and ironically told the committeemen they had better persuade the workmen to abandon their plan of a procession to the palace.

Thus rebuffed, the committeemen proceeded to M. Witte's residence. M. Witte received them affably and offered tea to them, which they declined. Having heard them, M. Witte expressed himself with great sympathy, but maintained that all measures had been decided without consulting him, adding: "I am nothing in the administration."

M. Witte then referred them to Minister Sviatopolk-Mirsky, regretting his inability to do anything, and advising them to get the demonstration abandoned. He said the workmen had taken a wrong course, which was incompatible with autocracy. The Emperor could only receive a deputation by application through proper channels.

He then telephoned to Minister Sviatopolk-Mirsky and tried to persuade him to receive the committee. The Minister, however, still declined, and the deputation departed.

Late last night at a conference of editors of St. Petersburg newspapers it was agreed to address to the censorship administration a protest against the censorship of the day's events, and it was also resolved to send a deputation to negotiate with the workmen's union regarding the resumption of work by the printers.

DAY OF TERROR IN CZAR'S CAPITAL

Troops Slay Women and Children with Men.

LED BY PRIEST TO DEATH

Workmen Force Guards to Fire to Stop Them.

BARRICADES IN STREETS

A General Killed and Other Officers Attacked—Crowds Shout "Down With the Czar."

ST. PETERSBURG, Jan. 22.—This has been a day of unspeakable horror in St. Petersburg.

Minister of the Interior Sviatopolk-Mirsky presented to his Majesty last night the invitation of the workmen to appear at the Winter Palace this afternoon and receive their petition, but the Emperor's advisers had already taken the decision to show a firm and resolute front, and the Emperor's answer to the 100,000 workmen trying to force their way to the Palace Square to-day was a solid array of troops who met them with rifle, bayonet, and sabre.

The priest Gopon, the leader and idol of the men, in his golden vestments, holding aloft the cross and marching at the head of thousands of workmen through the Narva Gate, miraculously escaped a volley which laid low half a hundred persons.

The figures of the total number killed or wounded at the Narva Gate, the Moscow Gate, at various bridges and islands, and at the Winter Palace vary. The best estimate is 500, although there are exaggerated figures placing the number as high as 5,000.

Many men were accompanied by their wives and children, and in the confusion, which left no time for discrimination, these shared the fate of the men.

One Regiment Mutinied.

The troops, with the exception of the Moscow Regiment, which is reported to have thrown down its arms, remained loyal and obeyed orders.

The military authorities had a firm grip on every artery in the city. At daybreak guard regiments, cavalry, and infantry held every bridge across the frozen Neva, the network of canals which interlace the city, and the gates leading from the industrial section, while in the Palace Square, as the storm centre, were massed Dragoon regiments, infantry, and Cossacks of the Guards.

Barred from the bridges and gates, men, women, and children crossed the frozen river and canals on the ice by twos and threes, hurrying to the Palace Square, where they were sure the Emperor would be present to hear them.

But the street approaches to the square were cleared by volleys and Cossack charges. Men and women, infuriated to frenzy by the loss of loved ones, cursed the soldiers while they retreated.

Strikers Built Barricades.

Men harangued the crowds, telling them that the Emperor had foiled them and that the time had come to act. Strikers began to build barricades in the Nevsky Prospect and at other points, using any material that came to hand, and even chopping down telegraph poles.

Fighting meantime continued at various places, soldiers firing volleys and charging the mob. The whole city was in a state of panic. Women were running through the streets seeking lost members of their families. Several barricades were carried by the troops.

Toward 8 o'clock in the evening the crowds, exhausted, began to disperse, leaving the military in possession. As they retreated up the Nevsky Prospect the workmen put out all the lights.

The little chapel at the Narva gate was wrecked.

On Kaminostov Island all the lights were extinguished.

Every officer wearing the uniform of the Emperor who was found alone was mobbed. A General was killed on the Nicholas Bridge, and a dozen officers were seized, stripped of their epaulets, and deprived of their swords.

Troops Spared Father Gopon.

There was a very dramatic scene at the Narva Gate when Father Gopon, in golden vestments and bearing aloft an ikon, and flanked by two clergymen carrying religious banners, approached at the head of a procession of 8,000 workmen.

Troops were drawn up across the entrance. Several times an officer called upon the procession to stop, but Father Gopon did not falter. Then an order was given to fire, first with blank cartridges. Two volleys rang out, but the line still did not waver.

Then, with seeming reluctance, an officer gave the command to load with ball, and the next volley was followed by shrieks of the wounded.

As the Cossacks followed up the volley with a charge the workmen fled before them, leaving about 100 dead or wounded.

It was evident that the soldiers deliberately spared Father Gopon. One of the clergymen by his side was wounded, but he escaped untouched and hid behind a wall until the Cossacks passed. He was then spirited away by workmen.

The Scenes in Palace Square.

The most harrowing scenes of the day were around the Palace Square.

This enormous place back of the Winter Palace is surrounded by gardens fronting the Admiralty and by a vast semi-circular building containing the offices of the General Staff, the Ministry of Finance, and the Foreign Office. In the centre of the block is cut an arched gateway surmounted by a bronze quadriga. The gateway serves as an entrance to the Grand Morskaia, one of the most fashionable streets of the city, which crosses the Nevsky Prospect.

Beyond the semi-circular building is a wide space leading to the Moikal Canal, and beyond this stands an enormous square building, the headquarters of the St. Petersburg Military District. From this building the Grand Duke Vladimir had issued orders for the whole military preparations, and from it he directed the day's operations.

In the centre of the square stands a great granite column supporting a statue of Victory, commemorating the defeat of the Napoleonic invasion, at which a veteran guard in the uniform of the period of Alexander I. stands sentinel.

Like a Military Camp.

When The Associated Press correspondent arrived at the Palace Square early this morning he found a considerable crowd of demonstrators already lining the railings of the Admiralty Gardens and the Boulevard. The square itself presented the appearance of a military encampment.

Several companies of the Pavlovsky and Preobrajensky Guards had piled their arms, while the men were sitting around campfires or stamping on the snow to keep warm. Beyond the infantry stood squadrons of the Chevalier Guards and the Horse Guards, without their lances, cuirasses, or the usual gay trappings.

The men carried carbines slung across their shoulders, and their stirrups were covered with felt or straw to keep off the cold. All the soldiers wore bashliks, or hoods, to protect their ears from the keen, searching wind. A field kitchen steamed merrily, disseminating the odor of viands.

Many of the men wrestled or boxed, cracking jokes as one or another rolled on the snow.

A whole row of ambulances drawn up near the palace served as a grim reminder of the stern business on hand.

Meanwhile pickets were stationed at all the entrances of the palace, and cavalry patrols kept promenaders moving along the sidewalk. Sleigh traffic continued uninterrupted till the time came for the cavalry to charge.

The crowd of strikers in and outside the Admiralty Gardens continued to grow hourly, swelled by arrivals from the Nevsky Prospect, which debouches upon the boulevard skirting the Gardens.

Constantly Reproached Troops.

The strikers manned and held a small edifice at the corner of the Gardens and poured out constant objurgations and reproaches at the troops. It was in vain that officers requested them to disperse.

"We have come to present our homage and grievances to the Emperor."

"Let the Emperor come out and hear us; we do not wish to do harm."

"Long live Nicholas II.! If he only listens to our grievances we are sure he will be just and merciful!"

"We cannot longer endure our sufferings. Better die at once and end all!"

Such were the cries repeatedly heard.

Many strikers brought their wives and children. "You soldiers are our brothers; you cannot shoot these little ones," they exclaimed. But as the pickets and patrols continued driving off the people the demonstrators began to give way, and the bitterest insults and oaths, in which the Russian vocabulary is particularly rich, became frequent.

"We are not Japanese; why brutalize us? Will you shame the mother who bore you, who was a Russian like ourselves?" were some of the cries that were heard. Later such expressions as "Scoundrels!" "Mercenaries!" "Dogs!" and worse were heard. A long-haired student among the crowd hurled an insulting epithet at an officer, who sent a couple of men to arrest him.

The crowd tried to rescue the student, but he was dragged and kicked across the sunlit square, his long hair tossing in the wind. The crowd broke out into a storm of hoots and hisses. Then a young workman jeered at a soldier, who applied his rifle butt, and, with the help of comrades, dragged the workman, despite his piteous pleadings, to the lock-up.

Every time the troops moved the crowds hissed them. Strikers also gathered at the entrance of the Grand Morskaia and of the avenue leading to the Moika. The crowd at the latter place swelled to huge proportions, blocking the bridge across the canal.

Ordered to Disperse Crowd.

The order came at 1:30 P. M. to clear off the crowd. The Colonel commanding the Horse Guards uttered a short, sharp command; the troopers drew their swords and advanced at a quick trot, and then broke into a gallop, heading straight for the Moika, where they were lost in a cloud of snow.

Shrieks from the wounded resounded. Then came silence, broken only by the galloping of ambulance horses.

The next twenty minutes passed without incident. Nothing indicated the approach of the horrible butchery which was destined to stain the corner of the Admiralty Gardens with human blood.

The crowd there persisted in refusing to move on, clamoring for the Emperor and continually hurling abuse at the troops, but attempting no violence.

Two companies of the Preobrajensky Guards, of which Emperor Nicholas himself was formerly Colonel, which had been standing at ease in front of the Palace, formed up and marched at double quick toward the fatal corner.

Events followed with awful swiftness.

The commanding officer shouted "Disperse! Disperse! Disperse!"

Many in the crowd turned to flee, but it was too late. A bugle sounded and the men in the front ranks sank to their knees and both companies fired three volleys, the first two with blank cartridges and the last with ball.

A hundred corpses strewed the sidewalk. Many women were pierced through the back as they were trying to escape.

The Associated Press correspondent, standing behind the troops, saw mangled corpses of persons of all ages and both sexes strewing the ground. One boy of thirteen had his skull pierced and rent by bullets. Great splashes and streams of blood stained the snow.

Only a few of the victims remained alive, for the fatal volley was fired at a distance of not more than twenty paces, and so the ambulances had little to do.

Sleighs Carried Off the Dead.

The police recruited a large number of sleighs to carry off the dead.

Heartrending scenes were witnessed as wives, husbands, and mothers came up to claim their dear ones and were carried off with them in the sleighs.

Meanwhile the crowd had drifted up the Nevsky Prospect, yelling, "Murderers! Murderers!" and the square resumed its calm aspect, the troops returning to their stations.

It was now the turn for the crowd stationed at the Morskaia entrance to the square, where the Horse Guards repeated the exploit with which they had cleared the Moika, and drove the people pell mell down the thoroughfare.

From thenceforward the Palace Square ceased to be the centre of interest. The Associated Press correspondent went to the Grand Morskaia, and stood a whole hour near the corner of the Nevsky Prospect. The fashionable hotels on either side of the Grand Morskaia were crowded, but the doors were closed except to well-known visitors. Fashionable jewelers' and other stores were barred, but mostly unshuttered. Quite a number of prominent personages stood on the sidewalks watching the developments.

Secretary Spencer Eddy of the American Embassy chatted with Grand Duke Boris, who had driven up in a stylish sleigh, drawn by a magnificent trotter. M. Bompard, the French Ambassador, drove past with his wife. As a couple of squadrons of red-capped hussars trotted by the officers gave the command, "Use the flats of your swords."

Then the troopers moved off and disappeared down the street, the crowds shrieking "Murderous dogs!" but quickly vanishing before them. A few who were wounded were picked up and conveyed to a drug store on the opposite corner of the Grand Morskaia and the Nevsky Prospect.

An Impromptu Oration.

No troops were visible for as much as half an hour. A crowd quickly formed outside the drug store, and an orator was found for the occasion. Standing on the steps of the drug store, he addressed the impromptu meeting thus:

"Comrades: We came humbly and peacefully to meet the Emperor and lay our grievances before him; but the Emperor refuses to see us, and instead soldiers were sent to shoot us down. Then all I can say is he is no Emperor." "Down with the Emperor!" shouted the crowd. The orator proceeded:

"We have suffered under the sway of the Chinovniks." ("Down with the Chinovniks!" exclaimed the crowd.) "We hoped for redress, but hope is no longer possible; we can win our rights only by fighting." ("Down with the autocracy!" yelled the crowd.)

"Our only chance of redress is from representatives of the people." ("Long live the Constitutional Assembly!") "Then all I have to say is, To arms, comrades, to arms!"

"To arms!" was the thunderous response.

The crowd, now aroused to a state of frenzy, at the sight of the wounded who were being brought out of the drug store and placed in ambulances, saluted them as martyrs. Every head was uncovered as the victims were conveyed away.

The wilder element in the crowd had now obtained the upper hand and pro-

INDEX TO DEPARTMENTS.

[illegible]ed to attack every officer in sight. [A] General driving up the Nevsky Prospect was mobbed, with shouts of "Murderer!" His sword was captured as a trophy, the crowds shouting "Hurrah!" [A]nother General was nearly dragged from his sleigh, but clutched the driver desperately, and in escaping was struck on his bald head by a glass bottle and stunned.

Swords were wrenched from several passing officers, and the crowd shouted "Break their swords, but do not beat them."

The appearance of several companies of infantry restored order, but the crowds refused to disperse and several volleys were fired and a number of people killed.

Half a dozen policemen were surrounded by a crowd in a neighboring side street. The policemen drew their revolvers and fired, and one of them was killed by a comrade's misdirected fire.

THE RIOTERS' LAST STAND.

Barricades Erected on Island—Thirty of the Defenders Slain.

ST. PETERSBURG, Monday, Jan. 23.—The Associated Press correspondent was present when the first barricades were constructed on Vassili Ostrov Island, where fighting occurred late last night, resulting in the killing of thirty of the defenders of the barricades.

The strikers, driven from the river front, had gathered in front of the union headquarters, out of sight of the soldiery, and, buzzing like a nest of angry hornets, a hundred men brandished handleless sabre blades secured from some junk shop, which were the only weapons seen in the hands of the strikers during the day. Others swarmed up poles and cut down telegragh, telephone, and electric light wires, which they strung from lamp post to lamp post across the street to break up charges of cavalry.

At first none of the leaders seemed to have any plans. Suddenly two men appeared carrying ladders, and others pushed up with more ladders, timber, and lumber from incomplete buildings, and old sleighs. In the twinkling of an eye a substantial barricade had been constructed, bound together with wires and ropes. On it water was poured, which immediately froze.

As a last contribution, Christmas trees were added to the pile, and the crowd rushed to repeat the process at the other end of the block. Meanwhile others were bringing on bricks for missiles.

When the troops advanced the strikers lined the barricades and offered what resistance they could; but while half the infantry rested their rifles on a barricade and volleyed the others demolished the obstruction and marched over the street, which was then encumbered with fifty dead or wounded, and the snow on which was crimsoned with human blood.

Among the rumors curent last night was one that the workmen on Vassili Ostrov had seized a dynamite factory, and another that they were pillaging shops. The island was in darkness, neither gas nor electricity being available.

PROOF OF WIDE DISCONTENT.

But London Times Takes Conservative View of Russian Outbreak.

Special Cable to THE NEW YORK TIMES.

LONDON, Jan. 23.—The Times, referring editorially to the terrible events of yesterday in St. Petersburg, says:

"With our present information it is quite impossible to gauge the importance of these events. They would be grave at any time, but are doubly grave at this moment, when the country whose capital they convulse is engaged in a great and disastrous war at the furthest extremity of Asia.

"They prove the existence of widespread and profound discontent among the working classes of St. Petersburg, for no Socialist intrigues or harangues could have led thousands of workingmen to confront death unless they were convinced that their lives under autocracy had become unbearable. How far the discontent may extend throughout the other cities of Russia and into the rural districts we have little means of ascertaining.

"The gravity of the position depends on factors with which we are at present unacquainted. The French seem disposed to recognize in it the beginning of a great upheaval, comparable with that which marked the downfall of their own ancient monarchy and their historic system of society. They may be right or they may be wrong. The differences between France at the close of the eighteenth century and Russia at the beginning of the twentieth are at least as numerous and striking as the resemblances.

"We can but say that for the present it seems to us their alarm for the immediate future of Russia may perhaps be as much exaggerated as the extravagant confidence they have hitherto professed in her future. What that future may be we dare not venture to forecast. We stand face to face with a great possibility which time alone can [illegible]cure and unfold."

REVOLUTION, LONDON THINKS.

Belief That a New Chapter in Russia's History Has Begun.

LONDON, Monday, Jan. 23.—Such [illegible]es as these, extracted from editorial articles in the London morning newspapers, sufficiently indicate the opinion held here of yesterday's events in St. Petersburg:

"Revolt has been quelled, but revolution has begun."

"The Bureaucracy has declared its policy [illegible] is the policy of the Blagovestchensk [illegible]."

"[illegible] inevitable reaction has begun, and with it a new chapter in Russia's history and probably also in the history of Europe and Asia."

"The revolutionary movement in Russia has received its baptism of blood, its crown of martyrdom."

"Is there a Mirabeau or even a Danton in Russia to-day?"

"A very grave responsibility lies today at the door of the Czar, who has failed to grasp his unique opportunity."

"The 'Little Father' has become the murderer of his people, and it remains with him to save the country from disaster. Even at the eleventh hour he may do so, but only by recognizing that autocracy has gone forever."

Temper of Masses Attested.

It is pointed out that the fate of Russia does not depend upon the people of St. Petersburg alone, but on the masses throughout the country, and it is considered that the events of recent months connected with the agitation for constitutional reform sufficiently attest the people's temper.

Some of the special dispatches from St. Petersburg this morning comment upon the unexpectedly determined attitude displayed by the Russian workmen yesterday as revealing a new phase in the character of the patient masses.

PARIS DEEPLY IMPRESSED.

Situation in Russia Everywhere Discussed—Revolution Feared.

PARIS, Jan. 22.—The news of the bloody events in St. Petersburg has caused a profound sensation here. The newspapers issued special editions throughout the evening giving dramatic details of the street fighting, and these were eagerly read and discussed on the boulevards, at the theatres, and in other public places, the tragedy being the universal subject of comment. The newspaper offices were surrounded by crowds awaiting bulletins.

Officials here have received advices practically the same as those made public. The general view, including that of officials, is one of the deepest apprehension that the events of to-day may precipitate in Russia a period of revolution such as France has witnessed.

The Temps's St. Petersburg special correspondent to-night makes a graphic comparison between the position of Emperor Nicholas II. and King Louis XVI. on the eve of the Reign of Terror. After a careful analysis of the situation the correspondent concludes that most of the military forces of Russia will remain loyal to the Emperor, although he foresees prospects of some of the artillery regiments playing the same rôle that the regiment of the French Guards took on the fall of the Bastille at the outbreak of the French Revolution. The correspondent also points out that Emperor Nicholas's withdrawal to Tsarskoe-Selo places twenty-one kilometres between him and the excited populace.

The prevailing tone here is one of awe at the magnitude of the horror. The Socialist journals do not disguise a strong sentiment in favor of the people and of indignation against the course of the Government.

PRAYERS IN WASHINGTON.

Offered for Czar and His People in Many of the Churches.

WASHINGTON, Jan. 22.—Fervent prayers were offered in many of the churches to-day for the Russian Emperor and for his people. Intense interest in the struggle at the Russian capital was manifested.

Count Cassini, the Russian Ambassador, arrived here to-night from New York and was driven at once to the Embassy, accompanied by Col. Raspopoff, the Russian military attaché. Immediately upon the Ambassador's arrival copies of the latest press dispatches were shown to him. Count Cassini was never more calm than as he carefully scanned their contents. Officially the Ambassador has heard nothing of the situation, and for this reason he would make no comment.

"Apparently there is a serious strike in St. Petersburg," he remarked, "but I have no news except that which has reached me in these dispatches."

CROWDS READ BULLETINS.

The Cynic, the Workman, and Tolstoy—The Czar and the Auto.

The bulletins posted every few minutes yesterday afternoon and evening drew large crowds to the front of the Times Building. Interesting, and, in some cases, amusing, were the comments made by persons who stopped to read the condensed items of intelligence from mob-ridden St. Petersburg.

One woman, after a glance at the bulletin boards, remarked as if surprised:

"There seems to be something doing in Russia after all."

"The world of letters," announced a cynical individual, waving his cane at the bulletins, "is about to be enriched with another essay by Count Tolstoy."

This remark bore fruit of another kind. A man who had all the appearance of a laborer said:

"That's no dream, either, and there's a whole lot to it. Tolstoy is the man in Russia to-night. And he's the man in the east side of New York, too. There's hardly a Russian or a Pole comes into New York who hasn't a cheap copy or a pamphlet by Tolstoy stowed away somewhere in his sack o' belongings. Bein' in a free country they can afford to howl with him, and they do it, too!"

An automobilist slowed up his machine and stopped at the curb opposite the window where the bulletins were being posted every few minutes. After carefully reading and digesting the latest news, he turned to a woman in the auto and said:

"I can see a picture of the Czar rushing through the Nevsky Gate, his crown under one arm, a gripsack under the other, and shouting at the top of his voice: 'A bubble! A bubble! My kingdom for a bubble!'"

While the automobilist heard the Czar yearning to exceed the speed limit a Broadway stroller—one of the type which knows everything about Manhattan and nothing about anything outside of it—gave a contemptuous glance at a dispatch marked "St. Petersburg, 10:50 P. M.," and posted here at 8:05 P. M., and said:

"That's the worst o' them up-to-date noospapers."

FIRE ON HUNGARIAN MOB.

Gendarmes Kill Four Persons at Riot of Liberals.

BUDAPEST, Hungary, Jan. 22.—The gendarmerie were called out to-day to quell a disturbance following a meeting of local Liberals at the village of Turopolya.

The gendarmes fired on the mob, killing four, and wounding one.

REVOLUTION PARTY HERE HAILS NEWS WITH JOY

Scenes of Enthusiasm at Convention of Russian Refugees.

GLOOM AT THE CATHEDRAL

Ambassador Cassini Attends Service and Hears the News from St. Petersburg—Priest Speaks of Russia's Ill-Luck.

Nowhere in this city did the news of the uprising in the Czar's capital create such a profound impression as on the lower east side. In that part of the city thousands of men and women who have cared and suffered for the cause of Russian freedom, have found a haven, and there was not one of these who did not feel a personal share in the events of which the cable told.

When the first bulletin was posted outside the offices of the east side newspapers and the first extra was sent out, it was as though a tocsin had rung. All the highways and byways of that crowded section of the city at once became filled with men and women, a series of unbroken processions converging on the offices of the Jewish newspapers in East Broadway.

These organs, of course, did not have a foreign cable service at all commensurate with the occasion or the demand for news, but they did the best they could under the circumstances. The Vorwaerts, the organ read by the Russian immigrants of revolutionary tendencies, at noon gave out an extra in which were presented in brief outline the happenings in the Russian capital. There was an attempt at a bulletin service at all the offices of the east side newspapers, but what news reached the crowds in this manner was merely sufficient to whet their appetite for more. And during the entire afternoon and evening the very editorial sanctums of these newspaper offices were constantly invaded by men and women who with shining eyes demanded news.

East Side Cafes Ablaze.

On the street corners and in the parks, wherever two or three met, the one topic of conversation was the St. Petersburg revolt. And in the little cafés and restaurants on the east side, where the east side middle class love to congregate of a Sunday evening, they dined last night to the tune of the "Marseillaise" and the Russian National anthem woven into melody, while the guests went frantic with excitement.

Next to the overshadowing question of what the present uprising meant, and what it was going to accomplish for Russian freedom, there was another question that came up for discussion whenever the uprising itself was discussed. That question was:

Who is Father Gopon?

And surprising as the fact may seem, despite the hundreds of underground channels that lead from Russia to the Russian exiles on the lower east side, there did not seem to be a man or a woman there who could identify the priest.

Call Gopon God's Own Man.

"Who knows, little brother?" said a recent arrival to these shores. "Who knows where God finds His agents? I have never heard of Father Gopon, but I know now that he must be God's own man, since he took no weapon and met the Cossacks with nothing but a cross raised aloft."

One needed only to go among the men and the women of the east side last night to find that there were many among them who ascribed what had occurred to supernatural intervention. There were many who insisted on seeing more than a mere coincidence in the fact that the Russian New Year had been marked by the surrender of Port Arthur, and the members of the bund pointed in the strange irony of fate to the fact that the uprising in the Russian capital should occur on the day when they were holding their annual convention.

Work of Russian Agitators Here.

The annual convention of the "Bundists" went into session on Saturday night. They have an organization which is represented in all the large cities of the United States where Russians live in any great number. They are closely allied with the mother organization in Russia.

The principal purpose of the organization in this country is to raise funds for their brethren who are fighting for the cause in Russia. During the half dozen years it has been in existence, though it is made up largely of men and women with incomes that leave little or no margin when the expenses of livelihood have been defrayed, it has sent $500,000 to Russia.

Most of this has been used for revolutionary literature, and among this the staple has been copies of the American Constitution printed in the Russian language and made up so as to fit into the Russian prayer books that are provided in the Orthodox churches. Through their Russian agents the Bundists have been so successful in smuggling them into the Russian places of worship that they insist that the present demand for a constitution in that country is largely due to the familiarity Russians have attained in recent years with the charter of American liberty.

At the noon recess the delegates attending the convention obtained news of what was going on in St. Petersburg. This news was of a meagre nature, and had not been amplified to any extent when a TIMES reporter was conducted into Clinton Hall, in Clinton Street, near Grand, where the convention was held, late yesterday afternoon, bringing the details contained in cable dispatches from the Russian capital.

Morris Lewinsohn, an east side physician, was in the chair. The discussion was a proposition to decrease the expenses of the organization here, so as to be able to make better provision for the cause in Russia. Of the delegates, sixty-six in number, most were recent arrivals, unable to speak English. Half their number had been incarcerated in Russian prisons or exiled to Siberia for the part they had taken in the revolutionary movement there.

The TIMES reporter was soon surrounded by a group of delegates clamoring for news. To Dr. Morris Winchevsky, an east side physician, an outline of the latest news was given, including the report that a regiment of infantry had declined to fire on the mob which attempted to cross the Nikolovsky Bridge.

"This is the greatest news of all," said Jacob Marinoff, a delegate from Denver. "The dynasty is lost. The day of freedom has dawned upon Russia."

Bundists Frantic with Joy.

Dr. Winchevsky then mounted the platform and told the news in Russian. Time and again he was interrupted by enthusiastic demonstrations. When he reached the Nikolovsky Bridge incident the convention was swept from off its feet by the wild demonstration that followed.

First there were cheers upon cheers, while the men threw their hats toward the ceiling and women got to their feet, waving handkerchiefs. Then by degrees a hush fell upon the audience, and in the midst of it a woman's voice rang clear through the hall:

Siberian Refugees Heard From.

"I knew it, I knew it! They are our brothers, too. I knew it all the time," she cried in Russian. The next moment she fell into the arms of another woman delegate who stood near by, and both sobbed convulsively. Other women followed their example, and the men looked on with shining eyes.

The woman whose voice startled the convention was none other than Jenny Hourwitch. She is not yet thir.y years ofa ge, but since she was sixteen she has been in the ranks of revolutionary Russia. Ten years ago she was sent into exile in a distant part of Siberia, but with some others succeeded in making her escape.

One could almost have heard a pin drop, so deep was the silence in the room when a moment later a tall rugged man arose well up toward the front rows of seats. It was Isadore Merriam. His face bore two deep scars received in the Gomel riots, which followed closely on the heels of the Kishineff tragedy. He was later immured and tortured in a prison in the Government of Mogilieff. He burrowed his way to freedom under the prison walls with a spoon.

"When I felt American soil under foot," he said, "I made a vow and I have kept, it, and to-day I have my reward. I have every day taken 5 cents from the price of my breakfast, which costs ten, and I have given this to the Bund. But I eat another meal besides, and from now on I will take 5 cents from that, too, to help our friends in Russia."

A wave of emotion again swept through the audience, and as it was found impossible to go on with the regulaar business of the session Dr. Peskin, another of the delegates, proposed the taking up of a collection then and there. Considering the aggregate wealth of those in attendance and the conditions under which they live, a more generous collection was never taken up, even in the most fashionable Fifth Avenue Church, nor was one ever more ungrudgingly given. The men and women present made a rush for the platform, and the result was a hatful of bills.

Many of the delegates expressed their belief that some time last night the prisons of Petropalovsk and Schlusselberg would be stormed. These prisons are full of political offenders, and the latter especially is known to the revolutionists as an abode of terror.

The Russian Social Democrats also held crowded meetings yesterday afternoon and evening. They met at Grand Lyric Hall, 85 Forsyth Street, adopting resolutions of sympathy with the revolutionists and pledging financial and moral support. The meeting was largely a celebration until the news of the many killed and wounded in the Cossack charges cast a gloom over the gathering, but there were many who spoke of returning to Russia, despite the risk involved. Strangely enough the Anarchists made little or no demonstration.

A vivid contrast to the effect produced on the lower east side, and generally in the quarters where Russian Jews live in any great numbers, was witnessed in the Russian Cathedral. The news reached there just as the Right Rev. Alexander A. Hotovitzky, Archpriest of the cathedral, was intoning solemn high mass.

At the same time Count Cassini, the Russian Ambassador at Washington, entered the church. Count Nicholas de Ladygensky, the Russian Consul General here, who is a regular attendant of the church, met him at the door. A moment later the American and Russian flags were fluttering from the flagstaffs on the priest's residence, as is always the custom when Count Cassini visits the church, which was named for the Czar.

The Russian Ambassador came to New York to attend the Russian Symphony Concert at Carnegie Hall, and had intended to return to Washington yesterday forenoon, but went to church instead. He was accompanied by Commander Boutakeff, the Naval Attaché of the embassy; Col. Raspopow, the Military Attaché, and M. Vilenkin, the financial agent of the Russian Government in this country. The Ambassador and his party occupied seats near the altar. Safonoff, the Russian conductor, also attended the service and shook hands sadly with Count Cassini and his party.

In the service prayers were chanted for the success of the Czar in the Far Eastern struggle, and in the sermon Archbishop Hotovitzky made an address to the congregation which had been prompted by the news from the Russian capital, saying:

Priest Speaks of Riots.

"Only a few days ago we heard how our Imperial Master, the Czar, came near being killed in his own imperial city, where he is well loved. This year, 1905, seems to be an unlucky one for Russia. It opened with disaster in the Far East. And to-day the mobs are fighting in the streets of the capital. We may well ask what has Russia done, what sins have her sons committed to incur the wrath of God? What shall we do to propitiate Him? God save Russia. God save Russia."

There was a hush in the church when the address was brought to a close, and the chant of the "Mnogaya Lyeta"—"The Grand Many Years," as it would be rendered in English—was intoned by the singers in the choir loft. This is a sacred chant, used only on special occasions.

Count Cassini took luncheon at the Archpriest's residence, and then drove to the Waldorf-Astoria. There, through his private secretary, he gave out the following statement:

"Count Cassini has no official information of the strike riots reported from St. Petersburg. Under the circumstances, he is not in a position to make any statement, except to say that he deeply deplores the disturbances, and is confident that everything will be adjusted before long."

Count Cassini seemed quite ill when he reached the hotel. He retired to his apartments at once, and remained there until his departure for Washington on the Congressional Limited.

GAYNOR DENOUNCES CZAR.

Wants Nations to End His Rule, If Russians Do Not.

Justice William J. Gaynor of the Supreme Court, speaking last night at the annual meeting of the Hebrew Educational Society, in the society's building on Pitkin Avenue, in the East New York section of Brooklyn, declared that the Czar was the tool and victim of a corrupt and avaricious Church and aristocracy, and that if the downtrodden people of Russia did not end this rule the combined civilizations of the world would have to interpose, as did the United States in the case of Cuba.

"The children whom this society educates," said Justice Gaynor, "come from despotic Russia, many of them fleeing from the fury of race bigotry. The Government which in this age permits such conditions to exist—and in the name of Christianity at that—should not be permitted to exist."

The society re-elected all of the present officers.

REFUGEES FROM PORT ARTHUR

Arriving at Che-Foo in Junks—Little Looting in Fortress.

CHE-FOO, Jan. 22.—Twenty-seven men and women, comprising the first party of refugees from Port Arthur, arrived here in a junk to-day. They stated that twenty-two other junks, bearing over 500 non-combatants, were also coming. Several launches immediately left with the idea of assisting the junks in reaching Che-Foo.

These refugees, including men, women, and children, had been waiting for a steamer at Pigeon Bay. They were without shelter and were obliged to sleep on the sand. The expected steamer failing to arrive, permission was secured for them to use junks.

The refugees say that since the first few days following the surrender of Port Arthur there has been practically no looting, the Japanese officers dealing sternly with all offenders. The Chinese were more culpable than the Japanese, who generally confined themselves to taking small articles, which they probably wanted chiefly as souvenirs. The consensus of opinion is that the soldiers behaved with remarkable self-restraint, compared with others in similar conditions in history.

Rough[illegible] lost their [illegible]

EUROPE APPREHENSIVE OF RUSSIAN REVOLUTION

Momentous Political Consequences Looked For by the Powers.

AFFECTS WHOLE HEMISPHERE

Profound Sensation in the Balkans Caused by Port Arthur's Fall—Other Ominous Signs in Near East.

The momentous possibilities—nay, probabilities—of the great liberal movement in Russia have for some time been recognized in all the principal countries of the Eastern hemisphere—save perhaps in Russia itself.

As defeat followed defeat in the Far East the discontent ever latent in the mighty empire of the Czar became increasingly manifest. Sullen, dumb, inert at first, it was, under the spur of agitation and the voicing of the national sentiment and aspirations, roused to open expression in all the Russias, accompanied by resistance that no longer was passive.

The anxious powers, keenly observant, saw the movement gathering momentum and, a force so ominously formidable that it bade fair to become irresistible, spread beyond the borders of Russia and overwhelm all Europe.

In an article published a fortnight ago on the general situation in Russia The London Times's military correspondent said:

"Apart from the closing scenes of the great tragedy of Port Arthur the attention of Russia and of the civilized world has been almost wholly absorbed of late by the liberal movement, which has shaken the autocratic edifice from roof to basement and must necessarily have momentous consequences, since it is clear that the forces which have produced this political disturbance draw their strength from every class of the Russian community, from the highest nobles down through every intermediate class to the lowest of the peasants.

"This evolution can hardly fail to have a very decisive influence upon the duration of the war, since not only are men's minds in Russia wholly preoccupied with projects of internal reform, but they are also set upon the arrest of hostilities as a necessary preliminary to these reforms.

"The state of Poland, and the excesses committed by mobilized troops, which have been of a far more serious nature than has been allowed to transpire, all tend in the same direction.

"The great liberal movement in Russia is by far the most important event in the foreign politics of our time, and deserves every attention on the part of distant observers. Whether it will succeed, and, if so, what will be its effect upon foreign politics, is still hidden in the gloom of the future, but that it will necessarily entail a weakening of Russian power or a period of rest for Russia's neighbors is at present quite unproved.

"The French revolution was a great explosive force which produced results far beyond the borders of France herself. Far from thinking that a Russian revolution will be confined to the territories of the Czar, we should rather ask ourselves whether this great National movement may not entail political consequences transcending even those of the great revolt of France.

"When the Slav genius, hitherto trammeled and trodden down, finds scope at last for its superabundant energies and remarkable gifts, we may all be compelled to rearrange our ideas."

A writer in The Spectator of London, in discussing the international phase of the unrest in Russia, said:

"It is not only the future of Asia which is at stake, but much of the future of Europe. A paralysis of that great empire, which for more than a century has hung like a heavy cloud on the Eastern fronteirs of the really civilized section of the world, would, for example, leave Germany mistress of the Continent. It might shatter the Austrian Empire to pieces, for her Slav majority would no longer have to fear being 'buried in the Russian morass.' It would intensify in a high degree the quarrel always smoldering between the Ottomans and the remnant of their Christian subjects—a result of which Europe already perceives signs in the new arrogance which the Divan is displaying in the Balkans.

"French society would be shaken to its heart by a new liability to invasion, and with it fresh proclivity to panic. Even Great Britain, though still 'encompassed by her inviolate sea,' would feel the influence of the great change, for India would be as safe from invasion as herself, and being safe, would be apt to indulge in dreams of large ambition.

"While, however, we perceive this clearly, we do not understand so well why so many thoughtful men believe that the progress of the unrest will be fatal to the autocracy, or why they are so possessed with the notion that, if that great cataclysm occurs, Russia will be weaker for its occurrence.

"As yet all the symptoms point rather to a vast jacquerie than to what is commonly known as a revolution. From province after province of Russia come up stories which show that the suspicion of the proprietary class so long smoldering among the peasantry is breaking into flame; that chateau after chateau is menaced; that in district after district the landlords are sending their families, or flying themselves, for protection to the great cities. The plunder to which the Reservists so often betake themselves is as much an expression of hatred to the rich as of desire for a final revel, and is accompanied in many instances by a destruction of property which can in no way benefit the mutineers.

"It is admitted by the great landlords, themselves, who are promoting the movement of the Zemstvos toward greater liberty, that one at least of their motives is dread of an agrarian revolution as sanguinary as that of 1789-93 in France.

"We do not imagine that the Government would actively aid that revolution, though it must be remembered that whole classes of the smaller proprietors were ruined at a stroke by the decree of emancipation; but it is not impossible they would remember that their soldiers are peasants, and would passively watch a revolt that would end in a Russia composed of an absolute Czar and millions of small freeholders.

"Even anarchy in Russia might not destroy her strength except for a short period. There is much in the Slav of the French nervous excitability; much, also, of that craving for external repute which used to be the French motive power."

Similar views are held by other political experts. Significant of what might happen in the Balkans, "the powder magazine of Europe," is the effect of the fall of Port Arthur, as described by correspondents at Belgrade and Sofia.

The belief in Russian invincibility, which long had been an article of faith in the Slavonic States of the Balkan Peninsula, received a severe shock, the result of which was an evident increase in the fears of Austrian encroachments in Macedonia, which always have existed at Belgrade and which Servian policy for some time has been endeavoring to propagate in Bulgaria.

An even more serious cause for apprehension was a marked stiffening in the attitude of the Porte toward the reforming powers in Macedonia.

Russian Army and People.

The military correspondent of The London Daily Telegraph recently discussed the relation of the Russian Army to the rising excitement. The opinion had been expressed in Continental quarters that an insurrection as formidable as the French Revolution was impossible because of the nature of modern armaments. The writer in The Daily Telegraph, after pointing out that Louis XVI. had ample forces to cope with the revolt, took the view that possession of magazine rifles and quick-firing guns by the men marched to Versailles at the outset of the Revolution would not have influenced the issue in the smallest measure, because the fact was that the men would not have employed them. He continued:

"The question, therefore, of real importance in judging of prospects in Russia is, How far has the disturbance of men's minds, which the Czar has been frankly told in bold language now amounts to 'revolution,' reached the army? I am tolerably sure that no one whatever can really answer as yet, but there are very formidable facts which suggest that the thing, whatever you call it, is spreading in this deadly direction. Nothing to my mind is so significant as the address of the peasant communities of the Moscow district, in which they say that they are instructing their sons to allow themselves to be shot rather than to bear arms in the hateful war. We have already had cases very fully reported from the south, in which the troops have refused to fire. This announcement from the heart of the most purely Muscovite portion of the whole empire seems to be even graver than these.

The Officers of the Army.

"In order to officer the immense numbers of soldiers that are not being called in from civil life it has been necessary to summon every profession. Barristers have been practicing in the courts in uniform prior to their departure. Doctors have been taken from large, popular practices. Engineers have been hurried away from great contracts. Now these classes have been all under the same kind of moral pressure under which the Moscow peasants tell us that they have placed their sons.

"Every part of society, from top to bottom, being in this condition of ferment, I find it very difficult to believe that the same kind of process of assimilation between the homes and the cadets in the ranks as took place in France will not, sooner or later, result from it. How long the infection will take to spread no one can guess, but that the Czar's livery will not stop it I am very sure."

"All the News That's Fit to Print."

The New York Times.

THE WEATHER.
Fair to-day and to-morrow; rising southerly winds.

VOL. LV...NO. 17,617. NEW YORK, THURSDAY, APRIL 19, 1906.—TWENTY TWO PAGES. ONE CENT In Greater New York, Jersey City and Newark. | Elsewhere, TWO CENTS.

OVER 500 DEAD, $200,000,000 LOST IN SAN FRANCISCO EARTHQUAKE

Nearly Half the City Is in Ruins and 50,000 Are Homeless.

WATER SUPPLY FAILS AND DYNAMITE IS USED IN VAIN

Great Buildings Consumed Before Helpless Firemen—Federal Troops and Militia Guard the City, With Orders to Shoot Down Thieves—Citizens Roused in Early Morning by Great Convulsion and Hundreds Caught by Falling Walls.

SAN FRANCISCO, April 18.—Earthquake and fire to-day have put nearly half of San Francisco in ruins. About 500 persons have been killed, a thousand injured, and the property loss will exceed $200,000,000.

Fifty thousand people are homeless and destitute, and all day long streams of people have been fleeing from the stricken districts to places of safety.

It was 5:13 this morning when a terrific earthquake shock shook the whole city and surrounding country. One shock apparently lasted two minutes, and there was almost immediate collapse of flimsy structures all over the city.

The water supply was cut off, and when fires started in various sections there was nothing to do but let the buildings burn. Telegraph and telephone communication was cut off for a time.

The Western Union was put completely out of business and the Postal Company was the only one that managed to get a wire out of the city. About 10 o'clock even the Postal was forced to suspend.

Electric power was stopped and street cars did not run, railroads and ferryboats also ceased operations. The various fires raged all day and the fire department has been powerless to do anything except dynamite buildings threatened. All day long explosions have shaken the city and added to the terror of the inhabitants.

Following the first shock there was another within five minutes, but not nearly so severe. Three hours later there was another slight quake.

First Warning at 5:13 A. M.

Most of the people of San Francisco were asleep at 5:13 o'clock this morning when the terrible earthquake came without warning.

The motion of the disturbance apparently was from east to west. At first the upheaval of the earth was gradual, but in a few seconds it increased in intensity. Chimneys began to fall and buildings to crack, tottering on their foundations.

The people became panic-stricken, and rushed into the streets, most of them in their night attire. They were met by showers of falling bricks, cornices, and walls of buildings.

Many were crushed to death, while others were badly mangled. Those who remained indoors generally escaped with their lives, though scores were hit by detached plaster, pictures, and articles thrown to the floor by the shock. It is believed that more or less loss was sustained by nearly every family in the city.

Steel Frame Buildings Stand.

The tall, steel-frame structures stood the strain better than brick buildings, few of them being badly damaged. The big eleven-story Monadnock office building, in course of construction, adjoining the Palace Hotel, was an exception, however, its rear wall collapsing and many cracks being made across its front.

Some of the docks and freight sheds along the water front slid into the bay. Deep fissures opened in the filled-in ground near the shore, and the Union Ferry Station was badly injured. Its high tower still stands, but will have to be torn down.

A portion of the new City Hall, which cost more than $7,000,000, collapsed, the roof sliding into the courtyard, and the smaller towers tumbling down. The great dome was moved, but did not fall.

The new Post Office, one of the finest in the United States, was badly shattered.

The Valencia Hotel, a four-story wooden building, sank into the basement, a pile of splintered timbers, under which were pinned many dead and dying occupants of the house. The basement was full of water, and some of the helpless victims were drowned.

Fires Start in Many Places.

Scarcely had the earth ceased to shake when fires started simultaneously in many places. The Fire Department promptly responded to the first calls for aid, but it was found that the water mains had been rendered useless by the underground movement.

Fanned by a light breeze, the flames quickly spread, and soon many blocks were seen to be doomed. Then dynamite was resorted to, and the sound of frequent explosions added to the terror of the people. These efforts to stay the progress of the fire, however, proved futile.

The south side of Market Street, from Ninth Street to the bay, was soon ablaze, the fire covering a belt two blocks wide. On this, the main thoroughfare, were many of the finest edifices in the city, including the Grant, Parrott, Flood, Call, Examiner, and Monadnock Buildings, and the Palace and Grand Hotels.

At the same time commercial establishments and banks north of Market Street were burning. The burning district in this section of the city extended from Sansome Street to the water front, and from Market Street to Broadway.

Fires also started in the Mission, and the entire city seemed to be in flames.

Long Detours Around Fires.

The flames, fanned by the rising breeze, swept down the main streets until within a few hundred feet of the ferry station, the high tower of which stood at a dangerous angle.

The big wholesale grocery establishment of Weelman, Peck & Co. was on fire from cellar to roof, and the heat was so oppressive that passengers from the ferry boats were obliged to keep close to the water's edge, in order to get past the burning structure.

It was impossible to reach the centre of the city from the bay without skirting the shore for a long distance so as to get entirely around the burning district.

About 8 o'clock the Southern Pacific officials refused to allow any more passengers from trans-bay points to land, and sent back those already on the boats. The ferry and train service of the Key Route was entirely abandoned owing to damage done to the power house by the earthquake at Emeryville.

Lack of Dynamite Felt.

There was little dynamite available in the city. The Southern Pacific soon brought some in. At 9 o'clock Mayor Schmitz sent a tug to Pinola for several cases of explosives. He sent also a telegram to Mayor Mott of Oakland. At 10:30 he received this reply to his Oakland message:

"Three engines and hose companies leave here immediately. Will forward dynamite as soon as obtainable."

The town of San Rafael, despite its own needs, sent fire fighting apparatus here.

Mayor Schmitz gave orders to use dynamite wherever necessary, and the firemen and United States soldiers, who assisted them, blew down building after building. Their efforts, however, were useless, so far as checking the headway of the flames was concerned.

The shortage of water was due to the breaking of the mains of the Spring Valley Water Company at San Mateo. The water needed so badly in the city ran in a flood over San Mateo.

Burning of the Opera House.

The fire swept down the streets so rapidly that it was practically impossible to save anything in its way. It reached the Grand Opera House on Mission Street, and in a moment had burned through the roof. The Metropolitan Opera Company from New York had just opened its season there, and all the expensive scenery and costumes were soon reduced to ashes.

From the opera house the fire leaped from building to building, leveling them almost to the ground in quick succession.

The Call editorial and mechanical departments, in the handsome building at Third and Market Streets, were totally destroyed in a few minutes, and the flames leaped across Stevenson Street toward the fine fifteen-story stone and iron building of Claus Spreckels, which, with its lofty dome, was the most notable structure in San Francisco. Two small wooden buildings furnished fuel to ignite the splendid pile.

Thousands of people watched the hungry tongues of flames licking the stone walls. At first no impression was made, but suddenly there was a crackling of glass and an entrance was effected. The inner furnishings of the fourth floor were the first to go. Then, as if by magic, smoke issued from the top of the dome.

This was followed by a most spectacular illumination. The round windows of the dome shone like so many full moons; they burst and gave vent to long, waving streamers of flames. The crowd watched the spectacle with bated breath. One woman wrung her hands and burst into a torrent of tears.

"It is so terrible," she said.

The tall and slender structure which had withstood the forces of the earth appeared doomed to fall a prey to fire. After a while, however, the light grew less intense, and the flames, finding nothing to consume, gradually went out, leaving the building standing, but completely gutted.

At California and Sansome Streets stood the Mutual Life Building, a modern structure of architectural beauty, to which the flames were soon communicated. An attempt was made to save it, but the fire was irrepressible. The flames gained, and in a few moments the big building was beyond hope. The Anglo California Bank was swept by the flames and came down in a rush.

Time and again attempts were made with dynamite to clear a space which should prevent the flames from spreading to other buildings, but freely as the explosive was used the fire crept and climbed from one structure to another.

An unusually loud report showed that a gas house at Eighteenth and Market Streets had blown up. The fire caused by the explosion quickly communicated in various directions. As the gas house exploded a feeling of despair overcame the men who were performing the rescue work.

Scare at Palace Hotel.

The Palace Hotel, the rear of which was constantly threatened, was the scene of much excitement, the guests leaving in haste, many with only the clothing they wore. Finding that the hotel was surrounded on all sides by streets, and was likely to remain immune, many returned and made arrangements for the removal of their belongings, though little could be taken away owing to the utter absence of transportation facilities.

The Parrott Building, in which was located the chambers of the State Supreme Court, the lower floors being devoted to an immense department store, was ruined, though its massive walls were not all destroyed.

A little further down Market Street, the Academy of Sciences and the Jennie Flood Building and the History Building kindled and burned like so much tinder. Sparks carried across the wide street, ignited the Phelan Building, and the army headquarters of California, Gen. Funston commanding, were burned.

Still nearing the bay, the waters of which did the firemen good service along the docks, the fire took the Rialto Building, a handsome skyscraper, and converted scores of solid business blocks into smoldering piles of bricks.

Thousands Watch the Flames.

Banks and commercial houses, supposed to be fireproof, though not of modern build, burned quickly, and the roar of the flames could be heard even on the hills, which were out of the danger zone. Here many thousands of people congregated and viewed the awful scene.

Great sheets of flame rose high in the heavens, or rushed down some narrow street, joining midway between the sidewalks, making a horizontal chimney of the former passageway.

The dense smoke that arose from the entire business district spread out like an immense funnel and could have been seen miles out at sea. Occasionally as some drug house or place stored with chemicals was reached, most fantastic effects were produced by the centred flames and smoke which rolled out against the darker background.

One of the first orders issued by Chief of Police Dinan this morning was for the closing of every saloon in the city. This step is taken to prevent drink-crazed men from rioting in the streets.

Mayor Schmitz sent out word to the bakeries and milk stations throughout the city that their food supplies must be harbored for the homeless. Provisions were made to place tents in every park in the city, and those who have lost all will be given food and shelter.

Early in the morning the prisoners confined in the city prison on the fifth floor of the Hall of Justice were transferred in irons to the basement of the structure. Later they were removed to the Broadway Jail, and if necessity arises they will be taken to a branch county jail on the Mission Road.

The Mayor also established a base of rescue, and soon had forces out where they could accomplish most. Many men were sent down to the lodging house district near Market Street. There it was found that many frame buildings, packed with people, had collapsed, burying their occupants in the ruins.

The rescuers jumped into the wrecks and pulled out the dead, the dying, and the injured. Practically every physician in the city immediately volunteered his assistance, and soon there was a well-equipped medical corps organized which began ministering to the injured.

For hours bodies were taken out in the lodging house district, and hundreds of men volunteered to go into the ruins to get more.

The pretentious City Hall, bounded by Larkin and McAllister Streets and City Hall Avenue, was badly shattered by the earthquake, and the ruin later were burned. It took twenty years to build the City Hall, the pride of the coast. When the first shock was felt the building rocked and swayed until it cracked. Part of the interior fell and the ruins caught fire. An alarm was turned in and the firemen responded. Chief Sullivan, awakened by the shock at his quarters in a firehouse, hastened to put on his clothes. As he reached for them the tower of the California Hotel dropped upon his building and crushing through the roof killed him.

The firemen arrived at the City Hall, but were helpless. They hitched their hose to the fire plugs, but there was no water supply.

Every possible precaution has been taken to guard property. Immediately after the destructive shocks the police turned out on guard, and the Governor and Gen. Funston, commanding the Pacific Division of the United States Army, were asked to send troops.

A thousand men from the Presidio, sent by Gen. Funston, arrived downtown at 9 o'clock to patrol the streets. The Thirteenth Infantry, 1,000 strong, arrived from Angel Island a little later and went on patrol duty at once.

The soldiers were ordered to shoot down vandals caught robbing the dead and to guard with their lives the millions of dollars' worth of property placed in the streets to escape the flames.

The First California Artillery, 200 strong, two companies, was detailed to patrol duty on Ellis Street. Two more companies patrolled Broadway in the Italian section. The Ellis Street contingent of guardsmen were under the command of Capt. G. A. Grattan. Capt. William A. Miller commanded the forces on Broadway.

The city is under martial law, and all the downtown streets are patroled by cavalry and infantry. Details of troops are also guarding the banks.

Early this morning Mayor Schmitz, who established his office at Police Headquarters, named the following citizens as a Committee of Safety:

James D. Phelan,	Paul Cowles,
Herbert Law,	M. H. De Young,
Thomas Magee,	Claus Spreckles,
Charles Fee,	Rudolph Spreckles,
W. P. Herrin,	C. W. Fay,
Thornwell Mullalley,	John McNaught,
Garret W. Enerney,	Dent Robert,
W. H. Leahy,	Thomas Garrett,
J. Downey Harvey,	Frank Shea,
Jeremiah Dinan,	James Shea,
John J. Mahoney,	Robert Fisis,
Henry T. Scott,	T. F. Woodward,
I. W. Hellman,	Howard Holmes,
George A. Knight,	George Dillman,
I. Steinhart,	J. B. Rogers,
S. G. Murphy,	David Rich,
Homer King,	H. T. Cresswell,
Frank Anderson,	J. A. Howell,
W. J. Bartnett,	Frank Maestretti,
John Martin,	Clem Tobin,
Allan Pollock,	George Toumey,
Mark Gerstle,	E. D. Pond,
H. V. Ramsdell,	George A. Newhall,
W. G. Harrison,	William Watson.
R. A. Crothers,	

THE BUILDINGS DESTROYED.

A Partial List of the Structures Torn Down or Injured.

SAN FRANCISCO, April 18.—The following is an incomplete list of the buildings destroyed or injured:

Call Building, entirely destroyed.

Claus Spreckels Building, burned out.

Hearst Building, collapsed.

New Chronicle Building, hardly damaged.

The White House, walls badly cracked; all plate glass windows gone; every piece of stock in building removed before 9:30 A. M.

Winchester Hotel, Third Street, totally destroyed by earthquake shock.

Grand Opera House, entirely destroyed.

Claus Spreckels house and stables, Van Ness Avenue, badly damaged and will have to be largely rebuilt.

St. Luke's Episcopal Church, Van Ness Avenue, will have to be pulled down.

Mechanics' Library Building, Post Street, cornices fell to street; building slightly injured.

Crocker Building, Market and Post Streets, slightly damaged, principally around light shaft.

Lick House, walls and roof largely caved in.

Upham Building, Pine and Battery Streets, totally destroyed; loss, $550,000.

Fire house adjoining California Hotel in Bush Street; Chief Sullivan and wife, sleeping in engine house, severely bruised by bricks crashing through roof from hotel.

California Hotel, Bush Street, upper walls collapsed and upper floors wrecked.

The building in course of construction to be occupied by the Hamman baths will have to be rebuilt. It is in Post Street near the Olympic Club. The walls are badly warped and twisted and the roof has fallen in.

San Francisco Gas and Electric Company's Post Street plant, only slightly injured.

St. Francis Hotel, exterior slightly cracked and sea[med], but not seriously injured.

Pacific Union Club, Post and Stockton Streets, front injured and fissures in rear wall.

St. Dominic's Church in Pierce Street, total loss. The interior of the church is wrecked and there are fissures in the walls. The structure will have to be pulled down. The parochial house in the same block is nearly a wreck. It is estimated that the loss to the parish is $300,000.

The ornamental top on St. Dunstan's, the apartment house at Sutter Street and Van Ness Avenue, fell into the street.

The Concordia Club building in Van Ness Avenue has several fissures in the side, and rebuilding will be necessary.

The Hotel Grinado, badly damaged; stone coping about roof fell.

EARTHQUAKE'S AUTOGRAPH AS IT WROTE IT 3,000 MILES AWAY.

Tracing Made by the Seismograph Needle in the Office of State Geologist John M. Clarke, State Museum, Albany, Showing How the Earthquake Traveled Across Continent in 19 Minutes.

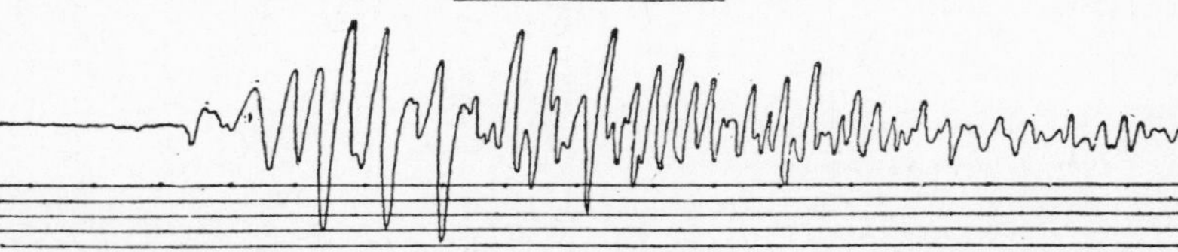

The drawing represents the vibration of the north and south pendulum of the seismograph during the time of the most intense activity, beginning in San Francisco at 5:13 A. M., in Albany at 8:32. In Albany the violent agitation ended at 8:43 A. M. The straight lines at the side of the wavy line indicate the normal condition of the record as the recording drum revolves, and this serves to show the contrast between the ordinary progress of the record and that during a disturbance. The spaces between the dots indicate lapses of one minute each.

The same violent disturbance was noticeable on the seismograph at Washington between 8:32 and 8:35 A. M., thus verifying the time of transit across the continent—19 minutes.

ALL SAN FRANCISCO MAY BURN; CLIFF HOUSE RESORT IN SEA

Flames Carried From the Business Quarter to Residences

PALACE HOTEL AND MINT GO; BIG BUILDINGS BLOWN UP.

Other Shocks Felt During the Afternoon—Insane Asylum Is Wrecked and Hundreds of Former Inmates Are Roaming About the Country—Reports of Heavy Loss of Life at San Jose.

SAN FRANCISCO, Thursday, April 19.—12:15 A. M. (3:15 A. M. New York Time.)—At midnight the fire still roars. Fleeing inhabitants can see from miles around the pillars of fire towering skyward. The crash of falling ruins and the muffled reports of the exploding dynamite reach the ear at regular intervals.

A disaster that staggers comprehension and in point of terror and damage is unprecedented on the coast has not yet reached its culmination.

The Merchants' Exchange Building, one of the handsomest and most substantial edifices in the city, is in flames, as is also the Crocker-Woolwarth Building.

The former building is a fourteen-story structure, seven floors of which are occupied by the Southern Pacific Railway Company as offices. The Crocker-Woolworth Building is a twelve-story terra cotta and granite structure and stood directly opposite the Palace Hotel.

The immense D. O. Mills Building is surrounded by fire and probably will burn. The Lick House, the Occidental Hotel, and the Russ House in this immediate vicinity are in immediate danger.

The exact loss of life never will be known. Hundreds have been incinerated. To-night the city resembles one vast shambles with the red glare of the fire throwing shadows across the worn and panic-stricken faces of the homeless.

At the morgue in the Hall of Justice fifty bodies lie. Before the eyes of an Associated Press reporter three thieves were shot dead.

The Japanese quarter has been burned and the people fled in terror, packing on their backs what household effects they could tie together.

At 9 o'clock to-night an Associated Press man who went to a high hill overlooking the city noted that the sky on the east and south sides was illuminated for a distance of four or five miles. The illumination on the southern side was in a duller glow, showing that the flames were not consuming property of such great proportions as was the case on the east side.

In the business district toward the water front the flames were either checked or blocked at about Washington Street, and at the corner of Kearny Street the Hall of Justice could be noted standing, but it was impossible to determine what damage had been done to the interior. From the Hall of Justice to the south the fire cut its way through some of the choicest buildings in the city, the Pacific Mutual and the Italian-American Bank Building being reduced to ashes.

Down Kearny Street on both sides at 10 o'clock the conflagration was still raging with fury, but the direction of the wind prevented its advance up the hills to the west toward the residence quarter.

To the west of Kearny, up to Dupont, most of the buildings were burned as far south as California Street. All around the new fourteen-story Merchants' Exchange Building the fire burned fiercely, licking the sides of the steel giant, but it resisted the influence of the heat.

Then came the destruction of the Western Union Building, at the corner of Pick and Montgomery Streets. In this building were the offices of the Associated Press. Earlier in the day the occupants had been ordered out by the authorities on account of danger, and The Associated Press established a temporary station in The Bulletin editorial rooms. Then the latter place was closed, and this dispatch is written on a doorstep near Chinatown, the illumination of the burning buildings furnishing light for the writer.

It appeared that the great Mills Building would block some of the southward sweep of the blaze, as it had already checked an advance northward earlier in the night. If this proves true the limits of the fire will be determined, but predictions on this point are as unreliable as the strong wind, which every five minutes is changing from one direction to another.

The city to-night in face of its appaling disaster, is fairly quiet and orderly. Liquor cannot be had anywhere and the formidable presence of Federal troops, militia and naval reserves has had its effect on the element that might be disposed to be disorderly.

The Mayor's proclamation authorizing the shooting of looters on sight has been scattered broadcast in circulars and few reports of thieving are received.

It is impossible to give anything like an accurate statement concerning the killed. Unquestionably many people were either killed outright, imprisoned or rendered unconscious in collapsed buildings which were afterward burned.

At 10 o'clock the Occidental Hotel began burning and the great Crocker Building containing the Crocker-Woolworth National Bank was ablaze.

On Geary Street the Albert Pike Memorial Temple of the California bodies of the Scottish Rites Masons, containing scenery that cost $20,000 and costumes valued at $15,000, collapsed. The new Jewish synagogue adjoining was cracked to its foundations.

While five dying men were taken from a collapsed building at Second and Jessie Streets Fathers Hogan, Rogers and Huber of St. Patrick's Church granted them the last rites of the Catholic Church. This ceremony was performed while a mass of coping overhead threatened to crush the priests to death. Three of the men died.

A shoemaker, Joseph Lindsay, was four hours in a demolished building and when dug out it was found that he had not been hurt.

The entire Larkin Street frontage of the City Hall for a distance of several hundred feet was thrown out into the street, and that thoroughfare for two blocks is piled high with boulders of mortared brick and twisted iron.

Latest reports from Leland Stanford University at Palo Alto indicate that the magnificent stone buildings of that institution have suffered severe damage. Many of the buildings were ruined by cracks that split them from cornice to foundation.

The University of California at Berkeley, across the bay, escaped serious injury. The buildings are intact. Only a few structures collapsed in Berkeley, the shock being slight there.

Artillerymen from the Presidio with their supply wagons and the army commissary wagons are aiding in getting the fleeing inhabitants and their baggage out of the threatened quarters.

270 Dead in an Asylum.

The insane asylum at Agnews is a total wreck, 270 of the inmates being killed. It is reported that the attachés of the institution who were about at the time of the earthquake were saved. The ruins took fire shortly after the collapse. One hundred and twenty bodies have been removed.

There were about 700 persons in the building. Hundreds of the inmates who escaped death are roaming about the country in a state of panic.

Half San Francisco Gone.

OAKLAND, Cal., April 18, 10 P. M.—It looks now as if the entire City of San Francisco would be burned.

At 10 o'clock to-night the fir

was unabated, and thousands of people are fleeing to the hills and clamoring for places on the ferryboats to cross the bay.

Correspondents are trying to get matter to Oakland by boat, but they are very uncertain. The Government is furnishing tugs, but the confusion is so great that they cannot be relied upon.

It will be impossible to send full details for several days.

From the Cliff House comes word that the greatest pleasure resort and show place of the city, which stood upon a foundation of solid rock has been swept into the sea. Not a thing stands to tell where the monster stone building once stood. It has been leveled to the foundation and only the rock lining the sea coast remains intact.

At this hour the fire is increasing in violence. It is spreading in all directions in both the business and residence quarters.

Practically the entire district south of Market Street, from the water front to the Mission, has been swept clean by the flames.

At 5 o'clock to-night, in the northern part of the downtown business section, the fire swept around the Hall of Justice and communicated to Chinatown, thence proceeding westward into the heart of that colony. It then began rapidly eating its way southward on both sides of Kearny Street, and at 7 P. M. was within a block of the California Hotel.

This point was near the plant of The Evening Bulletin, in which the three morning papers had agreed to join to issue a four-sheet paper to-morrow morning. The plan was abandoned, as The Bulletin lay directly in the path of the flames.

One of the big losses of the day was the destruction of St. Ignatius Church and College, at Van Ness Avenue and Hayes Street. This was the greatest Jesuitical institution in the world, and was built at a cost of $2,000,000.

At 7 o'clock the fire had swept from the south side of the town across Market Street into the western addition, and was burning houses at Golden Gate Avenue and Ootavia Street. This result was reached after almost the entire southern district, from Ninth Street to the eastern water front, had been converted into a blackened waste. In this quarter were hundreds of factories, wholesale houses and many business firms, in addition to thousands of homes.

On the north side, the fire to-night was not making such rapid headway as in the western addition, where there is a limited water supply available. The firemen were making desperate efforts to stop the flames.

Temporary headquarters were established in tents in Portsmouth Square this evening for Mayor Schmitz, Chief of Police Dinnan, and Gen. Funston, but this site became too dangerous about 6 o'clock and was abandoned. Later the flames swept the square.

Wide fissures have been made in the streets, street railways have been twisted out of line, sewers and water pipes have burst, and it is feared there will be an epidemic of disease.

Water Sold by the Glass.

Provisions are sold at fancy prices, and even water is vended by the glass. As the flames spread into the residence districts people left their homes and fled to the parks and squares. A series of rather severe earth shocks at 7 o'clock further increased the terror, and many left homes that were not in danger.

A Finance Committee, with James D. Phelan at the head, has been appointed, and Mayor Schmitz has been instructed to issue drafts for all funds needed on this committee. A general meeting of the Citizens' Committee has been called for to-morrow morning.

A message from President Roosevelt was received this morning, and it had a cheering effect. George Gould also telegraphed, offering assistance.

Throughout the city, wherever there is a public square, a scene of desolation is presented. Tents have been pitched by fortunate possessors of canvas, but most of the homeless people are huddled in frightened groups about the household belongings they managed to save from the general ruin.

From Golden Gate Park comes news of the destruction of the immense building covering a portion of the children's playground. The walls are shattered beyond repair. The roof has fallen in, and the destruction is complete. The pillars of the new stone gates at the park entrances are twisted and torn from their foundations. Some of them, weighing nearly four tons, were shifted as though they were constructed of cork.

Nearly every noted landmark that has made San Francisco famous has been laid in ruins or burned to the ground. Never has the fate of a city been more disastrous.

In Union Square Park, where a number of homeless now have temporary shelter, the mighty Dewey Monument has been shifted from its base. It now stands leaning at an angle of 10 degrees. There is danger of the immense stone structure falling.

No afternoon papers were issued, and it is doubtful if the morning papers will appear.

The papers in San Francisco estimate the dead at from 500 to 700, and 20,000 homeless.

The Palace Hotel is destroyed. The Postal and Western Union buildings and the magnificent new Union Trust Company Building, eleven stories high, have been dynamited.

It is reported that the Mint in San Francisco is ablaze, and from the outside indications it will be impossible to save it. The fire surrounds it on every hand.

A Western Union operator has just been along Montgomery Street to the section formerly occupied by the Western Union Building. He says that this whole section is aflame and is surrounded by United States troops. The block bounded by Montgomery, Bush, Pine and Sansome Streets is doomed. Fifteen or twenty blocks along the water front are now a mass of flames.

All efforts to prevent the fire from reaching the Palace and Grand Hotels were unsuccessful, and both were completely destroyed, together with all their contents.

Commissioner E. Myron Wolf has announced that the eighty-odd fire insurance companies interested had decided to pay dollar for dollar to every one insured with them. The companies will not discriminate between fire and earthquake, and every one insured will be paid to the extent of the loss. But two of the companies affected are Pacific Coast concerns, the others having principal offices in the East or in Europe, and all will stand the loss without danger of failure.

Another sharp shock of earthquake was felt on this side of the bay after 6 o'clock this evening. It was of short duration, lasting about five seconds.

The city is under martial law and precautions have been taken to prevent disorder and looting to-night. Four thieves were shot by soldiers to-day for looting. The soldiers have orders to shoot without warning any person acting in a suspicious manner.

The greatest destruction was wrought in that part of the city which was reclaimed from San Francisco Bay. Much of the devastated district was at one time low, marshy ground, covered by water at high tide. As the city grew it became necessary to fill in many acres of this low ground in order to reach deep water.

The Merchants' Exchange Building, a fourteen-story steel structure, was situated on the edge of this reclaimed ground. It had just been completed and the executive offices of the Southern Pacific Company occupied the greater part of the building.

The damage by the earthquake to the residence portion of the city, the finest part of which is on Nob Hill and Pacific Heights, seems to have been slight. On Nob Hill are the residences of many of the men who in the early seventies became wealthy through mining investments or the construction of the Central Pacific Railroad. They include the Stanfords, Huntingtons, Hopkinses, Crockers, Floods, and others.

The magnificent Fairmount Hotel, not yet completed, stands on the brink of Nob Hill, overlooking the bay. The hotel was not seriously damaged. The construction of the hotel was started by Mrs. Hermann Oelrichs of New York as a monument to her father, United States Senator Fair, but she recently sold it for $3,000,000. To the westward of Nob Hill, on Pacific Heights, are fine new residences, but little injury was done to any of them.

The Palace Hotel was a seven-story building, about 300 feet square. It was built thirty years ago by the late Senator Sharon, whose estate was in the courts for many years. At the time it was erected the Palace Hotel was the best-equipped hotel in the West.

The Post Office is a fine graystone structure, and has been completed less than two years. It covers half a block on Mission Street, between Sixth and Seventh Streets. The ground on which the building stands was of a swampy character, and some difficulty was experienced in obtaining a solid foundation.

The City Hall was a mile and a half from the water front. It was an imposing structure, with a dome 150 feet high. The building covered about three acres, and cost more than $7,000,000.

Best Theatres All Burned.

All of San Francisco's best playhouses, including the Majestic, Columbia, Orpheum, and Grand Opera House, are a mass of ruins. The earthquake demolished them for all practical purposes, and the fire completed the work of demolition.

The scene at the Mechanics' Pavilion in the early hours of the morning and up to noon, when all the injured and dead were removed because of the threatened destruction of the building by fire, was one of indescribable sadness. Sisters, brothers, wives, and sweethearts searched eagerly for some missing dear ones. Thousands of persons hurriedly went through the building inspecting the cots on which the sufferers lay in the hope that they would locate some loved one that was missing.

The dead were placed in one portion of the building, the remainder was devoted to hospital purposes. After the fire forced the nurses and physicians to desert the building, the eager crowds followed them to the Presidio and the Children's Hospital, where they renewed their search for missing relatives.

Up to a late hour this afternoon more than 750 persons who were seriously injured by the earthquake and the fire had been treated at the various hospitals throughout the city.

The front of the Bailey & La Costa Building on Clay Street, near Montgomery, fell in and three men and seven horses were killed.

Capt. Gleason of the Police Department was severely injured at noon by falling tiling.

The stereotypers and the pressmen of The Examiner and The Call, as soon as the shock was felt, rushed out of their buildings and found that the coffee house at Stevenson and Third Streets had collapsed. They immediately set to work with axes and other implements to rescue those inside.

The sheds over the Southern Pacific long wharf on San Francisco Bay completely collapsed. Many of the bunkers fell into the bay, carrying with them thousands of tons of coal. The long wharf was one of the most important shipping points about the bay, and freight traffic will be interrupted considerably.

At Eighteenth and Valencia Streets to-night there is a crevice six feet wide in the pavement, and the entire sidewalks are torn up. The street car tracks at this point are twisted into fantastic shapes.

When the time arrived for the banks to open this morning there was a rush by many depositors to withdraw their accounts. The banks, however, kept their doors shut, and would give money to none of the depositors.

The Board of Supervisors has been called together and will decide on the proper measures which should be immediately adopted to afford first aid to persons who have been driven from their homes.

A. W. Hussey came to the station at the Hall of Justice shortly before 10 o'clock this morning and told how, at the direction of a policeman whom he did not know, whose star number he gave as 615, he had cut the arteries in the wrists of a man pinioned under timbers at the St. Katherine Hotel.

According to the statement made by Hussey, the man was begging to be killed and the policeman shot at him, but his aim was defective and the bullet went wide of the mark. The officer then handed Hussey a knife, with instructions to cut the veins in the suffering man's wrists, and Hussey obeyed orders to the letter.

Chief of Police Dinan directed that Hussey be locked up. There has been no opportunity to investigate his story, but the police believe that the awful calamity rendered him insane and that the incident reported to them has no existence excepting in the imagination of the man who made the report.

Sixteen-year-old Otto Settner of 3234 Pierce Street rushed into the room of his father when the big shock came and shouted: "Oh, papa, I am dying!" The child fell dead in his father's arms.

Measures have already been taken for the care of the destitute. They will be fed and protected in Golden Gate Park and the public squares.

The Southern Pacific Railroad is carrying out of town all those who want to leave. No one is allowed to enter, and those who have left will not be able to get back for several days at least.

It is reported that while a building was being blown up with dynamite a premature explosion killed fifteen men.

The Terminal Hotel, at the water front and Market Street, fell to-day and buried twenty persons under the debris. They were incinerated and there is no possibility of learning their identity.

The Court House at Redwood City and other buildings collapsed. Menlo Park, Burlingame, and other fashionable suburban towns suffered. Santa Rosa, to the north; Napa, Vallejo, and all towns around the bay were damaged. These reports, alarming as they were, created little interest in San Francisco, where the people were in a frantic state.

To-day's experience has been a testimonial to the modern steel building. A score of these structures were in course of construction, and not one suffered from the earthquake shock. The completed modern buildings were also immune to harm from the seismic movements. The buildings that collapsed were all flimsy wooden and old brick structures.

The damage by earthquake does not begin to compare with the loss by fire. The heart of the business quarter of San Francisco has been destroyed by fire. Fire has done the great damage. An area of thickly covered ground of eight square miles has been burned over, and there is no telling when the fire will be under control.

The principal damage done in Oakland was caused by falling chimneys.

WASHINGTON, April 18.—The War Department has received the following message from the Western Union at San Francisco:

"Although water has been secured to the firemen in many sections, the fire is by no means under control. It is raging around Pine and Montgomery Streets, and the Western Union Building has been abandoned to its fate. At the Oakland ferry house, where the company has established an office, it is difficult to obtain information concerning current events."

LOS ANGELES, Cal., April 18.—Many rumors are in circulation that additional shocks occurred at San Francisco during the day. All wire communication with San Francisco was lost early to-day. The Postal Telegraph Company had two wires working to Oakland, across the bay from San Francisco.

A special train of four cars with about seventy-five doctors and nurses on board left Los Angeles for San Francisco over the Southern Pacific Railroad this evening. The train is due in San Francisco to-morrow forenoon.

An equal number of doctors and nurses who tendered their services was turned away on account of lack of accommodation on the train. Another special will leave to-night with more nurses, doctors, and policemen.

CHICAGO, April 18.—Henry Forsland, racing correspondent at San Francisco, wired his paper from Oakland this afternoon:

"All means of transit from San Francisco to Oakland closed. No one is allowed to enter the city from outside points, martial law having been declared. A number of racing folk said to have perished in the St. Nicholas Hotel."

FUNSTON ASKS AID.

Sends to Washington for Tents and Rations for 20,000 People.

WASHINGTON, Thursday, April 19.—The Secretary of War earl ythis morning received the following second dispatch from Gen. Funston:

"OAKLAND PIER, Cal., April 18, via Union Pacific special wire via New York.—We are doing all possible to aid residents of San Francisco in the present terrible calamity. Many are homeless, and I shall do everything in my power to render assistance, and trust to War Department to authorize any action I may have to take. Army casualties will be reported later. All important papers saved. We need tents and rations for 20,000 people.

"FUNSTON."

A dispatch received early this morning from Army Department Commissary Trauthoff, is as follows:

"Oakland Pier, Cal. April 18, via Union Pacific Railroad special wire, via New York.—Depot destroyed by fire. Everything lost. Local troops supplied. Will wire in reference to Manila shipments.

"TRAUTHOFF."

From Benica, Arsenal, Cal., comes the following addressed to the Chief of Ordnance:

"Damage by earthquake chiefly to chimneys and ceilings. Probably not over $1,500. Report will follow. No one injured here. BENET, Commanding."

This dispatch was sent to General Funston by Commissary General Sharpe:

"The Secretary of War has directed the Commissary at Vancouver Barracks to forward to the Depot Commissary at San Francisco 200,000 rations. Is the railroad open to Portland?"

WASHINGTON, April 18.—The first message received from Gen. Funston arrived here at 11:40 o'clock to-night. It was addressed to Secretary Taft, who had already retired. The message follows:

"Secretary of War, Washington:

"We need thousands of tents and all the rations that can be sent. The business portion of the city destroyed and about 100,000 people homeless. Fire still raging. Troops all on duty assisting the police. Loss of life probably 1,000. Best part of residence district not yet burned. FUNSTON."

Orders will go forward from the War Department to-morrow morning to the adjacent posts to carry out Gen. Funston's recommendations.

200 OR 300 DIE IN SANTA ROSA

10,000 Reported Homeless in That Town.

SAN JOSE LOSS HEAVY

News of Disaster in Many Other Towns.

Terrified Crowd Fled to the California Hills and Watched Santa Rosa Burn.

SACRAMENTO, April 18.—Dr. Stone, Superintendent of the Napa State Hospital, telephones the Governor's office that an automobile arrived there with news that Santa Rosa is ruined and that between 200 and 300 persons were killed.

LOS ANGELES, April 18.—A report from San José, fifty miles south of San Francisco, says that the Vendome Hotel annex was wrecked, ten or fifteen persons being killed there. The Doherty Block was burned and one woman was killed. Dr. Degrow was killed and his wife was injured.

Every business building in San José was damaged or demolished. The Mayor deputized 500 men to watch property. It is estimated that fifty persons wer killed in San José. The Post Office was nearly wrecked.

The First Presbyterian Church was demolished, and the Court House is a wreck.

Passengers from many other cities in California bring tales of death and disaster. Canta Cruz, Monterey, Gilroy, and Hollister, they say, are wrecked. The death list at Santa Cruz is reported to be large.

A report says that Santa Rosa is a wreck, 10,000 being homeless. The loss probably will reach into the hundreds. Main Street is piled many feet deep with fallen buildings. Not one business building is intact. The four-story Court House is a pile of broken masonry. Identification of the dead is impossible. What was not destroyed by the earthquake was swept by fire.

Citizens fled to the fields and hills to watch the destruction of Santa Rosa. The water system was destroyed by the earthquake.

Eight dead Italians were taken out of an Italian hotel at San Jose. At that place the Presbyterian Church, St. Patrick's Cathedral, and the High School were destroyed. The new Hall of Justice at San Jose, just completed at a cost of $300,000, was demolished.

At Loma Prieta, eighteen miles from Santa Cruz, a mine house slipped down the side of a mountain, burying ten men in the ruins.

STANFORD UNIVERSITY RUIN.

All But Two Buildings Demolished—Two Persons Killed.

OAKLAND, April 18, 8 P. M.—Reports from districts outside San Francisco indicate widespread damage. San José, fifty miles south, lost many buildings, and from fifteen to twenty persons were killed. The annex of the Vendome Hotel collapsed, and fires started. Stanford University and Palo Alto suffered.

At Stanford all but two of the fine buildings were demolished and two men were killed. One of them was Julius Robert Hanna of Bradford, Penn., and the other was Otto Gurb, a fireman.

Six students are lying in the Palo Alto Hospital with bruises, cuts, and internal injuries. These are Ross D. Howard of San Francisco, Henry L. Deering of Santa Ana, Cal.; —Frolic, Halburt R. Thomas of Los Angeles; Robert Westnick of Santa Barbara, and W. H. Masters of Portland, Ore.

IN OTHER TOWNS.

Enormous Loss of Property in Places Near San Francisco.

Oakland, which is across the bay from San Francisco, suffered considerable damage to property, but no fatalities were reported after the earthquake, according to a message sent to the New York office of the Western Union yesterday by one of its operators in Oakland. This operator reported that the trains were able to run in Oakland, but that they went very slowly.

STOCKTON Cal., April 18.—A sharp earthquake shock was felt here at 5:15 o'clock this morning. The Santa Fé bridge over the San Joaquin River settled several inches.

SAN FRANCISCO, April 18.—At Napa many buildings were shattered and the loss will amount to $300,000. No loss of life is reported.

In Vallejo the damage was slight in comparison with that suffered in other places. The loss will be about $10,000.

SALINAS, Cal., April 18.—At 5:15 o'clock this morning three earthquakes shook Salinas, lasting respectively five, three, and forty-two seconds. They came from the northeast and southwest. The damage is $2,500,000. No lives were lost in Salinas.

Among the buildings destroyed in Salinas are the Ford & Stanbury Building, dry goods; Elks' Hall, Masonic Building, the Knights of Pythias Building, armory, Porter & Irving store, Logan cyclery, Odd Fellows' Building, City Hall, and several smaller buildings. Every window in the city was broken. Chimneys toppled over and crashed through roofs. Spreckels's sugar factory, three miles from town, was destroyed, causing damage of $1,500,000. The High School Building was wrecked. Several stores lost their entire stocks. At 2:25 o'clock this afternoon another shock was experienced, but no lives were lost. Several men, women, and children were cut about the face by flying glass.

Salinas was cut off from wire communication with San Francisco, 118 miles north.

At Watsonville, the Moreland Academy was destroyed by fire and several buildings collapsed. At Monterey and Pacific Grove there was a slight shock that caused little damage.

At the Delmonte Hotel three chimneys fell through the roof, killing a bridal pair and a hotel servant, and injuring several other persons.

At Hollister, Granger's Union warehouse was restroyed. A Mrs. Griffith was killed, and her husband became crazed.

LOS ANGELES, April 18.—Los Angeles did not feel the earthquake to any extent. The nearest point where damage was done was 400 miles north of this city.

ALBANY GETS A RECORD OF THE PACIFIC SHOCKS

Earthquake Travels Across the Continent in 19 Minutes.

IS FELT MORE THAN AN HOUR

Violent Vibrations Caused a Quarter-Inch Swing in Seismograph at State Museum.

Special to The New York Times.

ALBANY, April 18.—State Geologist John M. Clarke obtained a complete record of the San Francisco earthquake on the recording seismograph in the State Museum this morning. The record is automatically inscribed on smoked paper and shows the exact time of the arrival and duration of the vibrations. As the disturbances lasted for one hour and twenty minutes, the record was many feet in length. The most destructive period was from 8:32 to 8:43. Mr. Clarke said:

"The first manifestation of the disturbance was received here at 8:21½ A. M., corresponding to 5:21½ A. M. Pacific time. The first waves to arrive were the slight tremors which travel much more rapidly than the destructive waves of great amplitude. These slight preliminary vibrations continued until 8:32½ A.M., when the first large waves arrived, followed immediately by shakings of the greatest intensity that lasted until 8:43. The amplitude of the most violent vibrations shown on the record is about two inches, but as the record is intensified about ten times the actual swings of the greater waves were one-quarter of an inch.

"After the intense shakings the vibrations gradually decreased, though they continued to be felt until 9:50 A. M.

"The heavy waves traveled at the rate of about 11,000 feet a second and the lighter preliminary and subsequent waves much more rapidly, about 40,000 feet a second."

It is evident that the first tremors felt in Albany were not noticed in San Francisco by the sleeping people. The shock, which at 5:13 set buildings to tumbling, was the one recorded here at 8:32. Therefore the disturbance took 19 minutes to cross the continent.

On April 10 the seismograph in the State Museum showed the prevalence of an earthquake which lasted fifty-five minutes. The disturbance was quite marked, but Mr. Clarke made no mention of it, thinking that perhaps the instrument might have been out of order. He has since had the shock confirmed by Baltimore and other places where he wrote for information.

This shock, he believes, was the forerunner of to-day's disturbance. Prof. Clarke says there are tremendous disturbances in the centre of the earth.

RECORD MADE IN WASHINGTON.

Needle Passes Off Sheet of Seismograph for Three Minutes.

Special to The New York Times.

WASHINGTON, April 18.—The San Francisco earthquake registered itself most accurately on the seismograph at the Weather Bureau in this city. For the first time since the discovery of the instrument by which earthquake waves could be measured the experts of the bureau were able to see the vibrations as they recorded themselves.

It was not until a telephone message was sent to the bureau that attention was directed to the seismograph, when it was at once noted that the indicator was moving violently from one side to the other of the sheet of paper on which the record is marked. Prof. Charles F. Marvin, who has charge of the instrument, and his assistants, at once concentrated their work for the day on the phenomena of the earthquake.

The seismograph consists of a cylinder on which a sheet of paper six inches by three feet, coated with parafine and soot, is placed and over which a needle or stylus hangs. This stylus marks most delicately as the cylinder moves, the line resulting from the difference between the earth waves and a mass of matter that as far as possible by all means known to science is immovable.

There are a dozen similar instruments in use throughout the world and the scientists of the various countries provide for such observations, and there is an international bureau at Strasburg, Germany, where all records are compared and the results reported back to the various corresponding bureaus in various parts of the world.

There is no seismograph on the Pacific Coast similar to the one here, but there is one of a different type at the Lick Observatory and another maintained by the Canadian Government at Vancouver. The coast survey has one at Baldwin, Kan., and there is one of the old type at Johns Hopkins University and one of the modern pattern at Albany recently installed.

The first disturbance on the seismograph here was noted at 8.19:20 o'clock. It appeared in minute wavering marks on the sooty paper. These kept on almost imperceptibly, increasing in size for several minutes, until at 8:25 they began to break into well-defined waves over a quarter of an inch long. From second to second they lengthened, and within an inch space as the cylinder moved on from the needle they gradually grew to be an inch and a half long. At 8:32 the waves had increased to be three inches long, and the needle passed off of one side of the sheet of paper.

For three minutes it remained off the sheet, and at 8:35 again came up on the bevel of the brass cylinder and began once more to mark the record of seismic disturbance. What movements the indicator made while off the paper can only be imagined. The waves may have been much longer during that period than at the time when the record was completed. The greatest length of the vibration or wave was four inches.

Under the old methods of fixing this basis of measurement a pendulum was used. This pendulum was sometimes made several hundred feet long. By means of levers this has been done away with, and a most acute and accurate means of measurement has been devised. The stylus makes a fine straight line around the cylinder when there is no disturbance.

The wave register continued for three hours, although the length of the waves had become again quite minute.

The Weather Bureau did not receive as usual the 5 o'clock observation which is taken every morning. This observation it is believed must have been taken before the earthquake occurred, but no dispatch could be sent reporting it. About noon a dispatch was received from Prof. McAdie, the Observer in charge of the San Francisco Weather Station, saying he and his three assistants were safe and well. The station was in the Mills Building, which was in the heart of the destroyed district, and went down with other buildings.

The scientists rely on the staff of the Lick Observatory to make the observations of the earthquake phenomena that will give its history.

Prof. Willis Moore of the Weather Bureau said to-day that the eruption of Vesuvius was recorded during its entire period on the magnetic instruments of the research station at Mount Weather, a few miles from this city in Virginia. He stated, however, that thi swas not an earthquake record, but rather that Vesuvius acted like a powerful wireless transmitter and Mount Weather as the receiver, Vesuvius with its eruptions there disturbing the electrical potentials which disturbances sent out electro-magnetic waves that encircled the earth. The records at Mount Weather were clear and distinct.

BALTIMORE, April 18.—The seismograph at the Johns Hopkins University shows a record of the earthquake at San Francisco which marks it as the most severe disturbance ever recorded in this city with the exception of the earthquake in Colombia, South America, last January.

The recording film shows the disturbance to have been most severe between 8:25 and 8:55 A. M., Eastern time, and that it had not ceased when the film was taken from the instrument at 11:30 o'clock.

VIENNA'S DISTINCT RECORD.

Observers Learn of Earthquake Soon After the First Vibrations.

VIENNA, April 18.—A telegram from the Government Observatory at Laibach says that from 2:25 to 2:59 o'clock this afternoon the seismograph recorded a distant earthquake of great force and destructiveness.

The indications showed that the disturbances were much more violent than those which recently occurred in Formosa.

The difference in time between San Francisco and Vienna is 9 hours and 6 minutes.

WASHINGTON WITHOUT NEWS.

War and Navy Departments Fear Their Depots Are Destroyed.

WASHINGTON, April 18.—Up to 10 o'clock to-night not a word of an official nature had reached the War Department from San Francisco. Secretary Taft has made repeated efforts to obtain some information from Gen. Funston, in command of the Department of California, but thus far without avail.

Quartermaster General Humphrey and Commissary General Sharpe to-night expressed the opinion that both the Quartermaster's depot and the commissary warehouse in San Francisco are destroyed. The description of the district burned over contained in the press reports includes that on which both the depot and the warehouse stand.

If this should prove to be correct, the War Department, it is said, would have no supplies available in San Francisco for relief work. There are various army stations along the coast, however, both north and south of San Francisco, which might be called on in an emergency to render some assistance in this direction.

The Navy Department is also without any advices from the naval station at Mare Island, California, and the officials are in ignorance as to what, if any, damage has resulted to the naval establishment there. This station is perhaps twenty-five miles from the City of San Francisco, and the officials hope that it has not felt any serious effects from the earthquake. Rear Admiral Bowman H. McCalla is in command there and his judgment is relied upon by Secretary Bonaparte and his assistants to take whatever action may be necessary to safeguard the Government interests.

Secretary Taft late to-night directed another message to be sent immediately to Gen. Funston urging him to advise the War Department of the conditions at San Francisco as soon as possible and to do everything in his power to let the public at large know of the actual state of affairs in the stricken city.

The War Department was advised that an officer who had an automobile had consented to make an attempt to reach Gen. Funston at once and carry the dispatches which have accumulated at Oakland and could not be sent because of lack of ferry accommodations. At 11:10 o'clock to-night Secretary Taft was without any official advices.

The War Department late to-night received a Western Union dispatch from Oakland saying that another sharp earthquake had just been felt on that side of the bay, but that it was of short duration, lasting about five seconds.

Upon hearing the news of the San Francisco earthquake, Assistant Secretary of War Oliver telegraphed Major General Greely, commanding the Pacific Division, with headquarters at San Francisco, instructing him to co-operate with the local authorities and use all resources at his command to assist in alleviating the situation there.

DEAD IN THE STRICKEN CITY.

A Partial List of Those Known to Have Perished.

SAN FRANCISCO, via Oakland, April 18.—Here is a partial list of the dead in the city itself:

BAKER, ——, Second and Stevenson Streets.
BRODERICK, PATRICK, Valencia Hotel.
BUNNER, STEVE, Police Sergeant; killed at door of City Hall.
BUSALACCHI, PHILIP, fish market, Seventh and Minna Streets.
BURGE, FRANK, native of England, 65 years old; killed by walls falling upon him at 235 Geary Street.
CARR, WILLIE, 1,547 Ellis Street.
CROWDER, Mrs. LENA, 14 Seventh Street.
DRUM, Mrs. HART.
FEBNER, MAX, policeman; killed at door of City Hall.
GETZ, ——, Sixteenth and Folsom Streets.
GUELLIMAN, WILLIAM, 110 Eddy Street.
HESLIP, Mrs. IDA, Geary and Stockton Streets.
HUSTEL, M. A., 2,527 Sutter Street.
ISHIDO, SAKIE, 420 Stevenson Street.
KING, ——, 920 Mission Street.
KORNFELD, W., 12 years old, 939½ Folsom Street.
KNOWE, WILLIAM, injured by falling wall; died in Mechanics' Pavilion.
LACKMANDA, T., 427 Stevenson Street.
LIND, PETER, Western Meat Company.
McGANN, Mrs.
McKENZIE, ——, 115 Haight Street.
MIYIKAI, F., 423 Stevenson Street.
PALADINA, LOUIS, Montgomery and Merchant Streets.
MINZE, MYRTLE, 258½ Langdon Street; killed by the collapse of a wall.
STAGMAN, GERONIMO, 518 Merchant Street.
STINSON, Mr., physician; killed in his room on the eighth floor of the California Hotel by collapse of wall.
SWINDETT, ADOLPH, and wife.
THRAPHY, JOHN, fish market, Montgomery and Sacramento Streets.
VAIL, WILLIAM, 4 years old, 280 Stevenson Street.
WEBSTER, ANNA, 14 Williams Street.
WHELAN, ANNIE, 2,782 Sacramento Street; killed while asleep by the falling of a chimney upon the roof of the cottage.
UNKNOWN—Three Chinese, two white women, man at Hayes and Polk Streets, man at Wilcox House, Second and Jessie Streets; father and son living at 157 [illegible] Street.

"All the News That's Fit to Print."

The New York Times.

THE WEATHER.

Generally fair to-day and to-morrow; wind variable.

VOL. LV...NO. 17,685 • • • • NEW YORK, TUESDAY, JUNE 26, 1906.—FOURTEEN PAGES. ONE CENT In Greater New York, Jersey City and Newark.

CAPT. WYNNE GUILTY, NAVAL COURT SAYS

Marine Officer May Be Dismissed from the Service.

THE PRESIDENT WILL DECIDE

Will Review the Findings in the Case of the ex-Postmaster General's Son.

If President Roosevelt approves the findings of the court-martial that recently tried Capt. Robert F. Wynne, United States Marine Corps, on charges of insubordination, Capt. Wynne will be dismissed from the service. The record of the court-martial is now in the hands of Secretary Bonaparte, and in a few days will be sent to President Roosevelt for final review.

Although it has not been officially announced, it is generally known in the service that the verdict of the court-martial is entirely against Capt. Wynne, the court finding him guilty on all three charges and fixing his punishment at dismissal. The charges on which the Captain was tried were, first, neglect of duty in not reporting the guard at quarters; second, willful disobedience of orders, and, third, conduct prejudicial to good order and discipline.

It has now been seventeen days since the court-martial, which was held on the armored cruiser Pennsylvania, at the New York Navy Yard, concluded its inquiry into the charges preferred against Capt. Wynne by Lieut. Commander Bryan, who, on the morning of May 21, the date of Capt. Wynne's alleged insubordination, was, in the absence of Capt. Samuel P. Comly, the senior officer on board the Alabama, the flagship of the Second Division of the First Squadron of the Atlantic Fleet.

President Roosevelt, with whom the final decision in the case rests, is a warm personal friend of Capt. Wynne's father, Consul General Wynne, who was Mr. Cortelyou's predecessor as Postmaster General.

Since the court-martial adjourned, Capt. Wynne has received numerous assurances of good will from his friends in and out of the service. There are many persons who have the deepest sympathy for the young officer. His father and mother, who sailed for London on the Atlantic Transport liner Minneapolis last Saturday, were with him on Friday last.

In addition to his court-martial Capt. Wynne also had to face a medical board of inquiry. This inquiry was held a few days after the court-martial adjourned, the board being composed of Medical Inspector Howard E. Ames of the battleship Maine, Surgeon John F. Uria of the armored cruiser Pennsylvania, and Passed Assistant Surgeon Richard B. Williams of the armored cruiser West Virginia. The medical examination was the result of the testimony offered at the court-martial to the effect that owing to a sunstroke Capt. Wynne suffered in the Boxer troubles in China he was not in a condition to appreciate his obligations to his superiors properly and that he should be retired from the service. Capt. Wynne appeared before the medical board and testified that on Aug. 6, 1900, while on the march to Peking for the relief of the legations, he had suffered a sunstroke near Yang-Tsun. In 1903, while at Guantanamo, Cuba, and again in March of this year, at the same place, he was prostrated in China.

The medical board found Capt. Wynne sane in every way, but it is understood to have recommended that in the future he should not again be assigned to service in the tropics. This report is a part of the record, which will in a few days be forwarded by the Secretary of the Navy to President Roosevelt.

Capt. Wynne was arrested on May 31 on the order of Lieut. Commander Bryan of the Alabama. Capt. Wynne at the time was assigned to duty on a Board of Inquiry, which duty he interpreted to mean that he was exempt from other service. Following this construction, on the morning of May 1 he failed to report when the call to quarters was sounded aboard his ship. Lieut. Commander Bryan noted his absence and sent to Capt. Wynne's quarters to ascertain why he had not appeared. Capt. Wynne sent back word that his assignment on the Board of Inquiry relieved him from any other duty and stayed in his quarters.

Lieut. Commander Bryan then directed an officer and two marines to bring Capt. Wynne on deck. Capt. Wynne refused at first to report, the situation finally becoming so serious that a subordinate officer, a friend of Capt. Wynne's, went to him and persuaded him to report to Lieut. Commander Bryan in order to avoid any further trouble.

PEABODY'S SPECIAL TRAIN.

New Yorker Hires One Rather Than Have His Party Rise at 5:30 A. M.

Special to The New York Times.

ATLANTA, Ga., June 25.—Because he did not desire to have the members of his party awakened in the early morning hours to take the southern train at 5:30 o'clock, George Foster Peabody of New York chartered a special train to make the trip, paying $668 for the cars and engine that were used.

The conductor and others of the crew were rewarded liberally for the special run they made.

INDEX TO DEPARTMENTS.

DOESN'T TAINT ALL TRADE.

London Times Editorially Defends Business Methods in This Country.

Special Cable to THE NEW YORK TIMES.
[Copyright, 1906.]

LONDON, Tuesday, June 26.—The Times this morning publishes a letter from an American correspondent protesting against the alleged readiness of Europe to condemn the whole American people and their business on account of the scandalous disclosures respecting American life insurance methods and the operations of the Chicago meat packers. Commenting on the letter editorially, The Times says:

"It would be a great mistake to suppose that every Englishman believes everything said by every newspaper. No sensible man believes that American business is rotten because some swindles have been exposed, any more than he thinks that all French business is rotten because there was a Panama scandal, or that all our own business is in the same condition because we have scandals from time to time and are aware of much that is wrong, though it may not yet have come in so striking a form before the world.

"Strong language about scandal is not to be taken to show that even those who use it suppose the whole business world in the country where it occurs to be corrupt. It is not their aim or business to offer a careful judicial view of American business as a whole. They are concerned with the scandal alone, and the general perspective must be left for adjustment on some other occasion.

"Americans may dismiss the idea, if they ever entertained it, that the people of this country regard them as all in the same boat with the Beef Trust, Standard Oil Company, dishonest railway managers, and people who control yellow dog funds. There are Pharisees and foolish individuals in all countries. We have some among us, and as they are generally very ready to talk, they probably do some mischief, but the mass of the people understand very well that the mass of American people are very like themselves, and that in America, as here and elsewhere, society is held together only by the saving remnant of which our correspondent speaks—the quiet, inarticulate people who still believe in probity and honor and try to do their duty and fulfill their obligations honestly."

TRUST MEN GO TO JAIL.

Five Ice Men Sentenced for Conspiracy in Ohio.

Special to The New York Times.

TOLEDO, Ohio, June 25.—After a consultation between the five convicted ice men and their attorneys this afternoon it was decided to make an effort to have a modification of the sentence of $5,000 fine and one year's imprisonment made in the morning. Pending the making out of the commitment papers which will send these five men—Joseph A. Miller, R. C. Lemmon, R. A. Beard, H. P. Breining, and P. H. Watters, all prominent in business and social circles—to the Toledo Workhouse, they are prisoners in the county jail, under the supervision of Sheriff Chambers. There is little hope held out to them by their attorneys for escaping all of their Workhouse penalty.

When Judge Kinkade sentenced the men this morning for being guilty of being members of a conspiracy in restraint of trade he told the prisoners and their counsel that when they brought to him papers showing that the money illegally exacted from the public since the 11th of March by the increase of prices had been returned to the public, and when they showed that the trust was broken and that prices would go back to the standard in existence prior to March 11, the date of the formation of the trust, he would listen to a plea of modification. He did not say that he would modify the sentence, or what the modification would be if he did so do.

He further told the prisoners that until he was relieved of a great congestion of criminal work that had piled up while he was hearing the ice trials he would not have time to listen to their statements, giving them to understand in this manner that they must stay at least a short time in the Workhouse.

In spite of this statement the lawyers are trying by every means known to their profession to get the Judge to hear them to-morrow so that their clients may be saved from the Workhouse. Friends of the convicted men have sent them their meals to-day, but on the strict order of the court no one has seen them since they returned from a visit to their counsel this afternoon. While making their trip to the lawyers several of the prisoners were seen. All were in the deepest despair. They had each expected a fine, and were prepared for a heavy one, but the imprisonment was unlooked for.

SHAW AND THE STEEL TRUST.

Leader Williams Asks Inquiry Into Alleged Tariff Favoritism.

Special to The New York Times.

WASHINGTON, June 25.—John Sharp Williams introduced in the House to-day a resolution calling on the Secretary of the Treasury for the correspondence and reports in the matter of certain rulings of the Treasury Department with regard to the levying of an additional 1 cent a pound on certain steel imports.

Mr. Williams is after the motive of the Secretary in insisting on the attempt to collect 2 cents per pound duty on strip steel, after the Board of General Appraisers of New York has repeatedly decided that such importations are subject only to the duty of 1.2 cents per pound provided in paragraph 135 of the Dingley act.

It is charged on information which Mr. Williams has obtained that the basis for the claim for the higher duty was made up, partly at the instigation of a man who had been an examiner at New York, but has now become an employe of the Steel Trust. This man, it is said, when he was examiner made several decisions contrary to what he is now upholding. The material that has been supplied to Mr. Williams charges Secretary Shaw, by inference, with making a ruling in favor of the Steel Trust and against independent manufacturers, and with insisting upon it after the courts have decisively turned him down.

Ohio's New Governor Better.

COLUMBUS, Ohio, June 25.—Gov. Harris returned to the capital from his home at Eaton this evening. He said that he was feeling much better.

MISS FULLER SUDDENLY DECIDES ON A WEDDING

Surprise When Chief Justice's Daughter Quietly Marries.

ENGAGEMENT NOT ANNOUNCED

Ceremony Was Planned for Next Winter, but Dr. Mason's Urgings Upset the Plans.

Special to The New York Times.

WASHINGTON, June 25.—With only a few relatives present and without the knowledge of their friends, Miss Frances Louise Fuller, daughter of Chief Justice Melville W. Fuller, was married at noon to-day to Dr. Robert French Mason of this city.

Their engagement had never been formally announced, and the few who knew of it had been told that the wedding would not take place till next season. Dr. Mason, however, did not wish their engagement to be so long and his urgings suddenly won the day, and no time was taken to prepare for an elaborate ceremony.

The marriage ceremony was performed in the home of the bride's father, in this city, by the Rev. Herbert Scott Smith, rector of St. Margaret's Episcopal Church. The wedding party was a small one, George L. Mason, brother of the bridegroom, acting as best man, and Mrs. White of Chicago, sister of the bride, acting as matron of honor and giving the bride in marriage. The only other guests were Mrs. Hugh Wallace, another sister of the bride; Mr. and Mrs. Benjamin S. Minor, brother-in-law and sister of the bridegroom, and Miss Margaret Mason, his sister. A few of the Fuller servants who remained in town to care for the house while the family were in their Summer home at Sorrento, Me., were also present.

After an informal breakfast following the ceremony the bride and bridegroom left for one of the coast resorts and Mrs. White returned to her home in Chicago. Dr. Mason and his bride will join the Chief Justice next month in Sorrento for a visit, after which they will temporarily live here at the Dupont, where Dr. Mason has lived for some time.

The wedding has thrown what remains of society here into a flutter. Friends of the couple had rested in the assurance that they would be present at the marriage next season.

After the departure of the Chief Justice and his daughter for Chicago, about two weeks ago, however, Dr. Mason became impatient, went on to Chicago, and gained the consent of his fiancée and her father to have the ceremony take place this month. Miss Fuller was unwilling to be married anywhere but in Washington, even though her father was not well enough to make the trip back again to witness the ceremony. Accompanied by her sister, the bride-elect arrived here on Saturday and all arrangements were made hurriedly.

Mrs. Mason has acted as hostess for her father since the death of her mother, two years ago. She was in Europe at that time, studying music, but came immediately home and has been at the head of the judicial household ever since. She discharged the duties of hostess with dignity, grace, and tact, although there have been no formal entertainments, owing to their deep mourning.

Miss Fuller has no own sisters, as the daughters of the Chief Justice who have previously figured so prominently in Washington society, all now married, were the daughters of his first marriage. They include Mrs. Nathaniel Francis and Mrs. Hugh Wallace of this city and Mrs. White of Chicago.

INDEPENDENT PLANTS BAD.

Chicago Inspectors Find Improvement in Some, However.

Special to The New York Times.

CHICAGO, June 25.—Sanitary Inspectors in a report to-day condemn independent packing plants of this city.

Filthy pens, rooms covered with dirt and clotted blood, decayed and neglected vats used daily, and general unsanitary conditions were found in some of the smaller plants. The worst conditions were discovered in the plant of David Levi & Co. at the Union Stock Yards. Chief Sanitary Inspector Perry L. Hedrick cites the details in his report delivered to Health Commissioner Whalen.

In the plants of H. Boore & Co., Boyd, Dunham & Co., and Henry Guth, efforts were being made to improve the conditions, and these places were generally clean. Aside from improper toilet facilities and walls and ceilings that need cleaning, signs of improvement were noticed.

In the Levi plant the Inspectors could find nothing to commend.

COREY TO FIGHT SUIT.

Answers Wife's Divorce Plea and Says He Didn't Desert Her.

RENO, Nev., June 25.—William Ellis Corey, President of the United States Steel Corporation, this afternoon filed an answer to the petition of Mrs. Corey for divorce.

He denies that she is a legal resident of Nevada, and further denies that he ever abandoned her. He asks that her suit be dismissed.

Special to The New York Times.

BRADDOCK, Penn., June 25.—The news that W. Ellis Corey had filed an answer to his wife's suit for divorce and that the answer showed fight in every line evidently came as a blow at the home here of his father, A. A. Corey, to-night. Mrs. Laura Cook Corey, wife of the steel man, is with her father-in-law, but she declined to be seen this evening.

Mrs. Gilman, mother of Mabelle Gilman, the actress, was in Pittsburg today. The rumor is that she and Mrs. Corey met this afternoon in Pittsburg, but that cannot be confirmed.

Curfew Law in Ballston.

BALLSTON, N. Y., June 25.—The Board of Trustees to-night passed a curfew law which forbids children to be on the streets after 9 o'clock at night under penalty of being taken home by the police.

REJECT ROCKEFELLER CASH.

Reformers of the Young Do Not Want His $5,000,000.

Special to The New York Times.

CHICAGO, June 25.—Judge Lindsey of the Denver Juvenile Court has pledged himself to refuse the $5,000,000 promised to him by John D. Rockefeller with which to finance a National Juvenile Improvement Association. His alternative was to take the money with the active condemnation of the leaders of different charities of the country having a like aim. Jane Addams of Hull House, Chicago, negotiated the affair while she and Judge Lindsey were in St. Paul at the biennial meeting of Women's Clubs just closed.

Judge Lindsey asked to have a convention of juvenile workers called in Chicago. Judge Mack issued the call. The convention was to be held in Hull House, Chicago. In the week previous, when both were in St. Paul, Jane Addams told Judge Lindsey that the other workers, herself included, could not federate with any association that was to be financed by John D. Rockefeller. She said she was sure Judge Lindsey would coincide with their views when they were put to him. Otherwise the leaders would refuse to attend the meeting in Chicago. It was an open revolt against Judge Lindsey's connection with Rockefeller's money.

"I do not know where we shall get the money to do the work of organizing and carrying out the plans, but I promise you I will not accept any money whatever from Mr. Rockefeller," was Judge Lindsey's reply.

Miss Addams immediately reported his pledge to her colleagues, and the convention in Chicago was attended with enthusiasm.

TO SPEND $20,000,000.

Pennsylvania Road Plans Big Increase in Equipment.

Special to The New York Times.

PHILADELPHIA, June 25.—More than $20,000,000 is about to be expended by the Pennsylvania Railroad Company for the purpose of equipment and for general construction work. This determination has been reached by President Cassatt, and a construction and equipment list will be submitted to the Board of Directors for its approval at the meeting to be held on Wednesday. The requisition will include the construction of 300 locomotives and not less than 15,000 freight cars.

The decision to spend such a large sum is the outcome of the coal investigation by the Inter-State Commerce Commission, and the belief held by Mr. Cassatt that the outlook for business is bright. The funds to pay for the improvements to be ordered by the Board of Directors will become available through the French loan of $20,000,000 and the $50,000,000 bond issue recently negotiated through Kuhn, Loeb & Co. of New York.

The $20,000,00 to be spent for locomotives, cars, and general construction work does not include the money that will be erquired to take over the 15,000 individual coal cars now being operated on the Pennsylvania system, and which Vice President Thayer announced it is the purpose of the management to buy as soon as plans have been worked out in detail.

JOHN D. CRIMMINS RALLIES.

Not Out of Danger, However, and Improvement Will Be Slow.

Special to The New York Times.

STAMFORD, Conn., June 25.—John D. Crimmins rallied to-day, and his condition to-night was reported as more hopeful. Dr. J. W. Avery, the attending physician, issued this bulletin to-night:

"Mr. Crimmins has had a comfortable day and is resting well this evening. He has made a slight improvement. No further complications have arisen, and the outlook is rather more hopeful, although he is by no means out of danger. His improvement will be slow, as his condition is one from which he cannot recover quickly."

SMOTHERED BY SAND SLIDE.

Two Laborers Dug Out Within Fifteen Minutes, but Life Was Extinct.

Special to The New York Times.

PEEKSKILL, June 25.—An unexpected slide of fine sand in one of James A. De Groat's sand banks at Jones's Point, opposite this village, this morning smothered two men to death. Another was slightly injured.

The other men on the gang escaped unhurt. The bodies were recovered within fifteen minutes after the sand had fallen, but life was extinct.

John Pesti, single, 29 years old, and Louis Suyoke, 24 years old, laborers, were the victims. Both men had been employed by De Groat for several years.

PRATT'S GIFT TO AMHERST.

New Yorker Gave $40,000 for Natatorium Dedicated Yesterday.

AMHERST, Mass., June 25.—The dedication of the new Pratt Natatorium, given to Amherst College by Harold I. Pratt, 1900, of New York, was the feature of today's observances of commencement week.

Mr. Pratt, Mortimer L. Schiff, '96, of New York; Dr. Edward Hitchcock, Athletic Supervisor, and President George Harris made addresses. The Brookline Swimming Club gave an exhibition in the large tank.

The building cost $50,000, of which $40,000 was given by Mr. Pratt for the natatorium, and $10,000 by Mr. Schiff for squash tennis courts on the upper floor of the structure.

TROOPS CONTROL ALLENTOWN

State Constabulary Take Charge in Presence of Car Strikers.

ALLENTOWN, Penn., June 25.—Following the strike of the motormen and conductors of the Lehigh Valley Transit Company, the corporation turned off its power at midnight, but resumed operations this morning, after the arrival of Troop C, State Constabulary, with thirty-four men, under Lieut. Smith.

PURE FOOD BILL CONFERENCE

Senate Objects to House Amendments—The House Insists.

WASHINGTON, June 25.—The House insisted to-day on its amendments to the Pure Food bill, and asked for a conference. The Speaker appointed as conferrees Mr. Mann, (Ill.,) Mr. Hepburn, (Iowa,) and Mr. Ryan, (N. Y.)

The Senate voted not to concur in the amendment of the House, but subsequently agreed to the conference, and Senators Heyburn, McCumber, and Latimer were appointed as conferrees.

THAW MURDERS STANFORD WHITE

Shoots Him on the Madison Square Garden Roof.

ABOUT EVELYN NESBIT

"He Ruined My Wife," Witness Says He Said.

AUDIENCE IN A PANIC

Chairs and Tables Are Overturned in a Wild Scramble for the Exits.

Harry Kendall Thaw of Pittsburg, husband of Florence Evelyn Nesbit, former actress and artist's model, shot and killed Stanford White, the architect, on the roof of Madison Square Garden at 11:05 o'clock last night, just as the first performance of the musical comedy "Mamzelle Champagne" was drawing to a close. Thaw, who is a brother of the Countess of Yarmouth and a member of a well known and wealthy family, left his seat near the stage, passed between a number of tables, and, in full view of the players and of scores of persons, shot White through the head. Mr. White was the designer of the building on the roof of which he was killed. He it was who put Miss Nesbit, now Mrs. Thaw, on the stage.

Thaw, who was in evening clothes, had evidently been waiting for Mr. White's appearance. The latter entered the Garden at 10:55 and took a seat at a table five rows from the stage. He rested his chin in his right hand and seemed lost in contemplation.

Thaw had a pistol concealed under his coat. His face was deathly white. According to A. L. Belstone, who sat near, White must have seen Thaw approaching. But he made no move. Thaw placed the pistol almost against the head of the sitting man and fired three shots in quick succession.

Body Fell to the Floor.

White's elbow slid from the table, the table crashed over, sending a glass clinking along with the heavier sound. The body then tumbled from the chair.

On the stage one of the characters was singing a song entitled "I Could Love a Million Girls." The refrain seemed to freeze upon his lips. There was dead silence for a second, and then Thaw lifted his pistol over his head, the barrel hanging downward, as if to show the audience that he was not going to harm any one else.

With a firm stride Thaw started for the exit, holding his pistol as if anxious to have some one take it from his hand.

Then came the realization on the part of the audience that the farce had closed with a tragedy. A woman jumped to her feet and screamed. Many persons followed her example, and there was wild excitement.

L. Lawrence, the manager of the show, jumped on a table and above the uproar commanded the show to go on. "Go on playing!" he shouted. "Bring on that chorus!"

Girls Too Terrified to Sing.

The musicians made a feeble effort at gathering their wits and playing the chorus music, but the girls who romped on the stage were paralyzed with horror, and it was impossible to bring the performance to an orderly close.

Then the manager shouted for quiet, and he informed the audience that a serious accident had happened, and begged the people to move out of the place quietly.

In the meanwhile Thaw had reached the entrance to the elevators. On duty there was Fireman Paul Broodin. He took the pistol from Thaw's hand, but did not attempt to arrest him. Policeman Debes of the Tenderloin Station appeared and seized his arm.

"He deserved it," Thaw said to the policeman. "I can prove it. He ruined my life and then deserted the girl." Another witness said the word was "wife" instead of "life."

A Woman Kissed Thaw.

Just as the policeman started into the elevator with Thaw a woman described as dark-haired and short of stature reached up to him and kissed him on the cheek. This woman some witnesses declare was Mrs. Thaw.

The crowd was then scrambling wildly for the elevators and stairs. The employes of the Garden who knew Thaw, and nearly all of them did, as he visited the place often, did not seem greatly surprised at the tragedy. When Thaw entered the Garden in the early part of the show he seemed greatly agitated. He strolled from one part of the place to another, and finally took a seat in a little niche near the stage.

He was half hidden from the audience, but could see any one who might enter. It is believed that he knew just where White would sit, and had picked out this place in order to get at him without interference.

Henry Rogers of 222 Henry Street was seated at the table next to the one at which White was sitting when he was killed. He says that Thaw fired when the muzzle of his pistol was only a few inches from White's temple.

Another witness said that after firing three shots and looking at White as if to be sure that he was stone dead, Thaw uttered a curse and added:

"You'll never go out with that woman again."

A Woman Sat Near White.

At another table adjoining that at which White was killed sat a woman dressed in white. It was believed for a time that she was a companion of White's, and it was reported that she leaned over and kissed the face of the dead man, but this could not be verified, and it is positive that White was alone when he entered the Garden.

Some one in the audience hurried to the fallen man to see if assistance was needed. A great pool of blood had quickly formed on the floor. The tables had been pulled back and in the bright glare of thousands of electric lights it was quickly seen that White was beyond any earthly help.

A number of the actors and actresses left the stage, and away from the calcium and the footlights their painted faces showed strangely in the group of employes and friends of Thaw and the dead man which formed as the last of the audience left.

Thought It a Stage Trick.

Two of them said that the reason the fright of the audience was not worse when the shots rang out was that just before the tragedy a dialogue concerning a burlesque duel had been carried on by two of the characters, and many people thought that the old trick of playing in the audience had been tried again.

As the lights of the Garden were dimmed, the body of White was straightened out, the arms brought to the sides, and the legs placed together. A sheet was obtained in one of the dressing rooms, and this was stretched over it.

While all of this was going on, Policeman Debes and his prisoner had reached the street entrance. Thaw never once lost his composure. His linen and his evening suit showed no signs of ruffling. Only the paleness of his face showed that anything had happened to excite him.

Wanted Mr. Carnegie to Know.

"Here's a bill, officer," he said to the policeman before he started for the station. "Get Carnegie on the telephone and tell him that I'm in trouble."

The policeman and prisoner then walked through the crowd to Fifth Avenue, up the avenue to Thirtieth Street. As they turned the corner at the Holland House a number of cabmen who knew Thaw tipped their hats to him and he recognised their salute in return.

The trip up Thirtieth Street, across Broadway and Sixth Avenue, was without any excitement, and the prisoner reached the station without the usual crowd of curious people following.

Thaw did not seem to be intoxicated, but walked in a sort of daze. He made few comments on the way to the Tenderloin Station. Sergt. McCarthy asked him what his name was, and he answered:

"John Smith, 18 Lafayette Square, Philadelphia."

"What's your business?" he was asked.

"I am a student."

No charge was made on the books against this "John Smith." The detectives were sent out to investigate fully before a charge was made. Sergt. McCarthy asked him:

"Why did you do this?"

"I can't say," he replied apathetically.

Cards found on the prisoner read "Harry Kendall Thaw, Pittsburg." He made no comment when they were pulled out of his pocketbook.

Thaw Sent for Two Friends.

Young Thaw walked dazedly to the back room. He waited a while, and then sent for Frederick W. Lowenfellow and Frederick Delafield. The reporters asked him to make a statement. He refused to do it.

Young Thaw had lighted a cigarette while he stood in front of the Sergeant's desk. In the back room he sat on a long bench that is used by reserves, between two big policemen. He pushed his hat back on his head, stretched out his feet, and lit another cigarette. His eyes had a far-away look.

A number of his friends hurried over to the station to talk with the prisoner, but they were not allowed to see him. William Thaw, a brother of his who is stopping at the Holland House, had not been to see him up to nearly 3 o'clock.

When the detectives put on the case had brought in the witnesses and they had been examined in Capt. Hodgins's room, Thaw was charged with homicide and was locked in a cell.

The following witnesses were detained until the arrival of Coroner Dooley:

Paul Brodin, a fireman, 697 Prospect Avenue, the Bronx; Lionel Lawrence, manager of the company playing at the Madison Square Roof Garden, 325 West Forty-second Street; Harry Silverstein, Marvin Pincher, 84 West Thirteenth Street; Warren Paxzen, 146 East Twentieth Street; Edward Carney, 467 Second Avenue.

Thaw Not Ready to Talk.

Coroner Dooley reached the Tenderloin Station at 1:30 this morning and asked to see the prisoner. Thaw had sent the doorman out to buy him some cigars. He was smoking and seemed calm when the Coroner entered.

"Have you any statement to make to me?" the Coroner asked after he had made himself known.

"I don't care to make any statement now," Thaw replied. "I would appreciate it if you would tell Burr McIntosh or ex-Judge Hornblower or Joseph H. Choate of what has happened."

"Mr. McIntosh is upstairs," he was told. "Do you want to see him?"

"No," he replied, "just tell him to call up Mr. Hornblower or Mr. Choate. Tell him not to call up Mr. Choate until morning. I would not like to get him out of bed."

Mr. Choate is at Stockbridge, Mass.

Mr. McIntosh took the message and left the station.

Coroner Dooley said that he found Thaw in good mental condition. He added that he believed the murder was done through jealousy.

When Thaw was searched in the station $125 in paper money, $2.36 in coin, two silk handkerchiefs, two gold pencils, a gold watch, and a little pocket combination mirror case were found. These were taken by the Sergeant.

Mrs. White at St. James, L. I.

Mrs. Lizzie Hanlon, housekeeper for Mr. White at his residence, 121 East Twenty-first Street, had not heard of the shooting when a reporter from THE TIMES called shortly before midnight. She expressed the utmost horror, and could suggest no explanation.

The house is one of the most magnificently decorated in the city. Standing amid elaborate Italian decorations with carved marble and graceful fountains on every hand, Mrs. Hanlon gave what information she could. She said:

"Mr. White has been alone in the house for some time. Mrs. White has been away in the West for about three weeks or a month, but is now at her country residence at St. James, L. I.

"Lawrence White, Mr. White's son, came down from Harvard the other day. Both he and his father came in and dressed for dinner to-night, but they did not go out together, Mr. White leaving alone a few minutes before his son. I do not know where either of them went."

"Has Mr. Thaw been to the house to see Mr. White recently?" Mrs. Hanlon was asked.

"Mr. Thaw? I never heard of him. As far as I know Mr. White did not have any visitors here to-day."

Young White, with a friend, Leroy King, dined with his father last night at the Café Martin. Mr. White, his son says, was in the best of spirits and said nothing about any trouble.

After the dinner the party entered an electric automobile and went up to the New Amsterdam roof garden. There the two boys asked the elder White to stay and see the performance.

He said: "No, I thank you," adding that he was going elsewhere.

That was the last they saw of him.

Meant to Go to Philadelphia.

Lawrence White says his father was thinking of going to Philadelphia last evening on a matter of business, and intended to up to the last possible moment, and only changed his plans in order to dine with the boys, who had just come down from Harvard.

"If he had only gone!" exclaimed the son in his grief.

Lawrence White said he had never seen Harry Thaw in his life and had never heard his father speak of him, and that he knew of absolutely nothing that could lead to such a tragedy.

He was then informed that his father was dead and that the body was still

Garden. He departed for that ce at once.

At 1:50 o'clock this morning Mr. White's body was removed to the undertaking establishment of J. Aldred & Son, at 359 Fourth Avenue.

It was said there that the body would be taken to his home in Twenty-first Street to-day.

Only One Bullet in Head.

After the body was taken to the undertaker's a hasty examination was made. Three wounds were found. The fatal bullet entered the left eye. The other two bullets grazed the shoulders, leaving a flesh wound on each. The top of the head showed a mark, this having been caused by striking the edge of the table as the body fell to the floor.

By a strange coincidence White and Thaw and his wife dined at the Café Martin last night. With White was his son, Lawrence, and Leroy King, a friend. This party had a table on the porch.

Inside the café Thaw dined with his wife and his father-in-law. At no time of the evening did the two parties meet. Both White and Thaw were well known by the employes, and when the news of the tragedy was being told over the tables by the after-theatre patrons this coincidence was recalled.

Detectives Look for Mrs. Thaw.

Mr. and Mrs. Thaw have been stopping at the Lorraine, Fifth Avenuee and Forty-fifth Street. Detectives were sent there to get her as a witness, but she had not returned at 3 o'clock this morning.

At that hour Policeman Debes, who arrested Thaw gave this account of what happened:

"I was on post at Twenty-sixth Street and Madison Avenue last night, and asked the manager of the Garden if there would be any shooting in the show. I did this because the use of firearms at Hammerstein's last week made me hurry and scurry for awhile, thinking the shooting was done on the street. He told me there was not.

"I heard three pistol shots and started for the Garden. I met the electrician of the place, who was on the run. He said that a man and a woman had been shot in the audience. I hurried upstairs and the first I saw was a woman who had fainted. Then I found Thaw with the fireman. I asked him if he had shot the man whose body I could see by the table?

"'Yes,' Thaw repied.

"Then he added that the man had ruined his life—or wife—I could not distinctly make out.

"'Is he dead?'" he asked.

"I told him he was.

"'Well, I made a good job of it and I'm glad,' he added. Then a woman, who Manager Lawrence told me was Mrs. Thaw, ran up and embraced him and kissed him.

"'I didn't think you would do it in this way,' she said. He whispered to her, patted her on the shoulder, and said that it would all come out all right.

"When we got to the street a number of women shook hands with the prisoner and sympathized with him. Some wanted to know why he had killed White but he did not answer."

A dispatch from Pittsburg last night said that Thaw and his wife were to have sailed for Europe to-morrow.

Mrs. William Thaw, mother of Mr. Thaw, sailed for London on the Atlantic Transport liner Minneapolis last Saturday. She is on her way to visit her daughter, the Countess of Yarmouth, who was Miss Alice Thaw.

WHAT WITNESSES SAY.

One Man Is Sure That Thaw's Wife Was There.

An eye witness thus described the shooting of Stanford White by Harry Thaw:

"Mr. Thaw had seats on the Twenty-sixth Street side of the theatre, down near the stage. A woman was near him. Thaw got up several times in the evening and walked around in the space in front of the stage.

"Mr. White entered about 11 o'clock. He had a little talk with Manager Stephens of the roof garden, and I heard him say to Mr. Stephens that he had just left the Manhattan Club. Mr. White took a seat just a few tables from Thaw. I saw Thaw walk up to Mr. White, say a word or two to him, and then pull a small pistol from his pocket and shoot at him three times.

"The wounded man dropped off his chair, tilting the table as he fell. The audience did not go into hysterics right away. One reason for that, I take it, was that Fuller Spice and Gustavus K. Hicks, two of the characters in the play, had just been having a dueling dialogue, and at the time of the shooting Spice was on the stage with six chorus girls. The audience seemed to think that the shooting was in the play.

"After a moment or two several women near Mr. White's table began to get hysterical. The orchestra seemed to have known what had taken place because of their proximity, but they tried desperately to keep the lively tune going. Now and then it would break, and the audience would shout, 'Go on, go on! What's the matter there?'

"The orchestra braced up several times, but the tune kept hitching more and more until finally it trailed off pitifully. By that time the audience seemed to know what had happened."

Still another man who was at the show said he was sure that the woman who rushed up to Thaw after the shooting was Mrs. Thaw. He added:

"As Mrs. Thaw passed the body of White, she turned to me and said:

"'Is he dead?'

"I ansyered, 'Yes.'

"She cried: 'My God, Harry, you've killed him.'

"Thaw said: 'Kiss me, dear, before I go down stairs.

"Thaw and his wife embraced each other, she kissing him several times. Then the woman cried: 'My God, Harry, he is dead.'

"Thaw again said, 'Kiss me, dear.' Once more his wife threw her arms about him and kissed him.

"I never saw a face more full of agony as she turned around.

"Then a policeman came and Thaw went down in the elevator."

Here is another story of the killing of Mr. White told by a man who sat a few feet from the table where the shooting occurred:

"The show was going along nicely. It was 'Mamzelle Champagne,' and my attention was on the stage until I noticed a strange-looking fellow who walked about in a nervous sort of way. His throat was muffled up, and it appeared to me that he was a man who seemed on the verge of delirium tremens. I said to the man friend who was with me that the fellow who was muffled up was either a prizefigher or an athlete in training, but when he came near us I saw that he was wildly excited.

"He muttered to himself several times and paced up and down the floor, turning now and then to see who was near him, as if he thought he was being followed. As he passed toward the rear of the place a woman near the man who was shot later leaned forward and whispered something. It seemed to me that she was afraid of somebody or something.

"A waiter came along and I called his attention to the muffled man, remarking that he seemed foolish. The waiter said he had noticed the fellow around all evening and that something was wrong with him.

"Just then the fellow walked over to the side of the building where the tables were and craned his neck forward as if he suddenly spied the person he was looking for, and quickened his pace.

"'That fellow's going to grab somebody,' I said, turning to my companion, and when I again looked in the direction of the fellow I saw him with pistol in hand and pointing it downward at the man at the table near by. Then he fired.

"Immediately after the shots were fired the man who did the shooting leaned forward and said something to the woman. It sounded like 'It's all right, don't worry. I'm not sorry I did it.'

"That settled the show. All about women were frantically pleading with their escorts to take them out of the place and into the street, but the escorts couldn't find a way out so easily.

"The woman who was sitting near the man who was shot evidently had lots of friends near at hand, for they got her away quickly. I think they took her behind the stage, for I saw a man leading her back.

"As that man who did the shooting had his neck muffled up, it seemed to me that he was trying to disguise himself while preparing to kill the other man."

WHITE AIDED MRS. THAW.

George W. Lederer Tells How He Gave Her Financial Assistance.

Special to The New York Times.

CHICAGO, June 25.—George W. Lederer, the theatrical manager, formerly of New York, now of the Colonial Theatre here, to-night told about the friendship between Stanford White and the former Miss Florence Evelyn Nesbit, now Mrs. Harry Thaw. Mr. Lederer introduced Miss Nesbit to the stage. He said:

"Miss Nesbit was the daughter of a Pittsburg lawyer, and when she was 11 or 12 years old her father died, leaving an estate much involved. His widow found it was necessary for her to pitch in and make a living, and she went to Philadelphia, where for a couple of years Evelyn posed as a model. Then she moved to New York, where she continued to pose.

"When she was only 15 or 16 years old she met Mr. White, and subsequently he became a close friend of her and of her mother's. I think that throughout his friendship for the girl was entirely platonic. He was a persistent first-nighter, and liked pretty girls.

"He took a strong personal interest in the Nesbits, assisted them financially, and made them comfortable in every way. Subsequently the girl went on the stage, first appearing in 'Florodora' in the Casino. Mr. White remained her very good friend and she in turn was grateful to him.

"She is of frivolous disposition and no doubt refused to break off her friendship for him after marrying young Thaw, who is a cigarette fiend, and always seemed half crazed to me when I saw him.

"Now Mr. White was a great 'rounder.' His close friends in the older days were 'Freddy' Gebhard and 'Tom' Clark, but from all I observed and from talking many times with Miss Nesbit's mother I am firmly convinced that his friendship for Miss Nesbit and the help he gave her grew out of sheer good-heartedness. Of course he was a man who always liked to talk to pretty girls and to be with them."

Friends of Mr. Thaw said last night that there had long been feeling between the men because of the interest that Stanford White had taken in the former Miss Florence Evelyn Nesbit, now Mrs. Thaw.

Mr. White was greatly interested in the stage, and was one of a group of men, young and old, who frequently were seen about the theatres where musical comedies were playing and at restaurants and other places with actresses. Mr. White cultivated the friendship of various theatrical managers, and for years had enjoyed the privilege of going behind the stage at various productions. He had befriended many young actresses, helping them to better themselves in their profession. In fact, it was known that a word from him would often get a girl a chance to come out from the back row of the chorus and play a part.

It was through this influence that Mr. White gave Miss Nesbit her first opportunity. She had been brought to New York by her mother, a Pittsburg widow, and had attracted the attention of several artists and photographers, who employed her as a model. It was through this employment, it is understood, that Mr. White became acquainted with her. He found that she had a leaning toward the stage, and helped to persuade her mother that she should have a chance to make a career.

When the consent of the mother had been gained Mr. White aided her to get into "Florodora." Afterward he asked George W. Lederer to engage her for "The Wild Rose," which was then about to be put on at the Knickerbocker. It was largely because of his friendship toward Mr. White that Mr. Lederer took up the young woman and boomed her as a new beauty. Her success was such that she soon had her pictures in the newspapers, and became popular with the young men who frequent stage doors.

Miss Nesbit, however, was grateful to Mr. White, and generally preferred to take any late suppers she might have in company with him and such friends as he might choose. Mr. White often went behind the stage at the Knickerbocker to see her. He helped her in learning the arts of the stage. They were seen together, with friends, driving and dining often.

It is understood that it was through the influence of Mr. White that Miss Nesbit was afterward taken up by Mrs. Robert Osborn, when she started Mrs. Osborn's Playhouse. Miss Nesbit was one of the beauties there, and it was said that Mr. White was one of the financial backers of the enterprise. At any rate, he was frequently seen at the playhouse, and again had the privilege of going behind the stage.

When Mr. Thaw entered the field as an admirer of Miss Nesbit the influence of Mr. White was eclipsed. After their marriage, however, the architect still let his friends understand that he felt the same friendship for the young woman and that he would be glad to aid her in any way possible in case the Thaw family should continue to frown upon her husband because of his marriage to her.

McKIM HORROR-STRICKEN.

"Thaw Must Be Crazy" Says the Dead Architect's Partner.

Charles F. McKim, head of the firm of McKim, Mead & White, first learned of the shooting at 11:45 o'clock through THE TIMES, when the news was telephoned to him at his residence, 9 East Thirty-fifth Street.

For a time Mr. McKim could only ejaculate, "My God—good God!" He at first said he couldn't believe it was true.

"Why," said he, "I was talking with him only three hours ago. He was then in our office. I talked with him over the telephone about some of our work. He had been in the office all day working hard."

At this point Mr. McKim was so overcome by his feelings that he could not speak for a brief time. Then he said:

"Thaw must be crazy."

He was assured that Thaw appeared perfectly sane and sober. This added to Mr. McKim's mystification.

"I cannot conceive of such an awful thing," continued Mr. McKim. "It is a horrible nightmare."

Mr. McKim was told what Thaw had said to Mr. White.

"I cannot conceive of any possible ground upon which such a statement could be made."

Mr. McKim said he didn't know Thaw.

PITTSBURG GREATLY SHOCKED.

Benjamin Thaw Too Ill to be Told of His Brother's Crime.

Special to The New York Times.

PITTSBURG, June 25.—Social and financial circles in Pittsburg were greatly shocked to-night by the news from New York that Harry K. Thaw had shot and killed Stanford White. The Thaws have for years been social leaders here. Harry Kendall Thaw, the husband of Florence Evelyn Nesbit, over whom Thaw and White are said to have quarreled, has for some years been the black sheep of the Thaw family. He is the son of Mrs. William Thaw of Lyndhurst.

Benjamin Thaw, a brother of the man who did the shooting, is lying seriously ill at his home. Josiah Copely Thaw, another brother, is out of the city. At the residence of Mrs. William Thaw, Jr., in Sewickley, to-night, a member of the family who declined to give her name said she was certain that there could have been nothing between Mrs. Harry K. Thaw and White to have provoked the shooting.

The Rev. W. L. McEwan of the Third Presbyterian Church of Pittsburg, the clergyman who married Harry Kendall Thaw and Miss Nesbit, said to-night when told of the tragedy:

"It is too awful to think or talk about. When I married those two young people life looked rosy for them. They had everything before them. Oh! that it should come to this!"

STANFORD WHITE'S CAREER.

He Designed Many of the Finest Buildings in This Country.

Stanford White was born in this city on Nov. 9, 1853. He was the son of Richard Grant White and Alexina B. Mease. His father was well known as a critic, journalist, and essayist, and for more than twenty years served as Chief of the United States Revenue Marine Bureau for the District of New York. His mother was a daughter of Charles Bruton Mease of this city.

The American head of the family was John White, who came to this country in 1632 from England, a passenger on the ship Lion, and settled at Cambridge, Mass. He became a freeman the second year after his arrival, and was then a salesman of the town. He removed to Connecticut with Pastor Hooker's company in 1636, becoming one of the founders and proprietors of Hartford. He later settled at Hadley, Mass., which place he represented in the General Court in 1664. He died in Hadley in 1683.

Stanford White's great-grandfather was Calvin White, for many years rector of the St. James Protestant Episcopal Church at Derby, Conn., but in his later years he became a Roman Catholic layman. His grandfather was Richard Mansfield White, a shipping merchant of New York City. Stanford White was educated in the private schools of New York and by tutors, and received the degree of A. M. from New York College in 1883.

He began the study of architecture in the office of Charles T. Gabrill and Henry H. Richardson. From 1878 to 1881 he traveled and studied in Europe, and on his return formed a partnership with Charles F. McKim and William R. Mead, under the firm name of McKim, Mead & White.

The name of this firm is associated with some of the most notable architecture of the country, many examples of which were designed by Mr. White himself. He was the architect of the Villard house, on Madison Avenue, now the property of Whitelaw Reid; of the Madison Square Garden, the Century and the Metropolitan clubhouses, the Washington Arch, on Washington Square; the New York University, the University of Virginia, and many private residences throughout the country.

Among his most conspicuous special works are the architectural features for the sculptures of Augustus Saint-Gaudens, notably the pedestal of the Farragut Statue, Madison Square; the pedestal for the Chapin Statue, Springfield, Mass., and the pedestals for the Lincoln and Logan Statues and the Adams Tomb, Washington, D. C.

He was the creator of interior designs which won great praise for him. Specimens of his work in this direction are shown in the Players and Metropolitan Club houses, the Villard residence, the Church of St. Paul the Apostle, and the Church of the Ascension, all of this city.

A work by which he will always be remembered, and which is considered by many of his friends as the best specimen of his genius, is the Marble House, which he built at Newport for Mrs. William K. Vanderbilt. Its construction marked the zenith of his fame. He received carte blanche as to material and decoration. His bust now stands on a pedestal in the hall as a recognition of the success he achieved.

He had charge of the interior decorations for the Metropolitan Club. When the time came for building the University Club the committee in charge called him in and told him that while the Metropolitan was superb they did not want him to copy it in the new structure.

Although only a few years had elapsed since the Metropolitan was completed, he had discovered certain things which he thought he could improve, and these he embodied in what is said by many to be the handsomest and most complete clubhouse in the world.

Mr. White was a member of the Institute of Architects, of the Metropolitan, University, Grolier, Players, Century, and Meadow Brook Clubs of New York City, and of many artistic and literary organizations throughout the country.

In 1884 he married Bessie, daughter of Judge J. Lawrence Smith of New York, a descendant of Col. Richard Smith, the original patentee of Smithtown, L. I., and of Gen. Nathaniel Woodhull, who fell at the battle of Long Island.

He leaves one son, Lawrence Grant White. Mrs. White is one of three sisters. The others are Mrs. J. Bloomfield Wetherell and Mrs. Prescott Hall Butler.

Mr. and Mrs. White have not been living together recently, and while the husband nominally retained his home at their house at Gramercy Park and Lexington Avenue, he spent but little of his time there.

Madison Square Garden, designed by him, and where he met his death, was known as his "pleasure house." When the Garden was nearing completion he stipulated that he should have a suite of apartments in the tall tower. He had had it ever since.

For a busy man, who worked hard and achieved notable things, he gave up a great deal of time to the pleasures of friendship and sociability. He had a very large acquaintance among actors and singers, lawyers and doctors and society folk. To them all he was known as "Stan."

He was never happier than when in the suite of apartments in Madison Square Garden, directly above the spot where he was killed. He was the supreme master and promoter of all the fun hatched there. It was an attractive place for suppers after the play or the horse show, and invitations to a function there were always highly prized.

WHO HARRY THAW IS.

The Life of the Pittsburg Man Who Wed Miss Nesbit.

Harry Kendall Thaw and Evelyn Florence Nesbit were married on April 4, 1905, in the parsonage of the Third Presbyterian Church, in Pittsburg. The marriage followed a reconciliation of Thaw with his family, from whom he had been estranged for some time on Miss Nesbit's account.

Thaw is about 36 years of age, and is the son of the late William Thaw, who was Vice President of the Pennsylvania Railroad lines west of Pittsburg. He was a graduate of the Western University of Pennsylvania. While in Pittsburg he made his home with his mother at Lyndhurst, on Beechwood Boulevard, in the east end of that city. After he was graduated from college and attained his majority, Thaw lived very little in Pittsburg, most of his time being spent in Europe.

His marriage came as the culmination of a romance with Miss Nesbit, which extended over three years, or back to the time when she appeared on the stage here as one of the "Florodora" sextet girls. It continued through various stages here and in Europe, until in October, 1904, the pair returned to this country from abroad and went to the Hotel Cumberland.

There Mr. Thaw refused to register Miss Nesbit as his wife, and they were asked to give up their rooms in the hotel. This stirred up a scandal. Thaw and the former chorus girl went from one hotel to another, finally going west to attend the St. Louis Exposition.

Several times during their journey they denied that they were married. Both dropped out of sight until just before the marriage, when the report came from Pittsburg that they had been summoned there by Mrs. William Thaw, the young man's mother, who had some time before declared that her son would not be given his income of $80,000 a year unless he gave up Miss Nesbit.

Miss Nesbit, or Mrs. Thaw, was born in Pittsburg, but did not know Thaw while she lived there. She came to this city about five years ago to earn her living. Before she became an actress she was one of the best known artists' models here. She first appeared in "The Wild Rose," as a show girl, but it was only for a short time. Her connection in a similar capacity in "The Girl from Dixie" was even more brief. She appeared for a time in "Florodora," and it was then that she met Thaw.

Miss Nesbit was one of a party, of which Thaw was also a member, that went abroad in the Spring of 1904. It was known then that they were often in each other's company. The gossip about them, however, did not become general until dispatches told of Thaw's arrest for speeding an automobile in Switzerland in company with his "wife."

Not long after that a story became current that they had been married abroad, and that Thaw's family was so annoyed at the reports that he could hope for no further advances from his father's estate until the provisions of the elder Thaw's will made it mandatory to turn over to him the $5,000,000 which was his share of the $40,000,000 left by his father when he died.

The story of the marriage was indignantly denied soon afterward by Thaw and Miss Nesbit when they returned to this country in October, 1904.

Few men in recent years have been so persistently in the public eye, on account of his escapades, as Harry Thaw. There were two things in which he remained firm—his objection to the marriage of his sister Alice to the Earl of Yarmouth, with whom he had previously had a bitter quarrel, and his devotion to Miss Nesbit.

In spite of the fact that his mother, who controlled his income of $80,000 a year, had previously cut down his allowance to $2,500 on account of his affair with the former model and chorus girl, Thaw remained fixed in his purpose to marry her and finally won his mother's consent to the match.

It was said in Pittsburg some time ago by members of the Thaw family that his mother had spent over $1,000,000 in her efforts to prevent an undesirable match. It was no secret that his family earnestly desired a union which would bring another coronet into the family.

Before he met Miss Nesbit Thaw gave a dinner in Paris to a score of famous beauties of Europe, at which he was the only man present. The banquet was one of the most elaborate affairs ever given there, and it was said to have cost no less than $50,000.

On the Saturday before his marriage Thaw came to Pittsburg from the East. In the evening he went to the Hotel Schenley. To some of his old associates that he met there he declared that before another week had passed he would be a benedict. The gathering was turned into a bachelor dinner, and the host then swore those present to secrecy, announcing that Miss Nesbit was to be his bride.

Miss Nesbit went to Pittsburg the day before her marriage. She was attended by a chaperon, Miss Pierce, and went to the home of her parents, Mr. and Mrs. C. J. Holman in Oakland.

The complete reconciliation of Thaw and his family was shown by those who attended the wedding, which was performed hastily and secretly. Those present were Mrs. William Thaw, the bridegroom's mother; his brother, Josiah Copley Thaw, and Frederick C. Perkins. Miss Nesbit was given away by her stepfather, C. J. Holman. Her mother was also there.

Pittsburg society refused in spite of the efforts of the elder Mrs. Thaw to receive Mrs. Harry K. Thaw. The young woman had good manners and tact, and it is said that lately these have helped her to overcome the barriers that had been raised against her.

Mr. Berlitz in the Academy.

M. D. Berlitz, the teacher of languages, whom President Loubet of France created a Chevalier of the Legion of Honor, has been made an officer of the French Academy. This is an honor which few Americans have obtained.

SPLIT ON WOODBURY REPORT.

Dady's Alderman Will Decide Whether It Shall Praise or Blame.

Two reports will be presented to the Board of Aldermen to-day by the committee which conducted the investigation into the affairs of the Department of Street Cleaning. One of the reports, it is understod, is severe in its criticisms, while the other is practically a "whitewash" for Major Woodbury's régime.

Chairman Grifenhagen of the Investigation Committee will present a report which has been prepared by William M. Ivins, counsel for the investigation. This will recommend the removal of Commissioner Woodbury and some of his subordinates. The other report clears the entire department. At present, however, the members are in doubt as to which report will be signed by a majority of the committee and which will be the minority report. There are five members of the committee, and a meeting will be held this morning to determine this point.

Chairman Grifenhagen and Aldermen Brown are strongly in favor of the Ivins report, while Alderman Dowling of Tammany Hall and Alderman Mulligan, Municipal Ownership League, are understood to favor the other statement, which is said to have been prepared by the counsel for Commissioner Woodbury. Alderman Downing, Col. "Mike" Dady's Alderman from Brooklyn, holds the deciding vote, and he has not as yet said which one he should approve.

SMALLPOX AT CATSKILL.

40 or 50 Mild Cases in River Town—Vaccinate, Says Darlington.

Dr. Darlington, President of the Board of Health, received a telephone message from Alexander H. Seymour, Secretary of the State Department of Health, yesterday, saying that there had been between forty and fifty mild cases of smallpox at Catskill-on-the-Hudson, and that of this number fourteen or fifteen cases are still remaining.

Dr. Darlington believes that the public should be advised of the conditions, so that all persons who intend going into that region for their Summer vacations may be vaccinated.

YESTERDAY'S FIRES.

2:10 A. M.—269 West 141st Street; M. Millman; damage, $5,000.
3:30 A. M.—Thirty-second Street and Ninth Avenue; New York Contracting Company; damage trifling.
3:30 A. M.—336 East Eighty-first Street; Adam H. Michael; damage, $500.
7:15 A. M.—111 Mott Street; Raphael Elio; damage, $10.
9:15 A. M.—221 Lexington Avenue; owner unknown; damage, $2,000.
9:50 A. M.—259 East Seventy-eighth Street; William Coppler; damage, $30.
10:45 A. M.—120 Elizabeth Street; owner unknown; damage, $200.
11:45 A. M.—357 Bowery; owner unknown; damage slight.
11:55 A. M.—608 Second Avenue; owner unknown; damage trifling.
1:50 P. M.—344 Grand Street; William Friedman; damage, $25.
2:50 P. M.—16 Doyers Street; owner unknown; damage, $10.
3:30 P. M.—226 Stanton Street; Max Gordner; damage, $10.
3:55 P. M.—3,966 Park Avenue; Drummill Railroad Lamp Works; damage, $25.
4 P. M.—171 East Ninety-ninth Street; Mrs. Annie Fitzgerald; damage trifling.
5:45 P. M.—38 Maiden Lane; Prier Brothers; damage, $50.
6:15 P. M.—126th Street and North River; New York Central Railroad; damage, $300.
6:45 P. M.—145 West Sixteenth Street; Helen Mitchel; damage, $500.
7:45 P. M.—3 Cherry Street; John Lyman; damage, $1,000.
8 P. M.—151 and 153 Cedar Street; William Moehring & Co.; damage, $2,000.
8:25 P. M.—66 Canal Street; Morris Cohen; damage, $50.
9:25 P. M.—212 to 216 Second Avenue; owner unknown; no damage.
10:05 P. M.—34 and 36 West Eighteenth Street; Elizabeth Shine; damage, $100.
10:30 P. M.—Hester and Essex Streets; Board of Education; no damage.

"All the News That's Fit to Print."

The New York Times.

THE WEATHER.
Fair to-day; fair, colder to-morrow; fresh westerly winds.

VOL. LVII...NO. 18,164. ** NEW YORK, FRIDAY, OCTOBER 18, 1907.—EIGHTEEN PAGES And Part I. of Autumn Review of Books. ONE CENT In Greater New York, Jersey City, and Newark. { Elsewhere, TWO CENTS.

BANK HERE IS SAFE IN HEINZE CRASH

Clearing House Committee Finds the Mercantile National in Sound Condition.

BUTTE BANK CLOSES DOORS

Otto Heinze & Co. Suspended from Stock Exchange—Ridgely Likely to Succeed Heinze in the Mercantile.

At the instance of the New York Clearing House Committee, which met late yesterday afternoon, an examination of the Mercantile National Bank, from the Presidency of which F. Augustus Heinze resigned in the morning, was made last night. For this work the committee selected James G. Cannon, Vice President of the Fourth National Bank; Edward Townsend, President of the Importers and Traders' Bank, and Walter E. Frew, Vice President of the Corn Exchange Bank. Early this morning they made a report, saying that the bank's capital was intact, and that it would open for business as usual this morning.

In addition to this move by the Clearing House, Mr. Heinze's resignation was followed by announcements of the suspension of Otto Heinze & Co. on the Stock Exchange and the closing of Heinze's Butte Savings Bank.

At the meeting at the Clearing House in the afternoon there were present J. Edward Simmons, President of the Fourth National Bank, and Alexander Gilbert, President of the Clearing House and of the Market and Fulton National Bank, besides three members of the official Clearing House Committee—William A. Nash, President of the Corn Exchange Bank; Dumont Clarke, President of the American Exchange National Bank, and Edward Townsend. James T. Woodward, President of the Hanover National Bank and Chairman of the Clearing House Committee, was out of town, as was also A. Barton Hepburn, President of the Chase National Bank and another member of the committee.

During the meeting the affairs of the Mercantile National and the events of the last few days in Wall Street, particularly the sensational incidents connected with the United Copper Company, were carefully gone over, and the resolution reached to make an examination of the Mercantile National at once, that institution being a member of the Clearing House, and therefore subject to examination by it. It was virtually decided that if the examination proved the bank to be in sound condition the Clearing House, which means all the great banks which are members of it, would stand by the Mercantile National and see it through any troubles which might follow the events of the last few days.

The committee, therefore, selected the bankers named to make the examination, and this committee went up to the Western Union Building, where the Mercantile National Bank offices are, and began an examination of its books, which lasted far into the night. Practically all the officers of the bank and the greater part of the clerical staff remained on hand to help the committee in the work.

Upon leaving the bank the committee went immediately to the home of J. Edward Simmons, at 28 West Fifty-second Street. At midnight the following statement was given out by Mr. Simmons:

"Mr. Nash, the Acting Chairman of the Clearing House Committee, states that the committee, with the full co-operation of the officers and Directors of the Mercantile National Bank, made an examination of its condition after the close of business to-day. The examination was very thorough, and was not completed until a late hour. Mr. Nash and his associates were convinced from the result of the examination that the bank was perfectly solvent and able to meet all its indebtedness. The capital of $3,000,000 is intact and with a large surplus."

Mr. Simmons was asked if this meant that the Clearing House had decided to stand by the bank in case there was a run.

"There certainly can be no other meaning to the action the Clearing House has taken," he said.

Mr. Simmons said the bank would open its doors this morning, as though nothing had happened.

"Has it been decided yet who will be the President of the Mercantile National?" Mr. Simmons was asked.

"There is little doubt that Mr. Ridgely will accept the Presidency," he replied. "He has not yet signified his intention of accepting, but I am quite sure he will take the position offered him."

Charles A. Hanna, the National bank examiner in this city, made arrangements to receive a duplicate report from the Clearing House Examination Committee for the purpose of informing Controller of the Currency Ridgely of the status of the bank.

Heinze Out; Offer to Ridgely.

An offer of the Presidency was made to Mr. Ridgely in Washington in the morning by telegraph, following the resignation of F. Augustus Heinze, who withdrew from the office after a protracted meeting of the Board of Directors. The Directors met at 11 o'clock in the morning and were in constant session until after 1 o'clock. It was then announced that Mr. Heinze had resigned the Presidency. In doing so he made the following explanation:

> In view of the difficulties in which my brother's firm finds itself, I have determined that it is proper that I should give liberally of my time in assisting them to straighten out their affairs. In aid of this, I have, after consulting with my fellow-Directors of the bank and my personal friends, and consulting as well my own personal interests as a large stockholder of the bank, this day resigned as its President, remaining, however, as a Director, and have joined with by fellow-Directors in a request that Mr. Ridgely accept the place made vacant by my resignation.

The condition of the Mercantile and the effects upon it of the developments of the last few days in the affairs of the copper company of its former President were carefully gone into. The discussion of the situation was vigorous, and there were plainly differences of opinion, but the final result of the meeting was

Continued on Page 4.

AMERICAN HOTEL FOR BERLIN.

It Hears of a Colossal Structure to be Run on Our Lines.

Special Cable to THE NEW YORK TIMES.

BERLIN, Oct. 17.—It is announced here that an American syndicate has acquired a block of choice property in Berlin at the corner of the Unter den Linden and Pariser-Platz, for the purpose of erecting a colossal building containing a palatial hotel, a grand opera house, and a roof garden, the whole establishment to be run upon American lines.

The opera house, it is stated, will have seating capacity for three thousand persons.

It is understood the plans for the colossal edifice will soon be laid before the Kaiser with a request for his approval of them. His assent will have to be given before the building can be erected. It is said the structure will cover more ground than is covered by the Waldorf-Astoria, and that it will exceed in magnificence any building of its kind in Europe.

AGED WOMAN'S BACK BROKEN.

Struck by an Auto While Returning from Father Mayer's Funeral.

Mrs. Amelia Greenblatt of 115 East Eighth Street attended the funeral yesterday of her late pastor, the Rev. John B. Mayer, in the St. Nicholas Roman Catholic Church in Second Street. The service ended at noon and Mrs. Greenblatt started from the church to go to her home.

She crossed the sidewalk and stepped into Second Avenue almost in front of an automobile driven by Rudolph Plain of 379 Gates Avenue, Brooklyn. Plain, who was driving from the Williamsburg Bridge toward Bond Street, sounded his horn loudly as he came down the avenue into which throngs were flocking from the church.

The loud blast of the horn startled Mrs. Greenblatt, who is 54 years old, and she stood still, apparently stupefied by her danger. Plain put on his brakes and tried to swing his machine to one side. Before he could stop the car, however, it had struck the woman and flung her to one side against the curbstone.

Women in the crowd screamed in horror. Policeman Burke of the Fifth Street Station lifted the woman in his arms and put her in the tonneau of the auto which Plain had succeeded in stopping. Then he ordered the chauffeur to drive up Avenue A to Bellevue Hospital at top speed.

The trip to the hospital of more than a mile was made in less than three minutes. Physicians who examined Mrs. Greenblatt said that her spine was broken.

The Rev. Father Mayer, whose funeral Mrs. Greenblatt had attended, died on Monday at the age of 56. He was born in Germany, came here in 1870 and was ordained a priest and assigned to the St. Nicholas Church seven years later. His long pastorate there endeared him to the German population of the parish over which he presided and hundreds visited the church yesterday.

PUMP THEM IN—KIPLING.

Immigration of Whites to Canada Will Keep Out Yellow Men.

TORONTO, Oct. 17.—"Pump in the immigrants from the old country; pump them in."

That is the solution Rudyard Kipling suggests for the Asiatic problem on the Pacific Coast. Mr. Kipling, accompanied by his wife, arrived here last night from a tour of the Canadian Northwest.

"Immigration is what Canada wants in the west," said Mr. Kipling. "You must have laborers there. You want immigration, and the way to keep the yellow man out is to get the white man in. If you keep out the white then you will have the yellow man, for you must have labor. Work must be done and there is certain work a white man won't do so long as he can get a yellow man to do it. Pump in the immigrants from the old country. Pump them in. England has five millions of people to spare."

Mr. Kipling expressed the opinion that both in the mother country and in Canada the labor party is opposed to immigration. "In England," he said, "the party is opposed to immigration because it would remove its great grievance with regard to the unemployed. In Canada there is a feeling in opposition to immigration because labor feels that it will be swamped."

Mr. Kipling, on being asked if the statement which appeared in a local paper that he was in Canada on behalf of the British Government and to formulate a scheme for their consideration as to Asiatic immigration was true, laughed and said: "I have still some sense of humor left." Pressed for an answer in the affirmative or negative, he said, laughing merrily: "Well, say that I am."

GOV. SMITH FREES SLAYER.

Atlanta People Think He Indorses the Unwritten Law.

Special to The New York Times.

ATLANTA, Oct. 17.—By granting a pardon to L. D. Strong of Macon to-day, Gov. Hoke Smith, in the opinion of many here, indorsed the "unwritten law."

Six months ago Strong, who is a prominent business man of Macon, killed Henry Smith, a Macon merchant, alleging, on the girl's confession, that Smith had mistreated Strong's 16-year-old sister. Strong went to Smith's place of business and shot him five times in the presence of many people. Smith lived a few minutes, and as he died, swore that he was innocent. Public sympathy was with Strong, but the jury convicted him and he was sent to the penitentiary. At once a movement for pardon was begun, and it culminated to-day when Gov. Smith, on the recommendation of a prison commission, gave him freedom.

MAGILL ON THE STAND.

Says Nagging of His Mother and Sister Caused Wife's Despondency.

DECATUR, Ill., Oct. 17.—Taking the stand to-day in his own behalf, Fred H. Magill, accused of murdering his first wife in order that he might wed Faye Graham, told in a matter-of-fact way of the events that led up to Mrs. Magill's death and the finding of her body by him the next morning.

Just before he retired that night, the witness said, his wife requested him to get her a bottle of beer. He got a bottle from the ice chest and then retired. In the morning when he awoke he saw his wife was not around. He made search of the house and found her in the spare room, lying with a blanket wrapped tightly around her head. He spoke to her, but got no reply, and upon examination he found she was dead. Witness said he detected the odor of chloroform.

Asked what, in his opinion, caused his wife's despondency he replied:

"Her headaches and the nagging of my mother and sister."

Magill was on the stand four hours. His testimony concluded the case for the defense.

CONRIED AND BOYD AT ODDS IN STOCKS

Opera Director's Brother Handled the Dealings of the Opera House Superintendent.

PROFIT FIGURES WIDE APART

$40,000, Says Boyd, Perhaps $300, Says Conried, and He'll Pay in Due Time.

Feeling that he was not getting rich enough from his salary as Superintendent of the Metropolitan Opera House and having heard of the many opportunities for obtaining money following the antics of the bulls and bears in Wall Street, Andrew Boyd who, besides having been Superintendent of the Opera House for many years is a close personal friend of Heinrich Conried, decided last January that he would take a little flyer in stocks with his savings. To-day he is a sadder, but wiser man. He met the same fate as many other lambs, though, he says, in a different way from many of them.

In his career in the theatrical business Mr. Boyd has always made it a practice to lay aside a little for a rainy day. This little he put in the bank from time to time until it grew to $1,000. Then he bought a bond. This nucleus made him all the more anxious to save, and another bond and yet others were added to the savings until the amount had reached about $10,000, all in interest bearing bonds.

Then, last January, when the stock market was active, Mr. Boyd grew interested in it through Alexander Conried, a stock broker, brother of Heinrich Conried, Director of the Metropolitan Opera Company.

Alexander Conried has no office, and, so far as known, he has no direct connection with any brokerage firm in "the Street." He is what is known as a "wandering broker," taking business from whom he can get it and putting it where he thinks it will be to his best advantage. Mr. Boyd says he gave Mr. Conried $6,000 to be used as margin in stock speculations.

The stocks that Conried bought for Boyd, copper being among the number, began to drop rapidly. The $6,000 in margins soon became $5,000, then $4,000, $3,000, $2,000, and $1,000, and when the $500 mark had been reached, according to Boyd, Conried told him he would have to advance more money if he would save the $6,000 he had already put up.

Then it is said he gave Conried $4,000 in bonds as additional margins. This money Boyd thought had saved the day for him. He watched the quotations in the papers, and each day he noticed, so he says, that his stocks were getting better and better. Finally he figured out for himself a large profit, and asked Mr. Conried for it. He says he didn't get it, and on this point Mr. Conried agrees with him, but adds that there were no such profits as Mr. Boyd had figured out.

Mr. Boyd took his side of the case to a lawyer yesterday. When Mr. Conried heard of this he consented to give his version of the affair, and it is a very different version, to a TIMES reporter.

"My trades for Mr. Boyd were just the same as trades for all other clients," he said.

"Mr. Boyd did put up margins for me to buy stocks for him, but it is absurd to say that I made $40,000 in the market for him and failed to turn it over to him. I bought copper around 118 and it went off. I bought other stocks for him and they went up. I really think that the amount of his winnings in the market would reach only about $300.

"It is quite true that when I closed out his account I owed him several thousand dollars, and could not pay it to him at the time the account was closed because the money was locked up in several other accounts, and I had to wait until they were straightened out. I have paid him a part of the money, and expect to close out the balance within a few days. The whole thing is really very greatly exaggerated."

J. VIPOND DAVIES HURT.

Consulting Engineer Stops Runaway and Saves Children—His Hip Broken.

J. Vipond Davies, chief consulting engineer of the Hudson Tunnel Company, who lives in 24 Bowne Avenue, Flushing, Queens Borough, had one hip broken and received internal injuries yesterday morning while preventing a team of runaway horses from running down a group of school children.

Mr. Davies was on his way through Amity Street, Flushing, to the Main Street railroad station to catch the 8:30 o'clock train for Long Island City, when two teams of horses hitched to moving vans, owned by G. Anderson & Son, which were backed against the sidewalk, took fright at an automobile driven by William Haak of Franklin Place. One of the teams became unmanagable and started off.

The horses were heading direct toward a group of school children when Mr. Davies sprang and caught the nearest horse by the bridle. He was swung from his feet, but managed to change the course of the team from the street toward the sidewalk.

Mr. Davies was clinging to the bridle when the team crashed into a tree. He was thrown against the tree and fell to the ground so that the front wheels of the van passed over his legs. The team was checked by the collision and the horses were quickly caught, while Mr. Davies was picked up and carried into the office of Dr. E. T. Lawrence at 147 Amity Street.

When Mr. Davies learned the extent of his injuries, at his own request he was taken to his home. His condition is said to be serious.

THIS ISSUE OF THE NEW YORK TIMES includes AUTUMN BOOK LIST NUMBER of The New York Times Saturday Review (FIRST SECTION)

Second Section To-morrow.

FIRST WIRELESS PRESS MESSAGE ACROSS THE ATLANTIC

Signalizing the Opening of the Marconi Service to the Public, and Conveying a Message of Congratulation from Privy Councillor Baron Avebury, Formerly Sir John Lubbock.

Form 168

THE WESTERN UNION TELEGRAPH COMPANY.
INCORPORATED
24,000 OFFICES IN AMERICA. CABLE SERVICE TO ALL THE WORLD.

This Company TRANSMITS and DELIVERS messages only on conditions limiting its liability, which have been assented to by the sender of the following message. Errors can be guarded against only by repeating a message back to the sending station for comparison, and the Company will not hold itself liable for errors or delays in transmission or delivery of Unrepeated Messages, beyond the amount of tolls paid thereon, nor in any case where the claim is not presented in writing within sixty days after the message is filed with the Company for transmission.
This is an UNREPEATED MESSAGE, and is delivered by request of the sender, under the conditions named above.
ROBERT C. CLOWRY, President and General Manager.

RECEIVED at 813 Sixth Ave. Corner 46th St.
TELEPHONE: 3907 BRYANT.

1B Lr Sn Dh & 53 Collect D, P R, Land lines,

London Via Marconi Wireless Glace Bay N S Oct 17th,

Times, New York.

This message marks opening transatlantic wireless handed

Marconi company for transmission Ireland Breton limited 50 words

only send one many messages received Times signalize event

quote trust introduction wireless more closely unite people states

Great Britian who seem form one Nation though under two Governments

and whose interests are really identical.

Avebury Marshall .... 1210 Am Oct17th

ALWAYS OPEN. MONEY TRANSFERRED BY TELEGRAPH. CABLE OFFICE.

The above message was immediately followed by others which appear in another column of The Times this morning.

MARCONI CONGRATULATES THE NEW YORK TIMES

GLACE BAY, NOVA SCOTIA, Oct. 17.—Mr. Marconi says: "Congratulate New York Times on having received first westward press message."

FROM THE PRIME MINISTER OF FRANCE.

WEST STRAND, London, Oct. 17, via Marconi Wireless Telegraph to Glace Bay, N. S.—THE NEW YORK TIMES's Paris correspondent forwards to me the following message for transmission across the Atlantic by Marconi wireless telegraph:

"Dans l'inauguration du prodigieux mode de communication mis désormais à leur disposition, les deux grandes républiques ne peuvent que trouver une heureuse occasion de se feliciter et de formuler les voeux les plus cordiaux pour le mantien de la paix dans le travail pour le bonheur des peuples dans la solidarité."
"CLEMENCEAU."

[Translation.]

In the inauguration of the marvelous means of communication put at their disposition from this time forward, the two great Republics could not but find it a happy occasion to congratulate themselves and to express the most cordial wishes for the maintenance of peace in the work for the happiness of the people in the joint responsibility.
CLEMENCEAU.

MISS VANDERBILT MUST TAKE CHANCES

By No Means Certain She Will Be Admitted to Austrian Court in Vienna.

A HIGH OFFICIAL SAYS SO

Unless Emperor Dispenses with Proof of Considerable Ancestral Nobility She Will Be Shut Out.

Special Cable to THE NEW YORK TIMES.

VIENNA, Oct. 17.—A Court official of high rank, of whom I inquired what would be Miss Gladys Vanderbilt's status with respect to the Court in the event of her marriage to Count Szechenyi, said:

"The lady in question would be received at Court in Budapest, but not in Vienna, unless the Emperor should dispense with the proof of nobility with respect to sixteen of her ancestors, which otherwise she would be required by Austrian Court etiquette to furnish.

"Such a concession is sometimes made, and very likely it would be made in the case we are speaking of, out of consideration for the social standing of Count Szechenyi and the importance of the Vanderbilt family."

It seems, in view of this authoritative statement, that Miss Vanderbilt, if she marries the Count, may find herself in a rather unpleasant predicament when she comes to live in Vienna.

NEWPORT, Oct. 17.—Miss Gladys Vanderbilt is not spending all the time with her fiancé, Count Szechenyi, although he is a guest at her mother's house. This morning she was at the Casino with a number of young women friends, the Count remaining at The Breakers.

At noon she drove about town in her basket phaeton with her chum, Miss Josephine Pearson. They had a "college ice" together in a Thames Street drug store. Miss Vanderbilt seemed to be thoroughly enjoying the absence of a crowd of curious sightseers, and to fully appreciate the fact that she was being left entirely unnoticed.

This evening Miss Vanderbilt and Count Szechenyi attended a dinner given in their honor by Mrs. Charles H. Baldwin at Snug Harbor, and later accompanied Mrs. Baldwin and her other guests to the Opera House to see William Collier in "Caught in the Rain." This was Miss Vanderbilt's first appearance at the Newport Opera House since her engagement, and she and the Count were naturally the centre of attraction between the acts.

H. P. WHITNEY ARRESTED?

Colorado Authorities Accues Visitors of Slaughtering Deer Wantonly.

Special to The New York Times.

DENVER, Col., Oct. 17.—Two men who say they are Frank Carnegie, nephew of Andrew Carnegie, and Harry Payne Whitney of New York, came to Colorado two weeks ago to hunt bear. They hired guides and started out with a pack of hounds. Reaching the game country, they began to slaughter deer promiscuously, both for the sport and for bait for traps.

Deputy Warden Bush finally arrested the hunters and their guides, took them before a Justice of the Peace, and prosecuted them for wanton destruction of deer. Bush says he had an offer of $300 to drop the case before the trial. After the trial began, he says, the Justice was called out of court by his wife, and when he returned he dismissed the case. The State Game Warden is investigating the case.

ROCKEFELLER TOO SAVING.

Supt. Jones of Forest Hill Resigns Because Expenses Are Cut.

Special to The New York Times.

CLEVELAND, Oct. 17.—Asserting that John D. Rockefeller wants to cut expenses too much, C. C. Jones, for some seven months superintendent of the Forest Hill estate, has resigned, and will leave for New York on Nov. 15. Jones says that Rockefeller insisted on curtailing expenses to such an extent that he could not keep up the place. He allowed some trimming of costs when he took the position, but recently, he says, Mr. Rockefeller wanted to reduce the pay of the men and he demurred. An argument followed and Mr. Jones resigned.

"When I came here I thought I was to run the estate," said Mr. Jones, "but soon found that such was not the case. Mr. Rockefeller insisted on changes and orders that I did not believe were for the best, and I found that I couldn't look after the place as it should be and follow the suggestion that he made, so I quit."

SAVED BY SENATOR SCOTT.

He Stops Runaway and Rescues Two Mexican Women.

Special to The New York Times.

CITY OF MEXICO, Oct. 17.—United States Senator Nathan B. Scott of West Virginia, here on a pleasure trip, made a daring rescue of two prominent Mexican women in a runaway accident in one of the principal streets here last evening.

Senator Scott, who is almost 65 years old, jumped from the sidewalk, seized the reins, and stopped the runaway horses after a desperate struggle.

Latest Shipping News.

Arrived—S. S. Emilia, Trieste, Sept. 4; S. S. Olinda, Nuevitas; S. S. Fagertun, Port Antonio.

DEUTSCHLAND STUCK CLOSE TO HER PIER

Capt. Kaempff Gives Up Attempt to Get Liner Off After Three Hours' Work.

PASSENGERS SENT TO BED

Hundreds of Friends Exchange Greetings with Them as Seven Tugs Strive in Vain.

The Hamburg-American liner Deutschland from Hamburg for this port, stuck in the mud last night in the Hudson River, with her big freeboard actually scraping against the end of her Hoboken pier. After waiting for nearly three hours in the hope that the big ship might be warped into her dock, her 500 cabin passengers and 300 steerage passengers reluctantly went to bed, convinced that it would be morning before they could set foot on American soil.

During the time that a flotilla of tugs struggled to pull the ship off the mud and up to her pier hundreds of persons waiting to welcome home-coming voyagers lined the pier, exchanging greetings with the marooned passengers, for though the boat touched her pier there was no way for the passengers to reach it except by sliding down a forty-foot rope ladder, and this Capt. Kaempff would not permit.

The accident came as a climax to a voyage replete with fog and rough weather. Soon after leaving Hamburg the liner ran into weather that compelled her to slacken speed, and soon after there followed forty-eight hours of dense fog. Delayed by these conditions, the Deutschland did not reach Quarantine until 9 o'clock last night, instead of early yesterday morning, when she was due.

It was an hour later before the big boat slowed down near her pier to let the tugs make their lines fast to her. Usually there are at least fourteen tugs employed to swing the steamship into her dock, but last night only seven answered Capt. Kaempff's call.

Six of these made lines fast to one side to pull the stern around, while the other made fast to her bow, against which it shoved, apparently without effect. The tugs puffed and steamed, but the ship scarcely moved, and in the meantime the tide was rapidly running out.

For half an hour the struggle was kept up, and then the Deutschland's keel touched bottom. Amidships, one side of the boat grated against the pier, while the bow and stern swung far away from the structure.

WIRELESS JOINS TWO WORLDS

Marconi Transatlantic Service Opened with a Dispatch to The New York Times.

MESSAGES FROM EMINENT MEN

Prime Minister Clemenceau, the Duke of Argyll, Lord Avebury and Others Send Greetings.

10,000 WORDS THE FIRST DAY

Marconi in Personal Supervision at Glace Bay and Greatly Pleased with the Results.

SIR HIRAM MAXIM'S TRIBUTE

His Message to Peter Cooper Hewitt in New York, Who Is Trying to Pick Up the Oversea Messages.

By Marconi Transatlantic Wireless Telegraph to The New York Times.

LONDON, Oct. 17.—This message marks the opening of the transatlantic wireless service. It is handed to the Marconi Company here for transmission to Ireland, and thence to Cape Breton, Nova Scotia, and New York. As it is limited to fifty words, I can send at present only one of the many messages received for transmission to The New York Times to signalize the event. This message, from Privy Councillor Lord Avebury, formerly Sir John Lubbock, follows:

"I trust that the introduction of the wireless will more closely unite the people of the United States and Great Britain, who seem to form one nation, though under two Governments, and whose interests are really identical. AVEBURY."

MARCONI'S CONGRATULATIONS.

The above message, received early yesterday morning, was quickly followed by one from The Times's correspondent at Glace Bay, as follows:

"Glace Bay, N. S., Oct. 17.

"Mr. Marconi says: 'Congratulate New York Times on having received first westward press message.'"

Then came in full the original message filed by The Times's correspondent in London, from which the short dispatch above was condensed, to meet the fifty-word limit imposed by the Marconi Company upon the first message transmitted. The full message follows:

MESSAGES FROM EMINENT MEN.

By Marconi Transatlantic Wireless Telegraph to The New York Times.

LONDON, Oct. 17.—This message marks the opening of the transatlantic wireless service. It is now eleven years since William Marconi, in May, 1896, announced in New York that he had discovered the secret by which messages might be flashed through space without the assistance of wires or cables such as were used in the ordinary methods of telegraphy at that time. Mr. Marconi's statements were received with skepticism, and his prediction of the wonders which he felt confident could be worked by means of his application of the Hertzian waves was openly disputed even by electricians, who ought, from their knowledge of the feats achieved by the electric spark, to have recognized that the limits of its potentialities had not been reached.

Mr. Marconi, as this message testifies, has now accomplished all that he expressed his confidence in being able to do. This message, which I have handed in at the Lon-den office of the Marconi Wireless Telegraph Company for transmission to New York by the Marconi system, speaks for itself.

There is pleasure in transmitting by wireless telegraphy the following messages from representative Englishmen, which have been furnished by the signatories for publication in The New York Times, in connection with one of the most remarkable achievements of modern science.

The Duke of Argyll's message is:

"The air message is an emblem of the kinship of two peoples who love freedom."

Privy Councillor Baron Avebury, formerly Sir John Lubbock, writes:

"I sincerely trust that the introduction of wireless telegraphy may still more closely unite the people of the United States and Great Britain, who seem to form one nation, though under two Governments, and whose interests are really identical."

Sir George Taubman Goldie writes:

"May this latest triumph of science consolidate the essential unity of the English-speaking nations, the forerunner of the unity of mankind."

Field Marshal Viscount Wolseley's message is:

"I rejoice that a new link between the United States and the mother country has been created. May it strengthen the union between all English-speaking races."

Alfred Austin, Poet Laureate, sends this:

"Let the Stars and Stripes and the Union Jack still float most high together."

The message of Sir Norman Lockyer, the distinguished scientist, is:

"All honor to the country where, beyond all others, the Central Government, the State Legislatures, and private citizens foster education and research as the true, and indeed the only, foundation of a nation's greatness. Such a nation will be the one to profit most from the future victories of science, which are certain to beggar the achievements of the present as wireless telegraphy pales the achievements of the past."

Marconi and His Wireless Stations at Glace Bay, N. S., and Poldhu, Cornwall

MARCONI STATION AT GLACE BAY. N.S.

FROM FRANCE'S PREMIER.

M. Clemenceau's Felicitations Upon the Opening of the New Service.

By Marconi Transatlantic Wireless Telegraph to The New York Times.

WEST STRAND, LONDON, Oct. 17.—The New York Times's Paris correspondent forwards to me the following message for transmission across the Atlantic by Marconi Wireless Telegraph:

"Dans l'inauguration du prodigieux mode de communication mis désormais à leur disposition, les deux grandes républiques ne peuvent que trouver une heureuse occasion de se féliciter et de formuler les voeux les plus cordiaux pour le mantien de la paix dans le travail pour le bonheur des peuples dans la solidarité.

"CLEMENCEAU."

[Translation.]

In the inauguration of the marvelous means of communication put at their disposition from this time forward, the two great Republics could not but find it a happy occasion to congratulate themselves and to express the most cordial wishes for the maintenance of peace in the work for the happiness of the people in the joint responsibility. CLEMENCEAU.

OPENING OF THE SERVICE.

About 10,000 Words Were Sent Between Nova Scotia and Ireland.

Special to The New York Times.

MARCONI WIRELESS STATION, GLACE BAY, N. S., Oct. 17.—Communication with Clifden, the Irish station of the Marconi Company, was established on schedule time this morning and has continued successfully across the Atlantic throughout the day.

The first message received here was a brief one addressed to THE NEW YORK TIMES, and was immediately followed by another containing 353 words. This message enjoyed the distinction of containing the greatest number of words of any telegram sent or received to-day. The first message transmitted from here was addressed to The London Standard by Sir Wilfred Laurier, and read as follows.

"Standard, London, Eng. Welcome new bond between Britain and Canada, one more triumph for Empire and Science. Wilfred Laurier." Invitations had been issued to a large number of guests, and many American and English newspaper men were present.

It has been a busy, tiring day for all hands, both at this station and at Clifden in Ireland. They have all been worked up to their full capacity. This afternoon the system was much overloaded, owing to the heavy filling of personal congratulatory telegrams.

Mr. Marconi permits me send to THE NEW YORK TIMES copies of the following messages dispatched and received by him:

To Lord Kelvin, 15 Eaton Place, London: Very happy to be able to send you and Lady Kelvin most cordial greetings transmitted through ether, from Canada to Ireland. MARCONI.

Lord Kelvin's reply, dated Largs, Scotland, read:

Marconi, Glace Bay: Heartiest thanks for your kind telegram and congratulations on your practical use of ether. KELVIN.

To Henneker Heaton, Esq., M. P., Bexhill on Sea: On occasion establishment regular transatlantic wireless service, send you best greetings, also express my sincere admiration for your untiring and successful efforts to promote facilities universal communication. MARCONI.

London advised that Henniker Heaton was on his way to Australia.

The Dublin Stock Exchange congratulated the New York Stock Exchange on the successful inauguration of a cheap telegraph system between Great Britain and the United States.

The Governor General of Canada sent a message of congratulation to his Majesty King Edward at Buckingham Palace, London. Up to this time, at 7:30 P. M., I estimate that 10,000 words have been exchanged, and many remain on hand at each end.

Mr. Marconi is satisfied with the day's work as indicative of what will be done after a few days running, when the organization is fully perfected. He has been present throughout the entire day, lending a helping hand wherever needed, and encouraging the staff to greatest exertions. He expresses his confidence in the great commercial future of the system and proposes to erect other stations to supplement the service established to-day.

His station at South Wellfleet, Cape Cod, Mass., will be immediately overhauled and refitted for the embodiment of the improvements in both the sending and receiving apparatus that have been so successfully adopted here.

Apart from the technical and commercial standpoints, Mr. Marconi expresses satisfaction in the belief that when wireless stations are universally in operation, as they are bound to be in the near future, this new method of communication will tend to bind different countries more closely together, a consummation which must inevitably conduce to better understanding between nations.

This belief is also unmistakably shared by many eminent people who to-day have used his system of wireless telegraphy in its expression. Mr. Marconi speaks in the warmest terms of praise of the great and unstinting efforts of his staff, who have most loyally supported him throughout the arduous work which to-day's inauguration has necessarily involved.

In the external appearance of the station there was nothing to indicate that to-day marked a new era of transatlantic telegraphy except that from the tops of the four towers now generally identified with Marconi high-power stations floated the national flags of Italy, Great Britain, Canada, and the United States.

In the operating house and engine room, however, all hands could be seen, each attending to his appointed task, hurrying here and there in its execution, with R. N. Vyvyan, the engineer in charge, keeping a watchful eye over everything.

At his signal the machinery was started in motion, switches thrown in, and all was ready for the transmission of the first message. The operator then pressed the key to an accompanying flash of light and a sharp musical report, quickly followed by others, which formed themselves into the characters of the Morse code, and one realized that a message was speeding to its destination on the other side of the broad Atlantic.

Then at a signal switches were thrown out and the receiving operator, wearing a telephone headgear, was observed busily engaged in taking down the business then being transmitted from Ireland. For the wonderful feat that is being accomplished, the apparent simplicity of the operation is astounding.

"I am entirely satisfied with the result," said Mr. Marconi to-night. "You can say that everything worked splendidly; we are going to operate a limited service for a while, but we have already handled from five thousand to ten thousand words to-day on account of it being a special day and a large number of congratulatory and press messages having been exchanged between London and New York. We did not transmit commercial or private messages as a rule to-day, as we made it a sort of press day.

"You cannot call it an inaugural or opening. We had our real opening two years ago, when telegrams were passed by our system between the President and the King. We have not, therefore, addressed anything to crowned heads, but we are just quietly starting to do a regular business between Europe and America in continuation of the old service. Sir Wilfrid Laurier sent two messages by our system this morning. One was addressed to the British people. We also received here a message from Lord Strathcona, the Canadian High-Commissioner in London. I am indeed pleased with the result."

TIMES GREETS LONDON MAIL.

Conditions at Clifden, the Irish Station, Were Perfect.

Special Cable to THE NEW YORK TIMES.

LONDON, Oct. 17.—The special correspondent of THE NEW YORK TIMES at Clifden, Galway, the Irish station of the Marconi transatlantic wireless system, telegraphed to-day that the first newspaper message transmitted to America was a dispatch to THE NEW YORK TIMES.

The last word of the message was tapped off at eight minutes past two, Irish time. Similarly, the first newspaper dispatch received at London was a NEW YORK TIMES message addressed to The Daily Mail, as follows:

"THE NEW YORK TIMES sends greetings to The London Daily Mail, with congratulations to Marconi on the inauguration of his wireless system.

"THE NEW YORK TIMES."

This was received at the Galway station at 11:48 A. M.

After this a goodly number of messages were received by the several newspapers. Very many applications to transmit dispatches were made at the offices of the Marconi Company, but they had to be refused as the service at present is confined entirely to press messages.

In reply to the specific question, "When shall you be ready to transmit private or commercial messages?" Mr. Knight, the traffic manager of the Marconi Company, said: "At the end of next week. In about ten days' time."

Asked if messages can be transmitted both ways simultaneously, Mr. Knight answered: "Yes. The receivers and transmitters are differently attuned and consequently there is no interference."

The correspondent at Clifden telegraphs that it was at 11:39 A. M., Irish time, Thursday, that W. S. Entwistle, the engineer in charge of the station there, gave orders to prepare to transmit the first public message.

The connection with the Glace Bay station was quickly made. Later Mr. Entwistle said: "I am satisfied with the way things have been going at Clifden. The transmission and reception seem to be very good, and at Cape Breton, too. Our hours, at first, for these messages will be between 6 and 8 P. M., English time."

Mr. Entwistle added that no attempt had been made to-day at speed, but that both transmission and reception were now being accomplished as a certainty.

LONDON AND NEW YORK?

Peter Cooper Hewitt Predicts an Early Connection Between the Cities.

The early connection of London and New York by wireless was predicted last night at midnight by Peter Cooper Hewitt in his electrical studio in the Madison Square Garden Building. He was endeavoring to pick up a message from England to the Marconi station at Glace Bay on his receiving instrument in the tower.

He had been able to get messages received at Cape Cod, but none received further north.

"This morning," said Mr. Hewitt, "I met Prof. R. A. Fessenden, who has been an indefatigable worker in the completion of wireless possibilities, and he told me that he had picked up messages from England yesterday. They were sent to Marconi at Glace Bay, and Prof. Fessenden's station is at Broad Rock, Mass."

"If the messages from the other side have been received by wireless as near New York as the Massachusetss coast," Mr. Hewitt was asked, "is there a probability or a possibility that they will in a short time be picked up here and handled in a way that will meet the demands of the times in intercontinental communication?"

"I should say that there is an extreme probability," he replied. "The only question is that of mastering atmospheric conditions, and Prof. Fessenden has discovered that a wave of 81,000 a second is less interfered with than any other wave length. With increased horse power generating the spark, and with the knowledge of the wave best measured to combat adverse atmospheric conditions, there will soon be direct communication of sufficient speed and accuracy between London and New York to meet demands of intercontinental communication between those cities."

One of the first messages to be received in New York yesterday was one to Mr. Hewitt. The message to Mr. Hewitt was from Sir Hiram Maxim, who sent it from London by Marconi service. It read as follows:

London, Via Marconi Wireless.
Glace Bay, N. S., Oct. 17, 1907.
Mr. Peter Cooper Hewitt, 51 Madison Avenue, New York, N. Y.:

I think that all of us who have dabbled in science sufficiently and who understand the difficulties that one has to encounter even with the ponderable should take off our hats to Mr. Marconi and congratulate him upon his almost unbelievable success in dealing with the imponderable. All honor to Marconi! Perhaps the next step will be to harness the whole energy of Niagara to make an attempt to communicate with the planet Mars. HIRAM MAXIM.
9:15 A. M.

"A great achievement for Marconi," he said. "He has fully crowned his ambition. It is a double pleasure to hear of his achievement and to be informed of it by Sir Hiram Maxim.

"It was thought very extraordinary when Marconi sent a message across the English Channel. Marconi's untiring work and endeavors perfected wireless telegraphy so that it became available for ships, and now his work is crowned by success in establishing transatlantic communication which, if considered from the information possessed even by scientists ten years ago, is a most marvelous achievement and one that will prove of far greater public utility than the communication between ships which he had already established.

"In this great epoch in wireless telegraphy, brought about by Marconi's untiring skill and development, it must not be forgotten that Hertz's appreciation and physical rendering of Maxwell's theorem rendered this possible."

Mr. Cooper was asked if he took Sir Hiram's suggestion as to the signaling of Mars seriously. He declined to discuss this matter.

"Would you like to know what's going on over the roofs of New York to-night?" Mr. Hewitt asked the reporter. He showed the way to his Marconi receiving instrument. In a glass inclosure glowed a blue light. Heavy magnets were balanced against the bottom of the glass, and overhead streamed many wires that led to the mast on the top of the tower near the gilded Diana. "Tuning" the instrument, Mr. Hewitt placed on his head a nickel band holding two receiving telephone ear cups. He handed another set of receivers to the TIMES reporter. The microphone immediately registered the sounds of the telegraph code.

The wireless operator at Galilee, N. J., was calling for a ship on its way across the Atlantic. Then an operator of another station began to tangle in and the Galillee man got sore. He said things in dots and dashes and then called for and got an answer from 42 Broadway. To the operator there he told of his futile effort to get the ship wanted and suggested that a station further north be tried. No. 42 Broadway began to call for Nova Scotia. In the meanwhile Mr. Hewitt had changed the key of his instrument and a message from a ship far out at sea was picked up. Then three tugs outside of New York were picked up, a Sound steamer, and in all ten different wireless operators were heard at their work in as many minutes.

"It would surprise the ordinary lay mind how large a business is being done in wireless right around him," said Mr. Hewitt. "Just listen how fast that man at Galilee is sending now."

Galilee had forgotten his grievance of a few minutes before and was hurling words with the speed of lightning through the air.

EXPERIMENTING SINCE 1678.

How the First Groping After Facts Culminated in Present Service.

In 1678, Christian Huygens, a Dutch mathematician, worked out a theory of the undulation of light in an ether, which was a conveying medium and which might explain the phenomena of light. Before he started on this theory of the undulation of the ether scientists and philosophers had worked over the problem of that transcendental thing which enveloped them and through which sounds were carried and images presented.

In the history of wireless telegraphy, by A. Frederick Collins, it is pointed out that at least a thousand years before Christ, the question was at issue whether the interstellar space was filled with a substance, a fluid-filling matter.

Huygens struck the first practical note, and Michael Farraday, in 1845, held to the Huygens undulatory theory by a firm belief in its eventual practical realization, began to experiment. He succeeded in establishing the fact of an all-pervading medium. Farraday was followed by James Clerk Maxwell who, in 1881, systematized Farraday's conception with his electro-magnetic theory of light, a theory which means that light, electricity, and magnetism are transmitted by the same ether at an identical rate of speed.

The next step towards wireless communication was made in the study of wave motions. Hertz was the first to employ the term electric radiation. He used the term, Collins points out, to describe the waves emitted from a Leyden jar. They have been called Hertzian waves ever since. Before Hertz's discovery Prof. Joseph Henry of Washington, D. C., had succeeded in magnetizing needles at a distance. He used a frictional machine on the floor of his house and magnetized needles on the floor below. This was sending electrical power through the air with a practical demonstration of its passing.

With the discovery that the air was a means of conveyance for electricity, came the effort to produce electric discharges. Sparks were produced as early as 1602, but they were so small that they could be barely seen with the naked eye. In 1745, came the discovery and development of a jar in which electricity could be stored—the Leyden jar. Then the sparks began to fly, and with them, the certainty among scientific investigators of the phenomenon of electricity, that the passing of a spark into the air meant a displacement of air and a consequent agitation that might be directed and used.

The sparks were made to grow, until Elihu Thomson in 1877 produced them 64 inches long.

To detect the electric air waves, meant the first attempt at control of the invisible, or, as Dr. Hiram Maxim called it yesterday in his Marconigram from England to Peter Cooper Hewitt in New York, the imponderable.

Guitard, in 1850, observed in dust-ladened air, when electrified, the particles of dust cohered into the forms of strings. Here was the first practical hint of a path through the void. A. S. Varley, in 1866, tried experiments with a loose mass of dust containing conducting material as if to blaze a highway through the wilderness of ether.

In 1879 Prof. Hughes sent a wireless signal a mile distant, using a microphonic carbon joint as a detector of the waves. Hertz, in 1888, devised a metal ring for the detection of induction. In 1894 the question of sending signals by the Hertz radiator and receiving them with his detector was one that engaged the minds of scientists. Lodge employed a device by which he discovered what he called the coherer. This was named as the result of his observation that the action of electricity on metal filings was coherence, that is a clustering of the particles together.

Marconi, a young man, just in his twenties, was studying electric transmission through the ether in 1897, and he worked over the Lodge device, developing it.

All the rest of the story of how the air was harnessed and made to serve the purposes of mankind in its communication from continent to continent is crammed in the last eventful decade. Marconi as a boy was interested in the Hertzian waves and their control. In his teens he experimented in the country place of his parents, near Pontecchio in Italy. The first practical system of generating and transmitting electric waves through the air was worked out by him in 1896. He immediately packed up and went to England, where he applied for his patent.

With sending and receiving instruments perfected there came out of the air and the brain of thinking humans the system that has stripped away from electricity the use of wire and cable as a conveyor, and the day that Ben Franklin sent a kite aloft to find that it attracted the lightning from the heavens had not resulted in only a futile experiment.

The meshes of wide spreading autamas at the Marconi stations to-day attract and hold for unriddling the dots and dashes started from across the ocean, just as did the brass key of the Philosopher Franklin, who little knew what his kite-flying would bring about. The inventive genius of the men following Franklin and their patience and sacrifice devised the receiving instrumtnts which hold the power that the key had unlocked from the heavens.

While Marconi has carried wireless telegraphy to its perfection with the results he achieved yesterday, he has not been, by any means, the sole toiler toward this achievement. After Clerk-Maxwell defined the ether waves Sir William Preece in 1885 managed to send currents between two insulated squares of wire a quarter of a mile apart. Sir Oliver Lodge obtained successful signalling results in 1889, and three years later Sir William Preece secured wireless communication for a distance of three and a third miles from Flatholm, in the Bristol Channel, and Lavernock, on the Welsh Coast.

Then Marconi came into the field, and, instead of signals, messages were sent until he began to labor at the task of sending messages from England to North America. In 1901 he managed to transmit the letter S from Cornwall to Newfoundland. In 1902 the S. S. Philadelphia kept in communication with the Marconi station at Poldhu when out 1,550 miles. At the end of that year communication between the continents was established, but it remained until yesterday to have it in operation so completely in accord with the demands of speed and accuracy, that it became a distinct commercial and economic factor in the life of to-day.

FIRST OVERSEA MESSAGE.

How the Historic Greetings Were Sent to England in 1902.

The following description of the sending of the first wireless message across the Atlantic to The London Times was written in January, 1903, by Dr. George A. Parkin, a Professor at Upper Canada College, and London Times correspondent.

The message was sent Dec. 16, 1902, from the present station at Glace Bay, Nova Scotia. The story of the message and the description of the station as it

Continued on Page 3.

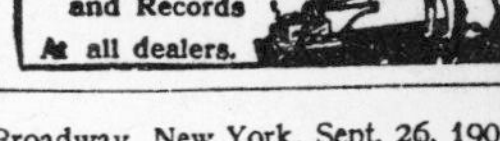

"All the News That's Fit to Print."

The New York Times.

THE WEATHER.
Fair to-day and probably Friday; wind light to fresh southwest.

VOL. LVII...NO. 18,492. * * * * NEW YORK, THURSDAY, SEPTEMBER 10, 1908.—SIXTEEN PAGES. ONE CENT In Greater New York, Jersey City, and Newark { Elsewhere, TWO CENTS.

BOSSES HAVE DECIDED TO ACCEPT HUGHES

Parsons, Whom the "Test" Results in Manhattan Surprised, Admits It.

RENOMINATION NOW SURE

The Governor Will Have 513 Delegates at Least, 8 More Than Are Needed—Woodruff Talks.

Developments in the Republican camp yesterday practically insure the renomination of Gov. Hughes at the Republican State Convention, which will meet in Saratoga next Monday.

While there was at first an effort among the Republican leaders who have opposed the Governor's renomination to magnify the opposition shown in the primary "tests" on Tuesday and to minimize the pro-Hughes sentiment, President Herbert Parsons of the Republican County Committee lost no time in climbing down from the fence and making a dash for the Hughes band wagon.

Republican State Chairman Timothy L. Woodruff gave out a long statement in which he sought to justify the objections of the anti-Hughes leaders to the Governor's renomination. Chairman Woodruff did not deviate yesterday from the position he has maintained for the last few weeks—that "the delegates must decide." It is asserted, though, that Mr. Parsons is not playing a lone game, but merely had the good sense to head a procession that may develop into a foot race of bosses and bosslets into the Governor's camp, and that Mr. Woodruff in all probability will be the second in line.

Test Made It Clear—Parsons.

President Parsons, who has been subjected to a great deal of pressure emanating from Oyster Bay and from the managers of the Taft campaign, made his first open statement on the question of the Governor's renomination yesterday. He said:

"The result of the test votes taken in this county shows that a considerable majority of the enrolled Republicans prefer that Gov. Hughes should be renominated. We took the test to put the question up to them, and, if their desires were explicit, to act accordingly. The test shows that there is some bitter opposition. But in view of the controlling sentiment in favor of the Governor's renomination, which the test has made clear, it is my opinion that a large majority of the delegates from New York County to the State Convention will favor Gov. Hughes's renomination."

Hughes Sure of 513 Delegates.

If President Parsons, who will control the delegation from New York County, makes good his statement, the renomination of Gov. Hughes is assured. New York County has 187 delegates in the State Convention. A simple majority of one from that number will give the Governor 94 of the New York delegates.

The number of delegates from up State either instructed for, committed to, or reliably classed for Gov. Hughes, number 362. Friends of State Chairman Timothy L. Woodruff, who is leader of the Republican organization in Kings County, admit that 57 of the delegates from Kings at least will go to the State Convention either pledged to or instructed for Gov. Hughes.

This will give the Governor a total of 513 delegates, according to the present line-up. Only 505 delegates are needed to nominate. And a dozen counties, with an approximate aggregate of 100 delegates, are in the doubtful column, with a probability that a majority will go to the convention to work for the renomination of Gov. Hughes when they learn that a large majority of the New York delegates will be for the Governor, and that nothing can be gained by opposing his renomination.

Those Pledged to Him Now.

Here is a list of up-State counties where the delegates have either been instructed for Gov. Hughes, stand committed to him, or can be depended upon to be for his renomination at the Saratoga Convention:

County		County	
Broome	12	Monroe	36
Cattaraugus	11	Nassau	9
Cayuga	12	Oneida	22
Chautauqua (2 A.D.)	8	Oswego	12
Chenango	7	Rensselaer	19
Clinton	7	Rockland	5
Cortland	6	Saratoga	11
Delaware	7	Schuyler	4
Dutchess (1 A.D.)	7	Steuben	15
Erie	39	Suffolk (2 A.D.)	3
Franklin	8	Tompkins	6
Greene	6	Westchester	20
Herkimer	9	Wyoming	6
*Jefferson	13	Yates	4
Lewis	5		
Total			362

*All of 1st and part of 2d A. D.

In the Doubtful Column.

Here are the counties placed by the leaders in the doubtful column:

County		County	
Essex	6	Seneca	5
Orange (1 A.D.)	9	Sullivan	5
Otsego	9	Ulster	14
Queens	18	Washington	9
St. Lawrence	18		
Total			93

The Anti-Hughes Force.

Here are the up-State counties which either have elected or will elect anti-Hughes delegates:

County		County	
Albany	28	Orange (1 A.D.)	8
Chemung	8	Putnam	3
Columbia	7	Richmond	8
Dutchess (part 2 A. D.)	7	Schenectady	11
		Schoharie	5
Fulton and Hamilton	5	Suffolk (2 A.D.)	7
		Tioga	6
Jefferson (2 A.D.)	1	Warren	6
Montgomery	8	Wayne	9
Niagara	13		
Ontario	9		
Total			143

These delegates have been instructed for Senator Horace White of Syracuse or Speaker James W. Wadsworth, Jr.:

FOR WADSWORTH.

County		County	
Allegheny	9	Livingston	7
Chautauqua (1 A.D.)	10	Orleans	6
Genesee	6		
Total			39

FOR WHITE.

County		County	
Onondaga	30	Madison	8
Total			38

Both State Chairman Woodruff and County President Herbert Parsons of the Republican County Committee said yesterday that it would be futile to attempt at this time to figure out to a mathematical certainty how many delegates from their respective bailiwicks would be against the Governor at the convention. These delegates, it would seem, constitute about the only element of uncertainty in the situation, but in the aggregate they will not have any effect on the result.

Self-Justification by Woodruff.

The analysis by State Chairman Woodruff of the result of the primary test was strangely in contrast with the statement of President Parsons, based on the returns from the districts in which the primary test was made. While President Parsons insisted that the returns disclosed a decided Hughes sentiment, Mr. Woodruff in his statement asserted that these same returns justified the declaration of the leader that the Governor was unpopular with the Republican voters. Mr. Woodruff said:

"The magnitude of the opposition man-

Continued on Page 2.

NO WATER TO FIGHT A FIRE.

Low Pressure Gives Brooklyn Factory Blaze a Dangerous Start.

Inadequate water pressure permitted a fire which started shortly before midnight last night on the third floor of the six-story factory building at 552 to 556 State Street, Brooklyn, to spread so rapidly that twenty minutes after the fire had been discovered Deputy Fire Chief Lally sent in five alarms.

For ten or fifteen minutes after their arrival the firemen were unable to throw streams of water into the flames, and even after that time the pressure was not up to the standard. The water tower threw a spray of water which might almost have come from an atomizer, so small was it.

By midnight every one of the six floors, which were occupied by the Empire Cork Specialty Company, was in flames, and fire was leaping out of all the windows and threatening momentarily to communicate the blaze to the tenements on either side of the factory or to those in the rear of it in Atlantic Avenue. The tenants in these buildings were ordered out by the police.

It took the reserves from five precincts to handle the crowds, which were record ones for Brooklyn. Deputy Commissioner Baker took charge of the police.

Chief Croker and Deputy Fire Commissioner Wise responded to the fifth alarm, and Chief Croker took command. By 12:30 o'clock he believed that it was under control. The tenements adjoining the burning building on both sides had been somewhat injured by flames.

The damage was estimated at $75,000 to the building and stock of the cork company. The factory is owned by Percy G. Williams, the theatrical manager.

The blaze tied up the trolley cars, which run through Atlantic Avenue or up Flatbush Avenue from Fulton and Livingston Streets. The lines affected included the Flatbush Avenue, Seventh Avenue, St. John's Place, Fifth Avenue, and Third Avenue.

TESTS CHURCH WELCOMES.

Minister, Disguised as Workingman, Cordially Greeted in All But One.

Special to The New York Times.

CHICAGO, Sept. 9.—To disprove the assertion of the Socialists that the churches only welcome the rich and scorn the workingman, the Rev. John Thompson, pastor of the McCabe M. E. Church, spent his August vacation disguised as a workingman and attending services at nine wealthy churches of the city.

In a threadbare and shiny blue serge coat, trousers that were worn at the edges, a cheap cotton shirt and tie, old shoes and a black felt hat, the minister was so well disguised that even his friends might have passed him by. In fact he sat in a street car beside one of the members of his own congregation and was not noticed.

"I made the experiment," he said to-day, "to find what, if any, truth there might be in the charge that the workingman and the poorly dressed visitor are not made welcome in our churches. I found, as I had hoped, that it was just the other way.

"In the nine churches that I visited I found the congregation always attentive, and in eight of the churches the ministers were cordial. In the ninth, I must say, I was surprised to see how crusty the minister was, and I was practically repulsed when I spoke to him at the end of the service."

THINK PRISONER IS MONROE.

Man in Trenton Jail Said to Answer the Desperado's Description.

Special to The New York Times.

TRENTON, Sept. 9.—"Samuel Worthington," who was arrested here for stealing a ride on a train and is now serving thirty days in jail, may prove to be "Bill" Monroe, the Orange County desperado, who is wanted for assault and arson at Middletown, N. Y.

Monroe has been chased in many directions by Sheriffs' posses. Only recently he attended the fair at Middletown, N. Y., disguised as a woman and tacked a notice on a tree stating that he had made such a visit.

"Worthington" gave his address as Middletown, and admitted that he had been arrested once for horse stealing and another time for assault. He said that he served time for these offenses in Pennsylvania.

Squire Manfred Naar, who committed Worthington to jail, communicated with the Sheriff of Orange County asking that some one who knows Monroe be sent to Trenton to see whether Worthington is the much-sought-for outlaw. A Deputy Sheriff of Orange County has started for this city for this purpose.

GLAD HE LED LYNCHERS.

Ex-Senator Sullivan Will Stand Consequences for Directing Shooting.

MEMPHIS, Sept. 9.—A special from Oxford, Miss., quotes former United States Senator W. V. Sullivan as follows with reference to the lynching last night:

"I led the mob which lynched Nelse Patton, and I'm proud of it. I directed every movement of the mob, and I did everything I could to see that he was lynched. Cut a white woman's throat! And a negro! Of course I wanted him lynched. I saw his body dangling from a tree this morning, and I'm glad of it.

"When I heard of the horrible crime I started to work immediately to get a mob. I did all I could to raise one. I was at the jail last night and heard Judge Roane advise against lynching. I got up immediately after and urged the mob to lynch Patton.

"I roused the mob and directed it to storm the jail. I had my revolver, but did not use it. I gave it to a Deputy Sheriff and told him to 'shoot Patton, and to shoot to kill.' He used the revolver and shot. I suppose the bullets from my gun were some of those that killed the negro.

"I don't care what investigation is made, or what are the consequences. I am willing to stand them. I wouldn't mind standing the consequences any time for lynching a man who cut a white woman's throat. I will lead a mob in such a case any time."

Claim of $1,000 Filed Against Thaw.

PITTSBURG, Penn., Sept. 9.—A claim of $1,000 was filed before Referee in Bankruptcy Blair against Harry K. Thaw to-day by Dr. Jackson R. Campbell of New York.

CROKER IS FOR BRYAN, ALSO FAVORS BETTING

Thinks Republican Anti-Trust Laws Have Not Helped Condition of the Individual Citizen.

GAMBLING IS HUMAN NATURE

America with Hughes Anti-Betting Laws Is a Free Country No Longer—King Edward the Finest Sportsman.

Special Cable to THE NEW YORK TIMES.

DUBLIN, Sept. 9.—"I am out of politics," said Richard Croker to the correspondent of THE NEW YORK TIMES, who saw him to-day in his beautiful Irish home some miles out from this city. "I know nothing of what is going on, and, anyhow, there is too much water between here and America for me to do anything. Moreover, anything I do say is so misrepresented. "Why," exclaimed Mr. Croker, indignantly, "only the other day it was said that I hoped Taft would win!"

"Your sympathies are with Bryan then?" he was asked.

"Certainly, I hope Bryan will win. He would make a fine President."

"What are his chances?"

"That I do not know, but there has been a great change in public feeling in recent years."

"How will the Republican anti-trust laws affect the issue?"

"They look very nice on paper, but how do they affect the individual? Have they lessened the cost of living or increased the wages of the individual? I say they have not. I judge things by their results, and I say the individual is no better off to-day. As a matter of fact, the cost of living has never been higher and wages are no better. That is the result which has been brought about under the Republican régime."

"What do you think the Democrats will do with regard to the New York Governorship?"

"That I don't know," replied Mr. Croker, and for a moment he contemplated the graveled walk upon which we were standing. Then, looking up with a gleam of scorn in his gray eye, he said:

"Look what they've been doing there! Why, they've broken up horse racing!"

Gov. Hughes's Anti-Betting law was, in Mr Croker's opinion, enough to damn any party.

"They are ruining the country; ruining the race tracks, in which a great deal of money is invested; ruining the breeders of horses, many of whom are breaking up their studs, and that in a free country! It is a free country no longer. You have more freedom over here. I go to race meetings here and I see a fine crowd of people, ladies and gentlemen, enjoying themselves, and King Edward himself at their head.

"King Edward is the finest sportsman in the world. If there was anything wrong in it do you think he would be at the head of all kinds of sport in this country? In London you have a national sporting club. They encourage all kinds of sport and are allowed to make a certain amount of money; the rest goes to hospitals and charities."

Mr. Croker added that he was not against a certain supervision of betting and gambling and would favor the introduction of the Paris mutuel system of betting, but he certainly would not endeavor to stop betting altogether. It was in human nature to gamble and in the spirit of free people.

"That's why it is tolerated over here; because it is the will of the people, and that's why the King is at its head."

Continuing his argument as to the ethics of gambling, Mr. Croker said it was in the very essence of human nature to gamble.

"If I insure this house," he said, indicating the beautiful mansion in which he lives, "I merely bet with the insurance company that it will be burned down, and the company bets it won't; and if I insure my horse, I bet he will break his neck, and the company takes the risk that he won't. It is the same, to a large extent, in business of all kinds."

"But, Mr. Croker, a man may bet with what he cannot afford to lose; he may mortgage his coat."

"That," replied Mr. Croker, "is his own affair. If he didn't put his money on a horse he would probably get rid of it some other way."

Mr. Croker added that there was no reason why gambling laws should not apply equally to the Stock Exchange and the race track.

"Gov. Hughes's policy," he said, "would get us back to the Puritanical days of the Know Nothings."

Mr. Croker hopes to visit New York in the Fall, but his mission there will have nothing to do with politics.

PARKER UNWILLING.

Doesn't Desire to Hold Public Office Again, He Says.

Alton B. Parker, who returned here from Washington yesterday, made it plain that, as THE TIMES indicated, he does not intend to run for Governor.

"I am not willing to run for Governor of New York," said Judge Parker. "I did not feel that the situation and the question presented justified me in saying more yesterday than that it is my desire never again to hold public office. My friends, I felt, would understand that I said precisely what I meant, and my answer was intended to inform them and no one else."

Judge Parker will entertain Mr. Bryan at dinner next Sunday.

OGDEN M. REID A REPORTER.

Starts on the Staff of His Father's Newspaper and Seems to Like It.

Ogden Mills Reid, only son of Whitelaw Reid, Ambassador to St. James's, is now hunting down the elusive political item as a reporter on his father's newspaper, The Tribune. He began yesterday, and last night he was waiting in vain at the Hotel Knickerbocker to form the acquaintance of William James Conners of Buffalo and the Democratic State Committee. Later, at an hour when the seasoned reporter would have called it a day's work, he cheerfully volunteered to go on a still hunt for Republican State Chairman Timothy L. Woodruff, who is a mighty difficult man to find after Republican State Headquarters has closed for the day.

"He takes to the work as a fish takes to water," said one of the veteran workers on The Tribune, in discussing young Mr. Reid's first day as a newspaper reporter.

Young Mr. Reid's appearance as an active worker on The Tribune staff recalls the story printed recently in THE TIMES that Whitelaw Reid had refused several offers to purchase his newspaper on the ground that he desired to leave it as a legacy to his son.

The latter is a Yale graduate of the Class of 1904. Subsequently he took a course at the Yale Law School. At the university he was chiefly noted for his interest in aquatic sports. In appearance he does not greatly resemble his father, the Ambassador.

MRS. LAWSON RESCUED AT SEA

Hangs On to Railing of Steam Yacht Capsized in Collision.

Special to The New York Times.

BOSTON, Mass., Sept. 9.—Mrs. Arnold Lawson's ability to maintain a hold on the railing of the steam yacht My Gypsy saved her from drowning this afternoon.

When the yacht was struck by the outward bound fishing vessel Boyd and Leeds Mrs. Lawson caught the railing as she was going overboard, and held on until rescued by the tug Metropolitan. At times she was immersed in the sweeping seas, but when the yacht had been righted from the effects of the collision she pluckily returned to it and informed the party of friends aboard that her experience was "nothing."

The My Gypsy, which is the yacht that Thomas W. Lawson gave his deceased wife, in charge of Capt. Crockstad, had just cleared for a short sail, and Mrs. Lawson was sitting at the stern of the boat on deck. Capt. Crockstad tried to run the My Gypsy across the bow of the schooner.

The bowsprit of the Boyd and Leeds caught the signal mast of the steam yacht. The yacht was suddenly careened to port.

Mrs. Lawson, when the boat began to capsize, was swept down the deck on her yacht chair. When the chair hit the rail she was thrown overboard, but managed to get a hold on the rail.

The big ocean tug Metropolitan closed in, and the crew reached out and hauled Mrs. Lawson aboard their boat.

THREAT TO BURN WHITEFACE.

Man Arrested for Attempt to Blackmail Mountain Lumber Company.

Special to The New York Times.

LAKE PLACID, N. Y., Sept. 9.—Probably never before has a mountain been made a medium for blackmail, but that is the use to which John St. Clair of Bloomingdale is charged with putting Mount Whiteface in a letter to the T. J. & J. Rogers Company of Ausable Forks, demanding the immediate payment of $200 under penalty of a fire, which, in addition to burning the company's holdings of about 15,000 acres of timber land about the base, would probably have swept the entire mountain, destroying forever the wonderful scenic beauty of Whiteface.

The letter was sent to the company over the name of L. H. Murphy. The company officials decided to set a trap for the man. A check for $100 was mailed to L. H. Murphy, at Bloomingdale. St. Clair, it is charged, called for mail in the name of Murphy, and he was followed to this village by ex-Sheriff S. W. Barnard. After an unsuccessful attempt to cash a check for $100 at the American House, the man succeeded in getting it cashed by a tradesman and was arrested by Deputy Sheriff Allen.

WANAMAKER BUILDING PLANS.

$6,000,000 Raised for Construction of Last Section of Philadelphia Store.

PHILADELPHIA, Sept. 9.—A mortgage for $6,000,000 on the Philadelphia store of John Wanamaker, including the property bounded by Chestnut and Market, Thirteenth and Juniper Streets, and the properties 1224 and 1226 Market Street, was recorded to-day. The mortgage, or trust deed, was to secure $6,000,000 worth of 5 per cent. five-year gold bonds, of which the Land Title and Trust Company is made trustee.

The purpose of Mr. Wanamaker is to borrow $6,000,000 and to issue 6,000 bonds of $1,000 each, secured by these properties. This, it is understood, is to complete financial arrangements by which Mr. Wanamaker will begin at once the construction of the last section of his store on the Chestnut Street side.

By the terms of the mortgage or trust deed Mr. Wanamaker can sell the old plant to replace it with the new one, but he must keep up the insurance on the properties and pay taxes, &c.

Officers of the trust company say all the bonds have been subscribed for at par by financial men of this city and New York.

TO BUY FRANKLIN HOUSE.

Say American Syndicate Has Option on Building in Paris.

PARIS, Sept. 9.—Michael J. Doyle of Philadelphia announced to-day that he had secured an option for an American syndicate upon the house in this city built and occupied by Benjamin Franklin when he was cultivating friendly relations with France during the American Revolution. The receptions given by Mr. Franklin in this house made it famous.

Subsequently Napoleon I. lived there for a time, and after his divorce from Josephine he turned the property over to her. Mr. Doyle declines to give the names of those interested or the purposes for which it is planned to use the property.

Special to The New York Times.

PHILADELPHIA, Sept. 9.—The Michael J. Doyle mentioned in a dispatch from Paris is probably Michael Francis Doyle, a well-known lawyer, who has been abroad for some time and is prominent in civic associations.

Nothing was known here of his intention to purchase the Franklin house, and if he was acting for a syndicate, it is probable that they have kept their plans secret for fear of enhancing the price.

AERONAUT AND TIGER FALL FROM BALLOON

Men, Women, and Children Flee in Terror as Animal Lands in Fair Grounds.

ATHLETE SERIOUSLY HURT

The Tiger, Uninjured by 100-Foot Drop, Takes Refuge in the Balloon Tent.

Nearly 15,000 persons, many of them children, yesterday being Children's Day at the Richmond County Fair, stood in the fair grounds at Dongan Hills, S. I., late in the afternoon looking up into the air, where young William Coby, in spangles and tights, sat smiling and bowing on a trapeze attached to a balloon which slowly rose above the heads of the crowd. The young trapezist had one arm around a pet tiger cub, which he supported on the trapeze, and which with him was soon to drop in a thrilling dive with a parachute.

Children shouted in delight, and men and women waved hats or handkerchiefs at the athlete. Suddenly from somewhere in the crowd there arose a cry. Instantly it was taken up by others, and presently the multitude were shouting to the trapezist:

"Look out! Your balloon's on fire."

Coby, looking downward, had not seen a spiral of flame which caught the eye of some one in the crowd as it ate its way around one of the hempen supports which attached the trapeze to the balloon. He was nearly 100 feet in the air, but perhaps the voices of the crowd reached his ears. At any rate he turned his eyes upward.

Then he leaped into activity. He tried to free his parachute and prepare for the leap which would enable him to float easily to the ground. But he was an instant too late, however. Before he could free the parachute the bar on which he stood working at the ropes with nervous fingers dropped from the supporting balloon.

A cry of horror arose from the crowd as Coby's figure whirled downward, spinning over and over in the air. Beside him in the downward dive shot the tiger cub, its paws and tail thrashing around in the air.

It was only a few seconds before Coby and his tiger cub struck the turf on the inside of the race track course from which they had ascended. Instantly the crowd pressed forward. But suddenly men and women, dragging children by the hands or carrying infants in their arms, turned back in a wild panic, and fled toward the grandstand, opposite which the balloon ascension had been made.

"The tiger! Look out for the tiger!" was the cry that went up.

Apparently uninjured by its fall the tiger cub made for the crowd in long leaps. Although the crowd did not know it, the animal's only object apparently was to gain the shelter of the tent used to house the balloon. Once within the tent it lay whimpering in terror.

Coby was carried to his dressing tent, and there Dr. Mord from the Smith Infirmary looked him over. He found that the man had received internal injuries and a severe concussion of the spine, and advised his immediate removal to the infirmary. He was taken there in an ambulance.

Coby is only 18 years old, and lives at 903 Bremer Street, Milwaukee. He is a professional balloonist and parachute jumper, and had been exhibiting daily at the fair since its opening on Monday. The police arrested his manager, Frank Robinson, later, asserting that he had not used proper precaution in seeing to it that the balloon and its apparatus were in proper shape before permitting the ascent. Robinson was bailed out by the officials of the fair. The balloon dropped near by, and was found to be only slightly damaged. Robinson wanted to reinflate it and make an ascent himself, but this was not allowed.

Samuel Haber of 209 Spring Street, Manhattan, got a fractured kneecap in the excitement following the fall of Coby and the tiger cub. He was running from the animal when he fell. He, also, was taken to the infirmary.

Yesterday was Democratic day at the fair, and among the visitors were Charles F. Murphy, Col. Henry Watterson, J. Hamilton Lewis, and State Chairman Conners.

HUMAN DYNAMO IN TEXAS.

Electrically Charged Boy Furnishes Power for Fan or Lights.

Special to The New York Times.

GALVESTON, Texas, Sept. 9.—A living storage battery is the only thing to which E. G. Atloy, an American born child of Russian parents, living with his widowed mother in Houston, Texas, can be compared. The boy, who is 7 years old, is a human magnet, and possesses all the electric properties of a dynamo engine in addition.

A metal filling had been put in one tooth, and when the boy came home he picked up the knob used to connect an electric fan with an electric light wire in his mother's residence and thrust it into his mouth.

A threaded metal cap was on the end which screws into the cup for the electric bulb. As the metal cap touched the metal tooth filling the boy's head jerked slightly and the fan began to revolve and then to buzz frantically at full speed. This kept up as long as the circuit was completed in the boy's mouth.

The mother was frightened and feared witchcraft, but the boy seemed pleased at the sensation.

A piece of iron held in the boy's hand for a few moments becomes highly magnetized. A hammer with an iron handle held in his hands will attract tacks at a distance of four feet.

The boy says that he feels only an agreeable sensation. He has red hair of the reddest possible hue, large freckles, and blue eyes.

FIREMAN'S SON STARTS A FIRE

Eight-Year-Old Boy Wanted to See the Engines Turn Out.

Acting Capt. Rehahn of the 152d Street Police Station was at a small fire in the cellar of the tenement at 2,805 Eighth Avenue last night, when he heard a boy say to another that he knew who started the fire. Rehahn grabbed the youth, who led him to Colonial Park, where in some bushes the policeman found eight-year-old William Donnelly, Jr., son of a fireman, who lives at 2,811 Eighth Avenue.

According to Rehahn, the boy admitted that he started the blaze to see the engines turn out. Young Donnelly was paroled in the custody of his father, who will take him to the Children's Court to-day to answer a charge of malicious mischief.

MRS. SAGE 80 YEARS OLD.

She Receives Many Flowers and Telegrams at Long Island Home.

Special to The New York Times.

LAWRENCE, L. I., Sept. 9.—An unusual number of parcels and telegrams came here yesterday for Mrs. Russell Sage. Most of the parcels contained flowers, and the telegrams and letters were for the most part congratulations upon her eightieth birthday.

Mrs. Sage spent the day quietly at her home. It is the cottage in which Mr. Sage died, and is one of the favorite houses maintained by Mrs. Sage.

Several friends called to pay their respects to Mrs. Sage on her birthday, but many did not know she was in town. She was pleased at the receipt of congratulations sent by institutions she had helped. She expects to remain in her Lawrence cottage thoughout September.

HARRIMAN IN FAST RUN.

Line Clear for His Special Train Speeding to Omaha.

OGDEN, Utah, Sept. 9.—E. H. Harriman's special train reached Ogden at 5:15 o'clock this afternoon. The train consists of several private cars and a baggage car. Every district on the Salt Lake Division has been kept clear during the day to give the special right of way for a record run. One of the fastest trips on record was made between these points.

After a stop of twenty minutes at Ogden, the Harriman party pulled out for Omaha, and another record run is scheduled for the thousand-mile journey.

BOSTON PAWNSHOPS BUSY.

Loans Taken Out on $425,000 Worth of Property in Two Days.

BOSTON, Sept. 9.—Personal property valued at $425,000, including more than 700 watches, was pawned in the City of Boston yesterday and to-day. O. W. Farley of the loan division of the Bureau of Criminal Investigation spent the busiest day in the history of the department recording the loans.

No reason for the unusual amount of pawning is known except that yesterday followed a holiday.

WILL BUY CHEYENNE CANYON.

New York Syndicate to Add to Attraction of Famous Scenic Resort.

Special to The New York Times.

COLORADO SPRINGS, Col., Sept. 9.—A syndicate of New York capitalists has secured an option on the famous South Cheyenne Cañon including the seven falls at the head of which Helen Hunt Jackson, the poet, was buried, also the cave of winds and the Manitou cliff dwellers' ruins.

The purchase price is given by Attorney R. S. Ellis, who represents the owners, as $500,000. Although a payment has been made, the names of the purchasers are withheld at present. The buyers plan considerable outlay to add to the attraction of these famous scenic environs, which are visited by thousands of tourists annually.

RETALIATE ON ERIE ROAD.

$2 a Mile Charge for Observation Engine Forces Inquiry by State Board.

Special to The New York Times.

TRENTON, Sept. 9.—The State Railroad Commission is indignant at the proposition of the Erie Railroad to the effect that it will charge $2 a mile for an observation engine for a tour of inspection by the commission over the Erie lines in this State. This would make the trip cost the State $800. The Commissioners aver that there must be something radically wrong with the Erie lines that the officials should seek to put such a price on an observation engine for the use of the three Commissioners to get the best possible view of the tracks, &c.

In retaliation the commission has put all of its force of inspectors on the Erie lines, and will order a thorough report of the Erie system at once.

Under the law the commission is entitled to ride free of expense on all lines in the State, but the law is silent on observation engines.

GUN FIGHT TO CATCH WOMAN.

Alleged Black Hand Agent Opens Fire on Officers Who Try to Capture Her.

BESSEMER, Mich., Sept. 9.—Mrs. Frank Galler, who, it is alleged, as a "Black Hand" agent, has for several weeks been terrorizing business men, was captured here to-day after a gun fight with officers. She is the wife of a miner.

Five officers were lying in wait at Powder Mill Creek, near a box where money was to be deposited. About 4 o'clock the woman cautiously crept along the road, grabbed the box, and ran. Upon being pursued by officers she drew a pistol and began a fusillade. The fire was promptly returned, until officers who were stationed at a turn in the road grabbed the woman and placed her under arrest. The woman's husband, Frank Galler, has also been jailed. The couple, with four children, came from Venice, Italy, five years ago.

POLICEMAN ARRESTS 15 MEN.

Overawes Fighting Striking Lamplighters and Strikebreakers with His Gun.

Alone and unaided Policeman McGrath of the West 152d Street Station arrested fifteen Italians at 185th Street and Broadway last night, thirteen of whom were striking lamplighters and the other two strikebreakers. McGrath, who was on a bicycle and in plain clothes, saw the thirteen attack the two, and threatening to shoot them he managed to make them all stand.

He was pondering over what to do with his prisoners when he saw Sergt. Kennison on the steps of his home near by. He called him and the two men managed to make the fifteen walk to the horse shed of a near-by roadhouse, where they kept them until they summoned the patrol wagon from the station.

All fifteen were taken to the station, where Frank Masietto of 2,515 Amsterdam Avenue and Joseph Maglieri of 570 West 103th Street, the strikebreakers, were held for carrying concealed weapons. The other thirteen, among whom the police said was the leader of the strikers, Joseph Vende of 517 West 168th Street, were all charged with disorderly conduct.

WRIGHT FLIES OVER AN HOUR

Follows 57-Minute Flight at Fort Myer with One of 62 Minutes 15 Seconds.

AMERICA RULES IN AVIATION

Lieut. Lahm Also Makes Trip with Wright and Record for "Doubles" Is Smashed.

PLANES OBEY EVERY TOUCH

In Early Morning Flight Aviator Outdoes Delagrange — Achievements Watched by High Officials.

Special to The New York Times.

WASHINGTON, Sept. 9.—In three successive flights in his aeroplane to-day, Orville Wright broke three world's records and wrested from France for America the laurels of the air.

In his first flight at an early hour this morning he drove his machine in circles over the Fort Myer parade ground for 57 minutes and 31 seconds, beating the previous endurance record made by Delagrange by 25 minutes 46 1-5 seconds.

In his second flight, late in the afternoon, he remained in the air for 62 minutes and 15 seconds, surpassing his own previous record by 4 minutes and [illegible] seconds.

His last flight was made with Lieut. Lahm of the Signal Corps in the seat beside him. Together they sailed for 6 minutes and 16 seconds, surpassing the record for doubles formerly made in Virginia by Orville Wright and his mechanician by 2 minutes and 36 seconds.

As far as altitudes attained were concerned the most spectacular flight of the day was the first. Then with few people to watch him Wright determined to familiarize himself with the upper air. From his normal course of some forty feet above the parade ground Mr. Wright turned the nose of his skimming craft upward for little runs at a height of 100 feet from the ground.

But as a demonstration of perfect mastery of his planes, and consequent mastery of the air, the long flight in which he broke his own and all other records for endurance was unequaled. When Mr. Wright descended from his morning flight he said that if he had known how near the hour limit he had come he would have stayed up longer, and there is no doubt that he would have done it. But the experience he gained in his 57 minutes of constant attention to the tricks of aviation in his early flight told its own story in the inventor's assurance in the afternoon, and in the perfect response to the slightest touch he made on his three levers.

Leading Officials Watch Flight.

The most representative company that has yet watched the daily experiments gathered this afternoon, following the report of Mr. Wright's early success. Gen. Nelson A. Miles came to Washington for the express purpose of watching the flights, and studied the manoeuvres of the inventor. Secretary of War Wright and Secretary of the Navy Metcalf were on the grounds long before the flight took place, and the army was represented by Gens. Oliver and Murray, Col. Hatfield, and many others. The French Military Attaché, Major Fournier, who recently witnessed some of Wilbur Wright's attempts at Le Mans, was also present. The crowd numbered several thousands.

It was 5:17:45 o'clock when the heavy weights dropped from the derrick and gave the forward impetus to the airship, waiting balanced on its monorail. Wright had taken his seat a moment before without the least apparent uneasiness, and in a businesslike way took hold of the controlling levers.

As viewed from behind at close quarters the enormous planes with the large twin propellers whirring with an irregular rattle behind them seemed to flutter off down the parade ground like a wounded bird. As the distance increased, however, the impression of irregular motion conveyed by the propellers was lost, and the machine seemed to be sliding over the grass on its skids like an iceboat over a frozen lake. The aeroplane was [illegible] yards from the starting point before [illegible] could be seen that it had left the ground and was skimming the highest [illegible] under its own power.

Then like a giant gull, snow white [illegible] the sunlight, the tips of the planes [illegible] to the left, and still on the rise the [illegible] plane passed over the aerodrome at the other end of the field, missing its [illegible] roof by only a few feet. Mr. Wright [illegible] his planes and rudder rigid until a complete half circle had been described, and then brought the ship back to an even keel as he sped up the field along the side of Arlington National Cemetery.

Dips Machine to the Crowd.

The crowd, intent on watching the start had given only a straggling cheer as the falling weights jerked the machine along the starting rail, and the cheer was quite lost in the whir of the propellers and the backward rush of a powerful current of air. But as Wright soared over the spectators crowded around the starting point, a long [illegible] told their spontaneous enthusiasm. The aviator did not move his hands from the levers to wave an acknowledgment, but instead he dipped the nose of the [illegible] like structure, swooped to within twenty feet of the ground, and returned [illegible] with a leap to a height not far short of 100 feet.

After the first few rounds Mr. Wright settled down to a methodical management of his machine. Time after time he circled the field, varying the diameter of his circle and the height of his course only enough to gain added experience at each turn. But it was in this steady flight that the beauty of his motion was most apparent.

The sun was just setting as the record-breaking flight ended. At each turn the low light caught the tilted canvas of the planes, and brought out their whiteness in startling relief. Each turning of the southeast corner in particular presented the full length of the ship as it tilted to an angle of thirty degrees, the lower wing of the planes cutting the heavy shadow of the trees in Arlington Cemetery. In showing the endurance of his craft, Mr. Wright circled the field fifty-five times.

The short flight with Lieut. Lahm showed that the requirement that two men shall be carried for the prescribed length of time is anything but a handicap to the inventor. Though the ship rose a trifle more slowly than with the lighter load, it rose with an evenness and steadiness that showed plainly that, with two men on board, the aeroplane would prove a more reliable support than with one.

Flight in the Moonlight.

The crowd had in great measure gone home before the second flight of the afternoon took place. The afterglow in the west had almost faded, and what light there was came from the rising moon, somewhat obscured by mists. Against the sky the ship showed almost black as it turned in short circles with its heavy load.

Even as the ship left the rail it became apparent that the added weight would be simply so much additional ballast. In former flights the lightness of the craft was so great that the unevenness of the matted weeds with which part of the parade ground is covered seemed to give the ship a dipping motion as it glided along at the start. But with the added weight the flight was majestic from the beginning.

On a perfectly even keel the ship rose at a gradual angle, attaining the height of about forty feet in the first circuit. Mr. Wright made no effort to go higher, but the short turns he took about the parade ground showed that his mastery over the heavily laden craft was perfect.

He came down directly in front of the entrance to the aerodrome at a distance of a hundred yards. The impact of the descent on the springy skids launched the ship into the air again. It rose about twenty feet on the rebound and settled gently to earth thirty yards nearer the shed.

Lieut. Lahm is confident that he will soon be able to run the ship by himself, and was enthusiastic over the possibilities for reconnoitring opened up by Mr. Wright's invention. There will be almost daily flights for several days to come, and Lieut. Lahm expects to accompany Mr. Wright on most of them.

The outcome of the day's work was as much a surprise to Mr. Wright as to any one else. When he took his narrow seat on the lower plane for his first flight to-day he had no idea of breaking any records. But as he soared easily aloft at heights he had formerly hesitated to try, his confidence increased. But even then, as he had no watch with him, he did not know to what extent he was surpassing himself and his brother.

The Morning Flight.

When Wright brought his machine to earth after the morning flight and crawled from his seat, he was pounced upon by Augustus C. Post, Secretary of the Aero Club of America, and Charles Taylor, the mechanician from the Wright factory. Both men were boisterous in their enthusiasm, and they pumped Wright's hands up and down, both talking excitedly and pouring out their congratulations.

"Fifty-seven thirty-one! Fifty-seven thirty-one!" Taylor repeated over and over. Post threw one arm around Wright's shoulders and talked excitedly.

"Fifty-seven thirty-one, as much as that?" questioned Wright, quietly. "If I'd known it was that close to the hour I would have remained up full time."

Wright was apparently as calm as though he had done nothing out of the ordinary. His quiet smile did not broaden perceptibly, although he plainly showed his satisfaction with the performance of his machine. When he could escape from the congratulations of his friends he made his way to the aerodrome, doffed his cap, put on his straw hat, and in company with Post strolled unconcernedly off in the direction of the car that was to take him to Washington.

Not more than twenty persons were present at the parade grounds when Wright made his ascent in the morning. It was exactly 8:25 when the aeroplane shot along the rising track, skimmed out over the ground and rose abruptly in the air. A handful of newspaper men, several cavalrymen from the fort, one or two photographers, and Mr. Post were grouped at the north end of the field.

At Express Train Speed.

The aeroplane swept down the stretch until just above the aerodrome it turned and in an abrupt curve headed east. With the speed of an express train it sailed toward the grove that shelters the graves in Arlington National Cemetery, and when almost within the shadows of the trees it effected another spectacular turn and rushed north. Thus the first round was completed.

As he increased his number of circuits, Wright seemed to enter the wild spirit of the test. The aeroplane, time and again, swooped from an altitude of between 75 and 100 feet toward earth until it was a scant 10 feet above the tops of the waving grass. Then in response to the turn of its forward planes it soared aloft for long stretches and skimmed as true as any arrow.

Early in his flight Wright began to climb higher and higher, until he was sailing at a height of more than 150 feet. At that altitude the big white aeroplane showed not the slightest effect of counter air currents. There was no rocking nor diving perceptible, and it maintained its course as steadily as a ship on a Summer sea.

Once well up above the ground, Wright increased the radius of his flight. He drove his ship down the field far past the aerodrome and into the broken country beyond. Over the roofs of the post buildings he sailed, and he looked down on the graves in Arlington through the tree tops ninety feet beneath.

Tempted to Venture Afield.

When he alighted Mr. Wright acknowledged that the temptation to leave the open ground and venture over the wooded and hilly country beyond was almost irresistible. On several occasions he did dash out of bounds and manoeuvred over small forests of maple and oak, but although these excursions were frequent, they were brief, for the danger from the motor stopping was uppermost in the aviator's mind. The machine would probably have been ruined if it had landed in the thickets.

While he maintained a speed estimated variously at from thirty-eight to fifty miles an hour, Wright did not put his motor to the test. The compact little machine that drives the two big rear propellers was running only at three-quarters speed, no change having been made since the flights of yesterday. There is no doubt that the contract speed of forty miles an hour will be met easily, and what the aeroplane could do on a straightaway dash with its motor working to the limit is a matter of conjecture. Under favorable conditions it is probable it could reach and maintain a velocity of from sixty-five to seventy-five miles.

That the flight was not an official one accounts for the failure to make accurate data. The instruments for recording distance and time attached to the aeroplane were of little assistance, for they were gauged only for a flight of ten kilometers. On such a long flight they were practically of no use whatever.

THE WRIGHT BROTHERS AND THEIR AEROPLANE.

WILBUR WRIGHT.

ORVILLE WRIGHT.

Average Distance Covered.

Competent observers estimate that the average distance covered in each of the fifty-seven circuits of the drill ground was approximately three-quarters of a mile. This is really guesswork, however, for Wright put his machine through so many manoeuvres and varied his flights to such an extent that it was practically impossible to make any close estimate. It is generally conceded that he covered forty miles in the fifty-seven minutes and thirty-one seconds he was up, thus making an average speed of about forty-two miles an hour.

The landing made by the machine was as easy and successful as in the previous flights. Rushing along toward the aerodrome on the fifty-eighth lap, Wright shut off his motor, deflected his planes, and the great white aeroplane swooped downward. Within a few feet of the ground, the planes were raised gently and it rose for a second, when it again settled, touching the earth with its circular understructure and settling once more. This time it slid gracefully for six or seven feet and stopped.

When Wright crawled out of his seat he was plainly cramped from his long trip. He was cold also, the rushing air in the reaches having chilled him to the bone. He was surrounded almost immediately.

"There is little I can tell you about the flight," he said, "except that at no time was the aeroplane anything but under perfect control. I am getting better acquainted with the machine in every flight, and its possibilities, so far as I can see now, are limited only by the amount of the fuel we can carry."

Post to Make Official Record.

There were witnesses enough to the flight to-day to make an official record. Augustus C. Post is to take steps at once to provide for this, and the Aero Club, it is confidently expected, will accept the figures.

By his wonderful flight Orville Wright practically doubled the best official record ever made by a heavier-than-air machine.

It was only Sunday last that Leon Delagrange, President of the Aviation Club of France, established a new world's record up to that time by remaining in the air 29 minutes 54 4-5 seconds. He circled the field at Issy, near Paris, fifteen and a half times, and covered a distance of fifteen and one-quarter miles.

Monday Delagrange, after installing a fuel tank of increased capacity on his machine, made a flight of thirty-one minutes. But the record wasn't allowed to stand, three minutes being deducted on account of the machine having touched the ground while making its first round of the field.

The preparatory flights of Wilbur Wright on the field of Le Mans, France, had promised notable achievements. But the American aeroplanist had been able to remain in the air less than twenty minutes, when Delagrange succeeded in establishing new figures both as to duration of flight and distance covered.

The sensation caused by the Frenchman's performance, however, has in no way disconcerted Wilbur Wright, who still expresses confidence that he will be able to fulfill the condition of the French competition.

BADEN-POWELL'S COMMENT.

Aerial Navigation Without Aid of Gas Now an Accomplished Fact.

LONDON, Sept. 9.—Major Baden Baden-Powell, who invented man-lifting kites in 1894 and for several years was President of the Aeronautical Society, and who is considered the greatest expert in England on aerial navigation, was much pleased when he learned of Mr. Wright's exploit to-day. With reference to to-day's record-breaking flights he said:

"Another step has been achieved and more will surely follow it. It now may fairly be said that aerial navigation without the aid of gas is an accomplished fact. The ability to remain floating in midair for an hour is something more than a mere experiment. Such an achievement has practical uses of the greatest import."

The Aero Club was almost deserted this evening, a large number of the leading members having gone to France to watch Wilbur Wright's flights, but those at the club were enthusiastic over the possibilities demonstrated by Orville Wright's exploit.

DELAGRANGE TO TRY AGAIN.

"Neither Jealous Nor Discouraged," He Says—French Aeronauts Pleased.

PARIS, Sept. 9.—French aeronauts are unanimously of the opinion that the great flights made by Orville Wright in his aeroplane in the United States to-day mark a great advance in the conquest of the air, and welcome his feat particularly on account of the valuable stimulus which it will impart to the efforts of aeroplanists of all nations. Mr. Wright's record-breaking performance comes most opportunely at a moment when the various Governments are beginning seriously to consider the question of extending financial and other support to experimenters in aerial navigation. It doubtless also will have the effect of increasing public interest in the promotion and establishment of associations similar to that recently organized by M. Quinton, which would be of incalculable value in fostering and encouraging the new science.

M. Bleriot, the noted French aeroplanist, said that after what he had seen at Le Mans, where Wilbur Wright is making his trials, the performance of the latter's brother to-day did not cause him the slightest astonishment. He was perfectly satisfied, he added, that the Wright brothers' machine was the best aeroplane yet constructed. He was convinced that it could fly much longer than an hour, but in the absence of complete details he was unable to make any definite comment on the incidents connected with the two splendid performances.

He would be greatly interested, he said, to see the Wright machine make a long flight against a strong wind, as he understood that the work to-day was in a dead calm. He was not discouraged, however, at the stride ahead made by the American competitors. On the contrary, both he and M. Delagrange intended to redouble their efforts to catch the Wrights and if possible to outdistance them.

M. Delagrange, when informed of the record-breaking flight, said:

"I am neither jealous nor discouraged; on the contrary, weather permitting, I will try to fly an hour myself. Wright's apparatus is neither inferior nor superior to mine; it flies, so does mine.

"The Wrights have had ten years' experience and training. I have had eighteen months; that makes a difference."

NOT SURPRISED IN BERLIN.

Capt. von Hildebrandt Says Aeroplane's Value Has Been Proved.

BERLIN, Sept. 9.—The news of Orville Wright's record flight did not reach Berlin until too late for publication, but a number of aeronauts at the Aero Club when informed of the event expressed delight but not astonishment, as since the experiments of Wilbur Wright in France the conviction has prevailed that the Wright brothers were capable of great things.

Capt. von Hildebrandt of the balloon battalion, one of the most prominent experts in aeronautics in Germany, summed up the general view. "Orville Wright's latest performance," he said, "means a great step forward in flying technique. Nobody now can further doubt the reports of the earlier feats of the Wright brothers. These long trips which have just been accomplished prove that the machine is so solidly built that it can remain in the air as long as the benzine lasts, while from the number of turns made it can be seen that the steering gear is excellent and that the machine answered every movement with precision.

"After this most successful exploit, no one can doubt the practical value of the flying machine, even although it still needs special apparatus for starting. Henceforth technicists must devote more attention to the aero dynamic machine, in which we are destined soon to see great improvements."

WORK OF WRIGHT BROTHERS.

Began Study of Aerial Navigation in 1896 as Mechanics in a Bicycle Shop.

It was in 1896 that the brothers Wright first became interested in the solving of the problem of constructing a man-lifting machine which should not depend upon a gas bag for sustentation, but should gain its support directly from the inertia of the air. They were then engaged as expert mechanics in the manufacture and repair of bicycles at Dayton, Ohio. Wilbur Wright, in telling how he and his brother became interested in the conquest of the air, said:

"In 1896 my brother and I saw a press dispatch telling of the death of Lilienthal, the German aeronaut, by a fall from his machine. This started our first active interest in the problem of aerial navigation. Up to 1900 we merely studied and made laboratory experiments, and then, in that year, started the actual work of building a flying machine."

In their early efforts they received great encouragement from Octave Chanute of Chicago, an ex-President of the Western Society of Engineers, and himself an enthusiastic believer in the future of the flying machine. After many experiments a machine was built which made its first flight on Dec. 17, 1903. During all the time the two brothers were working hard and secretly stories of their wonderful invention leaked out, but even in the highest aeronautical and engineering circles, both at home and abroad, were treated with the utmost skepticism.

Wilbur Wright, who is at present at Le Mans, France, conducting experimental flights, is the elder of the two brothers, having been born on April 16, 1867, while Orville Wright was born Aug. 19, 1871. They are the sons of Bishop Milton Wright of the United Brethren Church.

MR. HERRING'S AEROPLANE.

Succeeds in Making Light Motor—May Build Machine for 5 Persons.

A. M. Herring, notwithstanding the fact that he is in some respects a rival of the Wright brothers, in that he also has a contract to furnish a practical aeroplane to the United States Government, was enthusiastic over the record-breaking flight of Orville Wright.

"I am perhaps not as surprised as many others," said Mr. Herring last evening, "for I have kept close watch of the Wright brothers' progress for years, and I have been sure that their recent tests both here and in France would result in some unusual flights. They will undoubtedly do better yet. I am particularly glad that the Wrights have achieved this success at this time because it will demonstrate conclusively to the world that the brothers all along knew what they were talking about when they claimed they made flights of over twenty miles three years ago at Dayton, Ohio."

Mr. Herring's machine was to be delivered to the Government officers for tests by the end of this week, but he stated yesterday that he had been obliged to ask for a little more time, owing to necessary work on some of the small parts of the machine.

"My aeroplane is practically completed," he added, "and if absolutely necessary I could put it together this week and make a flight, but I prefer to wait until I am perfectly satisfied with it in every minor detail. With two or three weeks more time I will be in condition for the most arduous test, and by the end of this month or the first week of October I hope to be at Fort Myer."

It is known that Mr. Herring's machine will be radically different in many important respects from all previous aeroplanes, but just what new ideas are embodied have been kept carefully guarded. Mr. Herring, however, did say yesterday that he had succeeded in making an unusually light motor. His machine will be equipped with two motors of five cylinders each. Their combined horse power will be 44, and yet their weight is only 30 pounds.

As to what Mr. Herring may do in the near future it may be interesting to state that in a recent conversation with a friend he stated that he would be willing to take a contract to build an aeroplane that would carry five persons.

SCHOOLBOARD FIGHTS EDSON'S RE-ELECTION

Supt. Maxwell's Chief Assistant Lacks Seven Votes and Final Result Goes Over.

MISS RICHMAN EXONERATED

Complaint of East Side Residents Dismissed — Schoolship St. Mary's to be a Nautical Museum.

Much to the surprise of most members of the Board of Education, at its session yesterday, the first since July 8, a fight was made on the re-election of Andrew W. Edson, Associate City Superintendent, who ranks next to Dr. W. H. Maxwell.

Mr. Edson, who receives a salary of $6,500 a year, was scheduled for re-election, and notices to that effect had been sent to all members, but Commissioner Higgins moved that action on the matter be deferred until the next meeting. Commissioner Barrett opposed the motion, and it was lost. Friends of Mr. Edson then tried to get a re-election by acclamation, but Commissioner Partridge opposed this. The ballot showed only 17 votes for Mr. Edson, when 24 were necessary, 7 being in opposition, with 5 others blanks. The motion for postponement, then renewed, was adopted.

Some significance attaches itself to the fight on Mr. Edson for the reason that, apparently, it comes from those members who are quite generally regarded as opposed to the policies and administration of City Supt. Maxwell. It is understood also that Mr. Higgins and Commissioners siding with him do not regard Mr. Edson as enthusiastic regarding technical and vocational schools as they would like.

Miss Julia Richman, District Superintendent in charge of schools on the lower East Side, was for the second time exonerated by the board, charges having again been preferred against her in a petition signed by fifty-four residents of the east side.

James C. Monaghan, long an American Consul in Germany, was elected principal of Stuyvesant evening trade school, the first of its kind in Manhattan. He is at present connected with the Department of Commerce and Labor at Washington.

As indicated in THE TIMES yesterday, the board adopted the new budget asking the Board of Estimate for $33,031,484.65 for expenses of 1909, an increase over the appropriation of 1908 of $6,258,521.06.

The old schoolship St. Mary's is to become a museum and workship for the Nautical School if Gov. Hughes can prevail upon the Secretary of the Navy to assign her to the Nautical School alumni for that purpose.

CLASH ON TREASURY THEFT.

State and Federal Authorities in Conflict Over Papers in Chicago.

CHICAGO, Sept. 9.—The hearing of the case of George W. Fitzgerald, charged with the theft of $173,000 from the local Sub-Treasury, set for this morning, was unexpectedly postponed till afternoon when Judge Chetlain called the case today.

The postponement was at the request of Sub-Treasurer Boldenweck, acting, it is said, on telegraphic instructions from Washington. Mr. Boldenweck refused to discuss the matter.

When the case came up this afternoon it developed that the telegram from Washington had been sent by L. A. Coolidge, Assistant Secretary of the Treasury, to Capt. Porter of the Chicago branch of the Secret Service. The telegram called attention to a rule that information or documents in the possession of Federal authorities bearing on State cases should not be turned over except on order from headquarters at Washington. It was ordered that this rule be observed in the Fitzgerald case. Consequently, when attorneys from the State Attorney's office called upon Capt. Porter, Mr. Boldenweck, and District Attorney Sims, no information was forthcoming.

Judge Chetlain this afternoon, however, issued subpoenas calling into his court to-morrow various Federal employes supposed to have knowledge of the case.

WASHINGTON, Sept. 9.—Both the Department of Justice and the Treasury Department disclaim any knowledge of any instructions regarding the postponement of the trial of George W. Fitzgerald for alleged Sub-Treasury theft at Chicago, and point out that as the trial is before a State court this Government is not attempting to interfere in any way.

Rumor That David Shellard Is Indicted

It was rumored in the Kings County Court House yesterday afternoon that the Grand Jury had found an indictment against ex-Policeman David Shellard in connection with the death of Barbara Rieg, who was found dead from a shot on the night of July 21 in the shelter house in Irving Square Park. Shellard, who had known the girl for some time, is alleged to have been in the shelter house with her shortly before the discovery of the tragedy. He was arrested at the time, but a Coroner's jury found that the woman was a suicide. Shellard is now out on $10,000 bail.

BOSSES HAVE DECIDED TO ACCEPT HUGHES

Continued from Page 1.

ifested to Gov. Hughes in New York County, and particularly in Kings County, certainly justifies the position which I have taken, that we would have to await the gathering of the delegates at Saratoga to enlighten us as to the exact situation in all the Assembly districts, which are the units of representation. Ardent supporters of the Governor's renomination have insisted that I, as the head of the State organization, should declare for him on the ground that there was little or no opposition to him. I have, of course, recognized the very large and earnest sentiment in his favor among many classes, and the very best classes of Republicans, but could not be blind to the opposition which, for the first time, was made evident yesterday to the public.

"Some district leaders in New York and Kings Counties and some State leaders have been vehemently criticised for their opposition, on the theory that it was founded purely upon personal antipathy to the Governor. It must certainly now be admitted by all fair-minded men that Judge Brenner and Mr. Jaquillard in Brooklyn and Mr. Levinson, Mr. Blake, and Mr. Nedjedly in New York, whose combined five districts showed 682 for and 2,533 against Gov. Hughes, were justified in believing, as it has been stated in the press they did, that some other man should be the party's candidate for Governor.

Remember Dix, Says He.

"The only Republican Governor who has been nominated to succeed himself since Fenton was renominated at the close of the civil war, with the sole exception of Gov. Odell, was Gen. John A. Dix, and incidentally it should be said that he was disastrously defeated. My only reason for referring to this is to call the attention of some of the too aggressive advocates of the Governor's renomination, who think a political leader is almost a criminal who has not already declared for his renomination, that the renomination of Republican Governors is quite the exception and not the rule.

"The convention, which will assemble next Monday, will settle this controversy deliberately and wisely. There the majority of the party's duly elected representatives will rule. Whatever the result may be I for one will accept it as the party's will in the best of spirit, and I sincerely hope and believe every other true Republican will do the same. The nominee, whoever he may be, Gov. Hughes or any one else, will receive the most loyal and earnest support of the State organization and of every county organization affiliated with it. There is altogether too much at stake in this Presidential year for any Republican to allow his prejudices, or even his personal desires, to impair the present prospects of a splendid Republican victory in the Nation and the State."

Primary Test Surprised Bosses.

It was learned yesterday that the results of the primary test in Manhattan and the Bronx came as a complete surprise to Mr. Parsons. The New York County President, it was said, had not expected a majority for the Governor's renomination in any except the Nineteenth and Twenty-fifth Assembly Districts. The Governor's friends came off victorious in six out of the nine districts where the test was made.

State Chairman Woodruff and Mr. Parsons spent some time in earnest conference before Mr. Parsons made public his statement conceding a large majority of the New York delegation to the Governor. There were reports last night that State Chairman Woodruff was viewing this action on the part of Mr. Parsons with perfect complacency.

During the remainder of the week the Republican leaders will busy themselves with the making up of a slate for the State ticket. Only one nomination has been definitely decided upon. Judge Albert Haight of the Court of Appeals, whose term expires on Dec. 31, will be renominated for another term.

For the State Ticket.

There is an abundance of material from which to select candidates for the various places on the State ticket. Here are the names of the candidates now under consideration:

For Lieutenant Governor—Senator Horace White of Syracuse, Speaker James W. Wadsworth, Jr., Senator John Raines of Canandaigua, Assemblyman Edwin A. Merritt, Jr., Frank A. Dudley of Niagara Falls, ex-Senator John Lewis Childs of Floral Park, L. I., and Senator W. W. Armstrong of Rochester.

For Secretary of State—Ex-Senator William D. Barnes of Rensselaer, ex-District Attorney John S. Maxwell of Amsterdam, Mayor Samuel A. Carlson of Jamestown, and James A. Lavery of Poughkeepsie.

For State Controller—Mayor Gaus of Albany, Register William A. Prendergast of Brooklyn, Congressman William N. Calder of Brooklyn.

For State Treasurer—County Treasurer Brush of Suffolk County, Republican County Chairman George A. Lewis of Nassau, and Homer A. Moore of Queens.

For Attorney General—Julius M. Mayer of this city, Gilbert D. Hasbrouck of Ulster, and Senator Harvey D. Hinman of Binghamton.

For State Engineer and Surveyor—Ex-Deputy State Engineer Frank M. Williams of Madison, Lloyd Collis of New York, and ex-Deputy State Engineer Arthur O'Brien of Utica.

THREE BOYS AT PLAY RUN DOWN BY AUTO

One Is Killed and Another Receives Injuries from Which He Is Expected to Die.

TAKEN IN AUTO TO HOSPITAL

Owner of the Car Then Surrenders to the Police and Is Held on a Homicide Charge.

A five-year-old boy lost his life yesterday, and his two companions of about his age were badly hurt, one of them perhaps mortally, in an apparently unavoidable automobile accident on the Richmond Turnpike, Tompkinsville, S. I. The dead boy was William Schumacher, who lived at 11 Brook Street, Tompkinsville. Almer Meyer, also 5 years old, of the same address, had his right arm fractured in three places, and six-year-old John Perrine of 1 Brook Street, had his right leg and arm, as well as his skull, fractured. He will probably die.

All three of the children were run down by an automobile driven by Richard Agar, an export merchant, with offices in lower Broadway, Manhattan, who lives in Tompkins Avenue, Tompkinsville. In the car with Mr. Agar were his wife and a chauffeur.

The accident occurred at a point where the Richmond Turnpike makes a steep decline. Mr. Agar was running carefully, when about half way down he had to turn out for a wagon. Just as his car got well abreast of the wagon, Mr. Agar was horrified to see the three little boys step out from behind it, directly in the path of the automobile.

The youngsters were playing horse, and the Perrine boy was driving his two small companions with reins made of clothes line. The small driver appeared to be frightened so by the sudden appearance of the automobile bearing down upon him that he could not move. His companions tried to run to one side, but the Perrine boy strained on the home-made reins and held them back.

Mr. Agar shut off his power and jammed down the brakes on his auto. The rear wheels skidded over the road, tearing up the surface, but even this force was not enough to bring the car to a halt before it was upon the Perrine boy. Mr. Agar tried to turn out, but despite his efforts the automobile struck the boy, flinging him twenty feet away into the ditch beside the road. The youngster's grip on his reins dragged the Schumacher and Meyer children backward and directly under the wheels of the automobile before Mr. Agar could stop the car.

All three children were unconscious. Mr. Agar and his chauffeur, Herbert Peach, sprang from the car and lifted them into it, Mrs. Agar making room for them in the tonneau beside her.

Mr. Agar climbed in beside his wife and supported the Schumacher boy while Peach drove the car at full speed to the Smith Infirmary, about a quarter of a mile away. At the hospital Mr. Agar climbed from the tonneau with the Schumacher child in his arms, but a single glance told the surgeons that the boy was dead. He had died on the ride from the scene of the accident to the hospital.

The other two children were placed in wards immediately, but the surgeons held out little hope for the recovery of the Perrine boy. After seeing that the children were cared for, Mr. Agar gave himself up to the police and soon afterward was arraigned before a Magistrate. He was held in $1,000 bail to await the action of the Grand Jury on a charge of homicide. A friend went on his bond.

Both Mr. Agar and his wife were almost prostrated by the shock of the accident.

MOTORCAR HITS A BOY.

Autoists Stop, but Drive Away Before Police Arrive—Victim in Hospital.

A heavy touring car swung swiftly out of Prospect Avenue into Jennings Street, the Bronx, shortly after 3 o'clock yesterday afternoon and ran into a group of boys playing in the street, hitting Morris Burns of 753 Jennings Avenue. The automobile, in which were several men and women, stopped a short distance away, but was driven on again before a policeman arrived.

Policeman Thomas of the Tremont Avenue Station called an ambulance from the Lebanon Hospital and the injured boy was taken to that institution. He had internal injuries, but was not fatally hurt.

A boy gave the police a card on which was the name of Charles S. Towle, a civil engineer with offices at 7 East Forty-second Street, who lives at Mamaroneck, N. Y. The police did not learn how the boy got the card, and they do not know it was Mr. Towle's auto that hit young Burns.

COURT WARNS GAMBLERS.

Tells 29 Arraigned for Policy Playing That Reform Wave Will Get Them.

Twenty-nine persons were arraigned before Judge Swann, in General Sessions, yesterday, on the charge of being concerned in the game of policy. He gave a warning to them in particular, and to all gamblers, saying:

"You people had better look out. A wave of reform is sweeping over the whole world. I saw it in France and Belgium, where I was for two months. All over the world they are forcibly stopping gambling."

Twenty-three of the twenty-nine pleaded guilty. The others, it is expected, will plead to the indictment on Friday. Ten were sentenced to pay a fine of $15 or serve a day for each dollar. They had no money and went back to the Tombs.

There were two women among the prisoners—Ada Black of 164 Eldridge Street and a negro woman named Mary Nicolese, who, after pleading, suddenly sprang to her feet and said:

"Judge, I have a little baby at home. If you send me to prison he will die. There is no one to care for him."

The Judge allowed her to go under promise to appear on Friday.

"All the News That's Fit to Print."

The New York Times.

THE WEATHER.

Fair, warmer to-day; clouding to-morrow; light, variable winds.

VOL. LVIII...NO. 18,854. * * * NEW YORK, TUESDAY, SEPTEMBER 7, 1909.—EIGHTEEN PAGES. ONE CENT In Greater New York, Jersey City, and Newark { Elsewhere, TWO CENTS.

GAYNOR, UNPLEDGED, CONSENTS TO RUN

Writes Business Men He Will Accept Support of Any Party, but Make No Promises.

SAYS TAMMANY IS FOR HIM

Assured by Leaders of the Nomination, He Declares—Is for War on Machine Control and "City Spoliation."

Supreme Court Justice William J. Gaynor of Brooklyn has announced his willingness to become a candidate for Mayor in a letter written to a committee of influential Brooklyn citizens, who urged him soon after his return from Europe to enter the fight. The long-awaited declaration of his position was made public last night together with the names of the committee of citizens and their letter to the Brooklyn jurist.

Justice Gaynor reviews the entire Mayoralty situation, assails "mere political control," which has resulted in "spoliation of the city treasury." He declares, however, that he has reason to believe that he will receive the Democratic nomination and Republican support, as well as that of the Independence League.

An interesting part of the letter is that in which Justice Gaynor refers to the printed statements that he would not receive the indorsement of the Republican organization unless he made some definite pledge of his position. While declaring that he does not believe that the majority of the organization demand any such condition of him, he emphatically states that he will pledge himself to no organization.

"I shall not take a nomination from any organization to which is annexed any pledge, promise or condition whatsoever other than to be Mayor in fact, and do my duty if elected," says he.

In referring to his expectation of welcoming all voters to his standard, Justice Gaynor says: "When an organization or party vouches for one and nominates him and wants him elected I have always understood that it welcomes help from any and all quarters to elect him."

Promises from Tammany.

He goes on to make the significant declaration that he has received assurance from influential Democrats that the Tammany City Convention will give him an "unconditional nomination" and that "no one can prevent the election of delegates who will nominate me." He states that he is aware that there is opposition to him in the organization, but that he does not believe "an undivided delegation can be brought into the convention opposed to my nomination."

"As to the Independence League," he continues, "inasmuch as it has always stood for the uplifting of city government, I think I may justly expect its support."

Justice Gaynor concludes with a solemn pledge to discharge his trust with fidelity and honesty, ending with the words, "No party or party machine can drag us down if we stand fast together: on the contrary, we may lift city politics up in all parties, and make the spoliation of the city's treasury, through mere machine political control, a thing impossible in the future."

Here is Justice Gaynor's answer:

Justice Gaynor's Letter.

Sept. 4, 1909.

"Messrs. Abraham Abraham, James McMahon, Archibald R. Watson, Judson G. Wall, Michael H. Drummond, James Creelman, Charles M. Higgins, M. M. Belding, Jr., and Frank J. Price:

Dear Sirs—Your letter added to my very great anxiety, already caused by similar letters and requests and public discussion, but has finally helped to enable me to see my way through it. I put myself in your hands, and consent to be a candidate for nomination for Mayor. No doubt you have observed that several bodies of citizens have nominated me already. I specially note your statement, 'We do not care who, or what party convention, joins in nominating and voting for you if you will give us your consent to run,' etc. It requires me to say something of recent occurrences in order that there may be no misunderstanding, and I trust I may say it without a bit of unkindness to any one.

The Republican City Committee has met since your letter was written and apparently give out a statement that the Republican City Convention will not nominate any one who will not pledge himself in advance not to accept a nomination from the Democratic City Convention also. Although published in all of the newspapers, and in no way questioned, I have doubted whether it was in fact authorized. I know that many Republicans will not acquiesce in it. As is well enough known, I have long been of those who look upon such extreme partisanship in city or local elections as most unfortunate. Its main result is to play everything year after year into the hands of party machines.

In years gone by I have worked shoulder to shoulder with Republicans and Democrats alike and together in efforts to prevent official wrongdoing and lift the city Government up and make it intelligent and decent. I so worked successfully with those who prevented the fraudulent purchase of the water company, and other even worse things, still in general remembrance, and with those who moved upon and destroyed John Y. McKane and his corrupt control, results and benefits from which were accepted by leaders and the machines of both parties in turn through series of years.

We never paused then to inquire of one another's politics, or to put any ban or bar on one another because of politics, and we shall not do the like now. Must I now in order to run for Mayor first get up and unjustly offend men who so worked with us then, and thousands of others who gave us their good-will and sympathy in such work, by saying that I shall not suffer the city convention of their party to also nominate me? If I should do so I could not expect their votes.

The great bulk of the voters here who are Democrats in National politics are in favor of intelligent and good local government the same as the corresponding bulk of Republican voters are. How much better it would be for the city if they should work together instead of proscribing and ostracizing each other.

Base Men in the Minority.

Base men are in the minority in all parties and everywhere. There are 75,000 or more voters in this great city who now never allow National politics to influence their votes in city elections. What,

Continued on Page 7.

HARRIMAN SUFFERS RELAPSE.

Diagnosed as Acute Indigestion—His Physician Says, 'We Hope for the Best.'

Special to The New York Times.

TURNER'S, N. Y., Sept. 6.—That E. H. Harriman has had a relapse was admitted this afternoon by Dr. W. M. Gordon Lyle, his physician, at the Harriman home here. Acute indigestion is Dr. Lyle's diagnosis of his patient's trouble.

The attack came on yesterday after Mr. Harriman had appeared to be doing nicely for several days. A telephone message was sent from the Harriman home in the early hours of this morning to Miss Taylor, Superintendent of St. Luke's Hospital nurses' registry, at 214 West 108th Street, Manhattan, asking her to send her best nurse here with all speed. The nurse arrived within three hours.

According to Dr. Lyle, Mr. Harriman is resting easily to-night. He said that it was he who sent for the nurse. There is a report that there are four other nurses here, but this could not be confirmed. Certain it is that Mr. Harriman's state of health is such that both day and night nurses are required.

When Dr. Lyle was seen this afternoon he was much perturbed over the presence here again of newspaper men. It was pointed out to him, however, that they were withdrawn on the understanding that the press was to be apprised of any change in Mr. Harriman's condition through his office at 120 Broadway. He was told that nothing could be learned from that source to-day.

"It is true," said Dr. Lyle, "that Mr. Harriman has had a relapse. Yesterday he had a sharp attack of indigestion, but he is better to-day, and is now resting comfortably. We hope for the best."

Mr. Harriman's entire family is at Tower Hill, while Judge Robert S. Lovett, general counsel to most of the important Harriman interests, was summoned to Arden and arrived last night. It is said that two of the physicians who were called into consultation with Dr. George W. Crile, the Cleveland surgeon, shortly after Mr. Harriman's return from Europe, are again at Arden. They are Dr. Walter B. James of 17 West Fifty-fourth Street and Dr. George E. Brewer of 61 West Forty-eighth Street.

Dr. Lyle gave out this bulletin at 4 P. M.: "Mr. Harriman had an attack of acute indigestion at 11 P. M. last night, having partaken of a dinner a little heartier than his strength would allow. His condition is improved to-day, although there are still slight indications of a bad stomach."

At Dr. Brewer's home last night it was said that the doctor was at Cedar Camp in the Adirondacks, so far as any of his household here knew. He may have gone to Arden from there, however. There was no response to the telephone when a TIMES reporter tried to reach Dr. James's house over the wire.

DYNAMITE HOUSE AND PLANT.

Official Who Had Discharged Men Kicks Explosive to the Ground.

Special to The New York Times.

TYRONE, Penn., Sept. 6.—The handsome residence of Thomas Calderwood, an official of the American Lime and Stone Company, and all of the buildings of the company at the quarry near here, were completely wrecked and one unidentified fire engineer was killed by explosions of dynamite early to-day.

Calderwood some time ago discharged some foreign employes of his company, and it was the general belief here that the explosions were acts of revenge.

Mr. Calderwood arose at 5 o'clock and smelled something burning. Upon investigation he found a large bundle of dynamite securely bound with wire on his kitchen window. He immediately tore the window open, and kicked it to the ground, and shouted for his wife and daughter to run for their lives. They had barely reached the street before the explosion occurred. Every window in the house was smashed to atoms. The doors and walls were badly damaged. Windows for blocks were broken.

At the quarries a ton of dynamite had been stored. The whole amount was exploded, completely destroying the buildings about the works, and blowing a large steel car 100 feet from the tracks.

The home of Harry Houck, near the quarries, was completely destroyed. The scales used for weighing cars were wrecked, and windows were broken in the houses within a radius of five miles.

HUGHES'S DEPUTIES AT RACES

Make No Secret of Their Mission, but Find No Betting at Sheepshead Bay.

Four investigators of race-track conditions from Albany visited the Sheepshead Bay race course yesterday, as the representatives of Gov. Hughes, after presenting themselves, with credentials which were accepted, to Sheriff Hobley of Kings County.

The investigators made no secret of their mission, but made no claim to official standing of any kind, except to say that they came to observe what was going on and ascertain the conditions concerning betting at the race track for a report to the Governor.

The visitors watched the proceedings of the holiday crowd through the afternoon, and agreed that they saw nothing fitting the description of race-track betting published in an afternoon newspaper early last week, which report caused Gov. Hughes to request reports from the New York police officials and the officials of Kings County on the matter of race-track bookmaking.

MISS STEWART A PRINCESS.

Emperor Francis Joseph Confers the Rank in Her Own Right.

VIENNA, Sept. 6.—Emperor Francis Joseph has conferred upon Miss Anita Stewart, whose marriage to Prince Miguel of Braganza will take place Sept. 15, the rank of Princess in her own right.

Miss Anita Stewart is the daughter of Mrs. James Henry Smith by her first husband, William Rhinelander Stewart, whom she divorced in South Dakota to marry Mr. Smith. When Mr. Smith died in Kobe, Japan, he left his stepdaughter an income of $40,000 a year, to which her mother will add another $40,000 a year on her marriage to Prince Miguel next month in London.

In order to get the consent of his father, Dom Miguel, the Prince had to renounce all claim to the throne of Portugal in favor of his younger brother, Prince Francis Joseph.

LONDON APPLAUDS PEARY'S EXPLOIT

Instant Acceptance of His Report a Contrast to Skepticism Toward Dr. Cook.

HAD AWAITED HIS VERDICT

Admiral Nares Thinks It Peculiar That the Announcements Should Come So Close Together.

Special Cable to THE NEW YORK TIMES.

LONDON, Sept. 6.—The news that Commander Robert E. Peary had reached the north pole was made known throughout London by late editions of the evening papers, which displayed the brief announcement, under headlines which suggested none of the reservations with which the reports of the discovery by Dr. Cook have been received.

In marked contrast with the skepticism with which Dr. Cook's reports were printed is the immediate and whole-hearted acceptance of Peary's dispatch. Nothing could show this better than a comparison of headlines upon the two announcements.

A Difference in Headlines.

"North pole reached by Peary. Official news that the American flag was hoisted April 6, 1909." That is the way in which Commander Peary's dispatch is presented to its readers by a London paper which headed Dr. Cook's report as follows: "The north pole reported discovered. American explorer's statement."

With the general public a similar readiness to accept Commander Peary's statement is strikingly apparent and bears out the saying frequently heard here recently to the effect that had it been Commander Peary instead of Dr. Cook who had come forward with a bare announcement of the discovery of the pole not a single voice would have been raised in question. It is a testimony to Commander Peary's high reputation as a man and an explorer that the world accepts his word without a shadow of hesitation.

Had Awaited Peary's Testimony

Mr. Peary's announcement is hailed with peculiar satisfaction, because, throughout the controversy that has been raging in the last few days, it has been stated again and again that Mr. Peary's testimony would settle the question definitely. "Peary will know the truth," it was said. Thus, Peary is the witness for whom the whole world is waiting. There was a consensus of opinion among the people with whom I talked to-night that if Commander Peary contests the claims put forward by Dr. Cook, the latter will find it an extremely difficult task to establish his pretensions to be the discoverer of the pole, even should the "proofs" which he is now withholding prove to be as good as he says they are.

Cook Expects Confirmation.

Dr. Cook, on being informed in Copenhagen to-night of the news from Mr. Peary, said:

"I hope it is true, for Peary's reports will confirm all my claims."

An arctic explorer to whom to-night I showed Mr. Peary's message to THE NEW YORK TIMES, saying, "I have the pole," made the comment that Mr. Peary, by implication, denied any other claim to the honor of discovering the pole, and that, consequently, it was to be inferred that the confirmation which Dr. Cook expects from Mr. Peary is hardly likely to be forthcoming.

Peculiar Coincidence, Says Nares.

Sir George Nares, who led the arctic expedition of 1875-6, when interviewed to-night with regard to Commander Peary's message announcing the discovery, said:

"It is difficult to avoid the conclusion that Commander Peary's Eskimos at Etah must have known that Dr. Cook had crossed Smith's Sound and passed Etah last Winter to reach Ellsmere Land. Dr. Cook, then," continued the Admiral, "gets down from his Eskimo headquarters at Annotook to Upernavik by a Greenland route never before traversed, passing all the sea glaciers in Baffin Bay just in time to catch a Danish Government vessel which leaves Upernavik early in the year before the whaling vessels are due.

"My first impression was that Dr. Cook had got hold of Commander Peary's Eskimos in some way or other and ought to have communicated either with Commander Peary or with the Eskimos at Etah.

"The question now arises how it comes about that Cook and Peary announce at practically the same time the discovery of the north pole. Is it not a peculiar fact that this coincidence takes place, in view of the possibility of news having reached Etah of the success of one or the other of the men?"

Capt. Scott of the exploring ship Discovery stated to-night that Commander Peary's message put it beyond doubt that the Stars and Stripes was the first flag to fly at the north pole.

The Proper Witness Arrives.

"Just at the very moment when men were saying that only the evidence of an independent witness who had himself visited the north pole could estab-

Continued on Page 2.

In order not to miss The New York Times of to-morrow, in which will be printed exclusively Lieut. Peary's own story of his discovery of the North Pole, order a copy from your newsdealer early to-day.

COOK GLAD PEARY REACHED THE POLE

Unmoved When, Wreathed with Flowers at Banquet, He Hears the News.

HOPE NOW FOR OTHERS

Believes More Expeditions Will Reach the Pole Within the Next Ten Years.

COPENHAGEN, Sept. 6.—Copenhagen was electrified to-night by the report of Commander Peary's announcement that he had reached the north pole. Dr. Cook was immensely interested and said:

"That is good news. I hope Peary did get to the pole. His observations, and reports on that region will confirm mine."

Asked if there was any probability of Peary's having found the tube containing his records, Dr. Cook replied:

"I hope so, but that is doubtful on account of the drift. Commander Peary would have reached the pole this year, probably, while I was there last year. His route was several hundred miles east of mine. We are rivals, of course, but the pole is good enough for two.

"The fact of two men having reached the pole along different paths," continued the explorer, "should furnish large additions to scientific knowledge. Probably other parties will reach it in the next ten years, since every explorer is helped by the experience of his predecessors, just as Sverdrup's observations and reports were of immeasurable help to me.

"I can say nothing more concerning Commander Peary's success without knowing further details, than that I am glad of it."

While Dr. Cook was conversing casually this morning with some friends, a possibility of the dénouement which electrified the world to-day was laughingly suggested. Dr. Cook remarked:

"It is quite possible that Peary will turn up now. He is about due to get back if he carries out his plans."

Those who have had the best opportunities to become acquainted with Dr. Cook here believe that he is not likely to enter into a controversy with Commander Peary.

It is doubtful if history furnishes a more dramatic episode than the breaking of the news to Dr. Cook that Peary had realized the goal of his life's ambition and repeated struggles. Dr. Cook was seated at a dinner, surrounded by explorers and correspondents, in the gilded ballroom of the Tivoli Casino. Around his neck was hung a garland of pink roses, according to the Scandinavian method of honoring heroes, which the explorer wore blushingly and with visible embarrassment. Several speeches, acclaiming him, had been given and repeated toasts to him drunk with clamorous cheers.

Amid this scene a whisper went around that Peary had planted the Stars and Stripes at the pole. Cook was perfectly cool and unmoved. He made a striking speech, in which he paid high tribute to the work of Svërdrup, who sat near, to whose discoveries he largely owed his success; to John R. Bradley, who had financed the expedition; to "the intelligence, endurance, and faithfulness" of the Eskimos who had assisted in the preparations, and those who had accompanied him. The whole story of the expedition, he said, has not come out, and will not come out for some time, nor will it come out in installments, but only when it is completed.

Dr. Cook did not permit the whispers which came to his ear of Peary's success to move him in the least, but when he had finished he was surrounded by correspondents who looked for some sign of emotion, but the explorer said smilingly: "I am glad."

Nothing but arctic exploration has been thought of here for the last few days. The people at first refused to believe that such a report as that telling of Peary's success had been received. They thought it must be a canard or a practical joke. The Danish news agency, which received the telegram from London, feared that it had been imposed upon and cabled to London for confirmation before it would circulate the report.

Minister Egan characterized it as one of the most dramatic events of history. The rumor spread that Peary was returning by way of Denmark, and this made an immense sensation. Some questioned the authority of the Peary telegram on the ground that it was improbable that a scientific man would use such dramatic language.

After the dinner to-night Dr. Cook stood about talking with Sverdrup and the other guests in a most unconcerned manner. Later, with the roses still decorating his shoulders, his hosts led him through the Casino grounds to an automobile. A crowd of several hundred, half of the number being women, surrounded and followed him, cheering, but the people were not able to get near enough to shake hands, because of a cordon of police.

PEARY DISCOVERS THE NORTH POLE AFTER EIGHT TRIALS IN 23 YEARS

Notifies The New York Times That He Reached It on April 6, 1909.

HE WIRES FROM LABRADOR

Returning on the Roosevelt, Which He Reports to Bridgman Is Safe.

IS NEARING NEWFOUNDLAND

Expects to Reach Chateau Bay To-day, When He Will Send Full Particulars.

McMILLAN SENDS WORD

Explorer's Companion Telegraphs Sister: "We Have the Pole on Board."

SEVEN VAIN EXPEDITIONS

Many Years Consumed in Learning the Feasible Route—Picked Men Were His Assistants.

Commander Robert E. Peary, U. S. N., has discovered the north pole. Following the report of Dr F. A. Cook that he had reached the top of the world comes the certain announcement from Mr. Peary, the hero of eight polar expeditions, covering a period of twenty-three years, that at last his ambition has been realized, and from all over the world comes full acknowledgment of Peary's feat and congratulations on his success.

The first announcement of Peary's exploit was received in the following message to THE NEW YORK TIMES:

> Indian Harbor, Labrador, via Cape Ray, N. F., Sept. 6.
> THE NEW YORK TIMES, New York:
> I have the pole, April sixth. Expect arrive Chateau Bay, September seventh. Secure control wire for me there and arrange expedite transmission big story. PEARY.

Following the receipt of Commander Peary's message to THE NEW YORK TIMES several other messages were received in this city from the explorer to the same effect.

Soon afterward The Associated Press received the following:

> INDIAN HARBOR, Via Cape Ray, N. F., Sept. 6.—To Associated Press, New York:
> Stars and Stripes nailed to the pole. PEARY.

To Herbert L. Bridgman, Secretary of the Peary Arctic Club, he telegraphed as follows:

> Herbert L. Bridgman, Brooklyn, N. Y.:
> Pole reached. Roosevelt safe. PEARY.

This message was received at the New York Yacht Club in West Forty-fourth Street:

> INDIAN HARBOR, Via Cape Ray, N. F., Sept. 6.—George A. Carmack, Secretary New York Yacht Club:
> Steam yacht Roosevelt, flying club burgee, has enabled me to add north pole to club's other trophies. (Signed) PEARY.

Cipher Shows Authenticity.

The telegram to Mr. Bridgman was sent in cipher. The cipher used was a private one and indicated clearly that the dispatch was undoubtedly from Commander Peary.

Commander Peary also sent a message to his wife at South Harpswell, Me., where she has been spending the Summer.

"Have made good at last," said the explorer to his wife. "I have the old pole. Am well. Love. Will wire again from Chateau."

The message was signed simply "Bert," an abbreviation of Robert, Commander Peary's first name. Mrs. Peary sent a wife's characteristic reply, with love and a blessing and a request for him to "hurry home."

By a strange coincidence, Mrs. Frederick A. Cook, too, was in South Harpswell, Me., when she received the first news from her husband.

Peary's Companion Reports.

Two messages were received in this country also from Donald B. McMillan, who accompanied Peary. Mr. McMillan was an instructor in mathematics and physical training at the academy in Worcester, Mass., until the close of school last year, when he obtained a leave of absence of two years to go on the Peary expedition.

In addition to his message to Dr. D. L. Abercrombie, Principal of the academy, Mr. McMillan sent the following to Mrs. W. C. Fogg, his sister, who is Postmistress at Freeport, Me.:

> Indian Harbor, Sept. 6, 1909.
> Mrs. W. C. Fogg, Freeport, Me.:
> Arrived safe. Pole on board. Best year of my life. BEN.

Follows Cook's Report Quickly.

These messages, flashed from the coast of Labrador to New York and thence to the four corners of the globe while Dr. Frederick A. Cook is being acclaimed by the crowned heads of Europe and the world at large as the discoverer of the north pole, added a remarkable chapter to the story of an achievement that has held the civilized world up to the highest pitch of interest since Sept. 1, when Dr. Cook's claim to having reached the "top of the world" was first telegraphed from the Shetland Islands.

The two explorers, Dr. Frederick A. Cook and Commander Robert E. Peary, both Americans, had been in the arctic seeking the goal of centuries, the impossible north pole, whose attainment has at times seemed beyond the reach of man. Both were determined and courageous, and both had started expressing the belief that their efforts would be crowned with success.

Peary the Better Known.

Peary was well known to both scientists and the general public as a persistent striver for the honor of reaching the "farthest north." Dr. Cook, on the other hand, had held the public attention to a lesser degree. He made his departure quietly and his purpose was hardly known except to those keenly interested in polar research.

Then suddenly, and with no word of warning, a steamer touched at Lerwick, in the Shetland Islands, and Dr. Cook's claim to having succeeded where expedition after expedition of the hardiest explorers of the world had failed was made known. Dr. Cook's announcement was that he had reached the pole on April 21, 1908.

Three days later Dr. Cook arrived at Copenhagen and received a welcome such as no explorer had ever received before.

Peary Announces Success.

Five days after the receipt of the Lerwick message, almost to the hour, came the sensational statement from Indian Harbor, Labrador, that Commander Peary also had been successful on his third expedition to the coveted goal, the date being April 6, 1909.

He filed his brief messages and continued on his way to the south, leaving the world to marvel at a dramatic situation such as has seldom been recorded—the double achievement of a purpose that for almost ten centuries had baffled the endeavor of man and had taken many an explorer to his death in the frozen north.

It is almost certain that Commander Peary did not know of Dr. Cook's announcement when he sent his messages from Indian Harbor.

Under ordinary circumstances Commander Peary's announcement would have evoked world-wide interest, but the existing conditions conspired to add many times to the importance of his communication.

According to Dr. Cook's account of his expedition, he buried the American flag at the pole in a metal tube; Peary's words would indicate that the Stars and Stripes were raised by him and left standing.

How the News Came.

The message from Commander Peary to THE NEW YORK TIMES was received in New York at 12:39 yesterday through the Postal Telegraph Company. It was handed in at Indian Harbor, Labrador, and was sent from there by wireless telegraph to Cape Ray, Newfoundland, and from Cape Ray to Port aux Basques by the Newfoundland Government land lines; thence to Canso, Nova Scotia, by cable, and to New York from there over the lines of the Commercial Cable Company.

PEARY REPORTS TO THE TIMES

ANNOUNCES HIS DISCOVERY OF THE POLE AND WILL SEND A FULL AND EXCLUSIVE ACCOUNT TO-DAY.

Indian Harbor, Labrador, via Cape Ray, N. F., Sept. 6.

The New York Times, New York:

I have the pole, April sixth. Expect arrive Chateau Bay September seventh. Secure control wire for me there and arrange expedite transmission big story.

PEARY.

PEARY'S MESSAGE TO HIS WIFE.

SOUTH HARPSWELL, Me., Sept. 6.—Commander Robert E. Peary announced his success in discovering the North Pole to his wife, who is summering at Eagle Island here, as follows:

INDIAN HARBOR, via Cape Ray, Sept. 6, 1909.

Mrs. R. E. Peary, South Harpswell, Me.:

Have made good at last. I have the old Pole. Am well. Love. Will wire again from Chateau.

(Signed) BERT.

In replying Mrs. Peary sent the following dispatch:

SOUTH HARPSWELL, Me., Sept. 6, 1909.

To Commander R. E. Peary, Steamer Roosevelt, Chateau Bay:

All well. Best love. God bless you. Hurry home.

(Signed) JO.

CONFIRMED BY FELLOW-VOYAGER.

INDIAN HARBOR, Labrador, Sept. 6, 1909.

Dr. D. W. Abercrombie, Worcester Academy, Worcester, Mass.:

Top of the earth reached at last. Greetings to Faculty and boys.

(Signed) D. B. McMILLAN.

DR. COOK CABLES THE TIMES.

To the Editor of The New York Times:

COPENHAGEN, Sept. 6.

Glad Peary did it. Two records are better than one, and the work over a more easterly route has added value.

COOK.

WASHINGTON CREDITS PEARY.

Believes Cook, Too, but Has Said That He Must Produce Records.

Special to The New York Times.

WASHINGTON, Sept. 6.—There was instant acceptance among the geographers in Washington of the assertion in Commander Peary's laconic cable message that he had discovered the north pole. And there was just as ready rejoicing for Peary is popular with the scientific men in the National capitol, and they are ready to take his word at its face value without examination or delay.

In the manner of their acceptance of this announcement of a second discovery of the point that has baffled discovery for so many years there is a sharp contrast to the attitude of the same men toward the announcement from Dr. Cook. Most of them, indeed, accept Cook's assertion, and announce their belief that the Brooklyn man actually did reach the north pole in April, 1908. But there

Commander Robert E. Peary and His Ship, the Roosevelt.

LIEUTENANT PEARY.

PEARY'S SHIP THE ROOSEVELT.
COPYRIGHT 1909 BY UNDERWOOD & UNDERWOOD.

Where Peary Filed the News of His Discovery.

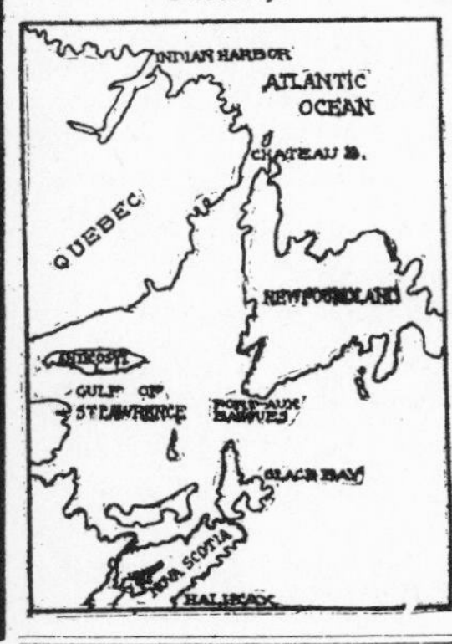

PEARY, ON THE DECK OF THE ROOSEVELT.

Men Who Shared in Peary's Search for the Pole.

CREW OF THE "ROOSEVELT" (LEFT TO RIGHT)—JOHN BARNES, JOHN CADY, HENRY JOHNSON, JOHN MURPHY, 2ND MATE, DENNIS MURPHY, THEODORE GUSLIN, 1ST MATE, JOSEPH WHITE.

CAPTAIN SAM BARTLETT OF THE ROOSEVELT

have been many references to the necessity imposed upon Dr. Cook of promptly producing records and observations which should constitute proof of the authenticity of his claim.

No such remarks greeted the announcement from Peary this afternoon. It was taken for granted at once that as soon as he reaches the United States full data of his journey over the polar ice will be forthcoming, and that the documentary evidence will not only be complete but unquestionable.

The officials of the National Georgraphic Society were greatly pleased at the news of Commander Peary's success. Dr. Willis J. Moore, President of the society, did not care to comment extensively upon the announcement in advance of more detailed information, but he unhesitatingly expressed the belief that both Peary and Cook had reached the long-sought goal.

"I believe that Dr. Cook and Commander Peary have both accomplished their object," said Prof. Moore this afternoon. "It is gratifying that the strange coincidence should have occurred. For scores of years men of different nations have been striving to reach the north pole, but now within a few days comes the news that two Americans have succeeded.

"Such wonderful achievements as this make epochs in the history of the world," declared Capt. Veeder, in charge of the United States Naval Observatory, "and I have no doubt that this discovery will add immeasurably to the sum of human knowledge." Capt. Veeder greeted the announcement of Peary's attainment of the pole with a hearty "Good!" and added that he was immensely pleased to know that the American Navy was at least second in the race, if not first.

"Peary adds still another name to the long list of American heroes," said Prof. Asaph Hall of the observatory. "I did not know him personally, but I had come to have the greatest admiration for him. The energy he has displayed, his persistence, and the intelligence he has brought to bear on this great problem, which have at last been crowned with success, are worthy of all commendation."

Those persons who had associated with Peary here spoke of him to-day as a man of wonderful capacity for doing things, and they instantly accepted the statement that he had discovered the pole. They had expected him to eventually win in his struggle, and so it was no surprise to them when word came that he had succeeded.

Rear Admiral W. S. Cowles, Chief of the Bureau of Equipment of the Navy, expressed his delight.

"It was my understanding," he said, "when he left here that it was his hope to reach the pole about this time. Peary is a most deserving officer. He has pursued his purpose under all sorts of adverse conditions, and only a man of his energy and persistence could hope to win so great an undertaking. Peary had an exceptionally fine equipment. Very much money was spent on his outfit, and he has been able to take advantage of all of the mistakes and successes of his predecessors. It would be no great wonder at all if he has at last achieved what he set out to do."

Admiral Cowles also said he believed that Dr. Cook discovered the pole last year. "At any rate," he said, "I believe, in the interest of fair play, that adverse judgment should be suspended until it has been demonstrated that he has not made the discovery he claims."

"That dispatch from Peary means that he has finally achieved what he has so long been after," said Henry Gannett, an old friend of Peary, and Vice President of the National Geographic Society. "I am awfully glad that he has gotten to the north pole, whether he was the first to reach there or not. He certainly worked hard enough to get there. Such a dispatch from Peary would signify only his own achievement. Even if Cook was there first, whatever he left there would have floated miles away. I always thought that Peary had the best chance of all of the men who have gone out in the effort to reach the north pole. He was fitted by long experience and by his well-known high qualities."

PARIS BELIEVES PEARY.

Feels Friendly to Dr. Cook and Thinks He Will Be Upheld.

PARIS, Sept. 6.—Commander Peary's announcement that he has carried the American Flag to the north pole has caused a profound impression in France. The momentous dispatch arrived too late to be printed in the Paris evening papers, and the bulk of the people will not hear the news until to-morrow morning. Nevertheless, the announcement circulated rapidly, and it was with a genuine thrill that people discussed the dramatic incident of two American explorers reporting within a few days of each other the attainment of the goal for which man has been struggling for centuries.

Peary, more than Cook, is known to the French people, but the fact that Peary was seeking the pole somehow had been forgotten in the eager discussion of the achievement of Dr. Cook. Public opinion might be summarized in the statement that belief in Peary's success probably would tend to destroy many doubts entertained concerning Cook's claims, since it is felt that weather and ice conditions very likely rendered the voyages of both successful.

Prominent French scientists, who have already expressed their views, are of the opinion that Commander Peary's prominence as an explorer, and his glorious achievements in the past, will undoubtedly mean that the announcement of his success will be immediately accepted without question, in contradistinction to that of Dr. Cook, whose unobtrusive and solitary voyage raised doubt at once in some quarters. In the meantime Peary's story is awaited with the keenest interest, for the situation not only appeals to the French mind from a dramatic standpoint, but also arouses intense scientific curiosity to compare the narratives of the two explorers.

The attitude of the French press has been entirely friendly to Dr. Cook. For the most part the newspapers have accepted his claims, with some tendency, as in the case of the Temps, to place a question mark over each day's headline pointing to the discovery of the north pole. To-night expressions are heard on the sides of a warmly congratulatory nature on the determination of America's representatives to plant the flag at the pole, and the feeling here is one of unreserved homage to the Stars and Stripes.

The news of Peary's achievement was conveyed to the distinguished geographer, J. J. A. Bouquet de La Grye, of the Academy of Sciences, who clapped his hands and cried:

"Then it is surely done. We do not doubt Cook, but somehow we feel that if Peary flashes back word of victory it means that the man, with his vast polar experience, will be able to prove to the world that the goal has at last been attained. It is certain also, that Peary's success will lend moral support to the truth of Cook's claim."

M. Lemesof, Librarian of the Geographical Society, recalled how only to-day he had pointed out that it was to be regretted Cood did not wait several days at the pole to make thorough examinations and observations.

"I am convinced the explorer reached the north pole," M. Lemesof had said, "but his difficulty will come in establishing his claim. It is a pity that Cook did not remain longer at the pole, make a thorough examination of the territory, and secure observations extending over many days, as did Commander Peary and others, when they reached their limit of progress.

"There is this possibility, however, instead of arriving at the pole itself, Cook may have mistakenly circled around it and then headed homeward, figuring that he had reached the goal and was then leaving it behind him. But we should await Dr. Cook's observations. Perhaps he will be able to convince scientists, and then again, perhaps he never will."

"It would seem," added Mr. Lemesof to-night, "as if the almost simultaneous discoveries mean that nature's pathway has become easier for the footsteps of the explorer, and that the geographical secret has at last reached a solution."

Another scientist said that he was glad Peary had succeeded, like Cook, for Peary's tenacity of purpose and dogged determination to contribute to the world's scientific history had won the admiration of all scientists.

COMMENT IN BERLIN.

Newspapers Call It the Most Remarkable Coincidence in History.

BERLIN, Sept. 6.—The announcement that Commander Peary had reached the north pole was received here with immense astonishment. It was pointed out on all sides that this was the most remarkable coincidence in human history, the long and protracted struggle to reach the pole at last ending in two almost simultaneous discoveries.

The first dispatches awakened considerable misgivings, some being inclined to see a practical joke intended to give sensational surroundings to Dr. Cook's story, but a later dispatch from New York, which stated that Peary had also sent a telegram in cipher left room for no doubt that the first message had originated with Peary.

The news reached Berlin too late to appear in all the morning papers and too late for any of them to get the views of scientists, but the editorial comment indicates the immense sensation the news has made in Berlin.

The Lokal Anzeiger says that scarcely room exists to doubt the authenticity of Peary's dispatches, or that he also reached the pole. The paper calls it "a unique coincidence, without parallel in the world's history."

The Tageblatt thinks that the two discoveries mutually confirm each other, both explorers having set out in the same region and apparently having encountered similar meteorological conditions. "It will remain a memorable event," says the newspaper. The Tageblatt concludes by saying the civilized world will congratulate America upon the success of her sons, to whom equal honors are due, since both equally possess the qualities which make most for "the progress of humanity, intelligence, energy, and self-sacrifice."

The Vossiche Zeitung says; "It is one of the most wonderful accidents that two explorer succeed almost at the same time in solving the polar problem, which has occupied the attention of the race for centuries."

The Boersen Courier calls it an astonishing occurrence. Some of the newspapers, not being cognizant of the dates of Peary's start and discovery, raise the question as to which man reached the pole first.

PEARY'S MESSAGE CHEERED.

American Theatre Audience Pleased When The Times Dispatch Is Shown.

There was great applause from the large audience in the American Theatre in West Forty-second Street last night, when a copy of the message sent by Commander Peary to THE NEW YORK TIMES, announcing the discovery of the north pole, was thrown upon the screen just ahead of the moving pictures.

Apparently the fact that the explorer had successfully reached the goal of his life-long ambition was not generally known to the men and women in the theatre, and there were marked expressions of satisfaction as they left the building at the close of the performance.

LONDON APPLAUDS PEARY'S EXPLOIT

Continued from Page 1.

lish beyond question or cavil the claim of Dr. Cook," says The Daily Mail editorially, "that very witness arrived in Commander Peary, an explorer whose statements will be accepted by the whole scientific world without doubt or hesitation."

The editorial continues:

"The warmest congratulations of the British public will go out to the explorer who has devoted his life to the siege of the pole and whose efforts now at last, after incredible toil and suffering, have been crowned with a magnificent success. Baffled, beaten back time after time, he has known how to win victory in the end. Indomitable has been his perseverance, iron his fortitude, heroic the spirit which led him to laugh at every disappointment, and thus by sheer strength of character to reach his self-appointed goal.

"As the glory of attaining the north pole has been denied to British effort, all in this country will rejoice that it has fallen to one of our kinsmen over the sea, and to such a kinsman. America may well be proud of sons like Commander Peary.

Doubts of Dr. Cook Persist.

"Greatly as Commander Peary's achievement would have moved the world at any time, coming at this moment it has a special, absorbing interest. Only a few days have passed since the claim of Dr. Cook to have reached the north pole was made known to the public. The long message in which he recounted his journey was by general consent pronounced unconvincing. Further particulars which he has communicated since landing at Copenhagen have not removed all ground for doubt. Though Danish scientists of high reputation accept his claim, a large section of the public still entertains doubts and asks why it is that he has not brought with him his journal and detailed observations to establish the truth of his statements.

"Now, on the very eve of the day on which Dr. Cook will receive the gold medal of the Danish Geographical Society, a witness comes from the unknown who has looked upon the pole."

Hails Peary as Discoverer.

"Commander Peary must," in the words of the leading editorial article in The Standard, "be hailed and congratulated as the discoverer of the north pole, subject only to the reservation that a prior claim has been advanced and remains to be verified."

Before arriving at this conclusion, after a careful review of the situation, The Standard points out that in the matter of the value of services rendered to science by each of the two explorers, there can be no comparison.

With reference to Dr. Cook's claims this journal declares that "amazement was, and still is, tempered with some incredulity. The form in which the intelligence first reached the civilized regions could not fail to suggest a suspicion, not necessarily as to the explorer's veracity but as to the accuracy of his records. Even now that Dr. Cook has landed at Copenhagen and submitted himself to a cross-examination, he very frankly allows that overwhelming proof of his success is now before the public.

"Peary's exploit is received generally with no reserve. The Stars and Stripes float literally or metaphorically in the coveted breezes at the northernmost point on the globe. We have this in the most definite terms, straight from Peary himself, who, in one of his messages, with a pardonable touch of humor, invites us to imagine him nailing the banner of his country to the north pole itself."

Cook's Delay in Question.

The London Times editorially congratulates Mr. Peary on his triumph, saying:

"The whole world is glad to receive certain information that the dogged devotion to arctic exploration which he has displayed on no fewer than eight expeditions has been crowned by the attainment of the supreme goal."

"The record of Mr. Peary's achievement," adds The Times, "raises some interesting comparisons with the details of his own journey which so far have been supplied by Dr. Cook, who claims to have reached the pole very nearly a year earlier. It is rather remarkable that no news of the departure of Dr. Cook from Etah with his Eskimos in the early Spring of 1908 appears to have been sent home to America by the members of the Peary expedition. Those critics who still view Dr. Cook's account with an obdurately skeptical eye will doubtless be encouraged by the report of Mr. Peary's success to inquire very exactly into the course of Dr. Cook's wanderings between April, 1908, when he claims to have reached the pole, and the date of his return to the Greenland settlements."

Wants Peary to Clear Darkness.

The Daily Telegraph, in the course of an editorial congratulating Commander Peary on planting the Stars and Stripes at the north pole, makes the sarcastic suggestion that Peary may have found the bottle at the north pole in which Cook says he imprisoned the record of his discovery, or may be able to explain "the darkness in which his reputed predecessor worked despite the sun which never sets between the Spring and Autumn equinoxes."

In another article by a scientific contributor this paper, which makes a special feature of the Peary news with three columns of cabled matter, points out several circumstances which may have made Dr. Cook wrong in his reckonings.

PEARY'S FRIENDS ELATED.

Members of New York Arctic Clubs Expect a Bitter Controversy.

The message from Commander Peary stating that he had reached the north pole excited great enthusiasm yesterday among his friends and backers in this city. Their joy at hearing of his success was only heightened by the fact that it arrived so soon after the report from Dr. Cook that he had discovered the pole, but both they and the Cook adherents seemed to look to a heated controversy when the explorers came to make their observations and data public.

Dr. Roswell O. Stebbins, 4 East Forty-third Street, who in 1894 sailed on the Miranda expedition under Dr. Cook, was startled by the news.

"That is truly extraordinary," he said, "if it is really true. That the pole should be twice discovered in that short space after all these years of failure on failure is most remarkable. It is what I had been hoping earnestly for ever since Dr. Cook sent in his report—that Peary would succeed. Then the matter could be settled, once for all; they could corroborate each other; Cook's story could be verified by Peary's.

"But I hoped that their reports would come in quite independently of each other; that when Peary reported it would be without the knowledge that Cook had reported. I am afraid that is not the case. Peary must have heard at Etah that Cook had come back with his story of success, and this will awaken intense controversy, I am afraid. Peary made his expedition in an extraordinarily short space of time. He must have come upon remarkable conditions for covering ground.

"With the knowledge that there is enmity between the two men over that difficulty regarding the blue fox skins, and the anger Peary's friends feel that Dr. Cook should have profited from Peary's hints as to the best course, and should have taken over the dogs and Eskimos Peary planned to use, I foresee trouble. Had they filed quite independent reports it would have been different, but Peary must have heard of Cook from Harry Whitney, who was at Etah, so that when he sent his story he knew of Cook's."

Thinks the Time was Short.

Limond Corbin Stone, a member of the Arctic Club, who went on Peary's expedition of 1901 when Dr. Cook was surgeon, and who therefore knows both explorers personally, was most enthusiastic over Peary's success.

"If Peary sent the message," he said, "it is certainly all right. I am overjoyed at the news. I only regret that he did not get there first. It's a great thing for this country. Some people are surprised at the speed that Peary made in getting up there and back. I am not, really. The time is certainly rather short, but not exceptionally so. Why, in the expedition of 1901 he started out over the ice on his actual dash for the pole early in February, as I take it he did this time. Then, of course, he failed, but he pushed on up north over the islands of Greenland, to Cape Morris K. Jesup—it was then he gave it that name—and returned to Etah before the 5th of August. He had covered as much ground and undergone as much hardship then as this expedition required of him, fully.

"Now in this case, he probably set out around the first of February on his dash for the pole. Well, if he reached the pole, or the place from which he began his return trip by April 6, he would, according to previous experience, have had plenty of time to reach Etah again by early August. If he had not returned to Etah earlier even than the middle of August he would, according to my figuring, have had time to get to Indian Harbor by the date he gives.

"Probably he did find smoother ice than he ever before came upon, and better conditions generally, but if I had figured the thing out I should place him now just where his cablegram shows he is, somewhere around Indian Harbor. It does not sound well to say I told you so, but I did feel sure that Peary would succeed this time, and so did all his friends in the Peary Club and out of it.

"I believe that both Dr. Cook and Peary succeeded. I know them both for honest men, absolutely honest men. There is, of course, the chance that Dr. Cook made some miscalculation; examination would show that. As for the insinuation made by some of Cook's friends that Peary is making an incorrect report, that is absolutely absurd. He is a man of highest integrity; he would not vary his report a minute.

"I put no stock in the story of personal enmity between Cook and Peary. I know there is feeling between their friends; there is likely to be more now, I am afraid; there is likely to be hot and fierce discussion."

Friends Were Prepared to Wait.

Gen. Thomas H. Hubbard of 16 West Fifty-eighth Street, member of the Peary Arctic Club, and closely identified with all of Peary's explorations, said last night that he was much surprised to hear the news, and that it was so good that he could not make up his mind to accept it as definite until he heard more regarding it.

"Of courrse as soon as I am sure that Peary sent the cablegram," he said, "I am sure that the report is true. It is perfectly possible, but the time is rather short. I had not expected to hear anything for, say, another thirty days or a little less. That would have given him the average time. Yes, we did expect Peary to succeed on this expedition, but we were prepared to wait for success a couple of years more.

"As for Dr. Cook, I know little about him. I don't care to say anything in criticism of his statements, for they may easily have become confused in some respects before they come out in print. Any insinuation by any one at all that Peary is not telling the truth is beneath consideration. Commander Peary is no faker; what he says is right."

Does Not Believe Peary.

The first actual murmuring of a possible controversy originated yesterday in the rooms of the Arctic Club of America, the club which comprises most of the Cook contingent. Capt. B. S. Osbon, Secretary of the club, stated flatly that he did not believe Commander Peary was making a true report.

"I doubt if he reached the pole," said he. "I want far stronger proof of it than this bare word. I do not see how he could possibly have made the entire expedition in so short a time. If he did he must have encountered truly ideal conditions—smooth ice and much open water. Under those circumstances it would be possible that he returned to his ship, and made the coast of Labrador, but conditions would have had to be excellent.

"When he got to Etah he must have found Harry Whitney there, and from him he would have heard of Dr. Cook's exploit. I am, of course, a Cook man, but I repeat that I do not believe that Peary reached the pole. He would have required most extraordinaryly good fortune to do it."

SCIENTISTS HAVE NO DOUBTS.

Philadelphians Are Elated Over the Report from Peary.

Special to The New York Times.

PHILADELPHIA, Sept. 6.—News of Commander Peary's achievement was greeted everywhere with enthusiasm among scientists in this city. Nowhere was there a suspicion of doubt as to the truth of his announcement, and all agreed that he had earned the honor he had strived so hard to win for the last fifteen years. A peculiar aspect of the case was the general belief which has been held that he would reach the goal.

Peary has been well known to Philadelphia scientists since 1892, and on his several journeys to the arctic before he attempted the pole he took scientists from this city in his party. They naturally began to know the man intimately, both as a scientist and as a leader, and all who accompanied him to the Far North acknowledge his ability as a scientist and his natural qualities as a commander.

He has always been a strict disciplinarian, and those who went north with him also found him to be a hard worker, as well as one who desired unremitting labor, in their several capacities, of all in his party.

He is an honorary member of almost every scientific body in Philadelphia, and his contributions to science are to be found in the journals of those societies which issue such publications. Consequently his word that he has reached the pole is accepted without question, for, as a scientist remarked: "We know the proof will be forthcoming, if Peary has been there."

News of the discovery has been expected here for a month, and all those scientists who followed Peary's attempts express themselves as having been confident that he would be heard from this Summer. While they felt certain that, if it were at all possible, Peary would push to the pole, they, knowing the uncertainty of arctic exploration, were not sure he would succeed this time, although at his start he declared this would be his last attempt.

Prof. Charles L. Doolittle, Director of the Flower Observatory of the University of Pennsylvania, was on a thirty-mile bicycle spin when he heard the news of Peary's discovery, but he was resting after his trip when a reporter called. His son, Prof. Eric Doolittle, assistant director of the observatory, who is equally interested in the news, when questioned as to the probable value to science of the discovery, said that astronomically it would have but little value.

"We know the weight of the earth now and know the position of the stars over the pole, but it might be interesting to stand at the pole and look up at the North Star. Of course, we know where it is. That has all been calculated long ago," he said.

"Peary probably will bring back a lot of data of much value in the study of climatology and meteorology, and his observations will be of the greatest value. He undoubtedly took observations very frequently. On his previous trips his observations were very accurate, and I have no doubt that his observations taken during his latest journey will be of the greatest value to geologists and meteorologists."

PREDICTED PEARY'S RETURN.

"We'll Hear from Him Soon," Said Nansen the Day Before.

CHRISTIANIA, Sept. 6.—Capt. Nansen, who is visiting in Bergen, refused tonight to make any statement regarding the discoveries of Dr. Cook and Commander Peary, but in an interview yesterday he said:

"In some few days we shall hear from Peary."

This recalls his utterance on his return from his own expedition in 1896, having left the Fram seventeen months before. When fears were expressed concerning the fate of those left behind, he added:

"Be easy about the Fram; Sverdrup will come shortly."

Sverdrup returned a week later.

"All the News That's Fit to Print."

The New York Times.

THE WEATHER.
Fair, warmer Sunday; rain probably Monday; moderate south winds.
For full weather report see Page 10, Part 3.

VOL. LX...NO. 19,419. ** NEW YORK, SUNDAY, MARCH 26, 1911.—90 PAGES, In Eight Parts, Including Picture Section and Review of Books. PRICE FIVE CENTS.

LIMANTOUR, VICTOR, PROMISES REFORMS

He Remains in Mexican Cabinet and de la Barra Will Displace Creel.

FORCE WILL MEET FORCE

Minister, However, Appeals to Mexicans and Nations to Believe in the Government's Good Faith.

FROM VICE PRESIDENT CORRAL.
Mexico City, March 25.
To the Editor of The New York Times:

The resignation of Gen. Diaz's Cabinet has been well received, because its object is to make it easier for the President to introduce reforms in public administration which it is thought will contribute to reestablish peace.

RAMON CORRAL.

FROM MINISTER OF WAR COSIO.
Mexico City, March 25.
To the Editor of The New York Times:

I am not in a position to answer your question since it is for the public to discuss the effects of the resignation.

G. COSIO.

Señor Limantour seems to have gained full sway in the Mexican Government. He is to remain as Minister of Finance. Ambassador de la Barra, with whom he had long consultations in New York, has been summoned from Washington to be Minister of Foreign Affairs in place of Enrique Creel, Limantour's rival. Four other new names are on the Cabinet slate.

Señor Limantour in an interview appeals to all Mexicans to rally to the Government. He promises needed reforms, but declares force will be met with force.

The Maderos, who were in New York, have gone to Texas to be nearer to Francisco I. Madero, the rebel leader.

Insurrectos have appeared at new and widely scattered places. Successful operations are reported in Coahuila and Neuvo Leon in the North and Guerrero and Oaxaca in the South.

APPEAL BY LIMANTOUR.

Assures Mexicans of Reform and Appeals for Their Support.

Special to The New York Times.

MEXICO CITY, March 25.—Señor José Yves Limantour, whose return to this city has been followed by the upsetting of the Diaz cabinet, and who is expected to be a figure of great importance in the new Ministry, in an interview with the correspondent of THE NEW YORK TIMES this afternoon outlined the policy which he believes will be followed by the Government. Señor Limantour, whose resignation went in with those of his colleagues, spoke as an individual.

"I hope and earnestly trust," he said, "that the present difficulties will soon be solved in the best interests of the country and to the satisfaction of all reasonable and patriotic citizens; and I feel that I can say that the administration of Gen. Diaz is prepared to take such measures and implant such reforms as will satisfy the best public opinion of the country; and that, while meeting force with force, it will leave nothing undone in the present circumstances to unite all good Mexicans.

"A united Mexico is our watchword. I ask all patriotic and progressive Mexicans to be patient, and while the Government is working at the problem before it that they practically display the love of the fatherland, which has been and must be the basic principle of Mexico's proud position in the world. The putting aside of all personal resentments is imperatively demanded and a common cause to overcome a national difficulty is a necessity.

"If the citizens and friends of Mexico will continue to prove their devotion to the glorious past and the promising future of this nation in a brief time all complexities can readily be overcome. The Mexican people and the Governments friendly to us must believe—and I say this in all solemnity of verity—that the Government is determined to properly and progressively satisfy all legitimate demands for reformative measures, and that it is doing this in its line of duty as a representative Government, honestly, sincerely, and fearlessly."

The resignation of the Cabinet yesterday is taken as an indication that Señor Limantour's policies are prevailing with President Diaz. Señor Limantour's recognized value in his present office and his unfamiliarity with diplomatic duties is advanced as a strong argument against a change in his office, and he will remain as Finance Minister.

While high officials will not admit that Gen. Bernardo Reyes has been recalled from Europe, it can be stated with practical certainty that the summons has gone to him. To Gen. Reyes, who has long been called the "idol of the Mexican Army," may be intrusted the task of handling the rebellion, as Minister of War and Marine. He will succeed the aged Gen. Cosio, who has been severely criticised for the campaign so far conducted. Gen. Reyes, who has long been abroad on a mission to study the military methods of Europe, was last heard from in Rome, whence he had gone from Paris.

Six Chosen For Ministry.

MEXICO CITY, March 25.—Although no official announcement has been made, it is known that five of the new members of President Diaz's Cabinet have been chosen and it is almost certain that Jose Yves Limantour will remain as Minister of Finance. Other selections besides that of Señor de la Barra as Minister of Foreign Relations, are:

DEMETRO SODI, Judge of the Supreme Court, Minister of Justice, succeeding Justino Fernandez.

NORDBETT DOMINGUEZ, Postmaster General, Department of Communications, succeeding Leander Fernandez.

MANUEL MAROQUIN, well-known civil engineer, Department of Fomento, succeeding Olegario Molina.

JORGE VERA ESTANOL, attorney, Minister of Education, succeeding Justo Sierra.

So far as official announcement of the

Continued on Page 9.

TO-DAY'S SUNDAY TIMES CONSISTS OF

Part I. Pictorial Section.

WIRELESS NEWS BY KITES.

Got Calls 4,000 and 6,000 Miles Away, Say San Francisco Men.

SAN FRANCISCO, March 25.—Notable achievements in wireless telegraphy are reported by a party that conducted experiments in receiving messages with the aid of high-flying kites on a beach near the Golden Gate last night.

The experimenters say they have distinctly heard calls from San Juan, Porto Rico, Washington, D. C.; Key West, Fla.; Brooklyn Navy Yard, Colon, Guantanamo, Cuba, and the station at Otichishi, Japan, which is 4,900 miles distant. They also detected an indistinct Marconi spark, which they believe was sent from Cornwall, England, a distance of 6,500 miles.

The receiving aerials were strung between two pairs of 16-foot kites, which rose to a height estimated at 1,500 feet.

To-day reports of the experiments are being prepared for transmission to the War Department, together with suggestions for the use of such an appliance for the detection of distant activities of enemies.

SENDS WIRELESS 2,500 MILES.

The White Star Liner Megantic Forwards a Message to England.

HALIFAX, N. S., March 25.—What is said to be an entirely new feat in direct wireless communication, the sending of a message over the Atlantic a distance of 2,500 miles from a ship at sea to England, was reported by the White Star Dominion liner Megantic, which arrived to-day from Liverpool.

While off the coast last night Purser Pomeroy of the Megantic sent a wireless dispatch to Liverpool via Poldhu, Cornwall. The message was received and to-day when the ship docked a reply by cable was handed to the purser.

Hitherto messages from ships in this part of the Atlantic have gone by way of Cape Race or Glace Bay and a range of 600 miles has been considered as practically the limit.

RAILROAD STRIKE IS OFF.

kQueen & Crescent Firemen Return to Work, Both Sides Yielding Points.

Special to The New York Times.

CINCINNATI, Ohio, March 25.—The strik eof firemen on the Queen and Crescent road, which caused considerable loss of freight and passenger service, was called off late to-night following a conference of the road's officials and representatives of the Firemen's Union. Both parties found it necessary to concede points of difference.

The company retains the right to employ such firemen as are now in service between Oakdale and Chattanooga, and to give them one-half the passenger and preferred freight runs.

It is understood that the strike, which has lasted sixteen days, has cost the company at least $250,000, besides the cost of operating trains with new firemen.

It is significant that the agreement is not signed by Vice President Powell of the road, who took the matter out of the hands of General Manager Baker. It is signed by Baker for the road and Vice President H. O. Teat, Chairman J. L. Payne, Vice Chairman G. A. Odenwald, and Secretary-Treasurer J. L. Fetterman of the Firemen's Union.

TALK OF CHARGES AGAINST THE MAYOR

Civic Organizations Taking Up Magistrate Corrigan's Attack—Want Police Control Shifted.

MAY GO TO THE GOVERNOR

Former District Attorney Philbin Says the Force Is Demoralized and Gaynor Doesn't Understand It.

An attempt was made yesterday to start an official investigation of police conditions in this city. Various civic organizations communicated with Magistrate Joseph E. Corrigan, who in a letter to the newspapers described the situation as intolerable and put the blame directly upon Mayor Gaynor.

It is the intention of the organizations to find out if things are as bad as has been set forth by Magistrate Corrigan and to have the responsibility placed somewhere.

Magistrate Corrigan has been asked to submit all the information and data relating to the subject he has on hand or can get, and he will comply with the request. This is as far as the Magistrate will go, he said, as he considers that he has done his duty in drawing the attention of the public to the abuses.

"I have nothing to add to what I stated in my letter," said Magistrate Corrigan yesterday, "but I am ready to stand by everything I wrote. My deductions are more than borne out by the letters which I receive by every mail. Most of these are from responsible people and contain specific instances of how the police of New York City are demoralized. These letters I am willing, with the consent of the owners, to turn over to any investigating committee, with any other information which I possess. I hope a full investigation will be made, either by the Grand Jury or some civic body."

Magistrate Butts Takes Notice, Too.

It was reported that the civic organizations will endeavor to have police control taken entirely out of the hands of the Mayor. It was said that they will even go so far as to bring charges before the Governor against the Mayor if he does not remedy defects of his own accord.

City Magistrate Butts substantiated in a measure yesterday the charges of Magistrate Corrigan. On Thursday Magistrate Butts praised Magistrate Corrigan's sincerity and courage, and he was not invited to the meeting of Magistrates on Thursday evening at which thirteen Magistrates disclaimed sympathy with Magistrate Corrigan's attack.

Magistrate Butts's position was defined when two policemen from the West 126th Street Station offered newspaper clippings in the Harlem Court describing proceedings at the Polo Athletic Club as a basis for warrants for the boxers. They said they had been unable to get into the club.

"It is a barefaced confession of the general inefficiency of the Police Department for you to offer me such evidence," said Magistrate Butts. "It reflects small credit on the police affairs of the city. How absurd it is for you men to come here and ask for a warrant or even a summons, when you make no straight charge based upon any real evidence that a crime has been committed.

"Now, understand me! I do not blame you two men or your Lieutenant or your Captain, but it certainly shows inexperience, if not stupidity, in the police administration of the City of New York. The court is powerless to put in motion its processes on such 'evidence' as this. The application for a warrant is denied."

Among those who openly backed up Magistrate Corrigan's charges yesterday were former District Attorney Eugene A. Philbin, who helped to break up the old police "system," convicting a number of Captains for neglect of duty and forcing others to retire from the department.

Force Demoralized, Says Philbin.

"I consider the police force of New York the finest body of men in the world for its size," said Mr. Philbin. "For the most part it is made up of splendid fellows, but they are now working purely under the stimulus of their own innate virtue. The force as a force is demoralized; never in my time has it been in such a state, and I believe that whether his statement was judicious and well timed or not, Magistrate Corrigan was entirely correct in his description of the conditions.

"Men are afraid of their commanding officers, not in the old sense of knowing that they must obey them, but in the sense of having no confidence in them. They are afraid to make an arrest, almost to call their souls their own. Of course, such a condition is intolerable.

"A Captain in the old days was held strictly accountable for what happened in his precinct, and although an honest patrolman, with a grievance or a wrong to report, did not have a chance in the world if he went to Headquarters with it, the discipline was splendid and New York was protected. I did my best to destroy that old system while I was in the District Attorney's office, thinking that thereby I could do a permanent good to the city. It seems, however, that I really did an injury, as so far nothing has been found as a substitute for what was called the police 'business.'

Criticisms of the Mayor.

"I do not believe that Mayor Gaynor is fully informed on police matters, or so thoroughly conversant with them as those who have studied them for years. In my opinion the only solution is to appoint a Police Commissioner for a long tenure of office, say fourteen years, so that he may be free from all influence.

"I am convinced that all the Magistrates who signed the statement condemning the action of Magistrate Corrigan, though they believed it impolitic and, perhaps, tending further to upset the discipline and efficiency of the force, really agreed with him."

James Forbes, Secretary and Director of the National Association for the Prevention of Mendicancy and Charitable Imposture, who is well acquainted with police conditions in New York, also supports Magistrate Corrigan.

"There is no question about it," he said, "the whole police force of the city is utterly demoralized. The police realize that the Mayor dislikes the police, mistrusts them, takes every opportunity to side against them.

"Now, the police force is a peculiar body, with a psychology all its own. They are very closely bound together, so that the slightest influence spreads at once through the entire force, and the Mayor's constraint, which has been carried to the extent of persecution, has simply wiped out their spirit."

Letters to Corrigan.

Letters from all kinds of people praising him for the stand he has taken in regard to the police continue to pour in on Magistrate Corrigan. The following is from a prominent lawyer:

"I congratulate you on having at last brought the public to a realization of present conditions. Whatever the other

Continued on Page 8.

141 MEN AND GIRLS DIE IN WAIST FACTORY FIRE; TRAPPED HIGH UP IN WASHINGTON PLACE BUILDING; STREET STREWN WITH BODIES; PILES OF DEAD INSIDE

The Flames Spread with Deadly Rapidity Through Flimsy Material Used in the Factory.

600 GIRLS ARE HEMMED IN

When Elevators Stop Many Jump to Certain Death and Others Perish in Fire-Filled Lofts.

STUDENTS RESCUE SOME

Help Them to Roof of New York University Building, Keeping the Panic-Stricken in Check.

ONE MAN TAKEN OUT ALIVE

Plunged to Bottom of Elevator Shaft and Lived There Amid Flames for Four Hours.

ONLY ONE FIRE ESCAPE

Coroner Declares Building Laws Were Not Enforced—Building Modern—Classed Fireproof.

JUST READY TO GO HOME

Victims Would Have Ended Day's Work in a Few Minutes—Pay Envelopes Identify Many.

MOB STORMS THE MORGUE

Seeking to Learn Fate of Relatives Employed by the Triangle Waist Company.

The Burning Building at 23 Washington Place.

Three stories of a ten-floor building at the corner of Greene Street and Washington Place were burned yesterday, and while the fire was going on 141 young men and women—at least 125 of them mere girls—were burned to death or killed by jumping to the pavement below.

The building was fireproof. It shows now hardly any signs of the disaster that overtook it. The walls are as good as ever; so are the floors; nothing is the worse for the fire except the furniture and 141 of the 600 men and girls that were employed in its upper three stories.

Most of the victims were suffocated or burned to death within the building, but some who fought their way to the windows and leaped met death as surely, but perhaps more quickly, on the pavements below.

All Over in Half an Hour.

Nothing like it has been seen in New York since the burning of the General Slocum. The fire was practically all over in half an hour. It was confined to three floors—the eighth, ninth, and tenth of the building. But it was the most murderous fire that New York has seen in many years.

The victims who are now lying at the Morgue waiting for some one to identify them by a tooth or the remains of a burned shoe were mostly girls of from 16 to 23 years of age. They were employed at making shirtwaists by the Triangle Waist Company, the principal owners of which are Isaac Harris and Max Blanck. Most of them could barely speak English. Many of them came from Brooklyn. Almost all were the main support of their hard-working families.

There is just one fire escape in the building. That one is an interior fire escape. In Greene Street, where the terrified unfortunates crowded before they began to make their mad leaps to death, the whole big front of the building is guiltless of one. Nor is there a fire escape in the back.

The building was fireproof and the owners had put their trust in that. In fact, after the flames had done their worst last night, the building hardly showed a sign. Only the stock within it and the girl employes were burned.

A heap of corpses lay on the sidewalk for more than an hour. The firemen were too busy dealing with the fire to pay any attention to people whom they supposed beyond their aid. When the excitement had subsided to such an extent that some of the firemen and policemen could pay attention to this mass of the supposedly dead they found, about half way down in the pack, a girl who was still breathing. She died two minutes after she was found.

The Triangle Waist Company was the only sufferer by the disaster. There are other concerns in the building, but it was Saturday and the other companies had let their people go home. Messrs. Harris and Blanck, however, were busy and their girls—and some men—stayed.

Leaped Out of the Flames.

At 4:40 o'clock, nearly five hours after the employes in the rest of the building had gone home, the fire broke out. The one little fire escape in the interior was never resorted to by any of the doomed victims. Some of them escaped by running down the stairs, but in a moment or two this avenue was cut off by flame. The girls rushed to the windows and looked down at Greene Street, 100 feet below them. Then one poor, little creature jumped. There was a plate glass protection over part of the sidewalk, but she crashed through it, wrecking it and breaking her body into a thousand pieces.

Then they all began to drop. The crowd yelled "Don't jump!" but it was jump or be burned—the proof of which is found in the fact that fifty burned bodies were taken from the ninth floor alone.

They jumped, they crashed through broken glass, they crushed themselves to death on the sidewalk. Of those who stayed behind it is better to say nothing—except what a veteran policeman said as he gazed at a headless and charred trunk on the Greene Street sidewalk hours after the worst cases had been taken out:

"I saw the Slocum disaster, but it was nothing to this."

"Is it a man or a woman?" asked the reporter.

"It's human, that's all you can tell," answered the policeman.

It was just a mass of ashes, with blood congealed on what had probably been the neck.

Messrs. Harris and Blanck were in the building, but they escaped. They carried with them Mr. Blanck's children and a governess, and they fled over the roofs. Their employes did not know the way, because they had been in the habit of using the two freight elevators, and one of these elevators was not in service when the fire broke out.

Found Alive After the Fire.

The first living victim, Hyman Meshel of 332 East Fifteenth Street, was taken from the ruins four hours after the fire was discovered. He was found paralyzed with fear and whimpering like a wounded animal in the basement, immersed in water to his neck, crouched on the top of a cable drum, and with his head just below the floor of the elevator.

Meantime the remains of the dead—it is hardly possible to call them bodies, because that word suggests something human, and there was nothing human about most of these—were being taken in a steady stream to the Morgue for identification. First Avenue was lined with the usual curious east side crowd. Twenty-sixth Street was impassable. But in the Morgue they received the charred remnants with no more emotion than they ever display over anything.

Back in Greene Street there was another crowd. At midnight it had not decreased in the least. The police were holding it back to the fire lines, and discussing the tragedy in a tone which those [illegible] death seldom use.

"It's the worse thing I ever saw," said one old policeman.

Chief Croker said it was an outrage. He spoke bitterly of the way in which the Manufacturers' Association had called a meeting in Wall Street to take measures against his proposal for enforcing better methods of protection for employes in cases of fire.

No Chance to Save Victims.

Four alarms were rung in fifteen minutes. The first five girls who jumped did so before the first engine could respond. That fact may not convey much of a picture to the mind of an unimaginative man, but anybody who has ever seen a fire can get from it some idea of the terrific rapidity with which the flames spread.

It may convey some idea, too, to say that thirty bodies clogged the elevator shafts. These dead were all girls. They had made their rush their blindly when they discovered that there was no chance to get out by the fire escape. Then they found that the elevator was as hopeless as anything else, and they fell there in their tracks and died.

The Triangle Waist Company employed about 600 women and less than 100 men. One of the saddest features of the thing is the fact that they had almost finished for the day. In five minutes more, if the fire had started then, probably not a life would have been lost.

Last night District Attorney Whitman started an investigation—not of this disaster alone but of the whole condition which makes it possible for a firetrap of such a kind to exist. Mr. Whitman's intention is to find out if the present laws cover such cases, and if they do not to frame laws that will.

GIRLS JUMP TO SURE DEATH.

Fire Nets Prove Useless—Firemen Helpless to Save Life.

The fire, which was first discovered at 4:40 o'clock on the eighth floor of the ten-story building at the corner of Washington Place and Greene Street, leaped through the three upper stories occupied by the Triangle Waist Company with a sudden rush that left the Fire Department helpless.

How the fire started no one knows. On the three upper floors of the building were 600 employes of the waist company, 500 of whom were girls. The victims—mostly Italians, Russians, Hungarians, and Germans—were girls and men who had been employed by the firm of Harris & Blanck, owners of the Triangle Waist Company, after the strike in which the Jewish girls, formerly employed, had become unionized and had demanded better working conditions. The building had experienced four recent fires and had been reported by the Fire Department to the Building Department as unsafe, on account of the insufficiency of its exits.

The building itself was of the most modern construction and classed as fireproof. What burned so quickly and disastrously for the victims were shirtwaists, hanging on lines above tiers of workers, sewing machines placed so closely together that there was hardly aisle room for the girls between them, and shirtwaist trimmings and cuttings which littered the floors above the eighth and ninth stories.

Girls had begun leaping from the eighth story windows before the firemen arrived. The firemen had trouble bringing their apparatus into position because of the bodies which strewed the pavement and sidewalks. While more bodies crashed down among them, they worked with desperation to run their ladders into position and to spread firenets.

One fireman, running ahead of a hose wagon, which halted to avoid running over a body, spread a firenet, and two more seized hold of it. A girl's body, coming end over end, struck on the side of it, and there was hope for an instant that she would be the first one of the score who had already jumped to be saved.

Thousands of people, who had crushed in from Broadway and Washington Square and were screaming with horror at what they saw, watched closely the work with the firenet. Three other girls, who had leaped for it a moment after the first one, struck it on top of her, and all four rolled out and lay still upon the pavement.

Five girls who stood together at a window close to the Greene Street corner held their places while a fire ladder was worked toward them, but which stopped at its full length two stories lower down. They leaped together, clinging to each other, with fire streaming back from their hair and dresses. They struck a glass sidewalk cover and crashed through it to the basement. There was no time to aid them. With water pouring in upon them from a dozen hose nozzles the bodies lay for two hours where they struck, as did the many others who leaped to their deaths.

One girl, who waved a handkerchief at the crowd, leaped from a window adjoining the New York University Building on the westward. Her dress caught on a wire, and the crowd watched her hang there till her dress burned free and she came toppling down.

Many jumped whom the firemen believe they could have saved. A girl who saw the glass roof of a sidewalk cover at the first-story level of the New York University Building leaped for it, and her body crashed through to the sidewalk.

On Greene Street, running along the eastern face of the building, more people leaped to the pavement than on Washington Place to the south. Fire nets proved just as useless to catch them and the ladders to reach them. None waited for the firemen to attempt to reach them with the scaling ladders.

All Would Soon Have Been Out.

Strewn about as the firemen worked, the bodies indicated clearly the preponderance of women workers. Here and there was a man, but almost always they were women. One wore furs and a muff, and had a purse hanging from her arm. Nearly all were dressed for the street. The fire had flashed through their workroom just as they were expecting the signal to leave the building. In ten minutes more all would have been out, as many had stopped work in advance of the signal and had started to put on their wraps.

What happened inside there were few who could tell with any definiteness. All that those who escaped seemed to remember was that there was a flash of flames, leaping first among the girls in the southeast corner of the eighth floor, and then suddenly over the entire room, spreading through the linens and cottons with which the girls were working. The girls on the ninth floor caught sight of the flames through the windows, up the stairway, and up the elevator shaft.

On the tenth floor they got them a moment later, but most of those on that floor escaped by rushing to the roof and then on to the roof of the New York University Building, with the assistance of 100 university students who had been dismissed from a tenth story classroom.

There were in the building, according to the estimates of Fire Chief Croker, about 600 girls and 100 men. The bodies of those killed and burned to death were found principally on the ninth floor, where over 50 perished in front of a closed doorway, which they had jammed shut; in the two elevator shafts 30 or more were piled up in the bottom after the elevator had ceased running; at the bottom of a single iron fire escape in an air shaft in the building's rear and on the fire-proof stairways between the eighth and ten stories, up which the fire from the burning sewing machines on the eighth floor went with a rush of air toward the roof.

When the Fire Was Discovered.

Samuel Bernstein, the waist factory's foreman, and Max Rothberg, his first assistant, were standing together on the eighth floor when the screams of girls attracted their attention to the southeast corner of the large room. They rang for the elevators, of which two were in the south side of the building, and Rothberg telephoned to the Fire Department and Police Departments. Two hundred girls were working on that floor, most of them still at their machines in the narrow aisles that gave them hardly room to move about. Dynamos, used to operate the sewing machines were in the corner from which the fire was spreading.

The two men attacked it with buckets of water, feeling confident at first they would be able to put it out. In the meantime the girls, screaming loudly and in a panic, rushed for the elevator shaft and the staircase, where they encountered a closed door.

Dora Miller of 10 Cannon Street got the door part way open, but it was jammed shut again by the press of people behind her. She struck a glass panel in it with her fists until she had made a hole large enough to climb through, and she escaped. Twenty others followed her before the flames reached them, and the rest of those caught on the floor were only discernable as a mass of charred bones when the firemen at last worked their way up the staircase.

Bernstein and Rothberg escaped by way of the elevator on its last trip to the floor.

Factory Owners Escape.

The two partners, Harris and Blanck, were both in the building, Harris being on the ninth floor and Blanck on the eighth. With Blanck, according to a statement of Joseph Zito, an elevator man, were his two daughters and a governess. He was telephoning for a taxicab to take them home when the alarm was sounded.

Blanck told Zito, the latter declares, to keep his elevator running and take out the women first.

The two passenger elevators, in charge of Zito and another operator named J. Gaspar, made several trips, but never went above the eighth floor, as they found more than enough people surrounding the entrance on that floor each time they reached it.

One of the men—which one was not made clear in the various versions of the affair offered—deserted his elevator and ran away, crying "Fire" as he ran.

Max Steinberg, a New York University law student, saw him running through Washington Place, and at the same time saw a girl leap from an eighth story window. He pulled a fire alarm box in Washington Square East and then ran to the building, where he entered the deserted elevator and ran it for four more trips before the heating of the cables put it out of commission.

Trapped on the Ninth Floor.

On the ninth story, which like the eighth was filled with sewing machines and was used for cutting and sewing shirtwaists, the girls fared worse than those on the floor below. They crowded about the elevator shaft, but no cars responded to their frantic ringing of the bell. Time after time they saw the cars approach, only to be filled at the eighth and go down again.

Girls who rushed to the staircase were met with flames which bore them down before they could retreat. Those who reached the windows and waited there for firemen saw the ladders swing in against the building two stories below them.

The one little iron fire escape, leading from a rear window, was pitiably inadequate, and it was from this floor that most of those came who fell like paper dolls, end over end, to the pavement.

There were about 20 men on the ninth floor. Calmer than the girls, they lined the southerly tier of windows first and tried to force the girls back to prevent them from jumping. Several girls they dragged back, after they had reached the window sills, and some they induced to lift themselves in again after they had climbed outside and were clinging only with their hands.

Zito, the elevator man, said that on his last trip down he could hear the thud of bodies striking the roof of his car as women jumped from the ninth floor after giving up hope that he would reach them. He heard the rattle of silver from their pay envelopes as it came through the iron grating into the car.

The loss on this floor was not known to the firemen and police until nearly 7 o'clock, when Deputy Fire Chief Binns reached it on the concrete stairway, which remained perfectly solid and unharmed. Binns found the bodies of fifty or more women, those who had not been burned beyond recognition seeming to be mere girls. They were lying in heaps upon the floor, as if they had huddled together near the stairway and the elevator shaft, and had been overtaken there by the flames. Money from the pay envelopes was strewn about close to them.

The tenth floor was the only one on which men were employed in any numbers. On this floor was the packing room, where the finished shirtwaists were prepared for shipment, and the showroom, where customers were made welcome.

Students Save Some Lives.

The men and women on this floor rushed for the roof. The smoke issuing from the windows was seen by Prof. F. Somner, who was teaching twenty-five young men the principles of the New Jersey Code on the tenth floor of the law school.

Prof. Somner ordered his students to rush to the roof and lower ladders to the roof of the factory building. The New York University building is one story higher than the waist factory building. One ladder was procured and a student named Kremmer descended on it to the roof of the building on fire. Another student, at the top of the ladder, grasped the women as they climbed toward the top, while Kremmer kept them from blocking the bottom rungs.

Men, panic-stricken, fought with the women to get to the ladder, but Kremmer shoved them away and let the women out of the danger zone first. Over 100 women and 20 men escaped this way. Another hundred reached a building north of the burning one, whose roof was only five feet higher and could be reached without a ladder.

How many reached the streets through the stairways nobody knew, as they were foreigners who spoke little English and fled for their homes in the lower east side as soon as they gained the sidewalk.

The task of the police and firemen outside the building was hardly started before the fire had caused its full damage in loss of life. The three burned stories, after it was all over and Fire Department searchlights played upon them, were seen to be wholly intact except for their wooden window trim and wooden floor coverings. Red tiling flashed the searchlight glow back to the street below from all the ceilings, and steel and concrete layers made the floors as firm to the tread of the firemen as if they had been newly built.

East Side of Building—40 Bodies on Sidewalk.

One Hour After This Picture Was Taken Two of the Victims Were Discovered to be Alive.

Police and Firemen Arrive.

The call to the police reached Headquarters over the telephone in a brief message that said girls were jumping from the Triangle Waist Company windows. The police were familiar with the place, as it had played a centre rôle in the opening phases of the shirtwaist strike.

Headquarters, from First Deputy Commissioner Driscoll and Chief Inspector Schmittberger to the last clerk and doorman, emptied itself, at Driscoll's orders, into the fire zone. Inspector Daly and twelve Captains reported to Schmittberger a few moments after he arrived.

Capt. Dominick Henry of the Mercer Street Station had preceded Driscoll and Schmittberger, and was attempting to establish fire lines when they arrived. Twenty-five patrol wagons from all the downtown precincts and 150 men came into the fire zone. They made one line on Washington Square East, forcing the people to the west side of the street, another line at Broadway, and cross-street lines at Waverly Place and on Fourth Street.

The second, third and fourth fire alarms were turned in before any apparatus had appeared, on the receipt of information at Fire Headquarters that there were twenty or more dead on the sidewalks. Chief Croker arrived in time to see his men spreading hopelessly their small and one or two large life nets, and saw many jump to their deaths.

Ambulances from Bellevue and New York and St. Vincent's Hospital—twenty or more in number—lined the street in Washington Square East and in Washington Place.

Ten surgeons from Bellevue, under Drs. Byrne, Read, and Kempf, threaded their way among the firemen gathering up the dead. They worked at this task from 6 o'clock until 7, and then policemen came to their assistance. The bodies found on Greene Street were taken to the east sidewalk, while those in Washington Place were laid in lines on both sidewalks.

Tarpaulins, laid over them, protected them somewhat from the deluge of water which, pouring from the high-pressure towers like a miniature niagara, flowed down the side of the building and into foot-deep flood along the pavement.

The surgeons could offer little aid except to cover over the bodies of the dead. Here and there from near-by stores reports came of injured, and a few ambulances drove away with these to the hospitals. Mostly all there was to do was to determine that life was extinct in the bodies on the pavement, and cover them over.

Deputy Police Commissioner Driscoll sent in an order at 6:30 o'clock for seventy-five coffins, and later another order for seventy-five more. It was not known to the firemen and policemen at first that the death roll would reach anything like its final proportions.

How Many Died.

A thirteen-year-old girl hung for three minutes by her finger tips to the sill of a tenth floor window. A tongue of flame licked at her fingers, and she dropped to death.

A girl threw her pocketbook, then her hat, then her furs from a tenth-floor window. A moment later her body came whirling after them to death.

At a ninth-floor window a man and a woman appeared. The man embraced the woman and kissed her. Then he hurled her to the street and jumped. Both were killed. Five girls smashed a pane of glass, dropped in a struggling tangle, and were crushed into a shapeless mass.

A girl on the eighth floor leaped for a fireman's ladder, which reached only to the sixth floor. She missed, struck the edge of a life net, and was picked up with her back broken. From one window a girl of about 13 years, a woman, a man, and two women with their arms about one another threw themselves to the ground in rapid succession. The little girl was whirled to the New York Hospital in an automobile. She screamed as the driver and a policeman lifted her into the hallway. A surgeon came out, took one look at her face and touched his hand to her wrist.

"She is dead," he said.

One girl jumped into a horse blanket held by firemen and policemen. The blanket ripped like cheesecloth, and her body was mangled almost beyond recognition.

Another dropped into a tarpaulin held by three men. Her weight tore it from their grasp and she struck the street, breaking almost every bone in her body.

Almost at the same moment a man somersaulted down upon the shoulder of a policeman holding the tarpaulin. He glanced off, struck the sidewalk, and was picked up dead.

Chief Croker thought at first it would not go over twenty-five. Then he placed the number at sixty-five—the total on the streets and reported from the inside. At 7 o'clock, over two hours after the firemen had come, the dead on the ninth floor were found, and those in the elevator shaft, each find sending the total up beyond the largest estimates previously made.

In getting out the bodies, the task proved so formidable that it was late in the night before it was reasonably complete.

Taking the Bodies Away.

Coroner's Physician O'Hanlon, with Coroners Holtzhauser and Lehaene, arrived at 6:45 o'clock along with District Attorney Whitman and several of his assistants. O'Hanlon explained that he had cared for the dead from the Slocum disaster on the recreation pier, and it would be better to handle these in the same manner, as the Morgue would prove hopeless to the task of accommodating them. He said he had still some of the tags such as were used in the Slocum disaster, and he proposed that each body be tagged exactly where it lay, and that records be made by number. He was told by Coroner Holtzhauser to proceed in this manner, and did so with the assistance of 100 or more policemen.

As fast as bodies had been looked over for identifications and tags fastened to them, coffins were brought from a supply depot established in East Washington Place. In these rude wooden boxes, coverless, the bodies were placed in patrol wagons and driven away.

At 7:45 o'clock the searchlights from four Fire Department engines were playing in the upper windows, and a glow came out of them from torches carried within by firemen. Suddenly a black shadow swung out of the ninth-story window, and the creaking of pulleys and a rope and tackle began, as the black mass descended speedily toward the ground. Firemen in windows on the lower floor guided the ropes. It was the beginning of the work of bringing out the bodies from the floor where the death roll was the largest.

The pulley system worked for an hour, each body being lowered after it had been wrapped in black cloth and tied securely until it resembled just such packages as go up and down daily in the business district, rope-and-pulley fashion.

Coroner's Statement.

The scene was more than Coroner Holtzhauser could stand. Sobbing like a child, the Coroner, who was first to open the fireplace where Ruth Wheeler's body was incinerated in the Wolter flat, said that that scene was easy to stand compared with this.

"And only one miserable little fire escape!" he said. "I shall proceed against the Building Department along with the others. They are as guilty as any. They haven't been insistent enough, and these poor girls who were carried up in the elevator to work in the morning—now they come down on the end of a rope."

That investigations from many centres would be started was early made apparent. Building Department officials, who arrived at 7:20 o'clock, said they would begin one this morning. Fire Marshal Beers said he would begin another. The District Attorney made a list of witnesses that he will question.

Chief Croker's View.

Fire Chief Croker, after the fire had flickered down to a few embers still glowing here and there, spoke vigorously against the men who have opposed his plans for better fire protection. "Look around everywhere," he said, "nowhere will you find fire escapes. They say they don't look sightly. I have tried to force their installation, and only last Friday a manufacturers' association met in Wall Street to oppose my plan and to oppose the sprinkler system, as well as the additional escapes."

"This is just the calamity I have been predicting," said Chief Croker. "There were no outside escapes on this building. I have been advocating and agitating that more fire escapes be put on factory buildings similar to this. The large loss of life is due to this neglect."

He said that there was only one fire escape from the building. An old-time perpendicular affair, he said, leading to the courtyard in the centre of the block of buildings, which would only allow of one person's escape at a time. When he examined this escape, he said, he found on the upper floors that it had become very loose, and it was a dangerous matter to escape by that route.

"A repetition of this disaster is likely to happen at any time in similar buildings," he said. He advocated balcony fire escapes with a wide iron staircase.

The staircases in the building, the Chief said, were of the ordinary three feet six inches wide type, but he believed that if escape had been sought by that route, the death list would not have been so appalling.

There were rumors that the fire started by a gasoline explosion, but the survivors said that they had heard no explosion.

Fire Commissioner R. Waldo being out of town yesterday, the fire was in charge of Deputy Commissioner Arthur J. O'Keefe, in charge of Brooklyn and Queens, who is taking the Commissioner's place

He and Coroner Holtzhauser had a dispute concerning the cause of the fire at 11:20 o'clock. Holtzhauser remarked that there was terrible responsibility for the Fire Department to meet.

"And for some other departments, too," O'Keefe replied. "Commissioner Waldo to my certain knowledge had reported this place to the Building Department within the past three months as a building unsafe for use as a factory, since there were insufficient means of egress by stairways, and there were not sufficient fire escape facilities.

"Oh, that makes a difference, then," Holtzhauser concluded.

Winfield R. Sheehan, Commissioner Waldo's secretary, joined the group at that juncture. He said that he personally had mailed the protest to the Building Department and knew of Commissioner Waldo's anxiety because of the unsafe condition of the building and his inability to force the making of changes.

Alfred Ludwig of the Department of Buildings was acting in the capacity of Superintendent during the absence of Supt. Rudolph P. Miller, who was out of town last night.

The building which was burned, it was said by one of the members of the department who stands near to the Commissioner but who refused to be quoted, was one of several thousand which had been recommended by the Fire Department for additional fire escapes.

"These recommendations," said the official, "were made several weeks ago after a thorough investigation by members of the Fire Department of all office, manufacturing, and loft buildings in the five boroughs. These investigations were made by the Fire Department at the request of Commissioner Waldo, although according to law this department had no control over the construction and means of escape on the many large factory buildings in the city.

"There was not one building in the city which escaped the eyes of the Fire Department, each place being investigated by the foreman of the engine company in the district in which it was situated.

"The investigation lasted weeks, and after a report had been made to the Commissioner it was forwarded to the Building or the Tenement House Department. Many of the recommendations which were made by the Commissioner were at once attended to, but this one seems to have been neglected."

Fire Chiefs and others connected with the department seemed to believe that the large loss of life could have been avoided had the operators not become panicstricken. The work of the elevator men was spoken of by members of the department with praise, who seem to think had they not kept their heads the total loss of life might have been doubled.

The building, Chief Croker said, was all that could be wished for in the way of fireproof construction. "But it isn't the building that's going to give us fireproof conditions," Croker said to the dripping firemen and others crowded around him. "The lesson of the fire is that a building is just as fireproof as the stuff within it—fireproof walls, fireproof floors, and fireproof stairways—then rooms packed with flimsy cloth and trimmings and run by electric dynamos about which waste and oil were allowed to accumulate."

The Edison Company strung lights between 8 and 9 o'clock through every floor in the building, to aid the firemen in their search for bodies.

The cloud of smoke from the fire was visible in all parts of Manhattan. It rose straight in the air above the roof, and then for a time between 5 and 6 o'clock tongues of flame illumined the darker mass above. The firemen could not reach it with their hose streams, and even the high pressure towers had difficulty in throwing their streams above the ninth floor. No water went over the roof until firemen made their way up the staircase after the fire fighting had become a matter of detail and small burning sections.

It leaped across an open areaway into the New York University Law School, destroying the Faculty room and damaging two classrooms. Students carried many valuable books to safety out of the library and helped with buckets to wet down woodwork that was beginning to smoke in the intense heat.

Nowhere in the building except on the three upper floors were people at work. The other concerns in the building had dismissed their forces at 3 o'clock, and only the shirtwaist makers were continuing at work. These were Meyer, Crown & Wallace, clothiers, on the sixth and seventh floors; Morris Blum, clothier, on the fifth and sixth floors; Harris Brothers, clothiers, on the third and fourth floors, and the Hatters' Exchange, and Martin Bates, Jr., on the first and second floors.

The superintendent of the building, who refused to give his name, or identify himself other than that he was employed by J. J. Asch of 725 Broadway, the owner, said there were two freight elevators in the rear on which the owners had partly depended to get the shirt waist makers out in case of fire. Whether anyone had tried to use them, or if anyone had come down on them he did not know.

The building was roped off at 10:30 o'clock, and the police lines withdrawn.

Continued on Page 3.

"All the News That's Fit to Print."

The New York Times.

THE WEATHER.
Fair to-day; probably fair to-morrow; moderate west winds.
For full weather report see Page 11.

VOL. LX...NO. 19,470. * * * NEW YORK, TUESDAY, MAY 16, 1911.—TWENTY-TWO PAGES. ONE CENT In Greater New York, Jersey City, and Newark. { Elsewhere, TWO CENTS.

DIAZ NOW READY TO QUIT AT ONCE

Is Believed to Have Informed Madero That He and Corral Are Prepared to Resign.

WANTS TO NAME 4 MINISTERS

While Madero's New Demands Include Resignation of Diaz and the Entire Cabinet.

FEDERALS ABANDON SONORA

Troops Concentrating in Mexico City—Hermosillo Evacuated—Rebels Get Another Border Town.

BY STEPHEN BONSAL.
Special Correspondent of The New York Times.

MEXICO CITY, May 15.—The statement from an insurgent leader to THE NEW YORK TIMES, republished here by The Diario del Hogar, a paper with a wide circulation and with an anti-Diaz policy, created a great sensation this afternoon.

It is apparent that the light seen by every one else has not escaped those at the Palace.

The principal demands of Gen. Madero were received this morning. The revolutionary leader states that they are greater than they were before the capture of Juarez, but only commensurate with the proportions of that victory. He demands the immediate resignation of Diaz: secondly, the issuance of orders for new elections; thirdly, the resignation of the whole Cabinet.

These demands are under consideration. While they have not been rejected and Madero's threat to march upon Mexico City if they are rejected is obviously exerting great weight, a counter-proposition has been made by the Federal Government here to Madero through Judge Carbajal.

If my information is correct, Gen. Diaz offers to resign immediately without any further delays, and promises the same for Vice President Corral, but he asks Madero to consent that four members of the present Cabinet, or rather four Ministers whom he may select, shall remain.

These are understood to include Señor de la Barra, Minister of Foreign Affairs, and Señor Vera Estanol, Minister of Education and the Interior. Further, Gen. Diaz sets great store upon Gen. Reyes being appointed Minister of War immediately upon his arrival in this country, possibly on May 21.

It is thought here in circles sympathetic with the revolution that, for the purpose of stopping bloodshed and reestablishing law and order at the earliest possible moment, Gen. Madero may accept the Diaz counter-proposition.

With the good news that the negotiations are progressing and bid fair to have success, the atmosphere of the capital has cleared wonderfully and the city wears a more cheerful aspect. Business, of course, is practically at a standstill, but the tension in the foreign colony, as well as among the Mexicans, is greatly relaxed.

An incipient riot in the Bolsa district last night was suppressed so quickly that we have no means of discovering its character, if it had any.

From outside the city, however, cumulative news continues to pour in of the peaceful advance of the revolution. Town after town has fallen, no resistance being offered, nor was law and order interrupted. Pachuca, only three hours away from the capital, was attacked this morning. Half the town seems to be in the possession of the revolutionists, and it is expected that the conquest will be completed to-night.

The railway from Puebla to Oaxaca, after many interruptions and robberies, committed apparently by unattached bandits to the detriment of passengers and freight patrons, has suspended operations, but the main railway communication with the southern part of the republic is uninterrupted.

The plight of Americans on the wing is deplorable. Many instances are heartrending. There are 600 at Vera Cruz awaiting transportation, and this does not include about forty distressed citizens who, I am informed, have applied at the consulate there for transportation, if possible, or relief in any event.

Fifty American families, members of the railroad colony, have left Aguas Calientes in the last forty-eight hours, leaving only four families there. The American Smelting and Refining Company there is advancing money to all its married American employes who are leaving for the United States by many routes, and thus the whole colony is deserted.

A similar exodus is taking place in other sections of the republic, of which, however, owing to the interrupted wires and difficulty of communication our information is very meagre. Americans on the Pacific side seem concentrating at Colima, from which place

Continued on Page 7.

THE FIRST AERO-TAXI.

Will Carry Passengers from Lucerne at a Fixed Rate a Kilometer.

Special Cable to THE NEW YORK TIMES.

PARIS, May 15.—According to the Temps, the first aero-taxi will be put into service in a few days at Lucerne.

The innovation is due to the enterprise of the Compagnie Trans-Aerienne, which has just sent to Lucerne a biplane fitted with a taximeter. The aeroplane will be piloted by the aviator Erbster, and will carry passengers on cross-country flights at so much per kilometer registered on the dail.

It is calculated that the aero-taxi will ultimately become a far cheaper conveyance than the streets taxicab, owing to the bee-line route it will be able to follow in the air, where, furthermore, trouble owing to congested traffic is non-existent.

SHACKLETON NOT A RIVAL.

Not Going to Crocker Land—Glad to Hear of American Expedition.

Special Cable to THE NEW YORK TIMES.

LONDON, May 15.—Sir Ernest Shackleton has no intention of leading an expedition to Crocker Land and cannot understand how his name came to be connected with such a report. When THE NEW YORK TIMES correspondent questioned him concerning it, he said:

"I cannot understand who originated the story. I expect some private conversation has been retailed for public consumption. I have discussed privately among people I know possible expeditions ranging from New Guinea and the Amazon to the Kara Sea.

"It is interesting to hear that the Museum of Natural History in New York is sending an expedition to Crocker Land, because it is certainly a tract that ought to be explored. I have no intention of butting in anywhere on any other expedition, and, anyhow, I am not going anywhere this year. I wish success to the Americans."

Sir Ernest thinks highly of the prospects of the American expedition.

FIREMEN OVERCOME RIOTERS.

Two Thousand Strikers, After Fierce Battle, Driven Back by Water.

Special to The New York Times.

GRAND RAPIDS, Mich., May 15.—A score of men and women were injured and many members of a mob of 2,000 striking furniture workers and sympathizers were hurt in a riot at the plant of the Widdicomb Furniture Company to-night. Several of the injured may die.

After a fierce battle with revolvers, clubs, stones, and missiles of almost every description, in which the police were badly beaten, a fire engine company attacked the mob with streams of water, and succeeded in quelling the disturbance to a certain extent. Many women were active among the rioters.

The trouble [illegible] when a mob of about 300 men, women, and boys attacked a closed automobile driven by Ralph Widdicomb of the furniture company, who was taking several strikebreakers from the factory. One of the policemen on guard at the plant attempted to make an arrest, and the mob closed in on him. Other policemen with drawn revolvers quickly arrived, but were overwhelmed.

A squad of reserves was rushed to the scene and soon began firing, and the fire was returned by the rioters. Several police officers were knocked senseless by missiles hurled by women.

Mayor Ellis made a fruitless attempt to quell the riot before the Fire Department was summoned. A terrific battle ensued as the firemen began to lay their lines. The mob was finally broken up and the strikebreakers were spirited away.

CORNER ERMINE MARKET.

St. Louis Firm Puts Up Prices for the Coronation.

Special to The New York Times.

ST. LOUIS, Mo., May 15.—Owing to the scarcity of ermine on the European market, St. Louis controls an important feature of the coronation festivities. A St. Louis concern, the F. C. Taylor Fur Company has been quietly cornering the catch of the trappers of Alaska and Canada and are now preparing to ship 100,000 of the little white skins to London. The value of this shipment is estimated at $175,000.

The Taylor Company has been working so quietly that even the agents for the Royal Furriers, who visited St. Louis several months ago, did not know that there was a supply here. The world was scoured by this agent and every one of the available furs bought up.

After the English agent left St. Louis the fur company began getting their skins out of storage, and when they counted up found that they had more than 200,000. Six weeks ago they shipped about 80,000 skins, and within the next week will have sent out about 100,000 more.

The furs are not being shipped directly to London, but they will eventually reach that place, probably by the first of June. The wholesale price of the skins has risen from about one dollar each to almost double that price.

MRS. DODGE SENTENCED.

Not Less Than Four Nor More Than Six Years in Vermont State Prison.

GUILDHALL, Vt., May 15.—A sentence of not less than four nor more than six years in the State prison at Windsor was imposed to-day upon Mrs. Florence L. Dodge, who was convicted on Saturday of manslaughter in shooting William Heath at her home at Lunenburg on Sept. 17.

Mrs. Dodge received the sentence without the slightest evidence of emotion. Her counsel stated that they would take no exceptions to the sentence. Mrs. Dodge will probably be taken to the State prison to-morrow.

When asked by the court if she had anything to say, Mrs. Dodge replied:

"I have nothing further to say than I have said all the time: 'I am innocent.'"

$250,000 FOR RIOT LOSS.

United States Express Company Sues Jersey City.

TRENTON, N. J., May 15.—In an effort to recover $250,000 damages as the result of rioting incident to the recent strike, Edward T. Platt, Treasurer of the United States Express Company, brought suit in the Supreme Court here to-day against the Mayor and Aldermen of Jersey City.

It is charged that the Mayor and police failed to suppress the mobs and rioting and the city is held to be responsible for the damage done to the company's property and for the interference with its business.

COUNTERFEIT PLANT TAKEN IN A RAID

Four Men and a Woman Captured on Charges of Making Bogus Indian-Head Bills.

ALL READY TO LEAVE TOWN

Band Said to Have Made Plans to Flood Alaska with the Bad Five-Dollar Bills.

Through the arrest yesterday of four men and a woman, the seizure of a lithographic stone, upon which had been engraved a fac simile of the Indian head five dollar bill, many engraving tools and printing apparatus, the Secret Service men believe they have ended a plot which had for its object the flooding of Alaska with counterfeit money.

For weeks the Government sleuths have been watching the band and they swooped down upon them yesterday when the experimental printing plant had been closed, the apparatus packed ready for shipment and those charged with being interested in the making of bad money had their tickets already purchased for Chicago.

The prisoners are James Glenard, his wife, and Marko Pagonich of 216 East Sixteenth Street; Samuel Pekovich of 216 Eleventh Avenue, and Miahailo Karahasvick, an engraver, of 433 East Sixth Street. With the exception of the Glenards, the prisoners are from Montenegro. Pagonich's card sets forth that he is President of the Alaska King River Mining Company of Douglas, Alaska. Glenard said he had been for fifteen years a member of the New Orleans police force. Three years ago, he said, he left there and went to San Francisco, where he and his wife ran a boarding house. The pair came to New York six months ago. Mrs. Glenard has two gold upper front teeth in each of which is set a diamond.

After weeks of shadowing, Richard H. Taylor, in charge of the local Secret Service, with John Henry and Frank Burke and others of the force, went to the Glenard house about noon yesterday. On the way they arrested Karakasvick. They told those in the Glenard flat that they were Government agents and demanded to know why the band had pawned so much jewelry lately. Nothing was said about counterfeiting and the three men and the woman readily consented to go to the Secret Service office in the Custom House. While this was going on other Secret Service agents went to 6 Paterson Street, Hoboken, and seized the plant. Those arrested were confronted with the evidence and each was questioned separately. After the examination they were locked up, some in the Old Slip and others in the Greenwich Street station.

The development of the plot has been carefully watched by the Secret Service men. Karakasvick, it is said, had been under suspicion before in connection with the counterfeiting of Austrian notes. In watching him the agents say they discovered the identity of the others.

The plot started six weeks ago, when some of those under arrest lived at 462 Eighth Avenue. Five weeks ago the Glenards moved to 216 East 16th Street and that became the headquarters. It took weeks of patient work to complete the lithograph stone. This was ready three weeks ago and those engaged in the plot rented and furnished a floor in the Hoboken house. They furnished it, bought a fine hand press, paper, ink and other necessaries. Two days ago the first proofs were run off on the press. Then everything was packed up preparatory to moving to Chicago. The proofs are now in the hands of Taylor and his men. The sleuths say the work is remarkably good. The stone was engraved to imitate the silk fibre as in a genuine bill.

While the preparatory work was in progress the funds of the band ran short, and it was then they had resorted to pawning their jewelry. Their returns would have been quick, for had they decided to print here, the agents say, they could have turned out at least sixteen bills an hour.

Glenard protests that he was forced into the plot by threats against himself and his wife. At first, he said, he believed that the other men were engaged in making stock certificates for the Alaska mine. He admits that toward the last he knew that bad money was to be made and when he wanted to back out threats were made against his life.

TO SELL "SPENDTHRIFT" FUND

There's a Chance That the Purchaser May Profit 1,000 Per Cent.

Special to The New York Times.

CAMBRIDGE, Mass., May 15.—Hammond Braman, college man, former banker and broker of this city, stands to lose the $50,000 "spendthrift trust fund" created for him by his father unless he bids it in or has it bid in to-morrow when it is put up at auction.

In the Boston papers to-day appeared an announcement that the auction would take place to-morrow by order of the Board of Trustees in Bankruptcy. Further particulars were to be obtained from Clarence W. Rowley, attorney at law. The advertisement was headed as follows:

> Win or lose a $50,000 fortune,
> Now tied up in a Spendthrift Trust.
> If the man dies without a child, you get the whole. If the man dies leaving a child, you get nothing. He hasn't any child now and we don't think he ever will have any.

Braman went into bankruptcy about three years ago. The Old Colony Trust Company is trustee of the Braman fund. If Hammond Braman dies without issue those who take a chance in the auction may realize 1,000 per cent. on their investment. Braman is the son of Grenville T. W. Braman, formerly a member of the firm of Braman & Dow.

PROF. WHEELER RESIGNS.

Instructor at Yale, Divorced for Cruelty, Leaves the College.

Special to The New York Times.

[illegible]HAVEN, Conn., May 15.—Prof. [illegible]ard Wheeler of the Sheffield Scientific School, Yale, forwarded by telegraph from Chicago his resignation to [illegible]ity corporation at its May [illegible]day, which was attended by [illegible] members except President Taft [illegible]dwin.

[illegible] given out by Secretary [illegible] the corporation to-night says [illegible]signation was received, and [illegible]cepted, in accordance with a [illegible] requires a professor's resignation [illegible] upon the table for one meeting.

[illegible]ment adds that "it will be [illegible] the next meeting, and, in [illegible], he will not exercise his [illegible] professor at the university. [illegible]er's classes were to-day [illegible] other instructors during [illegible] of the school year.

MRS. TAFT BETTER; NO ALARM FELT NOW

President Returns to Washington, Gets Reassuring Telegram, and Goes to Theatre.

WIFE LEAVES THURSDAY

Daughter Will Act in Her Place at White House Social Events for a Time.

Mrs. Taft, whose illness caused the President to return to New York Sunday night to see her at his brother's house, 36 West Forty-eighth Street, was so much improved yesterday morning that the President took an early train for Washington. In the evening, when he received a reassuring telegram, he went to the theatre. The telegram said that Mrs. Taft would return to Washington on Thursday afternoon.

Announcement was made at the White House that the programme which Mrs. Taft has mapped out for the Spring will be adhered to. The dinner to the Fur Seal Commissioners on Thursday night and the garden party Friday evening will be given. Miss Helen Taft, who is now with her mother, will act as mistress of the White House on both occasions.

Dr. Evan W. Evans, Henry W. Taft's family physician, called at the house yesterday morning to see the wife of the President, and remained about half an hour. Mrs. Taft was getting along so nicely that it was not thought necessary to issue a formal bulletin. She is rapidly recovering from her nervous attack.

The President had two callers before he left his brother's house yesterday morning. Henry L. Stimson, who is to join the President's Cabinet as Secretary of War, came to talk over matters connected with his appointment. Mr. Stimson was to have been sworn in as Secretary of War this week, but it was announced yesterday that he would not take the oath until next Monday.

The other caller was Postmaster General Hitchcock, who had been spending the week-end in New York. When he read of Mrs. Taft's illness he drove to the house to inquire about her.

The President, accompanied by Major Butt and Henry W. Taft, came out of the house at 9:40, and entered a waiting automobile. The presence of a squad of police and secret service men outside the door served to attract a small crowd, who cheered when the President came down the steps, smiling broadly as he raised his grey Fedora hat.

The President's automobile was preceded down Fifth Avenue by two bicycle policemen and followed by two automobiles containing detectives and secret service men. The President sat with his brother. At the Pennsylvania station he boarded the private car Ideal, which was attached to the 10:08 train.

PRIEST ARRESTS A BOY.

Crap Player Tried to Strike Father Brann, the Latter Declares.

Father Henry A. Brann of St. Agnes's Church, at 143 East Forty-third Street, was seated at a front window of the rectory yesterday afternoon when he noticed a group of boys playing dice on the sidewalk opposite. He quietly left the building, but five of the lads saw him and ran. Isadore Berkowitz, 15 years old, a telegraph messenger living at 1,571 First Avenue, however, endeavored to seize 8 cents they abandoned on the sidewalk and was caught by the priest.

Near Lexington Avenue and Fifty-first Street the boy attempted to strike the priest, but Father Brann managed to hold the youngster until the arrival of Patrolman McMahon.

The priest accompanied the prisoner and the patrolman to the East Fifty-first Street Station, where the boy was charged with juvenile delinquency and sent to the Children's Society. He denied that he had tried to strike the priest, but said his coat was pulled half off and he was endeavoring to get it upon his shoulders.

MUCKRAKING TO CEASE.

President Cannon of Fourth National Bank Tells a Western Audience So.

Special to The New York Times.

OMAHA, May 15.—There is to be an end of muck-raking and the magazines which have heretofore devoted so much space to articles of this character are to take up religion and "play up" theology as it has never been done before, according to James G. Cannon, President of the Fourth National Bank of New York, who to-day addressed the Omaha Ministerial Union on the subject of the "Forward Movement." Mr. Cannon said:

"If there is not the greatest ingathering in the churches it will be the fault of the men in charge, for we are going to have the subject of religion so 'played up' in the papers and magazines that the man who wants to promulgate religion will not have a single excuse for failing to get busy among his friends and neighbors.

"The magazine editors who have been muckraking all their lives are seeing that the thing must end, and that the only step toward progress consists in building man up."

WEAPON BILL PASSES.

Only Seven in Assembly Vote Against It and It Goes to Governor.

Special to The New York Times.

ALBANY, May 15.—By a vote of 123 to 7, the Assembly to-night pased the Sullivan dangerous weapon bill. The bill makes the sale or carrying of dangerous weapons without a permit a felony, and provides that dealers in such weapons must keep a register, in which the name of a purchaser must be recorded.

The bill has already passed the Senate, and now goes to the Governor.

STANDARD OIL COMPANY MUST DISSOLVE IN 6 MONTHS; ONLY UNREASONABLE RESTRAINT OF TRADE FORBIDDEN

And of Such Unreasonable Restraint the Supreme Court Finds the Standard Guilty.

DECISION PLEASES TAFT

Decision Reads "Unreasonable" Into Law and Is What Trusts Wanted, Says La Follette.

LOWER DECISION MODIFIED

More Time Given and Injunction Against Doing Business Meanwhile Is Removed.

JUSTICE HARLAN DISSENTS

Objects to Limiting the Sherman Law by the Use of the Term "Unreasonable."

WHAT STANDARD WILL DO

Chicago Counsel Says It Will Go On as Usual After Changes Are Made.

Special to The New York Times.

WASHINGTON, May 15.—Final decision was returned late this afternoon by the Supreme Court of the United States in one of the two great trust cases which have been before it for so long—that of the Standard Oil Company. The decree of the Circuit Court for the Eighth Circuit directing the dissolution of the Oil Trust was affirmed, with minor modifications in two particulars. So far as the judgment of the court is concerned the action was unanimous, but Justice Harlan dissented from the argument on which the judgment was based.

The two modifications of the decree of the Circuit Court are that the period for execution of the decree is extended from thirty days to six months, and the injunction against engaging in inter-State commerce on petroleum and its products pending the execution of the decree is vacated. This latter modification is made distinctly in consideration of the serious injury to the public which might result from the absolute cessation of that business for such a time.

Broadly speaking, the court determines against the Standard Oil Company on the ground that it is a combination in unreasonable restraint of inter-State commerce. For the first time since it has been construing the Sherman Anti-Trust act the court takes that position, and thus definitely reads the word "unreasonable" into the law. It was on this ground that Justice Harlan dissented. This decision, therefore, is a practical reversal of the position taken by the court in the trans-Missouri case, one of the first cases under the Sherman law.

In that case Justice White joined with the late Justice Brewer in a dissenting opinion, while Justice Harlan was with the majority of the court. That decision held, as Justice Harlan now holds regarding the Standard Oil Company, that the combination complained of was in restraint of inter-State commerce and therefore under the inhibition of the statute. Justices White and Brewer then held that the combination complained of was an "unreasonable" restraint of commerce, and so brought itself under the ban of the law.

Justice Harlan sharply criticised the majority of the court for taking this position. He declared it to be a menace to the institutions of the country. He said it was amending the Constitution by judicial interpretation, and was unjustified. And he asserted that one of the greatest dangers to the country was the willingness of the courts to take such action.

How Decision Was Received.

The decision was received with varying emotion by the crowd in the little court room. Attorney General Wickersham hailed it as a victory for the Administration. Frank B. Kellogg, the Assistant "Trust Buster," who has had the chief management of the case from the Government from its inception, was of similar opinion. Progressive Senators like La Follette openly expressed distrust of the effect of the decision, and Senator Kenyon, who only a few weeks ago left the Department of Justice to enter the upper house of Congress, spoke of it as a "dangerous decision."

While in the Department of Justice, Mr. Kenyon was in charge of the prosecution of the Beef Trust, the members of which will be indicted individually on the criminal count. The department hopes to bring these cases to trial in the near future.

Trust lawyers who were in court did not display any willingness to comment on the decision. But among the lawyers who heard the Chief Justice deliver his epitome of the opinion, which he did without referring to the printed text of the decision, and who were not connected with this case, the opinion prevailed that the decision was distinctly favorable to "big business." For a long time there has been open expression of the hope on the part of "big business" that when the decision in the oil and tobacco cases did finally come down, they would at least point a way under which the big corporations could continue to do business, and that the present general method would not be utterly d[illegible]

President Taft himself, in messages to Congress and in public speeches, has declared himself earnestly in favor of retaining the economy and efficiency of combinations and of destroying merely those practices which unduly restrained inter-State commerce and stifled competition. There was a time when the President was in favor of some amendment to the Sherman law in the effort to reach this situation. But he finally came to the conclusion that it was impracticable to write the word "unreasonable" into the law, and pointed out that more and more the Supreme Court was tending toward the point where its decisions in trust cases would be based on that construction of the statute.

Way Out for Corporations.

Now it seems to have been done, and the forceful personality of Chief Justice White has so impressed itself upon the court that he has carried seven of the other Justices with him. Representatives of "big business" who heard him this afternoon did not hesitate to declare emphatically that the decision was all that the big corporations could ask. They regarded with especial favor the establishment of the proposition that a combination must be in "unreasonable" restraint of commerce to be unlawful.

This they believe points out the way by which the big corporations in the country can continue to exist. They recalled with satisfaction the fact that President Taft has specifically declared that it is not mere size which puts a corporation or combination under the ban of the law; it is not the breadth or scope of its operations, or the amount of its capitalization, but whether or not it does two things; fixes prices and controls output.

The representatives of corporations here to-day find in Chief Justice White's decision a practical agreement with the position of President Taft. They have been satisfied with that position and have realized for a long time that business must conform to such standard. Now they find relief in the decision of the highest court in the country, and some of them expressed the opinion this evening that the effect on the general business situation would be good.

There is very little difference in the views of the progressives and those of big business men here as to the effect of the decision. But whereas the corporation representatives regard it with favor, the progressives find in it cause for distrust and dissatisfaction. This view was especialy emphasized by Senators La Follette and Kenyon.

La Follette Not Satisfied.

"In the light of what Justice Harlan in his dissenting opinion said of the Chief Justice's decision," said Senator La Follette, "I think that if it is true that the court holds that the law applies only to unreasonable restraint of trade it is a very dangerous decision. In that view of it I should say it is precisely what the trusts want, and they, more than any others, will be pleased with the decision. The court has amended the Sherman anti-trust law just as it was attempted over and over in the Senate to do it. What they did not get in the Senate they have now got from the court.

"If Justice Harlan interprets the decision correctly we shall have a plenty to do now with the law so amended. Every trust will now come into court and claim justification on a special set of facts going to support the claim that it is not restraining trade unreasonably, and it is to be expected that courts will make use of a sliding scale of reasonableness to apply to each case. I fear that the court has done just what the trusts have wanted it to do and what Congress has refused steadfastly to do."

Senator Kenyon of Iowa took a view similar to that of Senator La Follette. He said:

"I think the court has amended the anti-trust law, and it will lead to trouble. The courts will now be obliged to consider the reasonableness or unreasonableness of trust operations, and to-day's decision will prove to be only the beginning of a long and hard fight. It suggests that legislation will be demanded by the people to make good what has been taken from the law, but it is not easy to see just what legislation will fit the situation.

"I am inclined to feel that nothing short of jail sentences will accomplish any positive results. There has been discussion of the limitation of investments, with safeguards against stockholders being in more than one corporation, but all that is probably far in the future, and I do not care to talk about it. I do not hesitate to say, however, that there is danger in this decision."

On the other hand the decision was regarded by many as a great victory for the Government. Among these were Senator Cullom of Illinois, who sat through the greater part of the Chief Justice's delivery of the decision, and also through Justice Harlan's dissenting opinion. Senator Bailey of Texas manifested great pleasure in the decision. He went in and out of the court chamber several times in the afternoon, and after the adjournment of the court walked out through the Capitol and stood for several minutes talking with a group of Justices, including Chief Justice White, Justice Holmes, and Justice Van De Water.

"It is a correct interpretation of the law," said Senator Bailey, "and no corporation will be able under its operation to organize a trust or engage in business in violation of law. I think the Supreme Court has now made it impossible for a corporation to defy the law."

What Wickersham Says.

Attorney General Wickersham and Solicitor General Lehmann were surrounded as soon as the court adjourned by those who wanted to learn their views of the decision. Mr. Wickersham commented very briefly and then went to the Department of Justice, where he promptly withdrew into his private office and prepared a statement in which he formally expressed his view of the victory won by the Government. The statement says:

"The Attorney General stated, with respect to the decision in the Standard Oil case rendered by the Supreme Court to-day, that the court unanimously affirms the decree rendered by the Circuit Court in favor of the Government in every particular save that it gives the defendants six months instead of thirty days' time in which to comply with the decree.

"Substantially every position contended for by the Government in this case is affirmed by the Supreme Court. In the reasoning by which the Chief Justice reaches the conclusion in which the whole court concurs he expresses the view that only contracts, combinations, &c., which in any way unreasonably or unduly restrain inter-State trade and commerce or which are unreasonably restrictive of competitive conditions are within the prohibition of the first section of the Sherman act. Justice Harlan, on the other hand, dissents from this view and contends that every contract, &c., which does restrain trade and commerce is within the inhibition of the statute, but he concurs with the whole court in the decree of affirmance.

"The Chief Justice further holds that the second section of the act seeks, if possible, to make the prohibitions of the act all the more complete and perfect by embracing all attempts to reach the end prohibited by the first section that is, restraint of trade by any attempt to monopolize or monopolization thereof, even although the acts by which such results are attempted to be brought about, or are brought about, be not embraced within the general enumeration of the first section. He further hold that the criterion by which it is to be determined in all cases, whether a contract, combination, &c., is a restraint of trade within the meaning of the law, is the direct or indirect effect of the acts involved."

> **OPINIONS ON THE DECISION.**
>
> Attorney General Wickersham: "Substantially every proposition contended for by the Government is affirmed."
>
> Frank B. Kellogg, counsel for Government: "It is a complete victory for the Government."
>
> Senator Kenyon, formerly Assistant Attorney General: "I think the court has amended the anti-trust law, and it will lead to trouble."
>
> Senator La Follette: "I fear that the court has done what the trusts wanted it to do, and what Congress has steadily refused to do."
>
> Alfred D. Eddy, Standard Oil counsel in Chicago: "The business of the Standard Oil Company will go on as usual, although changes will be made."

Courtroom Crowded.

It has been a long time since there [illegible] scene in the Supreme [illegible] afternoon. [illegible] at all, and [illegible] con[illegible] attrac[illegible] the Capitol [illegible] many more [illegible] trust cases [illegible] in the restricted quarters of the great court.

Long before noon there was a long line of waiting men and women in the corridor before the door of the courtroom, a line that extended clear across the rotunda of the Capitol. And despite the oppressive atmosphere of the courtroom very few of those who managed to get in left and made room for others.

As the afternoon waned there were many significant nods about the room and gestures at the big clock over the head of the Chief Justice, showing how the audience took note of the fact that it had got beyond the hour of closing for the Stock Exchanges. Every Justice on the bench had at least one opinion to deliver, and they prosed along through them until it began to look as if there would be no trust case to-day.

At length it came the turn of the Chief Justice. The aged Justice Harlan had lingered a weary time over a number of railroad cases, and when Chief Justice White began to read, and it was seen that he was delivering not an opinion, but the orders of the court on certain motions, it began to look as if the trust cases would surely go over for another fortnight. Then the Chief Justice announced that he had the opinion and judgment of the court in a case, and there was a rustle of sudden expectancy. But instantly it appeared that it was not a trust case.

This decision dragged along to its close and the audience of Senators and Congressmen scattered about inside the rail, along with the Attorney General and the representatives of the Department of Justice, and the trust lawyers shuffled wearily, as if thinking that they had wasted a day for nothing. Then the Chief Justice plunged into the great decision. With an added note of solemnity in his manner he said:

"I have the opinion and judgment of the court in No. 358," and everbody in the room knew that the Standard Oil decision was coming.

Chief Justice Reads Decision.

The Chief Justice did not read the long opinion, but, speaking extemporaneously, delivered a synopsis of the decision. He spoke, as usual, rapidly and with great variation in volume of voice, so that at times his words were distinctly audible in every part of the room and at other times even the stenographers directly in front of him were unable to catch a syllable. Several times Justice McKenna, who sits at his left hand, leaned over and suggested that he raise his voice so that he could be heard. Once or twice on such suggestions the Chief Justice repeated what he had said, and then for a time would speak forcibly, so that all could hear.

Always with earnestness and conviction the Chief Justice spoke, often accompanying his words with a gesture. When he discussed the motive of the men who enacted the Sherman law his voice rang through the courtroom as he said:

"The writers of that law were legislating for freedom."

It was just one minute to 4 o'clock when the Chief Justice began speaking in the Standard Oil case. He was forty-nine minutes delivering his synopsis.

It was just twelve minutes of 5 o'clock when the Chief Justice concluded, and the audience gathered in the crowded courtroom breathed a sigh of relief at the final gratification of a nation-wide curiosity in regard to the fate of one of the most gigantic business organizations known in the world's history. The Chief Justice gathered up his papers, flung his silken

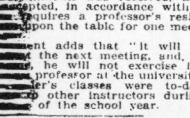

FULL TEXT OF THE SUPREME COURT DECISION IN THE STANDARD OIL CASE

robe up over one shoulder and then over the other, and sank back in his chair and closed his eyes to rest. The other Justices, who had been craning around in their seats to listen to him, moved restlessly in their chairs, and seemed relieved that the mighty decision was at last out.

Justice Harlan Critical.

The next moment Justice Harlan was heard to speak and it was known that he had a dissenting opinion to deliver. The venerable Justice, like the Chief Justice, spoke off hand and with frequent gestures and decided animation. He launched at once into sharp criticism of the decision delivered by the Chief Justice and several times alluded sarcastically to the Chief Justice's reference to the application of the "light of reason" to the case. He then cited the decision of the court in the Hopkins case in 1896, later in the Trans-Missouri Traffic Association case and the Western Traffic Association case.

"Fifteen years ago," he said, "this court laid down the law and construed the Sherman Anti-Trust law and three times since the passage of the act the court has gone on record in regard to it. And in two of the cases the present [illegible] Justice dissented from the decision of the court."

Justice Harlan went on to urge that if laws were to be amended, those who seek that result should go to Congress, and not to the courts.

"I declare," he said, with emphasis, "without hesitation that to-day the greatest danger to our free institutions is the disposition of courts to encroach on the domain of the legislative branch."

The elaborate exposition given by the Chief Justice of the appication of the common law to the broad fundamental principle that every man should have his equal chance in the business world, Justice Harlan said, had no proper place in the decision of the case.

"Governments are entitled," he said, "to be judged by their statute laws rather than by the common law in a matter that goes like this case vitally to the welfare of the Nation."

Referring to the stubbornly fought controversy over the questions involved in the trans-Missouri case, and the decision made in that case by the late Justice Peckham, to which Chief Justice White dissented, Justice Harlan named over the eminent counsel who appeared for the defendant in that noted cause—John G. Johnson of Philadelphia, E. J. Phelps of Vermont, ex-Senator George F. Edmunds, and others—and declared that the court knew that those great lawyers went into every nook and cranny of the law in that case and failed to establish to the satisfaction of the court that there should read into the anti-trust the limitation as to unreasonable and reasonable restraint of trade.

He then pointed out that the court was reversing itself and that it was not only doing that, but was taking in the Standard Oil case opposition ground to that laid down in the case of the United States against the Chicago, Burlington & Quincy Railroad decided to-day, in which the Federal law requiring carriers engaged in inter-State commerce to provide safety appliainces on their cars to protect the life and limb of employes, was upheld. The court in that case had held that the carrier must make sure that every inter-State car before starting out was provided with the appliances required by the mandatory language of the law. It was not sufficient that these were reasonably calculated to accomplish the result sought; they must accomplish that result absolutely if the carrier desired to continue in the operation of an inter-State business.

Objects to Such Construction.

Justice Harlan then went on to say:

"The decision to-day means practically that the courts may by mere judicial construction amend the Constitution of the United States and the statutory laws. The anti-trust law of 1890 was passed when this country was in a crisis arising out of the accumulation of capital in a few hands and out of combinations which had their hands upon the throat of this country. The question before Congress at that time was what shall we do?

"Many things in this opinion may alarm the country. Who are the men moving about in darkness? And who have the light of reason? There was no doubt in the mind of the men who enacted the law of 1890 as to the meaning of the language they employed. They sought a remedy for the conditions then existing and thought they had found it. It has long been the contention of those who have questioned the meaning of the statute that Congress did not intend to restrain reasonable trade agreements, but only unreasonable restraint of trade.

"We have heard a good deal about common law, and it is not new to hear it asserted that common law did not restrict reasonable combinations in the business world. But it has been the uniform rule laid down in this court and followed until to-day that the law of 1890 prohibited all contracts in restraint of trade, and made no exceptions. The reading of the law is plain. It says, 'Every contract is declared to be illegal—every contract combination in the form of trust or conspiracy, in restraint of trade or commerce among the several States or with foreign nations, is hereby declared to be illegal.' Congress is the body to amend the law, and not the court by a process of judicial legislation wholly unjustifiable.

"Now, for another time the same arguments are employed by great men who come to us asking us to decide the same question in direct opposition to the conclusions reached on the trans-Missouri case.

"There has been no session of Congress since 1896 that somebody in the interest of opposite views to what this court has said in its decisions to date, has not applied to Congress to get the law amended. It has not been amended. There is probably no man in the country to-day who believes it will be amended. These people do not give up as long as they can fight. Whenever the chance offers, they raise the question and seek a construction of the law of 1890.

Criticises Judicial Delay.

"The most alarming tendency of this age, in my judgment, so far as institutions are concerned, is the tendency of judicial delay. When men of vast interests are concerned and cannot get the law-making power to enact legislation they desire they bring up some case in an attempt to have the Constitution or the statutes construed to mean what they want them to mean. The courts are full of cases which involve attempts to have the laws reconstructed.

"We have announced our views of the act of 1890. They have been accepted and acted upon. And I suppose millions of property have changed hands under the decisions in 1890 and 1889. Prosecutions have been instituted and people have been sent to jail under these constructions of the law. Now the court in the opinion in this case says that this act of Congress applies to only those contracts in restraint of trade which are unreasonable. That is what the combinations said fifteen years ago."

In conclusion the venerable Justice said that he had sought simply to review the reasoning laid down by the Chief Justice as to express his mind in opposition to the step taken by the court. Later he said he should commit his remarks to writing, with the exposition of the fundamental cases in which the court had during the last fifteen years made its record on the anti-trust law.

It was twenty-five minutes past 5 when Justice Harland filed his opinion and gave way to the Chief Justice, who proceeded immediately to entertain motions for the admission of candidates to the Supreme Court bar.

The audience arose and began to make its way out into the cooler and purer air of the corridors and rotunda. Knots of lawyers gathered here and there discussing the decision and its effect on the future of trust litigation and upon the business of the country. All the afternoon messengers kept running from the courtroom to the telegraph offices, carrying dispatches to law offices and brokers' firms in all parts of the country.

Rule of Reason Laid Down for Trust Cases in Future

Supreme Court, in Decision, Holds That Congress Struck at Monopoly but Did Not Seek to Forbid Contracts Not Unduly Restrictive—Lower Court to Enforce Its Decree Against Standard Oil.

Special to The New York Times.

WASHINGTON, May 15.—The text of the decision of the Supreme Court to-day, in which the Standard Oil combination was declared to be a violation of the Sherman anti-trust law, is as follows:

The Standard Oil Company of New Jersey and thirty-three other corporations, John D. Rockefeller, William Rockefeller, and five other individual defendants, prosecute this appeal to reverse a decree of the court below. Such decree was entered upon a bill filed by the United States under authority of Section 4 of the act of July 2, 1890, known as the Anti-Trust act, and had for its object the enforcement of the provisions of that act.

The record is inordinately voluminous, consisting of twenty-three volumes of printed matter, aggregating about 12,000 pages, containing a vast amount of confusing and conflicting testimony, relating to innumerable, complex, and varied business transactions, extending over a period of nearly forty years. In an effort to pave the way to reach the subjects which we are called upon to consider we propose at the outset, following the order of the bill, to give the merest possible outline of its contents, to summarize the answer, to indicate the course of the trial, and point out briefly the decision below rendered.

The bill and exhibits, covering 170 pages of the printed record, was filed on Nov. 15, 1906. Corporations known as Standard Oil Company of New Jersey, Standard Oil Company of California, Standard Oil Company of Indiana, Standard Oil Company of Iowa, Standard Oil Company of Kansas, Standard Oil Company of Kentucky, Standard Oil Company of Nebraska, Standard Oil Company of New York, Standard Oil Company of Ohio, and sixty-two other corporations and partnerships, as also seven individuals, were named as defendants. The bill was divided into thirty numbered sections, and sought relief upon the theory that the various defendants were engaged in conspiring "to restrain the trade and commerce in petroleum—commonly called 'crude oil'—in refined oil, and in the other products of petroleum, among the several States and Territories of the United States and the District of Columbia and with foreign nations, and to monopolize the said commerce."

Charge of Original Conspiracy.

The conspiracy was alleged to have been formed in or about the year 1870 by three of the individual defendants, viz., John D. Rockefeller, William Rockefeller, and Henry M. Flagler. The detailed averments concerning the alleged conspiracy were arranged with reference to three periods, the first from 1870 to 1882, the second from 1882 to 1899, and the third from 1899 to the time of the filing of the bill.

The general charge concerning the period from 1870 to 1882 was as follows:

> That during said first period the said individual defendants, in connection with the Standard Oil Company of Ohio, purchased and obtained interests through stock ownership and otherwise in and entered into agreements with various persons, firms, corporations, and limited partnerships engaged in purchasing, shipping, refining, and selling petroleum and its products among the various States for the purpose of fixing the price of crude and refined oil and the products thereof, limiting the production thereof, and controlling the transportation therein, and thereby restraining trade and commerce among the several States and monopolizing the said commerce.

To establish this charge it was averred that John D. and William Rockefeller and several other named individuals, who, prior to 1870, composed three separate partnerships engaged in the business of refining crude oil and shiping its products in inter-State commerce, organized in the year 1870, a corporation known as the Standard Oil Company of Ohio, and transferred to that company the business of the said partnerships, the members thereof becoming, in proportion to their prior ownership, stockholders in the corporation.

It was asserted that the other individual defendants soon afterward became participants in the illegal combination and either transferred property to the corporation or to individuals to be held for the benefit of all parties in interest in proportion to their respective interests in the combination; that is in proportion to their stock ownership in the Standard Oil Company of Ohio. By the means thus stated it was charged that by the year 1872 the combination had acquired substantially all but three or four of the thirty-five or forty oil refineries located in Cleveland.

Extension of the Combination.

By reason of the power thus obtained and in further execution of the intent and purpose to restrain trade and to monopolize the commerce, inter-State as well as intra-State, in petroleum and its products, the bill alleged that the combination and its members obtained large preferential rates and rebates in many and devious ways over their competitors from various railroad companies, and that by means of the advantage thus obtained many, if not virtually all, competitors were forced either to become members of the combination or were driven out of business, and thus, it was alleged, during the period in question the following results were brought about:

> (a) That the combination—in addition to the refineries in Cleveland which it had acquired as previously stated and which it had either dismantled to limit production or continued to operate—also from time to time acquired a large number of refineries of crude petroleum, situated in New York, Pennsylvania, Ohio, and elsewhere. The properties thus acquired, like those previously obtained, although belonging to and being held for the benefit of the combination, were ostensibly divergently controlled, some of them being put in the name of the Standard Oil Company of Ohio, some in the name of corporations on limited partnerships affiliated therewith, or some being left in the name of the original owners who had become stockholders in the Standard Oil Company of Ohio and thus members of the alleged illegal combination.
>
> (b) That the combination had obtained control of the pipe lines available for transporting from oil fields to the refineries in Cleveland, Pittsburg, Titusville, Philadelphia, New York, and New Jersey.
>
> (c) That the combination during the period named had obtained a complete mastery over the oil industry, controlling 90 per cent. of the business of producing, shipping, refining, and selling petroleum and its products, and thus was able to fix the price of crude and refined petroleum and to restrain and monopolize all inter-State commerce in those products.

Interests Centred in Trustees.

The averments bearing upon the second period, 1882 to 1899, had relation to the claim:

> That during the said second period of conspiracy the defendants entered into a contract and trust agreement, by which various firms, corporations, limited partnerships, and individuals engaged in purchasing, transporting, refining, shipping, and selling oil and the products thereof among the various States turned over the management of their said business, corporations, and limited partnerships to nine Trustees, composed chiefly of certain individuals defendant herein, which said trust agreement was in restraint of trade and commerce and in violation of law, as hereinafter more particularly alleged.

The trust agreement thus referred to was set out in the bill. It was made in January, 1882. By its terms the stock of forty corporations, including the Standard Oil Company of Ohio, and a large quantity of various properties which had been previously acquired by the alleged combination and which was held in diverse forms, as we have previously indicated, for the benefit of the members of the combination, was vested in the Trustees and their successors, "to be held for all parties in interest jointly." In the body of the trust agreement was contained a list of the various individuals and corporations and limited partnerships whose stockholders and members or a portion thereof became parties to the agreement. This list is in the margin.

Concerns Taken Into Trust.

[List of corporations the stocks of which were wholly or partially held by the Trustees of Standard Oil trust.]

	Capital Stk. Standard Oil.	Trust Ownership.
NEW YORK STATE.		
Acme Oil Co., manufacturers of petroleum products	$300,000	Entire
Atlas Refining Co., manufacturers of petroleum products	200,000	Entire
American Wick Mfg. Co., manufacturers of lamp wicks	25,000	Entire
Bush & Denslow Mfg. Co., manufacturers of petroleum products	300,000	50 p. c.
Chesebrough Mfg. Co., manufacturers of petroleum products	500,000	2,661–5,000
Central Ref'g Co., (Limited,) manufacturers of petroleum products	200,000	1—67.2 p.c.
Devoe Mfg. Co., packers, manufacturers of petroleum	300,000	Entire
Empire Ref'g Co., (Limited,) manufacturers of petroleum products	100,000	80 p. c.
Oswego Mfg. Co., mfrs. of wood cases	100,000	Entire
Pratt Mfg. Co., mfrs. of petroleum products	500,000	Entire
Standard Oil Co. of New York, mfrs. of petroleum products	5,000,000	Entire
Stone and Fleming Mfg. Co., (Limited,) mfrs. of petroleum products	250,000	Entire
Thompson & Bedford Co., (Limited,) mfrs. of petroleum products	250,000	80 p. c.
Vacum Oil Co., mfrs. of petroleum products	25,000	75 p. c.
NEW JERSEY.		
Eagle Oil Co., mfrs. of petroleum products	350,000	Entire
McKirgan Oil Co., jobbers of petroleum products	75,000	Entire
Standard Oil Co. of New Jersey, mfrs. of petroleum products	3,000,000	Entire
PENNSYLVANIA.		
Acme Oil Co., mfrs. of petroleum products	300,000	Entire.
Atlantic Refining Co., mfrs. of petroleum products	400,000	Entire.
Galena Oil Works, (Limited,) mfrs. of petroleum products	150,000	86½ p. c.
Imperial Refining Co., (Limited,) mfrs. of petroleum products	300,000	Entire.
Producers' Consolidated Land and Petroleum Co., producers of crude oil	1,000,000	65-132 p. c.
National Transit Co., transporters of crude oil	25,455,200	9? p. c.
Standard Oil Co., mfrs. of petroleum products	400,000	Entire.
Signal Oil Works, (Limited,) mfrs. of petroleum products	100,000	38¾ p. c.
OHIO.		
Consolidated Tank Line Co., jobbers of petroleum products	1,000,000	57 p. c.
Inland Oil Co., jobbers of petroleum products	50,000	50 p. c.
Standard Oil Co., mfrs. of petroleum products	3,500,000	Entire
Solar Refining Co., mfrs. of petroleum products	500,000	Entire
KENTUCKY.		
Standard Oil Co., jobbers of petroleum products	600,000	Entire
MARYLAND.		
Baltimore United Oil Co., mfrs. of petroleum products	60,000	5,059—6,000
WEST VIRGINIA.		
Camden Consolidated Oil Co., mfrs. of petroleum products	200,000	51 p. c.
MINNESOTA.		
Standard Oil Co., jobbers of petroleum products	100,000	Entire
MISSOURI.		
Waters-Pierce Oil Co., jobbers of petroleum products	400,000	50 p. c.
MASSACHUSETTS.		
Beacon Oil Co., jobbers of petroleum products	100,000	Entire.
Maverick Oil Co., jobbers of petroleum products	100,000	Entire.
MAINE.		
Portland Kerosene Oil Co., jobbers of petroleum products	200,000	Entire.
IOWA.		
Standard Oil Co., jobbers of petroleum products	600,000	60 p. c.
Continental Oil Co., jobbers of petroleum products	300,000	62½ p. c.

The agreement made provision for the method of controlling and managing the property by the Trustees, for the formation of additional manufacturing, &c., corporations in various States, and the trust, unless terminated by a mode specified, was to continue "during the lives of the survivors and survivor of the Trustees named in the agreement, and for twenty-one years thereafter."

The agreement provided for the issue of Standard Oil trust crtificates, to represent the interests arising under the trust in the properties affected by the trust, which, of course, in view of the provisions of the agreement and the subject to which it related, caused the interest in the certificates to be coincident with and the exact representative of the interest in the combination, that is, in the Standard Oil Company of Ohio.

Soon afterward, it was alleged, the Trustees organized the Standard Oil Company of New Jersey and the Standard Oil Company of New York, the former having a capital stock of $3,000,000 and the latter a capital stock of $5,000,000, subsequently increased to $10,000,000 and $15,000,000, respectively. The bill alleged "that pursuant to said trust agreement the said Trustees caused to be transferred to themselves the stocks of all corporations and limited partnerships named in said trust agreement and caused various of the individuals and copartnerships, who owned apparently independent refineries and other properties employed in the business of refining [illegible] in and among said various States and Territories of the United States as aforesaid, to transfer their property situated in said several States to the respective Standard Oil Companies of said States of New York, New Jersey, Pennsylvania, and Ohio, and other corporations organized or acquired by said Trustees from time to time.

Concerns Controlled in 1888.

For the stocks and property so acquired the Trustees issued trust certificates. It was alleged that in 1888 the Trustees "unlawfully controlled the stock and ownership of various corporations and limited partnerships engaged in such purchase and transportation, refining, selling, and shipping of oil," as per a list which is excerpted in the margin.

> [The list given by the court is:
>
> 1. All the stockholders and members of the following corporations and limited partnerships, to wit: Acme Oil Company, New York; Acme Oil Company, Pennsylvania; Atlantic Refining Company of Philadelphia; Bush & Co., (Ltd.;) Camden Consolidated Oil Company, Elizabethport Acid Works, Imperial Refining Company, (Ltd.;) Charles Pratt & Co., Paine, Ablett & Co., Standard Oil Company, Ohio; Standard Oil Company, Pittsburg; Smith's Ferry Oil Transportation Company, Solar Oil Company, (Ltd.;) Stone & Fleming Manufacturing Co., (Ltd.,) also all the stockholders and members of such other corporations and limited partnerships as may hereafter join in this agreement at the request of the Trustees herein provided for.
>
> 2. The following individuals, to wit: W. C. Andrews, John D. Archbold, Lide K. Arter, J. A. Bostwick, Benjamin Brewster, D. Bushnell, Thomas C. Bushnell, J. N. Camden, Henry L. Davis, H. M. Flagler, Mrs. H. M. Flagler, John Huntington, H. A. Hutchinson, Charles F. G. Heye, A. B. Jennings, Charles Lockhart, A. M. McGregor, William H. Macy, William H. Macy, Jr., Estate of Josiah Macy, William H. Macy, Jr., executor; O. H. Payne, A. J. Pouch, John D. Rockefeller, William Rockefeller, Henry H. Rogers, W. P. Thompson, J. J. Vandegrift, William T. Wardell, W. G. Warden, Joseph L. Warden, Warden, Frew & Co., Louise G. Wheaton, H. M. Hanna, and George W. Chapin, D. M. Harkness, D. M. Harkness, trustee; S. V. Harkness, O. H. Payne, trustee; Charles Pratt, Horace A. Pratt, C. M. Pratt, Julia H. York, George H. Vilas, M. R. Keith, Trustee; George F. Chester. Also such individuals as may hereafter join in the agreement at the request of the Trustees herein provided for.
>
> 3. A portion of the stockholders and members of the folowing corporations and limited partnerships, to wit: American Lubricating Oil Company, Baltimore United Oil Company; Beacon Oil Company, Bush & Denslow Manufacturing Co., Central Refining Company of Pittsburg, Chesbrough Manufacturing Company, Chess Carley Company, Consolidated Tank Line Company, Inland Oil Company, Keystone Refining Company, Maverick Oil Company, National Transit Company, Portland Kerosene Oil Company, Producers Consolidated Land & Petroleum Company, Signal Oil Works, (Ltd.,) Thompson & Bedford Company, (Ltd.,) Devoe Manufacturing Company, Eclipse Lubricating Oil Company, (Ltd.,) Empire Refining Company, (Ltd.,) Franklin Pipe Company, (Ltd.,) Galena Oil Works, (Ltd.,) Galena Farm Oil Company, (Ltd.,) Germania Mining Company, Vacuum Oil Company, H. C. Vantine & Co., (Ltd.,) Waters Pierce Oil Company. Also stockholders and members, (not being all thereof) of other corporations and limited partnerships, who may hereafter join in this agreement at the request of the Trustees herein provided for.]

Fight Against Trusts in Ohio.

The bill charged that during the second period quo warranto proceedings were commenced against the Standard Oil Company of Ohio which resulted in the entry by the Supreme Court of Ohio, on March 2, 1892, of a decree adjudging the trust agreement to be void, not only because the Standard Oil Company of Ohio was a party to the same, but also because the agreement in and of intself was in restraint of trade and amounted to the creation of an unlawful monopoly.

It was alleged that shortly after this decision, seemingly for the purpose of complying therewith, voluntary proceedings were had apparently to dissolve the trust, but that these proceedings were a subterfuge and a sham because they simply amounted to a transfer of the stock held by the trust in 64 of the companies which it controlled to some of the remaining 20 companies—it having controlled before the decree 84 in all—thereby while seemingly in part giving up its dominion, yet in reality preserving the same by means of the control of the companies as to which it had retained complete authority. It was charged that especially was this the case as the stock in the companies selected for transfer was virtually owned by the nine Trustees or the members of their immediate families or associates.

The bill further alleged that in 1897 the Attorney General of Ohio instituted contempt proceedings in the quo warranto case based upon the claim that the trust had not been dissolved as required by the decree in that case. About the same time also proceedings in quo warranto were commenced to forfeit the charter of a pipe line known as the Buckeye Pipe Line Company, an Ohio corporation, whose stock, it was alleged, was owned by the members of the combination, on the ground of its connection with the trust that had been held to be illegal.

Resort to a Holding Concern.

The result of these proceedings, the bill charged, caused a resort to the alleged wrongful acts asserted to have been committed during the third period as follows:

> That during the third period of said conspiracy and in pursuance thereof the said individual defendants operated through the Standard Oil Company of New Jersey as a holding corporation, which corporation obtained and acquired the majority of the stocks of the various corporations engaged in purchasing, transporting, refining, shipping, and selling oil into and among the various States and Territories of the United States and the District of Columbia and with foreign nations, and thereby managed and controlled the same, in violation of the laws of the United States, as hereinafter more particularly alleged.

It was alleged that in or about the month of January, 1899, the individual defendants caused the charter of the Standard Oil Company of New Jersey to be amended, "so that the business and objects of said company were stated as follows, to wit":

> To do all kinds of mining, manufacturing, and trading business; transporting goods and merchandise by land or water in any manner; to buy, sell, lease, and improve land; build houses, structures, vessels, cars, wharves, docks, and piers; to lay and operate pipe lines; to erect lines for conducting electricity; to enter into and carry out contracts of every kind pertaining to its business; to acquire, use, sell, and grant licenses under patent rights; to purchase or otherwise acquire, hold, sell, assign, and transfer shares of capital stock and bonds or other evidences of indebtedness of corporations, and to exercise all the privileges of ownership, including voting upon the stock so held; to carry on its business and have offices and agencies therefore in all parts of the world, and to hold, purchase, mortgage, and convey real estate and personal property outside the State of New Jersey.

The capital stock of the company, which since March 19, 1892, had been $10,000,000, was increased to $110,000,000, and the individual defendants, as theretofore, continued to be a majority of the Board of Directors.

Without going into detail, it suffices to say that it was alleged in the bill that shortly after these proceedings the trust came to an end, the stock of the various corporations which had been controlled by it being transferred by its holders to the Standard Oil Company of New Jersey, which corporation issued therefor certificates of its common stock to the amount of $97,250,000. The bill contained allegations referring to the development of new oil fields—for example, in California, Southeastern Kansas, Northern Indian Territory, and Northern Oklahoma—and made reference to the building or otherwise acquiring by the combination of refineries and pipe lines and the new fields, for the purpose of restraining and monopolizing the inter-State trade in petroleum and its products.

Devices to Maintain a Monopoly.

Reiterating in substance the averments that both the Standard Oil Trust from 1882 to 1899 and the Standard Oil Company of New Jersey since 1899 had monopolized and restrained inter-State commerce in petroleum and its products, the bill at great length additionally set forth various means by which during the second and third periods, in addition to the effect occasioned by the combination of alleged previously independent concerns, the monopoly and restraint complained of was continued. Without attempting to follow the elaborate averments on these subjects, spread over fifty-seven pages of the printed record, it suffices to say that such averments may properly be grouped under the following heads:

Rebates.

Preferences and other discriminatory practices in favor of the combination by railroad companies.

Restraint and monopolization by control of pipe lines and unfair practices against competing pipe lines.

Contracts with competitors in restraint of trade.

Unfair methods of competition, such as local price cutting at the points where necessary to suppress competition.

Espionage of the business of the competitors.

The operation of bogus independent companies and payments of rebates on oil with the like intent.

The division of the United States into districts and the limiting the operations of the various subsidiary corporations as to such districts so that competition in the sale of petroleum products between such corporations had been entirely eliminated and destroyed.

And, finally, reference was made to what was alleged to be the "enormous and unreasonable profits" earned by the Standard Oil Trust and the Standard Oil Company as a result of the alleged monopoly; which presumably was averred as a means of reflexly inferring the scope and power acquired by the alleged combination.

Remedies Sought by Government.

Coming to the prayer of the bill, it suffices to say that in general terms the substantial relief asked was: first, that the combination in restraint of inter-State trade and commerce and which had monopolized the same, as alleged in the bill, be found to have existence, and that the parties thereto be perpetually enjoined from doing any further act to give effect to it; second, that the transfer of the stocks of the various corporations to the Standard Oil Company of New Jersey, as alleged in the bill, be held to be in violation of the first and second sections of the Anti-Trust act, and that the Standard Oil Company of New Jersey be enjoined and restrained from in any manner continuing to exert control over the subsidiary corporations by means of ownership of said stock or otherwise; third, that specific relief by injunction be awarded against further violation of the statute by any of the acts specifically complained of in the bill. There was also a prayer for general relief.

Of the numerous defendants named in the bill, the Waters-Pierce Oil Company was the only resident of the district in which the suit was commenced and the only defendant served with process therein. Contemporaneous with the filing of the bill the court made an order, under Section 5 of the Anti-Trust act, for the service of process upon all the other defendants, wherever they could be found. Thereafter the various defendants unsuccessfully moved to vacate the order for service on non-resident defendants or filed pleas to the jurisdiction. Joint exceptions were likewise unsuccessfully filed, on the ground of impertinence, to many of the averments of the bill of complaint, particularly those which related to acts alleged to have been done by the combination prior to the passage of the Anti-Trust act and prior to the year 1890.

Denial by the Defendants.

Certain of the defendants filed separate answers, and a joint answer was filed on behalf of the Standard Oil Company of New Jersey and numerous of the other defendants. The scope of the answers will be adequately indicated by quoting a summary on the subject made in the brief for the appellants:

> It is sufficient to say that, while admitting many of the alleged acquisitions of property, the formation of the so-called trust of 1882, its dissolution in 1892, and the acquisition by the Standard Oil Company of New Jersey of the stocks of the various corporations in 1899, they deny all the allegations respecting combinations or conspiracies to restrain or monopolize the oil trade; and particularly that the so-called trust of 1882, or the acquisition of the shares of the defendant companies by the Standard Oil Company of New Jersey in 1899, was a combination of independent or competing concerns or corporations. The averments of the petition respecting the means adopted to monopolize the oil trade are traversed either by a denial of the acts alleged or of their purpose, intent, or effect.

On June 24, 1907, the cause being at issue, a special examiner was appointed to take the evidence, and his report was filed March 22, 1909; it was heard on April 5 to 10, 1909, under the expediting act of Feb. 11, 1903, before a Circuit Court consisting of four Judges.

The court decided in favor of the United States. In the opinion delivered all the multitude of acts of wrongdoing charged in the bill were put aside, in so far as they were alleged to have been committed prior to the passage of the Anti-Trust act, "except as evidence of their (the defendants) purpose of their continuing conduct and of its effect." (173 Fed. Rep. 177.)

Lower Court Against the Trust.

By the decree which was entered it was adjudged that the combining of the stocks of various companies in the hands of the Standard Oil Company of New Jersey in 1899 constituted a combination in restraint of trade and also an attempt to monopolize and monopolization under Section 2 of the Anti-Trust act. The decree was against seven individual defendants, the Standard Oil Company of New Jersey, thirty-six domestic companies, and one foreign company, which the Standard Oil Company of New Jersey controls by stock ownership, these thirty-eight corporate defendants being held to be parties to the combination found to exist

Counsel for appellant says: "Of the thirty eight corporate defendants named in Section 2 of the decree and as to which the judgment of the court [illegible] four have not appealed, to [illegible] cana Refining Company, Manh[illegible] Company, Security Oil Compan[illegible] Pierce Oil Company, and one, [illegible] ard Oil Company of Iowa, has [illegible] dated and no longer exists."

The bill was dismissed as [illegible] corporate defendants, thirty-th[illegible] ber, it being adjudged by [illegible] of the decree that they "hav[illegible] proved to be engaged in t[illegible] on or carrying out of the comb[illegible] Of the dismissed defendants [illegible] were natural gas companies and t[illegible] companies which were liquidate[illegible] ased to exist before the filing of [illegible] tion. The other dismissed defend[illegible] en in number, were: Florence [illegible] ining Company, United Oil Com[illegible] water Oil Company, Tidewater [illegible] pany, (Limited,) Platt & Wash[illegible] efining Company, Franklin Pipe Company, and Pennsylvania Oil Company.

The Standard Oil Company of New Jersey was enjoined from voting the stocks or exerting any control over the said thirty-seven subsidiary companies and the subsidiary companies were enjoined from paying any dividends as to the Standard Company or permitting it to exercise any control over them by virtue of the stock ownership or power acquired by means of the combination; the individuals and corporations were also enjoined from entering into or carrying into effect any like combination which would evade the decree. Further, the individual defendants, the Standard Company, and the thirty-seven subsidiary corporations were enjoined from engaging or continuing in inter-State commerce in petroleum or its products during the continuance of the illegal combination.

Disposes of Two Minor Points.

At the outset a question of jurisdiction requires consideration, and we shall also, as a preliminary, dispose of another question, to the end that our attention may be completely concentrated upon the merits of controversy when we come to consider them.

> First—We are of the opinion that in consequence of the presence within the district of the Waters-Pierce Oil Company, the court, under the authority of Section 5 of the anti-trust act, rightly took jurisdiction over the cause and properly ordered notice to be served upon the non-resident defendants.
>
> Second—The overruling of the exceptions taken to so much of the bill as counted upon facts occurring prior to the passage of the anti-trust act—whatever may be the view as an original question of the duty to restrict the controversy to a much narrower area than that propounded by the bill—we think by no possibility in the present stage of the case can the action of the court be treated as prejudicial error justifying reversal. We say this because the court, as we shall do, gave no weight to the testimony adduced under the averments complained of except in so far as it tended to throw light upon the acts done after the passage of the anti-trust act and the results of which it was charged were being participated in and enjoyed by the alleged combination at the time of the filing of the bill.

We are thus brought face to face with the merits of the controversy.

Wide Scope of the Problem.

Both as to the law and as to facts the opposing contentions pressed in the argument are numerous, and in all their aspects are so irreconcilable that it is difficult to reduce them to some fundamental generalization, which by being disposed of would decide them all. For instance, as to the law. While both sides agree that the determination of the controversy rests upon the correct construction and application of the first and second sections of the anti-trust act, yet the views as to the meaning of the act are as wide apart as the poles, since there is no real point of agreement on any view of the act. And this also is the case as to the scope and effect of authorities relied upon, even although in some instances one and the same authority is asserted to be controlling.

So also is it as to the facts. Thus, on the one hand, with relentless pertinacity and minuteness of analysis, it is insisted that the facts establish that the assailed combination took its birth in a purpose to unlawfully acquire wealth by oppressing the public and destroying the just rights of others, and that its entire career exemplifies an inexorable carrying out of such wrongful intents, since it is asserted the pathway of the combination from the beginning to the filing of the bill is marked with constant proofs of wrong inflicted upon the public and is strewn with the wrecks resulting from crushing out, without regard to law, the individual rights of others.

Indeed so conclusive, it is urged, is the proof on these subjects that it is asserted that the existence of the principal corporate defendant—the Standard Oil Company of New Jersey—with the vast accumulation of property which it owns or controls, because of its infinite potency for harm and the dangerous example which its continued existence affords, is an open and enduring menace to all freedom of trade and is a byword and reproach to modern economic methods.

Powerful Plea of the Defense.

On the other hand, in a powerful analysis of the facts, it is insisted that they demonstrate that the origin and development of the vast business which the defendants control was but the result of lawful competitive methods, guided by economic genius of the highest order, sustained by courage, by a keen insight into commercial situations, resulting in the acquisition of great wealth, but at the same time serving to stimulate and increase production, to widely extend the distribution of the products of petroleum at a cost largely below that which would have otherwise prevailed, thus proving to be at one and the same time a benefaction to the general public as well as of enormous advantage to individuals.

It is not denied that in the enormous volume of the proof contained in the record in the period of almost a lifetime to which that proof is addressed, there may be found acts of wrongdoing, but the insistence is that they were rather the exception than the rule, and in most cases were either the result of too great individual zeal in the keen rivalries of business or of the methods and habits of dealing which, even if wrong, were commonly practised at the time.

And to discover and state the truth concering these contentions both arguments call for the analysis and weighing, as we have said at the outset, of a jungle of conflicting testimony covering a period of forty years, a duty difficult to rightly perform, and, even if satisfactorily accomplished, almost impossible to state with any reasonable regard to brevity.

Departure from Ordinary Decisions.

Duly appreciating the situation just stated, it is certain that only one point of concord between the parties is discernable, which is that the controversy in every aspect is controlled by a correct conception of the meaning of the first and second sections of the Anti-Trust act. We shall therefore, departing from what otherwise would be the natural order of analysis, make this one point of harmony the initial basis of our examination of the contentions, relying upon the conception that by doing so some harmonious resonance may result adequate to dominate and control the discord with which the case abounds.

That is to say, we shall first come to consider the meaning of the first and second sections of the Anti-Trust act by the text, and after discerning what by that process appears to be its true meaning, we shall proceed to consider the respective contentions of the parties concerning the act, the strength or weakness of those contentions, as well as the accuracy of the meaning of the act as deduced from the text in the light of the prior decisions of this court concerning it. When we have done this we shall then approach the facts. Following this course, we shall make our investigations under four separate headings:

> 1. The text of the first and second sections of the act originally considered and its meaning in the light of the common law and the law of this country at the time of its adoption.
>
> 2. The contentions of the parties concerning the act, and the scope and effect of the decisions of this court upon which they rely.
>
> 3. The application of the statute to facts, and,
>
> 4. The remedy, if any, to be afforded as the result of such application.

Meaning of the Sherman Act.

1. The text of the act and its meaning.

We quote the text of the first and second sections of the act, as follows:

> Section 1.—Every contract, combination in the form of trust or otherwise conspiracy in restraint of trade or commerce among the several States, or with foreign nations, is hereby declared to be illegal. Every person who shall make any such contract, or engage in any such combination or conspiracy, shall be deemed guilty of a misdemeanor, and, on conviction thereof, shall be punished by fine not exceeding $5,000, or by imprisonment not exceeding one year, or by both said punishments, in the discretion of the court.
>
> Section 2.—Every person who shall monopolize, or attempt to monopolize, or combine or conspire with any other person or persons to monopolize, any part of the trade or commerce among the several States, or with foreign nations shall be deemed guilty of a misdemeanor, and, on conviction thereof, shall be punished by fine not exceeding $5,000, or by imprisonment not exceding one year, or by both said punishments, in the discretion of the court.

The debates show that doubt as to whether there was a common law of the United States which governed the subject in the absence of legislation was among the influences leading to the passage of the act. They conclusively show, however, that the main cause which led to the legislation was the thought that it was required by the economic condition of the times, that is, the vast accumulation of wealth in the hands of corporations and individuals, the enormous development of corporate organization, the facility for combination which such organizations afforded, the fact that the facility was being used and that combinations known as trusts were being multiplied, and the widespread impression that their power had been and would be exerted to oppress individuals and injure the public generally. Although debates may not be used as a means for interpreting a statute (United States v. Trans-Missouri Freight Association, 166 U. S. 318, and cases cited) that rule in the nature of things is not violated by resorting to debates as a means of ascertaining the environment at the time of the enactment of a particular law, that is, the history of the period when it was adopted.

Monopolies and the English Law.

There can be no doubt that the sole subject with which the first section deals is restraint of trade as there in contemplated, and that the attempt to monopolize and monopolization is the subject with which the second section is concerned. It is certain that those terms, at least their rudimentary meaning, took their origin in the common law and were also familiar in the law of this country prior to and at the time of the adoption of the act in question.

We shall endeavor then, first to seek their meaning, not by indulging in an elaborate and learned analysis of the English law and of the law of this country, but by making a very brief reference to the elementary and indisputable conception of both the English and American law on the subject prior to the passage of the Anti-Trust act.

(a) It is certain that at a very remote period the words "contract in restraint of trade" in England came to refer to some voluntary restraint put by contract by an individual on his right to carry on his trade or calling. Originally all such contracts were considered to be illegal because it was deemed they were injurious to the public as well as to the individuals who made them. In the interest of the freedom of individuals to contract this contract doctrine was modified so that it was only when a restraint by contract was so general as to be coterminus with the kingdom that it was treated as void. That is to say, if the restraint was partial in its operation and was otherwise reasonable the contract was held to be valid.

(b) Monopolies were defined by Lord Coke as follows:

> A monopoly is an institution, or allowance by the King by his grant, commission, or otherwise to any person or persons, bodies politic or corporate for the sole buying, selling, making, working, or using of anything, whereby any person or persons, bodies politic or corporate, are sought to be restrained of any freedom or liberty that they had before, or hindered in their lawful trade. (3 Inst. 181.)

Hawkins thus defined them:

> A monopoly is an allowance by the King to a particular person or persons of the sole buying, selling, making, working, or using of anything whereby the subject in general is restrained from the freedom of manufacturing or trading which he had before. (Hawk. P. C. 1 c. 79.)

The frequent granting of monopolies and the struggle which led to a denial of the power to create them, that is to say, to the establishment of the doctrine that they were incompatible with the English Constitution, is known to all, and need not be reviewed. The evils which led to the public outcry against monopolies and to the final denial of the power to make them may be thus summarily stated:

1. The power which the monopoly gave to the one who enjoyed it to fix the price and thereby injure the public.

2. The power which it engendered of enabling a limitation on production, and.

3. The danger of deterioration in quality of the monopolized article which it was deemed was the inevitable resultant of the monopolistic control over its production and sale.

Law Against Power of Persons.

As monopoly as thus conceived embraced only a consequence arising from an exertion of sovereign power, no express restrictions or prohibitions obtained against the creation by an individual of a monopoly as such. But as it was considered, at least so far as the necessaries of life were concerned, that individuals by the abuse of their right to contract might be able to usurp the power arbitrarily to enhance prices, one of the wrongs arising from monopoly, it came to be that laws were passed relating to offenses such as forestalling, regrating, and engrossing by which prohibitions were placed upon the power of individuals to deal under such circumstances and conditions as, according to the conception of the times, created a presumption that the dealings were not simply the honest exertion of one's right to contract for his own benefit unaccompanied by a wrongful motive to injure others, but were the consequence of a contract or course of dealing of such a character as to give rise to the presumption of an intent to injure others through the means, for instance, of a monopolistic increase of prices. This is illustrated by the definition of engrossing found in the statute 5 and 6 Edward VI., Ch. 14, as follows:

> Whatsoever person or persons shall engross or get into his or their hands by buying, contracting, or promise-taking, other than by demise, grant, or lease of land, or tithe, any corn growing in the fields, or any other corn or grain, butter, cheese, fish, or other dead victual, whatsoever, within the realm of England, to the intent to sell the same again, shall be accepted, reputed, and taken an unlawful engrosser or engrossers.

As by the statutes providing against engrossing the quantity engrossed was not required to be the whole or approximate part of the whole of an article, it is clear that there was a wide difference between monopoly and engrossing, &c. But, as the principal wrong which it was deemed would result from monopoly, that is, an enhancement of the price, was the same wrong to which it was thought the prohibited engrossment would give rise, it came to pass that monopoly and engrossing were regarded as virtually one and the same thing. In other words, the prohibited act of engrossing, because of its inevitable accomplishment of one of the evils deemed to be engendered by monopoly, came to be referred to as being monopoly or constituting an attempt to monopolize. Thus Pollexfen in his argument in East India Company vs. Sandys Skin, 165, 169, said:

> By common law, he said that trade is free, and for that cited three inst. 81 F. B., 65; 1 Roll. 4, that the common law is as much against monopoly as engrossing; and that they differ only, that a "monopoly" is by patent from the King, the other is

Continued on Page 3.

"All the News That's Fit to Print."

The New York Times.

VOL. LXI...NO. 19,767 * * * NEW YORK, FRIDAY, MARCH 8, 1912.—TWENTY-TWO PAGES. ONE CENT In Greater New York, Jersey City, and Newark. } Elsewhere, TWO CENTS.

THE WEATHER.

Increasingly cloudy, rain to-night and on Saturday; colder Saturday night; wind variable.

For full weather report see Page 21.

MRS. W. W. JACOBS IS SENT TO PRISON

Wife of Novelist Sentenced to Month's Hard Labor for Smashing Windows in London.

"DUTY TO HER CHILDREN"

Her Defense and Husband's Plea Fail—More Suffragette Window-Breaking Yesterday.

By Marconi Transatlantic Wireless Telegraph to The New York Times.

LONDON, Friday, March 8.—Undeterred by the hard labor sentences passed by the Magistrates on suffragists earlier in the week, a number of women early yesterday morning waited in the West End for the taking down of the shutters in front of the shops, and as soon as the glass was exposed smashed the expensive windows of some big establishments. Among the windows destroyed were some of the largest in London. Half a dozen of the "militants" were arrested, and doubtless heavy sentences await them.

The latest prominent convict-recruit to the ranks of the militant suffragettes is Mrs. Eleanor Jacobs, wife of W. W. Jacobs, the novelist, who was sentenced to a month's imprisonment at hard labor by Magistrate Fordham at the West London Police Court yesterday for breaking four windows in the Earl's Court Road Post Office on Wednesday afternoon. When asked by the Magistrate what she had to say, she replied:

"I have done this because I think it is my duty as the mother of five children."

"Was it your duty as the mother of children to smash property?" asked the Magistrate.

"Yes, that is the only way we can protest against the action, or rather the inaction of the Government in refusing us justice," responded Mrs. Jacobs.

The Magistrate remarked that her statement was absurd and started to remand her for eight days to have a doctor report on her state of mind.

The defendant smilingly replied:

"My mind is quite sound. I have done my duty to my children for twelve years. I think my daughters, when they grow up, should have equal rights and responsibilities and duties with my sons."

Later in the afternoon Mr. Jacobs appeared before the Magistrate and pleaded for his wife, saying that she had taken this attitude because she conceived it her duty to her children that she should support the movement. He asked the Magistrate to consider that for a long time persons like his wife had been under the influence of two leaders of the movement, Mr. and Mrs. Pethick Lawrence.

He said he could not speak too highly of her as a wife and mother, and hoped the court would extend leniency to her and not inflict on her the hardships which very properly, no doubt, had been inflicted on many of these misguided women. His wife, he said, could not stand hardship, and if called upon to endure it her health would be permanently affected; she did not realize what she was doing.

He wished to say that if the Government had not played with the question, his wife and those other unhappy women would not have been brought into their present position.

The Magistrate, while expressing sympathy with the novelist, said there was no reason why he should deal more leniently with Mrs. Jacobs than with a vagabond who broke a window for a night's lodging, and passed sentence of one month's imprisonment at hard labor.

LONDON, Friday, March 8.—The extent to which the window-smashing raids of the suffragettes has aroused public feeling against them was evidenced by the large force of foot and mounted police necessary to protect them from a great mob, carrying an effigy of Miss Christabel Pankhurst, which gathered outside Oscar Hammerstein's London Opera House, where the militant section of the suffragists held a meeting last night. The speeches at the meeting were tame and there was a noticeable absence of all incitement to violence.

One woman speaker said that, if any woman desired to judge the panic the latest actions of the suffragettes had caused, let her go to the nearest store and try to borrow a hammer.

A large band of medical students created disorderly scenes outside the Opera House.

The excitement into which London has been thrown by the activity of the suffragettes is indicated by the instructions last night that ladies will not be admitted to Buckingham Palace for the Court tonight unless they present their invitation cards, and also by the announcement that both Houses of Parliament will be closed to the public to-day.

The public was practically asked yesterday to help the police catch the window smashers. The Commissioner of Police issued a circular calling attention to the fact that under the common law anybody is empowered to restrain persons attempting to do such damage and to hold them until a policeman arrives, and, similarly, persons detected after the damage is done.

WOULD SMASH IN PHILADELPHIA

Militant Suffragist Threatens Violence Like That in London.

Special to The New York Times.

PHILADELPHIA, March 7.—Miss Lida Stokes Adams, prominent in the National Women's Suffrage Association, declares that unless the women of Pennsylvania get the ballot the suffragette riots of London may be repeated in this city.

Miss Adams is a militant suffragist. She believes that the women of this country are seeking the ballot in too mild a manner and that if they would use a little muscle instead of voice for argument the cause would advance in a more rapid manner.

FOUR DEAD IN TRAIN WRECK.

Thirty Also Hurt in Wabash Crash—Six Coaches Off the Track.

Special to The New York Times.

LAFAYETTE, Ind., March 7.—The Continental Limited No. 1 of the Wabash Railroad, which left Lafayette an hour and a half late, was wrecked at Redwood Curve, a mile and a half west of West Lebanon, Ind., thirty-five miles from here, at 5 o'clock this afternoon, and as the accident tore down all wires, communication with the scene of the wreck was difficult.

Four persons were killed and thirty injured.

The dead are Mrs. U. G. Good, who boarded the train at Fort Wayne, Ind., en route to St. Louis, and died almost instantly, her back being broken; Mrs. Grant, en route from Adrian, Mich., to Kansas City; a Pullman porter, name unknown, and an unknown youth about 18 years old.

The seriously injured are Mrs. Paul Triesce, Danville, internally hurt; May Hudson, Sidney, Ill., cut and bruised; Fred Henschen, St. Louis, traveling auditor Wabash Railroad, hurt about head. Among those less seriously hurt are William P. Howell, Indianapolis; W. C. Thoms, Toledo; Sherman Sayres, Lafayette, Ind.; A. R. Kitsero, Peru, Ind.; Charles Rhodenburg, Dallas, Texas; E. F. Jennings, Buffalo, N. Y.; E. C. Kohl, Crawfordsville, Ind.; L. H. Robinson, Camden, N. J., and F. Barker, Elmira, N. Y.

The entire train of six coaches left the track, but the engine remained on the rails. A wreck train with physicians on board hurried to the scene.

A broken rail is believed to have caused the wreck. The coaches are piled in confusion on the side of a thirty-foot embankment. The tracks are all blocked, and other trains are detouring.

LONE WINDOW SMASHER HERE

Staten Island Girl Takes a Cue from the London Suffragettes.

Miss Annie Glisman, 22 years old, whose home is between Prince's Bay and Pleasant Plains, S. I., has been deeply interested in reading of the exploits of the London suffragettes, and last night she started out on a lone window-smashing crusade.

Miss Glisman first made her way to the home of Alderman Charles Cole, in Prince's Bay, and, after announcing her presence by breaking a window with a stone, rang the doorbell. The Alderman opened the door, and to him the young woman announced that she was a suffragette and had come to demand her rights. She did not explain what she deemed her rights, but declared that if the Alderman did not do something she would stone the house.

Mr. Cole tried to calm her and cautioned her against violence. Then he called his wife to the door to talk to the young woman while he went to the telephone to notify the police. While he was at the telephone the young woman went away, but she was soon heard from in the neighborhood. Stopping in front of several houses, she hurled stones through the windows.

Detectives responded to the call of Alderman Cole, but Miss Glisman eluded them for some time. Finally she was taken to the station, and from there was sent to the City Farm Colony in New Springville, where she will be examined as to her sanity.

OLD MAN-O'-WAR IN CHAIRS.

Daedalus, Sea-Fighter of a Century Ago, Done Into Furniture.

Timbers from the man-o-war Daedalus, which was an aristocrat of the British Navy a century ago when fighting ships were wearing oak armor belts, have been lying for the past month in the wood yard of F. Eckenroth & Son, 921 East Fifth Street.

They were brought over from England several weeks ago in the Mesaba, of the Atlantic Transportation Company's line to be worked up into household furniture for a residence which is being built at 46 East Seventeenth Street for Stephen C. Clark, a real estate dealer at 149 Broadway.

The timbers were square sawed stanchions of oak fourteen and sixteen inches in thickness, which had acted as supports to the main deck of the man-o'-war. It took several weeks to get them ready for the saw by drawing out the spikes and bolts with which every piece was found to be loaded.

The timbers, cut up, were taken yesterday to Sherwin & Co., wood workers, at 287 East 137th Street, where they will be finished into chairs, tables and trimmings for the dining room and library of Mr. Clark's house.

Mr. Clark said last night that seasoned oak had been ordered from England and that it was purely accidental that the wood purchased had been part of a dismantled warship.

JUMPS INTO NIAGARA RAPIDS.

Man on Freight Train Seeks Death in the Whirlpool.

Special to The New York Times.

BUFFALO, N. Y., March 7.—An unidentified man jumped from a Michigan Central freight train to death in the Niagara whirlpool rapids late this evening. The train was on its way from Canada, and it is believed by the Niagara Falls police that the suicide boarded the train at the Canadian end of the bridge.

When the train was about half way across the cantilever bridge and directly over the whirlpool one of the crew saw a man climb to the top of a car, jump over the low rail a few feet away, and disappear.

NEW OIL CAPITAL $30,000,000.

Standard Company of Indiana Arranging for Increase of Stock.

WHITING, Ind., March 7.—The stockholders of the Standard Oil Company of Indiana to-day voted to increase the capital stock of the Indiana corporation from $1,000,000 to $30,000,000.

After the increase has been referred to the Indiana State authorities and a certificate issued by the Secretary of State the Directors of the Standard Oil Company of Indiana will direct the distribution of the stock of the company in accordance with the reorganization plan approved by the United States Court.

HONORS FOR MRS. ROOSEVELT

Costa Rica Government Put Special Train at Her Disposal.

SAN JOSE, Costa Rica, March 7.—Mrs. Theodore Roosevelt and her daughter, Miss Ethel, arrived at Port Limon this morning.

The visit of the wife and daughter of the ex-President of the United States was a surprise to the Government, which took steps immediately to place a special train at their disposal to bring them to San José. Preparations are being made by a women's Reception Committee to entertain the visitors.

TREATIES, SHORN, PASS SENATE, 76 TO 3

Clause Invading Senate's Rights Is Eliminated and Other Restrictions Are Added.

ROOSEVELTIAN VOTES DECIDE

Four Such Senators Defeat Taft's Arbitration Aims—Existing Treaties Suffice, Say Opponents.

Special to The New York Times.

WASHINGTON, March 7.—The Senate brought the debate on the general arbitration treaties with Great Britain and France to an end to-day by unanimous consent, and then proceeded to take from the treaties nearly everything that marked their least advance on the fifteen treaties drafted in 1908 and 1909, when Senator Root was Secretary of State. The single point of advance left in the treaties provides for a Joint High Commission of Inquiry to investigate disputes and their arbitrability, but gives the commission no powers of award. As amended, the treaties were ratified by a vote of 76 to 3.

The turn of affairs adverse to the textual integrity of the treaties came as a surprise to the leaders of the Senate and the supporters of the Administration. It had been known that the ratification of the treaties by the Senate could be obtained only by means of some device like the Lodge resolution of ratification, which, while leaving the treaties unamended internally, so construed them as to deprive the Joint High Commission of its final powers of sending disputes to arbitration and reserved the Senate's full powers of advice and consent. But it had been hoped that the appearance of victory would be saved to the Administration by retaining unimpaired the language in which the treaties were submitted to the Senate.

The defeat of Mr. Taft's plans resulted from the defection of four Roosevelt Senators, who, with two other Republicans, joined the almost solid Democratic vote in insisting upon the elimination bodily from the treaties of the third clause of Article III., which made the decisions of the High Commission final as to the arbitrability of differences.

Col. Roosevelt has sharply assailed the treaties in editorials and speeches. In general, it can be said that the amendments seeking to weaken the treaties had the support of the Democrats, Roosevelt Republicans, and a few unclassified Republicans. But by a strange coincidence the only Senator who voted throughout for every proposal to weaken the treaties was William Lorimer of Illinois, who is Mr. Roosevelt's bitterest enemy in the Senate. At the last it was he who, with Mr. Reed of Missouri, and Mr. Martine of New Jersey—two radical Democrats—voted against ratification.

Bone of Contention Removed.

The test vote came as soon as debate ended. It was on the original amendment reported last Summer from the Committee on Foreign Relations eliminating Clause 3 of Article III., which has always been the bone of contention. The clause was stricken out by a vote of 42 to 40.

The vote for the amendment was made up of thirty-six Democrats and six Republicans. The vote against the amendment was made up of thirty-seven Republicans and three Democrats. The Republicans who voted to strike out the important clause were Mr. Borah of Idaho, Mr. Bourne of Oregon, Mr. Bristow of Kansas, and Mr. Dixon of Montana—all Roosevelt sympathizers—and Mr. Lorimer of Illinois and Mr. Smith of Michigan. The Democrats who voted for the retention of the clause were Mr. Rayner of Maryland, Mr. Thornton of Alabama, and John Sharp Williams of Mississippi.

Then Mr. Culberson of Texas offered an amendment to the body of the treaties exempting from its terms all questions of vital interest, independence, honor, or the interests of third parties. That amendment failed by a vote of 37 to 45, though subsequently the object of the amendment was accomplished in an amendment to the resolution of ratification. Mr. Bacon then unsuccessfully offered to the body of the treaties the amendment, subsequently adopted as part of the resolution of ratification, exempting from the operation of the treaty all questions of immigration, State bonds, Territorial integrity, the Monroe Doctrine, and all issues of American policy. As an amendment to the body of the treaty this motion was lost by a tie vote, 41 to 41.

The second change actually made in the text of the treaties was contained in an amendment offered by Mr. Chamberlain, a Democrat from Oregon. He excepted from the operation of the treaties all questions concerning the admission of aliens to the schools of the several States or their admission into the United States. This amendment, which, of course, has no bearing upon the present treaties, but looks merely to the possible negotiation of similar treaties with Japan and China, was adopted by a vote of 40 to 38.

The question of final ratification then came up, and Mr. Lodge, after explaining that the elimination of Clause 3 of Article III. made his carefully worded resolution of ratification unnecessary, withdrew it and offered instead a simple resolution declaring the treaty with Great Britain ratified. To that Mr. Bacon of Georgia offered his former amendment, and by the change in half a dozen votes it was adopted, 46 to 36. The amended resolution was then adopted, a two-thirds vote being necessary. All votes affecting the British treaty were then voted to apply to the French convention.

Treaties' Purpose Destroyed.

The language of the Bacon amendment shows how completely the significance of the new treaties has been destroyed. It reads:

> Resolved further, That the Senate advises and consents to the ratification of the said treaty with the understanding, to be made a part of such ratification, that the treaty does not authorize the submission to arbitration of any question which affects the admission of aliens into the United States, or the admission of aliens to the educational institutions of the several States, or the territorial integrity of the several States or of the United States, or concerning the question of the alleged indebtedness or moneyed obligation of any State of the United States, or any question which depends upon or involves the maintenance of the traditional attitude of the United States concerning American questions, commonly described as the Monroe Doctrine, or other purely Governmental policy.

The debate was significant from the fact that all the opponents of the pending treaties, declared their belief that the treaties already in force as negotiated by Mr. Root as Secretary of State were superior in phraseology and definiteness. Mr. Root himself made a striking address in behalf of the treaties, though, like Mr. Lodge, who also supported them, he favored the Lodge resolution of ratification on striking out the plenary powers of the Joint High Commission.

TRIES TO KILL GIRLS, BLOWS HIMSELF UP

Coachman George Mead Terribly Beats Young Women with Steel Molding, Then Ends His Life.

USED A STICK OF DYNAMITE

Fancied Injury by the Girls' Father, the Rev. Frank Hartfield, Cause of Tragedy Near Brewsters, N. Y.

Special to The New York Times.

BREWSTERS, N. Y., March 7.—In their home, Stonehenge Cottage, in Sodom, twelve miles from here, the Misses Ruby and Amy Hartfield, daughters of the Rev. Frank Hartfield, rector of the Episcopal Church here, and granddaughters of Mrs. Seth B. Howes, widow of a wealthy showman and owner of a large estate known as the Castle, about a mile and a half from this village, are recovering from the attack made on them yesterday by George Mead, their grandmother's coachman and the caretaker of her house, in her absence.

All that remains of Mead was taken to-day from the morgue to the little cottage near the Howes estate, to which he brought his bride less than six months ago. Mead, facing capture at the hands of employes of H. H. Vreeland, former head of the Metropolitan Street Railway Company, blew himself to pieces with a stick of dynamite. His young wife is prostrated.

Miss Ruby Hartfield is 20 years old, and her sister is 18. Mead was 32 years old, having entered the employ of Mr. Howes 16 years ago.

Apparently, Mead intended to kill both the girls and perhaps himself at the same time, to avenge a fancied wrong at the hands of their father. Mead is known to have believed it was by the rector's advice that Mrs. Howes, on leaving for the Winter, four months ago, refused to allow him the use of her automobiles, that he might learn to be a chauffeur, and also reduced his coachman's wages of $45 a month to $30 a month for acting as caretaker. No later than Tuesday Mead threatened to "get square" with the rector.

The attack on the girls was made at about 8 o'clock, when they reached The Castle, after a twelve-mile drive from home, bringing keys to the place, in response to a telephone message from Mead that the wind had blown loose a shutter and he must enter the house to repair this. The girls drove into the stable, from an upper window of which they had seen Mead peering as they ascended the driveway. The man was down the stairs almost before the girls were in the stable, and he bolted the door behind them.

Struck Girls Down.

Both girls were alarmed at his action, but alighted from their pony carriage. Ruby stepped toward Mead to hand him the keys, and he sprang at her, bringing up a steel moulding which he had held behind him, and striking her on the head. As the girl sank, he caught her and struck her again and again.

As Mead dragged Ruby into a washroom, Amy stood, too frightened to scream. Then she rushed toward Mead, crying:

"If you are going to kill her, kill me, too."

Mead dropped the elder sister and sprang at Amy. He struck her once on the head, and the girl fell to her knees. Evidently believing that he had stunned her, Mead jumped back to the other girl. Amy, however, staggered to the stable door, pushed it outward a few inches, and screamed.

Her cries were heard by Dennis Hogan, gardener on the Vreeland estate, who hurried to the stable. Amy faltered an explanation. On the floor of the washroom he found Ruby, her face covered with blood. Mead was not to be seen, but a door into the carriage house showed how he had escaped.

Hogan raised the girl, and carrying her started toward the Vreeland place with Amy clinging to his arm. They had nearly reached the road when they were prostrated by an explosion.

The report reached the ears of A. B. Yates in the Vreeland stable, and he hurried to the scene. With Hogan he got the girls to a safe place, and telephoned to Dr. F. Robert Ritchey, who came with Constable Arthur Brown and Deputy Sheriff H. S. Brown.

The officers found the front of the building almost blown to pieces. Every window was shattered and the south wall bulged outward. Within, the flooring was blown into splinters, but the pony and the cart stood unharmed in the wreckage. The post to which the pony had been tethered was torn from the floor. The two-inch oak partition, which separated the washroom from the main stable, was blown out.

Man Blown to Pieces.

In a corner of the washroom lay Mead's head, neck, part of his left shoulder, and his left arm. His body had been blown to pieces, and his legs and right arm were found in different corners of the room. Most of the damage was confined to the washroom. In the stable two horses, besides the pony, were unhurt, and both of Mrs. Howes's automobiles were not damaged.

On a shelf in the washroom the officers found two sticks of dynamite. One end of the shelf on which they rested was blown away, but the sticks had not exploded. It was with one like these, it is believed, that Mead killed himself. He had the dynamite there to blow up stumps on the place.

Mead's body was taken to the morgue here and afterward claimed by his young wife. Coroner Smith said he would hold an inquest as soon as the Misses Hartfield were well enough to appear before him as witnesses.

Seven stitches were taken in Amy's scalp and thirteen in patching up wounds on the head of Ruby. The girls are still confined to their bed.

PREDICT STOCKING FAMINE.

White Costumes Will Be Incomplete Unless the Retailers Hurry Up.

The increased demand for white dress fabrics for summer is regarded in the New York hosiery market as an infallible indication that white hosiery will be popular.

Many of the stocking mills are preparing to meet the expected demand, which it is believed will exceed that of last year. It is predicted that the failure of retail buyers to appreciate this will cause a shortage in the supply before the season is very far advanced. At the present time buyers are ordering sparingly, and it is said that the rush of orders later on will overwhelm the mills.

AMUNDSEN REACHES THE SOUTH POLE; STAYS FOUR DAYS, DEC. 14 TO 17, 1911; PARTY ALL WELL, HE TELLS THE TIMES

Norwegian Explorer Sends Word of His Success From Tasmania.

NO NEWS FROM CAPT. SCOTT

London Waits Anxiously for Word That He, Too, Has Attained the Goal.

AMUNDSEN'S FULL STORY

Will Be Published Exclusively in The New York Times, Probably To-morrow.

SHACKLETON GIVES PRAISE

Believes Norwegian Was Aided by Good Weather and His Special Equipment.

EXPLORERS MAY HAVE MET

Possible That Their Parties Came Together on the Routes Converging Toward the Goal.

WARNING.

For the protection of Capt. Amundsen, who has risked his life in the attainment of the south pole, and whose chief material reward must be the proceeds of the sale of his narrative, The New York Times, which has purchased the rights thereto for the United States, to be duly protected by copyright, gives notice that it will prosecute any infringement whatsoever of such copyright.

AMUNDSEN ANNOUNCES HIS DISCOVERY

Special Cable to The New York Times.

Christiania, Norway, March 7.

I have received the following message:

HOBART, Tasmania, Thursday, March 7, 1912—Pole attained, fourteenth—seventeenth December, 1911. All well. ROALD AMUNDSEN.

(Signed) LEON AMUNDSEN.

(Photograph, American Press Association.)

Roald Amundsen

He Discovered the Northwest Passage, and To-day His Triumphant Attainment of the South Pole Is Announced.

SHACKLETON ON THE FEAT.

Famous Antarctic Explorer Analyzes the Performance of Amundsen.

By SIR ERNEST SHACKLETON.

Specially Contributed to The New York Times and London Chronicle.

Special Cable to THE NEW YORK TIMES.

LONDON, March 7.—Analyzing the somewhat brief cable to hand, announcing Capt. Amundsen's attainment of the south pole, one, from previous experience, would assume that the journey was done with extreme rapidity and under very favorable conditions as regards the weather.

Capt. Amundsen has attained the geographical south pole, the long-sought-for spot, and that finishes record breaking as far as the ends of the earth are concerned.

Assuming that the latitude of Amundsen's Winter quarters was 74° 44', that is only 676 geographical miles from the south pole. This place was named Bay of Whales by me on my expedition, and was formerly known as Balloon Bight. If Amundsen did fifteen miles a day and reached the south pole on Dec. 14, he would have started south about the beginning of November, but it is much more likely that he did not travel at that rate, especially for the first hundred or two odd miles, so we may assume that he started for the pole about the beginning of October.

There is no indication in the cable whether Amundsen followed the route of my expedition in reaching the mountains that guard the approach to the pole. It may be possible that he found a new route and an easier one up to the plateau which lies about 9,000 to 11,000 feet above sea level. He may have had good weather.

Took Three Days to be Sure.

The words of the cablegram, "Pole attained, Dec. 14 to 17," evidently mean that on reaching the geographical pole, so that no uncertainty should exist as to his exact position, he waited three days, taking noon observations so as accurately to determine his position.

The advantage of taking three days of continuous observations at the pole are as follows:

Assuming that an explorer took a noon observation of the altitude of the sun and found that he was at the pole, a degree of uncertainty would still exist because of the slow movement of the sun, which completes the circle with hardly any perceptible rise or fall. If an observation is taken for the second day at the same spot, and the difference of declination of the sun in its north or south path corresponds with his observation of the day before, and it does this for the third day, he may safely assume that his position is accurate.

A flying snapshot is not as reliable as a continuous series of observations. If he were using a theodolite, undoubtedly the most accurate instrument, there is no doubt that he could ascertain the position of the pole to one mile.

If Capt. Amundsen left the pole on Dec. 17 he would very likely, with a fair wind behind him, return to Winter quarters in about forty-five days. We left our "furthest south," which was, roughly speaking, 100 miles north of the pole, on Jan. 9, and reached our Winter quarters on Feb. 28. They were 650 geographical miles from the pole, approximately the same length of journey that Amundsen would have covered from the pole to his Winter quarters, as they were ninety miles further south than ours.

We then assume that Capt. Amundsen reached Bay of Whales at the end of January. He would take two or three days loading up and getting under way with the Fram. He would then presumably go north and work to the westward of Cape Adare, and then get into the westerly winds and make Hobart, Tasmania. The Fram, being a slow vessel, doing about five knots, it would take quite a month, unless there were strong winds behind her, to reach Hobart.

Did Scott Reach the Pole?

The question naturally arises in one's mind, did Capt. Scott reach the pole before Dec. 14?

If so, the honor flies with the British flag, but the same endurance, the same skill, and the same meed of endeavor must be granted to Capt. Amundsen as the Norwegian people would grant to Capt.

Scott if the positions were reversed.

It would be quite possible that the two expeditions, having reached Beardmore Glacier, would be in touch with each other, or would come across depots which would indicate the advance or return of either party, and if Scott had left a party at the foot of the glacier they would naturally be acquainted with Amundsen's movements, as Amundsen's men would be had Amundsen left a party or depot in the same position.

There may have been a more dramatic situation still. The two parties, crossing the glacier and converging toward the coveted spot from different directions, may have met at the pole itself.

Amundsen Well Equipped.

Capt. Amundsen's equipment, though not so large as Capt. Scott's, has peculiar advantages when you consider the nationality of the expedition. The Norwegians who accompanied Amundsen are accustomed to driving dogs, and are born ski runners. The broad stretches on the plateau and the level stretches on the barrier surface, would be excellent for skiing. The dogs will keep up the rapid pace which ski runners are able to adopt, and this is naturally faster than the slow-plodding foot movements of ponies.

Capt. Amundsen had 112 dogs at the start, all first-class and well broken in, and their numbers may have been supplemented by births during the long polar nights, so that his team may have been considerably increased before he started on his dash to the pole.

Capt. Scott's party, on the Terra Nova, who found Amundsen at Bay of Whales, described the dogs as being wonderfully trained, stopping or going on at the sound of a whistle.

No matter which party reached the pole first, both will have done much to unveil the mystery of the south and increase the interest and desire for further work in this great, unknown continent.

ERNEST SHACKLETON.

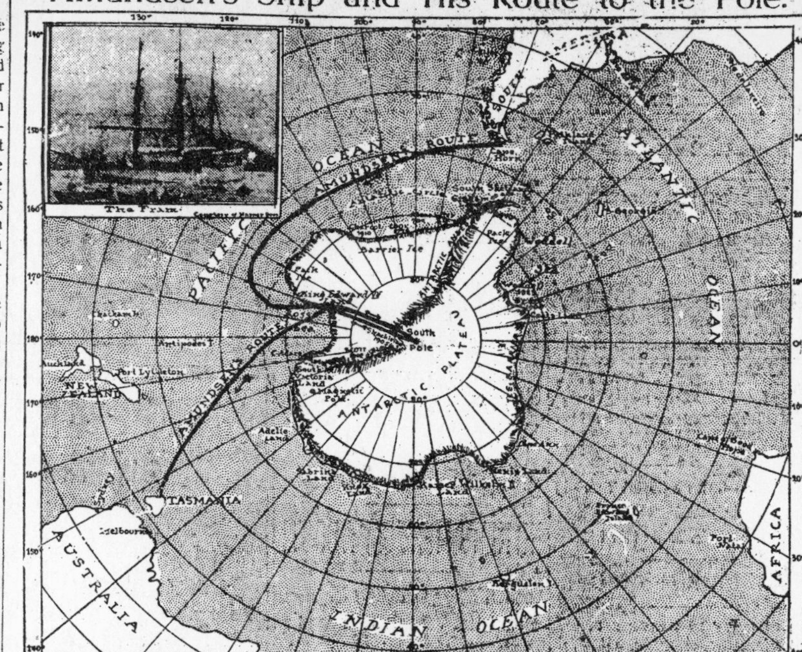

Amundsen's Ship and His Route to the Pole.

LONDON'S ONLY REPORT.

Printed by The Chronicle, Which Shares It with The New York Times.

Special Cable to THE NEW YORK TIMES.
Copyright, 1912, by The New York Times Co.

LONDON, Friday, March 8.—The Daily Chronicle this morning says:

"After nearly 140 years of heroic endeavor, the south pole has been discovered. The news of the brilliant achievement was received in The Chronicle office at a late hour last night. The details of Capt. Amundsen's feat and the difficulties he had to surmount are not yet to hand, but The Chronicle has secured Capt. Amundsen's story, and it will appear exclusively in London in these columns. Capt. Amundsen will cable direct from Hobart, and his narrative will be commenced in The Chronicle to-morrow."

The Chronicle copyrights Capt. Amundsen's first brief dispatch, and prints conspicuously the following notice:

"The newspaper and magazine copyrights for the entire world in the above cable and further cables in which Capt. Amundsen will describe his historic achievement have been acquired by The Daily Chronicle. Copyright for the United States is vested in THE NEW YORK TIMES, and for France in Le Matin by arrangement with The Daily Chronicle. The Liverpool Daily Post and The Yorkshire Post have the exclusive use of Capt. Amundsen's narrative for the British provinces."

The Chronicle says editorially: "Our first thoughts (though we may have wished that Commander Peary's hope had come true that 'the world should whirl between the ensigns of the same Anglo-Saxon race') will compel Britons, who have striven so heroically for the prize that has been won, to congratulate heartily that great explorer and his nation, to whom the honor of the discovery of the south pole has so deservedly fallen."

The Chronicle adds: "England will wait most anxiously for news of the Scott expedition. Though robbed of its crowning glory, geography and science will undoubtedly profit from it. Capt. Amundsen's expedition, which has now ended successfully, was originally planned for the conquest of the north pole, but hearing the news which Peary brought back, Amundsen showed his resource and promptness of decision by at once steaming south to the region which still offered a similar prize. He has won that prize. To England the glory of discovering neither the north nor the south pole has fallen, but in the story of the exploration of the great ice continents, his country played a splendid part, and we can join heartily with the whole world to-day in offering to the conqueror and to Norway a meed praise which is so well deserved. The prize has been finely won. It has also been grandly lost."

THOUGHT SCOTT HAD WON

But Mrs. Scott Wouldn't Accept What Proved to be False News.

Special Cable to THE NEW YORK TIMES.
Copyright, 1912, by The New York Times Co.

LONDON, Friday, March 8.—London was in a fever of excitement all day yesterday and during the evening over the result of the race to the south pole. An early report from Wellington, New Zealand, had credited Capt. Roald Amundsen with the statement that his English rival, Capt. Robert F. Scott, had reached the pole. At that hour no news direct from Capt. Amundsen had been received by THE NEW YORK TIMES, which has obtained exclusive American and Canadian rights for the Norwegian explorer's first dispatches and the narrative of his expedition, or by the King of Norway, to whom Capt. Amundsen naturally wished to send an early report of the result of his dash to the pole. THE NEW YORK TIMES office in Pall Mall was besieged by inquiries, and the general interest displayed completely dwarfed that in the coal strike and the suffragettes.

Throughout the evening the question of whether Scott or Amundsen had reached the pole continued the absorbing topic. The last editions of the evening papers added nothing definite to the stock of available information.

At 7 P. M. THE NEW YORK TIMES's London office and The London Daily Chronicle received a cipher message from Leon Amundsen, the explorer's brother, in Christiania, which intimated that the Norwegian had been heard from and that the message was on its way to London. This dispatch was worded in such a way as to suggest the inference that Capt. Amundsen was returning victorious, but even yet the secret as to the exact measure of success he had attained was not disclosed.

Shortly afterward an agency dispatch from Christiania stated that a cipher message had been received there from a private individual aboard the Fram to the effect that Amundsen had reached the south pole, but right on top of this came another agency message from the Norwegian capital, declaring that a message had been received by a private person there from Capt. Amundsen himself, in which he stated that Capt. Scott had reached the pole.

So one report followed another, and the speculation grew keener. One contribution to the ever-growing budget of "information" was a New York dispatch, saying that special correspondents of the American papers in Auckland and Wellington, New Zealand, reported that they had succeeded in communicating with Amundsen and that he announced that Capt. Scott had reached the south pole.

The News by Cipher.

Eventually, some little time before midnight, after an exchange of cipher messages between Christiania and London, THE NEW YORK TIMES on the American Continent and The Chronicle in Europe were in possession of the actual news of the results of Capt. Amundsen's dash into the antarctic zone. I have already cabled you the text of the cipher message received from Leon Amundsen, Roald's brother. The cipher isn't one that would puzzle an expert, but as far as can be judged from what is known here, it served its purpose in preserving the secrecy of the contents of the message. It was the simple method of reading the letters of the alphabet backward, Z in the cipher representing A in plain language and Y standing for B. Translated in plain language the cipher dispatch read:

Christiania, Norway, March 7.

The following telegram received:

HOBART, Tasmania, March 7.—Pole attained, fourteenth-seventeenth, December, 1911. All well. ROALD AMUNDSEN.

(Signed) LEON AMUNDSEN.

The signature, Leon, was that of Roald's brother. There was one error in the cipher, Amundsen's name, as transmitted in the cipher, spelling out as Amundrsen.

Mrs. Scott Hesitated to Believe.

All the evening papers had displayed flaring posters, accepting the report of Capt. Scott's success as correct. One of them printed an interview with Mrs. Scott, who said that no news had reached her which confirmed the report.

"How," she asked, "could Capt. Amundsen know of it, even assuming it to be correct?"

"Wasn't it true that Amundsen was said to have got the start on Capt. Scott, and taken him by surprise in some way?" Mrs. Scott was asked.

"Yes, that is true."

"Then, is it not possible that he finds that after all he has not left Capt. Scott in the rear so successfully as he thought?"

"Does Amundsen say he reached the pole himself?" Mrs. Scott asked.

"No, the message simply is 'Scott reached pole,' which suggests that he found himself supplanted."

"But, I do not see how he could know that unless he had been there himself," Mrs. Scott declared.

"Could he have met Scott's expedition returning?"

"I cannot see how that could be, because Capt. Scott would return the way he went, and that would not bring him face to face with the Amundsen expedition."

"I do not think," Mrs. Scott went on, "that Capt. Amundsen can possibly know anything about it, and even if he did he had no right to disclose the news before Capt. Scott made it known."

"Should it be true, Mrs. Scott, what would be your feelings?"

"Well, feelings of joy and intense relief, of course, but I don't say I feel either, because I have no information to justify it."

"I think, too," she went on, "you should publish the statement of Capt. Amundsen with great reserve. If it is not true, it will injure Capt. Scott and bring discredit on the country. Other nationalities are striving to find the South Pole, and if you say that Capt. Scott has succeeded, and it later on turns out to be not true, there is probably no end to what jealousy will prompt them to say. I hope it is true, but at present I dare not believe it."

In conversation with THE NEW YORK TIMES correspondent later, Mrs. Scott reiterated the doubts she had expressed in the earlier interview, adding:

"I would take my oath my husband would not have intrusted the news to anybody."

Geographers Skeptical.

At the Royal Geographical Society, skepticism was the prevailing note. It was pointed out that one reason for distrusting the accuracy of the Wellington report and the statement attributed to Amundsen was that the Norwegian was at Hobart and not at Wellington.

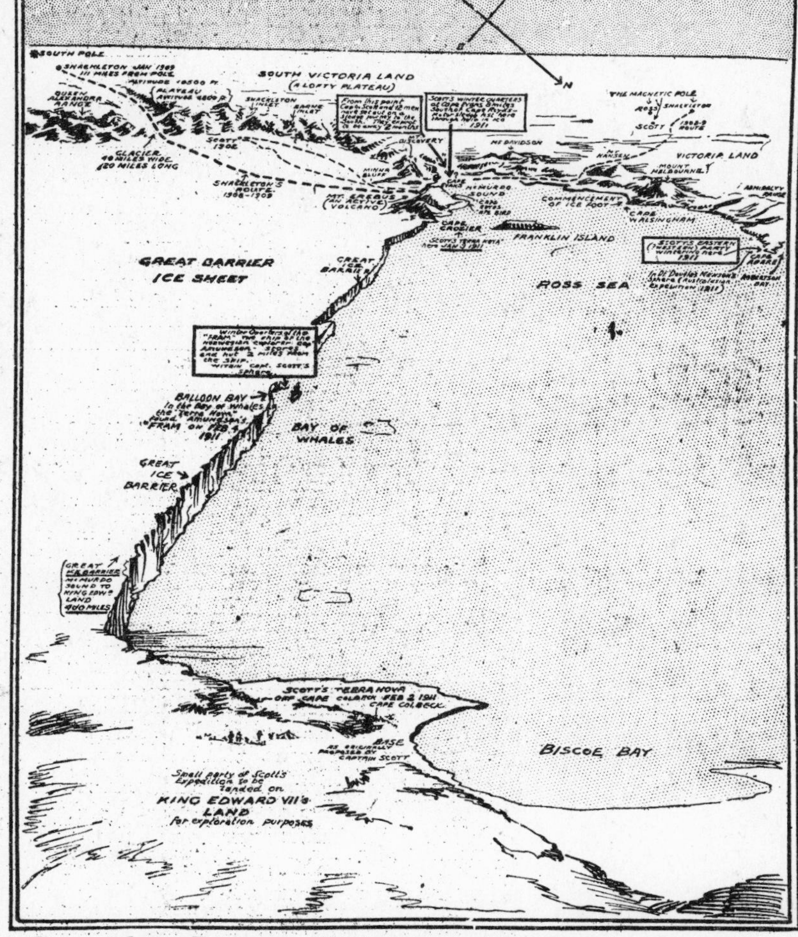

Great Ice Barrier Guarding the Southern Pole.

Dr. Scott Keltie, Secretary of the Royal Geographical Society, said:

"I can't think of Capt. Amundsen as making such a statement even if it is true. Personally, I don't think the report is true.

"There is just the possibility that Amundsen may have reached the pole himself, only to find that Capt. Scott got there ahead of him and left some record of his feat behind, and that Amundsen, feeling somewhat conscience-stricken at the rather rough deal he gave Capt. Scott over the matter of the rival expedition, sought to make some reparation by acknowledging Capt. Scott's victory at the earliest possible moment. Then there is another possibilty that Capt. Amundsen, having failed himself, put in at Capt. Scott's base on the return journey and learned the news there, for, it will be remembered, Amundsen's ship left a month earlier than Scott's to bring him back.

"Whatever has happened, one thing seems apparent by Capt. Amundsen's attitude, namely, that he hasn't been successful himself.

"As a matter of fact, we hadn't expected to hear from Capt. Scott for at least another two weeks, judging by previous expeditions, and it may be longer than that, for if Capt. Scott has not been successful he is certain to remain in the Antarctic another year, although his ship will return with a full account of what has been accomplished."

During their talk Dr. Keltie referred to what he called the "pleasant position" of THE NEW YORK TIMES in having the exclusive American rights to the stories of both Amundsen and Scott.

"It's a great piece of journalism," he said, "for you come out on top whoever wins."

The mention of Scott and Amundsen, of course, brought up the Peary-Cook controversy, and Dr. Keltie laughed heartily when he learned that Dr. Cook is suing THE NEW YORK TIMES for libel.

"And what's Peary doing?" he asked. "Isn't he suing Cook? Have you read Cook's latest book? He calls Peary almost every name in the calendar, but I suppose Peary thinks it more dignified to take no notice of it. Some things in it are extraordinary; for instance, the picture of Cook with a sextant, showing him making observations with the instrument at 40 degrees when 6 or 7 degrees was proper."

"In a way," remarks The Evening News, "this is something like the Cook-Peary drama—with a difference."

A Christmas Day Meeting.

Reckonings by experienced polar explorers some months ago showed that it was possible for Capt. Scott to have reached the South Pole on Dec. 22, and that Capt. Amundsen might have been there about the same date. A meeting at the pole on Christmas Day was, therefore, possible, and one of Jules Verne's most fantastic dreams would thus have been realized—one explorer reaching the pole and finding another already in possession.

Describing such a scene in a Christmas Day article, Sir Ernest Shackleton, the polar explorer, wrote:

"I picture to myself Scott and Amundsen on a high plateau, about 10,000 feet above the level of the sea, close to the pole, but whether fighting their way toward it or on their way back after the discovery, who can say? I imagine a strong, biting southerly wind, with the temperature about 40 degrees below zero, warm clothes, frozen sleeping bags, and thin tents which just serve in keeping out the wind, but not the cold. I think it quite possible that Scott or Amundsen, or both, have already succeeded, especially as the competition between them is in the nature of a race."

London Left in Doubt.

None of the London papers this morning, with the exception of The Chronicle, has any definite news of the result of the race for the south pole. The Times contains the following comment:

"It can only be a few hours now before we learn the facts. It is known that the Fram, Capt. Amundsen's ship, left Buenos Aires at least a month before the Terra Nova sailed from New Zealand to Capt. Scott's headquarters. If the ice were favorable Amundsen would then be able to start back long before Scott. On his way back he might well have called at Scott's headquarters to learn the news and so ascertain whether Scott had reached the pole, or he may himself have reached the pole, only to find that he had been forestalled by his English rival. He himself may have miscalculated the difficulties and failed in his attempt to outrun Scott. His route was an untried one, and no one knew what impediments might bar the way.

"The main point at present is that there is no reason to doubt that Amundsen might well have learned what Scott had done and may have been generous enough to reveal the good news even before he cabled his own tale, but it is all conjecture, and we can only hope that early information may assure us of the Englishman's victory."

Lieut. Evans, Secretary of the British antarctic expedition, which Capt. Scott led, has issued the following statement:

"No authoritative news whatever regarding the success, or otherwise, of Capt. Scott's expedition has yet reached here."

"South Pole Mystery" is the heading put in The Standard upon its news dispatches, which begin: "Has the south pole been reached by Scott or by Amundsen, or by both?"

The Standard says that surprise is expressed in exploration circles at the fact that the news should have been telegraphed by Amundsen from Hobart to Wellington, 1,393 miles away, pointing out that there is no direct cable communication between Hobart and Wellington, and that the news would have had to go to Sydney in the first instance, and then be transmitted to Wellington from there. Thus the mystery of the Wellington dispatch to The Daily Express thickens.

The Standard editorially says:

"Fortunately there is no reason to suppose that we shall have any repetition of the unseemly and unpleasant controversy which attended Peary's discovery of the north pole. Capt. Amundsen is an explorer of a different kind from the ingenious Dr. Cook, nor would he attempt to dispute his English rival's claim to the prize if he really obtained it. There is nothing incredible in the supposition that such news could have reached the Norwegian explorer in his own dash for the pole from the Bay of Whales. He must have come very close to the Terra Nova. He might easily have fallen in with some of Scott's sledge parties, and even may have met the chief of the British exploring expedition himself on his return after reaching his goal.

"If so, Amundsen, knowing that the honors of that quest had gone elsewhere, might have seen no reason to continue his southward journey and hastened to emancipate himself from the icy region as speedily as possible. Scott, having completed his exploration, would come back less rapidly.

"Amundsen at least forestalled his other competitors, the Australians, Japanese, and Germans, in being the first to announce, if he has announced, the news to the world of almost the last great victory that was left for geographical science to gain."

"Antarctic mystery," is the heading of The Daily Telegraph's article, in which it is said:

"The statement is made at Christiania, on good authority, that Amundsen failed in the attempt to reach the south pole. Moreover, King Haakon of Norway has so far received no report from Amundsen regarding the expedition. His Majesty has displayed deep interest in the Norwegian explorer's dash to the pole, and it does not seem likely that if Amundsen attained his objective he would have failed to inform his sovereign of his success. That would constitute a great triumph for Norwegian enterprise, already so adorned by the brilliant exploits of Fridtjof Nansen."

The King Probably Told.

I have reason to believe this statement about King Haakon is incorrect, in so far as it relates to his having received no report. On the contrary, his Majesty probably was the first recipient of the news of his loyal subject's triumph, but realizing that the financial rewards of the exploration will be chiefly derived from the disposal of the exclusive news to the newspapers, with great consideration he decided against making his information public, leaving that rôle to the newspapers which paid heavily for the privilege.

A Christiania dispatch under Thursday's date says:

"The first telegram from Capt. Amundsen arrived here this morning, addressed to the King, and will be published to-morrow in two morning newspapers, the Aftenposten and the Tidens Tegn, which contracted for the exclusive right of first publication.

"The evening newspapers express confidence that Amundsen reached his goal and explored the interior of the unknown continent. The general impression of scientific authorities here is that Amundsen, even if he has not actually reached the pole, accomplished a magnificent performance.

"His brother, Leon Amundsen, states it was the explorer's intention, before starting on the expedition to south polar waters, to make a lecturing tour in Australia and Europe. In any case, the Fram, after undergoing necessary repairs, will proceed to San Francisco, where Amundsen will meet her in 1913. It is expected that Amundsen will publish the details of his report in the near future."

HISTORY OF CAPT. AMUNDSEN.

First Sailor to Take Ship Through the Northwest Passage.

Roald Amundsen, who is now only 40 years old, has long been considered one of the most competent of the northern explorers. He is the first and only man so far to accomplish the long-attempted feat of taking a ship from the Atlantic to the Pacific Ocean by way of the Northwest Passage, which, by the way, Columbus was looking for when he accidentally hit upon America. He made, at a point within a short distance of the magnetic north pole, the only set of complete polar magnetic observations taken before Peary's discovery of the north pole. These achievements were accomplished in 1903 and 1905.

Amundsen's expedition at the time was made at a cost of only $30,000, in a tiny whaling sloop, the Gjoa, only seventy feet long and of only forty-seven tons burden.

Amundsen was born in Sarpsburg, Norway, on July 16, 1872, and in his childhood moved with his parents to Christiania. His father was Jens Amundsen, a skipper; his mother's maiden name was Sahlquist. His parents destined him for the medical profession, but after studying medicine for one year at the University of Christiania, on the death of his mother, he went at the age of 19 to sea, cruising for several years as a whaler and sealer on Norwegian vessels. He is a tall, spare man with a rusty red beard, and the appearance of a typical Scandinavian sailor. He is a bachelor.

He had his first real taste of exploration when in 1897 he went as first officer with the Belgica on Gerlach's Belgian south polar expedition. It was this trip, which lasted from 1897 to 1899, that filled him with aspirations to make discoveries in the arctic region, and especially to discover the long-sought Northwest Passage. First he decided to prepare himself by studying two years in Hamburg under Neumayer, the expert on magnetism, and finally at Wilhelmshafen under Borgen in the meteorological station.

Then he proceeded to raise the modest funds necessary for his expedition. A large part of the $30,000 was Amundsen's own money. Frithjof Nansen, the Norwegian polar explorer, a close friend of Amundsen, helped him raise another part.

Amundsen was finally able to put out from Christiania in the Gjoa on June 17, 1903. He sailed around the north end of America, reaching the mouth of the Mackenzie River about Sept. 3, 1905, and then by way of Baffin's Bay, Lancaster Sound, Barrow Strait, Peel Sound, James Ross Strait, and Rae Strait. Twice the Gjoa wintered in the ice. For many months Amundsen maintained an observatory on King William's Land, within ninety miles of the magnetic pole, taking daily observations.

The Northwest Passage was for more than three centuries the lure of adventurous sailors of all lands. Martin Frobisher, 300 years ago, had declared it the only thing that still remained to be discovered in the world. Perhaps it was John Cabot who first set out for it, in an endeavor to find a new way East by sailing West. As far back as 1553 Sir Hugh Willoughby and Richard Chancellor sailed from England to search for that same passage; Frobisher followed in 1576. John Davis in 1585, Barents of Amsterdam, in 1596, and scores of others, including Sir John Ross in 1818, and Sir John Franklin in 1859.

Amundsen sailed from Christiania, Norway, on June 16, 1903, in the little Gjoa, a mere eggshell of a vessel, with but eight men all told upon her. The Gjoa registered only 47 tons, and was 70 feet long and 20 broad.

Amundsen made his way through Lancaster Sound to Beechy Island, and sailed to Cape Adelaide, thence eastward of King William Land by entering Ross Strait. He reached Gjoa Harbor, in latitude north 68 degrees and 95 minutes, on the south coast of King William Land, on September 17, 1903. There the vessel was laid up safely for the Winter.

From that time until Aug. 13, 1905, Amundsen made daily observations of magnetic conditions, day and night for twenty months.

On Aug. 13, 1905, the Gjoa started on her westward way. She had come some 770 miles from Baffin Bay, and only 760 remained to Cape Bathurst, the American whaling station, and the completion of the Northwest Passage. At one point in Simpson Strait there was barely room for her to pass, and at another point there was water to a depth of only three fathoms. Dense ice was encountered in Victoria Strait, but she elbowed her way through.

On Aug. 26, after passing through Dolphin and Union straits, the Gjoa, somewhat east of Cape Bathurst, met the first American whaler.

An accident to the propeller of the ship necessitated Amundsen's wintering with the Gjoa at King Point, 69 degrees 10 minutes north, 138 degrees west. But Amundsen, taking sledge, arrived at Eagle City, Alaska, on Dec. 12, 1905, bringing the first news of his successful achievement of the Northwest Passage to the world.

He returned to the Gjoa that winter and brought her safely through the Behring Strait, the first ship to make the Northwest Passage. He had also determined the magnetic pole by observations covering nearly two years in its immediate vicinity.

The Northwest Passage trip brought Amundsen great renown, but soon afterward he turned his thoughts toward the north pole, and once announced his plan of drifting around the polar sea. He received strong backing from his countrymen, King Haakon of Norway heading the list of subscribers in support of his project.

In 1909, when Dr. Cook returned to America with his yarn of how he discovered the north pole, Amundsen declared he saw no reason to doubt the doctor's story. A little later he himself announced his project of drifting around the polar sea to the north pole—a plan which was a little Cookish jest of his own, apparently for he switched off toward the south pole instead.

FRAM, STRONGEST SHIP AFLOAT

Amundsen's Craft Withstood the North Pole Ice Packs in 1895.

The Fram, the ship in which Capt. Amundsen made his expedition to the antarctic and on which he is now returning to civilization, is the vessel in which Dr. Fridtjof Nansen, the Norwegian explorer achieved his "farthest North" in 1895. The word Fram means "Forward."

The ship was built especially for arctic ice-bucking at Colin Archer's shipyard, at Larvik, by Dr. Nansen, after his return from his Greenland voyage in 1889, and it is considered the strongest small craft ever constructed, her power of resistance to a crush of ice being greater

Continued on Page 3.

"All the News That's Fit to Print."

The New York Times.

THE WEATHER.
Unsettled Tuesday; Wednesday, fair, cooler; moderate southerly winds, becoming variable.
For full weather report see Page 23.

VOL. LXI...NO. 19,903. NEW YORK, TUESDAY, APRIL 16, 1912.—TWENTY-FOUR PAGES, ONE CENT In Greater New York, Jersey City, and Newark. Elsewhere, TWO CENTS.

TITANIC SINKS FOUR HOURS AFTER HITTING ICEBERG; 866 RESCUED BY CARPATHIA, PROBABLY 1250 PERISH; ISMAY SAFE, MRS. ASTOR MAYBE, NOTED NAMES MISSING

Col. Astor and Bride, Isidor Straus and Wife, and Maj. Butt Aboard.

"RULE OF SEA" FOLLOWED

Women and Children Put Over in Lifeboats and Are Supposed to be Safe on Carpathia.

PICKED UP AFTER 8 HOURS

Vincent Astor Calls at White Star Office for News of His Father and Leaves Weeping.

FRANKLIN HOPEFUL ALL DAY

Manager of the Line Insisted Titanic Was Unsinkable Even After She Had Gone Down.

HEAD OF THE LINE ABOARD

J. Bruce Ismay Making First Trip on Gigantic Ship That Was to Surpass All Others.

The admission that the Titanic, the biggest steamship in the world, had been sunk by an iceberg and had gone to the bottom of the Atlantic, probably carrying more than 1,400 of her passengers and crew with her, was made at the White Star Line offices, 9 Broadway, at 8:20 o'clock last night. Then P. A. S. Franklin, Vice President and General Manager of the International Mercantile Marine, conceded that probably only those passengers who were picked up by the Cunarder Carpathia had been saved. Advices received early this morning tended to increase the number of survivers by 200.

The admission followed a day in which the White Star Line officials had been optimistic in the extreme. At no time was the admission made that every one aboard the huge steamer was not safe. The ship itself, it was confidently asserted, was unsinkable, and inquirers were informed that she would reach port, under her own steam probably, but surely with the help of the Allan liner Virginiar, which was reported to be towing her.

As the day passed, however, with no new authentic reports from the Titanic or any of the ships which were known to have responded to her wireless call for help, it became apparent that authentic news of the disaster probably could come only from the Titanic's sister ship, the Olympic. The wireless range of the Olympic is 500 miles. That of the Carpathia, the Parisian, and the Virginian is much less, and as they neared the position of the Titanic they drew further and further out of shore range. From the Titanic's position at the time of the disaster it is doubtful if any of the ships except the Olympic could establish communication with shore.

Titanic Sank at 2:20 A. M. Monday.

In the White Star offices the hope was held out all day that the Parisian and the Virginian had taken off some of the Titanic's passengers, and efforts were made to get into communication with these liners. Until such communication was established the White Star officials refused to recognize the possibility that there were none of the Titanic's passengers aboard them.

But by nightfall came the message from Capt. Haddock of the Olympic to Cape Race, Newfoundland, telling of the foundering of the Titanic and of the rescue of 655 of her passengers by the Cunarder Carpathia, which, the wireless message said, reached the position of the Titanic at daybreak. All they found there, however, was lifeboats and wreckage. The biggest ship in the world had sunk at 2:20 o'clock yesterday morning.

Mr. Franklin admitted late last night that the Parisian and the Virginian, though they were among the first to answer the Titanic's calls for help, could not have reached the scene before 10 o'clock yesterday morning, seven and a half hours after the big Titanic buried her nose beneath the waves and pitched downward out of sight. The Carpathia, so the wireless dispatch from Capt. Haddock to Cape Race announced, reached the scene of the Titanic's foundering at daybreak, several hours before the expected arrival of the Virginian and the Parisian.

1,465 Lives Lost First Report.

It is unbelievable, so White Star Line officials were compelled to concede finally, that the Carpathia should have failed to pick up every lifeboat which still floated on the waves. If they failed to pick up more than 655 passengers, it was because the others of the ship's complement had gone with her to the bottom.

But it was not until nearly nightfall that the extent of the disaster was realized. Before that the reassuring nature of the bulletins issued by the White Star line was sufficient to quiet the fears of those who had relatives or friends aboard the unfortunate ship and to prevent widespread belief in a serious disaster.

Capt. Haddock's message from the Olympic, which is printed in another column of THE TIMES, strongly indicated that none but the 655 taken from life boats by the Carpathia had been saved. This message was relayed immediately to the White Star offices, but Mr. Franklin positively declined to make the text of the message public. He offered still the hope that passengers were aboard the Parisian and the Virginian, and even when the admission was wrung from him that there seemed little hope of the saving of any others than the 655 aboard the Carpathia, he clung to the hope that in some unexplained way there were other passengers abroad the two Allan liners.

First Reported Titanic in Tow.

Throughout the day there had been reassurances that the Titanic was being towed to port by the Virginian, and when Capt. Haddock's message proved this to be untrue only the admission was made at the White Star offices that the Titanic had sunk. Mr. Franklin said that Capt. Haddock's message was brief and "neglected to say that all the crew had been saved." But the inference was not that all the passengers had been saved. Rather it was that many of them had died, and presently Mr. Franklin admitted the fear that there had been a terrible loss of life on the Titanic.

This version of Capt. Haddock's wireless had been given at the White Star offices:

> Capt. Haddock of the Olympic sends a wireless message to the White Star offices here that the steamer Titanic sank at 2:20 A. M., after all the passengers and crew had been lowered to life boats and transferred to the Virginian. The steamship Carpathia, with several hundred passengers of the Titanic, is now en route to New York.

At 9 o'clock, however, he modified this statement, declaring:

> As far as we know the situation, there have been rumors from Halifax that three steamers were at the scene of the Titanic's sinking, namely, the Virginian, the Parisian, and the Carpathia. We have heard from Capt. Haddock of the Olympic, who says that the Titanic sank at 2:20 o'clock this morning. Haddock also informs us that the Carpathia has 675 survivors on board. It is very difficult to say whether the Virginian and the Parisian have any survivors on board until we can get a report from those vessels.

Fears Serious Loss of Life.

> We have asked for that report from Capt. Haddock, and we are expecting a reply at any time. The Carpathia is proceeding to New York direct. We very much fear that there has been serious loss of life, but it is impossible for us to say definitely concerning this sad part of the situation until we are able to reassure ourselves whether or not any of the Titanic's passengers are aboard the Allan liners.
>
> We are hopeful that the rumors which have reached us by telegraph from Halifax that there are passengers aboard the Virginian and the Parisian will prove to be true, and that these vessels will turn up with some of the passengers. It is the loss of life that makes this thing so awful. We can replace the money loss, but not the lives of those who went down.

Another version of the message from the Olympic was current last night and included the sentence: "Loss likely total 1,800 souls." This sentence was not in the message received by THE TIMES from Cape Race nor in that sent to the White Star line offices.

Continued on Page 2.

The Lost Titanic Being Towed Out of Belfast Harbor.

CAPT. E. J. SMITH,
Commander of the Titanic.

THE PROBABLE LOSS.

Number Aboard.	
First cabin	325
Second cabin	285
Steerage	710
Crew, (estimated)	800
Total	2,120
Saved.	
By the Carpathia	866
Probably drowned	1,254

PARTIAL LIST OF THE SAVED.

Includes Bruce Ismay, Mrs. Widener, Mrs. H. B. Harris, and an Incomplete name, suggesting Mrs. Astor's.

Special to The New York Times.

CAPE RACE, N. F., Tuesday, April 16.—Following is a partial list of survivors among the first-class passengers of the Titanic, received by the Marconi wireless station this morning from the Carpathia, via the steapship Olympic:

Mrs. JACOB P. ——— and maid.
Mr. HARRY ANDERSON.
Mrs. ED. W. APPLETON.
Mrs. ROSE ABBOTT.
Miss G. M. BURNS.
Miss D. D. CASSEBERE.
Mrs. WM. M. CLARKE.
Mrs. B. CHIBINACE.
Miss E. G. CROSSBIE.
Miss H. ROSEBIE.
Miss JEAN HIPACK.
Mrs. HY. B. HARRIS.
Mrs. ALEX. HALVERSON.
Miss MARGARET BAYS.
Mr. BRUCE ISMAY.
Mr. and Mrs. ED. KIMBERLEY.
Mr. F. A. KENNYMAN.
Miss EMILE KENCHEN.
Miss G. F. LONGLEY.
Mrs. A. F. LEADER.
Miss BERTHA LAVORY.
Mrs. ERNEST LIVES.
Miss MARY CLINES.
Mrs. SINGRID LINDSTROM.
Mr. GUSTAVE J. LESNEUR.
Miss GIORGETTA A. MADILL.
Mme. MELICARD.
Mrs. TUCKER and maid.
Mrs. J. B. THAYER.
Mr. J. B. THAYER, Jr.
Mr. HENRY WOOLMER.
Miss ANNA WARD.
Mr. RICHARD M. WILLIAMS.
Mrs. F. M. WARNER.
Miss HELEN A. WILSON.
Miss WILLARD.
Miss MARY WICKS.
Mrs. GEO. D. WIDENER and maid.
Mrs. J. STEWART WHITE.
Miss MARIE YOUNG.
Mrs. THOMAS POTTER, Jr.
Mrs. EDNA S. ROBERTS.
Countess of ROTHES.
Mr. C. ROLMANE.
Mrs. SUSAN P. ROGERSON. (Probably Ryerson).
Miss EMILY B. ROGERSON.
Mrs. ARTHUR ROGERSON.
Master ALLISON and nurse.
Miss K. T. ANDREWS.
Miss NINETTE PANHART.
Miss E. W. ALLEN.
Mr. and Mrs. D. BISHOP.
Mr. H. BLANK.
Miss A. BASSINA.
Mrs. JAMES BAXTER.
Mr. GEORGE A. BAYT—
Miss C. BONNELL.
Mrs. J. M. BROWN.
Miss G. C. BOWEN.
Mr. and Mrs. R. L. BECKW—
Miss RUTH TAUSSIG.
Miss ELLA THOR.
Mr. and Mrs. E. Z. TAYLOR.
GILBERT M. TUCKER.
Mr. J. B. THAYER.
Mr. JOHN B. ROGERSON.
Mrs. M. ROTHSCHILD.
Miss MADELEINE NEWELL.
Mrs. MARJORIE NEWELL.
HELEN W. NEWSOM.
Mr. FIENNAD OMOND.
Mr. E. C. OSTBY.
Miss HELEN R. OSTBY.
Mrs. MAMAM J. RENAGO.
Mlle. OLIVIA.
Mrs. D. W. MERVIN.
Mr. PHILIP EMOCK.
Mr. JAMES GOOGHT.
Miss RUBERTA MAIMY.
Mr. PIERRE MARECHAL.
Mrs. W. E. MINEHAN.
Miss APPIE RANELT.
Major ARTUR PEUCHEN.
Mrs. KARL H. BEHR.
Miss DESSETTE.
Mrs. WILLIAM BUCKNELL.
Mrs. O. H. BARKWORTH.
Mrs. H. B. STEFFASON.
Mrs. ELSIE BOWERMAN.

The Marconi station reports that it missed the word after "Mrs. Jacob P." In a list received by the Associated Press this morning this name appeared well down, but in THE TIMES list it is first, suggesting that the name of Mrs. John Jacob Astor is intended. This supposition is strengthened by the fact that, except for Mrs. H. J. Allison, Mrs. Astor is the only lady in the "A" column of the ship's pasenger list attended by a maid.

NAMES PICKED UP AT BOSTON.

BOSTON, April 15.—Among the names of survivors of the Titanic picked up by wireless from the steamer Carpathia here to-night were the following:

Mr. and Mrs. L. HENRY.
Mrs. W. A. HOOPER.
Mr. MILE.
Mr. J. FLYNN.
Miss ALICE FORTUNE.
Mrs. ROBERT DOUGLAS.
Miss HILDA SLAYTER.
Mrs. P. SMITH.
Mrs. BRAHAM.
Miss LUCILLE CARTER.
Mr. WILLIAM CARTER.
Miss CUMMINGS.
Mrs. FLORENCE MARE.
Miss ALICE PHILLIPS.
Mrs. PAULA MUNGE.
Mrs. JANE ———
Miss PHYLLIS O. ———
HOWARD B. CASE.
Miss MINEHAN.
Miss BERTHA ———

Biggest Liner Plunges to the Bottom at 2:20 A. M.

RESCUERS THERE TOO LATE

Except to Pick Up the Few Hundreds Who Took to the Lifeboats.

WOMEN AND CHILDREN FIRST

Cunarder Carpathia Rushing to New York with the Survivors.

SEA SEARCH FOR OTHERS

The Californie Stands By on Chance of Picking Up Other Boats or Rafts.

OLYMPIC SENDS THE NEWS

Only Ship to Flash Wireless Messages to Shore After the Disaster.

LATER REPORT SAVES 866.

BOSTON, April 15.—A wireless message picked up late to-night, relayed from the Olympic, says that the Carpathia is on her way to New York with 866 passengers from the steamer Titanic aboard. They are mostly women and children, the message said, and it concluded: "Grave fears are felt for the safety of the balance of the passengers and crew."

Special to The New York Times.

CAPE RACE, N. F., April 15.—The White Star liner Olympic reports by wireless this evening that the Cunarder Carpathia reached, at daybreak this morning, the position from which wireless calls for help were sent out last night by the Titanic after her collision with an iceberg. The Carpathia found only the lifeboats and the wreckage of what had been the biggest steamship afloat.

The Titanic had foundered at about 2:20 A. M., in latitude 41:46 north and longitude 50:14 west. This is about 30 minutes of latitude, or about 34 miles, due south of the position at which she struck the iceberg. All her boats are accounted for and about 655 souls have been saved of the crew and passengers, most of the latter presumably women and children.

There were about 2,100 persons aboard the Titanic.

The Leyland liner California is remaining and searching the position of the disaster, while the Carpathia is returning to New York with the survivors.

It can be positively stated that up to 11 o'clock to-night nothing whatever had been received at or heard by the Marconi station here to the effect that the Parisian, Virginian or any other ships had picked up any survivors, other than those picked up by the Carpathia.

First News of the Disaster.

The first news of the disaster to the Titanic was received by the Marconi wireless station here at 10:25 o'clock last night [as told in yesterday's New York Times.] The Titanic was first heard giving the distress signal "C. Q. D.," which was answered by a number of ships, including the Carpathia,

Side View of the Lost White Star Liner Titanic, the Largest Steamship Ever Launched.

Length over all, 882 feet 6 inches.
Breadth over all, 92 feet 6 inches.
Breadth over boat deck, 94 feet.
Height from bottom of keel to top of captain's house, 105 feet 7 inches.
Height of funnels above casing, 72 feet.

Height of funnels above boat deck, 81 feet 6 inches.
Distance from top of funnel to keel, 175 feet.
Number of steel decks, 11.
Number of Watertight bulkheads, 15.

Passengers accommodated, 2,500.
Crew, 860.
Tonnage, registered, 45,000.
Tonnage, displacement, 66,000.
Approximate cost, $7,500,000.

the Baltic and the Olympic. The Titanic said she had struck an iceberg and was in immediate need of assistance, giving her position as latitude 41.46 north and longitude 50:14 west.

At 10:55 o'clock the Titanic reported she was sinking by the head, and at 11:25 o'clock the station here established communication with the Allan liner Virginian, from Halifax for Liverpool, and notified her of the Titanic's urgent need of assistance and gave her the Titanic's position.

The Virginian advised the Marconi station almost immediately that she was proceeding toward the scene of the disaster.

At 11:36 o'clock the Titanic informed the Olympic that they were putting the women off in boats and instructed the Olympic to have her boats ready to transfer the passengers.

The Titanic, during all this time, continued to give distress signals and to announce her position.

The wireless operator seemed absolutely cool and clear-headed, his sending throughout being steady and perfectly formed, and the judgment used by him was of the best.

The last signals heard from the Titanic were received at 12:27 A. M., when the Virginian reported having heard a few blurred signals which ended abruptly.

The Virginian Still Searching.

ST. JOHNS, N. F., April 15.—The steamer Virginian will proceed from the scene of the wreck after daylight to-morrow morning, bringing such survivors of the steamship Titanic "as she may be able to rescue," according to wireless advices received here late to-night.

These advices did not clear up the uncertain point as to whether or not the Virginian had on board any of the passengers or crew of the Titanic. The message was taken as indicating in the words "which she may rescue" that there were no survivors aboard at the time.

The only information received here to-night regarding the Titanic disaster was that the Carpathia had 675 persons aboard, including passengers and some of the crew, and was proceeding to New York with them.

The steamers Parisian and Virginian were reported searching for others of the Titanic's people. The Virgnian was to give up her search after daylight and proceed here on her way to Liverpool. Being a mail boat, she is forced to make the utmost haste to her destination.

Other Ships Probably Too Late.

MONTREAL, April 15.—The two Allan Line steamships Virginian and Parisian, which were reported as having steamed toward the scene of the Titanic disaster, had not reported to the company here up to 10 o'clock to-night any definite news of what they had done.

The report that the Virginian had sent a wireless to the effect that she had rescued a number of passengers and then had retransferred them to the Carpathia was not confirmed.

George Hannah, General Passenger Agent of the line, is of the opinion that the Virginian arrived on the scene too late to be of any assistance, and, being a mail boat, she proceeded on her voyage. She may not be in touch with the world until she nears the Irish coast.

Mr. Hannah thinks that the Parisian may have arrived in time to be of assistance to the Titanic. If she did not, he thinks she would probably have spent some time cruising around in search of persons clinging to wreckage, and it is possible that some were saved in this way.

Sir Montague Allan, head of the Allan Line, stated to The New York Times's representative to-night:

"We have heard no word from the Virginian, and have received no official message as to the whereabouts of the passengers. We have received, however, a Marconigram dispatched to New York stating that the Carpathia had arrived on the spot where the Titanic had been, that all the Titanic's boats had been accounted for, and that 655 of the passengers had been saved, but that the rest had gone down with the Titanic. This is not official and we have no official news yet. I shall be very glad to make public the text of any official news we receive."

LINER'S GRAVE TWO MILES DEEP

Location of Titanic's Deathbed Placed by Canadian Marine Official.

HALIFAX, April 15.—The deathbed of the ten-million-dollar steamer Titanic, and of probably many who must have been dragged down with her, is two miles, at least, below the surface of the sea.

The calculation was made by an official of the Government Marine Department, who finds that depth on the chart at a point about 380 miles from Halifax and about 70 miles south of the Grand Banks, where he believes the Titanic went down.

This location is midway between Sable Island and Cape Race, and in line with those dangerous sands, which, however, might have proved a place of safety had there been time to run the Titanic there and beach her.

The Canadian warship Niobe, which has one of the most powerful wireless equipments of any vessel in this vicinity, was unable to get in tune with any of the ships in the vicinity of the Titanic disaster, and the Government station at Camperdown heard only fragmentary relays of messages.

Lloyds agent here had not received late to-night any official notification of the loss of the Titanic.

EXCITED CROWDS AT WHITE STAR OFFICE

Continued from Page 1.

Mr. Franklin said it was an error, and that the loss would certainly not reach that figure if the Carpathia had saved the number reported. THE TIMES dispatch reported that number as 655.

It may be relied upon that everything that reached Cape Race concerning the loss of the Titanic is contained in THE TIMES dispatch from that point.

Mr. Franklin admitted at 10 o'clock last night that he had not ben able to get into communication with the Parisian or the Virginian. He admitted then for the first time that Capt. Haddock's message had held out little hope that passengers had been taken aboard these steamers.

"What Capt. Haddock did say," conceded Mr. Franklin, sadly, "was discouraging to such a belief."

Vincent Astor Weeps in Office.

So reassuring was the tenor of the first reports of the accident and so late was it before the truth concerning the disaster became known, that up to 11 o'clock last night there were few visitors at the White Star offices, though the telephones there were constantly in use answering inquiries of anxious friends and relatives of the Titanic's passengers.

Several frightened women, crying with anxiety, were among the first visitors, and presently Vincent Astor, son of Col. John Jacob Astor, arrived at the offices. He and A. J. Biddle, who accompanied him, were closeted with Mr. Franklin for some time, and when they left young Mr. Astor was crying. He refused to answer questions as to what he had heard about his father.

Vincent Astor reappeared in the offices of the steamship company shortly after 1 o'clock to-day. When told no list of the survivors had been received he buried his face in his hands and sobbed.

Sylvester Byrnes, private secretary to Isidor Straus, was another visitor at the offices. He said Jesse Straus, a son, was on the Hamburg-American liner Amerika and probably at that moment was passing the spot where the vessel carrying his father had sunk. Another son, Herbert, said Mr. Byrnes was on his way to Halifax, where, it had been at first reported, the passengers of the Titanic would be landed. He will not learn until this morning that the Titanic is at the bottom of the sea.

Shortly before midnight last night a brother of Frederick M. Hoyt, Commander of the Larchmont Yacht Club, who, with his wife, was a passenger on the Titanic, made inquiry at the offices of the steamship company, as did Leo Greenfield of 1,239 Madison Avenue, whose wife and son were in the ill-fated steamer.

A young man and woman, who declined to make known their identity, entered the offices of the company just before midnight.

"Is it true that the Titanic has sunk—are the stories in the evening papers true?" the young man inquired of a clerk.

He was told that the steamship had gone to the bottom.

"My God!" he exclaimed; "we are ruined. They are all lost."

The young woman became hysterical.

A Mr. Mardhoff also called to inquire whether Arthur Ryerson and the latter's family were safe. Mr. Ryerson, his wife, two daughters, and a son were coming back from England to attend the funeral of another daughter in Philadelphia, Mr. Mardhoff said.

J. B. Fourman called to ask for news of his brother.

Notables on the Steamer's List.

Notable passengers on the Titanic, whose faith was in doubt in the lack of definite advices as to the identity of the survivors, were Mr. and Mrs. John Jacob Astor, Major Archibald Butt, Aid to President Taft; Charles M. Hays, President of the Grand Trunk Pacific of Canada, his wife and daughter; W. T. Stead, Benjamin Guggenheim, F. D. Millet, the artist, and J. G. Widener of Philadelphia; Mr. and Mrs. Isidor Straus, J. B. Thayer, Vice President of the Pennsylvania Railroad, J. Bruce Ismay, President of the International Mercantile Marine, Henry B. Harris, the theatrical manager, and Mrs. Harris, and Col. Washington Roebling, builder of the Brooklyn Bridge.

A ray of hope appeared shortly before 11 o'clock last night in a message to New York from the operator of the Marconi wireless station at Sable Island, near the scene of the disaster. Answering an inquiry regarding the delivery of wireless messages to the passengers of the Titanic, the operator reported that it was difficult to deliver them, "as the passengers are believed to be dispersed among several vessels."

Even this faint indication that other vessels than the Carpathia had picked up survivors of the Titanic was eagerly seized upon by thousands of relatives and friends of those who had set sail on her.

Solomon Guggenheim, Robert and Mrs. Robert G. Guggenheim with Miss Nettie Gerstle and Louis Rothschild, heard of the sinking of the Titanic as they left a Broadway theatre last night. Benjamin Guggenheim was a passenger on the Titanic, and his relatives had believed him safe. They hurried to the White Star offices, but could get no information beyond the statement that 675 persons were on the Carpathia.

Among those who made inquiry in the offices of the company last night was Miss Wheelock of 317 Riverside Drive, who requested information relative to the safety of her brother-in-law and sister, Dr. and Mrs. D. W. Marvin, who, she said, were returning in the Titanic on a honeymoon trip.

Shortly after 11 o'clock last night Mr. Franklin said he had received a dispatch stating that the Carpathia rescued survivors from a small fleet of lifeboats at 10:30 o'clock yesterday morning, more than eight hours after the Titanic is reported to have sunk. In his opinion, the Carpathia is hastening with all possible speed to New York City, in order that the persons taken from the lifeboats, who were suffering from exposure, might obtain medical attention with the least possible delay. In the cabins were 230 women and children, but it is not known how many there were among the 710 third-class passengers. In the first cabin there were 128 women and 15 children, and in the second cabin 79 women and 8 children.

The rush to the White Star's offices will come to-day. Then the public will know of the disaster to the Titanic, and White Star officials prepared last night to receive the throngs they expect to-day.

Not until Thursday night, however, and possibly not until Friday morning, can first hand knowledge of the wreck be obtained, for it is not until then, Mr. Franklin said last night, that he expected the Carpathia to reach this port. Already he has wired to Capt. Haddock and has tried to reach the Carpathia to obtain a list of those who were rescued. This will probably be obtained by wireless before the Carpathia reaches port. What names may appear upon it none can tell except that Mr. Franklin and steamship men in general realize that of all the 655 there probably will be the name of only a man or two.

The "rule of the sea," that law by which the women and children are always first taken from a sinking ship, is frequently written of in romances of the sea. There is no such rule that seafaring men recognize, but there needs no rule to cause men to stand aside in time of danger, said Mr. Franklin last night.

"It is a matter of courtesy extended by the stronger to the weaker, on land as well as on sea," he added, "and we know, therefore, that mostly women and children—perhaps only women and children—are passengers aboard the Carpathia. Capt. Smith, I am sure, went down with his ship. Capt. Haddock said no word of him, but I know Capt. Smith. He is that kind of a man."

So far no details have been received as to how such passengers as were rescued were taken from the doomed steamer. All these must wait until the Carpathia reaches here or until she gets within wireless range.

Capt. Haddock's wireless telling of the sinking of the ship and the records of the Cape Race wireless station which received the Titanic's first call for help afford some idea of what must have happened aboard the now sunken vessel.

The Titanic struck at 10:25 o'clock Sunday night in latitude 41.16 north and longitude 50.14 west. The huge iceberg with which she collided stove in her bow plates, and just half an hour later the big ship flashed out over the sea the news that she was sinking by the head. From then until 12:27 o'clock yesterday morning the Titanic's wireless flashed news of her condition and appeals for immediate help out over the water. Then the last crash of the instrument died out in an indistinguishable blur.

Did the Titanic sink then? It is just possible she did, for until that instant the sending of the operator aboard the big steamer had been clean cut and deliberate. His touch was as sure and steady as though his ship was in no danger, and his brother operators at Cape Race are certain that while the ship rode the waves and his instruments were intact the Titanic's operator would have kept up his massages to the world.

If the vessel disappeared from sight then, however, such of her lifeboats as had put off from the ship must have been at a safe distance to escape the suction of the huge steamer as she passed out of sight. It was at exactly 11:36 o'clock that the Titanic's wireless notified the Olympic, then speeding to her rescue that the women and children were being put off in boats. With the work started at this time there remained time for the life boats to be propelled far from the sinking vessel in the fifty-one minutes that intervened.

There is the chance, however, that the smaller boats could not live in the ice field into which the Titanic had run, or keeping afloat there, could not be driven through a sea as thick as molasses to a safe distance from the Titanic. Some of them may have been drawn down with the mother ship. The bigger vessel's extraordinary powers of suction were exemplified when she left her Southampton pier and jerked the steamer New York from her moorings. But for the occupants of such lifeboats as lived the scene must have been almost as terrible as for those whose lot it was to stay aboard the doomed vessel.

It was night, and the darkness must have redoubled the terrors of embarking in lifeboats in a sea of ice. From the Titanic it is probable that rockets were sent up and Coston lights burned to cast their wierd light over the scene, and as boat after boat, loaded to its capacity with women and children, was pushed off from the side, the attempts at cheers which must have gone up from those left behind only can be imagined until the survivors reach here to tell of it.

Wives and sisters must have sat in the small boats, slowly drawing away from the wounded leviathan, from whose decks husbands and brothers waved farewells. At the gangways there must have been partings like those in a death-chamber, for the fate of those who remained aboard must have been known. With the Titanic in such shape that it was necessary to send off the women and children within an hour of the time the steamer struck, there could have been none aboard so optimistic that he could see hope of relief.

Capt. Smith and his officers must have known that their vessel, the biggest one afloat, was gasping and straining in her last effort to keep her bow above water. They must have felt in the shiverings and trembling of the big vesel that the end was a matter of minutes only, and yet knowing this, Capt. Haddock's dispatch says simply that the women and children were put off. There is no rule of the sea, but the courtesy of the sea must have been observed by cabin passenger and steerage traveler alike.

What provision had been made to meet such a catastrophe aboard the Titanic is not known here. Mr. Franklin admitted that he did not even know the number of lifeboats the big steamer carried, except that they were in such number as were required by the British law.

Satistics of the Titanic's life-saving equipment were not available at the office of the Local Steamboat Inspecting Service, for the vessel had not yet entered this port, the cruise which had ended beneath an ice covered sea off Newfoundland being the Titanic's maiden voyage for this port. The statistics for the Olympic, the Titanic's sister ship, were available, however, and it is probable that there was very little difference in the equipment provided for the Titanic and that of the Olympic, for the vessels are almost identical in size and capacity.

These are the figures for the Olympic. She carries sixteen lifeboats and four collapsible boats, or rafts. These are calculated to carry at least 1,180 people. The requirements do not make it obligatory for a vessel to carry accommodations sufficient for its complete passenger and crew list. It would be an impossibility to do so, it was pointed out yesterday, for it would be impossible to carry such a number of lifeboats and the rafts in positions where they could be quickly lowered into the water.

The life preserver requirement demands a sufficient number to accommodate passengers and crew, even when the vessel is filled to capacity. The Olympic carries 3,455 life preservers and 48 life buoys. This fulfills the requirements of the British Board of Trade, and the United States Inspection Service simply sees that each vessel meets the requirements of its own Government.

But the life preservers and buoys which the Titanic carried can have been of little service in the emergency which the big ship encountered. Between the time she collided with the iceberg and the probable time that the big vessel sank there were just two hours and two minutes to transfer all of her passengers and crew, 2,120 persons all told, into the lifeboats. The sixteen lifeboats and four collapsible rafts were calculated to accommodate 1,171 persons, more than one-half of those who awaited rescue aboard the Titanic. There was time for every one to leave the ship, but the means of taking them off were lacking.

Had it been possible for the Carpathia, the Parisian, the Virginian, or the big Olympic to reach her in time, the Titanic might have relayed her passengers to any of these boats in the two hours and two minutes of life which remained to her after the collision.

But it was not until daybreak that the Carpathia arrived on the scene, and she was the first by probably five hours to get there. Just what the Carpathia found will not be known in detail until she gets within wireless range or reaches this port. It can be imagined readily, however, that what her crew and passengers saw when they drew close to the scene of the collision, was several small boats in a sea of ice, jammed to overflowing with women and children, and with only men enough aboard to handle the craft. About them floated bits of wreckage from the giant Titanic, and besides this only ice.

It would not have been until they were almost upon the small boats that the Carpathia's crew could have seen them, but those in the lifeboats must have strained their eyes, peering through the lifting gloom for a glimpse of smoke which should tell them that rescue was at hand. It was about daybreak when the Carpathia sighted the survivors.

With the last of her life the big ship screamed out her location that all might hear and hasten to the spot. Steamers from every point of the compass had heard and had heeded her wireless calls. Those in the small boats could not but know that from all sides help was coming as fast as power could be generated to drive the engines.

For hours in the darkness the small boats must have drifted about, their helmsmen bringing them back over the scene of the disaster as fast as they fell away, and as the first dim rays of daylight began to break up the black covering of night, there must have been eyes in every boat sweeping the sea in all directions for a glimpse of the ship that was to save them.

What caused the big steamer to sink may never be known. Probably those who could tell with authority carried the secret of the vessel's sinking to the bottom with them. She struck the iceberg bow on. So much is known from the first wireless which the Titanic sent out, and from this very fact it was concluded at first that the big steamer was in no danger.

Mr. Franklin called her unsinkable, and last night when he knew at last that the pride of his line was beneath the ocean he could not seem to comprehend that the steamer had sunk.

"I thought her unsinkable," he declared, "and I based by opinion on the best expert advice. I do not understand it."

Nor can any one else ashore say now what sent the big vessel to the bottom. It may have been that the shock deranged the mechanism by which her water-tight compartments are closed. Another conjecture advanced last night was that there was a spur of the iceberg under water on to which the Titanic ran when she collided with the visible part of the berg, and that this spur opened holes in plates further back along the keel. Either or both of these things may have happened.

Where the Titanic Hit the Iceberg, and Where She Foundered, and How Other Liners Answered the Wireless Calls for Help.

LONDON WENT TO BED THINKING ALL SAVED

Only the Latest Morning Newspapers Contained an Inkling of Real Disaster.

LLOYD'S HAD TRYING DAY

Debate on the Relative Safety of Big Ships is Started by the Recent Accidents.

Special Cable to THE NEW YORK TIMES.

LONDON, Tuesday, April 16.—After a day of great anxiety Londoners went to sleep last evening believing that all the passengers of the Titanic were certain to be saved, and that even the great ship herself might yet be brought to port.

All the leading morning papers carry editorials on the Titanic disaster, though all were written on the assumption that the vessel would be saved and no lives lost. In each case much praise was devoted to the triumph of the wireless. Not one paper up to 3 o'clock even suggests the loss of life, although news is now coming in which tells of the extent of the disaster.

It is interesting to relate that THE NEW YORK TIMES office was probably the first to be informed of the disaster. It made the news known to the principal hotels, where it was received with incredulity at first, and caused the greatest consternation and anxiety until later afternoon dispatches brought some reassurance.

Most of the excitement during the day centred about Lloyds'. Describing the scene, The London Telegraph says:

"When the room opened there was a rush among some underwriters who had heavy lines to get rid of their liability, and for this they had to pay 50 guineas per cent., at which a considerable amount of business was done. Before luncheon the rate rose to 55 guineas, and after 2 o'clock it reached 60 guineas.

"The ideas of the experts were many and varied, but the fact that had most influence in taking the rate to 60 guineas for a steamer so splendidly equipped with water-tight compartments as the Titanic, was the sudden cutting off of the wireless messages, which some thought might mean that the vessel was sinking, while others imagined that the shock of the collision might have brought down the pole of the wireless apparatus.

"Just before 4 o'clock a telegram was received at Lloyds to the effect that the Titanic was being towed toward Halifax. On this the rate dropped to 25 guineas, giving those who had written earlier in the afternoon a profit of 35 guineas."

Great commiseration is expressed for Capt. Smith, who is one of the best-known shipmasters of the North Atlantic. It is pointed out here as a coincidence that the Baltic should have been called on to perform a similar service to the Titanic as she did to the ill-fated Republic. In each instance the Baltic had passed the distressed vessel, being about two hundred miles away, when called on to turn back and go to her assistance. As a further coincidence it is stated that R. L. Barker, purser of the Titanic, was also purser on the Republic when she went down.

One of those who keenly felt the Titanic's loss was the Right Hon. Alexander Carlisle, who had charge of the building of the Titanic and who affectionately dubbed it "the last of my babies." He intended making the voyage in her, but decided not at the last moment. He was dreadfully upset by the news, but preferred to wait until the receipt of more details before discussing it, although he had insisted from the first that the boat was unsinkable.

Another representative of Harland & Wolff, when interviewed, said that if the liner had sunk, the collision must have been of great force, for the aim of Lord Pirrie and his colleagues had been to make the vessel practically unsinkable.

The suggestion that suction was in any way responsible for the present accident to the Titanic is scouted by those able to judge. Sir William White, the famous ex-Director of Naval Construction and Assistant Controller of the Royal Navy, in conversation last night said:

"In these cases speculation regarding the cause of the accident is premature. I think that until the circumstances are known in greater detail there can be no question of suction in the case of the Titanic. Moreover, suction depends upon relative speeds. Now an iceberg is a very slow-moving thing, almost stationary as you might say. There is so much under water that it is not at all like a ship.

"No, it seems that the Titanic simply struck an iceberg. It is not an unknown thing."

The disaster to the Titanic following the misfortune to her sister ship, the Olympic, has caused the question to be raised whether these mammoth liners can be handled as safely as the smaller vessels which they are so rapidly displacing. It is recalled that disaster was only narrowly averted when the Titanic left Southampton on Wednesday, the American Line steamship New York, which was only about one-fifth of her tonnage, having been torn from her moorings as the Titanic was passing, and almost drawn into collision. On the other hand, there is a definite theory among shipbuilders, founded on exact mathematical calculations, that vessels even twice the size of the Titanic would be as perfectly safe as any of the smaller liners that have crossed and recrossed the Atlantic without ever having a single accident.

A distinguished shipping authority, discussing this aspect of the disaster, expressed the following interesting opinion:

"The disaster to the Titanic hardly affects the question of size in respect to safety. A collision with an iceberg is an accident that might happen to any vessel.

It rather shows that the bigger the liner the greater is the safety in such a case. A smaller ship would probably have sunk almost immediately. The Titanic, however, with its watertight bulkheads and appliances for safety was at least able to keep afloat for a certain time.

"If she was going at anything like full speed the impact must have been terrific. Had it been a collision with any other ship, she would not have been in any danger of sinking, but the impact against an iceberg or rocks must be much more violent than against another vessel, which is a yielding substance to some extent.

"In regard to weather, too, the bigger the liner the more is she exempt from the troubles that affect smaller vessels. The larger vessels are, it is true, more difficult to work out of narrow waters but with tenders and tugboats, both ahead and astern to aid, and with the help of their own engines, it is wonderful how they can move about even in narrow channels."

The main topic of discussion on the Stock Exchange was the Titanic disaster, and each new edition of the evening newspapers was eagerly snapped up as it arrived in Throgmorton Street. The news of the disaster, however, did not produce any widespread effect on the markets, although it was quite possible that investment securities would be thrown on the market in large lines if a heavy burden were thrown upon the shoulders of Lloyds' underwriters.

Preference shares of the International Mercantile Marine Company, the big American Shipping Trust, which has controlling interest in the Oceanic Steam Navigation Company, owners of the Titanic, were very flat, falling 2 points, to 22¾ nominal. International Marine common shares, too, were weak, dropping ½ to 5¾. The company's 4½ per cent. bonds at 72¼ showed a loss of half of 1 per cent. The loss in capital value, involved by the fall of these three securities, is quite out of proportion even to the total loss of the steamer, and even if the total loss were to be borne by the International Mercantile Marine Company.

There were 3,418 bags of mail on the Titanic when she left Southampton, and it is stated that the proportion of registered packets was heavier than usual. There were no parcels for Canada on the ship, but the letters consisted of the usual midweek mail for North and South America, Canada, and the islands in the Pacific, a total of 563 bags.

Much of the Titanic's cargo was destined for New York stores for their Spring display of European fashions. These goods comprised expensive laces, the finest silks, and an immense consignment of cotton material from Manchester. In addition there was a considerable stock of wines.

LONDON, April 16.—In addition to a valuable shipment of diamonds which was said to be aboard the Titanic, it was declared to-night that among almost priceless jewels carried by the passengers were pearls belonging to an American woman valued at $800,000. The steamer also carried a large amount in bonds and a valuable registered mail.

It is stated that the owners were unable to insure the Titanic to the full amount because the British and European markets were not big enough to swallow the sum.

By Marconi Transatlantic Wireless Telegraph to The New York Times.

LIVERPOOL, Tuesday, April 16.—The Titanic disaster has caused widespread consternation in Liverpool, deep sympathy being expressed for the White Star Line.

Although Liverpool people had no opportunity of seeing the giant liner before she took her place in the Southampton service, they are proud of the fact that the company's headquarters remain here, and naturally follow its fortunes with keen interest. Therefore among leading officials of other Atlantic companies genuine regret was expressed yesterday, even before the appalling extent of the disaster was known.

Up to a late hour last night no direct official news had reached the White Star Company's Liverpool office. The officials seemed to derive comfort from the fact that J. Bruce Ismay, head of the line, was on board the Titanic. The limited range of the wireless installation was said to account for the absence of direct news in Liverpool, as communicating vessels were too far west. Liverpool, therefore, depended chiefly for news on the New York and Canada reports.

Although most of the Titanic's crew reside in Southampton, many have relatives in Liverpool, and these made anxious inquiries at the White Star offices. The officials tried to reassure them, saying that no ordinary collision would sink the Titanic, which was specially strengthened amidships to insure steadiness in heavy seas. Her transverse bulkheads numbered fifteen, any two of which might be flooded without involving the safety of the ship. The watertight doors were electricaly controlled.

As far is ascertainable, nobody living in Liverpool was included in the Titanic's saloon list.

Atlantic liners arriving here report the presence of extensive icefields in the North Atlantic. Last Saturday the Cunard Company received a cablegram from its New York office reporting a wireless message on Friday from the Carmania, stating that she had passed numerous icebergs and "growlers," and an extensive field of ice in almost the exact latitude where the Titanic struck.

The Canadian-Pacific liner Empress of Britain, which arrived at Liverpool on Sunday from Halifax, also reported the presence of immense quantities of ice in the western Atlantic. Last Tuesday, when three days out from Halifax, she encountered an icefield 100 miles in extent with enormous bergs. This caused her to steer wide of her course. Fortunately the Empress of Britain had previously received a wireless message from the Allan liner Virginian warning her of the presence of the ice. The icefields appeared as an enormous white line on the horizon.

Experienced sailors regard so much floating ice at this early period as quite exceptional. Atlantic liners are still on the Winter route.

The Titanic disaster recalls the loss of the White Star cargo steamer Naronic in February, 1893, with seventy-four lives. She left Liverpool on her maiden voyage, and was never again heard of. It is believed that she was sunk by an iceberg.

Liverpool marine offices are involved in Titanic insurance to a limited extent.

GREAT GRIEF IN BELFAST.

Lord Pirrie, Who Designed the Ship, Called Her His Last Effort.

Special Cable to THE NEW YORK TIMES.

BELFAST, April 15.—Nowhere has the news of the disaster to the Titanic been received with greater regret than in Belfast, the birthplace of the world's mightiest ship. Every stage of her construction, as in the case of her predecessor, the Olympic, was followed with the keenest interest and local pride. Her launching was the occasion of a general holiday.

To no one will the news come with greater shock than to Lord Pirrie, Chairman of Harland & Wolff, and designer of the vessel, who is recovering from a severe operation. When the Titanic was launched he remarked that she would be his last and supreme effort in marine architecture.

GREAT ANXIETY IN PARIS.

Americans Besieged the Steamship Offices, Wild for News.

Special Cable to THE NEW YORK TIMES.

PARIS, April 15.—The accident to the Titanic caused a very great sensation in Paris to-day. The first news received about midday and for an hour or so, when it was reported that the vessel had gone down with all hands, the offices of the White Star line and all other possible sources of information were soon besieged by friends and relatives of the passengers. It was not till 3 o'clock that it was known that some of the passengers were saved.

Paris just now counts a very large number of rich American visitors, and the scenes of intense anxiety in many of the hotels during the day are not easily to be forgotten.

The Titanic embarked 150 first-class passengers at Cherbourg, together with 40 second class.

One passenger, Mrs. J. C. Hogeboom, has had unusually hard luck. She first booked passage on the Oceanic some time ago, but as the boat did not sail she was offered passage on the Olympic. She preferred, however, to remain for the first trip of the Titanic.

Interior Views Showing the Luxury of the Titanic's Furnishings.

FIRST CLASS SMOKING ROOM

PARISIAN CAFE

RESTAURANT RECEPTION ROOM

FIRST CLASS STATE ROOM

SUNKEN LINER WAS $7,500,000 PALACE

Titanic, Really a Fifteen-Story Floating Hotel, Represented the Height of Luxury.

BIGGEST OF ALL SHIPS ALSO

Carried a Crew of 800 Men and Had Accommodations for 2,500 Passengers.

The Titanic, although built as a sister ship to the Olympic, set sail on this, her maiden voyage, as queen of the seas, the largest and most luxurious vessel afloat. Her registered tonnage was 45,000, like that of the Olympic, but officers of the White Star Line declare that she measured 45,328 tons. Capt. E. J. Smith, who was assigned to command her after her spectacular launching from Belfast on May 31, was until then in command of the Olympic.

The cost of the Titanic has been officially estimated at $7,500,000. She was 882½ feet long, 100 feet more than any other save the Olympic, and if set on end would have reached high above the Metropolitan Tower as well as the new Woolworth Building. From stem to stern she provided a walk equal to four city blocks. In size she exceeded that of a battleship by 5,000 tons; she was twice as big as the dreadnought Delaware. She was built for an average speed of 21 knots, and for rich tourists and lovers of luxury. Two suites on the Titanic each cost $4,350 for a single trip.

Her dimensions were as follows:

	Ft.	In.
Tonnage, registered		45,000
Tonnage, displacement		66,000
Length over all	882	6
Breadth over all	92	6
Breadth over boat deck	94	0
Height from bottom of keel to boat deck	97	4
Height from bottom of keel to top of Captain's house	105	7
Height of funnels above casing	72	0
Height of funnels above boat deck	81	6
Distance from top of funnel to keel	175	0
Number of steel decks		11
Number of water-tight bulkheads		15
Passengers carried		2,500
Crew		860

The Titanic presented the appearance of a great fifteen-story floating palace, splendid and gigantic in every detail, built to be the last word in speed, power, size, and equipment. In safety, too, it was believed, the last word had been uttered in the construction of the Titanic. Her hull was divided into fifteen water-tight compartments, the doors of which could be closed simultaneously by throwing a single lever on the bridge. Through this arrangement of bulkheads it was believed the vessel was absolutely unsinkable, even though half of the ship be filled with water.

Her interior represented more that of a hotel than a ship, with heavy balustraded wide stairways, elevators running up and down for nine stories, great saloons and restaurants, a miniature theatre, squash and tennis courts, swimming pools and Turkish and electric baths; great smoking rooms, card rooms, beautiful music rooms, sun parlors, Winter gardens, palm courts, gymnasium, and on the top of its twelfth deck, even a miniature golf links. There were tennis courts thirty by twenty feet in size, with a coach aboard to teach those who could not play.

Each stateroom had its own bathtub, with hot and cold water. There was a servants' hall for the valets, maids, and other domestics of the voyagers, where they were supposed to stay, even if they traveled first-class, while not in attendance upon their employers.

For these, there were provided sitting rooms in some suites as large as fifteen by fifteen feet. The restaurant was larger than that on the Olympic, and had as an innovation a private promenade deck on the starboard side. The main promenade deck had an unbroken sweep of 190 yards on either side of the ship. Its value was calculated at about $40 a front foot for a six-day's voyage, since suites on it cost $1,350 as against $2,300 for similar suites off it.

The main dining room, with a capacity of nearly 550 passengers, provided an a la carte service for those who preferred not to be held to regular hours for dining, night suppers, and dinner parties.

The main reception room was separated from this dining room by glass, through which at night dazzled brilliant electric light clusters, giving the whole the appearance of a fairyland. The scene was described in the official booklet as follows:

"Upon a dark richly carpeted cloth which will further emphasize the delicacy and refinement of the paneling and act as a foil to the light dresses of the ladies, this company will assemble, the apotheosis, surely, of ocean-going luxury and comfort. What more appropriate setting than this dignified Jacobean room, redolent of the time when the Pilgrim Fathers set forth from Plymouth on their rude bark to brave the perils of the deep."

Some idea of the immensity of the vessel, aside from its splendor, can be gained from a few figures. In her double bottom alone there are 500,000 rivets, 1¼ inches in diameter, the weight of which alone amounted to 270 tons. The plates in the bottom weighed 4¼ tons each, and were 36 feet long. The stern frame weighed 70 tons, the rudder 100 tons, and the boss arms 73½ tons aft and 45 tons forward. The largest beam in her was 92 feet long and weighed more than 4 tons. In binding her massive steel plates 3,000,000 steel rivets were used, the total weight of which was 1,200 tons. Each link in her anchor chains weighed 175 pounds.

The floors of the Titanic's fifteen stories were called the bottom, double bottom, bed plates, lower orlop, orlop, lower, middle, main, saloon, upper, promenade, upper promenade, boat, and sun decks, and the extra compass platform. The private promenades connected with the most luxurious suites on the ship. These suites were situated about amidships, on either side of the vessel, and each was about 50 feet long. Each comprised a sitting-room, two bedrooms, and a bathroom, with a "front garden" on the promenade, railed off in front of the suite.

The Titanic, like the Olympic, was a four-funnel ship, the distance from keel to the top of the funnels being 175 feet. More than 2,000 sidelights and windows were put into the vessel to provide a maximum of light and air. The ship was built under the direct supervision of Alexander M. Carlisle, general manager for Harland & Wolff, the Belfast shipbuilders, whose distinction in shipbuilding is such that he has been made a Privy Councillor to the King of England.

"All the News That's Fit to Print."

The New York Times.

THE WEATHER.
Increasing cloudiness, warmer, probably snow; Wednesday, clearing; brisk southeasterly winds.
For full weather report see Page 22.

VOL. LXII...NO. 20,107. ... NEW YORK, TUESDAY, FEBRUARY 11, 1913.—TWENTY-FOUR PAGES. ONE CENT In Greater New York, Jersey City, and Newark. | Elsewhere, TWO CENTS.

SCOTT FINDS SOUTH POLE; THEN PERISHES WITH FOUR MEN IN ANTARCTIC BLIZZARD; BODIES FOUND AFTER EIGHT MONTHS

ARMED TRUCE IN MEXICO CITY; MADERO RETURNS

Called Upon by Diaz for His Resignation, the President Cries, "I Will Die First!"

REBEL LEADER INSISTENT

Says He Held Off to Prevent Slaughter, but the Federals Have Not Done the Same.

BATTLE PREDICTED TO-DAY

Both Sides Have Been Strengthening Their Positions and Seeking Reinforcements.

FOREIGNERS NOT MOLESTED

Executions Take Place at the Palace—Son of Reyes Kills Himself.

NORTHERN GENERALS WAITING

Washington Hurries Warships to Convenient Ports to Watch Events in Republic.

General Diaz to The Times.

By Cable to the Editor of THE NEW YORK TIMES.

MEXICO CITY, Feb. 10.—The revolt is in progress and in a few hours will have to be decided. All the chances are in our favor. I will protect all your citizens and properties.

FELIX DIAZ.

Special Cable to THE NEW YORK TIMES.

MEXICO CITY, Feb. 10.—The city at 10 o'clock to-night was quiet.

The Federals and Revolutionists still held their positions. The Government was taking ammunition to the palace under a heavy guard.

Gen. Diaz says he delayed battle in order to avoid slaughter of non-combatants, but as the Government has not refrained from hostile movements he has about lost patience.

Fighting, it is expected, will begin at daybreak.

Special Cable to THE NEW YORK TIMES.

MEXICO CITY, Feb. 10.—An armed truce prevailed between the Federals and the revolutionists all day.

Gen. Diaz still held the arsenal and had practical control of all the heavy artillery. He is equipped with rifles and machine guns and has an unlimited supply of ammunition. According to reports, he is arming and drilling several hundred men in the arsenal.

A conference was held this morning between Gen. Diaz, two of his suporters, and Cabinet Ministers at a café in the centre of the city. What occurred at the conference was not made public, but after it was over a red flag was raised on the arsenal, and war without quarter was declared.

Several cannon were taken from the arsenal last night to the suburbs. They were placed where they would command the Chapultepec Castle. Officers in the castle say they will raze it if necessary to save it.

The movements of President Madero are kept secret. It is reported that he went to Cuernavaca last night and returned to the city at dawn this morning. Gen. Felipe Angeles, commander of Cuernavaca, it is said, is at Contreras, twelve miles south of the capital, with about a thousand Madero troops.

Gen. Angeles, it is said, has some heavy artillery.

The populace is maintaining neutrality.

A small riot in the Colonia del Carmen early this morning was stopped by mounted police.

The number of dead has not been reported, as it is impossible to pass the lines.

Genovevo de la O and Felipe Nerl, rebel leaders from the State of Mexico, occupy a position within ten miles of the capital at Tlalpam and Xicpimilco, awaiting the orders of Gen. Diaz to enter he capital. Tlalpam is five miles beyond the Country Club. Foreigners are leaving that place.

Messengers were sent to Gen. Diaz this morning, protesting loyalty to him and asking permission to enter and join his forces. He sent an officer with instructions to take the positions and wait further orders.

Higinio Aguilar and Gaudencio de la

Continued on Page 8.

EDISON 66 YEARS OLD TO-DAY

Wife Will Make Him Quit Work Long Enough to Dine with Friends.

Special to The New York Times.

WEST ORANGE, N. J., Feb. 10.—Thomas A. Edison, who will be 66 years old to-morrow, will pass the day just as he does the other 364 in the year, with the exception of an occasional Sunday, when he yields to the insistence of Mrs. Edison and goes to church. He will work in the laboratory and offices, but has promised to "knock off" in the evening to be the guest at a family dinner party which Mrs. Edison is arranging.

The employes of the works will observe the day by wearing buttons or pins bearing the numerals "66." The workers at the Edison plant are grateful because since Edison took charge of the commercial branches in December many of the pay envelopes of the humbler employes have been fattened.

The production of the kinetophone, the further perfection of the storage battery, and the development of the disk phonograph record are among the achievements of the inventor during the past year. For his storage battery Edison received the Rathenau medal, donated by Emile Rathenau of Berlin.

"I feel like twenty-five," said Edison this afternoon. "I'm sure I'm going to keep right at it, too, for a good many years more."

POPE DECORATES EDITORS.

Medals to Cardinal for Those Who Compiled Catholic Encyclopedia.

Cardinal Farley received from Pope Pius X. yesterday the "Pro Ecclesia et Pontifice," an important decoration, to be bestowed upon the Board of Editors of the Catholic Encyclopedia. The order was instituted by Pope Leo XIII., July 17, 1888, and the decoration was made a permanent distinction only in October, 1898. It is to reward those, who, in a general way, deserve well of the Pope. The medal is made of gold, silver, and bronze. It is cross shaped, made rectangular in form by fleurs de lis, fixed in the angles of the cross. In the centre of the cross is a small medal with an image of its founder, Pope Leo XIII. The ribbon is purple, with delicate lines of white and yellow on each border. The decoration is worn on the right side of the chest.

The Board of Editors of the Catholic Encyclopedia consists of Charles G. Herbman, Ph. D., L. L. D., Professor of Latin Language and Literature at the College of the City of New York; Edward A. Pace, Ph. D., D. D., Professor of Philosophy at the Catholic University in Washington; Conde B. Pallen, Ph. D., L. L. D., of New Rochelle; Mgr. Thomas J. Shahan, D. D., rector of the Catholic University, Washington, and the Rev. J. J. Wynnee, S. J.

Dr. Pallen has just returned from Rome, where he presented the Pope with a set of the Vatican edition of the encyclopedia.

LEFT CHANGE FOR $50 BILL.

Clerks Wonder if Their Customer Was Absent-Minded or Crazy.

All day yesterday the clerks at the Broadway and Thirtieth Street store of Hackett Carhart & Co. expected to see a wild-eyed man run in and demand if any one had seen on Saturday a perfectly good $50 bill. No such person turned up, and last night as the employes put out the lights they wondered if there really could be any one in this city who cared so little for money.

On Saturday afternoon a customer asked to be shown some neckties. He seemed perfectly rational and betrayed no more than the proper amount of interest in the adornment of his person. He selected ties worth $4.50 and handed the salesman a $50 bill. This was sent on its way to the cashier for change and the ties were wrapped up. The man took his parcel, put it in his pocket, and quit the store. When the salesman received the change he had gone. The man ran out into Broadway, but the customer had disappeared.

The salesman reported the incident and the cashier decided at once that the note must be a counterfeit. But examination proved that it was genuine.

SOON TO WED, DISAPPEARS.

Rockfellow's Friends Unable to Account for His Sudden Departure.

Special to The New York Times.

PLAINFIELD, N. J., Feb. 10.—Rowland C. Rockfellow, son of the late Mayor George W. Rockfellow, disappeared from his home on Saturday, leaving two notes for his mother, who was prostrated by his absence. His wedding to Miss Rae Warnock, daughter of Mr. and Mrs. W. W. Warnock, was set for Tuesday night, Feb. 18, and one of the letters addressed to his mother said:

"I wil lnot be responsible for any debts unless contracted by myself." The wedding invitations had been issued when the young man disappeared.

Mrs. Rockfellow said to-day that she could not account for her son's action. She exhibited the other note he had left, which read:

> Dear Mother: I have been a good boy. I am not dishonest, but I can't help going away. Don't blame me.

W. R. Causbrook, district manager of the Public Service Corporation's local office, where Rockfellow was employed as cashier, said this afternoon that his accounts were correct. His fiancee, Miss Warnock, said she had not had any quarrel with Rockfellow. The first intimation she had had of his absence, she asserted, was on Saturday night when he failed to appear at a dinner party given to them.

WILSON WON'T SEE CASTRO.

Declines Request of ex-President of Venezuela for an Interview.

TRENTON, N. J., Feb. 10.—Representatives of ex-President Castro of Venezuela came to Trenton to-day to obtain an interview for the General with President-elect Wilson. Castro wished to see the Governor, but Mr. Wilson declined to receive him on the ground that he would not mix in any affairs of the Taft Administration before his inauguration as President.

Castro has been building hopes on the possibility of friendly action by Mr. Wilson. He has said that if Mr. Wilson was President instead of Mr. Taft he would have no trouble in obtaining admission to this country. When Mr. Wilson visited Ellis Island some time ago the ex-President expressed much regret that he had been unable to see him. One of Mr. Wilson's companions on that trip, Mrs. J. Borden Harriman, did ask Commissioner Williams to let the Governor's party talk with Castro, but Mr. Williams refused the request curtly. Mr. Wilson seemingly did not know of Mrs. Harriman's request at the time it was made.

SCOTT'S LAST MESSAGE TO THE WORLD.

Not Faulty Organization, but Misfortune, Caused the Disaster Which He Foresaw—Asks Aid for Families of the Dead.

MESSAGE TO THE PUBLIC.

The causes of this disaster are not due to faulty organization, but to misfortune in all the risks which had to be undertaken. One, the loss of pony transport in March, 1911, obliged me to start later than I had intended, and obliged the limits of stuff transported to be narrowed. The weather throughout the outward journey, and especially the long gale in 83 degrees south, stopped us. The soft snow in the lower reaches of the glacier again reduced the pace.

We fought these untoward events with will and conquered, but it ate into our provisions reserve. Every detail of our food supplies, clothing and depots made on the interior ice-sheet and on that long stretch of 700 miles to the pole and back worked out to perfection. The advance party would have returned to the glacier in fine form and with a surplus of food but for the astonishing failure of the man whom we had least expected to fail. Seaman Edgar Evans was thought to be the strongest man of the party, and Beardmore glacier is not difficult in fine weather. But on our return we did not get a single completely fine day. This, with a sick companion, enormously increased our anxieties. I have said elsewhere that we got into frightfully rough ice, and Edgar Evans received a concussion of the brain. He died a natural death, but left us a shaken party, with the season unduly advanced.

But all the facts above enumerated were as nothing to the surprise which awaited us at the Barrier. I maintain that our arrangements for returning were quite adequate, and that no one in the world would have done better in the weather which we encountered at this time of the year. On the summit, in latitude 85 degrees to 86 degrees, we had minus twenty to minus thirty. On the Barrier, in latitude 82 degrees, 10,000 feet lower, we had minus thirty in the day and minus forty-seven at night pretty regularly, with a continuous headwind during our day marches.

These circumstances came on very suddenly, and our wreck is certainly due to this sudden advent of severe weather, which does not seem to have any satisfactory cause.

I do not think human beings ever came through such a month as we have come through, and we should have got through in spite of the weather but for the sickening of a second companion, Capt. Oates, and a shortage of fuel in our depots, for which I cannot account, and, finally, but for the storm which has fallen on us within eleven miles of the depot at which we hoped to secure the final supplies. Surely misfortune could scarcely have exceeded this last blow!

We arrived within eleven miles of our old One Ton camp with fuel for one hot meal and food for two days. For four days we have been unable to leave the tent, the gale blowing about us. We are weak.

Writing is difficult, but for my own sake I do not regret this journey, which has shown that Englishmen can endure hardships, help one another, and meet death with as great a fortitude as ever in the past. We took risks. We knew we took them. Things have come out against us, and therefore we have no cause for complaint, but bow to the will of Providence, determined still to do our best to the last.

But if we have been willing to give our lives to this enterprise, which is for the honor of our country, I appeal to our countrymen to see that those who depend on us are properly cared for. Had we lived, I should have had a tale to tell of the hardihood, endurance, and courage of my companions, which would have stirred the heart of every Englishman.

These rough notes and our dead bodies must tell the tale, but surely, surely, a great, rich country like ours will see that those who are dependent on us are properly provided for.

March 25, 1912.

(Signed) R. SCOTT.

INDICT WALSH, NEWELL AND FOYE

True Bills Found Against Police Captain and Lawyer on Bribery Charge.

WHITMAN AFTER HOCHSTIM

Ready Now to Indict One of the Heads of Syndicate Running Disorderly Hotels.

WALDO HUNTING DOWN GRAFT

Big Police Official Reported Called for Examination To-day—Costigan Aids Curran Inquiry.

The Extraordinary Grand Jury returned indictments yesterday against Police Capt. Thomas W. Walsh, Patrolman Charles E. Foye, and Edward J. Newell, the lawyer. Walsh and Newell were charged with bribery and against the lawyer there was a second indictment charging him also with misdemeanor. The first bill found against Newell a fortnight ago was dismissed and the new ones returned. Foye was charged with perjury because of his sworn testimony before the Curran Committee that Chairman Curran had tried to persuade him not to press a charge against a saloonkeeper whom he had arrested.

The witnesses against Walsh and Newell were Thomas J. Dorian and Nathan J. Michaels, the managers of the Hotel Avenel; George A. Sipp, and Patrolman Eugene Fox. All of them were willing witnesses except Michaels. Sipp's story, covering five years of paying graft to Capt. Walsh for protection, was corroborated by Dorian before the Curran Committee, and then Dorian fled the city. District Attorney Whitman made a long and fruitless effort to find him. It was learned that he was receiving his weekly pay from the hotel syndicate that employed him, and a search began for evidence to show that these payments were really made to keep Dorian away.

Mr. Whitman threatened to proceed against the syndicate and to indict Dorian. Then Dorian returned and told a story to Mr. Whitman that not only confirmed the confession made by Fox, but gave information that showed that the disorderly hotel syndicate had paid graft to the police for many years in the many districts in which they owned hotels. It was discovered that there were several of these hotels in various sections of the city. Yesterday Mr. Whitman said that he was ready to submit enough evidence before the Grand Jury to indict at least one of the leading spirit of the syndicate.

Whitman After Hochstim.

The man that Mr. Whitman is after is Max Hochstim, who, with Philip Blau, Jacob Spielberg, and a man named Fromberg, composed the Baltic Hotel Company that owns the Hotel Avenel and other hotels of the same character. Mr. Whitman learned yesterday that Mrs. Hochstim owns thirty-nine shares of the Baltic Hotel Company, and that Hochstim owns one share. The sixty other shares are scattered. Some of the information against the syndicate was gathered yesterday in the course of the investigation in connection with police graft bearing upon the cases directly aimed against Walsh and Newell.

The moment the indictment against Newell was returned Justice Goff issued a bench warrant for his arrest. It was served by Detective Flood of Mr. Whitman's office, who found Newell in his office at 42 Broadway. He was brought before Justice Goff and his bail on the bribery charge was fixed at $2,000, while the $1,000 on which he was held on the misdemeanor charge was continued. A surety company furnished the bail, and Newell went about his business. Foye is away on a vacation. He will be taken into custody this morning as soon as he returns and bail will be set. If he fails to furnish it he will be locked up. No action was taken against Capt. Walsh because of his illness. As soon as he is physically able to go abroad he will be arraigned and released on bail.

W. M. K. Olcott, Newell's lawyer, had a talk with Mr. Whitman between the time of Newell's indictment and his arraignment in court. Before Mr. Whitman went home last night it was said that there were prospects that Newell would tell all he knew of his connection with Sipp and Capt. Walsh.

It was explained that if he told all he knew it would be to the effect that a well known lawyer handed him $1,000 to give to Sipp in return for Sipp's promise to remain out of this State until after Jan. 1, 1914; that he held out $300 to pay himself for the services he had rendered Sipp while the latter was a prisoner at Atlantic City on the charge made against him by the police and that the money came originally from Capt. Walsh. But if Newell's story goes beyond this transaction it might reach a point where the system of the police to get legal services from certain influential sources, directly or indirectly, would be uncovered.

Newell Proved Obdurate.

When Newell was indicted first for a misdemeanor, under Section 2,441 of the

Continued on Page 9.

Death Wipes Out Brave Party on Return Trip to Winter Quarters

LEAVES MESSAGE TO PUBLIC

Disaster Not Due to Faulty Organization, but to Misfortune, His Last Word.

THREE BODIES IN ONE TENT

There Scott, Wilson, and Bowers Succumbed to Starvation and Exhaustion.

OATES BRAVED DEATH ALONE

Knowing His Fate, He Marched Out Into the Blizzard—"Brave Soul," Wrote Scott.

EVANS KILLED BY A FALL

Storm Wrecked Last Hope of Saving Themselves When Only 11 Miles from a Food Depot.

REACHED POLE JAN. 18, 1912

Found Amundsen's Records There—Perished March 29, 1912, and Bodies Were Found in the Following November.

By Lieut. E.R.G.R. EVANS, R.N.
Second in Command of the Scott Expedition.

Special Cable to THE NEW YORK TIMES.

CHRISTCHURCH, New Zealand, Feb. 10.—Capt. Robert F. Scott's antarctic ship, the Terra Nova, on Jan. 18, this year, arrived at Cape Evans, the base on McMurdo Sound, where it was to meet the explorers on their return from the expedition in search of the south pole and bring them back, if they were ready. It was learned from the shore party found at this base that Capt. Scott and the four men with him had reached the pole on Jan. 18, 1912, but all had perished on the return journey, about the end of March. Their bodies were not found until a searching party discovered them on Nov. 12, nearly eight months after the disaster.

Capt. Scott, Dr. Edward A. Wilson, chief of the scientific staff, and Lieut. H. R. Bowers had made their way back to within 155 miles of Cape Evans, when they were caught in a blizzard and were overcome about March 29. They were then within eleven miles of One Ton Depot, where they would have found shelter and supplies.

Previously Petty Officer Edgar Evans and Capt. L. E. G. Oates of the Inniskillen Dragoons, who had been in charge of the ponies and dogs, had succumbed. Evans was the first to give way, dying from concussion of the brain due to a fall on Feb. 17. Oates died from exposure on March 17.

Found Amundsen's Records.

The records of Capt. Scott were recovered by a relief expedition. They showed that he and his party had reached the south pole on Jan. 18, 1912. There they found the tent and records left by Capt. Roald Amundsen when he quit the pole on Dec. 17, 1911.

Six other men of the Scott expedition who had been through a perilous experience were found to be safe and well. They composed Lieut. V. L. A. Campbell's expedition, which had been sent to make geological investigations to the east of Cape Evans. The Terra Nova has been unable to take the men off the year before on account of ice, and they were left to spend another Winter in the antarctic. In this party were Dr. Levick, Priestly, Abott, Browning, and Dickerson.

Relief Party Had to Return.

Before the Terra Nova sailed for New Zealand last March Surgeon Atkinson, who had been left in charge of the western party until Capt. Scott's return, dispatched Garrard and Demetri with two dog teams to assist the southern party, whose return to Hut Point was expected about March 10, 1912. Atkinson would have accompanied this party, but was kept back in medical charge of Lieut. Evans, the second in command, who, it will be remembered, nearly died from scurvy.

This relief party reached One Ton Depot on March 3, but was compelled to return on March 10, owing primarily to the dog food running short, also to persistent bad weather and the poor condition of the dogs after the strain of a hard season's work. The dog teams returned to Hut Point on March 16, the poor animals being mostly frostbitten and incapable of furthe work.

Garrard collapsed through an overstrained heart. His companion was also sick. It was impossible to communicate with Cape Evans, the ship having sailed on March 4, and the open sea lying between Atkinson and Keohane.

The only two men left sledged out to Corner Camp to render any help that might be wanted by the southern party. They fought their way out to Corner Camp against the unusually severe weather, and, realizing that they could be of no assistance, they were forced to return to Hut Point after depoting one week's provisions.

In April, when communication with Cape Evans was established, a gallant attempt to relieve Lieut. Campbell was made by Atkinson, Wright, Williamson, and Keohane. This party reached Butter Point, when they were stopped by open water. Their return was exciting and nearly ended in disaster, owing to the sea ice breaking up.

Search Party's Journey.

The search party left Cape Evans after the Winter on Oct. 30 last. The party, which was organized by Surgeon Atkinson, consisted of two divisions, Atkinson taking the dog teams with Garrard and Demetri, and Mr. Wright being in charge of a party including Nelson, Gran, Lashley, Crean, Williamson, Keohane, and Hooper, with seven Indian mules. They were provisioned for three months, as they expected an extended search.

One Ton camp was found in order, and all provisioned.

Proceeding along the old southern route, Wright's party sighted Capt. Scott's tent on Nov. 12. Within it were found the bodies of Capt. Scott, Dr. Wilson, and Lieut. Bowers. They had saved their records, hard pressed as they were.

From these papers the following information was gleaned:

The first death was that of Seaman Edgar Evans, petty officer

Capt. Robert Falcon Scott.

The continuation of the authentic narrative of Capt. Scott's expedition will appear exclusively in The New York Times to-morrow.

Map of Capt. Scott's Route, Showing Point at Which He Died.

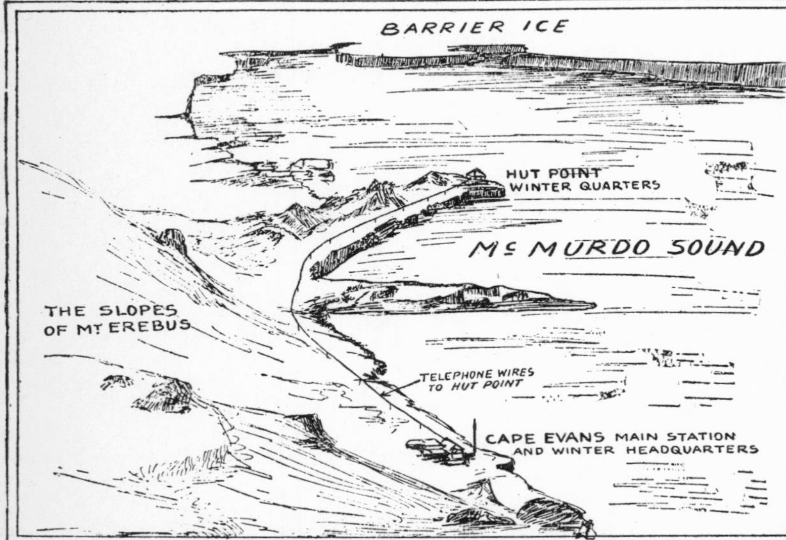

Where the Survivors of the Scott Party Were Found.

of the Royal Navy, official number 160,225, who died on Feb. 17 at the foot of the Beardmore Glacier. His death was accelerated by a concussion of the brain sustained while traveling over the rough ice some time before.

Capt. L. E. G. Oates of the Sixth Inniskillen Dragoons was the next lost. His feet and hands had been badly frostbitten from exposure on the march. Although he struggled on heroically, on March 16 his comrades knew that his end was approaching. He had borne his intense suffering for weeks without complaint, and he did not give up hope to the very end.

Oates Went Out to Die.

Capt. Scott wrote in his diary this tribute to Capt. Oates:

"He was a brave soul. He slept through the night, hoping not to wake, but he awoke in the morning. It was blowing a blizzard. Oates said: 'I am just going outside and may be some time.' He went out into the blizzard, and we have not seen him since."

Another passage read: "We knew that Oates was walking to his death, but, though we tried to dissuade him, we knew it was the act of a brave man and an English gentleman."

On March 16 Oates was really unable to travel, but the others could not leave him and he would not hold them back. After his gallant death Scott, Wilson and Bowers pushed on northward when the abnormally bad weather would permit them to proceed. They were forced to camp on March 1, in latitude 79 degrees 40 minutes south, longitude 169 degrees 23 minutes east, eleven miles south of the big depot at One Ton Camp.

This refuge they never reached, owing to a blizzard, which is known from the records of the party at Cape Evans to have lasted nine days, overtaking them. Their food and fuel gave out and they succumbed to exposure.

In Capt. Scott's diary Surgeon Atkinson found the following, which is quoted verbatim:

Scott's Message to the World.

"Message to the public:

"The causes of this disaster are not due to faulty organization, but to misfortune in all the risks which had to be undertaken.

"One, the loss of the pony transport in March, 1911, obliged me to start later than I had intended and obliged the limits of the stuff transported to be narrowed.

"The weather throughout the outward journey, and especially the long gale in 83 degrees south, stopped us. The soft snow in the lower reaches of the glacier again reduced the pace.

"We fought these untoward events with a will, and conquered, but it ate into our provisions reserve.

"Every detail of our food supplies, clothing, and depots made on the interior ice sheet and on that long stretch of 700 miles to the pole and back worked out to perfection.

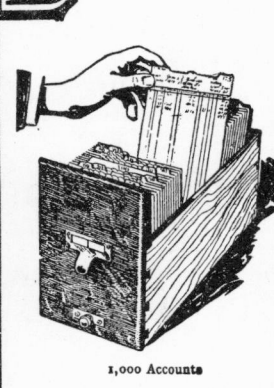

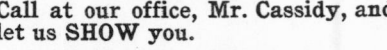

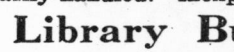

Strongest Man First to Go.

"The advance party would have returned to the glacier in fine form and with a surplus of food but for the astonishing failure of the man whom we had least expected to fail. Seaman Edgar Evans was thought the strongest man of the party, and the Beardmore Glacier is not difficult in fine weather. But on our return we did not get a single completely fine day. This, with a sick companion, enormously increased our anxieties.

"I have said elsewhere that we got into frightfully rough ice, and Edgar Evans received a concussion of the brain. He died a natural death, but left us a shaken party, with the season unduly advanced.

"But all the facts above enumerated were as nothing to the surprise which awaited us on the Barrier. I maintain that our arrangements for returning were quite adequate, and that no one in the world would have done better in the weather which we encountered at this time of the year. On the summit, in latitude 85 degrees to 86 degrees, we had minus twenty to minus thirty. On the Barrier in latitude 82 degrees, 10,000 feet lower, we had minus thirty in the day and minus forty-seven at night pretty regu-

Continued on Page 3.

SCOTT FINDS POLE, THEN PERISHES

Continued from Page 2.

arly, with continuous headwinds uring our day marches.

"It is clear that these circum tances came on very suddenly, nd our wreck is certainly due to his sudden advent of severe weather, which does not seem to ave had any satisfactory cause.

The Final Disaster.

"I do not think human beings ver came through such a month s we have come through, and we hould have got through in spite f the weather but for the sickening of a second companion, Capt. Oates, and a shortage of fuel in ur depots, for which I cannot account, and, finally, but for the torm which has fallen on us within eleven miles of this depot, at which we hoped to secure the final upplies.

"Surely misfortune could scarcely have exceeded this last blow!

"We arrived within eleven miles of our old One Ton camp with fuel for one hot meal and ood for two days. For four days e have been unable to leave the ent, the gale blowing about us. We are weak.

"Writing is difficult, but for my own sake I do not regret this journey, which has shown that Englishmen can endure hardships, elp one another, and meet death with as great a fortitude as ever n the past. We took risks. We new we took them. Things ave come out against us, and herefore we have no cause for omplaint but bow to the will of Providence, determined still to do ur best to the last.

"But if we have been willing o give our lives to this enterrise, which is for the honor of ur country, I appeal to our ountrymen to see that those who epend on us are properly cared or. Had we lived I should have ad a tale to tell of the hardihood, ndurance, and courage of my ompanions which would have tirred the heart of every Englishman.

"These rough notes and our ead bodies must tell the tale, but urely, surely, a great rich country ke ours will see that those who re dependent on us are properly rovided for.

(Signed) R. SCOTT,
March 25, 1912.

A Cross Over Their Graves.

Surgeon Atkinson and his pary gathered the records and efects of the dead men and read he burial service over their odies and erected a cairn and cross to their memory over the nner tent in which they buried hem. A record of the finding of their bodies was left attached to he cross.

The party then searched for twenty miles south, endeavoring to discover the body of Capt. Oates. It was not found, but another cairn and record were left in the vicinity to his memory.

It should here most certainly be noted that the southern party nobly stood by their sick companions to the end, and in spite of their distressing condition they had retained every record and thirty-five pounds of geological specimens, which proved to be of the greatest scientific value. This emphasizes the nature of their journey.

The search party then turned northward, having decided to direct their efforts next to the relief of Lieut. Campbell and the northern party.

The remainder of this tragic narrative will be published tomorrow.

INTENSE GRIEF IN LONDON.

News Announced at Special Meeting of Geographical Society.

By Marconi Transatlantic Wireless Telegraph to The New York Times.

LONDON, Tuesday, Feb. 11.—News of the death of Capt. Robert F. Scott, one of the most heroic and intrepid explorers who ever adventured into the arctic or antarctic, in a disaster which is described as the greatest and most tragic in the history of polar exploration since the death of Sir John Franklin, was received here yesterday and has come as a terrible shock to the English nation.

Capt. Scott and His Men on the Terra Nova.

The news was received with consternation in naval and exploration circles and was the one theme of conversation yesterday in all the clubs. The tragedy is regarded as all the more sad because fate overtook the explorers after they had reached the goal of their ambition, the south pole.

The members of the Royal Geographical Society met with heavy hearts last night at a special meeting of the society. Half an hour before the meeting began the theatre was packed. A notable figure present was Sir Allen William Young, the veteran arctic explorer. He was navigating officer of the Fox, which went to look for Franklin in 1857.

Profound silence fell upon the audience as the Chairman, Douglas W. Freshfield, Vice President of the society, rose to speak of Capt. Scott's fate. His voice faltered several times in the course of his speech, while his hearers listened with bowed heads.

They met, he said, under the shadow of a great calamity. He was not in a position to give any complete or consecutive account of the disaster. He could only piece together such scraps of information as, through the courtesy of the Central News, had been put into his hands.

Tells the Society of the Tragedy.

Mr. Freshfield then announced that not only had Capt. Scott lost his life, but also Dr. E. A. Wilson, Lieut. H. R. Bowers, Capt. L. E. G. Oates, and Petty Officer E. Evans.

Capt. Scott's party, said Mr. Freshfield, found Capt. Amundsen's tent and records at the south pole. On the return trip, about March 29, 1912, eleven miles from One-Ton Depot, a blizzard overwhelmed them. They had suffered greatly from hunger and exposure, and the death of Scott, Bowers, and Wilson was virtually due to that. They died soon after the blizzard swept down on the party.

Oates died from exposure a few days later. The death of Evans resulted from a fall. The other members of the expedition were reported to be in good health. A searching party discovered the bodies and records some time later. Mr. Freshfield went on to say:

"We know no more to-night. Tomorrow, doubtless, will make the sad story clear. We shall learn how their comrades learned of the deaths of the pioneers and how their records were recovered, for it is evident, from the fact that we learn they found Capt. Amundsen's records, that their own must have been preserved.

"No arctic or antarctic party, I believe, was ever sent out better equipped or better fitted by the gallantry or experience of its members, from Capt. Scott downward, to meet with the ordinary perils of the pole, but arctic travel would not be what it is—a training ground for the highest qualities of the British race—if these perils were altogether avoidable.

"And of all the dangers of the region of snow and ice there is none so terrible, so overwhelming, as the blizzard. Even on European mountains it has counted its victims by the thousand. We can imagine how these terrors are multiplied a hundredfold on the icy uplands 10,000 feet above sea level in the heart of the antarctic. Under these conditions, unless shelter is at hand, human powers, even the toughest, cannot long maintain the struggle against the malignant forces of nature. The end must come, and as a rule it comes speedily and not unmercifully."

"Farewell to a Band of Heroes."

More formal expression of the society's deep regret and heartfelt sympathy must be left to a later day, said Mr. Freshfield, adding:

MRS. R. F. SCOTT.

"All I can say to-night is, farewell to a band of heroes whose names will shine as examples of the endurance which is the highest form of courage and as noble evidence of the qualities of Englishmen. Not once or twice in our rough island story have these qualities been shown, but never more conspicuously than by the members of this ill-fated expedition.

"Capt. Scott lives in all our minds, and will live in our memories as the ideal of the English sailor of our age, a man intellectually gifted as well as brave and resourceful in all emergencies, full of scientific zeal and enthusiasm.

"Nor do his companions deserve less honor. They were equal in their daring, their endurance, their deaths. Of their accomplished work we shall hear hereafter. For the moment we can think only of the price that has been paid for it."

A message of sympathy to the Royal Geographical Society from the King was read. In it his Majesty said:

"I am deeply grieved to hear the very bad news you give me of the loss of Capt. Scott and four of his party just when we were hoping shortly to welcome them home on their return from their great and arduous undertaking. I heartily sympathize with the Royal Geographical Society in the loss to science and discovery through the death of these gallant explorers. Please send me further particulars."

To a press representative after the meeting Sir Allen Young said he had never himself experienced a blizzard of the kind that would overwhelm such a plucky party.

Dr. W. Bruce of the Oceanographical Laboratory, Edinburgh, who achieved considerable distinction in antarctic exploration, regards the reports that scurvy broke out among the supporting party after it left Capt. Scott as rather significant. He says this might indicate that Scott's advance party was also afflicted with scurvy, and consequently weakened and unable to resist the severity of an antarctic blizzard as a healthy party would have done.

Expedition Splendidly Equipped.

The Scott expedition was the finest ever sent into the southern regions. It comprised a splendid band of devoted scientists. It was in October, 1909, that Capt. Scott made public his project for reaching the pole. At a Mansion House meeting in support of his scheme he gave a detailed statement of the objects of the expedition. The amount he asked for was £40,000, ($200,000.) The sum was based on the cost of the discovery expedition, which cost £92,000, out of which £51,000 was expended on building the Discovery. That left about £40,000, which kept the Discovery expedition for three years and a quarter.

Out of the £40,000 which he trusted he would obtain, said Capt. Scott, he proposed to purchase a ship for £12,000, and he hoped with the remaining £28,000 to pay the same expenses as were paid for in the Discovery expedition for £40,000. The main items of expenditure were salaries and ship expenses.

It was quite possible, Capt. Scott said, to man a ship to-morrow and equip an expedition with gentlemen who would be prepared to go without salary at all, but it was no use to take a geologist who knew no geology or a cook who could not cook. Every man was worthy of his hire, and the best policy was to pay good wages, facing the position manfully.

Capt. Scott said to the meeting: "My supporters, or the country at large, need never fear that the dignity of the country will suffer from anything which may be done by our expedition. We may fail, but they shall have no reason for doubting the story which we tell."

These word read ominously in the light of yesterday's tragic messages.

Scott's belief, as disclosed at the same meeting, was that the majority of the British people, while envying no nation what it possessed, would dearly like to see the Union Jack floating at the south pole. He said it was not his wish to bring another exploration into the international arena, but he was strongly of the opinion that such an expedition should form the subject of national enterprise.

Dec. 22, 1911, was fixed by Capt. Scott as the date on which he intended, if possible, to plant the British flag at the south pole. Every detail of the voyage and the subsequent march over the ice, so far as such matters could be arranged beforehand, had been mapped out, all dates had been fixed, and these Capt. Scott mentioned in the course of a lecture at the Royal Institution.

He said, however, that he was too familiar with unexpected happenings on such an adventure to suppose that plans could be exactly, or even closely, followed, and he did not wish it to be supposed that he failed to contemplate the possibility of circumstances that might upset some, if not all, of his calculations.

The whole-hearted sympathy of the British nation goes out to Mrs. Scott, now on the high seas between San Francisco and New Zealand, where she expects to meet her husband and where news of the calamity awaits her.

CAPT. ROBERT SCOTT — LIEUT. H. R. BOWERS — L. E. G. OATES — E. A. WILSON

Four of the Five Men Lost in the Scott Expedition.

SCOTT'S MOTHER TOLD.

His Wife Went to Fetch Him—Little Son Waiting for Return.

Special Cable to THE NEW YORK TIMES.

LONDON, Feb. 10.—"I am going to fetch him home."

These were Mrs. Scott's farewell words to Peter, her blue-eyed, fair-haired boy, aged 3½ years, when she started for New Zealand on Jan. 4.

"I will get to New Zealand at the end of next month," ran one of her last communications to England, and she wistfully added: "I hope you don't miss Peter as much as I do."

Peter, who has already begun to take a great interest in antarctic exploration, would look at a photograph of his father, whom, of course, he does not remember seeing in person, and would talk with his mother about him. He would study the map of the antarctic regions, helping his mother with tiny flags placed in it to indicate the progress of the expedition. He also had a map of his own, and his mother would show him "where daddy is," and teach him the names of the places.

The boy was quite excited when he was told that his father would be home soon, and, after Mrs. Scott left England, he solemnly announced to some members of the household:

"Mother has gone to fetch him back. Then she is going to bring him home, and then I am going to meet him at the station."

In 1911, in order that Scott might see how his son was progressing, Mrs. Scott had cinematograph pictures taken of Peter at play in the garden. These were sent out to the first base of the expedition, but whether Scott ever saw them is not known.

The last message Mrs. Scott received from her husband came in March of last year, dispatched before the dash for the pole which had begun the previous November.

Mrs. Scott is a great favorite in social circles, not only for her accomplishments, but also because of her charm of disposition. She had great faith in her husband's ability to reach the South Pole, and when the news was received of Amundsen's success she calmly remarked to a friend she would await Scott's return.

Her boy, who is described as the image of his father and a bright, cheerful little fellow, is now staying with Capt. Scott's aged mother.

The news of Scott's death reached his relatives through cablegrams to newspapers. Lady Ellison Macartney, the explorer's sister, was the first to hear of his fate and she broke the news to her mother gently by telephone. Mrs. Scott has not felt any apprehension for the fate of her son, and bore up very bravely, her grief being somewhat tempered by the fact that he died in an effort to advance the world's knowledge.

Special to The New York Times.

SAN FRANCISCO, Feb. 10.—Mrs. Scott, widow of the antarctic explorer, had a good time in San Francisco while she was waiting for the steamer Aorongi to sail for New Zealand. She received many invitations to social functions and she was bade good-bye by Mayor Rolph. Just before the steamer sailed she said:

"Capt. Scott will not reach civilization for at least two months. Consequently, I expect to reach the antipodes in ample time to greet him and hear his story of his three years' experience in the south pole regions. Our meeting probably will take place at one of the South New Zealand ports.

"Of course, you all know as much about my husband's doings during his absence in the South as I do, but I am confident that, while Capt. Amundsen beat his expedition to the pole, it was no fault of Capt. Scott. No one will be quicker to congratulate Capt. Amundsen, especially as he has endured the same hardships as Capt. Amundsen and can so readily appreciate the emotions of that sturdy Norwegian when he realized he had won the race to the south pole."

MEAGRE NEWS IN LONDON.

Times Again Denies That Scott and Amundsen Raced for the Pole.

LONDON, Tuesday, Feb. 11.—The press and public are entirely dependent upon THE NEW YORK TIMES-Central News copyrighted dispatches for news of the fate of Capt. Scott, and further details are anxiously awaited. The newspapers devote many columns to the expedition and to Capt. Scott's career, while their editorial articles contain many tributes to the lost explorers. The Times says:

"Never since the loss of Franklin has such a disaster befallen British polar explorers. * * * It is possible for us in this temperate clime to realize something of the horror, terror and irresistible vehemence of an antarctic blizzard if we recall the description which we gave on Nov. 19 last from the pen of Dr. Simpson, who was for a time lent by the Indian Government to be chief physician of the expedition. He tells of a gale which blew continuously for six days 'at over-gale strength' more than thirty-eight miles an hour, rising at different times to fifty-two, sixty-six and eighty miles an hour, the temperature marking between 31 and 35 degrees below zero.

"We shall never know what degree of violence was attained by the blizzard which was fatal to Capt. Scott, but it may be assumed that it was as bad as this or worse.

"In judging Capt. Scott and his friends, let us put out of our minds all gossip which from time to time has been circulated about a race between him and his friendly rival, Capt. Amundsen. That this explorer should have diverted his course from the north to the south pole was an accident, and so was the almost simultaneous arrival of the Danish vessel and the Terra Nova in those southern waters.

"As long since pointed out in these columns by one of Capt. Scott's companions, Herbert Ponting, he never raced, never headed a mere dash to the pole. He went forward with a scientific expedition, and if he had not had the misfortune to lose nine of his nineteen invaluable ponies he might very probably have arrived first, and, what is of much more importance, might not have found it necessary to send that memorable dispatch when the Terra Nova first came to fetch him away: 'I am staying in the antarctic another year in order to continue and complete my work.'"

The Daily Mail says: "It is a tragedy as overpowering, as moving in the dignity and heroism of its victims, as Franklin's end in the arctic more than sixty years ago. Victory is swallowed up in death. Scott and his companions died for the honor and greatness of their country as truly as any seaman or soldier who falls in battle, and by her they will ever be lamented and their memory cherished as a sacred inheritance."

Both The Times and The Daily Mail end their editorials with an adaptation of Tennyson's famous lines on Franklin.

The Daily Chronicle says: "To-day the deepest sympathy of England and the world will go out to Mrs. Scott in the heart-breaking bereavement which has fallen upon her. It will be something to her to know that the sympathetic thought of an Empire is with her in the dark hour of sorrow and trial, that England says 'Well done' of a life spent in England's service, and that in saying that the best that can be said is said."

A FRIEND'S TRIBUTE.

Such a Death as the Explorer Would Have Desired, He Writes.

Special Cable to THE NEW YORK TIMES.

LONDON, Feb. 10.—An intimate friend of Scott, in an appreciation contributed to The Daily Telegraph, says:

"Robert Falcon Scott met such a death as he himself would have desired. He met his fate on the heights of the southern iceland, which, as he told me often, he had come to love.

"He himself would be the last to regret his end and the manner of its coming, for it came, it appears, after the task which he had set himself had been accomplished.

"A quiet man who loved not talking of himself, a man who endured more hardship than falls to the usual lot even of mariners, he appreciated greatly the calmness of his own English home. No one but Robert Falcon Scott and one other can have any idea of the wrench he must have felt at parting from the wife he but lately married, even though it was to go on the quest the fulfillment of which was the dream of his life.

"I remember sitting with him in his pretty little drawingroom on the first floor of his tiny house in Buckingham Palace Road the night after the news of Shackleton's successful rush to the South had come through. He had just come in from a day's hard work at the Admiralty, and he was enthusiastic in his quiet way over the success of his one-time lieutenant and former colleague. From the little table he picked up his pipe. Mrs. Scott brought in a map of the South Polar regions, and, seated before the fire in a deep armchair, with his wife kneeling on the rug beside him, her head resting against the husband who was soon to leave her forever, he traced on the map the route which Shackleton and his men must have followed, sometimes with his finger, sometimes with his pipe, and, as he traced step by step the perilous journeys, he described the awesome nature of the Antarctic peril. Man's great joy in achievement came out as he talked, while the wife's love of and pride in her husband became more and more manifest as the talk went on. For three hours we sat and chatted, and all the time the longing to go South again kept coming uppermost.

"Are you going again?" I asked him, and he shook his head gently as he looked at his wife, but in his eyes shone the fire of the explorer—the man who does not like to be beaten—while one could see that Mrs Scott, like her husband, had pride in his being first, and one felt that he would go again, and that his wife, loving him so dearly that she would put his reputation before her affection, would cheer him forth on the dangerous journey.

"Within a very few weeks I knew Scott was going south again, but I know and Mrs. Scott knows also that the journey was resolved upon one evening when we sat and talked of Shackleton.

"In his direct honesty this big seaman had much of the schoolboy in him, and it was with something of schoolboy's shamefacedness he admitted to me some weeks later he was making arrangements to give up his Admiralty appointment so as 'to make another try for the pole.'

"One fly there was in amber, and that I learned when he admitted to me with a wry smile that all the appliances which were being taken were not British, the gyroscopic compass, which was a part of the equipment, being of foreign manufacture. His men, however, were British right through, and his pride in them was great, almost beyond belief.

"Aptly was he christened Falcon, for, like the falcon, he aimed high, and is happy in his death, inasmuch as his quarry was reached and the end came too late to rob him of victory."

"All the News That's Fit to Print."

The New York Times.

THE WEATHER

Local showers today: Tuesday, fair; fresh, shifting winds, becoming northwest.

For full weather report see Page 17.

VOL. LXIII...NO. 20,610. ... NEW YORK, MONDAY, JUNE 29, 1914.—EIGHTEEN PAGES. ONE CENT In Greater New York, Jersey City and Newark. Elsewhere TWO CENTS.

HEIR TO AUSTRIA'S THRONE IS SLAIN WITH HIS WIFE BY A BOSNIAN YOUTH TO AVENGE SEIZURE OF HIS COUNTRY

CALIFORNIA GOES ON ROCKS IN FOG

Tory Island, Off Northwest Irish Coast, Scene of Mishap to Anchor Liner.

IN NO IMMEDIATE DANGER

Bows Badly Stove In and Ship Taking Water Through Two Holes in Hold.

PASSENGERS STILL ABOARD

Ship Carries 1,000 Persons—Rescue Vessels, Called by Wireless, Standing By Throughout Night.

Special Cable to THE NEW YORK TIMES.

LONDON, June 28.—The Anchor liner California, with more than 1,000 persons aboard, has gone ashore on Tory Island, off the northern coast of Ireland. The destroyer Swift, the fastest and largest vessel of her class in the world, and other vessels have gone to her assistance in response to wireless calls for aid.

The ship is said to be in no immediate danger.

The accident to the California occurred in a thick fog. The latest news received early this morning was that although the position of the liner was serious, no lives had been lost.

In reply to a wireless message, the Captain sent the following details:

> California ran ashore Tory Island in fog, about half mile from lighthouse. Did not hear foghorn blowing. Quiet sea. No danger. Three men of war and steamer Cassandra standing by to transfer passengers.

The California went on the rocks with such force that the lower part of her bows were badly stove in, and the two front holds soon filled with water. She is in five fathoms of water forward and seven fathoms aft. There was no panic on board.

News has been received from Londonderry that the landing of the Irish passengers may be expected before noon today.

News of the stranding was caught by the Malin Head wireless station and the entire torpedo boat destroyer flotilla which was for duty off the Ulster voast looking for gun runners, was called up and wireless orders were given to all the destroyers from the cruiser Hecla in Lough Swilly to hurry with all speed to the scene of the accident.

Subsequently orders were received by all the telephone and telegraph stations on the coast from Bangor to Bunbeg, County Donegal, to keep their offices open all night.

By 11 o'clock six destroyers were making for Tory Island.

LONDONDERRY, June 28.—In a thick fog and rain which rendered Tory Island invisible from the mainland, the Anchor Line steamer California, bound from New York for Glasgow, went ashore tonight on the rocks off that island. Wireless calls for help brought speedy assistance from a number of small gunboats and torpedo boats which were patrolling the Northwest Irish Coast for gun runners in connection with the Ulster movement.

The latest news received here is that the California is stuck fast on the rocks, but is in no immediate danger. She struck with such force that the lower part of her bows was badly stove in, and she is making water through two holes in her forehold and second hold.

The steamer, which has on board 121 saloon and more than 300 second cabin passengers, lies in five fathoms of water forward and seven fathoms aft.

The passengers and crew are still on board. There was no panic when she struck the rocks.

Several steamers, including one liner, and the gunboats are standing by, and other vessels are expected to arrive at the scene during the night.

LONDON, June 28.—Capt. Coverley of the California late tonight sent out this wireless dispatch:

"Ran ashore in fog about half mile from the lighthouse. Did not hear foghorn. Sea quiet. Three men-of-war and steamer Cassandra standing by to transfer passengers."

CARRIED 841 PASSENGERS.

Place Where California Struck Ten Miles Out of Her Course.

The California sailed from New York at noon on Saturday, June 20, for Glasgow via Moville with 116 first-class, 350 second-class, and 375 third-class passengers. She signaled Malin Head yesterday afternoon, and should have been off Moville about 8 o'clock. Tory Island is more than ten miles out of her course.

The California carried a crew of 240 officers and men, and was commanded by J. A. Coverley, one of the most experienced Captains in the Anchor Line service. This was his second voyage on the California after having been twelve years on the Calabria in the New York-Mediterranean service, and more recently in command of the liner Elysia in the Indian service of the Anchor Line.

The California is the second largest vessel of the Anchor Line in the New York trade, and was built at Glasgow by D. & W. Henderson Bros. in 1907. She is 470 feet long, with a beam of 58 feet 2 inches and a depth of hold of 23 feet 6 inches. She is a twin-screw steamer, with an average speed of 15 knots.

The Captains and other officers of the Anchor Line are accustomed to fog around the coasts of Scotland and Ireland and always keep a man on the lookout on the foc'sle head, as well as

Continued on Page 3.

STAYS IN AIR 21 HOURS.

Berlin Aviator's Feat Held to be a World's Record.

BERLIN, June 28.—Herr Landmann, an aviator, today concluded a non-stop flight of 21 hours 49 minutes.

It is asserted that this flight constitutes a world record.

Twenty-one hours would be almost enough to carry the seaplane America either to the coast of Ireland, or to the Azores. Plans for the forthcoming trans-Atlantic flight are based on the America's reaching the Azores in twenty hours.

DEWEY IN CANAL PARADE.

Will Be Invited to Make Trip Aboard His Old Flagship Olympia.

Special to The New York Times.

WASHINGTON, June 28.—Admiral George Dewey may take his old flagship, the Olympia, through the Panama Canal next March in the naval parade. Rear Admiral Clark, retired, has been ordered to take command of his old ship, the Oregon, for the occasion, and Secretary Daniels said this afternoon that he had decided to invite Admiral Dewey to take part. If the Admiral does not feel like making the journey via the canal, he may go overland to San Francisco and go aboard the Olympia upon the arrival of the pageant fleet there.

The President and Secretary Daniels will make addresses upon the arrival of the fleet at the exposition city. It is likely that Admiral Dewey and Admiral Clark also will speak. The entire brigade of midshipmen will be taken to San Francisco for the occasion. This will probably take the place of their annual cruise.

The Oregon and the Olympia will be moored at a specially constructed wharf and will be on exhibition throughout the entire exposition. Behind them will be anchored seven typical modern naval ships—a dreadnought of the New York or Oklahoma type, a battleship of the Connecticut or Minnesota type, an armored cruiser of the Tennessee or Montana type, one of the three scout cruisers, a destroyer, a submarine, and a collier, each of the latest build. In addition, the entire Atlantic Fleet will remain throughout nearly the whole of the exposition.

Neither Admiral Dewey nor Rear Admiral Clark has been aboard his ship since relinquishing their commands shortly after the close of the Spanish-American war.

A NEW GAME FOR BROADWAY.

But Auto Owners Hope Trundling Stolen Tires Won't Become Popular.

Harry E. Sullivan with his brother and two women rode up to Shanley's Restaurant, in West Forty-third Street, last evening in a limousine auto with a new white tire strapped like a life preserver to the back. Two men who had the appearance of chauffeurs came down the street after the owners of the auto entered the restaurant. With businesslike briskness they unbuckled the new white tire and trundled it down the street. The taxicab starter at Shanley's scratched his head. Then he spoke to Patrolman Louis Fick.

"They did it so natural," he explained, "that I didn't think to bother them."

The patrolman jumped into an auto and started in pursuit of the tire. By its tread-prints on the damp pavement he followed it down to Ninth Avenue, up to Forty-fourth Street, around the corner, and there the artful dodgers foiled him by rolling it into the street where its trail was lost in a maze of tire tracks. The tire was worth $75.

"If it's as easy as that," said Mr. Sullivan when he heard of his loss, "rolling rubber hoops in Broadway is apt to become a popular pastime. The first rule of the game is: 'A rolling tire must gather no moss.'"

SCORES BRYAN AND TREATY.

Francis B. Loomis Calls Colombian Agreement "Stupendous Blunder."

Special to The New York Times.

SAN FRANCISCO, June 28.—Bryan's proposed treaty between the United States and Colombia is vicious as to motives and purpose, says Francis B. Loomis, former Assistant Secretary of State. In a statement here tonight Mr. Loomis said:

"Bryan's Colombian treaty is a covert attempt to loot the United States Treasury by lobbyists and political brigands, into whose hands the Secretary of State is playing.

"Bryan and the President are trying to besmirch and discredit the achievement of the previous Administration, which made the canal a reality.

"The treaty is one of the most stupendous blunders made by Bryan, who is running wild with his 'world peace' theories. The United States owes Colombia nothing, either by treaty or otherwise.

"Mr. Bryan's contention that the people of Latin America feel aggrieved because we refuse to permit the Colombian troops to cross the Isthmus for the purpose of engaging in bloody encounters, and closing the lines of transit is not supported by ascertainable facts. The truth is the important Governments of South America such as Argentina, Brazil, and Chile care nothing about Colombia, and they deplore her misdeeds as much as we do."

STATE'S TOLL OF ACCIDENTS

Automobiles Killed Nearly Half as Many as Railroads in April.

Special to The New York Times.

ALBANY, June 28.—There were nearly half as many deaths in New York State from automobile accidents during April as there were from railroad accidents. This is shown in the vital statistics issued by the State Department of Health for April. The deaths resulting from railroad accidents numbered 58, from automobiles 25, from street cars 15, and other vehicles 20. Landslides killed 12 individuals, and 3 others died from injuries inflicted by animals. There were 128 suicides during the month and 35 homicides.

The other external causes of death ran the total up to 735 for the month.

$120,000 FOR SHACKLETON.

Sir James Caird's Gift for His Antarctic Expedition.

Special Cable to THE NEW YORK TIMES.

LONDON, June 28.—Sir James Key Caird, the millionaire jute manufacturer of Dundee, has given $120,000 toward the expenses of the Shackleton antarctic expedition.

Sir James made the gift after Sir Ernest Shackleton had personally explained to him the programme which he hoped to carry out.

Sir Ernest says the gift puts the expedition on a sound basis, and there is now no fear that it will not start well equipped.

FEDERALS DESERT AGUASCALIENTES

Town South of Zacatecas Evacuated by Huerta's Forces, but Villa Turns Back.

IS CAMPAIGN ABANDONED?

Border Hears His Ammunition Is Exhausted — Row with Carranza Will Not Down.

ENVOYS WAIT ON CARRANZA

Rebel Chief Said He Must Consult Generals—Reply Called Favorable.

ZACETAS, June 27, via El Paso, June 28.—Aguascalientes, capital of the States of the same name, has been evacuated by the Federals, according to information reaching Gen. Villa's headquarters today.

Owing to this, his plan of campaign has been changed, and the troops of the division are returning to Torreon.

Part of the division left last night. The rest will leave for the north today. Gen. Villa will follow his troops during the day. Last Wednesday it was announced that the Villa troops would be taken toward Aguas Calientes overland.

Late reports show that the losses of the Federals here were much greater than at first supposed. The number of prisoners taken by Villa's troops exceed 4,300. The number of killed was close to that figure.

The latest casualty report of the Constitutionalists was over 700 dead and 1,100 wounded, but these figures are not complete.

EL PASO, June 28.—Gen Villa's campaigns are apparently postponed indefinitely.

Lack of ammunition is given as the principal cause, but recent developments, still concealed in the Carranza-Villa estrangement, are believe by partisans of trangement, are believed by partisans of the quiet situation below this point.

The victory of Zacatecas, won by Villa last week, occasioned the expenditure of nearly all his ammunition during the four days of almost continuous fighting.

Since then Villa has not been able to replenish his supply from the United States on account of the strict embargo by United States troops along the frontier. It is said that he has not been assisted in this regard by Gen. Carranza, who could draw on the arsenals at Monterey and Saltillo.

He has only the little ammunition left after the fighting at Zacatecas and an unstated quantity captured from the Federals there.

Gen. Villa returned today to Torreon, according to telegrams from him dated from that place. Some matters connected with his relations with Carranza, it is stated, will be taken up by Villa as well as the obtaining of ammunition for his army.

The statements of Alfredo Breceda, one of Carranza's agents at Washngton, fell here today as oil on the fire.

Carranza and Villa adherents are now outspoken in their views of the recent estrangement, and regard Breceda's statements as an additional indication that discussion of the matter will not subside for some time. Breceda's remarks closely followed in effect those made a few days previously by Roberto Pesqueira. Constitutionalist confidential agent. The Villa men have remained silent.

CARRANZA-HUERTA DEAL?

Report of Peace Negotiations Comes from Mexico City.

VERA CRUZ, June 28.—Secret peace negotiations between Gen. Carranza and President Huerta have been in progress in the capital, according to Antonio Magnon, an American who arrived from Mexico City today. Mr. Magnon said it was positively known that representatives from Carranza had been in the capital for several days in conference with President Huerta, but that the details of the discussions had been kept secret.

It was thought in the capital that a peace agreement between Huerta and Carranza based upon Huerta resignation, was certain to come soon, Carranza having been forced to make some concessions because of his disagreements with Gen. Villa and Gen. Angeles.

It is reported in Mexico City that supporters of Villa and Carranza have been fighting near Monterey.

Mr. Magnon said also that President Huerta's volunteer forces at San Luis Potosi, including all the noted chieftains, such as Gen. Pasquale Orozco and Gen. Antonio Rojas, had refused to cooperate further with the regular army or to withdraw toward the capital, but would fight the Constitutionalists in that region. The volunteer leaders, most of whom are veterans of the three years' border warfare, and all frontiersmen, and, according to Mr. Magnon, say that the Federal recruits are hopeless as soldiers and only hamper the actions of the veteran volunteers.

Gen. Joaquin Maass, Federal commander at San Lois Potosi, went to the capital last Friday to confer with President Huerta, Mr. Magnon said, and was still there when Magnon left Saturday. Mr. Magnon said Gen. Maass, whom he had known for years, confirmed the reported action of the volunteers.

The Federals are fortifying Aguascalientes against a Constitutionalist advance, but it is understood in the capital that Gen. Villa plans to direct his next blow against Queretaro, cutting both the National and Central Railways and compelling the abandonment by the Federal forces of much territory in order to prevent themselves from being cut off from the capital.

Mr. Magnon said that he learned at Soledad that the Federals were gathering railway equipment for the narrow

Continued on Page 5.

Propose Pan-American Memorial to Columbus

A splendid tomb topped by a great light is proposed to be erected in Santo Domingo, in the Caribbean Sea, by subscriptions from peoples of all lands. See

NEXT SUNDAY'S TIMES.

OUR GUNS FIRE ON SANTO DOMINGO

Few Shots from the Machias Stop Bombardment of Puerto Plata by President Bordas.

WARNED BY CAPT. RUSSELL

Told Not to Endanger Foreigners in Attack on Rebels There—Refugees Taken Off by Our Boats.

Special to The New York Times.

WASHINGTON, June 28.—Following general instructions from the Navy Department to protect the lives and property of Americans and foreigners in Santo Domingo, the little American gunboat Machias on Friday afternoon entered the inner harbor of Puerto Plata, and with a few shots from her main battery silenced a battery of President Bordas's forces that was bombarding the town.

The bombardment was in violation of emphatic orders from Capt. Russell, commanding the American squadron, that the attack on the city, which is in the hands of rebels, be conducted in such a way as not to imperil the lives of foreigners.

Capt. Russell is in personal command of the first line battleship South Carolina, that was detached from service at Vera Cruz when conditions in Santo Domingo became threatening. His dispatch to the department, which, like all dispatches from Santo Domingo, took two days to come, makes no mention of casualties. His dispatch follows:

> PUERTO PLATA, June 26, 1914.
>
> This afternoon, about 5:30, when the Bordas artillery ashore fired shells into the city of Puerto Plata, the Machias anchored in the inner harbor and with some shots from her main battery stopped the artillery fire into the city, after which there was no further firing. We have the situation well in hand, and no additional vessels, either United States or foreign, will be needed to prevent the bombardment of Puerto Plata. The prompt stopping of the artillery fire into the city this afternoon will have a very reassuring effect upon the Americans and other foreigners in the city, who have recently displayed great anxiety about their protection and safety.
>
> At 8:30 P. M. Friday the revenue cutter Algonquin took on board forty-two persons for passage to San Juan, thirty-three being Porto Ricans and nine Americans, ten men, thirteen women, and nineteen children, and then steamed for San Juan. The Clyde Line steamer Seminole, from Norfolk en route to Santo Domingo City, arrived at 3 P. M. Friday, and after delivering mail took away from Puerto Plata four persons—one French, two Spanish, and one Chinaman. The Clyde Line steamer Algonquin, en route to New York, arrived at 7 P. M. Friday and took away from Puerto Plata twenty-four persons—five Americans, thirteen British, three French, and three Cubans. These passengers were put on board the three vessels named by the South Carolina boats. RUSSELL.

The Navy Department today was emphatic that Capt. Russell's summary enforcement of his orders indicated no change in policy, and that the silencing of President Bordas's battery did not mean that American intervention on a wider scale would be undertaken. The orders had been emphatic, and the attacking forces seemed to think they could be disregarded with impunity. The United States has never indicated its sympathies as to the contending forces, though as under the treaty it was responsible for the Custom House at Puerto Plata, its obligation in this instance was clearly not to encourage attack by the Government's troops.

The Machias is a gunboat of 1,177 tons, 204 feet in length, and with 32 feet beam. Her main battery consists of eight guns of about 4-inch calibre and four smaller guns. She was formerly used by the Naval Militia of Connecticut.

Secretary of the Navy Daniels said the other day that there was no intention to send more ships to the island, and Friday's incident is not thought to have changed his mind on that score.

$500,000 FIRE AT DOVER, N. J.

Incendiaries Destroy Richardson & Boynton Stove Plant.

DOVER, N. J., June 28.—All of the plant of the Richardson & Boynton Company, except the shipping department building, was destroyed by fire today. The firm manufactured stoves and ranges, and its plant, which was Dover's largest industry, covered thirty acres of ground. The loss is $500,000, partly covered by insurance. The works, which ordinarily employ 1,100 men, were shut down three weeks ago for repairs.

Charles Helfer, a night watchman, says he made the rounds of the works at 6:30 A. M. and found everything all right. At 7:30 o'clock he saw smoke coming from the trimming shop. Men who were in the street say they saw flames in three or four different places at the same time.

Dover's two steamers and an auto chemical engine and truck manned by the Volunteer Fire Department responded to the general alarm. All the buildings were frame except the shipping building, which is built of concrete. The water pressure was inadequate, and the flames spread rapidly to the casting and cleaning shop, the mounting, boiler, patent filing, drill and patternmakers' shops, each in a separate building. Three Lackawanna Railroad box cars in the yard near the shipping building were burned. All the finished stock on hand was in the shipping building. The firemen concentrated their efforts to save that building.

For an hour or two there was fear the flames might spread to the town. The firemen successfully defended the nearest buildings.

Incendiarism is suspected. Secretary and Treasurer W. L. R. Lynd, who is also Mayor of Dover, said he couldn't account for the fire. There was no fire in any building of the plant, and the engines had been cold since the shutdown. It is recalled that a threatening letter was sent to Mayor Lynd demanding he should prevent the delivery of the Slattery anti-Catholic lectures. He declined to interfere, and the lectures were delivered on May 15 and 16 last.

The plant will be rebuilt at once. At noon a gang of laborers was put to removing the débris. The company has offices in New York.

Francis Ferdinand Shot During State Visit to Sarajevo.

TWO ATTACKS IN A DAY

Archduke Saves His Life First Time by Knocking Aside a Bomb Hurled at Auto.

SLAIN IN SECOND ATTEMPT

Lad Dashes at Car as the Royal Couple Return from Town Hall and Kills Both of Them.

LAID TO A SERVIAN PLOT

Heir Warned Not to Go to Bosnia, Where Populace Met Him with Servian Flags.

AGED EMPEROR IS STRICKEN

Shock of Tragedy Prostrates Francis Joseph—Young Assassin Proud of His Crime.

Special Cable to THE NEW YORK TIMES.

SARAJEVO, Bosnia, June 28. (By courtesy of the Vienna Neue Freie Presse.)—Archduke Francis Ferdinand, heir to the throne of Austria-Hungary, and his wife, the Duchess of Hohenberg, were shot and killed by a Bosnian student here today. The fatal shooting was the second attempt upon the lives of the couple during the day, and is believed to have been the result of a political conspiracy.

This morning, as Archduke Francis Ferdinand and the Duchess were driving to a reception at the Town Hall a bomb was thrown at their motor car. The Archduke pushed it off with his arm.

The bomb did not explode until after the Archduke's car had passed on, and the occupants of the next car, Count von Boos-Waldeck and Col. Morizzi, the Archduke's aide de camp, were slightly injured. Among the spectators, six persons were more or less seriously hurt.

The author of the attempt at assassination was a compositor named Gabrinovics, who comes from Trebinje.

After the attempt upon his life the Archduke ordered his car to halt, and after he found out what had happened he drove to the Town Hall, where the Town Councillors, with the Mayor at their head, awaited him. The Mayor was about to begin his address of welcome, when the Archduke interrupted him angrily, saying:

"Herr Burgermeister, it is perfectly outrageous! We have come to Sarajevo on a visit and have had a bomb thrown at us."

The Archduke paused a moment, and then said: "Now you may go on."

Thereupon the Mayor delivered his address and the Archduke made a suitable reply.

The public by this time had heard of the bomb attempt, and burst into the hall with loud cries of "Zivio!" the Slav word for "hurrah."

After going around the Town Hall, which took half an hour, the Archduke started for the Garrison Hospital to visit Col. Morizzi, who had been taken there after the outrage.

As the Archduke reached the corner of Rudolf Street two pistol shots were fired in quick succession by an individual who called himself Cavrio Princip. The first shot struck the Duchess in the abdomen, while the second hit the Archduke in the neck and pierced the jugular vein. The Duchess became unconscious immediately and fell across the knees of her husband. The Archduke also lost consciousness in a few seconds.

The motor car in which they were seated drove straight to the Konak, where an army Surgeon rendered first aid, but in vain. Neither the Archduke nor the Duchess gave any sign of life, and the head of the hospital

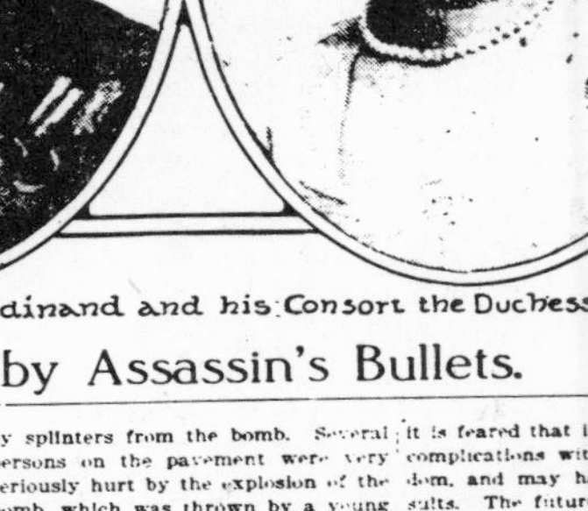

Archduke Francis Ferdinand and his Consort the Duchess of Hohenberg Slain by Assassin's Bullets.

could only certify they were both dead.

The authors of both attacks upon the Archduke are born Bosnians. Gabrinovics is a compositor, and worked for a few weeks in the Government printing works at Belgrade. He returned to Sarajevo a Servian chauvinist, and made no concealment of his sympathies with the King of Servia. Both he and the actual murderer of the Archduke and the Duchess expressed themselves to the police in the most cynical fashion about their crimes.

ARCHDUKE IGNORED WARNING.

Servian Minister Feared Trouble if Heir Went to Bosnia.

Special Cable to THE NEW YORK TIMES. [Dispatch to The London Daily Mail.]

VIENNA, June 28.—When the news of the assassination of the Archduke Francis Ferdinand and the Duchess was broken to the aged Emperor Francis Joseph he said: "Horrible, horrible! No sorrow is spared me."

The Emperor, who yesterday left here for Ischl, his favorite Summer resort, amid acclamations of the people, will return to Vienna at once, in spite of the hardships of the journey in the terrible heat.

The Archduke, who was created head of the army, went to Bosnia to represent the Emperor at the grand manoeuvres there. This was the first time the Archduke had paid an official visit to Bosnia. The Emperor visited the provinces immediately after their annexation, in 1908, and the manner in which he mixed freely with the people was much criticised at the time, as those in his party were always afraid lest some Slav or Mohammedan fanatic might attempt the monarch's life. The Emperor's popularity, however, saved him from all danger of this kind.

Before the Archduke went to Bosnia last Wednesday the Servian Minister here expressed doubt as to the wisdom of the journey, saying the country was in a very turbulent condition and the Servian part of the population might organize a demonstration against the Archduke. The Minister said if the Archduke went himself he certainly ought to leave his wife at home, because Bosnia was no place for a woman in its present disturbed state.

The Minister's word proved correct. The people of Sarajevo welcomed the Archduke with a display of Servian flags, and the authorities had some difficulty in removing them before the Archduke made his state entry into the city yesterday, after the conclusion of the manoeuvres. In these manoeuvres were the famous Fifteenth and Sixteenth Army Corps, which were stationed on the frontier throughout the recent Balkan war, and they carried out the evolutions before the Archduke.

Greeted with Cheers.

The details of the tragedy, as received in Vienna, were as follows: The Archduke was driving in a motor car toward the Town Hall in Sarajevo, with the Duchess of Hohenberg by his side. A large crowd assembled to watch them go by. The Archduke, raising his hand to his military cap, acknowledged the cheers, while the Duchess was smiling and bowing, her pretty face framed by her blonde hair.

Suddenly the Archduke's sharp eye caught sight of a bomb hurling through the air. His first thought was for his wife, and he threw up his arm in time to catch the bomb, which thus was turned aside from its course and fell on the pavement and exploded. The Archduke's motor car hastened on its way, its occupants unharmed, but the two Adjutants who were seated in the next motor car were injured by splinters from the bomb. Several persons on the pavement were very seriously hurt by the explosion of the bomb, which was thrown by a young man named Tabrinovitch, (Gabrinovics,) who is a typist from Trebenje, in Herzegovina, and is of Servian nationality. He was arrested some twenty minutes later.

The Archduke and his wife left the Town Hall, intending to visit those who had been injured by the bomb, when a schoolboy 19 years old, named Prinzip, who came from Grahovo, fired a shot at the Archduke's head. The boy fired from the shelter of a projecting house.

Wore Bullet-Proof Coat.

The boy must have been carefully instructed in his part, for it was a well-guarded secret that the Archduke always wore a coat of silk strands which were woven so densely, so that no weapon or bullet could pierce it. I once saw a strip of this fabric used for a motor-car tire, and it was puncture-proof. This new invention enabled the Archduke to brave attempts on his life, but his head naturally was uncovered.

The Duchess was shot in the body. The boy fired several times, but only two shots took effect. The Archduke and his wife were carried to the Konak, or palace, in a dying condition.

Later details show that the assassin darted forth from his hiding place behind a house and actually got on the motor car in which the Archduke and his wife were sitting. He took close aim first at the Archduke, and then at the Duchess. The fact that no one stopped him, and that he was allowed to perpetrate the dastardly act indicate that the conspiracy was carefully planned and that the Archduke fell a victim to a political plot. The aspiration of the Servian population in Bosnia to join with Servia and form a great Servian kingdom is well known. No doubt today's assassination was regarded as a means of forwarding this plan.

Break News to Children.

The Archduke's children are at Glumex, in Bohemia, and relatives already have left Vienna to break the news to them. The Duke of Cumberland motored to Ischl immediately upon receipt of the news and was received by the Emperor, who will arrive in Vienna at 6 o'clock tomorrow. The bodies of the Archduke and his wife will not be brought to Vienna until tomorrow a week.

The Archduke Charles Francis Joseph, the new heir to the throne, is at Reichenau, near Vienna, with his wife, Princess Zita of Parma, and their little son and daughter. He is expected in Vienna tonight.

When the first news of the assassination became known in Vienna, early this afternoon, crowds collected in solemn silence and discussed the report, which was not credited at first. Every one connected with the press was stormed by crowds asking whether confirmation had been received, and on hearing the truth they said, "How awful!" and then dispersed, to go about their ordinary business or pleasure. The newspapers are getting out extra editions, and the whole city talks of nothing else.

New Heir Popular.

The Archduke Charles Francis Joseph, who is now heir to the throne, always has enjoyed great popularity. He was trained for the throne from the first, although he was kept somewhat in the background, being sent to country garrisons. He was not allowed to undertake to act as the representative of the Duchy of Vienna to as great an extent as the Viennese would have wished. This, however, did not detract from his popularity, while the Princess Zita, his wife, won all hearts before she married the heir to the throne, and the birth of a son two years ago completed her popularity, if, indeed, anything was lacking.

General opinion here connects the assassins with the Servian faction, and it is feared that it will lead to serious complications with that unruly kingdom, and may have far-reaching results. The future of the empire is a subject of general discussion. It is felt that the Servians have been treated too leniently, and some hard words are being said about the present foreign policy.

All the public buildings are draped in long black streamers and the flags are all at half-mast.

BRAVERY OF ARCHDUKE.

Gave First Aid to Those Wounded by the Bomb.

SARAJEVO, Bosnia, June 28.—Archduke Francis Ferdinand, heir to the Austro-Hungarian throne, and the Duchess of Hohenberg, his morganatic wife, were shot dead in the main street of the Bosnian capital by a student today while they were making an apparently triumphant progress through the city on their annual visit to the annexed provinces of Bosnia and Herzegovina.

The Archduke was hit full in the face and the Duchess was shot through the abdomen and throat. Their wounds proved fatal within a few minutes after they reached the palace, whence they were hurried with all speed.

Those responsible for the assassination took care that it would prove effective, as there were two assailants, the first armed with a bomb and the other with a revolver. The bomb was thrown at the royal automobile as it was proceeding to the Town Hall, where a reception was to be held, but the Archduke saw the deadly missile coming and warded it off with his arm. It fell outside the car and exploded, slightly wounding two aids de camp in a second car, and half a dozen spectators. It was on the return of the procession that the tragedy was added to the long list of those that have darkened the pages of the recent history of the Hapsburgs.

As the royal automobile reached a prominent point in the route to the palace, an eighth grade student, Gavrio Prinzip, sprang out of the crowd and poured a fusillade of bullets from an automatic pistol at the Archduke and the Duchess. Both fell mortally wounded.

Prinzip and a fellow-conspirator, a compositor from Trebinje, Nedeljo Gabrinovics, barely escaped lynching by the infuriated spectators and were finally seized by the police, who afforded them protection. Both men are natives of the annexed province of Herzegovina.

Wards Off the Bomb.

The first attempt against the Archduke occurred just outside the Girls' High School. The Archduke's car had restarted after a brief pause for an inspection of the building, when Gabrinovics hurled the bomb. This was so successfully warded off by the Archduke that it fell directly beneath the following car, the occupants of which, Count von Boos-Waldeck and Col. Merizzo, were struck by splinters of iron.

Archduke Francis Ferdinand stopped his car, and after making inquiries as to the injuries of his aids and lending what aid he could, continued his journey to the Town Hall. There the Mayor began the customary address, but the Archduke sharply interrupted and snapped out, "Herr Burgomeister, we have come here to pay you a visit and bombs have been thrown at us. This is altogether an amazing indignity."

After a pause, the Archduke said: "Now you may speak."

On leaving the hall the Archduke and his wife announced their intention of visiting the wounded members of their suite at the hospital on their way back to the palace. They were actually bound on their mission of mercy when, at the corner of Rudolf Street and Franz Josef Street, Prinzip opened his deadly fusillade.

bullet struck the Archduke in the face. The Duchess was wounded in the abdomen and another bullet struck her in the throat, severing an artery. She fell unconscious across her husband's knees. At the same moment the Archduke sank to the floor of the car.

Plunges Into River.

After his unsuccessful attempt to blow up the imperial visitors Gabrinovics sprang into the River Miljachka in an effort to escape, but witnesses plunged after him and seized him.

A few yards from the scene of the shooting an unexploded bomb was found

WIDESPREAD POLITICAL PLOT THOUGHT TO HAVE INSPIRED KILLING OF ARCHDUKE

ich, it is suspected, was thrown away an accomplice after he had noted the ccess of Prinzip's attack.

he assassins were questioned by the lice during the course of the afternoon, and both seemed to glory in their ploit. Prinzip said he had studied for time at Belgrade. He declared he had g intended to kill some eminent person from nationalist motives. He was aiting the Archduke at a point where knew the automobile would slacken ed, turning into Franz Josef Street. e presence of the Duchess in the car used him to hesitate, but only for a ment. Then his nerve returned and emptied his pistol at the couple. He nied that he had any accomplices.

Prinzip is 18 years old and Nedeljo brinovics is 21. Gabrinovics told the lice that he had obtained the bomb m Anarchists at Belgrade, whose mes he did not know. He similarly nied that he had accomplices and nded the whole tragedy with cynical ifference.

Anti-Servian demonstrations began tonight. The crowds knelt in the streets d sang the national anthem. The yor of Sarajevo issued a proclamation to the inhabitants of the city denouncing the crime, and declaring that the confessions of the assassins it s shown beyond all doubt that the b thrown at the Archduke's car from Belgrade.

It is said that after the attempt with bomb the Duchess tried to dissuade Archduke from venturing in the car again. To allay her fears M. tiorek, Governor of Bosnia, said: t's all over now. We have not more one murderer in Sarajevo," whereupon the Archduke decided to go on.

meeting of the provincial Diet today the President of the Chamber expressed Bosnia's profound sorrow and ignation over the outrage and paid a ing tribute to the Archduke and the chess. He also declared his devotion the Emperor and the ruling house.

FRANCIS JOSEPH PROSTRATED.

Aged Emperor Takes to His Room on Hearing of the Tragedy.

ISCHL, June 28.—Emperor Francis Joseph suffered a profound shock when was informed of the assassination the Archduke Francis Ferdinand and Duchess, and retired immediately his private apartment after giving [illegible] that everything should be in [illegible] for his return to the palace Schoenbrunn on Monday. The Duke Cumberland paid a visit of condolence this afternoon.

The three young children of the Archduke and the Duchess, who remained with the aged Emperor when their ents went to Bosnia, were playing the gardens of the palace when the ws came. Nobody had the heart to orm them of their bereavement.

The succession, if no change is made reafter, now passes to Archduke arles Francis, son of the late Archduke Otto, and a nephew of Francis rdinand, who married Princess Zita Parma. They have one son and one ughter.

VIENNA, June 28.—The assassination Archduke Francis Ferdinand and the chess of Hohenberg caused a profound sensation here. The streets were ckly thronged, and anxious inquiries re made regarding the details of this, latest addition to the list of tragedies that have befallen some of the most inent members of the imperial ily during the present reign.

Immediately the assassination became wn, the authorities took possession the telegraphic and telephonic facilities Sarajevo and shut off unofficial communications.

The utmost sympathy is expressed where for the venerable Emperor cis Joseph, who only yesterday Vienna for Ischl, upper Austria, to uperate after a serious illness.

Archduke Francis Ferdinand and his left the capital on Wednesday in best of health and spirits for a tour Bosnia and Herzegovina, where the chduke was also to take command important manoeuvres. According to orts received here, they had met with enthusiastic reception everywhere. mors of a plot against the life of the r to the throne had been in circulation for the past few days, and the police thought they had taken effective cautions to safeguard the Archduke the Duchess.

It is feared that the Sarajevo tragedy still further embitter the none too ndly relations existing between Austria and Servia. Both the youth who d the fatal shots and the bomb wer are Servians, with close associations with Belgrade. The bombs also e from Belgrade. It is likewise remarkable that the first news of the assassination received at Budapest came the Servian capital.

The effect of the tragedy on the stock ket was the subject of discussion by kers, but tomorrow being St. Peter's St. Paul's Day, and a holiday, will e the Boerse an opportunity to recover before the opening on Tuesday.

Telegrams are being received tonight all parts of the kingdom announcing the immense sensation caused by the e. All public festivities have been celed.

Anti-Servian demonstrations occurred ght outside the Servian Legation. stones were thrown at the residences of prominent Servians. Troops e ordered out to suppress the disorders.

It is reported here that several Bosnians and Serbs have been arrested at ajevo for complicity in the plot, ch is said to have wide ramifications. The newspapers have issued special editions with black borders, expressing abhorrence at the crime.

The Wiener Zeitung pays high tribute the extraordinary zeal and devotion the empire displayed by the Archduke to whose indefatigable care, it were due the great developments recent years in the Austrian army navy.

POPE MUCH DEPRESSED.

Spends a Long Time in Prayer—Italian Foreign Office Anxious.

Special Cable to THE NEW YORK TIMES.

ROME, June 28.—The terrible crime Sarajevo, though not a personal to the Italian sovereigns as they not know the Archduke Ferdinand, causing considerable anxiety at the eign Office. Although the Archduke was considered unfriendly to y, being very clerical and also under the influence of the military party successor is an unknown quantity, and might not be such a stanch porter as the aged Emperor of the ple Alliance.

The Pope was much depressed by crime. At first his entourage intended to withhold the news, but Cardinal Merry del Val broke it as gently possible to the Pope who every is less able to withstand the [illegible]

[illegible] SEND CONDOLENCES.

[illegible] States Government Notified of Assassination by Embassy.

[illegible]

Prince Maximilian Charles of Hohenberg

Princess Sophie of Hohenberg

Prince Ernest of Hohenberg

CHILDREN OF THE LATE ARCHDUKE.

WARSHIP SPEEDS TO TELL THE KAISER

Found on Racing Yacht, He Returns, Deeply Affected, to Kiel Harbor.

LEAVES FOR BERLIN TODAY

Kaiserin Motors to Join Him—German Emperor Recently Guest of the Dead Archduke.

Special Cable to THE NEW YORK TIMES.

KIEL, June 28.—"The regatta will continue; I myself leave for Berlin tomorrow." This, uttered in low tones, was the first observation of the Kaiser on returning, grave-faced, to the yacht Hohenzollern at 6:30 o'clock tonight after having learned while racing in the Baltic the terrible fate of Archduke Ferdinand and his consort.

As soon as the news reached Kiel, about 4:30 o'clock, the fastest torpedo boat at the station was dispatched to pick up the Meteor. The Kaiser ordered the race broken off forthwith, and the yacht taken in tow of the torpedo boat. He stood silent on the deck but acknowledged the salutes offered to him en route. How deeply he was affected could plainly be seen by those on the British flagship King George V., which the Meteor passed at close range.

Before proceeding to the harbor the Kaiser sent a wireless from the torpedo boat canceling a large dinner party on the Hohenzollern tonight. Previously all German and British warships had placed their flags and the Austrian royal standard at half-mast, the sudden appearance of the mourning emblem being the first inkling the vast Sunday crowds on the quayside had of the day's dread happening at Sarajevo.

Prince Henry of Prussia, who was addressing the Danish war veterans at Sonderburg, canceled his stay there and telegraphically ordered the garden party, to be held at his castle at Kiel at sundown, abandoned. Then the Prince hurried to Kiel by motor.

The Kaiserin was spending the week end at her ancestral home at Grünholz, in Schleswig-Holstein. She also motored to Kiel and joined the Kaiser on the Hohenzollern. The Kaiserin accompanies her husband to Berlin.

The Emperor will of course proceed to Vienna for the funeral, and would doubtless be prepared to go sooner if he thought his presence could comfort Emperor Francis Joseph.

The tragedy has a special poignancy for the Kaiser owing to his Majesty's having been a guest of his assassinated ally, together with Admiral von Tirpitz, at Konopischt, Bohemia, the first week of June. The Archduke was an ardent advocate of a forward naval policy for Austria-Hungary, and it was supposed he sought the experienced counsel of von Tirpitz in connection with future projects.

By The Associated Press.

BERLIN, Monday, June 29.—The Berlin press comment in serious vein on the killing of Emperor Francis Joseph's heir.

The Tageblatt thinks the crime will further intensify the already tense situation in the dual monarchy.

The Tages Zeitung says the shooting is directly connected with the Servian discontent at Austria's assistance in the creation of an Albanian State. It calls the death of the Archduke "a great loss to Austria, removing a strong figure, upon whom the hopes of all patriots rested."

The Morgen Post says:

"General opinion will ascribe the crime to the Pan-Slavistic propaganda, and great efforts will be necessary to prevent it from having as eventful results for Europe as did the events at Prague preceding the thirty years' war."

The Vorwaerts says that the fatal shots are a fearful warning to Austria-Hungary and that the Archduke fell as a sacrifice to the Austro-Hungarian policy toward the Balkans.

ENGLISH COURT MOURNS.

No Officials in London to Receive Report of Assassination.

Special Cable to THE NEW YORK TIMES.

LONDON, Monday, June 29.—News of the assassination of Archduke Ferdinand and his wife, the Duchess of Hohenberg, reached London early yesterday afternoon, and was speedily made public by a special edition of a weekly paper. Official and diplomatic persons in many cases were apprised of the tragedy long after it was widely known among the general public, for, as usual on a Summer Sunday, practically all the official world had gone out of town.

Nobody was at the Foreign Office to receive the news, and up to after 7 o'clock last evening inquiries at the Austro-Hungarian Embassy elicited the response that nothing official to confirm the reports was known there. Further investigation showed this meant merely that no member of the embassy staff was on hand to open the dispatches which poured into the embassy. An attaché arrived just [illegible]

Two future Emperors of Austria. Archduke Charles Francis Joseph and his Son, the Archduke Francis Joseph Otto.

The New Heir and the Present Ruler.

Emperor Francis Joseph of Austria

received official dispatches confirming the reports of the double tragedy.

King George himself received the first news through the good offices of a newspaper. The Daily Mail telephoned Buckingham Palace early yesterday afternoon and imparted the information to a member of the royal household, who conveyed it to King George. His Majesty immediately dispatched Sir Charles Cust to the Austrian Embassy, where the royal messenger learned that Count Mensdorff was in the country, and all the members of his staff likewise out of town.

The King has given orders that the state ball which was to be held at Buckingham Palace this evening be postponed, and that court mourning be observed for one week. The King's levee arranged for tomorrow morning has not been countermanded, as it is regarded merely as an official function and not a festivity.

At Marlborough House, Queen Alexandra's residence, the news came as an especial shock, for not only were the Archduke and Duchess well known there, but one of Queen Alexandra's guests is Queen Olga of Greece, whose husband, Queen Alexandra's brother, died at the hand of an assassin last year.

The chief note struck by all editorial comment is the tragic history of the Emperor Francis Joseph.

The London Times says:

"His public successes have always been overshadowed by his private griefs. The death of his brother Maximilian in Mexico, the tragedy of the Crown Prince Rudolf, the crowning blow of the assassination of the Empress Elizabeth, and now this last dreadful occurrence make a story of woe for which history furnishes few parallels.

"The sympathy of the whole world will go forth to the bereaved Emperor and all Englishmen will pray he may be able to bear this final affliction with the fortitude he has never failed to show in his deepest trial.

"We should say the events of yesterday will probably tend to strengthen the dual system, at any rate for a time, but the more the southern Slavs see their hopes recede the greater will be the danger of an ultimate explosion. Already they grow restive under repression, and if their dreams are thwarted in one direction they may turn in another. For the moment the horror of the assassinations engrosses thought, but they must assuredly add fresh clouds to the political outlook in Austria-Hungary."

Speculation is rife in London as to the effect of the assassination upon the aged Emperor. No love was lost between the Kaiser and his heir. Indeed, after Francis Joseph's recovery from his recent illness, at one time expected to prove fatal, it was a current saying among the Viennese that the Emperor was helped to pull through by his keen desire to spite his nephew and delay his accession to the imperial and royal throne as long as possible.

Among the Viennese the Archduke was highly unpopular. His manner was brusque and occasionally overbearing. He possessed none of those qualities of frank bonhomie and democratic good-fellowship which characterised his uncle.

With the Hungarians the Archduke was even less of a favorite. Despite his marriage to the Hungarian Countess Chotek, the Archduke's sympathies were never with the Magyar faction of his future subjects. The great nobility of Budapest on their side rather resented the marriage which raised a woman belonging to one of the smaller families above their heads, and the possibility of the Duchess of Hohenberg's children succeeding to the Hungarian Throne while debarred from the Austrian imperial throne was not considered a compliment by the Magyars.

Notwithstanding Francis Joseph's personal dislike to his nephew, the shock of today's news is likely to exercise a prejudicial effect upon the physical health of a man of 84.

LONDON, June 28.—The Archduke Ferdinand and his wife were almost as great favorites in England as they were in German Court circles. They were [illegible]

from being officially recognized for the reason that she was not of royal blood.

Last year the Archduke and the Duchess visited King George and Queen Mary at Windsor and received every possible attention.

It was generally believed that upon the Archduke's accession Hungary would recognize the Duchess as Queen of Hungary, and that in time the Archduke would succeed in getting Austria to do likewise, although their children could never hope to ascend the throne.

Those who met them on their visits to England describe the Archduke and his wife as a much attached couple, entirely free from any affectation. They moved about among friends in England, and besides visiting at the royal palaces, spent many weeks at different times in English country homes.

The Archduke's successor as heir to the throne, Archduke Charles Francis, is likewise a popular figure in England and other countries. He represented Austria at the Coronation of King George, as Archduke Francis Ferdinand would not attend because his wife could not take her place by his side. Archduke Charles, besides speaking English and German fluently, has a thorough knowledge of the Slav tongue. He is of athletic build and carriage, and shows distinct traces of his military training. With Austria and Hungary alike, he is immensely popular, and the close study of Slavonic and Balkan problems to which he has devoted himself should be of good service when he comes to the throne.

In unofficial London the opinion seems to prevail that the crime could not be attributed to any political intrigue, but rather to the inherent hatred of the Serbs for their Austrian neighbors, which has become more bitter since the recent events in the Balkans, in which the Serbs charge Austria with taking part against Servia.

"There is no more pathetic figure in Europe today," said one official, "than the venerable Emperor, the sunset of whose days has been clouded by this last of the dreadful calamities which have befallen the tragic Hapsburg line."

Archduke Francis Ferdinand's death is certain to have considerable effect upon the European situation. Rightly or wrongly, he was credited with having ambitions for the further extension of Austrian territory toward the Gulf of Salonika, which would, if attempted, lead to a conflict with Austria's neighbors and thus again cause a rupture between the dual monarchy and Russia.

The Archduke's friendship for the German Emperor also gave his enemies in Europe an opportunity to accuse him of favoring an aggressive policy, and it had been a fetish in the continental capitals that when he came to the throne there would be an end to the peace that had prevailed among the great powers.

Where he was better understood, however, the Archduke received credit for being an ardent patriot, whose only ambition was to maintain the greatness of his country, which he believed could only be accomplished by making the army and navy such as to be feared by the strongest enemy.

PARIS PRESS FEARS WAR

But Thinks There Will Be an End of Ferdinand's Projects.

Special Cable to THE NEW YORK TIMES.

PARIS, Monday, June 29.—The French press devotes a great deal of space to Archduke Ferdinand's assassination. The general tone indicates a belief in the end of his projects and reputed intention to make Austria a greater Slav power. Combined with the admitted hostility of Servia and the opposition of Russia, French interests caused him to be regarded as the European stormy petrel.

A note of genuine regret is that, deprived of the Archduke's strong personality, Austria inevitably will be more subject to German influence. Several journals express the fear that the consequences will be sufficiently serious again to plunge the Balkans, if not Europe, into a conflict.

PARIS, Monday, June 29.—[illegible]

TRAGEDY MAY ALTER POLITICS OF EUROPE

Late Archduke's Ambitions Regarded with Distrust in Many of the Capitals.

WANTED A TRIPLE EMPIRE

And His Designs on Slavic Territory Had Long Threatened to Bring About Trouble.

Special Cable to THE NEW YORK TIMES.

LONDON, Monday, June 29.—A new situation has been created in Europe by the tragedy at Sarajevo. While the crime cannot but arouse universal horror and indignation for the assassin and sympathy for the victims, there are political considerations which make it an event of as high importance from that point of view as in its personal dynastic aspects.

In Russia, England, and France the Archduke Francis Ferdinand was regarded as one of the most serious dangers to European peace. Even in Germany his accession to the throne was viewed with apprehension. A man of strong opinions and great will power, he already, as heir to the throne, exercised a potent influence upon Austrian policy. He was a strong supporter of Aerenthal, whose tenure of the Austrian Foreign Office saw Europe on the verge of war, and throughout the more recent developments in the Balkans some of the difficulties encountered by European statesmen in limiting hostilities to Southeastern Europe arose from the Archduke's insistence on what he regarded as the full measure of Austria's rights.

Russian diplomacy for some time past has been convinced that Francis Ferdinand's policy ultimately would bring about a crisis in Austro-Russian relations, and military movements in the great Slav empire which only a few months ago created a sensation in the Continental press were defended by Russian newspapers on the ground that they were necessary precautions against Austria.

Germany, which in 1909 threatened a mobilization of her army unless Russia agreed to Austria's annexation of Bosnia and Herzegovina, afterward used her influence in a contrary direction, and Kaiser Wilhelm's counsels of moderation to his Austrian ally undoubtedly were not without their effect upon the course of events immediately preceding and following the Balkan war.

The dead Archduke's dream was what is known in Austria-Hungary as trialism. His object was to prevent that disruption of the dual monarchy which it has so often been predicted would follow the death of Emperor Francis Joseph. Trialism is a device for consolidating the empire, which at present is a dual State, controlled in Austria by Germans and in Hungary by Magyars.

In this disposition of nationalities the Slav elements of the population do not play their proper rôle in the body politic of the empire. Trialism aims at reconstituting the State with three instead of two populations, one of them predominantly Slav, just as one is now predominantly German and the other predominantly Magyar. A necessary corollary of trialism is the increase of the Slav populations of the empire by the inclusion of Slavonic races of the Balkans.

Whether such an ambition ever could be realised is open to doubt. The actually existing hatred of Austria by Servia and other Slav peoples of the Balkans would have to disappear first or be ground out under the heel of a military despotism.

The effort to develop these ambitions by the latter process naturally would be alarming to Russia, which dreams of a Slav empire extending over the Balkan States.

It is a curious instance of the irony of fate that the Archduke, whose ambition was the annexation of a Slav kingdom, was stricken by the hand of a youthful enthusiast, who dreamed of "a greater Servia" that would unite under one sceptre Servians of the present kingdom of that name and their Slavonic brethren of Bosnia, Herzegovina, Dalmatia, and Croatia.

While the importance of the Archduke's assassination in the field of international politics is thus seen to be great it may also have vast effects upon the internal fortunes of Austro-Hungary.

The new heir apparent, while popular in Vienna, is described as a young man of no remarkable ability, and the process of disintegration of the empire might very well be helped by a régime the head whereof was a weakling. The oft-repeated prediction respecting the breaking up of the empire on the death of Francis Joseph, however, is discredited by well-informed observers of Austrian affairs. In the conscriptional army the Government possesses not only a weapon to repress separatist movements, but an instrument whose power may weld together the various elements of which the dual kingdom is composed.

MAY MEAN INTERVENTION.

Grave Consequences of a Change of Ferdinand's Policy.

A couple of revolver shots probably never before formed a connection between such a line of complicated causes and such an infinite variety of possibly still more complicated effects as those which yesterday killed Archduke Ferdinand and his wife, the Duchess of Hohenberg.

Since the absorption of Herzegovina and Bosnia in 1908 by Austria, the ambition of Servia has been to keep that Empire in check, and to secure for herself a strip of coast line on the Adriatic. Keeping pace with that ambition has been that of Austria to extend her narrow coast line southward, and to absorb all the Slav territory possible. This last ambition has often found expression in the words of the ill-fated heir presumptive to the Austrian throne.

He realised that the days of the dual monarchy might end, through German or Russian intervention, with the death of the venerable Francis Joseph, and to preserve the entity of the empire he conceived the idea of a triune empire made up of Magyar, Slav, and German States.

It was in pursuance of this policy that Herzegovina and Bosnia were added to the Slav territory of the Empire and caused guns to be leveled across the Danube six years ago.

But these guns did not then explode. At the time it seemed as though Servia, backed up by Russia, might force Austria to withdraw, when Germany came to the rescue of her ally and caused Russia to dismiss her Foreign Minister and abolish her Pan-Slavonic policy. A state of armed neutrality then ensued until the Balkan war.

The maintenance of the Turk in Europe had long been acknowledged by the powers to be a vital necessity—not because of any particular desire to befriend the Turk, but solely because the downfall of the Turkish Empire would mean a disruption of the relative strength of the mutual bond on which reposed the peace of Europe.

Aside from the Pan-Slavonic force represented by Russia tending to destroy this equilibrium was the other force represented by Austria-Hungary and the Archduke Ferdinand's scheme for a triune empire.

But while Russia would have gained access to the Mediterranean by the destruction of European Turkey, Austria-Hungary would have left that territory as a rampart against Russia on the east and have forced her way through the heterogeneous mass of Macedonia to the Aegean or the Strait of Otranto. In other words, Austria would have liked the land north of Greece as a Slav appendage to her German and Magyar nationalities.

It is no wonder, therefore, that the Austro-Hungarian scheme found more sympathy in the chancelleries of Western Europe than the Russian, which the defeat of Turkey by the little Balkan nations in the late war has perceptibly strengthened.

One power, however, kept Austria in line, and has continued to keep her in line, even in the present Albanian imbroglio. That power is Italy, to whom Austrian control of the Adriatic would be fatal.

The foregoing shows how Austria was able to exercise such an influence at the Congress of London eighteen months ago, and still later at the Congress of Bokharest, and, while preventing Servia from gaining territory on the Adriatic, was able quietly to appropriate the Sanjak of Novi Bazar.

The Kingdom of Albania was created by the powers so that neither Austria nor Servia should have access to the sea at that point. All that Russian influence could do for Servia was to prevent Albania from becoming a protectorate of Austria-Hungary.

These are the principal points in the causes which led up to the two revolver shots. Now for their possible effects:

The great exponent of a Magyar-German-Slav Empire is dead. Austria-Hungary has today a population of over 50,000,000, thus classified: 30,300,000 Cisleithanians and 20,000,000 Transleithanians. The former are divided as follows: Germans, 10,000,000; Slavs, 18,000,000; Latins, 1,000,000. Transleithania or Hungary has about 20,000,000 inhabitants, including about 700,000 Germans scattered through Presburg, Temesvar, and Transylvania.

In other words, about one-fourth of the entire population is German, one-fourth Slav, and one-half Magyar. The first have already come under the Pan-Teutonic influences of Berlin, the second under the Pan-Slavonic influences of St. Petersburg. There remain only the Magyars, who have usually been found ready to take care of themselves.

There are formidable reasons why intervention from either Germany or Russia may arrive in the present crisis unless the tradition of the late Archduke's tri-une empire be conserved and strengthened by united action at Vienna and Budapest.

Both in Germany and in Austria herself there has long been a desire for German intervention. Germany needs the agricultural products of German Austria and also free access to the Adriatic. Austrian Germans are no longer the controlling influence in Austria-Hungary; they have lost confidence in themselves, but not in the principles of Pan-Germanism as construed in Berlin.

This same is true of the Austrian Slavs in regard to the principles of Pan-Slavism as expressed in St. Petersburg, and, in a milder form, in Belgrade, Sofia, and Bukharest.

The situation caused by the revolver in the hands of the Servian student is one of infinite possibilities.

HOW AUSTRIA ENCROACHED ON THE BALKANS.

overshadows the feeling of horror and reprobation over the assassination and the deep sympathy for the aged Emperor in the comments of the morning papers. The opinion is expressed that the tragedy will intensify the Serbophile feelings and draw Servia and Russia closer and place Austria more under the dependency of Germany.

President Poincaré telegraphed condolences to Emperor Francis Joseph, and Premier Viviani sent expressions of regret to the Austrian Premier.

NEW HEIR IS POPULAR.

Charles Francis Joseph a Young Man of Good Impulses.

Special Cable to THE NEW YORK TIMES.

LONDON, June 28.—Archduke Charles Francis Joseph, the new heir to the throne of Austria-Hungary, is a nephew of Archduke Francis Ferdinand, and a great-nephew of the Emperor. He is a son of the late Archduke Otto and Princess Marie Josepha of Saxony, and is only 26 years old. In 1911 he married a distant cousin, the Archduchess Zita of Parma. He is a typical young Austrian officer, very gay, very popular, and extremely devoted to his wife, who is a great favorite with the Emperor.

The Archduke's slender, tall figure was recently seen at many Court functions. His predominant characteristics are tact, graciousness, and gracefulness of demeanor, which explain his popularity. Like most members of the House of Hapsburg, he is an excellent shot and is fond of hunting. He also is an eager motorist and has often been known to drive his own car. Of dancing he is exceedingly fond, but a skating accident some years ago prevents him from waltzing.

When he is in Vienna he is to be seen constantly at the opera and theatres, rarely missing a night. He has a preference for light music, and excels as a linguist, speaking not only German, Hungarian, French, English, and Italian well, but also Polish. His English is particularly good, as in his childhood he was under the care of an English governess.

The Archduke holds the rank of Major in the Thirty-ninth Infantry Regiment, and is an honorary officer in various Prussian, Saxon, and Bavarian regiments. He has one child, the Archduke Francis Joseph Otto, 2 years old. He takes the child out with him in his motor car with a perambulator packed at the back of the car, and, to the amusement of the Viennese, he is often seen wheeling the little Archduke in the perambulator.

The Archduke Charles Francis Joseph, now next in succession to the Austrian throne, is the eldest son of the Archduke Otto, who was the younger brother of Francis Ferdinand. Archduke Otto was born at Graz in 1865 and died in Vienna in 1906. He was married at Dresden in 1886 to Maria Josepha, Princess of Saxony, who is still living at Vienna. The only children of the marriage are the Archdukes Charles Francis Joseph and Maximilian Eugen Ludwig, the latter of whom is 19 years old and a student of law.

Charles Francis Joseph was born at Persenbeug on Aug. 17, 1887. He attended the Vienna public schools, [illegible]

Bourbon house of Parma. The Duchy was made a part of the Kingdom of Italy after the war of 1859, and since that time the principal residence of the family has been at the castle of Schwarzau, not far from Vienna. It was here that the Princess Zita was married on Oct. 21, 1911. Her half-brother Henry is now head of the house. Their father, Duke Robert, who died in 1907, was married first to Princess Maria Pia of the Two Sicilies, and second to Princess Maria Antonia of Parma, who still lives at Schwarzau. Princess Zita is a child of the second union and was born at the Villa Pianore, near Viareggio, on May 9, 1892.

Of her nineteen brothers and sisters many are feeble-minded, but the Archduchess Zita herself has always been extremely healthy and of considerable mental brilliancy. She received an old-fashioned convent education, but is fond of tennis, hunting, and outdoor sports in general, and already has made a position for herself at the imperial court. At a ball at Schoenbrunn Palace last March she took for the first time a place at the head of the Archduchesses.

As usual, it is said that her union with the Archduke was the result of a love match. In this case some color seems to be lent to the theory by the strong belief that the Emperor had wanted Charles Francis Joseph to marry a daughter of the Archduchess Maria Valeria, his own favorite daughter, who was married in 1890 to the Archduke Franz Salvator of Hapsburg-Tuscany. Aside from his reputed disappointment at the failure of this plan, the old Emperor is said to have been reluctant to see his grandnephew marry into the family of Parma, which contains so many subnormal members. The Princess Zita, however, impressed him so favorably after he had begun to make her acquaintance that the Emperor, thinking of his dead wife, is said to have exclaimed that Zita would be a second Elizabeth.

The Archduchess Zita now has two healthy sons, the older of whom, Francis Joseph Otto, was born at the Villa Warthols, near Reichenau, on Nov. 20, 1912.

MANY RULERS FELL AT FANATICS' HANDS

Like Ferdinand and Duchess, They Were Victims of the Misguided National Spirit.

A CENTURY'S LONG LIST

Anarchy, Revolt from Tyranny and Dynastic Strife Each Inspired Assassins' Deeds.

To national spirit, seeking fanatical vengeance, is to be ascribed the assassination of Francis Ferdinand and his wife. Bosnia was restive under Austro-Hungarian rule, and the discontent of late had grown in intensity.

There have been many assassinations of rulers due to this spirit. Chief of the victims was President Abraham Lincoln, shot and mortally wounded on April 14, 1865, in Ford's Theatre, Washington, by John Wilkes Booth. The conspiracy of which Booth was a member was formed by Southerners, maddened by the fall of the Confederacy, and embraced all the higher officers of the Federal Government in its scope. William H. Seward, Secretary of State, was the only other man whom the conspirators succeeded in attacking.

Mehemet Ali Pasha, another victim of this spirit, was a Prussian expatriate who had become a Turkish General. He was murdered by Albanian nationalists in 1878. Yi Wan Yon, Korean Premier, was killed in December, 1909, on account of political animosities growing out of the impending annexation of Korea by Japan.

Lord Cavendish, Chief Secretary for Ireland, and Thomas Burke, Under Secretary, were murdered by Irish nationalists in Phoenix Park, Dublin, in 1882.

Nationalist murders have been numerous in the Czar's dominions, where Poles, Finns, and others are in constant revolt. Among the higher officers killed for nationalist reasons in recent years were Gov. General Bobrikoff of Finland, in 1904; Lieut. Gov. Boguslavsky of the Caucasus, in the same year; Procurator Johnson of the Finnish Senate in 1905; August von Hennings, Assistant District Chief of Courland, in 1906; Gen. von Liarpiarski, acting Military Governor of Warsaw, in 1906; Prince Dixhavakoff and family, in Transcaucasia, in 1909.

An extraordinary number of assassinations of rulers and persons high in authority have occurred in the last hundred years. Besides the rulers who have been killed by anarchists who believe in militant tactics, several have been assassinated by fanatics who believed themselves appointed instruments of fate for the removal of some one who had been denounced by agitators.

Of this latter sort was the assassination of President McKinley by Czolgosz at Buffalo, in September, 1901. Czolgosz was an anarchist who had heard on many sides that McKinley ought to be removed, and finally came to believe himself the one to do it. King Humbert of Italy, on the other hand, was killed as the result of a carefully laid anarchistic plot said to have originated in Paterson, N. J. He was shot at Monza on July 29, 1900, by Angelo Bresci.

Sadi Carnot, President of France, was stabbed by an Italian anarchist named Caserio on June 24, 1894, and died the next day. The Empress Elizabeth of Austria was murdered by the French-Italian anarchist Lucchenl at Geneva on Sept. 10, 1898. Antonio Canovas del Castillo, Premier of Spain, was killed by an anarchist on Aug. 23, 1897.

King George of Greece was shot mortally at Salonika a few days after his triumphal entry into the town, on March 18, 1913. His murderer was a Greek named Aleko Schinas, who probably was half demented. In the same class, presumably, was the man who killed Spencer Perceval, Prime Minister of England, in the lobby of the House of Commons in 1812.

It was left to the [illegible] ever, to furnish the [illegible] killed by a disappointed [illegible] President Garfield was shot in a railroad station in Washington on July 2, 1881, by Charles J. Guiteau, and died some months later. Guiteau's declaration that he wanted to obtain the succession of Vice President Arthur generally has been taken as a mere attempt to cover a personal grudge.

Prince Danilo of Montenegro was assassinated by a personal enemy in 1860, and the Earl of Mayo, Governor General of India, while on a visit to the penal settlement in the Andaman Islands in 1872, was slain by a convict, who broke away from the guards.

Dynastic strife, perhaps the most frequent cause of the assassination of sovereigns in time past, has led to few murders since the beginning of the nineteenth century. The chief instances are in Servia. Prince Michael Obrenovitch was killed in 1868 by partisans of the house of Karageorgevitch, and on June 11, 1903, King Alexander and Queen Draga were slain by a group of military conspirators, who proceeded to put Peter Karageorgevitch on the throne.

The murder of rivals for the Presidency or dictatorship has been frequent in some of the lesser Latin-American republics, and the instance of the killing of Francisco Madero, "while attempting to escape," has many precedents. Nearly all of the Presidents, dictators, or Emperors of Haiti have been killed by assassins, successful rivals, or mutinous troops, or have committed suicide to escape the fate that threatened prisoners.

Liberal revolt against tyrannous or unduly repressive government has accounted for more killings than all the other causes together. Chief among the nations in this respect is Russia, where Alexander II. was slain by terrorists in 1881, in spite of the fact that he had instituted many reforms. He was believed to be going back into the hands of the reactionaries. The Czar Paul was killed in 1801 by a group of Court officials, who had found his tyranny unbearable.

Premier Stolypin was killed in 1911, and M. von Plehve, Minister of the Interior, in 1904. The Grand Duke Sergius, uncle of the Emperor Nicholas, was slain in the Kremlin in 1905; and there is hardly a Russian Emperor, Grand Duke, or high official in the history of the last one hundred years who has not again and again had narrow escape from violent death.

In Italy the Duke of Parma was killed by Liberals among his subjects in 1854. Nasr-ed-din, Shah of Persia, was assassinated in 1896; Sultan Abdul Aziz of Turkey was forced to abdicate by a constitutionalist rising in 1876 and a few days later either killed himself or was murdered; Nazim Pasha, Commander in Chief of the Turkish Army, was killed on Jan. 23, 1913, in a military revolution carried through by the Young Turk Party. Stefan Stambuloff, who did probably more than any other man to create the Bulgarian nation of today, was slain on the streets of Sofia in 1895, with policemen standing by. He had had violent disagreements with King (then Prince) Ferdinand, and it was generally believed that the country had become too small to hold them both.

Juan Prim, Marshal of Spain and a leader in the liberal movement in that country in the middle decades of the nineteenth century, was [illegible]

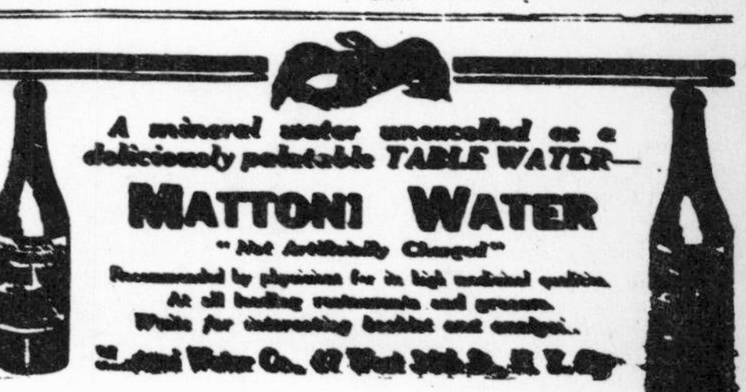

"All the News That's Fit to Print."

The New York Times.

THE WEATHER
Fair today and Thursday; fresh north and northeast winds.
For full weather report see Page 15.

VOL. LXIII...NO. 20,640. NEW YORK, WEDNESDAY, JULY 29, 1914.—EIGHTEEN PAGES. ONE CENT In Greater New York, Jersey City and Newark. Elsewhere TWO CENTS.

AUSTRIA FORMALLY DECLARES WAR ON SERVIA; RUSSIA THREATENS, ALREADY MOVING TROOPS; PEACE OF EUROPE NOW IN KAISER'S HANDS

MME. CAILLAUX FREED BY JURY

Wild Tumult in Court After the Verdict—Mobs in Streets Display Anger.

'MURDERESS!' CRIES CROWD

Spectacle of Opposing Counsel Embracing Calms the Uproar for a Moment.

MME. CAILLAUX RECEIVES

Attired in an Evening Gown, Is Congratulated by Her Friends —Says Labori Obtained Acquittal.

Special Cable to THE NEW YORK TIMES.

PARIS, July 28.—The jury in the trial of Mme. Henriette Caillaux, wife of the ex-Premier and ex-Minister of Finance, tonight acquitted her of the charge of murdering, on March 16, Gaston Calmette, editor of the Figaro. The jury had been out for fifty minutes. Although no one expected a severe sentence, the verdict for the moment stunned all in the courtroom except a crowd in the extreme rear, which apparently had a premonition of what was going to happen and was prepared to voice its emotions in loud cheers.

M. Caillaux evidently had a similar vision, for exactly at the moment when the jury left the court room to go through the form of meditating and deliberating its verdict the large Caillaux limousine, stocked with pillows, rugs, and attendants, drew aside to the entrance to the prisoners' exit of the Conciergerie.

By the time the angry crowd left the court room and a mob of several thousand in the street had realized what had happened, the released woman had signed the book at the Conciergerie and had been safely driven away.

A cordon of gendarmes surrounded both the prison and the Palais de Justice adjoining it from early evening, but the crowd broke the ranks and a wild fight ensued.

Mobs Shout "Assassin!"

The boulevards until a late hour were filled with mobs numbering thousands, yelling "Assassin!" and "Down with Caillaux!" The crowds were finally dispersed by dragoons.

There was pandemonium in the courtroom from the time the jury went out until the guards cleared it half an hour after the verdict was returned. It was impossible for anybody to sit, see, or hear. Free fights occurred all over the place, even within the rail marking the space reserved for the court officials. When the jury returned the noise reached the climax, Judges and guards trying to produce order.

It was several minutes before the foreman of the jury could be heard. After the verdict Mme. Caillaux, who had been lying back in her chair, threw her arms about her counsel, Maitre Labori. M. Caillaux was not in court, but was in his car outside.

The demonstrations in the courtroom were chiefly against the verdict, there being "boos" and hisses and cries of "Assassin!" Finally there was a round of cheers for Maitre Labori and another for Maitre Chenu, counsel for The Figaro, who smiled grimly as the verdict was read.

The day's session was devoted to the summing-up speeches of the barristers. There were few incidents, except at the beginning, when the crowd, which was bigger than on any preceding day, became unruly.

At a critical moment of Maitre Chenu's speech—just as he began to describe the scene of the shooting—Mme. Caillaux had another fainting spell, and was carried from the prisoners' inclosure.

There were many arrests of boulevard demonstrators tonight. The trouble would probably have been more serious had not the war situation attracted the greater attention.

Prisoner Falls on Labori's Neck.

PARIS, July 28.—Mme. Caillaux was acquitted after a trial lasting nine days. The announcement of the jury's verdict was followed by the wildest tumult. Mme. Caillaux tottered and fell on the neck of her counsel, Fernand Labori, and embraced him. Her hair was undone and fell over her shoulders. Her hat dropped to the floor. The spectators stood up on desks and chairs. "Caillaux!" "Labori!" and cries of "Caillaux! Assassin!" merged into one.

The din was deafening. Several groups of barristers came to blows and Republican Guards, in an endeavor to separate them, joined in the mêlée. The spectacle of Maitre Labori and Maitre Chenu, the latter counsel for the Calmette family, embracing each other, calmed the tumult for a moment, but it was redoubled when they left the building with Mme. Caillaux.

Failing to make himself heard, the presiding Judge, followed by the other Judges, marched out of the room. The advocates took complete possession of the court, and some of them mounted the Judges' desks and harangued the crowd. The guards then cleared a portion of the court, and, comparative quiet being re-established, Presiding Judge Albanel returned and read the judgment, ordering the release of Mme. Caillaux.

Much shaken with emotion, Mme. Caillaux departed by the witnesses' door, the guards making a lane through the crowd. She covered her face with her hands as if to shield herself from the furious cries of "murderess!" by way of a number of narrow corridors and back staircases, reaching a small side door in the Palace of Justice, where an automobile was waiting, and she drove off unobserved.

M. Caillaux left the building by the main entrance on the arm of his devoted friend, Deputy Pascal Ceccaldi, amid mingled cheers and hoots.

Thus ended the most sensational trial that the Paris courts have had to deal with in years. Each day provided its dramatic thrill, and although the verdict has been pronounced the ultimate outcome cannot be foretold.

The session of the court today was devoted to speeches by counsel. Mme. Caillaux had come into the prisoner's dock pale and worn, and she collapsed in the course of the address of Maitre Chene, who denounced her bitterly.

Prosecutor's Speech Mild.

The speech of the Procurator General, Jules Herbaux, was unusually mild in tone. To the jurors he said: "Your duty, as the defenders of the interests of society, requires you to find a verdict of guilty, but no one expects you to be pitiless."

Maitre Labori, who came last, delivered a masterpiece of passionate eloquence. He concluded amid tempestuous applause:

"My wish is that Mme. Caillaux shall leave here acquitted, and that the press shall be purified. Let us keep our anger for our enemies abroad. Let us leave this court resolute and united to face the perils which threaten us!"

Mme. Caillaux had been becoming visibly weaker as the sitting continued today, and appeared unconscious of what was taking place in court. A hot-water bottle was placed beneath her feet and a cushion at her back soon after she entered the court.

Meanwhile Maitre Edward Seligman, one of the attorneys representing the family of the murdered editor, continued his address. He said:

"The sons of Gaston Calmette asked us to bring them to this court to seek justice. We refused to do so, but do not forget, gentlemen of the jury, with what anguish the orphans await your verdict. You have heard witness after witness speak in praise of the late M. Calmette. There has been only one discordant note, and that came from M. Caillaux. What connection with the case has the fortune of the murdered man? How many millions must a man have in order to permit his being assassinated with complete impunity?"

Following Maitre Seligman came Maitre Chenu, and his cutting analysis of the actions of Mme. Caillaux on the day of the tragedy was too much for the prisoner. She collapsed and fell in a heap on the floor of the prisoners' enclosure.

At the moment Mme. Caillaux swooned Maitre Chenu was saying:

"I will speak of nothing except the assassination of M. Calmette. I will ask the accused whether, when she spoke of her love for her daughter, she thought of the two children of M. Calmette, whose pictures never left him. I shall not attempt to go into the biography of Mme. Caillaux. She is a cool, sensible woman, without emotion or pity. She has tears only for herself. She worked with tenacity to break up her lover's home. You see the result—the mistress triumphed over the lawful spouse. They are bound up in each other—in their happiness, in their hopes, even in their murder plans.

"M. Caillaux is a man of inordinate and limitless ambition, whose power rests on his own audacity and on the fear he inspires.

"M. Caillaux omitted to tell his wife of the assurances given by President Poincaré that Calmette was incapable of printing private letters. They did not fear that. What they feared was the publication of the report by Victor Fabre on the Rochette swindle.

"The husband's violent words at the lunch table decided the wife to substitute herself for him, and she prepared the assassination with as much calm as a society woman fitting in calls between two tea parties."

"Down With Caillaux!"

Demonstrations against the Caillaux verdict occurred in several places tonight. In the Boulevards excited crowds discussing the merits of the case, grew to large proportions, and when the jury's verdict became known there were shouts of derision and cries of "Down with Caillaux!"

In one section the mob became so disorderly that mounted Republican Guards were hastily summoned to assist the police in quelling the disturbances. A large number of police and rioters were injured, and many arrests were made.

Maurice and Jean Rostand, sons of the dramatist, were among those taken into custody.

The Figaro office was also the scene of a demonstration.

After dining at home with her husband and a few friends Mme. Caillaux attired in a handsome evening gown, received a number of intimate acquaintances.

"It is Maitre Labori," she said, "to whom I owe the good fortune to be finally free. He pleaded today with all his fine talent, and I am profoundly grateful to him."

Press Condemns the Verdict.

Special Cable to THE NEW YORK TIMES.

PARIS, Wednesday, July 29.—The acquittal of Mme. Caillaux rouses scanty but hostile comment. The Eclair says: "When the news was published yesterday Paris growled." Echo de Paris says: "The country will attribute the result to the baneful influence of politics."

The Figaro says: "It is the most enormous scandal of our epoch and covers the radical republic with mud and blood. It is an abominable parody of justice. Mme. Caillaux has torn an acquittal from a dazed jury, a terrified Government, and sold Judges."

The Matin gives an account of the incidents following the acquittal and refrains from comment, as does The Journal.

STORY OF THE CRIME.

Shooting Due to Calmette's Newspaper Campaign Against Caillaux.

The Caillaux case, the most celebrated French trial since the Dreyfus case, began on the evening of March 16, when Gaston Calmette, editor of The Figaro, was shot in his office by Mme. Henriette Caillaux, wife of Joseph Caillaux, ex-Premier and Minister of Finance in Premier Doumergues's Cabinet. He died a few hours later. The shooting was the consequence of a vigorous newspaper campaign carried on by Calmette against Caillaux.

Caillaux is an excellent financier and campaign manager. He was Premier in 1911, holding office during the Morocco crisis, and resigning in January, 1912, on account of popular dissatisfaction at the settlement made with Germany at that time.

Calmette's attacks charged, among other things, that Caillaux had used his influence to delay the trial of the swindler, Henri Rochette, in 1906, so as to give him time to escape to Mexico, and that as Minister of Finance he had promised to certain claimants against the Government $1,200,000 on condition that they subscribe 80 per cent. of that sum to the Radical campaign fund. It is said that Calmette had various letters in his possession charging that Caillaux was a tool of Germany in the Morocco crisis, which he had not yet published at the time of his death.

WARBURG IS WON, HITCHCOCK THINKS

Expects Nominee for the Reserve Board to Appear Before Committee.

SECRET CONFERENCE HERE

Banker Is Made to Understand There Is No Discrimination Against Him.

TECHNICAL POINT EXPLAINED

Charles R. Crane Called to White House, Presumably to Get Offer of Jones's Place.

Senator Gilbert M. Hitchcock of Nebraska, who has been acting as Chairman of the Banking and Currency Committee during the absence of Senator Owen in Europe, had an unofficial conference in this city last night with Paul M. Warburg in which he urged on Mr. Warburg that he should appear before the committee, which has under consideration his nomination for membership in the Federal Reserve Board.

Senator Hitchcock was found at the Pennsylvania Station just as he was leaving for Washington at midnight. He seemed greatly pleased with the result of his conversation with Mr. Warburg, and said he saw no reason now why Mr. Warburg should not consent to appear before the committee.

"Did Mr. Warburg say whether or not he would do so?" Senator Hitchcock was asked.

"No," the Senator replied, "but he seemed to understand after our talk just how the committee felt toward him, and that there had been no discrimination against him, and he indicated in every way that he would be willing to appear. I believe Mr. Warburg's attitude has been changed by the explanation I have been able to make to him. I think it has been made clear to him that it is the wish of President Wilson that he should understand that no desire to discriminate against him was intended."

Senator Hitchcock had been down to Southampton, L. I., to visit his family and stopped over in the city a few hours on his way to Washington. He would not say where the interview was held.

No Discrimination Intended.

"I think Mr. Warburg's attitude," he said, "was due to the feeling that there was some discrimination in the committee against him, but generally a committee always has the privilege of inviting before it for investigation men who are nominated to Judgeships and other high offices. This is due only to a desire on the part of the Senate to acquaint itself fully with these men and what they have done.

"Personally I know that Mr. Warburg is an important man in the business and financial world, and has been connected with big things, but he has been in this country only a comparatively short time, and it is to inform itself further of his achievements that the committee has invited him before it. I think the Senate feels the same way toward Mr. Warburg as the committee feels.

"The reason Mr. Warburg felt that he had been discriminated against was probably because three of the five nominees for members of the Federal Reserve Board were readily confirmed. Two of these were officials in Washington, and there was little that could be asked of them that was not already known in official life in Washington. The third man was W. P. G. Harding of Birmingham, Ala. He wrote out for the committee a complete history of his life, and this was sufficient for its purposes."

SUGGEST A. BARTON HEPBURN.

Administration Still Hopeful of Warburg's Confirmation.

Special to The New York Times.

WASHINGTON, July 28.—While the Administration is hopeful that Paul M. Warburg will appear before the Senate Committee on Banking and Currency to testify in regard to his appointment on the Federal Reserve Board, nothing definite has been heard from Mr. Warburg on the subject.

While the impression prevails that Mr. Warburg would be confirmed if he found it consistent with his dignity to accept the committee's invitation to appear, his continued refusal has resulted in the suggestion of others to take his place. A. Barton Hepburn of the Chase National Bank of New York was the most prominently mentioned today, though there is nothing official indicating that serious consideration has been given to any candidate other than Mr. Warburg.

Senators of the Committee on Banking and Currency were mildly shocked today to learn that Chairman Owen favored for the place his lifelong friend, the Rev. Dr. J. M. T. Johnston, a retired minister now in the banking business in Kansas City. At Mr. Owen's request Dr. Johnston appeared before the committee last Summer in support of the Owen-Glass Currency bill. Much of the anecdotal part of his testimony has been stricken from the committee's record. Quickly wearying of the academic topic assigned to him, the Rev. Dr. Johnston branched out into stories of an intimate domesticity that were received in silent astonishment by his mixed audience.

C. R. CRANE CALLED BY WILSON

Chicago Capitalist May Be Offered Jones's Place.

Special to The New York Times.

CHICAGO, July 28.—Charles R. Crane, who is about to retire from the Presidency of the Crane Company, has been invited to Washington by President Wilson.

The action of the President is taken to mean that Mr. Crane will be offered the place on the Federal Reserve Board made vacant by the withdrawal of the nomination of Thomas D. Jones.

According to the intimate friends of Mr. Crane, he is not disposed to undertake the duties of a member of the Federal Reserve Board, since they would tie him to Washington. Should the President persuade him, however, to take the position, it is declared he undoubtedly would be of service in the organization and administration of the new banking and currency systems, as his long business experience would be invaluable in this connection.

President Wilson is to see Mr. Crane at the White House tomorrow.

Notice Sent to the Powers of the Opening of Hostilities.

SERVIAN VESSELS SEIZED

Sharp Fighting Begins Along the River Drina on the Bosnian Frontier.

COUNTER INVASION PLAN

Montenegrin and Serb Armies to Invade Bosnia and Start a Rebellion There.

GREY'S PEACE PLAN FAILS

Kaiser Declines to Join in Conference to Exert Pressure on Austrian Ally.

BUT REPLY IS CONCILIATORY

And London Still Has Faith That His Influence Will Avert General Conflict.

Special Cable to THE NEW YORK TIMES.

LONDON, Wednesday, July 29.—Austria-Hungary declared war on Servia yesterday. The declaration was made at noon to the Servian Government by means of an open telegram. The Austro-Hungarian forces followed up the declaration by seizing two Servian vessels at Orsova, on the Danube, together with a number of boats.

The question whether the Austro-Servian war can be localized and a European Armageddon can be avoided now depends, so far as anything can depend on one man, upon Emperor William.

THE NEW YORK TIMES correspondent referred yesterday to the hopes of the British Foreign Office that the Kaiser's personal influence would be exercised for peace. Now that Germany has refused to accept Sir Edward Grey's suggestion of an ambassadorial conference and Austria has declared war on Servia, the only hope of avoiding that greater conflict, which the whole world apprehends, lies in the conversations that are proceeding directly between Vienna and St. Petersburg, and particularly the turn which can be given them by the German monarch.

The Kaiser's Role.

THE TIMES correspondent is informed on the best authority that great hopes are based on Emperor William's influence in this direction. This information is reflected in The Times editorial this morning, which says:

"There is reason to believe that in the most exalted quarter of Germany the maintenance of European peace is warmly and honestly desired. The pressure from all manner of influential personages and groups is doubtless being exerted to overcome the pacific leanings of the Emperor. It may tax his powers of resistance severely, but in foreign affairs he is the undoubted master and he has often shown that he has a will and judgment of his own. We still hope with some confidence that they will be exerted on the side of that peace which it has often been his honorable boast he helped to keep for six and twenty years.

"Our Paris correspondent repeats that grounds exist for the belief that Germany has already given a better proof of her wish for peace than is known to France."

In London Germany's reply to Sir Edward Grey's proposal is not looked upon as a diplomatic rebuff. The tone of the reply was conciliatory, and Prince Lichnowsky, the German Ambassador here, explained that Germany, while most anxious to co-operate with Great Britain in the attempt to find a settlement, was unable to accept the rôle of a mediator so far as the Austro-Servian dispute was concerned, as she must eschew anything calculated to create the impression that she was not in entire harmony with her Austrian ally. The German Ambassador particularly insisted on the weight which Germany attaches to co-operation with Great Britain, with a view to localizing the conflict.

The conversations at St. Petersburg between Count Szapary, the Austrian Ambassador, and Premier Sazonoff, are understood to be proceeding on a tone which gives good hope that it will be found possible to prevent the conflagration spreading beyond the present limits.

Up to a late hour this morning no definite confirmation had been received here of the various reports that Russia had begun a general mobilization.

Statements that the army corps in the west and southwest of Russia were being brought up to their war strength were accepted without hesitation as part of the precautionary measures which every country in Europe, big or small, with the exception of Spain, Portugal, and Switzerland, considered necessary. The news of the issue of orders for a general mobilization of Russian forces would mean that a great European conflict would be precipitated.

May Strike First at France.

Berlin dispatches state that Germany has made it quite clear in St. Petersburg that even "a partial mobilization" will be answered immediately by the mobilization of the German Army, which, according to one dispatch, "nothing could then hold back."

This is in accordance with what is known of the German war policy. The German General Staff does not contemplate simultaneous campaigns on a great scale against both France and Russia. France can mobilize nearly as quickly as herself. Russia takes some weeks to mobilize and more weeks to move her armies from mobilization centres to the frontier.

Germany's safety lies in taking advantage of the slowness of Russian mobilization. She will content herself with a comparatively slight screen of troops along her Eastern frontier to hold back the Russians and will launch all her striking force against the French lines of defense, hoping to pierce them and break the back of the French armies before Russia is ready to act.

The next few hours is likely to show whether Germany thinks the extensive military movements which are taking place along the Russian side of the German-Austrian frontiers constitutes a partial mobilization.

In this connection extreme importance attaches to the statement made in a special dispatch to THE NEW YORK TIMES from St. Petersburg that Russia will declare a general mobilization if Austria occupies Belgrade.

A military expert who is acquainted with the European situation said, when shown the dispatch, that he hoped the correspondent's forecast was incorrect, for such a step would precipitate an Armageddon, as Germany could not aford to throw away the advantage which the slowness of Russian mobilization, the chief weakness of the Dual Alliance, gave her, and would immediately strike at France.

Probable Plans of Opposing Armies.

The Servians are reported to have formed a division in the Sanjak of Novi Bazar and to be concentrating strong forces on the River Lim, which runs through the Sanjak. Montenegrin troops are stated to be in close contact with the Servian forces.

The object of these movements, according to The London Times, is apparently to threaten Herzegovina and Bosnia, where the nature of the ground is favorable for guerrilla operations.

Rumors of fighting on the Drina River that forms the frontier between Bosnia and Servia, were circulated in Vienna and Berlin. Part of the Austro-Hungarian forces is expected to advance across the Drina in the direction of Kraguoyevatz. The Servian forces, on the other hand, are expected to cross into Bosnian territory with the object of raising an insurrection among the Bosnian Serbs.

It is stated on Austrian authority that the object of Austria-Hungary is to crush and disarm Servia and, in particular, capture the Servian artillery and compel Servia to reduce her army in future to inoffensive proportions.

Austria-Hungary also is determined to sieze Mount Lovtchen, a Montenegrin stronghold, which commands the important naval base of Bocche di Cattaro, despite the opposition which Italy is expected to offer to this proceeding.

Three Italian training ships now on a visit to the Clyde have been recalled.

Austrian naval concentration has been ordered at Fiume.

Black Sea Lights Out.

The Russian authorities have ordered all lights along the Russian Black Sea coast extinguished, with the exception of the Chersonesf Lighthouse near Sebastopol harbor. Sebastopol itself is open only to Russian warships.

Russia has ordered the mobilization of fourteen army corps in the neighborhood of the Austrian frontier, but these orders are understood to be merely preparatory, not final. In diplomatic circles it is stated that Germany will not reply to this partial mobilization unless a Russian army is mobilized also in the north.

Two French Cabinet councils were held yesterday. No mobilization order has been issued, but considerable military preparations are being made. All officers and men on leave have been recalled to the colors. The French Socialists have issued a manifesto calling upon the Government to use its influence in Russia in favor of peace.

Military preparations are proceeding in Holland and Belgium, with the view of maintaining the neutrality of those countries against an attack by the great powers.

Hungarian Diet Enthusiastic.

Great enthusiasm prevailed in the Hungarian Chamber when Count Tiza, the Prime Minister, announced the outbreak of war and declared the situation demanded a deed of arms, not words. Count Apponyi, leader of the Opposition, supported the Premier. The Parliament was prorogued by royal decree.

Patriotic demonstrations took place in St. Petersburg, the crowds cheering the friendly embassies and legations, including those of Great Britain and Servia.

The Times St. Petersburg correspondent reports the growth of pessimism in official circles. News of the Austro-Hungarian occupation of Belgrade would inflame public feeling. Russian statesmen are convinced that England alone can save the situation, and that Sir Edward Grey's proposals by no means exhaust all his possibilities of persuasion.

Captured Passengers Detained.

BELGRADE, July 28, (by Indirect Route.)—The Servian steamers Deligrad and Morava were seized today at Orsova, on the Danube, by Austrians. The Servian colors were hauled down and the Austrian flag hoisted. The passengers were detained.

Many Servian families have left the capital for the country districts in spite of the advice of the authorities, while there has been a great exodus of Austrians and Hungarians from Belgrade and other parts of Servia.

Perfect order prevails in the capital, the police duties having been undertaken by a corps of volunteers composed of students.

Military preparations are being carried out with feverish activity. The troops have been concentrated in fortified positions. The headquarters of the army has been established at Kragouyevatz, but in the event of necessity will be transferred to Krushevatz, ninety miles southeast of Belgrade.

Two Army Corps at the Border.

BERLIN, July 28.—Reports from the Austrian border today state that the transport of the Eighth and Ninth Austrian Army Corps from Bohemia toward the Servian frontier began yesterday, and that there was no other traffic on the Bohemian railroads except troop trains. The two army corps in Bohemia consist of thirty-two battalions of infantry with a large number of quick-firing machine guns, six regiments of cavalry, two regiments of field artillery, and two regiments of the Army Service Corps.

An unconfirmed dispatch from Gumbinnen, Eastern Prussia, to the Taegliche Rundschau, today says Russia has occupied Wirballen, Russian Poland, with a force of engineers, cavalry, artillery, and two regiments of infantry while Russian guards have been placed along all roads on the frontier. The dispatch adds that a squadron of German Uhlans has advanced to Eydtkuhnen on the Russian frontier.

AUSTRIA MAY PAUSE.

Suggestion in Paris That She May Take Some Territory and Wait.

PARIS, July 28.—According to what is believed to be responsible opinion, there remains the possibility that when Austria has occupied some Servian territory she will in a day or two announce her intention not to proceed further, but to hold what she has taken until Servia gives competent guarantees that she will observe Austria's wishes. Russia would not then be likely to intervene, it is argued, except diplomatically, and negotiations appear to be going on at the present time between Austria and Russia.

On the announcement of war tonight Paris became animated. There were patriotic demonstrations in the capital and many other cities throughout the republic, but there were also demonstrations against the war.

A large number of noted French aviators, led by Roland Garros, in a letter to the Minister of War, have offered their services.

Maurice Barres, member of the Chamber of Deputies and President of the League of Patriots, has issued a call for a big demonstration on the arrival at Paris of President Poincaré to signify affirmation of the Triple Entente and readiness for the service of France.

Text of Austria-Hungary's Declaration of War.

VIENNA, July 28.—Austria-Hungary's declaration of war against Servia was gazetted here late this afternoon. The text is as follows:

"The Royal Government of Servia not having replied in a satisfactory manner to the note remitted to it by the Austro-Hungarian Minister in Belgrade on July 23, 1914, the Imperial and Royal Government finds itself compelled to proceed itself to safeguard its rights and interests and to have recourse for this purpose to force of arms.

"Austria-Hungary considers itself, therefore, from this moment in a state of war with Servia.

(Signed) "COUNT BERCHTOLD,
"Minister of Foreign Affairs of Austria-Hungary."

Russia Announces Its Wish to Remain at Peace Yet Is Determined to Guard Its Interests.

ST. PETERSBURG, July 28.—The Russian Government tonight issued the following official communication:

"Numerous patriotic demonstrations of the last few days in St. Petersburg and other cities prove that the firm pacific policy of Russia finds a sympathetic echo among all classes of the population.

"The Government hopes, nevertheless, that the expression of feeling of the people will not be tinged with enmity against the powers with whom Russia is at peace, and with whom she wishes to remain at peace.

"While the Government gathers strength from this wave of popular feeling and expects its subjects to retain their reticence and tranquillity, it rests confidently on the guardianship of the dignity and the interests of Russia."

CZAR'S FORCES MASS ON EASTERN BORDER

His Capital Expects War and Counts Confidently on England's Aid.

MOBILIZATION ORDER READY

German Official Says Its Issue Would Mean Launching of Kaiser's Army.

Special Cable to THE NEW YORK TIMES.

ST. PETERSBURG, July 28.—With the actual opening of the war the localization of the conflict becomes impossible. Even if Austria-Hungary goes no further than the occupation of Belgrade by the troops thrown across the Save at Semlin, Russia will declare a general mobilization.

Already rapid mobilization is proceeding in the west and southwest, virtually from the German frontier to the Black Sea.

The gravity of the situation is reflected in the diplomatic movements in this capital. The Emperor today gave audience to both the Foreign Minister and the War Minister.

A strong opinion prevails here that in the event of the outbreak of a general European war England would actively support Russia and France, her co-partners in the Triple Entente.

ST. PETERSBURG, July 28.—The fact that Austria had declared war became known here late this evening.

Thousands of persons then gathered, and, cheering wildly, marched through the main streets to the British and French Embassies, where there were scenes of enthusiasm.

Mounted police eventually scattered the crowds, without great disorder.

Says Germany Will Strike Hard.

BERLIN, July 28.—No confirmation had been received up to a late hour this evening by the German Foreign Office or the Russian Embassy of the mobilization of army corps in Russia reported in dispatches to London.

A German official said flatly that any Russian mobilization against Austria, partially or otherwise, meant war. German mobilization orders would then, he said, immediately be issued, and when these once had been sent there would be no possibility of recalling them or of Germany resting on her arms while negotiations continued, as the strategic necessities of war on her two fronts would force Germany to strike immediately and hard.

The opinion was expressed tonight in well-informed Russian circles, however, that partial mobilization of Russian troops along the Austrian frontier was quite probable as an answer to the Austrian declaration of war on Servia.

Servian officials here appeared to think that such a step could be undertaken without evoking a German counter mobilization.

PEACE CONGRESS PROTEST.

Meeting Place to be Changed from Vienna to Berne.

BRUSSELS, Belgium, July 28.—The International Peace Association, at the request of the American delegates now here, has called a meeting for next Friday.

As a protest against the warlike action of Austria the association has decided to change the meeting place of the Universal Peace Congress in September from Vienna to Berne.

Austrian Emperor to Take Command at Vienna Headquarters.

WAR FEVER AT CAPITAL

Crowds Cheer Outbreak of Hostilities and Demonstrate at Friendly Embassies.

OUTBREAK OF FOOD RIOTS

Prices Soar as Hostilities Are Declared and the Government Steps In to Regulate Them.

MANIFESTO FROM EMPEROR

Forced to Grasp the Sword, He Says, to Defend the Honor of His Monarchy.

FRANCE FEARS A GREAT WAR

Army Moves to the Frontier—Belief in Paris That Russia Will Not Desert Servia.

Special Cable to THE NEW YORK TIMES.

VIENNA, July 28.—Upon the issue of the formal declaration of war against Servia today Emperor Franz Josef gave orders for the removal of the Summer Court from [illegible] capital. His entourage [illegible] suade him that Vienna air would [illegible] suit him, but the aged Emperor [illegible] plied:

"I do not want the air of Vienna. I want the atmosphere of headquarters."

The opening of the war has caused the imposition of all kinds of restrictions upon public business. All the railways, of course, are under military control, and the telegraphs are being reserved entirely for the service of the State.

The hope is still entertained here that the war will be confined to Austria-Hungary and Servia. The report that Russia and France have intervened in Vienna is incorrect. In official circles here it is maintained that any action by those powers must be supported by the third party to the Triple Entente, namely, Great Britain. It is known that Great Britain and France do not want a European war. Peace among the great powers or war among the great powers must depend on the action of St. Petersburg.

At the Foreign Office here it is freely stated that now that war has begun Austria-Hungary will be bound to no more conditions such as she propounded prior to the outbreak of hostilities.

Food Prices Up in Vienna.

There was an abnormal rise in the price of provisions today, which caused great indignation on the part of the public, who flocked to the markets to lay in stores in anticipation of a possible scarcity. Vegetables in many cases trebled in price. Feeling ran so high that in many instances stallkeepers in the markets were mobbed or assaulted, and the police had to be called out to restore order. The authorities declare that the sudden increase in the prices of provisions and vegetables is totally unwarranted.

A permanent committee appointed to deal with the question of provisioning the country, sat today to discuss the regulation of prices in order to prevent the public being cheated. A similar meeting with the same object also was held in the Diet.

It was officialy asserted that there was no reason for [illegible] with regard to the food suply, and that it was needless for citizens to start the accumulation of stores of provisions. The only effect of such procedure, it was added, would be to still further raise prices.

Official arrangements have been made to take care of families of reservists called to the colors. In the event of a reservist being killed or reported missing an allowance of about 25 cents per day for each adult and 12 1-2 cents a day for children will be continued for six months.

The Declaration of War.

By The Associated Press.

VIENNA, July 28.—It is with a feeling of intense relief that the people in the dual monarchy look forward to the war with Servia, which for several days has seemed to be inevitable, and

WAR DRUMS BEATING ALONG THE DANUBE—MANIFESTO BY THE EMPEROR

which was today announced in the following formal declaration:

The Royal Government of Servia not having replied in a satisfactory manner to the note remitted to it by the Austro-Hungarian Minister in Belgrade on July 23, 1914, the Imperial and Royal Government finds itself compelled to proceed itself to safeguard its rights and interests and to have recourse for this purpose to force of arms.

Austria-Hungary considers itself, therefore, from this moment in a state of war with Servia.

(Signed) COUNT BERCHTOLD,
Minister of Foreign Affairs of Austria-Hungary.

The Minister of Foreign Affairs addressed a verbal note to the foreign representatives, informing them of the declaration of war, and announcing that Austria would, on the assumption of similar observances on the part of Servia, adhere to the provisions of The Hague conference of Oct. 15, 1908, and the Declaration of London of Feb. 26, 1909.

Manifesto by the Emperor.

A manifesto issued by the Emperor, after stating that it had been his fervent wish to dedicate his declining years to preserving the empire from the burdens and sacrifices of war, says:

"Providence has decreed otherwise. The intrigues of a malevolent opponent compel me in defense of the honor of my monarchy and for the protection of its dignity and the security of its possession to grasp the sword after long years of peace."

The manifesto refers to the ingratitude of Servia for the support the Emperor's ancestors afforded to Servian independence; how Servia for years has pursued a path of open hostility to Austria-Hungary; how Austrian annexation of Bosnia and Herzegovina, which injured no Servian rights, called forth in Servia outbreaks of the bitterest hatred.

"My Government," continues the Emperor, "then employed the handsome privileges of the stronger, and with extreme consideration and leniency only requested Servia to reduce her army to a peace footing and promise to tread the paths of peace and friendship."

Then recalling that it was Austrian forbearance two years ago that enabled Servia to reap the fruits of the struggle against Turkey, the Emperor says:

"The hope that Servia would keep its word has not been fulfilled; the flame of its hatred for myself and my house has blazed always higher. The design to tear from us by force inseparable portions of Austria-Hungary has been manifested with ever-lessening disguise."

Criminal Propaganda Denounced.

The manifesto then dwells on the "criminal propaganda, which has extended over the frontier, aiming at the destruction of the foundations of order and loyalty in the southeastern part of the monarchy and the leading astray of growing youth and inciting it to deeds of madness and high treason."

It continues:

"A series of murderous attacks in an organized and well-carried-out conspiracy, whose fruitful success wounded me and my loyal people to the heart, forms the visible and bloody track of those secret machinations which were operated direct in Servia."

Declaring that a stop must be put to these intolerable provocations, the honor and dignity of the monarchy protected, and its political, military, and economic developments guarded from continuous shocks, he says:

"In vain did my Government make a last attempt to induce Servia to desist. Servia rejected the just and moderate demands of my Government and refused to conform to the obligations forming the natural foundations of peace in the life of peoples and States. I must, therefore, proceed by force of arms to obtain those indispensable pledges which alone can insure tranquillity to new States within and lasting peace without.

"In this solemn hour I am fully conscious of the whole significance of my resolve, and my responsibility before the Almighty. I have examined and weighed everything and with serene conscience I set out on the path that duty points. I trust in my people, who throughout every storm have always rallied in united loyalty around my throne and have always been prepared for the severest sacrifices for the honor, greatness and might of the fatherland.

"I trust in Austria-Hungary's brave and devoted forces and in the Almighty to give victory to my arms."

The Emperor's manifesto is addressed to all his people.

Wouldn't Accept Compliance Now.

The Foreign Office declared today that even should Servia now comply with the demands contained in the Austrian note the Government of the dual monarchy would not be satisfied. Officials at the Ministry stated that Servia's reply had made it impossible for Austria-Hungary to adhere to her former standpoint, and compliance by Servia with the demands made on her could no longer influence the course of action of the Austro-Hungarian Empire.

The news of the formal declaration of war ran through the city before the extra editions of the papers could reach the vendors' hands, and was everywhere greeted with a spirit which might be described as close to religious exaltation. A great crowd which constantly increased in numbers assembled before the War Ministry and cheers greeted the appearance of military officers and the Ministry officials.

Willing to Localise Conflict.

The evening papers published the following inspired statement:

"In well-informed circles the view is that, so far as Sir Edward Grey's proposal is to localise the conflict between Austria-Hungary and Servia, the former can declare herself entirely agreed with Sir Edward Grey's remarks, but, regarding what he has said concerning the suppression of military operations, things have proceeded much too far to allow anything to be done in this direction.

Whether the war will be confined to the two countries cannot yet be said, but the feeling on this point in high official circles is optimistic. Even the certain knowledge, however, that Russia would intervene would not cause Austria to hesitate a moment or alter her course in the slightest.

Vienna is absolutely without news of the numbers of the troops, which the papers naturally are forbidden to print. A sharp censorship has been established over the press and all means of communication.

Advices from Belgrade say that the Servian capital is now situated at Nish, where the Skupshtina (National Assembly) met today. All the servians between 18 and 60 years able to bear arms have been called out, and mobilization is proceeding rapidly, although the peasants, who will have to leave their harvesting, are reported to be much discontented.

The Militaerische Rundschau reports sharp fighting along the River Drina, Servian volunteers attempting to cross the river being opposed by Austrian frontier troops. It also reports that the Servians fired on their own river transports by mistake, killing and wounding a number of Servian soldiers.

GERMANY REJECTS PLAN.

Doesn't Approve of English Proposal for a Conference.

Special Cable to THE NEW YORK TIMES.

BERLIN, July 28.—Germany has practically refused to consider Sir Edward Grey's peace proposal. She bases her action on the ground that the project constitutes an unwarranted interference with the action which Austria-Hungary has begun and which she must be allowed to carry through to the bitter end.

No scheme for the cessation of hostilities, which it is declared here could only result to the advantage of Servia, could claim the support of the Kaiser's Government. The German view is that the time for outside intervention in Austria's quarrel with the Serbs will not arrive until the Dual Monarchy has extorted full expiation for the crime of Serajevo and everything therewith associated.

Designed as Counter-Proposal.

Germany's reply to Sir Edward Grey, which is designed as a "counter-proposal," is couched in more conciliatory terms than those described, but is essentially negative in its tenor. The counter-proposal takes the form of suggesting that the cause of peace would be better advanced if the "mediatory negotiations which already have commenced with the best success" were continued among the different European Governments.

Direct negotiations between the Russian, Austrian, and German Foreign Offices, it points out, are still proceeding, and this Government is of the opinion that if the efforts of the powers are concentrated at the points of chief importance, namely, St. Petersburg and Nish, the goal desired will be attained in the quickest possible manner. Germany, in the meantime, will continue to remain in close exchange of views with all the other Cabinets, with the object of preserving European peace.

It is insisted that, grave as the situation undoubtedly is, nothing has arisen to compel the view that it is entirely hopeless. "So long as Russia has not mobilized or taken any other aggressive action," was the statement made in an authoritative quarter tonight, "it would be beyond the mark to give way to utter pessimism."

Conferences at Potsdam.

The Kaiser, who is still at Potsdam, has been in conference unbrokenly throughout the day with the political, military, and naval chieftains. The Imperial Chancellor was closeted with his Majesty alone for a long time this forenoon, and had another conference with him in the afternoon, together with Gen. von Falkenhayn, the Minister of War.

The opinion prevails in Potsdam that mobilization of the German Army and war are imminent. Unusual movements of troops through Berlin are noticeable. Great lines of infantry, clad in their new gray field uniform, marched across town from the Doeberitz camp today. It is stubbornly denied that "extraordinary measures" of any sort have thus far been taken, but it is palpable that far-reaching precautionary dispositions of a preliminary nature are in full progress.

The war spirit in Berlin has cooled off, so far as "demonstrations" are concerned. The police today decided to prohibit further processions through the streets, on the ground that they interfere with traffic. The shop windows in the Unter den Linden display prints of famous German battles. The pavements are thronged with people, who gape at the pictures by the hour. The city continues feverishly excited over the prospect of war, and extra editions of the newspapers are eagerly grabbed.

Anti-War Meetings Fall Flat.

The anti-war demonstrations of the Socialist Party throughout Greater Berlin tonight fell somewhat flat. Twenty-seven meetings were held, and they were attended by about 60,000 persons, but the denunciations against Austria and protests against Germany's participation in the war were greeted only with mild enthusiasm.

The semi-contempt in which the German Army appears to hold the army of Russia is set forth in a remarkable communiqué in today's official Military Gazette. The article says:

"Just as Europe frequently underestimates the Austrian-Hungarian Army, so is the fighting efficiency of the Russian Army usually overestimated. Nobody denies that the Russian Army numerically is extraordinarily strong, but numbers, as the wars of Frederick the Great fortunately teach, do not decide. Far more important factors are the morale of the troops, leadership, armaments, equipment, topographical conditions, railway facilities, and public sentiment.

"It is perhaps not inappropriate to call attention at this hour to the fact that Russia alone never yet won a victory over an army of equal strength. In 1877 she would not even have overthrown Turkey without the help of Prince Carol of Rumania. Against the modern army of Japan in the Manchurian war Russia suffered a serious defeat. It may be interpolated here that recent press reports of the creation of five new Russian army corps is incorrect. These corps do not exist.

"Without discussing the armies of any other great powers, it can be said without boasting that the German war establishment since 1870-71 has been developed incessantly, with the utmost intensity and sleepless zeal. All military preparations for war, of no matter what sort, have been made with Germany's well-known thoroughness. It may be said without exaggeration that Germany can contemplate the gravest events with entire equanimity, in confidence in God and her own strength."

Trips of Americans Spoiled.

Berlin is full of tourists, including many Americans bound to Carlsbad, Marienbad, and other well-known Austrian spas. They were informed today that the last through trains for Austrian destinations are leaving German points tonight. After tomorrow no guarantee can be given that passengers can be transported beyond the Austrian frontier, owing to occupation of the railway lines by military trains.

Numbers of prominent German seaside resorts are being depleted of visitors, who are hurrying back home in expectation of the outbreak of war.

German Fleet Concentrated.

By The Associated Press.

BERLIN, July 28.—The German Admiralty today ordered the concentration of the German fleet in home waters.

The gathering of Ambassadors at the weekly reception of the German Foreign Minister, Herr von Jagow, late this afternoon was decidedly pessimistic, although most of the envoys had no knowledge of the Austrian declaration of war. The British Ambassador, Sir Edward Goschen, visited the Imperial Chancellor, Dr. von Bethmann-Hollweg, as well as the Foreign Minister, and it was surmised that he was pressing upon the German Government the necessity of action to preserve peace.

After the Socialist mass meetings tonight the crowds that had attended them converged in processions to the centre of the city, singing the workmen's "Marseillaise" and shouting "Down with war." The intention was to hold meetings in the Unter den Linden and Wilhelmstrasse, but the police had made extensive preparations to cope with this and had cordoned off Wilhelmstrasse early in the evening and several hundred foot and mounted men occupied the Unter den Linden. An enormous crowd of patriotic people, however, had jammed this section before the arrival of the Socialists and drowned their songs and cries with patriotic airs and cheers for Austria and forced the Socialists to beat an ignominious retreat.

The police were able to prevent the crowds from forming processions, but they were fully occupied in keeping them away from that end of the avenue in which the Russian and French embassies are situated.

HAGUE RULE INEFFECTIVE.

Refers Only to Naval War—Might Be Important if Greece Joins Servia.

Special to The New York Times.

WASHINGTON, July 28.—Unless Montenegro, Greece, or some other nation with a coast line takes sides with Servia, Austria's proposal that the Declaration of London apply to the present war would have very little effect. That declaration relates exclusively to naval war and contraband on the high seas, and as Servia is without a navy, a merchant marine, a port or seacoast, the declaration could interest her only in regard to shipments destined for Servia through the ports of another country.

In that limited degree Austria's offer seems to give slight favor to Servia, while no benefit in return accrues to the Dual Monarchy except from public opinion. The declaration would limit the things that might be counted as contraband of war, and that might therefore be seized by Austria on neutral merchant ships. But Servia under no circumstances would be able to seize anything destined for Austria.

If Montenegro and Greece join Servia, however, all this will be changed, and the possibility would be at once raised of Austria's capturing the American battleships Idaho and Mississippi, already sold to Greece and now in process of being turned over to their new owner. The Idaho has been transferred at Villefranche to a Greek crew and renamed the Memnos. The Mississippi, under her new name, Kilkis, is now at Newport News, Va., and will sail for Piraeus in a few days. One of her higher officers will be Louis Brown, for several years a newspaper man in Washington, who attended the Naval Academy at Annapolis.

Map Showing Frontiers of Continental Nations Which May Be Involved in War.

FRANCE EXPECTS TO BE DRAWN IN

Officials Believe That Russia Will Not Sacrifice Prestige by Deserting Servia.

ARMY MOVES TO FRONTIER

Paris Police Ordered to Arrest Everybody Who Cries Down with Anybody or Anything.

Special Cable to THE NEW YORK TIMES.

PARIS, Wednesday, July 29.—A "big war" is almost certain, according to French opinion. This is not yet altogether reflected in the press, but is learned from the highest inside authoritative sources. The conviction is growing that there is a possibility that within ten days the Triple Entente and the Triple Alliance may be testing each other's strength.

Gold is already withdrawn by the Bank of France, and last night there were no signs of the yellow metal anywhere. It is impossible to obtain anything but huge five-franc silver pieces in exchange for banknotes.

An unobtrusive movement of troops toward the eastern and northern frontiers is progressing rapidly. All leave has been withdrawn everywhere. Notice of mobilization is liable to be posted on the streets at any time. Already the main line railway stations are heavily policed, and soldiers exercise surveillance of all persons traveling to the frontiers.

However, the populace, aside from hoodlums, who have been creating nightly disturbances, is almost apathetic. Demonstrations on the boulevards in no way reflect the real feelings of calm and security. There has been no run on the savings banks, as in Berlin. Everywhere are heard expressions of complete confidence in the preparedness of the French Army.

To Stop All Demonstrations.

Prefect of Police Hennion last night decided to end what Le Temps calls "disgraceful exhibitions" by giving orders to arrest everybody who cries down with anything or any one.

THE NEW YORK TIMES correspondent learns from a high financial source that they have been secretly informed that the outlook for peace is not encouraging. This feeling was also expressed in a high foreign diplomatic quarter.

The opinion of those in authority is that if Russia allows Austria any definite military action against Servia she will lose tremendous world prestige. They do not believe for a minute that she intends to lose it, and therefore the Triple Entente is bound to act. No one here believes that Russia has not been ready to avenge the Austrian aggresive policy in the Balkans for the last ten years. The idea that she is likely to remain inactive now, as at the time of the Bosnia incident because of military unpreparedness, is received scornfully.

Russia Now Ready to Act.

It is pointed out that at the time of the Bosnia incident Russia talked much, but did nothing because she was hardly convalescent from the blows of Japan. Now Russia is saying little, but dispatches from St. Petersburg indicate that more than 1,000,000 men are already in the process of mobilization.

THE NEW YORK TIMES correspondent is able to state that the official feeling is that Germany is the only country in a position to restrain Austria without bloodshed. This same opinion is very skeptical that such is German intention.

Up to last night, according to the Foreign Office, no official communication had been received that fighting had commenced. Le Temps said last night:

"What does Germany want? Is it peace or war? For the third day in succession we are obliged to repeat the question. Russia will not allow the independence of Servia to be destroyed. France and England stand by Russia. On the basis of this clearly defined certainty the Cabinets of Berlin and Vienna must gauge their activities."

Press Jibes at Germany.

This morning's press is somewhat less temperate. The Eclair says:

"Admitting that Germany wants at least a postponement of war, if not definite peace, nevertheless she is perhaps not displeased to put our patience to a rude test.

"We are forced to suspect that behind the quarrel between Vienna and Belgrade is a complicity which singularly enlarges the question."

The Figaro says:

"Though Germany ostensibly does not wish war, she is clearly not acting in the interest of peace. Her game is exceedingly dangerous, if she is hoping for diplomatic success by reason of Russian apathy."

The Matin says:

"If Russian calm makes European safety, it is German reserve that causes European anxiety. All the French parties are united in the effort to limit what the Socialist Party yesterday called an enterprise of violence without precedent, which will one day turn against imperialist Germanism the abuse it makes of brute force."

The Journal says:

"Germany's unwillingness to accede to Sir Edward Grey's proposals indicates clearly a desire to gain the time necessary for military preparations."

The Petit Journal says: "May it not be possible that the answer to the German puzzle is a premeditated plea for a general war? Do they wish to settle, not the Servian question, but the Slav question?"

FRANCE HAS 800,000 READY.

Considers Her Force the Equal of Germany's, Though Smaller.

Special Cable to THE NEW YORK TIMES.

PARIS, July 28.—In view of the concentration of French troops near the German frontier, I collected particulars as to this country's war strength. In the event of a European war France would be able to put about 800,000 men into the field immediately.

For some time past there have been huge concentration of troops at Verdun, Toul, Epinal, and Belfort, the first class strongholds forming the advance line along the German frontier, and the garrisons or second line such as Maubeuge, La Fere, Rheims, Langres, &c., also contain large bodies of men to be moved forward at a moment's notice.

Although a large number of the men now with the colors are not yet thoroughly trained soldiers, they nevertheless have enough military experience to form valuable fighting line material. Should it become necessary to utilize the field army, the total strength would be about 1,300,000. There are twenty-one army corps, besides thirty-six complete reserve divisions and some reserve cavlary.

Though the French army is nominaly inferior to Germany's, military experience, considered with the greater fighting value of the French unit, compensates for that disadvantage.

FRENCH SOCIALISTS PROTEST.

Urge the Government to Disregard "Occult Agreements."

PARIS, July 28.—Fifty Socialist deputies of the extreme group which has 104 members in the Chamber of Deputies met today and discussed the relations of France to the Austro-Servian conflict. Afterward they issued a declaration to the effect that the intervention of Russia would extend and aggravate the evils of war without offering any sure guarantees of benefit to Servia.

The declaration says that France, which has foregone for forty years in the interest of peace, her desire to recover Alsace-Lorraine ought not now, because of "occult agreements," allow herself to be drawn into conflict over Servia.

A committee consisting of Jean Jaurès and others was appointed to call on Bienvenu Martin, Acting Premier, with a copy of the declaration and to ask him his intentions concerning the calling of an extra session of Parliament.

The manifesto was made entirely representative of the party by all the extreme Socialist Deputies signing it.

Bienvenu Martin replied that the calling together of Parliament immediately would be useless because the Government had no statement to submit to it. He said the Cabinet was endeavoring to make effective the English proposal for mediation which sought the best means of avoiding an extension of the conflict.

Baron von Schoen, the German Ambassador, had a conference with Bienvenu Martin, Acting Premier, at the Foreign Office in the morning and the members of the Cabinet were summoned to meet later in the day.

René Viviana, the French Premier, who is on board the battleship La France in the North Sea, today kept in frequent wireless communication with the Foreign Office here. He is returning to France as rapidly as possible, and is due to arrive at Dunkirk tomorrow morning.

Abel Ferry, Under Secretary of State for Foreign Affairs, left Paris immediately after the Cabinet meeting to meet President Poincaré and Premier Viviani at Dunkirk.

BRITAIN PREPARES HER NAVY.

Crews of Second Fleet Filling Up—Navy Yards Are Active.

Special Cable to THE NEW YORK TIMES.

LONDON, July 28.—Precautionary measures are being taken by the British naval authorities. There was great activity at Portsmouth today, chiefly in getting ships of the second fleet ready to answer a quick call. The crews are being filled and all leave is stopped. Strong infantry detachments are guarding all the magazines.

There is also considerable naval activity on the Humber. The eighth destroyer flotilla arrived and coaled. Submarines and a cruiser took up stations at the mouth of the Humber.

The tanks of the Admiralty's oil fuel depot at Killingholme have been spotted with green, black, and red paint to render them unobservable from the sea.

A flotilla of submarines and three seaplanes have arrived in Dover naval harbor.

ITALY MASSING FLEET.

First and Second Fighting Squadrons to Concentrate at Gaeta.

ROME, July 28.—It is reported that the first and second naval squadrons are forming to concentrate at Gaeta, forty miles northwest of Naples.

Italian Warships Ordered Home.

GLASGOW, July 28.—Three Italian warships, visiting the Clyde, were ordered today to return immediately to Italian waters.

WAR DRUMS BEATING IN SERVIAN CAPITAL

King Peter Ventures Back, Then Hurries to Nish to Assume Direction of Affairs.

ALL SERVIANS CALLED OUT

Business Suspended in Belgrade, but Only Hostilities Known Are Stray Shots of Border Patrols.

By MARTIN H. DONOHUE.

Special Cable to THE NEW YORK TIMES.

SEMLIN, Hungary, July 28.—Here at the heart of the war area no active hostilities have taken place up to the time of wiring to signalize the existence of a state of war except a few exchanges of shots between patrols on the banks of the frontier rivers, the Danube to the eastward from here and the Save to the westward.

King Peter of Servia has been back in Belgrade, his capital, on the opposite bank of the Save from here, but remained only long enough to hold a conference with his Ministers, after which he left for Nish, 150 miles south of Belgrade, there to resume full control of the affairs of state.

The Treasury, the state documents, and the Parliament have already been transferred to Nish.

The legislative body, sitting at Nish, is issuing a proclamation calling to the colors all able-bodied Servians, irrespective of age.

The streets of Belgrade today resound with the beating of drums. It is a martial city. All civil business is suspended and the banks, offices, and hotels are closed.

The last of the foreign residents of that city, mostly Germans, Austrians, and Hungarians, but including two English, have just crossed to this side of the river on a steamer flying the neutral flag of Rumania.

Belgrade is nestling in the sunshine, as if it was sleeping profoundly. But Semlin and Belgrade, though within hailing distance, are not on speaking terms. The Save severs them now as the frontier of war.

Meanwhile the Servian Army gives no sign of life. No trace can be found of the existence of such an army. Several search parties which have been out have come back, unable to locate the elusive Serb. This seems to be a campaign which is to be carried out under revised rules of war. It might not inappropriately be called a game of hide-and-seek, wherein up to now the Servians do the hiding.

Belgrade is now defenseless, and could be taken at any moment by simply rowing across, by taking a steamer, or, still easier, by traversing the railway bridge, but no move has been attempted.

The enemy's capital is dominated completely by Austrian guns. The Servian artillery could be put out of action within the first day if firing should begin, but no gun is heard.

The only sign of activity I can observe in Belgrade is that displayed by the Government arsenal, the tall chimney of which throws out smoke day and night.

There is "a partial state of siege" proclaimed in Semlin. Two hundred Servian refugees from Southern Hungary are here, penniless and clamoring to be sent across to their own country. The authorities here are deliberating as to what course to pursue with regard to them, while the refugees squat by the quayside, looking across the dun-colored Save River at beloved Belgrade, so near and yet so far.

WAR RISKS ARE RAISED.

Large Amount of Insurance Done—U. S. Figures in Quotations.

Special Cable to THE NEW YORK TIMES.

LONDON, Wednesday, July 29.—The Times this morning says:

"Underwriters yesterday did a large amount of insurance against war risks. The inquiries made were many times in excess of the previous day. There were reports of many exceptional rates being paid, but inquiries in well-informed circles showed that in many cases the same rates as ruled on Monday were being paid. These were 15 guineas per cent. against any of the four powers, Great Britain, France, Germany, or Russia, being involved in war within the next six months, 20 guineas for six powers, Austria and Italy in addition to the above, for three months, and the same rate for three months, covering eight powers, the additions being Japan and the United States.

"Later in the day, on the receipt of graver news, the rates stiffened and ranged from those quoted to 5 per cent. higher in each case.

"To cover a cargo to East Australia and New Zealand via Suez 5 shillings per cent. is charged for any nationality except Russian and Austrian. For wool and produce from Australia and New Zealand the rate was 5 shillings per cent. for British vessels and 10 shillings for others except Austrian and Russian. From India the home rate was the same as for Australia.

"For produce from Russian Baltic ports by British steamers to the United Kingdom a rate of 10 shillings per cent. was quoted.

"Of particular interest was the fact that specie and coin, shipped on German liners for Hamburg from the United States, were covered at the rate of 5 shillings per cent. The usual rate in connection with the latter is about 1 shilling per cent."

GERMANY TO ROUMANIA.

Wants to Know How That Country Stands in the Dispute.

ROME, July 28.—Authoritative advices received here from Bucharest state that Germany has asked for positive assurances from Rumania of her intentions in connection with the Austro-Servian situation.

BRITISH STRIFE FORGOTTEN.

Nation Averse to Conflict, but Ready to Aid Ally.

LONDON, Wednesday, July 29.—There is absolutely no enthusiasm in England for war—no desire for this particular war, which confronts Great Britain, yet there is a general belief that her obligations to her partners in the Triple Entente, as well as her interests as a great European power, will force her to support Russia and France in any steps they may take.

The dark developments of the day were received without excitement, but with the deepest gloom. The immediate effect of the war cloud is likely to be a compromise on Home Rule, as all parties feel that domestic dissensions must be settled at all costs in the face of peril from without. The demands of the Conservative papers for a general election have been wholly hushed. The Foreign Office has become the most important branch of the Government, and no one wants to risk the possibility of losing Sir Edward Grey, with his exceptional influence in the councils of Europe.

The Government is confronting the situation with calmness. There is no sign of unusual events at the Foreign Office, except that the Prime Minister, Mr. Asquith, who seldom visits that office, called there this evening and conferred with Sir Arthur Nicolson, Permanent Under Secretary, and the Austrian Ambassador, who came to make formal announcement of the declaration of war.

The morning newspapers realize the gravity of the menace threatening Europe. Editorially they admit that Austria is justified in chastising Servia, but they argue that any attempt to destroy Servia's sovereign rights would plunge the whole of Europe into war.

The Daily Telegraph says the German Emperor holds the fate of Europe in the hollow of his hand.

"We have before us," it adds, "the appalling spectacle of a first-class power rushing to arms, and Europe, convulsed and sick with anxiety and fear, watching impotently the conflict she will be unable to control."

The Morning Post asks:

"If Austria does not want to annex Servian territory, what is the political purpose of her war? There must be some other motive than mere revenge. It seems that Austria is deliberately challenging Russia with the approval of Germany. It is a struggle between the Triple Alliance and the Triple Entente, and it seems difficult to decide which would be the greater misfortune—Europe's acceptance of the challenge, which would be followed by a great war, or non-acceptance and the consequent domination of the Triple Alliance."

"All the News That's Fit to Print."

The New York Times.

THE WEATHER
Generally fair today and Monday; gentle to moderate south winds.
For full weather report see PAGE 5, SPORTS SECTION.

LXIII...NO. 20,644. .... NEW YORK, SUNDAY, AUGUST 2, 1914.—88 PAGES, In Seven Parts, Including Picture and Rotogravure Section, Real Estate Directory, and Review of Books. PRICE FIVE CENTS.

...ERMANY DECLARES WAR ON RUSSIA, FIRST SHOTS ARE FIRED; FRANCE IS MOBILIZING AND MAY BE DRAWN IN TOMORROW; PLANS TO RESCUE THE 100,000 AMERICANS NOW IN EUROPE

...orts for Refugees ...g Considered by ...te Department.

CHARTER VESSELS

...iation Will Probably Be ...from Congress to Res- ...Stranded Americans.

SEND OVER GOLD

...eve Those Unable to Get ...h on Paper or to ...Obtain Passage.

...ARSHIPS NOW THERE

...Being Confronted with ...ny Urgent Calls for Assistance.

...S INQUIRIES POUR IN

...ton Can Only Reply That ...presentatives Are Instruct- ...Give All Possible Aid.

...NGTON, Aug. 1.—The Ad- ...ion has under consideration ...ing of army and navy trans- ...bring American refugees back ...rope, and a special request to ... for an appropriation is ex- ...be made.

...resident and Mr. Bryan dis- ...everal plans, but will not make ...decision until tomorrow, when ...ll confer again and get the ...of the bankers who usually ...e State Department abroad in ...imes.

...essary the Washington Gov- ...is prepared to send Amer- ...ssels abroad with gold for ...of of Americans. Immediate- ...r the conference with the ...t Mr. Bryan cabled all con- ...legations and embassies to ...o pains in caring for Ameri- ...ho remain in the war zones, ...give every facility to those ...shed to leave.

...Department officials admit- ...t a most serious problem was ...ting them in the plight of ...ans abroad. They estimated ...least 100,000, and possibly ...y as 300,000, were scattered ...out Europe. The disorganiza- ...European exchange has made ...ctically impossible to cash ...or letters of credit. American ...tes, legations and embassies ...oid of funds for the emergency ...has suddenly confronted them. ...re being besieged on all sides ...quests for financial assistance.

...the cancellation by several ...hip lines of their sailings many ...ans find themselves unable to ...ssage on the overcrowded boats ...rican register. American war- ...would be of little use, as they ...ardly any capacity for passen- ...Naval officers have suggested ...he Government could charter ...rtely some of the big ocean ...foreign register to bring ...ns home.

...ecial arrangement, officials be- ...he American Government could ...the use of foreign ships, secur- ...xemption from seizure if used ...r transportation of Americans.

...only American warships in Eu- ...waters are the little gunboat ...on, station ship at Constantino- ...d the battleship Maine at Ville- ...e, with Annapolis midshipmen ...e officers and crew of the bat- ...Idaho taken over at that port. ...Greek Government. The Maine ...ave Villefranche today for An- ...s.

...pecial appropriation would be ...ed to charter steamships to ...Americans home. Congress al- ...has acted promptly in such ...encies, and is expected to do so

...y applications were received at ...tate Department from persons ...United States desirous of hav- ...merican Consuls investigate and ...upon the safety of their friends ...elatives in Europe. The State ...tment is returning the uniform ...r that under their general in- ...ions the Consuls will look after ...eport the case of any Americans ...tress in their respective districts, ...onsequently that no special in- ...ions are needed.

ENGLAND HESITATES WHAT COURSE TO TAKE

Grey Wants to Throw the Weight of Great Navy at Once in Favor of Russia and France.

Special Cable to THE NEW YORK TIMES.

LONDON, Sunday, Aug. 2.—Great Britain's rôle in the European war now begun is now a great question. THE TIMES correspondent learns on good authority that the Cabinet is practically divided into equal parts on the question whether to take immediate action or await developments in the hope of remaining outside of the struggle.

Sir Edward Grey, according to this information, heads the party which believes that it is England's duty and interest to throw the weight of her navy at once into the scales on behalf of France and Russia.

Lloyd George leads the other faction, which believes that this country can with honor and advantage hold itself outside and not engage in a European conflict.

One statement, which is given for what it is worth, is that the Chancellor of the Exchequer thinks that England and the United States can together intervene at a propitious moment in such fashion as to reduce to some extent the horrors of a Continental Armageddon. In passing it may be mentioned that the wildest reports have been current on all aspects of the situation for a week past. THE TIMES correspondent refrained from chronicling them because the actual facts of the situation require no sensational embroidery.

Cabinet to Meet Tonight.

A special meeting of the Cabinet has been summoned for the unprecedented hour of 11 o'clock tonight. Most of the Ministers are remaining in town till then, and none is going out of reach. Some hope to get a day's golfing as a respite.

The Cabinet Council sat for two and a half hours yesterday. Sir Edward Grey left in the middle of the proceedings for the Foreign Office.

With reference to the Cabinet's position, The Observer this morning says:

"France and Germany have cast the die on their frontiers. Before nightfall, or even before these lines see the light may be fired in the western and decisive theatre of war the first shots of a tremendous struggle that will decide the destinies of the Old World for generations. The first great actions may decide the final issue, first in the West and then in the Near East.

"If after the lamentable wavering of last week we hesitate one day more we shall be too late to influence an arbitrament which indirectly but surely will decide our own fate no less than that of France. Our hours are numbered. If the Ministry decides today to desert France, then they will strike us out of the list of nations that any power can trust."

Fleet Ready for a Blow.

It is said that the Cabinet is likely to reach a decision tonight. One factor that will probably influence the decision is the total absence of indications of any of that anti-German sentiment which has been a feature of the spurious agitation of recent years. In the event of the Cabinet deciding upon war, speculation is rife as to what the fleet will do first.

The First Home Fleet, which sailed under sealed orders, is believed to be off the coast of Holland or in the neighborhood of Denmark. A high official of the Admiralty said to THE TIMES correspondent tonight:

"It is idle to speculate. Only three men in England know what its orders are."

Thanks to the recent Spithead review by the King, Great Britain's navy is practically ready for war, and a proclamation of mobilization would only really affect the second line. Its ability to strike a sudden, serious blow is not doubted in England, and, as is evident from the orders given to German liners, the blow is apprehended in Germany.

The Admiralty is, of course, in wireless touch with the commanding officers, and to prevent any possibility of interference with the radio communications stringent instructions have been issued that all amateur or private wireless systems must be stopped.

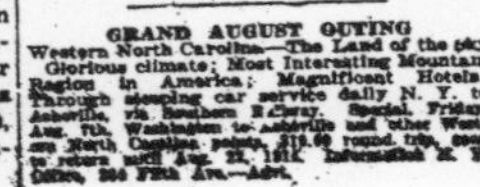

France Orders Mobilization After Germany Asks Her Intentions.

DELCASSE WAR MINISTER

Germany's Old Enemy Heads Army Organization — Once Nearly Caused Conflict.

CLEMENCEAU IN CABINET

President and Cabinet Issue a Manifesto to French Nation.

PLAIN WORDS TO GERMANY

"You Are Mobilizing; We Know It," Says Prime Minister to German Envoy.

ORDERS TO FOREIGNERS

Americans May Stay on Getting Permits—Austrians and Germans Liable to Arrest.

PARIS, Aug. 1.—An official decree orders a general mobilization of the French Army, beginning tomorrow.

The mobilization, according to the official decree, is to be completed at 11:59 o'clock Sunday night.

The wildest enthusiasm was manifested on the Paris boulevards when the news of the order became known. Bodies of men, formed into regular companies in ranks ten deep, paraded the streets, waving the Tricolor and other national emblems and cheering and singing the "Marseillaise" and the "Internationale," at the same time throwing their hats in the air.

Here and there the cry, "On to Berlin!" was raised.

On the sidewalks were many weeping women and children. All the stores and cafés were deserted.

Relations Not Yet Severed.

The decree of mobilization of the French Army, which was followed by a proclamation by the President and the Cabinet to the nation, has, however, not terminated diplomatic relations between France and Germany. Conversations between the powers, notably between Russia and Austria and between France and Germany, continued this evening.

Up to a late hour tonight, it was stated, the German Ambassador was still in Paris.

A rumor in circulation here tonight was to the effect that there were some waverers in the Cabinet yesterday on the question of ordering the mobilization, but that the views of those who asserted that it would be suicidal to allow Germany to put France to further expense with regard to war preparations without actual mobilization prevailed.

The course of diplomatic events since yesterday afternoon can be stated briefly as follows:

Baron von Schön, the German Ambassador to France, called on the French Premier, René Viviani, at 7 o'clock last evening and formally notified him that Germany had addressed an ultimatum to Russia, desiring to know by noon today whether the St. Petersburg Government would discontinue the mobilization of the Russian Army.

Baron von Schön was directed by his Government to ask what were the intentions of France should Russia's reply to Germany be a refusal to demobilise.

The German Government fixed "before 1 P. M. today" as the period within which France must answer. Baron von Schön called at the French Foreign Office at 11:40 A. M. to receive France's reply. Premier Viviani made an earnest appeal to the German Ambassador, asking if Germany could not yet do something to avert war.

The Baron promised to communicate with Berlin and to return to the Foreign Office at 4 P. M., which he did.

"You Are Mobilising. We Know It."

In the course of their second interview today Premier Viviani said to the German Ambassador:

"You are mobilizing. We know it."

Baron von Schön did not reply, and M. Viviani continued:

"This attitude of your Government has dictated ours. We were compelled to take precautions similar to yours. Our peaceful intentions remain unchanged. We wish peace, and the best proof we can give you of this is that at the present moment the French Parliament has not been convoked. Under our constitution we should be compelled to convoke it if our intentions were not peaceful."

Baron von Schön said: "But frontier incidents are unfortunately to be feared."

Premier Viviani replied:

"How can you suppose such things? Our troops are five miles from the frontier. We are, in fact, exposed to the violation of our frontier, and there is not another power in the world which would have consented to do such a thing."

This refers to the withdrawal of the French troops from the immediate frontier.

The Premier proceeded to point out that the German troops were at the very foot of the frontier posts, and said he concluded from this that if incidents occurred they could only be provoked by the German military forces.

The German reply was submitted to a French Cabinet Council, which, within a few minutes afterward, ordered a general mobilization of the French Army.

The date of the mobilization was set for tomorrow, but it really begins immediately. The men are called out in classes at intervals of days, according to the year in which they entered the army. Precise instructions are always in the possession of every man, so that he may know what to do when a general mobilization is posted.

Reservists Obey Instantly.

The response to the order of mobilization was instant, and the stations of all the railways, particularly those leading to the eastward, were crowded tonight with departing reservists. Many women accompanied the men until close to the stations, where, the women softly crying, farewells were said.

The Russian Ambassador, M. Iswolsky, called on Premier Viviani at 11 o'clock tonight and informed him that Germany had declared war on Russia.

Nothing is known among the general public as to what is going on behind the screen which fell along the German frontier at about 4 o'clock yesterday afternoon.

Arrangements were made last night by Myron T. Herrick, the American Ambassador, acting under instructions from Washington, to take over the affairs of the German Embassy, while Alexander H. Thackara, the American Consul General, is to look after the affairs of the German Consulate.

All foreigners may leave Paris or France before the end of the first day of mobilization by train, but not by automobile. Those deciding to leave France may do so by certain trains, the time tables of which are posted on the walls of Paris tonight, or by sea.

American citizens or British subjects may remain in France, except in the regions on the eastern frontier and near certain fortresses, provided they make declarations to the police and obtain special permits.

No foreigner will be permitted to leave France after the first day of mobilization without a passport signed by a Prefect. Americans, Englishmen, and other foreigners may remain in Paris by obtaining special permits from the police.

Delcasse War Minister.

LONDON, Aug. 1.—A Paris dispatch to the Central News by indirect route reports that Premier Viviani has made changes in the Cabinet.

Théophile Delcassé becomes Minister of War, and Georges Clemenceau, the ex-Premier, joins the Ministry.

M. Delcassé is one of the bitterest enemies of Germany among French statesmen. He nearly caused a war with that country in 1905.

Cabinet Council in Session Till 4 A. M.

PARIS, Sunday, Aug. 2.—The Council of Ministers, which held a late night session to discuss the European situation, adjourned shortly after 4 o'clock this morning. It will continue its discussion of the situation this afternoon. No announcement of the result of the delibera- [illegible]

Poincare Orders Mobilization, Telling France It Is Not War Yet

PARIS, Aug. 1.—President Poincaré and the members of the Cabinet today issued the following joint proclamation to the French nation:

For some days the States of Europe have been considerably aggravated, and, notwithstanding the efforts of diplomacy, the horizon has darkened. At the present hour a greater part of the nations have mobilized their forces. Even the countries protected by neutrality conventions have deemed it their duty to take this measure as a precaution.

The powers whose constitutional or military legislation differs from ours have, without issuing a decree of mobilization, begun and carried on preparations which, in reality, are equivalent to mobilization, and are but the anticipated execution of it.

France, who always has affirmed her desire for peace, who on many a tragic day has given to Europe counsels of moderation and a living example of decorum, and who has multiplied her efforts to maintain the peace of the world, has now prepared herself for all eventualities, and has taken from henceforth her first indispensable dispositions for the safeguarding of her territory.

But our legislation does not permit the completion of these preparations without a decree of mobilization. Conscious of its high responsibility, and feeling that it would fail in its sacred duty if it did not take this measure, the Government has signed the decree.

Mobilization is not war. Under the present circumstances it would appear, on the contrary, to be the best means of assuring peace with honor.

Strong in its ardent desire of arriving at a peaceful solution of this crisis, the Government under cover of these essential precautions will continue its diplomatic efforts, and still hopes to succeed. It counts upon the coolness of the people not to give itself up to unjustified emotion. It counts upon the patriotism of every Frenchman, and it knows that there is not a single one who is not ready to do his duty at this hour.

There are no longer any parties. There is an eternal France—a France peaceful and resolute. There is a fatherland of peace and justice, all united in calm vigilance and dignity.

KAISER SIGNS ORDER MOBILIZING HIS ARMY

"Let Your Hearts Beat for God and Your Fists on the Enemy," Cries Chancellor.

BERLIN, Aug. 1.—Emperor William, at 5:15 o'clock this evening, signed an order mobilizing the German Army.

A semi-official statement says that the threatening danger of war necessitates that military measures be taken for the protection of the German frontier and railway lines. Restrictions, therefore, on the postal, telegraph, and railway services are inevitable, owing to the requirements of the military authorities.

It was officially announced that the time limit of the German ultimatum to Russia expired at noon.

An official communication published in the North German Gazette says the Russian Emperor on July 29 telegraphed to Emperor William urgently requesting him to help in averting the misfortune of a European war and to try to restrain his ally Austria-Hungary from going too far.

Emperor William replied that he would willingly take up the task of mediator, and accordingly diplomatic action was initiated in Vienna.

While this was in progress the news that Russia was mobilizing arrived in Berlin, and Emperor William telegraphed to the Emperor of Russia that his rôle as mediator was by this endangered, if not made impossible.

The communication adds that a decision was to have been taken in Vienna today in regard to the mediation proposals in which Great Britain had joined Germany, but that meanwhile Russia had ordered the full mobilization of her forces. Upon this Emperor William addressed a last telegram to Emperor Nicholas emphatically declaring that his own responsibility for the safety of the German Empire had forced him to take defensive measures.

War Speech by Chancellor.

The German Imperial Chancellor, Dr. von Bethmann-Hollweg, addressed a huge procession of demonstrators today from the window of his official residence, making a stirring speech, in which he said:

"At this serious hour in order to give expression to your feelings for your Fatherland you have come to the house of Bismarck, who with Emperor William the Great and Field Marshal von Moltke welded the German Empire for us.

"We wished to go on living in peace in the empire which we have developed in forty-four years of peaceful labor.

"The whole work of Emperor William has been devoted to the maintenance of peace. To the last hour he has worked for peace in Europe, and he is still working for it. Should all his efforts prove vain and should the sword be forced into our hands we will take the field with a clear conscience in the knowledge that we did not seek war. We shall then wage war for our existence and for the national honor to the last drop of our blood.

"In the gravity of this hour I remind you of the words of Prince Frederick Charles to the men of Brandenburg:

"'Let your hearts beat for God and your fists on the enemy.'"

Enthusiastic cheers and the singing of the national anthem greeted the close of the Imperial Chancellor's speech.

Germany's War Challenge Delivered to Russia at 7:30 Last Evening

EMBASSY THEN DEPARTS

Enrollment of Reservists Begun Throughout the Czar's Vast Empire.

STIRRING SCENES ATTEND IT

Hardly a Family but Loses a Protector, Yet They Take the Call Submissively.

FRANCE HAS TILL MONDAY

Reply to Germany Due Then, but Issue May Be Forced Earlier.

ITALY REMAINS NEUTRAL

Triple Alliance Obligations Not Touched, She Says—Feared a Revolution.

LUXEMBURG INVADED.

Germans Seize a Neutral State Between Them and Paris.

LONDON, Aug. 2.—The Germans have invaded the Duchy of Luxemburg. They seized the Government offices and telephones. The news reached here in a Reuter telephone message from Brussels at 4 A. M. New York time.

Luxemburg is a neutral State southward of Brussels, with its borders on Germany and France. A straight line drawn between Berlin and Paris would pass through the heart of the Duchy of Luxemburg.

Special Cable to THE NEW YORK TIMES.

LONDON, Sunday, Aug. 2.—The news that Germany had declared war against Russia reached London from St. Petersburg late last evening, only half an hour after a Central News dispatch from Paris had raised the hopes of all by the statement that Germany had extended for forty-eight hours, that is, until Monday noon, the period in which Russia and France could reply to the German ultimatums.

The first of these ultimatums was one demanding that Russia cease the mobilization of her army in twelve hours.

The second was a note presented by Baron von Schoen, the German Ambassador in Paris, to Foreign Minister Viviani calling upon France to inform Germany whether in the event of the outbreak of war between Germany and Russia, France would remain neutral.

These notes were regarded as diplomatic skirmishing, designed to cover the hard fact that Germany was bending all her energies to the delivery of the first blow, which might affect the whole course of the war, now officially begun.

In the history of modern warfare an official declaration of war is either accompanied or preceded by an actual stroke of war.

In London this morning it is believed Germany would not officially declare war upon Russia unless her plans for a rapid attack had been entirely completed. Where or how the first blow will be struck is a matter of the widest speculation.

France Next to Be Involved.

France's reply to the German request as to the former's attitude in case Germany engaged in war with Russia is stated to have proved unsatisfactory to Berlin. It was bound to be. Germany could count confidently on it being so. Therefore, according to speculation in London this morning, the eventual news is likely to show that Germany has taken an unsatisfactory reply from France for granted, and while declaring war on Russia has struck or has made her chief preparations to strike at France. This, of course, is pure speculation, and THE NEW YORK TIMES correspondent mentions it for what it is worth.

The established facts, bearing on the crisis in yesterday's developments, are important to note. The first is that the effort made by King George to bring influence to bear on the Czar in favor of peace failed of effect.

The terms of the King's telegram are guarded as the strictest secret. All information THE TIMES correspondent could obtain was that the message was of a highly personal and confidential nature. It followed an interview with Premier Asquith at 2 o'clock yesterday morning.

Italy Feared a Revolution.

The second development was a confirmation of the report that Italy would remain neutral as long as she was assured that her interests were not menaced.

From an official source THE TIMES correspondent learns that the Italian Government was practically forced to this decision by the apprehension that the taking up of arms on behalf of Austria in a quarrel, precipitated by the hereditary enemy of Italy, would have caused an immediate revolution in Italy.

Italy's abstention is a serious blow to the Triple Alliance and may yet prove an important factor in determining, if not the issue of peace or war, at least the duration of the conflict.

One of the ways suggested to prevent the outbreak of war was that Italy and Great Britain should combine and declare themselves on the side of France and Russia. The suggestion utterly disregarded the treaty by which Italy was bound to the Triple Alliance, but it was given some color of vraisemblance by the fact that the British and Italian Ambassadors in various capitals have been working together in a manner which indicated that the Italian Government preferred any peaceable solution of the war to the treaties which bound her to Germany and Austria.

The third important development of the night was the news that the French Government had issued orders for general mobilization.

This came a few hours after the severance of telephonic communications between London and Paris. The French Government informed the British authorities that the telephone was cut for ordinary communication in order to prevent any leakage of news.

Up to 2 o'clock this morning practically no news beyond the announcement of the mobilization had been received here from Paris

The fullest confirmation of the general mobilization was obtained in London by the issue of a notice to the French Embassy here. This called upon all Frenchmen liable to military service to return to France within twenty-four hours. The news speedily became known in Soho, the French quarter of London, and this morning bands of enthusiastic Frenchmen paraded through Leicester Square.

The almost [illegible] telegraphic and [illegible] communication with Paris [illegible] fact that a London paper which had made most elaborate arrangements to obtain a special wire, under a guarantee that nothing in the nature of leakage of military secrets could possibly occur, had not received a word out of Paris up to 3 o'clock this morning.

Telephonic and telegraphic communications with the Continent were generally interrupted.

GERMANY'S DECLARATION

Served by the Retiring Ambassador as Russian Enrollment Begins.

ST. PETERSBURG, Aug. 1.—The German Ambassador, in the name of his Government, sent a declaration of war to the Russian Minister of Foreign Affairs at 7:30 o'clock this evening. Count von Pourtales and the entire staff of the German Embassy then left St. Petersburg.

Martial law has been proclaimed in the capital and its suburbs.

Announcement of the declaration of war was made to the people two hours after it had been received. The city immediately presented a spectacle of extraordinary animation. The Nevsky Prospect and all [illegible] leading thoroughfares are [illegible] processions carrying portraits of the Emperor, with flags waving and torches blazing. From time to time there is an outburst of cheering, followed by singing.

Speakers fired with patriotic fervor harangue the crowds. In front of the Kazan Cathedral each procession halts and a sudden hush falls over the processionists, then the strains of the national anthem, sung in perfect harmony by a section of the procession, are heard, and the crowds listen silently with bared heads. On the conclusion of the hymn the procession moves forward and the demonstrations are resumed with greater ardor.

Enrollment of the reservists started at a hundred centres in St. Petersburg at 6 o'clock this morning and was accompanied by stirring scenes. Crowds of women and children accompanied their husbands and fathers to the assembling stations, while priests everywhere blessed the reservists as they marched through the streets singing hymns.

The Municipal Council of Warsaw has voted 1,000,000 roubles (about $500,000) for the Red Cross service of Russia and friendly powers.

The Fateful Red Posters.

Special Cable to THE NEW YORK TIMES.

ST. PETERSBURG, Aug. 1.—All attention is now concentrated on the mobilization of the troops. During the night bills were posted in all parts of the city summoning the whole of the reservists to the colors, and the population awoke to read the startling news on posters printed in red.

Women wept, but the men took it for the most part quietly and seriously, in sad submissiveness.

"I don't care for my life," said one peasant to me, "but I am sorry for the children."

[illegible] are frequent on all hands. Hardly a house, hardly a fam-

Chronology of Yesterday's Fateful Events

12 Midnight—Germany demands that Russia cease mobilization and gives a twelve-hour limit.

2 A. M.—King George of England, after an audience with Premier Asquith, telegraphs to the Czar, making a strong appeal for peace.

12 Noon—The time limit of Germany's ultimatum to Russia expires.

5:15 P. M.—Emperor William signs an order for the mobilization of the German Army.

7:30 P. M.—The German Ambassador at St. Petersburg delivers to the Russian Government a declaration of war in the name of Germany and leaves St. Petersburg.

First Shots Fired in the Russo-German War.

BERLIN, Aug. 1.—A German patrol near Prostken was fired on this afternoon by a Russian frontier patrol. The Germans returned the fire. There were no losses.

Prostken is a village of 2,300 inhabitants, in East Prussia. It is situated about two and one-half miles west of the international boundary line, on the Konigsberg & Lyck Railroad. The nearest Russian village is Grajevo, about three miles across the international boundary.

Kaiser Forgives Enemies, Prays for Victory

BERLIN, Aug. 2.—The Emperor again spoke from a window of the Castle tonight to a crowd of 50,000 beneath, who cheered and sang patriotic songs until he appeared. He said:

"I thank you for the love and loyalty shown me. When I enter upon a fight let all party strife cease. We are German brothers and nothing else. All parties have attacked me in times of peace. I forgive them with all my heart. I hope and wish that the good German sword will emerge victorious in the right."

The speech was thrice interrupted by vociferous cheering. At its conclusion the Kaiser bowed in all directions, retiring amid a frenzied demonstration.

The Imperial Chancellor also addressed the assembly, saying:

"All stand as one man for our Emperor, whatever our opinions or our creeds. I am sure that all the young German men are ready to shed their blood for the fame and greatness of Germany. We can only trust in God, Who hitherto has always given us victory."

An imperial decree convokes the Reichstag on Aug. 4.

ITALY DECIDES TO REMAIN NEUTRAL—GERMANY TRIED TO HALT AUSTRIA

...ty is untouched. Workmen, shop assistants, clerks, cabmen, porters, tradesmen, in fact the whole male population between 20 and 40 years of age liable to service have had to abandon their occupations immediately, and tomorrow morning at 6 o'clock they will gather at the appointed meeting places and be apportioned to the various regiments.

St. Petersburg on Sunday will be like a camp, with ovens in the streets and temporary night shelters, and this will be going on not only here but in Moscow and every town in Russia. More than that, all over the plains peasants are being taken from the fields amid the harvest, and old men, boys, and women will have to do the reaping.

Never has there been such a mobilization in Russia. It is a tremendous effort, and here in St. Petersburg the people are displaying extraordinary calmness and restraint. Even the heavy-hearted manifest remarkable tenacity of purpose, and on all sides public opinion shows hardly a dissentient voice.

GERMANS TRY TO CUT CABLE.

Great Invading Fleet Gathering at Entrance to Baltic.

COPENHAGEN, Aug. 1.—German torpedo boat destroyers operating outside the Danish sea territory made an unsuccessful attempt today to cut the cable communication to Russia by way of Rodvig, Denmark.

The Fehmarn Belt is crowded with German dreadnoughts and other big vessels, which are accompanied by transport vessels. A number of Russian vessels also have been observed in that vicinity.

Nearly all the steamship lines between Germany and Denmark have been stopped.

The large military force concentrated on Seeland, the largest and most important of the Danish islands, and containing the capital, was increased tonight by 20,000 men for the protection of Copenhagen.

The Danish Parliament met tonight in extraordinary session for the purpose of passing legislation necessitated by the situation.

The [illegible] Government has ordered the immediate return of all the German automobiles, numbering 800, at the Malmoe (Sweden) exhibition.

ANTWERP, Aug. 1.—A dispatch from Flushing, Netherlands, to The Metropole says that a tug met in the North Sea tonight seventeen units of the German Fleet proceeding toward the Skagerrak with lights out. Later they turned back.

At the present time there are several British squadrons cruising north of Flushing.

Shelling of Belgrade Renewed?

ATHENS, Greece, Aug. 1.—Austrian monitors on the Danube this morning renewed the bombardment of Belgrade and its surroundings according to a telegram from Nish, Servia.

Despatches from Semlin and other sources on Thursday last announced that the Austrian Army had occupied Belgrade after bombardment.

It must therefore be assumed that the news contained in above cablegram from Athens, if reliable, either is belated or that the Servians who on Friday were reported to have checked the Austrians in their attack on the pass into the Morava River Valley at Semendria, have succeeded in recapturing their capitol.

LONDON TAKES NEWS COOLLY.

Extension of Warfare Feared as Peace Hopes Die.

LONDON, Sunday, Aug. 2.—Pleasure-loving Londoners, issuing by thousands from the theatres last night, were confronted by newspaper placards announcing that Germany had declared war on Russia. For the first time the full significance of the fate, overhanging Europe, appeared to strike the ordinary citizen with full force, and he began with seriousness to ask himself what part England was to play in the great drama.

People stopped on the sidewalks in anxious groups, discussing the unexpected news, but there were no unusual demonstrations, except here and there collisions between little knots of Germans and Frenchmen, arising from patriotic ardor, of which it takes a deal to excite the phlegmatic Englishman.

The greatest excitement was observed in the foreign restaurants of the West End, especially in the German haunts, where crowds cheered Emperor William and sang "The Watch on the Rhine," and other patriotic songs.

The French element was less in evidence, owing to the fact that large numbers of Frenchmen have returned to France in the last few days.

The Russians in London are rather negligible in quantity and most of these are refugees from Russian oppression. They showed little emotion over the news that Germany and Russia were at war.

There was no cessation of diplomatic activity in London throughout the day. [illegible] evening Premier Asquith gave a [illegible] dinner party at his residence in Downing Street, the guests including the Russian Ambassador. Sir Edward Grey remained at the Foreign Office until a late hour and then went to Buckingham Palace to consult King George. The Japanese Ambassador had a long conference with Sir Edward Grey during the afternoon.

It is a question whether Belgium and Holland will be able to maintain their neutrality against their powerful neighbors, and whether Great Britain will not find herself compelled to send an expeditionary force to attempt to preserve that neutrality.

Another factor, which as yet has not received much consideration, is the attitude of Turkey. If she has sufficiently recovered from the effects of her war with Italy and the Balkan States, she may be able to throw considerable weight into the scale. It is generally understood that Germany has an effective understanding with Turkey, which may lead to interesting developments.

The German Emperor and his advisers maintained to the last that they had made supreme efforts for the sake of peace, and say that the last of the series of earnest appeals from Emperor William to Emperor Nicholas was a telegram repudiating responsibility for the calamity threatening the world, on the ground that while Germany was mediating with Austria-Hungary at Russia's request, Russia, by her general mobilization, was threatening Germany's safety.

Previous to the announcement of Germany's action hope still survived here that some way might be found to avert the threatened catastrophe.

This resulted in part from the announcement that King George, in a final effort to prevent the outbreak of a general war, had sent a dispatch to Emperor Nicholas, making a strong appeal for the preservation of peace.

Following this, many pessimistic reports reached here.

A Daily News dispatch from Berlin, timed at 2 o'clock yesterday morning, said Germany had addressed an ultimatum to Russia, demanding that mobilization be stopped within twelve hours. It was also stated that a question had also been addressed to France in regard to her attitude in certain contingencies. One report said France had received a time limit of eighteen hours.

At the German Embassy reference was made to a mention of French neutrality in Germany's note to the French Government, [illegible] said that this [illegible] would not

ITALY TELLS KAISER SHE WILL BE NEUTRAL

Considers Obligations Under Triple Alliance Apply Only to Defensive War.

500,000 MEN UNDER ARMS

Fleet Also Ready for Action in Case Nation's Interests Should Be Infringed.

PARIS, Aug. 1.—The following dispatch was received here this evening from Rome:

It is authoritatively announced that the Marquis di San Giuliano, Italian Foreign Minister, has informed the German Ambassador at Rome that Italy will remain neutral, her obligations under the Triple Alliance treaty applying only to a defensive war. Italy therefore considers herself released from her engagements, the war waged by Austria-Hungary, supported by Germany, being essentially an offensive war.

ROME, Aug. 1.—The German Ambassador to Italy today asked to be informed as to Italy's attitude in the event of war between Germany and Austria-Hungary on the one side and Russia and France on the other.

The Marquis di San Giuliano, the Foreign Minister, said he would reserve his reply until he had consulted Premier Salandra. According to the Messagero during the interview which followed between the Marquis di San Giuliano and Premier Salandra the two Italian statesmen were in complete agreement as to the line of conduct to be pursued by Italy in the present crisis.

The Messagero declares that as it is not a question of a defensive war on the part of Germany and Austria-Hungary, the other two members of the Triple Alliance, Italy has decided to confine herself to pointing out to her allies that her treaty obligations with them do not oblige her to take up arms in the present crisis, and that she will remain neutral. The newspaper adds that it is not certain this neutrality will last until the end of the war, but Italy will stand aloof from hostilities as long as she is convinced that her interests are not being infringed.

King Victor Emmanuel is keeping in close touch with events, and is said to be in frequent direct communication with other European rulers, especially the German Emperor.

Meanwhile the Italian Government is preparing to meet any eventuality. About 500,000 soldiers are under arms, including those who can be withdrawn from Tripoli and other places, as just before the Austro-Servian outbreak 100,000 reservists had been called to the colors.

All the fortifications along the eastern frontier have been hurriedly put into a state of war, while the various squadrons of the fleet have assembled at their naval stations.

The Pope is said to have made strenuous efforts to prevent the war, as since the recent concordat between the Vatican and Servia his feelings are very friendly toward that country. The signature of the concordat is said in some quarters to have been one of the causes of Austrian resentment against Servia. Speaking on the subject to the Austrian Ambassador, the Pontiff informed him that he considered the Austrian attitude toward the Servian concordat unfair, and added that he must "protect his children wherever they are."

Special Cable to THE NEW YORK TIMES.

ROME, Aug. 1.—Italy is facing one of the most difficult situations that has ever arisen in her history. This is a result of her unnatural alliance with the dual monarchy, forced upon her by the unfriendly attitude of France, and now after more than thirty years' existence is bearing fruit.

The people of Italy cannot reconcile themselves to the idea of standing by Austria, their traditional enemy, in case of a European conflagration.

AUSTRIANS A UNIT FOR WAR.

Bent on Ending Campaign of Hate by Sword and Cannon.

NEW YORK TIMES-London Chronicle Special Cable Dispatch.

VIENNA, July 31, (Delayed in Transmission.)—To Austria-Hungary this is no sudden war. For long years a conspiracy of hatred and malice has been directed against the dual monarchy from Servia.

Diplomacy failed to remove the danger, and now the sword, rifle, and cannon must do the work which peaceable means during all these years found itself unequal of achieving.

This long-overdue war, the Austro-Hungarian journals point out, is showing the whole world that this country is not, as has often been said, a mere geographical expression or an anachronism of statecraft, but, after all, a united nation with a bond of common interest and a cement of common determination, which appears strong enough to see her through the stormy days ahead.

There is no doubt that the whole nation is behind the Emperor and his advisers. There is no discordant note. The demonstrations in the streets continue to grow in enthusiasm, and tremendous popular demonstrations, with all the country's veteran warriors present, are now taking place in front of the City Hall.

At the stations pathetic but brave scenes are witnessed when wives and sweethearts of the soldiers are admitted to say goodbye to the departing troops.

Four Nations of Europe Now at War.

The Boundaries of Germany, Russia, Austria-Hungary and Servia, and the Scene of the First Shots Between Germany and Russia.

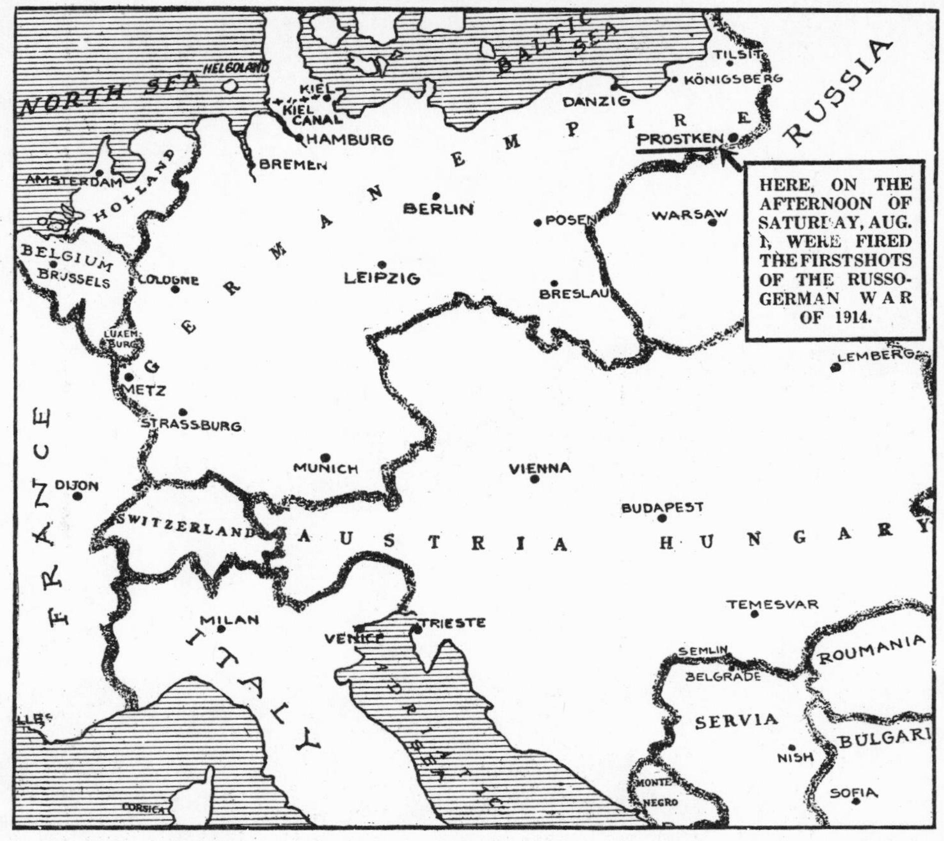

GERMANY PRESSED AUSTRIA TO LIMIT

Rebuked Her for Refusal to Discuss Matters with the Russian Government.

WANTED TO LOCALIZE WAR

Caused Reopening of Negotiations, but Czar's Mobilization Broke Them Off Again.

Special Cable to THE NEW YORK TIMES.

LONDON, Aug. 1.—An important contribution to the diplomatic history of the present crisis is contained in a Berlin dispatch to The Westminster Gazette. This says in part:

"When the Russian Government made it known that it considered itself threatened as to its interests by Austria's proceeding against Servia the German Government did everything possible to bring about an understanding. Notwithstanding the wide-embracing military measures that Russia had already taken against Austria, the German Government continued the intervention in Vienna and with very pressing proposals went to the utmost limit possible with a sovereign State and ally."

The correspondent then cites a dispatch sent by the German Chancellor, Dr. von Bethmann-Hollweg, to the German Ambassador in Vienna on Thursday, in which he said:

"Austria's refusal to exchange views with St. Petersburg would be a grave mistake. We are ready to fulfill our duty as an ally. However, we must refuse to be drawn into a world conflagration through Austria disrespecting our advice."

Austria thereupon reopened the conversations at St. Petersburg, which were abruptly ended by the Russian mobilization.

By The Associated Press.

LONDON, Aug. 1.—The full text of the telegram from Chancellor von Bethmann-Hollweg of Germany to the German Ambassador at Vienna, sent after the receipt of a message from St. Petersburg stating that Austria-Hungary had declined Russia's request to enter into direct negotiations, is thus given in The Westminster Gazette:

> The report of Count von Pourtales, German Ambassador at St. Petersburg, does not harmonize with the account your Excellency has given of the attitude of the Austro-Hungarian Government. Apparently, there is a misunderstanding, which I beg you to clear up.
>
> We cannot expect Austria-Hungary to negotiate with Servia, with whom she is in a state of war. The refusal, however, to exchange views with St. Petersburg would be a grave mistake.
>
> We are indeed ready to fulfill our duty as ally. We must, however, refuse to be drawn into a world conflagration owing to Austria-Hungary not respecting our advice.
>
> Your Excellency will express this to Count von Berchtold, Austro-Hungarian Foreign Minister, with all emphasis and great seriousness.
>
> VON BETHMANN-HOLLWEG.

In reply to this communication Count von Berchtold told the German Ambassador that there was in fact a misunderstanding and that the Austro-Hungarian Ambassador at St. Petersburg had been instructed to begin negotiations with Sergius Sazonoff, the Russian Minister.

A statement given by the German Foreign Office to the correspondent concludes:

"These negotiations, as well as the intermediary action of the German Government, were ended by the mobilization of all arms in Russia on sea and land."

The declaration of the Foreign Office was admittedly given, according to the correspondent, "in the hope yet of preventing a world war, and as an alternative of justifying G[illegible] to England, whose friendship she still desires."

The Gazette said the Austro-Hungarian Government sent a communication to St. Petersburg Friday, declaring that Austria-Hungary had no intention of annexing Servia, extinguishing the sovereignty of Servia, or reannexing the Sanjak of Novibazar.

Latest Estimates of the Land Forces of the Four Powers Now Engaged in War

Russia.

In European Russia.	
Infantry	838,000
Cavalry	304,000
Artillery	98,000
Total	1,240,000
In Asiatic Russia	300,000
On first reserve (estimated)	1,500,000
Grand total	3,040,000

(It is thought that Russia could mobilize for effective use in Europe about 1,240,000 men.)

Servia.

Five brigades, consisting of	
Infantry	97,680
Artillery	8,880
Cavalry	3,390
Engineer Corps	4,685
Ambulance	4,855
Ammunition	5,750
Commissary, &c.	5,935
One cavalry brigade, including horse batteries, mountain artillery, &c.	20,764
Garrison troops	16,562
Total	168,501
First reserve troops, who have served in the army within the past 12 years	99,451
Second reserve troops, who are held subject to call for 6 years after passing from the first reserve	56,678
Grand total	324,630

Germany.

Infantry	487,874
Rapid-fire gun corps	24,021
Cavalry	85,703
Field artillery	91,409
Heavy artillery	34,699
Scouts	24,045
Railroad and other corps	48,669
Total	795,930
First reserve (trained troops)	454,000
Landwehr	600,000
Grand Total	1,849,980

Austria.

Infantry	196,957
Cavalry	47,151
Field artillery	37,069
Heavy artillery	9,934
Auxiliary corps	20,841
Total	312,552
Austrian Reserves—	
Infantry	41,157
Cavalry	4,400
Artillery	3,002
Hungarian Reserves—	
Infantry	27,430
Cavalry	5,623
Artillery	3,191
Grand Total	399,361

In time of war this strength can be doubled, but the above listed troops are immediately available.

GERMANS HURRY TO TSING-TAU

All Reserves Proceeding to Their Fortified Port.

SHANGHAI, Aug. 1.—German reserves throughout China are proceeding with all haste to Tsing-tau, the fortified port in the German territory of Kiao-chau.

The American steamship Hanamet, with a cargo of cattle and foodstuffs, which left Tsing-tau yesterday for Vladivostok, returned to Tsing-tau today under orders from the German authorities.

OUR DIPLOMATS WILL AID.

Country's Agents Abroad Instructed to Look Up All Tourists.

Special to The New York Times.

WASHINGTON, Aug. 1.—The United States Government has ample machinery at its disposal to care for the safety and comfort of American travelers in Europe, and to give information to persons in this country who have relatives or friends in the present or prospective war area. American diplomatic and Consular officers in Europe have been instructed by the State Department to obtain lists of Americans in their several districts and to these officers anxious persons in this country may apply by cable for information or requests to the State Department by telegraph or letter will receive attention at once.

The list that follows includes the names and stations of American diplomatic officers, and the stations where the United States has Consular officers, not only in countries likely to be affected by hostilities, but in other countries in Europe in which Americans may seek safety.

EMBASSIES AND LEGATIONS.

Austria-Hungary—Frederic C. Penfield, Ambassador, American Embassy, Vienna.

Belgium—Brand Whitlock, Minister, American Legation, Brussels.

Bulgaria—Charles J. Vopicka, Minister, American Legation, Bucharest, Rumania. (Mr. Vopicka is also Minister to Rumania and Servia.)

Denmark—Maurice Francis Egan, Minister, American Legation, Copenhagen.

France—Myron T. Herrick, Ambassador, American Embassy, Paris.

Germany—James W. Gerard, Ambassador, American Embassy, Berlin.

Great Britain—Walter H. Page, Ambassador, American Embassy, London.

Greece—American Legation, Athens.

Italy—Thomas Nelson Page, Ambassador, American Embassy, Rome.

Luxemburg—Henry Van Dyke, American Legation, The Hague, Netherlands.

Montenegro—American Legation, Athens, Greece.

Netherlands—Henry Van Dyke, Minister, American Legation, The Hague.

Norway—Albert G. Schmedemann, Minister, American Legation, Christiania.

Portugal—Thomas H. Birch, Minister, American Legation, Lisbon.

Rumania—Charles J. Vopicka, Minister, Bucharest.

Russia—Charles J. Wilson, Charge d'Affaires, American Embassy, St. Petersburg.

Servia—Charles J. Vopicka, Minister, American Legation, Bucharest, Rumania.

Spain—Fred M. Dearing, Charge d'Affaires, American Embassy, Madrid.

Sweden—Jefferson Caffery, Charge d'Affaires, American Legation, Stockholm.

Switzerland—Pleasant A. Stovall, Minister, American Legation, Berne.

Turkey—Henry Morgenthau, Ambassador, American Embassy, Constantinople.

Consular Offices.

The following are places where there are Consular offices:

Austria-Hungary—Consul General, Vienna; Consul General, Budapest; Consul, Carlsbad, Bohemia; Consul, Fiume, Croatia; Consul, Prague, Bohemia; Consul, Reichenberg, Bohemia; Consul, Trieste.

Belgium—Consul General, Antwerp; Consul General, Brussels; Consul, Ghent; Consul, Liege.

Denmark—Consul General, Copenhagen.

France—Consul General, Paris; Consul, Bordeaux; Consular Agent, Bayonne; Consul, Calais; Consular Agent, Boulogne-sur-Mer; Consul, Cognac; Consul, Grenoble; Consul, Havre; Consular Agent, Cherbourg; Consul, Limoges; Consul, Lyons; Consular Agent, Dijon; Consul General, Marseilles; Consular Agent, Bastia, Corsica; Consular Agent, Cette; Consul, Nantes; Consular Agent, Brest; Consul, Nice; Consul, Reims; Consul, Roubaix; Consular Agent, Dunkirk; Consul, Rouen; Consular Agent, Amiens; Consular Agent, Dieppe; Consul, St. Etienne.

German Empire—Consul General, Berlin; Consul, Aix la Chapelle; Consul, Barmen; Consular Agent, Sorau; Consul, Bremen; Consular Agent, Brake; Consular Agent, Bremerhaven; Consular Agent, Emden; Consul, Breslau; Consul, Chemnitz; Consul General, Coburg; Consular Agent, Sonneberg; Consul, Cologne; Consul General, Dresden; Consul, Erfurt; Consul General, Frankfort-on-the-Main; Consular Agent, Cassel; Consular Agent, Wiesbaden; Consul General, Hamburg; Consular Agent, Cuxhaven; Consular Agent, Kiel; Consular Agent, Lubeck; Consul, Kehl; Consul, Leipzig; Consular Agent, Gera; Consul, Magdeburg; Consul, Mannheim; Consular Agent, Neustadt; Consul General, Munich; Consul, Nuremberg; Consul, Plauen; Consular Agent, Markneukirchen; Consul, Stettin; Consular Agent, Danzig; Consular Agent, Konigsberg; Consular Agent, Swinemunde; Consul, Stuttgart.

British Possessions on Continent—Consul, Gibraltar; Consul, Malta.

Greece—Consul General, Athens; Consular Agent, Kalamata; Consul, Patras.

Italy—Consul General, Rome; Consul, Catania; Consul, Florence; Consul, Genoa; Consul, Leghorn; Consular Agent, Carrara; Consul, Milan; Consul, Naples; Consular Agent, Bari; Consul, Palermo; Consul, Tripoli; Libya; Consul, Turin; Consul, Venice.

Netherlands—Consul General, Rotterdam; Consul, Amsterdam; Consular Agent, Flushing; Consular Agent, Luxemburg; Consular Agent, Scheveningen.

Norway—Consul, Bergen; Consul, Christiania; Consular Agent, Christiansand; Consular Agent, Trondhjem; Consul, Stavanger.

Rumania—Consul General, Bucharest; Consular Agent, Sofia. (Bulgaria.)

Russia—Consul General, Moscow; Consular General, St. Petersburg; Consul, Odessa; Consular Agent, Rostoff-on-Don; Consul, Riga; Consular Agent, Libau; Consular Agent, Helsingfors, Finland; Consular Agent, Reval; Consul, Warsaw.

Servia—Consul, Belgrade.

Sweden—Consul [illegible], Stockholm—Consul, G[illegible] Agent, Malmo; Consular [illegible]

Switzerland—[illegible] Consul, Berne; Consul, Ge[illegible] Vevey; Consul, S[illegible] Zurich; Consular Agent, Locarno.

GREECE MOBILIZES; MAY FIGHT BULGARS

They Cannot Agree on Boundary Question, but Rumania Is Trying to Settle Squabble.

MONTENEGRIN-SERVIAN PACT

Prince Peter, King's Youngest Son, Announces They Will Fight Side by Side.

NEW YORK TIMES-London Chronicle Special Cable Dispatch.

MILAN, Aug. 1.—A special evening edition of the Secolo makes the announcement from Bucharest that Montenegro intends to fight side by side with Servia. Prince Peter of Montenegro, who arrived in Bucharest yesterday, said in an interview:

"Union between the two countries will now undoubtedly be realized. I may say before my departure to Cettinje that a project of military and financial union has already been agreed upon. Each country will retain its own King and its own sovereignty.

"The union already exists in fact. All that is now necessary is a formal announcement to the world at large."

The same journal's special correspondent at Salonika states that the Graeco-Bulgarian commission which is now sitting to settle the boundary dispute abruptly terminated its sittings through inability to reach an agreement, and another war looms up on the horizon. Negotiations, however, are still proceeding between Athens and the Rumanian capital to devise a means of preserving the treaty of Bucharest, but the Greek Government, hard pressed, has ordered a general mobilization as a precautionary measure.

All the State archives at the Franco-Servian Bank have been transported to Salonika under strong escorts of Servian officials and soldiery.

EXPECTS TURKEY TO FIGHT.

Her Ambassador Looks for Hostilities with Servia.

SWAMPSCOTT, Mass., Aug. 1.—A. Rustem Bey, the Turkish Ambassador, who is spending his vacation here, said tonight that in his opinion Turkey soon would become involved in war with Servia.

He expressed the opinion that a general European war was probable, and notwithstanding the fact that Turkey recently had signed a treaty with the Serbs, his country would again be arrayed in arms against them.

WILL RESPECT BELGIUM.

France Promises It Unless Other Power Violates Neutrality.

BRUSSELS, Aug. 1.—Antony Klobukowski, French Minister to Belgium, called today on M. Davignon, the Minister for Foreign Affairs, and informed him that the French Government would respect the neutrality of Belgium in the event of war, in conformity with its previous declarations.

Should Belgian neutrality be violated by another power, France, he said, would then take the necessary measures.

Norway Will Keep Out.

CHRISTIANIA, Aug. 1.—A Government decree, issued today, [illegible] complete neutrality of Norway.

PARIS HAS GIVEN UP ALL HOPE OF PEACE

Cheering Crowds Wave the Tricolor and Flags of the Allies as Troops Move.

GERMAN ENVOY IS LEAVING

Up to Midnight There Had Been Hope of Averting a Clash—Troops Guard the Stations.

Special Cable to THE NEW YORK TIMES.

PARIS, Sunday, Aug. 2.—Remarkable scenes were witnessed in Paris tonight after the order for mobilization was issued. At this moment, 2 A. M., armored troops, autos, and provision wagons are rumbling along Rue Lous Legrand, beneath the windows of THE NEW YORK TIMES Paris office.

The last ray of hope that war could be averted has flickered out.

The crowds in the boulevards are waving the Tricolor. English, Russian, and also Italian and Japanese flags are carried in the friendly wave of patriotism that has been sweeping the city ever since the general mobilization order was announced.

From the hills about the city the searchlights are sweeping the heavens, but the Eiffel Tower wireless station is dark.

With as dramatic suddenness as has marked every move in the crisis has come the climax—the announcement just made of Germany's declaration of war against Russia.

The German Ambassador is leaving Paris, though the news is not yet generally known.

Mobilization is in full swing and has kept all Paris up for the last night before the enforcement of martial law.

Bodies of soldiers are constantly moving toward the railroad station. Trudging along beside them I see old men, veterans of the Franco-Prussian War, urging on youngsters. At the rear of each detachment, women follow, some cheering, others silent, some quietly weeping.

At sunrise the city has the status of an entrenched camp. Until midnight there appeared to be a faint, last hope of peace—it was rumored in official circles that word had come from Russia that they would demobilize if the other powers would agree. This perhaps explains the word received from the Foreign Office earlier that the German Ambassador was not leaving.

Clemenceau and Delcassé were in the Cabinet council today, and there is a report that there will be a War Ministry with these two in high positions.

Nearly all the taxis, wagons, and buses have now been requisitioned. The Gare de l'Est is picketed by troops at the gates. Guns, troops, and munitions are being entrained. THE NEW YORK TIMES correspondent counted twenty-five motor buses filled with soldiers inside.

Dense crowds in the boulevards are making patriotic speeches and singing patriotic songs. The police are keeping the crowds moving, but are not otherwise interfering. A huge crowd cheered England before the offices of The London Daily Mail.

Germans are being hustled and buffeted all over the city, numbers hiding in their apartments.

The Gare de Lyon took passengers, but not baggage, until 9 o'clock and then shut up shop. Street vendors have done a rushing business all day, selling "The Siege of Paris, 1870," and also war maps.

At nightfall all the cafeterias were permanently closed, the famous Cafe de la Paix closing for the first time in thirty years.

From the hour within which general mobilization was declared until the last trains at midnight thousands were literally streaking across the city to the stations in taxis, and wagons of all descriptions were piled high with luggage, families trying to escape to the country, where the living is likely to be cheaper. It is almost impossible now to secure salt. Under military rule the prices which soared today will go back to normal, the Government punishing any tradespeople who are offenders.

Tonight the police took possession of several retail provision houses because the proprietors had seized the advantage to make money and also sold in excess of the Government allowances.

From all the stores a constant stream of people were carrying today as much as they could pack along.

At the Ritz, Continental, and Edward VII. hotels dinner was served tonight by chambermaids, all the waiters having joined the colors.

OFFICERS TO OBSERVE WAR.

Col. Reber, Aviation Expert, Going to Europe at Once to View Battles.

Special to The New York Times.

WASHINGTON, Aug. 1.—Naval and army officers will be sent to Europe to watch the operations of the fleets and armies in the field and report their observations to the American Government. Although no actual designations have yet been made by Secretaries Garrison and Daniels, names are informally under consideration by each department, and the officers to be sent will be selected at the proper time.

The War Department is sending Col. Samuel Reber, an expert in aviation, to Europe to make a special study of that arm of the service there. Congress recently passed an act organizing the Aviation Corps of the American Army and providing for its enlargement. Col. Reber is under orders to visit Paris and other points to study the latest development in aeroplanes and military aviation. He will pay particular attention to the use of air craft in actual warfare. Col. Reber hopes to be able to sail next week. The date of his sailing has been interfered with by the orders given to transatlantic liners to remain in their ports until further notice. He is not certain what steamer he will now be able to find a booking on. He will go first to London and then to Paris.

Gossip in military circles is that the military representative to be sent to Europe to make a special report on the war probably will be Major Gen. Hugh L. Scott, Assistant Chief of Staff, or Lieut. Col. Henry T. Allen, of the General Staff. Both are distinguished officers. Gen. Scott is a cavalry expert and was until recently in command of the army on the Texas frontier. Lieut. Col. Allen is also a cavalry expert. He served as military attache to Sweden and then to Russia just before the Spanish war. After that he went to the Philippines and organized the Philippine constabulary. Col. Allen speaks and writes the Russian, German, French and Spanish languages.

The military and naval attaches now in Europe also will watch the progress of military events and report to the War and Navy Departments. There are fourteen military and naval attaches representing this Government in Europe.

FOUR WARSHIPS AT HAVANA.

British Cruiser Among Them and Two German Vessels Near.

Special Cable to THE NEW YORK TIMES.

HAVANA, Aug. 1.—Four warships now in Havana Harbor are prepared to leave momentarily. The British cruiser Berwick, which came in yesterday and took on a large supply of coal, stripped for action and took out sailing papers this evening. The German cruiser Bremen is expected here momentarily, and the German cruiser Karlsruhe was heard talking by wireless 200 miles out. The Italian cruiser Calabria took out papers this evening and expects to sail tonight.

A Dutch cruiser and the French naval oil tankers in the harbor said they did not know whether they would sail at all.

The effect of the war was strongly felt here this afternoon, when the Tobacco Trust shut down its factories, putting 9,000 men out of work.

SWISS TAKE PRECAUTIONS.

Parliament Summoned to Guard Republic's Independence.

BERNE, Aug. 1.—The Swiss Federal Parliament has been summoned to meet on Monday, to consider measures to safeguard the independence of Switzerland and to appoint a commander in chief of the army of 175,000 men called to the colors by a mobilization order.

The house will also deal with a measure for the issue of five-franc notes.

German Officials Hurry Home.

CAPE TOWN, Aug. 1.—The German Consul General, with his staff, left for England today on the steamer Saxon. The offices of the Consulate General have been closed.

Sweden Declares Its Neutrality.

STOCKHOLM, Aug. 1.—The Swedish Government today issued an official notification of its strict neutrality in the European conflict.

"All the News That's Fit to Print."

The New York Times.

EXTRA 5:30 A. M.

VOL. LXIV...NO. 20,923. NEW YORK, SATURDAY, MAY 8, 1915.—TWENTY-FOUR PAGES. ONE CENT In Greater New York, Jersey City and Newark | Elsewhere TWO CENTS

LUSITANIA SUNK BY A SUBMARINE, PROBABLY 1,260 DEAD; TWICE TORPEDOED OFF IRISH COAST; SINKS IN 15 MINUTES; CAPT. TURNER SAVED, FROHMAN AND VANDERBILT MISSING; WASHINGTON BELIEVES THAT A GRAVE CRISIS IS AT HAND

SHOCKS THE PRESIDENT

Washington Deeply Stirred by the Loss of American Lives.

BULLETINS AT WHITE HOUSE

Wilson Reads Them Closely, but Is Silent on the Nation's Course.

HINTS OF CONGRESS CALL

Loss of Lusitania Recalls Firm Tone of Our First Warning to Germany.

CAPITAL FULL OF RUMORS

Reports That Liner Was to be Sunk Were Heard Before Actual News Came.

Special to The New York Times.

WASHINGTON, May 7.—Never since that April day, three years ago, when word came that the Titanic had gone down, has Washington been so stirred as it is tonight over the sinking of the Lusitania. The early reports told that there had been no loss of life, but the relief that these advices caused gave way to the greatest concern late this evening when it became known that there had been many deaths. Although they are profoundly reticent, officials realize that this tragedy, involving the loss of American citizens, is likely to bring about a crisis in the international relations of the United States.

It is pointed out that the sinking of the Lusitania is the outcome of a series of incidents that have been the cause of concern to this Government in its endeavor to maintain a strictly neutral position in the great European war.

Nation's Course in Doubt.

It is impossible to say tonight what effect the loss of American lives on the Lusitania will have on the Government. Judged from the little that can be learned it is a safe prediction that President Wilson will endeavor to ascertain all the facts, including evidence as to whether a German submarine was responsible for the sinking of the vessel, before proceeding to determine the course to be pursued. The news that many lives had been sacrificed, probably as many as a thousand, was given to him at the White House about 10 o'clock this morning, but no word came from him as to what effect this intelligence had on him.

The State Department tonight sent instructions to the American Embassy in London to send the names of any Americans who might have been killed or injured in the disaster. A bulletin from THE TIMES, saying probably 1,000 lives had been lost, was sent to the White House as soon as received and laid before President Wilson. The news that two torpedoes had been fired into the Lusitania by a submarine and that the Lusitania sank fifteen minutes afterward was also sent to the White House, but reached there after the President had gone to bed. The President retired about 11 o'clock.

On account of the many inquiries it had received from friends and relatives of passengers on the Lusitania and the intense public interest in the tragedy, orders were given tonight to the telegraphers and cipher clerks in charge of the telegraph office in the State Department to remain at their posts all night. They also had instructions to make public any messages bringing official details regarding the Lusitania's passengers. Usually the telegraph office closes at midnight.

Rumors of Congress Session.

There were reports this evening that Congress would be called in extra session, but these were not justified and the most that can be said is that while the Government is greatly concerned over the situation, it has shown no inclination toward excitement or taking hasty action.

Senator W. J. Stone, Chairman of the Committee on Foreign Relations, said tonight:

"I cannot comment on a supposed

Continued on Page 4.

The Lost Cunard Steamship Lusitania

X Where the First Torpedo Struck. XX Where the Second Torpedo Struck.

Cunard Office Here Besieged for News; Fate of 1,918 on Lusitania Long in Doubt

Nothing Heard from the Well-Known Passengers on Board—Story of Disaster Long Unconfirmed While Anxious Crowds Seek Details.

Official news of the sinking of the Lusitania yesterday reached New York in fragmentary reports, and several hours elapsed between the first unverified rumor of the disaster and the cable messages that told at night of the saving of some of the passengers and gave meagre details of the most sensational incident of its kind in the war.

The early accounts that indicated all on board had been saved reassured hundreds of friends and relatives of passengers. Later, it was made known that lives had been lost and probably many persons had been injured.

Among the prominent passengers rescued was George A. Kessler. The list of those of whom no word was received included A. G. Vanderbilt, Charles Frohman, Charles Klein, Justus Miles Forman, and Elbert Hubbard, besides persons widely known in society.

A cablegram sent to Farley Hopkins of The Yale News staff at New Haven, by his father, who was aboard the Lusitania, stated that the vessel was sunk, not beached, that three hundred persons had been already landed, and that the rest in small boats were making for shore. The message reached New York at 8:15 o'clock and was signed "Lee Higginson & Co., London."

Word of the safety of Charles E. Lauriat, Jr., of Boston, Mass., a member of the firm of Charles E. Lauriat & Co., booksellers, who was a first-cabin passenger, reached relatives there in a cablegram early this morning. The message, dated at Queenstown, 2:40 A. M. Read simply:

> Charles E. Lauriat, Jr., safe and well.

For more than half a century it was the boast of the Cunard Line that it never had lost a life. The Oregon was sunk in collision near Fire Island in 1886, but no lives were lost until five passengers were swept off the Campania's forward deck by a wave on Oct. 5, 1905. The sinking of the Lusitania is the first big disaster the Cunard Line has had.

Message to Cunard Office.

The first word of the sinking of the Lusitania received here reached the local offices of the Cunard Line, 21 State Street, at 11:41 o'clock yesterday morning, but was not made public until late in the afternoon. The message, which was sent from the head office in Liverpool, read:

> The Lusitania, we regret to advise, an unconfirmed report states to have been torpedoed by a submarine at 2 P. M., Friday, ten miles from Kinsale, and sunk at 2:30. There is no news as to the safety of passengers or crew.

Following this dispatch there was a message which had been picked up by the wireless station at Land's End evidently a distress call from the liner, which said:

> Come at once. Big list. Position ten miles west Kinsale.

A third dispatch from Queenstown stated:

> All available craft in harbor dispatched to assist. Weather here beautifully fine. Wind southeast, light.

By 3 o'clock in the afternoon the news of the sinking of the Lusitania had been spread in the city and the Cunard offices were besieged by relatives and friends of the passengers on board. Owing to the alterations in and additions to the passenger list on sailing day, last Saturday, it took some time to get the correct figures, which were finally given out as 290 first, 601 second, and 362 third class passengers. Of the cabin passengers thirty-six had been transferred fro mthe Cameronia on Saturday morning. This delayed the Lusitania's departure from 10 o'clock to 12:28.

1,918 Persons on Board.

The officers and crew numbered 665 men instead of the usual complement of 860, on account of fewer men being carried in the engineers' and stewards' departments. Thus there were in all 1,918 persons on board.

The Cunard agents told all inquirers that they would give out the messages as fast as they were received and had no intention of keeping back the news from the public. Several bulletins were received from the Liverpool office, but few of them contained any definite statements and they were cancelled, in some instances, within an hour. One received at 4 P. M. read:

> Motor fishing boats towing two boats filled with passengers, probably fifty. Tug Stormcock making Kinsale. Some passengers on board. Many rescue vessels are now apparently making Queenstown.

The first dispatch stating positively that the Lusitania had sunk reached the Cunard office at 5 P. M. It read:

> Old Head Kinsale Station reports about twenty boats, all belonging to Lusitania, are in vicinity where sunk. About fifteen boats are making for the spot to rescue.

An unconfirmed report was received late in the afternoon that all the passengers and crew had been saved in small boats and rafts. This information was given out to the people waiting in the Cunard office, and many of them went home. It was estimated that fully 500 inquiries were received by telephone and telegraph in the afternoon from relatives and friends of passengers on board. Long-distance calls were received from St. Louis, Atlanta, Montreal, and Toronto.

The next bulletin made public at the Cunard office was the following:

> Liverpool, May 7.
> 1:51 P. M. (New York Time.)
> Following received by Admiralty, Galley Head, 4:25 P. M. Several boats, apparently survivors, southeast nine miles. Greek steamer proceeding to assist.

The next bulletin was:

> Liverpool, May 7.
> 2:33 P. M. (New York Time.)
> Queenstown wires Old Head: Large steamer just arrived in vicinity apparently sending assistance. Tugs, patrols, &c.,

Continued on Page 3.

List of Saved Includes Capt. Turner; Vanderbilt and Frohman Reported Lost

LONDON, Saturday, May 8.—5:30 A. M. The Press Bureau has received from the British Admiralty at Queenstown a report that all the torpedo boats and tugs and armed trawlers, except the Heron, which went out from Queenstown to the relief of the Lusitania have returned.

These vessels have landed 595 survivors and forty dead. Fifty-two more survivors are reported aboard a steamer, while eleven others and five bodies have been landed at Kinsale, making the total number of survivors 658, besides forty-five dead. The numbers will be verified later, and it is considered possible Kinsale fishing boats may have rescued a few more.

Among the survivors is the Captain of the Lusitania, William T. Turner. Some of the survivors at Queenstown say that Alfred Gwynne Vanderbilt was drowned. Every effort to find Mr. Vanderbilt and Charles Frohman, the theatrical manager, among the survivors has failed.

The Central News says that the number of the Lusitania's passengers who died of injuries while being taken to Queenstown will reach 100.

QUEENSTOWN, Saturday, May 8, 4:45 A. M.—The list of the Lusitania's survivors, as far as compiled, follows:

TURNER, Captain.
MATHEWS, A. T., Montreal.
ABRAMOWITZ, S.
LANE, G. B.
MEYERS, W. G. E.
TRIMMINS, J. T.
WITHERBEE, Mrs. A. F.
MACKWORTH, Lady.
ADAMS, Mrs. HENRY, Boston.
RANKIN, ROBERT, New York.
SHARP, SAMUEL.
BYRNE, M. B., New York.
DAVIS, EMILY.
WALKER, ANNIE.
HOUSNELL, E.
CROSS, A. B.
YOUNG, PHILIP, Montreal.
VASSAR, W. A. F., London.
STEELE, GEORGE.
CROSLEY, CYRUS.
PARKER, JAMES.
COLEBROOK, the Rev. R.
MORRIS, H. C. S.
FISH, Mrs., and two children.
MARTIN, Miss R.
GAUTLETT, F. J., New York.
MAYCOCK, Miss MAY.
HENDERSON, VIOLET.
MARDERUD, UNO.
LEVIN, THOMAS D.
THOMAS, D. A., Cardiff, Wales.
EVANS, T. J. M.
CLARKE, A. R.
BURGESS, W. G.
CHARLES, J. H., and daughter, Toronto.
LONEY, Miss, New York.
HERRIS, JOHN.
HOLLAND, Miss.
BRANDELL, Miss JOSEPHINE, New York.
PERRY, F. K. A.
GRAB, O. H.
MOSLEY, G. G., New York.
BROOKS, J. H., New York.
JEFFRY, A. M.
CAIRNS, M.
HAMMOND, O. H., New York.
MANLEY, A.
NEATH, H.
NORTH, Miss.
WINTER, Miss.
WINTER, Miss.
DUGUID, GEORGE.
MOORE, DANIEL.
McCONNELL, JOHN W., Memphis, Tenn.
SHARPE, Miss.
CONNER, Miss.
DALY, H. M.
CLIFFE, PATRICK.
BOHAN, JAMES, Toronto.
CROSLEY, Mrs. CYRUS.
BRETHERTON, Mrs. CYRIL H., and two children, Los Angeles, Cal.
HOPKINS, A. L., New York.
LASSETTER, Mrs. H. B., of Sydney, Australia, wife of General Lassetter.
LASSETTER, Master P.
LAURIAT, CHARLES E., Jr., Boston, Mass.
PAYNTER, Miss IRENE, Liverpool, England.

KINSALE, Ireland, May 8.—Eleven survivors of the Lusitania have been landed here, together with the bodies of five persons who were dead. Among the survivors are:

SMITH, J. RESTON, New York.
BOTTOMLEY, FREDERICK.
BOYLE, N. L.
HOTCHKISS, CHARLES.
HARRIMAN, CORNELIUS.
LIVERMORE, VERNAR.
SULLIVAN, Mrs. F.

Consul's List of Saved.

WASHINGTON, May 8.—Consul Lauriat at Queenstown sends this report:

"Total saved of all nationalities, 700. The following are American survivors of Lusitania; other names will follow:

CRAB, O. S.
PEARL, Major and Mrs., and two children.
SMITH, Mrs. JESSIE TAFT.
HARDWICK, CHARLES C.
EARL, STUART D.
PEARL, AMY.
STANLEY, Mrs.
LINES, L. B.
HILL, C. T.
RANKIN, ROBERT.
LONEY, Miss.
DOHERTY, Mrs. WILLIAM, and infant.
PHILLIPS, THOMAS.
McADAMS, WILLIAM.
HOUGHTON, J. H.
SWEENEY, JOHN M.
HAMMOND, OADEN H.
BROOKS, J. H.
JEFFRY, CHARLES T.
LUND, Mrs. C. H.
SHEPPERDSON, ARTHUR.
MOORE, Dr. D. V.
BERNARD, CLINTON.
LIGHT, HERBERT.
LINNSON, J., Jr.
WILLIAMS, EDITH.
LEARY, JAMES J.
SLIDELL, THOMAS.
WOLFENDEN, Mrs. JOHN.
HOLLAND, Mrs. NINA.
MESH, Mrs. THOMAS.
KESSLER, GEORGE A.
McMURRAY, L.
KAY, ROBERT.
LOCKHART, R. F.
CANNON, OWEN.
HARRIS, DURIGHT C.
JUDSON, FRED S.
COLLIS, ED M.
WRIGHT, R. C.
GAUNTLET, F. J.
KNOX, S. N.
O'DONNELL, PATRICK.

Saw the Submarine 100 Yards Off and Watched Torpedo as It Struck Ship

Ernest Cowper, a Toronto Newspaper Man, Describes Attack, Seen from Ship's Rail—Poison Gas Used in Torpedoes, Say Other Passengers.

Queenstown, Saturday, May 8, 3:18 A. M.

A sharp lookout for submarines was kept aboard the Lusitania as she approached the Irish coast, according to Ernest Cowper, a Toronto newspaper man, who was among the survivors landed at Queenstown.

He said that after the ship was torpedoed there was no panic among the crew, but that they went about the work of getting passengers into the boats in a prompt and efficient manner.

"As we neared the coast of Ireland," said Mr. Cowper, "we all joined in the lookout, for a possible attack by a submarine was the sole topic of conversation.

"I was chatting with a friend at the rail about 2 o'clock when suddenly I caught a glimpse of the conning tower of a submarine about a thousand yards distant. I immediately called my friend's attention to it. Immediately we both saw the track of a torpedo followed almost instantly by an explosion. Portions of splintered hull were sent flying into the air, and then another torpedo struck. The ship began to list to starboard.

"The crew at once proceeded to get the passengers into boats in an orderly, prompt, and efficient manner. Miss Helen Smith appealed to me to save her. I placed her in a boat and saw her safely away. I got into one of the last boats to leave.

"Some of the boats could not be launched as the vessel was sinking. There was a large number of women and children in the second cabin. Forty of the children were less than a year old."

Poison Fumes from Torpedoes.

From interviews with passengers it appears that when the torpedoes burst they sent forth suffocating fumes which had their effect on the passengers, causing some of them to lose consciousness.

Two stokers, Byrne and Hussey of Liverpool, gave a few details. They said the submarine gave no notice and fired two torpedoes, one hitting No. 1 stoke hole and the second the engine room. The first torpedo was discharged at 2 o'clock. In twenty-five minutes the great liner disappeared.

Signals have been received at Queenstown that an armed trawler, believed to be the Heron, and two fishing trawlers are bringing in 100 more bodies.

The Cunard Line agent states that the total number of persons aboard the Lusitania was 2,160.

Loss of the Lusitania Fills London With Horror and Utter Amazement

Special Cable to THE NEW YORK TIMES.

LONDON, Saturday, May 8.—Stupefaction is the word which best describes the first impression created by the news of the sinking of the Lusitania. People seemed unable to realize that at this stage of the world's progress such a deed could be committed as an act of war.

"I have no words for it," said Lord Rosebery, and everyone one found the same sentiment repeated.

[illegible]

Continued on Page 3.

SOME DEAD TAKEN ASHORE

Several Hundred Survivors at Queenstown and Kinsale.

STEWARD TELLS OF DISASTER

One Torpedo Crashes Into the Doomed Liner's Bow, Another Into the Engine Room.

SHIP LISTS OVER TO PORT

Makes It Impossible to Lower Many Boats, So Hundreds Must Have Gone Down.

ATTACKED IN BROAD DAY

Passengers at Luncheon—Warning Had Been Given by Germans Before the Ship Left New York.

Only 650 Were Saved, Few Cabin Passengers

QUEENSTOWN, Saturday, May 8, 4:28 A. M. Survivors of the Lusitania who have arrived here estimate that only about 650 of those aboard the steamer were saved, and say only a small proportion of those rescued were saloon passengers.

Official Confirmation

WASHINGTON, May 8.—A dispatch to the State Department early today from American Consul Lauriet at Queenstown stated that the total number of survivors of the Lusitania was about 700.

LONDON, Saturday, May 8.—The Cunard liner Lusitania, which sailed out of New York last Saturday with 1,918 souls aboard, lies at the bottom of the ocean off the Irish coast.

She was sunk by a German submarine, which sent two torpedoes crashing into her side at 2:30 o'clock yesterday afternoon while the passengers, seemingly confident that the great, swift vessel could elude the German underwater craft, were having luncheon.

The great inrush of water caused the liner to list heavily to port, so that she could not launch many of her lifeboats.

About 1,260 of those on board the great ship, including many Americans, apparently went down with her, as a statement issued late this morning by the Admiralty says the total number of survivors is only 658.

There were 1,253 passengers on board the steamship, including 200 who were transferred to her from the steamer Cameronia. The Americans totaled 188. The crew numbered 665.

It is believed that only a few first class passengers were saved as they thought the ship would remain afloat, and made little effort to escape.

There appears to be a large proportion of the ship's crew among the survivors landed at Queenstown. Only a few offi-

PRESIDENT WILSON SHOCKED AND WASHINGTON FEARS THE DISASTER MAY CAUSE A CRISIS

Longitudnal Section of the Lusitania, Showing Her Construction and Where She Was Hit

x Where the first torpedo struck. xx Where the second torpedo struck.

NO. 1—Navigating Bridge, Officers' Rooms, Roofs of Public Rooms, Marconi House and Docking Bridge.

A, OR BOAT DECK—Captain's Rooms, First Class Library, Grand Entrance, Passenger Elevators, First Class Lounge, Music Room, Smoking Room and Veranda Café, Second Cabin Promenade and Lounge.

B, OR PROMENADE DECK—Forecastle Head, Head Front of Promenade Deck, Observation Corridor, First Class Staterooms, Regal Suites, En Suite Rooms, Grand Entrance and Passenger Elevators, First Class Staterooms, Dome of Dining Saloons, Second Cabin Promenade, Drawing Room, and Second Cabin Smoking Room.

C, OR UPPER DECK—Forward Capstan and Windlass Machinery, Third Class Smoking Room and Ladies' Room, Third Class Covered Promenade, Third Class Main Entrance, First Class Children's Dining Saloon and Nursery, Grand Entrance and Passenger Elevators, First Class Grand Dining Saloon, Engineers' Quarters, Second Cabin Main Entrance, Second Cabin Staterooms and Promenade.

D, OR SALOON DECK—Stewards' Quarters, Third Class Main Dining Saloon, First Class Staterooms, Grand Entrance and Passenger Elevators, First Class Grand Dining Saloon, Galleys and Pantries, Second Cabin Dining Saloon, Second Cabin Staterooms, Stewards' and Cooks' Quarters.

E, OR MAIN DECK—Seamen's Quarters, Third Class Cabins, Grand Entrance and Passenger Elevators, First Class Staterooms, Firemen's Quarters, Second Cabin Staterooms, Stewards' Quarters.

F, OR LOWER DECK—First Class Baggage Rooms, Third Class Cabins, Coal, Stores, Wine Rooms, Firemen's Quarters, Mail Room, Mail Sorting Room, and Stewards' Quarters.

BELOW DECK F—Boilers, Engine Room, Pump Room, Tanks, and Shaft Tunnels.

the starboard side, one forward and another in the engine room. They caused terrific explosions.

"Captain Turner immediately ordered the boats out. The ship began to list badly immediately.

"Ten boats were put into the water, and between 400 and 500 passengers entered them. The boat in which I was, approached the land with three other boats, and we were picked up shortly after 4 o'clock by the Storm Cock.

"I fear that few of the officers were saved. They acted bravely.

"There was only fifteen minutes from the time the ship was struck until she foundered, going down bow foremost. It was a dreadful sight."

At the time this dispatch was sent from Queenstown two other vessels were approaching the port with survivors.

The Cunard Line received a message saying that a motor boat, towing two boats containing fifty passengers, and two tugs with passengers, was passing Kinsale. A majority of the rescue boats are proceeding to Queenstown.

An Admiralty report states that between 500 and 600 survivors from the Lusitania have now been landed, many of them being hospital cases. Several of them have died. Some also have been landed at Kinsale, but the number has not yet been received.

Hit 10 Miles Off Kinsale Head.

This greatest sea tragedy of the war, because of the terrible loss of lives of non-combatants and citizens of neutral nations, took place about ten miles off the Old Head of Kinsale about 2 o'clock in the afternoon.

A dispatch to the Exchange Telegraph from Liverpool quotes the Cunard Company as stating that "the Lusitania was sunk without warning."

According to a Queenstown dispatch the Lusitania was seen from the signal station at Kinsale to be in difficulties at 2:12 P. M. and at 2:33 she had completely disappeared.

This indicated, the dispatch added, that the liner was afloat twenty-one minutes after what evidently was the beginning of her trouble.

Official announcement was also made here last night by the Cunard Line that the Lusitania remained afloat at least twenty minutes after being torpedoed, and that "twenty boats were on the spot at the time." Sixteen more boats, officials of the line said, had been dispatched to the scene for rescue work.

As soon as the Lusitania's wireless call for assistance was received at Queenstown at 2:15 o'clock, Admiral Coke, in command of the naval station, dispatched to the scene all assistance available.

The tugs Warrior, Stormcock, and Julia, together with five trawlers and the local life boat in tow of a tug, were hurried out to sea. It was thought it would take most of them about two hours to reach the spot where the Lusitania was reported to be sinking.

One dispatch received here said the liner was eight miles off the Irish coast when she finally went down.

London Torn With Anxiety.

All the afternoon, following the first startling message from Ireland and the fragmentary bulletins, indicating a possibility of heavy loss of life, London waited with intense anxiety for further news.

This anxiety grew steadily through the evening as hour after hour passed without any definite statement from an authoritative source as to the extent of the disaster.

The Cunard offices, which will remain open throughout the night, were besieged by a great crowd, largely composed of women, many of them weeping bitterly as the hours passed and no definite news came of those aboard the Lusitania.

Accommodation was provided inside the offices for those who had relatives or friends on the steamer, while hundreds waited outside, eagerly reading the scanty bulletins which told of rescue boats arriving at Kinsale and Queenstown, but gave no names of the saved, and consequently did not allay the anxiety.

Flickering Gleam of Hope.

There was a gleam of hope in the general gloom soon after 8 o'clock, when this announcement was made unofficially:

> The Cunard Company has definitely ascertained that the lives of the passengers and the crew of the Lusitania have been saved.

This was speedily proved untrue, however, but the more optimistic still refused to credit the early reports of the swift sinking of the big liner. It was believed that her watertight bulkheads would tend to keep her afloat, and if she floated a reasonable length of time before going down, it was possible that rescuing ships got to her side in time to save all on board.

Owing to the fact that all the news of the Lusitania came through the Admiralty, and that only fragments filtered through at intervals, the crowds got increasingly more impatient, though the Cunard officials posted quickly all bulletins received.

Late in the evening the Admiralty felt compelled to give out notice that it was not holding back any known facts, but did not feel justified in giving out rumors.

Americans Besiege Embssy.

The American Embassy and Consulate and the American newspaper offices were flooded with telephonic inquiries from Americans as to the fate of the passengers on the Lusitania, but there was no definite news there until after midnight, and the only hope that could be held out was that some boats had landed survivors and others had been seen making for the shore. The Embassy decided to remain open all night, so that any news that was received could be made public.

Up to 1 o'clock no news tending to allay the public anxiety had been received in the city. Then dispatches, issued by the Admiralty, indicated that among the survivors landed at Queenstown were some injured, presumably by the explosion.

A later dispatch from the same source increased the apprehensions in this direction. Those wounded are being sent to the naval and military hospitals.

A press dispatch from Queenstown reported that 400 pasesngers and crew had been landed at Kinsale. This stated that none of the first-class passengers had been saved, but this is proved not true by private dispatches.

An Admiralty statement states, however, that the survivors from the Lusitania landed at Kinsale numbered about eleven.

A private telegram from Clonakiety to Dublin says that several hundred passengers had landed that from the Lusitania.

DOUBLE BOTTOM

Cross Section of the Lusitania.

FEARED FOR LINER'S SAFETY.

Washington Heard Alarming Rumors Before the News Came.

WASHINGTON, May 7.—Information gathered among officials of the Government and in diplomatic quarters confirms the belief that plans for the destruction of the Lusitania were made several weeks ago. First, the German Embassy was instructed to advertise in the leading newspapers of the United States warning passengers against traveling on ships belonging to enemies of Germany. Anonymous warnings then were said to have been sent to individuals who proposed sailing on the Lusitania. Most significant of all were letters received here from officials in Germany by individuals saying that the Lusitania surely would be destroyed.

From the day the ship sailed from New York officials here have received inquiries from many sources almost daily as to the safety of the vessel. One official was told with mpch positiveness today that this was the day selected for the destruction of the vessel.

The naval radio station at Arlington has been on the alert for news, and from time to time has been reported as having picked up messages saying the vessel was sunk. Inquiry at the Navy Department each time failed to confirm the reports, and they were not circulated because it was feared they would sprad unnecessary alarm.

At the German Embassy, while no comment was made as to whether it was known that the vessel was to be destroyed, it was said the Embassy knew the Lusitania carried arms and ammunition and, being advised of the resolution of the German Admiralty to attack ships that carried, officials had believed she would be attacked. At the embassy and among diplomats friendly to Germany there was a general satisfaction amounting almost to relief when the first reports came that no lives were lost, for it was urged that the purpose the German submarine campaign was only to destroy British commerce and ships, but no lives. There was a disposition on the part of the Germans to inquire also wether the Lusitania carried any guns on her decks, which might place her in the class of a warship and make unnecessary, according to the rules of international law, the giving of warning.

BULLETINS STIR UP WAR SYMPATHIZERS

Arguments and Fights Follow Sinking of the Lusitania —One Arrest.

The first reports of the sinking of the Lusitania, by a German submarine posted on the bulletin boards around the city caused great crowds to gather and stirred heated arguments and a number of personal encounters. The police stationed at these places had their hands full keeping the peace.

When Paul Zeider of 416 West 126th Street passed Times Square at 6:30 o'clock last evening he saw on the bulletin board the news that the Germans had sunk the Lusitania. He shouted: "Hurragh for the Germans!" and threw his hat in the air. There was an angry outcry, and a dozen men rushed for him. When Traffic Policeman MacDonald, stationed at Broadway and Forty-third Street, had shoved his way into the centre of the small riot, he had to call Patrolman Foley to help rescue Zeider. The German sympathizer failed to appreciate this service, and began struggling with the policemen. He was then taken to the West Forty-seventh Street Police Station and locked up on a charge of disorderly conduct.

In front of THE TIMES bulletin board, in Herald Square, in Park Row, and, in fact, everywhere people congregated to talk about the sinking of the Lusitania, there were angry arguments.

WILSON SHOCKED AT TORPEDO BLOW

Continued from Page 1.

the Shoreham Hotel when the first bulletin was received here. With him were Secretary Garrison, Secretary Daniels, Secretary Lane, Secretary Wilson, and Mr. Tumulty, the Secretary to the President. As the party finished luncheon and was leaving the dining room a newspaper man handed Mr. Bryan the bulletin telling of the sinking of the big Cunarder.

Bryan Hurries to Office.

It was read eagerly by all the Cabinet officers and Mr. Tumulty. Secretary Bryan nurried to the State Department and asked if any official news of the disaster had been received. Nothing had come, however. It was an hour later before the official news reached the Department.

This was in the form of a cable message from Walter H. Page, the American Ambassador in London, received at 3:05 P. M., and was as follows:

"The Lusitania was torpedoed off the Irish Coatst, and sunk in half an hour. No news yet of passengers."

This message was repeated to the White House over the Government telegraph wire.

No other official information came until after 9 o'clock tonight, when the State Department received this message from Consul Frost at Queenstown, Ireland:

"Lusitania sunk at 2:30. Probably many survivors. Rescue work progressing."

Secretary Bryan declined to comment on the Lusitania disaster when he was questioned by newspaper men. He expressed satisfaction over the reports that no lives had been lost, but he declined to go beyond that. His reticence was typical of the attitude displayed throughout official circles, where there was an evident appreciation of the seriousness of the situation.

May Group Protests.

In the absence of any authoritative statement of the Government's position, opinion here is inclined toward the view tha the United States will group the Lusitania case with those of the American tank steamer Gulflight and the British passenger steamer Falaba. In the sinking of the Falaba by a German submarine Leon C. Thrasher, an American citizen, lost his life. Two members of the crew of the Gulflight jumped overboard and were drowned when tha vessel was torpedoed, and the Gulflight's Captain died of heart failure sixteen hours afterward.

No representations have ever been made by the United States to Germany on the subject of Thrasher's death. An investigation is now being made by American officers in England and Germany in an effort to get at all the facts connected with the Gulflight affair, with the primary purpose of determining whether a German submarine was responsible for the attack on the vessel. It was suggested here this evening that when the Government came to make representations to Germany concerning the death of Thrasher it probably would include in its note references to the explosion against the bow of the Gulflight, provided evidence was obtained to show beyond a reasonable doubt that the injured had been done by a German torpedo, and to the sinking of the Lusitania, granted also that there was evidence of a German attack.

In grouping these three incidents the Government, it was said, would be in a position to maintain the contention that Germany had disregarded the warning of the United States concerning attacks by German submarines on American merchant vessels and on foreign vessels carrying American citizens.

In that warning, which was addressed to Germany in the form of a diplomatic note pertaining to the German war zone order, with its consequent submarine warfare against merchant vessels, this Government said that if a German war vessel should destroy on the high seas an American vessel or the lives of American citizens, "it would be difficult for the Goernment of the United States to view the act in any other light than as an indefensible violation of neutral rights which it would be hard, indeed, to reconcile with the friendly relations now so happily subsisting between the two Governments."

The War Zone Order.

To obtain an idea of the bases of the position that may be assumed by the United States Government, it is necessary to keep in mind the several diplomatic notes and certain occurrences that have to do with the German war zone order, which provided for hostile operations by German submarines against merchant ships of Germany's enemies. The points of these bases may be set forth as follows:

1. The German Government issued a decree providing that food supplies of the civilian population of the empire should be taken over and distributed by the Government.

2. Great Britain construed this action as meaning that all food supplies in Germany, or shipped to Germany for the use of the civilian population, were to be taken over by the German Government for the use of its armed forces. Great Britain then took action indicating that she intended to prevent any foodstuffs from going to Germany. Up to that time she had permitted foodstuffs for the civilian population to go to Germany if carried in neutral vessels.

Our Flag Protest.

3. Following the action of the British Government in detaining the Wilhelmina, an American ship loaded with food suplies from the United States for the civilian population of Germany, the German Government issued its war zone order, providing that a submarine warfare should be waged against British, French, and Russian ships within a prescribed area of water adjacent to the coast of the British Isles, and warned neutral nations that they should keep their merchant ships away from the war zone, on account of the danger that they might be mistaken for ships of the enemy and made to suffer the consequences.

4. The Lusitania, the vessel sunk today, flew the American flag on a voyage from New York to England, and Germany took advantage of this incident to justify the war zone order. The use of the flag was the subject of a protest by the United States to Great Britain.

5. The United States Government protested against the war zone order as far as it might apply to American ships, and insisted that the well-defined right of visit and search to determine the nationality, destination, and cargo of a merchant vessel should be exercised by Germany in order to prevent the possible sinking of an American vessel by a German submarine or other warship. At the same time, this Government warned Germany that friendly relations between Germany and the United States might be severed if a German warship should destroy an American vessel or cause the loss of American lives through sinking a vessel of other nationality with Americans on board.

6. The war zone order caused the British Government to issue the Order in Council providing for stopping all supplies to Germany, even if carried in neutral bottoms and intended for civilians.

7. The British passenger ship Falaba, bound for Africa, was torpedoed by a German submarine and Leon C. Thrasher, an American citizen, was drowned.

8. The American ship Gulflight was sunk off the Scilly Isles, supposedly by a torpedo fired by a German submarine, and two members of the crew were drowned. All others on the Gulflight were saved except the Captain, who died from heart failure.

Modus Vivendi Failed.

After the issuance of the German war zone order, and the promulgation of the British Order in Council, which carried into effect the practice of the British Government in nolding up neutral vessels with cargoes of foodstuffs for Germany the United States Government endeavored to effect an arrangement in the form of a modus vivendi by which American foodstuffs were to be permitted to go to Germany under a guarantee from the United States that they would be distributed only to non-combatant civilians. These negotiations failed.

Examination of the official British Admiralty chart of the south coast of Ireland in the Navy Department late this afternoon in connection with the various bulletins from London, Liverpool, and Queenstown threw considerable light on the difficulties that would be encountered in rescuing the 1,900 persons constituting the passengers and crew of the Lusitania. According to the only message that appears to have come from the Lusitania in the form of distress calls received by the Land's End wireless station the position of the Lusitania was given as ten miles south of Kinsale. Interpreted in the light of subsequent messages, this message from the Lusitania was accepted as meaning that her position was about ten miles south of Old Head of Kinsale, a rocky promontory on the Irish coast about six and one-half miles due south of the town of Kinsale, which stands in from the coast on a narrow harbor.

Struck in Deep Water.

The point given by the Lusitania is located in water 49 fathoms, or 294 feet, deep. The 40-fathom line, within which the water is less than 240 feet deep, is nearly 4½ miles from the coast at Old Head of Kinsale, the nearest point of land to the accident. The 30-fathom line, behind which the water is not over 180 feet deep, runs 1 2-3 miles from the coast at Old Head of Kinsale. The 20-fathom line, behind which the water is not over 120 feet deep, is a mile from Old Head of Kinsale, and the 10-fathom (60 feet depth) is a half a mile from Old Head. These measurements based on official soundings by the British Admiralty are sufficient to show the precipitous shelving of the ocean depths and the difficulty that would be encountered in trying to beach the Lusitania.

If the Lusitania was struck ten miles from Old Head of Kinsale, as indicated by the Lusitania's message, it would have been necessary for the giant Cunarder to travel not less than 8¼ miles in order to reach water in which there would be a depth of 20 fathoms, or 120 feet, and this water would be too deep for beaching. The nearest point at which the Lusitania could reach water of not more than ten fathoms, 60 feet depth, would be 9½ miles from the point of torpedo attack, and within a half mile of Old Head of Kinsale. It is not thought that the Lusitania could have been beached at all off Old Head of Kinsale, the shores of which are of rock and almost vertical. To beach the Lusitania its Captain would have been compelled to steer into Courtmacsherry Bay, a large arm of the ocean, west of Old Head of Kinsale, and bounded on the west by a promontory known as Seven Heads. To be beached in Courtmacsherry Bay the Lusitania would have been forced to travel not less than twelve miles after being struck.

Twenty-eight Miles from Queenstown.

The air-line distance by water from Queenstown to the place where the Lusitania was struck is shown by the British Admiralty chart to be twenty-eight miles from Queenstown. This means that vessels sent in the rescue fleet from Queenstown had to travel about sixty miles in making the round trip, and this could not be done in less than about six hours.

The three nearest points of the Irish coast to the point where the Lusitania was torpedoed were the promontories of Old Head of Kinsale, Seven Heads, and Galley Head. Old Head of Kinsale is fifteen miles southwest of Roche Point, the entrance to Cork Harbor, which leads to Queenstown and Cork. Seven Heads is seven miles west-southwest of Old Head of Kinsale and ten miles northwest of the point where the Lusitania was torpedoed.

Galley Head is ten miles west southwest of Seven Heads, and seventeen miles west-northwest of the point where the Lusitania was struck. Some of the wireless messages received at Liverpool came from the Admiralty wireless station at Galley Head, which is on the Galley Head promontory, just mentioned. One of the cable messages received by the Cunard Company in New York this afternoon from Liverpool stated that a Cork newspaper reported that 300 passengers had landed at Clonakilty.

This probably means that these passengers landed at Clonakilty Bay, which is situated between Galley Head and Seven Heads and fifteen miles from the point where the tragedy occurred. The town of Clonakilty is two miles inland from the head of this bay. There are two landing coves in Clonakilty Bay. These are Dunnycove Bay, on the west side of Clonakilty Bay, three and one-half miles south of the town of Clonakilty, and Barry Cove, on the east side of Clonakilty Bay, five miles southeast of the town of Clonakilty.

No Railroad There.

No railroad touches the shore of Clonakilty Bay. Any passengers landing on that bay would have to travel over rocky roads to Clonakilty, the end of the Clonakilty branch of the Cork and Bandon Railway. Once at Clonakilty these passengers, in order to reach Queenstown, woud travel over this branch railway to Clonakilty Junction, a distance of eight miles, then go eastward through Bandon to Cork, about twenty-two miles, and thence by rail about ten miles to Queenstown.

One of the Cunard Line's messages from Liverpool said the Admiralty wireless station at Galley Head reported having sighted several boats apparently containing survivors nine miles southeast and that a Greek steamer was proceeding to assist. Nine miles southeast of Galley Head would mean that these boats had gone considerably off their course, and would mean that their boats had drifted a little south of west about ten miles from the place where the Lusitania was struck.

The nearest point of approach to shore for persons in boats making away from the place where the Lusitania was struck would be Courtmacsherry Bay, ten miles distant from the point of attack, and five miles nearer than Clonakilty Bay. Courtmacsherry Bay is between the promontories of Seven Heads and Old Head of Kinsale, and there are many places on its shore where passengers in small boats might safely land. Arms of Courtmacsherry Bay are Seven Heads Bay, Boat Harbor, Garylucas, Ringalurisky Point, and West Holeopen Bay. Those who may have succeeded in landing on the west side of this bay would take the Owenkeagh Railroad from the town of Courtmacsherry to Ballinascarty, on the Clonakilty Branch Railway, and then go through Bandon to Cork. Those landing on the east side of this bay would have to travel by highway to the town of Kinsale, whence they could proceed by the Kinsale Branch of the Cord and Bandon Railway to Cork and Queenstown.

A high Government official, who is an expert in nautical and maritime matters, ventured the suggestion tonight that perhaps only half of the lifeboats of the Lusitania could have been used in the circumstances of the loss of the vessel as reported.

"The press and official dispatches agree that the Lusitania sank in half an hour," he said. "To have sunk so rapidly the Lusitania probably listed quickly and heavily. Otherwise the vessel, constructed as she was, would have gone down very slowly if she had settled straightaway without any heavy list. If complete developments show that the vessel listed rapidly it will probably be found that the lifeboats on one side were not used, or only part of them used. If the vessel listed to the starboard very quickly it would have been difficult to use the lifeboats on the port side because these boats would not reach the water. They would strike the side of the vessel and turn over. The lifeboats on the starboard side could have been, of course, used while the vessel was listing to starboard. The Lusitania was heavily bulkheaded. There were coal bunkers built along both sides to protect the machinery against shell attack.

But this coal would not give protection against torpedo attack. A torpedo tearing a great hole in the side of a vessel would let in the water, but if the hole were near the bunkers the coal would impede the inflow of the water somewhat. If the Lusitania settled straightaway without listing, I think it would have been possible to get off the 1,900 persons in half an hour, but it would be quick work and depend altogether on conditions met at the time. With the vessel listing, if only half of the lifeboats were used, that would account for heavy loss of life."

"All the News That's Fit to Print."

The New York Times.

THE WEATHER

Fair Sunday; Monday partly cloudy; light, variable winds.

For full weather report see Page 23.

VOL. LXV...NO. 21,281. NEW YORK, SUNDAY, APRIL 30, 1916.—96 PAGES, In Seven Parts, Including Picture and Rotogravure Section and Review of Books. PRICE FIVE CENTS.

CONFEREES OPEN MEXICAN PARLEY; VIEWS CONFLICT

Obregon Asks for Withdrawal of Our Troops and Scott for Co-operation.

BOTH QUESTIONS DEFERRED

Long Discussion Over the Conditions in Territory Where Pershing's Men Are.

CORDIALITY SHOWN AT END

Impressive Military Display Marks Reception of Obregon and Staff in El Paso.

From a Staff Correspondent.

Special to The New York Times.

EL PASO, Tex., April 29.—The first conference between the representatives of the United States and Mexico began at 5 o'clock this afternoon in the Mexican Customs House in Juarez, and at exactly 7 o'clock, when the four American Army officers and six Mexican representatives left the building, General Scott was seen to pat General Obregon on the shoulder as they went down the steps.

Both the American Chief of Staff and the Mexican Minister of War were smiling, and the conferees of both sides shook hands with one another. Beyond this manifestation of cordiality, they disclosed nothing that had occurred at the discussion of the operations of the American punitive expedition in Mexico, but THE NEW YORK TIMES correspondent is able to state with authority that this is what occurred at the first conference:

General Obregon communicated to General Scott what amounted to a demand that all American troops be withdrawn from Mexico. This was discussed for a few minutes, then it was practically tabled.

Scott's Counter-Proposal.

General Scott presented then the counter-proposal that the Carranza Government co-operate with the American force in Mexico in further pursuit of the Villista bandits. After brief discussion this counter-proposal was tabled to be taken up again at a later conference.

It was agreed between the representatives of the two Governments that these two proposals could not be passed on until there had been discussion regarding the actual conditions prevailing in Mexico in general, and particularly in the State of Chihuahua. Thereupon a prolonged discussion of conditions in the northern State in which the American troops are now situated began. This discussion lasted throughout the remainder of the conference.

General Scott said after the first conference:

"You may say for me that the meeting was very satisfactory. I will notify General Obregon as to the time of our next meeting."

The Mexican representatives have with them the Civil Governor of Chihuahua, Ignacio Enriquez, a clean-cut young Mexican who was educated at the University of Illinois. He is here practically as a "witness in the case."

In presenting their arguments in the discussion of conditions in the North of Mexico, the official representatives will call Enriquez to bear testimony that the State is now under the control of Carranza. And the reports of Mexican secret agents are already here, to be introduced as documentary evidence to the same end.

Mexicans Prepare a "Brief."

The Mexicans have prepared their case like a lawyer's brief. Another "witness" will be Luis Gutierrez, Military Governor of Chihuahua. From sources which THE TIMES correspondent is unable to disclose it was learned authoritatively tonight that General Obregon has complete authority to conduct the conferences without awaiting new instructions of any sort from General Carranza.

General Scott, however, will communicate each day while the conferences are in progress with the Washington Administration and receive new instructions with which to enter the next session.

General Scott is communicating the result of the first conference to Washington this evening, and expects further instructions by tomorrow morning.

The next conference was tentatively set for tomorrow to be held in the same room in the Mexican Custom House. The time is undecided. General Scott will set the hour after hearing from Washington. Those in a position to know estimated tonight that the conferences would last at least four or five days, and probably longer.

The officials who attended the conference this evening were:

Representing the United States, General Hugh L. Scott, Chief of Staff; General Frederick Funston, Lieut. Col. R. E. L. Michie of the General Staff, and Captain Fitzhugh Lee, General Funston's Aid.

Representing Mexico: General Obregon, the Minister of War; General Jackinto Trevino, commander of the Department of the Northeast; General Luis Gutierrez, General Plutarco, and General Elias Calles, Military Governor of Sonora.

The Mexicans also had present as an interpreter Andreas Garcia, their consul at El Paso, and there was an American interpreter with General Scott.

General Calles arrived here this morning. He had not been included in the list of conferees at first, but yesterday telegraphed a request that he be allowed to attend, and was invited by General Funston. The representatives of both countries agreed at this evening's conference that they would make no official statements for publication until all of the conferences were over.

Obregon and Suite Received.

The first official conference, which did not begin until 5 o'clock this afternoon, followed an exchange of formal visits on the part of the representatives of the two Governments. The American officials took the initiative and made the first call last night, motoring across the international bridge and visiting General Obregon and his associates in the Juarez custom house.

The Mexican officials paid a return visit this morning, General Obregon and his large retinue of Generals and minor officers calling on Generals Scott and Funston in their private car parked near the railroad station here. But before they reached the car the Mexicans had an opportunity to learn that despite the fact that about 12,000 American troops are now in Mexico there is still an impressive number of them at this particular point of the border.

Since the Americans crossed the

Continued on Page 6.

VILLISTAS SMASHED, ARMY OFFICERS THINK

Americans' Hard and Frequent Blows Have Taken Fight Out of Scattered Bandits.

By FRANK B. ELSER.

Special Correspondent of The New York Times.

RANCHO PROVIDENCIA, Chihuahua, Mexico, April 28, (by Carrier to Headquarters of General Pershing, Namiquipa, thence by Wireless to Columbus, N. M., April 29.)—Officers of the Seventh Cavalry arriving at this camp this afternoon from Minaca, Santo Tomas, and other towns in the Guerrero district were of the opinion that Villa forces in the Sierra Madre, in broken up bands, had been hit so hard and so often since the Americans came into the country that all the fight had been taken out of them.

These officers said that to the Americans had been given valuable assistance by the Carranzistas during the thirty-day campaign, which closed with the defeat of the last band of Villistas of considerable size at Temachi on Saturday, April 22.

Carranzistas, with large reinforcements from Torreon and from Zacatecas, San Luis Potosi, and other States in the southern part of the Republic, began to arrive today. As they have nothing in common with the natives of this region, it is now believed that they are in a position to keep Villistas from reassembling in numbers sufficiently large to do damage or levy tribute.

The opinion prevails among men arriving from the west that Villa is dead. This opinion is said to be entertained by natives regardless of political leanings.

CONFEREES DEADLOCK ON ARMY BILL ITEM

Can't Agree on Number of Regulars, on Volunteer Reserve or on Nitrate Plant.

WASHINGTON, April 29.—Conferees of the House and Senate, after three days of deliberation on the Army Reorganization bill, the first of the big preparedness measures, have come to a complete deadlock over several important features. It was strongly intimated tonight that they would report a disagreement and ask their respective branches of Congress for further instructions.

"Hopelessly apart on the size of the regular army, on the proposals for a volunteer reserve army, and on a Government nitrate plant," was the report of one member of the conference tonight, and he declared Congress would be asked in the near future to pass again on these features of the measure.

The Senate conferees are insisting determinedly upon the provision in the Senate bill for a regular army of 250,000 men and Representative Kahn, the Republican House conferee, is standing with them. Representatives Hay and Dent, however, are insistent upon the House provision for 140,000 men.

Representative Kahn pointed out to the conferees today that his amendment for an army of 200,000 had been defeated by only a small majority when the House had the bill under consideration. Since that time, big army men contend, international developments have caused a change of feeling on the part of many representatives. Some Administration leaders think the House might now be brought to accept the 250,000 Senate proposal should the conferees fail to agree.

It was said tonight that should a disagreement be reported the Senate might agree to give up its volunteer army plan and accept instead the National Guard reserve provision of the House bill, and might also abandon the Government nitrate plant provision, which, it is conceded generally, never will be accepted by the House.

900 RECRUITS A WEEK ARMY'S AVERAGE NOW

5,417 Men Enlisted in Last 44 Days—18,413 Applicants Rejected.

WASHINGTON, April 29.—Figures compiled by the War Department based on reports from recruiting stations in all parts of the country show that 5,417 recruits have been obtained for the army in the last forty-four days. This is a fraction over one-fourth of the total of 20,000 men to be added to the regular army under the Hay emergency resolution, which was passed by Congress immediately after the Pershing expedition went into Mexico. At the present rate of enlistment it will take all Summer to obtain 20,000 recruits.

During the forty-four days in which the enlistment has been pushed under high pressure the recruiting officers have received applications from 23,830 young men. Of this number the applications of 18,413 were rejected on account of failure to measure up to the high standard required by the recruiting officers.

Every five days the War Department receives telegraphic reports showing the progress in recruiting, the last of these periods having ended at noon yesterday. These reports show that the recruits are being obtained at the rate of about 900 a week. To date the enlistment record has been as follows, for each of the periods:

Period Ending	Applications.	Acceptances.
March 20	2,453	550
March 25	2,653	840
March 31	3,863	551
April 5	2,880	620
April 14	4,068	1,048
April 21	3,573	772
April 28	3,438	718
Total	23,850	5,417

Chicago has been the banner recruiting centre for the country, reporting that during the last forty-four days there have been 2,449 applications and 521 recruits accepted. San Francisco ranks second with 2,762 applicants and 484 recruits accepted, while New York City is third, with 2,122 applicants and 392 recruits accepted. St. Louis stands fourth with 884 applicants and 242 recruits accepted, while Philadelphia has a records of 582 applicants, of whom 221 were accepted.

COMPULSION VOTE GROWS.

Scottish Trades Union Congress Now Stands 66 to 46 Against.

GLASGOW, April 29.—The Scottish Trades Union Congress, by a vote of 66 to 46, today declared its opposition to compulsory military service.

The vote is considered significant, as heretofore the Scottish trades unionists have been virtually unanimous against compulsory service.

8,970 BRITISH AT KUT SURRENDER TO TURKISH FOES

Tigris Force Which Gen. Townshend Led Almost to Bagdad Is Starved Out.

RELIEF FORCE 20 MILES OFF

Hordes of Turks, Strongly Intrenched, Twice Defeated Efforts to Reach Town.

FLOODS ALSO HALT ADVANCE

England Laments Surrender, but Praises Commander for His Brilliant Defense.

LONDON, Sunday, April 30.—The British Tigris army under the command of Major Gen. Charles Townshend, which has been besieged at Kut-el-Amara, has surrendered to the Turkish foes. Exhaustion of supplies compelled the force to yield.

This official announcement was made here yesterday:

> After a resistance protracted for 143 days and conducted with a gallantry and fortitude that will be forever memorable, General Townshend has been compelled by the final exhaustion of his supplies to surrender.
>
> Before doing so he destroyed his guns and munitions.
>
> The force under him consists of 2,970 British troops of all ranks and services, and some 6,000 Indian troops and their followers.

The eventual surrender of General Townshend had been expected since the recent failure of the forces under Lieut. Gen. Gorringe and General Keary to break through the Turkish position at Sannayyat, about twenty miles below Kut-el-Amara on the Tigris River, and an unsuccessful attempt to send to the blockaded army provisions by steamers. It had been touch and go with the small British force for many days.

The location of Kut-el-Amara, on a peninsula extending into the Tigris River, made it impossible to send supplies by air as there was no landing place for aeroplanes.

While a supply vessel a few days ago got beyond the main Turkish lines at Es-Sinn, it was a forlorn hope, as the Turks investing the city, advised of her coming, could have easily sunk her from shore, even if she had escaped the artificial barriers in the river.

As for the forces, which attempted to relieve General Townshend, they met with almost continual misfortunes. Several times when it was believed they were on the point of success, rising waters made further progress impossible. After penetrating Turkish positions they were compelled to fall back or remain stationary, owing to the impossibility of attacking the position at Sannayyat, which was surrounded by water. The British troops did actually attack the prepared position there, after wading through mud and water waist deep, but while meeting with some success, failure at other points made their sacrifices futile.

The British public never lost faith in General Townshend, and even now that he has been forced to capitulate after destroying everything at Kut-el-Amara that might be valuable to the Turks, they look back upon his campaign as a brilliant one.

END OF 10 MONTHS' CAMPAIGN.

Surrender Is a Climax of Disasters to British Forces.

The surrender of General Townshend's army to the Turks is one of the few instances of the war in which an entire fighting unit of important numbers has laid down its arms. It is one of the largest body of troops of the Entente Allies which has surrendered at one time and larger than any other captured French or British force.

Signs have not been wanting for a month that the Anglo-Indian force at Kut-el-Amara was in sore straits. Communication had been kept up by aeroplanes, but the official British statement of Friday that a vessel loaded with food had grounded four miles below the city was a strong indication that the force had lacked supplies to a dangerous degree.

A recent Turkish official bulletin said the position of the British at Kut-el-Amara was critical and that they were expecting to receive small supplies of food by aeroplane.

Up to a late day General Townshend had kept alive the hope that he would be relieved. King George sent a message of encouragement to him several weeks ago, and in a message sent out as late as April 7 the General said he expected to be relieved soon.

Less than a score of miles away down the Tigris is a relief army which for months had been attempting to reach the besieged forces. A few weeks ago several successes over the Turks were announced and hope then ran high in England that the mission would succeed.

The Kut-el-Amara disaster is an unfortunate ending of a campaign which for a short time promised to be crowned with remarkable success by the capture of Bagdad.

It was early in June, 1915, that General Townshend, moving northward on his way to Bagdad, captured Kut-el-Amara with the Turkish force of 730 men and the Governor.

Led 40,000 Men Northward.

Townshend had with him two divisions of Anglo-Indian troops, or a few over 40,000 men. There are no towns deserving the name between Kut-el-Amara and Bagdad, and, receiving fresh supplies the following week, Townshend

Continued on Page 2.

Turks Report That the Kut Garrison Numbered 13,300 And That Surrender Was Made Without Conditions

LONDON, April 29.—A Constantinople dispatch, received by way of Berlin, says that the Vice Chief Commander of the Turkish Army announces that the British garrison at Kut-el-Amara, under General Townshend, which surrendered unconditionally, numbered 13,300 men.

Although the British report puts the size of the surrendered garrison at 8,970 men, it refers to the Indian troops "and their followers." This may account for the additional 4,300 reported from Constantinople and the seeming discrepancy between the British and the Turkish official reports of the surrender.

ROOSEVELT STIRS CHICAGO AUDIENCE

"I'm Proud of You!" He Cries as Diners Cheer His Plea for Preparedness.

WANTS UNIVERSAL SERVICE

Objects to Uncle Sam with a Chinese Pigtail, and Liberty as a Female Huckster.

Special to The New York Times.

CHICAGO, April 29.—Into the Middle West, territory classed by many political leaders as only lukewarm toward his doctrines of preparedness, Colonel Roosevelt today brought from New York his views, conceded to be preliminary to an avowed Presidential candidacy.

If his political chances are to be judged by the warmth of his welcome, his most ardent friends could not have been disappointed. For the reception he got from the time he stepped off the Twentieth Century Limited this morning until he had concluded his address before the Illinois Bar Association tonight was enthusiastic, and bore all the appearance of spontaneity.

He came to Chicago to address the jurists on "National Duty and International Ideals" in a 4,000-word speech, which was interpreted as a straight-out declaration of the issues on which the Roosevelt-for-President campaign shall be based.

A crowd of 1,000 or more greeted the Colonel when he arrived at the La Salle Street Station and thousands cheered him as he passed through the streets in his motor car. On every side the slogan: "We want Teddy! We want Teddy!" adopted by hundreds of delegates to the Republican National Convention of 1912, was chanted. In many ways the scenes enacted were not unlike those witnessed at the time of the 1912 convention upon the arrival of the Colonel, only the situation was more tense then and the crowds greater in size.

If the reception today was a manufactured one, it was well staged and the Roosevelt adherents, far from admitting that it was arranged in advance, assert that little publicity was given to the fact that the Colonel was to arrive here at a certain hour.

The cordiality of the earlier reception was repeated tonight at the Illinois Bar Association dinner at the Hotel La Salle, which was attended by Governor Dunne and hundreds of prominent jurists and attorneys of the State. In all more than 1,300 obtained seats, and the entire nineteenth floor was given over to the affair.

Hundreds of applicants were turned away. It was the biggest dinner ever held in Chicago, according to the management, and this gave an inkling of the interest which the Colonel has aroused in the campaign he has undertaken.

He Assails Wilson's Policies.

The jurists and their guests gave the Colonel a rousing reception and listened with the deepest attention to his carefully prepared address, much of which was in the form of an attack upon the Wilson Administration and the country's policies in handling international problems. If it has accomplished nothing else, the trip has served to place Colonel Roosevelt before the people of the Middle West as openly and uncompromisingly a candidate for the Republican nomination. Where there were a number, and among them several political leaders of prominence, who found it difficult to believe that Colonel Roosevelt actually hoped to capture the Republican Convention after sending the Republican ticket to defeat four years ago there are none now.

"Yes, Teddy's in it for sure," was a remark frequently heard from the lips of those who watched his strenuous entry and heard his address.

Colonel Roosevelt, by his appearance here, has unquestionably created a new atmosphere in connection with national preparedness. He has added, also, a new "punch" to the pre-convention campaign, and where it was lagging a bit has set it ahead at least two weeks in this section. Where many had given little heed before to the fact that the National Convention was only a few weeks off they have been brought to a full realization of the fact that the decision must soon be made, and that if Roosevelt is to be headed off the job must quickly be undertaken.

The greatest demonstration came tonight at the dinner when the jurists, attorneys, and their guests rose and shouted themselves hoarse when the Colonel placed himself on record for universal service founded on a modified form of the Swiss system.

From the moment that he began to speak the Colonel had the crowd with him, and his words were interrupted a score of times by applause. At the final outburst, spontaneous and sustained, with the diners on their feet, waving napkins and shouting, the Colonel gave way to the emotions he felt.

"My heart is thrilled," he exclaimed when his voice could be heard above the din. "I know you are sound. I knew the West meant business—that you would stand for the nation.

"By George, I'm Proud of You!"

The cheering was redoubled and drowned out the Colonel's voice for more than a minute, and he stood there, his face glowing.

"I can't do you the good you have done me," he continued, pounding with his clenched fist to emphasize his feelings. "But I'll go on with my head up and my heart strong to preach preparedness to the people.

"By George, I'm proud of you—it's great! And I can't tell you how glad I am that you showed your feelings in this manner when I spoke of universal service in which all of us would take our man's part in upholding the welfare of this nation.

"I did not know how you'd take it when I said that but I believe in it with all my heart, and I didn't care a darn what the effect would be, I was going to tell you what I thought and felt. I'm proud of you as American citizens. I can't tell you how proud I am."

And the demonstration did not end there. At the conclusion of the

Continued on Page 3.

GERARD APPRISED OF KAISER'S STAND

Berlin Believes the Ambassador Has Been Told What Germany's Reply Will Be.

WASHINGTON GETS NO WORD

Awaits Envoy's Report on Visit to the Emperor—President Will Allow No More Parleying.

BERLIN, April 29.—Ambassador Gerard was received in audience by Emperor William last night and conferred with other leaders of the Empire. No intimation has been given as to when the German reply to the American note will be ready, except a hint contained in a Berlin dispatch to the Cologne Gazette, which said:

"The consultations at Great Headquarters probably are near a conclusion. The visit of the American Ambassador was designed to permit him to consult with persons in authority there over the situation. It is assumed their final decision also will be communicated to him there."

The Tageblatt explains this morning that its statement that the basic features of the answer already have been settled was misunderstood. The paper asserts it meant only to say that a draft of the answer had been made, but that a decision had not yet been reached. The wording of this morning's statement indicates clearly, however, that there was no misunderstanding on the part of the readers, but that the Tageblatt made an error yesterday.

There is virtually no comment in the press upon the situation except that from the pen of Count Ernst von Reventlow, who still appears to believe a breach with the United States is inevitable.

The official organ of the Hansabund, the organization of commercial interests, refers to the gravity of the decision to be reached. It says the representatives of commerce, industry, and trade belonging to the Hansabund are certain the decision will be reached with the dispassionate care which it demands, but are equally certain that Germany's dignity as a nation and its freedom to use all weapons of defense will be fully regarded.

The Hansabund hopes, however, it is declared, that an honorable and peaceful understanding will be reached, but that if such a solution proves impossible all Germans will stand united behind the Emperor.

PRESIDENT WILL NOT PARLEY.

Germany Must Comply or Break Will Follow—Optimism Abating.

Special to The New York Times.

WASHINGTON, April 29.—The feeling of optimism that has prevailed here over the indications that Germany would meet the American demands for the abandonment of present methods of German submarine warfare began to wane today on account of the view that appeared to prevail in Berlin that the issue would be discussed between the two Governments before the German answer was transmitted. This Government wants no discussion. It holds that the time for discussion has passed. There is every reason to believe that President Wilson has determined to break relations with Germany if his demand is not complied with literally.

The supposition in some quarters that Emperor William asked Ambassador Gerard to convey a message to President Wilson which would suggest a modification of the American attitude or permit a discussion of the principle involved, has not tended to increase the hopefulness of those who understand the President's position. Even the Kaiser's personal request along such lines would not influence the President, it is gathered, to consent to further exchanges concerning the merits of the submarine controversy.

Much of the optimism that has prevailed here has been based on information to the German Embassy that the Berlin Government would endeavor to meet the desires of the United States. In German circles this optimism continues, and it is shared to a great extent by officials of the Washington Government. But those officials in a position to know the inside of the situation are not indulging in any high hopes. They know the determination of President Wilson to have a settlement of the submarine issue one way or the other, and realize that he has made up his mind that a severance of diplomatic relations must come if Germany attempts to evade the American demand by suggestions of parley or otherwise.

The President, there is good reason to believe, has decided irrevocably that he will take the course set forth in the note to Germany if a satisfactory answer is not forthcoming, and will not be influenced by opposition in Congress or elsewhere. The pro-German deluge of telegrams to Senators and Representatives has not had the slighest effect on the President. If anything, this phase of the German propaganda has made the President and his advisers even more determined to adhere to the course they have outlined.

Mr. Gerard was expected to have reached Berlin on his return from his visit to the Kaiser some time today. At the State Department just before the closing hour it was said that no message had come from the Ambassador as to his conference with the German Emperor and none was expected today on account of the unusual delays in telegraphic transmission of cipher dispatches. The department has not heard from the Ambassador since he cabled that he had been invited by the Kaiser to visit him, and was leaving Berlin for the front on Thursday.

It was reported today that the Administration was becoming anxious over the failure of the German Government to respond to its demand, which called for a declaration "immediately" that present methods of German submarine warfare had been abandoned and made effective, but nothing to bear out that impression was obtained in official quarters. The Administration has no inten-

Continued on Page 3.

DUBLIN REVOLT IS NEAR COLLAPSE; POST OFFICE REBELS SEIZED IS BURNED; WIMBORNE TELLS STORY OF RISING

Redmond Tells Nationalists to Aid the Troops in Suppressing Revolt

LONDON, April 29.—John Redmond, leader of the Irish Nationalists, has placed himself absolutely at the disposal of the authorities and is in constant touch with them. He has instructed Nationalist supporters in all parts of Ireland to hold themselves at the disposal of the military authorities.

In many places besides Dublin the Nationalist voters have already, on their own initiative, mobilized in support of the troops. At Tipperary yesterday volunteers offered their services.

Irish Rebels Proclaimed Republic; Seven Headed It, Wimborne Says

Failure to Cut Wire to Curragh Camp a Fatal Error—Sailors Landed from Fleet to Aid Troops in County Galway.

DUBLIN, April 29.—Baron Wimborne, Lord Lieutenant of Ireland, expressed to The Associated Press at the Viceregal Lodge today the assurance that the seditious movement would be suppressed in the course of a few days.

The Viceroy was full of praise for the loyalty displayed by the great majority of the Irish people, and considered the momentary success gained and the damage done by the rebels as small when viewed in connection with the surprise of the outbreak and the evident preparations made for it.

The country outside of Dublin, except for a few isolated places, has, he declared, remained peaceful.

Requested to give an account of what had happened since the rebels had proclaimed an Irish republic last Monday afternoon, Baron Wimborne said:

"The outbreak began Monday morning about 11:30 o'clock. About that time information was received that Dublin Castle had been attacked, Stephens Green occupied, and the Post Office seized by the rebels. Telephonic communication with the Curragh Camp was immediately obtained by the authorities and the reserve troops there were brought to Dublin that night and the following morning.

"Meanwhile the situation at the Castle, which had never been captured by the rebels, was strengthened. The only casualty there was the shooting of a policeman at the gate. A very few hours after the outbreak large forces had been assembled in the Castle, which, however, was never in real danger.

Failed to Cut Wire to Curragh.

"The rebels had cut telegraphic communications with the country districts and England, but had not succeeded in discovering a telephone wire which connected the Curragh Camp with headquarters. This was one of their great mistakes. They did not cut communication with North Ireland, with which we have at all times been able to converse.

"At one time the rebels had possession of the Broadstone Railway Station, which was not protected.

"On Tuesday morning all the reinforcements we had called from Curragh had reached Dublin, and since that moment the rebels have not attempted anything except sniping from certain localities and houses. It is so easy for them to abandon houses by back doors and to get away to other advantageous positions.

"The military cannot distinguish the rebels from other citizens. Sometimes they leave their houses after hiding their rifles and cartridges and mingle with the ordinary inhabitants. After taking observations of the soldiers' positions they return to commence sniping again. Most of the houses they occupy they have entered by force, and not because the householders sympathize with their movement. As a matter of fact, the general run of people do not sympathize with them.

"Since the number of troops has increased, the position of the rebels has remained the same. When their activities at any point become too lively the troops throw a few shells into the houses they occupy and such explosions have caused fires, while other fires have been started by the rebels themselves.

"They have barricaded Sackville Street and are in possession of all the houses there, but they were shelled out of Liberty Hall by a gunboat on Tuesday, and we occupied their headquarters immediately. They burned Linen Hall barracks, and other small fires have occurred.

"In the early stages of the revolt the Sinn Feiners fired on the members of the fire brigade, but later we cleared the area around the fires, and the firemen were able to extinguish the flames.

"Wednesday the military arrangements were completed by the arrival of further reinforcements, and the rebels were hemmed in in Sackville Street. The work of disposing of the troops to deal with the snipers occupied a lot of time and much care, but eventually this district and other rebel quarters were surrounded. Everything done has been carried out according to plans.

"A big cordon has been drawn all around Dublin and shorter cordons around the inner districts.

Fighting in Galway.

"Regarding the situation in the provinces on the whole, it is very good. We were naturally apprehensive lest there might be some response there to the Dublin movement. Fighting occurred in Galway near Athenry, where the police are now in possession of the town, but the rebels are encamped in a ruined castle. There also has been fighting in a Galway town which the rebels attacked and compelled us to land men from the fleet to support the military.

"Encounters took place at Enniscorthy, County Wexford, and there were certain rebellious assemblages in Meath and Louth, but on the whole reports are quiet. This applies also to Cork, Limerick, Kerry, Clare, Kilkenny, Mayo, Sligo, Tipperary, Leitrim, Kildare, Roscommon, and all of Ulster."

When asked concerning the origin and connections of the rebel movement with the Germans, the Viceroy said there was an absolute certainty the rebellion was timed to take place with the knowledge of Germany, and was intended to bring about the withdrawal of troops from England to Ireland.

"As to the landing of Sir Roger Casement," said Baron Wimborne, "that was all arranged in Germany with the connivance of the Sinn Feiners. On the night of his arrest a motor car upset into a river and the occupants, who were drowned, both wore Sinn Fein badges. The Germans do not seem to have supplied the rebels with arms, which are of all descriptions, even including fowling pieces.

"A proclamation issued by the rebels announcing the foundation of the Irish Republic was signed by seven persons, including J. T. Clark, Connolly, Pearce, and MacDermott."

Augustine Birrell, the Chief Secretary for Ireland, who was present during the interview with the Viceroy, supplemented his remarks by saying the situation would be dealt with according to martial law, which now is in full operation in Ireland, and deprives the citizens of the right of a civil trial. Mr. Birrell was not overwilling to give information as to occurrences, but he said he was satisfied that the situation was well in hand and that the suppression of the movement was a matter of a short time.

The visit of The Associated Press Correspondent to the Viceregal Lodge followed a long drive in an open motor lorry through the disturbed sections of the city and past barricades, where soldiers knelt or lay down in replying to the rebel snipers. Occasional bullets whistled overhead and the rattle of a machine gun salvo was heard.

No soldier is permitted to walk about without a rifle, as such a proceeding would bring almost certain death. Citizens stood behind curtains and windows as the automobile of the correspondent dashed by. Only a few venture onto the porches, and they fear to go to the stores to obtain provisions.

Boys Shot in Bread Line.

This fear was fully justified, as The Associated Press Correspondent saw two small boys shot while waiting at a bakery for bread during the morning. In other parts of the city, also, many civilian casualties were caused, but the number either of the soldiers or civilians killed or wounded could not be obtained.

The rebels today have been confining their activities to sniping in various parts of the city. The scenes of their operations have been circumscribed to the districts about Sackville Street, the cattle market, and Stephen's Green, where they are surrounded by vigilant troops in complete cordons, while the city itself is cut off from approach by another cordon whose limits are around the circular road which surrounds the city.

Every civilian is regarded with suspicion, and passage through the lines can be obtained only with the best of credentials and passes.

Outside the three areas already mentioned as being in possession of the rebels, numbers of isolated snipers occasionally fire pot shots at passing soldiers. These snipers are difficult to locate. At a hotel on the north wall dozens of shots went through windows and struck walls, while spent bullets dropped everywhere in the streets.

BANK SAVED BY STUDENTS.

Trinity College Opened Heavy Fire on Rebels and Drove Them Off.

LIVERPOOL, April 30.—How Trinity College students saved the Bank of Ireland is told by a resident of Liverpool who has just arrived from Dublin.

"It was the intention of the Sinn Feiners," he said, "to take this institution and its valuable contents, and a body of rebels came along with the express purpose of putting this intention into execution. Opposite the bank stands famous Trinity College, where an officer's training corps of students is stationed, and the young officers had a warm reception in readiness.

"The rebels came along in great style, anticipating no trouble and shooting down the half-dozen soldiers always on guard at the bank. But as they advanced there was a rifle volley, and some of the attacking party dropped to the ground.

"The college had been transformed into a veritable fortress. In the windows were sandbags, loopholed, behind which the officers were waiting to give battle. The insurgents were stupified, and for a moment hesitated as to what they should do. Then several sprang forward, shouting to their comrades, and the rebels pressed on.

"Again came a volley from the windows of Trinity College. More men fell and the rebels broke in disorder and fled."

LEADER CONNOLLY KILLED

Artillery Used Against Dublin Section in Which Rebels Are Corralled

CASUALTIES EXCEED 100

Sackville and Grafton Streets Reported to Have Been Set on Fire.

MANY LADS IN THE REVOLT

Old Men, Too, Joined the Ranks—Little Disorder in Other Parts of Ireland.

LONDON, Sunday, April 30.—Field Marshal Viscount French, commander of the home forces, reports that the General Post Office at Dublin, which has been the principal stronghold of the Sinn Feiners, has been burned down.

James Connolly, one of the leaders of the rebels, is reported to have been killed.

It is said Connolly undertook to issue to persons desiring to leave Dublin passports bearing the words: "Pass bearer. James Connolly, Commandant General of the Irish Republican Army."

Many of the rebels have been made prisoner, and the revolt in Dublin is on the verge of collapse.

In the rest of Ireland the situation is generally satisfactory.

It is reported that the casualties in the street fighting in Dublin exceed 100, and that the troops have been compelled to resort to cannon in one section. A dispatch received yesterday afternoon said that Sackville and Grafton Streets were in flames, and that artillery was being used on the houses, the inhabitants having been removed.

The recent news that the rebels have been driven out of St. Stephen's Green with bombs, suffering heavy losses in killed, wounded, and prisoners, has not been confirmed officially.

From inquiries made among the military authorities at Dublin, the correspondent of The Evening Star concludes that there probably are not more than 1,500 or 2,000 men and lads actually engaged in the rebellion, so far as the central part of the city is concerned. Among them are quite a number of old men who were closely associated with the Fenian troubles, and some youths of 16 or 17. This is shown, the correspondent says, by the appearance of the prisoners already brought in.

Of the situation outside Dublin little is known beyond the official admission that the disaffection has spread to various localities in the west and south of Ireland. Field Marshal French's statement of Friday night described these disturbances as local in character, and so far as has been revealed by information which has passed the censorship they have not been attended by heavy fighting.

A dispatch from Tralee yesterday said that Austin Stack, commander of the Tralee corps of Sinn Feiners, and Cornelius Collins, an accountant in the General Post Office at Dublin, who are charged with abetting in the importation of arms from the enemy, were taken from the Tralee jail under a strong military and police escort and removed on a train to an unknown destination. There was no demonstration.

SCENES IN EMBATTLED CITY.

Newspaper Men Landed with Birrell in Midst of the Fighting.

DUBLIN, Thursday, April 27, (via London, April 29.)—Fifteen hundred or so armed men of the Sinn Fein had a hold on Ireland's capital today. After four days of fighting their rebel flag still flew from a number of central points.

Since Monday some of the chief positions in the city have been in the hands of the rebels. In defending these strongholds against regular troops and Irish Nationalist Volunteers the rebels are fighting with desperation for their lives, which they know may be forfeited on the charge of treason.

Regulars now command all the rebel positions, the fall of which is merely a question of time.

The streets of Dublin were deserted today, except for sentries and military guards. Business was at a standstill. Civilians peeped anxiously from behind curtained windows. Field guns were barking, machine guns rattling, and rifle fire was pattering, apparently from every quarter at the same time.

Birrell Landed with Newspaper Men.

When The Associated Press correspondent landed early this morning at the quay near the Custom House the pinging of bullets from rifles of snipers in the vicinity was frequent. Augustine Birrell, the Secretary for Ireland, had made the passage from England with the newspaper men. As he stepped ashore he shouted cheerily: "I wish you luck, gentlemen! I don't know what will happen to you, now that you are here!"

Soldiers and rebels fired at each other from street corners, wharves, roofs, and windows. Sentries with fixed bayonets on loaded rifles, stationed every few yards, shouted their commands to halt. Naval guns joined in and added to the deafening gunfire.

From the quay the respective positions could be seen. The rebels were holding a square section of territory from the point where Liberty Hall stood before a gunboat destroyed it as far as Sackville Street to Stephen's Green and the Four Courts district, and along the southern side of the river to the Butt and O'Connell bridges. They also held isolated positions in a flour mill and a disused distillery opposite the Northwall Station.

Over all this section there was considerable fighting the whole day. The distillery was the scene of one of the sharpest little battles of the uprising. The rebels were forced out of the flour mill by bombardment and many of them were seen, covered with flour, making their way to the distillery. Once there they hoisted the rebel flag, which floated from the corner of a square tower.

Rebel Flag Defies Shells.

Soon a naval gun opened fire. The first shot hit the tower, and then half a dozen in succession struck the roof around it. The flag still flew and the rebels replied with rifles and a machine gun. The bombardment ceased after a dozen shots, but was renewed later. Hit after hit was scored, but the flag remained hanging from its pole. One shot hit a water tank just below it and for a time there was a miniature cascade down the walls of the distillery. When night fell and all firing except with rifles ceased, the flag was still flying defiantly over the side of the little tower.

Another brief artillery bombardment was directed against barricades in Sackville Street. Clouds of thick smoke soon rose around various prominent objects in that part of Dublin as the shells burst, while between times the rattle of the machine guns seemed like a continuation of the reverberation of the heavy pieces.

So closely guarded were the approaches to the fighting zone that it was impossible to gauge accurately what damage was done, and attempts by correspondents to pass along a street leading toward the centre of the city brought upon them a detachment of soldiers with weapons ready for use. The troops had early in the rebellion learned to distrust civilians, some of whom were found to be evidently in sympathy with the Sinn Feiners, if not in league with them. Wearing khaki meant just the same as a sentence of death.

When the revolt began, at 1 o'clock Monday afternoon, the soldiers walking about the city were, as usual, unarmed, and numbers of them paid the full penalty without being able to defend themselves.

Other governmental uniforms brought discomfort for their wearers. The Dublin metropolitan police were exposed to somewhat similar treatment to that of the soldiers by the rebels and most of the policemen went to their homes and changed to civilian clothing.

Postmen on duty at the general post office, which was the first building seized by the Sin Feiners and later became their headquarters, were sent away and told to come back in a week for their wages, which would be paid to them in Irish republican coinage. The rebels cut all of the wires, destroyed the apparatus, and seized all the money they could find.

All Foreseen Except Failure.

Everything except failure seemed to have been foreseen by the rebels who, when they started the revolt, were as well uniformed as were the regular soldiers. Their clothing, arms and equipment were good and they were even provided with intrenching tools, which they used when they marched on Stephen's Green.

The ammunition supply of the rebels appeared to be plentiful and was used unsparingly. Some bullets which entered the hotel where the correspondents assembled were certainly of German manufacture. Other weapons used by the rebels were twelve-bore shotguns and cartridges filled with ugly leaden slugs.

The battle was thickest today around an entire block of business houses in the Sackville Street quarter. These buildings had been occupied by the rebels at the start, and breaches had been made in a party wall between the stores so that the men could retreat, fighting, from one room to another in the event of the place being stormed.

Tonight the Irish capital is brilliantly lighted by the flames from an important central block of houses a couple of acres in extent. Frequent explosions occurred, followed by salvos of machine gun and rifle fire turned on the rebels, who were making their way from one building to another.

No exact idea of the number of casualties was obtainable, but many bodies were lying about the streets unburled. Houses contained many others. The authorities said the troops had not suffered nearly as much as had the rebels, whose strongholds were under fire at all times, both day and night.

Women and Children Shot.

A Belfast dispatch to The Evening News says:

"Strangers who traverse some parts of the central portion of Dublin take their lives in their hands. In one or two instances rioters shot down women and children. Opposite the Shelbourne Hotel still lies the carcass of a horse shot on Tuesday, as this region has been too dangerous to permit of its removal. At the law courts the rebels indulged in an orgy of destruction. They sacrificed many valuable books from the reference library and tore up quantities of documents."

A correspondent in Dublin of the Exchange Telegraph Company says:

"The Post Office is barricaded on the inside with bags of papers and all available books. Around Jacobs' factory the trouble is accentuated by women taking sides. Their attempts to get provisions in to the besieged rebels are resisted by co-workers who remain loyal, and many free fights among the two factions of women are reported."

THINK GERMANS SENT ARMS.

Countess Markievicz Reported to Have Shot a Castle Guard.

LONDON, April 29.—"The thing that surprises me the most about the uprising in Dublin is the supply of munitions in the hands of the rebels," said an Irishman who arrived in London this morning. He is an engineer in the War Department. He spent ten hours in Dublin on Tuesday and, departing that evening, remained until last night in Kingstown.

"There is little doubt in the popular mind that Germans have been landing arms from submarines for months," he continued, "and it is even said—though I don't believe it—that a few Germans also landed and organized.

"I learned that the rebels made prisoners of a large number of policemen and a few stray soldiers at the Royal Irish Constabulary depot and at Phoenix Park.

"I heard that the Countess Markievicz, the sister of an Irish Baron who was prominent in the Larkin strike and a leading figure in the present movement, shot dead a guard in front of Dublin Castle in an effort to capture the castle. This effort proved abortive.

"I heard a report, which I could not verify, that Alderman Kelly, a large tobacco dealer and a member of the Sinn Fein, was killed when the rebels were driven from his place. A report also was current that James Connolly, a Sinn Fein leader, had been killed.

"There was some looting by the rabble following in the wake of the rebels. Afterward I saw $5 shoes selling from carts in the streets for 10 cents and upward, while silk hats, blouses, and fine lingerie were equally cheap. There was no looting by the rebels themselves, further than the throwing out to poor women in the streets of sacks of flour and biscuits from a biscuit factory."

WATERFORD AWAITS NEWS.

All Quiet There and the Rising in Dublin Is Generally Condemned.

WATERFORD, April 28, (via London, April 29.)—Southern Ireland today was in the grip of a stern military censorship which virtually cut it off from all news of the stirring events now occurring in Dublin. The newspapers here have been permitted to publish only the briefest official reports, and the people of this section are awaiting with keen expectancy the details of the uprising.

The busy city of Waterford, although quiet prevails here, has been cut off from all wire communication with outside points with the exception of the direct wire with London, and so rigid is the military rule that even telephonic communication from house to house has been forbidden. The situation here is said to be a good example of the conditions prevailing under military rule in other sections of Ireland.

Waterford hears that Dublin is surrounded by a great cordon of troops and that railway traffic from Southern Ireland to Dublin has been suspended as far as the public is concerned beyond points approximately thirty miles from the city. Various disquieting but unconfirmed rumors regarding events in various parts of Ireland outside of Dublin have been received by word of mouth. With all these reports, however, is coupled the statement that the military have the situation well in hand, and that sporadic outbreaks have been quickly crushed.

The Sinn Fein, which is credited with fathering the uprising, has an organization of considerable extent, but is said to be strongest in Cork, Kerry, Wexford, and Dublin. Of these organizations that in Wexford appears quite active, but Cork is said to be quiet. No report has been received here from Kerry. Waterford has only a small body of Sinn Feiners, but every precaution is being taken. The post office, which controls the wires to London, was guarded all last night by a large body of police, and the big bridge over the river was lifted, presumably to prevent a possible invasion of the main section of the town from the direction of Wexford.

On every hand one hears eager queries for news and strong condemnation of the revolutionists.

8,970 BRITISH AT KUT SURRENDER

Continued from Page 1.

pushed on northward, part of his force following the old caravan trail and part the river, where his troops were transported by boats, most of which had been brought from India and were as primitive as those which the Turks and Arabs brought to oppose them.

The British van on Nov. 22 reached Ctesphon, eighteen miles from Bagdad. There it was attacked by an overwhelming force, and, although on the following day it recovered the ground lost, Townshend saw nothing but a siege before him and no prospect of being reinforced for several weeks.

His water supply also gave out and the order was given to retreat southward. This retirement, accomplished under extraordinary disadvantages, was hailed in England as a remarkable achievement. Not only did General Townshend ward off the pursuing Turks with comparatively small losses, but he succeeded in taking with him all his wounded.

The main body pushed ahead, but on Dec. 5 Townshend determined to make a stand with the rear guards, at the scene of his previous victory, Kut-el-Amara. This guard, consisting of something over 10,000 men, made an intrenched camp around the place, while the remainder of his force passed on down the Tigris.

Major General Charles Townshend.

Kut-el-Amara is nothing but a mud collection of ramshackle houses on somewhat raised ground. Behind the river front are a mosque and a collection of one or two storied Arab houses.

Three days after he began to intrench, (that is, on Dec. 8,) Townshend's communications with the main body of troops were cut off, and ever since then he has been besieged, although few actual assaults have been made against his defenses since the middle of January.

Before that time almost daily attacks were made by the Turks. Townshend is said to have captured over 8,000 Turks and Arabs by sorties.

When it became evident that Townshend was so beset that he could not fight his way out, steps were taken to send a relief expedition. Thirty thousand Indian troops were dispatched and two Anglo-Indian divisions, which had been fighting in France were transported to the head of the Persian Gulf, making, with the remnants of Townshend's main expedition, a relief force of 90,000 men. General Sir Percy Lake was placed in command of the entire forces, in succession to Sir John Nixon, and command of the relief expedition itself was given to Major Gen. Aylmer.

This expedition was poorly supplied in regard to transport and river gunboat service and Aylmer's march up the river again turned to a retreat after the first dash. The march began on Jan. 6, when the advanced guard left Gherbi, about eighty miles by river southeast of Kut-el-Amara. By Jan. 8 he had reached Sheikh Saad, forty miles to the north, where he defeated the Turks in two pitched battles. Between Jan. 13 and 19 he reached Orah, and on Jan. 21 he was at El Gussa, only eight miles from Kut-el-Amara. On the following day he attacked the Es Sinn intrenchments, which the Turks had built across the river, but failed to take them. Floods came to add to the trouble, due to lack of equipment, so that his position became almost as precarious as was Townshend's at Ctesiphon. Like him, Aylmer retreated.

Colonials Sent to Help.

Up to this time the campaign had been under the direction of the India Office, but the War Office in London now took a hand and a large body of Colonials, including the Thirteenth Division of Gallipoli fame, with full equipment and supplies was sent from Egypt, together with a flotilla of gunboats. In February Aylmer again started from his base at Gherbi and General Lake himself joined the expedition.

By the middle of March the expedition was near El Owasa and defeated the Turks there, after having met with a reverse at Felahie.

On April 5 the British force carried by assault the Turkish intrenched position at Umm-el-Henna, twenty-two miles from Kut-el-Amara. The next day the capture of Felahie was officially announced. Even then the relief expedition was about fifteen miles further away from Townshend's beleagured force than it was on Jan. 21. Formidable masses of Turks were gathered on both sides of the Tigris below the invested town, holding intrenched and strongly fortified posts to contest the further advance.

The fighting in this region has been severe ever since, but the relief force, although gaining some ground, was never able to win a decisive victory.

The losses on both sides recently have been heavy. On April 14 it was admitted that the Tigris army had lost 8,100 men up to that time. Since then there have been several battles between the Turks and the relief expedition. In one engagement alone, according to the Turkish accounts, the British lost 4,000 men.

Serious floods in the river added to the great difficulties met by the relief force in the form of an alert and relentless foe.

Some idea is given of the circumstances under which Aylmer's men have worked by a letter from a South African officer, published in The Cape Times. In part he says:

"The River Tigris plays the deuce with the surrounding country when it gets above itself from melting snows coming down from the Caucasus, when it frequently tires of its own course and tries another. The river is the only drinking water, and you can imagine the state of it when Orientals have anything to do with it. A sign of its fruity state is the fact that sharks abound right up to Kurna.

"We have all kinds of craft up here, improvised for use higher up. His Majesty's ship Clio, a sloop, was marked down in 1914 to be destroyed as obsolete, but she, with her sister ships, Odin and Espiegle, have done great work in the battles to date. Now that we have got as far as Amara and Nasariyeh, the vessels that give the greatest assistance are steam launches with guns on them, flat-bottomed Irrawaddy paddle steamers. For troops we have 'nakelas,' a local sailing vessel, and 'bellums,' a long, narrow, small cone-shaped thing, holding from fifteen to twenty men; barges for animals, &c. Rafts have been used higher up to mount guns on. Here we also have motor boats. * * *

"The difficulties as we advance are increased to a certain extent, though country and climate are improving. Our lines of communication will lengthen out, and we shall have to look out for Arab tribes raiding. Our aerial service is increasing; we have now a Royal Navy flight section, which has hydroplanes as well."

General Townshend's Career.

Major General Charles Vere Ferrers Townshend, who commanded at Kut-et-Amara, is heir presumptive to the Marquisate of Townshend. He is the great-great-grandson of the George Townshend who fought with distinction at the Heights of Abraham, in 1759, when Quebec was stormed and Wolfe died in the arms of victory.

The present Townshend is 54 years of age and married to the Countess Louise Cahen d'Anvers of France, has had a distinguished career beginning with the Royal Marine, in which he made the Nile expedition. He was then transferred to the Indian Army and distinguished himself by defending Chitral with splendid tenacity.

Scene of the Tigris Campaign Which Has Ended in Surrender

JAMES LARKIN IN CHICAGO.

Labor Agitator Refuses to Comment on the Irish Revolt.

CHICAGO, April 29.—James Larkin, a leader in the Dublin strikes in 1913, who is now living here, refused today to comment on the present situation in Ireland.

Over the telephone from his home he said:

"I have nothing to say on the Irish question."

Further efforts to question him were unavailing.

CONNOLLY ONCE HERE.

Dead Irish Leader Believed to Have Been Editor of The Harp.

SAN FRANCISCO, April 29.—The rebel leader Connolly mentioned in London dispatches as having been killed in the Dublin fighting is believed here to have been James Connolly, formerly editor of The Harp, an Irish Socialist paper in New York, and known here and throughout the country as a lecturer for the Socialist party.

About 1910 James Connolly removed the office of his paper to Ireland.

IRISH LEAGUE TO REDMOND.

Assures Him of Support and Condemns the Revolt in Ireland.

Following the meeting of the New York Council of the United Irish League of America, held at 624 Madison Avenue Friday night, Stephen McFarland, President of the council, sent the following cablegram to John Redmond, the leader of the Irish Parliamentary Party in the House of Commons:

> Mass meeting of Municipal Council of the United Irish League of America again assures you and party of our absolute and unflinching support under the unprecedented circumstances caused by the present regretable outbreak, which is fraught with the greatest dangers to all the best interests of Ireland. We strongly condemn the conspiracy which has been conceived and engineered by men who never had and never will have the welfare of Ireland at heart. We extend our sympathy to our misguided brethren, whose mistaken sense of patriotism and duty has allowed them to be led into such a deplorable position by selfish, unscrupulous, and cunning propagandists.

The editor of an Irish publication in New York who a few days ago printed in his paper an attack on the President issued a two-column statement yesterday, in the course of which he charged that "somebody inside" of the office of United States District Attorney Marshall had divulged to the newspapers the contents of the papers seized in the office of Wolf von Igel, the former von Papen aide, who is to be arraigned tomorrow on the charge of having conspired with von Papen and others to destroy the Welland Canal.

"In last Saturday's Washington dispatches," the statement says, "there is a statement that the Department of Justice is going to start a nation-wide investigation into the activities of Irishmen in connection with the Irish revolt. This means that the Administration is undertaking openly to do England's work. It is the Administration that should be investigated by Congress, but, failing that, a lot of investigation and exposure of wrongdoing can be made through the courts."

A German publication of this city prints in its issue of yesterday a picture of Sir Roger Casement and underneath is the caption "The Irish Liberator." It also prints an editorial describing Sir Roger as the "War's great Irish hero." Incidentally, the same paper prints a signed article by William Jennings Bryan in the course of which the former Secretary of State says that "if we must have war it is better to postpone it until after this war is over."

SHE PRAISES COUNTESS.

Woman Leader of Revolt an Idealist, Says Mlle. de Holthoir.

Mlle. Beatrice de Holthoir of 115 West Seventy-first Street, who spends much time in Ireland and is an intimate friend of Countess Markievicz, the leading female figure in the Irish revolt, told a reporter for THE NEW YORK TIMES yesterday of the characteristics and ideals of the woman of noble birth and her followers, who have startled the world by their Irish revolt.

"Although the revolt and the activity of so many prominent persons in it seem strange to people so far away," said Mlle. de Holthoir, "it is more easily understood if one knows any of the leaders and is familiar with their views and grievances. None of those who have been named in connection with the riots is given to harboring fancied injuries. They would not turn against the mother country at the time when she is weakest if they did not feel it is their only course. They are thinking people who have gained nothing during the years and years they have struggled for home rule, and have now determined to strike while England is weakest in one great effort to get what they have asked for.

"There has never been a common bond between the two countries, nor can there ever be, for they are as divergent as though they were situated in entirely different parts of the world. While the Irish have always been considered romantic and idealists they are progressive, and in the face of every obstacle have proved themselves capable of engaging in the world commerce and of directing their own destiny.

"These are a few of the many reasons why Countess Markievicz, the dominant leader of the artistic circles in Ireland, has cast her lot with the majority of her countrymen, and all her friends and admirers are following her lead. She has always been averse to capitalists, and has practically given up her life to the interests of the working classes.

"Knowing the Countess as I do, the reports in the papers do not surprise me. She is a woman of superior intellect, with unusual patriotism, and long ago made her decision as to the stand she should take in such a crisis. Being impulsive she has now been carried away on the wave of enthusiasm in the cause for which she has fought. She was one of the chief sympathizers of John Larkin, who has often voiced his views at her salons.

"One of the gravest mistakes of England in dealing with Ireland has been in allowing the subjects such freedom of speech, for this has been the greatest influence in causing unrest."

CRAZY OVER IRISH TURMOIL.

Tarrytown Porter Breaks Straitjacket and Wrecks Hospital Ward.

Special to The New York Times.

TARRYTOWN, N. Y., April 29.—John Dalton, a 200-pound Irish porter employed by Allen Lehman, who has leased Mrs. Charles J. Gould's estate here, went crazy today from brooding over the Irish rebellion and news which he had received from relatives in that island which led him to believe they might be endangered. The Lehman family were all away from the house at the time and the servants fled from the place in terror when Dalton took off all his clothes, put on a black domino mask, and turned on all the gas in the house.

Chief of Police William J. Bowles, accompanied by Police Surgeon C. W. Fairchild and Overseer of the Poor William W. Brown, came out to the Lehman house and overpowered Dalton after a hard fight, in which Chief Bowles was struck in the face several times. They put a straitjacket on him and took him to the Tarrytown Hospital, but after an hour or so Dalton managed to break the straitjacket and succeeded in wrecking the ward where he was confined before the police again overpowered him. He is now securely fastened in the hospital and under guard.

CASEMENT'S SISTER PLEADS

Wants President to Receive Her and Intercede for Sir Roger.

Special to The New York Times.

WASHINGTON, April 29.—A telegraphic request of Michael F. Doyle, a Philadelphia lawyer, that President Wilson receive Mrs. George Newman, sister of Sir Roger Casement, who hopes to obtain the President's intercession with the British Government in order to prevent the execution of her brother, was sent today to the State Department by Joseph P. Tumulty, Secretary to the President, to whom it was addressed. The State Department will advise the President as to what course he should take.

Officials indicated today that there appeared to be no ground for the exercise of the good offices of this Government in Sir Roger Casement's behalf, and it was inferred that the President would feel obliged to refuse to see Mrs. Newman.

If Sir Roger Casement were a subject of one of the belligerent countries which had intrusted its interests in enemy territory to the care of the American Government, it would be proper for this Government to intervene, provided he was held in enemy territory. But in this case, it was explained, he is held in the territory of his own Government, and no cause for American interference exists. The British Government, it was said, might well resent any interference by the United States.

Pope Wires Archbishop of Dublin.

PARIS, April 29.—A Rome dispatch to The Matin says that Pope Benedict granted an interview of an hour to Cardinal Gasquet, a British prelate, after which the Pope sent a long telegram to the Archbishop of Dublin.

OPPOSE BRITISH WAR CRITIC.

Some Auditors Question Sincerity of Noel Pemberton-Billing.

LONDON, April 29.—Noel Pemberton-Billing, the former army aviator who was elected to the House of Commons on an aviation service reform program recently, met with some opposition in addressing a mass meeting in Albert Hall today on the question of aerial supremacy.

Mr. Pemberton-Billing's criticisms of the Government met with emphatic opposition from a small part of the audience, who made it evident that they were not in agreement with his remarks with regard to the Government's conduct of the war, and were questioning his sincerity in his critical attitude.

German Steel Output for March.

BERLIN, April 29, (via Sayville.)—During the month of March, according to the statement given out by the Overseas News Agency, the German steel output amounted to 1,361,502 metric tons, as compared with 1,236,845 metric tons in February.

TODAY'S SUNDAY TIMES

Consists of 96 Pages, as follows:

GERARD APPRISED OF KAISER'S STAND

Continued from Page 1.

tion of attempting to force Germany's hand while it is in ignorance of the character of the communication of the Kaiser to Ambassador Gerard.

President Wilson followed his usual practice on Saturday of not transacting official business and went for a motor ride in the afternoon.

Senator La Follette today introduced a bill providing for an advisory vote by the people as to whether the United States should declare war against any nation with whom the President had severed diplomatic relations. He did not ask for immediate action on it.

SAW A TORPEDOED CRUISER.

Skipper Tells of Clash at Sea in Which U-Boat Was Sunk.

The war has lifted the monotony from Atlantic voyages, according to reports brought here by Captains, officers, and engineers of freight steamships trading between this port and England or France.

The Captain of a freighter which has just arrived from the other side said that when he was passing through the Downs off Deal he saw a fight between a German aeroplane and two British monoplanes. All three aviators were using their machine guns. So far as he could judge, the German was not hit and managed to get away over the North Sea toward the Belgian coast.

About sixty miles off the southwest coast of Ireland the ship came up to a disabled British cruiser which had been torpedoed by a German submarine and had a hole about six by eight feet in her starboard side near the engine room.

"The water had rushed in," the Captain continued, "and about half the hole was above the water line. An officer came off from the cruiser and asked if I could tow her into Queenstown. After consulting with the Chief Engineer, I decided that we had not sufficient power to tow the warship, which was well down in the water, and, besides, there was the danger of the submarine still lurking around. The Lieutenant said the cruiser had sunk the submarine, because her periscope was seen to be knocked away.

"Finally I suggested that the Lieutenant should use my wireless and call for help and I would stand by until it arrived. The cruiser had her own apparatus, but had no sending power, the big dynamo having been wrecked.

"An answer was picked up from a third-class battleship, which arrived three hours later, and, I understand, managed to tow the damaged cruiser to Queenstown." The Captain added that there was no name or identification mark on the bow or stern of the warship.

PARIS SEES CLOSE OF VERDUN BATTLE

Germans Are Sending Heavy Guns Away, It Says, Probably to British Front.

PETAIN'S HONORS A SIGN

Crown Prince's Efforts East and West of Meuse on Friday Are Reported Futile.

LONDON, April 29.—Despite the energetic renewal of German operations last night on some portions of the Verdun front, French military critics are already beginning to believe that the campaign against that fortress is virtually at an end.

Heavy German batteries in considerable number, according to Paris advices, have been withdrawn from before Verdun and sent to a distant point, which, the French official judge, from the increasing activity there, to be the portion of the line held by the British.

The expectation in Paris is that the Germans will gradually reduce the frequence and intensity of their bombardments and infantry attacks on the Verdun front until normal conditions of trench warfare have been restored there.

The announcement of the decoration of General Petain and other high officers who have taken part in the battle is thought in Paris to be an indication that the high authorities share the view that the task of defending Verdun has been brought to an end.

The Germans showed activity on both sides of the Meuse last night. After a violent bombardment of French positions near Avocourt and Hill 304 on the west of the river, the Crown Prince's troops massed for an assault, according to the afternoon bulletin from Paris. French troops with hand grenades attacked them and prevented a charge.

On the east of the river a vigorous attack was made on French trenches east of Thiaumont Farm, but the Germans were repulsed with heavy losses, Paris says.

Berlin has nothing to say about the fighting in this section except to record futile French counterattacks near Dead Man Hill.

The British official report records considerable German artillery activity along the lines in France and tells of an attempted German attack near Hulluch, wherein a gas cloud was wafted back into the Teuton ranks and apparently caused some casualties.

The afternoon bulletin of the French War Office reads:

> In the Argonne district a surprise attack, executed last night at a point to the north of Four de Paris, made it possible for us to clean up some of the enemy trenches and bring back some prisoners.
>
> On the left bank of the River Meuse yesterday at 5 o'clock in the afternoon German troops were massed in the communicating trenches to the north of Hill 304, with the idea of attacking our lines. They were at once attacked with hand grenades and prevented from coming out, and then dispersed. Our artillery caused the explosion of a depot of munitions in the same region.
>
> During the night there was a general bombardment in this sector, the fire being particularly spirited in the regions of Avocourt, Esnes, and Hill 304.
>
> On the right bank of the River Meuse yesterday afternoon, after a violent preparatory artillery fire directed against our first lines, together with a curtain of fire of great intensity, the Germans delivered an attack against our trenches to the east of Thiaumont Farm, in which they employed flaming liquids. Cut down by the shells of our artillery and the fire of our machine guns, the enemy was repulsed with heavy losses.
>
> At the same hour an attack upon our positions between Douamont and Vaux also was checked by our fire. The remainder of the night passed in relative quiet on this part of the front.
>
> In Lorraine we have repulsed a strong reconnoitring party of the enemy in front of the wood of Banal, to the south of Domevre.
>
> In the Vosges a small German attack with grenades against one of our trenches at La Chapelotte was effectively checked by our curtain of fire.

The official bulletin issued by the French War Office tonight says:

> The day has been marked only by artillery actions, especially spirited in Belgium to the south of Bixschoote, and in the Argonne in the sector to the north of La Harazée.
>
> In the region of Verdun the enemy bombarded our positions in the Avocourt Wood, on Hill 304, in the region to the south of Haudromont, and in the sector at the foot of the Meuse Hills. Our artillery everywhere shelled the enemy batteries.
>
> One of our long-range guns shelled in the Heudicourt station (northeast of St. Mihiel) a train, several cars of which were destroyed.
>
> Aviation.—Last night one of our aerial squadrons bombarded a factory in full operation at Hayange, Lorraine, and bivouacs to the east of Azannes. This operation, carried out in spite of a very violent wind, constituted the hundredth bombardment by this squadron.

The British official communication says:

> There was considerable hostile artillery activity today against our trenches near Fricourt and Souchez and west of the Ypres-Pilkelm Road. Small mines were exploded during the day on both sides of the front at Souchez, southeast of Cabaret Rouge, and near Neuville, St. Vaast, and the Hohenzollern redoubt.
>
> Last night we raided German front line trenches about Crassier Double at Loos, causing several casualties among the enemy.
>
> Early this morning, after a heavy bombardment and under cover of gas, the enemy made two small attacks opposite Hulluch, but was driven back. The gas broke back over the enemy trenches and running to the rear on a front of about 700 yards. Judging by the number of ambulances seen coming up to Hulluch, the enemy must have suffered considerable casualties from our artillery and his gas. The ground behind the enemy lines was colored by gas on a front of about 1,000 yards to a depth of 3,000 yards.
>
> The fine weather yesterday resulted in much successful air work. There was a marked decrease in the number of hostile machines seen yesterday. Only four combats in the air occurred, with no loss on our side.
>
> Two German aeroplanes were brought down behind our lines today.

The Belgian official communication reads:

> The artillery actions were less intense than on the preceding day. In the sectors of Ramscapelle, Dixmude, and north of Steenstraete there has been a reciprocal bombardment.

BERLIN, April 29, (by wireless to Sayville.)—The German headquarters statement today reads:

> Between La Bassée Canal and Arras there were lively, continuous mine engagements, which resulted successfully for us.
>
> In the sector of Givenchy-En Gohelle our advance is progressing. Two British hand grenade counter-attacks were sanguinarily repulsed.
>
> In the Meuse sector new French counterattacks at Dead Man's Hill and to the eastward failed.
>
> German anti-aircraft guns south of Caronvillers brought down a French biplane whose occupants were dead.
>
> First Lieutenant Boelke, south of Vaux, shot down his fourteenth aeroplane.

LOST 20,000 MEN IN APRIL.

British Casualties This Month Exceeded Those in March.

LONDON, April 29.—British casualties this month, as compiled from published lists, are slightly in excess of those in March. The total from all fields of operation is 1,255 officers and 19,256 men, compared with 1,107 officers and 19,317 men in March.

CHILE GETS THREE SHIPS.

Germany Allows the Use of Vessels for Coast Traffic.

SANTIAGO, Chile, April 29.—Germany has acceded to the petition of the Government of Chile to allow three German steamers held now in Chilean ports to be used for travel along the coast of Chile.

Chile, like most countries, has felt the loss of freight carriers by the disappearance of the German merchant marine from the seas and by the contraction of British freighters due to Germany's submarine campaign. Several times rumors have gone the rounds of shipping circles to the effect that, like Italy and Portugal, the Chilean and Brazilian Governments were about to take over the German ships contained at their ports.

The ships at Chilean ports belong to the Kosmos Steamship Company and the Roland Line, and, according to reports reaching here when the war began, were twelve in number.

Prior to that time the annual number of steam vessels entering and clearing at Chilean ports was about 15,000, of 27,000,000 tons register. It has now been reduced to less than one-half.

As Chile depends largely on imports for maintenance, the country was brought face to face with a commercial crisis which the Government has been vainly trying to remedy by a subsidized revival of agriculture. This was difficult, as the best of the land was held by wealthy landowners, and few farming implements were manufactured at home.

In desperation the Chilean press often demanded that the Government take over and employ the German ships tied up in port, particularly as the German Government had not seen fit to apologize for the insult offered Chile at the time the German cruiser Dresden was sunk in Chilean waters.

On March 20 the Chilean Government, almost simultaneously with that of Brazil, declared that Chile would take no step which would bring her neutrality into question. It was also stated that negotiations were pending between Berlin and Santiago, inspired by the Chamber of Commerce of Valparaiso, for the peaceful taking over of some of the German ships to be used in domestic trade exclusively—for Chile has few railways, and since the war began her ports have been practically isolated.

BOMB IN BULGAR LEGATION.

Berlin Reports Plot to Blow Up Athens Building Failed.

BERLIN, April 29, (by Wireless to Sayville.)—By order of King Constantine the Greek Master of the Horse has visited M. Passarow, the Bulgarian Minister, and congratulated him on the failure of the recent attempt to blow up the Bulgarian Legation by means of a bomb, according to a dispatch from Athens, given out today by the Overseas News Agency.

Premier Skouloudis and Minister of the Interior Gounaris also paid visits to the Bulgarian diplomat.

"Experts, after examining the unexploded bomb, declared that it was of French origin," says the News Agency dispatch.

AUSTRIANS DROP BOMBS.

Aviators Busy on Italian Front—Artillery Fighting Goes On.

BERLIN, April 29, (by Wireless to Sayville.)—Today's Austro-Hungarian Army Headquarters report says:

> On the Italian front Italian artillery shelled the Doberdo Plateau and the Gorizia bridgehead, and also several villages behind our front.
>
> Our airmen dropped heavy bombs on the railroad stations at Gormona and San Giovania di Manzano.
>
> There were active artillery engagements at several places on the Dolomites front.
>
> An enemy attack against our position on the Col di Lana ridge was repulsed.

PLOT AT MUNITION PLANT?

35 Sticks of Dynamite Found Under Indiana Factory.

LEBANON, Ind., April 29.—Thirty-five half-pound sticks of dynamite were found here today under the building of the Columbia Conserve Company. The company has been manufacturing war munitions, but the plant has been closed down for some time.

It has been reported that the company would reopen and start operations again within a few days.

SWEDEN PLANS DEFENSE.

Ask for $15,250,000 to Strengthen the Army and Navy.

STOCKHOLM, April 29.—The Swedish Government has asked the Riksdag for a vote of 40,000,000 kroner for the army, 12,250,000 kroner for the navy, and 4,000,000 kroner for hastening the construction of destroyers and submarines, a totarl of about $15,250,000.

The army expenditure is proposed principally for the heavy artillery, engineering and supply services, and for the equipment of the landsturm.

GERMAN PRISONERS ESCAPE.

Six Tunnel Out of a Detention Camp at Alberta.

LETHBRIDGE, Alberta, April 29.—Six German prisoners escaped from the detention camp here, it was learned today, by tunneling a passage four feet under ground and 110 feet long.

Details regarding the escape and the charges against the prisoners were not permitted by censors.

"All the News That's Fit to Print."

The New York Times.

THE WEATHER
Fair today; tomorrow rain or snow; moderate northwesterly winds.
For full weather report see Page 19

VOL. LXVI...NO. 21,601. NEW YORK, FRIDAY, MARCH 16, 1917.—TWENTY PAGES. ONE CENT In Greater New York. | TWO CENTS New England and Middle States. | THREE CENTS Elsewhere.

REVOLUTION IN RUSSIA; CZAR ABDICATES; MICHAEL MADE REGENT, EMPRESS IN HIDING; PRO-GERMAN MINISTERS REPORTED SLAIN

RAILWAY STRIKE ORDERED TO BEGIN TOMORROW NIGHT

Managers and Heads of Brotherhoods End Final Conference, Both Defiant.

WILSON NOW THE ONLY HOPE

President Seems to Have No Authority, but May Make Appeal to Patriotism.

FIVE DAYS' GRACE FOR MILK

Travelers to Have Time to Get Home—Appeals for the Public's Approval.

The eight-hour fight between the 250 railroads of the United States and the 400,000 trainmen has placed the country again face to face with a nationwide railway strike.

The National Conference Committee of the Railways yesterday defied the ultimatum of the four brotherhoods that the eight-hour day should be put into effect at once, and the labor chiefs formally served notice that their strike order stood and that a progressive strike program would begin tomorrow night at 7 o'clock. Freight alone will be affected at the start.

As was the case last Fall, when the railroads and the unions broke off diplomatic relations, the only hope of averting a strike lies with President Wilson, and both the managers and the brotherhood leaders remained in New York overnight in the expectation that Mr. Wilson would take a hand in the situation. However, it is a moot question what steps the Government could take to prevent paralysis of transportation facilities and consequent weakening of the nation's resources in the international crisis. The general opinion among officials in Washington last night seemed to be that the President could do little beyond appealing to the patriotism of both sides. A provision to empower him to take over the roads in such an emergency was among the Administration recommendations for railway legislation which failed at the last session of Congress.

Daniel Willard, President of the Baltimore & Ohio, and a member of the National Defense Council, who has been watching the strike developments in New York for the last three days, left late yesterday afternoon for Washington.

Last August after the two sides broke, President Wilson sent the members of the United States Board of Mediation and Conciliation to New York to bring the two sides together. The board failed, and when a strike order was about to be issued, the President sent his Secretary, Joseph P. Tumulty, to New York, with a request that the managers and the labor leaders come to the White House. It was after he kept the two sides in Washington all during the month of August that the Adamson law was passed after a call for a national strike, effective Sept. 4, had been issued. Both sides as represented here now are in readiness to go to Washington.

Monday is decision day for the Supreme Court, and if it should hand down a decision on the Adamson law then it might lead to a renewal of conferences between the two sides regardless of the strike situation. The railroad managers have all along expressed the opinion that the law would be held invalid. The haste of the brotherhoods in forcing the issue has caused the managers to believe that the labor leaders also think the law will be thrown out. While the brotherhood heads say the action of the court one way or the other will not affect their demands, the railroad managers believe that the invalidating of the Adamson law would give them an advantage.

The word of the deadlock here yesterday was flashed to all parts of the country last night, and notices of embargoes and strike preparations were put out by nearly all of the railroads. Appeals to the patriotism of the men were made by many roads. President Wilson was among the first to get notice of the break.

Joseph Hartigan, City Commissioner of Weights and Measures, was quick to appeal to the brotherhoods to permit the movement of food trains into this city. In reply to his plea he received this letter, signed by the chiefs of the four organizations:

"Every indication now seems to warrant the statement that the freight train, engine, and yard employes on certain railways entering this city will peaceably withdraw from service at 7 P. M., Saturday, March 17, and that the employes on other lines will continue in service for several days thereafter, making it possible, in our opinion, to furnish this city food and fuel supplies for several days after the strike becomes effective.

"We regret exceedingly the necessity

Continued on Page 20.

Government Heads Hold a Mysterious Conference

Special to The New York Times.

WASHINGTON, March 15.—A conference surrounded with much mystery took place late this afternoon in the office of the Secretary of State. In addition to Secretary Lansing, it was attended by Mr. Baker, the Secretary of War; Mr. Gregory, the Attorney General; Mr. Daniels, the Secretary of the Navy; Mr. Polk, the Counsellor of the State Department, and Mr. Woolsey, personal legal adviser to the Secretary of State.

After the conference it was said by one of those who attended it that no particular subject had been discussed. It had been devoted, he indicated, to many questions that naturally came up for discussion at this critical period in the international relations of the United States. Elsewhere, however, the impression was given that the conference was called to consider matters of rather pressing importance.

FRYATT'S FATE FOR OUR GUNNERS

German Threat to Put to Death Crews of Any Armed American Ships They Capture.

WARNING IN MUNICH PAPER

Assumes That President "Realizes Fate to Which He Is Subjecting His Artillerymen."

BERNE, Switzerland, March 15, (via Paris.)—The crews of armed American merchantmen who venture to fire upon German submarines before a state of war exists between Germany and the United States, must expect to meet the fate of Captain Fryatt, warns the Munich Neueste Nachrichten, a copy of which has reached Berne, in commenting on the announcement of the State Department that American merchantmen will be armed.

"We assume," the newspaper says, "that President Wilson realizes the fate to which he is subjecting his artillerymen. According to the German prize laws it is unneutral support of the enemy if a neutral ship takes part in hostilities. If such a ship opposes the Prize Court then it must be treated as an enemy ship. The prize rules specify as to the crews of such ships. If, without being attached to the forces of the enemy, they take part in hostilities or make forcible resistance, they may be treated according to the usages of war.

"If President Wilson, knowing these provisions of International law, proceeds to arm American merchantmen, he must assume responsibility for the eventuality that American seamen will meet the fate of Captain Fryatt."

The Captain Fryatt referred to in the foregoing dispatch was Captain Charles Fryatt of the Great Eastern Railway steamer Brussels. He was tried before a German naval court-martial in July, 1916, and sentenced to death, on a charge that he had attempted to ram the German submarine 7-33. The sentence of the court-martial was executed.

STONE ASKS FOR LIST OF AMERICAN SHIPS

Senate Adopts His Resolution, Which Causes Much Speculation in Washington.

Special to The New York Times.

WASHINGTON, March 15.—Senator Stone of Missouri caused some comment at the Capitol today by introducing a resolution directing the Secretary of Commerce to give the Senate a full list of sea-going vessels applying for American registry between Jan. 1, 1916, and March 15, 1917; the name and character of such vessels before and after registration, the names of the ships' owners, and the precise date of application for registry and date of receiving it. The resolution was read and adopted without discussion, and Secretary Redfield will forward the information tomorrow.

There was a good deal of speculation as to why Mr. Stone, Chairman of the Committee on Foreign Relations, should want this information made public. One suggestion was that he might think that some belligerent nation was permitting its ships to be registered in the United States, so that through the later torpedoing of these ships by German submarines the United States might be drawn into the war. It was suggested that if Mr. Stone wanted the information for his own use, he could have got it by telephoning the Department of Commerce.

Mr. Stone showed no desire to explain his resolution and seemed prepared to rebuff questioners. He said that his resolution spoke for itself. When asked if the changes in the ownership of the Algonquin had prompted his resolution, the Senator said that he would not be interviewed.

LONDON HAILS REVOLUTION

Expected Czar's Overthrow and Sees Brighter Prospects for the Allies.

THINK THE COUP DECISIVE

Well-Informed Observers Believe the Patriotic War Party Has Made Its Control Secure.

FEAR NO SEPARATE PEACE

With Weak Ruler Deposed and Pro-German Advisers Ousted, They Predict New Victories.

Special Cable to THE NEW YORK TIMES.

LONDON, Friday, March 16.—It is the belief in well-informed circles here that the Provisional Government which has been set up in Russia by the military party will be able to keep the upper hand in maintaining a policy that means the uninterruptedly vigorous prosecution of the war to a victorious end.

The overthrow of the Czar was expected, and observers here are confident that the Grand Duke as regent will have the solid support of the war party, while they are equally sure of the elimination of any element with a pro-German taint.

An Anti-German Uprising.

As the situation is explained to THE NEW YORK TIMES correspondent, the revolution simply means that German sympathizers within the Russian Government have been overthrown, and that no chance remains for a separate peace being secretly arranged with Germany. This, it is felt, is the real basis of the revolution that has worked such a sudden change in Russian politics.

This revolution, which has been on the verge of boiling over for months, reached its crisis three days ago, when the military leaders, with the Duma behind them, started outbreaks in Petrograd and Moscow. It is evident from the way in which the uprising was conducted, says THE NEW YORK TIMES correspondent's informant, that it had been carefully planned and skillfully executed.

"After it got under way," he says, "there was no hesitation of movement until the members of the military party were masters of the situation. The details of what occurred in Petrograd and Moscow are lacking, but enough is known to show that they have been in a fever of sanguinary revolution for the last three days.

"Dashes of troops against the headquarters of the pro-German leaders, with the capture of Protopopoff and Stürmer as prisoners of war, were conspicuous features of the revolution. The houses of German sympathizers were burned in both cities, and the occupants either taken captive or forced to flee.

"Now that the military party is in control the situation is said to be settling down, with every prospect that the aim of the Revolutionists will be accomplished."

In fact, the situation was described last night as being "entirely satisfactory."

For months, said the informant of THE NEW YORK TIMES correspondent, Great Britain had been expecting an outcome of the Russian political crisis that would mean the solid intrenchment of the war party and the downfall of those seeking a separate peace with Germany. Now it may be confidently expected that Russia will play her part in the war with even greater vigor than before.

German-Born Czarina Blamed.

The Daily Chronicle in its leading article says:

"From a very early period the German-born Czarina and the clique of pro-German reactionaries whom her influence made powerful with the Czar were bent on ending the war prematurely in the interests of reaction. The Ministers set up under these auspices have for over two years acted in defiance of public opinion. Their policy was not obscure; they hampered the army in respect of munitions disorganized the country in respect of its distributive services, brought about artificial famine in a land which is one of the world's chief food producers, and themselves, through police agents, tried to stir up abortive revolts in order that they might plead military failure and internal revolution as a reason for withdrawing from the war.

"The people foiled them for long by magnificent and much enduring patriotism. When the Government left the army without munitions the local authorities—the zemstvos and unions of towns—stepped in and organized their

Continued on Page 2.

Duma Appeals to the Army for Unity Against Foe; Gives Pledge of No Weakening or Suspension of War

LONDON, March 15.—The Reuter correspondent at Petrograd telegraphs under date of yesterday:

"The Military Committee of the Duma has asked all the officers not yet employed by the committee to undertake the organization of the soldiers who joined the people, and help guard the capital. The committee issued a statement, pointing out that at the present moment, when facing an enemy who wished to take advantage of the temporary weakness of the country, it was absolutely necessary to make every effort to maintain the power of the army. It added that the blood of the Russians who had died during the two and a half years of war pledged the people to do this.

"The President of the Duma sent telegrams to the commanders of the Baltic and Black Sea fleets, to the chiefs of the armies on the northern, southwestern, western, Rumanian, and Caucasus fronts, and to the Chief of the General Staff, requesting that the army and navy preserve absolute calm, and to be sure that the struggle against the foreign enemy was not suspended or weakened even for a single moment. The telegram sent these commanders added:

> As hitherto, the army and navy must continue firmly and valiantly to defend the country, and while the Provisional Committee is aided by the military element in the capital and with the moral support of the people in restoring calm and regular activity, each officer, soldier, and sailor should fulfill his duty.

"The officers of the Petrograd garrison at a general meeting unanimously agreed to recognize the authority of the Executive Committee of the Duma until the formation of a permanent Government.

"An imperial bodyguard regiment rode into Petrograd today. It is estimated that there are now 60,000 troops in the capital."

People in Revolt Burn and Slay in Streets of Russia's Capital

Fashionable Hotel Riddled by Machine Guns When Pro-German Shoots at Crowd—Count Fredericks's Home Set on Fire and Family Ill-Treated—General de Knorring Shot.

Stuermer and Protopopoff Reported Assassinated

Special Cable to THE NEW YORK TIMES.

LONDON, Friday, March 16.—The Exchange Telegraph's Copenhagen correspondent sends the following:

"A telegram to the Extrabladet reports that the Russian Consul in Haparanda states that the pro-German ex-Prime Minister, Boris Stürmer, and Minister of Home Affairs Protopopoff have been murdered."

Special Cable to THE NEW YORK TIMES.

LONDON, Friday, March 16.—Belated dispatches from Petrograd, giving details of the revolution in Russia, are arriving here. A dispatch to The Morning Post, dated Wednesday, says:

"Every weapon save only heavy artillery has been freely used in Petrograd streets for four days past, and today there is still considerable firing at various points at intervals. Rifles, revolvers, machine guns, and armored motors—all have been used and are still in use.

"The military hotel, formerly the Astoria Hotel, which lodged exclusively officers from the front, their wives and families, with the majority of officers present here as representatives of the Allies, was subjected to a heavy fusillade from machine guns on armored motors, entirely as the result of what was represented as provocation on the part of a pro-German resident, who fired upon the people from the windows.

General's Daughter Wounded.

"The daughter of the Russian General Prince Tumanoff, who is now commanding a cavalry division at the front, was severely wounded in the neck, and her rooms were ruined by the fusillade. A mob of armed men—soldiers, sailors, and civilians—thoroughly searched the Astoria, and disarmed all the Russian officers, but showed marked consideration for the allied officers.

"Similar scenes have been enacted throughout Petrograd, while in the transpontine regions occupied by the factory population, heavy fighting has been in progress for days, until the alleged excessive cruelty of the police caused the Cossacks and soldiery to espouse the side of the people.

"The ease with which the whole of the capital fell into the hands of the revolutionaries very greatly mitigated the bloodshed inevitable in civil tumults, but the butcher's bill is undoubtedly heavy enough."

Supplementing this by a telegram dated Thursday the same correspondent says:

"Precisely one week ago peaceful street demonstrations, at first largely composed of women and children, were made in protest against the inadequate supply of black bread. The police, unable to cope with the movement, which they felt bound to crush by the usual police methods, called in the aid of the Cossacks.

"The workmen, who had held aloof from the overt demonstrations as organized bodies and who were at first represented only by the younger, irresponsible workingmen, were enraged at the rough treatment by the police of their women and children and were encouraged by the obvious reluctance of the Cossacks and soldiery generally to back up the police oppression. Finally the Cossacks turned on the police, who fled before them, and there was a pandemonium of irregular shooting.

"Matters were not improved by the setting at liberty of political prisoners and criminals and the burning of prisons. On the whole, however, the bloodshed, compared with the magnitude of the achievement, has been infinitesimal. Regiment after regiment, brought in from outside the capital, promptly joined their comrades on the side of the people, and when a special body of lifeguards known as the Imperial Convoy also came in it felt that the old régime had fallen indeed.

Rowdy Element Breaks Loose.

"In the meantime the red revolutionary parties were preaching anarchy in all its forms, and the rowdy elements of the population of the great city were busy indulging their professional instincts.

"Happily the worst incentive to violence—alcohol in all its forms—was almost unprocurable, and the disciplined sense of the soldiery, who now formed the majority, was against excesses which disgraced what was now felt to be the great cause of national freedom.

"M. Rodzianko, at the head of the Duma Committee, soon issued commonsense orders for the disarming of civilians and for the checking of red revolutionary manifestations. The soldiers and people themselves put a stop to the looting. Throughout the city a careful search was made for stores of foodstuffs, which were promptly put on sale. The results warrant the belief that unscrupulous profiteering on an incredible scale had long been prevalent.

"At the present moment a careful search is being made for higher military officers and other functionaries, who are being induced to accept the new conditions and carry on their public duties or undergo arrest. The secret police, that scourge of the Russian nation whose service is despised by all, and which has been for a generation past the refuge for defaulters and detected miscreants of all other public services receive no mercy, but the ordinary police are being merely put under arrest.

Police Stations Destroyed.

The Petrograd correspondent of The Daily Chronicle sent the following, bearing Wednesday's date:

"In Moscow, Kiev, and Kharkoff the troops have signified adherence to the new movement, and in Moscow the police have surrendered of their own accord. The Department of Police in Petrograd has been rifled and the building of the secret police, that hotbed of political intrigue, has been burned, and all police stations in town looted and their contents burned or scattered.

"The ordinary and political police, in some cases, were killed. In other cases, they were dragged from their hiding places and lodged in dark cells in the fortress of St. Peter and St. Paul, where so many have suffered martyrdom for Russian freedom. The political prisoners, victims of the old régime, have been freed from the jails, and many are now taking part in the reorganization of the Government."

Count Fredericks's Home Burned.

LONDON, Friday, March 16.—The Times Petrograd correspondent describes the sacking of the residence of Count Fredericks, Minister of the Imperial Court and Aide de Camp to the Emperor, as one of the most deplorable incidents of the revolt.

Count Fredericks's house was set on fire. His aged wife was carried out fainting. His daughter, who is frail, rushed out, carrying her favorite dog. The girl was ill-treated by the drunken mob, and the dog was killed. Both women eventually were taken to a place of safety.

Count Fredericks is now in attendance upon former Emperor Nicholas.

General de Knorring was ordered to report to the Duma, but refused to comply with the summons. On the contrary, he armed himself and the janitor

Continued on Page 2.

ARMY JOINS WITH THE DUMA

Three Days of Conflict Follow Food Riots in Capital.

POPULACE TAKE UP ARMS

But End Comes Suddenly When Troops Guarding Old Ministers Surrender.

CZAR FINDS CAPITAL GONE

Returns from Front After Receiving Warning from Duma and Gives Up His Throne.

Empress Reported Under Guard or Hiding From Angry People

Special Cable to THE NEW YORK TIMES.

PETROGRAD, March 14. (Dispatch to The London Daily Chronicle.)—The Empress of Russia has been placed under guard.

LONDON, March 15.—According to information received here the Russian people have been most distrustful during recent events of the personal influence of Empress Alexandra. She was supposed to exercise the greatest influence over Emperor Nicholas.

It is stated that her whereabouts is not known, but it is believed she is in seclusion, fearing the populace.

The Empress Alexandra before her marriage to the Emperor of Russia in 1894 was the German Princess Alix of Hesse-Darmstadt.

PETROGRAD, March 15.—Emperor Nicholas of Russia has abdicated, and Grand Duke Michael Alexandrovitch, his younger brother, has been named as Regent.

The Russian Ministry, charged with corruption and incompetence, has been swept out of office. One Minister, Alexander Protopopoff, the head of the Interior Department, is reported to have been killed, and the other Ministers, as well as the President of the Imperial Council, are under arrest.

A new national Cabinet is announced, with Prince Lvoff as President of the Council and Premier, and the other offices held by the men who are close to the Russian people.

Petrograd has been the scene of one of the most remarkable risings in history, beginning with minor food riots and labor strikes last week Thursday. The people's cry for food reached the hearts of the soldiers, and one by one the regiments rebelled, until finally those troops which had for a time stood loyal to the Government gathered up their arms and marched into the ranks of the revolutionists.

Duma President Leading Figure.

Michael V. Rodzianko, President of the Duma, was the leading figure among the Deputies, who unanimously decided to oppose the imperial order, issued last week, for a dissolution of the House. They continued their sessions, and M. Rodzianko informed the Emperor, then at the front, that the hour had struck when the will of the people must prevail.

Even the Imperial Council realized the gravity of the situation, and added its appeal to that of the Duma that the Emperor should take steps to give the people a policy and government in accordance with their desires and in order that there should be no interference with carrying on the war to a victorious ending.

The Emperor hastened back to the capital, only to find that the revolution had been successful and that a new Government was in control.

The Empress, who, it is alleged, has been influential in the councils opposed to the wishes of the people, is reported to have fled or to be in hiding.

Although considerable fighting took place, it is not believed that the casualties are large. One report says that they do not exceed 200.

A few defenders of the old régime put up a last feeble defense last night from the roofs of the wrecked Astoria Military Hotel and St. Isaac's Cathedral, facing on two sides of the same square.

The city is now quiet and perfect order prevails. So far as is known, no foreigners were injured.

The Imperial Palace at Tsarskoe-Selo is said to have been in a state of siege, but thus far no firing has been reported between the guards defending the palace and the revolutionists and troops.

According to one report the Emperor expected trouble to follow from his decree dissolving the Duma, and so warned the residents of Tsarkoe-Selo to arrange to remain in the suburb for an indefinite period.

Began From Strikes a Week Ago.

The most phenomenal feature of the revolution was the swift and orderly transition whereby the control of the city passed from the régime of the old Government into the hands of its opponents.

The visible signs of revolution began on Thursday, March 8. Strikes were declared in several big munitions factories as a protest against the shortage of bread. Men and women gathered and marched through the streets, most of them in an orderly fashion. A few bread shops were broken into in that section of the city beyond the Neva, and several minor clashes between strikers and police occurred.

Squads of mounted troops appeared, but during Thursday and Friday the utmost friendliness seemed to exist between the troops and the people.

This early period of the uprising bore the character of a mock revolution, staged for an immense audience. Cossacks, charging down the street, did so in a half-hearted fashion, plainly without malice or intent to harm the crowds, which they playfully dispersed. The troops exchanged good-natured raillery with the working men and women, and as they rode were cheered by the populace.

Long lines of soldiers stationed in dramatic attitudes across Nevsky Prospect, with their guns pointed at an imaginary foe, appeared to be taking part in a realistic tableau. Machine guns, firing rounds of blank cartridges, seemed only to add another realistic touch to a tremendous theatric production which was using the whole city as a stage.

On Saturday, however, apparently without provocation, the troops were ordered to fire on people marching in Nevsky Prospect. The troops refused to fire, and the police, replacing them, fired rifles and machine guns.

Then came a clash between troops and police, which continued in desultory fashion throughout Saturday night and Sunday. The Nevsky Prospect was cleared of traffic by the police and notices were posted by the commander of the Petrograd military district warning the people that any attempt to congregate would be met by force.

Until Sunday evening, however, there was no intimation that the affair would grow to the proportions of a revolution. The first serious outbreak came at 5 o'clock, when the men of the Volynsky Regiment shot their officers and refused when they received an order to fire upon striking workingmen in one of the factory districts.

Another regiment detailed against the mutineers also joined the revolt. The news spread rapidly to the other barracks and four more regiments went over. Some of the revolting troops marched to the St. Peter and St. Paul Fortress on the left bank of the Neva, and after a brief skirmish with the garrison took possession of it.

Dissension spread among the troops, who did not understand why they should be compelled to take violent measures against fellow-citizens whose chief offense was that they were hungry and were asking the Government to supply bread. Several regiments deserted. A pitched battle began between the troops who stood with the Government and those who, refusing to obey orders, had mutinied, and even slain their officers.

A long night fight took place between the mutinous regiments and the police at the end of St. Catharine Canal, immediately in front of the historic church built over the spot where Alexander II. was killed by a bomb. The police finally fled to the rooftops all over the city and were seen no more in the streets during the entire term of the fighting.

Turning Point in Revolution.

Still, on Monday morning the Government troops appeared to control all the principal squares of the city. Then came a period when it was impossible to distinguish one side from the other. There was no definite line between the factions. The turning point appeared to come about 3 o'clock in the afternoon. For two hours the opposing regiments passively confronted each other along the wide Liteiny Prospect in almost complete silence.

From time to time emissaries from the revolutionary side rode to the opposing ranks and exhorted them to join the side of the people. For a while the result seemed to hang in the balance. The troops appeared irresolute, awaiting

Leading Figures in Russian Revolution.

Czar Nicholas II who has Abdicated — Czarevitch Alexis (12 Yrs old) who will succeed to the Throne

Grand Duke Michael Alexandrovitch who has been named Regent — Michael Rodzianko, Head of the Revolution and the Temporary Government

Prince Lvoff Heads Cabinet; Milukoff Foreign Minister

PETROGRAD, via London, Friday, March 16. The members of the new National Cabinet are announced as follows:

Premier, President of the Council, and Minister of the Interior—Prince Georges E. Lvoff.

Foreign Minister—Professor Paul N. Milukoff.

Minister of Public Instruction—Professor Manuiloff of Moscow University.

Minister of War and Navy, ad Interim—A. J. Guchkoff, formerly President of the Duma.

Minister of Agriculture—M. Ichingareff, Deputy from Petrograd.

Minister of Finance—M. Tereschtenko, Deputy from Kiev.

Minister of Justice—Deputy Kerensky of Saratoff.

Minister of Communications—N. V. Nekrasoff, Vice President of the Duma.

Controller of State—M. Godneff, Deputy from Kazan.

the commands of their officers, who themselves were in doubt as to what they should do.

Desultory firing continued along the side streets, between groups of Government troops and revolutionists. But the regiments upon whose decision the outcome rested still confronted each other, with machine guns and rifles in readiness.

Suddenly a few volleys were exchanged: there was another period of silent suspense, and the Government regiments finally marched over to join the revolutionists. A few hours after the first clash, this section of Petrograd, in which were located the Duma building, artillery headquarters, and the chief military barracks, passed into the hands of the revolutionary forces, and the warfare swept like a tornado to other parts of the city, where the scene was duplicated.

At first it seemed a miracle that the revolutionists, without prearranged plan, without leadership or organization, could in such a short time, with comparative ease, achieve a complete victory over the Government. But the explanation lay in the reluctance of the troops to take sides against the people and their prompt desertion to the ranks of those who opposed the Government.

Workingmen and Clerks Fight.

The scenes in the streets were by this time remarkable. The wide streets, where the troops were stationed, were completely deserted by civilians, except for a few daring individuals, who, creeping along walls and ducking into courtyards, sped from one side to the other. But the side streets were choked with people.

Groups of students, easily distinguished by their blue caps and dark uniforms, fell into step with rough units of rebel soldiers, and were joined by other heterogeneous elements, united for the time being by a cause greater than partisan differences.

Unkempt workingmen, with ragged sheepskin coats covering the conventional peasants' costume of dark blouse and top boots, strode side by side with well groomed city clerks and shopkeepers.

This strange army of people, mustered at the street corners, shouldered their newly acquired rifles and marched out to join the ranks of the deserting regiments.

The economic and industrial life of the city came to a complete standstill. Street car service was supended from the beginning of the disorders and stores were closed. The two leading hotels which housed officers were wrecked. Others restricted their service to regular patrons. In response to an appeal by the revolutionist committees, citizens distributed food to the soldiers.

Duma Declares Government Ended.

On Monday the Duma members, except the Rightists, met in executive session, notwithstanding the order of the Czar dissolving their body. The result was a virtually unanimous vote to place the Duma squarely on the side of the revolution and to authorize the Executive Council of that body to declare the present Government overthrown, and organize a provisional Government.

President Rodzianko, who presided, sent a telegram to the Emperor, informing him of the developments and calling on him to listen to the voice of the people.

"The hour has struck," he said, "when the will of the people must prevail."

It was further stated in the telegram to the Emperor that a special committee, composed of the leaders of the various parties in the Duma, would submit a list of names for the new Cabinet.

Members of the Imperial Council also sent a message to Emperor Nicholas, outlining conditions and recommending a change in the internal policy in accordance with the decision of the Duma, dismissal of the present Cabinet and its reorganization in accordance with the desires of the people and their representatives. The message bore twelve signatures.

Simultaneously it was reported that all the Ministers except M. Protopopoff had resigned.

The following were named as the "staff of the temporary Government": Michael V. Dodzianko, H. V. Nekrasoff, I. Konovaloff, L. I. Dmitrukoff, A. Kerenski, M. S. Pshkeidze, V. V. Shulgin, S. I. Shidlovsky, Paul N. Miluff, M. A. Makarauloff, V. N. Lvoff, A. Rjevsky, and Colonel Englehard.

Remarkable Scene at the Duma.

The scene at the Duma before the revolution was in full flame was extraordinary. The members stood about the broad corridors talking calmly, the various priest members in long black gowns, with flowing hair, and members from the provinces in top boots and blouses mingling with well-groomed and frock-coated representatives.

At the front gates the troops began to assemble. They were without arms. They were the revolting regiments. One body in marching order entered the gate and halted before the entrance. A Duma member spoke from the steps, explaining the attitude of that body and assuring the regiments that the Duma was with them.

Auto trucks packed with men, soldiers, and civilians, with and without arms, rolled up the circular drive and stopped before the door, while some occupant delivered a lurid oration, and then went on cheered by the crowds.

Then came a small army of citizen soldiers, factory workers, clerks, students armed with rifles taken from the captured arsenals, their pale faces and black Winter clothing forming a strange picture against the snow piled high in the Duma garden.

For an hour they stood in more or less military formation before the building, and at dusk marched away toward the centre of the city, followed by the revolting soldiers. The crowd was extremely orderly. A group of a dozen soldiers pushed into the corridor of the building and demanded to be allowed to address the members. A mild-mannered young civilian of the student type took them in hand with a little difficulty and led them into the open. A delegation asked for food. Immediately waiters from the Duma restaurant were sent out with trays of tea and food until the place was cleaned out.

Last Stand of Old Regime.

At nightfall on Monday only one small district of the city, containing the War Office, the Admiralty Building, St. Isaac's Cathedral, and the Military Hotel, still resisted the onslaught of the revolutionary forces, and the battle for the possession of Petrograd came to a dramatic conclusion. In the Admiralty building the Council of Ministers secretly gathered for a conference, and the last regiments loyal to the old Government were drawn up as a guard.

While the Council sat in the last meeting which they were destined to hold, the building was surrounded and the besiegers poured rifle and machine gun fire upon the defenders.

For a few hours the fiercest battle of the day continued: the streets were swept by a steady fusillade and the crowds scattered for the nearest shelter, some of the people being compelled to spend the night in courtyards or corridors of office buildings or wherever they first found refuge.

Toward morning (Tuesday) there was a sudden lull, broken by exultant shouts, which deepened into a roar, and were succeeded by the Russian revolutionary "Marseillaise." The regiments defending the Admiralty had surrendered and gone over to the side of the rvolutionists.

The Ministers in the Admiralty Building were then arrested and the Russian national colors were replaced by the red flag of the revolutionists.

During the day revolutionary publications appeared in the streets, with the simple caption "News." These contained a résumé of developments, and they were eagerly read by all classes. Rodzianko's telegrams to the Emperor and others to the commanders of the troops at the front were reproduced. The first message to the Emperor read:

> The situation is grave. Anarchy reigns in the capital. The Government is paralyzed. The transport of provisions and fuel is completely disorganized. General dissatisfaction is growing. Irregular rifle firing is occurring in the streets. It is necessary to charge immediately some person trusted by the people to form a new Government. It is impossible to linger, since delay means death. Praying God that the responsibility in this hour will not fall upon a crowned head.

Later President Rodzianko sent the following to the Emperor:

> The position is becoming more serious. It is imperative that immediate measures be taken, because tomorrow will be too late. The last hour has come when the fate of the fatherland and the dynasty are being decided.

Similar telegrams were sent to all the commanders at the front with an appeal for their support before the Emperor of the Duma's action. General Alexis Brusiloff, Commander in Chief of the armies of the southwestern front, and General Nicholas Ruzsky, Commander of the northern armies, replied promptly. General Brusiloff sent this message:

"Have fulfilled duty before fatherland and Emperor."

General Ruzsky's reply read:

"Commission accomplished."

Petrograd Resuming Wonted Calm.

Today the city emerged from the week's nightmare of revolution and figuratively smiled under a brilliant flood of sunshine, following a series of gray days, ending with a snowstorm last evening.

Planks were pulled down from windows long closed. Stores, banks, and business establishments of every description reopened their doors for the resumption of ordinary activities as confidence in the new Government gained in force.

With the reopening of bread, sugar, tea, and meat shops queues of women with shopping bags and baskets lined up often to the length of a block to replenish stores exhausted by the long siege.

Truck sledges and little sleighs for hire, the most widely appreciated conveniences of Russian cities, began to appear again in the streets, which for six days had been absolutely void of any means of private transportation.

No newspapers, with the exception of the revolutionary publications, which sprang into life with the success of the revolt, have yet appeared.

The only visible signs of the clash of authority which turned the city into a battleground were the charred ruins of the jail, which are still pouring a cloud of smoke skyward, and here and there the remains of other police institutions and the homes of the few individuals who were regarded as offenders against the rights of the people.

In front of other Government institutions, which apparently it was not seen fit to destroy, were piles of charred embers, showing where wreckage and documents had been dumped and consumed.

Spark that Started Conflagration.

It is evident that the strike of workingmen Thursday of last week provided the spark which set aflame the growing unrest and angry discontent with the Government that, pervading the entire population of Russia, had reached the ignition point.

Thus the small manifestations of hungry factory workers, crying for bread, changed in a single day into a revolution which swept the whole city, spread to the Government troops who had been called to hold the crowds in check, and, supported by the Duma, ended in the downfall of the Government.

The revelations in the Duma of Government stupidity and corruption, and the allegations of treason against the chief members of the Cabinet, sent a wave of protest through the country, and all political factions, except a small reactionary group, still cherishing traditional ideas of the old regime which existed before Russia received a constitution, declared themselves firmly against the sinister influences which had been undermining the best efforts of the country successfully to carry on the war.

Even the Imperial Council, which never before in the history of the country had allied itself with the popular will, held special meetings, in which attention was called to the "serious conditions to which the country had been brought by the unscrupulous designs of governmental heads."

People Against Government.

With unanimity unprecedented the entire population presented a solid front against the Government. The belief prevailed everywhere and was expressed that pro-German Court circles and the Government were doing everything in their power to interfere with the proper conduct of the war and to bring about a separate peace.

Stürmer, Rasputin, and Protopopoff formed a picturesque trio, known as "the dark forces" against which the chief animosity of the country was directed, but powerful as they were, these figures were declared to be only symbols of German influence which was "militating against the patriotic desire of the mass of the Russian people for war until victory."

After the assassination of Rasputin and the removal of Stürmer from the Premiership, the same Ministerial influence, wearing a new mask in the form of a changed Cabinet, Duma officials declared, still flourished with undiminished strength. Direct appeals were made to the Emperor by all sorts of representative bodies and influential officials to save the country from the disaster which threatened it and to appoint a new Cabinet which would have the confidence of the people.

But the Government, except for empty concessions and compromises, remained obdurate to all appeals and showed not the slightest inclination to change the direction of its policy or accede to the demands more and more loudly expressed.

It was the opinion of the majority of the Deputies in the Duma that, despite this state of affairs, an open revolution was impossible, as the country realized that a revolution would seriously interrupt the work of the war and would be playing into the hands of those who had this very end in view.

Open letters were printed in the Petrograd newspapers from popular Duma leaders, and proclamations were posted in the streets, urgently begging the population not to create demonstrations or cause disorders which might lead to interruption of the manufacture of munitions or paralyze the industrial activity of the city.

People at Last Convinced.

Manifestations already arranged for March 6, including a general strike and the marching to the Duma of a deputation of workingmen, were in this way averted. But the moment was only postponed. The people, who had been long vaguely disturbed by the political unrest and were convinced that they were being exploited by the hostile Government, received what they regarded as the last proof of the inefficiency and corruption of their own Government when they were apprised that the already insufficient supply of food had become still more meagre and that for some days it would be necessary to go without bread altogether.

Patient and long suffering by nature, this was too much for the population of Petrograd, who knew that the interior of Russia was stored with immense quantities of grain and all kinds of provisions, and, without other motive at first than to voice a demand for bread, the people paraded the streets and the demonstrations began which soon kindled into a revolution.

REVOLT SPREADS FROM THE CAPITAL

Kronstadt Joins the Cause—Moscow Has Bloodless Revolution and Seethes with Joy.

LONDON, Friday, March 16.—The suddenness and complete success of the revolutionary movement in Russia are emphasized in the dispatches from Petrograd that are reaching London after three days of absolute silence.

All the evidence goes to show that the revolution was well prepared and broke out almost simultaneously in Petrograd and Moscow.

Details of the present conditions outside these cities are still meagre, but Kronstadt, the fortress and seaport at the head of the Gulf of Finland, twenty miles west of Petrograd, has joined the revolutionary movement, according to a Reuter dispatch. Two Deputies, Pepelauff and Taskine, on instructions from the Duma committee, proceeded to Kronstadt, where the troops placed themselves at the disposal of the Duma. M. Pepelauff was appointed commandant of Kronstadt, which is Russia's great naval station.

"The cities of Kharkov and Nijni-Novgorod, the latter the capital of the province of the same name, have declared for the new Government," the Reuter correspondent in Moscow telegraphs. He adds:

"Moscow resounds with popular rejoicing over the overthrow of the Government. The officers have rallied to the new national Government, and a military committee has been formed to preserve order and regulate food supplies. The committee is backed by a brigade of artillery, five regiments of infantry, and the armed militia.

"General Drosovsky, commander of the troops in the Moscow district, has been arrested. More than a thousand police and gendarmes also have been arrested and brought to the town hall. All the political prisoners in the great Butynky Prison have been released."

All pro-German reactionaries are being rounded up everywhere by the new Government, which is assuming power under a mandate to push the war against the Central Powers.

Former Premier Stürmer and the Chief of the Council of the Empire were imprisoned.

The Government of Petrograd is now in the hands of a committee consisting of representatives of the Duma, the Zemstvoes, and municipalities, presided over by President Rodzianko of the Duma. The "Push the War" party is in complete control.

Strict military rule prevails, and the army has the situation so well in hand that it is not expected adherents of the late Government will be able to offer any serious resistance, even in remote provinces.

The revolution was comparatively bloodless and, as far as is known here, no prominent persons were killed.

In Petrograd one bridge was blown up and some houses belonging to suspected pro-German reactionaries were burned. The people of Moscow adhered to the revolutionary movement without bloodshed.

The British and French Ambassadors have established official business relations with the Executive Committee of the Duma.

The Reuter correspondent at Petrograd says that the Grand Duke Cyril informed the Duma that he would place at its disposition the marines under his orders, and afterward visited M. Rodzianko in the Duma and told him that he was entirely at Rodzianko's orders.

Not a Word Against War.

The correspondent sends this dispatch under date of Wednesday:

"Your correspondent has been in the streets both night and day for the last three days. He has seen long lines of hungry men, women, and children, and has seen the wanton firing of rifles, machine guns, and civil war in the main thoroughfares, but has not heard a single word against war.

"A shortage of food, the lack of organization, and the neglect of the most elementary precautions are popularly ascribed to German influences. This is a word of provocation on every lip. With combined fervor warriors, religionaries—all Russians—resolved on the extermination of these influences.

"The killing of Rasputin was the match that set fire to the vast heap of patriotic determination that Russia would deserve well of her allies if she would give herself the chance. The fire quickly spread, ran from class to class, from civilians to troops. It smouldered in Petrograd on Saturday, burst into flame on Sunday, and to a conflagration yesterday.

"This morning your correspondent hears that its purpose has been achieved. All of the regiments in Petrograd have declared for the Duma and the people, and the naval barracks have been opened to enable the sailors to make common cause."

The news of the Russian revolution was not altogether a surprise to London. The sudden dissolution of the Duma and the Council of the Empire, together with reports of food riots in the Russian capital, caused considerable suspicion here as to how events were progressing.

The proclamation by the Military Governor in Petrograd forbidding street assemblages and declaring that disorders would be suppressed made it apparent that affairs were graver than the dispatches allowed by the Russian censorship would indicate.

Then came nearly three days of absolute silence from Petrograd, which extended even to official war bulletins, and rumors began to circulate here that some kind of a revolution was happening. Although these reports, circulating from the Scandinavian capitals were declared to be groundless, suspicion remained here.

The struggle between the Duma and the reactionary party in Russia has been known to be proceeding with great bitterness for a long time, and repeated changes in the ministerial ranks showed that matters were far from settled. Little was permitted to appear in the English papers, but from time to time news percolated from different quarters as to how liberal Russia was struggling against pro-German influence in the persons of Sturmer, Protopopoff, and other high personages.

"The hated Kreaty Prison was seized by the revolutionists after a short resistance by its guards. All the political prisoners held there, including the members of the workmen's group arrested a month ago, were liberated. The same course was followed at the preliminary detention prison and the women's prison. Detective Headquarters was demolished and burned with all the archives relating to political personages and organizations.

"Among those arrested were Bishop Pitrim, the Metropolitan of Petrograd; M. Kurloff, who was in charge of the police arrangements at the time of the murder of Premier Stolypin, and whose activities have been renewed recently, and General Soukhomlinoff, former Minister of War."

FINNISH RAILWAYS TORN UP.

Cossacks in Petrograd Sided with People, Slew Police Chief.

Special Cable to THE NEW YORK TIMES.

LONDON, Friday, March 16.—The Exchange Telegraph's Stockholm correspondent, in a dispatch dated Thursday, which has just reached here, says:

"The afternoon papers report from Haparanda that all communication between the frontier and Petrograd has ceased owing to the Finnish railways being torn up at several places.

"A traveler who witnessed Saturday's events in Petrograd declares in an interview in the journal Allebanda that the authorities from the first feared to employ troops against the revolutionists, and the soldiers were only used as guards. The fighting between the populace and the police, supported by some Cossacks, was very sanguinary. Nevertheless, a part of the Cossack regiment took sides with the people, and when the Superintendent of Police in the Viborg quarter, north of the Neva, ordered the Cossacks to intervene, he was cut down."

Special Cable to THE NEW YORK TIMES.

COPENHAGEN, March 14.—A message from Stockholm tonight says that Petrograd, as the first result of the events of the last few days, has obtained municipal self-government, for which the city has struggled for fifteen years. The townsmen themselves are now able to arrange the provision question.

Bridge Over Neva Blown Up.

STOCKHOLM, March 14, (via Berlin and wireless to Tuckerton, March 15.)—Reports of serious disturbances in Russia are published in Swedish newspapers. The Tidningen of Sundsvall publishes a statement that a railroad bridge over the Neva River, in Petrograd, has been dynamited by revolutionists.

The Nyheter of Haparanda prints an interview with a Swedish business man who arrived in Petrograd on Saturday morning from Moscow. This man is quoted as saying there had been open revolution in many cities of Russia since Thursday of last week. Especially violent riots are reported to have occurred in Petrograd on Saturday, shops being stormed by mobs. According to this information, publication of newspapers was suspended and the authorities posted placards warning the people to remain indoors to avoid danger.

The Nyheter says that other travelers from Petrograd report that similar disturbances occurred there on Friday, that the soldiers were compelled to use their sabres, and that many persons were wounded.

COMMONS TOLD OF ABDICATION

Revolution Due to Russian Purpose to Fight War Out, Says Bonar Law.

LONDON, March 15.—Announcement of the abdication of Emperor Nicholas of Russia was made in the House of Commons tonight by Andrew Bonar Law, the Chancellor of the Exchequer, in these words:

"Only tonight a message has been received from our Ambassador to the effect that a statement from the Duma announced that the Emperor had abdicated and that Grand Duke Michael Alexandrovitch had been appointed Regent.

"There is some comfort for us in the comparative tranquillity with which this change was conducted. Here is also real comfort that all the Government's information shows that the movement was not in any sense directed toward an effort to secure peace by Russia.

"On the contrary, the discontent was not against the Government for carrying on the war, but for not carrying it on with that efficiency and energy which the people had expected."

Mr. Law's statement was made in the course of a reply to Sir James Henry Dalziel, Liberal, who had asked about the situation in Russia. In part the Chancellor said:

"I quite agree that in a matter of this gravity it is the Government's duty, if it is in their power, to give the House all the information which could be safely imparted. I am strongly of the opinion that the House of Commons is the proper place where information of this kind should be communicated to the country.

"The first news the Government had of any serious trouble in Russia came by telegram Friday night. It was to the effect simply that there were disturbances in the streets. Since then the Government has had daily telegrams giving more or less tentative information.

"By degrees it became plain that Petrograd was becoming more or less under ordered rule and that that rule was the rule over which the President of the Duma was exercising control.

"Almost from the outset the soldiers and sailors have taken the side of the Duma in the revolution. The result has been, so far as information has reached the Government, that there has not been any serious loss of life."

A telegram received by the naval attaché of the Russian Embassy in Paris reported that the railways and public services in Petrograd had resumed work, Mr. Law added.

CROWD CHEERS FOR ALLIES.

Recognizes British Ambassador and Escorts Him to Embassy.

Special Cable to THE NEW YORK TIMES.

LONDON, Friday, March 16.—The Petrograd correspondent of THE TIMES, telegraphing yesterday evening, says:

"Sir George Buchanan paid his usual call at the Foreign Office this morning, walking thither with M. Paléologue, the French Ambassador, undeterred by the activity of police snipers concealed in garrets. He was recognized by the people near Winter Palace, who greeted him with cheers and escorted him back to the embassy, where they gave a rousing demonstration in honor of the Allies."

LONDON HAILS RUSSIAN REVOLT

Continued from Page 1.

supply. When police agents tried to bring about riots and strikes, the workmen's own leaders prevented their breaking out. When secret negotiations were opened up with Germany the Duma blasted them by public exposure on the popular side.

"The Duma's demand for sympathetic and really national Government was enforced, first, by the Council of the Empire, normally the stronghold of high officialdom, and then by the Congress of Nobles, which represents the landed aristocracy.

"With the nobility, much of the bureaucracy, the army, the navy, the Duma, the professional classes, and the working classes all ranged against them, the 'dark forces' held obstinately on their way. The murder of the Czarina's favorite, the infamous Rasputin, only intensified the reaction, though its story and sequel showed significantly how far many members of the Imperial family were from supporting the reigning head and his consort in the policy which was jeopardizing the dynasty. But the Czar's blindness was incurable. In a kind of panic he got rid of every remaining progressive Minister; a nonentity of no importance from the Czar's personal circle was made Prime Minister, and the real power fell to Protopopoff, the strong man of the camarilla, who was to see their design through."

London Overjoyed at the News.

LONDON, Friday, March 16.—The news that "Great Russia" had joined the democracies of the world, and that one of the three great absolutist rulers of the world had resigned his throne in accordance with the demands of his people was received here with unmixed joy. There has been no illusion about Russia here. Particularly in the last year it had been well understood that the situation there has been the people against the throne.

"The people and the army are all for the war and against Germany," has been the word which came from Russia through all channels repeatedly. That the Court has been enshrouded in a pro-German atmosphere, and that the Emperor was a weak man, under the thumb of his wife and also under the domination of several members of the bureaucracy, some of whom were influenced only by the tradition of the old régime and others of whom were in the pay of German diplomats, had also been reported.

The men now in control of the destinies of the great empire of Eastern Europe are Russians who are anti-German and pro-Russian to the core, as the Russian developments are regarded here as wholly to the benefit of the Entente Powers in the war.

The revolution is commented upon editorially here with enthusiasm, mainly as a great triumph for the Entente and a great disaster for the Central Powers. The press describes it as the death of German hopes and a more crushing and more far-reaching blow than Germany has yet received. The Liberal papers also welcome it as a triumph of democracy, presaging great influence on the cause of liberty throughout the world.

There is a note of anxiety in some of the comments that troublesome developments may occur, but this note is not emphasized. Pity and sympathy are expressed for the Emperor, of whom the worst said is that he lacks intellectual and moral strength. Tributes are paid to his generous and lovable disposition and his ardent desire to serve his people, while his abdication is described as an act of unselfish patriotism, which it is hoped has saved his country from civil war and Petrograd from anarchy.

CZAR AS RULER SHOWED TIMIDITY

Believed in Autocracy, but Modified Father's Stern Repressive Measures.

CALLED HAGUE CONFERENCE

Japanese War the Beginning of His Troubles—Empress Suspected of Pro-German Leanings.

Nicholas II., Czar of Russia, has abdicated his throne following a Liberal revolution. He has had to surrender it because he was unwilling, or unable, to lend his influence with sufficient intensity to the successful prosecution of a foreign war. If he had died three years ago he would probably have gone down in history as the man who called the first Hague Conference, and who gave Russia her first Constitutional Government.

Yet the paradox is not as great as it appears, for the whole career of Nicholas has shown him as a man of excellent intentions, but vacillating resolution; with no very great understanding, with a spirit that comes easily under the sway of others without any critical examination of their character or motives; a weak and timid man, who now and then nerves himself to some act of determination which apparently exhausts all his resolution and leaves him weak and helpless for a long time afterward.

He came to the throne on Nov. 1, 1894, following the thirteen years of reaction under his father, Alexander III. In temperament and aspirations Nicholas seems to have occupied a middle position between his father and his grandfather, the murdered Alexander II. Like his father, he firmly believed in autocracy; he had few, if any, of the liberal tendencies which made his grandfather's murder, in 1881, the greatest misfortune of the Russian liberal movement. But he had not the temperament, perhaps not the power, to initiate and continue the stern measures of repression which his father had carried out.

Softens Repressive Measures.

Instead, the first years of his reign showed him an Emperor of mildness and amiability—rather a dreamer, disinclined to a vivid personal interest in public affairs, with something of the mystic about him, but withal a moderate and benevolent ruler. The entente cordiale with France, entered into under his father, was strengthened to a close alliance; the repressive measures of bureaucracy and police that had dealt such blows to the revolutionary parties of earlier decades were modified, and finally, at the beginning of 1899, the autocratic ruler of one of the world's greatest military empires took the initiative in calling a conference to discuss disarmament and arbitration.

Perhaps a man of different temperament would have devoted more of his attentions to trying to settle some of the outstanding causes of international dispute. But political activity has never been one of the Czar's principal interests. He called The Hague conference. He did not originate the idea; as in most of the other dramatic acts of his life, he took the immediate and decisive action which his position made possible after he had been fired by the ideas of other men.

Even though it was realized very soon that the hopes entertained by enthusiasts for The Hague conference would not be realized, it undoubtedly forwarded the cause of arbitration, if not of disarmament.

The War with Japan.

Meanwhile, Russian interests were drifting steadily toward the war with Japan. In February, 1904, the war actually broke out, and the cumulative disasters due to official incompetence or dishonesty not only ruined for the time being Russia's standing as a great power, but set fire to the internal dissension that had been growing under cover for many years. The general strike in Petrograd in September, 1905, was the first token that here was a real revolution to reckon with; and the demoralization of the Russian army and bureaucracy was so great that observers compared conditions to those in France in 1789. Fearful that he might go the way of Louis XVI., the Czar hastily gave out the ukase of Oct. 30, which promised a representative assembly and other reforms couched in vague terms.

The result was disastrous both for the liberals and for the Czar. The first two Dumas were elected on a rather liberal suffrage and were strongly radical. They wanted more than any legislative assembly could have got at once in any nation; and their summoning gave the bureaucrats a chance to recover their nerve. The possibility of liberal legislation in the Duma was hampered by the naval revolts at Kronstadt and Sebastopol and by the street fighting in Moscow in December, 1905. The suppression of each of these revolts gave the conservatives a stronger hold on the reins of government, and the loss of life and property did much to shake the hold of the revolution on persons of moderate sympathies.

The result was that in a year or so the Duma was prorogued; the revolution, leaderless and unorganized, weakened by the defection of the moderates who hoped to find all that Russia needed in the legislative assembly, had been beaten down into an epidemic of sporadic assassinations, and the Czar, who if no liberal at the outset of his reign was certainly not a severe reactionary, seems to have been thoroughly frightened with the possibilities of popular government. When the third Duma was assembled, in 1907, it was based on a much more restricted suffrage and was of a distinctly conservative tinge. The Russian revolution had again been quelled, to find its further immediate results only in the inspiration of the younger writers.

Hardly had Nicholas again become secure in his position as ruler of an empire with nominal liberal institutions, but actually in the hands of the reactionaries, when events in the Balkans turned the course of Russian history in another direction. The advocates of an understanding with Austria and a vigorous policy in the Far East had been answered by the victory of Japan. Now the proclamation of Bulgarian independence, followed by the Austrian annexation of Bosnia and Herzegovina, challenged Russian influence among the southern Slavs.

War at that moment was averted by the dramatic entrance of the German Emperor on the side of Austria, and it is credibly reported that this appearance "in shining armor" was never forgotten by Nicholas.

When the Germans had again come to Austria's aid in the last week of July, 1914, one of the strongest factors in Russian determination to fight, if necessary, is believed to have been the Emperor's insistence that the Germans should not be allowed to bluff successfully again.

Internal Dissension Grows.

Internal dissension was brewing in Russia again when the Balkan wars finally broke up the unstable equilibrium that had been precariously preserved in Europe since 1878, and the Empire was on the eve of a general strike when the war broke out in 1914. At this time, as has been said, the Emperor seems to have been one of the strong forces which led the Russians to determine that if any one was going to win on a bluff, it must be Russia.

Here Nicholas appears as the champion of national and Slavic aspirations; in the telegrams exchanged with the German Emperor and King George of England, just before the war broke out, he insists on the impossibility of stopping the mobilization. And when war had actually started, on Aug. 15, 1914, he issued the famous manifesto which proclaimed the autonomy of a reunited Poland as one of the things for which Russia was fighting. Later came his manifesto holding out hope to the Jews. So far Nicholas was in line with some of the cardinal principles of Russian liberalism—resistance of German aggression, promotion of the smaller Slavic nationalities, liberal treatment of the subordinate peoples within the empire. Yet after two years he has been brought to abdication.

The explanation, apparently, lies in Court intrigues and camarillas, with their implications of superstition, mysticism, and cruelty which have in recent months been stigmatized in many quarters as Oriental; which, it has been said, could have occurred nowhere but in Russia. Yet the circuitous politics within the Russian Court differs only in degree, not in kind, from matters which have not been unknown in England and Germany, which have even been hinted at from time to time in countries republican in name and form.

"Dark Forces" an Element.

The growth in the Russian Court of the influence of the "dark forces" against which the Liberal revolution has fought seems to have been due in great part to the personal temperament and personal relations of Nicholas. Treason was rife from the first among a large section of the Baltic nobility, which holds many of the highest posts in the bureaucracy, and still more in the upper circles of Court ceremony. That this influence was sufficient, apparently, to paralyze the Emperor himself on more than one occasion may perhaps be attributed to the Empress, to the psychological reaction of the revolution of 1905 on the Czar, and to his religious mysticism.

The Empress of Russia, Alexandra Feodorovna, was Princess Alixe of Hesse-Darmstadt. For years common rumor has held that she was unhappy in the Court of Russia, that her temperament and that of her husband were not in sympathy, despite the lack of any open scandal in the imperial household. Since the war began the assertion has been made freely, even in some of the countries allied with Russia, that the Empress sympathized with that portion of the nobility of Germanic stock which would regard a German victory as not undesirable in a struggle which the Russian people had made their own.

That the Emperor feared and distrusted liberalism more than ever since the uprisings that followed the Japanese war is generally accepted, and he, too, could not have failed to take alarm at the growing strength of the Duma, at the evidence that a Russian victory, the possession of Constantinople, must bring with it more in the way of liberal reform than the autonomy of Poland and the removal of restrictions on the Jews.

The Emperor has been credited, too, with fears that success in the field might have the result of alienating the sympathy of the people from his own personality, never of the sort to hold the imagination or arouse instinctive enthusiasm, and make the great national hero his uncle, the Grand Duke Nicholas Nicholaievitch, who commanded the army during the successes of the first year of the war.

But still a stronger influence, according to the belief which has settled already into almost a certainty, was the monk Rasputin, the last of a long series of religious wonder-workers who had held ascendancy over the Czar. It was in this field that the Oriental characteristics of Nicholas II., the Oriental possibilities of his office made themselves most apparent. He seemed as credulous in the presence of a monk who had gained some local reputation for religious power as any mujik.

Philippe Landard, the Frenchman, was followed in his favor by the monk Theophile; he by Iliodor, the "mad monk" of Tsaritsin; and finally came Gregory Rasputin, who gained his influence with the Emperor, according to general belief, through his ascendancy over the Czarina.

It was only in January that Rasputin was murdered in Petrograd by a small group of liberally minded nobles, who are said to have included in their masked circle at least one Grand Duke. The killing of Rasputin was followed by some action—not as strong as might have been supposed—to punish his murderers and to suppress the liberal party that they represented. It seems to have been this reaction that sealed the fate of Nicholas.

More than once there had been evidence that diverse forces were fighting for the soul of the Emperor. His firm stand for the popular crusade against the Germans and for some of the reforms demanded by the Liberals at the outset of the war had been followed now and then by evidences that at times he could shake off the "dark forces" that beset the palace. Most notably did this occur in September, 1915, when, after four months of continuous disaster in the field, the Czar transferred the Grand Duke Nicholas to the Caucasus and took personal, even if only nominal, command of his armies.

This act at once made it plain to the Russian people that the Czar was with them, that it was still his war and their war, the war for Holy Russia. But in the end suspicion of the Liberals, fear of what the people might do, and the influence of the Empress, the Baltic Germans, and Rasputin seem to have aligned the Czar on the side of those who believed that a German victory was the lesser of two evils.

In personal appearance Nicholas closely resembles his cousin, George of England. As to his personal character, aside from his amiable desire to do something beneficial, his superstition, and the ease with which he has been deluded by persons preying on his feelings, there is little evidence. He has been regarded as weak and timid; and the evidence of Prince George of Greece, an eyewitness of the first attempt to assassinate him, made in Kyoto in 1891, who told how "Nicky ran down the street, into a shop and out of it again," to get away from the Japanese fanatic who had struck at him with a sword, seems to have been a fair forecast of a character which had not within it the strength needed by the Emperor of a great nation engaged in the war of 1914.

PEOPLE IN REVOLT BURN AND SLAY

Continued from Page 1.

of his house with revolvers and fired upon the guardsmen, killing two of them.

The guardsmen thereupon shot General de Knorring, whose body was dragged to the quay and thrown into the river.

HOW THE BLOODSHED STARTED

Guards Fired on People, but Latter Showed No Animosity.

Special Cable to THE NEW YORK TIMES.

LONDON, Friday, March 16.—The Times Petrograd correspondent, telegraphing Monday and describing Sunday's scenes on the crowded Nevsky Prospect, says:

"Warnings not to assemble were disregarded. No Cossacks were visible. Platoons of guardsmen were drawn up here and there in courtyards and side streets. The crowd was fairly good-humored, cheering the soldiers and showing themselves ugly only toward a few visible police.

"Shortly after 3 P. M. orders were given to the infantry to clear the streets. A company of guards took up station near the Sadovaya and fired several volleys in the direction of the Anitokoff Palace. Something like 100 people were killed or wounded. On the scene of the shooting hundreds of empty cartridge cases are littered in the snow, which is plentifully sprinkled with blood.

"After the volleys the thoroughfare was cleared but the crowd remained on the sidewalks. No animosity was shown toward the soldiers. The people shouted 'We are sorry for you, Pavlovtsy; you had to do your duty.' The same company later returned to its barracks, situated in the Champ de Mars near the British Embassy. I had just called on Sir George Buchanan and I was walking through the Summer gardens when bullets began to whistle over my head.

"The Pavlovtsy Guards on approaching their barracks on the other side of the Field of Mars found the way blocked by another crowd, who cheered them, but refused to disperse. The Colonel in command ordered the men to lie down so as to avoid killing the people. After several volleys the crowd gave way, and, sending his men forward, he, himself, superintended the removal of the wounded.

"Following his men, he then crossed the canal bridge; two individuals, apparently disguised, one as a student, the other as an officer, barred the way.

Strikes Colonel with Own Sword.

"The student wrested the Colonel's sword from him and slashed him savagely over the arm and head, causing serious but not dangerous wounds."

The correspondent says the worst scenes of Sunday occurred around Nicholas Station and the adjoining Ligovskaya. Here the police had machine guns, and from roofs and garrets of surrounding edifices poured down a murderous fire upon the crowd.

On Monday the insurgents took possession of the Law Courts and sacked the Ministry of the Interior and office of the Commandant of City, while indiscriminate shooting progressed in various quarters.

Telegraphing on Tuesday morning, the correspondent says:

"The district surrounding the Admiralty, including the Winter Palace, the Ministry of Foreign Affairs, the central telephone exchange, and the post and telegraph offices, remain partly in the hands of the Government, but are fiercely besieged by troops of the nation.

"All the Ministers took shelter under the protection of machine guns posted on the Admiralty spire. Armored cars, which all appear to be in the hands of the revolutionaries, are fusillading the Government machine guns. At the hour of telegraphing the fire from the Admiralty has ceased and the building appears to be in the hands of the revolutionaries. The Government thus are surrounded and completely isolated, and it would seem to be merely a question of hours before they are captured by the people.

"On a rough computation four-fifths of the city is in the hands of the troops, who have gone over to the Duma. Moreover, a huge number of inhabitants are armed with rifles, revolvers, and swords. The fortress of St. Peter and St. Paul, containing the tombs of the Romanoffs, the Imperial Mint and the prison where political prisoners are detained, fell into the hands of the people on Monday and became the headquarters of the revolutionary armies. Its guns command all the bridges and crossings over the Neva."

Rodzianko Addresses Troops.

"One of the most impressive scenes of the revolution was the arrival of the Preobrajensky Guards with their Colonel and officers at the Tauride Palace. The men, all of giant stature, were drawn up in ranks four deep the whole length of the enormous Catherine Hall. The President of the Duma came out to greet them. On the appearance of M. Rodzianko the Colonel's voice rang out, "Preobrajensky, attention!" and the whole regiment stood at salute. M. Rodzianko saluted them as follows:

"'Soldiers of the true faith, let me as an old soldier greet you according to our custom. I wish you good health.'

"'We wish good health to your excellency,' came the thunderous response.

"The President continued:

"'I want to thank you for coming here to help the members of the Imperial Duma to establish order and to safeguard the honor and glory of our country. Your comrades are fighting in the trenches for the might and majesty of Russia, and I am proud that my son has been serving since the beginning of the war in your ranks. But in order that you should be able to advance the cause and interests which have been undertaken by the Duma you must remain a disciplined force. You know as well as I do that soldiers are helpless without their officers. I ask you to remain faithful to your officers and to have confidence in them just as we have confidence in them. Return quietly to your barracks and come here at the first call when you may be required.'

"'We are ready,' answered the Preobrajensky Guards. 'Show us the way.'

"'The old authority is incapable of on condition that you obey my orders, leading Russia the right way,' was the answer. 'Our first task is to establish a new authority in which we could all believe and trust, and which would be able to save and magnify our mother Russia.'

"The soldiers marched out, shouting, 'Hurrah!'

"M. Rodzianko greeted in the same manner the officers and men of the Grenadier Guards and the officers and troopers of the Ninth Cavalry Regiment.

"After the President's speech to the troopers their Colonel, addressing them, said:

"'Men, I intend to carry out all orders given to me by the President of the Imperial Duma. I remain with you. Hurrah for the President of the Imperial Duma!'

"The troopers cheered loudly.

Councillors Petition the Czar.

"A group of twenty-two elected members of the upper house, including Gutchkoff, Stakhovitch, Prince Trubetskoi, and Professors Vassilieff, Grimm, and Vernaudski, yesterday addressed a telegram to the Czar in which, after reviewing the circumstances which had brought the people to a state of utter despair and led to the downfall of the Government in Petrograd, they say:

"'The maintenance of this old Government in office is tantamount to the complete overthrow of law and order, involving defeat on the battlefield, the end of the dynasty, and the greatest misfortunes for Russia. We consider that the only means of salvation lie in complete and final rupture with the past, the immediate convocation of Parliament, and the summoning of a person enjoying the confidence of the nation, who shall form a new Cabinet capable of governing the country in full accord with the representatives of the nation.'

"M. Protopopoff came down last night to the Duma and surrendered himself, proclaiming his desire to work for the welfare of his country."

GERMAN VERSION OF THE REVOLUTION

Petrograd Population Resuming Normal Activities at Request of Duma Committee.

BERLIN, March 15, (by Wireless to Sayville.)—There has been a successful revolution in Russia, according to the Overseas News Agency, (the official German news bureau,) which gave out the subjoined statement today:

"The following official report was issued in Petrograd on March 14 about the successful Russian revolution:

"'The population of Petrograd, incensed by the complete disorganization of transport services and of alimentation, have been irritated for a long time against the Government and had become restless. The population held the Government responsible for all its sufferings. The Government, expecting trouble, took measures on a large scale in order to maintain order, and, among other things, ordered the dissolution of the Council of the Empire and the Duma.

"'The Duma, however, on March 11, decided not to accept the imperial ukase, but to continue its meetings. The Duma immediately instituted an executive committee, presided over by M. Rodzianko, President of the Duma. That committee declared itself to be a provisional Government, and issued the following appeal:

"'The Executive Committee rested itself upon the population of the capital, which was in full revolution, and upon the army, completely united with the revolutionists. It arrested all the Ministers and sent them to jail. The Duma declared that the Ministerial Cabinet no longer existed.

"'Today, on the third day of the revolution, the capital, where order is returning swiftly, is completely in the hands of the Executive Committee of the Duma and of the troops which garrisoned Petrograd, and numbered more than 30,000, which troops support the revolution. Deputy Engelhard, Colonel of the Great General Staff, has been appointed commander of Petrograd by the committee.

"All the News That's Fit to Print."

The New York Times.

THE WEATHER
Generally fair today and Sunday; moderate west to variable winds.
For full weather report see Page 19.

VOL. LXVI...NO. 21,665. NEW YORK, SATURDAY, MAY 19, 1917.—TWENTY PAGES. ONE CENT In Greater New York. | TWO CENTS Elsewhere N. Y. State, N. J., Conn. | THREE CENTS Other States.

PRESIDENT CALLS THE NATION TO ARMS; DRAFT BILL SIGNED; REGISTRATION ON JUNE 5; REGULARS UNDER PERSHING TO GO TO FRANCE

WILL NOT SEND ROOSEVELT

Wilson Not to Avail Himself of Volunteer Authority at Present.

COMMENDS THE COLONEL

But Declares the Business at Hand Is Scientific and for Trained Men Only.

SAYS RESPONSIBILITY IS HIS

Sending of Pershing Division Believed to be in Direct Response to France's Call.

Special to The New York Times.

WASHINGTON, May 18.—Announcement was made at the War Department tonight by Secretary Baker that an expeditionary force of approximately one division of regular troops, under Major General John J. Pershing had been ordered to proceed to France on as early date as practicable. General Pershing and his staff will precede the troops to the fighting area.

Shortly before this announcement came from Secretary Baker, the White House gave to the press a statement from President Wilson in which he said that he would not avail himself, "at any rate at the present stage of the war," of the authority conferred by the Military Selective Draft act, which he had just approved, to organize volunteer divisions.

While referring in complimentary terms to Colonel Roosevelt's public service and gallantry, the President made it plain that he was entirely out of sympathy with the Roosevelt proposal that volunteers be sent to France without delay.

"Politically, too," said the President, "it would no doubt have a very fine effect and make a profound impression," but he added that "the business now at hand is undramatic, practical, and of scientific directness and precision." The President indicated that he did not regard Colonel Roosevelt as a military expert. He also stressed the point that upon the Executive rested the responsibility for the successful conduct of the war, and that he intended to be influenced by considerations along that line and let everything else wait.

It is apparent from President Wilson's statement that his present state of mind is strongly opposed to sending Colonel Roosevelt or any volunteer force to France.

The official announcement that an expeditionary force of regular troops would be sent to France "at as early date as possible" was handed to newspaper men at the War Department by Major Douglas MacArthur of the General Staff at 9:30 o'clock with the injunctions that it was not to be published through extra editions or otherwise until 10 o'clock. The statement containing this important announcement follows:

"The President has directed an expeditionary force of approximately one division of regular troops under command of Major Gen. John J. Pershing to proceed to France at as early a date as practicable. General Pershing and staff will precede the troops abroad. It is requested that no details or speculations with regard to the mobilization of this command, dates of departure, composition, or other items, be carried by the press, other than the official bulletins given out by the War Department relating thereto."

The President's Statement.

The President's statement regarding Colonel Roosevelt follows:

"I shall not avail myself, at any rate at the present stage of the war, of the authorization conferred by the act to organize volunteer divisions. To do so would seriously interfere with the carrying out of the chief and most immediately important purpose contemplated by this legislation, the prompt creation and early use of an effective army, and would contribute practically nothing to the effective strength of the armies now engaged against Germany.

"I understand that the section of this act which authorizes the creation of volunteer divisions in addition to the draft was added with a view to providing an independent command for Mr. Roosevelt and giving the military authority an opportunity to use his fine vigor and enthusiasm in recruiting forces now at the Western front.

"It would be very agreeable to me to pay Mr. Roosevelt this compliment and the Allies the compliment of sending to their aid one of our most distinguished public men, an ex-President who has

Continued on Page 2.

A Proclamation by the President of the United States

Executive Mansion, Washington, D. C., May 18, 1917.

Whereas, Congress has enacted and the President has on the 18th day of May, one thousand nine hundred and seventeen, approved a law, which contains the following provisions:

SECTION 5.—That all male persons between the ages of 21 and 30, both inclusive, shall be subject to registration in accordance with regulations to be prescribed by the President: And upon proclamation by the President or other public notice given by him or by his direction stating the time and place of such registration it shall be the duty of all persons of the designated ages, except officers and enlisted men of the regular army, the navy, and the National Guard and Naval Militia while in the service of the United States, to present themselves for and submit to registration under the provisions of this act: And every such person shall be deemed to have notice of the requirements of this act upon the publication of said proclamation or other notice as aforesaid, given by the President or by his direction: And any person who shall willfully fail or refuse to present himself for registration or to submit thereto as herein provided, shall be guilty of a misdemeanor and shall, upon conviction in the District Court of the United States having jurisdiction thereof, be punished by imprisonment for not more than one year, and shall thereupon be duly registered; provided that in the call of the docket precedence shall be given, in courts trying the same, to the trial of criminal proceedings under this act; provided, further, that persons shall be subject to registration as herein provided, who shall have attained their twenty-first birthday and who shall not have attained their thirty-first birthday on or before the day set for the registration; and all persons so registered shall be and remain subject to draft into the forces hereby authorized unless excepted or excused therefrom as in this act provided; provided further, that in the case of temporary absence from actual place of legal residence of any person liable to registration as provided herein, such registration may be made by mail under regulations to be prescribed by the President.

SECTION 6.—That the President is hereby authorized to utilize the service of any or all departments and any or all officers or agents of the United States and of the several States, territories, and the District of Columbia and subdivisions thereof in the execution of this act, and all officers and agents of the United States and of the several States, territories, and subdivisions thereof, and of the District of Columbia; and all persons designated or appointed under regulations prescribed by the President, whether such appointments are made by the President himself or by the Governor or other officer of any State or territory to perform any duty in the execution of this act, are hereby required to perform such duty as the President shall order or direct, and all such officers and agents and persons so designated or appointed shall hereby have full authority for all acts done by them in the execution of this act by the direction of the President. Correspondence in the execution of this act may be carried in penalty envelopes, bearing the frank of the War Department. Any person charged, as herein provided, with the duty of carrying into effect any of the provisions of this act or the regulations made or directions given thereunder who shall fail or neglect to perform such duty, and any person charged with such duty or having and exercising any authority under said act, regulations, or directions, who shall knowingly make or be a party to the making of any false or incorrect registration, physical examination, exemption, enlistment, enrollment, or muster, and any person who shall make or be a party to the making of any false statement or certificate as to the fitness or liability of himself or any other person for service under the provisions of this act, or regulations made by the President thereunder, or otherwise evades or aids another to evade the requirements of this act or of said regulations, or who, in any manner, shall fail or neglect fully to perform any duty required of him in the execution of this act, shall, if not subject to military law, be guilty of a misdemeanor, and upon conviction in the District Court of the United States, having jurisdiction thereof, be punished by imprisonment for not more than one year, or, if subject to military law, shall be tried by court-martial and suffer such punishment as a court-martial may direct.

Now, Therefore, I, Woodrow Wilson, President of the United States, do call upon the Governor of each of the several States and Territories, the Board of Commissioners of the District of Columbia, and all officers and agents of the several States and Territories, of the District of Columbia, and of the counties and municipalities therein, to perform certain duties in the execution of the foregoing law, which duties will be communicated to them directly in regulations of even date herewith.

And I do further proclaim and give notice to all persons subject to registration in the several States and in the District of Columbia in accordance with the above law, that the time and place of such registration shall be between 7 A. M. and 7 P. M. on the fifth day of June, 1917, at the registration place in the precinct wherein they have their permanent homes. Those who shall have attained their twenty-first birthday and who shall not have attained their thirty-first birthday on or before the day here named are required to register, excepting only officers and enlisted men of the regular army, the navy, the Marine Corps, and the National Guard and Naval Militia, while in the service of the United States, and officers in the Officers' Reserve Corps and enlisted men in the Enlisted Reserve Corps while in active service. In the territories of Alaska, Hawaii, and Porto Rico a day for registration will be named in a later proclamation.

And I do charge those who through sickness shall be unable to present themselves for registration that they apply on or before the day of registration to the County Clerk of the County where they may be for instructions as to how they may be registered by agent. Those who expect to be absent on the day named from the counties in which they have their permanent homes may register by mail, but their mailed registration cards must reach the places in which they have their permanent homes by the day named herein. They should apply as soon as practicable to the County Clerk of the county wherein they may be for instructions as to how they may accomplish their registration by mail. In case such persons as, through sickness or absence, may be unable to present themselves personally for registration shall be sojourning in cities of over 30,000 population, they shall apply to the City Clerk of the city wherein they may be sojourning rather than to the Clerk of the County. The Clerks of counties and of cities of over 30,000 population in which numerous applications from the sick and from nonresidents are expected are authorized to establish such agencies and to employ and deputize such clerical force as may be necessary to accommodate these applications.

The Power against which we are arrayed has sought to impose its will upon the world by force. To this end it has increased armament until it has changed the face of war. In the sense in which we have been wont to think of armies, there are no armies in this struggle, there are entire nations armed. Thus, the men who remain to till the soil and man the factories are no less a part of the army that is France than the men beneath the battle flags. It must be so with us. It is not an army that we must shape and train for war; it is a nation.

To this end our people must draw close in one compact front against a common foe. But this cannot be if each man pursues a private purpose. All must pursue one purpose. The nation needs all men; but it needs each man, not in the field that will most pleasure him, but in the endeavor that will best serve the common good. Thus, though a sharpshooter pleases to operate a trip-hammer for the forging of great guns and an expert machinist desires to march with the flag, the nation is being served only when the sharpshooter marches and the machinist remains at his levers.

The whole nation must be a team, in which each man shall play the part for which he is best fitted. To this end, Congress has provided that the nation shall be organized for war by selection; that each man shall be classified for service in the place to which it shall best serve the general good to call him.

The significance of this cannot be overstated. It is a new thing in our history and a landmark in our progress. It is a new manner of accepting and vitalizing our duty to give ourselves with thoughtful devotion to the common purpose of us all. It is in no sense a conscription of the unwilling; it is, rather, selection from a nation which has volunteered in mass. It is no more a choosing of those who shall march with the colors than it is a selection of those who shall serve an equally necessary and devoted purpose in the industries that lie behind the battle line.

The day here named is the time upon which all shall present themselves for assignment to their tasks. It is for that reason destined to be remembered as one of the most conspicuous moments in our history. It is nothing less than the day upon which the manhood of the country shall step forward in one solid rank in defense of the ideals to which this nation is consecrated. It is important to those ideals no less than to the pride of this generation in manifesting its devotion to them, that there be no gaps in the ranks.

It is essential that the day be approached in thoughtful apprehension of its significance, and that we accord to it the honor and the meaning that it deserves. Our industrial need prescribes that it be not made a technical holiday, but the stern sacrifice that is before us urges that it be carried in all our hearts as a great day of patriotic devotion and obligation, when the duty shall lie upon every man, whether he is himself to be registered or not, to see to it that the name of every male person of the designated ages is written on these lists of honor.

In Witness Whereof, I have hereunto set my hand and caused the seal of the United States to be affixed. Done at the City of Washington this 18th day of May in the year of our Lord one thousand nine hundred and seventeen, and of the independence of the United States of America the one hundred and forty-first.

Woodrow Wilson

By the President:
ROBERT LANSING, Secretary of State.

PLANS FOR NATIONAL ARMY

First Draft of 500,000 Men to be Divided Into Sixteen Divisions.

MILITIA SIMILARLY PLACED

Arrangement of Concentration Camps Will Be Near Home Regions of Units.

CALLS OUT NATIONAL GUARD

Entire Force to Mobilize and Recruit to War Strength, Beginning on July 15.

Special to The New York Times.

WASHINGTON, May 18.—President Wilson, tonight at 10 o'clock, issued his proclamation fixing June 5 as the day on which registration is to take place for the national army of 500,000 men to be drafted under authority of the Draft bill, which he signed tonight. On this date all men in the country between the ages of 21 and 30 years, inclusive, will be required to present themselves for registration. Those away from home will register by mail, according to the terms of the proclamation. The registration date for Hawaii, Alaska, and Porto Rico will be announced later.

The President's proclamation sets forth in detail the plans for registration and was telegraphed tonight by the War Department to all parts of the country for official posting and publication. It is so as to have the widest publicity. It is expected that the registration will occupy about five days. After that those entitled to exemption will be excluded from the draft. About 10,000,000 men between 21 and 30, inclusive, are expected to be registered. After the registration and exemptions have been completed, those declared to be eligible for drafting will have their names placed in jury wheels and 500,000 will be drafted for Federal service in the formation of the new national army.

Plans for the formation of the new army have been completed. It will be divided into sixteen divisions, each to consist of 28,000 men. They will be mobilized in sixteen concentration camps, the names of which soon will be announced. The draft army will be officially known as the National Army, in contradistinction to the regular army and the National Guard army. These National Army divisions will be numbered consecutively from one to sixteen.

New York and Pennsylvania will furnish enough men in the draft to form three National Army divisions, exclusive of what they will furnish for the regular army and the National Guard army. New York and Pennsylvania will each furnish about a division and a half for the National Army. The only other State to furnish as much as a division for the National Army will be Illinois. Seven Pacific Coast States, where the population is not so dense, will furnish the sixteenth National Army division.

Distribution of Divisions.

The distribution of the divisions, according to the States that will form them, will be as follows:

First—Massachusetts, Maine, Connecticut, Rhode Island, Vermont, and New Hampshire.
Second—Lower New York State and Long Island.
Third—Upper New York State and Northern Pennsylvania.
Fourth—Southern Pennsylvania.
Fifth—Virginia, Maryland, Delaware, New Jersey, and District of Columbia.
Sixth—Tennessee, North Carolina, and South Carolina.
Seventh—Alabama, Georgia, and Florida.
Eighth—Ohio and West Virginia.
Ninth—Indiana and Kentucky.
Tenth—Wisconsin and Michigan.
Eleventh—Illinois.
Twelfth—Arkansas, Mississippi, and Louisiana.
Thirteenth—North Dakota, South Dakota, Nebraska, Minnesota, and Iowa.
Fourteenth—Colorado, Kansas, and Missouri.
Fifteenth—Arizona, New Mexico, Texas, and Oklahoma.
Sixteenth—Washington, Oregon, Idaho, Montana, California, Nevada, and Utah.

Calls Out the Guard.

President Wilson also issued orders today for the mobilization of the entire National Guard of the country. Instructions were sent to the Adjutant General of the States to the effect that the National Guard not now in Federal service and enlisted men of the National Guard Reserve would be drafted into the Federal service on various dates, ranging from July 15 to Aug. 5. All National Guard coast artillery will be drafted on July 15. The organizations will be held at their rendezvous for about two weeks and will then be sent to concentration camps in the Southern, Southeastern, and Western Departments for training.

There are now 60,000 National Guardsmen in Federal service. There are more than 100,000 not yet in Federal service. These are to be called into Federal service under the orders issued today. New National Guard units will also be formed and all the guard units will be expanded until 400,000 men have been obtained. This will be designated the National Guard Army, and it will com-

Treasury Plans to Let the Banks Keep Funds Paid for Liberty Bonds

Institutions Subscribing $100,000 Favored—Subscriptions for the Bonds Increase Here—Bank of Commerce Takes $10,000,000 of the Issue.

Special to The New York Times.

WASHINGTON, May 18.—To avoid any disturbance of the money market in placing the Liberty Loan of 1917, the Treasury Department today, in behalf of Secretary McAdoo, who is out of town, issued a circular to banks and trust companies urging that they should buy Treasury certificates in as large amount as practicable, and at least to half their estimated subscriptions, for the new bonds. In the circular, to which his name was signed, Secretary McAdoo also suggested that banks having to make payments for $100,000 or more of bonds, and having qualified as depositaries, will be permitted to cover their payments, in excess of the amount of Treasury certificates taken by them, by placing credit on their books to the account of the Treasurer of the United States.

An indication of the extent to which employers of large forces of men and women are buying Liberty Loan bonds for their employes and permitting payments in small installments was given today when it was learned from one distributing firm in New York that fifty-two corporations either have adopted this plan of aiding their employes or were considering it. Of the fifty-two corporations, thirty-nine reported their number of employes as approximating 168,327. The other thirteen did not report the number of their workers.

California Takes $500,000.

The State of California set an example for other States today by subscribing to $500,000 of the Liberty Loan. Accompanying the application for the bonds was a statement to the effect that the State would take more later.

A subscription for $300,000 of Liberty Loan bonds was made by the Driggs-Seabury Ordnance Company of Utica, N. Y., and Sharon, Penn., makers of the Lewis machine gun, which has large contracts with the Government.

The Treasury circular, issued today, which was signed by Secretary McAdoo, was as follows:

"Banks and trust companies having payments to make on account of subscriptions, and which have qualified as depositaries, may make payment upon such subscriptions on June 28 as to any amounts not paid in Treasury certificates of indebtedness by credit on their books to the account of the Treasurer of the United States, of which credit notice will be given in duplicate to the Treasurer and to the Federal Reserve Bank of the district on or before June 28.

"The amounts so credited will be withdrawn from time to time as required. How long they may be permitted to remain will depend in large measure on the extent to which the privilege of prepayment for the bonds of the Liberty Loan on or before June 28 is availed of. It will be necessary that the early installments paid upon subscriptions to the loan be devoted largely to the payment of the short-term Treasury certificates of indebtedness, which have been and will be placed throughout the country chiefly for making loans to Governments engaged in making war against Germany, and in part to meet unusual war expenditures of our own Government.

Shifting of Credits.

"As practically all the proceeds of the Liberty Loan, whether advanced to foreign Governments or expended directly by departments of the United States, will be spent in this country in payment of indebtedness heretofore or hereafter incurred, the bank resources of the United States as a whole will not be diminished, and the operation involves only a shifting of credits.

"Because of the great amount of work involved in passing upon the qualifications and securities of the banks and trust companies, which will have payments to make, it is deemed necessary until after July 1 to limit to those banks and trust companies having payments to make on subscriptions for $100,000 or more bonds, the provision for making payment by credit, the object in providing for payment by credit being to avoid any disturbance in the money position which might result from large payments being made from June 28 to Monday, July 2, a period when there is customarily a heavy movement of funds due to corporate interest and other payments.

Proceeds to Be Redeposited.

"As soon after July 2 as practicable the qualifications and securities of other banks and trust companies desiring to participate in redeposits will be passed upon, and after provision has been made for the immediate disbursements which the United States will have to make, up to and including July 1, the proceeds of the loan received from time to time, in full or installment payments, will be redeposited with qualified banks and trust companies in a proportion, yet to be determined, based upon the amounts of bonds of the Liberty Loan for which

Continued on Page 11.

Bethmann and Czernin to Confer With the Kaiser

BERLIN, May 18, (via London.)—Chancellor von Bethmann Hollweg and Dr. Zimmermann, the Foreign Minister, left today for German Great Headquarters, where they will meet Count Czernin, the Austro-Hungarian Foreign Secretary. They will continue the conference begun at Vienna recently, when Dr. von Bethmann Hollweg visited there.

The Tageblatt says that it understands that the Polish question and details in connection with the proclamation issued on Nov. 5, 1916, concerning Poland will be discussed.

The Reichstag will reconvene on July 5 for a three days' session, which will comprise the Summer legislative period.

CAMERONIA SUNK; 140 ON BOARD LOST

10,000-Ton Anchor Liner Had Been Used as a Troopship by the British Admiralty.

STAYED AFLOAT 40 MINUTES

Troops Escaped by Jumping to Destroyers—Announcement of Loss Long Delayed.

LONDON, May 17, (Delayed by Censor.)—The British Admiralty announced today that the transport Cameronia has been sunk. The statement follows:

"The British transport Cameronia, with troops, was torpedoed by an enemy submarine in the Eastern Mediterranean on April 15. One hundred and forty men are missing and are presumed to have been drowned."

The survivors of the Cameronia say the vessel was torpedoed in fine, calm weather in the afternoon. The submarine was not seen.

A large number of casualties were due to the explosion of the torpedo, which struck where there happened to be many soldiers. There was some excitement and confusion at the outset after the torpedo had struck, but discipline soon prevailed. The boats were launched, but one of them was smashed, and many lives were lost.

The Cameronia was afloat for forty minutes after she was torpedoed, which enabled several destroyers to run alongside. Soldiers from the Cameronia jumped on these boats in disciplined succession. The destroyers ceased taking on men as soon as they had ob-

Continued on Page 3.

SEA-AND-AIR FIGHT IN THE ADRIATIC

Austrian Light Cruisers Raid Allied Drifter Line and Sink 14 British Minesweepers.

CHASED TO THEIR OWN PORT

Italian Airmen Aiding—British Cruiser Torpedoed and an Italian Destroyer Sunk.

LONDON, May 18.—The British Admiralty announced today that fourteen drifters had been sunk in a raid by Austrian light cruisers in the Adriatic Sea and that the British light cruiser Dartmouth was torpedoed in a subsequent engagement with the Austrian warships, but reached port safely.

The Admiralty said that the British warships Dartmouth and Bristol pursued the Austrian vessels to a point near Cattaro when, battleships coming to their assistance, the British vessels were compelled to withdraw. The text of the statement reads:

"The Admiralty announces that from reports received from the Rear Admiral commanding the Adriatic squadron, supplemented by the Italian official communication, it appears that cruisers, subsequently reinforced by destroyers, raided the allied drifter line and succeeded in sinking fourteen British drifters, from which, according to the Austrian communication, seventy-two prisoners were taken.

"His Majesty's ship Dartmouth, with the Italian Rear Admiral aboard, and H. M. S. Bristol immediately chased the

Continued on Page 3.

Committee Rejects McAdoo's Plan to Levy $445,000,000 More Taxes

Zone Postal Plan May Be Stricken from the Taxation Bill—House Approves Higher Excess Profits and Retroactive Income Imposts.

Special to The New York Times.

WASHINGTON, May 18.—Prior to the convening of the House today the Committee on Ways and Means decided that it would not attempt to raise, at this time, the additional $445,000,000 in indirect taxes requested yesterday in Secretary McAdoo's communication to Chairman Kitchin. Republican members of the committee, as well as some Democrats, rebelled against the proposal to revamp the War Taxation bill and greatly add to its total after the committee had spent weeks in preparing a measure to produce $1,800,000,000.

The House when it met showed a disposition to stand by the bill as presented by the committee. The retroactive income tax section was approved by a vote of 123 to 54, all proposed amendments being rejected. The House likewise approved the excess profits tax carried in the bill, defeating various amendments to reduce and to increase the tax.

That a majority of the members of the Ways and Means Committee have practically reached the conclusion that there should be a change in the second-class mail postage rates recommended in the bill was learned today. Before the bill is put on final passage the committee is to hold another meeting to consider a revision of these rates. The indications are that the "zone system" rates will be stricken from the bill, and the committee will offer an amendment carrying out the suggestion of Chairman Moon of the House Committee on Post Office, reading as follows:

Strike out the section (the zone system section) and insert: Upon all newspapers, magazines and other publications regularly admitted as matter of the second class, when mailed by the publisher and no other, 1 cent per pound. Provided, that parcel post rates shall be charged upon all that portion of such newspapers, magazines or other publications which is devoted to paid advertising matter when addressed to any Post Office in the third, fourth, fifth, sixth, seventh, or eighth zones.

Certain members of the committee believe that the Moon amendment will not only produce more revenue, but that it also has a better chance of approval in the House than the original committee proposal, which calls for a flat rate on all second class matter, fixed by zones, ranging from 2 to 6 cents a pound. In the general debate on the Revenue bill the argument was repeatedly made that the Government was carrying advertising matter at a great loss, and the levy in postage should be against the advertising rather than the news sections of publications.

If the Moon amendment should be adopted the postal rate legislation will be less burdensome upon newspapers than magazines. Newspapers circulating within a comparatively limited field would not be materially affected. Periodicals and magazines with a country-wide circulation and a surplus of advertising matter would be hard hit by a levy of parcel post rates against the aggregate weight of all the advertising columns.

Excess Profits Tax Approved.

The House made fair progress today in its consideration of the tax measure. It approved the excess profits section and those portions of the bill levying additional taxes on beverages and tobaccos. The House reached but did not dispose of the sections imposing a 5 per cent. tax on various articles, including automobiles and musical instruments.

The Ways and Means Committee has agreed to consider the advisability of modifying the 5 per cent. levy on automobiles. This proposed tax has been strongly opposed by the automobile interests. No assurance has been given by the committee, however, that it will agree to a modification of the tax, but the question will be taken up in committee tomorrow, according to present plans.

Representative Madden of Illinois led an unsuccessful fight against the retroactive tax on incomes. This section provides that there shall be assessed against incomes for the calendar year 1916 an additional tax of one-third of the tax already paid. Under the section each person who has paid a tax on 1916 incomes would have to pay prior to Sept. 15 next, an amount equal to 33 1-3 per cent. of the original levy. Nevertheless the House adopted the retroactive tax which the Ways and Means Committee estimates will produce $108,000,000.

Wet and Dry Forces Clash.

Wet and dry forces clashed for almost two hours today over an amendment by Representative Howard of Georgia, designed to eliminate the liquor tax increases. Representatives Howard, Cooper of Ohio, Hersey of Maine, and others maintained that the liquor interests were indorsing the proposed increases, hoping thus to strengthen their position against absolute prohibition. The amendment was overwhelmingly defeated. The section as it was approved increases the tax on whisky from $1.10 to $2.20 a gallon and that on beer from $1.25 to $2.50.

Only a perfunctory fight was made on the excess profits tax section. Its opponents will carry their objection to the Senate. Representative Good of Iowa made the chief opposition, offering an amendment patterned somewhat after the English law, but it was decisively beaten.

list of sixteen divisions, to be designated as the fifth to the twentieth, inclusive.

The approximate dates for drafting the National Guard are:

July 15—New York, Pennsylvania, Ohio, West Virginia, Michigan, Wisconsin, Minnesota, Iowa, North Dakota, South Dakota, and Nebraska.

July 25—Maine, New Hampshire, Vermont, Massachusetts, Rhode Island, Connecticut, New Jersey, Delaware, Maryland, District of Columbia, Virginia, North Carolina, South Carolina, Tennessee, Illinois, Montana, Wyoming, Idaho, Washington, and Oregon.

Aug. 5—Indiana, Kentucky, Georgia, Florida, Alabama, Mississippi, Arkansas, Louisiana, Oklahoma, Texas, Missouri, Kansas, Colorado, New Mexico, Arizona, Utah, California.

"All National Guard organizations," said an official War Department announcement tonight, "both in and out of the Federal Service, will be recruited at once to full war strength. The necessary arms, equipment, and clothing for recruits is not at present on hand, but it is hoped all supplies will be available by the time the troops are sent to their concentration camps.

Like the regular army and the national army the National Guard army is to be organized on a divisional basis. New York, Pennsylvania, and Illinois will each supply sufficient guardsmen to form its own army division. The other divisions are to be formed by brigading and other wise amalgamating the units of groups of two or more States. The original National Guard mobilization plan called for the formation of only twelve divisions, numbered from five to sixteen, inclusive. The plan now adopted, which allows for formation of new units and great expansion of the present National Guard force, calls for the formation of sixteen divisions.

These divisions will be formed out of the various troops of the different States as follows:

Fifth—Maine, Massachusetts, Vermont, New Hampshire, Connecticut, and Rhode Island.
Sixth—New York.
Seventh—Pennsylvania.
Eighth—New Jersey, Delaware, Maryland, Virginia, and District of Columbia.
Ninth—Tennessee, North Carolina, and South Carolina.
Tenth—Georgia, Alabama, and Florida.
Eleventh—Michigan and Wisconsin.
Twelfth—Illinois.
Thirteenth—North Dakota, South Dakota, Nebraska, Iowa, and Minnesota.
Fourteenth—Kansas and Missouri.
Fifteenth—Texas and Oklahoma.
Sixteenth—Ohio and West Virginia.
Seventeenth—Kentucky and Indiana.
Eighteenth—Arkansas, Louisiana, and Mississippi.
Nineteenth—California, Nevada, Utah, Colorado, Arizona, and New Mexico.
Twentieth—Washington, Oregon, Idaho, Montana, and Wyoming.

32 Concentration Camps.

It will be necessary to establish thirty-two concentration camps to take care of the thirty-two army divisions to be formed out of the national army and the National Guard army. All camps for the National Guard divisions will be in the Southern, Southeastern, and Western Departments of the army. The plan for the distribution of the National Guard divisions and the National army divisions in concentration camps was announced today as follows:

Northeastern Department—First National Army Division.
Eastern Department—Second, Third, Fourth, and Fifth National Army Divisions.
Southeastern Department—Sixth, Seventh, and Twelfth National Army Divisions; also the Fifth, Sixth, Seventh, Eighth, Ninth, Tenth, Sixteenth, Seventeenth, and Eighteenth National Guard Divisions.
Southern Department—Fifteenth National Army Division; also the Eleventh, Twelfth, Thirteenth, Fourteenth, and Fifteenth National Guard Divisions.
Western Department—Sixteenth National Army Division; also the Nineteenth and Twentieth National Guard Division.
Central Department—Eighth, Ninth, Tenth, Eleventh, Thirteenth, and Fourteenth National Army Divisions.

Thus it will be seen that all of the National Guard army divisions, with the exception of two, will be trained and sheltered south of Mason and Dixon's line in the Southern and Southeastern Departments. The two exceptions will be the Nineteenth and Twentieth National Guard Divisions, which will be trained in the Western Department of the army.

Big Command for Wood.

Thus it is evident that Major Gen. Leonard Wood, by his transfer from the old Department of the East, with headquarters at New York City, to the newly formed Southeastern Department, with headquarters at Charleston, S. C., May 1 put him in line to command what is now becoming the most important military division of the country in the number of men to be concentrated in cantonments for training purposes in connection with the formation of the new armies. There will be twelve concentration camps in General Wood's department. Each will shelter an army division of 28,000 men. Three of these will be divisions of the new national draft army, while the other nine will be divisions of the expanded National Guard army.

All of the thirty-two concentration camps have not been selected. They are being chosen by the department commanders. But the location of six of the camps was announced today. These will be at Ayer, Mass.; El Paso, Texas; American Lake, Wash.; Atlanta, Ga.; Augusta, Ga., and Columbia, S. C. Three of them, those at Atlanta, Augusta, and Columbia are in General Wood's department.

The selection of all the cantonment sites is being rushed, and in some instances boards appointed by the department commanders are inspecting possible locations for the purpose of making recommendations to the departmental commander, who makes the selection. Their will be no public hearings, as there was said to be no time for these.

The requisites of a camp site were said to be: Space, good sanitary conditions, such as absence of marshes, with natural advantages for drainage; proximity to lines of transport, a good water supply.

The War Department is assembling vast quantities of supplies for the construction of the thirty-two camps, each of which will be a complete town, with sewerage, water works, lighting systems, streets, &c. The construction of the cantonments will be started immediately after the selection and approval of sites.

MILITIA WILL NEED 10,000 MORE RECRUITS

Some New York Regiments Must Increase 50 Per Cent. to Reach War Strength.

Officers attached to Division Headquarters of the National Guard saw yesterday that there would be no difficulty in putting the militia of this State on a war footing by July 15. Approximately 10,000 more men are needed to raise the force to the required war strength. This will mean an increase of 50 per cent. or even more in some of the regiments, which are now even below the designated peace strength.

Further than the newspaper announcements from Washington that the War Department has issued mobilization orders for the entire militia of the country, officers at New York headquarters received no official communication upon which they could act. They expect to receive official orders from Governor Whitman today, after which they will proceed to prepare the National Guard for Federal service.

Five regiments and a squadron of cavalry of the New York National Guard are already in Federal Service. These contingents are the Second, Third, Twenty-third, Forty-seventh, and Seventy-first Infantry, and a squadron of the First Cavalry. The organizations which are still in State service are the First, Tenth, Seventh, Fourteenth, Fifteenth, Sixty-ninth and Twelfth Infantry Regiments; Squadron A, the Twenty-second Engineers, eight troops of the First Cavalry, First Battalion Signal Corps, First, Second, Third and Fourth Field Hospitals, First, Second, Third and Fourth Ambulance Companies, Eighth, Ninth, and Thirteenth Coast Defense Commands, and the First and Second Field Artillery.

To assist in recruiting the National Guard to war strength representatives of about eighty trades and professions, including many prominent bankers, lawyers, and manufacturers held a meeting in the Bankers' Club at 120 Broadway yesterday and organized themselves into the Citizens' Preparedness Association. In the main they were the same men who, under the leadership of Colonel Charles H. Sherrill, organized the preparedness parade last Spring.

Sherrill Heads Movement.

Among those who were present were Colonel Thomas Denny of Denny, Pomroy & Co., bankers; Paul H. Cravath, Chairman of the Lawyers' Defense Committee; De Lancey Nicoll, Henry W. Taft, Michael Friedsam, head of Altman & Co.; Herbert H. Straus, Dr. W. J. Schieffelin, Bertrand H. Borden, and George T. Adee. Colonel Sherrill presided and was elected President of the Citizens' Preparedness Association, with Roger W. Allen as Secretary and Warren Barber as Treasurer.

The organization which was formed yesterday grew out of a movement started two weeks ago by Colonel Sherrill to swing all the trades of the State into an energetic recruiting campaign for the National Guard. He announced yesterday that eighty trades had responded to the call and were making every effort to fill the quota which was assigned by Colonel Sherrill to each trade to make up a grand total of 10,000 men, which would put the Guard on a war footing. Although these quotas were assigned arbitrarily, none of the trades has complained against having too much of a burden and some of them have even promised to raise more than the designated number of men.

All of the trade papers of the State are participating in the movement, and the work is being carried on with so much enthusiasm and energy that Colonel Sherrill said yesterday that not only 10,000 men, but twice or even three times that number would probably be raised for National Guard service by July 15. He read the following telegram which he received from Governor Whitman praising the movement and requesting the various trades to continue their organization throughout the war:

"I am very glad to learn that you have organized in over sixty trades for a Statewide movement to aid recruiting in response to General Stotesbury's telegram. I appreciate more than I can tell you all you have already done. Of course, the State must look to men of the character of those who compose your membership in her effort to respond to the requirements of the Federal Government. I suggest that these committees continue throughout the war, so that I may count on their advice and assistance when needed."

Bankers Issue Call.

It was announced at the meeting that the bankers and brokers' section had been fully organized with the following committee in charge of enrollments for that section: Col. Thomas Denny, Chairman; M. E. de Aguiro, President of the Consolidated Stock Exchange; Major H. K. Bird, Director of the Harriman National Bank; M. N. Buckner, President of the New York Trust Company; Oliver B. Bridgman, Captain Jay F. Carlisle, C. Douglass Green, Gates W. McGarrah, President of the Mechanics and Metals Bank; E. R. McCormick, H. G. S. Noble, President of the New York Stock Exchange; Major R. A. de Russy, and Lieutenant Howard C. Smith. The committee issues a call to the bankers and brokers of New York State, naming the following inducements for joining the guard:

Enlistments are voluntary as against conscription which is to follow:

Individuals will have an opportunity to select their commands and serve with their friends.

Voluntary service will be recognized as having prior claim to advancement over enforced service.

The guard age is from 18 to 45. The conscription age 21 to 30.

The names of all enlisted men reported to this office will be published in the Bankers and Brokers' Honor Roll in the trade publications.

Assurances have been given that militia regiments mustered into service will be promptly mustered out at the close of the emergency.

The call ends with the following statement:

"The realization that this war and its successful prosecution means life, health, and happiness to our State and nation and those we hold dear must be an impelling force for co-operation and self-sacrifice and an ambition to serve among us all. Employers and individuals alike must recognize the public call."

ATHLETES FOR MARINE CORPS.

Fifty College Men Will Take Examinations for Commissions.

Four hundred more men are needed to fill the First Reserve Engineer Regiment, which is being recruited in this city for immediate service in France. A preliminary detachment of the regiment will go into camp at Fort Totten on Tuesday and prepare the ground for the rest of the division. Recruiting for the regiment has not been very rapid in the last three days. Yesterday's enlistment totaled only forty men, but the recruiting officers are still hopeful of having the regiment completed by Tuesday.

Captain Frank Evans, in charge of marine recruiting for New York, announced yesterday that fifty college athletes would take examinations for commissions in the United States Marine Corps at the Brooklyn Navy Yard on Monday. These men were all recommended for commissions by Presidents of various Eastern universities. Among the Yale men are Harry Le Gore, the football star; John W. Overton, Captain of the track team, and Louis A. Ferguson, Captain of the swimming team. Princeton is represented by William D. Jewett, champion heavyweight wrestler, Harold B. Hoskins, Captain of the soccer team, and William A. Eddy, Captain of the basket ball team.

The Marine Corps recruited twenty-five men from New York yesterday. The Navy enlisted by 6 P. M. a total of fifty men from the greater city, and the regular army about seventy men.

G. F. Glover, superintendent of St. Luke's Hospital on Morningside Heights, announced yesterday that the Norrie Pavilion of the Hospital, which had never before been occupied, would be opened on Monday for the treatment free of charge of men who had tried to enlist in the army or navy and had been rejected because of defects which could be readily corrected under proper medical care.

RECRUITING FOR ARMY TAKES FURTHER DROP

Only 1,482 Men Enlisted on Thursday—Pennsylvania Is Still the Banner State.

Special to The New York Times.

WASHINGTON, May 18.—A still further falling off in the daily recruiting for the army was shown by complete reports of Thursday's enlistments. Only 1,482 joined the colors, which is a falling off of more than 25 per cent. from the daily average maintained for the past few weeks. The total number of recruits since April 1 now is 74,933 men.

Pennsylvania continues to be the banner State in daily recruiting with its record of 208 men obtained Thursday. The daily statement of recruiting as issued by Adjt. Gen. McCain follows:

	Obtained May 17.	Total to May 17.		Obtained May 17.	Total to May 17.
Alabama	14	529	Nebraska	15	1,435
Arizona	..	121	*Nevada	6	389
Arkansas	13	537	N. H.	32	213
California	60	2,390	N. J.	39	1,924
Colorado	24	681	N. M.	12	122
Connecticut	7	545	New York	114	5,544
Delaware	..	43	N. Car.	18	647
D. of Col.	..	170	N. Dak.	..	225
Florida	9	546	Ohio	52	2,557
Georgia	19	2,132	Oklahoma	19	1,103
Idaho	10	434	*Oregon	22	1,867
Illinois	130	7,390	Penn.	208	5,139
Indiana	51	5,177	Rhode Isl.	3	221
Iowa	39	2,258	S. Car.	22	490
Kansas	44	2,033	S. Dak.	..	459
Kentucky	18	1,304	Tennessee	12	1,034
Louisiana	10	847	Texas	53	3,067
Maine	..	311	*Utah	9	541
Maryland	4	758	*Vermont	2	46
Mass.	63	2,261	Virginia	6	709
Michigan	78	3,738	Washington	12	815
Minnesota	25	1,598	West Va.	38	764
Mississippi	11	374	Wisconsin	18	898
Missouri	83	3,447	Wyoming	14	203
Montana	7	292			

*Quota obtained.
Total quota, 183,898.
Total obtained for May 17, 1,482.
Total obtained since April 1, 74,933.

PERSHING WON FAME IN MORO CAMPAIGNS

Jumped Over 862 Officers from Captain to Brigadier General by Roosevelt.

FOUGHT SIOUX AND APACHES

"Black Jack" Was Youngest West Pointer Ever Made General in Peace Times.

Maj. Gen. John J. Pershing, the famous "Black Jack" of the regulars, will go down in history as the first American army officer to command troops on the battlefields of Europe. He (Pershing) is one of the officers who were picked by Colonel Roosevelt, when the Colonel was President, for rapid promotion to the highest of army commands.

General Pershing was just a dashing, much-loved Captain of cavalry when in 1906 Colonel Roosevelt startled the country by sending his name to the Senate for confirmation as a Brigadier General. The other officers advanced by Colonel Roosevelt were Major Gen. Leonard Wood and Major Gen. J. Franklin Bell, the latter of whom recently succeeded General Wood as commanding officer of the Eastern Department, on Governors Island.

Pershing is a West Pointer of the West Pointers, as a classmate of his expressed it not so very long ago. He was graduated into the regular service as a Second Lieutenant of cavalry in 1886 and he began to make himself heard of before he had been in the saddle a year. It was to the Sixth United States Cavalry that Pershing was assigned shortly after he received his diploma from the Military Academy.

In the first few years of his service Pershing fought in the fierce border campaigns against the Apache Indians of Arizona, and he was again heard of when in 1890 he led his sturdy troopers in the turbulent Sioux wars of the early nineties. He was in the thick of the fighting that marked the brief warfare that was waged by the regulars against the Spaniards in Cuba in 1898, and shortly after the Treaty of Paris was signed and the Philippines came under the American flag he was among the first to be ordered to duty in the new possessions.

Arriving in the Philippines, General Pershing, then a Captain, was promptly ordered into the Moro country, where as one of the leaders against the then fierce and intensely anti American Moros he was soon to gain fame and honor and win the single star of a Brigadier. At the time of his nomination for that rank in 1906 he was the youngest West Pointer ever named as a General of the regular army in a time of peace. In order to reward Pershing President Roosevelt jumped him over 862 officers who were his seniors in rank.

Eleven years ago the big problem in the Philippines was still the pacification of the Moros. Those splendid warriors, hundreds of whom are now serving in the crack organization known as the Philippine Scouts, fought inch by inch the Americans and refused to take word of Governors and commanders sent to mollify them that the United States was their friend.

Pershing was ordered to finish the Moro campaign and was named Governor of Mindanao and commander of the troops operating in that part of the province where the Moro opposition was still a problem of the first magnitude. From a distance of several thousands of miles the job did not sound big at the time, but a more difficult task has seldom, if ever, been placed on the shoulders of an officer of the regular army. He gritted his teeth and undertook the work with his famous smile. He had a picked lot of regulars under him, every man of whom he knew and trusted and every one of whom knew and loved "Black Jack."

The Moros that Pershing was called upon to bring to terms had mobilized in the crater of an extinct volcano called Bud Dajo, on the island of Jolo. To drive them out had been a task with which the army had contended since 1906. Pershing announced to his men that the Moros were coming out of the crater if it took him ten years to accomplish the job.

There were 600 Moros—every one a Mohammedan fanatic—in the crater fortification when Pershing started "to clean out the mountain hole." Without Bud Dajo safely and securely in American control the Moro problem could never be solved.

With a thousand men, half of them his own trusted troopers, and the others picked Filipino scouts, the campaign for Bud Dajo began. The Americans and the scouts had to proceed through miles and miles of dense jungles, opposed every yard of the way by the fierce Moros. But Pershing kept on, and finally he fought his way to the foot of the mountain.

Pershing's jungle fighters cut a trail around the mountain, and, fortifying themselves from attack from above, began the siege. The soldiers formed a complete cordon around the mountain and calmly instituted a campaign of watching for the first sign of the Moros leaving the crater, and waiting a chance to get them when they tried to cut through the cordon.

In their retreat to the crater the Moros had been so hotly pursued that for once they had been unable to take with them the supplies that would make possible a long stand. At last the "iron ring" began to make itself felt, and in small detachments the Moros tried to gain the open jungle by dashes through the American cordon. Every dash was frustrated, the fanatics rushing forth to certain death. Finally, on Christmas Day, 1911, the 400 Moros still in the crater did something a Moro seldom does—they marched down the mountainside and surrendered. A few reached the jungle, but the regulars pursued, beat the brush, and in the end these desperadoes paid the penalty of their daring.

With Bud Dajo captured, Pershing set about to finish his job. On Jan. 11, 1912, there followed on Lake Seit a stiff engagement, which resulted in the death of eighteen Moros and the serious wounding of two Americans, one of the latter Lieutenant H. H. McGee, U. S. A. For nearly eighteen months more the campaign lasted. Every day or two there was a skirmish of some sort, but Pershing kept on, determined never to stop until the Moros had been completely subdued and American authority recognized.

General Pershing was still in the Philippines in 1913, finishing up the pacification of the Moros. That task may be said to have been accomplished when he won the Battle of Bagsag in June, 1913. The Moros had made a last stand, and the Sultan of Jolo, who commanded them, had told them that victory meant that he would become lord of the United States as well as of Jolo in the event the Americans were defeated.

At dawn, June 12, 1913, General Pershing ordered his artillery to open fire and then followed the charge of his cavalry and infantry forces. The battle ended with the complete triumph of Pershing's men and the breaking finally of Moro opposition to American rule.

In January, 1916, General Pershing returned to the United States, and was assigned to the command of the Eighth Brigade of the regular army, with headquarters at El Paso. There he remained until the Villa raid on Columbus, N. M., when President Wilson ordered a punitive expedition into Mexico, and placed General Pershing in command.

The way in which Pershing handled the Mexican problem met with the entire approval of President Wilson. No officer in the army stands higher in the estimation of the President than does General Pershing, and army officers have been predicting ever since war was declared on Germany that he would lead the first American troops sent to Europe.

On the death of Major Gen. Funston, who was General Pershing's immediate superior on the border, President Wilson nominated General Pershing as successor and assigned him to the command of all troops on the Mexican border. That command he retained until a few days ago, when he was ordered to Washington to receive instructions and the command of the first American troops ever ordered to fight on European soil.

In June, 1916, General Pershing wrote an article for THE NEW YORK TIMES, in which he made a plea for universal military training in this country. On the day that his appointment to the European command is announced he sees the system he urged made a law.

"With general military training in this country," wrote General Pershing, "there would be less talk of hyphenated Americans, because their military education would make them an integral part of our body politic. The assimilation of the thousands of foreigners who come to America would be much more rapid if given military training, especially if they could have service in the army. Young men would go through it together and become comrades and friends. Compulsory military training would cement and unify the various classes of foreign and native population as no other process yet proposed. In such a school they would not only receive military instruction, and learn our language and our ways, but, better still, their association with native Americans would inspire them with American ideals.

"Whether native or foreign born, military training should be made an important part of the education of every young man and should be a prerequisite to his exercise of the right of suffrage. From the sole viewpoint of its effect upon the foreign element, it is time for every American who is concerned in the destiny of his country to give deep thought to the question of universal military training."

General Pershing is a son-in-law of United States Senator Warren of Wyoming. Two years ago he suffered a great bereavement when his wife and two little daughters were burned to death at the Presidio of San Francisco. His little son alone was saved, and Congress awarded the Medal of Honor to a soldier for saving the life of little "Jack" Pershing, Jr.

(Photo © International Film Service.)

General John J. Pershing

Who Will Command Our Regulars Soon to Go to France.

PERSHING TO LEAD TROOPS TO FRANCE

Continued from Page 1.

rendered many conspicuous public services and proved his gallantry in many striking ways. Politically, too, it would no doubt have a very fine effect and make a profound impression. But this is not the time or the occasion for compliment or for any action not calculated to contribute to the immediate success of the war. The business now in hand is undramatic, practical, and of scientific definiteness and precision. I shall act with regard to it at every step and in every particular under expert and professional advice from both sides of the water.

Need All Trained Officers.

"That advice is that the men most needed are men of the ages contemplated in the draft provision of the present bill, not men of the age and sort contemplated in the section which authorizes the formation of volunteer units, and that for the preliminary training of the men who are to be drafted we shall need all of our experienced officers. Mr. Roosevelt told me, when I had the pleasure of seeing him a few weeks ago, that he would wish to have associated with him some of the most effective officers of the regular army. He named many of those whom he would desire to have designated for the service, and they were men who cannot possibly be spared from the too small force of officers at our command for the much more pressing and necessary duty of training regular troops to be put into the field in France and Belgium as fast as they can be got ready.

"The first troops sent to France will be taken from the present forces of the regular army, and will be under the command of trained soldiers only.

"The responsibility for the successful conduct of our own part in this great war rests upon me. I could not escape it if I would. I am too much interested in the cause we are fighting for to be interested in anything but success. The issues involved are too immense for me to take into consideration anything whatever except the best, most effective, most immediate means of military action. What these means are I know from the mouths of men who have seen war as it is now conducted, who have no illusions, and to whom grim matter is a matter of business. I shall centre my choice upon those means and let everything else wait.

"I should be deeply to blame should I do otherwise, whatever the argument of policy for a personal gratification or advantage."

Sending Colonel Roosevelt or any force of volunteers to France was strongly, even bitterly, opposed by the General Staff, and it is supposed that the General Staff's views were communicated to President Wilson by Secretary Baker. The definite decision not to send Colonel Roosevelt to France or accept the authority conferred to raise volunteers was [illegible] in the [illegible] regular meeting of the Cabinet this afternoon. The decision to send to Europe a division of regular troops without delay was the outcome of a compromise between the expressed wish of the French Government and the view of the General Staff. The General Staff as a whole was opposed to sending any troops to the fighting areas until the War Department had completed the organization and equipment of the army of regulars, National Guard, and drafted men, amounting approximately to 1,200,000 men of all three classes in the first increment.

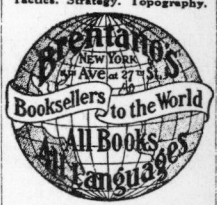

The French Government, however, virtually appealed to this Government, at first informally, and later in a way to show that compliance with the appeal was regarded as vital, to send troops to the battle front with the least possible delay. Marshal Joffre made known this desire of France to representatives of American newspapers soon after he reached Washington, and his words were emphasized in the statement furnished to THE NEW YORK TIMES this week by General Pétain, the new Commander in Chief of the French armies in the field. It was obvious from what General Pétain said that what France needed was men; in fact, he said so in as many words.

President Responsive.

To these appeals the President has been responsive, although in taking the action announced tonight, with reference to the Pershing expedition, he went contrary to the ideas of a majority of the members of the General Staff, who contended that an untrained army or a small army would be useless in the trenches. There was a disinclination in some quarters, however, to concur in the opinion of the General Staff that it was desirable to wait a year while the new army was being trained before attempting to send an expedition across the Atlantic. According to the General Staff view the French Government wanted Americans to fill up the gaps in the French ranks.

It was contended by military critics here that the scheme advanced by General Pétain through the columns of THE NEW YORK TIMES did not contemplate having the American volunteers for whom he called serve as a single unit under the Stars and Stripes, but distributed among the French troops under the tricolor of France. [illegible]

Under the voluntary censorship [illegible] the formation of the Pershing expedition. [illegible] its departure for France will not be long delayed.

Until the War Department announcement cleared away doubt, it was supposed that the first expedition would be composed of National Guard organizations as well as regulars. There had been indications that National Guard forces were being prepared for service abroad, but the War Department declined to furnish any information.

General Pershing arrived in Washington last week from El Paso, Texas, where he established his headquarters after his return from the punitive expedition sent into Mexico to disband the Villistas. He has been [illegible] that he would be placed in command of the first military expedition sent from this country to the theatre of conflict in Europe.

Mr. Balfour and members of the British War Mission were also of the opinion that American troops should be sent to France without delay. Their reasons, however, were not entirely similar to those advanced by French representatives. It was apparent that the main reason for the anxiety of France to have Americans on the battle front was that stated so frankly by General Pétain: "But what is imperative now is men," he said.

"What France needs most is men—infantry." All that was said by the French representatives in Washington bore out that statement. The British, on the other hand, stressed that the presence of American troops in the trenches would have a marked psychological effect upon the French and British forces in the field, and would cause a corresponding lowering of the morale of the German armies. There is also reason to believe that the British observers here reached the conclusion that America needed something to awaken it to a realization that it was actually engaged in the bloody European conflict, and that nothing would better accomplish this than the sending of an expeditionary force to France. The knowledge that American soldiers were fighting in the trenches would stimulate American enthusiasm, with all that that would mean, in the opinion of some of the British visitors.

The Pershing expedition may be said to have been ordered to Europe for two reasons—to strengthen the French battle line and to produce the desired psychological effect in all the allied countries, including the United States. In these days a division of American troops, consisting of about 28,000 men, is a mere handful in comparison with the enormous armies that have been engaged in the present conflict. But it was felt by the Administration that it would be well to have the Stars and Stripes shown on the battle line and at the same time furnish France with some assistance in carrying out the great offensive in which her armies are engaged in combination with those of Great Britain.

Expect Criticism in Congress.

What effect will be produced in Congress by the refusal of President Wilson to send Colonel Roosevelt to Europe could not be ascertained with any degree of accuracy tonight for the reason [illegible] the Senators and Representatives interested in the Colonel's cause could not be found. Their course is problematical. But the question as to what was likely to follow a decision by the President not to send Colonel Roosevelt to France has been discussed here with animation in the past several days.

It is not doubted that the President will be criticised by friends of Colonel Roosevelt in the Senate and the House. The President understood the intent of the Senate and the House was admitted by him in the statement he issued tonight, and after that admission he proceeded to give his reasons for believing it unwise to form a volunteer force or to appoint Colonel Roosevelt to any command.

It has been suggested here within the past few days that if the country should obtain the idea that President Wilson unfairly treated Colonel Roosevelt it would cause widespread indignation that [illegible] way of suggestion as to the effect of adverse action by the President on the desire of Colonel Roosevelt to go to France.

The opinion was expressed tonight that friends of Colonel Roosevelt might take umbrage at some of the comments of the President in his statement on the ground that he was ironical at the Colonel's expense. The reference to the "very fine effect" and "profound impression" that might be made politically by sending the Colonel to Europe was mentioned, as was the statement that "the business now at hand is undramatic."

Pershing Promoted by Roosevelt.

Elsewhere there is a disposition to contend that President Wilson turned a very clever political trick when he combined the selection of General Pershing to command the first American expedition to France with his announcement of his refusal to send Colonel Roosevelt there with a volunteer contingent.

It was recalled in this connection that General Pershing owed his first military boost to Colonel Roosevelt, then President of the United States. General Pershing was a Captain of the regular army, who was making an enviable record in the Philippines insurrection when President Roosevelt promoted him to the grade of Brigadier General, a tremendous jump over many officers senior to Captain Pershing in years and service.

President Roosevelt was severely criticised for this action. It was contended that he had been influenced in doing so by the fact that Captain Pershing was the son-in-law of Senator Francis E. Warren of Wyoming, then Chairman of the Senate Committee on Military Affairs.

The nomination was confirmed by the Senate, and since then General Pershing has given great satisfaction to the War Department. It is asserted in some quarters that Colonel Roosevelt has been placed in a position where he cannot criticise the selection of the commander of the expeditionary force, and by some this is held to be an advantage to President Wilson in any controversy that might arise over the contention that the President has acted unfairly to Colonel Roosevelt and ignored the wish of Congress.

ROOSEVELT SILENT ON WILSON'S ACTION

Refuses to Discuss Plans for Going to France—Had Wired Offer to President.

Special to The New York Times.

OYSTER BAY, May 18.—Colonel Roosevelt was told tonight of President Wilson's decision not to allow the expedition to France. He showed acute interest, but refused to make any comment for publication until he had had time to study the full text of the President's statement.

The decision of the President came with sharply defined force, for this afternoon, after receiving information that the measure was before the President for final action, the Colonel sent a telegram to the White House tendering his services.

"I sent to President Wilson this afternoon a message offering to raise a division at once, or if it seemed desirable to him, two divisions," said the Colonel.

"No, no; not tonight," he replied to requests to make a statement as to what his plans would be with regard to going to France. He would not say whether he would contemplate any plan for offering his services in other capacities. He received an offer of a Major Generalship in the New York National Guard from Governor Whitman.

Earlier in the day Colonel Roosevelt expressed hearty approval of the suggestion of General Pétain, as printed in THE NEW YORK TIMES Wednesday morning, that France have American volunteers at once, to be trained in France by French officers.

"I, of course, emphatically agree with General Pétain that American volunteers should be sent abroad at once," he said, "and if I am allowed to take them over I should welcome the chance to have them given intensive training by the use of French officers in whatever way would most quickly and efficiently produce results."

While the Colonel took interest in the suggestion of General Pétain, it is said that he has been advised that the French and British Governments would be very slow to accept the services of any body of Americans who did not come to the arena of war with the approval of President Wilson.

There, of course, remains open to the Colonel the chance to accept the commission Governor Whitman has offered him, which in due course would bring him face to face with Federal service. At that he would have to be acceptable to the General Staff before he could go to France to fight. Friends of the Colonel say that he is not anxious for rank, but merely wants to have a part in whipping Germany. Incidentally he is 58 years old, and it would [illegible] come under the age limit.

Right up to tonight the Colonel continued to receive offers from well-known men to raise forces for his proposed division. He said today that Adjt. Gen. Barber of New Jersey offered to raise a full regiment in New Jersey, or two battalions. Governor Edge also offered to recruit a regiment. General Barber is an ex-army officer, and served in the Philippines with a volunteer regiment. The Colonel has received offers from members of Congress of several Northwestern States to raise regiments. Offers of two regiments have also come from Tennessee.

Colonel Roosevelt was asked to reply to statements published this week that he was only a paper army.

"I say," he replied, "that I can raise four divisions, two of them at once."

The Colonel probably will hold a meeting in a few days with the men who have been leaders in his plan to raise a volunteer division, after which he is expected to make an announcement of his intentions with regard to the war.

Special to The New York Times.

ALBANY, N. Y., May 18.—Governor Whitman declined tonight to discuss President Wilson's statement that Colonel Roosevelt would not be sent to France, and that no volunteers would be sent at this time. The Governor recalled that he had offered a Major Generalship to Colonel Roosevelt to recruit in this State. It was pointed out that this commission was only good in the State, and that if Colonel Roosevelt should accept it and recruit a division it would be necessary to get Federal permission before he could go to France.

HOSPITAL UNIT IS NOW IN ENGLAND

First American Expedition, Dispatched Secretly, Will Go to the Front Promptly.

FIVE OTHERS TO FOLLOW

Physicians, Nurses, and Many Hospital Corps Enlisted Men Included in the Personnel.

Special Cable to THE NEW YORK TIMES.

LONDON, May 18.—The first contingent of the American Army to reach this country arrived at a British port today. It is a unit of the Medical Corps with a personnel of 200 to 300, and includes a staff of surgeons, about sixty-five nurses, and three companies of enlisted men. The men looked smart in khaki uniforms, as did the nurses in blue uniforms with a red cross over the left breast of the cloak. The contingent was greeted on its arrival in port by the British General and his staff. This officer mounted a rostrum on the saloon deck, with the Stars and Stripes on one side and the Union Jack on the other, and addressed the corps. He welcomed the contingent to these shores on behalf of the British Army, and thanked its members for what they had done and for what they were about to do.

Colonel Bradley, from the American Embassy, also addressed the men while the officers were greeted by the American Consul.

Major Harry L. Gilchrist, leader of the unit in an interview, said:

"It is quite true that we are the first contingent of the American army to arrive, but you may be sure there are more to follow. The men of America simply are crazy to be over here and in the game. It was a very difficult job when we came to select from the hundreds that presented themselves at few hours' notice. They all wanted to come, but we were limited to the requirements of one unit, and so some had to be rejected."

Questioned about the trip across, Major Gilchrist said that it could not have been better, and added: "When we were preparing to come all the papers were full of the success of the German submarines, so we did not want the Germans to know anything, or they would have been after us for sure. At a certain point we were met by an American destroyer, which brought us into port. We saw nothing of any enemy submarines, and altogether had a very pleasant trip."

The contingent after disembarking passed on to another town where it received a civic reception. Led by their commander, the contingent gave lusty cheers for King George. The Mayor of the town then led in three cheers for President Wilson. During the reception the band played "The Star-Spangled Banner" and "God Save the King," while the Americans stood at salute. The American flag was flown side by side with Union Jack over all public buildings.

LONDON, May 18.—The American Hospital unit which reached England today is the first of six which are going to France. After a brief stay in England, the unit will be sent to the Continent, where it will take charge of a base hospital behind the British front. The hospital will have accommodations for 500 patients and be fully equipped by the British hospital service.

Sir Alfred Keogh, Surgeon General of the British Army, in making the foregoing announcement to The Associated Press, today said that the arrival of the American unit was the result of plans completed by Secretary of War Baker and Colonel T. H. Goodwin of the British hospital service, whom Surgeon General Keogh recently sent to the United States to confer with the army medical authorities there. Surgeon General Keogh said that it had been decided to send from America six units, comprising about 1,500 persons.

WASHINGTON, May 18.—The American hospital unit whose safe arrival in England is reported in the foregoing dispatches is Base Hospital No. 4 of Cleveland, commanded by Major Harry L. Gilchrist, Medical Corps, United States Army, and under the direction of Dr. George W. Crile. It is understood that it will be in the war zone in a day or two.

It is the first of six army base hospitals which have been ordered abroad for service in France, the movements of which have been kept secret by the War Department. Each includes, besides the officers in command and the directors, 24 physicians, 2 dentists, 65 Red Cross nurses, and 150 enlisted men of the Army Medical Corps.

Major Elbert E. Persons, Army Medical Corps, has been ordered to Philadelphia to organize motor ambulance companies for service in Europe in connection with American army hospital units, either now on the way to the front or soon to be sent. Major Percy L. Jones, Medical Corps, will assist in organizing the companies.

Today's army orders show that many officers have been ordered to duty from the Medical Officers' Reserve Corps and assigned to Base Hospital No. 21 at St. Louis and other army hospital units, including Base Hospital No. 10 at Chicago and No. 12 at Philadelphia.

MORE MEDICAL UNITS GOING.

Three, Totaling 600 Surgeons and Nurses, Await Transport.

Three units from Chicago, Philadelphia, and St. Louis, respectively, totaling 600 surgeons, nurses, and enlisted men of the United States Army Medical Corps and National Red Cross, have arrived at a city on the Atlantic coast ready to embark on two steamships, which will convey them to a British port. This will be the fourth detail to sail carrying the Stars and Stripes to the European war zone and making altogether 1,340 surgeons, nurses, and enlisted men, who will act abroad as ambulance drivers, stretcher bearers, and hospital orderlies.

There are still thirty-six units remaining in the country. Six of these are composed of staffs drawn from New York. Each unit comprises twenty-five surgeons, fifty nurses, and the remainder the administrative staff, consisting of orderlies, chauffeurs, and litter bearers, most of the latter being recruited from the colleges.

Before they leave for France undergraduates of Marietta College, Ohio, who have formed the Marietta section of the American Ambulance Corps, will be tendered a reception on Thursday, May 24, in the Astor Gallery of the Waldorf-Astoria by the Ohio Society of New York. The students will bring twenty ambulances with them, which they will operate in the fighting zone. At the reception delegations from the Daughters of Ohio, National Society of Ohio Women, Marietta College men, and the Miami University alumni will be present.

James S. Alexander, Jr., son of James S. Alexander, President of the National Bank of Commerce, is going to France to join the field service of the American Ambulance Corps. He is 20 years old, and is a senior at Williams College. A degree has been conferred upon him in anticipation of the regular commencement exercises in June.

FRENCH OFFICERS EXPECTED

Cadets at Madison Barracks May Receive Special Instruction.

Special to The New York Times.

SACKET HARBOR, N. Y., May 18.—Though nothing official has yet been received at camp, it is thought more than likely that French officers will be detailed here, probably early in July, to conduct a special course in the military tactics formulated by the war. Part of the instruction, it is said, will consist of trench work and explanation of the French methods of repelling gas and liquid fire attacks.

Right now the men are working harder than most of them ever toiled before, and when they look ahead at the elaborate program slated for the next two months, they apparently wonder what is going to happen. One source of grumbling has been eliminated with the complete construction of the cadet barracks. Early today the last of them were finished, and the men, up to now, paired off in other quarters, picked up their cots and equipment and moved in. There is still plenty of room for improvement in the bathing facilities, but it is understood that this part of the camp will soon be up to standard as the result of a recommendation made by Major Gen. Bell. When the General inspected the baths he is reported to have said there should be forty showers where there are now eight.

Another step forward has been the establishment of separate mess for each of the ten student quarters, and the mess is excellent.

In between the regular drills and practice marches the entire corps, except three companies, who will be treated tomorrow, was taken to Surgeon Chamberlain and inoculated against smallpox and typhoid. Tonight with sore arms and the usual slight fever, sick call was largely attended. The post hospital, which was built to accommodate the cases that might develop among 800 men, will be greatly enlarged. Work has already been started on an annex large enough for two additional wards.

In preparation for the cavalry and field artillery drills, about 350 horses are expected here. In the absence of any regular army field artillery post in this department, it is possible that several batteries from either the First or Second Field Artillery, N. G. N. Y., may be ordered here with their guns. New York City may also be asked to furnish the all-necessary band, as the present music is made up of sixteen musicians from the Third Infantry, N. G. N. Y., and so far their place in the military musical world is remarkable only for one thing—the fact that there aren't instruments enough to play the "Star-Spangled Banner" in the proper rousing way.

LET MORE GUARDSMEN GO TO PLATTSBURG

War Department Rescinds Order Limiting the Number That Might Attend the Camp.

Special to The New York Times.

PLATTSBURG, May 18.—The National Guard contingent from New York and New England which was expected here tomorrow will not arrive until Monday, according to word received today at camp headquarters. There will be 460 New England guardsmen and 313 from New York State. This number is in addition to the 2 per cent. of the National Guard's strength already permitted to enroll in the Plattsburg course.

It has been found that there were more men from the guard in camp than the allotted quota, notably from Squadron A and the Seventh Regiment of New York and the First Corps of Cadets of Boston. Because of this fact these men feared they might be ordered home. Colonel Wolf sent a list of the men in excess of the quota to the War Department, and yesterday received an order from Washington to the effect that these men would be deducted from the number arriving Monday. Today, however, came a wire countermanding this order. The guardsmen will be permitted to remain where they are, while the contingent which detrains Monday will bring its allotted strength. The addition of the guardsmen will bring the camp's enrollment up to 5,700.

The work at the camp is steadily increasing, as the instructors assert that if the men are driven as hard in the first as in the last weeks of the camp many will grow stale before the three months are up. Ponchos, packs, and intrenching tools were issued today, although the men will have no use for the latter two articles until later. A short hike of about three miles was taken in the morning.

Conferences were held in the afternoon, taking up sighting exercises with the rifle and the manual of interior guard duty. These conferences are usually held outside company barracks, the company instructor using the doorway for a rostrum with the men seated on the ground in a semicircle. A thundershower drove the students into their barracks, and the men listened to the lecturer sprawled on the floor or seated on the double decked bunks.

A baseball game is scheduled at the camp on Sunday between the Newark and Montreal teams of the International League. Plattsburg has always been considered a live baseball town, and the attraction will draw many visitors to the camp.

Forty-two Coast Artillerymen are expected at the camp to assist the single cavalry troop now at the barracks in garrison duty. The cavalrymen have been so much in demand as orderlies and buglers that all the drills they are likely to receive will be their target practice on the rifle range.

TO END CONSCRIPTION 4 MONTHS AFTER WAR

Senate Puts Limit on Draft Act by Amending the Army Deficiency Bill.

Special to The New York Times.

WASHINGTON, May 18.—Through an amendment which the Senate tacked to the Army and Navy Deficiency bill the period of conscription is to be limited to four months after the end of the war. This was accomplished by making the amendment a part of the budget. The amendment was put in by Senators Hoke Smith and McKellar and passed by a viva voce vote.

When the Senate began consideration of the bill Senator Smith, who had failed, along with Senator Stone and other supporters, to have the limited period clause placed in the draft bill, opened up a fight for it.

The amendment provides that the service of all persons selected by draft and all enlistments under the provisions of the act to increase the military establishment, "shall be for the period of the war, unless sooner terminated by discharge or otherwise." It adds that "whenever the war shall cease and at the conclusion of peace between the United States and its enemies in the present war, the President shall so declare by proclamation to that effect, and after four months from the date of the said proclamation the provisions of said act, in so far as they authorize compulsory service, shall cease to be in force and effect."

Before this amendment was adopted Senator Hitchcock of the Senate Military Committee offered another to muster out the drafted men six months after the war, but the Smith-McKellar amendment prevailed.

"All the News That's Fit to Print."

The New York Times.

THE WEATHER
Fair today and tomorrow; moderate northwest to north winds.

VOL. LXVII...NO. 21,839. NEW YORK, FRIDAY, NOVEMBER 9, 1917.—TWENTY-TWO PAGES. ONE CENT In Greater New York. | TWO CENTS Within Commuting Distance. | THREE CENTS Elsewhere.

REVOLUTIONISTS SEIZE PETROGRAD; KERENSKY FLEES; PLEDGE IS GIVEN TO SEEK "AN IMMEDIATE PEACE"; ITALIANS AGAIN DRIVEN BACK; LOSE 17,000 MORE MEN

WOODS MUST GO AS POLICE HEAD, HYLAN DECIDES

Mayor-Elect Will Ask Him to Retire if He Fails to Resign.

SUCCESSOR NOT YET FOUND

Murphy Will Refrain from Interference, Congressman Smith Declares.

HYLAN SHOCKS JOB HUNTERS

Announces Delay in Considering Appointments—Craig Against Pay-as-You-Go Plan.

Insists Emperor Charles Will Be Polish Ruler

Special Cable to THE NEW YORK TIMES.

THE HAGUE, Nov. 8.—In spite of recent denials, the Lokal-Anzeiger repeats that the Austrian Emperor is to be named King of Poland. It says this was decided on at a Crown Council on Monday.

Poland is to be joined to Austria, and Galicia is to belong to the future Kingdom of Poland. Lithuania and Courland will be separate States, such as Prussia, and be represented by Grand Dukes. The paper points out that in Austria even the Germanic parties appear to approve this, but that special emphasis is laid on and guarantees demanded for "the strengthening of Germanic-Austria."

The paper seems to question whether German interests have been sufficiently considered in this settlement.

THREAT OF DICTATOR IN GERMAN SNARL

Government Attempts to Force Dropping of Demand for Radical Vice Chancellor.

HERTLING DENIES PROMISES

Opposition to Attack Chancellor as Soon as Reichstag Meets Unless He Yields.

OTTO H. KAHN TALKS FINANCE WITH WILSON

New Yorker at the White House Discusses Economic Condition of the Country.

CADORNA IS OUTFLANKED

A General Among the Troops Cut Off on the Middle Tagliamento.

INVADERS CAPTURE 80 GUNS

Berlin Reckons Total at More Than 2,300; That of Prisoners Over 250,000.

ROME ADMITS WITHDRAWAL

Official Report Shows That Rearguard Actions Are Proceeding West of the Livenza.

British Government Denies Lack of Concern for Italy

LONDON, Nov. 8.—The following official announcement was issued tonight

"A statement from a correspondent of The Associated Press at Italian Headquarters appeared in the British press today. This statement set out to remind the Allies that something more than assurances were needed for getting reinforcements in men and munitions to the threatened Italian lines, and purported to reflect the feeling of Italians, who were represented as distrusting the allied efforts to help them. It was also stated that the enemy masses were so overwhelming that nothing but effective reinforcements would turn the tide.

"This alarmist statement is absolutely uncalled for and is calculated to do grave harm by suggesting that the seriousness of the military situation in Italy is not appreciated by her allies, and that the latter are not giving her the support she requires. There is no truth whatever in these assertions. The statement that the enemy masses are overwhelming is an absurd exaggeration."

The Associated Press issued this statement last night:

"The dispatch to which the foregoing British official statement refers was sent by The Associated Press correspondent at Italian Headquarters on Nov. 7. This correspondent is an American Staff man, who was present at the beginning of the Italian retreat and accompanied the Italian Army back to its present position.

"The dispatch in question was passed by the Italian military censors at General Cadorna's headquarters, and, as it was sent through France, also passed the French censorship."

LONDON HAILS OUR WAR MISSION

Comes at Critical Period of the War with New Assurance of Victory.

ENVOYS MAKE BRISK START

Begin Conferences on First Day—Benson Visits Jellicoe—Trip Was Uneventful.

AWAITS LIGHT FROM RUSSIA

Washington Reserves Judgment, Hoping Revolt Is Only Local.

EXPECTS A COUNTER-MOVE

Kerensky, with Conservatives and Perhaps the Army Behind Him, May Save the Country.

DARK DAYS SEEN AHEAD

And Allied War Conference Faces Another Huge Problem—Bigger Burden for Us.

Reverses Cited as Showing Greater Need Than Ever For Unified Direction of Allied War Policy

By CHARLES H. GRASTY.

Copyright, 1917, by The New York Times Company.

Special Cable to THE NEW YORK TIMES.

ROME, Nov. 8.—My observations here confirm previous insistence upon the urgent need of centralized methods of managing the war. At bottom this war is the biggest business enterprise ever undertaken, and, while the Kaiser handles his end of it as such, each of the Allies is more or less playing its own separate game. With an infinity of resources, they have discussed and postponed critical decisions until the advantage has been lost.

To mention one recent instance: If the Korniloff movement had been handled by the Allies as the Kaiser would have handled such an opportunity, the Russian situation might have been stabilized and the Italian drive rendered impossible.

There has not been a single allied action, with the exception of the battle of the Marne, ranking as a great aggressive stroke. The Allies are not organized to initiate and execute big policies. Instead of looking ahead and planning on a big scale, they yield where pressure is applied, with the result that usually they trail along a few days or weeks behind Germany. Purely local and political matters divide and divert attention in the allied Chancelleries.

Coming on top of many previous heartbreaking lost opportunities, the present menace in Italy is quite serious enough to rally the Entente Powers at last into substituting for the town meeting some plan under which they can see the war situation as a whole and concentrate with foresight, originality, and driving power, as we understand these things in America.

In a word, after three years, it is time to quit playing amateur against professional. If America gives the lead, all the rest will follow, as there are directed against us none of the petty jealousies peculiar to Europe, and all the allied countries have complete confidence in our disinterestedness and sound leadership.

Plans for the conduct of the war on the basis of a unified western front extending from the North Sea to the Adriatic are now under consideration by Premiers Lloyd George and Painlevé and other high civil and military officials in conference in Rome.

STOCKS TUMBLE ON RUSSIAN NEWS

Flood of Liquidation Hits Exchange, Heightened by Action of Short Sellers.

NEWS CHECKS BROAD RISE

No Action Considered Yet in Regard to Publishing Proportion of Short Sales.

HOPE STRONG MAN WILL RULE RUSSIA

Zemstvos' Agent Here and Herman Bernstein Agree That Kerensky Must Go.

GREAT REACTION EXPECTED

Sakhnovsky Thinks Revolt May Lead to Constitutional Monarchy.

MINISTERS UNDER ARREST

Winter Palace Is Taken After Fierce Defense by Women Soldiers.

FORT'S GUNS TURNED ON IT

Cruiser and Armored Cars Also Brought Into Battle Waged by Searchlight.

TROTZSKY HEADS REVOLT

Giving Land to the Peasants and Calling of Constituent Assembly Promised.

PETROGRAD, Nov. 8.—With the aid of the capital's garrison complete control of Petrograd has been seized by the Maximalists, or Bolsheviki, headed by Nikolai Lenine, the Radical Socialist leader, and Leon Trotzky, President of the Central Executive Committee of the Petrograd Council of Workmen's and Soldiers' Delegates. Their action has been indorsed by the All-Russia Congress of Workmen's Councils.

visional Government was accom-
ned without bloodshed.
ie Petrograd Council of Work-
's and Soldiers' Delegates solemnly
comes the accomplished change and
claims the authority of the Mili-
Revolutionary Committee until
creation of a Government by the
rkmen's and Soldiers' Delegates.
nnouncing this to the army at the
t, the Revolutionary Committee
upon the revolutionary soldiers to
ch closely the conduct of the men
ommand. Officers who do not join
accomplished revolution immedi-
y and openly must be arrested at
e as enemies.
e Petrograd Council of Workmen's
Soldiers' Delegates considers this
e the program of the new author-

irst—The offer of an immediate
nocratic peace.
econd—The immediate handing over
large proprietarial lands to the
sants.
hird—The transmission of all au-
rity to the Council of Workmen's
Soldiers' Delegates.
ourth—The honest convocation of a
stitutional Assembly.
he national revolutionary army
st not permit uncertain military de-
hments to leave the front for Pe-
grad. They should use persuasion,
where this fails they must oppose
such action on the part of these
achments by force without mercy.
he actual order must be read im-
diately to all military detachments
all arms. The suppression of this
er from the rank and file by army
anization is equivalent to a great
ne against the revolution and will
punished by all the strength of the
olutionary law.
oldiers! For peace, for bread, for
d, and for the power of the peo-
! (Signed)
E MILITARY REVOLUTIONARY
COMMITTEE.

elegates from the three Cossack reg-
nts quartered here declared they
ld not obey the Provisional Gov-
nent and would not march against
Workmen's and Soldiers' Delegates,
that they were prepared to main-
public order.

Council Welcomes Lenine.

e Petrograd Council of Workmen's
Soldiers' Delegates held a meet-
at which M. Trotzky made his dec-
tion that the Government no longer
ted; that some of the Ministers had
n arrested, and that the preliminary
liament had been dissolved. He in-
luced Nikolai Lenine as "an old
rade whom we welcome back."
enine, who was received with pro-
ged cheers, said:
Now we have a revolution. The
sants and workmen control the Gov-
nent. This is only a preliminary
toward a similar revolution every-
re."
outlined the three problems now
re the Russian democracy. First,
ediate conclusion of the war, for
ch purpose the new Government
t propose an armistice to the bellig-
ts; second, the handing over of
land to the peasant; third, settle-
t of the economic crisis.
the close of the sitting a declara-
was read from the representatives
he Democratic Minimalist Party of
Workmen's and Soldiers' Delegates,
ing that the party disapproved of
coup d'état and withdrew from the
ncil of Workmen's and Soldiers'
egates.
ter it was announced that the split
he Council had been healed and that
ll had been sent out for a delegate
each 25,000 of the population to ex-
s the will of the Russian Army.
owing is the text of this document:

All Army Corps and Divisional
Committees:
oday there is a reunion of the
orkmen's and Soldiers' Delegates.
e army committees are ordered to
d delegates for expressing the will
the army. We suggest to you to
d delegates immediately from your
ist. To refuse to take part in de-
ing the destiny of the revolution is
in which history will not pardon.
ct a delegate from each 25,000 and
d them to the reunion.
igned)
E PETROGRAD WORKMEN'S
ND SOLDIERS' DELEGATES.

Congress of Councils Approves.

bsequently the General Congress of
kmen's and Soldiers' Delegates of
Russia convened with 200 out of 560
gates in attendance. The Chairman
ared that the time was not propi-
s for political speeches, and the
r of business of the congress ap-
ed was as follows:
irst—Organization of power.
econd—Peace and war.
hird—A constituent Assembly.
e officers elected comprise fourteen
imalists, including Nikolai Lenine
M. Zinovieff, an associate of Le-
, and Leon Trotzky. In addition
n revolutionary Socialists were ap-
ted.
delegation was named to initiate
e negotiations with the other revo-
nary and democratic organizations
h a view to taking steps to stop
dshed."
resolution proposed by the Minima-
that an effort would be made to
h an agreement with the Provis-
l Government was voted down.
the 560 members of the Congress,
are Bolsheviki, 150 Socialist revo-
nists, sixty Minimalists, fourteen of
Minimalist-Internationalist group,
of the Nationalist-Socialist group,
e non-party Socialists, the others
g independent.
e official news agency today made
lic the following statement:
The Congress of the Councils of
rkmen's and Soldiers' Delegates of
Russia, which opened last evening,
ed this morning the three following
clamations:
All Provincial Councils of Workmen's and Soldiers' and Peasants'
Delegates.
All power lies in the Workmen's and
ldiers' Delegates. Government com-
ssaries are relieved of their func-
ns. Presidents of the Workmen's
d Soldiers' Delegates are to com-
unicate direct with the Revolution-
y Government. All members of ag-
ultural committees who have been
rested are to be set at liberty im-
diately and the commissioners who
rested them are in turn to be ar-
sted.
The second proclamation reads as
ows:
The death penalty re-established at
e front by Premier Kerensky is
olished and complete freedom for
litical propaganda has been estab-
hed at the front. All revolutionary
ldiers and officers who have been
rested for complicity in so-called
litical crimes are to be set at lib-
ty immediately.
The third proclamation says:
Former Ministers Konovaloff, Kish-
n, Terestchenko, Malyanovitch, Nik-
in, and others have been arrested
the revolutionary committee.
Mr. Kerensky has taken flight and
l military bodies have been empow-
ed to take all possible measures to
rest Kerensky and bring him back
Petrograd. All complicity with Ke-
nsky will be dealt with as high
eason.

Capture of the Winter Palace.

While the All-Russian Congress of
uncils had been deliberating the Gov-
nment forces, including the Women's
ttalion, which had been guarding the
nter Palace had been driven inside
the course of a lively machine-gun
d rifle battle, during which the cruiser
rora, that had been moored in the
va at the Nicolai Bridge, moved up
thin range, firing shrapnel, and
mored cars swung into action. Then
guns of the Fortress of St. Peter
d St. Paul, across the river, opened
the structure.
he palace stood out under the glare
the searchlights of the cruiser and
ered a good target for the guns.
e defenders held out for four hours,
lying as best they could with ma-
ne guns and rifles, but at 2 o'clock
s morning were compelled to sur-
der.
Meanwhile there had been spasmodic
ing in other parts of the city, but
Workmen's and Soldiers' troops took
ery means to protect citizens, who
re ordered to their quarters. The
dges and the Nevsky Prospect, which
rly in the afternoon were in the hands
the Government forces, were captured
d held during the night by the Work-
n's and Soldiers' troops.

LONDON, Nov. 8.—The opinion is ex-
essed in Russian circles in London
at M. Kerensky, who early was ad-
ed of the intentions of Nikolai Lenine
grasp power, is removing the seat
Government to Moscow, and from
ere will endeavor to unite the mod-
ates against the Maximalists and al-
ally to his support Cossacks and
ch other troops who have not already
ne over to the Extremists.

TROTZSKY IN EXILE LIVED IN THE BRONX

Hurried Home to Russia When the Czar Fell, After Three Months' Residence Here.

REAL NAME IS BRAUNSTEIN

Radical Socialist and Active in 1905 Revolution—Now Suspected to be in German Pay.

Leon Trotzsky, the active if not the real head of the new Maximalist revolt, was the most prominent of the Russian radicals who returned to their native land from exile in this country after the revolution of March. Trotzsky was living in the Bronx, on Vyse Avenue, when the Czar was overthrown; but he had been in this country less than three months, having previously been expelled from Germany, France, Switzerland, and Spain.

The real name of the Maximalist leader is Leber Braunstein, and he was born in a town in the Russian Government of Kherson, near the Black Sea. He became an extreme Socialist, and being gifted with a forceful literary style won distinction and prominence among the revolutionary leaders before the end of the nineteenth century.

In the revolution of 1905 Trotzsky published a book which practically set the sky as the limit for the Russian revolution then apparently on its way to a favorable issue. He demanded the application of the full program of socialism, not only in Russia but everywhere, and until this was accomplished revolution must never rest. The collapse of the movement in the following year sent him to Siberia, but after several years he was released, resumed his revolutionary activity, and was compelled to go abroad.

At the beginning of the war he was in Berlin, but the radical teachings of his writings there were too much for the Berlin Government, which had no taste for Socialist programs except in foreign parts. He was compelled to go to Switzerland, but here, too, he found the atmosphere chilly. After a time he landed in Paris and edited a newspaper there, but the French Government refused to allow his doctrines to be spread after Russian troops arrived in France, and he moved on to Spain.

Shanghaied From Spain.

Spain became too hot for him last Winter.

Everywhere he went he was not only a centre and leader of radicalism, but one of its most vigorous journalistic propagandists, and Spain was no more hospitable to his extreme social theories than other countries. According to a New Yorker who knew him well, he was practically shanghaied in Spain, and awoke after being taken captive to find himself on board a steamer whose destination he did not know till he was several days out.

The steamer was bound for Cuba, but Cuba was too small a country for Trotzsky's energies. He sailed at once from Havana for New York, and reached here on Jan. 14 last. Trotzsky was welcomed not only by the most radical faction of Russian Socialists, but by the German Socialists, too. Leaders of radicalism on the east side and in Harlem contributed furniture for the house where he established himself in the Bronx, and it caused considerable feeling among them when he eventually left town in such haste that none of the contributors were notified, and the furniture was left to take care of itself in the empty house for a considerable time.

While here he wrote many articles for the Vorwärts, the Jewish Socialist paper, and was for a considerable time the principal editor of Novy Mir, organ of the Russian Socialists. Novy Mir has since come under the ban of the Post Office Department and has been refused mailing privileges for its extreme pacifist attitude, but at that time a majority of the Board of Managers were not in favor of Trotzsky's propaganda for immediate peace, and, according to men who knew him, he was eventually asked to resign.

He was in active relation with both German and Russian Socialists, and American opinion is divided as to whether or not he has been an agent of Germany since the outbreak of the revolution. In view, however, of the fact that Lenine was accused by Kerensky of being in German pay, and that Trotzsky is apparently acting as a vizier of Lenine, the presumption that he is in German pay has been increased by recent events. It is said that just before he left last March a German Socialist group at a hall in Harlem gave a dinner for him, not the first time he had been so honored by radicals of that nationality in New York.

Detained by the British.

Trotzsky sailed from New York for a Scandinavian port on March 27, but was taken off the ship at Halifax by the British authorities, who knew his record. There were loud and vigorous protests from American radicals at this action, and eventually the first Russian Provisional Government, apparently unaware at that time of the strength and tendencies of the Bolsheviki, was induced to ask for his release. The British thereupon permitted him to go on his way.

Upon his arrival at Petrograd he joined the radical faction, which was busy denouncing America and the Allies and scheming to overthrow the Provisional Government and bring about immediate peace. Trotzsky has denied that he is for a separate peace, and says that if the Germans refuse to revolt against their Government and to fraternize with the Russians the latter must defend the revolution. But the fraternizing must be begun by the Russians wherever possible, officers are to be elected by the soldiers, and every order of any higher command must be submitted to a referendum before being carried out.

Leon Trotzky

Head of the New Revolutionary Government in Russia.

LENINE THE REAL POWER.

Believed to Have Plotted Present Rising While in Hiding.

Nikolai Lenine, denounced by moderate liberals the world over as the evil genius of the Russian revolution, and accused by General Brusiloff as a paid German agent, appears to be the directing power behind the present outbreak, as he was openly the leader of the Maximilist rising in Petrograd on July 16, which was suppressed after several hundred of the civil population had been massacred by machine gun troops following his leadership. This revolt, which followed close on the collapse of the Russian armies in Galicia after the successful offensive led by Alexander Kerensky, came near putting the Bolsheviki in command of Petrograd and resulted in the resignation of George Lvoff as Premier and his replacement by Kerensky.

Since then Lenine has been in hiding. Orders for his arrest were issued at once, and it was reported that he was captured in Finland, near the Swedish border, a few days later, but was retaken by his friends. After that he was reported to be in hiding in Sweden, or even in Switzerland, but recently it has been said that most of the time he was in Finland, and in constant telephonic connection with Trotzsky and other Maximalist leaders. At all events, he intended to put in his appearance at the democratic congress in Moscow in September, and the Bolsheviki had the effrontery to ask Kerensky for a guarantee that he would not be arrested. This the Premier refused to do, so Lenine remained in hiding; though it appears that any determined effort to find him would probably have been successful had Kerensky dared to use summary measures.

His Name an Alias.

Lenine, like most of the prominent Russian agitators, had to use an alias in his revolutionary activity. His real name is Vladimir Ilyitch Uulyanoff; he was born of a noble family at Simbirsk, on the Volga, about 1870. An older brother was executed for complicity in a plot to kill Emperor Alexander II. shortly before that ruler was actually assassinated in 188[illegible]. Lenine became prominent in the early nineties as a leader of the radical Social Democrats, who insist on the literal application of the Marxian theories, as against the more nationalistic view, with greater attention paid to the peasants and their actual condition, which was entertained by the Socialist revolutionists, the party of Kerensky. His most noted book is "The Development of Capitalism in Russia."

He was elected to the second Duma after the revolution of 1905, but was compelled to go into exile, a thing he had often done before, when the reaction triumphed. At the beginning of the present war he was in Cracow and was interned as an enemy alien, but was shortly released and allowed to proceed to Zimmerwald, in Switzerland, where a colony of Russian revolutionists was already established.

After the revolution the Provisional Government of Russia entered into an agreement with Germany by which the Russian revolutionists in Switzerland were allowed to return through Germany in return for the release of German civilians in Russia. Lenine headed the party which returned by this route, and his social program, which he has been advocating ever since, was drawn up as he passed through. He reached Petrograd on April 16, just after the pacifists in the Council of Workmen's and Soldiers' Delegates had forced the resignation of Milyukoff, and at once began to preach immediate peace and general confiscation.

His Rise to Power.

At first the Government seems to have underestimated him; Tcheidze said that probably the revolution would absorb him, and that if it did not there was little difference. But soon his newspaper, the Pravda, featuring violent attacks on England and France, became influential, and the tolerance of the Government was now based on the theory that arrest would make him a martyr. Certainly at first there was general disapprobation of his extreme views, but gradually he began to gain in power and to become the centre of the radical pacifists, despite the constantly reiterated charges that he was in the pay of Germany. A peace plan of his advanced in a speech was publicly denounced as given verbatim in a wireless message of Prince Leopold of Bavaria, and no satisfactory denial was ever made of Brusiloff's accusation.

Nevertheless, he gained in power. Seated in the palace which had formerly belonged to the dancer Kshesinskaya, the favorite of Nicholas, protected by the First Machine Gun Regiment, which was constantly loyal, he resisted all attempts to oust him until failure in the July rising drove him to temporary hiding, in which he appears to have plotted the new outbreak.

WASHINGTON AWAITS LIGHT ON RUSSIA

Continued from Page 1.

ical elements in Petrograd would not mean a separate peace for Russia or result in a material weakening of her fighting frontier.

Radicals Have Little Hold on Country.

The recent local elections throughout Russia were cited today to show the low esteem in which the Bolsheviki and other extremists were held in the country at large. They were defeated almost everywhere, the vote for their candidates being insignificant. They had likewise failed, it was pointed out, to control the situation in any city except Petrograd, where the radical and lawless elements of the nation have their headquarters.

The Bolsheviki recently obtained control of the Petrograd Council of Workmen's and Soldiers' Delegates, and this they are now using as a lever to bring all Russia to their views, by chauvinistic appeals to the masses. They have promised a millenium to the nation. They have pledged lands to the peasants and workingmen, a distribution of wealth such as would abolish the bourgeois and bring all the people to a common level and peace. They have been opposed by a minority of the Socialists, who were unable, however, to meet the extravagant promises of the Maximalists, which the ignorant of Petrograd and no less ignorant members of the council, believed the Bolsheviki could fulfil.

The Bolsheviki are international Socialists, professing to believe in no national lines, and it has been one of their fictions that they did not believe in a separate peace, because such a peace would be a recognition of nationalism, which they deny.

The State Department, it was authoritatively stated late today, did not accept as authentic the news dispatches describing events in Petrograd and would await official advices before expressing any opinion.

Emphasis was laid on the fact, however, that the press dispatches did not mention difficulties in other parts of Russia, and that an ending of the crisis in Petrograd might present itself.

There is a possibility, it was hinted in one quarter, that if the Bolsheviki are finally able to seize power in the nation, Russian diplomatic representatives throughout the world may refuse to recognize them as the legal authority. Should they convene the constituent assembly, it was thought that that assembly would refuse to recognize their authority.

Most observers think that in the last analysis the decision of the army will determine whether Russia is to remain in the war, as well as whether the Bolsheviki shall control the political situation. The radical coup is everywhere regarded as the triumph in Petrograd of German machinations.

Kerensky May Appeal to Korniloff.

By The Associated Press.

WASHINGTON, Nov. 8.—Discouragement felt here over the news of the overthrow of the Kerensky Government is tempered by the hope that the extreme radicals at the capital may not be able to extend their control. The suggestion was voiced here today if Kerensky, fleeing from the capital, could bring to his support General Korniloff, the strong man of the Russian Army, with his Cossack backers, he might set up a stronger government at Moscow.

An obstacle to the success of such a plan is found in the possibility that Korniloff, embittered by the treatment he received at the hands of Kerensky, might refuse to risk his future further upon such an uncertain leader.

In view of the intense Democratic spirit developed in Russia since the overthrow of the Czar, it is difficult to conceive of the appearance of any other form of Government than a republic, yet in diplomatic circles, where the temperament of the Russian masses is understood, the opinion was expressed that out of sheer weariness with revolutions and anarchy, the people might suddenly decide to confide their destinies in a dictator.

Inasmuch as even the Bolshevikis themselves have declared for "a democratic peace," which is opposed to the German idea, it is thought hardly possible that on this basis Germany could entertain proposals from the Maximalists for either a peace or an armistice.

It is pointed out also that even if the Germans did make a separate peace with the Maximalists, the fact that this party represented only a small section of the Russian people would make it necessary for the Central Powers to continue to maintain a large military force on the border to guard against an offensive from the other elements.

Therefore, it is hoped that the military situation will not change materially for the worse for the Entente Powers and America as a result of these latest developments. If a considerable portion of the Russian Army can be kept in the trenches, the advent of Winter will prevent the German troops who face them from taking advantage of temporary weakness to start an offensive.

Problem for Allied Conference.

Nevertheless, the Allies' war conference, just about to assemble in Paris to arrange a co-ordination of fighting forces, is faced with a great problem at its very outset. Coming close on the Italian reverses, the Russian débâcle brings the Allies, including the United States, face to face with the necessity of rearranging their fighting power to deal the heaviest possible blows on the battlefronts while Russia works out her destiny and Italy tries to hold back the invader pouring through the Alps.

Some idea of what Russia faces on her fighting lines is gained from the latest report to the Russian Embassy here, dated last Friday. This stated that the Russian troops were engaging 147 divisions of enemy troops, including Germans, Austrians, Bulgarians, and Turks, probably in all some 2,000,000 men. The possibility of those troops, or part of them, being released for a drive against the western front, to join the invaders in Italy, or even for Balkan service, is one of the questions which the allied conference will have to consider.

The immediate effect upon the part which the United States must take as the shifting of world events puts the burdens of war more and more on the American people cannot be assessed accurately at this time. The Treasury has authorized credits of $325,000,000 to Russia, and of that amount probably half has been drawn upon for supplies bought in this country.

An American commission of eminent railroad men is bringing order out of chaos on Russia's transportation systems. Millions of dollars worth of supplies have been piling up at Vladivostok, and the Americans have been applying the best methods to move them across Siberia.

A Question of Japan's Helping.

A factor in the situation which has been reluctantly discussed heretofore now comes to the front. It is the possibility that Japan might send troops into Russia to support the Provisional Government and help restore order. No one here, who would be authorized to speak on the subject, cares to do so, although it has been discussed by Japanese elsewhere. The consensus of their opinions, as published, has been that Japan would find difficulties in supplying an army for Russia. Moreover, the argument has been advanced that Japan's forces were needed to preserve order in the Far East.

LONDON STILL HAS HOPE.

Belief That Russian Moderates Will Assert Themselves.

LONDON, Nov. 8.—Chancellor Andrew Bonar Law informed the House of Commons this afternoon that the Government had no news of the latest developments in Russia. The Russian Embassy also was without advices. The only news of the deposition of the Kerensky Government thus far has been received from the Russian wireless and the semi-official Petrograd News Agency, both of which are now controlled by the Maximalists.

The Russian Chargé d'Affaires said that the world must regard with a certain degree of reserve the news which was evidently coming from a controlled source. It should be borne in mind, he said, that the Petrograd garrison by no means represented the whole Russian Army.

There is hope here that there may be another side to the picture. It is considered possible that the Kerensky faction may not have been turned out of power as completely as the Maximalists represent, and that the Conservatives may be able to reassert themselves without a general civil war. The army holds the key to the situation, and the issue appears to hang upon how far the soldiers respond to the Maximalist proclamation.

'RUSSIA OUT,' SPURS SPARTANBURG BOYS

Tired Soldiers Speed Up Drill When They Hear That Petrograd Is Moving for Peace.

ANXIOUS FOR THE FRAY

Two More Brigades to be Made of Skeleton Guard Units and Men from Yaphank.

Special to The New York Times.

CAMP WADSWORTH, Spartanburg, S. C., Nov. 8.—Just before sundown a company from the former Second Infantry was wearily going through close order drill out on the parade ground.

The officers, dust from shoes to hats, were hoarse from shouting commands all afternoon and the men, tired of toting their heavy equipment back and forth, were eager for the word to quit. A couple of men from the 102d United States Engineers with nothing to do until mess idly stood by enjoying the grilling of the infantrymen.

Soon a newsboy selling a Spartanburg afternoon paper ambled along and one of the engineers bought a paper. With one last, satisfied grin at the toiling "dough boys," the ex-Twenty-second man languidly glanced at the first page headlines telling the bad news from Petrograd. As they say in the movies, he registered keen and amazed interest, then discipline was forgotten and the engineer shouted at the laboring company:

"Hey, fellows, here's news—Russia is out."

The fagged and dusty company heard the announcement just as they came to a halt. While the Lieutenant drilling the infantrymen indignantly scowled at he excited and offending engineers, there was talking in the ranks. Then the Lieutenant ran the company off into another evolution. He said afterward it was like leading another set of men. The fatigue was gone and until "recall" sounded the company went through the drill freshly and with vim.

News Gives Them Spirit.

Afterward the top Sergeant explained the reason for the change of spirit, thus: "When that guy said that Russia had dropped out, every fellow in the company knew that it was up to the United States to take her place. And, believe me, if you had been doubling over that drill ground for weeks and fairly aching for the welcome word 'Embark,' you'd think any drill was light, too."

A similar sentiment throughout the division was found tonight when the 200 company units were canvassed to find out what the men thought about the news. Everywhere the men were enthusiastic about their chances for quick action. Somewhere in the camp some strategist figured out that if Russia really went out, Germany could throw all the troops now on the Russian front to the Western theatre and the Allies would have need of reinforcements at once.

This "reliable, inside information" went over the camp like all reports, quickly and thoroughly, and as the newspapermen were assured tonight, the Twenty-seventh being the "best division anywhere," the soldiers became exceedingly optimistic over the outlook.

Headquarters announced tonight the formation of two additional brigades, to be made up of regiments heretofore in the second line. This order was construed to be in line with Secretary Baker's announcement that all soldiers would have an opportunity to see service in France.

The brigades will be composed of all of the skeleton regiments, and for the present will be known as the First and Second Provisional Infantry Brigades. Brig. Gen. William Wilson, until recently in command of the Fourth Separate Brigade, New York National Guard, will command the First Brigade, which will be formed by the Tenth and Forty-seventh Infantry Regiments. The Tenth is a separate company organization with units scattered through the Hudson River Valley section, while the Forty-seventh hails from Brooklyn.

Colonel Bates to Command.

The Second Brigade will be composed of the men left in the First, Twelfth, Fourteenth, Seventy-first, and Seventy-fourth. Each of the units now enrolls about 200 men. Command of this brigade has been given to Colonel William G. Bates, who, as commander of the old Seventy-first, was the senior Colonel of the guard. Aside from General Wilson and Colonel Bates, the only officer yet appointed to the new formation is Major Leonard Smith, Fifty-second Field Artillery, who will be Brigade Adjutant.

It was explained that for the present each of the regiments to be in the new brigades would continue to bear its present designation. The regiments are to be filled up with drafted men who are to come here from Yaphank at a date not announced. Later the built-up units will be redesignated to conform with the War Department's series of regimental numerals.

The first official figures of the amount of insurance applied for disclosed that upward of $40,000,000 had been taken in four days. The leading units and the amounts follow:

107th Infantry	$11,256,000
102d Engineers	6,711,000
106th Field Artillery	4,456,500
108th Infantry	4,452,000
104th Field Artillery	3,314,500
105th Machine Gun Battalion	2,378,500
102d Sanitary Train	1,875,000
106th Machine Gun Battalion	1,388,000
Tenth Infantry	1,236,000

Reserve officers on temporary duty with the division got a hint of War Department plans today when several of them were transferred to another camp. First Lieutenant Fay M. Scott and Second Lieutenants Harold Banks, Raymond E. Cox, Everest Haight, Jesse Hoyt, Arthur L. Hawtrey, Waldo S. Kemp, and James W. Lillie were transferred to Chickamauga Park.

Sergeant H. M. Ladd, Jr., and Corporals John G. Davis and Wayne Marshall, all of Company L, 107th Infantry, tonight received commissions as provisional Second Lieutenants in the regular service.

RUSSIAN ENVOY HOPEFUL.

Says Petrograd Events Do Not Represent Russia's Views.

MEMPHIS, Tenn., Nov. 8.—"The intent and spirit of Russia as a whole should in no way be judged by the news from Petrograd," declared Boris A. Bakhmeteff, Russian Ambassador to the United States, when The Associated Press dispatches relative to the reported overthrow of the Russian Provisional Government were shown to him.

"Until just now I did not have any personal or official information on the subject, and therefore you cannot expect any official opinion," he continued. "But I can tell you that Petrograd is not the whole of Russia, and has never been, and that the spirit prevailing in Petrograd is not representative of the Russian spirit as a whole.

"The extremist element has always been strong in Petrograd, but as to the whole of Russia, the late elections in the provincial and county local bodies has shown the Maximalist feeling very weak. Less than 10 per cent. of these extremists were elected."

The Ambassador declined to comment further, reserving his opinion until he is supplied with official information from his Government. It was gathered, though, that it is his belief that Premier Kerensky represents the real spirit of Russia.

SEES RUSSIA STILL IN WAR.

Petrograd Radicals Do Not Represent Nation, Says H. P. Davison.

Special to The New York Times.

CHICAGO, Ill., Nov. 8.—Henry P. Davison of J. P. Morgan & Co., General Director of the American Red Cross, who arrived in Chicago today, expressed the belief that the revolt at Petrograd would not overthrow the purpose of the Russian people, and that they would be in the war to the finish.

"Despite the distressing news from Petrograd," he said, "I am still optimistic. Russia is not out of the war. The great mass of the Russian people outside the cities remain loyal to the allied cause. Their trouble now is that they are unorganized, and no man strong enough has yet appeared to organize them. They will work out their salvation without help, but it will take time. In spite of the dispatches, I can't see that their position in the war has been materially altered. The Russian people will not fail.

"With regard to Italy, its situation, too, is distressing, but not cause for alarm as to the ultimate outcome. The Italians will rally and will stem the enemy tide. Our workers already are in Northern Italy, and the desperate condition there means a greater task for us.

"We are preparing for a long war, although we hope it will be a short one. But there is no indication but that it will be a long one."

MEYER LONDON'S VIEWS.

Congressman Says Russia Will Never Make Separate Peace.

Meyer London, the Socialist Congressman from New York City, yesterday explained the causes and results of the Russian revolution and expounded the ideals and hopes of the Russian people before an audience of over a thousand at the Social Problems Club of the College of the City of New York.

"The causes of the revolution were many," he said. "For instance, on the eve of the war there was not even forty-eight hours' supply of food or ammunition in the country. But this was not the primary cause. General discontent with the incompetence of the Government was, perhaps, the chief cause."

He asserted that Russia would never consent to a separate peace with Germany.

"They have suffered in misery for centuries," he said, "but they are willing to suffer centuries more because they realize that if they stop they will endanger the rest of the world's safety. They demand, however, that the objects of the war be made clear, and that they be not asked to fight for the selfish purposes of other nations."

SCOUT IDEA OF PEACE.

Yale Professors Say Russia Will Not Lay Down Her Arms.

Special to The New York Times.

NEW HAVEN, Conn., Nov. 8.—"A long civil war is ahead for Russia if the Maximalists compel a separate peace with Germany," said Professor Alexander Petrunkevitch of Yale tonight. He is son of the first President of the Russian Duma, and has recently received messages from Russia confirming the trend of affairs toward internal volcanic outbursts.

"Russia's real leaders," he continued, "do not want peace on terms that Germany can offer. A group of extremists have gained the ascendency, and they are putting out feelers for peace, but this does not mean that the Russian people will support any treachery to the allied cause. Only civil war can follow today's action, and this will cost the people of Russia dearly."

Professor Charles Winslow of Yale, who has just returned from Russia with the American Red Cross Mission, said:

"Russia will not lay down arms till German militarism is crushed. She is passing through the throes of the most tremendous political and social revolution the world has even known, but Russia as a whole stands firm. She knows the German by bitter experience, and she will never lay down her arms till the menace of this domination is removed."

SEES CIVIL WAR CERTAIN.

Russian Paper Here Says Cannon Will Crush Revolt.

The Russkoye Slovo, (Russian Word,) a daily in New York City, publishes this morning an editorial article signed by its editor, Leo Pasvolsky, in which he says:

"The Bolsheviki calls this a coup d'état, a revolution. But it is neither the one nor the other. It is a rebellion, pure and simple. It is a revolt against the legal, established Government, recognized by the Russian people. It is treason to the people of Russia, and Russia will regard the actions of Trotzky and of his companions as a rebellion, as high treason.

"Russia will not follow the mad Petrograd. It is impossible that the Russian giant should not awaken from its terrible sleep, should not cast away from its eyes that bloody curtain which blinds its vision and darkens its mind. The Bolshevik Government in Petrograd will re-enact the bloody Paris Commune. But this commune of our days will be shattered to splinters by cannon and machine guns. The rebellion will be crushed, and then the country will again come out upon the road that leads to the Constituent Assembly."

STOCKS TUMBLE ON RUSSIAN NEWS

Continued from Page 1.

ed to be completely bare of bidders, and much the same condition prevailed in the market for Italian exchange. A dollar would buy 8.38 lire for check transfer, a new low record for all time, compared with 8.05 the day before, and a normal quotation of 5.1826.

Brokers who stood in the midst of the avalanche of selling orders in stocks said after the market closed that renewed liquidation from all parts of the country appeared to supply most of the offerings. Outside of the Russian influence, the day brought forth nothing new as a factor to promote selling. There were none of the rumors which were common before the Stock Exchange took action last week to control short selling, and Governors of the board said at the end of the day that close observation of the character of business failed to show any deliberate efforts to force quotations down.

Discounts News from Russia.

In view of the fright among owners of stocks over the downfall of Kerensky, the attitude of prominent bankers was interesting. One big banker said:

"In my opinion, the rise of the revolutionists in opposition to the Russian Government is by no means so adverse a matter as the situation in Italy. While Russia will probably be filled with disturbance for some time, reports received from persons lately returned indicate that the Russian people themselves are not inclined toward peace, and, in my opinion, Russian opposition to Germany will not come to an end. The retreat of the Italian armies, while discouraging, is not hopeless by any means. There is the possibility of General Cadorna turning upon the Germans when they are far from their base, with extended lines of communication, and repeating the battle of the Marne."

A returned traveler from Russia, whose trip had to do with Government matters, said that the overturn of the Kerensky Government was likely to be temporary, the result of a "political explosion." The activities of the revolutionists were confined to Petrograd, he asserted, and did not reflect the real feelings of the people, who were determined to oppose the Germans, and were held back chiefly by the workings of pro-German intrigue.

The bankers were not disturbed by the outbreak in the stock market. Bank loans, they pointed out, were well guarded and demands for additional collateral sent out to brokers where necessary were met with immediate action. While the theory was held in commission houses that strong banking support had been accorded stocks, especially Steel, when the decline became most violent, no confirmation could be obtained among the bankers themselves. Their attitude continued as before that liquidation must run its course, reflecting conditions brought about by the war.

The Committee on Business Conduct of the Exchange continued the examination of names reported to them by brokers of stocks borrowed this week for customers. Governors said that no action had yet been considered in regard to public announcement of the proportion of short sales to sales of long stock.

HOPE STRONG MAN WILL RULE RUSSIA

Continued from Page 1.

continue in his present position. He has tried to be gentle with the Bolsheviki, in the confidence that they would appreciate his position and treat him as he treated them. Now there must be leaders who will know how to handle them. It has been well established that Lenine is in the German pay, and there is no doubt that the present rising is supported by German funds.

"The ideal of Trotzsky and Lenine is what Trotzsky calls 'the permanent revolution,' a revolution continuing until the maximum Socialist program is in force throughout the world. I don't think there is much likelihood that this program will win, but there is certain to be considerable disorder if the reports so far are correct. One thing I am afraid of is that there will be more pogroms. Trotzsky is a Jew, and unfortunately there are a number of Jewish leaders among the most radical faction. Of course, it is very far from being a wholly Jewish affair. Lenine himself, whose real name is Ulyanoff, comes of an old and noble Russian family, and there are plenty of other Russian leaders. But the prominence of a few Jews is, I am afraid, likely to be avenged on the entire race.

"One thing worthy of note is that the Bolsheviki have learned a point from the procedure of the original revolutionists. You will remember that the revolutions of March seized the telegraph and cable offices, so that after a few days of no news from Petrograd there came out of a clear sky the story of the completed revolution and the full list of Ministers of the Provisional Government.

"This had a great effect in bringing into line the provincial cities and the country districts which might have hesitated if there had come full accounts of the indecisive fighting of the first two or three days. Lenine overlooked this point in his July revolt, but Trotzsky's promptitude in seizing the means of communication at present indecates a desire to try to swing the provinces to the support of a fait accompli in the same manner."

WORKS OF ART.

Photographic reproductions of famous portraits by Lorenzo di Credi, Domenico Ghirlandaio and Angilo Bronzino, in the Rotogravure Section of The New York Times next Sunday. Order today.—Advt.

"All the News That's Fit to Print."

The New York Times.

THE WEATHER
Fair today and Tuesday; diminishing northwest winds.
For weather report see next to last page.

VOL. LXVIII...NO. 22,206. NEW YORK, MONDAY, NOVEMBER 11, 1918. TWENTY-FOUR PAGES. TWO CENTS Metropolitan District 50 Mile Radius | THREE CENTS Within 200 Miles | FOUR CENTS Elsewhere

ARMISTICE SIGNED, END OF THE WAR! BERLIN SEIZED BY REVOLUTIONISTS; NEW CHANCELLOR BEGS FOR ORDER; OUSTED KAISER FLEES TO HOLLAND

SON FLEES WITH EX-KAISER

Hindenburg Also Believed to be Among Those in His Party.

ALL ARE HEAVILY ARMED

Automobiles Bristle with Rifles as Fugitives Arrive at Dutch Frontier.

ON THEIR WAY TO DE STEEG

Belgians Yell to Them, "Are You On Your Way to Paris?"

LONDON, Nov. 10.—Both the former German Emperor and his eldest son, Frederick William, crossed the Dutch frontier Sunday morning, according to advices from The Hague. His reported destination is De Steeg, near Utrecht.

The former German Emperor's party, which is believed to include Field Marshal von Hindenburg, arrived at Eysden, [midway between Liége and Maastricht,] on the Dutch frontier, at 7:30 o'clock Sunday morning, according to Daily Mail advices.

Practically the whole German General Staff accompanied the former Emperor, and ten automobiles carried the party. The automobiles were bristling with rifles, and all the fugitives were armed.

The ex-Kaiser was in uniform. He alighted at the Eysden station and paced the platform, smoking a cigarette.

Many photographs were taken by [of?] the members of the Imperial party. On the whole the people were very quiet, but Belgians among them yelled out "En voyage a Paris." (Are you on your way to Paris?)

Chatting with the members of the staff, the former Emperor, the correspondent says, did not look in the least distressed. A few minutes later an imperial train, including restaurant and sleeping cars, ran into the station. Only servants were aboard.

The engine returned to Visé, Belgium, and brought back a second train, in which were a large number of staff officers and others, and also stores of food.

The preparations began for the departure at 10 o'clock this morning, but at 10:40 o'clock the train was still at Eysden. The blinds of the train were all drawn.

The Daily Mail remarks that, if the party arrived in Holland armed, all of them must be interned.

While other dispatches con-

Continued on Page Three.

Kaiser Fought Hindenburg's Call for Abdication; Failed to Get Army's Support in Keeping Throne

By GEORGE RENWICK.

Special Cable to THE NEW YORK TIMES.

AMSTERDAM, Nov. 10.—I learn on very good authority that the Kaiser made a determined effort to stave off abdication. He went to headquarters with the deliberate intention of bringing the army around to his side. In this he failed miserably.

His main support consisted of a number of officers, nearly all of Prussian regiments, who formed themselves into two regiments and placed themselves at his Majesty's disposal. To do anything with such support was seen, of course, to be Gilbertian.

During the night the Kaiser called the Crown Prince, Hindenburg, and General Gröner to him, and the consultation lasted a couple of hours. Both officers strongly pressed the Kaiser to bow to the inevitable, and Hindenburg informed him that any more delay in coming to a decision to abdicate would certainly have the most terrible consequences and lead to serious events in the army. For those consequences Hindenburg said he must refuse responsibility.

The Crown Prince, it is said, was the first to give way. General Gröner fully supported Hindenburg's view, but when the conference broke up the Kaiser remained unconvinced of the advisability of abdication. He is said to have come to his final decision an hour or so later, after several communications had reached him from Berlin and after another short and stormy talk with Hindenburg.

Meanwhile, his son-in-law, the Duke of Brunswick, for himself and his heir, had abdicated. "Brunswick's Fated Chieftain" was forced without fighting to abdicate. Reports have it that the republican movement in Brunswick, which long before the war was chafing under autocratic conditions, began to be noticed even before it was set in motion at Kiel.

Kaiser Shivered as He Signed Abdication

LONDON, Nov. 10.—Emperor William signed his letter of abdication on Saturday morning at the German Grand Headquarters in the presence of Crown Prince Frederick William and Field Marshal Hindenburg, according to a dispatch from Amsterdam to the Exchange Telegraph Company.

The Crown Prince signed his renunciation of the throne shortly afterward.

Before placing his signature to the document, an urgent message from Philipp Scheidemann, who was a Socialist member without portfolio in the Imperial Cabinet, was handed to the Emperor. He read it with a shiver. Then he signed the paper, saying:

"It may be for the good of Germany."

The Emperor was deeply moved. He consented to sign the document only when he got the news of the latest events in the empire.

The ex-Kaiser and former Crown Prince were expected to take leave of their troops on Saturday, but nothing had then been settled regarding their future movements.

GERMAN DYNASTIES BEING WIPED OUT

King of Wuerttemberg Abdicates—Sovereign of Saxony to Follow Suit.

PRINCES MAY BE EXILED

Socialists Are Demanding That Every Sovereign in the Empire Shall be Dethroned.

LONDON, Nov. 10.—A Havas dispatch from Basle says:

"Wilhelm II., the reigning King of the monarchy of Würtemberg, abdicated on Friday night."

A Wolff Bureau dispatch from Stuttgart, by way of Amsterdam, says that the King has issued a proclamation saying that his person would never serve to hinder the development of the wishes of the people.

According to a report received from Berne, the German Socialists are demanding that every dynasty in Germany be suppressed and all the Princes exiled. It is reported that the Kings of Bavaria and Saxony intend to abdicate soon.

Here is a list of the rules, until several days ago, of the various parts of the German Empire. Those who have abdicated and those reported to be on the point of abdication are marked by an asterisk:

ANHALT—Duke Edward, son of the late Duke Friedrich of Anhalt and of Princess Antoinette of Saxe-Altenberg. Succeeded his brother April 18, 1861.

BADEN—Friedrich II., succeeded to

Continued on Page Two.

MORE WARSHIPS JOIN THE REDS

Four Dreadnoughts in Kiel Harfor Espouse the Revolutionary Cause.

GUARDSHIPS ALSO GO OVER

Those Protecting Mines in the Great Bolt and the Baltic Abandon Their Posts.

LONDON, Nov. 10.—The crews of the German dreadnoughts Posen, Ostfriesland, Nassau, and Oldenburg, in Kiel Harbor, have joined the revolution, says a Copenhagen dispatch. Marines occupied the lock gates at Ostmoor and fought down a coast artillery division which offered resistance.

According to the British Wireless Service three German destroyers have anchored outside of Stockholm. All the guardships in the Baitic, it is said. have joined the revolutionary movement.

Six more cruisers flying the red flag arrived at Hamburg last night, says a Wolff News Agency dispatch received in Copenhagen.

An Amsterdam dispatch states that the Berlin Vossische Zeitung and Vorwärts confirm the fact that the inception of the revolution at Kiel was mistaken for the idea that a cruise had been ordered and that it was intended to give battle to the British fleet.

Up to Friday night the number of persons killed at Kiel was twenty-eight, according to information re-

Continued on Page Three.

BERLIN TROOPS JOIN REVOLT

Reds Shell Building in Which Officers Vainly Resist.

THRONGS DEMAND REPUBLIC

Revolutionary Flag on Royal Palace—Crown Prince's Palace Also Seized.

GENERAL STRIKE IS BEGUN

Burgomaster and Police Submit—War Office Now Under Socialist Control.

LONDON, Nov. 10.—The greater part of Berlin is in control of revolutionists, the former Kaiser has fled to Holland, and Friedrich Ebert, the new Socialist Chancellor, has taken command of the situation. The revolt is spreading throughout Germany with great rapidity.

Dispatches received in London today announce these startling developments. The Workmen's and Soldiers' Council is now administering the municipal government of the German capital.

The War Ministry has submitted, and its acts are valid only when countersigned by a Socialist representative. The official Wolff telegraphic agency has been taken over by the Reds.

The red flag has been hoisted over the royal palace and the Brandenburg Gate. The former Crown Prince's palace is also in possession of the revolutionists.

There was severe fighting in Berlin between 8 and 10 o'clock last night and a violent cannonade was heard from the heart of the city.

Burgomaster and Police Join.

A Copenhagen dispatch states that Dr. Liebknecht, the famous Socialist, who spent many months in prison for antagonizing the German Imperial Government and who was recently released, has issued the following announcement in Berlin in behalf of the Workmen's and Soldiers' Council:

"The Presidency of the police, as well as the Chief Command, is in our hands. Our comrades will be released."

A dispatch from Berne states that the Burgomaster of Berlin has placed himself and his staff at the disposal of the new Government.

Some German newspapers describe the movement as Bolshevism. The people are shouting "Long live the Republic!" and singing the "Marseillaise."

Officers Shelled by Reds.

When revolutionary soldiers attempted to enter a building in Berlin in which they supposed that a number of officers were concealed shots were fired from the windows. The Reds then began shelling the building. Many persons were killed and wounded before the officers surrendered.

When the cannonade began the people thought the Reichsbank was being bombarded, and thousands rushed to the square in front of the Crown Prince's palace. It was later determined that other buildings were under fire. Among those killed in the fighting at the "Cockchafer" Barracks was one of the workmen's leaders known as "Comrade" Habersroth.

The Reds, at last reports, were maintaining order.

Berlin was occupied by forces of the Soldiers' and Workmen's Councils on Saturday afternoon, according to a Wolff Bureau report received in Copenhagen. News of Emperor William's abdication was received in the city on that afternoon with general rejoicing, which was tempered by the fear that it had come too late.

Russians Aid in Outbreak.

How far the example of the Russian Bolsheviki influenced the German upheaval is an interesting question. Red flags figured frequently in the various risings and Chancellor Ebert's motor car floats the international emblem.

The shoulder straps were torn from the uniforms of officers in a number of German cities and even the soldiers' insignia were stripped from them. Russian prisoners played a part in the demonstrations in two or three towns.

Delegates of the revolutionary German navy arrived in Berlin on Friday, according to a dispatch from Copenhagen. They conferred for several hours with the Minister of Marine and with members of the Reichstag majority parties.

It is stated that Hugo Haase, a Socialist leader in the Reichstag, has the situation at Hamburg in hand.

It is officially announced from Berlin, according to a Copenhagen dispatch, that the War Ministry has placed itself at the disposal of Chancellor Ebert. This action was for the purpose of assuring the provisioning of the army and assisting in the solution of demobilization problems.

Serious food difficulties are expected in Germany, owing to the stoppage of trains. The Council of the Regency will take the most drastic steps to re-establish order.

In the new German Government there will be only three representatives of the majority parties, namely, Erzberger, Gothein, and Richthofen, says a dispatch from Copenhagen. The other posts will be occupied by Socialists and independents.

Reds Announce Success.

BERLIN, Nov. 9, (German Wireless to London, Nov. 10)—(Associated Press.)—The German People's Government has been instituted in the greater part of Berlin. The garrison has gone over to the Government.

The Workmen's and Soldiers' Council has declared a general strike. Troops and machine guns have been placed at the disposal of the Council. Guards which had been stationed at the public offices and other buildings have been withdrawn.

Friedrich Ebert (Vice President of the Social Democratic Party) is carrying on the Chancellorship.

The text of a statement issued by the People's Government reads:

In the course of the forenoon of Saturday the formation of a new German People's Government was initiated. The greater part of the Berlin garrison, and other troops stationed there temporarily, went over to the new Government.

The leaders of the deputations of the Social Democratic Party declared that they would not shoot against the people. They said they would, in accordance with the People's Government, intercede in favor of the maintenance of order. Thereupon in the offices and public buildings the guards which had been stationed there were withdrawn.

The business of the Imperial Chancellor is being carried on by the Social Democratic Deputy, Herr Ebert.

It is presumed that, apart from the representatives of the recent majority group, three independent Social Democrats will enter the future Government.

Scheidemann Exhorts Calm.

Deputy Scheidemann, (leader of the majority Socialists in the Reichstag,) in a speech today. said:

"The Kaiser and the Crown Prince have abdicated. The dynasty

Continued on Page Four.

Socialist Chancellor Appeals to All Germans To Help Him Save Fatherland from Anarchy

BERNE, Nov. 10, (Associated Press.)—In an address to the people, the new German Chancellor, Friedrich Ebert, says:

Citizens: The ex-Chancellor, Prince Max of Baden, in agreement with all the Secretaries of State, has handed over to me the task of liquidating his affairs as Chancellor. I am on the point of forming a new Government in accord with the various parties, and will keep public opinion [illegible] informed of the course of events.

The new Government will be a Government of the people. It must make every effort to secure in the quickest possible time peace for the German people and consolidate the liberty which they have won.

The new Government has taken charge of the administration, to preserve the German people from civil war and famine and to accomplish their legitimate claim to autonomy. The Government can solve this problem only if all the officials in town and country will help.

I know it will be difficult for some to work with the new men who have taken charge of the empire, but I appeal to their love of the people. Lack of organization would in this heavy time mean anarchy in Germany and the surrender of the country to tremendous misery. Therefore, help your native country with fearless, indefatigable work for the future, every one at his post.

I demand every one's support in the hard task awaiting us. You know how seriously the war has menaced the provisioning of the people, which is the first condition of the people's existence. The political transformation should not trouble the people. The food supply is the first duty of all, whether in town or country, and they should not embarrass, but rather aid, the production of food supplies and their transport to the towns.

Food shortage signifies pillage and robbery, with great misery. The poorest will suffer the most, and the industrial worker will be affected hardest. All who illicitly lay hands on food supplies or other supplies of prime necessity or the means of transport necessary for their distribution will be guilty in the highest degree toward the community.

I ask you immediately to leave the streets and remain orderly and calm.

COPENHAGEN, Nov. 10.—The new Berlin Government, according to a Wolff Bureau dispatch, has issued the following proclamation:

Fellow-Citizens: This day the people's deliverance has been fulfilled. The Social Democratic Party has undertaken to form a Government. It has invited the Independent Socialist Party to enter the Government with equal rights.

WAR ENDS AT 6 O'CLOCK THIS MORNING

The State Department in Washington Made the Announcement at 2:45 o'Clock.

ARMISTICE WAS SIGNED IN FRANCE AT MIDNIGHT

Terms Include Withdrawal from Alsace-Lorraine, Disarming and Demobilization of Army and Navy, and Occupation of Strategic Naval and Military Points.

By The Associated Press.

WASHINGTON, Monday, Nov. 11, 2:48 A. M.—The armistice between Germany, on the one hand, and the allied Governments and the United States, on the other, has been signed.

The State Department announced at 2:45 o'clock this morning that Germany had signed.

The department's announcement simply said: "The armistice has been signed."

The world war will end this morning at 6 o'clock, Washington time, 11 o'clock Paris time.

The armistice was signed by the German representatives at midnight.

This announcement was made by the State Department at 2:50 o'clock this morning.

The announcement was made verbally by an officila of the State Department in this form:

"The armistice has been signed. It was signed at 5 o clock A. M., Paris time, [midnight, New York time,] and hostilities will cease at 11 o'clock this morning, Paris time, [6 o'clock, New York time.]

The terms of the armistice, it was announced, will not be made public until later. Military men here, however, regard it as certain that they include:

Immediate retirement of the German military forces from France, Belgium, and Alsace-Lorraine.

Disarming and demobilization of the German armies.

Occupation by the allied and American forces of such strategic points in Germany as will make impossible a renewal of hostilities.

Delivery of part of the German High Seas Fleet and a certain number of submarines to the allied and American naval forces.

Disarmament of all other German warships

under supervision of the allied and American Navies, which will guard them.

Occupation of the principal German naval bases by sea forces of the victorious nations.

Release of allied and American soldiers, sailors, and civilians held prisoners in Germany without such reciprocal action by the associated Governments.

There was no information as to the circumstances under which the armistice was signed, but since the German courier did not reach German military headquarters until 10 o'clock yesterday morning, French time, it was generally assumed here that the German envoys within the French lines had been instructed by wireless to sign the terms.

Forty-seven hours had been required for the courier to reach the German headquarters, and unquestionably several hours were necessary for the examination of the terms and a decision.

It was regarded as possible, however, that the decision may have been made at Berlin and instructions transmitted from there by the new German Government.

Germany had until 11 o'clock this morning, French time, (6 o'clock, Washington time,) to accept. So hostilities will end at the hour set by Marshal Foch for a decision by Germany for peace or for continuation of the war.

The momentous news that the armistice had been signed was telephoned to the White House for transmission to the President a few minutes before it was given to the newspaper correspondents.

Later it was said that there would be no statement from the White House at this time.

Armistice Courier Was Much Delayed.

LONDON, Nov. 10, (British Wireless Service.)—The German courier bearing the text of the armistice conditions arrived at German headquarters at 10 o'clock this morning, according to the official announcement from Paris. The courier, Captain Helldorf, was long delayed while the German batteries persisted in bombarding the route he had to follow.

On Saturday morning the German delegates suggested that the courier's mission might be attempted by airplane. The French High Command saw no objection to this and offered to furnish a machine on condition that the German High Command pledge itself that the airplane would not be fired at. A rapid message was sent to German headquarters, which was replied to without delay as follows:

"We grant free passage to the French airplane bringing our courier. We are issuing orders that it shall not be attacked by any of our machines. For the purpose of recognition it should carry two white flags very clearly marked."

The orders from the German headquarters staff, however, were inoperative as regarded the land batteries, for on La Capelle road the enemy's fire, despite reiterated requests to desist, went on without intermission.

A French airplane, piloted by an officer of the French Air Service, was soon available, and the pilot was ordered to hold himself ready to start on his journey. About that time a message came from General Headquarters, announcing that orders for the cessation of fire had been given to the batteries directed against La Capelle Road, and that Captain Helldorf was at liberty to start by automobile. Almost immediately the German fire ceased, and the courier set out on the road for Spa at 3:20 o'clock in the afternoon.

German headquarters was notified of his departure, and informed that he might be expected to arrive in the evening. But the road was long and hard, and many delays occurred.

PARIS, Nov. 10.—"It is possible," says the Temps, after recording the delayed arrival of the German courier at Spa with the armistice conditions, "that, owing to this delay, due to material circumstances, the seventy-two hours' grace may be prolonged. Such prolongation may be necessary through the events which are occupying Germany."

BERLIN, Nov. 10, (By Wireless to London, 8:50 P. M.)—The arrival of the armistice conditions in Berlin is expected hourly.

LONDON, Nov. 9.—The German armistice terms, The Daily Express says it understands, are even more stringent than those forecast on Oct. 31. Germany will be absolutely deprived, the newspaper adds, of further military power or action on land and sea and in the air.

The British War Cabinet sat late tonight, Premier Lloyd George having returned purposely from the country.

Mr. Balfour, the Foreign Minister, had an audience today with the King, who, on account of the armistice situation, has postponed his projected tour of the provinces.

A message from the German Commissaries to the German High Command, transmitted by the French Government wireless, says:

"We acknowledge receipt of two radios announcing the arrival of the four Commissaries (delegates?) and their probable delay for some hours."

HARDEN PREDICTED TRUCE BY YESTERDAY

Versailles Terms Hard, He Said, but Germany Must Not Forget Her Record in 1871.

By GEORGE RENWICK.

Copyright, 1918, by The New York Times Company. Special Cable to THE NEW YORK TIMES.

AMSTERDAM, Nov. 8.—"I believe by Sunday the guns will be at rest," said Maximilian Harden in a lecture on Wednesday in Berlin. Minute-long applause followed the statement. Reason had triumphed, he went on, and though the conditions formulated at Versailles would be hard, Germany must not forget that forty-seven years ago the Germans at the same place set forth iron-hard terms.

Dealing with the problem, who was to blame for the sorry position wherein Germany now found herself, Harden said that civilians might be acquitted of guilt for what was done in August, 1914. It was the military régime which was to blame for the war.

In August last, he went on, Ludendorff, for the first time, recognized the impossibility of victory, and advised von Hintze to make peace. Though Harden termed Ludendorff the "German Bonaparte," and said he accomplished great things, "it cannot be hidden," he added, "that he was completely deceived regarding the economic and technical strength of the Entente. But things would not have happened as they have, had not Hindenburg and Ludendorff for four years kept the German people in a maze of falsehood and deception as to the actual situation. The policy of the military leaders has suffered the most complete shipwreck."

Harden supported the demand for the abdication of the Kaiser, and warned the Government that it was necessary to protect the country against Bolshevism.

TAKES OVER WOLFF BUREAU

'Comrade William Karle' in Control of Semi-Official Agency.

BERLIN, Nov. 10, (via London.)—An official communication issued today says the Wolff Bureau, the semi-official news agency, has been placed under control of "Comrade William Karle."

No records showing who William Karle is are available. If he is a journalist his name has not appeared among those who have been writing for the German press during the war.

American Flier Drowned Off England

LONDON, Nov. 8.—Lieutenant George Nelonsbe, an aviator from California, fell with his machine into the sea on Wednesday night and was drowned.

NEWS OF ARMISTICE FLASHED TO CITY

Signing of Truce Tidings Wafted Afar by Searchlight on Times Building.

CROWDS GATHER IN STREETS

Whistles Throughout City Proclaim Glad News, and Thousands Awake to Get the Tidings.

When the first bulletin of the signing of the armistice, with the acceptance of the terms of the Allies, came into the office of THE NEW YORK TIMES shortly before 3 o'clock this morning orders were given immediately for the lighting up of both The Times Building and The Times Annex, and they remained lighted throughout the rest of the hours of darkness.

A few minutes after the first word had reached the newspaper office the searchlight on the tower of The Times Building played its rays all over the city. It had been put into operation to announce the results of the election on last Tuesday, and the flashing of more momentous news attracted crowds to Times Square.

In such a few minutes that it was almost beyond the belief of persons who have never seen a great city rejoicing over the greatest of former victories and over events of a magnitude to stun the mind, the Square was filled with many hundreds of persons. It was a mystery to all where they came from. Many came out of the subway, others came out of the restaurants, cigar stores, and other places that remain open all night.

This throng was increased by drivers who left their milk wagons, their newspaper wagons, by men on their way to work, by taxicab chauffeurs, by street car conductors, and by many other folk who had heard the tooting of sirens in their neighborhoods and who arose from their beds to find out just what was the latest event of a day that will be marked forever in history.

The display of large bulletins in the windows of The Times Building saying that the armistice had been signed, together with the news in the earlier editions of the paper that the former German Kaiser had fled from just retribution, moved these many hundreds to full-throated and full-lunged jubilance.

The same bulletins were displayed in the windows of the offices of THE TIMES in other parts of the city, and soon they were the centre of crowds that had forgotten completely that the city had already had one day of celebration over what had been a false report of the event all longed for.

Celebration began all over again, and at that late hour it looked as if the city would outdo its "fake rumor" day, or London's Mafeking Day, and every other day where millions rejoiced.

Police sirens and bells all over the city again took up the Swan Song of the Kaiser, of militarism, and thousands were waked from their slumbers by the din. Hundreds got up from their beds and walked the streets in tousled clothes to get confirmation of the news they had been expecting. Other hundreds saw the flashing of the searchlights from the tower of THE TIMES and telephone calls by the hundreds began to pour into the newspaper office.

The invariable question was: "Has the armistice been signed?" and when the question was answered with the affirmative, with the additional information that the Kaiser's right to rule had passed with him in unroyal flight, there were cheers at the other end of the wire.

Among the hundreds around the bulletin boards in Times Square were many sailors and soldiers who had service stripes on their sleeves, some of them having more than one stripe. Many had medals, and many more had scars, scars put upon them by the soldiers of the man whose downfall was reported.

At first these men were unable to comprehend the news. The crowds of civilians were not so slow. They seized the soldiers and sailors and made them prisoners to admiration. The crowd waltzed the soldiers and sailors on their shoulders and bounced them around, pounded them on the backs, cheered them, set them down and tried to force them to make speeches, and then drowned their first words with cheers.

Groans and cries went up from the crowd when the name of William Hohenzollern was mentioned. "Poor Bill! He tried to pinch off the world! He's gone! Bill's dead," one man cried. The man who was taken seriously only a few weeks ago had suddenly become a joke because the allied armies had beaten him so decisively and because he had run away, with his Crown Prince, his General Staff, and a train full of food.

PARIS CONVINCED WAR IS FINISHED

Germans Must and Will Surrender, Is Prevalent Feeling in Boulevard Throngs.

Copyright, 1918, by The New York Times Company. Special Cable to THE NEW YORK TIMES.

PARIS, Nov. 10.—Are the Germans manoeuvring for a further military struggle or are they prepared to surrender, no matter what the terms?

That is a question the French people are asking themselves. But putting the question apparently is more for the sake of speculative interest than because of doubt. There is remarkable unanimity in the answer to the effect that Germany must and will surrender.

The thought that is in the air all over Paris is, "The war is finished." You can feel it. You can see it in the faces in the street. It is just as tangible a thing as was the gloom last Spring and Summer, before the beginning of the great victory of July 18.

It is many weeks since things have fallen out of the sky to kill Parisians and damage property. Today things are going up, instead. I mean toy balloons. This is worth mentioning, because, if anything is symbolic of festive cheer, it is the sight of old men and women in the crowds with bunches of red and blue balloons over their shoulders to sell to the children.

There are such crowds today in the Place de la Concorde and the Champs Elysées looking at the hundreds of captured German cannon and gleefully commenting on the coming of a white flag from the armies that were so recently using those same cannon with deadly effect against the allied troops.

There are thousands of these cannon of all kinds and all calibers clustered thickly in the centre of the Place de la Concorde, where the guillotine was set up a little over a century ago, and spreading out in long lines along the Seine, in the Tuileries Gardens and up the Champs Elysées.

In one short block I counted 130 big cannon pointing at one another on opposite sides of the street.

On a smaller scale it is the same way throughout the towns all over France, where captured cannon are being given to municipalities for public squares as rewards for their good showing on Liberation Loan subscriptions.

There are no rope guards around the captured guns in the Paris streets. Children are allowed to swarm over them, play horse on them, fight imaginary battles, and monkey with the mechanism that raises and lowers the muzzles to their hearts' content.

Thousands of pairs of little breeches in Paris are no doubt streaked with rust from climbing over the cannon today. But no boy gets scolded. The war is finished, says the crowd, and the great victory is ours; nothing else matters for the moment.

More seriously there is much comment on the personnel of Germany's truce quartet. Von Winterfeld is thought as little of in Paris as a Bernstorff or von Papen would be in New York.

But inasmuch as Foch will do all the talking at the armistice conferences nobody cares much about the personality of those who bear the white flag. The developments of the last few days, the Austrian surrender and the German surrender being almost taken for granted, seem to have done much to change that portion of French public opinion which was adverse to conversations between Washington and Berlin.

AUSTRIA SENDS BACK 250,000 ITALIANS

Released Prisoners Say They Found Little Violence, Except in Hunger Strikes.

ITALIAN ARMY HEADQUARTERS IN NORTHERN ITALY, Nov. 10, (Associated Press.)—More than a quarter of a million Italian prisoners of war held in Austria have been returned to Italy. Sick and wounded men will be returned later by way of Switzerland.

The repatriated soldiers say that violent conditions are not prevalent in Austria, except disorders due to hunger strikes. They declare that the civilians desire heartily to see the return of their own men home. The soldiers in Austria are indifferent or else express happiness that the war is over.

Italian officers returning from Austria express the opinion that for the present there will be no disturbances in Austria like those in Russia.

GERMAN DYNASTIES BEING WIPED OUT

Continued from Page 1, Column 2.

the throne as Grand Duke Sept. 28, 1907.

*BAVARIA—King Ludwig III., proclaimed Nov. 5, 1913.

*BRUNSWICK—Duke Ernest Augustus.

HESSE—Grand Duke Ernest Ludwig, succeeded at the death of his father March 13, 1892.

LIPPE—Prince Leopold IV. Leopold assumed the Regency in succession to his father, Sept. 27, 1904, but the right of succession was claimed by Prince Georg of Schaumburg-Lippe, and the dispute was settled in Leopold's favor by a judicial court at Leipsig, Oct. 25, 1905.

MECKLENBURG - SCHWERIN — Grand Duke Friedrich Franz IV. succeeded on the death of his father, April 10, 1897.

OLDENBURG—Grand Duke Friedrich August succeeded at the death of his father, June 13, 1900.

PRUSSIA—Wilhelm II. succeeded his father, June 15, 1888.

REUSS, (Elder Branch) — Prince Heinrich XXIV. succeeded his father, April 19, 1902.

REUSS, (Younger Branch)—Prince Heinrich XXVII. succeeded his father, March 29, 1913.

SAXE-ALTENBURG—Duke Ernest II. succeeded to the throne, Feb. 7, 1908.

SAXE-COBURG AND GOTHA.—Duke Charles Edward, succeeded his uncle, Alfred, July 30, 1900.

SAXE-MEININGEN. — Duke Bernhard, succeeded on the death of his father, June 25, 1914.

GRAND DUCHY OF SAXE-WEIMAR-EISENACH.—Grand Duke Wilhelm Ernst, succeeded his grandfather, Jan. 5, 1901.

*KINGDOM OF SAXONY. — King Friedrich August III., succeeded to the throne on the death of his father, Oct. 15, 1904.

SCHAUMBURG-LIPPE. — Prince Adolf, succeeded his father, April 29, 1911.

SCHWARZBURG - RUDOLSTADT—Prince Gunther succeeded his cousin Jan. 19, 1890.

SCHWARZBURG - SONDERHAUSEN—Since the decease on March 28, 1909, of Prince Karl Gunther, this principality has been united with Schwarzburg-Rudolstadt by a personal bond of union under the government of Prince Gunther.

WALDECK — Prince Friedrich succeeded at the death of his father, May 12, 1893.

*WURTTEMBERG — King Wilhelm II. ascended the throne Oct. 6, 1891.

Had Reigned Since 1891.

Wilhelm II., King of Württemberg was born Feb. 25, 1848, the son of Prince Friedrich of Württemberg and of Princess Katharine of Württemberg. He ascended the throne Oct. 6, 1891. He married twice. His first wife was Princess Katharine of Württenberg. He died April 30, 1882, leaving a daughter, Princess Pauline, born Dec. 19, 1877. His second wife was Princess Charlotte of Schaumburg-Lippe, who died April 8, 1886.

The former Duchy of Württemberg became, with a large increase of territory, an electorate in 1803 and was created a kingdom by the Peace of Pressburg, 1805, and by a decree of Jan. 1, 1806. Württemberg is a constitutional hereditary monarchy, the Constitution of which bears the date of Sept. 25, 1819, but changes were made in 1906.

Friedrich August III. was born May 25, 1865, the son of King George, and succeeded to the throne on the death of his father, Oct. 15, 1904. He married Princess Luise of Tuscany Nov. 21, 1891, and the marriage was dissolved Feb. 11, 1903. Children born of the marriage were Prince George, Prince Friedrich Christian, Prince Ernst Heinrich, Princess Margarethe, Princess Marie Alix and Princess Anna Monica.

The royal house of Saxony is one of the oldest reigning families in Europe. Saxony included the Governmental divisions of Dresden, Leipsig, Bautzen, Chemnitz, and Swickau. Its estimated population in 1914 was 4,984,500, and its area is 5,787 square miles.

Although the religion of the royal family is Catholic, the vast majority of the inhabitants are Protestants. In proportion to its size Saxony is the busiest industrial State in the German Empire.

The house of Saxony dates back to Heinrich of Eilenberg, of the family of Wettin, who was Margrave of Meissen, 1089-1103. The house spread subsequently into numerous branches, the elder of which, called the Ernestine Line, is represented by the ducal families of Saxe-Altenburg, Saxe-Coburg-Gotha, and Saxe-Meiningen, and the grand ducal family of Saxe-Weimar, while the younger, the Albertine line, lives in the rulers of the Kingdom of Saxony. In 1806 the Elector Friedrich August III., on entering the Confederation of the Rhine, took from Napoleon the title of King of Saxony, which was confirmed by the Congress of Vienna in 1815.

PEACE CONFERENCE NOW LONDON TOPIC

Speed a Prime Requisite, it Is Believed, in Bringing Plenipotentiaries Together.

QUESTION IS "WHAT NEXT?"

Germany Not Thought Likely to Go to the Extremes Seen in Russia and Austria.

Copyright, 1918, by The New York Times Company. Special Cable to THE NEW YORK TIMES.

LONDON, Monday, Nov. 11.—While it will necessarily take some time to arrange the preliminaries for a peace conference, since America's plenipotentiaries, for instance, could hardly arrive with requisite agenda under a month, and in some quarters a much longer period is expected to elapse before the conference gets to work, there is a profound feeling here that the utmost expedition is desirable.

The expectation here is that the first step will be to summon a more or less informal conference of the Allies to settle the preliminaries. Much, however, will depend on the question as to what enemy Governments will be in existence to deal with.

The conclusion of hostilities finds England with greatly enhanced prestige in the world and with power such as she never before wielded. The Chronicle says:

"By her alliance with America she is indeed arbiter of war and peace in the universe. Satisfaction is profound in this country that the peace is in every sense a British peace, responding exactly to our desires and providing, if such is possible, some compensation for our sacrifices."

However, the lengths to which the revolution will go in Germany will influence to a large extent the character of the peace. Some fears are expressed that no durable government may at first rise out of the ashes of imperialism. On the other hand, a wide extension of the revolution does not necessarily portend Bolshevism, as it is considered that the natural discipline of the German people will restrain them from excesses, provided the morale of the army is not too hopelessly compromised by the sweeping movements of the allied troops.

It is clearly within the power of any General who retains the confidence of his troops to restore quiet by suppressing outbreaks. An analogy between Russia and Germany is by no means complete, for the Germans are educated and accustomed to self-control.

The weakness of the position, however, resides in the fact that the middle classes lack initiative and have depended in the past entirely upon the Government.

They are therefore little likely to contribute materially to the re-establishment of order. Again there is not the same reason why Germany should follow the example of Austria and break into constituent parts.

There are no racial differences to accentuate the political divisions in the German Empire, yet there are undoubted signs of separatism. The effort to form a republic in Schleswig-Holstein is due largely to racial causes, for the Danish element is notoriously anti-German.

Though Ebert belongs to the majority Socialists, who until recently supported the Government in all its proceedings, there is evidence elsewhere that minority Socialists such as Haase and Ledebour at Hamburg are themselves co-operating to restore order. The danger is that tomorrow the public, maddened by its sufferings and by deceptions practiced upon it, will proceed to extreme lengths.

OLD NORTH CHIMES RING.

Bells Which Have Pealed for Great Historical Events Again Sounded.

BOSTON, Nov. 10.—The chime of bells in the tower of the Old North Church, Salem Street, which for 180 years has pealed in celebration of great historical events, again rang out today in celebration of the announced abdication of the German Emperor.

Patriotic airs were chimed from 10:15 to 10:45 A. M. These chimes were played before the Revolution by Peter Faneuil and Paul Revere. They pealed out the glad news when the Stamp Act was repealed in 1776, and informed Boston of the Declaration of Independence in the same year.

Polish Republic Announced; Galicia Is Taken Over

AMSTERDAM, Nov. 9.—A message from Cracow announces the formation of a Polish Republic under the Presidency of Deputy Daszynski.

AMSTERDAM, Nov. 10.—Professor Lammasch, the Austrian Premier, has received official notification, says a dispatch from Vienna, that Poland has assumed sovereignty over Galicia.

Galicia is a crownland of Austria-Hungary north of the Carpathians. It has an area of 30,307 square miles and in normal times had a population of some 7,000,000.

TRAVEL FROM HOLLAND TO PARIS BY AUTO

Americans Find German Electric Barrier Destroyed and Vast Stores Abandoned.

By CHARLES H. GRASTY.

Copyright, 1918, by The New York Times Company. Special Cable to THE NEW YORK TIMES.

PARIS, Nov. 10.—An automobile journey overland from Holland to Paris has just been completed by Gilman Paul, Secretary, and Captain Robert Goelet, Assistant Miliary Attaché of the American Legation at The Hague. They left there a little over a week ago and made their way from The Hague to Flushing and ferried across the Scheldt to Breskens, where they were met by a French military motor.

Crossing the Dutch frontier at Sluis, they were compelled to make a detour via Zeebrugge to Bruges, the direct road having been blown up by the Germans.

The actual time occupied was two days, but several days were spent on the way taking observations.

Paul and Goelet say that the electric fence which the Germans maintained between Holland and Germany, with its 4,000 volts of current, has been destroyed and that work is progressing on road repairs, so that within a few days an auto trip from Paris to Holland can be completed in twenty-four hours.

They saw mountains of material that had been abandoned by the German Army in the retreat.

Mr. Paul and Captain Goelet came to Paris to prepare for a weekly courier service overland between Paris and The Hague.

PARIS CROWDS CHEER NEWS.

Await the Armistice Bulletin While Rejoicing in Fresh Victories.

Copyright, 1918, by The New York Times Company. Special Cable to THE NEW YORK TIMES.

PARIS, Nov. 9.—The moonlit boulevards and streets of Paris were filled tonight with joyous crowds, waiting momentarily for expected news of the armistice. In the meantime, all other good news was received with shouts, and it is coming fast. Hardly had the crowds finished cheering over the request of Prince Maximilian made to be relieved of the Chancellorship when newspaper office bulletins recorded the fact that the Kaiser had abdicated.

Almost simultaneously Paris learned that Romanoues had become Premier of Spain and General Coanda Premier of Rumania. Both these men are firm friends of the Allies. Coanda's wife is a Frenchwoman.

But all these big things, even to abdication itself, which had been discounted, were looked upon only as the curtain-raisers for the big fact yet to come of the ending of the war. No details have been received here as to who will succeed the Kaiser, but it is taken for granted that the German Socialists are in the saddle.

TOWNSHEND REACHES PARIS

British General Captured at Kut Shows Signs of Privations.

Copyright, 1918, by The New York Times Company. Special Cable to THE NEW YORK TIMES.

PARIS, Nov. 10.—General Townshend, the British commander captured by the Turks at Kut, arrived in Paris today. He will remain here for some time. He shows signs of the severe treatment he experienced, together with his fellow-prisoners, at the hands of the Turks.

"All the News That's Fit to Print."

The New York Times.

THE WEATHER
Fair today; Thursday cloudy; mild temperature; wind southeast.
For weather report see next to last page.

VOL. LXVIII...NO. 22,278. NEW YORK, WEDNESDAY, JANUARY 22, 1919. TWENTY-TWO PAGES TWO CENTS Metropolitan District 50 Mile Radius | THREE CENTS Within 200 Miles | FOUR CENTS Elsewhere

NEW YORK TO ASK COURTS TO ANNUL NEW PHONE RATES

Service Board Orders Attorney to Join Other States in Fight on Burleson's Order.

JERSEY AND MICHIGAN SUE

Governor of Massachusetts Declares That State's Rights Should Be Protected.

PLEA FOR PRIVATE CONTROL

National Association of State Commissions Opposed to Present Management.

Special to The New York Times.

ALBANY, Jan. 21.—At its session here today the Public Service Commission of the Second District directed its counsel to begin an action, either by mandamus or injunction, to restrain the New York Telephone Company from putting into operation its new tariff of rates under the order of the Postmaster General. The telephone company, it is stated, is now charging substantially increased rates for services.

The new tariff has not been filed with the commission, and it is the opinion of that body that the telephone company is violating Section 92 of the Public Service Commission law. Attorney Ledyard P. Hale will at once proceed against the telephone company under the commission's authority.

"The commission delayed taking action," said Chairman Hill today, "because it was thought that its position would be stronger by waiting until the Postmaster General had put the order into effect. The new rates were promulgated by the Postmaster General with the statement that they brought about a decrease in charges, but analysis by the commission gives the same results as those made by the commissions in Illinois, Ohio, Nebraska, New Jersey, Indiana, Missouri, and other States; that is, that the increase in rates varies from 20 to 100 per cent.

"The general effect of the order of the Postmaster General is to increase charges for certain telephone service covering the bulk of traffic and making charges for certain services which were heretofore free."

Stands for State's Rights.

BOSTON, Jan. 21.—The action of the New England Telephone and Telegraph Company in putting into effect today the new telephone toll rates determined by the Postmaster General was called to the attention of Attorney General Attwill by the Public Service Commission, with a request that proceedings looking to a suspension of the rates be instituted in the State Supreme Court. The commission alleged that the company had violated the laws of the State in ignoring an order of the commission.

"I see no reason," said Governor Coolidge, "why any of the States should surrender any of their rate-making powers to the Federal Government. In times of war emergencies may arise making it advisable not to stand upon the Constitution, but at the present time I feel that the State's interests should be fully protected. I feel strongly that the Public Service Commission, as in the past, should continue to make rates for Massachusetts patrons."

Michigan Asks an Injunction.

LANSING, Mich., Jan. 21.—First steps to test the right of Postmaster General Burleson to fix long-distance telephone rates in Michigan were taken today by Attorney General Groesbeck in petitions in the Circuit Court for an injunction. Separate petitions were filed for each of the companies involved. They ask in addition to the restraining writ, an order requiring the companies to continue the present rates "until they are legally modified."

Order Obtained in Jersey.

TRENTON, N. J., Jan. 21.—Postmaster General Albert S. Burleson, the New York Telephone Company, the Delaware and Atlantic Telephone and Telegraph Company, and the American Telephone and Telegraph Company were ordered tonight, through an order issued by Judge John Rellstab, in the United States court, to appear and show cause at 10:30 o'clock on Monday morning next, in the Federal court here, why an injunction should not issue to restrain the Postmaster General and the telephone companies from continuing in force the order of the Postmaster General increasing telephone rates in New Jersey. These new rates, effective today, should first be approved by the Public Utility Commission, it is alleged.

Judge Rellstab, however, refused to issue a restraining order which would prohibit the immediate continuance of the new rates until the court had had an opportunity to pass upon the application for an injunction.

The petition was presented by Alfred N. Barber, Secretary of the State Utility Commission, through L. Edward Herrmann, counsel for the commission. Mr. Barber contends that the board is empowered by the State laws to have supervision, regulation, and control over all public utilities in the State. He also asserts the board has power to fix "just and reasonable" rates and may require every public utility concern in the State to file with it complete schedules and classification of rates.

The petition sets forth that the Utility Board issued an order yesterday directing the suspension of the new rates in

Continued on Page Four.

France Had 5,192,372 Men Mobilized on Jan. 1, 1918

LYONS, Jan. 21, (Havas.)—The number of effectives mobilized by France from the outbreak of the war is given as follows in the report of Deputy Benazet on the war budget:

Aug. 15, 1914.—Officers, 92,828; soldiers, 3,780,000.

Feb. 15, 1915.—Officers, 97,753; soldiers, 4,900,000.

Jan. 1, 1916.—Officers, 109,814; soldiers, 5,060,000.

Jan. 1, 1917.—Officers, 115,004; soldiers, 5,026,000.

Jan. 1, 1918.—Officers, 128,372; soldiers, 5,064,000.

On Jan. 1, 1918, the infantry numbered 2,106,775; artillery, 899,645; aviation, 59,285; cavalry, 166,422; engineering corps, 185,110.

TREASON CHARGE AT WIRE INQUIRY

Moon Accuses Reynolds, Postal Official, Because He Fought Burleson's Plans.

AID FOR SMALL SYSTEMS

Mackay Manager Insists Control Is in Interest of Crippled Companies and Western Union.

Special to The New York Times.

WASHINGTON, Jan. 21.—Because Edward Reynolds, Vice President and General Manager of the Postal Telegraph-Cable Company, would not comply with orders issued by Postmaster General Burleson, Chairman Moon of the House Post Office Committee this afternoon charged Mr. Reynolds with "treason" at the committee hearing on the bill Judge Moon has written to extend the period of Federal control over the telegraph and telephone system. Trembling with indignation Mr. Reynolds resented the accusation, while members of the committee protested against Judge Moon's treatment of the witness.

The hearing was marked with bitterness all day. Witnesses representing the Minnesota State Railroad and Warehouse Commission, whom Representative Steenerson of that State presented, were accused by Judge Moon of being actuated by the desire to retain their places, which, he said, would be eliminated by Government regulation. There was distinct line-up in the committee, headed by Judge Moon on one side, and Representatives Steenerson and Madden of Illinois, both Republicans, on the other. Solicitor William H. Lamar of the Post Office Department sat beside Judge Moon and coached the Chairman with questions during the session.

It developed during the testimony that Mr. Reynolds had been dismissed on Dec. 1 because he indorsed a letter written by one of his subordinates urging delay and obstruction to the Federal plan of control.

"You were dismissed, were you?" asked Judge Moon.

"I certainly was," replied Mr. Reynolds.

"Because you were treasonable?"

"I take exception to that," exclaimed Mr. Reynolds, while members at the other end of the table shouted "No, No!" One of them, Mr. Madden, interjected:

"That should certainly be stricken from the record."

"You were disloyal to Mr. Burleson," continued Judge Moon.

"My daughter and son are in France and I won't permit you or any one else to impugn my loyalty," responded Mr. Reynolds.

"I think we should proceed with the hearing as if the witness was a human being," said Mr. Madden. "There's no reason that the power of Government should be used to bulldoze the witness."

Produces Reynolds's Letter.

Judge Moon explained that Mr. Reynolds, in his opinion, had been disloyal to the Postmaster General. The letter in question was of few lines and indorsing one in which a district superintendent said that, "as the war was over" the Postmaster General's plans should be rearded, and added, "Thank God for a Republican House and presumably a Republican Senate." Mr. Reynolds said:

"I sent the letter out to some eight officials. It came into the hands of Mr. Burleson, and he dismissed me."

Mr. Reynolds testified he had started with the Postal Company thirty years ago as a messenger and read a prepared statement, in the course of which he said:

"Mr. Burleson's Operating Committee, consisting of a Western Union man, two Bell Telephone men and one Independent Telephone man, has within the last few days tried to get the Postal Company to agree to increased telegraph rates and the Postal Company has refused.

"I am reliably informed that most of the independent telephone companies were making money at the time the Government took them over, and I am also informed that they wish their properties returned at once, notwithstanding the statements made to this committee to the contrary.

"Public sentiment is opposed to retaining the wires, and no one is willing to admit he wishes the Government to keep the telephone lines in order to bring about Government ownership, except Mr. Burleson, himself, because that purpose is a perversion of the purpose for which Congress authorized the seizure of the lines.

"The whole situation looks to me like a scheme for the raising of telephone rates and the financing of crippled tele-

Continued on Page Four.

LIBERAL GROUPS GAIN IN RETURNS OF GERMAN VOTE

Predicted in Berlin That a Socialist-Democratic Alliance Will Control Convention.

EBERT PARTY FACES FIGHT

May Be in a Minority if the Opposition Combines, Copenhagen Estimates.

RHINELAND FOR CENTRISTS

Weimar Reported to Have Been Selected as Meeting Place of National Assembly.

BERLIN, Jan. 20, (Associated Press.)—Full election returns from all sections of Germany are coming into Berlin slowly because of the work in apportioning the vote among the six leading parties.

Based on incomplete returns available at 8 o'clock tonight, the Majority Socialists had from 43 to 45 per cent. of the total vote. With the Independent Socialists and the German Democrats, the Majority Socialists will constitute the Left of the National Assembly, with 65 per cent. of the seats.

The Democratic Party has made an excellent showing, and may outstrip the Centrists (Christian People's Party) in the final count.

The Independent Socialists made a strong eleventh-hour rally in Berlin, and probably will get four out of the fourteen seats from Greater Berlin. The Majority Socialists will get five seats from Greater Berlin, the Democrats two, and the three parties of the Right one each.

Socialists Outvoted in Wurttemberg.

The combined bourgeois parties in the Kingdom of Württemberg and the Province of Hohenzollern, Prussia, elected ten delegates to the National Assembly. The Majority Socialists seated seven and the Independent Socialists none. The combined popular vote of the Socialists was 506,000, and of the bourgeois parties 920,000.

In Mecklenburg and Lübeck the combined bourgeois parties elected three delegates and the Socialists three.

The Majority Socialists appear to have made big gains in East Prussia.

In Hanover and Bremen the Socialists had a large majority over the Independents.

The Independent Socialists in Leipsic polled 195,000 votes against 95,000 for the Majority Socialists.

At Frankfort-on-the-Oder the Majority Socialists elected four delegates, the German Democrats two, the National People's Party two, while the Independent Socialists, the German People's Party, and the Centrists failed to get a seat.

In the Magdeburg-Anhalt district the German Democrats got three delegates, the Majority Socialists seven, the National People's Party one, and the Independent Socialists, German People's Party, and Centrists none.

May Get Final Count Today.

The official final count of the national vote probably will not be available before Wednesday. Numerous votes in Berlin are being contested by the Independent Socialists, who charge the Majority Socialists with having used an illegal caption on their party ballot.

It is probable that former Chief of

Continued on Page Three.

Denial That Root or Taft Will Be Wilson's Alternate

By RICHARD V. OULAHAN.

By Wireless to The New York Times.

PARIS, Jan. 21.—Statements from New York printed in the Paris afternoon newspapers that Elihu Root or William Howard Taft will succeed President Wilson on the American delegation when the President returns to America are said by those close to the President to be unfounded, although no authoritative statement has been issued.

These reports are entirely contrary to the President's announced intentions when he left America. He had arranged then that Secretary Baker should come to France to take his place in the plenipotentiary panel, and there is every reason to believe that there has been no change in his plans. The system for the rotation of plenipotentiaries was adopted, it is understood, partly to fit Mr. Baker's case.

MANUEL READY TO RESUME CROWN

Has Placed Himself Entirely at Disposal of Portugal, His Lord-in-Waiting Says.

ROYALIST CABINET FORMED

Revolt Successful in North, Spanish Government Hears—Lisbon Remains Loyal.

Special Cable to The New York Times.

LONDON, Jan. 21.—Viscount Asseca, Lord-in-Waiting to former King Manuel of Portugal, received The Daily Chronicle representative tonight at the hotel in London where the ex-King is staying. When the latest message from Vigo was shown to the Viscount he made the following statement:

"At the beginning of the war King Manuel made it distinctly understood that there was to be no movement in his favor in Portugal and that his country was to devote the whole of its energies to prosecution of the war. The assassination of the President in December altered the situation and seemed to threaten the country with chaos.

"In the circumstances a new situation was opened up, the possibility of which before was out of the question. The King's position was this, that he placed himself entirely at the disposal of Portugal. If his country wished him to return he would at once do so without any reference to difficulties or dangers that the course would involve.

"He has been treated with infinite kindness in this country, where he has greatly enjoyed his stay, but he has lived with no other idea than to return to his throne."

MADRID, Jan. 21.—The monarchist movement in Portugal, headed by Paiva Conceiro, has been successful in Northern Portugal, and a Government has been formed at Oporto, according to a report received by the Spanish Government yesterday from the Governor of the Province of Ponte Vedra, in Northwestern Spain, who added that Lisbon was believed to have joined the movement.

The monarchical Government, it was said, was constituted with Paiva Conceiro as President of the Council and Food Minister; M. Saleri, Minister of Home Affairs; Viscount Barro, Minister of Justice and Instruction; Magalhaes Lima, Minister of Foreign Affairs; Silva Ramos, Minister of Communication and Public Works; Count Asevedo, Minister of Labor, and Tamagnini Barbosa, Minister of War.

Advices from another source state that the telegraph and telephone lines between Lisbon and Oporto have been cut, and declare that Manuel has also been proclaimed King in Lisbon.

Direct news from Lisbon, received here in an official message, however, states that the Government controls the

Continued on Page Two.

Latest Returns of the German Election Show Socialist Lead for Assembly Seats

The following table shows the definite elections to seats in the German National Assembly, as shown by the latest cabled returns:

	Maj. Soc.	Ind. Soc.	Democrats.	People's.	Chris. People's.	National.	Comb'd Anti-Soc.
Berlin	5	4	2	1	1	1	..
Saxony	17	3	6	2	..	4	..
Württemberg	7	..	..	..	..	..	10
Mecklenburg and Lübeck	3	..	..	1	1	1	..
Baden	5	..	3	..	5	8	..
Hamburg	7	1	3	..	..	..	..
Magdeburg-Anhalt	7	..	3	1	..	..	..
Frankfort-on-Oder	4	..	2	2	..	..	..
Totals	55	8	19	7	7	14	10

Estimated distribution of seats in the National Assembly, based on incomplete returns: Majority Socialists, 184; Majority and Independent Socialists and German Democrats combined, 266; other parties, 144. Total seats in the Assembly, about 410.

Total popular vote so far announced in detail—5,791,430.

Party Totals—Majority Socialists, 1,593,366; Independent Socialists, 548,795; Democrats, 688,315; Christian People's Party, 707,730; People's Party, 198,373; National Party, 218,635; Bavarian parties, 410,224, in Württemberg only. Combined Socialists, 506,000; Combined Anti-Socialists, 920,000.

A Copenhagen compilation of the vote gives a total of 6,082,311, of which the Majority Socialists are said to have received 2,603,422.

The Majority Socialists are the party of Premier Ebert, from which the radical element split and formed the Independent Socialist Party.

The Democratic Party is a radical combination of the former National Liberals and Progressives.

The People's Party is the Pan-German element.

The Christian People's Party is the old Centrist or Catholic Party, now joined by many Protestants.

The National Party is made up of former Conservatives.

IRISH ASSEMBLY PROCLAIMS THE IRISH REPUBLIC

Declaration of Independence Read to First Sinn Fein Assembly in Dublin.

MEETING AT MANSION HOUSE

Evacuation of Ireland by the Garrison of British Troops Is Demanded.

APPEAL TO FREE NATIONS

Urges Recognition of National Status and "Right to Vindication" at Peace Conference.

DUBLIN, Jan. 21, (Associated Press).—Twenty-five members of the Sinn Fein Society elected to the British House of Commons assembled here this afternoon and formally constituted themselves the "Dail Eireann," which is Irish Gaelic for "Irish Parliament."

They elected Charles Burgess, whose Irish name is Cathal Brugha, Speaker. They also adopted a declaration of independence and an address to the free nations of the world and appointed a committee consisting of Count Plunkett, Arthur Griffiths and Professor Edward De Valeera to present the claims of Ireland to self-determination to the Peace Conference at Paris.

The two last named being in British prisons, only the venerable Count Plunkett can proceed to Paris, and then only provided the British Government consents to give him passports.

Proceedings Were Dull.

The walls of the hall were quaintly embellished with classic statues in plaster and coats of arms. Past Lord Mayors have witnessed many more exciting dramas, notably in recent years the conventions of the Nationalist Party, when there were impassioned speeches and hot party contests. That today's proceedings seemed tame by contrast was due to the fact that they were conducted in the dead language of the Irish tongue. This was a tribute to sentiment, but it was deadening to interest. Few of the 2,000 auditors understood the addresses.

Oratory was killed by the process of reading all the speeches, and even some of the delegates had trouble in following them on their manuscripts. The only concession to popular interest was the translation of the declaration of independence and the address to the free nations in English and French, and this was a wearisome process.

It should not be inferred there was any lack of emotion or want of feeling or responsibility on the part of the delegates. They evidently felt themselves men playing great parts in a solemn sacrament.

A crowd of perhaps a thousand, including many women and children, wearing green, white and yellow ribbons, pressed around the door of the Mansion House, watching the delegates enter. Only two policemen were visible, but the Sinn Fein had its own police—youths wearing white arm bands—to keep order.

Another crowd of different type was on hand—repatriated war prisoners of the Dublin Fusiliers. They had been entertained at luncheon in the Mansion House, and their friends and the public generally were waiting outside to cheer them.

This combination furnished the possibilities of a clash. But none occurred.

A Dingy Meeting Place.

The rotunda of the Mansion House, where the congress met, is a dingy old place, lighted by stained glass windows overhead. The platform and half the floor were fitted with tables for officers and delegates. The remainder of the floor and the circular gallery were reserved for the public, admission being by ticket.

A large proportion of the audience consisted of women. The number of young priests was conspicuous. One of the popular figures arriving first was Father O'Flanagan, who recently was dismissed from his parish by the Bishop on account of his political activity.

There was a brief demonstration when the delegates advanced down the centre aisle, the people standing on their seats and applauding them.

The youthfulness of the Sinn Fein leaders was their most noticeable characteristic. There were hardly a half dozen gray heads in the group. Count Plunkett, Member of Parliament and one of the leaders of the party, introduced in a few terse sentences Charles S. Burgess, a young man who acted as Chairman and who made a short speech which was much applauded. Most of the members of the party crossed themselves frequently during the prayer of the Rev. Father O'Flanagan.

The roll call was made in English. It included all the Members of Parliament elected from Ireland to the British Parliament. Naturally a majority of these men failed to respond, as they are in prison.

Mention of the name of Sir Edward Carson, leader of the Ulsterites, was the cause of much merriment during the session. The most striking feature of the program was the reading of the Declaration of Independence. First in Irish, with the delegates standing, and afterward in English and French, "Ireland's address to the free nations" was read. It began:

"The nation of Ireland, having her national independence, calls through her elected representatives, in Parliament as-

Continued on Page Two.

COUNCIL TO DECIDE ON RUSSIA TODAY; COMPROMISE INQUIRY PLAN EXPECTED; WON'T RECEIVE ANY PARTY SPOKESMAN

See in Reinforcement of Polish Army A Means of Checking Russian Bolshevism

By Wireless to The New York Times.

LONDON, Jan. 21.—The Daily Chronicle's diplomatic correspondent, discussing the Russian problem now before the Peace Conference, says that the telegrams exchanged between Great Britain and America alone on this portentous subject would fill a volume.

"The opinion obtains here," he says, "that if any intervention is sanctioned it will take the form of reinforcing the Polish Army, which would thus offer a wall to Bolshevism from the east to the west. Polish forces hitherto employed in the west would be strengthened by the addition of two American divisions."

The correspondent proceeds to point out that the weak point in this proposal is the uncertainty as to the disposition of the populace, and whether Bolshevism can be fought by such means. Premier Paderewski's difficulties are considerable, and are as great in the economic as in the political field. The question is how Poland can exist without close economic relations with Russia, since she cannot hope to find a market for her manufactures in the German or Austrian States. The correspondent proceeds:

"The interdependence of Poland, Esthonia, and other constituent parts of the old empire inspire the belief in many quarters that the only real remedy for the present anarchy is federation. Such a solution will probably receive sympathetic consideration from the conference. It is obvious that Russia is too large a territory to be administered from one centre, and its interests also are too diverse. Federation, then, seems to be the most workable system."

DOMINIONS SEEK TO ENTER LEAGUE

British Colonies Want Admission, with Same Status as Other Nations.

EARNED IT, SAYS HUGHES

Nationhood Won by Australia's Efforts in War—Natural Outcome, Says Borden.

PARIS, Jan. 21, (Associated Press.)—Canada, Australia, and the other self-governing Dominions of Great Britain have begun an effort for individual representation in the projected League of Nations. They claim the right to enter the league with the same status as other nations.

The question is now being discussed by the British and Dominion officials, and it will be for the British Government to say whether it shall ask the Peace Conference to accord the Dominions individual membership in the League.

The admission by the Peace Conference of the right of the Dominions to a separate representation at the sessions is held to have been in itself tacit recognition of their nationhood. The new proposal, however, goes further, and it is considered that its acceptance would be a formal acknowledgment by the world of the Dominions existing autonomously within the British Empire and of their equality with other nations. Unofficially it is stated that England will probably approve the plan, although the matter is still the subject of grave discussion.

Premier Hughes of Australia, discussing the claims of the dominions with The Associated Press, said:

"We have earned the right by our sacrifices and efforts in this great war to a place in the family of nations. We expect to come in with the same status as any other nation. So far as I understand it, President Wilson's conception of the League of Nations is that all nations shall come in on a basis of equality, the nations to come in as entities and retain their sovereign rights as nations.

"That being so, of course, once the status of nationhood is established, the Dominions would come in as the other nations and would be accorded whatever right they have."

Sir Robert L. Borden, Premier of Canada, gave to The Associated Press tonight the following statement regarding the claims of the Dominions:

"In the Imperial War Council in 1917 I had the honor of moving in behalf of Canada a resolution which was accepted by the United Kingdom and the other dominions and which declared that the readjustment of the constitutional relations of the component parts of the British Empire should be based on the full recognition of the dominions as autonomous nations of the Imperial Commonwealth.

"The principle thus established has been illustrated and carried into effect by the Peace Conference, in which the several Dominions have distinctive representation as members of the world-wide Britannic commonwealth, which, in open sense, is itself a League of Nations.

"The resolution of 1917, to which I have alluded, declared in emphatic terms the right of each Dominion to an adequate voice in the foreign policy and foreign relations with which the proposed League of Nations is intimately and vitally concerned.

"It is neither necessary nor desirable to forecast the exact method by which this essential purpose shall be fulfilled in framing the constitution of the proposed league."

Canada, Australia, and New Zealand have for several years claimed for themselves absolute independence, so far as the conduct of internal affairs was concerned, but this principle has never been formally admitted by England. The Dominions, it is said, will now ask for formal recognition of it.

The announcement of the aspirations of the Dominions is being discussed with the keenest interest in official circles in Paris. The question is being frequently asked whether this present important step is to be followed later by insistence on the part of the Dominions of a right as nations to have a full share in dictating the foreign policy of the empire as far as it affects the Dominions.

"The British Empire is in one sense a national entity and in another a League of Nations in itself," was the way one high personage summarized the situation tonight.

The Italian Government has nominated Senator Scialoja, former Minister of Justice, as the Italian member of the international committee in Paris to study the question of the League of Nations. Leon Bourgeois and Lord Robert Cecil are the French and British members respectively.

LICHNOWSKY PLEA FOR A JUST PEACE

German Diplomat Expresses His Faith in Wilson and British Statesmen.

ANXIOUS ABOUT FRONTIERS

But Believes Germany's Rights Will Be Respected, "Especially in the East."

BERLIN, Jan. 21, (Associated Press.)—Prince Lichnowsky, former German Ambassador to Great Britain, today gave the following statement to The Associated Press:

"A peace of right and justice, provided it is not merely to be a phrase behind which a peace of violence conceals itself as a Pax Britannica, can only be such a peace as neither enslaves nor mutilates the conquered and which leaves him the possibility of recuperating, of paying his debts and of entering with complete confidence into the peaceful competition of a Society of Nations. A League of Nations which has its roots only in statutes and is not in the hearts of peoples is worthless.

"Just as the conquerors hundreds of years ago treated France forbearingly and left in its possession its old borders, including even German Alsace, which had earlier been taken away from us just as forcibly as we later took it back, so I believe there will be left to us, especially in the East, our borders which are indispensable for us politically and economically.

"Not only ethnography, but also geography, should be taken into consideration in establishing borders. The Poles and Czechs have no more right to our mixed-language territories, which owe their prosperity alone to German organization and to the German market, than we have to all the German territories outside the empire, including the German parts of Alsace-Lorraine.

"Hence a peace of justice would be only such a one as neither boycotts us nor lays upon us intolerable financial burdens which would make us dependents for all time, nor one which creates untenable borders and robs us of lands which we require geographically and economically.

"Mr. Wilson and the British statesmen have announced their war aims to be the abolishing of autocracy and militarism and making good the harm the war has done to Belgium and France. I expect confidently that they will now demonstrate the uprightness of their intentions and that they will not create the impression that a war psychosis now rules them, just as it ruled with us during the war."

STEVENS TO BE HEAD OF TRANS-SIBERIAN

Russian General Horvath to be Co-Director—Allies to Speed Up Work on Road.

VLADIVOSTOK, Jan. 20, (via Montreal.)—The agreement for Allied control of the Trans-Siberian Railway gives the Americans control of the line from Pogranichana to Omsk, a distance of 3,000 miles; the British will have charge of the line from Omsk to the fighting front; the French will control the Khabarovsk line, and the Japanese the line from Blagoviestchensk to Chita.

The administrative positions are to be filled by Russians and Americans in equal numbers. There are to be Russians only on the working staff. John F. Stevens, head of the American Railway Commission to Russia, is to be chief administrator of the railway, with the Russian General Horvath as co-director. Americans are to guard the line.

Cars and engines are being supplied from the United States. Great workshops are being opened in Vladivostok, and every effort is to be made to speed up operations.

AGAINST DEAL WITH SOVIETS

Danish Diplomat Emphasizes the Futility of Treating With Them.

CALL WILSON REACTIONARY

Red Leaders Scoff at the President and Lloyd George, Council Is Told.

OUR LEAGUE PLAN UP SOON

Wilson Expected to Present Memorial at Full Session Late This Week.

PARIS, Jan. 21, (Associated Press.)—The Supreme Council of the Great Powers hopes to formulate a concrete proposal on Russia at tomorrow's meeting. This was the definite official announcement of the communiqué issued tonight after the council had been considering the Russian situation continuously for two days.

It can be added that, while this concrete proposal was not finally decided upon and reduced to writing, its main features were agreed upon in principle. The members came from the session, however, feeling that there was no sovereign remedy insuring a certain cure for the difficult and dangerous situation, and that it would be desirable to embody several lines of action in the proposal.

The first effect of this decision will be that neither Sergius Sazonoff, the Russian Minister of Foreign Affairs before the revolution, nor any Soviet agents will be received in Paris as exponents of Russian affairs, but that some form of inquiry or investigation of political conditions in Russia will be made without considering the presence in Paris of the champions of either side of the dispute. This determination is largely the result of a strong sentiment in some quarters against having any direct dealings with the Bolsheviki.

Early indications were that Premier Lloyd George's proposal to M. Pichon, the French Foreign Minister, would again take form in having Soviet agents come here, and three names of prominent leaders were mentioned as possible emissaries. But this is now said to have been definitely superseded by a plan of inquiry or investigation without involving the presence of Soviet agents.

Dane's Testimony Against Soviets.

The Danish Minister to Russia, Harold Scavenius, who took charge of French interests on the departure of the Ambassador, made a statement before the executive session of the council today on conditions in Russia, which also had a strong influence in determining that Soviet representatives should not come to Paris. He was the last of the Ministers to leave Petrograd, and today he emphasized the futility of trying to conduct any intercourse with the Soviet leaders.

He read an article written by one of the Soviet chiefs declaring that Premier Lloyd George and President Wilson were too conservative and reactionary for the Soviets to deal with.

He also gave exact data on the Bolshevist forces, showing that they did not exceed 90,000 armed men, the remainder being without arms or ammunition, clothing or shoes. He said also that the Red Army was largely recruited from the famished peasants, who took this means to obtain food and the pay the Soviet seemed able to give them.

Polish Question Up Today.

The Polish question will come up at tomorrow's session as well as the matter of Russia. It is understood in this connection that President Wilson has received information concerning the spread of the Bolshevist movement in Poland, where the Russian Red Army is nearing Warsaw. It is expected that proposals will be renewed for the allied armies to help the Polish Army with war material, but this has not yet been decided.

The official communiqué tonight also announces that the question of procedure of the conference was again discussed. The nature of this discussion was in determining the appointment of two committees, the first to deal with reparation for the damages of the war, the second to deal with the subject of the League of Nations.

Another full session of the Peace Conference will probably be held next Friday or Saturday for the purpose of the presentation of a memorial on the League of Nations by President Wilson. The English and French me-materials on the League will probably be presented at the same time, and the committee proposed today will then work out the details, while the full conference may enunciate some general expression of principle on the plan.

The council at 12:30 o'clock took a recess until 3 P. M. M. Scavenius finished his statement at noon and withdrew. The council, however, continued its consideration of the Russian question and planned to resume it at the afternoon session.

At the close of the morning session President Wilson and Premier Lloyd George had an earnest discussion of ten minutes' duration in an antechamber.

The Supreme Council's afternoon session lasted from 3 to 5 o'clock.

Text of the Official Statement.

The official statement regarding the council's proceedings says:

> The President of the United States, the Prime Ministers and Foreign Ministers, assisted by the Japanese representatives, met today at the Quai d'Orsay from 10:30 A. M. to 12:45 P. M. in the morning, and in the afternoon from 3 to 5 P. M.
>
> In the morning M. Scavenius, Danish Minister to Russia, gave all the information at his disposal on the various parties in Russia.
>
> In the afternoon the discussion of this question was continued. Very great progress toward an agreement was made, and it is hoped to formulate a concrete proposal on this subject tomorrow. The question of the procedure of the conference was then discussed.

The next meeting will take place at 11 o'clock tomorrow morning.

M. Sazonoff, former Russian Foreign Minister, has been in conference with some members of the American delegation, urging the admission to the conference of delegates from the Omsk Government in Russia, which he represents here.

The attitude of the various powers toward Russia is summed up today by L'Information, which states that the situation stands as follows:

"France and Italy heretofore have been for intervention on condition that the Allies were unanimous for it. Great Britain, through Premier Lloyd George, has expressed a desire to see intervention limited to the coasts of the Caspian Sea, leaving to Russia the adjustment of her own affairs in the interior. President Wilson seems to agree with the latter conception, and to be still hoping to see the Bolsheviki, in the process of evolution, establish a régime less resembling an anarchical one. Japan has not yet agreed to consider the possibility of prolonging the action she has undertaken in Siberia."

FRENCH NOW UNWILLING TO INTERVENE IN RUSSIA

See Futility of Acting Alone, While the Italians Cannot Spare Troops.

By CHARLES A. SELDEN.

By Wireless to THE NEW YORK TIMES.

PARIS, Jan. 20.—The proceedings before President Wilson and the Premiers and Foreign Ministers of England, France, Italy, and Japan at the Quai d'Orsay today and tomorrow may be likened very closely to an investigation by a Grand Jury. The first witness, so to speak, called today was M. Noulens, the recently returned French Ambassador to Russia. Tomorrow he will be followed by M. Scavenius, the Danish Minister to Russia.

To the testimony of these men the great powers will add all available information on every phase of the Russian situation, political, economic, military, and social. This is the first and one of the greatest tasks of the Peace Conference.

No one pretends yet to say what the finding of this Grand Jury will be, but it is admitted that one of three courses must be followed. These are:

First—To fight the Bolsheviki outright and directly by sending a powerful military force of American and allied troops into Russia.

Second—To fight the Bolsheviki indirectly and by proxy, that is, not by sending in troops, but by furnishing adequate supplies—guns, ammunition, food ,and money—to the Russian Governments which are anti-Bolshevist, and aiding them in every possible way short of sending troops, but leaving the actual fighting to save Russia from her present plight to Russians themselves.

Third—To give up fighting the Bolsheviki altogether, and to try to arrive at a working arrangement with the Soviet Government whereby the Bolshevist leaders would pledge themselves to cease warfare and terrorism and to give the Allies an opportunity to relieve the present starvation conditions in Russia and assist in the reorganization of the transportation and industrial systems as a preliminary to restoring commercial and diplomatic relations with the rest of the world and putting the Russian people in a position to decide upon their form of government.

No Chance of Intervention.

There seems to be hardly one chance in a million that the first of these three possible courses will be adopted. The anti-intervention policy of America is well known. Furthermore, France herself, formerly the chief advocate of sending a big allied military force into Russia to exterminate the Bolsheviki, no longer feels that she is able to undertake such a task at the end of a long war and in the face of public clamor for speedy demobilization. France surely would not undertake the enterprise alone, and there is no trace of encouragement or co-operation from any other nation. Italy, who is keeping up full mobilization in case of the emergency of war with the Jugoslavs, would send no troops for a Winter campaign in Russia.

So practically there are really only two possible courses open: either to supply the anti-Bolshevist Russians with munitions to keep up the war on the Lenine forces, or to treat with the representatives of the Bolsheviki, as has already been proposed by Lloyd George. France is the only Government which has declared itself against this proposal from the British Premier, and the only other declared opposition to it is that from the committee of Russian statesmen and diplomats in Paris striving to be accepted by the Peace Conference as the only representatives of Russia with whom the other powers may safely deal.

It has been assumed by France that Italy would stand by her in this matter, and that America and Japan would consent to the Lloyd George plan. But the Orlando Government has given no sign to indicate its Russian policy for the immediate future, and Italy dares not go too far in antagonism to what may be America's attitude, for she is absolutely dependent on the continuance of loans from the United States.

Hope for Lloyd George's Plan.

So it is well within the range of possibility and even probability that the Lloyd George proposal which, when revealed to the world the other day by Pichon's vehement rejection of it, caused such a sensation in international politics, may after all be adopted by the Peace Conference, before which the Bolsheviki would thus have an opportunity to state their case and promise to cease their atrocities till the conference could finally pass on their case.

It should be remembered that the proposal which Lloyd George passed on to the Foreign Offices of other countries came originally from the Bolsheviki themselves in the shape of a request of Litvinoff, who assured Lloyd George that Bolshevist terrorism would cease if he and his associates could get a chance to appear before the Peace Conference.

The adoption of this last of the three possible courses would involve the cessation of the present hostilities against the Bolshevist Government which the Allies are now carrying on in Northern and Southern Russia and Siberia and the withdrawal of the comparatively small military forces now engaged in those campaigns, after satisfactory assurance had been obtained from the Bolsheviki that they also would cease all fighting.

This would not mean formal recognition by the powers of the Bolshevist Government. On the contrary, the Lloyd George plan would provide for the Peace Conference listening to representatives of the other Governments of Russia which are now struggling to maintain themselves against Bolshevism and eventually to unite themselves into one democratic Government of all Russia.

As I cabled you last week, the whole Lloyd George plan is strongly opposed by the Russian committee in Paris on the ground that the Bolsheviki, who represent the destruction of nations, should have no place in a conference based on the idea of democratic States, and that the representatives of the other Governments of Russia should not be received as representing separate States, for the purpose of all those States is to be united, and the truest representation of the real Russia which they are all striving for is in the personnel of this Paris committee consisting of Sazonoff, Lvoff, Bakhméteff, Maklakoff, and Tchaikovsky. These men will be heard before the decision is reached.

Lenine's Power Seems Waning.

Paris sees vague, wavering signs of hope in the situation because of evidence of the breaking down of the Bolsheviki's strength. Deaths from starvation at the rate of a thousand daily are occurring in Petrograd alone, and the population of that city has been cut in half in the last fourteen months by removal, death, and massacre. Every form of enterprise by which men live has been completely paralyzed; and, because of all this, Lenine's power is diminishing rather than increasing.

Lenine apparently realizes this. It was with his approval, of course, that Litvinoff asked for parleys with the Allies, and he has already gone so far as to propose to the Soviet Congress a surrender to the Allies. Two hundred delegates voted on this proposal, and it was defeated by a majority of only twelve. On the other hand, Lenine still has good control of the Red Army, now estimated at 300,000, and the advocates in Paris of making working arrangements with the Bolsheviki say that is the only way, because every threat of military intervention from without simply increases Lenine's power.

REDS SPEND BILLIONS, CAN'T COLLECT TAXES

Soviet Government Faces Probable Deficit of 43,000,000,000 Rubles for 1918.

STOCKHOLM, Jan. 21.—The financial statement of the Russian Bolshevist Government for 1918, according to a Petrograd dispatch, shows that the expenditures for the year were 47,000,000,000 rubles, and that there would be a probable deficit of 43,000,000,000 owing to the inability of the Government to collect the property tax.

From July to December the Soviet Government spent 7,773,000,000 rubles on the Ministry of War, compared with 644,000,000 rubles in the preceding six months.

NEED 350,000 TONS OF FOOD.

Allied Investigator Finds 5,000,000 Poles Must Have Relief.

PARIS, Jan. 21.—Dr. Vernon Kellogg, of the international relief organization, who has just returned to Paris from making a food survey of Poland on behalf of the Supreme Food and Relief Council, says that there are between 4,000,000 and 5,000,000 people there who must be supplied with 350,000 tons of food for the six months until the next harvest.

Food, he reports, is imperative to fortify the new Government and check disorders in Warsaw, Lemberg, Lodz, and other large cities. Danzig is the key to the Polish relief situation, and under the armistice it is open to the Allies, as well as the territory leading into Poland. Dr. Kellogg urges the immediate shipment of quantities of milk for the starving children in Lemberg, but says extensive relief is impossible until the Danzig avenue is thoroughly organized. A shipload of food bought in New York by Polish and Jewish committees is now on the way to Danzig. Other food will be rushed from Copenhagen and Rotterdam when money for it is available.

Dr. Kellogg says that shipments of raw materials also are necessary to afford employment.

REDS SEEK PEACE WITH UNITED STATES

Ask for a Conference to Discuss Withdrawal of American Troops from Russia.

SEND NOTE TO WASHINGTON

State Department Forwards It by Wireless to Paris to be Dealt with There.

STOCKHOLM, Jan. 20.—Maxim Litvinoff, former Bolshevist Ambassador in London, who is in Stockholm, forwarded on Saturday to the American State Department a note sent by Bolshevist Foreign Minister Tchitcherin, in which it was pointed out that the original reasons for allied intervention in Russia, as restated recently in the American Senate by Senator Hitchcock, do not exist any more. The note expresses willingness to come to an understanding with the American Government.

Foreign Minister Tchitcherin asked the American Government to fix a date and place for Soviet representatives to meet emissaries of the United States. Tchitcherin made the assertion that American officers and soldiers "do not any longer understand why they are in Russia."

WASHINGTON, Jan. 21.—American representatives at the Peace Conference, it was said today at the State Department, have under consideration the note of Bolshevist Foreign Minister Tchitcherin, proposing that the United States fix a date and place for a conference between Soviet representatives and American emissaries to discuss withdrawal of American troops from Russia.

The note was forwarded promptly to Paris after its receipt at the State Department by wireless, so that it might be considered along with other aspects of the Russian situation.

ESTHONIANS RETAKE NARVA FROM REDS

Capture Many Prisoners and Guns —Trotzky Said to Have Escaped From City.

LONDON, Jan. 21.—A notable success has been won against the Bolsheviki by Esthonian troops operating to the northeast of Lake Peipus, according to an Esthonian official statement received by wireless at Stockholm today and transmited here. They have taken the town of Narva, on the Reval-Petrograd Railway line, together with a large number of prisoners.

Finnish troops co-operated with the Esthonians, the statement says. A quantity of booty fell into the hands of the victorious forces, including guns, provisions, and armored trains. The prisoners included division and regimental staffs.

Leon Trotzky, the Bolshevist War Minister, it is stated, was present in Narva during the fighting and fled after the Bolshevist defeat.

STOCKHOLM, Jan. 21.—Swedish military missions which have returned here from Lithuania and Esthonia have reported favorably regarding the sending of a volunteer military expedition into Lithuania, where the Lithuanian forces are unable to stem the Bolshevist advance. The missions report against an expedition to Esthonia, owing to the lack of economic resources there.

The first Swedish detachment probably will start for Libau this week.

COPENHAGEN, Jan. 21.—A majority of the members of the Lithuanian Cabinet, headed by the Premier, arrived at the Danish Island of Bornholm, in the Baltic Sea, Monday. They left Libau because of the Bolshevist invasion of Lithuania.

URGES SEIZURE OF LIVONIA.

Prof. Jeanneret Says It Is Source of Red Army's Chief Strength.

By Wireless to THE NEW YORK TIMES.

GENEVA, Jan. 20.—M. Philippe Jeanneret, the Swiss professor who has just returned from Russia, where he was a teacher at the college in Khasan for many years, has joined the Czechoslovak Corps in Russia. He has had personal experience in fighting the Bolsheviki.

"The organization of the Bolshevist Army," he says, "has been effected chiefly by Letts and Hungarians. In the early days of our campaign the Red Guards were merely bandits who pillaged villages and murdered defenseless peasants, but took to their heels when we attacked them. But quite suddenly there was a complete change, and we found ourselves opposed to well-disciplined regular troops.

"Lenine and Trotzky, realizing their danger, had incorporated thousands of Hungarian prisoners, whom they paid and fed well, in their army, and reorganized it with the help of Lett officers. The Letts and Hungarians today form the backbone of the Bolshevist forces. Lenine and Trotzky draw most of their strength from Livonia, which the Allies should occupy without delay if they wish to strike a mortal blow against Bolshevism in Russia.

"The cruelty and bestiality of the Letts, who hold nearly all the important posts under the Bolshevist Government, surpass belief. The horrors at Khasan, where 250 men, women, and children were walled up in a cellar and left to starve, were perpetrated by order of the Lett Commissary with the Bolshevist Army."

After his tragic experiences, it is natural that the Swiss professor's spirit is overshadowed by the menace which to him appears very real of a Bolshevist invasion of Europe.

"Take strong measures before it is too late," he earnestly advises. "Otherwise Europe will once more be plunged in a sea of blood. Here in the West no one seems to dream of danger. Victory and peace have filled everybody with joy and hope, but the last act of the great drama has not yet been played. Those who, like myself, have been face to face with Bolshevism, are terrified by what they see creeping nearer day by day."

PADEREWSKI NOT WOUNDED.

Warsaw Denies Stories of Disorders, Says Germans Circulate Them.

WARSAW, Jan. 20, (Associated Press.) —Polish troops in arresting more than 200 Bolshevist agitators fired a dozen shots today in the Jewish quarter of the city. The incident at once gave rise to a report that pogroms had occurred. The Jewish newspaper of Warsaw says, however, that only three persons were wounded. Another newspaper says that two of those wounded were Polish women and that the third was a Jewish cabman, who was shot accidentally.

Members of allied missions who are arriving here from Switzerland and France say that wild rumors about disorders in Poland have been in circulation in allied countries. One rumor had to do with the alleged wounding of Ignace Jan Paderewski.

Most of the reports of disorders can be dismissed as having a German origin. There are also innumerable stories circulated here regarding conditions in the outside world, and these are only contradicted when travelers arrive or when Paris or London newspapers reach Warsaw two or three weeks after the alleged incidents were said to have occurred.

A Vienna dispatch received in Copenhagen and transmitted to London on Jan. 12 said that M. Paderewski had been wounded slightly by an assassin at Warsaw. There never was any confirmation of this report from Warsaw direct.

POLES STILL HOLD OUT IN BESIEGED CITIES

People of Lemberg and Przemysl Resist Ukrainian Troops Despite Fierce Bombardment.

WARSAW, Jan. 20, (Associated Press.)—The Polish population is heroically defending Lemberg from capture by the Ukrainians. Women and boys are taking part in the spirited fighting.

For the last month Lemberg has been surrounded by the Ukrainians, and the railway has been cut.

Przemysl is also being shelled by six German nine-inch guns, and airplanes are dropping shells upon the town daily, but the Ukrainians have not been successful in capturing it.

MOVES TO DECLARE HAMMERLING AN ALIEN

Citizenship of Head of Foreign Language Newspapers May Be Revoked by Court.

Special to The New York Times.

SCRANTON, Penn., Jan. 21.—By direction of the Department of Justice the United States District Attorney for this Federal district is preparing to present a petition to the United States District Court for the revocation of the naturalization papers of Louis N. Hammerling, President of the Association of Foreign Language Newspapers in the United States, with offices in the Woolworth Building, New York.

The evidence seems to be, so far as the investigation has proceeded, that when Hammerling applied for his second papers he swore that he was born in Hawaii. It is alleged that this statement was not true.

It was said at Mr. Hammerling's home, 104 East Fortieth Street, last night that he was out of town and it was not known when he would return.

PLAN REVOLTS IN FAR EAST.

Bolsheviki Prepare Propaganda for China, India, and Persia.

LONDON, Jan. 21, (via Montreal.)—The Russian Bolshevist Government for a long time has been organizing an extensive propaganda for revolutions in China, India, and Persia and is now ready, as soon as the opportunity offers, to send agents with large sums of money to stir up trouble throughout Asia, according to reliable advices received here.

A great obstacle facing the revolutionary plans of the Bolsheviki is the existence of the army of the Omsk Government, which at present effectively bars the road to Asia by way of the Ural front. If, however, it is pointed out, Admiral Kolchak's army becomes weakened and disintegrates through lack of support and encouragement, the Bolshevist plans would very seriously threaten the peace of Asia.

CONSIDERING PLANS TO RELAX BLOCKADE

American Delegates Contemplate Allowing Enemy Countries to Import Foodstuffs.

PARIS, Jan. 21.—(Associated Press.)—Owing to pressure of more urgent problems before delegates to the Peace Congress, various economic delegations are studying, each for itself, the blockade and kindred problems. It is probable that they will start joint discussions this week.

American opinion contemplates a certain relaxation of the earlier "watertight" blockade, which would allow the entry of foodstuffs, lubricants and other materials into enemy countries. This, it is held, would permit the restoration of distributing systems, flour mills and other agencies involved in the preparation of food supplies. The blockade, however, would otherwise be as rigidly enforced as ever, because of its value as a weapon to force the enemy to accept the peace terms that will be presented.

The relaxation of the blockade as regards foodstuffs is already effective in a part of the former Hapsburg domains. Food is being sent into Vienna as well a to liberated regions, and will be supplied to Germany under the terms of the armistice extension agreement signed at Treves last Friday.

American experts are said to believe that babbitt metal for bearings, lubricants, repair parts for locomotives and flour mills and other articles fall in virtually the same category as foodstuffs, since it is obvious that enemy countries have no adequate facilities for milling flour and distributing food after it is imported.

Some American economic experts advocate for enemy countries, at least Austria-Hungary, and possibly Germany, a further relaxation of the blockade to permit the importation of limited quantities of raw materials. These imports, however, would not be enough to permit the Central Powers to resume international commercial competition while the allied countries were still laboring under the handicap of the devastation of their chief industrial regions, the spoliation of industrial plants, the transformation of the great bulk of their remaining factories into war plants, and the absence of industrial laborers who are still under arms.

The manufacture of textiles, for example, is urgently required to meet the needs of enemy populations, and the production of other materials is held to be absolutely indispensable. This would, it is said, facilitate relief measures and alleviate conditions of unemployment upon which Bolshevism thrives, particularly in Hungary.

TELLS OF BISMARCK'S AIM.

Memorandum Quotes Him as Saying He Expected to Crush France.

PARIS, Jan. 21.—Prince Bismarck contemplated a second war by Germany against the French which would result in the virtual destruction of France, according to a document published in the Petit Parisien today.

The document purports to be a note made by an ex-counsellor of the then King of Hanover, summing up a conversation with Bismarck, and is said to have been found recently among the papers of a French literary man.

"I am positive that if I live long enough I am destined to destroy France," Bismarck is quoted as having said, "for in another war I will take from her her colonies and her fleet, not to mention billions, and will dismember her a second time. For this purpose I am going to prepare the German people to become more powerful."

ARABS LOOK TO US FOR INDEPENDENCE

Prince Feisal of Hedjaz Says Eyes of the Whole East Are Turned Toward America.

PRESENTS CLAIMS AT PARIS

Proposes a State Comprising Hedjaz, Syria, Mesopotamia, Yemen, and Nejd.

PARIS, Jan. 21, (Associated Press.)—Prince Feisal, son of the King of Hedjaz, whom he represents at the Peace Conference, is pressing his claims for the recognition of the Arab State of Hedjaz.

"The Arabs have long enough suffered under foreign domination," he said to The Associated Press today. "The hour has at last struck when we are to come into our own again. We have, I believe, an even greater right to become free and independent than any of the new States to be formed through the war, since we are the oldest democracy in the world.

"The country is inhabited almost exclusively by a homogeneous set of Arabs, all descending from a common stock, while the foreign element is infinitesimal, certainly smaller than in any other country I know of. There are only about two thousand Turkish officials and no Turkish population in a land containing three and one-half million Arabs. Why then should not the Arabs rule the country where they live and have lived for countless generations? Why should we not be masters in our own house?"

The Prince then explained that the provinces they claimed as constituting the proposed State are Hedjaz, Syria, Upper and Lower Mesopotamia, Yemen and Nejd. He made it clear that he was here officially only as the representative of the Kingdom of Hedjaz.

"But," he added, "I am also the representative of the whole Arab army, which was recruited from each and all of these States, and I can truthfully say that the Arabs are unanimous in claiming their independence. If the Peace Conference should doubt this statement, or lend ear to the rumors that Syria prefers the French, or Palestine the British, let them send a commission to investigate. If they find that any portion of Arabia would prefer to be ruled by China, Japan, Chile or any other power, then I shall not have another word to say.

"As a small struggling nation we have already done much. King Hussein, my father, commonly called 'the Grand Old Man of the East,' declared war against Turkey when she was at the height of her military glory, and invited volunteers to his standard. Soon quite a considerable army collected, which, under my personal leadership, inflicted on the Turks a series of defeats, culminating in the taking of Medina last week.

"The Arab Army acted as the British right wing, and in the last offensive, in addition to taking 40,000 prisoners, by a rapid march cut the Turkish line of retreat, enabling the British to capture 70,000 more.

"The two usual objections made to our ambitions," continued the Prince, "are: 'Have your people reached a high enough standard of civilization to govern themselves?' and 'Will you have enough money to carry on your State?'

"To the first I unhesitatingly say 'Yes.' The world must not forget that it is Arabs who largely govern the country at this very moment, and all over the world Arabs have shown their worth as merchants and administrators. There must be some six or seven thousand Arabs fighting in the American Army, as there are about 250,000 Arabs in America.

"As for the second question, I also answer in the affirmative. Our country is a rich one. It contains large quantities of copper, iron, mineral oils, and a little coal, while, when properly irrigated, it is perhaps one of the most fertile in the world. That, I think, is enough to tempt capital, and we intend to welcome all foreigners who come with the intention of investing capital or teaching us something. The only stipulation we make is that there shall be no intrigue, no foreign control, but complete freedom for the Arabs.

"I address this appeal to the American people," said Prince Feisal in conclusion, "because I believe American public opinion to be the chief factor in deciding our fate. I also address them because I have complete faith in them. Even in the furthest corner of my own distant country the word has spread that America is the friend of all oppressed and the enemy of all oppressors, that to her all oppressed may come, sure of finding patient ears to listen and strong arms to uphold the weak if the claims are found to be just.

"At this moment the eyes of the whole East are turned toward America. It is up to her now to show that our faith is not misplaced."

Officers Lead Revolt at Budapest.

AMSTERDAM, Jan. 21.—It is reported that there have been counter-revolutionary demonstrations led by officers at Budapest, and that there have been conflicts with the police in which bloodshed resulted.

Uhlans Sent to Polish Border.

BERLIN, Jan. 20, (Associated Press.)—A squadron of the 3d Guard Uhlans, according to the Lokal-Anzeiger, left Potsdam this morning for the Polish front.

MANUEL READY TO RESUME CROWN

Continued from Page 1, Column 4.

situation, and that the republican leaders are united in defense of the present régime.

Other messages report Lisbon quiet, with strong police forces guarding the palace of the Civil Governor.

The commander at Coimbra has received orders to march upon Oporto, Braga, and Viscus.

PARIS, Jan. 21.—Circumstances of the outbreak of the monarchical revolution in Portugal are given in an agency dispatch from Lisbon filed at 11:45 A. M. on Monday. It says:

"The Minister of War, with a number of officers, took a special train to Oporto and arrived there yesterday. They were received at the station by officers of the garrison, who conducted them to headquarters. They were informed that a monarchy was about to be proclaimed in Oporto.

"The Minister and his suite were able to take a train for Lisbon. On their way they received confirmation of the proclamation of a monarchy in Oporto.

"The monarchist manifesto calls upon the population to fly the old blue and white royalist banner.

"The Cabinet has taken vigorous measures to maintain order. A state of siege has been proclaimed throughout the country. The warships Vasco da Gama and Guadiana have been called home, and two other war vessels have been sent to Oporto. At Coimbra two divisions of the reserves have been called to the colors.

"The Lisbon garrison remains loyal to the Government."

The message states that the troubles are not of a Bolshevist nature, but are merely due to interparty quarrels.

"From a conversation between Premier Barbosa and Ayres Ornellas, chief agent in Portugal of ex-King Manuel," adds the message, "it appears that the former King considers the present moment inopportune for an attempt to restore the monarchy."

DIFFICULT TO ADJUST ALLOTMENT TREATIES

American Delegates Strongly Favor Recasting of Secret Programs Framed in Wartime.

By Wireless to THE NEW YORK TIMES.

LONDON, Jan. 21.—A. P. Nicholson, the Paris correspondent of The Daily News, telegraphs:

"As the question of the secret treaties made during the war is referred to from time to time, it is of interest to state that I am hearing on trustworthy authority that the view taken by the Allies who signed such treaties is this:

"The treaties signed between the other powers and Russia are abrogated by the Russian revolution only so far as those parts relating to Russia are concerned, while the parts concerning the remaining signatories hold good as treaty obligations. At the same time the view is taken in British circles that so much has happened since—America's entry into the war and later events—that it is profoundly desirable that the conference as a whole should regard such agreements as modified by these later events.

"America, which was not a party to such agreements, takes the strong line that this is so, and will make that view felt.

"The agreement between France and Russia of February, 1917, which provided for the Rhineland as an autonomous and neutral State, of course falls to the ground.

"The Treaty of London of 1915, signed by Great Britain, France, Russia, and Italy, is what the Italian claims are founded on. The Russian clauses drop out, but the clauses remaining prescribe a smaller territory to the Jugoslavs, though Fiume was allotted to them. To Italy went the Trentino, Istria, Southern Tyrol, Gorizia, Gradisca, the Dalmatian province, a number of the Adriatic islands, and the Dodecanese Islands.

"The agreement of the same Allies with Rumania in February, 1918, included the Rumanian claim to the Banat, which is now opposed by the Serbians.

"A memorandum on Turkey in the Spring of 1916, made by Great Britain, France, and Russia, holds good diplomatically between Great Britain and France except for the dropped Russian clauses. It was by this that France claimed the coastal strip of Syria and the vilayet of Adana, and Great Britain South Mesopotamia, with Bagdad and the Syrian ports of Haifa and Acre.

"The Persian and China agreements fall out, but I understand that there is an agreement of Japan with the Allies giving Japan possession of the Caroline and Marshall Islands in the Pacific. This is strongly opposed by Australia.

"It will be seen from this outline what far-reaching modifications will be required in the interests of a common agreement."

DEPUTIES' WORK FOR PEACE.

Committee of the Chamber Planned to Co-operate with Clemenceau.

PARIS, Jan. 21.—Premier Clemenceau having appealed to the Chamber of Deputies to co-operate in the task of making peace, Maurice Damour, supported by 100 Deputies, has introduced a motion in the Chamber for the appointment of a committee on the subject to give its opinions on various matters and to prepare reports for submission to the Chamber.

By the adoption of this method M. Damour points out, the Parliament would be kept in close touch with the negotiations and would afford the negotiators needed moral support. The Chamber thus would also be able to study the preliminaries of the peace before they were submitted for ratification.

WOMEN CRY FOR JUSTICE.

French Petition Asks Peace Conference to Avenge Their Wrongs.

PARIS, Jan. 21.—Frenchwomen have addressed a petition to the members of the Peace Conference asking justice in the name of thousands of women, young girls, and children who, it is set forth, were systematically torn from their families and subject to various forms of ill treatment at the hands of the Germans during the war. The petition adds:

"In order forever to prevent the recurrence of such atrocities we ask that those who executed them and those who ordered them be condemned as criminals of the common law."

WHOLE NAVY FORCE SOON TO BE SENT HOME

F. D. Roosevelt Says That Fewer Than 3,000 Men Will Remain Abroad After Feb. 15.

LONDON, Jan. 21.—Franklin D. Roosevelt, Assistant Secretary of the Navy, after a conference with Admiral Sims on plans for the demobilization of the American navy in European waters said tonight that he was confident that with the exception of about 3,000 men the American navy would be out of Europe not later than February 15.

When the armistice was signed there were 70,000 American sailors in European waters. Today there are approximately 25,000. Several thousands are at aviation stations in France and Ireland, but are being sent home as rapidly as possible.

One of the present difficulties in the way of complete demobilization is the uncertainty at this time as to just how many German passenger ships will be allotted to carry American soldiers home and as to when the ship will be delivered. These ships will be manned and operated by the American navy and their advent into troop service will require the services of men at the ports from which they will sail.

The navy is having little difficulty in disposing of the vast amount of material and supplies in France, England and Ireland. The material in England and Ireland is being sold largely to the British Admiralty and the British Air Department. The little that the British government organizations are not taking is of small value and is being sold at auction. In France the navy is selling some material to the American army while the international relief organization also is getting some. The navy also has lent 250 men for relief work in Belgium.

Assistant Secretary Roosevelt is here with full authority to clear up demobilization details and will remain until Feb. 1. His presence obviates the delays which would be necessary should many questions have to be referred to Washington.

LONDON STRIKE GROWING.

Public Services Threatened with Tieup in Fight Over Hours.

LONDON, Jan. 21.—A strike which would close down all the engineering works and nearly every class of public service in London is threatened today. Already 15,000 workers are out, and as the men and the employers broke off negotiations for a settlement during the day it is expected that at least 250,000 men engaged in the engineering trade will cease to work before the end of the week.

The trouble arises out of the operation of the forty-seven-hour week, which has just been granted. When the new hours came into operation the employers decided that forty-seven hours meant forty-seven hours' work and withdrew certain privileges that had been previously allowed, such as ten minutes for refreshments in the morning, and a few minutes of the employers' time for men engaged in rough work to wash their hands.

Similar troubles are occurring in other parts of the United Kingdom.

DOUBTFUL OF PEACE LEAGUE

Representative Kahn Would Train Every Boy to be a Soldier.

At the dinner of the National Garment Retailers' Association, held last evening at the Waldorf, Representative Julius Kahn of California told of his plans for reconstruction and of his hope "that there would soon be written on the statute books of this country a law for the universal training of our young men." Other speakers were the Rev. H. Percy Silver, former chaplain of West Point, and Anson H. Ball of Best & Co.

"I am one of those who have not become convinced that the millennium has dawned," said Mr. Kahn. "I contend that war is not a thing of the past, much as we all would like to have it so. Man is a fighting animal. He cannot help it. He was born that way. It is his very nature.

"Many well-meaning and highly educated persons seem to think that you can prevent war with a scratch of the pen by international agreements. I wish I could bring myself to that belief. They hope that, at the Peace Conference, the nations will agree to a plan of disarmament. These good intentioned dreamers seem to forget some of the lessons of history.

"That plan of disarmament was tried by the great Napoleon, who was undoubtedly the greatest military genius of modern times, against the very power that we have been fighting during the past eighteen months.

"It would be, in my opinion, the height of folly to neglect our own preparations for possible wars of the future, and the defense of our rights as a vigorous, independent, and progressive nation. For that reason I am strongly in favor of universal training for American youth. I consider such a policy the best form of insurance for peace."

IRISH PROCLAIM IRELAND A REPUBLIC

Continued from Page 1, Column 5.

sembled, upon every free nation to support the Irish Republic by recognizing Ireland's national status and her right to vindication at the Peace Conference."

It declared that Ireland was radically distinct from England in race, language, customs, and traditions. Ireland, it said, was one of the most ancient nations of Europe. She had preserved her national integrity and vigor intact through seven centuries of foreign oppression and never had relinquished her national rights, which she had defiantly proclaimed every generation throughout the era of English usurpation, "down to her last glorious resort to arms in 1916."

It concluded with an announcement of the "complete independence of the Irish Republic against the arrogant pretensions of England, founded in fraud and sustained only by an overwhelming military occupation."

The meeting lasted only ninety minutes.

Probably no country except Ireland could present an episode as remarkable as the assembly of the "Irish Parliament." Perhaps no writer except an Irishman like George Bernard Shaw could do justice to the paradoxical nature of the proceedings.

Many Members in English Jails.

About half the Sinn Feiners elected to membership in the British Parliament participated, the other half being in various English prisons, charged with sedition, or merely held on suspicion under the spacious and elastic provisions of the Defense of the Realm act. The Sinn Feiners met under the shadow of Dublin Castle, where presides Field Marshal Viscount French, the First Viceroy in many years to give Ireland a purely military government. They met with his full knowledge and tacit consent to take measures which are purely seditious and in direct violation of explicit law.

This is one paradox. Another is that these Sinn Feiners, elected by about half of the voters in Ireland on a platform of independence from the British Empire, were chosen members of the British Parliament, but specifically refused to recognize that body and to call themselves members of the British Parliament. They occupy Mansion House by the permission of the Lord Mayor of Dublin, who himself is a Home Ruler, but not so much of a Separatist that he does not expect to accept what most of his predecessors have accepted—a knighthood from the British Government.

In the shabby Sinn Fein headquarters, situated in a decayed old house which was at one time one of Dublin's finest mansions, courteous young women secretaries gave cards of admission to today's meeting quite impartially to friend and foe; to supporters of the Sinn Fein and to correspondents of English newspapers which hold the Sinn Fein and all its works anathema. Cardinal Newman had his residence in this house during his unhappy incumbency of his high ecclesiastical post in Dublin, concerning which he was reported to have said afterward that his days in Dublin should be subtracted from his term in purgatory.

Today's program in "Independence Hall" differed in one respect from the solemnities of 1776 at Philadelphia. They were carried out in the Irish language, which is virtually a dead tongue, so dead that the Sinn Feiners have been obliged to rehearse their parts and were compelled to lapse occasionally into boycotted English terms because they could not find Irish words to fit modern parliamentary procedure.

Ireland is a country of the unexpected but no one predicts any trouble or disorder. The Government has revoked the order, made last July, requiring official authorization for public meetings and processions, which order had been suspended for some time. The revolutionary flag floats quite freely over the homes of Sinn Feiners in Dublin. Members of the party expect protection from the authorities of the nation whom they are defying. Once they would have looked to the United States for sympathy and help, but now they think they do not command American support.

They do not talk of, and apparently do not contemplate violence. Dublin had an unhappy and fruitless experience in the insurrection of 1916, an experience which cost rows of buildings on Sackville Street, once pointed to with pride as one of the finest avenues in Europe.

The Constitution of the new Irish Republic, declared yesterday by the Sinn Fein Assembly at Dublin, will be in accordance with the highest American ideals of personal and religious liberty, Diarmuid Lynch, Secretary of the Friends of Irish Freedom, and recently elected member of the British Parliament, predicted in New York last night.

"From my intimate knowledge of the men elected to the Dail Eireann," he added, "I am satisfied that they will secure the respect and co-operation of the Ulster minority and will bring honor and prosperity to their country in a measure unattainable while the British connection lasted."

Although the members of the "Dail Eireann" or "Irish Parliament" are conducting their business in Gaelic, they will undoubtedly make concessions to those who do not speak the Irish language, Mr. Lynch said.

GOMPERS HOLDS ALOOF FROM BERNE MEETING

But Goes to Paris to Continue Organization of World Labor Congress.

LONDON, Jan. 21.—An adjourned conference of leaders of British labor with Samuel Gompers and other American labor delegates now in England has reached an agreement to form a nucleus for an International Trades Union Congress. A committee of five will be appointed to represent British labor at the new Congress and to aid in organizing it. Mr. Gompers will confer with the British committee in the next few days to formulate plans for the Congress and to select an early date for the meeting in order that the Congress may meet simultaneously with the Peace Conference.

Mr. Gompers and the other American delegates will go to Paris tomorrow, where, Mr. Gompers said tonight, it is hoped to discuss the new movement with French labor leaders in advance of the next meeting with the British committee.

The British Trade Union Congress is committed to the idea of an international Socialist and Labor conference. This conference was first set for Lausanne, but recently was changed to Berne. Arthur Henderson is now at Berne as the representative of British Labor in making the arrangements for the meeting. Mr. Gompers said tonight, however, that the Trades Union Congress would be divorced entirely from the meeting at Berne.

BERNE, Jan. 21.—It is announced that Austria will be represented at the labor conference being arranged in Berne by at least two delegates. Deputy Seitz, a Social Democrat leader, and Deputy Allenburg have been designated by the Austrian labor party. German delegates are expected, but there is no indication yet as to who will be the representatives.

The attitude of Samuel Gompers, the President of the American Federation of Labor, in remaining aloof from the Berne conference mystifies the labor leaders here, more so, they say, because he has been quoted as saying that American labor would have nothing to do with Bolshevism. The Socialists here for the conference, it is declared, not only are opposed to Bolshevism, but are hated cordially by the Bolsheviki.

MANNING LEFT $9,000,000.

Executors Ask Permission to Sell Securities to Pay Expenses.

The estate of John B. Manning, retired broker, who died April 23 last at the age of 83, after he had settled for $100,000 a suit for $1,000,000 for breach of promise brought by Miss Honora May O'Brien, now the wife of an Irish farmer, left an estate valued at $9,000,000, according to a petition filed in the Surrogate's Court yesterday by the executors asking permission to sell securities to pay inheritance taxes and other expenses of the estate. The inheritance taxes will amount to between $1,500,000 and $2,000,000, the Federal inheritance tax will be $150,000, and the debts and funeral expenses about $200,000. The estate has already sold $1,800,000 of securities under a court order to meet expenses and a further sale is necessary to raise $600,000 needed.

The will left the estate to six children and three grandchildren of the decedent. Guardians for the grandchildren oppose the present sale of the securities because of market conditions, but the adult heirs favor the sale and believe no sacrifice of the securities will be necessary. The heirs will receive the securities in nine equal parts after all expenses are paid.

Mr. Manning held stocks and bonds in about 100 corporations. Among the larger holdings of stock are: Consolidated Gas, $156,520; Consolidated Coal, $207,000; Northwestern Railroad, preferred, $146,250, and common, $549,275; Jersey Central, $252,500; Corn Exchange Bank, $171,900; Chemical National Bank, $189,420; Lackawanna Railroad, $680,535; Illinois Central, $285,950; First National Bank, $154,860; Manhattan Railway, $115,862; Chicago & St. Louis Railroad, $129,580; Pullman Company, $288,963; Reading Railroad, $621,000; Union Pacific, $214,650; Southern Pacific, $121,000; New York Central, $196,350; Liberty bonds, first issue, $152,837, second issue, $207,782. Surrogate Cohalan reserved decision.

Section 1

"All the News That's Fit to Print."

The New York Times.

THE WEATHER
Cloudy, probably rain Sunday; Monday clearing; southeast winds.
For full weather report see Page 22.

Section 1

VOL. LXVIII...NO. 22,282. • • • NEW YORK, SUNDAY, JANUARY 26, 1919.—108 PAGES, in Nine Parts, Including Picture and Magazine Sections (Rotogravure) and Book Section. FIVE CENTS In Greater New York

LEAGUE OF NATIONS PLAN IS ADOPTED; PEACE CONFERENCE ACTS ON WILSON PLEA, STRONGLY SUPPORTED BY LLOYD GEORGE

MOVE TO CANCEL 15 BILLIONS IN WAR EXPENSES

House Bill Revokes $7,179,156,944 in Contracts and $8,221,029,294 in Authorizations.

AFFECTS ARMY AND NAVY

Committee Has Not Yet Found Time to Cut Allotments to Other Departments.

BIG SAVING IN THE ARMY

Reduction in Ordnance Department Alone $9,217,648,304, and Quartermaster $3,756,135,307.

Special to The New York Times.

WASHINGTON, Jan. 25.—The cessation of war saved the nation billions of dollars through the cancellation of contracts and authorizations. In the deficiency bill reported to the House by the Appropriations Committee, today, contracts for $7,179,156,944 are ordered canceled and authorizations amounting to $8,221,029,294 are withdrawn. If the war had continued another six months it is estimated that the expenditure of both these amounts, or more than $15,000,000,000 would have been necessary.

The bill carries recommendations for appropriations of $295,244,329.45 for the various services of the Government, divided as follows: War Department, $6,473,782.68; Navy Establishment, $280,762,225.36; Civil Service, $7,853,750.57; Navy Department, $154,570.84.

The largest items for which appropriations are recommended follow:

War Department — Temporary employes, $4,000,000; disposition of remains of officers and men, $2,473,782.68.

Navy Department: Bureau of Navigation, $1,531,178.64; Bureau of Yards and Docks, $6,100,000; Bureau of Construction, $15,000,000; Bureau of Steam Engineering, $4,330,882.

Representative Swagar Sherley, Chairman, in his report said:

"The repeal of appropriations and withdrawal of authorizations has been confined to the military and naval establishments, not because funds voted to other departments are all required, for such is not the fact, but because the magnitude of the task made impossible at this time a review of the other departments, and it is hoped that in connection with the Sundry Civil and other bills many of these surplus funds may be dealt with. The committee in recommending that various sums shall be covered into the Treasury does not mean to affirm in any sense that the total of the moneys left with the various bureaus is needed or should be expended, or to approve or disapprove various activities set forth in the hearings. There should, and doubless will be, large savings made from these balances.

"What the committee has endeavored to do is to cover into the Treasury such sums that plainly are not needed, but as it is necessarily uncertain just to what extent the Government may be able by cancellation of contracts and discontinuance of projects to reduce its obligations, the committee has deemed it wise to leave funds amply sufficient to meet such obligations. To have undertaken to pass judgment on remaining activities would have been to usurp the prerogatives of many of the committees and would have required a detailed examination that would have taken many additional months.

"The labors of the committee have been greatly added to because of the absence of any uniform system of keeping accounts by the various departments, and it desires to express the hope that Congress may provide soon for such a system of accounting. While the work of the committee by some may be thought unnecessary on the ground that the departments probably would not have expended the sums anyway it was the judgment of the committee that it was wise directly to provide against their expenditure, and it cannot be doubted that the examination of their balances and survey of their activities and needs by the various corps of the army and navy brought about by the action of the committee should enable these departments to make savings of many millions."

The following table shows the savings in cancellation of contracts and authorizations:

ARMY ESTABLISHMENT.

Purpose.	Appropriations.	Authorizations.
Sig. Serv....	$83,373,206.04	$45,000,000.00
Mil. Aeron..	85,000,000.00	....
Airc'ft prod.	402,000,000.00	....
Qm. Corps...	3,740,385,307.76	15,750,000.00
Med. Dept...	54,145,513.73	65,000,000.00
Eng. Corps..	792,580,435.76	200,000,000.00
Ord. Dept...	1,503,369,009.75	7,714,279,294.70
Chem. Warf.	183,932,610.86	150,000,000.00
Total army	$6,844,795,077.70	$8,190,029,274.70

NAVAL ESTABLISHMENT.

Aviation	$98,000,000.00	....
Navigation ..	[illegible],500,000.00	....
Ordnance ...	164,833,843.69	$31,000,000.00
Public Works	2,173,627.00	....
Sup. and Ac.	23,096,000.00	....
Steam Eng..	1,420.33	....
Marine Corps	42,216,975.06	....
Total navy	$334,361,866.98	$31,000,000.00
Grand total army and navy	$7,179,156,944.68	$8,221,029,294.70

Combined appropriation and authorization, $15,400,186,239.38.

Text of the Resolution to Create a World League As Unanimously Adopted by Peace Conference

PARIS, Jan. 25.—Following is the text of the resolution relating to the creation of a League of Nations, which was adopted by the plenary session of the Peace Conference today:

The conference, having considered the proposals for the creation of a League of Nations, resolved that:

It is essential to the maintenance of the world settlement which the associated nations are now met to establish that a League of Nations be created to promote international obligations and to provide safeguards against war.

This league should be created as an integral part of the general treaty of peace and should be open to every civilized nation which can be relied on to promote its objects.

The members of the league should periodically meet in international conference and should have a permanent organization and secretaries to carry on the business of the league in the intervals between the conferences.

The conference therefore appoints a committee, representative of the associated Governments, to work out the details of the constitution and the functions of the league and the draft of resolutions in regard to breaches of the laws of war for presentation to the Peace Conference.

Responsibility.

That a commission, composed of two representatives apiece from the five great powers and five representatives to be elected by the other powers, be appointed to inquire and report upon the following:

First—The responsibility of the authors of the war.

Second—The facts as to breaches of the laws and customs of war committed by the forces of the German Empire and their allies on land, on sea, and in the air during the present war.

Third—The degree of responsibility for these offenses attaching to particular members of the enemy's forces, including members of the General Staffs and other individuals, however highly placed.

Fourth—The constitution and procedure of a tribunal appropriate to the trial of these offenses.

Fifth—Any other matters, cognate or ancillary to the above, which may arise in the course of the inquiry and which the commission finds it useful and relevant to take into consideration.

Reparation.

Following is the draft of a resolution in regard to reparation which the conference adopted:

That a commission be appointed, which shall comprise not more than three representatives apiece from each of the five great powers and not more than two representatives apiece from Belgium, Greece, Poland, Rumania, and Serbia, to examine and report:

First—On the amount of reparation which the enemy countries ought to pay.

Second—On what they are capable of paying, and,

Third—On the method, the form, and time within which payment should be made.

International Legislation.

A resolution in regard to international legislation on industrial and labor questions was passed. It reads:

That a commission, composed of two representatives apiece from the five great powers and five representatives to be elected by the other powers represented at the Peace Conference, be appointed to inquire into the conditions of employment from the international aspect and to consider the international means necessary to secure common action on matters affecting conditions of employment and to recommend the form of a permanent agency to continue such inquiry and consideration, in co-operation with and under the direction of the League of Nations.

This resolution was adopted regarding international control of ports, waterways, and railways:

International Control.

That a commission composed of two representatives apiece from the five great powers and five representatives of the other powers be appointed, to inquire and report upon the international régime for ports, waterways, and railways.

CROMWELL DEATHS NOW CONFIRMED

Bordeaux Police Chief Reports That Young Women Committed Suicide.

PARIS, Jan. 25, (Associated Press)—The Commissioner of Police at Bordeaux confirms the report of the suicide of the Misses Gladys and Dorothea Cromwell.

The American Red Cross Headquarters here, in answer to inquiries, says it has been informed that the Misses Cromwell sailed on the French steamer La Lorraine. Friends of the twin sisters accompanied them to the pier.

The officer in charge of the Red Cross party on board the ship sent by wireless to the Red Cross a copy of the note found in the stateroom occupied by the sisters in which they said they intended to commit suicide.

The drowning of the Misses Dorothea and Gladys Cromwell from the French liner La Lorraine soon after the vessel sailed from France is still a mystery to members of their family in New York.

Seymour L. Cromwell, the only brother of the young women, discredits the reports and declared last night at his residence, 169 East Seventy-fourth Street, that he believed a mistake had been made, because of the conflicting dispatches and a cheerful letter he had received from his sisters less than a week ago.

Mr. Cromwell said late last night:

"Not only I, but the State Department and of course the Red Cross have sent cables to France endeavoring to find out some definite explanation. As yet I have received no satisfying word, but I was given to understand when the cables were sent that no answer would be forthcoming for thirty-six hours.

"The only thing that can convince me that such a thing could ever have happened would be to receive a wireless from the liner Espagne stating that my sisters were not aboard that vessel. Returning from France on La Lorraine is one of my most intimate friends and also two close friends of my partner in business. Wireless messages have been sent to these friends, but as yet no answer has come."

The Misses Cromwell were 32 years old and not 22 as first reported.

SEEK TO INSTALL STATE SOCIALISM

North Dakota Nonpartisan League, Controlling Legislature, Plans Legislation.

Special to The New York Times.

BISMARCK, N. D., Jan. 25.—Seven million dollars would be invested by North Dakota in the establishment of a State bank and a system of terminal elevators and flour mills under the industrial program introduced in the State Legislature by the Nonpartisan League, which controls both houses.

Complete revision of the State's scheme of taxation, by which the taxation burden would be transferred from personal property to corporations, incomes, and land, also has been proposed, and has the support of the league majorities, which are bound by a caucus pledge to pass all legislation indorsed by such caucus.

The abandonment of the old system of appointive State officials for fixed terms also is due, with the substitution of the Socialist plan, by which officers such as State Tax Commissioners, educational directors, charitable institution directors, &c., may be removed at will.

These, in a general way, are the big problems which confront the Legislature, now twenty days old, and which William Lemke, Vice President of the Nonpartisan League, says will be adjourned by Feb. 10.

This is the first State Legislature completely controlled by the nonpartisans. They have more than two-thirds of the members of the House and Senate, and by using emergency clauses in their administration measures they will come very near to beating referendum of their bills, as 30,000 signatures are required to refer bills to which emergency clauses are attached, and the State has only about 100,000 voters all told.

In carrying out their program for industrial enterprises, the nonpartisans

Continued on Page Five.

REDS WANT PARLEY NEARER

Tchitcherin, Foreign Minister, Says Princes' Islands Are Too Remote.

BUT WILL CONSIDER PLAN

Promises to Do So on Receipt of Confirmation of Council's Reported Decision.

TAKES A SUPERCILIOUS TONE

Invitation Comes, He Says, When Soviets Have Settled Internal Troubles of Russia.

PARIS, Jan. 25.—M. Tchitcherin, the Bolshevist Foreign Minister, has sent a wireless message to the Soviet representative in Sweden asking for confirmation of the decision of the Supreme Council of the Peace Conference to send a mission to confer with representatives of the different factions in Russia on Princes' Islands.

M. Tchitcherin's message says that the islands are too remote for such a meeting. He objects to the isolation of the islands as tending to surround the conference with secrecy, and also objects to leaving to the Entente the choice of participants.

This proposition of the Supreme Council, the message says, is made at a time when the Bolsheviki are victorious over their opponents and the internal situation of Russia has been settled, but the Soviet Government, on receipt of the confirmation requested, will carefully consider the proposal.

More Russians Enter Protests.

The Council of the national and democratic bloc of Russian political organizations abroad has sent a strongly worded protest to Premier Clemenceau against the decision of the Supreme Council to call a conference of the Russian factions.

"We would be men without honor and courage if we accepted for a single moment a truce such as proposed to us while all that are dear are in danger of death—violent death by execution or assassination or slow death through hunger," the protest says.

"The interest of humanity in general and democracy in particular requires the establishment in Russia of a régime based on the sovereignty of the people freely expressed. An improvised meeting at the Princes' Islands cannot be an expression of this sort. Russia has long clamored for the free election of a Constituent Assembly. The attempt was stifled by the Bolsheviki by force of arms, and they are today asked to make the voice of Russia heard!"

The Russian Bolshevist Government at Moscow, according to information received by the Socialist newspaper L'Humanité, is surprised that the suggestion made by the allied and associated Powers for a conference between the Russian factions comes at a time when the Bolsheviki are victorious in the field. The Bolsheviki, however, the advices add, do not reject the principle of a conference.

Vladimir Bourtzeff, a well-known Russian revolutionist, in an article in the Matin says that the Russian parties opposed to the Bolsheviki will positively refuse to attend the conference on Princes' Islands, because they look on the Bolsheviki as traitors to the fatherland and as murderers who have dishonored Russia.

Vasili Maklakoff, the latest Russian Ambassador accredited to France, according to the same article, says that all Russians in Paris feel deeply humiliated by the proposal of the allied and associated Powers. The Ambassador adds that a party truce and cessation of hostilities, as requested by the Allies, could have only one result—the hampering of the armies which are about to liberate Northern Russia—without putting an end to the reign of terror. The Ambassador is also quoted as declaring that only the Bolsheviki will profit by such a conference.

Alluding to the decision of the Supreme Council of the Peace Conference to send a delegation to meet representatives of the various Russian factions, which decision has been objected to in some Russian quarters as not in the real interest of the Russian people, M. Maklakoff said yesterday:

"The presence of France and America at the Peace Conference is a guarantee that any unfriendly intention toward Russia, even if there were such, would not be countenanced. It is most strange, however, that France, which on Dec. 29, in alluding to Bolshevism while stating her attitude toward Russia, declared that she would 'never have anything to do with crime,' should now have joined in the proposal to hold a discussion with Bolshevist delegates at the Princes' Islands."

It may be noted in connection with the attitude of Ambassador Maklakoff to-

Continued on Page Three.

Text of Wilson's Speech to Peace Conference Pointing Out Need of a League of Nations

PARIS, Jan. 25.—President Wilson's address before the Peace Conference today was as follows:

Mr. Chairman—I consider it a distinguished privilege to be permitted to open the discussion in this conference on the League of Nations. We have assembled for two purposes, to make the present settlements which have been rendered necessary by this war and also to secure the peace of the world, not only by the present settlements but by the arrangements we shall make at this conference for its maintenance.

The League of Nations seems to me to be necessary for both of these purposes. There are many complicated questions connected with the present settlements, which perhaps cannot be successfully worked out to an ultimate issue by the decisions we shall arrive at here. I can easily conceive that many of these settlements will need subsequent consideration; that many of the decisions we make shall need subsequent alteration in some degree, for if I may judge by my own study of some of these questions they are not susceptible for confident judgments at present.

It is therefore necessary that we should set up some machinery by which the work of this conference should be rendered complete.

We have assembled here for the purpose of doing very much more than making the present settlements that are necessary. We are assembled under very peculiar conditions of world opinion. I may say, without straining the point, that we are not the representatives of Governments, but representatives of the peoples.

It will not suffice to satisfy governmental circles anywhere. It is necessary that we should satisfy the opinion of mankind.

The burdens of this war have fallen in an unusual degree upon the whole population of the countries involved. I do not need to draw for you the picture of how the burden has been thrown back from the front upon the older men, upon the women, upon the children, upon the homes of the civilized world, and how the real strain of the war has come where the eyes of the Government could not reach, but where the heart of humanity beats.

We are bidden by these people to make a peace which will make them secure. We are bidden by these people to see to it that this strain does not come upon them again. And I venture to say that it has been possible for them to bear this strain because they hoped that those who represented them could get together after this war and make such another sacrifice unnecessary.

It is a solemn obligation on our part, therefore, to make permanent arrangements that justice shall be rendered and peace maintained.

This is the central object of our meeting. Settlements may be temporary, but the action of the nations in the interest of peace and justice must be permanent. We can set up permanent processes. We may not be able to set up a permanent decision.

Therefore, it seems to me that we must take as far as we can a picture of the world into our minds. Is it not a startling circumstance, for one thing, that the great discoveries of science, that the quiet studies of men in laboratories, that the thoughtful developments which have taken place in quiet lecture rooms have now been turned to the destruction of civilization? The powers of destruction have not so much multiplied as they have gained facilities.

The enemy, whom we have just overcome, had at his seats of learning some of the principal centres of scientific study and discovery, and he used them in order to make destruction sudden and complete. And only the watchful and continuous co-operation of men can see to it that science, as well as armed men, is kept within the harness of civilization.

In a sense the United States is less interested in this subject than the other nations here assembled. With her great territory and her extensive sea borders, it is less likely that the United States should suffer from the attack of enemies than that other nations should suffer. And the ardor of the United States—for it is a very deep and genuine ardor—for the society of nations is not an ardor springing out of fear or apprehension, but an ardor springing out of the ideals which have come in the consciousness of this war.

In coming into this war the United States never for a moment thought that she was intervening in the politics of Europe, or the politics of Asia, or the politics of any part of the world. Her thought was that all the world had now become conscious that there was a single cause of justice and of liberty for men of every kind and place.

Therefore, the United States should feel that its part in this war should be played in vain if there ensued upon it abortive European settlements. It would feel that it could not take part in guaranteeing those European settlements unless that guarantee involved the continuous superintendence of the peace of the world by the associated nations of the world.

Therefore, it seems to me that we must concern our best judgment in order to make this League of Nations a vital thing—a thing sometimes called into life to meet an exigency—but always functioning in watchful attendance upon the interests of the nations, and that its continuity should be a vital continuity; that its functions are continuing functions that do not permit an intermission of its watchfulness and of its labor; that it should be the eye of the nations, to keep watch upon the common interest—an eye that did not slumber, an eye that was everywhere watchful and attentive.

And if we do not make it vital, what shall we do? We shall disappoint the expectations of the peoples. This is what their thought centres upon.

I have had the very delightful experience of visiting several nations since I came to this side of the water, and every time the voice of the body of the people reached me, through any representative, at the front of the plea stood the hope of the League of Nations.

Gentlemen, the select classes of mankind are no longer the governors of mankind. The fortunes of mankind are now in the hands of the plain people of the whole world. Satisfy them, and you have justified their confidence not only, but have established peace. Fail to satisfy them, and no arrangement that you can make will either set up or steady the peace of the world.

You can imagine, I dare say, the sentiments and the purpose with which the representatives of the United States support this great project for a League of Nations. We regard it as the keynote of the whole, which expressed our purposes and ideals in this war and which the associated nations have accepted as the basis of a settlement.

If we return to the United States without having made every effort in our power to realize this program, we should return to meet the merited scorn of our fellow-citizens. For they are a body that constitute a great democracy. They expect their leaders to speak; their representatives to be their servants.

We have no choice but to obey their mandate. But it is with the greatest enthusiasm and pleasure that we accept that mandate. And because this is the keynote of the whole fabric, we have pledged our every purpose to it, as we have to every item of the fabric. We would not dare abate a single item of the program which constitutes our instructions; we would not dare to compromise upon any matter as the champion of this thing—this peace of the world, this attitude of justice, this principle that we are the masters of no peoples, but are here to see that every people in the world shall choose its own masters and govern its own destinies, not as we wish, but as they wish.

We are here to see, in short, that the very foundations of this war are swept away. Those foundations were the private choice of a small coterie of civil rulers and military staffs. Those foundations were the aggression of great powers upon the small. Those foundations were the holding together of empires of unwilling subjects by the duress of arms. Those foundations were the power of small bodies of men to wield their will and use mankind as pawns in a game. And nothing less than the emancipation of the world from these things will accomplish peace.

You can see that the representatives of the United States are, therefore, never put to the embarrassment of choosing a way of expediency, because they have had laid down before them the unalterable lines of principles. And, thank God, these lines have been accepted as the lines of settlements by all the high-minded men who have had to do with the beginning of this great business.

I hope, Mr. Chairman, when it is known, as I feel confident it will be known, that we have adopted the principle of the League of Nations and mean to work out that principle in effective action, we shall by that single thing have lifted a great part of the load of anxiety from the hearts of men everywhere.

We stand in a peculiar cause. As I go about the streets here I see everywhere the American uniform. Those men came into the war after we had uttered our purpose. They came as crusaders, not merely to win a war, but to win a cause. And I am responsible to them, for it falls to me to formulate the purpose for which I asked them to fight, and I, like them, must be a crusader for these things, whatever it costs and whatever it may be necessary to do in honor to accomplish the object for which they fought.

I have been glad to find from day to day that there is no question of our standing alone in this matter, for there are champions of this cause upon every hand. I am merely avowing this in order that you may understand why, perhaps, it fell to us, who are disengaged from the politics of this great continent and of the Orient, to suggest that this was the keystone of the arch, and why it occurred to the generous mind of your President to call upon me to open this debate. It is not because we alone represent this idea, but because it is our privilege to associate ourselves with you in representing it.

I have only tried in what I have said to give you the fountains of the enthusiasm which is within us for this thing, for those fountains spring, it seems to me, from all the ancient wrongs and sympathies of mankind, and the very pulse of the world seems to beat to the fullest in this enterprise.

CONFERENCE ACTS SWIFTLY

Hears Speeches in Favor of League and Gives Quick Approval

FIRST ADDRESS BY WILSON

Lloyd George Warmly Voices Great Britain's Support of the Proposal.

ORLANDO ALSO BACKS IT

Wilson and House Are American Members of Commission to Draft League Plan.

Delegates of Great Powers on Peace League Commission

PARIS, Jan. 25.—The delegates of the Great Powers on the League of Nations, it was learned tonight, will be:

For the United States—President Wilson and Colonel Edward M. House.

For Great Britain—Lord Robert Cecil and General Jan Christian Smuts.

For France—Leon Bourgeois and Ferdinand Larnaude, Dean of the Faculty of Law of the University of Paris.

For Italy—Premier Orlando and Viterio Scialoia.

For Japan—Viscount Chinda and K. Ochiai.

The delegates of the small nations will be announced later.

PARIS, Jan. 25, (Associated Press.)—The plenary session of the Peace Conference today unanimously adopted the project to establish a League of Nations and name a commission to draft the complete plan.

President Wilson and Colonel House are the two American members of the commission.

The session of the conference began at 3 o'clock in the afternoon in the Salle de la Paix of the Foreign Office with the same imposing setting as the first session, but with little ceremony and a manifest purpose of business.

M. Clemenceau was again in the chair, with President Wilson and the full American delegation at his right, and Premier Lloyd George and the British delegation at his left.

When the session opened it was addressed by President Wilson on the subject of the proposed world league.

The President declared that the conference had solemn obligations to make a permanent settlement.

With great earnestness he asserted that the conference could not complete its work until some further machinery of settlement should be set up.

"We are not here alone," he went on, "as representatives of Governments, but as representatives of peoples, and in the settlements we make we need to satisfy, not the opinions of Governments, but the opinion of mankind."

League Must Have Continuity.

The President contended that a League of Nations must be a vital thing and not casual or occasional. It must have continuity.

"It should be the eye of nations, an eye which never slumbers," he added.

On his travels, the President said, people everywhere had greeted the league as the first thing in their interest.

"Select classes of men no longer direct the affairs of the world," said the President, "but the fortunes of the world are now in the hands of the plain people."

The wish of the people, therefore, must be heard. The war had swept away those old foundations by which small coteries had "used mankind as pawns in a game." Nothing but emancipation from the old system, he contended, would accomplish real peace.

The President said he had seen American soldiers in the street—soldiers who had come, not alone for war, but as "crusaders in a great cause." He added, "And I, like them, must be a crusader, whatever it costs to accomplish that end."

After declaring that the conference was for the purpose of a settlement arising out of the war and to make peace for the world, the President said:

"A League of Nations seems necessary for both purposes. There are many questions which we feel cannot ultimately be worked out here, that may require subsequent consideration, subsequent alterations even to some degree."

He described how the war burden was borne by the people as well as by the armies, and said:

"We are bidden by these sufferers to make peace secure for them and see to it that the strain need never be borne again."

Britain for It, Says Lloyd George.

Following the reading of a translation of President Wilson's speech, Premier Lloyd George said:

"I rise to second this resolution. After the noble speech of the American President, I feel that no observations are needed in order to commend this resolution to the Conference, and I should not have intervened at all, had it not been that I wished to state how emphatically the people of the British Empire are behind this proposal.

"And if the national leaders have not been able during the last five years to devote as much time as they would like to its advocacy, it is because their time and their energy have been absorbed in the exigencies of a terrible struggle.

"Had there been the slightest doubt in my mind as to the wisdom of this scheme, it would have vanished before an irresistible appeal made to me by the spectacle I witnessed last Sunday. I visited a region which but a few years ago was one of the fairest in an exceptionally fair land. I found it a ruin and a desolation.

"I drove for hours through a country which did not appear like the habitation of living men and women and children, but like the excavation of a province, shattered and torn. I went to one city, where I witnessed a scene of devastation that no indemnity can ever repair—one of the beautiful things of the world disfigured and defaced beyond repair.

"And one of the cruelest features to my mind was what I could see had happened—that Frenchmen, who love their land almost beyond any nation, in order to establish the justice of their cause had to assist the cruel enemy in demolishing their homes, and I felt that these are the results—only part of the results.

"Had I been there three months ago, I would have witnessed something that I dare not describe. But I saw acres of graves of the fallen. And these were the results of the only methods, the only organized methods, that civilized nations have ever attempted or established to settle disputes amongst each other. And my feeling was: Surely it is time that a saner plan for settling disputes between peoples ought to be established than this organized savagery.

"I don't know whether this will succeed. But if we attempt it, the attempt will be a success, and for that reason I second the proposal."

Italy's Premier Indorses Plan.

The Italian Premier, Vittorio Orlando, followed Lloyd George. He declared that no people were readier to accept the League of Nations in its entirety than the Italian people.

Leon Bourgeois, a veteran French supporter of the League of Nations, spoke next, pledging the French to do everything "that can help to put us on the road which has been pointed out by President Wilson."

"I should like to ask," said Premier Hughes of Australia, "if we are to have an opportunity to discuss this scheme when it is finished."

"Without any doubt," responded M. Clemenceau.

The Chinese delegates added their support to the resolution, saying that China associated herself in the lofty ideals expressed. The Polish delegates and Camille Huysmans, head of the Belgian delegation, added their strong approval.

"Is there any objection to the resolution?" asked M. Clemenceau. There was no response and he declared the resolution unanimously adopted.

M. Clemenceau then announced the composite committee, and the order of the names as announced makes President Wilson Chairman.

Louis Klotz of the French delegation proposed a financial section to the League of Nations, but the proposal finally went over.

M. Clemenceau proposed another plenary session on Monday for the selection of committees, and without division this was adopted. At 6 o'clock the council adjourned until 3 o'clock Monday afternoon.

Small Powers Make Demands.

The first sign of a division in the conference was when it proceeded to consider the four resolutions framed by the Council of the Great Powers, providing for committees on labor, responsibility for the war, reparation for damages, and ports, railways, and waterways.

Camille Huysmans, in behalf of Belgium, asked for two members on the Committees of Labor, Reparation, and the League of Nations, and one each on the others. Serbia made a similar request.

Brazil was more emphatic, declaring against "a cut-and-dried program," and saying that the conference should be master of its own decisions.

M. Venizelos said that Greece was entitled to membership on the Committees of Reparation and Ports. M. Bratiano, for Rumania, and Dr. Benes, for Czechoslovakia, as well as the delegations representing Portugal, China, Siam, and Poland, also asked for places on the committees.

It looked for a time as if the small nations had formed a bloc and would contest the decisions of the great powers to restrict the committees.

"We will have something to say," declared Dr. Benes, "in winding up the Austro-Hungarian Empire, and it is difficult to understand how any committee can act without information that the Czechoslovaks alone can give."

M. Bratiano added:

"The smaller nations have greater interests at stake than the great powers on many of these questions."

M. Clemenceau finally, in a good-tempered speech, said that the council had not imposed its decision, but had simply convoked the conference to consider the plan.

"After forty-eight years of public life," he said, "I am satisfied that the larger the committee is, the less it accomplishes. I beg the delegates not to waste time on questions of procedure when millions of men are waiting to be demobilized. Let us organize the committees at once, and so get to work. We have no desire to be unjust to any one, but wish to devise a procedure leading to rapid results."

M. Clemenceau's assurance that the council would consider the questions raised finally prevailed, and Belgium, on behalf of the smaller powers, withdrew the protests, saying that the position having been cleared they trusted to the fairness of the council.

The resolutions were adopted without change.

PARIS, Jan. 25, (Havas.)—At the Peace Conference this afternoon, the permanent Chairman, M. Clemenceau, read a resolution on the League of Nations to the effect that such a league was to be organized by international co-operation for the purpose of making secure international obligations and safeguarding the nations against war. The league would be an integral part of the peace treaty and would be open to all civilized nations favoring its aims.

The Conference appointed a commission representing the Associated Governments to elaborate a constitution for the league, including its prerogatives.

LEAGUE PLAN TO MOVE FAST.

Wilson Ready to Work Ten Hours a Day, He Tells Delegates.

PARIS, Jan. 25.—Rapid and substantial strides toward the real objects of the Peace Conference are expected as a result of today's session.

With the League of Nations question formally before them for discussion, the delegates are expected to work continuously at the task, possibly ten hours a day. President Wilson, it is said, has told the delegates he would be willing to work ten hours a day until tangible results are ready for announcement to the world.

While much of the ensuing discussion will be in secret, according to the rule of procedure now in force, there is reason to believe that more sessions may be public than had been expected, especially while a League of Nations is being discussed.

Without any official outline of the President's plan for a league before the public, a comparison of what Premier Lloyd George has in mind with what the President may propose is only partly in order, but it may be said, on the authority of those in a position to know what is in the President's mind, that the British outline very generally accords with the principles toward which the American group has been working.

The outstanding principle, expressed in the British outline which declares that a distinction must be realized between justiciable disputes and non-justiciable disputes and that each State must be the final judge whether or not a dispute is justiciable, is taken in American circles to be quite in line with the developing opinion among all delegates. It has been reported previously that the point has been passed where the creation of a super-sovereignty had been considered feasible.

The general outlines of the British plan are taken in American quarters to be in consonance with the generally crystallizing idea here that the league probably will be projected as a sort of a guardianship for smaller nations, extending international assistance for the development and preservation of economic and financial, as well as military, sovereignty. It is pointed out in American circles, however, that a full measure of comparison cannot be made until President Wilson makes a statement on his own ideas, and that he is considering some phase which is not expressed in the British outline.

President Wilson has been giving the proposition almost continuous study, even though engaged in the study of the Russian question and other issues before the Supreme War Council, and has, it is said, his ideas definitely reduced to form in which they can be placed before the Peace Conference.

SEES ERA OF FORCE ENDED.

London Times Applauds Warning to Claimants by Supreme Council.

LONDON, Jan. 25.—Commenting on the action of the Supreme War Council in issuing a warning to those who are using armed force in Europe and the East to enlarge their possessions before claims are finally adjusted, The Times says:

"The decisions of the Conference will rest on two sets of considerations and two only. The first set is the result of the war that was terminated by the armistice of November. The armistice ended once and for all the argument of force and for any of the parties to the great suit in international justice which is now opening in Paris to continue to appeal to force is contempt of court.

"The second set of considerations is made up of claims of justice. Various rival nationalities, who are now crying out their claims, are harking back to an era definitely closed by the defeat of Germany in which might was held to determine right. The great powers in the conference, having at the cost of incredible exertions and sacrifices overthrown that old band and set up a new tribunal of justice, must assert their authority against all appeals by violence. We do not mean that all claims that are being put out are necessarily claims that in themselves are unjust. But just or not they will be prejudiced by a continuance of violence. He who asks for justice must come into court with clean hands."

The Manchester Guardian welcomes the action of the Council. It says that some of the "many instances" referred to are notorious. It is well understood, the paper says, that it is painful to have to wait for satisfaction of national aspirations, often of long standing, "until the grain to feed them has been ground by such slow grinding mills as those of the Peace Conference."

"Great Britain's decision to leave such questions as the future of Mesopotamia, Palestine, and the German Colonies to the League of Nations is profoundly important," says The Daily News. "The adoption of such a policy by the British delegation has established the League in its true place in relation to the Peace Congress and invests the whole proceedings of the Congress with an atmosphere of confidence and good will, created by the refusal of a great nation to take advantage of the accident of military possession of valuable territory.

"If Great Britain is ready to give such an effective pledge of her faith in the League of Nations, no other power is left with an excuse for holding back. The decision may well prove to be the greatest victory of the war."

WOULD HAVE LEAGUE STATE SUFFRAGE VIEWS

But Wilson Tells Frenchwomen He Does Not Favor Putting Subject on League Program.

PARIS, Jan. 25.—President Wilson told a delegation of women, representing the working women of France, who called upon him today to urge that the Peace Conference include woman suffrage among the points of settlement, that, much as he sympathized with their cause, he felt that it was entirely a domestic question for the several nations.

He said that he believed that it would be regarded as quite outside the province of the conference if it "undertook to dictate to the several States what their internal policy should be."

The same situation, he added, applied to the question of labor, and it seemed to him that the conference would take some action by expressing its sentiments on these subjects.

"The conference," said the President, "is turning out to be a rather unwieldy body—a very large body, representing many nations, large and small, old and new, and the method of organizing its work successfully will, I am afraid, have to be worked out stage by stage. Therefore, I have no confident prediction to make as to the way in which it can take up questions of this sort."

The President, in his address to the women, paid tribute to the efforts of all women in winning the war, repeating that, as it had been a people's war, he stood for a people's peace. He added that the efforts and sacrifices of the women of France particularly had won the admiration of the world. He continued:

"The people won this war, not the Government, and the people must reap the benefits of this war. At every turn we must see to it that it is not an adjustment between Governments merely, but an arrangement for the peace and security of men and women everywhere. Little obscure sufferings daily, unknown privations and unspoken sufferings of the heart are the tragical things of this war. They have been borne at the home, and the center of the home is woman.

"I welcome this opportunity to bring you this message, not from myself merely, but from the great people whom I represent."

LAST WARNING GIVEN TO FIGHTING ALLIES

Paris Council Will Use "the Big Stick" to Curb Boundary Disputes.

ITALY'S TRYING POSITION

Associated with Other Allies in Forbidding Hostilities While Her Troops Confront Jugoslavs.

By CHARLES A. SELDEN.

Copyright, 1919, by The New York Times Company.
Special Cable to THE NEW YORK TIMES.

PARIS, Jan. 24.—The statement issued by the five big powers, warning all nations to cease fighting among themselves over territory the rightful claims to which are to be determined by the Peace Conference itself, is based on the fact that the "firing of the last shot" in Europe on Nov. 11 was merely a pleasant figure of speech.

Literally, many shots have been fired every day since then in numerous boundary disputes among new and old States which technically are friends and Allies. If all the fighting that has been going on since the armistice had been concentrated between two nations it would make a very sizable war in itself, as measured by the standards existing prior to August, 1914.

But it has all been for nothing. Every drop of blood shed this Winter to push the claims of any State one inch beyond the limitations fixed tentatively on Nov. 11 has been shed in vain. More than that, there comes now the warning that "possession gained by force will seriously prejudice the claims of those who use such force."

I asked a French authority if any secret warnings had been given before this public one was sent out to the whole world.

"No," he said significantly, "this is the first and will be the last. It is what you call in America 'the big stick.' It is a very 'big stick.'"

Italy's troops are now opposed to those of the Jugoslavs on territory for which both have conflicting claims which must be settled by the Peace Conference in Paris, and nowhere else, and in no other way. The Italians and Jugoslavs have already had two actual encounters with bloodshed.

Another situation in which Italy figures, and from which hostilities were feared when the warning was given, grows out of her contest with Greece over Albania and the northern half of Epirus. Greek and Italian troops in both of these regions have been perilously near a clash because of the conflicting claims of their Governments.

Other nations to which the warning particularly applies, with a brief statement of the offending acts of each, are as follows:

The Czechoslovaks have been invading parts of Galicia in conflict with the Rumanians. The Rumanians and Serbians are fighting for possession of the disputed Province of the Banat, north of the Danube.

The Poles are invading German Poland, or Posen. This is entirely unnecessary, because Poland will undoubtedly get Posen when the time comes. It is pointed out here that she would have been making better use of her troops if she had used them in a more vigorous effort to hold back the Bolshevist invasion.

The King of the Hedjaz, who will get his Arabian State by peaceful means from the Paris Conference if he will only be patient, has not been fighting yet, but has offended by sending out military expeditions to take possession of territory before the boundaries of his kingdom have been determined.

Although the warning applies technically only to friendly nations, it is supposed to affect Hungary, who is also trying to use some force to save what she can from Rumanian-Czechoslovak encroachments.

This is also a supplementary warning to the various Russian Governments, which have been told that they must cease hostilities as a preliminary to the Marmora Conference. The representatives of several of those Governments in Paris have already intimated that they will disregard the action of the conference and will not participate in any parleys with the Bolsheviki.

Our Troops Barred from Disputes.

PARIS, Jan. 25.—The warning issued yesterday by the Supreme Council that territorial claims must come before the Peace Conference unprejudiced by attempts at possession by force is very widely discussed here. It seems to be generally acknowledged that President Wilson was the author of the warning, and that he has a deep feeling in the matter because in at least one instance where small bodies of American troops were under other command they were used to push forward into a territory where the native population would not have tolerated the forces of any European power, but hailed the coming of the Americans with joy. In some of these cases, after the welcome had died down, the population awoke to find that the American troops had departed, and that their towns were in the possession of troops of another nationality.

The President, it is known, took summary action to prevent the use of American forces for such purposes. He has now obtained an agreement in the Peace Conference to warn all nations against such steps.

COSSACKS "LOSING SPIRITS."

Russian Embassy Says They Vainly Await Aid of Allies.

Special to The New York Times.

WASHINGTON, Jan. 25.—The Russian Embassy today received and made public an offical cablegram from the All-Russian Government at Omsk to the effect that Bolshevist disorders in Siberia have been crushed; that the situation there is good and confidence in the new Government being strengthened, but the dispatch added that Cossacks on the southern Russian front are losing their "splendid spirit, having vainly awaited aid from the Allies for a year."

"The general situation at the front is favorable," the calegram read. "On the Perm front, the Siberian troops are going splendidly. On the Ufa front temporary reverses were caused, owing to the troops lacking arms. This, however, has been remedied.

"On the southern front the situation is difficult. Orenburg is threatened by the Bolsheviki. The Cossacks there are losing their splendid spirits, having vainly awaited aid from the Allies for a year. To improve their morale, it is desirable that at least small detachments of foreign troops be sent to their assistance. This necessity is being brought to the attention of the Allies, but does not seem to be met with favor by them.

"The interior situation is good and the Government is gaining strongly owing to these favorable developments: Recognition of the Omsk Government by Denikin, (Commander in Chief of the Volunteer Army in the southern regions, with headquarters at Yekaterinodar,) who united all southern Russia; appointment of General Janin, (as commander of the forces of the Omsk Government, and formerly French commander of the Czechoslovak forces); favorable solution of the question of relations between General Janin, General Knox, and Admiral Kolchak; agreement as to allied assistance relative to the railways, which are badly disorganized; appointment of Sazonoff, (Foreign Minister of the Yekaterinodar Government as Foreign Minister of the Omsk Government,) and, finally, the expected settlement of the Semenoff inciden.

"Confidence in the Government is strengthening on behalf of political parties, owing to the recent declarations which determine the political course and are favorably adopted by all.

"Feeble Bolshevist disorders which have occurred in several towns indicate that Bolshevism has been entirely crushed. The greatest difficulties still arise owing to the lack of monetary signs of merchandise and disorganization of transportation."

The embassy made public also the following cablegram from the Government of the Northern Regions at Archangel:

"By order of Tschaikovsky, President of the Provisional Government of the Northern Regions, Lieut. Gen. Miller has been appointed Governor General of the Northern Regions. Mr. Ignatieff has been appointed member of the Provisional Government in the capacity of Chief of the Department of the Interior.

"Governmental monopoly of leather has been abolished. Important measures concerning adjustment of land problems are being undertaken. Mobilization is being continued, non-commissioned officers being called up to 30 years of age. The victory of the Siberian troops has been solemnly celebrated in all the churches. The commissary arriving from Siberia communicated that Siberian troops were advancing toward the River Petokora and that their junction with the northern troops will take place shortly.

"Tschaikovsky is leaving for Paris to attend the conference there."

SAYS FRANCE FACES TRADE WAR WITH FOE

Hurley Predicts All German Energy Will Go Into Commerce—Sure France Can Compete.

PARIS, Jan. 25.—France now faces a commercial struggle with Germany, Edward N. Hurley, Chairman of the United States Shipping Board, said at a Franco-American dinner tonight, and must prepare to meet German competition which will be organized with the energies formerly devoted to making war. The end of the war, Mr. Hurley added, cannot be considered as having come until France is entirely rehabilitated commercially.

For twenty-five years, Mr. Hurley said, Germany devoted 50 per cent. of her efforts toward commercial lines and the rest to building up her great military machine. As no such machine will be permitted in the future, he added, all her efforts will be devoted to commerce.

"Say what you will about her methods," he declared, "she has demonstrated her efficiency in commerce, and with her whole effort devoted in the future to trade, the other nations of the world will always have a formidable competitor, no matter what restrictions it becomes advisable to put in her path. To solve this problem France must organize, as she cannot meet it by relying on isolated individual efforts."

French products, Mr. Hurley proposed, should be protected with a "Made in France" trade mark, vigorously protected against infringement. Shipping, he said, must be furnished at fair and equal rates in order to give all nations an equal footing in manufacturing and selling genius. The American Shipping Board, he hoped, would be of assistance to France by furnishing ships to increase the French merchant marine.

"The commerce and authority of France," Mr. Hurley concluded, "are now free to make her a greater nation than she ever was before. You will, with your energy and skill, place her in a position in which the world wants her to be—one of the leading nations of commerce and industry. If the people of France will enthusiastically support their commercial and industrial leaders as they supported their gallant army, I have no fear that her devastated regions will be quickly rehabilitated and her trade and commerce restored as important factors throughout the world. Your commercial future and supremacy are before you. You have another duty to perform—to reorganize, to cooperate, to make the wheels of French industry turn again and thus become a great commercial power."

INSIST ON RHINE FRONTIER.

Even French Literary Men Express Annexationist Views to Wilson.

By CHARLES A. SELDEN.

Copyright, 1919, by The New York Times Company.
Special Cable to THE NEW YORK TIMES.

PARIS, Jan. 24.—A sample of the things that the French insist upon in their talks with President Wilson, as he receives one small group after another, is afforded by the conversation that four members of the Society of Men of Letters had with him on Wednesday. The four were: Georges Lecomte, President of the society; General Malleterre, the Abbé Wetterle, who represented Alsace-Lorraine for many years in the German Reichstag, and Firmin Roz.

Like so many others who have seen him, they told him that the Germans must be pushed back beyond the Rhine, not only in Alsace-Lorraine and the Sarre Valley immediately north, but from the entire left bank region. They told him they needed peace for their efforts as thinkers and their tasks as writers.

They believed his League of Nations was one safeguard of peace, but France, which had been invaded four times in a century, needed other security for its future, which could be afforded only by ridding the whole left bank in perpetuity of all German soldiers and fortifications.

Mr. Wilson made no comment.

WILSON TO VISIT RHEIMS TODAY

Plans Another Short Trip to the Battle Area Between Conference Sessions.

MAY SEE VERDUN NEXT

Mrs. Wilson and Admiral Grayson to Accompany Him—French Officer as Guide.

PARIS, Jan. 24.—President Wilson will have his first view on Sunday of the havoc wrought in Northern France by the Germans. On that day he will make the first of a series of short trips by going to Rheims, from which he will tour the surrounding district in an army motor car.

Later the President expects to make another visit to the battle area, probably the region of Verdun. He will go on a Sunday or some other day between the sessions of the Peace Conference when he feels he is not taking the time he thinks he should devote to business.

The President will take a very small party. It will include Mrs. Wilson, Rear Admiral Grayson, and a French Army officer who is familiar with the field and military operations that took place there, and who will explain the situation to the President as they go along.

Although the President has been strongly urged by the French authorities to visit the devastated districts as one of the first events of his visit to France, he has not considered that he has had the time until now. His views on the question of reparation by Germany have been fairly well defined by those about him, and what effect, if any, his visit to the ruined regions may have on his opinions in that regard is the subject of lively discussion among Frenchmen.

AMERICA AND BRITAIN AS HOPE OF OPPRESSED

Balfour's Vision of a Heart Union of the English-Speaking Peoples.

Special Cable to THE NEW YORK TIMES.

LONDON, Jan. 25.—Arthur J. Balfour makes a striking pronouncement on the services which the United States and the British Empire can render to small and oppressed nations as joint trustees of civilization in a foreword which he has contributed to the first number of The Landmark, the new organ of an English-speaking union.

"That we shall always be friendly countries," he says, "I do not doubt, but that does not content me in the least. I want something much more than that. I want every member, every citizen of the British empire whether he lives in this small island or whether he belongs to the great British dominions over seas, and every citizen of the great American republic to feel that they are joint trustees for civilization and the world of those principles of peace and of liberty for which we are all struggling at this moment and I believe that that is what will happen, and I believe thatt the time will come when all small and oppressed nations will instinctively look, and not look in vain, to the all powerful protection of international arrangements of which the heart—the very heart and core—will be the union of soul, the union of sentiment, the union of belief of the great free English-speaking community now scattered over the whole world."

STRAUS OFF TO CONFERENCE

Will Represent League to Enforce Peace at Paris Discussions.

The White Star liner Lapland sailed at 2 o'clock yesterday afternoon for Liverpool with 368 first, 241 second, and 235 third class passengers, which is the largest number taken from this port on any one steamship since the armistice was signed on Nov. 11.

One of the first cabin passengers was Mrs. Whitelaw Reid, widow of the former Ambassador to England, who is returning to continue her work there with the American Red Cross. Oscar S. Straus, Chairman of the League to Enforce Peace, who was accompanied by his wife, said that he was going over by invitation to confer with representatives of the league in England, France, and Italy.

Mr. Straus said that he expected to meet Lord Bryce, former British Ambassador to the United States; Lord Grey, and M. Bourgeois, former Premier of France.

When asked about his plans for the Peace Conference discussions at Paris, Mr. Straus replied:

"We shall stand behind the plan of President Wilson for a League of Nations and report to the league here, of which former President Taft is the head, in order to aid them in their propaganda throughout the United States, which begins soon. It is our purpose to translate victory in war into a victory in peace for our children and our children's children.

"I think yet it will serve its purpose, for the League of Nations was built on The Hague Conference, but now it has the sanction of power behind it."

There were also on the Lapland a number of bankers, merchants, and business men including Frank Vanderlip, President of the National City Bank; Albert Strauss, Vice Governor of the Federal Reserve Bank, who said they were going over on a mission at the request of Secretary of the Treasury Carter Glass. Other passengers were C. F. Kelley, President of the Anaconda Copper Mine; R. L. Agassiz, President of the Calumet and Hecla Mining Company, and S. R. Guggenheim of the American Smelting and Refining Company, who said that it was the first time in four and a half years that any member of his firm had been to Europe.

An industrial commission appointed by Secretary of Labor Wilson to study industrial conditions abroad also sailed. The Secretary was at the pier to see the party off. The commission is headed by E. T. Gulacho of Chicago.

Just before the Lapland got away the liner Belgic, which had on board 100 American and British officers, 4,000 sacks of mails, and 18,000 tons of cargo, also got away for Liverpool.

NORTHCLIFFE ATTACK SEEN AS AID TO WILSON

Regarded as Club to Help Him Speed Up Work of Peace Conference.

BY CHARLES H. GRASTY.

Copyright, 1919, by The New York Times Company.
Special Cable to THE NEW YORK TIMES.

PARIS, Jan. 24.—The Northcliffe press editorial attack on the Peace Conference, including a side thrust at President Wilson, created a mild sensation, but in American circles this criticism was taken smilingly. Every one knows that President Wilson has been working sleeplessly to speed up action, and he is probably not disappointed at his inclusion in Northcliffe's general criticism of delay.

Until he went South for reasons of health, Northcliffe was working hand in glove with Colonel House, and it is shrewdly suspected that the present criticism is a piece of finesse with a club to help Wilson in his fight on procrastination in such a way as not to create feeling against the President among the dilly-dallying European diplomats. Wilson and Northcliffe share the same opinion regarding the danger of delay.

Today's communiqué's reference to the grab game being played in Southeastern Europe takes the bull by the horns in matters that have been causing serious concern for weeks past. The plain terms in which the Peace Conference deals indicate that patience at last is exhausted and that acts committed in the intoxication of victory no longer will be tolerated.

It is believed that the tumult produced by the action of the conference in dealing with the Bolsheviki will soon subside and that the Prinkipos program will be duly carried out. The Russian problem is so difficult that whatever is done is bound to encounter objection.

Bolshevism is now considered the paramount peril, and inasmuch as military intervention is a measure from which every ally flinches, some other way out must be found.

In this connection there is apparent a slightly changed feeling regarding Germany and a disposition to watch the progress of movements there with an approach to an interest that is not bitterly hostile.

German stabilization on a democratic basis would undoubtedly be a big point in the game. It would confine Bolshevism within Russian limits. Any sticks are good enough to beat the dog with.

The forecast cabled you a week ago, showing the progress in American plans and predicting early results of a substantial character, is borne out by the growing confidence of insiders.

President Wilson has gained a strong position here, and such criticism as that of Senator Harding impairs it less than it would have done a month ago. In some ways such attacks actually help Wilson as suggesting that unless Europe receives help from the President she needn't expect it from any other quarter.

FILE NEW RUSSIAN PROTEST.

Loyal Organizations Here Will Continue to Fight Bolshevism.

The decision of the Peace Conference to propose parleys with all the Russian Governments is asserted to be a fatal and historical error in an advertisement published today and signed by the Executive Board of the General Committee of Russian National Defense, the Voluntary Association of the Russian Army and Navy Officers in the United States, and the Union of Russian Engineers.

The advertisement is in the form of a resolution, and it says that the decision of the allied Governments is likely to strengthen the Bolshevist cause at the very moment when Trotzky's régime is on the verge of complete collapse; "that, notwithstanding the decision of the Supreme Council, the loyal Russian organizations feel their duty and will continue their fight against the Russian Bolshevist traitors." "We are deeply convinced," it continues, "that the loyal Russian delegates should meet the Allies' representatives either in Paris or nowhere."

The statement asserts that it is the opinion of the organizations issuing it that the Bolsheviki in signing the Brest-Litovsk treaty committed treason to Russia; that it has been proved that Russian Soviet officials were on the payroll of the Imperial German Government; that the Bolsheviki have instituted a reign of terror; that they have abolished all the fundamental principles of liberty and civilization in Russia, and that it is contrary to the national dignity of the people of Russia to meet the allied representatives "somewhere in the back yard of Europe."

TODAY'S SUNDAY TIMES

Consists of 108 Pages,
as follows:

Section 1

"All the News That's Fit to Print."

The New York Times.

THE WEATHER
Fair and continued cool Sunday; fair Monday; moderate winds.
For full weather report see Page 23.

Section 1

VOL. LXVIII...NO. 22,434. NEW YORK, SUNDAY, JUNE 29, 1919. 122 PAGES, In Nine Parts, including Picture and Magazine Sections (Rotogravure) and Book Section. FIVE CENTS In Greater New York | Elsewhere SEVEN CENTS

PEACE SIGNED, ENDS THE GREAT WAR; GERMANS DEPART STILL PROTESTING; PROHIBITION TILL TROOPS DISBAND

WILSON PROMISES TO ACT

Must Wait Until Complete Demobilization, His Word from Paris.

THIS WILL TAKE 7 WEEKS

President Calls Attention of Congress to His Request for Repeal.

LIQUOR MEN UNPREPARED

Had Hoped Until Announcement That Executive Would Intervene at the Eleventh Hour.

Special to The New York Times.

WASHINGTON, June 28.—President Wilson will not lift the ban which provides for war-time prohibition until the demobilization of the army has been terminated.

But when demobilization has been completed, the President will lift the ban. Formal announcement to this effect was made at the White House tonight. The President is in agreement with A. Mitchell Palmer, his Attorney General, that he cannot at this time lift the ban on wartime prohibition. He agrees with the Attorney General that the language of the law is such that he will be free to act on his own initiative, without Congressional action, not immediately after the signing of the treaty of peace, but when the army has been demobilized. As the army has not yet been demobilized, and there are yet a million men in the army, called into service under the emergency of war, the President, in the failure of Congress to vest him with power to call off wartime prohibition, takes the position that he cannot interfere with the putting of wartime prohibition into effect.

The responsibility for putting wartime prohibition into effect is put squarely up to Congress by the President. He takes the position that the law calling for wartime prohibition was an act of Congress, that its terms are clear, and that he had asked Congress to provide for the repeal of the legislation. Congress, having failed to act so far, has left the President's hands tied with legal strings so far as lifting the ban is concerned, and he makes this situation very plain in a cablegram sent to the White House just before he left Paris today.

President Wilson's cablegram was made public at the White House at 8 o'clock tonight by Joseph P. Tumulty, the Private Secretary to the President.

In his message the President said that he could not act until the army had been completely demobilized, and since there were still a million men in the service there was no chance of his taking immediate action. He called attention to the fact that the present difficulty could have been obviated if Congress had heeded his recommendation of several months ago.

The President in his message left no doubt as to what action he will take when demobilization is terminated.

"When demobilization is terminated," says the final sentence of his cablegram, "my power to act without Congressional action will be exercised."

When demobilization has been terminated will be determined by the President upon information to be supplied to him by Secretary Baker and by Attorney General Palmer. The prospects are that six, or perhaps seven, weeks will elapse before demobilization is terminated, which means that the President will probably not be in position, under his construction of the law, to act before the middle or latter part of August in lifting the ban.

It means that wartime prohibition will go into effect on July 1, even though there is no adequate provision legally made for its real enforcement, and that it will remain in effect until the termination of demobilization unless Congress meanwhile adopts the President's request for a repeal of the legislation which provided for the institution of wartime prohibition.

Congress is free at any time to enact the necessary legislation. So far all attempts to bring about repeal have failed on Capitol Hill and there is no present indication that Congress intends to change.

Not only has the President asked Congress to repeal the legislation standing in the way of lifting the ban, but in his cabled statement of today the President declares without equivocation that he will exercise his power to act when demobilization is terminated, and makes it clear he will then lift the ban unless Congress by repealing the act of Nov. 21, 1918, does away with wartime pro-

Continued on Page Eleven.

President Sends A Prohibition Message; Says He Will Act When Demobilization Ends

WASHINGTON, July 28.—The following message from President Wilson, stating his stand on the prohibition question, was made public at the White House tonight by Secretary Tumulty:

> I am convinced that the Attorney General is right in advising me that I have no legal power at this time in the matter of the ban on liquor. Under the act of November, 1918, my power to take action is restricted. The act provides that after June 30, 1919, "until the conclusion of the present war and thereafter until the termination of demobilization, the date of which shall be determined and proclaimed by the President, it shall be unlawful, &c." This law does not specify that the ban shall be lifted with the signing of peace, but with the termination of the demobilization of the troops, and I cannot say that this has been accomplished. My information from the War Department is that there are still a million men in the army under the emergency call. It is clear, therefore, that the failure of Congress to act upon the suggestion contained in my message of the twentieth of May, 1919, asking for a repeal of the act of Nov. 21, 1918, so far as it applies to wines and beers, makes it impossible to act in this matter at this time. When demobilization is terminated, my power to act without Congressional action will be exercised.
>
> WOODROW WILSON.

VIOLENCE GROWS IN BERLIN FERMENT

Bomb Hurled at Building in Which Officials Were Conferring on Strike.

SHOTS FIRED AT MINISTERS

Railway Strikers Ignore Orders from Noske and Union Chiefs to Resume Work.

Special Cable to THE NEW YORK TIMES.

BERLIN, June 28, (via Copenhagen.)—Vorwärts, even Die Freiheit and also Ledebour, in his first speech after his release from prison, earnestly warn the people against riots and political revolt which, in view of the enormous military strength gathered in Berlin, can only lead to awful bloodshed.

Doubtless the big leaders of the Independent Socialists do not wish any outbreaks at present. Nevertheless the air is charged with the spirit of rebellion, and nobody here would be surprised if tomorrow there were a repetition of the events of January and March on a much larger scale.

The minor leaders of the Independents, Communists and Sparticides desire to inflame this unrest, communicating it to ever-growing circles of the workers, and inciting the lawless elements to the most audacious and wholesale crimes. Unknown parties shortly after 2 o'clock this morning threw a bomb against the façade of the building of the Public Works Department. It exploded with a terrific noise, shattering about 200 windows. Nobody was hurt. Later, when the ministers and the railway employes' delegates left the building, after trying vainly all night to reach an agreement, unknown persons fired revolvers at the government members, without hitting any one.

Incite Lawlessness in Berlin.

Though ten or more members of the Executive Committee of the Berlin Soldiers' and Workers' Councils, after being arrested yesterday on suspicion of conniving with the Hamburg revolutionists for the overthrow of the Federal Government, have been released for lack of evidence nobody doubts for one moment that telephone congratulations were exchanged between them and the Hamburg revolutionists, as overheard by officials, but the identity of the man who answered the Hamburg announcement of the successful revolt with "Bravo!" and promised the Executive Committee's aid in starting a revolt against the Government in Berlin could not be established.

Members of that Executive Committee have never made any secret of their intention to overthrow the Government at the first opportunity, and doubtless the weaker heads among them yesterday believed that the time had come. The lawless element believe this, and it cannot be denied that they are quite right, if the absence of any effective policing of the capital is any justification.

Insecurity has reached an incredible degree. Lately men disguised as officers have been ascending street cars and, with pointed revolvers, collecting pocketbooks and jewels from the passengers in true Wild West fashion. This

Continued on Page Three.

DUTCH UNWILLING TO GIVE UP KAISER

Majority of the People Firmly Opposed to Yielding to Allies' Demand.

HOPEFUL AT AMERONGEN

Troelstra Says Chamber Would Surrender Ex-Ruler to Germany Only.

Special Cable to THE NEW YORK TIMES.

THE HAGUE, June 27.—The question of the delivery of the ex-Kaiser is again on the tapis here. There is no doubt that a majority of Netherlanders are already forgetting Germany's and the ex-monarch's record and violently oppose his surrender.

Appeals such as the recent one from the German Officers League and echoes from the German press only serve to strengthen these feelings. The officers' appeal stated that the German officers would be dishonored forever if Holland delivered the ex-Kaiser to the Allies, and ended with the statement: "It is even yet not certain whether a German can be found to sign the peace treaty."

The NEW YORK TIMES correspondent questioned Pieter Troelstra, the Socialist leader, the report emanating from Germany that the Dutch Social Democrats opposed the surrender of the ex-Kaiser. Troelstra replied:

"Our party has taken no official attitude. As we have not yet considered the question officially no resolution has been taken and no official correspondence carried on.

"It is true that we are against his surender on principle and would oppose it. I consider that we must wait until we receive the allied demand, so that the matter is not urgent.

"I can certainly say that as Socialists we believe in the right of asylum. English Socialists defend the right of asylum and London has always been a city for political refugees. Switzerland and the Netherlands have been free for centuries and it is a matter of tradition."

When asked if the question were put to a vote in the Dutch Chamber other parties would oppose the delivery of the ex-monarch, Troelstra replied in the affirmative.

"It is impossible," he said, "to deliver a refugee to an enemy. It is against all rights. If Germany should demand the Kaiser it would be another question. We should be in favor of that. I feel nothing but antipathy for his personality, but only his own Government has a right to demand him. I believe that all parties would vote in favor of a demand from the German Government."

Plead Ties with Dutch Queen.

Special Cable to THE NEW YORK TIMES.

BERLIN, June 28.—The League of Officers of the Former Prussian Army and German Navy has addressed a message to the Dutch Queen pleading that she had refused to extradite the "all highest war lord, our beloved unforgettable King, his Majesty Kaiser Wilhelm, who because of high treason in his own country, and not forced by the enemy's arms,

Continued on Page Three.

LEAGUE OPPONENTS UNITING

Republican Senators Now Seem Agreed on Policy of Reservations.

McCUMBER IS WON OVER

But North Dakota Senator Opposes Any Action Nullifying the Covenant.

SHANTUNG ACTION ASSAILED

Borah Calls It Indefensible—Norris Demands a Reservation Regarding It.

Special to The New York Times.

WASHINGTON, June 28.—With unexpected swiftness the Republican opposition in the Senate to the League of Nations covenant, as embraced in the Treaty of Peace, began to crystallize today, after the cables had brought word that Germany had signed the treaty, and that the President, in his message to the American people, had expressed the hope that the treaty would be "ratified and acted upon in full and sincere execution of its terms."

The President's message, coupled with his statement in interviews at Paris that he hoped the Senate woud ratify the treaty with the League of Nations covenant in it, without amendment, had the effect, it appeared, of bringing closer the elements of opposition among the opponents of the League. Instead of influencing wavering Senators toward an attitude favoring the ratification of the League of Nations covenant, the President's appeal appeared to have exactly the opposite effect.

While the opponents of the covenants, before Germany signed, were admittedly divided as to a policy to pursue in fighting the covenant when the treaty should come before the Senate, they seemed, for the first time since the League fight started, to have come to some general agreement.

Every Republican Senator to whom THE NEW YORK TIMES correspondent talked said decisively that he believed that, if the League covenant was to be accepted by the Senate some character of qualifying resolution would have to be passed, along with the treaty ratification, to express dissent from features objected to.

Even Senator McCumber of North Dakota, the one Republican member of the Foreign Relations Committee who has all along advocated adoption of the covenant, after the President's message had been read in the Senate, said that he believed it would be necessary for that body to adopt "explanatory reservations" in the ratification of the treaty, respecting features involved in the covenant. Mr. McCumber spoke of such reservations being necessary as to the Monroe Doctrine and the right of the United States to determine its purely domestic questions, like immigration, racial equality, and the tariff.

The North Dakota Senator made it clear that he would not favor any resolution of reservation that would have the effect of nullifying the covenant. He wanted the treaty of peace ratified, with the League of Nations included. But he insisted that the Senate should not hesitate to express its dissent from features that affected purely American affairs. If this were not done, he said, there might come some development in the future that might impel the Senate to take action which, in effect, would take America out of the League.

McNary for Interpretation.

Senator McNary, Republican, Oregon, who only a few days ago announced himself as favoring the League of Nations, declared today that he would not oppose a resolution that would enable opponents of the covenant to make clear their dissent from matters to which they objected. This, he said, might be done through a resolution of "interpretation," which was another way of saying one of "qualification."

At the same time Senator McNary agreed with Senator McCumber that no resolution ought to be adopted that would have the effect of rejecting the League of Nations covenant.

Talk of direct amendment of the covenant was not so insistent today among the more radical Senators. They appeared to be willing now to stand behind qualifying resolutions that would amply set forth the features subject to objection. They maintained, however, that Article X., guaranteeing the territorial integrity of members of the League, should come out. On this point

Continued on Page Five.

Wilson Says Treaty Will Furnish the Charter for a New Order of Affairs in the World

WASHINGTON, June 28.—The following address by President Wilson to the American people on the occasion of the signing of the Peace Treaty was given out here today by Secretary Tumulty:

> My Fellow Countrymen: The treaty of peace has been signed. If it is ratified and acted upon in full and sincere execution of its terms it will furnish the charter for a new order of affairs in the world. It is a severe treaty in the duties and penalties it imposes upon Germany; but it is severe only because great wrongs done by Germany are to be righted and repaired; it imposes nothing that Germany cannot do; and she can regain her rightful standing in the world by the prompt and honorable fulfillment of its terms.
>
> And it is much more than a treaty of peace with Germany. It liberates great peoples who have never before been able to find the way to liberty. It ends, once for all, an old and intolerable order under which small groups of selfish men could use the peoples of great empires to serve their ambition for power and dominion. It associates the free Governments of the world in a permanent League in which they are pledged to use their united power to maintain peace by maintaining right and justice.
>
> It makes international law a reality supported by imperative sanctions. It does away with the right of conquest and rejects the policy of annexation and substitutes a new order under which backward nations—populations which have not yet come to political consciousness and peoples who are ready for independence but not yet quite prepared to dispense with protection and guidance—shall no more be subjected to the domination and exploitation of a stronger nation, but shall be put under the friendly direction and afforded the helpful assistance of governments which undertake to be responsible to the opinion of mankind in the execution of their task by accepting the direction of the League of Nations.
>
> It recognizes the inalienable rights of nationality, the rights of minorities and the sanctity of religious belief and practice. It lays the basis for conventions which shall free the commercial intercourse of the world from unjust and vexatious restrictions and for every sort of international co-operation that will serve to cleanse the life of the world and facilitate its common action in beneficent service of every kind. It furnishes guarantees such as were never given or even contemplated for the fair treatment of all who labor at the daily tasks of the world.
>
> It is for this reason that I have spoken of it as a great charter for a new order of affairs. There is ground here for deep satisfaction, universal reassurance, and confident hope.
>
> WOODROW WILSON.

DEPORT THIRTY 'RED' AGITATORS

Fifteen Have Been Shipped Away in a Week—18 More Waiting at Ellis Island.

MOST OF THEM ANARCHISTS

Number Includes Some Suspected of Having a Hand in Plot Against Officials.

The deportation of alien agitators and conspirators who have abused their sojourn in America by preaching the overthrow of the United States Government, some of them coming under suspicion of the Secret Service for plots against President Wilson and other high public officials, has begun. Within the last seven days, fifteen of these disturbers, among them the editors of two anarchist newspapers, have been deported from New York, and eighteen others are now on Ellis Island awaiting the sailing of ships that will return them to the lands of their nativity.

The Secret Service agencies of the Government have been quietly, but thoroughly, at work for weeks, and every day or two a new batch of aliens who have urged the destruction of American institutions are rounded up and their records submitted to the proper authorities with a view to immediate deportation.

In the last four weeks thirty anarchist, I. W. W., and Bolshevist agitators have been deported by way of Ellis Island. This number does not include the Seattle and Spokane I. W. W. disturbers and other radicals who were sent East for deportation as a result of Bolshevist strikes in the Pacific Northwest several months ago. Some of those agitators also have been deported, and the cases of several others, recommended for the "homeward voyage," are soon to be decided by the courts.

Most of the deportations have taken place since bombs were set off at the homes of Attorney General Palmer and

Continued on Page Nine.

AMERICA GREETED BY KING GEORGE

"Brothers in Arms Will Continue Forever to be Brothers in Peace."

SENDS MESSAGE TO WILSON

"We Lay Down Our Arms in Proud Consciousness of Valiant Deeds Nobly Done."

LONDON, June 28, (Associated Press.)—King George has sent the following message to President Wilson:

"In this glorious hour when the long struggle of nations for right, justice and freedom is at last crowned by a triumphant peace, I greet you, Mr. President, and the great American people in the name of the British nation.

"At a time when fortune seemed to frown, and the issues of the war trembled in the balance, the American people stretched out the hand of fellowship to those who on this side of the ocean were battling for a righteous cause. Light and hope at once shone brighter in our hearts, and a new day dawned.

Together we have fought to a happy end; together we lay down our arms in proud consciousness of valiant deeds nobly done.

Mr. President, it is on this day one of our happiest thoughts that the American and British people, brothers in arms, will continue forever to be brothers in peace. United before by language, traditions, kinship, and ideals, there has been set upon our fellowship the sacred seal of common sacrifice. GEORGE, R. I.

After news of the signing of peace had been received here the following was issued over King George's signature:

The signing of the treaty of peace will be received with deep thankfulness throughout the British Empire. This formal act brings to its concluding stages the terrible war which has

Continued on Page Three.

ENEMY ENVOYS IN TRUCULENT SPIRIT

Say Afterward They Would Not Have Signed Had They Known They Were to Leave First by Different Way.

CHINA REFUSES TO SIGN, SMUTS MAKES PROTEST

These Events Somewhat Cloud the Great Occasion at Versailles—Wilson, Clemenceau, and Lloyd George Receive a Tremendous Ovation.

President Wilson Starts for Home

PARIS, June 28, (Associated Press.)—President Wilson left Paris on his homeward journey tonight. His train started from the Gare des Invalides for Brest at 9:45 P. M.

Mr. Wilson's party was accompanied to Brest by General Leorat and Colonel Lobez, the President's French aids, and also by Stephen Pichon, French Foreign Minister; Georges Leygues, French Minister of Marine, and Captain André Tardieu, a member of the French peace delegation. Ambassador Wallace, General Pershing, Premier Clemenceau, and Colonel House were at the station to say good-bye.

The crowd in the station, numbering upward of a thousand, wildly cheered the departure of the President, who raised his hat to cries of "Vive Wilson." Mrs. Wilson threw kisses to the crowd as the train departed.

The superdreadnought Oklahoma will accompany the George Washington to the United States.

VERSAILLES, June 28, (Associated Press.)—Germany and the allied and associated powers signed the peace terms here today in the same imperial hall where the Germans humbled the French so ignominiously forty-eight years ago.

This formally ended the world war, which lasted just thirty-seven days less than five years. Today, the day of peace, was the fifth anniversary of the murder of Archduke Francis Ferdinand by a Serbian student at Serajevo.

The peace was signed under circumstances which somewhat dimmed the expectations of those who had worked and fought during long years of war and months of negotiations for its achievement.

Absence of the Chinese delegates, who at the last moment were unable to reconcile themselves to the Shantung settlement, struck the first discordant note. A written protest which General Smuts lodged with his signature was another disappointment.

But bulking larger than these was the attitude of Germany and the German plenipotentiaries, which left them, as evident from the expression of M. Clemenceau, still outside of formal reconciliation and made the actual restoration to regular relations and intercourse with the allied nations dependent, not upon the signature of the "preliminaries of peace" today, but upon ratification by the National Assembly.

To M. Clemenceau's warning in his opening remarks that they would be expected, and held, to observe the treaty provisions loyally and completely the German delegates, through Dr. Haniel von Haimhausen, replied after returning to the hotel that had they known that they would be treated on a different status after signing than the allied representatives, as shown by their separate exit before the general body of the conference, they never would have signed.

Under the circumstances the general tone of sentiment in the historic sitting was one rather of relief at the uncontrovertible end of hostilities than of complete satisfaction.

The ceremony had been planned deliberately to be austere, befitting the sufferings of almost five years, and the lack of impressiveness and picturesque color, of which many spectators, who had expected a magnificent State pageant, complained, was a matter of design, not merely omission.

The actual ceremony was far shorter than had been expected, in view of the number of signatures which were to be appended to the treaty and the two accompanying conventions, ending a bare forty-nine minutes after the hour set for the opening.

Premier Clemenceau called the session to order in the Hall of Mirrors at 3:10 P. M.

The signing began when Dr. Hermann Müller and Johannes Bell, the German signatories, affixed their names. Herr Müller signed at 3:12 o'clock and Herr Bell 3:13 o'clock.

President Wilson, the first of the allied delegates, signed a minute later. At 3:49 o'clock the momentous session was over.

The most dramatic moment connected with the signing came unexpectedly and spontaneously at the conclusion of the ceremony, when Premier Clemenceau, President Wilson and Premier Lloyd George descended from the Hall of Mirrors to the terrace at the rear of the palace, where thousands of spectators were massed.

GREAT DEMONSTRATION FOR ALLIED LEADERS.

With the appearance of the three who had dominated the councils of the Allies there began a most remarkable demonstration. With cries of "Vive Clemenceau!" "Vive Wilson!" "Vive Lloyd George!" dense crowds swept forward from all parts of the spacious terrace. In an instant the three were surrounded by struggling, cheering masses of people, fighting among themselves for a chance to get near the statesmen.

It had been planned that all the allied delegates would walk across the terrace after signing, to see the great fountains play, but none of the other plenipotentiaries got further than the door.

President Wilson, M. Clemenceau and Mr. Lloyd George were caught in the living stream which flowed across the great space, and became part of the crowd themselves. Soldiers and bodyguards struggled vainly t-clear the way. The people jostled and struggled for a chance to touch the hands of the leaders of the Allies, all the while cheering madly.

Probably the least concerned for their personal safety were the three themselves. They went forward smilingly, as the crowd willed, bowing in response to the ovation, and here and there reaching out to shake an insistent hand as they passed on their way through the château grounds to watch the playing of the fountains—a part of the program which had been planned as a dignified State processional of all the plenipotentiaries.

Every available point of vantage in the palace and about the grounds was filled with thousands of people, who, less hardy than their comrades, had not been able to join the procession. No more picturesque setting could have been selected for this drama.

The return of President Wilson, M. Clemenceau, and Lloyd George toward the palace was a repetition of their outward journey of triumph. As they reached the château, however, they turned to the left instead of entering. The crowd was in doubt as to what was intended, but followed, cheering tumultuously.

Nearby a closed car was waiting and the three entered this and they drove from the grounds together amid a profusion of flowers which had been thrust through the open window.

All the diplomats and members of their parties who attended the ceremony of treaty signing wore conventional civilian clothes. Outside of this also there was a marked lack of gold lace and pageantry, with few of the fanciful uniforms of the Middle Ages, whose traditions and practices are so sternly condemned in the great, seal-covered document signed today.

One spot of color was made against the sombre background by the French Guards. A few selected members of the Guard were there, resplendent in red-plumed silver helmets and red, white and blue uniforms.

A group of allied Generals, including General Pershing, wore the scarlet sash of the Legion of Honor.

As a contrast with the Franco-German peace session of 1871, held in the same hall, there were present today grizzled French veterans of the Franco-Prussian war. They took the place of the Prussian guardsmen of the previous ceremony, and the Frenchmen today watched the ceremony with grim satisfaction.

The conditions of 1871 were exactly reversed. Today the disciples of Bismarck sat in the seats of the lowly, while the white marble statue of Minerva, Goddess of War, looked on. Overhead, on the frescoed ceiling, were scenes from France's ancient wars.

GERMAN PROTEST AT THE LAST MINUTE.

Three incidents were emphasized by the smoothness with which the ceremony was conducted. The first of these was the failure of the Chinese delegation to sign. The second was the protest submitted by General Jan Christian Smuts, who declared the peace unsatisfactory.

The third, which was unknown to the general public, came from the Germans. When the program for the ceremony was shown to the German delegation, Herr von Haimhausen of the German delegation went to Colonel Henri, French liaison officer, and protested. He said:

"We cannot admit that the German delegates should enter the hall by a different door than the Entente delegates; nor that military honors should be withheld. Had we known there would be such arrangements before, the delegates would not have come."

After a conference with the French Foreign Ministry it was decided, as a compromise, to render military honors as the Germans left. Otherwise the program as originally arranged was not changed.

Secretary Lansing was the first of the American delegation to arrive at the palace, entering the building at 1:45 o'clock.

The Peace Treaty was deposited on the table at 2:10 o'clock by William Martin of the French Foreign Office. It was inclosed in a stamped leather case.

Premier Clemenceau entered the palace at 2:20 o'clock.

Detachments of fifteen soldiers each from the American, British and French forces entered just before 3 o'clock and took their places in embrasures of the windows, overlooking the château park, a few feet from Marshal Foch, seated with the French delegation at the peace table.

The American soldiers who saw the signing of the treaty were all attached to President Wilson's residence. They were: George W. Bender, Baltimore; Stanley Cohek, Chicopee, Mass.; George Bridgewater, Palestine, Texas; Harlan Hayes, Green City, Wis.; J. S. Horton, Lexington, Miss.; William R. Knox, Temple, Okla.; Albert E. Landreth, Portsmouth, Va.; Sergeant Sam Lane, Prosper, Texas; George Laudance, Philadelphia; M. D. Mary, Havre, Mon.; Fred Quantz, Cleveland; Hubert Ridgeway, Mo.; Raymond Riley, Baltimore, and Frank Wilgus, Allentown, Penn.

With the thirty poilus and Tommies they were present as the real "artisans of peace" and stood within the enclosure reserved for plenipotentiaries and high officials of the conference as a visible sign of their rôle in bringing into being a new Europe.

Premier Clemenceau promptly stepped up to the French detachment and shook the hand of each man. The men had been selected from those who bore honorable wounds, and the Premier expressed his pleasure at seeing them there and his regret for the sufferings they had endured for their country.

Delegates of the minor powers made their way with difficulty through the crowd to their places at the table. Officers and civilians lined the walls and filled the aisles.

President Wilson entered the Hall of Mirrors at 2:50 o'clock. All the allied delegates were then seated except the Chinese, who did not attend.

The difficulty of seeing well from many parts of the hall militated against demonstrations on the arrival of the chief personages. Only a few persons saw President Wilson when he came in, and there was but a faint sound of applause for him.

An hour before the signing of the treaty those assembled in the hall had been urged to take their seats, but their eagerness to see the historic ceremony was so keen that they refused to remain seated, and crowded toward the centre of the hall, which is so long that a good view was impossible from a distance. Even with opera glasses, correspondents and others were unable to observe satisfactorily, as the seats were not elevated; consequently there was a general scramble for standing room.

German correspondents were ushered into the hall just before 3 o'clock and took standing room in a window at the rear of the correspondents' section.

When Premier Lloyd George arrived many delegates sought autographs from the members of the Council of Four, and they busied themselves for the next few minutes signing copies of the official program.

At 3 o'clock a hush fell over the hall, and the crowds shouted for the officials, who were standing, to sit down, so as not to block the view. The delegates showed some surprise at the disorder, which did not cease until all the spectators had seated themselves or found places against the walls.

MULLER AND BELL SHOW GREAT COMPOSURE.

At seven minutes past 3 Dr. Müller, German Secretary for Foreign Affairs, and Dr. Bell, Colonial Secretary, were shown into the hall, and quietly took their seats, the other delegates not rising.

They showed composure, and manifested none of the uneasiness which Count von Brockdorff-Rantzau, head of the German peace delegation, displayed when handed the treaty at Versailles.

Dr. Müller and Dr. Bell had driven early to Versailles by automobile from St. Cyr instead of taking the belt line railroad, as did the German delegates who came to receive the terms of peace on May 7. Their credentials had been approved in the morning.

In the allotment of seats in the ceremonial chamber places for the German delegates were on the side of the horseshoe table, where they touched elbows with Japanese plenipotentiaries on their right and the Brazilians on their left. Delegates from Ecuador, Peru, and Liberia faced the Germans across the narrow table.

M. Clemenceau, as President of the Conference, made this address:

"The session is open. The allied and associated powers on one side and the German reich on the other side have come to an agreement on the conditions of peace. The text has been completed, drafted, and the President of the Conference has stated in writing that the text that is about to be signed now is identical with the 200 copies that have been delivered to the German delegation.

"The signatures will be given now and they amount to a solemn undertaking faithfully and loyally to execute the conditions embodied by this treaty of peace. I now invite the delegates of the German reich to sign the treaty."

There was a tense pause for a moment. Then in response to M. Clemenceau's bidding the German delegates rose without a word and, escorted by William Martin, master of ceremonies, moved to the signatory table, where they placed upon the treaty the sign manuals which German Government leaders declared until recently would never be appended to this treaty.

They also signed a protocol covering changes in the document and the Polish undertaking.

It was too distant to see, even with glasses, the expression on the faces of the German plenipotentiaries during the ceremony, but observers among the officials say that the Germans fulfilled their rôles without apparent indications of emotions such as marked Count von Brockdorff-Rantzau's dramatic declarations at the first meeting.

President First Leader to Sign.

When they regained their seats after signing, President Wilson immediately arose and, followed by the other American plenipotentiaries, moved around the sides of the horseshoe to the signature tables.

President Wilson, and not M. Clemenceau, thus had the honor of signing as first of the leaders of the world alliance, but the honor was due to the alphabet, not other considerations, as the signatures occur in the same French alphabetical order as the enumeration of the allied and associated powers in the prologue of the treaty—the same order which determined the seating of the delegations at the plenary sessions of the interallied conference.

Premier Lloyd George came next, after the American envoys, with the English delegation. The British dominions followed.

The representatives of the dominions signed in the following order: For Canada—Charles J. Doherty, Minister of Justice; Sir George Foster, Minister of Trade and Commerce, and Arthur L. Sifton, Minister of Customs. For Australia—Premier William M. Hughes and Sir Gilbert Cook, Minister for the Navy. For New Zealand—W. F. Massey, Prime Minister and Minister of Labor. For the Union of South Africa—Premier Louis Botha and Jan Christian Smuts, Minister of Defense. For India—Edwin S. Montagu, Secretary for India, and the Maharaja of Bikanir.

Surprise Over Smuts's Protest.

A murmur of surprise passed around the hall when it became known that General Smuts, representing South Africa, signed under protest and filed a document declaring that the peace was unsatisfactory.

He held that the indemnities stipulated could not be accepted without grave inury to the industrial revival of Europe. He declared that it would be to the interests of the allied powers to render the stipulations more tolerable and moderate.

General Smuts asserted that there were territorial settlements which he believed would need revision, and that guarantees were provided which he hoped would soon be found out of harmony with the new peaceful temper and unarmed state of the Central Powers. Punishments were also foreshadowed, he said, over which a calmer mood might yet prefer to pass the sponge of oblivion.

M. Clemenceau, with the French delegates, were the next in line for the signing, then came Baron Saionji and the other Japanese delegates. The Italians came after the Japanese, and they, in turn, were followed by the representatives of the smaller powers.

During the attaching of the signatures of the great powers and the Germans a battery of moving picture machines and cameras clicked away so audibly that they could be heard above the general disorder.

At 3:45 the booming of cannon in celebration of the peace broke the monotony in the Hall of Mirrors, where the crowd had already tired of watching the signing.

China's failure to send her delegates to the ceremony created much comment. The vacant seats of the Chinese were noted early in the proceedings, but it was expected that the delegates would arrive later. Then the report was circulated officially that the Chinese would not sign without reservation on Shantung, and would issue a statement this evening on their position.

Some Confusion About Arrangements.

While the formal proceedings moved with system and complete adherence to program, the same cannot be said for other arrangements, which detracted markedly from the impressiveness of the event. So many spectators had, in one manner or another, gained access to the hall that the struggle for points of vantage at times approached the stage of a brawl, and the few officials intrusted with keeping order had the greatest difficulty in obtaining a semblance of it.

Cries of "Down in front!" which were probably never before heard at a gathering of similar importance, were addressed quite as often to officials of the Conference as to unofficial spectators. The stage for the ceremony was as crowded as the spectators' inclosures, giving a picture of crush and confusion. The plenipotentiaries and attachés, instead of arriving in delegations, formally introduced by ushers, as had been planned, drifted in individually as at the earlier sessions.

Among the American witnesses of the signing were Mrs. Wilson, accompanied by Miss Wilson and Mrs. Lansing, Mrs. House, Mrs. Wallace, Mrs. Scott, and several other wives of delegates and officials; Herbert Hoover, Bernard M. Baruch, Vance McCormick, John W. Davis, Ambassador to Great Britain; Hugh C. Wallace, Ambassador to France; Henry Morgenthau, and about seventy of the more important attaches of the Peace Commission.

The close of the ceremony came so quickly and quietly that it was scarcely noticed until it was all over. M. Clemenceau arose almost unremarked, and in a voice almost lost amid the confusion and the hum of conversation, which had sprung up while the minor delegates were signing, declared the conference closed and asked the allied and associated delegates to remain in their places for a few minutes—this to permit the German plenipotentiaries to leave the hall and the building before the general exodus.

None arose as they filed out, accompanied by their suite of secretaries and interpreters, just as all the plenipotentiaries had kept their seats when Dr. Müller and Dr. Bell entered. This was regarded as an answer to the action of Count von Brockdorff-Rantzau in reading his speech seated at the first meeting, but even more as an expression of sentiment at the German attitude toward the acceptance of peace.

Germans White-Faced as They Left.

Beyond the demonstration for the allied leaders the main interest of the people about the palace was centred in the arrival and departure of the Germans. Few people witnessed the arrival of the Germans, but, despite the precautions of the soldiers, great crowds gathered about the rear of the palace when the envoys from Berlin left after signing the treaty.

There was no audible demonstration against the Germans, but there was a distinct current of hostility evident among the crowd which jammed close to the cars. The Germans were white-faced and quite apparently suffering strong emotion, but whether it was fear, anger, or chagrin one could only surmise.

The scene around the palace had been an animated one from an early hour. All day yesterday workmen and officials were busy in the château putting final touches on the arrangements, but the Hall of Mirrors was not yet ready. Much remained to be done at the last moment.

The peace table—a huge hollow rectangle with its open side facing the windows in the hall—was, however, in place, its tawny yellow coverings blending with the rich browns, blues, and yellows of the antique hangings of the room and the rugs covering the dais. The mellow tints of the historical paintings in the arched roof of the long hall completed the picture.

Last minute changes were made today in the program to expedite the signing of the treaty. Two additional tables were placed beside the large one within the Hall of Mirrors. One of the new tables held the Rhine Convention and the other the protocol, containing changes in and interpretations of the treaty. The arrangement of the tables thus enabled three persons to be engaged simultaneously in affixing their signatures.

Most of the seventy-two plenipotentiaries had to write their names only twice, once on the treaty and once on the protocol. The convention covering the left bank of the Rhine and the treaties regarding the protection of minorities in Poland was signed only by delegates of the great powers.

Because of the size of the treaty and the fragile seals it bore, the plan to present it for signing to Premier Clemenceau, President Wilson, and Premier Lloyd George was given up.

A box of old fashioned goose quills, sharpened by the expert pen pointer of the French Foreign Office, was placed on each of the three tables for the use of plenipotentiaries who desired to observe the traditional formalities.

Tables for the secretaries were placed inside the table for the plenipotentiaries.

Chairs for the plenipotentiaries were drawn up around three sides of the table, which formed an open rectangle fully eighty feet long on its longer side. A chair for M. Clemenceau, President of the Peace Conference, was placed in the centre of the table facing the windows, with those for President Wilson and Premier Lloyd George on the right and left hand, respectively. The German delegates' seats were at the side of the table nearest the entrance which they could take after all the others had been seated.

This arrangement was made to permit the Germans to leave after the signature of the treaty before the allied delegations, not waiting for the procession of allied delegates to the terrace to witness the playing of the fountains.

Crowds Gathered Early.

This morning was cloudy, but just before midday the clouds began to break.

People began to gather early in the neighborhood of the palace. As the morning wore on the crowds kept increasing in size, but the vast spaces around the château swallowed them up at first.

By noon eleven regiments of French cavalry and infantry under command of General Brecard had taken positions along the approaches to the palace, while within the court on either side solid lines of infantry in horizon blue were drawn up at attention.

Hours before the time set for the ceremony an endless stream of automobiles began moving out of Paris up the cannon-lined hill of the Champs Elysées, past the Arc de Triomphe, and out through the shady Bois de Boulogne, carrying plenipotentiaries, officials, and guests to the ceremony. The thoroughfare was kept clear by pickets, dragoons, and mounted gendarmes.

In the meantime thousands of Parisians were packing regular and special trains upon the lines leading to Versailles and contending with residents of the town itself for places in the park where the famous fountains would mark the end of the ceremony.

Long before the ceremony began a line of gendarmes was thrown across the approaches. While theoretically only persons bearing passes could get through this line, the crowds gradually filtered into and finally filled the square.

Within this square hundreds of fortunate persons had taken up positions at the windows of every wing of the palace.

The automobiles, bearing delegates and secretaries, had reserved for their use the Avenue du Paris, the broad boulevard leading direct to the château's court of honor, French soldiers being ranged along the highway on both sides.

At the end of the court a guard of honor was drawn up to present arms as the leading plenipotentiaries passed, this guard comprising a company of Republican Guards in brilliant uniform. The entrance for the delegates was by the marble stairway to the "Queen's Apartments" and the Hall of Peace, giving access thence to the Hall of Mirrors.

This formality was not prescribed for the Germans, who had a separate route of entry, coming through the park and gaining the marble stairway through the ground floor.

How Our Delegates Signed.

VERSAILLES, June 28, (Official report transmitted from Hall of Mirrors to State Department.)—President Wilson and the American delegation completed signing the Peace Treaty at 3:14 o'clock, Paris time. The American delegation signed in this order: Secretary Lansing, Henry White, Colonel House, and General Bliss.

SIGNING PROVIDES BRILLIANT PAGEANT

Ceremony Staged in Gorgeous Setting of "All the Glories of France."

STORM OF CHEERS FOR FOCH

Wilson Received with Enthusiasm—Doughboys and Tommies in the Vast Throng.

By WALTER DURANTY.

Special Cable to THE NEW YORK TIMES.

VERSAILLES, June 28.—There could have been found no nobler setting for the signing of peace than the palace of the greatest of French kings, on the hillcrest of Versailles. To reach it the plenipotentiaries and distinguished guests from all parts of the world, who motored to their places in the Hall of Mirrors, drove down the magnificent, tree-lined Avenue du Château, then across the huge square—the famous Place d'Armes of Versailles—and up through the gates and over the cobblestones of the Court of Honor to the entrance, where officers of the Garde Républicaine, in picturesque uniform, were drawn up to receive them.

It was a few minutes after 2 when the first automobile made its way between dense lines of cavalry backed by a double rank of infantry with bayonets fixed—there were said to be 20,000 soldiers altogether guarding the route—that held back the cheering crowds.

The scene from the Court of Honor where I was standing was impressive to a degree. The Place d'Armes was a lake of white faces, dappled everywhere by the bright colors of flags and fringed with the horizon blue of troops whose bayonets shone like flames as the sun peeped for a moment from behind heavy clouds. Above airplanes—a dozen or more—wheeled and curvetted.

The entrance to the palace courtyard is usually barred by great gilded gates. Today, in the words of the hymn, it was "flung open wide the golden gates and let the victors in," Up that triumphal passage, fully a quarter of a mile long, between the wings of the palace to the entrance to the Hall of Mirrors, representatives of the victorious nations passed in flag-decked limousines—hundreds, one after another, without intermission — for fifty minutes.

Midway down the courtyard is a big bronze statue of Louis XIV. on horseback, and all along its sides are statues of the Princes and Governors, Admirals and Generals, that made him Grande Monarque of France.

At the entrance, just inside the gates, General Bricker, commander of the Sixth Cavalry Division, was sitting on a splendid chestnut, hardly less immobile than the Great King, save when he flashed his sword up to salute a guest of especial distinction. And, as if to typify the whole scene, there were the inscriptions on the façade of the twin temple-like structures on either side of Louis XIV.'s statue: "To All the Glories of France." It was the supreme dedication of the palace to the greatest day that all its glorious history has known.

Torrent of Cheers for Foch.

One of the earliest to arrive was Marshal Foch, amid a torrent of cheering, which broke out even louder a few moments later when the massive head of Premier Clemenceau—for once with a smile on the Tiger's face—was seen through the windows of a French military car. To both, as to other chiefs, including Wilson, Pershing, and Lloyd George, the troops paid the honor of presenting arms all around the courtyard.

After Clemenceau they came thick and fast, diplomats, soldiers, Princes of India in gorgeous turbans, Japanese in immaculate Western dress, Admirals, flying men, Arabs, and a thousand and one picturesque uniforms of the French, British, and Colonial Armies.

Once amidst terrific enthusiasm a whole wagonload of doughboys, themselves yelling "their heads off," drove up the sacred slope of victory, but instead of proceeding right to the entrance swung around the Louis statue in the middle of the courtyard and went out by a side gateway, where the rest of the automobiles also went after depositing their passengers. Ten minutes later a camion laden with British Tommies arrived and got a cordial reception.

Whoever was responsible for it had a good thought, that the rank and file who had suffered and sweated most should share in the glorious finale, and it was every one's regret that a load or two of poilus had not equally participated.

It was 2:45 o'clock when Balfour, bowing and smiling, heralded the arrival of the British delegates. Lloyd George was just behind him, for once in the conventional high hat instead of his usual felt.

Warm Welcome for Wilson.

At ten minutes of 3 came President Wilson in a big black limousine, with his flag, a white eagle on a dark blue ground. The warmth of welcome accorded him bore witness to the place he still holds in French hearts and the people's appreciation of the stand he took in the past few weeks against altering the treaty in Germany's favor.

By 3 o'clock the last visitor had arrived, and the broad ribbon road stretched empty between the lines of troops from the gates of the palace courtyard. The Germans had already taken their places—to avoid a possible unpleasant incident they had been conveyed from the Hôtel des Reservoirs Annex through the park.

It is impossible to tell what the day meant to the people of Versailles. To them, even more than to the rest of France, it was the wiping out of the ancient stain whose shame they had felt more deeply than any other. At the entrance of the crowded dining hall of the Hôtel des Reservoirs the old aunt of the proprietor stood with swimming eyes.

"I saw them dine here," she said, "on the night before the other treaty. And now this—thank God I have lived for it!"

At the side entrance to the courtyard there was a pathetic incident. An old woman, supported by two sons, one in the uniform of a Major of Chasseurs, the other in civilian clothes, but with an armless sleeve and the Legion of Honor and War Cross ribbons in his buttonhole, came up to the stern guardians and begged admittance, although without a ticket.

"Just let me inside the courtyard," she pleaded. "When the Germans were here a General was quartered in my house. I shared the defeat; let me share the victory."

The orders were strict and absolute, but for her they made an exception.

President Thanks France for Her Hospitality

PARIS, June 28.—President Wilson today, on the eve of his departure from France, made the following statement:

As I look back over the eventful months I have spent in France, my memory is not of conferences and hard work alone, but also of innumerable acts of generosity and friendship which have made me feel how genuine the sentiments of France are toward the people of America and how fortunate I have been to be the representative of our people in the midst of a nation which knows how to show us kindness with so much charm and so much open manifestation of what is in its heart.

Deeply happy as I am at the prospect of joining my own countrymen again, I leave France with genuine regret, my deep sympathy for her people and belief in her future confirmed, my thought enlarged by the privilege of association with her public men, conscious of more than one affectionate friendship formed, and profoundly grateful for unstinted hospitality and for countless kindnesses which have made me feel welcome and at home.

I take the liberty of bidding France godspeed as well as goodbye, and of expressing once more my abiding interest and entire confidence in her future.

(Signed) WOODROW WILSON.

THREE TENSE MINUTES AS GERMANS SIGNED

Murmurs Hushed as They Entered — Their Signatures Ended the Tension.

By CHARLES A. SELDEN.

Special Cable to THE NEW YORK TIMES.

VERSAILLES, June 28.—The stillest three minutes ever lived through were those in which the German delegates signed the Peace Treaty today. Contrary to expectation, the Germans signed first, after a brief speech by Premier Clemenceau, in which he said the treaty provisions must be faithfully and loyally adhered to. The Germans had been ushered into the Hall of Mirrors, where all the other delegations, with the exception of the Chinese, awaited them.

The Chinese were not present to sign because they were not allowed to make reservations in reference to Shantung. Despite the French opposition to protests or reservations of any kind, however, General Smuts issued a long protest immediately on giving his signature for South Africa.

To return to the utter silence of those first three minutes, in the audience outside the space reserved for delegates there was just the beginning of a murmur when the Germans appeared, but it was quickly hushed and spontaneously.

It recalled another historic incident at the battle of Santiago when Captain Philip of the American Navy restrained his men. This time it would be, "Don't cheer, boys. They're signing."

The tensity of the occasion ended with the Germans finishing their work at the writing table.

The American delegates, led by President Wilson, signed next to the Germans. Then followed the British and the long procession of other delegates.

TODAY'S SUNDAY TIMES

Consists of 122 Pages,
as follows:

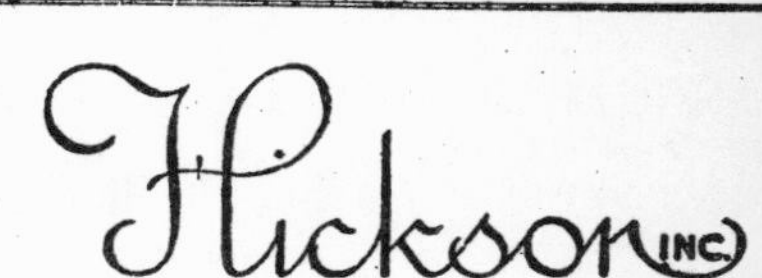

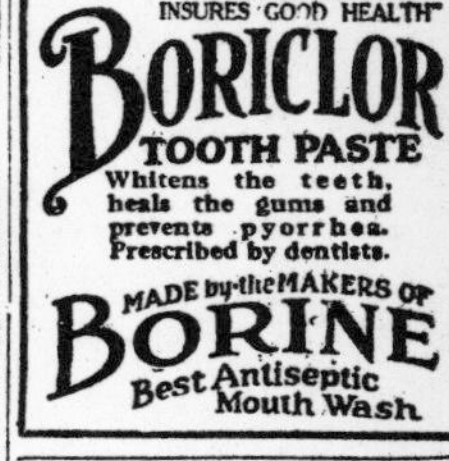

"All the News That's Fit to Print."

The New York Times.

THE WEATHER
Fair today, with diminishing north-west winds; Friday fair, warmer.
For weather report see next to last page.

VOL. LXIX...No. 22,580. NEW YORK, THURSDAY, NOVEMBER 20, 1919. THIRTY-TWO PAGES. TWO CENTS Metropolitan District 50 Mile Radius | THREE CENTS Within 200 Miles | FOUR CENTS Elsewhere

SENATE SESSION ENDS, TREATY IS DEFEATED; THREE VOTES TAKEN, 39 TO 55, 41 TO 50, 38 TO 53; MAY BE REVIVED AT THE DECEMBER SESSION

PRINCE SPENDS DAY SEEING NEW YORK; 'HAVING FINE TIME'

Mingles Democratically with People and Wins Their Hearts with His Smile.

ENJOYING EVERY MINUTE

Visits Movies, Wall Street, and Woolworth Tower, and Says He Will Come Again.

WALKS UNNOTED ON AVENUE

Tops Off His Busy Day Dining with Fellow-Britons and Dancing with Our Debutantes.

The second day of the visit of the Prince of Wales to New York, during which many thousands of Americans and hundreds of his own countrymen lavished attentions upon him, served to lift to new levels the high favor with which he was received when he arrived. Not only did he endear himself to countless new friends, but with his simple enjoyment, his quick response, he contrived to seem a very old friend indeed to those who had known him for all of two days.

New York, which was curious and interested when he arrived and frankly approving by the time he had made his first tour of the city and uttered his first little speech, had, in the words of one of the many speakers who paid him honor, "quite capitulated to him" by the time he reluctantly left the last of a series of brilliant functions last night.

Nor was the Prince reticent about letting the city know he reciprocated all its warmly expressed feeling. As on the day of his arrival, he talked on each occasion seriously for a few moments of the part he hoped to play in deepening the ties of friendship between the United States and Britain.

But each time he digressed long enough to assure his hearers that he was "having a fine time," and each time he became a little more emphatic in his assurances—which impressed his listeners as being meant as much as anything to convince himself—that he was coming back soon and would stay longer when he came.

Though he was never entirely out of the willing hands of his American hosts during the day, they did surrender him to a degree in the evening that he might enjoy the hospitality of those over whom he some day is destined to rule. The members of seven British societies, most of whom doubtless saw him for the first time, felt the appeal of his clean, bright youth just as quickly and as warmly as have Americans, and lost no opportunity to give noisy and hearty evidence that they liked his looks and his actions and the way he talked.

Enjoys Day Heartily.

With the more formal ceremonies of welcome out of the way, the Prince had a better time of it and found the long program laid out for him less exacting. He was treated to a variety of experiences, he met all sorts of people, he was not called upon to do a great deal of talking, and he gave himself up heartily to those opportunities to play which the wise elders who surrounded him had interspersed in his day.

At that, he was tired and, at times, a bit nervous. But that seemed to make no difference. The smile—one might almost call it a grin—which has earned for him the popular title of "the smiling prince," was seldom absent.

And when he reached the Madison Avenue home of Mrs. Whitelaw Reid, late last night, to be the guest of honor at a great ball she gave him, in which all of society's best participated, he was about the last man present to manifest any willingness to quit dancing and go home.

He danced with many of the débutantes of the season, and with a fair share of the matrons of earlier ones. The slim figure in evening clothes with the broad blue ribbon of the Order of the Garter slashing the white shirt front, topped by that unmistakable mop of smooth blond hair, was an active, a conspicuous, and a popular one.

Proves Himself Real Democrat.

Edward Albert found every opportunity during the day to exhibit that democracy for which he has expressed so much liking, both here and in Canada, and which many of those who have admired him have ascribed as one distinct source of his own appeal. He was called upon to meet and to mingle with many elements, to respond, as it were, to a great variety of stimuli, and he proved equal to each occasion, leaving every function he attended with a trail of good wishes behind him.

The city showed itself anything but

Continued on Page Three.

Panama Canal Toll Records Broken by October Traffic

PANAMA, Nov. 19.—The tolls collected from ships passing through the Panama Canal during October exceeded those of any previous month.

They amounted to $661,000 as compared with the next highest month, May, 1918, when $644,000 was collected.

Commercial vessels to the number of 196 passed through the canal in October.

HARDING BLAMES THE SPECULATORS

Break in Stocks, He Said, Followed 'Unbridled Speculation' in the Market.

WARNINGS WERE UNHEEDED

Reserve Board Refused to Withhold Credit from Commerce and Industry for Stock Trading.

WASHINGTON, Nov. 19.—The recent break in the New York stock market was due to "unbridled speculation," Governor Harding of the Federal Reserve Board said in a letter tonight to Senator Owen of Oklahoma, who had asked for a direct explanation of the price crash.

Speculators took no heed of warnings issued by the Board and by the Federal Reserve Bank at New York that reserves were declining and that a halt must be called, Mr. Harding said, and the speculative movement continued. These circumstances, he added, then forced the New York bank to call the attention of rediscounting banks to the situation, in order that demands of regular customers for call money in handling commercial transactions might be protected.

Text of the Letter.

The text of Governor Harding's letter follows:

"My Dear Senator: Receipt is acknowledged of your letter of the 14th instant.

"The Federal Reserve act is intended for the benefit of commerce and industry and not for the stimulation of the investment market or of speculative movements. The short title of the act reads, as follows: 'An act to provide for the establishment of Federal Reserve banks, furnish an elastic currency, to afford means of rediscounting commercial paper, to establish a more effective supervision of banking in the United States.'

"Section 13 of the act provides in part that Federal Reserve Banks may discount notes, drafts, and bills of exchange arising out of actual commercial transactions: That is, notes, drafts, and bills of exchange issued or drawn for agricultural, industrial, or commercial purposes, or the proceeds of which have been used, or are to be used, for such purposes. It provides further that nothing contained in the act shall be construed to prohibit such notes, drafts, and bills of exchange, secured by staple agricultural products, or other goods, wares or merchandise from being eligible for such discount 'but such definition shall not include notes, drafts, or bills covering merely invstments or issued or drawn for the purpose of carrying or trading in stocks, bonds, or other investment securities, except bonds and notes of the Government of the United States.'

"The Board has repeatedly called attention to the fact that resources obtained from the Federal Reserve banks should not be used for speculative purposes, and at various times when there has been unusual speculative activity it has issued public warnings as to the bad effect of such activities upon the banking situation. The first warning of this kind was issued as long ago as October, 1915, and the warning has been repeated on several occasions since that date when conditions made it necessary. On June 10, 1919, the Board made public a letter which it had addressed to all Federal agents, reading as follows:

"'The Federal Reserve Board is concerned over the existing tendency towards excessive speculation, and while ordinarily this could be corrected by an advance in discount rates at the Federal Reserve Banks, it is not practicable to apply this check at this time because of Government financing. By far the larger part of the invested assets of Federal Reserve Banks consists of paper secured by Government obligations, and the board is anxious to get some information on which it can form an estimate as to the extent of member bank borrowings on Government collateral made for purposes other than for carrying customers who have purchased Liberty Bonds on account, or other than for purely commercial purposes.'

"This letter was sent out for the purpose of ascertaining to what extent Government obligations were being used to secure loans from Federal Reserve Banks

Continued on Page Two.

DEADLOCK ON COAL CONTINUES DESPITE GARFIELD'S APPEAL

New Joint Sub-Committee Meets but Operators Fail to Present Counter-Demands.

SAYS PUBLIC IS PARAMOUNT

Fuel Administrator Asserts People Will Not Stand Excessive Prices or Prolonged Tieup.

COAL SHORTAGE GROWING

Supplies to Cleveland Plants Cut Off—Kansas City Coal Scanty.

Special to The New York Times.

WASHINGTON, Nov. 19.—Conferences between the coal operators and miners of the Central Competitive field were again adjourned tonight without anything like a definite agreement having been reached, despite the fact that Fuel Administrator H. A. Garfield made an address before the joint session of the scale committees this morning, in which he said that the public, "the chief party in interest in the present controversy, was not in a mood to tolerate either excessive prices or prolonged stoppage of production."

The most hopeful note was sounded this evening by representatives of the operators after a session of a committee of sixteen, formed of eight representatives of the Scale Committee of the operators and eight acting for the miners. The operators said that some progress had been made and that there would be another joint session at 10 o'clock tomorrow morning.

John L. Lewis, Acting President of the United Mine Workers, upon leaving the conference said that the miners were still in a receptive mood, but that no proposal had been submitted by the operators as yet. He did not discourage those who expressed the hope that some result might be approached at tomorrow's renewal of the conference but said that nothing "concrete" had, as yet, been accomplished.

It had been hoped that the address by Dr. Garfield, which was delivered at an open meeting in the morning, would bring immediate results. In this, at least, the situation was disappointing. Once behind closed doors, the representatives of the operators and miners again locked horns and fenced for advantage. Dr. Garfield's address had carried the conviction that the Government did not intend to permit a heavy increase in the price of coal to the consumer and the operators felt that they wanted further time to consider their proposal in view of that situation.

Garfield May Speak Again.

As the situation stands now, it seems probable that the Fuel Administrator, as the representative of the public, will have something further to say within the next forty-eight hours unless the end of the disagreement is in sight.

Attorney General Palmer announced today that he had summoned the operators and miners of Alabama and of the New River District of West Virginia, to meet with him tomorrow to discuss charges made by the miners that union men who want to return to work in these districts are being discriminated against. The operators have made the charge that the order recalling the strike order was not issued in proper form, with the seal of the union attached.

In regard to the latter charge Mr. Palmer said today that the Department of Justice was satisfied with the manner in which Acting President Lewis and other officials of the United Mine Workers of America had complied with the instructions of the court. An investigation, he said, showed that the order recalling the strike order had been issued in proper form.

Garfield Explains His Purpose.

WASHINGTON, Nov. 19 (Associated Press).—Dr. Garfield, addressing the joint session of the Scale Committees in the morning, explained that his purpose was to furnish the conference with the data which he would use in determining what wage advances, if any, agreed to by the operators and miners could be borne properly by the public.

"I represent the people of the United States in a different sense from the Secretary of Labor," he said. "It is part of Mr. Wilson's function to effect conciliation. It is my sole function to exercise those powers conferred on the Fuel Administration; to see that an adequate supply of coal is furnished the people of the United States, and to

Continued on Page Five.

Public Opinion Is Trying Unions, Says Gov. Roberts

NASHVILLE, Tenn., Nov. 19.—Governor A. H. Roberts issued a statement here today declaring Tennessee labor unions were on trial at the bar of public opinion. When the toiler "becomes an anarchist or engages in lawlessness," he said, "he then forfeits his right to the sympathy of the law-abiding man.

"No man can fight under two opposing flags. The people should awake to a realization of the dangers confronting them.

"The coal miners have utterly disregarded the order revoking the strike because it is said to have been printed on plain paper, signed with a typewriter, and did not have the seal of the union. No one would be foolish enough to believe that this was not a mere accident."

PLOT TO PUT BOMBS IN CHRISTMAS MAIL

Philadelphia Police Report Discovery of Nation-Wide Red Conspiracy.

AIMED AT HIGH OFFICIALS

Explosives Were to be Concealed in Ribbons and Holly Marked as Gifts to Victims.

Special to The New York Times.

PHILADELPHIA, Nov. 19.—Discovery of a Red plot to slay officials with explosive Christmas mail packages was announced this afternoon by James Robinson, Superintendent of Police.

Information of the plot, which he considers reliable, indicates it is nationwide, and directed against Federal, State and city authorities who took part in the national roundup of radicals planning the overthrow of the Government.

Immediate steps were taken to prepare Federal investigators, postal authorities, and the police of the large cities for action against the mail plot, which is scheduled to begin operation just before and during the Christmas holidays.

Evidence that bombs were to be sent through the mail concealed in ribbons and holly was reported to Superintendent Robinson by Andrew Emanuel, head of the bomb squad, who said he unearthed it during his investigation of radical activities here. The information was verified, according to Emanuel. The information is believed to have emanated from an anarchist "squealer."

A memorandum issued by the Bureau of Police is as follows:

"Superintendent of Police Robinson is in possession of reliable information that the members of a certain radical organization with headquarters in the principal cities of the United States, are preparing to send out, prior to and during the Christmas holidays, packages of neat appearance, which would probably be considered as Christmas gifts by the persons who receive them, to the United States Government officials and officials of the States and cities whose duties have required them to take an active part in the suppression of Bolshevist and anarchist movements.

"The radicals say that when the officials receive and open the packages they will be greatly surprised, as an explosion will result.

"The superintendent has sent the information to the Government officials in this city, and to Chief of Police Quigley of Rochester, N. Y., who is chairman of the Board of Governors of the National Bureau of Criminal Identification, and President of the International Association of Chiefs of Police, with the request that the matter be given wide publicity."

Todd Daniel, District Superintendent of the Department of Justice, and George A. Leonard, Chief Postal Inspector, were apprised of the plot. The city's Bomb Squad has been doubled, and determined efforts are being made to arrest the organizers of the conspiracy before it begins operation.

WASHINGTON, Nov. 19.—Department of Justice officials said tonight they were without information as to the discovery by the Philadelphia police of a nation-wide plot to kill Federal, State, and municipal officials by means of bombs sent through the mails at Christmas time. The Bureau of Investigation of the department, however, immediately asked its Philadelphia agents for details of the Reds' conspiracy as gathered by the police there. Officials also began checking over the long list of radicals who are under surveillance by the department to ascertain their latest activities.

EXPECT TO REVIVE TREATY

Hitchcock Believes Wilson Will Send It to Senate Again.

PEACE RESOLUTION BACKED

Republicans Count on Putting Through Plan at the Session Next Month.

TO TEST PUBLIC SENTIMENT

Situation May Be Changed if the Opinion of the Country Asserts Itself.

Mr. Taft Still Hopes For a Compromise

When ex-President William Howard Taft, who is staying at the Hotel McAlpin, was told last night of the defeat of the Peace Treaty he made this comment:

"I'm longing for a compromise. That's all I have to say tonight. Why not agree on a preamble and not sacrifice so much?"

Mr. Taft indicated to his questioner that he had no further statement to make at the time.

Special to The New York Times.

WASHINGTON, Nov. 19.—After the Senate had adjourned late tonight Senator Hitchcock, who has led the fight for the Administration forces, declared that the treaty was not dead and that he believed the President would resubmit it at the next session of Congresss in December.

"The President can send it back," he said. "I do not, however, know what course he will follow, as I have not discussed that with him, and have not been in communication with the President since the action taken by the Senate tonight."

Senator Lodge, Chairman of the Foreign Relations Committee, admitted that the President could resubmit the treaty if he saw fit, but added that the Republicans' attitude would be unchanged. He was asked if he considered the treaty dead.

"It is dead in this Senate," he said. "They killed it, just as I told them they would if they voted against it," he added, with an emphatic gesture.

Senator Lodge said that he did not care to discuss at length the action taken, which spoke for itself. He did, however, express the belief that, by refusing to accept the majority reservations, the Administration Senators must accept the responsibility for the treaty's defeat at this session.

In his opinion, Senator Lodge said, the President would have to wait until Congress reconvened in December to withdraw the treaty. The action of the President in withdrawing the treaty, Mr. Lodge held, would be an admission on the President's part that it had been rejected.

It is understood that Senator Lodge will press the adoption of his concurrent resolution declaring that a state of peace exists at the opening of the regular session of Congress in December. The Republicans express confidence in their ability to put the resolution through.

The text of the Lodge resolution is:

Whereas, by resolution of Congress, adopted April 6, 1917, and by reason of acts committed by the then German Government, a state of war was declared to exist between that Government and the United States; and,

Whereas, the said acts of the German Government have long since ceased; and

Whereas, by an armistice signed Nov. 11, 1918, hostilities between Germany and the Allied and Associated Powers were terminated; and

Whereas, by the terms of the Treaty of Versailles, Germany is to be at peace with all the nations engaged in war against her whenever three Governments, designated therein, have ratified said treaty; now, therefore,

Be it resolved by the Senate, (the House of Representatives concurring) that the said state of war between Germany and the United States is hereby declared to be at an end.

It is understood that Administration leaders will fight this plan for ending the war, and there is a constitutional question whether Congress can do so by a resolution not requiring the President's signature.

After the Senate adjourned it was admitted on all sides that the future treaty situation was decidedly mixed. Senator Hitchcock was asked whether President Wilson was likely to call the Senate immediately in special session for a reconsideration of the treaty. Mr. Hitchcock answered that he thought the President would not show quite so much

Continued on Page Two.

President Wilson's Final Appeal to Democrats That Helped to Defeat the Lodge Reservations

WASHINGTON, Nov. 19—Following is the text of the President's letter, addressed to Senator Hitchcock and read at the Democratic conference this morning:

My Dear Senator—You were good enough to bring me word that the Democratic Senators supporting the treaty expected to hold a conference between the final votes on the Lodge resolution of ratification and that they would be glad to receive a word of counsel from me.

I should hesitate to offer it in any detail, but I assume that the Senators only desire my judgment upon the all-important question of the final vote on the resolution containing the many reservations of Senator Lodge. On that I cannot hesitate, for, in my opinion, the resolution in that form does not provide for ratification but rather for nullification of the treaty. I sincerely hope that the friends and supporters of the treaty will vote against the Lodge resolution of ratification.

I understand that the door will then probably be open for a genuine resolution of ratification.

I trust that all true friends of the treaty will refuse to support the Lodge resolution.

Cordially and sincerely yours,

WOODROW WILSON.

URGED THE SENATE TO SAVE EUROPE

Gen. Smuts, in Belated Message, Pleaded That We Not Blast the World's Hopes.

SPOKE FOR HIS PEOPLE

South African Leader Said League Alone Could Prevent Dissolving Civilization.

JOHANNESBURG, Union of South Africa, Nov. 19 (Associated Press).—Lieut. Gen. Jan Christian Smuts, British member on the League of Nations Commission, in "a message from South Africa to America," appeals to America "not to blast the hopes of the world" through non-ratification of the treaty covenant by the Senate.

[This appeal was received in the offices of the New York newspapers just a few moments after word came from Washington that the Senate had adjourned without acting on the treaty.]

General Smuts says:

"I am told that the League is in danger in the American Senate. I can scarcely believe it. But if so, may I send a message from South Africa to America.

"My people are a small people, my voice in their behalf is weak. But the greatest leaders in America before now have listened to me.

"I trust my appeal will not be resented. I appeal to America not to blast the hopes of the world. America has established a great record in the war. She has shown herself capable of the highest altruism. When human freedom was endangered and appealing hands were stretched out, America rose to the height of her great opportunity, shamed the cynics who believed she was merely bent on money-making and rushed whole-heartedly to the rescue of those great human ideals for which the Allies were fighting. Her great act of unselfishness and moral idealism in the most critical stage of the war saved world democracy.

"Today the world is no less endangered, the machinery of the League is wanted to save civilization from dissolving into fragments, from falling into decay. It alone can save tottering Europe.

"No nation put more faith, more effort into the construction of the League than America. It now only remains to ratify and pass the covenant. Other nations have approved it. Even distant Asia is represented. Japan has given her approval, while America alone hesitates and falters.

"Will the great leaders now lag behind the racks? I cannot believe it. I cannot believe that America will, after all, block the way, that the purely American viewpoint will be allowed to override the wider interests and necessities of our own civilization in the greatest crisis in history.

"America has proved true to the best ideals of free and peaceful Government, and can only be true to herself by remaining true to these ideals as embodied in a League for the whole human race. It is in the power of America to lift the heavy weight of despair which today is bearing down Christendom. We all pray to her to do so. We pray her to sign the great covenant and complete the work for humanity which she so unselfishly set out in the war to do."

EXECUTE MOROCCAN REBELS

Spaniards Put to Death 21 Tribesmen Who Slew Officers.

MADRID, Nov. 18—Twenty-one Moroccan tribesmen were executed at Tetuan, east of Tangier, this morning following their conviction by a courtmartial of killing their officers while the tribesmen were in the service of the Spanish Government, according to advices received here.

'NULLIFICATION,' SAID PRESIDENT

Asked Democrats Through Hitchcock to Defeat the Lodge Treaty Plan.

PARTY CONFERENCE AGREED

Lodge Retorted, Declaring the Senate Had Equal Responsibility for Treaties.

WASHINGTON, Nov. 19.—A letter from President Wilson advising Senators to vote against ratification of the treaty with the Foreign Relations Committee's reservations embraced in it was laid before a conference of the Administration forces in the Senate this morning by the Democratic leader, Senator Hitchcock, and had much to do with swaying the minority.

In his letter the President declared that the Lodge resolution really meant "nullification" of the treaty.

The decision of Democratic friends of the treaty to vote against a ratification resolution containing the Lodge reservations was affirmed at the conference of Democrats. Senator Hitchcock announced that enough Democrats to insure its defeat had agreed to vote against the Lodge resolution.

No compromise plan was drafted by the Democrats but it was suggested that after the prospective defeat of the Lodge reservations a committee of Democrats would be appointed to confer with the Republicans to that end.

Democrats who attended the conference were not bound by any conference agreement and said they were willing to accept many of the majority's reservations, but could not accept the preamble or those dealing with Article X, Shantung, equality of voting and one or two others. If the majority declined to compromise, it was said, responsibility for failure of the treaty would rest on that side of the chamber. Various compromise measures were considered at the conference.

Republican Leader Lodge in a formal statement predicted that the Senate would "not obey the orders" of President Wilson with regard to the treaty.

"The Senate has equal power and responsibility with the President in the making of treaties," said Senator Lodge. "They will not, in my opinion, obey the orders of the President, who undertakes to command the Senate to ratify the treaty without the reservations adopted by a large majority of the Senate, which Americanize it and make it safe for the United States. What he commands will not, in my judgment, be done."

It was learned that a proposal to modify the preamble reservation of the committee so that the reservations would not require affirmative acceptance by the other powers had been under serious consideration by the Republican leaders. They were said to have manifested a willingness to insert a proviso by which the reservations could be accepted by the other powers by merely "not objecting" to them.

Just before the Senate convened and while the Democratic Senators were meeting, Senator Lodge held a conference with Will H. Hays, Chairman of the Republican National Committee.

SWISS ACCEPT THE LEAGUE.

Decision of the National Council Subject to Referendum.

BERNE, Nov. 19.—Switzerland's adhesion to the League of Nations was voted by the Swiss National Council today. The vote came after eight days of debate, the count being 124 in favor of joining the League to forty-five against.

The decision of the council is subject to a referendum.

LODGE RESOLUTION BEATEN

Lost by 39 to 55 the First Time and 41 to 50 Afterward.

FULL RATIFICATION FAILS

Defeated by 38 to 53—All Attempts at Compromise Are Beaten.

PEACE DECLARATION MOVED

Lodge Proposal Goes Over to Next Session—11 Hours of Tense Struggle.

Special to the New York Times.

WASHINGTON, Nov. 19.—The treaty of peace with Germany, after a long and bitter parliamentary struggle, came to a vote in the Senate tonight and in each of three tests was defeated. The first vote was on the question of ratification with the Lodge reservations. Thirty-nine Senators voted for ratification on these terms and 55 voted against. The second vote was on the same question, revived by a motion to reconsider, and this time 41 Senators voted for and 50 against. The third and final vote was on the question of ratification without reservations of any kind; 38 Senators voted "yes" and 53 "no." The Senate then adjourned sine die at 11:10 o'clock.

Immediately after the last vote, which spelt the doom of the treaty as far as this session of Congress is concerned, Senator Lodge, the majority leader, offered a concurrent resolution declaring peace to exist between Germany and the United States, this being done so as to pave the way for an independent treaty with Germany.

As the House had adjourned sine die, the Lodge resolution had to go over until the next session of this Congress, which meets December 1.

After the Democrats for the second time had voted down the Lodge resolution of ratification, Senator Underwood, Democrat, of Alabama, offered the substitute resolution of ratification without reservations. Although Senator Lodge and those working with him had blocked all previous efforts of the Democrats to obtain a vote on any resolution of their own through parliamentary points of order, Mr. Lodge allowed the Underwood resolution to come to a vote.

Seven Democratic Senators voted against it and one Republican Senator, Mr. McCumber of North Dakota, voted for it. The vote on the resolution ended the efforts of the minority to save the treaty.

Proposes Notice to Wilson.

After the Senate had voted, Senator Fletcher, Democrat, of Florida, suggested that the Senate communicate word of its action to President Wilson. Upon this Senator Penrose, Republican, of Pennsylvania, exclaimed:

"Oh, he'll know about it well enough."

Senator Lodge remarked that the President would undoubtedly take official cognizance of the action of the Senate. He referred to the procedure under other treaties where Presidents had done this.

The Democratic forces made repeated efforts to obtain a vote upon substitute resolutions of ratification with mild reservations. At every point in this struggle the Democrats were outvoted by the Republican majority. Throughout the last stages of the fight Senator Lodge held his forces solidly together, with the single exception of Senator McCumber, who voted for the Underwood substitute.

The middle-ground Senators who had been counted upon by Mr. Hitchcock to come to his relief at the last moment and bring about a parliamentary twist by which the Democrats could substitute their reservations, declined all overtures for compromise. Senators Lenroot, McCumber, Kellogg, Edge and others of the so-called mild reservationists told the Administration Senators during the last hour of the fight on the Senate floor that the Administration leaders had lost their opportunity for compromise, and that they intended to stand by the majority program.

Hitchcock's Efforts Fail.

Appeals were made by the Democratic leader for the Republicans to leave the way open for compromise, but these were abruptly thrust aside. Senator Hitchcock implored the middle-grounders not to shut the door to agreement.

During the final moments of the fight Senator Swanson, Democrat of Virginia, walked over to Senator Lodge while the minority moves for substitute resolutions were in progress, remarking:

"For God's sake, can't something be done to save the treaty?"

"Senator, the door is closed," replied Senator Lodge. "You have done it yourselves."

The defeat of the treaty was witnessed by crowded galleries which followed the various manoeuvres with acute interest. Crowds stood in the corridors leading to the galleries unable to get into the Senate chamber.

In the votes on ratification, the full voting strength of the Senate was recorded except that of Senator Fall, who was at his home in New Mexico. He would have voted to reject the treaty.

One of the last moves of the minority forces was that of Senator Pomerene, Democrat, of Ohio, to appoint a "committee on conciliation," headed by Senators Lodge and Hitchcock, to redraft the resolution of ratification containing reservations that would be acceptable to both sides. This was voted down.

Force Sidetracking of Treaty.

After the defeat of the Underwood substitute resolution the Democrats endeavored to keep the treaty from being sidetracked through a motion by Senator Pittman of Nevada, providing that the treaty remain before the Senate. Senator Lodge raised a point of order against this just as he had done upon other motions made by the Democratic leaders during the night. Vice President Marshall remarked that he had been overruled three times in sustaining the minority on points of order and said he would rule the Pittman motion out of order. It was then abandoned.

Following this, Senator Lodge had recourse to a parliamentary move often used in the House of Representatives, by which measures are finally disposed of after twice being voted down. Mr. Lodge, to do this, moved that the vote by which the Underwood substitute was defeated be reconsidered and that, at the same time, the motion to reconsider be laid upon the table.

Just before Senator Lodge put his motion for the Senate to adjourn sine die, Senator Cummins of Iowa moved that the Senate upon reconvening at once proceed to consideration of the pending bill to restore the railroads to private ownership. The Cummins motion was agreed to.

The attitude of the Democratic minority in voting to reject the treaty with the Lodge reservations imbedded in it was inspired by a letter written by President Wilson to Senator Hitchcock which was read at a conference of the minority Senators early in the day, the President taking the viewpoint that the treaty could not be accepted in any such form.

Vote on Lodge Resolution.

The vote on the Lodge resolution of ratification came at 5:30 P. M., after the Senate had debated the treaty for five and a half hours. Senator McCumber of North Dakota had just made a four-minute speech, in which he told the Administration forces that, by assuming their attitude for unequivocal ratification of the treaty, they were "scuttling their own ship." As he sat down cries of "vote, vote, vote," came from all over the chamber.

No other Senator arose to speak and the Vice President ruled that the majority resolution of ratification was "now before the Senate for vote."

The crowded galleries sat in tense silence as the roll was called. A murmur swept through them as the vote was announced, 55 to 39, by which the resolution was defeated.

In the vote in favor of rejection, twelve "irreconcilable" Republicans aligned themselves with forty-three Democrats. Voting for the resolution were thirty-five Republicans and four Democrats, the latter being Gore, Shields, Smith of Georgia and Walsh of Massachusetts.

The vote on the Lodge resolution was:

FOR THE RESOLUTION—39.

Republicans—35.

Ball,	McCumber,
Calder,	McLean,
Capper,	McNary,
Colt,	Nelson,
Cummins,	New,
Curtis,	Newberry,
Dillingham,	Page,
Edge,	Penrose,
Elkins,	Phipps,
Frelinghuysen,	Smoot,
Hale,	Spencer,
Harding,	Sterling,
Jones, Wash.,	Sutherland,
Kellogg,	Townsend,
Kenyon,	Wadsworth,
Keyes,	Warren,
Lenroot,	Watson.
Lodge,	

Democrats—4.

Gore,	Smith, Ga.,
Shields,	Walsh, Mass.

AGAINST THE RESOLUTION—55.

Republicans—13.

Borah,	La Follette,
Brandegee,	McCormick,
Fernald,	Moses,
France,	Norris,
Gronna,	Poindexter,
Johnson, Cal.,	Sherman.
Knox,	

Democrats—42.

Ashurst,	Overman,
Bankhead,	Owen,
Beckham,	Phelan,
Chamberlain,	Pittman,
Culberson,	Pomerene,
Dial,	Ransdell,
Fletcher,	Reed,
Gay,	Robinson,
Gerry,	Sheppard,
Harris,	Simmons,
Harrison,	Smith, Ariz.,
Henderson,	Smith, Md.,
Hitchcock,	Smith, S. C.,
Johnson, S. D.,	Stanley,
Jones, N. M.,	Swanson,
Kendrick,	Thomas,
King,	Trammell,
Kirby,	Underwood,
McKellar,	Walsh, Mon.,
Myers,	Williams,
Nugent,	Wolcott.

The Senate was in a stir when Senator Reed moved that the vote by which the resolution was defeated be reconsidered. This was intended to bring the resolution immediately back, to be voted on again.

The vote on Senator Reed's motion to reconsider the vote defeating the Lodge resolution was:

FOR THE MOTION—62.

Republicans—19.

Capper,	Lenroot,
Colt,	McCumber,
Curtis,	McLean,
Dillingham,	McNary,
Edge,	Nelson,
Hale,	Smoot,
Jones, Wash.,	Spencer,
Kellogg,	Sterling,
Kenyon,	Townsend.
Keyes,	

Democrats—43.

Ashurst,	Owen,
Bankhead,	Phelan,
Beckham,	Pittman,
Chamberlain,	Pomerene,
Culberson,	Ransdell,
Dial,	Reed,
Fletcher,	Robinson,
Gay,	Sheppard,
Gerry,	Shields,
Gore,	Smith, Ariz.,
Harris,	Smith, Ga.,
Harrison,	Smith, Md.,
Henderson,	Smith, S. C.,
Hitchcock,	Stanley,
Johnson, S. D.,	Swanson,
Jones, N. M.,	Trammell,
King,	Underwood,
Kirby,	Walsh, Mass.,
McKellar,	Walsh, Mon.,
Myers,	Williams,
Nugent,	Wolcott.
Overman,	

AGAINST THE MOTION—30.

Republicans—29.

Ball,	McCormick,
Borah,	Moses,
Brandegee,	New,
Calder,	Newberry,
Cummins,	Norris,
Elkins,	Page,
Fernald,	Penrose,
France,	Phipps,
Frelinghuysen,	Poindexter,
Gronna,	Sherman,
Harding,	Sutherland,
Johnson, Cal.,	Wadsworth,
Knox,	Warren,
La Follette,	Watson.
Lodge,	

Democrat—1.

Thomas.

Senator Hitchcock, springing from his seat, moved that the Senate adjourn. This move was desired by the Administration forces so as to give them an opportunity, over night, of working with the Republican middle-grounders in an effort at compromise.

The Senate voted down this motion, 51 to 42, it being substantially a partisan alignment, with Senators Reed, Gore and Shields of the Democrats voting with the majority.

Vice President Overruled.

With the minority's effort at adjournment defeated, Vice President Marshall ruled that the treaty was now back in Committee of the Whole, instead of the Senate, where the Lodge resolution had been voted down, and that it was open to any amendments or reservations or substitute resolutions of ratification that might be offered.

This ruling of the Chair, if sustained, would have meant that the minority would have an opportunity to put in substitute reservations in an effort to wean the support of middle-ground Senators and thus save the treaty from being defeated.

Senator Lodge raised a point of order against the Vice President's ruling, his motive being to obtain a vote to override it. Mr. Lodge questioned the ruling of the Chair, by which the treaty was held to go back to the Committee of the Whole. He argued that the majority resolution, upon the vote to reconsider, was once more before the Senate and that this alone could be voted on.

This juncture in the treaty fight had long been anticipated by the majority and it was evident that Senator Lodge was ready for the emergency, the Senator in advance having had the assurance of the Republicans that they would stand with him. Without debate the point of order against the Vice President's ruling was sustained by a vote of 51 to 42, exactly the same as upon Senator Hitchcock's motion to adjourn.

Senator Hitchcock attempted at this point to offer a substitute resolution of ratification without qualification. Senator Poindexter raised a point of order against it. The Vice President overruled the point. In doing so, Mr. Marshall once more asserted the right of Senators to offer any resolution or reservations or amendments to the treaty. Upon appeal from the decision of the chair, the Vice President was overruled by a vote of 50 to 43.

McCumber Compromise Move Fails.

Senator McCumber offered an amendment to the preamble or committee reservation No. 1, providing for the acceptance of all reservations adopted by the Senate by three of the principal signatories, the McCumber amendment eliminating the provision for acceptance. Senator McCumber offered this in an effort to bring the Democrats to the support of the treaty, the preamble which had been adopted as reservation No. 1 having been denounced by President Wilson as impossible of acceptance.

Senator Poindexter raised a point of order against the McCumber amendment and, upon the chair sustaining Senator McCumber the Senate overruled the Vice-President by a vote of 50 to 43. In ruling that the McCumber amendment was in order, the Vice-President remarked with a smile:

"It will take three votes like this to convince me."

Senator McCumber, in another effort to save the treaty from final rejection, moved to reconsider the vote by which the preamble had been adopted by the Senate. Senator Penrose raised the point of order that Senator McCumber could not make the motion inasmuch as he had not voted with the prevailing side when the preamble was adopted. Senator McCumber subsided, making no effort to press the amendment.

After this the Democrats made frantic efforts to avoid being forced to another vote on the Lodge amendment. Hurried conferences among the Democrats were in progress in the chamber. Postmaster General Burleson, who had been in the Senate, while the votes were being taken, participated in them.

Senator Robinson, Democrat, of Arkansas, insisted that the Senate was "violating all precedents," in its handling of the treaty.

"Having voted down the Lodge resolution," said Senator Robinson, "the Senate with a thorough disregard of parliamentary precedents, is now being called upon to vote once more on the identical proposition. We might continue indefinitely along this line and reach nowhere. Unless the Senate comes to a vote on a substitute resolution it will never reach an agreement on the treaty of peace."

Senator Lenroot, replying to Senator Robinson, declared that the Senate was proceeding under parliamentary procedure and that there was no other way.

Senator Underwood, Democrat, of Alabama, in a vigorous speech, declared that the Republican Party would be to blame if the treaty were defeated.

"This side of the Chamber," he said, pointing to the Democratic side, "is not responsible to the country for the action the Senate may take. The control is in the hands of the Republicans. The Republican Party is responsible to the people for the peace of the nation. What a spectacle is presented to the nation tonight by the way the Republicans are exercising the power entrusted to them by the people of the United States!"

Senator Underwood asserted that the vote on the Lodge resolution was a repudiation of Republican leadership.

"We shall maintain that we are entitled to offer other resolutions of ratification," Senator Underwood said. "The Vice-President already has ruled correctly that we have that right, but a majority of the Senate destroyed his ruling. When this resolution (of Senator Lodge) is voted down again we must face the fact whether a partisan majority, which intends to destroy this treaty, can be controlled, or by indirect measures say to the Senate 'You shall ratify as we present it or not at all.'

"That is the issue. I am prepared to meet it and the American people will know who aims to ratify this treaty and who to destroy it."

Senator Harding, Republican, of Ohio, insisted that the blame for defeat of the treaty would lie with the Democrats for having rejected efforts at compromise. Senator Fletcher implored the Republicans not to block an effort to reach agreement on the treaty.

Senator Lenroot, his face flushed, angrily replied to Senator Fletcher:

"There will be no compromise. If the President wants this treaty, he must take the reservations substantially as adopted today."

Reject Conciliation Plan.

Senator Pomerene, Democrat, of Ohio, who in the meantime had been in conference with the Administration leaders, moved that the treaty, along with the majority resolution of ratification, be referred to a "Committee of Conciliation," composed of six Senators to be appointed by the President of the Senate. Those on the committee, he proposed, should comprise the majority leader, Senator Lodge, who would be Chairman of the committee; Senator Hitchcock, the minority leader, and four other Senators to be named by the Chair.

Under Senator Pomerene's proposal "the Committee on Conciliation" would "prepare and report to the Senate such a resolution of ratification and reservation as, in their judgment will meet the approval of not less than two-thirds of the Senate."

Senator La Follette, Republican, of Wisconsin, moved to lay the resolution on the table and his motion was carried, 48 to 42.

In asking for adjournment, Senator Hoke Smith said that he would vote for the Lodge resolution if it came up again but he believed another attempt should be made at compromise before final action was taken. He said that if the treaty were rejected the President could bring it up again at the next session.

The vote which gave a second defeat of the Lodge resolution was:

FOR THE LODGE RESOLUTION—41.

Republicans—34.

Ball,	McCumber,
Calder,	McLean,
Capper,	McNary,
Colt,	New,
Cummins,	Newberry,
Curtis,	Page,
Dillingham,	Penrose,
Edge	Phipps,
Elkins,	Smoot,
Frelinghuysen,	Spencer,
Hale,	Sterling,
Harding,	Sutherland,
Jones (Wash.),	Townsend,
Kellogg,	Wadsworth,
Keyes,	Warren,
Lenroot,	Watson,
Lodge,	

Democrats—7.

Gore,	Shields,
Myers,	Smith (Ga.),
Owen,	Walsh (Mass.)
Pomerene,	

AGAINST THE LODGE RESOLUTION—50.

Republicans—13.

Borah,	La Follette,
Brandegee,	McCormick,
Fernald,	Moses,
France,	Norris,
Gronna,	Poindexter,
Johnson (Cal.),	Sherman.
Knox,	

Democrats—37.

Ashurst,	Overman,
Bankhead,	Phelan,
Beckham,	Pittman,
Chamberlain,	Ransdell,
Dial,	Reed,
Fletcher,	Robinson,
Gay,	Sheppard,
Gerry,	Simmons,
Harris,	Smith (Ariz.),
Harrison,	Smith (Md.),
Henderson,	Smith (S. C.),
Hitchcock,	Stanley,
Johnson (S. D.),	Swanson,
Jones (N. M.),	Thomas,
Kendrick,	Trammell,
King,	Underwood,
Kirby,	Walsh (Mon.),
McKellar,	Williams,
Nugent,	Wolcott.

The vote by which the substitute resolution of unconditional ratification of Senator Underwood was defeated was:

FOR THE UNDERWOOD MOTION—38.

Republican—1.

McCumber.

Democrats—37.

Ashurst,	Overman,
Bankhead,	Owen,
Beckham,	Phelan,
Chamberlain,	Pittman,
Dial,	Pomerene,
Fletcher,	Ransdell,
Gay,	Robinson,
Gerry,	Sheppard,
Harris,	Simmons,
Harrison,	Smith, (Ariz.),
Henderson,	Smith, (Md.),
Hitchcock,	Smith, (S. C.),
Johnson (S. D.),	Stanley,
Jones, (N. M.),	Swanson,
Kink,	Underwood,
Kirby,	Walsh, (Mon.),
McKellar,	Williams,
Myers,	Wolcott.
Nugent,	

AGAINST THE MOTION—53.

Republicans—46.

Borah,	Lenroot,
Brandegee,	Lodge,
Calder,	McCormick,
Capper,	McLean,
Colt,	McNary,
Cummins,	Moses,
Curtis,	New,
Dillingham,	Newberry,
Edge,	Norris,
Elkins,	Page,
Fernald,	Penrose,
France,	Phipps,
Frelinghuysen,	Poindexter,
Gronna,	Sherman,
Hale,	Shields,
Harding,	Smoot,
Johnson, (Cal.),	Spencer,
Jones, (Wash.),	Sterling,
Kellogg,	Sutherland,
Kenyon,	Townsend,
Keyes,	Wadsworth,
Knox,	Warren,
La Follette,	Watson.

Democrats—7.

Gore,	Thomas,
Reed,	Trammell,
Shields,	Walsh, (Mass.)
Smith, (Ga.),	

Lodge Opens the Debate.

When Senator Lodge, at the beginning of the session, offered his resolution of ratification, he remarked that any substitute which the minority might have to offer would be in order at that time. Senator Hitchcock thanked the Senator for the suggestion, but said that the minority would prefer to offer its substitute after the Lodge resolution had been voted on.

Senator Hitchcock asked if the Lodge resolution contained the preamble as agreed upon by the majority of the Senate. He started to read from a copy he held in his hand and, after reading the first line, said that his copy was a misprint. Mr. Lodge sent to his office for another copy and started reading that to the Senate.

This copy, in different phraseology from the majority preamble as adopted, contained a clause providing that acceptance by the three principal signatories of the reservations adopted by the Senate could be made "either without objection or by exchange of notes." This draft, it appeared, was one drawn by middle-ground Senators a day or so ago in an effort to come to a compromise with the Administration forces on the preamble, so as to make it acceptable to President Wilson.

Senator Lodge, evidently aggravated over having started to read this compromise preamble to the Senate, tossed the copy to his desk, remarking:

"That is a mistake."

Eventually Mr. Lodge got the right preamble as adopted by the Senate and read that one. He renewed his suggestion that the minority might offer a substitute resolution of ratification, saying that it could be voted on before the vote on his resolution.

"This is the time for any resolution the minority leader wishes to put in," urged Senator Lodge. "If he wants a vote on a resolution without qualification, he can get it now."

Senator Hitchcock protested that as the majority Senators appeared to be bound by pledge to their leader to vote for their resolution, the vote on that resolution ought to come ahead of any substitute. If the latter were offered first, he said, it would be voted down by the majority forces.

"If the Senator from Nebraska thinks that the majority of the Senate will not keep their pledge to support the majority reservations after the majority resolution is defeated by the minority, he is mistaken," replied Senator Lodge. "They intend to stand together to support the majority resolution and the Senator might as well understand it."

Wilson Letter Put in Record.

Senator Hitchcock, declining to offer the minority resolution, produced from his pocket the letter of President Wilson to him, urging defeat of the majority resolution, and had it read into the record.

"Comment on that letter is superfluous," observed Senator Lodge when the clerk had read the letter.

Senator Hoke Smith of Georgia, who had voted with the majority on several of its reservations, arose to say that he intended to vote for the Lodge resolution regardless of any urging to the contrary.

"I regard the treaty as having been vastly improved through the reservations," said Mr. Smith. "I dislike to disagree with my party associates, but I feel that I would be faithless to my obligations as a Senator if I failed to support the reservations as put into the ratifying resolution."

Senator Thomas, Democrat, of Colorado, announced that he would vote against the Lodge resolution, but wanted to let the Senate know that his mind had been "made up long ago."

Senator Robinson, Democrat, of Arkansas, also opposed the Lodge resolution, saying that he believed the reservations embodied in it would mean the "death of the treaty." He asserted that foes of the treaty had been successful, temporarily at least, "in accomplishing indirectly what they would not do openly" and had "planned to alienate the nations who were allies in the war. Yet Senators who say they want the treaty" he declared "are aiding in this plan, which gives comfort only to those who want to see the treaty killed."

Senator Robinson objected especially to the preamble, the Shantung provision, that regarding Article X of the League covenant and the one on withdrawal from the League.

"The friends and not the enemies of the treaty," said the Senator, "should dictate the terms of ratification."

He added that "it is plain that our self-respecting allies would not accept" the Lodge terms.

Sherman Calls Treaty "Vicious."

Senator Sherman, Republican, of Illinois, one of the irreconcilables, would vote against the Lodge resolution, he explained, because the treaty, with or without reservations, was a "vicious instrument."

"For the first time since the armistice was signed I find myself in agreement with the Administration Democrats in the position I take for rejection of the treaty," said Mr. Sherman.

Senator Shields, Democrat, of Tennessee, said he intended to vote for the Lodge resolution because of the pledge he took on assuming the office of Senator to "uphold the Constitution."

"Without the majority reservations I think the Senate would do right in rejecting the treaty," said Mr. Shields. "We cannot, with conscience, take the traty as written."

Senator Edge, Republican, of New Jersey, who participated in the conference of middle-ground Senators yesterday, when compromise with the Administration forces was considered, told the Senate that he regarded the time was past when compromise could be effected.

"As far as I am concerned," said Senator Edge, "the time for further changes in the resolution of ratification, the preamble or in any of the reservations, has gone. I have no patience with the argument that a word must be changed here, or a word must be changed there, in order that compromise may be effected. It appears to me that the reason back of it is mere party or personal pride rather than the necessity for the compromise."

Senator Lenroot of Wisconsin, who had taken a leading part in the efforts of middle ground Senators to reach a compromise with the Administration forces at various stages of the treaty fight, denounced the minority for, as he said, having abruptly declined to deal with the middle grounders.

"If the Senators on the other side of this chamber want to take a position against the integrity and the independence of the United States, they may do so," said Mr. Lenroot. "For myself I would rather resign my place in the Senate than accept the treaty without such reservations as protect America. Those that have been adopted ought to stay in the resolution of ratification, and I intend to vote for it."

Senator Kellogg of Minnesota, one of the mild reservationists, then explained his position. He said, in part:

"The passionate appeal of the Senator from Nebraska asking the Senators on this side to compromise and get together on reservations comes a little late and with bad grace. I want to ask him if that has been his attitude for three months when he stood here and announced time after time that this treaty would be ratified without any reservations whatever; if that has been his attitude when, in the public press and in speeches, he has stated that the treaty must be accepted as it is and the Senate must abdicate its right to make reservations or pass upon this great document?

"These reservations have not been sprung upon the Senate as he intimates. They have not been drawn by the enemies of the treaty. They have been drawn by its friends who want to save it and who want to leave a real effective League of Nations and a treaty of peace with Germany.

"The people of the United States are generous. We are willing to join a League of Nations to insure a world peace, but we are not willing to give up the control of our domestic questions; we are not willing to pledge this nation to go to war and to send its sons abroad without the judgment of the American people, which must be expressed through their Congress.

"This Republic is the hope of the world and are we going to surrender our aspirations and our Government to the dictation of foreign nations? It is not necessary for a League of Nations to preserve peace."

Senator Brandegee, Republican, of Connecticut characterized the League of Nations idea as a "pipe dream," saying that "all the reservations in the world would not make it worth while."

Hitchcock Appeals to Republicans.

Senator Hitchcock at this point made a strong appeal to the "friends of the treaty" on the Republican side not to adhere to any program that would kill it.

"I appeal to those Senators who would save the treaty not to be bound by convention or caucus rules in their pledge to support a program that means the rejection of the treaty," said Mr. Hitchcock. "I know there are Republicans who do not want the treaty thrown out. It is possible, I am positive, to reach a compromise that will save it."

The majority's reservation on Article X, Mr. Hitchcock said, was obnoxious in its phrasing in "assuming no obligation" under the treaty provision affected. The minority, he said, was willing to compromise on a reservation that would assert the privilege of the United States to determine, through Congress, when and where its armed forces might fight under any decision of the League of Nations.

Senator Borah of Idaho, in an impassioned speech, called upon the Senate to reject the treaty. Mr. Borah said he was "not misled by the insistence of the minority that the treaty would be rejected if the Lodge reservations were upheld by the majority. He predicted that the minority eventually would swing in line and vote for the Lodge resolution.

Senator McCumber, the last to speak on the resolution of ratification before the vote came, said that he had "just four minutes left" of the hour allotted to him.

"I want to make an earnest plea to the other side of the chamber in that time," he said, addressing the Democrats. "Will you stand by what we have offered you or will you scuttle your own ship? It is up to that side of the chamber. You have known since the beginning that reservations were inevitable, and those in the committee resolution are as mild as could be offered."

The Vice President's gavel banged, interrupting Senator McCumber.

Cries of "Vote," "Vote," "Vote" arose from both sides of the chamber.

Senator Lodge arose, moving a vote on the majority resolution, and the treaty passed to the voting stage.

May Feel Out Other Powers.

WASHINGTON, Nov. 19.—It was suggested tonight among Democratic Senators that President Wilson might be asked during the recess to feel out the other powers as to their attitude on reservations with the idea of bringing the treaty to some sort of a ratification after Congress reassembles.

OUR GERMAN TRADE HINGES ON TREATY

Experts Say That Failure to Ratify It Will Mean Heavy Business Loss.

By EDWIN L. JAMES.

Copyright, 1919, by The New York Times Company.

By Wireless to THE NEW YORK TIMES.

PARIS, Nov. 19.—Without membership on the Reparation Commission, which becoming a party to the Versailles Treaty will give to America and which not becoming a party to it will prevent America from having, American business might as well forego any hopes of a proper share in the trade with Germany for some years. This is the opinion of American experts here who are thoroughly familiar with the treaty and with the plans for its enforcement.

For years to come the Allied Reparation Commission will control the finances of Germany. This commission, which will assess the amount that Germany must pay the Allies, and which will have most to do with watching to see that it is paid, is to be the world's most powerful financial organ. Not only can it influence what the German Government may do with its finances, but it can influence what German individuals can do when it comes to importing and exporting.

America cannot sell goods to Germany if Germany cannot pay, and Germany will not be able to pay unless the European Allies let her pay. America will find it difficult to buy goods in Germany if the Reparation Commission decides that those goods may best pay Germany's debt by going elsewhere.

ALLIES MAY GO ON WITHOUT AMERICA

Britain and France Drawn Closer Together by Action of Senate on Treaty.

BALK AT RESERVATIONS

British Leaders Comment on "Refusal" of United States to Assume Share of Burdens.

Copyright, 1919, by The New York Times Company.

Special Cable to THE NEW YORK TIMES.

LONDON, Thursday, Nov. 20.—Speaking last night at a dinner of the Anglo-French Society, Lord Burnham said the refusal—he was afraid that was the only word which could be used—of the United States to take upon its broad shoulders any of the liabilities arising out of the war made it more incumbent on France and Britain not to allow anything to prevent them accomplishing the ends they had in view. It would be an incentive to Britain and France to grip one another's hands more tightly.

Lord Denbigh, who also spoke, referred to the bad blow which the Senate had given to the treaty, and said that if the verdict were not reversed the only effect could be that Britain and France would be thrown more and more on their own resources, and it would be all the more necessary for them to be firm allies.

The Daily Express Lobby Correspondent says:

"Discussion took place in Government circles yesterday on the bearing of America's attitude on the future of the peace treaty. The view of Lord Robert Cecil was that the reservations made by America are so extensive as to amount almost to repudiation. Repudiation of the covenant means repudiation of the treaty as signed in Paris by America. It would not affect the validity of the treaty between Germany and the other associated powers which ratify or have ratified it.

"What new process of peace-making may be rendered necessary would only affect Germany and America. The treaty will have full force as soon as ratifications are exchanged by three great powers. France, Japan, Britain and Italy are putting their final ratifications in order and present delay is believed to be due to France not having been able to complete certain machinery for giving the treaty full effect."

NEW YORK PRESS COMMENT.

Sun Thanks God That the Senate Killed the Treaty.

New York morning newspapers, commenting on the Senate's action, said:

The Sun: "Thank God this treaty is dead and we are still a free and independent nation!"

The World: "The United States helped to win a victorious war. It helped to negotiate a victorious peace. If the United States cannot ratify that peace the Senate has made itself a menace to the welfare of mankind and the United States stands discredited as a nation."

The Herald: "This is an American victory for the present. The victory cannot be gainsaid. It may be less oppressive to President Wilson if he recalls the treaty, substitutes a new one, or agrees to an American treaty in accordance with the Senate."

OUR PEACE MISSION TO SAIL DEC. 5 OR 6

Other Delegations Are Likely to Leave Paris at About the Same Time.

By EDWIN L. JAMES.

Copyright, 1919, by The New York Times Company.

Special Cable to THE NEW YORK TIMES.

PARIS, Nov. 19.—Frank L. Polk, Chairman of the American peace delegation, announced this afternoon that the American delegation would leave Paris the first week in December, sailing from Brest on the America Dec. 5 or 6. Mr. Polk notified the Supreme Council to this effect today.

While formal action has not been taken by the council, it is presumed that it will declare in a day or so that the Peace Conference will end about Dec. 1. The British will withdraw their representation the first week in December, the Italian and Japanese delegations, as well as numerous minor delegations, will get away from Paris about the same time as the Americans.

It has not been announced whether or not the Allied ratifications of the Peace Treaty will be deposited before the conference adjourns. It is not necessary that this be done if the Conference sees good reasons for further delay. On what Washington does in the next ten days probably depends the action to be taken.

The Supreme Council, on the adjournment of the Conference, will turn over to a committee of Ambassadors its unfinished business. The chief features of this program are the Hungarian treaty, the Adriatic, Baltic, and probably the Rumanian situations. The Ambassadors will have no duties to discharge with respect to Russia or Turkey. The Russia problem will be left to the Foreign Offices of the different nations, and the Turkish treaty will be drafted by a new Peace Conference, which will probably be called in March.

It is not yet definitely decided whether the American Ambassador will sit on the Ambassadors' committee. Final advice is awaited from Washington. His presence is desired by other Powers. He will in any event be able to keep the State Department informed as to the diplomatic negotiations in Paris, even if he has no say in them.

EXPECT TO REVIVE TREATY

Continued from Page 1, Column 5.

"humor" as this would imply, but he admitted that he had not discussed the subject with the President and had no idea of what the President's course would be.

The Senate and the House will assemble in regular session required by the Constitution twelve days hence and what little was said tonight indicated a belief that the President would not call an extra session in the interim.

Just before adjourning, the Senate agreed to a motion of Senator Cummins that the first business to be taken up at the next session would be the pending bill providing for the return of the railroads to private ownership. A treaty, however, is a privileged matter that may receive preference over all other business. The same principle applies to the resolution offered tonight, to declare the war with Germany at an end.

If the resolution were adopted, it is held, the Versailles Treaty of Peace with its League of Nations covenant would be killed. Nobody was in a position tonight to indicate exactly what would be the Senate's course when the regular session begins less than two weeks hence. If in the brief interim public opinion should assert itself in criticism of the action of the Senate in refusing to ratify the treaty, the whole situation might be changed.

Senator Hitchcock accepted the Senate's action without any display of ill-humor.

"The Republicans," he said, "have worked themselves into an awkward position. They are split in the Senate and split in the country on this proposition. The Democrats remained practically sound. I think we made a pretty good showing."

"Considering that they had all Summer and Fall," he added, "to work on the matter, I think it is not very comforting to them that a bare third of the Senate voted for the resolution of ratification with the majority reservations attached."

PALMER AND M'ADOO BOOMS ON IN ILLINOIS

Both Men Likely to Figure in Primary Presidential Preference Vote.

Special to The New York Times.

CHICAGO, Nov. 19.—Attorney General A. Mitchell Palmer and William G. McAdoo, former Secretary of the Treasury, are almost certain to be rival candidates for the Democratic Presidential preference vote in Illinois at the April primaries, according to a report current here today.

Quietly but definitely plans have been made by Illinois representatives of the two aspirants for the nomination to enter them for the support of the fifty-eight Illinois delegates in the Democratic National Convention. Chicago party leaders have been informed that headquarters for each of them will be opened here not later than the Christmas holiday week.

Their confidential agents have been and are now negotiating for the active support of Roger C. Sullivan and the regular party organization in Cook County. Thus far Mr. Sullivan and his political lieutenants have given no indication of their intentions.

Mr. Sullivan is on record as favoring the renomination of President Wilson.

FIGHT IN DEMOCRATIC CLUB.

Insurgent Ticket Headed by Major John P. Lee Is Nominated.

Insurgency is rampant again in the National Democratic Club. An independent Nominating Committee, composed of a hundred club members, has placed an opposition ticket in the field against that headed by John M. Riehle, candidate for re-election as President for a sixth term. Major John P. Leo, Chairman of the Board of Standards and Appeals and, according to advance notice of the coming conflict sent out last night by the insurgents, "one of the biggest men in the Mayor's administration," is the opposition candidate for President.

There was a club fight some years ago in which Tammany Leader Charles F. Murphy was the issue, but this year he does not figure. "The committee of the insurgents and the regulars have called on Mr. Charles F. Murphy and he has promised to be entirely neutral in the fight," the press agent of the insurgent movement explained in his statement of last night. The insurgent ticket is made up as follows:

President, John P. Leo; Second Vice President, Thomas Rush; Secretary, William Jasper; Treasurer, Herman A. Curiel; Corresponding Secretary, Leonard McGee; Governors, John B. Hasslocher, Thomas F. Smith, John F. Galvin, James F. Donnelly, Charles S. Guggenheimer, John F. O'Brien, and Mark Elsner. Thomas F. Smith is Secretary of Tammany Hall.

The insurgents, who will meet at the club this evening, accuse the "regulars" of an attempt to block the meeting by inviting all club members to attend a pink tea at the Biltmore at the same hour as guests of the Riehle leaders.

HARDING BLAMES THE SPECULATORS

Continued from Page 1, Column 2.

for other than commercial purposes or for carrying subscriptions.

"In its monthly publication, the Federal Reserve Bulletin, the board has called attention repeatedly since that date to the dangerous speculative tendencies which have been prevalent.

"In a printed statement during the Summer, the board made the specific announcement that it would not sanction any policy which would require the Federal Reserve Banks to withhold credits demanded by commerce and industry for the processes of production and distribution in order to enable member banks to furnish cheap money for speculative purposes.

"In ordinary circumstances and normal times one check would have been to advance discount rates, but owing to the fact that the Government has sold over $21,000,000,000 of Liberty bonds and Victory notes, many of which securities have been sold to persons who were unable to pay for them in full, but were obliged to pay for them in installments out of savings or accrued incomes, it was felt that an advance in the discount rate on notes secured by Government obligations should so far as possible be avoided.

"The speculative movement continued; its demands on the banks for credit coming on top of commercial requirements, of the seasonal crop moving demand and of demands arising out of the unusual congestion of export commodities at ports owing to the delays in transportation. As a consequence of these conditions, the reserves of the Federal Reserve banks began to decline, and those of the Federal Reserve Bank of New York, in particular, dropped to such an extent that the board, about two weeks ago, approved an increase in discount rates of that institution averaging about one-half of one per cent. All other Federal Reserve Banks shortly afterward expressed the desire to put into effect a similar advance in their rates, which the board approved.

"The Federal Reserve Bank of New York, on Nov. 2, the date on which the advance in its rates was made public, issued the following statement, supplementing the repeated warnings of the board:

"'The reason for the advance in rates announced today by the Federal Reserve Bank of New York is the evidence that some part of the great volume of credit, resulting from both Government and private borrowing which war finance required, as it is released from time to time from Government needs, is being diverted to speculative employment rather than to reduction of bank loans. As the total volume of the Government's loans is now in course of reduction corresponding reductions in bank loans and deposits should be made in order to insure an orderly return of normal credit conditions.'

"Notwithstanding this notice, activities on the exchanges continued and the reserves of the Federal Reserve Bank still declined. During the week ending Nov. 8, the Federal Reserve Board sold to other Federal Reserve Banks ninety million dollars of acceptances for account of the Federal Reserve Bank of New York, but in spite of this action the reserves of the New York bank fell to 40 per cent. In these circumstances, in order to prevent further expansion, it became necessary to call the attention of the large rediscounting banks to the situation.

"The high rates for call money which have prevailed continuously for the last two weeks, and intermittently for several months past, were in themselves very clear indication of the strained position into which the unbridged speculation had thrown the stock market and rendered a readjustment inevitable unless the resources of the Federal Reserve banks were to be indirectly drawn upon for stock market purposes. The public has had ample notice of the board's policy.

"You are so familiar with the Federal Reserve act that it is hardly necessary to call your attention to that paragraph of Section 4 which treats of the duties of the Board of Directors of a Federal Reserve Bank and which provides that 'said board shall administer the affairs of said bank fairly and impartially and without discrimination in favor of or against any member bank or banks, and shall, subject to the provisions of law and the orders of the Federal Reserve Board, extend to each member bank such discounts, advancements, and accommodations as may be safely and reasonably made with due regard for the claims and demands of other member banks.' This would, of course, afford means for a strict rationing of credits should such an extreme course ever become necessary. It is interesting to note that there no longer exists in the mind of the public or in fact a connection between call money rates and the commercial paper market, and it must be gratifying to all those interested in sound banking methods that the events of the last week have had no effect upon the market for commercial paper.

"Very truly yours,

"W. P. G. HARDING, Governor."

"Hon. R. L. Owen,

United States Senate."

"All the News That's Fit to Print."

The New York Times.

THE WEATHER
Fair today and probably Saturday; no change in temperature; gentle variable winds.
For weather report see next to last page.

VOL. LXIX...No. 22,861. NEW YORK, FRIDAY, AUGUST 27, 1920. TWO CENTS In Greater New York | THREE CENTS Within 200 Miles | FOUR CENTS Elsewhere

SOVIET WAIVES DEMAND TO ARM WORKERS; ANSWERS ANGLO-ITALIAN NOTE ON POLAND; POLES PRESS PURSUIT, TAKE OSSOWETZ

BACKDOWN PLEASES LONDON

Soviet Says It Acts in Interest of World's Peace and Welfare.

PRESS ASSAILS LABOR PARTY

Council of Action Accused of Going Behind Country's Back in Critical Negotiations.

POLES TO SHIFT PARLEY

Unable to Communicate Freely with Envoys at Minsk, They Will Select Another City.

LONDON, Aug. 26 (Associated Press).—M. Tchitcherin, the Russian Soviet Foreign Minister, has sent a note to Mr. Balfour replying to the Italo-British ultimatum respecting changes in the peace terms offered to Poland. The Soviet Government accepts the British proposals.

The note opens with a comment on the unusual tone of the Anglo-Italian Governments' communication, which, it says does not tend to help permanent good relations and world peace.

It calls attention to the action of those Governments which had so often accused the Russian Government of interfering in the internal affairs of other States, and charges that, in this communication "they have issued peace propaganda directed against our institution, which constitutes an act of interference in Russian affairs sufficient to justify corresponding action by us."

M. Tchitcherin says, however, that despite natural resentment the Soviet Government has decided not to insist upon this point, but to meet fully the wishes of the Anglo-Italian Governments in the interest of the establishment of permanent good-will.

Expressing surprise that the question of the interpretation of principle should have caused such difficulty, M. Tchitcherin proceeds to argue that after the imitation of Poland's army to 50,000 was recognized by the British Government as a just peace term, it was a concession on the part of Russia to admit the formation of civil militia, which, he asserts, "is, in fact, a supplementary armed force," and adds: "We, therefore, find it astonishing that this should arouse the British Government's indignation.

"Seeing that Great Britain declares peace through Eastern Europe to be its aim, we can point to the fact that the workers in Poland for a long time have been the one force steadfastly opposed to the Polish Government policy, and have in repeated resolutions demanded peace with Russia. If, nevertheless, the British Government so forcibly opposes strengthening of this fundamental pillar of peace, it clearly shows with what distrust it regards the workers.

"If the British Government indeed thinks that the workers by nature are animated by the doctrine of Bolshevism, such a point of view will undoubtedly be welcomed by those who look forward to spreading Bolshevism in Great Britain."

The Proposed Civic Militia.

Alluding to the proposed civic militia, he says:

"Although our interpretation of this point in our peace terms is thoroughly justified, we nevertheless are willing to remove this, the only point of divergency, in order to establish a full understanding between us and the above Governments.

"As to the terms of peace with Poland, we first of all declare we never considered our terms as an ultimatum and are still, as we have been all the time, willing to discuss them with the Polish Government with whom alone we are treating for peace. Any undertaking we may give thereanent will, therefore, be given to Poland alone.

"In view, nevertheless, of our earnest desire to obtain important results for the world's welfare and peace arising from a peace with Great Britain, we are willing to inform the British Government that the Russian Government is resolved to make a concession on this point. It will not insist upon the clause referring to the arming in Poland of a workers' civic militia, thus securing full agreement with Great Britain as to all the terms of peace with Poland."

The Soviet Foreign Minister continues: "It is not the custom of the Russian Government to mix practical business transactions with theoretical pointless and discussions of principles. The British Government, however, has launched against the Soviet régime the strange accusation of being an oligarchy."

There then follows quite a disquisition to the effect that all States whose Soviet are obviously true oligarchies because they are States in which an immense majority toil for a privileged few while in Soviet Russia the whole nation works for the whole nation's benefit.

Leads Soviet System.

M. Tchitcherin contends that the system of local workers' councils, in whose hands rests control of the whole Soviet fabric, gives the masses much more power than the parliamentary system, and concludes, that, being a truly popular

Continued on Page Eight.

Poland's Reply to Colby Called "Not Disappointing"; Washington May Make Full Details Public Today

Special to The New York Times.

WASHINGTON, Aug. 26.—The Government of Poland has made reply to Secretary Colby's communication of Saturday, Aug. 21, in which the hope was expressed that Poland would find it agreeable to issue a declaration of its intention to abstain from any territorial aggression against Russia, and asking Poland to state its purpose to remain within the ethnic boundaries indicated by the Paris Peace Conference, pending an agreement as to its eastern frontier.

It was stated that the Polish communication has not yet been fully transmitted over the wires and that, therefore, it was impossible to make official comment concerning it. The statement was authorized, however, that the note, as far as could be ascertained, did not appear to contain anything that might be construed as disappointing to this Government. Full information regarding the reply will probably be disclosed tomorrow.

It is known to have been anticipated by this Government that Poland would accept the admonition of the United States, forwarded last Saturday, in friendly spirit. It is felt, therefore, from the statement that the Polish reply appears to contain nothing which would be disappointing to this Government, that the Polish Government has accepted the suggestion conveyed in the American communication.

POLES FOLLOW UP PURSUIT OF REDS

Northern Army Occupies Fortress of Ossowetz and Continues Dragnet Operations.

REPORT BUDENNY WOUNDED

Germans at Frontier Fire on Russians and Drive Many Back Into Poland.

WARSAW, Aug. 26 (Associated Press) —Ossowetz, the fortress northeast of Lomza, was taken by the Poles Tuesday afternoon, according to a communication issued today. There are no details. The communication adds that the centre army is continuing its progress beyond Ostrolenka.

The Polish cavalry on the southern front, after a short hand-to-hand fight, wiped out the 722 Bolshevist Brigade and made prisoners of many of the men, including the brigade Chief of Staff.

A Bolshevist brigade of 4,000 which crossed the Dniester River before Herodenka and reached the Sereth River was surrounded and surrendered to the reinforced Polish that are clearing out the region south of the Dniester and the left bank of the Bug on the Galician front.

The Bolsheviki no longer are grouped on a continuous front, but isolated fighting is continuing. Groups that reach the right bank of the Dniester are driven back or surrounded and captured. These Red detachments are said to be composed largely of Caucasians or Turkestans. It is reported that they have done much pillaging but have not displayed ardor in fighting for the Soviets.

Remnants of the 4th Bolshevist Army, which were cut off by the Polish advance in the region of Kolno, succeeded in cutting their way through to the eastward after a battle lasting ten hours, an official statement issued here last night reported. The Soviet troops carried out a regrouping manoeuvre and succeeded in making their way out of the trap which had closed upon them, but were surrounded by more numerous forces of the 4th Polish Army.

The 5th Polish Army continues its work of rounding up detachments of Bolshevikl in the region west of the railroad running from Novo Georgievsk to Mlawa.

On the central front the Poles have carried out a flanking movement to the north and occupied Knyszyn, fifteen miles northwest of Bialystok, and Stawiski, twelve miles northeast of Lomza. Occupation of these towns, with the capture of Kolno, completed the work of forging a ring around the Fifteenth Bolshevist Army. Other Soviet forces have reassembled at various places and are making repeated attacks in their attempts to break the Polish cordon. Nine attacks were made in the region of Kolno, but all are said to have been repulsed with enormous losses. Among the captives is the commander of a Bolshevist division.

Russians Bringing Up Reserves.

Fresh Bolshevist forces released from the Finnish frontier have been rushed toward Grodno in an endeavor to head off the Polish advances and, if possible, to rescue thousands of the Red army hemmed in by the Poles. Owing to the Soviet-Finnish peace treaty thousands of Reds, it is reported, are being transferred to the Polish front. The Poles are expected to reoccupy Grodno at an early date.

The Bolsheviki who have escaped the Polish armies are overrunning the East Prussian frontier to such an extent that the German military authorities are said to have called out extra border forces to guard the scattered points and prevent further crossing. It is estimated that between 25,000 and 30,000 Reds have sought refuge in Prussia. At several places the Germans, it is asserted, fired on the Reds, driving them back into Poland, where thousands are gradually being surrounded by the Poles in their northern sweep.

The official communiqué issued tonight says that the Bolshevist committee from

Continued on Page Eight.

WRANGEL TO FIGHT TILL PEOPLE RULE

Says Civil War Will Cease When They Are Able to Form the Government.

HIS NAVY NOW ORGANIZED

Forces on All Fronts Well Equipped—Take Novorossisk and Donetz Coal Basin.

SEBASTOPOL, Crimea, Aug. 23 (Associated Press).—Civil war in Russia would cease immediately if the Russian people were free to organize a government according to their own wishes, General Baron Wrangel, who was recognized as head of the South Russian Government by France a few days ago, declared here yesterday. They are not able to do this at present, however, because of the domination of the Soviet leaders, and the fight must go on until Russians are free to take matters in their own hands, he continued.

General Wrangel expressed the gratification he felt over the note sent to Italy by the United States Government relative to the Russian situation and declared recognition of the South Russian Government by France was the "just expression of one ally's appreciation of another's sacrifice in the common cause." He asserted that his forces on all fronts were well equipped, and that the naval arm of the service was at last able to assist in the struggle against the Bolsheviki.

General Wrangel, who leaves tomorrow to personally direct the organization of forces rallying against the Bolsheviki, received the correspondent of the Associated Press at his home in this city and gave him an exclusive interview.

Bolshevism Hateful to Cossacks.

"Ever since the South Russian Army honored me by placing itself under my command, leaders of various Cossack organizations have been urging us to send expeditions into the Caucasus and Kuban regions to assist in throwing off the tyranny of the Bolsheviki," he said. "Soviet domination has always been hateful to the Cossacks, but it was not until the last fortnight that it was possible to meet their appeals. We have been too busy organizing here and establishing our northern fronts to do anything else.

"Various Cossack expeditions we have sent to Yeisk and other points in Kuban and the Don territory are advancing eastward, being heartily supported and joined by local Cossacks. Our navy is now restored to a point where it can effectively support our troops in any possible sea action, and, consequently, the time is propitious for giving the Don, Kuban, Astrakhan and Terek Cossacks the organization needed for utilizing their unlimited resources against their oppressors.

"The Cossacks have men, foodstuffs and animals sufficient for a long fight, and the spirit with which they have joined the expeditions sent to help them indicates they will soon hold all important ports and railways to the Georgian border."

"What effect will recognition by France have on the Crimean Government?" he was asked.

General Wrangel's eyes brightened as he responded promptly: "The note of France was a chivalrous and just expression of one ally's recognition of another's self-sacrifice in the common cause.

"I cannot conceal my surprise," he continued after a moment's hesitation, "that other allies have not given the same generous recognition of the blood shed, not for Russia alone, but to protect the entire civilized world against plunder, murder and despotism. It is not only Russia's battle which is being fought in South Russia."

"May I ask," said the correspondent, "what impression the American note to Italy on the attitude of the United States toward Bolshevism created?"

"It was most favorable," he replied. "It was very gratifying to me personally, and I am sure to all right-minded Russians, that the United States should thus officially have expressed its

Continued on Page Eight.

Edward R. Stettinius, Stricken Suddenly In Morgan Office, Undergoes An Operation

Edward R. Stettinius, member of J. P. Morgan & Co., was operated upon for appendicitis last night in Roosevelt Hospital. According to the operating surgeons, Mr. Stettinius rallied at once from the operation and late last night he was reported to be progressing favorably.

Mr. Stettinius was purchasing agent in America for the Allies before this country entered the war. In that capacity Mr. Stettinius was said to have spent more than five billion dollars, principally for Great Britain, his purchases running up to $100,000,000 a month at certain times. When the United States entered the war the banker was appointed Surveyor General of Supplies, became a member of the War Council and bought everything the army acquired.

The banker, who lives at 1,021 Park Avenue, has been spending the Summer at his country place near Oyster Bay, L. I. He came to the city yesterday morning at his usual hour and when he arrived at the Morgan offices apparently was in the best of health. A short time after he began his work, however, he experienced severe pains in the stomach. Mr. Stettinius thought at the time that he merely had an attack of acute indigestion. The pain, however, grew steadily more severe, and finally the banker, on the advice of his physician, consented to go to Roosevelt Hospital.

After an examination at the hospital his illness was diagnosed as appendicitis and an operation was regarded as imperative. The banker's preparation for the ordeal was begun at once and at 7 o'clock he was placed on the operating table. Dr. James I. Russell and Dr. Henry Cave performed the incision, which, they declared, had been successful in every respect.

Mr. Stettinius, a St. Louisan, is 55 years old. He was graduated from St. Louis University, and his first five years in business was a stock broker. He developed a talent for organization and became Director and Vice President of the Babcock & Wilcox Company and President and organizer of the Diamond Match Company. He became a Morgan partner on Jan. 1, 1916.

LORD MAYOR DYING; REPORT IRISH CRISIS

Viceroy's Council in Dublin Said to be in Sharp Disagreement with Cabinet.

FIERCE FIGHTING IN BELFAST

Some Killed, Many Wounded and Scores of Incendiary Fires Mark New Outbreaks.

LONDON, Aug. 26.—It is stated tonight that King George has consulted with responsible Ministers, but that the policy of the Government remains unchanged with regard to Lord Mayor MacSweney, now dying from hunger strike in Brixton Prison.

Redmond Howard sent another long appeal to the King, complaining that the Home Secretary had refused to see him today.

When told of King George's telegram replying to the appeal of Redmond Howard, nephew of the late John Redmond, Father Dominic, the Lord Mayor's private chaplain, said: "I am glad, but I am afraid it is too late to hope for the Lord Mayor's recovery now. He is resigned to his fate."

Father Dominic, interviewed by the Press Association, said that Mr. Howard was acting without any authority from the Irish Republican Party. The party, he declared, did not agree with Mr. Howard's statement in his telegram to the King about the murders committed in Ireland. The Republicans did not admit that any murders whatever had been committed.

Mary MacSweney, the Lord Mayor's sister, today replied to the telegram which Premier Lloyd George sent her from Lucerne. She said:

"I made no appeal to you for exceptional treatment for my brother. I warned you of your responsibility in event of his death. He and his comrades demand their freedom as a right.

"If my brother or any of his comrades must die to win that freedom, they do so willingly, and we are proud of them, but their death lies on you and your Government. Self-determination, for which you say England went to war, is as much Ireland's right as Poland's. We claim it and will have it, even if you have decided that my brother is to die."

Suffers Collapse During Night.

Lord Mayor MacSweney, despite two serious collapses during the night, was brighter today when visited by Father Dominic, his private chaplain. He was too weak to speak more than a few words, however.

Mayor MacSweney's visitors also included his two sisters and Bishop Cohalan of Cork.

It was officially stated today that thirteen policemen were injured, none seriously, during last night's disturbances outside Brixton Prison, when a crowd engaged in a free fight with the police.

Extra large forces of police cordoned Brixton Prison tonight to prevent a repetition of disorderly demonstrations. Relatives visited the Lord Mayor this evening and found his condition without change since this morning, when he suffered two brief collapses.

The Evening Standard's Dublin correspondent says:

"Divisions of opinion between the Irish Executive and the Cabinet have reached an acute stage, culminating in Sir Hamar Greenwood's visit to Premier Lloyd George at Lucerne. The Viceroy's position, as well as that of the responsible members of the executive, is in the balance, and it is stated here that the next few days will bring definite announcement of a more liberal ameliorative policy in Ireland or resignations that must vitally alter the personnel of the Irish administration.

"The fact is that MacSweney and other hunger strikers have been more or less the cause of precipitating the present crisis, but the situation has been ripening for months.

"Viscount French and his counsellors frankly oppose the policy of drastic repression, and while fully prepared to enforce law and order they hold that conciliatory measures should immediately be given a more particular trial than hitherto.

"While Sir Hamar Greenwood sympathizes with this view, and is prepared to support it, he feels that his share in the Irish administration must necessarily take its direction from the Cabinet."

Radicals Hold Demonstration.

Copyright, 1920, by The New York Times Company.
Special Cable to THE NEW YORK TIMES.

LONDON, Aug. 26.—What the Socialist Daily Herald described this morning in advance as a monster labor demon-

Continued on Page Three.

COLBY PROCLAIMS WOMAN SUFFRAGE

Signs Certificate of Ratification at His Home Without Women Witnesses.

MILITANTS VEXED AT PRIVACY

Wanted Movies of Ceremony, but Both Factions Are Elated —Wilson Sends Message.

Special to The New York Times.

WASHINGTON, Aug. 26.—The half-century struggle for woman suffrage in the United States reached its climax at 8 o'clock this morning, when Bainbridge Colby, as Secretary of State, issued his proclamation announcing that the Nineteenth Amendment had become a part of the Constitution of the United States.

The signing of the proclamation took place at that hour at Secretary Colby's residence, 1,267 K Street Northwest, without ceremony of any kind, and the issuance of the proclamation was unaccompanied by the taking of movies or other pictures, despite the fact that the National Woman's Party, or militant branch of the general suffrage movement, had been anxious to be represented by a delegation of women and to have the historic event filmed for public display and permanent record.

Secretary Colby did not act with undue haste in signing the proclamation, but only after he had given careful study to the packet which arrived by mail during the early morning hours containing the certificate of the Governor of Tennessee that that State's Legislature had ratified the Congressional resolution submitting the amendment to the States for action.

No Suffrage Leaders See Signing.

None of the leaders of the woman suffrage movement was present when the proclamation was signed.

"It was quite tragic," declared Mrs. Abby Scott Baker of the National Woman's Party. "This was the final culmination of the women's fight, and, women, irrespective of factions, should have been allowed to be present when the proclamation was signed. However, the women of America have fought a big fight and nothing can take from them their triumph."

Leaders of both branches of the woman's movement—the militants, headed by Miss Alice Paul, and the conservatives, led by Mrs. Carrie Chapman Catt—some of whom had been on watch nearly all night for the arrival of the Tennessee Governor's certification, visited the State Department, and the militants sought to have Secretary Colby go through a duplication of the signing scene in the presence of movie cameras. This Mr. Colby declined to do, on the ground that it was not necessary to detract from the dignity and importance of the signing of the proclamation by staging a scene in imitation of the actual signing of the proclamation.

In informal conversation with newspaper men late this afternoon Secretary Colby said that "effectuating suffrage through proclamation of its ratification by the necessary thirty-six States was more important than feeding the movie cameras."

At the same time Mr. Colby congratulated the women of the country on the successful culmination of their efforts in the face of discouragements, and declared the day "marks the opening of a great and new era in the political life of the nation."

"I confidently believe," said the Secretary, "that every salutary, forward and upward force in our public life will receive fresh vigor and reinforcement from the enfranchisement of the women of America. To the leaders of this great movement I tender my sincere congratulations. To every one, from the President, who uttered the call to duty, whenever the cause seemed to falter, to the humblest worker in this great reform, the praise not only of this generation but of posterity will be freely given."

Reads Message from President.

Speaking tonight at the woman's suffrage meeting in Poli's Theatre, Secretary Colby made the following references to President Wilson:

"There never was a man more deeply or profoundly convinced of the justice of the suffrage cause than Woodrow Wilson. And there never was a party leader who held his party with more stern, austere and unbending insistence to the performance of a duty dictated by high principle:

"The President called me on the telephone this morning. It is a private wire

Continued on Page Three.

51 CITIES ASSESSED FOR $8,145,000 FUND, COX CHARGES AGAINST THE REPUBLICANS, SAYS TOTAL FOR COUNTRY WILL BE DOUBLE

Republican Quotas for 51 Cities in 27 States On List Produced by Gov. Cox as Official

Special to The New York Times.

PITTSBURGH, Aug. 26.—Following are the quotas for fifty-one cities in twenty-seven States, totaling $8,145,000, which Governor Cox in his speech here tonight said were on an official list distributed at a meeting of the Republican Ways and Means Committee in Chicago as the assessments levied on these cities for the Republican campaign fund:

City	Quota	City	Quota
New York City	$2,000,000	Rochester	50,000
Chicago	750,000	Kansas City	50,000
Philadelphia	500,000	Denver	50,000
Detroit	450,000	New Haven	50,000
Pittsburgh	400,000	Omaha	50,000
Cleveland	400,000	Scranton	50,000
Boston	300,000	Spokane	50,000
Cincinnati	250,000	Syracuse	50,000
St. Louis	250,000	Bridgeport, Conn.	50,000
Buffalo	250,000	Washington, D. C.	50,000
San Francisco	150,000	Louisville	50,000
Los Angeles	150,000	Des Moines	50,000
Indianapolis	125,000	Schenectady	50,000
Toledo	100,000	Portland, Ore.	50,000
Columbus	100,000	Birmingham	50,000
Seattle	100,000	Canton, Ohio	40,000
Minneapolis	100,000	Worcester, Mass.	25,000
St. Paul	100,000	Lowell, Mass.	25,000
Providence	100,000	Lynn, Mass.	25,000
Newark	100,000	Albany, N. Y.	25,000
Youngstown	80,000	Atlanta	25,000
Akron	80,000	Memphis	25,000
Oakland	75,000	Duluth	25,000
Milwaukee	75,000	Jersey City	25,000
Dayton	60,000		
Baltimore	50,000	Total	$8,145,000
New Orleans	50,000	Population approximately 25,500,000.	

NOMINEE READS OUT QUOTAS

Says They Were on Official List Distributed by Republicans.

NEW YORK ON FOR $2,000,000

Declares Upham's Bulletins Called for Secrecy and Urged "Boys Get the Money."

SOME OVERSUBSCRIPTIONS

Cox Repeats His Charges and Asserts Harding and Hays Indorse Huge Fund.

Special to The New York Times.

PITTSBURGH, Pa., Aug. 26.—Quoting from official documents of the Republican Party organization, Governor James M. Cox placed before the people at a great mass meeting here tonight some of the evidence which he offers in substantiation of his charge that a campaign fund of not less than $15,000,000 is being raised by the Republicans, most of it from business interests, with which to attempt to "buy the Presidency."

Governor Cox produced a typewritten sheet giving, he said, quotas assessed at a meeting of the Ways and Means Committee of the Republican National Committee on fifty-one cities in twenty-six States. The total assessment for these cities alone, he said, was $8,145,000. The sheet of paper which he held in his hand, Governor Cox declared, was one of several which had been distributed to the Republican leaders who attended the meeting. He asserted that Will H. Hays, Chairman of the Republican National Committee, was present and had addressed the gathering.

Statements of this kind were received with great applause by the crowd in the hall where the meeting was staged.

Developing his charges, Governor Cox quoted several extracts from pamphlets labeled "Official Bulletin, Treasurer's Office, Republican National Committee," and bearing the name of Fred W. Upham, Treasurer of the committee. In these bulletins it was stated that many communities which had been assigned quotas in the list of quotas had subscribed or oversubscribed their amounts.

There were also many quotations from "official bulletins" concerning the manner in which the workers were exhorted to get out and do their duty, which caused laughter and applause on the part of the big crowd. As a climax to the charges Governor Cox quoted from a letter written for an issue of the bulletin by Senator Harding in which the Senator gave thanks and indorsement.

Gives New York Quota as $2,000,000.

On the sheet of paper produced by Governor Cox, New York City was put down for $2,000,000, Chicago for $750,000, and Philadelphia for $500,000. The Governor called attention to the fact that these assessments had been laid on business and industrial centres and offered this as substantiation of his charges that big banking and financial interests were prepared to subscribe heavily in order to have the Republican Party under financial obligation should Senator Harding be elected.

Governor Cox, after his speech tonight, said that he "intended to pass this evidence" on to the Senate subcommittee investigating campaign expenditures, which reopens its hearing at Chicago Monday morning.

He cited the fact that, according to The Wall Street Journal, Mark Hanna spent $16,500,000 in 1896. "Nothing approaching it," he added, "has been attempted until now."

He contended that his charge that the Harding campaign fund would reach $15,000,000 was a modest one. In concluding his address, Governor Cox quoted Will H. Hays as having said, when the charges of a great campaign fund were under discussion: "If, at the instance of our adversaries, this campaign is finally resolved into a financial discussion, we will know of no reason aside from natural distaste why we should not meet that issue as readily as any other."

"I renew the charges and accept the challenge," Governor Cox declared, and the crowd cheered.

There was a big parade upon the arrival of Governor Cox here. Thousands turned out to meet him.

Speech of Governor Cox.

In producing his evidence Governor Cox said:

"I have charged the leaders who have taken over the official affairs of the Republican Party organization with raising a stupendous campaign fund, so stupendous as to exceed the realm of legitimate expense, which means but one thing, imminent danger of an odious and corrupt campaign.

"In order that the present situation might be properly placed in the public understanding, we should be reminded that the contribution of large sums of money by business interests brought the Newberry Senatorial contest in Michigan. When accusations were made, general denial was forthcoming

HARDING RECEIVES MESSAGE FROM ROOT

Herrick, Who Brings It, Says International Court Meets Views of Europe.

PREPARE CAMPAIGN ISSUE

Senator, in Talk to Teachers, Says America Will Do Its Share if Republicans Win.

Special to The New York Times.

MARION, Ohio, Aug. 26.—Elihu Root's return from Europe, where he has been organizing an International Court of Justice, will be followed by an "announcement of very important accomplishments that will go far toward clarifying the entire international situation," Myron T. Herrick, former Ambassador to France, said today.

Asked whether the results of Mr. Root's work will have any bearing on the Presidential campaign, Mr. Herrick replied that he anticipated they would be of "very great political significance."

It is generally believed here that Mr. Herrick, who saw Mr. Root in Paris, brought to Senator Harding either a message from Mr. Root or an outline of the organization of the international court. Only last week Senator Harding intimated that the Root court plan might play a big part in Republican attacks on the League of Nations.

The Senator has announced that Saturday's speech will define clearly his foreign policies; that he will clear up all doubts then as to whether he stands for an "association of nations," adopting or rejecting some of the provisions of the League of Nations.

Today in an extemporaneous speech to a delegation of school teachers from Marion County, Senator Harding said that the foreign policies he contemplated did not propose that America should remain aloof from international affairs, but rather that this country should remain free to act in accordance with American instead of international principles.

Opponents of the Treaty of Versailles, the Senator concluded his talk today, were anxious for America to play her part in the world. She was willing, he told them with real satisfaction, but that the greatest service this country could perform was by maintaining freedom of action and standing before the world as an example of popular representative Government.

Root Court as League Substitute.

In speeches and in interviews since his notification, Senator Harding has centred his opposition to the League of Nations upon the executive and legislative features of the covenant. In his acceptance speech he proposed an association of nations based on justice and moral ties alone, and this declaration, in view of Senator Harding's intimations regarding the political significance of the Root court, is regarded as an indication that he will propose for the nations of the world to give up the League and unite upon an international tribunal of justice.

Further evidence to support the belief that the principles of the Root court will be found embodied in Senator Harding's speech next Saturday, was found in the fact that Mr. Herrick, only back in this country four days,

Continued on Page Two.

HAYS TO DISCLOSE FUND TO KENYON

"Governor Cox Will Have to Prove His Case There," Chairman Declares.

SAYS HE WILL BARE NAMES

And Wants to Know Democratic Sources of Revenue—Blair's List Called Tentative.

Will H. Hays, chairman of the Republican National Committee, declined to comment directly last night upon Governor Cox's speech at Pittsburgh, in which the Democratic nominee declared that he offered proofs of his charge that "sinister influences had contributed millions to buy an underhold on the Presidency."

Mr. Hays had made it clear earlier in the evening that he did not intend to reply to the speech of Governor Cox offhand. When told that Governor Cox had promised to make public evidence to corroborate his charge that the Republicans were raising a campaign fund of $15,000,000, Mr. Hays said:

"It does not make any difference what Candidate Cox may say at Pittsburgh relative to campaign contributions. I hope he divulges the source of the funds received by the Democratic National Committee and by other agencies to be used in an effort to elect him. Every activity of the Republican National Committee in connection with the raising and spending of money will be shown in full next week before the Senate Investigating Committee of which Senator Kenyon is Chairman. Incidentally, Mr. Cox will have an opportunity to do likewise.

"He has charged that millions have been paid into the Republican National Committee with which to corrupt the electorate. That charge he will have to prove. It is an insult to the thousands of good citizens all over the country who have contributed to the Republican Party. The name of every single contributor of every single dollar will be given to the Senate Committee next week, and the quality of the citizenship which constitutes that list will be such a condemnation of the veracity and judgment of Cox that the whole country will know it."

Fred W. Upham, Treasurer of the Republican National Committee, was said at Republican headquarters to have left for Chicago last night. Mr. Upham has been treasurer of the committee since the 1916 campaign, and the details of the money-raising plans were said to have been within his jurisdiction rather than that of the Chairman.

Harry M. Blair, assistant to Mr. Upham, mentioned in Governor Cox's speech as having prepared the quota list for fifty-one cities, upon which Governor Cox largely based corroboration of his charge, was originally from Cleveland, Ohio. He was formerly Secretary to the Roosevelt Memorial Association, and is credited with great success in money-raising campaigns for the Y. M. C. A. and the War Camp Community Service. He was later attached to the Chicago headquarters of the Republican National Committee.

Well-informed Republicans said, after learning details of Governor Cox's speech, that all his information, with one exception, seemed to have been ob-

Continued on Page Two.

STILL LEAD JAPAN IN NAVAL BUILDING

United States Battle Fleet Will Continue to be Superior in 1923.

TOKIO HAS BIG PROGRAM ON

It Calls for Construction of Eight Superdreadnoughts and Eight Battle Cruisers.

Special to The New York Times.

WASHINGTON, Aug. 26.—Much interest has been aroused in this country over the Japanese naval building program which calls for the construction of eight superdreadnoughts and eight battle cruisers—the eight-eight program, as it is termed. Information at hand shows that the battle cruisers of the Akagi and the Amagi type, are to be smaller by more than 3,000 tons than the American dreadnought battle cruiser Saratoga and her class.

The Akagi and the Amagi are in a class of four under construction, the others being the Atago and the Atako. Four similar vessels are projected. Figures obtainable show the following comparative measurements of the Akagi class with the Saratoga class:

Akagi class—full load displacement, 40,000 tons; speed, 30 knots per hour; main battery, eight 16-inch guns; shaft horsepower not definitely known. One report is that the shaft horsepower is 250,000, but this is not believed, as the larger vessels of the Saratoga class are to be faster than the Akagi class with much less horsepower than 250,000.

Saratoga class—full load displacement, 43,500 tons; speed, 33.25 knots per hour; main battery, eight 16-inch guns; shaft horsepower, 180,000.

The Japanese dreadnoughts Negato and Mutsu are compared with the ships of the American Colorado class in that they are of the same classification and almost of a size. The Japanese vessels will have a slight advantage over the Colorado class in displacement and more than two knots better speed. The comparison follows:

Colorado—Full load displacement, 33,590; speed, 21 knots; main battery, eight 16-inch guns.

Negato and Mutsu—Full load displacement, 33,800; speed, 23.5; main battery, eight 16-inch guns.

The Japanese vessels are supposed to be four-turbine ships. Te Negato, was launched on Nov. 16, 1919. The Mutsu was launched on May 31, 1920. The material for two other vessels of this class is being assembled. Four others are scheduled for completion in 1929. Of the battle cruisers of the eight-eight program two are being built to be completed by 1923, two others have been authorized and four are projected. These last mentioned six should be completed by 1927.

A comparison of the United States and Japanese battle fleets in 1923 will show the following:

United States—Battleships, 17; 14-inch guns, 84; 16-inch guns, 104; displacement, 624,074 tons.

Battle cruisers, 6; 14-inch guns, 0; 16-inch guns, 48; displacement, 261,000 tons.

Total weight of broadside fire of American battle cruisers, 98,304 pounds.

Japan—Battleships, 8; 14-inch guns, 48; 16-inch guns, 32; displacement, 258,860 tons.

Battle cruisers, 6; 14-inch guns, 32; 16-inch guns, 16.

Total weight of broadside fire of Japanese battle cruisers, 76,704 pounds.

In the seventeen battleships of the American fleet, built and building, are six vessels of more than 40,000 tons displacement. All are included in the program to be completed by 1923. In addition to these the United States is building four battleships of more than 33,000 tons.

All the new super-dreadnoughts of more than 33,000 tons and more than 43,000 tons will carry batteries of 16-inch guns, the four ships of the Colorado class having eight each and the six ships of the South Dakota class having twelve each.

The Saratoga class of battle cruisers, which the Navy Department hopes to complete by 1923, comprises six vessels. The American navy has no battle cruisers in commission.

Under the intensive Japanese building program, eight battleships and six battle cruisers are to be completed by 1923 and it is expected that the rest of the Japanese program for capital vessels—those capable of going into the first battle line—will be completed in 1927 with twelve battleships and twelve battle cruisers added to the fleet. In addition, the Japanese program calls for eight high speed cruisers of 6,000 tons, twenty-four light cruisers of 5,000 tons, thirty-two destroyers of 1,300 tons, thirty-two destroyers of 850 tons, twenty-four submarines of 1,300 tons, forty submarines of 800 tons, and twelve special duty ships of about 12,000 tons.

MRS. SKEFFINGTON A JUDGE.

Appointed by Sinn Fein 'Parliament' to 'Supreme Court of Ireland.'

Mrs. Hannah Sheehy Skeffington, whose husband died in the Easter rebellion, has been appointed a Justice of the "Supreme Court of Ireland," by the Sinn Fein "Parliament," according to a cablegram received here yesterday from Mrs. Skeffington. The message was addressed to Mrs. Cathleen O'Brennan at the Hotel Ansonia.

"Will the newly enfranchised American women," Mrs. Skeffington asked in her message, "show their love of freedom and justice by asking their Government to prove its good faith to the democracy of the world by stopping the murder of Mayor MacSweney?"

Mrs. O'Brennan announced last night that Mrs. Gertrude Corliss, who was one of the British Embassy pickets a short time ago, would head a delegation to Washington today to interview Secretary of State Colby on the Justice's suggestion. Miss Helen Pinkerton of Tacoma, Wash., will start East at the same time for the same purpose.

While Washington is being besought, the pickets at the British Consulate, 44 Whitehall Street, will be continuing their exercise.

Tonight a mass meeting to show indignation against the treatment accorded MacSweney will be held in the Lexington Theatre.

NUGENT WINS IN PRIMARY.

Idaho Democrats Renominate Senator—Republicans for Gooding.

IDAHO FALLS, Idaho, Aug. 26.—United States Senator John F. Nugent of Idaho was renominated for that office Wednesday at the Idaho State Democratic Convention. T. A. Walters, of Caldwell, was unanimously nominated for Governor.

Mrs. Nell K. Irions, of Sand Point, nominated for Congress from the First District is the first woman to be named for a Congress in the State. Mayor W. P. Whitaker, of Pocatello, was nominated for Congress from the Second District.

Mrs. Sarah E. Melvin, of Lemlin County was nominated for State Treasurer.

POCATELLO, Idaho, Aug. 25.—F. R. Gooding of Gooding, Idaho, won the nomination for United States Senator in the State Republican Convention today. Congressman Burton L. French, of the First District and Addison T. Smith, Second District, were renominated, as was Governor . . W. Davis.

De Valera to Talk on MacSweney.

Circumstances surrounding the arrest, trial and hunger strike of Terence MacSweney, Lord Mayor of Cork, whom Premier Lloyd George has declined to free from his prison cell in Brixton, will be described at a public meeting here tonight by Eamonn de Valera, "president of the Irish Republic," and three members of the Irish "parliament." Addresses will be made to acquaint the American public with "the facts in the case," it was announced. The meetings, to be held under the auspices of the American Committee on Irish Independence, was called by Frank P. Walsh, Chairman.

COLBY PROCLAIMS SUFFRAGE CHANGE

Continued from Page 1, Column 5.

that connects the office of the Secretary of State with he library of the President. And he asked me if I had been invited to address this meeting tonight. He expressed his pleasure when I told him that I had, and said: 'I hope you will let nothing interfere with your attendance.' He said:

"'Will you take the opportunity to say to my fellow citizens that I deem it one of the greatest honors of my life that this great event, the ratification of this amendment, should have occurred during the period of my administration.'

"And he said, further:

"'Please say also that nothing has given me more pleasure than the privilege that has been mine to do what I could to advance the cause of ratification, and to hasten the day when the womanhood of America would be recognized by the nation on the equal footing of citizenship that it deserves.'"

Present Memorial to Wilson.

Late this afternoon Mrs. Carrie Chapman Catt, head of the National American Woman's Suffrage Association, and Mrs. Helen H. Gardiner, another active worker in that organization, were received at the White House by President and Mrs. Wilson. The National Woman's Party, known as the militants, and a rival organization to that headed by Mrs. Catt, was not represented.

Mrs. Catt and Mrs. Gardiner presented to the President a memorial of appreciation in the form of a bound volume, a page coming from each State, for the work he did for suffrage. They had expected to receive from the President a written message to be read tonight at the big mass meeting and jubilee at Po' s Theatre over the ratification of the amendment, but the President informed them he had handed it to Secretary Colby and that the latter would include it in his remarks to the women at the mass meeting.

One page of the volume presented to the President is taken up with the tribute from the New York organization, the first paragraph of which reads:

"Dear Mr. President: The women of this organization of a million and a quarter enrolled members have a special reason for loyalty and gratitude. Your stalwart advocacy of our campaign last year contributed materially to our victory in New York State."

This is signed:

"New York State Woman Suffrage Party, Harriet Burton Laidlaw, Mary Garret Hay, Laura J. Starke Belknap, Narcissa Cox Vanderlip, Muriel Rosalie Edge, Katrina Ely Tiffany."

The mass meeting was attended by women from every section of the country and a number of officials of the administration, including members of the Cabinet, were present.

Factions Dispute Over Ceremony.

Differences between the rival organizations of suffragists as to who should be present at the signing of the proclamation developed yesterday, and as no agreement could be brought about between them, it is believed that Secretary Colby decided to sign the proclamation in his own home to avoid a clash at his offices.

"It was decided," said the Secretary in a statement this afternoon, "not to accompany this simple ministerial action on my part with any ceremony or setting. This secondary aspect of the subject has regretfully been the source of considerable contention as to who shall participate in it and who shall not. Inasmuch as I am not interested in the aftermath of any of the friction or collisions which may have been developed in the long struggle for the ratification of the amendment, I have contented myself with the performance in the simplest manner of the duty devolving upon me under the law."

Representatives of both factions visited the State Department this morning. Mrs. Catt and members of her party were photographed by movie operators as they left the State Department. Miss Alice Paul and her associates of the militant wing of the suffragists waited in the corridor of the State Department to be seen by the Secretary of State, who sent word he would receive them, but at this moment the Spanish Ambassador arrived and took precedence over the delegation of militants.

As time wore on the militant delegation thinned and finally left the department without having an audience with the Secretary of State.

Secretary Colby late this afternoon was asked by newspaper men to picture the scene that took place at his home when the final chapter of the story of ratification was reached.

Colby Describes the Signing.

"The package containing the certified record of the action of the Legislature of the State of Tennessee," said Mr. Colby, "came in on a train which reached Washington some time during the early morning hours. I was awakened by Charles L. Cooke of the State Department at about a quarter to 4 o'clock this morning, who said that the packet from the Governor of Tennessee had arrived. I told him to bring it to me."

Secretary Colby was then asked whether Mr. Cooke brought the packet to him forthwith.

"He brought it to me in about ten minutes," replied the Secretary. "There were some legal matters connected with the ratification that I wished to have examined by the chief law officer of the State Department, so I sent the papers to F. K. Nielsen, the solicitor of the State Department, with instructions to bring the papers to me at my home at 8 o'clock this morning.

"I had received a large number of messages asking me to act on the amendment with insistent promptitude. Fear was strong in some minds that the 'antis' would effect some sort of injunction from the courts to interfere with my proclamation of the completion of the act of ratification. While it was not my opinion that it would be becoming for me to resort to undue eagerness to avoid an opportunity for judicial interference, I saw no reason whatever why I should conspicuously loiter.

"I confess to a disinclination to signing it in the wee morning hours of the night, believing that would not be conducive to a dignifed function of so important a character, and thought that 8 o'clock in the morning would be a fair hour for action in the matter."

Secretary Colby was asked whether he had eaten breakfast before he signed the proclamation.

"Breakfast is an unimportant function with me," replied the Secretary with a smile. "I may say that I had time to partake of about one and one-half cups of coffee before I signed the proclamation."

"Then," the Secretary continued, "that about concludes the odyssey of the morning's proceedings."

Paraphrases Dewey at Manila.

"You remember," he continued, "the simple way in which the late Admiral Dewey went about the opening of his battle at Manila Bay, how he waited until morning to enter Manila Bay, went up on deck, wiped the egg stains of breakfast from his moustache, observed the disposition of the enemy's ships and of his own, which had crossed the mines during the night, and then taking out a cigar, turned to one of his Captains and said: 'When you are ready, you may fire, Gridley.' So I turn to the women of America and say: 'You may now fire when you are ready. You have been enfranchised.'"

Secretary Colby in response to other questions said that he had used no golden pen prepared for the occasion, but an ordinary steel pen, in signing the proclamation. It was one of his regular pens, he explains, and when asked to whom it would be given, replied: "I have promised it to dozens of persons."

Asked whether he would give the pen to the National American Woman's Suffrage Association, the National Woman's Party, or send it to the Smithsonian Institution, Secretary Colby said with a smile, "I should not be surprised if it found its way there."

Immediately after the announcement that Secretary Colby had signed the proclamation, Alice Paul said:

"August 26th will be remembered as one of the great days in the history of the women of the world and in the history of this republic.

"All women must feel a great sense of triumph and of unmeasurable relief at the successful conclusion of a long and exhausting struggle.

"The suffrage amendment is now safe beyond all reasonable expectation of legal attack. This opinion was secured from high legal authorities by officers of the National Woman's Party, who devoted their efforts after the signing of the ratification proclamation to discover what further steps, if any, would be necessary to protect the amendment.

"Pending injunction cases were automatically thrown out of court by the signing of the proclamation according to the consensus of legal opinion. The only possible legal attack is now through a taxpayers' suit to prevent the women in an individual State from voting."

National headquarters of the Woman's Party will be maintained. A national convention of its members will be called to decide upon the party's future policy. Alice Paul will go to New York probably on Saturday to hold a meeting of the Executive Committee to discuss plans and a date for the convention, it was said.

McAdoo Sends Congratulations.

William G. McAdoo was one of the first to congratulate the Woman's Party on the signing of the proclamation in a message to Mrs. Abby Scott Baker, political Chairman of the party. He said:

"I know how justly elated you and all the splendid women who have been working so devotedly with you are today over the consummation of the great thing for which you and they have fought. You have had a conspicuously influential part in the triumphs of woman's suffrage. I know with what intelligence and courage you have gone at the task. I am rejoiced not alone for you, but for all the women of America, at this colossal achievement for humanity and civilization."

Francis J. Heney of Los Angeles wired Mrs. Abby Scott Baker:

"Hearty congratulations on success which is yours. The victory is due to the inconquerable fighting spirit of your little band of irreconcilables. More power to all of you."

"There is absolutely nothing that can be done now to upset or nullify the ratification of suffrage by the Tennessee Legislature," said Mrs. Harriet Taylor Upton, Vice Chairman of the Republican National Executive Committee, and President of the Ohio Suffrage Association. "I regard the suffrage victory in Tennessee as perfectly safe right now and nothing can undo it. Otherwise Mrs. Catt and I would never have left Nashville and come to Washington.

"And right here I want to publicly give credit to those stalwart mountaineer Republicans of the Tennessee Legislature who stood pat on suffrage from start to finish and who made suffrage possible. Had it not been for their faithfulness and their devotion to what they believed was right suffrage would never have won out in Tennessee. You can quote me on that and make it as I really believe."

Mrs. Upton, accompanied by Mrs. Carrie Chapman Catt, President of the International Suffrage Association, came to Washington from Nashville to confer with Secretary Colby and with officials of the Department of Justice and also to attend the suffrage jubilee held here tonight.

SAYS STATE DID NOT RATIFY.

Speaker of Tennessee Wires Colby House Vote Was Nullified.

Special to The New York Times.

NASHVILLE, Tenn., Aug. 26.—With the exception of a telegram to Secretary of State Colby from Speaker Seth M. Walker of the Tennessee House of Representatives, there have been no new developments in the fight for the ratification of the Susan B. Anthony Suffrage Amendment in the Tennessee Legislature today.

Suffrage workers regard the proclamation of Secretary of State Colby as final and are content to leave the matter of ratification to the decision of the courts.

Speaker Walker's telegram to Secretary Colby follows:

"Tennessee has not ratified Nineteenth Amendment. Motion to reconsider House vote was duly entered on journal, and no quorum was present under Constitution of Tennessee on Aug. 21, 1920, when motion to reconsider was attempted to be acted upon.

"Under decision of Judge Lurton in 87 Tennessee reports, 137, effect of motion to reconsider was to nullify prior vote until said motion was acted on by Constitutional quorum of 66 members. This has not been done. Legislature acting as Parliamentary body under provision of Tennessee Constitution, see Haire vs. Rice 204, United States 291.

"This Legislature has no power to act and, furthermore, has not acted. The Governor's certificate in effect leaves these two questions up to you to decide, which you can lawfully do.

(Signed) "SETH M. WALKER.
"Speaker of the Tennessee House of Representatives."

DECATUR, Ala., Aug. 26.—Members of the Tennessee Legislature on a filibuster here, joined today in a statement saying that notwithstanding the proclamation by Secretary Colby mass meetings called for Saturday would be held in Tennessee "to condemn the high-handed action" of Governor Roberts and "the other politicians who were instrumental in influencing members to vote for the amendment in violation of their oaths and contrary to the wishes of their constituents."

AUGUSTA, Me., Aug 26.—Governor Milliken issued a proclamation tonight calling a special session of the Legislature to meet on Aug. 31 for the purpose of enacting Legislation to enable women to register in time to vote at the State election on Sept. 13.

GOV. ROBERTS SIGNING SUFFRAGE CERTIFICATE

(From left to right) Senator L. E. Grimin, A. S. Singgart, Assistant Attorney General; Major Daughtry, Secretary to the Governor; Miss Holt, stenographer; Miss Williams, Vice Chairman National Democratic Executive Committee; Miss Cullom, stenographer.

(In circle) Mrs. Guilford Dudley of Nashville, Third Vice President of the National American Woman's Suffrage Association, who led the fight in Tennessee.

Text of the Proclamation Signed by Colby Certifying Ratification of 19th Amendment

WASHINGTON, Aug. 26.—Following is the proclamation certifying the ratification of the Suffrage Amendment, signed by Secretary of State Colby today:

Bainbridge Colby,
Secretary of State of the United States of America.

To all to whom these presents shall come, greeting:

Know ye, That the Congress of the United States at the first session, sixty-sixth Congress begun at Washington on the nineteenth day of May in the year one thousand nine hundred and nineteen, passed a resolution as follows:

To wit:

Joint resolution.

Proposing an amendment to the Constitution extending the right of suffrage to women.

Resolved by the Senate and House of Representatives of the United States of America in Congress assembled (two-thirds of each House concurring therein), that the following article is proposed as an amendment to the Constitution, which shall be valid to all intents and purposes as part of the Constitution when ratified by the Legislatures of three-fourths of the several States.

ARTICLE.

"The right of citizens of the United States to vote shall not be denied or abridged by the United States or by any State on account of sex.

"Congress shall have power to enforce this article by appropriate legislation."

And, further, that it appears from official documents on file in the Department of State that the amendment to the Constitution of the United States proposed as aforesaid has been ratified by the Legislatures of the States of Arizona, Arkansas, California, Colorado, Idaho, Illinois, Indiana, Iowa, Kansas, Kentucky, Maine, Massachusetts, Michigan, Minnesota, Missouri, Montana, Nebraska, Nevada, New Hampshire, New Jersey, New Mexico, North Dakota, New York, Ohio, Oklahoma, Oregon, Pennsylvania, Rhode Island, South Dakota, Tennessee, Texas, Utah, Washington, West Virginia, Wisconsin and Wyoming.

And, further, that the States whose Legislatures have so ratified the said proposed amendment, constitute three-fourths of the whole number of States in the United States.

Now, therefore, be it known that I, Bainbridge Colby, Secretary of State of the United States, by virtue and in pursuance of Section 205 of the Revised Statutes of the United States, do hereby certify that the amendment aforesaid has become valid to all intents and purposes as a part of the Constitution of the United States.

In testimony whereof, I have hereunto set my hand and caused the seal of the Department of State to be affixed.

Done at the City of Washington, this 26th day of August, in the year of Our Lord one thousand nine hundred and twenty.

BAINBRIDGE COLBY.

SEEK ASSEMBLY SESSION.

Connecticut Attorney General Sees Need of Revising Statutes.

HARTFORD, Conn., Aug. 26.—A special session of the General Assembly is necessary to bring the election statutes into harmony with the suffrage amendment, in the opinion of Attorney General F. E. Healey.

The suffragists say that if the Governor does not, within a few days, call a special session so that the period for enrolling women as voters may be lengthened, a formal request for the calling of the General Assembly will be made to him.

Executive Secretary John Buckley said that as soon as official notification comes from Secretary of State Colby of the ratification of the amendment, the Governor will consider "the advisability for, and need of, a special session."

Ratification Pleases White.

George White, Democratic National Chairman, expressed gratification over the proclamation of the ratification of the woman suffrage amendment by Secretary of State Bainbridge Colby, following official certification of favorable action by Tennessee, the thirty-sixth State. "I am particularly pleased," he said, "that a Democratic State brought final ratification and that the proclamation was issued by a Democratic Secretary of State."

GOV. SMITH TO GREET MRS. CARRIE C. CATT

Governor Smith, who issued the call for the special session of the New York State Legislature which ratified the woman suffrage amendment, will be among the first to greet Mrs. Carrie Chapman Catt, President of the National American Woman Suffrage Association, upon her return from Nashville, Tenn., this afternoon. Governor Smith will go to the Pennsylvania Station, where Mrs. Catt will be met by hundreds of suffragists when she arrives at 2:06 this afternoon, city time.

With Mrs. Catt will be Mrs. Harriet Taylor Upton of Ohio, Vice Chairman of the National Republican Executive Committee, and Miss Charl Williams of Tennessee, Vice Chairman of the National Democratic Executive Committee. Both of these women were active in Tennessee during the fight for ratification, as representatives, respectively, of Senator Harding and Governor Cox in the efforts of the two Presidential nominees to gain a thirty-sixth ratifying State.

The suffragists will assemble at Thirty-first street and Seventh Avenue, from which place they will accompany Mrs. Catt to the Waldorf-Astoria. The procession will proceed up Seventh Avenue to Thirty-fourth Street and across Thirty-Fourth Street to the hotel. The order of the procession will be:

Mounted police; Seventy-first Regiment Band; standard bearers; automobile carrying Mrs. Catt, Mrs. Upton, Miss Williams and Miss Mary Garrett Hay, Vice-President of the association; officers of the National American Woman Suffrage Association; officers of the State League of Women voters; officers of the City League of Women Voters; delegation of Connecticut women; delegation of New Jersey women, and suffragists.

LORD MAYOR DYING; REPORT IRISH CRISIS

Continued from Page 1, Column 4.

stration in favor of the release of the Lord Mayor of Cork was held tonight in the neighborhood of Brixton Prison. The demonstrators did not get near enough to the prison for any sound of theirs to penetrate to the cells. The police in strong force held all approaches to the prison and forced the demonstrators to place their wagon platform a quarter of a mile away.

The meeting was organized by The Daily Herald and a huge banner advertising the Socialist-Labor newspaper and its editor, George Landbury, completely overshadowed a small placard referring to the Lord Mayor. One Sinn Fein flag was also displayed on the platform and there was another at the back of the crowd, while green blouses and hat trimmings were conspicuous among the women who listened to the speeches.

Perhaps one thousand people attended the proceedings. The platform had been set in a side street about a hundred yards from the main road, and in front of it the real sympathizers with the Lord Mayor and revolution were packed to hear fiery speeches and pass bloodcurdling resolutions. Behind them stood two policemen quietly chatting. To THE NEW YORK TIMES representative one remarked: "There are a lot of people here, but they are very young."

As he spoke a row of schoolboys perched on a wall, in a shrill treble, broke into a popular song. On the main road all Brixton was out to see the event. It is a popular London suburb, and men, women and children found the demonstration interesting. They were entirely good tempered.

One burly workman told THE TIMES representative:

"Last night one fellow shouted 'Up rebels!' Then one policeman got up and the fellow ran. The fellow said he 'wished he had him (the policeman) in Ireland, he did, then he would shoot him.' The policeman was not listening."

The police lines had a particular fascination for the crowd, which kept parading past, watching half a dozen officers, who blocked the way to the prison, and a dark mass of reserves twenty yards behind.

One man became abusive. A solitary policeman stepped into the crowd and bade him pass along. He refused, and the policeman shoved him down.

An inspector in charge nodded to ten sergeants and they quietly worked their way through the throng to their comrade's aid. Then three more, and then another ten were sent after them, with the result that the crowd gathering around the first were quietly and efficiently shepherded along far away from the point where trouble might have broken out. Vigilance was undoubtedly necessary. In a gathering as large as this there were plenty of young men who might have been violent if they got out of hand, but they seemed unorganized and completely submerged by Brixton, out for a Summer evening's diversion.

DUBLIN, Aug. 26.—Replying to the appeal of the Irish Dominion Conference in behalf of Lord Mayor MacSweney, Home Secretary Shortt telegraphed today:

"I am very sorry. The decision is the decision of the Cabinet, and I cannot alter it."

An announcement was made at Dublin Castle this evening that eleven hunger striking prisoners in the Cork jail had been transferred from cells to the prison hospital.

The announcement added that no prison regulations were to be allowed to stand in the way of any possible palliative treatment.

A large creamery at Knocklong, County Limerick, was burned today. A creamery at Shanheiden was set on fire, but the flames were extinguished.

PARIS, Aug. 26.—George Gavan Duffy, Irish Member of Parliament, who is the "Irish Republican Envoy" in France, today published a letter he sent to Premier Millerand yesterday, appealing to France to intervene for the release of Lord Mayor MacSweney.

The letter says that France saved the British Empire by her sacrifices during the war, and "were a suggestion made to the London Government it would save the life of an Irish patriot."

MOBS OVERRUN BELFAST SHOOTING AND BURNING

Some Killed and Many Wounded in New Outbreaks—Soldiers Fire Into Crowds.

BELFAST, Aug. 26 (Associated Press)—Serious rioting broke out in Belfast tonight, during which there was considerable shooting and some incendiarism.

A number of wounded persons were taken to hospitals.

Early today Sinn Feiners in Ballymacarret sniped the military, who returned the fire. Fraser McCann was shot dead and another man was wounded.

Tonight's rioting began in the Falls District of West Belfast, the scene of the deadliest fighting in the July disturbances. It started with revolver firing near the Kashmir Road, of evil memories. Albert Street, in the Falls area, situated in the populous mill locality, mainly inhabited by Nationalists, became the new storm centre.

During the trouble an armored car appeared and fired on the rioters, a number of whom were taken to hospitals suffering from machine-gun wounds. Crowds of shipyard workers appeared from the side streets, waving union jacks.

The military was [illegible] as was a section of [illegible] which was summoned fo[illegible] fire at the foot of Sea[illegible] Street. A few minutes after the fi[illegible] started the whole block of buildings was a seething mass of flames. There was much looting.

At 8 o'clock the riots had extended to Grosvenor Road, a long thoroughfare running from the heart of the city to the Falls, where two spirit stores were looted. The military was obliged to disperse the rioters.

Rioting of the fiercest nature began at the city end of Ballymacarrett about 6 o'clock this evening in Vulcan Street and immediate vicinity. Many were injured among the rival factions. Later the trouble extended to Newtonards, thirteen miles from Belfast, involving the shipyard workers.

"Belfast could be no worse," said a high police official of the conditions in Belfast tonight.

Fierce fighting occurred this afternoon in Clonallon Street, East Belfast. The military fired volleys at the crowd and a number of persons were seen to fall. The Fire Brigade was caught between hostile stone-throwing mobs and had to return to its station.

Rioting was renewed at noon in Wolff and Foundry Streets. The police quelled the outbreak.

During last night's rioting the casualties were reported as one person killed and twenty injured, including two young women. One of the latter is in a critical state.

The Fire Brigade reported twenty-eight incendiary fires in the twelve hours ended at 7 o'clock this morning. Thirty-nine persons were arrested for rioting and kindred offenses.

The rioting originated in a report that Nationalists yesterday stoned children leaving the Comber Street national school at Ballymacarret, a Belfast suburb.

Robert Caldwell, Principal of the school, denied that the pupils were attacked, but there was no doubt that the report was believed by both sides and that it acted like matches to tinder, especially since the recollection was still fresh of the stoning of a Sunday school excursion at Castle Dawson, which precipitated a great riot following the Larkin engineering strike in 1907.

As the report spread that the children had been stoned, mothers flew to the scene and excitement, already inflamed by the Bisburn events, rose to fever heat. Word reached the shipyards and many workers left in a mood for the events which followed.

The authorities banned a meeting which the carpenters' executive had called at the suggestion of headquarters in England to consider the question of expelled Sinn Fein workers. Believing such a meeting would have been marked by intense feeling, the ban was announced, the authorities resolving not to allow anything which would further embitter the situation.

"All the News That's Fit to Print."

The New York Times.

THE WEATHER
Fair today and Thursday; no change in temperature; north winds.
Temperature yesterday—Max., 40; min., 30.
For full weather report see Page 23.

VOL. LXXI....No. 23,328. NEW YORK, WEDNESDAY, DECEMBER 7, 1921. TWO CENTS In Greater New York | THREE CENTS Within 200 Miles | FOUR CENTS Elsewhere

IRELAND TO BE A FREE STATE WITHIN THE BRITISH EMPIRE; AGREEMENT SIGNED GIVING HER A STATUS LIKE CANADA'S; ULSTER CAN STAY OUT; PARLIAMENT CALLED TO RATIFY

Text of Agreement to Establish the Irish Free State

LONDON, Dec. 6 (Associated Press.)—The text of the agreement signed this morning by the British Government and the Irish representatives follows:

Article I.—Ireland shall have the same constitutional status in the community of nations known as the British Empire as the Dominion of Canada, the Commonwealth of Australia, the Dominion of New Zealand and the Union of South Africa, with a Parliament having powers to make laws for peace and order and good government in Ireland, and an executive responsible to that Parliament, and shall be styled and known as the Irish Free State.

Article II.—Subject to provisions hereinafter set out, the position of the Irish Free State in relation to the Imperial Parliament, the Government and otherwise shall be that of the Dominion of Canada, and the law, practice and constitutional usage governing the relationship of the Crown or representative of the Crown and the Imperial Parliament to the Dominion of Canada shall govern their relationship to the Irish Free State.

Article III.—A representative of the Crown in Ireland shall be appointed in like manner as the Governor General of Canada and in accordance with the practice observed in making such appointments.

Article IV.—The oath to be taken by the members of the Parliament of the Irish Free State shall be in the following form:

"I do solemnly swear true faith and allegiance to the Constitution of the Irish Free State as by law established, and that I will be faithful to his Majesty King George V., and his heirs and successors by law, in virtue of the common citizenship of Ireland with Great Britain and her adherence to and membership of the group of nations forming the British Commonwealth of Nations."

Article V.—The Irish Free State shall assume liability for service of the public debt of the United Kingdom as existing at the date thereof and toward the payment of war pensions as existing on that date in such proportion as may be fair and equitable, having regard for any just claims on the part of Ireland by way of set-off or counter-claim, the amount of such sums being determined, in default of agreement, by the arbitration of one or more independent persons being citizens of the British Empire.

Article VI.—Until an arrangement has been made between the British and Irish Governments whereby the Irish Free State undertakes her own coastal defense, defense by sea of Great Britain and Ireland shall be undertaken by his Majesty's imperial forces, but this shall not prevent the construction or maintenance by the Government of the Irish Free State of such vessels as are necessary for the protection of the revenue or the fisheries. The foregoing provisions of this article shall be reviewed at a conference of representatives of the British and Irish Governments to be held at the expiration of five years from the date hereof with a view to the undertaking by Ireland of a share in her own coastal defense.

Article VII.—The Government of the Irish Free State shall afford to his Majesty's imperial force (a) in time of peace such harbor and other facilities as are indicated in the annex hereto, or such other facilities as may from time to time be agreed between the British Government and the Government of the Irish Free State, and (b) in time of war or of strained relations with a foreign power such harbor and other facilities as the British Government may require for the purposes of such defense, as aforesaid.

Article VIII.—With a view to securing observance of the principle of international limitation of armaments, if the Government of the Irish Free State establishes and maintains a military defense force, the establishment thereof shall not exceed in size such proportion of the military establishments maintained in Great Britain as that which the population of Ireland bears to the population of Great Britain.

Article IX.—The ports of Great Britain and the Irish Free State shall be freely open to the ships of the other country on the payment of the customary port and other dues.

Article X.—The Government of the Irish Free State agrees to pay fair compensation, on terms not less favorable than those accorded by the Act of 1920, to Judges, officials, members of the police forces and other public servants who are discharged by it or who retire in consequence of the change of government effected in pursuance of the hereof paragraph.

Provided that this agreement shall not apply to members of the auxiliary police force or persons recruited in Great Britain for the Royal Irish Constabulary during the two years next preceding the date hereof. The British Government will assume responsibility for such compensation or pensions as may be payable to any of these excepted persons.

Article XI.—Until the expiration of one month from the passing of the Act of Parliament for the ratification of this instrument, the powers of the Parliament and Government of the Irish Free State shall not be exercisable as respects Northern Ireland, and the provisions of the Government of Ireland Act of 1920 shall, so far as they relate to Northern Ireland, remain of full force and effect, and no election shall be held for the return of members to serve in the Parliament of the Irish Free State for the constituencies of Northern Ireland unless a resolution is passed by both houses of Parliament of Northern Ireland in favor of holding such elections before the end of said month.

Article XII.—If before the expiration of said month an address is presented to his Majesty by both houses of Parliament of Northern Ireland to that effect, the powers of the Parliament and Government of the Irish Free State shall no longer extend to Northern Ireland, and the provisions of the Government of Ireland Act of 1920 (including those relating to the Council of Ireland) shall, so far as they relate to Northern Ireland, continue to be of full force and effect, and this instrument shall have effect, subject to the necessary modifications;

Provided, that if such an address is so presented, a commission consisting of three persons, one to be appointed by the Government of the Irish Free State, one to be appointed by the Government of Northern Ireland, and one, who shall be Chairman, to be appointed by the British Government, shall determine in accordance with the wishes of the inhabitants, so far as may be compatible with economic and geographic conditions, the boundaries between Northern Ireland and the rest of Ireland, and for the purposes of the Government of Ireland act of 1920, and of this instrument the boundary of Northern Ireland shall be such as may be determined by such commission.

Article XIII.—For the purpose of the last foregoing article the powers of the Parliament of Southern Ireland under the Government of Ireland Act of 1920, to elect members of the Council of Ireland, shall, after the Parliament of the Irish Free State is constituted, be exercised by that Parliament.

Article XIV.—After the expiration of said month, if no such address as mentioned in Article XII. hereof is presented, the Parliament of the Government of Northern Ireland shall continue to exercise as respects Northern Ireland the powers conferred upon them by the Government of Ireland Act of 1920, but the Parliament of the Government of the Irish Free State shall in Northern Ireland have in relation to matters, in respect of which the Parliament of Northern Ireland has not the power to make laws under that act (including matters which, under said act, are within the jurisdiction of the Council of Ireland), the same powers as in the rest of Ireland, subject to such other provisions as may be agreed to in the manner hereinafter appearing.

Article XV.—At any time after the date hereof the Government of Northern Ireland and the Provisional Government of Southern Ireland, hereinafter constituted, may meet for the purpose of discussing provisions, subject to which the last of the foregoing article is to operate in the event of no such address as is therein mentioned being presented, and those provisions may include: (a) Safeguards with regard to patronage in Northern Ireland; (b) safeguards with regard to the collection of revenue in Northern Ireland; (c) safeguards with regard to import and export duties affecting the trade and industry of Northern Ireland; (d) safeguards for the minorities in Northern Ireland; (e) settlement of financial relations between Northern Ireland and the Irish Free State; (f) establishment and powers of a local militia in Northern Ireland and the relation of the defense forces of the Irish Free State and of Northern Ireland, respectively, and if at any such meeting provisions are agreed to, the same shall have effect as if they were included among the provisions subject to which the powers of Parliament and of the Government of the Irish Free State are to be exercisable in Northern Ireland under Article XIV. hereof.

Article XVI.—Neither the Parliament of the Irish Free State nor the Parliament of Northern Ireland shall make any law so as either directly or indirectly to endow any religion or prohibit or restrict the free exercise thereof or give any preference or impose any disability on the account of religious belief or religious status, or affect prejudicially the right of any child to attend school receiving public money without attending the religious instruction of the school, or make any discrimination as respects State aid between schools under the management of the different religious denominations, or divert from any religious denomination or any educational institution any of its property except for public utility purposes and on the payment of compensation.

Article XVII.—By way of provisional arrangement for the administration of Southern Ireland during the interval which must elapse between the date hereof and the constitution of a Parliament and a Government of the Irish Free State in accordance therewith, steps shall be taken forthwith for summoning a meeting of the Members of Parliament elected for the constituencies in Southern Ireland since the passing of the Government of Ireland act in 1920 and for constituting a Provisional Government. And the British Government shall take steps necessary to transfer to such Provisional Government the powers and machinery requisite for the discharge of its duties, provided that every member of such Provisional Government shall have signified in writing his or her acceptance of this instrument. But this arrangement shall not continue in force beyond the expiration of twelve months from the date hereof.

Article XVIII.—This instrument shall be submitted forthwith by his Majesty's Government for the approval of Parliament and by the Irish signatories to a meeting summoned for the purpose of members elected to sit in the House of Commons of Southern Ireland, and, if approved, it shall be ratified by the necessary legislation.

Signed on behalf of the British delegation:

LLOYD GEORGE.
AUSTEN CHAMBERLAIN.
BIRKENHEAD.
WINSTON CHURCHILL.
WORTHINGTON-EVANS.
GORDON HEWART.
HAMAR GREENWOOD.

On behalf of the Irish delegation:

ART OF GRIOBHTHA (ARTHUR GRIFFITH).
MICHAEL O. O. SILEAIN (MICHAEL COLLINS).
RIOBARD BARTUN (ROBERT C. BARTON).
E. S. DUGAN (EAMON J. DUGGAN).
SEORSA GHABGAIN UI DHUBHTHAIGH (GEORGE GAVAN DUFFY).

Dated the 6th of December, 1921.

ANNEX.

An annex is attached to the treaty. Clause 1 specifies that Admiralty property and rights at the dockyard port of Berehaven are to be retained as at present date and the harbor defenses and facilities for coastal defense by air at Queenstown, Belfast, Lough and Loughswilly to remain under British care, provision also being made for oil, fuel and storage.

Clause 2 provides that a convention shall be made between the two Governments, to give effect to the following conditions: That submarine cables shall not be landed or wireless stations for communication with places outside of Ireland established, except by agreement with the British Government, that existing cable rights and wireless concessions shall not be withdrawn except by agreement with the British Government, and that the British Government shall be entitled to land additional submarine cables or establish additional wireless stations for communication with places outside of Ireland, that lighthouses, buoys, beacons, &c., shall be maintained by the Irish Government and not be removed or added to except by agreement with the British Government, that war signal stations shall be closed down and left in charge of care and maintenance parties, the Government of the Irish Free State being offered the option of taking them over and working them for commercial purposes, subject to Admiralty inspection, and guaranteeing the upkeep of existing telegraphic communication therewith.

Clause 3 provides that a convention shall be made between the two Governments for the regulation of civil communication by air.

HARDING PROPOSES FLEXIBLE TARIFF AND LABOR REGULATION

Asks Congress to Extend the Powers of the Present Tariff Commission.

WOULD FUND FOREIGN DEBT

Will Not Denounce Trade Treaties and Wants Merchant Marine Act Changed.

AGAINST TAX-EXEMPT BONDS

Many Arms Conference Delegates in Throng Which Listens to President's Address to Congress.

Special to The New York Times.

WASHINGTON, Dec. 6.—In an address which President Harding pointed out was not only a message to the Congress but to the people of the entire country he made an appeal today for the united support of his party in the accomplishment of legislation that he considers vital to the peace, prosperity and security not only of the United States but of the world. Senators and Representatives of both parties agreed that it was a very frank expression of the views and hopes of the Chief Executive. In much that he said the President won the outspoken approval of the Democrats as well as the Republicans.

[The full text of the message is published on Page 8.]

Not since the war days has a more representative audience listened to an address by a President on the opening of Congress. Occupying seats of honor directly in front of the rostrum from which the President spoke were statesmen of Europe and the Orient who are representing their respective countries at the Conference for Limitation of Armament. They were an intensely interested body of men who, observing the strictest decorum, did not join in the applause that continually interrupted the delivery of the address.

Behind the diplomats and foreign delegates were grouped the members of the Senate and House, Secretary Hughes and the other members of the Cabinet being in the first row of seats in the House reservation. There were just two uniformed personages on the floor. One was General Pershing and the other his aid, Major Quekemeyer.

Refers Twice to Arms Conference.

Twice in the course of his address, once at the beginning and again as he concluded, the President referred to the Conference for Limitation of Armament in session in Washington.

"It is gratifying to report," he said at the start, "that our country is not only free from every impending menace of war, but there are growing assurances of the permanency of the peace which we so deeply cherish."

"Agreeable to your expressed desire," he said, in concluding his address, "and in complete accord with the purposes of the executive branch of the Government, there is in Washington, as you happily know, an international conference now most earnestly at work on plans for the limitation of armament, a naval holiday, and the just settlement of problems which might develop into causes of international disagreement.

"It is easy to believe a world hope is centred on this capital city. A most gratifying world accomplishment is not improbable.

Procedure to Avoid Strikes.

Discussing at considerable length the problem of capital and labor, the President pointed out that the right of labor to organize is as necessary and as fundamental as is the right of capital to organize, and that the right of labor to negotiate through its chosen agents is as essential as is the right of capital to organize to maintain corporations and to limit the liabilities of stockholders. But, he added, just as it is undesirable that a corporation shall not be permitted to impose undue exactions upon the public, it is just as essential that labor shall not be permitted to exact unfair terms of its employers, or subject an innocent public to distress in order to gain its end.

In the same way that nations are seeking procedures to settle their difficulties without resort to war, the President suggested, some procedure should be found whereby labor and capital can reach agreements without resort to those forms of warfare" which are recognized as strikes, lockouts, boycotts and the like.

"Inescapable" World Relationship.

Other outstanding features of the address were the earnestness and the unqualified positiveness with which the President asserted the "inescapable relationship" of the United States to the affairs of the world in finance and in trade. The United States, he declared, would be unworthy of its best traditions. "if we were unmindful of social, moral and political conditions which are not of direct concern to us," but which

Continued on Page Nine.

B.R.T. DIVIDENDS PAID DAY OF RECEIVERSHIP

Checks for $236,250 Mailed by Operating Company Just Before Garrison Took Charge.

HECTIC HOLIDAY FOR HEDLEY

Got $1,000,000 on New Year's Eve to Stave Off the Failure of Interborough.

Stories of quick shifts of millions between holding companies and subsidiaries in both the Interborough and Brooklyn Rapid Transit systems on the eve of receiverships were told in the Transit Commission's hearing yesterday by James R. Sheffield, trustee in bankruptcy for the Interborough Consolidated Corporation, and Howard Abel, Controller for the B. R. T.

On Dec. 31, 1918, a few hours before Lindley M. Garrison was appointed receiver for the New York Consolidated Railroad Company, which operates the subway and elevated lines of the B. R. T. system, the companys officers rushed out checks for the last payment of a 1¼ per cent. dividend on $18,900,000 of stock, amounting to about $236,250. The dividends had been declared in the preceding September. As holder of approximately 96 per cent. of the stock of the New York Consolidated, the Brooklyn Rapid Transit Company received the larger part of this payment.

A year later President Frank Hedley and other officers of the Interborough were spending a "hectic New Year's Eve," and finally obtained a loan of $1,000,000 from its bankrupt holding company, the Interborough Consolidated, to aid in averting a receivership for the subway and elevated lines of Manhattan and the Bronx.

A few days before this New Year's Eve loan the Interborough Rapid Transit Company had finished paying back to the Interborough Consolidated $800,000 borrowed from the treasury of the holding company the day before it went into bankruptcy in March, 1919. Mr. Sheffield, trustee in bankruptcy for the Interborough Consolidated, had demanded the return of that $800,000 on the ground that the loan was "illegal."

He also had demanded from the Interborough payment of a note for $500,000, due on April 1, 1919, but which was

Continued on Page Five.

German Explosion Kills 100, Sets Dynamite Works Afire

BERLIN, Dec. 6 (Associated Press).—It is reported that 100 persons lost their lives today as the result of the explosion of an oil tank in the Nobel Dynamite Works at Saarlouis, Rhenish Prussia.

The works are burning.

SAYS UNION ABUSES RAISE BUILDING COST

Witness Tells Lockwood Committee of Expenses Piled Up by Labor Inefficiency.

The Lockwood committee opened a new phase of its housing inquiry late yesterday afternoon by examining witnesses in an endeavor to learn to what extent housing construction was loaded with high costs due to the inefficiency of labor. C. G. Norman, Chairman of the Board of Governors of the Building Trades Employers' Association, detailed a long list of abuses he alleged existed in building trade unions, resulting from severe membership and production restrictions demanded by the organizations.

Patrick J. Crowley, successor of Robert P. Brindell as Chairman of the Building Trades Council, having jurisdiction over 115,000 workers, explained the inefficiency of labor by the phrase "more pay, more pep," and declared he had heard no complaints lately regarding the inefficiency of labor.

Samuel Untermyer, senior counsel to the committee, and Henry Mayer, assistant counsel, again took up the affairs of Inside Electrical Workers' Union 3, which is said to have collected $250,000 a year on "permit" cards which enabled non-union journeymen to work on union jobs if they paid $2.50 a week for journeymen's cards and $1 a week for helpers' cards. Mr. Untermyer examined Joseph Lawlor, Treasurer of the union, concerning the $26,000 of the funds alleged to be missing, but Lawlor became involved in confused statements, saying he believed that William A. Hogan, the financial secretary, had turned the money over to the union, and then that he did not know whether Hogan turned the money over to him or not, finally returning to his original statement.

In introducing the examination of

Continued on Page Six.

America Will Enter No Alliance; Three More Chinese Advisers Out

No Treaty on Far East Likely, but a Less Formal Agreement—Project Shaping Slowly.

By EDWIN L. JAMES.

Special to The New York Times.

WASHINGTON, Dec. 6.—Whatever plans are being worked out for an international treaty, protocol, resolution, agreement, or understanding among three, four, five, six, seven, eight or nine powers to establish a Far Eastern policy do not now form a proper subject for public consideration, according to the official view of the American delegation to the armament conference.

It is stated by spokesman for the delegation that much progress has been made in the working out of a Far Eastern agreement. But just what that "progress" means and just what it is purposed to commit the nation to the Amerlaen representatives are not yet prepared to say.

While reports originating from other delegations are being published all over the world, emphasizing the idea of an alliance of the United States with other nations, the Ameriacn delegates think the time is not fit to present the American views on what might be a suitable arrangement.

Efforts made today to induce the American representatives to set correspondents on the right path amid the eddies of conflicting rumors as to what was being done brought only the instructive statement that what had been been published about treaties and alliances was not within gunshot of the truth. But just what the truth is—that is not forthcoming.

Observers, and many visiting diplomats, have commented frequently upon the secrecy of the conference since its first days. Not a few of the old-school diplomats who are here and at work feared that the Americans were going to stage the conference doings in the open. It is probable that there was a general expectation that some of the real negotiations would be done at public meetings. It even looked that way just after the first two open sessions.

But the fears of the old school diplomats have proved groundless. For two weeks there has not been a plenary session, and it has become evident that the plenary sessions will be full-dress occasions for announcing decisions previously reached.

While there is no official statement on the subject, there appears no reason to suppose that the American delegation is going to undertake to involve this country in an alliance to take the place of the Anglo-Japanese alliance or to serve any other purpose. Nor will there, in all probability, be any treaty, three-

Continued on Page Four.

Attaches of Delegation Resign in Protest Against 'Negative Results' of Conference.

Special to The New York Times.

WASHINGTON, Dec. 6.—As a protest against "negative results" of the conference concerning China's aspirations, three additional attachés of the Chinese delegation to the Washington conference, two of them superior advisers, today tendered their resignations. This action followed that of Dr. Philip K. C. Tyau, Secretary General of the delegation, yesterday.

Those who resigned today are Yuho M. T. Liang, ex-Minister of Foreign Affairs; Tzu-Chi Chow, ex-Minister of Finance, superior advisers, and Vice Admiral Ting-Kan Tsi, associate director of the revenue council and adviser to the delegation. He was an adviser to the office of the President of China during the incumbency of the late Yuan Shih-Kai. A report that Lieut. Gen. Fu Hwang, adviser to the delegation, also had resigned, was denied.

It was uncertain tonight whether the resignations would be accepted.

China's attitude was criticised by an American official, who said that China had nothing to gain by such a course. He pointed out that the conference was making great progress, and that China found herself in a very strong position, face to face with all the nations interested in the Far East, with their representatives disposed to do everything possible to aid in restoring China's integrity and rehabilitating her finances.

There is divided opinion in the Chinese delegation as to the situation that that country is facing in the conference. One Chinese adviser, deprecating the resignations, said that the action had been premature and would fail of the expected effect. Some of them resigned for the political effect at home, while others, it was said, were absolutely sincere in the course taken.

Another spokesman for China counseled a more determined attitude on the part of China and an insistence that the Shantung Railroad dispute be adjusted first, rather than the minor differences now under consideration in the parley. He said he was in a position to say that the leaders in the conference had decided just how far the Far Eastern matters should be settled and that China would be forced to take what was given her. In his opinion, the conference leaders have agreed not only upon a naval ratio but upon other matters. China, he said, would not be allowed to change her tariff treaties and most of the things in dispute would be left to a commission to study and report upon to another conference.

"We are not too sensitive about the

Continued on Page Four.

Carson Sees for Britain Day of 'Abject Humiliation'

Special Cable to THE NEW YORK TIMES.

LONDON, Dec. 7.—The Morning Post says that after reading the terms of the Irish agreement the comment of Lord Carson, former Ulster leader, was:

"I never thought I should live to see a day of such abject humiliation for Great Britain."

CANADIAN ELECTION LIBERAL LANDSLIDE

Premier Meighen Loses His Seat and His Protection Policy Is Repudiated.

OTTAWA, Dec. 6.—Premier Meighen was defeated in his home constituency, Portage La Prairie, Manitoba, in the Canadian general election today. His opponent was Harry Leader, Progressive.

Returns received tonight indicated the defeat of the Meighen Government and a landslide for the Liberals, led by W. L. Mackenzie King. Seven members of the Cabinet were defeated.

Mr. King, the Liberal leader, was elected in North York, Ontario, a division normally Conservative, by 1,000 majority. T. A. Crerar, leader of the Progressive Party, was elected in Marquette, Manitoba.

In the eastern part of the dominion the Liberals made a clean sweep. Quebec, with sixty-five members in Parliament, will be represented entirely by Liberals. Five of the seven defeated Cabinet members were candidates in Quebec constituencies.

Nova Scotia, with sixteen seats, gave them all to Liberals, two members of the Government going down to defeat in that province. Liberals were reported elected in three out of the four Prince Edward Island divisions, and in six of the eleven constituencies in New Brunswick.

The Cabinet members defeated were F. B. McCurdy, Minister of Public Works, Colchester, N. S.; E. K. Spinney, Minister without portfolio, Yarmouth, N. S.; L. P. Normand, President of the Privy Council, Three Rivers, Quebec; C. C. Ballantyne, Minister of Marine and Fisheries, Montreal, Quebec; A. Fauteux, Solicitor General, Terre Bonne, Quebec; L. G. Belley, Postmaster General, Charlevoix, Quebec; Rudolphe Monty, Secretary of State, Beauharnois, Quebec.

Premier Meighen issued the following

Continued on Page Twelve.

ULSTER RESERVED; DUBLIN REJOICES

Craig Cabinet Begins Sessions to Consider the Terms of the Agreement.

NORTH DISLIKES THE OATH

But Waits to See if Sinn Fein Is Really Friendly—Dail's Acceptance Predicted.

Special Cable to THE NEW YORK TIMES.

BELFAST, Dec. 6.—News that the settlement had been achieved between the British Government and the Sinn Fein delegates caused some surprise in Belfast, particularly in view of De Valera's declaration at Galway in regard to allegiance. The disposition of Ulster people is not to enter upon any hasty criticism or comment, but to wait until the terms are revealed. Should the position of Ulster be safeguarded and southern Ireland accept allegiance and a recognized position within the British Empire there will be a general feeling of satisfaction in the north that the strife in Ireland has been brought to an end.

A specially convened meeting of the Ulster Cabinet was held today. After considering the terms for two and a half hours the Cabinet adjourned further consideration until tomorrow.

Colonel Spender, Secretary to the Northern Cabinet, was asked for the Cabinet's first impression of the terms of settlement. He said they were somewhat puzzled and were anxious to have certain points cleared up. Colonel Spender added that if the proposed changes in area affected any great tract of territory or meant any great disturbance of population they would not be acceptable to Ulster. He understood, however, that they really meant small adjustments along the frontier.

Asked if the form of oath was acceptable, Colonel Spender said that the Ulster people did not like it, but if it were acceptable to the British people they could not object. He regarded with suspicion the fact that the Sinn Feiners were not prepared to take the ordinary form of oath.

Likes the Option for Ulster.

In one form, Colonel Spender remarked, the latest proposals meant an advance, because the former ones provided for forcing Ulster to go in under an all-Ireland Parliament while these gave an option. If the good-will of the Sinn Fein was forthcoming, he added, and there was an intention on their part

Continued on Page Two.

'IRISH FREE STATE' CREATED

All of Ireland Outside of Ulster to Have Dominion Rule.

ULSTER CANNOT STOP IT

Redrawing of Her Frontiers to Follow if She Finally Refuses to Join.

NAVAL RIGHTS RESERVED

Control of Finances, Land Forces and Powers of Council of Ireland Given to New State.

Special Cable to THE NEW YORK TIMES.

LONDON, Dec. 6.—"Ireland shall have the same constitutional status in the community of nations known as the British Empire as the Dominion of Canada, the Commonwealth of Australia, the Dominion of New Zealand and the Union of South Africa, with a Parliament having powers to make laws for the peace and order and good government of Ireland and an Executive responsible to that Parliament, and shall be styled and known as the Irish Free State."

Such is the first article of the "treaty between Great Britain and Ireland" which was signed some minutes after 2 o'clock this morning on behalf of Great Britain by Lloyd George, Austen Chamberlain, Lord Birkenhead, Winston Churchill, Sir L. Worthington-Evans, Sir Hamar Greenwood and Sir Gordon Hewart, and on behalf of Ireland by Arthur Griffith, Michael Collins, Robert Barton, E. J. Duggan and Gavan Duffy.

The signatures were affixed to the document in that historic room of 10 Downing Street on whose walls hang the portraits of the greatest British Premiers of the past and of one American, George Washington, the Father of His Country.

It was that same room, Lord Birkenhead pointed out today, which "witnessed the fateful and melancholy discussions that preceded the final recognition on the part of the statesmen of this country that the American colonies were lost. It was in that room," said the Chancellor of the Exchequer, "in which the anxieties, uncertainties and vicissitudes of the war met with daily reflection, that yesterday was entered upon, in my judgment, a new phase which promises, after all these bitter centuries and generations, that at last an era may dawn which will enable us, of our day and generation, to say that we have not achieved less in settlement here at our own doors of the issue which seems, but is not, domestic than we achieved in the fields of arms when we preserved the security and existence of these islands from the greatest menace that assailed them since the Napoleonic period."

The Cabinet met this morning and approved the agreement reached between the British and Sinn Fein delegates. The Premier was heartily congratulated.

Parliament to Meet Next Week.

Now that the treaty of settlement has been signed the next step will be to submit the terms to the British Parliament for approval. For this purpose both Houses have been summoned to meet on Wednesday next, Dec. 14, by which time it is hoped the agreement as signed by the Sinn Fein delegates will have been ratified by the Dail Eireann.

This meeting of Parliament will be the first of a new session, and this will give added importance to the opening ceremony.

The King will open the session in person and in full state. The greatest emphasis will thus be laid upon it as a great historic occasion, on which the King's speech will no doubt lay due stress. There will be no other business to place before the Houses at this stage, and a day or two would be enough to secure the object in view. Then Parliament would adjourn until the date of assembly previously fixed, Jan. 30, unless there should appear a reason for a meeting a week or two earlier. But the preparation of the necessary bill for giving effect to the Anglo-Irish agreement will require time and its completion before the end of January is unlikely.

The terms of the agreement were carried to Dublin by E. J. Duggan, one of the Sinn Fein plenipotentiaries, and Desmond Fitzgerald, Dail Minister of Publicity.

Meanwhile at the house in Hans Place occupied by the delegates and at the Secretariat in Cadogan Gardens the process of packing up began. There was noticeable slackening in the care with which doors had been guarded ever since the Sinn Feiners came to London; and women secretaries were bustling about packing up big files of documents and getting their own baggage ready. Formal orders had not yet been issued to them, but they expect to leave by the mail train tomorrow night, arriving in Dublin on Thursday morning.

None of the delegates was ready to discuss the settlement, and equal reticence was shown by the rest of the party. They seemed, however, confident that the agreement would be accepted by the Sinn Fein generally, and when it was suggested that De Valera's speeches in the last day or two looked rather ominous, one of the secretaries declared he thought his utterances on Monday quite moderate.

A poster of The Freeman's Journal

with the one word "Peace" upon it was being shown around at the Cadogan Gardens with a great deal of satisfaction, and all seemed pleased with the outcome of their mission. The women, too, were glad to be going home, but they admitted they had some regrets as "you do get so fond of London."

Arthur Henderson, M. P., made the following statement tonight in behalf of the National Labor Party:

"The whole British labor movement will welcome the news of the settlement not only with joy but with great satisfaction."

It was Lord Birkenhead, it may now be stated, who a little after 2 o'clock this morning brought out from that historic Cabinet room of No. 10 to a waiting group of newspaper men the glad news that an agreement had been reached. There was a time not long ago when the present Lord Chancellor was nicknamed "Galloper Smith," because of his semi-martial activities among the Ulster die hards. Irish Nationalists and British Liberals were united in obloquy of the "Galloper." Now it is the last ditch Unionists who revive the nickname as a synonym of betrayal.

Birkenhead Announced Signing.

Lord Birkenhead, along with Austen Chamberlain, has worked with Lloyd George in the cause of peace with courage and determination, to which the fullest tribute should be paid. Birkenhead's announcement this morning had all the dramatic force of the utmost simplicity. It gave the result achieved in a single brief sentence. It told nothing of what had gone before in the council chamber, and some time must elapse before it will be possible to lift the veil which shrouds the happenings around the long green-baized covered table on which the treaty was signed. There are details that it is impossible to print as yet, while it is uncertain whether the treaty will be accepted without cavil by all elements in Southern Ireland.

There is, it is feared, at least a small section of Irishmen who will not be content with less than a republic in the fullest sense of the word, who would rather be the enemies of England to the death than accept terms of peace and amity and association with the hereditary enemy, and to whom the treaty signed this morning will appear as a betrayal. Consequently to give any details regarding the attitude taken by individual members of the Sinn Fein delegation would be to expose them to danger of fanatical vengeance. It required courage to be the first to say, "I agree and I will sign this treaty."

To the credit of all the Irish delegates it can be stated that when once one of their number had thus given the lead the others showed no hesitation in following. Then the signatures were written and the treaty became a document pledging the Dail Eireann and its Cabinet and the British Government to observance of the provisions which will undoubtedly be criticised in many quarters, but which, on the whole, it is believed by those best qualified to judge on both sides, will meet with general approval of the peoples of Great Britain and Ireland.

Before the agreement was reached there had been many tense moments in the three hours during which the night conference lasted. When the afternoon conference was adjourned on the understanding that the Sinn Fein delegates would return with a final reply at 10 o'clock after communication with Dublin, the outlook was as black as it could be. Lloyd George had insisted on the reply delivered that night being final. It was to be "Yes" or "No." He had pledged himself to Sir James Craig to "deliver the goods" by Tuesday if there were any goods to be delivered. No further delay could be brooked. There had been enough of discussion. The British delegates and the Sinn Fein delegates had gone fully into every phase of the question. When the Irish delegates came back to Downing Street at 10 o'clock they must bring a definite answer with them.

Sudden Turn in the Negotiations.

The British delegates were on hand at 10 o'clock. It was an hour and twenty minutes later when the Irish delegates appeared. Many telephone messages had been exchanged between Dowhing Street and the Irish headquarters. Requests for a little more time, owing to the difficulties of communication with Dublin, had been granted. On the British side there was every desire to give all the time available within the time limit that the answer, one way or another, must be given early enough to permit of Sir James Craig being notified on Tuesday of the outcome of the negotiations.

The British Ministers waited, with what patience or impatience may be imagined. At last word came that the Irish degelates were on the way.

The secrets of this final conference may not yet be revealed. That the Sinn Fein delegates did not come prepared to say either yes or no without further question is obvious from the fact that the night meeting lasted practically three hours. The question of allegiance was still the main difficulty. Suggestions were made, arguments advanced, points of view thrashed out.

The proceedings seemed to be caught in a vicious circle when the British Prime Minister, standing up at the table, summed up the whole discussion calmly but trenchantly. Great Britain had gone as far as it was possible to conceive of her going. No British Government which could be imagined could go further. Unless this island underwent a political upheaval, the end whereof was anarchy, its people would never willingly abdicate its title to security. Ireland could have peace now. Ireland was offered everything that Britain could give. Britain did not want war, and would not wage war upon Ireland except in its own self-defense. But the question inevitably must become one of peace or war.

"You can have peace now," Lloyd George may be imagined to have said. "Do you want war? We do not; we want peace."

Thus peace was won, or at least appears to be won, for it is not considered that either the extremist elements in South Ireland or the die-hards of Ulster will be in a position to upset the agreement arrived at. Even on the unlikely assumption that the Dail Eireann should refuse to ratify the treaty it would undoubtedly become necessary to hold a referendum and it is believed there would be found an overwhelming majority of moderate Irishmen in favor of the settlement.

Free State Equals Republic in Gaelic.

A number of extremists, it is also suggested, are likely to be placated by the fact that the Gaelic equivalent of free state is said to be republic.

Ulster, on its side, can do nothing detrimental, at least by constitutional means within its power. Whether there may be dissatisfaction enough to precipitate disorders on a great scale remains to be seen.

The provision relative to the demarkation of new boundaries between the Irish Free State and Northern Ireland is not expected to meet with much opposition from Ulster, as a strong section of public opinion in that province is in favor of getting rid of some the disaffected population of Tyrone and Fermanagh who would be embodied in the Southern Ireland Government.

When the treaty had been signed G. H. Shakespeare, one of Lloyd George's secretaries, was entrusted with the mission of taking a copy post haste to Sir James Craig in Belfast. Shakespeare started in a fast motor car for Euston Station at 2:30 A. M. There a special train was waiting for him and steamed for Holyhead at 2:50.

The line had been cleared of all traffic and Holyhead was reached at 8:26 A. M. A naval pinnace was waiting at the quayside to take Shakespeare aboard the 35-knot destroyer Salmon, which reached Belfast at 2:30 o'clock this afternoon.

Sir James Craig at 2:25 in the afternoon telegraphed to Lloyd George that no communication had reached him, but just half an hour later Shakespeare met the Ulster Premier at the Assembly College and handed him the terms of the treaty between Great Britain and the Irish Free State.

From all parts of the Empire today Lloyd George received a multitude of telegrams of congratulation.

Special Provisions for Ireland.

LONDON, Dec. 6.—(Associated Press) The centuries-old quarrel between England and Ireland was ended, as had been fervently hoped, in the small hours of Tuesday morning by the signature in the Prime Minister's Cabinet room of "a treaty between Great Britain and Ireland," consisting of eighteen articles, giving Ireland the title of the Irish Free State and the same constitutional status as Canada, Australia and other overseas dominions.

Ireland is treated as a single entity in the provisions of the treaty, with special clauses providing against the possibility that Ulster should refuse acquiescence in the settlment, in which case the Government of Ireland act of 1920 will remain in force so far as the northern parliament is concerned, but the stipulation that a special commission shall determine new boundaries for northern Ireland.

Provisions also are made for the cooperation of the two parliaments in providing certain safeguards in the event of Ulster remaining out of the new free State. Neither Parliament, however, will be permitted, under the treaty, to make laws endowing any particular religion, or to impose any religious disability.

The treaty looks to Ireland in the future undertaking its own coastal defence and provides that Ireland shall in time of war give the British forces necessary harbor and other facilities. It further, by providing against international limitation of armaments, recognizes the Irish free state's right to maintain its own military defence force.

Premier Lloyd George is the recipient of universal congratulations for having successfully rescued the negotiations from what appeared to be a complete impasse. The general belief, however, is that Lord Birkenhead, who came to the Government's rescue when the question of renewal of the Anglo-Japanese treaty had reached a critical stage, is this time responsible for the formula overcoming the allegiance difficulty.

Chamberlain Appeals to Ulster.

Austen Chamberlain, who is leader of the Government in the House of Commons and of the Unionist Party, speaking at Birmingham tonight expressed the conviction that before Christmas peace and good-will would be established between "the parent races of teh British commonwealth," and he appealed with emotion to Northern Ireland to join the new free State.

The signing occurred in the historic Cabinet Room, the Prime Minister and Arthur Griffith being the first to sign for either side, after which all the members shook hands all around with the greatest cordiality. At 3 o'clock in the morning the Premier sent a special message to the King at Sandringham and also a copy of the agreement.

The Irish delegates are returning home with the result of the negotiations. They expect some opposition in the Dail Eireann, but with the influence of Arthur Griffith and Michael Collins, as well as the other delegates, they have little apprehension as to the outcome. In the first place their "saor statt" (Gaelic for free State, there being no word in Gaelic for republic, is acknowledged by the Government, which will go a long way with the rank and file among the Sinn Feiners.

In the next place Mr. Lloyd George, Mr. Collins and Mr. Griffith are given the greatest credit for the success of the conference, though the Premier had the loyal support of Austen Chamberlain and Lord Birkenhead, the latter heretofore being looked upon as a "die-hard" supporter of Ulster's claims. The two chief Sinn Fein negotiators came here with the reputation of being bitterly opposed to any agreement with England, they turned out to be more moderate than their colleagues, Robert Barton, who is an Englishman, and George Gavan Duffy, who has practiced at the English bar.

Lieutenant Commander Erskine Childers and John Erskine, English ex-service men attached to the Irish delegation, are said to have been more insistent in their demands for South Ireland than either Mr. Collins or Mr. Griffith, who were supported by Eamon J. Duggan, and with Barton and Duffy were opposed to submitting the Government's previous terms, which were taken to Dublin last week, to the deision of the Dail Eireann Cabinet, asserting that they were not worthy of consideration.

Arrangements are already being made for prayers of thanksgiving in the churches of England. Cardinal Bourne has arranged for a service in Westminster Cathedral on Thursday at the Feast of the Immaculate Conception, when Viscount Fitzalan, Viceroy of Ireland, and other English Catholics are expectd to attend. The other churches have decided to hold special services on Sunday next.

Austen Chamberlain and Lord Birkenhead both addressed meetings at Birmingham tonight on the settlement. Mr. Chamberlain asserted that the Government had been true to the letter and spirit of its pledges. The settlement provided all essential conditions of national and imperial security. Ulster was mistress of her own fate, but he appealed to Sir James Craig and his colleagues in deciding between the two alternatives to consider whether they could not, while safeguarding their own interests, serve the cause of imperial unity

Lord Birkenhead said he had risked everything on his belief in the good faith of the Irish delegates. This issue was the most vital upon which a British Cabinet had pronounced for 240 years.

"We have made up our minds, rightly, we believe," he added. "We have put everything to the hazard. What a world we shall inherit if it is proved that we have not been too sanguine!

"When this settlement is accepted there will meet at Downing Street a new partner of the empire; her spokesman, the Irish Prime Minister, will meet on equal terms with the Prime Minister of Great Britain in determining the fortunes of that greater whole, the empire, of which Ireland is not the least illustrious partner."

Arthur Henderson, the Labor leader, says that the whole British Labor movement will welcome the settlement with joy and great satisfaction.

Michael Collins, who had planned to go to Dublin tonight, changed his mind and remained here with Mr. Griffith and his other colleagues. Eamon de Valera, so far, has declined to comment on the settlement.

GREATEST OF EVENTS, SAY BRITISH PRESS

London Daily Chronicle Thinks Irish Agreement More Vital Than Victory in War.

LLOYD GEORGE IS LAUDED

Wide Influence of Decision on General World Peace Is Predicted by Some Papers.

Special Cable to THE NEW YORK TIMES.

LONDON, Dec. 7.—The terms of Irish settlement meet with general approval of the London newspapers. The Daily Chronicle says:

"We shall be reminded soon enough that all the difficulties are not yet over, but victory is definitely won and we regard it in all moderation as a greater thing than our victory in war. That saved us from ruin, but this new victory is a rich and positive contribution to the wholesomeness of the world's politics. That left us weak and exhausted, but this victory will mean almost from the outset a new accession of strength.

"Viewed even in terms of power, it is a great stroke for England to have converted our ablest and most persistent enemies in half the countries of the world into warm friends, and as a reinforcement of our moral power it adds to us the equivalent of a new dominion."

Discussing the settlement in detail, The Chronicle says:

"If we turn to the famous offer of July 20 last, we shall see that the settlement conforms broadly to the lines there laid down, but certain of the stipulations have been waived and some others have been rendered less formidable by processes of restrictive definition, the most noticeable withdrawn being that of the claim for free trade 'between all parts of these islands,' in view of the Southern Irishmen's strong theoretic leanings to protection."

As regards Ulster's position, the Chronicle says she has two alternatives, either to go into the Irish Free State retaining her present Belfast Parliament for its present purposes and enjoying certain other guarantees, or to remain exactly where she is, sending members still to the Parliament at Westminster and subject to no other authority save that conferred by last year's act on the Council of Ireland. In the latter event a boundaries' commission will modify the frontiers and certain matters arising out of the formation of the Irish Free State will be settled by negotiation between it and the Ulster Parliament.

Praises Lloyd George.

The Daily Express says:

"We may rejoice with little or no fear of our joy turning to bitter disillusion. The British peoples al lover the world will see to it that this settlement goes through, and in our own Parliament there will certainly be no difficulty.

"The Prime Minister has done many great things: none has been greater than this.

"Thus we emerge as a still united empire from darkness to light. We face the new future with fetters struck from our body politic. If God so wills, it shall be a time of true regeneration for us and for all men.'

The Daily Telegraph hails the signing of the agreement as the greatest event that has happened in the internal affairs of Great Britain for generations. It goes on:

"It is an accomplished fact that changes as if by magic the whole political prospect and bids us hope more confidently for a fortunate outcome from other difficulties that seem no more insoluble than did that of Ireland so short a time ago.

"We do not say, we may not think, that the path to the actual establishment of the Irish Free State will not run wholly smooth. One cannot expect miracles, but the ship has weathered the point of disaster, and with good pilotage will come to the harbor safe.

"The Prime Minister in signing this agreement has written his name among the greatest in our history. The achievement is his far more than any others. Today he stands on a peak of his attainment. Much as he may do for his country in the future, he can accomplish nothing greater than the curing of this deadliest of all its political troubles."

"Broad and Generous Conception."

The Daily News says:

"The British Government may fairly claim the respect which is due not merely to a broad and generous conception, but to the tact and patience and adroitness which alone could have surmounted the enormous difficulties in the way of its execution.

"The Prime Minister's talents have never been used to better purpose. It is the crowning triumph of his career as a diplomatist."

The Daily Mail says:

"This plan of Irish settlement establishes clearly before the world the British love of liberty and desired to extend it widely. An Ireland at peace within the empire is a consummation which we have long devoutly wished and which must have far-reaching effects and profoundly enhance the moral status of this country throughout the world."

The Westminster Gazette says:

"The Sinn Fein have consented to swear allegiance to the empire, which has imposed upon them as the price of freedom sufferings which it is impossible for them so soon to forget. Undoubtedly they are wise in their own interests to make the sacrifice, but that is no reason why its magnitude should be overlooked. In the circumstances it is a concession which outweighs all our concessions.

"The outstanding virtue of the terms of settlement is that they are independent of Ulster's consent. She may come in or she may stay out as she chooses."

The London Times says:

"Viewed as the world will view them, these are, indeed, fitting peace terms to mark the close of an age of discontent and mistrust and the beginning of a new era of happinqss and mutual understanding. They proclaim that the genius of the British nation for Government is not dead and that our statesmen have not lost the ancient secret of our national greatness."

Morning Post Is Critical

A discordant note in the chorus of praise comes from The Morning Post, which says: "A surrender is always a surrender and a betrayal a betrayal and a condonation of crime a participation in the sin of the criminal, though these things be called peaceful settlements and hopes for the future and dawning of a new era and so forth. The event of yesterday is but the culmination of the steady policy of yeilding to threats and of intriguing with rebels. It is is hailed as a co-triumph we wish we could join in these very natural, but deluded transports. * * *

"Never before in modern times has a British Government qualied before armed rebellion and organized assassination; acknowledged itself impotent to enforce English law and English justice and totally forsaken the loyal subjects of the King."

Criticising the terms of the settlement, The Morning Post says:

"The most important point to Great Britain is, we suppose, its effect upon the security of our country in war, because it is by the test of war that all statesmanship is tried. It is proposed to leave the defence of Ireland on land to an Irish army or militia. British forces, it would seem to follow, are to be withdrawn from Ireland, so that the only armed force in the south and west will be the present gunmen or their successors.

"How the harbors can be secured to our navy with an independent Irish army in occupation of the land behind we are bound to say we cannot comprehend, but if the position of Great Britain in Ireland is thus placed at the hazard of a hostile force, what of the case of the Loyalists in Ireland who have always lived in the belief that they have a right to the protection of the forces of the Crown? Are they now to be abandoned to the mercy of those who have up till now shown themselves their implacable enemies?

LONON, Dec. 6 (Associated Press).—The Manchester Guardian characterizes the settlement as a splendid achievement, reflecting the utmost credit on the patience and reasonableness of the negotiators, and that "it may frankly be admitted that only a coalition of the great Government parties could have carried it through."

This newspaper expresses the hope that Ulster for its own sake will come into the agreement, but says that whether it does or does not Ireland is secure and will certainly in due course include the whole of the Irish territory.

MOVED BY IRISH CLAIM.

Ireland Granted Recognition as an "Ancient Parent State."

BIRMINGHAM, Dec. 6 (Associated Press).—The Lord Chancellor, Lord Birkenhead, in an address here today, explaining the Irish settlement, said:

"One of the Irish delegates said across the conference table: 'You can not quite dismiss us and our claims and our history in that way. We, too, are an ancient parent State, and we have through the centuries flung our sons and our settlers into every corner of the habitable civilized globe.' That claim is true. That claim has modified the fundamental view which we have adopted and by which we stand."

In discussing the financial phases of the agreement, he said. "In matters of finance there again the Parliament to be set up is supreme in its own house. They [the Irish delegates] have recognized that it is necessary to strike a balance between this country and Ireland in financial matters. On such a balance being struck, they shall pay us a due proportion, having regard for any set-off or counterclaim they may think proper to put forward—a due proportion of our national debt and our expenditure on war The amount of this will be determined by arbitrators to be chosen from among the citizens of this country, and who, I hope, will include a distinguished colonial Judge.

"In the opinion of all my colleagues the interests of Ireland itself and of the empire as a whole will be forwarded. Should it become possible in the near future for the inhabitants of Northern Ireland to adhere to a general Parliament, which on matters not by existing legislation, reserved for the decision of the Northern Ireland Parliament alone still require decision and obviously affect the interests of Ireland taken as a unit and as a whole.

"The representatives from Sinn Fein are prepared to recommend to the Dail Eireann that the newly constituted Irish Free State shall not merely make a treaty of association with the British Empire but shall enter into the British Empire for all purposes. The fidelity of the Irish Free State to be constituted will be declared in plain, unequivocal language, in the constitution as created by this instrument, to the commonwealth of nations and to King George.

"The Dail will be summoned at an early date, and the terms will be placed before them. The terms will be placed before both houses of Parliament in the new year.

"If they do not assent, the people of England will have an early opportunity of deciding."

Lord Birkenhead, who was one of the signers of the epoch-making agreement, declared the conferees had made secure the safety of Great Britain and Ireland, and that they had put their names to a documents representing a sane and reasonable settlement.

KING IS "OVERJOYED."

Royal Congratulations Sent to Lloyd George on the Irish Settlement.

LONDON, Dec. 6.—King George telegraphed Prime Minister Lloyd George this afternoon the royal congratulations on the reaching of the Irish agreement. The message read:

"I am overjoyed to hear the splendid news you have just sent me. I congratulate you with all my heart on the successful termination of these difficult and protracted negotiations, which is due to the patience and conciliatory spirit which you have shown throughout, and I am indeed happy in some small way to have contributed by my speech in Belfast to this great achievement."

THINKS ULSTER WILL ACCEPT.

Earl Granard, Here, Pleased by the Irish Settlement.

Earl Granard, K. P., arrived yesterday on the White Star liner Olympic, accompanied by his cousin, Miss Violet M. de Trafford, to meet the Countess, who has been visiting her father, D. O. Mills. When he heard of the Irish settlement Earl Granard said:

"That is good news, although I have not heard the terms. From what I learned recently during my five weeks' stay in Ireland, I think Ulster will accept. The blockade had done a great deal of harm to trade in the north of Ireland. Belfast used to be the centre for shipping goods to England and abroad, but it has been doing practically nothing. This is one reason why I think Ulster will fall into line. The business people there are tired of the blockade and the political squabbling."

AUSTRALIANS REJOICE.

Irish Agreement Welcomed Enthusiastically by the Press.

Copyright, 1921, by The Chicago Tribune Co.

SYDNEY, Australia, Dec. 6.—The Irish settlement is enthusiastically received by the Australian press. The Telegraph says that no news could have been more welcome to the English-speaking world, and that the result will be beneficial to the whole empire, doing more to improve relations between Great Britain and the United States than all the speeches ever made.

The Herald says that Ireland has had a miraculous deliverance, and that nowhere is the news received with greater relief than in the dominions.

IRISH LEADERS HERE SEE NEW ERA DAWN

Settlement Hailed With Delight and With Praise for de Valera and Lloyd George.

SOME ANXIETY OVER ULSTER

Doheny Says American Sympathizers Used Influence to Soften Extreme Demands.

Prominent Americans who have been leaders in the movement to help Ireland in her struggle for freedom said last night they were pleased with the terms of settlement in so far as they had been able to study them. It was generally believed that the action of American sympathizers in exerting their influence in recent months for a moderate settlement had helped to prevent Sinn Fein leaders from holding out for a republic.

In this connection it was recalled that when Bryan L. Kennelly, banker and real estate operator and one of the trustees of St. Patrick's Cathedral, recently returned from a trip abroad he announced that he had advised Eamon de Valera that if a dominion form of government was not accepted by the Sinn Feiners Americans who had always contributed heavily to the Irish cause would withdraw their financial support.

Edward L. Doheny, President of the Mexican Petroleum Company and National President of the American Association for the Recognition of the Irish Republic, who has been a liberal financial supporter of the independence movement, said:

"It is only fair to say that the greater number of Americans having sympathies with the aspirations of the Irish people have tried to get them not to be too extreme.

Anxious Concerning Ulster.

"The accomplishment of the Irish Free State is what I have hoped for. I have had the utmost faith that the conference would result in it. I have believed that Lloyd George and his Ministry were sincerely working for a settlement, and knew that the aims of de Valera and his associates were the same. We were and are anxious about the attitude of Ulster, but we believe that a real conciliatory feeling pervades the political atmosphere over there and that even Ulster will eventually be satisfied or at least reconciled.

"It is a great event throughout the British Dominions, but nowhere more portentous than here in America. It removes the greatest obstruction to a frank and friendly intercourse between this country and Great Britain. It makes for a better feeling among the English-speaking peoples everywhere. It should have a beneficial and cohering effect upon the deliberations of the conferees now meeting in Washington.

"Perhaps the most glorious effect of the agreement is the peace which it brings to the war-wracked people of Ireland, the liberty it brings to thousands of prisoners and the chance it gives to all the people of that great country under the new system which will obtain."

New Era Dawns, Says Kennelly.

Bryan L. Kennelly, President of Bryan L. Kennelly, Inc., and Vice President of the Harriman National Bank, said:

"The congratulations of the entire world are due Eamon de Valera, the able Irish statesmen and those gallant patriots who stood by him during all the trying days of the past few years. They have won a great victory and no tribute can adequately do justice to their achievement.

"I see in their victory the early restoration of world-wide peace, the revival of world-wide commerce and the return of world-wide prosperity. dream of centuries has in part come true; the daring and sacrifice, the eloquence and appeals, and the sufferings and hopes of the Irish people have at last borne fruit. Many have been the willing feet that have followed the Irish cause, many have been the strong hand to defend it, and many have been the warm hearts to love and cherish and bless the land of a sturdy and useful and enduring race.

"In the establishment of an Irish Free State I see the dawn of a new era. I sense the coming of a new and better age. All honor and glory to those Irishmen who had the courage to enter the breach and the fortitude to see the peace negotiations through to a triumphant finish."

Ambiguous, Says Conboy.

Martin Conboy of the American Committee for Relief in Ireland said: "It is difficult to talk about the settlement, because the terms have not become fully known. Just what a Free State is is somewhat ambiguous without further information to judge by. It would appear that the negotiators have produced a form of government that is unique—a governmental institution diferent from anything that has hitherto been devised. The agreement apparently is acceptable to all the contracting parties, and apparently recognizes the right of Ireland to choose its own form of government. The most significant feature is that it is an implicit recognition of the right of determination."

Step Toward World Peace.

Major Eugene Kinkead, active leader of the American Association for the Recognition of the Irish Republic, said: "Any treaty entered into between Ireland and Great Britain and signed by Eamon de Valera, Michael Collins, Arthur Griffith and Robert Barton will vitalize in its operation the principle of government by the governed. I venture to predict that the people of Ireland, living under a government functioning in harmony with this basis American principle, will develop their latent industrial and commercial possibilities in a manner which will surprise the world. The artificial differences between the strong, energetic son of Ulster and the courageous, indefatigable South, will vanish with the removal of British intrigue from Ireland, and a new progressive and constructive force firmly attached in its every part to the doctrines of Christ will contribute to the world's civilization. The settlement of this international problem is the most forward step toward world peace since the signing of the armistice."

Judge Alfred J. Talley of the Court of General Sessions said: "Ireland's struggle and sacrifice amidst tremendous odds for the ideal of freedom has been an inspiration in these days of sordid materialism. For centuries she has been compelled by a persecution unparalelled in history to be a nation of exiles, and what has been Ireland's loss has been a rich contribution in statesmanship, in eloquence, in literature and art, in the bravery of her men and the virtue of her women, to the upbuilding of the other nations of the world, especially our own. These influences she can and now will devote to the welfare of her country and to the realization of her own destiny. America, which loves liberty, should rejoice the most at the return of Ireland to the family of free nations."

K. of C. Prayers Approved.

James A. Flaherty, Supreme Knight of the Knights of Columbus, said: "We feel that the prayers of the Knights of Columbus for a settlement of the Irish question have been approved. Until official word is received from Eamon de Valera no positive statement can be issued, but the reports from London indicate that the happy solution has been reached—that Ireland will receive autonomy to the fullest extent compatible with victorious membership in the hegemony known as the British Empire, which with the inclusion of Ireland, and upon that condition alone, becomes an association of free nations."

The Rev. John J. Wynn, editor of the Catholic Encyclopedia: "The patience and forebearance shown by the Sinn Fein and Cabinet parties to the conference will, no doubt, prevail with the third party to come peacefully into the same agreement. It is a lesson in peacemaking for all the world, and its happy termination comes auspiciously during our own disarmament conference and in this season of good-will."

"If an Irish settlement is made according to the published terms," said Dudley Field Malone, "Ireland will have the mastery of her affairs and the control of her economic and cultural life. Such a settlement would be a tribute to the genius and courage of Sinn Fein and to the good-will of the English people under the statesmanship of Lloyd George."

Morgan J. O'Brien Lauds Lloyd George.

Morgan J. O'Brien, a member of the American Committee for Relief in Ireland, said: "This extraordinary event, which is to settle a problem 700 years old, marks today as one of the greatest days in the history of the modern world. Four questions are practically settled with the disarmament conference coming to a successful close, the Near East problem practically settled, the German reparations question clearing up and Ireland made a free State. Lloyd George is one of the greatest men in history. He alone could solve the Irish question with his infinite tact and patience."

John W. Goff, former Justice of the Supreme Court and former Recorder, who is Vice President of the American Association for Recognition of the Irish Republic, refused to comment on the settlement, saying he did not know enough about it. John Devoy, editor of The Gaelic American, refrained from comment for the same reason.

Mgr. James W. Powers of All Saints' Roman Catholic Church, Vice President of the American Association for the Recognition of the Irish Republic, said: "It is a great victory. I believe the two nations will live together in peace and understanding. Ultimately, I believe that Ireland will get complete independence. The Ulster question will settle itself in time. I have absolute faith in President Eamon de Valera."

Great Victory, Kelly Asserts.

Major Michael Kelly of the Irish Veterans' Association said: "From the Irish fighting man's point of view the settlement is a great victory. It is due to the unconquerable spirit of the Irish race, which has at last prevailed. We are all happy to learn that a settlement has been reached and that peace reigns in Ireland. We have no doubt that the heritage of the Irish race will be safeguarded by President de Valera and his associates in the peace treaty that is to be signed."

Supreme Court Justice Daniel F. Cohalan, President of the Friendly Sons of St. Patrick and spokesman for the Friends of Irish Freedom, declined last night to comment, but said he might have something to say later. "I desire to wait until all the details have been made known," he said.

At a meeting of the Delaware Club of the Fourteenth Assembly District held last night in the clubhouse, at 320 East Seventy-second Street, more than eight hundred members enthusiastically approved a message of congratulation to be sent by cable to Eamon de Valera. The message, which was sent after the meeting by William C. Blaney, President of the club, follows:

"Congratulations. Your fight for freedom has been crowned with success."

A discordant note was sounded by the Irish-American Labor League in a statement issued through its secretary, Thomas J. O'Flaherty, saying it was up to the workers to set up Soviet republics in Ireland and Great Britain.

ULSTER RESERVED; DUBLIN REJOICES

Continued from Page 1, Column 7.

to treat Northern Ireland as one part of the British dominions should treat another, then the situation might be easier.

The Belfast News Letter says:

"There is one point which it will be difficult for the Northern Parliament to accept, and that is the revision of the boundaries of Northern Ireland by a commission. According to Lord Birkenhead, the basis on which this commission would proceed would be population, taking into consideration economic and geographical considerations. The counting of heads is not the only factor in the matter, and the boundaries question is one, to our mind, that Northern Ireland cannot agree to as it is disclosed in this settlement with the Sinn Fein."

Relief in South of Ireland.

Special Cable to THE NEW YORK TIMES.

DUBLIN, Dec. 6.—News that an agreement on the Irish question had been arrived at was received in Dublin and the country generally with astonishment. The public was certainly not prepared for the announcement, on the contrary, it was prepared for the worst. A semi-official report had been circulated in Dublin that the negotiations had broken down.

Astonishment that was still greater prevailed during the afternoon when an outline of the terms of settlement became known. Even de Valera, who returned to Dublin from Limerick today, when he learned from the newspapers of the over-night settlement, expressed surprise, but would make no statement.

A feeling of great relief pervades the city and there is much satisfaction that the terms are considered so wide and generous in their scope. The whole situation has so suddenly assumed a change within a few hours that the public cannot yet measure the full significance of the offer by Great Britain.

Gratification was apparent on all sides that the end of the long-drawn out struggle was at last within measurable distance of a great and amicable settlement. Hopes were expressed that no obstacles would now stand in the way of a consummation of Mr. Lloyd George's work.

Many messages reached here this evening from Cork, Limerick and other centres in the southwest and the Midlands, and also from many towns north of the Boyne, indicating that the news had been received with intense satisfaction.

Acceptance by Dail Expected.

Messrs. Dugan and Fitzgerald arrived in Dublin this evening from London, bringing with them the official draft of the terms. In well-informed circles it is confidently believed that the terms will be accepted by the Dail Eireann, a special session of which will be summoned immediately.

The Freeman's Journal says:

"Ireland needs no assurance that the terms are in harmony with the principles for which she stands. She was aware from the first that these principles contained no menace to the real interests of Great Britain. This fact appears at last to be clear to British statesmen. Ireland has given the strongest of all proofs of her will to peace. She looks to Lloyd George and his colleagues to do their part in insuring that the opposition of a fanatical minority shall no longer prevent peace with honor."

DUBLIN, Dec. 6.—The Irish Times says:

"If this treaty is ratified, if Irishmen of all creeds and parties combine and administer it in a spirit of broadminded patriotism, if it bridges the gap between the North and South, if it reconciles Ireland to the empire, it will be one of the most glorious and fruitful achievements of modern statesmanship; it will give the rising generation in Ireland scope for effort and prospects for happiness their fathers never knew."

COLLINS PROPOSES ALL-BRITISH LEAGUE

Sinn Fein Minister Asks if America Would Not Join Such a Group of Nations.

Special Cable to THE NEW YORK TIMES.

LONDON, Dec. 6.—In an article which he contributes to The Manchester Guardian, Michael Collins says:

"General Smuts has given warning that South Africa will be restive in any association which is not a league of free nations. The colonies can only be kept if they are themselves on a free and mutual footing, and if such footing is also conceded to Ireland as a free partner in the group. If Ireland were free all the component nations of the group would be bound more firmly together.

"Into such a league might not America be willing to enter? By doing so America would be on the way to secure the world ideal of free, equal and friendly nations on which her aspirations are so firmly fixed."

BOLAND THANKS AMERICANS.

Believes Agreement Will Be Received Here With Great Joy.

WASHINGTON, Dec. 6 (Associated Press).—Harry J. Boland, representative of the Provisional Irish Government in Washington, issued the following statement tonight upon the agreement reached in London:

"After centuries of conflict the Irish nation and the British have composed their differences. A treaty of peace has been signed and an agreement reached between the representatives of the Irish nation and the representatives of the British Empire—an agreement which restores Ireland to the comity of nations. The last phase of the conflict was serious and bloody. The determination of the Irish people to be free faced Great Britain with the alternative of an honorable peace or a war of extermination.

"The agreement will be submitted to the Parliaments of both nations for ratification. America has contributed in large measure to the present happy position by generous financial support given without stint, by many expressions of sympathy and support coming from Congress and from State Legislatures and by the organized opinion of liberty loving Americans.

"This great moral force was thrown behind the people of Ireland and was of incalculable benefit to them in their struggle. The support thus given was offered freely and we feel sure that the agreement reached between Britain and Ireland will be received in America with great joy. America can be assured that Ireland will not be ungrateful and will not forget the assistance she received from this generous land in her hour of trial."

SAYS PREMIER SHOWED IRISH FUTILITY OF ARMS

Knew Sinn Fein Would Not Negotiate Until it Had Tried Strength and Failed.

Special Cable to THE NEW YORK TIMES.

LONDON, Dec. 6.—"If we could look into the back of Mr. Lloyd George's mind," writes a contributor to The Daily Chronicle, who has had exceptional opportunities of performing such a feat, "we should probably find he is quite as proud of the settlement of the Irish question as he is of his part in winning the great war."

In the course of the article the writer makes a disclosure calculated to cause comment. Referring to Mr. Lloyd George's attempts to solve the Irish problem, he says:

"At the end of 1919 he took up the Irish question once more. By that time the situation had grown much worse. Sinn Fein had swept the board at the 1918 election. It had swallowed up every other movement in Southern Ireland. It was busily organizing on military lines.

"At Christmas Mr. Lloyd George introduced the 1919 Home Rule bill, basing it upon what he regarded as the three cardinal elements in the Anglo-Irish question: The impossibility of Great Britain agreeing to an Irish republic, repudiation by Nationalist Ireland of membership in the United Kingdom, and the refusal of Ulster to come into an all-Ireland Parliament.

"It was no secret to Mr. Lloyd George's associates that he doubted whether this act would succeed. He felt that Sinn Fein was out for a fight and would not and, indeed, could not consistently with its pledges and its principles negotiate until it had tried its strength and learned that it could not succeed in getting a republic by force of arms. In the light of the experience of the last six months it is difficult to say that Mr. Lloyd George was not right.

"Early in 1920 the Sinn Fein started on its campaign of unlimited violence. By July, 1920, it had succeeded in confining the police to a few large barracks and was practically in control of rural Ireland. The British Government was faced with the alternatives of surrender or new methods.

"Mr. Lloyd George, whose eye was always on an ultimate settlement, voted unhesitatingly against a policy of surrender and for a policy of standing up to the Sinn Fein with whatever weapons were necessary to defeat their attempt. Hence the policy of reprisals. From this time onward, the whole question in Mr. Lloyd George's mind was, when would the time come when all parties would be so tired of violence that a frame of mind would exist that would make an agreement possible? The struggle was protracted. The attempt to make a truce at Christmas failed.

"Then came the opening of the Northern Parliament by the King. Such an opportunity was not to be missed and the Government made the famous offer to Ireland on July 6 of a settlement on a dominion basis.'

POPE GREATLY PLEASED.

He Expresses Satisfaction Over the Irish Agreement.

WASHINGTON, Dec. 6 (Associated Press)—Pope Benedict, a message from Rome said today, expressed great satisfaction on learning that an agreement had been reached by the British and Sinn Fein delegates affording a basis for settlement of the Irish question.

The Irish struggle has been one of the greatest anxieties for the Pontiff, representatives of both sides having had active friends in Rome.

He did not conceal his sympathy with what he regarded as the just claims of the Irish people, but condemned the use of violence on both sides.

"All the News That's Fit to Print."

The New York Times.

THE WEATHER
Fair and cold today and Sunday; northwest winds.
Temperatures yesterday—Max. 35; min. 12.
For weather report see last page.

VOL. LXXII....No. 23,765. ••• NEW YORK, SATURDAY, FEBRUARY 17, 1923. TWO CENTS In Greater New York | THREE CENTS Within 200 Miles | FOUR CENTS Elsewhere

TUT-ANKH-AMEN'S INNER TOMB IS OPENED, REVEALING UNDREAMED OF SPLENDORS, STILL UNTOUCHED AFTER 3,400 YEARS

ESSEN IS COWED AFTER WOUNDING OF TWO SOLDIERS

Fight in Beer Hall Causes the French to Turn Out a Stronger Military Display.

CITY NOW WITHOUT POLICE

Chief Arrested, Men Disarmed and Records Seized—Frequent Clashes Elsewhere.

JAIL FOR 2 BURGOMASTERS

Electric Plant Director Is Fined 5,000,000 Marks—Berlin Supplies Funds for Strikers.

Special Cable to THE NEW YORK TIMES.

DUESSELDORF, Feb. 16.—Every day is adding more and more to the casualty list of the Ruhr occupation.

Last evening in a beer hall at Essen two French soldiers were slightly, and one German policeman gravely, wounded.

At Gunkenrath a French sentinel fired on and killed a German workman who was trespassing on the railroad track.

At several points last evening sentries and posts fired shots as warnings and with every rifle discharged the tension is growing.

The affair at Essen was the most important as affecting the situation in the town. It began, as trouble may at any time begin, trivially enough. Eight French soldiers and two Belgians went into the beer house and called for drinks about 9:30 in the evening. As usual the landlord refused to serve them and the soldiers, as has become their habit, began to draw beer themselves. In protest the landlord called in the German policeman on duty at the door, and, according to all accounts of both the Germans and the French, this policeman entered excitedly with his revolver in his hand crying "Hands up!"

At once the affair which had been a burlesque became serious. The French soldiers instead of obeying such a peremptory order began to draw their revolvers. Then the German fired. Before he could be overpowered he had wounded two men slightly and it was not till he fell with a bullet through his body that he stopped firing.

Attracted by the noise the German police patrol entered at that moment and prevented further fighting.

Police Headquarters Raided.

Today the affair had an aftermath. With armored cars and machine guns a detachment of French troops rode through the town and wheeled sharply into the police barracks before it was known what was intended. They arrested the chief of police, disarmed eighty men in the station and took possession of all records.

Everywhere throughout town patrols have been moving about all day, and as if in warning to the nationalist trouble makers, the French are displaying their strength.

Yesterday the town was silent, depressed and suspicious. Today it is cowed. The French have the whip hand and even the most ardent nationalist must admit it.

All through the province the measures of the French for repressing organized resistance and propaganda are increasing in severity. Over half the newspapers in the Ruhr have now been suspended for one cause or another, police who do not salute, being arrested in batches, and with every new batch the penalty is being increased.

To all this tightening up the Germans are making as yet no new reply. The telephones of Düsseldorf, Essen and several other places are still suspended.

At Bochum the municipal employes today struck for four hours as a protest against the arrests which have been made in the town and against the requisitioning of automobiles. The only return to work was at Duisburg, where the tramway employes have been granted a 110 per cent. increase in wages at a time when the mark is improving by leaps.

Yesterday for the first time the effect of the export prohibition order became apparent. As fewer freight trains are leaving the district fewer are coming in, and from 200 the number out and in has fallen to about 40. If that falling off continues a food shortage, which always threatened, may become a reality, and both the French and Germans are doing their utmost to deal with the situation when it arises, each with the hope that their efforts will rally the masses to their support. The Germans are organizing storage and distribution centres as if for a siege, and at the same time the French are accumulating all the food they can in the district. The number of military trains has been largely increased and food is being brought from France far in excess of what is needed by the troops.

To counter all this effort to obtain local support among the workers the Germans have now nearly completed their arrangements for payment of workers forced out of employment by the prohibition of exports. Big firms are prepared themselves to stand a loss, but to small firms the Government, through the Employers' Association and the Reichsbank, is prepared to give all the help that is needed. The total wages roll which it is estimated will have to be met is something like 50,000,000 gold marks a month, and the Government, which in November last asked for a moratorium in reparation payments, seems now prepared to pay this sum to workmen in order to support resistance to the French. So far there has, however, been little or no closing down, and except at the coalpits where little or nothing is being done except for repairs and local consumption work, the Ruhr seems almost normal.

Quick Retaliation by French.

ESSEN, Feb. 16 (Associated Press).—Following the wounding of two French soldiers by German security police in a café brawl last night, Essen was the

Continued on Page Three.

89 M. P.'s Ask Harding's Aid; 'One Hope of Saving Europe'

By Wireless to THE NEW YORK TIMES.

LONDON, Feb. 16.—Signed by eighty-nine Labor and Co-operative members of the British Parliament, the following cablegram was sent to President Harding today:

"America with Britain unwittingly made France's present destructive action possible. We appeal for American co-operation today as the one hope of saving Europe."

Among those who have signed the message are Arthur Henderson, George Lansbury, R. E. Buxton and John Hodge.

$500,000 GEM THEFT SUSPECT ARRESTED

"Marshall" Held as Leader of Gang That Robbed Mrs. Schoellkopf at Drinking Party.

CAUGHT ON MONTREAL TRAIN

Another Arrest Here Said to Have Furnished Clue—Companion Also in Custody.

Inspector John D. Coughlin at Police Headquarters last night announced that the debonair "Marshall," alleged leader of the gang that robbed Mrs. Irene Schoellkopf of $500,000 worth of jewelry in an apartment at 64 West Fifty-second street early on the morning of Jan. 1, had been arrested yesterday on a train between Schenectady and Troy. The arrest was made by Detectives Daly, Horan and Buckley of Inspector Coughlin's staff. They caught "Marshall" when he was attempting to return from Montreal and took him to a house at 73 Lancaster Street, Albany, which he said was his home, to look for the stolen jewels. The detectives reported to Inspector Coughlin by telephone from the Lancaster Street house that they had not found the booty.

The man alleged to be "Marshall" was traveling under the name of M. D. Biddulph. According to the police, his full name is Matthew Darian Biddulph. The police say that he is an ex-convict, and that he is known to the police all over the country under the aliases of R. H. Matthews, R. H. Harrison and John F. Derby. According to the police, his photograph is No. 17,553 in the Rogues' Gallery at San Francisco, and he has been arrested many times, and convicted several times.

Inspector Coughlin said the man was wanted in Los Angeles and San Francisco on the charge of passing worthless checks.

Search of the records at Police Headquarters last night showed that "Marshall" had been arrested for passing a worthless check at the Yale Club in New York City in 1917, but had got off with a suspended sentence.

"Marshall," when arrested, said he was 27 years old and gave his occupation as traveling salesman and actor. Under the name of Biddulph, Inspector Coughlin said, the man had had some success as a moving picture actor, appearing in Universal photoplays. By a coincidence, the last film in which he is known to have appeared was called "Wanted at Headquarters," in which he played a "heavy" part—in other words played a movie villain. This was in 1919.

Companion Also Arrested.

The detectives arrested with "Marshall," a man who identified himself as George F. Daley of 83 Clinton Street, Albany. As far as known, Daley had no connection with the Schoellkopf case, but the police are holding him to investigate why he was traveling with "Marshall." Daley is said to be a New York billposter, with an address in the vicinity of Broadway and 82d Street.

The arrest of "Marshall" and Daley followed a few hours after Horan, one of the detectives who made these arrests, had locked up a man named Charles Curtis in New York. Horan and his partner, Detective Owens, have been detached from all other duty to work exclusively on the Schoellkopf case for several weeks. In the line-up at Police Headquarters yesterday morning, Horan and Owens recognized Curtis, who had been arrested as a suspect in another case, as a man they had been looking for as a friend of one of "Marshall's" alleged confederates in the Schoellkopf robbery.

Curtis was released from the charge on which he was first held, but Horan immediately rearrested him on the charge of suspicion of burglary in another jewel theft—the robbery of Mrs. Lillian Myers of $50,000 worth of jewels in her apartment at 300 West Forty-ninth Street on July 21 last. Curtis is believed to have given the information on which Horan and the other

Continued on Page Six.

ANDERSON ENRICHED BY REALTY TRADING, IS STORY TO PECORA

Prosecutor Quotes Him as Saying $24,700 Came, in Currency, From Deals.

CONTRADICTS HIS AFFIDAVIT

Report to Anti-Saloon Directors in 1919 That Money Came From Loans Is Recalled.

GRAND JURY MOVE HINTED

Inquiry Will Be Pressed "in Some Other Way," Brackett Is Warned in Letter.

In a letter to ex-Senator Edgar T. Brackett, counsel for William H. Anderson, State Superintendent of the Anti-Saloon League, Acting District Attorney Ferdinand Pecora yesterday indicated that unless Mr. Anderson answered questions relating to the source and expenditure of the publicity fund of $24,700, he would take Grand Jury action. Mr. Pecora's letter was in reply to a reiteration by Mr. Brackett that Mr. Anderson should not submit replies to questions pertaining to the fund, details of which Mr. Anderson professes to have withheld from the Board of Directors of the League.

Intimating that he questioned the accuracy of statements made by Mr. Anderson, Mr. Pecora disclosed that Mr. Anderson had asserted he had obtained the money through realty investments negotiated by a friend at a time when he was earning $4,000 a year as an official of the League in Maryland. Mr. Pecora quoted Mr. Anderson as saying that the profits were in excess of $24,700, the sum which he alleged he had loaned the League here for its work when the necessary expenditures exceeded the income. Mr. Pecora pointed out that Mr. Anderson was unable to give the location of any of the realty and declined to divulge the name of his investor friend. Mr. Anderson told the Acting District Attorney that he had received the profits in currency, which he placed in his safe rather than in a bank, according to the letter to Senator Brackett.

Text of Pecora's Letter.

Mr. Pecora's letter follows:

Feb. 16, 1923.

Hon. Edgar T. Brackett, 120 Broadway, New York City.

Dear Senator Brackett:

Much as I regret your adherence to your advice to Mr. Anderson to refuse to answer certain questions which I have asked him as to the sources from which he obtained the sum of $24,700.00, which he claims to have expended on behalf of the Anti-Saloon League during the years 1913 and 1914, and details of such expenditure, I recognize fully your unquestioned right to advise him as his counsel in such manner as you may deem to be in accordance with his own interests.

You express the view that it would seem grotesque to base any prosecution of Mr. Anderson on the facts which have been shown. You also recognize that the ascertainment of the sources from which Mr. Anderson obtained the $24,700, and the methods by which he expended the same, properly comes within the scope of the inquiry which this office is making in so far as light may be shed on the question as to whether the representations which Mr. Anderson made to the Directors of the league in connection therewith are true or false.

In connection with his expenditure of $24,000, Mr. Anderson has declared to me, among other things, that the monies were paid out by him in currency from time to time to certain persons whose identities he will not disclose; that these payments were made for publicity work on behalf of the league; that he has no vouchers or written records of any kind which would show the respective dates and specific amounts of such payments, and that he cannot from memory give such data; that he cannot produce a single copy or piece of printed matter that was used in such publicity work; that all of said monies came from his personal means which he did not keep in any bank or other such depositary, but which he kept in a safe in the office of the respective headquarters of the league in the States of Maryland and New York; and that he made such expenditures upon his own initiative and judgment; and without his having consulted the Board of Directors of the league in New York with regard to them.

Tried to Trace Money.

In view of the unusual circumstances under which, according to his own statements, Mr. Anderson made

Continued on Page Four.

Idaho Assembly Bars Japanese From Leasing Any Lands There

BOISE, Idaho, Feb. 16.—The Assembly of the Legislature, by a vote of 54 to 6, today passed a measure to prohibit the leasing of lands in the State to Japanese. The measure, according to its author, Representative Gillis, while aimed primarily at the Japanese, is applicable to all aliens.

Speaking to the Assembly, Representative Gillis said he feared an influx of Japanese and other aliens to Idaho through refusal of the Federal Government to re-lease land now occupied in Washington, and because of other States passing anti-leasing laws.

ENGINEER AMBUSHED AND SLAIN AT DOOR

Earl Remington of Los Angeles, Who Made Planes in War, Is Found Dead in Driveway.

WIFE ASLEEP IN THE HOUSE

Victim, Shot as He Stepped From Automobile, Met Death He Had Feared.

LOS ANGELES, Feb. 16.—Earl Remington, wealthy electrical engineer, found dead from gunshot wounds in the yard of his home here early today, had lived in fear of death for the last week, according to his wife, who was so prostrated with grief that she could not be seen until late today.

Two persons took active parts in the slaying of Remington, according to police conclusions announced late tonight.

Mrs. Remington said her husband had been acting strangely and showed extreme nervousness. Noises outside the house, particularly at night, seemed to distress him, she said. Remington had offered their home, which is in an exclusive residential district, for sale, the widow stated, but had instructed her never to permit any stranger to enter the house.

Although Remington telephoned to his wife yesterday that he was going to their ranch near Chino and would not return until late, it has been established, according to the police, that he did not go to the ranch.

Detectives are attempting to trace his movements yesterday in the hope of finding some clue to the slaying. They stated they had found two friends of the dead man who said they saw him at 5 o'clock yesterday afternoon.

That Remington was slain by some one having a grudge against him is the opinion expressed by the detectives.

Whether an attempted burglary of the office of the safe company of which Remington was the head, on Oct. 15, 1922, had anything to do with the engineer's death also is being investigated. Two of the company's safes were broken into, according to a report, but nothing of value was taken. The police are working on the theory that papers may have been taken at that time which were used later in a blackmailing plot against Remington.

Remington evidently was murdered at about last midnight. A dozen neighbors heard the fatal shot, and his wife lay sleeping within a few feet of him; but the body was not found until 6 o'clock this morning, when Charity Dawson, a negro maid, started downstairs to light the gas heating plant of the house at 1,400 South St. Andrews Street; a fashionable neighborhood.

There was a trail of blood on the driveway and a riddled leather portfolio which Remington had carried. The maid called Mrs. Remington, and the whole neighborhood was soon aroused by their screams.

Remington left his offices early in the afternoon for a trip to his Chino ranch. He was not seen thereafter by either employes or family until his body was found. He rang up his wife at 3:30 P. M. and told her he was going to Chino, according to the maid.

Remington, the police believe, drew up in his Ford coupé at the side of his house, perhaps at the order of his assailant. He stepped around to the back of the car, shifting the leather portfolio now high, now low, in front of his body in an effort to shield himself.

There was a loud report, perhaps two. One charge from the shotgun tore its way to the engineer's heart.

As he staggered away from the machine he fell on his back, arms spread out.

Mrs. Remington, according to the maid, did not hear the report of the gun. As her husband lay dying she was asleep in a bedroom in the northeast corner of the house, directly above the driveway. From her window she could have looked down on the struggle.

Neighbors playing cards heard the shots but thought they were automobile engines backfiring, or tires exploding. If the Remington dog had not been chloroformed for rabies about two weeks ago, the engineer might still be alive, according to the maid. She believes the dog might have awakened the family. Remington had no children.

"The motive may have been robbery, it may have been revenge," said Detective Sergeant Cline after talking with Mrs. Remington.

Remington was Vice President of the International Electric Protective Association, and had a wide reputation as a safe and bank designer.

Aviation was his sporting diversion, and he was adept at stunt flying. During the war he organized and was general manager of an aviation company here.

Charge Hawaiian Coolie Labor Plot.

Special to The New York Times.

WASHINGTON, Feb. 16.—Charges were made today by the Executive Council of the American Federation of Labor that for two years there had been an intensive agitation for the importation of 50,000 Chinese coolies into the Hawaiian Islands, where they would be placed under bond making them "debt slaves" for five years or less if they became rebellious. The council instructed the Federation's legislative representatives to do all in their power to prevent any enactment of laws that would in any degree open the gates to this character of immigration.

SENATE APPROVES BRITISH DEBT BILL; FINAL VOTE, 70-13

46 Republicans, 24 Democrats Favor It—Borah Among the Four Republicans Opposed.

BITTER DEBATE TO FINISH

Many Assail "British Victory," but Glass Wins Applause by Recalling Allies' Sacrifices.

ONLY ONE AMENDMENT

Settlements With Other Allies Must Have Congress Approval—Bill Now Goes to Conference.

Special to The New York Times.

WASHINGTON, Feb. 16.—The Senate passed the British Debt Refunding bill tonight by a vote of 70 to 13, forty-six Republicans and twenty-four Democrats voting to ratify the settlement as agreed to by the Debt Funding Commission, while nine Democrats and four Republicans were recorded in favor of repudiating the settlement.

The final roll-call was ordered at 7:20 o'clock tonight. The Administration victory was much more impressive than had been anticipated, it having been predicted that between fifteen and twenty Senators would oppose the bill when the vote on passage was reached.

The measure passed with only one amendment—that proposed by Senator Robinson of Arkansas, which gives to Congress the right to pass on settlements that may be arrived at in the future with other debtor nations. An amendment to equalize the interest rates and require Great Britain to pay the same interest as the United States itself pays on the loan was defeated, 61 to 21.

It is expected that the House will promptly accept the Robinson amendment and that the bill will be in the hands of the President early next week.

All efforts to amend the bill with regard to interest rates or in other important particulars were signally defeated. An amendment proposed by Senator Harris of Georgia, which authorizes the appointment of three Democrats on the Funding Commission, would undoubtedly have carried, but was withdrawn when the Republican leaders promised to give this matter early consideration when it is presented to the Senate in the form of an independent bill. The Republicans appear as anxious as some of the Democrats to have the minority share the responsibility of adjusting the more than $11,000,000,000 debt now due this country by its former associates in the European war.

Sharp Debate Continued All Day.

Eight lively hours preceded the passage of the bill. At times the debate was spirited to the point of bitterness, but the clean-cut Administration victory was never in doubt. The defeat of the Hitchcock amendment to maintain the British interest charges at a rate as high as rates paid by this Government and a speech by Senator Glass of Virginia broke the back of the opposition. The impassioned plea of the Virginia Senator for favorable action and his fervid defense of Great Britain came near the close of the long day. When Senator Glass concluded it appeared for a minute or two as if the session might have to suspend while Senators, Republicans as well as Democrats, pressed forward to shake his hand and congratulate him.

The leaders of the opposition were La Follette, Reed of Missouri, McKellar, Heflin, Trammell and Norris, while Smoot, Lenroot, Glass and Underwood commanded the defending forces. La Follette made the longest of all the speeches, a carefully prepared utterance in which he denounced Secretary Mellon, ridiculed the President and assailed the majority membership of the Finance Committee for what he charged was its undue and unwarranted haste in rushing the bill to a final vote.

The last day arguments of the opposition were based principally on the claim that the United States, in agreeing to fix the interest Great Britain will pay at 3 per cent. for the first ten and 3½ per cent. for the remaining fifty-two years, had, in fact, canceled what they claimed was approximately $1,666,000,000 of the interest charges.

La Follette Ridicules Harding.

Opening the debate, Senator La Follette recalled the White House dinner of a year ago, which was attended, among others, by J. Pierpont Morgan, Charles H. Sabin and Secretary Mellon, all of them, declared the Wisconsin Senator, of the international banking group.

Continued on Page Five.

KING TUT-ANKH-AMEN,
wearing the crown and royal vestments, as he appeared to his contemporaries. From a multi-colored decoration on the walls of the tomb of Huy, his Viceroy, discovered some years ago near the tomb of the King.
Courtesy Metropolitan Museum of Art.

KING IN NEST OF SHRINES

Series of Ornate Covers Enclose Pharaoh's Sarcophagus.

WHOLE FILLS LARGE ROOM

Mortuary Chamber Opens Into Another Room, Crowded With Great Treasure.

EXPLORERS ARE DAZZLED

Wealth of Objects of Historic and Artistic Interest Exceeds All Their Wildest Visions.

Special Cable to THE NEW YORK TIMES.

LUXOR, Egypt, Feb. 16.—This has been, perhaps, the most extraordinary day in the whole history of Egyptian excavation. Whatever any one may have guessed or imagined of the secret of Tut-ankh-Amen's tomb, they surely cannot have dreamed the truth as now revealed.

The entrance today was made into the sealed chamber of the tomb of Tut-ankh-Amen, and yet another door opened beyond that. No eyes have yet seen the King, but to practical certainty we know that he lies there close at hand in all his original state, undisturbed.

Moreover, in addition to the great store of treasures which the tomb has already yielded, today has brought to light a new wealth of objects of artistic, historical, and even intrinsic value which is bewildering.

It is such a hoard as the sanguine excavator can hardly have pictured, even in visions in his sleep, and puts Lord Carnarvon's and Mr. Carter's discovery in a class by itself and above all previous finds.

Official Opening Sunday.

Though the official opening of the sealed mortuary chamber of the tomb has been fixed for Sunday, it was obviously impossible to postpone until then the actual work of breaking in the entrance. This was a job involving some hours of work, because it had to be done with the greatest care, so as to keep intact as many of the seals as possible, and also to avoid injury to any of the objects on the other side which might be caused by the falling of material dislodged.

All this could not be done on Sunday while the official guests were kept waiting in the singularly unpleasant atmosphere of the tomb, so an agreement was made with the Egyptian authorities by which the actual breaking through of the wall should be done in their presence today.

Consequently, Howard Carter was very busy inside the tomb all morning with Professor Breasted and Dr. Alan Gardiner, whose assistance has been invaluable from the beginning of the work of examining seals and deciphering and copying inscriptions of all kinds. They had finished by noon, and the tomb was closed till after luncheon, at which Lord Carnarvon, Mr. Carter and Lady Evelyn Herbert entertained all those invited to be present today.

Official Story of Inner Tomb.

It was after 1 o'clock when the official party entered the tomb, and the operation was begun which was to result in such astounding discoveries, of which I am able to give the following authoritative description:

Today between the hours of 1 and 3 in the afternoon the culminating moment in the discovery of Tut-ankh-Amen's tomb took place when Lord Carnarvon and Howard Carter opened the inner sealed doorway in the presence of Lady Evelyn Herbert, Abdel Hamid Salimân Pasha, Under Secretary of Public Works; Pierre Lacau, Director General of the Antiquities Department; Sir William Garstin, Sir Charles Cust; Mr. Lythgoe, the curator of the Metropolitan Museum of Art of New York; Mr. Winlock, Director of the

GOV. REILY RESIGNS PORTO RICO OFFICE

Tells President Ill Health Forbids Him to Resume Executive Duties.

HAD BEEN LONG UNDER FIRE

Offended by His Inaugural Address, Unionists Made Many Charges Against Him.

WASHINGTON, Feb. 16 (Associated Press).—The resignation of E. Mont Reily as Governor of Porto Rico was received at the White House early this evening, but no announcement was made concerning it, although there was every indication that it would be accepted.

The text of the cablegram of resignation, as made public at the White House, follows:

Hon. Warren G. Harding, President of the United States:

On account of very serious injury while in the States, my trip to Porto Rico prostrated me, and I have been confined to my bed since, not being able to resume my official duties. My physicians inform me it will be several months before I can recover and I must have complete change and rest, free from all care. This being the case, I feel that I should resign and look after my health first.

I would like for my resignation to become effective April 1, believing that by that time I will be able to travel, and if I am not can be taken to a hospital here until I am able to do so.

In offering my resignation, I cannot do so without expressing to you and Secretary Weeks my appreciation of the unfailing loyalty and support you have both continually given to me in my arduous and trying work here.

Your recent statement to me that you were for me 100 per cent. had its echo in the great demonstration tendered me on my return, and shows that the work of your Administration in Porto Rico has not been in vain, but has been appreciated. It was a complete vindication of our American policies instituted in the islands two years ago.

A delegation composed of men of all political parties called on my Secretary yesterday, requesting that I withhold my resignation until you could be communicated with. I have notified them my resignation was irrevocable. Ninety per cent. of the people of the Island are for you and the things you stand for, and are pleading that no backward step be taken in-

Continued on Page Five.

GOETHALS DEMANDS COAL FOR UP-STATE

"We Want Action, Not Conferences," He Says in Message to Federal Fuel Distributer.

SEIZURE IS THREATENED

Insists Shipments to Canada Be Diverted—People Will Get Coal, He Asserts.

General George W. Goethals, State Fuel Administrator, serving notice on the Federal Fuel Distributer that "we want action, not conferences" for the relief of suffering localities in Northern New York, suggested in two telegrams yesterday immediate authorization by the Federal officials of drastic relief measures.

Diversion to up-State towns of coal now moving to Canada, priority of New York shipments over shipments to Canada and seizure of cars en route to Canada were some of the measures suggested.

"The people in that part of the State are going to get coal," General Goethals asserted in making public the telegrams. "I am awaiting action from Washington on the telegrams. In case I don't get it, I am not saying what I am going to do."

The seizure of one car of coal consigned to Canada for use of the Saratoga Springs Hospital was authorized yesterday by the shipper, John F. Bermingham, President of the Lackawanna Coal Company. General Goethals called this to the attention of F. R. Wadleigh, Federal Fuel Distributer, in one of his telegrams and asked why the Government could not require the Delaware & Hudson Railroad "to supply our needs."

Reports from Mr. Kilmer to the State Fuel Administration offices yesterday were that people up-State were "on the point of taking coal off the tracks." The people were ready "to take the law in their own hands," he stated and added that "no juries in the afflicted communities would ever vote for conviction."

Predictions of epidemics from influenza and pneumonia unless coal arrived at some of the up-State points today were made by Mr. Kilmer.

General Goethals told reporters that priority must be given both to an emergency shipment of 20,000 tons, which is required immediately, and to future regular allotments.

Schools at many points in the Saratoga district have been closed for lack of fuel, reports to the State Fuel Administration said. Two schools in Corinth have been closed, and unless some coal arrives before Monday, or the school authorities can get some wood, the high school also will close. The school at Schuylerville was ordered closed yesterday for an indefinite period because of the lack of fuel.

Louis Cohen, a landlord of 514 West 152d Street, was sentenced to thirty days in the workhouse in the Court of Special Sessions yesterday for failing to supply sufficient heat and hot water for the house at 522 West 146th Street.

Probation officers reported that the building was badly in need of repairs. Window panes were out and doors were loose, they said, and the temperature recently had been several degrees below the legal minimum.

Mrs. Bertha Becker, who owns a building at 324 West 151st Street, was fined $250 on a similar charge in Special Sessions.

Won't Stop Coal to Canada.

WASHINGTON, Feb. 16.—The proposal for an embargo on anthracite exports, especially to Canada, has been carefully considered and definitely abandoned, it was said today at the White House.

In the view of high Government officials an embargo would have no material effect on the coal shortage which is being experienced in sections of New York and New England.

Doctor and Chauffeur Killed When Train Wrecks Ambulance at Jersey Grade Crossing

A fatal grade crossing accident occurred last evening at Hackensack, N. J., where a train running forty miles an hour, on the New Jersey and New York branch of the Erie Railroad, smashed into an ambulance, crushing a hospital interne and a chauffeur to death. James Reape, 38 years old, of 90 Nassau Street, Brooklyn, the chauffeur, was instantly killed. Dr. Louis Nishawitz, 25, of 830 Kelly Street, the Bronx, an interne at the Hackensack General Hospital, was mortally injured. His skull was fractured and his left leg and right arm were cut off. He died in the hospital half an hour after the accident. The ambulance was wrecked.

Dr. Nishawitz lost his life in the performance of his duty, as he was answering a call to take a sick woman to the hospital from her home on Hudson Street, Hackensack. After the accident a second ambulance was sent for the woman, but the delay had been fatal, and she was dead on its arrival.

The accident occurred about 5:50 P. M. at the Essex Street crossing. The train was a Haverstraw express, carrying commuters from New York.

Owing to a sharp curve south of Essex Street, the engineer could not see the crossing until he was close to it. The crossing gates should have been lowered, but were not. John Burke of Pearl River, N. Y., the gate tender, said the gates were frozen and out of commission. According to Burke, he stood in the middle of the road and swung a red lantern, but the ambulance driver did not heed. Burke was arrested on a technical charge of manslaughter.

Dr. Nishawitz was the son of Max Nishawitz, a shoe merchant in the Bronx. The physician was a graduate of De Witt Clinton High School and the Long Island College Hospital.

Harding Threatens to Cut Shipping Fleet Unless Congress Passes the Subsidy Bill

WASHINGTON, Feb. 16.—The Administration Shipping bill was restored tonight to its former place as the unfinished business of the Senate, after having been laid aside since early in the week to allow consideration of the British debt settlement legislation. This was done on motion of Senator Jones of Washington after advocates of the measure had demonstrated their superior strength by voting down, 38 to 30, a motion by Senator Robinson of Arkansas to adjourn.

The vote on adjournment was not regarded as an accurate test of the strength of the forces supporting and opposing the Shipping bill, as several Senators on both sides were absent.

Opposition of the shipping measure are expected, when the Senate meets tomorrow, to counter with a proposal to lay the bill aside again in favor of the Capper Truth-in-Fabrics bill, and it was considered possible that a test vote on the merchant marine legislation may result.

Although the future of the subsidy bill in the Senate has not been clearly indicated in the face of claims and counter-claims on the possibility of its passage, it was said at the White House today that President Harding would not call a special session of Congress to consider the merchant marine situation if the Shipping bill should fail.

Mr. Harding was said to feel that the necessity for action looking to a solution of the shipping problem had been clearly demonstrated, and to have reached the decision that if the Shipping bill is not enacted the Government will proceed at once to take such steps as will diminish in a very great degree the present losses of the Government's fleet.

Detailed reports on the operation of Shipping Board vessels, showing net losses on individual voyages running as high as $100,000, had been studied by the President and his advisers, it was said, and the consensus of opinion was that the losses would be wiped out under the necessary economies which would follow the return of the shipping to private ownership.

Egyptian expedition of the Metropolitan Museum, together with other representatives of the Government.

The process of opening this doorway, bearing the royal insignia and guarded by the protective statues of the King, had taken several hours of careful manipulation under the intense heat. It finally ended in a wonderful revelation, for before the spectators was the resplendent mausoleum of the King, a spacious and beautifully decorated chamber completely occupied by an immense shrine covered with gold inlaid with brilliant blue faience. This beautiful wooden construction towers nearly to the ceiling and fills the great sepulchral hall within a short span of its four walls. Its sides are adorned with magnificent religious texts and fearful symbols of the dead and it is capped with a superb cornice and a tyrus molding like the propylaeum of a temple, in fact, indeed, the sacred monument.

Another Shrine Within.

On the eastern end of this shrine are two immense folding doors, closed and bolted. Within it, is yet another shrine, closed and sealed, bearing the cipher of the Royal Necropolis. On this inner shrine hangs the funerary pall, studded with gold, and by the evidence of the papyrus of Rameses IV. there must be a series of these shrines within, covering the remains of the King lying in the sarcophagus.

Around the outer canopy, or shrine, stand great protective emblems of a mystic type finely carved and covered with gilt, and upon the floor lie seven oars for the King's use in the waters of the other world.

In the further end of the eastern wall of this sepulchral hall is yet another doorway, open and never closed. It leads to another chamber, the store chamber of the sepulchre. There at the end stands an elaborately and magnificently carved and gilded shrine of indescribable beauty. It is surmounted by tiers of uraei and its sides are protected by open-armed goddesses of the finest workmanship, their pitiful faces turned over their shoulders toward the invader. This is no less than the receptacle for the four canopic jars which should contain the viscera (brain, heart, &c.) of the King.

Immediately at the entrance to this chamber stands the jackal god Anubis, in black and gold, upon his shrine, which again rests upon a portable sled, strange and resplendent. Behind this again is the head of the bull, emblem of the underworld.

Stacked on the south side of the chamber in great numbers are black boxes and shrines of all shapes, all closed and sealed, save one with open doors in which are golden effigies of the King standing upon black leopards. Similarly at the end of the chamber are more of these cases, including miniature coffins, sealed, but no doubt containing funerary statuettes of the monarch, servants for the dead in the coming world. On the south side of the deity Anubis is a tier of wonderful ivory and wooden boxes of every shape and design, studded with gold and inlaid with faience, and beside them yet another chariot.

This sight is stupendous and its magnificence indescribable, and as the time was fast creeping on, and dusk was falling, the tomb was closed for further action and contemplation.

The foregoing narrative is necessarily hasty and may be subject to correction in details as a result of future investigation. The truth is that all those who were privileged to share in today's unparalleled experiences were and still are so bewildered that it is not easy for any of them to give a consecutive narrative. All, however, agree in describing as overwhelming the impression produced by the discovery of the great shrine, or canopy, splendid in its blue and gold and almost filling the entire space of the new chamber.

Observer Gives More Details.

Another informant gave me the following further particulars:

"As soon as it was possible to see through the opening which was being made by Mr. Carter and Mr. Callender it became evident that some large obstacle blocked the way inside. It looked like a screen of gold inlaid with blue, in the decoration of which I noticed the well-known so-called buckle of Isis.

"In fact, it was the great shrine, or canopy, or tabernacle, or whatever you call it, made of wood, carved and gilded, and almost filling up the entire interior of the new chamber. It reached nearly to the ceiling and the space between it and the walls at the sides may have been eighteen inches. That is quite enough to permit the passage of the old Egyptian workmen and others scantily clad and slimmer than we of today, but it was narrow for us to squeeze through in our clothes.

"On entering one turned to the right, which would be to the north, and then along the east side, the passage being still as narrow as at first. I noticed that the interior of the walls of the chamber were decorated, but the painting has much deteriorated and looked to me of inferior quality. The door into the shrine, or tabernacle, is in the eastern side and has heavy bronze hinges and was opened with some difficulty. When opened it only showed another wooden wall or screen, being the exterior of a second inner tabernacle, a box inside a box.

"The interior faces of the wall of the outer tabernacle are all carved and decorated with religious texts, and so far the outer face of the inner tabernacle is similarly gilded and decorated, and I can make no attempt to describe the feelings of awe, wonder and mystery with which the spectacle inspired one.

"On the door of the inner tabernacle the original seals seem yet unbroken. The robbers do not appear to have penetrated it. We made no attempt to open it today, simply because it was impossible. Apparently the inner door will not be opened until the outer wall is removed. It must have been shut and sealed and the outer wall then erected around it. It will, therefore, I conjecture, be necessary to pull down the outer screening wall before the inner shrine is opened. This will be quite an undertaking in the narrow space.

"Among the individual objects I noticed besides the oars, or paddles, for the use of the deceased in the hereafter, were some alabaster vases, seemingly of the finest quality, and a piece of some sort of jewelry lying huddled on the floor, where one may suppose they had been thrown by robbers."

From the foregoing it will be evident that we have really arrived at the sepulchre of an old Egyptian King unviolated by robbers and undisturbed through 3,000 years. In the official narrative given above, reference is made to the papyrus of Ramses IV. Egyptologists will remember that this papyrus gives a sketch of the ground plan of the tomb, which shows the resting place of the sarcophagus to be inside a series of concentric boxes, or tabernacles, painted to imitate wood, precisely such as was found today.

Of Great Historic Interest.

The historical interest of the discovery is, therefore, enormous.

What also may be taken as reasonably certain is that the construction of these successive tabernacles, which successfully baffled the ancient robbers, makes the immediate opening of them impossible. The actual sight of King Tut-ankh-Amen where he lies will have to be postponed to some time indefinite. The period of his long and lonely watch is not yet ended.

Each of those who entered today is enthusiastic, if rather incoherent, in admiration of the new hoard of articles lying in the further chamber. This is merely a room hewn out of the rock, never having had a door built in it. So it has always been open to access from the chamber containing the tabernacles. The view, therefore, of its contents is unobstructed.

What especially struck all who saw it was the shrine spoken of above with the four guardian goddesses, all with their faces turned to the entrance as if pleading not to be disturbed. The workmanship of this is most beautiful. The greatest admiration is also expressed for some alabaster vases, said to be much lovelier even than the lovely ones formerly discovered. They are apparently white, not having become yellow by age. The statuettes and so forth seen are undoubtedly of the greatest beauty and value, while the number of unopened boxes with their seals unbroken give promise of an unprecedented harvest of precious things.

Great Problem Faces Discoverers.

With the contents of the annex to the outer chamber still awaiting attention added to this new and amazing store of wonders the mere embarrassment of riches confronts Lord Carnarvon and Mr. Carter with a serious problem, even though no attempt is made to touch for awhile the tabernacle of the King. The immensity of the whole thing makes one gasp.

The actual ceremony of breaking through the sealed door started at 1:45 P. M. Luncheon was over a little after I and the party, led by Lord Carnarvon and Sir William Garstin, made their way from the staff dining room in a cache to the tomb, into the well of which all descended.

A short interval elapsed for the arrival of M. Lacau, with Abdel Hamid Soliman Pasha, Under Secretary for Public Works.

After various introductions Mr. Callender removed the grille and descended the passage in order to unlock the steel gate. All present then proceeded to take off their coats, for not only was the opening process likely to be lengthy, but the atmosphere was certain to be sultry, to say the least of it.

There was a slight hitch owing to the failure of the electric current. A few moments were full of tense suspense, and even those watching from the parapet could sense the suppressed excitement which possessed each of those standing below at the top of the steps, on the lookout for the signal when they were to descend to experience the moment for which they had waited three months, when, before their eyes, the crumbling wall would reveal the mystery that had lain behind it for 3,000 years.

At last Mr. Callender sent up word that the light was on, and Mr. Carter and then Lord Carnarvon, with Lady Evelyn Herbert close at hand, followed by Sir William Garstin, Abdel Hamid Soliman Pasha, M. Lacau, Mr. Engelbach, Professor Breasted, Dr. Gardiner, Mr. Lythgoe and others, descended into the antechamber. There were twenty in all, to whom must be added the laborers who carried down huge trays for the reception of seals, &c.

Carter Eulogizes Carnarvon.

Before the actual work started Mr. Carter made a little speech in which he stated that all that had been done and anything that the wall might reveal was entirely due to Lord Carnarvon. He thanked every one for coming to the ceremony and expressed his gratitude to the Metropolitan Museum for the great assistance it had given, and also the Egyptian Government. They had still most important work to do, he said, and much might be damaged if improperly handled. He hoped that they would be allowed to carry it to completion in peace, for after all they were all working for the sake of science.

Lord Carnarvon followed with a few words, likewise expressing thanks to those present, to the Egyptian Government, and particularly to Mr. Lythgoe and the Trustees of the Metropolitan Museum for their ready assistance and sympathy and the loan which they made of their experts, who were probably the best experts in the world, for carrying out a very important and delicate work and dealing in a proper and in a scientific manner with the treasures of this tomb.

Lord Carnarvon concluded by saying that it was entirely due to Mr. Carter that they made this scientific discovery, for Mr. Carter, by his unquenchable faith and indomitable perseverance, had "bucked him up" in the face of the many previous disappointments they had experienced.

Mr. Carter then turned to the sealed wall and began breaking it with a chisel and mallet. In a short time he had removed a large piece, which revealed the wooden lintel of the door. By about 3 o'clock sufficient had been removed to enable Mr. Carter to enter, and shortly afterward a large portion of the wall came away, revealing to the dazzled and spellbound gaze of the spectators the wonderful spectacle described above.

The Queen of the Belgians and Prince Leopold, traveling incognito as the Countess de Rethy and Count de Rethy, and accompanied by Professor Cappart, arrived by special train this morning, having come through direct from Alexandria without changing, and with but a few minutes' halt at Cairo. She was met at the station by Abdel Azez Bey Yeha, Governor of the province, with the Sub-Governor and other officials, and Colonel J. K. Watson. The Queen is staying at the Winter Palace Hotel. This is the Queen's second visit, the first being in 1911, when she came with the King and stayed about two months, while he went to the Sudan on a shooting expedition.

ONLY FIVE ENTERED THE TOMB.

Watchers Outside Shared the Excitement of the Discoverers.

Special Cable to THE NEW YORK TIMES.

LONDON, Saturday, Feb. 17.—Description of the scenes about the tomb of Tut-ankh-Amen yesterday are cabled to London papers by special correspondents at Luxor.

The Daily Telegraph's correspondent in his description of the scene outside the tomb when the party was about to enter, says:

"Mr. Callender opened the massive dungeon door leading from the entrance to the steps and a number of chairs were taken down.

"'We are going to have a concert. Carter is going to sing a song,' said Lord Carnarvon very audibly, glancing up at the pressmen whose presence seemed to disconcert him. He sent for a representative of a London newspaper and held a consultation with him and Suliman Pasha, finally descending into the tomb, saying in French to Mr. Lacau, 'give me some gendarmes with some naboots [heavy sticks] I will be satisfied.'

"The press men, however, had no intention of trying to storm the tomb, but watched events with the closest attention. For the next three hours every sound and every incident was noted and interpreted. Sometimes it was a piece of masonry that was brought up, sometimes Lady Evelyn's exclamation, sometimes the sound of chisel blows or hammering of wood.

"The excitement of the watchers on the parapet grew intense as they saw laborers carry out blocks of masonry and baskets of minor debris. After an hour Lord Carnarvon came up for a breather, his forehead dripping with perspiration and his face pale with excitement, he lighted a cigarette, rested two minutes then threw it away and went back, unable to control his impatience.

"It was five minutes past 2 when the first piece of masonry came up. Gradually the blocks were piled up neatly. They were mostly squarish or oblong with a corner missing where seals had been sliced off.

"Mr. Lacau, who came up once for a drink from a flask, pointed out curious brown markings on blocks, indicative of damp below.

"Only once was a seal brought out. It was round and greenish, about six inches in diameter, with corrugated markings. Later on a mattress, pillows and wadding were taken down and the parapet watchers knew the find had been made.

"Professor Breasted, in congratulating Lady Evelyn Herbert when they had all come out at 5:30 P. M., said: 'It is perfectly marvelous and I speak as an expert.'

"Mr. Carter undertook the most delicate and arduous task of battering down the wall. He entered first and Lord Carnarvon followed. He was in the seventh heaven of delight, waving his arms and uttering exclamations of bewilderment.

"The only other persons to enter the mortuary chamber were Lady Evelyn Herbert, Suliman Pasha and M. Lacau. The tomb was reclosed until Sunday's official opening, when Field Marshal Viscount Allenby will be present.

PRAISES CARNARVON'S WORK.

The London Times Says He Is Out of Pocket on His Explorations.

Special Cable to THE NEW YORK TIMES.

LONDON, Saturday, Feb. 17.—The London Times, in an editorial, says:

"Men and women in all lands who take an interest in history and in the achievements of successive civilizations will join in congratulating Lord Carnarvon and his assistants, Howard Carter and Mr. Callender, upon the marvelous additions they have made to the knowledge and to the high pleasures which the increase of knowledge brings.

"Their congratulations will be warmer by reason of the discreditable and unfounded aspersions which have been cast in certain quarters upon Lord Carnarvon's work. He has been charged with creating a monopoly in news from Luxor and even with 'commercialism.'

"No charges could be more false. He supplied the news through The London Times solely because that was the best way and, in fact, the only practical way of supplying it fully and independently to all the newspapers throughout the world who wished to take it. The nature of the work compelled him to distribute it through an agent. Had he attempted to do it himself it would have swamped his labors as archaeologist.

"The imputation of commercialism is without a shadow of foundation. Lord Carnarvon has devoted very large sums to the exploration which has just been crowned with a success so signal. He has spent them for the love of science and a little for the sporting delights of the quest. He has reaped a very great and very satisfying reward, but it is not a money reward or a commercial reward. His labors will leave him very heavily out of pocket."

TESTIMONY OF THE SEALS.

London Expert Finds Proof Tomb Has Been Untouched Since 1340 B.C.

Special Cable to THE NEW YORK TIMES.

LONDON, Saturday, Feb. 17.—Professor Percy E. Newberry in an article in The Morning Post discussing the opening of the inner chamber of Tut-ankh-Amen's tomb, says:

"The seals removed from the plaster of the walled up entrance were, apparently, of three kinds. The Necropolis seal, which was impressed upon plaster just as the ordinary Englishman of today seals up an important letter, is no evidence of date, since the same seal, a jackal couchant upon nine bound prisoners, was used as late as Ptolemaic times a thousand years after Tut-ankh-Amen.

"The seal of Tut-ankh-Amen can only have been used by the royal undertakers just after his death. The third seal used seems to have been that of Hor-em-Heb, which was a stamp on plaster that covered up the hole made by robbers. Consequently it is clear that the inner chamber, opened yesterday, had been entered by no one since the days of Hor-em-Heb, 1340 B. C. The furniture in the outer chamber of the tomb seems definitely to have been that used by the king during his life. If there is another complete set it may be simply funerary furniture made for the tomb.

"There are a number of new and fascinating features in the description telegraphed by The Morning Post correspondent. The most interesting is the account of the double canopy, apparently made of gilded wood, which covered the sarcophagus. Something of the same kind was brought to light from the chamber which contained the coffin and body of Akh-n-aten. This canopy, made of wood and covered with stucco, had collapsed over the coffin. But we know of no instance of a double canopy apart from yesterday's discovery.

"The sarcophagus is sealed and undoubtedly contains the mummy of Pharaoh in its swathing bands, possibly with all his protective amulets upon him.

"The scenes on the brilliantly painted walls should be of most profound interest. The sarcophagus chamber of the King who followed Tut-ankh-Amen, has scenes upon it unlike any others in the valley. They represent the King in his daily life and this has previously been unique. For instance, he is shown following the chase in a papyrus marsh. The interior of the sarcophagus chamber is usually decorated and covered with religious inscriptions, but scenes such as those in the tomb of this King have so far no parallel. The presence of the cat (the goddess Bast) is remarkable. So far as I know it has never previously been found in a royal tomb.

"The fact that one of the Caponic jars appears on the floor outside the Caponic box is probably due to tomb robbers. Such jars are always found in sets of four and contained the viscera of the deceased.

"The sarcophagus chamber is called in the payri 'the hall of gold wherein the King rests,' and this appellation seems to be fully justified by the correspondent's description. It was also known as the chariot hall, and four chariots, not dismantled, but upon their wheels were found in Tut-ankh-Amen's sarcophagus chamber, whereas in the outer chamber they were dismantled.

"The name of Chariot Hall was known from a papyrus in Turin with a plan of a royal tomb, but now for the first time chariots have actually been found in situ.

"Unquestionably this discovery is the most important of its kind ever made and its full value will only be apparent after many months of study and investigation."

TUT-ANKH-AMEN ON HIS THRONE,
as shown in an elaborate decoration which covers the walls of the tomb of Huy, his Viceroy for Ethiopia.
Courtesy Metropolitan Museum of Art.

EXPECT NEW FACTS FROM INNER TOMB

Experts Think It May Give a Version of the Flood and of the Oppression of the Jews.

MAY TELL OF ATEN HERESY

It Is Also Counted On to Reveal, if Untouched by Robbers, Splendor of Pharaonic Mummies.

No mortuary chamber of a Pharaoh tomb has hitherto been found untampered with and no sarcophagus, the outer stone coffin, has hitherto been found unplundered by robbers, according to Dr. Ambrose Lansing, Egyptologist of the Metropolitan Museum of Art. The antechamber, and its annex, of the tomb of Tut-ankh-Amen were entered by the dynastic robbers, probably in the reign of Tut-ankh-Amen's successor, Hor-em-eb, but they evidently had to make a hasty retreat after stripping some of the gold from the funerary objects and looting some of the boxes of jewels and other small portable treasures, but the treasure left behind far exceeds in value and interest anything ever before found. Th treasures in the inner chambers may be still greater and more important, according to Dr. Lansing, who hopes that these chambers escaped the looters entirely. If so, it is the only tomb of a Pharaoh known to have escaped.

If the inner tomb of Tut-ankh-Amen did escape, and it now seems that it did, it would be almost the only tomb of any great ruler or great personage of antiquity to have had such luck. Prehistoric tombs and early historic tombs in Asia, Africa, Europe and the Americas, almost without exception, have been plundered. Grave-robbing is one of the oldest and most universal crimes. It has the most ancient pedigree of all crimes, except murder the primal malefaction, according to the Bible.

According to Dr. Lansing, it will be months and perhaps a year before public curiosity can be fully satisfied about the contents of the inner chambers. The jewels on the mummy may be the most complete and interesting specimens of the work of the Egyptian jewelers, who were great masters. Literary treasures also are likely to be found. Because of the high artistic achievement indicated in the other finds in the tomb, it is believed that the paintings in "The Book of Dead," which is expected to be found, may be the finest of their kind. Papyri relating to the "Aten" heresy which Tut-ankh-Amen rejected may be discovered.

Hopes for Information on the Flood.

Dr. Elliot Smith, the noted British archaeologist, has expressed the hope that legends in the inner chamber may throw a new light on the origin of the narrative of the flood. The destruction of the world because of the wickedness of man, as told in Genesis, is also read in Babylonian records and is suggested in certain tomb inscriptions in ancient Egypt, according to Dr. Smith, who believes the account originated in Egypt.

Arthur Wiegall, former Inspector General of Antiquities to the Egyptian Government, and others have put forward the theory that Tut-ankh-Amen was the Pharaoh of the oppression, whose army was overwhelmed in attempting to pursue the Jews in their miraculous passage through the waters of the Red Sea.

Historians and archaeologists will have the keenest possible interest in the papyri that may be found in the tomb, hoping that something will be discovered to give the Egyptian version of their relations with the Jews. So far no reference has been found, in all the early records of Egypt, to the sojourn of the Jews in that country, to the seven years of famine and the seven years of plenty, to the seven plagues, or to the destruction of the army which Pharaoh sent to recall the Jews after permitting them to depart from Egypt.

One of the leading objects of searches for papyri in recent years has been to find corroboration from Egyptian sources for the stay in Egypt and the exodus, but these events, which make so large a figure in Jewish history, are a blank in the Egyptian records which have been recovered so far. Egyptian history, tradition and literature were never consolidated and preserved, and have been pieced together only in modern times and from fragments. The Jews are believed to have been a comparatively small tribe at the time and Egypt a highly populous country, so that the Jewish contact with Egypt has been represented by some historians as a thing of slight consequence to the Egyptians, who would regard it as the deportation or withdrawal of a handful of aliens. The series of terrible plagues, described in the Old Testament are not touched upon in any Egyptian material so far recovered.

Connects Moses with Aten Heresy.

Mr. Wiegall's theory is that Moses, who had risen in the Egyptian Government service, had succeeded in inaugurating the worship of Jehovah, so that the "Aten heresy" would in reality be the Jewish religion.

The belief that Tut-ankh-Amen was the Pharaoh of the persecution is based on chronological grounds and on the belief that, since the "Aten" heresy was repudiated during his reign, Moses and his people, who were responsible for it, may well have had their troubles with the Egyptians at this time. Tut-ankh-Amen's tomb is a short distance from the burial-place of Meneptah, who is generally believed to have been the persecutor of the Jews and the "Pharaoh of the Exodus."

But it will be months, according to Dr. Lansing, before the curtain can be raised on these and other possibilities.

"I received a letter from one of the workers," he said, "indicating that the tomb will probably be looked over and then cemented up until next season. Things will be examined in place, inventoried and photographed, but they cannot very well be taken out of the tomb this season. The heat becomes very severe in March, and it is impracticable to continue at work. The things must be studied where they are. Much mischief would be caused by any hasty attempt to transport them. It will be very difficult to remove the heavy sarcophagus. Everything is much safer in the place where it has been preserved for more than thirty-two centuries.

"No other Pharaoh, I believe, has ever been found untouched in the original sarcophagus. The robbers in all other cases smashed the stone lid and took the jewels and valuable things which were buried with the body. As this has invariably happened to the other Pharaohs, we do not know exactly what their funerary equipment was, but it probably consisted of a number of fine pieces of jewelry among other things.

"Many unsmashed sarcophagi have been found, but on being opened, it was discovered that the mummies had been transferred there after having been plundered in earlier sarcophagi. In such cases, the necropolitan authorities had rewrapped the mummies, and re-equipped the bodies, but with less splendor.

"If the mummy is found as originally buried, we might expect to find many valuable articles, such as collars of gold, probably ornamented with stones, gold bracelets and anklets and perhaps some kind of a crown. I don't believe there would be anything like a breastplate, but there would probably be a pectoral, which is something like the modern lavalliere.

"Judging from the reports, these pieces might be set with stones, especially lapis lazuli, carnelian and turquoise, which are about the oldest precious stones. This was long before the use of pearls or diamonds as jewelry. There might be found some imitations of lapis lazuli and other stones in glass. Glass was highly esteemed at that early stage in the art of making it, but it was used only for imitations of the precious stones, and on the whole it is probably unlikely that jewels ornamented with glass will be found.

Mummy May Wear Mask.

"Whatever the jewels are, they will probably be found, not next to the body, but wrapped in among the folds of the cloth in which the mummy is wound. There will probably be no robes or articles of clothing, outside of the plain cloth wrapping. There might be a covering of tapestry or something of the kind in the sarcophagus, but that is doubtful. It is expected that there will be a mask on the face. This will probably be made of stucco placed on linen, formed like a human face and then gilded."

The theory of Professor Flinders Petrie is that the richness of the treasures in Tut-ankh-Amen's tomb is due to the fact that he was the last of his line and had, therefore, no heirs to whom his treasures could be passed, and as a result that most of his personal estate, in the way of jewelry and art, was buried with him. Professor Petrie believes that objects of this kind which he had inherited from generations of ancestors were probably buried with him. On this hypothesis the inner chamber might be exceptionally rich in heirlooms which would make a splendid addition to the treasury of art and archaeology already found in the outer chamber.

"But this is a moot question," said Dr. Lansing. "The other Pharaohs were so badly plundered that we do not really know how much or little may have been originally buried with them. Several couches, chariots and other furniture have been found in other tombs."

It is not expected that any more trussed fowl and such objects will be found in the inner chambers, which are supposed to be devoted mainly to magical things which were expected to speed the soul of the dead on its way to its eternal home. It is in conection with this that valuable literary remains are expected.

One of the trappings of a splendid funeral in ancient Egypt was the illuminated papyrus roll known as "The Book of the Dead." This was a religious document in the form of a scroll which might approach 100 feet long, with religious writings, elaborate pictures of the hereafter, as some Dante of ancient Egypt had portrayed it. This was supposed to have a magical function, being a sort of religious Baedeker, outlining the pilgrimage which lay before the Pharaoh. The most interesting point expected in "The Book of the Dead" which is thought almost certain to be found with Tut-ankh-Amen is some reference to the Aten heresy.

This papyrus may indicate alterations in "The Book of the Dead" as a result of the change of religion made by Khu-n-aten. The prayers and magical formulae of "The Book of the Dead" are almost certain to have been changed during the Aten period, and it is possible that some change may be retained in the document buried with Tut-ankh-Amen. Whether changed or not, it is likely to be a fine and splendidly illuminated document.

Drawings Have Magic Purpose.

Some of the drawings of "The Book of the Dead" and their purpose are described as follows by E. Wallis Budge in his Egyptian history:

"The Theban and Saite Recensions of 'The Book of the Dead' are full of spells, accompanied by magical drawings. Thus the Chapter of the Ladder and the drawing of it would secure for the deceased the use of the famous ladder whereby Osiris had climbed up from earth into heaven. The Chapter of the Ferryboat and a picture of it would provide a boat for the deceased when he wished to sail across the Nile of the Other World. Each part of the spell possessed a magical name, which is given in the text of the spell, and when all the names of the parts were properly pronounced by the deceased the boat would sail to any place to which he wanted it to go. The Judgment scene, which represented to the initiated the deepest and most fundamental truths in the religion of Osiris, was, to the ordinary Egyptian, a magical picture drawn on funerary papyri with the view of making the gods declare those for whom it was drawn to be truth seekers. If drawings of Osiris, Ra, Isis and Nephthys, the four gods of the wind, were painted on a coffin, they would enable its occupant to enter each of the four quarters of heaven."

An Egyptian version of the story of the "flood," according to Dr. Elliot Smith, was in one case at least told of the wall of a tomb, to assist the soul of the inmate of the tomb.

Suggesting that the walls or contents of the tomb of Tut-ankh-Amen might throw further light on the origin of the Biblical narrative, Professor Smith declared:

"Inscribed on the walls of the tomb of Seti I. in the Theban necropolis—less than seventy years after the burial of Tut-ankh-Amen—is the remarkable story of the Destruction of Mankind. In spite of the fact that it was inscribed in this tomb as recently—in comparison with the Sumerian story—as 1300 B. C., the strange confusion of archaic reference which has made it so unintelligible to most modern scholars reveals the fact that its origin must be referred back to the fourth millennium. Although the destruction is not brought about by the flood, it is clear that the Egyptian and Mesopotamian stories have a common origin and a common motive. For the essential incident in the latter is not the flood, but the destruction of mankind which it brought to pass.

"If it be asked why this venerable story should be inscribed in the tomb of an Egyptian Pharaoh, the answer is that its aim was to secure for the dead king those boons the attainment of which was the central motive of the tale."

What was done in the Babylonian legend by the flood was accomplished in the Egyptian variation, according to Dr. Smith, by the slaughter of all Egyptians by an ancient king. The legend indicates that the kings of old were executed when they began to show signs of age, because the belief prevailed that the prosperity of early Egypt waxed or waned with the physical condition of the king. The monarch of this legend began to show symptoms of age. His subjects began to murmur that it was time for the king to die. But the king hit on the plan of killing his subjects and renewing his youth by drinking their blood. He finally killed them all.

"But when the king had slaughtered them," Dr. Smith cotninued, "and had attained a renewal of his youth, he was overcome by the boredom of too prolonged an existence upon earth. So he mounted upon the back of a celestial cow and so reached heaven and attained immortality."

"All the News That's Fit to Print."

The New York Times.

THE WEATHER
Showers today and tomorrow; fresh south and southwest winds.
Temperature yesterday—Max., 73; min., 69.
For weather report see Page 22.

VOL. LXXIV....No. 24,651. *** NEW YORK, WEDNESDAY, JULY 22, 1925. TWO CENTS In Greater New York | THREE CENTS Within 200 Miles | FOUR CENTS Elsewhere in the U. S.

LONG STEP TO PEACE IS SEEN BY BRITAIN IN GERMANY'S REPLY

Chamberlain to Consider With Briand Chances of a Parley in August.

WANTS COMPACT PRESSED

Meanwhile the French Think There Are Traps in the Berlin Note.

GERMANS LOOKING TO US

They Want Americans Made Members of the Arbitration Tribunal.

By EDWIN L. JAMES.

By Wireless to THE NEW YORK TIMES.

LONDON, July 21.—The British Government regards the German security note as a distinct step toward making the Rhine peace compact. While less favorable than London had hoped Dr. Stresemann's communication is seen as opening the way to early negotiations between the Allies and Germany.

Here one finds the belief that some of the most troublesome passages in the German Foreign Minister's note were written for home consumption, especially the section relating to article XVI. of the Covenant of the League. Following the action of the League Council notifying Germany that no special conditions could attend her entry, it is thought here that Dr. Stresemann wrote this part of the note with full knowledge that it was doomed to failure but in the hope of mollifying opposition in the Reich.

As the British see it, the last paragraph of the note is the most important one, in which Berlin says: "On essential points a significant rapprochement of the views of the two sides has already taken place," and in which the German Government hopes for a settlement of outstanding differences and expresses a wish for speedier discussions. That, the British say, really sums up what the Reich's note means, namely, that the matter should be gone ahead with.

Think French Should Be Reassured.

The declaration of the Germans that they have no prime intention of bringing about revisions of the Versailles Treaty is seen here as a passage which should calm French fears, even though the Germans cling to the provision of the League covenant providing for a revision of antiquated treaty provisions.

Likewise, the German statement relative to changing conditions in Rhineland occupation are regarded here as very mild, in view of the report from Berlin that the Reich would demand quick evacuation of the Coblenz and Mayence bridgeheads as part of the compact arrangement.

It was expected that Germany would object to the provisions of M. Briand's note for exceptions and possible Allied crossing of the Rhine peace zone. London does not believe that Germany seriously means the suggestion that the allies should renounce any and all sanctions for possible violations of the Versailles Treaty, especially in regard to reparations, but it is recognized that Berlin has raised a disputable issue in questioning the French claim to the right to guarantee arbitration treaties between Germany and Czechoslovakia.

The only lack of cordial spirit the British see in the German note is the manner in which Berlin refers to Germany's entry into the League. Knowing all along that the allies regarded the Reich's joining the League as an essential part of the bargain, Berlin's condescending agreement to consider the proposal favorably is regarded as slightly in bad taste.

Germany's suggestion for a temporary arrangement of Article XVI until universal disarmament brings other nations' armies down to the level of Germany's is seen as a rather clever move to raise during the coming negotiations the issue of the strength of the French army. The disposition here is not to regard this part of the German note as stating any essential position but rather as intended to seek a bargaining position.

Mr. Chamberlain will at once discuss with M. Briand the conclusions to be drawn from the German note and in particular will consider whether arrangements should be made to invite the Germans to a security conference at Brussels on Aug. 15 or thereabouts. Mr. Chamberlain is anxious to have the security negotiations in shape to be able at Geneva in September to offer the League Assembly something to replace the Geneva protocol work of last year's assembly, which was killed by the unfavorable attitude of the present British Government.

British Press Divided on Note.

The morning papers differ pretty much over the note, according to their political stand. The pro-Government papers find it good and the Opposition press finds it bad.

The Daily Telegraph sees in the friendly tone of the note its chief value. In the arguments raised by the Berlin document this paper perceives an indication of difficult negotiations but fair prospects of success. In the German request for consideration of modifications of the Treaty of Versailles The Telegraph finds the chief stumbling block, but considers the tone of the note indicates a desire for a Rhine compact, and says

Continued on Page Six.

Party Goes South on Yacht To See Dredging by Beebe

The Vanadis, the yacht of Harrison Williams, 60 Broadway, left New York early yesterday morning for Cape Hatteras, where William Beebe and the New York Zoological Society Expedition on the Arcturus are expected Friday afternoon.

A party of friends of Mr. Williams are on board the Vanadis, and George Palmer Putnam, William Beebe's publisher, left New York by rail yesterday morning to join the party at Cape May at the invitation of Mr. Williams.

Beebe, returning from the Sargasso Sea, has notified the New York Zoological Society that he is on his way back to New York and will stop at a designated place off Hatteras to trawl and dredge. This point will be the rendezvous of the Arcturus and the Vanadis.

The Vanadis will also accompany the Arcturus on its return to New York on Saturday. Mr. Williams is chief patron of the zoological society's expedition.

MOB CLUBS DEPUTY, FOE OF THE FASCISTI

Giovanni Amendola, Leader of Aventine Opposition, Is Attacked on Country Road.

BOOED OUT OF MONTECATINI

Assault Follows Siege of Hotel, Peace Truce and Flight From Town of Water Cures.

By Wireless to THE NEW YORK TIMES.

ROME, July 21.—Deputy Giovanni Amendola, perhaps the most important leader of the Aventine opposition to the Fascist régime, was attacked and clubbed by unidentified persons presumed to have been Fascisti, while fleeing by motor car toward Pistoia from Montecatini, where a Fascist crowd, after besieging him in his hotel for several hours, eventually booed and hissed him out of town.

Deputy Amendola suffered several bruises and superficial wounds on various parts of the body, and will have to remain twenty days in a hospital, it was said at Pistoia, where he went for first aid. He was later brought to Rome by rail accompanied by members of the Fascist railroad police, who guarded him from further attacks.

About half way between Montecatini and Pistoia Signor Amendola's motor car was obliged to halt by two other motor cars drawn up across the road. As soon as Amendola slackened speed fifteen or more individuals who had been hiding behind the hedge sprang up and rushed at the Opposition leader, striking at him with sticks they carried. They then re-entered their motor cars and headed toward Montecatini at a rapid pace.

Amendola, though bleeding from several cuts, was not seriously wounded and ordered the car driven to Pistoia.

Had Gone for Water Cure.

Signor Amendola had gone to Montecatini in order to take a water cure for which the town is famous, but no sooner was his presence known than the hotel was completely surrounded by thousands of Fascist citizens, some even having come from surrounding villages. The crowd booed and hissed lustily.

When that form of amusement began to become monotonous efforts were made to break through the cordons of carabineers which the police officials in order to forestall trouble had placed across each entrance to the hotel.

After several determined rushes had been stopped by the carabineers, the Fascisti succeeded in penetrating into the hotel and chased Deputy Amendola to the fourth floor of the building, where he took refuge in his room, bolting the door. His secretary, who had not been equally fleet of foot, had his eye blackened.

Further hostilities were prevented by the intervention of Fascist Deputies, who prevailed upon the Fascisti to leave the Deputy alone and to enjoin their companions outside the hotel.

The local Fascist leaders and several

Continued on Page Five.

ALL POLICE BELOW 14TH ST. JOIN HUNT FOR A MISSING BOY

Comb East Side Tenements Aided by Forty Detectives for Robert Perles.

ABANDON DROWNING THEORY

Marine Division Fails to Find Clue in River—Lad Seen by Man at 5 P. M. on Sunday.

LITTLE GIRL ALSO SAW HIM

Says She Played With Him but Can Tell No More—Sewers and Intakes to Be Searched Today.

Forty detectives from lower east side precincts and all the uniformed patrolmen between the Battery and Fourteenth Street, on the east side, were brought into the hunt yesterday for Robert Perles, 4 years and 6 months old, who disappeared last Sunday after he had left his home at 272 East Third Street to visit a relative at 95 Ridge Street. Following the abandonment of their first theory that the boy had been drowned in the East River near the recreation pier at the foot of East Third Street, the police decided on an intensive search. Policemen from the Marine Division in launches had dragged the waters in the vicinity of this pier in the forenoon without uncovering any clue that might justify the theory.

A conference of detectives in charge of the quest in the Fifth Street Station at noon led to the issuance of an order to mobolize all detectives from the Old Slip, Beach Street, Oak Street, Mercer Street, Clinton Street and Fifth Street Stations in the block bounded by Delancey, Rivington, Attorney and Ridge Streets, in which lives Mrs. Annie Levine, aunt of the boy, and in which he was last seen playing in front of Public School 4. Mrs. Levine lives in a five-story tenement four blocks from the East River. At 11 A. M. Sunday, she said, she saw her little nephew playing with Daniel Blitz, a companion.

The decision to search every house in this block from cellar to roof was brought about when Lieutenant Detective Louis Dittman recalled that on Oct. 26, 1923, four-year-old Irving Pickelny had disappeared just as mysteriously from in front of his home at 358 Grand Street, and his body had been found in the cellar of the tenement at 71 Suffolk Street a month later.

Detectives Comb Tenements.

The Pickelny home was less than a quarter of a mile from the homes of the parents of the missing Perles boy and his aunt. Detectives were assigned in pairs to comb thoroughly the neighboring tenements as well as the cellar of the public school and tenements in the vicinity of the Perles home in East Third Street, a short distance away.

When they reported after four hours that not a trace of the boy had been found Chief Inspector William J. Lahey then caused an order to be issued from Police Headquarters to all the uniformed men of the section between Fourteenth Street and the Battery to be especially vigilant and arrest any one of subnormal appearance found acting suspiciously.

While the hunt for the boy by the detectives was in full swing hundreds of children and grown-ups were questioned in the hope of obtaining a clue. Samuel Perles, father of the boy, took an active part in this questioning.

As in the hunt for the slain Pickelny boy, the excitement attendant on the police activity aroused the imaginations of many children and much time was lost running down reports of the missing boy's having been seen at various places in the neighborhood, even up to yesterday forenoon.

One witness, however, gave the police information which led them to believe that Robert was alive at 5 P. M. last Sunday. This witness was Max Slissen, who lives on the third floor of 91 Ridge Street, two doors north of the Levine home. Slissen was encountered by Detective Morgan Callahan of the Missing Persons Bureau, who had been assigned

Continued on Page Four.

Buck M'Neil, Saver of 40 Lives, Gets First Honors on Tablet

"Buck" McNeil, the Battery Dock Master, who has saved more than forty persons from drowning off the sea wall at Battery Park, will be the first "Honor Man" to have his name engraved on a tablet to be placed in the office of Dock Commissioner Cosgrove, it was announced yesterday.

The tablet will be a memorial to the late Charles F. Murphy, who served as Dock Commissioner from 1898 to 1902. It will be presented by Charles F. Murphy, a nephew of the Tammany leader. Annually a Dock Department "Honor Man" will have his name engraved on the tablet. McNeil will also be presented with a medal by members of the department. He already has more than three dozen medals for saving life.

COAL STRIKE THREAT IS WIRED TO HOOVER

Miners' Official Warns of General Tie-Up Over West Virginia Wage Fight.

SEEKS ROCKEFELLER AID

Charges Assaults by Armed Guards—Anthracite Conferees Make Little Headway.

Special to The New York Times.

ATLANTIC CITY, N. J., July 21.—While the anthracite operators and miners spent an afternoon in fruitless bickering over a new wage agreement, representatives of the bituminous coal miners here today drew up plans for an intensive campaign against soft coal operators in Northern West Virginia. Van A. Bittner, chief representative of the United Mine Workers in that territory, sent an identical telegram to Secretary of Commerce Hoover and Secretary of Labor Davis denouncing the Bethlehem Mines Corporation, a subsidiary of the Bethlehem Steel Corporation, and the Consolidation Coal Company for their alleged violation of the Jacksonville agreement. He declared that "unless something is done to prevent this abrogation of wage agreements it will be necessary for the miners of the entire State of West Virginia to join with the United Mine Workers of America of the rest of country in a general strike."

At the same time Mr. Bittner, after conferring at the Hotel Ambassador with Thomas C. Townsend, chief counsel for the miners in Northern West Virginia, sent telegrams to John D. Rockefeller Jr. and Samuel Untermyer, alleging that eviction proceedings have been started against hundreds of miners and their families, and that armed guards have assaulted miners. Mr. Untermyer is appealed to because of his large interest in the Bethlehem Steel Corporation, in control of the Bethlehem Mines Corporation. Mr. Rockefeller is supposed to be interested in the Consolidation Company.

Warns of Nation-Wide Strike.

Here is the telegram sent by Mr. Bittner to Secretaries Hoover and Davis:

Several large coal companies in Northern West Virginia, among whom are the Bethlehem Mines Corporation, a subsidiary of the Bethlehem Steel Corporation, and the Consolidation Coal Company, which is controlled by the Rockefeller and Watson interests, have abrogated their wage contracts with the United Mine Workers of America and are attempting to put into effect a wage reduction approximating 50 per cent.

Defenseless miners, their wives and little children are being evicted from their homes by these coal companies because the miners will not agree to violate and abrogate the terms of the wage agreement which is effective until March 31, 1927. Hundreds of armed gunmen are being employed to intimidate, coerce and force our people to accept this reduction in wages.

In the interest of the coal miners and all the people of our country the time has arrived when the Government of the United States should take a definite position against abrogation of wage contracts by the coal operators of Northern West Virginia.

The miners do not propose to have their wage agreements broken down by this method of guerrilla warfare on the part of the Northern West Virginia operators, and unless something is done to prevent this abrogation of wage agreements it will be necessary for the miners of the entire State of West Virginia to join with the United Mine Workers of America of the rest of the country in a general strike.

The United Mine Workers of America are forced to take this position due to the action of the coal operators who have been so unfaithful to our wage agreements solemnly made to insure peace in the coal mining industry.

Ask Rockefeller's Aid.

The following telegram was sent to John D. Rockefeller Jr.:

I wrote you several days ago informing you that the statement made by President Lewis of the United Mine Workers of America that your company in Northern West Virginia, the Consolidation Coal Company, had abrogated its agreement with the United Mine Workers of America was absolutely correct and the Consolidation Coal Company is using every means known to corporate greed to make effective a wage reduction of approxi-

Continued on Page Three.

HYLAN REFUSES BAIT TO GO ON BENCH AND QUIT MAYOR'S RACE

Foes Realize Need for Keeping Him on Ticket to Block Third-Party Plan.

McCOOEY CALLS LEADERS

Brooklyn Chief Confers With Olvany, but Both Refuse to Tell What Was Said.

HEARST EMISSARY ACTIVE

Meeting of Borough Leaders on Mayoralty Situation Is Put Off Until Next Week.

In a final attempt to avert an open break and keep him in line for the ticket, Democrats who do not believe Mayor Hylan could make a winning fight for a third term, yesterday sent friendly emissaries to the Mayor, who now are bringing all their persuasive powers to bear with a view to inducing him to quit the Mayoralty race and accept a nomination for the Supreme Court in the Second Judicial District.

Up to last night these envoys of the anti-Hylan forces had not been able to budge Mayor Hylan from his determination to make a fight for the Mayoralty again. It was stated, however, that the pressure would continue, and that when the Mayor awakened to a realization of his loss of popularity with the voters there was hope that he would yield to their representations.

In the meantime the anti-Hylan forces are sparring for time. It was announced yesterday that the conferences of the five Democratic borough leaders, at which the Democratic city slate is to be decided upon, would be deferred until next week. This announcement was made after John H. McCooey, the Democratic leader in Brooklyn, which is Mayor Hylan's home borough, had met George W. Olvany, the Tammany chieftain, at the Hotel Vanderbilt, where they discussed the tangled Mayoralty situation for an hour or more over luncheon.

Neither Mr. Olvany nor Mr. McCooey would disclose any part of their conversation, except to say that it had been wholly informal and that naturally no decision of any kind had been reached. Prior to meeting Mr. Olvany, the Democratic leader in Brooklyn had talked for almost an hour with James P. Sinnott, one of his district leaders and a high spokesman for Mayor Hylan himself.

Confer in McCooey's Office.

This conference was held in Mr. McCooey's office at the Hall of Records in Brooklyn. What they talked about can only be surmised, for there was no announcement after their meeting. It was presumed, however, that the sole topic was Mayor Hylan's chances to get a renomination for Mayor.

Mr. McCooey is likely to be subjected for the next few days to pressure from sources both friendly and unfriendly to the Mayor and his third term aspirations. An emissary of William R. Hearst arrived in this city yesterday, showing every desire that his presence on the scene of strife should not be bruited about.

The emissary was William A. De Ford, a member of Mayor Hylan's Board of Transportation, and head of the legal department of the Hearst publications in the East. Mr. De Ford had interrupted a vacation to return to the city at a time which may prove crucial to Mayor Hylan's political future. Word had preceded him from Atlantic City, where he has been spending part of his holiday, that he was coming to town for important political conferences. Mr. De Ford when questioned yesterday, declared that he was aware of no such conferences in which he was to be a participant, and that his return at this time was to attend a meeting of the Transportation Board.

Hearst Expected Soon.

That the visit of Mr. De Ford was occasioned by reasons purely political, however, was the general opinion among politicians who learned of his presence in the city. Mr. De Ford has been one of Mr. Hearst's political advisers for the last couple of years. He is conversant with all the plans of the editor-politician in relation to the candidacy of Mayor Hylan. Mr. De Ford declined

Continued on Page Fourteen.

Search All London for Wisconsin Professor; He Had $3,000 and Family Suspects Foul Play

Special Cable to THE NEW YORK TIMES.

LONDON, July 21.—Joseph Victor Collins, Professor of Mathematics at Wisconsin University and candidate in 1910 for the United States Senate, is missing in London and foul play is suspected by his wife and daughter.

Scotland Yard circulated a description and photographs of the missing man, and detectives spent yesterday combing London and hospitals are carrying out a systematic search for him.

Once during the day it was believed he was found and his daughter was called to St. George's Hospital and endured the ordeal of inspecting a suicide's body. It wasn't that of her father.

Professor Collins, when he disappeared, had in his pockets American Express checks and loose change of a value of over $3,000, and the suspicion is that he fell in the hands of sharpers.

With his daughter he boarded an omnibus which passed the corner of a street where his hotel is. The daughter alighted, but the father continued to the railroad station to secure sleeping accommodations for the journey to Edinburgh to the educators' sessions there. That was the last seen of him.

His daughter, in interviews, said she thought he was followed. There were several suspicious-looking men on top of the omnibus, she said. He was the last man in the world, she said, to go off voluntarily, for he had heard all about London gangsters and American visitors.

Mrs. Collins also said she was sure there was foul play behind the disappearance.

EDINBURGH, July 21 (AP).—Professor Collins has not arrived here for the sessions of educators, and no room has been reserved for him in Edinburgh.

Special to The New York Times.

STEVENS POINT, Wis., July 21.—Professor Joseph V. Collins is 66 years old and a member of the Faculty of the Stevens Point State Normal School. He is a widely known mathematician. He was a candidate for State Superintendent of Schools in 1903 and for the United States Senate in 1910.

Members of the Normal School Faculty suggest the disappearance of the professor was due to the fact that he is near-sighted and had wandered into an unknown quarter of London. They think he may have broken his glasses, without which he cannot distinguish a person a few feet away.

Professor Collins had $20,000 in his possession. He has been an instructor at the Normal School since it was organized in 1894.

Girl, Saved by Dog, Shoots Her Assailant; Negro Again Shot by Posse Before Capture

Special to The New York Times.

NEW BRUNSWICK, N. J., July 21.—Shot twice, once by Miss Barbara Long, who lives with her brother Nicholas on a farm near the Lincoln Highway a few miles from here, and a second time by one of a posse which pursued him through the fields after he is alleged to have attacked Miss Long, Jess Williams, a negro, was arrested today on a charge of atrocious assault. After his wounds had been treated at the Middlesex General Hospital he was taken to the New Brunswick Jail.

Miss Long was saved from serious harm by the intervention of a large shepherd dog which made the negro take to his heels through the fields. The negro begged for food, and as Miss Long was preparing it he forced his way into the kitchen of the farmhouse and began to choke her. Miss Long managed to break his grasp on her throat. She screamed and the dog sprang at him. The negro ran from the place and Miss Long fired both barrels of a shotgun at him as he fled. The man was hit, but kept running.

Nicholas Long, the girl's brother, ran to the house when he heard his sister's screams and the shots. He took the gun and followed the negro, being joined by several men working in the fields near by. One man jumped into an automobile and intercepted the negro, who had been wounded a second time by a shot from one of his pursuers.

The negro was later arraigned before Justice of the Peace C. W. Sedam and committed to jail without bail. According to the police, he said he did not intend to harm the girl, but merely tried to rob the place.

SCOPES GUILTY, FINED $100, SCORES LAW; BENEDICTION ENDS TRIAL, APPEAL STARTS; DARROW ANSWERS NINE BRYAN QUESTIONS

Both Sides Speed Procedure for Scopes Appeal; Defense Cost $25,000, With Lawyers Serving Free

Special to The New York Times.

KNOXVILLE, Tenn., July 21.—With the conviction of John Thomas Scopes, attorneys for the defense at Dayton began at once to formulate their plans for the appeal. The case will come before the Supreme Court when that tribunal sits in Knoxville in September. Attorneys for both sides today agreed to expedite the appeal procedure in order to assure a hearing of the issues at that session.

Clarence Darrow, chief of the defense staff, is expected to argue the case before the Supreme Court here. Frank Spurlock, prominent attorney of Chattanooga, assisting the defense, will also plead for Mr. Scopes, being well versed in the peculiarities of Tennessee law. John R. Neal of Knoxville also is expected to take an important part in the appeal proceedings.

For the State, Attorney General Stewart and Ben G. McKenzie doubtless will carry the burden.

The defense's appeal will consist of two main points: First, that the Anti-Evolution law is unconstitutional; second, that even though the law were valid, Mr. Scopes did not violate it, and that the defense was prohibited from proving this at the Dayton trial.

DAYTON, Tenn., July 21 (AP).—A misdemeanor case carrying as a penalty to the guilty offender a fine of $100 and costs of the trial brought an expenditure to the defenders of John Thomas Scopes of about $25,000.

The actual court costs are estimated at well over $300, or more than treble the fine assessed.

The greatest expense of the trial was the cost of bringing expert witnesses, who were not allowed to testify. Defense counsel estimated that cost to be $20,000 to $25,000.

Attorneys on both sides bore their own expenses and served without fees.

In addition several hundred dollars was paid out by the county in preparing the Court House for the trial.

G. G. HAVEN A SUICIDE, DUE TO ILL HEALTH

Banker and Opera Patron Shoots Himself After Vain Struggle to Recover.

FRIEND DISCOVERS BODY

Dr. E. Eliot Finds Him Dead in His Room While Wife Is Away Shopping.

George Griswold Haven, senior member of the banking firm of Strong, Sturgis & Co. of 11 Wall Street and President of the Metropolitan Opera and Real Estate Company, which controls the Metropolitan Opera House, committed suicide by shooting himself through the head with a revolver at his residence, 6 East Fifty-third Street, yesterday morning.

Mr. Haven, who was 59 years old, had been suffering from a nervous disorder for eighteen months. His mind was clear, but for a year and a half he had been inactive in business and had rested and traveled, seeking to regain his health.

Once or twice recently, according to friends of Mr. Haven, he had expressed himself as despairing of recovery and had shown that he had thoughts of ending his life. He gave no warning of any kind yesterday and left no note or statement explaining his act.

Married Five Months Ago.

Yesterday morning he rose at 8 o'clock and appeared his usual self. He had breakfast with his wife, formerly Miss Dorothy James, daughter of Henry A. James of this city. They were married last February at St. George's Church in this city. The first Mrs. Haven had died two years before.

After breakfast Mrs. Haven went shopping and her husband went to his room on the fourth floor. At 10:30 o'clock yesterday morning Dr. E. Eliot of 34 East Sixty-seventh Street called at the Haven residence. He was an old personal friend of Mr. Haven, but had not been treating him professionally. A servant informed Dr. Eliot that Mr. Haven was in his room.

"I'll go up and see him," said Dr. Eliot. He found Mr. Haven lying dead on his bed. There was a revolver beside him. He had shot himself through the jaw. The bullet had lodged in the brain, killing him instantly. He had been dead about half an hour when Dr. Eliot discovered the body. The revolver was one

Continued on Page Ten.

BONAPARTE GIVES PROPERTY TO WIFE

Great-Grandnephew of the Emperor Signs Away All but $5,000 a Year.

AGREEMENT ENDS HER SUIT

Referee Files Report and Recommends That Leon Jacobs, Lawyer, Get $5,000 Fee.

The details of the settlement of the suit brought by Jerome Napoleon Bonaparte, great-grandnephew of the Emperor, against his wife, Blanche Bonaparte, to set aside an agreement transferring all of his property to her, became known in the Supreme Court yesterday, when a report was filed by Emanuel B. Cohen, appointed referee to determine the amount of the fee to be paid to Leon R. Jacobs, who acted as attorney for Mr. Bonaparte. The referee recommended that the fee be fixed at $5,000, although counsel for Mrs. Bonaparte contended that $250 should be enough.

The report of the referee states that on Dec. 23, 1922, Mr. Bonaparte entered the Craig House, a sanitarium at Beacon, N. Y., "to endeavor to restrain himself of a habit which he had unfortunately contracted." He was discharged as cured on April 21, 1923. Mr. Bonaparte alleged in the suit filed in his behalf by Mr. Jacobs that while he was ill his wife induced him to go to the office of her attorney, William M. K. Olcott, and sign an agreement putting all his property in her hands, and reserving only a small part of the income for himself.

The referee states that Mr. Bonaparte went alone to the office of Attorney Olcott and signed the assignment of his property dictated by Mr. Olcott, whereby he was to get only $5,000 of the income, and the remainder was to go to his wife. The agreement also set forth that he had made a will leaving all of his property inherited from his father and grandparents to his wife.

Value of the Property.

The instrument stated that the property consisted of a half interest in rents from Baltimore property owned by his grandmother, Suzane M. Bonaparte, valued at $165,000; an interest in rents from property owned by his great-grandmother, Elizabeth Patterson, valued at $30,000; a half interest in a deed of trust executed by his father, Jerome Napoleon Bonaparte, in 1877, amounting to $11,000; a life interest under the will of his father, from which the income in 1924 was $10,452; a half interest in property owned by his father in Baltimore valued at $3,000, and a claim for a further quarter interest in his father's property, in litigation, which, if successful, would add $30,000 to his income.

The referee states that Mr. Bonaparte, after being released from the sanitarium, made several requests to his wife for the return of his property, but that she refused to return it and also refused to pay his bills at the Craig House. Mr. Bonaparte then consulted Attorney Jacobs as to taking legal action, and in the course of ten weeks saw him twenty times. At these interviews he stated that the value of his property was $500,000. Mr. Jacobs accordingly brought suit to set aside the transfer on the ground that the plaintiff did not realize what he was doing at the time he signed the agreement.

The attorney last saw his client when they called at the Hotel St. Regis to see

Continued on Page Eight.

FINAL SCENES DRAMATIC

Defense Suddenly Decides to Make No Plea and Accept Conviction.

BRYAN IS DISAPPOINTED

Loses Chance to Examine Darrow and His Long-Prepared Speech Is Undelivered.

HIS EVIDENCE IS EXPUNGED

Differences Forgotten in the End as All Concerned Exchange Felicitations.

Special to The New York Times.

DAYTON, Tenn., July 21.—The trial of John Thomas Scopes for teaching evolution in Tennessee, which Clarence Darrow characterized today as "the first case of its kind since we stopped trying people for witchcraft," is over. Mr. Scopes was found guilty and fined $100, and his counsel will appeal to the Supreme Court of Tennessee for reversal of the verdict. The scene will then be shifted from Dayton to Knoxville, where the case will probably come up on the first Monday in September.

But the end of the trial did not end the battle on evolution, for not long after its conclusion William Jennings Bryan opened fire on Clarence Darrow with a strong statement and a list of nine questions on the basic principles of the Christian religion. To these Mr. Darrow replied and added a statement explaining Mr. Bryan's "rabies." Dudley Field Malone also contributed a statement predicting ultimate victory for evolution and repeating that Mr. Bryan ran away from the fight.

The end of the trial came as unexpectedly as everything else in this trial, in which nothing has happened according to schedule except the opening of court each morning with prayer. It was reached practically by agreement between counsel in an effort to end the case, which showed signs of going on forever, although all the testimony offered before the jury took only two hours.

Young Scopes, in his shirt sleeves, his collar open at the neck, his carrot-colored hair brushed back, stood up before the bar with a gold epauletted policeman beside him, and Judge Raulston had pronounced sentence before his counsel could suggest that Mr. Scopes might have something to say.

"Oh," exclaimed Judge Raulston, "Have you anything to say, Mr. Scopes, as to why the Court should not impose punishment upon you?"

Scopes Calls Statute Unjust.

Mr. Scopes, who is hardly more than a boy and whose pleasant demeanor and modest bearing have won him many friends since this case started, was nervous. His voice trembled a little as he folded his arms and said:

"Your Honor, I feel that I have been convicted of violating an unjust statute. I will continue in the future, as I have in the past, to oppose the law in any way I can. Any other action would be in violation of my ideal of academic freedom, that is, to teach the truth as guaranteed in our Constitution, of personal and religious freedom. I think the fine is unjust."

No one had expected such a quick ending. Mr. Darrow came into court full of the pleasant anticipation of another "go" at Mr. Bryan, whom he questioned to the delight of hundreds the day before. But the court had no sooner opened than Judge Raulston decided that there would be no further questioning, and then ordered Mr. Bryan's testimony expunged from the record.

Mr. Bryan, who had contented himself with the thought that he would have an opportunity to put Mr. Darrow on the stand and tear into him, was somewhat chagrined at this turn of the case, and announced that he would have to appeal to the fairness of the press to give prominence to the questions which he would have asked Mr. Darrow.

"I had not reached the point where I could give my statement to answer the charges made by the counsel for the defense as to my ignorance and bigotry," he said, bitterly.

Sparrow Poses as Dove of Peace.

But before the day's session was over a dove of peace hovered over the court room in the form of a frightened sparrow, which had strayed in through an open window, and everybody exchanged felicitations except Mr. Bryan and Mr. Darrow. Judge John Raulston declared that the Word of God, "given to man, that man may use it as a waybill to the other world," was an indestructible thing, and prayed God that he had decided right the questions raised in the trial. A minister pronounced a benediction and court adjourned.

The general gratification of the people at the end of a good show was shown by their applause whenever any member of either side, or the visiting spectators, rose to thank Dayton for its hospitality and kindness. And there was a further manifestation of the remarkable change in sentiment which has taken place since this trial began.

The defense faced a unitedly hostile audience when they started. There were

Scopes Trial Ends Abruptly, but Evolution Fight Rages in Statements

clamors against Clarence Darrow, the agnostic, and resentment that outsiders should come in and tell Tennessee how to run its schools.

The tide turned when Dudley Field Malone made his first speech and won the hearts of Dayton, for Tennesseans love a fiery speaker, and rounded, eloquent periods delight them. Mr. Darrow ended by winning their respect by his courage in the face of hostility, and when today both sides spoke briefly their appreciation of courtesies, and Mr. Bryan defended his position, it was a repudiation of Mr. Bryan's charges by Mr. Malone and the denunciation of bigotry by Mr. Darrow that won the most fervent applause.

That does not mean that the majority was with them. It was not. But they had caught the fancy of the crowd, which has learned a lot about evolution from the scattered fragments presented to them. Many people of the State crowded around Mr. Darrow after court was over to thank him for his defense of Mr. Scopes and to say that they were ashamed of the Anti-Evolution law.

There was no doubt that the ruling of the Court against further examination of counsel on either side was as much a disappointment to Mr. Bryan as it was to Mr. Darrow. Mr. Bryan was obviously full of wrath at the position in which he had been placed, with no opportunity of justifying himself on the court record, and Mr. Darrow had come into court with the pleasant anticipation of learning what else Mr. Bryan knew about the Bible.

There was a council of war by the forces of the State last night, and whatever desire Mr. Bryan had of going on with his examination so that he could rip into Mr. Darrow and his colleagues, and brand them as agnostics or infidels, was suppressed by Attorney General Stewart, who has maintained an indignant, though dignified, opposition to the events of the last few days. He was anticipated, however, by the Court.

"Since the beginning of this trial the Judge of this court has had some big problems to pass upon," said Judge Raulston as soon as court opened. "Of course, there is no way for me to know whether I have decided these questions correctly or not until the courts of last resort speak. If I have made a mistake, it was a mistake of the head and not the heart.

"There are two things that may lead a Judge into error. One is prejudice and passion, and another is an over-zeal to be absolutely fair to all parties. I fear that I may have committed error on yesterday in my over-zeal to ascertain if there was anything in the proof that was offered that might aid the higher courts in determining whether or not I had committed error in my former decrees. I have no disposition to protect any decree that I make from being reversed by a higher court, because, if I am in error, I hope to God that somebody will correct my mistake.

"I feel that the testimony of Mr. Bryan can shed no light upon any issues that will be pending before the higher courts. The issue now is whether or not Mr. Scopes taught that man descended from a lower order of animals. It isn't a question of whether God created man as all complete at once, or it isn't a question as to whether God created man by the process of development and growth. Those questions have been eliminated by this Court, and the only question we have now is whether or not this defendant taught that man descended from a lower order of animals.

"As I see it, after due deliberation, I feel that Mr. Bryan's testimony cannot aid the higher court in determining that question. If the question before the higher court involved the issue as to what evolution is, or as to how God created man, or created the earth, or created the universe, this testimony might be relevant, but those questions are not before the Court, and so, taking this view of it, I am pleased to expunge this testimony given by Mr. Bryan yesterday from the records of this court, and it will not be further considered."

"Of course I am not at all sure that Mr. Bryan's testimony would aid the Supreme Court, or any other human being," said Mr. Darrow, "but he testified by the hour there and I haven't got through with him yet."

General Stewart objected to an argument, and Mr. Darrow took an exception from the Court's ruling, announcing that he would try to get from the Supreme Court a writ certifying the testimony. Then Mr. Darrow threw up his hands and ended the case.

"We have all been here quite a while, and I say it in perfectly good faith, we have no witnesses to offer, no proof to offer on the issues that the Court has laid down here," he said, "that Mr. Scopes did teach what the children said he taught, that man descended from a lower order of animals. We do not mean to contradict that and I think to save time we will ask the Court to bring in the jury and instruct the jury to find the defendant guilty. We make no objection to that and it will save a lot of time and I think it should be done."

Hays Again Offers Proof.

Arthur Garfield Hays then made again his offer of proof for the record.

"We offer to prove by Mr. Bryan that the Bible was not to be taken literally," he said, "that the earth was a million years old, and we had hoped to prove by him further that nothing in the Bible said what the processes were of man's creation. We feel that the statement that the earth was a million years old, and nothing said about the processes of man's creation, that it was perfectly clear that what Scopes taught would not violate the first part of the act."

All Mr. Hays's arguments brought nothing but exceptions, and then Mr. Bryan rose to his feet, a great weariness in his voice and with the look of a tired and disappointed man.

"At the conclusion of your decision to expunge from the testimony the testimony given by me upon the record I didn't have time to ask you a question," he said. I fully agree with the Court that the testimony taken yesterday was not legitimate or proper. I simply wanted the Court to understand that I was not in position to raise an objection at that time myself, nor was I willing to have it raised for me without asserting my willingness to be cross-examined. Now the testimony has ended and I assume that you expunge the questions as well as the answers."

"Yes, sir," said Judge Raulston.

"That it isn't a reflection upon the answers any more than it is upon the questions," continued Mr. Bryan in his dispirited voice.

"I expunge the whole proceedings," said the Court.

"Now, I hadn't reached the point where I could make a statement to answer the charges made by the counsel for the defense as to my ignorance and bigotry," said Mr. Bryan, turning to glare at Mr. Darrow, who hunched up his shoulders and said:

"I object, your Honor! Now, what's all this about?"

"Why do you want to make this, Colonel Bryan?" asked the Court.

"I just want to finish my sentence."

"Why can't he go outside on the lawn?" growled Mr. Darrow.

Judge Raulston said he would hear what he had to say, and Mr. Bryan continued:

"I shall have to trust to the justice of the press which reported what was said yesterday to report what I will say, not to the Court, but to the press, in answer to that charge scattered broadcast over the world, and I shall also avail myself of the opportunity to give to the press, not to the Court, the questions that I would have asked had I been permitted to call the attorneys on the other side."

"I think it would be better, Mr. Bryan," said Mr. Darrow, "for you to take us out also with the press and ask us the questions, and then the press will have both the questions and the answers."

"The gentleman who represents the defense not only differs from me," continued Mr. Bryan, "but he differed from the Court very often in the matter of procedure. I simply want to make that statement, and say that I shall have to avail myself of the press without having the dignity of its being presented in this court, but I think it is hardly fair"—his voice rose as he lifted his clenched hand—"to bring into the limelight my views on religion and stand behind a dark lantern that throws light on other people but conceals themselves. I think it is only fair that the country should know the religious attitude of the people who come down here to deprive the people of Tennessee of the right to run their own schools."

"If your Honor please," interrupted Mr. Malone, who manages to get into every argument, "I wish to make a statement if statements are in order."

"If your Honor please," added Mr. Malone, who has taken joy in standing up for the religious principles of all those on the side of the defense, "the attorneys for the defense are hiding behind no screen of any kind. They will be happy at any time in any forum to answer any questions which Mr. Bryan can ask along the lines that were asked him yesterday."

Attorney General Stewart, whose Fundamentalism has been the cause of much embarrassment to him all during the case, stopped fidgeting and suggested that the jury be brought in and the case ended. Mr. Darrow and Mr. Stewart, with Judge Raulston, then agreed that the jury be brought in and instructed by both sides to bring in a verdict of guilty.

When the jury were present Judge Raulston charged them that all they had to do was to determine whether or not Mr. Scopes taught that a man descended from a lower form of animals and that if they so found beyond a reasonable doubt they should bring in a verdict of guilty.

"May I say a few words to the jury," said Mr. Darrow. He stood before them, as plain a looking person as any one among them, his suspenders standing out against his shirt, his arms folded so that he grasped his shoulders, and smiled benignantly at them.

"We are sorry we have not had a chance to say anything to you. We will do it some other time," he said. "Now, we came down here to offer evidence in this case and the Court has held under the law that the evidence we had is not admissible, so all we can do is take an exception and carry it to a higher court to see whether the evidence is admissible or not. As far as this case stands before this jury, the Court has told you very plainly that if you think my client taught that man descended from a lower order of animals you will find him guilty, and you heard the testimony of the boys on that question and heard read the books, and there is no dispute about the facts.

"Scopes did not go on the stand, because he could not deny the statements made by the boys. I do not know how you may feel, I am not especially interested in it, but this case and this law will never be decided until it gets to a higher court, and it cannot get to a higher court very well unless you bring in a verdict. I do not want any of you to think we are going to find any fault with you as to your verdict.

"We cannot explain to you that we think you should return a verdict of not guilty. We do not see how you could. We do not ask it."

"What Mr. Darrow wanted to say to you was that he wanted you to find his client guilty," said Mr. Stewart to the Judge, "but did not want to be in the position of pleading guilty because it would destroy his rights in the Appellate Court."

Bryan's Speech Is Undelivered.

And that's all there was to that. Mr. Bryan did not get his chance to make the summing up he had been working on so long, the speech that was to rival his "Cross of Gold" speech of many years ago, which made him a candidate for the Presidency. He knew he would not get this into the records soon after court opened, and it was one of his great disappointments. He is said to have been writing it for three months. He never would have gotten a chance to make it even if the verdict of guilty had not been found by agreement, because the defense had planned to let the State open the summing up, and then refuse to argue, which would have shut off anything except the verbal onslaught of Sue Hicks, who was scheduled to talk first for the prosecution.

After Mr. Scopes had been found guilty and fined, Judge Raulston set bail in $500, which was furnished by The Baltimore Sun. The case will come up before the State Supreme Court in September, and Judge Raulston allowed thirty days for preparation of the appeal.

Then followed the felicitations, started by Mr. Malone, who said:

"Your Honor, may I at this time say on behalf of my colleagues that we wish to thank the people of the State of Tennessee, not only for their hospitality, but for the opportunity of trying out these great issues here."

He was applauded liberally by the crowd. One of the visiting spectators got up to thank Dayton for its hospitality. Gordon McKensie of the prosecution, thanked the defense for bringing into Tennessee new ideas.

"We have learned to take a broader view of life since you came," he said. "While much has been said and much written about the narrow-minded people of Tennessee, we do not feel hard toward you for having said that, because that is your idea. But we people here want to be more broad-minded than some have given us credit for, and we appreciate your coming and we have been greatly elevated, edified and educated by your presense, and should the time ever come when you are back near the garden spot of the world we hope that you will stop off and stay a while with us here in order that we may chat about the days of the past when the Scopes trial was tried in Dayton."

Dr. John R. Neal of the defense spoke, and then Mr. Bryan rose again and said the people would decide this issue.

"I don't know that there is any special reason why I should add to what has been said, and yet the subject has been presented from so many viewpoints that I hope the Court will pardon me if I mention a viewpoint that has not been referred to," he said. "Dayton is the centre and seat of this trial largely by circumstance. We are told that more words have been sent across the ocean by cable to Europe and Australia about this trial than has ever been sent by cable in regard to anything else doing in the United States. That isn't because the trial is held in Dayton. It isn't because a school teacher has been subjected to the danger of a fine of from $100 to $500, but I think it illustrates how people can be drawn into prominence by attaching themselves to a great cause.

"Causes stir the world, and this cause has stirred the world. It is because it goes deep. It is because it extends wide and because it reaches into the future beyond the power of man to see. Here has been fought out a little case of little consequence as a case, but the world is interested because it raises an issue, and that issue will some day be settled right, whether it is settled on our side or the other side. It is going to be settled right. There can be no settlement of a great cause without discussion, and people will not discuss a cause until their attention is drawn to it, and the value of this trial is not in any incident of the trial, it is not because of anybody who is attached to it, either in an official way or as counsel on either side.

"Human beings are mighty small, your Honor. We are apt to mignify the personal element and we sometimes become inflated with our importance, but the world little cares for man as an individual. He is born, he works, he dies, but causes go on forever, and we who have participated in this case may congratulate ourselves that we have attached ourselves to a mighty issue.

"Now, if I were to attempt to define that issue I might find objection from the other side. Their definition of the issue might not be as mine is, and, therefore, I will not take advantage of the privilege the Court gives me this morning to make a statement that might be controversial, and nothing that I would say would determine it.

"I have no power to define this issue finally and authoritatively. None of the counsel on our side has this power, and none of the counsel on the other side has this power. Even this honorable Court has no such power. The people will determine this issue. They will take sides upon this issue, they will state the questions involved in this issue, they will examine the information—not so much that which has been brought out here, for very little has been brought out here, but this case will stimulate investigation and investigation will bring out information, and the facts will be known, and upon the facts as ascertained the decision will be rendered, and I think, my friends and your Honor, that if we are actuated by the spirit that should actuate every one of us, no matter what our views may be, we ought not only desire but pray that that which is right will prevail, whether it be our way or somebody else's."

Darrow Makes Final Retort.

His words brought a last retort from Mr. Darrow. He thanked Dayton for its hospitality and courtesy and liberality and thanked the Court for not sending him to jail, which aroused laughter.

"Of course there is much that Mr. Bryan has said that is true," he continued. "And nature—nature, I refer to—does not choose any special setting for mere events. I fancy that the place where Magna Charta was wrested from the barons in England was a very small place, probably not as big as Dayton. But events come along as they come along.

"I think this case will be remembered because it is the first case of this sort since we stopped trying people in America for witchcraft, because here"—and he thundered out the last words—"we have done our best to turn back the tide that has sought to force itself upon this modern world of testing every fact in science by a religious dictum. That is all I care to say."

Judge Raulston was moved to join the proceedings.

"I recently read somewhere what I think was a definition of a great man, and that was this: That he possess a passionate love for the truth and has the courage to declare it in the face of all opposition. It is easy enough, my friends, to have a passion to find a truth, or to find a fact, rather, that coincides with our preconceived notions and ideas, but it sometimes takes courage to search diligently for a truth that may destroy our preconceived notions and ideas.

"The man that only has a passion to find the truth is not a complete and great man; but he must also have the courage to declare it in the face of all opposition. It does not take any great courage for a man to stand for a principle that meets with the approval of public sentiment around him, but it sometimes takes courage to declare a truth or stand for a fact that is in contravention to the public sentiment.

"Now, my friends, the man—I am not speaking in regard to the issues in this case, but I am speaking in general terms—that a man who is big enough to search for the truth and find it, and declare it in the face of all opposition, is a big man.

"Dayton has been referred to, that the law—that something big could not come out of Dayton. Why, my friends, the greatest Man that has ever walked on the face of the earth, the Man that left the portals of Heaven, the Man that came down from Heaven to earth that man might live, was born in a little town, and he lived and spent his life among a simple, unpretentious people.

"Now, my friends, the people in America are a great people. We are great in the South, and they are great in the North. We are great because we are willing to lay down our differences when we fight the battle out and be friends. And, let me tell you, there are two things in this world that are indestructible, that man cannot destroy, or no force in the world can destroy.

"One is the truth. You may crush it to the earth, but it will rise again. It is indestructible, and the causes of the law of God.

"Another thing indestructible in America and in Europe and everywhere else, is the Word of God, that He has given to man, that man may use it as a waybill to the other world. Indestructible, my friends, by any force because it is the Word of the Man, of the forces that created the universe, and He has said in His Word that 'My word will not perish,' but will live forever.

"I am glad to have had these gentlemen with us. This little talk of mine comes from my heart, gentlemen. I have had some difficult problems to decide in this lawsuit, and I only pray to God that I have decided them right.

"If I have not the higher courts will find the mistake. But if I failed to decide them right, it was for the want of legal learning and legal attainments, and not for the want of a disposition to do everybody justice."

The meeting was about to break up when Arthur Garfield Hays rose and called out to the Judge, laughingly:

"May I, as one of the counsel for the defense, ask your Honor to allow me to send you the 'Origin of Species' and the 'Descent of Man,' by Charles Darwin?"

There was a roar of laughter as the Judge said he would be glad to receive them.

"We will adjourn," said the Court, "and Brother Jones will pronounce the benediction."

Benediction was pronounced, and it was followed by a rush to the doors.

French Scientists Protest Tennessee Law As an "Odious" Effort to Suppress Thought

Special Cable to THE NEW YORK TIMES.

PARIS, July 21.—The anti-evolution trial at Dayton may be regarded as a source of amusement in some places, but not so in France, where prominent scientists today formally launched a protest against Tennessee's attempt to suppress the teaching of the Darwinian theory.

The protest bears the signatures of the leading members of the Academy of Science and is based on the conviction that the Dayton proceedings constituted not only an attack on "the most prolific acquisition to biology in the nineteenth century" but also an "odious" attempt to limit freedom of thought.

Among the leading signators of the protest are Mme. Irene Curie, co-discoverer of radium; Paul Appell, rector of the University of Paris, and such noted figures in French science as Professors A. d'Arsonval, A. Aulard, Ferdinand Brunot, Jacques Hadamard, Dr. Imbeaux, Paul Janet, Paul Langevin, Louis Lumiére and General Sebert, each one representing a record of valuable achievements in important branches of scientific research.

The protest reads as follows:

"The undersigned vigorously protest against the violation of freedom of thought which the proceedings at Dayton represent. They believe that if the Darwinian theories at some points remain open to dispute it is impossible to withhold them from the knowledge of modern man. These theories have contributed greatly to the formation of contemporaneous scientific thinking and the idea of evolution which they have projected on the double terrain of observation and experience is one of the most prolific acquisition of biology in the nineteenth century.

"Among all forms of oppression that which would limit the imprescriptible right of freedom of thought is the most odious and most futile.

"If it be the right and duty of each individual to dispute the conclusions of science it is not within the province of any one to prohibit him from formulating them and submitting them to the judgment of men.

"No power, political or religious, can arrogate to itself the right to proscribe any form whatever of human thinking.

"In raising against the Dayton trial the protest of men of science we seek to defend not only one of the most valuable of scientific theories but also, and especially, freedom of thought, which never has been disavowed by the great American nation."

EVOLUTION BATTLE RAGES OUT OF COURT

Bryan Denounces Opponent as Product of Evolution—Says Bible Is Vindicated.

DARROW RETORTS IN KIND

Explains the Commoner's "Rabies" as Due to Exposure of "Ignorance" on Stand.

Special to The New York Times.

DAYTON, Tenn., July 21.—The conflict between William Jennings Bryan and Clarence Darrow was continued out of court today after John Thomas Scopes was found guilty and the trial ended. Disappointed in his desire to question Mr. Darrow as to his belief in the divinity of Christ, the immortality of the soul and his conception of God, Mr. Bryan propounded nine questions to Mr. Darrow in typewritten form, and Mr. Darrow answered them with his agnostic's creed, "I do not know," except where he could deny them with his belief in natural, immutable law.

[The text of Mr. Bryan's questions and of Mr. Darrow's replies to them will be found in another column on this page.]

Although the contest of the champions, which included long statements, was at long range, carried on through the intermediary of newspaper reporters—far different from the proceedings of the day before when Mr. Bryan lost his temper on the stand under Mr. Darrow's prodding questions—it was none the less bitter.

Mr. Bryan called Mr. Darrow "the finished product of evolution," embodying "all that is cruel, heartless and destructive in evolution."

"He is our Exhibit A," said Mr. Bryan, "and proves the criminal folly of entrusting to the tempestuous sea of life an intellectual ship without a moral rudder."

Bryan Sees Bible Vindicated.

The Tennessee trial has proved that the Bible is true, Mr. Bryan stated, and has awakened people to "the insidious attacks which have been made, under cover of a scientific hypothesis, upon the authority of the Bible by unbelievers."

Mr. Darrow answered that he could not believe in the God believed in by Mr. Bryan, "a magnified picture of a man," but that he had never said he did not believe in God, and was an agnostic willing to receive light.

"Far be it from me to determine between Mr. Bryan and myself as to who has the greatest love of man," said Mr. Darrow. "Mr. Bryan's statement throws some light upon his feelings. I fancy no one in need of a friend or help would have any uncontrollable impulse to fly to him."

Mr. Bryan's "rabies," Mr. Darrow said, were due to his having been placed upon the witness stand, and added:

"I cannot help having some pity for Mr. Bryan being obliged to show his gross ignorance by the simple and competent questions asked him on the witness stand. However, I am inclined to think the public would forget it sooner if he stopped raving about it."

Dudley Field Malone said that the defense had accomplished its purpose in obtaining a record full of reversible error which would declare the law unconstitutional, and declared that Mr. Bryan was trying to raise a smoke screen "to cover the shameless exhibition of ignorance and bigotry which he has given throughout this trial." Mr. Bryan had run from the issue, he said, and added:

"There is more of philosophy and love of Jesus Christ in Clarence Darrow than there is in the pretensions of William Jennings Bryan.

Text of Bryan's Statement.

Mr. Bryan's statement follows:

"The trial is over; the State has won its case. The Tennessee law has been vindicated and sentence pronounced on the young school teacher who violated it. The State has not lost a point from the beginning of the trial to the end.

"The issue is so large that individuals and localities are relatively unimportant. It dwarfs all other issues now under consideration by the people of the United States and of the world. Is the Bible true? is the question raised by the Tennessee law, and that question is answered in the affirmative as far as this trial can answer it.

"Believing as I do in revealed religion—that is to say, in Christianity built upon the Word of God—I rejoice that the followers of our Lord and Saviour Jesus Christ are at last awakened to the insidious attacks which have been made, under cover of a scientific hypothesis, upon the authority of the Bible by unbelievers of every grade and class. The attack upon the authority of the Bible is organized, deliberate and malignant, and had only to be uncovered to be understood.

"Mr. Darrow's entrance into the case has been most fortunate for the Christian Church. He is the most conspicuous of the outspoken opponents of religion in the nation. He is the finished product of evolution—the most perfect that has yet developed in the United States. He embodies all that is cruel, heartless and destructive in evolution. He is our Exhibit A and proves the criminal folly of entrusting to the tempestuous sea of life an intellectual ship without a moral rudder and without a compass.

"He does not believe that there is a God—he is an avowed agnostic—and, therefore, has no sense of responsibility to God, as love of fellow-man has no other foundation than love of God, as set forth in the two Commandments, 'Thou shalt love the Lord thy God with all thy heart, and thy neighbor as thyself.' He has no basis upon which to build an unselfish interest in anybody or in anything. In this trial he has been true to his unbelief from beginning to end.

"He objected to the customary opening of the court with prayer and insisted on the removal of a sign, 'Read your Bible.' He has slurred the Bible, insulted the Court, has shown his contempt for everything Christian and, everybody identified with Christianity as it is taught in orthodox churches, and 'the ruling passion strong in death,' closed the after-trial meeting in the court room with a sneer when all the other participants had spoken in a spirit appropriate to the occasion.

To Continue His Attack.

"In the speech which I prepared for delivery before the jury [I was honored by the State with the privilege of making the closing speech] I shall set forth the State's side of the case in defense of the law and in explanation of the purpose of the good people of Tennessee, whose will it expressed. This speech will be ready for next Sunday morning's papers. I shall prepare for the papers on Thursday morning an answer to Mr. Darrow's charge that I am an ignorant bigot.

"I am not vain enough to think that this compliment—for, coming from him, it was a compliment—was intended for me alone. While it was addressed to me, it was intended for all who dare differ from him to the extent of believing in the Bible, the God whom it reveals as the supernatural Christ of whom it tells. I shall answer for all Christians as well as for myself, but I feel that the answer will receive more consideration if it is separated from the proceedings of today. I shall, therefore, extend this article only far enough to include the questions that I would have submitted to Mr. Darrow and the counsel associated with him.

"When Mr. Darrow summoned me as a witness yesterday I might have refused to testify, but knowing that his purpose was to impose upon the people outside the courtroom rather than to try the case, I consented to testify in order that he might not be able to charge me with unwillingness to face his questions. He did not ask a single question that was proper or that would have been permitted had I objected to it. The Judge permitted them to be asked only because I was willing to answer, and later, upon reflection, expunged both questions and answers from the record.

Says Attack Was on the Bible.

"In accepting the invitation to testify, I did so on condition that I might question the attorneys on the other side in the same way. When the Court reached the conclusion that such testimony was incompetent and expunged it from the record, I was precluded from asking the questions which I had prepared. I give them below. It will be seen that they are the same in purpose as his questions; namely, they seek to bring out the religious attitude of the person to whom they are addressed. They are as improper for the trial as his, but as proper for the newspapers. If the gentlemen are as honest as they constantly protest that they are, they will not object to a frank statement of their views. Their real purpose can better be ascertained from their views on religion than from any professions that they make as to their reasons for appearing in the case.

"Before the Court and in the proffer of evidence, they contended that the theory of evolution is consistent with the Bible. If so, why was the case not conducted by conspicuous champions of Christianity? If their answers show that they do not accept the Bible in its orthodox interpretation as it is accepted by the people of Tennessee, then the public will be compelled to believe that instead of defending free speech or religious liberty, they are attempting to force the views of a minority—whether those views be described as religious or irreligious—upon the children of the majority in the public schools.

"For the first time in history, so far as I have been able to learn, a militant minority, made up of atheists, agnostics and other dissenters from orthodox Christianity, is seeking to use the court to compel the majority to pay teachers to undermine the religious faith of the children of the taxpayers who employ teachers."

Text of Darrow's Reply.

Mr. Darrow's statement follows:

"Mr. Bryan has done me the honor to say I am the finest product of evolution. I do not believe I am. I hope there are many finer products, both living and still to come. If I am the finest product of evolution I am the direct antithesis to him. Mr. Bryan is not a product of evolution, but comes under the classification of those who revert to type.

"Whether Mr. Bryan and I are typical examples of what should be the outcome of real religion I am not able to say. I fancy neither of us is the best that could be done. Far be it from me to determine between Mr. Bryan and myself as to who has the greatest love of man. Mr. Bryan's statement throws some light on his feelings. I fancy no one in need of a friend or help would have any uncontrollable impulse to fly to him. As to my entrance into this case being unfortunate to the Christian Church, I did not come into it until he volunteered, and which one's entrance was most unfortunate must be determined by religionists. I am inclined to think that most intelligent religionists would like to get rid of Mr. Bryan.

"I have never said I did not believe in a God. I have never been able to satisfy myself of a first cause. As to that, I am an agnostic—ready to receive light from any one who has anything to give.

"Mr. Bryan, although he has been as long out of court as ever, knows perfectly well that it is not customary to open court with prayer. It was especially out of keeping in this case. While Mr. Bryan insisted this was a trial between the Bible and evolution, likewise no one who had any sense of justice in such a trial would have approved of such a sign, ten feet long and fourteen inches high, tacked up before the jury, enjoining them to read the Bible.

Why He Put Bryan on Stand.

"Mr. Bryan's rabies seem due to the fact that I placed him on the witness stand. I offered to place on the witness stand eminent Christian scholars to interpret the meaning of the story in Genesis and the Bible as to the creation of Man. Mr. Bryan objected to this testimony, with a sneer at all colleges, institutions of learning and Biblical scholars, and told the Court that a jury in Tennessee, most of whom had little education, knew more about the Bible than all the eminent scholars we sought to call.

"The Judge excluded this testimony on Mr. Bryan's request from the hearing of the jury, but permitted us to put it in the record for examination by the Supreme Court on the question of whether the trial court erred in excluding the evidence. On the same theory we called Mr. Bryan to the witness stand as an expert on the meaning of the Bible. Very likely we were wrong in this, as he was probably not an expert, but we had in mind that for several years the newspapers of this country had carried his Sunday preaching to the world, and we thought he ought to know.

"We had a perfect right to offer his evidence as to whether the Bible in all cases should be literally interpreted. How much Mr. Bryan knows about the Bible or any other subject can best be determined by reading his answers. However, he did say he believed the literal days of creation mentioned in the first book of Genesis were probably not literal days, but were vast periods of time, which would seem to me to warrant the inference that if Mr. Bryan could place his interpretation on the meaning of a day which opened in the morning and closed in the evening, it might not be an evidence of original sin if some one else placed an interpretation on the method by which God made man.

"Of course, I cannot help having some pity for Mr. Bryan's being obliged to show his gross ignorance by the simple and competent questions asked him on the witness stand. However, I am inclined to think the public will forget it sooner if he stops raving abot it.

Says Bryan Invited Inquiry.

"I was led to believe that Mr. Bryan was perfectly willing to permit evidence as to the correct interpretation of Genesis and likewise as to what evolution meant, by the fact that I was reliably informed by a dozen newspaper men of high standing whose reports were generally printed that he had invited the fullest investigation of the case of evolution and religion. The justice of such an investigation was very plain because only one member of the jury had ever read of evolution, and the rest had never heard anything of it until Mr. Scopes was arrested.

"Mr. Mryan informed us that he will soon make a statement of what he would have said, if he had said it, 'for all Christians.' I assume he has the authority to speak 'for all Christians.'

"Mr. Bryan is not the best judge of whether my questions were not competent. It is enough to say he answered them in the presence of the Court. It is interesting to note that on the morning after his answers that the Court on its own motion, before anything was said, shucked the testimony from the record. I could not help wondering why the Court helped Mr. Bryan out of his dilemma so early in the morning before any protest was made in open court.

"Mr. Bryan has seen fit to ask me to answer nine specific questions. Of course this has nothing whatever to do with the case, but I have no objection to answering them. Of course I speak for myself and myself alone, and I speak of my present opinions, which I am always ready to change.

"I have never tried to impose my views of religion on any human being that ever lived. I have a right to my own views and would fight as hard to protect every other man's views as I would fight to protect my own."

Malone Sees Ultimate Victory.

Mr. Malone's statement in part reads:

"Our objects in coming to Tennessee have been fulfilled. Though Professor Scopes has been convicted, we have made a record filled with reversible error, which will, we believe, ultimately declare the Tennessee evolution law unconstitutional.

"But a greater result has been achieved. Mr. Bryan has been organizing, through political and church organizations, a campaign to control the educational system of the country by dogmatic religion and to organize sufficient church and political power to create a State religion in the United States. It has been necessary to expose the objects and pretentions of Mr. Bryan's present leadership.

"After his examination by Clarence Darrow yesterday no intelligent person in America can believe that Mr. Bryan is an authority on science, education or the Bible. Mr. Bryan announced to the country that this trial would be the forum in which would be fought the battle of science against religion, but when the witnesses for science were produced, Mr. Bryan, out of fear, opposed their testimony, and out of cowardice, ran from the issue which he had made."

Text of Bryan's Nine Questions on Religion And Darrow's Replies to the Commoner

Special to The New York Times.

DAYTON, Tenn., July 21.—The text of the nine questions which William Jennings Bryan asked Clarence Darrow this evening and Mr. Darrow's replies to them was as follows:

I—The Existence of God.

Q.—Do you believe in the existence of God as described in the Bible?

A.—I do not know of any description of God in the Bible, although we are informed in one part of it that He is a spirit. If Mr. Bryan would describe what he means by God I could probably tell whether I believe in his God. The question of what is meant by the Word was directly put by counsel for the defense, and one of counsel for the State, in Mr. Bryan's presence, said he believed God was like man and was a magnified picture of a man. I do not believe in this kind of God. As to the origin of the universe and what is back of it I do not pretend to know. I haven't the intimate acquaintance with it that Mr. Bryan says he has.

II—The Bible.

Q.—Do you believe that the Bible is the revealed will of God, inspired and trustworthy?

A.—I think that there is much of value in the Bible. I do not believe that it was written or inspired by God. I believe it should be taken as every book and the portions of every great book made sublime by great figures of speech, may be called inspired. I might even say this of Mr. Bryan's book "In His Image," if I could find any such portion.

III—Christ.

Q.—Do you believe in the supernatural Christ, foretold in the Old Testament and revealed in the New Testament?

A.—I do not believe any supernatural Christ was foretold in the Old Testament and revealed in the New. I believe that the Christ that was prophesied in the Old Testament was a great Jew who should deliver the Jews from their physical bondage and nothing else.

Mr. Darrow answered questions 4, 5, 6 and 7 collectively.

IV—Miracles.

Q.—Do you believe in the miracles recorded in the Old and New Testaments?

V—Reasons Asked.

Q.—If you believe in some, but not all of them, please name a few of those which you accept and those you reject, with the reasons for same?

VI—Virgin Birth.

Q.—Do you believe that Christ was conceived of the Holy Ghost and born of the Virgin Mary as recorded in Matthew and Luke?

VII—The Resurrection.

Q.—Do you believe that Christ rose from the dead, as described in the four Gospels?

A.—As to Questions 4, 5, 6 and 7, I do not believe in miracles. I believe that the universe acts and always has acted in accordance with immutable law, and whatever may be back of the Universe has never violated these laws.

VIII—Immortality.

Q.—Do you believe in the immortality of the soul?

A.—I have been searching for truth of this all my life with the same desire to find it which is incidental to every living thing. I have never found any evidence on the subject.

IX—Origin of Man.

Q.—If you believe in evolution, at what point in man's descent from the brute is he endowed with hope and promise of a life beyond the grave?

A.—I have no knowledge on the question of when man first believed in life beyond the grave. I am not at all sure whether some other animals have not the same hope of future life. The origin may have arisen in vivid dreams concerning the return of the dead, or, for all I know, from actual evidence of the return of the dead.

AUTHOR OF LAW DISAPPOINTED.

Thinks Scopes Should Have Been Fined More—Studies Evolution.

Special to The New York Times.

DAYTON, Tenn., July 21.—John Washington Butler, the Lafayette farmer who is the author of Tennessee's anti-evolution measure, said today that he was sorry that John Thomas Scopes was not fined more than $100 for violating the law.

"I am well satisfied," he said, "with the verdict of guilty, but I think a fine of $500 would have been more in keeping with the gravity of the offense.

"This has not been a test case of the law. Other school teachers who violate will be brought to trial and fined.

"As for myself, I am busy now reading evolution, but so far I have learned nothing that makes me disbelieve my Bible."

CROWD AT THE END SURGES TO DARROW

Tennessee Fundamentalists Pay a Spontaneous Tribute to His Courage.

ALL CONGRATULATE HIM

It Is Only Later That Thought Is Given to Bryan and the Other Figures in the Trial.

Special to The New York Times.

DAYTON, Tenn., July 21.—When John Thomas Scopes, the young school teacher, was found guilty today of teaching the theory of evolution, as every one had expected, a strange thing happened in the Rhea County Court House, where so many strange things have happened since the strange trial started.

The so-called Fundamentalists of Tennessee, who had seemed so overwhelming in favor of the law, who had cheered the utterances of counsel defending faith in the Bible against the "heresies" of scientists, stormed Clarence Darrow, the agnostic, to shake his hand.

Men and women rushed behind the bar the moment Judge Raulston adjourned court. They surged about Mr. Darrow, pushing each other to get at him. They brought up their children, who also wanted to shake his hand, and members of the jury came up smiling and offered their hands.

In a moment Mr. Darrow was holding a reception and for a little while William Jennings Bryan, the Fundamentalist leader, seemed forgotten. Presently, after the crowd had shaken Mr. Darrow's hand, it went more leisurely to Mr. Bryan, but for a half hour the group about the Chicago lawyer was undiminished. He was congratulated for his rationalism, his utterances and his courage, and from many came invitations to visit other Tennessee communities to speak, and from the jury came regrets that they did not hear him.

R. L. Gentry, the juror who is a country school teacher and farmer, a little middle-aged man with a long drooping mustache, like that of the old Indian fighter, seemed to speak for all the jurors.

"We were sorry we didn't get a chance to hear you," he said. "We all wanted to hear what you had to say, and we heard practically nothing."

Those who had seen Mr. Darrow only "in action" this half hour of repose when he was receiving the greetings of the country folks, got another picture of the man whose demeanor in the court room had been so skeptical, so pessimistic, so sardonic in his references to "Mr. Bryan's religion." They saw the stern, yellow face with the disillusioned eyes soften into smiles, while the eyes lighted up with pleasure. He was as delighted as a boy and seemed as shy, and when a small boy was brought up to shake hands with him he put his arm about the lad's shoulders and held him close as if from the child he got strength to bear up under the adulations of the grown-ups.

But the congratulations did not come to Mr. Darrow alone. Dudley Field Malone and Arthur Garfield Hays of counsel for the defense also held little receptions in the court room. Mr. Malone has become popular with the Tennesseans. They have liked his smiling manner. They had applauded almost every utterance he made, and they will remember him a long time through the speech he made last week asking Mr. Bryan why the Fundamentalists "were afraid" to permit the introduction of scientific evidence.

The conclusion of the trial was a "love feast." Every one spoke well of every one else. Mr. Bryan softened and spoke to the Court of "the side which was right" eventually winning. So also in a different vein spoke Mr. Darrow. Newspaper correspondents thanked the Court and the town for their hospitality, Tennessee lawyers "welcomed" the lawyers from other States to help the "settlement of a great issue" and, finally, Judge Raulston, with his "I pray to God I have decided these questions right," adjourned the trial.

The crowd was greater even than yesterday when Mr. Bryan was questioned on the reasons for his beliefs, for nearly all expected he would be placed again on the stand, and nearly all were stunned when, so suddenly, the case was ended by both sides waiving their rights for summation. But such as were inside got some of the humor and some of the pathos that has characterized the case.

Kelso Rice, the Chattanooga policeman who has acted as court officer, announced a moment after he had called the room to order for the opening of court that the session had started early "on account of the Judge's watch."

"The Judge is not fast," he added; "it's just his watch."

And then, a little later, after the Judge had been out to prepare his charge to the jury, they saw him pose so seriously before the cameras with the charge in his hand as if he were reading it, his usual smile gone, the hand with which he so often stroked his chin still.

Neither did the Judge smile when he got up to expunge from the record the testimony Mr. Bryan gave yesterday. Attorney General Stewart had objected vainly yesterday to the continuance of the examination. The Judge had sought to give Mr. Bryan an opportunity to escape it, but Mr. Bryan had insisted on remaining on the stand and the State felt "matters had been allowed to go too far." So Judge Raulston expunged it from the record, his face a blur of features as he intoned in a sing-song voice his reasons for the action, while Mr. Stewart sat looking at the floor.

Soon the trial was over, John Thomas Scopes, standing beside a gold-braided policeman, was convicted of teaching that "man descended from a lower order of animals in contradiction to the Bible," and the Tennessee crowd rushed at his defenders with congratulations and encouragements.

ENGLISH RIDICULE BRYAN.

London Star Calls Scopes Trial a Farce.

By Wireless to THE NEW YORK TIMES.

LONDON, July 21.—In a parting shot at the Scopes trial The Star ridicules William J. Bryan's child-like belief in the Bible, and says that if the Bible had said that Jonah swallowed the whale he would have believed that with equal credulity.

"The gem of yesterday's proceedings," says The Star, "is Mr. Bryan's reply to the evidence of the rector of the Episcopal Church in Tennessee, who held that when the Bible says that little hills skipped like young rams no one is expected to accept the statement literally. But it would take more than that to daunt the credulity of Mr. Bryan, for has he not heard of earthquakes and landslides?

"When called to the witness chair he placidly asserted that everything should be accepted as given. He believed the story that the whale swallowed Jonah. In the face of credulity like that we are not surprised to learn that the floor of the court house showed signs of giving way. Mr. Bryan's faith might not move mountains, but it is quite sufficient to shake the flimsy foundations of a shack in Tennessee.

"The reflection is not upon the Bible, but upon Mr. Bryan, whose fantastic excuses are degrading a legimate controversy into sheer farce. One more example of what Mr. Bryan can swallow and the arboreal instincts of the natives will reassert themselves. They will take to the branches of trees."

Commenting on the Scopes verdict, Sir Oliver Lodge said he thought that it was a mistake, but so long as it was the law it was bound to be observed. He did not regard the case as a trial of evolution.

2,000,000 WORDS WIRED TO THE PRESS

Western Union Sent Vast File From Dayton on Time Under Many Difficulties.

120,000 TO THE TIMES

Five Direct Wires Used to Get 19,500 Words on a Single Day—100 Reporters at Trial.

Special to The New York Times.

DAYTON, Tenn., July 21.—Nearly 1,500,000 words were sent over the commercial wires of the Western Union Telegraph Company to the newspapers of the United States on the Tennessee evolution trial. This was exclusive of the private wires operated by four press associations during the ten days the trial was in progress and over which, it was estimated another 500,000 words were carried in day and night reports.

The Western Union had twenty-two telegraphers here under the direction of T. S. Bogan of Nashville, District Commercial Manager; J. W. Ware of Atlanta, Division Traffic Supervisor, and W. P. Shearer, Division Wire Chief. They worked under difficulties in a storeroom separated from a grocery by a partition. Into this room ventilation came only through the doorway.

The heavy traffic was carried for the most part during an unusually heated spell, when the operators worked in a temperature of nearly 100 degrees. On two nights they worked against electrical storms which interrupted wires to the east and they had to reroute the press circuits by way of Chicago.

On another night, the heaviest of the trial, when 202,000 words were filed, the operators worked by candlelight because the town's electric light plant was out of use. Yet despite all these difficulties there were no complaints about slow service.

There were more than 100 reporters here, two of them from London who sent daily cables. The average daily press file when court was in session was 165,000 words.

News of the Scopes trial telegraphed to THE NEW YORK TIMES by its special correspondents at Dayton, totaled 120,000 words in a period of twelve days. Although the daily average was 10,000, the reports on a single day thrice exceeded 15,000 words, and once rose close to 20,000.

The largest number of words handled was telegraphed on July 16, when in addition to all the other features of the day's developments, THE TIMES carried the full text of Mr. Bryan's argument against the admission of evidence by scientists and scholars. To get the bulk of that text into the first edition, with all the other trial news of the day and all of it in succeeding editions, five telegraph wires were used. These wires ran direct from the Western Union office in Dayton to the telegraph room in The Times Annex, so that at the peak ten men—five at each end—were engaged in the telegraphic transmission of a single story.

Almost as great a problem confronted THE TIMES on Monday, when there were put into the court record a series of papers by scientists and scholars, outlining the case for evolution as against special creation, as well as all the other news of the trial, including the examination of Mr. Bryan by Mr. Darrow. There came from Dayton on that day 16,788 words and at times four wires were used to get them all into the office on time. The third largest file was on July 13, when 15,248 words were handled.

"All the News That's Fit to Print."

The New York Times.

THE WEATHER
Fair and slightly warmer today; tomorrow possibly rain or snow.
Temperature yesterday—Max. 31, min. 16.
For weather report see Page 35.

VOL. LXXVI....No. 25,186. NEW YORK, SATURDAY, JANUARY 8, 1927. TWO CENTS In Greater New York | THREE CENTS Within 200 Miles | FOUR CENTS Elsewhere in the U. S.

NEW YORK AND LONDON TALK FREELY, OPENING NEW RADIOPHONE SERVICE; FIRST PRIVATE CALL TO NEW YORK TIMES

MEXICO INVOLVED AS BORAH ASSAILS NICARAGUAN POLICY

White House and Kellogg Point to Aid Mexicans Are Giving Sacasa Forces.

DON'T ACCUSE GOVERNMENT

Administration Stands Firm in Its Support of the Diaz Regime.

BORAH CONSULTS COOLIDGE

His Attack Follows Frank Interview With President—He Supports Sacasa as Legal Executive.

Special to The New York Times.

WASHINGTON, Jan. 7.—The smoke that has enveloped the Government's attitude in Nicaragua's civil war lifted further today to reveal forks of flame indicative of an underlying blaze of considerable proportions, while a back-fire of opposition added to the over-heated atmosphere.

Senator Borah, Chairman of the Committee on Foreign Relations, after having it out with President Coolidge face to face, put himself in a position of hostility to the President before he made his exit from the White House door. His utterances to newspaper men concerning the President's policy were provocative of the first declaration in any public way from an authoritative source that the effort to overthrow the Government of President Diaz of Nicaragua, which the United States has recognized and is supporting, was being augmented from Mexico.

This assertion, or suggestion, or whatever it may be termed, came guardedly from the White House as well as the State Department, with the implication in the latter case that it reflected what had been said by Frank B. Kellogg, Secretary of State, although there was careful avoidance of any accusation that outside fomentation of the Nicaraguan revolutionary movement involved the Mexican Government.

"Intervention," Borah Calls It.

When he left President Coolidge's office Senator Borah told newspaper men that our policy in Nicaragua was "intervention." In a prepared statement after his return to the Capitol he contended that the constitutional President of Nicaragua was Juan Sacasa, whose belligerent campaign to oust the Government recognized by the United States as "constitutional" is meeting with opposition from the Washington Administration, which takes the position that Sacasa is seeking to usurp authority to which he is not entitled.

The Administration, however, stood flatly on its policy of supporting President Diaz against Sacasa and gave no sign of bending under the storm of criticism that its course has aroused.

Chief interest in Washington concerns the question whether the Administration will seek to justify its Nicaraguan policy by a public declaration that the Mexican Government, headed by President Calles, who has no love for President Coolidge and Secretary Kellogg, is furnishing arms and ammunition to the Sacasa forces with a view to setting up a Nicaraguan Government hostile to the United States.

So far only informal hints from Administration sources have furnished a clue to the underlying reason for the several steps taken by the State Department and the Navy Department in seeking to uphold the hands of President Diaz. Today's utterances by Secretary Kellogg and the White House, while they fell short of actual accusation of the Calles Government, marked a step nearer official specification along that line.

At the White House it was said that there was no doubt that arms had gone from Mexico to Nicaragua, a statement qualified by a disclaimer that this implied an accusation against the Mexican Government. When Secretary Kellogg, a bit more cautious, was asked whether it was not known that Mexico had been supplying Sacasa with arms, he returned that "everybody knew where the ships came from and where the landed arms in Nicaragua."

Administration's Course Explained.

It was made known at the White House that the broad foundation of the Administration's course in Nicaragua was furnished by two recognized principles.

One was what is known as the Evarts doctrine, enunciated by William M. Evarts when he was Secretary of State in 1878 in a communication to John W. Foster, then Minister to Mexico. This doctrine, read textually to newspaper representatives at the White House, laid down that it was the first duty of a Government to protect life and property; that this duty was incumbent on a Government whose nationals were menaced by the neglect of a Government in whose territory they resided; that the United States Government was not solicitous about the methods to accomplish this protection of its imperiled nationals in a foreign land and that "protection in fact to American lives and property is the sole point upon which the United States is tenacious."

The other fundamental has a more intimate relationship to the present Nicaraguan situation. It is the outgrowth of efforts made by Charles E. Hughes when Secretary of State to bring the Central American republics into formal agreement that they would take certain measures to put a stop to their frequent revolutionary tendencies, and to this end to recognize only those Governments in Central America which

Continued on Page Four.

F. W. Savin, Banker, to Wed Again at 76; Maid in His Home to Be Fourth Wife Today

Frank W. Savin, millionaire banker and the second oldest living member of the New York Stock Exchange, is to be married for the fourth time, probably today, this time to a Czechoslovakian maid employed on his estate at Port Chester.

City Clerk Sanarcoe of Port Chester issued a license to the couple yesterday. Mr. Savin gave his age as 76 and his bride to be, Anna Mary Schleis, on her affidavit said she was 41 years old. She was born in Czechoslovakia and came to this country some years ago.

City Clerk Sanarcoe said last night he understood the marriage ceremony would be performed today by the Rev. Hugh F. Gilmartin, pastor of the Roman Catholic Church of Our Lady of Mercy. Father Gilmartin said last night he knew nothing about it.

Mr. Savin's first wife, to whom he was married in 1871, was Arriba Wheat, the daughter of a New Haven doctor. The couple had two children, Josephine and Frank W. Savin Jr.

Mr. Savin's second wife was Sadie West, who figured in the Lexow investigation into police conditions. She died on Sept. 8, 1911, and is buried under an apple tree on the Savin estate.

His third wife was Mrs. Sarah Munroe Treadwell, whom he married on Feb. 3, 1912. She had been companion and housekeeper for the second Mrs. Savin.

The third Mrs. Savin died on Dec. 17, 1925.

While his second wife was alive Mr. Savin adopted a four-year-old girl, Muriel Elizabeth Withnall, an orphan. Soon after he married his third wife he adopted her brother-in-law, Charles Edy Monroe, who was then 43 years old. He is still living on the Savin estate. Mr. Savin had previously disinherited his two children by his first wife.

It was understood last night that the reason for Mr. Savin's fourth marriage was his advancing age and that as Miss Schleis had been caring for her employer for some time, he decided she would be a suitable person to look after him and suggested that she become his wife, whereupon she consented.

SHADOW LAWN RAZED BY $1,250,000 BLAZE

Mansion Where Woodrow Wilson Conducted His Front-Porch Campaign Destroyed.

ART TREASURES ARE LOST

H. T. Parson, Woolworth Head, Owned Estate—Flames Visible 20 Miles.

Special to The New York Times.

LONG BRANCH, N. J., Jan. 7.—Shadow Lawn, the home of Hubert T. Parson, President of the F. W. Woolworth Company, in the Norwood district of West Long Branch, from which the late President Woodrow Wilson conducted a "front porch" campaign in 1916, was destroyed by fire tonight.

The fire started in the basement about 6 o'clock while a dozen or more servants were dining and, fanned by a high wind, the flames swept through the wooden structure. By 10 o'clock all that remained of the magnificent building were two chimneys that towered above the glowing ashes. The loss, which included valuable tapestries, rugs, pictures and furnishings, was estimated at $1,250,000. Mr. and Mrs. Parson were in New York at the time of the fire.

The cause of the fire was not learned definitely. It was said to defective wiring by some and by others to an overheated furnace. The servants, including Josephine Fitzgerald, Lucy Clarke, Katherine Paterson and Catherine Graham, were dining in the kitchen when they noticed smoke coming from the basement. They hurriedly searched the first floor, then went to the basement. Thick clouds of smoke met them.

Caretaker Sends In Alarm.

Meanwhile, John Thompson, caretaker, who lives in a cottage nearby, had seen the smoke. He ran to the corner of Norwood and Cedar Avenues, which border on the fifty-eight acre estate on which the house was situated, and turned in an alarm to the West Long Branch Fire Department.

While the firemen were hastening to the scene Miss Clarke and Miss Fitzgerald braved the thick smoke in the basement to connect a fire hose there and send a stream of water on the fire. Soon the flames grew higher and forced them to flee. With the other servants they had to vacate the mansion without their belongings they could gather in a few moments and seek shelter in other buildings on the estate.

By the time the West Long Branch firemen reached the house the flames were mounting swiftly and alarms were turned in quickly for aid from the Fire Departments of Long Branch, North Long Branch, Eatontown, Elberon, Deal, Allenhurst and Asbury Park.

Flames Seen for Twenty Miles.

Situated on a knoll that looks over the ocean about one mile away, with carefully laid out lawns, orchards and groups of shrubs stretching away from it, the mansion soon blazed into a torch that lit up the sky and was seen for twenty miles. Large crowds from the surrounding neighborhood hurried toward the estate in their automobiles. At one time there were nearly 1,000 cars parked on Norwood Avenue.

The increased force of firemen was powerless to check the roaring flames. They had a hard time saving nearby barns and stables. Finally there was nothing left but the walls and that was left of the mansion were the two chimneys and the mass of embers. Mr. Parson was notified in New York and left for Long Branch at once.

Built by Insurance Man.

Shadow Lawn was erected in 1902 by the late John A. McCall when he was President of the New York Life Insurance Company. It was said that he spent $1,000,000 in establishing the estate. After he had lived there two years he died. Abraham White then acquired it, but failed in trying to make it a Summer colony of the estate and in 1908 a syndicate, headed by Myron H. Oppenheim, took it over with a similar intention. This project also failed to materialize. In 1909 J. B. Greenhut, New York department store owner, purchased it.

Already Shadow Lawn had been considered as a Summer White House, at least by certain New Jersey residents, who put forth the plan of buying it and presenting it to the Government as a Summer residence for the President, who was then William Howard Taft. The sale ended this plan, but in 1916, when Mr. Wilson was engaged in the campaign against Charles Evans Hughes, he occupied it and used it as a headquarters for his operations. It was there that he received the election returns that brought him victory.

In 1917 Mr. Greenhut sold the estate to the Harson-Leighton Corporation which a year later sold it to Mr. Parson. Mr. Parson spent large sums improving the house and the land. He and Mrs. Parson were accustomed to spend many week-ends there.

FOUR DIE IN PLUNGE OF FALLING DERRICK

Seven Others Hurt When Huge Mast Drops on Structure Next to Morgan Office.

WALL STREET FRIGHTENED

Crash Heard Through Financial District—Three Investigations Seek Cause of Accident.

A falling steel derrick mast on the site of the old Mills Building, at Broad Street and Exchange Place, adjoining the offices of J. P. Morgan & Co., carried two men to their death yesterday afternoon about 2 o'clock. Two more died in hospitals later in the day. Seven others were injured. Three investigations failed to reveal the cause of the accident.

The crash was heard by thousands, and many in the financial district, fearing another Wall Street explosion, rushed out to see what had happened. Iron workers and riggers for the Thompson-Starrett Company, which is building an office structure for the Equitable Trust Company on the site, had just erected the mast. Held by new steel one and three-quarter inch cables on a platform of 14 by 16 inch timbers, it was perpendicular and was thought to be secure.

Two Were Perched on Top.

The two who were killed outright were expert riggers. They had climbed its latticed sides and were perched near the top preparing to run the cables through the blocks. Iron workers were on the platform below them, sixty feet above the concrete and rock floor of the excavation.

Then the base of the mast slipped. There was a warning shout. Men sought cover where they could—all but the two on the mast—as the six tons of steel swayed for an instant and then fell toward Broad Street, carrying away the heavy timbers and twisting heavy steel I-beams from their riveted sockets into scrap iron. Fifteen feet of the tip of the mast snapped off against the concrete wall of the basement. Fellow-workers picked up the dead men and the injured from where they had been thrown. Dead and injured were taken in taxicabs and ambulances to B oad Street and Beekman Street hospitals. The complete casualty list follows:

The Dead.

BEAUVAIS, JACK, 36 years old, 409 West Twenty-first Street; fractured right wrist, possible fractured skull; Beekman Street Hospital.

KRAFT, WILLIAM, 51 Weston Avenue, Maspeth, Queens; fractured skull and internal injuries; Broad Street Hospital.

MONICK, JAMES, 400 West Forty-eighth Street; fractured skull and internal injuries; Broad Street Hospital.

PAUL WALTER, 30 years old, 331 Pearl Street, Brooklyn; possibly fractured skull and internal injuries; Broad Street Hospital.

The Injured.

GAGNON, EDWARD, 30 years old, 137 West 125th Street; contusions; Broad Street Hospital.

MEYER, WILLIAM, 41 years old, 133 West 133d Street; contusions; Beekman Street Hospital.

MITCHELL, ANGUS, 30 years old, 177 Park Place, Brooklyn; abrasions, contusions; Broad Street Hospital.

RASMUSSEN, R., 58 years old, 452 Senator Street, Brooklyn; possibly fractured skull and scalp lacerations; Broad Street Hospital.

RICE, PETER, 31 years old, 331 Pearl Street, Brooklyn; injuries to back; Beekman Street Hospital.

SNOW, JOSEPH, 25 years old, 150 Schermerhorn Street, Brooklyn; scalp lacerations; Broad Street Hospital.

VALCOURT, ARTHUR, 28 years old, 206 Sixty-first Street, Brooklyn; contusions of right leg and lacerations; Broad Street Hospital.

Patrolmen Keegan, Grace and Eichell of the Old Slip Station, who were on post near by, telephoned the hospitals and Police Headquarters for rescue workers and reserves. Squads from Police and Fire Departments responded and searched for injured men, while the more seriously hurt were carried away and surgeons dressed minor injuries in the street.

Three Investigations Begun.

George Ellis, foreman in charge, was questioned by detectives and later taken to the office of Assistant District Attorney William P. Ryan of the Homicide Bureau. Action will be withheld, Mr. Ryan said, until Benjamin Hickey, an engineer attached to the District Attorney's office, completes an investigation. Inspectors from the Bureau of Buildings, after a preliminary examination, requested from Thompson-Starrett Company to guard broken pieces of the derrick for a more searching investigation.

Peter Eller, Assistant General Superintendent, made a preliminary survey for the company. Mr. Eller said that his examination was informal, as he had been assigned to look after the injured.

"In some manner," he said, "although fastened by new, strong steel cables, the base appears to have slipped. Competent engineers will make

Continued on Page Ten.

PRESIDENT'S FORCES BEAT BIG NAVY MEN ON CRUISER FUNDS

By Vote of 183 to 161 the House Refuses Appropriation to Build 3 Ships Now.

LEADERS DIVIDE ON VOTE

Longworth Joins Opponents of Coolidge Policy, Making a Speech From the Floor.

DIRIGIBLE STAYS IN BILL

Advocates of New Construction Predict Senate Will Adopt Their Cruiser Program.

Special to The New York Times.

WASHINGTON, Jan. 7.—A cry of "Stand by the President!" raised by a group of Republicans, combined with taunts from Democrats that the Old Guard leadership had definitely broken with President Coolidge on the naval increase issue, turned a threatened defeat for the Administration into victory today, when the House, by a vote of 183 to 161, rejected the Tilson amendment for an appropriation of $450,000 to begin work on three cruisers of the 1924 program, which Mr. Coolidge wished to hold up pending negotiations for another arms limitation conference.

Today's fight was one of the most picturesque waged in the House in a long time. Party lines were knocked helter-skelter, Democrats joining Republicans to uphold the President's desire for a halt on naval building, as indicated in his budget message. The La Follette Republicans from Wisconsin and most of the members of the farm bloc stood by the Administration.

On the other hand, Speaker Longworth, Republican Leader Tilson, Chairman Snell of the Rules Committee and Representatives Mills and Fish of New York, all dyed-in-the-wool party men, aligned themselves with the opposition.

The day was made notable by the appearance in debate of Speaker Longworth, who took the floor to aid the navy bloc and declared it was the duty of Congress to see to it that the navy did not drop below the 5-5-3 ratio contemplated by the Washington treaty. It was the first time that a Speaker had taken part in a House debate since Champ Clark made his protest in 1917 against President Wilson's recommendation for draft legislation.

Say Longworth Seeks Presidency.

In the opinion of Democrats, this was the first step of Mr. Longworth in the direction of placing himself in the field as a candidate for President in 1928.

"It means that Mr. Longworth is ready to throw his hat into the ring, and he made no mistake in utilizing the occasion today to make known his intentions," said Representative Loring M. Black Jr., a Tammany member from Brooklyn.

Representative Tilson of Connecticut, the Republican floor leader, summarized the reasons that led to today's victory for the Administration when he said:

"I think we all have a right to be very much surprised at the vote. The pacifist sentiment in the House is greater than was expected."

Speeches by Representatives Burton of Ohio, Green of Iowa and French of Idaho, who was in charge of the Naval bill, all Republicans, and Garrett of Tennessee, the Democratic leader, were credited with the development of events favorable to the Administration. Messrs. Burton, Green and French pleaded with the House to stand by the President on the "peace" issue, while Mr. Garrett's ironical references to the alleged break of Speaker Longworth, Mr. Tilson, and others identified with the Republican organization on the Navy bill, in the opinion of many, aroused resentment among enough Republicans to turn the scale.

Dirigible Appropriation Stops.

The forces arrayed against the Administration on the naval issue saved something from the mêlée. They succeeded in holding in the bill the Begg amendment, informally approved yesterday authorizing an appropriation of $200,000 to begin work on a $4,500,000 dirigible. This was adopted today by a vote of 185 to 105. In his budget message the President suggested that this construction be postponed pending conclusion of experiments being made by naval experts.

While House leaders declared tonight

Continued on Page Six.

Prince of Wales Leaps as Horse Stumbles; Sprains Wrist, but Continues in the Hunt

Special Cable to THE NEW YORK TIMES.

LONDON, Jan. 7.—The Prince of Wales met with another hunting accident today. He was out with the famous Quorn hunt in the neighborhood of Melton Mowbray when his horse stumbled at a difficult fence and fell. The Prince was able to jump clear, but in doing so badly sprained his left wrist and his wrist watch was smashed to atoms.

The horse, which had galloped away, was recaptured and restored to the Prince, who, although evidently in pain, pluckily remounted and completed the day's sport.

The Prince was not the only follower of the Quorn hunt to meet with an accident today. Violet, Duchess of Westminster, had an alarming experience. Her horse fell and she did a complete somersault, but escaped injuries.

Captain Greenall was also thrown and his horse broke its neck. Captain Hornby had a severe fall and broke an arm and his collarbone.

Less than a month ago, while hunting with the Quorn hounds, also near Great Dalby, the Prince of Wales was unhorsed when his favorite hunter fell at a formidable hedge. The Prince was thrown over the horse's head, but fell clear of the animal and kept hold of the reins. In a moment he had remounted and, covered with mud, continued to follow the chase.

LONDON HAILS NEW TIE

Radiophone Is Seen as Equal in Importance to Opening of Cable.

SERVICE IN GREAT DEMAND

Business Houses Are Among the First to Take Advantage of Quick Intercourse With Us.

SIMPLICITY STIRS WONDER

Reception Appears to Be Better Than That Experienced Here —Talks Continued at Night.

Special Cable to THE NEW YORK TIMES.

LONDON, Jan. 7.—London hailed today the first public telephonic conversations between New York and the British capital as an event of equal importance to the opening of the first transatlantic cable sixty-eight years ago or the first demonstration of the telephone itself eighteen years later.

So great was the demand for communication that at the last moment it was decided to keep the service open until 11 o'clock tonight (London Time).

Thrilling as were the inferences from the event, in its material details, the opening was quite matter-of-fact. It took place at 1:45 o'clock, London time, in exact accordance with the schedule.

Sir Evelyn Matter of Fact.

Sir Evelyn Murray, Secretary General of the British Postoffice, sitting in his usual chair at his desk at that time, heard his telephone ring and lifted the receiver. The first words he heard were: "This is American service calling," and New York's response.

A conversation between the two officials then took place, after which the service was thrown open to the public.

The first private transatlantic telephonic conversation—it started only five minutes by London Time after the inauguration of the service—was that between Adolph S. Ochs, publisher of THE NEW YORK TIMES, and Geoffrey Dawson, editor of The London Times. The London Times says in its account of the conversation:

"Mr. Ochs's voice was loud and distinct. After expressing his pleasure at being in direct verbal communication across 3,000 miles of space, he gave a message to the editor of The London Times, of which the actual text is recorded here."

There follows a report of Mr. Ochs's remarks [printed elsewhere in this issue of THE NEW YORK TIMES].

Reply of London Editor.

The editor of The London Times said to Mr. Ochs, in reply:

"Hearty greetings to yourself and to the whole staff of THE NEW YORK TIMES. It is right that the first telephone message sent across the Atlantic from Printing House Square should be addressed to the great newspaper which not only bears the same name but pursues so steadily the same ideal of the close cooperation of English-speaking nations. A happy new year to you all!"

Throughout the day the officials of the new transatlantic branch of the telephone service were busy handling private calls, most of which had been applied for weeks ahead. One of the early calls made was the advertising representative of THE NEW YORK TIMES in London to the New York office for the purpose of telephoning two advertisements, one on behalf of Edward Baron of the Carreras Tobacco Company and the other for Sir Charles Higham. THE NEW YORK TIMES man in London heard the voice of T. D. Palmer who answered the call from THE TIMES office in New York with perfect clearness. In fact, the whole conversation as far as the London reception was concerned was much more audible than a telephone message from Paris and fully

Continued on Page Two.

Times Wide World Photo.

His Honor of New York Telephones to London's Lord Mayor.

31 CALLS ARE MADE IN DAY

Static Troubles Users Slightly, but Voices Usually Are Distinct.

TIME EXTENDED TO 6:30 P. M.

Sir Evelyn Murray and W. S. Gifford Call Phone New Link Between Nations.

SOCIAL AND BUSINESS CALLS

Two Advertisements Also Cross Ocean to The Times—Service Continues at 8:30 A. M. Today.

"Hello, London."

These two simple words, spanning the Atlantic on electric waves traveling with the speed of light, heralded the opening of the radio telephone between New York and London yesterday morning, the most remarkable communication service yet devised by man.

They were spoken by Walter S. Gifford, President of the American Telephone and Telegraph Company, in the directors' room of the company on the top floor of 195 Broadway. He was talking to Sir G. Evelyn P. Murray, Secretary of the British Postoffice, over a circuit of 850 miles of land line and 6,300 miles of ether path. And so eager were persons on both sides of the Atlantic to have a part in the events of this first amazing day of public wireless transatlantic talking that from the time Mr. Gifford officially declared the system open to the public until it closed late in the afternoon there was a steady stream of conversation flowing through the air.

So many were the calls that the service was kept open until 6:30 o'clock, although there were interruptions in the middle of the day due to static.

Interrupted by Static.

For two long periods no messages could be sent or received, although the interference was much worse in sending from London than from this end. The English day is shorter than that in this country at this time of the year, and at sunset, when static raises an almost impenetrable curtain against the electro-magnetic waves, the operators were forced to turn the system over to the technical men for readjustment and sometimes for the application of greater power. For a time the English operators wished to discontinue, but were persuaded to keep going in the hope, later fulfilled, that the service would become better.

Conditions were worse yesterday than they have been for a month, much to the disgust of the operators, who had hoped for a good day. Rating the normal freedom from static—there is always some static—as 100 per cent., it was estimated at the offices of the company that yesterday conditions were only 25 per cent. of normal. Thirty-one calls were put through, not counting Mr. Gifford's, between 8:37 A. M. and 6:30 P. M., when the service was discontinued for the day. It will be resumed this morning at 8:30 o'clock and continued probably until 1 o'clock.

Fifty Hear Gifford Speak.

In the directors' room of the American Telephone and Telegraph Company at least fifty persons were in chairs ranged about a table and along the walls when the service opened. Each chair was equipped with a pair of headphones. Among those waiting for the epoch-making opening were Mr. Gifford, who sat at the head of the table; D. F. Houston, J. J. Carty, Bancroft Gherardi, F. B. Jewett, E. S. Wilson A. W. Page, E. K. Hall, C. M. Bracelen, N. T. Guernsey, C. P. Cooper, all Vice Presidents of the company; J. D. Ellsworth, assistant to the President; C. A. Heiss, Controller; H. Blair-Smith, Treasurer; A. A. Marsters, Secretary; J. S. McCulloh, President of the New York Telephone Company; C. G. Du Bois, Chairman of the board of the Western Electric Company; E. S. Bloom, President of the Western Electric; H. D. Arnold, director of research of the Bell Telephone Laboratories, and other officials.

There was a little delay in opening the system, the time for which had been set at 8:30 o'clock. It was found at once that the percentage of audibility, as the telephone men say, was very low at the high end, but after the technical men had eliminated static as much as possible Mr. Gifford picked up the radio telephone and said:

"Please connect me with Sir Evelyn Murray in London."

His voice was pitched in a low, conversational tone. So matter-of-fact did he seem, so lacking in excitement was the atmosphere of the room in which he sat, that the radio receiver was the centre of attention, that it did not seem possible that the miracle of projecting voices through the air for more than 3,500 miles was actually taking place. It was hard to realize the momentousness of the occasion.

Reply Comes Distinctly.

There was a slight buzzing on the wire, a slight click, and then the reply came back, distinctly:

"Hello, is that you, Mr. Gifford?"

The incredible had been accom-

$6,000,000 IN DEALS OVER RADIOPHONE

Wall Street Houses Talk to London on Foreign Exchange Transactions.

SCORE USE NEW SYSTEM

International Acceptance and Midland Banks Make Deals— A. T. & T. Stock Rises.

Wall Street was a heavy user of the new wireless telephone system between New York and London at the inauguration of service yesterday. More than $6,000,000 of foreign exchange transactions were effected, the details of a large financial reorganization were relayed to European correspondents of a New York banking house and Stock Exchange news was transmitted both ways over the ocean. In addition to the actual business transacted, executives of many banking houses conversed with men with whom they do business in London and discussed conditions there. At least a score of Wall Street houses made some use of the new system during the day.

$5,000,000 Transfer Put Through.

The largest deal of the day involved the transfer of £1,000,000 sterling and was put through by the foreign exchange department of the International Acceptance Bank, speaking to an official of the Overseas Branch of the Midland Bank of London. The conversation was carried on from an ordinary desk telephone in the bank's office, and the call was put through without confusion or delay. Later the International Acceptance Bank renewed its conversations with the Midland Bank and put through trades in four different Continental currencies. The total of the transactions of these two banks over the wireless telephone for the day was about $6,000,000. Arrangements for the deals had been made in advance and they were consummated without a hitch.

Strupp & Co., an international banking house, was in communication with London early in the day. After several offers and counter-offers, this firm and a London exchange trading concern put through several deals in Spanish pesetas and other currencies.

Stock Sells at New High.

Mainly in response to the success of the new communications system, stock of the American Telephone and Telegraph Company sold at its highest price since before the war. Ordinarily rather an inactive stock with average transactions around 1,500 shares a day, the stock made a net gain of 1⅜ points, and 4,200 shares changed hands. It closed at 151⅞, the highest it has touched since 1911, when sales were made at 153⅛.

Representatives of Speyer & Co. and J. & W. Seligman & Co., the banking firms which have acquired control of the Victor Talking Machine Company, telephoned the details of the new financing to the Central News, Ltd., of London, for distribution to British and Continental centres. The time occupied by the radio telephone was 6 minutes and 19 seconds. A large part of the new Victor securities will be distributed by European banking houses.

Both of the principal financial news agencies, Dow, Jones & Co. and the New York News Bureau, talked with their London correspondents. Reviews of the London Stock Exchange movements were received here, and New York developments were telephoned to London.

Results Good, Bankers Say.

Bankers who used the new system said that favorable results were obtained. Most of them foresee a suc-

Continued on Page Three.

WALKER HAS HIS FUN OVER LONDON CHATS

"Just Like Talking to Albany," Is His Comment After Holding Conversations Across Sea.

GREETS THE LORD MAYOR

Tells an Editor They Had Better Be Confidential With Many Millions Listening In.

Mayor James J. Walker had two talks with London over the transatlantic radio telephone yesterday, and apparently enjoyed them. His first talk was with Mr. Nichol, editor of The London Evening News, and his second with the Lord Mayor of London, Sir Rowland Blades. The conversations were delayed by static, and the Mayor seemed inclined to poke a little fun at the radio telephone, for he assured Mr. Nichol that the conversation must be more or less confidential, as probably millions of people were listening to it.

The conversation between the Mayors of the two largest cities in the world lasted five minutes, from 4:21 to 4:26 P. M. It was supposed to have begun at 1:30 o'clock, and the Mayor sat in his office, figuratively champing at the bit because of the delay. The call was made by The World to The World's office in London. At London the connection was made between The World office and the Lord Mayor's home, and in New York between The World office and the City Hall.

Talk With Lord Mayor

The conversation with the Lord Mayor follows:

The Lord Mayor—Hello.

Mayor Walker—Is this your Lordship?

The Lord Mayor—Yes.

Mayor Walker—This is the Mayor of New York, your Lordship. My compliments to you and the compliments of the City of New York to you and to the people of the City of London.

The Lord Mayor—(Not clear).

Mayor Walker—I didn't hear that, your Lordship.

The Lord Mayor—It is very kind of you to ring me up.

Mayor Walker—It is a great delight to me. I suppose we are both to be congratulated. Are you pretty well?

The Lord Mayor—Yes. (Rest of sentence not clear.)

Mayor Walker—Beg pardon?

The Lord Mayor—It gives me sincere pleasure to receive your kind message and I cordially reciprocate your friendly sentiments. I regard this a wonderful new method for communication between America and Great Britain. Direct phone intercourse will not only be immensely convenient to the commercial men of our two cities, but of immeasurable comfort and relief to those thousands of visitors from America who, to our great delight, come here during the season and may wish to get into personal touch with their families in America.

The same applies to our British visitors to the United States. Its influence in maintaining our friendly understanding, both socially and commercially, will be incalculable. I am proud to be the first Lord Mayor to speak to New York's principal citizen in this way. If we cannot meet face to face, a phone chat now and then will be the next best way of bringing us into direct communication. Accept London's good wishes for the New Year for yourself and your great city.

Mayor Walker—You can be assured, sir, that we have quite the same sentiments.

The Lord Mayor—This accomplishment will be of great commercial advantage to the two cities. I am proud to be the first Lord Mayor to speak in this way. Can you hear me?

Mayor Walker—I can hear your Lordship very well.

The Lord Mayor—I want you to ac-

Continued on Page Two.

Static Fails to Prevent the Success of the First Day's Transatlantic Phone Service

plished. Voices had raced around a circuit of 7,150 miles at a speed of 186,000 miles a second. They had traversed space on the band of an invisible wave, flashed through complicated apparatus silently, and been made articulate again at the other end.

"Yes, this is Mr. Gifford," replied the composed man at the head of the table. A tiny crash of static obliterated some of Sir Evelyn's words, and Mr. Gifford said, "I beg pardon."

"Just coming over now," was the reply of the British official. "Good morning."

"Do you hear me all right, sir?" asked Mr. Gifford.

"Yes," said Sir Evelyn.

Those about the room clutched their head phones a little tighter to their ears. Comprehension of what this conversation meant, the quiet impressiveness and fascination of magic become commonplace, took hold of them. Mr. Gifford glanced, smiling, around the room and then began his brief words of welcome to his colleague on the other side of the ocean.

New Channel of Communication.

"Today, as the result of very many years of research and experimentation, we open a telephonic channel of speech between New York and London," he said. "Thus, the people of these two great cities will be brought within speaking distance. Across 3,000 miles of ocean, individuals in the two cities may, by telephone, exchange views and transact business instantly as though they were face to face. I know that it is your aim, as it is ours, to extend this service so that in the near future any one in either of our countries may talk to any one in the other.

"No one can foresee the ultimate significance of this latest achievement of science and organization. It will certainly facilitate business; it will be a social convenience and comfort; and through the closer bond which it establishes it will promote better understanding and strengthen the ties of friendship. Through the spoken word, aided by the personality of the voice, the people of New York and the people of London will become neighbors in a real sense, although separated by thousands of miles.

"We are glad to have cooperated with you in this notable enterprise and shall actively continue to work with you in extending and improving the service. I congratulate you upon your successful solution of your problems and wish to extend to you and to your associates the greetings and good wishes of the officers and staff of the American Telephone and Telegraph Company and of their associates in the Bell telephone system."

Sir Evelyn's Reply.

As Mr. Gifford closed the voice of Sir Evelyn, stronger than it had been at first, began his prepared speech. He said:

"The opening of a public telephone service across the Atlantic between London and New York is a conspicuous milestone on the road of telephone progress and marks the beginning of a new epoch in the development of communication between our two countries. Personal conversation between Great Britain and the United States has emerged from the stage of experiment into a practical reality, and we are confident that the service which we are inaugurating today will be a boon to both nations, whether as an aid to commerce or as a medium of social and domestic intercourse, and will tend to strengthen the bonds which unite the two communities.

"I am charged by the Postmaster General to take this occasion to acknowledge the notable contributions which your company has been able to make through its engineering and research organization toward the solution of the many baffling problems which have been encountered. We recognize, as we believe you recognize, that there are difficulties still to be overcome before the transatlantic service can attain the standard of regularity and reliability at which we aim, but we are convinced that there is no better means of solving these difficulties than by putting the service to the crucial test of daily use, and we hope that before long transatlantic conversation will be available not only to the citizens of London and New York, but to every telephone subscriber in both countries.

"We of the British Postoffice look back with pleasure upon the cordial cooperation with the American Telephone and Telegraph Company, which has led to the success so far achieved, and on behalf of the Postmaster General and the officers of the General Postoffice I warmly reciprocate your greeting and good wishes. I now declare the service opened to the public."

London Times Greets N. Y. Times.

The first private conversation put through as soon as Mr. Gifford finished was between Adolph S. Ochs, publisher of THE NEW YORK TIMES, and Geoffrey Dawson, editor of The London Times. The connection was made and conversation began at 8:57 o'clock New York time.

Mr. Gifford finished speaking at 8:49 o'clock. Two minutes earlier Miss Mary A Timmons on the switchboard in THE NEW YORK TIMES office was told to be ready to receive a London call. Six minutes after Mr. Gifford had finished she was notified that the call was ready, and at 8:57 Mr. Ochs picked up the telephone in his office in the Times Annex and said:

"Good morning, Mr. Dawson. This is Mr. Ochs in New York. Can you hear me?"

Mr. Dawson replied that he could hear very well. The words from far-off London came through as distinctly at this time as on any long distance call in this country, only a little buzzing on the line indicating the static which later was to play havoc with communication.

"It is thrilling to greet you in this manner," continued Mr. Ochs. "Salutations to you and your associates on The Times. I wish you all a happy and prosperous New Year and ever increasing service to the public.

"Who now has the temerity to say that prayers are not heard in Heaven?

"Let me give you this pleasant bit of information as the first message by telephone. There is an ever-increasing sentiment throughout the United States, which is becoming more and more articulate, in favor of a reconsideration of the foreign interallied debts, after the French ratify their agreement, to the end that they may be adjusted on a higher moral and political basis, for peace and good-will throughout the world.

A Bell Prophecy Recalled.

"Yesterday I witnessed the exhibition of a new invention at Fox's studio in this city. It is called a Movietone, whereby sound is synchronized with motion pictures tending to verify what Dr. Alexander Graham Bell said about twenty years ago on the occasion when I gave a dinner at THE TIMES office in honor of Mr. Moberly Bell, then manager of The London Times. The inventor of the telephone then said that the day was not long distant when you could see as well as hear a person at a far distant point.

"I am being photographed as I am talking to you. I shall send you a copy of the picture by wire.

"Good-bye. Hope to hear often from you."

Heard Radiophone Talks, Johannesburg Amateur Says

JOHANNESBURG, South Africa, Jan. 7 (AP).—A local wireless amateur has put forth the claim that he was able to listen in on the radiophone conversations which inaugurated the transatlantic radiophone system between London and New York today. He says that he was able to hear distinctly during the time he was "tuned in."

A message was sent to The London Times telling of the manner in which Mr. Dawson's call was received. The talk lasted five minutes. While Mr. Ochs was speaking a flashlight photograph was taken and sent by radio to London. This was reproduced in The London Times this morning.

During the conversation a picture of Mr. Dawson was on Mr. Ochs's desk.

$5,000,000 Deal Handled.

Immediately after this message the flood of calls started from other newspapers, financial firms in Wall Street—one of which involved a $5,000,000 deal in foreign exchange—from moving picture executives, men in many lines of business, as well as reciprocal greetings between Mayor James J. Walker and the Lord Mayor of London. One firm received by the new telephone system an order for 100 carloads of lumber. Another announced to London a merger of business interests.

Shortly after 5 o'clock another message from London came to THE NEW YORK TIMES office. A telephone rang in the office of Rollo Ogden, editor of THE TIMES, and when he answered the telephone operator's voice said:

"London Chronicle calling. Here's your party."

At the London end was Ernest A. Perris, editor of The London Daily Chronicle, who had exchanged with Mr. Ogden a series of questions each was to answer.

"This is Mr. Perris speaking," came the voice from London, and Mr. Ogden replied:

"This is Mr. Ogden. Can you hear me?"

His voice traveled seventy miles by wire to the powerful radio station at Rocky Point, L. I., by radio to Wroughton, England, and a final eighty miles by wire to London, in the tiniest fraction of a second.

"I hear you perfectly," replied Mr. Perris.

"This is a great historic occasion," he continued. "We must make the most of our time. First let me wish you and all the readers of THE NEW YORK TIMES good health and good fortune for 1927."

"I wish heartily to reciprocate your good wishes, both personal and public," said Mr. Ogden.

Gives Causes for Our Prosperity.

Mr. Perris then asked Mr. Ogden to what he attributed the marvelous prosperity of the United States in the last few years. Mr. Ogden replied that he attributed it partly to good luck, partly to free trade over all the territory of the United States, abundance of money and credit, a surplus of exportable food and raw materials, standardization and high wages.

Is a purity crusade needed in the moving picture cities of California, Mr. Perris then asked, and Mr. Ogden said the trouble in the film cities was vulgarity, not impurity. They then decided to abandon the formal conversation, and Mr. Perris wanted to know how the weather was in New York.

"A very fine day but quite cold," Mr. Ogden told him, and after a few more pleasantries they said good-bye and broke the tenuous chain of electric waves linking them.

First Ads Phoned From London.

Among the early calls yesterday came one to the advertising department of THE NEW YORK TIMES, when two advertisements were telephoned by its London office. They came at 9:20 o'clock, and were advertisements of Indian tea and Craven tobacco. It took seven minutes to transmit them, and the cost was $175.

Last night, after the advertisements telephoned from London were in type here for publication today, THE TIMES received the following wireless from the sender, Sir Charles Higham, in London:

London, Jan. 7.

Editor, THE TIMES, New York:

Heartiest congratulations on being the first American newspaper to receive advertisements from England by telephone. That I should be the first advertising agent to send an advertisement by telephone from England naturally pleases me.

SIR CHARLES HIGHAM.

Other Calls to Newspapers.

In quick succession after the talk between Mr. Ochs and Mr. Dawson there were calls from Ralph D. Blumenfeld, editor of The London Daily Express, for Ralph Pulitzer of The World, and calls for The New York American, The Associated Press and The Herald Tribune. It soon developed that there are apt to be just as many transatlantic bromides as there are over the average local telephone line. Inquiries as to health and what the weather was in London were not overlooked, even by Mayor Walker in his two talks. One man was reported to have whistled to test the system. And it was also learned that only one woman talked during the whole day.

One of the most satisfactory results was the ease with which figures were transmitted, many stock quotations and figures of foreign exchange being received without much difficulty, although they occasionally had to be repeated, and in many cases firms took the precaution of sending a confirmation by cable or wireless telegraph. Service went on briskly until 11 o'clock, fifteen conversations having been completed by that time, and then trouble started.

Static broke over the waves with such force that even the technical men trying to restore the system to normal had great difficulty in conversing, sometimes not getting anything through. The worst interruptions were from 11:42 until noon, and from 1 o'clock until 1:45 P. M. In this interval from soon after 11 until after 2 o'clock only a few messages were forced through the static disturbance.

Average Talk Five Minutes.

The average message yesterday seemed to be about five minutes, but it is expected that the calls will get longer as the use of the new system becomes more common, particularly among large financial houses. There are more than enough calls registered to keep the system busy this morning, and telephone officials expect this demand to keep up. The company officials said they believed the first day had proved the system to be a success despite the worst static in a month. Whether it is extended to other cities will depend entirely on public demand.

The variety of the messages yesterday was due largely to the desire to talk on the first day, no matter on what subject, even the business calls being largely in the nature of "stunt" performances. Elmer Anderson, President of the Southeast Lumber Company, of 15 William Street, talked with A. P. Bamberger, a London lumber dealer, and received from him an order for 100 carloads of lumber valued at $100,000. Timber trade papers of England also talked with timber publications in New York.

The first call between London and Newark was from Sir Woodman Burbidge, of Harrods, Ltd., the department store of London, to Louis Bamberger, President of L. Bamberger & Co. Sir Woodman said "Hello," and Mr. Bamberger, not to be outdone in international courtesy, answered in the English fashion, "Are you there?" Sir Woodman said he was there. Sir Arthur Worley of London called C. F. Shallcross, United States manager of the North British Mercantile and Insurance Company, and announced that he would use the radio telephone frequently.

Rodman Wanamaker Talks.

Rodman Wanamaker spoke to his London store, and the message was relayed by telephone to the Paris branch of Wanamaker's. He also received a message from a Mr. Hodges of the Goldsmiths and Silversmiths Company of London, extending New Year greetings. One of the first persons to carry on a conversation was Adolph Zukor, President of the Famous Players-Lasky Corporation, who, at 10:50 A. M., was connected with John Cecil Graham, the company's Managing Director in London. Photographs of Mr. Zukor were taken and plans made to transmit them to London.

A message from London to California was sent over the radio telephone and relayed from New York. It was received from Castleton Knight in London by Major Edward Bowes, Managing Director of the Capitol Theatre, and relayed by him over land wire to John Gilbert of the Metro-Goldwyn-Mayer studios in Culver City, Cal., a distance of 7,000 miles.

NEWS BY RADIOPHONE.

Associated Press Gets a Sample From Its London Bureau.

The first news dispatch to be received by The Associated Press over the newly inaugurated radiophone commercial service between London and New York came from its London bureau at 10:02 A. M. yesterday, when the New York headquarters obtained a connection with the British Postoffice.

The London bureau dictated the following news dispatch to New York:

"LONDON, Jan. 7 (AP).—Official announcement that the Prince of Wales will visit Canada and the United States next Summer is expected to be made at Ottawa, Canada, soon. The Prince of Wales desires to accept the Canadian Government's invitation to attend the jubilee celebration in July. The Prince is expected to visit New York and the Middle West."

["Official announcement" that the Prince of Wales would visit Canada next Summer was carried in Associated Press dispatches from Ottawa, dated Dec. 10.]

Greetings Are Exchanged.

When the connection with London was established Carl S. Brandebury, an editor in the New York office, was advised. Over the receiving apparatus came first the roar and clicking of static and New York called:

"Hello, London A. P."

"Hello, New York office. This is Frank King talking. How are you?" came the voice, which rose and then faded away to almost a whisper as the static storm off Houlton, Me., beclouded the circuit.

"What's your big news?" asked the New York editor.

"Here it is," replied King. "I'll dictate it to you."

"Go slow," replied the A. P. editor in New York, "and I'll take it on a noiseless typewriter."

Then King dictated his dispatch on the projected visit of the Prince of Wales. At times his voice faded so that it was quite impossible to understand his dictation. Then it came clear again as the roar of the static passed. Sometimes it was only a blur of jumbled words and Brandebury had to call for several repetitions.

Some Words Unintelligible.

Some words, wholly unintelligible, were interspersed between three or four words that sounded as clearly as if they might have been uttered from some near-by local station.

So the news of the Prince's visit was carried while the static elements sputtered and cracked as if to fight man's commercial entrance into its aerial domain. The dispatch concluded, King asked to be remembered to everyone in the New York office and Charles Stephenson Smith, the chief of staff of the London office, came in on the wire.

"Hello, Brandebury; this is Smith talking. How is everybody in the New York office?"

"Fine," replied Brandebury, "and everybody wants to be remembered to you and the staff."

Then Brandebury, remembering that these radio telephonic amenities were running at the rate of $25 a minute, cheerily said "Good-bye," and Smith replied, "Good-bye, old man." And the first commercial call of The Associated Press to its London bureau was over.

Prepare for the Call.

It was 9:20 o'clock when the long-distance operator in the New York office notified The Associated Press to hold itself in readiness for a call to London within a few minutes.

There was a scurrying of copy boys around the switchboard with a vain hope that they might catch in some way a word or two that might come from the English capital. A noiseless typewriter was quickly placed within a telephone booth with a headset placed over the editor's ears.

There was a long wait of forty minutes before the voice of the London operator came weakly over the new circuit that the London call was ready.

Outside the telephone booth in the New York office the rataplan of telegraph instruments and mechanical sending machines dispatching to all points of the compass the news of the world added in small measure to the hum of the static on the London connection.

Getting Used to It Already.

Editors and operators peered into the telephone booth from time to time, but to them it was only another mechanical event and step toward the perfection of instantaneous and efficient transmission of the news of The Associated Press.

While the dispatch was the first to be transmitted over the Atlantic Ocean by commercial radiophone, The Associated Press received the first news dispatch transmitted by voice through the air from London to New York on March 7, 1926.

In that experimental dispatch Ambassador Alanson B. Hougnton, who was sailing on the steamer President Roosevelt from London, disavowed persistent rumors to the effect that he was returning to the United States to take the place of Secretary of State Kellogg.

LONDON, Jan. 7 (AP).—Only urgent demands for the presence of the Prince of Wales in England on official duties, it is understood, will prevent an American visit this year, news of which was sent by radiophone from London today.

After the Prince attends the jubilee celebration at Ottawa in July, he plans to spend a vacation on his ranch in Alberta, the to revisit mid-Western United States and later to go to New York for the Anglo-American polo matches before returning home.

DESCRIBES RADIO PROGRESS.

Gifford Tells of Experiments Leading to Transatlantic System.

An outline of the research work which has made possible the transatlantic radio telephone was made by Walter S. Gifford, President of the American Telephone and Telegraph Company, yesterday morning to those assembled in the directors' room of the company to witness the opening of the service.

In 1915, Mr. Gifford said, the company undertook experiments in the field of radio telephony, and, within a few months, engineers had built radio telephone equipment which enabled them to transmit the voice across the Atlantic to Paris and across the American continent and out into the Pacific as far as Hawaii.

"There are certain aspects of that important experiment of 1915 that I should like to mention," he said. "For one thing, we had to borrow an antenna which would be large enough to transmit over the long distances we hoped to attain. One of the few such antennas on the Atlantic Coast was that at Arlington, Va., belonging to the navy, and the use of that antenna was generously granted.

"At Paris, in spite of the war, permission was also generously granted for our engineers to equip the Eifel Tower with our radio telephone receiving apparatus. The ten-minute period immediately following 2 A. M., which the French assigned us, was favorable so far as atmospheric conditions were concerned, but interference from high-powered telegraph stations throughout Europe presented an almost impenetrable barrier to our faint speech signals coming from Arlington.

First Words Are Heard.

"After weeks of fruitless listening, success came at last. One night, just as they were ceasing their efforts, our engineers in Paris caught the words 'and now, Shreve, good-night.' There was no mistaking the origin of those words, and within a few minutes a cablegram was on its way to New York telling of the success.

"On following evenings, reception proved better and was heard with as much gratification by the French engineers invited to be present as by our own. Although 1,500 miles further away, Honolulu had picked up our messages from Arlington much sooner than Paris because of better receiving conditions.

"Following the close of the World War experimentation was again begun, and new lines of development were undertaken, with the result that many notable improvements were perfected. Time does not permit enumeration of these, but to illustrate the kind of thing that was done I will mention a new water-cooled vacuum tube which to the eye is very little larger than the tube used in 1915, but which is about 400 times as powerful.

"The 'single side band' type of transmission, which also was developed then, utilizes the power of the apparatus some five times as efficiently, and our developments in methods of receiving signals further improved transmission. To summarize, we are today employing about 100 times the power that our apparatus of 1915 could handle, and utilizing this power to many times as good advantage.

Voices Recognized in 1923.

"The effectiveness of these developments was first illustrated publicly in a test of January, 1923, during which, officials of our company speaking in New York, were, by prearrangement, heard in London by a large gathering of engineers and scientists. The test continued for some four hours, and frequent cable replies stated that as different speakers came to our microphone not only their words but their voices as well were recognized by the listeners.

"Today our engineers are providing the novel arrangement of simultaneous transmission eastward on long waves of 5,000 meters and short waves of 22 meters. These are both available to the receiving operator in London, who chooses whichever gives the better reception. Our short wave transmission is directive, such as is sometimes called 'beam' transmission.

"Even with these alternate wave transmissions, however, the natural disturbances to which radio transmission is subject are sometimes too great for us. We cannot claim, therefore, that the problem of transoceanic telephony is entirely solved; but our efforts have reached such a stage that we believe progress can now most rapidly be made by having commercial use and further research studies go on together."

At the top is a picture of the interior of the radiophone station at Houlton, Me. The unit receiving the radio waves from London is at the right and the telephone testboard and amplifier for the wire circuit to New York is shown at the left.

At the lower left is the huge bank of amplifier tubes used in transatlantic telephony.

In the oval are the antennae of the Rocky Point (L. I.) transmitting station.

LONDON HAILS NEW OVERSEAS PHONE

Continued from Page 1, Column 5.

as audible as an ordinary local call in London itself.

That was the general experience of others in London who either telephoned or were telephoned to by New York subscribers. The London reception appears to have been generally better than at New York.

However, the British Postoffice announced tonight that although the new service opened satisfactorily, radio reception deteriorated after sunset on account of bad atmospheric conditions. As a result, it was found impossible to complete all calls which had been booked. Conditions as regards atmospherics are said to have been exceptionally bad.

Big Deals Transacted.

Hundreds of thousands of pounds, it is estimated, were involved in calls which took place before closing service at 6 o'clock, bankers and brokers dividing with newspapermen the privilege of being pioneers of the new era of communication. On one conversation depended a £250,000 contract between Sir Walter Gibbons of the Capitol Film Theatre in London and the Fox Film Company. Another provided an opportunity for the Lord Mayor of London and the Mayor of New York to exchange greetings.

Those who had arranged for calls experienced little delay and were unanimous in their approval of the service provided. The proceedings were in fact so simple that it was difficult for subscribers to realize that they were participating in a revolution of transatlantic communication.

London business houses were among the first to take advantage of the new facility, for, although cabled replies can be received within a few minutes by Stock Exchange houses engaged in arbitrage business, this is less suitable for some purposes than telephone service. The Midland Bank was one of the first business houses to engage telephonic service to New York, its oversea branch carrying on two conversations with the International Acceptance Bank of New York and executing important exchange transactions in dollars, francs, lire, guilders and marks.

Sir Woodman Burbridge, managing director of Harrods, Ltd., the big London department store, spoke to Louis Bamberger, President of Bamberger & Co., in Newark.

"We are living in great days," said Sir Woodman. "I don't like to prophesy, but it seems to me that long before the wireless telephone has had a chance to grow old-fashioned, it will have proved itself one of the most wonderful friends of peacemakers this world has ever known."

Sir Arthur Worley, general manager of the North British and Mercantile Insurance Company, had occasion to communicate with the American manager of the company in New York on an important matter and was able to obtain the use of the new service.

The London Times put through a second call to its correspondent in New York. It was much severer than the test call, which had been strictly limited to six minutes. It was used to dictate two messages, 545 words long, which were received without difficulty. The messages were dictated at the rate of a hundred words a minute and there were not more than half a dozen pauses for repetition. The excellence of the communication left nothing to be desired. It was noticeable that the very strength of the speaker's voice occasionally tended to blur its clearness.

The Daily Express in the course of its wireless talk with New York had a photographic record of part of the message received made in The Express office with the "audiometer," invented by Professor A. M. Low, which prints a record.

Several unauthorized listeners participated in today's telephone conversations to the extent of hearing them. They were owners of wireless sets who were able to pick up calls with such clearness that one declared he could hear the popping champagne cork drawn in a London office so that the caller could celebrate the occasion.

LONDON PRESS HAILS EVENT.

Radiophone Called Triumph—Papers See Great Future.

Special Cable to THE NEW YORK TIMES.

LONDON, Jan. 7.—London newspapers devote a great deal of editorial space to today's demonstration of the radiophone.

"As our correspondent tells the story," writes The London Times, "telephony across the Atlantic seems as natural a proceeding as it can be, and so did it seem to all in London who participated in the same formalities or spoke to friends in New York on private business afterward. It was, in fact, no more difficult to speak to New York than to the next room, provided the ears are attuned to possible differences in accent or intonation and there is no atmospheric interference.

"A great triumph, the fruit of much research and almost infinite resourcefulness, has been achieved and a process has been initiated which henceforward will take its place in the regular apparatus of life. Ultimate developments may be impossible to foresee. More than one who 'dipped into the future' yesterday and 'saw the vision of the world' looked to the provision of universal facilities from every private telephone in the two countries while Mr. Ochs spoke of the nearness of the visages being added to the voice. But for the time being progress must be gradual."

The Daily News, under the caption "On Wings of Wireless," states editorially:

"Through the good offices of a member of The Daily News staff a lady enjoyed the felicity yesterday of telephoning a kiss from London to our resident correspondent in New York."

The newspaper continues that wireless telephony must in the long run stimulate and enormously cheapen international business transactions, although until a directional beam system is developed so as to eliminate the factor of publicity people will prefer the cable for confidential messages.

"World wireless telephony," The Daily News concludes, "is a force which will make for progress, understanding and peace. It is perhaps not too much to say that if in 1914 the statesmen of Europe had been able to talk to one another as intimately as men talked yesterday across the Atlantic, there would have been no World War."

Sees Space Annihilated.

"The imagination boggles," says The Daily Express, "at the events which took place during a few minutes yesterday while Great Britain was at lunch. Space was annihilated. Distance became of no account. The world was constricted into the confines of a suburb. Jules Verne and H. G. Wells were suddenly turned into prophetic dwarfs. To what will it lead? No one can say."

The Westminster Gazette thinks radiotelephony will "facilitate business, be a great social convenience and let us hope it will do much to promote that better sympathy and understanding between the English-speaking peoples which is devoutly to be wished."

The Daily Chronicle, which put in a call to THE NEW YORK TIMES and was not able to get it through until late this evening, was the first of today's users of the new service to proclaim anything but complete satisfaction with it.

"London's first day of wireless telephony talking with New York," says The Chronicle, "was only partially successful. For two and a quarter hours the service worked very well, indeed, and then came a devastating attack of 'fading,' that unexplainable phenomenon of twilight, which obliterated all calls and left the ether telephonically a howling wilderness. At any time the 'fading' period is a difficult one in long-distance wireless transmission, but yesterday it was at its very worst, and many people who had booked calls were grievously disappointed. During a quiet period The Daily Chronicle rang up THE NEW YORK TIMES and matters of political, industrial and domestic interest were discussed without interruption."

The Chronicle, which submitted to Rollo Ogden, editor of THE NEW YORK TIMES, a list of questions on prosperity, prohibition, the League of Nations and other subjects of common interest and which in turn answered questions proposed by THE TIMES, gives great prominence to these questions and answers in its pages.

Officials Sure of Success.

Post Office officials, when asked whether they were satisfied with the first day's service, answered, "The service was splendid all afternoon until 4 o'clock, when the signals began to fade away. Finally they were swallowed up by atmospheric conditions. The cause, of course, was the twilight periods across the Atlantic. Twilight reaches New York about 9 o'clock, Greenwich time, after which improvement normally should set in. We were bothered by particularly trying atmospheric conditions this afternoon, and after 4 o'clock we were able to get through only one or two moderately successful calls. We have no fear, however, regarding the success of the service."

A high official of the Western Union was asked by THE NEW YORK TIMES whether the cable companies expected keen competition from the new service.

"No," was his reply. "The maximum number of calls that could be handled with the present apparatus is thirty, whereas the cable companies can send thousands of messages. Then, too, a man who wishes to telephone to New York has to remain by his telephone until his number is secured, whereas he can send a cablegram and have a reply sent to him anywhere he wishes. The greatest obstacle to transatlantic telephoning is the difference in time between England and the United States. We don't see how there can be any great extension of telephoning, since the number of available wave lengths must be becoming more and more limited."

WALKER HAS HIS FUN OVER LONDON CHATS

Continued from Page 1, Column 7.

cept London's good wishes for the new year to you and your great city.

Mayor Walker—Thank you.

The Lord Mayor—I had the pleasure yesterday (rest of sentence not clear).

Mayor Walker—I didn't quite get that. You can be assured, however, that my sentiments are quite the same as yours.

The Lord Mayor—Yes.

Mayor Walker—It is a very great accomplishment and a great feat—bringing London and New York together. It is a noteworthy step that will be of material advantage to our commercial and industrial relations and bring us that much closer together.

The Lord Mayor—Fine.

Mayor Walker—I hope this will reflect upon the peace and goor fortunes of the entire civilized world, marking a great occasion for you and me, and making me just a bit anxious to meet you fact to face. If fortune smiles on us, I am looking forward to a time when I will meet you in your jurisdiction. Be assured that the people of New York would be very happy should you decide in the very near future to pay us a visit.

The Lord Mayor—Yes, sir.

Mayor Walker—Congratulations of New York again to you and the wishes of all our people for a very happy and a prosperous new year.

The Lord Mayor—Yes, sir; fine.

The Mayor—Thank you, very much, again. My compliments and congratulations, and please be assured I find this a great delight to talk to you.

The Lord Mayor—I would like to say—(rest of sentence not clear).

Mayor Walker—Hello, there.

The Lord Mayor—I would like to say a personal friend of mine, Lord Burnham——

Mayor Walker—Is he coming over? I hope to see more of him. Thank you, very much, your Lordship, and good-bye.

The Lord Mayor—Good-bye.

The earlier conversation between the Mayor and Mr. Nichol was as follows:

The Mayor—Hello, Mr. Nichol, this is the Mayor talking.

Mr. Nichol—It is very kind of you.

The Mayor—We have been waiting for more than five hours, but we are compensated now with this great accomplishment.

Mr. Nichol—What sort of a day did you have in New York?

The Mayor—It is a very delightful day, a sunshiny day, with a temperature of 35.

Mr. Nichol—It is raining here now. Did you get that book I left for you?

The Mayor—Yes, I did. I haven't got to it but I am going to digest it very shortly. I want you to know of the very intense interest that this telephone call has found in New York City.

Mr. Nichol—I am attending a dinner of Columbia, given at a restaurant.

The Mayor—Very good; and I am at the City Hall, surrounded by the representatives or correspondents of all our great newspapers, who have taken a most lively interest in the accomplishment of this great feat. They have been very generous in their reports and their stories.

Mr. Nichol—Yes.

The Mayor—All the newspapers here in New York and the entire city are listening in by radio now, so that you and I, aside from the personal delight I find in talking to you, are probably heard by millions of people. That is why this conversation must be more or less confidential.

Mr. Nichol—Thank you.

The Mayor—It has been a genuine delight to have talked with you, sir, and I hope very soon it will be at a closer distance.

Mr. Nichol—Thank you so much.

The Mayor—Compliments of New York City to you, and thank you very much.

Mr. Nichol: Thank you so much.

The Mayor: Bye-bye.

When Mayor Walker had finished speaking to Mr. Nichol, he turned around and ruminated a moment over the great invention, and said it was just like talking to Albany.

"It's raining over there, boys," he said to the newspaper men gathered near him. That message delivered, he thought again, remembered that Mr. Nichol was dining in a restaurant, and suddenly exclaimed:

"Gee, I forgot to tell them to be in by 3 o'clock curfew."

"All the News That's Fit to Print."

The New York Times.

THE WEATHER
Increasing Cloudiness today; rain with rising temperature tomorrow.
Temperatures yesterday—Max., 50; min., 38.
For weather report see Page 30.

VOL. LXXVI....No. 25,276. *** NEW YORK, FRIDAY, APRIL 8, 1927. TWO CENTS in Greater New York | THREE CENTS Within 200 Miles | FOUR CENTS Elsewhere in the U. S.

FAR-OFF SPEAKERS SEEN AS WELL AS HEARD HERE IN A TEST OF TELEVISION

LIKE A PHOTO COME TO LIFE

Hoover's Face Plainly Imaged as He Speaks in Washington.

THE FIRST TIME IN HISTORY

Pictures Are Flashed by Wire and Radio Synchronizing With Speaker's Voice.

COMMERCIAL USE IN DOUBT

But A. T. & T. Head Sees a New Step in Conquest of Nature After Years of Research.

Herbert Hoover made a speech in Washington yesterday afternoon. An audience in New York heard him and saw him.

More than 200 miles of space intervening between the speaker and his audience was annihilated by the television apparatus developed by the Bell Laboratories of the American Telephone and Telegraph Company and demonstrated publicly for the first time yesterday.

The apparatus shot images of Mr. Hoover by wire from Washington to New York at the rate of eighteen a second. These were thrown on a screen as motion pictures, while the loudspeaker reproduced the speech. As each syllable was heard, the motion of the speaker's lips and his changes of expression were flashed on the screen in the demonstration room of the Bell Telephone Laboratories at 55 Bethune Street.

When the television pictures were thrown on a screen two by three inches, the likeness was excellent. It was as if a photograph had suddenly come to life and begun to talk, smile, nod its head and look this way and that. When the screen was enlarged to two by three feet, the results were not so good.

Phone Hides His Face.

At times the face of the Secretary could not be clearly distinguished. He looked down, as he read his speech, and held the telephone receiver up, so that it covered most of the lower part of his countenance. There was too much illumination also in the background of the screen. When he moved his face, his features became clearly distinguishable. Near the close of his talk he turned his head to one side, and in profile his features became clear and full of detail.

On the smaller screen the face and action were reproduced with perfect fidelity.

After Mr. Hoover had spoken, Vice President J. J. Carty of the American Telephone and Telegraph Company and others in the demonstration room at Washington took his place and conversed one at a time with men in New York. The speaker on the New York end looked the Washington man in the eye, as he talked to him. On the small screen before him appeared the living face of the man to whom he was talking.

Time as well as space was eliminated. Secretary Hoover's New York hearers and spectators were something like a thousandth part of a second later than the persons at his side in hearing him and in seeing changes of countenance. The faces and voices were projected from Washington by wire. It was shown a few minutes later, however, that radio does just as well.

Similar Test by Wireless.

In the second part of the program the group in New York saw and heard performances in the Whippany studio of the American Telephone and Telegraph Company by wireless. The first face flashed on the screen from Whippany, N. J., was that of E. L. Nelson, an engineer, who gave a technical description of what was taking place. Mr. Nelson had a good television face. He screened well as he talked.

Next came a vaudeville act by radio from Whippany. A. Dolan, a comedian, first appeared before the audience as a stage Irishman, with side whiskers and a broken pipe, and did a monologue in brogue. Then he made a quick change and came back in blackface with a new line of quips in negro dialect. The loudspeaker part went over very well. It was the first vaudeville act that ever went on the air as a talking picture and in its possibilities it may be compared with the Fred Ott sneeze of more than thirty years ago, the first piece of comedy ever recorded in motion pictures. For the commercial future of television, if it has one, is thought to be largely in public entertainment—super-news reels flashed before audiences at the moment of occurrence, together with dramatic and musical acts shot on the ether waves in sound and picture at the instant they are taking place at the studio.

The next number from the studio at Whippany was a regular radio program piece—a short humorous dialect talk by Mrs. H. A. Frederick of Mountain Lakes.

Before and between the acts the announcer of the Whippany studio made

Continued on Page Twenty.

Voorhis Hopes When He Is 100 To Visit Smith in White House

Hope that he might celebrate his one hundredth birthday with Governor Smith in the White House was expressed yesterday by John R. Voorhis, veteran Grand Sachem of the Tammany Society and President of the Board of Elections. Mr. Voorhis will be ninety-eight years old next July and, if Governor Smith should be nominated for and elected President, his one hundredth birthday would occur in July, 1929, a few months after the inauguration.

"As near as I can determine, it looks as though Governor Smith would be nominated," Mr. Voorhis said. "The opposition to him is diminishing and the general sentiment for him is increasing. So far as his election is concerned, it is too far ahead to tell much about it."

Mr. Voorhis, who is still remarkably active, was seen at Tammany Hall. He stopped there on his return from a trip to Brownsville, where he went to inspect quarters sought by the Board of Elections for the storage of voting machines.

$840,000 FUR STRIKE AUDIT WAS HOPELESS

Accountants at Bribe Inquiry Testify Meagre Data Failed to Show Where Money Went.

REIGN OF TERROR KEEPS UP

Pickets Still Make Trouble, Says Frayne, Although There Is No Strike Now.

Accountants engaged by the American Federation of Labor's special committee to check up the expenditure of $840,000 by the Communist-led Joint Board of Furriers during last year's strike testified yesterday at the John Doe inquiry into allegations of police bribery that they could not find a single original voucher which specifically stated the use to which the money was put. Instead of original vouchers they said a forged cash book was furnished to them and not the book of original entry, as well as a large number of checks made out to "bearer," endorsed by the late Abraham Goodman, the Joint Board's counsel, and others.

The General Strike Committee handling the funds of the union checked out the money to counsel and to chairmen of various committees such as hall and picket committees, and the furthest the accountants were able to penetrate into the tangle of checks was to obtain some of the "receipts" for the money signed by subcommittee officers who received it from the Strike Committee, they asserted. They told Magistrate Joseph E. Corrigan, presiding at the inquiry, that they were never able to learn to whom the committee chairmen paid the money or whether some of it went for relief and court fines and how much was expended in this way.

Says Audit Was Hindered.

Every obstacle was placed in the way of the accountants by the Joint Board officers, according to the witnesses, until finally the union demanded individual receipts for every scrap of paper supplied for examination, with the understanding that

Continued on Page Nine.

THEFT OF 300 PAPERS ON MEXICO REVEALED BY FORGERY INQUIRY

Secret Military Reports Among Documents Stolen in Wholesale Diplomatic Robberies.

SOME WERE "DOCTORED"

Calles Turned Them Over to Us When It Became Known That We Knew He Had Them.

SUBJECT OF MYSTERY NOTE

Many Papers Believed Stolen From Our Embassy in Skillful Plot—Washington Disclaims "Leak."

By RICHARD V. OULAHAN.
Special to The New York Times.

WASHINGTON, April 7.—Pilfering of the United States Government's confidential correspondence relating to Mexico has been established through investigation which dovetails with the subject matter of the "mystery note" delivered to the Mexican Foreign Office recently by James R. Sheffield, the American Ambassador in Mexico City.

This pilfering was conducted on a wholesale scale, as nearly or quite 300 documents belonging to the United States Government were stolen. These documents were turned over to President Calles of Mexico, who, when the fact that he had them became known to the United States Government, delivered them to the State Department.

Included in this large batch of confidential papers was a considerable number of reports of a military nature, most of them supposed to have been taken from the office of the military attaché of the embassy in Mexico City.

Some time ago rumors were circulated in Washington that a "leak" in the State Department had been discovered and that an employe of the department had been dropped from the rolls in connection with the alleged "leak."

No "Leak," Officials Believe.

It is now being asserted that the alleged "leak" was associated with the established fact that confidential documents of the United States Government relating to Mexico had come into the possession of the Mexican Government.

While Government officials today maintained their attitude of silence concerning the pilfering of confidential diplomatic and military papers, it was indicated that there had not been any leak in the State Department. The denial took the form of a statement, in answer to inquiries, that it was not believed that any such leak had existed.

Officials showed a disinclination to discuss the matter and would not go further than to express that belief, with the additional information that they had not heard of any leak.

Other reports are that confidential military papers of the United States relating to Mexico had been offered for sale for $50,000. Another report is that official documents, presumably belonging to the Mexican Government, had been offered for sale to the American Embassy in Mexico City.

Signs of Skillful Plotting.

From what is known of the matter it is evident that a skillfully arranged effort to obtain confidential documents pertaining to the relations of the United States and Mexico has been in progress for some time. There are features of it as intriguing as elements of a fantastic novel having to do with international plotting.

It has been established, according to information obtained, that some of the stolen documents were "doctored" by having forged words and phrases inserted in them with the suspected intention of making it appear that the Coolidge Administration had hostile in-

Continued on Page Four.

Caruso Convicted of First Degree Murder; Killed Doctor After Death of Little Son

A jury in the Kings County Court late last night brought in a verdict of guilty of murder in the first degree against Frank Caruso for the killing of Dr. Casper S. Pendola of Maspeth in February.

Caruso, 36 years old and the father of five children, killed the physician when he found his 9-year-old son, Joseph, who was being treated by Dr. Pendola for diphtheria, had died.

The jury returned to the court room at 11:51 o'clock, after most of those who had listened all day to the trial had left the room. The defendant heard the foreman's announcement with little visible concern. He arose at the call of the clerk, walked a few steps forward and gave his pedigree in an even tone.

Caruso said he had been sixteen years in this country. He was a native of Italy. He lived at 36 Third Street, Brooklyn, and had been convicted and fined $100 eight years ago for having a pistol.

The case went to the jury at 6 P. M. Twice the jury returned to the court room, once to inquire about the different degrees of murder, and again to have a part of Judge McLaughlin's charge read. In the first hour of its deliberation a report reached the Court that it stood 7 to 5 for first degree murder.

After the verdict was announced Judge McLaughlin, turning to the jury, said: "I thank you for the careful consideration you have given to this case. The verdict will make for law and order. Any other finding would have been a miscarriage of justice."

In summing up George Voss, attorney for Caruso, declared that the defendant was moved to the frenzy that resulted in the killing because Dr. Pendola laughed when he heard that Caruso's son had died following treatment for diphtheria. He told the jurors that under the same circumstances they would have felt the urge to kill. He asked them not to class Caruso with the cold-blooded gangsters who murder with deliberation. He raised the technicality that the doctor had been killed by strangulation instead of stabbing, as charged in the indictment.

In his summing up Chief Assistant District Attorney Joseph V. Gallagher said that the testimony of a Holy Family Hospital ambulance surgeon and the autopsy report of Assistant Medical Examiner Gregory Robillard showed that Dr. Pendola had been stabbed to death. He said that the two knife wounds indicated that the murder was premeditated.

County Judge McLaughlin, in his charge to the jury, said the murder was neither legally justifiable nor excusable. After explaining the distinction between first and second degree murder he cautioned the jury to abandon all sympathy and sentiment in deciding the case.

Caruso will be sentenced on April 18.

HUGE POTASH 'TRUST' UNDER FEDERAL FIRE

Tuttle Sues French and German Groups, Alleging Scheme to Monopolize Markets Here.

$50,000,000 ANNUAL TRADE

American Concern Also Named in Complaint—Case Second Under Wilson Tariff Act.

Acting under instructions from the Department of Justice, United States Attorney Charles H. Tuttle began yesterday an injunction suit against a German syndicate called the Deutsche Kalisyndikat Gesellschaft, to restrain it from carrying out an alleged plan to create in the United States a monopoly in the sale of potash. It is charged that the plan violates the Sherman Anti-Trust law and the Wilson Tariff act and that a group of German and French producers of potash are now in this city to complete arrangements with certain American distributing agencies to make the monopoly complete and effective.

It is charged that the German companies have an exclusive selling agency in this city which operates under the name of the Potash Importing Corporation of America, that the French companies have a similar agency, and that these two groups have agreed to divide the business in this country and to handle the product with a single agency at prices to be agreed upon between them.

Danger to Our Interests Seen.

The danger of such a monopoly to the interests of the people in this country is indicated by Alexander B. Royce, a special assistant to the United States Attorney, in charge of trust cases, who said:

"The Government petition charges that beginning May 1, 1927, the French and German companies have agreed to continue the division of the United States business. It is also charged that these two groups have been dividing the sales of potash in this country since August, 1924. The complaint alleges that because the mines of the French and German companies constitute the only source of a large supply of potash, users in the United States are almost wholly dependent upon them."

It is explained that the syndicate is a combination of the owners of all the potash mines in Germany, that their headquarters and principal office is in Berlin, and that associated with them are the French companies which own potash mines in Alsace, the greater part of the product being shipped to the United States. From the close of the war until 1924 the French companies, it is asserted, sold potash to importers in this country independently of each other and free from agreements on prices, quantities, or conditions.

The Defendants Named.

The corporate defendants are the German syndicate, the Société Commerciale de Potasses d'Alsace, Mines Domaniales de Potasse d'Alsace, the Société Anonyme des Mines de Kali Sainte-Thérèse and the Potash Importing Corporation of America. The individual defendants are Dr. Maximilien Kempner, Dr. Oskar Eckstein, A. Diehn, Robert Kunze, Dr. Ernst Frohnknecht, all of whom are officers and employes of the syndicate; le Cornee, whose Christian name is not known, and René Gide, who are described as active in the control of the French potash industry; E. K. Howe, H. A. Forbes, Walker B. Howe and René Gide, a resident of this city, especially interested in the product of the Société Commerciale des Potasses d'Alsace. The latter is evidently a son or other relative of the René Gide first mentioned.

That the Government has been aware of the alleged negotiations by the defendants to monopolize the potash trade in the United States is indicated by the fact that it has been known that all the German defendants are guests at the Hotel Plaza, and all of the French defendants have quarters at 25 West Forty-third Street, and because certain movements of representatives of the two factions are known.

Mr. Royce said 1,000,000 tons of pot-

Continued on Page Three.

WARNS NIGHT CLUBS OF COMING CLEAN-UP

Banton Declares New Theatre Padlock Measure Also Applies to Them.

SURE OF PUBLIC SUPPORT

He Will Act on Complaints, He Says—Playhouse Owners Are Perturbed Over New Bill.

Governor Smith's approval of the Wales Theatre Padlock bill caused District Attorney Banton to announce yesterday that the bill was as directly applicable to night clubs and cabarets as to theatres, and to declare that "women in night clubs had better put on clothes, too." Mr. Banton, who drew the bill and enlisted the support necessary for its passage, said it was backed by the public, which would make convictions easy.

The District Attorney, while denying that he would spy on either the theatres or the night clubs, intimated strongly that the public as well as the police would report violations, said he would act promptly upon complaints of private citizens or policemen, and that clean entertainments would soon result. He added that, "as in all cases where a moral principle is involved, the Governor was found on the side of right-thinking people."

Theatrical producers and managers, for the most part, expressed disappointment over Governor Smith's action in signing the bill. Arch Selwyn, declaring that it had been a "very, very foolish thing for the Governor to do" expressed the opinion that the bill would mean "new graft in various departments of the city." An exception was A. L. Erlanger, who expressed approval of the Governor's action.

Banton Issues Statement.

In a statement issued soon after he had learned that Governor Smith had signed the bill, District Attorney Banton said:

"The producers and managers of plays now before the public had better go through them (the plays) and cut out their dirty lines and scenes. Authors of plays yet to be produced had better keep in mind this new law.

"We now have the right kind of law and the law is backed by the public. Public sentiment, when aroused, makes it easy for us to get convictions against indecent shows. Without it we find it hard to get convictions. Under this new law we shall find that theatre owners will be the best kind of censors of plays produced in their theatres—and that, after all, is what is effective in keeping the stage clean.

"This new law increases efficiency in the administration of the statute against obscenity in the theatres in the following particulars:

"First—Heretofore it has been necessary to proceed against the play as a whole. The amendment permits the arrest of those who interject into the play an obscene act.

"Second—All plays, or parts thereof, which depict or in any way deal with the subject of degeneracy are prohibited.

"Third—Therefore the owner of the theatre, like the ostrich, could hide his head in the sand and pretend not to know what was going on about him, and conviction of the owner or lessee of a theatre has been next to impossible, as in the case of John Cort, who for eleven months was one of the principal owners of the theatre in which 'Sex' was produced. From now on the owner or lessee of the property will be held responsible for a violation on his property, and on conviction of the actors or producers, the licensing authority may revoke the license and refuse to issue a new license for a period not exceeding one year."

Law Called Unconstitutional.

Commenting on a statement by William H. Klein, attorney for the Shuberts, that the new law was unconstitutional, Mr. Banton said:

"The license granted by a public official is only a privilege and the power to grant such license implies the power to revoke it. It is within the legislative power to define just what that official power is. This new law places the licensing power, in the case of the theatrical performance, on a par with any other licensing power in ex-

Continued on Page Eight.

2 Boys Killed, 5 Hurt, When Truck Hits Auto On Which 10 Were Riding Home From School

Two school boys were killed and five others were injured yesterday when a truck crashed into a coupe on which they were riding at Beverly and Rugby Roads, Brooklyn.

The boys killed were Lawrence Moen, 11 years old, of 360 East Seventh Street, and Caesar Saiya, 10 years old, of 698 Coney Island Avenue. Attilio Saiya, 14, brother of Caesar, received internal injuries and was sent to the Kings County Hospital, with Nicholas Demarinio, 13, of 239 East Ninth Street, whose right leg was fractured, and Timothy Barlow, 11, of 240 East Ninth Street, who was badly cut and bruised. John Ledischi, 13, of 260 East Ninth Street, was cut and bruised. After being treated at the hospital he was sent home. Columbus Saiya, another brother of the dead boy, received similar injuries, but ran home before a doctor reached the scene. He was treated at home last night.

The boys, with three others, were leaving Holy Innocents Parochial School, at Beverly Road and East Seventeenth Street shortly after 4 o'clock, when one of them hailed a friend driving past in a coupe. The boys had attended a confirmation class for confirmation next Sunday.

In the coupe were Stephen J. Collins of 1,042 Flatbush Avenue, and his wife. Asked if he could give them a ride home Mr. Collins told the boys to climb on. Those who could not find places on the running board clambered on the back of the car.

When the coupe reached Rugby Road, a short distance away, the boys' shouts of pleasure changed suddenly to screams of fright. As the coupe started across Rugby Road a truck driven by Frank Whalen of 646 Seventy-fourth Street, bore down on it and before Collins could get the coupe out of the way the truck crashed into it, striking Moen and Caesar Saiya, who were standing on the running board. Moen was instantly killed. The coupe was whirled around and hurled across the street. As it slammed against the curb five of the boys were thrown off. Collins, his wife and the other boys were only slightly injured.

The Saiya boy was hurried to the hospital, but was dead when he got there. Collins and Whalen were questioned by Assistant District Attorney Bernard Becker, who directed that both men be held for the action of the Brooklyn homicide court this morning. Collins said he did not see the truck coming because his vision was obscured by the boys standing on the running board of his car.

SMITH APPROVES THEATRE PADLOCKS; VETOES GAS CUT-OFF

Governor Declares Majority of the People and Producers Desire a Clean Stage.

APPLIANCE BILL A PUZZLE

Tempted to Sign It Because of Graft Talk, He Finally Rejects It as Too Broad.

30-DAY BILLS CLEANED UP

Port Authority, Sewage Plant and Salary Measures Approved—One Baumes Proposal Vetoed.

By W. A. WARN
Special to The New York Times.

ALBANY, April 7.—Although less than two weeks have elapsed since the Legislature adjourned sine die, Governor Smith today finished work on the huge mass of legislative measures the lawmakers sent to his desk for veto or approval, for the consideration of which the Governor is allotted thirty days under the law. The speed with which the thirty-day bills were disposed of is thought to establish a State record.

The Governor left this evening for New York City, where he will remain until Monday, when he will go to the Sea View Golf Club at Absecon, N. J. for an indefinite stay, accompanied by Mrs. Smith and other members of his family. He is badly in need of rest, having worked under high pressure for weeks.

Among the bills approved by the Governor today were the Theatrical Padlock bill, on which a hearing was held yesterday; the bill giving the Governor veto power over New York State members of the Port Authority Commission; the bill authorizing the State to surrender the northern end of Ward's Island to the New York City authorities as a site for a modern sewage disposal plant; a bill approving the New York-New Jersey-Pennsylvania compact for developing new water supply facilities on the Delaware River and a number of bills providing salary increases to be paid out of the New York City treasury to judges and some other county officials within the city.

Important Bills Vetoed.

Governor Smith vetoed the Thayer bill, which would have repealed the aldermanic ordinance under which a certain patented gas cut-off appliance must be installed in all buildings above a certain height and which was denounced by spokesmen for New York City realty interests at a hearing yesterday as prolific in graft to the promoters. The Governor said this measure had been so loosely drawn and would have such far-reaching disastrous effects that he felt compelled to withhold his approval.

Among other measures vetoed were a bill that would have enabled the Montauk Riding and Driving Club in Brooklyn to disregard vital provisions of the Tenement House law in the erection of a "club apartment" structure in Brooklyn, designed to have on the ground floor a huge arena for horse shows and driving meets; a bill which would have permitted osteopaths to perform minor operations and one which would have conferred the title of doctor on optometrists.

In all 3,401 bills were introduced at the recent session of the Legislature. Of these 861 reached the Governor's desk. Out of this number he approved 731, which now will take their place on the statute books. He vetoed 130. Approximately 400 bills were among the thirty-day lot.

Of forty-six bills permitting claim suits to be brought against the State in the Court of Claims, Governor Smith vetoed twenty-four and approved twenty-two. Some pension and retirement bills affecting New York City were among the measures which the Governor failed to give his approval. In a so-called omnibus veto were included forty bills rejected by the Governor as unnecessary or faultily drawn.

About the most important measure in this batch was one of the Baumes Crime Commission measures, providing for the establishment of bureaus of criminal identification in all cities with

Continued on Page Twelve.

SOVIET OFFICES IN TIENTSIN RAIDED BY CHINESE POLICE; NOW CUT OFF IN SHANGHAI

Court Banishes Man for Life From State of North Carolina

Special to The New York Times.

DANVILLE, Va., April 7. – J. H. Anderson of this city was banished from the State of North Carolina for life today by Judge W. E. Haring, sitting at Yanceyville. Anderson also was told by the Court that if he was found within 200 miles of Danville henceforth he would be arrested and required to serve two years on the roads.

A jury had convicted him after twenty-four hours' deliberation of an assault on a young woman. Anderson was permitted to choose between sentence or exile, and he chose the latter.

DAWES CONTINUES REED COMMITTEE

Declares It Has Legal Authority to Function During the Recess of Congress.

FESS TAKES GOFF'S PLACE

Naming of Ohio Senator Instead of Shortridge of California Surprises Washington.

CHICAGO, April 7 (AP).—Vice President Dawes, guided by a Supreme Court decision, today held that the Senate Campaign Fund Investigating Committee retains its powers although Congress has adjourned, and appointed Senator Simeon Fess, Republican, Ohio, to succeed Senator Guy D. Goff, Republican, West Virginia, who resigned as a member of the committee.

The Vice President followed the opinion of the high court in the recent case against Mal Daugherty, whose testimony was wanted by a Senate committee.

The filibuster in the expiring hours of the Senate of the Sixty-ninth Congress and the failure of the resolution of Senator James A. Reed of Missouri, the Chairman, to continue the committee, and the resignation of Senator Goff, left the decision to the Vice President.

Senators Goff, Borah, Republican, Idaho, and Walsh, Democrat, Montana, all expressed opinions that the committee continued legally to exist. Senator Keyes, Republican, New Hampshire, Chairman of the Committee on Audit and Control of the Contingent Fund of the Senate, held that the committee was dead and that he should not approve further expenditures from the fund by the committee.

Gives Reasons for Decision.

Vice President Dawes returned here yesterday from a vacation trip to Panama and late today advised Senator Fess of his selection to the Goff vacancy on the committee. At the same time the Vice President made public his action and basis for it in a statement in part as follows:

"In my judgment the Supreme Court of the United States in the case of John J. McGrain, Deputy Sergeant-at-Arms of the United States Senate, appellant, v. Mal S. Daugherty, rendered Jan. 17, 1927, conclusively disposes of the question in the affirmative. The Supreme Court was passing on the question of the powers of a Senatorial committee authorized by a resolution 'to sit and perform its duties at such times and places as may be deemed advisable or necessary by said committee.'

"It held that this language of the resolution extended the powers of the committee beyond the Congress which passed the creating resolution. Senate resolution 195, Sixty-ninth Congress, creating the present Senatorial Investigating Committee, contains the following language:

" 'Said committee is hereby empowered to sit and act at such time or times and at such place or places as it may deem necessary.'

"The holding of the Supreme Court,

Continued on Page Two.

MORE DOCUMENTS SEIZED

Permission for Tientsin Search Is Given by French Consul.

THREAT TO MOVE EMBASSY

Soviet Consul General, Before Isolation at Shanghai, Says It May Go to Hankow.

PEKING EXPECTS RUPTURE

Wellington Koo Resigns as Premier in North—American Missionary Is Missing.

Special Cable to THE NEW YORK TIMES.

TIENTSIN, China, April 7.—The Chinese police, with the sanction of the French Consul, raided today the Soviet bank [the Dah Bank] and also the offices of the Chinese-Eastern Railway and other Soviet offices, all in the French concession, and seized documents.

The raid was prompted by the discoveries in the Soviet buildings at Peking yesterday.

TIENTSIN, April 7 (AP).—Chinese police this afternoon entered the French concession, with permission of the Consul, and searched the Dah Bank and various Soviet trade missions. The Chinese detained all persons pending the search and removed documents for examination.

French police took no direct part in the raid, but maintained order outside.

Shanghai Consulate Under Guard.

SHANGHAI, April 7 (AP).—Police, assisted by White Russian volunteers, late today surrounded the Soviet Consulate in the international settlement with orders to prevent any one from entering or leaving the premises.

No reason for this action was given but it was stated that there was no present intention to raid the Consulate.

Among the visitors whom the police held up was the Chinese Commissioner of Foreign Affairs, who was informed that he would not be allowed to enter unless he consented to be searched. The Commissioner refused to permit this and left.

The possibility of the removal of the Soviet Embassy at Peking to Hankow, the seat of the Cantonese or Nationalist Government, was suggested today by Wilhelm F. Linde, Soviet Consul here, as a result of yesterday's raid by Northern soldiers on buildings attached to the Russian Embassy.

Mr. Linde said that such a removal was not impossible in discussing the incident with newspaper men after he had called upon the Norwegian Consul General, Dean of the consular corps in Shanghai, to announce that he would hold the consular body responsible if the Soviet Consulate here were raided also.

The Soviet Consul General also declared that if the Peking raid was carried out with the approval of the diplomatic corps, it would set a precedent that would endanger the foundation of diplomatic prerogatives. In this connection he said that he understood that permission for the entry of the Chinese troops and police into the legation grounds at Peking had been granted solely by the Dean of the diplomatic corps and not from all the members.

Yangtse Evacuation Goes On.

While interest continued to centre here on the international possibilities of the Peking raid in so far as it may cause serious repercussions in Moscow, foreigners in various sections of China are steadily evacuating the areas where anti-foreign agitation has been spreading.

Hankow, scene of a growing tenseness, was the centre of riotous anti-foreign outbreaks over last week-end, resulting in further plans for a rapid departure of the comparatively few remaining foreigners.

"Situation growing worse steadily" was a wireless message received from there today.

With lawlessness in the city apparently increasing, the commander of the United States Yangtse River patrol is urging Americans still in the city to leave as soon as possible. Japanese are leaving the city in increasing numbers, while German and Russian nationals are preparing to leave soon.

Dr. C. P. Triberg of St. Peter, Minn., a member of the Augustana Synod Mission of the American Lutheran Church, was reported missing today and it is feared he has been captured by bandits. All the members of the mission, which was centred in the Province of Honan, are leaving China, fifty-four of the ninety-four members leaving tomorrow on the President Pierce.

In line with the decision to bring all British gunboats out of the upper Yangtse area, the British consuls and the remainder of the British communities at Chung-king, I-chang,

Earl Carroll's Friends Will Seek a Parole; No Pardon Is Asked; Term Starts Tuesday

Special to The New York Times.

WASHINGTON, April 7.—Inquiries at the Department of Justice today indicated that friends of Earl Carroll, New York theatrical producer, who was sentenced to a term of a year and a day at Atlanta for perjury in connection with the famous bath tub case, will attempt to obtain a parole for Mr. Carroll at the appropriate time if executive clemency is refused before the sentence begins, as now seems assured.

Up to date no application for the exercise of executive clemency in behalf of Mr. Carroll has been received at the Department of Justice, which handles such matters before they are sent to the President for consideration. It was explained to friends of Mr. Carroll that executive clemency is rarely extended before the execution of a sentence, and then only in cases where precarious health or facts tending to throw doubt on the guilt of persons accused are cited.

In most instances the Attorney General will not consider recommending a pardon until at least one-third of the sentence of a person convicted has been served. A prisoner likewise is not eligible for parole until he has served one-third of the time for which he has been sentenced.

Under the mandate of the New York Court Mr. Carroll's sentence will begin on April 12, and as things now stand he will have to surrender himself to the custody of the authorities on that date.

Television Triumphs in Its First Demonstration Between New York and Washington

Continued from Page 1, Column 1.

a motion picture appearance. He was seen as well as heard.

Phone Girl Is Seen, Too.

In the Washington part of the demonstration the telephone girl was visible. She appeared on the miniature screen and asked to whom the caller wished to talk. This one was a good-looking girl with fluffy hair, and as cool and efficient as if she had been at the television-telephone switchboard all her life.

A coincidence is that "Metropolis," the German film now showing what purports to be the New York of a century or centuries hence, has a make-believe screen in connection with the telephone—a case of a prophecy being fulfilled about as soon as it started.

The demonstration of combined telephone and television, in fact, is one that outruns the imagination of all the wizards of prophecy. It is one of the few things that Leonardo da Vinci, Roger Bacon, Jules Verne and other masters of forecasting failed utterly to anticipate. Even interpreters of the Bible are having trouble in finding a passage which forecast television. H. G. Wells did not rise to it in his earlier crystal-gazing. It is only within the last few years that prophets have been busy in this field. Science has moved ahead so rapidly in this particular line that one of the men, who played a major part in developing the television apparatus shown yesterday, was of the opinion four years ago that research on this subject was hopeless. More than twenty years ago, however, Dr. Alexander Graham Bell, the inventor of the telephone, predicted at a gathering in the tower of the Times Building that the day would come when the man at the telephone would be able to see the distant person to whom he was speaking.

Light Squares Put on Wire.

The demonstration began yesterday afternoon at 2:15 with General Carty at the television apparatus in Washington. As he held the transmitter in his hand and talked the light of an arc lamp flickered on his face. Small circles of light were moving across his face, one after another, but they were traveling at such high speed that they seemed to bathe his face in a uniform bluish light. By a complicated process these lights were dividing his face into fine squares. Each square traveled as a telegraph signal from Washington to New York. Here, with inconceivable rapidity, these squares were assembled as a mosaic. Each square differs in its amount of illumination. These differences of illumination traced the countenance in light and shadow and registered the least changes of expression. The squares rushed across the wire from Washington at the rate of 45,000 a second. The face was done over every eighteenth part of a second. About 2,500 squares—or "units," as they are called—make up each picture.

As General Carty talked his face was thus dissected by light in Washington and reconstructed on the small screen in New York. President Walter S. Gifford of the American Telephone and Telegraph Company was on the New York end of the wire.

"How do you do, General? You are looking well," said Mr. Gifford.

The face of General Carty smiled and his voice inquired after the health of the speaker on the New York end.

"I am instructed to make a little conversation," said President Gifford, "while they are getting the loudspeaker ready. They are having a little power trouble."

"We are all ready and waiting here," said General Carty." Mr. Hoover is here."

"You screen well, General," said Mr. Gifford. "You look more handsome over the wire."

"Does it flatter me much?" General Carty asked.

"I think it is an improvement," was the reply.

Hoover's Voice Heard.

Mr. Hoover was then called on to take a seat before the light which divides the sitter into 45,000 squares a second, and he was informed of the slight delay. A few seconds later, the power trouble was conquered, and the voice of Secretary Hoover was heard over the loudspeaker, as his face appeared on the large screen.

The illuminated transparent screen seemed somewhat corrugated. This is due to the fact that the squares which make up the picture are arranged in fifty rows, one on top of the other. In the centre of the screen appeared a white glare, surrounded by darker markings. As the eye became accustomed to looking at the screen in the darkened room, the large luminous patch took shape as the forehead of Secretary Hoover. He was leaning forward in such a way that the forehead was taking up too much of the picture, while his mouth and chin were blotted out behind the telephone transmitter. When he moved, however, the picture became clearer.

The face was easily recognizable, although the features, which had been sharp and distinct on the miniature screen, had become considerably blurred by the enlargement. It was plain that, enlarged to the size of an ordinary motion picture film, the detail would have been completely lost. The invention is admitted to be far from the motion picture house stage.

Secretary Hoover's Speech.

The face looked up from the manuscript, the lips began to move and the first television-telephone speech started as follows:

"It is a matter of just pride to have a part in this historic occasion.

"We have long been familiar with the electrical transmission of sound. Today we have, in a sense, the transmission of sight, for the first time in the world's history.

"Human genius has now destroyed the impediment of distance in a new respect, and in a manner hitherto unknown. What its uses may finally be no one can tell, any more than man could foresee in past years the modern developments of the telegraph or the telephone. All we can say today is that there has been created a marvelous agency for whatever use the future may find, with the full realization that every great and fundamental discovery of the past has been followed by use far beyond the vision of its creator.

"Every school child is aware of the dramatic beginnings of the telegraph, the telephone and the radio, and this revolution in electrical communications has perhaps an importance as vital as any of these.

"This invention again emphasizes a new era in approach to important scientific discovery, of which we have already within the last two months seen another great exhibit—the transatlantic telephone. It is the result of organized, planned and definitely directed scientific research, magnificently coordinated in a cumulative group of highly skilled scientists, loyally supported by a great corporation devoted to the advancement of the art. The intricate processes of this invention could never have been developed under any conditions of isolated individual effort.

A "Dramatic" Achievement

"The world is under obligation to the American Telephone and Telegraph Company for its vision in the establishment and support of these laboratories, and does tribute to all those who have played their part in this development.

"These laboratories have produced a long list of additions to the telephonic art and a constant contribution to

President Walter S. Gifford of the American Telephone and Telegraph Company in first public demonstration yesterday of television. Mr. Gifford is talking to Secretary Hoover in Washington and is able to see Mr. Hoover on the screen immediately in front of him. At right of picture, Dr. Herbert Ives, who superintended the development of television for the A. T. & T.

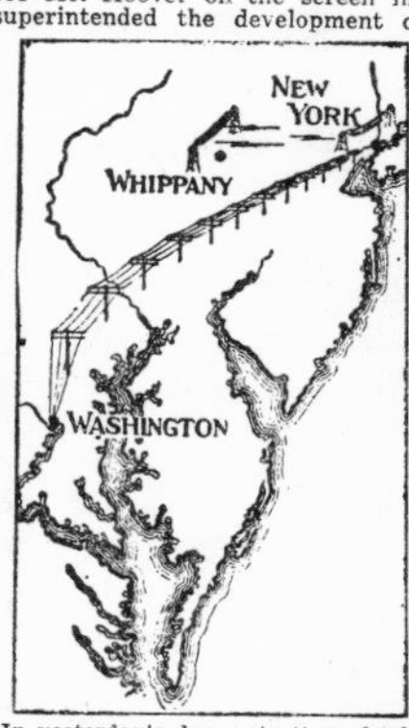

In yesterday's demonstration of television living pictures were sent to New York by wire from Washington and by radio from Whippany, N. J.

This telephoto from Washington shows Mr. Hoover talking to his New York audience. With him, left to right, are General J. J. Carty and A. E. Berry, telephone officials, and Judge Stephen Davis, Solicitor of the Department of Commerce.

other arts, but no one of them more dramatic or more impressive than this.

"I always find in these occasions a great stimulation to confidence in the future. If we can be assured a flow of new and revolutionary inventions to maintain thought, stimulate spirit, and provide a thousand new opportunities for effort and service, we will have preserved a vital and moving community."

Mrs. Hoover took a seat before the machine which projects living pictures of the sitter and talked to Mr. Gifford.

"What will you invent next?" she said. "I hope you won't invent anything that reads our thoughts."

Half a dozen newspaper men were called to the telephone one after another to talk with men in the demonstration room at Washington. THE TIMES reporter in New York talked to David Lawrence. On the small screen Mr. Lawrence was pictured perfectly. He looked like an excellent daguerreotype which had come to life and started to talk. Even the crinkle of his hair registered perfectly. In these small motion pictures, projected by television, the detail of the face appears in clear-cut black lines against a shining gold background, due to the orange light from neon, which is used in reproducing the pictures.

The pictures were projected only one way yesterday—from Washington to New York. Two-way television-telephone conversations will be held later.

Commercial Use Uncertain.

The Bell Laboratories have been directed to concentrate on developing television with all possible speed, although the American Telephone and Telegraph Company has no idea today whether it will ever be commercially valuable. The corporation's attitude is that it wants to know all about the subject, in spite of the fact that its future is vague. Discussing the future possibilities of television yesterday, President Gifford said:

"I'll have to leave that to your imagination."

Dr. Frank B. Jewett, Vice President of the American Telephone and Telegraph Company, said yesterday that television was further advanced now than transoceanic telephony was in 1915 when the company held its first successful radio telephone tests from Washington to Paris and Honolulu. Eleven years of development followed that first test in 1915 before transatlantic telephony was placed on a commercial basis.

The television demonstration of yesterday is far in advance of anything that is claimed for any other invention in the same field. John L. Baird, the Scotch inventor, has been considered the leader in television research, but his work is alleged to be crude in comparison with the Bell system. The Alexanderson television project is still in the laboratory, having never been given any public demonstration, and most other television systems are in the talking stage.

Process Is Simple in Detail.

The process by which yesterday's results were achieved appears infinitely complicated and difficult on first encounter, but becomes fairly simple when traced step by step.

The thing that chiefly staggers the mind is that all that traveled over the wire from Washington to New York or over the ether from Whippany to New York is a series of electrical impulses.

Speed and exactitude are the tremendous achievements in the process. Dots of light are put together at the rate of 45,000 a second to form the motion pictures. Each dot has to be in its exact place. The mosaic of square would be a jumble—the picture would be completely "pied"—if there was an error of one ninety-thousandth part of a second in the synchronization between the sending apparatus in Washington and the receiving apparatus in New York.

Putting aside the terrific speed, the problem seemed quite simple, as it was explained yesterday by Dr. Herbert E. Ives, who has been chief of the research work which has resulted in television.

The process begins when the sitter takes his position in front of the television apparatus and the arc light is turned on. Most of this light is shut off from the sitter by a disk. In the disk are a series of holes. As the disk is turned, the light strikes the sitter through the hole nearest the rim. This spot of light travels across the top of his head. The second hole is further from the rim of the disk. The second spot of light travels across the sitter's face, just below the first, the third just below the second, and so on. There are a total of fifty holes and fifty spots of light travel across the sitter or the scene to be photographed, one beneath the other.

If the process could be slowed down infinitely, it would begin with the action of the visible spot of light. In practice, however, the spots move so quickly that the subject seems to be flooded by a steady illumination. There is never more than one spot of light on his face at a time, but the entire fifty spots cross the face or thing to be photographed eighteen times a second.

Spots Vary in Brightness.

The lines and contours and colors of the face cause variations in the brightness of the spots they reflect. These variations are turned into variations of electrical current. Facing the sitter are three large photo-electric cells. The moving spots of light are reflected from the face or scene into these cells, where they cause electron showers. The showers are strong or weak, as the light is strong or weak. Electron showers are nothing but electrical current, so that these cells cause a current which constantly varies according to the characteristics of the face or scene to be pictured.

This current is amplified 5,000,000,000,000,000 times before it is strong enough for the work required. Then it is sent, either by wire or radio, to the receiving television station.

This current is a flying picture. Every change in volume is a feature of a scene or portrait. But the question is to make every bit of this flying picture land in the right place.

Arriving at the receiving apparatus, the current is carried to a "brush" or an electrical contact apparatus, which is mounted on a wheel.

As it revolves on this wheel, the "brush" makes and breaks electrical contact approximately 2,500 times. Each contact is made with one of 2,500 wires which are mounted on a circle in which the wheel turns.

Each wire snatches a bit of the electric current or flying picture. To each one of these wires must be delivered eighteen times a second exactly the bit of the picture which is intended for it. The most minute error would scramble the portrait completely.

Neon Gas is Lighted.

Each wire carries its bit of current to a square of tin foil behind the television screen. These squares of tin foil are arranged fifty in a row. There are fifty rows. When the bit of current—or fragment of picture—reaches one square of tin foil, it leaps from the tin foil to a wire. It makes the leap through the gas called neon. This is instantaneously illuminated by the passage of electrical current through it. Eighteen times a second there is a flash of neon in front of each of the 2,500 patches of tin foil. The flash is strong or feeble, according to the light or shadow on one particular part of the face or scene. These tiny flashes—occurring at the rate of about 45,000 a second—build up the face on the screen.

The receiving and transmitting of the picture—that is, the taking to pieces of the picture at one place and its reassembling at another—is synchronized by a special system which causes every one of the 2,500 squares or unit to fall in its proper place eighteen times a second. This control involves the use of two wires. In the case of radio television—one wavelength is used for sending the picture and two for the synchronization process. Dr. Ives emphasized the difficulty arising here, in view of the congested condition of the "air."

It would take several hundred times as many dots of light a second, under equally perfect control, to make television practical on a large screen for motion picture house purposes. There is one big difficulty here. Television cannot be used on a larger screen without using a more powerful light on the person or object sent. The light which is now thrown on the sitter is strong enough to be uncomfortable after a short time. Whether this factor will prove a heavy obstacle is doubtful. A more sensitive photo-electric cell may be developed which would enable television to be extended further without the use of stronger lighting.

How the Eye Is Deceived.

Dr. Ives called the human eye "a television system." Instead of having only 2,500 wires, the eye has more than a million nerve fibres which carry light impulses to the brain.

As in motion pictures, it is the phenomena of "persistence of vision" which cause the flickering squares of light to fuse together so that the eye sees them as objects in motion. Motion pictures really consists of still pictures shown at the rate of eighteen per second. The eye blends the stills into motion. In television, the eye is even more deceived. Here there is only a series of spots of light flashing on and off, but each spot maintains its effect on the human eye long enough for the brain to comprehend them as an organized picture.

Some of the others who played important parts in the research ending in yesterday's achievement were Dr. Frank Gray, H. M. Stoller, E. R. Morton, R. C. Mathes, J. W. Horton.

Dr. Ives has behind him many years of fruitful research into physical problems. After graduating from the University of Pennsylvania in 1905, he studied three years at Johns Hopkins, receiving the degree of Doctor of Philosophy. During the next ten years as research physicist for a number of organizations he developed, among other things, an "artificial eye" for use in photometry; a method for the description of colors in precise numerical terms; and the first practical lamp for the production of artificial daylight. This lamp is now in general use in retail stores for color comparisons. Another elaborate research was the demonstration of the "mechanical equivalent of light," a fundamental factor in comparing efficiencies of lamps of different kinds. Early in his career, Dr. Ives took up the study of the photoelectric cell, and applied it to a simulation of the eye for experimental work on the human response to light flashes. Conclusions drawn from this study have been applied in the development of the television system.

Dr. Ives's Service in the War.

As a captain in the Signal Corps, Dr. Ives during the war had charge of three laboratories for the development of airplane photography. His book on this subject is regarded as the classical work in its field.

Returning to civil life, he entered Bell Telephone Laboratories. When Bell System executives decided that the time was ripe to develop a practical picture-transmission system, Dr. Ives was placed in charge of the work. In addition to general supervision, Dr. Ives was specifically responsible for the optical aspects of the problem, and for the photoelectric cell. He also continued the study of photoelectric cells and of related problems which have led up to the development of the television system.

Dr. Ives was born in Philadelphia, the son of Frederick E. Ives, scientist and inventor of the halftone process of reproduction.

NEW 'CONQUEST OF NATURE.'

But Television's Practical Use Is Still Uncertain, Gifford Says.

In opening yesterday's demonstration of television, President Walter S. Gifford of the American Telephone and Telegraph Company said:

Today we are to witness another milestone in the conquest of nature by science. We shall see the fruition of years of study on the problem of seeing at a distance as though face to face. The principles underlying television, which are related to the principles involved in electrical transmission of speech, have been known for a long time, but today we shall demonstrate its successful achievement. The elaborateness of the equipment required by the very nature of the undertaking precludes any present possibility of television being available in homes and offices generally. What its practical use may be I shall leave to your imagination. I am confident, however, that in many ways and in due time it will be found to add substantially to human comfort and happiness.

It is our constant aim to furnish this country with the most complete telephone service possible. In connection with that aim, we endeavor to develop all forms of communication that might be supplemental to the telephone. With that in view we shall continue our work on television, which, although not directly a part of telephone communication, is closely allied to it.

Jewett Tells of Research.

Vice President Frank B. Jewett of the American Telephone and Telegraph Company said:

The demonstration of television which you have been invited to witness today is to be in fact what the name implies—"far vision." You will see and converse with people as far away as Washington and with others not so distant. That those with whom you converse will not see you is primarily because for this demonstration it did not seem necessary to provide the equipment for complete two-way working, and not because of any inherent obstacle.

As Mr. Gifford has stated, the general principles underlying television have been known for a long time. It is one thing to appreciate general principles, however, and frequently quite another to realize them practically. In the case of television many of the elements long recognized as essentials to success were not possible of attainment until general science had been further advanced. But even when recently fundamental research work developed new knowledge, new materials and new methods, the problem of successful television demanded a vast amount of coordinated research and development work to crystallize scientific possibilities into practical realities.

The research and development functions of the Bell System, of which these laboratories are a most important part, are organized for the solution of just such problems. The American Telephone and Telegraph Company has organized its scientific work to provide in one great coordinated science institution every facility needed for the solving of intricate problems of distant electrical communication. Scientists competent to develop new knowledge work in close associaation with other scientists and engineers seeking practical solutions for a host of problems.

When some years ago it began to be evident that scientific knowledge was advancing to the point where television was shortly to be within the realm of the possible, we took up seriously a study of the problems involved. Under the supervision of Dr. Ives, research and development on the various elements of terminal equipment and connecting channels was undertaken. As a result of this coordinated work we are today in position to view scenes and actions at a distance and to employ in their transmission either telephone wires or radio waves. To accomplish this result much fundamental research work was required, many new things had to be devised any many old principles were applied under the guidance of recently acquired scientific knowledge. Principal in all this has been the knowledge obtained during the past few years in the research and development which has made possible ttranscontinental and transoceanic telephony and telephotography.

GUESTS AT NEW YORK END.

Business Executives, Bankers and Editors See Demonstration.

The invited guests at the New York end of the television demonstration yesterday were:

OWEN D. YOUNG, Chairman the General Electric Company.
GERARD SWOPE, President the General Electric Company.
Gen. JAMES G. HARBORD, President the Radio Corporation of America.
DAVID SARNOFF, Vice President the Radio Corporation of America.
GUY E. TRIPP, Chairman the Westinghouse Electric and Manufacturing Company.
EDWIN M. HERR, President the Westinghouse Electric and Manufacturing Company.
SOSTHENES BEHN, President International Tel. and Tel. Company.
HERNAND BEHN, Vice President International Tel. and Tel. Company.
CLARENCE H. MACKAY, President Postal Telegraph-Cable Company.
JOHN L. MERRILL, President All America Cables.
NEWCOMB CARLTON, President Western Union Telegraph Company.
JAMES L. McQUARRIE, Vice President International Tel. and Tel. Company.
WILLIAM R. HEARST, President The New York American.
ARTHUR BRISBANE, Editor New York Evening Journal.
OGDEN REID, President the Herald Tribune Publishing Company.
B. H. RIDDER, President the New York Staats Zeitung.
ADOLPH S. OCHS, President THE NEW YORK TIMES.
ARTHUR HAYS SULZBERGER, Vice President THE NEW YORK TIMES.
RALPH PULITZER, President The New York World.
C. H. K. CURTIS, President The New York Evening Post.
W. T. DEWART, President The New York Evening Sun.
D. P. SCRIPPS, President The New York Telegram.
C. W. BARRON, President The Wall Street Journal.
J. F. FROST, President The Brooklyn Citizen.
H. F. GUNNISON, President The Brooklyn Eagle.
R. F. HUNTSMAN, President The Brooklyn Standard Union.
F. C. PECK, President The Brooklyn Times.
E. W. SCUDDER, owner Newark News.
ARTHUR J. SINNOTT, managing editor Newark News.
FRANK B. NOYES, President Associated Press.
KENT COOPER, general manager Associated Press.
CARL A. BICKEL, President United Press Association.
M. KOENIGSBERG, President International News Service.
F. S. FERGUSON, President Newspaper Enterprise Association.
ALBERT SHAW, American Review of Reviews.
MERLE THORPE, Nation's Business.
GEORGE HORACE LORIMER, Saturday Evening Post.
WILLIAM SEAVER WOOD, Literary Digest.
ROBERT BRIDGES, Scribner's.
THOMAS B. WELLS, Harper's.
ELLERY SEDGWICK, Atlantic Monthly.
CARL DICKY, World's Work.
LAWRENCE ABBOTT, Outlook.
MERLE CROWELL, American Magazine.
RONALD MILLAR, Liberty.
J. M. PATTERSON, Liberty.
WILLIAM L. CHENERY, Collier's.
ARTHUR POUND, Assistant Editor Independent.
Dr. HENRY GODDARD LEACH, Forum.
C. C. CHESNEY, President A. I. E. E., General Electric Co., Pittsfield, Mass.
M. I. PUPIN, Past President A. I. E. E., Columbia University.
K. T. COMPTON, President American Physical Society, Princeton University.
W. E. FORSYTH, President American Optical Society, Nela Park, Ohio.
J. P. SOUTHALL, Past President American Optical Society, Columbia University.
HOWARD McCLENAHAN, Secretary Franklin Institute, Philadelphia.
A. W. GOODSPEED, Secretary American Philosophical Society, University of Pennsylvania, Philadelphia.
L. B. STILWELL, consulting engineer.
GANO DUNN, President J. G. White Engineering Corporation.
ELMER A. SPERRY, President Sperry Gyroscope Company.
PROFESSOR GEORGE B. PEGRAM, Dean of the School of Engineering, Columbia University.
PROFESSOR W. L. SLICHTER, Professor of Electrical Engineering, Columbia University.
CLAYTON H. SHARP, Electrical Testing Laboratories.
JOHN W. LIEB, Vice President New York Edison Company.
PROFESSOR THEODORE LYMAN, Professor of Mathematics, Harvard University.
DR. R. A. MILLIKAN, California Institute of Technology, Pasadena, Cal.
DR. GEORGE E. HALE, Mount Wilson Observatory, Pasadena, Cal.
WALDEMAR KAEMPFFERT, scientific adviser, New York Times.
E. E. FREE, consulting engineer.
W. H. ONKIN JR., editor Electrical World.
COLONEL G. S. GIBBS, signal officer, U. S. A., Governors Island.
LIEUT. COM. A. V. LANPHIER, district communication officer, Third District, U. S. N.
O. D. MUNN, Scientific American.
J. McK. CATTELL, science.
J. S. ALEXANDER, Chairman of the Board of Directors of the National Bank of Commerce.
GEORGE F. BAKER, Chairman of Board of Directors First National Bank.
GEORGE F. BAKER JR., Vice President First National Bank.
J. I. WATERBURY, banker.
DANIEL WILLARD, President of Baltimore & Ohio R. R.
CHARLES F. ADAMS, lawyer, Boston.
CHARLES F. CHOATE JR., lawyer, Boston.
W. CAMERON FORBES, associate in the University Museum, Boston.
GEORGE P. GARDNER, Vice President of Coastwise Transportation Corp., Boston.
WILLIAM A. GASTON, lawyer, Boston.
EDWIN S. GREENE, President of Lockwood, Greene & Co., Inc., Boston.
HENRY S. HOWE, Director of American Bell Telephone Co., Boston.
ARTHUR LYMAN, lawyer, Boston.
PHILIP STOCKTON, President of Old Colony Trust Co., Boston.
EUGENE V. R. THAYER, Director of American Telephone & Telegraph.
PROF. J. C. HUBBARD, New York University.

WASHINGTON HAILS THE TEST.

Operator There Puts Through the Calls as Scientists Watch.

Special to The New York Times.

WASHINGTON, April 7.—The first practical demonstration of television, which in the opinion of Federal authorities presages the early introduction of visual radio, was staged between Washington and New York today by the American Telephone and Telegraph Company and the Bell Laboratories.

The apparatus for the television demonstration was set up at the Washington end of the line in a small brick building at 1,208 H Street, Northwest, and it was there that Secretary Hoover spoke. His movements were synchronized perfectly while he talked to President Gifford of the A. T. and T. in New York.

In addition to Secretary Hoover, the Washington group attending the demonstration today included Stephen Davis, solicitor of the Department of Commerce; George Akerson, confidential secretary to Mr. Hoover; Vernon Kellogg, of the National Research Laboratories; Albert E. Berry, President of the Chesapeake and Potomac Telephone Company, and other local telephone officials. Also present was Mrs. Gilbert Hovey Grosvenor, wife of the President of the National Geographic Society, and who was formerly Miss Elsie May Bell, a daughter of the late Dr. Alexander Graham Bell of telephone fame. Mrs. Grosvenor was one of those who spoke over the wire to New York.

Miss Edna Horner of the Chesapeake & Potomac Company, had the distinction of being the first woman whose likeness was seen through television. She answered the New York calls as various persons present here were requested to come to the phone for conversation with persons in the Bell Laboratories. Mrs. Herbert Hoover was the second woman whose likeness was so seen. After the earlier demonstration a number of scientists were invited late in the afternoon to come to the local studio. Both Secretary and Mrs. Hoover returned with this group and the Secretary again conversed with New York.

Mrs. Hoover's Comment.

Mrs. Hoover, in speaking to Mr. Gifford, laughingly said: "I don't know whether this is a good invention or not. There are times when I talk over the phone and wouldn't want any one to see how I look."

The group of scientists and officials at the second demonstration here included: Major Gen. McK Saltzman; Dr. George K. Burgess, director of the Bureau of Standards; Dr. C. G. Abbott, Secretary of the Smithsonian Institution; Dr. J. C. Merriam, Carnegie Corporation; Dr. E. E. Slosson, Science Service; Dr. Gilbert Grosvenor, President of the National Geographic Society; James Stokely, Science Service; Charles J. Bell, President of the American Security and Trust Company; Captain Ridley, U. S. N.; Colonel Harrison Brand and John W. Childress, Chairman of the District of Columbia Public Utilities Commission.

Radio Board Interested.

The Federal Radio Commission is much interested in television with the idea that in the comparatively near future it may be utilized in broadcasting programs. In an order recently issued the commission permits invasion of the top part of the amateur broadcast band by experts who desire to experiment with television and other innovations related to radio transmission.

Colonel Dillon, a member of the commission, expressed the opinion that "television is imminent" in connection with radio service, and that it was incumbent on the Government to afford it every facility to assure perfection at the earliest possible date.

Television was discussed at hearings before the Radio Commission last week by C. Francis Jenkins, Washington inventor, who said that the practical use of the invention by which the eye as well as the ear may be served through the medium of radio was about to be realized. He declared that the practical introduction of visual radio was "not a matter of years but of months." The Federal Commission has been advised that great progress has been made by experimenters with visual radio in England and Scotland.

Man's Triumphs Reviewed.

The astounding number of man's conquests over nature in the past thirty years was curiously brought out in the personal record of one of the men whole physical image was carried with his voice over the telephone in the demonstration of television this afternoon. That man is Dr. C. G. Abbot, Acting Secretary of the Smithsonian Institution. During his thirty-two years with the institution, Dr. Abbot remarked at the demonstration, he has chanced to be closely associated with a number of extraordinary developments.

The first of these was aviation. During the pioneering work on mechanical fight of Samuel P. Langley, as Secretary of the Smithsonian Dr. Abbot had occassion to test some of the apparatus used by Langley in connection with his measurements of speed.

When the second disastrous test of Langley's large man-carrying airplane was made in December, 1903, Dr. Abbot stood in the high tower of the Smithsonian Building with his eye glued to a telescope watching the take-off from a houseboat on the Potomac.

One of the first samples of radium chloride purified by M. and Mme. Curie came to the Smithsonian Institution, so that Dr. Abbot was among the first in America to have in his hand a tube of this new marvel. A year or two earlier he had translated for the Smithsonian report of 1897 Roentgen's epoch-making account of his discovery of the X-ray, which transmits pictures through the human body as television now transmits pictures through the air.

In connection with his solar radiation investigations on Mount Wilson in California Dr. Abbot was, he believes, the first person to whom Dr. George E. Hale told of his discovery of magnetism in the sun. Dr. Hale overtook Dr. Abbot on the way to luncheon after a morning spent at the tower telescope and announced his great discovery by the few quiet words: "I think I have it!"

Speaking of power telescopes recalled to Dr. Abbot Hale's quaint expression in regard to the 150-foot tower on Mount Wilson which he desired to protect from shaking by the wind. He did so by enclosing every member of the steel tower which supported the instruments by a box-like member of a separate tower standing on a different foundation. Of this contrivance Hale said to Dr. Abbot when he first conceived it: "I am going to put pants around it."

The Fossil Discoveries.

Again, Dr. Abbot was among the first at the Smithsonian to whom the late Secretary Walcott described his epoch-making discoveries of fossils which proved the existence of life upon the earth at a period variously estimated at from fifty to one hundred million years earlier than had previously been supposed.

"All these achievements," said Dr. Abbot, "and now this present one of being seen in one city while telephoning from another, as well as many more striking discoveries which have wonderfully illuminated the past thirty years, form a story of such absorbing interest and reflect such a glory on the achievements of the human mind as men of few generations have been privileged to be witness to.

"It will be recalled that the first Secretary of the Smithsonian Institution, Joseph Henry, while yet at his laboratories in Albany and afterward at Princeton, was able to send signals with electro-magnetic apparatus through several miles of distance. It was from the principles which he discovered that later on the electric-magneto telegraph of Morse was developed.

"Again, nearly fifty years later, Dr. Alexander Graham Bell, who was for many years, up to his death, a regent of the Smithsonian, invented the telephone and was encouraged by Henry himself in the self-sacrificing course of experiment which led up to the invaluable discovery.

"Now, about fifty years later still, comes this new discovery by which the human face may be seen in one city while the human voice is speaking in another.

"These inventions have been named the telegraph, the telephone and the television. Perhaps fifty years hence there may be other developments, needing no apparatus whatever, by means of which human thought may be transmitted at the will of the sender by the process which now we dimly recognize as telepathy."

H. HUGHES NOT TO QUIT WORK ON "THE CREOLE"

Lecturer at Columbia Denies University Officials Have Got Him to Drop Play.

A published report that pressure by officials of Columbia University had caused Hatcher Hughes to abandon work on a play called "The Creole," was branded as completely false yesterday by Mr. Hughes.

Mr. Hughes, who won the Pulitzer prize several seasons ago with his "Hell Bent fer Heaven," lectures at Columbia on dramatic subjects. "The Creole," which was written by Samuel Shipman and Kenneth Perkins, was played on the Coast a few months ago with Richard Bennett as its star, and at that time attracted police attention. Mr. Hughes recently contracted with Albert Lewis, who controls the play, to make certain revisions in it.

Mr. Hughes declared that there had been no intimation, either official or unofficial, that the university regarded his association with the play as undesirable, and that he did not think university officials were even aware that such play existed. He branded the entire report as "a sensational story," but added that it was quite possible that "something might be started" as the result of it.

Mr. Lewis, producer of the play, said late in the afternoon that he understood "everything had been straightened out," but that he was quite willing to release Mr. Hughes from his obligation to work on the play. All that he had asked Mr. Hughes to do, Mr. Lewis said, was to eliminate from the play everything of an objectionable nature.

THEATRICAL NOTES.

"Big Lake" will open tonight at the American Laboratory Theatre.

"Hit the Deck" will open at the Belasco Theatre on April 19, instead of the 18th.

June Walker, Henry Hull and Geoffrey Kerr will appear together in vaudeville this Summer in a sketch, "This Way Out," by Frank Conlan. They will open on May 2.

The annual Summer production at the Columbia Theatre will open on Saturday night of next week, for an indefinite run. It will be entitled "Let's Go."

Grace George's revival of "The Legend of Leonora" will end its engagement at the Ritz Theatre next Monday night, instead of this Saturday.

There will be a benefit performance at the Times Square Theatre on Sunday night in aid of the Riverside Congregation.

The Shubert-Riviera Theatre and the Bronx Opera House will be dark next week.

Howard Thurston, the magician, will begin an engagement at the Central Theatre on April 18 instead of April 25, as previously announced.

Sophie Tucker will continue with "Gay Paree" on tour.

Section 1

"All the News That's Fit to Print."

The New York Times.

THE WEATHER
Generally fair today and tomorrow; moderate to fresh southerly winds.
Temperature yesterday—Max., 66; Min., 53.
For weather report see Page 31.

Section 1

VOL. LXXVI....No. 25,320. NEW YORK, SUNDAY, MAY 22, 1927. Including Rotogravure Picture Section in three parts, Magazine and Book Sections in Rotogravure. FIVE CENTS In Manhattan, Bronx and Brooklyn | Elsewhere TEN CENTS

LINDBERGH DOES IT! TO PARIS IN 33½ HOURS; FLIES 1,000 MILES THROUGH SNOW AND SLEET; CHEERING FRENCH CARRY HIM OFF FIELD

COULD HAVE GONE 500 MILES FARTHER

Gasoline for at Least That Much More—Flew at Times From 10 Feet to 10,000 Feet Above Water.

ATE ONLY ONE AND A HALF OF HIS FIVE SANDWICHES

Fell Asleep at Times but Quickly Awoke—Glimpses of His Adventure in Brief Interview at the Embassy.

LINDBERGH'S OWN STORY TOMORROW.

Captain Charles A. Lindbergh was too exhausted after his arrival in Paris late last night to do more than indicate, as told below, his experiences during his flight. After he awakes today, he will narrate the full story of his remarkable exploit for readers of Monday's New York Times.

By CARLYLE MACDONALD.

Special Cable to THE NEW YORK TIMES.

PARIS, Sunday, May 22.—Captain Lindbergh was discovered at the American Embassy at 2:30 o'clock this morning. Attired in a pair of Ambassador Herrick's pajamas, he sat on the edge of a bed and talked of his flight. At the last moment Ambassador Herrick had canceled the plans of the reception committee and, by unanimous consent, took the flier to the embassy in the Place d'Iena.

A staff of American doctors who had arrived at Le Bourget Field early to minister to an "exhausted" aviator found instead a bright-eyed, smiling youth who refused to be examined.

"Oh, don't bother; I am all right," he said.

"I'd like to have a bath and a glass of milk. I would feel better," Lindbergh replied when the Ambassador asked him what he would like to have.

A bath was drawn immediately and in less than five minutes the youth had disrobed in one of the embassy guest rooms, taken his bath and was out again drinking a bottle of milk and eating a roll.

"No Use Worrying," He Tells Envoy.

"There is no use worrying about me, Mr. Ambassador," Lindbergh insisted when Mr. Herrick and members of the embassy staff wanted him to be examined by doctors and then go to bed immediately.

It was apparent that the young man was too full of his experiences to want sleep and he sat on the bed and chatted with the Ambassador, his son and daughter-in-law.

By this time a corps of frantic newspaper men who had been madly chasing the airman, following one false scent after another, had finally tracked him to the embassy. In a body they descended upon the Ambassador, who received them in the salon and informed them that he had just left Lindbergh with strict instructions to go to sleep.

As Mr. Herrick was talking with the reporters his son-in-law came downstairs and said that Lindbergh had rung and announced that he did not care to go to sleep just yet and that he would be glad to see the newspaper men for a few minutes. A cheer went up from the group who dashed by Mr. Herrick and rushed upstairs.

Expected Trouble Over Newfoundland.

In the blue and gold room, with a soft light glowing, sat the conqueror of the Atlantic. He immediately stood up and held out his hands to greet his callers. THE NEW YORK TIMES correspondent being first to greet him.

"Sit down, please," urged every one with one voice, but Lindbergh only smiled again his famous boyish smile and said:

"It's almost as easy to stand up as it is to sit down."

Questions were fired at him from all sides about his trip across the ocean, but Lindbergh seemed to dismiss them all with brief, nonchalant answers.

"I expected trouble over Newfoundland because I had been warned that the situation there was unfavorable. But I got over that hazard with no trouble whatsoever."

Sleet and Snow for 1,000 Miles.

"However, it wasn't easy going. I had sleet and snow for over 1,000 miles. Sometimes it was too high to fly over and sometimes too low to fly under, so I just had to go through it as best I could.

"I flew as low as 10 feet in some places and as high as 10,000 in others. I passed no ships in the daytime, but at night I saw the lights of several ships, the night being bright and clear."

Everyone then wanted to know if the flier had been sleepy on the voyage.

"I didn't really get what you might call downright sleepy," he said, "but I think I sort of nodded several times. In fact, I could have flown half that distance again. I had enough fuel

Continued on Page Two.

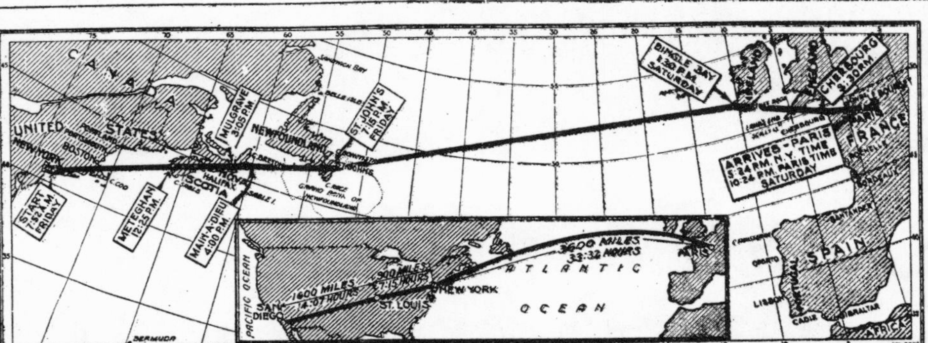

MAP OF LINDBERGH'S TRANSATLANTIC ROUTE, SHOWING THE SPEED OF HIS TRIP.

LEVINE ABANDONS BELLANCA FLIGHT

Venture Given Up as Designer Splits With Him—Plane Narrowly Escapes Burning.

BYRD'S CRAFT IS NAMED

Lindbergh Cheered at Ceremony—Commander, Now Last in Field, Waits on Weather.

Through no fault of his own, Clarence D. Chamberlin, who with Bert Acosta established a world non-stop flying record a few weeks ago, will not fly the record-breaking monoplane in an attempt to establish a second New York-Paris non-stop flight.

G. M. Bellanca, designer of the plane, and Charles S. Levine of the Columbia Aircraft Company, owner of the ship, came to the parting of the ways last night and the designer finally severed his connection with the promoter. Then Levine issued a statement that the proposed flight, which has been talked of for weeks, was off.

The statement said:

"Due to the crowning blow of Mr. Bellanca's resignation, the plane will be placed in the hangar. Mr. Bellanca's resignation causes us to abandon plans for the New York-Paris flight for the present."

At the very moment that the statement was issued the plane was near the runway at Roosevelt Field with gas tanks filled and oil and equipment aboard ready for the start for Paris.

Plane Threatened by Fire.

A few minutes later, as it was being wheeled off, preparatory to being housed for the night, it narrowly escaped being destroyed by fire. When the word came to the field that the flight was definitely off mechanics were ordered to empty one gasoline tank to lighten the machine. The gasoline spilled on the ground and while the ship was being towed away a careless spectator threw the stub of a lighted cigarette down.

In an instant there was a terrific flare and a dense burst of smoke as the gasoline blazed up.

"The Bellanca's gone," was the cry that rose from thousands of spectators who had gathered at the field.

Word was flashed to the army air station at Mitchel Field that there had been an accident and ambulances and fire-fighting apparatus were sent across the road. An ambulance from the Nassau County Hospital at Mineola was also sent to Roosevelt Field, as well as fire apparatus from Mineola.

The plane, however, was beyond the danger line and was not injured.

It had been announced that the Columbia would take off at 8 o'clock and Chamberlin was in his flying clothes ready to climb into the cockpit with the unnamed pilot who was to have accompanied him on the trip.

With the elimination of the Bellanca monoplane, only Lieut.

Continued on Page Four.

Times Wide World Photo

CAPTAIN CHARLES A. LINDBERGH,
Who Flew Alone Across the Atlantic, New York to Paris, in Thirty-three and One-half Hours.

New York Stages Big Celebration After Hours of Anxious Waiting

Harbor Craft, Factories, Fire Sirens and Radio Carry Message of the Flier's Victory Throughout the City—Theatres Halt While Audiences Cheer.

New York bobbed all day yesterday with excitement and expectancy, first yearning for word of Captain Lindbergh, then half-doubting, gaining confidence as the afternoon progressed and finally acclaiming the victory of the young aviator with street demonstrations where the crowds were thickest, in which the ancient phrase, "I told you so," was often repeated. It was evident during the day that New York had confidence in the lad from the West.

On the streets and elsewhere Lindbergh was the one topic of conversation the whole day long. In the subway, on the elevated, in trains and cars, motion-picture houses, theatres, wherever a few had gathered, or even where one man could find another to talk to, one heard "Lindbergh — Lindbergh — Lindbergh."

And such expressions as this:

"He'll make it, all right."

"Some baby!"

"Well, if he's hit Ireland, he's safe anyway."

"He's away ahead of his time."

"What's the difference in time between here and there, anyway?"

Confused On Difference in Time.

To this latter question there were some amazing answers. One woman who had the aviator's running time mixed with the difference in time between New York and Paris solemnly informed her companion that there was thirty-six hours difference in time between the cities. He said it with an air which signified: "I don't mean maybe." A surprising number of persons insisted that the difference in time was three hours.

Early in the day, even before there was any good reason why there should be definite news, the interest of the people was demonstrated in two ways. At every news stand there were little groups scanning the headlines and buying newspapers. In every newspaper office the switchboards were literally swamped with inquiries. It was not sufficient that the operator said there was no word, or, later, that Lindbergh's plane had been seen over Ireland. The inquirers wanted specific information:

"Well, when will you get the first news?" they asked. And later:

"If he's over Ireland how long will it be before he gets to Paris?"

"Is he all right?"

The questions that were asked, considering that no news could possibly come direct from Captain Lindbergh before he landed, were as surprising as the guesses at the difference in time.

The Times Gets 10,000 Phone Calls.

The telephone inquiries came from all sorts of people and all directions. Not a few rang up THE TIMES office and apologetically explained that they were on golf links or elsewhere at a distance, and hence could not

Continued on Page Three.

LINDBERGH TRIUMPH THRILLS COOLIDGE

President Cables Praise to "Heroic Flier" and Concern for Nungesser and Coli.

CAPITAL THROBS WITH JOY

Kellogg, New, MacNider, Patrick and Many More Join in Paying Tribute to Daring Youth.

Special to The New York Times.

WASHINGTON, May 21.—The triumph of Captain Charles A. Lindbergh in flying from New York to Paris without a stop created a tremendous sensation in the national capital and found immediate response in a host of official messages and statements congratulating the daring aviator upon his achievement.

President Coolidge expressed his admiration in a message transmitted through Ambassador Herrick in Paris for delivery to the young flier in person.

With a single possible exception, this city has never been more thrilled since the armistice, when Woodrow Wilson mingled with noisy thousands in celebrating the end of the war. The exception was when Walter Johnson arose from apparent defeat and won the deciding world series baseball game in 1924.

"The American people," the President said, "rejoice with me at the brilliant termination of your heroic flight. The first non-stop flight of a lone aviator across the Atlantic crowns the record of American aviation, and in bringing the greetings of the American people to France you likewise carry the assurance of our admiration of those intrepid Frenchmen, Nungesser and Coli, whose bold spirits first ventured on your exploit, and likewise a message of our continued anxiety concerning their fate."

Secretary Kellogg, in a message similarly transmitted, said:

"I heartily congratulate you on the success of your great adventure in accomplishing a non-stop flight from New York to Paris. It is a great step in the advancement of aviation. Every one in the United States is proud of your accomplishment."

Knew Lindbergh as a Boy.

In a statement issued here Mr. Kellogg referred to his personal friendship for Lindbergh, whom he has known for years through the young man's late father, a Representative in Congress from the Secretary's home State of Minnesota.

"News has just reached me," Mr. Kellogg said, "of the success of Lindbergh in completing his flight from New York to Paris. It is an achievement of which every American can justly be proud. I have known Lindbergh since he was a boy and rejoice at this culmination of his ambitions, which could only have been gained by scientific knowledge, superb courage and physique and sterling character. Our rejoicing in Lindbergh's success, however, is tempered by our continued ignorance of the fate of Nungesser and Coli, whose courage and valor have now been equaled, but cannot be surpassed."

Hanford MacNider, Acting Secre-

Continued on Page Four.

CROWD ROARS THUNDEROUS WELCOME

Breaks Through Lines of Soldiers and Police and Surging to Plane Lifts Weary Flier from His Cockpit

AVIATORS SAVE HIM FROM FRENZIED MOB OF 100,000

Paris Boulevards Ring With Celebration After Day and Night Watch—American Flag Is Called For and Wildly Acclaimed.

By EDWIN L. JAMES.

Special Cable to THE NEW YORK TIMES.

PARIS, May 21.—Lindbergh did it. Twenty minutes after 10 o'clock tonight suddenly and softly there slipped out of the darkness a gray-white airplane as 25,000 pairs of eyes strained toward it. At 10:24 the Spirit of St. Louis landed and lines of soldiers, ranks of policemen and stout steel fences went down before a mad rush as irresistible as the tides of the ocean.

"Well, I made it," smiled Lindbergh, as the little white monoplane came to a halt in the middle of the field and the first vanguard reached the plane. Lindbergh made a move to jump out. Twenty hands reached for him and lifted him out as if he were a baby. Several thousands in a minute were around the plane. Thousands more broke the barriers of iron rails round the field, cheering wildly.

Lifted From His Cockpit.

As he was lifted to the ground Lindbergh was pale, and with his hair unkempt, he looked completely worn out. He had strength enough, however, to smile, and waved his hand to the crowd. Soldiers with fixed bayonets were unable to keep back the crowd.

United States Ambassador Herrick was among the first to welcome and congratulate the hero.

A NEW YORK TIMES man was one of the first to reach the machine after its graceful descent to the field. Those first to arrive at the plane had a picture that will live in their minds for the rest of their lives. His cap off, his famous locks falling in disarray around his eyes, "Lucky Lindy" sat peering out over the rim of the little cockpit of his machine.

Dramatic Scene at the Field.

It was high drama. Picture the scene. Almost if not quite 100,000 people were massed on the east side of Le Bourget air field. Some of them had been there six and seven hours.

Off to the left the giant plane lighthouse of Mount Valerien flashed its guiding light 300 miles into the air. Closer on the left Le Bourget Lighthouse twinkled, and off to the right another giant revolving phare sent its beams high into the heavens.

Big arc lights on all sides with enormous electric glares were flooding the landing field. From time to time rockets rose and burst in varied lights over the field.

Seven thirty, the hour anounced for the arrival, had come and gone. Then 8 o'clock came, and no Lindbergh; at 9 o'clock the sun had set but then came reports that Lindbergh had been seen over Cork. Then he had been seen over Valentia in Ireland and then over Plymouth.

Suddenly a message spread like lightning, the aviator had been seen over Cherbourg. However, remembering the messages telling of Captain Nungesser's flight, the crowd was skeptical.

"One chance in a thousand!" "Oh, he cannot do it without navigating instruments!" "It's a pity, because he was a brave boy." Pessimism had spread over the great throng by 10 o'clock.

The stars came out and a chill wind blew.

Watchers Are Twice Disappointed.

Suddenly the field lights flooded their glares onto the landing ground and there came the roar of an airplane's motor. The crowd was still, then began a cheer, but two minutes later the landing glares went dark for the searchlight had identified the plane and it was not Captain Lindbergh's.

Stamping their feet in the cold, the crowd waited patiently. It seemed quite apparent that nearly every one was willing to wait all night, hoping against hope.

Suddenly—it was 10:16 exactly—another motor roared over the heads of the crowd. In the sky one caught a glimpse of a white gray plane, and for an instant heard the sound of one. Then it dimmed, and the idea spread that it was yet another disappointment.

Again landing lights glared and almost by the time they had flooded the field the gray-white plane had lighted on the far side nearly half a mile from the crowd. It seemed to stop almost as it hit the ground, so gently did it land.

And then occurred a scene which almost passed description. Two companies of soldiers with fixed bayonets and the Le Bourget field police, reinforced by Paris agents, had held the crowd in good order. But as the lights showed the plane

European Capitals Rejoice in the Success of the Daring Trip of Lone American Flier

landing, much as if a picture had been thrown on a moving picture screen, there was a mad rush.

Soldiers and Police Swept Aside.

The movement of humanity swept over soldiers and by policemen and there was the wild sight of thousands of men and women rushing madly across half a mile of the not too even ground. Soldiers and police tried for one small moment to stem the tide, then they joined it, rushing as madly as anyone else toward the aviator and his plane.

The first people to reach the plane were two workmen of the aviation field and half a dozen Frenchmen.

"Cette fois, ca va!" they cried. (This time, it's done.)

Captain Lindbergh answered:

"Well, I made it."

An instant later he was on the shoulders of half a dozen persons who tried to bear him from the field.

The crowd crushed about the aviator and his progress was halted until a squad of soldiers with fixed bayonets cleared a way for him.

It was two French aviators—Major Pierre Weiss and Sergeant de Troyer—who rescued Captain Lindbergh from the frenzied mob. When it seemed that the excited French men and women would overwhelm the frail figure which was being carried on the shoulders of a half dozen men, the two aviators rushed up with a Renault car and hastily snatching Lindy from the crowd, sped across the field to the commandant's office.

Then followed an almost cruel rush to get near the airman. Women were thrown down and a number trampled badly. The doors of the small building were closed, but the windows were forced by enthusiasts, who were promptly ejected by soldiers.

Five Minutes of Cheering for Nungesser.

Spurred on by reports spread in Paris of the approach of the aviator, other thousands began to arrive from the capital. The police estimate that within half an hour after Captain Lindbergh landed there were probably 100,000 storming the little building to get a sight of the idol of the evening.

Suddenly he appeared at a window, waiving his helmet. It was then that, amid cheers for him, came five minutes of cheering for Captain Nungesser.

While the gallant aviator was resting in the Aviators' Club part of the crowd turned toward his airplane. It had landed in the pink of condition. Before the police could intervene the spectators turned souvenir mad, had stripped the plane of everything which could be taken off, and some were even cutting pieces of linen from the wings when a squad of soldiers with fixed bayonets quickly surrounded the Spirit of St. Louis and guarded it while mechanics wheeled it into a shed, but only after it had been considerably marred.

While the crowd was waiting, Captain Lindbergh was taken away from the field about midnight, to seek a well-earned repose.

The thing that Captain Lindbergh emphasized more than anything else to the American committee which welcomed him, and later to newspapermen, was that he felt no special strain.

"I could have gone one-half again as much," he said with conviction.

Excited Crowds Block Paris Traffic.

Not since the armistice of 1918 has Paris witnessed a downright demonstration of popular enthusiasm and excitement equal to that displayed by the throngs flocking to the boulevards for news of the American flier, whose personality has captured the hearts of the Parisian multitude.

Thirty thousand people had gathered at the Place de Opera and the Square du Havre, near St. Lazare station, where illuminated advertising signs flashed bulletins on the progress of the flier. In front of the office of the Paris Matin in the Boulevard Poissonniere the crowds quickly filled the streets, so that extra police details had the greatest difficulty in keeping the traffic moving in two narrow files between the mobs which repeatedly choked the entire street.

From the moment when the last evening editions appeared, at 6:30 o'clock, until shortly after 9 there was a curious reaction, due to the fact that news seemed to be at a standstill. The throngs waited, hushed and silent, for confirmation.

It was a tense period when the thought in every mind was that they were witnessing a repetition of the deception which two weeks ago turned victory into mourning for the French aviators Nungesser and Coli. Suppose the news flashed from the Empress of France that the American flier was seen off the coast of Ireland proved false, as deceiving as the word flashed that Nungesser's White Bird had been sighted off Nova Scotia!

Wait Tensely for News.

During a long, tense period no confirmation came. The people stood quietly, but the strain was becoming almost unbearable, permeating through the crowd. Pessimistic phrases were repeated. "It's too much to think it possible." "They shouldn't have let him go." "All alone, he has no chance if he should be overcome with exhaustion."

To these comments the inevitable reply was, "Don't give up hope. There's still time."

All this showed the French throng was unanimously eager for the American's safety and straining every wish for his ultimate victory.

A French woman dressed in mourning and sitting in a big limousine was seen wiping her eyes when the bulletins failed to flash confirmation that Lindbergh's plane had been sighted off Ireland. A woman selling papers near-by brushed her own tears aside exclaiming:

"You're right to feel so, madame. In such things there is no nationality—he's some mother's son."

Something of the same despair which the crowds evinced two weeks ago spread as an unconfirmed rumor was circulated that Lindbergh had been forced down. Soon after 9 o'clock this was turned to a cheering, shouting pandemonium when the Matin posted a bulletin announcing that the Lindbergh plane had been sighted over Cherbourg.

Crowd Delirious With Joy.

The crowd applauded and surged into the street, halting traffic in a series of delirious manifestations which lasted for ten minutes with cries of "Vive Lindbergh," "Vive l'Americain." The new was followed by a general rush for taxicabs and subway stations, thousands being seized simultaneously with the idea of going to Le Bourget to witness the arrival of the victorious airman.

All roads leading toward the air field were jammed with traffic, though thousands still clung to their places before the boulevard bulletin boards. Other throngs moved toward the Etoile, lining ways of access to the hotel where it had been announced the American's rooms were reserved, in the hope of catching a glimpse of the international hero, the first to make Paris from New York by air, as he passed in triumph from the airdrome.

Landing Excites Crowd to Frenzy.

Ovation after ovation followed the news of Lindbergh's startling progress through France, the crowds steadily augmenting until they filled the entire block. The throng was estimated at 15,000 people. After Cherbourg word was flashed that the plane had traversed Louvirs, then the outskirts of Paris.

In a perfect frenzy the huge crowd hailed the announcement that Lindbergh had landed at Le Bourget. Straw hats sailed in the air, handkerchiefs fluttered and a roar of cheers and clapping spread through the throng and was carried along down the boulevards, where the crowds seated in the cafe terraces rushed into the streets and joined in the demonstration. The cheering was renewed again and again.

Stars and Stripes Wildly Applauded.

From the tops of motorbuses, stopped in the traffic, joyful figures demonstrated their glee, the police abandoning their efforts to restrain the throng and joining in the general elation.

From the first recheering of "Vive l'Americain" rolled up a mighty shout, "The flags," the same cry which two weeks ago gave rise to the false rumor of an anti-American demonstration, when it was falsely reported that a mob demanded the removal of the American flags from the Matin office.

"Vive l'Americain" the Cry.

For several minutes this cry was renewed until the proprietor of a motion picture house unfurled a little American flag, which was greeted with cheer upon cheer and which became the mightiest pro-American demonstration seen in France since the days of the war, when, as the Yankee troops landed, three large American flags beside the French Tricolor hung from Le Matin's window in the glare of searchlights.

There could be no mistaking the sincerity of these cheers, which were prolonged as a Frenchman in the crowd rushed up to the American demonstrators, wringing their hands in congratulations.

Extra papers telling the tale of the American's triumph in bulletin form sold as fast as the newsmen could distribute them.

The throng slowly dispersed in a general procession toward Montmartre, where many hundreds were to spend the remainder of the night in a celebration.

Flier's Navigation Called Uncanny.

What appealed to the French aviators as the uncanny part of Captain Lindbergh's performance was his lack of navigating instruments. Old and experienced airmen, in conversations during their wait for him said he had one chance in a thousand because, while he might head in a given compass direction in leaving America, the winds might put him many hundreds of miles out of his path.

Guesses were made that he might land in Spain, in Portugal, in Northern Africa or in Ireland or even Norway. But the flier landed at Le Bourget as simply as you please and as accurately as if he had half a dozen navigators aboard.

Traffic to Le Bourget in Record Jam.

When the news of Captain Lindbergh's arrival reached Paris tens of thousands of people started for Le Bourget Field. They met the crowds starting to come home and there ensued the worst traffic tangle the French Capital has had. The police estimate that 12,000 automobiles became involved in the tangle and many of the cars did not get back to the city until after 3 o'clock this morning.

For two hours there was a hopeless mixup with no movement in any direction. The emergency traffic police brought from Paris worked nearly all night in straightening out the mess.

French papers estimated that at midnight 150,000 people were trying to get to or from Le Bourget and there were frequent exhibitions of temper which acted as a great contrast to the enthusiastic joy which greeted the arrival of the American hero.

Soon after Lindbergh landed an employe of the Bourse telegraph office arrived with more than 700 cablegrams for him, but the employe was unable to get within half a mile of the addressee.

Greeted by Herrick and French Officials.

By The Associated Press.

PARIS, May 21.—Captain Charles A. Lindbergh, the young American aviator who hopped off from New York yesterday morning all alone in his monoplane, the Spirit of St. Louis, arrived in Paris tonight safe and sound.

After a battle with the mob the Reception Committee got Captain Lindbergh into the Administration building, where he was officially greeted by Ambassador Herrick and high French officials.

But Lindbergh was too weary seemingly to know what it was all about. He smiled and said: "Thank you, I am awfully happy," and then his fatigue could be fought off no longer and he seemed to go to sleep standing there on his feet.

Outside the crowd was howling for a sight of the hero who has won the heart of France as no American probably had before. Brilliant searchlights were focused on the balcony of the building, into which Lindbergh had been carried. But the crowd had to be disappointed—Lindbergh could do no more.

The American Ambassador came to the balcony and waved the aviator's helmet at the crowd, and held aloft a great bunch of flowers, obviously presented to the flier.

"Nobody Knows Me Here," Says Flier.

Lindbergh, asleep on his feet, was lifted up and carried to an automobile and hurried to Paris, a few miles away, to sleep after so many hours when ever to close his eyes for a moment might have meant death.

Before he went to bed, however, Captain Lindbergh informed Ambassador Herrick that he had brought two or three letters of introduction with him, because, he explained, "This is a new country to me and nobody knows me here."

ORTEIG AND PAINLEVE LAUD FLIER'S FEAT

Donor of Prize Commends Lindbergh's Modesty and War Minister His Bravery.

Special Cable to THE NEW YORK TIMES.

PARIS, Sunday, May 22.—Raymond Orteig, donor of the $25,000 prize which Captain Lindbergh won yesterday, arrived in Paris last evening half an hour after Lindbergh had alighted at Le Bourget airdrome on his flight from New York.

"Lindbergh has accomplished a magnificent feat, and I regret that I was not there to welcome him when he touched French soil," Mr. Orteig said.

"What is so admirable is the modesty of this hero, who in silence prepared for his magnificent effort."

In a statement issued this morning M. Painlevé, Minister of War, said:

"The victory of Lindbergh is a magnificent human triumph. It takes a place in the history of aviation beside the wonderful crossing of the Mediterranean by Garros.

"I cannot imagine anything more moving than those hours of absolute solitude between the sky and the immense ocean when, leaning upon the guiding bar, this daring human bird communicated with the world only by his periscope and stoically followed the path which had no returning.

"These marvelous accomplishments are a stimulant for invention and for progress. They increase the mastery of men over matter, over time and over space.

"Some heroes die, and others, coming after them, succeed. Those who die are not sacrificed in vain. Lindbergh has triumphed in the great flight undertaken by Nungesser and Coli. All honor to Lindbergh!"

PARIS SPENT DAY WISHING SUCCESS

Bulletins of Lindbergh's Progress Dominated the News as Extras Were Issued.

ALL FACILITIES PREPARED

Enthusiasm Called Answer to Reports That False Nungesser News Aroused Hatred.

Special Cable to THE NEW YORK TIMES.

PARIS, May 21.—The French could not have shown toward Lindbergh's flight a more kindly, more sympathetic, more enthusiastic attitude. All during the day one heard only expressions of the most sincere hope that he would be successful and declarations of the greatest admiration for his brave effort.

Liberté, the most Nationalist of the French newspapers, said this afternoon:

"Paris, which carries in its heart mourning for Nungesser and Coli, is preparing to receive the brave American aviator. We shall give to him the same welcome America would have given our heroic pilots had they succeeded. Facts will answer the stupid reports that the public opinion of Paris was hatefully unloosed against America when it found out all the telegrams announcing Nungesser's success were lies.

"Paris, always impassioned by courage, Paris which has not forgotten its emotion of joy when, in 1917, it saw the first American regiments in the streets, will unite this evening in one fervent thought the names of Lindbergh, Nungesser and Coli.

"If Lindbergh should disappear in the immensity of the ocean we shall think of his mother and shall join in the same pious thought—mother of Lindbergh, mother of Nungesser, mother of Coli."

Le Quotidien hails Lindbergh as more of a sporting American than any other of the potential United States candidates.

The newspapers this morning as well as this afternoon displayed news of the flight as the predominating item. It was about 2 o'clock when a report that the Empress of Scotland had sighted Lindbergh reached the French capital. Within a few minutes extras were on the streets. Soon afterward came the news that the gallant aviator had been sighted 200 miles off the Irish coast.

These messages were displayed in big type on the front pages of all the afternoon papers with the exception of the Temps, which, apparently remembering the telegrams relative to Nungesser's flight, published the news of Lindbergh "sous toutes"—with reserve. At 4 o'clock the news reached Paris that Lindbergh had been sighted over the South of Ireland.

Early this morning the Government gave orders that everything possible should be done at Le Bourget to facilitate the arrival of Lindbergh. Preparations were made to light the French-English air route in the event that the American had not arrived by nightfall. Also orders were given to prepare the airfield at Cherbourg as well as airlights at the Sain. Ingelevert, Berck, Abbeville and Beauvais, and finally the great light on Mount Valerien, visible for 250 miles.

In view of the handling of the great crowd expected at the Paris airport, an extra regiment was placed at the disposal of the Commandant at Le Bourget. He gave orders that no airplane should be allowed in the air in the vicinity of Le Bourget this evening, keeping the air route perfectly clear for Lindbergh.

So hazardous was considered the flight of Lindbergh that several well-known French aces gave interviews this afternoon to the papers, expressing doubts and urging against too great optimism. Lecointe said:

"It is a magnificent effort and I hope with all my heart that the courageous American will succeed. Crossing the Atlantic is a terrible undertaking, as the fate of Coli and Nungesser showed."

Pelletier Doisy, known as the nerviest French aviator, expressed great admiration for the American.

"'The Flying Fool,' if he arrives, will be nothing short of fantastic," he said. "Certainly he had nerve and no one knows what he will do. I certainly hope the brave boy succeeds."

ARRANGE FOR RECEPTIONS.

Lindbergh Will Be Guest of Many Organizations.

Special Cable to THE NEW YORK TIMES.

PARIS, May 21.—Once he has indicated he is thoroughly refreshed, Captain Charles Lindbergh will receive friends and official callers in the reception rooms and make his response as to whether he will attend the functions which already are being organized in his honor.

Principal among these receptions is one set for 5 o'clock Monday in the magnificent salons of the Aero Club de France, where the American hero will be greeted with a tremendous ovation by representatives of the French Navy, military and civil fliers and of every organization in France interested in aviation.

The officials preparing this function are already besieged with requests for invitations from private individuals, including the leading statesmen of France, Deputies and members of the army.

Another reception is planned by the Paris chapter of the National Aeronautic Association of the United States, which also is having difficulty in filling demands for places.

Raymond Orteig, donor of the $25,000 prize for the first New York-Paris flight, is expected to attend the American Club luncheon Tuesday noon in the immense dining hall of the new Hotel Ambassador which, it is expected, will be jammed with Lindbergh admirers. Club members will have the preference for seats after the invited guests. Club members are limited to one guest each. The remaining seats will be open to the public.

Miss Ederle Sends Congratulations.

ATLANTA, Ga., May 21.—Gertrude Ederle tonight cabled the following message to Captain Lindbergh in care of Ambassador Herrick at Paris: "Heartiest congratulations from one pioneer to another. Your courageous feat is another brilliant page in history. I, too, was told it could not be done when I attempted the Channel. However, youth will be served."

COULD HAVE GONE 500 MILES FARTHER

Continued from Page 1, Column 8.

left to go 1,000 miles, I think—certainly 500—although I had no time to examine my fuel tanks, the crowds were so terrific.

"If it wasn't for the soldiers and two French aviators I think I might have been injured by wild enthusiasts in the throng. Anyway, I paid no attention to economy of fuel during the voyage."

Saw Flares Forty Miles From Le Bourget.

Ambassador Herrick then asked the young aviator if he had any difficulty finding his way once he reached Europe.

"Well, you know this is my first trip to Europe, and I just had to take a chance," was his reply.

He added with another of his smiles, that he liked what he had seen of Paris and he wanted to stay as long as he could.

The American youth said that never once during the trip had he doubted his eventual success, and when he was over Cherbourg, or what he thought was Cherbourg, he knew he would make it.

"About forty miles away from Paris," he continued, "I began to see the old trench flares they were sending up at Le Bourget. I knew then I had made it, and as I approached the field with all its lights it was a simple matter to circle once and then pick a spot sufficiently far away from the crowd to land O. K.

"I landed perfectly. Then the crowd descended on me, and it was all over but the handshaking."

Lindbergh refused to take seriously the problem of flying the Atlantic, when he was asked how he had performed the almost unbelievable feat.

"You know, flying a good airplane doesn't require near as much attention as a motor car," he explained.

Ate Sandwich and a Half on the Way.

"I had four sandwiches when I left New York," he said. "I only ate one and a half during the whole trip and drank a little water. I don't suppose I had time to eat any more, because you know it surprised me how short a distance it is to Europe."

By this time the interview had lasted for seven or eight minutes and Mr. Herrick insisted that it would involve too much strain on the flier to submit him to further questioning. Every one then withdrew, and with a cheery "good night" and a final handshake with the Ambassador, Lindbergh hopped into bed like a schoolboy after a hard day's play, and before this correspondent left the embassy word came downstairs that Lindbergh was sound asleep.

Herrick Cables Lindbergh's Mother.

Immediately after this Mr. Herrick sent the following cable to Linbergh's mother in Detroit:

"Warmest congratulations. Your incomparable son has honored me by becoming my guest. He is in fine condition and sleeping sweetly under Uncle Sam's roof.

"MYRON HERRICK."

Lindbergh brought no baggage, so a hasty wardrobe was assembled for him at the embassy from the personal effects of Ambassador Herrick and his son, Parmely.

The young flier, however, did bring three letters, the only excess baggage he carried. Two were from Theodore Roosevelt for Ambassador Herrick and his son, and the third was addressed to the Ambassador and was from Charles Lawrence of the Wright firm that built the motor for the Spirit of St. Louis.

BULLETINS RECORD PROGRESS OF FLIER

First Sighted Yerterday by a Vessel About 500 Miles West of Ireland.

MARKS SEEN IN SOUTH ERIN

Lindbergh Was Flying High Over Plymouth, England—Over the French Coast at 8 P. M.

The progress of Captain Lindbergh's flight from the time he was sighted 500 miles west of the Irish coast yesterday morning until he landed at Le Boruget last night is told briefly in the following bulletins:

HALIFAX, May 21 (AP).—The Canadian Government wireless station at Cape Race, N. F., has picked up a wireless from the steamer Hilversum, sent at 12:10 Greenwich Time (7:10 A. M., Eastern Standard Time), saying: "Lindbergh sighted 500 miles from Irish coast. Plane keeps full speed."

VALENTIA, Ireland, May 21 (AP).—The Government wireless station is advised by the steam collier Nogi that she sighted a gray airplane heading east-southeast while the Nogi's position was about 52.45 north latitude, 12.5 west longitude. The plane was flying rather low.

LONDON, May 21 (AP).—A Dublin dispatch to the Press Association at 2:50 o'clock this afternoon quotes a message from Valencia, Southwestern Ireland, as saying that Lindbergh's plane was sighted 100 miles off that point.

Identified at Dingle Harbor.

BELFAST, Ireland, May 21 (AP).—Lindbergh's plane was reported sighted over Dingle Harbor, County Kerry, Southwestern Ireland, at 5:30 o'clock this afternoon, flying in the direction of Cork.

Lindbergh was first sighted by a Hallyfernter civic guard, who notified Tralee and Dingle that it was possible to identify the markings on the plane, NX-211.

All eyes in the little Kerry towns crossed in the passage of the plane were turned to the sky, but observation opportunities were slight, as Lindbergh was traveling very rapidly and at a height of about 1,000 feet.

The wind was from the west and the weather sunny, with occasional showers.

Flying High Over Plymouth.

By Wireless to THE NEW YORK TIMES.

LONDON, May 22.—A British Admiralty report from Admiral Bentick says that Lindbergh's plane passed Plymouth at an altitude of between 6,000 and 8,000 feet.

Reaches the French Coast.

The French Cable Company announced receipt of official advices, The Associated Press in New York reported at 3:25 P. M. yesterday, saying that Captain Lindbergs's plane passed over Bayeux on the French coast at 8 o'clock last night, French time.

Bayeux, near the coast of Seine Bas, an arm of the English Channel, is about 150 miles by air line from Paris.

CHERBOURG, May 21 (AP).—An airplane, believed to be Captain Lindbergh's, passed over Cherbourg in the direction of Paris at 8:30 P. M.

The machine passed at a very high altitude, and it was impossible in the gathering dusk to see its identification marks. It came from the direction of the open Atlantic.

Passage of the machine, a monoplane, was signaled from the semaphore stations at Jobourg and Onglet on the coast. The fishing boat Jean Marc messaged the plane's passage across the Channel.

Paris Hears of Passing Ireland.

Special Cable to THE NEW YORK TIMES.

PARIS, May 21.—News has been received at Le Bourget airdrome that Captain Lindbergh was seen passing over Southwest Ireland at 3:35. The Cherbourg aerdrome has been warned to have an escort in readiness. The wind reported to be blowing hard, considerably aiding Lindbergh and increasing his speed by fully thirty miles an hour.

Special Cable to THE NEW YORK TIMES.

LE BOURGET, May 21, 9:15 P. M.—Many thousand people are packed on all the roofs and in the windows of Le Bourget air port awaiting the arrival of Lindbergh. As yet there is no official news, however. An unconfirmed report has been received that the airplane was seen passing over the Plymouth (England) district two hours ago and over Cherbourg at 8:45.

Darkness has fallen. All Le Bourget's searchlights are sweeping the sky and rockets are being sent up at regular intervals. The wind has moderated and the sky is clear.

Special Cable to THE NEW YORK TIMES.

PARIS, May 21, 10:21 P. M.—An unknown airplane has appeared over Le Bourget. It is believed to be Lindbergh. There is great excitement.

Special Cable to THE NEW YORK TIMES.

PARIS, May 21.—Lindbergh alighted at Le Bourget at 10:24 P. M.

Special Cable to THE NEW YORK TIMES.

PARIS, May 21, 10:35 P. M.—Le Bourget has confirmed the arrival of Lindbergh at 10:24. From a height of 10,000 feet he landed on a lighted field almost unexpectedly. Four minutes from the time the sound of his motor was heard he was on the ground.

A crowd of many thousands broke down the iron railings around the field as though they were paper and poured out onto it.

Ambassador Herrick was among the first to welcome and congratulate the hero.

LINDBERGH VICTORY THRILLS ENGLAND

Universal Enthusiasm Spreads Over British Isles as News Is Flashed From France.

PEOPLE SCAN SKY ALL DAY

Lucky Ones on American's Course See Plane Sweep Over on Memorable Voyage.

Special Cable to THE NEW YORK TIMES.

LONDON, May 21.—London followed Captain Lindbergh on his tremendous adventure with an interest scarcely less keen and hopes equally as sincere as those entertained for his success in New York from the time he set forth till he reached Paris, where his flight was crowned with deserved success tonight.

All day today English eyes scanned the blue spaces of the skies for the tiny black speck whose appearance would indicate that the ocean's expanse at least had been safely spanned. During the afternoon men eagerly read the rapidly succeeding editions of the evening papers for fresh information and keenly canvassed the chances of this young knight errant of the air in his lone joust with death.

The fact that two Royal Air Force officers were simultaneously engaged in an attempt to break the world's long distance non-stop flight record by flying from London to India added to rather than detracted from the interest. The sheer audacity of Captain Lindbergh's feat alone was enough to capture the general imagination.

The offices of the Sunday newspapers were bombarded tonight by excited queries whether the flight had been successful, and so many were the telephone inquiries to Paris that an hour's delay prevailed between the two capitals.

Progress Over British Isles.

Captain Lindbergh, according to the Dublin correspondent of THE NEW YORK TIMES, was first definitely sighted off the Irish coast by the French trawler Nogi at 3:30 P. M., English time. He was steering east-southeast and flying rather low at latitude 52.45 north and longitude 12.5 west. He reached the Irish coast 100 minutes later, passing over Three Sisters, County Kerry.

He then crossed Dingle Bay and was seen flying south-southwest toward the coast in the direction of Kenmare, apparently with the idea of making direct for Paris.

He passed Baltimore, County Cork, at 5:45. He was then flying seaward at a very high altitude.

Then the news arrived that the big white airplane had been seen over England. At 7:40 P. M. it was visible over St. Germain's, Cornwall about nine miles west of Plymouth, from which point a transatlantic flight of a different kind once set forth to American shores. Five minutes later it was sighted over Prawle Point, South Devon. It was then flying very high and very fast.

The next news was the flash from Paris announcing that the airman had been sighted from France, and hot on the heels of this came the news of his arrival.

British airmen, who knew the difficulties with which Lindbergh's attempt was beset, were almost speechless in their admiration of the pluck and skill that pulled the young pilot through.

Sir Alan Cobham, the distinguished British flier, whose recent flight to Australia and back was an air epic, said tonight that he was thrilled by Lindbergh's achievement and could not understand how he had been able even to keep awake.

"Well Done!" Says Prince of Wales.

"Well done!" exclaimed the Prince of Wales on hearing of Lindbergh's success.

Mr. Houghton, the American Ambassador, said:

"We are all proud of Lindbergh—who is no 'flying fool' after all. It is a wonderful achievement."

The Sunday papers are full of praise for the young airman. The Weekly Dispatch says:

"Every British heart will swell with the impulse of sincere joy in the exploit of the flying fool whose non-stop flight from New York to Paris has well-nigh eliminated the word impossible from the dictionary of aerial adventure. Lindbergh's achievement is truly epoch-making in the heroic sense of the word.

"From the merely practical viewpoint it is a most astonishing feat which has been performed in this fight for mastery over the air. His was a flight of the imagination, which imagination, translated in terms of pluck and skill, made real. Doubtless there will be emulators, but the first glory belongs to him and to America, and we cheerfully pay our tribute of praise and admiration. Well done, Captain Linbergh!"

The Sunday Express says:

"Lindbergh is no ordinary man. He is the stuff heroes are made of. He defied death and snatched his reprieve and pardon. His daring dazzles the world. It is difficult to imagine anything more desperately heroic than his solitary flight across the ocean. The exploit entailed continuous navigation hour after hour without rest or respite. It involved a ceaseless call upon every nerve. Probably the airman lived through the whole adventure in a state of exaltation and ecstasy governed by iron self-control and steely courage."

The Observer says:

"It is a magnificent achievement of sheer courage and self-reliance. It stands perhaps alone in the spectacular records of airmanship. The chief fear for Lindbergh was that he had overestimated his powers of physical endurance. Evidently he knew himself."

TOWN WILD OVER LINDBERGH

Cheers and Tears Mingle in Celebration of Little Falls, Minn.

LITTLE FALLS, Minn., May 21 (AP).—Pandemonium broke loose here when a crowd jammed in front of the local newspaper heard the announcement that Charles A. Lindbergh, who grew to manhood here, had successfully completed his New York-Paris airplane hop.

Cheers, back-slapping and here and there a tear ended the tension that has gripped this town of 7,000 since "our Charley" took off. A blaring band added to the din, whistles shrieked and bells rang.

"All the News That's Fit to Print."

The New York Times.

THE WEATHER
Showers today, probably tomorrow; not much change in temperature.
Temperature yesterday—Max. 80, min. 59.
For weather report see Page 15.

VOL. LXXVII....No. 25,714. *** NEW YORK, TUESDAY, JUNE 19, 1928. TWO CENTS in Greater New York | THREE CENTS Within 200 Miles | FOUR CENTS Elsewhere in the U. S.

AMELIA EARHART FLIES ATLANTIC, FIRST WOMAN TO DO IT; TELLS HER OWN STORY OF PERILOUS 21-HOUR TRIP TO WALES; RADIO QUIT AND THEY FLEW BLIND OVER INVISIBLE OCEAN

RITCHIE WITHDRAWS IN FAVOR OF SMITH, URGING PARTY UNITY

New Yorker's Nomination Will Assure Democratic Victory, He Asserts.

DIRECTS APPEAL TO SOUTH

Smith as President Would Restore Popular Government, Maryland Executive Says.

TURNS OVER HIS DELEGATES

Sees Struggle of 1924 Avoided at Houston—Reed Still in Race, Backer Declares.

Special to The New York Times.

BALTIMORE, June 18.—Governor Albert C. Ritchie tonight withdrew as candidate for the Democratic Presidential nomination, with the announcement that he would instruct the Maryland delegation to cast its sixteen votes at the National Convention at Houston next week for Governor Smith of New York.

In a formal statement, Governor Ritchie urged the Democratic Party to unite behind Governor Smith. The New York Executive, he declared, was "fitted by experience, character and ability to assume the leadership of the party and had the best chance to win in the November election.

"His record is a guarantee that with him as President, honesty in Government would take the place of corruption in Government," he said of Governor Smith.

Governor Ritchie expressed his gratitude that Maryland had advanced his own name for the Presidential nomination. "The great majority of the Democratic Party in every section of the country" was ready to back Governor Smith, however, he said, and he felt a responsibility to the party so to declare himself.

Makes Especial Plea to South.

Mr. Ritchie directed his plea in behalf of Governor Smith particularly to the South. The national situation demanded, and pointed to, the success of the Democratic Party as the champion of self-government and popular self-rule, principles which the South through the Democratic Party had saved to the nation, he asserted.

He, "as a son of the South," had fought enthusiastically for these principles. As an American and as a Democrat, he now urged a "united and unbroken front" by the party to assure its success next Fall.

"Every Democrat should subordinate himself to this higher call for party unity," he said, to re-establish in national life those principles of which Governor Smith was the "exponent."

Governor Ritchie asserted that, in dropping his candidacy for the Presidential nomination, he also took himself out of the running for second place on the party ticket.

"I have not the slightest thought of the Vic. Presidency, nor expectation of it being offered to me, or accepting it if it is," he said. "In taking this action, I do so without any ulterior motive whatsoever. It emanates from a profound sense of duty to the nation and to the Democratic Party, with which the country's well-being is inseparably bound up."

Governor Ritchie's Statement.

The following is Governor Ritchie's statement in full:

I am profoundly convinced that no consideration of self or of personal advancement on any one's part should be allowed to stand for one moment in the way of the success of the Democratic Party, which is the natural champion of self-government and popular self-rule.

These principles are challenging the attention of the country today as they have not done for years. To them I have dedicated such political effort as I am able to exert. Faith in them saved the South during the dark days of reconstruction and made possible a reunited and happy nation; and as a son of the South I have brought to the struggle for these principles the enthusiasm and the loyalty which came to me from ancestors who were ready to die, and some of whom did die, for the cause in which they believed.

As a Democrat I have regarded this struggle as a duty, and as an American I believe that the dictates of patriotism require the reestablishment of these principles in our national life.

That my own State should think me worthy to be the standard-bearer of the Democratic Party is a distinction for which I never can sufficiently express my gratitude, nor can I adequately express it to my friends elsewhere in the coun-

Continued on Page Ten.

President of Porto Rican Senate Stabbed And Badly Hurt by a Maniac Anarchist

Wireless to THE NEW YORK TIMES.

SAN JUAN, Porto Rico, June 18.—Antonio Barcelo, President of the Porto Rican Senate, was stabbed with a chisel at the close of a welcoming demonstration at City Hall today and probably owes his life to the fact that he is fat.

The chisel made a four-inch wound, then was deflected by a rib.

Justo Matos, 35 years old and believed to be demented, who attempted the assasination with the unusual instrument, was himself shot through the abdomen by an unidentified bystander after police, they say, actually had him in custody. The condition of Matos is considered critical.

In their efforts to protect Matos police were unable to detect who had shot him.

The assault on Señor Barcelo took place at the close of a noisy welcome while hundreds of persons surged about him with greetings. Señor Barcelo was just returning home from New York where Columbia University gave him an honorary degree of Doctor of Laws and President Butler had referred to him as "captain of his island people."

By The Associated Press.

SAN JUAN, Porto Rico, June 18.—Señor Barcelo tonight was in a hospital undergoing treatment for his wound. Matos was in prison, heavily guarded to protect him from an outraged populace.

A huge crowd met Señor Barcelo at the docks and escorted him to the Plaza, where on a balcony overlooking the promenade he addressed them.

It was while he was speaking that Matos edged through the crowd, pushed his way onto the low balcony and wielded his chisel. The crowd apparently did not comprehend what had happened. There was a shot from somewhere and Matos was seen to fall, writhing in pain, on the street level, where police took charge of him.

At the hospital, where Señor Barcelo was taken, doctors declined to state whether the wound was likely to prove fatal.

The motive for Matos's action is not known. Some in the crowd who noticed him before his deed said he remarked he was ill, and then added that he could kill ten Porto Ricans willingly.

The stabbing itself, perhaps by coincidence, followed the statement in Señor Barcelo's speech that he was not a member of any political party or faction but a Porto Rican, and was proud of the honor accorded him by Columbia University not so much for his own sake as that it went to a citizen of his country.

La Democratica, Señor Barcelo's newspaper, this afternoon said Matos had visited their office and the Barcelo home for a week asking whe the legislator would return here. Other afternoon papers refer to him as a "Socialist fanatic," and one calls him a "confessed anarchist."

SMITH SUPPORTERS SEE A QUICK VICTORY

Hope Ritchie's Withdrawal in Favor of Governor Will Be Followed by Others.

AIDES START FOR HOUSTON

Van Namee, Sure of Success, Says "Steam-Roller" Methods Will Not Be Used.

With George R. Van Namee, manager of Governor Smith's preconvention campaign for the Democratic nomination, speeding toward Houston to open headquarters in the Hotel Rice, Smith supporters here were jubilant last night at the announcement by Governor Ritchie of Maryland that he would advise the sixteen delegates from that State to cast their votes for New York's Governor on the first ballot.

Mr. Van Namee predicted, just as he boarded the train at Grand Central Station yesterday noon, that Governor Smith would be nominated on "an early ballot." The more optimistic Smith supporters contended last night that the first ballot would show a strength of 704 votes, or 29 1-3 short of the number required for nomination. The hope was expressed that Governor Ritchie's action might swing other State delegations into line before the voting starts at Houston, in which event Governor Smith might be nominated on the first ballot.

Rules Out "Steam Roller" Plan.

While declining to name the ballot on which he believed Governor Smith would be nominated, Mr. Van Namee declared that with 650 delegates already instructed and many others known to favor the Smith candidacy, his nomination was practically assured. The Smith forces, Mr. Van Namee declared, would not attempt any "steam-roller" methods at Houston and would seek in no way to prevent any candidate from presenting his claims to the nomination. The Smith forces, he added, are concerned with promoting party harmony.

With Mr. Van Namee were Mrs. Van Namee, Howard Cullman of the Port of New York Authority and George C. Norton. Norman E. Mack, Democratic National Com-

Continued on Page Nine.

12 INJURED BY BOMB 'PLANTED' IN DETROIT

County Building Shaken, Windows Shattered and Hundreds Panic-Stricken.

'PURPLE' GANG SUSPECTED

Darrow Attending Court Case Is Jarred—Jokes With Judge About Blast.

Special to The New York Times.

DETROIT, June 18.—A devastating blast which injured twelve county employes, two seriously, shattered dozens of panes of glass and rocked the Wayne County Building to its foundation this afternoon is believed by police to have been another attempt at intimidation of the courts by sympathizers with the "Purple" gang, nine members of which are now on trial on charges of conspiracy to extort.

"The dynamite bomb evidently was intended for the Municipal Courts Building, where the 'Purples' are on trial," Police Inspector John T. Doyle of the First Precinct declared, "but as usual in such cases some stranger was hired to plant the bomb and probably mistook the county building for the City Courts building.

"It is a miracle no one was killed. The bomb was a powerful one. If it had exploded in the confined space of the rest room instead of in the courtway, I believe it would have wrecked the building and killed many persons."

The explosion occurred at about 2:50 o'clock. The bomb was left in the men's room on the first floor and was found by Frank Stolpa, a constable, who tossed it into the areaway in the centre of the building and was trying to extinguish it with water when it exploded.

One May Lose an Eye.

Stolpa and Arthur Vercrusse, another constable, who also helped in the efforts to extinguish the bomb, were struck in the face by flying glass and bits of iron from the bomb and taken to Receiving Hospital for treatment. Vercrusse, according to the physicians, may lose the sight of his right eye.

About 100 men and women clerks,

Continued on Page Fourteen.

Keel Laid for Biggest Ship, 1,000 Feet Long; 60,000-Ton 'Oceanic' to Cost $30,000,000

Wireless to THE NEW YORK TIMES.

LONDON, June 18.—The biggest ship in the world was begun today at Harland & Wolff's shipyards in Belfast, when the keel was laid for a giant White Star liner to cost $30,000,000. She will be more than 1,000 feet long, with a beam of 100 feet and tonnage of about 60,000.

The ship will not be ready for sailing until 1932, and experts have yet to decide what type of machinery will be installed in her.

When the new ship is added to the White Star fleet she will be called the Oceanic. The six largest steamships in service at the present time, all in the Atlantic trade, are:

The Leviathan of the United States Lines, 59,957 gross tonnage, 907 feet long and 100 feet 3 inches beam.

The Majestic of the White Star Line, claimed by some to be the largest liner afloat, on the basis of the builder and designer's pre-war measurements, which are 56,551 gross tons, 915 feet 5 inches long and 100 feet 1 inch beam.

The Cunarder Berengaria, 52,226 gross tonnage, 883 feet 5 inches long and 98 feet 3 inches beam.

The White Star Olympic, 46,439 gross tonnage, 882 feet 5 inches long, 92 feet 5 inches beam.

The Cunarder Aquitania, 45,647 gross tonnage, 868 feet 7 inches long and 97 feet beam.

The new French liner Ile de France, 43,500 gross tonnage, 757 feet 8 inches long and 91 feet 8 inches beam.

NOBILE VAINLY HAILS FLIERS CIRCLING OVER BUT NOT SEEING HIM

General Radios Base Ship That Rescue Planes Were Over Stranded Men an Hour.

SECOND FLIGHT ALSO FAILS

This Time Italia Castaways Sight One of Planes Piloted by Riiser-Larsen and Holm.

SAVOIA REACHES KINGS BAY

Big Italian Seaplane Ready for Dash North—French and Swedish Craft on Way.

By The Associated Press.

ROME, June 18.—The two Norwegian fliers, Captain Riiser-Larsen and Lieutenant Luetzow Holm, today made a second unsuccessful attempt to find General Umberto Nobile and the party with him north of Spitsbergen. They returned to the icebreaker Braganza without having sighted the marooned men.

Nobile, however, informed the base ship Citta di Milano by wireless that he had seen one of the planes fly within two kilometers of him.

Snow Hides Frantic Signals.

Copyright, 1928, by The Associated Press.

KINGS BAY, Spitsbergen, June 18.—High overhead yesterday General Umberto Nobile saw two seaplanes sent to rescue him and his five comrades from the Arctic ice-floes, but frantic efforts to signal the planes or make known their existence below failed, and, after an hour's reconnaissance above, the craft were seen to disappear in the grim Arctic horizon, flying back toward Spitsbergen.

This news came to the base-ship Citta di Milano today by wireless from the stranded Italia commander, who for days has been awaiting on slowly moving floe ice sight of some one from the outside world who might aid in returning him and his mates on the Italia to civilization and home.

Sunday they thought their days of watching perhaps over. But they failed to count on the trickiness of the snow with visibility, and when help had passed them by their situation was if anything more difficult than before.

Good Visibility of No Avail.

The two seaplanes were those piloted by Captain Riiser-Larsen and Lieutenant Leutzow Holm, the Norwegian fliers. Both set out early Sunday and took a course over Beverly Sound, North Cape and Cape Platen, keeping at a height of from 750 to 900 feet. Both planes carried provisions and clothes for the stranded men.

Visibility was good, but when they returned to Spitsbergen they had not seen a trace of the Italia's commander and the remnant of his crew or of the silk tent he had painted red to aid them. This despite the fact that messages from General Nobile indicated that they had remained above him and in the vicinity for more than an hour.

Today Captain Riiser-Larsen and Lieutenant Holm set out for further reconnaissance, intending, if there were to be variations at all in their course, to keep between their route yesterday and the coast of Northeast Land.

No Chance to Land Amid Ice.

The fliers, on returning yesterday, said that in the area where the fliers are supposed to be they found the ice much too rough for landing. They said that the ice floes were openin. considerably, but that the cracks and openings were still too narrow for landing attempts by the seaplanes. They were such, however, as to foster progress by the ice breakers.

In his message to the Citta di Milano conveying the tragic irony of the situation, General Nobile, to aid further searches, gave his present position as 88.33 north and 17.12 east. This would put him about five miles to the east of Foyn Island.

Savoia's Arrival Raises Hopes.

The hydro-airplane Savoia-55, piloted by Major Maddalena, arrived here at 10:45 o'clock tonight. She was the first of the four big seaplanes en route to Spitsbergen to reach the Northern base.

Fine weather was in evidence as the big machine settled in the harbor. Her arrival and the news that at least two others of large cargo and passenger capacity were en route, raised hopes of the watchers here who for weeks have been trying to get into direct touch with General Nobile and the other survivors of the Italia.

It was a bit uncertain as to whether

Continued on Page Six.

Photo copyrighted by G. P. Putnam.

FIRST WOMAN TO FLY THE ATLANTIC.
Amelia Earhart, Co-pilot of the Airplane Friendship, Photographed in Boston, Just Before She Started on Her Great Adventure.

Eager Crowds Imperil Miss Earhart As They Welcome Fliers at Burry Port

Police Aid Weary Trio to Battle Way to Refuge in Zinc Works—Friends Fly From Southampton to Greet Them and Hear Story of Their Adventures.

By ALLEN RAYMOND.

Special Cable to THE NEW YORK TIMES.

BURRY PORT, Carmarthenshire, South Wales, June 18.—The first woman to cross the Atlantic successfully by air, Miss Amelia Earhart, Boston settlement worker, alighted in the seaplane Friendship here this morning on the broad expanse of Loughor estuary, after a flight of 20 hours and 40 minutes elapsed time from Trepassey.

Few persons saw the gilt-winged Fokker monoplane descend on the Welsh coast, but this evening, when friends rushing from Southampton brought Miss Earhart ashore, she was the recipient of so enthusiastic a reception by the 2,000 inhabitants of this town that it seemed for a few minutes as if she would not outlive her triumph.

Eager Crowds Imperil Aviatrix.

The arrival of the Friendship was the greatest event this remote district has had since the end of the World War when the town's boys came home. Miss Earhart was nearly crushed by the anxiety of the crowd of men, women and children to touch the hem of her flying suit, get her autograph on a slip of paper, wring her hand and congratulate her upon her triumphant passage over the Atlantic.

The High Sheriff of Carmarthenshire, who had rowed out to greet her; the town's three policemen and a couple of friends had to form a ring with locked arms about the latest popular heroine and literally to fight their way a hundred yards from the shore to the office of the local zinc works, where they found shelter back of locked doors.

"You must remember," the local Police Chief said apologetically, "that our people never saw anything to compare with this. I advise you to remain here until we get extra police."

The Friendship's crew were marooned within the walls of the Frickers Metal Company an hour and a half before police reinforcements arrived and cleared a way to two motor cars to take them to a distant hotel where rest, food and sleep could be obtained after their arduous journey.

Poor Visibility Forced Landing.

Poor visibility forced the plane to come down on the Welsh coast after the first tentative objective—Valentia, Ireland—had been left far behind, but the possible goal of Southampton not yet reached.

Except for the first hour over the Atlantic after leaving the rugged shores of Newfoundland, the fliers never saw sea or land until they had winged their way to the Eastern Irish coast. They flew through fog, rain and snow most of the time, fighting for altitude and clearer weather, but they came fast with the wind behind of twenty to thirty miles per hour speeding them on.

They probably had plenty of gasoline left, when they descended, to reach Southampton—seventy-five gallons—but were struggling in the midst of dense fog and knew they were somewhere off the southern coast of Britain. With their object attained—that of making Miss Earhart the first woman to complete a transatlantic crossing—they decided to take no further risks.

They will go on to Southampton tomorrow.

Stultz and Gordon Elated.

The full story of the flight has yet to be told. The two airmen, Stultz and Gordon, who had the major responsibility and labor of getting the Friendship safely across the ocean, were soon fast asleep after battling their way to the hotel. Both ejaculated their joy at their success and chuckled together over the moments in mid-ocean when they seemed dubious of the outcome.

Miss Earhart, who came through her experience in fine condition and

Continued on Page Two.

FOUGHT RAIN, FOG AND SNOW ALL THE WAY

Miss Earhart Says Motors Spat and Gas Ran Low, But She Had Neither Fear Nor Doubt of Success.

PASSED OVER IRELAND WITHOUT EVEN SEEING IT

Wind Aided Plane—Girl Credits Feat to Stultz and Gordon—She Flew Because It Would Have Been 'Too Inartistic to Refuse.'

By AMELIA EARHART.

Special Cable to THE NEW YORK TIMES.

BURRY PORT, Carmarthenshire, South Wales, June 18.—I have arrived and I am happy—naturally.

Why did I do it? When one is offered such a tremendou adventure it would be too inartistic to refuse it. I have been a flier for years. I had planned to spend my vacation flying. I knew the moment this chance came to me that if I turned it down I would never forgive myself.

My trip across the Atlantic aboard the airplane Friendship was all I had imagined it to be as pleasure, and much more though pretty uncomfortable at times. This is my first trip to England, and it is rather funny dropping in by airplane Nevertheless I hope to make the trip again some day and mak it in the same way by air. What I wanted to demonstrate in this flight was that this type of travel was comparatively saf and ought to be developed.

Gives Great Credit to Companions.

I was a passenger on the journey—just a passenger. Everything that was done to bring us across was done by Wilme Stultz and "Slim" Gordan. Any praise I can give them the ought to have. You can't pile it on too thick.

Transoceanic flying has to be done by pilots who can fl by instruments alone I am afraid that some accidents whic marred past flights have been caused by pilots not too sure c instrument flying.

Despite the fact that the weather reports promised us fir visibility and fair weather, we had fog, rain and even snow practically all the way across. We only had clear weather fo one hour out of the twenty-two we were on the way.

The reason we came down here was because we could no see anything. We had just about enough gasoline left, w reckoned, to make Southampton, but we did not dare attemp it because we were flying blind and we knew we had com across. We will go on there tomorrow.

Calls Waiting the Worst Part.

To go back to the beginning, the hardest strain of all thi flight in a way was the waiting at Trepassey. The flight, c course, was a climax piled on top of this worry. That is wha made it so tiring. But we had been trying so much to tak off at Trepassey that all I can remember thinking of when w took off was that at last we were on the way. I was not reall sure till we had flown for half an hour along the coast an headed against the open sea, because I knew that if everythin was not all right Bill would go back.

When we started there was such a burst of spray that th outside motors started cutting out. I was afraid we had mad another false start, but the motors picked up again, and a though they stammered once in a while on the flight when coate with snow, I never had a moment of real trepidation about the and never doubted that we should arrive.

I did not do much. I did not handle the controls onc although I have had more than 500 hours' solo flying and onc held the women's altitude record. When Bill Stultz left th controls to work the radio "Slim" would take them.

Thought of Fishing in Newfoundland.

We got two messages from ships on the way, and when found out what ships they were I did a lot of thinking an jotted down a lot of notes about my feelings, which I hope t expand some day, perhaps.

Leaving the American coast, it was beautiful weathe The jagged coastline beneath us had a grandeur one never for gets, and passing over Newfoundland one could see lots of lake where they told me there were good trout. I hope to fish the some time.

Beneath us the water was wonderful greens and blues, an everything was serene, though, of course the first thing w did was to start looking for the fog which we knew would mee us off Newfoundland. The first hour over the open sea was th only time we saw it. We did not even see Ireland, though w passed right over it, but when we knew we were over Souther England we could not establish any landmarks and our radi had quit us. We do not know yet how it got out of order, bu it was all right when Bill worked it last night and no good whe he tried it this morning.

Marvelous Colors in the Clouds.

Last night was gorgeous. The billows of fog shot wit pink seemed like a vast sunlit desert, and even when night can there was an interesting color effect. There was the glow

Wales and England Join to Greet Intrepid Fliers

our exhausts. At times we seemed to be flying straight into rings of all the colors of the rainbow. Once there were three rings at the same time.

The air was not very bumpy and we had a good following wind. When we got above the clouds and flew very high the stars had a tremendous brilliance. Once we were 11,000 feet up, and it was pretty cold. Most of the time I lay close to the fuselage writing in my little book or talking to Bill or "Slim."

Every time Bill came back from the radio he would tell me what he had received. He got a call from CEV, and I found out that this was the Chilean boat named Bet-Chala. It gave us its bearings. Then we got the position of the British ship Regent close by. That was 20:45 Greenwich Mean Time [4:45 P. M. New York Daylight Saving Time, Sunday], and I remember that the position was about 48 north and 39 west.

Magnetic Compass Seemed the Better.

I watched the petrol consumption and noticed that we kept climbing. Our earth inductor compass did not seem to work so well as our magnetic compass, and the radio went completely out.

For food we carried half a dozen oranges, two vacuum bottles of coffee, one sweetened but without milk, some water, three hard-boiled egg sandwiches and spare rations of chocolate, malted milk tablets and pemmican.

I ate three oranges and half a dozen malted milk tablets. I drank nothing and somehow did not feel hungry. I do not think I dozed at all. I did not need coffee to keep me awake.

Although it has been somewhat of a strain, naturally, I am feeling contented and very fit now that I am here. I did not train for the flight because I had planned to fly quite a bit during my vacation but had not known till six weeks before we started that I was going on such an adventure. One always likes real adventure on a vacation, and I am pretty fit physically. I do some horseback riding and last Winter took up fencing.

Brought Only Her Flying Clothes.

The only clothes I have brought with me are these flying clothes which I borrowed from a friend in Boston before I started. I lack toilet articles and will send out to buy clothes here. We were cutting down every ounce.

I do not know how long I am going to stay abroad this time. I am due back pretty soon at Denison House from my vacation. Of course, I should like to browse around London and see all the old things one reads and dreams about, but perhaps the flight is enough of a good dream come true.

Summing up, the trip thus far has been full of hardship because it is not comfortable aboard the floor of a plane. I cannot exactly call it thrilling. It was a wonderful experience—probably that is the best description—an experience not to be missed if one is offered the chance. I never had any real doubt of the outcome.

The Friendship has just had a great reception from the townspeople of the little Welsh village where we alighted. But I am not looking forward particularly to the repeated crowds which it seems likely we shall meet.

It is all too recent, this flight, for me to compose my exact impressions or even to remember exactly what happened and when. But I know I would not have missed it for anything.

Although I did not handle the controls, I believe a woman could if she were trained. I do not believe women lack the stamina to do a solo trip across the Atlantic, but it would be a matter of learning the art of flying by instruments only, an art which few men pilots know perfectly now. Among the masters I should rank my two friends, Bill and "Slim," who brought me over.

In tomorrow's issue Miss Earhart will continue her story, telling of her experience during the long wait at Trepassey, Newfoundland.

Eager Crowds Imperil Miss Earhart As They Welcome Fliers at Burry Port

By ALLEN RAYMOND.

Continued from Page 1, Column 6.

spirits, struggled against weariness to narrate her experience before she, too, sought sleep.

The adventurers, after five false starts in the Harbor of Trepassey, succeeded in lifting the plane only after dropping fifty gallons of gasoline and cutting down the supply to 700 gallons as against 1,000 they had meant originally to carry. Even with the lightened load they barely lifted the plane skyward with two motors cut out because dashed with spray, but soon they were lifting its weight gradually along the Newfoundland coast till Stultz felt sure the engines were running smoothly.

Weather Good Only at Start.

They headed for the open sea in excellent weather only to run into continuous fog after an hour's flight.

As gasoline was used, lightening the plane, they were enabled to soar 5,000 to 11,000 feet, where most of the way above the clouds they traveled amid a sea of blazing stars, heading, it seemed, into a series of rainbow rings. They received bearings twice from a ship before the radio was out of commission, and encountered bad weather until over Queenstown, Ireland.

There they saw ships and tried to drop notes to find their exact location, but failed to obtain an answer.

Stultz turned correctly southward, however, and headed toward Southampton.

Meanwhile, headed by the Hon. Mrs. Frederick E. Guest, backer of the flight, with her husband, Captain Guest, a member of Parliament and international polo player, and Raymond Guest, former captain of the Yale polo team, there was a large gathering at Southampton awaiting the fliers' arrival. A plane bearing Captain Guest cruished intermittently from noon till 3 P. M. on the lookout. A fast motor launch owned by Hubert Scott Pain, Director of the Imperial Airways, and a noted British sportsman, scudded at a 40-mile an hour gait over the lower harbor awaiting to escort the crew of the Friendship to land.

After hours of anxiety, during which the plane was believed overdue, the watchers at Southampton received the welcome word at 2:45 P. M. that the Friendship was down on the Welsh coast.

Race to Coast by Plane and Auto.

A race to reach her by plane and high-powered automobile began instantly. A seaplane carrying Captain H. H. Railey, European director of the flight, and THE NEW YORK TIMES correspondent, was the first to drop alongside the ocean fliers in Loughor estuary after a three-hour jaunt cutting across Southern England. There were still traces of fog which cut the ocean journey short, but flying low the occupants of the seaplane descried the gilt wings of the Friendship bobbing at a buoy offshore here.

A final run by motor boat brought the fliers in sight. As Miss Earhart looked from the open doorway of the fuselage and recognized one of her visitors as Captain Railey, he, ending a two weeks' vigil to welcome her, cast his hat skyward with a shout of jubilation and let it float off down the tide.

There was an exultant reunion. After a consultation it was decided by Stultz to taxi the plane into the shelter of the Burry Port quays and there the hospitable attack of the Welsh throng began.

Before it was ended Miss Earhart had appeared thrice, in the manner of royalty, at a window of the zinc factory to acknowledge the cheers of the dense crowd below; had been served with tea by the wife of the factory foreman and finally battled and tricked her way to a roadside inn near the village as darkness was nearing and the clock struck 9.

She had been thirty hours en route to her first comfortable resting place.

"Tired and hungry, but cheerful," she commented, lounging in her wooly coat and breeches and stout leather boots. "And we got here all right. There wasn't any race with Miss Boll, but, of course, I'm glad to be the first woman across."

Stultz Tells of Difficulties.

Captain Wilmer Stultz was the first to come ashore after the Friendship had alighted at Burry Port. He declared he was dead tired and explained that he had only enough gasoline left to enable the Friendship to taxi another ten miles.

"No one was more thankful than I was," he admitted, "to see the Welsh coast. We had a very bad trip right through and most of the way I was flying blind. I was at the joystick throughout the whole trip and had considerable difficulty in keeping on my course because of the fog and rain. After realizing that we were getting short of gasoline I resolved to come down as soon as a favorable opportunity offered.

"Then I saw the estuary, which I now know to be Burry Port, and after circling to make sure everything was clear I landed on the strip of water and fastened up to a buoy.

"We are all well, but very, very tired. Miss Earhart is resting on the seaplane, but I came ashore to see about gasoline. At the moment I have not enough to allow us to rise again.

"The trip? Well, I dont' want to discuss it at the moment. It wasn't a pleasant experience, although everything went perfectly. I had to steer solely by the instruments, and luckily none of them went wrong. We flew at a fair height, but flew blind. When we approached the Welsh coast I had to come down to the ground to see where we were."

"Tremendous Triumph," Says the Hon. Mrs. Guest.

Captain Guest, who was formerly Minister of Air, and the Hon. Mrs. Guest, who partially financed the Friendship's flight and originally intended to participate in it, were at Southampton when the news arrived that the plane was down at Burry Point.

"I regard the flight as a tremendous triumph," Mrs. Guest said, "and hope it will be another link in the chain of Anglo-American friendship. That is why I named the machine 'Friendship.'"

Sir Samuel Hoare, Air Minister, sent the following telegram to the United States Ambassador in London:

> Please accept and convey to Miss Earhart and Wilmer Stultz and their companion the Air Council's warm congratulations on the successful completion of their Atlantic flight."

PLANE ESCAPES DISASTER NARROWLY

Misses Copper Works Chimney by Few Yards Only While Alighting at Burry Port.

CROWDS CHEER THE FLIERS

Rush to Give Them Enthusiastic Welcome and Little Girl Offers Kitten as Mascot.

BURRY PORT, Wales, June 18 (AP).—The first woman ever to cross the Atlantic Ocean in an airplane, and the two men who aided her in the crossing, tonight sought well earned repose in this little Welsh town.

It was shortly after noon that watchers on the Welsh coast saw an airplane approaching from the southwest like a great black bird. As it drew nearer the drone of its three powerful engines became audible, but it was not until the big ship flew low over Llanelly Railway Station (four miles from Burry Port) that it dawned on the curious crowds that this was the Friendship and that aboard it was the first woman to cross the Atlantic in an airplane.

The Stars and Stripes painted on its fuselage and the printed letters of its name could be seen, and once Burry Port had seen this insignia it was transported with excitement.

After circling gracefully over the town the plane continued at a low altitude along the river to the coast, and there narrowly escaped disaster when it passed only a few yards to the side of the Bury Port copper works chimney stack. Observers held their breath, but the plane slipped by to make a graceful landing a few minutes later in the estuary. The tide was almost dead low when the plane skimmed the water, taxiing up to a buoy, where the fliers made fast while launches and boats from the shore scurried out to greet them.

MRS. STULTZ EXCITED AS FRIENDSHIP LANDS

Sleepless, Endless Vigil Leaves Her Still in No Mood to Stop and Take a Rest.

One of those most overjoyed to hear of the successful arrival of the airplane Friendship in England was Mrs. Wilmer Stulz, wife of the pilot of the machine that carried Amelia Earhart across the Atlantic. For days and nights the hour-to-hour strain of wondering at what moment her husband would take off on the hazardous flight had reduced her sleeping to restless winks at long intervals.

At 9 o'clock last night after a day spent in excited comment and chat with friends and with her husband's associates, she was still in no mood for slumber.

"Oh, I don't know when I'll get some sleep," she laughed. "What do I care about sleep? What does a mere matter of sleep amount to after an event like this?"

At that time she had received no word from her husband, although Stultz landed in Wales early yesterday. But no others on this side had received direct word of the transoceanic fliers, and she was not in the least dismayed.

"He's got plenty to do," she said. "Besides, he must be so tired; I hope he is getting a little sleep himself right now."

She did not know as yet whether she would await him in New York or would go to Europe to meet him, she declared, but was waiting for information about the plans of the Friendship crew before determining.

"I am so happy and relieved I can't make plans anyway," she added.

GARDEN CITY, N. Y., June 18 (AP).—A telegram of congratulation from Mrs. Gertrude Goldsborough, widow of Brice Goldsborough, who was lost with Mrs. Frances Wilson Grayson in a transatlantic flight attempt, was among nearly a hundred messages received today by Mrs. Wilmer Stultz, wife of the man who piloted the monoplane Friendship from Newfoundland to Wales.

"It was the sweetest message of them all," Mrs. Stultz said.

The flier's wife also received a wire from her mother at Middletown, N. Y., suggesting that she come home for a rest after the strain of awaiting news of her husband's safety on the long flight.

STULTZ HOME CELEBRATES.

Williamsburg Stages Big Parade, Led by Flier's War "Buddy."

Special to The New York Times.

ALTOONA, Pa., June 18.—Williamsburg, the Blair County birthplace and home of Wilmer Stultz, 28-year-old co-pilot of the Friendship, today staged its greatest celebration in honoring a fellow townsman, a mammoth parade being held to mark the success of his flight.

Factory whistles were blown and sirens shrieked during the morning when it was announced that Stultz and his party were safely landed, and immediately plans went forward to stage a parade. Joseph Bechtol, World War veteran, and "buddy" of Stultz, was Chief Marshal. Mayors and Burgesses of all Blair County towns participated.

The parade came to a halt in front of the home of Mrs. Clara Stultz, mother of the flier. Her house was elaborately decorated by townspeople, and it was the scene of a big gathering all day.

Two sisters, Mrs. John Stratiff and Miss Mabel Stultz of Williamsburg, and a brother, Ellwood, of Huntingdon, were at the home awaiting word from the flier. Mrs. Stultz had kept a vigil throughout the night and was happy and relieved over the success of the flight.

Cablegrams of congratulation were sent by the Williamsburg Business Men's Club, the Altoona Chamber of Commerce and Altoona Business Club.

FRENCH REJOICE AT GIRL'S SUCCESS

Foch on Hearing News of Landing Phones Wife at Once—Lauds American Women.

RUTH ELDER EXPRESSES JOY

French Aviatrices Weep and Ask for Plane in Which to "Do as Well" as Miss Earhart.

Special Cable to THE NEW YORK TIMES.

PARIS, June 18.—Interest in the flight of Miss Earhart and pleasure at its success was everywhere general in France. A member of THE NEW YORK TIMES staff, who had had the news of the landing from London by telephone, happened to call a few minutes later on Marshal Foch. The Marshal's first question was:

"What is the news from Miss Earhart?"

And when told that she had succeeded he telephoned at once to tell his wife.

"That is wonderful," he said. "These American girls never let the men keep their laurels long without challenge."

Among French girls the same spirit is not lacking. Maryse Bastie and Denyse Collin, two French women who have the best flying record in France, almost dissolved in tears when told the news.

"Won't somebody give us a machine and we will do as well," said Mlle. Bastie.

Their chagrin will be even more bitter if the negotiations now going on for Ruth Elder to be Dieudonné Costes's flying partner on his westward flight succeed. Then, indeed, they will conclude that all luck lies with Americans.

Recalls Gladiators' Salute.

In the press there is, however, that usual word of caution which Frenchmen like to attach to exploits which are purely spectacular.

"That finest of all aids to progress, emulation, is behind this struggle to be first or next to cross the Atlantic," writes Camille Aymard in the Liberté. But the palpitating interest of the world in these great adventures comes from the same taste for agony and death which all humanity shares from that dark frenzy which long ago pushed the Romans to watch the bloody spectacles of the arena and which still takes the Spaniard to the arena.

"If the passage of the Atlantic was less perilous how much less would be public interest. Miss Earhart's farewell message to the American people is of just such a kind as the gladiators used to address to Caesar in his purple-garlanded throne. Today it is the people who are sovereign, and Miss Earhart made no mistake."

Ruth Elder Congratulates Her.

Ruth Elder was one of the first people to send congratulations to Miss Earhart. She was just finishing luncheon when the news reached Paris that the Friendship had landed safely in Wales, and immediately she send the following telegram:

"Congratulations on history-making flight. I was with you every minute in spirit and thought. I know only too well what a grand exploit it was and am so glad that the first woman to cross the Atlantic by air was an American girl."

"Of five of us who have tried, only Miss Earhart and myself have lived," Miss Elder said afterwards, "and I very nearly didn't. I am so glad for her sake that she has succeeded, and also because aviation and transatlantic flying need successes, not tragedies."

Friendship Circles Steamer, Drops Notes but Misses Deck

S. S. AMERICA, June 18 (AP).—The Friendship was sighted from the deck of the steamship America a little after 10 o'clock this morning about seventy-two miles southeast of Cobh [Queenstown].

Captain George H. Fried, telling of his efforts to communicate with the plane, said:

"I saw the plane rapidly approaching. She dropped to an altitude of a few hundred feet above the ship, circled around twice and dropped a message each time, but the messages fell 200 yards from the liner and sank immediately.

"We were able to discern with the naked eye the name 'Friendship' and the markings on the plane. We were only just then receiving a message that the Friendship had started. I ordered the wireless operator to communicate immediately and he sent repeated calls, but received no reply.

"I also instructed that the ship's name and position be chalked on the deck, but the plane made off rapidly northward before this was completed. Later we observed the plane veer eastward and disappear.

"Our position was 51 north and 7:18 west. It was 10:30 A. M."

OUTFITTER GRATIFIED BY FRIENDSHIP'S FEAT

Robert E. P. Elmer Spent Two Months Equipping Plane With All Modern Devices.

Special to The New York Times.

CHICAGO, June 18.—Robert E. P. Elmer, former naval aviation officer, sat in the Chicago offices of the Vacuum Oil Company today and read with great satisfaction of the successful completion of the monoplane Friendship's flight across the Atlantic. Mr. Elmer had followed the fortunes of Amelia Earhart and her co-pilots with more than ordinary interest because he had entire charge of fitting the plane with the last word in flying, navigating and radio equipment in preparation for the flight.

Mr. Elmer had just returned from two months spent in the East fitting the Friendship with everything needed to make it, as he says, the safest plane that ever undertook a long over-water flight. A classmate of Commander Richard E. Byrd at Annapolis, Mr. Elmer was recommended by Byrd when Mrs. Frederick Guest of New York, backer of the Friendship's flight, wanted some one with experience to fit the plane with the latest aids to flying and navigation.

"When we first took over the Friendship it was equipped only for ordinary flying, and very little of that," Mr. Elmer said today. "It had been built in Fokker's plant in Holland, and the few instruments it had were virtually obsolete. Pontoons had to be fitted to make it a seaplane and complete instruments equipment arranged to the best advantage. Then it all had to be tested, which is about the biggest job of all.

"I think the Friendship was the safest and best equipped airplane ever to attempt an ocean flight. It had everything. Besides two magnetic compasses there was an earth inductor compass, wind drift instruments, smoke bombs to determine directions and velocity of the winds, flares, a kite for radio communication in event of a landing at sea, and all the other instruments used in ordinary flying as well as in advanced aerial navigation.

"The flight of the Friendship was undertaken as a sporting-scientific proposition. There was no desire for sensational publicity by either the backer or the crew. That was one reason Miss Earhart was chosen as the woman to go along. She is sincerely interested in aviation and is a good pilot. Wilmer Stultz is a veteran naval flier and knows his business in all sorts of weather, while the mechanic, Gordon, also is a pilot."

COURAGE HER IDEAL.

The spirit of indomitable courage in which Miss Amelia Earhart set forth upon her hazardous flight across the North Atlantic was intimately revealed in verse from her own hand embodied in an article by Marion Perkins, by whom she was employed as a settlement worker, made public yesterday by the Survey Graphic.

Miss Earhart described her outlook on life thus:

Courage is the price that Life exacts for granting peace,
The soul that knows it not
Knows no release from little things:

Knows not the livid loneliness of fear,
Nor mountain heights where bitter joy can hear
The sound of wings.

How can Life grant us boon of living, compensate
For dull gray ugliness and pregnant hate
Unless we dare

The soul's dominion? Each time we make a choice, we pay
With courage to behold resistless day,
And count it fair.

"All the News That's Fit to Print."

The New York Times.

Copyright, 1929, by The New York Times Company.

THE WEATHER
Cloudy and warmer today; tomorrow colder, with showers.
Temperature yesterday—Max., 64; min., 43.
U. S. Weather Forecast—Details on Page 31.

VOL. LXXVIII....No. 25,993. ***** NEW YORK, MONDAY, MARCH, 25, 1929. TWO CENTS In Greater New York | THREE CENTS Within 200 Miles | FOUR CENTS Elsewhere Except 7th and 8th Postal Zones

RUM BOAT SKIPPER TELLS OF SINKING UNDER FIRE IN GALE

Captain of I'm Alone, Now a Prisoner and Wounded, Admits Liquor Trade.

ON THE HIGH SEAS, HIS PLEA

Disputes Coast Guard Claim and Says It Was Cowardice to Fire on Him.

CAPTORS' ACTS ARE UPHELD

Washington Officials, Following Report, Declare Sinking Was Commendable.

Special to The New York Times.

NEW ORLEANS, March 24.—Manacled and under heavy guard, Captain John T. Randell and the crew of the British schooner I'm Alone, which was sunk Friday, as a rum-runner, off the Louisiana coast by Coast Guard patrol boats, were brought here today on the Dexter and the Walcott, which had captured them when their vessel went down.

The prisoners were taken to the Custom House and were examined there throughout the day by customs inspectors and United States District Attorney Talbot. Reporters were not allowed to talk with either members of the schooner's crew or members of the crew of the Coast Guard craft.

The British Consul, Mr. Tom, declared this morning that he would insist upon having a representative present while the schooner's crew was being examined, and a vice consul was permitted to attend the proceedings.

Captain Randell's Statement.

According to the customs authorities, Captain Randell made the following statement to H. S. Creighton, supervising customs agent at New Orleans.

"I am 49 years of age and was born in Trinity, N. F. My present home is at Liverpool, N. S. I am a Canadian citizen since 1899. My family consists of a wife and two children, and they live at Liverpool. I am a master mariner and carry a master's 'C. O. and C.' license, issued at Cardiff, England.

"I have known of the I'm Alone for about two and one-half years. About that long ago I saw some reference in the newspapers to her being engaged in the rum-running business off the Atlantic coast. Early in the Spring of 1928, to my knowledge, the I'm Alone was bought by one of the firm of Robin, Jones & Whitman of Lunenberg, N. S., from the people who owned her when she was a notorious runner.

"My information was that a man who called himself Rogers had previously owned this boat. In October, 1928, she was bought by the Eastern Seaboard Steamship Agencies, Ltd., of Montreal. Their business address is in either the Montreal Building or the Coristine Building. Their cable address is Essalmo.

"I was employed by the Eastern Seaboard Steamship Agencies, Ltd., as master of the I'm Alone and took this ship at Lunenburg either Oct. 30 or Nov. 1, 1928. I have received my instructions in the operation of this vessel from Mr. George Hearn, general manager of the Eastern Seaboard Steamship Agencies.

Tells of First Liquor Cargo.

"In November, 1928, we cleared from Lunenburg to Halifax. Leaving Halifax about Nov. 5, 1928, we cleared in ballast for St. Pierre, where we arrived about Nov. 10, 1928. At St. Pierre, we took on a cargo of approximately 1,400 cases of assorted liquors. This was received from the Great West Wine Company.

"Before clearing from St. Pierre, an employe of the Great West Wine Company delivered to me the one-half part of twelve or fifteen American one dollar bills. At this time he gave me instructions to take my ship to a position thirty miles due south of the Trinity Shoals light buoy off Louisiana. He also instructed that I should deliver my cargo to the person who presented to me the other half of the first numbered one of my dollar bills.

"I cleared from St. Pierre for Belize, British Honduras, soon after Nov. 10, 1928. I came to the agreed position south of the Trinity Shoals life buoy. Before I discharged my cargo the American Coast Guard cutter Walcott picked me up and remained in my vicinity for about forty-eight hours. I cannot be positive of the exact date that the Walcott picked us up, but you have stated that they encountered us on Nov. 28, 1928, and that date is probably correct.

"After I encountered the Walcott I went to Belize, remaining there one or two days and cleared again, this time for Nassau. You have stated that on this occasion I cleared from Belize Dec. 6, 1928. I have no data to verify that date but that is probably correct. When I cleared from Belize on this date I still had on

Continued on Page Twenty-two.

Prince of Wales Will Attend Foch Rites Instead of Brother

Special Cable to THE NEW YORK TIMES.

LONDON, March 24.—The Prince of Wales will represent King George at Marshal Foch's funeral instead of Prince George, who was originally deputized to represent the monarch.

"In view of the special desire of the Prince of Wales to attend the funeral," states The London Times, "the King has authorized the change of arrangements, and the investiture ceremonies the Prince of Wales was to have conducted on behalf of the King on March 26 have been postponed."

GOULD'S DIARY GIVES EPIC OF ANTARCTIC

Byrd's Geologist Reveals Day-to-Day Life Struggle of Three on Mountain in Storm.

WIND BLAST LIKE GUNFIRE

Near Freezing, All Worked Desperately to Save Plane as Only Hope for Escape.

Wireless to THE NEW YORK TIMES.

LITTLE AMERICA, Antarctica, March 24.—The following is the diary of Laurence M. Gould, geologist and geographer of the Byrd Antarctic Expedition, written in his tent in the Rockefeller Mountains during the days of storm which culminated in the blowing away and wrecking of the airplane.

This isolated him and his companions, Bernt Balchen and Harold June, 135 miles from the base, with only a hand sled for returning. They were rescued, however, by Commander Byrd after a hazardous flight.

By LAURENCE M. GOULD.

MARCH SEVENTH.

A fairly good morning. Four dog teams are hurriedly getting their gear ready to start laying bases for this Fall. They left the base this afternoon—Vaughan with Goodale, Crockett, Bursey with their teams, Joe De Ganahl navigating and Pete [Carl Peterson] with the radio.

Haines said the weather was O.K. for our mountain trip. Balchen had gone out in the morning with Braathen to set flag markers across the bay ice for the dog teams. He returned about noon. I told him to get ready for the flight; June, too, as radio man.

We took off with a fairly clear sky and bright sky in the direction of our mountains, almost due east. A high head wind made flying rather slow. We were in the air two hours and ten minutes. We landed about a mile from the base of one of the highest peaks and established camp, secured the plane and turned in.

MARCH NINTH.

Out early this morning. We went out and measured a base line and located all the peaks in this part of the group.

The wind was blowing quite hard and it was cold, so we hurried into camp, where we had to stay until late afternoon. Then we three went to the mountain nearest and climbed part way up its face. Granite—all granite.

MARCH TENTH.

When I woke up at 6:30 and prepared to get up I found it was snowing and blowing pretty hard—too hard to do any work.

We stayed in bed until about 11. Balchen got up and so then did I. We prepared breakfast and fed June in bed.

The wind was growing stronger. Suddenly the two tent guys that had been fastened to the airplane skis let go. We thought they had broken. Balchen looked out of the tent.

"The plane has moved!" he shouted.

We both hurried out and started shovelling frantically. The wind was growing stronger and the plane

Continued on Page Twenty.

PARIS PAYS HOMAGE TO MARSHAL FOCH AT ARCH OF TRIUMPH

Mighty Host Files Past His Gun-Carriage Bier Beside the Unknown Soldier's Tomb.

PETAIN REKINDLES FLAME

Procession Is Led by 100 War-Blinded, With Americans Next—Many Hurt in Crush.

BODY IS MOVED AT NIGHT

Silent Crowds, Many Kneeling in Prayer, See Coffin Borne Through City to Notre Dame.

By P. J. PHILIP.

Special Cable to THE NEW YORK TIMES.

PARIS, March 24.—Under that Triumphal Arch which Napoleon planned to celebrate his victories and through which nearly ten years ago Foch rode in the midst of the Allied troops on their great day of glory, the body of the Marshal has lain all day today beside that other body of one of those who fought and died unknown in that army of millions which he commanded.

To him there—to both of them, great commander and unknown soldier—the people of Paris have all day paid homage. It has been no ordinary spectacle. An immense sympathy and such comradeship as there is seldom among men seemed to fill these people as by thousands after thousands they came from all ends of the city up the triumphal way to bow their heads before their two dead.

Man Killed, Many Hurt in Crush.

But the solemn march past of these hosts was not without the tragic side that seems inseparable from such occasions.

So great was the crowd in the Place de l'Etoile in the late hours that the press toward the arch became uncontrollable. Women and old men were thrown down and trampled upon and others were hurt by being crushed against the arch or lampposts. One aged man, a cobbler and former soldier, died before a space could be cleared to give him first aid. Many of the injured were taken to hospitals.

Order finally was restored and the crowd resumed its reverent march past the bier.

It was always in the minds of the multitude that there were two warriors lying there under the arch—one who had been their leader, their man of destiny, on whom during agonizing months their hopes were fixed, in whose hands they were; and the other who had been one of themselves, who had fought in the mud of Flanders and Verdun, who had suffered with them, who had known the cold and filth of the trenches, who had felt fear clutch him and gone on, who had fought mutely with the common courage of all in that struggle out of which the man who today lay beside him was to build victory.

Body Escorted from House.

It was Palm Sunday, a day of glorious Spring sunshine. In the Champs-Elysées the buds of the chestnut trees had just begun to burst into life. In the streets there were only early churchgoers, each carrying a sprig of palm, when they brought the dead Marshal from his home to lie there in state. An escort of cavalry waited near the house.

One by one his most intimate friends, General Weygand, Major L'Hopital and General Gouraud, came and stood in those few last moments beside Mme. Foch and her two daughters. Some members of the government were there.

Suddenly that battlecry of France, "Aux Champs," blared out on the trumpets. Six men were carrying the coffin out of the house into a waiting hearse. On it were laid his kepi with its triple crown of oak leaves, his sword and his marshal's baton.

Continued on Page Four.

Zeppelin Starts 5-Day, 5,000-Mile Flight Over the Mediterranean and the Holy Land

Wireless to THE NEW YORK TIMES.

FRIEDRICHSHAFEN, Monday, March 25.—The dirigible Graf Zeppelin took off at 12:45 this morning on its five-day 5,000-mile non-stop flight over the Mediterranean and the Near East.

Dr. Hugo Eckener, commander of the airship, announced before the departure that he would adapt himself to weather conditions in selecting the route to be traversed. He intends to cross from Marseilles to Genoa and then to Rome, Naples and Palestine, returning by way of Constantinople.

A duly authorized postoffice has been installed aboard the Graf Zeppelin, which will postmark mail carried from here and drop it overboard at Jaffa and Athens.

The unusual spectacle of the giant German dirigible—once an instrument of war—floating over the cradle of Christendom during Holy Week will be afforded to the inhabitants of Palestine if the Graf Zeppelin flies true to form.

It was recalled in this connection that the last time sky-gazers in the Near East beheld a German airship was in 1917, when a war dirigible set out from a military base in the Balkans to fly along the headwaters of the Nile on a relief expedition to the German colonials led by General Lettow-Vorbeck in German East Africa.

At 11 o'clock last night Dr. Eckener spread gloom among his twenty-seven passengers and guests by announcing that the flight would have to be postponed for a full day, as the gusts of wind which puffed in from Lake Constance interfered with hauling the Graf Zeppelin out of the hangar.

He even advised his friends to go to sleep, but Paul Loebe, President of the Reichstag, who is an inveterate optimist, continued to take farewell puffs at his cigar and refused to be persuaded that the postponement was inevitable. Dr. Eckener himself was keen for a take-off tonight, as a delay of several hours would have meant the loss of a full day because the French demanded that he fly over France at night.

Half an hour after midnight the dirigible suddenly poked its nose out of the hangar and at the same time Dr. Eckener ordered the passengers and baggage aboard. Shouting "All aboard for Jerusalem!" the twenty-seven passengers scrambled into the gondola, while several thousand jubilant townsfolk swarmed over the Zeppelin grounds, yelling vociferous farewells which were completely drowned out by Dr. Eckener's "Let go!" the signal which sent the airship upward.

It was soon over Lake Constance, heading for the Franco-Swiss frontier, and lost to the view of the villagers, who caught intermittent farewell glimpses of its silvery hull as the cloud-strewn moonlight beamed upon it.

With greater mileage to negotiate than that covered on its first Atlantic cruising last Autumn and a larger list of passengers and crew aboard, German aeronautic circles believe the Zeppelin present non-stop flight will afford a more impressive index to the dirigible's capacity to meet the most exacting scientific, technical and practical tests than did the two Atlantic crossings.

The airship is carrying a crew of forty-one and 5,000 pieces of mail. Among the passengers are Drs Koch and von Guerard, the former being Minister of Transportation, and three engineers of the Zeppelin works who were assigned to the flight for the purpose of studying the craft's performance.

FOX IN TALKIES ONLY; SIGNS 200 SHOW FOLK

Drops Silent Films After 18 Months' Preparation for New Policy at $15,000,000 Cost.

BROADWAY TO LOSE STARS

Will Rogers, Willie Collier and George Jessel Among Them—Other Studios May Follow.

After eighteen months of preparation and the expenditure of upward of $15,000,000 on new studios, machinery and technical experimentation, William Fox announced yesterday that the Fox Film Corporation, beginning today, would produce dialogue and musical pictures exclusively.

The revolutionary change is expected to have a repercussion on the entire field of public entertainment. The legitimate theatre also will be affected. Will Rogers, William Collier, George Jessel and other stars, stage directors, dramatists, musical comedy producers, scenarists and dancers are among 200 of Broadway's "show folk" who have been placed under contract by Winfield Sheehan, the company's vice president and general manager.

The policy of signing up stars of the legitimate theatres wholesale, together with dramatists and musical comedy personnel will make it possible for patrons of every crossroad village movie house equipped with sound machinery to see and hear high-priced Broadway performers in pieces mounted by the foremost directors. The quips of Will Rogers will be heard by audiences gathered in motion picture houses from coast to coast.

Hollywood is expected to become the international centre for stage producers, singers, actors, dancers, comedians and writers for the stage.

Sheehan Goes West Tomorrow.

Mr. Sheehan will leave for California tomorrow to take charge of the new $10,000,000 studio at Fox Hills, known as Fox Movietone City. Twenty-five complete recording units are now in operation on the sound-proof stages at this new 180-acre plant. The silent-picture studios in Sunset Boulevard have also been soundproofed and electrified to meet the new production requirements, with the addition of a $500,000 movietone laboratory and sound-reproduction rooms.

The announced plans call for filming one complete feature-length talking or musical production every week, including comedies, musical comedies, operettas, dramas, melodramas and spectacular dramas.

The statement by Mr. Fox, president of the corporation is expected to speed up plans now being discussed in other motion picture organizations for similar drastic changes in output. It was thought for a time that the requirements of the foreign market would postpone indefinitely the radical change in Fox policies given out yesterday. Gossip in Hollywood has been that the foreign demand for silent pictures might prove an obstacle. It was decided by the Fox executives, however, that, with the production of silent films for foreign markets a year and a half ahead, the time was favorable for the change to the audible film.

While Mr. Sheehan would not discuss the plans of his organization concerning the foreign field, where English language talking-pictures cannot be sold, he said that the problem had been carefully considered. He indicated that European eventualities such as the possible manufacture of talking-pictures by foreign producers, and their further development in this country during the next year, would govern future action.

The announcement yesterday was confined only to the four Fox units, one in New York, two in Hollywood

Continued on Page Sixteen.

SAMUEL REA DIES IN HIS 74TH YEAR

Former Head of Pennsylvania Railroad Had Been Ill for Several Weeks.

WORKED UP WITH SYSTEM

Bringing Road Into Manhattan Climax of 54 Years' Service, Ending in Retirement in 1925.

Special to The New York Times.

PHILADELPHIA, March 24.—Samuel Rea, former president of the Pennsylvania Railroad, and an outstanding transportation executive and engineer, died at his home in Gladwyne, a suburb, this morning after an illness of several weeks. He was in his seventy-fourth year.

Influenza, followed by a heart attack, had vitally taxed Mr. Rea's strength.

At the death bed were his wife, Mrs. Mary B. Rea, and daughter, Mrs. George Junkin; a daughter-in-law, Mrs. George B. Rea, widow of an only son who died several years ago, and his granddaughter, Miss Ann Thorp Rea.

Funeral arrangements have been made for Tuesday, and special trains will be operated by the Pennsylvania Railroad to Bryn Mawr, where the service will be held at 4 P. M. in the Presbyterian Church. The burial will be in Bryn Mawr.

Started as Rod Man on P. R. R.

With fifty-four years of almost continuous service with the Pennsylvania system to his credit, during which he rose from chain man and rod man to the presidency, Mr. Rea retired from the latter post on Oct. 1, 1925, nine days after he had celebrated his seventieth birthday. He was the first president of the railroad to retire under its seventy-year pension rule.

But the man whose engineering genius was largely responsible for the Pennsylvania's New York City extension, including the construction of the river tunnels, the passenger station in Manhattan, and the Hell Gate Bridge and New York connecting railroad forming the link between the Pennsylvania and the New Haven systems, was not satisfied to lead an inactive life after his retirement.

He retained the directorships of the Pennsylvania and subsidiary lines and was interested in projects of a civic and political nature. One of the last occasions in which he drew public attention came during the Presidential campaign, when he accepted the chairmanship of a committee of leading business and professional men of Philadelphia who supported Governor Smith. Mr. Rea, while regarded as independent in politics, looked upon himself as a Democrat.

Just before John J. Raskob, chairman of the Democratic National Committee, came to Philadelphia to aid in organizing this committee, Mr. Rea issued a public statement in support of the Democratic nominee. He said he was a member of the Association Against the Prohibition Amendment and therefore favored Smith's liberal views on prohibition and that he always had been inclined to prefer "revenue tariff" to the Republican protective tariff.

Mr. Rea had been active in the last few years in regional planning work in Philadelphia and vicinity. In 1926 he received the Franklin Medal from the Franklin Institute, one of the highest awards that can be conferred upon an engineer. A year ago he was elected an honorary member of the Institute of Civil Engineers of London, being the only such member in the Western Hemisphere.

Messages of sympathy to the family, containing high tributes to Mr. Rea, began to reach the home soon after his death became known.

General W. W. Atterbury, Mr.

Continued on Page Eleven.

FLIERS FAIL TO FIND 4 IN MISSING PLANE AFTER ALL-DAY HUNT

Army, Navy, Marines, Coast Guard Aid in Search From Here to Norfolk.

FEAR IT WAS BLOWN TO SEA

But Airmen Say It Might Have Crashed on Coast and Not Be Found for Days.

CONTINUE FLIGHTS TODAY

Craft of Type That Was Carrying Sportsman From Miami Reported Seen Dropping in Jersey.

More than a score of planes and several Coast Guard cutters searched fruitlessly yesterday the bays and inlets, rivers, swamps and forests between New York and Norfolk, Va., for the Sikorsky plane in which T. Raymond Finucane, Rochester business man and sportsman, and three others left Norfolk for Curtiss Field last Friday morning. The searchers dropped down at Curtiss and Mitchel Fields here, at Bolling Field in Washington and other airports last night just before darkness with the same discouraging reports. They had seen so sign of the plane. The search will be continued today.

Early in the evening Washington ordered the Los Angeles to join the search, but late last night it was announced at the naval air station at Lakehurst, N. J., that the order had been rescinded shortly before midnight. Officers at the air station would say nothing concerning the order itself or the reasons for the cancellation of it.

Weather reports for the day were unfavorable, and both the private and governmental agencies engaged in the search were dubious last night as to how thorough a hunt could be conducted today from the air.

Plane Reported Seen in Jersey.

From Atlantic City came reports that a plane of the type of the Sikorsky had been seen. J. A. Walk of Atlantic City, N. J., told Coast Guardsmen there that on Friday afternoon between Toms River and Atlantic City he saw a large amphibian come down in the woods about a mile from the road on which he was driving. Walk, with guardsmen, planned to try to find the spot this morning, and the naval officials at Lakehurst were notified last night.

Walk said that it was about 4:30 o'clock in the afternoon when he saw the plane near Waretown, N. J. If Walk saw the missing amphibian, it was hours overdue, for it should have arrived at Curtiss Field before noon on Friday.

At Linwood, about ten miles from Atlantic City, two boys reported having seen a plane glide down into the woods near Patcong Creek on Friday afternoon.

The boys saw the ship from different places and arrived home with their stories at different times. Both gave corresponding descriptions of the craft and both gave the probable landing spot as "behind the Dennis farm near Patcong Creek."

A search was started in the vicinity tonight, but without result.

Reward of $500 Offered.

Curtiss Flying Service, Inc., which owns the big amphibian piloted by Harry Smith which Mr. Finucane had chartered on a wager in Miami, offered a reward of $500 last night for information that would lead to its discovery. Besides Finucane and Smith, the plane carried Frank Abels and J. A Boyd, Curtiss mechanics. They left Miami on Thursday, twelve hours after a train carrying friends of the financier, among

Continued on Page Twenty.

REBELS SUFFER HEAVY LOSS IN REPULSE AT MAZATLAN; FEDERAL AID NEARS PORT

Hoover to Take Fishing Trip Just Before Congress Meets

Special to The New York Times.

WASHINGTON, March 24.—President Hoover is planning to get his first trout fishing early next month before Congress meets in special session.

The trout season opens on April 1 in both Virginia and Maryland, where fishing accommodations have been provided for him in the Shenandoah Park and at Catoctin Manor.

His present plans are to fish in the Maryland streams, probably on April 6. There his secretary, Lawrence Richey, has eight miles of streams.

The estate is twelve miles beyond Frederick and can be reached in an hour and a half by motor.

TAMMANY PROPOSES TRIUMVIRATE RULE

Gilchrist, Wagner and District Leader Suggested for Places on Temporary Body.

FAVORED AS COMPROMISE

Would Enable Organization to Gain Services of Senator, Who Refuses Olvany Post.

The selection of a triumvirate to rule the destinies of Tammany, in case of continued difficulty in choosing a successor to George W. Olvany, has been suggested and will receive the consideration of the "Big Four" and the committee of seven, it was learned yesterday.

The election of a triumvirate, it was said, would only be brought about by a deadlock in trying to choose a new leader, as there was a general agreement that it would be better to enter a city campaign with an undivided leadership. The triumvirate idea, however, gained some ground as a possible last-resort measure, and was sufficiently definite to contain the specific proposal that it should consist of a district leader, Senator Robert F. Wagner and John F. Gilchrist, former chairman of the Transit Commission and close friend of former Governor Smith.

Plan Favored as Compromise.

The principal argument for the triumvirate was that it might be a very effective compromise and that it would enable Tammany to have the services of Senator Wagner, who, it was learned, had refused to permit consideration of his name for the leadership after it had been suggested by influential members of the organization. Senator Wagner, it was said, felt that his official duties and his law practice took all his time and that he did not believe he should be called upon to carry the duties of the Tammany leadership in addition. It was said that he might not have the same objection to being one of a trio to govern Tammany.

The naming of a triumvirate also would compose, at least temporarily, the fight between those who still insist that an Assembly district leader must be named as Judge Olvany's successor and those who favor the selection of an outsider. Martin G. McCue of the Twelfth District and John F. Curry of the Fifth were said to regard themselves as still among the leaders in the contest for the

Continued on Page Twenty-two.

ATTACKERS RETIRE TO HILLS

The Government Is So Advised, Though Rebels Claim Gains.

CALLES PUSH DUE TODAY

Advance in Chihuahua Thought Likely to Bring Battle There This Week.

INSURGENTS STILL STRONG

Rebel Tactics Appear to Be Achieving Purpose of Forcing Federals to Divide.

Developments in Mexico.

Mexican Federal defenders of Mazatlan reported yesterday that defeated rebel attackers had retired to positions in near-by hills after heavy casualties.

Federal reinforcements arrived within forty miles of Mazatlan and expect to raise the city's siege today.

General Calles expects to renew his advance on Chihuahua today.

By L. C. SPEERS.

Staff Correspondent of The New York Times.

Special Cable to THE NEW YORK TIMES.

MEXICO CITY, March 24.—Government troops continue today in undisputed control of the defenses of Mazatlan after driving off rebel attacks, while the main force of insurgents, under Generals Roberto Cruz and Ramon F. Iturbe, has retired to positions several kilometers further from the first-line trenches of the Federals, according to official reports to Chapultepec Palace.

General Jaime Carillo, commanding the Federals, in a report to President Portes Gil declared that this morning found only a small force of the enemy in hills in the vicinity of Mazatlan. The main rebel units took up new positions in the course of the night along the highways leading to the city, more out of range of the Federal guns ashore and afloat than was the case with their previous positions, from which the unsuccessful assaults of Friday night and yesterday were directed.

The troops of General Cruz, in the opinion of General Carillo, suffered heavy losses in killed and wounded. However, at the time he made the report he was unable to estimate the total casualties. General Carillo did not give his own losses, but the tenor of reports to Chapultepec Palace all lead to the conclusion that they were small in comparison to those of the revolting forces.

During lulls in the night the rebels busied themselves in removing their wounded out of range of the Federal guns, said General Carillo, who added that at no time from sundown to dawn was there any severe fighting. There was only infrequent firing, he explained, involving only the outposts of the contending forces.

The new positions of the main rebel force are far enough back, the Carillo report said, to justify calling it a retreat.

It goes without saying that this morning's bulletins from the Mazatlan front occasioned the greatest satisfaction in high government quarters, who are confident that the rebel threat against the nation's principal Pacific port is practically eliminated.

Reinforcements Near Mazatlan.

The vanguard of the Federal reinforcements for Mazatlan was forty miles from the nation's most important Pacific port tonight, and Chapultepec Palace considers that the rebel menace to that city is definitely ended.

The news that the Federals were so unexpectedly close to their objective came to President Portes Gil in a message from General Evaristo Perez, commanding the advance of the reinforcements ordered to Sinaloa by General Calles, with instructions to crush the rebellion not only in the Mazatlan district but in all of Sinaloa.

A late bulletin on the advance of the Perez column makes a reference to the capture of Rosario by his troops. It was not previously understood that the place was in control of the rebels. There were no details as to the capture.

At the same time there was made public a report from General Calles to the President in which General Calles says he is informed that $600,000 in Mexican and American money was looted at Torreon and sent to El Paso to deposit either by General Escobar or persons close to him. Whether an actual deposit was made was not disclosed.

It is believed certain that the first Federals will reach Mazatlan before noon tomorrow, by which time, in

Made No Feuds, Won Friends, Says Coolidge, In Assessing Results of His Administration

Special to The New York Times.

WASHINGTON, March 24.—Former President Coolidge is quoted in an article by John H. Lambert in the coming issue of The Nation's Business as saying:

"I believe I am leaving the government of my country in good condition.

"I have made no feuds. I have made many new friends. My only regret now is severing myself from the companionship of my friends here."

The article tells of Mr. Coolidge contributing a book to "Dick Hall's House" at Dartmouth College. This is an infirmary built by Mr. and Mrs. E. K. Hall of Montclair, N. J., as a memorial to their son, who died in 1917. There are several thousand books in the library. Each carries on the flyleaf an inscription by the donor. Mr. Coolidge wrote in the volume that he gave:

"To Edward K. Hall:

"In recollection of his son and my son, who have the privilege by the grace of God to be boys through all eternity.

"CALVIN COOLIDGE."

SPRINGFIELD, Mass., March 24 (AP).—Only silence met efforts of reporters today to obtain comment from former President Coolidge on an editorial in a Boston newspaper urging him to run for the Senate in 1930. His secretary informed inquirers that Mr. Coolidge could not be reached for comment, although a moment before she had asked what question they wished she should ask him.

The reply was interpreted as a diplomatic manner of saying the former President "did not choose" to comment on the editorial.

Father Saves Son, Then Drowns in Boat Upset; Restless on Fishing Trip, Boy Caused Accident

Special to The New York Times.

LONG BEACH, L. I., March 24.—Alexander Jordan, well-to-do insurance man of Island Park, L. I., his son, Alexander Jr., and their dog Bobbie went fishing in a rowboat this afternoon in Reynolds Channel, about 300 feet from shore. Weather conditions were ideal. A light breeze was blowing, just enough to ruffle the surface of the water. The air was balmy, the sunshine brilliant.

But the fish were not biting and the son soon grew restless. His father cautioned him to be quiet, but as the minutes passed without even the promise of a "bite," Junior's activity increased. Something in the water caught his attention. He left his seat and started forward. The small craft rocked perilously.

The father warned him again and at the same time arose and grasped the boy's arm. The craft tilted, shipping water. Without relaxing his grasp, the man tried to right the boat by shifting his weight to the other side. He lost his balance and fell, upsetting the rowboat.

Although Jordan had been partly stunned by a blow from the overturning boat he still clung to his son. The cold water revived him and, holding the lad's head above water with his left arm, he struck out for shore. From time to time he paused to shout for help. But the place is isolated and his cries went unheeded until he was within fifty feet of land. Then several men plunged into the water and took the boy from his arms.

Junior was none the worse for his experience, but when his rescuers dragged him ashore and looked around for Jordan the latter had disappeared. Five minutes later the rescuers found him and dragged him ashore. He was dead. Artificial respiration was tried without success and at the end of half an hour efforts to resuscitate him were abandoned. Later the boat was towed ashore and the dog was found safe in an air pocket beneath the overturned hull.

John Kopec, 18 years old, of Bayonne, N. J., was drowned yesterday in the Kill Van Kull, a half mile from Elm Park, S. I. Kopec had gone rowing with William Creedon, 18, of Bayonne. When the boat overturned, Creedon, who could swim, kept afloat until rescuers arrived. Kopec sank instantly.

DECLARES GENIUS IS WORLD'S NEED

Dr. Harlow Shapley Would Create "Seductive Dignity" for Intellectual Life.

SPECIALIZING PERIL SEEN

Dr. Alexis Carrel, in Philosophic Survey, Seeks Coordination of Science and Social Effort.

Special to The New York Times.

PHILADELPHIA, March 24.—Views of six memoers of the American Philosophical Society on the intellectual needs of the modern world, as expressed in letters to Dr. Francis X. Dercum, the society's president, endorsing its recently announced intellectual stock-taking, were made public here tonight.

Dr. Dercum's letter outlining the plan was sent to 435 members of the society in this country and abroad, as the first step in a survey designed to guide the society in the promulgation of a program of continuing and expanding service to all branches of learning. The letters made public were among the first 100 received and others will be given out from time to time as they are reviewed and collated, Dr. Dercum said.

"The world's intellectual need today, as always, is genius," wrote Dr. Harlow Shapley, astronomer and director of Harvard College observatory.

"Lacking that (and we generally do lack it) an important need is an epidemic of broad intellectual sympathies and a third need is the promotion of a seductive dignity for the intellectual life, especially where academic dignity is more solemn and repulsive than alluring."

Dr. Alexis Carrel of the Rockefeller Institute for Medical Research declared that the world "imperatively needs the advent of great intellectual leaders who know the requirements of spiritual life as well as the sciences concerned with inanimate and living matter," and warned that there was peril in specialization unless it was properly directed.

Sees Some Bad Effects.

"A better coordination of scientific and social effort," he wrote, "would render a distinctive service in preventing some of the bad effects of specialized knowledge. When only one aspect of a problem is taken into consideration, the solution is generally effective.

"Architects are constructing cities which are of an impressive beauty, but totally unfit for the proper sheltering and breeding of human beings. Physicians, as well as industrialists and bankers, often do not realize that men are not mere machines, while priests may forget that they possess bodies.

"The desire for the immediate welfare of the individual seems to obliterate in many educators the supreme interests of the nation and of the race.

"The danger of a narrow intellectual education is evident. But high culture cannot be given to all. The more gifted children should be protected against the leveling influence of the high or preparatory schools. If some of the best university students were segregated they could be given a more active and encyclopedic training and taught that early specialization is not desirable."

Dr. James R. Angell, president of Yale University, wrote:

"I should say that perhaps the most pressing intellectual need is such poise as comes from a genuine coordination of the great sub-divisions of thought. These sub-divisions have become so highly specialized, so separatistic and so self-conscious, not to say self-complacent, that the genuinely philosophical outlook of life and its problems, an outlook which presupposes inclusive vision and genuine insight, has become utterly impossible.

Calls for Creative Scholarship.

"In our own American world I think there is a crying need of more just evaluation of the human and social import of creative scholarship—indeed, a scholarship of every kind. At present it enjoys only the most meagre recognition."

Dr. David Starr Jordan, Chancellor emeritus of Stanford University, said in his letter that "stock-taking is good business," and added: "I approve of your intellectual stock-taking."

"More attention should be paid to the histories of the past civilizations and their influence on us through continuity," wrote Dr. E. A. Wallace Budge of the British Museum.

Dr. W. W. Keen of Philadelphia, a former president of the American Philosophical Society, who celebrated his ninety-second birthday on Jan. 19, wrote that in his opinion the day's intellectual need is "a sense of dependence in God."

HAGUE GOES ON STAND AT TRENTON TODAY

Jersey City Mayor Need Not Open Bank Records and May Not Face Contempt if He Balks.

Special to The New York Times.

TRENTON, N. J., March 24.—What is expected to be the high spot of the legislative investigation of Hudson County is scheduled for tomorrow when Mayor Frank Hague of Jersey City is put on the witness stand at Trenton by the McAllister Commission.

When he was first subpoenaed, the Mayor appealed successfully to the Court of Chancery against the summons. He accepted the second subpoena, however, which was much modified. He will not have to produce his personal bank records, nor those of his wife, and it is even said that he will not face contempt proceedings if he refuses to answer any questions.

Mayor Hague will be asked as to disclosures developed by the inquiry, but Senator McAllister, the chairman, will not permit him to be pressed for answers.

The Legislature will reassemble tomorrow night with the Senate at peace as result of the scolding administered by Governor Larson. The Governor will forward the letters demanding the resignations of the members of the Civil Service Commission, and if they are not forthcoming he is prepared to have the Legislature remove them. It is expected that Mr. Larson will name United States District Court Judge Joseph L. Bodine of this city as successor to the late Supreme Court Justice Frank S. Katzenbach.

LOCAL OPTION BILL ATTACKED AS 'TRICKY'

H. H. Curran Declares It Would Cause Double Prosecutions Under Jones Law.

The local option bill pending in the Legislature, which would enable counties to elect individually whether they would take measures for the enforcement of prohibition, was attacked yesterday in a statement by Henry H. Curran, president of the Association Against the Prohibition Amendment. He called it a "tricky bill, dealing with dynamite."

"Every legislator who votes for the so-called county option bill," he said, "votes to settle upon the people of the State of New York the infamous Federal Jones law, by which a man may be put in jail for five years for carrying home a bottle of beer. If such an unlucky citizen should escape the clutches of the county jail, he could then be locked up at once by the Federal prohibition agents. He thus incurs the double jeopardy against which our Constitution has for 140 years protected him.

"Furthermore, there is no option in this bill. If a dry county wants to take unto itself the Jones law, then a wet county should be able to rid itself of the Jones law entirely. But a wet county cannot do so. The whole thing is heads I win, tails you lose in favor of the prohibitors. We shall oppose this bill and those who vote for it with all our strength.

REMER BILL VETO ASKED.

Civil Service Body Opposes Clerks for Judges Exempt From Rules.

Governor Roosevelt has been urged to veto the Remer bill, which seeks to create the positions of "clerks to judges" in the municipal courts, such positions to be exempt from civil service requirements, in a letter sent to him by the Civil Service Reform Association, and made public yesterday.

The Remer bill, it is explained in the letter, was introduced after the Appellate Division had ruled that such "clerks to judges" could not be appointed by the judges themselves under the existing law, but would have to be taken from civil service lists. Fifty such positions had been filled prior to the Appellate Division's decision, and the association charges that the sole purpose in attempting to establish the new class of clerical offices was to increase political patronage.

SLAIN IN BOOTLEG FEUD.

Body of Man Killed With Hatchet Found in Camden (N. J.) Park.

CAMDEN, N. J., March 24 (AP).—His head almost severed by a hatchet the body of Gaeto Agodia, 30 years old, was found today in Forest Hill Park. The police expressed the belief that he had been slain as the result of a bootleg gang feud.

Beside the body, police found the hatchet with which Agodia had been killed. A few feet away in the rain-soaked sod were the imprints of a woman's shoes and those of a man. A diamond ring and several dollars in cash were untouched in the victim's pockets.

Letters in the man's clothing led to his identification by relatives from Atlantic City. They said they had not seen Agodia for three years.

FOX WILL PRODUCE SOUND FILMS ONLY

Continued from Page 1, Column 4.

and one in Westwood, Cal. The Metro-Goldwyn-Mayer and Loew Film companies, recently acquired by the Fox company, are not affected by the announcement.

According to the Fox executives, the step was taken as a result of public response to the talking films, which indicated that patronage was being thrown enthusiastically toward the innovation. The matter was tentatively decided a year and a half ago, it was said, and $10,000,000 has been spent on studios, $5,000,000 on machinery and a large amount of money on experimental work.

The stage celebrities signed by Mr. Sheehan will not appear again in Broadway productions until their contracts expire. Mr. Rogers has a two-year contract and Owen Davis has written the comedian's first talking picture. George Jessel, who has a three-year contract, will begin production soon on a musical play with an Italian background. Among others who have been engaged are J. Harold Murray, singer; Edward Royce, stage director; Seymour Felix, dancer and director; Lester Lonergan, actor and director, and B. G. De Sylva, Lew Brown and Ray Henderson, musical comedy song writers.

The change in Fox policy will affect thousands of actors, title writers, directors and supervisors. Screen favorites unable to measure up to the new vocal requirements will probably lose out as a result of the altered production policies, but new importance is expected to accrue to speaking actors, singers, stage experts, song and dance directors, lyricists, composers and dialogue writers.

Other Negotiations Under Way.

Mr. Sheehan admitted that negotiations with important stage, musical and literary celebrities were under way, and indicated that many new personalities would be heard by motion picture audiences as a result of the radical departure in production. He announced that Oscar Straus, a Viennese operetta composer, had written a musical play, "Married in Hollywood." Dave Stamper, former composer of Ziegfeld shows, has completed a musical comedy for film production.

"Fox Movietone Follies, now in the editing stage, has been produced as the first of an annual series of musical revues," the announcement stated.

Other productions will be "The Passing of the Third Floor Back," by Jerome K. Jerome; "Cameo Kirby," by Booth Tarkington and Harry Leon Wilson, with Warner Baxter in the title rôle; "Behind That Curtain," by Earl Derr Biggers, and "The Cock-Eyed World," based on a story by Laurence Stallings and Maxwell Anderson, with dialogue by Billy K. Wells.

Plays now in production or soon to be produced are "King of the Khyber Rifles" by Talbot Mundy; "The Man Who Came Back," "Conquistador," "The Mad Song" and "Frozen Justice."

Among the film actors whose movietone tests have been successful and who will be heard in Fox Movietone features will be Janet Gaynor, Mary Duncan, Lois Moran, Sue Carol, Mary Astor, June Collyer, Louise Dresser, Sharon Lynn, Charles Farrell, Warner Baxter, Victor McLaglen, Edmund Lowe, Nick Stuart, David Rollins and Paul Muni.

Directors who during the past six months have been learning the new technique and will now direct exclusively talking and musical films include Frank Borzage, Raoul Walsh, John Ford, F. W. Murnau, Irving Cummings, Allan Dwan, Benjamin Stoloff, David Butler, James Tinling, Alfred Werker, Berthold Viertel, Howard Hawks, George Seitz, Marcel Silver, Norman Taurog, William K. Howard and John Blystone.

Additional directors, recruited from the stage, include A. H. VanBuren, Clarke Silvernail, Frank Merlin, Frank Tasselt, Campbell Gullan and Bobby Connolly.

Broadway playwrights who are writing dialogue at the Fox studios in Hollywood include Paul Gerard Smith, Harlan Thompson, Walter Weems, Billy K. Wells, Edwin Burke and Tom Barry. Dialogue writers who are now in Hollywood working on movietone features include George S. Brooks, S. K. Lauren, Zoe Akins, John Hunter Booth, Gilbert Emery, Clare Kummer, George Middleton and Elliott Lester.

THEATRE MEN UNRUFFLED.

Declare Many Successful Shows Do Not Depend on "Names."

The announcement of William Fox that his company's policy of making only singing and talking pictures in the future would rob Broadway of many well-known actors, playwrights and composers did not disturb theatrical men yesterday.

Arthur Hammerstein said that the established "names" obtained by the talking pictures might make a difference for a short while, but that when these persons returned from Hollywood producers would be able to engage them more cheaply than before. He said that the majority of his musical productions had been staged without great stars in the casts, and that some of the most successful musical shows produced on Broadway recently showed how little they depended on the actors by the success with which they had been duplicated by other casts.

"I can't understand how Mr. Fox expects to succeed with some of his productions which have not been tried out on the public," Mr. Hammerstein asserted. "We musical comedy producers get one success out of five or six tries. And the public is going to be just as skeptical about talking and singing pictures as it is about musical shows."

Charles L. Hertzman, general manager for Laurence Schwab and Frank Mandel, both of whom are away from New York, expressed doubt that the talking and singing pictures would hurt musical shows here and in the larger cities. He said that the companies of "Good News" and "The Desert Song," which his firm had on tour, had run into such film opposition in several places and had not yet been affected by it. He declared that Schwab and Mandel and other producers now specialized in shows that did not require stars and "names" in their casts.

Neither Lee nor J. J. Shubert was in town yesterday, it was stated at their offices. E. Romayne Simmons, one of their casting executives, said he did not regard Mr. Fox's Broadway inroads as serious.

Frank Gillmore, acting president of the Actors' Equity Association, reiterated his opinion that the talking pictures as a whole would have no more than a temporary effect on the theatre, and said that neither he nor his organization was at all alarmed as to the future of the spoken drama or musical plays. He added that the wholesale importation of Broadway talent to Hollywood would make no difference to Equity from an economic viewpoint, as actors would be needed to fill the places of those who had left New York.

ZIEGFELD "NOT WORRIED."

Does Not Believe Sound Films Will Ever Replace Legitimate Shows.

Special to The New York Times.

PALM BEACH, Fla., March 24.—Florenz Ziegfeld, commenting here today on the announcement that the Fox Film Corporation would henceforth produce sound movies only, said:

"I don't believe the singing and talking movies will ever take the place of presentations by flesh and blood actors in the legitimate theatre. Beauty in the flesh will continue to rule the world and no better way will ever be found to glorify beauty than the stage.

"I believe the time is not far off when it will be possible to take movietones of musical presentations and thereby make it possible for the entire world to hear and see such productions, but never equal to the originals by flesh and blood actors, although acceptable presentations.

"I have decided and am now concluding arrangements to duplicate as near as possible all my productions, future and past, in movietone and will devote considerable of my own time in making these movietone productions.

"No matter how much money may be spent, producing ability is what movietones lack more than anything else, and material that makes up success will be their greatest difficulty. But let me repeat, no movietone will ever hurt the legitimate theatre, but movietones cannot exist successfully without the legitimate theatre and if they hurt that they only kill themselves. The first movietone producer who helps the theatre is the one who will find himself with successful movietone productions.

"We will see what we will see. I am not worried."

K. of C. Holds Communion Breakfast

The Knights of Columbus Evening High School held its annual communion breakfast yesterday at the K. of C. Hotel, Fiftieth Street and Eighth Avenue. More than 175 members of the school, residing in Manhattan, Brooklyn, the Bronx, Staten Island, Westchester and New Jersey, received communion, in a body, before the breakfast at St. Malachy's Roman Catholic Church. Among the speakers at the breakfast were the Rev. Thomas B. Kelly, pastor of the Church of St. Thomas the Apostle; Dr. James J. Walsh, Catholic historian and physician, and Thomas J. Gray, chairman of the New York Chapter, K. of C.

PARALYZED ARTIST HERE.

Robert Reid, 69, to Show Two Pictures Painted With Left Hand.

Robert Reid, 69-year-old American painter who overcame the handicap of paralysis two years ago by learning to paint with his left hand, has arrived in New York to attend the Spring exhibition of the National Academy of Design, now open at the Fine Arts Building, 215 West Fifty-seventh Street, where two paintings which he executed with his left hand are on exhibition.

Accompanied by a nurse, Mr. Reid made the trip from the Clifton Springs, N. Y., Sanitarium where he has been a patient since he was stricken and where the two pictures, a figure of a girl and a portrait of the superintendent of the sanitarium, were painted. He will return to the sanitarium in a few days. Mr. Reid is a member of the National Academy of Design and the National Institute of Arts and Letters and has pictures in the permanent collection of a number of galleries including the Metropolitan Museum in New York, the Corcoran and National Galleries in Washington, and the Albright Gallery in Buffalo.

Compares "Spirit" to Electricity.

"Electricity is the best agent known by which we can illustrate the working of the Holy Ghost," the Rev. Dr. Robert A. Brown declared in a sermon yesterday morning, in the Glad Tidings Tabernacle, Thirty-third Street near Eighth Avenue, of which he is the pastor. "Electricity can do almost anything, but only when in conformity to law," he said. "The same is true of the Holy Ghost."

"All the News That's Fit to Print."

The New York Times.

Copyright, 1929, by The New York Times Company.

THE WEATHER
Cloudy, probably rain today and tomorrow; warmer tomorrow.
Temperatures yesterday—Max. 49, min. 38.
U. S. Weather Forecast—For details see Page 50.

VOL. LXXIX....No. 26,212. * * * * NEW YORK, WEDNESDAY, OCTOBER 30, 1929. TWO CENTS In Greater New York | THREE CENTS Within 200 Miles | FOUR CENTS Elsewhere Except 7th and 8th Postal Zones

STOCKS COLLAPSE IN 16,410,030-SHARE DAY, BUT RALLY AT CLOSE CHEERS BROKERS; BANKERS OPTIMISTIC, TO CONTINUE AID

GRUNDY FOR CURBING 'BACKWARD STATES' ON THE TARIFF BILL

Veteran Republican Lobbyist Tells Senate Inquiry the West Needs "Silencing."

PENNSYLVANIA KNOWS BEST

"Unfortunate," He Holds, That the Constitution Gives Equal Voice to States in Senate.

BATTLES INVESTIGATORS

He Assails Borah—Would "Hate to Tell" His Opinion of Wisconsin.

Special to The New York Times.

WASHINGTON, Oct. 29.—Joseph R. Grundy, president of the Pennsylvania Manufacturers' Association, told the Senate Lobby Committee today that certain "backward" States of the West, through their Senators, had been altogether "too vocal" in the consideration of the current tariff bill, and that some method should be found to "silence" them at times when legislation affecting the economic welfare of the United States is under way.

Mr. Grundy declared it "unfortunate" that the framers of the Constitution had seen fit to grant to the States equal rights and representation in the Senate, as the effect of the arrangement was to give sections slow in developing their resources an equal voice in legislation directly involving such great reservoirs of wealth and taxation as Pennsylvania.

Mr. Grundy was recalled today for cross-examination on testimony he gave before the lobby committee on Oct. 24. Last week Mr. Grundy and the Senate investigating committee got along very well, and that session was decorous and orderly in contrast with today, when the witness and his questioners appeared to be antagonistic from the outset.

Criticizes Senator Walsh.

At one stage Mr. Grundy sharply described a series of questions put by Senator Walsh of Montana as "impertinent." There were frequent references to the Vare case, to the party service which Mr. Grundy had performed in the collection of Republican campaign funds, and to the relations of the witness with public men and his activities here as a part of the tariff lobby.

At times the hearing resembled a hot political debate, in which the five members of the committee were arrayed against the witness. Mr. Grundy was once reproved by Senator Blaine of Wisconsin, a member of the committee, for alleged evasion, and Mr. Blaine exclaimed heatedly:

"Look me squarely in the eye and answer my question."

The hearing was marked by frequent spats between Mr. Grundy and Senators Borah, Caraway and Walsh, and in one interchange with the witnesses Mr. Borah denied emphatically a statement that he had opposed the debenture plan at the Kansas City convention.

Chairman Caraway repeatedly indicated that the witness was not frank with the committee and that, while it might be "smart" for him to "sidestep," eventually the investigators would get what they were after.

Hit at "Most Vocal" States.

Mr. Grundy was impelled to enter into a discussion of his belief that "backward Western States" should be silenced on the tariff by questions asked by Senator Walsh. The Senator read from a statement submitted to the committee a week ago, in which Mr. Grundy asserted that if "volume of voice" in the Senate were proportioned to population, productive power or the total contributed toward the national upkeep, some of those States "which are now most vocal would need amplifiers to make their whispers heard."

Mr. Grundy also had declared that "such States as Arizona, South Dakota, Idaho and Mississippi, &c., do not pay enough toward the upkeep of the government to cover the costs of collection." As a result of Mr. Walsh's examination, Mr. Grundy finally included Arkansas and Montana in his list of "backward" States, thus bringing in three of them having representation on the lobby committee.

"You have not mentioned Wisconsin in your list," suggested Senator Walsh. "What do you think about that State?"

"What I think about Wisconsin I'd hate to tell you," replied the witness. This evoked an outburst of laughter in the audience, in which the committee joined.

Favors a Few Concessions.

Mr. Grundy again caused laughter when he said that he would permit the "backward" States, through their Senators, to have their say on questions affecting "Junior Red Cross work and outdoor relief," but that, generally speaking, they should be required to "hold their peace" on

Continued on Page Eighteen.

Von Opel, Rocket Flier, Weds Woman Pilot Who Advised Him

Wireless to THE NEW YORK TIMES.

BERLIN, Oct. 29.—Fritz von Opel, the first to fly a rocket plane, and who intends to sail for New York the beginning of November to study and work at General Motors plants, was married on Saturday to Frau Sellnik, née Loewenstein, the former wife of a Wiesbaden actor. For many months she has been von Opel's professional adviser on aviation and she herself is one of Germany's six woman pilots, flying her Handley Page plane with the greatest skill.

Frau von Opel, who is also a daring automobilist, is handsome, slender and blonde. When the airman landed safely from his rocket flight she was the first to congratulate him, shedding tears of joy. She will accompany him to the United States.

COALITION FIGHTING MOVE TO KILL TARIFF

Will Try to Force Through Bill, While Reed Favors Ending Session Nov. 15.

WATSON QUITTING CAPITAL

Departure for Florida Tomorrow for Health Leaves Jones as Republican Senate Leader.

Special to The New York Times.

WASHINGTON, Oct. 29.—Faced by Old Guard Republican willingness to leave the Smoot-Hawley tariff bill to its fate, the Democratic-Progressive coalition was today more determined than ever to drive the bill through the Senate and force the conservatives to accept it in a completely rewritten form.

Coalition strategy was centred upon fixing on the Old Guard leaders any responsibility for abandonment of the remodeled bill with the Simmons-Norris flexible amendment to the farm debenture plan. To those old-line Republicans who are now ready to desert the measure, the coalition applied the unflattering comparison of "rats and a sinking ship."

The administration Republicans refused to be stirred by such criticism. Senator Reed of Pennsylvania reiterated his conviction that the bill would never emerge from conference. Senator Moses announced that he would vote against the bill in the Senate, before it ever went to conference. The Republicans were so dismayed that they even seriously considered a motion to adjourn the Senate about the middle of November until the regular session starts on Dec. 2.

To add to their disorganization it was revealed that Senator Watson, Republican floor leader, would leave for Florida on Thursday to rebuild his shattered health.

McNary to Act as Aide.

Old Guard lieutenants hurriedly announced that Senator Jones of Washington, assistant leader, would take charge in Mr. Watson's absence, aided by Senator McNary of Oregon, who is popular with all Senate factions, has a fine record as a conciliator and more influence than most regular Republicans with the farming public.

When it was first announced that Senator Watson was going to Florida, reports spread that his illness was so serious that he might never return to the Senate as floor leader. His friends, however, denied this. They admitted that he was an ill man and needed a complete rest for a time, but asserted that he would return to assume his duties.

There was some assumption that Mr. McNary would be made temporary leader, because Senator Jones had not sufficiently recovered from the effects of a recent operation, but Mr. Jones assured Old Guard members that he felt capable of taking over the task.

While pessimistic, Senator Watson, who is dropping work by his physician's orders, would not admit that the outlook for passing the tariff bill by the end of the special session was absolutely hopeless. He did not share the view that the session might as well be adjourned, which Senator Reed may propose for about Nov. 15.

Instead, Mr. Watson will work until his departure to bring about "some sort of agreement for some sort of bill," basing this plea on the idea that the coalition must concede increases on industrial as well as agricultural rates.

Says Action Would Aid Business.

"It would have a quieting effect on business to pass the tariff bill," asserted Senator Watson. "Tariff bills are always the occasion of some unrest, though this bill has caused less agitation than usual because a Republican tariff is to be superimposed on a Republican tariff and everybody knows that if this bill fails the country would continue to be prosperous.

"It is true that there ought to be changes in agricultural rates to meet new conditions, but it is equally true

Continued on Page Fifteen.

KAHN REFUSES POST IN SENATE CAMPAIGN; CALLS CHOICE UNWISE

He Writes to Moses to Withhold His Name for Treasurer Due to 'Divided Reception.'

WAS RELUCTANT, HE SAYS

Recalls He Told Senator of His Stand, but Yielded as a Duty to His Party.

HOLDS VIEWS CONFIRMED

Declares He Is a Wall St. Man but a Liberal in Politics—Friends See Him Put in False Light.

Otto H. Kahn in a letter to Senator George H. Moses of New Hampshire, chairman of the Republican Senatorial Campaign Committee, made public yesterday, declined the post of treasurer of that committee because of the "divided reception" which the announcement of his designation as treasurer had met.

Announcement of the selection of Mr. Kahn was made by Senator Moses at the dinner given last Thursday evening at the University Club here by Jeremiah Milbank for Claudius H. Huston, the new chairman of the Republican National Committee. Publication of this announcement, together with the report that speakers at the dinner attacked the members of the Progressive Republican group in the Senate, brought protests from some of these Senators against the selection of Mr. Kahn.

Mr. Kahn in his letter to Senator Moses declared that, while a Wall Street man, he was a liberal in politics. He said some of the interpretations placed on his designation were erroneous, but added that the way it had been received justified his earlier feeling that he was not the right man for the position. No formal action for the appointment of a treasurer of the Senatorial committee has yet been taken, and Mr. Kahn requested Senator Moses not to present his name to the committee.

Mr. Kahn's Letter.

Mr. Kahn's letter follows:

Oct. 28, 1929.

My dear Senator:

When you did me the honor to ask me to act as treasurer of the Republican Senatorial Campaign Committee I told you that I feared your kindly sentiment toward me, springing from a long friendship, was swaying your judgment, that I felt sure that I was not the right man for the position, that, moreover, I was overwhelmed with demands upon my time and energies and that I hoped very much you would not persist in your request.

You argued to the contrary and, among other things, pointed to the fact that, while a Wall Street man, I was known to be, as indeed I am, a liberal in politics. You repeated your invitation when I had the pleasure of seeing you at Mr. Milbank's dinner last Thursday.

I thereupon stated that, though my views were unchanged, I felt that if we want effective party government, such as our political system requires, every citizen should be willing to make good his professions of party allegiance by submitting to being drafted, within the limits of reason and possibility, and that if the leaders of the party to which I belong demanded of me a service which did not conflict with my other duties and responsibilities I was not at liberty to refuse, however reluctant I was to accept.

You regarded this answer as tantamount to an acceptance in principle, as you were perfectly justified in doing, and at what was supposed and intended to be a strictly private dinner, you made informal reference to that acceptance.

Sees His Doubts Confirmed.

But the divided reception with which the report of the appointment of a separate treasurer for your committee and of my designation as such treasurer has met, however erroneous some of the interpretations placed thereon, appears to have confirmed the validity of the doubts which I ventured to express when you offered that position to me, and to justify me in concluding to abstain from occupying it.

I understand that no formal action has been taken as yet by the National Republican Senatorial committee concerning the appointment of a treasurer, and I am making free to write these lines to request that you will please refrain from bringing my name before the committee for appointment to the treasurership.

Believe me, dear Senator,
Very faithfully yours,
OTTO H. KAHN.

Hon. George H. Moses, The Senate, Washington, D. C.

Influential Republicans expressed regret that Mr. Kahn had decided not to take the post of treasurer of the Republican Senatorial committee. It was recalled that he was re-

Continued on Page Fourteen.

Newark Man, 4 Feet 10, Says He Was Smallest in A. E. F.

WASHINGTON, Oct. 29 (AP).—Nicholas Casale of Newark, N. J., wants to be known as the smallest man who went to France with the American Expeditionary Forces.

He has appealed to Representative Hartley of Kearny to establish that fact. Casale recently secured an affidavit from the Veterans' Bureau certifying that he was 4 feet 10 inches tall and weighed 106 pounds when he enlisted. The bureau has refused to declare him the "smallest man," saying it would require months for clerks to scan the record of every man who served with the A. E. F.

It was not explained how Casale secured enlistment when the minimum requirements are 5 feet and 110 pounds.

MISSING AIRLINER BROUGHT IN SAFELY

Pilot Lands Western Express Ship at Albuquerque After Being Forced Down.

WOULD NOT RISK STORM

Passengers Tell of Cold Night in Deserted Ranch House as Snow Swirled Round.

Special to The New York Times.

ALBUQUERQUE, N. M., Oct. 29.—Lost for more than twenty-four hours while marooned on a bleak New Mexico mesa, Western Air Express tri-motored liner 113 escaped today from the snow-swept stretch where it was forced down Monday and landed here with its crew of three and two passengers, chilled but safe.

Caught in a blinding swirl of snow Monday at 10:15 A. M., the plane was forced down near Trechado, seventy-five miles southeast of Gallup, N. M. The crew and passengers found refuge in an abandoned ranch house.

The passengers are Dr. A. W. Ward of San Francisco and W. E. Merz of Mount Vernon, N. Y. The crew includes James E. Doles, chief pilot, of Los Angeles; Allan C. Barrie, co-pilot, of Burbank, Cal., and R. L. Britton, steward, of Los Angeles.

Employes of the airport and pilots of two planes waiting for the weather to clear to resume the search for the 113 stood amazed as the big craft glided along the runway. They rushed out to the plane and as the group of men who had been given up for dead stepped out they danced around them, clapped them on the back and hugged them in delight.

Wild Night of Intense Cold.

Despite their fatigue, Dr. Ward and Mr. Merz were lighthearted and stepped jauntily from the plane. They regretted only the loss of time but joined in praise of Pilot Doles for his skillful manoeuvring to save the ship in the storm when further progress could not be risked.

They told of a harrowing night which followed the forced landing, of tramping through snow to find shelter, of sleeping on an old bed spring covered with seat cushions from the plane and of shivering in intense cold while they took turns in keeping up a fire.

"A half frozen rabbit and a rabbit's foot brought us good luck," Dr. Ward said.

"The half-frozen rabbit had been captured in the bushes by co-pilot Barrie. The rabbit's foot was worn by steward Britten. He had bought it the day the T. A. T. plane City of San Francisco crashed."

Suddenly Enveloped by Storm.

"We left Holbrook, flying east," Doles said, "and were about one hour out when we had to dodge a storm. I nosed her down towards St. John's. Suddenly the storm seemed to break over us all at once, and a landing became a necessity.

"I found a small spot, and it

Continued on Page Seventeen.

Navy Paymaster Leads Way to $47,000 Loot, Dug Up by Night in Washington Chicken Yard

Special to The New York Times.

WASHINGTON, Oct. 29.—Led by Lieutenant Charles Musil, a navy paymaster accused of embezzling $54,600, naval authorities, in a search late at night, recently uncovered $47,000 of the loot buried in a chicken yard in Southeast Washington on the grounds of the Home of the Aged and Infirm.

When Lieutenant Musil voluntarily surrendered himself, on Oct. 14, to the naval authorities at New York, after having disappeared on Sept. 28 from his post as paymaster for Destroyer Division 40 at Charleston, S. C., he is said to have turned over $1,500 to Captain C. T. Owens, commanding the receiving ship Seattle.

This leaves $6,100 unaccounted for and naval officers, in announcing today the discovery in the chicken yard, said they were trying to locate the rest of the money, although they had scant hope of success.

According to the story told to the officers by Lieutenant Musil, he came here directly from Charleston and buried the money in the yard of his former home. He then left for Chicago, where he bought some stock, and went to Detroit and into Canada. From there he proceeded to New York, where he became conscience-stricken and gave himself up.

He was held at the Brooklyn Navy Yard, but when he told his story of the buried money he was brought here to direct the search for it. He is now awaiting general court-martial on specifications covering embezzlement.

Lieutenant Musil was born in Illinois in 1893, enlisted in the navy twenty years ago and was commissioned in 1921. He has a wife and 9-year-old son in New York City.

LEADERS SEE FEAR WANING

Point to 'Lifting Spells' in Trading as Sign of Buying Activity.

GROUP MEETS TWICE IN DAY

But Resources Are Unable to Stem Selling Tide—Lamont Reassures Investors.

HOPE SEEN IN MARGIN CUTS

Banks Reduce Requirements to 25 Per Cent—Sentiment in Wall St. More Cheerful.

Resources of the banking group which was organized last Thursday to stabilize conditions in the stock market were utilized yesterday to break the force of the terrific flood of selling which accompanied the biggest day, from the point of view of volume, ever experienced on the New York Stock Exchange.

Despite the drastic decline, sentiment in Wall Street last night was more cheerful than it has been on any day since the torrent of selling got under way. Periodic "lifting spells" which developed between intervals of extreme weakness were cited by bankers at the close of the market, as testifying to the presence of investment buying. The public is in some measure regaining its senses and the unreasoning fear which has prompted the sacrifice of securities for any price they would bring is at length subsiding.

While even the tremendous buying power of the banking group was unable to turn the tide of selling in yesterday's market, the group did not relax its concern over the situation on the Exchange. Two meetings were held during the day, one at noon and one at 4:30 P. M., the latter lasting until 6:30 P. M.

Will Continue Support.

After the evening meeting Thomas W. Lamont of J. P. Morgan & Co. spoke to reporters.

"I want to take occasion," Mr. Lamont said, "to explain again, as heretofore, that the banking group was organized to offer certain support in the market and to act as far as possible as somewhat of a stabilizing factor.

"It was not the intention of the group to attempt to maintain prices, but to maintain a free market; in other words, to correct the condition that prevailed last Thursday.

"The group has continued and will continue in a cooperative way to support the market and has not been a seller of stocks."

The statement was issued at the request of reporters to quiet rumors which had been abroad that the banking group had been selling stocks instead of supporting them.

These rumors were, of course, without foundation, for the group is known to have purchased heavily in directions where the force of its buying power would be most effective in stemming demoralization. It was reliably reported that in many instances when no bids could be obtained on the floor for large blocks of stock forced on the market the group had supplied the necessary bids and in other instances had acted as a stabilizing influence upon the list as a whole.

At the noon meeting of the group Owen D. Young, chairman of the General Electric Company, director of the Federal Reserve Bank of New York and head of the Young committee on reparations which recently developed the Young plan, joined the

Continued on Page Three.

240 Issues Lose $15,894,818,894 in Month; Slump in Full Exchange List Vastly Larger

The drastic effects of Wall Street's October bear market is shown by valuation tables prepared last night by THE NEW YORK TIMES, which place the decline in the market value of 240 representative issues on the New York Stock Exchange at $15,894,818,894 during the period from Oct. 1 to yesterday's closing. Since there are 1,279 issues listed on the New York Stock Exchange, the total depreciation for the month is estimated at between two and three times the loss for the 240 issues covered by THE TIMES table.

Among the losses of the various groups comprising the 240 stocks in THE TIMES valuation table were the following:

Group.	Number of Stocks.	Decline in Value.
Railroads	25	$1,128,686,488
Public utilities	29	5,135,724,327
Motors	15	1,689,840,902
Oils	22	1,332,617,778
Coppers	15	824,403,820
Chemicals	9	1,621,697,897

The official figures of the New York Stock Exchange showed that the total market value of its listed securities on Oct. 1 was $87,073,630,423. The decline in the 240 representative issues therefore cut more than one-sixth from the total value of the listed securities. Most of this loss was inflicted by the wholesale liquidation of the last week.

U. S. STEEL TO PAY $1 EXTRA DIVIDEND

American Can Votes the Same and Raises Annual Rate From $3 to $4.

BIG GAIN IN STEEL INCOME

Earnings for Nine Months Are $15.82 a Share, Against $8.17 a Year Ago.

Two leading industrial companies yesterday declared extra dividends of $1 a share on the common stock, as a result of their earnings through the Summer months. The companies were the United States Steel Corporation and the American Can Company, whose interests touch every section of the country. Their action caused the Wall Street district to accept the extra dividends as final proof of the prosperity of the country, despite the breaks which have occurred in the stock market.

While the directors of neither of the companies referred to present conditions in the stock market as a reason for taking the extra dividend action at this time, the opinion was expressed that the directors chose this time to declare the extras as reflecting their belief in the fundamental soundness of industry.

Directors of the American Can Company, in addition to declaring the $1 extra disbursement, also increased the regular dividend rate on the common stock from $3 a year to $4 a year, committing themselves to this payment for the future.

The United States Steel directors contented themselves with announcing that earnings for the first nine months of this year were nearly double those of the same period for 1928, namely, $15.82 a share on the common stock outstanding, compared with $8.17 for the nine months of 1928.

Steel Surplus Up $22,909,447.

Earnings of the United States Steel Corporation for the three months ended on Sept. 30 were reported as $72,009,666, equivalent to $5.57 a share on the common stock outstanding, and the extra dividend makes the disbursements for the quarter less than half of the actual earnings. The operation for the three months, after the preferred and common stock dividends, including the extra dividend, increased the surplus of the company by $22,909,447.

September was the lowest for the three months which enter into the quarterly earnings. The amount reported for this month was $21,794,450, which compares with $25,298,059 in August and $24,917,157 for July. The total earnings for the quarter after deducting all expenses incident to operations, including those for ordinary repairs and maintenance of plants, taxes, including the reserve for Federal income taxes, and the interest on bonds of subsidiary companies, amounted to $70,173,713. Allowances for depreciation, depletion and obsolescence took away another $16,819,393, leaving the net income for the three months at $53,354,320. The interest for the quarter on the bonds of the company outstanding amounted to $1,778,970, and the payment of the 1¾ per cent dividends on the preferred stock amounted to another $6,304,919.

Extra Due to Rise in Earnings.

The official statement issued by the company after the meeting of the directors read as follows:

"The United States Steel Corporation's earnings for the first nine

Continued on Page Six.

RESERVE BOARD FINDS ACTION UNNECESSARY

Six-Hour Session Brings No Change in the New York Rediscount Rate.

OFFICIALS ARE OPTIMISTIC

Mellon Also Attends Cabinet Meeting, but Declines to Discuss Developments.

Special to The New York Times.

WASHINGTON, Oct. 29.—The further decline in stock market prices today passed without expressed apprehension on the part of Federal officials. The situation was watched intently by the Federal Reserve Board, which held a continuous session from 10 A. M. until 4 P. M., with Secretary Mellon in attendance.

Secretary Mellon, as ex-officio chairman of the board, attended the early part of the meeting before going to the White House for the Cabinet meeting. It could not be learned whether the market situation was discussed by the President and the Cabinet.

At 2:30 P. M. Mr. Mellon returned to the Reserve Board meeting, and remained until near its close. During the day he had conferred with Under-Secretary Ogden L. Mills and Roy A. Young, Governor of the Reserve Board. After the board adjourned, neither Secretary Mellon nor Mr. Young would even intimate the nature or scope of the discussions.

The Federal Reserve Board was so absorbed in studying the financial problems facing the country as the result of another violent stock fluctuation that most of its members did not leave the board room for luncheon.

Board Reviews Credit Situation.

Members of the board, while admitting that the market situation was under discussion, declared at the end of the day that there was no change which called upon the board for action relative to credits.

There was a report that the board had reviewed the credit situation to determine whether the time had come to lower the rediscount rate to ease credit for business ventures.

The board has hesitated to act on the rediscount rate during the stock market decline, fearing that lowered rates might be employed to bolster up the market. The board's policy is not to aid in speculation, but it feels that the rediscount rate should be lowered to stimulate credits for business when it is apparent that such action would not be accepted as assistance to speculative loans.

Mr. Young said there was no change in financial conditions which the board thought called for its action.

Cut in Discount Rate Expected.

It is thought the question of lowering rediscount rates may come before the Federal Reserve Board shortly. The Boston Federal Reserve Bank directors will meet tomorrow and the New York directors on Thursday. It is possible that one of these banks may suggest a lowering of the rates.

Some observers believe that a reduction in rediscount rates might have a strong psychological effect not only upon business but the market as well. There was no official indication that such a move was imminent, although some observers thought such action might come if suggested by the New York bank directors, since the rate there is 6 per cent as against 5 per cent in other regions. Some thought the New York rediscount rate might be reduced to 5 per cent soon.

Today's session of the board was the longest since the financial flurry

Continued on Page Six.

CLOSING RALLY VIGOROUS

Leading Issues Regain From 4 to 14 Points in 15 Minutes.

INVESTMENT TRUSTS BUY

Large Blocks Thrown on Market at Opening Start Third Break of Week.

BIG TRADERS HARDEST HIT

Bankers Believe Liquidation Now Has Run Its Course and Advise Purchases.

Stock prices virtually collapsed yesterday, swept downward with gigantic losses in the most disastrous trading day in the stock market's history. Billions of dollars in open market values were wiped out as prices crumbled under the pressure of liquidation of securities which had to be sold at any price.

There was an impressive rally just at the close, which brought many leading stocks back from 4 to 14 points from their lowest points of the day.

Trading on the New York Stock Exchange aggregated 16,410,030 shares; on the Curb, 7,096,300 shares were dealt in. Both totals far exceeded any previous day's dealings.

From every point of view, in the extent of losses sustained, in total turnover, in the number of speculators wiped out, the day was the most disastrous in Wall Street's history. Hysteria swept the country and stocks went overboard for just what they would bring at forced sale.

Efforts to estimate yesterday's market losses in dollars are futile because of the vast number of securities quoted over the counter and on out-of-town exchanges on which no calculations are possible. However, it was estimated that 880 issues, on the New York Stock Exchange, lost between $8,000,000,000 and $9,000,000,000 yesterday. Added to that loss is to be reckoned the depreciation on issues on the Curb Market, in the over the counter market and on other exchanges.

Two Extra Dividends Declared.

There were two cheerful notes, however, which sounded through the pall of gloom which overhung the financial centres of the country. One was the brisk rally of stocks at the close, on tremendous buying by those who believe that prices have sunk too low. The other was that the liquidation has been so violent, as well as widespread, that many bankers, brokers and industrial leaders expressed the belief last night that it now has run its course.

A further note of optimism in the soundness of fundamentals was sounded by the directors of the United States Steel Corporation and the American Can Company, each of which declared an extra dividend of $1 a share at their late afternoon meetings.

Banking support, which would have been impressive and successful under ordinary circumstances, was swept violently aside, as block after block of stock, tremendous in proportions, deluged the market. Bid prices placed by bankers, industrial leaders and brokers trying to halt the decline were crashed through violently, their orders were filled, and quotations plunged downward in a day of disorganization, confusion and financial impotence.

Change Is Expected Today.

That there will be a change today seemed likely from statements made last night by financial and business leaders. Organized support will be accorded to the market from the start, it is believed, but those who are staking their all on the country's leading securities are placing a great deal of confidence, too, in the expectation that there will be an overnight change in sentiment; that the counsel of cool heads will prevail and that the mob psychology which has been so largely responsible for the market's debacle will be broken.

The fact that the leading stocks were able to rally in the final fifteen minutes of trading yesterday was considered a good omen, especially as the weakest period of the day had developed just prior to that time and the minimum prices for the day had then been established. It was a quick run-up which followed the announcement that the American Can directors had declared an extra dividend of $1. The advances in leading stocks in this last fifteen minutes represented a measurable snapback from the lows. American Can gained 10; United States Steel common, 7½; General Electric, 12; New York Central, 14½; Anaconda Copper, 9½; Chrysler Motors, 5¼; Montgomery Ward, 4¼, and Johns Man

Bank and Trust Stock Prices Crumble in Record Trading

ville, 8. Even with these recoveries the losses of these particular stocks, and practically all others, were staggering.

Yesterday's market crash was one which largely affected rich men, institutions, investment trusts and others who participate in the stock market on a broad and intelligent scale. It was not the margin traders who were caught in the rush to sell, but the rich men of the country who are able to swing blocks of 5,000, 10,000 up to 100,000 shares of high-priced stocks. They went overboard with no more consideration than the little trader who was swept out on the first day of the market's upheaval, whose prices, even at their lowest of last Thursday, now look high in comparison.

The market on the rampage is no respecter of persons. It washed fortune after fortune away yesterday and financially crippled thousands of individuals in all parts of the world. It was not until after the market had closed that the financial district began to realize that a good-sized rally had taken place and that there was a stopping place on the downgrade for good stocks.

Third Day of Collapse.

The market has now passed through three days of collapse, and so violent has it been that most authorities believe that the end is not far away. It started last Thursday, when 12,800,000 shares were dealt in on the Exchange, and holders of stocks commenced to learn just what a decline in the market means. This was followed by a moderate rally on Friday and entirely normal conditions on Saturday, with fluctuations on a comparatively narrow scale and with the efforts of the leading bankers to stabilize the market evidently successful. But the storm broke anew on Monday, with prices slaughtered in every direction, to be followed by yesterday's tremendous trading of 16,410,030 shares.

Sentiment had been generally unsettled since the first of September. Market prices had then reached peak levels, and, try as they would, pool operators and other friends of the market could not get them higher. It was a gradual downward sag, gaining momentum as it went on, then to break out into an open market smash in which the good, the bad and indifferent stocks went down alike. Thousands of traders were able to weather the first storm and answered their margin calls; thousands fell by the wayside Monday and again yesterday, unable to meet the demands of their brokers that their accounts be protected.

There was no quibbling at all between customer and broker yesterday. In any case where margin became thin a peremptory call went out. If there was no immediate answer the stock was sold out "at the market" for just what it would bring. Thousands, sold out on the decline and amid the confusion, found themselves in debt to their brokers last night.

Three Factors in Market.

Three factors stood out most prominently last night after the market's close. They were:

Wall Street has been able to weather the storm with but a single Curb failure, small in size, and no member of the New York Stock Exchange has announced himself unable to meet commitments.

The smashing decline has brought stocks down to a level where, in the opinion of leading bankers and industrialists, they are a buy on their merits and prospects, and brokers have so advised their customers.

The very violence of the liquidation, which has cleaned up many hundreds of sore spots which honeycombed the market, and the expected ability of the market to right itself, since millions of shares of stock have passed to strong hands from weak ones.

Bids Provided Where Needed.

One of the factors which Wall Street failed to take into consideration throughout the entire debacle was that the banking consortium has no idea of putting stocks up or to save any individuals from loss, but that its sole purpose was to alleviate the wave of financial hysteria sweeping the country and provide bids, at some price, where needed. It was pointed out in many quarters that no broad liquidating movement in the stock market has ever been stopped by so-called good buying. This is helpful, of course, but it never stops an avalanche of liquidation, as was this one.

There is only one factor, it was pointed out, which can and always does stop a down swing—that is, the actual cessation of forced liquidation. It is usually the case, too, that when the last of the forced selling has been completed the stock market always faces a wide-open gap in which there are practically no offerings of securities at all. When that point is reached, buying springs up from everywhere and always accounts for a sharp, almost perpendicular recovery in the best stocks. The opinion was widely expressed in Wall Street last night that that point has been reached, or at least very nearly reached.

Huge Blocks Offered at Opening.

The opening bell on the Stock Exchange released such a flood of selling as has never before been witnessed in this country. The failure of the market to rally consistently on the previous day, the tremendous shrinkage of open market values and the wave of hysteria which appeared to sweep the country brought an avalanche of stock to the market to be sold at whatever price it would bring.

From the very first quotation until thirty minutes after 10 o'clock it was evident that the day's market would be an unprecedented one. In that first thirty minutes of trading stocks were poured out in 5,000, 10,000, 20,000 and 50,000 share blocks at tremendous sacrifices as compared with the previous closing. The declines ranged from a point or so to as much as 29½ points, and the reports of opening prices brought selling into the market in confused volume that has never before been equaled.

In this first half hour of trading on the Stock Exchange a total of 3,259,800 shares were dealt in. The volume of the first twenty-six blocks of stock dealt in at the opening totaled more than 630,000 shares.

There was simply no near-by demand for even the country's leading industrial and railroad shares, and many millions of dollars in values were lost in the first quotations tapped out. All considerations other than to get rid of the stock at any price were brushed aside.

Brokerage Offices Crowded.

Wall Street was a street of vanished hopes, of curiously silent apprehension and of a sort of paralyzed hypnosis yesterday. Men and women crowded the brokerage offices, even those who have been long since wiped out, and followed the figures on the tape. Little groups gathered here and there to discuss the fall in prices in hushed and awed tones. They were participating in the making of financial history. It was the consensus of bankers and brokers alike that no such scenes ever again will be witnessed by this generation. To most of those who have been in the market it is all the more awe-inspiring because their financial history is limited to bull markets.

The machinery of the New York Stock Exchange and the Curb market were unable to handle the tremendous volume of trading which went over them. Early in the day they kept up well, because most of the trading was in big blocks, but as the day progressed the tickers fell further and further behind, and as on the previous big days of this week and last it was only by printing late quotations of stocks on the bond tickers and by the 10-minute flashes on stock prices put out by Dow, Jones & Co. and the Wall Street News Bureau that the financial district could get any idea of what was happening in the wild mob of brokers on the Exchange and the Curb.

Ticker Finishes at 5:32.

In the afternoon trading the tickers got more than an hour behind. Current tape prices were 5, 10 and 20 points away from those on the floor of the Exchanges. The Exchange ticker did not tap out the final quotation on stock prices until 5:32 P. M. The Curb tickers completed their task at 6:17. In most cases no attempt was made to keep up records in the Exchange board rooms, and only the last prices received from the Exchange floor by the ticker services were posted.

The following table shows the lag of the Exchange ticker during the day and the selling price of United States Steel common during the intervals of the day:

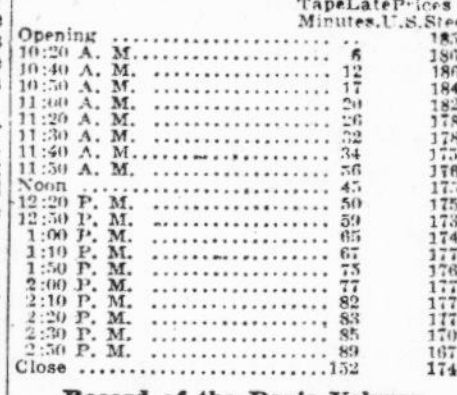

	Tape Late Minutes.	Prices of U.S. Steel.
Opening	..	185⅝
10:20 A. M.	6	186
10:40 A. M.	12	186
10:50 A. M.	17	184
11:00 A. M.	20	182
11:20 A. M.	26	178
11:30 A. M.	32	178¾
11:40 A. M.	34	175⅛
11:50 A. M.	36	176¼
Noon	45	175¼
12:20 P. M.	50	175½
12:50 P. M.	59	173
1:00 P. M.	65	174⅜
1:10 P. M.	67	177
1:50 P. M.	73	176
2:00 P. M.	77	177
2:10 P. M.	82	177
2:20 P. M.	83	177⅜
2:30 P. M.	85	170½
2:50 P. M.	89	167½
Close	152	174

Record of the Day's Volume.

Just how the tremendous total of more than 16,000,000 shares was built up in a five-hour trading day, a record likely to stand for a long while, is reflected in the following table, which shows the volume at intervals yesterday as compared with the previous day:

	Tuesday.	Monday.
10:30	3,259,000	815,600
12:00	8,378,200	3,135,200
1:30	12,652,000	5,547,900
2:10	13,838,000	6,328,500
3 P. M.	16,410,030	9,212,800

All low records, as measured by THE NEW YORK TIMES average of fifty representative stocks, were broken in the drastic liquidation, and prices on the average now are lower too than they were during last October. As measured by these statistics, the average of twenty-five railroad shares declined 6.29 in yesterday's trading and the average of twenty-five industrials was off 43.03. The combined average of fifty representative stocks showed a decline at the close of 24.66.

Table of Declines.

The largest declines in the leading issues on the New York Stock Exchange are reflected in the following tables:

	Monday's Low.	Yesterday's Low.	Yesterday's Close.	Net Decline.
Air Reduction	135	108¼	120	25
Allied Chem. & Dye	231	204¾	210	35
Am. & Foreign Power	72¾	50	55	22½
Am. Mach. & Fdy	201	175¼	175¼	25¾
Am. Tel. & Tel	232	204	204	28
Atch., Top. & Santa Fe	251	221	234	17
Auburn Automobile	175	120	130	60
Beatrice Creamery	100	80	80	20
Brooklyn Union Gas	146	100	112	34
Burroughs Add. Mach.	58¾	29	37⅝	20⅝
Columbian Carbon	158⅝	119	119	38⅝
Delaware & Hudson	170	141½	144⅝	25⅜
Drug, Inc.	91¼	71	72¼	19
Du Pont	150	80	116	34
El. Auto Lite	92⅛	50	50	45
Gen. Electric	250	210	222	28
Hershey Chocolate	112	86	86	26
Houston Oil	50⅛	26	34	16⅛
Int. Tel. & Tel	85	61	71	17
Johns-Manville	130	107	115	17
Louisville & Nashville	139	110	110	20
Macy (R. H.) Co	160	120½	128	33
Marlin Rockwell	50	30	30	20
Nash Motor	60	40	45	15
National Biscuit	180	142	165	15
Nat. Dis. Prod.	32⅛	15	15	17⅛
N. Y., N. H. & H	108	87	89⅜	18⅛
North American	96½	70	70	27½
Pub. Serv. of N. J.	87⅛	73	73¼	14
Purity Bakeries	89½	55	55	44½
Safeway Stores	138¼	115	115	23¼
Sears-Roebuck	111	95	95	16¼
Stand. Gas & El.	105½	79	80¼	25¼
Stone & Webster	105¼	81	90	20
Unit. Aircraft & Trans.	60⅛	40	41	19⅛
U. S. Ind. Alcohol	151	125½	125⅝	26⅜
U. S. Steel	185	166½	174	12
Westinghouse E. & M.	141	100	126	39

Losses on Curb Market.

Among the leading losses on the Curb market were the following:

	Low Monday.	Low Yest.	Close Yest.	Net Dec. Day.
Ainsworth	30	20	20	10
Allied Power & Light	43⅜	29	31¾	11⅝
Aluminum Co. Amer	299¾	225½	225½	74¼
Aluminum Co. Ltd	145	100½	100½	45
American Cigar	133	100	100	33
Amer Cities P & L, B	29	10	15	14⅝
Amer & For Pow war	57	25¾	30¼	29¾
Amer Gas & Elec	125½	110⅛	110⅛	15
Assoc G & E A	42⅛	35⅛	35⅛	10⅞
Blumenthal (S.)	60	29	29	31
Cent. P. S., A	46	20	25	13
Com. Edison	315	273	273	42
Con. Gas Balt	102	71	90	13
Firestone T. & R.	200	172	172	28
Elec. Bd. & Share	83	50	59⅞	23½
Elec. Invest	115	75	85	40
Fokker Aircraft	25⅛	8	9⅞	17
Goldman Sachs	60	35	35¾	24⅜
Gulf Oil Pa	146¼	121⅛	132	20⅛
Humble Oil	95	75	80	15
Hydro Elec. Service	45	35⅛	35⅛	14⅞
Insull Util	64½	26	40	26
Lehman	90	80	82	10
Midwest Util	275	130	190	85
No. States Power, A	180	115¼	115¼	64¾
Stand. Oil of Ohio	90⅛	60	60	30⅛
Stand. Pow. & Lt	103	66	66	37
Tri. Cont. Allied	70	50	50	20
Tubize Artif. Silk, B	216	150	230	19
U. S. Foil, B	41	19⅝	24	18⅜
U. S. Gypsum	66¼	48	48	18¼

Peaks Reached in September.

The bull market, the most extensive in the history of the country, started in the Coolidge Administration and reached its height with a tremendous burst of speculation in the public utility issues, the flames of speculation being fed by mergers, new groupings, combinations and good earnings.

The highest prices were reached in early September. At that time the market had a quick break and an equally rapid recovery. Then started a slow sag. Two developments, not considered important at the time, served to start the ball rolling downhill. The first of these was the refusal of the Massachusetts Public Service Commission to permit the Boston Edison Company to split its shares; the second was the collapse of a pool in International Combustion Engineering shares on the Stock Exchange, an over-exploited industrial which had been pushed across 100 by a pool and which crashed when the corporation passed its dividend.

In the meanwhile, the Hatry failure abroad had diverted a tremendous volume of selling to the United States, and under these influences the market continued to sag until it literally crumpled of its own weight.

CURB STOCK DROP LARGEST ON RECORD

7,096,300 Shares Sold, With Declines Ranging From 2 to 99 Points.

TRADING WIDEST IN HISTORY

New Lows for the Year Set by Most Issues—Biggest Loss by Tubize Silk.

In the widest trading it has ever experienced, the Curb Exchange yesterday suffered the most severe decline in its history. Few stocks missed the setting of low records for the year. Utilities and investment trusts were the heaviest issues on the list, but no group escaped the widespread selling, which rolled up a total turnover of 7,096,300 shares, compared with 6,337,415 last Thursday.

Losses were from 2 to 99 points, the latter occurring in Tubize Silk in an inactive market, contrasted with the heavy volume in other issues. Other severe losses occurred in Aluminum Company of America and Aluminum, Ltd., Atlas Plywood, E. W. Bliss, Colgate-Palmolive-Peet, Deere & Co., Ford of Canada A, Glen Alden Coal, General Baking preferred, Lane Bryant, Newmont Mining, Noranda Mines, Powdrell & Alexander, United States Foil B and Walgreen.

In the utility section sharp declines occurred in Allied Power and Light, American and Foreign Power warrants, American Cities B, American Light and Traction, Central States Electric, Commonwealth Edison, Baltimore Gas, Duke Power, Eastern Gas and Fuel, Electric Bond and Share, Electric Investors, Electric Power and Light option warrants, Indian Territory Oil, Northern States Power A, Standard Power and Light, Tampa Electric and United Gas.

New lows were established by Cities Service, Associated Gas, Central Public Service, American Gas and Electric, American Superpower, Middle West Utilities, Niagara Hudson Power, United Corporation warrants and United Light and Power A. Most of the stocks ended above the lowest marks.

In the oil group the declines principally affected Lion Oil, Humble Oil, Imperial Oil, Petroleum Corporation, Standard of Indiana, Standard of Kentucky and Vacuum Oil, which went to record lows for the year.

Bottom marks in the investment trust group were shown by Blue Ridge, Marine Midland, Insull Utility Investments, Haygart, Graymur, Goldman Sachs, Electric Shareholdings, Electric Power Associates, National Investors, Pennroad, Prudential Investors, Selected Industries, Shenandoah, Utility Equities, Utility and Industrials, Transamerica, Tricontinental, Tricontinental Allied and other less active issues.

Fokker Aircraft, Anchor Post Fence, Cord Corporation, Crocker Wheeler, Thermoid, Doehler Die and many other issues reached new lows in the decline.

CHICAGO CRASH CONTINUES.

Stocks Drop $1 to $75 a Share in Heavy Selling—Gain in Last Hour.

Special to The New York Times.

CHICAGO, Oct. 29.—Chicago stocks cracked again today as another selling wave engulfed the market. Prices sank $1 to $75 a share as large blocks of securities were thrown into the mêlée.

Commonwealth-Edison took the brunt of the battle as it sold off to a low and close of $235, after sales of 3,500 shares, a decline in value for the day of $75. Middle West Utilities registered the biggest individual turnover of the day with sales of 156,700 shares. This stock closed $6.50 lower.

The market had a ray of hope in the last hour when seventy-six issues closed higher than the lows for the day. The recoveries from the bottom prices ranged from $1 to $20 a share.

Three stocks finished with net gains on the day. These were led by Midland United, which sold up nearly $2.50 to $24, on sales of 6,100 shares. Swift International and United Reproducers were up fractionally, National Standard closed unchanged at $34, and Central Illinois Securities held its loss to 25 cents.

The rallies from the darkest moment were led by Auburn Automobile. This stock dropped $50 to a low of $120 and then worked up to $140 to cut the loss to $30.

Although wheat prices on the Chicago Board of Trade opened 2½ to 6⅞ cents a bushel lower, in sympathy with the break in stocks in New York and a decline in Liverpool, an extremely nervous feeling prevailed and price changes moved within a range of 5 cents during the day. The market, traders said, acted surprisingly well, all things considered. The break in prices brought large buying by foreigners, and especially by millers who have made large sales of flour for domestic use and export. Export sales have increased and bids on hard Winters at the gulf are within 1 to 2 cents of the December price in Chicago, the best relative bids this season.

SAN FRANCISCO BANKERS AID.

Stocks Rally at Noon When Reassuring Statement Appears.

SAN FRANCISCO, Oct. 29 (AP).—Caught in a whirl of frenzied selling stock prices tumbled headlong in early transactions on the San Francisco Exchanges today and then rallied sharply around noon as hysteria gave place to bargain hunting. No basis for the widespread alarm shown by traders was manifest along Montgomery Street outside the action of the market itself.

Transamerica, no longer supported by its president, A. P. Giannini, dropped more than 32 points cutting its market quotation in half, then recovered 18 points, settling again and steadying around 41 as 74,000 shares changed hands in less than three hours.

A statement signed by six leading San Francisco bankers and read on the floor of the San Francisco Stock Exchange added impetus to the recovery. The bankers said that business conditions on the Pacific Coast and throughout the country are sound and they recommended cool judgment of values.

RECORD PHILADELPHIA SALES.

500,000 Shares Traded on Exchange With Losses Up to 22 Points.

Special to The New York Times.

PHILADELPHIA, Oct. 29.—With sales of more than 500,000 shares, surpassing all previous records, securities on the Philadelphia Stock Exchange joined in another great decline today. Total losses exceeded those made on any other one day on the local board, the declines in individual stocks ranging from a fraction to twenty-two points. There was some recovery before the end, but advances from the lowest prices of the day were very small.

Margin calls sent out by local brokers last night were said to have met with prompt and generous response, yet prices continued to sag until the new commitments were wiped out. More than forty stocks on the Exchange tumbled to new low marks.

Interest again was centred on the public utility issues and especially on United Gas Improvement new stock. This issue fell steadily to below 24, and although it moved up a little before the close, it showed a net loss of more than five points for the day.

BIG LOSSES AT BOSTON.

Investment Trust Stocks Lead Selling, With Many New Lows of Year.

Special to The New York Times.

BOSTON, Oct. 29.—Prices were slashed unmercifully on the Boston Stock Exchange again today, the investment trust group, which is the principal trading section of the local list, bearing the brunt of the selling. Nearly all the stocks in this group were hammered to new low points for the year. Several of the industrials and specialties were also thrown overboard in the scramble to get out of stocks.

The most spectacular drop was in American Founders, which sold down to 66, a maximum loss for the day of 29 points, and closed at 80 for a net loss of 15. United Founders also showed a wide loss, selling at 31 all day, for a net decline of 17½ points. General Capital, which did not open until 2 o'clock, sold down to 20, closing at 30 for a loss of 25 points.

In the industrial group Bigelow Hartford lost 6½ to 85, United Shoe dropped 6 points to 60, Libby-McNeill was off 3¼, Hy-Grade Lamp 5½ and Union Twist Drill 3¾.

Coppers were heavily liquidated all day, Quincy being the leader, with a decline of 10 points to 20. In the utilities New England Telephone was the chief sufferer, showing a decline of 19 points to 140. Boston Elevated common slipped 5 points to 67.

RECORD DROP IN MONTREAL.

New Lows in 51 Exchange Issues and 20 in Curb Stocks.

MONTREAL, Que., Oct. 29.—Stock values on the Montreal Stock Exchange crashed today and new records were made for volume of trading, 540,151 shares, and fifty-one stocks dropped to new low prices for the year or longer. Twenty fresh minimums were created on the curb.

Nickel and Brazilian together furnished seven-tenths of the turnover. International Nickel sold off to the new low of 29½, and closed to 30¾, for a net decline of 3¼ points, while Brazilian dropped to the fresh bottom of 39, and closed at 43½, for a net loss of 7 points.

Utilities were weak, Montreal Power suffering the most severely. Equipments, papers and implements showed many sharp breaks. The close was weak.

MANY WIPED OUT IN TORONTO.

New Lows Made by 62 Stocks—Reassurances From Officials.

Special to The New York Times.

TORONTO, Ont., Oct. 29.—A new sales record for the Toronto Stock Exchange was made today when new lows for 1929 were set for sixty-two stocks. More than a hundred issues were carried downward. The leaders bore the brunt of the selling, losses reaching 50 points. The sales totaled 331,109 shares.

The day meant the end of hundreds of small traders. In view of the liquidation, A. E. Phipps, president of the Canadian Bank Association, and Sir Thomas White, a vice president of the Canadian Bank of Commerce, and a former Dominion Minister of Finance, issued statements telling Canadians that business conditions were sound. MacKenzie King, Prime Minister of Canada, also issued a reassuring statement from Ottawa.

Time to Buy Stocks, Says Raskob; Sees Only Temporary Effect on Business

John J. Raskob, one of the country's leading industrial and political leaders, declared last night in a statement to THE NEW YORK TIMES that many stocks are selling at bargain prices and that he and his friends are buyers of stocks. It may be stated in this conection that Mr. Raskob has been out of the stock market for many months and did not reenter it until he believed that stocks had reached a level at which they could be purchased with safety.

His statement, written at his desk last night, was as follows:

"Many of us have long felt great concern because of the inflated condition of the stock market during the past several months. Huge amounts of money have been loaned in the call money market at most attractive rates during this period by people who ordinarily would have this money invested in securities. The present decline in the stock markets of this country has carried prices, in many instances, to levels ridiculously low, with the result that nearly all of the standard railroad stocks are cheap and the industrial list is filled with stocks selling at real bargain prices.

"In a panic, whether in a theatre fire or the stock market, people lose their heads and go too far, which always results in needless and unnecessary suffering.

"Prudent investors are now buying stocks in huge quantities and will profit handsomely when this hysteria is over and our people have opportunity in calmer moments to appreciate the great stability of business by reason of the sound fundamental economic conditions existing in this great country.

"The pendulum has swung too far. The list is filled with bargains and my friends and I are all buying stocks."

Mr. Raskob was asked if he believed that the decline in the stock market would have great effects on business. He answered that he did not believe the effects would be other than temporary, lasting probably two or three months, and that he did not believe that the effects would be drastic in other than luxury industries.

Hundreds Added to Forces To Speed Delivery of Stocks

The various stock delivery, transfer and clearing agencies of Wall Street were stepped-up to an extraordinarily high rate of speed yesterday to cope with the unsurpassed volume of transactions on the New York Stock and Curb Exchanges, while hundreds of additional runners were obtained from the telegraph companies to assist the regular staffs.

The Stock Exchange advanced the delivery time for securities from 2:15 to 2:45 o'clock to permit the runners to deliver the huge stacks of securities at their proper destinations. The delivery time was advanced to 2:30 the day before.

The Stock Exchange Clearing Corporation reported yesterday that the work arising from Monday's 9,212,800-share day was completed in record time and that adequate preparations had been made to take care of yesterday's 16,410,030-share volume.

BANK STOCKS BREAK IN RECORD DEALINGS

National City Is Off 120 From Monday, First National 1,600, at a Closing Low Bid of 5,200.

BARGAIN HUNTERS ACTIVE

Trusts and Investment Trusts Hit Also in the Unlisted Market—Many Issues Neglected.

A demoralized market in unlisted securities culminated yesterday in what was said by some dealers to be the largest selling of bank stocks on record. For the greater part of the forenoon, bids were highly erratic, if obtainable at all. Gradually, however, a definite selling wave developed in the bank and trust issues and spread to the investment trusts. Other groups were practically neglected as a result of the attention focused on these issues.

Since trading in unlisted securities is carried on by telephone between dealers' offices instead of on a central trading floor, accurate estimates of the volume of sales were unavailable. For that reason, one unlisted house spokesman expressed the opinion that the sales of bank stocks yesterday, while admittedly greater than those of Monday or Thursday, had been exceeded one day last year. The general opinion, however, seemed to be that the bank stocks changed hands in unequaled volume.

Bank Stock Bargains Hunted.

The unlisted market was described as a field day for bargain hunters in bank stocks. These sharpshooters provided a moderate rally around 2 o'clock which, in the case of some dealers, proved short-lived. One house asserted that it had plenty of bids at the close, but others reported a lack of buying support at that time. This house said it had plenty of bids in for bank stocks and that its closing orders were higher than the prices at which it sold bank stocks earlier in the day.

Selling of the bank shares was again ascribed to a need for funds by holders who sought to protect their commitments on the open market exchanges against yesterday's slump. Yesterday, however, the further break in bank stocks was attributed in part to a growing conviction that the bank stocks had been inflated in value and could be obtained at lower prices than had prevailed in recent markets.

National City Bank led in activity. This issue sold as low as 300, and the best bid at the close was 325, a net loss of 120 from Monday. The greatest loss was made by First National, which, owing to its high price, fluctuates more widely on fewer sales than do other bank stocks. First National closed at a low bid of 5,200, down 1,600 points from Monday's closing bid. Among trust companies, Brooklyn Trust led in weakness, closing at a bid of 800, down 860 points from Monday.

Chase National Bank sold as low as 135 and closed down 38 points at 150. Chatham-Phenix sold as low as 110 and closed at 120, off 10. Bank of United States sold as low as 85 and closed down 27 at 98. Bankers Trust touched 130 and closed 135, down 35. Central Hanover's low was 280 and its close 330, down 40. Equitable Trust touched 425 and closed at 450, down 110. Guaranty sagged to 580 and closed at 625, down 175.

One house claimed to have bids for these banks and trust stocks from 5 to 10 points above these closing figures. However, houses which specialize in bank and trust issues said these figures represented their prices.

Investment Trust Issues Hit.

Next to the bank and trust issues, the wave of selling in unlisted trading showed its greatest influence on investment trust issues. British Type Investors sold as low as 5 and closed at a bid of 10 for a loss of 13¼ points. United Founders Corporation touched 20 and closed at 33 for a net loss of 20.

As was the case Monday, most of the trading interest in the unlisted market was absorbed by the bank and trust shares. Insurance shares, which showed some activity Monday, lapsed into comparative inactivity yesterday, although high-priced insurance stocks that did appear were hard hit.

CURB FIRM IS SUSPENDED.

John J. Bell & Co. Admits Inability to Meet Obligation.

The selling flood that has almost inundated the stock market brought its first brokerage house failure yesterday when John J. Bell & Co. at 40 Exchange Place, members of the New York Curb Exchange, was suspended from the exchange because of its admitted inability to meet its obligations.

The announcement of the suspension was made by the Exchange soon after the market opened. There was no statement of assets or liabilities, but it was said last night that a statement would be made today. No petition in bankruptcy has been filed by the firm.

MARGINS CUT TO 25% ON LOANS ON STOCK

Bankers Meeting in Morgan Offices Decide Deflation Has Been Sufficient.

FRESH BUYING POWER SEEN

Impaired Accounts Can Be Better Protected Also by Move, It Is Believed.

Following a meeting in the offices of J. P. Morgan & Co. at noon yesterday of the banking group organized last Thursday to support the stock market, it was announced that the banks composing the group, together with several other banking institutions of the city, had agreed upon a reduction of the margin required on security collateral loans to 25 per cent of the market value. This announcement meant that brokers were enabled to borrow up to 75 per cent of the market price of the securities offered as collateral.

It has been the custom for the banks to establish a base price considerably below current market quotations and to lend from 60 to 70 per cent of this base. Yesterday's move indicates that the banks believe security values have been so far deflated as to make unnecessary the enormous margins maintained during the advances in stocks. The action of the bankers was promptly followed by leading brokerage houses, which informed their customers that their accounts would be carried on a 25 per cent margin.

While the banks displayed a much more liberal attitude toward collateral loans, they continued to exercise a keen discrimination as to the class of security they would accept in loan envelopes.

Two Statements by Brokers.

The easing of marginal requirements was explained in two statements issued on behalf of the banking pool.

The first statement, issued at J. P. Morgan & Co. at noon, follows:

"It is learned this morning that many of the leading institutions, including the following: J. P. Morgan & Co., National City Bank, First National Bank, Chase National Bank, Bankers' Trust, Equitable Trust Company, New York Trust Company, Irving Trust Company and Bank of America, are stating to their customers that for the present they plan to require the maintenance of only 25 per cent margin on the Street demand loans."

A statement issued later was as follows:

"There is no money problem involved in the present situation. There is plenty of money and it will be loaned freely.

"As indicating that bankers are feeling that present price levels are safe, it may be said authoritatively that certain of the larger banks in the Wall Street district revised margin requirements as of last night (Monday), making a requirement of only 25 per cent margin on closing quotations, instead of the previous practice of 40 per cent margin or of setting arbitrary prices from which a somewhat lower margin was required.

"It is understood also that many Stock Exchange houses have also followed the change."

While many other banks than those named in the statement took like action, a few others did not commit themselves to any hard and fast rule, preferring to exercise discretionary judgment.

Loan Value Reductions Not Severe.

The marking down of loan values yesterday was not severe, according to the best opinions available on the subject, and it was expected that the tendency was to accept leading stocks at prices closer to market quotations than formerly on the theory that the compression in market values would automatically curtail the extent of any drops in standard issues.

It was explained that the reduction of margin requirements on the lower price levels was intended to build up fresh buying power as well as to save impaired accounts so far as it was possible, and in leading brokerage houses it was reported that buying of stocks yesterday had resulted from the establishment of 25 per cent margins.

The heavy declines of Thursday, Monday and yesterday, estimated at approximately 30 per cent, with respect to the average level of Stock Exchange stocks, has been accompanied by large reductions in brokers' loans, the contraction having been especially noteworthy yesterday. The prediction was ventured by several leading firms that brokers' loans would show this week a reduction of as much as one billion dollars since last Wednesday, when the last Federal Reserve Board figures were compiled.

It was ascertained that Stock Exchange houses had little difficulty with respect to the loan situation and that the measures taken by the banks to reduce their margin requirements had greatly helped to protect impaired accounts.

6-DAY STOCK TAX $1,500,000

State Income From Transfers Exceeds All Previous Marks.

ALBANY, Oct. 29 (AP).—Unparalleled trading in stock markets in the last six days will put close to $1,500,000 in the coffers of the State, officials of the Department of Taxation said tonight.

This income, derived from the stock transfer tax, said Frank S. McCaffrey, Deputy State Commissioner, breaks all records since the tax was first levied, nearly a quarter of a century ago.

The State imposes a tax of 2 cents per $100 of par value of all stocks. Stocks with no par value are taxed 2 cents a share.

"All the News That's Fit to Print."

The New York Times.

LATE CITY EDITION

Copyright, 1932, by The New York Times Company.

VOL. LXXXI....No. 27,066. NEW YORK, WEDNESDAY, MARCH 2, 1932. TWO CENTS

JAPANESE ROUTING CHINESE IN FIERCE SHANGHAI BATTLE; DEATH TOLL EXCEEDS 2,000

WHOLE CHINESE LINE FLEES

Pressure From North of Fresh Japanese Troops Forces Quick Move.

PURSUERS LEFT BEHIND

Tachang, Miaoshin and Chapei Fall Before Advance Made Behind Smoke Screen.

TRUCE EXPECTED AT ONCE

Chinese Are Stunned by Sudden Blow—Say Retreat Meets Terms of Japanese.

By HALLETT ABEND.
Wireless to THE NEW YORK TIMES.

SHANGHAI, Wednesday, March 2.—The Chinese were routed this morning by the Japanese in the most sanguinary battle since the World War.

The Japanese killed and wounded before 10 o'clock admittedly exceeded 300. Yesterday's advance in this region totaled two kilometers (more than a mile) and the Japanese losses up to midnight officially were admitted to be slightly in excess of 300 killed and wounded, while the bodies of 1,800 Chinese soldiers were discovered this morning on the ground won yesterday.

Brief reports from General Kenkichi Ueda's headquarters report that the Chinese retreat is degenerating into an utter, panicky rout and the rapid Japanese advance is finding difficulty in maintaining contact with the fast fleeing Chinese soldiers.

The pall of smoke from burning Chinese villages and towns was thickening over Shanghai. Immense exultation was manifested in Japanese circles and the Chinese were stunned by the suddenness and magnitude of the military disaster.

The Japanese captured Tachang at 12:30 today.

Chinese in Pell Mell Retreat.

Early this afternoon the Japanese forces were rapidly approaching from beyond Taching and the Chinese were in pellmell retreat. There was great confusion at Nantao, where Chinese soldiers were attempting to evacuate in railway trains to Hangchow.

The Nineteenth Route Army has voluntarily withdrawn from Chapei, is abandoning other fronts and concentrating at Chenju, according to official oral notification given at 12:30 by the secretary of Mayor Wu Te-chen to United States Consul General Edwin S. Cunningham in his capacity as senior consul.

This withdrawal, the official notification said, also means the evacuation of all Chinese soldiers from Nantao ad Lunghua, but Mr. Cunningham was assured there was danger of disorders at Nantao because 2,000 regular police and 600 picked volunteers already have taken over the maintenance of law and order. It is understood that Chinese will not attempt to police Chapei, declaring "that is dependent upon the Japanese."

Truce Expected Soon.

Presumably the crumpling of the Nineteenth Route Army will be quickly followed by the signing of a truce and by further retirement of the Chinese forces, since Chenju is inside the twenty-kilometer zone which the Japanese insist must be evacuated.

Between 7:30 and 10 o'clock this morning the Japanese had pushed forward to within two kilometres of Tachang. A vast area was being bombed and shelled with unparalleled intensity and the region was dimmed with smoke from huge conflagrations.

The Chinese began the day's hostilities by using two batteries of big guns, firing from Chapei into the Japanese naval headquarters area in Hongkew Park, where many large fires are now burning. For an hour and a half the Chinese batteries kept the city rocking and the roar of their detonations made sleep impossible.

The Japanese had made exceedingly important gains at 10 o'clock toward Tachang, although the terrain is even more difficult than around Kiangwan, with a multitude of vertical banked creeks and sloughs

Continued on Page Twelve.

Settlement Stores Reopen And Shoppers Flock to Them

Special Cable to THE NEW YORK TIMES.

SHANGHAI, March 1.—Acting upon the request of General Tsai Ting-chai three of the largest Chinese-owned department stores on the Nanking Road of the International Settlement reopened today and many smaller stores and shops followed suit. This action contributed largely to a return to approximate normalcy in general business conditions.

SHANGHAI, March 1 (AP).—Stores and offices in the International Settlement reopened today and bargain hunters turned out in droves.

The three big department stores were crowded with shoppers, but the service staff was considerably depleted. Many of the clerks used to live in Chapei and Hongkew and nobody knows where they are now.

JAPAN WILL OFFER NEW TRUCE TERMS

Accepts League Proposal for Armistice at Shanghai With Reservations.

CHINA AFFIRMS AGREEMENT

Plans for Special Assembly at Geneva Tomorrow Await Outcome of Negotiations.

By CLARENCE K. STREIT.
Special Cable to THE NEW YORK TIMES.

GENEVA, March 1.—Naotake Sato this evening gave Joseph Paul-Boncour, President of the League Council, Tokyo's definite acceptance of the latter's so-called "President's plan" for a Shanghai truce and a round-table discussion. Mr. Sato added that the "details"—which is to say, the truce—were to be worked out in Shanghai. Later he confirmed his oral communication in a brief note.

The note merely said Japan was "happy to accept the plan the President has submitted. It mentioned none of the reservations which Mr. Sato gave M. Paul-Boncour orally regarding the details of the truce to be settled on the spot, apparently because Japan thought the terms of the "President's plan" included such reservations.

At any rate, these reservations not merely still stand, but it is understood Mr. Sato explained to M. Paul-Boncour that Japan, instead of accepting Admiral Kelly's armistice terms, was making a counter-proposal.

The United States delegation preferred to reserve comment on Tokyo's reply.

Diplomatic Move Seen.

There is a suspicion in Chinese and Soviet circles that, if Japan does really accept the truce terms, she will then try to win through diplomacy what she failed to win on the battlefield by seeking to have the boundaries of the International Settlement at Shanghai extended to include some districts largely populated by Japanese. There is nothing, certainly, in either the "President's plan" or Mr. Sato's declaration yesterday to prevent such a manoeuvre, for they bar merely any concession or move which exclusively favors the Japanese.

The wording of the second point of the president's plan" and the whole of Mr. Sato's declaration, especially the third point, appear to some to be designed to facilitate such a plan by their references to strengthening the international character of the Settlement.

The Chinese appear to regard the United States as the only one in the group on which they can count not to take advantage of the present situation to try to block China's old fight on the whole question of extraterritoriality.

New Settlement Status Hinted.

There is also some significant, although still vague, talk of the need of improving the status of the Shanghai International Settlement and possibly of putting it under League jurisdiction, like Danzig.

Although the skepticism here is pointed chiefly toward Japan, some are skeptical too of the Chinese Government being able to keep its troops to the terms of the armistice.

Pending definite developments with regard to the armistice and the

Continued on Page Thirteen.

145 in House Force Vote on Dry Law Test; Texan, Last Signer, Rolls Up in Wheelchair

Special to THE NEW YORK TIMES.

WASHINGTON, March 1.—An outright vote on whether the House shall consider a proposal to return liquor control to the States was assured today when the necessary 145 members had signed a petition to cite the Judiciary Committee for discharge from further study of the measure.

The vote probably will be taken on March 14, the first "discharge" day on the calendar.

The wets hailed it as the greatest day since prohibition when the last signature necessary was obtained soon after noon. The 145th member affixing his signature was Representative Mansfield, Texas Democrat. Mr. Mansfield, who is crippled, rolled up to the desk in his wheel chair, while Representative Blanton, Democrat, of Texas, a militant dry, was on his feet chiding the wets for their "failure" to get the required signatures.

The House was set into an uproar when at that moment it was found that Mr. Mansfield, from Mr. Banton's own State, had made the "wet failure" a literal "howling success." Some observers were quick to remark that March 2 is the Independence Day of Texas, the anniversary of its Declaration of Independence from Mexico.

Representative La Guardia of New York, a wet, was taking Mr. Blanton to task for his remarks when the news was broadcast that Mr. Mansfield had signed.

"Any time that this House has the experience of seeing the distinguished gentleman from Texas (Mr. Blanton) get unduly excited," Mr. La

Continued on Page Two.

SALES TAX ACCEPTED BY ADMINISTRATION, MILLS ANNOUNCES

Secretary Pledges Cooperation on New Bill Despite Changes in Treasury Plan.

$625,000,000 NOW IS GOAL

Basis for Manufacturers' Levy Is Widened as Subcommittee Completes Draft.

Special to THE NEW YORK TIMES.

WASHINGTON, March 1.—Acceptance by the administration of the new tax measure, including a general sales tax applicable to practically every manufacturing industry in the country, was assured today by Secretary Mills.

Mr. Mills told a Ways and Means subcommittee that, even though the original treasury plan had been changed at nearly every major point, the administration would cooperate to the fullest extent in setting in motion and administering the new tax increases.

The subcommittee completed the new tax bill, excepting one or two minor administrative features, this afternoon.

The manufacturers' tax provisions, as agreed on, exempt only a few articles, chiefly commodities for the "poor man's breakfast table" and his daily paper, and the farmer's products, his magazines and periodicals.

The final meeting of the subcommittee resulted in a decision to recommend an even wider base for the manufacturers' levy. Yesterday the subcommittee tentatively agreed to frame the tax so as to produce around $550,000,000 in additional revenue. Today it decided to extend the scope so as to produce $625,000,000.

The additions to the sales tax base were understood to have been made by adding commodities which were being held "in reserve" for special excises.

Members of the subcommittee declined to discuss details, but it was the prevailing idea that gasoline and industrial alcohol had been included in their definition of "manufactured products."

If this is true, gasoline and industrial alcohol would be subject to the 2 per cent general tax instead of the special excises of one cent a gallon as proposed originally.

Agree on Excess Levies.

Final decision on the special excise levies was reached today. Committeemen likewise declined to discuss these, holding that to mention them would be to let loose an "avalanche" of protests on members of Congress.

Other excises most prominently mentioned in discussions of the measure were a 5 to 10 per cent consumers' levy on electric energy and illuminating gas; a tax on oil, with a differential upward on oil imports, and an increase of 3 cents a share on stock transfers.

The bill probably will be presented to the full Ways and Means Committee tomorrow afternoon and may be offered to the House for action by Saturday night, according to Representative Crisp of Georgia, acting chairman.

Actual passage in the House by the end of next week was the confident hope of authors of the measure.

Representative Crisp, fatigued from his strenuous work on the bill, was buoyed in spirit today with the hope that it might even be introduced in the House tomorrow. He will offer the measure as soon as the Ways and Means Committee has agreed to it. It will then be referred back to the committee, which immediately will go through the routine of making a formal report.

Being a revenue bill, it will have priority in the House and, according to Mr. Crisp, will be called up as soon as possible for action.

He mentioned next Tuesday as a

Continued on Page Four.

SENATE BODY ACTS FOR BROAD INQUIRY ON SHORT SELLING

Banking Committee Will Go Beyond Hoover Idea in Stock Exchange Investigation.

EFFECTS ON TRADE SOUGHT

Subcommittee Named to Go Into Long and Short Sales and Interstate Phase.

Special to THE NEW YORK TIMES.

WASHINGTON, March 1.—An investigation of the New York Stock Exchange was recommended today by the Senate Banking and Currency Committee. A subcommittee, headed by Senator Walcott, Republican, of Connecticut, immediately began drafting a resolution requesting authority for such an investigation from the Senate.

The subcommittee was instructed by the full committee to include in the resolution authorizations covering studies of both long and short selling, the effect of speculation on interstate commerce, the use of interstate communications systems by speculators and the value of a proposed stock transfer tax as a check on speculation.

This decision went far beyond the action believed to have been requested by President Hoover Friday when he called Senator Walcott to the White House for a conference on "bear raiding." No intimation of an investigation of trading other than short selling has come from the White House.

The subcommittee was chosen after an executive session, during which the committee members argued the constitutional right of the Senate to investigate the Stock Exchange.

The full committee finally agreed generally that such authority does exist, and the subcommittee, charged with considering this point in more detail, reached the same conclusion late this afternoon.

Regulation Not Contemplated Now.

Leading members of the full committee, including Senator Walcott, indicated that no regulatory measure affecting the Stock Exchange is contemplated at this time. The committee intends to run to the ground rumors about the Stock Exchange and, if questionable practices are found, to suggest means of correcting them, preferably through the action of the governors of the Stock Exchange itself.

"I hope this will not result in Federal legislation," Senator Walcott told newspaper men. "We have no legislative plans. However, the committee feels that if we can by investigation persuade the Stock Exchange to draw such regulations as will abolish bear raids, bull raids and dangerous pool operations, then we will have done the country good service.

"There is not a man on that committee who wants the Stock Exchange abolished. But we want to see what abuses exist. There is so much talk about the Exchange, and we are just as anxious to clear the Stock Exchange of any unwarranted misrepresentations as we are to uncover abuses in security dealings."

The subcommittee was appointed by Senator Norbeck, Republican, of North Dakota, chairman of the full committee, who named Senators Steiwer, Republican, of Oregon, and Bulkley, Democrat, of Ohio, to serve with Senator Walcott.

What sides were taken by committee members on the question of constitutionality was not revealed, but Senator Norbeck said that eventually "almost every member agreed there is authority under some provision or other." The principal point at issue was whether the Stock Exchange could be considered as engaging in interstate commerce or whether its business should be considered as confined to New York.

The committee's executive session

Continued on Page Thirteen.

LINDBERGH BABY KIDNAPPED FROM HOME OF PARENTS ON FARM NEAR PRINCETON; TAKEN FROM HIS CRIB; WIDE SEARCH ON

FOUR STATES JOIN HUNT

Wire Systems Flash Out Alarm on First Word of Kidnapping.

NEW YORK CAR IS SOUGHT

Roads Are Scoured for Pair Said to Have Inquired Way to the Lindbergh Home.

AUTOS STOPPED ON ROAD

Hunt Here Is Led by Mulrooney—Underworld Haunts Visited in Scores of Cities.

The Baby's Description.

HOPEWELL, N. J., March 2 (AP).—A chubby, golden-haired boy closely resembling his famous father—that is the description given Charles Augustus Lindbergh Jr.

He is 20 months old, has blue eyes, curly hair, fair complexion. He is about normal size for a child his age. He has just begun to toddle and is learning to talk.

At 10:40 o'clock last night Colonel Charles A. Lindbergh telephoned the New Jersey State Police Headquarters at Trenton that his son had been kidnapped from the Lindbergh home in Hopewell, N. J. Within ten minutes every communication method of modern science had been utilized to broadcast the alarm and to mobilize the police systems of four States and scores of communities in the search.

Colonel Lindbergh had scarcely poured out his tale when the vast machinery of cooperating police systems began to function. While one man was calling the State police barracks at Lambertville, N. J., ten miles from Hopewell, on the telephone, another was writing out this message to be flashed over the police teletype system:

"Colonel Lindbergh's baby kidnapped from Lindbergh home at Hopewell between 7:30 and 10 P. M. Boy, 19 months, dressed in sleeping suit. Search all cars."

Pair in Stolen Car Hunted.

Shortly before 1 o'clock this morning the Princeton Police Department sent over the network of wires the first message containing anything approaching a definite clue. It read as follows:

"Information received that two men in blue or black sedan bearing New York license plates stopped a man working on highway and asked to be directed to the Lindbergh home in Hopewell."

Relayed to every outpost, this message gave the searchers their first indication of the possible description of the kidnappers' car. It was so vague, however, that they did not permit it to stop them from questioning the occupants of cars of other descriptions.

As the first alarm was being typed out the telephone connection with the Lambertville barracks had been established and Lieutenant Arthur Keaten, in command of that post, had been informed of the situation. With every man who could be spared, he started at once for Hopewell.

Upon their arrival Corporal Joseph Wolf, at Lieutenant Keaten's direction, telephoned back confirmation of the kidnapping, but he was not at that time able to add further details to the few which had been furnished by Colonel Lindbergh.

Meanwhile picked detectives were sent on the rounds of known underworld haunts to see if they could pick up any clues as to the identity of the kidnappers.

Window Found Open.

An open window in the nursery of the Lindbergh home at Hopewell indicated how the kidnappers had gained entrance to the house. A close watch has been kept on the baby since it was born, but apparently no member of the family dreamed of the possibility of a kidnapping and no one remained in the nursery last night after the nurse had placed the child in his crib and made sure he was asleep.

The small force under Lieutenant Keaten at once began a careful search of the woody areas surrounding the Lindbergh home, on the possibility of uncovering some clue to the

Continued on Page Three.

The Lindbergh baby photographed a year ago. Left to right are Mrs. Dwight W. Morrow, the baby's grandmother; Mrs. Charles Cutler Long, the great-grandmother; Charles Augustus Lindbergh Jr., and Mrs. Charles A. Lindbergh, his mother.

KIDNAPPING OF BABY SPEEDS FEDERAL LAW

Demand in Capital for Statute Providing Death Penalty Expected to Increase.

OFFICIALS HINDERED NOW

Can Act in Almost Any Other Interstate Crime—Patterson Assails "Filthy Act."

Special to THE NEW YORK TIMES.

WASHINGTON, Wednesday, March 2.—Immediate pressure for early passage of the measure making kidnapping a Federal offense is held certain to be the result of the kidnapping of Colonel Lindbergh's son.

Senator Patterson of Missouri recently introduced a bill to this effect. It provides a death penalty. The measure would give authority to the government when the kidnapped person is removed from one State to another. The bill was approved unanimously two weeks ago by the Senate Judiciary Committee and its supporters are confident that it will be adopted by the Senate.

A companion bill introduced by Representative Cochran of Missouri, chairman of the Committee on Expenditures, has been before the Judiciary Committee in that branch for about ten days. The hearings were scheduled for completion soon and the portents, before this morning's news, were for a favorable report.

Patterson Denounces Crime.

"It is a shock to me to hear of this outrage," said Mr. Patterson this morning when informed by THE NEW YORK TIMES. "I hope the child will soon be returned to its parents. This filthy act will aid us in passing the needed legislation, and I am sorry it will not be retroactive, so that the Lindbergh kidnappers can be dealt with by the Federal Government."

On Jan. 23 a telephone message was received by Senator Patterson from Chicago to the effect that there was a plot to kidnap General Charles G. Dawes, who had just been appointed president of the Reconstruction Finance Corporation. Mr. Patterson then said that this information came from a newspaper correspondent. It created excitement in Washington official circles, although the General refused to take it seriously. However, it spurred the efforts of those behind the legislation.

Action Urged in Chicago.

As a result, when the House Judiciary Committee began hearings, Colonel Isham Randolph of Chicago, head of the "Secret Six" of that city, and former Representative Cleveland A. Newton of St. Louis came to Washington to urge early action. Mr. Newton gave the following list of kidnappings which he said had

Continued on Page Three.

FATHER SEARCHES GROUNDS FOR CHILD

Lindbergh and Troopers Hunt With Flashlights for Clues on Big Estate.

NEWS ROUSES COUNTRYSIDE

Hundreds of Autos Rush to the Home in Lonely Woodland, Clogging Narrow Road.

Copyrighted, 1932, by The Associated Press.

HOPEWELL, N. J., Wednesday, March 2.—Charles Augustus Lindbergh Jr., 20-month-old son of the flying Colonel, was kidnapped last night from his nursery in the Lindbergh country home near here. The child, clad in a blue sleeping robe, was put to bed at the usual hour, 7:30 P. M. At about 10 P. M. someone peered into the nursery. The crib was empty.

Beneath the nursery window, footprints showed in the soft earth. These indicated that the kidnappers, moving with such stealth that the Lindberghs, although in the house, heard no sound, had removed their shoes before climbing a ladder to the window. The trail of the shoeless footprints was followed by The Associated Press reporter to the rutted lane, where police believe a waiting car was parked. Feminine footprints, as well as those of a man, were found.

The first news the Lindberghs had of the crime was when the frightened nurse ran downstairs, screaming that the baby had been kidnapped.

The first newspaper man to reach the home was an Associated Press reporter, who ran a mile over muddy, rut-cut roads to reach a phone to send the first direct news from the residence. This was at 12:00 A. M.

Colonel Lindbergh, bare-headed as usual, was pacing the grounds, while troopers and detectives went over the place with flashlights, seeking clues.

Mrs. Lindbergh, who telephoned the news to her mother, Mrs. Dwight W. Morrow, at the Morrow home in Englewood, N. J., was inside the house. A close friend of Mrs. Lindbergh said she was expecting another child within three months.

The house, glowing with lights from top to bottom, was the only bright spot in the wooded, gloomy district. Wishing to get complete privacy, the Lindberghs picked the site from the air and it is almost inaccessible to the outside world. A winding, muddy lane—their private property—leads to the new house from a country highway, called the Stoutsburg-Wertsville Road. The entrance to the Lindbergh road is more than four miles from Hopewell and there are few neighbors near enough to be of any aid in time of

Continued on Page Three.

CHILD STOLEN IN EVENING

At 10 P. M. Nurse Finds Boy, 20 Months Old, Gone, in Nightrobe.

FOOTPRINTS IN THE ROOM

Muddy Trail Leads to Ladder in Wood and Half Mile to Highway, Where Car Waited.

WOMAN BELIEVED INVOLVED

Parents, Distraught, Guarded in Home—Police Deny Report of Ransom Note.

Charles Augustus Lindbergh Jr., 20-month-old son of Colonel and Mrs. Charles A. Lindbergh, was kidnapped between 8:30 and 10 o'clock last night from his crib in the nursery on the second floor of his parents' home at Hopewell, near Princeton, N. J.

Apparently the kidnapping was carried out either while Colonel and Mrs. Lindbergh were at dinner, or soon afterward. The baby's nurse, Miss Betty Gow, visited the nursery about 8:30 o'clock and found everything in order there. When she returned at 10 o'clock, however, the crib was empty.

Muddy footprints that trailed across the floor from the crib to an open window bore mute testimony as to how the baby had disappeared. Miss Gow dashed downstairs. "The baby's been kidnapped!" she shouted. Colonel Lindbergh raced to the nursery, followed closely by his wife. Mrs. Lindbergh recalled that earlier in the day she had tried to fasten a screen on the window that had been opened and had been unable to do so.

Satisfied that there was no mistake and that the baby actually was gone, Colonel Lindbergh telephoned Chief of Police Charles Williamson at Hopewell. Williamson drove to the house accompanied by another officer. Outside the door they met the Colonel. He was bareheaded, and wearing an old black leather jacket such as he frequently wears on his flights.

Footprints Under Window.

Briefly he told Williamson what had occurred. The chief telephoned first to State Police Headquarters at Trenton. Then he, his fellow officer and the Colonel began searching the grounds. Beneath the nursery window were marks where a ladder had stood and the footprints of one person. There were no shoe prints. The kidnapper, apparently, had worn socks or moccasins.

Sixty feet away in rocky ground at the edge of a wood the Colonel and Chief Williamson found a makeshift ladder. Its rungs were caked with mud. Colonel Lindbergh could not say whether it belonged on the premises. He thought it might have been left there by the builders while the house was being constructed during his flight to the Orient last Summer with Mrs. Lindbergh.

The searchers had no difficulty in following the footprints across the muddy ground. A second set of tracks joined them near the edge of the woods. They were much smaller. The two officers thought they might be those of a woman.

The search was interrupted by the arrival of a detachment of State Troopers sent from the barracks at Lambertville and the hunt began anew. The tracks were followed to the main highway, about half a mile from the house, where they disappeared. The kidnappers evidently had entered an automobile at that point.

Lindbergh Aids Search.

Carrying a flashlight, Colonel Lindbergh stayed with the searching party until long after midnight. Once or twice he returned to the house, but he declined to discuss the kidnapping with newspapermen. Instead, he referred them to Major Schoeffel of the State Police, who told the story in detail.

"I hope you boys will excuse me,"

Continued on Page Three.

Four States Search for Lindbergh Baby, Kidnapped at Night From Parents' Home

THE LINDBERGHS, THEIR INFANT SON AND THE SCENE OF THE KIDNAPPING.

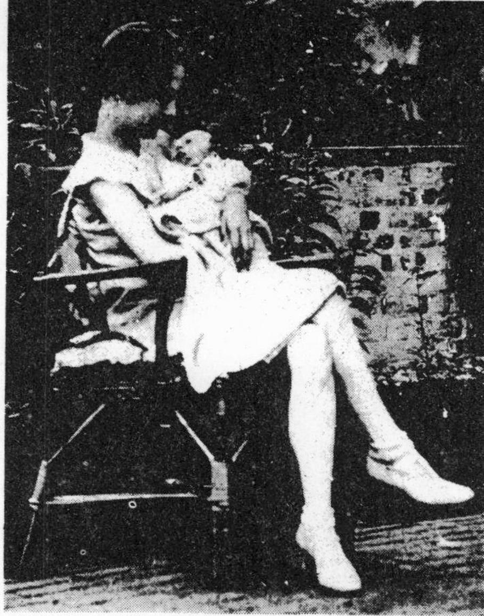

Times Wide World Photo.
Mrs. Lindbergh Holding Her Baby Son.

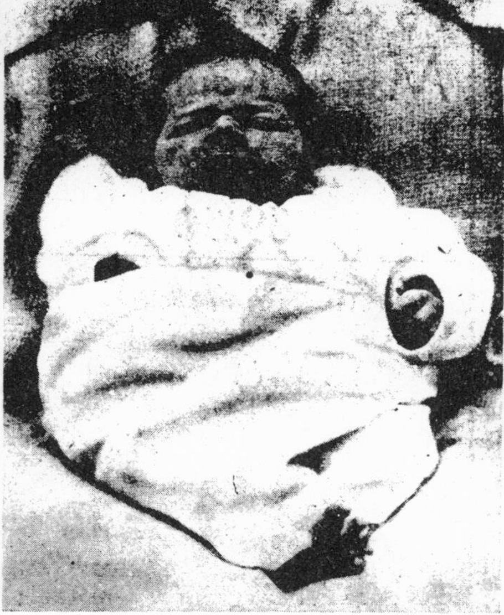

Times Wide World Photo.
First Picture Taken by Colonel Lindbergh of His Infant Son.

Times Wide World Photo.
Colonel and Mrs. Lindbergh After One of Their Flights.

Aero Service Photo.
The New Home Built by the Lindberghs Near Princeton, From Which Their Child Was Kidnapped Last Night.

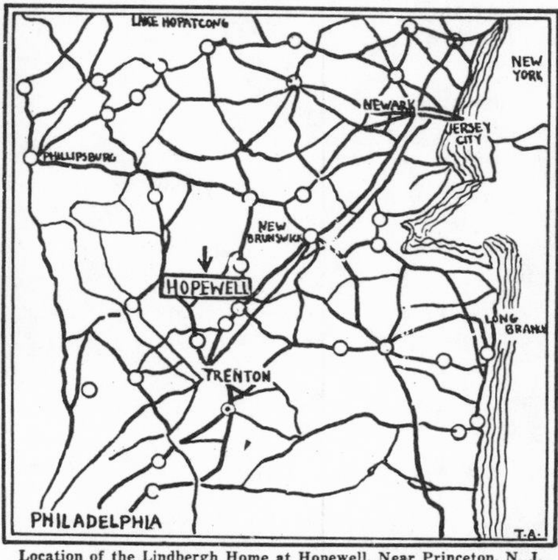

Location of the Lindbergh Home at Hopewell, Near Princeton, N. J.

WORLD HAILED BIRTH OF LINDBERGH'S SON

Wires and Radio Flashed News, Bringing Flood of Messages From All Over Globe.

BORN AT THE MORROW HOME

"Cutest Thing You Ever Saw," Said Will Rogers After Visit Two Weeks Ago.

Charles Augustus Lindbergh Jr. was born at the home of Mrs. Lindbergh's father, the late Ambassador Dwight W. Morrow, in Englewood, N. J., on June 22, 1930. It was Mrs. Lindbergh's twenty-fourth birthday and an occasion for double celebration.

Perhaps nowhere in the world, at any time in history, had a child been the object of such wide public interest as was the Lindbergh child.

At 3 P. M. on the twenty-second of June the news was announced. The Lindbergh baby, weighing between seven and one-half and seven and three-quarter pounds, blinked at the bright Summer sunlight, and the word went flashing round the world by telegraph, cable and wireless.

Reporters who had waited in legions at the gate of the Morrow estate for several days used motor cars to get to the nearest telephones and to the nearest telegraph offices. Radio broadcasters stepped to their microphones and sent the message out over chains of stations.

Strangers Drove to Gate.

Within an hour after the child was born messages began to pour into the Morrow home from everywhere, from people in all walks of life, rich and poor alike. Everybody was interested in the birth of the son of the most famous young man in modern history. Strangers came in long motor processions to the gate of the estate to offer their congratulations.

An hour after the news of the birth of the baby Lindbergh became known, a song based on his arrival was sung from one of the broadcasting stations.

From Mexico City, where Lindbergh wooed and won Miss Anne Morrow for his bride, the telegrams were countless. President Ortiz Rubio sent his personal congratulations and the congratulations of his people. And in far-off France, where the name of Lindbergh was cheered whenever it was mentioned, the nation "adopted" the Lindbergh baby for its own. It was the favorite topic on the boulevards and in thousands of French homes.

Children Brought Flowers.

The long road leading to the Morrow gate became like a path to some sacred shrine, the day after the story of the baby's birth was published. Little children from the town of Englewood and neighboring districts picked bouquets of daisies and other wild flowers, and clutching them in damp palms carried them to the guards for "Lindy's baby."

But the guards had orders to admit no one, even children. Messengers could not get beyond the gate. Only the most intimate friends of the Morrows and the Lindbergs were allowed through. One ingenious individual tried to get by with a brand new baby carriage, but when the guard telephoned to the house the man was turned away. No carriage had been ordered, Colonel Lindbergh said.

For a month the waiting world got few details about the famous baby, but late in July the Colonel said that he and his wife, contemplating a flying trip to the Morrow Summer home in Maine, might take the child with them. The nation waited expectantly, but the trip was finally made without the baby. Mr. and Mrs. Lindbergh changed their plans at the last moment.

Cheated of the vicarious thrill of reading about the baby's flight, mothers throughout the land watched hungrily for other details of its development. Was it to be trained as their children were? A dispatch from Washington in September, 1930, gave the first clue. The baby's first book was to be "The Painted Pig," a work of his grandmother, Mrs. Elizabeth Morrow.

A month later Colonel Lindbergh announced that when the baby reached the proper age he would be permitted to choose his own life work. At the same time it was learned that so many gifts were sent to the child, when news of its birth was broadcast, that the Lindberghs could not find room for them all. They came from every part of the world.

"To acknowledge them individually," said a magazine writer who had interviewed Colonel Lindbergh, "was completely out of the question. To have returned them without a personal explanation to those who sent them would have seemed an ungracious act, while to send the gifts of others to charitable organizations might also have appeared as a signal lack of appreciation." The baby's toys became a real problem and they kept mounting with each new batch of mail from the more distant corners of the globe.

On Oct. 17, 1930, Colonel and Mrs. Lindbergh moved into the home of Harold M. Van Horn near Princeton, N. J., to stay there until the home they were building near Hopewell should be completed.

The child's first birthday, coming with his mother's twenty-fifth, was celebrated at the Morrow Englewood estate. By that time he was a chubby little fellow passing much of his time in the daylight hours on the velvety, spacious lawns.

While his parents were on their flying tour in the Orient last Summer, the child spent part of the season at the Morrow Summer home in Maine and during July, August and September was back at Englewood, awaiting their return. In October he returned with the Morrows to Maine.

Will Rogers, after a visit to the Morrow family two weeks ago, wrote: "The Lindbergh baby is the cutest thing you ever saw, walking, talking, and disgraced the Lindbergh name by crying to come away with Mrs. Rogers and I in the car."

STOLEN CAR CLUE FAILS IN KIDNAPPING SEARCH

Sedan Taken in Atlantic City and Linked to Lindbergh Case Found Near Scene of Theft.

Reports that a green sedan owned by Herbert W. Allen of Margate, N. J., had been used by the kidnappers, gave the police a hope last night that they had a definite clue on which to work, but the hope faded at 1:30 A. M. today when the Allen car was found on Arkansas Avenue at the beach in Atlantic City, a few blocks from where it had been stolen at 9:30 P. M.

Mr. Allen and his wife drove to the Capitol Theatre in Atlantic City from their Margate home, at 8 o'clock last night. When they came out at 10 P. M. the car, a six-cylinder 1924 model, with a top speed of fifty miles, was gone from its parking place in Atlantic Avenue at Maryland Avenue. They rushed to the police station and were reporting the theft just as the teletype alarm telling of the kidnapping was coming through.

Just what happened that gave the impression that the Allen car was used by the kidnappers is not clear. Apparently it was due to some mixup on the telephone. At 11 P. M. reports were broadcast that a dark green sedan, 1924 model, had been seen speeding away from the Lindberghs' Hopewell estate. The reports even contained the license number of the Allen car.

While Mr. Allen, head electrician for the Marlborough-Blenheim Hotel in Atlantic City, was patiently trying to explain that it was physically impossible for any one to have stolen his car at 9:30 P. M.—the time fixed by a cigar store clerk near the theatre who had seen two men get into the sedan—and to have reached Hopewell, ninety miles away, in time to have taken the baby, a report came in that his car had been found.

KIDNAPPERS STEAL THE LINDBERGH BABY

Continued from Page One.

Colonel Lindbergh explained to the reporters, "but I would rather the State Police answered all questions. I am sure you understand how I feel." Mrs. Lindbergh, though greatly shocked by the baby's disappearance, was reported to be bearing up as well as could be expected.

Within a few minutes after word of the kidnapping reached State Police Headquarters at Trenton, all available troopers were ordered out to search automobiles along the highways and an alarm was flashed over the police teletype system in New Jersey and adjacent States.

Guards were posted along all main arteries of traffic leading from New Jersey into New York and Pennsylvania. City and county police cooperated with State troopers in searching all automobiles leaving the State, as well as cars on highways for miles around the Lindbergh home.

The unusual excitement in the vicinity of the Lindbergh home spread rapidly through the neighborhood. When news got abroad that the Lindbergh baby had been kidnapped George Jennings, a laborer, drove to police headquarters in Princeton and told the police how two men in a dark sedan bearing a New York license had stopped him in Washington Road, Princeton, yesterday afternoon and inquired the way to the Lindbergh home. An alarm for the car was sent out over the teletype.

The Philadelphia police were also called into the hunt. New Jersey State troopers requested them to question a man living in Philadelphia. When detectives called at his home, however, they were advised by relatives that he had not been there for two or three days. Asked regarding his whereabouts, the relatives are said to have replied that he was in "a small town near Philadelphia." They explained, too, that the man's absence was nothing unusual since his business often kept him away for several days at a time.

When word reached New York, Police Commissioner Mulrooney, who was at home in bed, was notified. He hurried to Police Headquarters to take personal charge of the hunt here. He ordered special guards posted at once at the entrance to the Holland Tube and the George Washington Memorial Bridge, as well as at all ferry terminals. He also mustered all available Police Department cars and sent them out with orders to search automobiles whose occupants looked suspicious.

Meanwhile the Lindberghs had notified Mrs. Dwight W. Morrow, mother of Mrs. Lindbergh, at her home in Englewood, N. J., and Mrs. Evangeline L. Lindbergh, Colonel Lindbergh's mother, at her home in Grosse Pointe, a suburb of Detroit.

Troopers Guard Home.

Long after last midnight the Lindbergh home at Hopewell was ablaze with lights, while Colonel Lindbergh was kept busy discussing the kidnapping with officials of the State and county police. A trooper stood guard at the entrance of the lane which leads back from the highway to the house. Two more troopers guarded the entrance to the house, while at least a score of others were scattered over the vicinity hunting clues.

Report of a Ransom Note.

The ladder was being carefully examined for fingerprints and the grounds searched for anything that might possibly serve to indicate the identity of the kidnappers. It was reported that a note demanding randemanding ransom had been left by som had been left by the kidnappers in the nursery, but State police denied all knowledge of it.

Colonel Lindbergh agreed with the police that the persons responsible for the kidnapping had been well acquainted with the layout of the house. Neither he nor Mrs. Lindbergh nor any other of the occupants of the house had heard any sounds of prowlers, he said.

Major Schoffel announced that he would obtain from the contractor who built the Lindbergh home a list of every man employed there during the building, and that all of these men would be questioned today by police.

Grandparents Receive Word Of the Lindbergh Kidnapping

ENGLEWOOD, N. J., March 1 (AP).—Mrs. Dwight W. Morrow received the news that her grandson, Charles A. Lindbergh Jr., had been kidnapped shortly before midnight tonight. Mrs. Anne Lindbergh telephoned her mother the news. At the Morrow residence it was said that Mrs. Morrow could not discuss the kidnapping and that she was undecided whether to leave immediately for the Lindbergh home in Hopewell.

DETROIT, March 1 (AP).—Mrs. Evangeline L. Lindbergh, mother of Colonel Charles A. Lindbergh, received word of her grandson's kidnapping tonight and left at once for an unannounced destination.

At her home in suburban Grosse Pointe it was said she was greatly disturbed. It could not be learned whether she would go to New Jersey.

PAIR STABBED AT 42D ST.

Father and Son Lay Attack at Elevated Station to Strikers.

Samuel Kursmer, 60 years old, and his son, Leo, 26 years old, of 2,179 Washington Avenue, the Bronx, were attacked early last night on a stairway of the I. R. T. elevated station at Third Avenue and Forty-second Street, by three men who had trailed them from Brooklyn. Both were stabbed several times. They managed to get into a taxicab and were taken to Flower Hospital in serious condition. Their assailants escaped in the crowd.

At the hospital the elder Kursmer told detectives that he and his son were employed as pressers in the shop of the Miami Dress Company at 3,515 Twelfth Avenue, Brooklyn. They are right-wing union workers, he said, and left-wing union workers from the shop are on strike. They believed the assailants were hired thugs.

FOUR STATES HUNT FOR MISSING BABY

Continued from Page One.

kidnappers and the remote hope that perhaps somehow the baby had managed to make its way out of the house alone.

Troopers meanwhile were speeding from the barracks at Morristown to the north, and from Trenton, to augment the searchers on the scene, while additional details were posted at every cross road to complete a cordon about the neighborhood and stop all cars for questioning.

Through the agency of the teletype the alarm reached the police of New York, Newark, Jersey City, Elizabeth, Camden, and Philadelphia within a few minutes of the receipt of the first alarm at Trenton. All of them quickly swung into action, as did the New York and Pennsylvania State police.

The word reached Police Headquarters here at 10:45 P. M. and was immediately relayed to Commissioner Mulrooney, Chief Inspector John O'Brien, and Assistant Chief Inspector John J. Sullivan, in command of detectives, all of whom rushed to headquarters to direct the New York efforts to assist in the search.

Orders were flashed to every precinct by the police telegraph system to be on the alert for suspicious cars, while the new police radio station, WPEG, flashed word to the shortwave station of the patrolling detective cars to join in the watch.

Similar steps, though on a smaller scale, were being repeated simultaneously in every city for many miles around the Lindbergh home. Posses of motorcycle and bandit squad policemen from Philadelphia, and Pennsylvania and New Jersey State troopers, clamped down a heavy guard on every bridge over the Delaware River.

The special police who patrol the Holland Tunnel and the new George Washington Bridge over the Hudson took similar precautions here last night.

Meanwhile through the "major control" of the State signal system at Hawthorne, N. Y., the word was being relayed to all the up-State cities

STOLEN CARS HELD CLUES.

Police Send Out Alarm for Sixteen in Kidnapping Hunt.

The police expressed the belief early today that the automobile in which the Lindbergh baby was kidnapped was undoubtedly a stolen machine. A list of sixteen automobiles reported stolen from different parts of New Jersey between noon yesterday and midnight was broadcast early today. The list, with license numbers, follows:

Chysler sedan, E-70,794 N. J., stolen in Newark.
Chevrolet coach, H-5,866 N. J., stolen at Camden.
Graham-Paige, C-21,917, N. J., stolen at Camden.
Buick sedan, E-24,437 N. J., stolen at Camden.
Franklin sedan, U-60,940 N. J., stolen at Irvington.
Willys-Knight sedan 1-E-8,361 N. J., stolen at Newark.
Chevrolet sedan, E-71,624 N. J., stolen at Belleville.
Buick sedan, E-13,840 N. J., stolen at Newark.
Hudson sedan, 1-E-54,006 N. J., stolen at Newark.
Buick coupe, K-34,607 N. J., stolen at Newark.
Buick sedan, 096,009 N. J., stolen at Lakewood.
Pontiac sedan, Z-12,852 N. J., stolen at Sweedesburg.
Ford coach, C-25-377 N. J., stolen at Camden.
Buick sedan, C-22,899 N. J., stolen at Camden.
Auburn sedan, C-24,837 N. J., stolen at Hammond.
Chrysler sedan, A-1,153 N. J., stolen at Atlantic City.

FATHER SEARCHES GROUNDS FOR CHILD

Continued from Page One.

trouble. Almost surrounding the house are dense woods.

The police, dashing pell-mell to the place, were delayed by the muddy roads. It was an hour before they reached the house, which is perched on the second highest eminence in New Jersey in an isolated region.

Rummaging around the ghostly estate, the Associated Press reporter ran into a party of four men near the entrance to the Lindbergh's private road, a mile from the house. Each of the group had flashlights and were shooting their beams in all directions in an effort to pick up more clues. An old deserted house stood near the entrance but it revealed nothing.

"Are you State police?" the reporter questioned.

"Who are you?" was the answer, and the reporter recognized Colonel Lindbergh. He showed the strain of the ordeal, but shook hands with the reporter when he had introduced himself.

"I'm sorry, but I can't tell you anything now," the Colonel said.

The Lindbergh baby is described as a golden-haired replica of his famous father. He is chubby, with blue eyes and curly hair. He was of about normal stature for his age, had begun to toddle about and was learning to talk.

His nursery, filled with every device for childish joy, is in the right-hand corner of the second floor of the big house. The window near his crib, which was open when his nurse went into the room, is thirty feet from the ground. A three-piece ladder was found a hundred feet from the house, as if it had been dropped in a hurry, and police believe this was used to reach the window, which looks out on the private road.

Besides the Lindberghs, the only persons in the house at the time of the kidnapping were Betty Gow, the baby's nurse; the butler, Ollie Wheatley, and his wife. It had been the Lindberghs' custom to spend week-ends only at the country place, but on Saturday they decided to remain all this week.

As news of the kidnapping spread through the friendly countryside, automobiles raced to the scene. Two hundred police were stationed in the vicinity in an effort to keep the traffic from clogging, but, even so, many machines came to a standstill in the narrow road.

State Trooper Michael Hullfish of Hopewell was foreman of the construction gang when the home was built and gave police the names of fifty men employed on the job, all of whom will be questioned.

AUNT OF BABY NOTIFIED.

But News of Kidnapping Is Kept From Great-Grandmother.

CLEVELAND, March 1 (AP).—Mrs. Dwight W. Morrow, grandmother of the missing Lindbergh baby, late tonight notified her sister, Miss Anne Spencer Cutter, over long-distance telephone from the Morrow home in Englewood, N. J., that her grandson had been kidnapped.

The news was withheld for the time being from Mrs. Morrow's mother, Mrs. Charles Long Cutter, in the fear that the shock might have serious effects because of her advanced age. Miss Cutter said she was undecided about going East.

Mrs. Morrow told her sister she could furnish no details because she had been unable to reach the Lindbergh home at Hopewell, N. J., by telephone.

SIX STATES IN DRIVE AGAINST KIDNAPPING

Promoters Declare Abduction Syndicate Is Ranking Racketeering Body in the Country.

CHICAGO, March 1 (AP).—The kidnapping of the young son of Colonel and Mrs. Charles A. Lindbergh comes at a time when civic and law enforcement officials of a half dozen States, aroused at the depredations of organized extortionists, are clamoring for Federal intervention.

Headed by Colonel Robert I. Randolph, former head of the Chicago Association of Commerce, Walter B. Weisenburger, president of the St. Louis Chamber of Commerce and others, these authorities have petitioned Congress for legislation making kidnapping a Federal offense. The system of relaying victims from one State to another employed by the allied extortion gangs hampers prosecution due to State extradition red tape, once the gangsters are apprehended, they contend.

Chief of Police Joseph Gerk of St. Louis, one of those who appeared before the House postal committee last week in behalf of the proposed legislation, has gathered statistics listing 208 kidnappings for ransom officially reported in 1931 and "at least ten times that number not reported." The kidnapping syndicate has been termed the ranking racketeering body of America today.

Describing its efficient organization, Alexander Jamie, chief investigator of the "Secret Six," said one of the gangs usually selects a victim in a town where it has headquarters but passes the word along to an allied combine to carry out the actual abduction. If local officials pick up the trail, the kidnappers immediately move their victim into another State and give him into the keeping of another gang. If the investigation proceeds with any degree of success, the victim may be relayed to various gangs in several States and, as usual, when likely suspects are picked up and the rendezvous of known kidnappers raided, no evidence which would aid in conviction is found.

In the metropolitan Chicago area alone, where more than a hundred such abductions have occurred in the past two years with losses to victims of millions of dollars, evidence substantial enough to warrant indictments has been gathered against only seven suspects.

The enormity of kidnapping operations in the United States was shown in a statement by Colonel Randolph and other leaders in the drive against it. They estimated that 2,000 persons paid ransom for release from abductors in the past two years.

LINDBERGH HOME FINISHED LAST FALL

Stone Structure Stands on a Hill-Top Overlooking Hopewell 3 Miles Away.

DISTRICT HEAVILY WOODED

Several Other Estates Located in Surrounding Area, Known as Sorrel Mountains.

The home of Colonel and Mrs. Charles A. Lindbergh, near Hopewell, N. J., from which their 20 months old son, Charles Augustus Lindbergh Jr., was kidnapped last night, is on Sourland Mountain, about ten miles north of Princeton in the centre of the Colonel's 350-acre estate.

Built of native field stone, covered with a white cement wash, the house, a rambling two and a half story structure, overlooks Hopewell, which is three miles away. It was not completed until late last October and the Lindberghs did not move into it until about five months after they had cut short their Asiatic tour after the death of Mrs. Lindbergh's father, the late Senator Dwight W. Morrow.

The interior is simply furnished, in keeping with the distaste of both Colonel and Mrs. Lindbergh for display. The house contains ten rooms, including several bedrooms overlooking the Hopewell Valley. On the ground floor are the living rooms, connected through French doors with a large porch, a dining room and a wing in which the kitchen is located.

For miles around the territory is densely wooded, very little of the district, known officially as the Sorrel Mountains, being cultivated. A number of other estates are in the neighborhood. Two small clearings of farm land are contained in the Lindbergh estate.

The Lindberghs picked the site of their home from the air as they were flying together over the Jersey forests seeking a suitable spot. It was selected for complete privacy, an aim which was achieved. It is far off the regular highways and can be reached only by dirt and gravel roads which wind through the dense woods. The only immediate neighbors are farmers, who live a simple rural existence and with whom the Lindberghs have had little to do.

In back of the house are dense woods, through which passage can be made only by following the long unused paths. In front and on both sides is open country. A quarter of a mile from the structure the meadows form a natural landing field for airplanes. However, the Colonel has made it a practice to motor back and forth to his New York office.

Fifteen miles to the west is the Delaware River, which is bridged there at Lambertville. A few miles to the south two of the main highways, Routes 29 and 31, cross. Also a few miles away to the east is the old main line road which connects New Brunswick and Princeton.

KIDNAPPING OF BABY SPEEDS FEDERAL LAW

Continued from Page One.

taken place in the Middle West and West:

California, 25; Indiana, 20; Illinois, 49; Kansas, 8; Michigan, 26; Oklahoma, 9; Wisconsin, 8; Nebraska, 6; Massachusetts, 15, and New Jersey 10.

Representative Cochran early this morning declared that the government was powerless, and said this act would undoubtedly result in the early passage of his bill in the House.

"The Federal authorities can punish a person who takes an automobile across a State line, or they can punish violators of the Mann act. But when they take a human across a line for the purpose of demanding ransom the authorities are helpless. The kidnappers can even use the mail to demand ransom from the Lindbergh family tomorrow if they want to, yet nothing can be done to punish them."

Attorney General Mitchell, whose department is expected to cooperate in the attempted apprehension of the kidnappers, said he could not comment at so late an hour.

Kidnapping Rumors a Year Ago.

ENGLEWOOD, N. J., Wednesday, March 2 (AP).—Just a year ago reports were broadcast that Constance Morrow, youngest sister of Mrs. Anne Morrow Lindbergh, was in danger of kidnapping. Details of the suspected kidnapping plot were never divulged, but it was understood that for weeks Miss Morrow was under constant special guard.

"All the News That's Fit to Print."

The New York Times.

LATE CITY EDITION
WEATHER—Fair and slightly warmer today and tomorrow.
Temperatures Yesterday—Max., 46; min., 37.

VOL. LXXXII....No. 27,401. Entered as Second-Class Matter, Postoffice, New York, N. Y. NEW YORK, TUESDAY, JANUARY 31, 1933. **** TWO CENTS In New York City. | THREE CENTS Within 200 Miles | FOUR CENTS Elsewhere Except in 7th and 8th Postal Zones

HITLER MADE CHANCELLOR OF GERMANY BUT COALITION CABINET LIMITS POWER; CENTRISTS HOLD BALANCE IN REICHSTAG

GROUP FORMED BY PAPEN

Nationalists to Dominate in Government Led by National Socialist.

DR. HUGENBERG GETS POST

Frick In Interior Ministry to Control Police, but Army Has Non-Partisan Chief.

REDS URGE STRIKE TODAY

Cabinet Stresses That It Will Not Attempt Monetary or Economic Experiments.

By GUIDO ENDERIS.

Special Cable to THE NEW YORK TIMES.

BERLIN, Jan. 30.—Adolf Hitler, leader of the National Socialist party, today was appointed Chancellor of Germany after being twice rejected last year for that office.

Herr Hitler was manoeuvred into heading a coalition government of National Socialists and Nationalists by Lieut. Col. Franz von Papen, former Chancellor. The new Cabinet is a compromise between a Presidential and a Parliamentary government.

The composition of the Cabinet leaves Herr Hitler no scope for gratification of any dictatorial ambition. He accepted the Chancellorship on less sweeping terms than he laid down in his audiences with the President in August and November of last year. He swore obedience to the republican Constitution today after the President had accepted Colonel von Papen's Cabinet slate.

The New Cabinet.

The new Cabinet is composed as follows:

Chancellor—Adolf Hitler.
Vice Chancellor and Reich Commissioner for Prussia—Lieut. Col. Franz von Papen.
Foreign Minister—Baron Constantin von Neurath.
Interior Minister—Dr. Wilhelm F. Frick.
Defense Minister—General Werner von Blomberg.
Finance Minister—Count Lutz Schwerin von Krosigk.
Economy and Food Minister—Dr. Alfred Hugenberg.
Labor Minister—Franz Seldte.
Transportation Minister—Baron Paul Eltz von Ruebenach.
Aviation Minister—Hermann Wilhelm Goering.
Employment Commissioner — Guenther Gereke.

Dr. Frick, former Interior Minister of Thuringia, and Herr Goering are Hitler's leading aides. Baron von Neurath, Count Schwerin von Krosigk and Baron von Ruebenach are holdovers from the Cabinet of Lieut. Gen. Kurt von Schleicher, which fell Saturday. Herr Goering also will be Acting Minister of Interior of Prussia. Herr Seldte is a leader of the Stahlhelm (Steel Helmet veterans' society) and stands far to the Right politically.

Ultimatum From Hindenburg.

President von Hindenburg had no personal contact with Herr Hitler during the negotiations leading to formation of the Cabinet, but informed quarters say the President threatened to precipitate a Presidential crisis unless Herr Hitler and Dr. Hugenberg made peace and got down to business. This ultimatum enabled Colonel von Papen to round up his new Cabinet without further parleys and march it before President von Hindenburg shortly after noon. It was immediately sworn in.

The speed with which it was projected into office is said to have bewildered Herr Hitler even more than its other members and left him cogitating on whether he had been stampeded into taking the Chancellorship on anything but his own terms.

Colonel von Papen kept his plans so secret that most of the afternoon papers, including Herr Hitler's official organ, were compelled to make over their regular evening editions to tell of the formation of the new Cabinet.

The National Socialists are in a minority in the Cabinet. The Chancellor's activities are severely limited through the presence in his Cabinet of Colonel von Papen, Baron von Neurath, Count Schwerin von Krosigk, Dr. Hugenberg and Herr Seldte. The preponderance of Conservatives is believed to have de-

Continued on Page Three.

Hitler Pledges Fight in Cabinet

By the Associated Press.

BERLIN, Jan. 30.—A proclamation emphasizing that the present Cabinet is not truly representative of Hitlerism and the nation was issued today by the new Chancellor, Adolf Hitler. In it the Nazi leader announced a determination to "carry on the fight within the government as tenaciously as we fought outside."

"After a thirteen-year struggle the National Socialist movement has succeeded in breaking through to the government; the struggle to win the German nation, however, is only beginning," the proclamation said.

"The National Socialist party knows that the new government is no National Socialist Government, but it is conscious that it bears the name of its leader, Adolf Hitler. He has advanced with his shock troops and has placed himself at the head of the government to lead the German people to liberty.

"Not only is the entire authority of State ready to be wielded, but in the background, prepared for action, is the National Socialist movement of millions of followers united unto death with its leaders. Our historic mission is now in the field of political economy."

Calling Herr Hitler's appointment "historic," the document lauded President von Hindenburg with these words:

"In this hour we wish to thank President von Hindenburg, whose immortal fame as a Field Marshal in the battlefields of the World War binds his name perpetually to that of young Germany, which is striving with burning heart to gain its liberty."

MODERATE CABINET PLANNED IN FRANCE

Daladier Is Unable to Get Socialist Support and Turns to Centre.

HITLER IS MADE AN ISSUE

Premier-Designate Rejects Left Demands for Cut in Military Budget on Berlin News.

By P. J. PHILIP.

Wireless to THE NEW YORK TIMES.

PARIS, Tuesday, Jan. 31.—France this morning was moving rapidly toward a new governmental alignment. Balked by the demands of the Socialists in forming a Cabinet with a Left orientation, Edouard Daladier, the Radical Premier-designate, turned with greater success to the Centre parties for collaboration.

M. Daladier announced at 1 A. M. that he expected to complete his Cabinet during the morning and to submit the list to President Lebrun this afternoon. In addition to the Premiership, he expects to take the portfolio of War, which he held in the fallen Cabinet of Joseph Paul-Boncour. M. Paul-Boncour, in the new line-up, would be Foreign Minister.

Other selections announced by M. Daladier are Georges Bonnet as Finance Minister, Lucien Lamoureux as Minister of the Budget, Camille Chautemps as Minister of the Interior, Henri Queuille as Minister of Agriculture, Georges Leygues as Minister of Marine, Anatole de Monzie as Minister of Education and Laurent Eynac as Minister of Posts and Telegraphs.

Hitler's Rise a Factor.

The shift in party alignment is undoubtedly due in part to the selection of Adolf Hitler as Chancellor of Germany, but there are two other big factors. The first is the discontent which has been growing strongly in this country during the past two months against Parliamentary government and the second is the definite split which occurred today between the Radicals and the Socialists.

Twice within six weeks the Socialists, by withdrawing their support, have overthrown radical Cabinets. Today they imposed unacceptable conditions for their collaboration or support.

Whether M. Daladier can form a Cabinet independent of the Socialists and whether, if he succeeds, he will be able to get sufficient support on the Right in Parliament remain uncertain. Even within his own party there is a strong faction opposed to association with the Right. Furthermore, there is no certainty the Centre will accept a Cabinet under such a strongly Radical leader. But M. Daladier has strong support in the Senate, which is controlled by the Radical party.

Yesterday was spent in negotiations between M. Daladier and the Socialist leaders and among the Socialists themselves. M. Daladier first, however, took the precaution to discuss the budget situation with the finance leaders of his own party, Georges Bonnet, Lucien Lamoureux and Louis Malvy. Then, on sure ground as to the extent to which his party would go in meet-

Continued on Page Six.

HOOVER SKEPTICAL OF SUCCESS ON DEBT

Sees Roosevelt Making Wrong Approach—Holds Economic Topics Should Come First.

QUICK ACTION HIS AIM

He Favored Joint Stand With Britain at World Parley—London Discusses Debts.

By ARTHUR KROCK.

Special to THE NEW YORK TIMES.

WASHINGTON, Jan. 30.—Since the visit of Sir Ronald Lindsay, British Ambassador, to President-elect Roosevelt at Warm Springs, President Hoover has necessarily taken a back seat in the making of arrangements for the coming of the representatives of Great Britain to Washington after Mr. Roosevelt takes office. The fact that the journey was undertaken on the suggestion of the President-elect, who wished to make his position clear to the British Cabinet through the Ambassador instead of through Mr. Hoover's State Department, virtually eliminated the President and Secretary Stimson as active factors.

Mr. Hoover and those who have worked with him closely on the war debts problem have scrupulously kept the pledge of silence made at the White House conferences, so far as the press is concerned. No amount of questioning has induced them to discuss the fundamental difference in method between the administration and Mr. Roosevelt. They have declined even to talk about it in confidence with their newspaper friends.

But, in a situation like this one, certain facts become known to under-officials, and they slowly emerge. It was in this way that THE NEW YORK TIMES correspondent learned that Norman H. Davis had been responsible for adding the clause in the joint communiqué from the White House that extended the invitation to British "representatives" to come here for a concurrent discussion of economic problems of mutual interest to the two nations at the same time the debt "representative" was asked to appear in Washington.

More Facts Transpire.

By the same route other facts about the Roosevelt-Hoover debt situation have now become known, although Mr. Hoover and Secretaries Mills and Stimson continue to refuse to confirm, deny or privately converse about what has passed between "the two Presidents" and Mr. Stimson. Among these facts are:

The President feels that his successor has been going about the debt-discussion business in the wrong way and that he has got himself into a "hole." From the first it has been Mr. Hoover's position that economic topics of common Anglo-American interest should be discussed first between British and American representatives. Tentative agreement having been reached, it was the President's plan that the two nations should then move promptly into the World Economic Conference

Continued on Page Four.

NEW BRITISH RATES AFFECT U. S. GOODS FINISHED IN CANADA

After April 1, 50 Per Cent 'Empire Content' Is Required for Preferential Duty.

1,000 PLANTS INVOLVED

Many Expected to Be Moved to England or Withdrawn to United States.

HUGE CAPITAL AT STAKE

$1,500,000,000 Invested in Factories in Dominion—Political Struggle There Foreseen.

Special Cable to THE NEW YORK TIMES.

LONDON, Jan. 30.—United States manufacturers who apply minor finishing touches on their goods in Canada and then send them to Great Britain under imperial tariff preferences as "empire goods" will lose that privilege under an order issued by the Board of Trade tonight.

"Certain classes of empire goods imported into Britain," the order says, "in order to qualify for the imperial preferences agreed upon at Ottawa, must contain in the future a minimum of 50 per cent of empire material and labor instead of 25 per cent as at present."

The regulation will go into effect April 1. The list of goods affected is being withheld.

The Board of Trade regulations are being published as "Import Duties [Imperial Preferences] No. 1 Regulations, 1933." Copies, including a schedule of the goods on which the increased percentage applies, will soon be issued by the government printer.

William Watson, chairman of the industries committee of the Scottish National Development Council, recently said he had heard Canadian manufacturers refer to the British tariffs as a "huge joke." One hundred and fifty American companies, he added, had established branch plants in Canada in the last fifteen months, and, since the empire labor content required only 25 per cent, the activities of these factories in the majority of cases were purely nominal. The Laborite Daily Herald says the new regulation is aimed primarily at the United States.

1,000 Plants Involved.

The order of the British Board of Trade raising the empire content on goods exported from Canada to the United Kingdom from 25 to 50 per cent strikes a blow at the more than 1,000 American branch plants in Canada which have been established across the border in order to enjoy the advantages of preferences granted on exports from Canada to Britain. These branch plants, owned by the greatest industrial organizations in the United States, represent an investment estimated by some at $1,500,000,000.

The raising of the quota of empire content on goods to enjoy imperial preference was a heatedly debated question at the Imperial Economic Conference at Ottawa last August. While the Canadians demanded that the British requirement be raised to meet the Canadian, which ranges between 50 and 60 per cent, the British were not inclined to meet this demand, regarding it as excessive.

The conference finally agreed to take no official action on the matter but to leave it to the discre-

Continued on Page Four.

MORTGAGEES STAY $200,000,000 DEBT OF IOWA'S FARMERS

Insurance Companies Here Act to Suspend Foreclosures Pending Legal Relief.

GOVERNOR'S PLEA HEEDED

Policy Announced by New York Life Followed by Other Eastern Organizations.

NEBRASKA NAMES BOARD

Bryan Appoints Seven Conciliators as Debtors' Resistance Drive Spreads Through West.

In the most extensive private effort to cooperate with the owners of mortgaged farms ever made, a number of the leading Eastern life insurance companies, with nearly $200,000,000 invested in Iowa farms, have decided to suspend foreclosure activities throughout that State until the Legislature can enact its program to improve the position of the debtors.

This decision became known yesterday after the publication of an announcement of such a policy in behalf of his own company only, by Thomas A. Buckner, president of the New York Life Insurance Company. This company has been the object of stormy criticism in Iowa.

Although the other companies are not planning any formal statement, it was revealed that Mr. Buckner's announcement substantially outlined the general procedure for the present.

Yesterday's action came partly as a result of the recent proclamation by Governor Clyde Herring of Iowa, asking all holders of realty mortgages to refrain from foreclosing until the Legislature has had time to act, and partly as a gesture on the part of the Eastern underwriters to overcome some of the bad feeling toward them that has been engendered in the last month.

No Action on Other States.

As far as could be determined, the insurance companies are not at present planning similar action with respect to mortgages in other States. They regard the Iowa situation as peculiar to that State, because of certain laws now on the statute books there which make it possible for holders of chattel mortgages and other liens, which are in reality secondary to the first mortgages, to foreclose.

In defense of the forced sales of Iowa farms in the last month, insurance officials said many of these had been brought about, not through any effort on their part or any desire to foreclose, but because of the demands of the holders of secondary claims.

It is contended that with public sentiment in Iowa running as strongly against the Eastern insurance companies as it is, it has become extremely difficult to obtain the cooperation with individual mortgagors which is necessary for effecting renewals, and that, of course, such renewals are impossible where local holders of second mortgages and other liens insist on pressing their claims.

The attention of the East was first drawn to the situation generally when a group of 800 farmers forced the New York Life Insurance Company to raise its bid from $3,000 to $33,000 on a farm being sold at

Continued on Page Eight.

Roosevelt, at 51, Celebrates His Birthday; Cuts 80-Pound Cake for Georgia Children

Special to THE NEW YORK TIMES.

WARM SPRINGS, Ga., Jan. 30.—Franklin D. Roosevelt today celebrated his fifty-first birthday anniversary by cutting an eighty-pound birthday cake in the presence of 150 patients and staff members of the Warm Springs Foundation and by a dinner at his cottage, which was attended by members of his family and James A. Farley, Frank C. Walker, Edward J. Flynn and Henry Morgenthau Jr.

The ceremony of cutting the birthday cake brought much pleasure to nearly ninety crippled patients, who regard Mr. Roosevelt with great affection. The cake, the gift of the four sons of the President-elect, was placed in the centre of a long table in the dining room of Meriwether Inn, around which were crowded some of the older patients in wheeled chairs and all the children.

As Mr. Roosevelt entered and took his seat the patients began to chant, "A happy birthday, Mr. Roosevelt." The shrill voices of children rose high.

After photographers had taken pictures of Mr. Roosevelt, Mrs. Roosevelt and the group, the President-elect, addressing the children particularly, said:

"Now let's all blow together, and blow out the candles."

This was accomplished with the expenditure of much childish breath and much laughter.

"You may think that there is only one surgeon here, but I am going to show you that there are two," said the President-elect, wielding a large knife on the cake.

The first slice went to Mrs. Roosevelt, and he continued cutting until the waiters had served every person in the room.

Mr. Roosevelt, as cheers resounded, announced the gift of a check of $1,000 from an anonymous donor for the patients' aid fund. He remained at the hotel for more than an hour, chatting with the patients. The dinner at his cottage was private.

LEHMAN ASKS $84,000,000 IN NEW TAXES, 1% ON '33 GROSS INCOMES, ¾% ON SALES; STATE BUDGET CUT 23% TO $234,998,531

Gov. Lehman's Revenue Proposals

Special to THE NEW YORK TIMES.

ALBANY, Jan. 30.—Governor Lehman's chief proposals on the budget included the following:

INCOME TAXES—Lowering of exemptions for a single person from $2,500 to $1,000 and a married person from $4,000 to $2,500, the $400 exemption for dependents to remain unchanged. Emergency rate to be continued. Establishment of a 1 per cent gross income tax, no personal exemption allowed, on every single person whose income is $1,000 or more and every married person whose income is $2,500 or more. Capital gains and losses excluded, and interest, bad debts, contributions and other actual losses subtracted. This tax, an emergency levy for one year, to be in addition to the regular State income tax. Both the lowered exemption and the emergency tax to be applicable on 1933 incomes, payable in April, 1934.

SALES TAX—Enactment of a three-quarter of 1 per cent levy on retail sales of all tangible personal property, exclusive of food products and motor fuel, effective from April 1, 1933, to June 30, 1934.

MOTOR FUEL TAX—An increase of 1 per cent per gallon, as an emergency levy effective from April 1, 1933, to June 30, 1934, making the tax per gallon 4 cents.

SALARIES—Reductions for State employes receiving more than $2,000 a year of from 6 per cent on the first $2,000 to 33.9 per cent on that portion of a salary exceeding $15,000.

FEES FOR PAMPHLETS—Reports and other documents of departments to be charged for on a basis to cover the cost of preparation and publication.

PUBLIC SERVICE FEE—Authorization for the commission to charge against a company investigated a part of the cost of such inquiry.

MACHADO SAYS FOES STIR CUBAN UNREST

President Accuses Them of Killing Innocent Persons in Terror Campaign.

DENIES HE IS A DICTATOR

Opposition Is Open, Courts Are Free and Curbs Are Bar to Anarchy, He Asserts.

By RUSSELL PORTER.

Special Cable to THE NEW YORK TIMES.

HAVANA, Jan. 30.—President Machado, in an interview at the Presidential Palace today, denied that his government is a dictatorship and insisted that a majority of the Cuban people are supporting him. He promised to hold an honest Presidential election next year, at which, he said, he would not be a candidate for a third term.

Replying to charges of the Opposition that he is trying to perpetuate his own régime by illegal, unconstitutional and repressive methods, General Machado asserted he would resign his office "tomorrow" if he could do so without endangering peace and order. To charges that hundreds of political prisoners have been killed after arrest by his secret police, that hundreds have been kept in prison incommunicado for months and other hundreds exiled, he replied that those killed were members of a radical terroristic group who had attacked police, that only ten or fifteen political prisoners are now in prison and that those in exile had left the country voluntarily.

Opposed to Intervention.

President Machado declared himself unequivocably opposed to any intervention by the United States to straighten out the tangled situation here.

The above is a summary of written answers which the President returned through a government press attaché to a questionnaire which this reporter was required to submit in order to obtain an interview. The President granted a brief personal interview, which was attended by Dr. Orestes Ferrara, the Secretary of State, and an interpreter, as General Machado speaks only a few words of English.

In an informal oral interview before the questionnaire was answered, President Machado conceded that he had committed some unjust acts. Every head of a State sometimes had to do unjust things as well as just ones, he argued. But he had received many injustices as well as given them, he continued, and he thought the things he had done for the good of Cuba more than balanced the injustices. In everything he had done, he said, he had done his duty to Cuba as he saw it, in the same spirit and on the same ground as his service for Cuba in the Army of Liberation in the rebellion against Spain.

Machado Mild in Appearance.

President Machado is an inscrutable, enigmatic person, who is the

Continued on Page Six.

NEW POLICE FEES TO BRING IN $791,404

O'Brien Approves Mulrooney's Proposal to Raise Present Charges and Add Others.

TAXI LICENSES DOUBLED

Mayor and Tremaine Confer on Water and Finance—Justices Take 10% Cut.

Mayor O'Brien took the first definite step yesterday toward building up new revenues for the city when he approved suggestions for increasing old fees charged by the Police Department and for adding new charges. The changes will provide altogether an increased revenue of $791,404.

Police Commissioner Mulrooney listed his suggestions in response to a letter from the Mayor last December in which all city department heads were asked to submit proposals to increase the city's revenues this year. Mayor O'Brien said the Police Commissioner's proposals were covered in a general way in the findings of the Mayor's committee on new sources of revenue, but he emphasized that the credit for them went to Mr. Mulrooney.

Present fees will be increased in accordance with Mr. Mulrooney's schedule, to provide an added return amounting to $502,704 a year, while the new charges will bring in $288,700. Mr. O'Brien said that ordinances would be prepared where necessary to put the charges into effect. The Police Department can increase some of the fees without such action.

$50,000 From One Levy.

Among the new fees is a $5 charge for testing low-pressure boilers in hotels and apartment houses. No charge is now made by the Police Department. The levy is expected to bring in $50,000 a year. The department also proposed a fee of $1 for qualifying examinations for various classes of stationary and portable engineers and firemen, estimating the yield at $2,500 a year from this source.

Certificates for the successful candidates approved by the Police Department for these positions are to be charged for at the rate of $5 each, producing new income estimated at $10,000 a year. Renewal certificates issued each year would be subject to a new charge of $1 each, bringing the city $10,900.

The department makes about 60,000 searches of its records every year for private corporations. Mr. Mulrooney suggested a fee of $1 for the first five years on this service and 25 cents for each succeeding year. He estimated the income at $60,000.

Suburban real estate buses, which pay no fees to the Police Department, will be charged $10 each for the privilege of using the city streets. The estimated receipts are $2,000 a year.

Law firms desiring transcripts of police arrest records, previously fur-

Continued on Page Eleven.

CENT ADDED ON GASOLINE

Sales Impost Proposed on All Retail Items Except Food.

FOR LOWER EXEMPTIONS

Governor Suggests Drop of $1,500—Pay Cut for State Employes Urged.

BUDGET SMALLEST SINCE '25

Deficit of $105,900,000 and Relief Measures Partly Offset Big Cuts in Appropriations.

Text of Governor Lehman's Budget Message, Pages 12 and 13.

By W. A. WARN.

Special to THE NEW YORK TIMES.

ALBANY, Jan. 30.—New or additional taxes, of an aggregate of $84,000,000, were recommended by Governor Lehman in his annual budget message, which was transmitted to the Legislature this evening with his constitutional budget bill, calling for total appropriations for the next fiscal year from all funds and for all purposes of $234,998,531, a decrease of 23.7 per cent.

The principal new revenues would be derived from drastic increases in the personal income taxes, estimated at $46,000,000; from a retail sales tax, with an estimated yield of $23,000,000, and an increase of 1 cent per gallon in the State tax on motor fuel, calculated to produce $15,000,000.

The increase in personal income tax consists of a lowering of exemptions to the Federal levels and establishment of a new 1 per cent emergency tax on gross income, without exemptions, but with some deductions. These changes would affect incomes of the calendar year 1933 on which tax would be paid in April, 1934.

The budget message contained no figures on a prospective beer tax. Upon consideration, the Governor said, he had decided not to include any estimate of revenues from that source, inasmuch as Congress had not yet acted favorably on the proposal to legalize beer.

"I reserve the right to submit amendments to this revenue program if and when Congress legalizes the sale of beer," the Governor said.

"In the event that Congress modifies the Volstead act so as to make possible the sale of beer, a considerable amount of revenue—although probably not so much as many assume—can be realized on the sale of that beverage."

To Meet $105,000,000 Deficit.

The Governor pointed out in his message that, although this year's budget total would be lower than any since 1925, new revenues would be necessary to dispose of an accumulated net deficit on June 30, the end of the current fiscal year, estimated at 105,900,000, and leave something like an adequate cash surplus on June 30, 1934, the end of the fiscal year for which the present budget is made will expire.

This is necessary even though the estimated intake from taxes already in force during the intervening period should leave about $24,000,000 in excess of the amounts appropriated which could be applied toward wiping out the deficit.

The amount of additional taxes asked is considerably below forecasts made which in some instances have run well in excess of $100,000,000. Governor Lehman himself recently estimated the latter figure would be necessary.

The comparatively low budget was made possible by material reductions in appropriations made for the administrative departments including graduated cuts in all salaries above $2,000, received by State officials and employes not protected by the Constitution in their salary rights, together with reductions in amount of State aid to the common schools and for county and town highway purposes.

The Governor himself, whose salary is fixed by the Constitution, largely as an example to other State officials, has ordered a volun-

Continued on Page Thirteen.

HITLER PUTS ASIDE AIM TO BE DICTATOR

German Cabinet Also Reveals Shift by Conservatives Who Once Barred Him.

NAZI'S RISE WAS RAPID

Imprisoned for Munich Revolt in 1923, He Later Led 6,000,000 in National Election.

LONG AN ALIEN IN REICH

Industrialists of Rhineland and the Ruhr Are Believed to Have Forced Coalition Rule.

Adolf Hitler's acceptance of the German Chancellorship in a coalition with conservatives and non-partisans marks a radical departure rom his former demand that he be nade "the Mussolini of Germany" s a condition to his assumption of overnment responsibility. It represents at the same time a recession rom their former position by President Hindenburg and the Conservatives, who hitherto had been set gainst entrusting the Chancellorship to Hitler although willing to ermit him to participate in the overnment. The net result is not ltered thereby.

For the first time in his spectacular and tempestuous career Hitler now called upon to prove in deed hat he has been promising in word the many millions of his supporters. He takes office at a time hen his own party is passing hrough a severe internal crisis, expressed in a bitter factional struggle etween extremists who have insted on extra-constitutional action nd the more moderate elements ho have maintained that the party ould not continue in the Opposion forever and could survive only hrough constructive participation the government.

This factional struggle, in which e Nazi leader had tried to placate oth sides, assumed acute form last ecember with the resignation of e leaders of the more moderate ction, Gregor Strasser and Gottied Feder. Strasser was Hitler's hief executive. Feder was the arty ideologist credited as being e real founder of the party.

Both resigned in protest against eir chief's refusal to participate the government unless the owers of a dictator were given to m. This position, critics in the ationalist Socialist party argued, as responsible for the loss of bout 2,000,000 votes in the Reichsg elections last November.

Party Declined Since August.

Ever since Hitler first refused the hancellorship in a Coalition Cabiet in August, 1932, there has been constant dribbling away from his arty. The elections in Thuringia, hich followed the losses suffered the party in the last Reichstag ections, served to emphasize this oint.

A powerful group of industrialists the Federation of German Industries recently gave indications of sharp change of attitude toward e National Socialists because of eir radical trend. This group in e Federation of German Industries has been inclined in recent onths to withdraw its support om the party and return to a poly of understanding with the German trade unions.

At the same time, however, a oup of Nazi industrialists in the hineland and the Ruhr, who have en among Hitler's chief financial ackers, have urged him to drop s uncompromising attitude and in the government. According to cent dispatches from Berlin, forer Chancellor von Papen was the friendly broker" between the National Socialists and this group of dustrialists.

Recent Berlin dispatches indicate so a deal between Papen and itler for the overthrow of Genera n Schleicher, who roused the diseasure of the Rhineland-Ruhr instrialists by his inclination to al leniently with labor and to seek e support of the trade unions. In is policy, these industrialists forew the abandonment of the ecomic program laid down by Papen Schleicher's predecessor in the ancellorship.

Long Without Citizenship.

Outstanding is the dramatic element of Hitler's accession to power the age of 43. The new Chanlor began as the son of poor parts in Austria. For a long time he as not even a German citizen, but man without a country. His political career began in a very unomising manner in 1921.

The Nazi leader went to Germany 1914 at the outbreak of the war d enlisted in the German Army. this act he sacrificed his Ausan citizenship. He had a good ar record, being gassed, wounded d winning a silver war service edal.

The advent of the German Revotion with the military collapse of ermany in 1918 found him a bitr opponent of the revolutionary heaval. He hated the republic from the day it was born and vowed that he would never rest until he had brought about a counter-revolution against the men and the parties whom he considered responsible for the downfall of the empire.

With General Erich von Ludendorff, who was one of his early supporters but with whom he parted company in later years, he attempted a revolution in Munich, which was easily suppressed by the Bavarian Government on Nov. 8, 1923.

The uprising was to have been the signal for a general monarchist revolution. The collapse of the movement led to the sentencing of Hitler to five years in prison. He was liberated after serving a year in a Bavarian fortress.

He resumed activities on a large scale in 1928. From that time his movement, stimulated by the economic depression, progressed fast. By 1930 the National Socialist party had won 107 seats in the Reichstag. In July, 1931, this number was increased to 230.

Hitler received his first official political recognition in 1932 when Chancellor Heinrich Bruening consulted him on a proposal to extend the term of President von Hindenburg by act of Parliament to avoid the disturbance of a Presidential contest. The Nazi flatly refused. He became a candidate against von Hindenburg but was defeated by more than 6,000,000 votes.

In that election Hitler reached the peak of his strength, polling more than 13,000,000 votes. The reversal of the tide came with the Reichstag elections a few months later, when the National Socialists suffered a loss of about 2,000,000 votes.

LEADING FIGURES IN THE NEW COMPROMISE GOVERNMENT WHICH TOOK OFFICE IN GERMANY YESTERDAY.

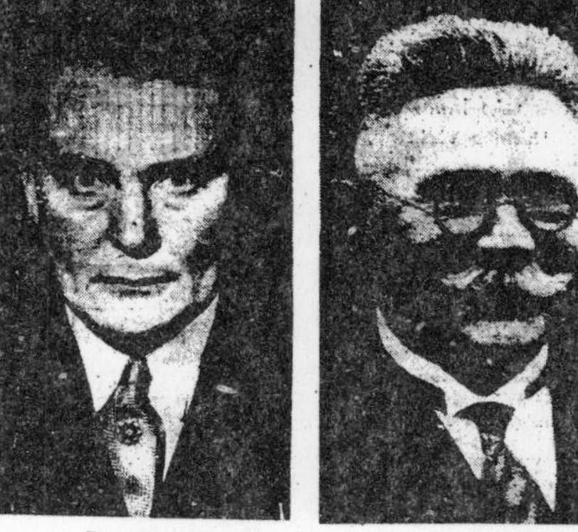

Times Wide World Photo.
HERMANN WILHELM GOERING, Aviation Minister.

Times Wide World Photo.
DR. ALFRED HUGENBERG, Minister of Economy and Food.

Times Wide World Photo.
ADOLF HITLER, Chancellor.

Times Wide World Photo.
FRANZ VON PAPEN, Vice Chancellor.

Times Wide World Photo.
LIEUT. GEN. VON BLOMBERG, Minister of Defense.

Times Wide World Photo.
DR. WILHELM F. FRICK, Minister of the Interior.

Berlin Hears of Army Plot For Monarchist Directorate

By The Associated Press.

BERLIN, Jan. 30.—It was reported today that a group of high army officers headed by General von Schleicher had threatened to take the law into their own hands and set up a "directorate" as a prelude to restoration of the monarchy. This rumor, emphatically denied in official circles, was offered in explanation of the haste with which the Hitler Cabinet was formed.

HITLER NEWS FAILS TO STIR WALL ST.

Reaction of Markets Is Mild—Marks Off 5 Points, Bonds Decline Moderately.

Events in Germany appeared to be moving too rapidly yesterday for Wall Street bankers concerned with German credits to appraise the significance of the appointment of the leader of the Nazis as Chancellor of the Reich, but the financial markets, on the whole, took the news calmly. German marks fell 5 points to 23.75 cents, but in view of the nominal character of the market this was not regarded as important. German bonds listed on the New York Stock Exchange reacted from a fraction to 5¾ points, but there was no great selling pressure.

The German Government 7s, known as the Dawes Plan bonds, sold off 2 points to 82½, while the 5½s, the Young Plan bonds, were down ¾ point to 59½. In view of the fact that these issues have been advancing steadily for several weeks the reaction was considered mild.

The American stake in Germany is estimated by the Statistical Office of the Reich at about $2,480,000,000, or 40 per cent of the total German foreign indebtedness of $6,200,000,000. This includes both short and long-term credits, external and internal bond issues held abroad, and real property in Germany owned by foreigners. The credits covered by the "standstill" agreements now amount to only about $800,000,000, of which about half is being extended by banks in this country.

GERMAN 'ADVENTURE' WATCHED IN BRITAIN

Reich's Attitude on Arms to Be Awaited With Misgiving, Says The London Times.

Special Cable to THE NEW YORK TIMES.

LONDON, Jan. 30.—Progress of Germany's "great political adventure" is being watched here in an atmosphere of doubt as to whether history will fix the new Chancellor as a mountebank or a hero. At the same time the British public is warned it is not the time to start rocking their own political boat in the turbulent European waters.

The London Times editorially says:

"The President has taken a great risk, that is obvious, but to return to the von Papen Cabinet, opposed by the vast majority of the German people, might well have involved the Reich in a crisis of the first magnitude."

The experiment, The Times adds, will be followed with some anxiety in foreign countries, particularly France where "resignation to the inevitable is far from implying satisfaction and in Poland which has been one of the chief targets of Nazi propaganda."

"In Britain, however, as in France, the effect of the change in government on the German attitude toward armaments will be watched with some misgivings," the editorial continues.

ITALIANS ACCLAIM THE HITLER REGIME

Press Is Joyful, Expecting Aid to Clarification of European Situation.

FOREIGN FEARS SCOUTED

World Too Much Changed to Permit Repetition of Past Errors, Says Fascist Paper.

Wireless to THE NEW YORK TIMES.

ROME, Jan. 30.—The National Socialist movement in Germany has given so many indications of sympathy for the Italian Fascist régime that the appointment of Adolf Hitler to the Chancellorship of Germany could not but produce sentiments akin to joy throughout Italy.

This universal feeling of pleasure is reflected in the entire Italian press, which hails the appointment of Herr Hitler with unfeigned enthusiasm and asserts the action not only will contribute powerfully to clarification of the European situation but that the appointment in itself marks a milestone in the reconstruction of Europe.

Sees End of Weimar System.

The newspapers are unanimous in the opinion that the accession of Herr Hitler to power means the end of the German political system founded on the Constitution of Weimar. It is predicted that his government will have not only strong anti-Communist leanings but equally strong anti-democratic tendencies and will closely resemble Italian Fascism in these respects.

Therefore, the event is interpreted here as greatly transcending in importance a mere change in government. It is regarded as offering additional evidence of a profound constitutional crisis affecting all European countries in varying degrees. La Tribuna says:

"The Chancellorship of Hitler, though legitimate, for he is the head of the party which electorally and in parliament is most numerous, is nevertheless the constitutional investiture of the National Socialists and those other parties which have always proclaimed a wish to create a constitutional power in deep contrast to that under the Constitution of Weimar."

Scout Fear of Militarism.

Fears expressed in some quarters that the Hitler government may mark a return of the militarist and expansionist spirit of Germany are scouted by the Italian press.

"Every time there has been a possibility of Hitler coming into power," says Il Lavoro Fascista, "there have been people outside of Italy who expressed the fear of an aggressive return of the pre-war militarist and imperialist Germany. We are convinced these fears are unfounded. The whole atmosphere of the world is too profoundly changed to permit a repetition of such past errors."

The possibility of a strong Communist reaction to the Hitler régime, however, is foreseen.

"The new Germany that now advances," writes Il Giornale d'Italia, "means a decided turn against communism and all the subversive elements tolerated and developed by the democratic régime. These negative forces certainly will not resign themselves to passive defeat. The new régime must, therefore, look forward to bitter internal battles, in which, however, it will have the support of all that part of Germany which is still strong and healthy and which, after the desolating experience of the last ten years, again appreciates the value of a strong, upright and constructive national government."

Expects German Revival.

Il Giornale d'Italia concludes its comment thus:

"Italy cannot but greet with profound cordiality the new German Government and reaffirm her thoughts about Hitler, which have been repeatedly expressed at the time of his bitterest struggles. In Hitler's movement and similar movements which today are united in a single force we Italians see, above all, a powerful means for the political restoration of Germany for the reconstruction of her strength as a nation and as a power of international importance.

"Italy, far from fearing, hails the development of this new force for the contribution it can make to European civilization and stability and for the collaboration it can offer in the expansion and reconstruction ideas of all States and nations."

Eckener Reaches Batavia.

THE HAGUE, Jan. 30.—Dr. Hugo Eckener of Germany, who is making studies of an airship route from Europe to the East Indies, has arrived at Batavia, Dutch Java. He thinks a fortnightly service between Marseilles and Batavia, with a flying time of five days, could be established within eighteen months.

POLAND SEES REICH SHOWING TRUE FACE

Holds Europe Will Soon Know the German Danger and the Sooner the Better.

Wireless to THE NEW YORK TIMES.

WARSAW, Jan. 30.—Adolf Hitler's access to power is rather welcomed here as a sound development in German politics. Political circles here hold that undiluted German nationalism should take full responsibility for the Reich's decisions and that Germany's true face should be shown to the world. Europe will soon know the German danger, it is believed, and the sooner the better it will be for Poland.

A favorable conclusion of the armaments conference at Geneva is now thought impossible here. The rapporteur of the Polish budget for the next year, in a speech today in Parliament, said in referring to the heavy war expenditure, amounting to nearly 35 per cent of the budget, that Poland could not reduce her army nor cut her war expenses in view of the growing menace of a Germany seeking revenge.

Poland's eyes are now on France, where a national government is expected to be formed to deal with the international situation.

EX-KAISER REMAINS CALM.

Crown Prince, Also at Doorn, Declines to Discuss Hitler.

Special Cable to THE NEW YORK TIMES.

DOORN, Jan. 30.—If Chancellor Hitler had full power, former Kaiser Wilhelm's hopes of regaining his throne probably would be higher than they are tonight. He seems to have taken the news of Herr Hitler's appointment without excitement, according to members of his household, and, like the former Crown Prince, who is his guest here, declines to talk politics.

Some say the former Crown Prince is urging his father to demand restoration of the monarchy, but presumably the former Kaiser will await developments. He has aged considerably lately and still is suffering from the effects of influenza.

Special Cable to THE NEW YORK TIMES.

LONDON, Jan. 30.—According to The Daily Herald's Doorn correspondent the ex-Kaiser spent all morning telephoning Major von Sell, representative of the Hohenzollerns in Berlin. The former Crown Prince, The Herald's correspondent says, has great influence over Herr Hitler and will try to persuade the Chancellor to open the door for his father.

CONTRASTS MARK HITLER'S CABINET

Hugenberg, Fiery Nationalist, Is in Discord With Economic Doctrines of the Nazis.

BLOMBERG JUST A SOLDIER

Defense Minister Has Not Been in Politics—Goering Is a Former Exile to Rome.

Special Cable to THE NEW YORK TIMES.

BERLIN, Jan. 30.—Next to Chancellor Adolf Hitler, the most sensational member of the new Cabinet is Alfred Hugenberg, who holds the portfolios of Economy and Food. Consolidation of these Ministries has been his pet scheme. He is an arch-capitalist—though with leanings toward antarchy—financier, industrialist and newspaper publisher, and has been called the German Northcliffe. A fiery Nationalist politician and Hohenzollen devotee, Dr. Hugenberg is abhorrent to labor unions and is in strongest discord with the economic doctrines of the Nazi movement.

Born at Hanover on June 19, 1865, he is the Cabinet's senior member. After studying law and spending a few years in the government service, chiefly the Finance Minstry, he devoted himself to banking and business enterprise, and in 1909 became chairman of the board of directors of the Krupp works at Essen. He held this post until the end of 1918, when he first entered politics.

Dr. Hugenberg sat as a Nationalist delegate in 1919 in the Constitutional Assembly at Weimar and has been a member of every Reichstag since the first. From the beginning one of the moving spirits of the German Nationalist party—the old "diehards"—he strove to make it more militant and acquired a string of newspapers for his propaganda.

Moderates Were Overborne.

He finally overbore the more moderate elements, ousted Count Westarp from the party leadership and himself became its head in October, 1928.

Dr. Hugenberg was one of the most ardent spokesmen for a plebiscite against the Young Plan in 1929 and at all times has vehemently protested against reparations. Of late he has extended his arguments against "foreign tribute"—in part at least—also to Germany's private debt abroad. He was the originator of the "Harzburg front" of October, 1931, which soon broke up to be patched together only now in this Cabinet. Because of this he has been regarded by some as an incubus on the German Nationalist party.

In strongest contrast with Dr. Hugenberg is the new Reichswehr Minister, Lieut. Gen. Werner von Blomberg, who is simply a soldier and has never been in politics. He was born at Stargard, Pomerania, in 1878. During the World War he served as a staff officer.

He attained his present military rank in October, 1929, when placed in command of the important Koenigsberg army district. He has visited the United States at the invitation of the American Army and had been chief of Germany's military advisers at the Geneva disarmament conference.

Reputation as an Expert.

The General served two periods in the Reichswehr Ministry as a department head and has a reputation as a military expert of great ability and clear and unprejudiced judgment.

Hermann Wilhelm Goering, Reich Minister without portfolio and Acting Minister of Interior for Prussia, has been Chancellor Hitler's personal representative in Berlin since 1930. He is 40 years old and was born in Upper Bavaria. Trained for a professional officer, he distinguished himself during the World War as a flier, was repeatedly decorated, and, toward the end, commanded the famous Richthofen Squadron.

Early associating himself with Herr Hitler, Herr Goering took part in the Munich uprising of 1923 and was slightly wounded in street fighting. To escape imprisonment, he fled across the border and became an exile, spending two of the years in Rome studying Italian Fascism. He returned to Germany under the amnesty of 1927. He was elected to the Reichstag in 1928, and is president of the present Reichstag as he was also of its short-lived predecessor.

Wilhelm Frick, Minister of Interior, is a lawyer by profession. He was born on March 12, 1877, in the Palatinate—it is a curious fact that of the three Nazis in the Cabinet, one is an Austrian and the two others are South German. Herr Frick is also one of the early Hitlerites.

At the time of the 1923 rising in which he was implicated he had a post in the Munich Police Presidency. Arrested and sentenced to a term in military prison, he was subsequently retried and acquitted.

Nearly two years Minister of Interior or Thuringia, Herr Frick has been a member of the Reichstag since 1924 and belongs to Chancellor Hitler's Inner Council.

Franz Seldte, Labor Minister, is a manufacturer of Magdeburg, where he was born in June, 1882. His claim to distinction rests almost solely on his having founded in 1919 and since having presided over the Stahlhelm (veterans' organization). He was in propaganda for an anti-Young Plan plebiscite, the idea of which originated with the Stahlhelm.

In 1931, Herr Seldte fathered an ill-fated initiative movement for creating a State Presidency for Prussia and consolidating it with the Reich Presidency. After the Presidential election in March, 1932, when the Stahlhelm put up Theodor Duesterberg as a Nationalist rival candidate with Herr Hitler against President von Hindenburg, Herr Seldte "withdraw the Stahlheim from politics."

HITLER IS NAMED REICH CHANCELLOR

By GUIDO ENDERIS.

Continued from Page One.

cided President von Hindenburg to accept the Nazi chief as Chancellor after his former rejections of him.

The only key post held by the National Socialists is the Interior Ministry, which has jurisdiction over the police. General von Blomberg, Defense Minister, is an army officer who has not been involved in politics. This portfolio was coveted by the Nazis.

Money Experiments Barred.

Dr. Hugenberg, Nationalist leader, has financial and economic aims opposed to those of the National Socialists and others in the Cabinet. But Colonel von Papen announced for the new government that "It will not indulge in any economic or currency experimentation."

Some Liberals welcome the new Cabinet. They reason that Herr Hitler has been removed from the street and saddled with the responsibility of office in a setting which will severely circumscribe his liberty of action.

The government will go before the Reichstag Feb. 7. It can survive only with Centrist votes because it has the backing of only 197 National Socialists and 51 Nationalists.

While the Centrist leaders say they were not consulted by Colonel Papen during his scouting expedition in the past two days, it is believed they will be neutral because of the expectation that the Hitler-Papen régime will collapse soon through withdrawal of the National Socialists. It is predicted the Nazis will discover the anomaly of their position in a government in which they hold a minority position with conflicting political groups.

The Socialists are confident Herr Hitler soon will "blow up and be disposed of definitely." But they and the Communists are prepared for repressive measures with Dr. Frick occupying the Interior Ministry. They count on the Reichstag being dissolved if Chancellor Hitler meets a no-confidence vote next week.

Newspapers Show Anxiety.

Newspaper comment, except among National Socialists, reflects general anxiety. "A leap in the dark" is a frequently recurring characterization of the new government.

The Frankfurter Zeitung emphasizes the necessity of rallying "to the defense of the rights of the working population, the fundamentals of democracy, freedom of thought and justice and social and economic rationality."

The Berliner Tageblatt forecasts reaction vieing with Fascism for power. The Democratic party's official bulletin is less alarmed. It says:

"There is the Socialist Hitler under the business supervision of the foxy capitalist Hugenberg and an ex-corporal amidst a Count and four Barons. This Cabinet is better than Papen's because it has some sense at least, namely the disenchantment that will now come to Hitler's followers."

The Nazi utterances naturally are full of elation. "The triumph of tenacity!" exclaims Der Angriff. It continues:

"This is not a mere change in government but is an event like nothing that has preceded in Germany's post-war evolution. With a strong National Socialist advance guard our leaders have moved into the government to clear the road to freedom for the German people."

The Centrist newspaper Germania emphasizes that the Cabinet attempts to unite "the most thoroughgoing capitalism, embodied in Hugenberg, landholding feudalism and Hitler's Socialism." Germania sees benefits because the new Cabinet "has established clearness and unequivocal responsibility in the political situation."

The Koelnische Zeitung hopes Chancellor Hitler will obtain the Centre's toleration "so a Cabinet of national concentration may bring Germany the tranquillity she so urgently needs."

Dr. Hugenberg and the extreme reactionary press are rather restrained considering the circumstances. The Boersen Zeitung admonishes the national front to stand together this time. Dr. Hugenberg's Der Tag deprecates excessive jubilation.

Cabinet Bars Experiments.

BERLIN, Jan. 30 (AP).—Presiding over the first session of his Cabinet of "national concentration," Chancellor Hitler tonight put through unanimous motions against all policies of suppression, economic adventures or financial experimentation.

He adjured his fellow Cabinet members "under no circumstances to disappoint the manifestation of faith and trust which today found spontaneous expression among the rank and file of the German people."

Later, in a press conference, the Chancellor, through Interior Minister Frick, assured German and foreign correspondents that "the new government seeks to live in peace and friendship with all the world."

Dr. Frick further asserted that the Hitler Cabinet intends to govern strictly constitutionally, adding that it does not even desire to govern with the aid of Article 48 of the Constitution, which grants the administration drastic powers in times of emergency.

Walther Funk, new government press chief, told foreign correspondents the Nazis were opposed to any financial or economic experiments.

"We are opposed to all experiments of a financial or economic nature and we shall not endanger the fruits of our political history by playing with economic standards," Herr Funk said.

BERLIN REDS URGE STRIKE.

Two Killed in Riots During Nazi Celebrations in Germany.

BERLIN, Tuesday, Jan. 31 (AP).—Police in Berlin were forced to use clubs to disperse crowds in the working class districts, which were flooded with Communist handbills urging that a general strike begin at 7 A. M. today in protest against the Hitler Cabinet.

At 1 A. M. a policeman, a member of a detail escorting 100 Nazis home after a demonstration in Wilhelmstrasse, was slain by shots from a darkened house. Later a Nazi was killed. Scores of smaller fights occurred throughout the capital.

At Königsberg, Nazis and Socialists and Communists engaged in a fight after the Communists' newspapers had been banned. A Nazi celebration in Mannheim was marred by a fight with knives. One victim was believed to be dying.

Scenes of wild jubilation at Hitler's appointment were reported last night at various Nazi strongholds in the country. Coburg City Hall flew the Nazi swastika banner and there was a torchlight procession. All Thuringia, where Dr. Frick formerly was Minister of Interior, flew flags.

Berlin's Nationalist-minded citizens rendered homage to President von Hindenburg and Chancellor Hitler in a gigantic demonstration such as has not been witnessed here since the days of the revolution, when President Fritz Ebert reviewed the masses from a balcony of the Presidential Palace.

Throngs of singing and chanting civilians jubilantly hailed the storm troops who gathered in the Siegesallee for a torchlight parade. Column after column, with waving swastika banners, swung through the Brandenburg Gate down Unter den Linden, which was jammed with jubilant crowds of Nazi sympathizers.

President von Hindenburg stood in a lighted window of the Chancellery as the singing, ecstatic crowds gave him the Fascist salute. Chancellor Hitler stood with Aviation Minister Goering at another window.

PRAGUE IS UNRUFFLED BY NEWS IN GERMANY

Accepts Hitler Appointment as Inevitable, but Hopes the Chancellor Will Fail.

Wireless to THE NEW YORK TIMES.

PRAGUE, Jan. 30.—Czechoslovak opinion accepts the nomination of Adolf Hitler to the German Chancellorship without special excitement, considering that he has been made a prisoner of the so-called Harzburg front by President von Hindenburg through the President's appointment of Franz von Papen and Lieut. Gen. Werner von Blomberg to important posts with him.

Private opinion considers it desirable that Herr Hitler as the leader of the strongest German party should get the opportunity of becoming a positive factor in German policy, so that it may be possible to estimate his capacity for government.

This calm acceptance of the new situation means only acceptance of the inevitable. It is the undisguised wish of Czechoslovaks that Herr Hitler may fail, but they recognize he must have a sporting chance to prove his worth. It is expected that Germany's international position will be weakened by Herr Hitler's appointment. It is felt that with such a Cabinet he cannot effect any important changes.

The National Socialist revolution, it is said here, is ended by the new appointment, but even though Herr Hitler has failed to obtain control of the Reichswehr he has through Captain Hermann Wilhelm Goering obtained control of the Prussian police. Only the extreme nationalist Czech press is agitated over Herr Hitler's appointment.

NRA — We Do Our Part

"All the News That's Fit to Print."

The New York Times.

LATE CITY EDITION

WEATHER—Rain and warmer today; tomorrow fair and colder.

Temperatures Yesterday—Max., 44; min., 34.

VOL. LXXXIII....No. 27,710. Entered as Second-Class Matter, Postoffice, New York, N. Y. NEW YORK, WEDNESDAY, DECEMBER 6, 1933. MP TWO CENTS In New York City. | THREE CENTS Within 200 Miles | FOUR CENTS Elsewhere Except in 7th and 8th Postal Zones

PROHIBITION REPEAL IS RATIFIED AT 5:32 P. M.; ROOSEVELT ASKS NATION TO BAR THE SALOON; NEW YORK CELEBRATES WITH QUIET RESTRAINT

LINDBERGHS AT SEA ON BRAZIL FLIGHT; 'O.K.' SHE REPORTS

630 MILES FROM AFRICA

Breeze Starts Fliers After Twenty Attempts in Dead Calm.

MOON LIGHTS THEIR WAY

10,000 Natives See Take-Off as Motor's Roar Stirs Them From Slumber.

RIDE THROUGH SQUALLS

Wife Radios Every Fifteen Minutes of Progress on 1,800-Mile Flight.

Colonel and Mrs. Charles A. Lindbergh were flying across the South Atlantic from Africa to Brazil this morning, reporting their progress by radio every fifteen minutes and their location every half hour.

At 2:20 A. M., New York time, five hours and twenty minutes after taking off from Bathurst, Gambia, in bright moonlight, they were 630 miles on their way across the Southern Ocean.

The first message from the plane was picked up by the Miami, Fla., station of Pan American Airways soon after 9:02 P. M. last night, New York time. It reported that the plane had taken off from Bathurst at that time. At 10 P. M., New York time, another message picked up by the Bahia, Brazil, station of Pan American Airways advised that the plane was flying Course 224 true, and gave its position, which Pan American officials estimated to be about 115 miles southwest of Bathurst. At 10:40 P. M. another message, also picked up by the Bahia station, reported "everything O. K.," and said the plane's position would be given every half hour and a progress O. K. sent out every fifteen minutes. The first progress O. K. was received by the Pan American station at Miami at 11 P. M., New York time.

Made 240 Miles in Two Hours.

At 11 P. M., the Bahia station also picked up a message. It gave for the plane a position approximately 240 miles southwest of Bathurst and right on her course. The operators at Bahia said that in her first message, Mrs. Lindbergh reported considerable static. But her messages, they said, were coming into Bahia strong, fast and clear, as if they were being sent by an experienced wireless operator.

The next message was received by the Pan-American station at Para, Brazil, at 11:50 P. M., New York time. It reported that the plane was flying at an altitude of 2,000 feet and making about 100 knots. There was unlimited visibility, the message said, with the sky about one-tenth overcast, and a quartering ten-knot tail wind.

At 12:30 this morning, the Pan American radio station at Miami and the Chatham, Mass., station of the Radiomarine Corporation each picked up a message from the plane giving a position approximately 446 miles southeast of Bathurst. The message said the plane was flying at an altitude of 1,200 feet, that there was visibility of about ten miles, that the sky was nine-tenths overcast, and that there was a quartering tail wind of 10 knots.

Squalls Met at Daybreak.

A message was received at 1:27 this morning at Pará, Brazil, reporting "skies eight-tenths overcast, scattered squalls, visibility three miles, daybreak; all's well."

At 1:50 A. M. the Bahia station picked up a message, "All's well."

At 2:20 A. M. a message was received at the Pará station reporting the plane's position as 630 miles southwest of Bathurst, flying at 1,000 feet, the skies nine-tenths overcast, frequent squalls, calm seas and no wind. That position indicated the Lindberghs had covered about one-third of the distance to Natal.

Natives Awaken for Start.

Special Cable to THE NEW YORK TIMES.

BATHURST, Gambia, Wednesday, Dec. 6.—With bright moonlight turning the waters around the little island of St. Mary, on which

Continued on Page Twenty-six.

Lindbergh Flight to Fame Twice as Long as New Hop

On the morning of May 20, 1927, six years and six months ago, Captain Charles A. Lindbergh, a mail pilot, left Roosevelt Field for Paris.

He flew alone, and veteran pilots shook their heads when they saw him take off. His silver plane, dripping with rain, lumbered slowly—too slowly—down the muddy runway. It gathered speed, bounced from the ground and settled back again. It barely cleared a tractor at the end of the runway and just climbed over low telephone wires at the end of the field.

Thirty-three and a half hours later the young mail pilot brought his gray plane down at Le Bourget. That famous flight covered 3,610 miles. The present flight, also in a single-engined plane, is about 1,875 miles.

PWA READY TO BAR CITY SUBWAY LOAN

Security for $25,000,000 Advance to Finish System Is Held Inadequate.

BANKERS' PACTS A FACTOR

Officials Here Say Attitude of Washington Is Based on a Misunderstanding.

Special to THE NEW YORK TIMES.

WASHINGTON, Dec. 5.—Inability of New York City to furnish security satisfactory to the Public Works Administration has caused the latter to abandon the allotment of $25,000,000 for completion of the Eighth Avenue subway.

New York officials have not been notified, but it was learned from reliable sources that the application for the loan would be refused.

At his press conference today Secretary Ickes said there was "nothing new" to report on the loan. He added, however, that the matter was held up by the question of security.

Senator Wagner announced virtual assurance of the loan more than two weeks ago. Since then the matter has been before the Special Board of Public Works, while PWA engineers and lawyers were investigating.

Application Signed by Mayor.

The application, for $25,000,000, signed by Mayor O'Brien, was on a loan and grant basis, 30 per cent of the cost of materials and structure to be an outright grant and the rest a loan on security furnished by the city.

The amount of money which completion of the subway would require is indefinite. Public Works Administration officials have scaled the sum down to some $22,500,000 under one estimate.

The money would be applied to equipping, tracking and finishing some eighteen miles of subway already dug, mainly in Brooklyn and Queens, and to the building of stations. Seven thousand men would obtain work through the Winter, it was estimated, and large supplies of capital goods would be purchased.

The allotment was discussed at the recent conference between Secretary Ickes and Mayor-elect La Guardia, but it was not gone into in any detail.

The attitude of the PWA, it was learned, is that the city has tied up the revenues of the subway by its financing agreements with the banks, and would be operating on a margin too slender to enable it to guarantee any return on the investment, even if the PWA funds allowed the subway to open miles of route and thus tap new sources of revenue.

Unification Another Problem.

The PWA feels that the situation is further complicated by the competition of the other New York subway lines. If the other lines were taken over by the city under the unification plan, a campaign promise of the Mayor-elect, the PWA feels that there would be a general scaling down of the demands of creditors and a consequent loss to the government on its investment. The question of the 5-cent fare is not worrying the administration, Secretary Ickes has said.

While Mr. Ickes has already ex-

Continued on Page Twenty-seven.

TAX PLAN OFFERED TO CURB EVASIONS, RAISE $237,000,000

House Subcommittee Urges a Check on Personal Holding Concerns by 35% Levy.

WOULD INCREASE SURTAX

Normal Income Tax of 4% and Revision of Capital Gains Are Also Proposed.

Special to THE NEW YORK TIMES.

WASHINGTON, Dec. 5.—Broad tax reforms designed to increase the Federal revenue $237,000,000 a year and prevent "the avoidance and evasion of the internal revenue laws" were recommended today in a report submitted to the House Ways and Means Committee by a subcommittee.

The full committee immediately began study of the suggestions, and Representative Doughton, the chairman, said a completed bill would probably be ready for presentation soon after Congress meets next month.

Changes sought are aimed principally at persons whose incomes are in the higher brackets, as well as at corporations now legally permitted to take advantage of what committee members said were "unfair but legal" provisions of the revenue laws.

Some discord was apparent within the committee, but no member would publicly express his feelings.

"It isn't law yet, and it is not even past the committee," said one member. "It must go to the House and Senate."

Nine Changes are Urged.

Nine phases of the present law were recommended for modification as follows:

1. Establishment of a normal income tax rate of 4 per cent, instead of the present 4 per cent on the first $4,000 and 8 per cent on the remainder of net income, and revision of the surtax rate on a graduated scale, with the brackets reduced from 53 to 27; estimated to increase revenue $36,000,000 annually.

2. Change for three years in the depreciation and depletion section of the 1932 Revenue Act by reducing allowances by 25 per cent; estimated to add $85,000,000 for each of the three years.

3. Revision of the capital gains and losses section by revising the method of adjustment and prescribing a scale-length of ownership; estimated to add $30,000,000.

4. Amendment of the personal holding companies' section to prevent persons with large incomes from forming companies to evade taxes; estimated to add $25,000,000.

5. Abolition of certain sections of the "exchanges and reorganization" provisions to "close the door to one of the most prevalent methods of tax avoidance"; estimated to add $18,000,000.

6. Imposition of a tax on dividends paid out of corporation earnings accumulated before March 1, 1913; estimated to add $6,000,000.

7. Amendment of the foreign tax credit sections of the 1932 act; estimated to add $10,000,000.

8. Withdrawal of permission for corporations which are affiliated through 95 per cent stock ownership to file consolidated returns; estimated to add $20,000,000.

9. Revision of the partnership losses section of the 1932 Revenue Act; estimated to add $7,000,000.

Eager to expedite the "major problems," the subcommittee passed over a group of minor matters, according to the chairman, Representative Sam B. Hill of Washington. He said the subcommittee would continue study of these problems.

Continued on Page Fourteen.

State House Bootlegger Is Barred in Maryland

Special to THE NEW YORK TIMES.

ANNAPOLIS, Md., Dec. 5.—Wet legislators here will patriotically support legal liquor. The State House bootlegger received formal notice today to discontinue his trade. The notice was served by a policeman on duty at the Capitol.

Throughout this session, the bootlegger has conducted a thriving business; a business which, he says, has been especially arduous because of the sudden demands made on him by legislators and their desire for prompt service.

While his services were cut off eight hours before post-prohibition stuff could be bought, the bootlegger thought the legislators had obtained a sufficient reserve to carry them through until evening and legal liquor.

RATIFYING BY UTAH ENDS PROHIBITION

With Impressive Ceremony, the 36th State Follows Ohio and Pennsylvania in Day.

CONVENTIONS ALL SOLEMN

Moderation Pleas Are Made at Columbus—Hush Greets Vote at Harrisburg.

Special to THE NEW YORK TIMES.

SALT LAKE CITY, Dec. 5—The Eighteenth Amendment to the Constitution of the United States passed out of existence officially at 3:32½ o'clock this afternoon, Mountain standard time (5:32½ New York time) with the ratification of repeal by the convention of Utah, the thirty-sixth required State.

The passing of national prohibition was marked by impressive ceremony in the hall of the House of Representatives in the State Capitol here.

To Delegate S. R. Thurman, a repeal leader of Salt Lake City, whose father was a member of the State's constitutional convention in 1895 before Utah was admitted to the Union, fell the honor of being the last to record his vote, the roll being called in alphabetical order.

His "Yea," placing the Twenty-first Amendment to the Constitution in effect, was greeted by enthusiastic applause from the audience of a few hundred persons.

About ninety seconds later Ray L. Olson of Ogden, president of the convention, who had been manager of the repealists' campaign, brought down his gavel and announced that the repeal amendment had been ratified. Notification was transmitted immediately to the White House by a special wire from the Capitol.

At the same time Delegate A. S. Brown, former president of the Salt Lake Chamber of Commerce, sent out word to President Roosevelt over the Columbia Broadcasting System. He congratulated the President on the successful culmination of the repeal movement.

The whole proceedings were in keeping with the historic aspect of the occasion. Besides high officials

Continued on Page Five.

Italy to Quit League Unless It Is Reformed; Demands Altered Aims and Set-Up at Once

By ARNALDO CORTESI.

Wireless to THE NEW YORK TIMES

ROME, Wednesday, Dec. 6.—At the end of a long sitting lasting far into the night, the Fascist Grand Council, which had been convoked to decide on Italy's relations with the League of Nations, passed a suspended sentence on Geneva.

After having discussed every aspect of the probable effect of Italy's withdrawal, the Grand Council decided "to render Italy's further participation in the League dependent on radical changes in that organization to be brought about within the shortest possible time, which changes must affect the League in its constitution, in its methods and in its objectives."

At the same time the Grand Council reached a temporizing decision also in the matter of payment to the United States of the debt instalment due on Dec. 15. In view of the impossibility of conducting negotiations on the debt problem, the Grand Council decided "to effect on Dec. 15 a token payment of $1,000,000 as renewed proof of Italy's good-will, while awaiting a final settlement of this whole question."

Since the breakdown in the disarmament negotiations Premier Mussolini has been advocating efforts outside Geneva and the League of Nations. He has favored action under the Four-Power Pact initiated by Great Britain, France, Italy and Germany, or at any rate negotiations by the leading powers including the United States.

As to reforms in the League, the press has suggested that the League be divorced from the Versailles Treaty, and that its constitution be revised to give the larger powers a freer hand in directing its affairs.

CITY TOASTS NEW ERA

Crowds Swamp Licensed Resorts, but the Legal Liquor Is Scarce.

CELEBRATION IN STREETS

Marked by Absence of Undue Hilarity and Only Normal Number of Arrests.

MANY SPEAKEASIES CLOSE

Machine Guns Guard Some Liquor Trucks—Supplies to Be Rushed Out Today.

Slowly gathering momentum from the time when the news began to spread just at nightfall that national prohibition was no more, the public rejoicing at the end of the long dry reign was carried on last night with restraint and absence of undue hilarity.

Throngs of New Yorkers ventured into Times Square and other centres of the metropolis and many of the thousand restaurants, hotels and clubs fortunate enough to have received their licenses for the sale of alcoholic beverages were swamped.

But gay as were their spirits, they were well-behaved. With the city's entire police force of 19,000 men mobilized to guard against overexuberant celebrants, arrests did not exceed the normal number for any day of the last five years. Incidentally, official word that repeal was a fact did not go out to the police until 9:20 P. M., just about four hours after Utah acted.

Stores Fail to Get Stocks.

The thronging to places of public entertainment was enhanced by the fact that only a handful of New Yorkers was able to drink a toast to the occasion with lawful liquor in their own homes. Because Utah did not make repeal effective until 5:32½ P. M., retail liquor stores with only two exceptions were unable to obtain wines and whiskies from the warehouses in the brief time left.

Indeed, the supply of lawful liquor even in the licensed places was woefully scant. Only fifty-four truckloads of bonded liquor were released from the warehouses before they closed last night, and the two largest warehouses shut their doors before the Twenty-first Amendment displaced the Eighteenth.

With 3,000 places licensed to dispense the newly legalized beverages in the metropolitan area and 2,000 more up-State, hardly one in a hundred was able to move in a stock in the few hours available. Some of the others, of course, had had the foresight to lay in supplies under medicinal permits during the dying days of prohibition.

Bootleggers and speakeasies came to the rescue, however, despite a stern warning from Police Commissioner Bolan that his men would not tolerate any such activity. They operated with a little more caution than usual, but nevertheless they took advantage of the occasion to dispose of a large part of their unlawful stocks. The raids threatened by Mr. Bolan proved few and on little known places.

Many Cordial Shops Close.

Cordial shops and other neighborhood dispensaries during the long drought showed fear of police activity last night for the first time in years. Hundreds of them closed their doors, others dealt only with long-known and trusted customers, and only a scattering number, principally in downtown Manhattan, carried on business as usual. Some of them carried signs promising to open as licensed liquor stores in a few days.

There was every indication, however, that New York's long reliance on contraband cheer was near its end. The warehousemen promised deliveries on a large scale would begin today, with 400 trucks licensed to speed legal liquors throughout the city and its suburbs.

A cargo of 6,200 cases of assorted wines and spirits worth about $170,000 arrived on the White Star liner Majestic from France and England late in the afternoon, but the ship was delayed five hours by

Continued on Page Two.

The Repeal Proclamation

Special to THE NEW YORK TIMES.

WASHINGTON, Dec. 5.—The text of the proclamation by William Phillips, Acting Secretary of State, certifying to the adoption of the Twenty-first Amendment repealing prohibition, follows:

WILLIAM PHILLIPS,

Acting Secretary of State of the United States of America.

To all whom these presents shall come, greeting:

KNOW YE, That the Congress of the United States, at the second session, Seventy-second Congress, begun and held at the city of Washington on Monday, the fifth day of December, in the year one thousand nine hundred and thirty-two, passed a joint Resolution in the words and figures as follows:

To wit—

JOINT RESOLUTION.

Proposing an amendment to the Constitution of the United States.

Resolved by the Senate and House of Representatives of the United States of America in Congress assembled (two-thirds of each House concurring therein), That the following article is hereby proposed as an amendment to the Constitution of the United States, which shall be valid to all intents and purposes as part of the Constitution when ratified by conventions in three-fourths of the several States:

ARTICLE.

Section 1. The Eighteenth Article of Amendment to the Constitution of the United States is hereby repealed.

Section 2. The transportation or importation into any State, Territory, or Possession of the United States for delivery or use therein of intoxicating liquors, in violation of the laws thereof, is hereby prohibited.

Section 3. This article shall be inoperative unless it shall have been ratified as an amendment to the Constitution by conventions in the several States, as provided in the Constitution, within seven years from the date of the submission hereof to the States by the Congress.

And, further, that it appears from official notices received at the Department of State that the amendment to the Constitution of the United States proposed as aforesaid has been ratified by conventions in the States of Arizona, Alabama, Arkansas, California, Colorado, Connecticut, Delaware, Florida, Idaho, Illinois, Indiana, Iowa, Kentucky, Maryland, Massachusetts, Michigan, Minnesota, Missouri, Nevada, New Hampshire, New Jersey, New Mexico, New York, Ohio, Oregon, Pennsylvania, Rhode Island, Tennessee, Texas, Utah, Vermont, Virginia, Washington, West Virginia, Wisconsin and Wyoming.

And, further, that the States wherein conventions have so ratified the said proposed amendment constitute the requisite three-fourths of the whole number of States in the United States.

NOW, therefore, be it known that I, William Phillips, Acting Secretary of State of the United States, by virtue and in pursuance of Section 160, Title 5, of the United States Code, do hereby certify that the amendment aforesaid has become valid to all intents and purposes as a part of the Constitution of the United States.

In testimony whereof, I have hereunto set my hand and caused the seal of the Department of State to be affixed.

Done at the city of Washington this fifth day of December in the year of our Lord one thousand nine hundred and thirty-three.

WILLIAM PHILLIPS.

Roosevelt Proclaims Repeal; Urges Temperance in Nation

President's Announcement Is in Accordance With the Instruction of Congress Contained in the Recovery Act—Declares Social Evils of Liquor Shall Not Be Revived.

Special to THE NEW YORK TIMES.

WASHINGTON, Dec. 5.—President Roosevelt's proclamation of the repeal of the Eighteenth Amendment was as follows:

By the President of the United States of America.

A Proclamation.

Whereas the Congress of the United States in the second session of the Seventy-second Congress, begun at Washington on the fifth day of December in the year one thousand nine hundred and thirty-two adopted a resolution in the words and figures following: to wit—

JOINT RESOLUTION.

Proposing an amendment to the Constitution of the United States.

Resolved by the Senate and House of Representatives of the United States of America in Congress assembled (two-thirds of each House concurring therein), That the following article is hereby proposed as an amendment to the Constitution of the United States, which shall be valid to all intents and purposes as part of the Constitution when ratified by conventions in three-fourths of the several States:

ARTICLE.

Section 1. The Eighteenth Article of amendment to the Constitution of the United States is hereby repealed.

Section 2. The transportation or importation into any State, Territory or possession of the United States for delivery or use therein of intoxicating liquors, in violation of the laws thereof, is hereby prohibited.

Section 3. This article shall be inoperative unless it shall have been ratified as an amendment to the Constitution by conventions in the several States, as provided in the Constitution, within seven years from the date of the submission hereof to the States by the Congress.

Declares Amendment Repealed.

Whereas, Section 217 (a) of the Act of Congress entitled "An act to encourage national industrial recovery, to foster competition and to provide for the construction of certain useful public works, and for other purposes," approved June 16, 1933, provides as follows:

Section 217 (a) The President shall proclaim the date of ——

(1) the close of the first fiscal year ending June 30 of any year after the year 1933, during which the total receipts of the

Continued on Page Two.

FINAL ACTION AT CAPITAL

President Proclaims the Nation's New Policy as Utah Ratifies.

PHILLIPS SIGNS DECREE

Orders 21st Amendment in Effect on Receiving Votes of Three Final States.

RECOVERY TAXES TO END

$227,000,000 a Year Automatically Dropped—Canadian Whisky Quota Is Raised.

Special to THE NEW YORK TIMES.

WASHINGTON, Dec. 5.—Legal liquor today was returned to the United States, with President Roosevelt calling on the people to see that "this return of individual freedom shall not be accompanied by the repugnant conditions that obtained prior to the adoption of the Eighteenth Amendment and those that have existed since its adoption."

Prohibition of alcoholic beverages as a national policy ended at 5:32½ P. M., Eastern Standard Time, when Utah, the last of the thirty-six States, furnished by vote of its convention the constitutional majority for ratification of the Twenty-first Amendment. The new amendment repealed the Eighteenth, and with the demise of the latter went the Volstead Act which for more than a decade held legal drinks in America to less than one-half of 1 per cent of alcohol and the enforcement of which cost more than 150 lives and billions in money.

Earlier in the day Pennsylvania had ratified as the thirty-fourth State and Ohio as the thirty-fifth.

Proclamation by President.

President Roosevelt at 6:55 P. M. signed an official proclamation in keeping with terms of the National Industrial Recovery Act, under which prohibition ended and four taxes levied to raise $227,000,000 annually for amortization of the $3,300,000,000 public works fund were repealed.

But the President went further. Accepting certification from Acting Secretary of State Phillips that thirty-six States had ratified the repealing amendment, he improved the occasion to address a plea to the American people to employ their regained liberty first of all for national manliness.

Mr. Roosevelt asked personally for what he and his party had declined to make the subject of Federal mandate—that saloons be barred from the country.

"I ask especially," he said, "that no State shall, by law or otherwise, authorize the return of the saloon, either in its old form or in some modern guise."

Makes Personal Plea.

He enjoined all citizens to cooperate with the government in its endeavor to restore a greater respect for law and order, especially by confining their purchases of liquor to duly licensed agencies. This practice, which he personally requested every individual and every family in the nation to follow, would result, he said, in a better product for consumption, in addition to the "break-up and eventual destruction of the notoriously evil illicit liquor traffic" and in tax benefits to the government.

The President thus announced the policy of his administration—to see that the social and political evils of the preprohibition era shall not be revived or permitted again to exist. Failure of citizens to use their new freedom in helping to advance this policy, he said, would be "a living reproach to us all."

He expressed faith, too, in the "good sense of the American people" in preventing excessive personal use of relegalized liquor. "The objective we seek through a national policy," he said, "is the education of every citizen toward a greater temperance throughout the nation."

As a means of enforcing his policy, the President has the Federal Alcohol Control Administration ready to take control of the liquor traffic and regulate it at the source of supply.

In its first major step today, the

Continued on Page Two.

Movies and Radio Record Formal Ending of Prohibition

SIGNING CEREMONY BRIEF, COLORFUL

Phillips First Reads Repeal Proclamation for Movies and Radio.

USES AN ORDINARY PEN

Excitement Reigns in Usually Calm State Department as States Send In Notifications.

Special to THE NEW YORK TIMES.

WASHINGTON, Dec. 5.—William Phillips, Acting Secretary of State, signed the proclamation repealing the Eighteenth Amendment at 49 and one-half minutes after 5 o'clock this afternoon, thus ending a brief but colorful ceremony.

Seated at a black, baize-covered table in the reception room of the Secretary of State, Mr. Phillips took up a pen such as might have been bought for 5 cents anywhere and quickly inscribed his name, dotting each of the four "i's" with great care. The document was taken into another room where the great red seal of state was affixed after a few minutes of unexpected delay, due to "mechanical" difficulties with the seal itself.

Mr. Phillips's signing was the climax of a day of interest and excitement at the customarily solemn State Department. Apparently little ordinary business was transacted, for all eyes were fixed on repeal.

Wait for Utah Vote.

At 12:52 P. M. notification of ratification by Pennsylvania arrived two minutes after the State convention acted. It came by telegraph. Duplicates were sent in an airplane piloted by Major Dowlin, in a motorcycle driven by J. J. Haggerty, a Pennsylvania State policeman, and by registered mail. Major Dowlin's copy of the notification was picked up by a State Department car at the airport, but Haggerty came roaring up to the department himself. Beaming broadly, he was introduced to Mr. Phillips by Dr. David Hunter Miller, historical adviser of the department.

Ohio's notification was received at 2:53 P. M., two minutes after the State convention acted. The telegram was received directly in the State Department's communication room.

Then the department turned its attention westward and waited for Utah, on whose notification the actual signing depended. As time went on, it became certain that the Utah decision would be recorded between 5 and 6 P. M., and accordingly the stage was set in the reception room.

About 5 o'clock Mr. Phillips, trim and dignified in his dark, double-breasted suit, entered the room, faced a battery of Klieg lights and posed for motion-picture and still photographers. Behind him stood Jefferson Caffery and Francis B. Sayre, two Assistant Secretaries of State, with Dr. Miller.

Reads for the Movies.

Over and over Mr. Phillips read portions of the proclamation in his neat, clipped English, while the cameras clicked and ground. A Bostonian, he threw a heavy broad "a" into words like "passed," and pronounced the last syllable of his name to rhyme with the first syllable of "ipso."

The movie men wanted Mr. Phillips to stop once on the word "conventions," but he maintained that this did not carry the meaning—and won his point.

The camera men through, Mr. Phillips retired while Assistant Secretary Caffery listened in on the Utah convention, being broadcast by radio. With a telephone at his ear, he entertained State Department officials, newspaper correspondents, radio broadcasters and camera men with frequent bulletins.

In a few moments Mr. Phillips was ready for the final act. He seated himself at the table, put his glasses on his nose and read the proclamation once again, this time in full, into the microphones of the two great broadcasting systems. From the walls, five former Secretaries of State, Hughes, Lansing, Colby, Stimson and Kellogg, looked down out of their gilded frames.

As he spoke the final words of the proclamation applause broke out, Mr. Phillips rose, bowed, removed his eyeglasses and started to leave the room. Michael J. McDermott, chief of the Division of Current Information, caught Mr. Phillips's arm and murmured something. Hastily the Acting Secretary resumed his seat, replaced his glasses and picked up a black wooden pen with a cork grip.

He thrust the pen into the inkstand, set it to the paper and rapidly wrote his name.

When the proclamation was taken into another room the discovery was made that while the iron Seal of State stood ready for use, there was no large, red wafer ready. In a few minutes one was obtained, and the seal was registered.

The seal is a brilliant red and bears the inscription, "Department of State, United States of America." The pen used by Mr. Phillips will probably be placed with other historic pens in the Library of Congress.

RAISES STATE TAX FIGURE.

Graves Now Estimates Liquor Revenue at $15,000,000.

ALBANY, Dec. 5 (AP).—Mark Graves, president of the State Tax Commission, today raised by $2,500,000, the amount of the revenue which will come to the State and its communities from the first year of hard liquor sales. Commissioner Graves said he now expects to collect $15,000,000 a year.

The State will not begin to collect liquor taxes until January. The taxes are to be paid monthly.

Troopers Get Liquor Laws.

Special to THE NEW YORK TIMES.

PLEASANTVILLE, N. Y., Dec. 5.—Captain Christopher Kemmler of Troop K, New York State police, has received copies of the new State Liquor Laws for his 102 troopers, to aid them in the task of enforcement. This was disclosed today at the headquarters of the troop in Hawthorne, N. Y. Troop K patrols Westchester, Putnam, Dutchess, Orange and Rockland Counties.

Times Wide World Photo.

THE OFFICIAL END OF PROHIBITION.

Acting Secretary of State William Phillips signing the certification that thirty-six States had ratified the repeal amendment, making it a part of the Constitution of the United States.

President's Proclamation

Continued from Page One.

United States (excluding public-debt receipts) exceed its total expenditures (excluding public-debt expenditures other than those chargeable against such receipts), or

(2) the repeal of the Eighteenth Amendment to the Constitution, whichever is the earlier.

Whereas it appears from a certificate issued Dec. 5, 1933, by the Acting Secretary of State that official notices have been received in the Department of State that on the fifth day of December, 1933, conventions in thirty-six States of the United States, constituting three-fourths of the whole number of the States had ratified the said repeal amendment;

Now, therefore, I, Franklin D. Roosevelt, President of the United States of America, pursuant to the provisions of Section 217 (a) of the said Act of June 16, 1933, do hereby proclaim that the Eighteenth Amendment to the Constitution of the United States was repealed on the fifth day of December, 1933.

Legal Purchases Asked.

Furthermore, I enjoin upon all citizens of the United States and upon others resident within the jurisdiction thereof, to cooperate with the government in its endeavor to restore greater respect for law and order, by confining such purchases of alcoholic beverages as they may make solely to those dealers or agencies which have been duly licensed by State or Federal license.

Observance of this request, which I make personally to every individual and every family in our nation, will result in the consumption of alcoholic beverages which have passed Federal inspection, in the break-up and eventual destruction of the notoriously evil illicit liquor traffic and in the payment of reasonable taxes for the support of government and thereby in the superseding of other forms of taxation.

I call specific attention to the authority given by the Twenty-first Amendment to the government to prohibit transportation or importation of intoxicating liquors into any State in violation of the laws of such State.

I ask the whole-hearted cooperation of all our citizens to the end that this return of individual freedom shall not be accompanied by the repugnant conditions that obtained prior to the adoption of the Eighteenth Amendment and those that have existed since its adoption. Failure to do this honestly and courageously will be a living reproach to us all.

Urges People to Sobriety.

I ask especially that no State shall by law or otherwise authorize the return of the saloon in its old form or in some modern guise.

The policy of the government will be to see to it that the social and political evils that have existed in the pre-prohibition era shall not be revived nor permitted again to exist. We must remove forever from our midst the menace of the bootlegger and such others as would profit at the expense of good government, law and order.

I trust in the good sense of the American people that they will not bring upon themselves the curse of excessive use of intoxicating liquors, to the detriment of health, morals and social integrity.

The objective we seek through a national policy is the education of every citizen towards a greater temperance throughout the nation.

In witness whereof, I have hereunto set my hand and caused the seal of the United States to be affixed.

Done at the City of Washington, this fifth day of December, in the year of our Lord nineteen hundred and thirty-three, and of the Independence of the United States of America the one hundred and fifty-eighth.

By THE PRESIDENT.

WILLIAM PHILLIPS,
Acting Secretary of State.

SAYS NORTH CAROLINA MUDDLED DRY VOTE

Former Governor Gardner, Here, Holds Repeal Lost Because It Was Tied to State Issue.

Although in favor of national prohibition repeal, the people of North Carolina voted against it in the last election because the wets there wanted repeal of State liquor restrictions as well, former Governor O. Max Gardner of North Carolina declared in an interview here yesterday. The former Governor is in New York on business.

Had North Carolina adopted Virginia's method of presenting two separate issues to the electorate, one on national repeal and the other on preserving existing State statutes restricting liquor, it would have voted wet on the national issue, he said.

Former Governor Alfred E. Smith and other critics of President Roosevelt's monetary policies were assailed by Mr. Gardner, who said the only thing they were doing was hindering recovery. He declared he felt the American people were overwhelmingly in favor of the President's program.

A real business revival is taking place in the South, Mr. Gardner said. He reported that furniture, textile, tobacco and other factories had been running almost continuously for the last five months and that hundreds of thousands of new workers had been employed.

DOMESTIC WINES LIMITED.

Stock of 25,500,000 Gallons Expected to Last Till Spring.

There is enough domestic still wine 2 years old or more in warehouses in this country to supply the United States until next Spring, according to a statement issued yesterday for the Italian-Swiss winegrowers of California, who wished to offset a recent estimate that there would be no more good domestic wine after Christmas.

The existing domestic stock of such aged still wine is 25,500,000 gallons, compared to an annual American wine consumption of 50,000,000, the statement declares. When this is gone in the Spring, however, it was admitted that the 1932 crop of 16,000,000 gallons would be only coming of age, while the 1933 crop of 25,000,000 gallons would be below the 2-year age limit heretofore respected. The supply of sparkling wine is admitted to be much lower.

The difference between supplies and demand will have to be imported from countries where wine culture has been unimpeded.

CITY CELEBRATES REPEAL QUIETLY

Continued from Page One.

bad weather and did not dock until after the customs had closed, delaying the unloading until this morning.

In New Jersey, one of the strongholds of wet sentiment through the long years of dry dominance nationally, the end of the Eighteenth Amendment was celebrated without benefit of State or local liquor regulation. Governor Moore vetoed control law, which he charged was unconstitutional.

Jersey Lacks Control Law.

This action, which prevented any further legislative enactment until after midnight, was accompanied by a message from the Governor, in which he asserted that "liquor has been sold illegally in New Jersey for the past thirteen years and it will not hurt if this is done for a few days more until we get a proper control law."

In the hotels, restaurants and clubs which were able to serve their patrons with legal liquor last night the after-effects of the fourteen years of prohibition were plainly noticeable. Perhaps the most striking departure from pre-prohibition days was the absence of bars, except those of the service variety.

To satisfy those who like to watch their drinks mixed, however, many of the hotels instituted perambulating bars, which were wheeled through their cafés. Their popularity with the feminine part of the festive crowd showed the influence of the high-class speakeasy.

Bloomingdale's department store said it was the first to make a retail sale of liquor here. The store had obtained a stock of liquor under a medicinal permit and had arranged an elaborate set-up for relaying the news to its liquor department when the radio flashed Utah's action. It dispensed a bottle of port and a pint of rye to its first customer.

The Association Against the Prohibition Amendment celebrated the final realization of victory in its long fight at a dinner of its directors at the Waldorf-Astoria, at which it voted to disband. Tribute was paid by the speakers there to Captain William H. Stayton, its founder and guiding spirit, as the real captain of the victory.

Thomas E. Dewey, United States Attorney, announced that 600 padlock cases which had been pending would be dropped, in line with his announcement of Monday that only the most flagrant violations of the prohibition laws would be prosecuted in order to free the local United States court for important matters.

Machine Guns Guard Liquor.

The few trucks that got under way from bonded warehouses and distilleries last night bore mute evidence of another effect of prohibition in the presence of armed guards, and in the case of some trucks bound for Connecticut, of machine guns, to guard against possible hijackers.

A note of warning, however, was sounded by Jouett Shouse, president of the association, against the Federal code, which, he asserted, had been "forced upon the distilling industry" by government officials. Mr. Shouse maintained that it opened the way to "possible dangers of corruption and of political favoritism far beyond the opportunities created by the Eighteenth Amendment."

Replying on behalf of the Federal Alcohol Administration, its recently named director, Joseph H. Choate Jr., assured the diners that there need be no "fears for the great reform" while President Roosevelt remains in the White House.

Radio and other public addresses of leading proponents of the repeal were numerous, and in the midst of the general approval one voice was raised in bitter comment. Fred A. Victor, State Superintendent of the Anti-Saloon League, denounced drinkers as "moral cowards" and "inadequate, if not plain yellow."

Speakeasies Give Away Their Prohibition Stock

Many speakeasies that had obtained licenses found themselves without a supply of legal liquor last night. They gave away their old prohibition stock in free drinks with dinners at an average price of about $2.50. In places where drinks were sold the prices were lowered from $1 to 50 cents.

Members of the 21 Club, also known as Jack and Charley's at 21 West Fifty-second Street, helped to bring in a legal stock of liquors from warehouses that were unable to make deliveries. The club has a license for exclusive membership.

The Stork Club, which also has a club license, gave away their old stock when they found it impossible to obtain new supplies. Other places on Fifty-first and Fifty-second Streets were in similar situations.

PROCLAIMS THE END OF PROHIBITION LAW

Continued from Page One.

FACA moved to make available a better supply of whisky so that immediate heavy demands might not continue the bootlegging evil. The particular move was to establish an extra import quota for Canadian whiskies of American types, rye and bourbon, suitable for blending with newer whiskies recently manufactured in this country.

A statement issued by the FACA read:

"A temporary liquor import committee, having regard for the special circumstances as to American bourbon and rye type which is suitable for blending purposes, has decided to issue immediately permits for substantial quotas of liquor of this category."

It was tacitly understood that practically all these "substantial quotas" would come from Canada.

Administration officials reiterated their confidence that the country would have an adequate supply of good liquors and wines within the next few days. Reports streamed into the FACA offices relative to the last-minute movements of liquor shipments to strategic wholesale points and every effort was being made to facilitate the issuance of import permits for the 4,800,000 gallons already allowed under foreign quotas.

Would Prevent Profiteering.

The chief concern of officials relative to the supply was that profiteers should not reap the advantage of the immediate post-repeal demand, and that consumers, in resentment at higher prices, should not continue to patronize the bootlegger.

State Department officials, bent upon an appropriate ceremony for proclaiming the Twenty-first Amendment in effect, were taken somewhat aback when it was reported that Utah, determined to be the thirty-sixth State to ratify, would not act until about 9 P. M., Eastern standard time.

The Utah officials, according to advices reaching Washington, apparently had the idea that either Pennsylvania or Ohio might delay its convention a few hours so as to claim the distinction. However, when Pennsylvania certified its ratification before 1 o'clock and Ohio followed before 3, Utah had no further doubts.

Acting Secretary Phillips was at the White House at a meeting of the Executive Council when word reached his office that Utah would vote around 5 P. M. He hurried the last-minute preparations for the certification ceremony and had only a few minutes to wait before the telegraph wires in the State Department sounded the few ticks that told of prohibition's end.

While prohibition was thus ended nationally, many of the States remain dry and, doubtless, not a few will continue so. Only about a score had elected, up to this afternoon, to avail themselves of the new freedom allowed by the Twenty-first Amendment, although legislative processes are understood to be under contemplation in a number of others whereby liquor will be made legal.

To Protect Dry States.

The new amendment makes it mandatory upon the Federal Government to protect these dry States from wet invasions.

Announcement was made at the Department of Justice this afternoon that the former force of 1,300 prohibition agents would be employed for the time being in that service. Attorney General Cummings changed the name of the force, however, from the Prohibition Division of the Bureau of Investigation to the Alcoholic Beverages Unit of the same bureau.

Legal divisions of a number of bureaus were still at work today making the adjustments necessary to repeal. Lawyers at the Industrial Alcohol Bureau, which passes tonight into the Bureau of Internal Revenue, said there would be no trouble about diverting stocks of medicinal liquor into commercial channels.

Repeal of the amendment carried with it repeal of the medicinal liquor laws, they said, adding that liquor sold in drugstores throughout the country, except in strictly Federal territory and States that forbid it, may be sold for beverage purposes. Concentration warehouses, they said, may release liquor to persons having permits to distribute it without any formal notice of repeal being sent to field agents.

Dry Leaders' Comment.

At the final accomplishment of prohibition repeal today dry leaders hailed again their cause, with some of them predicting that the United States would return to some such method of liquor control.

In the absence from Washington of Dr. F. Scott McBride, general superintendent of the Anti-Saloon League of America, the following comment was made by O. G. Christgau, executive assistant:

"Legalized liquor is now on tap and also on trial. The people will render their verdict after they see the difference between prohibition and legalized liquor sales.

"From now on the sponsors of repeal must accept responsibility for the evils of liquor. It is up to them to try to keep their promises, and when they fail there will be a change. It is unfortunate for the wets that they won during hard times because liquor is bad enough in good times. Also it is tragic that repeal should have come just before Christmas.

"Repeal of the Eighteenth Amendment will not solve the liquor problem nor end the fight for prohibition. It's impossible to make liquor good by law and so long as the liquor traffic exists the battle against this intolerable evil will go on.

"By the time the Anti-Saloon League convention meets in Washington during the second week of January liquor sales systems will have been in effect in many of the States and there will have been a test of the promises to protect dry territory and keep out the saloons. The results will be reported and studied as a basis of a new dry program to combat the liquor evil.

"Meanwhile, the league insists that it is smarter not to drink at all than to drink legal liquor, especially if you drive an automobile."

ENFORCEMENT UNIT FACES TRIPLE TASK

It Must Guard Dry States, Aid Tax Collections and Fight Smuggling.

CORPS NOW TOTALS 1,300

No Increase Is Expected in Hurly's Force—Codes May Spur Rum-Running.

Special to THE NEW YORK TIMES.

WASHINGTON, Dec. 5.—John S. Hurly, deputy chief of the Department of Justice's Bureau of Investigation, in charge of prohibition enforcement, said today that the present force of 1,300 would remain as now deployed in the dry and wet States until the Treasury set up its machinery of internal revenue agents for enforcement of the revenue laws.

Attorney General Cummings said at the same time that the name of this enforcement arm would be changed to the Alcoholic Beverage Unit.

Under this agency the Department of Justice agents in the wet States will operate chiefly for the protection of the government's revenue in cooperation with Treasury agents. It is assumed that Mr. Hurly's men will be withdrawn from wet States as soon as the proper machinery for tax collection is formulated by the Treasury.

No great increase in the personnel of the Internal Revenue Bureau, it is said, will be necessitated by the new taxes on liquor. The collections will be handled by collectors of internal revenue in the various districts.

In the dry States the Department of Justice agents will function to protect them, under the Webb-Kenyon Act, from an inflow of liquor from their wet neighbors.

What detailed action as to the protection of dry States will be taken must result from experience, officials said today. Some doubt was expressed whether the force of 1,300 agents would be sufficient for the purpose, even when withdrawn from wet territory.

Most officials expressed the belief that no increase in the forces was likely and that the dry States would be forced to cooperate for their own protection.

For the time being at least the alcoholic unit will cooperate with the Coast Guard and customs service to prevent liquor smuggling.

Officials differ in opinion as to the difficulties that will be encountered with smugglers. Prior to prohibition, when liquor taxes and tariffs were nominal and there were no code restrictions on imports, the smuggling problem was not of great importance.

Establishment of the codes, however, may stimulate smugglers to activity, although most officials do not believe that the problem will be comparable to that from 1920 to repeal.

The present fleet of the Coast Guard is greatly reduced under that prior to the economy drive and hardly would be sufficient to meet any substantial drive on the part of smugglers.

Joint regulations were issued today by Guy T. Helvering, Internal Revenue Commissioner, and J. Edgar Hoover, director of the Division of Investigation, relative to the effect of repeal in the District of Columbia, Hawaii, Puerto Rico and other Territories and possessions.

"All the News That's Fit to Print."

The New York Times.

LATE CITY EDITION
WEATHER—Showers today; tomorrow fair, somewhat cooler.
Temperatures Yesterday—Max., 91, Min., 73

Section 1

VOL. LXXXIII....No. 27,917. Entered as Second-Class Matter, Postoffice, New York, N. Y. NEW YORK, SUNDAY, JULY 1, 1934. Including Rotogravure Picture, Magazine and Book Sections. F TEN CENTS | TWELVE CENTS Beyond 200 Miles. Except in 7th and 8th Postal Zones.

HITLER CRUSHES REVOLT BY NAZI RADICALS; VON SCHLEICHER IS SLAIN, ROEHM A SUICIDE; LOYAL FORCES HOLD BERLIN IN AN IRON GRIP

EXCHANGE, LABOR BOARDS NAMED; FARM BILL SIGNED

KENNEDY IN 'CHANGE POST

The Others Are Mathews, Landis, Healy, Pecora for Varying Terms.

WIRE BOARD IS CHOSEN

Members Are Sykes, Brown, Case, Stuart, Payne, Gary and Walker.

RAIL PENSIONS APPROVED

Clark Howell Heads Air Study —Moffett Made Administrator of the Housing Act.

President Clears His Desk

On the eve of his departure this evening on the cruiser Houston for a month's cruise, President Roosevelt cleared his desk last night.

He named the two commissions to regulate the Stock Exchanges and the operations of telegraph, telephone and radio companies.

He signed the Frazier-Lemke bill setting up new methods for the compromising of agricultural indebtedness.

He signed the railroad employes' pension bill.

He appointed James A. Moffett of New York, prominent oil executive, Administrator of the Housing Act.

He appointed an Aviation Commission, with Clark Howell as chairman.

He created an impartial Labor Relations Board, abolishing the old one and eliminating the NRA from a rôle in settling labor disputes.

Picks Exchange Board

Special to THE NEW YORK TIMES.

WASHINGTON, June 30.—As his last act tonight in cleaning up essential business before sailing from Annapolis for a month's holiday today, President Roosevelt named the personnel of the Securities and Exchange Commission.

He did not designate a chairman, there being some doubt as to his authority to do so, but it was understood in well-informed quarters that responsibility for the commission's work under the sweeping Stock Exchange Control Act would fall upon Joseph P. Kennedy, New York financier, who was designated to serve for five years. Four other commissioners were named for periods varying from one to four years.

The personnel of the commission follows:

JOSEPH P. KENNEDY of New York, five-year term.

GEORGE C. MATHEWS of Wisconsin, four-year term.

JAMES M. LANDIS of Massachusetts, three-year term.

ROBERT E. HEALY of Vermont, two-year term.

FERDINAND PECORA of New York, one-year term.

Messrs. Mathews and Landis are members of the Federal Trade Commission. Mr. Pecora was counsel for the Senate Banking and Currency Committee during the period in which it aired publicly for the first time in twenty years the manifold operations of securities exchanges and investment banking houses. As committee counsel he played a large part in shaping the law under which the commission will operate.

The naming of the Securities and Exchange Commission came after President Roosevelt, in a day of intensive work, had also named the Communications Commission and a commission to plan coordination of aircraft development, and had issued statements announcing the signing of the Frazier-Lemke Farm Mortgage Bill and the Railroad Pensions Bill.

Kennedy Close to Farley.

The membership of the Securities and Exchange Commission had been pretty generally forecast, but even so its composition was full of surprises, particularly the obvious placing in line for the chairmanship of Mr. Kennedy.

This is the first emergence of the New Yorker from what seemed to be political eclipse since the campaign of 1932, when he was distinguished both as a heavy contributor and important raiser of campaign funds, and because of his

Continued on Page Twenty-one.

Major Sports Results

Track—Bill Bonthron of Princeton broke the world's record for the 1,500-meter run in the national A. A. U. championship meet at Milwaukee. Timed in 3:48.8, he beat Glenn Cunningham by two feet. It was the fifth meeting between the stars and the triumph gave Bonthron the edge with three victories.

Tennis—Four Americans advanced at Wimbledon. Frank Shields defeated Christian Boussus of France and George M. Lott Jr. halted Harry Hopman of Australia. Miss Helen Jacobs conquered Mlle. Jacqueline Goldschmidt of France and Miss Sarah Palfrey beat Miss J. Jedrzejowska of Poland.

Baseball—Routing Carl Hubbell, the Dodgers stopped the Giants, 8— before 12,000 at the Polo G ds. At Washington the Yank es were leading the Senators, 4—1, when rain caused the game to be called off in the fifth inning.

(Full details in Sports Section.)

JOHN JACOB ASTOR WEDS ELLEN FRENCH

Notables Fill Newport Church for Ceremony Climaxing Weeks of Social Activity.

ONLOOKERS PACK STREETS

Crowd Delays Both Bride and Bridegroom—Astor's Mother Sits in a Front Pew.

By RUSSELL B. PORTER.

Special to THE NEW YORK TIMES.

NEWPORT, R. I., June 30.—Two of America's oldest families, prominent in both landed wealth and in social position, were united in marriage here today at the wedding of John Jacob Astor 3d and Miss Ellen Tuck French.

The bridegroom is the third of his name in American life. The first John Jacob Astor, fur trader, founded the family in early American days. The second lost his life in the sinking of the Titanic, and the third John Jacob Astor, today's bridegroom, was born .. few months later. He is a half-brother of Vincent Astor, and inherited with the latter the great Astor fortune.

The bride is a granddaughter of Amos Tuck French and is related to the Vanderbilt family.

These young members of old families, the bridegroom only 21 years old and the bride 18, were joined together in a setting replete with symbols of early American traditions.

They were married according to the ancient simple ritual of the Protestant Episcopal Church, whose worshipers came to New England with the first settlers, in old Trinity Church, a long, narrow, weather-beaten white clapboard building with a towering white steeple and gilded spire and weather vane. It was all just as it was when the church was built more than two centuries ago, in 1726, eighty-seven years after the founding of Newport in 1639.

Shading the high steeple was a fine, old elm tree, as tall as or taller than the spire itself, with its great spreading branches almost speaking aloud the story of New England. The tree itself was as old or nearly as old as the church.

Church Recalls Colonial Days.

On the other side of the church, so that the wedding procession walked between it and the old tree to enter the building, was the old burying ground with its plain weather-beaten granite headstones bearing the names of men and women who played leading parts in shaping the history of the colonies and of the first days of the Republic.

All around the church, which is right in the centre of this fine old city, old frame buildings of Colonial architecture, with Grecian columns, steeply slanting roofs and gables, crowding close to the building line of the street, bespoke Newport's history.

The time joined with the place in celebrating the event with appropriate ceremony, for not only was it in the midst of the Summer season, when Newport's social colony is always in full swing, but it was coincident with a visit of a large part of the United States fleet. From time immemorial the navy has been associated with Newport, and

Continued on Page Eighteen.

FORD WILL ACCEPT NRA AND ITS CODE, JOHNSON IS TOLD

General Announces He Awaits Signed Certificate From Auto Maker.

SAYS HE ASKED CHANGES

Recovery Head Asserts His Suggestions Have Been Approved in Detroit.

Special to THE NEW YORK TIMES.

WASHINGTON, June 30.—General Johnson believed tonight that he was nearing such a settlement of his ten months feud with Henry Ford as would let the NRA put another feather in its cap and at the same time allow the automobile maker to re-enter the fertile field of government business.

General Johnson today read a copy of an unsigned letter purporting to be from the Ford Motor Company to a local dealer, setting forth the claims that that firm had been complying and would continue to comply with "pertinent" provisions of the Automobile Code.

The Recovery Administrator s. that if the letter, with certain revisions which he suggested, were returned to him signed by Henry Ford or any other authorized executive of the Ford Motor Company, he would consider it a certificate of compliance, would call off his "crack-down" campaign against the company and recommend to President Roosevelt that it be allowed to resume bidding on government contracts.

A large order of motor trucks for the army, which War Department officials prefer should be Ford products, is said to be the immediate stake in negotiations between the NRA and Mr. Ford. Harry H. Woodring Assistant Secretary of War, has made overtures to General Johnson within the last thirty-six hours to learn what the Ford company would have to do to qualify to bid.

Representative Kvale of Minnesota, active in the House Military Affairs Committee investigating War Department purchases, accompanied the Ford dealer when he called to show the unsigned letter to General Johnson this afternoon.

Talks To Ford Adviser.

General Johnson believed the letter to be entirely authentic and to have originated at the Detroit offices of the Ford Company despite the circumstances under which it was shown to him. This belief was intensified by a telephone conversation which he had with William J. Cameron, editorial adviser to Mr. Ford, regarding the suggested revisions.

The letter, according to General Johnson, was addressed to the Northwest Motor Company of Bethesda, Md., the local dealer that has tried so consistently to keep in contractual relations with the governmental departments regardless of Mr. Ford's refusal to sign a compliance certificate for his code.

In its original form the letter said that although the company had complied and would continue to comply with the provisions of the automobile compact, it reserved its "constitutional rights" as guaranteed by the fundamental law.

This was the section to which General Johnson objected. He told R. P. Sabine, president of the Northwest Motor Company, and Representative Kvale that President Roosevelt would not stand for

Continued on Page Twenty-two.

POLICE FILL THE STREETS

Goering's Forces Keep Curious Throngs on Constant Move.

MACHINE GUNS MOUNTED

Public Buildings on Unter den Linden and Wilhelmstrasse Are Heavily Guarded.

NEWS IS AT A PREMIUM

Rumors Are Rampant as Only a One-Sheet Paper Provides Authentic Information.

Copyright, 1934, by The Associated Press.

BERLIN, June 30.—With the peaceful cool of a Summer evening made strangely tense by squads of armed police and the presence of machine guns, this capital city was facing tonight the possibility of a new unnamed, undefined political event.

Crowds of curious spectators, only partly informed as to events through limited press dispatches, surged up and down Wilhelmstrasse, where public buildings were massed with police ever ready to keep them on the move.

In front of the home of Captain Ernest Roehm, suicide deposed leader of the storm troops, were bristling truckloads of Prussian Premier Hermann Goering's special police. They formed an impressive barricade separate from the thousands who dragged their feet in slow response to demands that streets and sidewalks be kept clear.

Show of Force Excites Crowds.

The presence of police everywhere one turned was a direct stimulant to the excitement of the street and thoroughfare. Never in the history of Berlin, it was pointed out, had so many police appeared in the streets at one time with such obvious readiness for action. In addition to the regular police force, augmented by armed reserves, there was the steel-helmeted, green-clad police of Premier Goering.

The sudden appearance of a police machine gun detachment, with ammunition ready, in historic Potsdammer Platz brought a final touch to the grimness of the situation. The sight of another similar detachment riding up and down Unter den Linden left no doubt in the public mind as to the nature of the emergency.

Men and women rushed like hounds on the scent wherever carriers appeared with copies of one newspaper which had printed one page only for free distribution. This carried a brief account of Captain Roehm's discharge by Chancellor Hitler.

Reactions to the news were various and could be read at will on the faces of newspaper readers. Persons obviously of a conservative mind wreathed their faces in smiles as they read what had happened.

Continued on Page Three.

THREE OF THE LEADERS WHO DIED IN THE REICH MUTINY.

Times Wide World Photo.
Captain Ernst Roehm, ousted Storm Troop head, who committed suicide.

Associated Press Photo.
Karl Ernst, Berlin Storm Troop leader, arrested and later shot.

Times Wide World Photo.
General Kurt von Schleicher, slain by arresting officers.

STORM TROOP CHIEFS DIE

Killed or Take Own Lives as Chancellor and Goering Strike.

REACTIONARIES ALSO HIT

Wife Shot With Schleicher as He Resists Police—Head of Catholic Action Slain.

HITLER FLIES TO MUNICH

Tears Off Rebels' Insignia and Arrests and Ousts Roehm —Papen Held but Freed.

By FREDERICK T. BIRCHALL.

Wireless to THE NEW YORK TIMES.

BERLIN, June 30.—On the eve of a self-proclaimed month of peace Germany has passed today through the throes of a violent purging that must profoundly affect her future. It is neither a revolution nor a coup d'état nor a counter-revolution but authoritative action intended to head off any of the three.

Chancellor Hitler in Munich, backed by General Hermann Wilhelm Goering, Premier of Prussia, in Berlin, has struck simultaneously at the rebel elements in his own Storm Troops and at certain reactionary elements temporarily allied with them or suspected of being so allied for their own ends in an attempt to upset the present régime in Germany.

When the day was over many Storm Troop leaders had been shot to death or had committed suicide.

In addition, General Kurt von Schleicher, Herr Hitler's predecessor as Chancellor, had been slain while resisting police who attempted to seize him as one of the plotters.

[Captain Ernst Roehm, chief of staff of the Storm Troops, committed suicide after having been ousted by Chancellor Hitler, according to The Associated Press, while Heinrich Klausener, chief of the Catholic Action, was shot to death by a Nazi special guard.]

The Official Version.

The official version is that the attempt was a joint effort "to bring pressure" on the government with a threat of violent action behind it. There is mention of a "foreign power" as being involved. The discerning interpret this reference as being to Russia and the ultimate aim of the rebels as a new national bolshevism.

Whatever the cause, Chancellor Hitler has acted swiftly and decisively. Flying to Munich in the early hours of this morning from Bonn, where he had been ostensibly inspecting work camps, he assembled his trusted special guards in that city and proceeded to gather in the suspected leaders, who had already proceeded to preliminary action.

Captain Roehm, the leader of the conspiracy, was arrested in his bedroom in his country house outside Munich by Herr Hitler himself and then and there deposed from all his offices. His fellow-conspirators were gathered in by the dozen in Munich and around it.

The official story told to foreign correspondents by General Goering this afternoon says that some of them, both in Munich and in Berlin, committed suicide and others were shot while resisting.

Goering Acts Swiftly.

Almost simultaneously in Berlin General Goering, by arrangement with Chancellor Hitler, was taking similar action. It came swiftly and unexpectedly just before noon. But here the members of the reactionary group believed to be acting with the rebel Storm Troop leaders were equally the objects of the assault.

Karl Ernst, group leader of the Berlin Storm Troops, was traced to a house near Bremen and surrounded there. He is dead and the official version is that he was shot while resisting arrest. The unofficial version is that he was brought by airplane to Berlin and executed on his arrival.

Police and special guards at the very outset sought to put General von Schleicher under arrest at his villa outside Potsdam. It is said that he attempted to draw a pistol. A volley of shots brought him down and his wife died with him.

Vice Chancellor Franz von Papen, who seems to have been under sus-

Continued on Page Two.

HITLER COMMANDS NAZI ABSTINENCES

Forbids the Troopers to Spend Money on Banquets and Bans Moral 'Debauches.'

WANTS 'MEN, NOT APES'

Chancellor Asserts All Must Be on Best Behavior or Be Expelled From Ranks.

Wireless to THE NEW YORK TIMES.

BERLIN, June 30.—Chancellor Adolf Hitler issued these eleven commands today to Viktor Lutze, new Chief of Staff of the Storm Troops:

In naming you Chief of Staff of the Storm Troops I expect that you will accept the series of duties that I herewith inform you of.

1—I demand of a Storm Troop leader, just as from a Storm Trooper, blind obedience and unquestioning discipline.

2—I demand that every Storm Troop leader recognize, like every other political leader, that his behavior and reputation must be an example for his organization and for our whole body of followers.

3—I demand that Storm Troop leaders, exactly as in the case of political leaders, be expelled from the Storm Troops without hesitation as soon as their behavior disgraces them in the eyes of the public.

Demands Simplicity.

4—I demand specially from the Storm Troop leader that he be an example of simplicity, not of display. I do not desire Storm Troop leaders to give costly dinners or that they attend such dinners. There was a time when we were not invited to such affairs, and we have nothing to seek there now. Millions of our fellow citizens have not even the necessaries of life. They are not oblivious of those whom fortune has favored, but it is unworthy of a National Socialist to increase the gulf between fortune and misery, which is already great enough.

I prohibit the use of Storm Troop or party funds for festivals and the like. It is shameless to stage debauches with the pennies of our poorest citizens. The luxurious headquarters in Berlin, in which it has now been discovered that some 30,000 marks monthly were spent for banquets, is to be done away with immediately.

State Dinners Excepted.

I prohibit for all party groups banquets and dinners paid for with any variety of public funds. I forbid all party and Storm Troop leaders to partake of such banquets. The only exceptions are functions necessary for reasons of State, notably those for which the Reichspresident and the Reich Foreign Minister are responsible. I forbid all party leaders and Storm Troop leaders to give so-called diplomatic dinners. A Storm Troop leader does not need to engage in representation, but simply to do his duty.

5—I do not desire Storm Troop leaders to undertake business trips in expensive limousines or cabriolets, or to employ public funds for such trips. The same

Continued on Page Two.

Hitler Alone Had Power To Order Shooting of 7

Special Cable to THE NEW YORK TIMES.

BERLIN, June 30.—Over its report of the deaths of seven storm troop leaders who yesterday were in power in German, the Völkischer Beobachter, Chancellor Hitler's own newspaper, carried the headline, "Seven Storm Troop Leaders Shot. End of Convicted Traitors."

The German words used for the verb and adjective taken together in this connection carry a wider meaning than the English equivalent, as is the case with so many German words. They imply that the men were proved guilty and executed.

These men were shot on the spot without trial on the mere allegation of their guilt by order of a higher authority. The only authority which could give an order for their execution unchallenged was Adolf Hitler, who, according to the same article in this newspaper, "is the supreme conscience of the German people."

GOERING POLICE NET CATCHES LEADERS

Suicides and Killings Follow Raids on Homes of Notables in Berlin and Vicinity.

By OTTO D. TOLISCHUS.

Wireless to THE NEW YORK TIMES.

BERLIN, June 30.—General Kurt von Schleicher, former Premier, was killed with his wife while "resisting arrest with a weapon in his hand," according to an official communiqué.

The communiqué was one of a long series issued throughout the day as the criminal police of Premier Hermann Goering of Prussia rushed about Berlin and its vicinity, leaving a heavy wake of arrests, suicides and killings among prominent persons.

General von Schleicher met death at his villa in Neubadelsberg, between Berlin and Potsdam. His wife, Frau Elisabeth von Schleicher, it is stated, fell while trying to shield him with her body during an exchange of shots.

From that point tragedy quickly spread. One squad of General Goering's police rushed to the office of Vice Chancellor Franz von Papen in Vos Strasse, next to the Chancellery, and asked the Vice Chancellor to accompany them to his home. There they kept Colonel von Papen under house arrest, and questioned him regarding his relations with General von Schleicher. The amenities were preserved, and later it was stated Colonel von Papen was "at liberty."

Von Papen Visitors Barred.

Visitors to Colonel von Papen's house, however, were not allowed to see him. His secretary and a Reichswehr officer assured every one that Colonel von Papen was in good spirits, had just finished tea and was smoking his afternoon cigar.

His office meanwhile had been occupied by black uniformed special guards, men with field equipment, rifles and hand grenades. To inquirers they insisted they were merely Colonel von Papen's regular guard, placed there to protect him. Visitors noted, however, that all doors of the building stood open, as if a whirlwind had swept through.

In the face of this action, Colonel

Continued on Page Eight.

NAZI CHIEFS TELL OF ENDING REVOLT

Hitler and Lutze Appeal to the Storm Troops to Be Faithful to Their Movement.

RAID DESCRIBED BY PARTY

Leader of War Veterans Urges Them to Be Calm and to Be Loyal to Government.

Wireless to THE NEW YORK TIMES.

BERLIN, June 30.—A series of statements was issued today by German leaders on their success in crushing the radical Nazi revolt.

NAZI PARTY STATEMENT.

A communiqué from the National Socialist party read:

Munich, June 30.

For many months individual elements have been trying to drive a wedge and produce conflicts between the Storm Troops and the party, as well as between the Storm Troops and the State. Suspicions of this became more and more confirmed, but it was also plain that these endeavors were to be charged to a limited clique of certain leanings.

Chief of Staff Roehm, in whom the leader placed an exceptional amount of confidence, not only did not oppose these endeavors but undoubtedly sponsored them. His well-known unfortunate characteristic gradually led to intolerable burdens which drove the leader of the movement and the Highest Leader of the Storm Troops [Hitler] into most serious conflicts of conscience.

Chief of Staff Roehm established contacts with General von Schleicher without the knowledge of Der Fuehrer [the Leader]. His go-betweens were another Storm Troop leader and an obscure person well known in Berlin, to whom Der Fuehrer had always strongly objected.

Since these negotiations also led —of course without the knowledge of Der Fuehrer—finally to contacts with a foreign power, or rather to its representative, it was not possible to avoid intervention both from the standpoint of the party and the State.

Provocative incidents brought about according to the plan caused Der Fuehrer to fly from Bonn to Munich at 2 o'clock this morning, after visiting labor camps in Westphalia, in order to remove and arrest the most seriously compromised group of leaders. Der Fuehrer himself went with only a few companions to Wiessee in order to still any attempts at resistance.

The execution of the arrests revealed such immorality that any trace of pity was impossible. Some of these Storm Troop leaders had taken male prostitutes along with them. One of them was even disturbed in a most ugly situation and was arrested.

Der Fuehrer gave orders for this plague to be done away with ruthlessly. In the future he will not permit millions of decent people to be compromised by a few of such sick men. Der Fuehrer instructed Premier Goering of Prussia to take similar action in Berlin and especially to arrest the reactionary accomplices of this political plot.

At noon today Der Fuehrer

Continued on Page Four.

Dillinger Raids Bank in South Bend, Ind., Reported Shot; Officer Slain, Loot $28,000

By The Associated Press.

SOUTH BEND, Ind., June 30.—A bandit quintet with John Dillinger reported to be in command, stormed the Merchants' National Bank today, scooped up $28,439 and fled in a wild barrage of bullets, leaving a slain policeman and four wounded men in their wake.

The ruthless raiders engaged in gun battles with a detective, two officers and a jeweler as they fled from the bank and made their way to the escape car a half block away. More than fifty shots raked the street in the heart of the city.

Detective Harry Henderson, who identified the bandits' leader as Dillinger, said he believed that he had shot the long-sought gunman as the quintet's car sped away.

Patrolman Harold Wagner encountered the three gangsters who carried out the actual robbery as they were hurrying from the bank. He was fatally wounded before he could reach his pistol.

Those wounded were P. G. Stahley, manager of the Birdsell Manufacturing Company; Jake Soloman, Delos N. Coen, a cashier, and Samuel Toth. At Epworth Hospital it was found that a bullet had struck Soloman in the hip and coursed upward. His condition was described as critical. Toth was wounded in the eye as a bullet smashed the windshield of his automobile.

Leaving an outpost, believed to be John Hamilton, on guard at their automobile, and another bandit closer to the bank, the man identified by a police detective as Dillinger, with two henchmen, one of them believed to be "Baby Face" Nelson, rushed into the bank about noon. Cowing the twenty-five customers with a machine gun, the man identified as Dillinger took up a strategic post and sent a score of slugs into the ceiling while his confederates snatched up $28,439. C. W. Coen, vice president of the institution, who took cover under a desk three feet from the gunner, declared he was positive the leader was the desperado Dillinger.

Bundling their loot, the three commandeered Stahley, Coen and several other patrons and used them as human shields as they marched out the door. Wagner ran toward them from across the crowded street. The machine gunner shot him down, three bullets entering the policeman's body.

Today's News Index

Automobile Exchange
MOTOR BOATS
SECTION 8.

Swift Blows by Nazi Leaders Crush Radical Plot in Reich

HITLER SMASHES A RADICAL REVOLT

By FREDERICK T. BIRCHALL.

Continued From Page One.

picion of some connection with General Schleicher, although they were not friends, was temporarily arrested and questioned as to his relations with the reactionaries. He was, however, left at his home under guard, and after answering questions was no further molested.

Secretary Is Arrested.

He was quite calm under examination and thoroughly convinced his questioners. However, his secretary and mouthpiece, Herr von Bose, was arrested and is said to be still in custody.

Police and special guards armed with rifles were placed around the homes of Cabinet Ministers. All public buildings were occupied and everywhere around important points were visible the rifle-bearing green-clad bodyguards of the Prussian Premier.

But apparently neither in Berlin nor Munich, except in isolated cases of individuals, was there the least resistance. Not only was the action so unexpected that it took the conspirators by complete surprise, but they appeared to have no really substantial following even among the storm troops themselves.

The dead are alleged tonight to include General von Schleicher and his wife and these six storm troop-leaders:

District Group Leader August Schneidhuber of Munich.

District Group Leader Edmund Heines of Silesia.

District Group Leader Karl Ernst of Berlin.

Group Leader Wilhelm Schmid of Munich.

Group Leader Hans Hayn of Saxony.

Group Leader Hans Peter von Heidelbreck of Pomerania.

Hard to Paint Full Picture.

It is difficult within a few hours of events like these taking place over so wide an area as Germany, from news sources that have lost the habit of collecting news and aided only by newspapers restricted to official outgivings, to paint a complete picture of all that has happened today.

Fortunately, official utterances have been fairly liberal and ostensibly frank and themselves convey a fairly clear idea of developments in this great day of Germany's internal struggling.

The fullest account was supplied by General Goering to foreign correspondents summoned to his office early in the afternoon. This was supplemented in what purported to be an official text of what he said, given out this evening, by a further illuminating passage that no one present remembered having been spoken then. It was probably added as an afterthought. Here it is:

"The main go-between in the conspiracy was former Reich Chancellor General von Schleicher, who made conduction between Captain Roehm and a foreign power and those eternally dissatisfied figures of yesterday. I expanded my task by delivering a stroke against those dissatisfied ones also.

"It was self-understood that General von Schleicher had to be arrested. While being arrested, he attempted to make a lightning assault upon those men who were to arrest him. Thereby he lost his life."

Unofficial Versions.

This is the sole authoritative version of General von Schleicher's death. Unofficial versions have it that the attempt to arrest him was made as he was leaving his villa near Potsdam with his wife to enter their motor to drive to Berlin and that she fell beside him under the rain of bullets that greeted his supposed attempt to draw a pistol.

But the most dramatic of all the scenes in this national drama were enacted near Munich and the outstanding figure in them was Chancellor Hitler himself. It seems that all along he had known of the conspiracy and his secret police were closely watching it. For several nights he had gone sleepless reading reports and giving instructions while awaiting the moment to strike.

After his interview with Franz Seldte, commander of the Stahlhelm, on Thursday, he went yesterday to the wedding of one of his followers near Essen merely to throw the conspirators off guard and assure them that all was well. After the wedding he inspected several labor camps, all the time keeping in touch with Premier Goering, who was the centre of information as to what was going on.

Early in the evening at Bonn the Chancellor ordered an airplane to be ready at the flying field at 2 o'clock in the morning, and at that time he started on his trip to Munich.

Arriving there at dawn, he learned that the storm troops in Munich and around had already been mobilized by the leaders who were in the conspiracy. They had circulated this slogan:

"The leader is against us, the Reichswehr opposes us. Comrades, to the streets!"

Adolf Wagner, the Bavarian Minister of the Interior, had been alarmed by the resulting influx the night before. He had sent some groups home and deposed some of the leaders. Chancellor Hitler sought out Herr Wagner.

In the meantime news of the Chancellor's arrival had spread like wildfire and the group leaders hurried to him, some voluntarily and some brought by an urgent summons. It was then barely 5 o'clock in the morning.

Chancellor Hitler called in his guards and ordered the arrest of the known rebels, himself tearing the insignia from their uniforms. Leaving them in custody, he motored on at top speed to Bad Wiessee, a resort outside Munich, where Captain Roehm was resting in his country house, and Herr Heines, Silesian leader and chief of police of Breslau, was spending the night. Captain Roehm was ill abed. It was only 5:30.

Strides In Unannounced.

Unannounced, Herr Hitler with his guards strode into Captain Roehm's bedroom and himself declared that his Storm Troop chief of staff was under arrest. Captain Roehm made no protest and attempted no resistance. While he dressed for his transfer to prison, Herr Hitler walked across the hall to the chamber of Herr Heines, who was there with a youthful male companion.

"The scene that took place on Chancellor Hitler's arrival," says the official account, "is indescribable." Herr Hitler's own indignation was overwhelming. Herr Heines is listed tonight among the dead, but as to how he came to his death the official records are silent.

Most of the possessions of both Captain Roehm and Herr Heines were taken into custody. The proceedings at the country house lasted almost two hours. At 8 o'clock the bodyguards of the two leaders arrived in motor trucks. But it was all over. They accepted the situation.

Herr Hitler motored back to Munich where, in the meantime, his special forces had been busy. Most of the storm troopers' leaders in Southern Germany were in the city. They had been ordered there for a conference. Suspects were hunted down and arrested at their lodgings, in their cars, on the streets and some even at railway stations as they sought to flee.

Hitler Issues Decree.

Herr Hitler went to the Bavarian Ministry of the Interior, where he joined Herr Wagner and General von Epp, Governor of Bavaria. There the Chancellor issued a decree announcing the deposing of Captain Roehm and his expulsion from the party and the appointment of Chief Group Leader Viktor Lutze as Chief of Staff of the Storm Troops.

After dictating and signing the decree, Herr Hitler addressed a letter to his new Chief of Staff, who is Governor of Hanover. He has spent all his life there and had never before been brought to the attention of the German public at large. In the letter the Chancellor praised Herr Lutze as a "true and ideal Storm Troop leader" and declared he wanted the Storm Troops developed into "a true and strong link in the National Socialist movement."

Informed over the telephone of his sudden elevation, Herr Lutze quickly accepted his task. The spirit in which the new chief of the Storm Troops has undertaken it may be gathered from the initial order of the day that he addressed to them on assuming office. It demanded from them unconditional faithfulness, the severest discipline and self-sacrificing devotion.

Goebbels With Hitler.

Chancellor Hitler remained in Munich until evening. Then he flew back to Berlin. His plane landed at Tempelhof at 10 o'clock on a flying field illuminated literally like day in honor of his coming.

With him was a little group of trusted intimates including Dr. Paul Joseph Goebbels, the Minister of Propaganda, and it then came out that Dr. Goebbels had been with his leader throughout the whole exciting period in Munich. He had been summoned yesterday to meet Herr Hitler in the Rhineland, had flown there from Baden and had remained at his side.

Dr. Goebbels's hand can be seen in an official party communiqué describing the events of the morning which was issued in Munich in the afternoon. This official version stressed that Captain Roehm had taken part in an anti-Hitler plot and had caused other difficulties for the Chancellor. It also reported Herr Hitler's appeal for loyalty from the Storm Troops.

It is quite notable that the Reichswehr has not stirred. The purging has been accomplished only by the Nazi special guards with some aid from the police. Herr Hitler's foresight in creating this trusted special guard force, carefully selected and specially uniformed, is the subject of much commendation tonight.

Stahlheim Stands Ready.

Nevertheless, there is little doubt that should action by the Stahlhelm have been called for the veterans would have been ready. Their headquarters in Berlin have been open all day and their leaders have been receiving bulletins from branches all over the country. The bulletins were all of the same tenor—no disturbances anywhere and general quiet prevailing.

The Stahlhelm is quite content with the outcome. Everything has gone its way. The Stahlhelm men have no sympathy with General von Schleicher or with the conspiracy. Late this afternoon their leader, Herr Seldte, issued an order directing his men to refrain from wearing their uniforms until further notice and affirming loyalty to Chancellor Hitler and President von Hindenburg.

The Hitler Cabinet stands virtually intact. It is announced that there will be no changes except the substitution of Herr Lutze, the new chief of staff of the Storm Troops, for Captain Roehm as Minister Without Portfolio.

Colonel von Papen, whose speech defending the right of criticism, although a small thing, undoubtedly encouraged the malcontents to hasten their plans because of the encouragement it received, remains at his post. Dr. Goebbels, who fought him and had been rated as the intellectual leader of the radicals, goes through this at his leader's side.

Tomorrow and afterward may bring real revelations as to what has gone on behind the scenes before this battle was fought out in the open. It has lent new significance to the declaration of General Werner von Blomberg, the Defense Minister, Friday that the Reichswehr was the servant of the State with no share in party politics.

It has brought to sight a new future for a smaller and more carefully sifted Storm Troop aggregation. And it has put monarchist reaction on the one hand or a lapse to pseudo-bolshevism on the other far into the background. But what its other effects will be must be left to the future to determine.

Roehm Commits Suicide.

Copyright, 1934, by The Associated Press.

BERLIN, Sunday, July 1.—Captain Ernst Roehm, chief of staff of the Nazi Storm Troops and for years Adolf Hitler's closest friend, committed suicide yesterday after he had been arrested, deposed and expelled from the Nazi party.

In the crushing of the meeting, of which he was one of the chief leaders, seven Storm Troop leaders were shot to death in Munich.

Heinrich Klausener, leader of the Catholic Action group, was also shot to death here by a Naiz special guard.

Count Wolf Heinrich Helldorf, Nai pzolice president of Potsdam, ally of Captain Roehm, was killed, ostensibly while resisting arrest.

The rebellious Nazis had planned virtually to kidnap Chancellor Hitler and force him to sign a document turning the streets over to the Storm Troops for three days. In Tiergarten Strasse, the street in Berlin on which the American, Japanese and Turkish embassies are located, bomb throwers hideouts had been placed.

Captain Roehm and former Chancellor von Schleicher, who were slain resisting arrest, had been charged with plotting with a "foreign power" to end the Hitler régime. Representations came to the German Foreign Office from at least one embassy asking that the "conspiring" power be named so that other embassies in Berlin might no longer be under suspicion.

Vice Chancellor Franz von Papen, who was held in custody temporarily yesterday and later subjected to questioning by the secret police, remained extremely enigmatic. Rumors were circulated that he had been shot and that both he and his staff had been arrested again early totday.

Associated Press Photo.

HITLER'S HEADQUARTERS IN MUNICH UNDER GUARD.

The Birthplace of the Nazi Organization, Known as "The Brown House," Which Has Been Placed Under the Protection of the Reichswehr.

ROEHM CASE RECALLS 1907 COURT SCANDALS

Prince Philip and Associates of Round Table Were Accused of Immoral Practices.

Charges of homo-sexuality against Ernst Roehm, commander of the Nazi Storm Troopers, yesterday, recalled a scandal which shook the court of Kaiser Wilhelm II more than a quarter of a century ago. The central figure of that scandal was His Serene Highness Prince Philip zu Eulenburg, who died, disgraced but unpunished, in 1921.

Prince Philip, an intimate adviser of the Kaiser, had been Ambassador to Vienna in 1907 when Maximilian Harden, the noted publicist and friend of Bismarck, published a veiled reference in his newspaper The Zukunft, to the practices and orgies indulged in by the Prince and his associates of the Round Table, as the group was called.

This group constituted one of the most powerful factors in the German Government. The German nation was shocked at the revelations about the nature of the friendship which held the group together, but even more shocked at the knowledge that M. Lecompte, first secretary of the French Embassy, had been admitted to the Round Table where State secrets were common property.

Among those involved in Harden's charges was General Count Kuno von Moltke, former military governor of Berlin. He brought suit against Harden for defamation of character but the editor was acquitted. At the instigation of the Kaiser, Harden then was charged with criminal libel and Prince Philip appeared as a witness against him, denying the practices charged.

Harden was convicted and sentenced to prison. Subsequently, a former servant of Prince Philip produced evidence in support of Harden's charges and in response to popular demand that he be punished, the Prince was arrested for perjury.

His trial began in the Summer of 1908. After about three weeks it was adjourned indefinitely on the ground that he was ill. It never was resumed.

HITLER COMMANDS NAZI ABSTINENCES

Continued From Page One.

applies to leaders of the political organization.

Demands "Exemplary" Behavior.

6—Storm Troop leaders or political leaders who become intoxicated in public are unworthy of being leaders of our people. The prohibition of nagging criticism demands exemplary behavior. Storm Troop leaders who behave themselves publicly in an unseemly fashion are to be expelled from the Storm Troops without hesitation. I make the authorities responsible for carrying out this order.

I expect that the State authorities will punish such misdemeanors more severely than in the case of non-National Socialists. A National Socialist leader, especially a Storm Troop leader, shall enjoy an exceptional position. For the same reason he has exceptional duties.

Insists on "Clean" Troops.

7—I expect of all Storm Troop leaders that they will cooperate in preserving the Storm Troop as a clean and upright institution. Every mother should be able to place her son in a Storm Troop, in the party and in the Hitler Youth without any fear that he could be morally ruined. I expect accordingly that every Storm Troop leader will take the greatest care to assure the instant dismissal from the party and from the Storm Troop any one guilty of a breach of Section 175 [dealing with homosexual crimes]. I desire men in the party, not absurd apes.

8—I demand of every Storm Troop leader th' he return my loyalty with equal loyalty. In particular, I demand from them that they use their strength in fields that belong to them and not in other undertakings.

Courage a Requirement.

Before all, I expect of a Storm Troop leader that he will not demand more courage and sacrifice of those under his command than he is willing to display himself. I demand, therefore, that he show himself a genuine leader, friend and comrade in his dealings with his German fellow-citizens under his command. I expect as well that he will value in his group virtue more than numbers.

9—And I expect of you as Chief of Staff that the old party member, the old party warrior in a Storm Troop must not be forgotten. I do not desire to see thousands of unnecessary but expensive staffs created, and I expect promotion to be made not so much on the basis of abstract knowledge as for natural capacity for leadership, loyalty and readiness to sacrifice.

Halls His Followers.

In my Storm Troops I have an invaluable corps of the truest and bravest followers. These men have conquered Germany, not the late-comers of 1933.

10—I demand that a Storm Trooper be trained intellectually and physically to be a most thorough National Socialist. Alone in the philosophy of the party is to be found the unequal strength of this organization.

11—I demand that in this organization loyalty and fellowship be the ruling principle. Just as every leader demands obedience of his men so I demand of my Storm Troops' leaders respect for the law and obedience to my commands.

HITLER CALM AMID RAIDS.

Rebel Storm Troop Leaders Are Seized at Munich Railroad Station.

Wireless to THE NEW YORK TIMES.

MUNICH, June 30.—Chancellor Hitler was calm as he went about the business of crushing what seemed here like an incipient rebellion. He had arrived at dawn.

The Union Station was heavily guarded throughout the morning. Rebellious Storm Troop leaders, arriving to confer with Captain Ernst Roehm or attempting to leave after they had arrived here were arrested. Other rebel leaders came in their automobiles and were met on the road by Chancellor Hitler's guards.

In the evening, having finished his task in Munich, Herr Hitler rode back to the flying field on which he had landed at 4 A. M. and took off for Berlin.

Streicher Not Arrested.

Special Cable to THE NEW YORK TIMES.

BERLIN, June 30.—A news agency report carried all over the world tonight had it that Julius Streicher, Nazi leader in Franconia and publisher of the anti-Semitic newspaper Der Stürmer, was among those arrested in today's revolt. It is not true.

GOERING IS NOTED FOR RUTHLESSNESS

Prussian Premier and Hitler Aviation Minister, at 41 Is Known as 'Iron Man.'

WAS FLIER DURING WAR

Recently Urged Expansion of Germany's Air Force and Received Huge Budget.

General Hermann Wilhelm Goering, Minister for Aviation and Premier of Prussia, who was Chancellor Hitler's chief aid against the mutineers, is known as the iron man of the Nazi government. He is only 41 years old. He is said to hold more official posts than any one else in the government. As the founder and head of the Nazi secret police he had a reputation for ruthlessness.

Goering is the Nazi leader in Prussia and his appointment as Prussian Premier April 11, 1933, by Hitler, followed the resignation of Colonel Franz von Papen, who remained as Vice Chancellor in the Hitler Cabinet.

Big, blond, beardless and Teutonic, Goering has a brilliant war record. During the war he succeeded to the command of Baron von Richthoven's famous air circus. He won credit for twenty allied planes. Born in Rosenheim, Upper Bavaria, Jan. 12, 1893, he was the son of a Bavarian State official.

Large Air Force Urged.

As Minister for Aviation Goering was quoted recently as saying that Germany required an air force 30 to 40 per cent as great as the combined forces of Poland, Czechoslovakia and France, her nearest neighbors. A huge organization for air defense is reported to have been developed. Flying clubs have been formed throughout the country and all private aviation is supervised by the Air Sports Federation. The Air Ministry has been granted in the 1934-35 budget $83,600,000, compared with $28,000,0[illegible] in 1933-34.

One of the high lights in Goering's stormy, dramatic career was his appearance before the German Supreme Court in the trial of Communists for the burning of the building of the Reichstag, of which he was president. Goering made an emphatic denial of charges that he had ordered the building fired.

Goering and von Papen served together as Hitler's representatives in conferences with Premier Mussolini in 1933. Recently, in May, he made a tour through the Balkans, during which, it was reported, he failed to receive very cordial welcomes.

Discontent Admitted.

Goering, on June 18, admitted that discontent was growing in the Third Reich, and in an address to the Prussian State Council at Potsdam he said it was for Hitler to decide whether there should be a "second revolution." This followed von Papen's criticism of the Nazi régime by a day.

Mutiny was reported in the last week in Goering's personal bodyguard of 400 men. To quiet the reports, the office of the Premier announced that the bodyguard had been incorporated into the Field Hunters Corps, which comprises the Nazi military police. Last March an attempt to assassinate Goering was rumored when a hand grenade exploded in the Unter den Linden shortly after his automobile had passed. It was reported that Karl Ernst, who was killed yesterday resisting arrest, was in the car with Goering.

Goering's forty-first birthday was celebrated in Berlin. Police paraded and bands played in the streets. Newspaper stories hailed him as the iron man of the Nazi régime who had established security in the new State by crushing Marxism with "brutal energy" and who had laid the groundwork for Reich reform by abolishing elective self-government in Prussia.

VINDICATION IS SEEN FOR DOLLFUSS POLICY

Austria Predicts More Trouble for Germany From Nazis—Hopes Habicht Is Muzzled.

Wireless to THE NEW YORK TIMES.

VIENNA, June 30.—"Austria is feverishly awaiting news from Germany but is still lacking a reasonable explanation of today's events," the Foreign Office told your correspondent tonight.

"All we can say at present," it was added, "is to emphasize that events have justified Chancellor Dollfuss's policy to keep Nazism out of Austria. The Nazis have evidently split into hostile camps and probably will be a source of further incalculable troubles.

"We ignore what rôle Theodor Habicht and other Austrian Nazi exiles played in the Munich events. If, however, the new Nazi orientation would result in the abandoning of the present terrorist campaign against Austria, we would greatly welcome it."

The Vienna public, which, under the present press régime refuses to read its dull uniform newspapers, bought all the extras available and excitedly discussed on street corners the prospects of further German developments.

Vienna Nazis evidently are greatly disappointed. They first insisted alleged reports from Germany were the fabrications of the Austrian Government propaganda service. Later they learned the truth in a German broadcast.

The usual Nazis bombings here stopped this evening.

Frontier traffic between Austria and Germany has been suspended since morning.

Late night reports from Salzburg and Kufstein indicated order prevailed in Bavaria. German frontier guards were closely watching traffic, evidently having received orders to prevent the escape of plotters to Austria.

PRAGUE HEARS OF 'PUTSCH'

Roehm Said to Have Cached Arms in Secret Depots.

Special Cable to THE NEW YORK TIMES.

PRAGUE, June 30.—The Czechoslovakian press declares today is a turning point in the history of German Nazism.

The official Prager Presse's Berlin correspondent reports that Captain Ernst Roehm had organized a putsch extremely carefully and had hidden arms depots unknown to Chancellor Hitler or Defense Minister Werner von Blomberg.

"All the News That's Fit to Print."

The New York Times.

LATE CITY EDITION
Cloudy, mild, with occasional rain today; clearing, colder tonight. Tomorrow colder.
Temperature Yesterday—Max., 53; Min., 35

VOL. LXXXVI....No. 28,811. Entered as Second-Class Matter, Postoffice, New York, N. Y. NEW YORK, FRIDAY, DECEMBER 11, 1936. P TWO CENTS In New York City. | THREE CENTS Within 200 Miles. | FOUR CENTS Elsewhere Except in 7th and 8th Postal Zones.

EDWARD VIII RENOUNCES BRITISH CROWN; YORK WILL SUCCEED HIM AS GEORGE VI; PARLIAMENT IS SPEEDING ABDICATION ACT

CODE FOR INDUSTRY VOTED HERE TO BACK AIMS OF NEW DEAL

Association of Manufacturers Pledges Cooperation for 'Era of Good Feeling.'

ASKS FOR CENSUS OF IDLE

Moley Urges Business Join in Federal Planning—McCarl for Industrial Board.

LABOR GIVES 30-HOUR PLAN

Industrial Progress Council in Washington Hears Program for a Shorter Week.

Industry and New Deal

The National Manufacturers Association meeting here adopted a code for industry pledging "era of good feeling" and cooperation with social aims of New Deal. The text of the code is on Page 30.

The Council for Industrial Progress in Washington heard labor's plan to promote employment by a thirty-hour week and Federal regulation of working conditions. Employers did not oppose new labor laws, but spokesmen insisted that they should conform to the Constitution. Page 33.

Code Is Adopted Here

A declaration of principles for American industry, calling for an era of good feeling both at home and abroad, pledging cooperation with the government in the national interest and embracing, at least in principle, some of the most important social reforms of the New Deal, was adopted yesterday afternoon at the final session of the forty-first annual convention of the National Association of Manufacturers, held in the Waldorf-Astoria Hotel.

The declaration was in harmony with the keynote speech delivered at Wednesday's session by Colby M. Chester, chairman of the General Foods Corporation and president of the association, and in striking contrast to the bitter criticisms of the New Deal uttered by industrialists at previous meetings.

In closing the convention Mr. Chester asserted his belief that it had "written a new, sound and progressive note in the industrial life of this nation in its declaration of principles," and predicted that it would have the support of "a united industry" within the year.

Census of Idle Is Urged

Resolutions were adopted urging a government census of unemployed and opposing governmental ownership of the railroads or any transportation system.

Addresses were made by Raymond Moley, editor of the magazine Today; John R. McCarl, former Controller General; George H. Mead, president of the Mead Corporation and chairman of the business advisory council to the Department of Commerce, and James A. Emery, general counsel of the association.

Mr. Moley urged joint economic planning by the government and business. He warned industry that it must recognize the meaning of the election returns—that the people voted for security of wages and living standards—and offer them a rational plan to attain these ends if it does not wish to be compelled to submit to impractical and drastic legislation.

A balanced budget through the reduction of relief expenditures and other government spending was advocated by Mr. McCarl. He urged industry to accept the responsibility for reducing the need for relief by giving more jobs. He also suggested that business organize a National Industrial Board to cooperate with the government in the "collective" solution of social and economic problems.

According to Mr. Mead, business wants "constructive regulation," contrary to a general public impression, although it is opposed to "government ownership or control." Business also believes in economic security, he said, adding that a "practical" economic security and

Continued on Page Thirty-one

4,336,000,000 Francs Set As French Budget Deficit

Wireless to THE NEW YORK TIMES.

PARIS, Dec. 10.—There will be a deficit of 4,336,000,000 francs in the French budget during the coming year, according to figures put before the Chamber of Deputies this morning by the finance commission.

The ordinary expenditure under the budget is estimated at slightly more than 48,000,000,000 francs and the income at 43,685,000,000 francs. With these figures before them, the Deputies began to vote in rapid succession for most of the 140 articles in the law having to do with the collection of revenue despite the protest of one Right Deputy who argued that to vote revenues before expenditures was contrary to all good sense and logic.

JAPAN WITHDRAWS DEMANDS ON CHINA

Indicates Dropping of Moves for Anti-Red Cooperation and Autonomy of North China.

ARMY IS UNDER CRITICISM

Foreign Office Wants Public to Know the Military Interfere With Major Policies.

By HUGH BYAS
Wireless to THE NEW YORK TIMES.

TOKYO, Dec. 10.—Withdrawal of all the Japanese demands regarding North China autonomy and of that for cooperation against communism was implied in a statement issued to the press today by Eiji Amau, Foreign Office spokesman.

Japan asks Nanking to fulfill the agreements already reached on lesser points, but the request is not accompanied by a threat or warning except that if Japanese lives or property are endangered or Japanese rights violated the government will take "adequate measures."

Ambassador Shigeru Kawagoe's failure to obtain satisfaction from China, even in minor matters, is explained as due to Chinese indignation over the invasion of Suiyuan Province by Mongols and Manchukuoans.

Mr. Amau said nothing to connect the Japanese Kwantung Army with these events, but the public was already aware that Manchukuo's Premier had proclaimed sympathy with the Mongolian rising and knew he would not have taken such a step without being prompted.

Mr. Amau's statement, read in conjunction with Foreign Minister Hachiro Arita's answer to the Privy Council yesterday, suggested that the Foreign Office wants the public to know how the Kwantung army interferes with major policies which all branches of the Tokyo government have agreed.

The statement claims that a definite agreement was reached with China regarding suppression of anti-Japanese movements—including revision of the control of the Chengtu Kuomintang (Nationalist party) branches—engagement of Japanese advisers, control of Korean exiles and reduction of tariffs.

Consulate Involved

China further agreed to reopening of the Chengtu Japanese Consulate and accepted most of Japan's demands for settlement of recent incidents.

A hitch occurred over air services. No agreement was reached regarding joint defense against communism though both sides concurred on several items.

Economic cooperation in North China was agreed on in principle. This stage having been reached, the Chinese, "taking advantage of the Suiyuan affair," broke off negotiations, threatened to repudiate all the concessions already made and evaded Ambassador Kawagoe's repeated requests for a further interview with Foreign Minister Chang Chun. Mr. Kawagoe was said to have handed Mr. Chang a note embodying the agreed points, requesting that they be put into effect.

"Japan is now watchfully waiting for China's response and is prepared to take adequate measures if China fails to control anti-Japanese movements or if Japanese life and property interests are jeopardized," said the statement.

It is pertinent to recall that Mr.

Continued on Page Twelve

CROWDS IN LONDON CALM

News Is Received With British Reserve as Thousands Gather.

QUEEN MARY IS CHEERED

Many Break Through Police Lines When She Calls at Home of Duke of York.

TENSION OF WEEK ENDED

People Sad at Losing Edward but Relieved the Suspense at Last Is Over.

Wireless to THE NEW YORK TIMES.

LONDON, Dec. 10.—As the news of King Edward's abdication sped to the far corners of the empire this afternoon Britain received confirmation of her worst fears with mixed emotions, sadness at losing so popular and beloved a sovereign and relief that the gnawing suspense of the last week at last had drawn to an end.

Massed thousands stood silently outside the towering iron gates of Parliament while the terse, restrained statement of the first monarch in England's history ever to renounce the throne voluntarily was read to the House of Commons. Presently, as the twilight shadows of Westminster Abbey lengthened over Parliament Square, word sped from mouth to mouth that the reign of Edward was coming to an end.

Although the atmosphere a few minutes before had been highly charged with tension and anxiety the news was received calmly and with typical British reserve. There was no demonstration and no show of feeling save for the serious, strained faces in the crowd and the flutter of women's handkerchiefs here and there.

Crowds Gather Throughout Day

Throughout the day, from dawn until after midnight, crowds of varying proportions gathered outside all the buildings associated with the historic happenings of the day. People clustered about No. 10 Downing Street, the Houses of Parliament and all the royal residences, standing stolidly and silently when allowed or moving along without protest if required. If any emotion was perceptible that could be described as a corporate reaction, it was one of bewilderment and incredulity that such a thing ever could actually happen.

A throng composed mostly of women, which at times reached 10,000 or more, stood on the pavement before Buckingham Palace forming

Continued on Page Twenty

Edward Plans Radio Talk To British Empire Tonight

Special Cable to THE NEW YORK TIMES.

LONDON, Dec. 10.—King Edward will broadcast to the empire tomorrow night at 10 o'clock immediately after he has signed the Abdication Act and ceased to be King, in the character of a private person. It is expected Parliament will have disposed of its business by then.

[American networks will broadcast the message at 5 P. M., Eastern Standard Time.]

The British Broadcasting Corporation has arranged for a worldwide hook-up.

Many persons feel the King's decision to broadcast is not wise. He has already sent a message to Parliament with a penciled note to the Prime Minister, commending the Duke of York to the support of the whole empire. These will be broadcast four times tonight and printed in every British newspaper.

MRS. SIMPSON CRIES LISTENING AT RADIO

Shaken and Exhausted by the Climax in Career of King Who Forsook Throne for Her.

WILL REMAIN AT CANNES

Edward Will Not Visit Her Now—Britons in France Question Her Course.

Wireless to THE NEW YORK TIMES.

CANNES, France, Dec. 10.—With tears streaming down her face, Mrs. Wallis Warfield Simpson, for whose sake Edward VIII has abdicated as King and Emperor of the greatest empire the world has ever known, listened today as did all the rest of the world to the news over the radio from the scene in the British Parliament.

She heard the words announcing that the King Emperor of whom so much had been expected had laid down his scepter and crown so as to be free to marry her some months hence and live the life of an ordinary mortal.

Says King Won't Go to Riviera

At 1 o'clock this afternoon the following statement was made by Herman L. Rogers, at whose villa Mrs. Simpson is staying:

"There is definitely no change so far as Mrs. Simpson's plans are concerned. She will stay here until after Christmas. She is now at the villa and in the best of health. There has been no change in the household.

"It cannot be stated if she has

Continued on Page Twenty

Soviet Orders Militia Punished for Arrests Without Warrants in Spite of New Charter

Special Cable to THE NEW YORK TIMES.

MOSCOW, Dec. 10.—The first charges of violating the new Constitution were brought at Kazan today in connection with the arrests of eleven persons there by the militia on its own initiative.

According to the new Constitution, "no one may be subjected to arrest except upon the decision of a court or with the sanction of the prosecutor." Apparently no such authorization was obtained, and Moscow authorities have called the Kazan militia's action an "outrageous violation" of the Constitution and ordered that the guilty be suitably punished.

According to an investigation in Kazan, a doorman at a restaurant was arrested this week purely on suspicion. When he failed to arrive home his mother made inquiries, and on finding his son in jail complained to the public prosecutor. The latter showed little interest.

A correspondent of the Moscow newspaper Izvestia then took up the matter and spurred the prosecutor to visit the jail, where he found eleven persons arrested without warrants.

Today also the first Soviet death sentence for the infringement of private ownership and personal property and the murder of a private individual was imposed in a Moscow court.

Two employes of a State antique shop had been selling valuable old books to two highly paid ballet dancers. Thus the employes had learned their clients had money and valuables. They invaded the young dancers' home in their absence, killed their mother and cook with a brass pestle and looted the apartment. The criminals were traced, arrested, convicted and tonight they will be shot.

Hitherto the death penalty has been imposed in murder cases only where the safety or welfare of the State was involved, the normal penalty for an ordinary murder being not more than ten years.

Nikolai V. Krylenko has assumed his duties as head of the All-Union Commissariat for Justice, newly created under the Constitution. Today he began reorganizing the whole legal profession of the country into voluntary associations, which will give legal aid to any accused persons demanding their services. Any accused person is entitled to free legal counsel if he desires. Legal aid offices are also being established by trade unions.

Because of the new legal guarantees many more lawyers than hitherto will be needed. Accordingly steps are being taken to enroll thousands more students in the law schools already established, and plans are being formed for the creation of many more schools in the various republics.

BALDWIN TELLS OF EVENTS

Relates to the Commons How He Warned King Against Marriage.

DENIES ANY BITTERNESS

Says Ruler, Far From Feeling Resentment, Had Become a Firmer Friend to Him.

LEGAL ISSUE IS REFUTED

Churchill Declares It Is Now Clear That There Was Never a Constitutional Crisis.

By CHARLES A. SELDEN
Special Cable to THE NEW YORK TIMES.

LONDON, Dec. 10.—The momentous session of Parliament that received today King Edward's message of abdication was best described by Prime Minister Stanley Baldwin himself when he said near the close of his narrative of the crisis:

"This House of Commons today is a theatre which is being watched by the whole world."

Never since the first British Parliament was called by Simon de Montfort 672 years ago had it been the theatre for such an impressive tragedy as that enacted today.

There have been greater political issues, perhaps, and more fateful struggles between Crown and Commons. There have been long Parliaments, short Parliaments and rump Parliaments. But there has been no precedent for today's enactment of the tragedy in which a monarch signed away his sovereignty over an empire of 500,000,000 people for his love of a woman.

And while the play was on, the wars of one hemisphere and the efforts in the other hemisphere to end wars were merely side shows.

Extra Police on Hand

Standing room only was the situation in the legislative chamber itself, while there was not even standing room left in the acres of lobbies and for many blocks outside on the streets that lead to the Houses of Parliament.

So many extra companies of police were assigned to duty around the buildings that it was feared serious disorder was anticipated by the authorities, but nothing could have been further from the fact. There was as much decorum in witnessing this self-effacement of Edward VIII as there was last January when the multitudes gathered to mourn for his father and to proclaim him.

Needless to say, the House itself was filled as it had not been since the session at which war was declared in 1914. In the diplomatic gallery, every seat was taken by Ambassadors and Ministers from nearly all nations.

What little daylight sometimes seeps into the Commons chamber on a Winter afternoon was completely shut out by a dense fog, so there was nothing but mellow illumination from the lights above the stained glass ceiling.

House Is Ill at Ease

The House was ill at ease during the hour's interval prior to the great moment when Prime Minister Baldwin entered with the King's message of abdication. The familiar cry, "Prayers are over," after the customary, brief devotional exercise with which every session opens, was followed by many involuntary, at least unusual, "Amens," suggestive of a devout wish that for this once they might be answered quickly.

There were no "King's men" in this House. But it was equally true there were no anti-King men.

The King's own message was received in sorrow and sympathy. When Mr. Baldwin made his long statement of the events that preceded the decision to abandon the throne, there vanished the last trace of the bitterness that had developed in the last week from fear that the Crown might try to override the Commons.

"We are not judges," said Mr. Baldwin, and it was one of his utterances to which members gave their warmest assent.

"While there is not a soul among us who will not regret this from the bottom of his heart," said the

Continued on Page Sixteen

Associated Press Photo.

SUCCESSOR TO THE BRITISH THRONE
The Duke of York

YORK GETS OVATION AT HOME IN LONDON

Cheering and Singing Theatre Crowds Surge About His Car While Auto Horns Salute.

HE DOFFS HAT TO THRONG

New Monarch Expected to Use Name 'George' as Symbol of Strength and Steadiness.

Special Cable to THE NEW YORK TIMES.

LONDON, Dec. 10.—Thousands of Londoners shouted a welcome tonight to a shy and awkward young man who was ready to step into the dazzling light of the greatest throne on earth.

With the abdication of King Edward VIII, the 41-year-old Duke of York was about to take his place on the world wide stage as the latest in the long line of English sovereigns. And tonight, in front of his town house at 145 Piccadilly, the crowds had their first chance to show him that they were glad.

A surging throng of theatre-goers on the way home surrounded his car as he returned after having dinner with Edward at Fort Belvedere. Cheering and waving hats, they filled the wide roadway in front of the house and blocked traffic so completely police were powerless to keep it moving.

Before the Duke entered the house he turned to the crowd and raised his hat several times. That was the signal for a great demonstration. Hundreds of motorists set up a deafening salute with their horns, while the crowd began singing the national anthem and "For He's a Jolly Good Fellow."

Popular Reign Indicated

It was a demonstration of some importance in the story of the British throne, for it showed that the Duke may be a popular King even without any of the brilliant qualities of his elder brother.

Tomorrow night he will become King, and Saturday morning his accession will be proclaimed with the stately pageantry that has come down unchanged from medieval times. For individual kings may come and go, but the British monarchy that has survived many shocks before this will keep its place as the keystone of the vast and loosely jointed empire.

Heralds in uniforms of gold will

Continued on Page Eighteen

EDWARD CHEERFUL AFTER TAKING STEP

Reported Like Man Who Has Had Crushing Load of Worry Lifted From Shoulders.

PACKS FOR HIS DEPARTURE

Knowledge That He Will Not Be Barred From Returning to England Relieves Him.

By FERDINAND KUHN Jr.
Wireless to THE NEW YORK TIMES.

LONDON, Dec. 10.—The blue and white flag of the Duchy of Cornwall fluttered slowly to the foot of its mast at 10 o'clock this morning on the high turret over Fort Belvedere.

It was a signal that made history, for at that moment King Edward was renouncing the greatest throne on earth so that he could marry the woman he loved. With his three brothers as his only witnesses, he signed the instrument of abdication as his "final and irrevocable decision" to retire into private life.

He will remain King until tomorrow afternoon, when the Abdication Bill is expected to reach him from Parliament. As soon as he signs it, however, his unhappy days as King will come to an end after the shortest reign in 453 years. The Duke of York will come to the throne as George VI and Edward will leave England as the first man in all the 1,000 years of the British monarchy to have left the throne of his own accord.

Edward Again Cheerful

Although he has not shown himself to the public for almost a week, it was reported on good authority tonight that he was like a man who had had a crushing load of worry lifted from his shoulders.

The depression and jumpiness of the last few days had vanished and the King was said to be cheerful and purposeful, superintending the packing of his belongings dealing with State papers, which arrived incessantly from London, and looking forward to more happiness than he has known in a long time.

Workmen and tractors were busy all day on Edward's private flying field at Smith's Lawn in Windsor Great Park, apparently preparing it for the take-off of an important airplane. Four police cars were on duty and a cordon of police and

Continued on Page Sixteen

KING MAKES HIS DECISION

Chooses Woman Over Throne After 'Long and Anxious' Thought.

FINALE LIKELY TOMORROW

New Reign, Expected to Bring Back Calm of George V's, Is to Be Proclaimed Then.

CROWNING PLAN MAY HOLD

Edward Can Use Either of Two Titles, Earl of Rothesay or Baron of Renfrew.

Edward's letter, the Abdication Bill, Baldwin's speech, Page 17.

By FREDERICK T. BIRCHALL
Special Cable to THE NEW YORK TIMES.

LONDON, Dec. 10.—Some time Saturday morning, perhaps even as soon as tomorrow night, Edward VIII will cease to be King and Emperor. He has made his choice between a woman and a throne and the woman has won.

Today at Fort Belvedere, his country home near Windsor Castle, and in the presence of his three brothers, the Dukes of York, Gloucester and Kent, the King signed a message to his Ministers announcing his determination "after long and anxious consideration" to renounce the throne to which he had succeeded on the death of his father. This, said the message, is "my final and irrevocable decision."

The message was carried by Prime Minister Stanley Baldwin this afternoon to a crowded session of the House of Commons and there read, not without emotion, by the Speaker.

Bill Introduced in House

There is no question of whether the House should accept it. Under the British Constitution there can be none, for it was an expression of the King's will and the King rules, though he does not govern, Britain and the empire. But immediately afterward, as soon as the Prime Minister in a speech that will be memorable for the restrained feeling it expressed and the leaders of the Opposition each after his fashion had voiced their regret, a bill was introduced that will implement the monarch's decision.

Tomorrow this formal bill of abdication will be rushed through all its stages in both houses, Commons and Lords. It will then be carried to the King for his royal assent. The moment he signs it he ceases to be King and his brother, the Duke of York, who is nearest to him, will reign in his stead.

The new King will take the throne, according to the best information available tonight, as George VI and for that choice there is a reason. It is desired, now that this storm is over and the skies are clearing, to get back to the ordered peace and quiet stability of the monarchy under the last King George, to leave behind this brief era of conflict between will and duty and to concentrate anew on the empire and its common destiny.

Proclamation Likely Tomorrow

Another era will begin probably at noon on Saturday when the accession of the new King is proclaimed from the balcony of St. James's Palace, again at old gray Charing Cross and finally from the steps of the Royal Exchange in the City of London, each time with all the pomp and ceremony that the monarchy has upheld here throughout a thousand years. Kings may change but the old order remaineth; that is to be Britain's watchword still.

And thus, in circumstances that will arouse wonder and pity as long as history continues to be written, ends the brief reign of King Edward VIII. It has lasted ten months and twenty-two days before this strange storm that love of woman created has brought it to a close, and the empire still endures. Even a newcomer can

Continued on Page Sixteen

Britain, Seeing 'Sunlight Ahead,' Hopes to Carry Out Original Coronation Plans

BILL SPED TO GIVE ABDICATION EFFECT

Edward Still King Until He Signs Act to Be Rushed Through Commons Today.

ONLY MAXTONITES FIGHT IT

Names Successor, Bars Royal Veto of the Exiled Monarch's Marriage.

Special Cable to THE NEW YORK TIMES.

LONDON, Dec. 10.—Edward VIII is still King and will remain so until he gives his assent to a bill giving effect to his declaration of abdication.

This bill received first reading in the House of Commons tonight and will be rushed through all stages tomorrow, with the only opposition expected from four members of the Independent Labor party, headed by the fiery Clydesider, James Maxton.

The broad effect of the bill, which has no parallel in modern political history and was hastily drawn up, is to remove King Edward and his heirs, if any, from succession to the British throne; second, to declare that as soon as the bill receives royal assent the member of the royal family next in succession to the throne, namely, the Duke of York, shall succeed, and, third, that the Royal Marriages Act of 1772, which empowers the ruling monarch to approve or disapprove the intended marriage of any member of the royal family, shall not apply to King Edward after his abdication nor to issue, if any, of Edward or descendants of that issue.

Thus the Duke of York, when he becomes King, will be relieved of any responsibility of approving or disapproving Edward's proposed marriage to Mrs. Wallis Simpson.

Under the terms of the new bill a "demise of the crown" will occur when the royal assent is given, and one effect of this is that all appointments made by Edward will continue to have effect. Had this provision not been included, there would have been considerable confusion and uncertainty over these appointments.

Late tonight Mr. Maxton, in behalf of his colleagues of the Independent Labor party, gave notice of this amendment to the second reading of the bill:

"This House declines to give second reading to a bill which has been necessitated by circumstances which show already the danger to his country and the British Commonwealth of Nations inherent in a hereditary monarch at a time when the peace and prosperity of the people require a more stable and efficient form of government of the republican kind, in closer contact with and more responsive to the will of the mass of the people, and which fails to give effect to the principle of popular election."

Leaders of the other parties in the Commons for their part expressed determination to respect Edward's wish that there should be no delay of any kind in giving effect to the instrument of abdication, the signing of which will be his last official act.

ITALY SEES TROUBLE FOR ALL MONARCHIES

Thinks Abdication Is Not End of Crisis for the British—Sympathy for Edward.

Wireless to THE NEW YORK TIMES.

ROME, Dec. 10.—King Edward's abdication, though expected here, did not fail to create an enormously deep impression on the Italian public.

The young King, whom the people here still remember on the Italian front during the World War, was very popular in Italy and sympathy for him is expressed on all sides.

If the collective opinion of the Italian people can be put into words, it is that Edward as a man came out of the trial with increased stature, but that as a King he has been found wanting. Italians think a greater King than Edward would have sacrificed himself and his love for his empire.

The monarchical system, it is felt, has been shaken, not only in Britain but in all other kingdoms. Italians think, however, that the worst blow has been suffered by the British Empire, and not a few of those who are still embittered by the part Britain played in League of Nations sanctions against Italy are not sorry for Britain's discomfiture.

The general opinion in Italy is that Edward's abdication may have vast, unpredictable repercussions throughout the British Empire and that the real crisis, far from being at an end, is just beginning. Most people concede, however, that British patriotism is so powerful a force that it will enable the difficult times ahead to be overcome without disaster.

BERMUDA'S INTEREST KEEN

Has Followed London Situation Through American Newspapers.

Special Cable to THE NEW YORK TIMES.

HAMILTON, Berumda, Dec. 10.—Great Britain's oldest self-governing possession, Bermuda, which, by reason of its proximity to the United States, regularly imports American newspapers, probably has been better acquainted with the details of King Edward's situation than any other British territory. Yet the news of the King's abdication created as much interest here as if it had been unexpected.

Bermuda's only daily newspaper, The Royal Gazette and Colonist, published today an illustrated extra edition. All sources of information were besieged with telephone calls, asking for the latest news.

The government issued the official text of King Edward's statement, including the abdication document. It foreshadowed early publication of the proclamation of the Duke of York as King.

DO NOT FORGET The Hundred Neediest.

EDWARD VIII, THE WOMAN FOR WHOM HE RENOUNCED THE THRONE, AND EVENTS IN HIS SHORT REIGN

Times Wide World Photo.

King Edward VIII

© Times Wide World Photo.

Mrs. Wallis Warfield Simpson

Times Wide World Photo.

Saluting his mother as she left Armistice Day ceremonies

Times Wide World Photo.

Presiding at the royal garden party last July

Times Wide World Photo.

Proclaiming Edward King of Great Britain

Times Wide World Photo.

Leaving Parliament in November after his first visit as King

EDWARD CHEERFUL AFTER TAKING STEP

Continued From Page One

park rangers was drawn around the field to keep sightseers away.

It was thought that the King might leave Saturday morning for Switzerland, where the bracing Winter climate would restore his health and where he would be brought near Mrs. Wallis Warfield Simpson, who is still on the Riviera.

His position as ex-King will be full of uncertainties, but apparently they are not weighing heavily on him. He does not know for one thing whether or when he can marry Mrs. Simpson, although there is an impression in London tonight that the decree absolute will be expedited in a perfectly legal manner so that she can marry again at the end of January.

Edward's financial position will also be uncertain for several weeks. It is understood that he will not be allowed to retain the revenues of the Duchy of Cornwall and that a new civil list providing a monetary grant for him and other members of the royal family will not be drawn up by Parliament until early in the New Year.

But it was reported tonight that Queen Mary and her other children had agreed to contribute something out of their personal fortunes until the nation has made some provision for its former King and Prince of Wales. Neither Parliament nor the royal family wants to leave him unprovided with funds, and Edward probably feels safe in the knowledge that he will not be penniless.

One source of relief to him is the knowledge that he will not be barred from returning to England. No promise to stay away from the British Empire was exacted from him during the complicated negotiations that preceded his abdication.

No doubt he will keep away until the bitter emotions of the moment have disappeared, but there is not the slightest reason, according to persons in close touch with Downing Street, why he should not return later as a visitor or even as an ordinary private resident of the country he once ruled.

Arrival of Three Brothers

By The Associated Press.

LONDON, Dec. 10.—After a quiet night and early morning in which no vehicles left or arrived at Fort Belvedere, King Edward's country estate, except speeding dispatch riders, the King's three brothers came in dramatic succession for a final conference.

The Duke of York, in a chauffeur-driven car, was slumped down in the rear seat looking pale and tired.

The Duke of Gloucester's visit was his first to Fort Belvedere since the crisis began.

The Duke of Kent, who has spent a great deal of time with Edward and the Duke of York in the distressing hours, was at the wheel of his own car.

It was apparent that the guards at the side gates on Ascot Road, which the brothers used to avoid the crowd gathered about the main entrance in the cold fog, were unprepared for the sudden gathering of the house of Windsor. When the Duke of York's car appeared it was forced to haul up a moment as the gate was only half-opened in time.

The three brothers looked haggard, dejected and as if their heads hadn't touched a pillow all night.

An unconfirmed report circulated in London tonight that Edward would purchase a castle in Denmark, about fifty miles from Copenhagen. The castle the abdicating King was said to have in mind is owned by the Princess Erik.

Edward's calmness and courage throughout the dispute over Mrs. Wallis Warfield Simpson have deeply impressed his staff, a member of the royal household said tonight.

"His Majesty faced the supreme issue of his life with quiet dignity and perfect coolness," this source asserted. "Once his mind was made up he remained like the Rock of Gibraltar.

"The King never showed outwardly the slightest sign of the intense physical and mental strain he was undergoing. He was his usual gracious, kindly, considerate self to every one who came in contact with him, whether personal friends, official staff or servants."

Dunkirk Prepares Guard

DUNKIRK, France, Dec. 10 (AP).—The chief of special police of the port of Dunkirk said tonight that he had received orders to station extra guards at the waterfront in preparation for the possible arrival of King Edward.

"We are anxious to know definitely if he is coming here," the chief said. "When we do know we will put even more police on duty."

APPEAL TO THE KING REVEALED TO PEERS

Vain Effort to Change Ruler's Mind Shown in Letter of the Cabinet—Loss Is Deplored.

LONDON, Dec. 10 (AP).—Viscount Halifax, Lord Privy Seal, moving the reply to the King's message in the House of Lords, read correspondence that passed between the Cabinet and King Edward vainly seeking to change his "irrevocable" decision.

The white-haired Archbishop of Canterbury then rose and in a choked voice said:

"This is an occasion when our thoughts are too deep for tears and certainly too deep for words."

"The Queen mother, as I well know," he added, "during these weeks of tension and anxiety has borne herself with all the dignity, calmness and courage which have given her a place so secure in the hearts and minds of her people."

The Marquis of Salisbury described the King's abdication as a wound in the body politic.

"It is a disaster," he cried, "that leaves it mutilated and torn. When we think of all the qualities of King Edward, and that he has abandoned all these responsibilities, we can only bow our heads in sorrow."

South Africa Voices Sympathy

CAPE TOWN, South Africa, Dec. 10 (AP).—The Cape Town public and press voiced sympathy and sorrow for King Edward on his abdication today but heartily welcomed his brother, the Duke of York, as his successor.

BALDWIN RELATES STORY IN COMMONS

Continued From Page One

Prime Minister, "there is also not a soul among us here today that wants to judge."

That was true. The harsh criticism of yesterday was stilled, at least for the moment. In its place there welled up all the old affection that the people had for Edward during his years as Prince of Wales and at his accession.

"The House must remember, though it is difficult to realize," said Mr. Baldwin, "that His Majesty is not a boy. He looks so young. We have all thought of him as our Prince."

That note of the grieved, but still affectionate, father struck a responsive chord in the House. Nearly every member of it thinks the King who "looks so young" has erred and flouted the traditions of the throne that he has abandoned. But there is no anger about it tonight.

Mr. Baldwin saw to that. When he entered the House and announced "a message from the King, signed by his own hand," it was the signal for beginning a ceremony and service of poignant farewell probably never equaled. The Commons had established its supremacy over the Crown beyond all trace of doubt, but there was no gloating over the victory.

Events Are Recounted

After the Speaker had read the royal message, Mr. Baldwin, showing in his face and his voice the great strain he had been under, gave his remarkable chronicle of the events since he first talked with the King last October about his attachment to Mrs. Simpson and warned him against the danger that his course would destroy respect for the monarchy. His quotation from Hamlet beginning with, "His soul is not his own," was Mr. Baldwin's measure of the restraint the King should have put on himself but did not.

In all the frankness of the vital conversations between the King and the Prime Minister, which were revealed today, there was no suggestion of personal rancor. And there was as much evidence in Mr. Baldwin's speech of Edward's regret over what he had done as of his stubbornness in going on with it.

All through his announcement, which required nearly an hour to deliver, Mr. Baldwin received many signs of approval from the whole House. But the greatest cheers came when he ended with this:

"Now let us rally behind the new King."

By The Associated Press.

LONDON, Dec. 10.—Cheering crowds greeted Prime Minister Stanley Baldwin today as he arrived at the House of Commons to deliver what was expected to be a final explanation of the controversy between King and Cabinet over Mrs. Wallis Simpson.

Mr. Baldwin drove into the carriage entrance at 2:34 P. M. after a quick trip by automobile from 10 Downing Street.

Continuous cheers sounded as the Prime Minister's car moved from the official residence into Whitehall and under the Commons entrance.

After the Commons session opened, what had taken place in the past days of anxiety was revealed by Mr. Baldwin, the man who told the King he must not marry against the dictates of his Ministers, subjects and Dominions.

Drawing aside the curtain that had cloaked the drama of a King and a commoner, the Prime Minister, in conversational terms, told all.

It was he, Mr. Baldwin said, who first had informed the King of the gravity with which the King's Ministers viewed the divorce decree nisi granted to Mrs. Simpson from Ernest A. Simpson in October. It was he who first told the monarch of his conviction that the British Empire would not countenance any union whatsoever between the King and the twice-divorced woman. It was he who first received from the King's own lips assurance that he was determined to marry Mrs. Simpson.

The Prime Minister contraverted reports that the strong wills of both men had engendered bitterness during the grave hours of discussion. If anything, he said, their mutual respect and friendship had become more firm by their ordeal.

"I would like to tell the House when I begin," the Prime Minister said, "that when I said good-bye on Tuesday night at Fort Belvedere, we both knew and felt and said to each other that that friendship, so far from being impaired by discussions this week, bound us more closely together than it ever had, and would last for life."

Mr. Baldwin, who throughout his speech continually assumed full responsibility for forcing Edward to choose between his throne and Mrs. Simpson, said he first became disturbed in the middle of October, when "two things disquieted me."

The first, he said, was the "vast volume of correspondence" which "expressed perturbation and uneasiness on what was then appearing in the American press."

The second, said Mr. Baldwin, was his "awareness" that in the near future "a divorce case was coming, the results of which made me realize that possibly a difficult situation might arise later."

"I felt it was essential," he explained, "that some one should see His Majesty and warn him of the difficult situation that might arise later if occasion was given for continuation of this kind of gossip and criticism—that might come if this gossip and criticism spread from the other side of the Atlantic to this country.

"I felt doubly bound to speak, as it was my duty as I conceived it, to the country and my duty to him, not only as a counselor but as a friend."

Insisting that he approached the Monarch on his responsibility alone, Mr. Baldwin said:

"I consulted—I am ashamed to say it, but they have forgiven me—none of my colleagues."

He first sought and obtained an interview with Edward in October, Mr. Baldwin continued in his chronology of the drama.

"There is nothing I have not told His Majesty," Mr. Baldwin said, "of which I felt he ought to be aware, but never has His Majesty shown any signs of offense, of being hurt at anything I have said to him, and the whole of our discussions have been carried through with an increase, if possible, of that mutual respect and regard in which we stood."

House in Second Session

The House of Commons adjourned for a time and reconvened at 6 P. M. to consider legislation carrying out Edward's abdication and the succession of the Duke of York.

The decision of the sovereign was accepted for the most part with sorrowful resignation, although in the night Parliament session, Winston Churchill, Colonel Josiah Wedgwood and other stanch champions of Edward expressed regret that the dénouement might not have been otherwise.

James Maxton, Left winger, evoked a round of boos when he asserted the monarchial system "now has outlived its usefulness." Mr. Maxton urged a republican form of government for Britain.

Clement R. Attlee, the leader of the Opposition, praised the passing monarch in a speech and then said:

"We hoped it would not come to abdication, but the King has made his decision. He is resolved to abide by it. We can do no other than accept it."

EDWARD GIVES UP THE BRITISH CROWN

Continued From Page One

sense tonight's feeling of relief that the solution has brought.

"For a brief bad moment," says The Times editorially, "it felt like an earthquake. Yet it was only a storm. It has blown over—not without leaving its traces. But the black skies are now behind and there is sunlight ahead."

The British determination that the King's abdication shall not becloud this new prospect is seen in various arrangements now being made.

It is even planned that if possible the preparations for the coronation shall go forward so that it will take place on the day and under the conditions originally set. It is not yet certain whether this can be accomplished, but if it possible it will be done. Another King with a Queen of British blood, who is a respected wife and mother, will be crowned. That is all. Otherwise it will be the same ceremony under the conditions already arranged.

In this the cynical may find evidence of that curious British practicality that underlies so much of the sentiment and ceremony that make of Britain a country apart. Fear of delay in the coronation ceremony has already produced heavy losses. Its definite postponement for any length of time might entail costs totaling millions of pounds sterling. One estimate has put the total as high as £50,000,000. So it will go as planned if determination and ingenuity can arrange it.

Edward Retains Titles

As to King Edward's future, little is known for the present about that. He will not, however, become plain "Mr. Windsor" as some, ignorant of British practice, might imagine.

In his own right he is already both Earl of Rothesay and Baron of Renfrew. He retains those titles. It is believed probable, moreover, that one of the new King's first acts will be to create his elder brother a Duke, although under what style and title is understood to be still undetermined. The title may be neither Cornwall nor Lancaster, these being appanages of the Crown. But nothing in this respect is certain.

It is probable that for a time at least the retiring King will live abroad. He is not expected to join Mrs. Wallis Warfield Simpson at the villa in Cannes where she has been temporarily enjoying the hospitality of her American friends, Mr. and Mrs. Herman L. Rogers. One report current tonight portrays the King's intention as being "to go cruising" for a while, probably in the Mediterranean. Another is that Switzerland for a while may be the scene of his self-imposed exile. Mrs. Simpson is expected to move to Italy.

Wedding in Spring Probable

Whatever else happens, it is taken for granted they will be together and since no impediment to their marriage can now arise, once Mrs. Simpson's divorce decree is made absolute, it is probable their marriage will take place some time next Spring.

The British public will be mildly interested, but that is all. One curious fact about the present situation is the extent to which Mrs. Simpson, although the situation arose entirely from her personality and history, has dwindled as a factor in its developments. The issue involved became far greater than the original cause.

Utterances in the House of Commons today made that plain. For ultimately the issue was whether the King's personal inclinations should come before his duty to his people and to the empire, and in this case inclination and duty were incompatible. His own words seem to accept that interpretation of the case:

"It should be remembered that the burden which constantly rests upon the shoulders of a sovereign is so heavy that it can only be borne in circumstances different from those in which I now find myself. * * * I am conscious that I can no longer discharge this heavy task with efficiency or with satisfaction to myself."

People Regretfully Agree

There seems to be almost unanimous, though regretful, agreement and there is consequent acquiescence in his decision. A King who can no longer discharge his heavy task with efficiency or self-satisfaction unless he has a particular woman whom empire sentiment pronounces unsuitable beside him to share his burden has lost the magic of rulership for the proud and self-reliant peoples over whom it has been his task to reign.

Sorrowfully, as if over a monarch taken from it by death, the empire is turning tonight toward the new King-Emperor. It does not know him very well except as a good husband, a devoted father and a conscientious prince, but it hopes for the best. He carries onward the tradition of Victoria and George V and for the present that is enough.

In his "instrument of abdication" today the retiring King declared himself:

"I, Edward VIII of Great Britain, Ireland and the British Dominions Beyond the Seas, King, Emperor of India."

He omitted "Defender of the Faith," which by usage comes before "Emperor of India." It may have been inadvertence, although such omissions are usually taken to mean something. Whether it was or not George VI can put it back, for he assuredly has nothing in mind that sets at naught the tenets and practices of the established church. Britain cleaves to established customs.

Departs Forever as King

And the retiring King departs forever as King, whether he returns to live in England or not. It is a curious coincidence that James II, the last British ruler to abdicate his throne—which he did in fact by a hasty departure if not by an official document—fled to France exactly 248 years ago today. And neither he nor any member of the House of Stuart was able to come back as King, although attempts were made.

Solid is the British structure and great is the capacity of its public opinion to overcome and absorb political changes. A year hence the man who is now Edward VIII may walk along Piccadilly looking into the shop windows and freely mix with his present subjects without receiving any more attention than any other distinguished member of London's divorcified society.

"All the News That's Fit to Print."

The New York Times.

LATE CITY EDITION
Fair today, temperature unchanged.
Tomorrow fair, little change in temperature.
Temperatures Yesterday—Max., 71; Min., 55

VOL. LXXXVI.....No. 28,958. Entered as Second-Class Matter, Postoffice, New York, N. Y. NEW YORK, FRIDAY, MAY 7, 1937. P TWO CENTS In New York City. | THREE CENTS Within 200 Miles. | FOUR CENTS Elsewhere Except in 7th and 8th Postal Zones.

HINDENBURG BURNS IN LAKEHURST CRASH; 21 KNOWN DEAD, 12 MISSING; 64 ESCAPE

ANARCHISTS RENEW BARCELONA STRIFE; 5,000 LEAVE BILBAO

Revolters, Regaining Part of Catalan Capital, Demand Shock Troop Dissolution

SOCIALIST MINISTER SLAIN

Insurgents Reported Gaining Unresisted in Aragon as Foes Withdraw 12,000

EVACUATION IN NORTH SPED

British Warships Protect Craft Taking Women and Children From Bilbao to France

The Spanish Situation

PERPIGNAN—Anarchists were reported to have regained positions in Barcelona and to have demanded the dissolution of the government's shock troops. Withdrawal of 12,000 men from the Aragon front, to deal with the situation, was also reported, leading to an advance by the Rebel armies. Page 1.

ROME—A heavy concentration of Rebels, including Italians, to rescue the Italians cut off at Bermeo, was under way on the Bilbao front. Page 10.

BILBAO—Five thousand women and children were taken from the city, and vessels carrying them to France were guarded by British warships. More refugees were preparing to leave. (Follows the above.) Page 10.

LONDON—Foreign Secretary Eden revealed that the British Government had evidence that Guernica was destroyed by airplanes. He favored a neutral inquiry. Page 10.

Anarchists Give Ultimatum

Special Cable to THE NEW YORK TIMES.

PERPIGNAN, France, May 6.—The Anarchists are reported to have regained control in parts of Barcelona this afternoon after the Catalan Generalidad believed it had dominated the situation.

The Anarchists issued an ultimatum to the government demanding the dissolution of the shock troops patroling the city, the government's chief support, within twenty-four hours and declaring that otherwise they would take matters into their own hands and use every means in their power to suppress the shock troops.

The Anarchists also have obtained the upper hand at Junquera in addition to Figueras, according to news received here, and threaten, it is alleged, to use asphyxiating gas unless their ultimatum is obeyed.

Anarchist broadcasts have been picked up here stating that the casualties in the disorders in Barcelona since the Anarchist rebellion Tuesday amounted to 400 dead and 2,000 wounded. Declaring that "enough blood has flowed," the broadcasts continue to appeal for calm every ten minutes, and it is therefore believed that trouble still persists in Barcelona.

French Consulate Menaced

The French Consulate was threatened by Anarchists, who asserted that Rightist sympathizers had taken refuge there. The consul appealed to French warships in the harbor and 200 armed sailors reinforced the consulate guard.

Telephonic communication with Barcelona is still cut off tonight, and telegraphic and telephonic communication with the interior of Catalonia, which was re-established yesterday, was again interrupted this morning.

The Spanish Consul at Perpignan has recommended that Frenchmen and others should not go further than Figueras, and trains do not proceed beyond Gerona.

Francisco Ascasso, leader of the Anarchists in the Aragon Government, is reported to have been murdered.

Rebels Gain on Aragon Front

By The Associated Press.

PERPIGNAN, France, May 6.—Reports of an unresisted Insurgent advance along the whole Aragon front of Northeastern Spain and of the withdrawal of 12,000 government troops from it to keep the peace in troubled Barcelona, put a new and serious face on the Catalan Anarchist insurrection tonight. The reports emanated from Insurgent

Continued on Page Ten

Judge Sentences Himself By Signing Papers Unread

Wireless to THE NEW YORK TIMES.

MOSCOW, May 6.—A judge on one of the most important benches of the Moscow District Court who has the bad habit of signing unread any document placed before him has just sentenced himself to jail.

The court clerks, deciding he needed a lesson in "Bolshevik vigilance," presented to him a sheaf of papers including one reading: "To the chief of Butyrky prison: Under Magistrate Abramson is sent to you for further detention." Judge Abramson signed all the papers and picked up his newspaper again.

The clerks, of course, extracted the sentence and were passing it around laughingly when the judge found out about it. He destroyed it in a rage, declaring such jokes tended to undermine Soviet justice.

The government learned about it, however, and today Izvestia delivered to Judge Abramson a stinging rebuke for perfunctoriness, reminding him that he dealt not in inanimate goods but in human fate.

HUGHES SEES CHOICE IN LAW OR TYRANNY

Courts Must Be Maintained, He Tells Law Institute, or We Replace Reason by Force

TEST OF BAR TO ROOSEVELT

Stewardship Is Questioned by Laymen, He Writes in Warning of 'Critical Audience'

Text of Chief Justice Hughes's address is on Page 17.

Special to THE NEW YORK TIMES.

WASHINGTON, May 6.—Chief Justice Hughes made what his hearers construed as a reference to the Supreme Court when he told the American Law Institute today that if society is to choose the processes of reason as opposed to the tyranny of force, "it must maintain the institutions which embody those processes." It was the second time that the Chief Justice of the United States has broken his silence since the controversy over reorganization of the Supreme Court started three months ago.

Vigorous applause, lasting more than a minute, followed the Chief Justice's words, with which he concluded a speech in which he avoided any direct reference to the court issue.

President Roosevelt in a message to the institute likewise refrained from any positive statement about the Supreme Court, but remarked that "law interpreters," among other legal experts, are facing a sometimes critical audience.

President on Lawyers' Position

"I am happy to greet you members of the bench, the bar and the law school faculties who have assembled for the fifteenth annual meeting of the American Law Institute," the President stated.

"I have followed with interest your accomplishments within recent years in the restatement of the law and your proposals for improvement in the administration of criminal justice.

"Today our stewardship as lawyers is being questioned. The laymen of America are not, perhaps, quite so disposed to make a complete delegation of law matters to law men. At least the layman asserts his right to evaluate us.

"Law scholars, law practitioners, lawmakers, law administrators and law interpreters have the stage today. But more significant, they must play their rôles before an intense and sometimes critical audience.

"But this is well. The virtue of the common law was its adaptability to growth and improvement. In generations present and future the lawyer likewise will be measured by the same test.

"It is encouraging today that so many outstanding leaders of the profession assemble to give service in the important and worth-while task to which the American Law Institute is dedicated. I extend again my warm and cordial greetings to your membership and my best wishes for continued success."

Only at one other time since President Roosevelt made his recommendations to Congress on Feb. 5 has the Chief Justice made any

Continued on Page Seventeen

NOTABLES ABOARD

Merchants, Students and Professional Men on the Dirigible

LEHMANN IS A SURVIVOR

Veteran Zeppelin Commander, Acting as Adviser on Trip, Is Seriously Burned

CAPT. PRUSS IS ALSO SAFE

C. L. Osbun, Sales Manager, Who Survived a Plane Crash, Escapes Second Time

Notables from many walks of life were among the passengers on the ill-fated Hindenburg. They included merchants, students and business and professional men and women.

Many of the survivors owed their lives to the fact that they were apparently near windows in the dirigible when the accident happened and were able to leap through them to the ground in safety.

Among the survivors listed were Captain Ernst Lehmann, veteran Zeppelin commander; Captain Max Pruss, the new Hindenburg commander; Herbert O'Laughlin of Chicago, employed by the Consumers Company of Elgin, Ill.; Clifford L. Osbun, export sales manager of the Oliver Farm Equipment Company of Chicago, and Ferdinand Lammot Belin Jr. of Washington, D. C.

Lehmann's Condition Grave

Early this morning Dr. E. G. Herbener, staff surgeon at the Paul Kimball Hospital in Lakewood, said that Captain Lehmann was on the doubtful list. Captain Lehmann is suffering from shock and second and third degree burns of the face and body. Captain Pruss is suffering from second and third degree burns of the face, forehead and arms and will probably recover, Dr. Herbener said.

Among the passengers who were still unaccounted for were John Pannes, passenger traffic manager of the Hamburg-American Line and North German Lloyd at New York, and his wife; Ernst Rudolf Anders, partner of the firm of Seelig & Hille, tea merchants of Dresden, Germany, and his son, R. Herbert Anders, and Hermann Doehner of Mexico, D. F.

Captain Lehmann and Captain Pruss were in the control gondola when the crash occurred. Both officers, together with several other members of the crew, leaped through the gondola windows to safety.

Lehmann an Adviser

Captain Lehmann, who was serving as adviser aboard the Hindenburg, had been commander of the ship until this year. He has had long experience with the lighter-than-air craft, and has been associated with Hugo Eckener, world-famous authority on Zeppelins, since 1921.

He was born March 12, 1886, at Ludwigshafen, on the Rhine, the son of a chemist. He became a naval cadet in 1905 and later entered the Polytechnic Institute at Charlottenburg, a borough of Berlin.

During the World War Captain Lehmann received the German Iron Cross award. After the war, as second in command to Eckener, he brought the dirigible Los Angeles to Lakehurst in 1924. When the Hindenburg was completed in 1936 Captain Lehmann was placed in command, a position he held until recently, when Captain Pruss was elevated as commander of the ship.

Mr. Osbun's escape from the disaster marked the second time that he had narrowly missed death as the result of a flying accident. Last year he was aboard a transport plane when it was forced down en route from Puerto Rico to Buenos Aires. Soon after he was transferred to a motorboat with other passengers and the motorboat blew up. Mr. Osbun escaped injury, but two other passengers were seriously burned.

Mr. Osbun declared that he was talking to fellow passengers in the dining salon, looking down through the observation window watching the ship being moored, when the disaster occurred. He was apparently blown through the window and thrown to the ground, suffering injuries. He was taken to the Paul Kimball Hospital in Lakewood, where his condition was said to be not serious.

Mr. Osbun is 37 years old, the fa-

Continued on Page Nineteen

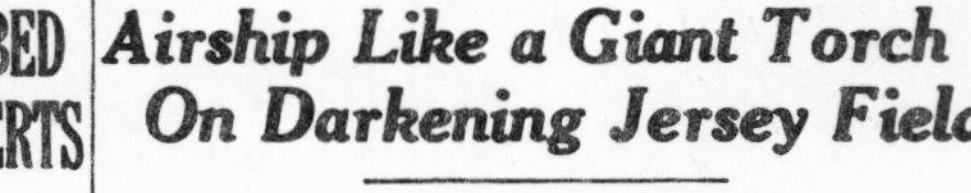

Associated Press Photo.

THE HINDENBURG IN FLAMES ON THE FIELD AT LAKEHURST

The giant airliner as she settled to the ground near her mooring mast at 7:23 o'clock last night

SHIP FALLS ABLAZE

Great Dirigible Bursts Into Flames as It Is About to Land

VICTIMS BURN TO DEATH

Some Passengers Are Thrown From the Blazing Wreckage, Others Crawl to Safety

GROUND CREW AIDS RESCUE

Sparks From Engines or Static Believed to Have Ignited Hydrogen Gas

A page of photographs of the disaster and survivors Page 20.

By RUSSELL B. PORTER

Special to THE NEW YORK TIMES.

NAVAL AIR STATION, LAKEHURST, N. J., May 6.—The zeppelin Hindenburg was destroyed by fire and explosions here at 7:23 o'clock tonight with a loss of thirty-three known dead and unaccounted for out of its ninety-seven passengers and crew.

Three hours after the disaster twenty-one bodies had been recovered, and twelve were still missing. The sixty-four known to be alive included twenty passengers and forty-four of the crew. Many of the survivors were burned or injured or both, and were taken to hospitals here and in near-by towns.

The accident happened just as the great German dirigible was about to tie up to its mooring mast four hours after flying over New York City on the last leg of its first transatlantic voyage of the year. Until today the Hindenburg had never lost a passenger throughout the ten round trips it made across the Atlantic with 1,002 passengers in 1936.

Two Theories of Cause

F. W. von Meister, vice president of the American Zeppelin Company, gave two possible theories to explain the crash. One was that a fire was caused by an electrical circuit "induced by static conditions" as the ship valved hydrogen gas preparatory to landing. Another was that sparks set off when the engines were throttled down while the gas was being valved caused a fire or explosion.

Captain Ernst Lehmann, who commanded the Hindenburg on most of its flights last year and was one of tonight's survivors, gasped, "I couldn't understand it," as he staggered out of the burning control car. Captain Max Pruss, commanding officer of the airship, and Captain Albert Sammt were also among the survivors.

Captain Lehmann was critically burned and injured; the other officers were also burned, but less seriously.

Experts in lighter-than-air operations who saw the accident said tonight that when the two landing lines were dropped by the dirigible at 7:20, they were immediately made fast to the mooring cars on the circular track about the mooring mast. The crew began to make the lines taut, but the ship had gathered too much momentum, according to these observers, and drifted several hundred yards past the mast. The starboard line pulled hard as the nose of the ship passed over the mooring mast at the top.

Order Not Heard

Captain Pruss, making his first trip in command of the dirigible, signaled and shouted, "Pay out!"

This order was heard by the operator on one mooring car, but not by the other, as the shout went against the wind and could not be heard. Consequently, one mooring car paid out and the other did not. The result was that the ship was thrown off its balance and lost the perfect equilibrium it had previously had.

Its nose dipped, forward ballast was dropped and the elevators were set to raise the ship. Instead the ship was held tight by one yaw line. The nose was pulled over and the elevators had an effect opposite to that which they were intended to have, according to this version. The tail dropped sharply and the bottom rudder hit the

Continued on Page Nineteen

DISASTER ASCRIBED TO GAS BY EXPERTS

Washington Sees Dangerous Combination of Hydrogen and Blue Gas as Cause

Special to THE NEW YORK TIMES.

WASHINGTON, May 6.—Washington airship experts and Congressional leaders received the news of the Hindenburg disaster with amazement and expressions of sorrow. But in every instance those who commented pointed out that the three disasters of the United States Navy were structural, while that of the German craft was due to the use of a combination of hydrogen and blue gas, the most dangerous of all gases for inflation of airships.

Dr. Hans Luther, the German Ambassador, said the disaster must not cause the world to lose faith in dirigibles and that it could not have been caused by technical defects.

"It is terrible," the Ambassador said. "I was horrified by the news, but it could not have been a technical matter. It must not cause us to lose faith in dirigibles because the Graf Zeppelin has operated safely and efficiently for eight years on the run from Europe to South America and elsewhere."

Secretary Hull sent the following message tonight to Konstantin von Neurath, the German Minister of Foreign Affairs:

"I extend to you and to the people of Germany my profound sympathy at the tragic accident to the dirigible Hindenburg and the resultant loss of life to passengers and crew."

"It is too terrible to believe," Admiral A. B. Cook, Chief of Naval Aeronautics, said. "From what I

Continued on Page Twenty-one

Airship Like a Giant Torch On Darkening Jersey Field

Routine Landing Converted Into Hysterical Scene in Moment's Time—Witnesses Tell of 'Blinding Flash' From Zeppelin

By CRAIG THOMPSON

Special to THE NEW YORK TIMES.

LAKEHURST, N. J., May 6.—The Hindenburg, giant silver liner of the air, suddenly became a torch above the naval air station here tonight. What began as a routine landing of the transatlantic airship ended in a holocaust.

The ground crew, officials of the naval air base, spectators, reporters and press photographers were going about their customary business of aiding or watching the ship nose into the mooring mast.

Two ground lines had been dropped from the nose. These, attached to the cars running on a circular track around the mast, were holding the ship nose down at a thirty-degree angle, and helping it jockey into a position favorable with the wind for a mooring.

A thunderstorm had passed over the field a short time before and a drizzly rain was still falling. Twilight was beginning, although the visibility was still good.

So suddenly that it left spectators on the verge of hysteria for some time afterward, the ship burst into flame. Some one in the ground crew yelled "Run for your lives!" and the crew did. The stern of the ship settled and the photographers, squinting through the view finders of their cameras, ran toward the ship.

The occurrence sounded, witnesses said, like two explosions, one following the other about thirty seconds apart. Some said they saw one burst of flame, others two, but the noises they described as explosions gave way to the sounds of human screams.

In the "heavier-than-air" hangar, the pilot of an American Air Lines plane, waiting to ferry passengers from the airship into Newark, watched from a window.

"It seemed to happen so fast that I didn't think anybody could escape," he said afterward.

He was wrong, for about at that moment a man ran into the hangar.

"His face was black, but he seemed to be all right otherwise. He wanted to telephone his mother in Chicago."

The passenger was Herbert James O'Laughlin of Chicago.

On the field was an army detachment from Philadelphia, detailed there for just such an emergency. This detail promptly went to work, trucks scurrying over the field seeking the injured, while in the hangar telephone calls were being put through to all points in New Jersey and New York City calling for ambulances, doctors, nurses, medicine.

All this occurred while the flames spread toward the uptilted nose of the ship, while the stern sank to the ground to be followed shortly by the entire length, girder and strut, the bared ribs of the ship from which the skin had disappeared.

Robert Seelig, Murray Becker and Larry Kennedy, all newspaper camera men, related what they had seen.

"There was a noise that sounded like bullets coming out of the gondolas," Seelig said. "I saw nobody

Continued on Page Twenty-one

GERMANY SHOCKED BY THE TRAGEDY

At First Disbelieving, Line's Officials Tell of Receiving Message of Landing

Special Cable to THE NEW YORK TIMES.

BERLIN, Friday, May 7.—It was a few minutes after 1 o'clock this morning when the first news of the disaster to the Hindenburg reached Berlin by telephone from The New York Times Bureau in London. The bureau forwarded the brief bulletin to the effect that the airship had been destroyed while making its landing. No details were given.

At that hour the German newspapers were without news. Several first editions, in fact, had reported the Hindenburg's supposedly safe arrival on the strength of an erroneous telegram received by the company in Frankfort on the Main. It was almost two hours later before the news of the disaster with some few details reached the newspapers through the medium of the German official news agency.

Facts Difficult to Get

In the meantime such facts about the airship and its passengers proved difficult to obtain. The Frankfort and Berlin offices of the Zeppelin company were closed and no complete list of the passengers or crew was available. A list of twenty-one names comprising foreign passengers out of a total list of thirty-nine was obtained by telephone from Frankfort, where this correspondent had retained it since the sailing day.

Dr. Hugo Eckener, veteran chief of the Zeppelin service, was in Austria, where he had lectured last night in Vienna. The Vienna bureau of THE NEW YORK TIMES traced him to Graz and obtained his ad-

Continued on Page Nineteen

Great Crowds Here Watched Ship, With Many Notables Aboard, Sail to Her Doom

THOUSANDS IN CITY SAW LAST FLIGHT

Crowds in Times Square Gazed in Admiration, With No Thought of Disaster

AIRSHIP GLEAMED IN SUN

Dipped Low for Benefit of the Sightseers—Planes Gayly Flew Beside It

Thousands of persons craned their necks in Times Square yesterday afternoon as the Hindenburg, a familiar sight to this area, soared above the tall buildings in a brilliant sun.

From windows, rooftops, sidewalks, fire-escapes and other points of vantage they viewed the giant airliner, little realizing it was the last time they were to see the ship.

Traffic was impeded in some sections of the city as throngs choked thoroughfares and chauffeurs stopped their automobiles, left the steering wheels and gazed skyward as the ship, its motors roaring and swastikas gleaming, passed over the city.

Not only in the metropolitan area but in other sections the ship was greeted by the tooting of automobile horns. Crowds turned out to see the airship at Portland, Me.; Boston, New London and other places over which it flew at a comparatively low altitude.

After it had hove into sight near City Island on Long Island Sound, word was flashed to Manhattan by telephone to be on the watch for the airship.

As was customary in other flights of the Hindenburg, the commander, Captain Max Pruss, in charge of the westbound flight across the Atlantic for the first time, soared over the city for the sightseers' benefit.

At 3:12 P. M. the ship, which left Frankfort at 3:19 P. M. Monday, passed southward on the west side of Times Square.

Leaving Times Square, the dirigible, accompanied by several planes, including the big twin-motored Burnelli flown by Clyde Pangborn, which appeared like an ant moving beside an elephant, traveled to Brooklyn, where additional thousands dropped their work and looked up to see the Hindenburg for the last time.

At Ebbets Field, where the Brooklyn Dodgers were playing the Pittsburgh Pirates, the baseball fans temporarily took their minds off the game and stood up to gaze skyward.

Swinging the ship back toward the north, Captain Pruss headed for Manhattan, where throngs in the narrow downtown streets, attracted by the roar of the motors of the airship and the escorting planes, gathered on street corners and on the steps of the Treasury Building in Wall Street for a glimpse of the pride of the German air fleet.

Amateur photographers, perched at vantage points on the Empire State Building observation towers and atop Rockefeller Center, snapped pictures as the silvery ship swung by. Other pictures were snapped by newspaper photographers in airplanes.

Finally, after a return visit to midtown New York, the huge craft turned just south of the Empire State Building and began the flight that was to have ended with the landing at Lakehurst.

Passing over the Hudson River on the way to Staten Island, the passengers and crew of the Zeppelin were greeted for several minutes by a deafening roar of steamboat and other harbor vessel whistles.

BIRGER BRINK, EDITOR, OF SWEDEN, MISSING

Planned to Visit Governor Earle of Pennsylvania—Passenger Tells of His Escape

Special to THE NEW YORK TIMES.

LAKEHURST, N. J., May 6.—Birger Brink, one of the editors of the Stockholm Tidningen, whose body is believed to be among those buried in the twisted framework of the Hindenburg, was making a brief visit to this country to interview Governor George H. Earle of Pennsylvania and Dr. John H. Finley.

Having planned to return on the Hindenburg at midnight, Mr. Brink found the delayed arrival of the airship would interfere with his plans, so he sent a radiogram to Governor Earle requesting him to meet him in Philadelphia. The Governor agreed to do this, and to facilitate the interview sent a plane to meet the Hindenburg at Lakehurst in order that Mr. Brink would lose no time.

Dr. Amandus Johnson, director of the Swedish-American Historical Museum of Philadelphia, accompanied the pilot of the plane to Lakehurst. Einar Thulin, New York correspondent for the Tidningen, also was at Lakehurst to welcome the Swedish editor.

Mr. Thulin was about to enter his car, parked near the hangar, when the explosion occurred. It threw him to the ground. Then he ran toward the burning wreckage, hoping to find Mr. Brink among those stumbling from the twisted girders.

He was unable to find the editor, but Rolf von Heidenstam, whom he had known in Sweden, stumbled into his arms and collapsed. Mr. von Heidenstam had been watching the landing manoeuvres from one of the dirigible's windows, he explained. According to Mr. Thulin, Mr. von Heidenstam was so dazed he could remember little of his experience.

Mr. von Heidenstam was badly burned about the head and was suffering from an injured back. Mr. Thulin was unable to learn to which hospital he had been taken.

By The Associated Press.

PHILADELPHIA, May 6.—Governor George H. Earle heard the news of the Hindenburg explosion as he waited here to confer with Dr. Birger Brink of Stockholm, a passenger on the ship.

Roosevelt Sends Hitler Message of Sympathy

Special to THE NEW YORK TIMES.

GALVESTON, Texas, May 6.—Shocked by the Hindenburg disaster at Lakehurst today, President Roosevelt tonight sent from his yacht The Potomac a message of sympathy to Adolf Hitler, the German Chancellor.

His message to Herr Hitler follows:

"His Excellency, Adolf Hitler, Reich Chancellor, Berlin.

"I have just learned of the disaster to the airship Hindenburg and offer you and the German people my deepest sympathy for the tragic loss of life which resulted from this unexpected and unhappy event."

At the same time, the President issued the following statement:

"I am distressed to hear of the tragedy of the Hindenburg, and extend my deep sympathy to the families of the passengers, officers and crew who lost their lives."

Both messages were sent to the temporary White House offices here for transmission, from the yacht on which the President is enjoying a fishing vacation.

NOTABLES ABOARD ILL-FATED LINER

Continued From Page One

ther of three daughters, Jean, 10 years old, Suzanne, 5, and Sally, 3, and lives at Parkridge, a suburb of Chicago. He was just concluding a three-month tour for his company which took him to South America, England and Germany.

A somewhat similar experience was had by Mr. O'Laughlin, who later told Dr. Jerome Kaufman of the Newark Hospital, who treated him on the scene for minor injuries, that he was in the main cabin of the ship with about fifteen other passengers when the ship "started to rock." He said he heard a "terrific noise" and that he jumped through a window to the ground. The ship at that time, he said, was only about fifteen feet from the ground.

Mr. O'Laughlin, who lives at 914 Bonnie Brae, River Forest, Chicago suburb, was returning to this country from a short European vacation which he started on April 11. His first act, when he was rescued, was to send a telegram to his mother in Chicago announcing that he was safe.

An early report listed Colonel Ira Nelson Morris, former United States Minister to Sweden from 1914 to 1922, as among the passengers. Colonel Morris called THE NEW YORK TIMES office last night and said that he was not aboard the ship, although his name headed the passenger list as given out by the Hamburg-American line.

Mr. Morris suggested that there might have been some confusion between his name and that of a nephew, Nelson Morris, who had been in Europe and had returned on the Hindenburg. The latter was among the survivors and was taken to a hospital for medical care.

Mr. Pannes, who had been employed by the Hamburg-American Line more than thirty years, was returning on the airliner with his wife. They had left here about one month ago on the Bremen for the purpose of returning on the Hindenburg.

Studied Air Service

Active in recent developments in the air traffic branch of this service since the first round-the-world flight of the Graf Zeppelin in August, 1929, Mr. Fannes made a special trip about one year ago on the Hindenburg to study the transit problems created by the entry of this airliner in transatlantic travel.

At that time he was engaged by the North German Lloyd Line in combining the regular shipping activity of the line with the duties of booking agent for the air line.

Mr. Belin Jr. is the son of a former American diplomat who has lived in Washington since his retirement from the foreign service. He was returning on a holiday visit to his home from Paris, where he had been a student at the Ecole des Sciences Politiques, in preparation for taking the examinations to enter the foreign service.

Mr. Doehner was general manager of the drug firm of Beick, Felix & Co., Mexico, D. F. His wife also was reported as missing, but their three children were listed as saved.

Business Man Missing

Another passenger on the ship who was unaccounted for last night was George Hirschfeld, a member of the Chamber for Industry and Trade of Bremen, Germany, and chairman of the committee for cotton. He was arriving to study the possibilities of developing business under the barter agreement recently made effective under which American cotton is shipped into Germany in exchange for German merchandise brought into this country.

Mr. Morris, member of the Chicago packing family, is the grandson and namesake of the founder of Morris & Co., which was merged several years ago with Armour & Co. He is 45 years old. His home in Homewood, a Chicago suburb, is regarded as one of the show places of that district.

Mr. Morris had been visiting in France with his wife, the former Blanche Bilboa, French actress, and was returning to Chicago on a business trip. He had intended to rejoin his wife in France. He was taken to the Paul Kimball Hospital in Lakewood following the disaster.

Other passengers who were still unaccounted for early this morning were the following:

Edward H. Douglas, who since 1930 has been living in Frankfort, Germany, where he was in charge of European agencies of the H. K. McCann Corporation, Ltd., an advertising firm. Mr. Douglas was born in Newark, N. J., in 1898 and served during the war as a petty officer in the United States Navy.

Moritz Feibusch, 57 years old, operator of the M. Feibusch Company, canned products and exporting firm of San Francisco. Mr. Feibusch had been on an extensive business trip to Europe. He lived at 2,201 Lincoln Way, San Francisco, which caused the passenger lists hastily compiled to give him a Lincoln, Neb., address on the first reports.

Times Wide World Photo.

THE HINDENBURG ABOVE TIMES SQUARE A FEW HOURS BEFORE THE DISASTER

The big ship passing over the Times Building late yesterday afternoon on her last flight

HINDENBURG FALLS IN FLAMES AT FIELD

Continued From Page One

earth. The ship bounded up again, then suddenly burst into flames and dropped to the ground.

It is understood that this version of the accident will be investigated by the naval board of inquiry convened for tomorrow and the Department of Commerce. The official investigation will also look into conflicting reports as to whether the fire was accompanied or preceded by explosions. Although most observers reported hearing a series of explosions, some insisted that there were no explosions until after the ship was almost destroyed by fire.

F. E. Fagg, head of the Bureau of Aeronautics of the Department of Commerce, flew in from Washington late tonight and conferred with Commander Charles E. Rosendahl, in charge of the air station. Mr. Fagg announced that Commander Rosendahl would preside over the board of inquiry to open tomorrow.

Commander Rosendahl, together with the 200 members of the ground crew, which had started to walk the dirigible to its mooring place, narrowly escaped injury when the Hindenburg fell in flames.

The catastrophe was witnessed by several hundred spectators, including several who had booked passage on the return trip of the Hindenburg to Germany, which had been scheduled to start at midnight tonight.

Delayed on Voyage

At the time of the crash, the Hindenburg was more than twelve hours late, having been due here at 6 o'clock this morning. Head winds delayed it coming across the Atlantic and down the coast from Labrador. On its last day it flew at reduced speed along the coast, waiting for dusk, as landing conditions are best at dawn and dusk.

After its scheduled landing tonight, it was to have been refueled quickly in preparation for the return voyage.

The airship was sighted here about 4:15 o'clock this afternoon. It flew over the landing field at a good altitude, but because of a strong wind, did not try to land. After circling the reservation, it pointed toward the coast again and disappeared. Shortly afterward thunderstorms blew up over the field and continued until about 7 o'clock.

A light rain was falling and the ground was well soaked when the Hindenburg reappeared, flying in from the coast at an altitude of about 500 feet.

Too high to land, the Hindenburg circled the field and came back at an altitude of about 150 feet. It flew over the mooring mast, doubled back and came in again heading slightly southwest, against the wind, with two lights in its bow against the gathering dusk.

During this turn over the field, the ship had begun to valve gas slightly and had dropped ballast twice to lighten its load for mooring. It was exactly 7:20 P. M. daylight saving time, according to official timing by company and naval authorities, when it dropped two lines to the ground crew.

Observers here said that the wind shifted just before the Hindenburg attempted to land, and that this made it difficult for the ground crew to manoeuvre her. A company representative said that normally the ship would have been expected to be perfectly safe the moment she dropped her lines.

Lined up on the field below the silvery cone-shaped airship, the ground crew grasped the lines and began to walk it the 100 yards to the mooring mast.

Muffled Boom Heard

At 7:23 o'clock those on the ground heard a low report or boom from the ship. Almost simultaneously there was a flash which lighted up the twilight, and sent a thrill of terror through the onlookers.

This was followed quickly by the bursting of flames from the rear gondola on the port side, where the engines had been throttled down in preparation for mooring. Then the flames spread forward, and in a moment the gigantic ship seemed to be enveloped in fire.

Horror gripped the spectators as the airship buckled aft of midships and began to settle slowly down to the ground in a mass of red flames and black smoke.

There was no sound from the ship except the crackling of flames as they crept forward and ate up the outer fabric so that her duralumin ribs could be seen before she struck the ground.

As the stern struck the earth there was another explosion. Then there was a series of explosions as the ship crumpled up and lay burning on the ground, with leaping forks of flame and billowing clouds of smoke rising into the air. There was something strange about the slow and gradual descent of the blazing ship. She came down so deliberately and settled upon the earth so quietly that spectators said afterward that they could not realize for a moment that a tragedy was taking place before their eyes.

This was but a momentary impression, for the shock of the sight, together with the scorching heat from the flames, drove the crowd running back several hundred feet. There were screams from women spectators, including Mrs. Rosendahl, who feared that her husband had been struck and killed by the falling airship.

Running around the ship until they could approach with the wind and not against the flames, rescuers dashed toward the burning dirigible. They included naval officers and sailors, company representatives and newspaper reporters and photographers.

Many of the survivors owe their lives to the heroic work of the volunteer rescue battalion. Others climbed out of the airship unaided, or were thrown clear when the ship grounded.

Some were hurled through the long isinglass strip on the side of the airship, through which passengers in the observation salon formerly looked out to see the country over which they were flying.

It was explained that the three ranking officers of the airship were saved because they were in the control car forward, whereas the original explosion or fire occurred aft, as did the buckling of the ship just before she dropped to the ground.

Because of this, the stern struck the ground first, and the flames, which enveloped the after part of the ship almost instantaneously, were comparatively slow in reaching the bow. This gave the officers in the bow, and more than half of the passengers, who were standing forward to watch the landfall, their chance to escape.

Had the slow fall of the ship taken much longer, however, nearly everybody aboard might have been burned to death, for a few moments after the bow struck the earth the whole ship was a mass of fire and soon nothing but a skeleton framework could be seen.

Can't Tell What Occurred

Passengers and crew members who were interviewed after the accident were unable to give much information as to the cause of the accident or the manner in which it occurred. Most of them said that it happened too quickly, and they were too stunned by the crash, to be able to tell exactly what had happened.

Commander Rosendahl took charge of the rescue work and summoned ambulances and fire engines from a wide area. Late tonight ambulances filled with doctors and nurses were still arriving here, from as far distant points as Jersey City.

While firemen fought the scorching flames rescuers dragged out injured persons and bodies of the dead. The burned and injured were carried from the wreck to a near-by road, where ambulances pulled up and took them aboard for hurried trips to the naval hospital here and hospitals in near-by cities. As the bodies were recovered they were taken to an improvised morgue on the naval reservation.

At midnight, although the flames had been put out, the embers were so hot that the rescuers were unable to complete their search of the wreckage. It was believed that additional bodies would be discovered tomorrow when the search is finished.

Coroner Raymond A. Taylor of Lakewood came here tonight and made plans for an inquest, which probably will be held tomorrow after all the bodies have been recovered. A hangar was being used as an impromptu morgue.

Commander Rosendahl ordered a cordon of sailors around the wreckage to keep sightseers away, and also set up guards outside the reservation to keep everybody out who did not have business inside. State troopers and marines were stationed at all cross-roads within a one-mile radius of the air station, closing the roads to all except police, officials, rescue workers and newspaper men.

Immediately after the disaster, special details of police cleared all highways to make way for doctors and nurses speeding to the scene from other points. Heavy fire engines and police emergency trucks clanging to the scene helped to keep the roads clear.

But while the rescue work was under way thousands of motorists converged toward the scene on all highways leading to Lakehurst. Before many of the injured had been taken from the first-aid stations on the field, lines of automobiles clogged the road for nearly ten miles on the main arteries to the north and south of the air station.

Harassed rescue workers and ambulance drivers complained that the press of the advancing crowd was so great that it was seriously hampering their work. As many policemen as could be spared were sent from the scene to patrol the surrounding roads and keep them clear.

A detail of National Guardsmen from Fort Monmouth took up stations on the main highways several miles from the air station and ordered motorists to turn back.

List of Saved and Missing

Following is an incomplete list of survivors, injured and missing in the Hindenburg disaster:

Survivors

At Fitkin Memorial Hospital, Neptune:

Eric Knocker.
Richard Kalmer, machinist in crew.
Ergin Brentele, machinist in crew.
Mrs. Elsa Ernst.
Philip Lentz, Frankfort on Main, Germany.
Herbert Dowe, wireless operator.

At the Royal Pines Hotel and Clinic, Pinewald:

Mrs. Mary Kleenmen, 51, Frankfort on Main, Germany.
Hans Fiund, 31, Frankfort on Main, Germany.
Alfred Grocinger, 20, Frankfort on Main, Germany.
George Grant, 63, London, England.

At Paul Kimball Hospital, Lakewood:

Captain Max Pruss, commander.
Captain Ernst Lehmann, former commander, condition critical.
Philip Mangone, 145 West Fifty-eighth Street, New York.
George Hirschfeld, Bremen and New York.
Colonel Nelson Morris, Chicago.
Otto C. Ernst, Hamburg, Germany.

And the following, unidentified as passengers or crew members: Albert Summit, William Stett, Theodore Ritter, Frank Herzog (condition critical), William Luthenberg, Hans Hugo, Adolph Fisher, Ray Fields Stahler, Joseph Lebrecht.

At Point Pleasant Hospital:

Mrs. Herman Doehner of Mexico, D. F., and her two sons, Walter and Werner; injuries reported not serious.

Survivors not at hospitals:

Mr. and Mrs. Leo Adelt, Berlin, Germany.
Pierre Belin, Washington, D. C.
Clifford Osburn, Chicago, Ill.
Joseph Spahs, Douglaston, L. I.
Herbert James O'Laughlin, Chicago, Ill.
Carl Otto Clemens, Bonn, Germany.
Irene Doehner.
Rolf von Heidenstamm.
Claus Rinkelbein.
Erich Knoscher.
Mrs. Margaret Mather.
Captain Albert Stampf.
Henry Bauer.
Walter Zeigler.
Radio Officer Speck.
Max Zabel.
Dr. Reudiger, ship's physician.
Staff Captain Wittemann.
Hans Hugo Witt.
Hinkel.
Emil Stoeckle.

Crew, Hospitals Unknown

Bulla.
Bahnolzer (critical).
Kurt Bauer.
Boetius.
Bernhardt.
Deeg.
Deutschler.
Iberflein.
Franz.
Felber.
Freund.
Henneberg.
Schneuble.
Staeb.
Schaedler.
Stoeffler.
Keppel.
Klein.
Kubis.
Lau.
Lens.
Zavier Maier.
Nunnenacher.
Nielsen.
Sauter.
Scweikard.
Scoenherr.

Listed as Missing

Among the passengers listed as missing are the following:

John Pannes, New York City.
Mrs. John Pannes, New York City.
Ernst Rudolf Anders, Dresden, Germany.
Herman Doehner, Mexico, D. F.
Edward Douglas, New York City.
H. Jackson, Dusseldorf.
Otto Reichhold, Vienna.
Hans Vinholt.
James Young.
Moritz Feibusch, San Francisco.
Birger Brink.
Burtis Dolan.
Fritz Erdman.

Identified Dead

Ludwig Feldber, crew.

HINDENBURG 129TH IN HONORED LINE

First Lighter-Than-Air Craft to Fly on Regular Schedule From Europe to the U. S.

TOOK TO AIR IN MARCH, '36

Landed at Lakehurst Year Ago After Flight of 61 Hours—18 Crossings Set This Year

Prior to establishing the first regular passenger service for lighter-than-air craft across the Atlantic, the Hindenburg, originally known as the LZ-129, first took to the air on March 4, 1936, for a trial flight over Lake Constance from her base at Friedrichshafen, Germany. She was manoeuvred about the sky for three hours and then was set down for final adjustments after meeting all technical requirements.

On March 26, 1936, about two weeks before the start of her maiden flight to the United States, the huge dirigible, which was twice as long as the Graf Zeppelin, had a minor accident as she was leaving the hangar. A sudden gust of wind grabbed her and set her down sharply, damaging one of the vertical stabilizers.

With the exception of this minor accident and the failure of one of her four sixteen-cylinder Daimler-Benz Diesel motors while crossing the Mediterranean during a South American trip, the Hindenburg had functioned well throughout her brief career. There have been several tense moments at her mooring masts when the big craft swayed dizzily under the velocity of high winds and when her ground crews found their task almost more than they could cope with, but she always came through safely.

Started First Flight Year Ago

Carrying fifty-one passengers and a crew of fifty-six the Hindenburg took off from Friedrichshafen at 4 P. M. on May 6, a year ago, for her first voyage to this country. With her gas volume of 7,000,000 cubic feet and a gross lifting capacity of 418,000 pounds she soared easily and pointed her nose westward for the 3,885 statute miles ahead.

Her four engines, which developed 4,400 horsepower, carried her swiftly over the Atlantic to Lakehurst, N. J., where she landed at 6:08 A. M. on May 9, after receiving a welcoming reception over this city that only New York knows how to give. When her nose was moored to the mast her log showed that the trip had been negotiated in 61 hours 35 minutes from her home base. This record was bettered several times on succeeding trips. As an indication of the comparative speed, the Los Angeles made her best crossing in 81 hours back in 1924.

The Hindenburg, the 129th in her line since Count Zeppelin, her namesake, soared over Lake Constance more than fifty years ago, had planned to make eighteen crossings this year. The schedule called for but a one-day stopover each time in Lakehurst. On her next proposed return flight from Germany, first planned for May 11 and later set for May 12 to arrange for coronation passengers, she had made arrangements to pick up photographs and news reels at London to be rushed to the United States.

Dr. Eckener Planned Service

Dr. Hugo Eckener, who was the Hindenburg's commander on most of her trips, first conceived the plan of transatlantic crossing in 1929 and hoped at that time for Germany and the United States to enter into a joint ownership of the line. This hope was shattered first by the depression and then by the crash of the Akron, the Macon and the British dirigible R-101, which fell in France. These things "created doubt" in some minds, Dr. Eckener afterward said.

During ten westward flights the Hindenburg averaged under sixty-four hours and on the eastward flights fifty-one hours. Some of her stop-overs were less than seven hours at Lakehurst.

The Hindenburg had a cruising range that would permit a flight from New York to China or a round trip between New York and Germany. On some of her stops here she was able to turn around and go back with scarcely any replenishing of her supplies outside of the fuel.

On her last successful crossing from Lakehurst to Frankfort on July 17, 1936, she carried fifty-seven passengers, which was a little better than average. Her smallest booking was twenty-one passengers for the westward flight on July 2, last year.

In five westward voyages last year she averaged better than forty-one passengers, 687 pounds of mail and 628 pounds of express. On the eastward trips the average number of passengers was more than fifty-two, with averages of 692 pounds of mail and 665 pounds of express. Her cargo has included such things as an airplane and a piano.

Despite the fact that the airship had been delayed by headwinds along the North Atlantic seaboard, preparations had been rushed at Lakehurst for refueling the airliner so that she could leave as scheduled. Standing at sidings were many railroad cars filled with more than 10,000 gallons of fuel waiting to be pumped aboard.

If the dirigible had left last night at 10 P. M., which was two hours after the original time set for the take-off on the return trip, it would have made the shortest stay in this country in its history.

Last year the Hindenburg made what were regarded as short stops when she left at midnight after arriving at dawn. In July of last year the Hindenburg made her fastest flight from this country to Germany, when she arrived over her German base forty-five hours and forty-three minutes after leaving Lakehurst.

On this trip the Hindenburg was carrying a ship's doctor for the first time. Also on board were two members of the United States Naval forces, Lieutenant Commander F. W. Reichelderfer and Lieutenant Richard W. Antrim.

Before her last eastward passage for the 1936 season the Hindenburg cruised for ten hours over six of the Eastern States as a farewell gesture, prior to her midnight sailing for home. The mammoth ship glistened in the sunlight for the edification of thousands on a roughly elliptical course from Boston to Philadelphia. Dr. Eckener said at the time it was done in appreciation of the welcome given the ship in this country. Guests on this trip included three admirals, the German Ambassador and representatives of the Department of State, the Department of Commerce and the press.

The Hindenburg carried passengers ranging in age from 6 months to 98 years. The child, the first so young to make the voyage, was the son of Melvin K. Whiteleather, a member of the Berlin staff of The Associated Press. The other extreme was a German professor who made the trip from Frankfort to Friedrichshafen, to hold the record as the oldest man to fly in lighter-than-air craft.

Ship Enlarged for Eighth Crossing

The ship was enlarged for passengers prior to her eighth crossing last year. On that voyage she carried her 1,000th passenger on the regular transatlantic service. In all there were 122 persons on board, including 72 passengers. Previously she could accommodate but 50 passengers and a crew of 55.

During the Winter months when the Lakehurst trip was not possible, the Hindenburg joined her sister ship the Graf Zeppelin in regular weekly trips to Rio de Janeiro. The weekly three-day service reached the market centers of Latin America.

The Hindenburg, always a matter of news when she was in flight, acquired special interest for readers the world over last September when she ferried three round-the-world reporters across the Atlantic on the first leg of their journey. Her performance on this trip was slightly disappointing owing to storms at sea but she negotiated the voyage without incident despite the fact that she arrived late, preventing the reporters from making planned connections on the Continent.

Performance Dispelled Doubt

The Hindenburg was built by the Luftschiffbau Zeppelin Company, which set up an operating company known as the Deutsche Zeppelin Reederei. Dr. Eckener, chairman of the board, and the American representative, F. W. von Meister, arranged for the docking facilities at Lakehurst, the western terminus.

Although there was considerable skepticism because of past performances of lighter-than-air craft, the Hindenburg schedule was carried out almost perfectly throughout the year. The courses were charted to suit the weather. Sometimes the ship would go as far north as Greenland and on other trips went south to the vicinity of the Azores but in the main adhered rather closely to the Great Circle.

Although the demand for travel this novel way increased with every trip, requiring the expansion of passenger accommodations, there was disappointment in the mail loads. The ship started off its regular flights by carrying 2,380 pounds of mail but this dropped gradually until it reached 167 pounds on one trip. The rates were forty cents for each half ounce. In the same way, freight cargoes varied from a peak of 2,380 pounds to sixty-three on the last successful westward journey.

The success of the Hindenburg and the frequent conferences based on this showing reached such proportions that it appeared America would again forget past disasters and once again engage in the lighter-than-air craft field.

GERMANY SHOCKED BY THE TRAGEDY

Continued From Page One

dress, whereupon this correspondent succeeded in awakening him and gave him the news by telephone. This was after the Zeppelin officials in Frankfort and Berlin, on the strength of their erroneous telegram reporting the ship's arrival, had been inclined to discredit any story of disaster.

Appeal to German People

Later brief details began to trickle in to newspapers and were used in the late editions, which devoted their entire front pages to the news.

All the newspapers feature an appeal to the German people, sent out by the official government service to "stand up under the blow." The government agency asserts that "the young and strong nations" can bear such disasters, and points out that a sister ship to the Hindenburg now is under construction in Friedrichshaven and soon will "take the place of the Hindenburg as ambassador from continent to continent, carrying the German flag over the ocean."

It is recalled that after preliminary trials the Hindenburg made its first long flight in company with the Graf Zeppelin in March of last year to propagandize for Hitler's plebiscite. It crossed the ocean ten times last Summer. It had made one flight to South America this year besides a number of trial flights in South Germany. This was the initial flight to New York for the season.

Film Plan for Airship

The loss of the Hindenburg occurred on the very day an interesting agreement was reached between the Zeppelin company and a group of American news photograph and film concerns. Under this agreement the airship was to have been instrumental in making a friendly German gesture toward Great Britain.

The next western trip was to have been delayed twenty-four hours to enable the airship to carry photographs and movie films of the British coronation ceremonies to New York.

The deal has been arranged by Berlin news bureaus of THE NEW YORK TIMES and The Associated Press.

Only Two Britons Aboard

Special Cable to THE NEW YORK TIMES.

LONDON, Friday, May 7.—The only two British passengers aboard the Hindenburg were said to be Captain Allen Charles Higgins, an army officer, and George Grant, steamship agent, both of London.

Officials of the Air Ministry and the German Embassy were appalled when THE NEW YORK TIMES telephoned to them the information of the disaster soon after 12:30 A. M. The Hindenburg was regarded here as the last word in safety and sound construction, and its series of successful transatlantic journeys with well-paying loads and keeping an accurate schedule had revived financial interest in the organization of a British airship service, which had been abandoned after the disaster to the R-101. It was revealed in a Berlin dispatch only last night that part of the duralumin metal framework had been salvaged from the R-101, re-rolled and embodied in the Hindenburg. In the minds of experts consulted the most astonishing feature of the disaster was that the airship had burst into flames.

Doehner Prominent in Mexico

Special Cable to THE NEW YORK TIMES.

MEXICO, D. F., May 6.—Mr. and Mrs. Hermann Doehner of this city, who were aboard the Hindenburg with their three children, were prominent members of the German colony here.

This correspondent had a difficult task in breaking the news of the accident to the mother of Mr. Doehner by telephone. After thanking him for the news Mrs. Doehner burst into tears and hung up.

Going to the home later with further details of the accident, the correspondent talked briefly with Hermann Jr., a son. Near tears the youngster, about 15 years old, said he had been born in Mexico, his family having lived here for some time, but he was so broken up that he was unable to talk further.

"All the News That's Fit to Print."

The New York Times.

LATE CITY EDITION
Showers early, generally fair and warmer today. Tomorrow generally fair, possibly thunder showers.
Temperatures Yesterday—Max., 76; Min., 58

VOL. LXXXVI.....No. 29,015. Entered as Second-Class Matter, Postoffice, New York, N. Y. NEW YORK, SATURDAY, JULY 3, 1937. PP TWO CENTS In New York City. | THREE CENTS Within 200 Miles. | FOUR CENTS Elsewhere Except in 7th and 8th Postal Zones

PHILADELPHIA DRIVERS STRIKE IN A.F.L. HOLIDAY AGAINST C.I.O.; BITTER LABOR ROW IN HOUSE

ALL TRUCKS HALT

Newspapers Suspend as the Strike Brings City Near Paralysis

MILK SHORTAGE IS FEARED

Mayor Ready to Add 10,000 Police—Other A. F. L. Groups Uphold Contracts

TAXI MEN REFUSE TO QUIT

C. I. O. Pacts Signed by Two Bakeries Cause Issue—NLRB Elections Demanded

Day's Strike Developments

Teamsters' council called a "holiday" for 25,000 drivers, halting the movement of food, freight, merchandise and newspapers in Philadelphia. Page 1.

Republic Steel mills at Massillon, Ohio, were reopened under protection of National Guardsmen. Page 6.

Johnstown remained quiet on eve of tomorrow's strike rally while Mayor and State police prepare for gathering of 40,000. Page 6.

A bitter attack by Representative Cox on Representative Maverick as defender of C. I. O. was vigorously applauded in the House. Page 1.

Members of Senate Civil Liberties Committee saw pictures of Chicago Memorial Day strike riot. Page 5.

Third Avenue system signed C. I. O. contract covering bus and trolley operators. Pay rises and preferential shop granted. Page 11.

Labor War in Philadelphia

Special to THE NEW YORK TIMES.

PHILADELPHIA, July 2.—A "general holiday" of 25,000 American Federation of Labor truckmen, called in a test of strength with the C. I. O., brought business activity in Philadelphia and its surrounding area to the edge of paralysis tonight.

The immediate occasion of the "holiday" was what the A. F. of L. leaders called an "invasion" of the truck union field by the C. I. O. through the signing of contracts with the Ward and Freihofer Baking Companies after the expiration of A. F. of L. contracts Wednesday night.

Eight hours after the "holiday" began at 2 P. M. today, virtually all deliveries were suspended. In the commission market district of the city between $1,500,000 and $2,000,000 worth of foodstuffs lay in warehouses, with little probability that they would be distributed before much of them spoil.

This evening at least a temporary milk shortage threatened. A statement by the Joint Teamsters Council, A. F. of L. organization which controls almost all the Philadelphia truckmen, promised that emergency milk and bread deliveries would be made tomorrow.

But parents who feared their children might go without food had bought up a large part of the milk supply immediately available.

Newspapers Suspend

At 10:30 this evening, after a conference of the publishers of all Philadelphia newspapers, it was agreed to suspend publication in line with the suggestion of Mayor Wilson "in order not to endanger the lives of citizens or policemen."

Conferences of the publishers were held in the office of Robert McLean, publisher of The Evening Bulletin, and the announcement was made after first editions of morning newspapers had been printed, though not generally distributed, because of the lack of trucks.

The suspension of publication, it was announced, will be indefinite. The Philadelphia newspapers affected are The Bulletin, The Daily News and The Evening Ledger, evening publications, and The Inquirer and The Record, morning newspapers. Their total circulation is about 1,500,000 copies. In Camden, N. J., The Camden Post and The Camden Evening Courier also suspended.

A statement released by the publishers and broadcast through radio stations and news services not affected by the "holiday" said that

Continued on Page Five

Cox Assails Maverick on the C.I.O. Amid Cheers of Representatives

Georgian Calls Texan More of a Buffoon Than a Public Servant and Asks if He Favors 'Terrorism'—Latter Angrily Defends Lewis and Warns 'Hysteria' Brought on Civil War

Special to THE NEW YORK TIMES.

WASHINGTON, July 2.—Supporters and opponents of the C. I. O. labor movement staged the bitterest debate of the session in the House today and suggestions were made that fist fights would result unless "these insulting remarks" were discontinued.

Representatives Maverick of Texas and Cox of Georgia were principals in the tussle, aided by Representatives Hill of Washington and Hoffman of Michigan.

After Mr. Maverick had answered Mr. Cox's speech of Wednesday attacking the C. I. O. movement as one which, if not halted, might plunge the country into civil war, the Georgia Representative took the floor for a speech in which language he used was bitterly objected to by Mr. Maverick.

The House, however, on a demand for a determination of the matter by Mr. Maverick, overwhelmingly voted to leave intact in the record Mr. Cox's words describing the Texan as "more interested in provoking amusement by his extravagance and buffoonery than in molding sound public sentiment."

In a parliamentary move rarely resorted to, Mr. Maverick had demanded that "the gentleman's words be taken down," after which it becomes the privilege of the House to determine whether the member's words reflect upon the integrity, character or standing of the offended colleague.

After the House, by a voice vote, had backed Mr. Cox, Mr. Maverick shouted that "a quorum is not present—they can put this on record if they want to." But Mr. Maverick withdrew his point of no quorum after Speaker Bankhead, striving to maintain order and enforce the rules, had observed that there obviously was no quorum present.

Mr. Maverick had defended the C. I. O. movement and had asserted Mr. Cox was "one of those" who sought to oppose the President in some points of his program.

"I want to think better than well of the gentleman (Mr. Maverick)," Mr. Cox said in reply. "However, it would be difficult for me to esteem him as highly as he might wish. I do want to believe, Mr. Speaker, that the gentleman loves his government and would not willingly lend himself as an instrument to its overthrow."

Quoting Andrew Jackson's words, "Our Federal Union, it must be preserved," Mr. Cox continued:

"Then I want him (Mr. Maverick) to join with me in asking the ques-

Continued on Page Six

PRIAL AND TAYLOR IN CONTROLLER RACE

Democrats Face Hard Fight in Primaries as Both Announce Candidacies in Day

LABOR COOL TO WAGNER

Party Reported to Be Loyal to La Guardia—Republicans Considering Smith

A primary fight for the Democratic nomination for Controller was indicated yesterday when former Deputy Controller Frank J. Prial announced his candidacy for that office and Controller Frank J. Taylor declared that he would be a candidate for re-election on his record.

Mr. Prial's announcement came just before the five Democratic county leaders, James J. Dooling, leader of Tammany; Frank V. Kelly of Brooklyn, Secretary of State Edward J. Flynn of the Bronx, James C. Sheridan of Queens and William T. Fetherston of Richmond, met in secret conference to prepare a slate for the Democratic city ticket. These five leaders were reported to be united on Senator Robert F. Wagner as the candidate for Mayor if he would consent to run.

There was no such unanimity on the candidate for Controller. Mr. Dooling was reported to favor the designation of Mr. Prial as the organization candidate in the interest of party harmony. Mr. Kelly was said to have insisted upon the designation of Controller Taylor. With agreement seemingly impossible, a bitter primary fight was in prospect with every indication that Mr. Prial would receive strong Tammany support.

The leaders made no definite decision. Mr. Sheridan insisted that the organization designate William F. Brunner, President of the Board of Aldermen, as its candidate for President of the new City Council.

Owen J. Brady, secretary of the Amalgamated Irish Societies, announced that this organization had sent a message to Mr. Dooling protesting against the nomination of Senator Wagner. The message read:

"Amalgamated Irish Societies of Greater New York strongly oppose nomination of Robert Wagner, consistent enemy of Irish race and leading advocate of American membership in League of Nations and World Court."

"I have decided to run for Controller," was Mr. Prial's laconic announcement, which he declined to amplify.

"Have you anything to add to this?" he was asked.

"No," he replied.

Mr. Taylor's declaration of his

Continued on Page Six

TREASURY DEFICIT IS $2,707,000,000 NET

Roosevelt Estimate In April Exceeded by $150,000,000 in Year-End Figures

DEBT ROSE $2,646,000,000

Receipts Up $1,178,000,000 —Outlay Exceeded Estimate by $220,000,000

Special to THE NEW YORK TIMES.

WASHINGTON, July 2.—The government ended the fiscal year on June 30 with a net deficit of $2,707,000,000 and a gross public debt of $36,425,000,000, according to final figures made public today by Secretary Morgenthau. The deficit was about $150,000,000 more than estimated by President Roosevelt on April 20. The debt was an increase of $2,646,000,000 for the fiscal year.

General receipts will be $5,294,000,000, exceeding those for 1936 by $1,178,000,000, and about $70,000,000 more than estimated in April. Total expenditures exclusive of $104,000,000 for statutory debt retirement were $8,001,000,000, or about $220,000,000 over the April estimate.

In addition to the gross public debt, Secretary Morgenthau said, the government has certain contingent liabilities in guarantees as to principal and interest on outstanding obligations of the Reconstruction Finance Corporation, Federal Housing Administration and the Home Owners Loan Corporation amounting as of June 30 to about $4,725,000,000, as compared with a total of $4,750,000,000 on June 30, 1936.

$3,889,000,000 of Assets Held

On May 31 the government held net assets in loans and other investments of governmental corporations and credit agencies of about $3,889,000,000, a decrease of $406,000,000 from May 31, 1936, the reduction representing mainly net recoveries by the government.

Daniel W. Bell, Director of the Budget, said he felt the government would come very close to the forecasts of a balanced budget in the year 1938 if revenues held up to estimates and Congress did not place any further burdens on the Treasury. The earlier forecasts had been for a deficit in 1938 of about $400,000,000, which it was hoped could be wiped out by economies.

Should that objective substantially be attained, it was estimated, with receipts of around $1,000,000,000 from social security legislation about $600,000,000 of outstanding government securities could be retired in the year. There would be issued, however, a like amount of special government securities which would be a charge against the public debt. Actual reduction of the

Continued on Page Twenty-six

NEW COURT BILL OFFERED IN SENATE TO END CONFLICT

Leaders Abandon President's Program in Effort to Save Him From Defeat

RETIRING AGE SET AT 75

Measure Limits Appointments to One a Year—Opponents Reject Compromise

The text of the new Court Bill will be found on Page 4.

By TURNER CATLEDGE

Special to THE NEW YORK TIMES.

WASHINGTON, July 2.—A substitute court bill, providing an addition of one justice a year to the Supreme Court to supplement those passing 75 years of age and refusing to retire, was introduced in the Senate today by Senate leaders, formally abandoning the President's original program.

It was presented by Senator Logan in the name of himself and Senators Ashurst and Hatch, but it represented the results of three weeks or more of negotiations by Senator Robinson, which he started when President Roosevelt gave him full authority to salvage what he could out of his judiciary reorganization plan and end the five-month controversy over the issue.

At the same time it started a drive to win such a compromise as might save Mr. Roosevelt from utter defeat on this most bitterly contested of all his measures to date.

Friends and foes of the proposal to enlarge the Supreme Court by the immediate addition of six new justices to replace or supplement those over 70½ years of age agreed that the new bill would be passed by a comfortable majority if it should ever reach a vote in the Senate.

This left a large "if," however, for opponents of the original six-justice bill vowed anew their determination to fight any increase in the membership of the high tribunal and boasted that they would filibuster for weeks to prevent the compromise plan from coming to a vote in the Senate.

Fighting "On Principle"

They said they were fighting the bill on a matter of principle, and that the principle was the same whether it increased the court by one or a dozen, if to increase it was to attempt to interfere with its line of decisions.

Whether the court-enlargement foes would attempt to make good on their threat, or whether, if they did, the administration leaders would try to ride out a filibuster were other unknown quantities in the equation. Any definite forecast of what might happen was, therefore, impossible.

The substitute bill will be brought up early next week, according to present plans. It may be debated for several days, possibly two or three weeks, without any suggestion of obstructionist tactics.

Should a filibuster then develop, however, it would be for the Senate leaders to determine whether they would attempt to ride it out, which most observers agreed they could do if they were willing to stay in session indefinitely, or whether, in the interest of early adjournment and greater harmony in the Democratic party, it would be better to postpone the matter indefinitely and recommit the bill to the Judiciary Committee for further study.

In view of all the circumstances

Continued on Page Four

SOVIET WITHDRAWS FORCE FROM AMUR AT SCENE OF FIGHT

Japanese-Manchukuoan Guard Also Gone, So Danger of New Clash Is Removed

PARLEYS WILL FIX BORDER

Tokyo Hails the Settlement as Evidence That Recent Purge Weakened Moscow

By HAROLD DENNY

Wireless to THE NEW YORK TIMES.

MOSCOW, Saturday, July 3.—The Commissariat of Defense issued an order early today for the withdrawal of Soviet armed patrols and naval cutters from Amur River islands, the ownership of which is in dispute between the Soviet Union and Japanese-controlled Manchukuo.

The islands were the scene of recent fighting with losses to both Soviet and Japanese forces. The ownership of the contested land will be determined by future negotiations.

Thus another threatening Far Eastern crisis appears to have blown over. The Soviet's order for withdrawal of its forces followed a half-hour conference at the Foreign Office late last night between Foreign Commissar Maxim Litvinoff and Mamoru Shigemitsu, the Japanese Ambassador, at which the envoy informed the Commissar that he had received telegraphic information from Tokyo that Japanese-Manchukuoan cutters had been withdrawn from the islands. He added that he expected the Soviet naval land and air forces would be promptly withdrawn also.

Both Statements Agree

According to the Soviet Foreign Office communiqué, the content of which was in harmony with the Japanese Ambassador's account of the conversation, Mr. Litvinoff agreed that the Japanese-Manchukuoan withdrawal met the suggestion he had previously made, that both sides withdraw and take up the sovereignty issue later. He promised immediately to inform military authorities so they could give the necessary orders.

The communiqué then continued:

"To the Ambassador's question as to whether the withdrawal would establish the status quo ante Mr. Litvinoff answered affirmatively. Explaining it would restore the status quo of both parties laying claim to the islands, he said that after the restoration of order it would be possible to start to review those claims.

"The Ambassador agreed that in the future it would be possible to begin demarcation of the border line on the Amur. Mr. Litvinoff made clear that such demarcation would determine the possession of the islands by one or the other party."

Border Issue Is Difficult

The solution, though it seems to dispose of the immediate danger, leaves the basic question of the Amur boundary unsettled. There are indications that will be a knotty problem. In the past two years the Soviet Union and Japan made proposals and counter-proposals for demarcation commissions without approaching agreement. The Japanese insisted the commission should be composed of three members, a Soviet citizen, a Manchukuoan and a Japanese. To this the Soviet objected that it would be tantamount to giving Japan two representatives to the Soviet's one.

Japanese Embassy officials asserted before Mr. Shigemitsu's confer-

Continued on Page Two

A. A. U. Declines Invitation to Germany; Religious Persecution Is Cited by Mahoney

Special to THE NEW YORK TIMES.

MILWAUKEE, Wis., July 2.—In the first rebuff given to a foreign nation in the half century of its existence, the Amateur Athletic Union of the United States tonight declined to permit a track and field team to compete in Germany this Summer.

The decision was made by the combined executive and foreign relations committee and the vote was unanimous. That part of the tour by a ten-man team that took it to Sweden, the Netherlands and Hungary was approved, but the athletic invasion of the Reich was banned.

In announcing the move, President Jeremiah T. Mahoney said.

"This is consistent with the stand that I have always taken. I do not believe that our American athletes should go to a country where freedom of speech, religion and action have been abolished. Since I first started the fight to keep our fine young boys out of a land that persecuted the Jews, the Nazis have begun to attack and stifle Catholicism and Protestantism as well. Nazi ideology cannot conform with American democracy."

The same leaders who made the unsuccessful fight to keep the United States out of the Olympic Games last Summer were behind tonight's move with reinforcements from other quarters.

Judge Mahoney was the ex-officio chairman of the double committee meeting. Others there were Jack Rafferty of Houston, Texas; Charles L. Ornstein of New York, Louis Di Benedetto of New Orleans, George W. Graves of Detroit, John J. Magee of Bowdoin College, Daniel J. Ferris of New York, Raymond N. Sellon of Milwaukee, Ward Haylett of Kansas State College and Charles F. Hunter of San Francisco.

The Houston convention last December saw this group come back into power in A. A. U. affairs after the Avery Brundage forces had held control in the Olympic year.

Mr. Ferris, as secretary-treasurer of the world's largest sport governing body, cabled to other inviting countries that their bids had been approved and to Germany that her offer had been declined.

MISS EARHART FORCED DOWN AT SEA, HOWLAND ISLE FEARS; COAST GUARD BEGINS SEARCH

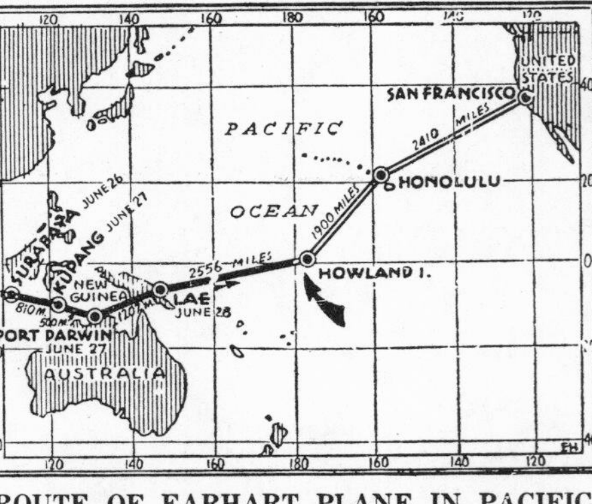

ROUTE OF EARHART PLANE IN PACIFIC

The flier took off from Lae, New Guinea, at 8 P. M., New York time, Thursday, and was in the vicinity of Howland Island at 4:43 P. M. Friday, when she was in communication with the Coast Guard cutter Itasca. She had intended to fly from this island to Honolulu and thence to the mainland for the completion of her world tour.

FUEL HAD RUN LOW

Fliers Were Near Goal When Last Reported but Saw No Land

PLANE EQUIPPED TO FLOAT

Has Sealed Gasoline Tanks and a Rubber Lifeboat for Emergency at Sea

RADIO BELIEVED HEARD

Los Angeles Amateurs Pick Up Weak Signals on Frequency Assigned to the Plane

By The Associated Press.

WASHINGTON, July 2.—Coast Guard headquarters was advised tonight that Amelia Earhart was believed to have alighted on the Pacific Ocean near Howland Island shortly after 5 P. M. Eastern daylight time today.

A message from the cutter Itasca, stationed in the vicinity of the island in the mid-Pacific, said:

"Earhart unreported at Howland at 7 P. M. [E. D. T.]. Believe down shortly after 5 P. M. Am searching probable area and will continue."

Admiral William D. Leahy, chief of naval operations, instructed the commandant of the naval station at Honolulu tonight to render whatever aid he may deem practicable in the search for Miss Earhart.

Plane Joins in Search

[A navy flying boat hopped off from Honolulu late last night for Howland Island, 1,900 miles distant, to join the cutter Itasca hunting for Miss Earhart, The Associated Press reported. Two Los Angeles radio amateurs were said to have picked up weak signals on the frequency assigned to the Earhart radio.]

Coast Guard headquarters had received information that Miss Earhart probably overshot tiny Howland Island because she was blinded by the glare of an ascending sun. The message from the Coast Guard cutter Itasca said it was believed Miss Earhart passed northwest of Howland Island about 3:20 P. M. [E. D. T.], or about 8 A. M., Howland Island time. The Itasca reported that heavy smoke was billowing from its funnels at the time to serve as a signal for the flyer. The cutter's skipper expressed belief the Earhart plane had descended into the sea within 100 miles of Howland.

Husband Asks Assistance

In a message to Washington, the flier's husband, George Palmer Putnam, who is awaiting her return to this country at the Oakland, Cal., airport, said:

"Technicians familiar with Miss Earhart's plane believe, with its large tanks, it can float almost indefinitely. With retractable landing gear and smooth seas, safe landing (on the sea) should have been practicable.

"Request such assistance as practicable from naval aircraft and surface craft stationed at Honolulu. Apparently plane's position not far from Howland.

"The plane's large wing and empty gasoline tanks should provide sufficient buoyancy if it came to rest on the sea without being damaged.

"There was a two-man rubber lifeboat aboard the plane, together with lifebelts, flares, a Very pistol and a large yellow signal kite which could be flown above the plane or the liferaft."

Mr. Putnam said his wife had planned to take emergency food rations and plenty of water on the hazardous flight, the most dangerous on her trip around the world.

Earlier the Coast Guard had ordered the cutter Roger B. Taney to proceed from Honolulu to Howland Island to aid the cutter Itasca in the search for Miss Earhart. A message from Honolulu, however, said the Taney was undergoing repairs and could not participate.

Amateurs Pick Up Signals

LOS ANGELES, July 2 (AP).—Two amateur radio operators claimed to have picked up signals tonight on frequencies officially assigned to the plane of Amelia Earhart.

Walter McMenamy said he picked up weak signals on 6210 kilocycles

Continued on Page Three

SOVIET 'LIQUIDATES' 120 MORE AS SPIES

Disclosure Indicates Others May Have Been Shot as the Agents of Estonia and Poland

AVIATOR IS AMONG THEM

Government Is Now Trying to Check Persecution of the Innocent in Campaign

Wireless to THE NEW YORK TIMES.

MOSCOW, July 2.—The detection and "liquidation" of two large groups of alleged spies—one of seventy members, said to be in the service of Estonia, and the other of fifty to seventy members, said to be in the service of Poland—were disclosed today by Leonid Zakovsky, chief of the Leningrad district of the Commissariat of Internal Affairs [the secret police department].

Mr. Zakovsky received the Order of Lenin on June 26 for "self-sacrificing fulfilment of most important orders of the government." The nature of the orders was not disclosed.

The detection of these groups apparently occurred in the past year, although many members were accused of having carried on activities for many years. Mr. Zakovsky did not say in so many words that all these 120 or more had been shot, but the plain inference is that they were.

Gives Details on Seizures

Mr. Zakovsky's disclosures, giving far more details than usual in such cases, are contained in an article he wrote for Komsomolskaya Pravda, Young Communist newspaper, instructing youth on the necessity of being on guard against foreign spies who invidiously worm their way into confidences.

He said the alleged Estonian group was led by the son of a Kulak [individualist farmer] in the Leningrad region and that that leader after training by the Estonian General Staff, returned to Russia and installed a secret radio station in a forest in the Leningrad region. By that means, it is said, he received and sent code messages.

Gradually, he recruited bands of saboteurs and spies in villages, factories and even in the Red army, but at length he was caught with the radio in the forest, resisted and was shot by secret police officers.

Mr. Zakovsky declared the Polish Intelligence Service organized bands in White Russia who, on the outbreak of war, were to become "Polish partisan rioters" commanded by Polish officers who would arrive on Soviet soil a few days before the outbreak of war.

Among other instances of alleged spying there was the case of a Soviet military aviator, who, Mr. Zakovsky said, became involved with a woman whose husband was a foreign spy. The husband and wife, after gaining important military information from him, blackmailed him into becoming a full-fledged spy and finally into organizing within his squadron a sabotage group that put planes out of repair, causing a number of accidents. The aviator was discovered and shot.

Indications that authorities are trying to check the distortion of the hunt for "spies" and wreckers

Continued on Page Three

VALERA FAR AHEAD IN IRISH ELECTION

His Return to Power in Dail Seems Assured by Early Count in Free State

VOTE ON CHARTER CLOSE

Heavy Adverse Sentiment Is Indicated—Larkin, Labor Leader, Wins Seat

Special Cable to THE NEW YORK TIMES.

DUBLIN, Irish Free State, July 3.—The first returns in the Free State general election received tonight indicate that the De Valera party, the Fianna Fail, is running ahead in many constituencies and the Cosgrave party faring badly.

Lord Mayor Alfred Byrne was the first candidate to gain election when he headed the poll in Northeast Dublin, far ahead of all other candidates. He received 12,068 votes. Next to him came Oscar Traynor, President Eamon de Valera's Minister for Posts and Telegraphs, with 9,693. The quota to insure election was 9,051.

Larkin Wins Seat

This constituency provided an election sensation when James Larkin, a labor leader, and once an inmate of Sing Sing prison in New York, won the third seat here by defeating General Richard Mulcahy, one of ex-President William Cosgrave's most effective front benchers. General Mulcahy was chief of staff of the Republican army during the fight against the British, and later was Minister for Defense in the Cosgrave administration. Subsequently he was a Minister in the local government. His defeat by Larkin is a big blow to the Cosgrave party.

Mr. de Valera easily headed the poll in Clare, where he was elected with 14,012 votes on the first count of a total of 63,000. This figure actually shows a decrease in de Valera's poll, compared to the 1933 election, when he received 18,000 votes of a total of 55,000. The decline is attributed to local dissensions over the selection of Fianna Fail candidates for this constituency.

In Cork City Mr. Cosgrave fared much worse than Mr. de Valera. Of a total of 53,019 votes the former President polled only 9,000-odd votes against the 14,863 he received in the 1933 election of a total of 68,000. Mr. Cosgrave headed the poll and was elected on the first count, but generally his party fared badly.

Results in Cork

His party's second candidate, Alderman William Desmond, polled only 2,008 and defeated the Labor candidate. On the other hand, the Fianna Fail held both its seats in Cork City with the return of Hugo Flinn, Parliamentary Secretary, and Thomas Dowdall. Already, before one-fourth of the results have been announced, the Cosgraveites have suffered two heavy defeats in Dublin and Cork.

In two other Dublin constituencies where results were available tonight the de Valera candidates headed the polls. Sean MacEntee, the Minister of Finance, was elected in Dublin Township on the first count with 10,124 votes.

Next to MacEntee came Cosgrave's former Attorney General, John Costello, with 8,418, who also was returned. In Dublin County

Continued on Page Two

PLANE IS BELIEVED TO HAVE BUOYANCY

Earhart Craft Also Carried Rubber Boat and Other Emergency Devices

HAUSNER FLOATED 8 DAYS

American Woman Dogged by Ill Fortune in Plan to Fly Around the World

Miss Amelia Earhart's monoplane, although a land ship without special flotation apparatus, has good buoyancy for that type of craft, it was pointed out last night. The buoyancy is obtained especially from the wing tanks and the general construction of the wings.

How long the plane would stay afloat if she were forced down on the water was said to be problematical. The tanks in which extra fuel was carried, when empty would act as pontoons for the fuselage. Check valves on the tanks do not admit water. The late Stanislaus Felix Hausner, Polish-American aviator, floated on a half-sunken land plane, also a monoplane, for eight days in the Atlantic before his rescue by a ship in 1932. In 1931 Rody, Johanssen and da Costa Veiga floated in their land plane off Newfoundland for seven days.

Safety Devices on the Plane

The safety devices on Miss Earhart's plane included a collapsible rubber boat that could be quickly inflated, an orange kite for use as a distress signal in the event of a forced landing and a flare pistol and flares. The auxiliary radio equipment, besides a standard motor-driven generator unit, included an emergency wind-driven generator that could be stuck out of the cockpit window to generate power if the regular generator failed.

Miss Earhart's plane, a twin-engined Lockheed Electra, was designed for modern transport and later modified under her direction to suit research and other special purposes to which she put it. It was constructed entirely of light alloys and was known as the model 10-E of 1936. At an altitude of 10,500 feet it had a cruising speed of well over 200 miles an hour. It was powered by two Pratt & Whitney Wasp engines of the latest type and was equipped with constant speed propellers.

Called a "flying laboratory," the ship has been dogged by ill fortune. It was wrecked in a crash at Honolulu on March 20 in an attempted take-off on a round-the-world flight projected by the woman flier. The plane later was returned to the United States for repairs.

It suffered another mishap last May 21, when an overheated engine caused a slight blaze just after she had landed at Tucson, Ariz., after a test flight from Burbank, Calif.. On the globe-girdling flight, at several stages of the journey trouble developed in various instruments, causing delays for adjustments.

Had Many Aids to Flight

Miss Earhart had had the ten passenger chairs in a transport removed. In their places she substituted extra fuel tanks and installed almost every known device to aid navigation, to facilitate high altitude flying, to test engine and plane performance and to keep records of flight details automatically.

The craft had a wing span of 55 feet, an overall length of 38 feet 7 inches and a height of 10 feet with its retractable undercarriage extended. Ranking officers of the United States Navy use similar models as transport planes. Fully loaded, the monoplane weighed more than 10,000 pounds.

The ship was called the flying laboratory of the School of Aeronautics of Purdue University because Miss Earhart conducted experiments in the plane, acting in her capacity as a member of the faculty of Purdue.

FAMOUS AVIATRIX REPORTED DOWN IN THE PACIFIC ON AROUND-THE-WORLD FLIGHT

Associated Press Photo.

Amelia Earhart, with her husband, George Palmer Putnam, in front of her plane at Los Angeles before she left on her first globe-encircling attempt, which ended in an accident in Honolulu. They are displaying the kites which she had planned to use as distress signals to aid searchers in finding her in the event of an emergency.

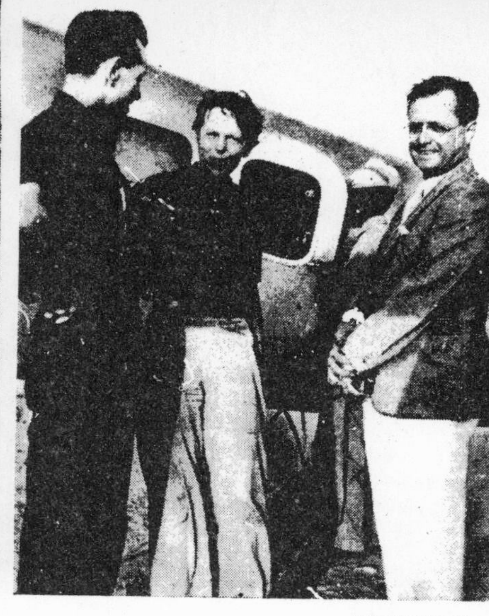

Times Wide World Photo.

Miss Earhart as she landed at the Karachi airport in India on June 15. This is one of the latest photographs of her to reach the United States. At the left is Fred J. Noonan, her navigator, and at the right is Viscount Sibour of the Standard Oil Company.

New York Times Studio Photo.

A recent portrait of Miss Earhart

Her plane—The Flying Laboratory

Times Wide World Photo.

EFFORT WAS SECOND BY FLIER THIS YEAR

Miss Earhart's Plane Was Wrecked at Honolulu in Take-Off Last March

WEATHER FORCED CHANGE

West-to-East Course Adopted for Her Second Attempt After Craft Was Overturned

Amelia Earhart and her navigator, Fred J. Noonan, left Lae, New Guinea, at 10 P. M. Thursday (New York daylight time) on the most perilous leg of their projected flight around the world—a 2,556-mile jump to Howland Island, tiny dot of land rising only a few feet above the sea, two miles long and half a mile wide. They expected to cover the distance in eighteen hours, at an average speed of 150 miles an hour.

The hop was to take them over a route never before traveled by an airplane, but the Coast Guard cutter Itasca and the United States Navy tug Ontario stood by to help. The Ontario was stationed halfway between Howland Island and New Guinea to keep in touch with Miss Earhart's plane by wireless or to go to her assistance if necessary.

At Howland a crew of men prepared to shoo flocks of huge birds from runways constructed months ago on America's frontier in the South Pacific in anticipation of commercial flying between the United States and Australia.

Her Second Attempt This Year

Miss Earhart's round-the-world jaunt via a route near the equator was her second attempt at the feat this year. In March her first attempt began at Oakland, Calif., and ended in near-disaster at Honolulu. On March 17 she took off from Oakland, Calif., in her $80,000 "flying laboratory" for Honolulu, with Paul Mantz, relief pilot; Captain Harry Manning, navigator, and Mr. Noonan, co-navigator.

The aviatrix and her companions reached Honolulu safely the next day in the record time of 15 hours 51½ minutes. They had clipped 1 hour 6½ minutes from the previous mark for the 2,410-mile flight, made by the Hawaii Clipper last December. Two days later, however, the plane crashed when taking off from Honolulu for Howland Island, ending her attempt to fly around the world. The right tire of the twin-engined ship blew out as the plane was taking off. The plane swerved, the landing gear collapsed and both propellers were smashed. The lives of all aboard were saved by the woman pilot's quick action in "cutting the switches."

Undaunted, Miss Earhart almost immediately set to work to plan a second attempt. Returning to the United States by steamship, she had her plane overhauled. The delay caused by this, however, meant that by the time she and Mr. Noonan, her only companion this time, were ready to begin a second attempt weather conditions around the world had changed and they had to plot a route different from their original one.

Finally, about the middle of May, all was in readiness. On May 21 Miss Earhart and Mr. Noonan left Burbank, Calif. They flew to Tucson, Ariz., then to New Orleans and then to Miami. On June 1 they hopped off from Miami to San Juan, Puerto Rico, which they reached the next day. Thence by easy stages they dipped down to Natal, Brazil, via Carpito and Paramaribo.

Crossed South Atlantic

They hopped off from Natal June 7, crossed the South Atlantic and landed, June 8, at St. Louis, Senegal. Then they crossed Africa via Dakar, Gao, Fort Lamy, El Fasher and Khartoum and landed at Assab, Eritrea, June 14.

After their take-off from Assab, on the Red Sea, they made a 1,900-mile flight to Karachi, India, where they landed June 14. Three days later they were in Calcutta, after a 1,390-mile jump from Karachi. From there they flew over jungles and lonely stretches of sea to Port Darwin, Australia, via Rangoon, Singapore, Bandoeng, Surabaya and Kupang.

They landed at Port Darwin, on the northern coast of Australia, last Sunday. Monday saw them at Lae, after a 1,207-mile flight from Port Darwin.

The flight from Lae to Howland Island was over equatorial seas dotted with tropical islands that, supposedly, still are peopled with savage or cannibalistic natives.

The late Sir Charles Kingsford Smith was the only flier ever to have made a flight over the Pacific comparable to that attempted by Miss Earhart from Lae to Howland Island. Sir Charles flew from California to Hawaii, then to Suva, Fiji Islands, and then to Australia.

MANAGUA OUSTS HONDURAN

Exile Blames Fear of President Carias of Revolt in Honduras

Special Cable to THE NEW YORK TIMES.

SAN JOSE, Costa Rica, July 2.—In accordance with apparent cooperation among Central American dictators, Rafael Medina Raudales, a lawyer and Honduran political exile, has been expelled from Nicaragua.

Mr. Raudales said that without warning he was arrested in Managua Wednesday, placed in an airplane against his will and arrived here yesterday. He had been expelled from Honduras by President Tiburcio Carias and believed his expulsion from Nicaragua was at the request of President Carias, who feared a revolutionary move.

EARHART AIRPLANE PROBABLY ON SEA

Continued From Page One

at 6 P. M. [10 P. M. Eastern daylight time] and heard the letters "L-a-t" which he took to mean latitude. The letters were followed by undecipherable figures.

The signals continued for some time. Mr. McMenamy expressed belief they came from a portable transmitter. He received other signals from a Coast Guard boat, presumably the cutter Itasca, requesting listeners to "stand by and listen on all frequencies."

At 8 P. M. [midnight Eastern daylight time], Carl Pierson, chief engineer of the Patterson Radio Corporation, picked up similarly weak signals on 3,105 kilocycles, Miss Earhart's daytime frequency. He said they were erratic and undecipherable.

Both Mr. McMenamy and Mr. Pierson said the signals came from a hand-cranked generator. Miss Earhart carried one in her plane.

Within 100 Miles of Goal

HONOLULU, July 2 (AP).—Amelia Earhart, the world's best known aviatrix, and her navigator, Fred J. Noonan, were believed forced down at sea today in their $80,000 "flying laboratory" somewhere near tiny Howland Island on a daring attempt to span the South Pacific.

Apparently headwinds had exhausted their gasoline within 100 miles of the end of a projected 2,556-mile flight from Lae, New Guinea.

The alarming silence of the plane's radio spurred into search the Coast Guard cutter Itasca from Howland Island when Miss Earhart's estimated gasoline deadline of 8 P. M. [E. D. T.] passed without word.

A message from the globe-girdling plane, the time of which was translated at Washington by Coast Guard headquarters as 3:20 P. M. [E. D. T.] said she had only a half hour's gasoline and had not sighted land. A later incomplete message was reported at 4:43 P. M. [E. D. T.] Earlier at 2:46 P. M. [E. D. T.] the plane was approximately 100 miles from the island.

The cutter Itasca set out at 8:30 P. M. [E. D. T.] to hunt the missing plane. Coast guardsmen here expressed the belief that aviation's "first lady" and her companion had overshot the minute island and come down somewhere in the vast mid-Pacific region far removed from regular shipping lanes. The cutter prepared to search the little known area northwest of Howland Island.

Bound around the world on an equatorial trail of more than 27,000 miles, Miss Earhart had flown since May 21 from Oakland, Calif., in relatively leisurely stages.

Arriving at Lae, New Guinea, June 28, she awaited favorable weather for the attempt to negotiate the unflown miles to Howland Island, the dot of land that represents the United States' frontier in the South Pacific and is regarded as a potential stepping stone on an air line between the Pacific Coast and the Antipodes.

She left Lae at 10 A. M. local time July 2, which was 8 P. M. yesterday, Eastern daylight time, expecting to complete the flight in eighteen or twenty hours.

The navy tug Ontario stood by half-way between New Guinea and Howland Island, but was not heard from. The Itasca, waiting to receive Miss Earhart at the island, received only the barest reports of her progress until the message came that her fuel was about gone.

The next nearest land to Howland is Jarvis Island, a similar mid-Pacific dot forty miles north. Aside from these virtual sandbars there is nothing but water for hundreds of miles.

Howland Island is many hours behind Eastern time, and daylight still existed there, with a smooth sea and good visibility prevailing.

The Coast Guard reported receipt of the following message from the Itasca:

"Earhart contact at 3:30 P. M. [E. D. T.]; reported half hour fuel and no landfall. Position doubtful.

"Contact 2:46 P. M. [E. D. T.]; reported approximately 100 miles from Itasca, but no relative bearing. Sea is smooth, visibility perfect, ceiling unlimited. Understand she will float for limited time."

Coast Guard officers consulted the army commanders in Honolulu concerning the possibility of sending land or sea planes from Honolulu, but officials said this was unlikely.

Officers aboard the cutter reported they estimated 8 P. M. [E. D. T.] was the latest the plane could stay aloft and that if it had not arrived by then a search would be started in the northwest quadrant from Howland Island "as the most probable area."

Headquarters officials said they could not understand the discrepancy between Miss Earhart's report that she had only a half hour's fuel and the Itasca estimate that she could remain in the air until 7 P. M. They added, however, that the Itasca officers might have taken into account a reserve fuel supply aboard the plane.

Information was sought concerning the sea, whether it was smooth enough to aid the fliers in keeping afloat until the Itasca could locate and rescue them or whether it was rough enough to endanger them immediately.

The Itasca radioed Washington the sea was smooth with visibility perfect.

Mrs. Noonan Confident

OAKLAND, Calif., July 2 (AP).—Mrs. Frederick Noonan, wife of the navigator of Amelia Earhart's world-girdling plane, called The Oakland Tribune this afternoon to ask whether the plane had landed safely at Howland Island in mid-Pacific.

An Associated Press dispatch was read to the effect that Miss Earhart and Mr. Noonan probably were forced down in the open sea.

Take-off Weather Perfect

SYDNEY, Australia, July 2 (AP).—Amelia Earhart took off at 8 P. M. yesterday [E. D. T.] across 2,550 miles of the South Seas from Lae, New Guinea, toward Howland Island on what she described as "the worst section" of her leisurely flight around the globe."

Weather conditions were perfect as Miss Earhart lifted her monoplane into the air. A run of nearly 900 yards was necessary before the plane left the ground with its heavy load of gasoline.

Howland Island Claimed For U. S. Two Years Ago

By The Associated Press.

WASHINGTON, July 2.—Howland Island, near which Amelia Earhart's plane was believed to have been forced down, is a one-and-a-half-mile-long treeless sandspit, strategically located on the direct air route between Hawaii and Australia. It is nearly 2,000 miles southwest of Honolulu.

Uninhabited until two years ago, it came into public notice when the Commerce Department took possession of it along with two other Pacific islets, Baker, forty miles to the north, and Jarvis, more than 1,000 miles to the east. For more than two years relays of Hawaiian schoolboys have lived on each, making meteorological observations and maintaining title for the United States.

SOVIET LIQUIDATES 120 MORE AS SPIES

Continued From Page One

into a campaign of reckless persecution of innocent people were seen in an editorial rebuke by the newspaper Pravda today to the district Communist party newspaper of Western Siberia.

The latter paper, under the heading, "Let us open fire on idiotic carelessness and kulak sabotage," denounced nine chairmen of lagging collective farms as "enemies of the people" and demanded that they be immediately investigated and tried for failure to take advantage of good weather for mowing hay. The paper called this alleged failure "economic and political hooliganism."

Pravda declared there was no evidence whatever of kulak sabotage and called the district party committee itself guilty of political hooliganism by complicating the government's hunt for real enemies of the people.

"The newspaper that irresponsibly soils the reputations of our people does counter-revolutionary work," said Pravda. "Libel in the newspapers is a form of wrecking that must be fought with all determination."

Izvestia today also assailed a Rostov paper for venomously attacking a world-known surgeon, Professor Bogoraz, for allegedly accepting bribes. The charges boiled down to the fact that Professor Bogoraz had charged fees to private patients which he treated in a State clinic.

Fees at Clinics Are Legal

Such charging of fees is entirely legal even under the Soviet's socialized medical system, and as Professor Bogoraz lacks both legs it is not practical for him to treat patients at their homes. The Rostov paper accused the surgeon of "pletneffism"—after Dr. Pletneff, Moscow heart specialist, who recently was sensationally denounced in the Soviet press, beginning with a Pravda statement that was followed by the customary inspired resolutions of indignation.

Dr. Pletneff was accused of an indescribable sadistic crime against a woman patient, but the charges were widely discredited by the public. The newspaper campaign against him suddenly ceased.

Recent disclosures of the abuse of peasants, whom the government has tried zealously to placate in recent years, have resulted in a series of trials of local government and party officials.

In the Archangel district eleven officials, including chairmen of village soviets, have just received sentences of from one to five years for unwarranted foreclosures of peasants' personal property for debts. In the past two years 1,000 individual peasants and collective farmers underwent confiscation of their property at forced sales. The possessions were bought up for a song for these very officials, according to Izvestia's report today.

A local tax collector was accused of instructing his agents to administer collections of the agricultural tax in a manner to "make feathers fly."

Ten officials near Kiev were sentenced to varying terms for confiscating peasants' property and virtually giving it to "useful" people.

In a district of the Don region two agricultural executives are going on trial on charges of organizing such mismanagement and confiscation that collective farmers in protest started a mass slaughter of cattle and fowl and 2,300 peasants withdrew from the farms.

27 KILLED IN BLASTS IN BRITISH COAL MINE

18 in Rescue Party Wiped Out on Way to Aid Men Trapped a Mile Underground

Wireless to THE NEW YORK TIMES.

LONDON, July 2.—Struggling through gas and smoke to aid a party of miners trapped a mile underground in the Brymbo colliery in Staffordshire today, a rescue group of eighteen was wiped out by a second explosion. Altogether twenty-seven lost their lives and many were injured.

Among the dead in the rescue party were John Cocks, 57, joint managing director of the Shelton Iron Company; H. Finney, senior government inspector of mines in that area; J. Bloor, subinspector, and H. L. Adkins, assistant manager.

Two hundred men were at work when the first blast came.

The mine is now blazing and may be flooded.

CANADA'S PAVILION AT PARIS FAIR OPENED

Mackenzie King and Lapointe Stress Good Neighborliness With U. S. and France

Wireless to THE NEW YORK TIMES.

PARIS, July 2.—In opening the Canadian pavilion at the International Exhibition here today, Prime Minister Mackenzie King said that no country was more fortunate in its relations with other countries than Canada. He said he previously had attended the Imperial Conference in London, where representatives of all the associated dominions of the British Empire met with those of the mother country in perfect freedom and independence, but had united in a determination to keep their freedom jointly if necessary.

Canada lived with the United States on the most cordial terms of a good neighborhood, he declared, and between Canada and France there was a sentimental link that would never die.

Canada, he said, was proud to take a small part in the exhibition, which was designed to show how the peoples of every country lived by genius and effort with men of all races and how essential each nation was to the other.

Ernest Lapointe, Canadian Minister of Justice, said that despite recent tendencies in international life, Canada had remained loyal to the principles of freedom of exchange of produce, of service and of thought, by which alone peace could be secured and maintained.

The Prime Minister and Mr. Lapointe were entertained at luncheon by Premier Camille Chautemps. Later Mr. King laid a wreath on the grave of the Unknown Soldier at the Arc de Triomphe and another on the grave of the scientist Pasteur.

BULGARIA HOLDS FASCISTS

140 Seized at Interior Minister's Orders for Varna Bombings

Wireless to THE NEW YORK TIMES.

SOFIA, Bulgaria, July 2.—Interior Minister M. T. Krasnovsky caused the arrest of 140 Bulgarian Fascists today in Varna, a Black Sea resort. The Fascists, who have anti-Semitic tendencies, committed six bombings last week. No one was hurt but much damage was done.

The police did not take energetic measures against the Fascists so the Mayor appealed to the Interior Minister, who went to Varna.

TOKYO ASAHI OBJECTS TO A TIMES EDITORIAL

Regrets Inability 'to Recognize the Justice of Japan's Policy in Manchukuo' Since 1931

Special Cable to THE NEW YORK TIMES.

TOKYO, July 2.—The newspaper Asahi objected today to Thursday's editorial in THE NEW YORK TIMES on the recent clash between Soviet and Japanese-Manchukuoan forces on the Amur River. The Asahi says:

"THE NEW YORK TIMES suggests that the Soviet may welcome the present incident as a means of arresting the downfall of the Soviet régime. This comment may be right, as far as the Soviet is concerned, but in criticizing Japan THE TIMES says the Manchurian affair in 1931 broke out at a time when Europe faced many difficulties and that the present incident appears in similar circumstances—when France faces a financial crisis and the European powers are disturbed by the Spanish war and Russia's weakness has been exposed.

"This interpretation of Japan's action is made without going into the circumstances of these affairs. Though lack of space may have prevented THE TIMES from entering detailed arguments, we regret, in view of its influence on American public opinion, that it has been unable to recognize the justice of Japan's policy in Manchukuo since the 1931 incident."

The Asahi's comment on the present Amur River affair is:

"The Soviet's illegal invasion of the southern waterway was part of continuous Russian activities along the Siberian-Manchukuoan border which show the Soviet Union's insincerity in connection with frontier demarcation."

PROGRESSIVE JEWS MEET

International Congress in Amsterdam to Draft New Rules

Wireless to THE NEW YORK TIMES.

AMSTERDAM, The Netherlands, July 2.—The International Congress of World Union for Progressive Judaism opened here today. Delegates from the United States, Great Britain, France and Germany met to devise new religious rules and general lines of conduct for liberal Jewry.

The movement, which originated in Germany, is strongly opposed by Orthodox Jews here. In recent years, however, because of the German persecution the movement has spread considerably among Jews who had abandoned their faith.

"All the News That's Fit to Print."

The New York Times.

LATE CITY EDITION
Generally fair and warmer today. Tomorrow mostly cloudy, mild temperatures, colder at night.
Temperatures Yesterday—Max., 46; Min., 36

Copyright, 1938, by The New York Times Company.

VOL. LXXXVII.. .No. 29,267. | Entered as Second-Class Matter, Postoffice, New York, N. Y. | NEW YORK, SATURDAY, MARCH 12, 1938. | PP | TWO CENTS In New York City. | THREE CENTS Within 200 Miles. | FOUR CENTS Elsewhere Except in 7th and 8th Postal Zones.

NAZIS SEIZE AUSTRIA AFTER HITLER ULTIMATUM; GERMAN TROOPS INVITED TO MAINTAIN ORDER; SEYSS-INQUART CHANCELLOR; POWERS PROTEST

A. E. MORGAN DEFIES PRESIDENT'S AIRING OF TVA BOARD ROW

Again and Again He Declines at Hearing in Roosevelt's Office to Give 'Facts'

SAYS IT IS UP TO CONGRESS

He Is Told He Should Resign if Not Willing to Support Accusations He Made

TWO COLLEAGUES HEARD

Lilienthal and H. A. Morgan Put Before Chief Executive Data Defending Their Course

A summary of Mr. Roosevelt's inquiry in TVA on Page 8.

By TURNER CATLEDGE
Special to THE NEW YORK TIMES.

WASHINGTON, March 11.—President Roosevelt met open defiance today in his efforts to investigate dissension in the Tennessee Valley Authority when Arthur E. Morgan, chairman of the board, refused to submit evidence in support of his charges against his fellow-directors and reiterated, instead, his demand for a Congressional investigation.

Chairman Morgan sat with the other board members, Dr. Harcourt A. Morgan and David E. Lilienthal, for six hours in the President's office, the most unusual meeting of its kind ever held in Washington.

Time and time again the TVA chairman heard the President repeat demands for him to bring forth evidence to back his charges. He heard the other directors spread before the President the grounds on which they had countercharged that the chairman was undermining the TVA and that they could work with him no longer.

Dr. Morgan even heard the suggestion from the President's lips that he should resign if he were unwilling to support with facts his accusations that "fairness" and "decency" were impossible in the TVA administration with the other two members on the board.

Says He Is an "Observer"

Except for rare intervals when he defended himself with a sentence or two against the charges of his associate directors, Chairman Morgan remained openly defiant of the proceedings. Throughout, he maintained the position he had stated shortly after 11 A. M. when he marched into the President's office behind the others:

"I am an observer and not a participant in this alleged process of fact finding."

As the conference temporarily ended early tonight, President Roosevelt told the three TVA board members that it was their duty to the country not to continue their "personal" row any longer. He told them that if they could not reach a settlement among themselves, it was the duty of those who could not see their way to do so, to resign. He gave them until 11 A. M. next Friday to submit any other statements or evidence to prove their charges, and, furthermore, to determine whether they would be able to compose their differences without a resignation.

This statement from the President was widely interpreted in Washington as an ultimatum to Chairman Morgan either to drop or substantiate his statement by next Friday or quit.

Expect Morgan to Resist

Simultaneously the Presidential statements aroused wide speculation as to whether Mr. Roosevelt had the power to remove Chairman Morgan or any of the other two TVA directors. From Dr. Morgan's attitude, observers concluded that he would resist any effort at ouster until his case was heard before a Congressional committee.

Various data concerning the dispute were brought into the open at the Presidential hearing and the two groups made it plainer than ever that they are separated by a chasm of professional and personal feeling which will require little short of a political miracle if it is to be patched up.

Opening the meeting with a statement of the necessity, in the public interest, of disclosing the facts upon which Chairman Morgan had based his charges against the other directors, the President turned to Dr. Morgan for a reply, but received, instead, a refusal to answer.

The President read the accusations made in recent statements by Chairman Morgan and at the end of each asked for specifications. As often as Mr. Roosevelt demanded "facts," Dr. Morgan stood on his previous statement, in which he had said in effect that he would have nothing to do with the President's personal inquiry.

The questioning revealed that Dr.

Continued on Page Nine

Flower Peddler Freed By Defiant Magistrate

In defiance of a letter from Chief Magistrate Jacob Gould Schurman urging city magistrates to impose heavier fines on flower vendors, Magistrate Sabbatino suspended sentence yesterday on a peddler in Coney Island Court, declaring that "nobody can tell me what to do except my Creator, through my conscience."

After releasing Thomas Hyden, 23-year-old peddler, of 357 Eighty-seventh Street, Brooklyn, Judge Sabbatino made public the letter from his chief. Terming the instructions "insulting," he said:

"In the letter I received, I was told that I should sentence floral peddlers to pay fines of $5 or to serve two-day jail terms, and should be even stricter with second offenders. The people of this city should heed the many robberies that are committed instead of worrying about floral peddlers."

WHITNEY ARRESTED ON SECOND CHARGE

Accused by the State of Using $109,384 Yacht Club Fund to Get a Loan

BAIL PLACED AT $25,000

Prompt Indictment Will Be Sought—Bennett-Dewey Feud Is Revealed

For the second time in two days Richard Whitney, senior partner of the brokerage film which bears his name and former president of the New York Stock Exchange, was arrested, fingerprinted, photographed, haled into court and held in bail yesterday on a charge of grand larceny in the first degree.

This time he was accused of the theft of bonds with a face value of $153,209 and present market value of $109,384 belonging to the New York Yacht Club, of which he had custody as treasurer of the club, and their use as collateral for a personal loan of $450,000 from the Public National Bank and Trust Company of New York without the permission or knowledge of the club. He was released in $25,000 bail on this charge after arraignment in the Felony Court before City Magistrate Thomas A. Aurelio, who held him for the grand jury.

The penalty fixed by law for conviction on the charge of grand larceny in the first degree is from five to ten years in State's prison for each offense.

Total Bail $35,000

Mr. Whitney now has his liberty on $35,000 bail, as he was freed in $10,000 on Thursday by Judge William Allen in the Court of General Sessions on the charge of stealing $105,000 in securities from the estate of his father-in-law, George R. Sheldon, of which he was an executor and trustee, and of which his wife, his sister-in-law, the widow of Judge Daniel F. Murphy of the Court of Special Sessions; Harvard University and St. Paul's School at Concord, N. H., were the beneficiaries.

Ambrose V. McCall, Assistant State Attorney General, who has been conducting daily hearings on behalf of Attorney General John J. Bennett Jr. since the Whitney firm was suspended by the Stock Exchange on Tuesday, informed Magistrate Aurelio that his investigation had already shown shortages of nearly $1,000,000 in the Whitney accounts. He said that in view of this and other circumstances Attorney General Bennett regarded the $10,000 bail asked by District Attorney Thomas E. Dewey of New York County in the Sheldon estate case as entirely insufficient.

Feud Is Revealed

Mr. McCall's statements brought into the open a feud that has been developing behind the scenes since District Attorney Dewey called a witness from the Attorney General's inquiry before the grand jury and obtained the indictment in the Sheldon case by a surprise move.

Hurrying here from Albany yesterday morning, Attorney General Bennett made no secret of his resentment at Mr. Dewey's action. He said that a district attorney had never before stepped into a case while it was under investigation by the Attorney General, and that he saw no necessity of Mr. Dewey acting as he had done. In the ordinary course of events, Mr. Bennett explained, his office would have presented the Sheldon case to the grand jury and prosecuted it just as it intends to do with the yacht club case, under Article 23-A of the General Business Law. He said his office has concurrent jurisdiction with the county prosecutor.

In view of the indictment obtained by Mr. Dewey, the Attorney General said he did not intend to accept Mr. Whitney's offer to testify at the State investigation. If it had not been for Thursday's indictment, he added, the broker would have

Continued on Page Eighteen

TAX BILL IS PASSED BY HOUSE, 294 TO 97; SENATE TO SPEED IT

Three Hours of Continuous Voting on Amendments Precede House Action

'THIRD BASKET' IS OUT

Liquor, Pork Import Levies Replace It—Profits, Gains Imposts Are Retained

By CHARLES W. HURD
Special to THE NEW YORK TIMES.

WASHINGTON, March 11.—The House passed the new Tax Bill today after three hours of continuous voting, in which a roll-call confirmed its former informal action eliminating a special levy of 20 per cent on the income of large closely held corporations. Adopted in place of the "third basket" surtax were new taxes on liquor and imported pork products. Final passage was voted 294 to 97.

The bill, which is expected to yield between $5,000,000,000 and $5,300,000,000 annually was ordered sent to the Senate immediately. There the Finance Committee will begin studies of it on Monday in expectation of a quick report.

Final House action on the bill occurred in the presence of almost all members on the floor, that being in itself a rare occurrence.

These members, permitted by the leadership only to vote and not to debate, carried on loud conversation among themselves, laughed and occasionally applauded as some member shouted "Aye" or "Nay" in response to his name through the dreary succession of roll-calls, one teller count and one standing division.

New Corporation Clause Voted

The most important change in the bill, as compared with current tax laws, consists of readjusted rates and schedules for corporation taxes, reported in detail previously, which are expected to make their burden more equitable.

However, the House refused again today, by an overwhelming vote on a roll-call, to reconsider its action continuing in effect the much criticized undistributed profits tax and the capital gains tax.

The results of the roll-calls, in the order in which they were taken, follow:

The House adopted, 233 to 153, the McCormack Amendment which eliminated the "third basket" contained in Section 1B.

It adopted, 201 to 182, an amendment by Representative Thompson of Illinois placing a new excise of six cents a pound on imported pork and three cents a pound on imported pork.

It approved, 290 to 96, an additional tax of 25 cents a gallon on spirits, proposed by Representative Robertson, to be added to the $2 rate now in effect.

It defeated, 292 to 94, a motion by Representative Treadway of Massachusetts, to recommit the bill to the Ways and Means Committee with instructions to eliminate the undistributed profits tax and to modify the corporate gains.

The final roll-call was on adoption of the bill.

A teller vote resulted in approval, by 135 to 96, of an amendment by Representative Boileau to include Engleman spruce among woods ex-

Continued on Page Nine

Netherlands Likens Crisis To Invasion of Belgium

Wireless to THE NEW YORK TIMES.

THE HAGUE, The Netherlands, March 11.—The news of the dramatic events in Austria has seriously impressed The Netherlands, where it is considered the most alarming intelligence for smaller European countries since August, 1914, when German troops invaded Belgium.

Although German relations with The Netherlands are quite different from those with Austria, it is felt that some pretext or other might serve the Reich some day to intervene in The Netherlands' internal affairs as well.

The attitude of the British Government in the face of the new situation is impatiently awaited. In any case the lesson of Austria will not be lost on The Netherlands.

ROME CHECKS PARIS ON AID FOR VIENNA

Refuses to Cooperate With France and Britain for the Support of Austria

FAILURE FOR BLUM IS SEEN

Premier Designate Is Unable to Form Union Government From All the Parties

By P. J. PHILIP
Wireless to THE NEW YORK TIMES.

PARIS, March 11.—It was learned here tonight that yesterday the French and British Governments jointly sounded out Italy as to whether cooperation could be expected in maintaining Austrian independence and that they received a firm negative reply.

However, Nazi Germany's annexation of Austria this evening has profoundly affected the French political situation and, in the opinion of every political party, made the immediate constitution of a government essential. That being so, Premier-designate Léon Blum tonight, after a day of continuous negotiation and argument with one party and another, informed the press that toward noon tomorrow he will announce his decision and intentions.

It is believed that he hopes to be able to announce the formation of a national government including most, if not all, of the parties. Before then, however, he will meet the National Council of the Socialist party, which last January ran counter to his wishes and by a small majority opposed every Socialist Minister in the Chautemps Cabinet.

What course events will take depends on M. Blum's ability to persuade his own party that the time has come for them to take the lead in the formation of a government which will represent France and not

Continued on Page Two

ITALY GETS SHOCK

Visit of Hitler Probably Will Be Canceled as Result of the Coup

ROME-BERLIN AXIS SHAKEN

Parleys With Britain Likely to Be Speeded and Accord Is Now Thought Probable

By ARNALDO CORTESI
Wireless to THE NEW YORK TIMES.

ROME, March 11.—The news from Austria struck Italy with the impact of an exploding bomb and left the official world here aghast. An official spokesman told an unusually large audience of newspaper men this evening that the Italian Government considered the situation so grave that it did not feel it could make any statement at present.

The general impression is, however, that whatever Italy may decide to do she will not make any attempt to intervene in Austria militarily and will not concentrate divisions at the Brenner Pass as in July, 1934, after the assassination of Chancellor Engelbert Dollfuss. Certainly no troop movements have been reported.

The greatest uncertainty and confusion reigned in Italian quarters, where the day's developments apparently were entirely unexpected. But it seems clear that Chancellor Hitler's action in forcing Chancellor Kurt Schuschnigg to resign has shaken the Rome-Berlin axis to its very foundations. Whether the axis will be able to survive depends on the turn of events in the next few days and the explanations Berlin furnishes in reply to Rome's inquiries. Worth recording in any case are the widespread rumors that Hitler's visit to Italy in May will be canceled. Such a cancellation would be an unmistakable symptom that the axis was doomed.

No Hint to Rome

The very surprise and shock caused by Dr. Schuschnigg's resignation prove that Hitler acted without giving the Rome end of the axis the slightest inkling of his intentions. As late as last night Italian circles close to the government were still saying that the Austrian plebiscite would lead to a clarification, which Rome heartily favored. Now the latest developments have brought the Italo-German situation to a climax.

It is declared here that Hitler could not have chosen a better moment for a coup in Austria. The Anglo-Italian negotiations are not yet properly under way and therefore Italy cannot definitely count on British support in any action she might meditate in Central Europe. France is in the throes of a Cabinet crisis, while Russia also is going through a far from happy period internally.

The events in Austria are also likely to have deep repercussions on the Anglo-Italian negotiations. Italy obviously will now enter them in a much weaker position, since her principal strength in relation to Britain hitherto was that in the field of foreign politics she and Germany acted as a unit. The wabbling of the axis cannot but increase for Italy the necessity of reaching an understanding with Britain and thus deprive her of a considerable part of her bargaining points.

Agreement Facilitated

On the other hand, the events in Austria cannot but make both Italy and Britain more determined to reach an agreement as soon as possible.

Even if the Rome-Berlin axis survives this blow, it is doubtful whether it will ever again regain the strength it had hitherto. Public opinion is convinced Germany has betrayed Italy: therefore it is difficult to imagine that the atmosphere of perfect cordiality and mutual confidence existing hitherto can ever be restored. Perhaps an open break will be avoided so as to gloss over the fact that a pillar that has upheld the whole of Italian foreign policy in the last two years has fallen to the ground, but it seems that the process of a breaking up of the axis has begun.

No course appears open to Italy but to save what she can of her position in Central Europe by diplomacy. Germany today is very different in a military sense from the Germany of 1934, so the use of force can in all probability be ruled out.

Perhaps Germany still counts

Continued on Page Two

The Austrian Situation

Following an ultimatum from Berlin, the Schuschnigg government in Austria retired yesterday evening and was succeeded by one headed by the Nazi leader, Arthur Seyss-Inquart, as Chancellor. He immediately asked Germany to send troops to help in preserving order. Some 50,000 highly armed and mechanized forces marched to the border. Both Munich and Vienna report some crossed into Austria. Berlin denies this. Nazi mobs took possession of Vienna and raided the Jewish quarter. The swastika was flown over public buildings, and Fatherland Front forces were disarmed. There were similar demonstrations in other cities.

Europe was aghast at the coup of Hitler. His action struck Italy with the force of an exploding bomb. The impression was that Italy would not retort with force, but it was believed the Rome-Berlin axis had been shaken and that Hitler's visit to Rome might be canceled. No advance notice of Germany's intention is believed to have been given to Mussolini.

Britain delivered a sharp protest to Berlin, saying Germany's action was bound to produce "the gravest reactions, of which it is impossible to foretell the issue." Other warnings were delivered earlier, but Foreign Minister von Ribbentrop retorted that Germany saw no reasons to confer with Britain until her purposes had been achieved elsewhere.

In Paris it was understood Italy had been asked if she would join in a united effort to save Austria, but had refused. France, however, took action similar to that of Britain in protesting the Reich's action. The parties tried to get together to form a new Cabinet to deal with the situation, but they were still too deeply divided to make that accomplishment possible. It was believed Léon Blum would not be able to gain sufficient support to head a government. [All the above dispatches on Page 1.]

Premier Negrin of Spain announced that Italy and Germany had made unofficial proposals for some agreement with the Loyalists, but they were determined not to enter on negotiations. [Page 2.]

BRITISH APPALLED BY REICH METHODS

Government Sends to Berlin a Sharp Rebuke Assailing the Tactics Employed

LONDON NOT TO INTERVENE

German Troops Start Across Border While Ribbentrop Is Guest of Chamberlain

By FERDINAND KUHN Jr.
Special Cable to THE NEW YORK TIMES.

LONDON, March 11.—At the very moment when German troops were crossing the Austrian frontier the British Government tonight delivered to Berlin one of the sharpest protests it has yet made in its post-war relations with Germany.

[France also protested to Germany along the same lines as the British rebuke, it was reported in Paris.]

The strength of the protest showed how strongly the British Government felt over the day's events and particularly over the methods by which Germany had finally attained her ends in Austria.

Referring especially to the second German ultimatum that had preceded the actual invasion, the British described it as the "coercion, backed by force, of an independent State in order to create a situation incompatible with its national independence."

Such action, it was pointed out, was bound to produce the "gravest reactions of which it is impossible to foretell the issue."

The protest was delivered at the Wilhelmstrasse by Sir Nevile Henderson, the British Ambassador.

British Warning Disregarded

In invading Austria tonight Germany flatly disregarded the warnings of the British Government earlier in the day that threat or use of force would damage the prospects of the Anglo-German talks and threaten future chances for reconciliation in Europe.

The warning was delivered personally to Joachim von Ribbentrop, German Foreign Minister, by Prime Minister Neville Chamberlain and Foreign Minister Viscount Halifax after luncheon at 10 Downing Street.

But the British Minister's words produced no effect upon Herr von Ribbentrop or upon his master in Berlin. Herr von Ribbentrop is said to have told Mr. Chamberlain, indeed, that the Fuehrer saw no reason for starting negotiations for reconciliation with Britain until German purposes "elsewhere" had been achieved.

While these words were being spoken the German Army was rolling along the express highways leading to the Austrian border and Berlin was preparing the ultimatums that forced the Austrian Government from power.

Britain will, of course, do nothing in the way of intervention. At this late stage in the absorption of Austria there is little left for Britain

Continued on Page Two

REICH ARMY MOVES; 50,000 AT FRONTIER

Force of Infantry, Artillery and Engineers Said to Have Entered Austria With Planes

BUT BERLIN MAKES DENIAL

Bavarian Roads Choked, Cars Taken Over—Border Towns Fired by Excitement

Wireless to THE NEW YORK TIMES.

MUNICH, Germany, Saturday, March 12.—With a dramatic suddenness that stunned the world the German Army embarked yesterday on its first campaign beyond the Reich's borders and without firing a shot achieved a victory that laid Austria prostrate at its feet, transformed the European equilibrium and set the borders fixed by the peace treaties into motion for a readjustment, of which the end is not yet in sight.

All day yesterday German forces, some 50,000 strong, made up of infantry, cavalry, artillery, motorized divisions, air force units and engineers with bridge building materials were moving to the Austrian frontier. Their mission was to avenge what is termed in Germany "the betrayal of Berchtesgaden"—Chancellor Kurt Schuschnigg's recent proclamation of a plebiscite on Austrian independence.

Last night, following Dr. Schuschnigg's overthrow and a telegram from the new Chancellor, Dr. Arthur Seyss-Inquart, to Chancellor Hitler requesting German military aid in preventing bloodshed, German troops were reported to have marched into Austria in close formation at three points—Salzburg, Kufstein and Mittenwalde.

[According to an Associated Press dispatch from Vienna, German troops crossed also at Passau, on the way to Linz, Austria, and a contingent of Reich troops, numbering about 1,000 men in trucks, was expected to reach Vienna at 6 A. M., New York time.]

Orders No Resistance

Information given out at the Munich army headquarters said the troops had begun to cross the border shortly after 10 o'clock, although their coming had been heralded by Dr. Seyss-Inquart in semihourly broadcasts beginning soon after 7 o'clock. The broadcasts included instructions to the Austrian military and civil authorities and the population not to resist the troops.

Whether the statements of the Munich army headquarters are correct or whether insistent denials in Berlin of a German march into Austria are the real truth does not much matter, for, even if the troops did halt at the border without crossing it, theirs is still the victory. It was their march that turned the tide in Austria and, after a bloodless Sadowa, enabled the Austrian

Continued on Page Three

SCHUSCHNIGG GOES

Resigns After Threat of Invasion as Powers Fail to Back Him

PLEBISCITE IS CALLED OFF

Goering and Hess Expected in Vienna Today—Nazis Rule Streets, Rout Foes

Censorship Imposed

By The Associated Press.

VIENNA, March 11.—Censorship has started.

An order posted in the correspondents' room in the Central Telegraph Office tonight said all telephone conversations from the room must be in German.

Correspondents for the International News Service, an American organization, were detained against their will, without charges, at the office.

By G. E. R. GEDYE
Wireless to THE NEW YORK TIMES.

VIENNA, Saturday, March 12.—Under threats of force from Berlin, Chancellor Kurt Schuschnigg of Austria yielded last evening and resigned in dramatic circumstances. The Nazis, with Dr. Arthur Seyss-Inquart, Interior Minister in the Schuschnigg Cabinet, as Chancellor, are in power.

To an unprepared public listening over the radio to a typical program of pleasant Viennese melodies the voice of the man who may have been the last Chancellor of an independent Austria announced at 7:45 P. M. that, in his own words, he had "yielded only to force" to avoid bloodshed and that under the threat of a German invasion that was to start at the very moment he spoke, he had resigned his office.

Plebiscite Is Postponed

Apart from the statement in a broadcast at 6 o'clock that "the Chancellor and Fatherland Front Leader, in consultation with President Miklas, has decided to postpone the plebiscite," there was no warning for the public when the program was interrupted for the announcer to say, "An important declaration is just coming." Then, without even mention of Dr. Schuschnigg's name, his voice was heard at the microphone.

When Dr. Schuschnigg had finished, thousands of Nazis began swarming into Vienna's streets to take over control unopposed. An hour afterward Dr. Seyss-Inquart also addressed the nation over the radio, calling on every one to maintain order and declaring that there was no question of resistance if the German Army should march in.

Dr. Seyss-Inquart's first official act as Chancellor appears to have been a message to Chancellor Hitler requesting the speedy dispatch of German troops to his support. The message read:

"Following the retirement of the Schuschnigg government, the Provisional Government of Austria regards the restoration and maintenance of law and order in Austria as its first duty.

"To this end it urgently requests the German Government to support it in this undertaking and assist it in the prevention of bloodshed. I therefore appeal to the German Government for the earliest possible dispatch of troops."

Up to noon Dr. Schuschnigg had remained firm in the face of all threats. Then came the first ultimatum from Germany, conveyed by Dr. Edmund Glaise-Horstenau, Minister Without Portfolio in the Schuschnigg Cabinet, on his return from Berlin. Austria was to postpone the plebiscite or she would be invaded.

Final Ultimatum Delivered

At 4 P. M. an airplane landed in Vienna. It brought Dr. Schuschnigg a final and, this time, an official ultimatum. The man who delivered it was believed to have been Josef Buerckl, Nazi leader in the Saar.

At first it was rumored that Field Marshal Hermann Goering and Rudolf Hess, deputy leader of the German Nazi party, had arrived with the ultimatum and were going to speak to the crowds in the Karlsplatz at 10 P. M., but this proved untrue. It was stated later, however, that Marshal Goering and Herr Hess would arrive today.

In any event, this ultimatum was quite different from that Dr. Glaise-Horstenau had delivered. It was an

Continued on Page Three

Mechanic on New Army Planes Held as Spy; Trapped by Counter-Espionage in Plant

Following several days of intensified counter-espionage activities around Long Island air fields, Federal authorities yesterday arraigned Otto Hermann Voss, a naturalized German mechanic employed in the Seversky aircraft plant, for espionage. Waiving examination, Voss was held in $10,000 bail.

The government invoked the same severe World War statute under which two renegade soldiers and a German woman were held as German spies on Feb. 26. Voss was charged with delivering and inducing others to deliver "to agents of a foreign power certain documents, writings, code books, signal books, photographs, instruments and information relating to the defense of the United States." The maximum punishment for conviction is imprisonment for twenty years.

The Seversky Aircraft Corporation at Farmingdale, L. I., is now building pursuit planes for the army that have broken several world records at speeds over 300 miles an hour and are recognized as one of the best types of fighting ships.

The background of the case was not revealed beyond what appeared in the complaint and the few words spoken by Lester C. Dunigan, assistant United States attorney, at the arraignment before United States Commissioner Isaac Platt. Mr. Dunigan said that after a conference with John F. Dailey, Acting United States Attorney, it had been decided that any statement at this time "would be out of order."

It was reported, however, that four men who were poor mechanics worked near Voss for three weeks until two Department of Justice agents arrested him Wednesday. Then they disappeared. Voss worked in the "day-dreaming" or experimental, section of the plant's assembly division, where Major de Seversky tests new ideas and materials.

Voss, it was learned, visited Germany for about a month last Summer. His wife at their home at 225 Jericho Turnpike, Floral Park, was on the verge of collapse after two long sessions of questioning by Federal agents. They were at her home on Wednesday and Thursday. Mrs. Voss asserted her husband was innocent and believed he came under suspicion when his name was found in a paper on the person of a friend arrested as a spy suspect recently.

The defendant, 39 years old, was silent at his arraignment. He is 6 feet tall with old scars on both cheeks. Mr. Dunigan said Voss worked at the plant at intervals for several years. His alleged illegal activities were dated from Jan. 2, 1936.

Schuschnigg Held Out Until He Found He Could Not Get Outside Support

NAZI CROWDS ROUT ENEMIES IN VIENNA

Ex-Chancellor's Guards Doff Uniforms and Flee to Safety in Civilian Garb

SHOPS OF JEWS ATTACKED

Anti-Hitler Residents Hide in Their Homes—Tourists Rush for Frontiers

Wireless to THE NEW YORK TIMES.

VIENNA, Saturday, March 12.—Thousands of swastika banners are being carried by crowds of Nazis in the main streets of Vienna early today after a night of widespread demonstrations, which became violent shortly before midnight with the breaking of windows in Jews' shops.

Within a quarter of an hour of former Chancellor Kurt Schuschnigg's farewell broadcast last night the Nazis' revolution was in full swing.

Going out into the street from the building in which he had heard Dr. Schuschnigg speak, the writer encountered thousands of Nazis streaming into the city past the dazed and helpless police, some of whom knew and some of whom did not know there was no longer a government in Austria.

The mob swarmed first into Kaernsterstrasse, singing the German national anthems outside the German Tourist Office with its gigantic portrait of Chancellor Adolf Hitler. Nazis waving small swastika flags swarmed up any suitable eminence—chairs or the coping of statues—and began impromptu speeches.

The Nazis marched to Fatherland Front headquarters, which was quickly darkened, and to the headquarters of former Chancellor Schuschnigg's special elite unit, the Storm Troops, in Hasburgergasse.

Troopers Remove Uniforms

Police cars dashed through the streets, collecting Storm Troopers, Fatherland Front officials and other identifiable supporters of an independent Austria. The Storm Troopers were disarmed and instructed to give up their uniforms. In civilian garb, carrying their uniforms in bundles, they hastened through the streets to safety. Others were detained by the police, whether for their own protection or for arrest was not revealed.

The Nazis seized the Chancellery, Rathaus, general postoffice and most Ministries and hoisted swastika banners that had been long held in readiness. They tore badges in the Austrian colors from all officials who still had the courage to wear them.

Within five minutes after Dr. Schuschnigg's farewell speech foreign envoys were stormed with applications from tourists who sought to flee immediately. Streams of automobiles set out for the frontier, bearing foreigners and many Austrians.

At the sight of mobs of shouting Nazis carrying German banners, at the sound of German songs, other Viennese hastened to their homes last night and locked their doors. Dr. Schuschnigg's downfall arrived too suddenly for the workers to carry out their plan to be on the streets last night to end the Nazi demonstrations of the past three days.

In the vicinity of THE NEW YORK TIMES office, where the main procession with torches and swastikas passed and repassed, the Nazis celebrated their triumph in discipline without violence, though with frenzied enthusiasm.

The streets re-echoed shouts of "Sieg Heil!" [Hail Victory!], followed by the chorus "And now we are victorious!" and cries of "Heil Hitler!", "Thanks to Hitler!", "Thanks to our leader!" and "Away with Schuschnigg!"

At 10 P. M. an enormous torchlight parade along the Ring closed that street to traffic and cut off the Inner City from the outer districts. It was impossible for any traffic to enter or leave the Inner City.

Crowds of young people, mostly under twenty years, shouting "Heil Hitler!" and "One people, one Reich!" marched with swastika flags. Eventually bands joined the procession.

Groups ran about the streets tearing down Austrian badges and all slogans posted during the last few days by patriotic Austrians. Other Nazis opened the gates of the Hofburg, which had been closed earlier in the day, and marched through the grounds of the palace of the Habsburgs, their enemies, singing the "Horst Wessel Song."

Illuminated emblems over the door of the Patriotic Front headquarters were smashed and photographs destroyed. At Storm Troop headquarters flags were torn down and were trampled with a picture of Dr. Schuschnigg.

At the German Tourist Agency's office there were very different scenes. A long stream of men and women passed in with grave faces, paying homage to Hitler's picture.

By 11 P. M. the appearance of large numbers of Nazi Storm Troops, Hitler Youth and Hitler Girl detachments, uniformed and marching well together, gave an air of order to the scene. National Socialist party discipline seemed to have made itself felt.

The picture in Vienna was very much like that in Berlin in Jan. 30, 1933, the day the Nazis took power and it was reflected in the great provincial cities. By midnight all Austria had begun to settle down as a Nazi State.

Building Is Set on Fire

VIENNA, Saturday, March 12 (AP).—Firemen saved the Fatherland Front building last night when dozens of Nazis hurled torches inside. Quiet was restored to the area at 11 P. M., but disorders broke out again a half hour later.

A barracks of the Storm Troops, the anti-Nazi army, was stormed by the jubilant demonstrators. Eight Storm Troopers were injured. There was panic among Vienna's Jews, who kept to their homes. Seven torchlight processions went to the district inhabited by Jews. Other paraders surrounded newspapers friendly to Jews.

SCENES IN THE MAIN STREETS OF VIENNA YESTERDAY

Times Wide World Radiophoto

Police patrolling one of the main thoroughfares to prevent clashes between the Nazis and supporters of the government.

Associated Press Radiophoto

Followers of Dr. Kurt Schuschnigg distributing pamphlets in the streets of Vienna a few hours before the Chancellor resigned in accordance with the demands of the Nazi Government.

REICH ARMY MOVES; 50,000 AT FRONTIER

Continued From Page One

Mittenwalde in particular is the starting point toward Scharnitz and the Fern-Alpine passes leading to Innsbruck and beyond that city to the Brenner Pass, where, in 1934, Premier Mussolini lined up his Nazis to proclaim a pan-German Reich.

All the points where the troops were said to have crossed are on the southern border of Bavaria; troops to prevent the entry of German forces into Austria.

The troops involved are in the main the Seventh Army Corps stationed at Munich under the command of General Ritter von Schobert. But it also was noted that General Walter von Reichenau, known as the army's most National Socialist general, who had been Munich commander until the Feb. 4 shift, broke off his trip to the meeting of the International Olympic Committee in Cairo, Egypt, and stopped at Munich.

Mobilization of the Seventh Army Corps apparently took place during Thursday night together with mobilization of Elite Guard divisions, Storm Troops and the National Socialist Motor Corps. When Munich awoke in the morning it saw troops and Nazi auxiliary formations on the march. And soon all the new motor roads leading to the Austrian frontier were blocked with the units, while the roar of planes overhead became incessant.

Vehicles Are Commandeered

To move the troops swiftly most public and private conveyances in Munich were commandeered—automobiles and trucks of members of the National Socialist Motor Corps, municipal buses, brewery trucks and the special auto-train "Deutschland," comprising a fleet of hundreds of trucks and including wireless, canteen and hospital trucks. Even taxicabs apparently were pressed into service, for only a few of them remain in the streets.

This correspondent motored all day along border highways amid many difficulties and frequent submissions to questioning and search. On the road to Salzburg he overtook within one hour no fewer than 230 military conveyances. The road on which usually only one or two cars are visible at a time was one long trail of armored cars, motorized artillery, supply wagons, canteens and trucks full of infantry, together with steel-helmeted soldiers riding motorcycles with rifles slung across their shoulders.

Approximately 130 trucks and armored cars and more than 100 motorcycles took an hour to pass.

Some trucks, including those commandeered from Munich breweries, were loaded with bridge-building materials, pontoons and motor boats, indicating they were moving toward the Inn and Salzach Rivers, over which leads the path to Upper Austria and, of course, Vienna.

Both lanes of the double-track Reich motor road were often completely blocked by moving troops. And this column was merely a fraction of the host that had been traveling this road since before dawn.

One column turned off at the Reich motor road exit leading to Rosenheim and there took a country road to Kiefersfelden, right on the Austrian border one and one-half miles from Kufstein. A large number of other columns before and after continued along the motor road through to the border near Salzburg.

As one proceeded along this picturesque countryside between tall, snow-capped mountains flanking the River Inn near the border, signs of excitement, spreading like wildfire over the whole district, became evident. Chattering groups of villagers stood before inns watching the long trail of armored cars and men moving past.

Kiefersfelden is a small village from which only a few minutes' walk brings a traveler into Austrian territory either by the broad white high road or by ferry over the Inn or again by a little longer woodland trail leading up a steep hill, the summit of which separates the two States.

The oldest Kiefersfelden inhabitant had never seen this village look anything like it did yesterday. Troops moved in by road from early morning. Shortly after noon a freight train steamed into the Kiefersfelden station containing some 2,000 infantrymen and cavalrymen. Toward sunset 2,000 or 3,000 more men with armored cars and artillery arrived there by road—some from Munich, some from Rosenheim, which must have brought the total number of troops in Kiefersfelden to some 6,000 or 7,000.

Soldiers were everywhere. Here a group of cavalry stood holding horses, armed sentrics were posted at farmhouse gates. Machine guns and anti-tank guns stood on the high road. Officers dashed to and fro in automobiles and dispatch riders tore along the road. Kiefersfelden looked like a village occupied by a hostile army.

Clear against the blue sky old Kufstein castle stood out on the hill about which the Austrian frontier of Kufstein clusters. The quaint medieval fortress that once defied attack by armed forces was today a pathetic reminder of the progress of modern warfare.

Kufstein villagers had no doubt of what this mighty demonstration of forces at Austria's very gateway signified.

"Austria is finished," was commonly heard.

It was said the troops would remain there until Monday in the expectation that before then the Austrian plebiscite would be called off. They did not have to wait that long.

At Freilassing opposite Salzburg, at Mittenwalde and at Fuessen similar or greater forces were concentrated and by sunset the whole Salzkammergut and Tyrol frontier was ranged by an estimated 50,000 trained soldiers with all equipment.

Despite the fact that everybody near the border was aware of what was afoot, officials all day made every effort to conceal the real situation. It was described by one of them as large-scale manoeuvres. Travelers were held up and searchingly questioned by the police and frontier officials and sometimes temporarily detained. Bodies of newly called up recruits from neighboring villages marched along the highroads last evening toward the border.

As a result of these developments Munich was in an uproar all day. Although the press kept completely silent on all Austrian developments, especially on the mobilization, the news spread quickly and people gathered in the streets to discuss the situation. Women anxiously compared notes, attempting to ascertain the whereabouts of their men folk called suddenly for field duty. Rumors flew thick and fast. Later in the day all newspapers suspended publication because of the general economic paralysis caused by the shortage of men.

At midday children both in Munich and in the countryside were told that schools would be closed until further notice because they had been requisitioned for reservists. Some reservists had orders to report Saturday or Sunday.

A pathetic attempt at Austrian resistance became known here during the day. At Scharnitz Pass, where an electric railway crosses the frontier, Austrians affixed a wire to the overhead power conductor, then spanned it across the road on which it could be dropped by the turn of a lever, barring the road with a current of 2,000 volts. But it did not save Austria.

Starhemberg Followers Asked Him to Give Fight

By The Associated Press.

VIENNA, March 11.—Before Chancellor Schuschnigg stepped out, old Heimwehr men appealed to Fascist Prince Ernest Dudiger von Starhemberg, former Vice Chancellor, to return from his Swiss honeymoon and reorganize his now disbanded private army.

The Prince, who organized his army to fight Nazis and Socialists in Austria, married last December the Viennese actress Nora Gregor. Some political observers predicted he was out of politics for good.

About 10,000 unemployed laborers were being outfitted last night with Heimwehr uniforms and weapons.

Troops on Way to Vienna

VIENNA, Saturday, March 12 (AP).—German troops moved toward Vienna in the early morning hours today to back up Nazification of the Austrian State. The troops, numbering about 1,000 men in trucks, expected to reach the capital at noon [6 A. M. in New York]. They carried several pieces of light artillery, the gendarmerie commandant at Schoerding on the Bavarian border told The Associated Press by telephone.

They met no resistance and were heading first for Linz, where Nazis prepared an enthusiastic welcome. From there they were to proceed quickly to Vienna.

Berlin Denies Entry

Wireless to THE NEW YORK TIMES.

BERLIN, Saturday, March 12.—Reports that German troops had crossed into Austria were still denied in German official quarters at midnight. The denial was emphatic and unequivocal and was supplemented only by the statement that Chancellor Arthur Seyss-Inquart's appeal to Chancellor Hitler for German troops to maintain order and prevent bloodshed was being considered.

Official quarters definitely contradicted recurring reports from points along the Austrian border that German units had crossed from Freilassing, Mittenwalde and Passau, and reports from Munich that troops had entered Innsbruck to the populace's jubilant acclaim.

AUSTRIA IS SEIZED IN COUP BY HITLER

Continued From Page One

official statement from the German Government that unless Dr. Schuschnigg resigned by 7:30 P. M., 300,000 Germans would cross the frontier, headed by two motorized divisions.

Even so, up to the last moment Dr. Schuschnigg held out, pondering whether he should not at least offer formal resistance. The hesitation in Dr. Schuschnigg's farewell speech when he said first that the Austrian troops had been ordered to offer "no serious resistance" and then changed it to "no resistance" indicates pretty clearly that up to the last he had intended that some formal resistance should be offered in order to bring home to Germany her full guilt.

But the Austrian Chancellor was unable to obtain assurances of support from any of the countries that have always professed sympathy for "gallant little Austria." No one seemingly was prepared to back up fine words with brave deeds.

Immediately after Dr. Seyss-Inquart's speech it became known that one of the second ultimatum's conditions had informed Dr. Schuschnigg that whether he resigned or not the Austrian Legion would march in from Germany and assume part of the police duties.

New Cabinet Announced

At 1 o'clock this morning, while the Nazi celebration was still going full force, a Nazi speaker appeared on the great balcony of the historic Chancellery Building and announced to the 10,000 gathered below with their flags and torches that President Miklas had appointed a new Cabinet, as follows:

Dr. Arthur Seyss-Inquart—Chancellor and National Defense.
Dr. Edmund Glaise-Horstenau—Vice Chancellor.
Dr. Wilhelm Wolf—Foreign.
Franz Hueber—Justice.
Professor Oswald Menchin, former dean of Vienna University—Education.
Dr. Hugo Jury—Social Welfare.
Rudolf Neumayer—Finance.
Anton Reinthaler—Agriculture.
Dr. Hans Fischboeck—Commerce.

Michael Skubl, president of the Vienna police, remains Secretary of State for Security. Two Nazis are appointed Under-Secretaries of State—Ernst Kaltenbrunner, for Security, and Major Clausner, present leader of the Austrian Nazis, for Propaganda.

The Cabinet consists mostly of former Pan-Germans and pronounced Nationalists—who certainly may be called Nazis now—together with some Nazis of the new generation. It is regarded merely as a transition Cabinet. Its program was to have been given by Dr. Seyss-Inquart in a broadcast last night, but there have been no signs of it.

Mayor Richard Schmitz of Vienna, a strong Catholic, has been replaced by Vice Mayor Fritz Lahr, a former Heimwehr man. It is rumored, but not yet confirmed, that Herr Schmitz has been arrested by the Nazis because he allegedly furnished arms to labor unions.

Several leading politicians, such as Guido Zernatto, secretary general of the Fatherland Front, and former Minister of Commerce Fritz Stockinger, are reported to have fled to Czechoslovakia.

Prelude to Last Act

The prelude to the last act of the Austrian tragedy was full of tense moments. At 10 o'clock yesterday morning for the first time and thereafter at half-hour intervals throughout the morning it was broadcast that the unmarried men of the 1915 class of recruits, who had already served ten months, were to report immediately for duty.

The fact that this mobilization of reservists was declared to be intended to maintain order for Sunday's plebiscite concealed from nobody that little Austria was making her last preparation to face a Nazi Putsch or a German invasion—or both.

All the gates of the Hofburg were closed and strongly guarded. Truckloads of troops with rifles and steel helmets crossed Vienna in all directions. The militia was called out and was soon seen filling sleeping bags with straw in the courtyard of the City Hall.

In motor trucks steel-helmeted troops with rifles and machine guns were rushed to the various Ministries.

Alarming reports came in from the provinces. In Innsbruck at noon Nazis in full Storm Troop uniforms, accompanied by thousands of supporters, broke through the police cordon, but were held up outside the City Hall by barbed-wire entanglements and machine guns. Steel-helmeted police with fixed bayonets drove the Nazis into the side streets.

In Graz troops put up barbed wire and brought out machine guns. They cornered a violent Nazi demonstration in one of the principal squares and covered the demonstrators with rifles. The demonstrators refused to disperse, however, before the Graz Nazi leader, Professor Armin Dardieu, had spoken to them, admonishing them to go quietly.

There were reports, impossible to confirm, that Nazi Storm Troopers had occupied the hills close to Graz, armed with machine guns.

In Salzburg Thursday night Nazis attacked non-Nazi crowds cheering for Dr. Schuschnigg. Many persons were injured and taken to hospitals, but there were no dead.

German Frontier Closed

On the news that Germany had moved two motorized divisions to the frontier, the Austrians closed it Thursday night. An invasion was already expected, but at 7 o'clock yesterday morning the frontier was reopened. Then, however, came the news that the Germans had closed their side of the frontier, which made matters look extremely serious.

Dr. Schuschnigg still remained firm after the first ultimatum from Germany at noon and discussed calling out all the reserves to meet what he was convinced was a German bluff to prevent him from holding the plebiscite, which was expected to expose the Nazis' real numerical weakness.

Then came satisfactory news from the workers. The mobilization order had caused every one to realize the danger. Dropping their quarrel about trade union posts, the workers met in the factories at the lunch hour and decided to support Dr. Schuschnigg without reserve.

Patriotic resolutions poured in from every quarter—Catholics, monarchists, Socialists and even Communists declared their determination to stand for Austria's independence at the plebiscite.

At midday a deputation of Socialist trade union leaders appeared before Hofrat Weiser, head of the anti-Red secret police, who had examined many of them in the past as prisoners. They told him that, in the face of the Nazi peril and the apparent impossibility of the police's getting Dr. Seyss-Inquart's permission to keep order in Vienna, the workers were prepared themselves to go out last night and clear the Nazi demonstrators from the streets.

The police official thanked them, but of course refused. But he promised them that from 9 P. M. he would guarantee that there would be no Nazi demonstrations in Vienna's streets. In point of fact, at 9 P. M. there were no police on the streets, only Nazi demonstrators and Storm Troops.

At 4 P. M. came the second German ultimatum and Dr. Schuschnigg's hesitation, until he was unable to obtain the support of other powers.

At midday the writer had ascertained that the Czechoslovak view was that everything depended on Italy. Czechoslovakia could not come to the rescue of Austria single-handed. In France there was no government and in London no support.

Schuschnigg Left Helpless

If Italy had moved and the Austrians had put up a show of resistance Czechoslovakia herself would have marched, but the hours slipped by toward the expiration of the ultimatum and Dr. Schuschnigg was left alone to decide the terrible question whether the threat was a German bluff and defend his country's independence or take it seriously and resign in order to avoid bloodshed. He chose the second alternative.

Immediately after he had broadcast, President Miklas summoned a Council of State. As far as can be ascertained Dr. Miklas insisted that Dr. Schuschnigg withdraw his resignation in view of the news that had come of the joint démarche in Berlin by Great Britain, France and Italy.

Up to 11:30 P. M. Dr. Schuschnigg was apparently still nominally Chancellor. Then came another sudden change and it was announced over the radio that "Federal Chancellor Seyss-Inquart will shortly broadcast a statement."

There was yet a half hour's delay. Then, instead of Dr. Seyss-Inquart, his deputy in the Fatherland Front, Dr. Hugo Jury, came to the microphone.

It was immediately apparent that Dr. Seyss-Inquart after all was not yet Chancellor, for Dr. Jury said:

"The Federal Minister entrusted with the business of the Federal Chancellery, Dr. Seyss-Inquart, is with the Federal President discussing with him details of the department. After the end of the conversation the Federal Minister"—Dr. Jury carefully avoided the designation of Chancellor—"will broadcast statements as to the results of the conference.

"The whole population is obeying the demand to maintain public order in all circumstances. National Socialists, continue to maintain your exemplary discipline in this historic hour."

Then, for the first time, the Austrian radio broadcast Germany's second national anthem, the Horst Wessel song.

Old Austria Collapses

Special Cable to THE NEW YORK TIMES.

VIENNA, Saturday, March 12 (London Times Dispatch).—After a day of indescribable nervous tension the Austria of Dollfuss and Schuschnigg—the Catholic Fascist Austria that by force suppressed Parliament and the powerful working class movement four years ago—collapsed last night under the threat of force.

In the afternoon, when Chancellor Schuschnigg was presented with a German ultimatum to postpone the independence plebiscite Sunday that he had announced Wednesday, German troops already had been mobilized on the frontier. Dr. Schuschnigg agreed to the postponement on condition that the Nazis should in the future restrain from disturbing order in Austria.

Chancellor Hitler's reply to this was that Dr. Schuschnigg must resign the Chancellorship in favor of Dr. Seyss-Inquart, who had been appointed Interior Minister at the Fuehrer's behest after the Berchtesgaden agreement.

Other conditions made by Hitler were that two-thirds of the seats in the Cabinet should be handed over to the Nazis, that the National Socialist party in Austria must receive full and unrestricted liberty and that the Austrian Legionnaires—the force of some 30,000 Nazis who fled from this country at the time of the unsuccessful Nazi rising in July, 1934, and afterward were drilled and regimented in Germany—should return and keep order in Vienna.

Dr. Schuschnigg's capitulation followed, and by 10 P. M. the Austrian Government had entirely ceased to function. The Nazi flag was flying over the historic Chancellery on the Ballhausplatz, where Metternich spun his tangled webs and where the Congress of Vienna met. The Government press department, bereft of all officials, had been occupied by police wearing swastika armbands. All the police, who three hours before had still been obeying the orders of the last government, were now wearing swastika armbands or giving the Hitler salute.

In the afternoon machine guns had been trained on the bridges and approaches to the city, but at the news of Dr. Schuschnigg's resignation the soldiers and police were withdrawn. The swastika flag is flying from all public buildings.

Nobody even knows for certain whether the Germans are now moving along the great asphalt motor road from the frontier through Salzburg, the festival city, to Linz and Vienna, or whether the villagers on the way are turning out to watch them.

Dr. Seyss-Inquart left a small doubt about it. The words he used in his broadcast might have meant, "No resistance must be offered to the German Army now approaching," or "No resistance must be offered to the German Army if it approaches."

REICH ARMY REPORTED MARCHING INTO AUSTRIA

Munich headquarters announced troops had advanced through Salzburg, Kufstein and Mittenwald, but Berlin denied that any had crossed the border.

Schools Get a Holiday

VIENNA, Saturday, March 12 (AP).—The populace was asked to display the Nazi swastika flags country-wide today, and the schools were ordered closed.

A radio announcement said that Dr. Arthur Seyss-Inquart, the new Chancellor, had sent a message calling on Nazis to "preserve the excellent discipline that has been a fine example to the world in this historic hour."

The Vienna police chief disclosed that German secret police agents had taken control of telephone exchanges, equipped to listen to conversations.

For three hours during last night's conferences at the Chancellery no one left or entered it. Shortly after 10 P. M., Nazi Storm Troop formations replaced city police guarding the building. Among the Nazi guards were many who served prison terms for participation in the Nazi putsch that resulted in the assassination of Chancellor Engelbert Dollfuss in 1934.

A source close to Dr. Seyss-Inquart said that Dr. Kurt Schuschnigg, who resigned as Chancellor, was "being promised protection and we suppose he'll stay in Austria." Nazis said they would demand that Dr. Schuschnigg promise he would never participate again in politics.

The head of the Austrian official news agency resigned. He will be replaced by a representative of the official German news agency.

A run was started on Vienna savings banks before they closed yesterday. Depositors demanded any part of their accounts they could obtain.

JESUITS OPEN ASSEMBLY

General Convocation in Vatican City Is First in Fifteen Years

VATICAN CITY, March 11 (AP).—The Society of Jesus, the Catholic Church's famed, far-flung missionary organization, today opened its first general convocation in fifteen years.

The 171 Jesuit leaders gathered here will devote special attention to reverses suffered by the faith in Germany and in Spain, Jesuit spokesmen said.

The heads of the society usually meet only on the death of the Superior General to elect his successor. There was no indication, however, that the present Superior General, 71-year-old Father Vladimir Ledochowski, intended to resign.

NEW VIENNA RULER IS HITLER'S CHOICE

Seyss-Inquart Named to Head Security Services After Berchtesgaden Talk

FAVORS UNION WITH REICH

A Catholic With Legitimist Ties, He Is None the Less an Ardent Nazi Sympathizer

Dr. Arthur Seyss-Inquart is a Vienna lawyer of strongly nationalist sentiments who was appointed under the 1936 agreement as "conciliator" to bring about a rapprochement of the Fatherland Front followers in Austria with the Nazis.

He is a Catholic, and his brother, who is now a prison governor, was formerly a priest and at one time was former Empress Zita's confessor. Thus Dr. Seyss-Inquart has connections with both Nazi and Legitimist circles in addition to the church, which is dominant in the Fatherland Front groups.

Dr. Seyss-Inquart was named Minister of the Interior, with direction of the security services, on Feb. 16 by Chancellor Kurt Schuschnigg as a concession to Germany. Chancellor Adolf Hitler insisted at his meeting with Dr. Schuschnigg at Berchtesgaden on Feb. 12 that control of the police and security services, formerly in Dr. Schuschnigg's hands, be turned over to Seyss-Inquart, who up to two years ago was active as a Nazi, who sympathizes with the Nazis and who is an open supporter of the idea that Austria should surrender her independence to Germany through Anschluss.

Both President Wilhelm Miklas and Dr. Schuschnigg realized what handing over control of the police to a friend of the Nazis would mean. They tried to avoid it, vainly seeking Premier Benito Mussolini's aid and by offering Dr. Seyss-Inquart the Ministry of Justice. Hitler, however, insisted he was the one man in whom he had confidence. Within twenty-four hours of his appointment, Dr. Seyss-Inquart went to Berlin to confer with Nazi leaders about extending the influence of the Nazis in the Fatherland Front to domination of the coalition.

Dr. Seyss-Inquart, described in the German press as the man who "enjoys Hitler's especial confidence," conferred at length with Hitler in Berlin on Feb. 17. Two days later he denied he was "a Trojan horse" and that his instructions were to make the Fatherland Front a Nazi party. On Feb. 23 his Security Department issued a decree curbing Nazi propaganda somewhat, bringing acute disappointment to the Nazis.

Two days later, however, he also issued a decree curbing criticism of Germany in the press.

CABINET MEETS IN PRAGUE

Views Austrian Events Calmly—Refugees Enter Country

PRAGUE, Czechoslovakia, March 11 (AP).—The Czechoslovak Cabinet met in special session tonight to consider the general situation in connection with events in Austria.

President Eduard Benes presided. The Cabinet was represented as viewing the situation calmly.

The impression prevailed in some quarters that the nazification of Austria was not the private concern of that neighboring State, but a matter affecting all Western powers.

Reports from Bratislava, on the Austrian-Czechoslovakia border about forty miles from Vienna, said trains and automobiles arriving there were filled with refugees from Vienna.

NAZI FLAGS DISPLAYED

Are Draped on Couch on Which Dollfuss Died After Putsch

VIENNA, Saturday, March 12 (AP).—Toward midnight S. S. [Nazi guard troops] men spread a huge Nazi flag over the yellow sofa in the chancellery on which Chancellor Engelbert Dollfuss slowly bled to death in the attempted putsch of July 25, 1934.

Other Nazis draped swastika banners on the balcony from which Major Emil Fey, former head of the police, had appealed to the crowds during the Dollfuss crisis.

"All the News That's Fit to Print."

The New York Times.

LATE CITY EDITION
Fair with slowly rising temperature today. Tomorrow fair with temperature unchanged.
Temperatures Yesterday—Max., 55; Min., 40

Copyright, 1938, by The New York Times Company.

VOL. LXXXVIII...No. 29,510. Entered as Second-Class Matter, Postoffice, New York, N. Y. NEW YORK, THURSDAY, NOVEMBER 10, 1938. PP THREE CENTS NEW YORK CITY and Vicinity | FOUR CENTS Elsewhere Except in 7th and 8th Postal Zones.

COALITION IN CONGRESS TO HALT THE NEW DEAL URGED AS THE REPUBLICANS APPRAISE VICTORY; GAIN 80 IN HOUSE, 8 IN SENATE, 11 GOVERNORS

BRITAIN PROPOSES PALESTINE PARLEY; REJECTS PARTITION

Calls Arab-Jewish Conference as Woodhead Board Finds Division Plan Unworkable

MANDATE IS REAFFIRMED

Arabs in the Holy Land Are Angered by Statement—Jews Are Pleased

Summary of Palestine report and British statement, Page 4.

By FERDINAND KUHN Jr.
Special Cable to THE NEW YORK TIMES.

LONDON, Nov. 9.—A round-table conference of Arabs and Jews was proposed by the British Government today in its seemingly endless search for a settlement of the Palestine problem

Prime Minister Neville Chamberlain's harassed Cabinet fell back upon the idea of a conference after Sir John Woodhead's commission of inquiry had found last year's partition plan unworkable and had failed to agree upon an alternative.

So the same British Government that last year proclaimed partition to be "the best and most hopeful solution of the deadlock" has reversed itself again.

Accepting the verdict of the Woodhead commission, the government today announced the conclusion that "the political, administrative and financial difficulties involved in the proposal to create independent Arab and Jewish States inside Palestine are so great that this solution of the problem is impracticable."

More Delay Forecast

This was exactly the conclusion reached by the House of Commons in July of last year when it refused to endorse the partition scheme. Months of effort have been fruitless; more delay and perhaps more bloodshed and heartbreak in the Holy Land appear inevitable before a settlement is reached.

Apart from calling a conference, the government announced no decision today except to "continue its responsibility for the government as a whole of Palestine" and to "keep constantly in mind the international character of the mandate with which it has been entrusted and its obligations in this respect."

This was an additional assurance to the United Staets and the other countries that are concerned over the future administration of Palestine.

Decisions will not be taken until after the attempt has been made to bring the Arabs and the Jews together around the conference table in London. A Cabinet spokesman said today that it was so important to reach an understanding between the Arabs and the Jews that the government felt it worth while to postpone a decision "for another period."

Britain Has Own Proposals

But if the conference breaks down or if the Arabs and Jews refuse to meet, there is reason to believe the British Government will have proposals of its own for the future administration of Palestine.

No official or semi-official hint of these proposals has been given, but they are understood to involve the creation of Arab and Jewish zones or cantons under British control. Immigration into the Jewish zones would be relatively free and controlled by the Jewish Agency; immigration into the Arab areas would be curtailed if not cut off altogether.

The extent of the new areas has not been decided, however, and will provide still another bone of contention before the struggle is over. In any event, the British Government will not try to press a decision upon the Arab and Jewish leaders until after both sides have had their say at the conference table.

A round-table conference on Palestine has long been the favorite idea of Malcolm MacDonald, Secretary of State for the Colonies and Dominions, whose father, the late Ramsay MacDonald, was one of the firmest believers in the value of the conference table.

The device was used in South Africa after the Boer War, in Ireland after "the troubles," in Egypt after Nationalist disorders, and most spectacularly in the case of India after the civil disobedience movement, and in each instance it helped toward a settlement.

Neighboring States Invited

But the proposed conference on Palestine will be an innovation in more ways than one. For one thing, the British Government has taken the somewhat daring step of deciding to invite representatives of neighboring Arab States as well as the Palestinian Arabs.

This is the first official recogni-

Continued on Page Four

American Hymn of Peace Proposed by Salvadorean

Special Cable to THE NEW YORK TIMES.

SAN SALVADOR, El Salvador, Nov. 9.—A contest for words and music for an American hymn of peace will be suggested to the Pan-American Conference at Lima, Peru, in December by Joaquin Leiva, chief delegate from El Salvador.

To promote peace, he will suggest that the hymn be sung daily in American schools, that the schools have peace slogans on their walls and that teachers give peace talks.

He further proposes that American countries designate a day of peace to be observed officially and by schools and the people.

BERLIN RAIDS REPLY TO DEATH OF ENVOY

Nazis Loot Jews' Shops, Burn City's Biggest Synagogue to Avenge Paris Embassy Aide

Wireless to THE NEW YORK TIMES.

BERLIN, Thursday, Nov. 10.—Despite authoritative warnings against anti-Jewish excesses issued before news of the death of Ernst vom Rath, Third Secretary of the German Embassy in Paris, who died there yesterday afternoon as a result of shots fired at him by a young Polish Jew Monday, violent anti-Jewish demonstrations broke out all over Berlin early this morning.

Raiding squads of young men roamed unhindered through the principal shopping districts, breaking shop windows with metal weapons, looting or tossing merchandise into the streets or into passing vehicles and leaving the unprotected Jewish shops to the mercy of vandals who followed in their trail in an unprecedented show of violence.

While crowds were still touring the streets at 7 A. M. viewing the debris left behind in all the principal shopping districts, Berlin fire-fighting forces were striving to control the burning of the city's largest synagogue, in the Fasanenstrasse, in the fashionable West End.

The fire had been set by a group of vandals and the flames soon encompassed the wooden structure. Fire-fighting units from all over the city were intent on confining the flames to the synagogue.

While large crowds watched the destruction of the building, residents in the vicinity moved their automobiles from garages in the neighborhood to safer places.

Nazi Guards Watch Vandalism

The vandalism began in the downtown shopping district on the Leipzigerstrasse and Friedrichstrasse soon after 2 A. M. As if possessing a "premonition" that something might happen groups of uniformed Elite Guards were gathered at the corner of those two streets when the demonstrators arrived.

The raiding parties for the most part were composed of youths seemingly between 20 and 30, who arrived on the scene in large open automobiles of a model frequently used by leading party officials or their guards.

Many of the raiders in the downtown districts wore boots—which are worn by all party groups when in uniform—and they worked with a precision that was a tribute to "spontaneous demonstrations."

Alighting quickly from the cars, the vandals hacked away at windows, accompanied by the laughs and jokes of onlookers. The windows were destroyed, the goods were removed from the showcases and tossed into the streets or passing vehicles, and the vandals passed on to the next jewelry shop—easily recognizable because since the last anti-Jewish demonstrations in the early Summer all Jewish-owned shops must have the name of their proprietors whitewashed on the windows in large block letters.

On the corner of the Friedrichstrasse and the Leipzigerstrasse the large department store of Arnold Mueller was an easy target. A man, a non-Jew, was observed making some protest, but he was attacked by raiders who struck him with the metal weapons and he might have been seriously injured had not members of the police and other onlookers intervened.

In the fashionable West End shopping district similar events took place. Along the Tauenzienstrasse, most of whose shops are still in Jewish possession, the attacks began soon after 3 A. M.—when night club patrons were on their way home.

Jewelry Shop Looted

The writer observed three cases of looting after raiders had broken the windows of lingerie, fur and jewelry shops. The looters waited until the raiders had passed on to the next Jewish-designated shop and then quickly grabbed something from the show windows, after which they ambled unconcernedly away.

On the Nuernbergerstrasse a man took a handful of hats from a bro-

Continued on Page Ten

ROOSEVELT IS TOLD WAGES-HOURS LAW HIT 30,000 WORKERS

Andrews, in Report on Effect of the Act, Says Total Made Idle May Be 50,000

HE EXPECTS NET INCREASE

Aide Says the President Feels 'Very Cheerful' Over Election; 'Everything Is Grand'

Memorandum on wages and hours sent to President, Page 30.

By FELIX BELAIR Jr.
Special to THE NEW YORK TIMES.

HYDE PARK, N. Y., Nov. 9.—The number of industrial workers laid off since the effective date of the new Wages and Hours Law was estimated at 30,000 to 50,000 in a report made to President Roosevelt today by Elmer F. Andrews, administrator. Mr. Andrews pointed out that these were less than half of 1 per cent of the workers coming under the measure, and he gave it as his opinion that net employment had increased rather than declined "as a result of the act."

The report was made public at the temporary White House offices at a time when reporters were pressing Marvin H. McIntyre, Mr. Roosevelt's secretary, for some statement from him on the outcome of the elections that brought unexpected victories to Republican candidates.

"President Roosevelt says he is feeling very cheerful and that everything is grand," Mr. McIntyre said after communicating with the Chief Executive.

But beyond that Presidential aides would say only that it was not the custom of Mr. Roosevelt to comment on election results. So far as could be learned from those who usually speak for him, the President's reaction to the election results had not changed since last night when he authorized the statement that he was "very happy" over the trend of the balloting.

Report Dated Five Days Earlier

Bearing the date of Nov. 4, the Andrews report to the President was scheduled for publication several days ago, but it was not until reporters descended on the temporary White House offices seeking a Presidential statement on the election that the President was approached concerning publication.

Mr. Andrews told the President that many of the lay-offs reported "are not due primarily to the new act." Contributing factors were listed as seasonal changes in activity, substitution of efficient for inefficient workers, and curtailment of operations as an offset to abnormally increased activity before the act went into effect.

The significance of the lay-offs, Mr. Andrews stated, was "still further reduced by the fact that a large share of the total consist of marginal and handicapped workers, whose position in the economic system has long been insecure."

"Some of the inefficient workers laid off are already being replaced by more efficient workers able to earn the minimum hourly," he added, "this transfer process will operate to reduce further the net effect of the act on employment volume."

In thirty-two States from which reports had been received, no lay-offs were reported; in five there had been only one situation involving a furlough as a result of the legislation.

Lay-offs were reported concentrated in a very few industries in the South, "most of which are characterized by wretchedly low wage rates and other special conditions

Continued on Page Thirty

Two Senators Elected To 2 Months' Pay Only

By The Associated Press.

WASHINGTON, Nov. 9.—Two of the Senators elected yesterday are not likely to see Congress in session except as sightseers.

They are Miss Gladys Pyle of South Dakota and Alex G. Barry of Oregon. Both were elected as Republicans to fill terms that will expire when the new session of Congress convenes in January. Each replaces a Democrat.

J. Chandler Gurney of South Dakota and Rufus C. Holman of Oregon, both Republicans, will be sworn in for the six-year term at the opening of the new Congress.

The two short-termers will draw about two months' pay but if they come to Washington it will be at their own expense since mileage is allowed only to members traveling to and from a session of Congress.

LA GUARDIA TO CALL PROGRESSIVE RALLY

Will Invite Leaders in Nation to Solidify Their Forces After Election Setback

Outstanding Progressive leaders throughout the country will be invited to a conference with Mayor La Guardia in Washington next week at which an effort will be made to solidify Progressive forces in the face of the apparent setback they suffered in Tuesday's election.

Discussing the results of the election yesterday, the Mayor announced his intention of convening the Progressive leaders. He said he would invite Senator Robert M. La Follette of Wisconsin, George W. Norris of Nebraska and Governor Frank Murphy of Michigan, as well as a number of other leaders in the Progressive movement. He conceded that the election results were "a black eye for the New Deal," but said the damage might easily be repaired.

"One Must Be Realistic"

"As I analyze the results of the election," the Mayor said, "I believe one must be realistic about it and realize that the progressive forces in several of the States seemingly have been disintegrated.

"Eliminating New Jersey, where I do not think the question of progressivism enters at all, I am willing to admit that there has been a decided setback. That is because the political sashay has not been perfected.

"You have a situation of supporters of progressive, humane, economic welfare legislation being opposed by the old line parties; you have candidates in the Democratic party who are not sympathetic with progressive legislation, and you have progressive candidates in the Republican party who do not agree with the control and management of the party, and the result is an increased strength to the forces of reaction.

"That means but one thing—that the progressive forces in this country have got to get together. It also means that labor must adjust its differences, and it also means that there must be a well defined, clear, concise progressive program.

"As the matter now stands, it is a little too loose.

"The situation in New York State,

Continued on Page Fourteen

Dewey Returns to Desk, Silent on Politics, After 'First Good Night's Sleep Since June'

Declining to discuss the political future, Thomas E. Dewey returned to his desk in the District Attorney's office yesterday afternoon.

His secretary placed before him a sheaf of telegrams, several hundred of them, of which a typical one was. "Congratulations on your magnificent campaign. You rendered a great public service. The results are a personal tribute." He did not give the name of the sender.

Mr. Dewey was perturbed by a report in THE NEW YORK TIMES that he had made public his telegram to Governor Lehman, conceding defeat, prior to the time that it had been sent to the Governor. The telegram actually had been sent, he said, before he made known its contents to the newspaper men at his campaign headquarters.

Mr. Dewey arrived at his office at about 3 P. M. He said that he had slept eleven hours, the "first good night's sleep since last June," and had arisen at 1:30 P. M. He plans to go away, as soon as possible, for a rest of two weeks or so. He is going to Virginia.

Asked whether he would personally try the case of James J. Hines, Tammany district leader charged with participation in a policy-racket conspiracy, when it came up again, he said he would confer with his assistants before deciding.

The case has been prepared by Assistant District Attorneys Sol Gelb and Charles P. Grimes. Mr. Dewey pointed out that neither of the two men had had a vacation and both were tired. He said he planned to confer with General Sessions Judge Charles C. Nott Jr. on a date for the second trial, which will not begin until after the first of the year.

The District Attorney also plans to take part in the trial of Robert Irwin, now in progress in General Sessions Court. Assistant District Attorney Jacob Rosenblum is in charge of that case, in which Irwin is charged with murder and is making a plea of insanity as a defense.

STATE SENATE SHIFT

Republicans Gain Five Seats and a Working Majority of Two

PICK UP TWO IN ASSEMBLY

Lehman Confronted by Two Years' Opposition in Both Legislative Houses

Governor Lehman, who was re-elected Tuesday by a plurality of 67,506 with one district missing, will face a hostile Legislature in which the Republicans captured control of both houses.

With a single district in Lewis County to be heard from, the vote for the Governor was found yesterday to total 2,383,584, with 2,316,078 for District Attorney Thomas E. Dewey, the Republican nominee. United States Senator Robert F. Wagner led the Democratic candidates, his plurality over John Lord O'Brian, Republican, being 447,397, with 121 up-State election districts missing.

Despite the fact that the Governor and the rest of his ticket won, the Republicans, taking full advantage of large up-State majorities, increased by one seat their representation in the State Assembly and won five seats in the State Senate to wrest control of the upper house from the Democrats.

In the Senate, which previously was dominated by the Democrats by a 29-to-22 margin, the Republicans now have control by 27 seats to 24, a working majority of two votes, since twenty-six are necessary for a majority.

In the Assembly the Republicans have eighty-five seats, the Democrats sixty-four and the American Labor party one. Last session the Republicans had eighty-four, the Democrats sixty-one and the American Labor party five.

Governor Lehman is faced with a two-year opposition when the Legislature convenes in 1939. This year, the Assembly term was increased from one to two years to match the Senatorial term.

Pitcher to Be Named

As soon as it became definitely known that the Republicans had captured control of both houses, William S. Murray, Republican State Chairman, announced that State Senator Perley A. Pitcher of Watertown would be named majority leader and temporary president of the upper house. Senator John J. Dunnigan of the Bronx, during the Democratic control, has acted as majority leader for the last six years.

In the Assembly, Oswald D. Heck of Schenectady is certain to continue as Speaker while Irving M. Ives of Chenango County will retain his position as majority leader. Irwin Steingut of Brooklyn is the Democratic minority leader in the lower house.

In gaining control of the Senate, the Republicans defeated Democratic incumbents in the Seventeenth Senatorial District in New York City, the Twenty-sixth District in Westchester, the Forty-fifth and Forty-sixth Districts in Monroe County and the Thirty-eighth District in Onondaga County.

In the Assembly contests, the Democrats gathered what little solace they could from the fact that they picked up three seats throughout the State. In New York City, the Democrats increased their Assembly representation by six seats, but lost three seats to the Republicans up-State.

Labor Party Losses

The Democratic Assembly gains in the city were made almost entirely at the expense of the American Labor party who lost their entire five-man Assembly delegation which was seeking re-election. The Labor party continued to be represented in the Assembly by electing Oscar Garcia Rivera in the Seventeenth Assembly District in Manhattan. Mr. Rivera, who was elected last year on the Republican ticket, was refused renomination and ran solely as an American Labor candidate.

But the American Labor incumbents—Nathaniel M. Minkoff and Gerald J. Muccigrosso in the Bronx and Benjamin Brenner, Salvatore De Matteo and Frank Monaco in Brooklyn—all went down to defeat.

With the exception of the Republican victory in the Seventeenth

Continued on Page Thirteen

Ending of Labor Party Alliances To Follow Tactical Loss at Polls

Doubling of Vote Up-State and Giving of Safe Margins to Lehman and Wagner Spur Trend to Independent Action for Future

By WARREN MOSCOW

The American Labor party, while polling in the city and State a large "straight-line" vote for its candidates, suffered a tactical loss in Tuesday's elections and its future influence in the State would seem to depend on national trends rather than any local alliances.

The Labor party, which achieved a commanding position last year as a result of its election of five Assemblymen and its rolling up of 482,000 votes in the city and 31,000 up-State, lost all its sitting Assemblymen, though electing one other; failed to elect any of the Republican-Labor nominees and also failed to defeat John J. Bennett Jr. and Morris S. Tremaine, Democratic candidates for Attorney General and Controller, whose labor records it had assailed.

On the other hand, it polled 341,853 votes for Governor Lehman in the city, and its State-wide total was headed for more than 400,000 for all its candidates, including its independent nominees for Attorney General and Controller, Joseph V. O'Leary and Langdon W. Post. It doubled its last year's up-State vote of 31,000.

The Labor party vote furnished the actual margin for the re-election of Governor Lehman and the election of Charles Poletti as Lieutenant Governor, and gave Robert F. Wagner and James M. Mead most of their pluralities in the Senate contests. It will be a subject of dispute whether the Laborites would have held the balance of power had the Republican nominee for Governor been any one but Thomas E. Dewey, but on the actual returns they gave Mr. Lehman his election margin with nearly 350,000 votes to spare.

The Socialist party, which polled only 18,000 votes in New York City, lost its place as a recognized party in the State. There is reason to believe that the Socialist voters cast their votes for Mr. Lehman, possibly under the American Labor party emblem, because of the predicted closeness of the race, and that they might otherwise have

Continued on Page Twenty-five

STOCKS TAKE SPURT ON ELECTION NEWS

Gain 1 to 4 Points on Turnover of 3,098,000 Shares, the Heaviest Trading in Year

The stock market staged yesterday the greatest post-election rally in many years, opening higher and continuing to gain in a series of spurts throughout the day. Leading stocks were up 1 to 4 points on a turnover of 3,098,000 shares, the heaviest trading since Oct. 21, 1937.

A pace of 950,000 shares was set during the first hour of trading, compared with 290,000 shares traded in the first hour on Monday, but this was not maintained.

New high marks for the year were made by 201 issues, and virtually three-fourths of all shares traded advanced in price. One stock, however, hit a new low level.

Heavy industry shares starred in the price advances, which ranged from 1 to 4 points. United States Steel gained 3⅜ points, General Motors 1¾ points, Bethlehem Steel 3¾ points, Chrysler 2¾ points, Du Pont 4 points, General Electric 1½ points and Air Reduction 2⅝ points, all making new high marks during the day and closing near the best levels.

Gains in Rail Shares

Railroads to gain included Union Pacific, up 2¾ points; Southern Railway, up 1⅜; New York Central, up 1¼, and Atchison, up 2⅛. Public utilities shared modestly in the rally, Consolidated Edison closing 2 points higher and Public Service of New Jersey 2½ higher.

The market's reaction to the election was noted chiefly at the opening of trading, with blocks of 1,000 to 8,000 shares frequent for initial transactions. Several important issues were delayed in opening. Chrysler appearing at 86⅞, up 1¼ points on a block of 7,500 shares, followed by General Motors, up a point on a block of 7,500 shares, and a little later by United States Steel, 1⅝ points higher on a block of 8,000 shares.

The ticker service soon fell behind as a result of the rush of trading, and at the end of the first quarter hour was five minutes late. A little before that the New York Stock Exchange began to send out flashes of prices for leading stocks at brief intervals, and soon thereafter the ticker began to catch up with transactions. At 10:42 A. M. the tape was abreast of the market, but at 2.58 P. M. it fell a minute behind and at the close of trading was two minutes late.

Largest Since Munich News

Transactions during the first hour were the largest since news of the Munich conference was published. The gain on that day, Sept. 28, was 2.36 points.

Yesterday the average for fifty stocks closed at 110.09, a gain of 2.52 points and the highest figure since early October, 1937. The average for twenty-five industrial stocks was 194.89, up 4.19 points

Continued on Page Twenty

CONGRESS CHANGES ARE COUNTRY-WIDE

Republicans Wrest Seats From the Democrats in 24 States —Gains Mounting

By TURNER CATLEDGE

Congressional gains of at least eighty seats in the House and eight in the Senate were revealed yesterday on more complete returns to have accrued to the Republican party in Tuesday's election.

Neck-and-neck finishes were in progress in Senate contests in Iowa and Indiana, with indications that the Republicans might annex another seat in the latter and in the House race in Indiana.

With only these results finally to be tabulated, one in the House and two in the Senate, the Republicans already had turned in gains sufficient to guarantee a preponderance of conservatives in the next Congress and thus to confirm a swing away from the "Third New Deal" which started soon after President Roosevelt submitted his court-enlargement bill early in 1937.

Already the Republicans had assured themselves a contingent of 169 members of the new House, as contrasted with their present corporal's guard of eighty-eight. They had reduced the present Democratic membership from 328 to 261 and had carved other gains out of the small number of Farmer-Laborites and Progressives.

Raided Democratic Strongholds

They had raided Democratic strongholds in twenty-four different States, or a vast majority of those States outside of the "Solid South."

In the same count they had taken eight Senate seats and re-elected three Republicans standing for re-election. Already they had assured a Republican membership of the next Senate of at least twenty-three, as contrasted with the strength of fifteen in the Seventy-fifth Congress.

The present Senate membership is seventy-six Democrats, fifteen Republicans, two Farmer-Laborites, one Progressive and one Independent. There is one vacancy.

Republican successes in Senate races were recorded in Connecticut, Kansas, New Hampshire, New Jersey, Ohio, Oregon, South Dakota and Wisconsin. In each case a Republican nominee either unseated a Democrat or captured a seat held in recent years by a Democrat.

Most notable of the Republican Senate victories, both in point of present importance and significance for the future, were in Pennsylvania and Ohio, both of which States turned Republican after Democratic landslides in the two previous elections.

In Ohio the Republicans picked up at least eleven House seats in a campaign centering around Robert A. Taft, who unseated Senator Robert J. Bulkley, an arch-New Dealer. Mr. Taft's majority had gone well above the 150,000 mark,

Continued on Page Eighteen

TAXPAYERS REVOLT

Democrats Admit Loss of Former Enthusiastic Backers of New Deal

HOPE COURSE WILL CHANGE

Leaders Wish Roosevelt to Be Guided by Farley Instead of Present Aides

Tables of the election results are on Pages 22, 23, 24, 25.

By ARTHUR KROCK

The average taxpayers of the nation—the group which, for want of a better name, is called the "middle class"—restored the country's traditional two-party system in Tuesday's elections and set up an opposition to the overwhelming Administration majority in Congress and a guard on its control of the administrative agencies of the New Deal. This was the message to be read in the almost complete returns of the polling in the forty-eight States.

Republican gains in Congressional seats, governorships and local offices were scattered over twenty-four of the forty-eight States, all outside the South. But the South, dominated by the Democratic party, had previously rejected the President's attempts to require complete obedience from its members of Congress. Therefore the decisions of the twenty-four States on Tuesday were annexes to what the South, in party primaries, had previously indicated.

Late last night it was evident that the Republicans had gained eighty seats in the House of Representatives at Washington, fifty more than the Democratic leaders expected, added eight—perhaps nine—Senators, made great inroads in the Farm Belt and among the Northern Negroes, and added eleven Republican Governors in the nation, a number that may be increased to thirteen.

Curb on New Deal Urged

On this news the New York stock market rallied strongly and Republican leaders in the country began to suggest a Congressional coalition to prevent any further advance of New Deal programs. Among these leaders was Herbert Hoover, whom President Roosevelt defeated in 1932.

The impression grew, on a study of the returns, that the President's New Deal political combination, devised in 1932 and perfected in 1934 and 1936, had been broken by the uprising of the average American citizens. This combination was made up of farmers, organized labor, the Northern Negroes, the regular Democrats, intellectual independents and a wandering group of left-wing radicals.

On Tuesday in twenty-four States many farm votes were lost; there were visible divisions in organized labor; the Negro vote divided in Ohio and Pennsylvania; and, according to Alf M. Landon, the Republican Presidential nominee in 1936, many regular Democrats broke away from their party moorings. He made a statement to that effect.

The directness of the attack on the left-wing radicals, who have been allies or members of the New Deal, was particularly to be noted in Wisconsin, Michigan and Minnesota. In these States Republican nominees for Senator or Governor upset New Dealers, Progressives and Farmer-Laborites, sounding a knell for the third party of the La Follette brothers in Wisconsin, the Democratic-C. I. O. alliance in Michigan, and the Roosevelt-Benson coalition in Minnesota.

Left Wing Leaders to Confer

The trend implicit in these happenings sufficiently impressed Mayor Fiorello H. La Guardia of New York, a prime mover in the New Deal radical combination, and induced him to arrange to meet with Senator Norris of Nebraska, Governor Murphy of Michigan and the La Follette brothers soon in an effort to get the left-wing Democratic allies back into formation.

In their successful effort to regain major party status and erect a real opposition in Congress and the various States, many Republican candidates gave encouragement to the Townsend plan and other devices to pension elderly citizens. Most Republican candidates also endorsed the social objectives and many of the legislative expressions to that end of the New Deal, pu

Continued on Page Fifteen

BRITAIN PARALLELS U.S. STAND ON CHINA

House of Commons Is Told the Government Takes Identical View Toward Japan

CONTRARY RUMOR DENIED

Official Says Chamberlain Did Not Propose Aid to Tokyo After War, but to Chinese

Wireless to THE NEW YORK TIMES.

LONDON, Nov. 9.—Great Britain stands squarely behind the United States in its protest against Japanese attacks on the Nine-Power Treaty, Richard Austen Butler, Under-Secretary for Foreign Affairs, said today.

At the same time he told the House of Commons that the government had taken cognizance of widespread rumors in China that Prime Minister Neville Chamberlain's recent remarks meant Britain was prepared to aid Japan to dominate China. On the contrary, Mr. Butler said, what Mr. Chamberlain meant in his defense of British policy on China was that the British Government was ready to aid the Chinese to rehabilitate themselves after suffering from the present war.

It is not "that we are looking to the end of the war to lend money to Japan to enable her to complete the domination of China," Mr. Butler said. This remark, it is known, was made as a result of a recent conversation between Sir Archibald Kerr, British Ambassador to China, and Generalissimo Chiang Kai-shek, in which the Chinese leader asked for a clear denial of the different interpretation put upon Mr. Chamberlain's declaration on the Far East.

Mr. Butler's statement that his country continued to regard the Nine-Power treaty and the Open Door as the basis of the China question could not well have been stronger. Referring to Japan's contention that the Nine-Power treaty was obsolete, Mr. Butler said:

"There have been pronouncements recently in Tokyo regarding the formation of an economic and political bloc comprising Japan, Manchukuo and China.

"I would like to say that the position of Great Britain in this matter is governed by the Washington treaties and other international agreements to which His Majesty's Government in conjunction with a large number of other governments is a party.

"We should not, therefore, consider any alteration of the position, as laid down in the treaties, which has been brought about by unilateral action.

"On this matter our stand is the same as that which has been so clearly laid down by the United States Secretary of State in his statement of Nov. 4, which would serve equally to define the attitude of His Majesty's Government in the matter of the Washington treaties.

"The United States Government previously protested in their note to Japan of Oct. 6 against infringement of the policy of the Open Door in China.

"In this connection I would like to say that His Majesty's Government has on their part made a formal protest in the same sense as the United States Government to the Japanese Government in recent months and they have made their position quite clear."

The last remark might well be interpreted as referring, among other things, to the latest specific question that Britain has had to face in connection with the Sino-Japanese war—Japan's action in cutting off the Yangtze River to neutral shipping. It is believed here that Britain, France and the United States may already have made parallel diplomatic protests on this action.

Lloyd George Warns on Burma

LONDON, Nov. 9 (AP).—David Lloyd George, wartime Prime Minister, characterizing Britain foreign policy as always "complete surrender to the dictators," said today that as a result Japan intended to march to the boundaries of Burma.

"For the first time," he told the House of Commons, "they are right on our frontier, a great, aggressive, military empire commanding millions of soldiers.

"It is a very grave event for the British Empire. We have troubles in India which have revealed discontent with the concessions made and there are demands for greater concessions—for independence."

HOOVER ASSERTS VOTE MEANS NEW DEAL CURB

He Says Republicans Can Now 'Restore Faith in America'

PALO ALTO, Calif., Nov. 9 (AP).—Herbert Hoover said today that the Republican party was now in a position to "restore faith in America."

The former President issued this statement on yesterday's election:

"The returns indicate that a majority of the American people voted for Governors, Senators or Congressmen, either Republican, or Democrat, who are opposed to the New Deal.

"This protest should enable the beginning of the end of this waste of public money, these policies of coercion, political corruption and undermining of representative government.

"The re-invigorated Republican party is now in position to join effectively with the anti-New Deal democracy to check these policies in the Congress and thereby contribute to restore employment and agriculture, to re-establish confidence in business and, above all, ot restore faith in America.

"Over the next two years it is the duty of the Republican party not alone to join in this check but to develop a constructive program which will commend itself to the country for 1940."

Managua Building Postoffice

Special Cable to THE NEW YORK TIMES.

MANAGUA, Nicaragua, Nov. 9.—Nicaragua began today construction of a new postoffice here, to be the largest in Central America. The New York company that is building the National Bank of Nicaragua has the contract. The government will issue stamps to commemorate the birth of the humorist Will Rogers.

CHINESE ENGAGING FOE IN CANTON ZONE

Report Japanese Repulsed at Two Places—Guerrillas Are Also Harassing Them

CITIES IN HUNAN BOMBED

Invaders Raid Them in Hope of Finding Chiang Kai-shek —Drive Nearer to Yochow

Special Cable to THE NEW YORK TIMES.

HONG KONG, Nov. 9.—Amid conflicting reports it became known today that Japanese forces were being seriously engaged by Chinese along the West and East Rivers and in an area about twenty miles north of Canton.

Moreover, the Japanese pressing into the interior of Kwangtung Province from Canton are being continually harassed by Chinese guerrillas. In addition, there are further indications that the Chinese soon intend to make a serious effort to recapture Canton or at least oblige the Japanese to maintain a large garrison there.

Significance is seen in the fact that Chinese planes have dropped leaflets in the vicinity of Canton urging the people to take heart and promising that the Japanese will be driven out in due course.

Reliable Chinese reports tell of a counter-attack at Fatshan, southwest of Canton, that has held up a large Japanese force and inflicted serious casualties. It is also reported that an engagement at Samshui, on the West River west of Canton, resulted in driving back Japanese units despite reinforcements that came to their aid.

At least 1,000 guerrillas in the region of the Boca Tigris forts are actively harassing the Japanese, whose strength at present is insufficient to clean up the occupied areas.

Japanese Bomb Hunan Cities

Special Cable to THE NEW YORK TIMES.

SHANGHAI, Thursday, Nov. 10.—Chinese reports from Chungking say that Japanese bombers in Hunan Province on Tuesday killed 200 persons in Hengshan and thirty in Hengyang. Huge fires are said to have been responsible for many deaths in Hengshan, with scores trapped in ruins.

The Japanese were believed to be seeking Generalissimo Chiang Kai-shek, who was said to be in one of the Hunan cities.

Japanese reports of the raids say that twelve Chinese planes at the Hengyang airfield were destroyed. In a raid on Yuanchow, in Western Thunan, the Japanese reported downing six Chinese planes in dog fights. Two crippled Japanese planes were power-dived to the ground by the pilots, destroying anti-aircraft positions, according to the Japanese reports.

Meanwhile, Japanese press dispatches reported that Japanese troops last night had advanced down the Canton Railway to within ten miles of Yochow, eighty miles north of Changsha and 122 miles southwest of Hankow. Japanese commanders say that the fall of Yochow is "only a matter of time."

The Japanese encountered stiff Chinese opposition yesterday in advancing along the railway and in taking Tungcheng, a vital point along the new Chinese front extending from Yochow through Tungcheng, Hsiuhsui and Wuding. Tungcheng streets were said to have been littered with Chinese dead when the Japanese entered the city.

Japanese warships in the Yangtze River are keeping abreast of the army in the Yochow drive. Early yesterday they were twenty miles from the city.

A Japanese Army spokesman here said that it had been learned from a "trustworthy" source that the Chinese had executed General Yu Han-mou, who had been in charge of the defense of Canton.

Dispatches from Chungking say that inhabitants of that new Chinese capital are streaming to the hills in fear of air raids.

NAZI PRESS STRESSES ROOSEVELT'S DEFEAT

'Anti-Fascist Alibi' Declared Rejected by Voters

Wireless to THE NEW YORK TIMES.

BERLIN, Nov. 9.—Early results of the elections in the United States are interpreted here as a cold douche for President Roosevelt and the New Deal that dampens many exuberant Democratic hopes for 1940.

The newspapers print the results under headlines such as "Election Defeat for Roosevelt," or "Rise of the Republicans," and the turn in the voters' sentiments is regarded as all the more remarkable because it occurred despite the Administration's continued deficit expenditures for social welfare.

Some newspapers warn that despite this defeat the Democrats still control Congress, wherefore little change may be expected in the United States's domestic and foreign policies.

The Tageblatt says:

"For the European observer and for us Germans particularly it is especially interesting that the anti-Fascist slogans thrown into the election campaign with so much ruthlessness and tendentious intentions have fallen futilely to the ground before the traditional instinct of survival within the country itself.

"It appears as if those are going to be right who considered it impossible simply to lift America off its hinges during the present crisis and revamp it completely. The Number One democracy, constantly played off against the authoritarian States, follows now as ever its own American laws.

"In this respect the election results, which naturally cannot conjure back the liberalistic presuppositions of the prosperity period, might clarify the situation nationally and internationally. Beyond that the anti-Fascist alibi with which Roosevelt's friends sought to provide him has not been acknowledged by the voters."

BERLIN RAIDS REPLY TO DEATH OF ENVOY

Continued From Page One

ken shop front and walked leisurely away in full sight of three uniformed night watchmen.

In the West End large crowds followed the proceedings and were politely asked by the raiders and their accompaniers not to block the sidewalks.

However, that the onlookers were not wholly sympathetic to the proceedings was evidenced by the faces of some of them, as well as by the statements of three poorly dressed workers who at three different observation points, seeing the writer taking notes, said in different phrases but all to the same effect:

"Do not forget to write that it is not working people who are doing this."

From Munich this morning came reports of similar disorders when party veterans who were celebrating the anniversary of the 1923 beer cellar Putsch heard of Herr vom Rath's death. Added details indicated that uniformed Elite Guards and Storm Troopers urged onlookers to assist in the proceedings.

An official German News Bureau dispatch from Dresden yesterday said that "spontaneous demonstrations" against Jews had taken place there and that "police were sent to protect the Jews and despite their livid rage the masses restrained themselves, so no serious riots resulted."

There were also reports of a demonstration before the office of the official French tourist agency here yesterday afternoon, which, however, was quickly dispersed.

An Official Warning

All these demonstrations took place despite the issuance yesterday of an official German News Bureau statement following reports of the burning of a synagogue in Westphalia. The statement said:

"In informed circles it is explained, relative to demonstrations against synagogues and Jewish business houses resulting from the indignation of the population of Kurhessen following the murderous attack at the Paris Embassy, that despite all justification for this indignation authoritative quarters now as before take the stand that measures against Jews in Germany cannot occur on individual responsibility but must have legal bases.

"Official organs feel it to be their task to convince the aroused population of the necessity of comporting itself with discipline despite monstrous provocations such as that recently made from Jewish quarters in Paris."

This statement somewhat inhibited the violence of the press campaign against the Jews, but Herr vom Rath's death took precedence in the press before the commemoration ceremonies for National Socialism's "martyrs" yesterday and this most recent victim was acclaimed as one of them.

As a final honor Herr vom Rath was promoted to Embassy Counselor First Class by Chancellor Hitler just before his death. The promotion was telegraphed to him with a message of congratulation by Foreign Minister Joachim von Ribbentrop.

That further legal measures against the Jews are now being prepared is assumed to be a certainty. Some reports hint at drastic capital levies. As a preliminary step, rumors are current, Jewish cultural organizations and newspapers will be closed down.

The press demands not only "legal but also political expiation" for the murder, which is interpreted here as a demand on France to take action against Jewish refugees from Germany.

Chancellor Hitler telegraphed condolences to Herr vom Rath's parents in Paris. The French Chargé d'Affaires called at the Foreign Office to express his government's condolences.

Jews' Leader Deplores Shooting

BERLIN, Nov. 9 (AP).—An executive of German Jewry issued a statement today expressing the horror of his people over the shooting of the Third Secretary of the German Embassy in Paris by a young Polish Jew.

A Propaganda Ministry decree of yesterday, however, made publication of this statement impossible. The decree banned all Jewish publications until further notice.

Blood Transfusions in Vain

Wireless to THE NEW YORK TIMES.

PARIS, Nov. 9.—Ernst vom Rath, Third Secretary of the German Embassy here, who was shot by Herschel Grynszpan, a 17-year-old Polish Jew, Monday morning, died at 4:30 this afternoon at the Clinique de l'Alma after a fourth blood transfusion from French war veterans and personal aid from Chancellor Adolf Hitler's private doctor had proved unavailing.

The charge against Grynszpan will accordingly be changed to murder, which might entail death by the guillotine despite his youth and the motives for the crime.

In what was regarded as a direct outcome of Grynszpan's deed the Socialist party today announced that it would interpellate the government on the conditions of sojourn of foreign undesirables in France. The Socialists in the past have observed a liberal attitude toward political and racial refugees.

It is now expected that the check on those categories of foreigners will be exceptionally sharpened, which may again raise the question of transit permits for the international volunteers from Loyalist Spain who are scheduled to arrive in France this week-end.

Herr vom Rath died with his father and mother at his bedside without having been able to understand a communication to the effect that Herr Hitler had just promoted him to the rank of First Class Legation Counselor.

The death certificate, signed by Dr. Brandt, Herr Hitler's personal physician; Professor Georg Magnus of Munich University and Dr. Baumgartner, declared that a stomach wound had proved fatal. The body has been removed to the German Embassy, where it will lie in state.

In a further statement to the police Grynszpan tearfully exclaimed:

"Being a Jew is not a crime. I am not a dog, I have a right to live and the Jewish people have a right to exist on this earth. Wherever I have been I have been chased like an animal."

He added that he had attended a rabbinical school at Frankfort-on-the-Main but had had no intention of becoming a rabbi, only of studying the Hebrew language and literature.

"All the News That's Fit to Print."

The New York Times.

EXTRA

Partly cloudy and somewhat warmer today. Tomorrow generally fair with moderate temperatures.

Temperatures Yesterday—Max., 67; Min., 61

Copyright, 1939, by The New York Times Company.

VOL. LXXXVIII...No. 29,805. Entered as Second-Class Matter, Postoffice, New York, N. Y. NEW YORK, FRIDAY, SEPTEMBER 1, 1939. THREE CENTS NEW YORK CITY and Vicinity | FOUR CENTS Elsewhere Except in 7th and 8th Postal Zones.

GERMAN ARMY ATTACKS POLAND; CITIES BOMBED, PORT BLOCKADED; DANZIG IS ACCEPTED INTO REICH

BRITISH MOBILIZING

Navy Raised to Its Full Strength, Army and Air Reserves Called Up

PARLIAMENT IS CONVOKED

Midnight Meeting Is Held by Ministers—Negotiations Admitted Failure

By The Associated Press.

LONDON, Friday, Sept. 1.—The British Parliament was summoned to meet today at 5 P. M. [12 noon in New York].

British Call Up Forces

By FERDINAND KUHN Jr.

Special Cable to THE NEW YORK TIMES.

LONDON, Friday, Sept. 1.—All attempts to bring about direct negotiations between Germany and Poland appeared to have broken down tonight as Great Britain mobilized her fleet to full strength, stretched her other defensive preparations close to the limit and began moving 3,000,000 school children and invalids from the crowded cities into the safety of the countryside.

Censorship was established over cables after London had been cut off for hours from communication with the Continent.

It was the peak of the crisis, but a day of rumors had not shifted the fundamental issue nor given a conclusive answer to the question of peace or war.

At midnight the British Government was not yet convinced that Germany really intended to attack Poland and provoke a world war.

Terms Called Smoke Screen

All that had happened during yesterday, including the sudden broadcasting of Chancellor Hitler's sixteen-point demands, was interpreted here as a smoke screen rather than as the flash of guns.

After hearing Herr Hitler's "terms" officials here quietly announced tonight that "the government primarily interested in the proposals is, of course, the Polish Government."

Until the Polish Government has had time to consider them, it was said in Whitehall that "it would be highly undesirable for any comment to be made."

It was fully expected that Poland would reject them later today; indeed, Polish circles here were describing them tonight as "utterly unacceptable," for they would involve dismemberment of Poland and loss of Poland's capacity to defend her independence. In any event, there was no sign of any intention here to put pressure on Warsaw to accept.

Much might have been said about the German "proposals" here tonight if the government had not been so anxious to leave the first decision to Warsaw without any prompting. That the British regarded them as artful went without saying, since they conveyed a first impression of reasonableness that was not borne out by the terms themselves.

Until the announcement on the German wireless tonight, the British Government had not been told about them officially, and the Polish Government was not informed until Josef Lipski, Polish Ambassador to Berlin, visited Foreign Minister Joachim von Ribbentrop a few minutes before the broadcast took place.

Shortly after midnight last night, Sir Nevile Henderson, the British Ambassador in Berlin, had heard the "points" read to him by Herr von Ribbentrop, but the reading was so fast that the Ambassador could not even take notes of them in detail. In any event, he was told Herr Hitler's "points" were not being given to him or his government officially, on the ground that it was already too late.

Time Limit Expired

On Tuesday Herr Hitler had asked that a Polish negotiator should arrive in Berlin within twenty-four hours; and as nobody had arrived from Warsaw when the time limit expired, Sir Nevile was told that the "points" could not be communicated officially to London.

The German time table with the

Continued on Page Four

Bulletins on Europe's Conflict

London Hears of Warsaw Bombing

LONDON, Friday, Sept. 1 (AP).—Reuters British news agency said it had learned from Polish sources in Paris that Warsaw was bombed today.

French Confirm Beginning of War

PARIS, Friday, Sept. 1 (AP).—The Havas news agency said today that official French dispatches from Germany indicated that "the Reich began hostilities on Poland this morning."

The agency also reported that the Polish Embassy here had announced that "Germany violated the Polish frontier at four points."

"German reports of pretended violation of German territory by Poland are pure invention, as is the fable of 'attack' by Polish insurgents on Gleiwitz," the embassy announcement said.

Attack on Entire Front Reported

LONDON, Friday, Sept. 1 (AP).—A Reuters dispatch from Paris said:

"The following is given with all reserve: According to unconfirmed reports received here, the Germans have begun an offensive with extreme violence on the whole Polish front."

First Wounded Brought Into Gleiwitz

GLEIWITZ, Germany, Friday, Sept. 1 (AP).—An army ambulance carrying wounded soldiers arrived at the emergency hospital here today at 9:10 A. M.

The men, carried in a wagon, were on stretchers. One had on a first-aid field bandage. It could not be ascertained where the ambulance came from.

At about 9:30 a half-mile long truck train manned by the engineering corps drove through the heart of the city with pontoon bridge building material. In the train were caterpillar tread, twenty-passenger motor vans.

Obviously the train had been on the road for a considerable time. All equipment was thickly covered with gray mud.

A scouting plane of the air force was patrolling an area over Gleiwitz.

Early today Gleiwitz residents reported that artillery fire

Continued on Page Four

DALADIER SUMMONS CABINET TO CONFER

News of Attack on Poland Spurs Prompt Action— Military Move Thought Likely

By The Associated Press.

PARIS, Friday, Sept. 1.—Edouard Daladier, Premier and War Minister of France, informed that German troops crossed the Polish frontier today, summoned an urgent meeting of his Cabinet for 10:30 A. M.

It was probable that Parliament would be called tomorrow.

Reports of the German invasion came from Berlin and from the Polish Embassy here. The Ministers were called to the Elysee Palace to meet with President Albert Lebrun.

Upon receipt of word of the German operations M. Daladier rushed to the War Ministry and called General Marie Gustave Gamelin, supreme commander of land, sea and air forces, into consultation.

A little later Daladier summoned Foreign Minister Georges Bonnet.

The Polish Embassy said that Germans violated the Polish frontier at four points and at the same time it characterized German charges that Poles had crossed into Germany as "pure invention."

Havas, Frnch news agency, announced that "a German declaration of war against Poland probably will lead France and Great Britain to take new military measures."

Britain and France are committed to aid Poland in any fight to save her independence.

Ministers Stand Firm

By P. J. PHILIP

Wireless to THE NEW YORK TIMES.

PARIS, Aug. 31.—The Cabinet met with President Albert Lebrun for more than two hours this evening at the Elysée Palace. At the close of the meeting Minister of the Interior Albert Sarraut handed the press the following communiqué:

"MM. Edouard Daladier, President of the Council, and Georges Bonnet, Minister of Foreign Affairs, laid before the Cabinet a detailed account of the international situation as a whole.

"The Cabinet was unanimous in formally maintaining the engagements taken by France."

Later M. Daladier had further conversations with M. Bonnet, Fi-

Continued on Page Four

BRITISH CHILDREN TAKEN FROM CITIES

3,000,000 Persons Are in First Evacuation Group, Which Is to Be Moved Today

By FREDERICK T. BIRCHALL

Special Cable to THE NEW YORK TIMES.

LONDON, Friday, Sept. 1.—The greatest mass movement of population at short notice in the history of Great Britain is under way. It is an evacuation, under government order, of little children, invalids, women and old men from congested areas.

From London, Birmingham, Manchester, Liverpool, Edinburgh, Glasgow and twenty-three other cities the great exodus is going on as this dispatch is being written. The numbers are stupendous. More than 3,000,000 of these helpless human beings are being taken out of danger of German bombs.

Nothing like it has ever been attempted anywhere; yet it is going on without mishap—so far, indeed, without serious confusion.

Scenes everywhere were much the same whether in the aristocratic West End or the proletarian East Side, but one that this correspon-

Continued on Page Three

Soviet Ratifies Reich Non-Aggression Pact; Gibes at British and French Amuse Deputies

By G. E. R. GEDYE

Special Cable to THE NEW YORK TIMES.

MOSCOW, Aug. 31.—With Premier and Foreign Commissar Vyacheslaff M. Molotoff, working under high pressure—so suddenly applied without any previous indication and contrasting so sharply with earlier delaying tactics this week as to suggest German insistence that the matter be finally settled—the Supreme Soviet [Parliament] tonight unanimously ratified the Russo-German non-aggression pact.

Ratification, which was first foreshadowed at midday, was preceded by a speech by Mr. Molotoff so precise in its definition of Soviet obligations to refrain from participating on the side of Great Britain and France in any war against Germany, so voluble in its defense against charges of inconsistency against Communist Russia for embracing Fascist Germany, and so insistent on the inevitability of friendship between "not merely the governments but also the peoples" of Germany and Russia as to extinguish the last faint hopes of the western democracies that Moscow might yet find loopholes or excuses for joining them at some subsequent date in resisting German aggression against Poland.

Mr. Molotoff's speech contained nothing to justify constantly repeated suspicions of the existence of a secret German-Soviet pact entitling the latter to participate in a partition of Poland.

The Premier's speech contained much trenchant and seemingly irrefutable evidence of blunders by the British and French Governments in handling the question of Soviet cooperation. It was not diffi-

Continued on Page Eight

HOSTILITIES BEGUN

Warsaw Reports German Offensive Moving on Three Objectives

ROOSEVELT WARNS NAVY

Also Notifies Army Leaders of Warfare—Envoys Tell of Bombing of 4 Cities

By JERZY SZAPIRO

Wireless to THE NEW YORK TIMES.

WARSAW, Poland, Friday, Sept. 1.—War began at 5 o'clock this morning with German planes attacking Gdynia, Cracow and Katowice.

At Gdynia three bombs exploded in the sea.

The regular German Army started an offensive in the direction of Dzialdowka—in Upper Silesia and Czestochowa. The German plan apparently is to cut off Western Poland along the line of Dzialdowka-Lodz-Czestochowa.

The offensive is developing, from East Prussia, toward Silesia and northwards from Slovakia.

At 9 o'clock an attempt was made to bombard Warsaw. The planes, however, did not reach even the suburbs.

A military attack on the garrison at Westerplatte in the Danzig area was repulsed.

The Foreign Office at 8:45 A. M. issued a communiqué saying that military action had begun in Westerplatte in the Danzig area as well as in Buschkowa near Gdynia, and in Dzialowka, Chojnice and Lowa.

Hostilities have begun and Poland has been attacked, said the communiqué.

Three cities in Upper Silesia suffered artillery bombardment, particulars of which are lacking, it was said.

While this dispatch was being telephoned, the air-raid sirens sounded in Warsaw.

Danzig Fighting Reported

WARSAW, Poland, Friday, Sept. 1 (AP).—It was reported today that Tczew and Czestochowa were bombed by German airplanes early this morning.

There was no official confirmation of the bombing.

Fighting was reported at Danzig. It was reported officially that German troops had attacked Polish defenses near Mlawa, bordering the southern part of East Prussia. There was no announcement of the damage resulting from the bombing.

Mist and clouds were overhanging the city. A light drizzle apparently afforded momentary protection against air raids. Warsaw went to work as usual.

Roosevelt Warns Navy

WASHINGTON, Friday, Sept. 1 (AP).—President Roosevelt directed today that all naval ships and army commands be notified at once by radio of German-Polish hostilities.

The White House issued the following announcement:

"The President received word at 2:50 A. M. Eastern standard time

Continued on Page Five

FREE CITY IS SEIZED

Forster Notifies Hitler of Order Putting Danzig Into the Reich

ACCEPTED BY CHANCELLOR

Poles Ready, Made Their Preparations After Hostilities Appeared Inevitable

Special Cable to THE NEW YORK TIMES.

DANZIG, Friday, Sept. 1.—By a decree issued early this morning Albert Forster, Nazi Chief of State, proclaimed the annexation of the Free City to the Reich, thus settling by a fell stroke the original point of contention in the international crisis.

In a telegram to Chancellor Hitler Herr Forster explained his action as necessary to remove "the pressing necessity of our people and State." Herr Forster also issued a proclamation to the people of Danzig saying the hour awaited for twenty years had arrived because "our Fuehrer, Adolf Hitler, has freed us."

[A NEW YORK TIMES dispatch from Berlin this morning said Herr Hitler telegraphed Herr Forster today thanking him and all Danzigers, and stating:

"The law for reannexation is in effect immediately."

The Chancellor stated, furthermore, that Herr Forster was appointed head of the civil administration of the Danzig area.]

In a four-article decree Herr Forster declared the Constitution of Danzig no longer valid. He declared himself sole administrator of the Danzig part of the German Reich, and he declared that until the Reich's legal system had been introduced by command of Herr Hitler all laws except the Constitution remained in effect. Then Herr Forster immediately wired Herr Hitler of his action, begged the Chancellor to give his approval of the move and through Reich law complete the annexation.

The German flag is now flying everywhere over Danzig, Herr Forster said, and all church bells resound to the event. "We thank God," he declared, "that He gave the Fuehrer the strength and the possibility to free also us from the evil Versailles treaty."

Hitler Accepts Danzig

By The Associated Press.

BERLIN, Friday, Sept. 1.—The German official news agency, D. N. B., announced today that Albert Forster, Nazi Chief of State in Danzig, had proclaimed the reunion of the Free City with the Reich.

Herr Hitler today accepted the Free City of Danzig into the Reich.

"I acknowledge your proclamation of the return of the Free City of Danzig to the Reich," Herr Hitler's telegram said. "I thank you, Gauleiter Forster, and all Danzig men and women, for your loyalty which you have displayed for so many years.

"Greater Germany welcomes you with joy in her heart.

"The law of reunion will be enacted forthwith. I appoint you, Herr Forster, chief of the civil administration in the Danzig territory."

Forster's telegram to Herr Hitler read:

My Fuehrer.

I have just signed and then put into effect the following basic law, concerning the reunion of Danzig with the German Reich.

The basic State law of the Free State of Danzig and the reunion of Danzig with the German Reich is effective Sept. 1, 1939.

To lift the immediate distress of the people and State of the Free City of Danzig, I decree the following basic State law:

ARTICLE I

The Constitution of the Free City of Danzig has been suspended effective immediately.

ARTICLE II

All legal and administrative power will be executed exclusively by the head of State.

ARTICLE III

The Free City of Danzig with its territory and its peoples forms

Continued on Page Five

Hitler Acts Against Poland

The port of Gdynia, north of Danzig (toward top of map), was blockaded this morning. At Gleiwitz (shown by cross) artillery fire was heard after a Polish-German skirmish had been reported there. Cracow, to the east, was among Polish cities said to have been bombed.

Hitler Tells the Reichstag 'Bomb Will Be Met by Bomb'

Chancellor Vows 'Fight Until Resolution' Against Poland—Gives Order of Succession As Goering, Hess, Then Senate to Choose

Chancellor Adolf Hitler of Germany, in a world broadcast this morning, opened "a fight until the resolution of the situation" against Poland, announcing that "from now on bomb will be met by bomb."

At the same time he announced, to face any eventuality, that if anything "happened" to him, Field Marshal Hermann Goering was to be in charge; if to Marshal Goering, Rudolph Hess; if to Herr Hess, the Senate, which he proposes to appoint, will select a successor.

The Chancellor, after attempting to narrow the conflict with Poland by assuring the Western powers that he had no designs on their frontiers, by assuring the neutrality of the sideline powers and by acknowledging the friendliness of Italy and the new relations with Russia, issued a defy to Poland's allies.

Says He Will Carry on

"I shall carry on this fight regardless of against whom I may come," he declared.

At the same time he held the door open for Poland to capitulate to his demands, declaring that he did not intend to make war against women and children. He said that if a solution did not come from the present Polish Government, it would come from a future Polish Government.

The Chancellor expressed confidence, toward the close of his address, that his decision, which was being broadcast over amplifiers hastily erected by electricians at the last moment in the streets of Berlin and the provincial capitals, would be accepted by the German people.

The scene enacted in the Kroll Opera House in Berlin was carried over sound waves to most of the nations of the world. From Berlin hook-ups had been arranged with the three major networks of the United States, and, according to the announcer for the German broadcasting system, over the Italian, Hungarian, Spanish, Norwegian, Swedish, Danish, Yugoslav, British and French national networks.

The summons to the Reichstag ordered by Herr Hitler himself, had been sent out only a few hours before the meeting. Most of the members had been awaiting the signal, and when the opera house opened shortly before 10 o'clock [5 o'clock, New York time] this morning, they were dressed in the uniforms of their military formations.

After Herr Hitler finished speaking the deputies enacted a law incorporating Danzig into the Reich, declaring Danzig citizens were now Germans, voiding the Constitution of the Free City and extending to its territory the jurisdiction of German law.

At 5:10 A. M., Marshal Goering opened the meeting and turned the floor over to the Chancellor.

In the early part of his address, Herr Hitler electrified his audience with this declaration:

"We have all been suffering under the tortures that the Versailles treaty has been inflicting upon us."

Then, speaking with measured deliberateness of Germany's claims to the pre-war German areas, he announced, as he had on a previous occasion:

"The Treaty of Versailles is, for us Germans, and has been, for us Germans, not a law."

Anticipating what the announcement's reiteration would lead to, the Deputies roared applause. Then Herr Hitler, his indignation rising as he proceeded, set about building up the German case, asserting that his proposals for a peaceful solution of the problem of Danzig and the Polish Corridor had been rejected, and charging that the Poles had visited atrocities on Germans, especially women and children, "killing many of them."

SUMMARY OF SPEECH

A summary of Herr Hitler's speech was translated as follows:

"For months we have been suffering under the burdens of the Treaty of Versailles. Danzig was and is a German city. All these regions have only Germany to thank for their cultural development.

"Minorities in the Polish Corridor have been shamefully mistreated. Here, as in other respects, I have tried to solve the problems by peaceful means. In the fifteen years of National Socialism we have been

Continued on Page Three

HITLER GIVES WORD

In a Proclamation He Accuses Warsaw of Appeal to Arms

FOREIGNERS ARE WARNED

They Remain in Poland at Own Risk—Nazis to Shoot at Any Planes Flying Over Reich

By OTTO D. TOLISCHUS

Special Cable to THE NEW YORK TIMES.

BERLIN, Friday, Sept. 1.—Charging that Germany had been attacked, Chancellor Hitler at 5:11 o'clock this morning issued a proclamation to the army declaring that from now on force will be met with force and calling on the armed forces "to fulfill their duty to the end."

The text of the proclamation reads:

To the defense forces.

The Polish nation refused my efforts for a peaceful regulation of neighborly relations; instead it has appealed to weapons.

Germans in Poland are persecuted with a bloody terror and are driven from their homes. The series of border violations, which are unbearable to a great power, prove that the Poles no longer are willing to respect the German frontier. In order to put an end to this frantic activity no other means is left to me now than to meet force with force.

"Battle for Honor"

German defense forces will carry on the battle for the honor of the living rights of the reawakened German people with firm determination.

I expect every German soldier, in view of the great tradition of eternal German soldiery, to do his duty until the end.

Remember always in all situations you are the representatives of National Socialist Greater Germany!

Long live our people and our Reich!

Berlin, Sept. 1, 1939.

ADOLF HITLER.

The commander-in-chief of the air force issued a decree effective immediately prohibiting the passage of any airplanes over German territory excepting those of the Reich air force or the government.

This morning the naval authorities ordered all German mercantile ships in the Baltic Sea not to run to Danzig or Polish ports.

Anti-air raid defenses were mobilized throughout the country early this morning.

A formal declaration of war against Poland had not yet been declared up to 8 o'clock [3 A. M. New York time] this morning and the question of whether the two countries are in a state of active belligerency is still open

Reichstag Will Meet Today

Foreign correspondents at an official conference at the Reich Press Ministry at 8:30 o'clock [3:30 A. M. New York time] were told that they would receive every opportunity to facilitate the transmission of dispatches. Wireless stations have been instructed to speed up communications and the Ministry is installing additional batteries of telephones.

The Reichstag has been summoned to meet at 10 o'clock [5 A. M. New York time] to receive a more formal declaration from Herr Hitler.

The Hitler army order is interpreted as providing, for the time being, armed defense of the German frontiers against aggression. The action is also suspected of forcing international diplomatic action.

The Germans announced that foreigners remain in Polish territory at their own risk.

Flying over Polish territory as well as the maritime areas is forbidden by the German authorities and any violators will be shot down.

When Herr Hitler made his an

Continued on Page Three

BRITAIN MOBILIZES; LIMITS FOOD BUYING

Full Naval Strength and Army and Air Force Reserves Are Called to Colors

CENSORSHIP ESTABLISHED

Telephone Service Is Stopped —Civil Flying Banned and Stock Exchange Closed

Special Cable to THE NEW YORK TIMES.

LONDON, Aug. 31.—The British Government tonight publicly announced that "in continuation of measures already adopted" it was completing naval mobilization forthwith.

Furthermore, there were also called immediately to the colors the remainder of the regular army reserve, the supplementary reserve and a further number of the Royal Air Force volunteer reserve.

These men were summoned to depots by repeated calls over the radio and were warned not to wait for individual notices. The public listened to these official bulletins with quiet confidence.

It is impossible to estimate the numbers of men involved by these successive orders but it has been announced in Parliament and in the current army estimates that the effectives of all ranks on Jan. 1 in the army reserve totaled 139,600 men, and in the supplementary reserve 32,000. These figures have doubtless been increased in the past months of preparation.

Sailors Called Quietly

Under the new Reserve and Auxiliary Forces Act, which enables the government to call up troops without the publicity hitherto entailed by a royal proclamation, the Admiralty last month called, by individual notice, a large number of naval officers on the retired and emergency lists and the men of the Royal Fleet Reserve. The remainder of the same two classes of the fleet in reserve are now to join immediately while the other classes, with the Royal Naval Reserve and Royal Naval Volunteers, will receive further instructions when they are required.

A rush of other official orders also called up the Air Raid Precautions officers to their positions and the local authorities were instructed to complete the distribution of gas masks.

[In addition, according to The Associated Press, the government placed an unexpected censorship on all communications to and from the British Isles, establishing censors at cable offices and telephone exchanges, while "all telephone service with countries abroad and ships at sea" was suspended. The Stock Exchange was closed.]

Simultaneously with these new military preparations, half of Britain was banned to civil airplanes. No aircraft now may fly over England and Scotland, including their territorial waters, east of a line drawn near Poole, in Dorset, through Salisbury, Kingsclere, Oxford, Pershore near Birmingham, Aysgarth in Yorkshire to Stonehaven in Kincardineshire.

Other prohibited areas include the neighborhood of Invergordon, Weymouth, Plymouth and Scapa Flow. All land planes entering Britain must approach by specified routes, landing at Shoreham, Belfast, Liverpool or Perth and flying boats must enter the Poole or Pembroke Dock airports, thus eliminating Southampton.

Fixing one week's food supplies as a reasonable maximum limit of public requirements, in the absence of an actual shortage, an order under the defense regulations tonight forbade the hoarding of foodstuffs including tea, coffee and cocoa. The order makes it an offense for any one to buy more than one week's supply of any kind of food or to keep more than a week's supply, apart from the stocks already accumulated on earlier government advice.

Penalties Are Fixed

The defense regulations render offenders liable, on summary conviction, to three months imprisonment or £100 fine and on conviction by indictment to two years' imprisonment and £500 fine. The order gives the Board of Trade authority to enter and search any premises in which there is reason to believe that the order has been contravened.

These restrictions do not apply to shopkeepers but they are warned not to sell food to a customer if there is ground for believing that he is buying excessive quantities, the result of which would be to create a shortage in local shops.

Persons who have already built up reserves are urged to keep them intact as long as possible but to be prepared to use them should local deliveries at any time be temporarily disorganized, thereby leaving stocks in the shops for persons who have not been able to put by reserves.

It is officially pointed out that the "government's plans for food supply are designed to prevent any undue rise in prices, to maintain the flow of distribution and to provide every person regularly with his or her fair share."

Tonight, under the glare of acetylene flares, workmen were carrying out the government's order to prepare air-raid trenches for instant occupation. Five pamphlets, each of 15,000,000 copies, have now been issued giving the public information on what to do in the event of a raid.

It is officially estimated that, if fifty bombs of the largest size fell within an area of one square mile, any individual within that area would have something like a 100-to-1 chance of escaping what may be called direct-hit effects. By far the greatest number of casualties is expected to come from "secondary" effects of the explosions, such as splinters, shock of blast and falling debris. The authorities are taking the most active preparations to prevent these.

Squads of air-raid precaution men are erecting splinter-proof shelters in gardens in the poorer parts of London as fast as the corrugated metal arches that line the roofs of these shelters can be delivered.

Thousands of transport vehicles have been commandeered.

Censors in Cable Offices

There is no evidence yet that full wartime censorship machinery has been put into operation. Censors were stationed in cable offices, however, and all copy passed through their hands.

American newspapers and news agencies are affected by this British action. Most American papers file their stories from the Continent to Britain by telephone and thence by cable to New York. They were rushing through the Continent's reaction to the British naval mobilization early this evening when telephone service was suspended.

Customers of most London banks today received change of address notices indicating that rural spots had been chosen for the transaction of business should hostilities start. This "decentralization" of business is one of the most remarkable features of the present emergency and there is some speculation, should the crisis pass, whether many of these old country mansions that are ready to come under the auctioneer's hammer because of the high cost of upkeep, but now are being temporarily taken over by large London business houses, may be permanently occupied.

Censorship Is Set Up

LONDON, Aug. 31 (AP).—Acting under defense regulations, the government tonight established full censorship of all communications in and out of England, applied restrictions upon the purchase of food and upon flights of civil aircraft in the United Kingdom, and suspended all telephone service abroad.

At 6:57 P. M. censors walked into cable, telephone and wireless offices and halted all services. Shortly thereafter it was announced that cabled news copy must be submitted to the censor at cable offices. Meanwhile the telephone exchange refused all outgoing calls and said incoming calls also were subject to the censor.

The British Postal Department, which controls telephone and telegraph communications, announced that "all telephone services with countries abroad and ships at sea are suspended."

"During the present emergency, telegrams are liable to the risk of considerable delay as a result of heavy demands upon the service. The sender of every telegram, whether for a destination in this country or elsewhere, must until further notice insert his full name and address in a space provided on the telegram form for reference.

"Telegrams for ships at sea (with the exception of telegrams and radio telegrams on British Government service) can be accepted only if written in plain English or plain French and on the understanding that they are accepted at the senders' risk.

A LESSON IN WAR CONDITIONS FOR CHILDREN IN BERLIN

Teachers and pupils in the German capital equipped with gas masks preparatory to starting the day's work

Times Wide World Radiophoto

Hitler Speech Promises 'Fight to Resolution'

Continued From Page One

trying to solve problems peacefully.

"I have often made proposals for the righting of insufferable wrongs. All of these suggestions which I have made for peaceful solutions, including disarmament, redevelopment and limitation of warfare, have been rejected.

"The long list of proposals I have made, including disarmament and limitation of warfare, have been rejected. All have been in vain.

"An impossible situation has arisen. The Treaty of Versailles for us Germans is not a law. It is not fair to put a pistol to a man's head, starve him and then say you are acting under sacred law.

"As to Danzig and the Corridor, I have tried to effect a peaceful solution.

"An impossible situation has arisen. The Treaty of Versailles is not law; therefore we are not violating any law.

His Proposal Rejected

"I cannot be indifferent to the fate of Danzig. I have had formulated proposals, and I must say nothing could be more fair than these proposals. My proposals were rejected—by mobilizations and pressure on the German people in the Polish Corridor and in Danzig.

"I told the Polish Ambassador ten days ago that if this situation continued, if Danzig was persecuted and if attempts continued by Poland to ruin Danzig economically, the situation could not be tolerated.

"It has been maintained that persecutions have not been carried out by the Poles, but I would like to know what are persecutions if not the mistreatment of women and children, in many places where they have even been killed. I made one last effort to make a proposal for mediation to the British Government. I accepted the British proposal.

"I accepted the preparations for mediation and I waited for the Polish representative two days.

"If Germany should stand for such things, Germany has nothing left but to withdraw from the political stage. No one should confuse my patience for cowardice.

"The first answer I received as a reply from Poland was mobilization and the atrocities committed against German women and children.

"I have therefore decided to talk to Poland in the same language she has used toward us for such a long time. Not for one second shall I hesitate in fulfillment of my duty.

"I have offered England friendship and, if necessary, close cooperation. Germany has no interests in the West. The Westwall is and remains our border in the west.

"I should like to express at this time our thanks to Italy.

"Neutral powers have assured us of their neutrality and we have assured them they will be respected. We mean this.

Hails Pact With Russia

"I am happy to make an announcement. I see no reason why Russia and Germany should remain enemies any longer. Any war between our peoples would be of no profit to either. We have, therefore, decided that the use of force would give an advantage to others. We have resolved to draw up a pact to exclude the use of force for all time to come.

"Every attempt of the western powers to change the situation will fail. This pact means—for all time in the future—something definite and something we will stick to and hold by. I believe the whole German nation will greet this stand.

"Germany and Russia fought against each other in the World War, and that shall not occur again. The ratification of the German-Russian [non-aggression] pact was announced yesterday in Berlin. I can endorse, word for word, the address yesterday by Premier Molotoff. Adjustments must be made that will permit Germany and Poland to live side by side in peace.

"I am resolved to fight until the Polish Government arrives at the decision that a solution can be attained. I want to eliminate the element of uncertainty between Poland and Germany.

Promises Bomb for Bomb

"I do not want to fight women and children. The Poles have shot regular soldiers upon our territory, and from now on bomb will be met by bomb. He who fights with poison will be met with poison. He who departs from the rules of humane warfare can expect the same from us.

"I shall carry on thus, fighting until the situation is acceptable to Germany.

"For the last few years more than 90,000,000,000 marks have been applied to the reconstruction of the German Army. We have the best-equipped army. It is much better than the army of 1914.

"If I now call upon the German people to make sacrifices I have a right to do so. I am ready to make every personal sacrifice on my own part. I expect nothing from any German but what I also would do myself and would always be prepared to do. My life belongs to my people. I shall march as the first German soldier of the people.

"I have put on my old soldier's coat, and I will not take it off until we achieve victory.

"If anything happens to me, then there shall come Marshal Goering. And if to Marshal Goering, then shall come Herr Hess. You shall be duty bound to them as you have been to me.

"In case something happens to take away Herr Hess, the choice shall be by the German people.

"My whole life has been nothing but one long struggle, and there is one word I never learned to know: that is 'capitulate.' November of 1918 shall never be repeated in the history of Germany.

"As long as I am willing to sacrifice my life for the German people, then the German people should do the same. If not, then they should be branded as traitors.

"You [members of the Reichstag] are responsible for the sentiment in your districts and individual groups throughout the country. I expect discipline from the German women, too, in this struggle. We stand together. We will meet all obstacles. If your will is strong enough, then we cannot fail. Sieg Heil!"

After the resolution to incorporate Danzig in the Reich [it was adopted unanimously] Marshal Goering spoke to the Reichstag. He said the German people would stand by the Chancellor to a man. They are resolved, he said, to bring his aims to pass as he stands behind the people.

"We expect you to do your duty to the utmost," said Marshal Goering. "We shall fight to the bitter end against the Poles."

Marshal Goering then proposed the following resolution:

"The Reich promises to stand behind the Fuehrer." That was acclaimed by "Deutschland Uber Alles," ending the session.

GDYNIA BLOCKADED BY GERMAN FLEET

Continued From Page One

nouncement Berlin's streets were still deserted except for the conventional early traffic, and there were no outward signs that the nation was finding itself in the first stages of war.

The government area was completely deserted, and the two guards doing sentry duty in front of the Chancellery remained their usual mute symbol of authority. It was only when official placards containing the orders to the populace began to appear on the billboards that early workers became aware of the situation.

Border Clashes Increase

Wireless to THE NEW YORK TIMES.

BERLIN, Friday, Sept. 1.—An increasing number of border incidents involving shooting and mutual Polish-German casualties are reported by the German press and radio. The most serious is reported from Gleiwitz, a German city on the line where the southwestern portion of Poland meets the Reich.

At 8 P. M., according to the semi-official news agency, a group of Polish insurrectionists forced an entrance into the Gleiwitz radio station, overpowering the watchmen and beating and generally mishandling the attendants. The Gleiwitz station was relaying a Breslau station's program, which was broken off by the Poles.

They proceeded to broadcast a prepared proclamation, partly in Polish and partly in German, announcing themselves as "the Polish Volunteer Corps of Upper Silesia speaking from the Polish station in Gleiwitz." The city, they alleged, was in Polish hands.

Gleiwitz's surprised radio listeners notified the police, who halted the broadcast and exchanged fire with the insurrectionists, killing one and capturing the rest. The police are said to have discovered that the attackers were assisted by regular Polish troops.

The Gleiwitz incident is alleged here to have been the signal "for a general attack by Polish francs-tireurs on German territory."

Two other points—Pitschen, near Kreuzburg, and Hochlinden, northeast of Ratibor, both in the same vicinity as Gleiwitz, were the scenes of violations of the German boundary, it is claimed, with fighting at both places still under way.

The attackers were all said to be heavily armed and supported by details of the regular Polish Army. But it is further reported that German border guards repulsed all the attempts.

Polish insurrectionists and soldiers are alleged to have stormed the Hochlinden Custom House, which was recaptured by Germans after a battle lasting for an hour and a half. The number of dead and wounded was not determined because of darkness, but fourteen Poles, including six soldiers, were captured.

Many Casualties Reported

In the Pitschen incident a band of 100 Poles, including soldiers, were said to have been surprised two kilometers on the German side of the frontier. They are accused of opening the fire, which was returned, resulting in the death of two Poles and the capture of fifteen, while the Germans lost one dead and many wounded.

Since Saturday Neuberstisch, near Gleiwitz, is said to have been subjected daily to Polish rifle and grenade attacks. These have seriously damaged property and communications.

Polish bands assisted by soldiers are also said to have attacked the railroad station in the Alt Eiche district of Rosenberg in East Prussia. They were repulsed by German machine gunners, the Poles losing an unknown number of men, the Germans one dead and one wounded, says the report.

In Katowice a Polish customs official is accused of forcing a German woman into Polish territory, although her companion escaped. Nothing is known of the whereabouts of the supposedly kidnapped woman.

Poles are accused also of endeavoring to cross the border and attempting to set fire to German houses. Germans report many attacks against Germans within Poland.

Poles Charge Border Violation

WARSAW, Aug. 31 (AP).—Polish sources asserted tonight that German patrols had crossed the border into Polish territory at several points. They also asserted that a German bomber had flown over Polish Silesia and had been pursued by Polish planes.

Daniels Becomes Dean Of Diplomats in Mexico

Wireless to THE NEW YORK TIMES.

MEXICO CITY, Aug. 31.—Ambassador Josephus Daniels has become dean of the diplomatic corps in Mexico City with the departure of Abelardo Rocas, Brazilian Ambassador, who has been appointed to a European post.

Mr. Rocas represented his government in the Mexican capital since 1931. Mr. Daniels, next in seniority, presented his credentials to President Ortiz Rugio on April 24, 1933.

The whole diplomatic corps conveyed personal congratulations to Mr. Daniels. He was the principal speaker at a farewell dinner given in Mr. Rocas's honor by the diplomatic corps last night, at which the guests included also Ambassador Manuel Bianchi of Chile and Minister Henri Goiran of France, who are about to leave this capital for other posts.

NO WAR MOVES IN SPAIN

Government's Attitude Reflects Desire to Avoid Conflict

Wireless to THE NEW YORK TIMES.

MADRID, Aug. 31.—Although the closest reserve is maintained concerning calls by Marshal Phillipe Pétain and Sir Maurice Peterson, the British and French Ambassadors, on Foreign Minister Juan Beigbeder yesterday, there is still no indication that Spain plans to enter Europe's threatened conflict.

There is no news of troop movements at the frontier, and the prices of shares here remain steady while other financial centers are registering intense alarm.

However, for the past three days the newspapers have taken a much more critical line toward "the intransigence of Britain and Poland." The Arriba, organ of the Falange Española, for example, argues that compromise has been a cardinal feature of British policy and asked why Prime Minister Chamberlain is so unyielding. Other newspapers feature stories from Berlin describing the calm and courage of the German people.

32 Die as Swedish Bridge Falls

Special Cable to THE NEW YORK TIMES.

STOCKHOLM, Aug. 31.—The new bridge joining the cities of Lunde and Sandoe across the River Aangermann, which has the largest concrete span in the world, collapsed today, killing thirty-two workers who were completing the structure. Apparently the workmen were just closing the span, which measures 720 feet, when some temporary timber supports failed.

BRITISH CHILDREN TAKEN FROM CITIES

Continued From Page One

dent witnessed was typical both of the method and the neighborhood. This was in Myrtle Street, Whitechapel. Its school had 180 children to be evacuated. They ranged in age from 5 to 16. A large proportion was Jewish.

The children arrived at the school, most of them with mothers or elder sisters, just as the sun came over the eastern horizon about 5:30 this morning. The teachers were already waiting for them outside the school. One teacher at the gate kept the relatives outside it. Only the children were passed through.

All apparently were children of poor families, but for this exodus they had been spruced up so that all were neat and clean. Every one, boy and girl alike, carried a knapsack over the shoulders, but the quality of the haversacks varied. Some were of real leather or rubberoid. Some were made out of pillowslips. In each were a change of clothes, toilet articles and a food package sufficient for the day. But there was one invariable piece of equipment. Each child carried a gas mask.

As they arrived in the school yard the teacher fastened onto each child a stout label on which were the child's name, number and school. When they were duly labeled they were marshaled into the assembly hall. There the headmistress told them that they were going on a holiday and that it would be nice to begin it with a little prayer. This was the prayer solemnly chanted in the treble child voices:

"May God take us all in His keeping and bring us safe back to our mummies."

Singing as They Wait

After that the children settled down to await their marching orders, an informal little gathering of chatterers in which groups formed and dissolved, wandered about and formed new groups. From time to time the teachers would start a song. One sang "Tipperary," reminiscent of the last war, and another was something about a "puff choo" train.

At 7 o'clock came the evacuation order with a male guide who was to see the children safely to the station and onto the train. The teachers marshaled the children out and they went along in a ragged procession, the smallest ones hand in hand, with the bigger ones interspersed among them.

It was only four blocks to the station, but every block was lined with anxious mothers who ran alongside with cautions and last messages, which again threatened to upset decorum. So after one block the headmistress called a halt and primly told the disturbers to leave because the children were getting excited. Some obeyed, but others just couldn't.

All along the street windows were opened and faces leaned out, the women weeping and the men calling out: "Keep smiling! Keep your head up and keep your feet dry!" The children began to feel that this was a really good joke and forgot their tears.

Nevertheless, it took fifteen minutes to traverse those four blocks to the station, and there the little scene was soon ended. The children lined up along the platform. There were no more tears, for the weeping mothers had been left outside.

In a few minutes along came a cheerfully lighted train. The children were shepherded aboard and the train went off to collect more elsewhere. When it departed the children were happily singing. This excursion was really turning out to be a grand holiday.

It will be three or four days before the evacuation is complete.

London with its millions of children, invalids and aged is naturally the biggest problem. There are 1,300,000 names on the London dispersal list alone, including 650,000 school children—that is, a half million in London proper and the rest in the contiguous area. But the most thorough preparations have been made, and it is all going along excellently.

The nine principal highways leading out of the metropolis, north, south, east and west, have been made one-way thoroughfares for traffic during the evacuation period. Ordinary suburban services have been curtailed, and during early hours the underground railways [subways] are being given over to evacuation trains. Some stations are wholly devoted to the exodus. Sixty of these trains will depart today.

School children are going first. They were notified yesterday of the hour at which they are to assemble in their schools. There they are being inspected and lined up for the journey. Their parents will take leave of them at the school gates. About 22,000 teachers and as many more guides and organizers and more thousands of locomotive engineers, conductors and omnibus drivers were up long before dawn getting ready to take care of the children.

The preparations for the children's comfort are most thorough. This is what each child is taking along: A gas mask, change of underclothing, house shoes, night dress, spare stockings, comb, toothbrush, towel, soap, face cloth, handkerchief, warm coat or macintosh and a packet of food for a day. Each child's name is written on strong paper and sewn to his or her clothes.

It is expected that 400,000 children will have left London before the day is over, and pupils of each school are moving altogether. But neither the children nor their parents know precisely where they are going. When they arrive, each child will send a postcard home telling where he or she is. The postcards are being taken along, but there comfortable quarters already have been prepared for all.

In response to a government appeal more than 1,000,000 rooms in country homes have been thrown open to the refugees. Those not thus cared for will be accommodated in schools and institutions. But private homes will house most of the children.

From London 151,000 are going to East Sussex, 83,000 to West Sussex, 154,000 to Kent, 124,000 to Essex, 95,000 to Surrey and 84,000 to Hertfordshire and all neighboring counties. Wales is taking care of 216,000 from Liverpool and Merseyside; 247,000 leaving Manchester are going to country villages in Lancashire, Cheshire, Shropshire, Staffordshire and Derbyshire, and 127,000 from the crowded streets of Newcastle and Gateshead are being distributed all over the North country.

From noon tomorrow onward mothers with children under 5, invalids, expectant mothers and blind persons will be evacuated. On Sunday and, if necessary, Monday, the remainder of these mothers with children under school age and school children who are going away with their parents, will be dispersed.

Arrangements for the evacuation of hospitals have been made especially thorough. Long ago some 250 large excursion coaches were outfitted as ambulances. The seats were made movable and the vehicles were prepared to receive stretchers. In these, patients will be taken to railway stations, where special trains will carry them to the country.

Under the new law that permits the government to billet either soldiers or civilians anywhere, owners of large country houses have been notified to be ready to receive invalids. Thus the great country houses of England are being turned into convalescent homes.

Acute cases, of course, cannot leave the hospitals. These must stay, but convalescents, slight cases and those patients recovering from operations are all being turned out, leaving room for air-raid casualties.

Mothers accompanying young children have been warned to take sufficient baggage but none is being permitted to take more than a little. Posters in schools and evacuation centers tell them what to take. At their destinations emergency rations, sufficient for the next forty-eight hours, are in readiness. After that those evacuated will take care of their own feeding where they are able, or the government will provide for them if they are unable.

There is no panic, no terror about this evacuation. The government has been anxious from the outset to have it understood it did not imply that war was inevitable; it would rather be in the nature of a rehearsal.

Walter Elliot, Minister of Health, Elliot, "asked me tell you that this broadcasting last night made this clear.

"The Prime Minister," said Mr. evacuation does not mean war is certain. This is insurance—a thing which ought to be done now.

"It will require patience, skill and cheerfulness — especially cheerfulness. The nation has a task before it to call out its strength and all its sympathy. I am sure we shall rise to it.

"By Monday night, no later, we will have given the world another example of what a free people—a people that puts its back into the work and its heart into the job—can do."

In that spirit it is being taken. Never did the stout souls of British plain folk show to better advantage. Never did the innate courtesy and kindness of the whole populace and the generous hospitality and readiness to help of the well-to-do shine more clearly. It is typical of that spirit and of the real piety of this land that the British Broadcasting Company held over the radio tonight a short religious service in which God was besought to comfort parents separated from their children and give courage to children and invalids, many of whom are leaving home for the first time.

No American could hear that or could witness the scenes of cheerful fortitude at schools, in little homes, in streets and at railway stations unmoved. This is a stanch and true people. In any "war of nerves" it is not they who will falter.

Lists Evacuation Areas

LONDON, Aug. 31 (AP).—The British Ministry of Health announced tonight that evacuation of children and others would be from the following areas:

Greater London, which includes London County Council area, the county boroughs of West Ham and East Ham, the boroughs of Walthamstow, Leyton, Ilford and Barking in Essex;

The boroughs of Tottenham, Hornsey, Willesden, Acton and Edmonton in Middlesex; the Medway towns of Chatham, Gillingham and Rochester; Dagenham, Thurrock, Gravesend and Northfleet, Portsmouth, Gosport and Southampton, Birmingham and Smethwick, Liverpool, Bootle, Birkenhead, Wallasley and Crosby.

Manchester, Salford and Stretford, Sheffield, Leeds, Bradford, Hull and Rotherham, Newcastle and Gateshead, Runcorn and Widnes and in Scotland, Edinburgh, Glasgow, Dundee, Clydebank and Rosyth.

POINTS OF EVACUATION

The major population centers shown here are designated in Britain's order of evacuation, effective today. Associated Press

"All the News That's Fit to Print."

The New York Times.

LATE CITY EDITION
Partly cloudy today, showers tonight, little change in temperature. Tomorrow showers.
Temperatures Yesterday—Max., 64; Min., 53

Copyright, 1940, by The New York Times Company.

VOL. LXXXIX...No. 30,077. Entered as Second-Class Matter, Postoffice, New York, N. Y. NEW YORK, THURSDAY, MAY 30, 1940. THREE CENTS NEW YORK CITY and Vicinity | FOUR CENTS Elsewhere Except in 7th and 8th Postal Zones.

ALLIES ABANDONING FLANDERS, FLOOD YSER AREA; A RESCUE FLEET AT DUNKERQUE; FOE POUNDS PORT; ONE FORCE CUT OFF FROM THE SEA AS LILLE FALLS

PRESIDENT TO ASK $750,000,000 MORE FOR ARMY PROGRAM

Nazi Blitzkrieg Held to Show the $3,300,000,000 Allotted Fails to Meet Needs

FOR TANKS, GUNS, PLANES

Tax Bill to Be Offered in House Today—D. M. Nelson Named Procurement Director

By FELIX BELAIR Jr.
Special to THE NEW YORK TIMES.

WASHINGTON, May 29—On the eve of his first meeting with the reconstituted Council of National Defense, President Roosevelt was putting finishing touches today on a new request for $750,000,000 as a supplemental appropriation for further expansion and mechanization of the military establishment to take account of European war developments since he sent his preparedness message to Congress two weeks ago.

The projected increase in funds for the Army, over and above the omnibus $3,300,000,000 defense program already pending, was mapped by the President in a White House conference with Treasury and War Department officials.

It was the President's plan to send up the supplemental request in a few days. Subject to additions, the new program contemplates placing orders immediately for the following:

About 3,000 new pursuit and bombing planes.

Between 1,500 and 2,000 tanks.

About 500 heavy howitzers.

A supply of aerial bombs of various sizes, to cost between $20,000,000 and $30,000,000.

Other modern weapons of war which have been developed in Army laboratories, but not yet put into actual production.

German Drive Appraised

There was no official announcement on the results of the meeting, and Secretary Woodring, who acted as spokesman for the group, said only that they had reviewed "the whole military situation."

From others present, however, it was learned that the nation's military preparedness had been reappraised in the light of Germany's advances in Western Europe since the President's preparedness message was first submitted to Congress.

Other developments in the national defense program were:

1. The Senate Naval Affairs Committee brought out a measure increasing the air force limit of the Navy to 10,000 planes and 16,000 pilots, with a report warning that the "country at this time is facing the possibility that the Allies may be defeated and that we may have to defend ourselves in both oceans at the same time."

2. Senate leaders were planning to take up tomorrow the $1,500,000,000 bill providing an 11 per cent increase in under-age surface tonnage, with indications that the measure would be disposed of without delay.

Procurement Officer Named

3. Secretary Morgenthau named Donald M. Nelson, executive vice president of Sears, Roebuck & Co., as director of the Treasury's Procurement Division, thereby adding another business executive to the list of those on whom the administration is relying for the success of the defense program.

4. Administration - Congressional plans for placing emergency rearmament financing on a "pay-as-you-go" basis gathered momentum, with an announcement by Representative Doughton, chairman of the House Ways and Means Committee, that he would introduce tomorrow a measure raising the statutory debt limit by $3,000,000,000 and imposing upward of $656,000,000 in new defense taxes.

5. Secretary Hull modified aviation restrictions under the Neutrality Act to permit the delivery of American planes by American pilots to Halifax, N. S., thereby removing the ban on through deliveries over the Maritime Provinces.

6. White House sources explained that there would be the closest possible relations between Presi-

Continued on Page Eight

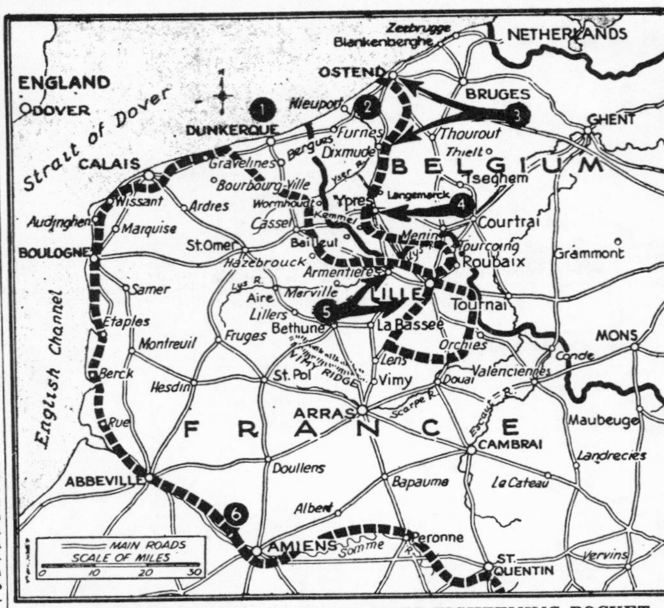

ALLIES STRIKE FOR COAST IN EVER-TIGHTENING POCKET

To keep the exit at Dunkerque (1) open French and British sea, land and air forces were waging a furious struggle yesterday; to retard the German advance the Allies were understood to have opened sluice gates on the Yser to flood the region below Nieuport (2). In the sector that had been held by the Belgians the Nazis pushed to Ostend and Dixmude (3). Farther south they were reported to have taken Ypres (4). Their most important operation of the day, however, was the bisecting of the pocket by the capture of Lille and Armentieres (5), thus cutting off from the sea the Allied forces in the lower section. Along the Somme the French eliminated a German bridgehead west of Amiens (6). The broken lines show the approximate battlefronts.

HULL ORDER SPEEDS PLANES TO ALLIES

Allows Our Pilots to Fly Craft Over Three Canadian Maritime Provinces

Special to THE NEW YORK TIMES.

WASHINGTON, May 29—The way was opened today for expediting deliveries of American airplanes to the Allied fighting lines when Secretary Hull modified regulations of the Neutrality Act to permit the delivery of such aircraft by American pilots to ports in the three eastern Canadian Provinces.

The step was designed to facilitate deliveries to the Allies because of the urgency of their military situation. It was taken at the request of the French Government.

Mr. Hull ruled that "American nationals may travel in belligerent aircraft over the Canadian Provinces of New Brunswick, Nova Scotia and Prince Edward Island." This means that pilots from the United States may fly new planes to Halifax, whence they will be flown across the Atlantic by pilots of the Allies or sent across by ship.

American pilots have been delivering planes in Ottawa and other Canadian cities. As before, they must still conform under the new order to regulations by pushing planes over the Canadian border from the United States.

Previously, while American pilots could fly planes over Canadian territory, once they were pushed over the border the fliers could not enter the three eastern maritime Provinces because American ships are barred from them and aircraft regulations conform to shipping rules. Newfoundland was excluded from the modification today because there was no actual need for including it.

The Department of Commerce announced that April shipments of aircraft and equipment to the Allies included 195 planes and 285 engines.

Of the planes, France received seventy completely powered craft and ninety-eight in a knock-down condition. The United Kingdom obtained twenty-three assembled and powered and Canada four.

Of the engines, 230 went to France, forty-three to Canada and twelve to the United Kingdom. The French plane acquisitions were valued at $9,176,538, those of the United Kingdom at $2,139,000 and those of Canada at $286,298.

With a variety of other equipment included, French purchases for the month totaled $14,443,071; those of the United Kingdom $2,908,621 and those of Canada $728,929.

The Department of Commerce announced that total exports of aero-

Continued on Page Ten

Berlin Exchange Slumps As Optimism Is Decried

Wireless to THE NEW YORK TIMES.

BERLIN, May 29—In what was apparently a strong reaction to warnings against over-optimism, which have been circulated generally among the population following the German victories in the West, the Berlin Boerse today took a sudden nose dive.

Most issues dropped between 1 and 4 per cent. In shipping, Hapag dropped 5 per cent and North German Lloyd dropped 3 per cent. Fixed interest securities were quiet and generally unchanged. The close was irregular, with call money at $1\frac{7}{8}$-$2\frac{1}{8}$.

Utilities, motor works and other heavy industries led the recession, while metal works in the Rhineland were among those that showed the maximum decline.

URUGUAY ON GUARD FOR FIFTH COLUMN

Check on Assembly, Increase in Army Urged—Nazis Take Bold Tone in Ecuador

Special Cable to THE NEW YORK TIMES.

MONTEVIDEO, Uruguay, May 29—The Uruguayan Government is frankly alarmed over Nazi fifth column activities.

After several Cabinet meetings at which the problem was closely studied, President Alfredo Baldomir has sent to Congress, with a request for urgent action, two bills. One provides for general rearmament and the other modifies Article 38 of the Constitution, which guarantees the right of assembly.

It has been rumored in well-informed diplomatic circles in more than one South American capital yesterday and today that Uruguay fears an invasion of Nazi fifth columnists from Southern Brazil. Official circles tonight emphatically denied any such fear and also denied that Uruguay had requested assistance from any other government.

The President's office earlier in the day, however, had published the details of the plans for rearmament and for modifying the constitutional guarantees.

Article 38 of the Constitution says that "all persons have a right to form themselves into associations," whatever may be the object sought, except they do not constitute an association declared by law to be illicit.

Since the law doesn't define what constitutes an illicit association, the bill that President Baldomir sent to Congress yesterday defines such il-

Continued on Page Six

ITALY BARS IMPORTS EXCEPT BY BARTER

Cancels Permits to Bring In Goods or to Buy Exchange for Payments Abroad

By HERBERT L. MATTHEWS
By Telephone to THE NEW YORK TIMES.

ROME, May 29—The Ministry of Foreign Exchange issued an order today to all banks and industrial firms canceling permits for importation and permission to acquire foreign currency to pay for imports. Thus Italy cuts herself off commercially from the world, except for barter agreements, and even there Italian ships coming in are not departing to bring back further imports.

This is the most serious indication yet given of the expectation of war, certainly as serious as the postponement of the sailing of Italian vessels announced last Friday.

The Conte di Savoia is due back from New York Sunday. No one expects her to depart, even on June 23, when she is scheduled to go. That will leave only the Conte Grande out of the Mediterranean among the large Italian ships. She sailed for South America a week ago.

[The steamship Roma arrived yesterday at Naples, according to The Associated Press, and is now expected to remain there instead of proceeding to Genoa, as scheduled. The Roma was to have left Genoa for New York June 29.]

Trade with the United States will suffer most heavily by the decision taken today. It has been possible for importers to acquire dollars at

Continued on Page Four

11,000 Times Speedier Way Found To Obtain Atomic Power Element

By WILLIAM L. LAURENCE

Development of a process that speeds up by 11,000 times the extraction of U-235, the element recently discovered to possess 5,000,000 times the power output of coal, promising to make it possible to utilize atomic energy as a new source of enormous power for all purposes, and to place in the hands of the nations at war, especially Germany, the most powerful fuel ever to be discovered, is to be announced in the forthcoming issue of Nature, leading British scientific weekly, advance proofs of which have reached THE NEW YORK TIMES.

Germany, more than any other European nation, has been concentrating on developing this power.

If the tests succeed the Allied blockade could be materially offset.

The new process for extracting U-235 that promises to revolutionize methods of power production and to usher in a new civilization based on the utilization of atomic power, was developed by Professor Wilhelm Krasny-Ergen of the Wenner-Grens Institute, Stockholm, Sweden, one of the leading scientific research institutions in Europe.

On May 5 it was announced that a tiny amount of U-235, a relative of uranium, had been isolated at the University of Minnesota and at the General Electric Company, and that pioneer experiments at the physics laboratories at Columbia University, under the direction of Professor

Continued on Page Eighteen

NAZIS TIGHTEN TRAP

They Drive a Line Across Pocket, Encircling Foes in South

SAY YPRES IS TAKEN

Zeebrugge and Ostend Fall—Large Stores Are Reported Seized

By GEORGE AXELSSON
Wireless to THE NEW YORK TIMES.

BERLIN, May 29—Remnants of the Allied Armies cut off in Flanders came a step nearer to being wiped out today when the Germans, simultaneously pressing from east and west toward the middle, managed to drive a wedge right across the pocket, thus separating the French and British divisions north of Lille from those in the south, who now are surrounded on all sides, no longer having access to the sea.

The Germans tonight claim to be in the city of Lille, in Ypres and Armentières and to have burned Dunkerque under heavy artillery bombardment. The Belgian capitulation permitted the Germans to take Bruges, Zeebrugge, Ostend and Thourout without a struggle.

Piercing the Allied lines at Lille, where, however, fortifications still seem to hold out, permitted the Germans to make two pockets out of the big one. The smaller of these, south of Lille, is square with the sides between nine and twelve miles long, and inside this narrow space are compressed the French divisions that only a few days ago tried to break the strong German hold at Valenciennes, as well as British contingents that figured in desperate resistance in the sector between Arras and Cambrai.

Refugees Also in Trap

Hemmed in with these troops is an incalculable number of refugees and other civilians, who are exposed to bombs and shell fire on the same terms as the soldiers fighting one another in this area.

The larger northern pocket reaches from Lille to the sea, and although it is some thirty miles wide the situation of the troops enclosed in it appears to be hardly less enviable than that of their comrades surrounded to the south. They are being hard pressed on three sides by withering German fire as well as from the air.

Their only chance of retreat, should they choose this way out, seems to be the narrow strip of coast between Dunkerque and Nieuport, but the Germans are said to be continuously shelling and bombing this district, making an exit, even if protected by Allied warships, seem most difficult.

Crowded together in an area bounded by Dixmude, Ypres—which the Germans claim to have taken by storm tonight—Armentières, Bailleul and Bergues, remnants of the British Expeditionary Force and whatever French and Belgians remain thereabout appear to have a choice only between death or surrender.

The situation up there, according to latest reports received in Berlin, indicates that the Allies have chosen to fight to the last. The Germans now stand before Dixmude, where the British are holding them, and a similarly bitter struggle is raging at

Continued on Page Four

The International Situation

On the Battle Fronts

The Battle of Flanders became yesterday a wholly rear-guard action, with the Allies trying to evacuate as many as possible of the troops caught in the German pocket. The trapped men fought on "desperately but not despairingly," Paris reported. [Page 1.]

The port of Dunkerque was still in Allied hands (although the Germans reported its embarkation area in ruins), as was Nieuport, just above the Belgian border. Ships were said to be waiting at the coast to take off the men who could get to them, although how they stayed afloat in the torrent of German bombing seemed a mystery. The British and French fleets were furiously bombarding German forces on the Channel, hoping to cover the withdrawal. The task of evacuation was made doubly difficult by a German force that, Paris reported, had straddled the Franco-Belgian border near Cassel and Mount Kemmel. The French said that defense flooding gates had been opened, inundating part of the area west of the Yser. On other fronts the French asserted that they had eliminated a German bridgehead on the Somme west of Amiens, and had repulsed a German thrust near Rethel, on the left flank of the invaders. [Included in the foregoing.]

The desperate situation of the Allied army of the north was made evident by Berlin dispatches telling of the success of the German effort to cut the opposing forces in two. The invaders drove a wedge between the two Allied wings to the north of Lille. Thus there are now two pockets; the forces south of Lille are completely surrounded, in a square-shaped area whose sides measure only nine to twelve miles. The pocket above Lille was greatly reduced by German advances pressing down from the north and up from the south. [Page 1.]

Early this morning shattered remnants of the British Expeditionary Force began arriving at British ports. Most of them were wounded. To the survivors still in Flanders King George sent a message saying they had displayed "gallantry that has never been surpassed in the annals of the British Army." [Page 1.]

The Allies recorded a victory in Norway. They took Narvik, and the Germans admitted its loss. The British said their warships had sunk seven German troop transports in the Narvik area in the last three days. [Page 1.]

Repercussions Elsewhere

Britain took drastic measures to guard against possible fifth column activities on the part of aliens. Beginning June 3, all aliens must be in their "ordinary place of residence" from 10:30 P. M. to 6 A. M.; they are forbidden to own bicycles, boats or aircraft without special permission. [Page 3.]

Italy, by decreeing an end to import and foreign currency permits, cut herself off from the world commercially, except for her barter arrangements. And even they have ceased to mean anything, as Italian vessels no longer are being sent abroad for cargoes. The new regulations gave the strongest indication yet of Italy's intention to join Germany in the field soon. [Page 1.]

Because Russia had refused to accept Sir Stafford Cripps, Left-Wing Labor member of the British Parliament, as a "special trade envoy," London conferred Ambassadorial status on him. Sir Stafford is in Athens, en route to Moscow. With offers of improved trade with Britain, he will seek to woo Russia away from Germany. [Page 4.]

The Nazi fifth-column technique stirred fears in South America. Uruguay's Congress received from President Baldomir two bills, one of which would provide for rearmament, the other modifying the Constitution to deny the right of assembly to anti-democratic organizations with foreign connections. [Page 1.]

What has happened in Flanders impelled a reappraisal in Washington of American defense plans, with the result that President Roosevelt decided to ask Congress for $750,000,000 (in addition to the $3,300,000,000 already projected) to be used to buy 3,000 pursuit and bombing planes, 1,500 tanks, 500 heavy howitzers and at least $20,000,000 in aerial bombs. [Page 1.]

The Senate Naval Affairs Committee, recommending House-adopted bills to speed air and naval preparedness, said the country's defense plans must be based on the possibility of defeat for the Allies. [Page 9.]

ALLIES GET NARVIK IN LAND-SEA FIGHT

Warships Support Troops in Final Thrust From Bels and Rombaks Fjords

By JAMES MacDONALD
Special Cable to THE NEW YORK TIMES.

LONDON, May 29—Narvik, Norway's important iron ore port, the prize of an unrelenting struggle ever since Germany invaded Norway on April 9, has been captured by Allied forces, the War Office and Admiralty announced in a joint communiqué today. The communiqué also announced the capture of Narvik Fagernaes, on the shore of Narvik Harbor, and Forsneset, five miles east of Narvik on the railway line over which Swedish iron ore reaches Narvik for shipment to Germany.

Fierce fighting by Norwegian, French, British and Polish forces continues in the district. An unofficial report received here today said British naval forces had sunk seven German troop transports in Narvik waters since Sunday.

British warships are reported high up in Rombaks Fjord, shelling German positions on the Ofoten railway. In a narrow part of the fjord the Germans have sunk four ships in an attempt to block off the British naval vessels.

Other reports reaching London today said German planes had raided Bodoe, at the entrance to Vest Fjord, about ninety miles south of Narvik, last evening, dropping 300 bombs and machine-gunning the town. Of the population of 6,000, it is said at least 5,000 are now

Continued on Page Five

HARRIED B. E. F. MEN ARRIVING IN BRITAIN

Many of Wounded Had to Wade Out to Boats Under Constant Fire of German Forces

By The United Press.

LONDON, Thursday, May 30—Shattered remnants of the British Expeditionary Force—blood-stained, muddy and walking like men asleep—began arriving in British ports early today.

Most of the first arrivals were wounded. They described a constant, pitiless German bombing and strafing bombardment of the French ports from which Viscount Gort is attempting to save his trapped divisions.

They said the shattered British forces were "sliding off a stretch of coast thirty miles long."

German bombs rained down continually, even on hospital ships, they said. Quays and harbor works of the French ports were under terrific German air attack, which went on all through last night.

Allied warships and the Royal Air Force worked and fought like beavers to aid the rescue of the battered armies of Flanders whose fate was teetered on the Channel's brink. Under a screen of intense curtain fire from long-range naval guns, the B. E. F. was backing out through the Dunkerque area.

Continued on Page Five

Dispatches from Europe and the Far East are subject to censorship at the source.

COAST FIGHT RAGES

Communications Lines and Bases Bombarded Constantly by Nazis

DUNKERQUE SHELLED

Allies Inflicting Heavy Losses as They Battle in Rear-Guard Actions

By G. H. ARCHAMBAULT
Wireless to THE NEW YORK TIMES.

PARIS, May 29—The full import of the Belgian defection during the course of the battle in Flanders may be gathered from the indication given tonight by a spokesman for the General Staff that King Leopold's army represented about half the Allied forces engaged on that front.

French and British in that area continue to fight desperately, though not despairingly yet, with the knowledge that at present at least little help can be given them. Their valor is described as very comforting in the circumstances, and it is added that whatever happens their honor will be safe.

Breaking the anonymity rule that has prevailed hitherto, it is announced this evening that, under General Georges Maurice Jean Blanchard's direction, General René-Jacques-Adolf Prioux is striving to fight his way to the coast in the general direction of Dunkerque, where Vice Admiral Jean Marie Abrial of the French Navy is cooperating and is holding that base, where he has organized a service of supplies with vessels of all kinds of tonnage.

Prioux a Cavalry Man

General Prioux was a corps commander at the beginning of the war; he is sixty-one years of age and comes from the cavalry arm.

No one has yet come from that inferno in Flanders to describe the scene; doubtless it baffles the imagination. For the battle is being waged on land, in the air, on the sea and under the sea. Every engine of death yet devised by man is in action and the fight never ceases day or night. Nor is it confined to the actual battlefield. All bases, all lines of communication are bombed continually on both sides, with the Germans concentrating a great effort on Dunkerque.

The communiqué issued from French General Headquarters this morning said that "information from accurate sources warrants the affirmation that the losses suffered by the Germans in the engagements yesterday and last night were particularly high."

The French and British are fighting mostly rear-guard actions against very superior numbers, but whenever any unit finds itself in approximately equal strength it counter-attacks "to progress over the enemy dead."

Position Very Critical

Nevertheless despite heroic deeds it cannot be gainsaid that the position of the Allied division is very critical.

The exact position of General Blanchard's forces is not known; his front in any case must be very fluid. Doubtless he has shortened his lines in order to constitute a sort of mobile fortress moving toward the sea and fighting every inch of the way. The tragic aspect of his situation lies in the fact that the prime task of Leopold's army was to cover the coast.

It is revealed today in this connection that it was at the Belgian King's repeated insistence that the Allies took up positions on the Scheldt to protect Antwerp and also that the order to retreat was deferred until May 15, although the Allied High Command had urged withdrawal on the eleventh or twelfth.

There is confirmation today of the indication given yesterday in these dispatches that before the capitulation there were French detachments between the Belgians and the sea. It is hoped that though relatively small they have acted effectively along the coast. It is believed, moreover, that it has been possible to flood part of the country west of the Yser River. Water lines of this sort proved of great value in the last war in this very region.

On the coast the Allies have lost Ostend. They hold Nieuport and

Continued on Page Two

BELGIANS FORMING AN ARMY IN FRANCE

Have Equipment for 60,000—Rump Parliament to Pass on Status Tomorrow

KING BELIEVED AT LAEKEN

Government Leaders Predict Pressure on Him to Set Up a Pro-Nazi Government

By P. J. PHILIP

Wireless to THE NEW YORK TIMES.

PARIS, May 29—King Leopold of the Belgians has, according to all accounts that have reached here from Belgian and other sources, returned to his palace at Laeken near Brussels, which his mother, Dowager Queen Elizabeth, had refused to leave even when Brussels was occupied by German troops.

Belgian informants say that his decision to surrender was taken on the advice of General van Overstraeten, who was known to be a Nazi sympathizer.

The King's children were, until two days ago, in the care of their father's aunt in a town in Central France. A report has been published since that they have arrived by road in Lisbon, Portugal, but this is believed unlikely.

Van Zeeland Back From U. S.

Former Premier Paul van Zeeland arrived in Paris today from the United States and had an immediate interview with the present Premier, Hubert Pierlot, at the Belgian Embassy.

Lieut. Gen. Henri Denis, the Defense Minister, has already taken in hand the recruitment and organization of a new army from among the refugees and the elements of the Belgian Army already in France.

In an interview this morning, Foreign Minister Paul-Henri Spaak reiterated what Premier Pierlot said yesterday: That any act of government attempted by King Leopold would be accounted null and that the only government that had the right to speak and act in the name of Belgium was that now situated in Paris.

"Our disagreement with the King," said M. Spaak, "was not on the issue of capitulation, because before we left he told us nothing of his intention to capitulate. But we left him with the impression that everything was finished between us. There was between him and us complete disagreement on everything."

See Nazi Pressure on Leopold

PARIS, May 29 (UP)—Adolf Hitler may attempt to persuade King Leopold to outlaw Belgium's refugee government and form a new Cabinet to cooperate with Germany, Belgian leaders claimed today.

It was said that any attempt by the 38-year-old King to get rid of the present Cabinet would be unconstitutional unless he could assemble a majority of Parliament in Brussels to effect the overthrow.

The Belgian rump Parliament will convene in the City Hall at Limoges Friday to define Belgium's status, fix Leopold's legal position and perfect plans for recruiting an army of 300,000 men. There are fifty Senators and Deputies in the French town now and at least fifty more are expected. [Belgium has 167 Senators and 203 Representatives.]

The rump Parliament steering committee took its initial act yesterday in unanimously endorsing Premier Hubert Pierlot's radio broadcast divesting Leopold of his royal powers and pledging to continue the war.

In the early days of the invasion the Belgian Government took the precaution of sending to France full army equipment for 60,000 men. It was said this equipment would suffice for the first new army units.

In addition to these supplies, the Belgian Government exported 23,000,000,000 francs in gold to the United States and England. It was said this sum would be sufficient to complete the new army's rudimentary equipment.

The Belgian Government last night informed Governor General Pierre Ryckmans of Belgian Congo that he was to ignore Leopold's surrender order and that Belgium was still at war.

It was believed the Cabinet would conscript all Belgian males of military age in France, estimated to total 250,000, and add to them 50,000 volunteers under and above military age. All able-bodied Belgians of military age have had their conscript training and thus would be ready for action sooner than the Czechs and the Poles, who required six months of special training.

It was foreseen that the Belgian Government would take a census of potential conscripts early next month and call the first batch of recruits to camp before the end of June.

BERMUDA WAR AID UP

Contribution to Britain Increased From £20,000 to £40,000

Special Cable to THE NEW YORK TIMES.

HAMILTON, Bermuda, May 29—The Assembly has increased to £40,000 its immediate war contribution to the Imperial Government, passing through second and third readings a bill that originally carried £20,000.

Several members strongly urged a contribution of £200,000, and sentiment in the Assembly appeared favorable. However, there was no agreement as to whether the full £200,000 should be voted immediately or spread over a period of years. The Assembly decided to wait until the commitee considering new taxation measures presented its report.

At present Bermuda has an unbalanced budget and new taxes are fully expected to be necessary before the end of this year.

French General's Sons Killed

PARIS, May 29 (AP)—Two aviator sons of General Victor Leon Ernest Denain, former Air Minister, have been killed in action within twelve days of each other. Jacques Denain was killed in a "dog fight" May 13. His brother, Jean, was shot down May 25 while returning from a reconnaissance flight.

The Texts of the Day's War Communiques

German

BERLIN, May 29 (AP)—The text of today's German High Command communiqué follows:

The fate of the French armies in Artois is sealed. Their resistance in the region south of Lille collapsed. The English Army, which was hemmed together in the region of Dixmude, Armentieres, Bailleul and Bergues, west of Dunkerque, also are facing destruction through our concentrated attack.

Bruges was passed in the swift advance through Northern Flanders, Ostend was taken and Dixmude reached. On the Yser [River] and the Yser Canal, north of Ypres, the enemy was still offering desperate resistance. The Reich's war flag is flying over the memorial of German youth at Langemarck, the scene of their courageous fights in 1914.

Lille has been reached in the attack from the east and west. The city has been taken. In an advance from the west, Armentieres was occupied. At Bailleul there is still fighting. East of Cassel, a fortified French border position that was defended by the opponent with a reversed front, was broken through and the Belgian border reached. At Wormhoudt the fighting is still in progress.

On May 28 the air force raided retreating columns and all kinds of troop concentrations and tanks. In the course of armed reconnaissance off the Belgian and French coast and in the Channel, three destroyers and two transports and two freighters were bombed and seriously damaged. One enemy submarine was sunk by a bomb in the Central North Sea. Destruction of an additional submarine was probable.

Despite unfavorable weather, German speedboats succeeded off Nieuport in sinking by torpedo hit a big enemy destroyer on flight to England. On the south front, isolated attacks by enemy infantry and tanks were repulsed.

The losses of the enemy in the air amounted to twenty-four planes on May 28. Of these, sixteen were shot down in an air fight and eight by anti-aircraft. Three German airplanes are missing.

Colonel Moelders scored his twentieth air victory. The number of enemy planes shot down by anti-aircraft in the period from May 16 to 25 increased from the hitherto announced 100 to 265, according to exact information.

The number of airplanes thus brought down by anti-aircraft since May 5 amount to 607. In addition, the air defense during the same period destroyed 101 enemy armored cars.

In Norway the enemy, supported by numerous warships, landed on the ore railway yesterday and entered Narvik from the north. German fighting units raided enemy naval forces lying there. One large battleship sustained a serious hit amidships and ceased firing after being enveloped in smoke. Three cruisers and one destroyer, as well as one freighter, were heavily hit by bombs. Troop debarkations at Ankenes were attacked with many bombs.

A special High Command announcement said:

Our troops, pressing their attack aimed at the destruction of the English Army, stormed Ypres and Kemmel.

British

LONDON, May 29 (UP)—An Admiralty-War Office communiqué issued today follows:

Information was received this morning that Narvik was captured last night by the Allied forces and that Fagernes and Forsneset are also in our hands.

LONDON, May 29 (AP)—The text of an Air Ministry communiqué follows:

The Royal Air Force continues to give all support in its power to the Allied armies in Northwestern France and Belgium.

Railways, roads, bridges and enemy troops were continuously attacked yesterday, last night and today by medium and heavy bombers. The enemy's advance has been considerably harassed and impeded by these attacks. One of our bombers has failed to return.

Our fighters have been engaged in offensive patrols over the French coast throughout today. Near Dunkerque this evening a formation of Hurricanes and Defiants engaged large forces of enemy bombers heavily escorted by fighters.

At least twenty-two enemy aircraft were shot down. All our aircraft returned.

French

PARIS, May 29 (AP)—The night French communiqué follows:

French and British fighting in the north of France are undergoing with a heroism worthy of their traditions a struggle of exceptional intensity.

For fifteen days they have been giving battle, cut off from the bulk of our armies by German forces constantly reinforced. Attacked incessantly on their two flanks, east and west, they are disputing the ground with the enemy, hanging on to the ground and counterattacking with both stubborness and bravery.

While they withstood these attacks the Allied [Belgian] Army that was under direct command of King Leopold III and defended the positions of the Escaut [Scheldt] River and the coast northeast of Ostend received from its King the order to cease firing, opening to the enemy the route to Ypres, Furnes and Dunkerque.

From that moment our troops under the command of Generals Blanchard and Prioux, and in close collaboration with the British Army of General Gort, have had to face increased danger. Displaying under these grave circumstances indomitable resolution, they are endeavoring to move toward the sea at the cost of the hardest fighting.

The French Navy is giving them powerful support in defense of ports and communication lines. Under the command of Admiral Abrial, the navy is employing a very great number of ships and is engaged in supplying the fortified camp of Dunkerque and the troops based on it.

Land and naval aviation are cooperating constantly.

On the Somme front fierce attacks by our troops allowed us today to reduce the bridgehead that the enemy had occupied to the south of the river. We took several hundred prisoners.

Nothing of importance to report on the rest of the front.

The High Command's morning communiqué said:

Our troops are resisting in the north with admirable courage against fierce efforts of the enemy.

Positive information permits affirmation that losses suffered by the Germans during combats yesterday and last night were particularly high.

On the Somme and Aisne [rivers] local actions were conducted with successes. An enemy raid was thrown back southwest of Chateau Porcien East of the Aisne there were no actions during the night.

COAST FIGHT RAGES AS ALLIES RETREAT

Continued From Page One

Dunkerque. The fate of Calais may be decided very soon since the Allies have only "some elements" there now. In these conditions the retreat logically should be toward a line of which Dunkerque marks the middle.

Prior to the Belgian defection the Allies held a line from Calais to Douai thence northward, encircling Lille, Roubaix and Tourcoing—a triple city which forms the heart of the French textile industry—to Menin on the Belgian border. Thereafter to the coast stood the Belgians. Their elimination necessitated a reduction of the front with the consequence that Lille, Roubaix and Tourcoing are now strongly menaced; fierce actions were fought today on their outskirts. [Here twenty-nine words were censored].

[The industrial city of Lille has been abandoned under intensive German attacks from two sides, The United Press reported.]

Meanwhile the French continue to apply pressure on the Somme. An action was begun by them yesterday morning with the object of eliminating a German bridgehead west of Amiens. The operation ended in complete success today with the capture of three villages and several hundred prisoners.

On the Aisne a German raid was repulsed southwest of Château Porcien in the vicinity of Rethel. Along the Maginot Line from the Moselle River to the Rhine all was quiet again today, but along the Rhine itself, especially in the upper portion of its course, French heavy guns were in action harassing lines of communication in Baden.

Battle Held Virtually Over

PARIS, May 29 (AP)—The Allies tonight gave up as lost the Battle of Flanders and, in a great retreat, opened the flood sluices around Dunkerque to guard their last port of escape on the sea.

The conflict in the north was all but over. The Germans thus were left substantially in control of France's northern industrial region and her northwest coast, across from England.

At least the battle had given the Allies time to build a strong southern front along the Somme and Aisne Rivers for 200 miles across France.

While the waters rose steadily in the vast system of streams around Dunkerque, French divisions fought to hold the rear while British troops defended the main points of passage for the main forces seeking the coastline.

The Allies brought on the inundation by opening the locks southwest and northeast of Dunkerque on the great canal that flows by the city and follows the coast for many miles.

In Dunkerque the last Allied resistance was rallied under Vice Admiral Jean Marie Abrial. The Allied armies, navies and air forces fought together in an effort to save as much as possible from the wreckage of Flanders.

Some Belgian units, refusing to lay down their arms despite their King's order to capitulate, were reported still fighting beside the British and French.

Airplanes Are Active

A single French division, which had been stationed with the Belgians as the backbone of their front, tried to hold back the Nazi rush in the Nieuport-Dixmude sector, a World War battlefield on the coast northeast of Dunkerque.

Suicide squads also held out on the eastern and southern sides of the Allied path to the sea. Some Allied units had to fight through German columns.

Airplanes tangled in the heavy clouds hanging over the battle area. Allied navy dive-bombers, using the low-flying tactics they employ against submarines and warships, plunged on German tanks.

American-made bombers, newly arrived, operated effectively, but too late to turn the tide.

The Germans made Lille, the industrial center of Northern France, and Calais, on the Channel Straits of Dover, particular battlegrounds. But their advance was slowed by Allied sharpshooters waging guerrilla warfare in thee fields and fighting in the streets of the cities.

And tonight, toward the vital city of Dunkerque, the bulk of an entrapped army of half a million was backing.

Supplies Held Adequate

The French admiral in command there reported that he was "satisfied with the supply situation," and at the same time ships were bringing in more and more food and munitions.

Also, while the French port of Calais—the nearest to England on the Strait of Dover—was reported partly occupied by the Germans, the French spokesman said some French troops still were holding out there.

Today the Germans had claimed the capture of Lille, an important fortified industrial city, and to have cut off in a subsidiary pocket to the south French troops previously isolated, in the large triangle held by the Germans, from their British comrades in arms.

Thus these twice isolated Frenchmen apparently had no specific objective toward which to fall back, but merely to retreat somewhere, or anywhere.

The main German attack was reported directed toward Cassel, northwest of Lille and about midway between that city and the English Channel. Cassel lies thirty miles southeast of Calais.

In the English Channel and the North Sea German torpedo speedboats went out to challenge British seapower, while German planes attacked from the sky.

German losses in aviation crews, particularly the young and insufficiently trained fliers manning dive bombers, along with the wear and tear of twenty days of Blitzkrieg, also were claimed to be slowing down the Reich army.

French military sources said that the Germans had now lost, since the beginning of the war, at least 2,000 tanks of an estimated total force of 5,000, as well as 2,000 planes—believed to be nearly half of the Nazi first-line strength.

During the day military dispatches summed it up with the philosophic report that the Germans appeared to be "getting out of wind."

Nazi Motor Cycle Troops Harry Allied Rear; 20,000 Sent Out to Disrupt Communications

By The Associated Press.

BERLIN, May 29—Chancellor Hitler has put soldiers mounted on motor cycles to new destructive uses behind Allied lines in carrying out his Blitzkrieg plans through Belgium and Northern France.

Dubbed "blue devils" by the French, the motor cyclists were sprung as a surprise on the Allies in the Picardy section of France, from Amiens to the Channel, north of the Somme.

Authorized quarters tonight said these motor cyclists, trained and used only for scouting duty, were estimated at 20,000 in number.

They were sent into Picardy during the encirclement operations against the Allies with orders to break all possible communication lines linking the Allied northern armies and those south of the Somme.

In addition they were to harass the enemy in every other possible way.

An authorized spokesman said the "blue devils" raced over the countryside fifty to sixty miles an hour in groups of eight and ten.

Each cycle has a sidecar. The crews are equipped with automatic pistols, carbines and light machine guns.

Without reducing speed they strafe enemy marching units and encamped troops alike.

The motor cycles throw off a thick blue exhaust which acts as a smoke screen and gives the riders their nickname.

Specialized motor cycle units follow the first squads. These latter machines are equipped with wire-cutting tools, hand grenades, and other destructive devices for use against power lines, transformers and other key objects.

Among the most ingenious instruments is a rope with a cutting edge. This rope can be thrown over a wire in such a way as to cut it by see-saw motion, although the users are insulated and safe.

The squads are composed of picked men who know the terrain to which they were assigned, either as a result of World War experience or special travel as tourists.

PORTUGAL LOOKING AHEAD

Hope Lies in War-Free Zones, Salazar Tells Soldiers

Special Cable to THE NEW YORK TIMES.

LISBON, May 29—In a war speech addressed to the Portuguese Army, Premier Antonio Oliviera Salazar, speaking as War Minister, said today:

"We have proceeded with our peace policy, conciliating with many efforts and circumstances such a policy with the nation's duties and interests. Portugal's present prestiges and friendships have kept war afar, but this attitude is not based on a sense of comfort or interest that in no case will be maintained. I believe that in the present condition of Europe it is God's gift that is keeping certain zones free from war, because it will be with such peace reserves that future peace will be built."

Cuban Group Honors Welles

The election of Sumner Welles, Under-Secretary of State, and Dr. Martinez Fraga, Cuban Ambassador to the United States, as honorary presidents of the Cuban Chamber of Commerce in the United States, Inc., was announced yesterday by the chamber. Lawrence Berenson has been re-elected president for a third term. Officers and directors chosen are José M. Bosch, Frank H. Hillery, Roscoe M. Greene and Gustavo Lobo, vice presidents; José Borrell, treasurer, and Manuel Rendueles, secretary.

KAISER'S GRANDSON BURIED WITH HONORS

200 Officers of Old Imperial Army at Potsdam Services

Wireless to THE NEW YORK TIMES.

BERLIN, May 29—Prince Wilhelm of Prussia, 34 years old and the eldest son of the former Crown Prince, was buried in Potsdam this afternoon with the military honors customary for a first lieutenant who dies as the result of wounds received in battle. The coffin was carried by noncommissioned officers, and one company of soldiers paid their comrade final honors. It was, however, not a customary funeral service.

Potsdam was crowded. Many of those here had come from Berlin and most of them were wearing mourning. There were, furthermore, some 200 officers of the former Kaiser's army, led by 90-year-old Field Marshall von Mackensen, all in imperial uniforms, and some twenty younger generals of the contemporary German Army.

The church service was held in Peace Church and among the many wreaths was one from Doorn from the former Kaiser with the single letter "W" upon the ribbon. The former Crown Prince and his two other sons also were present, while Wilhelm's widow walked on the arm of her father-in-law. Two army friends of Wilhelm also were present, which was unusual for wartime, for they had journeyed from the front for the funeral.

Field Marshal Hermann Goering also sent a wreath while Herr Hitler, Marshal Goering and Propaganda Minister Joseph Goebbels sent condolences. Among the other prominent persons present, representing their respective ruling houses, were the Danish Minister and the Greek Minister.

The body was placed in a sepulchre in the antique temple beside that of Wilhelm's grandmother, Victoria.

NAZIS SET UP DUTCH RULE

Seyss-Inquart Denies Intent to 'Conquer' Netherlands

BERLIN, May 29 (AP)—German administration of the Netherlands took definite form today with Arthur Seyss-Inquart, German Minister without portfolio, assuming full civil authority over the occupied territories. Aviation Gen. Frederich Christiansen assumed charge of military operations.

Herr Seyss-Inquart said in a brief address that the Germans occupied the Netherlands as a military necessity, not as "conquerors seeking to impose our political ideas" on the Netherland people. He added that Netherland laws would remain in force and the nation's institutions maintained.

7 in 10 of Parachutists Die

LONDON, May 29—The British Broadcasting Corporation reported today that of 10,000 Nazi parachutists landed behind the lines in the Netherlands, 7,000 had been killed.

BRITAIN WILL TAKE ALL EXCESS PROFIT

To Extend to Every Business the 100% Levy Recently Put on Those in War Trade

Wireless to THE NEW YORK TIMES.

LONDON, May 29—The already staggering burden of British taxation will be increased soon by a second budget, Sir Kingsley Wood, Chancellor of the Exchequer, indicated in the House of Commons today when he announced that a tax rate of 100 per cent on profits over a fixed limit would be imposed not only on concerns engaged principally in war production but on all trades and businesses. The tax will operate from April 1, when the fiscal year began.

These statements were made by Sir Kingsley in moving the second reading of the finance bill, the operating machinery for Sir John Simon's recent budget, which raised the income tax to seven shillings six pence to the pound—a tax based on an estimated war expenditure of £2,000,000,000 this year.

Since that estimate was made, Sir Kingsley said, the whole situation had undergone a vast change, the war's accelerated speed altering the fiscal picture.

Favors an Adjustment Period

Facing the question whether further taxation should be imposed immediately, the Chancellor of the Exchequer said he felt that it was essential that the country should have a brief period in which to adjust itself to the considerable load of new taxation already imposed.

"I am confident that the country will not flinch from carrying these burdens, which are little in comparison with the tasks that are being so bravely undertaken by our sailors, soldiers and airmen," he said.

Sir Kingsley reassured any nervous investors that nothing in the government's emergency powers gave it control which would endanger the savings money in any bank; these would be safe as they had always been. On the contrary, the greater the country's war effort the safer and more valuable they would be, he said. He emphasized the need for further lending to the State, and said he was considering what would be the best shape for a future war loan to take.

Voice for Labor on Budget

It is expected by Conservatives in the Commons that the next budget, which it is understood, will be introduced in the Autumn, will embody some ideas of the Laborites.

When Sir John Simon introduced his budget in the Spring, Labor pressed for a capital levy. The government did not deny the justice of a capital levy but took the position that to make such assessments in war time while capital values were changing would be impracticable.

Support for the belief that the Laborites are getting the government to sponsor some of their pet projects is seen in the announcement last night raising old-age pensions up to the level they demanded when in the Opposition, and in a report tonight that farm workers probably would get a minimum wage of forty-eight shillings a week, compared with the forty-two that was fixed recently.

MORE CITIZENS FOR REICH

All Nationals in Eupen and Malmedy Are Received

BERLIN, May 29 (AP)—Germany took into the Reich as citizens today all her nationals in Eupen and Malmedy, the Eastern provinces of Belgium reunited with the Reich in the first few days of invasion of the Low Countries.

Other residents of the provinces were declared German subjects.

Eupen and Malmedy were assigned to Belgium by the League of Nations on March 6, 1925, as part of the World War settlement. With them went the two-square-mile neutral district of Moresnet, together with a small portion of Prussian Moresnet. Altogether the territory amounts to 384 square miles, populated by 64,000 persons, five-sixths of whom are German.

Turkey's Budget Approved

ANKARA, Turkey, May 29 (AP)—The National Assembly tonight unanimously approved a national defense budget raising the year's expenditures for the armed forces to the record total of 350,000,000 Turkish pounds.

CANADA'S AIR PLAN AHEAD OF SCHEDULE

More Than 100 New Fields Are to Be Finished This Summer Instead of Over 2 Years

WHOLE EFFORT SPEEDED

In Airplane Industry 16,000 Men Will Soon Be Busy—Shortage of Mechanics

By Telephone to THE NEW YORK TIMES.

OTTAWA, May 29—Developments have shown that last week's war effort speed-up order here is being made effective far more rapidly than had been thought possible. From all quarters is coming evidence of a mighty effort to produce quick results.

The Commonwealth Air Training Plan, hitherto going according to set schedule, is an example. When it was drawn up last Autumn it provided for the building of new airports over a two-year period and even that, since an enormous job of construction over a wide territory was involved, was expected to tax the capacity of the Canadian building industry. But now, it is known, all the hundred-odd new airports are to be completed this Summer and indications are that the work will be done even in advance of schedule.

In the provinces the government holiday on highway construction is making available for airfield work the men and machines used hitherto for building roads. The cutting down of prairie farm rehabilitation has made available the men who worked on irrigation projects, a task not far removed from the leveling of land for air fields. Dominion and Provincial equipment, available at the centers of these activities, is just the thing for making air fields.

Work Begun on Eighty-One Units

Work has already started on eighty-one units in the Air Training Scheme and only thirty remain in the planning stage. The more there are under way the sooner will it be possible to speed up the training of Canadian pilots. Hitherto, the obstacle against rapid progress has been the difficulty of finding machines for them to fly. Aid from the United States will end all that.

Canada, herself, is also speeding up her airplane industry. Where there were 5,000 men building planes when Parliament assembled a fortnight ago, 16,000 will soon be employed in three shifts daily. The chief difficulty now is the scarcity of trained mechanics. Die makers, pattern makers, jig fixers and white metal workers are urgently needed, but 27,000 green hands are already enrolled in a training scheme to produce them, and of these some 20,000 have had sufficient instruction under a youth training plan to make them partly qualified.

It is the same story in other fields of the war endeavor. Canadian plants began work this week on additional special equipment for mechanical transport in the amount of $1,000,000. Additional facilities are being installed in many factories to increase the quantity and type of artillery shells. At present eight Canadian plants are engaged in producing 2,250,000 shells. The new provisions will add five or six companies to that number and double the quantity of shells produced.

60 Concerns Make Ammunition

Altogether sixty Canadian companies are now producing ammunition in various forms, including that for anti-aircraft guns, field guns and heavy howitzers, and $40,000,000 worth of orders have been placed. Another $30,000,000 is being spent in enlarging the capacity of plants making explosives. But here again the cry is for competent mechanics to produce machine tools. Thousands are required.

Announcement was made today of the appointment of W. F. Drysdale, who had been vice president of the Montreal Locomotive Works since 1932, as director of munitions under the Department of Supply. He is serving the government without pay.

In Parliament the bill providing $700,000,000 for war purposes in the current fiscal year had its final reading in the House, was approved by the Senate and has received the royal assent in record time for so large a sum.

16 MORE AMERICANS TO DRIVE IN FRANCE

Ambulance Volunteers Will Go to Front After Part in Memorial Day Service

FOUR HAVE BEEN CAPTURED

German Radio Says That Group Listed as Missing Is Now in Hands of Nazis

Wireless to THE NEW YORK TIMES.

PARIS, May 29—Sixteen American volunteers arrived from the United States by way of Italy today to join the third section of volunteer drivers sponsored unofficially by American Legion headquarters here.

They were in charge of Sedley Peck, former commander of the Paris Post of the American Legion, who drove an ambulance as a volunteer before the United States entered the World War. The drivers will participate tomorrow in the Memorial Day ceremonies and then will go immediately to the front.

Word has been received through Berne, Switzerland, today that four drivers who have been missing from the volunteers section for more than a week were captured and are held in German territory.

The American Volunteer Ambulance Corps said last night that a German radio announcement picked up in Paris reported that four American drivers and their ambulances had been captured by Nazi forces, the Associated Press reported in New York.

James Wood Johnson, president of the A. V. A. C. in New York, tentatively listed the captured men as Albert Raymond, Chicago; Lieutenant Louis Wehrle, Berne, Ind.; Murray Shipley, Cincinnati, Ohio, and Jan Glowacki, Jersey City, N. J.

They had been listed previously as missing—killed or captured.

Mr. Johnson said that Colonel J. V. Sparks, head of the A. V. A. C. in Paris, cabled this message.

"German radio announced four drivers our group loaned to Miss Anne Morgan taken prisoners together with their ambulances. Trying to confirm."

Mr. Johnson said that the men were in a group of ten ambulance crews of the Benjamin Franklin section working in the Ardennes district.

An unofficial announcement in Berlin last night said that Nazi troops had captured numerous American ambulances and equipment and were using them for their wounded.

Six more Americans, meanwhile, prepared to sail tomorrow on the United States liner Washington for Paris and front line service as drivers with the A. V. A. C.

They are John D. Wellborn of Washington, D. C., James J. Gardner of New Rochelle, N. Y., and four New York City residents—William M. Throop, Winslow Meadows, Herbert M. Witcombe and Carl Berthold.

Mr. Johnson said there was an urgent need for additional men as thirty-seven ambulances were idle in Paris because of lack of drivers. Another group will sail on June 15.

BRITONS BUYING JEWELRY

£24,000 Paid in Two Hours at Auction in London

Wireless to THE NEW YORK TIMES.

LONDON, May 29—Evidence of the growing tendency to invest large sums of money in jewels and negotiable commodities despite the government's efforts to divert savings to war loans was shown today when in two hours £24,000 was paid for jewelry in Christie's auction room.

The receipts included £4,000 for a single-stone diamond ring with a platinum hoop and sapphire-mounted shoulders. A pair of earrings with twin stone chains, each supporting a large circular diamond, changed hands for £2,500. Other high prices were realized for a necklace of seventy-one pearls with a diamond snap, which took £1,900; a specimen pink diamond ring, £1,180, and a diamond necklace, £1,650.

"All the News That's Fit to Print."

The New York Times.

LATE CITY EDITION
Partly cloudy, warmer today, followed by showers tonight. Tomorrow fair, temperature unchanged.
Temperatures Yesterday—Max., 76; Min., 65

VOL. LXXXIX...No. 30,093. Entered as Second-Class Matter, Postoffice, New York, N. Y. NEW YORK, SATURDAY, JUNE 15, 1940. THREE CENTS NEW YORK CITY and Vicinity | FOUR CENTS Elsewhere Except in 7th and 8th Postal Zones.

GERMANS OCCUPY PARIS, PRESS ON SOUTH; CAPTURE HAVRE, ASSAULT MAGINOT LINE; FRENCH ARMY INTACT; SPAIN SEIZES TANGIER

HITLER IS DOUBTED

Roosevelt Skeptical of Pledge He Will Not Cross Atlantic

HAS RECOLLECTIONS

U. S. Doing All It Can for Allies, He Asserts of French Appeal

By FELIX BELAIR Jr.
Special to THE NEW YORK TIMES.

WASHINGTON, June 14—President Roosevelt replied today to Adolf Hitler's reported denial of territorial aspirations in the Western Hemisphere with a reference to the German Chancellor's record of broken pledges to respect the integrity of European nations over a considerable period of time.

As a part of the same answer the President said the United States was doing and would continue to do everything in its power to give aid to the Allies. He said, in effect, that Chancellor Hitler's statement in an interview that he would confine his activities to Europe was to be taken with considerable quantities of salt.

The President followed up this with an announcement of plans to mobilize American scientific genius in the interest of national defense.

"That brings recollections," the President said when asked at his press conference for his reaction to statements credited to the German Chancellor in an interview published in Hearst newspapers today. Reporters were not permitted to quote directly the rest of the President's statement, in which he said his observation might be enlarged upon with dates and nations going back over quite a period of years.

Many Rumors in Washington

Mr. Roosevelt's press conference remark was the high point of a day in which Washington was thick with rumors of the formation of a new French Cabinet without Premier Reynaud, that France would soon seek a separate peace with the Germans and that the President had been asked by France or Great Britain to propose a declaration of war against the Nazi government.

Both the White House and State Department denied that any proposal had been received from the Allied governments that the United States declare war.

Secretary Hull was asked in connection with the French situation whether the question of a declaration of war by the United States had been projected or raised in any way. He replied that so far as he knew nothing was involved beyond the sale of supplies, under terms and conditions that every one knew.

The question was asked of the Secretary of State at his press conference, which was held at 1 o'clock. Mr. Hull said the appeal Premier Reynaud made to President Roosevelt was then being decoded, that he had not seen it, but he understood it was the same that the French Premier gave by radio last night. Later the French Ambassador, Count de Saint-Quentin, said he assumed it was that or its equivalent.

Day's Other Developments

These other developments in the legislative and executive branches during the day stood out:

1. The President let it be known, by inference, that no accumulation of circumstances in the European war would alter this country's determination to arm to the teeth.

2. The House passed and sent to the Senate a bill authorizing the Reconstruction Finance Corporation to organize and lend money to corporations for plant expansion and acquisition of strategic materials for nationl defense.

3. State Department officials made no secret of their belief that France would soon undertake negotiations with Germany looking to a separate peace and that reorganization of the French Government probably would be attempted with this in mind.

4. Administration sources said legislation would be introduced next week to embargo exports of scrap iron as a measure of national defense.

5. Attorney General Jackson

Continued on Page Ten

The International Situation

On the Battle Fronts

Paris was taken over yesterday by the German war machine.

Led by dust-stained tanks, followed by motorized divisions and then by infantry, the German Army marched down the Champs Elysées. Tense, grim-faced Parisians—the few who had remained behind—stood silently on the curbs as a hostile force marched through the famous boulevards of the "City of Light" for the first time since 1871. Shops were closed and shuttered. [Page 1, Column 7.]

In Berlin there were scenes of wild rejoicing. On Chancellor Hitler's orders church bells were rung for a quarter of an hour and the Nazi flag was ordered displayed for three days. [Page 2, Column 2.]

Berlin said that the fall of Paris—described as "catastrophic" morally and economically for the French—had completed the second phase of the war. The first was the Battle of Flanders. The third, the High Command communiqué said, was pursuit and "final destruction" of all the French forces. The chief drive of this "final" phase appeared to be directed against the flank of the Maginot Line through Champagne and the Argonne Forest—famous World War battlefield of American troops. Montmédy, western anchor of the line, was reported conquered. Spearheads had driven as far east as Vitry-le François, between Paris and Nancy. Verdun was said to be threatened. On the coast Havre's fall was claimed. [Page 1, Column 8.]

Hitler's personal press representative in the field with him said that the German leader considered the fall of Paris only an incident on his road of conquest and that he was not interested in peace now. [Page 2, Column 8.]

The French High Command said it had abandoned Paris because there was no "valuable strategical reason" why it should be defended and it did not want the city devastated. The communiqué said the French Army was retreating in good order. A slackening of the German drive was reported at several points, but the heavy push in Champagne, threatening the rear of the Maginot Line, was still in progress. The armament of the line is useless against an attack from the rear. A frontal attack on the line west of the Saar was reported repulsed. [Page 1, Column 5.]

High sources in London said that Britain had agreed to accept any military or political decision the French Government might make but would fight on whatever it was. [Page 1, Column 6.] If the war is to be waged successfully, however, informed sources said, every available piece of war material in the United States must be sent to the Allies at once. [Page 1, Column 4.]

The war appeared to be developing for Italy. First reports of action on her Alpine frontier were reported in a communiqué. It was divulged for the first time, too, that the Italian fleet was at sea in force. [Page 1, Column 3.] Attacks in Africa were reported, both by the Italian air arm and by Allied troops against Libya, Eritrea and Ethiopia. Successes were claimed by the Italians in all actions. [Page 4, Column 1.]

The French Government abandoned Tours as its provisional capital and started southward, apparently for the port of Bordeaux. It was the seat of the French Government for a short time in 1914. [Page 1, Column 6.]

Repercussions Elsewhere

Spanish troops yesterday took over control of Tangier, the small internationally-policed territory in Northern Africa fronting on the Straits of Gibraltar. Madrid said the action had been taken to "guarantee its neutrality" and had been done with the full consent of the other three guarantors—Britain, France and Italy. Berlin said the consent of the Allies was given after the act. Return of Tangier has been one of the most frequently expressed territorial demands of Franco-Spain. That of British-held Gibraltar is the other. [Page 1, Column 4.] In Washington Secretary Hull said the United States would insist on its extraterritorial rights in Tangier under the treaty of 1906. [Follows the foregoing.]

"That brings up recollections," President Roosevelt said at his press conference when a purported interview with Chancellor Hitler was shown to him quoting the German leader as saying he had no aspirations in this hemisphere. The President's reference was to similar statements made about European countries. Driving ahead with the American defense program, the President announced the appointment of a scientific research commission to work with the defense advisory commission. [Page 1, Column 1.]

COLONNA PROTESTS ON ITALIAN CHARGES

Envoy Sees Hull—Inquiry Here Widened—German Agent to U. S. Warns of Reprisals

Special to THE NEW YORK TIMES.

WASHINGTON, June 14—The Italian Ambassador, Don Ascanio dei Principi Colonna, protested to Secretary of State Cordell Hull today what he considered to be an unjustified effort to foment anti-Italian feeling in the United States.

The protest was directed specifically to the charges made in New York yesterday that the Italian Consulate General there, under orders of Premier Benito Mussolini, was seeking to promote fascism in this country by ideological propaganda. He also implied there were similar activities against Italy in other American cities.

His concern was especially manifested over publication of these charges by newspapers. The fact that the New York charges were issued through Police Commissioner Valentine apparently was not mentioned. No reference was made directly to President Roosevelt's Charlottesville address denouncing Italy.

In making the protest, Prince Colonna declared that Italian consuls in this country restrict their activities to their legal functions and that Italian nationals in the United States are careful to avoid

Continued on Page Nine

ITALIANS IN CLASH ON FRENCH BORDER

Report Attack Repulsed—Fleet Action Revealed—Coast Is Shelled

By HERBERT L. MATTHEWS
By Telephone to THE NEW YORK TIMES.

ROME, June 14—The war began to develop for Italy on land, sea and air, according to this morning's communiqué, with the first activity on the Italo-French frontier and an indication that the Italian Fleet was on its way on some great mission.

The taking of Tangier by the Spaniards is considered a first-rate victory for the Axis, but, of course, the fall of Paris dominates everything else.

Among Fascisti here there is rejoicing over the fate of Paris. The newspaper Lavoro Fascista cheers in an eight-column box whose sentiments are typical.

"C'est Paris," it says. "Capitalists, Jews, Masons and snobs all over the world are in mourning. The spiritual capital of all the old civilization has fallen. Paris has fallen. Paris itself 'la ville lumière—Paris tout entier.'"

As the war shapes up, even this early, the Mediterranean seems more than ever certain to become Italy's main theatre of operations. To be sure, there was some activity for the first time yesterday on the French frontier. There were clashes by patrols and "enemy, at-

Continued on Page Four

MOROCCANS MOVE IN

Spanish Troops Take Over Zone in Which U. S. Has Rights

'GIBRALTAR' NOW CRY

Madrid Students Parade and Shout for Return of the Famous Rock

By T. J. HAMILTON
Special Cable to THE NEW YORK TIMES.

MADRID, June 14—The Spanish Government announced early this afternoon that with the object of guaranteeing "the neutrality of the international zone" in Morocco, Moroccan troops entered Tangier this morning.

It was stated officially that the action had been taken in agreement with Great Britain, France and Italy, who are other guarantors of the zone under a convention of 1903. The United States, which is also a signatory to the convention, received a copy of the announcement in a note delivered to the United States Embassy here at 11 A. M.

The text of the communiqué follows:

"With the object of guaranteeing the neutrality of the international zone and the city of Tangier, the Spanish Government has decided to take charge provisionally of the surveillance, police and public safety services of the international zone; forces of Moroccan troops entered this morning with this object.

"All existing services are assured and they continue functioning normally."

Coveted by the Spanish

Next to Gibraltar, Tangier occupies the front rank in Spanish territorial aims. In the last few days newspapers have devoted special attention to it among African territories that the French, assertedly with the connivance of the British, took away from Spain.

Although the first extra newspapers did not appear on the streets until 4 P. M., word that Tangier had been occupied spread quickly. By noon flags were appearing on houses throughout Madrid and members of the Falange youth movement were marching in uniform through the streets.

The news helped to bring an extra welcome for General Franco when he arrived late in the afternoon to open an exposition showing accomplishments of the government in rebuilding devastated regions. The press confined itself to printing the text of the government communiqué and relating the history of the international zone.

However, there were four demonstrations during the day, in which university student Falangistas predominated, all shouting, "Tangier is ours!" Some of these demonstrations passed the French and British Embassies.

British circles emphasized tonight that the occupation of Tangier had taken place with the complete agreement of Britain and France, who along with Italy and Spain were guarantors of the interna-

Continued on Page Six

FRENCH NOTE LULL

Battle Continues Along Front—At Some Points Its Violence Abates

ATTACK IS REPULSED

Nazi Losses Are Heavy in Maginot Assault—Loire Next Barrier

By G. H. ARCHAMBAULT
Wireless to THE NEW YORK TIMES.

TOURS, France, June 14—Is there any significance in the fact that although the battle continued to be waged today all along the front from the coast to the Argonne, it was notable that at certain points its violence was abating?

That question is in every mind tonight, for it may contain confirmation of the belief that the Germans have now engaged the maximum of their available forces.

The communiqué issued tonight gives little information on the day's operations, but it implies that all the retreating French forces continue to fight rear-guard actions and that at several parts of the front they have, in addition, counter-attacked the advancing Germans.

The only reference to Paris is as follows: "The prescribed withdrawal has been effected in conformity with our plans."

But if there has been a relative lull on the main line of battle the Germans were very active in front of the Maginot Line, especially west of the Saar River. Early in the morning they launched a violent attack with the now customary accompaniment of tanks and dive-bombing planes. The French claim to have thrown back the attacking force, on which they inflicted heavy losses.

Present Front Uncertain

Manifestly this attack must be considered in correlation with the fighting in the Argonne, farther to the west.

It is impossible tonight to indicate the present front even approximately. It is really one long line of pockets and salients, a situation calling for great qualities of generalship in order to preserve cohesion of the French forces.

Meanwhile, with the withdrawal of the French troops charged with the defense of Paris the first phase of the Battle of France was ended in defeat. It may be called the Battle of the Seine. The next phase may be the Battle of the Loire.

The issue was clear from the moment it was decided to declare Paris an open city and the news of withdrawal cannot have surprised many. A communiqué issued this morning from French General Headquarters explained that there were insufficient strategic reasons for defending the capital to justify risking destruction of France's very heart.

From the military point of view it is clear now that a battle for Paris would merely have immobilized troops, added to the loss of life and brought about no com-

Continued on Page Three

British Call on U. S. for Munitions at Once; French Order 120 Bombers Here for 1941

By RAYMOND DANIELL
Special Cable to THE NEW YORK TIMES

LONDON, June 14—In circles close to the government it was said today that every gun, every ounce of war materials that the United States can spare was needed urgently and needed quickly if the cause for which the Allies were fighting was not to be lost on the battlefields of France. It is not a matter of months but of weeks, even days, it was added by those in a position to know the *facts*, of which the ordinary people in this country only now are becoming dimly aware.

Withdrawal of the battered French armies behind their abandoned capital and contemplation of the possibility that the Government of France may be forced to withdraw from Europe to Africa, led to expressions that made increasingly apparent the extent to which the

Continued on Page Four

After the Anglo-French Purchasing Commission yesterday had announced that French purchases of war material in the United States were being stepped up, the French signed a contract at 7 P. M. for 120 "flying fortresses" to be delivered in the second and third quarters of 1941. The planes are to be built by the Consolidated Aircraft Corporation.

In an interview earlier in the day a spokesman for the Anglo-French commission said that contracts for "many millions of dollars" had been placed during the day.

Instead of curtailing purchases following the capture of Paris by the Germans, France is sending more purchasing experts, this spokesman said. In response to a question relative to the ability to pay cash for purchases, he added:

"There is no immediate end of our

Continued on Page Four

Will Fight On, British Insist, Even if the French Capitulate

London Letting Ally Make Decision on the Immediate Course as Help Is Speeded—New Nazi Peace Offensive Expected

By The United Press.

LONDON, June 14—Britain has agreed to accept any decision France may make regarding military and political policy, but if France is lost as an ally the British will fight on alone against Chancellor Hitler's war machine, it was understood tonight.

The British Government was understood to have agreed this week to any choice the French Government might make in regard to these military and political matters, which weigh more heavily with each hour of Germany's increased drive, provided the choice had the approval of Generalissimo Maxime Weygand.

Foreign observers in London today regarded the German assault against the Maginot Line, particularly the strong flanking attack south of Montmedy around Vitry-le-François, as of far greater strategic importance than yesterday's German occupation of undefended Paris. Nevertheless, the psychological importance of the fall of Paris and the effect on French morale are not underestimated.

The impression prevails in foreign embassies in London that Herr Hitler would respond affirmatively to any possible French peace overture, but would impose harsh conditions as his price for ending the war in France. These conditions, it was felt, might range from dismantling the $500,000,000 Maginot Line to the return to Germany of Alsace-Lorraine and other territorial and economic and financial concessions.

There are strong indications, however, that Herr Hitler would refuse to negotiate with Britain, since he is intent on smashing Britain's financial and industrial power.

How far Germany would be prepared to bid for a completely Nazi-dictated peace presumably would depend upon the extent of the German losses suffered in the war.

If Britain should be compelled to fight on alone without France as an ally she would be able, it is felt in British quarters, to carry on until Autumn with United States aid. The British Navy is relatively intact despite Germany's claims to the contrary. Then, it is asserted, starvation might seriously menace Germany and Italy during the Winter, impairing their military strength and the security of their home fronts.

British morale appears to be firm,

Continued on Page Five

TOURS ABANDONED AS FRENCH CAPITAL

Government Is Expected to Make Seat at Bordeaux—U. S. Move Is Awaited

By P. J. PHILIP
Wireless to THE NEW YORK TIMES.

TOURS, France, June 14—Tours has ceased to be the substitute capital of France after a brief three-day career. Premier Paul Reynaud's speech last night and other symptoms showed clearly before we went to bed that that would be so.

There were already signs of packing up again in different administrations. Sleep seemed, however, more urgent than flight, especially as we ourselves had just obtained a bed—the first we had slept in since Sunday. In that we were luckier than most, although it does seem expensive to have had only one night's sleep in a two-room apartment rented for a month. However, it permitted a proper wash and a change of linen.

And now we and everybody else are on our way again. We don't know what is happening because the information service installed here with so much trouble on Monday has opened its wings and fled with a part of the censorship service. Press Wireless is functioning for a few hours and then good-bye to Tours.

Avalanche Advancing

The morning communiqué told the story of why this should be so—in part at least. The avalanche is advancing from all sides, closing around Paris and pushing forward in Champagne. The problem is where to go to escape it.

During the day, while we are on the road, things are likely to happen that will change the whole situation. It is too much now to hope that they will change it in any way that can be counted as satisfactory.

Along the roads through here the stream of civilian and military cars has recommenced. The embassies and legations have already pulled out. Wherever we go is going to be so congested that the remnants of that camping outfit with which we started are going to be invaluable.

Only 5,000 American bombers and fighters flying across the Atlantic in response to Premier Reynaud's desperate appeal could restore to the French people their belief that they are not alone in this terrible fight. Words and promises and the complicated explanation of political circumstances will not suffice. They will serve only to break further the dying hope there is today in every French heart.

For the British all the French feeling is as if they were of the

Continued on Page Three

REICH TANKS CLANK IN CHAMPS-ELYSEES

Berlin Recounts Parade Into Paris—Third of Citizens Reported Remaining

By The United Press.

BERLIN, June 14—German tanks today clanked across the Seine bridges, past the Arc de Triomphe and down the tree-lined Champs Elysées into the heart of Paris at the head of the first cavalcade of invaders to enter the French capital in nearly seventy years.

Flanked by armored cars, the dust-stained tanks swung triumphantly into Paris from the northwest at the head of Nazi units occupying the "City of Light," German accounts of the event said.

It was the ninth recorded invasion of Paris and the first since Bismarck's legions trod the broad boulevards in 1871. The jubilant German press proclaimed the fall of Paris to be the "symbol of decision" in Chancellor Adolf Hitler's Western offensive.

[Berlin Nazis expected Adolf Hitler to visit Paris June 21, the twenty-first anniversary of Germany's acceptance of the Treaty of Versailles, an Associated Press dispatch said.]

Entry From Northwest

The advance into Paris, through the suburbs of Argenteuil and Neuilly and into the aristocratic western part of the city began early in the morning, the Germans said. It was exactly five weeks after the massive western offensive began with the German drive into the Netherlands and Belgium.

The tanks rumbled between thin lines of tense and silent Parisians, the Germans said. Reports from the French capital estimated that probably a third of the city's normal population of 2,800,000 had remained in Paris.

Behind the tanks rolled anti-tank units, still dusty and laden with evidence of the furious fighting in which they had taken part to the north.

As the long shadows of the early morning retreated, more and more Nazi contingents streamed into the capital, evacuated by French Armies hoping to save their beloved Paris from the fate of Warsaw.

Motorized infantry, riding in steel-shielded trucks mounting machine guns to command the broad streets, converged from the Seine bridges to the Place de l'Etoile.

In that hub from which radiate eleven streets stands the Arc de Triomphe and its tomb of the Unknown World War Soldier, where flickers the Eternal Flame.

German reports indicated that the parade through Paris swung around

Continued on Page Two

2 FORCES TAKE CITY

Berlin Says Industrial Losses May Be Worst Feature for French

MONTMEDY CAPTURED

Anchor of Maginot Line Lost—Nazis Report Foe Is Routed

By C. BROOKS PETERS
Wireless to THE NEW YORK TIMES.

BERLIN, June 14—Today, for the third time within the last century and a quarter, victorious German troops marched into Paris. This time, however, the legions, the clatter of whose hobnailed boots resounds throughout Paris and the entire world, are more than just German soldiers. They are the bearers of a proposed new order for Europe and perhaps the world, a major tenet of which is to destroy the old one.

With the capitulation of Paris, the Germans claim that the destruction of the remaining French forces is but a matter of "the shortest time." Well-informed quarters in Berlin put that time at two weeks at most.

For the German High Command announced today that the second phase of the western campaign has been completed successfully, the resistance of the French northern fronts has been broken and the enemy is "in full retreat along the entire front from Paris to the Maginot Line near Sedan."

Retreat Called Rout

If the statements of German military officials in Berlin are correct, this "full retreat" is really a rout. For the French, forced from their positions, have had no time to construct new ones but are being constantly harassed by German tanks, other motorized units and planes as they move southward, it is reported.

Early this morning, the Germans declare, they unleashed a frontal attack on the Maginot Line along the entire Saar front. Farther east, the fall of Montmedy, "anchor" of the Maginot Line, was claimed as well.

The extreme right wing of the German forces was not idle either. For yesterday it captured Havre, Berlin heard, and thus added approximately another hundred miles to the stretch of French coast that already is in German hands.

Advance on Cherbourg

The lower Seine, moreover, according to the High Command, was crossed on a wide front. The extreme right wing, it is believed, now is advancing on Cherbourg further to cut France off from Great Britain and provide the Germans with still another base for a future raid on the British Isles.

The front is now about 300 miles long as the crow flies, Germans declare, from Havre to the Rhine.

Although no information has been officially released here relative to the progress of the attack on the Maginot Line, it was said in usually accurately informed quarters tonight that the force of the German drive in this sector already has borne fruit and that Reich troops have broken through in several places.

Escape Held Impossible

Forces of the German left wing are reported pushing forward in a southeasterly direction in what now appears to be a plan to storm the triangle of the Maginot fortifications from several sides, while an advance west of the fortifications to Belfort—southern tip of the Maginot Line—would cut off the avenue of escape for the French troops manning the line.

This German left wing yesterday was said to have captured Vitry-le Francois and crossed the Marne-Rhine Canal, which connects that town with Strasbourg. Still farther west another tentacle of the German left wing last evening was reported to have stormed the famous Hill 304 (Dead Man's Hill) northwest of Verdun, in which sector in 1916, Germans say, they lost 80,000 men.

The southern tip of the Argonne Forest also has been reached, Germans declare.

The Meuse defenses and Verdun

Continued on Page Two

HOLIDAY IN REICH MARKS PARIS FALL

Hitler Orders 3-Day Festival as Exultant Crowds Sing 'Deutschland Ueber Alles'

CHURCH BELLS JOIN FETE

Special Demonstration Held in Opera House—U. S. Party Was in Private Box

Wireless to THE NEW YORK TIMES.

BERLIN, June 14—The news that German advance troops had entered the French capital this morning reached the Berlin public at the noon hour and was again signaled through deafening radio fanfares at all important points of the city and in shops, stores, offices and factories.

"Deutschland ueber Alles," the national anthem, with "Die Wacht am Rhein" thrown in for good measure, resounded through the streets of the capital and the jubilation exceeded that accorded any other war event of recent weeks.

Flags were ordered out for three days and church bells will also peal at the Vespers hour.

While the capture of Paris was believed to be imminent the populace obviously did not expect it today.

Demonstration at the Opera

BERLIN, June 14 (AP)—Chancellor Adolf Hitler today declared a three-day holiday to celebrate the capture of Paris. Bands played. Crowds cheered hoarsely in Berlin.

Martial music filled the air and large crowds cheered after the High Command announced the German entry into Paris, the first time German troops have marched into the French capital since their conquest in 1871 in the Franco-Prussian War.

The Flanders victory earlier had been celebrated by eight days of flag flying.

There was a special demonstration at the State Opera House tonight over the fall of Paris.

Before the performance of Wagner's Die Meistersinger, one of Chancellor Adolf Hitler's favorites, the curtains parted and the entire cast was revealed on the stage, arms upraised in the Nazi salute.

The audience followed suit—with the exception of a party of Americans in the private box of United States Chargé d'Affairés Alexander C. Kirk. They stood.

Everyone else sang the twin national anthems—the Horst Wessel Lied and "Deutschland ueber Alles."

Church Bells Ordered Rung

BERLIN, June 14 (UP)—Today's announcement calling for German celebration of the conquest of Paris said:

"On the occasion of the great victory of German troops in France which today was crowned by the entry into Paris as well as the victorious ending of the fighting in Norway, the whole of Germany, at the Fuehrer's orders in honor of German soldiers, will be beflagged for three days. Church bells will ring for one-quarter of an hour."

Church bells in Berlin began ringing at 1:10 P. M. As the church bells pealed, radio announcers said that "today we think above all of the Fuehrer and our brave soldiers who made possible today's historic event."

U. S. SHIP LEAVES GENOA

Freighter Prusa Is Last American Vessel Due to Call in Italy

By Telephone to THE NEW YORK TIMES.

GENOA, Italy, June 14—The freighter Prusa left for the United States today, the last American steamer to go, following last night's departure of the American export liner Exochorda with 250 passengers aboard. The Prusa carries no passengers.

Aboard the Exochorda were about fifty Americans who resided in Egypt. Among the 200 Americans who left from Italy was Alan Rogers of the United States Embassy in Rome, who had been called to Washington.

GERMAN TANKS HEAD FOR THE FRENCH CAPITAL

GERMAN SOURCE: Armored reconnaissance units of the Nazi army pass a road marker designating the way to Paris.

Associated Press Radiophoto, passed yesterday by German censor

Texts of the Day's War Communiques

German

BERLIN, June 14 (AP)—The text of the first communiqué of the German High Command follows:

The complete collapse of the entire French front between the English Channel and the Maginot Line at Montmedy frustrated the original intention of the French command to defend the capital of France.

Thus Paris has been declared an open city.

At present victorious German troops are marching into Paris.

The text of the second communiqué follows:

The second phase of the gigantic campaign in the West is victoriously completed.

The power of resistance of the French northern front has collapsed. The Seine [River], southward from Paris, has been crossed on the broadest front and Havre taken. The enemy is in full retreat along the entire front from Paris to the Maginot Line at Sedan. At several points our tank and motorized divisions pierced through and overtook the retreat movement [French].

The enemy there fled leaving behind entire equipment. Infantry divisions broke through the defense lines of Paris. Enemy forces were no longer sufficient for protection of the French capital

Since this forenoon our victorious troops have been marching into Paris.

East of the Marne, Vitry-le Francois was taken. The Southern fringe of the Argonne forest was reached. Ridge 304 [Deadman's Ridge], northwest of Verdun was stormed yesterday evening.

Montmedy, strong pillar of the Maginot Line, is conquered.

The third phase of pursuit of the enemy until final destruction now has begun. This morning our troops on the Saar front also began a frontal attack on the Maginot Line.

Although hampered by weather, our fighting planes and dive-bombers destroyed units on June 13 and also supported armies in ground fighting at many points of the front.

Troop concentrations and marching and transport columns in the rear of the opponents were successfully bombed and machine-gunned.

Extensive destruction was carried out on airports, railroad stations and rail lines—especially in the region east of the Marne.

In the coastal region of Havre we succeeded in sinking two transports and an additional three were damaged, among which was one ship of 10,000 tons.

Anti-aircraft artillery north of Havre sank six enemy transports, considerably damaged an additional three, and forced one English destroyer to run away.

The opponent's air losses yesterday amounted to nineteen planes. Three were bagged in an air fight, three were shot down by anti-aircraft [guns] and the rest were destroyed on the ground.

Two of our own planes are missing. One submarine on June 13 sank the British auxiliary cruiser Scotstoun of 17,000 registered tons. Another U-boat succeeded in hitting and sinking from the most strongly protected convoy a 12,000-ton transport ship north of Hebrides.

French

TOURS, June 14 (UP)—The French High Command's morning communiqué said:

The enemy push on two sides of Paris has again been accentuated.

As the result of this advance, troops defending Paris are retiring on both sides of the city, conforming to orders received.

In renouncing direct defense of the capital, now declared an open city, the French Command wanted to spare the devastation that defense of the city would have entailed, and estimated that no valuable strategic reason justified the sacrifice of Paris.

On a vast front in Champagne enemy armies are progressing, fighting toward the South. Their most advanced elements seem to be pointed toward Romilly on one hand and St. Dizier on the other.

Our fighting and our movements are taking place in the greatest order.

TOURS, June 14 (AP)—The night French communiqué follows:

From the sea to the Argonne the battle continues on the whole front, although at certain points with less violence. The retirements ordered, notably that of the army of Paris, as announced in this morning's communiqué, have been carried out conforming to plans.

Our troops have counter-attacked several times.

The enemy this morning delivered a violent attack against our positions west of the Saar, using tanks and airplanes. They were repulsed with heavy losses.

During the night of June 13-14 a special formation of naval aviation commanded by Captain Daileire bombed and set fire to reservoirs of liquid fuels in the region of Venice.

Another formation dropped tracts on Rome.

Our warships bombarded industrial establishments and the railway line along the Italian coast.

Italian

ROME, June 14 (AP)—The text of today's High Command communiqué follows:

Activity of small detachments on some sectors of the Alpine front.

An enemy attempt to capture Galisia Hill was driven back.

In the central Mediterranean, enemy submarines attempted, without result, to oppose the movement of our fleet. Two enemy submarines were hit and one seriously damaged.

Continuing its action the air force carried out effective bombardment of air bases in the Tunis area.

An extensive offensive was carried out against the base of Hyeres with machine-gunning of planes of that airport from a low altitude and then bombing of military establishments, and against the base of Fayence in Provence and military installations of the Toulon base. One plane did not return to its base.

Intensive reconnaissance activity has been carried out over enemy bases and territories.

In Italian North Africa enemy attacks suported by tanks against our frontier posts on the Egyptian frontier were repulsed.

Prompt intervention of the air force destroyed several tanks and damaged others.

In Italian East Africa at dawn on June 11 enemy troops from Kenya [British colony] supported by artillery fire and aerial bombers attacked from the Moyale zone. The attack was completely driven back with slight losses. Among the prisoners taken by us were English officers and a non-commisisoned officer.

Our air force bombed Port Sudan and the port and airfield of Aden and an emergency landing field at Moyale. Two planes have not returned.

Enemy air attacks in Eritrea caused slight damage to war equipment. An enemy plane was shot down.

British

LONDON, June 14 (UP)—An Air Ministry communiqué today said:

Royal Air Force medium bombers bombed bridgeheads of the Seine and also troop concentrations east of Rouen all day Thursday. Five British planes are missing.

During the night large numbers of heavy bombers attacked lines of communication from Rouen to the Maginot Line and registered hits on bridges, railways, road junctions, freight yards, oil stores, convoys, ammunition dumps and forests occupied by troops. One British plane did not return.

LONDON, June 14 (AP)—An Admiralty announcement today said:

The Secretary of the Admiralty regrets to announce that the armed merchant cruiser H.M.S. Scotstoun (Captain O. K. Smyth) was sunk yesterday by a U-boat. Two officers and four ratings are missing and it is feared that they have lost their lives. The next of kin have been informed.

The remainder of the officers and ship's company have been landed at a British port.

A later Admiralty communiqué stated:

Aircraft of the fleet air arm carried out an attack on German naval units in Trondheim Fjord [Norway] early yesterday morning.

Information has now been received that one hit abaft the funnel was obtained with a heavy bomb on the battleship Scharnhorst. It is also reported that possibly a second hit was registered on the same ship.

An Admiralty communiqué tonight added:

Units of the Allied fleet have been to sea since the outbreak of war with Italy, carrying out sweeping operations in the Mediterranean with the object of protecting shipping and destroying enemy ships. No enemy has been sighted so far.

PRETORIA, South Africa, June 14 (AP)—A South African communiqué today said:

Yesterday our aircraft conducted bombing operations in the Chisimaio [Kismayu] area and scored direct hits on military camps.

Anti-aircraft opposition was encountered.

All our aircraft returned to their bases.

2 NAZI FORCES JOIN TO CAPTURE PARIS

Continued From Page One

are next in line in this sector, it is said in military quarters here. The objective of this push is stated to be the Maginot Line itself.

French Losses Cited

Germans also assert that what makes the defeat at Paris catastrophic for the French is that they have been forced in the retreat from this front to leave behind what the High Command calls their "entire military equipment." Following so closely on the heels of the Flanders debacle, with the heavy losses of equipment and men there, the latest losses, Germans claim, mean the end of the French Army. For it will have neither time nor opportunity to reorganize or re-equip, it is said here.

The High Command declares that the "third stage of pursuit of the enemy to his final destructions now has begun."

When the French are "destroyed" then it will be the turn of the British, Germans declare. For it is constantly reiterated here that the 874-year-old security of the British Isles, which hitherto had been provided by the kindness of Neptune, is about to be violated. Before July is past the Germans expect to be on British soil. Once there, German quarters confidently predict, a fortnight will be all they will require for their operations.

If one remonstrates and suggests that two weeks are not very much time, one is politely but firmly told that when the Germans said they would go through France according to schedule, foreign experts were inclined not too quietly to snicker.

Plans are all made for the invasion of England, it is added—and the entire campaign in the West will be concluded before the Autumn.

French Held Too Weak

The French capital, the High Command asserts, was surrendered only because the enemy no longer had sufficiently strong forces to defend it—not because the French desired to spare the city.

The German troops who marched into the French capital today were from the center of the German offensive. The advance on the city was made by two groups, one of which approached the gates from Pontoise. The other broke through the fortifications at Senlis. The capture of Paris, Germans declare, was not an easy task but was achieved by their infantry divisions only after bitter fighting.

The French capital fell exactly ten days after the Germans began the Battle of France and exactly five weeks after the initiation of the Western campaign. It is recalled that the Polish campaign began Sept. 1 and Warsaw did not surrender until the twenty-seventh.

Occupation of Paris by German troops cannot fail to have psychological and economic effects on France quite as devastating as are its military implications, in the opinion of the German press, which designates the French capital and its environs as the heart of the country's war and other industries.

Effect on Economy Noted

Economic writers point out that the paralyzing effect of the military loss of the metropolis is destined completely to disarrange the nation's economic organization, especially if Havre also is lost. The war and other industries situated in Paris and its immediate vicinity are estimated to support a population exceeding 6,000,000, and the social and political ramifications following the occupation of the city also must be taken into account.

Afternoon papers here contained only the bare statement that German troops had entered Paris. Details of the progress of the occupation still were lacking early this evening.

Neutral diplomatic circles in Berlin believe the loss of Paris in all probability is the prelude to a separate peace move by France to Germany. They profess to see no other choice for General Maxime Weygand, the French commander. Reports that France was prepared to take the lead for an armistice, current when the Flanders battle was definitely lost, were again in circulation today. Informed quarters believe Edouard Daladier's disappearance from the French Cabinet was primarily the result of his having advanced such a proposal.

Neutral opinion, so far as it could be gauged reliably today, appears to concur in predicting the collapse of France's military power in a fortnight at most now that the loss of Paris has left France only a torso, politically and economically.

The popular conception of Paris as the world's fashion center inclines many to minimize the capital's importance to the nation's industry, say German writers. They assert that despite stubborn attempts at decentralization the bulk of French key industries, especially automotive, motor and highly specialized branches, remained concentrated in and near Paris. Its capture therefore is appraised as even a greater victory than the Battle of Flanders and German military authorities frankly express gratification over General Weygand's decision to spare the capital a destructive bombardment.

Fort Communication Cut

It will be extremely difficult, if not impossible, for French troops in the Maginot Line to escape, military quarters in Berlin contend. The reason, they declare, is that the main lines of communication, particularly by rail, run from the Maginot Line in a westerly direction and already have been cut by the German advance.

French Army equipment, it is said here, is mostly designed for defense and its principal motorized units were destroyed in the Flanders battle, so that, it is argued, a protected retreat from the Maginot Line borders on the impossible.

By breaking the Maginot Line the Germans would acquire more direct connections between home bases and the Channel for the proposed invasion of Britain. The only thing that can prevent that invasion is a British surrender, it is said here.

Although the weather in France yesterday was reported to have been bad. German planes, said to see Allied planes very infrequently now, were described as assisting ground forces on all fronts. As in Poland, enemy troop concentrations behind the front, as well as retreating columns, were subjected to frequent surprise attacks, during which they were bombed and machine-gunned, Berlin reports asserted.

In the operations around Havre, Germans declare, their planes sank two enemy transports and damaged three others, one of which was of 10,000 tons. German anti-aircraft artillery, it is claimed, sank six enemy transports north of Havre, seriously damaged three others and forced a British destroyer to flee.

Allied plane losses yesterday totaled nineteen, the High Command declares, three of them shot down in dogfights, three by anti-aircraft artillery and the rest on the ground. Two German planes are reported missing. In spite of the arrival of additional planes of American manufacture in France, Germans declare they still are absolute and virtually uncontested rulers of the air.

LANDON CRITICIZES ROOSEVELT ON WAR

Opposes Sending Men Overseas as He Interprets the President's Speech

'TREAD SOFTLY,' HE URGES

Former Kansas Governor Warns That We Are Not Yet Well Equipped for Combat

TOPEKA, Kan., June 14 (UP)—Alfred M. Landon condemned tonight the President's Charlottesville speech promising aid to the Allies "as a course taken on his own responsibility that is in the direction of a war for which the nation is utterly unprepared and to which a vast majority of people are opposed."

He said the President showed "a disposition to take this country to the verge of war without regard to national opinion as expressed through Congress." He added: "It is the way of dictatorships, the way just taken by Mussolini."

He said the speech "was interpreted by the British press as bringing 'much neare. the United States' entry into battle.'"

Mr. Landon said he was in "thorough" agreement with the attitude of Senator Wheeler, who promised to take a walk from the Democratic party if it became a "war party."

In a statement Mr. Landon said:

"Senator Wheeler is an outstanding Democrat. But he announced in the Senate this week that he would 'break with the Democratic party' if it became a 'war party,' and he added that he would not support any Presidential candidate 'who is going to try to get us into war.'

"I thoroughly agree with Senator Wheeler's attitude on America and the war. Our sympathies are with the Allies. We believe their defeat would be a calamity to the world, and that it would be a menace to the United States.

Wheeler's Views Upheld

"Most of us are agreed that we should sell them all the material supplies we probably can. All of us are agreed on preparedness; on going the limit for national defense.

"But I am not ready to agree that we should go into war and send our boys overseas—for that is what going into war would eventually mean—and I am convinced that this is the view of the overwhelming majority of American people.

"The President has admitted our defenses have been so neglected that we must put all our energy into making them adequate. In this situation we should tread softly and not risk getting into a war for which we lack both essential equipment and trained men.

"What has disturbed Senator Wheeler and what has profoundly disturbed me has been the attitude of the President as disclosed most clearly in his Charlottesville (Va.) speech. It showed a disposition to take this country to the verge of war without regard to national opinion as expressed through Congress.

"The President has offered to the Allies 'the material resources of the nation.' He made this offer as if material resources of the nation were his to dispose of. This is not the way of democracy. It is the way of dictatorships—the way just taken by Mussolini.

Preparedness Held "Big Job"

"The speech was interpreted by the British press as bringing 'much nearer the United States' entry into the battle,' as meaning that America is about to enter the war. The President may not have meant to give this impression.

"Indeed he could not have meant to give it. He knows, if the British do not, that only Congress has the authority to declare war and that Congress has not the slightest notion of declaring war.

"Nevertheless his language was so emotional and so loose that it lent itself to this British interpretation. It would be cruel indeed to arouse false hopes in nations that are fighting for their existence.

"This is the time above all others for American people to keep their heads, to survey the world situation as calmly and dispassionately as possible. It is no time for whipping up national emotion.

"The big job facing us is preparedness. We have the greatest industrial organization in the world. In the last seven years the brains that constitute industrial leadership of this country have been driven into caves with a club waiting for them when they poke their heads out.

"The whole crux of the situation, as I said in January, 1939, is that, confronted by the might of totalitarian governments, we must not make the mistake of democracies in Europe. They were working less and playing more, while the people of totalitarian governments were playing less and working more."

4 POWERS COMPLETE MONETARY ACCORD

Netherlands Joins Belgium and Allies in Fixing Rates

Special Cable to THE NEW YORK TIMES

LONDON, June 14—A monetary agreement embracing Britain, France, Belgium and the Netherlands was completed today by the signing of the Netherlands. The official rate of exchange was fixed at 7.6 guilders to the pound, thereby establishing an effective union between the four currencies.

The original Anglo-French agreement stabilized the pound-franc exchange for the duration of the war and six months thereafter at 176½ francs to the pound. In a separate tripartite agreement with Belgium the value of the Belgian franc was fixed at the same level. The rate adopted for the guilder was the one provisionally adopted on the invasion of the Low Countries.

Britain and France will be able henceforth to buy the products of Netherlands Indies and Belgian Congo without the use of foreign exchange or gold. The Belgian and Netherland Governments will be able to make any payments to this country or France on the same basis.

All this, however, is not so important as stabilization of the rates for the dollar. It is reported negotiations have been going on between the Bank of England and United States representatives to establish an official sterling-dollar rate as the only one to be quoted in New York.

Latest Paris Surrender City's 9th Since 52 B.C.

German troops marched through Paris streets yesterday for the first time since the terrible siege of the city in 1871. It was the ninth foreign occupation in the long history of the city that had grown up in ancient times at the intersection of two great natural highways in the Seine Valley.

Julius Caesar captured the smoking ruins of the fortified town of the Gallic tribe of the Parisii during the Gallic War of Independence in 52 B. C.

Rebuilt as Lutetia, a Roman city, it was destroyed by the barbarian invaders of the third century, only to reappear as Paris.

The Franks under Clovis made themselves masters of Paris in the fifth century, the Danes in the ninth and Henry VI of England in 1422, an occupation that lasted until 1436.

Field Marshal Bluecher of Prussia led the Bohemians and Silesians into Paris in 1814 when the First Empire was overthrown and re-entered in 1815 after Waterloo.

The next fall of Paris was on Jan. 28, 1871, when the Germans, victors in the Franco-Prussian War, marched into the city, whose defenders had been decimated by a Winter of starvation and plague, by morale-shattering defeats of French troops elsewhere that provoked bloody riots and by an eighteen-day siege that had claimed one of the most frightful tolls in history.

REICH TANKS CLANK IN CHAMPS-ELYSEES

Continued From Page One

the Arc de Triomphe to move down the Champs-Elysées. Speculation had suggested that the honor of being the first to march beneath that historic arch might be reserved for Germany's self-styled first soldier, Adolf Hitler.

The great arch, started in the course of the Napoleonic triumphs, is a 160-foot pile of stones, each bearing the name of a victory or a hero in French military history.

Nazi officers at the head of the procession set their course for the headquarters of French officials still in the city, it was said, and formally took it over.

The French police, Fire Department and other city departments were said to have placed themselves at the disposal of the Germans. They offered to maintain order and discipline during the occupation of the capital, the Germans stated.

Germans Broadcast From Paris

Negotiations with the French officials in Paris were said to have been conducted by German officers without benefit of intermediaries.

One of the first acts of the Germans in Paris was to take over the radio stations, over which the playing of German music began immediately.

[A London dispatch said that the No. 2 radio station of Paris began broadcasting in German at 12:10 P. M. (7 A. M. New York time). The station is the one that took over the wave length of Radio Luxembourg after the Germans occupied the Grand Duchy.]

The last refugees left Paris at midnight. By orders of the Prefecture of Police, the city gates were closed by policemen and civil guards. The French troops fell back on both sides of the city, flowing around it and not going through it.

The authorities, left here for the bitter duty of surrendering the city, refused permission for any more people to leave it, in order to avoid confusion or a clash.

The first Germans to approach were motor cycle machine-gunners. They established their posts outside the gates and awaited the orders of their High Command.

The capital was like a city of the dead—shops closed, iron shutters in windows, those people who remained mourning in their homes and wondering what was coming.

Police and civil guards patrolled the streets slowly, almost alone. They had handed in their rifles and pistols. They were now a completely civilian force.

Parisians Report at Tours

TOURS, France, June 14 (AP)—The last hours of Paris as a free city of France were described sadly here today by a few of those civilians who had stayed on there almost to the end.

They told of small groups of men—unwilling to leave in the face of any disaster—still sitting in alternate sun and shadow at the boulevard cafes; of a city filled with a great and unaccustomed silence where only the police still stood guard.

Reports brought out from Paris a few hours before the German vanguards arrived said that anti-aircraft batteries had been dismantled and sandbag barricades removed, making the capital a completely undefended city.

Subways continued to function.

United States Ambassador William C. Bullitt spoke to crowds of Americans who swarmed to the embassy for information.

Many Americans decided to remain rather than tackle the refugee-choked roads leading from the capital.

Suburban Arms Plants Blasted

LONDON, June 14 (AP)—A Reuters (British news agency) dispatch from Paris today said big French armaments factories in the suburbs were blown up before the Germans entered the French capital.

Paris was almost a deserted city, the dispatch said. The French who remained while most of the population fled, stayed in their homes or sat in their shops with the shutters down.

All buildings and bridges, it said, were left intact.

Nine European Capitals Seized

BERLIN, June 14 (UP)—When German troops marched into Paris today they claimed for Adolf Hitler the ninth European capital occupied by his armed forces since March 12, 1938, when the Nazis took over Austria. Those capitals, in addition to Paris, are Vienna, Warsaw, Oslo, Prague, Copenhagen, Luxembourg, the Hague and Brussels.

AIDE SAYS HITLER SPURNS PEACE NOW

Fall of Paris Is Declared to Seem to Him Mere Incident in Road of Conquest

HIS GENERALSHIP PRAISED

Plan of Campaign Attributed to Chancellor Himself by Press Representative

WITH THE GERMAN ARMY, June 14 (UP)—The occupation of Paris, although naturally a cause for great rejoicing in Germany, is regarded by Chancellor Hitler as but an incident on his road of conquest, Otto Dietrich, his personal press representative, told foreign correspondents today.

This road, Herr Hitler is determined, shall see the end of the "domination" of the "plutocracies," Dr. Dietrich said. And Herr Hitler is not interested in peace now.

"So long as weapons are speaking, Germany has nothing to say of peace," Dr. Dietrich continued. "We have made repeated offers of a peaceful settlement. But now the issue has been joined for a decision.

"There has not been a single critical hour during which we were not certain which way the pendulum would swing. Everything has been done in accordance with our advance schedule. During my weeks in the Fuehrer's headquarters I have been astounded at the way in which the mechanism of a huge campaign has run with the precision of a watch."

He asserted that Herr Hitler, personally, was directing all phases of military operations and that the Paris battle plan was his, as was that for Poland last September.

"He created this army. He created its weapons. And he is its leader," Dr. Dietrich said.

In Field Since May 10

Herr Hitler has been in the field directing operations without a let-up since the blitzkrieg opened on May 10, Dr. Dietrich declared, adding that he keeps with him at his headquarters a small, trained staff whose members keep him in touch with all military and political affairs.

"The Fuehrer is a great field general," his press representative said. "I who have known him for years am astounded at the confident way in which he reaches military decisions. Once he has made a decision nothing changes it."

Then Herr Dietrich spoke of the political situation, in words that might have been his chief's because of their close personal association. He spoke almost contemptuously of the desperate efforts of the Allies to retrieve their position.

"We read of so and so many planes being delivered each week, of such and such preparations," he said. "We of all people know what it takes to build an army. We know that it cannot be built overnight.

"The forces that regenerated Germany and Italy were new forces. Who failed to understand that had to pay the price. Holland and Belgium—they were victims of fatal delusions, of the 'English sickness.'

"Poland could have been spared by accepting a plebiscite.

"For six months our press spared France. We wanted to build a bridge of peace, but it was no use.

"Our offers to England were also useless.

"And what now? Churchill [British Prime Minister] spoke of throttling Germans and now British troops are desperately trying to evade the iron grip of the German forces.

"Chamberlain [former Prime Minister] said he lived for the day when Hitler would be destroyed. Chamberlain today is a political corpse.

Blames Allied Leaders

"You have been to the front and are going again. You have seen what misery has been brought upon these peoples by their leaders. How can people accept such leaders with their empty, deceptive promises? How much longer will they tolerate them?"

Dr. Dietrich commented that it was difficult to describe Herr Hitler's average day at his headquarters—a secret one—as his activities depended upon particular developments. Generally speaking, he said, Herr Hitler requires little sleep. Each day he has certain set conferences with army leaders.

"The Fuehrer is in an extraordinarily good mode these days," Dr. Dietrich added. "He has benefitted from weeks of fresh air. He lives a simple life, as usual. He regularly follows the news in the world's leading newspapers. In fact, there is nothing of importance that appears in the world press that he does not know a few hours later."

Dr. Dietrich said Herr Hitler had revisited and recognized many places where he had fought as a lance corporal in the World War. Asked whether these visits had taken Herr Hitler into actual danger, Dr. Dietrich replied that it was difficult to express an opinion. But without having been in the actual front combat lines, he added, the Chancellor had visited various field operations around Ypres, Lille, Vimy Ridge, Arras and Cambrai and had witnessed fighting at Dunkerque.

VATICAN BROADCAST IS SET

Aim of Special Mass Tomorrow Is to Chart Post-War Society

By Telephone to THE NEW YORK TIMES.

ROME, June 14—The Vatican radio next Sunday will broadcast a special mass with Latin comment. The intention of the mass, it is stated, will be "so that human society may after the war be regulated on a basis of truth, justice and charity."

The mass will be celebrated in the Vatican Grotto on the altar placed over the tomb of St. Peter. The broadcast will be heard on the 31.06 and 19.84 meter bands at 11:30 A. M., daylight saving time [5:30 A. M. New York time]. Daylight time will be adopted by the Vatican simultaneously with Italy at midnight tonight.

On Sunday afternoon there will be another broadcast on the 31.06 meter band describing the beatification ceremony, in which the Pope will participate, of the Italian Capuchin lay brother Ignazio da Laconi.

"All the News That's Fit to Print."

The New York Times.

LATE CITY EDITION
Increasing cloudiness with rising temperature today. Tomorrow cloudy, somewhat colder.
Temperatures Yesterday—Max.,34; Min.,25

VOL. XCI No. 30,634. Entered as Second-Class Matter, Postoffice, New York, N. Y. NEW YORK, MONDAY, DECEMBER 8, 1941. THREE CENTS NEW YORK CITY and Vicinity

JAPAN WARS ON U. S. AND BRITAIN; MAKES SUDDEN ATTACK ON HAWAII; HEAVY FIGHTING AT SEA REPORTED

CONGRESS DECIDED

Roosevelt Will Address It Today and Find It Ready to Vote War

CONFERENCE IS HELD

Legislative Leaders and Cabinet in Sober White House Talk

By C. P. TRUSSELL
Special to THE NEW YORK TIMES.

WASHINGTON, Dec. 7—President Roosevelt will address a joint session of Congress tomorrow and will find the membership in a mood to vote any steps he asks in connection with the developments in the Pacific.

The President will appear personally at 12:30 P. M. Whether he would call for a flat declaration of war again Japan was left unannounced tonight. But leaders of Congress, shocked and angered by the Japanese attacks, were talking of a declaration of war on not only Japan but on the entire Axis.

The plans for action tomorrow were made tonight in a White House conference at which the President, surrounded by his Cabinet and by Congressional leaders of both parties, went through reports, some official, some unconfirmed, of the continued assaults of the Japanese upon American Pacific outposts.

Meet Far Into Night

The conference lasted until after 11 o'clock and at its close an official statement was issued. This said that the President had reviewed for his conferees the latest advices from the Pacific and declared:

"It should be emphasized that the message to Congress has not yet been written and its tenor will, of course, depend on further information received between 11 o'clock tonight and noon tomorrow. Further news is coming in all the time."

Congressional leaders asserted as they left the White House that they did not know what the President would say tomorrow.

"Will the President ask for a declaration of war?" Speaker Rayburn was asked.

"He didn't say," answered the Speaker.

Asked whether Congress would support a declaration of war, Mr. Rayburn observed:

"I think that is one thing on which there would be unity."

Politics Declared Dropped

"There is no politics here," said Representative Joseph W. Martin Jr., Minority House Leader. "There is only one party when it comes to the integrity and honor of the country."

"The Republicans," said Senator Charles L. McNary of Oregon, the Senate minority leader, "will all go along, in my opinion, with whatever is done."

Unless international developments and plans changed overnight, it was indicated, the Presidential recommendations would be directed for the present, at least, at Japan only. This was asserted authoritatively in the face of widespread expectation that any

Continued on Page Six

NEWS BULLETINS

are broadcast by The New York Times every hour on the hour over Station WMCA—570 on the dial.

WEEKDAYS
8 a. m. through 11 p. m.
SUNDAYS
9 a.m., 1 p.m., 5 p.m., 11 p.m.

TOKYO ACTS FIRST

Declaration Follows Air and Sea Attacks on U. S. and Britain

TOGO CALLS ENVOYS

After Fighting Is On, Grew Gets Japan's Reply to Hull Note of Nov. 26

By The Associated Press.

TOKYO, Monday, Dec. 8—Japan went to war against the United States and Britain today with air and sea attacks against Hawaii, followed by a formal declaration of hostilities.

Japanese Imperial headquarters announced at 6 A. M. [4 P. M. Sunday, Eastern standard time] that a state of war existed among these nations in the Western Pacific, as of dawn.

Soon afterward, Domei, the Japanese official news agency, announced that "naval operations are progressing off Hawaii, with at least one Japanese aircraft carrier in action against Pearl Harbor," the American naval base in the islands.

Japanese bombers were declared to have raided Honolulu at 7:35 A. M., Hawaii time [1:05 Sunday, Eastern standard time].

Premier-War Minister General Hideki Tojo held a twenty-minute Cabinet session at his official residence at 7 A. M.

Soon afterward it was announced that both the United States Ambassador, Joseph C. Grew, and the British Ambassador, Sir Robert Leslie Craigie, had been summoned by Foreign Minister Shigenori Togo.

The Foreign Minister, Domei said, handed to Mr. Grew the Japanese Government's formal reply to the note sent to Japan by United States Secretary of State Cordell Hull on Nov. 26.

[In the course of the diplomatic negotiations leading up to yesterday's events, the Domei agency had stated that Japan could not accept the premises of Mr. Hull's note.]

Sir Robert was summoned by

Continued on Page Five

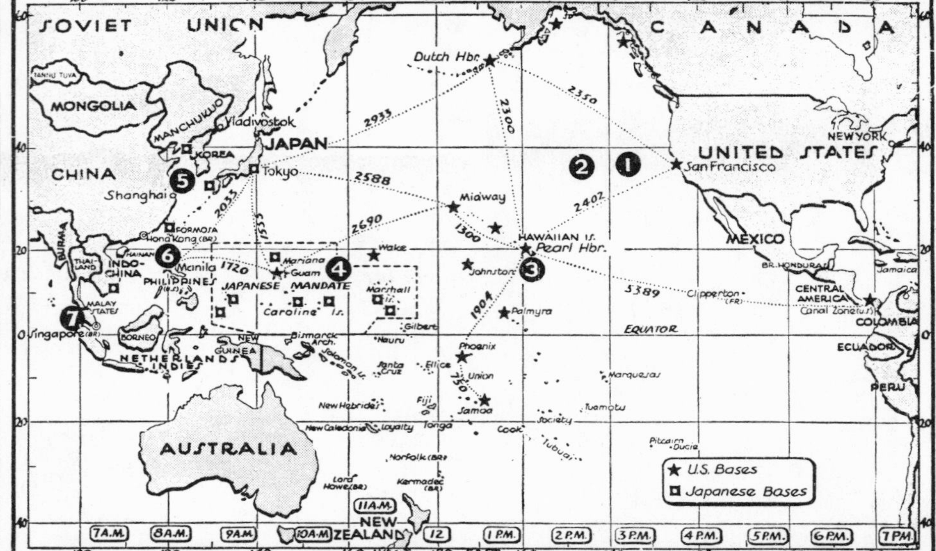

PACIFIC OCEAN: THEATRE OF WAR INVOLVING UNITED STATES AND ITS ALLIES

Shortly after the outbreak of hostilities an American ship sent a distress call from (1) and a United States Army transport carrying lumber was torpedoed at (2). The most important action was at Hawaii (3), where Japanese planes bombed the great Pearl Harbor base. Also attacked was Guam (4). From Manila (6) United States bombers roared northward, while some parts of the Philippines were raided, as was Hong Kong, to the northwest. At Shanghai (5) a British gunboat was sunk and an American gunboat seized. To the south, in the Malaya area (7), the British bombed Japanese ships, Tokyo forces attempted landings on British territory and Singapore underwent an air raid. Distances between key Pacific points are shown on the map in statute miles.

JAPANESE FORCE LANDS IN MALAYA

First Attempt Is Repulsed—Singapore Is Bombed and Thailand Invaded

By The Associated Press.

SINGAPORE, Monday, Dec. 8—The Japanese landed in Northern Malaya, 300 miles north of Singapore, today and bombed this great British naval stronghold, causing small loss of life among civilians and property damage.

About 300 Japanese troops landed on the east coast of Malaya and began filtering through jungle-fringed swamps and rice fields toward Kota Bahru airdrome, which is ten miles from the northern terminus of a railroad leading to Singapore.

An official report from the

Continued on Page Two

Tokyo Bombers Strike Hard At Our Main Bases on Oahu

By The United Press.

HONOLULU, Dec. 7—War broke with lightning suddenness in the Pacific today when waves of Japanese bombers attacked Hawaii this morning and the United States Fleet struck back with a thunder of big naval rifles. Japanese bombers, including four-engined dive bombers and torpedo-carrying planes, blasted at Pearl Harbor, the great United States naval base, the city of Honolulu and several outlying American military bases on the Island of Oahu. There were casualties of unstated number.

[The United States battleship Oklahoma was set afire by the Japanese attackers, according to a National Broadcasting Company observer, who also reported in a broadcast yesterday that two other ships in Pearl Harbor were attacked.

[The Japanese news agency, Domei, reported that the battleship Oklahoma had been sunk at Pearl Harbor, according to a United Press dispatch from Shanghai.

[Governor Joseph B. Poindexter of Hawaii talked with President Roosevelt late yesterday afternoon, saying that a second wave of Japanese planes was just coming over, and the Gov-

Continued on Page Thirteen

HULL DENOUNCES TOKYO 'INFAMY'

Brands Japan 'Fraudulent' in Preparing Attack While Carrying On Parleys

Texts of Secretary Hull's note and Japan's reply, Page 10.

By BERTRAM D. HULEN
Special to THE NEW YORK TIMES.

WASHINGTON, Dec. 7—Japan was accused by Secretary of State Cordell Hull today of making a "treacherous and utterly unprovoked attack" upon the United States and of having been "infamously false and fraudulent" by preparing for the attack while conducting diplomatic negotiations with the professed desire of maintaining peace.

But even before he knew of the attack, Mr. Hull had vehemently brought his diplomatic negotiations to a virtual end with an outburst against Admiral Kichisaburo Nomura, the Japanese Ambassador, and Saburo Kurusu, special envoy, because of the insulting character of the reply they deliv-

Continued on Page Eleven

ENTIRE CITY PUT ON WAR FOOTING

Japanese Rounded Up by FBI, Sent to Ellis Island—Vital Services Are Guarded

The metropolitan district reacted swiftly yesterday to the Japanese attack in the Pacific. All large communities in the area, including New York City, Newark, Jersey City, Bayonne and Paterson, went on immediate war footing.

One of the first steps taken here last night was a round-up of Japanese nationals by special agents of the Federal Bureau of Investigation, reinforced by squads of city detectives acting under FBI supervision. More than 100 FBI men, fully armed, were assigned to the detail.

The prisoners were sent to Ellis Island where they will be held pending action at Washington. It was indicated hundreds would be detained.

Earlier Mayor La Guardia had convened his Emergency Board and directed that Japanese nationals be confined to their homes pending decision as to their status and had their clubs and other meeting places closed and put under police guard.

A police sergeant and five policemen immediately went to the Japanese Consulate at 630 Fifth Avenue in Rockefeller Center where the Consul General, Morito Morishima, and his staff were preparing to leave, and posted a guard there. The Consul General and his staff were escorted to their homes when they left. They were not to move about the city without police in attendance.

Rear Admiral Adolphus Andrews, commander of the North Atlantic Squadron, told reporters at a conference in the Federal

Continued on Page Three

The International Situation

MONDAY, DEC. 8, 1941

Yesterday morning Japan attacked the United States at several points in the Pacific. President Roosevelt ordered United States forces into action and a declaration of war is expected this morning. [Page 1, Columns 7 and 8.] Tokyo made its declaration, as of this morning, against both the United States and Britain. [Page 1, Column 2.] The first Japanese assault was directed at Pearl Harbor Naval base in Hawaii. Many casualties and severe damage resulted. [Page 1, Columns 4 and 5; Map, Page 13.] United States Army aircraft took off from the Philippines this morning and some points in the Archipelago were bombed. [Page 8, Column 2.] Singapore and Hong Kong were bombed and a Japanese landing in Northern Malaya and a move on Thailand were reported. [Page 1, Column 3.] In Shanghai, Japanese marines occupied the waterfront; a British gunboat was sunk, a United States gunboat seized. [Page 9, Column 1.]

Factional lines dissolved as an angered Congress prepared to meet this morning. [Page 1, Column 1.] Secretary of State Hull accused Japan of having made a "treacherous and utterly unprovoked attack" after having been "infamously false and fraudulent." [Page 1, Column 6.] He released the text of diplomatic exchanges with Japan [Page 10].

while the President gave out the text of his fruitless appeal to the Japanese Emperor. [Page 12.] The White House was the hub of Washington activity and news bulletins were released there. [Page 12, Column 3.]

The Federal Bureau of Investigation was ordered to begin a round-up of some Japanese in this country [Page 6, Column 8.] As New York City went on a war footing and public precautions were taken, the FBI began the detention of Japanese nationals. [Page 1, Column 4.]

The unification of the country under the impact of the attack was swift. [Page 6, Column 6.] Formerly conspicuous isolationists indicated full support for the war effort. [Page 6, Column 4.]

Prime Minister Churchill notified Tokyo that a state of war existed. [Page 4, Column 1.] Declarations were made last night or early today by Australia, Canada [Page 14 Column 1], the Netherlands Indies [Page 7, Column 2] and Costa Rica. [Page 15, Column 1.]

Libya was the scene of a renewed tank battle and the Tobruk corridor was reported again clear of Axis forces. [Page 20, Column 2, with map.] On the Moscow front the German line was broken at two places, said Soviet sources. [Page 17, Column 2.]

Lewis Wins Captive Mine Fight; Arbitrators Grant Union Shop

The three-man arbitration board appointed by President Roosevelt to arbitrate the union shop dispute in the captive coal mines last night reversed the decision of the National Defense Mediation Board and ruled that all workers in the captive mines should be required to join John L. Lewis's United Mine Workers as a condition of employment.

The decision was made by a two to one vote, with Benjamin F. Fairless, president of the United States Steel Corporation, dissenting. Dr. John R. Steelman, who took a leave of absence from his post as director of the United States Conciliation Service to serve as chairman of the arbitration panel, and Mr. Lewis voted in favor of extension to the captive mines of the union shop provision of the standard Appalachian agreement.

Despite his dissent, Mr. Fairless promised that the coal mining subsidiaries of United States Steel would put the ruling into effect. All eight steel companies operating captive mines had given formal assurances before the decision was reached that they would accept it as binding.

The arbitration award ended a dispute in which Mr. Lewis had repeatedly defied the President by calling strikes that menaced the production of steel and that had had its repercussions in the enactment by the House of the Smith anti-strike bill.

In explaining his vote for the union shop, Dr. Steelman pointed out that 95 per cent of the 53,000 captive miners had voluntarily assumed membership in Mr. Lewis's C. I. O. union and that 99.5 per cent of all the miners in the nation were now members of the union.

Since the bulk of the industry, including many owners of captive mines, was already operating under the union shop, it could not be argued that the United Mine Workers was endeavoring to take

Continued on Page Forty-three

GUAM BOMBED; ARMY SHIP IS SUNK

U. S. Fliers Head North From Manila—Battleship Oklahoma Set Afire by Torpedo Planes at Honolulu

104 SOLDIERS KILLED AT FIELD IN HAWAII

President Fears 'Very Heavy Losses' on Oahu—Churchill Notifies Japan That a State of War Exists

By FRANK L. KLUCKHOHN
Special to THE NEW YORK TIMES.

WASHINGTON, Monday, Dec. 8—Sudden and unexpected attacks on Pearl Harbor, Honolulu, and other United States possessions in the Pacific early yesterday by the Japanese air force and navy plunged the United States and Japan into active war.

The initial attack in Hawaii, apparently launched by torpedo-carrying bombers and submarines, caused widespread damage and death. It was quickly followed by others. There were unconfirmed reports that German raiders participated in the attacks.

Guam also was assaulted from the air, as were Davao, on the island of Mindanao, and Camp John Hay, in Northern Luzon, both in the Philippines. Lieut. Gen. Douglas MacArthur, commanding the United States Army of the Far East, reported there was little damage, however.

[Japanese parachute troops had been landed in the Philippines and native Japanese had seized some communities, Royal Arch Gunnison said in a broadcast from Manila today to WOR-Mutual. He reported without detail that "in the naval war the ABCD fleets under American command appeared to be successful" against Japanese invasions.]

Japanese submarines, ranging out over the Pacific, sank an American transport carrying lumber 1,300 miles from San Francisco, and distress signals were heard from a freighter 700 miles from that city.

The War Department reported that 104 soldiers died and 300 were wounded as a result of the attack on Hickam Field, Hawaii. The National Broadcasting Company reported from Honolulu that the battleship Oklahoma was afire. [Domei, Japanese news agency, reported the Oklahoma sunk.]

Nation Placed on Full War Basis

The news of these surprise attacks fell like a bombshell on Washington. President Roosevelt immediately ordered the country and the Army and Navy onto a full war footing. He arranged at a White House conference last night to address a joint session of Congress at noon today, presumably to ask for declaration of a formal state of war.

This was disclosed after a long special Cabinet meeting, which was joined later by Congressional leaders. These leaders predicted "action" within a day.

After leaving the White House conference Attorney General Francis Biddle said that "a resolution" would be introduced in Congress tomorrow. He would not amplify or affirm that it would be for a declaration of war.

Congress probably will "act" within the day, and he will call the Senate Foreign Relations Committee for this purpose, Chairman Tom Connally announced.

[A United Press dispatch from London this morning said that Prime Minister Churchill had notified Japan that a state of war existed.]

As the reports of heavy fighting flashed into the White House, London reported semi-officially that the British Empire would carry out Prime Minister Winston Churchill's pledge to give the United States full support in case of hostilities with Japan. The President and Mr. Churchill talked by transatlantic telephone.

This was followed by a statement in London from the Netherland Government in Exile that it considered a state of war to exist between the Netherlands and Japan. Canada, Australia and Costa Rica took similar action.

Landing Made in Malaya

A Singapore communiqué disclosed that Japanese troops had landed in Northern Malaya and that Singapore had been bombed.

The President told those at last night's White House meeting that "doubtless very heavy losses" were sustained by the Navy and also by the Army on the island of Oahu [Honolulu]. It was impossible to obtain confirmation or denial of reports that the battleships Oklahoma and West Virginia had been damaged or sunk at Pearl Harbor, together with six or seven destroyers, and that 350 United States airplanes had been caught on the ground.

The White House took over control of the bulletins, and the Navy Department, therefore, said it could not discuss the matter or answer any questions how the Japanese were able to penetrate the Hawaiian defenses or appear without previous knowledge of their presence in those waters.

Administration circles forecast that the United States soon might be involved in a world-wide war, with Germany supporting Japan, an Axis partner. The German official radio tonight attacked the United States and supported Japan.

Axis diplomats here expressed complete surprise that the Japanese had attacked. But the impression gained from their attitude was that they believed it represented a victory for the Nazi attempt to divert lease-lend aid from Britain, which has been

Continued on Page Four

WHERE JAPANESE FORCES STRUCK THEIR OPENING BLOWS IN THE WAR AGAINST THE UNITED STATES

The harbor of Honolulu, on which Japanese airmen aimed their explosives The New York Times

Hickman Field, where 104 soldiers were killed and 300 wounded as a result of the attack. The structure is the new air corps barracks which houses about 3,000 men. Associated Press

Planes at Hickam Field ready for action Associated Press

Schofield Barracks, one of the points reported heavily bombed. Here the U. S. Army is shown staging a review in honor of the U. S. Navy. The New York Times

The United States naval air base at Pearl Harbor The New York Times

LA GUARDIA ACTS TO GUARD CITIES

Orders the Regional Civilian Defense Officials to Take Proper Steps at Once

Declaring that the Japanese attack upon Hawaii and the Philippines was the direct result of Nazi "master-minding" and an application of the "Nazi technique of mass murder," Mayor La Guardia took prompt and vigorous action yesterday in his dual capacity of Mayor and Federal Director of the Office of Civilian Defense.

In a press conference and two radio broadcasts, all originating at City Hall, the Mayor called upon citizens of New York to remain calm, assuring them that every precaution was being taken for their protection in the crisis, but warning them that they could not feel secure merely because they were on the Atlantic Coast and Japan's attack had been made in the Pacific area.

"We must be prepared for anything at any time," the Mayor said in his second broadcast. "We are not out of the danger zone by any means."

Word of the Japanese attack came to Mayor La Guardia in his home at 1274 Fifth Avenue as he listened to an early afternoon radio broadcast. By 5:45 P. M. he had taken the following steps:

Summoned his emergency board, consisting of key department heads, to a City Hall conference at 4:30 P. M., at which they were directed to put into operation immediately certain plans previously drawn to cope with war conditions.

Ordered the Police Department to see that all Japanese nationals remain in their homes pending determination of their status by Federal authorities.

Banned gatherings of Japanese nationals and ordered the Japanese Club closed and "supervised" pending Federal action.

Ordered police protection for the Japanese Consulate and for the persons of the Japanese Consul General and members of his staff, pending action in Washington on their official status.

Conferred by telephone with the White House, Army and Navy officials here and in Washington and representatives of the FBI.

Notified regional directors of the Office of Civilian Defense to get into touch with the Governors of States in their respective areas to map out intensified civilian defense training programs.

Instructed New York air raid wardens and Fire Department auxiliary forces to stand by for detailed instructions today, and served notice on local air raid wardens to be prepared for daily drills until further notice.

Speeding to City Hall in a police radio car, the Mayor found Police Commissioner Valentine, Fire Commissioner Patrick Walsh, Public Works Commissioner W. A. V. Huie and Dock Commissioner John McKenzie awaiting him there. The Mayor and his aides immediately went into conference.

While the conference was in session a telephone operator was busy putting the Mayor into contact with various Federal and local agencies. The plans the Mayor ordered put into effect were not made public, but are understood to relate to the protection of key facilities such as docks, power plants, water supply, public buildings and other city projects.

Broadcasting apparatus was hurriedly installed by WNYC, the municipal station, and at 5:15, at the close of a press conference, the Mayor went on the air. A little later he again went to the radio, his message this time being carried by the nation-wide networks of the Columbia, NBC and Mutual Broadcasting systems and station WHN.

In his press interview Mayor La Guardia declared that the Japanese attack had not come to him as a surprise and that the city was fully prepared to cope with the conditions created by that attack.

The Mayor urged that the public be on the alert from now on and that not too much comfort be taken from the fact that New York is on the Atlantic seaboard. Any one familiar with world affairs, he said, knew that Nazi "thugs and gangsters" were directing Japanese policy.

"I want to assure all persons who have been sneering and jeering at defense activities and even those who have been objecting to them and placing obstacles in their path, that we will protect them now," the Mayor said. "But we expect their cooperation and there will be no fooling."

In his second broadcast the Mayor emphasized more strongly his warning that New York and other Atlantic seaboard cities must not take too great comfort from the fact that Japanese aggression had been in distant Pacific waters. The situation, he said, was one of "extreme crisis" with anything to be expected.

All Private Planes Are Grounded by CAA; Pilot Licenses, Except on Lines, Suspended

By The Associated Press.

WASHINGTON, Dec. 7—The Civil Aeronautics Authority issued orders tonight grounding all private airplanes in the United States and its possessions, except commercial airliners.

The CAA suspended temporarily all pilot licenses except those held by pilots on regular air lines.

Robert Hinckley, chairman of the CAA Air Safety Board, sent telegrams to the Governors of the forty-eight States, Alaska and the Canal Zone asking them to assign police immediately to all known landing fields to protect facilities and to hold aircraft on the fields unless they were engaged in scheduled air transportation, were publicly owned or were operated under contract with the Federal Government.

This action was to remain effective, Mr. Hinckley said, until accredited representatives of the CAA or commanding officers of Army or Navy air fields issued instructions permitting specific planes to fly and until the Office of Civilian Defense issued further instructions for forming a civil air patrol.

The order suspending pilots' licenses, signed by D. H. Connolly, CAA Administrator, made provisions for reinstatement of private licenses in these cases:

Pilots at schools engaged in training operations for the government may regain their licenses when supervising Army, Navy or CAA officials are satisfied the holder "is an American citizen of unquestionable loyalty."

Pilots at aircraft manufacturing plants and at other defense manufacturing plants, upon certification by Army or Navy inspectors at the plants. This apparently applied to test pilots.

Pilots engaged in ferry activities (delivering planes under lease-lend agreements).

All other certificates may be reinstated only after satisfactory evidence of citizenship and loyalty accompanied by positive identification has been accepted by a designated representative of the CAA.

ENTIRE CITY IS PUT ON A WAR FOOTING

Continued From Page One

Building at 90 Church Street last night that:

"Every possible step has been taken to protect New York area from such an attack as surprised Pearl Harbor."

He told reporters that New York City is "a possible but not a probable danger zone."

Commissioner Valentine's men, at the request of Navy officials, checked and found no Japanese shipping in the harbor.

The Nippon Club at 161 West Ninety-third Street was closed by the police. Twelve Japanese who were there when the police came were escorted to their homes. Silent crowds watched their departure. There were no demonstrations.

Seven Japanese guests at International House at 500 Riverside Drive checked out late in the afternoon, apparently intent on making reservations for leaving the country.

On order from the State Department all Japanese reservations on planes out of New York were canceled. The police, on orders from the State Department, stopped all foreign sailings.

Twenty Japanese had reservations on the stratoliners, among them Mrs. Morito Morishima, wife of the consul general, and their two children. The reservations were made a week ago.

New York City policemen extended their visits to all Japanese restaurants in the five boroughs. They permitted diners to finish their meals, then escorted owners and their staffs to their homes.

Various Japanese commercial units seemed to have had some official signal of what was to come. Many did not renew leases. The Japanese Army officers of the Japanese Military Purchasing Commission, which had offices in the General Motors Building here, notified the superintendent Dec. 1 that they would not renew their lease.

The Japanese nationals were visited in their homes by FBI agents and detectives, told to take along a suitcase with traveling essentials, taken to a station house and booked as "prisoners of the Federal authorities," then removed in groups in patrol wagons and squad cars to the Federal Building at Foley Square. There, usually, their case histories were taken briefly, checked with official records already prepared, and then, in small groups, they were taken to the Barge Office at the Battery and to Ellis Island by ferry. A score, however, underwent extended questioning.

Most, if not all, of the estimated 2,000 to 2,500 Japanese nationals living in New York, some of whom are Japanese who were born in the United States, apparently were to be taken into custody, for in the West Side area from Eighty-sixth to 125th Street alone thirty-six Japanese subjects were sought. Small squads of FBI men joined squads of detectives in all precincts where Japanese are known to live.

All the prisoners were treated with every courtesy, although they were well guarded. They were allowed time to gather a traveling kit and each carried a suitcase or a traveling bag, apparently containing clothing enough for a stay on Ellis Island pending determination of their status and disposal by Federal authorities in Washington.

The round-up was not a wholesale arrest of Japanese, it was said at FBI headquarters. Known Japanese were being taken into custody on orders from Washington.

The first three Japanese to arrive at the Barge Office came at 11:45 P. M., shortly before armed Coast Guardsmen, under the command of Captain John Baylis, had thrown a cordon about the building.

Two of the prisoners refused to talk to newspaper men, but the third identified himself as Dr. S. Emy, 50 years old, a physician, who said he had been taken into custody at his home at 1035 Park Avenue at 8 o'clock last night. Dr. Emy, who is married and has a daughter, Josephine, said he had been in this country for thirty-five years and had been graduated from New York University in 1922. Remarking that he had not seen Japan since 1917, he commented, "This is an unfortunate situation."

Later newspaper men were not permitted to talk to the prisoners. In a later group was Kitadai Slughiro, president of a Japanese bank at 120 Broadway, who was taken into custody in his penthouse apartment at 70 Park Avenue shortly before last midnight.

Among others arrested were Keigi Hida, 48, a silk importer, living at the Hotel St. Mortiz, 40 Central Park South; Koji Matsuomoto, 39, a banker, and Sabino Tanji, 37, a Fifth Avenue silk and lace importer and exporter, both of the Hotel Barbizon-Plaza.

The FBI agents apparently acted according to a pre-arranged plan, after receiving instructions at their offices in the Federal Building. Federal stenographers and clerks were called in to take the pedigrees of the prisoners. The building was placed under heavy guard by squads of United States building guards, the public was excluded, and all persons, including Federal judges, were required to identify themselves.

Telephone operators also had to be called in as the FBI switchboard was swamped with telephone calls from citizens giving the bureau "tips" on activities by Japanese and other nationals that they considered suspicious. Similar calls were received by the police. All were investigated, although all, apparently, reflected overzealousness.

Some of the Japanese were crestfallen, some were smiling, but none offered resistance. Crowds were not permitted to collect, so there were no demonstrations.

No information about the round-up was given by Federal or local authorities. Early in the morning P. E. Foxworth, special agent in charge of this FBI district, saw reporters briefly and told them:

"We are at war and a censorship has been placed in Washington. I have received instructions to make no comments to the press."

At the Mayor's direction, Commissioner Valentine threw extra guards around communication points, the waterfront, power plants, defense industry units.

"Commanding oficers," said the Commissioner's order to borough commanders, "will direct members of the force to give particular attention and to be extra vigilant and alert in guarding all public utilities, electric, power, gas and steam plants, telephone and radio communication points and offices; armories, bridges, tunnels, water supply, ship yards, aviation fields, piers, defense manufacturing plants and other locations which may be affected in connection with defense industries and services and to supplement the present forces assigned if circumstances warrant."

Times Square crowds were tense and silent as they read the news bulletins on the Japanese attack. Only service men, chiefly sailors, seemed cheered by the information that Japan had declared war.

"We can whip them in no time," was a common remark sailors made.

The service men, in most cases, got their first word of the attack and the war declaration from policemen. Commissioner Valentine sent out a teletype order in mid-afternoon instructing all men on duty to tell sailors and soldiers to report to their ships, posts and stations.

Grand Central Terminal, Pennsylvania Station, the subways and buses were crowded with men in uniform hurrying back to their camps, ships and shore stations. There was some grumbling about broken furloughs, but in the main the men seemed eager to get back.

Newark, like New York City, went on war emergency footing immediately. Department heads were summoned to sudden conference and detailed plans for extra guards at all vital points were hastily mapped.

John B. Keenan, Public Safety Director of Newark, ordered policemen to board all trains in Newark and to take into custody "all suspicious persons of Oriental character." The same order applied to interstate buses.

Mayor Frank Hague in Jersey City, after a conference with his Commissioners, announced that "because of the present war crisis it was decided to be doubly certain that emergency conditions in Jersey City be covered until orders from the National Civilian Defense Director are received."

Jersey City at once sent extra details to the tunnels, waterfront and to defense industry plants.

Bayonne took the same steps. The guard was increased at the great oil plants and Navy shipbuilding yards.

Newark, Bayonne and most of the New Jersey communities immediately canceled fire and police leaves. This step was not taken in New York City. New York firemen, however, were instructed last night to be ready, any instant, for "recall" while off duty; never to get beyond range of a telephone or some other agency through which they might be reached in emergency.

Police stations throughout the city reported a spurt in volunteer enlistments in the air raid wardens' units.

Westchester County reported extra men assigned to the reservoirs at Croton, Ashokan and Kensico.

Aviation fields were barred to civilians lacking proper credentials. At Floyd Bennett Field in Brooklyn, policemen kept motor traffic on the Flatbush Avenue margin of the airport constantly moving.

"We're on a war basis," was their brief explanation.

Colonel William E. Larned, commanding the great Picatinny Arsenal at Dover, N. J., assured residents every possible safeguard against sabotage has been arranged.

Eleven shipyards in Brooklyn were put under extra heavy guard before night fell. Plants working on defense orders added to their guard personnel and in most cases drew extra city policemen.

TO STUDY CITY PROTECTION

750 Technical Specialists Will Begin Course Tonight

Tonight 750 technical specialists from departments of the city will begin study of municipal protection against bombardment at the Textile High School, 351 West Eighteenth Street. The course will be presented by New York University's College of Engineering in cooperation with the bureau of training of the Civil Service Commission.

Covering sixteen weeks, the course will include types and characteristics of explosive bombs, protection against sabotage, design and construction of bombproof buildings and protection against fire and disease.

The students will be drawn from engineering and architectural departments. The United States Office of Education is underwriting the expenses of the course.

The thirtieth annual appeal for the Hundred Neediest Cases is made in today's issue of The New York Times.

TOKYO INFORMED BRITAIN IS AT WAR

Churchill Instructs Craigie to Get Passports—Step Is Held Retroactive

CLOSE TIE TO U. S. IS SEEN

British Look for American Aid in Defeating Tokyo's Partners in Europe

LONDON, Monday, Dec. 8 (U.P.)—Prime Minister Winston Churchill, in the name of King George VI, has instructed the British Ambassador at Tokyo to declare to the Japanese Government the existence of a state of war between Great Britain and Japan, effective at the moment Japan started hostilities, it was understood today.

Sir Robert Leslie Craigie, the Ambassador, was instructed to ask the Japanese Foreign Office for his passports, it was understood.

Mr. Churchill was expected to announce his decision to the House of Commons at the opening of its session at 3 P. M. The House of Lords was summoned to meet at the same time.

The effect of the British decision was to make its recognition of a state of war with Japan retroactive to the moment Japan opened hostilities.

Formal Action Awaited

By CRAIG THOMPSON

Wireless to THE NEW YORK TIMES.

LONDON, Monday, Dec. 8—Britain was at war with Japan this morning, instructions for action having been flashed to the recently strengthened Far East Fleet, to the Singapore garrison and to other places where preparations for war had been made. Formal action awaited the message Prime Minister Winston Churchill will deliver to Parliament at 3 o'clock this afternoon.

It will be a special session of Parliament and it is the first time since the war against Germany began that the time of a Parliament meeting has been given in advance. The call for it went out last night shortly before it was known in London that the Japanese had made a declaration of war, but after Mr. Churchill, John G. Winant, the United States Ambassador, and others had gathered at 10 Downing Street to listen to or read every scrap of news of happenings in the Pacific they could obtain.

In the Japanese war Britain must look to the United States to take on the major operations, and this raises another problem. It is whether the scheduled shipments of lease-lend supplies to Russia and Britain will not be diverted for American needs. Unless the picture of American production has been badly understated to Britain, there are likely to be complications on this point.

Though the Japanese situation became serious while Britain was engaged in large-scale operations in Northern Africa, there has been no swerving of British policy. Months before it was unequivocally laid down by Mr. Churchill on Nov. 10, it had been made plain here that Britain would back up the United States to the fullest extent in whatever attitude was adopted toward Japan.

Mr. Churchill, however, put it on record in the strongest terms when he said, "Should the United States become involved in war with Japan the British declaration will follow within the hour."

Congress's expected declaration of war against Japan is regarded as the first step toward American involvement with Japan's European Axis allies. Many Britons have felt that the United States would be ranged alongside this country in actual hostilities and now that such expectations seem about to be realized, there is a stronger feeling of confidence in ultimate victory. A combination of the United States and Britain and her empire is regarded as unbeatable.

The Telegraph sees in the Japanese action "a carefully deferred answer to repeated representations of the United States Government in the interests of peace in the Far East up to and beyond the eleventh hour."

The Daily Mail denounces "Japanese treachery" and declares United States isolationism now gets its death blow.

The Express says Japan's "bluff" is over and the war that she "meant all these years in her dealings with Britain and America is an open war at last," adding that this is to Britain's advantage and will "not postpone the defeat of Hitler."

The Daily Herald says the United States knows she can count on Britain for the utmost support, and adds that Britain now has the opportunity "to repay America's comradeship by action."

The Manchester Guardian says the "United States and Britain, together with their Allies, must prepare themselves for a hard conflict in Pacific waters—a war mainly of naval and air power fought over great distances."

QUESTIONS JAPAN'S POWER

Tokyo's Acting Agent at Chicago Doubts Ability for Long War

CHICAGO, Dec. 7 (U.P.)—Kihachiro Ohmori, acting Japanese Consul General, said tonight that it was questionable how long Japan could continue at war with the United States.

"Japan is not wealthy," he said, as consulate attachés began burning office papers. "It is a question how long she could continue war with the United States."

WASHINGTON SCENE AS TIDE OF WAR SWEPT OVER NATION

A marine standing guard in front of the Capitol last night

Associated Press Wirephoto

Japan Starts War on U. S.; Hawaii and Guam Bombed

Continued From Page One

a Berlin objective ever since the legislation was passed and began to be implemented.

Secretary of the Treasury Henry Morgenthau Jr. announced that his department had invoked the Trading With the Enemy Act, placing an absolute United States embargo on Japan.

Robert P. Patterson, Under-Secretary of War, called on the nation to put production on a twenty-four-hour basis.

A nation-wide round-up of Japanese nationals was ordered by Attorney General Biddle through cooperation by the FBI and local police forces.

Action was taken to protect defense plants, especially in California, where Japanese are particularly numerous. Orders were issued by the Civil Aeronautics Authority to ground most private aircraft except those on scheduled lines.

Fleet Puts Out to Sea From Hawaii

The Navy last night swept out to sea from its bombed base at Pearl Harbor after Secretary of State Cordell Hull, following a final conference with Japanese "peace envoys" here, asserted that Japan's had been a "treacherous" attack. Neither the War nor the Navy Department had been able to communicate with its commanders in Manila.

Secretary of War Henry L. Stimson ordered the entire United States Army to be in uniform by today. Secretary Frank Knox followed suit for the Navy. They did so after President Roosevelt had instructed the Navy and Army to expect all previously prepared orders for defense immediately.

United States naval craft are expected to operate out of Singapore as soon as possible in protecting the vital rubber and tin shipments necessary to our national defense program.

Despite these preliminary defense moves, however, it was clear that further detailed discussions would soon take place between officials of the United States, Great Britain, China, the Netherlands and Australia to devise a total scheme of limiting the activities of the Japanese Fleet.

Immediate steps will be taken also to meet the increased menace to China's lifeline, the Burma Road. Reliable information indicates that the Japanese are preparing a large-scale assault on the road in the hope of cutting off American supplies before the Allies can transport sufficient forces into defensive positions.

Censorship was established on all messages leaving the United States by cable and radio.

In Tokyo United States Ambassador Joseph C. Grew obtained a reply to Secretary Hull's early message, according to dispatches from the Japanese capital.

The attack on Pearl Harbor and Honolulu began "at dawn," according to Stephen Early, Presidential secretary. Because of time difference, the first news of the bombing was released in Washington at 2:22 P. M. Subsequently it was announced at the White House that another wave of bombers and dive bombers had come over Oahu Island, on which Honolulu is situated, to be met by anti-aircraft fire again.

An attack on Guam, tiny island outpost, subsequently was announced. The White House at first said that Manila also had been attacked but, after failure to reach Army and Navy commanders there, President Roosevelt expressed the "hope" that no such attack had occurred. Broadcasts from Manila bore out this hope.

The Japanese took over the Shanghai Bund. Japanese airplanes patrolling over the city dropped some bombs, reportedly sinking the British gunboat Peterel.

Hawaii Attacked Without Warning

Reports from Hawaii indicated that Honolulu had no warning of the attack. Japanese bombers, with the red circle of the Rising Sun of Japan on their wings, suddenly appeared, escorted by fighters. Flying high, they suddenly dive-bombed, attacking Pearl Harbor, the great Navy base, the Army's Hickam Field and Ford Island. At least one torpedo plane was seen to launch a torpedo at warships in Pearl Harbor.

A report from Admiral C. C. Bloch, commander of the naval district at Hawaii, expressed the belief that "there has been heavy damage done in Hawaii and there has been heavy loss of life."

This was subsequently confirmed by Governor Joseph B. Poindexter of Hawaii in a telephone conversation with President Roosevelt. The Governor also said that there were heavy casualties in the city of Honolulu.

At the White House it was officially said that the sinking of the Army transport carrying lumber and the distress signal from another Army ship "indicate Japanese submarines are strung out over that area." Heavy smoke was seen from Ford Island near Honolulu.

In the raids on Hawaii Japanese planes were shot down, one bomber hitting and bursting into flames just behind a post-office on the Island of Oahu. It was reported without confirmation that six Japanese planes and four submarines were destroyed.

The second attack on Honolulu and its surrounding bases occurred just as President Roosevelt was talking to Governor Poindexter at 6 o'clock last evening.

There was no official confirmation of United Press reports from Honolulu that parachute troops had been sighted off Pearl Harbor.

Many Japanese and former Japanese who are now American citizens are in residence in Hawaii.

Saburo Kurusu, special Japanese envoy who has been conducting "peace" negotiations while Japan was preparing for this attack, and Ambassador Kichisaburo Nomura called at the State Department at 2:05 P. M. after asking for the appointment at 1 P. M. They arrived shortly before Secretary Hull had received news Japan had started a war without warning. Mrs. Roosevelt revealed in her broadcast last night that the Japanese Ambassador was with the President when word of the attacks was received.

The two envoys handed a document to Mr. Hull, who kept them waiting about fifteen minutes. Upon reading it, he turned to his visitors to exclaim that it was "crowded with infamous falsehoods and distortions."

President Roosevelt ordered war bulletins released at the White House as rapidly as they were received. A sentence or two was added to the story of the surprise attack every few minutes for several hours.

Cabinet members arrived promptly at 8:30 last evening for their meeting in the White House Oval Room. President Roosevelt had been closeted with Harry L. Hopkins in the Oval Room since receiving the first news. He had conferred with Secretaries Stimson and Knox by telephone and also with General George C. Marshall, Chief of Staff. Admiral Harold R. Stark, Chief of Naval Operations, was too busy to talk to the President even by telephone.

The first to arrive was Secretary of Commerce Jesse H. Jones. Secretary Knox came last. Secretary Hull was accompanied by two bodyguards.

Congressional leaders joining the Cabinet in the oval room at 9 P. M. included Senator Hiram Johnson of California, hitherto an isolationist and for long the ranking minority member of the Senate Foreign Relations Committee.

Others present were Speaker Rayburn, Representative Jere Cooper of Tennessee, representing Representative John W. McCormack, the House Majority Leader, who was not able to reach Washington in time for the conference; Chairman Sol Bloom of the House Foreign Affairs Committee and Representative Charles A. Eaton, ranking minority member; Vice President Wallace, who flew here from New York; Senator Allen W. Barkley, majority leader; Senator McNary and Senator Warren R. Austin, ranking minority member of the Foreign Relations Committee.

Cheering crowds lined Pennsylvania Avenue to see them arrive, another evidence of the national determination to defeat Japan and her Axis allies which every official is confident will dominate the country from this moment forth.

Senator W. Lee O'Daniel of Texas, of hillbilly band and hot biscuits fame, added a touch of inadvertent comedy to the scene when he arrived uninvited. He said he had come to "try to learn a few things" and "to make sure Texas is represented at this conference," thus ignoring the presence of Senator Connally.

Senator Barkley, who arrived in Washington by automobile about 7 P. M., said he did not find out about the Japanese attack until nearly 6 o'clock.

The formal positions of the United States and Japanese Governments toward the war were officially set forth by the release at the White House of the text of President Roosevelt's message of yesterday to Emperor Hirohito and by the Japanese document handed Ambassador Grew in Tokyo.

President Voiced Hope for Peace

The President's message expressed a "fervent hope for peace" and outlined the dangers of the situation.

"We have hoped that a peace of the Pacific could be consummated in such a way that the nationalities of many diverse peoples may exist side by side without fear of invasion," the President told the Emperor.

The President, recalling that the United States had been directly responsible for bringing Japan into contact with the outside world, said that in seeking peace in the Pacific "I am certain that it will be clear to Your Majesty, as it is to me, that * * * both Japan and the United States should agree to eliminate any form of military threat."

The Japanese document, despite the obviously carefully prepared attack on American bases, insisted that:

"On the other hand, the American Government, always holding fast to theories in disregard of realities and refusing to yield an inch on its impractical principles, caused undue delay in the [peace] negotiations."

Late last night, the United States Government announced that all American republics had been informed of the "treacherous attack" by Japan. It was stated that "very heartening messages of support" were being received in return.

The State Department statement on this matter said:

"All the American republics have been informed by the Government of the United States of the treacherous attack by Japan upon the United States. Immediately upon receipt of word of the attacks on Hawaii and other American territory, wires were dispatched to the American diplomatic missions, instructing them to inform the Foreign Offices at once. This government is receiving very heartening messages of support from the other American republics."

Senator Connally, as head of the powerful Foreign Relations Committee, predicted that world-wide war involving this nation probably depended on European developments within the next few days, according to The United Press.

Connally Promises Reply to "Treachery"

As Roland Young, committee clerk, took to Senator Connally's apartment drafts of the war declaration of April 2, 1917, Mr. Connally said:

"Professing a desire for peace and under the pretext that she coveted amicable relations with us, Japan stealthily concealed under her robe a dagger of assassination and villainy. She attacked us when the two nations were legally at peace.

"With rare and tolerant patience our government has striven to adjust our differences with Japan.

"Japan has now declared war upon the United States and on Great Britain. We shall resist this cruel and unjustifiable assault with naval power and all the resources of our country. We shall wreak the vengeance of justice on these violators of peace, these assassins who attack without warning and these betrayers of treaty obligations and responsibilities of international law.

"Let the Japanese Ambassador go back to his masters and tell them that the United States answers Japan's challenge with steel-throated cannon and a sharp sword of retribution. We shall repay this dastardly treachery with multiplied bombs from the air and heaviest and accurate shells from the sea."

Late last night American officers at the Mexican border were detaining all Japanese attempting to enter or leave the United States, according to a United Press dispatch from San Diego.

New York City, Chicago and other police forces acted to control Japanese nationals and with regard to consulates.

James L. Fly, chairman of the Federal Communications Commission and the Defense Communications Board, said further activity by amateur radio stations would be permitted only upon special governmental authorization.

He said he has been in constant touch with heads of all important communications companies with relation to execution of pre-existing plans for cooperation during any emergency.

GERMANY DELAYS AXIS PACT ACTION

Accusing U. S. of 'Provocation,' Berlin Puts Off Decision on Entering Japan's War

BERLIN, Monday, Dec. 8 (AP)—Obligated under the Axis Tripartite Pact to go to Japan's assistance if Japan was "attacked," Germany referred early today to hostilities in the Pacific as "clashes."

A special communiqué failed to clarify Germany's intentions, but termed President Roosevelt a "war-incendiary" or "war-monger."

The communiqué was divided into two sections. The first said:

"As a result of constantly increasing war-mongering of the American President Roosevelt in recent weeks, the first clashes between Japanese and United States armed forces occurred today."

Berlin's Comment on Roosevelt

The second part of the communiqué, devoted to comment, said:

"The war-incendiarist Roosevelt finally has reached his aim by also setting afire the Far East.

"Alongside Churchill he is one of those chiefly responsible for inciting this war. For years he tried to plot a war of Jews and plutocrats against the German Reich, which was revived by the revolution of the Fuehrer, and intentionally through his agents and middlemen worked toward the end of extending this struggle to other lands and other continents.

"The unwholesome role of Roosevelt confidents was made sufficiently clear by documents made public by Germans.

"He was the one who strengthened Poland to provoke the Reich.

"He gave France and England his promises of aid.

"He let the American public take over the financial burden of the English war after he committed perjury by breaking his election promise.

"Roosevelt sent his special envoy [Colonel William J.] Donovan, at the beginning of the year 1941 to capitals of the Southeast [Europe] and persuaded these lands against their considered judgment.

"Driven by blind hatred against the Reich of Adolph Hitler, he sent weapons and materials to British campaign areas and finally gave his fleet orders to fire on German warships.

"So Roosevelt ran after war like a demon until the Pacific Ocean also is inflamed. Dollar imperialism overcame the good sense of a wide circle of North American people."

Reich Awaiting Word From Japan

BERLIN, Monday, Dec. 8 (U.P.)—Belief was expressed here today that Germany would await Japan's version of the situation before action on the question of the invoking of the Tripartite Pact.

Berlin newspapers did not carry a line about the Japanese attacks. Informed quarters said it was possible there might not be any official action today.

Italy Predicts a Delay

By Telephone to THE NEW YORK TIMES.

BERNE, Switzerland, Monday, Dec. 8—"The cynical and sinister plan of Mr. Roosevelt was to oblige all the peoples of the world to furnish cannon fodder to serve the interests of the United States," the Italian radio said early today in a comment broadcast on the Japanese declaration of war against the United States.

"This has been the sole objective of the lease-lend act," the Italian radio went on. "However, thanks to the Japanese, the Americans, enemies of progressive humanity, must pay with their blood for the crimes of the Anglo-Saxon peoples."

The Italian radio also hurled invective against the United States to Italian émigrés in South America.

A Berlin radio announcement to the German nation at 11:04 o'clock last night [5:04 P. M. Eastern standard time] was heard here. It said:

"Following the provocations of the American nation, the first act of war has just occurred between Japan and the United States."

Article III of the Axis Pact

Under Article III of the Axis Tripartite Pact, signed by Germany, Italy and Japan at Berlin, Sept. 27, 1940, Germany could be called upon to war against the United States if the signers of the pact decided the United States "attacked" Japan. The article reads:

ARTICLE THREE—Germany, Italy and Japan agree to cooperate in their efforts on aforesaid lines (the New Order "leadership of Germany and Italy" in Europe and of Japan in Greater East Asia as set forth in Articles One and Two). They further undertake to assist one another with all political, economic and military means when one of the three contracting powers is attacked by a power at present not involved in the European war or in the Chinese-Japanese conflict.

Recruiting Stations Turn Many Away—Till Today

War spirit flashed up in the metropolitan district yesterday as bulletins came through from the Pacific.

Recruiting stations were closed for the day, but applicants for enlistment in the Army, Navy and Marine Corps were told to return today.

To the Federal Building in Newark, late in the afternoon, came a truckload of young men—about twenty—from the Oranges, seeking immediate enlistment.

These, like the rest, were told to come back today. Recruiting stations for the Marine Corps announced they would open at 7:30 A. M. today instead of at 9 A. M., the usual time.

NELSON SAYS NAZIS CAUSED THE ATTACK

Japanese Action Is in Reality an Assault on Us by the Axis Powers, He Says on Radio

Special to THE NEW YORK TIMES.

WASHINGTON, Dec. 7—The Japanese attack on the United States is only one phase of the war being waged against the United States by the Axis powers, Donald Nelson, Executive Director of the Supply, Priorities and Allocation Board, said tonight in a broadcast over the Mutual network.

"We must keep in mind," he said, "that though the attack has been made by the Japanese it is in reality an attack upon us by the Axis powers. It is, as you and I can see, part of a pattern. That pattern is designed to bring about, if possible, the extinction of democracy—of all freedoms everywhere.

"We are face to face with attack directed primarily from Berlin."

"Our goal for military victory," Mr. Nelson asserted, "is not only a job for the men of the Navy and of the Army, of the Air Corps and the Marine Corps. It is a job for each and every one of us."

"We, the citizens of the United States, have a vast stake in the Pacific," he went on. "This war that has now started thousands of miles from our shores comes directly home to all of us and at once. Many of the things we must have for peace and for war come from across the Pacific.

"I speak of rubber, tin, of tungsten, of manganese, of chromium.

"We must have these things in vast quantity to turn out the war goods our armed forces need to fight with and to keep our civilian economy running on a sound basis.

"Every one of us must begin at once to do his bit to conserve our vital supplies. Our men on the battle lines must be given every piece of fighting equipment they need for victory. You can help put that equipment in their hands—and make sure there are plenty of replacements—by doing your bit. Your bit multiplied by 130,000,000 other people doing their bit spells victory.

"All major elements of the Axis are now in action—direct military action—against the United States.

"No one can doubt that our military forces will show the world what this nation can do in a fight. Our Navy has already gone into action. But in a time such as this it is just as important that every civilian, every one of the 130,000,000 of us, mobilize ourselves at once, without doubt and without fear, behind the men who are out in front."

All Alaska Is Put on Guard

JUNEAU, Alaska, Dec. 7 (UP)—Governor Ernest Gruening today put the entire Territory on twenty-four-hour watch for protection of radio stations, telephone exchanges, oil tanks, public utilities and docks. Naval forces in the area previously had been ordered to duty.

FIRST LADY CALLS TO NATIONAL FAITH

Asks 'the Free and Unconquerable People' to Rise Above Their Personal Feelings

Special to THE NEW YORK TIMES.

WASHINGTON, Dec. 7—Sympathizing with the anxiety of parents who have sons in the services, Mrs. Franklin D. Roosevelt expressed today "a sincere hope that the certainty of what we must now meet will make you rise above personal feelings."

"We must go about our daily business more determined than ever before to do the ordinary things as well as we can and when we find a way to do anything more in our community to help others, to build morale, to give a feeling of security, we must do it," she said in her weekly radio talk over WJZ and a national network. "Whatever is asked of us, I am sure we can accomplish it; we are the free and unconquerable people of the U. S. A."

Mrs. Roosevelt said that "for months now the knowledge that something of this kind might happen has been hanging over our heads. That is all over now and there is no more uncertainty. We know what we have to face and we know that we are ready to face it."

Addressing a word "to the young people of the nation," she continued:

"You are going to have a great opportunity; there will be high moments in which your strength and your ability will be tested. I have faith in you. I feel as though I were standing upon a rock and that rock is my faith in my fellow citizens."

To "the women in the country tonight," she said:

"I have a boy at sea on a destroyer—for all I know he may be on his way to the Pacific; two of my children are in coast cities on the Pacific. Many of you all over this country have boys in the service who will now be called upon to go into action; you have friends and families in what has suddenly become a danger zone.

"You cannot escape anxiety, you cannot escape the clutch of fear at your heart and yet, I hope that certainty of what we have to meet will make you rise above these fears."

Mrs. Roosevelt opened her broadcast saying:

"I am speaking to you tonight at a very serious moment in our history. The Cabinet is convening and the leaders in the Congress are meeting with the President. The State Department and Army and Navy officials have been with the President all afternoon.

"In fact, the Japanese Ambassador was talking to the President at the very time that Japan's airships were bombing citizens in Hawaii and the Philippines and sinking one of our transports loaded with lumber on its way to Hawaii. By tomorrow morning the members of Congress will have a full report and be ready for action.

"In the meantime, we, the people, are already prepared for action."

Patterson Asks All Plants Guard Against Sabotage

Special to THE NEW YORK TIMES.

WASHINGTON, Dec. 7—The office of Robert P. Patterson, Under-Secretary of War, who is responsible for military procurement, sent out word by radio and telegraph today to managers of all factories making military supplies to make sure of the protection of their plants.

These factories are guarded by police forces organized and paid by the companies, but the personnel serve under government oaths and along lines devised by the Plant Protective Service of the War Department.

Further possible safeguards for such plants were arranged by the Provost Marshal General, Major Gen. Allen W. Gullion, when he requested all States to be on the alert with the Home Guards and "to take any other actions necessary."

LEHMAN ORDERS CAUTION

Tells Mayors to Move to Prevent Sabotage, Protect Japanese

ALBANY, Dec. 7 (AP)—Governor Lehman today instructed Mayors of New York State cities to take "all steps necessary to prevent sabotage," and ordered protection for Japanese nationals.

The text of the Governor's order, contained in telegrams to the Mayors, declared:

"You are directed to take all steps necessary to prevent sabotage in defense plants, public utilities, waterworks, bridges and all other places of strategic importance in your jurisdiction and to protect all Japanese nationals residing in your city."

TWO TRIBUTES TO SOVIET

Russians and Armenians Stage Separate Rallies Here

Russians and Armenians here paid tribute to the Soviet Union yesterday afternoon at Manhattan Center at two separate rallies, which filled two halls of the building almost to capacity. Three thousand persons attended a Russian-American meeting under the auspices of the American-Russian Committee for Medical Aid to the U.S.S.R., and 2,000 were present at a celebration of the twenty-first anniversary of the Armenian Soviet Socialist Republic.

Speakers at both meetings expressed confidence in the Red Army and resistance of the Soviet Union against Nazi aggression. At the Russian-American meeting, Dmitry Zaikin, Russian Vice Consul here, spoke for his government, and Dmitry Shiraeff presided. Prince Vladimir V. Koudasheff, committee chairman, told the audience that it represented the "real America and real humanitarianism."

At the Armenian rally, the "fighting Armenians" were hailed and a resolution was adopted in support of President Roosevelt's foreign policy.

15 Buried Seeking Tungsten

LISBON, Portugal, Dec. 7 (AP)—Fifteen Portuguese peasants, two of whom were rescued in a dying condition, were buried alive last night as they searched in an abandoned mine for wolframite. About fifty peasants sneaked by night into the long unused galleries at Lugar de Santo Oviedo hoping to extract the metal, much sought in wartime for use in the manufacture of steel. One gallery collapsed.

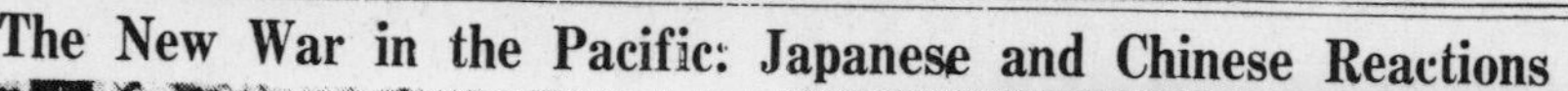

The New War in the Pacific: Japanese and Chinese Reactions

NEWSPAPERS CALL FOR MEETING FOE

Japan's Attack Is Recognized as War for Us, Bringing End to the Internal Strife

CHICAGO TRIBUNE IS FIRM

It Declares There Is No Time for Recrimination by Any One in This Crisis

Available newspaper comments on the attack by Japan, recognizing that it means war, call upon America to unite in defense. Excerpts from editorials are as follows:

NEW YORK CITY

Unity "at Hand" in Face of Peril

From The Herald Tribune.

In this solemn hour the first thoughts of every American will be of his country. "The drumming guns that have no doubts" have spoken. That union in face of peril which was grievously lacking is at hand.

Mr. Roosevelt and Mr. Hull deserve all praise for their patient efforts to preserve the peace. Since the clash now appears to have been inevitable, its occurrence brings with it a sense of relief. The air is clearer. Americans can get down to their task with old controversies forgotten.

That task is plainly not confined to the Pacific. If the ambitions of the Tokio militarists brought the issues of the Pacific to a bloody climax, they did so in the closest cooperation with their allies, the militarists of Berlin. We state no more than the simple truth when we declare that this war against our enemies—wherever they may be—will be fought to a victorious end with the last energy, the last resource and the last ounce of determination of every American man and woman.

Japan "Fired First Shot" in 1931

From The Journal of Commerce

The misguided nation which really fired the first shot in the new World War when it invaded Manchuria in 1931 now turns its guns upon the United States. Fortunately, this nation has proceeded far in preparing for such attack.

Japan's militarists must be defeated, and defeated decisively. However, this is no punitive war. The Japanese armies must return to their own territory and cease to range over the Asiatic mainland with fire and sword. Once disarmed, however, there is no reason why the Japanese nation should not be given the opportunity to work out its economic destiny to the full and remain the great industrial and commercial nation of the Orient.

"Reserving Right to Criticize"

From The Daily News.

The time has come for all of us to stand by the President in the general aim of winning the war, while reserving the right—as the British people and press have done throughout the rigors of this war to date—of criticizing government methods of all kinds pertaining to the war effort.

God knows the American people did not want this fight, any more than, we believe, the Japanese people wanted it. But now that we are in it, there is nothing for us to do but to see it through with everything we've got.

War Silencing Disunity

From The Mirror.

Henceforth, for all Americans, the fact of war with Japan must silence the voices of disunity. There is only one policy for all of us now: Decatur gave it to the United States 125 years ago—"Our country, right or wrong!"

BOSTON

War Brought to Doorstep

From The Herald

The surprise attack on Hawaii possessed a short-term cleverness. But the bombing of Hawaii did something which neither an invasion of Thailand nor even an assault on the Philippines could have done. It has brought the war to the doorstep of every American. It has unified the nation as could no Presidential proclamation or Congressional act.

PHILADELPHIA

"We Shall Not Falter"

From The Inquirer

Do the war-mad officials of the Japanese Government honestly believe they can get away with a crime like this? Or are they intent upon committing national hara-kiri?

We shall not falter now. Our great Navy and Air Force are on the line of battle. Japan has cast the die. Japan has invited just retribution. Japan has asked for it—let Japan have it!

ST. LOUIS

Attack Solidifying Unity

From The Globe-Democrat

By this attack upon Hawaii, Japan has adopted the most effective means of solidifying United States sentiment in a unity of defense that will prove triumphant. We are at war. Let the totalitarian prophets of force and slaughter and international rapine now learn how democracy can act in militant national harmony when grim issues challenge.

CLEVELAND

"Terrible Lesson" to Isolationists

From The Plain Dealer

The tragic events which have drawn this nation into war are a terrible lesson to two kinds of people, isolationists and the appeasers. The point should not be missed by those who still claim that the oceans are a barrier, that in order to attack Pearl Harbor the Japanese sent their ships and planes across an expanse of water that is several hundred miles wider than the Atlantic at its broadest point.

What the Japanese have done to Pearl Harbor on a small scale the Germans could and would do to Boston, New York, Philadelphia—and Cleveland—on a large scale should they once become masters of Europe and the British Isles.

CINCINNATI

"It Is a War We Shall Win"

From The Enquirer

Our turn to participate in the world-wide struggle has come with dreadful suddenness, even while the President was making desperate last-minute efforts to avert war by direct appeal to the Japanese Emperor.

Fortunately, we begin this long-anticipated war with powerful naval, air and land forces at hand, with strong allies in Britain, China, Holland and probably Russia. It is a war we can win, and shall win.

CHICAGO

To Strike With All Might

From The Tribune.

War has been forced on America by an insane clique of Japanese militarists who apparently see the desperate conflict into which they have led their country as the only thing that can prolong their power.

Thus the thing that we all feared, that so many of us have worked with all our hearts to avert, has happened. That is all that counts. It has happened. America faces war through no volition of any American.

Recriminations are useless and we doubt that they will be indulged in, certainly not by us. All that matters today is that we are in the war and the nation must face that simple fact. All of us, from this day forth, have but one task. That is to strike with all our might to protect and preserve the American freedom that we all hold dear.

[In addition to the editorial, The Tribune replaced at the masthead of its editorial page a slogan which it had carried for many years. It reads:

"Our country! In her intercourse with foreign nations may she always be in the right; but our country, right or wrong.—Stephen Decatur."]

Says but One Can Survive

From The Sun

It is war now, grim and to the death.

War to the death of Japanese and German militarism or to the death of the United States of America.

All that President Roosevelt foresaw and feared and worked against, all that lesser men refused to fear because they could not see, has come to pass. The thing of evil that is abroad in the world has coiled its ugly body and struck.

As Hitler struck at Europe, Japan has struck at America, cloaking words of peace in deeds of war and treachery.

Let no American think that this is a one-ocean war, a one-handed war or a war with one nation only.

It was Hitler who brought this war upon us, luring the Japanese with promises of aid and loot, filling their ears with tales of American weakness today and strength tomorrow.

The nation is one, or it is nothing. That means it is one, with a single will and purpose, a single heartbeat.

LOS ANGELES

"Act of a Mad Dog"

From The Times.

Japan has asked for it. Now she is going to get it. It was the act of a mad dog, a gangster's parody of every principle of international honor.

The attack on Honolulu by short-range bombers proves past dispute that it had been days if not weeks in deliberate preparation. The "peace negotiations" were mere play-acting to throw us off our guard.

The one respect in which Tokyo's "coup" differs from those of Hitler is that she has attacked no weak and defenseless nation. Instead, she has invited her own destruction by the swiftest and most ruthless means by which it can be encompassed.

SAN FRANCISCO

Call to Unite for Victory

From The Chronicle

By the act of Japan, America is at war. The time for debate has passed and the time for action has come. That action must be united and unanimous.

If war had to come, it is perhaps well that it came this way, wanton, unwarned, in fraud and bad faith, virtually under a flag of truce. For a war there can be only one side in action, and now there is only one in thought or feeling. Its slogan is "Americans Unite for Victory and Freedom!"

DO NOT FORGET
The Hundred Neediest.

Bonfire in Washington: Japanese lose no time in burning State papers on the grounds of their embassy
Associated Press Wirephoto

Police escort for Consul General: Morito Monishina leaving his office here last night.
The New York Times

Club closed: The steward at the Nippon Club, 161 West Ninety-third Street, carries out the orders of the police.
The New York Times

Thumbs up in New York: Chinese in front of the building at 630 Fifth Avenue, in which the Japanese Consulate is housed, express their reaction to the new turn of events.
The New York Times (by Sisto)

Hurried departure from New York: Officials leaving Japanese consulate
The New York Times

BURNING OF PAPERS WATCHED BY 1,000

While Japanese Embassy Staff Plies Fire Police Stand By, but Crowd Is Quiet and Orderly

Special to THE NEW YORK TIMES.

WASHINGTON, Dec. 7—As a crowd of more than a thousand looked on and Washington police stood by, the Japanese Embassy late today burned its official records and papers in the side yard of the embassy property.

This was done after the news was received of the attack on Hawaii and after Admiral Kichiburo Nomura, the Ambassador and Saburo Kurusu, special envoy, had returned to the embassy from the stormy meeting with Secretary Hull when they presented Japan's unsatisfactory reply to his proposal for a multilateral treaty of peace in the Pacific.

Fifteen containers were brought out of the embassy, piled up and lighted. The watching crowd grew and police details arrived, but all was peaceful. The only sound was the whirring of news cameras recording the scene.

The step was preparatory to departure of Admiral Nomura and his staff, presumably after the Ambassador has received his passports. Mr. Kurusu planned to go by plane to San Francisco. Joseph C. Grew, the American Ambassador in Tokyo and his staff, will return here as soon as arrangements can be made.

From what was said and from all that could be learned, both Admiral Nomura and Mr. Kurusu were astounded by the news of war. If several sources of information can be believed, they knew nothing of what their army and navy were preparing while they were conducting diplomatic negotiations.

These reports lent support to theories that the Japanese army and navy may have pulled out from under the foreign office, taken control and gone to war.

Admiral Nomura and Mr. Kurusu would say nothing. They sat glumly this afternoon in a room of the embassy and occasionally looked out at the growing crowd before the building, which stands in the fashionable section of Massachusetts Avenue in the Northwest section of the city. The embassy doors were locked at 5 P. M.

Meanwhile the State Department announced that "immediately upon receiving news of the Japanese attack on Hawaii the American Government took steps to see that absolute protection was accorded the Japanese official establishment and official personnel within the jurisdiction of the United States."

The protection applies to the property of the Japanese Embassy here, the two Japanese envoys and their staffs, and Japanese consulates and their personnel in the United States.

Tokyo Radio Broadcasts A Talk on 'Good Morals'

By The Associated Press.

LOS ANGELES, Dec. 7—The National Broadcasting Company's listening post said today that a Tokyo news broadcast at 6:20 A. M., Monday, Tokyo time [4:20 P. M., Sunday, New York time] had made no mention of the Japanese attack in the Pacific and had been followed by a lecture on "Good Morals" by a Tokyo university professor. These broadcasts were the first of the day from Tokyo.

ELECTIONS DEFERRED FOR SUPREME SOVIET

Powers Extended a Year as Presidium Issues Decree

Special Cable to THE NEW YORK TIMES.

KUIBYSHEV, Russia, Dec. 6 (Delayed)—Elections to the Supreme Soviet of the U. S. S. R., due to be held this month, were postponed by a decree of the Presidium of the Supreme Soviet, published today. Its powers, which include settling questions of war and peace, of admission of new republics into the U. S. S. R., of safeguarding security of the state and of foreign trade, are extended for one year.

No political significance has been attached to this announcement, which was caused by war circumstances—with millions under German occupation, evacuated or traveling to security, without mentioning those serving in the armed forces.

Members of the Supreme Soviet—the highest organ of state power in the Soviet Union—are elected every four years by the votes of all Soviet Union citizens over the age of 18 except those deprived of their rights. The elections would have been the second held since the system was introduced by the constitution of 1937.

Canada Limits Truck Manufacture

OTTAWA, Dec. 7 (Canadian Press)—Munitions Minister C. D. Howe announced tonight an order that all Canadian truck manufacturers be licensed as from Jan. 1. The order, issued by J. H. Berry, Motor Vehicles Controller, and approved by R. C. Berkinshaw, chairman of the Wartime Industries Control Board, calls for a "drastic" reduction in the 1942 output of light trucks and a limit on the manufacture of transports and buses.

TOKYO ACTS FIRST AND DECLARES WAR

Continued From Page One

Foreign Minister Togo fifteen minutes after Mr. Grew was called.

At the brief Cabinet session Premier Tojo reported on the progress of war plans against the British and American forces, according to Domei, and outlined the Japanese Government's policy.

Japanese Premier's Story

LOS ANGELES, Dec. 7 (U.P.)—Japanese Premier Hideki Tojo, in an address to the Japanese Empire as heard here by the National Broadcasting Company's Far Eastern listening post, announced that Emperor Hirohito had declared war on the United States and Great Britain.

"Japan has done her utmost to prevent this war," General Tojo said, "but in self-protection and for self-existence we could not help declaring war—considering the past attitude and acts of the United States."

General Tojo said that the rise or fall of East Asia "depends on this fight." He asserted that in the 2,600 years of Japanese history Japan had never lost a war.

"We therefore ask your cooperation," he said. "I hereby promise you that the final victory will be that of Japan. I ask that every individual in the island empire do his utmost to defend our country."

Urging the nation to be calm and collected, Premier Tojo said "there is nothing to fear in this war."

Silent on Roosevelt's Message

TOKYO, Monday, Dec. 8 (U.P.)—Before announcement here today that Japan was at war with the United States and Britain, both official and unofficial quarters were silent about President Roosevelt's message addressed to Emperor Hirohito, the existence of which was disclosed in Washington late Saturday. Japanese sources refused even to admit that it had been received.

The Cabinet Information Board, sole agency authorized to speak for the Government, said it had no official information about the message.

Even if the press reports known to foreign correspondents proved correct, an official added, "we would be unable to comment, because the matter concerns the two countries' highest authorities and therefore is beyond our province."

United States Ambassador Joseph C. Grew and other embassy officials also were silent. They would not say whether the message had been conveyed through the embassy here or through the Japanese in Washington.

All statements or comment about the message, they said, would have to come from Washington or the Japanese Government.

Premier Togo had been scheduled to open a three-day session of the Central Cooperative Council of the Imperial Rule Assistance Association, and newspapers had predicted he would clarify then Japan's "determination toward the United States."

ARMED CLASHES MARK BUENOS AIRES VOTING

Opposition Asks Nullification—One Person Is Killed

Special Cable to THE NEW YORK TIMES.

BUENOS AIRES, Argentina, Dec. 7—The election in the province of Buenos Aires took place today and gave rise to numerous complaints of irregular practices by the opposition parties. A number of armed clashes and incidents also occurred, but on the whole the elections went off fairly peaceably.

The worst incident took place in the small town of Quilmes, where one person was killed and one other gravely wounded.

Acting President Ramon S. Castillo stated late this evening that the election was, "on the whole, normal" and that over 70 per cent of the registered voters went to the polls. The Opposition, on the contrary, claimed that the election was the "most shameful in the whole of Argentine history" and demanded that it be annulled.

In view of Señor Castillo's statement it was considered unlikely that the opposition demand would be acceded to.

JAPAN OUT TO GET OUR CARGO SHIPS

Raiders in Pacific and Indian Oceans — Roosevelt Talks to Churchill on Phone

ALLIED CONFERENCE NEXT

Question Whether Russia Will Strike in Far East Weighed —U. S. Opinion United

By JAMES B. RESTON
Special to THE NEW YORK TIMES.

WASHINGTON, Dec. 7—Japan was reliably reported tonight to have sent "a number of commerce raiders" into the Pacific and Indian Oceans to attack unprotected merchant vessels carrying essential war materials to the United States and Great Britain.

It is understood that all Allied vessels have been warned against these raiders, which are evidently attempting to conduct a concerted attack against both British and United States vessels before the convoy system is put into effect in these areas.

President Roosevelt and Prime Minister Winston Churchill talked on the telephone today, and plans are now under way to "coordinate" the Allied defense in the Far East. Similarly, at both the Netherland and Australian legations tonight there were indications that those two countries were preparing to take part in the defense of the sea lanes leading to the United States and Great Britain.

Sea Routes Are Mined

The sea routes from Japan past the Malay Peninsula and the Netherlands Indies have already been mined effectively. The Japanese raiders, which have already passed into the Indian Ocean, are believed to have sailed south of Australia. Long-range patrols from Singapore, the Netherlands Indies and Australia, however, should make the safe return of these raiders more difficult.

To meet the menace of the Japanese raiders and to strengthen the defense of the Allied powers all over the world, British bases will from now on be available to the United States, whose warships are expected to operate out of Singapore as soon as possible in protecting the vital rubber and tin shipments necessary to the national defense program.

Despite these preliminary defense moves, however, it was clear tonight that further detailed discussions would soon take place between officials of the United States, British, Chinese, Netherland and Australian Governments to devise a total scheme of limiting the activities of the Japanese fleet.

Immediate steps will also be taken to meet the increased menace to China's lifeline, the Burma Road. Reliable information indicates that the Japanese are preparing a large-scale assault on the road in the hope of cutting off the American supplies before the Allies can transport sufficient forces into defensive positions.

In both official and diplomatic circles tonight the paramount question concerned the reaction of Russia to the spread of the war. It was felt that the cooperation of the Soviet Far Eastern armies against the Japanese would be of inestimable value in bringing a modern land army immediately up against Japan, but the general opinion was that the Allies should not count on such assistance in view of the Soviet Union's incomparable military commitments in the West.

It is an interesting coincidence that this particular question should arise a few hours after the arrival of Maxim Litvinoff, the new Soviet Ambassador to the United States.

Opinion in U. S. United

A Japanese attack on Thailand would probably have brought the United States into the war and would have created the diversion the Germans wanted, but at the same time such an attack would not, in the opinion of most observers here, have wiped away the divisions of opinion that have reduced the war effort of this country. Consequently, leading diplomats here believe that Japan has not only committed one of the most serious acts in her history but has done it in a manner most likely to assure the total opposition of the greatest industrial nation in the world.

Official observers in the capital expect the Japanese action to be followed by an all-out German attack in the Atlantic, with German submarines operating near the United States coasts. They expect, in other words, that Germany will abandon in the future what caution she has displayed in her dealings with American nationals and American ships in the past.

Although Japan's reckless technique was generally believed to have been determined by her own officers, the evidence of collusion between Germany, Italy and Japan is so clear that it is believed here that the United States will now sever diplomatic relations with the three Axis powers. Indeed, today's action was expected to clarify relations between many of the major powers of the world.

The Chinese Ambassador, Dr. Hu Shih, for example, said this evening that "there was no doubt" China would finally declare war on Japan if the United States formalized her state of war.

Burn Japanese Records in South

NEW ORLEANS, Dec. 7 (AP)—An attaché of the Japanese consulate began this afternoon to burn papers in the back yard of the consulate, around which a police guard had been placed. The smoke was visible from the street as the attaché piled papers on the flames.

"All the News That's Fit to Print."

The New York Times.

LATE CITY EDITION
Cloudy followed by clearing and colder today. Tomorrow fair and moderately cold.
Temperatures Yesterday—Max., 44; Min., 25

VOL. XCI..No. 30,635. Entered as Second-Class Matter, Postoffice, New York, N. Y. NEW YORK, TUESDAY, DECEMBER 9, 1941. THREE CENTS NEW YORK CITY and Vicinity

U. S. DECLARES WAR, PACIFIC BATTLE WIDENS; MANILA AREA BOMBED; 1,500 DEAD IN HAWAII; HOSTILE PLANES SIGHTED AT SAN FRANCISCO

TURN BACK TO SEA

Two Formations Neared City on Radio Beams, Then Went Astray

ALARM IS WIDESPREAD

Whole Coast Has a Nervous Night—Many Cities Blacked Out

By LAWRENCE E. DAVIES
Special to THE NEW YORK TIMES.

SAN FRANCISCO, Dec. 8—Two formations of "many planes," described as undoubtedly enemy aircraft, flew over the San Francisco Bay area tonight, it was announced officially by Brig. Gen. William O. Ryan, commander of the Fourth Interceptor Command, after a progressive blackout had blotted out naval and military establishments and whole cities along the Pacific Coast.

Conflicting reports spread, contributing to the "war of nerves," as the sirens wailed and broadcasting were silenced.

After another spokesman, through an error, had declared the blackout to be an air raid test, General Ryan said at the Presidio that it was no test but "the real thing."

The ships were detected first about 100 miles at sea, he said. In two formations they headed for the Monterey Peninsula, about eighty miles south of this city, and for San Francisco Bay itself.

Radio detectors plotted their course, bringing one formation in just north of the Golden Gate and the other to a point near Fort Barry, at the south end of the Golden Gate Bridge.

Planes Turn Back to Sea

After flying northward for some distance the planes turned south to a point thirty-five or forty miles down the peninsula section below San Francisco. Apparently trying to orient themselves, they flew about a while longer and then headed southwest to sea, General Ryan said.

The commanding officer, whose station is at Riverside and who said he just "happened" to be at the Presidio tonight, declared that the planes followed radio beams to these shores. When radio stations on the West Coast were silenced as part of the blackout the enemy craft apparently were not sure of their position.

No American planes were sent to the attack, he said, because "you don't send planes up unless you know what the enemy is doing and where he is going and you don't send planes up in the dark unless you know what you are doing."

Although there was no official explanation for the absence of anti-aircraft fire, it was indicated that the planes were hardly close enough for effective use of the guns.

Plane Carriers Rumored

Although General Ryan had no information, he said, as to the presence of enemy aircraft carriers hovering off the Pacific Coast, rumors of their presence had been broadcast during the day and this, it was acknowledged, would be the logical explanation for the appearance of the planes.

Lieut. Gen. John L. Dewitt,

Continued on Page Twenty-eight

NEWS BULLETINS

Please do not telephone The New York Times for war news. Every hour on the hour news bulletins are broadcast over Station WMCA—570 on the dial.

WEEKDAYS
8 a. m. through 11 p. m.
SUNDAYS
9 a.m., 1 p.m., 5 p.m., 11 p.m.

Philippines Pounded All Day As Raiders Strike at Troops

Air Base Near Capital Among Targets Hit by Japanese—Landing on Lubang With Aid of Fifth Columnists Reported

By H. FORD WILKINS
Wireless to THE NEW YORK TIMES.

MANILA, Tuesday, Dec. 9—After a day of widespread aerial attacks throughout the Philippines, Japanese bombers swept in over Manila Bay early this morning and attacked Nichols Field, the United States Army air base on the outskirts of this capital, and simultaneously reports were received of a Japanese landing on Lubang Island, off the northwestern tip of Mindoro.

This morning's attack, which began shortly after 3 o'clock, was the first in the Manila area. The damage was believed to have been slight, but some casualties were reported. [A National Broadcasting Company correspondent reported that an official statement issued in Manila after the raid said: "In the raid on Nichols Field, which was conducted by approximately ten Japanese bombers, one hangar was damaged and one officers' quarters was burned. The casualty list consists of one soldier killed and twelve wounded—all Americans."]

The reported landing on Lubang, sixty miles southwest of Manila, was not officially confirmed, but the reports received credence here. [Other unconfirmed reports, relayed by the Columbia Broadcasting System, told of landings in the Davao region, on the southern island of Mindanao.]

The Manila area's first experience with bombs was a climax to a day and night of tension and activity. The explosions could be

Continued on Page Nine

PLANES GUARD CITY FROM AIR ATTACKS

Army Interceptors Join the Navy Patrols—Anti-Aircraft Apparatus Set Up Here

While long lines of men of fighting age waited impatiently outside of every Army, Navy and Marine Corps recruiting office in the city yesterday, representatives of the city, State and Federal Governments went ahead with the grim business of making New York City ready for war.

Beginning at dawn yesterday Army fighting planes took off at regular intervals from Mitchel Field to maintain, in conjunction with a Navy patrol, a constant fighting force in the air, so there could be no repetition here of the surprise in Hawaii. At the same time the First Interceptor Command called to active duty 40,000 volunteer civilian aircraft spotters at 1,300 posts scattered through thirteen eastern coastal States and the District of Columbia.

Anti-Aircraft Guns Set Up

The Sixty-second Coast Artillery of Fort Totten, Bayside, Queens, set up anti-aircraft apparatus at vantage points around the city. One base was in Prospect Park, Brooklyn.

Air raid wardens went on duty at midnight in every part of the city, as a result of a series of conferences among Police and Fire Department officers and representatives of the Board of Education and the Department of Housing, at which it was agreed that air raid warnings would be broadcast by the blowing of the sirens of all police radio cars and emergency trucks and all Fire Department apparatus.

Alternating long and short blasts of the sirens will be sounded from the moment the Army notifies the Police and Fire Departments of the approach of an enemy and will be continued throughout the duration of the raid. The all-clear signal will be given by a series of short blasts from the sirens, it was agreed.

Teachers to Be Warned

The Police and Fire Departments, with their network of communications reaching into every neighborhood in the city, also undertook to advise the 800 public schools of an impending raid when the alarm is sounded, so the teachers can shepherd their pupils to their homes in accordance with plans already made.

Precautions against sabotage of bridges, tunnels, railroads, reservoirs, dams, power plants and other points of key importance throughout the city also were discussed at conferences of high police officials with Commissioner

Continued on Page Twenty-six

MALAYA THWARTS PUSH BY JAPANESE

Thailand Capitulates and Is Seen Virtually in Axis—Two Raids on Singapore

By F. TILLMAN DURDIN
Wireless to THE NEW YORK TIMES.

SINGAPORE, Dec. 8—The Japanese in the first eighteen hours of their attack on the Malaya peninsula have forced Thailand to capitulate, but do not now appear to have achieved any appreciable success in an invasion of British Malaya.

There was an air raid on Singapore this morning. Prai, on the mainland opposite Georgetown, more commonly known as Penang from the name of the island on which it is located, was also bombed, but damage was said to be slight.

[Bombs again started dropping on Singapore at 4 A. M. today, The Associated Press re-

Continued on Page Ten

1 BATTLESHIP LOST

Capsized in Pearl Harbor, Destroyer Is Blown Up, Other Ships Hurt

FLEET NOW IS FIGHTING

Aid Rushed to Hawaii—Some Congressmen Sharply Critical

By CHARLES HURD
Special to THE NEW YORK TIMES.

WASHINGTON, Dec. 8—The Battle of the Pacific spread tonight over a 5,000-mile "front" from Hawaii to the Philippines while a badly battered United States Fleet fought back at Japanese sea and air forces that launched severe attacks yesterday afternoon.

Tonight the Japanese were reported to be launching their main attack at the Philippines, particularly at Palawan, the greatest natural harbor in the archipelago. That attack was preceded today, according to reports from Manila, by an onslaught against the United States military air fields there, which put these out of commission for the time being and set fire to storage tanks containing vital gasoline for air operations.

The Japanese Sunday attack on Hawaii was reported in informed quarters to have been launched from the mandated islands, rather than from Japan proper, and aircraft carriers apparently approached undetected within 250 or 300 miles of Pearl Harbor.

3,000 Casualties on Oahu

The White House announced officially that the attack on the Island of Oahu, site of Honolulu and the Pearl Harbor naval base, probably has cost about 1,500 lives and resulted in an equal number of wounded persons.

To the toll of lives announced for this region, and undisclosed casualties in the Philippines and at other points, was added official word that one "old battleship" had capsized in Pearl Harbor, a destroyer had exploded and that several other

Continued on Page Four

The International Situation

TUESDAY, DECEMBER 9, 1941

The United States yesterday made a formal declaration of war on Japan after President Roosevelt had addressed a joint session of Congress. [Page 1, Column 8.] The Senate approved by unanimous vote [Page 6, Column 1] while one woman in the House of Representatives dissented. [Page 6, Column 4.]

In the national effort the Supply, Priorities and Allocations Board mapped expanding production [Page 36, Column 1], leaders of organized labor pledged support [Page 36, Column 4], and Mayor La Guardia issued a proclamation giving air raid defense instructions [Page 34, Column 1.]

In San Francisco two formations of enemy aircraft were sighted over the city, which was blacked out. [Page 1, Column 1.]

White House announcements indicated that the battle of the Pacific was raging with the United States still on the defensive. [Page 1, Column 4; Map, Page 4.] There were extensive air attacks in the Philippines [Page 1, Columns 2 and 3; Map, Page 9], raids on Hong Kong [Page 11, Column 1] and a Tokyo report that both Guam and Wake had been put under the Japanese flag. [Page 12, Column 1; with map.] The British were mopping up on a Japanese landing party in Malaya, but Thailand had yielded. [Page 1, Column 3; Map, Page 10.]

The small detachment of United States Marines at Tientsin and Peiping was disarmed and detained by the Japanese and they closed the United States Consulate in Shanghai [Page 3, Column 1.] Imperial Headquarters in Tokyo made sweeping claims of victory in the battle of the Pacific, listing great damage to the United States forces. [Page 1, Column 5.]

In London, Prime Minister Churchill announced Britain's declaration of war to Parliament and made a stirring address to the world. [Page 14, Column 1.]

The American nations began to line up behind the United States. A conference will be held, but seven countries have already declared war on Japan, two have broken diplomatic relations and several others are preparing to act. [Page 22, Column 3.] China decided to declare war not merely on Japan but on Germany and Italy as well. [Page 9, Column 4.] The various European governments in exile also supported the United States. [Page 18, Column 1.] Russia's position is obscure. [Page 2, Column 2.]

The United States accused Germany of having egged Japan on; said lease-lend aid would continue. [Page 1, Column 6.]

Berlin gave out word that Winter had stopped the Germans short of Moscow and that the capture of the Russian capital had been put off until Spring. [Page 1, Column 7.]

In Libya, the Axis armored forces were attacked from three directions by the British and what was expected to be a major engagement was eventually merely a rearguard action. [Page 24, Column 3.]

The President signs the declaration of war — Associated Press Wirephoto

LARGE U. S. LOSSES CLAIMED BY JAPAN

Tokyo Lists 2 Battleships, 1 Mine-Sweeper Sunk, 4 Capital Ships, 4 Cruisers Damaged

TOKYO, Tuesday, Dec. 9 (From Official Broadcasts, Distributed by The Associated Press)—Japanese Imperial Headquarters announced last night the sinking of two United States battleships and a mine-sweeper, severe damage to four other American capital ships and four cruisers and the destruction of about 100 American planes in Japan's surprise blows at Hawaii, the Philippines and Guam.

The official news agency, Domei, quickly interpreted "these magnificent early gains" as giving Japan naval mastery over the United States in the Pacific, and said that any force that the United States could muster now "would be regarded as utterly inadequate to accomplish any successful outcome in an encounter with the thus-far-intact Japanese fleet."

In addition, "many enemy merchant ships were captured" in the Pacific, it was announced, and the communiqué listed an unconfirmed report that a Japanese submarine had sunk an American aircraft carrier off Honolulu.

"No Japanese ships were lost during the fighting," it added.

Domei said today it was "understood that Japanese forces had destroyed more than 300 American planes, including 200 in dogfights and on the ground in Hawaii. The others, it said, were "believed" destroyed in the Philippines. Of the total, the news agency said, thirty were Fortress planes and thirty long-range bombers.

Japanese newspapers identified the two American battleships declared sunk Sunday at Pearl Harbor, Hawaii, as the 31,800-ton West Virginia, and the 29,000-ton Oklahoma. [An Italian broadcast, however, quoted Domei as listing the Oklahoma and the 33,100-ton Pennsylvania as lost. In Berlin, D. N. B. said in a Tokyo dispatch that an American transport ship carrying 350 men had been sunk off Manila.]

Japanese planes were reported to have again attacked the Philippines and British Hong Kong yesterday, inflicting "heavy damage" in a follow-up of the raids launched Sunday. "Twelve out of fourteen enemy planes on the ground were

Continued on Page Thirteen

The President's Message

Following is the text of President Roosevelt's war message to Congress, as recorded by THE NEW YORK TIMES *from a broadcast:*

Mr. Vice President, Mr. Speaker, members of the Senate and the House of Representatives:

Yesterday, Dec. 7, 1941—a date which will live in infamy—the United States of America was suddenly and deliberately attacked by naval and air forces of the empire of Japan.

The United States was at peace with that nation, and, at the solicitation of Japan, was still in conversation with its government and its Emperor looking toward the maintenance of peace in the Pacific.

Indeed, one hour after Japanese air squadrons had commenced bombing in the American island of Oahu the Japanese Ambassador to the United States and his colleague delivered to our Secretary of State a formal reply to a recent American message. And, while this reply stated that it seemed useless to continue the existing diplomatic negotiations, it contained no threat or hint of war or of armed attack.

Attack Deliberately Planned

It will be recorded that the distance of Hawaii from Japan makes it obvious that the attack was deliberately planned many days or even weeks ago. During the intervening time the Japanese Government has deliberately sought to deceive the United States by false statements and expressions of hope for continued peace.

The attack yesterday on the Hawaiian Islands has caused severe damage to American naval and military forces. I regret to tell you that very many American lives have been lost. In

Continued on Page Six

U. S. TO CONTINUE AID TO BRITAIN

White House Charges Nazis Sought Pacific War, but Will Fail to Gain Ends

Special to THE NEW YORK TIMES.

WASHINGTON, Dec. 8—A statement accusing Germany of having done everything in her power "to push Japan into the war" was issued this evening at the White House.

The statement declared that Germany's objective was "to put an end to the lease-lend program," which has aided the European enemies of Germany, including Britain and Russia and their allies and Turkey. It added that this program would continue "in full operation" and that the German attempt to end lease-lend shipments was "100 per cent" mistaken.

This statement took full cognizance of the belief in diplomatic circles here that Germany would carry out its pledges to Japan, its Axis ally, by declaring war on the United States and that Italy would

Continued on Page Seventeen

NAZIS GIVE UP IDEA OF MOSCOW IN 1941

Winter Forces Abandonment of Big Drives in North Till Spring, Berlin Says

By The Associated Press.

BERLIN, Dec. 8—Winter has stopped the Germans short of Moscow and the capture of the Soviet capital is not expected this year, a military spokesman declared tonight.

[A surprise Russian attack on Eastern Crimea from the Caucasus was revealed in a Moscow broadcast. A counter-attack from Sevastopol also was reported. The Soviet claimed important progress around Taganrog and on Moscow's defense lines.]

It seemed likely from the spokesman's statement that until Spring there could be no further major German offensive except along the extreme southern front. This word reduced the Russian campaign to secondary interest for the Germans for the first time, and attention focused instead on Ja-

Continued on Page Twenty-five

UNITY IN CONGRESS

Only One Negative Vote as President Calls to War and Victory

ROUNDS OF CHEERS

Miss Rankin's Is Sola 'No' as Both Houses Act in Quick Time

By FRANK L. KLUCKHOHN
Special to THE NEW YORK TIMES.

WASHINGTON, Dec. 8—The United States today formally declared war on Japan. Congress, with only one dissenting vote, approved the resolution in the record time of 33 minutes after President Roosevelt denounced Japanese aggression in ringing tones. He personally delivered his message to a joint session of the Senate and House. At 4:10 P. M. he affixed his signature to the resolution.

There was no debate like that between April 2, 1917, when President Wilson requested war against Germany, and April 6, when a declaration of war was approved by Congress.

President Roosevelt spoke only 6 minutes and 30 seconds today compared with Woodrow Wilson's 29 minutes and 34 seconds.

The vote today against Japan was 82 to 0 in the Senate and 388 to 1 in the House. The lone vote against the resolution in the House was that of Miss Jeanette Rankin, Republican, of Montana. Her "No" was greeted with boos and hisses. In 1917 she voted against the resolution for war against Germany.

The President did not mention either Germany or Italy in his request. Early this evening a statement was issued at the White House, however, accusing Germany of doing everything possible to push Japan into the war. The objective, the official statement proclaimed, was to cut off American lend-lease aid to Germany's European enemies, and a pledge was made that this aid would continue "100 per cent."

A Sudden and Deliberate Attack

President Roosevelt's brief and decisive words were addressed to the assembled representatives of the basic organizations of American democracy—the Senate, the House, the Cabinet and the Supreme Court.

"America was suddenly and deliberately attacked by naval and air forces of the Empire of Japan," he said. "We will gain the inevitable triumph, so help us God."

Thunderous cheers greeted the Chief Executive and Commander in Chief throughout the address. This was particularly pronounced when he declared that Americans "will remember the character of the onslaught against us," a day, he remarked, which will live in infamy.

"This form of treachery shall never endanger us again," he declared amid cheers. "The American people in their righteous might will win through to absolute victory."

Then, to the accompaniment of a

Continued on Page Five

President to Talk On Radio Tonight

By The Associated Press.

WASHINGTON, Dec. 8—President Roosevelt will make a radio address to the nation tomorrow night at 10 P. M., Eastern standard time, at which time the White House said he would make "a more complete documentation" of the Japanese attack than has yet been possible.

Stephen Early, Presidential secretary, announced that the Chief Executive would speak for half an hour and that the address would be carried by all networks.

Mr. Roosevelt began dictating the speech tonight in his White House study.

Japanese Aerial and Ocean Forces Strike in Widening War in the Pacific

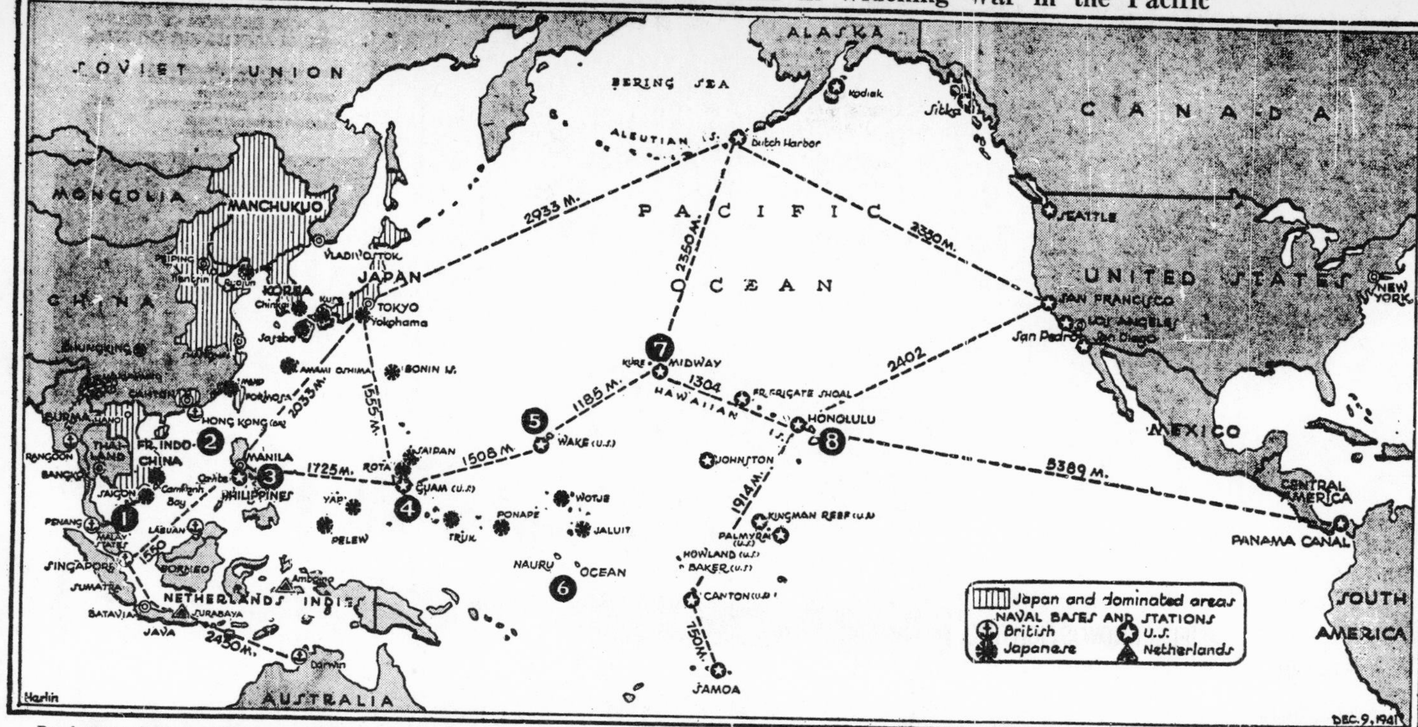

Developments in the Far Eastern hostilities included: the repulse of Japanese landing efforts in British Malaya (1), although landings were effected to the north in Thailand; raids on Hong Kong (2) and the Philippines (3); the Tokyo-alleged capture of Guam (4) and Wake Island (5); attacks on Australia's Nauru and Ocean Islands (6) as well as American-owned Midway Island (7) and the restoration of calm at Honolulu (8) after Sunday's raid. The map shows bases of the various Pacific powers and distances in statute miles between important centers.

1 BATTLESHIP LOST IN HAWAII ATTACK

Continued From Page One

vessels had been "seriously hit."

This information had the immediate dual effect of spurring war preparations and activities by the War and Navy Departments and numerous other official agencies.

The absence of official details as to losses and an equal absence of information as to the price exacted from the Japanese attackers caused worried speculation as to whether the United States had lost its edge of superiority in the Pacific. The White House announced only that "a number of Japanese planes and submarines have been destroyed."

Connally Is Critical

On Capitol Hill there was evident questioning criticism of the losses suffered, with Senator Tom Connally of Texas, chairman of the Foreign Relations Committee, commenting rather forcefully on this topic.

Senator Connally was asked by a reporter about reports that he had "given uncharted hell" to Frank Knox, Secretary of the Navy, at the White House conference last night. The Senator replied that he would "neither confirm nor deny the report," and then he asked: "Where were our airplanes and patrols in Hawaii, up in Baguio?" The reference was to a place celebrated as a resort in the Philippines.

Mr. Connally added that he would not ask for a Congressional investigation, because this was not the time for it.

"We are going to lose ships and fliers," he said. "I only hope that the Japanese lose more than we do. We have got to tighten up."

An official resume of the results of the attack on Hawaii and other related actions, issued today by Stephen Early, secretary to the President, read as follows:

"American operations against the Japanese attacking force in the neighborhood of the Hawaiian Islands are still continuing. A number of Japanese planes and submarines have been destroyed.

"The damage caused to our forces in Oahu in yesterday's attack appears more serious than at first believed.

"In Pearl Harbor itself one old battleship has capsized and several other ships have been seriously damaged.

"One destroyer was blown up. Several other small ships were seriously hurt. Army and Navy fields were bombed with the resulting destruction of several hangars. A large number of planes were put out of commission.

"A number of bombers arrived safely from San Francisco during the engagement—while it was under way. Reinforcements of planes are being rushed and repair work is under way on the ships, planes and ground facilities.

"Guam, Wake and Midway Islands and Hong Kong have been attacked. Details of these attacks are lacking.

"Two hundred marines—all that remain in China—have been interned by the Japanese near Tientsin.

"The total number of casualties on the Island of Oahu are not yet definitely known, but, in all probability, will mount to about 3,000. Nearly half of these are fatalities, the others being wounded. It seems clear from the report that many bombs were dropped in the city of Honolulu, resulting in a small number of casualties."

Reporters asked Mr. Early if there was an explanation for the manner in which the Pacific Fleet apparently was caught napping.

"No," he replied. "I don't know that there is any official explanation. The consensus of the experts is that probably some, if not all, of the planes that were attacking came from carriers. Apparently these planes were dive bombers.

"The attack came about daybreak or dawn. The carriers naturally would have all night under cover of darkness to approach. Planes would take off naturally and gain a high altitude and come in from the darkness. That is the consensus."

There was no official comment on reports in diplomatic circles that German planes and pilots, perhaps German staff work, assisted in preparation of the attacks.

Aid Rushed to Hawaii

WASHINGTON, Dec. 8 (AP)—The United States acknowledged today that its armed forces had suffered heavy losses from initial Japanese attacks and reported that fighting was continuing in the vicinity of Hawaii, in the Phillipines and at Guam, Wake and Midway Islands.

The progress of the battles at the widely scattered points was obscure, so far as official disclosures went, but the White House said reinforcements of planes were being rushed to Hawaii and that repair work was under way there on damaged ships, planes and ground facilities.

Irrespective of the conflicting reports, it was apparent that the audacious Japanese attacks had been carried out with a success that shocked many in high places in the capital.

But the grim, general feeling appeared to be—as one legislator put it—that Japan had had the first day of conflict: the United States would have the last one.

Some lawmakers openly wondered, however, why American forces had not detected the approach of the Japanese. Representative John D. Dingell of Michigan declared that he would demand the court-martial of the commandant of the Pacific Fleet and of the Hawaiian Department of the Army.

Tells of Japan's Attacks

WASHINGTON, Dec. 8 (U.P.)—Stephen Early, Presidential secretary, revealed today that Guam, Wake and Midway Islands and Hong Kong had been attacked in addition to Hawaii. While the Sunday battle raged at Oahu, "a number of bombers arrived from San Francisco," he said.

They presumably joined in the fighting.

Navy officials said the American forces launched a counter-thrust the moment the first enemy bomb exploded. Within a few hours the United States Fleet, its giant rifles stripped for action, steamed out of Pearl Harbor in search of the marauders.

Immediate objectives of the Pacific and Asiatic fleets are the Japanese naval units at large, particularly the aircraft carriers that nested the swarm of bombers that raked Oahu with death. There seemed no doubt that the aerial armada came from carriers that stole into position under cover of darkness.

Text of War Declaration

Special to THE NEW YORK TIMES.

WASHINGTON, Dec. 8—The text of the joint resolution adopted by Congress today declaring a state of war with Japan was as follows:

Declaring that a state of war exists between the Imperial Government of Japan and the Government and the People of the United States and making provisions to prosecute the same:

Whereas, the Imperial Government of Japan has committed unprovoked acts of war against the Government and the People of the United States of America; therefore, be it

Resolved, by the Senate and the House of Representatives of the United States of America in Congress assembled, that the state of war between the United States and the Imperial Government of Japan which has thus been thrust upon the United States is hereby formally declared; and the President is hereby authorized and directed to employ the entire naval and military forces of the United States and the resources of the government to carry on war against the Imperial Government of Japan; and, to bring the conflict to a successful termination, all of the resources of the country are hereby pledged by the Congress of the United States.

THE DAY IN WASHINGTON

WASHINGTON, Dec. 8—President Roosevelt arose at dawn, examined latest war dispatches, conferred with military and naval leaders, completed his draft of the message to Congress asking for a declaration of war against Japan, delivered the message and then signed the resolution for war adopted by Congress, and conferred with Mayor La Guardia on civilian defense on the Pacific Coast.

Announcements from the White House included those concerning the Japanese attacks, another condemning Germany for pushing Japan into the war and another that the President would speak to the nation on details of the war in the Pacific at 10 P. M. tomorrow.

The Senate adopted the war resolution, 82 to 0; received the Walsh bill to authorize $310,000,000 naval public works program, received the Andrews bill for $39,000,000 naval lighter-than-air development program; passed the bill authorizing extension of enlistments in naval forces; passed the bill prohibiting employment of certain maritime radio operators and adjourned at 2:05 P. M. until noon tomorrow. The Education and Labor Committee postponed consideration of labor legislation.

The House adopted the war declaration resolution, 388 to 1, and adjourned at 1:30 P. M. until noon tomorrow.

GREEK FAMINE TOLL RISING, ANKARA HEARS

200 Deaths Daily Reported—Italians Seize Beggars

Special Broadcast to THE NEW YORK TIMES.

ANKARA, Turkey, Dec. 8—Famine is sweeping through Greece and the death toll from starvation and disease through malnutrition is rising to an average more than 200 daily it is learned here from reliable foreign sources.

Eight hundred persons died in Athens and Piraeus last Monday, the majority of them collapsing in the streets, according to the reports.

Begging is commonplace and "fairly well-dressed skeletons" haunt the side streets and public places in the starving Greek capital, it is said. This is confirmed in detail by fugitives who have escaped from Greece and made their way to Turkey. Beggars are so numerous throughout Piraeus that the Italian troops of occupation have been ordered to arrest and punish any persons discovered soliciting food, it is reported. Hungry men, women and children roam the major Athens thoroughfares, but Italian military guards seize all beggars and loiterers are admonished to "keep moving."

Fifty thousand German soldiers, the majority of them suffering from head wounds, severe frostbite and bomb shock, are now hospitalized in Greece, according to military intelligence reports. There is a grave shortage of all medical supplies,

VICHY SURPRISED BY 'SUDDENNESS'

But Press Sees 'Orders Given Long Ago by Tokyo' to Prepare Moves

Wireless to THE NEW YORK TIMES.

VICHY, France, Dec. 8—"Yesterday the Japanese suddenly entered into war against the United States and Great Britain." This opening sentence of an editorial this evening in the Journal des Debats may be considered to reflect French opinion so far as it can be reflected in a controlled press.

The phrase may be all the more significant in view of the fact that newspapers this morning were restricted in their early editions to such headlines as "lively incidents in the Pacific."

The Journal des Debats alludes also to "warlike action without warning," to "orders given long ago by Tokyo," and to delays that "gave time to prepare military dispositions."

There is little doubt that the sudden opening of hostilities caused surprise here. The Japanese Ambassador this morning called on Admiral François Darlan, the Vice Premier, to give his government's views on the situation. On the American side there have been no diplomatic demarches yet.

The general feeling, in any case, is that the issue is now definitely joined between conflicting ideologies and that now the fight is to a finish.

Officially there is no reaction nor in the circumstances can there be, although developments in Indo-China are being watched closely.

All newspapers in the unoccupied zone give prominence to "a fine manifestation of Franco-American solidarity" in connection with ceremonies held at St. Maurice-de-Remens where the Quakers have housed a number of poor children from the city of Lyon.

Manila's Fate Worries Madrid

MADRID, Dec. 8 (AP)—Informaciones, the only Spanish newspaper to comment on the Pacific war, said today it hopes Manila would be "preserved for Christianity." It called the city "a fragment of the heart of Spain."

Plane Crash Kills One; 5 Missing

HALIFAX, N. S., Dec. 8 (AP)—One man was killed, five were missing and five injured today in the crash of a Royal Canadian Air Force flying boat into the sea off Halifax.

Surprise by Japan Repeats 1904 Tactics; Russia Also Was Struck Without Warning

Special to THE NEW YORK TIMES.

WASHINGTON, Dec. 8—When the Japanese began their naval and air attack on United States outposts Sunday they followed the same tactics of surprise attack without declaring war that they utilized when they attacked Russia in the Far East in 1904.

As in the present case, long and fruitless negotiations had been going on between the two nations, allegedly upon Japanese insistence on protecting "the independence and territorial integrity of Korea" from alleged Russian threats. The last note from Japan, sent on Feb. 5, 1904, said failure to obtain satisfactory assurance from Russia had "made it necessary for the Imperial Government to consider what measures of self-defense they are called upon to take."

A difference, however, is that Japan attacked Hawaii at or just before the time her last note to the United States was being delivered, but in 1904 it was three days later that the Japanese main fleet steamed into the harbor of Port Arthur, where the main Russian Far Eastern fleet was stationed, opened fire without warning and so badly damaged the Russian fleet that it never recovered.

Japan's war declaration came the day after.

A parody on a song, popular at the time, was recalled tonight to illustrate the sympathetic attitude of the United States of that day toward Japan. Sung by the late Cecil Lean, it ran:

What will Rojestvensky do?
All the people ask.
He can't cruise Nagasaki way,
For that's a hopeless task
He can't come out through the China Sea;
Why, he can't stir,
With Nogi here and Togo there
In Port Arthur.

Rojestvensky was the Russian admiral who took the Russian Baltic fleet from European waters in the Summer of 1904 on the long voyage to the Far East, where it was met and destroyed by Admiral Togo's Japanese fleet. General Nogi was the Japanese Army leader in the attack on Port Arthur.

New Zealand Lists Casualties

Wireless to THE NEW YORK TIMES.

WELLINGTON, New Zealand, Dec. 8—Additional evidence of the severity of the Libyan fighting was provided today with the issuance of the first three casualty lists, containing 458 names, and also by the fact that three more colonels' names were included. Lieut. Col. H. K. Kippenberger, whose conduct at Crete was described as a model of modern warfare, is listed as wounded and missing. Also wounded was Colonel G. D. Dittmer, one of the first New Zealanders named to a staff post.

DO NOT FORGET
The Hundred Neediest.

HISTORY IS HEARD: STUDIES HERE AS THE PRESIDENT ASKED FOR DECLARATION OF WAR

Barber

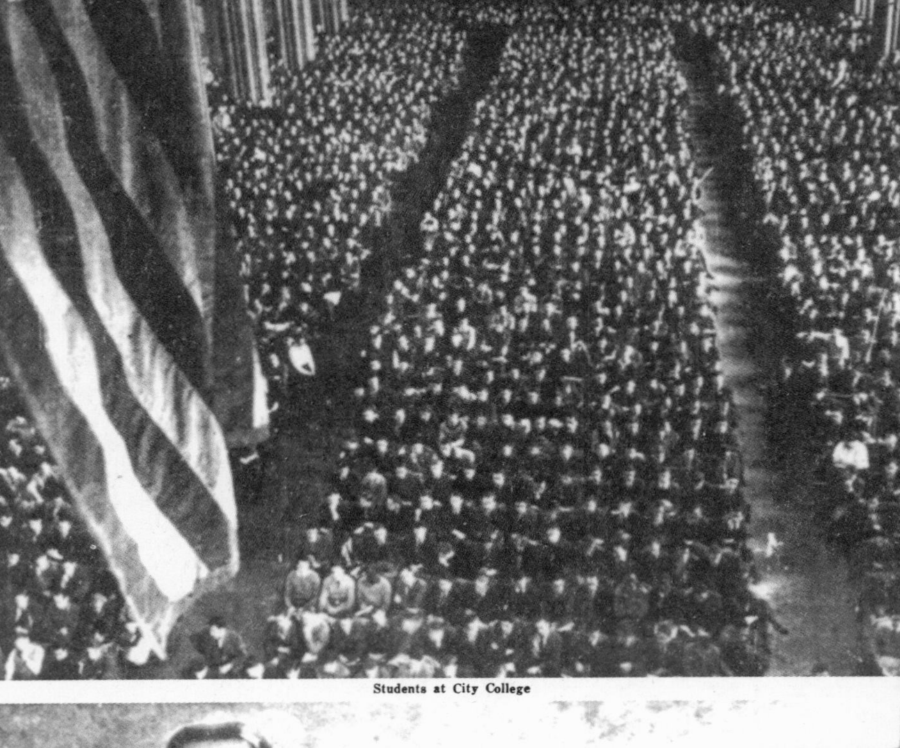
Students at City College

Bootblack

Pedestrians in Times Square

The New York Times

Laundryman

Capital Swings Into War Stride; Throngs Cheer for the President

Extraordinary Precautions Taken to Guard Him as Solemn Scene Goes Into History When He Calls on Congress to Act

By JAMES B. RESTON

Special to THE NEW YORK TIMES.

WASHINGTON, Dec. 8—The United States went to war today as a great nation should—with simplicity, dignity, and unprecedented unity. The deep divisions which marked this country's entrance into the wars of 1776, 1812, 1861, 1898 and 1917 were absent. Overnight, partisan, personal and sectional differences were shelved. The atmosphere of the Capital was grave, but for the first time in years there were no doubts.

It was clear from early morning that historic events were afoot. By sun-up workmen were pounding great stakes into the ground and straining a wire cable around the House wing of the Capitol to keep the crowds back. At the same time, barricades were being moved into place at the main entrances to the Capitol and attendants were tacking up signs reading "Show Your Passes."

By 11 o'clock, Marines with fixed bayonets, and Metropolitan and Capitol police were swarming all over Capitol Hill and guarding the White House. Streets leading to and from these two buildings were blocked off. By 11:30 two open cars full of Secret Service men had rolled up under the pillared portico of the White House with riot guns rigged along the sides.

Tempo of Capital Is Changed

Meanwhile, the whole tempo of the city had changed. There was very little of the sense of impending physical damage which dominated London on the outbreak of the war, but there was a sense of hurry. More cars were on the streets than at any time since Inauguration Day; everybody was evidently trying to do a great many things all at once; jammed telephones caused delays of as long as three hours on calls to New York; crowds were rapidly gathering at the White House and the Capitol.

Promptly at noon the big glass doors at the White House swung open, six limousines drew up, and President Roosevelt came out on the arm of his eldest son, Captain James Roosevelt, who was wearing the uniform of an officer of the Marines.

Mr. Roosevelt descended the steps without a word. The car, bearing the White House insignia, started at once for the Capitol.

Mrs. Roosevelt, Mrs. James Roosevelt, Mrs. Dorothy Brady, Mrs. Stephen Early, Grace Tully, the President's acting secretary, and General Edward M. Watson and Captain John Beardahl, the President's military and naval aides, were in the official party.

The crowds at the Capitol cheered as the official cars rolled up to a special entrance. Mr. Roosevelt went at once to the Speaker's entrance, where he waited for a few minutes before entering the chamber.

Meanwhile, the Army and police officials were taking elaborate precautions at all entrances. At every door stood a soldier of the Regular Army or a marine. As each person approached, the soldier snapped to present arms, blocking the door. Credentials were examined twice more at special barricades before any one was permitted to enter the chamber.

Even the Chinese Ambassador, Dr. Hu Shih, for whom this was an especially important occasion, was held up at the door until Senator Connally of Texas interceded for him, but he finally got in to join Dr. A. Loudon, the Minister of the Netherlands, and Viscount Halifax, the British Ambassador.

As the President waited in the Speaker's office, members of the Senate marched down the long corridor and through the rotunda to the House side and entered the chamber behind Majority Leader Barkley of Kentucky and Minority Leader McNary of Oregon.

As soon as the Senators were seated the members of the Supreme Court entered in their black robes and sat along the edge of the well of the House on the left of the rostrum. At 12:23 the members of the President's Cabinet arrived, in time to hear Speaker Rayburn rap for silence and announce:

"The President of the United States!"

Cheers Greet President

The members of both houses, their guests in the rear of the chamber, diplomats in the gallery, officials of the government, a handful of soldiers and the people who had managed to get seats in the galleries immediately rose to their feet. For an instant there was silence and then suddenly there was an ever increasing round of applause which terminated suddenly as Speaker Rayburn rapped with his gavel.

At that moment the President appeared. Then he received an ovation unmatched in his eight years as Chief Executive. Applause broke into cheering and lasted over a minute. Then, after a brief prayer by the chaplain, Mr. Roosevelt began to read his message while the movie lights blazed down on him from the galleries and the cameras whirred.

Seldom, if ever, in a message to the Congress has the President judged the temper of the representatives of the people better than he did in this speech. Two facts seemed to impress this gathering more perhaps than the simple words of the speech. By not the slightest inflection did he suggest that the facts of the world situation had finally justified his policy, as even his opponents were admitting today he might very well have done.

When he said that the United States would always remember the character of the Japanese attack, everybody stood and applauded, and he was interrupted repeatedly by cheering. Only at the end did he acknowledge this greeting. Then he looked up and smiled and waved his hand.

U. S. WAY OF LIFE HELD WORTH ANY SACRIFICE

Congregation Emanu-El Head Stresses Our Religious Truths

Confidence that neither men nor nations have the power to destroy the religious truths upon which this country is founded or the American way of life was expressed last night by Lieut. Comdr. Lewis L. Strauss, president of Congregation Emanu-El, in his report to the annual meeting of the congregation.

Commander Strauss's report was read in his absence by Sydney H. Herman, a vice president, because he had been called to his post at Washington in the war emergency.

"We are part of a pattern that is so much greater than the span of our own lifetimes," Commander Strauss wrote, "that even as we look backward with pride we can look forward with confidence into a world darkened with blackouts—secure in our conviction that the truths and the way of life which we are united to preserve are worth any sacrifice."

Mr. Strauss and Mr. Herman were re-elected. Others who will serve during 1942 are Roger W. Straus, vice president; Davis Brown, secretary; Walter S. Mack Jr., treasurer; Alfred R. Bachrach, Herbert S. Brussel, Saul F. Dribben, Mr. Mack, Carl Rosenberger and Frank L. Weil, trustees; Samuel Berliner, controller, and Samuel Berliner Jr., assistant controller.

Manchukuo Wars on U. S., Britain

The German radio announced yesterday that Manchukuo had declared war on the United States and Great Britain. The broadcast was heard by the National Broadcasting Company.

The thirtieth annual appeal for the Hundred Neediest Cases is made in today's issue of The New York Times.

WAR IS DECLARED AGAINST JAPANESE

Continued From Page One

great roar of cheering, he asked for war against Japan.

The President officially informed Congress that in the dastardly attack by Japan, delivered while the Imperial Japanese Government was expressing hope for continued peace, "very many American lives have been lost" and American ships reportedly have been "torpedoed on the high seas between San Francisco and Honolulu."

Mentioning one by one in staccato phrases the Japanese attacks on the Philippines, American Midway, Wake and Guam Islands, British Hong Kong and Malaya, he bluntly informed the people by radio and their representatives directly:

"Hostilities exist. There is no blinking the fact that our people, our territory and our interests are in grave danger. The people of the United States have already formed their opinions and well understand the implications to the very life and safety of our nation."

Victory May Take Time, He Warns

It may take a long time, Mr. Roosevelt warned, "to overcome this premeditated invasion," but of the unbounding determination of the American people and confidence in our armed forces neither he nor they had any doubt. Then he said:

"I ask that the Congress declare that since the unprovoked and dastardly attack by Japan on Sunday, Dec. 7, a state of war has existed between the United States and the Japanese Empire."

It was to a solemn Congress and to grim galleries that the President mentioned the casualties in Hawaii—officially estimated at 1,500 dead and 1,500 wounded.

Before him, on his left was the Supreme Court, its members clad in black robes. On the right in the front row sat the Cabinet, with Secretary Hull in the ranking position on the aisle. Behind the Cabinet were the Senators and then the members of the House.

Mr. Roosevelt spoke concisely, clearly and to the point to an already convinced audience already stirred to belligerency by the wantonness of the Japanese attack.

Extraordinaray precautions were taken by the Secret Service to guard the President during his short trip over the indirect mile and a quarter route from the Executive Mansion to the Capitol and back to the White House.

Crowds, solemn but determined, greeted the Chief Executive with cheers from the time he was driven out of the East Gate of the White House until he reached the rear entrance of the House after passing through crowded Capitol Plaza. The same crowds stood silently by as he returned.

Joint Session Is Ended

The two houses split up immediately after the address and passed the war resolution separately without debate, the time consumed being accountable to having the resolution officially introduced and in the physical problem involved.

Stephen T. Early, Presidential secretary, said that nothing official had been received by this government tonight on European reports that Germany and Italy were contemplating declaration of war against the United States. Germany, however, was widely expected to carry out its treaty commitments arranged by Hitler with Japan and to declare war on the United States with her Italian satellite following suit.

Since the Constitution provides that Congress alone can declare war, there was some doubt here as to whether the United States was officially at war with Japan from the time the House adopted the war resolution at 1:10 P. M., ten minutes after the Senate, or from the time the President signed the resolution at 4:10 P. M. Most attorneys consulted inclined to the belief the latter time marked the historic step.

It was just forty-seven minutes, at any rate, after Vice President Wallace affixed his signature at the Capitol until the President affixed his signature without great ceremony in the presence of Senate and House leaders.

The President shook hands with his guests, signed the document with an ordinary pen and promised the pen to Chairman Bloom of the House Foreign Affairs Committee. Besides officials, only an exceptionally large number of news reel and other photographers, including one in Army uniform, saw the ceremony.

Present at the ceremony in the Executive office were the following Congressional leaders: Vice President Wallace, Senators Barkley, Austin, McNary, Connally and Glass; Speaker Rayburn and Representatives McCormack, Martin, Bloom, Eaton and Luther A. Johnson of Texas.

The President went to the Capitol cheered by telegrams and messages in tremendous quantity all of which were said by Mr. Early to express "horror at this attack and full loyalty to the President and the government."

The messages came from Governors, Mayors, religious leaders, heads of civic movements, newspaper editors and radio broadcasters, many offering their personal services.

A Washington taxicab driver named Smith telephoned to the White House late last night, saying he had just finished paying for his cab, but that he offered it to the government and offered, further, to drive free of charge any government official needing transportation.

Alfred M. Landon, Republican Presidential candidate in 1936, telegraphed to the White House:

"The Japanese leave no choice. Nothing must be permitted to interfere with our victory over a foreign foe."

A committee to escort President Roosevelt into the House chamber was appointed by Speaker Rayburn. It consisted of Representative McCormack, House majority leader; Joseph W. Martin, House minority leader; Chairman Doughton of the House Ways and Means Committee; Senate Majority Leader Barkley, Senate Minority Leader McNary and Senator Glass of Virginia.

The President went from his automobile to the Speaker's room where he remained until he addressed the joint session at 12:30 P. M.

British Columbia Coast Blacked Out for Attack

By The Associated Press.

VICTORIA, B. C., Dec. 8—A complete blackout of coastal British Columbia and the lower mainland was ordered tonight because "the war situation is such that an attack by Japanese forces on the Paciifc Northwest coast is imminent."

All motor traffic on Victoria streets was halted at 6 P. M. by naval policemen. Drivers were told to go home.

The action followed an order of Mayor Andrew McGavin.

AIDS TWICE IN WAR STEPS

Man Who Took Declaration to White House Typed That of 1917

WASHINGTON, Dec. 8 (AP)—The man who delivered the declaration of war against Japan to the White House today for President Roosevelt's signature was he who typed the declaration of war against Germany in 1917.

Garrett Whiteside, now clerk of the Senate Committee on Enrolled Bills, was employed in the office of the House bill clerk in 1917. He said the chairman of the Foreign Affairs Committee stepped across the hall from the committee room and asked him if he could use a typewriter.

The Senator dictated the original draft of the 1917 declaration of war.

UNANIMOUS SENATE ACTS IN 15 MINUTES

13 Absentees Would Have Put Their 'Ayes' With Those of 82 Voting War on Japan

VANDENBERG SPEAKS OUT

Sets Record 'Clear' by Giving Nation's Answer to Foe and Making Pledge to President

By C. P. TRUSSELL

Special to THE NEW YORK TIMES.

WASHINGTON, Dec. 8—Months of controversy in the Senate over international and domestic issues ended today when by a vote of 82 to 0 it adopted the war resolution with such dispatch that some members, hurrying to their posts arrived too late to participate.

The resolution, formally accepting the battle challenge of the Imperial Government of Japan, was passed and on its way to the House for concurrence before an eager public could half fill the galleries to witness the historic proceedings.

All thirteen of the Senate absentees, some ill, some detained by official missions and a few on their way to the Capitol, later advised their colleagues, directly or through spokesmen, that they would have voted "aye" had they been present.

The vote recorded unanimous response as follows: Democrats, 56; Republicans, 24; Progressive, 1; Independent, 1.

Five Who Voted in 1917

In the chamber were nine members who had participated in the vote, taken April 4, 1917, which carried this country into the first World War. One of them, Senator George W. Norris, Independent, of Nebraska, voted "no" then, with five others. Today his vote was "aye."

Voting "aye" again, as they had voted in 1917, were Senators Peter G. Gerry of Rhode Island, Ellison D. Smith of South Carolina and Kenneth McKellar of Tennessee, Democrats, and Hiram Johnson, veteran Republican isolationist of California.

Also voting in the affirmative today, as in 1917, were four members of the Senate who cast their ballots in the House twenty-four years ago: Senators Alben W. Barkley of Kentucky, the majority leader; Tom Connally of Texas, chairman of the Foreign Relations Committee; Carter Glass of Virginia and Wallace H. White, Republican of Maine.

Senator Carl Hayden, Democrat of Arizona, who also served in the House in 1917 and voted "aye" on the war resolution, was unable to return in time to vote today.

Swift Pace of Legislation

At 12:51 P. M. the war measure was called up by Senator Connally, who had introduced it only a few minutes after President Roosevelt had delivered his message to the joint session. By 1:06 P. M. the roll had been called.

Three minutes later the Senate had passed and also sent across the Capitol a bill which would "freeze" into active service for the duration of the national emergency all enlisted men now in the Navy, the Marine Corps and the Coast Guard.

Then, after a brief question period, but without contest, it substituted for a House-adopted measure a bill of its own to put radio operators on merchant ships under personal control of the Secretary of the Navy, whose approval would be required for their employment.

The Senators then turned to measures for curbing defense strikes. During debate on this issue word was received from the House that it had concurred in the Senate draft of the war declaration.

This was at 1:37 P. M. Speaker Rayburn speedily signed the engrossed resolution at 3:15 and Vice President Wallace at 3:25, and then it went to the White House.

Defense Expansion Begun

War declared, preliminary expansion plans immediately went forward.

Chairman Walsh of the Naval Committee introduced a bill authorizing $310,000,000 for a naval public works program, including acquisition of Floyd Bennett Field in New York.

Almost simultaneously President Roosevelt sent the Senate a request for a supplemental appropriation of $33,750,000 in the pending $8,000,000,000 emergency money measure. Of this $18,500,000 would be used to buy Floyd Bennett Field and build new aviation facilities there and the remainder would go toward putting up a naval supply depot and storage facilities at Mechanicsburg, Pa.

Although the Senate took only fifteen minutes to adopt the war resolution, it fell behind the timetable which Senator Connally had charted. He had anticipated no speeches and had announced that he would make none. As he was about to call for a vote, however, Senator Vandenberg, Republican, of Michigan, a self-styled "isolationist," intervened.

Senator Vandenberg said that he desired "to make the record clear." Senator Connally observed that that was his privilege and yielded.

Vandenberg Gives Answer

"Out of peaceful Sunday skies—without a word of warning—yes, and even screened by the infamous treachery of pretended amity in pacific negotiations at Washington, like an ambushed murderer," Senator Vandenberg said, "Japan has violated our soil, killed our children, struck at our possessions, assailed our sovereignty and disclosed to us the pattern of a purpose which reeks with dishonor and with bloody aspirations.

"There can be no shadow of a doubt about America's united and indomitable answer to the cruel and ruthless challenge of this tragic hour—the answer not only of the Congress but also of our people at their threatened hearthstones.

"To the enemy we answer: 'You have unsheathed the sword and by it you shall die.'

"To the President of the United States we answer: 'For the defense of all that is America, we salute the Colors and we forward march.'

"I am constrained to make this brief statement, on my own account, lest there be any lingering misapprehension in any furtive mind that previous internal disagreements regarding the wisdom of our policies may encourage the despicable hope that we may weaken from within."

Here the Senator repeated to his colleagues the statement he made yesterday as war came to the Pacific and pledged his support to full prosecution of the war.

"For now it is enough that the attack has come," he added. "For nothing else will be enough except an answer from 130,000,000 united people that will tell this whole, round earth that though America still hates war, America fights when she is violated and fights until victory is conclusive. God helping her, she can do no other."

"The issue is clear, as just set forth by the President," said Senator Connally. "I ask for the ayes and nays."

The vote was taken.

The thirtieth annual appeal for the Hundred Neediest Cases is made in today's issue of The New York Times.

REPEATS HER ANTI-WAR VOTE

After the roll call Representative Jeanette Rankin of Montana waited in a telephone booth until the House corridors were cleared. Talking to her is Representative Joseph W. Martin Jr.

Associated Press Wirephoto

The President's Message

Continued From Page One

addition, American ships have been reported torpedoed on the high seas between San Francisco and Honolulu.

Yesterday the Japanese Government also launched an attack against Malaya.

Last night Japanese forces attacked Hong Kong.

Last night Japanese forces attacked Guam.

Last night Japanese forces attacked the Philippine Islands.

Last night the Japanese attacked Wake Island.

And this morning the Japanese attacked Midway Island.

Japan has therefore undertaken a surprise offensive extending throughout the Pacific area. The facts of yesterday and today speak for themselves. The people of the United States have already formed their opinions and well understand the implications to the very life and safety of our nation.

As Commander in Chief of the Army and Navy I have directed that all measures be taken for our defense, that always will our whole nation remember the character of the onslaught against us.

Victory Will Be Absolute

No matter how long it may take us to overcome this premeditated invasion, the American people, in their righteous might, will win through to absolute victory.

I believe that I interpret the will of the Congress and of the people when I assert that we will not only defend ourselves to the uttermost but will make it very certain that this form of treachery shall never again endanger us.

Hostilities exist. There is no blinking at the fact that our people, our territory and our interests are in grave danger.

With confidence in our armed forces, with the unbounding determination of our people, we will gain the inevitable triumph. So help us God.

I ask that the Congress declare that since the unprovoked and dastardly attack by Japan on Sunday, Dec. 7, 1941, a state of war has existed between the United States and the Japanese Empire.

HOUSE VOTES WAR, MISS RANKIN 'NAY'

Vote of 388 to 1 Comes Forty Minutes After Resolution Is Offered by McCormack

ISOLATIONISTS FOR STAND

Fish Is Among Those Pledging Unity—Martin Scores Attack as U. S. Sought Peace

By HENRY N. DORRIS

Special to THE NEW YORK TIMES.

WASHINGTON, Dec. 8—The House adopted today, 388 to 1, the resolution declaring war with Japan forty minutes after it was presented and would have done so sooner but for speeches by a few members, who pledged unity of action by this nation in winning the war.

The only member voting "no" was Miss Jeanette Rankin, Republican, of Montana, who, over a span of twenty-four years, kept her record of "no war" consistent. Miss Rankin was one of several in 1917 who voted in the negative when the war resolution was passed.

Going into session immediately after President Roosevelt and the Senate members left the chamber, Representative McCormack presented the resolution and asked that the rules be suspended so that it could be considered immediately.

Mr. McCormack made the request that the resolution be considered immediately and Miss Rankin rose to object. Speaker Rayburn observed that "there can be no objection," inasmuch as the vote was to be taken later.

Mr. McCormack presented the resolution with the simple statement:

"This is the time for action."

Representative Martin, minority leader, took the floor to pledge unity behind the war effort. He said:

"Our nation is today in the gravest crisis since its establishment as a republic. All we hold precious and sacred is being challenged by a ruthless, unscrupulous, arrogant foe.

"Treacherous Attack" Is Cited

"We have been the victim of a treacherous attack under cover of darkness. It came at a time when we were trying to establish a basis of peace through mutual understanding. Our ships have been sunk, our planes destroyed; many lives lost; cities and towns under the American flag have been ruthlessly bombed.

"No one hates war more than I. Every night I have uttered a silent prayer that America might be spared active involvement in a frightful war. I know the horrors which come with war, the loss of lives, the sacrifices which must be made by all, the sadness and desolation it always brings.

"America is challenged. That challenge comes in a ruthless way which leaves but one answer for a liberty-loving, self-respecting people. We are compelled by this treacherous attack to go to war. From now on there can be no hesitation. We must press the war with unstinted vigor and full efficiency.

"There can be no peace until the enemy is made to pay in full measure for his dastardly crimes.

"In view of the developments of the past forty-eight hours, the President's request has my support. When the historic roll is called I hope there will not be a single dissenting vote. Let us show the world we are a united nation; let us boldly proclaim we will not permit any force to strike down freedom and progress here in America or replace our way of life with slavery and dictatorship.

"God will give us the strength and the courage to drive to victory in a just cause, a cause which means all that makes life worth while to the people not only of America but in every country in the world."

Fish "Prepared" to Vote for War

Representative Fish, Republican, of New York, was recognized. He said that while he had consistently opposed our entrance into any war, unless the United States was attacked, he was prepared to vote for a declaration of war.

Representative Edith Nourse Rogers, Republican, of Massachusetts, declared that "Japan stabbed us in the back."

Representative Mary Byron, Democrat, of Maryland, said that her late husband, a member of Congress, had volunteered in 1917.

"I am willing to give my sons in their country's defense," she added.

Representative Luther A. Johnson, Democrat, of Texas, ranking member of the Foreign Affairs Committee, said that the Japanese attack, while peace negotiations were pending, was "a dastardly treachery."

America will present a united front, Representative Casey, Democrat, of Massachusetts, declared.

Representative Eaton, Republican, of New Jersey, said that the roar of Japanese cannon and bombs had been a clarion call to the American people for unity.

"All the News That's Fit to Print."

The New York Times.

LATE CITY EDITION
Continued moderately cool today; moderate winds.
Temperatures Yesterday—Max., 74; Min., 67
Sunrise, 6:29 A. M.; Sunset, 7:17 P. M.

Copyright, 1943, by The New York Times Company.

VOL. XCII..No. 31,274. Entered as Second-Class Matter, Postoffice, New York, N. Y. NEW YORK, THURSDAY, SEPTEMBER 9, 1943. THREE CENTS IN NEW YORK CITY

ITALY SURRENDERS, WILL RESIST GERMANS; ALLIED FORCES LAND IN THE NAPLES AREA; RUSSIANS IN STALINO, CLEAR DONETS BASIN

SOVIET TIDE RISES

Swift Red Army Blows Capture Key City, Free Rich Region

DRIVE NEARS DNIEPER

More Rail Hubs Fall—Thrust Toward Kiev Also Extended

By The United Press.

LONDON, Thursday, Sept. 9—The Red Army recaptured Stalino, Russia's twelfth city, yesterday and freed the Donets Basin, which before the war produced more steel than Japan and Italy combined, in a great surge that took it to Grishino, ninety miles east of Dniepropetrovsk on the lower Dnieper River.

While the armies of Gen. Rodion Y. Malinovsky and Gen. Fedor Tolbukhin drove the enemy from the rich Donets Basin, crowded with coal mines and factories, the army of Gen. Konstantin Rokossovsky drove to a point ninety-six miles northeast of Kiev by capturing Borzna, twenty-three miles west of Bakhmach.

Bakhmach and Romni, forty-two miles to the southeast, were surrounded on three sides, a Moscow radio bulletin reported, and thus the Bakhmach-Kremenchug railroad was cut. The roads leading from Bakhmach to Kursk and Gomel had been cut previously and only the lines to Kiev and Odessa remained open.

Picked Troops Take Stalino

Red Army shock troops, picked from the sixteen infantry divisions that had driven the Germans through city after city in six days of tireless fighting, took Stalino by storm.

The Russian communiqué said the Red Army troops drove in on Stalino throughout Tuesday night and yesterday morning. They fought through the suburbs and then stormed the city from north and south, routing the enemy in a street-by-street fight and capturing a great store of spoils.

Twenty-five miles northwest of Stalino the Russians took Krasnoarmeiskoye, a big railroad junction controlling two of four rail roads leading west from the basin.

In all the Russians took, in addition to Stalino, a city of 462,000 persons, more than 150 towns in the Donbas alone, twenty of them important, in gains of up to twelve and a half miles. During their Donbas offensive the Russians took twelve towns of more than 50,000 persons each.

The Germans at Krasnoarmeiskoye were so swiftly beaten that the Russians took nineteen planes and several loaded railroad trains.

March on Kiev Gains

On the Kiev front, the Russians took more than sixty towns in advances of up to twelve and a half miles. Their capture of Borzna in that area meant that the battle for the Dnieper River line had started. An advance of twenty-three miles to Nezhin would cut the only remaining German supply line east of the river. The Russians had already advanced 101 miles in nine days from Rylsk, half the distance to Kiev.

More than 1,000 Germans were killed at Borzna, and 1,000 were killed in another sector.

South of Bryansk the Russians advanced up to six miles to take several villages. They were reported only twenty miles south of Bryansk. The Soviet communiqué, recorded from the Moscow radio, reported that the Russians were advancing west of the Navlya railroad junction in this area, driving the Germans through dense forests.

West and southwest of Kharkov nearly four miles were gained in some sectors and about 1,200 Germans were killed.

The Germans were first to ad-

Continued on Page Twenty-two

New Fascist Regime Set Up, Nazis Report

By Cable to The New York Times.

LONDON, Thursday, Sept. 9—The German radio announced early today that a "National Fascist government has been set up in Italy and functions in the name of Benito Mussolini."

The announcement, called a "proclamation by the National Fascist Government of Italy," said "this Badoglio betrayal will not be perpetrated. The National Fascist Government will punish traitors pitilessly."

The broadcast, in Italian, said nothing about the whereabouts of Mussolini, who has been reported under arrest. It was preceded by the playing of "Giovinezza," the Fascist anthem.

FOE'S MARCUS LOSS 80%, NIMITZ SAYS

U. S. Carrier Planes Alone Hit at Japanese Isle—Hell Cat Fighter Excels in Test

By ROBERT TRUMBULL

By Telephone to The New York Times.

PEARL HARBOR, Sept. 8—Admiral Chester W. Nimitz, Commander in Chief of the Pacific Fleet, issued today a communiqué that gave the first details of the raid on Marcus Island Sept. 1. Coincidentally three naval air officers who participated in the action gave an interview covering all phases of the raid, which they said destroyed a surprisingly well-fortified Japanese air base.

Action Consisted of Bombing

Admiral Nimitz's communiqué said that a United States Pacific Fleet task force under command of Rear Admiral Charles A. Pownall attacked the little island, 1,185 miles southeast of Tokyo, at dawn Sept. 1. The air officers revealed that the action consisted entirely of bombing and strafing by carrier-borne aircraft.

They said that the new Grumman F6F Hellcat fighter was employed in combat for the first time in the

Continued on Page Twenty-two

IN HEART OF ITALY

American 7th Army Is Reported in Van of Naples Operation

MORE POINTS NAMED

Landings Rumored at Genoa, Pizzo, Gaeta and Leghorn

By Wireless to The New York Times.

ALLIED HEADQUARTERS IN NORTH AFRICA, Thursday, Sept. 9—The Allies have carried the land campaign against the Nazis in Italy to the vicinity of Naples in new operations announced within twelve hours of the disclosure by Gen. Dwight D. Eisenhower that the Italian armed forces had unconditionally surrendered.

The news was announced here a few minutes past 6:30 A. M. in the following thirteen words:

"Further operations have started on the Italian mainland in the vicinity of Naples."

In the absence of the slightest expansion of the communiqué, no details are available as to the forces participating. The single fact remained that the attack had been pressed near Italy's southern metropolis and port, second only to Genoa, in what obviously was a major amphibious thrust.

Naples is a city of more than 700,000 population—nearer 1,000,000 if the suburbs are included. The assault was launched eighty-three years and two days after Garibaldi entered the city alone in a dramatic liberation gesture, which culminated in the unification of the country ten years later.

Although there is no indication just how near the city itself the landing or landings were carried out, it is plain that Naples is the objective of the sea-borne invaders.

[This dispatch did not indicate the make-up of the landing parties. A Tunis radio broadcast

Continued on Page Four

U. S. SOLDIERS IN LONDON CHEER THE NEWS

Americans in front of the Red Cross Washington Club in the British capital when the news of Italy's surrender was announced.

Associated Press Radiophoto, passed yesterday by censor

Announcements of the Surrender

By Broadcast to The New York Times.

ALLIED HEADQUARTERS IN NORTH AFRICA, Sept. 8—The texts of the proclamations by Gen. Dwight D. Eisenhower and Premier Pietro Badoglio follow:

By GENERAL EISENHOWER

This is Gen. Dwight D. Eisenhower, Commander in Chief of the Allied Forces.

The Italian Government has surrendered its armed forces unconditionally. As Allied Commander in Chief, I have granted a military armistice, the terms of which have been approved by the Governments of the United Kingdom, the United States and the Union of Soviet Socialist Republics. Thus I am acting in the interest of the United Nations.

The Italian Government has bound itself to abide by these terms without reservation. The armistice was signed by my representative and the representative of Marshal Badoglio and it becomes effective this instant.

Hostilities between the armed forces of the United Nations and those of Italy terminate at once. All Italians who now act to help eject the German aggressor from Italian soil will have the assistance and the support of the United Nations.

By PREMIER BADOGLIO

The Italian Government, recognizing the impossibility of continuing the unequal struggle against the overwhelming power of the enemy, with the object of avoiding further and more grievous harm to the nation, has requested an armistice from General Eisenhower, Commander in Chief of the Anglo-American Allied forces. This request has been granted. The Italian forces will therefore cease all acts of hostility against the Anglo-American forces wherever they may be met. They will, however, oppose attack from any other quarter.

War News Summarized

THURSDAY, SEPTEMBER 9, 1943

Italy has surrendered unconditionally, and all hostilities between that country and the United Nations ceased yesterday. An armistice was signed last Friday, the same day that Italy was invaded, but the victors reserved the right to withhold announcement until the most favorable moment for the Allies. The armistice terms had been approved by the United States, Britain and Russia.

General Eisenhower, announcing the surrender, promised support to all Italians who helped fight the Germans. Marshal Badoglio issued a proclamation ordering all fighting against the "Anglo-American forces" to cease and commanding resistance to "attacks from any other quarter."

Allied radios and planes carried messages urging the Italians to take vengeance on their "German oppressors" and to prevent trains, ships and trucks from carrying German troops or supplies. [All the foregoing, 1:8; map, P.3.]

Landings in the Naples area followed only a few hours after the surrender announcement and it was believed the Allies were attempting to cut off German troops in southern Italy. The American Seventh Army was reported among the invading forces. [1:3; map, P. 4.] Earlier, the Italian Navy and merchant marine had been urged to take their ships to designated points and to scuttle the vessels as a last resort to keep them from the Germans. [7:4.]

Wild demonstrations of joy were reported from all over Italy, but in the north they gave way to sober realization of continued danger when the Germans occupied Milan and other cities and imposed martial law. [3:1.] No official comment came from Berlin, but the German radio, after withholding the news for hours, was furious at the "treachery." [1:5-6.]

Germany's Balkan satellites were so shaken by the Italian surrender that Bulgaria, Rumania and Hungary were reported ready to follow Italy out of the war. [10:3.]

President Roosevelt, in a radio address last night, termed the surrender a great victory for the Italian people as well as for the United Nations. But he warned: "The time for celebration is not yet. Our ultimate objectives in this war continue to be Berlin and Tokyo." [1:5-6.]

The actual fighting in Italy was of a minor nature. Land forces advanced on both coasts. [3:6.] Airfields were hit by Allied bombers and the Rome radio reported heavy raids on suburbs of the city. [4:1.]

With one Axis partner out of the war, the two others continued to be hit hard. The Red Army captured Stalino and cleared the Germans out of the Donets Basin. [1:1; map, P. 22.] Allied bombers from Britain struck enemy airfields in France and Belgium [23:2], while down in New Guinea Japanese troops were providing weak opposition as the Allies closed in on Lae. [22:1.]

The naval task force that raided Marcus Island Sept. 1 destroyed 80 per cent of the Japanese military installations. We lost three planes. [1:2.]

CITY 'JUMPS GUN' IN WAR BOND DRIVE

Rallies, Sales Begin on Vast Scale—State Savings Banks Will Invest $600,000,000

As President Roosevelt and Secretary of the Treasury Henry J. Morgenthau Jr. opened the Third War Loan Drive for $15,000,000,000 last night over the radio, it was announced here that in the campaign to raise the State's quota of $4,709,000,000 the mutual savings banks in the State would buy $600,000,000 in Government bonds. The United States Steel Corporation and its subsidiaries will buy $100,000,000 in Government securities, with parts of the total allocated to districts where the corporation operates.

Restive to get its drive under way, New York City held preliminary rallies yesterday as Army convoys took into the five boroughs Navy gunners who had been rescued at sea. The largest meetings were held in Times Square and on the steps of the Sub-Treasury Building at Wall and Broad Streets.

Burgess Hails Italy's Surrender

The thousands assembled in the streets for these two gatherings cheered wildly as speakers announced the capitulation of Italy. Ticker tape, confetti and torn paper were thrown from the windows of buildings where workers in the financial community were listening to the rally.

The unconditional surrender of Italy is "bullish news" and will be a great help in the bond drive, W. Randolph Burgess, chairman of the War Finance Committee for New York State, said later in the

Continued on Page Sixteen

President Hails Victory But Warns of Real Foes

By JOHN H. CRIDER

Special to The New York Times.

WASHINGTON, Sept. 8—President Roosevelt hailed the surrender of Italy tonight as "a great victory for the United Nations" and also "a great victory for the Italian people" against "their real enemies, the Nazis," but cautioned against over-optimism. Addressing the nation on the opening of the Third War Bond drive, the President said "the time for celebration is not yet" and added that "our ultimate objectives in this war continue to be Berlin and Tokyo."

Toward the middle of his speech the President interpolated three words which gave basis to reports that Allied armies already were on the move again in the Mediterranean when he spoke of troops in landing barges moving up to enemy coasts "at this moment."

"This war does not and must not stop for one single instant," he declared. "Your fighting men know that. Those of them who are moving forward through jungles against lurking Japs—those who are landing at this moment in barges moving through the dawn up the strange enemy coasts—those who are diving their bombs down on the target at roof-top level at this moment—every one of these men knows that this war is a full-time job and that it will

Continued on Page Seventeen

Germans Charge Betrayal by Italy In Plot With Russian Government

By GEORGE AXELSSON

By Wireless to The New York Times.

STOCKHOLM, Sweden, Sept. 8—Berlin's newspapers branded Italy's capitulation as cowardly treachery last night. The German press abounds in scatching denunciation of Premier Pietro Badoglio and King Victor Emmanuel, as well as the Italian people.

"Mussolini was too great a person for a nation like that," a German official said. This is the second time that Victor Emmanuel has broken his word, the newspapers say, because the King "left Germany in the lurch" in 1915 when he joined the Allies.

Forgetting its praise of the Italians during the heyday of their pact, Berlin now condemns the Italians as third-rate individuals. "The cowardly perfidy of Badoglio caps the crime," one paper said, "by being committed in collusion with the Soviet Government, which is treason not only against Italy and Germany but also against all Europe."

Berlin added that the Germans had no intention of giving up their entrenchments in Italy, where they hoped to offer efficient resistance. Italy, since last night, is German-occupied territory to the extent that the Germans have been able to gain a firm footing there. In the Italian provinces occupied by the Germans, Berlin boasts fascism will be revived even if "we leave it to the Italians in those provinces to organize themselves along fascist lines.

Official circles are reviving accusations of broken words of honor

Continued on Page Nine

GEN. EISENHOWER ANNOUNCES ARMISTICE

Capitulation Acceptable to U. S., Britain and Russia Is Confirmed in Speech by Badoglio

TERMS SIGNED ON DAY OF INVASION

Disclosure Withheld by Both Sides Until Moment Most Favorable for the Allies—Italians Exhorted to Aid United Nations

By MILTON BRACKER

By Wireless to The New York Times.

ALLIED HEADQUARTERS IN NORTH AFRICA, Sept. 8—Italy has surrendered her armed forces unconditionally and all hostilities between the soldiers of the United Nations and those of the weakest of the three Axis partners ceased as of 16:30 Greenwich Mean Time today [12:30 P. M., Eastern War Time].

At that time, Gen. Dwight D. Eisenhower announced here over the United Nations radio that a secret military armistice had been signed in Sicily on the afternoon of Friday, Sept. 3, by his representative and one sent by Premier Pietro Badoglio. That was the day when, at 4:50 A. M., British and Canadian troops crossed the Strait of Messina and landed on the Italian mainland to open a campaign in which, up to yesterday, they had occupied about sixty miles of the Calabrian coast from the Petrace River in the north to Bova Marina in the south.

The complete collapse of Italian military resistance in no way suggested that the Germans would not defend Italy with all the strength at their command. But the capitulation, in undisclosed terms that were acceptable to the United States, the United Kingdom and the Union of Soviet Socialist Republics, came exactly forty days after the downfall of Benito Mussolini, the dictator who, by playing jackal to Adolf Hitler, led his country to the catastrophic mistake of declaring war on France three years and three months ago this Friday.

Negotiations Begun Several Weeks Ago

The negotiations leading to the armistice were opened by the war-weary and bomb-battered nation a few weeks ago, it was revealed today, and a preliminary meeting was arranged and held in an unnamed neutral country.

The Italians who had approached the British and American authorities were bluntly told that the terms remained what they had been: unconditional surrender. They agreed, and the document was signed five days ago. But it was agreed to hold back the announcement and its effective date until the moment most favorable to the Allies.

That moment came today, when the Allied Commander in Chief, in a historic broadcast, announced the armistice. He concluded with the reminder that all Italians who aided in the ejection of the Germans from Italy would have the support and assistance of the United Nations.

One hour and fifteen minutes after the General's voice had gone out over the air, Marshal Badoglio faced a microphone in Rome and confirmed the armistice. He concluded with the promise that the Italian forces would oppose attacks "from any other quarter," although they were laying down the arms that they had taken up against the Anglo-American armies.

Military Aspect Emphasized

Although it was emphasized that the armistice was a strictly military instrument, "signed by soldiers," it was disclosed that it contained a clause binding Italy to comply with political, economic and financial conditions to be imposed at the Allies' discretion.

[It was believed that the armistice conditions were substantially the same as those imposed on France in 1940, which allowed the Germans to use all strategic French ports and military bases to wage war against Britain, The United Press reported.]

Immediately after the announcement of the armistice, the Allies made two appeals—one to the Italian people and one to the Italian Fleet—urging them to rally to a cause that was, in effect, the liberation of their own country. The appeal to the people was disseminated by radio and air-borne leaflet, while that to the Navy was broadcast by Admiral Sir Andrew Browne Cunningham, the Allies' Mediterranean naval commander.

The Italian people, particularly transport, railroad and dock workers, were asked not to give the slightest aid to the Germans. The men who man Italian ships received specific instructions how to bring their vessels into the protection of the United Nations.

Although the fear was proved unjustified by Marshal Badoglio's broadcast, the Allies had taken no chances of a German move to forestall his giving the news to the people. As a safeguard, they had obtained from the Italians an agreement to leave one senior military representative behind when the others returned to Rome. This man is now in Sicily and presumably, had Marshal Badoglio not gone on the air, his representative would have broadcast the decision to the Italian public.

As a further earnest of good faith, Marshal Badoglio had arranged to send the text of the proclamation that he made this evening to Allied Headquarters here. He kept his word.

1,181 Days at War and Losses

Italy quit the war after 1,181 days, during which she steadily lost territory and prestige. Last May 7, with the fall of Tunis and Bizerte, the last Italian soldier in North Africa was doomed. Since then, Sicily, part of Metropolitan Italy, was occupied in thirty-eight days.

The Italians endured two raids on military targets in Rome

Continued on Page Three

ITALIAN REJOICING GREETS SURRENDER

Crowds in Rome and Naples Reported Wild With Joy at News of 'End of War'

BUT NAZIS END 'TOLERANCE'

Hundreds of Hostages Picked Up by Germans—State of Siege Put in Effect

MADRID, Sept. 8 (U.P.) — The Italian people have gone wild with joy over the announcement that the government has withdrawn from the war, with huge crowds swarming through Rome and Naples in enthusiastic celebrations, the first reliable dispatches from the Franco-Italian frontier said tonight.

Despite the fact that the Germans have entrenched themselves in northern Italy and apparently intend to remain there until driven out by the Allies, scenes of immense rejoicing were reported under way in all major cities.

Rome and Naples were said to be the scenes of especially enthusiastic and loud demonstrations tonight, with crowds streaming into St. Peter's Square in the Eternal City to cheer Pope Pius.

Dispatches from France said that the Germans now probably would not permit Italian divisions stationed in the French Riviera and the Balkans to return to Italy. Preliminary speculation indicated the Nazis would disarm these troops, confiscate their equipment and compel them to serve in German labor corps.

By Telephone to THE NEW YORK TIMES.

BERNE Switzerland, Sept. 8—Unprecedented manifestations of joy throughout northern Italy with the announcement of "the end of war—against the Allies" were dampened tonight when German forces north of the Appenines unmasked their previous display of "tolerance." They openly took over in Milan and other large cities from the local civilian authorities, according to a broadcast from Guistizia e Liberta.

Curfew from 7 o'clock this evening "until further notice" was declared in all the large towns as local German commanders proclaimed a state of siege and ordered the complete stoppage of all civilian traffic.

Frontier sources, considerably hampered by the imposition of German control of Italian communications in the north were late in coming through with much information, and when it finally became available the information was conflicting on many points. It is presumed in northern Italy that a virtual state of war will now exist between Italy and the Reich. Far from withdrawing any men or matériel in that area, the German High Command has seen to it that "sufficient measures" have been taken to "counteract this long expected treacherous stab in the back."

While no official confirmation was forthcoming of many measures the Germans are understood to have taken, there seems to be good reason to believe one report that more than 4,000 "hostages" for the good behavior of the Italians were arrested within an hour after the radio announcement of the surrender.

Up to a late hour tonight the Italo-Swiss frontier remained technically open, guarded exclusively by the regular Italian customs guards. From Chiasso came a report, however, that numerous "civilian" officers with a pronounced German accent had arrived to "supplement" the regular complements there.

The Germans are making—as declared in an official DNB announcement tonight—all preparations to "hold that which has already been gained" as they continue in the "defense of Christian Europe" according to plan.

Mussolini's Fate Pending

ALLIED HEADQUARTERS IN NORTH AFRICA, Sept. 8 (U.P.)—The fate of Benito Mussolini and other ranking Fascist leaders probably will be settled under terms still to be concluded between Italy and the United Nations, it was revealed tonight.

Under terms of the armistice published today, the fate of Mussolini and his Fascist henchmen was not revealed.

It was explained that at present Allied leaders are preoccupied principally with taking measures to meet the inevitable German efforts to bolster their holdings in Italy.

Puppet Rule in Italy Predicted

Predicting that the Germans "will announce the arrest of King Victor Emmanuel and Marshal Badoglio," an NBC broadcast from Algiers last night said that the Germans planned to set up a puppet Fascist Government in Italy, or those parts of Italy that they succeed in holding. Roberto Farinacci, former Secretary of the Fascist party, is slated for the role of Italian Quisling.

Signor Farinacci was last reported, in Stockholm dispatches, to have been arrested by Italian authorities near Como during an attempt to escape from Italy.

Nicaraguans Hail Surrender

By Wireless to THE NEW YORK TIMES.

MANAGUA, Nicaragua, Sept. 8—The news of Italy's surrender was received here with great rejoicing. Sirens and fireworks informed the city that something unusual was happening and the streets were soon thronged.

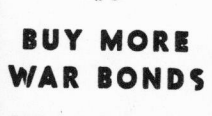

THE UNITED NATIONS DETACH ONE MEMBER FROM HITLER'S AXIS EUROPE

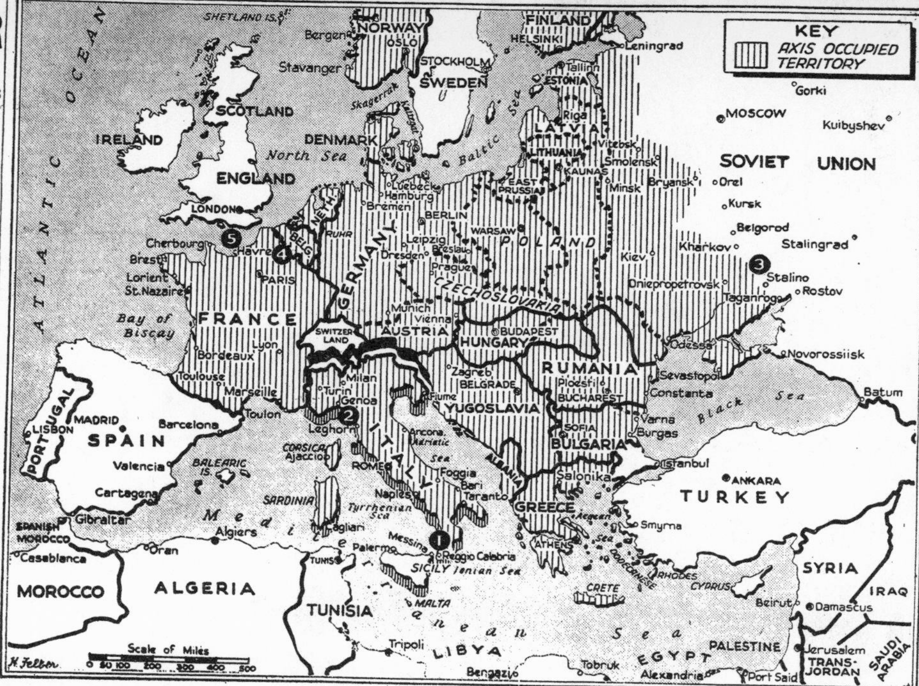

Sept. 9, 1943

As Italy's surrender was revealed yesterday the British and Canadians were making progress inland in Calabria (1). The Germans took over in north Italy (2). In between the Allies have made a landing in the vicinity of Naples. In other European theatres the Russians smashed into Stalino (3) and beyond (detailed map, Page 22); American and British fliers raked airfields and communications points in France and Belgium (4) and British light naval craft defeated five small enemy vessels in the English Channel not far from Havre (5). The shading on the map indicates Axis-occupied territory; in Italy, of course, German troops are occupying most of the country and are believed to be especially strong in the northern region.

Eisenhower Announces Armistice And Urges Italians to Assist Allies

Continued From Page One

and felt the weight of 20,000 tons of bombs on the mainland in the past six months. Of this total, 11,300 tons fell in August alone.

But, despite the abject condition of the nation today, it was emphasized here, the Germans were still expected to fight on in the worst way. It would be wrong and dangerously foolish to regard Italy as geographically out of the war, even though she is so politically. Thus the Allies kept up the air war against Italian airdromes yesterday even though the effective time of the armistice was almost at hand.

Despite rumors of negotiations of one kind or another ever since the fall of Benito Mussolini, it may be said that the news of the capitulation struck this area with stunning impact. It was known that Italian resistance and morale, as evidenced by the Sicilian and Calabrian campaigns, were dwindling, but complete capitulation was something of which few persons outside General Eisenhower's immediate circle had any idea.

Maj. Gen. Walter B. Smith, General Eisenhower's Chief of Staff, said at the close of the Sicilian campaign that one lesson had been never to give up possibility of achieving surprise. That apparently applied to the news of the armistice as well as to that of military developments.

Reserve Categories Abolished

ALLIED HEADQUARTERS IN NORTH AFRICA, Sept. 8 (AP)—An indication that Italy may already be beginning partly to demobilize her army was reported today in a Rome broadcast of a new decree abolishing several categories of reserve officers as "unnecessary."

A French officer at Allied Headquarters said that Italian occupation troops were being withdrawn from the Nice area in France and were being replaced by Germans.

German Troops Reported Halted

LONDON, Thursday, Sept. 9 (UP)—The Exchange Telegraph Agency reported today that the Algiers radio had said that the Italian Government had ordered all ships, trains and trucks carrying German troops in Italy to be held.

JAPANESE REPORTED CALM

Policy Said to Be Unaffected by Surrender of Italy

A Domei news agency dispatch broadcast by Tokyo radio said last night that Japanese official quarters had declared: "Japan's war policy remains unaffected by the latest development in the European theatre of war."

The Japanese determination to fight is unshaken, the dispatch said, and "meanwhile the Japanese public received the news of the Italian capitulation with complete calmness."

ARMISTICE CAST SHADOW IN SICILY

Mysterious Plane Made Two Trips to Allied Airfields in Palermo Region

By HERBERT L. MATTHEWS
By Wireless to THE NEW YORK TIMES.

AMERICAN SEVENTH ARMY HEADQUARTERS, Sicily, Sept. 3 (Delayed) — An incident whose clarification may have to await the end of the Italian campaign has been keeping northern Sicily agog for five days.

On Aug. 29, an Italian Savoia-Marchetti bomber flew to Palermo and landed on the airfield. Instructions had been sent all along the line that it was coming and was not to be shot at or molested. Out of it stepped an Italian colonel and another officer.

The next day the plane left, escorted by three Lightnings. On Aug. 31 the same mysterious order was sent around again and this time the plane landed at Termini Imerese, east of Palermo. The same officers were rushed to Palermo in closed cars.

This time they were not allowed to return, but a message was sent back stating that due note had been taken of the proposals made and it was expected that they would be carried out. If not, the officers were hostages and would have to pay the consequences.

It can be imagined what a sensation this incident caused among the thousands of Allied soldiers, who, of course, learned something about it immediately. Many had seen the plane come in. Rumors are always rife and lurid in all armies and this time they were like a strong forest fire. One soldier in Palermo asked whether the war was over. Others whispered solemnly that King Victor Emmanuel and Premier Pietro Badoglio had come to capitulate. None seemed to realize that the Allied task was to drive the Germans out of Italy and that the Italians had little to offer with the Germans sitting on their heads.

Still, something has been offered and some day we shall learn what it was.

NEWS BULLETINS
by The New York Times over Station WMCA—570 on the dial. Every hour on the hour 8 A.M. through 11 P.M.

PAYS EISENHOWER TRIBUTE

Jewish National Fund Lists Him on Jerusalem Honor Roll

The name of Gen. Dwight D. Eisenhower will be inscribed in the Sefer Ha'Zahav, the Jewish people's roll of honor in Jerusalem, as a salute to the commander of the Allied forces in North Africa, the Jewish National Fund announced here yesterday. The fund cabled its decision upon receipt of the news of Italy's unconditional surrender.

The Sefer Ha'Zahav, on the pages of which the names of the world's outstanding scientists, statesmen and military leaders of modern times have been inscribed in recognition of their achievements, is being preserved in Jerusalem. The fund said that the news of the unconditional surrender resulted in the receipt of many gifts.

ALLIES CONTINUE ADVANCE IN ITALY

Occupy Bova Marina in South and Push Beyond Palmi in West Coast Drive

NEW LANDING REPORTED

British Battalions Debark at Pizzo, 40 Miles to North, Germans Announce

By Wireless to THE NEW YORK TIMES.

ALLIED HEADQUARTERS IN NORTH AFRICA, Sept. 8—Moving ahead at their own pace in Calabria, the British and Canadian invaders of capitulated Italy advanced on both coasts of the Italian "toe" yesterday.

In the north a spearhead pushed past Palmi some five miles to the Petrace River, not far from Gioia Tauro. Gioia Tauro is the western terminus of the second and more important trans-peninsular road. It leads to Locri. The Allies already control the Bagnara end of the lower road, which crosses the Aspromonte area and zig-zags to Bora Marina.

[Late last night the British radio quoted a British correspondent as reporting that "bitter fighting is now in progress" between the British Eighth Army and German infantry on the Gioia plain north of Palmi, the National Broadcasting Company said.

[A German broadcast recorded by The Associated Press declared that Allied forces had swung forty miles up the coast to the north in a new landing at the Gulf of Sant' Eufemia on Tuesday night and "have been subjected to concentrated attacks since early today." A later broadcast said that four or five British infantry battalions had landed at Piggo, in the lower part of the gulf, pouring in more reinforcements afterward in a drive aimed to cut off "German rear guards to the south and southwest."]

Along the southern coast the troops have occupied Bova Marina, ten miles beyond Melito. The coastal strip in the Allies' hands now stretches about sixty miles, with inland salients jutting to San Stefano d'Aspromonte and Delianova.

Air Marshal Sir Arthur Coningham flew Gen. Sir Harold R. L. G. Alexander to the Italian mainland for a conference with Gen. Sir Bernard L. Montgomery forty-eight hours after the first landings on Sept. 3, it was learned today.

Day's Gains Fifteen Miles

ALLIED HEADQUARTERS IN NORTH AFRICA, Sept. 8 (AP)—The new advances reported by Allied headquarters covered some fifteen miles since yesterday's report.

The west coast advance carried five miles above Palmi to the mouth of the Petrace River. Here the invading troops were entering a small plain reaching some eight miles north to the Mesima River after hard travel in the mountains, slowed by enemy demolitions and skirmishes.

The firmly held Allied bridgehead is now defined by a line running from a point where the Petrace River enters the Gulf of Gioia, through Seminara, Delianova and San Stefano d'Aspromonte to the coastal area near Reggio Calabria, then paralleling the coast to Bova Marina, sufficiently inland to give the Allies full control of the coast road and railroad up to Bova Marina.

Front reports generally indicated a lowering of Italian troop morale. Civilians continued to greet the invaders. An account of a running battle between German and Italian troops in the mountains behind Reggio Calabria, three days before the British and Canadian invasion, reached Royal Air Force Headquarters here tonight.

It said that about 200 Germans and 100 Italians had been killed and wounded. The story, as told to the invaders in a resigned, friendly manner.

Such opposition as developed was easily routed, but extensive demolitions by the retreating enemy forces continued to make progress relatively slow.

The building up of Allied reserves of men and material on the Italian mainland, meanwhile, was being vigorously pursued by fleets of boats plying back and forth across the Strait of Messina under the protection of Allied warships and planes.

ROME, N. Y., WORKS ON

War Production Is Maintained as Italy's Rome Quits Conflict

ROME, N. Y., Sept. 8 (AP)—Rome, N. Y., took the fall of Rome, Italy, today without stopping one war production machine. All the large copper and brass fabricating mills and a huge Army air depot continued without pause for celebration of the unconditional surrender of Italy.

To thousands of residents of Italian extraction it meant their home towns would be spared the further scourge of war and their kinfolk in occupied Italy freed of the horrors of aerial destruction. The city has about 3,000 men in service, many of them of Italian extraction.

Vichy Gives Surrender News

The Vichy radio last night told the French people of the Italian capitulation by quoting a Nazi D. N. B. wireless transmission that had termed Marshal Pietro Badoglio's surrender "cowardly treason." Vichy characterized this as "the point of view of German circles." The domestic broadcast was reported by the United States Foreign Broadcast Intelligence Service.

"All the News That's Fit to Print"

The New York Times.

6 A. M. EXTRA

Partly cloudy and warmer today; moderate to fresh winds.

Temperatures Yesterday—Max., 67; Min., 51
Sunrise, 5:25 A. M.; Sunset, 8:34 P. M.

VOL. XCIII..No. 31,545. Entered as Second-Class Matter, Postoffice, New York, N. Y. NEW YORK, TUESDAY, JUNE 6, 1944. THREE CENTS IN NEW YORK CITY

ALLIED ARMIES LAND IN FRANCE IN THE HAVRE-CHERBOURG AREA; GREAT INVASION IS UNDER WAY

ROOSEVELT SPEAKS

Says Rome's Fall Marks 'One Up and Two to Go' Among Axis Capitals

WARNS WAY IS HARD

Asks World to Give the Italians a Chance for Recovery

The text of President Roosevelt's address is on Page 5

By CHARLES HURD

Special to THE NEW YORK TIMES.

WASHINGTON, June 5—President Roosevelt hailed tonight the capture of Rome, first of the three major Axis capitals to fall, as a great achievement on the road toward total conquest of the Axis. Rome, he said, marked "one up and two to go."

The President spoke for a quarter-hour on the radio, as had been announced yesterday, but his speech was notable for its lack of heroics. It was in no sense a speech of triumph, but rather a tribute to the United Nations forces and leadership that drove the Germans from Rome.

With this tribute he combined a solemn warning that much greater fighting lies ahead before the Axis is defeated, as well as high tributes to the Italian people, whom he again welcomed as a people into the family of nations opposed to the Axis.

"Italy should go on," Mr. Roosevelt said, "as a great mother nation, contributing to the culture and the progress and the good-will of mankind, developing her special talents in the arts, crafts, and sciences, and preserving her historic and cultural heritage for the benefit of all peoples.

"We want and expect the help of the future Italy toward lasting peace. All the other nations opposed to fascism and nazism ought to help to give Italy a chance."

Shrines Should Live, He Says

President Roosevelt saw considerable significance in the fact that Rome should be the first Axis capital to fall. He remarked its shrines, "visible symbols of the faith and determination of the early saints and martyrs that Christianity should live and become universal," and added that "it will be a source of deep satisfaction that the freedom of the Pope and of Vatican City is assured by the armies of the United Nations."

There is significance, too, he added, in the fact that Rome was liberated by a composite force of soldiers from many nations.

Reviewing the military picture, the President pointed out that "it would be unwise to inflate in our own minds the military importance of the capture of Rome." He cautioned his auditors that while the Germans have retreated "thousands of miles" across Africa and back through Italy "they have suffered heavy losses, but not great enough yet to cause collapse."

"Therefore," he added, "the victory still lies some distance ahead. That distance will be covered in due time—have no fear of that. But it will be tough and it will be costly."

Turning to the relief problem in the newly liberated portion of Italy, Mr. Roosevelt noted that some persons thought of the financial cost, but he maintained that the work would pay dividends "by eliminating fascism" and any future desire by Italians to "start another war of aggression." Relief has been planned, he added, but transport demands are so great that "improvement must be gradual."

He warned Italy that it "cannot grow in stature by seeking to build up a great militaristic empire,"

Continued on Page 5

Conferees Accept Cabaret Tax Cut

By The Associated Press.

WASHINGTON, June 5—A House-Senate conference committee agreed today to cut back the cabaret tax from 30 to 20 per cent, but eliminated a provision exempting service men and women from the levy.

The group decided to put the national debt limit at $260,000,000,000 as originally requested by the Administration.

The action is subject to House and Senate votes. The conferees met informally today, but members said that the decisions probably would stand as their final recommendation.

The House, at the insistence of a group of Republicans, passed a bill raising the debt ceiling only from $210,000,000,000 to $240,000,000,000. The Senate then put the figure at $260,000,000,000 and attached a rider reducing the cabaret tax from 30 to 20 per cent and exempting men and women in uniform from paying the tax on their checks.

Some tax experts argued that this exemption would make administration of the excise on night clubs impossible.

FEDERAL LAW HELD RULING INSURANCE

Supreme Court, 4-3, Decides Business Is Interstate and Subject to Trust Act

Special to THE NEW YORK TIMES.

WASHINGTON, June 5—The Supreme Court, by a four-to-three decision today, held that the insurance companies of the country, with assets of $37,000,000,000 and annual premium collections in excess of $6,000,000,000, are in interstate commerce and thus subject to the Sherman Anti-Trust Law.

The decision upset precedents which began with a contrary decision by the court more than seventy-five years ago and have been reaffirmed repeatedly since the adoption of the anti-trust law in 1890.

The majority decision, written

Continued on Page 13

PURSUIT ON IN ITALY

Allies Pass Rome, Cross Tiber as Foe Quits Bank Below City

PLANES JOIN IN CHASE

1,200 Vehicles Wrecked —Eighth Army Battles Into More Towns

By The Associated Press.

ROME, June 5—The Allies' armor and motorized infantry roared through Rome today without pausing, crossed the Tiber River and proceeded with the grim task of destroying two battered German armies fleeing to the north.

Fighter-bombers spearheaded the pursuit, jamming the escape highways with burning enemy transport and littering the fields with dead and wounded Germans. The enemy was tired, disorganized and bewildered by the slashing assault, which in twenty-five days had inflicted a major catastrophe on the Germans and liberated Rome almost without damage.

Railway Yards Bombed

Five hundred American heavy bombers blasted railway yards at five points in northern Italy between Venice and Rimini along which the Germans might attempt to move reinforcements and equipment to bolster their beaten armies. Hour after hour, the Allies' planes swept down on highways leading northward and tore the fleeing enemy apart. Twelve hundred combat vehicles were destroyed from dawn to dark yesterday, and hundreds more today. Farther north, medium bombers smashed bridges and rail facilities.

[The Germans have abandoned the entire left bank of the Tiber from Ostia, at its mouth, to Rome, according to a Vichy broadcast quoted by The Associated Press.

[The Germans are already entrenched in mountain positions

Continued on Page 2

FIRST ALLIED LANDING MADE ON SHORES OF WESTERN EUROPE

General Eisenhower's armies invaded northern France this morning. While the landing points were not specified, the Germans said that troops had gone ashore near Havre and that fighting raged at Caen (1). The enemy also said that parachutists had descended at the northern tip of the Normandy Peninsula (2) and heavy bombing had been visited on Calais and Dunkerque (3).

EISENHOWER ACTS

U. S., British, Canadian Troops Backed by Sea, Air Forces

MONTGOMERY LEADS

Nazis Say Their Shock Units Are Battling Our Parachutists

Communique No. 1 On Allied Invasion

By Broadcast to THE NEW YORK TIMES.

LONDON, Tuesday, June 6—The Supreme Headquarters of the Allied Expeditionary Force issued this communiqué this morning:

"Under the command of General Eisenhower, Allied naval forces, supported by strong air forces, began landing Allied armies this morning on the northern coast of France."

By RAYMOND DANIELL

By Cable to THE NEW YORK TIMES.

SUPREME HEADQUARTERS ALLIED EXPEDITIONARY FORCES, Tuesday, June 6—The invasion of Europe from the west has begun.

In the gray light of a summer dawn Gen. Dwight D. Eisenhower threw his great Anglo-American force into action today for the liberation of the Continent. The spearhead of attack was an Army group commanded by Gen. Sir Bernard L. Montgomery and comprising troops of the United States, Britain and Canada.

General Eisenhower's first communiqué was terse and calculated to give little information to the enemy. It said merely that "Allied naval forces supported by strong air forces began landing Allied armies this morning on the northern coast of France."

After the first communiqué was released it was announced that the Allied landing was in Normandy.

Caen Battle Reported

German broadcasts, beginning at 6:30 A. M., London time [12:30 A. M. Eastern war time] gave first word of the assault. [The Associated Press said General Eisenhower, for the sake of surprise, deliberately let the Germans have the "first word."]

The German DNB agency said the Allied invasion operation began with the landing of airborne troops in the area of the mouth of the Seine River.

[Berlin said the "center of gravity" of the fierce fighting was at Caen, thirty miles southwest of Havre and sixty-five miles southeast of Cherbourg, The Associated Press reported. Caen is ten miles inland from the sea, at the base of the seventy-five-mile wide Normandy Peninsula and fighting there might indicate the Allies' seizing of a beachhead.

[DNB said in a broadcast just before 10 A. M. (4 A. M. Eastern war time) that the Anglo-American troops had been reinforced at dawn at the mouth of the Seine River in the Havre area.]

[An Allied correspondent broadcasting from Supreme Headquarters, according to the Columbia Broadcasting System, said this morning that "German tanks are moving

Continued on Page A
Following Page 3

POPE GIVES THANKS ROME WAS SPARED

Voices Appreciation to Both Belligerents in Message to Throng at St. Peter's

By Wireless to THE NEW YORK TIMES.

VATICAN CITY, June 5—Pope Pius XII appeared on the balcony of St. Peter's at 6 P. M. today to thank God that Rome had been spared from the ravages of war while before him in the densely packed square of St. Peter's and the new broad Via Della Conciliazione tens of thousands of Romans cheered themselves hoarse.

It was the third time today that the Pontiff had showed himself to cheering crowds, as he had appeared twice at a window of his office this morning. But this was a solemn, sacred occasion and no one knowing anything about Pius XII can doubt the fervor of his thankfulness that Rome had been saved.

The Pontiff seemed strong and well and his voice carried far, though it was difficult to hear every word he said because of the crowd.

"We must give thanks to God for the favors we have received," said the Pope. "Rome has been spared. This day will go down in the annals of Rome."

He went on to say he hoped that Italians would be worthy of the grace shown them and put aside hatred and all personal vendettas. He then thanked both belligerents—the Allies and Germany—for having left Rome intact.

After a prayer of thankfulness to the Blessed Virgin and Saints Peter and Paul, guardians of Rome, the Pontiff gave his blessing, "urbe et orbis," as the immense crowd knelt before him.

[The Associated Press estimated the crowd was between 250,000 and 500,000.]

The world has changed for Rome but the Vatican goes on imperturbably as it has through so many other conquests in centuries gone by. It is neutral in fact and spirit. The Pope and all high officials went about their daily routine today as in the past. Except for the tanks and armored cars running along the street in front of St. Peter's one could never know what had happened today.

Continued on Page 5

Italy's Monarch Yields Rule To Son, but Retains Throne

By The Associated Press.

NAPLES, June 5—Victor Emmanuel III stepped aside as King of Italy today, as he previously had said he would do upon the liberation of Rome, and handed to his 39-year-old son, Crown Prince Humbert, all "royal prerogatives." Italian political pressure had been brought to bear against him since the occupation of Naples.

In a decree signed by himself and countersigned by Premier Pietro Badoglio, head of the Italian Liberation Government, the King named his son Lieutenant General of the Realm. The monarch, however, retained his title as head of the House of Savoy and remains as King without power.

[The first act of the Council of Ministers after the transfer of royal powers was a formal denunciation of the 1940 armistice treaty inflicted on France, The United Press said.]

Victor Emmanuel, who became King July 29, 1900, had announced last April 12 his "irrevocable" decision to withdraw from public life "on the day on which Allied troops enter Rome."

Little more than a figurehead since Benito Mussolini assumed the dictatorship of Italy, Victor Emmanuel had won a reputation in the first years of his reign as a sympathetic monarch, interested in his people and their problems.

Prince Humbert, tall and erect, opposed fascism in Italy at the start, but later made a truce with Mussolini. In effect, Humbert becomes the King's regent.

TEXT OF ROYAL DECREE

The King's withdrawal decree:

I, Victor Emmanuel III, by the grace of God and by the will of the nation King of Italy, in collaboration with the President of the Council of Ministers and with the agreement of the Council, have ordered and order as follows:

My beloved son, Humbert of Savoy, Prince of Piedmont, is nominated our Lieutenant General. In collaboration with responsible Ministers he will in our name superintend all matters of administration and exercise all royal prerogatives without exception, signing royal decrees which will be countersigned and authenticated in the usual way.

We order all concerned to observe this decree and to see that it is observed as the law of the State.

Given at Ravello June 5, 1944.
VICTOR EMMANUEL.
(Countersigned) PIETRO BADOGLIO.

The withdrawal was presented to

Continued on Page 4

ALLIED WARNING FLASHED TO COAST

People Told to Clear Area 22 Miles Inland as Soon as Instructions Are Given

By Cable to THE NEW YORK TIMES.

LONDON, Tuesday, June 6—The British Broadcasting Corporation began its 8 A. M. news bulletin this morning with quotations from a Supreme Headquarters' "urgent warning" to inhabitants of the enemy-occupied countries living near the coast.

Gen. Dwight D. Eisenhower has directed that whenever possible in France a warning shall be given to towns in which certain targets will be intensively bombed.

This warning, the broadcast said,

Continued on Page B

PARADE OF PLANES CARRIES INVADERS

Witness Says First 'Chutists Met Only Light Fire When They Landed in France

The first eyewitness account of the Allies' invasion of Europe was given in a pool broadcast from London this morning by Wright Bryan of the National Broadcasting Company, who accompanied the airborne troops in their landings.

His account said the first spearhead of Allied forces landed by parachute in northern France in the first hour of D-day.

"In the navigator's dome in the flight deck of a C-47, I rode across the English Channel with the first group of planes from the United States Ninth Air Force Troop Carrier Command to take our fighting men into Europe," Mr. Bryan said.

He added that just before he left French soil for the return trip he saw seventeen American paratroopers, led by a lieutenant colonel, jump with their arms, ammunition and equipment into German-occupied France."

He declared that his group at the head of the leading wing was met with "only scattering small

Continued on Page B

War News Summarized

TUESDAY, JUNE 6, 1944

The invasion of western Europe began this morning.

General Eisenhower, in his first communiqué from Supreme Headquarters, Allied Expeditionary Force, issued at 3:30 A. M., said that "Allied naval forces supported by strong air forces began landing Allied armies this morning on the northern coast of France."

The assault was made by British, American and Canadian troops who, under command of Gen. Sir Bernard L. Montgomery, landed in Normandy. London gave no further details but earlier Berlin had broadcast that parachute troops had landed on the Normandy Peninsula near Cherbourg and that invasion forces were pouring from landing craft under cover of warships near Havre. Dunkerque and Calais were being heavily bombed, the Germans said.

Later announcements from Berlin said that there was fighting between Caen and Trouville and that shock troops had swung into action to halt the invasion. [All the foregoing, 1:8.]

General Eisenhower, in an order of the day to each member of the "great crusade," told his men the enemy would fight savagely and added: "We will accept nothing less than full victory. Good luck." In a broadcast to the "Peoples of Western Europe," he said the day would come when he would need their full help. A special word to France added that Frenchmen would rule the country. [1:6-7.] Almost simultaneously it was announced that General de Gaulle had arrived in London. [6:2.]

The liberation of Rome in no way slowed the Allied pursuit of the tired and disorganized German armies in Italy yesterday. Armored and motorized units sped across the Tiber River to press hard upon the retreating enemy's heels. Five hundred heavy bombers joined with lighter aircraft to smash rail and road routes leading to northern Italy and to add to the foe's demoralization. The Eighth Army, despite heavy opposition, especially northeast of Valmontone, captured a number of strategic towns. [1:3; map P. 2.]

General Clark said that parts of the two German armies had been smashed. He doubted the ability of the German Fourteenth to put up effective opposition and declared that the Tenth had taken a bad beating. [3:1.]

King Victor Emmanuel fulfilled his promise and turned over all authority to his son, Crown Prince Humbert. [1:5-6.]

President Roosevelt warned the people of the United States in a radio talk last night not to over-emphasize the military significance of the liberation of Rome. "Germany has not yet been driven to surrender," he said. "Victory still lies some distance ahead. * * * It will be tough and it will be costly." The President appealed to the world to give Italy a chance to contribute her share to a lasting peace. [1:1.]

In the Pacific theatre Americans were converging on the Biak airfields. Allied planes sank one and damaged two Japanese destroyers and shot down at least eighteen aircraft. [8:1.]

Eisenhower Instructs Europeans; Gives Battle Order to His Armies

Following are the texts of a statement by Gen. Dwight D. Eisenhower broadcast to the people of western Europe and his Order of the Day to the Allied Expeditionary Force as recorded by The New York Times and the Columbia Broadcasting System:

People of western Europe! A landing was made this morning on the coast of France by troops of the Allied Expeditionary Force. This landing is part of the concerted United Nations plan for the liberation of Europe, made in conjunction with our great Russian Allies. I have this message for all of you. Although the initial assault may not have been made in your own country, the hour of your liberation is approaching.

All patriots, men and women, young and old, have a part to play in the achievement of final victory. To members of resistance movements, whether led by national or outside leaders, I say: "Follow the instructions you have received." To patriots who are not members of organized resistance groups I say, "continue your passive resistance, but do not needlessly endanger your lives until I give you the signal to rise and strike the enemy. The day will come when I shall need your united strength. Until that day, I call on you for the hard task of discipline and restraint."

Citizens of France! I am proud to have again under my command the gallant forces of France. Fighting beside their Allies, they will play a worthy part in the liberation of their

Continued on Page 3

The Texts of the Day's Communiques on Fighting in Various Zones

2 FLANKING DRIVES IN ITALY EXPECTED

One to East Along Highway to Pescara and Another to North Are Predicted

By DREW MIDDLETON

By Cable to THE NEW YORK TIMES.

LONDON, June 5—A new phase in the Italian campaign opened today when armored spearheads rumbled out of Rome in an attempt to cut off the retreating German Army.

Reports from Italy make it evident that the Allies intend to thrust simultaneously east along Highway 5 from Rome, to take in the rear of the German force remaining south of the road, and north into the Campagna, where they will be able to use their tanks most effectively. A rapid advance north from Rome will also constitute a wider outflanking movement than one along Highway 5.

Indeed, if this is rapid enough, it might become to some extent a pursuit on parallel lines, tending to drive a considerable proportion of the enemy's divisions into the dubious shelter of the Apennine Mountains. London observers believed that the Germans have lost 60 per cent of their effectives in the past twenty-four days. [The loss was estimated at 70,000 men, The United Press said.]

These tactics accord with the Allies' basic plan, to which the occupation of Rome is only an incident. They seek the complete destruction of the German Tenth and Fourteenth Armies, and today their reports show far more optimism that this will be achieved.

Since the opening of the offensive, the Allies have been cautious in their predictions, but now they seem to feel that the battle is "loosening up" and their chances of achieving their objective are improving hourly.

The drive to the northeast must, of course, be coordinated with steady pressure by the British Eighth Army against the enemy's rear guards. There has been brisk fighting along sections of the Eighth Army's front as the Germans strove to shield the withdrawal of their heavy equipment.

Such material must be salvaged if they are to form even a temporary line north of Rome. That it will be well north of the capital seems certain, for it is probable that the Fifth Army will reach the important junction of Rieti and perhaps even Terni, on Highway 4, before the enemy can establish defensive positions.

In view of the condition of the German troops and the proximity of the Allies' vanguard, it seems likely that the enemy will be unable to establish defensive positions until he has reached the Leghorn-Rimini line, 140 to 160 miles north of the Rome-Pescara position. This is a strong natural line. The Arno River, from Florence to Leghorn, forms the western hinge. The mountain features of Pratomagno and Bagno di Romagna are in the center and the Marecchia River, running to the Adriatic at Rimini, would be on the enemy's left flank.

PURSUIT ON IN ITALY FOR FLEEING NAZIS

Continued From Page 1

north of Rome, a German broadcast said. The German communiqué reported violent fighting northeast of Rome.]

Just twenty-four hours after the Allies' first troops had broken into the southeastern suburbs of the city at 8 A. M. yesterday, the leading elements had passed completely through the capital and the last German sniper had been killed or captured.

Eighth Army Fights Ahead

British Eighth Army forces advancing from the east continued to meet stubborn opposition, particularly northeast of Valmontone, where the Germans were fighting in fixed mountain defense positions. The enemy had been driven completely out of the Sacco Valley, clearing the towns of Fiuggi, Piglio, Paliano, Guarcino and Cave. Palestrina, astride an important retreat road four and a half miles north of Valmontone, was seized yesterday.

The British were encountering demolitions on a major scale. A spokesman said that the villages that they were being forced to storm were perched on rocky eminences several hundred feet high. The Germans had mined all the approaches and covered the roads with heavy fire.

Driving north along Highway 82 on the right, the Eighth Army closed in steadily on Balsorano, center of a strongly fortified area.

British troops on the coastal flank pressed within six miles of the Tiber below Rome. The hope of trapping the entire German force in this sector appeared to be bright, as few bridges over the Tiber were available. An Allied drive from Rome to the coast would seal their line of retreat.

Fifth Army troops pushing through the Alban hills captured the towns of Gottaferrata, Marino and Genzano and by-passed some enemy pockets of resistance. As evidence of the disorganization of the German forces in that area, it was disclosed that 377 prisoners taken at Velletri had represented fifty different companies.

Burned-out German combat vehicles in the streets of Rome offered abundant evidence that the enemy had turned the city into a battleground yesterday, at least to the extent of fighting a delaying action from block to block. Some inhabitants reported that the enemy had mounted guns on the roof of the Basilica of St. John Lateran, which is Vatican extraterritorial property, but this was not officially confirmed.

Delaying Actions Expected

It is generally assumed that the Germans will ultimately fall back about 150 miles north of Rome, where the northern Apennine Mountain range provides a formidable barrier. At no point short of that will they find a natural defense line comparable to the shattered Hitler and Gustav Lines. Beyond a doubt, they will fight any number of delaying actions as they fall back and will retard the Allies' advance with elaborate demolitions.

The capture of Rome did little to alter the situation as far as aerial operations was concerned, except to provide additional bases for operations of the Tactical Air Force.

Highways 1, 2 and 3, leading north of Rome, and a number of secondary roads were hit by fighter-bombers with virtually no opposition. Lightnings raked airfields and other targets in the Po Valley.

Medium bombers slashed rail and highway communications in the Florence area. Wellingtons and Liberators smashed at Terni, northeast of Rome.

United Nations

By Broadcast to THE NEW YORK TIMES.

LONDON, Tuesday, June 6—Supreme Headquarters, Allied Expeditionary Force communiqué 1:

Under the command of General Eisenhower, Allied naval forces supported by strong air forces began landing Allied armies this morning on the northern coast of France.

NAPLES, June 5 (AP)—A communiqué:

Allied armies in Italy have maintained their relentless pressure upon the enemy. Troops of the Fifth Army on June 4 entered the city limits of Rome, where sporadic resistance is being encountered. They control the whole of the Colli Laziali and have advanced in contact with the enemy toward the Lower Tiber. Our troops now dominate Highways 5, 6 and 7 leading into Rome.

Troops of the Eighth Army in contact with enemy rear guards have made considerable progress. The towns of Palestrina, Fiuggi, Piglio, Paliano, Guarcino and Cave are now clear of the enemy.

The total number of prisoners taken since the start of the attack now exceeds 20,000.

Motor transport, rail yards and bridges, highways and road bridges were attacked by aircraft of the Tactical Air Force north and west of Rome and in central Italy yesterday.

Medium and fighter-bombers as well as fighters also attacked rail and other military targets and shipping in Yugoslavia.

Strong forces of escorted heavy bombers struck at rail yards in northern Italy and important enemy communication lines along the French-Italian border.

From these operations two enemy aircraft were destroyed and eleven of our aircraft are missing. Seven enemy aircraft were sighted over the battle area yesterday during the daylight hours.

It is now known that one enemy aircraft was destroyed and one of ours is missing from night operations during the night of June 3-4.

The Mediterranean Allied Air Force flew approximately 2,000 sorties.

Last night our bombers attacked objectives in northern Italy.

By Broadcast to THE NEW YORK TIMES.

NAPLES, June 5—A special communiqué:

Troops of the Fifth Army occupied Rome on the night of June 4-5. The leading elements have passed through the city and are now across the Tiber in some places.

ADVANCED ALLIED HEADQUARTERS ON NEW GUINEA, Tuesday, June 6 (AP)—A communiqué:

NORTHWESTERN SECTOR

Halmahera: Our night air patrols bombed and sank an enemy destroyer and damaged two other vessels in waters to the east of Morotai Island. One of our air patrols shot down an enemy bomber in the area.

NORTHEASTERN SECTOR

Netherland New Guinea

Manokwari: Our night air patrols scored two direct hits on an enemy destroyer, leaving it dead in the water and probably in a sinking condition. Our attack planes struck enemy shipping and supply areas, sinking a small freighter and starting large fuel fires.

Numfor Island: Our medium units in a low-level attack destroyed two enemy troop-laden barges and damaged another. Our fighters shot down an enemy fighter over Mios Num Island.

Biak: Our ground forces continue their converging movement toward the airdromes. Our air patrols shot down ten enemy fighters and another, probably.

Sarmi-Maffin: Our heavy units at midday bombed enemy bivouac and supply areas, starting fires. Light naval units shelled coastal targets west of Maffin Bay.

British New Guinea

Wewak-Hansa Coast: Our medium units and attack planes and fighter-bombers continued the assault on the enemy's trapped garrisons at But, Wewak and Hansa Bay, dropping over six hundred tons of bombs on supply dumps and bivouacs. Many fires were started.

New Ireland

Our Solomons air patrols harassed Kavieng and coastal targets to the southeast.

New Britain

Our medium units and fighters from Solomons bases executed night harassing raids on Rabaul.

Bougainville

Our fighter-bombers attacked enemy lines of communication east of Matchin Bay and north of Kahili. Air patrols bombed coastal targets in scattered localities. Our light surface craft at night shelled enemy positions.

CAROLINE ISLANDS

Truk: Our heavy units from the Admiralties at midday dropped seventy-nine tons of bombs on Dublon and Eten Island, starting fires in hangar and repair areas. Seven of twenty enemy fighters attempting interception were shot down. We lost one plane. Air patrols harassed the area at night.

KANDY, Ceylon, June 5 (UP)—A communiqué:

Severe fighting continues at Myitkyina in the south of the town. Chinese-American forces to the southeast gained 200 yards and on the western outskirts 100 yards. Chindits continue to attack from the south at Waingmaw.

Kamaing now is more closely invested. Our units reached positions four and one-half miles east and six and one-half miles southeast of the town.

West of the Mogaung River Chinese forces thrusting south captured a village. In the extreme west the Japanese are withdrawing from Mansum.

North of Myitkyina levies raided Nsopzup. Our columns advancing in the Imphal-Ukhrul and Palel-Tamu road areas with artillery and air support captured several features on June 3. In the Bishenpur neighborhood we captured an important feature after an air strike.

Near Kohima vigorous patrolling continued. Northeast of Kohima our troops gained several more enemy positions and inflicted casualties.

In Arakan there was some shelling and patrols were active.

On June 3 USAAF and RAF fighters and fighter-bombers attacked Japanese positions, river craft, motor transport and barracks in the neighborhoods of Haka in the Chin Hills, Bishenpur, Kohima and northeast of Imphal, and also Moirang and the Somra Hill Tract. They destroyed barracks and motor transport and strafed Japanese troops and villages.

No Allied aircraft is missing.

United States

CHUNGKING, China, June 5 (AP)—A Fourteenth United States Air Force communiqué:

Flying in support of Chinese troops who are attempting to stem the advance of invading Japanese forces south of the Yangtze and the Tungting Lake area, planes of the Fourteenth USAAF on June 2 attacked enemy troop columns, motor transport, supply depots and river craft.

P-51's and P-40's attacked Tsungyang, causing large fires. They strafed five truck columns along the road near Pingkiang and a unit of Japanese cavalry, causing casualties and much damage.

Warhawks shot up river craft on Tungting Lake. Two Japanese fighters were intercepted and damaged by our top cover pursuit aircraft.

Later in the day P-40's and P-51's attacked Tsungyang a second time with unobserved results. They strafed the road to Tungcheng, causing an estimated 300 casualties and destroying thirty trucks.

Another flight of aircraft dive-bombed Tungcheng, starting large fires, one of which was reported to be a burning oil dump. Other P-51's bombed the city, causing casualties and destroying trucks.

P-40's operating in support of the Chinese offensive west of the Salween River attacked enemy positions and bridges at Watien in the vicinity of Tatangtzu on June 3. Transports dropped more than twenty tons of food and ammunition to Chinese ground troops.

Liberators on a river sweep over the Yangtze from Wuhu to Kichun bombed and sank three large barges.

Other B-24's attacked an enemy vessel in the South China Sea with unobserved results.

P-40's on a sweep over the Gulf of Tonkin strafed junks off the coast of French Indo-China. Other P-40's on offensive reconnaissance to Fort Bavard strafed and destroyed a Japanese fighter plane on the ground.

All our aircraft are accounted for.

WASHINGTON, June 5 (AP)—A Pacific Fleet announcement:

Several enemy patrol-type vessels were sighted west of Truk atoll on June 2 (west longitude date) and attacked by a single search plane. One was probably sunk and all were heavily strafed. On June 3 another search plane sighted the disposition and made an attack which resulted in the sinking of one of the auxiliaries and severe damage to another.

Liberators of the Eleventh Army Air Force bombed Ketoi Island in the Kuriles before dawn on June 4. No opposition was encountered. A single search plane of Fleet Air Wing 4 bombed Paramushiru Island before dawn on June 4.

All of our planes returned from these operations.

Navy communiqué 522:

PACIFIC AND FAR EAST

1. United States submarines have reported the sinking of sixteen vessels in operations against the enemy in these waters as follows:

One large transport, one large cargo vessel, seven medium cargo vessels, two small cargo vessels, four medium cargo transports, one small cargo transport.

2. These actions have not been reported in any previous Navy Department communique.

Navy communiqué 523:

ATLANTIC

1. The escort carrier U. S. S. Block Island was sunk in the Atlantic during May, 1944, as the result of enemy action.

2. The next of kin of casualties, which were light, have been notified.

LONDON, June 5 (AP)—A United States Strategic Air Forces in Europe communiqué:

Strong forces of B-24 Liberators and B-17 Flying Fortresses of the Eighth Air Force, escorted by medium forces of Thunderbolts and Mustangs of the same command, attacked German military installations in the Pas-de-Calais and Boulogne areas of France this morning.

No enemy aircraft were encountered. From this operation six of our bombers and two of our fighters are missing.

P-51 Mustang fighter-bombers and P-51 Mustangs of the Eighth Air Force attacked a German military convoy in France while P-38 Lightnings of the same Command conducted offensive patrol over enemy-held territory.

All our aircraft returned safely from these operations.

Four bombers previously reported missing in

British

LONDON, June 5 (AP)—An Air Ministry communiqué:

Last night aircraft of the Bomber Command attacked military installations along the French coast and objectives in Cologne. Mines also were laid in enemy waters.

None of our aircraft is missing.

An Admiralty communiqué:

His Majesty's submarines, continuing the offensive against the enemy and enemy-controlled shipping in the Mediterranean and Aegean, have sunk another two large supply vessels, two of medium size, twenty-two small supply ships and five naval auxiliaries. In addition, seven supply ships including two of medium size have been damaged.

Among the successes was the sinking of a large and strongly escorted supply ship bound for Crete with munitions. In the same area another large supply ship was torpedoed and sunk and a number of smaller vessels were destroyed by gunfire.

Naval auxiliaries destroyed by His Majesty's submarines included a medium-sized salvage vessel, a minesweeper and a heavily armed vessel believed to be a minesweeper.

During the course of these operations His Majesty's submarines successfully bombarded a number of shore targets including an oil refinery on the Italian coast, a railway goods yard and a seaplane hangar on the south coast of France and a radio station in Crete.

Chinese

CHUNGKING, China, June 5 (AP)—A communiqué:

In northern Hunan bitter fighting continued unabated yesterday south of the Milo River and in the area southwest of Pingkiang.

From morning until noon the enemy made fierce and continuous assaults on the front but was repulsed by our counter-blows. After noon the enemy in two columns attacked through gaps in the areas south of Sinshih. One of the two columns was thrown back after it reached a point about ten miles southwest of Sinshih. The other advanced by a roundabout route to a point seventeen miles south of Sinshih and launched vigorous attacks on our troops with heavy casualties to themselves.

In the meantime enemy troops at the west end of the Milo River made a southward advance along the Canton-Hankow Railway after passing through Kweiyi again. They were being hotly engaged.

Yesterday morning Japanese troops in the Tungting Lake sector in scores of armored boats forced a landing at points about ten and one-half miles north of Yiyang. They are being hotly intercepted by our troops.

In western Hupeh our troops south of the Yangtze River continued to pursue the retreating enemy after having recaptured Ansiang the night of June 3. Further progress was made.

The same day the enemy southeast of the Sungtze River attempted to force a crossing but was thrown back with heavy losses.

To the west, on the Yunnan front, our troops southwest of the Salween River, supported by artillery fire, at dawn yesterday vigorously attacked Mengliehchieh, east of Lungling (about five miles from Huitung Bridge and twenty-four miles from Lungling). The enemy offered stiff resistance. By 11 o'clock our attackers dislodged the enemy completely and recaptured the strong point. Remnants of the enemy were put to flight.

A later communiqué:

Chinese units south of the Yangtze, after beating the enemy back from points west of Ansiang and northeast of Hanshow, and frustrating a Japanese attempt to force a crossing of the Sungtze River from the east bank, launched a vigorous all-front counter-attack.

Our troops who recaptured Ansiang and pressed eastward continued an advance. Yesterday they reached points southwest of Nanhsien. Severe fighting broke out, with the enemy offering stubborn resistance. Chinese units, after recovering Yatzekang, northeast of Hanshow, continued to push vigorously northward and reached the Yukang region southwest of Nanhsien.

Our troops on the Sungtze River front yesterday morning totally smashed the resistance of the enemy on the east bank. Enemy remnants fled eastward in confusion. Our pursuing units advanced beyond the line linking Shataokwan and Michitai, both north of Kungan. Other strong Chinese units pressed on and opened attacks on Kungan. The enemy entrenched inside the city resisted savagely.

At noon today the attackers shattered the enemy's resistance completely and recovered Kungan. Enemy remnants fled in the direction of Owchihkow. At this moment various Chinese units operating in close collaboration are pursuing the retreating enemy.

An inventory is being taken of enemy troops killed and trophies captured at various points.

A later communiqué:

On the Yunan front our forces have captured several villages and, after crossing the Shweli River, have pushed to within twelve miles of Tengyueh, cutting the main enemy artery of supply to the north. Other Chinese units repulsed a Japanese attack from Nanchaikunfang and captured enemy outer defense positions east of the city.

In an artillery duel in the vicinity of Huitung Bridge [the Burma Road bridge over the Salween] two enemy guns were silenced, with our units suffering slight damage.

Our forces continue to hammer stubborn enemy defenses in the vicinity of Pingka in the south and Chiaotou in the north.

Russian

Yesterday's communiqué, as broadcast from Moscow to the Soviet Union and reported by the Federal Communications Commission:

During June 5 in the area northwest and north of the town of Jassy our troops successfully repelled attacks by large enemy infantry and tank forces. During June 4 in this area forty-one German tanks were destroyed and thirty-three enemy planes were brought down.

There were no changes in other sectors of the front.

During June 4 thirty-nine enemy planes were shot down in air combat and by anti-aircraft fire on all fronts.

During the night of June 4-5 our Air Force made a massed raid on the railway junction of Kishinev and military objectives of the town of Kishinev. At the time of the raid there were many enemy trains in the railway junction.

As a result of the bombing dozens of fires accompanied by explosions broke out. Railway engines, railway cars and freight cars laden with war equipment, and fuel tanks and military stores were burning.

One of our aircraft did not return to its airdrome.

LONDON, Tuesday, June 6 (UP)—The Russian Monday midnight supplementary communiqué, as broadcast from Moscow:

Northwest and north of the town of Jassy the enemy continued to attack our positions. Especially fierce battles occurred during the seond half of the day when the Germans threw fresh forces of infantry and tanks into battle. At first the Hitlerites succeeded in approaching our positions, but a counter-blow by Soviet tanks and infantry threw the enemy back. Soviet gunners successfully kept up their fire, destroying many enemy tanks and much manpower.

Units of X detachment in one day destroyed more than 600 Hitlerites and disabled or burned out twenty-one German tanks. In air combats Hero of the Soviet Union Ivan Kozhdub against distinguishing himself. In two days he downed five German aircraft.

Northwest of the town of Tiraspol, an enemy detachment in five boats attempted to cross the Dniester. Our battle guard fired on the Hitlerites with machine guns. Many Germans were killed or drowned in the river.

In one sector the enemy directed a whippet torpedo tank against our forward positions. Junior Lieutenant Dontseff, with a group of dare-devils, advanced to meet the whippet tank and cut wires dragging behind it. The whippet tank was delivered to base. All other German attempts to use torpedo tanks failed to yield any results. Our gunners shot up the whippet tanks and did not allow them to approach the forward positions of Soviet defenses.

Northwest of the town of Vitebsk groups of patrols under Senior Sergeant Vasilyev and Junior Lieutenant Drozdoff at night time made their way into German positions. The Soviet men suddenly broke into enemy trenches and in a fierce clash killed thirty Hitlerites. Our men captured prisoners and booty and returned to their units.

Six snipers of one of our units during the month of May killed fifty-three Germans. Junior Sergeant Skrylin and Private Kaganoff each destroyed twelve Germans, Privates Gogoleff and Vaturin ten each and Privates Rusakoff and Khotin nine each.

German

LONDON, June 5 (UP)—A German communiqué, as broadcast from Berlin and recorded by The United Press:

Despite the offer of the German Command not to involve the City of Rome in hostilities in order to maintain its cultural values, United States armored formations thrust into the inner part of the city at noon on June 4 in order to take possession of the Tiber bridges. Bitter fighting ensued which still was continuing in the evening.

On account of this attitude on the enemy's part, it was unavoidable that Rome should become a battlefield despite the clearly announced German intentions. The German High Command will, however, even now endeavor to limit the fighting in and around Rome to limits made absolutely necessary by hostilities.

Northeast of the city violent fighting with strong enemy assault groups is in progress.

In heavy fighting south of Rome flak formations of General of the Air Force Ritter von Pohl particularly distinguished themselves.

Near Cave and southeast of it, south of Guarcino and north of Sora our troops repelled strong enemy attacks supported by tanks and battle planes, inflicting losses on the enemy.

In the heavy fighting of the past few weeks the Seventy-first Infantry Division, commanded by Lieut. Gen. Raapke, particularly distinguished itself.

Italian torpedo-carrying planes last night attacked shipping targets in Gibraltar Bay, severely damaging four cargo boats totaling 30,000 tons, and scored hits on two more cargo boats.

Flak artillery of the Luftwaffe and naval flak downed nineteen enemy planes during United States bomber raids on northern Italy and over the front area.

One German U-boat sank one enemy submarine in the Aegean Sea.

On the eastern front the attack of German-Rumanian troops in the battle area northwest of Jassy gained further ground despite fierce enemy resistance and repeated counter-attacks. Strong Rumanian air forces continuously participated in the fighting with good effect and destroyed forty-two enemy planes in aerial combat.

Coastal patrol boats of the German Navy sank four Soviet motor torpedo boats and took prisoners in several night engagements in the Gulf of Finland.

Single British planes last night dropped bombs on the city area of Cologne.

Rumanian

Yesterday's communiqué, as broadcast domestically in Rumania and reported by the Federal Communications Commission:

On the Lower Dniester and in central Bessarabia no important events occurred. German and Rumanian troops continued to gain ground despite the enemy's stubborn resistance. Fighting continues.

The Rumanian and German air forces have supported with good effect operations on land and shot down forty-two enemy aircraft.

Finnish

Yesterday's communiqué, as broadcast domestically in Finland and reported by the Federal Communications Commission:

In Karelia and the Aunus Isthmus attacks made by an enemy combat patrol at four points, supported by artillery and infantry fire, were repulsed. There is nothing to report from our other land fronts.

Our coastal batteries fired on enemy units approaching the coast of the Karelian Isthmus. Two small craft were sunk.

In an air battle over the Karelian Isthmus three enemy fighter aircraft were shot down.

Japanese

No broadcast of a Japanese communiqué was recorded yesterday.

ALLIES PRESS ADVANTAGE AFTER THE CAPTURE OF ROME

June 6, 1944

Fanning out from the Italian capital, American and British troops crossed the Tiber River in pursuit of the Germans (1). Below the capital the British pushed to points six miles from the Tiber (2). An enemy report said the foe had withdrawn from the entire left bank between Rome and Ostia. But fighting persisted in the Alban Hills region, where the Fifth Army won Genzano, Marino, Grottaferrata and Palestrina (3). The Eighth Army took Paliano, Piglio, Fiuggi and Guarcino (4).

June 6, 1944

To compound the chaos of the German situation in Italy Allied fliers bombed five points along the railway between Ferrara (1) and Forli (2), as well as the key junction of Terni (3). As the enemy falls back from the present line (A), observers believe, he will not be able to make another effective stand short of a line running from Leghorn to Rimini via Mt. Pratomagno (B).

Fifth Army Pursuing Germans and Its Commander Entering Rome

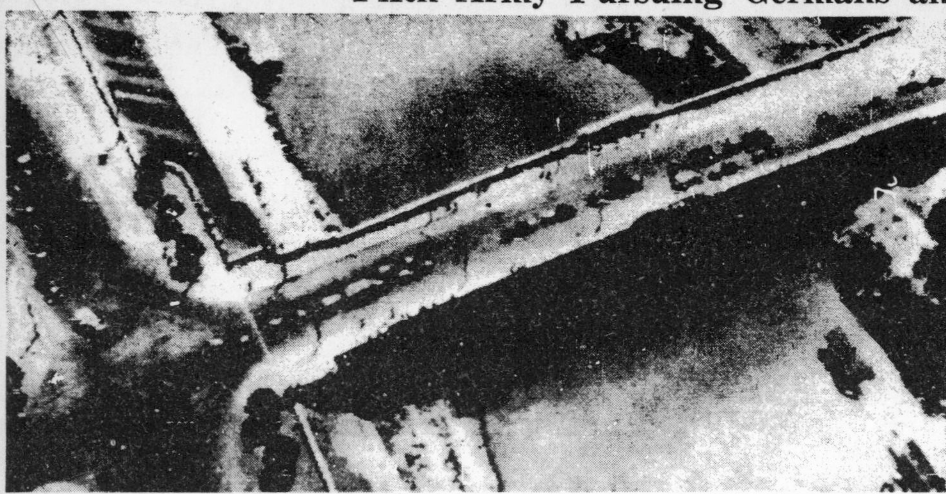

A troop convoy of the Fifth Army moving across a bridge over the Tiber River in pursuit of the enemy
The New York Times (U. S. Signal Corps Radiotelephoto)

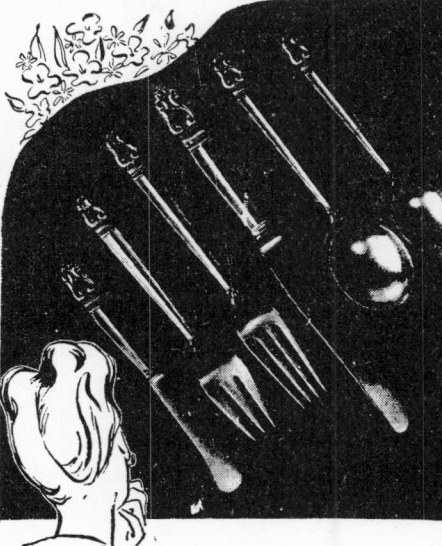

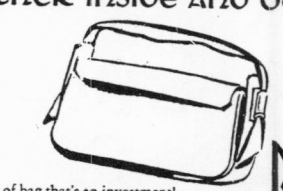

Lieut. Gen. Mark W. Clark is cheered as he rides past the Coliseum. Standing behind him is Maj. Gen Alfred M. Gruenther.
Associated Press Wirephoto (U. S. Signal Corps Radiophoto)

GEN. CLARK SEES 2 ARMIES BEATEN

Foe's 10th Smashed, 14th Unable to Give Effective Battle, He Says in Rome

By Wireless to THE NEW YORK TIMES.

ROME, June 5 — Lieut. Gen. Mark W. Clark was a happy man today, but, as he stood on the terrace of the Campidoglio, overlooking the Capitoline Hill, with his chief aides, the man who conquered Rome from the south for the first time in history did not speak loudly or even smile very broadly as he accepted congratulations.

For it was constantly obvious that the commander of the Fifth Army took his triumph with remarkable restraint. Perhaps it was partly fatigue, for, like every man in his hard-driving forces that made the final thrust into the city, General Clark was pretty tired. Probably another factor was a kind of numbness that crept over everyone today, keeping him from realizing the magnitude of the moment and from reacting too hysterically to it.

But there was still another factor in the case of the commanding general who stood quietly at the rail of Campidoglio, looking out over the British, American and Italian flags to the city below. It was the thought of his men who had helped him to gain historic glory at the cost of their lives.

Long, Bloody Fight

The Fifth Army had a long, bloody fight to Rome, and it had not ended even last night, when snipers were still killing Americans between the Centocelle suburb and the city. This loyalty to the men who could not be there to share his triumph was implicit in every word that General Clark said.

Leaning against the stone railing, the general remarked that he did not want to say much by way of direct comment. But later, in response to a direct request, he authorized a direct quotation of what he said.

"I asked that my corps commanders, General Truscott, General Keyes and General Juin, meet me here this morning at 10," the general said, "in order that we could coordinate our advance." He added that the army had been moving fast and communications could not always keep up. Then he resumed:

"This is a great day for the Fifth Army and for the French, British and American troops of the Fifth that have made this victory possible."

He thanked the air force for its share and then said: "And I want to say a word of tribute to the gallant men and women who made the supreme sacrifice that we could keep on going."

No Wacs Killed in Action

None of the Fifth Army's Wacs has been killed in action, but nurses and a Red Cross worker were killed on the beachhead. Somehow that was the peroration of General Clark's remarks and everyone present felt it.

Because General Clark has said that the destruction of the German armies was the primary, and the capture of Rome the secondary objective, General Clark and his aides told what they could of the effect of the smashing drive to Rome on the two German armies involved. General Clark said that the Allies had "smashed parts of two German armies." He alluded to the Tenth Army, which had fought on the main front, and the Fourteenth Army, which had tried vainly to root out our beachhead. He said that the Tenth Army had taken a bad beating and "I doubt if the Fourteenth is capable of effectively opposing us now."

Juin Joins Group

General Clark fingered his leather eyeglass-case and conferred with Maj. Gen. Lucian Truscott and Maj. Gen. Alfred M. Gruenther while, off to the right, a lone Italian guard stood out blackly against a white marble stairway. Then Gen. Alphonse-Pierre Juin arrived; he had been delayed.

"Congratulations," General Juin said to General Clark. "Congratulations to you," General Clark responded.

It was 10:17 A. M. The British and American Flags fluttered beside the Italian Flag. Immediately the French Tricolor was hoisted.

Below the terrace, the plaza of the Capitoline Hill swarmed with jeeps, command cars and light armored vehicles. One unshaven lieutenant watched the generals studying a map at the balcony rail. He leaned back and everything about his face and the way his helmet fit told how tired he was. "It took us a long time," he said, but he managed a smile as he said it.

WASHINGTON WAITS 3 HOURS FOR FLASH

Pershing Sees Victory in 'Like War of Liberation' Fought by Sons of 1918 Troops

Special to THE NEW YORK TIMES.

WASHINGTON, Tuesday, June 6—Washington learned officially of the invasion of Europe at 3:32 A. M. today when the War Department issued the text of the communiqué issued by the Supreme Headquarters, Allied Expeditionary Forces.

This flash was the climax of three hours of tense waiting that followed first German radio reports that hostilities off France had begun. Before that both the War Department and the Office of War Information said they had no information to confirm or deny the German reports.

The communiqué was handed newspaper men in the War Department by Maj. Gen. Alexander D. Surles, chief of the Army Bureau of Public Relations. With the communiqué was issued a statement by General of the Armies John J. Pershing which declared the sons of the American soldiers of 1917 and 1918 were engaged in a "like war of liberation" and would bring freedom to people who have been enslaved.

The capital awakened rapidly after the initial broadcasts. Lights flashed on and radios began to blare. Newspaper men hurried to their offices. Everybody was demanding to know whether it was "official."

If the White House was aware of the report, there was no outward indication. Only a few lights glowed there and the customary guards patrolled up and down monotonously.

Only a few hours earlier—at 8:30 P. M.—Mr. Roosevelt had addressed the world for fifteen minutes on the fall of Rome.

By 1:45 A. M., almost the entire public relations staff at the War Department had reported for duty.

Elmer Davis, director of the OWI, met about half a dozen news men in his office about 4 A. M. and told them the OWI had no assurance that the invasion was coming off this morning but thought that it might be. He said that OWI did not put out any of the German broadcast reports prior to official confirmation from General Eisenhower's headquarters.

Between the official flash and the time General Eisenhower began his talk, the OWI was transmitting the text of the communiqué.

The OWI director added that ABSIE, the agency's foreign radio, had broadcast General Eisenhower's speech in about twenty languages.

Pershing Sees Patriots Rising

WASHINGTON, Tuesday, June 6 (UP)—General Pershing, in a statement headed "American troops have landed in western Europe," said today that he had "every confidence" that the invasion would succeed.

The statement was released by the War Department.

"The overwhelming military might of the Allies advances," the aged general said. "It will be joined by the men of the occupied countries, whose land has been overrun by the enemy but whose spirit remains unconquered.

"Twenty-six years ago American soldiers, in cooperation with their Allies, were locked in mortal combat with the German enemy. Their march of victory was never halted until the enemy laid down his arms in defeat. The American soldier of 1917-1918, fighting in a war of liberation, wrote by his deeds one of the most glorious pages of military history.

"Today the sons of American soldiers of 1917-18 are engaged in a like war of liberation. It is their task to bring freedom to peoples who have been enslaved.

"I have every confidence that they, together with their gallant brothers-in-arms, will win through to victory."

McNaughton Prays for Invaders

MONTREAL, Tuesday, June 6 (Canadian Press) — Lieut. Gen. A. G. L. McNaughton, former commander of the Canadian Army overseas and the man who trained the Canadians for their part in today's invasion of the Continent, said early this morning that "all I'd like to say is that my prayers are with them."

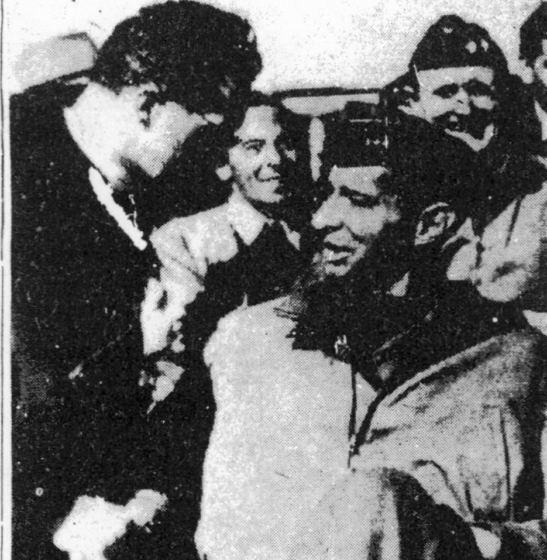

General Clark is greeted by a priest at the entrance to Vatican City. General Gruenther, chief of staff, is directly behind General Clark.
The New York Times (U. S. Signal Corps Radiotelephoto)

U. S. Troops Too Weary To Join in Celebration

By Broadcast to THE NEW YORK TIMES.

ROME, June 5—The doughboys who charged into Rome this morning were glad to be here but they were tired, too. They didn't come in all smiling, some of them were just fagged out, and it was hard for them to react in kind to the wild enthusiasm of the Romans.

They came in on foot, in jeeps, in tanks and in all sorts of military vehicles.

Pvt. Frank Balcor of 510 East Twelfth Street said it was a "great feeling to walk into this place. I never saw anything like this before."

But Pvt. Ed Cambra of 4½ Jane Street, Greenwich Village, couldn't even smile about it. Romans were milling all about him, including very pretty, cleanly dressed girls.

"My feet are just about swelled up. That's about all," was all he said.

BALKAN STATESMEN CONFER WITH HITLER

Antonescu Said to Be Seeking Return of Transylvania

BERNE, Switzerland, June 5 (UP)—Adolf Hitler is conferring with Balkan Quislings at Berchtesgaden at a meeting that may lead to a drastic revision of "the Vienna pact," whereby Transylvania was turned over to Hungary, according to information reaching Balkan diplomatic sources here today.

It is understood that Hitler and the German Foreign Minister, Joachim von Ribbentrop, had summoned Premier Dome Sztojay of Hungary, Premier Marshal Ion Antonescu of Rumania, Premier Ivan Bagrianoff of Bulgaria and his predecessor, Bogdan Philoff. It was said that Marshal Antonescu was attempting to get back Transylvania, after a reported similar offer from Russia should Rumania abandon the Axis camp, by threatening to resign unless the matter were settled in his country's favor immediately.

A Brazzaville broadcast heard by the Columbia Broadcasting System asserted that German troops had occupied all strategic points in Bulgaria and that the Gestapo had taken over the Ministry of the Interior, controlling the internal police. This broadcast, quoting information from Sofia, also said that new contingents of Bulgarian troops had been sent the Turkish border.

Airman Dies on Suffolk Field

WESTHAMPTON BEACH, L. I., June 5—Flight Officer Joseph R. Harvey of the Army Air Forces was killed early today when the fighter plane that he was flying crashed at the Suffolk Army air base near here. The flight officer's home was at 17 Round Hill Street, Jamaica Plain, Mass. He had taken the plane, alone, on a combat training mission.

Normandy Airdromes Wiped Out

LONDON, Tuesday, June 6 (UP)—The German DNB news agency today broadcast a dispatch, unconfirmed by Allied sources, that the most important airdromes in the area of the Normandy Peninsula of France had been wiped out.

LA GUARDIA PLEASED AT CHANGE IN ITALY

Says He Hopes That Abdication Means End of Hereditary Rule

Mayor La Guardia, before leaving by plane for Washington yesterday morning, called the Allied capture of Rome "very gratifying."

"It will tend to relieve the tension quite a bit," he added. "It looks to me that the Germans may retire to the Po River. We'll know in a few days. Incidentally, in the last war that was part of our strategy in the event we could not hold at the Piave River."

Upon his return from Washington at 6 P. M., the Mayor said he hoped the surrender of his powers of Government by King Victor Emanuel would mean the end of hereditary rule in Italy. The King had vested his powers in his son, Crown Prince Umberto.

"If that means that the power does not go to a hereditary prince, then indeed it is great progress and in keeping with what we are fighting for," the Mayor stated.

"I want to distinguish between a provisional or temporary government and a government by hereditary line. If this means that the power goes to the government, then the final say will remain with the people as to which form of government they will want when the time comes to make this decision."

ESPIONAGE TRIAL WEIGHED

Date for Doll Dealer's Case to Be Announced Tomorrow

The question of a date for the trial of Mrs. Velvalee Dickinson, 50-year-old doll dealer accused of espionage in behalf of the Japanese, was taken under advisement yesterday by Federal Judge Francis G. Caffey. He said he would announce tomorrow his decision on whether to grant a two-month adjournment sought by defense counsel or to put the case down for July 10 as requested by Edward C. Wallace, assistant United States attorney.

Maurice L. Shaine, Mrs. Dickinson's lawyer, disclosed that he was seeking release of 25,000 of the defendant's funds tied up by an income tax lien filed by the Bureau of Internal Revenue. A substantial part of it has been described by Mr. Wallace as evidence in the Government's case against Mrs. Dickinson.

3 RECOGNIZE ECUADOR

Brazil, Peru and Paraguay Set Up Links With New Regime

QUITO, Ecuador, June 5 (AP)—Brazil, Peru and Paraguay recognized the new Ecuadorean Government today and Casar Coloma Silva, Under-Secretary of Foreign Affairs, said communications received from other nations assured similar action by "all republics of the hemisphere."

Brazil was first to recognize the new regime.

Fleeing Nazis Take Labor Chief

ROME, June 5 (Reuter)—Bruno Buozzi, Italian trade union chief, was removed from Rome by the Germans on Saturday. He had been under arrest three months. The rest of Rome's leading Socialists and Liberals are safe in the city.

INVASION LEADERS OF ALLIES' FORCES

'Thumbnail' Sketches of Men Who Are Directing Blows Against Hitler's Westwall

By The Associated Press.

Supreme Allied Commander—Gen. Dwight David Eisenhower, 53 years of age, Texas-born, Kansas-reared; previously Allied commander of the forces in North Africa, Sicily and Italy.

Deputy Supreme Allied Commander—Air Chief Marshal Sir Arthur Tedder, 52, Briton who turned to the air after having been wounded as an infantryman in World War I; successful commander of Middle East and Allied Mediterranean Air Forces.

Allied Naval Commander—Admiral Sir Bertram Home Ramsay, 61, the man who brought the British Army home from Dunkerque, planner of sea participation in North African and Sicilian campaigns.

Allied Air Forces Commander—Air Chief Marshal Trafford Leigh Leigh-Mallory, 52, career airman son of British clergyman, formerly commander of all British-based Royal Air Force fighters.

British Ground Forces Commander—Gen. Sir Bernard Law Montgomery, 56, another clergyman's son, hero of Eighth Army victory at El Alamein and push across Africa and Sicily into Italy.

Senior American Ground Forces Officer—Lieut. Gen. Omar Nelson Bradley, 51, Missouri-born, quiet-mannered hero of American victory at Bizerte, called "Doughboys' General."

Commander of United States Strategic Air Forces—Lieut. Gen. Carl [Tooey] Spaatz, 53, Pennsylvania Dutch, endurance flier, founder of Eighth Air Force and commander of American air forces in Mediterranean victories.

Chief of Staff to General Eisenhower—Lieut. Gen. Walter Bedell Smith, 48, native of Indiana, General Eisenhower's Chief of Staff for North African invasion.

Commander of United States Eighth Air Force—Lieut. Gen. James H. [Jimmy] Doolittle, 47, one of world's most noted pilots, "the man who bombed Tokyo."

Commander of United States Ninth Tactical Air Force—Lieut. Gen. Lewis H. Brereton, 54, Pennsylvania-born, went to Annapolis but joined Army after graduation, was air commander in the Philippines, Java, India and the Middle East; noted for driving energy.

Commander of RAF Bomber Force—Air Chief Marshal Sir Arthur T. Harris, 52, took over present post in 1942 and has since been trying to bomb Germany out of the war by mass "saturation" technique which he organized.

Commander of British Second Tactical Air Force—Air Marshal Sir Arthur Coningham, 49, veteran of all kinds of air fighting, scored great success with RAF Desert Air Force and then commanded all Allied tactical operations in Tunisian and Sicilian campaigns; was cavalryman and fighter pilot in World War I.

Abbey Statue Stolen

NAPLES, June 5 (AP)—The theft of a costly altar statue from the Benedictine Abbey of Cassino for Reichs Marshal Hermann Goering has been proven by an order of the day issued on May 28 by Lieut. Gen. Richard Heidrich, commander of the German First Parachute Division, an official Allied source said today.

Davis Warns of German Trick

WASHINGTON, Tuesday, June 6 (UP)—Elmer Davis, director of the Office of War Information, warned the American public today that the German radio might be trying to build up a reputation for accuracy in its news reports of the invasion so that "they can put one over on the Allies later."

EISENHOWER GIVES ORDERS FOR BATTLE

Continued From Page 1

homeland. Because the initial landing has been made on the soil of your country, I repeat to you with even greater emphasis my message to the peoples of other occupied countries in western Europe. Follow the instructions of your leaders. A premature uprising of all Frenchmen may prevent you from being of maximum help to your country in the critical hour. Be patient. Prepare.

As supreme commander of the Allied Expeditionary Force, there is imposed on me the duty and responsibility of taking all measures necessary to the prosecution of the war. Prompt and willing obedience to the orders that I shall issue is essential. Effective civil administration of France must be provided by Frenchmen. All persons must continue in their present duties unless otherwise instructed. Those who have common cause with the enemy and so betrayed their country will be removed. As France is liberated from her oppressors, you yourselves will choose your representatives, and the government under which you wish to live.

In the course of this campaign for the final defeat of the enemy you may sustain further loss and damage. Tragic though they may be, they are part of the price of victory. I assure you that I shall do all in my power to mitigate your hardships. I know that I can count on your steadfastness now, no less than in the past. The heroic deeds of Frenchmen who have continued their struggle against the Nazis and their Vichy satellites, in France and throughout the French Empire, have been an example and an inspiration to all of us.

This landing is but the opening phase of the campaign in western Europe. Great battles lie ahead. I call upon all who love freedom to stand with us. Keep your faith staunch—our arms are resolute—together we shall achieve victory.

ORDER OF THE DAY

Soldiers, sailors and airmen of the Allied Expeditionary Force: You are about to embark upon a great crusade, toward which we have striven these many months. The eyes of the world are upon you. The hopes and prayers of liberty-loving people everywhere march with you.

In company with our brave Allies and brothers in arms on other fronts, you will bring about the destruction of the German war machine, the elimination of Nazi tyranny over the oppressed peoples of Europe, and security for ourselves in a free world.

Your task will not be an easy one. Your enemy is well trained, well equipped and battle-hardened. He will fight savagely.

But this is the year 1944. Much has happened since the Nazi triumphs of 1940-41. The United Nations have inflicted upon the Germans great defeats in open battle, man to man. Our air offensive has seriously reduced their strength in the air and their capacity to wage war on the ground.

Our home fronts have given us an overwhelming superiority in weapons and munitions of war, and placed at our disposal great reserves of trained fighting men. The tide has turned. The free men of the world are marching together to victory. I have full confidence in your courage, devotion to duty and skill in battle. We will accept nothing less than full victory. Good luck.

Let us all beseech the blessing of Almighty God, upon this great and noble undertaking.

General Eisenhower personally broadcast his statement to the peoples of western Europe, the Office of War Information reported.

His Order of the Day was distributed to assault elements after their embarkation. It was read by appropriate commander to all other troops in the Allied Expeditionary Force, the Columbia Broadcasting System, which recorded the order, said.

MEXICO ACCLAIMS 'SPIRITUAL VICTORY'

U. S. Troops' Prestige Rises With Fall of Italian Capital

Special to THE NEW YORK TIMES.

MEXICO CITY, June 5—The fall of Rome was welcomed with deep satisfaction by the Mexican Government and people. All morning newspapers today carried the news under streamers.

Miguel Aleman, Secretary of the Interior, and President Manuel Avila Camacho's closest collaborator, expressed the Government's attitude. He said:

"The liberation of Rome is more than a brilliant military victory; it is a spiritual victory which will spur the Allied armies and bring the final triumph nearer."

Archbishop Luis M. Martinez of Mexico said the capture of the Italian capital must have lifted a heavy weight from the minds of all Catholics.

"I thank God and hope that all Catholics in the world will do the same for having spared Rome from the danger of being bombed or destroyed," he stated. "It would have been most painful to all Catholics and the whole of mankind if the Eternal City—this marvelous religious, historical and artistic museum — had been partly or totally damaged. I also thank God for having spared from this danger the august person of His Holiness the Pope."

The fact that American troops were responsible for the fall of Rome has enhanced the prestige of the armed forces of the United States have had since the beginning of the Italian campaign.

A HANDY GLOSSARY OF INVASION TERMS

Brief Definitions of Military Designations Old and New Likely to Figure in News

Following is a list of military terms, both official and of slang derivation, that will undoubtedly be household words during the long-awaited invasion of western Europe. Some of the expressions date back to World War I and before, but most have found their way into military dictionaries and everyday civilian conversation since the invasion of Poland in 1939.

ACK-ACK (AA)—Anti-aircraft gun or shell fragments.

AIRBORNE TROOPS—Parachute, glider or "air landing" troops.

AIR LANDING INFANTRY—Troops transported by air; not specially trained as are parachute and glider troops.

BAZOOKA—Rocket-firing anti-tank gun fired from shoulder.

BEACHHEAD—Area on hostile shore, garrisoned, defended and organized to cover landings.

BEACHMASTER—Naval officer in charge of Navy beach party.

BEACH PARTY—Naval personnel sent ashore to control boats, marking of beaches, unloading of landing craft and communications seaward of high water mark.

BOOBY TRAP—Disguised device containing explosive that detonates when tampered with or moved.

BRIDGEHEAD—Works constructed to protect end of a bridge or defile nearest the enemy. Also applied to position held on side of river or lake nearest enemy.

BULLDOZER—Caterpillar tractor for leveling airfields and excavation operations.

CASEMATE—Shelter, usually concrete and steel, protecting a gun and its crew.

COMBAT TEAM—A unit, usually a battalion or regiment, reinforced by a battalion of field artillery, engineers, etc., but centered on infantry.

COMMANDO—Highly trained British amphibious assault unit; also, popularly, a member of such unit.

COMMAND POST (C. P.)—Forward headquarters of a commander.

D-DAY—Arbitrary symbol designating day on which an attack is to be initiated.

DRAGONS TEETH—Concrete posts used as anti-tank barriers.

DUCK—Army's amphibious truck; carries supplies or twenty or more men.

E-BOAT—Small, fast German 100-foot patrol boat, similar to United States PT-boat.

ELEMENT C—Grillwork of steel and cable forming anti-tank barrier.

FLAK—Abbreviation of German word "flugabwehrkanone" meaning anti-aircraft gun; also AA-shell fragments.

H-HOUR—The hour on D-day when an attack is to begin.

HALF-TRACK—Caterpillar-type vehicle with wheels in front.

LCC [Landing Craft, Control]—Directs other landing craft in invasion.

LCI (L) [Landing Craft Infantry, Large]—Ocean-going craft with twin landing ramps. Carries more than 200 equipped troops.

LCM (3) [Landing Craft, Mechanized; Mark III]—Ship-to-shore craft used chiefly to land bulldozers, tanks, guns, trucks, etc.

LCR (L) LCR (S) [Landing Craft, Rubber; Large and Small]—Used to land small infantry groups; also by Navy.

LCS [Landing Craft Support]—Used in van of other landing craft; blasts enemy shore with rocket or cannon fire.

LCT (5) LCT (6) [Landing Craft, Tank; Mark V and VI]—Transports tanks or trucks; also lends soldiers.

LCVP [Landing Craft, Vehicle, Personnel]—Small infantry and vehicle-landing craft.

LSD [Landing Ship, Dock]—A dock in itself; used after beachhead is secured.

LST [Landing Ship, Tank]—Ocean-going ramp-bowed vessel. Carries many tanks and trucks and heavy equipment directly to beachhead. Also carries smaller landing boats and is heavily armed with numerous AA guns.

LVT [Landing Vehicle, Tracked]—Amphibious vehicle, also called "Alligator," which carries assault troops or cargo.

LVT (A) [Landing Vehicle, Tracked; Armored]—Also called "Water Buffalo." it is really an amphibious tank with a 37-mm. cannon and two .50-caliber machine guns.

MAE WEST—Inflatable life belt.

MARSHALING YARD—Point on railroad where freight cars are formed into trains.

MINENWERFER—Small German trench mortar.

MORTAR—Pipe-like infantry weapon with high trajectory and short range.

NEBELWERFER—Powerful German multi-barreled rocket gun.

O'CLOCK—Term used, chiefly by fliers, to designate direction, with 12 o'clock indicating dead ahead; 3 o'clock directly to the right, etc.

OVER—Radio term indicating reply is awaited.

PARATROOPS—Specialized troops dropped by parachute behind enemy lines.

PT-BOAT—Fast torpedo-carrying Navy patrol boat.

RADAR—Radio device for locating and measuring distance to an object or target.

RANGER—United States counterpart of British Commando trooper.

ROGER—Radio term indicating message has been received and understood.

ROUND—The ammunition for a single discharge of a weapon.

SALIENT—Portion of a battle line that extends sharply in front of the general line.

SHORE PARTY—Normally a company of Army engineers who takes over beach control, supply, security, etc., from the Navy, landward of high water mark.

SORTIE—One flight or mission by one plane.

STRAFE—To shell or bombard fiercely; commonly applied to planes machine-gunning ground troops or installations.

TANK DESTROYER—A mobile gun firing armor-piercing shells.

WALKIE-TALKIE—Portable radio receiving and sending apparatus.

WILCO—Radio term indicating "will comply."

WHERE BERLIN SAYS INVASION FORCES ARE STRIKING

Germans announce that Havre is one of the focal points

An aerial view of the French port of Cherbourg — The New York Times

EISENHOWER ACTS IN GREAT INVASION

Continued From Page 1

the roads toward the beachhead" in France.]

The German accounts told of Nazi shock troops thrown in to meet Allied airborne units and parachutists. The first attacks ranged from Cherbourg to Havre, the Germans said.

[United States battleships and planes took part in the bombardment of the French coast, Allied Headquarters announced, according to Reuter.]

The weather was not particularly favorable for the Allies. There was a heavy chop in the Channel and the skies were overcast. Whether the enemy was taken by surprise was not known yet.

Eisenhower's Orders to Troops

Not until the attack began was it made known officially that General Montgomery was in command of the Army group, including American troops. The hero of El Alamein hitherto had been referred to as the senior British Field Commander.

In his order of the day, made public at the same time as the first communiqué, General Eisenhower told hs forces that they were about to embark on a "great crusade."

The eyes of the world are upon you, he said, and the "hopes and prayers of liberty-loving people everywhere march with you." The order, which reflected a full appreciation of the mighty task ahead and yet reflected the calm, sober confidence that permeates these headquarters, was distributed to assault elements after their embarkation. It was read by the commanders to all other troops in the Allied Expeditionary Force.

The news that has been so long and so eagerly awaited broke as war-weary Londoners were going to work. Hardly any of them knew what was happening, for there had been no disclosure of the news that the invasion had started in the British Broadcasting Corporation's 7 o'clock broadcast.

Even the masses of planes roaring overhead did not give the secret away, for the people of this country have grown accustomed to seeing huge armadas of aircraft flying out in their almost daily attacks against German-held Europe.

Details of how the assault developed are still lacking. It is known that the huge armada of Allied landing craft that crept to the French coast in darkness was preceded by mine sweepers whose task was to sweep the Channel of German mine fields and submarine obstructions.

Big Allied warships closed in and engaged the enemy's shore batteries.

Airborne troops landed simultaneously behind the Nazis' coast defenses.

Triphibious Strategy

Not only were the troops of the United States, Canada and Britain united in a single fighting team, but their huge land, sea and air forces operated as a perfectly integrated machine.

Today provided the first example in northwest Europe of "triphibious strategy" in which Navy and Air Forces first help the Army gain a foothold on enemy territory as the Army goes about the grim business of seizing airports and harbors for development of the attack.

Soon after his first communiqué and order of the day were published General Eisenhower broadcast a message to the underground movement of Europe, warning its members to stand fast and continue passive resistance but not to endanger lives "until I give you the signal to rise and strike the enemy."

In the coastal area where the Allies have landed little help is expected at the outset from French patriots because the Germans have been at pains to remove from there all but old men, women and children.

However, there was indication in General Eisenhower's broadcast that the Army of France would fight under the United Nations banner, for he said:

"Citizens of France, I am proud to have again under my command the armed forces of France."

Announcement of the great "triphibious" attack was undramatic in its setting. Correspondents assigned to the Supreme Allied Headquarters were summoned by telephone just as the official German news agency, DNB, was broadcasting the fact that the invasion had begun. To maintain the initiative in battle it was necessary to surrender the initiative in the war of words.

In a room, the walls of which were plastered with maps, the correspondents gathered at pine tables and listened to officers lay down the law on censorship and fill in the background of the manner in which the soldiers of Britain and America and all fighting services of the countries had been welded into one fighting unit.

Nazi Reports of Action

German broadcasts at 9 o'clock, London time, said:

"Combined landing operations of the Anglo-Americans, which were launched both from sea and air against the European west coast early today, extended over the whole coastal sector between Havre and Cherbourg.

"The main centers of air landing attacks are in the whole of Normandy as well as at the most important river mouths in the Seine Bight. Amphibious operations on a large scale were simultaneously begun between the Seine estuary and the mouth of Vire River, thirty miles south of Cherbourg.

"In addition to the numerous landing craft of various types, light naval craft of the Allies are being employed in considerable numbers," the Germans went on.

"Off the Seine estuary six heavy naval units and twenty destroyers were made out.

"German coastal batteries engaged (Allied) naval craft off shore.

"Considerable parts of the parachute formations that had to carry out the initial attack on western Europe against massed defense at the river mouth and near most important airfields on Normandy Peninsula already have been wiped out.

"According to preliminary reports the First British Parachute Division may already be considered badly mauled."

LEADS IN FRANCE

Gen. Sir Bernard L. Montgomery — The New York Times

RAF Bombers Out

By HAROLD DENNY

By Cable to THE NEW YORK TIMES.

LONDON, Tuesday, June 6—Early this morning Londoners, who at that time knew nothing of the invasion reports, were watching the sky as hundreds of Allied bombers and fighters roared overhead toward the southeast.

Just before 7 o'clock this morning the Royal Air Force announced "our bombers were over enemy-occupied territory in strength last night."

The whole Nazi-controlled French radio network went off the air at 7:25 A. M. today in the middle of a physical training broadcast.

Half an hour after Berlin had reported the Allied landings, Robert de Beauplay, Nazi spokesman on the Paris radio, was heard saying:

"It appears we have been given another month of grace before the invasion will start. A press report from Washington says Roosevelt will come to London at the end of June. Surely this indicates event will not start before then."

About the same time the German-controlled Calais radio station came on the air with the following announcement in English:

"This is D-day. We shall now bring music for the invasion forces."

The German people were not told of the supposed invasion in the first morning bulletin of the German home radio network. The Nazis' "achtung" service reported that "Germany is clear of raiders."

The Nazis' Paris radio said this morning that during last evening the outskirts of Paris were bombed again and two Allied planes were shot down.

The Paris broadcast said that "in addition to the Paris region the Departments of Nord and Pas-de-Calais were the main objectives of the Allies. Several places in Loire-et-Cher and the town of Saumur also were attacked."

'Beginning,' Says Sertorius

LONDON, June 6 (AP)—The German DNB commentator, Captain Sertorius, declared in a broadcast early today that the "great contest between the Reich and the Anglo-Americans has begun."

"The Allied landing in the west today has put the German armed forces in the mood which they express with a laconic 'they are coming.'

"At the present moment, when the Allied invasion of western Europe still is in its very first beginning, nothing can be said yet about the tactical and operational developments.

"We can only stress the single-mindedness with which the German Wehrmacht is facing the enemy's onslaught, for in war ethical values are at least as important as the number of soldiers and the quantity of their equipment."

This is the "year of decision" that Gen. Dwight D. Eisenhower, Allied supreme invasion commander, has set for the defeat of Germany.

With Allied armies rolling forward above Rome in Italy, and the Red Army massed with its might on the plains of Poland, the Germans have been expecting an imminent invasion by upward of 500,000 Allied troops.

These troops have been poised for months in England for just such a blow.

Transport Planes Fly

Huge transport planes filled with paratroopers and pulling air-borne troops in gliders roared over the German Atlantic Wall to drop their cargoes in the rear.

Just before they took off in the darkness the paratroops were wished godspeed by General Eisenhower.

He was accompanied by several other of his commanders and his face was tense but confident as he strode down the long lines of fighting men.

All night long London and England resounded to the roar of thousands of airplanes, some carrying bombs, some carrying men. Returning RAF bombers met big fleets of Flying Fortresses on their way out.

The forces thrown into operation were by far the greatest ever used in an amphibious operation. They had to be. An estimated million German troops waited in their fortifications for the great onslaught under crack Nazi Field Marshals von Runstedt and Rommel.

It was reported earlier this week that Adolf Hitler had a special train ready to rush him to France to take over personal command as he did on the East Front.

The world's greatest aerial bombardment has been rolling for months, blasting key communication lines leading to the coast, blowing up bridges, shattering locomotives, and keeping the Nazis guessing where the blow would fall.

NORMANDY'S SHORE OFTTIMES INVADED

Havre, Cherbourg and Lesser Ports of Region Are Gates on the Way to Paris

The coast of Normandy, which stretches along the English Channel from Tréport to Brittany and includes the Cotentin Peninsula on which Cherbourg is situated, has been the scene of several notable European invasions in the past. The Norsemen, from whom it gets its name, landed there in the tenth century and several British armies used it as a continental beachhead during the Hundred Years War.

With a number of good harbors and with rivers and canals available for inland water transportation, it has long been one of the principal maritime reaches of France. The chief ports are Havre and Cherbourg. Good secondary ports include Tréport, Abbeville, Dieppe and Caen, and a large number of fishing villages have harbors that can be used by small craft.

It is 205 miles from Havre along the Seine valley to Paris and 230 miles from the roadstead at Cherbourg to the French capital by way of Caen, Lisieux and Evreux. Caen is seventy-five miles nearer than Cherbourg.

In World War I the British demonstrated that it was possible to supply a large army in Normandy through use of specially designed barges that not only could navigate the treacherous Channel waters but could sail up canals and rivers to deliver their cargoes almost at the front.

The Contentin or Cherbourg peninsula is about seventy-five miles across at its base, a line running from Caen on the Orne estuary to Avranches on the mainland near the famed Mont St. Michel monastery.

Cherbourg, at the tip of the peninsula, is roughtly seventy-five miles from the base. Several good highways and a main rail line run out the peninsula to serve Cherbourg, which was one of the principal ports of call for transatlantic steamers in pre-war years.

Near the tip of the peninsula is a lateral ridge of high hills. A second ridge, somewhat higher, is found at the base of the peninsula. There are some high chalk cliffs along the northern side, but a good part of this coast is low with sandy beaches.

The Norman countryside greatly resembles that found in Britain.

Invasion Crowns Allied Reversal of Trend Set by Axis in World-Wide Aggressions

Allied troops, standing at the gates of western Europe today for the first time since the evacuation of Dunkerque in June, 1940, have set up another milestone—perhaps an almost final one—on the long road back from 1939, when Adolf Hitler's armored legions and his screaming Stukas crashed into Poland at the start of his attempt to make his "Aryan" Germany the ruler of the world.

It was on Sept. 1 of that year that Europe saw for the first time in war the deadly combination of air power, armored power and motor-carried infantry that captured bomb-scarred Warsaw in twenty-seven days and—with the Red Army moving in from the east—ended the Polish campaign in five days over a month.

A winter and an early spring of inconclusive fighting passed. Then Germany invaded Norway in April, 1940, and the Allies fought them off at Narvik before the tanks and the dive bombers launched their Blitzkrieg again. Then, while lesser German forces faced the French across the Maginot Line and the West Wall, major Nazi armies marched into the Netherlands, Belgium and Luxembourg on May 10.

The Netherlands surrendered on May 14. An armored column that pierced the French lines at Sedan reached the English Channel at Abbeville on May 21. Belgium, cut off from France, capitulated on May 28. Until June 4 Britons stood on the blazing beaches of Dunkerque, while fishing boats and pleasure craft—anything

Dunkerque

that would float—evacuated most of Britain's expeditionary force.

Three hundred and thirty-five thousand were taken off before the Germans seized the empty town. But France, fighting alone, was finished. June 10 saw the "stab in the back" as Italy declared war on France and Britain, and Mussolini's Black Shirts marched into Savoy and the Riviera. Paris fell on June 14. On June 22, forty-two days after the start of the campaign, the tanks and the Stukas had won. The armistice was signed. Hitler danced his little jig of victory, known to the newsreel audiences of the world. The dismal rule of Vichy and of the old Marshal, Henri Philippe Pétain, began. Hitler, in a year of easy victories, had swept into his "new order" no fewer than thirteen European nations.

In the chronology of the second World War, August and September, 1940, were Britain's crucial months. Tanks and mechanized artillery stopped at the Channel, but Reich Marshal Goering's Luftwaffe (the Marshal himself flew over London) set out to overcome the last remaining enemy.

France

Germany's weapon was severe daylight bombing of military objectives in England. The first mass raid was Aug. 8. It fired the vital London docks. More planes came daily, wave after wave, as they had attacked in battering Warsaw and Rotterdam. Hurricanes and Spitfires of the RAF went up to meet them. Sept. 15 saw the turning point. On that day 185 German planes went down in flames and the tactics that were to have left the military key points of England in wreckage and the island open to quick invasion had been defeated.

"Never," said Winston Churchill, "have so many owed so much to so few."

The Battle of Britain continued with "saturation" raids that wrecked the manufacturing center of Coventry, fired the city of London and struck at Birmingham, Sheffield, Manchester and the ports of Bristol, Plymouth, Liverpool and Southampton, through which supplies from the United States flowed into the embattled island—almost unarmed in land-power since Dunkerque. But hope of a speedy collapse of Britain faded from the Nazi calculations and the Wehrmacht turned eastward to the campaigns of Greece and Yugoslavia and the attack on Russia.

The war in 1941 had engulfed Europe, crossed the Arctic Circle, swung indecisively in Africa, and, with the German capture of Crete in June, pressed close to the borders of Asia Minor.

On Dec. 7, the conflict became global. Japan struck without warning at Pearl Harbor. The

Pearl Harbor

Arizona, the Utah and the Oklahoma, American battleships, were sunk by bombing at their piers. The balance of naval power in the Pacific shifted toward Japan. On Dec. 11 Germany and Italy declared war on the United States and the fighting fronts extended from the Philippines to the Black Sea.

In the Pacific the war began with a triumphal march for Japan, like that of Hitler in the west. First to be mopped up were the isolated bases. Guam fell Dec. 13 and Wake Dec. 24, after a historic defense by 378 marines, who fought off their first attackers and called by radio for "more Japs." Hong Kong capitulated Christmas Day.

On Dec. 10 the Japanese had made their first landing on Luzon and occupied Manila and Cavite Jan. 2. The long defense of Bataan began, to end with the surrender of the peninsula by disease-ridden troops on April 9 and the fall of Corregidor May 6.

The attack on Tokyo by Lieut. Gen. James H. Doolittle's bombers April 18 did not halt the march. "Impregnable" Singapore had been taken Feb. 15, after an attack down the jungles of the Malay Peninsula through occupied French Indo-China and acquiescent Thailand. Occupation of the Netherlands Indies was completed after the little Anglo-Netherland-American Far Eastern Fleet had waged the battle of Macassar Strait and been hopelessly damaged in the Java Sea. British and American troops with their Chinese allies, who had been fighting the Japanese since 1937, were driven from Burma. The march was checked only with the battles of the Coral Sea and Midway in May and June, and it was reversed for the first time when the marines landed at Guadalcanal on Aug. 7 to make the first recapture of Japanese-occupied land.

It was not in the Pacific but in far-off Africa

North Africa

that the United States struck its first full-scale blow at the Axis. There the war had seesawed back and forth along the Mediterranean coast since the collapse of the Italian Ethiopian and Red Sea colonies in 1941. Gen. Sir Archibald Wavell's drive beyond Bengazi was reversed in the spring of that year when troops were withdrawn for the Greek campaign. By July, 1942, Field Marshal Gen. Erwin Rommel and his Africa Corps had smashed to El Alamein, seventy miles from Alexandria. On Oct. 23 Gen. Sir Bernard L. Montgomery started the march back.

Then came two more big Allied victories that set a high-water mark to the Axis advances in the west and saw the armored wave begin to ebb. The first was the American landing in Africa, at Rommel's back; the second Stalingrad.

The African invasion began Nov. 8, 1942. From the greatest concentration of shipping ever assembled, American soldiers swarmed ashore at Algiers, Oran and Casablanca, meeting only slight resistance from the French at Admiral Darlan's orders. British forces joined them and, as General Montgomery pressed on, an iron ring was formed around Tunisia. On May 12, 1943, the last resistance ended and the disappearance of the last Axis soldier from Africa was the prelude to the capture of Sicily in July and August and the collapse of Mussolini and the invasion of Italy itself in September. Nine months later Rome fell.

Stalingrad was the turning point in Russia. Hitler, after tearing up his agreement with Premier Stalin, had crossed the Soviet border on June 22, 1941, and marched toward Moscow as the Red armies "traded space for time." The Moscow campaign failed at Vyazma, Kalinin and Mozhaisk, and a winter campaign drove the Germans back in 1942. The summer of that year, however, saw Germany resurgent in the east. The German tanks crashed into the Caucasus toward the Baku oil wells. Stalingrad, whose capture would have split the Russians north and south, was reached on Sept. 11.

In Stalingrad men fought from house to house, in cellars, as the houses fell, and then in heaps of rubble as even the cellars ceased to have a

Stalingrad

shape. Ten thousand men died daily, it was estimated. The Germans sickened of their infantry attacks, fell back on massed artillery and failed to take the town. The Russians cut around their flanks. Field Marshal Friedrich von Paulus and his German Sixth Army were encircled by Nov. 25, but at Hitler's personal orders, continued to resist. Then, on Feb. 2, 1943, the field marshal and 91,000 men yielded.

Three hundred and thirty thousand Germans had fallen in the Stalingrad campaign. The march to the Caucasus was broken and the Russian counter-attack began to move toward Rostov, Kharkov, Kiev and the Polish border, which the Russians crossed this year.

Africa, Sicily, Italy, Stalingrad and the Russian counter-drive were preludes to invasion. The curtain-raiser was bombing from the air. May 30, 1942, saw the beginning of the great Allied effort to smash German production and drive the Luftwaffe from the air. That was the date of the first 1,000-plane attack on Cologne.

Hamburg and Bremen, the great seaports; Essen and Duesseldorf, the great manufacturing centers; the Ruhr dams, kingpin of German power plants and waterways; Berlin, the capital—all felt such Allied blows in turn. American preci-

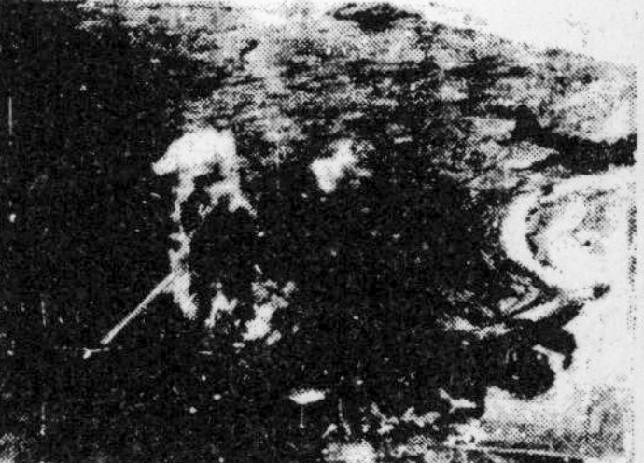

Air Invasion

sion daylight bombing supplemented the night attacks of the RAF. From the Foggia airfields, after the conquest of southern Italy, central Europe was opened to attack. Lighter bombers struck at the German fortifications along the European coasts in countless sorties.

An Allied invasion army stands on Continental soil today because of the promise of hundreds of thousands of Allied fliers to blast a beachhead for the ground troops and drive the Luftwaffe from the air. The long march back will show how well the promise has been kept.

"All the News That's Fit to Print"

The New York Times.

LATE CITY EDITION
POSTSCRIPT
Considerable cloudiness and milder today; moderate winds.
Temperatures Yesterday—Max., 51; Min., 37
Sunrise, 7:35 A. M.; Sunset, 5:45 P. M.

Copyright, 1944, by The New York Times Company.

VOL. XCIV No. 31,700. Entered as Second-Class Matter, Postoffice, New York, N. Y. NEW YORK, WEDNESDAY, NOVEMBER 8, 1944. THREE CENTS IN NEW YORK CITY

ROOSEVELT WINS FOURTH TERM; RECORD POPULAR VOTE IS CLOSE; DEMOCRATS GAIN IN THE HOUSE

2-DAY LUZON BLOWS SMASH 440 PLANES, 30 JAPANESE SHIPS

Halsey's Fliers Destroy 249 Aircraft, Sink Four Vessels in Sunday Sweep

MANILA FIELDS RAVAGED

Ports and Installations Hit Hard—Enemy Lines to Leyte Defenders Are Strained

By GEORGE HORNE
By Telephone to THE NEW YORK TIMES.

PEARL HARBOR, Nov. 7—Admiral William F. Halsey's Third Fleet carriers spread death and damage over southern Luzon Island in the Philippines for the second successive day on Sunday, sinking another five ships and destroying 249 additional enemy aircraft.

It was a major air strike, apparently an all-out effort to annihilate the Japanese air forces supporting enemy counter-attacks on Leyte, where American military leaders have reported the campaign nearing its final stages.

Over the two days, according to Admiral Chester W. Nimitz's communiqué today, the enemy has lost 440 aircraft, 327 of which were caught and destroyed on the ground and 113 shot down in the air. The principal plane concentrations were found on seven fields in the Manila network. They were Nichols, Clark, Nielson, Lipa, Tarlac, Bambam and Mabalacat.

[The two-day toll of enemy ships sunk or damaged was about thirty.]

Unable to Rise in Strength

As the widespread attacks continue, the enemy air opposition is becoming steadily weaker, as is evidenced by the fact that on the second day all but a few of the lost enemy aircraft were caught on the ground, unable to get into the air.

Terrific damage is being inflicted on port facilities and ground installations in and around Manila harbor. In addition to ships sunk and planes destroyed, many air and surface craft were listed as damaged. Reports on the action were still of a preliminary nature and there was no count of our own losses.

Admiral Nimitz said three oil storage areas were left blazing at the northern section of Clark Field and at the northeast of the field a tremendous explosion was observed, followed by fire. North of Malvar a railroad engine and five tank cars were blown up.

Five Ships Sunk at Manila

In the harbor of Manila the fighters, torpedo planes and dive-bombers sank three cargo ships and an oil tanker, probably sank a destroyer and damaged two destroyers, two destroyer escorts, a trawler and several cargo ships. Fourteen cargo ships were damaged during the two-day attack, in which wave after wave of American planes swept in from the sea to wipe out available enemy strength that might be used to bolster the hard-pressed Japanese forces on Leyte.

Meanwhile the steady attacks on the Bonins and Kuriles are continuing. On Sunday a Liberator of the Eleventh Army Air Force, flying hundreds of miles from our Aleutian bases, hit three small transports off Onnekotan Island in the Kuriles and other Liberators flying with it concentrated on land targets of the island base.

Seven enemy fighters fought the big bombers in a running battle, and guns from three Liberators brought down one and probably destroyed another. Two Liberators were damaged.

Otomari and Tori Island, also in the Kuriles, were attacked.

Seventh Air Force Liberators

Continued on Page 19, Column 2

War News Summarized

WEDNESDAY, NOVEMBER 8, 1944

Japanese Lose 440 Planes

Japanese air power in the Philippines received a staggering blow on Saturday and Sunday when Third Fleet carrier planes destroyed 440 enemy aircraft in the Manila and southern Luzon areas. Nearly thirty ships, including a number of warcraft, were also destroyed or damaged. Our fliers reaped their greatest harvest at seven airfields where they wiped out 327 planes on the ground. Port and ground installations suffered terrific damage. Reports were still incomplete and our own losses were not known. [1:1.]

Battle Joined on Leyte

American troops on Leyte were battling elements of four Japanese divisions in the hills north of Ormoc and repulsed three heavy attacks, inflicting great loss on the enemy. The area of Valencia, north of Ormoc, was under American artillery fire. [19:1, with map.]

Tokyo Sees B-29's

The jittery Japanese reported more Superfortresses on reconnaissance flights over Tokyo and surrounding territory. They also said that the Bonins and Volcanos had been bombed. [19:2.]

In China the enemy scored by driving to within twenty miles of Liuchow, but in Burma the British captured Kennedy Peak and threatened Fort White and Paletwa. [21:1.]

Grim Fight Below Aachen

The United States First Army fought its way back into the streets of Vossenack in some of the bitterest fighting of the war.

Luzon fields pounded from air

Three German counter-attacks from Schmidt were repulsed. The Sixth Army Group made important advances in the Vosges Mountains and in the Netherlands Allied troops were mopping up the liberated areas. [19:8, with map.]

Soviet Drive Forecast

Behind the lull on Russia's fighting fronts the Red Army was reported to be preparing for a great new offensive. [19:4.] The Athens radio announced that the Greek Government had ordered dissolution of the guerrilla bands Edes and Elas. [19:5.]

Robot Blows at U. S. 'Possible'

A joint Army-Navy statement said that it was "entirely possible" for flying bombs to reach the United States from Europe, but gave no indication such an attack was expected. [19:6-7.]

FISH IS DEFEATED; CLARE LUCE WINS

Congress Veteran Concedes Bennet's Victory—Close Finish in Connecticut

Special to THE NEW YORK TIMES.

NEWBURGH, N. Y., Wednesday, Nov. 8—Representative Hamilton Fish, for twelve terms a Republican member of the House and a leading isolationist and critic of President Roosevelt's foreign policy, conceded his defeat by Augustus W. Bennet just before 1 o'clock this morning.

"From reports I have received to date, it looks like I have lost the district by a 5,300 vote majority," he said.

"It looks as if the Republicans have lost the House, and if that is so, as much as I regret it, I have no great desire to continue to serve as a minority member, which I have for the last fourteen years in an uphill fight."

Mr. Bennet, in a victory statement, paid tribute to those who had supported him from all parties, "including the much-abused Political Action Committee." He hailed his election as the result of the citizens' determination "to eliminate Ham Fish from Congress."

Factors in the Result

Heavy Republican defections to Mr. Bennet in Orange County and strong support for Mr. Fish's opponent in the parts of the district in Rockland, Sullivan and Delaware counties sent the Republican nominee down to defeat in the bitterest Congressional election in this part of the State in years.

Complete returns from Orange County gave Fish 35,126 votes to 27,371 for Bennet, a majority for Fish of 7,755. This indicated that Mr. Bennet's majority for the whole Twenty-ninth Congressional District would be about 5,600.

Complete returns from Rockland County gave Bennet 19,706 votes to 12,323 for Fish, a majority of 7,383.

In Sullivan County, with twenty-four election districts missing, including those where Mr. Bennet was expected to run strongest, the vote was Fish 3,877, Bennet 3,776.

Continued on Page 2, Column 7

ROOSEVELT VICTORY CLAIMED IN JERSEY

Hague Spokesmen Also Say Wene Will Win—Constitution Revision Is Rejected

Despite greatly reduced pluralities in Hudson County, Democratic stronghold of New Jersey, lieutenants of Mayor Frank Hague of Jersey City, Democratic boss of the State, predicted shortly before 4 A. M. today that the State's sixteen electoral votes would be delivered to President Roosevelt, largely by virtue of an estimated plurality of 75,000 votes in Hudson. In 1940 Mr. Roosevelt carried the county by a plurality of 100,877.

Mayor Hague's spokesman also predicted victory for the party nominee for the United States Senate, Representative Elmer H. Wene, although by a close vote, and rejection of the proposed revised State Constitution by a substantial margin.

Mr. Hague himself left headquarters in Jersey City early today without making any statement.

The Jersey City predictions were made depsite the fact that eight of the twelve wards in the city had not reported returns up to that hour, but the estimates on the fate of charter revision appeared to be borne out by State-wide returns. At 4 A. M., with 1,311 of the State's 3,657 election districts missing, the vote for rejection was 480,503 to 381,686 for approval.

At the same hour Mr. Dewey was leading Roosevelt by a vote of 481,677 to 456,275, with 1,819 districts missing, and H. Alexander Smith, Mr. Wene's Republican opponent, was leading the Democratic nominee by a vote of 562,261 to 503,763, on the basis of returns from 2,226 districts.

Five Hudson Communities Bolt

The apparent failure of the Hague machine earlier to deliver the expected large Democratic plurality in the county had caused some political observers to place the State in the doubtful class.

Continued on Page 9, Column 4

GET 11 TO 20 SEATS

Victories Blast Hopes of Rivals to Control the House

SENATE UNCHANGED

Democrats Have 180 in House, Republicans 155, 98 in Doubt

By TURNER CATLEDGE

Democratic gains of from eleven to twenty seats in the House and a possible new place or two in the already one-sided Senate, appeared on returns received up to 5 A. M. today to have followed in the wake of yesterday's fourth-term landslide for President Roosevelt.

Republican hopes of controlling the House appeared to have been blasted beyond any possibility of realization and what in the earlier count seemed to portend a G. O. P. gain in the Senate began to fade with the later returns.

These same reports showed the defeat of Representative Hamilton Fish, Republican, of New York, one of the most controversial figures in the lower house; the possible defeat of Senator John A. Danaher, Republican, of Connecticut; a victory for Mrs. Clare Luce, Republican, in a close race in the Fourth Connecticut Congressional District; a trend in the early count against Senator Gerald P. Nye, Republican "isolationist" of North Dakota, and a neck-and-neck contest in which Senator James J. Davis, Republican, of Pennsylvania, was trailing his Democratic opponent, Representative Francis J. Myers, by a slight margin.

Leading Senators Re-elected

These returns also revealed the re-election of Senator Alben W. Barkley, Democratic Majority Leader, in Kentucky; of Senator Scott Lucas, Democrat, in Illinois; of Senator Robert A. Taft, Republican, in Ohio; of Senator Millard Tydings, Democrat, in Maryland, and numerous other sitting Senators, both Democratic and Republican.

With 98 House seats still in doubt, the Democrats had clinched 180 seats in the House of Representatives of the Seventy-ninth Congress; the Republicans were certain of at least 155; the American Labor party of 1 and the Progressives of 1.

Seventeen Senate places were still awaiting the decision of the final count, but the Democrats were certain of 49, or an actual majority. The Republicans appeared certain of thirty-one and the Progressives of one.

With the latest returns received the Democrats had garnered a net

Continued on Page 2, Column 5

ELECTED TO PRESIDENCY AND VICE PRESIDENCY

Franklin D. Roosevelt

Harry S. Truman

ROOSEVELT STRONG IN WAR VOTE TALLY

Partial Count of Ballots of Armed Forces Increases President's Majority

By CHARLES GRUTZNER Jr.

The majority given to President Roosevelt by civilian voters who went to the polls throughout the nation yesterday was increased by the count of war ballots marked, some of them as long as two months ago, by members of the armed forces in camps here and in far-flung theatres of operations.

The decisiveness of the President's victory over Governor Dewey removed the possibility that the outcome of the election might hinge on the soldier vote in some of the eleven States that delayed counting their war ballots, but partial returns from States that counted their war ballots yesterday made it clear that the support of the men and women in the armed forces would be a strong factor in building up the final majority of their Commander in Chief.

A breakdown of the vote into civilian and war ballots was slow in coming in from nearly all of the thirty-seven States that counted their soldier vote yesterday, because election officials were concerned chiefly with transmitting

Continued on Page 4, Column 2

New York for Roosevelt; Wagner Re-elected Senator

By JAMES A. HAGERTY

For the sixth consecutive time, four times as a candidate for President and twice as a candidate for Governor, President Roosevelt carried his home State of New York in yesterday's election and won its forty-seven electoral votes. With 3,609 of the 3,700 election districts in New York City and with 4,978 of the 5,421 election districts outside New York City reporting, President Roosevelt had an actual lead over Governor Dewey, his Republican opponent, of 300,831 and a plurality of about 283,000 for the President in the State was indicated.

Returns from 3,609 election districts out of 3,700 in New York City gave Dewey 1,240,216, Roosevelt 1,966,539. This is an actual plurality of 726,273 and an indicated plurality of 743,700 for Roosevelt.

Returns from 4,978 election districts out of 5,421 outside New York City gave Dewey 1,585,771, Roosevelt 1,160,329. This is an actual plurality of 425,442 and an indicated plurality of 460,785 for Dewey.

Re-elected in the sweep for the President was United States Senator Robert F. Wagner, who defeated Secretary of State Thomas J. Curran by a plurality probably greater than that for Mr. Roosevelt. Also elected was Associate Judge of the Court of Appeals, Marvin R. Dye, who defeated John Van Voorhis, Republican. The President, Senator Harry S. Truman, candidate for Vice President, Senator Wagner and Mr. Dye, all Democrats, also were nominees of the American Labor and Liberal parties.

Returns from 3,566 election districts of the 3,700 in New York City gave Curran 1,183,020, Wagner 1,957,026. This is an actual plurality of 774,006, and an indicated plurality of 802,900 for Wagner.

Returns from 4,797 of 5,421 election districts outside of New York City gave Curran 1,468,985, Wagner 1,086,736. This is an actual plurality of 382,249, and an indicated plurality of 433,680 for Curran.

Both Houses of the State Legislature remain Republican. Among the greatest upsets in the State was the defeat of former Mayor Rolland B. Marvin of Syracuse, Republican candidate for State Senator in the Forty-third Senatorial District, by Richard P. Byrne, Democratic and American Labor party nominee. On incomplete returns, Senator John J. Dunnigan, Democratic leader of the

Continued on Page 6, Column 4

DEWEY STATEMENT ADMITS HIS DEFEAT

Candidate Concedes Loss of Election at 3:12 A. M. and Congratulates Victor

Gov. Thomas E. Dewey, Republican candidate for President, conceded defeat at 3:12 o'clock this morning.

His statement was made at Republican National Headquarters in the Hotel Roosevelt, where both he and Herbert Brownell Jr., chairman of the National Committee, earlier had refused comment on the growing indication of a lopsided electrical college vote for his Democratic opponent, President Franklin D. Roosevelt.

Mr. Dewey said:

It is clear that Mr. Roosevelt has been re-elected for a fourth term, and every good American will whole-heartedly accept the will of the people.

I extend to President Roosevelt my hearty congratulations and my earnest hope that his next term will see speedy victory in the war, the establishment of lasting peace and the restoration of tranquillity among our peoples.

I am deeply grateful for the confidence expressed by so many million Americans for their labors in the campaign.

The Republican party emerges from the election revitalized and a great force for the good of the country and for the preservation of free government in America.

I am confident that all Americans will join me in a devout hope that in the years ahead Divine Providence will guide and protect the President of the United States.

President Roosevelt, from his Hyde Park home, acknowledged, at 3:28 o'clock this morning Gov-

Continued on Page 3, Column 2

Roosevelt Leads as Davis Trails, In Mounting Pennsylvania Count

Special to THE NEW YORK TIMES.

PHILADELPHIA, Wednesday, Nov. 8—On the basis of partial returns from all but three of the sixty-seven counties in Pennsylvania, it appeared early that President Roosevelt for the third successive time had captured the State's electoral votes.

Swept on the Roosevelt wave, it appeared, was Representative Francis J. Myers in his race to unseat James J. Davis, 71-year-old Republican Senator who was elected first in 1932 and re-elected six years ago.

Whether the Roosevelt impetus would be sufficient to sweep into office the Democratic candidates for the five State offices remained in doubt. Reports in these instances, lagging far behind the count on the top two contests, were inconclusive.

With 6,012 of 8,202 precincts reporting, President Roosevelt was leading Governor Dewey, 1,282,392 to 1,238,986. Among the returns were all the 1,338 precincts in this city where the President gained a lead of 117,000.

The returns showed that once again the soft coal miners in western Pennsylvania and the anthracite miners in the East repudiated John L. Lewis, president of the United Mine Workers of America, by turning in thumping pluralities for Mr. Roosevelt.

On the other hand, with less than half the precincts reporting and Governor Dewey reducing the President's lead, Republican leaders were hoping that late returns and a fair share of the soldier vote, to be counted on Nov. 22, would mean victory for the party in the State.

Although the President seemed

Continued on Page 8, Column 4

DEWEY CONCEDES

His Action Comes as Roosevelt Leads in 33 States

BIG ELECTORAL VOTE

Late Returns in Seesaw Battles May Push Total Beyond 400

By ARTHUR KROCK

Franklin Delano Roosevelt, who broke more than a century-old tradition in 1940 when he was elected to a third term as President, made another political record yesterday when he was chosen for a fourth term by a heavy electoral but much narrower popular majority over Thomas E. Dewey, Governor of New York.

At 3:15 A. M. Governor Dewey conceded Mr. Roosevelt's re-election, sending his best wishes by radio, to which the President quickly responded with an appreciative telegram.

Early this morning Mr. Roosevelt was leading in mounting returns in thirty-three States with a total of 391 electoral votes and in half a dozen more a trend was developing that could increase this figure to more than 400. Governor Dewey was ahead in fifteen States with 140 electoral votes, but some were see-sawing away from him and back again. Typical of these were Wisconsin, where he overtook the President's lead about 2 A. M.; Nevada, where Mr. Roosevelt passed him at about the same time, and Missouri.

In the contests for seats in Congress, the Democrats had shown gains of 11 to 20 in the House of Representatives, assuring that party's continued control of this branch. In the Senate the net of losses and gains appeared to be an addition of one Republican to the Senate, which would give that party twenty-eight members—far short of the forty-nine necessary to a majority. A surprise was the indicated defeat of the veteran Pennsylvania Republican, Senator James J. Davis.

Mrs. Luce's Opponent Concedes

The Congressional races were featured by a mass Democratic attempt, in which the President and Vice President Henry A. Wallace personally participated, to unseat Representative Clare Boothe Luce of Connecticut. But shortly after 3 A. M., following a night in which the lead had swung back and forth, her election was conceded by her opponent, Miss Margaret Connors. Some hours before, to his neighbors at Hyde Park, the President had expressed rejoicing over Mrs. Luce's "defeat." Her success is the vitriol in the Democratic honey.

Despite the great general victories by the Democrats, the popular vote will evidently show a huge minority protest against a fourth term for the President. Tabulations by the press associations indicated that the disparity between the ballots cast for the two candidates will be so small that a change of several hundred thousand votes in the key States, distributed in a certain way, would have reversed the electoral majority. At 4:40 A. M. The Associated Press reported 16,387,999 for Mr. Roosevelt and 14,235,051 for Mr. Dewey from more than one-third of the country's election districts. This ratio, if carried through, would leave only about 3,000,000 votes between the candidates.

One of the most interesting struggles for the Presidency was that in Wisconsin, where Mr. Dewey took an early lead, lost it and regained it again. Wisconsin is the State where the late Wendell L. Willkie made his stand for renomination, posing the issue of

Continued on Page 2, Column 2

ROOSEVELT VICTOR IN ILLINOIS VOTE

President Has a Lead of 232,193 With Half of State Figures Already Tabulated

LUCAS HAS LARGE MARGIN

Governor Green Is Trailing but May Pull Through on Late Down-State Ballots

Special to THE NEW YORK TIMES.

CHICAGO, Wednesday, Nov. 8—President Roosevelt appeared early this morning to have won a smashing victory over Gov. Thomas E. Dewey, his Republican opponent, in yesterday's contest for Illinois' 28 electoral votes.

At the same time, Senator Scott W. Lucas, Democratic incumbent, was assured of victory by a sizable margin over Richard J. Lyons, former State Senator, whom he had termed in his campaign as an "arch-isolationist."

With nearly half of the State's total precincts reported, Mr. Roosevelt maintained a lead of 243,462 over the New York Governor.

In Cook County, where he was supported by the powerful Democratic organization headed by Mayor Edward J. Kelly of Chicago, the President's lead over his opponent was 358,319.

Down-State, where huge predicted Republican majorities failed to materialize, Mr. Roosevelt was trailing Mr. Dewey by 115,084.

The vote at this hour from 5,029 precincts stood:

	D'nstate.	Cook Co.	Total.
Dewey	426,745	569,007	995,752
Roosevelt	311,661	927,326	1,238,987

Lucas Has Big Lead

Senator Lucas, who made his bid for re-election by supporting the President's plan for a world security organization with police powers, held a State-wide lead over Mr. Lyons of 240,071. The vote stood at 934,021 for Lucas and 693,950 for Lyons, with returns from 3,787 precincts.

Failure of down-State Republicans to come through with the expected hefty vote totals is expected to insure Mr. Lucas' re-election.

On the basis of these unofficial returns, Mayor Kelly late last night declared that President Roosevelt "will carry the State of Illinois by at least 200,000."

Projections by other experienced statisticians coincided with the Mayor's estimate. On the basis of present returns these statisticians set Mr. Roosevelt's plurality at about 250,000 with the expectation that when the "country" towns of Cook County, traditional Republican strongholds, are heard from about 50,000 will be cut from the Roosevelt total.

Governor Green Trailing

Gov. Dwight H. Green, seeking a second four-year term, was in a close battle with his Democratic challenger, Thomas J. Courtney, State's attorney of Cook County. Returns from 4,250 of the State's precincts gave Mr. Courtney 999,986 and Mr. Green 855,095. These included 1,419 downstate precincts, which gave Mr. Green 309,909 and Mr. Courtney 212,327.

Later reports from downstate and the traditional "country" towns in Cook County are expected by Republican party leaders to insure Mr. Green's re-election.

In the race for Representative at Large, Mrs. Emily Taft Douglas, Democratic newcomer to politics, and Stephen A. Day, Republican incumbent, were in a nip-and-tuck contest. Mrs. Douglas, who had denounced Mr. Day as an all-out isolationist and "the worst obstructionist in Congress," was trailing her opponent by about 1,000 votes.

With 608 precincts counted the vote stood: Day, 100,334; Mrs. Douglas, 99,066.

MARKS BALLOT UNDER FIRE

California Soldier Feels That It Is an Honor to Vote

SANTA MONICA, Calif., Nov. 7 (AP)—The significance of marking an American ballot while under fire on German soil was described by Corp. Roger M. Olsen of the United States Army in a letter to his wife here. The letter included the following:

"As I marked the little X's I could hear the thundering guns and big shells whistling through the air toward the enemy. Each little mark seemed to strengthen the chain of freedom which the enemy, a few miles away, had tried to break. It was indeed an honor to vote today."

VICTOR OVER FISH

Augustus W. Bennet
The New York Times, 1942

NEW YORKERS WENT TO THE POLLS EARLY YESTERDAY TO CAST THEIR BALLOTS

This line had formed by noon outside a voting booth at 108 East Forty-eighth Street — The New York Times

ROOSEVELT WINS HIS FOURTH TERM

Continued From Page 1

"isolationism" versus "internationalism." He ran last in the Presidential primary and expressed the belief, in then withdrawing from the race, that isolationism controlled the thinking of Wisconsin Republicans.

The close race between the President and Mr. Dewey, however, supported the view of others that Mr. Willkie was defeated by a combination between the followers of Mr. Dewey and Harold E. Stassen and that his contrary interpretation was not sound.

Stiff Fight in Pennsylvania

Pennsylvania was another scene of an intense struggle. Mr. Roosevelt got a much reduced majority in Philadelphia, but Allegheny County (Pittsburgh) exceeded expectations, and at 4 A. M. the State's thirty-five electors seemed moving toward Mr. Roosevelt's list.

In Ohio Mr. Dewey's early lead was being cut sharply by the President early this morning. New York's forty-seven electoral votes are certain for Mr. Roosevelt, and, with Illinois, Minnesota, Massachusetts, Connecticut and the 127 electors of the old Confederacy plus Tennessee in his column, the President was far beyond the 266 electors who constitute a majority.

The States in which Mr. Roosevelt was leading at 4 A. M. were:

Alabama, 11; Arizona, 4; Arkansas, 9; California, 25; Connecticut, 8; Delaware, 3; Florida, 8; Georgia, 12; Idaho, 4; Illinois, 28; Kentucky, 11; Louisiana, 10; Mississippi, 9; Maryland, 8; Missouri, 15; Montana, 4; Massachusetts, 16; Minnesota, 11; New Hampshire, 4; New Mexico, 4; New York, 47; Nevada, 3; North Carolina, 14; Oklahoma, 10; Pennsylvania, 35; Rhode Island, 4; South Carolina, 8; Tennessee, 12; Texas, 23; Virginia, 11; West Virginia, 8; Washington, 8, and Utah, 4—Total of 391.

Dewey Leads in New Jersey

The States with margins for Mr. Dewey were:

Colorado, 6; Indiana, 13; Iowa, 10; Kansas, 8; Maine, 5; Michigan, 19; Nebraska, 6; New Jersey, 16; North Dakota, 4; Ohio, 25; Oregon, 6; South Dakota, 4; Vermont, 3; Wisconsin 12; Wyoming, 3—a total of 140.

To win Mr. Dewey was obliged to effect a combination of Massachusetts (or Connecticut), New York (or Pennsylvania), the Border States, the Midwestern States and Oregon on the Pacific Coast. This is because the President, despite the midsummer "revolts" in Texas, South Carolina, Mississippi and Louisiana, was sure to start with 127 certain electors—the old South, plus Tennessee. Mr. Dewey failed to come within spyglass distance of this feat.

Wallace Proves Right

The popular vote ran so close until after 11 o'clock that even the most optimistic supporters of the President were cautious in their claims. But Mr. Wallace was not so timorous. He established a national record as a forecasting statistician by announcing at 9:30 P. M. that the President had been re-elected by a large electoral majority, that he had been given a Democratic House with a "mandate" to carry out his war and post-war program and that "bipartisan isolationism has been destroyed."

When Mr. Wallace issued this statement few were ready to accept his conclusion. But an hour later he had become a major prophet.

Hillman's Group Effective

Early in the day, throughout the United States, it became evident that the heavy registration was the true portent of a larger vote than was anticipated when the campaign began. Soon after the national conventions were held the predictions in both political camps were for a vote well below that of 1940, under 45,000,000 and perhaps little more than 40,000,000.

Faced with this prospect, Democratic spokesmen openly conceded that so light a vote meant the re-election odds would be against the President and that only with a tally of 45,000,000 or more could his true strength be registered—in which event they were confident of success.

But within a few weeks after the nominations, the Political Action Committee of the Congress of Industrial Organizations, under the chairmanship of Sidney Hillman, began its effort to bring out the vote. Pamphlets urging citizens to go to the polls, and making arguments for Mr. Roosevelt's re-election, were distributed in great numbers in all parts of the country, but particularly in the large cities and even more intensively in those areas where war industry had sprung up and the normal population was much enlarged.

When the registration periods arrived it was demonstrated that these activities of Mr. Hillman's group were very effective. By the end of this period a vote that may exceed 50,000,000 (including ballots from the armed services) was indicated, and Democratic hopes rose accordingly. Reports from the sections where CIO-PAC had been busiest accentuated the view that, in bringing out votes which otherwise might not have been registered, Mr. Hillman's committee had been more vigilant and more successful than the regular Democratic organizations.

One interesting phase of this new note in national political campaigns was that the Hillman group did not neglect the Solid South, where Democratic nomination is equivalent to election and the November vote accordingly is light. To make sure that the President's popular vote would represent his real November strength, and to avert any possibility of an electoral victory without a popular majority—or a popular vote far below the electoral vote of the Democratic national ticket in percentage—the CIO-PAC besought Southern Democrats, especially the war industrial workers, to go to the polls and swell Mr. Roosevelt's general totals.

Not until the returns are all in will it be possible to make an estimate of the degree to which this innovation materialized. But there was no doubt in the minds of the professional politicians, after registration, that in the areas of normally close party division the CIO-PAC has done notable work in preventing a light poll this year.

The proof of this in every large industrial city was received with mixed feelings by the regular Democratic organizations, which hitherto have had all the credit for the votes registered and cast for their ticket. They were obliged to accept a competitor which, they were certain, would not be hesitant in pointing to its contribution in the event of the President's election to a fourth term which, on analysis, would prove to have been achieved by the voters in the large industrial areas where the CIO-PAC is strong and has been very active. This would presage a rivalry for influence and reward in the next administration to which dispute Mr. Hillman and his group could bring impressive support of their claims.

For a space in the campaign, when the Republican orators and organizers concentrated their fire on Mr. Hillman, and he was put down as a liability, the Democratic National Committee subordinated the role of his group as best it could and declined to certify its members as official spokesmen of the President's re-election.

But as the voters turned out yesterday in unusual and unexpected numbers, the dispute was suspended in the mutual wish to win, to be resumed in the event of Mr. Roosevelt's re-election by citizens in PAC territory and demonstrably responsive to its influence. Before the campaign ended Robert E. Hannegan, chairman of the Democratic National Committee, was vigorously defending Mr. Hillman from the Republican attacks and making the PAC cause his own in so far as he could.

ELECTED SENATOR

The New York Times, 1938
Gov. Leverett Saltonstall

South Stays in the Democratic Fold

Special to THE NEW YORK TIMES.

AUSTIN, Tex., Nov. 7—The widely advertised political revolt in Texas failed to materialize and President Roosevelt was carrying the State by an overwhelming plurality by late tonight despite the bitter pre-election fight that developed within the Democratic party.

Voting results compiled by the Texas Election Bureau were indicative of the trend of the balloting—Roosevelt, 218,516; Governor Dewey, 37,698, and the Texas Regulars, who had a candidate, 37,676.

The Regulars, or the Roosevelt opposition, had conducted the largest campaign in the State, apparently putting forth a great deal of money in literature, newspapers and radio advertising. The Republicans, obviously realizing Texas was lost to the Democrats, made little effort.

All suggestions of merging the anti-Roosevelt vote in one column failed, and election day broke with the Republicans and Regulars castigating each other for failing to join forces.

The total late this evening was from 210 out of 254 counties with four of the tallies complete. The final total is expected to be large, exceeding 1940 when Mr. Roosevelt polled 840,151, against Wendell Willkie's 199,152. The 210 counties gave 459,142 votes to Mr. Roosevelt; 95,706 to Governor Dewey, and 71,670 to the Texas Regulars.

All the Democrats who were nominated for Congress in August were elected without contest. Neither of the Senators from Texas had contests this year.

ALABAMA

MONTGOMERY, Ala., Nov. 7 (AP)—President Roosevelt, Senator Lister Hill and other Democratic nominees got large majorities in unofficial returns from today's election in Alabama.

With ballots tabulated from 1,088 of the State's 2,300 boxes, President Roosevelt had 115,094 votes to 25,403 for Governor Dewey.

Senator Hill, on returns from 325 of 2,300 precincts, had 27,484 votes to 6,109 for John Posey, his Republican challenger.

GEORGIA

ATLANTA, Nov. 7 (AP)—Georgia voted strongly for the Roosevelt ticket in todays' election.

Returns from 587 of 1,735 precincts gave President Roosevelt 172,276; Governor Dewey, 29,499, and the unpledged Independent Democrats 1,887.

The State also re-elected, without opposition, Senator Walter F. George, chairman of the finance committee, and nine Democratic Representatives, including Carl Vinson, chairman of the Naval Affairs Committee.

Representative Robert Ramspeck, Democratic whip, beat Henry A. Alexander, Independent.

LOUISIANA

NEW ORLEANS, Nov. 7 (AP)—President Roosevelt held a four-to-one lead over Governor Dewey tonight in unofficial returns from today's general election.

The vote in 469 of the total 1,871 precincts gave 109,134 votes to President Roosevelt, and 25,395 to Governor Dewey.

This did not include any of the New Orleans vote, where the polls remained open until 9 P. M.

FLORIDA

TALLAHASSEE, Fla., Nov. 7 (AP)—Florida voters rolled up a two-to-one majority for President Roosevelt on the basis of unofficial returns from today's general election but made a close fight out of a proposed constitutional amendment to outlaw the closed union shop.

In the Presidential election, returns from 600 out of 1,498 precincts gave Mr. Roosevelt 148,312 and Governor Dewey, 67,597.

On the constitutional amendment, returns from 145 precincts gave 12,066 votes for, and 17,541 against.

The Democrats piled up votes for their Gubernatorial nominee, returns from eighty-two precincts giving Millard Caldwell 25,621 votes, and Bert Leigh Acker, Republican, 11,040.

Senator Claude Pepper, New Deal champion, seemed sure of re-election with 33,662 votes against Millard H. Draper, Republican, with 17,814.

MISSISSIPPI

JACKSON, Miss., Nov. 7 (AP)—Roosevelt-pledged Democrats, with their supplemental ticket, surged into the lead over party ticket bolters and Republicans in Mississippi on the basis of unofficial counts of today's election.

Returns from 695 of the State's 1,693 precincts gave 77,150 votes to President Roosevelt and 5,488 to Governor Dewey.

The Roosevelt vote included the combined vote of the solid pro-Roosevelt and regular Democratic tickets, the latter of which lists three Roosevelt bolters. The Dewey vote presented the combined vote of the regular and Indpendent Republican factions.

NORTH CAROLINA

RALEIGH, N. C., Nov. 7 (AP)—In 1,291 out of 1,922 precincts, North Carolina gave 382,029 votes to President Roosevelt in unofficial returns. Governor Dewey polled 158,379.

SOUTH CAROLINA

COLUMBIA, S. C., Nov. 7 (AP)—South Carolina, in 663 out of 1,282 precincts, gave 65,770 votes to President Roosevelt today by unofficial count. The Southern Democrats polled 5,766 for Senator Byrd, while the Republicans voted 3,648 for Governor Dewey.

VIRGINIA

RICHMOND, Va., Nov. 7 (AP)—Virginia, in 1,493 of its 1,714 precincts, gave President Roosevelt 213,876 votes today, against 128,510 for Governor Dewey.

4 Bay State Towns Cast Lighter Vote Than in '40

By The Associated Press.

SPRINGFIELD, Mass., Nov. 7—Votes of four small western Massachusetts towns tonight indicated a lighter turn-out than in the 1940 election.

New Ashford, Mt. Washington, Tolland and Montgomery gave today 132 votes for Dewey and 49 for Roosevelt, compared with 170 for Willkie and 54 for Roosevelt four years ago.

The 1944 total vote of these four was 181 against 224 four years ago.

DEMOCRATS GAIN NEW HOUSE SEATS

Continued From Page 1

gain of eleven. One of these was in the Fourth Maryland District, where George Z. Fallon, Democrat, defeated Daniel Ellison, the Republican incumbent; another was in the First Connecticut, where former Representative Herman P. Kopplemann, Democrat, unhorsed William J. Miller, Republican; the third in the First Pennsylvania, where William A. Barrett, Democrat, of Philadelphia, defeated Representative James Gallagher, Republican, and the fourth in the Fifth Pennsylvania, where William J. Green Jr., Democrat, unseated Frederick C. Pracht, Republican.

Gains In New York

Still other Democratic House gains were recorded in the Fortieth New York, where George F. Rogers, Democratic and American Labor nominee, apparently defeated Joseph J. O'Brien, Republican incumbent; in the Sixth Pennsylvania where Herbert J. McGlinchey, Democrat, turned out Representative Hugh D. Scott Jr., Republican; in the Third Connecticut where James P. Geeland, Democrat, defeated Representative Ranulf Compton, Republican; in the same state, where Joseph Ryter, Democrat, won the seat-at-large from Benjamin J. Monkiewicz, Republican; in the Second Connecticut where Mr. Chase Going Goodhouse, New London Democrat, defeated John D. McWilliams, sitting member from that District, and in the Fourth Kentucky, where Frank L. Chelf, Democrat, of Lebanon, nosed out the incumbent Chester O. Carrier.

The pro-Democratic tide in Connecticut swept out all Republican members with the exception of Mrs. Luce and Joseph E. Talbot, who was leading his Democratc opponent, Peter M. Higgins, in the Fifth District.

Other contests in which Democrats were making strong bids to occupy seats now held by Republicans were in, in Delaware where Philip A. Traynor was leading Earle D. Willey, incumbent Representative-at-Large; in the Fourth Minnesota where Frank T. Startey, Democrat-Farmer Laborite, was ahead of Melvin J. Maas, ranking Republican member of the House Naval Affairs Committee.

Bennet a Republican Gain

Although Mr. Fish was defeated in the Twenty-ninth New York, the victor, Augustus W. Bennet, had indicated that he would side with the Republicans in the organization of the House, therefore this result was not counted as a gain for the Democrats, regardless of their glee at the incumbent's defeat.

In the contest in Connecticut, Senator Danaher was trailing Brian McMahon, former United States Assistant Attorney General and outstanding internationalist.

In Iowa, on the other hand, a Republican, Governor Bourke Hickenlooper, was well ahead of a sitting Democrat, Senator Guy M. Gillette.

In Missouri, Governor Forrest C. Donnell, Republican, was leading State Attorney General Roy McKittrick, who defeated the sitting Senator Bennett Champ Clark in the Democratic primary of last August.

In New Jersey the Republicans were threatening, with H. Alexander Smith leading the Democratic candidate, Elmer H. Wene.

Governor Leverett Saltonstall of Massachusetts apparently had won an easy victory for the seat now occupied by Senator Sinclair Weeks, who succeeded Senator Henry Cabot Lodge by appointment of Governor Saltonstall when Mr. Lodge resigned to enter active military service.

Mr. Saltonstall apparently defeated Mayor John H. Corcoran of Cambridge, Democratic nominee for the post.

Out of the give and take in the Senate campaigns the Republicans seemed certain of annexing at least one seat, and possibly more, but they had not hoped of gaining control over the upper body.

Among the Democrats who appeared certain of election were incumbent Senators Lister Hill of Alabama, Walter George of Georgia, John Overton of Louisiana and Millard Tydings of Maryland; also Representative William J. Fulbright in Arkansas, Governor Olin Johnston in South Carolina and former Governor Clyde Hoey in North Carolina.

Other Republican Senators who seemed safely over the hump were all incumbents including Robert A. Taft of Ohio, Clyde Reed of Kansas, Charles W. Tobey of New Hampshire, Chan Gurney of South Dakota and George D. Aiken of Vermont.

In Illinois Senator Scott Lucas, Democrat, was leading his opponent, Richard Lyon, known in that State as the candidate of The Chicago Tribune, by a margin that made his re-election probable.

In New York, Senator Robert F. Wagner, Democrat, who started out behind, grew more and more hopeful of re-election as the count progressed. His rival was Thomas J. Curran.

On the early reports from California, Senator Sheridan Downey, Democrat, stepped off to a lead over Frederick F. Houser, Republican.

In Oregon Wayne L. Morse, former Republican member of the War Labor Board, who was supported by all elements of labor in that State, clung to a lead of his Democratic opponent, Edgar W. Smith.

In Idaho, Glen H. Taylor, who defeated Senator D. Worth Clark, New Deal critic, in the Democratic primary last summer, was ahead of the retiring Republican Governor, C. A. Bottolfsen.

In Wisconsin, Senator Alexander Wiley, Republican, maintained an apparently comfortable lead over two opponents, Howard J. McMurray, Democrat, and Representative Harry Sauthroff, Progressive.

In New Jersey the Republican, H. Alexander Smith, started off with and clung to a lead over the Democrat, Elmer H. Wene.

In Oklahoma Senator Elmer Thomas, Democratic incumbent, was leading William J. Otjen, Republican.

Before yesterday's balloting the House division stood: Democrats, 214; Republicans, 212; Progressives, 2; Farmer Labor, 1; American Labor Party 1, and vacancies 5. A gain of six seats would give the Republicans a majority of one, all that would be needed to elect a Speaker and establish control of all the committees which are so important to the conduct of business in the lower body.

This close division offered the minority party the best chance it had to regain mastery over the House, which it surrendered in the Democratic Congressional landslide in 1930.

The Republican hope this year was based largely on what party leaders considered the trend of the times which, in the case of the House, had been demonstrated in a slow but steady reduction in Democratic strength since the convening of the Seventy-Eighth Congress in January, 1943. At that time the party division was Democrats, 222, Republicans, 208; Progressives, 2; Farmer Labor, 1; American Labor Party, 1 and vacancies 1.

While the Republican chances of gaining control over the Senate organization were considered slim, the switch of several seats from the Democratic side was regarded as highly likely. Interest in Senatorial elections centered principally in contests where the international issue was raised, especially in North Dakota, where the outstanding "isolationist," Senator Gerald P. Nye, Republican, was fighting for his political life in a three-way race with the Democratic Governor, John Moses, and an independent, Lynn Stambaugh, whom Mr. Nye defeated for the regular nomination in the summer primary.

GAHAGAN RACE IS CLOSE

Actress in See-Saw Contest for Congress in California

LOS ANGELES, Nov. 7 (AP)—A see-saw contest developed tonight in the Fourteenth Congressional District between Helen Gahagan Douglas, Democration national committeewoman, and William D. Campbell, lawyer and Republican.

Tallies in 168 of the downtown district's 606 precincts gave the actress 7,006 votes to 6,889 for Campbell.

PRESIDENT AHEAD IN MASSACHUSETTS

Cities Reverse the Early Dewey Trend—Saltonstall Winning Seat in Senate

Special to THE NEW YORK TIMES.

BOSTON, Wednesday, Nov. 8—Massachusetts swung its sixteen electoral votes to President Roosevelt again early today and all indications from the unofficial returns were that the surge would give the commonwealth a Democratic governor for the first time since 1939.

Tabulations from 871 of the State's 1,852 districts gave Mr. Roosevelt 413,766 to Governor Dewey's 355,577.

Democratic Boston rolled up in all but two of 396 precincts 205,726 for the President against 125,326 for Mr. Dewey. In 1940, Boston gove the President a plurality of 90,000. His State plurality was more than 136,000.

The Roosevelt victory was foreseen as the larger cities of the Bay State recorded their vote, which reversed an early Republican trend.

Massachusetts was considered a close State by Democratic leaders last week, but they counted on the President's last major appearance here Saturday to swing the tide and offset Mr. Dewey's efforts here three days before.

Mayor Maurice J. Tobin of Boston was benefiting from the Roosevelt surge, running well ahead of Lieut. Gov. Horace T. Cahill, with 795 districts reporting, 373,419 to 304,987. The Democartic Mayor, however, was not keeping pace with the President in Boston, where 301 precincts showed 197,760 for Mayor Tobin and 133,511 for Mr. Cahill.

Governor Saltonstall was assured of a Senatorial seat from Massachusetts, literally swamping his Democratic opponent, Mayor John H. Corcoran of Cambridge.

Other candidates on the Republican ticket, including Robert F. Bradford, District Attorney of Middlesex County, running for Lieutenant Governor, appeared assured of election.

In one of the most confusing elections in the Bay State's history, President Roosevelt was badly cut in some Irish Catholic areas of Boston while running ahead of his 1940 vote in many Republican wards.

The Congressional races in the fourteen districts appeared to be going according to schedule, with nine Republicans and four Democratic incumbents re-elected.

MISSOURI CITIES PUT ROOSEVELT IN LEAD

ST. LOUIS, Wednesday, Nov. 8 (AP)—After trailing since early last night as rural precincts came in first President Roosevelt early today took the lead over Thomas E. Dewey when the big city vote from Kansas City and St. Louis began to roll in.

The vote in 3,043 of 4,543 precincts was Roosevelt 441,379, Dewey 438,719.

Forrest C. Donnell, Republican, was leading Ray McKittrick, Democrat, for Senator, and Jean Paul Bradshaw, Republican, was leading Phil M. Donnelly, Democrat, for Governor.

Phil M. Donnelly was building up an even larger lead over Jean Paul Bradshaw, his Republican opponent and fellow townsman from Lebanon, in their race for governor.

Gov. Forrest C. Donnell was the only Republican whose lead survived the onslaught of the big city vote. Running far ahead of the rest of his ticket, he maintained an impressive margin over Attorney General Roy McKittrick for United States Senator. In 3,097 precincts, Donnell had 458,363 and McKittrick 438,546.

The apparent closeness of the races indicated a possibility it might require the count of an estimated 85,000 absentee votes—mostly from soldiers—to decide the outcome. The absentees will not be counted unti Friday.

WINS IN CONNECTICUT

Mrs. Clare Boothe Luce
Associated Press, 1943

FISH IS DEFEATED; CLARE LUCE WINS

Continued From Page 1

indicating that Mr. Bennet would carry this section by a substantial plurality.

In forty-five districts out of sixty-two in Delaware County, the vote was: Fish 6,028, Bennet 8,842.

Mr. Bennet, who was defeated by Mr. Fish for the Republican nomination, appeared on the ballot under the labels of the Democratic, American Labor, Liberal and Good Government parties. Mr. Fish appeared as the candidate of the Jeffersonian Democratic party, as well as the Republican.

A leading member of the Foreign Affairs Committee of the House, Mr. Fish has been under attack from many Democrats, from President Roosevelt down, and from members of his own party, from Governor Dewey down, as an isolationist.

The basis of Mr. Fish's support has long been the Republican counties of Orange and Dutchess, where he had a strong personal following. Part of this following was lost when the section in Dutchess County, by the last redistricting, was placed in another Congressional district.

Mrs. Luce Is Re-Elected

Special to THE NEW YORK TIMES.

HARTFORD, Conn., Wednesday, Nov. 8—Representative Clare Boothe Luce, Republican, was re-elected yesterday in a close race. Miss Margaret Connors of Bridgeport, her Democratic opponent, conceded defeat just before 4 o'clock this morning.

The Hartford Courant, on the basis of its compilation, had declared Mrs. Luce the victor, although she was then trailing 97,287 to 97,660. Three towns, however, were missing and The Courant said that these would safely offset the margin of 373 held by Miss Connors.

These towns were Bethel, Trumbull and Wilton which went Republican in 1940 by about 700, 600 and 800 votes, respectively.

Mrs. Luce gained at one time last night a lead of nearly 9,000 votes, but returns from industrial centers of the county whittled this lead down. Bridgeport gave Miss Connors 38,398 votes to 23,625.

Mrs. Luce carried her home town of Greenwich 10,996 to 5,879. She had a margin of 896 in Norwalk. Stamford went to Miss Connors by a margin of 519.

Jaeckle Sees World Lesson

BUFFALO, Wednesday, Nov. 8.—Edwin F. Jaeckel, Republican State Chairman, commenting on the election, said early today that "all Americans should be proud of our unprecedented demonstration of the free processes of self-government in wartime, as "we have given the world a heartening lesson in government of, for and by the people."

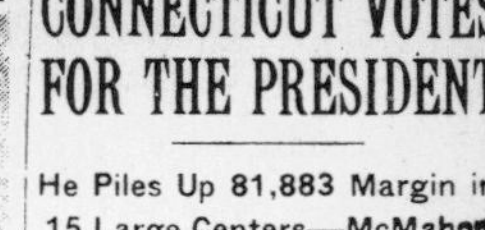

CONNECTICUT VOTES FOR THE PRESIDENT

He Piles Up 81,883 Margin in 15 Large Centers—McMahon Also Triumphs

Special to THE NEW YORK TIMES.

HARTFORD, Conn., Wednesday, Nov. 8—President Franklin D. Roosevelt maintained his monopoly on the vote of the fifteen large Connecticut cities by a lead of 81,883 in these industrial centers, to gain the eight electoral votes of the State in his quest for a fourth term.

The Dewey-dominated small towns were unable to cut into this advantage to any appreciable extent, thus giving the country's Chief Executive his third consecutive Connecticut victory in a national campaign. He was defeated by 8,000 votes here in 1932, but piled up a majority of 104,000 in 1936. This was reduced to a margin of 56,000 four years ago.

Results from 145 of the 169 cities and towns at 1:30 A. M. gave the President 417,660 votes to Governor Dewey's 367,978, a comfortable margin of almost 50,000. Brien McMahon, former Assistant United States Attorney General, ran some 3,000 ballots behind Mr. Roosevelt to upset the incumbent Senator, John Danaher. McMahon's total was 414,518 and Danaher had 364,766.

The Republican Governor, Raymond E. Baldwin, with 391,900 votes to the 377,318 of former Gov. Robert A. Hurley, appeared virtually assured of re-election. The Democrats, however, seemed to have elected the rest of the State ticket. Mr. Hurley definitely conceded his defeat shortly after 1:30.

The heavy Democratic vote in Hartford caused Representative William J. Miller, veteran of the first World War, to admit his defeat by his Democratic rival, Herman Kopplemann, about three hours after the polls closed at eight o'clock. The heavy Democratic margin in New Haven carried James P. Geelan to a Third District Congressional triumph over Representative Ranulf Compton.

The Republicans salvaged two of their six Congressional seats when Clare Booth Luce of Greenwich seemed to have defeated Margaret Connors of Fairfield and Joseph E. Talbot of Naugatuck triumphed over Peter B. Higgins of Torrington.

Mrs. Chase Going Woodhouse of New London, Democratic candidate for Congress from the Second District, won her contest with the incumbent, John D. McWilliams of Norwich, and Joseph F. Ryter, Democrat of Hartford, was victorious in the race for Representative-at-Large over the present office holder, B. J. Monckiewicz of New Britain.

With 155 of the 169 cities and towns in at 2 A. M., it appeared certain that President Roosevelt's majority would approximate that of 1940.

A 14,320 edge for President Roosevelt in Bridgeport, added to the 16,456 advantage which he obtained in New Haven and the sweeping 25,523 majority which he received in Hartford, gave the President an overall total of 56,299 in these big centers.

In Meriden, Mr. Roosevelt was victorious by a vote of 11,038 to Mr. Dewey's 9,152. Four years ago the President had a pluralty of 3,000 in Meriden. Mr. Roosevelt also ran behind his 1940 majority in Torrington; winning the city by 1,500 votes as against a 2,500 margin in the last national election.

Franklin P. Adams Trailing.

NEW HAVEN, Nov. 8 (AP).—Franklin P. Adams, of Weston, columnist, and expert on information Please, who promised to "campaign by keeping my trap shut," as Democratic candidate for the State Senate from the Twenty-fifth District, appeared early today to have been defeated by William H. Sheehy, Republican.

Late unofficial returns from seven of the district's nine towns gave Sheehy 19,886 votes and Adams 16,900.

"All the News That's Fit to Print"

The New York Times.

LATE CITY EDITION
Clearing and warm today.
Fair, continued warm tomorrow.
Temperatures Yesterday—Max., 74; Min., 54
Sunrise today, 6:21 A. M.; Sunset, 7:36 P. M.

VOL. XCIV...No. 31,856. Entered as Second-Class Matter, Postoffice, New York, N. Y. NEW YORK, FRIDAY, APRIL 13, 1945. THREE CENTS IN NEW YORK CITY

PRESIDENT ROOSEVELT IS DEAD; TRUMAN TO CONTINUE POLICIES; 9TH CROSSES ELBE, NEARS BERLIN

U. S. AND RED ARMIES DRIVE TO MEET

Americans Across the Elbe in Strength Race Toward Russians Who Have Opened Offensive From Oder

WEIMAR TAKEN, RUHR POCKET SLASHED

Third Army Reported 19 Miles From Czechoslovak Border—British Drive Deeper in the North, Seizing Celle—Canadians Freeing Holland

By DREW MIDDLETON
By Wireless to THE NEW YORK TIMES.

PARIS, April 12—Thousands of tanks and a half million doughboys of the United States First, Third and Ninth Armies are racing through the heart of the Reich on a front of 150 miles, threatening Berlin, Leipzig and the last citadels of the Nazi power.

The Second Armored Division of the Ninth Army has crossed the Elbe River in force and is striking eastward toward Berlin, whose outskirts lie less than sixty miles to the east, according to reports from the front. [A report quoted by The United Press placed the Americans less than fifty miles from the capital.] Beyond Berlin the First White Russian Army has crossed the Oder on a wide front and a junction between the western and eastern Allies is not far off.

[The Moscow radio reported that heavy battles were raging west of the Oder before Berlin, indicating that Marshal Gregory K. Zhukoff had launched his drive toward the Reich's capital. The Soviet communiqué announced further progress by the Red Army forces in and around Vienna.]

Paris is wild with excitement tonight. A special edition of the newspaper France-Soir carries a report by the radio station "Voice of America" that places American forces fifteen and five-eighths miles from Berlin after an airborne landing that had linked up with Lieut. Gen. William H. Simpson's forces advancing eastward from the Elbe. This would put American forces only seventy-five miles from the Red Army vanguard.

No Confirmation at Headquarters

There was no confirmation of this report at Allied Supreme Headquarters, which by its own admission was thirty-six hours behind developments on some sectors of the front.

Resistance was continuing only on the northern and southern flanks. The center had burst wide open. Weimar fell to Lieut. Gen. George S. Patton's infantry, and reports from the front said Erfurt also had been cleared. Schweinfurt and Heilbronn, two German bastions on the south, had fallen to United States Seventh Army forces, who were driving on Bamberg, while farther north Third Army forces were about thirty-five miles from the Czechoslovak frontier in the area east of Coburg.

[The German radio reported American Third Army forces at Lichtenberg, nineteen miles from the Czechoslovak border, The United Press said.]

The offensives to liberate the Netherlands and reduce the Ruhr

Continued on Page 12, Column 2

OUR OKINAWA GUNS DOWN 118 PLANES

Japanese Fliers Start 'Suicide' Attacks on Fleet, Sink a Destroyer, Hit Other Ships

By W. H. LAWRENCE
By Wireless to THE NEW YORK TIMES

GUAM, Friday, April 13—Japanese attempting to halt the American march to Tokyo, have started "desperate, suicidal" aerial attacks upon our ships and men in the Okinawa area, losing 118 planes on Thursday alone, Fleet Admiral Chester W. Nimitz announced today.

The Japanese succeeded in sinking a destroyer and damaging several other surface units, the communiqué said. All of the damaged vessels remained in action.

It was the first time that the Navy had revealed the suicidal nature of the Japanese air missions against our ships and men. The Japanese radio has been saying that this type of assault was being carried on by a "special attack corps" known in Japanese as "kamakazi," which, translated literally, means "divine wind."

Attack at Low Levels

The Japanese fliers launched their attacks upon our ships and men at a high speed and from low levels, diving directly into a ship or troop concentration to explode their bombs as they crashed.

There was no official estimate of the total number of enemy aircraft engaged in the Okinawa area attack other than the report of the 118 enemy planes destroyed.

Admiral Nimitz reported that the attacks began early on April 12 (Eastern Longitude time) with seven enemy planes shot down during the morning in the vicinity of the Hagushi beaches.

The tempo of the attack was stepped up in the afternoon as the Japanese bore in on our ships in wave after wave. Admiral Nimitz said that ships' guns, carrier aircraft and shore-based anti-aircraft shot down 111 of the attackers.

The revelation of the suicidal Japanese air attacks was the highlight of Admiral Nimitz' regular morning communiqué, which also disclosed the identity of two Marine and two Army divisions that have gone into action on Okinawa. These included the Twenty-seventh Army Division, formed from New York National Guard units, which are seeing action for the first time since the Saipan campaign and previously had engaged in the Gilbert Islands assault. It is com-

Continued on Page 13, Column 3

Army Leaders See Reich End at Hand

By The Associated Press.

WASHINGTON, April 12—High Army officials told Senators today that the end of organized fighting in Germany probably would come within a few days.

Describing the pell-mell dash of American Armies across Germany, General Staff officers expressed the opinion to members of the Senate Military Committee that a collapse of German arms was imminent.

Those who attended said the army chiefs declared that they were so sure of the results that orders had been drawn for a drastic reduction in shipments of durable equipment to Europe.

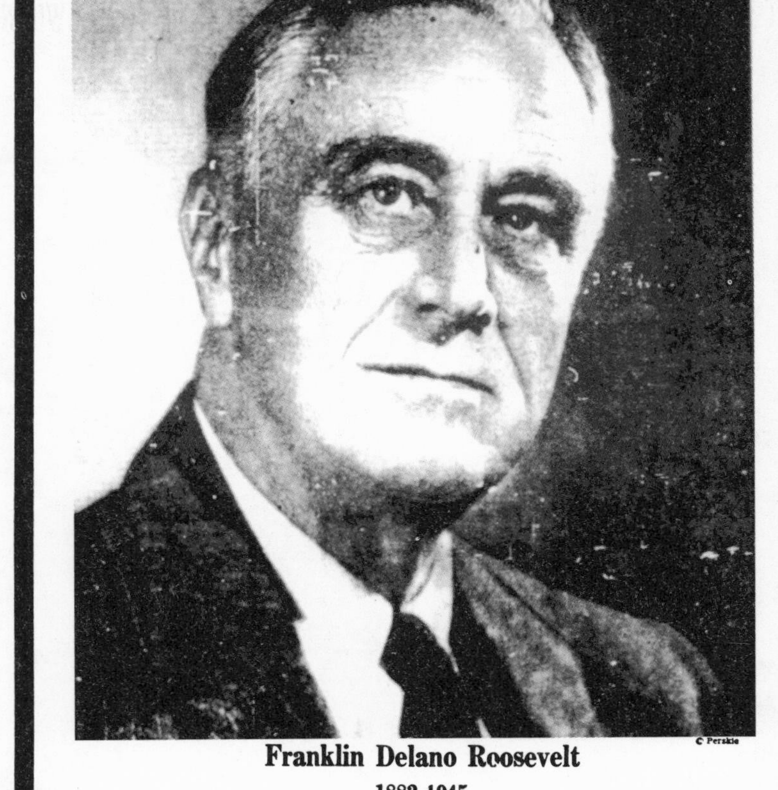

Franklin Delano Roosevelt
1882-1945

SECURITY PARLEY WON'T BE DELAYED

State Department Urges That World Be Shown We Plan No Changes in Policy

By JAMES B. RESTON
Special to THE NEW YORK TIMES.

WASHINGTON, April 12—The United Nations Security Conference will open in San Francisco on April 25, despite the death of President Roosevelt, Secretary of State Edward R. Stettinius Jr. announced tonight.

Mr. Stettinius said that he had been authorized by President Harry Truman to make this announcement after a meeting of the Cabinet at the White House.

Most of the overseas delegations to the San Francisco conference have either arrived in this country or are now on their way, but while this was said to have been a factor in the decision to proceed with the conference, State Department officials urged that every attempt be made to give immediate evidence to the world that President Roosevelt's foreign policy would be sustained by the new Administration.

President Roosevelt had planned to address the San Francisco conference. His interest in an international organization of nations to maintain peace and security had gone back to his service in the Wilson Administration, when he sat in the gallery of the Senate and listened to the debate that resulted in the rejection of the League of Nations Covenant. He had expressed to friends his desire to participate in the San Francisco conference and to see the United States enter the new league during his term in office.

The sudden elevation of Presi-

Continued on Page 2, Column 1

War News Summarized

FRIDAY, APRIL 13, 1945

President Roosevelt died yesterday afternoon, suddenly and unexpectedly. He was stricken with a massive cerebral hemorrhage at Warm Springs, Ga., on the eve of his greatest military and diplomatic successes—the impending fall of Berlin and the opening of the San Francisco Conference to set up a World Security Organization that would make the world free from martial and economic strife [1:7-8.]

Mr. Roosevelt had been sitting in front of the fireplace of his Little White House, having gone to Warm Springs on March 30 for a three-week rest. About 2:15 Eastern war time he said, "I have a terrific headache," lost consciousness in a few moments and died at 4:35. He was 63 years old. [1:6.]

The tragic word spread quickly around the world. Expressions of sorrow poured in from all sections. [4:5.] American soldiers and sailors refused to believe the reports until there was no longer doubt that their Commander in Chief had gone. [4:2-3.]

Harry S. Truman was sworn in as President at 7:09 o'clock last night, and a few minutes later Mrs. Roosevelt left for Warm Springs. [1:7.] The new President immediately called a Cabinet meeting and declared that Mr. Roosevelt's policies would be continued, that the war would be carried on until Germany and Japan surrendered unconditionally and that the San Francisco Conference would open April 25 as scheduled. [1:3.]

Some 500,000 American soldiers of the Third and Ninth Armies, and thousands of tanks, sped along a 150-mile front toward Berlin and Leipzig. The Ninth, surging across the Elbe, according to delayed reports was less than fifty miles from the German capital and 115 from the Russians along the Oder. The Third Army captured Weimar, home of the late German Republic, and was twenty-three miles below Leipzig, with the First closing a pincers from the north. [1:1-2; map P. 2.]

The Moscow radio reported that the Red Army was waging fierce battles east of Berlin, indicating resumption of the drive on that city. Elsewhere Russian troops scored wide gains and cut the last escape railroad from Vienna. [13:1.]

Open cities were ruled out and every German was ordered by Himmler to fight to the death, although Goebbels said "the war cannot last much longer." [12:6-7.]

The Ninth Air Force destroyed at least 117 more German planes yesterday. [11:8.]

In Italy the Eighth Army advanced along a thirty-mile front toward Bologna and the Po Valley; the Fifth Army also made good gains and was eleven miles from La Spezia. [13:8, with map.]

Japanese planes resumed their suicide attacks on American ships off Okinawa, sinking a destroyer and damaging several other vessels. One hundred and eighteen enemy planes were shot down. [1:2.] The Americal Division invaded Bohol, last of the enemy-held central Philippines. [18:6.] The B-29 attack on Koriyama, 110 miles north of Tokyo, set a new Superfortress distance record. [18:2.]

Secretary of State Stettinius and Secretary of War Stimson, denouncing Germany's "steadily increasing" mistreatment of American prisoners, said those responsible would be brought to justice. [13:6-7.]

Clashes between Right and Left wing elements in Iran were reported from Moscow. [13:2.]

LAST WORDS: 'I HAVE TERRIFIC HEADACHE'

Roosevelt Was Posing for Artist When Hemorrhage Struck —He Died in Bedroom

By The Associated Press.

WARM SPRINGS, Ga., April 12—President Franklin D. Roosevelt's last words were:

"I have a terrific headache."

He spoke them to Comdr. Howard G. Bruenn, naval physician.

Mr. Roosevelt was sitting in front of a fireplace in the Little White House here atop Pine Mountain when what was described as a massive cerebral hemorrhage struck him.

The President's Negro valet, Arthur Prettyman, and a Filipino messboy carried him to his bedroom. He was unconscious at the end. It came without pain.

Dr. Bruenn said that he saw the President this morning and he was in excellent spirits at 9:30 A. M.

"At 1 o'clock," Dr. Bruenn added, "he was sitting in a chair while sketches were being made of him by an artist. He suddenly complained of a very severe occipital headache (back of the head).

"Within a very few minutes he lost consciousness. He was seen by me at 1:30 P. M., fifteen minutes after the episode had started.

"He did not regain consciousness, and he died at 3:35 P. M. (Georgia time)."

The artist sketching Mr. Roosevelt was N. Robbins of 530 West 139th Street, New York.

Only others present in the cottage were Comdr. George Fox, White House pharmacist and long an attendant on the President; William D. Hassett, Presidential secretary; Miss Grace Tully, con-

Continued on Page 4, Column 3

END COMES SUDDENLY AT WARM SPRINGS

Even His Family Unaware of Condition as Cerebral Stroke Brings Death to Nation's Leader at 63

ALL CABINET MEMBERS TO KEEP POSTS

Funeral to Be at White House Tomorrow, With Burial at Hyde Park Home—Impact of News Tremendous

By ARTHUR KROCK
Special to THE NEW YORK TIMES.

WASHINGTON, April 12—Franklin Delano Roosevelt, War President of the United States and the only Chief Executive in history who was chosen for more than two terms, died suddenly and unexpectedly at 4:35 P. M. today at Warm Springs, Ga., and the White House announced his death at 5:48 o'clock. He was 63.

The President, stricken by a cerebral hemorrhage, passed from unconsciousness to death on the eighty-third day of his fourth term and in an hour of high triumph. The armies and fleets under his direction as Commander in Chief were at the gates of Berlin and the shores of Japan's home islands as Mr. Roosevelt died, and the cause he represented and led was nearing the conclusive phase of success.

Less than two hours after the official announcement, Harry S. Truman of Missouri, the Vice President, took the oath as the thirty-second President. The oath was administered by the Chief Justice of the United States, Harlan F. Stone, in a one-minute ceremony at the White House. Mr. Truman immediately let it be known that Mr. Roosevelt's Cabinet is remaining in office at his request, and that he had authorized Secretary of State Edward R. Stettinius Jr. to proceed with plans for the United Nations Conference on international organization at San Francisco, scheduled to begin April 25. A report was circulated that he leans somewhat to the idea of a coalition Cabinet, but this is unsubstantiated.

Funeral Tomorrow Afternoon

It was disclosed by the White House that funeral services for Mr. Roosevelt would take place at 4 P. M. (E. W. T.) Saturday in the East Room of the Executive Mansion. The Rev. Angus Dun, Episcopal Bishop of Washington; the Rev. Howard S. Wilkinson of St. Thomas's Church in Washington and the Rev. John G. McGee of St. John's in Washington will conduct the services.

The body will be interred at Hyde Park, N. Y., Sunday, with the Rev. George W. Anthony of St. James Church officiating. The time has not yet been fixed.

Jonathan Daniels, White House secretary, said Mr. Roosevelt's body would not lie in state. He added that, in view of the limited size of the East Room, which holds only about 200 persons, the list of those attending the funeral services would be limited to high Government officials, representatives of the membership of both

Continued on Page 3, Column 3

TRUMAN IS SWORN IN THE WHITE HOUSE

Members of Cabinet on Hand as Chief Justice Stone Administers the Oath

By C. P. TRUSSELL
Special to THE NEW YORK TIMES.

WASHINGTON, April 12—Vice President Harry S. Truman of Missouri, standing erect, with his sharp features taut and looking straight ahead through his large, round glasses, became the thirty-second President of the United States in a ceremony lasting not more than a minute in the Cabinet Room of the White House at 7:09 o'clock tonight.

The oath was administered by Chief Justice Harlan F. Stone two hours and thirty-four minutes after the sudden death of President Roosevelt at Warm Springs. Mr. Truman had picked up a Bible from the end of the big Cabinet conference table, held it with his left hand and placed his right hand upon the upper cover. After repeating the oath, he bowed his head, lifted the Bible to his lips and kissed it.

Even before he had taken the oath Mr. Truman had asked President Roosevelt's Cabinet to continue in service. He also authorized Edward R. Stettinius Jr., Secretary of State, to announce that the United Nations Conference for International Organization would go on as scheduled.

To the newsmen at the White House he sent this word, through Stephen Early, press secretary:

"For the time being I prefer not to hold a press conference. It will be my effort to carry on as I believe the President would have done, and to that end I have asked the Cabinet to stay on with me."

Soon after he became President, Mr. Truman left the White House for the five-room Connecticut Avenue apartment where he has resided with Mrs. Truman and their 20-year-old daughter, Mary Margaret, for four years. He said he was "going home, to bed."

It was shortly after he had finished presiding over the Senate debate on the United States-Mexican Water Treaty late this afternoon that Mr. Truman received word from the White House of President Roosevelt's death. This was at about 5:15 P. M., a half hour before the news was made public. Reaching for his hat, he dashed out of the office, calling back to his staff that he was going to the White House.

Arriving at the White House the

Continued on Page 3, Column 6

Byrnes May Take Post With Truman

Special to THE NEW YORK TIMES.

WASHINGTON, April 12—James F. Byrnes, recently resigned as Director of War Mobilization and Reconversion, known to be one of President Truman's warmest friends in official Washington, is expected to be called to the White House for consultation, and possibly to take an important post in the Cabinet, in the immediate future.

President Truman's admiration of former Justice Byrnes is well known here. He undoubtedly would have been Mr. Truman's choice as a successor to Cordell Hull as Secretary of State.

TRUMAN IS SEVENTH ELEVATED BY DEATH

New President Was Compromise for Second Place When Conservatives Fought Wallace

NATIONAL FIGURE 10 YEARS

But Senator Did Not Achieve Prominence Until He Headed War Investigating Group

Harry S. Truman is the seventh vice president of the United States to succeed to the Presidency upon the death of a Chief Executive. Like other Presidents, he rose to his position from humble beginnings and, although elected to the United States Senate in 1934, it was not until after this country had entered the second World War that he achieved national prominence through his effective chairmanship of the Senate war investigating committee.

Before entering the Senate as a protégé of "Big Tom" Pendergast, former boss of the Kansas City political machine, the strongest organization west of the Mississippi, Mr. Truman had played the role of an obscure Missouri politician, and had given little evidence of capacity for national leadership. During his chairmanship of the Truman committee, however, he was voted by Washington correspondents as the civilian who, next to President Roosevelt, "knew most about the war."

Spur to War Production

The direct and indirect benefits of the Truman committee's work were recognized throughout the country and gave him the necessary stature to be the running mate of President Roosevelt in his campaign for a fourth term. The early and sensational findings of the Truman committee enhanced the efficiency of war production and, indirectly, the committee's activities served as a stern warning against looseness and corruption in the execution of war contracts.

Throughout the period of Mr. Truman's chairmanship of the committee, it acted as a spur to the administration and leaders of the nation's armed forces. It exposed shortages in aluminum, rubber, zinc, lead, steel, manpower. It wielded a salutary influence in helping the President establish an efficient war production machine.

While steering clear of mere sensationalism, the committee did not hesitate to put the responsibility for shortcomings wherever the facts required it, not sparing the White House.

Because of this record, Mr. Truman became the logical compromise candidate for the Vice Presidency at the Democratic Convention in Chicago in 1944 in the bitter conflict between the conservative wing of the party and left-wing elements who had played so prominent a role in the earlier Roosevelt Administrations.

Henry A. Wallace, Mr. Roosevelt's third-term Vice President, was the undisputed first choice of the more radical elements backing Mr. Roosevelt. The conservatives had several candidates, of whom Mr. Truman was one. Others included James F. Byrnes, then heading the top home front agency of the Government, and Senator Alben W. Barkley of Kentucky, the Senate Majority Leader. There were others less widely known who were hopeful.

President's Letter a Factor

Mr. Truman pinned his hope of getting the nomination on White House support. Just before the convention opened, Mr. Wallace's friends were optimistic of victory. In a formal letter Mr. Roosevelt spoke highly of his 1940 running-mate and described him as his first choice in 1944 The Wallace hopes were dashed to the ground a short time later when it was disclosed that the President had written a secon letter, addressed to Robert E. Hannegan, Democratic national chairman, in which he declared that Senator Truman's nomination would be acceptable to him.

Between the first and second Roosevelt letters there had been a great deal of political maneuvering. Justice Byrnes was looked upon by many as the logical choice if Mr. Wallace were to be dropped. But before the convention opened he stated that he would not be a ca date at the request of the President. The understanding among observers was that Justice Byrnes was not satisfactory to Sidney Hillman, chairman of the Political Action Committee of the Congress of Industrial Organizations. While Mr. Wallace remained Mr. Hillman's first choice to the end, he told Democratic leaders that Mr. Truman would be satisfactory.

Thus it was that Mr. Truman became the compromise candidate for the vice presidency at a moment when many had feared that Mr. Roosevelt would not live out his fourth term.

Mr. Truman was born May 8, 1884, on a farm near Lamar, Mo., but grew up on a farm in Jackson County, about fifteen miles outside of Kansas City. Upon his graduation from high school he tried for appointment to West Point but was rejected because of a defective eye. Without funds to pay his way through college he took a job as porter and general utility man in a Kansas City drug store and enlisted in the Missouri National Guard. He then took a job with The Kansas City Star wrapping newspapers, shifting later to a position with a Kansas City bank.

Discouraged by the slow progress he was making in the city, he returned to his father's farm, five years after graduation from high school, where he was living when the first World War began and his National Guard company was ordered into Federal service.

He sailed for France as a lieutenant in the artillery, being promoted to captain soon after his arrival. He participated in the St. Mihiel and Argonne offensives and won the respect and admiration of his men by his consideration for their welfare. On the way home the men on his troopship voted to present him with a ten-gallon loving cup four feet high. He still has it.

Upon demobilization he married Miss Bess Wallace, and in partnership with an Army "buddy" invested his war service savings in a Kansas City haberdashery. The business failed to prosper, and the partners were forced to close it.

It was then that Mr. Truman turned to politics. In his new venture he was helped by a nephew of "Boss" Pendergast, who had served under Mr. Truman in the war and recommended Mr. Truman to his uncle as good political timber because of his fine record and popularity with his men.

Mr. Truman's first political job was an appointment as overseer of highways for Jackson County. A year later he was nominated and elected county judge for Jackson County, an office which under Missouri law does not require the holder to be a lawyer and which carried with it, in addition to judicial duties, supervision over many county expenditures. Believing that knowing a little law would "not hurt," Mr. Truman studied at night for two years in the Kansas City Law School. After serving one term as county judge he was defeated for re-election in 1924 but was returned to office as presiding judge of the court two years later.

As a member of the court, he supervised highway and public construction projects totaling $60,000,000, but throughout the roaring period of the rule of the corrupt Pendergast machine, whose chieftain was subsequently convicted and sent to jail, Mr. Truman, as is admitted even by enemies, remained clean.

Story of Senate Nomination

How he came to be nominated for the United States Senate in 1934 has been the subject of an oft-told anecdote. He went to Pendergast and requested appointment as collector of internal revenue, citing his faithful service in the $6,300 county job as justifying the promotion to the more lucrative post.

"The best I can do right now, Harry," Pendergast is quoted as having replied, "is a United States Senatorship."

Mr. Truman was elected, thus making his first appearance on the national arena.

His election to the Senate in a three-cornered race over Representative Jacob L. Milligan and Representative John J. Cochran was attributed, in part, to his modest appearance and simple manner of speaking. Describing himself as "a farm boy from Jackson County," he said it was his intention "to keep his feet on the ground, one of the hardest things to do for a United States Senator."

"All this precedence and other hooey accorded to a Senator isn't very good for the republic," he declared at a campaign rally. "If he isn't careful he ceases to be a citizen of his home State and becomes a foreigner. The association with dressed-up diplomats has turned the heads of more than one Senator, I can tell you."

During his first year in Washington, Mr. Truman declined an invitation to a $10 plate Jackson Day dinner.

"I am against the Democrats giving gold plate dinners," he said.

Mr. Truman attracted little attention in Washington during his first term in the Senate. He said little and voted for virtually all New Deal measures.

The overthrow of the Pendergast machine in Missouri and the conviction of Pendergast made Mr. Truman's campaign in 1940 difficult. He was re-elected by a margin of only 7,000 votes over Governor Lloyd Stark and Maurice Milligan, the man who prosecuted Pendergast and many of his henchmen.

Had he lost that election, he would not now be President of the United States.

Taking the Oath as the Thirty-second President of the United States

Harry S. Truman being sworn in by Chief Justice Harlan F. Stone in the Cabinet Room of the executive offices in the White House. Watching the solemn ceremony are, left to right: Secretary of Labor Frances Perkins, Secretary of War Henry L. Stimson, Secretary of Commerce Henry A. Wallace, War Production Board Chairman J. A. Krug, Secretary of the Navy James Forrestal, Secretary of Agriculture Claude R. Wickard, an unidentified person, Attorney General Francis Biddle, Secretary of State Edward R. Stettinius Jr., Mrs. Truman, Secretary of the Interior Harold L. Ickes, Speaker Sam Rayburn, War Mobilization Director Fred M. Vinson, Representative Joseph W. Martin Jr., House minority leader; Representative Robert Ramspeck and Representative John W. McCormack, House majority leader.

Associated Press Wirephoto

Truman's Home Town Takes the News Quietly

KANSAS CITY, April 12 (AP)—At near-by Lamar, Mo., birthplace of Harry S. Truman, news of President Roosevelt's death and Mr. Truman's rise to the nation's highest office was received quietly, according to Publisher Arthur Aull. He said he had not yet talked with townspeople, but added:

"People here think well of Harry Truman. They think he will do quite well."

At Independence, Mr. Truman's home town, people disappeared from the streets shortly after the news was received, presumably going into their homes or shops to listen to their radios.

ROOSEVELT IS DEAD; TRUMAN PRESIDENT

Continued From Page 1

houses of Congress, heads of foreign missions, and friends of the family.

President Truman, in his first official pronouncement, pledged prosecution of the war to a successful conclusion. His statement, issued for him at the White House by press secretary Jonathan Daniels, said:

"The world may be sure that we will prosecute the war on both fronts, East and West, with all the vigor we possess to a successful conclusion."

News of Death Stuns Capital

The impact of the news of the President's death on the capital was tremendous. Although rumor and a marked change in Mr. Roosevelt's appearance and manner had brought anxiety to many regarding his health, and there had been increasing speculation as to the effects his death would have on the national and world situation, the fact stunned the Government and the citizens of the capital.

It was not long, however, before the wheels of Government began once more to turn. Mr. Stettinius, the first of the late President's Ministers to arrive at the White House, summoned the Cabinet to meet at once. Mr. Truman, his face gray and drawn, responded to the first summons given to any outside Mr. Roosevelt's family and official intimates by rushing from the Capitol.

Mrs. Roosevelt had immediately given voice to the spirit that animated the entire Government, once the first shock of the news had passed. She cabled to her four sons, all on active service:

"He did his job to the end as he would want you to do. Bless you all and all our love. Mother."

Those who have served with the late President in peace and in war accepted that as their obligation. The comment of members of Congress unanimously reflected this spirit. Those who supported or opposed Mr. Roosevelt during his long and controversial years as President did not deviate in this. And all hailed him as the greatest leader of his time.

No President of the United States has died in circumstances so triumphant and yet so grave. The War of the States had been won by the Union when Abraham Lincoln was assassinated, and though the shadow of post-war problems hung heavy and dark, the nation's troubles were internal. World War II, which the United States entered in Mr. Roosevelt's third term, still was being waged at the time of his death, and in the Far East the enemy's resistance was still formidable. The United States and its chief allies, as victory nears, were struggling to resolve differences of international policy on political and economic issues that have arisen and will arise. And the late President's great objective—a league of nations that will be formed and be able to keep the peace—was meeting obstacles on its way to attainment.

Mr. Roosevelt died also in a position unique insofar as the history of American statesmen reveals. He was regarded by millions as indispensable to winning the war and making a just and lasting peace. On the basis of this opinion, they elected him to a fourth term in 1944. He was regarded by those same millions as the one American qualified to deal successfully and effectively with the leaders of other nations—particularly Prime Minister Winston Churchill and Marshal Joseph Stalin—and this was another reason for his re-election.

Yet the constitutional transition to the Presidency of Mr. Truman was accomplished without a visible sign of anxiety or fear on the part of any of those responsible for waging war and negotiating peace under the Chief Executive. Though the democratic process has never had a greater shock, the human and official machines withstood it, once the first wave of grief had passed for a leader who was crushed by the burdens of war.

President Truman entered upon the duties imposed by destiny with a modest and calm, and yet a resolute, manner. Those who were with him through the late afternoon and evening were deeply impressed with his approach to the task.

"He is conscious of limitations greater than he has," said one. "But for the time being that is not a bad thing for the country."

How unexpected was President Roosevelt's death despite the obvious physical decline of the last few months is attested by the circumstance that no member of his family was with him at Warm Springs, no high-ranking associate or long-time intimate, and that his personal physician, Rear Admiral Ross McIntyre, was in Washington, totally unprepared for the news.

Personal Physician Surprised

The Admiral, in answer to questions from the press today, said "this came out of a clear sky," that no operations had been performed recently on Mr. Roosevelt and that there had never been the slightest indication of cerebral hemorrhage. His optimistic reports of the late President's health, he declared, had been completely justified by the known tests.

This ease of mind is borne out by the fact that Mrs. Roosevelt was attending a meeting of the Thrift Club near Dupont Circle when Stephen Early, the President's secretary, telephoned her to come to the White House as soon as possible. Mrs. John Boettiger, the only daughter of the family, was visiting her slightly ailing son at the Naval Hospital at Bethesda, Md., some miles away.

While these simple offices were being performed by those nearest and dearest, the President lay in the faint from which he never roused. A lesser human being would have been prostrated by the sudden and calamitous tidings, but Mrs. Roosevelt entered at once upon her responsibilities, sent off her message to her sons and told Mr. Early and Admiral McIntire, "I am more sorry for the people of the country and the world than I am for us." When Mr. Truman arrived and asked what he could do for her, Mrs. Roosevelt rejoined calmly, "Tell us what we can do. Is there any way we can help you?"

Flag at Capitol Lowered

As soon as the news became a certainty the White House flag was lowered to half-staff—the first time marking the death of an occupant since Warren G. Harding died at the Palace Hotel in San Francisco, Aug. 2, 1923, following a heart attack that succeeded pneumonia. The flag over the Capitol was lowered at 6:30 P. M. Between these two manifestations of the blow that had befallen the nation and the world, the news had spread throughout the city and respectful crowds gathered on the Lafayette Square pavement across from the executive mansion. They made no demonstration. But the men's hats were off, and the tears that were shed were not to be seen only on the cheeks of women. Some Presidents have been held in lukewarm esteem here, and some have been disliked by the local population, but Mr. Roosevelt held a high place in the rare affections of the capital.

The spoken tributes paid by members of Congress, a body with which the late President had many encounters, also testified to the extraordinary impression Mr. Roosevelt made on his times and the unparalleled position in the world he had attained. The comment of Senator Robert A. Taft of Ohio, a constant adversary on policy, was typical. "The greatest figure of our time," he called him, who had been removed "at the very climax of his career," who died "a hero of the war, for he literally worked himself to death in the service of the American people." And Senator Arthur H. Vandenberg of Michigan, another Republican and frequent critic, said that the late President has "left an imperishable imprint on the history of America and of the world."

More Than Mere Words

These were not mere words, uttered in conformity to the rule of "nil nisi bonum." Mr. Roosevelt's political opponents did what they could to retire him to private life, and their concern over his long tenure was real and grew as the tenure increased. But ever since his fourth-term victory in 1944 they have felt sincerely that it would be best for the country if he were spared to finish the great enterprises of war and peace which the country had commissioned him to carry through. And when they called his death a national and international tragedy they meant it.

But this tribute paid, this anxiety expressed, they and the late President's political supporters and official aides turned their hearts and minds again to the tasks before the nation. No one said "On to Berlin and Tokyo!" For Americans do not speak dramatically. But that is what every one meant, and it was the gist of what President Truman said and did after the homely ceremony that made him the head of the State.

When the dignitaries were assembled with Mr. Truman for this solemn purpose, there was a slight delay until his wife and daughter should arrive. Then the Chief Justice, using a Bible borrowed from Mr. Roosevelt's office and speaking from memory, read the oath and the new President repeated it after him. Then he and Mrs. Truman called on Mrs. Roosevelt and, as the President said, went "home to bed."

He wore a gray suit, a white shirt and a polka-dot tie. His face was grave but his lips were firm and his voice was strong. He said through Mr. Early that his effort will be "to carry on as he believed the President would have done." And he arranged to meet with the Army and Navy chiefs tomorrow, to assure them as tonight he did the people that his purpose is to continue the conduct of the war with the utmost vigor and to the earliest possible and successful conclusion.

While these simple but dignified processes of democracy were in motion, preparations were being made to render fit respect to the memory of the dead President. It was decided that Mrs. Roosevelt, their daughter and other members of the family should fly to Warm Springs to accompany the remains to Washington, arriving Saturday.

Meanwhile, it was announced that the nation-wide series of Jefferson Day dinners have been canceled, and similar honors of observance will be paid at the Capitol, throughout the United States and at many places in the world that looked to Mr. Roosevelt as its leader from darkness to the light.

White House Statement

By The Associated Press.

WASHINGTON, April 12—The White House announced late today that President Roosevelt had died of cerebral hemorrage.

The death occurred this afternoon at Warm Springs, Ga. A White House statement said:

"Vice President Truman has been notified. He was called to the White House and informed by Mrs. Roosevelt. The Secretary of State has been advised. A Cabinet meeting has been called.

"The four Roosevelt boys in the service have been sent a message by their mother, which said that the President slept away this afternoon. He did his job to the end, as he would want to do.

"'Bless you all and all our love,' added Mrs. Roosevelt. She signed the message Mother.

"Funeral services will be held Saturday afternoon in the East Room of the White House. Interment will be at Hyde Park Sunday afternoon. No detailed arrangements or exact times have been decided upon as yet."

TRUMAN SWORN IN IN CABINET'S ROOM

Continued From Page 1

Vice President was taken to Mrs. Roosevelt. The President, she told him, had passed away.

"What can I do?" Mr. Truman asked.

"Tell us what we can do," Mrs. Roosevelt said. "Is there any way we can help you?"

Cabinet Sees the Ceremony

Mr. Truman then called the Cabinet to the White House, and members responded promptly. As word spread throughout the city and the Capitol, other officials and Congressional leaders converged upon the White House. The Chief Justice was called, and, in contrast with the oath-taking ceremony that inducted President Calvin Coolidge by lamplight in a Vermont farmhouse in August of 1923, the Cabinet room was filled with Washington officialdom.

Awaiting the arrival of the Chief Justice and Mrs. Truman, the Vice President conversed with Cabinet members and others present for his induction as President. Members of the White House staff stood in doorways leading to the big room. They remained to see the new President sworn in.

Mrs. Truman arrived soon after the Chief Justice. She had been informed of the death of President Roosevelt by her husband, who telephoned their apartment. Stunned, Mrs. Truman called Mrs. Oscar J. Ricketts, a close friend and manager of the apartment house, and asked her to come up. Mrs. Ricketts said later that Mrs. Truman was in tears, almost completely overcome.

Secret Service on the Alert

A White House limousine was sent for the new First Lady. She and Miss Truman left the apartment house by a back door and were rushed to the executive offices. Already a small crowd of neighbors had gathered before the front entrance of the apartment house. Secret Service men held them back.

Mrs. Truman's eyes were tear-stained as she went into the Cabinet room. As the oath was being administered she stood beside her husband, still putting her handkerchief to her eyes repeatedly.

It was announced at first that the new President had gone from the oath-taking directly to the Executive Mansion. It only appeared that he had started there, for his car quickly moved out the south gate and toward the home he soon will leave for the White House.

Jonathan Daniels, White House secretary, announced that the President would be at his White House desk at 9 o'clock tomorrow morning. Thus the former judge of Jackson County, Missouri, who aspired to become collector, but who was sent to the United States Senate instead, and who wanted to remain a Senator but became Vice President, was moved by fate into the White House, eighty-two days after having become what he frequently called "the V. P."

Hyde Park's Church Bells Give the News; Community to Miss Neighbor and Friend

Special to THE NEW YORK TIMES.

HYDE PARK, N. Y., April 12—The tolling of all the church bells in the town today brought the news to President Roosevelt's friends and neighbors in this little community that the nation had suffered a great loss.

As soon as the news was known the church bells were tolled and the flag on the Town Hall went to half staff. In Poughkeepsie, four miles away, the fire whistles were blown at intervals of ten seconds for a period of ten minutes to notify the people of the city and surrounding area that the President was gone.

There was little that Hyde Park could do. Late into the night groups stood around car radios listening to the news and talking quietly. Supervisor Elmer Van Wagener, personal friend of the President, announced that the schools would be closed today and that the regular meeting of the town board scheduled for last night had been dismissed.

At St. James Protestant Episcopal Church, known as the President's church, it was announced that the services Sunday would be conducted as memorial services for the President.

Supervisor Van Wagener, who had known the President well, said: "President Roosevelt was the greatest friend a fellow could have. We in Hyde Park will miss him more than ever as this is a small community and we were his neighbors and friends. He always took a great interest and pride in our little community of Hyde Park and he always loved to come back home and stay and rest with us. While the nation will miss him as a great President, we in Hyde Park will miss him as a neighbor. It will be quiet around here now, I guess."

Moses Smith, tenant farmer on President Roosevelt's estate broadcast from Poughkeepsie. He said that he had been a tenant farmer on the President's estate for twenty-five years and that the President's death was the greatest shock of his life. The President had visited his tenant regularly and Hyde Park Roosevelt-for-President meetings had been staged on the Smith lawn.

The Rev. W. George W. Anthony, in charge of St. James Church in the absence of the rector as a chaplain in the Navy, said:

"News of the death of the President was a tragic shock to all of us. President Roosevelt was a senior warden of this church for many years. We have lost a real neighbor. He was much loved by all, Republican or Democratic, in this community."

How to Display the Flag In Mourning Is Explained

When the American flag is displayed flat on a wall in a case of national mourning, a black crepe bowknot, either with or without streamers, is placed at the fastening point, it was pointed out last night at the Navy Public Relations Office. The blue field always must be uppermost and at the observer's left.

When displayed from an upright or horizontal mast, the flag is flown at half-staff, but never with the blue field down, as that signifies a distress signal.

'OUR GREATEST LOSS,' LA GUARDIA DECLARES

President Roosevelt's death was described by Mayor La Guardia "as the greatest loss peace-loving people have suffered in the entire war." Visibly shaken by the sudden passing of the Chief Executive, Mr. La Guardia, in a ten-minute extemporaneous broadcast over Station WNYC last night at 6:15 o'clock, urged "all New Yorkers to carry on."

It had been planned originally to have Mr. La Guardia accept from the New Yorw chapter of the Sons of the American Revolution, at its headquarters in the Plaza Hotel, a citation for the "patriotic services" rendered by the city station to the home front.

Instead, the Mayor paid tribute to the President, declaring that though "our leader had died, he lives on."

"His inspiration is with us," he said. "His leadership is with us. An additional duty and responsibility has now been thrust upon us, a duty to carry on.

"Franklin Delano Roosevelt is not dead. His ideals live. That pattern is so definite, it is so permanent, we cannot escape it; we must not escape it; we do not want to escape it.

"We cannot avoid it and we will not avoid it. Centuries and centuries from now, as long as history is recorded, people will know Franklin Delano Roosevelt loved humanity. I call upon all New Yorkers to carry on."

FRENCH VIEW NEWS AS 'GREAT' DISASTER'

By Wireless to THE NEW YORK TIMES.

PARIS, April 13 (Friday)—"A great disaster!" said Georges Bidault, the French Foreign Minister, early today when told of President Roosevelt's death. This expressed the feeling of the average Frenchman who heard the news by radio late last night.

The French people in general considered Mr. Roosevelt one of the great men of this age—not only because it was to him that they gave the great share of credit for the fact an enormous American Army landed in France to drive out the German conqueror, but also because it was to him that they looked to lead the United States and the world into new paths after this war.

Something of this feeling was in the expressions of sorrow one heard from all those in Paris who had learned the news. When a NEW YORK TIMES correspondent telephoned to Gen. Charles de Gaulle's house with the news a maid who answered asked what the call was about. "About the death of the President of United States," said the correspondent.

The maid's gasped "Oh," in a shocked tone was striking and a sufficient commentary. It was in a sense the voice of France.

DE GAULLE VOICES SORROW

He and Foreign Minister Are First to Call on Our Envoy

By Cable to THE NEW YORK TIMES.

PARIS, April 12—Ambassador Jefferson Caffery informed the American press tonight that the first persons who called on him to express sympathy over President Roosevelt's death were General Charles de Gaulle and Foreign Minister Georges Bidault.

"I am more shocked than I can say," he said. "It is a terrible loss not only for our country and me personally but also for all humankind."

Many Americans in Paris at first refused to believe the news. Correspondents received it mutely, with a deep sense of personal loss, when officers at Supreme Headquarters of Allied Expeditionary Forces called them together to give confirmation. Many received calls from French friends expressing sympathy.

General de Gaulle has ordered all flags in France and the empire at half-staff tomorrow.

TEXAN TELLS GRIEF OF 'YOUNG GUARD'

Rep. Johnson in Tribute Says 'President Was Never Afraid to Help the Little Guys'

Special to THE NEW YORK TIMES.

WASHINGTON, April 12—In a gloomy Capitol corridor, Lyndon B. Johnson, a 36-year-old Representative from Texas and a typical Representative, too, of a hundred formerly obscure young men whose leap into national prominence had been immeasurably aided by President Roosevelt's paternal coaching, stood with tears in his eyes tonight and said slowly:

"There are plenty of us left here to try to block and run interference, as he had taught us, but the man who carried the ball is gone—gone."

Mr. Johnson, a leading member of the Roosevelt "Young Guard," that is or has been made up by other such nationally known figures as Supreme Court Justice William O. Douglas, "Tommy" Corcoran and Ben Cohen, clamped a shaking jaw over a white cigarette holder and went on:

"I was in the Speaker's office (Speaker Rayburn) when it came. The phone rang, and the Speaker answered. He didn't say anything at all that I could hear—just a kind of a gulp. Then he hung up and looked at me. Finally, he said the President was dead.

Thought of "Little Folks"

"I was just looking up at a cartoon on the wall—a cartoon showing the President with that cigarette holder and his jaw stuck out like it always was. He had his head cocked back, you know. And then I thought of all the little folks, and what they had lost.

"He was just like a daddy to me always; he always talked to me just that way. He was the one person I ever knew—anywhere—who was never afraid. Whatever you talked to him about, whatever you asked him for, like projects for your district, there was just one way to figure it with him. I know some of them called it demagoguery; they can call it anything they want, but you could be damn sure that the only test he had was this: Was it good for the folks?"

Mr. Johnson, whose grief was the grief of the President's "young men" scattered in high positions all over Washington, came here as a Congressional secretary and in 1937 reached Congress in a campaign to fill a Texas vacancy in which he supported the President's plan to enlarge the Supreme Court.

Never Sorry For a "Yes"

Since that time, although an Administration man normally, he has many times voted against Roosevelt recommendations. He recalled:

"They called the President a dictator and some of us they called 'yes men.' Sure, I yessed him plenty of times—because I thought he was right—and I'm not sorry for a single 'yes' I ever gave. I have seen the President in all kinds of moods—at breakfast, at lunch, at dinner—and never once in my five terms here did he ever ask me to vote a certain way, or even suggest it. And when I voted against him—as I have plenty of times—he never said a word.

"A lot of people didn't really know him—not even people up here in Congress—and how thoughtful he could be right in the middle of all kinds of hell all around him.

"When my baby was born I never dreamed of mentioning it to him. But somewhow he found out about it and a White House car turned up out at my house and brought a book. It was a book about Fala, the President's dog, as a gift to my litlte daughter. The President had autographed it—they were calling him a 'master' then. He autoraphed it, 'From the master—of the pup.'

"I don't know that I'd ever have come to Congress if it hadn't been for him. But I do know I got my first great desire for public office because of him—and so did thousands of other young men all over the country.

Says "Little Guys Will Suffer"

"The people who are going to be crushed by this are the little guys—the little guy down in my district, say, who makes $21.50 a week driving a truck and has a decent house to live in now, cheap, because of Mr. Roosevelt."

As Mr. Johnson, a tall man who seemed very tired, stood talking reflectively, looking from a corridor window, Mr. Rayburn had left the silent Capitol. On a sheet of paper headed "Office of the Majority Leader," from the office of Representative McCormack of Massachusetts, Mr. Rayburn had written out with pen and ink, in a bold, old-fashioned hand:

"We know not how to interpret God in the way he performs. The world has lost one of the great leaders of all time. President Roosevelt's passing will shock and sadden good people everywhere. The American nation has been well led in every crisis. In Harry Truman we have a leader in whom I have complete confidence."

Mr. Johnson stood looking at the original copy of this farewell to President Roosevelt.

"God," he said, "God, how he could take it for us all."

MRS. TRUMAN 'GRIEVED'

Mother, 91, of President, Is Guarded From Interviews

GRAND VIEW, Mo., April 12 (AP)—Mrs. Martha Truman, 91, mother of Harry Truman, who succeeds to the Presidency of the United States, remained in seclusion at the home of her son tonight "deeply grieved" at the death of President Roosevelt.

Mrs. Truman's remarks were relayed by her daughter-in-law, Mrs. Vivian Truman, who said she feared to allow callers in the house because "the shock might be too bad for mother."

The daughter-in-law said she preferred not to ask Mrs. Truman's comment on her son's elevation to the Presidency at this time. She said:

"I don't believe it is best for anyone to talk to her now."

PRESIDENT HAILED AS WAR STRATEGIST

Some Military Observers Say He Exerted a Great Influence on War Movements

AND MADE VITAL DECISIONS

His Close Association With the Chiefs of Staff and His World Travels Are Stressed

By SIDNEY SHALETT

Special to THE NEW YORK TIMES.

WASHINGTON, April 12—As commander in chief of the United States Army and Navy, President Roosevelt was able to carry out his duties with a keen grasp of military and naval strategy, backed by a vast personal knowledge and enthusiasm for military subjects. Some military and naval observers in the Capitol suggested tonight that history would undoubtedly make it clear that President Roosevelt exerted more influence on military strategy than any previous wartime President.

From Casablanca to Teheran, from Quebec to Yalta, the President traveled great distances by air and sea to take part in momentous conferences that were of equal political and military importance. Wartime secrecy has masked many of his actions and observations in these historic discussions with the chiefs of staff of the United States and her principal allies in the war against the Axis, but hints dropped from time to time by men who have observed him at these conferences confirm that he made vital contributions to decisions affecting broad military strategy.

Left Details to Leaders

In a war in which the political and military issues often were so closely related, it has been hard to draw the line as to how the spheres of influence of political and military decisions were defined. One observer suggested that President Roosevelt's method of operating was to contribute all he could to discussions with his Chiefs of Staff leading up to military decisions, then to indicate in a broad sense what course he thought it wise to explore, but, after that, to leave the details to the military and naval leaders whose responsibility it was to execute them.

He kept in close touch with both the Joint (U. S.) Chiefs of Staff and the Combined (Anglo-American) Chiefs of Staff through his personal Chief of Staff, Fleet Admiral William D. Leahy, who sat on both bodies.

Leaders who had been with the President at some of the international war councils recalled his keen interest in any bold, new projects, particularly when revolutionary techniques and innovations were being introduced. Boldness was a keynote in his approach to such discussions, one observer stated. At the Quebec conference in August, 1943, for instance, the question of employing B-29 Superfortresses, then still in the experimental stage, from bases in China against Japan was introduced. The proposals were submitted to President Roosevelt, who asked questions about them in what was described as "extremely minute detail."

Later, in June 1944, the operations were begun in accordance with decisions in which the President had concurred.

Was Never "a Meddler"

One high-ranking officer commented that Mr. Roosevelt's approach to new military technique was "how is it going to work?" He wanted to understand the details, but his interest never was shown in what might be termed a "meddling sense," this observer stated.

President Roosevelt met many times with Prime Minister Churchill and on less frequent occasions with Marshal Stalin and other heads of state on military and political matters. His first war-time meeting with Mr. Churchill was in August, 1941, off the Newfoundland coast, when the historic Atlantic Charter was drawn up.

Soon after Pearl Harbor, Mr. Churchill came to Washington to see him. The British Prime Minister returned to his capital in June, 1942.

Mapped Italian Campaigns

In January, 1943, Mr. Roosevelt travelled 16,965 miles by plane, train and automobile to North Africa, via South America, for the Casablanca Conferences, at which the Sicilian and Italian campaigns were planned. Efforts were made then to compose the viewpoints of the two French military leaders, General Giraud and General De Gaulle.

Mr. Churchill came to Washington for a third time in May, 1943, and then, in August, for the important Quebec conferencees, at which vital decisions affecting the Pacific war were taken. Mr. Churchill came back to Washington with the President and they continued their talks.

In November, 1943, Mr. Roosevelt and Mr. Churchill met at Cairo with Generalissimo Chiang Kai-shek then flew to Teheran for conferences with Marshal Stalin. Then they returned to Cairo, and, on Dec. 4, met with President Inonu of Turkey.

In February, 1945, Mr. Roosevelt attended what was to be his last international conference—the Crimean Conference at Yalta, when the three powers, the United States, Britain and Soviet Russia, agreed on plans for "the final defeat of the common enemy."

Though nothing was revealed officially at the time about Russia's possible entrance into the Pacific war, it is generally believed that the spokesmen for the three powers explored this subject. It is significant that Russia's denunciation of her neutrality pact followed this last meeting of the "Big Three."

President Roosevelt's duties as Commander in Chief also carried him to Pearl Harbor last July for vital conferences with Gen. Douglas MacArthur and Admiral Chester W. Nimitz, affecting the Pacific war. He traveled far and wide in visiting Army installations in this country also, for he wanted to see at first-hand what the millions of men who had been inducted into the armed forces were doing.

Navy Interest Unflagging

The President was known for his keen interest in the Navy—his first love, since he had been Assistant Secretary of the Navy during the first World War. He was rarely happier than when cruising on a warship, and an old Navy cape was his favorite outer garment.

Yet he developed a similarly keen interest in the techniques of ground and air war. Some air officers, in fact, have commented in the past on Mr. Roosevelt's remarkable understanding of the theory and application of air power.

He has been credited with giving General H. H. Arnold, commanding officer of Army Air Forces, the green light prior to our actual entry into the war for drawing up a comprehensive air-war plan for use in case we became involved. General Arnold put some of his best planners to work on the matter, and thus, when war came, the AAF at least was ready with the plan of action it intended to follow.

His study at the White House constantly was being visited by Gen. George C. Marshall, Chief of Staff of the Army; Admiral Ernest J. King, Commander in Chief of the Fleet, and other prominent military figures. Every important field commander or admiral, here for conferences, reported at the White House to the Commander in Chief.

Often special messengers from the Army and Navy chiefs were sent to the White House at late hours to give the President personal reports on highly important developments.

War Heroes on Duty Here

Maj. Gen. Homer M. Groninger, port commander of the New York Port of Embarkation, Brooklyn, announced yesterday that nearly 4,000 combat veterans, 382 of them holders of the Purple Heart and forty-three others with awards ranging from the bronze star to the Distinguished Service Cross, are now on duty at the Army's New York Port of Embarkation.

SHE CARRIES BRAVELY ON

Mrs. Franklin D. Roosevelt — The New York Times Studio

Men at the Front Are Shocked by News; They Fear Effect on Peace Negotiations

By RICHARD J. H. JOHNSTON

By Wireless to THE NEW YORK TIMES.

WITH THE SEVENTH ARMY, Friday, April 13—Profound shock and deep concern for the strength of the United States position at the peace table were expressed by our troops along this front in the early hours this morning when the news of President Roosevelt's death was brought to them. It was with disbelief that many received the shocking report which was picked up on the radios and relayed by word of mouth from unit to unit up and down this front.

"This is a great tragedy and it will put a new slant on the peace conference," said Sgt. George Markel of Santa Ana, Calif.

Expressing disbelief, Corp. Israel Goldberg of St. Louis declared:

"I can't believe it. Were people at home prepared for this or told about it?"

"We are so close to victory it is a terrible time for this to happen," said Corp. Robert E. Viedt of South Dakota.

Pfc. John Lynch, Brooklyn, declared:

"I couldn't believe such a thing could happen.

"President Roosevelt was so important to us I can hardly believe he is gone."

By Wireless to THE NEW YORK TIMES.

GUAM, Friday, April 13—The deepest gloom settled over this advance headquarters of the Pacific Fleet as the word spread among Navy men that President Roosevelt had died suddenly at Warm Springs.

The men of the fleet knew that they had lost not only their Commander in Chief but a good friend—because the Navy always was close to Franklin Roosevelt's heart from his earliest years.

Officers who heard the news from correspondents who had received the Army news flash by radio could scarcely believe it.

"My God!" was the immediate and almost universal reaction, and most of them could say no more.

The President had been expected to come to the Pacific war theatre next summer on one of his periodic war inspection visits.

20-Year-Intervals Prove Fatal Election Harbinger

By The Associated Press.

President Roosevelt's death yesterday carried on an American tradition that Presidents elected at twenty-year intervals die in office.

The list included:

1840—William Henry Harrison.
1860—Abraham Lincoln.
1880—James A. Garfield.
1900—William McKinley.
1920—Warren G. Harding.
1940—Franklin D. Roosevelt.

ROOSEVELT CLOSED MIND AT SPRINGS

Set Pace in Fellowship as He Shed Cares of World, Superintendent Says

The President died in surroundings he probably loved nearly as much as his own home in Hyde Park.

In Warm Springs, where he went for complete relaxation, he apparently was able to close his mind to burdens of State and enter completely into the spirit of the sun-washed little colony of fellow "polio" sufferers.

In fact, the President himself set the pace and gave Warm Springs its tone, its spirit of fellowship and democratic association in which the affliction of infantile paralysis was a common and compelling bond.

This was the estimate of Louis Haughey, superintendent for the last five years of the Warm Springs Foundation, who is now in New York to take a post of wider scope with the National Foundation for Infantile Paralysis. On request, and pointing out that he was just an employe of the foundation who had had an opportunity to observe the President during his visits, he described Mr. Roosevelt's visits, and related how often he demonstrated at Warm Springs his infinite capacity for friendship.

Arrived on March 30

The President went to Warm Springs on March 30 and appeared to be in usual health, but looked worn and tired. Warm Springs itself is a tiny place of some 300 persons, and the foundation estate near by has a normal population of about 400. The President always entered into the easy life with great joy, driving about the rough wooded lanes, many of which he planned and supervised himself, going in his specially equipped car over terrain which, Mr. Haughey said, "I wouldn't drive any kind of car along." He called the patients and the doctors by name, and some of the old Negro attendants who worked around the buildings and gardens knew him as a gay and enthusiastic friend.

One hundred and thirty-three patients were there at the last count, and in the garden cottages were a number of persons who are no longer patients but who just like it and remain there. When the President came the foundation authorities usually had a week or ten days' notice to make arrangements, and when he came everyone knew that at least once during the visit the President would come over and eat with them in the main hall, telling stories, chatting with the children and welcoming new "guests" in his capacity as ranking old-timer.

Tireless Interest Recalled

"He was tirelessly interested in the foundation work and made employes accompany him on inspection tours," Mr. Haughey said. "We saw the most human side of the President. I am a dyed-in-the-wool Republican, but I just lost my heart to him personally. I've seen him go to a tenant farmer's—a man totally illiterate and pale with embarrassment and fright—and in a few minutes he'd be leaning on the side of the President's car, waving his arms and talking animatedly. More than any man I've ever known, he had the knack of making people feel at ease.

"Before the war the secretaries with him would go play golf and Mr. Roosevelt would drive along with them, making fun of their game. Before the war, which brought some restrictions, you would see him in the outdoor pool, with children and other adults splashing alongside, and the President having a grand time. At night he would get in his car and drive around and call on somebody, or find a party going on and join it. Politics and international affairs were taboo there, and they would not be mentioned at any of the gatherings.

"The President was amazingly able to forget his worries and take up playing. He was one of the few men who had absolute command of his thoughts, for it was obvious by the deep interest he showed in others and in the foundation that he was thinking at that time about them, and nothing else, with the big questions shut out or locked up in the back of his mind."

BRITAIN MOURNS AS FOR HER OWN

People Feel They Have Lost a Personal Friend and Worry Over the Future Peace

By CLIFTON DANIEL

Special to THE NEW YORK TIMES.

LONDON, Friday, April 13—Great Britain mourned for President Roosevelt today as deeply as if he had been one of her own great sons.

Shock, sorrow and fear were mingled in the faces of those who heard the news at midnight and afterward.

With Prime Minister Churchill, who was deeply affected, the people of Britain felt that they had lost a gallant personal friend. In the coming days this country will do honor to his memory in a way that will leave no doubt of her gratitude. It is the gratitude of a people who feel that the President was, in spirit and in fact, one of their saviors.

A great measure of the glory that Britain has felt in recent weeks in the triumph of Allied arms died with Mr. Roosevelt. No event since the military reverses of the summer of 1942 has left such a deep mark of depression on this country.

Faith Put in Triumvirate

Ever since the catastrophe of Pearl Harbor, which caused scarcely more pain in London than the news of the President's death, the British masses have put their faith and trust in the Allied triumvirate in which he was a partner.

By contrast with the high hopes raised by Yalta, doubts have been assailing people and politicians of Britain in the past few weeks—doubts especially about the ability of the United Nations to insure future peace.

As always, the people were beginning to turn again toward the "Big Three" to guide them out of their bewilderment. The loss of Mr. Roosevelt can, for the moment at least, only increase their concern.

It had been hoped by many in this country that Mr. Roosevelt, in his projected address to the San Francisco World Conference would have breathed inspiration into an assembly the value of which is now questioned by many.

Flynn and Baruch Get News

One of Mr. Roosevelt's oldest political associates, Edward J. Flynn, and one of his most intimate advisers, Bernard Baruch, were in the same hotel in London when the news of their friend's death reached them. Mr. Flynn immediately went to Mr. Baruch and they remained alone for some time.

Prime Minister Churchill had not retired when the news reached London just before last midnight. He had returned to No. 10 Downing Street only a short while earlier from a dinner party with British and Commonwealth delegates to the San Francisco conference.

There was no immediate statement from No. 10 Downing Street. It was explained that the Prime Minister, as was customary, would speak from the Commons and that, moreover, Mr. Roosevelt was his personal friend.

There was no doubt of the sadness which had fallen on the Prime Minister's residence.

Calls Pour in on No. 10

Within a few minutes after the bulletin reached London, telephone calls were pouring into No. 10 Downing Street. Between calls, the telephone girl there was heard to say: "Isn't it terrible!"

News of the President's death was conveyed to King George VI at midnight and the King received it with profound regret.

The elderly Jan C. Smuts, Prime Minister of South Africa, had gone to bed after the dinner party which Mr. Churchill had attended and at which Foreign Minister Anthony Eden was host, and his staff decided not to awaken him.

An American Air Forces major, who heard the news just as he was coming home after a gay evening on leave in London, could only say: "Oh, my God!"

One American woman, a friend of Mrs. Franklin D. Roosevelt, turned ashen and hid her face in her hands as she heard the news.

Ambassador John G. Winant was in London but was not immediately accessible. The American Embassy was deluged with telephone calls from the very moment that the news became known in London.

Prime Ministers Speak

Prime Ministers of the Dominions immediately expressed their great sense of loss and their sympathy. Prime Minister Fraser of New Zealand said:

"I deeply deplore the passing of a great and good man, a world statesman and leader. His death at this moment is a colossal loss to mankind. The deep and sincere sympathy of the Government and people of New Zealand go out to Mrs. Roosevelt and the family and to the whole American nation."

Deputy Prime Minister Forde of Australia said:

"The President's death is a very great loss to the American nation and the Allied cause. His personal contribution to the United States war effort marked him as one of the outstanding leaders of this age. His passing will be mourned not only by the people of the United States, but by the people of every freedom-loving nation. He will go down as one of the greatest American Presidents of all time.

"It is tragedy that as he worked so hard to save the peoples of the world from totalitarian dictatorships, he was not spared to rejoice in the great victory now within sight. He gave everything to the cause of freedom and liberty and did not spare himself."

There probably has never been—certainly not in modern times—a foreigner who was more loved in this country than was Mr. Roosevelt.

His Popularity Was Wide

His popularity as a war leader and statesman was second only to that of Mr. Churchill. His speeches were read and heard here with profound interest. The British people had faith in him as a defender of the oppressed, the inspiration of American military prowess, and the architect of the future.

There was a genuine and widespread wish in this country to see the President here at the end of the war. There is no doubt that he would have received a public ovation the like of which no other man before him had ever received.

Although the British have had their tiffs with their American Allies throughout the war, they never doubted that the President personally was their friend.

They remembered tonight that it was he who sent British soldiers and Home Guards rifles with which to defend these islands in the grim hour when Britain stood unarmed against Germany in the summer of 1940.

They felt that to him, as much as to any man, they owed such measures as the Lend-Lease Act which kept Britain from going hungry and unprotected in the direst period of her struggle to regain her strength.

Victory Spirit Dampened

Not only was Britain's victory spirit dampened by the news of the President's death, but also its hopes for the future were affected. Great reliance had been placed in Mr. Roosevelt, and his skill as an international negotiator as demonstrated so often in his meetings with Mr. Churchill and Marshal Stalin to help bring the world through the agony of reconstruction.

Recalling the miracle whereby a peaceful nation was turned almost overnight into a great "arsenal for democracy," the British had been hoping that the same genius would help bring order and assurance of future peace out of the chaos of a war-rent world.

The British people do not know President Truman. They not only knew Mr. Roosevelt but felt that through Mr. Churchill, who called Mr. Roosevelt by his first name, they shared a personal friendship.

The President and the Prime Minister talked by transatlantic telephone almost daily.

TRIBUTES IN LONDON PRESS

Daily Mail Says, 'Invalid in Strife Turned Forces Against Enemies'

By Cable to THE NEW YORK TIMES.

LONDON, Friday, April 13—Two words "Roosevelt Dead" formed the headlines on practically all London newspapers this morning. News of the President's end reached Fleet Street after the early evening editions had gone to press, and it was well after midnight before the first papers carrying the news reached the streets.

The Daily Mail and Daily Telegraph carried editorials in their later editions expressing shock over Mr. Roosevelt's death.

The London Times put "Death of Mr. Roosevelt" alongside the paper's name at top of page one. Although it carried no editorial in its later editions, The Times carried three columns of news and biography of Mr. Roosevelt. The Daily Express headlined the story with "Roosevelt Dead." with this subhead: "In the Hour of Victory, America Loses Her President. Tragic News at Midnight: Washington Cabinet Meets."

"Franklin Delano Roosevelt, the man who led America out of the depression, the man who led America through the war, lies dead on the very threshold of victory at a moment when the armies of the United States are almost in sight of Berlin," The Daily Mail said in an editorial headed, "The Great American."

Invalid in Strife

"This aristocrat in a democracy, this internationalist in a land half isolationist, this invalid in a world of strife, found the strength to check, to harness, to govern, and finally to turn the forces that threatened America with catastrophe and destruction into forces that created a healthier, sane people." Reviewing the President's accomplishments in the depression, in sponsoring lend-lease and carrying that legislation to a successful conclusion, The Mail paid tribute to the President's foresight. The paper added:

"Bitterly ironically, the author of American victory lies dead. But his work is done. To his wife, to the Roosevelt sons fighting in their country's armies across the seas, the sympathy of Britain goes out in full measure. And for Franklin Roosevelt's yet larger family—the hundred and thirty million American citizens to whom he spoke week by week—our sympathy is no less heartfelt."

"A Leader With Lincoln"

The Daily Telegraph said in its editorial that the President "will be remembered with Abraham Lincoln as a leader who set and kept his country on the path of true greatness with a steadiness of purpose and grandeur of vision unsurpassed in records of mankind. His passing leaves a gap in all our hearts and in the counsels of the Allies which it will be hard to fill. This country, in particular, owes him a debt which can never be repaid for his understanding, help and confidence in its darkest hours. When we had few confident friends he was an unremitting and undespairing one. That's why we venture to share with peculiar poignancy in the sorrow of the American people."

Fleet Street was itself stunned by the news of the President's passing. In city rooms of dailies those not engaged in writing about the President's death discussed the news. They offered condolences to American correspondents who visited the newspaper offices.

Mrs. Roosevelt Flies to Georgia; Was at Benefit When News Came

'Trouper to the Last,' Reporter Says as She Leaves—Sons, in Distant War Zones, Unlikely to Arrive for Funeral

Special to THE NEW YORK TIMES.

WASHINGTON, April 12—Six minutes after Vice President Harry S. Truman was sworn in as President, Mrs. Franklin D. Roosevelt, this nation's colorful First Lady for the last twelve years, entered a car under the White House portico and swung out of its driveway as a bereaved private citizen to fly to Warm Springs and get her husband's body.

At 7:15, a black-clad Mrs. Roosevelt and her daughter, Mrs. Anna Boettiger, in a red suit, appeared in the White House doorway and talked for a few minutes. Mrs. Boettiger walked with her mother as far as the waiting limousine. The President's secretary, Stephen T. Early, and his long-time personal physician, Rear Admiral Ross T. McIntyre, Surgeon General of the Navy, followed her into the car. Mrs. Roosevelt's tall figure was erect, and her step did not falter.

As she entered the car, she leaned over to bow to the little group of ushers, doormen and a few members of her press conference who stood there. A few hours before these newspaper women had been asking her questions on the pending United Nations conference and details of her week's activities.

"A trouper to the last," one commented.

The plane taking Mrs. Roosevelt, Mr. Early and Admiral McIntire to Warm Springs left Washington about 7:40 P. M.

First Lady at Thrift Shop

Word of President Roosevelt's death had come to the White House with complete suddenness.

"It was such a shock to all of us that none of us can take it in," said Miss Malvina Thompson, secretary to Mrs. Roosevelt. "It was absolutely out of the blue and we can't believe it yet."

She said that Mrs. Roosevelt had been attending a thrift shop benefit at the Sulgrave Club when a long-distance message came from Warm Springs, and she was called back to the White House to receive it.

To Mrs. Roosevelt fell the lot of finishing the last bit of business of her husband's Administration, informing the Vice President. Mr. Early told reporters that when Mrs. Roosevelt told Mr. Truman that the President had passed on, the Vice President asked:

"What can I do?"

"You can tell us what we can do," Mrs. Roosevelt replied.

Mr. Early later said that Mrs. Boettiger received the news while visiting her son, Johnnie, who is ill at the Naval Hospital in suburban Bethesda, Md. Mrs. Boettiger accompanied her father on many of his trips, including his recent journey to Yalta, but had not gone to Warm Springs because of her son's illness. She and her husband, Maj. John Boettiger, remained at the White House when Mrs. Roosevelt left for Warm Springs.

The word at the White House was that the large and widely scattered Roosevelt family probably would not be summoned for the funeral services because it would be impossible for the four sons, all overseas in the armed services to get here.

Three Sons in Pacific Area

Col. James Roosevelt, eldest son, is in the Pacific area with the Marines. Brig. Gen. Elliott Roosevelt, the second son, is in the European theatre. Lieut. Franklin D. Roosevelt Jr. and Lieut. John Roosevelt are with the United States Navy in the Pacific. Mrs. Franklin D. Roosevelt Jr., the former Ethel du Pont of the Delaware family, is the only daughter-in-law near by, as the wives of James, Elliott and John are in California.

The feeling at the White House was that since all thirteen of the grandchildren were here Inauguration Day they would want to remember their grandfather as he was then, and that no attempt would be made to bring them all here for funeral services and burial at Hyde Park. They are Sara and Kate, daughters of James Roosevelt; Anna Eleanor, Curtis and John, children of Anna; William Donner, Chandler, Elliott Jr. and David, children of Elliott; Franklin 3d and Christopher, sons of Franklin Jr., and Haven and Anne Sturgis, children of John.

Mrs. Roosevelt had had her busy schedule planned for the next week, including a speaking trip to New York, and she had set her next press conference for a week from tomorrow. It was to have been her last before her scheduled trip with her husband to the San Francisco conference.

Just a few moments before Mrs. Roosevelt left the White House another outstanding woman figure of this Administration, Secretary of Labor Frances Perkins, departed. She was the last Cabinet member to come out of the executive offices to her waiting car after the swearing-in ceremony. There were tears in her eyes.

Sorry for People

WASHINGTON, April 12 (AP)—Mrs. Roosevelt said, when informed of the death of the President:

"I am more sorry for the people of the country and the world than I am for us."

Sought Office Ten Times And Met Defeat Twice

Franklin Delano Roosevelt submitted his candidacy for public office to the voters on ten occasions during his career. He was successful on eight of the ten, but twice went down to defeat.

He scored his first victory in 1910, when he was elected to the New York State Senate, to which he was re-elected in 1912. In 1914 he was defeated by James W. Gerard in the Democratic primary for the nomination for United States Senator. He was defeated again in 1920 when he ran for the Vice Presidency on the Democratic ticket with James M. Cox.

Elected Governor of New York in 1928, Mr. Roosevelt was returned to that post in 1930 and then, of course, was elected President of the United States four times, in 1932, 1936, 1940 and 1944.

SHOCK, DISBELIEF ECHO IN CONGRESS

'Must Go Forward to Goal He Set,' Barkley Declares in Tribute to Roosevelt

By FREDERICK R. BARKLEY

Special to THE NEW YORK TIMES.

WASHINGTON, April 12—Expressions of shock, and sometimes even disbelief, echoed on Capitol Hill today at the news of President Roosevelt's death. Members of all parties joined in voicing these feelings.

Both House and Senate had adjourned for the day when the news came. The Senate had quit for an hour earlier, with a considerable number of its members out of town. The House, with only a corporal's guard present, had ended a pro forma session several hours earlier, as its members are generally on an unofficial Easter vacation.

"I am too shocked to talk," said Senator Alben W. Barkley, Senate majority leader. "It is one of the worst tragedies that ever happened to this nation or the world. But we must tighten our belts and go forward to the goal he set for us."

Representative Sam Rayburn of Texas, Speaker of the House, recently returned from a brief trip to Texas, said he was "too shocked and flustered" to make any comment whatever.

Later he issued the following statement:

"We know not how to interpret God in the way he performs. The world has lost one of the great leaders of all time. President Roosevelt's passing will shock and sadden good people everywhere. The American nation has been well led in every crisis. In Harry Truman we have a leader in whom I have complete confidence."

A Great Leader, Says White

Said Senator Wallace H. White of Maine, Republican leader in that body:

"The news is tragic. A great leader of our people and of world thought and effort has gone. He has had in amazing degree the loyalty and affection of countless millions here and throughout the world. Great as is his country's loss, his efforts in behalf of victory for our arms and for a just and peaceful world will continue. I express my deepest sympathy with his family."

The fact that the President's death came on the eve of the San Francisco conference he had promoted brought references to effect of his death on this world peace-making gathering.

Said Senator Tom Connally of Texas, a Senatorial delegate to this conference, and chairman of the Senate Foreign Relations Committee:

"My personal grief is tremendous. The people of the world who dream of a successful termination of the war and the erection of machinery for permanent peace and security will shed tears at his untimely death."

Representative Sol Bloom of New York, chairman of the House Foreign Affairs Committee, declined to speculate on what effect the President's death would have on the conference, but said:

"But we must carry through to win a peace that will be a monument to the President, who fought so long and hard for it and who died in that fight."

Vandenberg Cites Courage

Senator Arthur H. Vandenberg of Michigan, a Republican delegate to the conference, said:

"President Roosevelt leaves an imperishable imprint on the history of America and the world. Those who disagreed with him have always recognized his amazing genius in behalf of his always vigorous ideals. He mastered his own physical handicaps with a courage which never lapsed as he fought his way to an unprecedented pinnacle at home and to dominant influence around the world.

"His untimely death will be mourned at every hearthstone and on every battlefront where freedom wins the victory to which he literally gave his life. A successful peace must be his monument. A new President takes over tremendous responsibility in this critical hour. America moves on—mourning her tragic loss, pledging her loyalty to a new leader who shall be sustained with our united prayers."

Said Representative Clarence Cannon, Democrat, of Missouri, chairman of the House Appropriations Committee:

"My God, how terrible! The greatest man in the world." Representative Robert R. Ramspeck of Georgia, Democratic House Whip, made almost identical comment.

John W. McCormack of Massachusetts, Democratic House leader, said:

"President Roosevelt was one of the great men of all time—a builder of human values. He will go down in history as the savior of democracy. His death is an irreparable loss to the world."

MOST-FAMOUS SON MOURNED AT GROTON

Special to THE NEW YORK TIMES.

GROTON, Mass., April 12—Groton was shocked tonight by the death of its most illustrious son.

News of the sudden death of President Roosevelt, a member of the Class of 1900, came to the students and faculty as they sat down to supper. The Rev. John Crocker, headmaster, immediately led them into an adjoining school room where they offered prayers for the President, his family and for the nation. The flag at the school was lowered to half staff.

Special services will be held tomorrow at 8:30 A. M. when the 185 students gather for morning chapel.

President Roosevelt was preceded in death by his former teacher, the Rev. Dr. Endicott Peabody, who died last November at the age of 87, and of whom the President once said: "As long as I live his influence will mean more to me than that of any other people next to my father and mother."

Dr. Peabody was founder and headmaster of the school for fifty-six years, and had officiated at the marriage of President and Mrs. Roosevelt.

Last Words: 'Terrific Headache'

Continued From Page 1

fidential secretary, and two cousins, Miss Laura Delano and Miss Margaret Suckley.

Dr. Bruenn said that he called Vice Admiral Ross T. McIntire, White House physician, in Washington, and that Admiral McIntire in turn called Dr. James E. Paullin of Atlanta, an internal medicine practicioner and honorary consultant to the Navy surgeon general.

Dr. Paullin was present when Dr. Bruenn gave the statement of the cause of death to reporters of the three national news services.

News of the President's death spread quickly and caused many a tear among the 125 infantile paralysis patients at the foundation here.

Meyor Frank W. Allcorn of Warm Springs was giving a barbecue at his mountain cabin this afternoon for the President and about fifty other guests. Mr. Allcorn was awaiting the President's arrival when reporters got word through the Army Signal Corps radio telephone and summer White House telephone communication to rush to the foundation.

Miss Louise Hackmeister, veteran White House chief telephone operator, could hardly talk in her excitement to round up those who had to be informed.

Tears and quivering voices accompanied the announcement of the President's death by Mr. Hassett.

Miss Tully, Mrs. Alice Wineger, Mr. Hassett's secretary, and Mrs. Dorothy Brady, Presidential stenographer, sat tense on a sofa as Mr. Hassett gave the news. He said that the last piece of legislation Mr. Roosevelt signed was one to continue the Commodity Credit Corporation and increase its borrowing power.

"I Make a Law," President Said

Mr. Hassett added that as he did so, Mr. Roosevelt made his usual comment at such time:

"Here's where I make a law."

Mr. Hassett said that the President's mail was quite heavy on his last day, and that "it took him at least twenty minutes to sign papers."

Other papers Mr. Roosevelt signed among his last official acts were the appointments of a batch of small town postmasters, including one for Panaca, Nev., as well as several citations for the Legion of Merit.

The President went about his final work dressed in a blue suit with vest and a four-in-hand tie.

Needed More Weight

Mr. Roosevelt arrived at Warm Springs March 30. He had been under weight and his doctors wanted him to take it easy to see if he could regain the poundage at which he felt comfortable.

Rumors had been heard the last few days that the President was not picking up as much as his doctors would have liked.

He received reporters last Thursday and, in the presence of Sergio Osmena, president of the Philippine Commonwealth, told of his desire to grant full independence to the islands by autumn.

Mr. Roosevelt also outlined ambitious post-war plans for American participation in the Western Pacific to prevent further Japanese aggression.

He said that the United States and the other United Nations must accept trusteeships over Japanese-mandated islands, build new naval and air bases and help the Philippines rebuild, economically, after the commonwealth becomes a self-governing nation.

Report Was to Be Held Up

Reports of this news conference were to have been withheld for security reasons until Mr. Roosevelt returned to Washington.

The President had planned to stay here another week, then he was to return to the Capital and spend one day before taking a train to San Francisco to open the United Nations Conference on International Organization.

This was Mr. Roosevelt's second stay here in four months. He spent nineteen days here only last November-December.

White House reporters had recently noticed his gray pallor, and it had caused considerable comment among them.

Mr. Roosevelt's voice also had become weak in recent months, and he frequently asked reporters to repeat their questions.

This was attributable, according to those close to him, to a sinus leakage into the throat which caused slight constrictions.

The death announcement was made in the center of the 2,000-acre foundation for polio treatment which the President helped found more than twenty years ago. That was before he began serving his first term as Governor of New York.

SECOND TERM BEGAN WITH LABOR AT WAR

Budget Also Was Badly Out of Balance When Roosevelt Took Oath on Jan. 20, 1937

FIGHT ON SUPREME COURT

His Prestige Suffered in the Controversy, but Popularity Was Restored by 1940

In a great downpour of rain Franklin Delano Roosevelt was inaugurated President of the United States for his second successive term on Jan. 20, 1937.

This departure from the former inauguration date of March 4 was the result of the adoption of the Twentieth Amendment to the Constitution, known as the "lame duck" amendment, which shortened the period between the election and the assumption of office by the President and by members of Congress.

During the campaign President Roosevelt had had much to occupy him besides political matters. The national budget was badly out of balance, a gross Federal deficit of $2,096,966,300 being reported on Sept. 1 by Secretary of the Treasury Henry Morgenthau for the fiscal year 1936-37. This was nearly $1,000,000,000 more than was forecast in January although it was the lowest thus far under the New Deal.

Labor Strife Brewing

In addition, the President and the nation were confronted with the first indications of what was to be an epocal fight in the ranks of American labor. In August ten unio.. of the recently organized Committee for Industrial Organization (later the Congress of Industrial Organizations) were suspended from the American Federation of Labor after John L. Lewis, the CIO leader, and William Green, head of the A. F. of L., had failed to compose their differences concerning the craft union as against the industrial union. The President, who had pledged himself to the National Conference on Labor Legislation to support Federal and State minimum wage laws and the forty-hour week, for the time being adopted a hands-off policy in this fight, the implications of which were not yet fully foreseen.

Emergency relief still continued to be one of the most pressing problems confronting the President. Business was improving but employment indices were not keeping up with this improvement.

With his position described as "a little left of center," Mr. Roosevelt indicated at the outset of his second term that he would press forward along the liberal paths of his first administration.

In the face of a series of industrial outbreaks attending the efforts of Mr. Lewis to organize heavy industry under the banner of the CIO, Mr. Roosevelt kept silent for many months. This attitude was described by the President's opponents as due to Mr. Lewis' and the CIO's financial and ballot support at the polls. Organizing activities continued, labor-management strife and riots bordering on open warfare shook the nation.

Merchants and business men, many of whom had supported President Roosevelt at the last election, began to insist that the President use his influence to end the disorders that were causing hardship to labor and business alike. It was not until July that the President spoke. At a White House press conference he quoted the Mercutio of Shakespeare's "Romeo and Juliet": "A plague on both your houses."

Addressing a joint session of the Seventy-fifth Congress, on Jan. 6, 1938, President Roosevelt voiced his dissatisfaction with the attitude of the United States Supreme Court in declaring unconstitutional certain New Deal measures, among them the NRA and the AAA. The message said:

"It was their (the founders') definite intent and expectation that a liberal (Supreme Court) interpretation in years to come would give to the Congress the same relative powers as they themselves gave to Congress over national problems in their day."

In several addresses President Roosevelt had indicated that he was not particularly impressed by the functions of the United States Supreme Court. Nor was his regard for the high court increased when Chief Justice Charles Evans Hughes coldly declined his invitation to consult on legislative measures that might eventually come before the court.

Crisis in the Court Proposal

President Roosevelt formed a strong resolve to curb the court's power. Keeping his intentions a complete secret from his Cabinet, the Democratic leaders in Congress and his coterie of intimate advisers, he directed Attorney General Homer S. Cummings to work out several plans to clip the court's wings. When the plans were placed before the President he selected the one dearest to Mr. Cummings's heart.

The nation was not, however, prepared for the drastic program of Federal judiciary reform announced by President Roosevelt on Feb. 5. It precipitated a crisis such as the government had not known since the Civil War.

The battle raged for five months. Conservative Democrats and Republicans were ranged against Presidential prestige and power. In the midst of the strife, Justice Willis Van Devanter, one of the oldest, most often under attack as a "reactionary," retired. The court reversed itself, turning to a "more liberal interpretation of the Constitution." It upheld the Wagner Labor Relations Act and social security legislation. On July 22, by a vote of 70 to 20, the bill was killed in the Senate. Mr. Roosevelt had lost the battle, but he had won the war. Death, retirement and resignation permitted him, ultimately, to appoint more justices than had any other President.

The fury of the storm over the Supreme Court fight was revived in August of the same year, when the President sent to the Senate the name of Senator Hugo L. Black of Alabama as an associate justice of the Supreme Court to succeed Justice Van Devanter. The President picked Senator Black apparently with an eye toward selecting a loyal New Dealer, which the Senator was, and yet one whom the Senate would have to confirm, almost as a matter of Senatorial courtesy.

There were hints during the Senate debate that Senator Black had once been a member of the Ku Klux Klan. The Senate rejected the implications, and it was not until a month later that The Pittsburgh Post-Gazette produced documentary evidence that Justice Black had been a Klan member from 1923 to 1925. Justice Black, in a nation-wide radio address, admitted that he had been a member of the Klan, said he was no longer one, and took his place on the bench. He had been in Europe when the charges first were made, and the delay in answering them created an unfavorable impression around the nation. The storm, as others, died down eventually.

Danger of New Depression

John L. Lewis began his battle with the President about this time, accusing the Administration of indifference to the rights of workers in the strikes in the "Little Steel" plants in Ohio.

The President received another blow from Mr. Lewis early in September when the CIO chief warned him that he would lose the support of a large part of organized labor if he did not support the CIO.

Strengthened by his belief as a result of his Western trip that a majority of the country was still with him on New Deal reforms, the President issued a call for a special session of Congress to meet on Nov. 15 and take up legislation on wages and hours, crop-control, Government reorganization, anti-trust curbs and regional planning in the form of "seven little TVA's."

But the chief event of the month was the rapid drop in stock market prices, culminating in a decline that had been going on for several months, and that suddenly attracted public attention to the danger of another 1929. The same symptoms were visible as in the 1929-33 depression—a stock market crash, falling commodity prices, a business recession and growing unemployment.

The President immediately swung into action in an effort to stop the recession and prevent it from developing into a new depression. He called in business leaders and economists for advice, announced his intention to achieve a balanced budget as soon as possible, and called for a decline in the Federal spending policy of the last few years.

In an attempt to encourage business and industry to take the place of Federal spending with expansion policies of their own, the President promised a modification of taxes deemed harmful by business and instituted "peace negotiations" with the great public utility systems of the country, offering a modification of the Government's power program in return for pledges by the utility leaders to spend large sums for expansion of their facilities.

President Roosevelt was unsuccessful in his efforts to "purge" the Democratic party of conservative anti-New Dealers. He was widely criticized for using the Presidential office to bring pressure to bear for the election of New Deal candidates in the 1938 Congressional elections, but he insisted that, as head of the Democratic party, he had every right to speak out where his principles and policies were concerned.

The country saw it differently, and this was one of the reasons, together with the failure of economic recovery to proceed fast enough, the continuance of widespread unemployment, dissatisfaction with the working of the Wagner Labor Relations Act and disapproval of the Administration's failure to take a firm stand against the sit-down strike, among other things, that caused sweeping reverses for the New Deal at the polls in November, 1938.

Another result of the election was to remove the 1939 Congress definitely out of the category of a "rubber-stamp" assembly, as previous Congresses under the New Deal had been called. Without a formal coalition, Republicans and conservative Democrats joined forces in an effort to curtail the President's spending program, institute economies and start toward a balanced budget.

The new Congress did not reject all of the President's reforms, however, as it adopted a new farm bill, a Wages and Hours Law less drastic than the bill that previously had been defeated, and a modified form of the President's bill for the reorganization of the executive departments and agencies

Other Pictorial Chapters From the Life of Mr. Roosevelt

Son Elliott holds a large tarpon hooked by the President during a fishing trip in 1937

Associated Press

Relaxing during holidays from his duties. He is shown at Hyde Park in 1932.

The New York Times

Roosevelt Regime, From '33, Longest in Nation's History

Started in Economic Depression—Saw Us Faced With Gravest Problems and the World With Its Worst War

Franklin Delano Roosevelt, the thirty-first President of the United States, held that title longer than any man in history, and dealt, during his time, with the gravest problems, internal and external, which had faced the nation, and the world.

The internal crisis which existed at the time of his first inauguration, on March 4, 1933, when the nation's economic system was faltering and its financial organism paralyzed by fear, was followed in his third term by the global war, during which he and Winston Churchill emerged as leaders of the English-speaking world, and of much of the rest of it as well, regardless of language or customs.

The years between were packed with swift and drastic social and economic changes, to make Mr. Roosevelt the most controversial figure in American history. Beloved by millions, hated, admired, feared and scorned by countless adversaries, he did more to mold the future of the nation he headed, and the world he lived in, than anyone else. His character and his policies dominated.

The ultimate verdict of history upon Franklin D. Roosevelt will depend largely on the eventual outcome of the courses he selected—economic reforms at home, and the fight for democracy in the world, even when the latter involved a course that led to war.

Chose to Defy Dictators

So far as the war was concerned, with the bold confidence that was characteristic of him, he chose a policy of defiance of the dictators and aggressor nations, denunciation of efforts at appeasement and the unflinching extension of all-out material and moral support to the embattled democracies, which were locked in a death-grapple with the Axis powers that led to the attack on Pearl Harbor by the Japanese on Dec. 7, 1941.

It placed upon Mr. Roosevelt the responsibility of being Commander in Chief of the armed forces of the United States, of being, with Churchill and Stalin and Chiang Kai-shek, one of the guiding genii of the United Nations, when the responsibility was greatest, the armed forces the largest, and the alliance the most widespread, in history up to that time.

But had this last and greatest crisis of his life never arisen, there was still far more than enough in the life and deeds of Franklin D. Roosevelt to have filled a library of books. He had been prepared for his final ordeal by a public career of more than thirty years, which had given him an almost unrivaled schooling in the workings of government and a deep insight into the thought processes of the democratic masses of the country.

A State Senator Before 30

As a young New York State Senator who won nation-wide acclaim before he was 30 by a successful fight against Tammany; as Assistant Secretary of the Navy before and during our participation in the first World War; as the unsuccessful Democratic nominee for the Vice Presidency in 1920; and as Governor of New York for two terms beginning in 1928, he had achieved unusual honors even before his accession to the Presidency.

His public career was interrupted for several years by a sudden disaster that seemed at the time to have shattered it irretrievably. While he was swimming near his summer home at Campobello, N. B., in August, 1921, he was stricken with infantile paralysis. For months his life was in danger and it was almost a year before he could begin to get about on crutches. He never fully recovered the use of his lower limbs.

Mr. Roosevelt fought his ailment with the same courageous coolness that he displayed years later when, a few weeks before his first inauguration, he narrowly escaped assassination in Miami, Fla. He devoted his years of enforced leisure to wide reading, especially in the fields of American political and naval history, in which he was unusually well versed, and to carrying on an extensive correspondence with fellow-Democrats all over the United States.

Despite his physical handicap, which compelled him to lean on the arm of an aide while he was walking, Mr. Roosevelt enjoyed robust and vigorous health during most of his years of heavy burdens in his terms of office. Tall and broad-shouldered his weight varied only from 184 to 188. The cares of office put added lines into his handsome face, but never for long banished his smile from it.

A characteristic of the President that was remarked by all who were closely associated with him was his never-failing ability to dismiss from his mind even the gravest problems, once he had reached a decision. It was this capacity for relaxing as soon as the day's work was done that enabled him, his physicians said, to assume the burdens of presiding in wartime in at least as fine physical condition as he had known when he first entered the White House until comparatively recently.

Mr. Roosevelt was fortunate in other ways that helped his extraordinary career. He possessed unusual personal charm, which held to him many associates who questioned the wisdom of some of his policies. His distinguished bearing, made familiar to millions of people by countless news reel and newspaper pictures, was an asset. So was his richly timbred speaking voice, carried by radio into millions of American homes in countless fireside chats and formal addresses.

Gift for Vivid Phrases

He had a gift for vivid phrases that crystallized his policies for the multitude. In accepting his first nomination for the Presidency at the Democratic National Convention in Chicago on July 2, 1932, he pledged himself to "a new deal for the American people." Henceforth, through four Presidential campaigns and many stirring legislative battles, the term New Deal symbolized for his friends and foes alike the domestic policies he favored.

In the field of foreign relations he coined an almost equally well-known phrase when in his first inaugural he declared he would dedicate the nation to the policy of "the good neighbor." Eight years later, when he grimly resolved that this nation should furnish arms to Britain with which that country might fight for its life, he turned again to the simile of the good neighbor lending a garden hose to fight a fire, to justify his arms-loan plan to the American people.

In his bitterness, when the Supreme Court invalidated the National Recovery Act, he declared at a press conference that the court sought to relegate this country to "a horse and buggy age." His efforts on behalf of legislation designed to improve the social and economic lot of the less fortunate sections of the country were waged to the declaration that "one-third of this nation * * * is ill-fed, ill-clothed and ill-housed."

One of his battles with Congress in which he was defeated was in his attempt to reorganize the Supreme Court soon after his second inauguration. This precipitated a Congressional controversy unmatched in bitterness and in tense public interest since the fight over the League of Nations. And even in that instance his partisans asserted that he had won the substance if not the form of victory, when the court took a friendlier attitude toward New Deal legislation.

Won by Large Margins

Although the popularity of the New Deal with the people, as measured by mid-term Congressional elections and public opinion polls, waxed and waned, there never was any room for argument about the phenomenal and continuing personal popularity of Mr. Roosevelt. This was best illustrated by his success as the standard-bearer for the Democratic party, which, before his advent, had been the minority party in American politics for more than half a century.

In 1932, as the Democratic nominee opposing President Herbert Hoover, he carried forty-two States with 472 electoral votes, to six States with fifty-nine votes for his opponent. The popular vote was: Roosevelt 22,813,786, Hoover 15,759,266. In 1936 he carried every State but Maine and New Hampshire in defeating Governor Alfred M. Landon of Kansas. The electoral vote was 523 to 8; the popular vote was Roosevelt 27,751,612, Landon 16,681,913. In 1940 he defeated Wendell L. Willkie by an electoral vote of 449 to 82, and a popular vote of 27,243,466 to 22,304,755. In 1944 he defeated Governor Thomas E. Dewey of New York by an electoral vote of 432 to 99 and a popular vote of 25,602,505 to 22,006,278.

Even a brief recapitulation of the historic events of his Presidency would be a lengthy recital. The State papers and other documents of his public life alone fill a memorial library, erected at a cost of $250,000 on the Roosevelt family estate at Hyde Park, N. Y., as the gift of the historically minded President to the nation.

ROOSEVELT'S DEATH MOURNED BY IRISH

Dublin Newspapers Pay Tribute to Him as Great World Leader

By Cable to THE NEW YORK TIMES.

DUBLIN, Friday, April 13—The news of President Roosevelt's death reached here soon before midnight and caused profound regret. Throughout Ireland his great moral and spiritual qualities had won deep admiration, and he is mourned by all sections of the people.

The de Valera Government party's newspaper, "The Irish Press," paying tribute today in an editorial, says:

"No American of today had the stature of that remarkable man. For more than a generation he was a prominent figure in the political life of the United States, and the strength of his character was shown, when struck down by infantile paralysis, he refused to allow this personal calamity to drive him from what he regarded as his mission of public service.

"It was in 1932 that he was first elected to the Presidency. In those first years he showed courage and resource which have almost become a legend among a people whom he found in the midst of an economic panic bordering on despair, and whom he soon led back to self-confidence and self-reliance.

"As year followed year he established the worker and underprivileged in a position of security which they had not known previously in the history of their country.

"And finally he brought into this war a nation that had already been braced to meet its stresses, and whose vast material and manufacturing resources were already partially mobilized to fulfill the demands hitherto unknown to industry.

"The vigor of his leadership, his wide vision together with the gay courage of his character had made his fame known to every land. His death will bring the United States sympathy from many millions of peoples throughout the world and not the least sympathy of Irish men and women wherever they may be."

Irish Times says editorially, "He has died as he had lived, honored in varying but always in high degree by men of every nation. When clouds over the present sky have passed history will determine his true eminence. It has been said that Franklin Roosevelt was the greatest American since Abraham Lincoln, but he was something more, he was the first American president since Woodrow Wilson who was a great citizen of the world and a great lover of humanity.

"His untimely death deprives the American people of an inspiring as well as inspired leader. It has deprived the civilized world of a man whose name will shine for ever among the stars."

The Irish Independent says editorially, "His name will live in history high in the list of eminent statesmen whose achievements have left their mark not only in the progress of their own nations but also in international affairs."

Churchill Will Honor Roosevelt Today; Commons Expected to Adjourn in Tribute

By Cable to THE NEW YORK TIMES.

LONDON, Friday, April 13—Britain's official tribute to Mr. Roosevelt is expected to be paid by Mr. Churchill at the opening of the House of Commons this morning, and Commons probably will pay honor to the memory of the President by adjourning for a day as it does on the death of British leaders. The Prime Minister received the tragic news at 10 Downing Street immediately after the first news flash was received in London. The shock and great personal loss felt by Mr. Churchill were echoed by the Empire Conference statesmen gathered here for the preparatory talks to the San Francisco conference.

Most of them had returned to their hotels after a dinner given by Anthony Eden only a short while before BBC issued the bulletin in its midnight news summary. Mr. Eden was among numerous diplomats who phoned the American Embassy to convey condolences and sorrow of their countrymen.

Besides Mr. Churchill, leaders of the Labor and Liberal parties, many of whom had known the President personally, will speak in tribute in Commons today.

The news was broadcast over BBC and the German news agency said: "News of the death of President Roosevelt has, of course, made a deep impression in Berlin. German political circles refrain from drawing any conclusions on the possible effects which the death of the President may have on home and foreign policy of the United States."

The empire statesmen, told of the news, were literally stunned into silence for many minutes.

WASHINGTON, Friday, April 13 (AP)—Prime Minister Churchill said today that the death of President Roosevelt was "the loss of the British nation and of the cause of freedom in every land."

His voice breaking, Jonathan Daniels, one of Mr. Roosevelt's secretaries, read this message which Mr. Churchill sent Mrs. Roosevelt:

"I send my most profound sympathy in your grievous loss. It is also the loss of the British nation and of the cause of freedom in every land.

"I feel so deeply for you all. As for me, I have lost a dear and cherished friendship which was forged in the fire of war. I trust you may find consolation in the glory of his name and the magnitude of his work."

It was signed simply "Churchill."

Social, Economic Reforms Assailed, but Won Party Aid

Radicals Fought President's Taking Advice From Conservatives, but Course Brought Wide Backing

Early in the session the President announced that his program of social and economic reforms had been virtually completed, and that henceforth his Administration would concentrate on recovery rather than reform in domestic affairs.

Although he continued in close contact with the little group of Leftist advisers, headed by Tommy Corcoran and Ben Cohen who had replaced the original "brain trust," at the same time he accepted the advice of less radical men and acted more frequently as desired by conservative elements.

This brought down on his head a storm of protest from Communists and other radicals, who accused him of sabotaging his own New Deal and catering to the Wall Street and business interests he had previously flayed. They charged him with retreating in the face of insistent conservative demands for the amendment of the National Labor Relations Act and the Securities and Exchange Act.

Won Back Conservatives

Although business interests remained suspicious that the swing to the Right would only go a short way before the pendulum swung to the Left again, the President succeeded in winning back much support among the conservative elements of his own party, especially among the Southern Democrats and among middle-class people throughout the country.

This, with the widespread popularity of his foreign policy, which was in key with the overwhelming sympathy of the American people for the anti-Axis nations and their equally overwhelming desire to keep out of war, strengthened Mr. Roosevelt's political position.

Mr. Roosevelt, meanwhile, had been enlarging the scope of the defense program immeasurably. When THE NEW YORK TIMES on June 7 editorially called for enactment of compulsory military training the President made it known that he found the proposal most interesting. A few days later, on June 17, he disclosed his approval of a plan for some kind of government training for all youth, and at the same time he approved the construction of a two-ocean Navy at an ultimate cost estimated at $10,000,000,000.

While the delegates to the Republican National Convention were gathering in Philadelphia, the President set off a political bombshell on June 20 by announcing the appointment of two prominent Republicans to his Cabinet. Colonel Henry L. Stimson became Secretary of War, succeeding Secretary Harry Woodring, and Colonel Frank Knox succeeded Charles Edison as Secretary of the Navy. Both new appointees had been outspoken supporters of his pro-Ally foreign policy.

Definitely placing himself on record as favoring enactment of a selective compulsory military service law, Mr. Roosevelt in a message to Congress on July 10 asked for a further appropriation of $4,848,171,957 for military and naval expansion.

As delegates to the Democratic National Convention met in Chicago in mid-July, the President's silence on his third-term aspirations remained unbroken, although it was confidently expected in pro-New Deal quarters that he would accede to the movement to "draft" him as the nominee. Harry L. Hopkins, Secretary of Commerce, went to Chicago to act as liaison man with the White House, while Senator James F. Byrnes of South Carolina was the floor leader for the "draft" movement.

Mr. Roosevelt broke his long silence by a message to Senator Alben W. Barkley, permanent chairman of the convention, which the latter read to the assembled delegates on the evening of July 16, after the convention had concluded its organization. The President said that he had no wish to run again, and he released all delegates pledged to or instructed for him so that they might vote for any candidate they pleased.

In the face of the tremendous momentum that had been acquired by the "draft" movement, however, anything short of a positive refusal by the President to be a candidate was looked upon by all observers as an indication of his willingness to be "drafted." Accordingly, he was nominated on the first ballot on the evening of July 17, although Postmaster General Farley insisted on a roll-call, thus blocking an attempt by the "draft" proponents to make the nomination by acclamation.

While the convention was still in session, in the early morning hours of July 19, Mr. Roosevelt in a dramatic radio address from the White House announced his decision to run again. He said that he had hoped to be permitted to retire and that no "call of party alone" would have persuaded him to accept re-election, but that the national crisis had compelled him to change his decision.

Mr. Roosevelt, after personally choosing Edward J. Flynn of New York to act as Democratic National Chairman in place of Mr. Farley, made a series of personal tours of defense centers which, his opponents contended, were intended to dramatize himself against a popular background without engaging in debate of the issues with Mr. Willkie, the Republican nominee.

For the first time in the peacetime history of the United States, compulsory military training became established by law two weeks later when, on Sept. 16, Mr. Roosevelt affixed his signature to the Burke-Wadsworth bill.

Decides on Speeches

The political campaign, meanwhile, had been going forward with unusual intensity. As October advanced, some experienced political observers began to think that Mr. Willkie had a considerable chance for election. Although New Deal spokesmen ridiculed this contention, nevertheless, on Oct. 11, the Democratic National Committee announced that the President had decided to make a series of five political speeches.

In the first of these appearances, at Philadelphia on Oct. 23, Mr Roosevelt recalled that he had reserved the right to point out "deliberate falsifications of fact" by his opponents when he had announced his intention of not campaigning. He charged that the Republicans, borrowing the dictator techniques of propaganda, had made such falsifications.

John L. Lewis, president of the Congress of Industrial Organizations, who had played so prominent a part in the campaign for Mr. Roosevelt's election in 1936, astonished and dismayed his followers by bolting the Democratic ranks as the campaign reached its height. On Oct. 25, in a nation-wide radio address, he scored Mr. Roosevelt as seeking a dictatorship and as leading the nation toward war.

Other nationally prominent figures who had at one time or another supported Mr. Roosevelt, including former Governor Smith, John W. Davis, Democratic nominee for the Presidency in 1924; Lewis V. Douglas, director of the budget in the early part of the Roosevelt Administration, and John W. Haines, former Under-Secretary of the Treasury, came out during the campaign for Mr. Willkie.

These defections, however, and the inability of straw votes and public opinion polls to show a conclusive lead for either of the major candidates were swept away in another whirlwind tide of Roosevelt votes when election day came on Nov. 5.

SHIFTING ECONOMY TO WAR VAST TASK

Work of Mobilizing the Total Resources of America Was a Stormy Process

CRITICISM OFTEN SEVERE

Giant Production Goals Were Realized Despite Difficulties With Labor and Congress

On the home front during the war, President Roosevelt faced the task of providing the leadership for conversion of peace economy into an efficient war economy capable of delivering war materials when they were needed, in the amounts they were needed and where they were needed, staffing it with the manpower available after the needs of the armed services were satisfied.

This required total mobilization of American resources and the process was a stormy one, with the Administration, at frequent times, subject to wide criticism and contrary pressures. Out of it rose, however, the most powerful war economy of the time.

After the declaration of war, and during Prime Minister Churchill's visit to this country in the Christmas season of 1941, production and other plans were discussed. The President extended the draft to the group between 20 and 44, and ordered seemingly impossible production goals.

Airplanes were ordered boosted to 60,000 for the year, ship production to eight million deadweight tons, tanks to 45,000, while the plans for 1943, then laid down, called for 125,000 planes, 75,000 tanks and ten million tons of ships. For the beginning of this, Congress was asked to grant fifty-eight billions of dollars, which was done.

Trouble on Home Front

This was the real beginning of trouble on the home front, not that America resented the sacrifice, but that the program involved a vast dislocation of civilian economy, a labor shortage instead of a labor surplus, which, in turn, led to a food shortage, potential and to a great extent actual inflation and a vast series of governmental organizations, directives, decrees, set up to attempt to meet the problem. Labor, through the AFL and the CIO, gave the President a no-strike pledge a few days after Pearl Harbor, but there were "quickie" strikes, caused in some cases by irresponsible labor leadership, and in others by the attempts on the part of management to take advantage of the public sentiment against strikes in wartime.

Consistently, the President followed a lenient course toward labor, getting "tough" only with John L. Lewis, intransigeant leader of the coal miners. In several cases the Government, on Presidential order, took over the industry affected and the strikers returned to work.

The first eighteen months of the war saw production reach miraculous heights. It also saw the armed forces head toward the goal of 11,000,000 men; it saw fathers drafted, the age limits lowered to take in the 18 and 19-year-olds just leaving high school; it saw the automobile and the sirloin steak become rarities and luxuries, instead of the commonplace items of American life.

In all of this the President was the complete "boss." It was common knowledge in Washington that while he might set up McNutt as manpower boss, Ickes as controller of fuel, Henderson and later Prentiss Brown as heads of the price-control agencies, the final decisions rested with the President, also engaged in actual running and planning of the war.

Setback for New Deal

It led to criticism, and to the so-called "Battle of Washington" between rival agency heads whose conflicts took them, with frequency, to the White House for settlement. This led to weakness politically, and the elections of 1942 saw the first major setback for the New Deal at the polls.

The situation on the home front was complicated by the fact that the President, and his advisers, stuck to the policy of economic reform during the war period.

To meet criticism of conflicting governmental bureaus and statements the President appointed James F. Byrnes, previously functioning as director of economic stabilization, to head a new Office of War Mobilization, with powers previously exercised only by the President, and he gave to Mr. Byrnes as associates, but not as equals, Secretary of War Stimson, Secretary of the Navy Knox, Donald M. Nelson, head of the War Production Board; Fred M. Vinson and Harry L. Hopkins, closest personal adviser to the President, and holder of many official and unofficial governmental offices.

The coal strike in the spring of 1943, and the resultant drop in war production at a time when the armed forces were being increasingly successful, produced a real Congressional revolt. When the President vetoed, because of objection to several clauses in the measure, the Smith-Connally anti-strike bill, both Houses passed it over his veto, in a fit of anger, the same day, the Senate by 56 to 25 and the House by 244 to 108.

The Administration's war policy on public information was a frequent source of controversy. The President lost a major battle with the press as a preliminary to the International Food Conference at Hot Springs, Va., when he tried to restrict coverage, putting a number of obstacles in the way of obtaining more news than the Government was ready to release.

Strained Relations With Congress

The criticism continued, and the relations of the President and Congress were definitely strained as a result, midway through 1943.

The Roosevelt plan for food sub-

Continued on Following Page

"All the News That's Fit to Print"

The New York Times.

LATE CITY EDITION
Clearing and warmer today. Cloudy with moderate winds tomorrow.
Temperatures Yesterday—Max., 51; Min., 44
Sunrise today, 5:54 A. M.; Sunset, 7:53 P. M.

VOL. XCIV..No. 31,875. Entered as Second-Class Matter, Postoffice, New York, N. Y. NEW YORK, WEDNESDAY, MAY 2, 1945. THREE CENTS IN NEW YORK CITY

HITLER DEAD IN CHANCELLERY, NAZIS SAY; DOENITZ, SUCCESSOR, ORDERS WAR TO GO ON; BERLIN ALMOST WON; U. S. ARMIES ADVANCE

MOLOTOFF EASES PARLEY TENSION; NEW MOVES BEGUN

Russian Says Country Will Cooperate in World Plan Despite Argentine Issue

4 COMMISSIONS SET UP

They Will Deal With Council, Assembly, Court and Some General Problems

By JAMES B. RESTON
Special to THE NEW YORK TIMES.

SAN FRANCISCO, May 1—The United Nations Conference on International Organization has survived its first basic crisis and after six days of political maneuvering on secondary issues, it began to move at rapid tempo today toward its primary task—the creation of a world organization which would stop what Field Marshal Jan Christiaan Smuts called "this pilgrimage of death."

The test came last night. Rebuffed by the conference on his attempts to keep Argentina out of the conference and bring the Warsaw Poles in, Soviet Foreign Commissar Vyacheslaff M. Molotoff went late last night to Secretary Stettinius' penthouse at the Fairmont Hotel. He immediately made his position clear.

He still disapproved the conference actions on the Poles and the Argentine, but he wanted the conference to succeed; he would cooperate in its labors, and while he was under urgent pressure by the events in Europe to return to Moscow, he would remain at least for a few days until the major issues on the charter were thrashed out among the four sponsor powers. Then, he said, he would have to leave, probably at the week-end or early next week.

"Friendly Meeting" Is Held

Immediately, in what the Foreign Ministers of the United States, Great Britain and China described to their colleagues as "the most friendly meeting of the conference," the big four approved the formation of the working commissions and committees of the conference, and other committees began discussing, not the personalities or procedures of the conference, but the basic questions of creating an organization which would win the support, with the power, of the great nations without violating the rights and principles of all nations.

The three main developments of the day were as follows:

First, the conference approved four commissions to deal with the security council of the proposed organization, the general assembly, the judicial agency and general problems, and established twelve committees to study specific problems under these four commissions.

The heads of the four commissions were: Trygve Lie of Norway, Security Council; Field Marshal Smuts, General Assembly; Carraciolo Parra Rez of Venezuela, judicial organization; and Paul Henri Spaak of Belgium, general provisions.

Second, Field Marshal Smuts called on the four major powers to accept the special responsibilities which flow from the special authority given them under the Dumbarton Oaks proposals and urged all the nations here to pay more attention to the spiritual and economic aspects of the new charter than they had in the past.

Third, the Russians began studying in some detail the sixteen amendments to the Dumbarton Oaks proposals which were submitted by the United States. The other delegations started circulating amendments and exchanging views on proposals already circulated.

The facts on the crisis among the Big Three over Poland, Argentina, White Russia and the Ukraine can now be put down with assur-

Continued on Page 18, Column 6

Allies Invade North Borneo; Fighting Fierce, Tokyo Says

Australia Informed of Landing by Treasury Minister—MacArthur Reports Only Air Attacks and New Gains on Luzon

By The United Press.

MANILA, Wednesday, May 2—An official Australian announcement said yesterday that Allied troops had invaded Borneo, the world's third largest island, but Gen. Douglas MacArthur's communiqué early today reported only that heavy bombers were neutralizing enemy bases and airdromes on the oil-rich island.

Tokyo also reported the landings and said they had been made on the ten-square-mile island of Tarakan on the northeast coast, a region rich in oil wells, which the Netherlanders destroyed before the Japanese captured them in 1942. The enemy broadcast said "fierce fighting" was in progress.

[A later Japanese broadcast, picked up in San Francisco, reported that Allied units had landed on Tarakan Island at 6:30 A. M., Tuesday, Tokyo time. The broadcast said "the enemy had been bombarding the island since April 27, and on Monday morning began approaching the island in their landing attempts." It reported the landing force consisted of "about 5,000 soldiers" and said Japanese forces on the island "are holding secure their positions, obstructing the enemy's advance."]

General MacArthur announced that heavy bombers in attacks on Borneo had struck Kuching, Macassar and Kendari, while medium units and fighters had attacked Japanese gun positions on Tarakan.

General MacArthur announced that on Mindanao Island the Twenty-fourth Division, in another swift drive, had advanced eleven miles

Continued on Page 16, Column 2

REDOUBTS ASSAILED

U. S. 3d, 7th and French 1st Armies Charging Into Alpine Hideout

NEAR BRENNER PASS

British in North Close About Hamburg—Poles Gain in Emden Area

Von Rundstedt Caught

By The Associated Press.

WITH UNITED STATES SEVENTH ARMY, Wednesday, May 2—Field Marshal Karl von Rundstedt has been captured by United States Seventh Army troops.

The Seventh Army caught the former German commander in the west in its drive into the Nazis' southeastern redoubt area.

By DREW MIDDLETON
By Wireless to THE NEW YORK TIMES.

PARIS, May 1—The last defenses of the Third Reich were crumbling as Allied tanks and infantry swept almost unopposed into the northern and southern redoubts.

Gen. George S. Patton's United States Third Army has resumed its offensive into Austria, crashing to within twenty miles of Linz, and is only fifty-four miles from Amstetten, where Marshal Fedor I. Tolbukhin's Third Ukrainian Army was last reported. According to reports from the front, radio contact has been established between tanks of the United States Eleventh Armored Division and the vanguard of the Soviet armies.

Other armored columns of the

Continued on Page 14, Column 1

NAZI CORE STORMED

Russians Drive Toward Chancellery Fortress, Narrowing Noose

BRANDENBURG TAKEN

Stralsund Port Swept Up in New Baltic Gains—Vah Valley Cleared

By C. L. SULZBERGER
By Wireless to THE NEW YORK TIMES.

MOSCOW, Wednesday, May 2—Street battles within smoldering Berlin today entered their twelfth day since the Russians first broke into the city, with Nazi die-hards still holding grimly to the central part of the town, whittled down by yesterday's fighting, in which Marshal Gregory K. Zhukoff's First White Russian Army group completely occupied Charlottenburg and Schoeneberg and more than 100 blocks in the capital's central region.

Some 14,000 prisoners were taken within the city on Monday, the Russians announced. At the same time, the remnants of a hold-out group south of Berlin, part of which had been annihilated at Wendisch Buchholtz, was split in two and the survivors are being ground to death by Marshal Zhukoff's men.

Curiously enough, the midnight communiqué does not mention Marshal Ivan S. Koneff's First Ukrainian Army group, which has been working from the southwestern sector of the city toward the desperately defended Tiergarten.

Marshal Zhukoff's forward spearheads meanwhile struck deep into Brandenburg Province, capturing the city of Brandenburg, halfway to Magdeburg from Berlin.

While Gen. Andrei I. Yeremenko proceeded apace in his lightning

Continued on Page 3, Column 3

ADOLF HITLER
The New York Times, 1938

ADMIRAL IN CHARGE

Proclaims Designation to Rule—Appeals to People and Army

RAISES 'RED MENACE'

Britain to Insist Germans Show Hitler's Body When War Ends

By SYDNEY GRUSON
By Cable to THE NEW YORK TIMES.

LONDON, May 1—Adolf Hitler died this afternoon, the Hamburg radio announced tonight, and Grand Admiral Karl Doenitz, proclaiming himself the new Fuehrer by Hitler's appointment, said that the war would continue.

Crowning days of rumors about Hitler's health and whereabouts, the Hamburg radio said that he had fallen in the battle of Berlin at his command post in the Chancellery just three days after Benito Mussolini, the first of the dictators, had been killed by Italian Partisans. Doenitz, a 53-year-old U-boat specialist, broadcast an address to the German people and the surviving armed forces immediately after the announcer had given the news of Hitler's death.

[The British Foreign Office said that it would demand the production of Hitler's body after the end of hostilities, The Associated Press reported.]

First addressing the German people, Doenitz said that they would continue to fight only to save themselves from the Russians but that they would oppose the western Allies as long as they helped the Russians. In an order of the day to the German forces he repeated his thinly veiled attempt to split the Allies.

Radio Prepares Germans

Early this evening the Germans were told that an important announcement would be broadcast tonight. There was no hint of what was coming. The stand-by announcement was repeated at 9:40 P. M., followed by the playing of excerpts from Wagner's "Goetterdaemmerung."

A few minutes later the announcer said: "Achtung! Achtung! In a few moments you will hear a

Continued on Page 5, Column 4

NEW CIGARETTES FACE PRICE INQUIRY

OPA Calls on Manufacturers of 21-Cent Brands to Prove Quality Merits Charge

By JAMES E POWERS

Manufacturers of hitherto unheard of brands of cigarettes that have appeared on the market in recent weeks and are being retailed at four or more cents a package higher than ceiling prices for scarce popular brands will be called upon by the Office of Price Administration to show that the new products are of a quality rating the prices charged, it became known yesterday.

Daniel P. Woolley, regional OPA administrator, said an investigation was in progress as a result of complaints by smokers who said they had paid 21 cents a package for cigarettes "they had previously never heard of."

The United Wholesale Tobacco and Cigarette Distributors Association, a sub-jobbers' group, in a telegram to Senator William Langer of North Dakota, who recently introduced a resolution to set up a committee to look into the "black market" in cigarettes, demanded an immediate investigation of the entire cigarette shortage.

Mr. Woolley declared that as a result of OPA prosecution of violators of price ceilings, the black-market condition largely had been corrected here. He said he was centering on the pricing of the new cigarette brands.

Mr. Woolley added that studies were being made to determine

Continued on Page 40, Column 4

HARD COAL 'HOLIDAY' BRINGS WLB BAN

New Order by Board Asserts Output Is Urgent—Seizure Action Is Postponed

By JOSEPH A. LOFTUS
Special to THE NEW YORK TIMES.

WASHINGTON, May 1—The War Labor Board issued a new order tonight to the United Mine Workers and the operators to resume the production of hard coal. To give the UMW leaders an opportunity to act on the order it decided to defer for twenty-four to forty-eight hours a recommendation to President Truman for Government seizure of the mines.

The miners went on a holiday today after expiration of their contract at midnight.

Dr. George W. Taylor, WLB chairman, in a telegram to both parties took cognizance of the miners' traditional "no contract, no work" policy.

"The board's order provides for a continuing contract," he said. "It is urgent that production should be immediately resumed."

As in acting on the soft coal dispute a month ago, the WLB provided in the new order that any legal wage adjustment agreed upon or finally ordered be retroactive to the expiration date of the old contract.

Union spokesmen told the WLB at a brief hearing that the Tri-District Scale Committee had voted to advise the miners to return to work when the operators accepted the settlement proposal made by Secretary of Labor Perkins.

Dr. Taylor, in questioning John Owens of the UMW, noted that

Continued on Page 40, Column 3

Eisenhower Halted Forces at Elbe; Ninth Had Hoped to Storm Berlin

By The Associated Press.

WITH THE UNITED STATES NINTH ARMY, in Germany, April 26 (Delayed by Censorship)—A direct order from Supreme Allied Headquarters halted the United States Ninth Army's drive to Berlin at the Elbe River at a time when the most pessimistic officers were predicting that Lieut. Gen. William H. Simpson's forces could reduce the German capital in ten days, "even if the Germans fought hard."

General Eisenhower's order said the Ninth would halt on the Elbe and await the arrival of Russian forces from the east, thereby leaving the capture of the capital to the Red Army. It also was understood that the American First and Third and British and Canadian armies received similar orders to halt at the Elbe.

It was not clear whether General Eisenhower's order was dictated by political policy agreed upon by the Great Powers or in a belief that it was a military necessity.

It was felt by high staff officers in the field, however, that the Ninth and other American forces could push on to the capital without great difficulty. While the order disappointed some staff officers, it was not altogether unexpected. It was known that the Ninth Army had pushed past the eventual British-American occupation area when it crossed the Weser River.

While the staff officers were disappointed, the American doughboys and tankmen who had to do the fighting and dying to get to Berlin expressed no regret. Almost to a man, they felt they could do with-

Continued on Page 4, Column 4

War News Summarized

WEDNESDAY, MAY 2, 1945

Hitler is dead, according to the Hamburg radio, and on Monday, the day before he allegedly fell at his command post in the Chancellery in Berlin, he appointed Admiral Karl Doenitz to be the new Fuehrer. The head of the German Navy, who had made his mark directing the enemy's U-boats campaign, pledged continuance of the war. [1:8.]

Washington received the news, as did London, with some skepticism and a desire to see the body. Selection of Admiral Doenitz was considered logical in view of his strong Nazi feelings. [1:7.]

The new development was interpreted in London as a move to counteract Himmler's reported peace bid, but Prime Minister Churchill broadly intimated in the Commons that he might have "information of exceptional importance" to impart before Saturday. Peace will probably come before all enemy forces have surrendered, he said. [1:6-7.] Germany was reported to have begun evacuation of Denmark and to be ready to leave Norway. Count Bernadotte said in Sweden he had no new Himmler proposals, and the Nazis' Scandinavian withdrawals were related there to a prospective general capitulation. [11:1.]

Meanwhile, general Allied progress on the battlefields against slight resistance continued. The United States Third Army, on the day Hitler was declared to have died, captured Braunau, his birthplace. The drive into Austria was resumed and had reached to within twenty miles of Linz and fifty-four of the last known Russian position. The Seventh Army smashed through the Tyrol on a broad front and cleared Munich. The British Second Army, by-passing Hamburg, raced to within eighteen miles of the Baltic port of Luebeck. [1:4; map P. 14.]

General Eisenhower, it was revealed, personally ordered the halt of the Allied drive on Berlin from the west to permit the Russians to take the capital. [1:2-3.]

The Russians greatly cut down the German holding in Berlin, capturing the districts of Charlottenburg and Schoeneberg. West of the city they occupied Brandenburg and along the Baltic they seized Stralsund. [1:5; maps Pages 2 and 14.]

New Zealand troops in Italy made contact with Yugoslav Partisans at Monfalcone near Trieste and the British entered Udine. While the Eighth Army was closing a trap along the Swiss border, the Fifth neared France. [1:6-7; map P. 14.]

Mussolini and his mistress were buried in unmarked paupers' graves in Milan. [13:1.] Admiral Horthy, former Regent of Hungary, was captured. [4:3.]

Invasion of Borneo was officially disclosed in Australia, although no word of the break into the Japanese-held Netherlands East Indies had come from General MacArthur. On Mindanao in the Philippines, Americans were within six miles of the city of Davao. [1:2-3; map P. 16.]

Seventh Division troops on Okinawa resumed their southward advance, entering the village of Kuhazu. [15:1.] More than 400 starved, naked Allied prisoners of war were liberated by the British as they drove on Rangoon in Burma. [15:3.]

Good progress was made at the San Francisco Conference. Foreign Commissar Molotoff, after assuring Secretary of State Stettinius of his desire that the conference succeed, announced that pressure of events would compel his return to Moscow within a few days. [1:1.]

Clark's Troops Meet Tito's In General Advance in Italy

By VIRGINIA LEE WARREN
By Wireless to THE NEW YORK TIMES.

AT ADVANCED ALLIED HEADQUARTERS, in Italy, May 1—After advancing fifty-five miles in less than a day along the coastal road rimming the Gulf of Venice, units of one division of the Fifteenth Army Group made contact this afternoon with Marshal Tito's forces at Monfalcone while other troops under Gen. Mark W. Clark continued to sweep German remnants from the valleys of north Italy and to seal off the few remaining escape routes through the Alps.

No details of the meeting at the small seaport northwest of Trieste between Marshal Tito's men, who had driven fourteen miles from Trieste, and leading elements of the Eighth Army's Second New Zealand Division were given in tonight's communiqué.

On the other side of Italy another historic meeting was imminent as Fifth Army troops, continuing their drive along the Gulf of Genoa, advanced on the Aurelian Way to within sixty miles of the French border, which has already been crossed by French troops headed this way.

General Clark announced yesterday that the military power of Germany had virtually collapsed, but there still are drives for his two armies to make and engagements still to be won. The Germans, trying to regroup for their flight across the Alps, were deprived of two key road junctions leading to mountain passes west of Brenner when Belluno and Udine were occupied this afternoon by units of the Eighth Army.

Udine, which was taken by the British Sixth Armored Division, is twenty-eight miles southwest of Caporetto, the scene of the Italian disaster in World War I. The forces that entered Belluno went on five miles to Ponte nell 'Alpi, guardian of the approach to Italy's

Continued on Page 13, Column 5

DOENITZ' ACCESSION VIEWED AS A BLIND

Capital Lays His Designation to General Ignorance of His Allegiance to Party

By The Associated Press.

WASHINGTON, May 1—If Adolf Hitler really designated Grand Admiral Karl Doenitz his successor, military men here believe, he did so for the following reasons:

1. Doenitz is a Nazi supporter who could be counted on to keep German resistance going if possible.

2. But he is not associated in the Allies' minds with German atrocities and the extreme policies of the Nazi party. Therefore, Hitler probably figured that he might be able to get better treatment from the Allies when the hour of surrender came.

3. He is immensely popular with the German people.

There was a disposition here tonight to look for continued organized resistance whose core would now be centered in the Baltic and North Sea port areas. Those places are the homes of the German Navy and especially of the U-boat fleet that Doenitz commanded from 1936 until he succeeded Grand Admiral Erich

Continued on Page 5, Column 1

Copenhagen Writer Again Phones Story

By Cable to THE NEW YORK TIMES.

STOCKHOLM, Sweden, May 1—For the first time in more than five years THE NEW YORK TIMES correspondent in Copenhagen, tonight telephoned a story from the Danish capital. The Nazi-imposed censorship there has been lifted. Mr. Carstensen said:

"The Danes are overjoyed at their imminent liberation, but it is not noticeable on the Copenhagen streets.

"Anxious to avoid trouble on May Day, Copenhageners have been staying indoors. The blackout is still enforced and it is pitch dark in Copenhagen tonight. All Copenhageners are glued to radios listening to broadcasts on Hitler's death.

"We expect King Christian will resume his functions and name a new Cabinet any day now. In the meantime the strictest discipline is being observed so as not to give the Germans any excuses for starting more trouble."

On April 9, 1940, Mr. Carstensen was the first to give the world the news of the German invasion of Denmark in a wireless dispatch to THE NEW YORK TIMES. His dispatch was cleared less than an hour before the Nazis seized the radio station and was the last to be sent.

Churchill Hints Peace This Week; 2-Day Celebration Is Authorized

By CLIFTON DANIEL
By Wireless to THE NEW YORK TIMES.

LONDON, May 1—The general belief that peace with Germany will be announced this week persisted in Britain today, encouraged by Prime Minister Churchill himself and by Grand Admiral Karl Doenitz's announcement of the death of Adolf Hitler.

The War Cabinet again held a session tonight but so far as was known did not have any concrete proposal to consider. The chances that Heinrich Himmler ultimately will deliver an acceptable peace are now held in some official quarters to be only "fifty-fifty."

Nevertheless the buoyant Prime Minister told the House of Commons today that he might have "information of importance" to announce before Saturday.

The public's hopes were raised still further by a long Home Office circular giving the Government's views on how Britain should observe V-E Day, which the British, it appears, will be expected to celebrate strictly according to form.

[Stockholm reported, with the return there of Count Bernadotte, the "imminent liberation" of Denmark and Norway—already taking effect locally in Denmark—as a phase of a prospective general German capitulation that must be acceptable to the Allies' military commands.]

The hurrahing will begin with the announcement of the cessation of hostilities by Mr. Churchill over a nation-wide radio network. The King will speak at 9 o'clock that evening. And throughout that day

Continued on Page 10, Column 4

NAZI RUSE IS SEEN IN HITLER 'DEATH'

Writer Suggests the Report Is an Effort to Hide the Whereabouts of Leader

By LOUIS P. LOCHNER
Chief of the Former Associated Press Bureau in Berlin

WITH THE UNITED STATES SEVENTH ARMY, May 1 (AP)—I have just listened to the short-wave broadcast of Admiral Karl Doenitz' speech as the new Fuehrer of Germany, but I still find it difficult to believe that Hitler is really dead or that he remained in Berlin during the Russian assault.

The whole melodramatic build-up, beginning with Propaganda Minister Joseph Goebbels' announcement days ago that Hitler was personally conducting the defense of the capital, now reaching its climax in the claim that he met death in the Chancellery, of all places, looks like an effort to make good the Fuehrer's oft-repeated assertion: "I will never capitulate." Hitler could not afford to accept unconditional surrender, so what may prove to be the legend of his meeting a hero's death had to be staged.

Hitler may or may not be dead. If he is dead, it seems extremely unlikely that he died as the German radio says that he did. Having spent the past days in the very section of the country where Hitler rose to power, wrote "Mein Kampf" and conducted affairs of intrigue with the whole world from Munich, I still cannot escape the feeling that Hitler is some place where nobody expects him to be. From time to time people will claim to have seen him.

Doenitz' announcement by no means ends our troubles with Hitler. They may have only begun. There may be a state funeral for him, and photographers may have the opportunity to produce pictures of a dead man labeled Hitler. Then, some day much later, a "resurrected" Hitler may again stir the world.

The appointment of Doenitz as Hitler's successor indicates that the German leadership desires someone as chief of state who can possibly negotiate with the Allies. Doenitz had no experience in government and has no real hold on the affections of the German people. His appointment was obviously a political maneuver.

The course of the war is unlikely to be affected by his appointment.

YUGOSLAVS NAME ENVOYS

Stanoye Simitch Is Appointed Ambassador to Washington

Yugoslavia yesterday appointed new Ambassadors to the United States, Great Britain and the U. S. S. R., naming Stanoye Simitch, member of the Yugoslav delegation to the San Francisco Conference, as the Ambassador to Washington, the new Yugoslav telegraph service reported.

Maj. Gen. Vladimir Popovitch was appointed Ambassador to Moscow, a post formerly held by M. Simitch, and Dr. Lyuba Leontich was named Ambassador to London, said the English-language dispatch, as reported by the Federal Communications Commission.

Bozho Lyumovitch, former vice president of the anti-Fascist Assembly of National Liberation of Montenegro, was named Minister to the Polish Government at Warsaw, the dispatch said.

NAVY RESERVE SIGNS 223

College Students Begin 4-Month Officer Training Course

Special to THE NEW YORK TIMES.

ANNAPOLIS, May 1—Another group of university and college students, totaling 223, was enrolled at the Naval Academy today for four months of intensive instruction which will equip them for commissions as ensigns in the Naval Reserve. They are the twelfth class to report since the establishment of the reserves school in 1941.

The students will be apprentice seamen for a month, during which they will undergo indoctrination training in infantry, seamanship, ordnance and other branches. Those who qualify will become temporary midshipmen and go on with special training in engineering, leadership and discipline before receiving commissions as ensigns.

Doenitz the Spur of U-Boat War That Held Vast Threat for Allies

His Sea Policy of Destruction Gave Him Power in Reich—Spoke Ardently for Hitler After 'July 20 Plot' in '44

Grand Admiral Karl Doenitz
Associated Press, 1939

Grand Admiral Karl Doenitz, announced as crumbling Germany's new Reichsfuehrer, a severe, seamy-faced, beak-nosed little man who exhorted his seamen to "Kill, kill, kill!" and to avoid any act of humanity, became the Allies' most ruthless and formidable foe.

From the outbreak of war in 1939 to the middle of 1943, when our anti-submarine defenses became so efficient, it was clear even to the Germans that their Battle of the Atlantic was lost, his far-roaming U-boats came very near to adding years to the long war, and in fact did lengthen it more than any other single weapon in the Axis command.

Admiral Doenitz's once-vaunted Navy is defunct, hundreds of his submarines with their crews are rusting in the bottom of the Atlantic—in the later half of 1943 alone we sank more than 150 of them. His great battleship Tirpitz is a mass of wreckage, and the Bismarck, Scharnhorst, and Luetzow are wrecked or sunk along with most of the other ships that flew the swastika. Above all, his new job has a very short life-expectancy.

Prisoner of British in 1918

Karl Doenitz was born in Berlin-Gruenau on September 16, 1891, the son of an engineer.

Joining the German Navy at the age of 18, Doenitz became a U-boat commander in World War I after first serving on the warship Breslau. In October, 1918, when the U-88 was sunk by a British patrol in the Mediterranean, he was taken a prisoner to England. After the November, 1918, armistice he was confined to the Manchester lunatic asylum, having feigned insanity, according to estimates. He was later repatriated to Germany as insane.

His biographies disclose little of his activities in the years between the wars, but in 1935, after a cruise to the West Indies as commander of the cruiser Emden, he was placed in charge of the submarine service which Germany was then rapidly rebuilding.

Within a few months of the outbreak of hostilities in 1939, Doenitz, a rear admiral, was decorated by Hitler with the Knight Cross of the Grand Cross for his skillful operations of the submarine fleet. In September, 1940, he was promoted to vice admiral for his services in organizing and operating the U-boat warfare.

British losses to enemy submarines were beginning to mount and by early 1942 it was estimated that as many as thirty-four were operating off the Atlantic coast at one time. By 1943, when Doenitz was made commander in chief of the German Navy, with the rank of grand admiral, the Reich had between 300 and 700 submarines and was reportedly building a new one every day.

Built Up "Wolf-Pack" Tactics

In supplanting Grand Admiral Erich Raeder, Admiral Doenitz served notice on the Allies that "the entire concentrated strength" of his navy would be put into submarine warfare. Building was reportedly stopped on other classes of German fighting ships.

Doenitz had quarreled with Raeder, openly accusing his superior of issuing excessive figures on submarine sinkings and demanding that Gestapo and Storm Troop snoopers be stopped in their shadowing, interrogating and arresting of submarine men who, after the stress of long patrols, sometimes made statements that the Gestapo twisted into "sedition."

Described as hating the sea and advocating, rather than sea-power, the destruction of all sea-power by submarines, he fully expected to win the war with his U-boat fleets and their "wolf-pack" tactics that he originated.

Doenitz taught submarine skippers to prowl and attack together, an extremely effective method against convoys, and he built up a highly efficient radio communications system which linked him with every one of his ships no matter how far at sea. He developed the submarine tanker for supply, and spurred new building of electric submarines and the extension "breathing" equipment that permitted his U-boats to remain submerged for long periods.

But our rapidly growing fleet of escort carriers, patrol and escort craft, long-range patrolers of the air and helicopters beat the U-boat fleets, just as the Allied convoy system had bested them in 1918.

During 1942 it was all the American-British ship construction program could do to keep abreast of the sinkings and in some months the sinkings exceeded new construction. But in 1943 we had won the "most critical of all fighting fronts," in the Atlantic.

Acted as Hitler's Spokesman

In March, 1944, Admiral Doenitz took Hitler's place at the microphone and urged the German war machine to greater efforts. Reich Marshal Hermann Goering's air power was unable to stop the severe lashing of Allied bombers and the Reich armies were suffering badly in Russia. As D-day in Normandy approached Allied commanders expected the weakened enemy navy to make a suicide attack, but it failed to do so.

Last July, after the July 20 "plot" on Hitler's life, Admiral Doenitz spoke by radio to the German people and the world, assuring Hitler of his "sacred anger" and promising that the Reich Navy "stands firm." He ordered fanaticism in support of Hitler, and asserted that reorganized U-boat packs would renew war against the Allies.

These attacks never came in force, although U-boats are still in evidence in the Atlantic, in the areas where they once threatened the transportation of the armies and materials that are taking over Germany today.

DEATH OF HITLER ANNOUNCED BY FOE

Continued From Page 1

serious and important message to the German people." Then the news was given to the Germans and the world after the playing of the slow movement from Bruckner's Seventh Symphony, commemorating Wagner's death.

Appeals for Cooperation

Appealing to the German people for help, order and discipline, Doenitz eulogized Hitler as the hero of a lifetime of service to the nation whose "fight against the Bolshevik storm flood concerned not only Europe but the entire civilized world * * * It is my first task," Doenitz added, "to save Germany from destruction by the advancing Bolshevist enemy. For this aim alone the military struggle continues."

Clinging to the line of all recent German propaganda, reflected in Heinrich Himmler's reported offer to surrender to the western Allies but not to Russia, Doenitz said that the British and Americans were fighting not for their own interests but for the spreading of Bolshevism. He demanded of the armed forces the same allegiance that they had pledged to Hitler and he assured them that he took supreme command "resolved to continue the struggle against the Bolsheviks until the fighting men, until the hundreds of thousands of German families of the German east are saved from bondage and extermination." To the armed forces he described Hitler as "one of the greatest heroes of German history," who "gave his life and met a hero's death."

News tickers in the House of Commons lobby carried the news of Hitler's death just before the House rose tonight. The reaction of members and of the general public was much the same. Some doubted the truth of the announcement altogether, while others argued that there would have been no sense of making it if it were not true, since Hitler was perhaps the last person around whom the Germans still in unconquered territory would rally.

But there was an almost complete lack of excitement here. Those who believed the report seemed to accept it as a matter of course that Hitler would die. There was no official reaction.

The last reference to Hitler before tonight's announcement came in this afternoon's German communiqué, which said that the Berlin garrison had "gathered around the Fuehrer and, herded together in a very narrow space, is defending itself heroically." When Himmler offered his surrender to the Americans and British, it is reported, he told Count Folke Bernadotte, his Swedish emissary, that Hitler was dying of a cerebral hemorrhage. During the past week, Hitler was variously reported dead, dying or insane in Berlin, Salzburg or the Bavarian mountains.

Doenitz' self-proclaimed accession was believed in some quarters here to bear out reports of a recent split in the German hierarchy between the supporters of an immediate peace gathered around Himmler and the die-hard clique clinging to Hitler and his determination to fight to the very end.

It was noted that Doenitz commanded the last arm of the German military machine that could cause the Allies major difficulties, and his ability as an expert on submarine tactics is not belittled here.

He was one of the first military men to join the Nazis and his loyalty to the party and its ideology never wavered. Known as one of the most ruthless men in Germany, he has been a bitter enemy of Britain since his imprisonment during World War I, when he was confined to a Manchester asylum as a lunatic.

"Ghost" Interrupts Doenitz

LONDON, May 1 (AP)—When Doenitz declared on the radio that Hitler had died "a hero's death," a ghost voice immediately interrupted, shouting: "This is a lie!"

[The British Broadcasting Corporation subsequently reported that Hitler had actually died of a stroke, rather than in battle against the Russians, the National Broadcasting Company said.]

Hitler, who was 56 years old on April 20, was lauded by Doenitz as "one of the greatest heroes in German history." Here the ghost voice broke in: "The greatest of all fascists!"

"With proud respect and mourning, we lower our standards," Doenitz continued. "His death calls on us to act," the ghost voice interrupted. "Strike now!"

Doenitz launched into a pep talk to the German people and troops, only to be interrupted again by the ghost voice, crying: "Rise against Doenitz. The struggle is not worth while if crime wins."

Haw-Haw Repeats Message

After Doenitz had broadcast his message the Hamburg station played "Deutschland Ueber Alles" and the "Horst Wessel Lied." This was followed by three minutes of silence, then by a formal order of the day from Doenitz to the military services and then by funeral music. Then Lord Haw-Haw repeated the broadcast, including Doenitz' order of the day, in English.

The Foreign Office said that it believed that Hitler was dead, but it declined to comment on the accuracy of the Hamburg radio's report of how he died.

London Press Voluminous

London newspapers received the announcement of Hitler's death just as the early editions were going to press but the second editions went "all-out" on the news, with long obituaries of Hitler and briographical sketches of Doenitz, the British radio said early today, according to the Office of War Information.

The Times of London limited its comment to a five-column obituary of Hitler and another half-column of copy on Doenitz, with photographs of both. The Daily Express, on the other hand, said that it "rejoices to announce the report of Adolf Hitler's death," the broadcast said.

The Daily Herald commented that Hitler had "snatched power at a moment when moral conviction and mutual trust were at a low ebb among the governments of the democracies" and added: "It is up to the democracies to insure that no such moment shall occur again." The Daily Mail declared that the Germans would continue to "worship" Hitler.

DOENITZ' ACCESSION VIEWED AS A BLIND

Continued From Page 1

Raeder as Commander in Chief of the navy in 1943.

There may be some continued resistance in the southern pocket, but there are well placed officials who now say that there is no national redoubt area and never has been.

In proportion to the total strength of the services, there have been far more Nazi party members among German Navy officers than among Army officers. The reason appears to be this: After the First World War and the scuttling of the German Fleet at Scapa Flow, German navy men developed an inferiority complex. The rise of the Nazi party and its doctrines of world domination appealed to them even more strongly than to their brothers of the army.

The reports of Hitler's death caused a stir in Congress. Skepticism mingled with questioning whether it would make any difference in the final mop-up of German resistance.

Senator Edwin C. Johnson, Democrat, of Colorado, acting chairman of the Military Affairs Committee, said: "I hope it's so, but I would kind of like to have a look at the body before I believe it." Whether it makes any difference, Mr. Johnson said, depends not only on what attitude Doenitz takes but on what control he can exercise. "I doubt if it makes any difference," he added.

Senator Robert A. Taft, Republican, of Ohio, declared that it was "significant" and interesting that Hitler's death, if the report is true, should come with the complete collapse of his philosophy. Incidentally, it will save the Allies a lot of worry about dealing with a captured Fuehrer."

Hitler Fought Way to Power Unique in Modern History

Bent Most of Europe to His Will by Manipulating Chaos That Was Aftermath of the First World War

Adolf Hitler, one-time Austrian vagabond who rose to be the dictator of Germany, "augmenter of the Reich" and the scourge of Europe, was, like Lenin and Mussolini, a product of the First World War. The same general circumstances, born of the titanic conflict, that carried Lenin, a bookish professional revolutionist, to the pinnacle of power in the Empire of the Czars and cleared the road to mastery for Mussolini in the Rome of the Caesars also paved the way for Hitler's domination in the former mighty Germany of the Hohenzollerns.

Like Lenin and Mussolini, Hitler came out of the blood and chaos of 1914-18, but of the three he was the strangest phenomenon. Lenin, while not known to the general public, had for many years before the Russian Revolution occupied a prominent place as leader and theoretician, of the Bolshevist party. Mussolini was a widely known Socialist editor, orator and politician before making his bid for power. Hitler was nothing, and from nothing he became everything to most Germans.

Lenin dreamed of world revolution. Mussolini thundered of the coming world victory of fascism. Hitler actually challenged the earth to combat by unleashing another war of nations. Emerging from the field in 1918 as an obscure lance corporal, he led Germany twenty-one years later as supreme Fuehrer and War Lord.

Subdued Many Nations

Before the climax of a career unparalleled in history, he had subdued nine nations, defied successfully and humiliated the greatest powers of Europe, and created a social and economic system founded upon the complete subjection of scores of millions to his will in all basic features of social, political, economic and cultural life.

Sixty-five million Germans yielded to the blandishments and magnetism of this slender man of medium height, with little black mustache and shock of dark hair, whose fervor and demagogy swept everything before him with outstretched arms as the savior and regenerator of the Fatherland.

Austria, with 7,000,000 inhabitants, succumbed helplessly to his invasion. More than 2,000,000 Germans in the Sudeten country were added to his domain when he threatened to invade Czechoslovakia, and 10,000,000 Czechs and Slovaks were tied to his chariot wheel, their nation stripped of its defenses, their State destroyed, while all of Central Europe trembled before what appeared to be the irresistible advance of the goose-stepping Nazi hordes of his adopted country.

For more than six years after his advent to power in January, 1933, there seemed to be no one who would dare to challenge Hitler's progress from victory to victory until he met resistance from Poland, backed by the Anglo-French alliance.

Shortly after his dismemberment and subjugation of Czechoslovakia Hitler was reported to have said, "My time is short." His blow against Poland and challenge to France and England less than a year later were taken as indications that he had determined deliberately to stake all he had achieved and all that he still yearned for—domination of Europe—upon one card, war, sensing, perhaps, that time was against him, that he had unleashed forces of hatred and opposition throughout the world that might eventually destroy him.

Series of Broken Promises

Those who had hoped that success at home and extension of his power abroad would make him more circumspect and reluctant to pursue the program of conquest he had outlined for himself in "Mein Kampf" and in his speeches had abandoned that hope when, in violation of his promise to respect the integrity of Czechoslovakia after Munich, he marched on Prague and reduced that nation to a German protectorate.

It was not the first promise he had broken. His whole course at home and abroad had been marked by broken promises and he did not hesitate to massacre many of his own closest adherents, as he did in the purge of June, 1934, when he personally directed the killing of Capt. Ernst Roehm and a group of leading Nazis who had ventured to interfere in his plans for a closer association of the Reichswehr with the regime and insisted upon fulfillment of the original Nazi party promises in the economic field.

The world-wide condemnation of his methods was fed by the system of terrorism he had established at home and in the countries he had conquered, the jailing of scores of thousands in prisons and concentration camps, the secret murder of opponents and those suspected of opposition, the ruthless destruction of the Jews and the persecution of the Catholic and Protestant Churches in his drive for nazification of the nation.

Churches Persecuted Under Nazis' Paganism; Pastor Niemoeller Pre-Eminent in Opposition

It was not long after his coming to power that the churches found themselves at war with Hitler and his regime when they discovered that what he aimed at was no less than the substitution of a pagan German god for Christ.

Some brave representatives of the churches defied Hitler when all others had been broken. Of these Pastor Niemoeller was pre-eminent. In his prison cell Niemoeller became the symbol of Christianity struggling to maintain its truth and identity against the Nazi State.

Mass Unrest His Springboard

The social, political and economic conditions, as they developed in post-war Germany, smarting painfully under humiliation and defeat and struggling for nearly fifteen years with internal dissension and mass unemployment, supplied the springboard for Hitler's leap to power in 1933. Having become disappointed in all other parties, a sufficient number of Germans had accepted the Nazis when the latter, by means of force and propaganda ingeniously directed by Hitler, had maneuvered themselves into a position from which they could strike for seizure of the Government.

But an understanding of Hitler's conduct both before and after his advent to power has been sought by students of the man in study of his youth and family history.

One of the most striking contradictions was the discrepancy between the magnetism he exercised over millions and the unprepossessing appearance of this champion of Aryan race purity. Professor Max von Gruber, noted German authority on race hygiene, gave the following description of Hitler when he met him for the first time at a political trial in a German court in 1923:

"Face and head, bad—mongrel. Low, receding forehead, unhandsome nose broad cheekbones, small eyes, dark hair. Expression of the face not that of one commanding full self-control, but of one instantly excited. At the end—the expression of happy complacency."

Many who watched Hitler from the time when he first made his appearance on the political scene noticed his megalomania, his gambler's readiness to take risks, his habit of wild exaggeration and inability to grasp the full implications of things he said and did. It was this failure to measure the significance of his words and deeds that was considered responsible for the coolness he displayed at critical moments after violent outbursts of thought and temper, although on occasions he was reported to fall into tears and hysterics.

Propaganda a Basic Weapon

At the same time, however, he possessed an uncanny shrewdness in his estimate of the conduct and psychology of masses and individuals, and developed to a fine degree the art of swaying their emotions. The success he achieved in this field enhanced his contempt for the people, whom he called a "flock of sheep and blockheads," a "mixture of stupidity and cowardice." He was convinced that well-directed propaganda by a determined minority, backed by force at the strategic moment, constituted a sure road to victory.

"By shrewd and constant application of propaganda, heaven can be presented to the people as hell and, vice versa, the wretchedest existence as a paradise," he wrote in "Mein Kampf."

This contempt for the people and his unbounded capacity for hatred, which found expression in his merciless treatment of opponents and persecution of the Jews, according to psychologists who have studied the man's career closely, emanated in Hitler from the poverty, wretchedness and frustrations of his youth.

Hitler was born in an inn at Braynau, Austria, close to the German frontier, April 20, 1889. His father was Alois Schickelgruber, the illegitimate son of Alois Hitler. The future Fuehrer's parent was originally a peasant, but later entered the Austrian customs service. He was married three times, his third wife, who was also his niece and ward, being twenty years younger than her husband. She was the future dictator's mother.

Seven children were born of the three marriages contracted by Hitler's father, who died of pulmonary hemorrhage at the age of 66. His three wives died of weak chests. Two of Hitler's brothers and a sister died in childhood. A niece of the Fuehrer committed suicide. A half-brother had no progeny. The German dictator himself never married. At the age of 16 he suffered from lung trouble. On his mother's side there were several eccentrics in the family. In general, the family showed definite tendencies to illness and mental instability.

German Adherent From Youth

Unlike his father, who was a fervent supporter of the Austro-Hungarian monarchy and wanted his son to follow him in the Government service, Adolf Hitler was from early youth a strong adherent of Germany. He was convinced that it was the historic mission of the Germans to rule the Austrians and the complex of races inhabiting Franz Josef's land.

Hitler had no love for his father and resented his insistence that he prepare himself for the Government service. Not venturing to defy his father openly, he adopted a policy of passive resistance by idling away his time at school. At the age of 14, after his father's death, Hitler went to live with his mother at Linz. There he stayed until he was 19, pampered by his mother, who catered to his habit of idling.

Upon her death he found himself alone and friendless, without any means of earning a living and quite unprepared for the battle of life. He had been a failure at school and was unable to pass examinations. While his parents were still alive Hitler had gone for a short time to Munich, where he had taken some courses in drawing. With his mother's passing he betook himself to Vienna, where he applied for admission to the Academy of Arts. He thought of becoming an architect. The few drawings he presented to the director were so mediocre, however, that his application was denied for lack of qualification.

From 1909 to the outbreak of the First World War, Hitler led a wretched existence. For a while he lived in a Vienna "flophouse," among beggars and vagabonds. He spent nights on park benches, harassed by the police. He was an outcast among outcasts, eating at a monastery soup kitchen. This existence continued for three years, during which he managed to earn a precarious living by painting picture postcards for tradesmen and doing minor carpenter work.

Nevertheless, he considered himself to be an artist of talent and hated the world for not according him recognition. He spent his leisure hours day-dreaming and brooding over his frustration. He himself admitted in his autobiography that up to his twenty-fifth year he was what is known as a good-for-nothing, a spoiled idler. Moved by a sensitive ego, a restless spirit and a quick mind, he yearned passionately to make an impression, to gain recognition, to attain to great achievements, to know everything, to attract attention, to master the world.

Politics His Ruling Passion

His greatest passion was for politics. A shy and beaten youth, Hitler would become transformed as soon as conversation turned on matters political. His tongue would loosen and a torrent of words would rush from his lips. In those days before the First World War Hitler never formed friendships, male or female. He never communicated with his family, who thought him dead. Jeered at by acquaintances, he wept.

The one thing that gave him hope and courage was the disintegration of the Austro-Hungarian Empire, which he foresaw, and evidences of which had become apparent to many long before the war. Considering himself a German, he felt superior to those around him. For the Slavs of the empire he felt contempt. For the Jews he felt hatred. As for the workers, he believed them to be not much better. This feeling he expressed to Otto Strasser, one of his early collaborators in the Nazi movement, in 1930, when he said: "The workers, they want nothing but bread and games. In the great mass they are not worth consideration. We must build a master class from elements of a better race."

And it was he who would build that master class and lead it! In addition to dividing mankind into inferior and superior races, he divided it also into inferior and superior human beings. He stood out in his classification as the superman.

Long before he had dreamed of achieving power he had developed the principles that nations were destined to hate, oppose and destroy one another; that the law of history was the struggle for survival between peoples; that the Germans were chosen by destiny to rule over others, and that the great mass of the people were mediocrities immersed in a low materialism and destined to be dominated by a higher social type. The Jews he regarded as particularly inferior and a danger to all other peoples.

Violated His Party's Own Basic Principles Governing Society, Economics and 'Race'

These, it may be said, were the only principles to which Hitler remained true, for he violated the basic principles of the Nazi economic and social program, threw overboard the principle, so often proclaimed by him as Nazi party leader and Fuehrer, that what he desired was the union of all Germans and not the incorporation of other races in the Reich, and abandoned, temporarily, as a tactical maneuver his repeatedly proclaimed unalterable opposition to bolshevism, with which he consummated a treaty of non-aggression in the midst of the Polish crisis of August, 1939.

Hitler left Vienna in 1913 for Munich, where he supported himself by doing odd jobs as a painter and barely managed to earn his keep. He shared a room with a Viennese engineer, but had no real friends and no contacts with women. Those who came in contact with him were struck by his passion for politics and political wrangles. He drifted, unable to find regular employment of the kind his father had wanted him to have. Hitler himself disclosed later his father's prediction that no good would ever come of his son. He was poor, miserable and hopeless.

War Came as a Deliverance

Then came the war. It lifted Hitler from obscurity into a state of exaltation.

"To me those hours were like a deliverance," Hitler wrote of the outbreak of the war in "Mein Kampf." "I am not ashamed to say that, overcome by a storm of enthusiasm, I fell on my knees and thanked Heaven from an overflowing heart."

A year before, in Salzburg, the Austrian doctors had rejected him for military service because of physical weakness. He now volunteered for the German Army, and, when accepted, felt a sense of power and of great things to come. At the front, where he served as a dispatch carrier, he was friendless. No one wrote to him. No one sent him parcels. His services were recognized by his superiors, however, and he was rewarded with the Iron Cross.

Regarded as an eccentric by his comrades, he replied once, "You will hear much of me some day." Because his superiors did not take him seriously he was not advanced beyond the rank of lance corporal. He was gassed, and the end of the war found him in a hospital in Passewalk, Pomerania. He viewed with pain the collapse of the German Empire. His hour had not yet struck, but, enraged at the revolution and the revolutionists, bitter at the Kaiser and Field Marshal von Hindenburg because of their failure to suppress the revolution, he felt that his day would come. His confidence in himself was as great as his sense of frustration.

After the war Hitler did not return to civilian life. Though officially demobilized, he remained in the service of the Reichswehr. His work was in the political intelligence division. In those days the Reichswehr had already begun to dream of revenge. In addition to the illegal groups maintained inside the Reichswehr conspiring for the overthrow of the German Republic and planning for a military resurgence of the country, many officers and former officers attached themselves to various conspiratory "free corps" organizations formed for political purposes and the spreading of terrorism.

Some of these organizations helped stage revolts or "Putsches" against the Government, the most notable of which was the monarchist Kapp "Putsch" of August, 1920, when the insurgents captured Berlin, but were compelled to yield by a general strike proclaimed by the Ebert government. These "free corps" organizations were financed by some industrialists, who likewise sought to undermine the Government and thwart the work of the Inter-allied Military Commission established in Germany to keep her disarmed, in accordance with the provisions of the Versailles treaty.

A Spy for Conspirators Against Republic; Joined 'German Labor Party' Band in 1919

Hitler acted as an intelligence officer or spy for these "free corps" bands. He established relations with influential military circles both inside and outside the Reichswehr. When the latter suppressed the Communist regime in Bavaria in 1919, Hitler furnished information that led to the execution of many Communists and Socialists. The activities of the militarist insurgents led, among other things, to assassination of republican leaders, notably the killings of Erzberger and Rathenau.

In 1919 Hitler was assigned to the task of keeping an eye on a little band calling itself the German Labor party. Hitler joined this group and was followed soon thereafter by several hundred officers and former officers whom Ernst Roehm, at that time a captain on the staff of the Military Governor of Bavaria, had instructed to become members of the organization. This little party developed ultimately into the German National Socialist party, the organization forged by Hitler as the instrument for the achievement of power.

Among the men Hitler met when he joined the German Labor party was Dietrich Eckhart, a journalist, from whom he obtained the basic principles of the ideology later adopted by the Nazis. Eckhart died in 1923. Others whom Hitler met as members of the German Labor party were Rudolph Hess, who later became Deputy Fuehrer, and who was named second by Hitler in the line of succession to supreme power upon the outbreak of hostilities with Poland in 1939, and Alfred Rosenberg, another of those who subsequently played a leading role in the Nazi regime as ideologist and theoretician. Hess flew to England in 1941, presumably on a "peace mission," and remained there a prisoner.

Roehm also was a member of the organization. Altogether there were only six men in the German Labor party before Hitler joined it. These half dozen men, with Hitler in the lead, were the group that prepared the second world catastrophe of our time.

By force of eloquence, ruthless methods and daring of ideas, Hitler forged ahead in the movement founded by the little band. He went about making speeches bewailing the wrongs done to Germany, appealing to audiences and stirring them with the promise of new power and greatness to come.

The extremism of his utterances and promises made little impression at first. The poor lance corporal was treated as a circus performer. People laughed at him and his dreams. Germany lay crushed and prostrate after her defeat in a four-year war. Poverty and misery were abroad in the land. It seemed as if many decades would have to pass before the nation could pull itself together on the basis of a new order. But Hitler persevered.

Strategy Formula Simple

His strategy was based on a simple principle: to obtain the support of powerful and influential elements in the army, industry and finance and to buttress that with support among the masses. He addressed himself first to the middle classes, ruined by inflation, and managed to obtain some assistance from elements among the workers disappointed in the revolution.

To the middle classes he promised relief from what he called the tyranny of big business, particularly the department stores, with which small tradesmen found it difficult to compete. He promised them that when in power he would dissolve the department stores and abolish all interest. To the workers he promised dissolution of the trusts. Neither of these promises was kept.

Added to his economic program, designed to appeal to the ruined middle-class elements, he put forward his slogans of extreme nationalism and racism—the union of all Germans on the basis of self-determination in a greater Germany. It was not until 1928 that he came forward with a program for the farmers, who had become rich during the war on high prices resulting from the blockade. In 1932, when mass unemployment assumed unprecedented proportions in Germany, he promised work for all the unemployed.

Stubbornly, persistently, Hitler toiled at the task of building his movement. Believing the mission of national and social regeneration was to be realized by what he called a vigorous minority, a desperate élite, he gathered around him a group of intellectuals, officers, former officers, penurious students and ambitious youths without prospects in the Germany of that time.

All these were in the main men of humble origin who had gone through the war and found themselves socially shipwrecked when it was over. Like Hitler, they were ready for anything. They had nothing to lose and felt they had everything to gain if only they could grasp the instruments of power. Like Hitler, they were impelled in their thoughts and actions by a superiority complex, the satisfaction of which became the propelling ambition of their being. Like Hitler, they identified the regeneration of Germany with the realization of their dream.

They declared war on the republic, on the Versailles Treaty, on the Communists, whose methods of professional revolutionists, of propaganda and of force, they made their own. As Goebbels, who was to become Hitler's Minister of Propaganda and Enlightenment, explained it in later years, "Propaganda should not be decent—it should be effective," and "We fight with Marxist methods, but we shall do things better than the Marxists."

Munich Beer-Cellar Putsch of 1923 Failed; Imprisoned for Treason, He Was Soon Freed

In line with this conception, there was a distinct class element in the organization Hitler set up in those early years of his activity. All the officers and leaders were below the rank of major and captain. Army generals, active and retired, regarded him with suspicion because of his lowly origin and demagogic appeals to the middle classes. They joined him openly only after he had made an impression and showed that his chances of success were not to be minimized.

It was this distinction that was primarily responsible for the failure of Hitler's first "Putsch" on Nov. 8 and 9, 1923, in Munich, known as "the beer-cellar Putsch."

Believing his "Tag" had arrived, Hitler forced his way into an assembly of high-ranking Bavarian generals, Ministers, Government officials and politicians in the rathskeller of the Munich City Hall on the evening of Nov. 8 and, brandishing a revolver, fired a shot into the air, announcing that his revolution had begun. He called for a march on Berlin and pleaded with those present to give him their blessing. They were taken aback by this sudden move, for while they had pretended to encourage Hitler they knew that the time for action was not ripe and had made him promise that he would do nothing reckless and would not use violence that might endanger their own positions.

His action was a violation of his promise. But his men were outside, and, yielding to the importunities of General Ludendorff, who was among those present and with whom Hitler had made a working agreement, the Bavarian militarists and reactionaries, headed by von Kahr, Minister-President, and General von Lossow, Chief of the Bavarian Army, pretended to give their assent. The army and State officials returned to their offices and promptly proclaimed Hitler a traitor to the State.

There followed a skirmish next day in the center of the city between several thousand of Hitler's followers and the police, backed by Lossow's troops. Hitler was leading his men, waving his revolver, with Ludendorff beside him. Confident that the police would not fire upon seeing Ludendorff, Hitler marched on. But the police fired nevertheless. The thousands of Nazis scattered in all directions, with Ludendorff alone marching forward defiantly. He was arrested. Goering, who was also in the van, was wounded, but escaped and later fled the country. Hitler fell to the ground.

Testimony at the trial that followed the affair was almost unanimous that Hitler was the first man to get up and run for cover. He dashed toward his automobile and fled. He was caught, however, and tried for treason. The sentence was five years' imprisonment in a fortress. He served only a few months and was paroled, returning to political activity.

Rebuilt Power After Defeat

After the fiasco of the Munich "Putsch" it seemed as if Hitler's cause was irretrievably lost. Throughout the country he was the butt of ridicule. The Government and its supporters felt he could no longer be a danger and that there was no use making a martyr of him by keeping him in prison or taking special measures. For some time Hitler appeared to go into retirement. He was at work on "Mein Kampf," begun in prison, but at the same time continued quietly at the task of rebuilding his shattered group and developing the foundations for his mass movement.

Within the next seven years he obtained a huge following, which came to number 3,000,000. It was built along military lines, with army corps, regiments and companies. The men wore uniforms and were subject to strict military discipline. This army consisted of the Storm Troops, who were brown shirts, and the Black Guards, representing more carefully picked formations, wearing black shirts. These troops acted as the Hitler police at public meetings and demonstrations, attacked Jews in the streets of Munich, broke up meetings of the opposition, staged street brawls with Communists and republicans, beat up leaders of other parties and, in general, conducted a reign of terror with which the authorities found it increasingly difficult to cope, in proportion as the political aspect of the Nazi movement gathered strength.

The nation was thrown into a state of veritable civil war. The Socialists and Democrats took counter-measures by forming their semi-military Reichsbanner, while the Communists, fighting the Socialists and the republicans, organized their Red-Front Fighters League. The authorities in Bavaria, Thuringia and other German States openly sided with the Hitlerites and facilitated their work. Soon the authorities in Prussia began to find it more and more difficult to cope with them. Thus the movement gathered force as the final showdown was approaching.

Powerful Elements Allied

The same methods that Hitler subsequently used against other nations—intimidation, violent and abusive propaganda, coercion and terror—were applied by the Nazis to their political opponents in Germany. With increased support from the army and industrialists, a gigantic propaganda machine was set up, which, backed by millions of throats, blared wild accusations in an unending stream against the Government and leaders of other parties.

Men like Gustav Stresemann, to say nothing of Socialists and Democrats were denounced as traitors and held up to public ignominy. Their lives were in constant danger. An atmosphere of disorder was created with the intent of feeding popular demand for a "strong hand." All this was staged with tremendous dramatic effect by the able propaganda organization directed by Dr. Joseph Goebbels.

In the meantime, through Captain Roehm, Hitler strengthened his ties with the Reichswehr, which came to realize more and more that he could not be resisted without offending those millions of the population upon whom the Reichswehr itself, seeking the rearmament of Germany, had to depend. With a positive genius for political strategy of the kind necessary for his triumph, Hitler cemented the structure of his movement by amalgamating the support of the most powerful elements, the army and industrialists, with the enthusiasm and blind approval of his masses.

Reich Army Generals Became His Captives; His Political Power Increased After 1930

Already in those days, five years before his advent to power, the army generals had become his prisoners. Those who, like General von Schleicher, later attempted to withdraw to an independent policy, paid for it with their lives or with oblivion.

But great as were his successes in the years after the Munich putsch, it was not until 1930 that Hitler emerged definitely as a mighty political power in Germany. As late as 1928, in the Reichstag elections of that year, Hitler was able to obtain only twelve seats. But in the elections held in the fall of 1930 he received 6,000,000 votes and captured 107 seats.

It was one of the greatest upsets in the turbulent history of the struggling German Republic. By this time Hitler had become the veritable idol not only of the active Nazi party members but of the masses who cast their ballots for him.

The factor that gave his movement this great impetus was the economic crisis that broke over the world in 1929 and struck Germany with particular severity. Nearly 7,000,000 unemployed, added to the millions of impoverished middle-class people and the hundreds of thousands of professionals and jobless intellectuals, provided a setting made to order for Hitler.

Crisis Spurred Extremism

The crisis fed with unprecedented force the extremist elements on the right and on the left. The armies of Hitlerism and communism grew to proportions that made it increasingly difficult for the democratic republic to function. While professing uncompromising hostility to each other, the extreme Red and Brown elements cooperated in the Reichstag, the Prussian Diet and other provincial Legislatures in undermining the power and stability of republican institutions. In 1932 the Hitlerites and Communists worked together in staging a great transportation strike in Berlin.

Electoral Victory Followed by Careful Steps To Consolidate His Position With Military

After his electoral victory of 1930 Hitler moved to consolidate his position with the Reichswehr. Appearing as a witness at a trial of three Reichswehr officers for furthering a fascist plot in the army, Hitler made his famous declaration in which he flattered the army and promised that when his party attained power the "November criminals," those who made the German revolution and set up the Weimar Republic, would be exterminated, and that "heads would roll." In his testimony Hitler paid tribute to monarchist Germany, thus lulling the monarchists and their army generals into the belief that he planned to restore the old imperial order.

Meanwhile the government of Chancellor Heinrich Bruening, a Centrist leader, was fighting desperately to stem the tide of economic and political dissolution. For many months Bruening was ruling by decree based upon emergency laws hastily passed by the Reichstag. Social services were radically curtailed, taxes were raised to a degree never known before, and popular discontent continued to mount in ever more threatening degree.

There was talk of Hitler's being taken into the Government, but he persistently refused, saying he would not rule unless he was able to command all authority. At the same time, however, he declared that he would attain that power by "legal" means only, that he had no intention of carrying out a coup d'état.

In 1931 Hitler was received by President von Hindenburg for the first time. Until that moment the aged President had steadfastly refused to meet the man whom he regarded as an "upstart." Hitler took good advantage of that interview. He appeared to have won the President's confidence by speaking enthusiastically of the army and expressing his profound interest in its welfare, while pledging fealty to the aged executive. The "old man" was moved and subsequently tried to bring about some basis of unity between Hitler and Bruening, against whom the Nazis had been waging a vitriolic campaign.

Hitler Against Hindenburg

The situation became more acute when Hitler, despite his flattering of Hindenburg, who, he had hoped in vain, would call him to the Chancellorship, announced his own candidacy for the Presidency in the spring of 1932. In that campaign he intensified his agitation against the republic, the Versailles Treaty and the Government's fulfillment policy.

The whole world saw in the campaign a life-and-death struggle between the Nazis and the republic, as, indeed, it was. Hindenburg, running for a third term, emerged victorious, with 19,000,000 votes against 13,000,000 for Hitler. At the same time, however, Hitler registered his greatest electoral triumph from the point of view of votes received. From then on he was, indeed, a power not to be ignored.

The Bruening Cabinet fell shortly after the Presidential election and in the consequent Reichstag elections of July 31, 1932, the Nazis increased the number of their seats to 230, becoming the largest single political party. Twice before the end of the year Hitler demanded the Chancellorship, and each time Hindenburg refused. Hindenburg offered him a Cabinet post in a reconstituted Government but that was not enough for him. He was biding his time for the final blow at the republic. "The Chancellorship or nothing!" he demanded.

With the Reichstag unable to form a new Government because of the multiplicity of warring parties and the impossibility of agreeing on a coalition, it was again dissolved and new elections were called for Nov. 6, 1932. In that election the Hitlerites lost 2,000,000 votes, and it appeared as if the Nazi tide were receding.

What followed was a series of intrigues behind the scenes that ultimately landed Hitler in the Chancellorship. Bruening resigned and Franz von Papen, a Catholic and a diplomat remembered in the United States for his espionage and sabotage work during the First World War, was appointed in his place. Von Papen's Ministry was known as "the Cabinet of monocles." It had no basis of support in the Reichstag or in the population and was obviously a stop-gap.

General von Schleicher, army chief, fearing a union of the Hitlerites and Communists, against whom the army would be unable to stand, forced von Papen's resignation and himself assumed the Chancellorship. Von Schleicher's was "the second Cabinet of monocles." Powerful elements in the army and around von Papen, bent on helping Hitler to the Chancellorship, refused to support von Schleicher, however, who thereupon demanded another dissolution of the Reichstag and a general election. Hindenburg refused, and on the advice of his son, Oskar, and General von Blomberg who subsequently became Minister of War in Hitler's government, called Hitler to Schleicher's place. This was on Jan. 30, 1933. Hitler's goal was attained.

Upon calling Hitler to the Chancellorship, Hindenburg instructed him to form a coalition Government with other parties of the right. He was to observe the Constitution and rule only with the consent of the Reichstag. Hitler accepted these terms, with the proviso that new Reichstag elections were to be called so he might once more seek the approval of the electorate. Hindenburg was pleased by this ostensible desire of Hitler to seek the support of the majority. In fact, he was delighted.

The Reichstag was dissolved and in the campaign that ensued the Nazis unleashed a flood of propaganda eclipsing anything that had gone before. With the machinery of Government in their hands and in command of the National Treasury, with the prestige of authority behind them, the Nazis were able to terrorize the electorate and so cripple the campaign activities of other parties as to command the advantage.

In vain did the Nationalists, headed by Hugenberg, who suspected what was coming, object to the dissolution of the Reichstag and the calling of a new election. Having helped Hitler to power, they now saw themselves completely outmaneuvered by the Nazi chieftain.

The Burning of the Reichstag

One of the most shocking events in the history of the Nazi regime came on the evening of Feb. 27, 1933, a week before the elections. On that evening the Reichstag building suddenly went up in flames. Part of the building collapsed. The fire, it was determined, was of incendiary origin, for a great deal of inflammable material was used to start the conflagration. Hitler announced that Communists were the incendiaries, while Goering proclaimed that documents

Continued on Page 7, Column 2

THE SCHICKELGRUBER FAMILY

His mother

Adolf Hitler as a child

His father

Hitler (right) with two comrades during the first World War

The New York Times

Hitler's Role as a War Lord: Famous Meetings Before and During the Conflict

In Munich in 1938 when he won the consent of Britain and France to march into Czechoslovakia. Left to right: Prime Minister Neville Chamberlain, Great Britain: Premier Edouard Daladier, France: Hitler, Premier Mussolini, Italy, and Count Ciano, Foreign Minister of Italy. Associated Press

Another meeting. The Slovakian Premier Joseph Tiso at the Reich's Chancellory in Berlin just before Czechoslovakia was dissolved and taken under the "protection" of the Reich. Tiso, upon returning to his country, immediately asked for German "protection." Associated Press

The speech which started World War II. Hitler, on Sept. 1, 1939, announcing to the Reichstag that Germany was at war with Poland. Great Britain and France immediately declared war against Germany. Associated Press

At one of the Fuehrer's headquarters on the Russian front when the Nazis were pushing the Soviet Armies back toward the Urals. Left to right are Admiral Doenitz, then Chief of the German Navy; Premier Mussolini, Field Marshal Keitel, Hitler and Reich Marshal Hermann Goering. The New York Times

Congratulating his Gestapo Chief, Heinrich Himmler, when he appointed the latter Minister of the Interior in 1943. Associated Press

Getting a view of the battlefront from the window of his special plane Associated Press

Hitler in high and low spirits. In 1940 he danced his famous jig after the fall of France. At the right he looks over damage caused in a German town by Allied bombers. Associated Press

HITLER HEARTENED BY DEAL IN MUNICH

Sudeten Grab Strengthened Illusion He Could Act With Entire Impunity

The fortnight ending with the cession of the Sudeten region to Germany, at the end of September, 1938, and marking the prelude to the destruction of the Czechoslovak State, gave Europe the most acute crisis it has experienced up to that time since the end of the First World War. Encouraged by his triumph over France and England in the Sudeten dispute, Hitler occupied the whole of Czecholovakia less than six months later and began almost immediately to prepare for the showdown with Poland. The latter development brought him into armed conflict with the Western democracies and, ultimately, with the United States.

The Sudeten crisis was preceded by months of violent agitation by the Sudeten Nazis, under the leadership of Konrad Henlein. Originally the Henleinists demanded only autonomy with the Czechoslovak State. Gradually, however, under incitement from Berlin, they expanded their demands to a scope which made agreement with Prague extremely difficult, if not impossible.

Moved by the desire to facilitate a settlement in the hope of preventing a European war, for which the great democracies were unprepared, Great Britain dispatched Lord Runciman to Czechoslovakia with instructions to bring about an adjustment that would avert German armed intervention. He labored in vain for many weeks. Finally, it appeared that the Henleinists were determined to reject any plan of settlement except direct annexation of the Sudeten country to Germany. After fanning their agitation and disorders to the point of civil war, Henleinists informed Lord Runciman that the Sudeten question was no longer an internal one for Czechoslovakia.

Hitler Talks Self-Determination

At the same time, in an address at Nuremberg, Hitler frankly raised the question of "self-determination" for the Sudetens. It became clear that the conflict was one between Czechoslovakia and Germany. The situation reached a climax on Sept. 14, when the concentration of German troops on the Czech frontier made Hitler's invasion appear a matter of hours.

In a move unprecedented in British diplomacy, Prime Minister Neville Chamberlain rushed by airplane to Berchtesgaden for a conversation with Hitler in an effort to avert a military invasion of Czechoslovakia and the embroilment of England and France in war with Germany. Upon his return to London Mr. Chamberlain reported to the House of Commons that he had no doubt that "my visit alone prevented an invasion for which everything had been prepared." It appeared that the sole hope of averting a conflict that threatened to engulf Europe consisted in giving Hitler what he demanded, the incorporation of the Sudeten country into Germany.

A plan for effecting this transfer was then worked out by French and British experts, delimiting the new frontier. With this plan, to which Czechoslovakia was compelled to asset, Mr. Chamberlain returned to Germany. He again met Hitler, this time at Godesberg. To Mr. Chamberlain's surprise, Hitler was not satisfied with the plan of settlement. He simply handed to the Prime Minister a map indicating the territory he proposed to occupy beyond the confines embodied in the plan agreed to by the French and the British, together with a memorandum, which Mr. Chamberlain characterized as an ultimatum, announcing Hitler's intention to march into Czechoslovakia on Oct. 1. Nor was Hitler willing to agree to a guarantee of the integrity of the remaining parts of Czechoslovakia.

The last phase of the crisis followed quickly. It ended in Munich. Hitler got what he wanted, and in some sections of the territory in dispute even more. On Sept. 29 an agreement was signed ending the crisis. Within the next few days, marching in accordance with the conditions agreed upon at Munich, German armies occupied the Sudeten country and such other strips of territory as had been ceded by the Czechs. Shocked by these developments, the world sat back to see whether peace actually had been saved.

One immediate consequence of Munich was the resignation of the Czechoslovak Government, including President Eduard Benes. A new Government took over. The rest of the world hoped that within its narrower territorial confines Czechoslovakia would find it possible to live in peace.

A New Crisis Follows

But a new crisis soon made itsef manifest. It came from Slovakia, where the Hlinka party and Hlinka Guards, similar to Nazi Storm Troopers, agitated continually for autonomy, a demand which soon was extended to independence. German agents, active among the Slovaks, did their best to fan these sentiments, until finally, early in March, 1939, the Prague Government took steps to crush the Slovak movement. Slovak Premier Tiso, a tool of Germany, appealed to Hitler. Events then followed rapidly.

On March 12 anti-Czech demonstrations, provoked by German agents, broke out at Bratislava, Slovak capital. Simultaneously the German press and radio unleashed the usual blares of denunciation against the Czechs. Then Dr. Tiso, who meanwhile had been driven from office by the Czechs, took a plane for Berlin. He was received with full military honors. He conferred with Hitler. German troops were ordered to the Czech border.

On March 13, after a demand and served upon him by Hitler, President Hacha of Czechoslovakia summoned a meeting of the Slovak diet, assembled at Bratislava. The diet proclaimed the independence of Slovakia. Tiso became President. The Slovaks learned in astonishment that they were no longer part of Czechoslovakia. Hungary moved up into the Carpatho-Ukraine.

On March 14, on command from Berlin, President Hacha and Dr. Frantisek Chvalkovsky, Foreign Minister, arrived in Hitler's capital. They met with Hitler for three hours. There followed a communiqué declaring that President Hacha had "trustfully laid the fate of the Czech people and country into the hands of the Fuehrer of the German Reich."

Already German troops were across the border, marching into Bohemia on the excuse of restoring "order." The Czechs submitted under threat of aerial bombardment of Prague. Hitler proclaimed that Czechoslovakia "has ceased to exist." On the morning of the same day the German troops arrived in Prague, greeted with jeers from the populace. With them came the Gestapo. German clerks took over the National Bank. In the late afternoon Hitler himself arrived in the Czech capital to sleep in the Hradschin Castle, seat of the Bohemian kings, the Habsburgs and of the Czech democracy.

On March 15 Moravia and Bohemia were annexed to the Reich. They were made German protectorates. The Hitler swastika was raised over public buildings. Persecutions of Jews were unleashed. Mass arrests of prominent liberals began. From the Hradschin, Hitler issued a proclamation setting forth the new status of the country.

Bohemia and Moravia were proclaimed to be German protectorates on the ground that they were once, many centuries ago, part of the Holy Roman Empire. Germany now needed them for her "lebensraum." Meanwhile, Slovakia requested that she, too, be taken under Germany's rule as a protectorate. Hitler granted the "request."

Only one portion of Czechoslovakia thus remained outside the German Reich. This was the Carpatho-Ukraine, which Hungary now annexed, thus obtaining a common frontier with Poland. Hitler permitted the annexation because of the growing influence of the Nazis in Budapest. He was planning to do to Hungary what he did to Czechoslovakia.

On March 16, after a hurried tour of Bohemia and Moravia, Hitler rode into swastika-bedecked Vienna. Behind him, at Prague and in other Czechoslovak cities, stayed the Gestapo. Another wave of arrests, estimated at several thousand, followed. Many suicides of Jews and liberals were reported. The occurrences were a repetition of what happened with the annexation of Austria and the occupation of the Sudeten country.

On March 18 Hitler named the "Reich Protector" for Bohemia and Moravia. He was Baron Konstantin von Neurath, former Nazi Foreign Minister, president of the Nazi secret Cabinet Council.

Hitler Fought Way to Power Unique in Modern History

Continued From Page Six

umentary material to prove this charge would soon be made public.

The burning of the Reichstag produced a profound impression. Masses of people believed the Communists were actually responsible. More than ever they looked to Hitler as the savior of the nation, and, indeed, in the elections a week later he won his greatest victory, but with only 43 per cent of the votes cast.

Later, at a trial conducted by the Nazi Government itself, a group of Communists accused of starting the fire were acquitted. Among these were the German Communist leader, Torgler, and the Bulgarian Communist, Dimitroff. The latter subsequently became the general secretary of the Communist International. The only man convicted was Marinus van der Lubbe, a former Dutch Communist of distinctly queer mind, who was supposed to have been found in the Reichstag Building at the time of the fire.

Widespread belief in Germany and abroad, on the basis of extensive investigation, was that the Hitlerites themselves set fire to the Reichstag, with van der Lubbe as their tool, to enhance their chances in the election.

After the election Hitler proceeded at full steam toward establishment of his dictatorship. Decrees issued by him and Goering, who was Minister-President for Prussia, vested the Government with dictatorial power. All Communist members of the Reichstag were ordered arrested, as were many Social Democrats. They were thus prevented from attending the Reichstag session called for March 23. Bills were introduced affirming and extending the Government's absolute authority.

Storm Troopers, displaying pistols, were stationed in the Reichstag, meeting now in the Kroll Opera House, filling the aisles between the members' benches. "Choose between peace and war!" shouted Hitler to the terrorized representatives of the people as he demanded passage of the bills.

The Social Democrats alone voted in the negative, but Hitler had his majority. He was now the "legal" dictator of Germany. On June 27 he threw Hugenberg, leader of the Conservatives, out of the Government and the Nazis ruled supreme. Ostensibly, the dictatorial power wrested by Hitler from the Reichstag was for four years, until April 1, 1937, but actually it meant the end of democracy in Germany.

On March 12, 1933, President von Hindenburg decreed that the Nazi swastika, Hitler's party emblem, should be incorporated in the black-white-red ensign as part of the official flag of Germany.

With supreme power in his hands and millions of Storm Troopers ruling the country like an army of occupation, Hitler then proceeded to destroy the last vastiges of opposition. He abolished the Socialist, Communist and Democratic parties, smashed the trade unions, suppressed the entire opposition press, drove all Republicans from Government and civil service positions, filling all available posts with his party friends and supporters.

Even the Nationalist party, the party of the conservative Junkers and industrialists, was dissolved, while the Centrist party, the great party of German Catholics, announced its own "voluntary dissolution."

Arrests and Terror Established Control; Unity of Nazi Party and State Was Decreed

There were mass arrests of Socialists, Communists, liberals, Catholics and others, many of whom were taken to concentration camps, where they were severely beaten and maltreated in brutal fashion. Some of the leading statesmen and labor chieftains of Germany were among the prisoners. Many were murdered by prison guards and Storm Troopers.

At the same time a wave of anti-Semitic outrages spread all over the country. Decrees depriving Jews of civil rights, of property and the right to work in various professions were issued. These found expression later in even severer form in the Nuremberg laws.

On April 1, 1933, the Nazis carried out a one-day boycott on Jewish shops and stores, placing guards in front of the establishments and keeping customers from entering. Jews were degraded to an inferior position in German society and virtually deprived of opportunity for existence. Throughout the world, Jews, supported by Gentiles, countered with an economic boycott against Germany. This failed, however, to abate Hitler's merciless campaign.

One of the most shocking episodes of the early period of the Hitler regime was the burning of the books of outstanding German and foreign authors. The books consigned to funeral pyres in the streets and public squares of Berlin and other leading cities represented the scientific, artistic and liberal heritage of the ages. Their burning was supposed to symbolize the break between the new Nazi Germany and what the Nazis characterized as the "shameful" past. The spectacle served to emphasize the divorce of Nazi Germany from Western culture and civilization.

On Dec. 1, 1933, a decree proclaimed the "unity of the Nazi party and the State." By this decree Hitler meant that all labor organizations, youth organizations, universities, schools, parties and individuals had lost their identity and were merged, so far as the Nazis were concerned, in the State.

But despite the great power already wielded by him, his position was not yet entirely secure, not even in his own party, where the so-called left wing, led by Captain Roehm, was manifesting dissatisfaction over Hitler's inclination to seek coordination of the State with the army as against the Storm Troopers, who regarded themselves as the real force that carried the Nazi party to victory.

Around Captain Roehm, who at one time aspired to supreme leadership of the party, had gathered also Nazi elements disappointed in Hitler's failure to make good on his economic policies, policies akin to bolshevism, and his inclination to play politics with the big trusts and industrialists, against whom he had raged in the days when he was denouncing "capitalism" in efforts to gain the ear of the workers.

Fearing a revolt of the Storm Troopers, or rather of that group under Roehm that threatened a breach between the Reichswehr and the Government, Hitler announced in June, 1934, that the Storm Troop organizations would take a vacation for a month beginning July 1. During that period it was intended to disband those formations considered unreliable and reorganize the entire Brownshirt army. This met resistance and Roehm demanded a showdown.

On June 30 and the following day Roehm received it. Under Hitler's personal direction Roehm and his associates were murdered. Among the victims of the "purge" was also General von Schleicher.

In a Reichstag speech on July 13, Hitler sought to justify the purge as punishment for revolt against his authority and declared that the welfare of the German people required drastic action. He said the number killed was seventy-seven, but other sources declared it exceeded 1,000.

Scarcely had the consternation caused by these executions died down when the nation was treated to another surprise. On Aug. 2, 1934, President von Hindenburg died on his estate at Neudeck, Prussia. He had been ill for some time. Within a space of a few hours, Hitler announced that he had taken over the powers of the President in addition to those of Chancellor, thereby vesting himself autocratic authority never wielded by any German ruler. He proclaimed himself Fuehrer and ordered a plebiscite for approval of the consolidation of the powers of the President and Chancellor under that title. The plebiscite was held on Aug. 19. The approval vote was overwhelming.

From that moment Hitler embarked upon his bold program in the domain of internal and foreign affairs, a program that led to the mass rearmament of Germany, making her once more a great military power, reoccupation and militarization of the Rhineland, the annexation of Austria, the occupation of Czechoslovakia, the seizure of Memel, Danzig and the Polish Corridor, the destruction of Poland, seizure of Denmark and Norway, the conquest of Holland, Belgium, Luxembourg, France and the Balkans, the invasion of Russia, and the long domination of the European Continent by Nazi Germany.

It all ended, however, in the confirmation of Napoleon's dictum: "Empires die of indigestion."

With the fall of Hitler's empire under the blows of Allied arms Germany fell to the lowest estate experienced by any nation in modern times.

That was Hitler's contribution to the history of the "master race."

Hitler's 'Intuition' Strategy Helped Hasten Defeat of Germany on East and West Fronts

History will determine Hitler's exact degree of responsibility for the conduct of military operations during the war. It was known that he was frequently in disagreement with his generals, who had been inclined to urge greater caution than he had exhibited on many critical occasions. He was encouraged in his daring at crucial moments before the war by what appeared to him the unwillingness or unreadiness of France and England to enter into collision with Germany.

Thus it was at the time of the German invasion of the Rhineland, of the occupation of Austria and during the Czechoslovak crisis of 1938. It is probable that at the time of the diplomatic conflict with Poland, immediately preceding the outbreak of hostilities, Hitler felt that Britain and France would accept another Munich and yield to his demands on Poland. This may be regarded by the future historian as his first great mistake.

The long series of sweeping victories won by the German armies in the early years of the war buttressed his self-confidence, fanned by the adulation heaped upon him by his press, which pictured him as a great military genius. After the fall of France in June, 1940, he gave vent to his exultation by dancing an impromptu jig on the sidewalks of Paris, an act that the newsreels recorded for the entire world to see.

His personal responsibility for the invasion of Russia in June, 1940, was never denied. The great initial victories of the Germans in Russia were also attributed to his alleged uncanny military talents. Less than two years later, however, it had become clear that his invasion of Russia, which cost Germany millions of lives, was another and perhaps the greatest of his errors. For a few months it had seemed that his plans in Russia would be crowned with success, but after the reverses that compelled the German retreat from Moscow he sought to cover up the setback by placing the responsibility on the German generals, removing Field Marshal Gen. Walther von Brauchitsch as Commander in Chief and announcing that he would take personal charge of military operations.

The development of the campaigns in Russia led subsequently to one disaster after another. The loss of a German army of 300,000 at Stalingrad in February, 1943, was attributed directly to Hitler's bad strategy in ordering the German forces to hold on to the end when a timely retreat might have saved that army.

His declaration of war on the United States, in support of Japan and in agreement with Italy, on Dec. 11, 1941, marked another fateful day in his career. It was at least as grave a mistake as his invasion of Russia. He was apparently convinced that he would be able to bring Russia to her knees before the United States could make its power felt in Europe. Moreover, he believed that the United States would be too busy in the Pacific to take any decisive part in the European struggle. He was also reported to believe that Japan would strike at Russia immediately after Germany's declaration of war on this country and thus help drive Russia out of the war within a few weeks or months. Later he was reported to have accused Japan of treachery in not doing so.

As the military situation grew more ominous for Germany, Hitler swept aside the authority of his generals and announced that he would exercise complete direction of the war, guided by his "intuition." He minimized the importance of the Allies' landings in French North Africa in November, 1942, and tried to make his people believe that the invasion of Italy and the overthrow of Mussolini in July, 1943, would likewise fail to prevent German victory.

To buttress the tottering structure of the Italian front and repair the political blow dealt to the Axis in Italy he sent a squad of parachutists in September of that year to rescue Mussolini from his confinement behind the Allies lines. The rescue enabled Hitler to establish a puppet Mussolini government in northern Italy which functioned until the entire Italian front collapsed under Anglo-American blows. On April 28, 1945, Mussolini was captured by Italian Partisans and executed. At that very time Hitler was reported dead or dying in Berlin.

While Hitler's public appearances declined in frequency with the progress of the war toward the climax of Germany's defeat, his utterances against her opponents grew in violence and vituperation. He ridiculed the Allies' leaders as "military idiots" and boasted that their armies would never be able to land on the Continent.

Proof of the fatal effects of Hitler's interference with his generals in the conduct of military operations was obtained in documents captured by the Allies shortly after their invasion of Normandy on June 6, 1944. By the middle of 1944 it had become clear to German military and civilian leaders that their country had lost the war and that the elimination of Hitler was essential to salvage what was possible from the wreck. A group of conspirators resolved to remove him from the scene. On July 20, 1944, he was painfully burned by a bomb.

The assassination attempt was attributed to a band of generals and other officers. Hundreds of persons including some distinguished military men involved in the conspiracy were executed and the Government's terror against "defeatists" was intensified. Hitler gradually disappeared from view, although orders and proclamations continued to be issued in his name. In the last few weeks of the war it has become apparent that he had lost control of the situation.

"All the News That's Fit to Print"

The New York Times.

LATE CITY EDITION
Cloudy with showers today. Partly cloudy and cooler tomorrow.
Temperatures Yesterday—Max., 64; Min., 47
Sunrise today, 5:46 A. M.; Sunset, 7:59 P. M.

VOL. XCIV..No. 31,881. Entered as Second-Class Matter. Postoffice, New York, N. Y. NEW YORK, TUESDAY, MAY 8, 1945. THREE CENTS IN NEW YORK CITY

THE WAR IN EUROPE IS ENDED! SURRENDER IS UNCONDITIONAL; V-E WILL BE PROCLAIMED TODAY; OUR TROOPS ON OKINAWA GAIN

ISLAND-WIDE DRIVE

Marines Reach Village a Mile From Naha and Army Lines Advance

7 MORE SHIPS SUNK

Search Planes Again Hit Japan's Life Line—Kyushu Bombed

By WARREN MOSCOW
By Wireless to THE NEW YORK TIMES.

GUAM, Tuesday, May 8—In an island-wide American advance on Okinawa yesterday the First Marine Division drove south to the edge of Dakeshi Village, about a mile from Naha, the capital, straightening out the line on our right flank. In the center the Seventy-seventh Army Division used flame-throwing tanks for considerable advances, while the Seventh Army Division moved forward on the left flank.

[Airfields on Kyushu, southern Japan, were bombed Monday and Tuesday by Superfortresses, two of which were lost in heavy air opposition.

[Allied fliers started operating from the Tarakan airfield although fighting continued on that island off Borneo, and in the Philippines American troops made advances on Mindanao and Luzon.]

Japanese Dead at 36,535

As the United States forces on Okinawa resumed their drive, Fleet Admiral Chester W. Nimitz revealed that Japanese killed on the island had mounted to 36,535 on Monday, showing that the Americans were maintaining their rate of 1,000 a day.

The Americans have not yet taken the main Japanese artillery emplacements on Okinawa, which were the principal targets of the fleet off the island. The fleet's guns continued yesterday, along with carrier aircraft, to support the ground movements.

Meanwhile search bombers of Fleet Air Wing 1 continued to give an impressive demonstration of what the tightening air blockade of Japan will mean. Attacking at mast-head height with bombs and machine guns, these long-range aircraft, based in the Okinawa area, sank four more ships in waters off Korea and damaged five others.

The ships sunk were a large cargo ship, a medium cargo ship, a medium oiler and a large fleet tanker. Two small freighters were

Continued on Page 12, Column 2

The Pulitzer Awards For 1944 Announced

The Pulitzer Prize awards announced yesterday by the trustees of Columbia University included: For a distinguished novel, to "A Bell for Adano," by John Hersey; for an original American play of the current season, to "Harvey," by Mary Chase.

Among the newspaper awards were those to Hal Boyle, Associated Press war reporter, for distinguished correspondence; to James B. Reston of THE NEW YORK TIMES for his reporting of the Dumbarton Oaks Security Conference; to Joe Rosenthal, Associated Press photographer, for his photograph of marines raising the American flag at Iwo and to The Detroit Free Press for "distinguished and meritorious public service" in its investigation of legislative corruption at Lansing, Mich.

Further details of the awards will be found on Page 16.

MOLOTOFF HAILS BASIC 'UNANIMITY'

He Stresses Five Points in World Charter, but His View on One Is Questioned

By JAMES B. RESTON
Special to THE NEW YORK TIMES.

SAN FRANCISCO, May 7—The major allies who forced Germany's unconditional surrender have reached "unanimity" on the kind of world security organization which should be created at the United Nations conference to protect their newly won victory, Vyacheslaff M. Molotoff, Russian Foreign Commissar, said today.

While the delegates at the conference celebrated the end of the European war, and three Foreign Ministers, T. V. Soong of China, Paul Henri Spaak of Belgium and Trygve Lie of Norway left the conference to deal with urgent official business elsewhere, Mr. Molotoff told the press that the Soviet Union attached the "greatest importance" to five agreements reached by the heads of the Big Four delegations.

First, he said, these leaders agreed to support the principles of justice, international law, human rights and fundamental freedom for all.

Second, he added, the Big Four agreed not to make provision in the security charter for the revision of treaties.

His statement on this point was ambiguous and led to some speculation as to the unanimity of all four on the question.

Revision Power Called Danger

A reference in the United Nations charter to the necessity of revising treaties, Mr. Molotoff stated, "would play into the hands of enemy countries, which would certainly like to undermine and emasculate these treaties." Furthermore, he declared, to give the new League of Nations authority to consider revision of treaties would be a violation of national sovereign rights, which are guaranteed in the Dumbarton Oaks Charter.

For these reasons, he concluded, "the idea of revising treaties was rejected as untenable."

Third, Mr. Molotoff said, it was agreed among the Big Four that treaties directed against Germany, such as Russia's twenty-year alliances with Britain, France, Czechoslovakia, Yugoslavia and the Warsaw Poles, "should remain in force until such time as the Government concerned felt that the international security organization was really in a position to undertake the accomplishment of the tasks of

Continued on Page 15, Column 2

Leopold Rescued By 7th Army Troops

By The Associated Press.

WITH THE UNITED STATES SEVENTH ARMY, Tuesday, May 8—Léopold III, King of Belgium, and his wife, Princess Rethy, have been liberated by the Seventh Army, it was announced today.

They were found near Strobl, eight miles east of Salzburg. The Americans had been told of their whereabouts by civilians.

With the King and his wife were eighteen members of their staff and four children. All were in good health

Elements of the American 106th Cavalry Group had to overpower German Elite Guards to make the rescue. Seventh Army troops are now closely guarding the royal party.

GERMANY SURRENDERS: NEW YORKERS MASSED UNDER SYMBOL OF LIBERTY

Thousands filling Times Square in spontaneous celebration yesterday — The New York Times

PRAGUE SAYS FOES ACCEPT SURRENDER

Czechoslovak Radio Reports All Fighting in Bohemia Will Be Ended Today

By The Associated Press.

LONDON, Tuesday, May 8 — The Czechoslovak - controlled Prague radio announced today that the Germans in Prague and throughout Bohemia, a last major holdout pocket of German resistance, had accepted unconditional surrender.

The announcement came as the United States Third Army was reported to have advanced to the outskirts of the Czechoslovak capital, and three Russian armies hammered toward the same goal from the east and north.

"The German military plenipotentiary is negotiating with the Czechoslovak National Council on the modalities of unconditional surrender," said the broadcast, detailing what purported to be the

Continued on Page 11, Column 2

Wild Crowds Greet News In City While Others Pray

By FRANK S. ADAMS

New York City's millions reacted in two sharply contrasting ways yesterday to the news of the unconditional surrender of the German armies. A large and noisy minority greeted it with the turbulent enthusiasm of New Year's Eve and Election Night rolled into one. However, the great bulk of the city's population responded with quiet thanksgiving that the war in Europe was won, tempered by the realization that a grim and bitter struggle still was ahead in the Pacific and the fact that the nation is still in mourning for its fallen President and Commander in Chief.

Times Square, the financial section and the garment district were thronged from mid-morning on with wildly jubilant celebrators who tooted horns, staged impromptu parades and filled the canyons between the skyscrapers with fluttering scraps of paper. Elsewhere in the metropolitan area, however, war plants continued to hum, schools, offices and factories carried on their normal activities, and residential areas were calmly joyful.

One factor that helped to dampen the celebration was the bewilderment of large segments of the population at the absence of an official proclamation to back up the news contained in flaring headlines and radio bulletins. With the premature rumor of ten days ago fresh in everyone's mind, and millions still mindful of the false armistice of 1918, there was widespread skepticism over the authenticity of the news.

By mid-afternoon loudspeakers were blaring into the ears of the exulting thousands in the amusement district the news that President Truman's proclamation was being held up by the necessity of coordinating it with the announcements from London and Moscow, and that the formal celebration of the long-awaited V-E Day would be delayed until today.

This sobering note gradually

Continued on Page 7, Column 6

SHAEF BAN ON AP LIFTED IN 6 HOURS

Action Comes After Protests From Newspapers and Public —Writer Still Barred

Suspension of filing facilities of The Associated Press in the European theatre was clamped on by Supreme Headquarters, Allied Expeditionary Forces (SHAEF), yesterday in an unprecedented action and was lifted six hours and twenty minutes later.

The ban was continued, however, on all copy submitted for clearance by Edward Kennedy, chief of the press association's staff on the Western Front, who sent the momentous story announcing Germany's final surrender in a dispatch from Reims, France, which was received in New York over the AP wires at 9:35 A. M. (EWT).

It was not until seven hours and fifty-five minutes had elapsed aft-

Continued on Page 4, Column 2

Summary of News of the War and German Surrender

TUESDAY, MAY 8, 1945

The war ended in Europe yesterday after five years, eight months and six days of the bloodiest conflict in history. Grand Admiral Karl Doenitz surrendered unconditonally to the Allies in a little red schoolhouse at Reims, France. At 8:41 P. M. Sunday, New York time, Col. Gen. Gustav Jodl signed for the enemy and Lieut. Gen. Walter Bedell Smith, General Eisenhower's Chief of Staff, for the Allies. In the absence of any official announcement there was some confusion as to the compliance with the surrender. Fighting had been going on in Czechoslovakia and nothing had been heard from German pockets along the French coast. [1:7-8.]

President Truman planned a broadcast from the White House at 9 o'clock this morning. Washington, gratified that the war in Europe was over, was confused by lack of confirmation. [2:2.]

Prime Minister Churchill will also broadcast at 9 A. M. from London and Premier Stalin is expected to make a simultaneous announcement in Moscow. King George will talk over the radio six hours later. [2:8.] London will celebrate V-E Day today, but, unable to restrain its joy, staged many impromptu celebrations yesterday. [2:7.]

Most New Yorkers took the news calmly and thankfully, sobered by realization that the war in the Pacific was far from over. There were, however, noisy outbursts in such centers as Times Square and Wall Street. Scrap paper showers fluttered from roofs and windows. [1:4-5.]

German Foreign Minister Lutz Schwerin von Krosigk broke the news to his people. The future will be difficult, he warned, and then added: "We must make right the basis of our nation. In our nation justice shall be the supreme law and the guiding principle. We must also recognize law as the basis of all relations between the nations." This sudden, complete reversal in German policy was received with skepticism by the Allies. [3:1.]

Perhaps one reason for this was the announcement from Moscow that 4,000,000 men, women and children had been done to death by gas, shooting, famine, poisoning and torture in the German extermination camp at Oswiecim, Poland. [12:5.]

The actual situation in Czechoslovakia was obscure. Late last night a Patriot broadcast said the Germans were negotiating with the Czechoslovak National Council details of surrender in Prague and Bohemia. Fighting had continued throughout yesterday and German planes had bombed public buildings and hospitals. [1:3; map P. 11.].

The United States Third Army continued its general advance into Czechoslovakia and the Fifth and Seventh Armies joined again in the Alps. The British Second Army moved to Denmark and Poles entered the shattered port of Wilhelmshaven. [11:1.] Breslau fell to the Red Army after an eighty-four-day siege; 40,000 Germans were captured. [11:5.]

Japan accepted the surrender of her Axis partner with a statement that she never had expected German aid and would go on to victory without the Reich. [13:1.]

Infantry and marines on Okinawa scored another general advance after naval bombardment had pulverized Japanese strong points. Pacific Fleet planes sank or damaged thirteen more ships off Korea and Japan. [1:1; map, P. 12.] B-29's maintained their assault on Kyushu airfields. Two of the big planes were shot down. [14:3-4.]

On Tarakan Allied troops were within a mile and a half of the eastern shore. Americans gained on Mindanao and Luzon in the Philippines. [12:3-4.]

Foreign Commissar Molotoff said in San Francisco that unanimity on amendments to Dumbarton Oaks assured success of the conference. He declared that the Big Four consultations had ended. [1:2.]

GERMANS CAPITULATE ON ALL FRONTS

American, Russian and French Generals Accept Surrender in Eisenhower Headquarters, a Reims School

REICH CHIEF OF STAFF ASKS FOR MERCY

Doenitz Orders All Military Forces of Germany To Drop Arms—Troops in Norway Give Up —Churchill and Truman on Radio Today

By EDWARD KENNEDY
Associated Press Correspondent

REIMS, France, May 7—Germany surrendered unconditionally to the Western Allies and the Soviet Union at 2:41 A. M. French time today. [This was at 8:41 P. M., Eastern Wartime Sunday.]

The surrender took place at a little red schoolhouse that is the headquarters of Gen. Dwight D. Eisenhower.

The surrender, which brought the war in Europe to a formal end after five years, eight months and six days of bloodshed and destruction, was signed for Germany by Col. Gen. Gustav Jodl. General Jodl is the new Chief of Staff of the German Army.

The surrender was signed for the Supreme Allied Command by Lieut. Gen. Walter Bedell Smith, Chief of Staff for General Eisenhower.

It was also signed by Gen. Ivan Susloparoff for the Soviet Union and by Gen. Francois Sevez for France.

[The official Allied announcement will be made at 9 o'clock Tuesday morning when President Truman will broadcast a statement and Prime Minister Churchill will issue a V-E Day proclamation. Gen. Charles de Gaulle also will address the French at the same time.]

General Eisenhower was not present at the signing, but immediately afterward General Jodl and his fellow delegate, Gen. Admiral Hans Georg Friedeburg, were received by the Supreme Commander.

Germans Say They Understand Terms

They were asked sternly if they understood the surrender terms imposed upon Germany and if they would be carried out by Germany.

They answered Yes.

Germany, which began the war with a ruthless attack upon Poland, followed by successive aggressions and brutality in internment camps, surrendered with an appeal to the victors for mercy toward the German people and armed forces.

After having signed the full surrender, General Jodl said he wanted to speak and received leave to do so.

"With this signature," he said in soft-spoken German, "the German people and armed forces are for better or worse delivered into the victors' hands.

"In this war, which has lasted more than five years, both have achieved and suffered more than perhaps any other people in the world."

LONDON, May 7 (AP)—Complete victory in

Continued on Page 3, Columns 2 and 3

Members of the Combined Chiefs of Staff Who Planned Strategy That Defeated Germany and Italy

Admiral William D. Leahy
Chief of Staff to President
The New York Times (U. S. Navy)

Gen. George C. Marshall
Chief of Staff, U. S. Army
Associated Press

Admiral Ernest J. King
Commander in Chief of U. S. Fleet
The New York Times (U. S. Navy)

Gen. Henry H. Arnold
Chief U. S. Army Air Forces
The New York Times (U. S. Army Air Forces)

Field Marshal Maitland Wilson
Chief of British Joint Staff Mission
The New York Times (British Official)

Lieut. Gen. Macready
Chief of British Army Staff Mission
The New York Times

Admiral Somerville
Head of Admiralty Delegation
Chase-Statler

Air Marshal Douglas Colyer
RAF Representative
The New York Times (British Official)

FOREIGN MINISTER BIDS REICH TO HOPE

Schwerin von Krosigk Begins Campaign to Regain Freedom for Germany

By Wireless to THE NEW YORK TIMES.

LONDON, May 7—Having surrendered unconditionally, the skeleton German Government of Grand Admiral Karl Doenitz turned to post-war problems today and—if the words of its Foreign Minister can be believed—renounced Nazi principles and began a campaign to regain Germany's eventual independence.

Now that the Allies are in a position to dictate Germany's future, the Government appears to have been converted rather quickly to ideas of justice, international law and respect for treaties.

Broadcasting from Flensburg, Foreign Minister Count Ludwig Schwerin von Krosigk was the first to announce at 2 P. M. that Admiral Doenitz had ordered the unconditional surrender of all German forces. He stressed that because of the collapse of all physical and material forces Germany had succumbed and repeated that Germany had continued to fight as long as she had only to save as many men as possible from the Soviet Army.

Stresses Severe Terms

"No one," he added, "must be under any illusions about the severity of the terms to be imposed upon the German people by our enemies."

The severity of these terms is not known even to the public in Allied countries. The terms have been drafted over a period of months by the European Advisory Commission in London and were not supposed to be given to the Germans until unconditional surrender had been accepted.

Whatever the surrender terms may be, Count Schwerin von Krosigk called on the German people to "stand loyally by the obligations we have undertaken" and to preserve "the unity of ideas of a national community" that was manifested during the war.

In an appeal to Germany's conquerors he said:

"In our nation justice shall be the supreme law and the guiding principle. We must also recognize law as the basis of all relations between the nations. * * * Respect for concluded treaties will be as sacred as the aim of our nation to belong to the European family of nations. * * *

"Then we may hope that the atmosphere of hatred which today surrounds Germany all over the world will give place to a spirit of reconciliation among the nations, without which the world cannot recover.

Hopes for Freedom

"Then we may hope that we will again receive the freedom without which no nation can lead a bearable and dignified existence."

These forgive and forget sentiments sounded strange from a man who was from the beginning a member of the Government that denied equal justice to its own citizens, flouted international law and repeatedly violated its treaties.

The Foreign Minister apparently hoped that Germany, like Italy, would be allowed to work her way rapidly back to respectability. His speech followed the program outlined last week by Albert Speer, Armaments and Production Minister, for the restoration of transport and food distribution to prevent Germany from starving.

BRITAIN'S CENSORSHIP IS STILL UNRELAXED

By Wireless to THE NEW YORK TIMES.

LONDON, May 7—War correspondents' biggest headache—the censorship—has not yet been cured. A revised statement of censorship policy from London is expected to be issued Thursday, and until then every word written in this victorious capital must be passed by the censor, "for security reasons," before being transmitted across the Atlantic.

The British Government has promised in the past that censorship on non-military matter would end with the war in Europe. Military censorship will be continued until the end of the Japanese war and no news of the movement of naval or military formations will be passed for immediate publication.

SHAEF censors are still at their job as usual tonight and they are carrying on their usual routine until instructions from "high up" come through.

Your waste paper will buy extra comforts for wounded Veterans and speed Victory. Save yours and ask school children, Boy Scouts and P.A.L.'s about the V-V Waste Paper Program.

The War in Europe Is Ended; Nazis Sign Surrender Terms

Continued From Page 1

Europe was won by the Allies today with the unconditional surrender of Germany.

[The first announcement that Germany had capitulated came at 8:09 A. M., Eastern Wartime, when German Foreign Minister Count Lutz Schwerin von Krosigk stated in a broadcast over the Flensburg radio that Grand Admiral Karl Doenitz, new Chancellor of Germany, had ordered the unconditional surrender of all German armed forces.

[In his broadcast announcing the German surrender, Count Schwerin von Krosigk called upon the Germans "to stand loyally by the obligations we have undertaken."

["Then we may hope that the atmosphere of hatred which today surrounds Germany all over the world will give place to a spirit of reconciliation among the nations, without which the world cannot recover," he added. "Then we may hope that our freedom will be restored to us, without which no nation can lead a bearable and dignified existence."]

Germany's formal capitulation marked the official end of war in Europe, but it did not silence all the guns, for battles went on in Czechoslovakia.

Boehme Says Troops Were Unbeaten

In Norway, however, Gen. Franz Boehme, German Commander in Chief, broadcast an Order of the Day over the Oslo radio tonight commanding his troops to lay down their arms in obedience to Count Schwerin von Krosigk's "announcement of unconditional surrender of all German fighting troops."

The Norwegian garrison surrendered at the order of Boehme, who said that the capitulation "hits us very hard because we are unbeaten and in full possession of our strength in Norway and no enemy has dared to attack us."

"In spite of all that," he added, "in the interests of all that is German we also shall have to obey the dictate of our enemies. We hope that in the future we shall have to deal with men on the other side who respect a soldier's honor * * * clench your teeth and keep discipline and order. Obey your superiors. Remain what you have been up to now—decent German soldiers who love their people and homeland more than anything in the world."

He said he also "expected" that the Norwegian population "will keep the discipline with respect to the Germans that the German soldiers in Norway always kept toward the Norwegians."

Under the terms of the capitulation, the Germans will march across the border into internment in Sweden.

The Swedish Telegraph Agency in a broadcast said an Allied naval force of forty-eight ships had been sighted at the entrance of Oslo Fjord and a landing was expected "at any moment."

Sevez Says Negotiators Differed

By Wireless to THE NEW YORK TIMES.

PARIS, May 7—There was one official voice on the surrender heard in Paris tonight or rather it will be heard when the Figaro appears tomorrow morning. That was the voice of General Sevez who, in spite of the complete lack of other official confirmation of German's capitulation, told a reporter for the Figaro that it was he who had signed the capitulation for France.

General Sevez said that the discussion went on all afternoon and late into the night. German General Friedeberg seemed crushed by the emotional effect of the surrender, General Sevez said.

"Sometimes we were separated from the Germans and discussed questions among the Allies," he declared. "Sometimes the Germans took places facing us. Each point discussed led to further discussion.

"We were seated behind a narrow school table. General Smith had General [Lieut. Gen. Sir Frederick E.] Morgan and me at his right while General Susloparoff was at his left. When the Germans came in, we were already seated. All three Germans bowed before us without a word.

"Repeatedly the Germans went to a telephone booth connected directly with Doenitz. We did the same to talk with our superiors. Only General Smith remained in direct contact with General Eisenhower, whose residence was at Reims.

"When the capitulation was signed General Eisenhower received the three Germans. It was finished at 2:40 o'clock Monday morning. I was

Brig. Gen. Andrew J. McFarland
United States Secretary
The New York Times (U. S. Signal Corps)

Brigadier A. T. Cornwall-Jones
British Secretary
Associated Press

called by telephone by General Eisenhower who put a plane at my disposal to take me to Reims. Soon afterward I arrived in the small schoolhouse where the offices of the Supreme Command were."

General Sevez, who is Assistant Chief of Staff of the French Army, said he was called because the French Chief of Staff, Gen. Alphonse-Pierre Juin, was in San Francisco.

Surrender of Criminals Required

By Wireless to THE NEW YORK TIMES.

LONDON, May 7—The terms made ready for Germany by the European Advisory Commission are believed first of all to call for the disarmament of all forces, the surrender of war criminals and complete obedience to the orders of Allied Military Government authorities for restoring order in Germany.

At a time to be jointly decided by the Allies, the Allied Control Commission, composed of the Commanders in Chief of the British, American, Soviet and French forces in Germany, will take charge of the Reich.

The permanent shape of the future Reich is not expected to be decided until the peace conference is held, perhaps two years hence, but some adjustments of the German border in favor of Poland and the Soviet Union may take place in the interim.

One question that may be settled promptly is that of drafting labor from Germany to rebuild the devastated European countries. More than 10,000,000 men may soon be in Allied captivity and until peace has been signed they will remain prisoners of war and can be sent to work wherever they are needed.

The British and American forces will soon have captured more Germans than the total number of men in their own forces and consideration must be given to the reallocation of these prisoners.

GERMANS TO CROSS INTO SWEDEN TODAY

By Cable to THE NEW YORK TIMES.

STOCKHOLM, Sweden, May 7—Four thousand Germans marched up along the Swedish frontier northeast of Oslo today, and tomorrow they will give themselves up to the Swedish Army. They were directed toward the Swedish frontier four days ago, after the Swedish authorities were notified of their intention to cross the border.

Preparations for their reception have been completed. Two large tent camps in the townships of Ed and Mon in Dalanra, northwest of Stockholm, are now ready to receive the first contingent of the capitulating German soldiers.

A score of cars bearing German staff officers was observed on an inspection tour along the Norwegian frontier due east of the Norwegian town of Hamar yesterday and observers say they were arranging for troop quarters. It is now evident that the German troops in Norway will camp in this area, waiting for the signal to cross the Swedish border to be disarmed and interned.

The first 4,000 German soldiers will start crossing the border tomorrow morning when Swedish troops and customs officials will accept their weapons and other military equipment.

While extensive plans have been made for the entry of German troops into Sweden it is not yet known whether all the Germans in Norway—more than 200,000 including the civil administration—will be sent across the frontier, the Swedes have prepared for the reception of roughly that number.

DUBLIN HAILS NEWS; STUDENTS CELEBRATE

By Cable to THE NEW YORK TIMES.

DUBLIN, May 7—News of the end of the war in Europe was received here with relief. When the first editions of an evening newspaper carrying the story, with big banner headlines, appeared on the streets this afternoon they were quickly snapped up by crowds in O'Connell Street at premium prices.

In the streets, shops, cafes and taverns people spoke with elation over the good news. The legations and consulates of the United Nations or liberated countries flew their flags to mark the occasion.

Shortly after news of the German surrender came over the radio a party of Trinity College students emerged upon the roof of the main entrance of Trinity College in College Green and ran up two Union Jacks, the Stars and Stripes and the flags of France and the Soviet Union from the college flagstaffs, following which they sang "God Save the King" and "Rule Britannia."

A crowd gathered in College Green to witness the students' display, which lasted less than two hours when the flags were taken down and the students disappeared from the rooftops.

Royalty Welcomes Freed Kin

LONDON, May 7 (U.P.)—Viscount Lascelles, nephew of the King, and John Alexander, master of Elphinstone, nephew of the Queen, were welcomed home tonight by the royal family. Both were among "special hostage" prisoners held by the Germans who were liberated a few days ago.

PARIS CELEBRATES IN CARNIVAL SPIRIT

French Civilians and Allies' Troops Refuse to Wait for Official Confirmation

By HAROLD CALLENDER

By Wireless to THE NEW YORK TIMES.

PARIS, May 7—Parisians and Allied soldiers in Paris let themselves go with abandon tonight in celebration of what they thought was the end of the war in Europe, even though Supreme Headquarters here, like the Allies' Governments, refused to confirm that the Germans had capitulated.

The sirens that not long ago had announced enemy air raiders were all set to go off to announce the end of hostilities in Paris and throughout France, as soon as they should be officially authorized to do so. That authorization did not come and the sirens remained silent.

But this did not prevent joyful men, women and girls in a half dozen Allied uniforms and in civilian clothes from jamming the boulevards in seething carnival crowds. It did not prevent somebody's airplanes, apparently unauthorized, from soaring over the center of Paris and dropping flares as if in confirmation of the joyful but unofficial news.

Nor did it prevent others, unofficial persons, no doubt, from sending up fireworks that burst in the warm night air to the amusement of the crowds who thought that peace had come to Europe.

Nor did it prevent radio loudspeakers in the Place de l'Opéra from telling the crowds that hostilities had ended. Nor did it prevent the newspapers from describing the signing of the German capitulation which, they said, had taken place in Rheims at 2:45 A. M. today and was to become effective tomorrow.

Papers Issue Extras

Extras of the evening papers appeared this afternoon with large headlines announcing the capitulation on the authority of the German radio, which, the French thought, would hardly lie on that subject. The French official news agency distributed a Reuter dispatch from London saying that the surrender had been signed by Col. Gen. Gustav Jodl, new Chief of Staff of the German Army, in a small schoolhouse, as well as a dispatch quoting the Canadian radio to the same effect.

The British Broadcasting Corporation, to which the French listened so attentively during the German occupation, broadcast orders to German vessels to put into certain ports. But it was not officially authorized to say that Germany had capitulated, and so it did not say so.

It was as if everybody, including the Germans, testified to the complete defeat of Germany—except the Allies' Governments, which for some reason withheld this momentous news, as it seemed to the French.

The official reticence went so far here as to cause the police to seize the first extras of one evening paper announcing the German capitulation. But this practice was soon stopped. People in the streets bought the papers and read them calmly. They were not startled, since Germany had long been crumbling and they had read that Heinrich Himmler had asked for peace, though it took the Allies' Governments days to admit it.

Tonight the French radio told the nation that not only German but British and American broadcasts had all but officially announced the end of hostilities and that New York and London were celebrating. Meanwhile, Paris, which has a tradition of street demonstrations, began slowly to bubble over with pent-up feelings.

Liberation Day Repeated

It was liberation day over again in the sense that it was a city showing its sense of relief in a massive, noisy, carefree manner. It was liberation again also in the sense that American and British soldiers mingled with the French in a more comradely way than they have done in recent months. Groups of Britons in all uniforms marched through the boulevards singing "Tipperary." Americans strode along with French soldiers and girls. The Allied peoples represented in Paris seemed friendly once more at least for one night.

It took several hours for Paris to warm up—either because the people doubted the news or because it came somewhat as an anticlimax in view of the fortnight of reports of the impending fall of the Germans. The Café de la Paix turned out its lights at 9 P. M., following its ordinary wartime routine.

There were comparatively scant alcoholic aids to the warming up.

Champagne costs about $12 a bottle these days and the champagne ration promised for New Year's has not yet been distributed. Wines are very scarce. The French Government was to release an extra wine ration for the celebration of the German defeat, but it had not got around to it tonight. Maybe it was waiting for formal, official confirmation.

There were not many lights in Paris tonight either and the crowds milled about in half-darkened streets, for since the war is officially still going on, we have a kind of blackout in Paris still. Maybe a German plane or two may come over and drop a bomb.

Thus, it was in spite of many official handicaps and discouragements that Paris let itself go tonight and acted—like Paris.

It was as if the individualistic "frondeur" spirit of the capital, a spirit that consists in a lack of respect for authority, had taken hold of the city and was determined to show that people are more than Governments.

Gen. Charles de Gaulle was understood to be waiting to broadcast to the French nation to tell it that the war in Europe was over. But he, like the sirens, awaited the official cue that did not come. So the people celebrated without his blessing or inspiration. The newspapers will say tomorrow that the sirens will eventually howl for three minutes "to announce to all Frenchmen the end of the war by the capitulation of Germany."

The Government will declare a two-day holiday with pay in celebration of the event. As a special treat in honor of victory, the Government will distribute, beginning tomorrow, extra rations of potatoes, salt, wine, butter and American tinned goods.

The Reich Minister's Plea

LONDON, May 7 (U.P.)—The text of the broadcast by German Foreign Minister Lutz Schwerin von Krosigk, as recorded by the British Ministry of Information:

German men and women! The High Command of the armed forces has today at the order of Grand Admiral Doenitz declared the unconditional surrender of all fighting German troops.

As the leading Minister of the Reich Government which the Admiral of the Fleet [Doenitz] has appointed for the winding up of all military tasks, I turn at this tragic moment of our history to the German nation.

After a heroic fight of almost six years of incomparable hardness, Germany has succumbed to the overwhelming power of her enemies. To continue the war would only mean senseless bloodshed and a futile disintegration.

A government which has a feeling of responsibility for the future of its nation was compelled to act on the collapse of all physical and material forces and to demand of the enemy the cessation of hostilities.

It was the noblest task of the Admiral of the Fleet and of the government supporting him—after the terrible sacrifices which the war demanded—to save in the last phase of the war the lives of a maximum number of fellow-countrymen.

That the war was not ended immediately, simultaneously in the west and in the east, is to be explained by this reason alone.

We end this gravest hour of the German nation and its Reich.

In this gravest hour of the German nation and its Reich we bow in deep reverence before the dead of this war.

Their sacrifices place the highest obligations on us. Our sympathy goes first to our soldiers. It goes out above all to the wounded, the bereaved and to all on whom this struggle has inflicted blows.

No one must be under any illusions about the severity of the terms to be imposed on the German people by our enemies. We must now face our fate squarely and unquestioningly.

Nobody can be in any doubt that the future will be difficult for each one of us and will exact sacrifices from us in every sphere.

We must accept this burden and stand loyally by the obligations we have undertaken. But we must not despair and fall into mute resignation. Once again we must set ourselves to stride along the path through the dark future. These are the factors guaranteeing the best state: unity, justice and liberty.

From the collapse of the past, let us preserve and save one thing—unity, the ideas of the national community, which in the years of war have found their highest expression in the spirit of comradeship at the front and readiness to help one another in all the distress which has inflicted the homeland.

Shall we retain this unity and not again split up under the stress * * * [two or three words indistinct] can we get over the future hard times? We must make right the basis of our nation, In our nation justice shall be the supreme law and the guiding principle.

We must also recognize law as the basis of all relations between the nations: we must recognize it and respect it from inner conviction.

Respect for concluded treaties will be as sacred as the aim of our nation to belong to the European family of nations as a member of which we want to mobilize all human moral and material forces in order to heal the dreadful wounds which the war has caused.

Then we may hope that the atmosphere of hatred which today surrounds Germany all over the world will give place to a spirit of reconciliation among the nations, without which the world cannot recover.

Then we may hope that we will again receive the freedom without which no nation can lead a bearable and dignified existence. Let us devote the future of our nation to the meditation of the innermost and best forces of the German spirit, which has given the world lasting achievements and values.

To our pride in the heroic struggle of our nation let us link the determination—belonging as we do to the world of the Christian western civilization—to make to the honest work of peace a contribution which shall be worthy of the best traditions of our nation.

May God not leave us in our efforts. May He bless our dificult task.

Surrender News No Spur To Donations of Blood

Blood donors at the New York unit averaged the usual number, the New York chapter of the American Red Cross announced yesterday in an appeal to donors to continue giving blood until the end of the war with Japan.

Charles Keller, 39 years old, of 1922 Avenue N, Brooklyn, was the first Brooklyn donor to give blood after yesterday's surrender report. He made his thirteenth donation at 9:30 A. M., declaring that he would continue to give blood "as long as it is needed, but I hope our boys in the Pacific won't be needing it very long."

"All the News That's Fit to Print"

The New York Times.

LATE CITY EDITION
Partly cloudy, less humid today. Cloudy and warm tomorrow.
Temperatures Yesterday—Max., 72; Min., 66
Sunrise today, 5:57 A. M.; Sunset, 8:06 P. M.

VOL. XCIV..No. 31,972. Entered as Second-Class Matter, Postoffice, New York, N. Y. NEW YORK, TUESDAY, AUGUST 7, 1945. THREE CENTS IN NEW YORK CITY

FIRST ATOMIC BOMB DROPPED ON JAPAN; MISSILE IS EQUAL TO 20,000 TONS OF TNT; TRUMAN WARNS FOE OF A 'RAIN OF RUIN'

HIRAM W. JOHNSON, REPUBLICAN DEAN IN THE SENATE, DIES

Isolationist Helped Prevent U. S. Entry Into League—Opposed World Charter

CALIFORNIA EX-GOVERNOR

Ran for Vice President With Theodore Roosevelt in '12—In Washington Since '17

Special to THE NEW YORK TIMES.

WASHINGTON, Aug. 6—Senator Hiram Warren Johnson of California lifelong isolationist who helped prevent this country's entry into the League of Nations and fought all "foreign entanglements" through a second World War, died in his sleep this morning at Bethesda Naval Hospital, nine days after, ill but consistent, he had paired his vote against ratification of the United Nations Charter. Death was caused by a thrombosis of a cerebral artery. Mrs. Johnson was with him when the end came.

When word reached the Capitol of the passing of the oldest member of the Senate in point of service, save Senator Kenneth McKellar, the President pro tempore, the mourning was deep. With great personal affection colleagues paid humble tribute to his integrity of character, his liberalism and his steadfastness to his ideals and convictions. They joined in declaring that the country had lost a great statesman.

Senator Johnson, who was serving the fourth year of his fifth term in the Senate, would have been 79 years old on Sept. 2. Although his health had been failing during the last two years and though the thundering voice which had conveyed his eloquence through innumerable stirring debates had become little more than a whisper, friends believed he planned to seek a sixth term in 1947.

He went to the hospital July 18. Five days before that he had cast the lone vote in the Foreign Relations Committee, of which he was the ranking minority member, against reporting the new World Charter to the Senate without change. He did not participate in the floor debate on this document, which won Senate approval by a vote of 82—2. However, he clashed spiritedly with colleagues while the hearings were in progress.

Funeral arrangements awaited the arrival of the Senator's son, Lieut. Col. Hiram W. Johnson Jr., who was flying here from California.

Capper Becomes the Dean

The death of Senator Johnson made Senator Arthur Capper of Kansas, who last month marked his eightieth birthday, the Republican dean of the Senate. It also elevated him to the ranking minority membership on the Foreign Relations Committee, with which Senator Johnson had been so conspicuously identified through the many years of his unshaken position on foreign policy. Mr. Capper, too, with Senators McKellar, Carter Glass of Virginia, David I. Walsh of Massachusetts and Peter G. Gerry, was in the League fight of 1919 and 1920. He supported it, with reservations.

The career of Senator Johnson, from his entrance into the Senate from the Governorship of California in March of 1917, was one distinctly lacking in compromise or reservation. In 1912 he had bolted his party with Theodore Roosevelt and had become his running mate on the Bull Moose ticket. In 1932 he again bolted to support Franklin D. Roosevelt for the Presidency but broke bitterly with the President when he ran for his third term.

In 1919 Mr. Johnson joined with Senators Lodge, Borah, Reed,

Continued on Page 23, Column 4

Jet Plane Explosion Kills Major Bong, Top U. S. Ace

Flier Who Downed 40 Japanese Craft, Sent Home to Be 'Safe,' Was Flying New 'Shooting Star' as a Test Pilot

By The United Press.

BURBANK, Calif., Aug. 6—Maj. Richard Bong, America's greatest air ace, died today in the flaming wreckage of a jet propelled fighter plane which crashed while he was testing it.

Only 24 years old, he wore twenty-six decorations including the nation's highest award, the Congressional Medal of Honor. He had survived countless air battles and shot down forty Japanese planes without a scratch.

The knowledge he gained in those battles was too valuable to risk, so he was brought home to "safe" duty. He was on that "safe" duty today when his P-80, the Shooting Star, hurtled over a clump of trees and burst like a bomb in a field.

Witnesses did not agree on the cause of the crash. One Army flier said that Major Bong overshot the Lockheed airport. Another witness, John McKinney of North Hollywood reported that he saw something fall out of the plane's tail.

"The plane started to wobble up and down, then went into a left bank and hit the ground," he stated. "It exploded and burned and scattered wreckage over about a block square."

Major Bong was trying to get out of the ship when it crashed. He had released the escape hatch and was partly clear. He had pulled the ripcord to his parachute, and the silken folds lay about the body as the flames swept over it.

With a roaring sigh, the plane, like a giant blowtorch, shot over the airport just before 3 P. M. and then lurched over the trees and nosed down into the field, a mile away.

Smoke and flame surged up and crowds rushed from the airport. By the time anyone could reach the scene the ship had been almost consumed.

The crash scene was near the intersection of Cahuenga and Oxnard Boulevards and barely out-

Continued on page 15, Column 2

MORRIS IS ACCUSED OF 'TAKING A WALK'

Fusion Official 'Sad to Part Company'—McGoldrick Sees Only Tammany Aided

The No Deal ticket, headed by Council President Newbold Morris, "can only serve the interests of Tammany Hall," Controller Joseph D. McGoldrick, candidate for re-election on the Republican-Liberal-Fusion party slate, declared yesterday in a fresh attack on the third-party ticket injected over the week-end into the city Mayoralty campaign.

A short while later Gabriel A. Wechsler, general secretary of the City Fusion party, which supported Mayor La Guardia and Mr. Morris in previous city campaigns, accused Mr. Morris of "taking a walk away from the good government forces."

To both charges Mr. Morris declared he would stand on his statement of Sunday that he was not interested in "just taking votes" away from Judge Jonah J. Goldstein, Republican-Liberal-Fusion candidate for Mayor, or from William O'Dwyer, his Democratic-American Labor party opponent.

"I have no comment," he said, "since I stand on my statement of Sunday. We are waging an affirmative campaign."

Informed that Hyman Blumberg,

Continued on Page 19, Column 6

CHINESE WIN MORE OF 'INVASION COAST'

Smash Into Port 121 Miles Southwest of Canton—Big Area Open for Landing

By The Associated Press.

CHUNGKING, China, Aug. 6—Chinese troops have broken into the South China port of Yeungkong and cleared a fifty-mile stretch of the Chinese "invasion coast" west of Hong Kong, Generalissimo Chiang Kai-shek's headquarters said today.

Swaying block-by-block street fighting is raging in the strategic coastal highway town, 121 miles southwest of Canton, a communiqué said.

By breaking into Yeungkong Chinese forces won control of a fifty-mile coastal stretch leading west to Tinpak, which lies east of Luichow Peninsula on the South China Sea. The coastal area now is open to a virtually unopposed landing should American forces choose it for a staging point for supplies to the armies of South China.

West of Luichow Peninsula another 145-mile coastal stretch extending to the Indo-China frontier is under Chinese control and observers believe the Chinese soon may launch a concerted drive from the west and east that would seal off the Japanese on the Luichow

Continued on Page 2, Column 7

Turks Talk War if Russia Presses; Prefer Vain Battle to Surrender

By SAM POPE BREWER
By Wireless to THE NEW YORK TIMES.

ANKARA, Turkey, Aug. 6—Russo-Turkish relations weigh heavy on Turkish minds these days. All leading editors commented today on various aspects of the Russian claims against Turkey.

The Potsdam conference leaves the situation virtually unchanged so far as the Turks can see, but they seem to agree that they would go to war, however hopeless such a war might be, rather than yield before the threat of force. Suggestions from London and Washington that the Russians have been asked to moderate their demands give little reassurance here.

The Potsdam communiqué created more confusion than confidence and the Turks are still trying to decide whether the fact that the conference did not deal with certain specific questions means that it was a failure.

Many point out that all the really thorny questions still are unsettled. The Turks probably do not see a relative importance among world problems of Russian demands on Turkey, but point out that the important question of principle is involved. The general and apparently official argument is that the status of the Straits cannot he modified by a bilateral agreement but must be discussed at a conference of the signatories of the Montreux Convention, with America replacing Japan. The signatories were Great Britain, France, Russia, Japan, Turkey, Greece, Rumania, Yugoslavia and Bulgaria.

The grounds for the Russian claims to Kars and Ardahan are not clear, but throughout the Near and Mideast in recent months

Continued on Page 13, Column 1

KYUSHU CITY RAZED

Kenney's Planes Blast Tarumizu in Record Blow From Okinawa

ROCKET SITE IS SEEN

125 B-29's Hit Japan's Toyokawa Naval Arsenal in Demolition Strike

By FRANK L. KLUCKHOHN
By Wireless to THE NEW YORK TIMES.

MANILA, Tuesday, Aug. 7—More than 400 fighters and bombers, speeding at chimney-top level for two hours Sunday over Tarumizu in southern Kyushu in the largest single attack launched by Gen. George C. Kenney's Far East Air Forces to date, leveled that city's munitions factories and aircraft and munitions storage depots and waterfront installations.

Rockets and demolition bombs were poured by waves of B-26 Invaders, B-25 Mitchells and Mustangs and Thunderbolts of the Fifth and Seventh Air Forces from Okinawa, supported by a few B-24 Liberators carrying big bombs.

[Tarumizu, about 350 miles from Okinawa, appeared to be a site at which the Japanese might be preparing a rocket campaign against the American base, said a United Press dispatch. FEAF pilots reported seeing in the area, which has extensive cave construction, what seemed to be Japanese robot planes and also a huge catapult-like machine, extending over the water, that might be a rocket launcher.

[About 125 B-29's hit the Toyokawa naval arsenal of Japan in a demolition bombing Tuesday noon, Strategic Air Forces headquarters at Guam reported.]

The planes over Tarumizu met scant resistance, as our fliers took their time to assure the highest

Continued on Page 11, Column 2

REPORT BY BRITAIN

'By God's Mercy' We Beat Nazis to Bomb, Churchill Says

ROOSEVELT AID CITED

Raiders Wrecked Norse Laboratory in Race for Key to Victory

The text of Mr. Churchill's statement is on Page 8.

By CLIFTON DANIEL
By Wireless to THE NEW YORK TIMES.

LONDON, Aug. 6—The hitherto secret details of the grisly race between Germany and the Allies to find a weapon so destructive that it would insure absolute victory—a race not only between scientists but also between under-cover agents—were recounted in London tonight after it had been disclosed that the first atomic bomb had been dropped on Japan.

"By God's mercy British and American science outpaced all German efforts," said a statement by former Prime Minister Churchill written before he left office and issued from 10 Downing Street by his successor, Clement R. Attlee.

"The possession of these powers by the Germans at any time might have altered the result of the war," Mr. Churchill said, "and profound anxiety was felt by those who were informed."

The British Isles, which endured the terrors of flying bombs and rockets, did hear repeated rumors that Adolf Hitler's V-3 weapon was to be an atomic bomb, but they never knew until tonight how close they came to being the first victims of its destructive power. Much less did they suspect what

Continued on Page 9, Column 1

War News Summarized

TUESDAY, AUGUST 7, 1945

One bomb hit Japan on Sunday night, but it struck with the force of 20,000 tons of TNT. Where it landed had been the city of Hiroshima; what is there now has not yet been learned.

The attack, dramatically announced by President Truman sixteen hours after the missile had struck, was with an atomic bomb, a "harnessing of the basic power of the universe," he said. "The force from which the sun draws its power has been loosed against those who brought war to the Far East. And the end is not yet."

Details of the missile are closely guarded, but the 125,000 workers who saw materials pour into their factories never saw anything go out. The bomb is the result of pooling British-American scientific knowledge begun in 1940. "We have spent two billion dollars on the greatest scientific gamble in history—and won," Mr. Truman said, and warned:

"We are now prepared to obliterate more rapidly and completely every productive enterprise the Japanese have above ground in any city. It was to spare the Japanese public from utter destruction that the ultimatum of July 26 was issued at Potsdam. If they do not now accept our terms they may expect a rain of ruin from the air."

Secretary of War Stimson detailed the story of research and production and forecast improvements to increase the effectiveness of the "atomic bomb" several times. Congress will be asked to establish a committee to control peacetime use.

Hiroshima was a major military target, a city of 318,000 persons thickly settled around a quartermaster's depot, an embarkation port, armament and airplane parts plants. [All the foregoing 1:5.]

All production was in the United States at two plants at Oak Ridge, near Knoxville, Tenn., and one at Richland, Wash. A scientific laboratory was maintained in Sante Fe, N. M. [1:6.]

Former Prime Minister Churchill told of Britain's part, including costly attacks on German "heavy water" plants and the race to outstrip the Nazis. He praised American scientific achievement and gave full credit to President Roosevelt and his advisers. [1:5.]

Tokyo made no mention of what had happened to Hiroshima but rail service in that area was canceled. [1:7.]

Okinawa sent out 400 planes that left Tarumizu, on Kyushu's Kagoshima Bay, in flaming wreckage. About 125 "Superforts" bombed Toyokawa naval arsenal by daylight. [1:4; map p. 11.]

Chinese troops have broken into the port of Yeungkong and have cleared a large stretch of the south China coast west of Hong Kong and east of the Luichow Peninsula. [1:3; map P. 2.]

Moscow, moving to implement Potsdam decisions, has resumed diplomatic relations with Finland and Rumania. [11:4.]

The Germans received an opportunity to develop democratic talents when the United States and Great Britain authorized local trade unions and political parties in their zones of occupation. [12:2.]

France is expected to ratify the United Nations Charter and then the Bretton Woods monetary plan in the near future. [13:6.] Marshal Pétain was accused of having asked Hitler for help in regaining France's colonies. [13:1.]

Argentina has lifted the state of siege in effect since Pearl Harbor. [14:6.]

Steel Tower 'Vaporized' In Trial of Mighty Bomb

Scientists Awe-Struck as Blinding Flash Lighted New Mexico Desert and Great Cloud Bore 40,000 Feet Into Sky

By LEWIS WOOD
Special to THE NEW YORK TIMES.

WASHINGTON, Aug. 6—A blinding flash many times as brilliant as the midday sun and a massive, multi-colored cloud boiling up 40,000 feet into the air accompanied the first test firing of an atomic bomb on July 16, three weeks ago today. Set in the remote desertlands of New Mexico, the experiment was seen against a wild background where rain poured in torrents, and lightning pierced the sky up to the zero hour of the explosion at 5:30 A. M.

A steel tower from which the atomic weapon hung was vaporized. In its place was only a huge, sloping crater. At the moment of the explosion a mountain range three miles distant stood out sharply in brilliant light.

"Then," said the War Department in a description, "came a tremendous, sustained roar and a heavy pressure wave which knocked down two men outside the control tower (10,000 yards, or more than five miles, away.)"

Before the detonation scientists waited in tense expectancy. Minutes lengthened seemingly to hours. Lying face downward, with their feet toward the steel tower, the watchers waited, nearly breathless. They were "reaching into the unknown" and did not know what would happen.

On the instant that all was over these men leaped to their feet. The terrible tension ended, they shook hands, embraced each other and shouted in glee. Behind their triumph was sober consciousness of possessing the means to "insure the speedy conclusion of the war and save thousands of American lives."

The scene of the great drama was the Alamogordo Air Base, 1.. miles southeast of Albuquerque. Here the scientists strove to unlock the secret upon which $2,000,000,000 had been spent.

Graphic word pictures of the

Continued on Page 5, Column 1

ATOM BOMBS MADE IN 3 HIDDEN 'CITIES'

Secrecy on Weapon So Great That Not Even Workers Knew of Their Product

By JAY WALZ
Special to THE NEW YORK TIMES.

WASHINGTON, Aug. 6—The War Department revealed today how three "hidden cities" with a total population of 100,000 inhabitants sprang into being as a result of the $2,000,000,000 atomic bomb project, how they did their work without knowing what it was all about, and how they kept the biggest secret of the war.

One of these, Oak Ridge, situated where only oak and pine trees had dotted small farms before, is today the fifth largest city in Tennessee. Its population of 75,000 persons has thirteen supermarkets, nine drug stores and seven theatres.

A second town of 7,000 was built for reasons of isolation and security on a New Mexico mesa. The third, named Richland Village, houses 17,000 men, women and children on remote banks of the Columbia River in the State of Washington.

None of the people, who came to these developments from homes all the way from Maine to California, had the slightest idea of what they were making in the gigantic Gov-

Continued on Page 3, Column 2

TRAINS CANCELED IN STRICKEN AREA

Traffic Around Hiroshima Is Disrupted — Japanese Still Sift Havoc by Split Atoms

By The United Press.

WASHINGTON, Aug. 6—The Osaka radio, without referring to the atomic bomb dropped on Hiroshima, hinted tonight at the terrific damage it must have caused by announcing that train service in the Hiroshima and other areas had been canceled.

First mention of the bomb came in a Japanese Domei agency dispatch announcing that President Truman and Prime Minister Attlee had disclosed that the new missile had been dropped on Hiroshima.

The Office of War Information began telling the Japanese today what hit them. OWI branch transmitters in San Francisco, Hawaii and Saipan beamed President Truman's statement on the atomic bomb to Japan.

Edward Barrett, director of the OWI's overseas branch, said that the President's announcement and related information on the atomic bomb will dominate the OWI's normal Japanese transmissions for the next several days.

LONDON, Tuesday, Aug. 7 (U.P.)—The Japanese Domei news agency, in a dispatch recorded by the British radio, said today that

Continued on Page 7, Column 3

Reich Exile Emerges as Heroine In Denial to Nazis of Atom's Secret

Special to THE NEW YORK TIMES.

WASHINGTON, Aug. 6—How Germany twice narrowly missed the secret of harnessing atomic energy by splitting uranium atoms and releasing the most powerful destructive force on earth was recalled today in War Department reports on the atomic bomb.

Development of the bomb after more than ten years of experimentation and research marks the first time that Prof. Albert Einstein's theory of relativity has been put to practical use outside the laboratory: the equation by which he showed the existence of a definite relationship of matter, energy and the velocity of light.

That the new bomb may be far from its maximum devastating potential was indicated by the War Department's statement that said:

"The energy we are now able to utilize in the atomic bombs, at 100 per cent efficiency, constitutes only one-tenth of 1 per cent of the total energy present in the material. But even one-hundredth of 1 per cent is still the most destructive force by far on this earth."

The principal character in the dramatic story of the long search for a method of releasing atomic energy is Dr. Lise Meitner, a woman physicist whom the Nazis expelled from Germany as a "non-Aryan." With her associates, Dr. Otto Hahn and Dr. F. Strassmann, both chemists, she had been working in the Kaiser Wilhelm Institute in Berlin, bombarding uranium atoms with neutrons and then submitting the uranium to chemical analysis.

As the War Department tells the story:

To their amazement, they found the element barium in the debris of the smashed uranium atoms.

Continued on Page 7, Column 1

NEW AGE USHERED

Day of Atomic Energy Hailed by President, Revealing Weapon

HIROSHIMA IS TARGET

'Impenetrable' Cloud of Dust Hides City After Single Bomb Strikes

Truman, Stimson statements on atomic bomb, Page 4.

By SIDNEY SHALETT
Special to THE NEW YORK TIMES.

WASHINGTON, Aug. 6—The White House and War Department announced today that an atomic bomb, possessing more power than 20,000 tons of TNT, a destructive force equal to the load of 2,000 B-29's and more than 2,000 times the blast power of what previously was the world's most devastating bomb, had been dropped on Japan.

The announcement, first given to the world in utmost solemnity by President Truman, made it plain that one of the scientific landmarks of the century had been passed, and that the "age of atomic energy," which can be a tremendous force for the advancement of civilization as well as for destruction, was at hand.

At 10:45 o'clock this morning, a statement by the President was issued at the White House that sixteen hours earlier—about the time that citizens on the Eastern seaboard were sitting down to their Sunday suppers—an American plane had dropped the single atomic bomb on the Japanese city of Hiroshima, an important army center.

Japanese Solemnly Warned

What happened at Hiroshima is not yet known. The War Department said it "as yet was unable to make an accurate report" because "an impenetrable cloud of dust and smoke" masked the target area from reconnaissance planes. The Secretary of War will release the story "as soon as accurate details of the results of the bombing become available."

But in a statement vividly describing the results of the first test of the atomic bomb in New Mexico, the War Department told how an immense steel tower had been "vaporized" by the tremendous explosion, how a 40,000-foot cloud rushed into the sky, and two observers were knocked down at a point 10,000 yards away. And President Truman solemnly warned:

"It was to spare the Japanese people from utter destruction that the ultimatum of July 26 was issued at Postdam. Their leaders promptly rejected that ultimatum. If they do not now accept our terms, they may expect a rain of ruin from the air the like of which has never been seen on this earth."

Most Closely Guarded Secret

The President referred to the joint statement issued by the heads of the American, British and Chinese Governments, in which terms of surrender were outlined to the Japanese and warning given that rejection would mean complete destruction of Japan's power to make war.

[The atomic bomb weighs about 400 pounds and is capable of utterly destroying a town, a representative of the British Ministry of Aircraft Production said in London, the United Press reported.]

What is this terrible new weapon, which the War Department also calls the "Cosmic Bomb"? It is the harnessing of the energy of the atom, which is the basic power of the universe. As President Truman said, "The force from which the sun draws its power has been loosed against those who brought war to the Far East."

"Atomic fission"—in other

Continued on Page 2, Column 2

FIRST ATOMIC BOMB DROPPED ON JAPAN

Continued From Page 1

words, the scientists' long-held dream of splitting the atom—is the secret of the atomic bomb. Uranium, a rare, heavy metallic element, which is radioactive and akin to radium, is the source essential to its production. Secretary of War Henry L. Stimson, in a statement closely following that of the President, promised that "steps have been taken, and continue to be taken, to assure us of adequate supplies of this mineral."

The imagination-sweeping experiment in harnessing the power of the atom has been the most closely guarded secret of the war. America to date has spent nearly $2,000,000,000 in advancing its research. Since 1939, American, British and Canadian scientists have worked on it. The experiments have been conducted in the United States, both for reasons of achieving concentrated efficiency and for security; the consequences of having the material fall into the hands of the enemy, in case Great Britain should have been successfully invaded, were too awful for the Allies to risk.

All along, it has been a race with the enemy. Ironically enough, Germany started the experiments, but we finished them. Germany made the mistake of expelling, because she was a "non-Aryan," a woman scientist who held one of the keys to the mystery, and she made her knowledge available to those who brought it to the United States. Germany never quite mastered the riddle, and the United States, Secretary Stimson declared, is "convinced that Japan will not be in a position to use an atomic bomb in this war."

A Sobering Awareness of Power

Not the slightest spirit of braggadocio is discernable either in the wording of the official announcements or in the mien of the officials who gave out the news. There was an element of elation in the realization that we had perfected this devastating weapon for employment against an enemy who started the war and has told us she would rather be destroyed than surrender, but it was grim elation. There was sobering awareness of the tremendous responsibility involved.

Secretary Stimson said that this new weapon "should prove a tremendous aid in the shortening of the war against Japan," and there were other responsible officials who privately thought that this was an extreme understatement, and that Japan might find herself unable to stay in the war under the coming rain of atom bombs.

It was obvious that officials at the highest levels made the important decision to release news of the atomic bomb because of the psychological effect it may have in forcing Japan to surrender. However, there are some officials who feel privately it might have been well to keep this completely secret. Their opinion can be summed up in the comment by one spokesman: "Why bother with psychological warfare against an enemy that already is beaten and hasn't sense enough to quit and save herself from utter doom?"

The first news came from President Truman's office. Newsmen were summoned and the historic statement from the Chief Executive, who still is on the high seas, was given to them.

"That bomb," Mr. Truman said, "had more power than 20,000 tons of TNT. It had more than 2,000 times the blast power of the British 'Grand Slam,' which is the largest bomb (22,000 pounds) ever yet used in the history of warfare."

Explosive Charge Is Small

No details were given on the plane that carried the bomb. Nor was it stated whether the bomb was large or small. The President, however, said the explosive charge was "exceedingly small." It is known that tremendous force is packed into tiny quantities of the element that constitutes these bombs. Scientists, looking to the peacetime uses of atomic power, envisage submarines, ocean liners and planes traveling around the world on a few pounds of the element. Yet, for various reasons, the bomb used against Japan could have been extremely large.

Hiroshima, first city on earth to be the target of the "Cosmic Bomb," is a city of 318,000, which is—or was—a major quartermaster depot and port of embarkation for the Japanese. In addition to large military supply depots, it manufactured ordnance, mainly large guns and tanks, and machine tools and aircraft-ordnance parts.

President Truman grimly told the Japanese that "the end is not yet."

"In their present form these bombs are now in production," he said, "and even more powerful forms are in development."

He sketched the story of how the late President Roosevelt and Prime Minister Churchill agreed that it was wise to concentrate research in America, and how great, secret cities sprang up in this country, where, at one time, 125,000 men and women labored to harness the atom. Even today more than 65,000 workers are employed.

"What has been done," he said, "is the greatest achievement of organized science in history.

"We are now prepared to obliterate more rapidly and completely every productive enterprise the Japanese have above ground in any city. We shall destroy their docks, their factories and their communications. Let there be no mistake; we shall completely destroy Japan's power to make war."

The President emphasized that the atomic discoveries were so important, both for the war and for the peace, that he would recommend to Congress that it consider promptly establishing "an appropriate commission to control the production and use of atomic power within the United States."

"I shall give further consideration and make further recommendations to the Congress as to how atomic power can become a powerful and forceful influence toward the maintenance of world peace," he said.

Secretary Stimson called the atomic bomb "the culmination of years of herculean effort on the part of science and industry, working in cooperation with the military authorities." He promised that "improvements will be forthcoming shortly which will increase by several fold the present effectiveness."

"But more important for the long-range implications of this new weapon," he said, "is the possibility that another scale of magnitude will be developed after considerable research and development. The scientists are confident that over a period of many years atomic bombs may well be developed which will be very much more powerful than the atomic bombs now at hand."

Investigation Started in 1939

It was late in 1939 that President Roosevelt appointed a commission to investigate use of atomic energy for military purposes. Until then only small-scale research with Navy funds had taken place. The program went into high gear.

By the end of 1941 the project was put under direction of a group of eminent American scientists in the Office of Scientific Research and Development, under Dr. Vannevar Bush, who reported directly to Mr. Roosevelt. The President also appointed a General Policy Group, consisting of former Vice President Henry A. Wallace, Secretary Stimson, Gen. George C. Marshall, Dr. James B. Conant, president of Harvard, and Dr. Bush. In June, 1942, this group recommended vast expansion of the work and transfer of the major part of the program to the War Department.

Maj. Gen. Leslie R. Groves, a native of Albany, N. Y., and a 48-year-old graduate of the 1918 class at West Point, was appointed by Mr. Stimson to take complete executive charge of the program. General Groves, an engineer, holding the permanent Army rank of lieutenant colonel, received the highest praise from the War Department for the way he "fitted together the multifarious pieces of the vast country-wide jigsaw," and, at the same time, organized the virtually air-tight security system that kept the project a secret.

A military policy committee also was appointed, consisting of Dr. Bush, chairman; Dr. Conant, Lieut. Gen. Wilhelm D. Styer and Rear Admiral William R. Purnell.

In December, 1942, the decision was made to proceed with construction of large-scale plants. Two are situated at the Clinton Engineer Works in Tennessee and a third at the Hanford Engineer Works in the State of Washington.

These plants were amazing phenomena in themselves. They grew into large, self-sustaining cities, employing thousands upon thousands of workers. Yet, so close was the secrecy that not only were the citizens of the area kept in darkness about the nature of the project, but the workers themselves had only the sketchiest ideas—if any—as to what they were doing. This was accomplished, Mr. Stimson said, by "compartmentalizing" the work so "that no one has been given more information than was absolutely necessary to his particular job."

The Tennessee reservation consists of 59,000 acres, eighteen miles west of Knoxville; it is known as Oak Ridge and has become a modern small city of 78,000, fifth largest in Tennessee.

In the State of Washington the Government has 430,000 acres in an isolated area, fifteen miles northwest of Pasco. The settlement there, which now has a population of 17,000, consisting of plant operators and their immediate families, is known as Richland.

A special laboratory also has been set up near Santa Fe, N. M., under direction of Dr. J. Robert Oppenheimer of the University of California. Dr. Oppenheimer also supervised the first test of the atomic bomb on July 16, 1945. This took place in a remote section of the New Mexico desert lands, with a group of eminent scientists gathered, frankly fearful to witness the results of the invention, which might turn out to be either the salvation or the Frankenstein's monster of the world.

Mr. Stimson also gave full credit to the many industrial corporations and educational institutions which worked with the War Department in bringing this titanic undertaking to fruition.

In August, 1943, a combined policy committee was appointed, consisting of Secretary Stimson, Drs. Bush and Conant for the United States; the late Field Marshal Sir John Dill (now replaced by Field Marshal Sir Henry Maitland Wilson) and Col. J. J. Llewellin (since replaced by Sir Ronald Campbell), for the United Kingdom, and C. D. Howe for Canada.

"Atomic fission holds great promise for sweeping developemnts by which our civilization may be enriched when peace comes, but the overriding necessities of war have precluded the full exploration of peacetime applications of this new knowledge," Mr. Stimson said. "However, it appears inevitable that many useful contributions to the well-being of mankind will ultimately flow from these discoveries when the world situation makes it possible for science and industry to concentrate on these aspects.'

Although warning that many economic factors will have to be considered "before we can say to what extent atomic energy will supplement coal, oil and water as fundamental sources of power," Mr. Stimson acknowledged that "we are at the threshold of a new industrial art which will take many years and much expenditure of money to develop."

The Secretary of War disclosed that he had appointed an interim committee to study post-war control and development of atomic energy. Mr. Stimson is serving as chairman, and other members include James F. Byrnes, Secretary of State; Ralph A. Bard, former Under-Secretary of the Navy; William L. Clayton, Assistant Secretary of State; Dr. Bush, Dr. Conant, Dr. Carl T. Compton, chief of the Office of Field Service in OSRD and president of Massachusetts Institute of Technology, and George L. Harrison, special consultant to the Secretary of War and president of the New York Life Insurance Company. Mr. Harrison is alternate chairman of the committee.

The committee also has the assistance of an advisory group of some of the country's leading physicists, including Dr. Oppenheimer, Dr. E. O. Lawrence, Dr. A. H. Compton and Dr. Enrico Fermi.

The War Department gave this supplementary background on the development of the atomic bomb:

"The series of discoveries which led to development of the atomic bomb started at the turn of the century when radioactivity became known to science. Prior to 1939 the scientific work in this field was world-wide, but more particularly so in the United States, the United Kingdom, Germany, France, Italy and Denmark. One of Denmark's great scientists, Dr. Neils Bohr, a Nobel Prize winner, was whisked from the grasp of the Nazis in his occupied homeland and later assisted in developing the atomic bomb.

"It is known that Germany worked desperately to solve the problem of controlling atomic energy."

The Texts of the Day's War Communiques

JAPANESE LOSE ANOTHER PIECE OF THE ASIATIC COAST

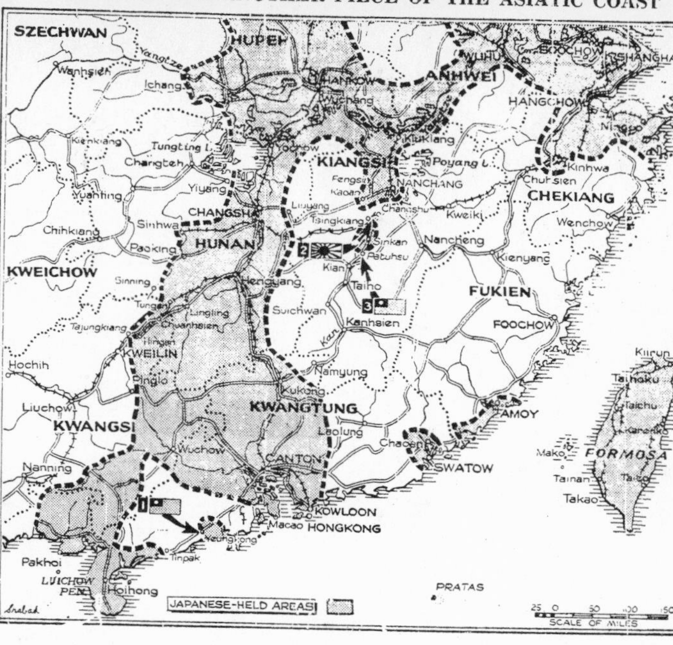

Aug. 7, 1945

Chinese entered the port of Yeungkong (1) and gained control of the coastline west to Tinpak. The Japanese troops in the Kiangsi "floating pocket" occupied Sinkan and advanced to the outskirts of Tsingkiang (2), while the pursuing Chinese captured the town of Patushu (3).

United Nations

MANILA, Tuesday, Aug. 7 (UP)—A communiqué:

JAPAN

Far East Air Forces bombers and fighters on Aug. 5 concentrated their attacks on the waterfront and factories at Tarumizu, on the eastern shore of Kagoshima Bay, in in southern Kyushu. Rockets, incendiaries, demolition and firebombs caused widespread destruction, leaving the entire target engulfed in flames, with smoke billowing 12,000 feet. Night patrol bombers over Tsushima Strait sank a large enemy transport and a medium freighter-transport.

FORMOSA

Seventh Fleet search planes ranging over the Formosa area sank a subchaser off the east coast and sank or damaged eight cargo craft near Takao and in the Pescadores.

ASIATIC COAST

Reconnaissance bombers of the Far East Air Forces and of the Seventh Fleet at night struck Gunzan city, in the south Korea, and scored a direct hit on five enemy junks off Hainan Island. Others by day bombed Tinghai airfields, in the Shanghai area, destroyed or damaged two river steamers near Hatien and silenced airfield defenses at Tourane, French Indo-China. Fighters shot down two enemy planes in the Singapore area.

BORNEO

Australian fighters bombed and strafed enemy concentrations in close support of ground operations in the Balik Papan sector. Search planes of the Seventh Fleet destroyed a freighter and two luggers and damaged shipyards at Kuching and Pontianak. A number of river craft were sunk along the east coast.

EAST INDIES

Thirteenth Air Force and Australian heavy bombers struck dispersal areas at Miti, Halmahera, and facilities in the vicinity of the Banjuwangi shipyards, in eastern Java. Surface elements of the Seventh Fleet sank a troop-laden barge in the Sangihi Islands, attacked enemy water craft and started fires among coastal installations in the Moluccas.

NEW GUINEA-BISMARCKS-SOLOMONS

Marine, Netherlands, New Zealand and Australian planes, on wide sweeps over enemy rear areas, attaked bivouacs at Manokwari and along the Sepik River, in New Guinea, as well as on New Ireland and Bougainville.

CALCUTTA, India, Aug. 6 (UP)—A communiqué:

LAND

Our troops operating in the flooded area between Myitkyo and the Sittang River bend met with continued enemy resistance. Heavy enemy fire was brought down on Gurkha troops who captured a bridge on the Pegu-Martaban railway two miles east of Abya. Our positions near the Abya railway station were shelled by the enemy.

South of Abya our patrols crossed the old Sittang channel and probed enemy positions. South of Myitkyo our artillery engaged the enemy.

British troops, operating on the Toungoo-Mawchi road advanced to Milestone 29 without meeting opposition.

AIR

Four direct hits and three near-misses were made on a 3,000-ton vessel in Chilachap Harbor on the south coast of Java by Liberators of the Air Command on Aug. 4. Quayside installations were also attacked. A 100-foot vessel and an 80-foot vessel were sunk off Pranburi on the Kra Isthmus by other Liberators on the same day. Damage was also caused to railway installations at Pranburi, which is on the Bangkok-Singapore railway.

A 100-foot barge blew up south of Kaw Samui Island off the Kra Isthmus after direct hits by a Sunderland which also strafed two schooners and twenty smaller craft.

Troops in the Kyaukkyi and Kyaikto area were bombed and strafed by Spitfires yesterday.

Detailed reports on Aug. 4 show that in Spitfire and Thunderbolt battle area strikes direct hits were scored on strong points and slit trenches while extensive damage was caused to buildings and jungle huts. Objectives were in the Nyaungkashe area, south of Myitkyo and near Kyaukkyi.

United States

CHUNGKING, China, Aug. 6 (AP)—A communiqué of the United States Fourteenth Air Force:

Two Japanese aircraft were damaged on the ground at the Tsinan auxiliary airfield Aug. 5 by Fourteenth Air Force P-51's.

North of the Yellow River fifty-nine enemy-operated locomotives were damaged in air attacks on Aug. 5 and in previously unreported missions Aug. 4. Continuing attacks on rail and shipping, planes knocked out five railroad bridges, three on the Tatung-Puchow railroad and two on the Peiping-Hankow railroad.

On Aug. 4 fighters in the Changsha area destroyed twenty-one sampans, damaged six more and destroyed a 150-foot barge. Sweeping the North River on the same day, P-51's damaged or destroyed supply-laden junks.

From all missions all our aircraft returned to base.

GUAM, Aug. 6 (UP)—Communiqué 4 of the United States Army Strategic Air Forces:

(1) At least 580 Marianas-based B-29 Superfortresses struck at Japan during the night of Aug. 5-6 dropping approximately 3,850 tons of incendiary and high explosive bombs on the Ube coal liquefaction company and on the industrial areas of Nishinomiya-Mikage, Imabari, Maebashi, Saga and mining the waters around Geijitsu, Tsuruga, Hagi-Oura and Rashin. Returning crews reported good to excellent results, with large fires observed in several of the target areas. Enemy fighter opposition was light and anti-aircraft fire was meager to moderate. One of our bombers failed to return.

(2) A small force of B-29's dropped forty-five tons of bombs on Moen Airfield No. 1 at Truk on the afternoon of Aug. 5. No opposition was encountered.

(3) A force of ninety-eight P-51 Mustangs from Iwo Jima [Island] strafed and launched rockets against airfields and targets of opportunity in the Tokyo area shortly after noon of Aug. 5. Returning pilots reported that they destroyed two enemy aircraft and six locomotives, probably destroyed one aircraft, set two oil tanks afire, and damaged one aircraft, several factory buildings, four locomotives, railroad stations and cars, seven small boats and various miscellaneous targets. Our force encountered one enemy interceptor, which fled, and anti-aircraft fire ranging from meager to intense. Two of our airplanes were damaged and three failed to return. One pilot has been rescued.

(4) Around noon of Aug. 3, P-51 Mustangs from Iwo Jima struck the Tokyo area with the following results:

Destroyed: Two enemy aircraft in the air and eight on the ground, fourteen locomotives, several trucks, gun emplacements and a transformer.

Damaged: Seven aircraft, six locomotives, fifty railroad cars, various hangars, buildings and factories, power lines and twelve to fourteen boats.

Our force encountered ten enemy interceptors and anti-aircraft fire ranging from moderate to intense. Of the ninety-seven mustangs which participated in the mission, five were damaged and six failed to return. One pilot is known to have been rescued.

(5) A small force of P-51 Mustangs from Iwo Jima made a neutralization strike against air installations on Chichi Jima the afternoon of Aug. 3, strafing the target and dropping four tons of bombs. All of our airplanes returned.

(6) The first photographs available on the results of the B-29 strike in the early hours of Aug. 2 show that the industrial area of Toyama was totally destroyed.

GUAM, Tuesday, Aug. 7 (UP)—Pacific Fleet communiqué 457:

(1). Aircraft of the Fourth Marine Aircraft Wing sunk two boats and damaged two buildings in the Palaus on Aug. 6. On the preceding day aircraft of this wing struck enemy targets in the Palaus, at Yap and in the Marshalls.

Japanese

No broadcast of a Japanese communiqué was recorded yesterday.

News of Weapon Electrifies Truman Ship; President Makes Announcement to Crew

ABOARD THE AMERICAN CRUISER Augusta, With President Truman, Aug. 6 (AP)—President Truman personally told the fighting men aboard this warship today of the release of the first atomic bomb over Hiroshima.

Soon after having received word of the success of the mission, the President, accompanied by Secretary of State James F. Byrnes, walked into the wardroom, where officers were at lunch.

"Keep your seats, gentlemen," he said in a voice terse with excitement. "I have an announcement to make to you."

Hesitating a moment as the officers waited, excited and puzzled, Mr. Truman continued:

"We have just dropped a bomb on Japan which has more power than 20,000 tons of TNT. It was an overwhelming success."

The applause and cheering had hardly died down when the President left as quickly as he had appeared, en route to repeat the news to members of the crew's mess in various parts of the ship.

The President gave a great share of credit for development of the new weapon to the persistence and determination of Secretary of War Henry L. Stimson. It was in connection with the successful culmination of years of work on the war's most powerful weapon that Mr. Stimson went to Potsdam to confer with the President.

The crew's reception of the news was uproarious. The word heard on every hand was, "I guess I'll get home sooner now."

Mr. Truman received word of the death of Senator Hiram Johnson of California and sent a message of condolence to Mrs. Johnson.

The Augusta is headed for an East Coast port from which the President will return to the White House. He expects to be in Washington by Wednesday. The time for his nationwide radio report on the Big Three meeting has not been set.

CHINESE WIN MORE OF 'INVASION COAST'

Continued From Page 1

Peninsula and on Hainan Island to the south.

Three hundred and seventy miles north of Hong Kong the Chinese High Command admitted further progress by a Japanese force, originally estimated at 20,000 troops, which has been withdrawing northward toward the enemy bastion of Nanchang, 160 miles southeast of Hankow.

A war bulletin said the Japanese were advancing up the east and west banks of the Kan River, under almost daily United States Fourteen Air Force bomber and fighter attacks. On the river's east bank the Japanese "floating pocket" occupied Sinkan, sixty-five miles south-southwest of Nanchang, and were said to have pushed on toward Changshu, only forty-four miles below the big Japanese-held river port.

On the west bank of the Kan the Japanese were reported to be advancing on Tsingkiang, fifty-three miles southwest of Nanchang, and were battling at the town's outskirts Saturday.

American fighter planes struck into the area west of the Kiangsi battlefront and destroyed or damaged twenty-seven Japanese sampans on the Siang River near Changsha, a United States communiqué said. North of the Yellow River other fighter-bombers blasted rail communications and struck into the far north, hammering a Japanese auxiliary airfield at Tsinan.

New word of Japanese barbarism meanwhile reached Chungking on the heels of official reports that 50,000 civilians were killed or missing in the Kanhsien area, 240 miles north of Hong Kong, after a six-month enemy occupation of the region.

An OWI correspondent reported from recently liberated Kweilin that the Japanese had sacked it. The destruction, he said, began twenty days before the city was abandoned July 27.

During those twenty days squads of Japanese soldiers systematically set sections of the city afire and looted it. Puppets and traitors received 3,000 Chinese dollars for each building they destroyed. Even trees lining the main streets were burned down.

Chinese troops are pushing northeast from Kweilin toward the former American air base city of Lingling.

Kian's Recapture Reported

CHUNGKING, China, Aug. 6 (U.P.)—The Chinese Central News Agency reported that Japanese troops had been cleared from Kian, 100 miles north of Kanhsien in Kiangsi Province. Chinese communiqués have not announced that Kian was occupied by the Japanese, but the news agency said Chinese troops recaptured the city Aug. 1. All buildings along the main street were destroyed or damaged by heavy street fighting, it was reported.

The news agency, commenting on reports that 50,000 Chinese had been killed or were missing from the recently liberated city of Kanhsien, said that most of the civilian group probably were hiding in the hills. Japanese troops, before fleeing the former American air base city, destroyed 509 houses and other property valued at more than 2,000,000 Chinese dollars, it was reported.

A Fourteenth United States Air Force communiqué said American pilots damaged fifty-nine locomotives in attacks Aug. 5 and in previously unreported missions Aug. 4. In continuing attacks against rail traffic, warplanes knocked out five railroad bridges.

Communists List Gains

A Chinese Communist radio dispatch from Yenan said yesterday that Communist troops had recaptured from the Japanese 2,535 square miles of territory with 404,900 population between May 12 and July 3. The dispatch, recorded by the FCC, added that "thirty-seven Japanese and puppet strongpoints were taken," according to the Associated Press.

NEW BURMA PUSH OPENS

British Smash to Within 17 Miles of Mawchi

CALCUTTA, India, Aug. 6 (U.P.)—Tank-led British infantrymen have smashed to within seventeen miles of Mawchi, Japanese headquarters east of the Sittang River and only forty miles from Thailand, Admiral Lord Louis Mountbatten said today.

British jungle veterans scored a two-mile gain along the Toungoo-Mawchi road and reached a point twenty-nine miles east of Toungoo. The advance opened an assault against a ring of outlying enemy bastions west of Mawchi. Thousands of enemy troops have fled the Irrawaddy-Sittang River sectors and concentrated at that point for a last-ditch stand before fleeing into Thailand. Recent communiqués have stated that Japanese artillery in that sector has been particularly active.

Meanwhile, British troops battled trapped remnants of the Japanese Twenty-eighth Army along a seventy-five-mile jungle stretch between the Rangoon-Mandalay railway and the Sittang.

Fierce charges by Japanese troops have limited Allied gains, the communiqué said. Despite heavy enemy fire, Gurkha troops seized a bridge on the Pegu-Martaban railway two miles east of Abya. British positions near the Abya railway station were shelled.

South of Abya British patrols crossed the old Sittang channel and probed enemy positions. In the Myitkyo sector, key strongpoints twenty-nine miles northeast of Pegu, Allied artillery battered enemy positions.

Four direct hits and three near misses were made on a 3,000-ton vessel in Tjilatja Harbor on the south coast of Java, Admiral Mountbatten said. Harbor installations also were blasted in the attack last Saturday.

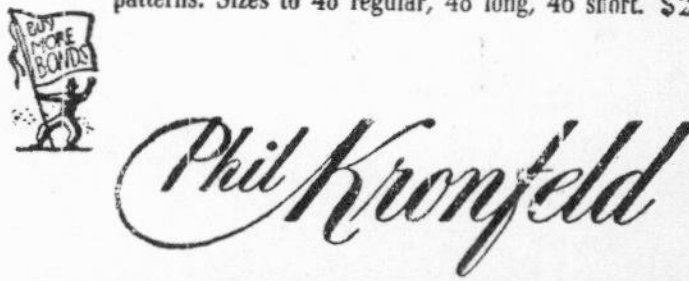

"All the News That's Fit to Print"

The New York Times.

LATE CITY EDITION
Clearing early today; cooler.
Clear and cool tomorrow.
Temperatures Yesterday—Max., 88; Min., 72
Sunrise today, 6:23 A. M.; Sunset, 7:26 P. M.

Section 1

NEWS INDEX, PAGE 33, THIS SECTION

VOL. XCIV..No. 31,998. Entered as Second-Class Matter, Postoffice, New York, N. Y. NEW YORK, SUNDAY, SEPTEMBER 2, 1945. Including Magazine and Book Review. TEN CENTS New York City and Suburban Areas (15c Elsewhere)

JAPAN SURRENDERS TO ALLIES, SIGNS RIGID TERMS ON WARSHIP; TRUMAN SETS TODAY AS V-J DAY

HOLIDAY TRAFFIC NEAR 1941 LEVEL; 'GAS' IS PLENTIFUL

Exodus From City Is Greatest Since Pre-War Days but Congestion Is Avoided

GOOD WEATHER PROMISED

Near-by Resorts Do Capacity Business—3 Persons Die in Queens Accidents

America's millions, deprived since 1941 of the chance to cruise the highways of their nation, hit the road in traditional Labor Day week-end style yesterday.

There was a plentiful supply of gasoline, the sun shone warm out of blue skies, and everyone felt free from war worries. This combined to roll up traffic that continued heavy all day.

New York City's heat-ridden population took to car, train, bus and plane. The exodus to near-by mountain and seashore resorts was the greatest since that of 1941.

The weather formed a perfect lure. Not even the thunder showers predicted by the Weather Bureau for late afternoon took place. Today's prediction is for clearing weather early, followed by cooler, with the highest temperature around 80 degrees, and with fresh to strong northwest winds. A clear and cool Monday is forecast by the bureau. The temperature yesterday reached 88 degrees at 3:30 P. M. with the humidity at 52 per cent. The all-time high for the date was set in 1924 with 92.5 degrees and the low in 1872 with 51.

Many Cars Come Into City

Travel in the city was two-way. As cars streamed out of the city over bridges, on ferries and through tunnels, out-of-towners poured in. The main idea for Labor Day seemed to be change of scenery.

Thousands of automobiles, many of them looking as though they had just been taken off the jacks for the first time in years, formed a continuous procession along the main highways leading up-State, out on Long Island and to the South Jersey shore.

The Port of New York Authority reported that 69,400 automobiles had crossed the George Washington Bridge into New Jersey. Forty-five thousand cars passed through the Holland Tunnel during the sixteen hours preceding 6 o'clock last night. Lincoln Tunnel police said traffic was heavier than usual.

Few serious accidents were reported. "Maybe it's because the cars just don't have the pep," remarked a Westchester County parkway policeman.

Sights along the parkways bore out his contention. Many cars became pathetically silent as their drivers resignedly hauled them over to the side of the road to patch up tires or to fume over engine repairs.

Gasoline Supplies Abundant

Assured of as much gasoline as they wanted, motorists traveled leisurely and did not cause congestion. Filling station pumps received their heaviest workout in years. Station operators estimated that demands for gasoline ranged from 10 to 30 per cent over last week-end, but they reported there was no difficulty in obtaining supplies.

The Cities Service Oil Company said it was having difficulty in meeting orders for premium gasoline, ordinarily accounting for 25 per cent of sales, as the supply was limited, but no company reported shortages of non-premium gasoline. No motorist was forced to stay in town because of lack of fuel.

Trains, buses and airlines were crowded, as they have been all through the war. The airlines re-

Continued on Page 30, Column 2

Times Sq. Takes V-J News Quietly

Times Square throngs, which had greeted Japanese capitulation explosively last month, took the formal signing of terms in much calmer fashion last night.

Two hundred policemen, including twenty-five mounted patrolmen, who had been assigned to the area in case of another outburst of feeling, reported that the street crowds took the flashing of the bulletin from Times Tower at 10:04 P. M. with a few cheers and good-natured remarks, and did not attempt to start a celebration.

In numbers the crowd was no larger than an average Saturday night, and of the persons present perhaps half or more were out-of-town visitors here for the Labor Day week-end, the police estimated. Other parts of the city were similarly quiet.

Mayor La Guardia had said earlier that the people "have had their big time and are satisfied." He decided not to hold a celebration in Central Park today as had been planned.

PRESIDENT STRESSES LABOR DAY OF PEACE

But He Warns That After Six Holidays of Hostilities Great New Problems Lie Ahead

Special to THE NEW YORK TIMES.

WASHINGTON, Sept. 1—President Truman hailed the first Labor Day of peace in six years today and declared a grateful world would always remember the workers of all free nations for their contribution to victory.

Secretary Forrestal and J. A. Krug, chairman of the War Production Board, also lauded the men and women of labor, and Philip Murray, chairman of the Congress of Industrial Organizations, told a radio audience that America's vast war plant must be put to work on peacetime products which would give prosperity unlimited to this country.

Mr. Truman's statement said that six years ago today the workers of the United States, and of the world, awoke to a Labor Day in a world at war, and added:

"We in the United States had two years of grace, but the issue was squarely joined at that hour, as we now know. There was to be no peace until tyranny had been outlawed.

"Today we stand on the threshold of a new world. We must do our part in making this world what it should be a world in which the bigotries of race and class and creed shall not be permitted to warp the souls of men.

"We enter upon an era of great problems, but to live is to face problems. Our men and women did not falter in the task of saving freedom. They will not falter now in the task of making freedom

Continued on Page 24, Column 3

HAILS ERA OF PEACE

President Calls On U. S. to Stride On Toward a World of Good-Will

SALUTES HEROIC DEAD

Cautions Jubilant Nation, Hard Jobs Ahead Need Same Zeal as War

Text of the President's address proclaiming V-J Day, P. 4.

By WILLIAM S. WHITE
Special to THE NEW YORK TIMES.

WASHINGTON, Sept. 1—President Truman, in remembrance of all who have fallen and in an appeal to all Americans to go forward now in hope and fraternity toward "a new and better world of peace and international good-will," tonight solemnly proclaimed tomorrow to be V-J Day.

The moment that he began to speak was, in the official and historical sense, the first moment of peace this country had known since a December day nearly four years ago, when, at a sudden, a harsh and an incredible blow the whole of the Pacific world went into flames.

Into the human calendar of great American holidays, like the Fourth of July and the Eleventh of November, the President thus entered another date, the Second of September, although it does not technically signify the end of the "duration" and will have no basis as a legal end of the war. The termination of hostilities, for purposes of computing military service, for setting the limit to war agencies and for all other like formalities, will be set only by final decision of Congress.

Japanese Surrender Signaled

But Mr. Truman's speech was a speech to the heart of a country that had had the skill to make the atomic bomb and could now "use the same skill and energy and determination to overcome all the difficulties ahead," rather than to the keepers of its books of law.

It was notice from the White House, so long awaited, that nearly four years of war, a struggle of sacrificial grandeur such as the United States had never known, had at last come to an end, and that the terrible ledger opened at Pearl Harbor had now been balanced and closed.

The President spoke in this mood, a mood of valedictory and of dedication, as he proclaimed "this . . . victory of more than arms alone . . . this . . . victory of liberty over tyranny." He had just received the signal from across the world that the Japanese had signed, aboard the great battleship Missouri, the last, humiliat-

Continued on Page 4, Column 1

JAPANESE FOREIGN MINISTER SIGNING SURRENDER ARTICLES

Mamoru Shigemitsu (right, seated), on behalf of Emperor Hirohito, affixes his signature to document as Gen. Douglas MacArthur (left) and Lieut. Gen. Richard K. Sutherland (center) look on during ceremony aboard the Missouri in Tokyo Bay.
Associated Press Wirephoto (via Navy Radio from U. S. S. Iowa)

BYRNES FORESEES A PEACEFUL JAPAN

Says People Are Expected to Force Development—World Amity Vital, Hull Warns

Special to THE NEW YORK TIMES.

WASHINGTON, Sept. 1—Secretary of State James F. Byrnes declared tonight that with Japan's surrender we have entered the second phase of our war—"what might be called the spiritual disarmament of that nation, to make them want peace instead of wanting war."

The intention of this Govern-

Continued on Page 5, Column 1

Japan's Surrender Ordered Over Militarist Opposition

By FRANK L. KLUCKHOHN
By Wireless to THE NEW YORK TIMES.

TOKYO, Sept. 1—In the rubble of this once-proud imperial capital the story of how the Japanese Army opposed the surrender and how the Emperor made the final decision to capitulate after having heard the opinions of all his advisers, and how War Minister Korechika Anami had committed suicide was unfolded today by one of a handful of those in a position to know without bias what occurred.

It was also learned how the Japanese reacted step by step to wartime developments and how propaganda that Japan could win had been continued to the last moment, thus leaving the industrious long-

Continued on Page 7, Column 1

TOKYO AIDES WEEP AS GENERAL SIGNS

Imperial Staff Chief Hastily Scrawls His Signature—Shigemitsu Is Anxious

By The Associated Press.

ABOARD U. S. S. MISSOURI in Tokyo Bay, Sunday, Sept. 2—The solemn surrender ceremony, on this battleship today, marking the first defeat in Japan's 2,600-year-old semi-legendary history, required only a few minutes as twelve signatures were affixed to the articles.

Surrounded by the might of the United States Navy and Army, and under the eyes of the American and British commanders they so ruthlessly defeated in the Philippines and Malaya, the Japanese representatives quietly made the marks on paper that ended the bloody Pacific conflict.

The Japanese delegation came aboard at 8:55 A. M., 7:55 P. M. Saturday, E. W. T., as scheduled. They reached the Missouri in personnel speed boats flying the American flag.

Foreign Minister Mamoru Shigemitsu led the delegation. He climbed stiffly up the ladder and limped forward on his right leg, which is artificial. He was wounded by a bomb tossed by a Korean terrorist in Shanghai many years ago.

On behalf of Emperor Hirohito, Mr. Shigemitsu signed first for

Continued on Page 9, Column 1

U. S. CHIEFS DIVIDED ON ITALY'S COLONIES

State Department Split Over Russia and Influence Zones Is Projected by Issue

By JAMES B. RESTON
Special to THE NEW YORK TIMES.

WASHINGTON, Sept. 1—A fundamental issue has developed in the Department of State over the future of the Italian colonies, particularly Eritrea, Libya and Italian Somaliland.

The issue is whether these colonies should go back to Italy as part of her sovereign territory, be taken from her and administered by the United States, Britain, France and the Soviet Union under the United Nations Organization or be administered by a neutral international commission under the United Nations.

The major powers that defeated Germany are soon to start draft-

Continued on Page 15, Column 1

World News Summarized

SUNDAY, SEPTEMBER 2, 1945

The rulers of Japan, who set the Pacific ablaze nearly four years ago with their surprise attack on Pearl Harbor and hoped to culminate that assault with a peace dictated in the White House, formally signed their unconditional surrender to the Allied powers in Tokyo Bay. Foreign Minister Shigemitsu signed the historic document for his country in the shadow of the sixteen-inch gun muzzles of the battleship Missouri. General MacArthur, who signed in behalf of the Allies, said mankind hoped a better world would result from the solemn occasion. [1:8; map P. 12.]

President Truman proclaimed today as V-J Day. He urged the nation to observe the day of victory over Japan in a spirit of dedication and as a symbol of "victory of liberty over tyranny." He also asked his countrymen to remember "our departed gallant leader, Franklin D. Roosevelt." [1:3.]

Japan's decision to surrender was dictated by Emperor Hirohito after he had overruled a strong faction within the Cabinet and the army that wanted to keep on with the war in the belief that the Japanese could defeat an invasion of the homeland, according to well-informed observers in Tokyo. [1:5-6.]

Medical "experiments" recalling medieval sadism were carried out on dying American prisoners of war by young Japanese Army doctors, two American physicians interned with their compatriots said aboard a United States hospital ship. [1:6-7.]

With the Foreign Ministers' Council scheduled to meet in London next week to begin consideration of peace terms, it was learned that a serious division of opinion over the disposition of the Italian colonies had developed in the State Department. [1:6.]

Former Secretary of State Stettinius said in London that the development of the atomic bomb emphasized the need for "the speedy creation of the United Nations Organization to keep the peace of the world" and predicted that as soon as the organization began functioning it would appoint a military staff to deal with the use of atomic bombs, as well as all other types of force, in preserving peace. [18:2.]

"ALL THE NEWS THAT'S FIT TO PRINT"

In the first eight months of this year, The Times published 6,092 more columns of news than any other newspaper. With World Peace still to be won, and reconversion a topic of daily import, The New York Times continues to print the complete news.

Public Gets Big Army Food Stocks; Whipping Cream Is Freed of Bans

Special to THE NEW YORK TIMES.

WASHINGTON, Sept. 1—The national food situation continued its steady improvement today as the Department of Agriculture, with four orders, increased the supplies of butter, canned salmon and ice cream and signalled the return of whipping cream.

This action was a direct consequence of the sharp reduction of military requirements of these foods. With the discontinuance of butter purchases by the armed forces, the Department explained, it is now possible to revoke the limitations on the sale of heavy cream and the use of butter fat in the production of all frozen desserts. Both these rulings will make whipping cream and ice cream of a higher butter fat content readily available.

In a simultaneous direction, the agency ordered released for civilian use all butter currently held by creameries and receivers for the armed forces and other Government buyers. Although as much as 20,000,000 pounds of butter may be returned to civilian consumers under this ruling, ration values will not be changed, it was indicated.

"At the time ration point values were established for September, the Office of Price Administration recognized the possibility of these

Continued on Page 35, Column 1

Enemy Tortured Dying Americans With Sadist Medical 'Experiments'

By ROBERT TRUMBULL
By Wireless to THE NEW YORK TIMES.

ABOARD THE HOSPITAL SHIP BENEVOLENCE, in Tokyo Bay, Sept. 1 — Seriously ailing American prisoners at Shinagawa, the only hospital serving 8,000 prisoners of war held in the Tokyo area, were guinea pigs for fantastic experiments recalling the sorcery and sadism of the middle ages, Drs. Mack L. Gottlieb and Harold W. Keschner, both of New York, told this correspondent today.

Both doctors are recuperating aboard this ship after their rescue from Shinagawa on Wednesday by a special Navy evacuation mission headed by Comdr. Harold A. Stassen, former Governor of Minnesota and now Assistant Chief of Staff and Flag Secretary to Admiral William F. Halsey, commander of the Third Fleet.

[In an interview in Tokyo the Japanese Army doctor to whom some of these practices were charged confirmed the cruel treatment of American prisoners.]

Dr. Gottlieb, who had his home and office at 307 East Forty-fourth Street, was a Naval officer captured at Guam. Dr. Keschner, of 451 West End Avenue, was taken with an Army force in the Philippines. Both are in good physical

Continued on Page 14, Column 1

WAR COMES TO END

Articles of Capitulation Endorsed by Countries in Pacific Conflict

M'ARTHUR SEES PEACE

Emperor Orders Subjects to Obey All Commands Issued by General

The texts of the surrender documents and statements, P. 3.

By The Associated Press.

ABOARD THE U. S. S. MISSOURI in Tokyo Bay, Sunday, Sept. 2—Japan surrendered formally and unconditionally to the Allies today in a twenty-minute ceremony which ended just as the sun burst through low-hanging clouds as a shining symbol to a ravaged world now done with war.

[A United Press dispatch said the leading Japanese delegate signed the articles at 9:03 A. M. Sunday, Tokyo time, and that General MacArthur signed them at 9:07 A. M.]

Twelve signatures, requiring only a few minutes to inscribe on the articles of surrender, ended the bloody Pacific conflict.

On behalf of Emperor Hirohito, Foreign Minister Mamoru Shigemitsu signed for the Government and Gen. Yoshijiro Umezu for the Imperial General Staff.

MacArthur Voices Peace Hope

Gen. Douglas MacArthur then accepted in behalf of the United Nations, declaring:

"It is my earnest hope and indeed the hope of all mankind that from this solemn occasion a better world shall emerge out of the blood and carnage of the past."

One by one the Allied representatives stepped forward and signed the document that blighted Japan's dream of empire built on bloodshed and tyranny.

First was Admiral Chester W. Nimitz for the United States, then the representatives of China, the United Kingdom, the Soviet, Australia, Canada, France, the Netherlands and New Zealand.

The flags of the United States, Britain, the Soviet and China fluttered from the veranda deck of the famed superdreadnaught, polished and scrubbed as never before. More than 100 high-ranking military and naval officers watched.

Pledges Justice and Tolerance

"As Supreme Commander for the Allied powers," General MacArthur told the Japanese, "I announce it my firm purpose, in the tradition of the countries I represent, to proceed in the discharge of my responsibilities with justice and tolerance, while taking all necessary dispositions to insure that the terms of surrender are fully, promptly and faithfully complied with."

All through this dramatic half hour, only those aboard the battleship knew of what was taking place, because the Missouri has no broadcasting facilities.

But recordings were rushed to the near-by communications ship Ancon, and the solemn words of General MacArthur beginning the ceremony—"We are gathered here, representatives of the major warring powers"—were flashed around the world.

The Japanese representatives were present at the command of Emperor Hirohito contained in a proclamation issued by order of the Supreme Allied Commander.

The Emperor further commanded his officials "to issue general orders to the military and naval forces in accordance with the direction of the Supreme Commander

Continued on Page 2, Column 3

4 FREE AMERICANS TO STAY IN JAPAN

2 Women Missionaries Plan to Go On With Work—2 Men Have Japanese Wives

By ROBERT TRUMBULL
By Wireless to THE NEW YORK TIMES.

TOKYO, Sept. 1—Navy evacuation parties today visited two establishments in and near Tokyo where Allied civilians were interned and found enthusiasm for liberation considerably diluted among the long-time residents of Japan.

Their treatment had been kind in great contrast to that given prisoners of war and only thirty-nine of the fifty-six internees accepted the Navy's offer of transportation out of the Empire.

There were three American men at a former Franciscan monastery at Urawa, thirty-two miles north of Tokyo, and three Americans were among women missionaries interned at Seibo Hospital in the capital. Only one American man and one woman elected to leave Japan. The other men are held by marital ties in the missions, while the two women desire to continue their missionary work among the Japanese.

After the almost hysterical welcome given our evacuation parties by emancipated prisoners of war we were taken aback to have a Canadian internee tell us, "Your arrival makes me feel almost like going back with you."

At Urawa, Father Edwen Ronan, former father superior of the Passionist Fathers at Norwood Park, Ill., expressed a desire to return to the Philippines, where he had been chief chaplain of the Philippine Army from 1937 until his capture on Mindanao after he had escaped from Corregidor in the last plane out.

Two Married to Japanese

The other Americans who prefer to stay are Charles Dreher, formerly of Tenafly, N. J., and Harry Stillman of Newark. Mr. Dreher was editor of a magazine, Japan Newsweek, and Mr. Stillman manufactured ultraviolet ray lamps. Both are married to Japanese and have homes here, to which they will return.

The monastery, a large, two-story frame building in a spacious suburban setting, also confined eleven Britons, three Belgians, two Netherlanders, thirty Canadians and seven Greeks.

The group included eleven Franciscan and nineteen Dominican clerical and lay missionary workers. The seven Greeks were sailors.

Thirty-nine of the fifty-six wished to be repatriated and happily loaded their possessions into commandeered Japanese trucks, with little Japanese gendarmes doing most of the lifting.

Except for a few isolated cuffings and kickings and, by European standards, poor food, these internees had fared well and their captors were friendly. The camp interpreter, Yoshiharu Kanda, turned out to be a classmate of mine at the University of Washington. His sister and brother still live in Seattle. Kanda is looking for a job now. He has a letter of recommendation as an interpreter signed by three inmates.

The Seibo Hospital is a large and apparently first-class institution, even by Western standards. It was undamaged by bombs, although five holes in the roof were made by food parcels when their parachutes failed to open. Seven Japanese were killed in these accidents. Inmates said that the Urawa building, officially known as the Saitama internment camp, also had a hole in its roof from the same cause.

Missionaries' Zeal Undimmed

Women interned at Seibo, also known as the Hospital of Our Lady, had lived through the war in a sheltered world where the love of the missionary for the flock burned undimmed.

Six women left the institution today, but only one was returning to the United States. The others were leaving because the hospital was a Roman Catholic institution and they were Protestant missionaries. The rest, Catholic nuns of various nationalities, remained.

Miss Lois E. Kramer of Naperville, Ill., a missionary of the Evangelical faith who spent twenty-eight years in Japan, is going home.

"We have been treated wonderfully," she said. "The Japanese have been kind gentlemen and we were treated exactly the same at various camps where we were interned before we were sent here. I love Japan and love my work. The people here have been good to me."

Miss Geneva Wells, formerly of Geneva, N. Y., elected to return to Yamaguchi, where she had a mission. She arrived in Japan forty-five years ago yesterday.

"I hope to stay at least fifty years," she said.

Her sister Florence teaches English at Thuda College in Tokyo and was not interned.

BRINGING A FORMAL END TO HOSTILITIES BETWEEN JAPAN AND THE ALLIES

A general view of the surrender ceremony aboard the American battleship

Associated Press Wirephoto (via Navy Radio from U. S. S. Iowa)

WAR COMES TO END AS JAPANESE SIGN

Continued From Page 1

of the Allied Powers." The Imperial General Headquarters issued the order later.

Thus Emperor Hirohito formally acknowledged that General MacArthur's word in Japan would come foremost of all Japanese officialdom during the Allies' occupation of the country, which never before had been occupied by an alien force.

"I command all my people forthwith to cease hostilities," the Emperor said, "to lay down their arms and faithfully to carry out all the provisions of the instrument of surrender and the general orders issued by the Imperial General Headquarters hereunder."

All issues have been "determined on the battlefields of the world and hence are not for our discussion or debate," General MacArthur said before he invited all representatives to sign the surrender instrument.

"Nor is it for us here to meet, representing as we do the majority of the peoples of the earth, in a spirit of distrust, malice or hatred," he added. "But rather it is for us, both victors and vanquished, to rise to that higher dignity which alone benefits the sacred purposes we are about to serve. * * *"

General MacArthur and Admiral Nimitz paid deep tribute to Allied dead and to the people of all Allied nations whose blood, work and sacrifices helped bring victory.

Admiral Nimitz said he took "great pride in the American forces which have helped to win this victory," and declared that "America can be proud of them."

"The officers and men of the United States Army, Navy, Marine Corps, Coast Guard and Merchant Marine who fought in the Pacific have written heroic new chapters in this nation's military history," Admiral Nimitz said. "I have infinite respect for their courage, resourcefulness and devotion to duty. We also acknowledge the great contribution to this victory made by our valiant allies. United we fought and united we prevail."

Admiral Nimitz observed that "the long and bitter struggle, which Japan started so treacherously on the seventh of December, 1941, was at an end.

Recalls Our Dark Days

General MacArthur touched obliquely on the bitter days of the early Philippine fighting when he said:

"As I look back on the long, tortuous trail from those grim days of Bataan and Corregidor, when an entire world lived in fear, when democracy was on the defensive everywhere, when modern civilization trembled in the balance, I thank a merciful God that He has given us the faith, the courage and the power from which to mould victory." General MacArthur told of the Allies' plans to help Japan take her place among peaceful nations.

The Japanese used the knowledge gained from Western science to forge "an instrument of oppression and human enslavement," he said. Freedom of expression, action and thought were denied the Japanese through "application of force," he declared.

"We are committed by the Potsdam Declaration of principles to see that the Japanese people are liberated from this condition of slavery," the Allied leader declared. "It is my purpose to implement this commitment just as rapidly as the armed forces are demobilized and other essential steps taken to neutralize the war potential."

He declared that "if the talents of the race are turned into constructive channels the country can lift itself from its present deplorable state into a position of dignity."

General MacArthur said that "in Asia as well as in Europe unshackled peoples are tasting the full sweetness of liberty," and asserted that "in the Philippines America has evolved a model for this new free world of Asia."

The United States granted the Philippines commonwealth status more than a decade ago, and the islands will in time become completely independent under an act of Congress.

"In the Philippines, America has demonstrated that peoples of the East and peoples of the West may walk side by side in mutual respect and with mutual benefit," the general said. "The history of our sovereignty there has now the full confidence of the East."

Kurihama Base Surrenders

KURIHAMA, Japan, Sept. 1 (AP)—This naval base, built at the site of Commodore Perry's landing on Japan in 1853, was formally surrendered today.

A United States marine artillery battery took possession of the base, including a training school and enough armament and ammunition for a major arsenal.

Only 523 Japanese officers and men were present when the Marines took over the barracks, which once quartered 20,000.

Official surrender was accepted by Lieut. Col. Walter S. Osipoff of San Diego, Calif., who received the Japanese naval captain's sword.

Kurihama, on the eastern side of Uraga Strait entering Tokyo Bay, was where Perry met the representatives of the Japanese Shogunate in his historic mission to open Japan to commerce.

Other Japanese officers' swords were surrendered to 1st Lieut. Robert H. Manning Jr. of Dubberly, La., and 1st Lieut. Robert T. Patterson Jr. of Rogers, Tex.

Armament seized included 5,000 rifles, fifteen five-inch rocket cannon, 257 anti-tank guns, fifteen coastal guns and many anti-air-weapons.

Communique

Russian

LONDON, Sept. 1 (AP)—A Soviet communiqué, as broadcast from Moscow and recorded by the Soviet monitor:

During Sept. 1 the troops of the Second Far Eastern Front, operating together with the ships and the units of the Pacific Fleet, occupied the islands of Kunashiri and Shikotan, in the southern group of the Kurile Islands, thus completing the clearing of the Japanese troops from all the Kurile Islands.

During Aug. 31, 13,000 Japanese troops and men and five generals surrendered to our troops.

SHIP IN FROM NEW GUINEA

700 Americans Reach Nassau After Hard 36-Day Trip

By Wireless to THE NEW YORK TIMES.

NASSAU, Bahamas, Sept. 1—The Netherlands troopship Bloemfontein, chartered by the United States, arrived from New Guinea last night after a hard trip with about 700 Americans aboard, including a woman and her three young daughters.

The vessel left New Guinea thirty-six days ago. She is taking on 1,000 Royal Air Force personnel here and is sailing for New York this afternoon.

"All the News That's Fit to Print"

The New York Times.

LATE CITY EDITION
Sunny with moderate temperatures today. Tomorrow cloudy.
Temperatures Yesterday—Max., 52; Min., 42
Sunrise today, 7:20 A. M.; Sunset, 4:48 P. M.
Full U. S. Weather Bureau Report Page 37.

VOL. XCV...No. 32,129. Entered as Second-Class Matter, Postoffice, New York, N. Y. NEW YORK, FRIDAY, JANUARY 11, 1946. THREE CENTS IN NEW YORK CITY

UNO OPENED; ATTLEE ASKS WORLD UNITY

SPAAK IS ELECTED

Belgian Is President of the General Assembly After Floor Fight

SOVIET LEADS OPPOSITION

U.S. Votes on Russian Side for Norwegian—Session Contrasts With League Meeting in 1920

Addresses at the opening of the UNO in London, Page 3.

By JAMES B. RESTON
By Cable to The New York Times.

LONDON, Jan. 10—The fifty-one nations of the greatest war-time coalition in history, representing four-fifths of the people in the world, started today another chapter in man's melancholy search for peace and security.

One hundred and forty-seven days after the close of the war that cost more than 20,000,000 casualties and left countless millions homeless and on the twenty-sixth anniversary of the ratification of the ill-fated League of Nations Covenant, the nations met this afternoon in the blue and gold auditorium of the Central Hall of Westminster for the first meeting of the United Nations General Assembly.

Greeting them on behalf of Britain, which served as the springboard for the final conquest of Germany, Prime Minister Attlee told them frankly that they would succeed in their new venture only if they brought "the same sense of urgency, the same self-sacrifice and the same willingness to subordinate sectional interests" with which they fought the war.

Spaak Elected President

Then, with a little less dignity than marks the balloting at a political convention at home, they proceeded to elect Paul-Henri Spaak, Belgian Foreign Minister, as President of the first General Assembly, despite a determined effort by the Soviet Union to replace him with the Norwegian Foreign Minister, Trygve Lie.

This election produced the only extraordinary incident of the day. When Dr. Eduardo Zuleta Angel of Colombia, chairman of the UNO Preparatory Commission and temporary president of the General Assembly, announced the balloting for the Presidency, the deputy chairman of the Soviet delegation, Andrei Gromyko, Russian Ambassador to Washington, asked to be recognized and strode to the microphone on the improvised modernistic blue and gold stage.

It was known at this point that the candidacy of M. Spaak would win, but Mr. Gromyko, assured that he was supported by the United States, told the General Assembly that his delegation attached great importance to the election and favored the Norwegian Foreign Minister because of his personal capacities and the active movements of his country in the war.

Pole and Ukrainian Back Lie

As soon as Mr. Gromyko had left the rostrum, Foreign Minister Wincenty Rzymowski of Poland asked to be recognized and he then seconded the Russian nomination. When he had finished, D. Z. Manuilsky, the Ukrainian People's Commissar for Foreign Affairs, a striking, white-maned figure with a booming voice, moved that Dr. Lie be elected by acclamation despite the fact that the rules of the Assembly call for elections by secret ballot.

After another short speech for Dr. Lie by Gustav Rasmussen, Danish Foreign Minister, the temporary president called for a vote on whether to decide the issue by secret ballot, but immediately Mr. Gromyko rose again and asked for a vote on the motion to elect Dr. Lie by acclamation.

Some confusion attended those motions during which Mr. Manuilsky voted both for the secret ballot and for the election of Dr. Lie by acclamation, but finally fifteen delegations voted for a secret ballot and only nine voted in favor of putting Dr. Lie in by acclaim. The

Continued on Page 3, Column 2

Delegates Welcome Copies of The Times

By Wireless to The New York Times.

LONDON, Jan. 10—Copies of yesterday morning's issue of THE NEW YORK TIMES were distributed to delegates to the United Nations Organization's General Assembly this evening and they received an enthusiastic reception from all, particularly the American representatives.

"This is about as useful, informative and happy a thing as has happened to an exiled American in a long time," Adlai Stevenson said. He has been here for four months working on the establishment of the UNO.

King George will be among the recipients. Buckingham Palace officials said that he was very happy to have the paper.

Copies are being sent to prominent Britons, including former Foreign Secretary Anthony Eden, Prime Minister Attlee and leading members of the Cabinet, and to the heads of each of the fifty-one delegations to the Assembly. The papers are being flown across the Atlantic.

PRESS STILL BESET IN 'FREE' RUMANIA

Russian and Union Censors Bar Liberal Chief's Effort to Use Grant Given by Moscow

By SAM POPE BREWER
By Wireless to The New York Times.

BUCHAREST, Rumania, Jan. 10—Even before United States Ambassador W. Averell Harriman took off for London at dawn today to report to Secretary of State James F. Byrnes at the United Nations Organization meeting on the Allied commission's work here, the great difficulty of getting a loyal execution of the Moscow communiqué's terms in this test case of Allied cooperation showed itself.

Though press freedom was promised and Rumanian censorship of the domestic press was officially dropped yesterday, first a Russian censor and then an unofficial typographical union censorship clamped down last night on an apparently inoffensive statement by Liberal Party Chief Constantin (Dinu) Bratianu on his party's conception of a "free press."

Mr. Harriman and Sir Archibald Clark Kerr, British Ambassador to Moscow, had a three-hour conversation last night with Premier Petru Groza in which the question of restoring the freedoms was discussed, among other things, but if the Premier's ideas on freedom are still the same as those expressed in the previous night's communiqué there is little likelihood that his "assurances" will be acceptable to the United States Government.

The outstanding flaw in M. Groza's statement was the assertion that the present Ministers of Justice, the Interior and Propaganda could be expected to protect such freedom, when it was under their aegis that flagrant abuses

Continued on Page 6, Column 2

CHIANG PROCLAIMS TRUCE AND REFORM AS COUNCIL BEGINS

Marshall Ends Deadlock With Early Meeting, Sends Word to Delegates' Session

TROOP MOVEMENT FROZEN

Civil Liberties, End of Police Abuses, Amnesty, New Voting Basis Promised China

Chiang's announcement of the truce appears on Page 10.

By TILLMAN DURDIN
By Wireless to The New York Times.

CHUNGKING, Jan. 10—Only a few moments before President Chiang Kai-shek proclaimed a sweeping series of political and democratic reforms in China, a formal truce order, hammered out by Gen. George C. Marshall and representatives of the Chinese Government and the Chinese Communist party, brought a cease-fire order to the civil war fronts.

The agreement provided for an immediate halt to hostilities, full restoration of all war-blocked communications and the establishment of a control organization, with American participation, to supervise the carrying out of the armistice compact. The continued movement of Government forces in Manchuria and south of the Yangtze River is not prejudiced under the terms of the agreement.

This agreement highlighted a day of historic happenings in Chungking, all tied together, with dramatic timing and with close political relationship.

Conference Assembles

The Political Consultation Conference, an assemblage of party leaders and non-party persons, dedicated to working out a program of political unity and democratization for China, met in its first session. The truce accord was reached after an emergency early morning meeting of the three negotiators just in time for President Chiang to reveal the agreement in his opening address to the conference.

In his speech President Chiang announced these far-reaching Government measures in the field of civil rights:

Steps to insure freedom of person, of conscience, of publication and of assembly.

Abrogation of secret police activity in assuring that rulings were being made under which only proper judicial and police authorities would be permitted to arrest, try or punish individuals.

Equality of "all legal parties before the law" and their right to open activity "within the law."

Release of all political prisoners "except traitors and those found to have committed definite acts injurious to the Republic."

Promotion of local self-government everywhere, with popular election to be held "according to law" and from "the lowest strata upward."

The supreme achievement of bringing at least an armistice and perhaps permanent peace to China came to fruition after a hitch in the discussion yesterday threatened to prolong if not seriously to endanger the negotiations. It is clear that the masterly mediation of General Marshall was a major factor in producing the final success.

Last night the three-man conference brought up a disagreement

Continued on Page 10, Column 2

Japanese Cabinet Has Resigned; Interest of Emperor Is Indicated

By Reuter.

TOKYO, Friday, Jan. 11—The Japanese Cabinet has resigned.

Japan's seven-day political crisis broke when ailing Prime Minister Baron Kijuro Shidehara, who is still confined to bed, informed the Cabinet through Foreign Minister Shigeru Yoshida that he had decided that the Cabinet should resign en masse as a result of General MacArthur's "political purge" directives of Jan. 4.

Mr. Yoshida, who earlier this morning called on the Emperor at the Royal Palace to inform him of the Premier's decision, is expected to make another call this afternoon, when it is believed that Hirohito will again give the resigning Baron Premier an imperial command to form a new Government.

The Premier's personal secretary stated that it would be several days yet before the Premier would be able to attend to state duties, but that the Cabinet would carry on in the meantime to give the Baron time to select a list of names of proposed new members to submit to General MacArthur's headquarters for approval.

By LINDESAY PARROTT
By Wireless to The New York Times.

TOKYO, Jan. 10—Emperor Hirohito will take a hand to break the Cabinet deadlock that has paralyzed Japan since General MacArthur's directive of Jan. 4 outlawed from public office all but two members of the Government of Baron Kijuro Shidehara, it was said in informed circles tonight.

Although the bulk of the Cabinet's members have been ordered ejected as members of former ultranationalist societies, it continues to cling tenaciously to its position. Faced with this situation, the Emperor, it is stated, will summon his personal advisers to ask them to find a solution, since the Japanese Government during the past week has, in effect, continued to func-

Continued on Page 10, Column 6

17.5% GM PAY RISE URGED BY BOARD; PHONE TIE-UP OFF UNTIL MONDAY; STEEL AND UNION PACT INDICATED

Appeal to Strikers By Union Leaders

Following is the text of the statement issued last night by the Association of Communication Equipment Workers asking its members to delay picketing until Monday:

"This is a special message to the members and officers of the Association of Communications Equipment Workers in all locals throughout the United States.

"Ernest Weaver, national president, and the bargaining committee composed of Messrs. Thornton, Massey and Barry request the officers to comply with a special request made by Secretary of Labor Schwellenbach not to establish picket lines at any location until Monday morning, Jan. 14.

"The Secretary of Labor has arranged a conference of the union and the company at 4 P. M., Friday, Jan. 11, in Washington, D. C. The members and officers of the ACEW are urged to comply with the request of the Secretary of Labor in consideration of the public, the long lines and other telephone workers. ACEW members will remain on strike."

GOVERNMENT TO USE ALUMINUM PATENTS

Alcoa Cedes Rights to RFC for Licensing to Reynolds Metals, Leasing Federal Plants

By WALTER H. WAGGONER
Special to The New York Times.

WASHINGTON, Jan. 10—The Aluminum Company of America agreed today to grant the Government free use of its patents for the production of aluminum together with the right to license them to its competitors acquiring Government-owned plants.

The decision by the country's

Continued on page 15, Column 5

PICKETING DELAYED

Union Calls on Locals to Change Plans After Schwellenbach Plea

PARLEY IN CAPITAL TODAY

Negotiations With Western Electric End Here After Rejection of Offer

By LAWRENCE RESNER

A postponement until Monday of picket lines that had threatened the disruption this morning of the nation's telephone service was ordered last night by leaders of striking telephone installation workers after a last minute appeal by Secretary of Labor Lewis B. Schwellenbach.

Despite this decision, which was announced at 11:20 P. M. by Ernest Weaver, president of the Association of Communications Equipment Workers, a certain amount of difficulty was anticipated in reaching all locals of the union to prevent all picketing.

To expedite a widespread announcement of the order, Mr. Weaver enlisted the aid of the nation's press and radio to publish and broadcast a message to the members of his union to delay action pending results of conferences with Secretary Schwellenbach scheduled to start at 4 P. M. today in Washington.

Leaders Urged to Comply

This message urged the members and officers of the ACEW "to comply with the request of the Secretary of Labor in consideration of the public, the long lines and other telephone workers."

Officials of Western Electric, against whom the installation workers' strike is directed, also agreed to join in the discussions

Continued on Page 13, Column 2

World News Summarized

FRIDAY, JANUARY 11, 1946

Fifty-one nations met in the first General Assembly of the UNO in London, yesterday, and heard Dr. Eduardo Zuleta Angel of Colombia, temporary president, and Prime Minister Attlee plead for international harmony. Paul-Henri Spaak, Belgian Foreign Minister, was elected President of the Assembly. The only incident arose when Soviet delegate Gromyko unexpectedly sought the election by acclamation of Norway's Foreign Minister Lie, but M. Spaak, backed by Britain, won on a secret ballot, 28 to 23. [1:1.]

Canada, Brazil and Poland are slated for two-year terms as non-permanent members of the Security Council, and the Netherlands, Mexico and Egypt for one-year terms. [3:1.]

The UNO Site Committee listened to a broadcast of the London proceedings in the library of the home of President Roosevelt. The members were impressed with Hyde Park. [2:6.]

Despite the Moscow parley's free press demand the Russian censors in Rumania emasculated a statement by Liberal leader Bratianu and the local typographical union, on some papers refused to print what was left undeleted. [1:2.]

Fighting between Iranian patriots and "autonomy" partisans broke out in the Russian-occupied zone between Azerbaijan and Teheran. Five persons were killed. [11:2-3, with map.]

A verbal tilt between Rabbi Stephen S. Wise and Chairman Hutcheson enlivened the Anglo-American Committee hearing. Non-Zionists said Palestine could not absorb all Jews seeking refuge. [2:2.]

The Cabinet in Japan resigned after getting word from Premier Shidehara. [1:2-3.]

In China following upon the Chungking - Communist truce, Generalissimo Chiang Kai-shek guaranteed equality for all political parties, freedom of speech and person, local elections, political amnesty and end of one-party government. [1:3.]

Korea, too, moved toward unity when the five major parties issued a joint statement praising the Moscow decision for self-government. [10:1.]

"We want to go home" demonstrations continued throughout the Pacific area. [4:1.] In Germany a soldier committee seemed satisfied with explanations offered at a conference with officers, but their comrades continued loud protests. [4:2-3.]

The Senate Military Affairs Committee appointed a subgroup to investigate demobilization. Hearings will start Monday and General Eisenhower may be called. [1:6-7.]

A general wage increase of 19½ cents an hour was recommended by the General Motors fact-finding board. This is six cents more than the company offered and 13½ less than the union demanded, but union acceptance is anticipated. The board said the increase was not inflationary. [1:8.]

Leaders of the United Automobile Workers were hastily summoned to a meeting in Detroit tomorrow. General Motors is expected to resume negotiations. Dealings with the other motor companies seemed to be making progress. [1:6-7.]

The General Motors decision added optimism to the resumed negotiations in this city between United States Steel and the union, the first time both sides had met since October. There was great hope that a strike might be averted. [1:6-7.]

What happens in the steel deliberations will largely determine whether 200,000 electrical workers walk out Tuesday. [12:2.]

The threatened disruption of the nation's telephone service scheduled for this morning was delayed until Monday on Labor Secretary Schwellenbach's plea to the Western Electric strikers. [1:5.] Cable operators refused to handle messages and money for soldiers reaching them through Western Union. [1:7.]

Meat packers rejected a Government offer to pay more for its meat without raising retail prices. There seemed little hope of halting a strike. [13:1.]

UAW to Consider Report During Week-End in Detroit

Executive Board and GM Union Committee Are Expected to Accept Federal Findings —General Motors Officials Silent

By WALTER W. RUCH
Special to The New York Times.

DETROIT, Jan. 10—Leaders of the United Automobile Workers, CIO, were summoned hastily today to come to Detroit for two week-end meetings to consider the report of President Truman's General Motors fact-finding board.

As soon as it became known that the report would be released today, R. J. Thomas, international president, requested members of the international executive board of the UAW to come here for a special meeting on Saturday morning.

Almost simultaneously, Walter P. Reuther, vice president of the UAW, and director of its General Motors division, sent out telegrams to the national General Motors committee of the union, scheduling a meeting for Sunday afternoon.

Recommendations were expected to flow from the Saturday meeting into that set for Sunday, with the ultimate outcome likely to constitute a new overture on the part of the UAW toward settlement of the fifty-one-day-old General Motors strike. The UAW, it was learned, was almost certain to take the report of the fact-finding commission as an acceptable compromise of its wage differences with General Motors.

The corporation, however, remained silent on the Washington report. This was not as disquieting as it might have been had the company not withdrawn from the proceedings rather than argue with the UAW over the "ability to pay" issue. One company official explained that the concern could hardly be expected to comment upon the result of a proceeding from which it had withdrawn as a party.

According to the best available sources here, the company now will proceed to sit down with the UAW, as in the past, to negotiate private-

Continued on Page 15, Column 7

Averting of Steel Strike Expected in Parley Here

By RUSSELL PORTER

Possibility of a settlement of the wage dispute in the steel industry without a strike increased yesterday afternoon when representatives of the United States Steel Corporation and the United Steel Workers of America, an affiliate of the Congress of Industrial Organizations, resumed collective bargaining negotiations in a three-hour conference, apparently held in a friendly atmosphere, and adjourned until 2 P. M. today for further discussion.

The conference is being held at the headquarters of the corporation at 71 Broadway.

The negotiations were interrupted last October, when the company refused any concessions to the union's demand for a $2-a-day wage increase unless a compensatory price increase was allowed by the Government. They were resumed after a price increase of about $4 a ton was authorized. The company had asked for $7.

Effect on Other Strikes Seen

Both sides refused comment on the progress of the negotiations after yesterday's meeting, but it was evident they were hopeful of an agreement that would avert the strike, scheduled to begin Monday, which would call out 700,000 workers throughout the industry.

Observers, meanwhile, felt a peaceful settlement of the steel dispute also would head off threatened CIO strikes in the electrical and packing-house industries and might influence compromise solutions of existing strikes in the automobile and other industries.

The recommendations of President Truman's fact-finding board for an increase of 19½ cents an

Continued on Page 12, Column 3

WIRE STRIKE STOPS MESSAGES TO GI'S

Funds Also Held Up Here as Pressure Becomes Severe—No Moves for Settlement

By A. H. RASKIN

Messages and money orders intended for soldiers and sailors overseas were piling up in cable offices here yesterday as the strike of 7,000 Western Union telegraph workers in New York, Long Island and northern New Jersey went into its third day.

With no moves for settlement of the strike in prospect, the pressure of the telegraph tie-up on business activity became increasingly severe. Many large companies, already handicapped by the virtual suspension of normal telegraphic service, reported that mechanical failures were interfering with the operation of inter-office communications between the home offices here and branches in other cities.

The Western Union management and the strikers differed as to the volume of traffic that was being kept up in the face of the

Continued on Page 12, Column 6

Senators to Inquire Into All Phases Of Demobilization of Armed Forces

By C. P. TRUSSELL
Special to The New York Times.

WASHINGTON, Jan. 10—Under pressure from Senators and the War Department, a special Senate Military Affairs subcommittee was created today to investigate the entire question of demobilization of the armed forces. It will begin work as soon as witnesses are available.

Public hearings, said Senator Edwin C. Johnson of Colorado, chairman of the subcommittee, will start Monday if either Kenneth C. Royall, Acting Secretary of War, or General Eisenhower, the first scheduled witnesses, was able to appear then.

Appointed to the subcommittee by Senator Elbert D. Thomas, chairman of the Military Affairs Committee, were, besides Mr. Johnson, Senators Frank P. Briggs, Democrat, of Missouri, and Chapman Revercomb, Republican, of West Virginia.

Senator Johnson, in a letter to Senator Thomas, urged the entire Military Affairs Committee to call General Eisenhower before it for public discussion and interrogation.

"It is distressing and humiliating to all Americans to read in every newspaper in the land accounts of near mutiny in the Army," Senator Johnson said. "The causes for this deplorable situation must be brought out in the open. No American Army must ever be permitted by the Congress to degenerate into a mob."

Senator Revercomb is the author of a resolution which would effect the immediate discharge, on an estimated basis, of any of an estimated 1,000,000 fathers who are still in the services here and overseas. He said today that he believed Congress should take over the demobilization program.

As plans for the investigation

Continued on Page 4, Column 4

REPORT TO TRUMAN

Fact-Finders Proposing Increase 12½% Short of Union Demand

FIRM OFFERED 13½ CENTS

President Lauds Board, Asks Adoption of Recommendation and End to Walk-Out

The text of the Fact Finding Board's report, Pages 14, 15.

By LOUIS STARK
Special to The New York Times.

WASHINGTON, Jan. 10—President Truman's fact-finding board in the General Motors dispute recommended today a general wage increase of 19½ cents an hour, or 6 cents more than the company offered.

The increase is about 17.5 per cent above present hourly rates as compared with the union demand for a 30 per cent rise.

The average wage in General Motors was estimated as $1.119 an hour. The proposed increase would bring this up to $1.314. The union requested $1.45 an hour.

Last November the Commerce Department estimated that the corporation was able to pay a wage increase of 15 per cent now and a further 10 per cent next year.

The President received the 12,000-word document from the board, headed by Lloyd K. Garrison, at noon and later issued a summary of the findings.

President Lauds Report

Praising the report as "a thorough and reasoned document," Mr. Truman said that he believed "it will commend itself to the good judgment of the American public." He added:

"I sincerely hope that the parties will follow the recommendations and bring about a speedy end to this most costly conflict. I am satisfied that if such a settlement is made the industrial skies will rapidly clear and American industry and labor will go forward to new heights of achievement in the interests of the whole country."

Outstanding in the report is the statement that the proposed wage increase is non-inflationary; that it will not require a price increase, and that it is well within the national stabilization policy.

R. J. Thomas and Walter P. Reuther, president and vice president of the CIO United Automobile Workers, hurried to New York to lay the board's findings before Philip Murray, CIO president, who resumed wage negotiations with the United States Steel Corporation today.

They issued no statement here, but it was said unofficially that the auto workers would accept the recommendations, which were also signed by the other board members, Milton E. Eisenhower, president of Kansas State Agricultural College, and Judge Walter P. Stacy of the Supreme Court of North Carolina.

There was no comment here from General Motors officials.

Report Tied to Steel Dispute

The report, coming as it did with renewal of the steel wage negotiations, caused speculation here to continue to be optimistic on the early settlement of the steel dispute, which threatens a strike of 700,000 workers Monday.

This union requested a wage increase of $2 a day, or 25 cents an hour. Steel union sources have indicated that the organization was prepared to accept $1.60, or 20 cents an hour, which would be slightly in excess of the General Motors recommendation.

Besides the wage recommendation, the Garrison Board proposed that "in line with the customary practice of American industry in similar situations," the status quo prevailing before the strike be restored by reinstatement of the 1945 contract which the company has canceled ("as it had a right to do").

After the contract is reinstated, the board suggested, the parties

Continued on Page 15, Column 1

HOLLAND TO ENTER SECURITY COUNCIL

Canada, Brazil, Poland, Egypt and Mexico Also Slated to Be in That Body

RIVALRY FOR OTHER UNIT

Economic, Social Membership Coveted—Ukraine Chairman of Committee on Atom

By SYDNEY GRUSON

By Wireless to THE NEW YORK TIMES.

LONDON, Jan. 10—The election of Belgium's Paul-Henri Spaak as President of the first United Nations General Assembly today assured the Netherlands of a place on the Security Council as the small power representative of Western Europe, it was learned tonight.

With this decided, it was reported a definite line-up of the non-permanent members of the Council to be elected tomorrow or Saturday had been agreed upon by the Big Five. Canada, Brazil and Poland will receive two-year terms and the Netherlands, Mexico and Egypt will get one-year terms. These six nations, along with the Big Five, will form the first composition of the body that has primary responsibility for the maintenance of international peace and security.

If M. Spaak had not obtained the Presidency Belgium would have vied with the Netherlands for the seat on the Security Council. In fact, Andrei A. Gromyko of the Soviet Union told M. Spaak tonight that Russia had proposed Belgium for this seat.

M. Spaak approached the Soviet delegate at a reception that Ernest Bevin, British Foreign Secretary, gave tonight for the delegates and said he was sorry that Mr. Gromyko had felt he had to oppose his election. But M. Spaak assured Mr. Gromyko that he would be a fair president.

Soviet Position Explained

Mr. Gromyko replied, in effect, that M. Spaak's election was all right with the Soviet Union and offered the explanation that he had not supported M. Spaak because he had proposed Belgium for the Security Council.

By Saturday afternoon it is hoped the first general Assembly will have elected, besides the membership of the Security Council, the membership of the Economic and Social Council and the officers who will make up the Assembly's Steering Committee.

There has been intense rivalry for positions on the Economic and Social Council, UNO's primary instrument to restore and maintain the world's physical well-being. There are thirteen seats to fill, the Big Five being charter members.

According to the best information available tonight six of these thirteen seats definitely will go to Canada, Colombia, Chile, Peru, Cuba and Czechoslovakia. The seven others most likely to be elected are Iraq, India, Australia, Turkey, Belgium, Norway and Greece, although the Netherlands may be included and Norway or Greece dropped. The steering committee, over whose composition the executive committee and the preparatory commission fought so long, will be made up of the Assembly's seven vice presidents, M. Spaak as president and the chairmen of the Assembly's six main committees.

The slate of chairmen had Big Five approval tonight but it may not have tomorrow on the basis of what happened over the presidency. However, there is little likelihood that any of them will be contested.

Ukraine's Chairmanship

The Ukraine will receive the chairmanship of the Political and Security Committee, where discussion on the atomic energy commission to be established under the UNO may provide fireworks. Senator Tom Connally is the United States representative on this committee. Poland is slated to receive the chairmanship of the Economic and Financial Committee; New Zealand the Social, Humanitarian and Cultural Committee; Uruguay the Trusteeship Committee, Syria the Administrative and Budgetary Committee, and Panama the Legal Committee.

The Big Five each will provide one vice president and the other two will come from India and Venezuela, according to present plans.

Thus on the Steering Committee, in addition to the Big Five, there will be two representatives of what is generally referred to here as the Soviet Union group, three Latin Americans, one small Western European power, one British Dominion and India. The Russian idea of equitable geographical representation has been followed in drafting the line-up.

BYRNES VISITS BEVIN

UNO Atomic Bomb Resolution and UNRRA Reported Topics

By Wireless to THE NEW YORK TIMES.

LONDON, Jan. 10—United States Secretary of State James F. Byrnes paid a brief visit to the Foreign Office today before the opening of the UNO General Assembly and talked with Foreign Secretary Ernest Bevin for half an hour.

They are believed to have discussed the United States interpretation of the atomic energy resolution and British proposals for expanding the work of the United Nations Relief Rehabilitation Administration and bringing the care of refugees under the direction of the UNO.

American Slav Head Is in Sofia

By Wireless to THE NEW YORK TIMES.

SOFIA, Jan. 10—At the invitation of the Bulgarian Slav Committee, Leo Krzycki, national president of the American Slav Congress, has arrived from Bucharest. After visits to Russia and Poland, he will stay in Sofia for several days to re-establish connections with the Bulgarian branch of the Slav World Unity.

Texts of Opening Addresses at UNO Assembly in London

LONDON, Jan. 10 (UP)—The texts of the address by Dr. Eduardo Zuleta Angel of Colombia, temporary chairman of the UNO Assembly, and Prime Minister Attlee of Britain follow:

By Dr. Zuleta

Determined to save succeeding generations from the scourge of war, which twice in our lifetime has brought untold sorrow to mankind, and imbued with an abiding faith in freedom and justice, we have come to this British capital, which bears the deep impress of heroic majesty, to constitute the General Assembly of the United Nations and to make a genuine and sincere beginning in the application of the San Francisco Charter.

That instrument having been freely and democratically debated, it has been unreservedly accepted by all in confident belief that the machinery set up under its provisions will prove adequate to the achievement of its historic purpose; in a word, the maintenance of peace and security by collective recourse, at need, to the use of land, sea and air forces, and the establishment, through cooperation in economic, social, educational and humanitarian fields, of those conditions of stability and well-being which will insure peaceful and friendly relations based on the principle of equal rights and self-determination among the nations of the world.

It is an arduous and difficult duty but one which we can and must discharge without delay, for the whole world which waits upon our decisions rightly—yet with understandable anxiety—looks to us now to master our problems and we cannot, with impunity, fail mankind again in the face of past sufferings, which have supervened upon the most terrible and devastating of wars.

Good-Will Ascendant

This we shall not do. An inner voice tells us that we can all lift up our hearts; that we can rise to the level of true understanding, humanitarianism and bring to bear on, at least some of the problems of peace, the spirit of cooperation, the tenacity of purpose, self-sacrifice and technical effort which, when applied to the dramatic problems of war, led us to the splendid triumph of the democracies that has brought us together here.

We knew that this is so from our memories of San Francisco, where the greatest difficulties were overcome in an atmosphere of good-will, lit up by the tragic glare of the European furnace. We feel it when we consider the ability shown and the harmony achieved by the Executive Committee and by the Preparatory Commission in accomplishment of their task. It is manifest in the remarkable interest which the Great Powers have evinced and the invaluable help they have provided to insure the working of the United Nations Organization—an interest eloquently displayed, so far as the present Assembly is concerned, in the presence of delegates of the highest standing and of greatest eminence.

It is evident above all in the determination which animates each one of us to fulfill the task, second to none in importance, nobility and grandeur, for there is no purpose to which leading statesmen can more worthily apply their intellect and will than that of maintaining the peace on the basis of full international cooperation and so alleviating the ills which beset mankind.

To the achievement of this task, all of us, great and small, strong and weak, will give our unqualified and unhesitating support.

The five great powers who, by virtue of Articles 24 and 27 of the Charter, and by the very nature of things, will shoulder the chief responsibility for the maintenance of peace and security, will bring to bear not only the immense weight of their military, financial and industrial resources but something more important, without which their very power would be nothing but the prelude to apocalyptic cataclysm. I mean good-will, divested of every shred of intrigue or trickery, and that spirit of cooperation which is so vital to maintain among them the harmony and unity which are the basic and unalterable foundations of the United Nations Organization.

An Era of Sacrifice

In signing the Charter, the other powers have already yielded up as their first contribution to this great undertaking a large part of that which they hold most dear and precious—their sovereignty. They made this sacrifice with deep emotion but without hesitation, realizing that here was the beginning of a new era in which their security would be adequately guaranteed by adequate and effective means and in which any violence or aggression against them would be ruthlessly put down.

They have, however, another obligation to fulfill: that of joining their efforts in good faith and lofty spirit to maintain harmony among the powers, knowing full well that any ill-advised action or policy likely to endanger their unity would be suicidal.

AT THE OPENING SESSION OF THE UNO GENERAL ASSEMBLY IN LONDON

Prime Minister Clement Attlee addressing the delegates in Central Hall yesterday — Associated Press Radiophoto

In this Assembly, which to use a well-known phrase is the "town meeting of the world," smaller powers will be able, year in and year out, to make their voices heard in as free and democratic atmosphere as that of San Francisco and London.

We must not, however, lose sight of the fact the weight their voices will carry and the influence they will exert will depend less on the terms of the Charter on functions and duties of the Assembly than on wisdom, judgment, spirit of cooperation and the sense of justice by which it is guided and inspired.

Founded on reason and actuated by real love of peace and mankind, its pronouncements will command the attention and respect of the Security Council, both for their intrinsic value and as essential factors in shaping the Council's decisions, which will necessarily be more effective the more accurately they reflect universal public opinion, freely, fully and democratically expressed.

Gentlemen: under Article 2 of the Charter, the organization is to be based on the principle of sovereign equality of all its members; and this is not inconsistent with the self-evident fact that those nations which bear the chief responsibility for the maintenance of peace are those who have the greatest resources for the purpose.

That this principle is not a dead letter in the Charter, and that it is not robbed of its force by the acknowledgment of this elementary truth, is evident by the fact, which may have occasioned some surprise, that the unique privilege of opening this Assembly of the United Nations, comprising so many eminent personalities, has fallen to an obscure delegate of a small Spanish-American republic which has no pretensions to military force or economic power, but which is none the less proud of its legal structure, its democratic organization and its love of freedom.

By Mr. Attlee

I have the honor today of welcoming to London this great Assembly of delegates of the United Nations.

I would like in the first place to thank you, Mr. President, for your speech and also to place on the record the appreciation which I am sure we all feel for the successful manner in which you have carried out the arduous and important duties of the President of the Preparatory Commission.

I know well from my colleagues how much that commission has owed to your guidance. Without your sense of business, readiness to accept responsibility, and the influence which you have exerted on your colleagues, we might not have been able to meet at this time with a procedure and program ready to hand.

I hope the proceedings of this conference will be animated by the same sense of urgency, the same practical spirit and the same cooperative atmosphere as has characterized the work of the Preparatory Commission.

I know that great questions were debated freely, even dispassionately, but at the same time there was a lively spirit of conciliation and good-will which led eventually to almost complete unanimity. I have said we welcome you here in London, and it will be our endeavor to make you feel at home in this, our capital city, so you may speak as freely and frankly as if you were meeting in some special territory under international control.

Enemy's Malice Evident

We shall do our best to make your stay here pleasant within the limit of our means. We wish we could do more, but I am sure that all of you in the course of your stay will realize that anything lacking in your entertainment is not due to any absence of good-will, but to the effect of the malice of our enemies wreaked upon this ancient city. Evidence of this you will see around you.

Last night we listened to an inspiring speech by His Majesty the King in which he set before us in a few words the nature of the task which we have to accomplish, the vital importance of the issues at stake and the keen desire of all nations of the British Commonwealth for whom he spoke to make this first meeting of the UNO a complete success.

I had the privilege of taking part in the discussions at San Francisco from which was evolved the Charter of the United Nations. The initiation of these discussions while our enemies were still in the field against us was at once an act of faith in our victory and an acknowledgment of the cause for which we were fighting.

The purposes and principles set down in the preamble and in an article of the Charter have the whole-hearted support of His Majesty's Government and, I believe, of the whole of the people of this country, to whatever political party they belong.

We realize that, as perhaps never before, a choice is offered to mankind. Twice in my lifetime a war has brought untold sorrow to mankind. Should there be a third World War, the long upward progress toward civilization may be halted for generations and the work of myriads of men and women through the centuries be brought to naught.

Paul-Henri Spaak, Belgian Foreign Minister, who was chosen president of the General Assembly. The New York Times, 1942

A Common Endeavor

The preamble to the Charter of the United Nations admirably sets out the ideals for which men and women laid down their lives during the war. But the affirmation of principles is easy; the translation into action and the making of a working reality out of an ideal is very difficult.

In the stress and strain of war it is possible to fuse an ideal aim with practical effort. When in the summer of 1940 this country was left open to imminent danger of invasion, the whole of the people were animated by one single aim, and that aim was immediately translated into action. Every man and woman leaped forward to serve wherever needed and the strength of that purpose endured through five years of war.

During those five years, as nation after nation joined in the struggle, efforts of the fighting forces, of workers behind the line, of resistance movements, were all coordinated and directed to the single purpose of victory. Private interests and individual national aspirations were sunk in common endeavor.

Now, today, when victory has crowned our arms, we have to bring to the task of creating permanent conditions of peace the same sense of urgency, the same self-sacrifice and the same willingness to subordinate sectional interest to the common good as brought us through the crisis of war. We must all, therefore, approach our work with the realization of its outstanding and vital importance.

The United Nations organization must become the overriding factor in foreign policy. After the First World War there was a tendency to regard the League of Nations as something outside the ordinary range of foreign policy. Governments continued on old lines, pursuing individual aims and following the path of power politics, not understanding that the world had passed through a new epoch.

In just such a spirit in times past in these islands, great nobles and their retainers used to practice private war in disregard to the authority of central government. The time came when private armies were abolished and when the rule of law was established throughout the length and breadth of this island. What has been done in Britain and other countries on a small stage has now to be effected throughout the whole world.

We must all now, today, recognize the truth proclaimed by the Foreign Minister of the U.S.S.R. at Geneva—"Peace is indivisible." Looking back on past years, we can trace the origins of the late war to acts of aggression, the significance of which was not realized at the time.

Failure to deal with the Japanese adventure in the Far East, and with acts of aggression of the Fascist rulers of Germany and Italy, led inevitably to a breakdown of the rule of law and the Second World War. In the last five years the aggression of Hitler in Europe drew eventually into a contest of men from all continents and from the islands of the sea. It should make us all realize that the welfare of every one of us is bound up with the welfare of the world as a whole, and that we are all members, one of another.

I am glad that the Charter of the United Nations does not deal only with governments and states, or with politics and war, but with the simple, elemental needs of human beings, whatever their color or their creed.

Human Rights Fundamental

In the Charter, we reaffirm our faith in fundamental human rights. We see the freedom of the individual in the state as an essential complement to the freedom of the state in the world community of nations. We stress, too, that social justice and the best possible standards of life for all are essential factors in promoting and maintaining the peace of the world.

I have said that the solution of the problem of peace from war is urgent and vital as never before. We, perhaps, in these islands which were for so long immune from attack behind the barrier of the sea, feel more than any others that we are living in a new age.

The development of powerful weapons of destruction operating from distant bases has destroyed the illusion of isolationism. The coming of the atomic bomb was only the last of a series of warnings to mankind that, unless the powers of destruction could be controlled, immense ruin and almost annihilation would be the lot of the most highly civilized portions of mankind.

I welcome therefore the decision to remit the whole problem of the control of atomic energy to a commission of the United Nations Organization. In this discovery we can see set clearly before us in tangible form the question that faces the modern world.

Here is an invention fraught with immense possibilities, on the one hand, of danger and, on the other, of advantage to the human race. It is for the peoples of the world, through their representatives, to make their choice between life and death.

I hope and believe that every delegate who is here today has come, not only in a spirit of determination, but in a spirit of hope. We have always with us skeptics and pessimists who will tell us that there always has been war and that there always will be war, who point to the failure of the League of Nations as a reason for skepticism as to the success of the United Nations Organization. But the progress of civilization has been one of continual failure and of learning by experience.

To take an example, the history of the trade union movement is marked by failure after failure. After every defeat the skeptics and the timorous said, "You cannot get workers to combine, the self-interest of the individual is too strong," but eventually unity was achieved.

Lesson of Past Mistakes

I have intense faith that we will make the United Nations Organization a success. We have learned from past mistakes. The old League of Nations suffered from many disabilities, most of all perhaps that two great nations, the United States of America and the Union of Soviet Socialist Republics, were not present in its formative stage.

Today as never before the world is united. Further, the Constitution of the new organization is essentially realist in that it provides for the sanction of force to support the rule of law.

I think too, that at the present time ordinary men and women in every nation have a greater realization of what is at stake. To make this organization a living reality we must enlist the support not only of governments, but of the masses of people throughout the world. They must understand that we are building a defense for the common people.

In the purposes of the United Nations Organization we have linked with the achievement of freedom from fear the delivery of mankind from the peril of want. To the individual citizen the specter of economic insecurity is more constant, more imminent, than the shadow of war. Every individual can be brought to realize that things that are discussed in conference here are the concern of all and affect the home life of every man, woman and child.

Without social justice and security there is no real foundation for peace, for it is among the socially disinherited and those who have nothing to lose that the gangster and aggressor recruit their supporters.

I believe, therefore, that, important as is the work of the Security Council, no less vital is it to make the Economic and Social Council an effective international instrument. A police force is a necessary part of a civilized community, but the greater the social security and contentment of the population, the less important is the police force.

Finally, let us be clear as to what is our ultimate aim. It is not just the negation of war, but the creation of a world of security and freedom, of a world which is governed by justice and the moral law. We desire to assert the pre-eminence of right over might and general good against selfish and sectional aims.

We who are gathered here today in this ancient home of liberty and order are able to meet together because thousands of brave men and women have suffered and died that we may live. It is for us today, bearing in mind the great sacrifices that have been made, to prove ourselves no less courageous in approaching our great task, no less patient, no less self-sacrificing. We must and will succeed.

UNO INAUGURATED WITH ATTLEE PLEA

Continued From Page 1

United States abstained on both those votes.

In the second balloting that followed, although M. Spaak had never been formally nominated on the floor, he received twenty-eight votes to twenty-three for Dr. Lie, the United States voting with the Russians for the Norwegian.

Thus the Assembly started with a show of strength by the Soviet Union, which is known to oppose M. Spaak because of his close friendship with Britain and his adherence to closer political ties among the Western European democracies—a movement that the Soviet Union has deprecated.

In reviewing this incident afterward some delegates showed interest in the silence of the United States. In the private preliminary discussions that preceded the session the United States had strongly supported Dr. Lie, but when delegates of the Soviet Union and her neighbors demonstrated for the Norwegian, Mr. Byrnes remained in his seat.

The incident, nevertheless, served to emphasize the great contrast between the opening of this General Assembly and the first meeting of the League of Nations General Assembly in Geneva in November, 1920.

Twenty-five years ago, in a peaceful neutral country, untouched by war, the theme was one of confidence in the power of moral force, and the only note of concern was over the absence of the United States and Russia.

In that opening speech twenty-five years ago Giuseppe Motta, speaking for Switzerland, was certain that the idea of country and the idea of humanity could be fused, that the United States would join the League, and that Russia, "cured of her madness and delivered of her misery," as he said, would come back to the fold.

There were other striking contrasts that indicated the changes of history and illustrated the form and structure of the new security organization. Twenty-five years ago Italy, Japan and Rumania were present because they guessed right about the outcome of the first German war, but today they were absent because they guessed wrong about the second German war.

Two Nations Watched

Today in this grim capital, bleak and scarred by the explosions of German aerial intruders, it was the two young and powerful nations, the United States and the Soviet Union, that held the stage, one by its speech and, the other by its silence.

Then, too late, the neutrals, Sweden and Portugal, were present because the League of Nations accepted the right of nations to remain neutral in war, but today they were absent because they were not invited and because they are not prepared to abandon their neutrality whenever the Security Council votes the UNO powers into action against an aggressor.

There were a few familiar Geneva faces in the Central Hall today—Viscount Cecil of Chelwood, who played so important a part in the drafting of the League Covenant, and Dr. V. K. Wellington Koo, Chinese Ambassador to London, who was the only delegate in the hall who played an important role in that first General Assembly meeting in Geneva.

But the differences were vastly greater than the similarities. The leading place on today's program was reserved for a Socialist Prime Minister of Britain—symbolical not only of the rise of the Socialists in Britain but of the swing to the left in many parts of the Allied world.

Incidentally, the role of France today was more obscure. Overrun in this war, she was allowed to sit in on the deliberations of the major powers over the elections of the officers, but her role was definitely secondary.

Even the speeches today were different in tone and structure. The League opened with much talk about governments and the morals of disarmament, of the sense of right and the virtue of pity. But today the British Prime Minister talked of the economic causes of war and he did not mention disarmament.

Tomorrow and Saturday the Assembly will get down to routine the work of electing chairmen of the six main Assembly committees, two vice presidents, the non-permanent members of the Security Council and thirteen of the eighteen members of the Economic and Social Council.

The election for the important post of secretary general will not take place until later. The Soviet Union favors Stanoje Simitch, Yugoslav Ambassador in Washington, for this post, but while some of the British Conservatives are beginning to talk about Anthony Eden and even Winston Churchill for the job, the trend still favors the election of Lester Pearson, Canadian Ambassador in Washington.

The Soviet Embassy said tonight that Andrei Y. Vishinsky, leader of the Russian delegation to the UNO Assembly, probably would remain in Sofia, Bulgaria, for two days and that it had no definite information as to when he would arrive in London. While he is absent from the sessions Mr. Gromyko, the Russian's UNO expert, with experience at Dumbarton Oaks, San Francisco and the executive committee and Preparatory Commission conferences here, is head of the Soviet delegation.

With Foreign Commissar Molotoff absent, other delegates have made no secret of the fact that they would be encouraged by Mr. Vishinsky's presence.

HISTORY REPEATED AT PEACE SESSION

But This Time Belgian Leader Is Named by Narrower Margin —Crowds Brave Rain

By Wireless to THE NEW YORK TIMES.

LONDON, Jan. 10—History repeated itself when a Belgian was elected president of the United Nations Assembly today. Twenty-five years ago in Geneva another Belgian, Paul Hymans, was elected president of the first Assembly of the League of Nations.

M. Hymans made the grade much more easily than did Paul-Henri Spaak this afternoon. At the League meeting the Belgian obtained thirty-six votes out of forty-five. M. Spaak was elected by twenty-eight votes to twenty-three.

* * *

A one-minute interview with Andrei A. Gromyko of the Soviet Union delegation:

"How did you like today's session, Mr. Ambassador?"

"That was good," Mr. Gromyko replied.

"But you didn't get your man elected."

Mr. Gromyko paused reflectively, then, with a characteristic shrug of his shoulders and raising his hands, commented: "That was bad."

* * *

It was gray outside Central Hall in the drizzling rain, but the crowd of several hundred Londoners who had come to see the arrivals and the flags of the fifty-one nations that flew over the hall made a brave showing for the opening of the new world peace agency.

The crowd was in good humor despite the rain, cheering alike for notables and the humble members of the public lucky enough to get in.

* * *

The queue for the public seats began to form fifteen hours before the first session started. At 1 A. M. 18-year-old Gordon Fairchild of Brighton became the first person in the line. He said he wanted to be present at the meeting because "I am very interested in international law."

* * *

As in San Francisco, the five Saudi Arabian delegates were the most colorful persons on the floor, in their native cloaks of brown and gold. The delegation was headed by Emir Feisal Ibn Abdul Azis, the second of King Ibn Saud's children, and beside him was his bodyguard, also in national costume and carrying a glittering dagger.

* * *

The Polish delegates had to dash straight from the airport to the Assembly. They had been scheduled to arrive yesterday, but bad weather forced their plane to return to Brussels after they were over Britain, because no landing field was open.

* * *

The Assembly met in Central Hall, the headquarters of the British Methodist Church, in a high-domed room whose blue, gold and cream color scheme relieved sharply the simplicity of the surroundings of the gathering place.

From a grille in the roof a huge chandelier of floodlights to aid the movie cameramen flung a garish white light over the historic scene, in which nearly 2,000 delegates, alternates and advisers were the main participants. They sat, crowded, in blue-covered chairs, the main delegates along long English oak tables set almost semi-circularly in three banks in front of a platform draped in blue and gold.

The emblem of the United Nations—the world almost encircled in gold laurel leaves—hung against the back curtain of the platform.

On the platform, before M. Spaak was elected president and formally opened the Assembly, sat Dr. Eduardo Zuleta Angel of Colombia, presiding as chairman of the Preparatory Commission in a throne-like red chair, with Gladwyn Jebb, British executive secretary of the Preparatory Commission, on his right and Andrew Cordier, United States chairman of the Assembly Secretariat, on his left.

Virtually everyone on the floor of the hall wore black, including Mrs. Eleanor Roosevelt.

Name French Envoy to Colombia

By Cable to THE NEW YORK TIMES.

BOGOTA, Colombia, Jan. 10—The Foreign Office announced today the appointment of Jacques Lecompte-Boinet as French Minister to Colombia.

PRAVDA IS TERSE ON UNO MEETING

But Russia Takes a Sincere Interest in Organization and Is Cooperative

By BROOKS ATKINSON

By Wireless to THE NEW YORK TIMES.

MOSCOW, Jan. 10—In eight lines Pravda announced today opening of the United Nations Organization's General Assembly. Five more lines reported Secretary of State James F. Byrnes' arrival.

As is well-known—to use a common Russian newspaper phrase—Foreign Commissar Vyacheslaff M. Molotoff is not attending the opening sessions. Andrei Vishinsky, his deputy, got only as far as Sofia last evening, although he may yet reach a London plane soon enough to check in at the conference hall.

But it is commonly believed that Moscow takes the UNO very seriously. It has taken its full share of the preliminary work and has consistently presented the UNO in newspapers and magazines as one of the possible guarantees of world peace and security.

Although Mr. Byrnes and Foreign Secretary Ernest Bevin are attending the opening session, M. Molotoff can genuinely plead overwork. He is very busy. Besides being Foreign Commissar, he has many government and administrative tasks. He performs the duties of Deputy Premier.

As Vice Commissar, Mr. Vyshinsky is well able to represent Moscow, being thoroughly conversant with the UNO's affairs. As a Russian expert on the Balkan countries he has been busy since the Moscow conference, when he and the American and British Ambassadors here rushed off to Bulgaria and Rumania without taking a rest. If he is delayed in reaching London, he may have a legitimate reason—concluding business that should be finished before the UNO's meeting

At first glance, the Russian Government's attitude toward the responsibility of the Big Three may seem more overbearing than ours but it may be only more candid. The New Times, which reveals considered political opinions, describes the Big Three as the "sponsors of the UNO" and adds that they have "assumed the chief responsibility for its success." World peace, it says, "requires that the victorious Anglo-Soviet-American coalition jointly conduct a firm and purposeful policy with regard not only to the vanquished foe but international affairs as a whole."

Nothing published here suggests that the Government regards the UNO as a substitute for a foreign policy or as a panacea for all international maladies. Russia probably prefers to wait and see. But there is plenty of evidence that she sincerely wants the UNO, hopes that it will succeed and intends to cooperate. As one of the Big Three and the Big Five, the Soviet Union has the power of life and death over the UNO, as have all the chief powers. In such affairs Russia is less bouncing and gay than we, but has a serious attitude toward all international affairs and a great capacity for serious work.

VISCOUNT CECIL ASKS SUPPORT FOR THE UNO

By Wireless to THE NEW YORK TIMES.

LONDON, Jan. 10—Viscount Cecil of Chelwood, one of the most prominent champions of the League of Nations and formerly British representative to various League assemblies, said tonight that the United Nations Organization was not the perfect instrument, but he warned that "we must not let a second peace child die."

Broadcasting to Sweden, Lord Cecil said that it was essential for every nation to recognize that "national patriotism has its best and most natural expression in the larger patriotism of peace. Since history began," he added, "the world has been made up of a number of competing nations, each based on a passionately loved sovereignty. But unrestricted national sovereignty is inconsistent with peace. If each nation is to be allowed to fight for what it conceives to be its right, war will continue.

"Can we build up behind the charter strong enough to make aggression impossible? If we can, peace is safe and with it the opportunity for progress. If not a relapse into barbarism seems inevitable."

"All the News That's Fit to Print"

The New York Times.

LATE CITY EDITION
Mostly sunny today. Fair and warmer tomorrow.
Temperatures Yesterday—Max., 54; Min., 45
Sunrise today, 5:52 A. M.; Sunset, 5:38 P. M.
Full U. S. Weather Bureau Report, Page 59

VOL. XCVI...No. 32,393. Entered as Second-Class Matter Postoffice, New York, N. Y. NEW YORK, WEDNESDAY, OCTOBER 2, 1946. THREE CENTS IN NEW YORK CITY

12 NAZI WAR LEADERS SENTENCED TO BE HANGED; GOERING HEADS LIST OF THOSE TO DIE BY OCT. 16; HESS GETS LIFE, SIX OTHERS ORDERED TO PRISON

SHIP OFFICERS QUIT, PARALYZING PORT 2D TIME IN MONTH

Never Before Have Masters Been Called From Bridges —Engineers Also Strike

WASHINGTON PLEAS FAIL

But Efforts to Settle Dispute Over Wages and Working Conditions Are Continued

By GEORGE HORNE

The cogs of the nation's merchant marine slowed to a standstill yesterday for the second time in a month as the unprecedented strike of licensed officers got under way.

It was unprecedented because never before in the country's shipping history have shipmasters—captains earning as much as $500 and $600 a month—been called from their bridges in a union action to enforce wage and working demands. But they were leaving their ships on order, along with brother engineer officers of the Marine Engineers Beneficial Association.

Reaction among the captains was mixed, and the situation affecting them at a late hour last night was obscure, after a welter of messages to and from the negotiating headquarters in Washington where Government authorities were still trying to effect a settlement before the walkout could settle down to a long-term affair.

Many Captains Not in Union

Many captains are not members of the National Organization of Masters, Mates and Pilots (AFL), even on such ships as have MMP contracts. Shipping operators said the captains, who are the owners' supreme representatives aboard, and as such considered beyond the call of strike action, were "being threatened."

They declared that Capt. Harry Martin, East Coast president of the MMP, had agreed in Washington yesterday to leave security watches aboard all ships, including a captain and a day and night mate for stand-by duty. But they said the pledge was not being honored.

At a special meeting of the AFL Maritime Trades Department at the office of the International Longshoremen's Association last night it was announced that "the status quo" remains. That meant that captains were being called off, whether they agreed or not. The AFL spokesman said the response among all MMP officers was excellent.

Ship operators took the position that the masters were "in the middle" and "behind the eight-ball," and they agreed that many would have to leave their ships at the union's call.

The MMP leaders have stood by their original conception of the walkout as being no strike. It was, the union leaders said, simply a case of the men not working

Continued on Page 4, Column 5

Cards Beat Dodgers In First Game, 4-2

Despite a muscle ailment, Howie Pollet pitched the Cardinals to a 4-2 victory over the Dodgers at St. Louis yesterday in the first of a three-game play-off series for the National League pennant. The Cards meanwhile routed Ralph Branca, first of five Brooklyn pitchers, with three runs in as many innings.

Howie Schultz momentarily tied the score for the Dodgers with his homer in the third and also batted in their second run with a single in the seventh.

The play-offs, first such in the history of major league baseball, will be resumed tomorrow at Ebbets Field, and the third contest, if necessary, will be played there Friday.

(Complete details on Page 35.)

12 Inches of Snow Blanket Several Up-State Areas

Flurries Are Reported as Far South as the Pennsylvania Line—Temperature Here Is Near Record Low for Date

By The Associated Press.

ALBANY, Oct. 1—Canadian-border areas of upper New York dug out tonight from more than a foot of snow as high winds churned the tail-end of the season's first storm into near-blizzard fury.

It was still snowing early tonight, but a United States weather forecaster described the pre-winter blast as a one-day storm. He predicted low temperatures for another 48 hours.

The storm, whipping across the Adirondack area from Canada, forced some schools to close, blocked secondary highways and disrupted power and communications lines in northern New York.

Although the brunt of the storm was felt in the upper Adirondacks, its effect was State-wide. Temperatures plummeted toward the freezing mark and snow flurries were reported in western and southern New York, along the Pennsylvania line.

Syracuse, reporting its earliest snow in forty-four years of official records, had a half-inch.

New York City's 45-degree temperature early this morning was within three degrees of the 1916 record low for the date.

Some up-State areas without snow had steady rain. Saratoga Springs reported a twenty-four-hour fall of 1.5 inches and Schenectady had 2.08 inches in the thirty-six hours ending at 8 A. M.

The villages of Malone in Franklin County and Potsdam in St. Lawrence apparently were hardest hit, with traffic crippled and heavy damage caused by falling trees and branches. Malone had 13 inches of snow and Potsdam a foot. Both were without electric power.

Malone's gas service was cut partly when a falling tree damaged a main. The Alice Hyde Memorial Hospital was without electricity all morning and gas most of the day. Power was re-

Continued on Page 27, Column 2

LEHMAN 'STRADDLE' CHARGED BY IVES

Says Rival Evades Wallace Foreign Policy Issue With Aim to Placate Left

Special to THE NEW YORK TIMES.

ALBANY, Oct. 1—Irving M. Ives, Republican candidate for United States Senator, charged tonight that former Governor Herbert H. Lehman, his Democratic opponent, had issued a "shadow doctrine" on foreign policy designed to placate both old-line Democrats and left-wing groups.

Mr. Lehman, he declared, straddled the issue and took a "vague and insecure" stand which had something to please "each of the political organizations and splinter parties he represents in this campaign."

In a State-wide radio broadcast he challenged Mr. Lehman to tell the people whether he agreed with Secretary of State James F. Byrnes or with former Secretary of Commerce Henry A. Wallace. He declared it impossible to side with both.

Challenge on "Enslavement"

"Mr. Wallace believes in drawing an iron curtain across eastern Europe," he said, adding:

"We have seen that wars arise when people are enslaved and the truth kept from them. Does my opponent favor a policy which would permit this condition to

Continued on Page 8, Column 3

11,236-MILE RECORD SET AS NAVY PLANE LANDS IN COLUMBUS

Truculent Turtle Smashes Old Mark by 3,300 Miles in Non-Stop Flight From Australia

UP 55 HOURS 15 MINUTES

Four-Man Crew, Fresh Despite Rough Hop, Is Disappointed at Not Finishing in Washington

By FREDERICK GRAHAM
Special to THE NEW YORK TIMES.

COLUMBUS, Ohio, Oct. 1—A non-stop flight distance record that surpassed the previous mark by more than 3,300 miles was set today when the Truculent Turtle, the Navy's new twin-engine, land-based patrol bomber, landed here to complete an 11,236-mile flight that started Sunday morning in Perth, Australia.

The plane touched down here at 12:25 P. M., Eastern standard time.

The time for the flight, which started in the warm spring weather of Australia and ended in chilly winds here, was 55 hours 15 minutes. Despite a heavy load of fuel and constant headwinds that averaged 11.5 miles an hour for the entire trip, the average speed of the plane was 203.4 miles an hour.

The old distance record, set by the four-motored Dreamboat, a Superfortress, in a flight from Guam to Washington, was 7,916 miles.

Like "Long Patrol Mission"

"You might say it was no tougher than a good, long patrol mission," Comdr. Thomas D. Davies, chief of the four-man crew that manned the flat-sided Lockheed plane, said when he dropped from the exit hatch in the belly of the fuselage and greeted Navy officers at the municipal field.

"We had turbulent air, headwinds and some instrument weather," Commander Davies con-

Continued on Page 12, Column 3

HULL, 75, STRICKEN AFTER PEACE PLEA

United Nations' 'Father' Calls on Powers to Renew Zeal—His Condition Serious

Text of Mr. Hull's statement appears on page 18.

By BERTRAM D. HULEN
Special to THE NEW YORK TIMES.

WASHINGTON, Oct. 1—Cordell Hull, former Secretary of State, suffered a stroke in the United States Naval Hospital at Bethesda, Md., last night, a few hours after he had completed a statement appealing to the Great Powers to compose their differences for the sake of world peace.

The stroke was officially described at first as "light," but the hospital announced later that Mr. Hull's condition had become "more serious during the day." Friends meanwhile had described him as extremely weak and had expressed grave concern. They considered his condition to be critical.

A hospital bulletin issued at 10 o'clock tonight said Mr. Hull remained in serious condition. "No improvement has been noted in his condition since the last bulletin," it said. "No change" was reported at midnight.

Nevertheless, the former Secretary's statement for world peace was issued on his behalf tonight, carrying out his instructions.

Continued on Page 18, Column 3

City's Search for Meat Supplies Fails to Uncover Any Hoarding

A meat search by three city departments was three-quarters finished yesterday and disclosed holdings in local slaughterhouses, storage plants and railroad cars of 13,312,880 pounds—not much compared to New York's normal consumption of 3,800,000 pounds a day.

With fewer than fifty of the city's 400 major repositories of meat still to be visited by the task force of 225 policemen and inspectors of the Health and Market departments, Mayor O'Dwyer said he saw nothing in the findings so far to warrant municipal action.

Meat supplies in retail stores, meanwhile, continued to shrink, and the Office of Price Administration reported that the black market was shrinking even faster than the supply of available meat. This did not seem any great victory to housewives, since the race was in the direction of a zero supply.

OPA enforcement agents, continuing their daily check on prices and, incidentally, supply, found only one out of ten butcher shops with meat to sell. Many were shut and many others sold only poultry. There was more sausage meat than any other kind. Last week the district OPA had reported one shop out of five selling meat.

Yesterday's report by the district enforcement staff was to the effect that only 5 per cent of the meat being offered for sale was at black market prices, whereas the same office had estimated last week that 20 to 35 per cent of the local sales were at over-ceiling prices.

The City Council, in a majority resolution sent to its rules committee, called upon the Federal Government to seize all cattle and meat in the country and blamed the meat industry for "open defiance to the American people by the creation of a meat famine." The resolution, which also urged that the Government make available to the public as an emergency health measure the meat so

Continued on Page 33, Column 3

RECEIVING THEIR FREEDOM FROM NUREMBERG COURT

Col. Burton C. Andrus, who headed the prison where the defendants were confined during their trial, handing out letters certifying their liberty to Hans Fritzsche (left), Franz von Papen (second from right) and Hjalmar Schacht (right).

Associated Press Radiophoto

GERMANY NOT FREE, SCHACHT COMPLAINS

Von Papen Says He Has Given Up Politics—Austria Seeks Extradition for Trial

By DANA ADAMS SCHMIDT
Special to THE NEW YORK TIMES.

NUREMBERG, Germany, Oct. 1—Franz von Papen said that his political career was "absolutely ended," Hans Fritzsche asked to be tried again by a German court and Hjalmar Schacht asked for chocolate for his two children today when the three men acquitted by the International Military Tribunal appeared before 200 representatives of the world press.

Schacht got his candy bars and all reaped a harvest of cigarettes

Continued on Page 20, Column 3

Russian and Jackson Object; Schacht Called a Swindler

By The Associated Press.

NUREMBERG, Germany, Oct. 1—Soviet Justice J. I. Nikitchenko tonight assailed the acquittal of three high Nazis by the International Military Tribunal, asserting that the opinion freeing Hjalmar Schacht, banker, was in "obvious contradiction to the evidence." [Justice Nikitchenko also declared Schacht a "swindler," according to a Reuters dispatch.]

The Russian Major General also dissented from the acquittal for the German General Staff, the Reich Cabinet and the decision imprisoning Rudolf Hess for life instead of giving him the death penalty.

Justice Robert Jackson of the United States, speaking for what he called the prosecutors of all nations, declared the decision on individuals were of secondary importance compared to the fact that the principle was established making aggressive war a crime punishable by death. However, Justice Jackson also assailed the Schacht verdict.

Justice Nikitchenko said Fritzsche, as a radio propagandist, "had a most basic relation to the preparation and conduct of aggressive warfare." The most detailed dissent was in the case of the German General Staff and High Command, of which Justice Nikitchenko said:

"Without their advice and active cooperation, Hitler could not have solved [his] problems. In the majority of cases their opinion was decisive. * * * The General Staff issued most brutal decrees and orders for relentless measures against unarmed, peaceful population and prisoners of war."

Justice Nikitchenko said bluntly

Continued on Page 24, Column 6

SLAV BLOC STALLS VOTING ON TRIESTE

Connally Disputes Vishinsky's Charge That U. S. Seeks to Violate Big Four Accord

By LANSING WARREN
Special to THE NEW YORK TIMES.

PARIS, Oct. 1—Making use of procedural entanglements in an atmosphere of raw nerves, the Slav States succeeded tonight in blocking a vote on the United States proposal to implement the Italian draft treaty's general clauses on a statute for Trieste.

During a tense discussion in the peace conference's Italian Political and Territorial Commission, Senator Tom Connally of the United States and Andrei Y. Vishinsky, Soviet Vice Foreign Minister, exchanged accusations and retorts. Other leading delegates made contradictory suggestions on procedure, and finally the lateness of the hour forced adjournment.

Mr. Vishinsky charged that the United States proposal was an adroit and deliberate effort to evade an agreement by the Big Four's Council of Foreign Min-

Continued on Page 17, Column 2

World News Summarized

WEDNESDAY, OCTOBER 2, 1946

Twelve high Nazi conspirators were sentenced by the International Military Tribunal in Nuremberg yesterday to death by hanging for the supreme crime of aggressive war; three received life sentences in prison, four received lesser terms and three were acquitted.

The men who will be executed not later than Oct. 16 are Goering, von Ribbentrop, Kaltenbrunner, Rosenberg, Frank, Frick, Streicher, Sauckel, Seyss-Inquart, Keitel and Jodl. Bormann was sentenced to death in absentia. Hess, Funk and Grand Admiral Raeder received life sentences, von Schirach and Speer twenty years, von Neurath fifteen years and Grand Admiral Doenitz ten years. Schacht, von Papen and Fritzsche were acquitted. [All the foregoing 1:8.]

The verdicts on Hess, von Papen and Schacht and the exoneration of the General Staff, Cabinet and Storm Troops as organizations brought a strong dissent from the Russian Justice, Maj. Gen. Nikitchenko. The chief American prosecutor, Justice Jackson, said he was "disappointed" in the liberation of von Papen and Schacht because it would adversely affect further prosecution of industrialists and militarists. [1:6-7.]

Russia accused the United States at a commission meeting of the Conference of Paris of attempting to change agreements reached by the Foreign Ministers Council on Trieste and the Slav bloc succeeded in delaying a vote. [1:7.]

Former Secretary of State Hull, who is 75 years old today, was stricken in Bethesda Naval Hospital shortly after completing a statement urging the Great Powers to compose their differences for the sake of peace. His condition is serious. "Incalculable disaster" would follow any irreconcilable division in this "most perilous juncture in history," Mr. Hull said. [1:3.]

A House committee, it was disclosed, has been quietly laying the basis to ask Congressional approval for this country's first integrated, permanent world-wide espionage and counter-espionage service. [13:1]

Iran, rejecting Britain's disavowals, has asked for the recall of a British Embassy secretary accused of conspiring to bring about a revolt of southern tribesmen. [11:1.]

Dmitri Shostakovich's new Ninth Symphony has been condemned in the Soviet press for ideological weakness and failing to reflect the true spirit of the Russian people. [31:3-4.]

Bernard M. Baruch characterized as "either misinformation or complete distortion" charges at a political rally by supporters of former Secretary Wallace that the United States expected other nations to give up their atomic energy secrets while this country withheld all information. [1:6-7.]

The American Merchant Marine was almost completely tied up by the strike of engineers and deck officers that began at midnight yesterday. Federal conciliation efforts continued without result. [1:1.]

No progress was made toward ending the Pittsburgh power walkout that has halted production on vital materials [2:2], and a strike of CIO warehouse and office workers threatens to paralyze the dress manufacturing industry in New York. [2:4.] Thirty-seven persons were injured in a picketing riot at Hollywood studios. [3:1.]

The Navy bomber Truculent Turtle landed at Columbus, Ohio, establishing a new world distance record of 11,236 miles in its non-stop flight from Perth, Australia. [1:4; map P. 12.]

Baruch Rebukes Wallace Groups For Distorting U. S. Atom Plan

By A. M. ROSENTHAL
Special to THE NEW YORK TIMES.

LAKE SUCCESS, N. Y., Oct. 1—In a sharp reply to followers of former Secretary of Commerce Henry A. Wallace, Bernard M. Baruch, American representative on the United Nations Atomic Energy Commission, categorically denied tonight that this country was asking the rest of the world to stop nuclear research and reveal its uranium resources while the United States retained complete freedom of action.

Mr. Baruch's strongly worded denial was the result of statements made in Chicago on Saturday at a conference of the National Citizens Political Action Committee, Independent Citizens Committee of the Arts, Sciences and Professions, and the Congress of Industrial Organizations' Political Action Committee. It was sent as a telegram addressed to Henry Morgenthau, Harold Ickes and Philip Murray, president of the CIO, who were speakers at the conference.

After noting that the conference had gone on record as saying that the United States was trying to have other nations accept "binding agreements" while keeping its technical knowledge to itself as long as it saw fit, Mr. Baruch declared:

"I say without reservation that this is either misinformation or complete distortion. Nowhere does any such statement occur in the American proposal."

Mr. Baruch followed his denial with a pointed request for a correction.

"I am sending this to you," he said in the telegrams, "in order that you may see that this is corrected immediately."

The Baruch statement was issued by the American delegation at 7 P. M., on the eve of a meeting tomorrow morning of the Atomic Energy Commission's Committee 2, which will discuss the

Continued on Page 16, Column 3

50-MINUTE SESSION

Tribunal Dooms Keitel, Ribbentrop, Streicher, Rosenberg, Jodl

SIX SAID TO APPEAL

Allied Council in Berlin Last Resort—Doenitz Gets Lightest Term

Verdicts in the Nuremberg trials are on pages 22, 23, 24.

By KATHLEEN McLAUGHLIN
Special to THE NEW YORK TIMES.

NUREMBERG, Germany, Oct. 1—Death by hanging was decreed this afternoon for twelve of the original twenty-four defendants indicted in the Nuremberg war crimes trials. Three others—Dr. Hjalmar Schacht, Franz von Papen and Dr. Hans Fritzsche—were acquitted by the International Military Tribunal over the dissent of the Soviet member of the court, Maj. Gen. Iola T. Nikitchenko.

Those who will die by the noose within fifteen days, unless reprieved through an appeal within four days to the Allied Control Council in Berlin, are Hermann Goering, Joachim von Ribbentrop, Field Marshal Gen. Wilhelm Keitel, Ernst Kaltenbrunner, Dr. Alfred Rosenberg, Hans Frank, Wilhelm Frick, Julius Streicher, Fritz Sauckel, Col. Gen. Alfred Jodl and Arthur Seyss-Inquart.

Martin Bormann, who succeeded Rudolf Hess as Deputy Fuehrer and who was tried in absentia, owing to the lack of conclusive evidence that he is dead, also was sentenced to death by hanging if and when he ever is apprehended.

Mitigation in von Neurath Case

Life imprisonment was meted out to Hess, Walther Funk and Grand Admiral Erich Raeder. General Nikitchenko dissented likewise from his colleagues' judgment on Hess, expressing the opinion that he had merited death by hanging.

Baldur von Schirach, formerly supreme leader of the Hitler Jugend, and Albert Speer, Reich Minister for Armament and Munitions and chief of the Todt Organization, received twenty-year terms.

Possibly in consideration of his advanced years, Baron Constantin von Neurath, former Foreign Minister, although adjudged guilty on all four counts, received the comparatively mild sentence of fifteen years' imprisonment. He is 73. The Tribunal said in mitigation that he had been dismissed by Adolf Hitler for having been too lenient in his administration as Protector for Bohemia and Moravia and that he had intervened to obtain the release of many Czechoslovaks who had been arrested.

The mildest punishment of all fell to Grand Admiral Karl Doenitz, once Commander in Chief of the German Navy and, during the last days of the war, successor to Hitler as head of the German Government. He must serve ten years in prison.

[Six of those convicted—von Ribbentrop, Frank, Seyss-Inquart, von Schirach, Speer and Doenitz—have appealed their sentences, the British Broadcasting Company said, quoting official sources. The BBC broadcast was recorded by the National Broadcasting Company.]

Pattern Is Similar

In the courtroom, which over the last ten months has echoed unceasingly to the testimony of the unprecedented horrors precipitated upon the world through the Nazi hierarchy, the profound drama of the concluding phase of the trial lasted only fifty minutes. Lord Justice Sir Geoffrey Lawrence, as presiding jurist, announced all the sentences to the eighteen convicted men as they were summoned singly before the tribunal. An atmosphere of utter solemnity prevailed throughout this grim interval.

Beginning with Goering, form-

Continued on Page 21, Column

12 NAZI WAR CHIEFS SENTENCED TO DIE

Continued From Page 1

chief of the Luftwaffe, each prisoner in turn stepped through the narrow door to face the tribunal from the rear of the prisoners' dock, flanked by two military police on each side. Headsets were handed them and adjusted to the German translation channel to insure their complete understanding of the court's decree. Sentence was pronounced and they turned and left by the same exit they had used so long.

With few exceptions, the pattern was almost identical. The spectators, all wearing earphones of the quadrilingual interpreting system, saw each defendant adjust the corresponding headset, saw him receive the pronouncement and heard the switch close. Each in turn paused as if uncertain, waiting. A few seemed stunned. Others plucked off the headset and flung themselves back through the [illegible]ing door, which closed with [illegible]cisive thud.

Hess alone took up his stance with his customary air of defiance, shaking his head negatively when a guard proffered the earphones. When the soldier attempted to put them on his head, Hess pushed his hand away angrily and for the last time went through his familiar motion of flinging up his head and staring about absently.

The probability is that Hess was unaware of what was said, although he may understand enough English to have comprehended the verdict of the Tribunal whose juristdiction he steadfastly has challenged.

Kaltenbrunner and Speer Bow

Kaltenbrunner, head of the secret police under Heinrich Himmler, on being sentenced to death, removed the earphones and saluted his judges with a typically military bow before retiring. Later, Speer, whose lighter sentence might well have inspired his gesture, also made a low bow before turning to leave.

Von Schirach, whose wife had made a direct plea for his life to members of the Tribunal, flung a baleful glance at his judges before turning on his heel. Sauckel, who directed the slave labor program, likewise paused in his departure for one fleeting, speculative look back at the jurists' bench.

None of the military—to whom death by hanging is the supreme ignominy—demonstrated any emotion whatever as they received their sentences, removed the headset and disappeared. They all stood characteristically at attention to hear their destiny pronounced and maintained their impassive attitudes to the end.

Frank, erstwhile Governor General of Poland, fumbled the longest in adjusting the receivers at his ears. His crippled left hand, useless since he slashed his wrist in an attempt at suicide, drooped limply from the wrist for a moment until he self-consciously lowered his arm and folded his hands before him. As Lord Justice Lawrence concluded his sentence, Frank remained motionless until a guard touched his arm and helped him remove the earphones.

When von Neurath, as the last in the line, had left the court room, the provisional death sentence against Bormann was read into the record by the Lord Justice, who then announced the request of General Nikitchenko to be recorded as dissenting on the judgments respecting Schacht, von Papen and Hess. The Soviet jurist further dissented from the findings of the remainder of the Tribunal with respect to the German Cabinet and General Staff, declaring himself of the opinion that they should have been branded as criminal.

This dissenting opinion, Lord Justice Lawrence said, will be entered in the record and published as soon as possible.

Thereafter the dissolution of the highest criminal court in the world was accomplished through the simple signal of the jurists' rising to retire. Once again free men the instant the court adjourned, the three who had been acquitted left their jail cells in the Palace of Justice building within two hours.

Their preparations were simple—the obtaining of documents certifying their discharge by the International Military Tribunal, which they will use until proper identification papers can be obtained from civilian authorities, and their joint appearance in the press room on the second floor of the court house for a mass interview by the international press, whose coverage of the trial Schacht has furiously resented.

However, he found himself being photographed again today by the same camera man at whom he had thrown a cup of hot coffee during a recess of the court recently. Even before the Tribunal had passed this morning to its review of Doenitz' case after announcing Schacht's acquittal, the former Reichsbank president received the first congratulations from his codefendants. Speer, who sat almost directly behind him throughout the historic trial, leaned across from his seat in the second row to extend his felicitations.

Fritzsche, energetic radio commentator and head of the wireless news service of Dr. Joseph Goebbels' propaganda bureau, was the most visibly affected of the three exonerated. He rose with the others as the judges left the bench at the end of the morning session, then collapsed back onto his seat for several minutes as if without strength to stand. He recovered himself before the afternoon session and appeared quite normal again as he joined Schacht and von Papen in the press room before leaving Nuremberg.

By order of the Allied Control Council, the execution of those condemned to death must take place within two weeks, which would bring the deadline to Oct. 16. It is considered probable that under the provision for appeal for clemency or mitigation of the sentences, some of those convicted will submit such requests, and particularly that the military men sentenced to death by hanging may seek at least a change to the extent of dying before a firing squad.

Yesterday's judgment, specifying the status of the various organizations that had been under indictment, was expected to clarify promptly the future of large numbers of individual members, who now can be either dismissed as cleared or brought to trial if they are member of the SS, Gestapo, Sicherheitsdienst or the Political Leadership Corps.

Of the remaining two men accused under the original indictment as the trial began last Nov. 20, one, Robert Ley, who headed the labor front, committed suicide last October in the Nuremberg jail. The other, Gustav Krupp von Bohlen under Halbach, was adjudged too ill to appear for trial and the proceedings against him were suspended indefinitely pending his possible recovery of his mental and physical faculties.

THEIR FATE WAS NOT IN THEIR HANDS

Hermann Goering and Rudolf Hess hear judgment of the War Crimes Tribunal in Nuremberg

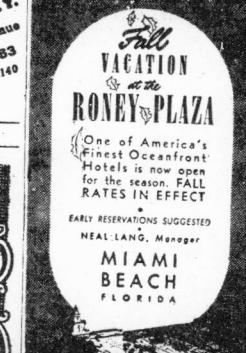

Associated Press Radiophoto

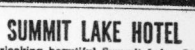

"All the News That's Fit to Print"

The New York Times.

LATE CITY EDITION
Increasing cloudiness, cold today. Snow, not so cold tomorrow.
Temperature Range Today—Max., 18; Min., 0
Temperature Yesterday—Max., 24; Min., 5.5
Full U. S. Weather Bureau Report, Page 31

Copyright, 1948, by The New York Times Company.

VOL. XCVII No. 32,879. Entered as Second-Class Matter. Postoffice, New York, N. Y. NEW YORK, SATURDAY, JANUARY 31, 1948. THREE CENTS IN NEW YORK CITY

MANY HOMES WITHOUT HEAT AS ZERO COLD IS DUE HERE; U. S. CUTS OIL EXPORTS 18½%

FUEL CRISIS GROWS

Hundreds of Families Reported Suffering in City Area

BAY STATE SEIZES PLANT

Bradford Acts When Walkout Threatens Boston Gas—Oil Diversion Denied Here

By WILL LISSNER

Hundreds of families in the city were reported by their landlords to be in cold homes for lack of fuel oil last night as temperatures dropped toward zero in Manhattan and toward subzero levels in the suburbs.

At 3 A. M. today the temperature dropped to 2.2 degrees, establishing a new low record for the season. The previous record was 5 degrees, registered last Saturday.

The winter's coldest weather gripped not only New York but the whole Northwest. The Midwest and South, however, got some relief yesterday from the protracted cold spell. The fuel situation was reported acute in many cities throughout the East.

Temperatures, after falling to points between zero and 5 degrees above in Manhattan and zero and 10 degrees below in the suburbs, are expected to rise today to 20 degrees. The cold is due to continue, according to the United States Weather Bureau, but whereas yesterday was sunny, increasing cloudiness was expected today. More snow is threatened tomorrow. The lowest temperature yesterday was 5.5 degrees at 9:50 A. M.

Yesterday's hourly temperatures were:

1 A. M.	23	2 P. M.	12
2 A. M.	23	3 P. M.	15
3 A. M.	22	4 P. M.	14
4 A. M.	18	5 P. M.	12
5 A. M.	13	6 P. M.	12
6 A. M.	9	7 P. M.	11
7 A. M.	8	8 P. M.	9
8 A. M.	7	9 P. M.	8
9 A. M.	6	10 P. M.	7
9:50 A. M.	5.5	11 P. M.	7
10 A. M.	6	12 M.	6
11 A. M.	8	1 A. M.	5
Noon	9	2 A. M.	4
1 P. M.	10	3 A. M.	2.2

Petroleum Exports Cut

As the fuel shortage produced critical conditions for many apartment and home owners in this and other cities, officials took steps to relieve the situation.

The Commerce Department announced in Washington that it had ordered exports of petroleum products cut 18½ per cent from 11,850,000 to 9,650,000 barrels during the first quarter of the year. Oil exports to Japan and the Ryukyus were cut from 1,600,000 barrels to 100,000. Exports will be allowed only from areas where fuel can be spared, the department said.

In Massachusetts Gov. Robert F. Bradford ordered the seizure of a gas plant in Everett where a walkout of 900 workers was threatened that would have effected service to sixty-four hospitals and 1,500,000 residents of Greater Boston. After seizure and issuance of a temporary injunction, union leaders ordered their followers to remain at work.

In Tennessee, Governor James McCord proclaimed a state of emergency and announced a voluntary fuel conservation program.

In Rochester, Sheriff's deputies and city policemen were organized to make emergency deliveries of fuel oil in extreme cases.

In Endicott, Mayor E. Raymond Lee declared an emergency due to the gas shortage and urged residents to conserve fuel. Many homes there and in Binghamton and Johnson City were without heat and residents sought emergency shelter.

Philadelphians Warned

Residents of Philadelphia were warned of a gas shortage caused by the oil shortage and were urged to restrict use of gas to the absolute minimum.

Police Commissioner Arthur W. Wallander of this city, regional fuel coordinator, sent telegrams asking eighty-six terminal dealers here to remain open today and tomorrow, because of the expected severe cold, to supply fuel oil to hardship cases.

Mayor O'Dwyer declared during the afternoon that it was not necessary at this time to proclaim a state of emergency and to divert

Continued on Page 12, Column 5

Petroleum Shipment Abroad Is Curbed to Ease Shortage

Department of Commerce Orders Quotas Reduced From 11,850,000 to 9,650,000 Barrels for Quarter—Slashes Japan

Special to THE NEW YORK TIMES.

WASHINGTON, Jan. 30—The Department of Commerce announced today that "in view of the serious shortage of fuel oils," in this country it had ordered an 18½ per cent cut in exports of petroleum products during the first quarter of this year. Its action will reduce from 11,850,000 to 9,650,000 the barrels of petroleum designated for overseas.

The Department also announced that it would limit licenses for export of petroleum products to shipments for those areas of the United States where the fuel can best be spared during the emergency.

In addition, it was disclosed that a separate quota of gas oil and distillate fuel oil had been established for the first quarter for shipments to Japan and the Ryukyus, drastically cutting their supply from 1,600,000 barrels to 100,000. The Department said that the difference would be met from oil producing areas outside the United States.

Proposals had been made in Congress to stop all shipments abroad except those going to American military forces. Bills designed to accomplish this end have been introduced in the House and the Senate.

Walter S. Hallanan, chairman of the National Petroleum Council, said today that the petroleum industry had taken "prompt and forthright action to alleviate the shortages of some petroleum products which have been rendered acute in certain sections by the severe cold weather." The industry "takes pride in the fact that it was the first to develop a voluntary agreement under the recent authorization of Congress," he added.

Canada Is Not Affected

WASHINGTON, Jan. 30 (AP)—The action today of the Depart-

Continued on Page 11, Column 4

Record 799-Million Budget Is Asked by Dewey for State

He Estimates Actual Outlay at 753 Millions for Next Fiscal Year, but Says No Rise in Taxes Is Needed—Warns on Inflation

By LEO EGAN

Special to THE NEW YORK TIMES.

ALBANY, Jan. 30—Governor Dewey submitted another record-breaking budget to the Legislature tonight, calling for appropriations of $799,600,000, including deficiencies for the current year, but estimating expenditures in the new budget year at a figure of $753,500,000. The Governor regards the lower figure as his "budget" total.

Appropriations recommended are $128,200,000 higher than those carried in last year's budget message but, because of supplemental grants for teacher pay, veterans' housing, college housing, central schools and rent control, only $53,400,000 higher than actual appropriations, which were $746,200,000.

The expenditures of $753,500,000 contemplated in Mr. Dewey's message compare with an actual total of $707,500,000 in the current year, according to revised estimates. The revised figure reflects increased relief contributions and higher food prices for inmates of state institutions which are being provided for in deficiency appropriations.

Allowing for continuance of the reductions made in 1946, which he recommended, the Governor estimated that existing regular taxes would produce $758,600,000 in the new budget year, enough to balance expenditures and leave a $5,000,000 surplus.

The regular tax structure does not include the additional one-cent-a-package levy on cigarettes or the 20 per cent increase in existing income tax rates which were voted to finance the $400,000,000 veterans' bonus. If the present return from these special levies continued, Mr. Dewey said, the bonus bonds might be retired in eight or

Continued on Page 9, Column 1

Text of Gov. Dewey's budget message will be found on pages 8 and 9.

REALTY VALUATIONS RISE $745,775,468 IN CITY FOR 1948-49

Higher Accrued Value Is Chief Factor in $17,684,240,921 Total, Biggest Since '33

By LEE E. COOPER

New York's land and buildings, regarded as the richest segment of real estate in the world, have risen in value to $17,684,240,921 on the city's tax books for the coming fiscal year.

Municipal assessors have chalked up a tentative increase of $745,775,468 over current figures on taxable properties for the year beginning July 1, 1948, to carry the aggregate valuations to the highest level since 1933.

A report submitted to Mayor O'Dwyer yesterday by Harry B. Chambers, president of the Tax Commission, showed an average rise of about 4½ per cent for the five boroughs, accounted for largely by an upswing in "accrued value" rather than by addition of new construction to the assessment rolls.

The report set the following ten-

Continued on Page 11, Column 3

GOP GROUP SHAPES SHARP ERP REVISION WITH FUND REDUCED

A Proposal to Sell U. S. Goods to Latin America for Food for Europe Wins Favor

By FELIX BELAIR Jr.

Special to THE NEW YORK TIMES.

WASHINGTON, Jan. 30—A fighting nucleus of eighteen Senate Republicans agreed late tonight to press for important changes in the Administration's European Recovery Program as the party's legislative leaders brushed aside President Truman's demand for approval of the full $6,800,000,000 asked for the first fifteen months of operations.

The group of eighteen Senators, in which Westerners predominated, called for a complete shift in emphasis of the Marshall Plan "from the underwriting of trade deficits to the support of specific production programs" in which financial aid would be contingent on increased output of food, coal, steel and transportation facilities.

Senator Joseph H. Ball of Minnesota said the principles agreed

Continued on Page 6, Column 2

GANDHI IS KILLED BY A HINDU; INDIA SHAKEN, WORLD MOURNS; 15 DIE IN RIOTING IN BOMBAY

MOHANDAS K. GANDHI

The New York Times

THREE SHOTS FIRED

Slayer Is Seized, Beaten After Felling Victim on Way to Prayer

DOMINION IS BEWILDERED

Nehru Appeals to the Nation to Keep Peace—U. S. Consul Assisted in Capture

By ROBERT TRUMBULL

Special to THE NEW YORK TIMES.

NEW DELHI, India, Jan. 30—Mohandas K. Gandhi was killed by an assassin's bullet today. The assassin was a Hindu who fired three shots from a pistol at a range of three feet.

The 78-year-old Gandhi, who was the one person who held discordant elements together and kept some sort of unity in this turbulent land, was shot down at 5:15 P. M. as he was proceeding through the Birla House gardens to the pergola from which he was to deliver his daily prayer meeting message.

The assassin was immediately seized.

He later identified himself as Nathuran Vinayak Godse, 36, a Hindu of the Mahratta tribes in Poona. This has been a center of resistance to Gandhi's ideology.

Mr. Gandhi died twenty-five minutes later. His death left all India stunned and bewildered as to the direction that this newly independent nation would take without its "Mahatma" (Great Teacher).

The loss of Mr. Gandhi brings this country of 300,000,000 abruptly to a crossroads. Mingled with the sadness in this capital tonight was an undercurrent of fear and uncertainty, for now the strongest influence for peace in India that this generation has known is gone.

[Communal riots quickly swept Bombay when news of Mr. Gandhi's death was received. The Associated Press reported that fifteen persons were killed and more than fifty injured before an uneasy peace was established.]

Appeal Made By Nehru

Prime Minister Pandit Jawaharlal Nehru, in a voice choked with emotion, appealed in a radio address tonight for a sane approach to the future. He asked that India's path be turned away from violence in memory of the great peacemaker who had departed.

Mr. Gandhi's body will be cremated in the orthodox Hindu fashion according to his often expressed wishes. His body will be carried from his New Delhi residence on a simple wooden cot covered with a sheet at 11:30 tomorrow morning. The funeral procession will wind through every principal street of the two cities of New and Old Delhi and reach the burning ghats on the bank of the sacred Jumna River at about 4 P. M. There the remains of the greatest Indian since Gautama Buddha will be wrapped in a sheet, laid on a pyre of wood and burned. His ashes will be scattered on the Jumna's waters, eventually to mingle with the Ganges where the two holy rivers meet at the temple city of Allahabad.

These simple ceremonies were announced tonight by Pandit Nehru in respect to Mr. Gandhi's wishes, although many of the leaders desired that his body be embalmed and exhibited in state. India will see the last of Mr. Gandhi as it saw him when he lived—a humble and unassuming Hindu.

News Spreads Quickly

News of the assassination of Mr. Gandhi—only a few days after he had finished a five-day fast to bring about communal friendship—spread quickly through New Delhi. Immediately there was a spontaneous movement of thousands to Birla House, home of G. D. Birla, the millionaire industrialist, where Mr. Gandhi and his six secretaries had been guests since he came to New Delhi in the midst of the disturbances in India's capital.

While walking through the gardens to this evening's prayer meeting Mr. Gandhi had just reached the top of a short flight of brick steps, his slender brown

Continued on Page 2, Column 1

All Britain Honors Gandhi; Truman Deplores Tragedy

By HERBERT L. MATTHEWS

LONDON, Jan. 30—Mohandas K. Gandhi, in death, has won the unanimous tribute of Britons—something he never hoped for or expected during his life. Nowhere outside of India has the shock of his assassination contained the feelings and emotions evident here today because Britain and Mr. Gandhi have been linked for good or evil over the last forty years.

In a special broadcast to the British people tonight the Prime Minister said:

"The voice which pleaded for peace and brotherhood has been silenced, but I am certain that his spirit will continue to animate his fellow countrymen and will plead for peace and concord."

[President Truman and Secretary Marshall expressed their grief and condolences in messages to India. Members of Congress were apprehensive. Leaders of many other lands joined in paying tribute and in deploring the manner of Mr. Gandhi's death.]

The sincerity of today's expressions of regret, which came from the King and Queen, the Prime Minister, the political parties—even the Communist—and from many humble Londoners who filed silently into India House this afternoon to pay tribute, cannot be doubted.

Those many quarrels when Mr. Gandhi fought with his passive resistance against the imperial power of Britain are truly things of the past. Mr. Gandhi himself paid high tribute to Britain for her policy of freeing India and of trying to help to keep the two dominions at peace with each other.

The British, on their side, have

Continued on Page 2, Column 2

U.S. WARNS CITIZENS IN PALESTINE FIGHT

Consulate General Says They Face Loss of Passports and All Protective Rights

By SAM POPE BREWER

Special to THE NEW YORK TIMES.

JERUSALEM, Jan. 30—United States citizens fighting in the armed services of the Jews or the Arabs will lose their passports and their right to protection, the United States Consulate General warned Americans in Palestine tonight. Furthermore, naturalized citizens, it was said, would lose their American nationality if they fought for a foreign power.

[Zionist hopes for getting United Nations help in arming a Jewish militia in Palestine were dimmed by the statement of Sir Alexander Cadogan, chief British representative, that the British Government would not allow formation of such forces before the end of the mandate.]

The consular warning is being twisted by Arab sources into a promise that those fighting for the Jews may have their passports back when the fighting ends. The relevant passage reads: "American passports valid only for direct

Continued on Page 4, Column 4

Hope Wanes in Sea Search For 28 Aboard Lost Airliner

By FREDERICK GRAHAM

The Atlantic area northeast of Bermuda was being searched last night for survivors of a British South American Airways plane that disappeared in the area early yesterday morning with a crew of six and at least twenty-two passengers, but hope had almost been abandoned.

The thirty-two-passenger plane, which listed among those aboard Air Marshal Sir Arthur Coningham, Royal Air Force, who commanded the Second Tactical Air Force of the Allies at the invasion of Normandy, was out of London and on the Azores-to-Bermuda leg of the flight when last heard from about 1 A. M. (EST) yesterday.

At least fifteen United States Air Force, Navy and Coast Guard planes plus three Coast Guard cutters, two commercial steamers and a British South American Airways plane worked over a large area about 400 miles northeast of Bermuda without success. More aircraft are scheduled to continue the search today.

The plane, a converted Lancaster bomber of the type used by the RAF for saturation bombing of Germany, had stopped in Santa Maria in the Azores to refuel. An Associated Press dispatch from Bermuda said the plane, believed to have been commanded by Capt. David Colby, radioed to Bermuda that it would arrive there at midnight Thursday, an hour and a half late. One hour later it reported to 440 miles northeast of Bermuda. that there was a moderate sea swell and that it was bucking strong headwinds. Nothing more has been heard from the plane.

The only other report that might

Continued on Page 10, Column 2

ORVILLE WRIGHT, 76, IS DEAD IN DAYTON

Co-Inventor With His Brother, Wilbur, of the Airplane Was Pilot in First Flight

Special to THE NEW YORK TIMES.

DAYTON, Ohio, Jan. 30—Orville Wright, who with his brother, the late Wilbur Wright, invented the airplane, died here tonight at 10:40 in Miami Valley Hospital. He was 76 years old.

Mr. Wright, who had been confined to a hospital in October, collapsed in his office on Tuesday. He was suffering from lung congestion and coronary arteriosclerosis.

At the bedside when Mr. Wright died were Horace A. Wright, a nephew; Mrs. H. S. Miller, a niece, and Delyle Myers, a nurse.

The announcement of his death was made by Dr. A. B. Brower, family physician.

Engrossing Amusement

In the early fall of 1900 fishermen and Coast Guardsmen dwelling on that lonely and desolated spot of sand dividing Albemarle Sound from the Atlantic Ocean on the coast of North Carolina called

Continued on Page 12, Column 2

Arms Get Atomic Energy Priority In Policy Set by Congress Group

By WILLIAM S. WHITE

Special to THE NEW YORK TIMES.

WASHINGTON, Jan. 30—The Joint Committee on Atomic Energy laid down today a firm policy that the production of atomic weapons, rather than work on peacetime applications of atomic energy, must be the "vital business" of the United States for the foreseeable future.

It declared also that "uninterrupted operation" of the "critical," or military, facilities of the Atomic Energy Commission was so essential to national security that an investigation was in motion to find a formula to assure "continuity of work" under all labor eventualities.

In its first report to Congress, the committee indicated some dissatisfaction "in a number of cases" with certain aspects of the handling of internal security within the personnel of the Atomic Energy Commission.

"In certain of these cases" the report went on, "the committee has requested that the commission outline in detail its security policy as applied to these specific instances.

"In the majority of these cases," it was added, the men in question had been employed while atomic energy still was under Army control.

As to the essential policy to be followed in atomic development, the committee declared:

"Until such time as an effective, enforceable and reliable program for the international control of atomic energy is in successful operation, the most vital business of the Atomic Energy Commission must be the meeting of the atomic requirements of national defense.

"The joint committee has been assured that those charged with these responsibilities are keenly aware thereof. This phase of the atomic energy program is of paramount

Continued on Page 6, Column 5

World News Summarized

SATURDAY, JANUARY 31, 1948

Mohandas K. Gandhi, 78-year-old spiritual leader of hundreds of millions of Indians, was shot in New Delhi yesterday as he walked toward a pergola to lead 1,000 of his followers in evening prayer. He died twenty-five minutes later. His assassin, a Hindu, was seized after he had fired three quick shots into the frail leader, who only recently had ended a hunger strike in protest against communal strife. [1:8.]

News of the tragedy shocked the world. In Bombay, it ignited a new outburst of rioting. [2:3.] United Nations officials at Lake Success feared this might be the beginning of a new wave of violence throughout India. [2:4-5.] President Truman said the whole world would mourn and expressed hope that the assassination would "not retard the peace of India and the world." [2:1.] Similar expressions of regret were voiced in London, where the King and the Queen and Prime Minister Attlee were among the many leaders to pay tribute to Mr. Gandhi. [1:6-7.]

The French National Assembly approved, 308 to 242, the Government's program to establish a free gold market and to allow Frenchmen to repatriate foreign assets by paying a tax. The Socialists reversed their previous stand and voted for the program. [1:6-7.]

Two recent Russian notes protesting the reopening for American use of an airfield in Tripolitania and the presence of American naval craft in Italian ports will be rejected by the State Department. [6:5.] The Navy announced that another 1,000 marines would go to the Mediterranean soon to replace an equal number now serving in that area. [6:4-5.]

The United States consulate in Jerusalem declared American citizens participating in the fighting would lose their passports and right to protection. [1:7.] Britain announced at Lake Success before the Palestine Commission that she could not allow the formation of any armed militia in Palestine before her mandate ends. [4:3.]

In Washington a group of eighteen Senate Republicans urged a change in the European Recovery Program to support specific production goals and brushed aside the Administration's request for approval of the full initial fund of $6,800,000,000. [1:5.]

An 18½ per cent reduction in exports of petroleum products was ordered by the Commerce Department in view of the "serious shortage" of oil in this country. [1:2-3.]

Also in Washington, the Joint Committee on Atomic Energy declared this nation must concentrate for the foreseeable future on the "uninterrupted" production of atomic weapons in preference to the peaceful utilization of atomic energy. [1:2-3.]

Governor Dewey asked the Legislature to appropriate $799,600,000 as he submitted another record-breaking budget. Appropriations last year totaled $746,200,000. [1:4-5.]

Winter's coldest weather hit the metropolitan area, with the thermometer hovering near zero in the city. In the suburbs the temperature was expected to fall to sub-zero levels during the night. Some homes suffered from a shortage of fuel oil. [1:1.]

A thirty-two passenger British plane was feared lost on its way to Bermuda. [1:2-3.]

Orville Wright, air pioneer, died in Dayton, Ohio, at 76. [1:2.]

France Votes Free Gold Market, Legalizes Hidden Assets by a Tax

By HAROLD CALLENDER

Special to THE NEW YORK TIMES.

PARIS, Jan. 30—Parliamentary sanction was given today for the Government's devaluation of the franc and its accompanying monetary policy.

By a vote of 308 to 242, the National Assembly passed the Government's bill to create a free gold market and to legalize the hitherto illegal possession of foreign securities held by Frenchmen, if those assets were repatriated and the owners paid a special tax of 25 per cent of the assets' value.

As a comparatively free market in dollars had already been established by decree—although its opening was delayed by the freezing of bank notes of 5,000 francs—today's vote by the Assembly completed the series of measures framed by the Government to derive maximum benefit from devaluation by getting possession of privately owned foreign securities and hoarded gold.

Estimates of the total of these illegal securities have been in the neighborhood of $300,000,000 in the United States alone, while official guesses have placed the value of the hidden gold in France at $2,000,000,000.

Apparently placated by the freezing of the bank notes, the Socialists once again switched their position and voted today for the gold market bill, which they had opposed bitterly Wednesday, although their Ministers had apparently accepted it in the Cabinet meeting last Saturday. They were not reluctant to switch, for they did not desire to upset the Government and wreck the "Third Force," hostile though they were to the Government's departure from a planned economy.

The freezing measure, taken when the Socialists had precipitated a Cabinet crisis by balking at the gold market, was considered mainly a political move. But René Mayer, Finance Minister, told the

Continued on Page 5, Column 2

FOUND the right cigar! Try PRINCE HAMLET all Havana Filler. 10c and 2 for 25c.—Advt.

WASHINGTON FEELS CONCERN FOR INDIA

Truman Calls Gandhi's Death an 'International Tragedy,' Issues Formal Statement

MARSHALL SENDS A NOTE

Addresses Himself to Nehru—Members of Congress Hear of Bombay Disturbance

Special to THE NEW YORK TIMES.

WASHINGTON, Jan. 30—The assassination of Mohandas K. Gandhi shocked the capital today. Fears were expressed that it might lead to serious complications in India.

In an immediate reaction released through Charles G. Ross, Presidential press secretary, President Truman said it was "a tragic loss to the whole world," adding:

"I regard the assassination as a great international tragedy. Notwithstanding the great sorrow this will cause the world I sincerely hope it will not retard the peace of India and the world."

Later in a formal statement Mr. Truman declared that all peoples would be inspired by "his sacrifice" to work with increased vigor toward the peace and brotherhood which he symbolized.

Message from Marshall

Secretary of State George C. Marshall in a message to Pandit Jawaharlal Nehru, Prime Minister and Foreign Minister of the Dominion of India, said:

"The United States has been shocked by the tragic news of the passing of Mahatma Gandhi, and shares with India a heavy burden of sorrow and loss. In his devotion to tolerance and the brotherhood of man, the Mahatma was one of those rare spokesmen for the conscience of all mankind. The sense of bereavement felt in this country evidences the close ties between the peoples of the United States and India."

The Indian Embassy placed its flag at half staff in token of sorrow.

Official opinion here as to the possible consequences of the assassination were reserved, pending further development. The State Department delayed any detailed comment until reports have been received from its diplomatic representatives in the area.

Statement by Truman

In his formal statement President Truman said:

This morning when I heard the tragic news of the assassination of Mahatma Gandhi I sent a message to Earl Mountbatten, the Governor General of India, expressing my condolences to him and to the people of India.

Gandhi was a great Indian nationalist, but at the same time was a leader of international stature. His teachings and his actions have left a deep impression on millions of people.

He was and is revered by the people of India and his influence was felt not only in affairs of government but also in the realm of the spirit. Unhappily he did not live to witness the full realization of those ideals for which he struggled. But his life and his work will be, through the years to come, the greatest monument to him. His selfless struggle for the betterment of his people, will, I am sure, endure as an example of India's leaders, many of whom are his disciples.

I know not only the peoples of India, but all peoples will be inspired by his sacrifice to work with increased vigor toward the brotherhood and peace which the Mahatma symbolized.

Note to Mountbatten

In a message to Earl Mountbatten, the President said:

I am deeply grieved by the news of the assassination of Mohandas K. Gandhi, and I send you and the Government and people of India my sincere condolences. As a teacher and leader, his influence made itself felt not only in India but everywhere in the world, and his death brings great sorrow to all peace loving people. Another giant among men has fallen in the cause of brotherhood and peace. I know that the peoples of Asia will be inspired by his tragic death to strive with increased determination to achieve the goals of cooperation and mutual trust for which the Mahatma has now given his life.

Congress Concerned

WASHINGTON, Jan. 30 (AP)—In Congress today members of both parties expressed concern that the effect of Mr. Gandhi's assassination on world peace prospects might not be good.

Senate Democratic Leader Alben B. Barkley of Kentucky said he hoped the "international tragedy" would not "retard the peace of India and the world."

Representative Arthur G. Klein, Democrat, New York, called Mr. Gandhi's death "a profound loss to civilization and progress and to a stable peace." However Senator Elbert D. Thomas, Democrat, Utah, said that Mr. Gandhi "may be a stronger force as a result of his death than he was alive" because "he put spiritual values into everything he did and, more and more, the world is beginning to see that it is the things of the spirit which ultimately have the greatest influence."

Government officials were silent on the repercussions that might follow the Indian leader's slaying but early reports of rioting did not encourage hopes that the subcontinent's internal strife would cease at once.

In the House, Representative Emmanuel Celler, Democrat, New York, proposed that Congress authorize a monument to Mr. Gandhi, to be built in Washingon by public subscription.

A New York Republican, Representative Kenneth B. Keating, asked the House to pause in tribute to "this great world figure."

Gandhi Received Huge Fee For a Phonograph Record

By The Associated Press.

LONDON, Jan. 30—Mohandas K. Gandhi was said to have received the largest fee ever paid for making a phonograph record.

Some sixteen years ago he signed a contract with the Columbia Phonograph Company by which he was to receive a minimum of $200,000 for recording a record entitled "The Justification of God." Proceeds went to the Indian National Congress party for use in the independence campaign.

His voice was clear and his English diction was declared to be perfect.

COMMUNAL RIOTING RECURS IN BOMBAY

News of Gandhi's Death Brings Swift Clash—Fifteen Are Killed, Many Injured

Special to THE NEW YORK TIMES.

BOMBAY, India, Jan. 30—The death of Mohandas K. Gandhi today revived the embers of communal antipathy that he latterly lived to extinguish. In the first short, sharp outburst of fierce communal rioting after news of his death today, six persons were killed and thirty-two admitted to hospitals with injuries in street fighting. [The day's toll was placed at fifteen killed and fifty-four injured, according to The Associated Press.]

Police fired repeatedly to suppress disturbances and rioting subsided only after a curfew was imposed. Armored cars and motorized police squads were patroling silent, deserted streets late tonight pending troop movements tomorrow.

All public entertainments were cancelled as Bombay went into mourning. Shops were closed and all transport disappeared. But before the traffic suspension was complete, scores of cars and buses were halted and their passengers ejected by impatient youths.

"Congress House," the party headquarters, became a temple of mourning. Hundreds congregated there and wept as Mr. Gandhi's favorite hymns were sung. Every head was bared and tears streamed down the worshippers' faces at the end of a spontaneous ceremonial service.

BOMBAY, Jan. 30 (UP)—Bloody rioting broke out in Bombay today a few minutes after the news of Mr. Gandhi's assassination spread.

A mob invaded the famous Hotel Taj Mahal, forcing it to close its doors and put out all its lights. A dinner dance and private parties scheduled tonight in the hotel were cancelled and all bars closed.

All of the victims were reported stabbed. The worst rioting was in the Golpitha, Nagpada and Girgaum districts, strongpoints of the Hindu extremist Mahasabha group, which never accepted Mr. Gandhi's advocacy of friendship with the Moslems.

Moslem shops were reported to have been looted in the Kaldabevi Road section, in the center of Bombay. Shopkeepers hastily locked and barred their doors.

When one Moslem woman, member of a prominent family, heard the news of Mr. Gandhi's assassination she cried: "God help us all."

The gathering mobs stalled all street car and bus service. Crowds in the downtown section yelled, "Close down!" to shopkeepers.

Police, despairing of breaking up the mobs, fired over their heads when they showed signs of getting out of control.

At 11 P. M. the police commissioner announced that "the situation is under control, but we will have to keep close watch tomorrow."

The Government ordered all its offices to close tomorrow as a mark of respect for the "departed father of the nation."

Newspapers in Bombay printed extras for the first time since the end of the war.

NANKING PRAISES IDEALS

Government Statement Calls Gandhi 'Spiritual Leader'

Special to THE NEW YORK TIMES.

NANKING, Jan. 30—The Chinese Government expressed "profound sorrow" tonight at the assassination of Mohandas K. Gandhi in a statement issued by Dr. Hollington K. Tong, official spokesman.

The statement eulogized Mr. Gandhi as a "great" Asiatic, a "great" spiritual leader and "architect" of Indian freedom.

Describing his death as a "staggering loss to his people," the Government statement added:

"Without his heroic leadership and self-sacrifice, his country would still be far from its goal. He symbolized in his own person the highest ideals of his people. Gandhi was struck down while he was leading his last noble fight for Indian unity. His death in the cause of a united India raises him to a pedestal of supreme greatness.

"China feel his loss with grief."

News Distresses Aga Khan

Special to THE NEW YORK TIMES.

CANNES, France, Jan. 30—The Aga Khan, leader of the Ismaili Moslems, showed distress tonight at the news of Mohandas K. Gandhi's death. "It is a terrible thing for India and for all the world," he said at his villa where he is spending the winter.

PAYING TRIBUTE TO GANDHI AT LAKE SUCCESS

The United Nations flag is lowered to half staff

The New York Times

U. N. Renders Tribute to Gandhi; Apprehension Felt at His Death

By A. M. ROSENTHAL

Special to THE NEW YORK TIMES.

LAKE SUCCESS, N. Y., Jan. 30—The uneasy fear that the death of Mohandas K. Gandhi would bring bloodshed and new disaster to India ran today like a thread through a day of gloom at the United Nations.

The Indian delegate unhappily told the Security Council that it was impossible to say what might happen in his country now that its "man of the great soul" was dead. And the Pakistani delegate looked around the Council table and said all India must unite or the assassination of the Mahatma would be just a taste of horror to come.

For weeks, India and Pakistan—the two Dominions that Mr. Gandhi wanted undivided—have appeared before the Council to quarrel over the future of the Princely State of Kashmir, to accuse each other of mass murder and systematic aggression. Today, however, there was no debate. The Council put aside the business of Kashmir to mourn for the Mahatma.

Delegates from every one of the eleven members of the Council spoke before a filled, quiet chamber to give condolences to India. They called the Mahatma a martyr, a symbol of peace, an apostle of brotherhood. They said hopefully that his death must bring India and Pakistan closer to the unity he represented. And then for the first time in the Council's history they stood in silence for thirty seconds.

Underlying Fear Felt

The assassination of Mr. Gandhi was felt outside the Council chamber, in the offices and corridors and delegates' lounge. Always, the underlying fear was that new riots would be touched off. Delegates and Secretariat members kept an ear to radios for word from India, and all through the day there were calls to newspaper offices with the same question:

"Is there rioting?"

For the Indian delegation, the day of mourning began at 7:45 A. M. when a reporter called their hotel to tell them the news. The delegate who first heard the story could not believe it, asked for a repeat, then hung up slowly and went to tell the others.

The United Nations went into mourning at the beginning of the work day. Acting Secretary General Byron Price ordered the white-on-blue flag of the world organization hung at half-mast for three days here, in New York and Geneva. None of the national flags of the fifty-seven United Nations will be raised for those three days.

At first there was talk that the Council would cancel its meeting out of respect for Mr. Gandhi but Fernand van Langenhove of Belgium, Council President, decided to hold a memorial session.

The delegates' lounge, where pre-meeting caucuses and informal talks take place, was a subdued room, with none of the usual high-pitched chatter and laughter. Sir Mohammed Zafrullah Khan Pakistan's Foreign Minister, was the first delegate to enter and he waited by himself at first.

Other delegates entered and waited—Andrei A. Gromyko of the Soviet Union, Warren R. Austin of the United States, Philip J. Noel-Baker of the United Kingdom. They talked quietly of the news.

The Indian delegation entered the room. It was led by N. Gopalaswami Ayyangar. His throat was wrapped in a muffler and he looked tired. First Sir Zafrullah and then the other delegates walked over and said how sorry they were and what a loss it was.

When the meeting started, the press galleries, photographers, newsreel and radio booths were filled. Most of the audience who heard the eulogies to the 78-year-old Mahatma were youngsters from Long Island and New York high schools.

The delegates from Pakistan and India spoke last, but everything else seemed like prelude. Everybody in the room knew that the actions of those two Governments would decide what would happen to the people of the subcontinent.

Sir Zafrullah told the Council that the death of the Indian leader meant as much to Pakistan as to India.

"He was the keystone of the arch that is now subject to many stresses," he said.

In plain language, then, the Pakistan Foreign Minister said that the "catastrophe" of Mr. Gandhi's death might "become the forerunner of great disaster in many fields."

"It is devoutly to be prayed for that in this hour of grief and distress leaders of all communities in India will unite to devote every effort toward averting these disasters," he went on.

Hopes For Improvement

Mr. Ayyangar, who had received a condolence call from Sir Zafrullah earlier in the day, seemed optimistic before the meeting. He was asked whether Mr. Gandhi's death would further complicate the already complicated Kashmir case and he said he hoped it would have an "opposite effect."

But when he spoke to the Council—slowly, heavily and pausing after each word—Mr. Ayyangar said that the possible reprecussions of the murder were "not easy to assess."

Mr. Ayyangar dwelt on the fact that Mr. Gandhi had stood for Indian unity and had opposed division. Looking across the table at Sir Zafrullah, Mr. Ayyangar said the Mahatma regretted nothing in his life's work so much as the fact that the struggle for Indian independence had led to partition.

The Indian delegate's voice was filled with sorrow as he spoke of "our biggest man, the tallest man in the world judged by moral standards." He said that Mr. Gandhi's life was one long dedication to truth, nonviolence, service to the poor and human dignity. All his life, said Mr. Ayyangar, the Mahatma had stood for returning good for evil.

GANDHI IS KILLED BY A HINDU YOUTH

Continued From Page 1

around the shoulders of his granddaughters, Manu, 17, and Ava, 20.

Someone spoke to him and he turned from his granddaughters and gave the appealing Hindu salute—palms together and the points of the fingers brought to the chin as in a Christian attitude of prayer.

At once a youngish Indian stepped from the crowd—which had opened to form a pathway for Mr. Gandhi's walk to the pergola—and fired the fatal shots from a European-made pistol. One bullet struck Mr. Gandhi in the chest and two in the abdomen on the right side. He seemed to lean forward and then crumpled to the ground. His two granddaughters fell beside him in tears.

Crowd Is Stunned

A crowd of about 500, according to witnesses, was stunned. There was no outcry or excitement for a second or two. Then the onlookers began to push the assassin more as if in bewilderment than in anger.

The assassin was seized by Tom Reiner of Lancaster, Mass., a vice consul attached to the American Embassy and a recent arrival in India. He was attending Mr. Gandhi's prayer meeting out of curiosity, as most visitors to New Delhi do at least once.

Mr. Reiner grasped the assailant by the shoulders and shoved him toward several police guards. Only then did the crowd begin to grasp what had happened and a forest of fists belabored the assassin as he was dragged toward the pergola where Mr. Gandhi was to have prayed. He left a trail of blood.

Mr. Gandhi was picked up by attendants and carried rapidly back to the unpretentious bedroom where he had passed most of his working and sleeping hours. As he was taken through the door Hindu onlookers who could see him began to wail and beat their breasts.

Less than half an hour later a member of Mr. Gandhi's entourage came out of the room and said to those about the door:

"Bapu (father) is finished."

But it was not until Mr. Gandhi's death was announced by All India Radio at 6 P. M. that the word spread widely.

Assassin Taken Away

Meanwhile the assassin was taken to a police station. He identifed himself as coming from Poona.

It was remarked that the first of three attempts on Mr. Gandhi's life was made in Poona on June 25, 1934, when a bomb was thrown at a car believed to be Mr. Gandhi's. Poona is a center of the extremist anti-Gandhi orthodox Hindu Mahasabha (Great Society).

The second possible attempt to assassinate Mr. Gandhi was by means of a crude bomb planted on his garden wall on Jan. 20 of this year.

The only statement known to have been made by the assassin was his remark to a foreign correspondent: "I am not at all sorry."

He is large for a Hindu and was dressed in gray slacks, blue pullover and khaki bush jacket. His pistol, which was snatched from him immediately after the shooting by Royal Indian Air Force Flight Sergeant D. R. Singh, contained four undischarged cartridges.

Lying on a wooden cot in his bedroom, Mr. Gandhi said no word before his death except once to ask for water. Most of the time he was unconscious. When he was pronounced dead by his physician weeping members of his staff covered the lower half of his face with a sheet in the Hindu fashion and the women present sat on the floor and chanted verses from the sacred scriptures of the Hindus. Those who could see these ceremonies through the windows knew then that Mr. Gandhi had expired.

Pandit Nehru arrived at about 6 o'clock. Silently and with burning eyes he inspected the spot where Mr. Gandhi was shot and then went into the house without a word. Later he stood high on the front gate of Birla House and related the tentative funeral arrangements to several thousand persons gathered in the street and blocking all traffic. His voice shook with grief and hundreds in the crowd were weeping uncontrollably.

Several thousand mourners formed orderly and quiet queues at all doors leading into Birla House and for a time they were permitted to file past the body. Later when it became evident that only a small fraction of the gathering would be able to view Mr. Gandhi's remains tonight, the body was taken to a second-floor balcony and placed on a cot tilted under a floodlamp so all in the grounds would see their departed leader.

His head was illuminated by a lamp with five wicks representing the five elements—air, light, water, earth and fire—and also to light his soul to eternity according to Hindu belief.

Pandit Nehru delivered Mr. Gandhi's valedictory in his radio address late this evening. In a quivering voice he said:

"Gandhi has gone out of our lives and there is darkness everywhere. * * * The father of our nation is no more—no longer will we run to him for advice and solace. * * * This is a terrible blow to millions and millions in this country. * * *

"Our light has gone out, but the light that shone in this country was no ordinary light. For a thousand years that light will be seen in this country and the world will see it * * * Oh, that this has happened to us! There was so much more to do."

Referring to the assassin Pandit Nehru said:

"I can only call him a madman."

He pleaded for a renewed spirit of peace, which had been Mr. Gandhi's last project, saying:

"His spirit looks upon us—nothing would displease him more than to see us indulge in violence. All our petty conflicts and difficulties must be ended in the face of this great disaster * * * In his death he has reminded us of the big things in life."

Enmity Incurred

Mr. Gandhi's pleas for tolerance since the far-reaching communal warfare of last August and September had earned him the enmity of extremist elements, notably the Hindu Mahasabha which condemned his fast for inter-religious unity and whose leaders refused to sign his peace pledge. There was also a widespread condemnation of Mr. Gandhi's forgiving attitude among the refugees who had suffered deeply at Moslem hands in the West Punjab.

More serious to India perhaps than loss of Mr. Gandhi's restraining influence on fanatic passions may be the political implications of his death. Though he held no office he was the central figure of India's dominant Congress party and the last of the "old guard" in the long struggle for liberation from foreign rule.

Some Indian observers were predicting tonight that Mr. Gandhi's death would inevitably be followed by a fission in the Congress party and the emergence of a new political pattern after a period of deep confusion.

JINNAH SORROWS FOR HIS HINDU FOE

KARACHI, Pakistan, Jan. 30 (AP)—Governor General Mohammed Ali Jinnah, leader of this Moslem Dominion, tonight expressed his deep sorrow over the assassination of Mohandas K. Gandhi and his sincere sympathy with Hindu India on the loss of a great man.

"I was shocked to learn of the most dastardly attack on the life of Mr. Gandhi, resulting in his death," Mr. Jinnah said.

"There can be no controversy before death. Whatever our political differences, he was one of the greatest men produced by the Hindu community and a leader who commanded their universal confidence and respect.

"I wish to express my deep sorrow, and I sincerely sympathize with the great Hindu community and his family in this bereavement at this momentous, historical and critical juncture so soon after the birth of freedom for Hindustan and Pakistan.

"The loss to the Dominion of India is irreparable, and it will be very difficult to fill the vacuum created by the passing away of such a great man at this moment."

Pakistan's Premier, Liaquat Ali Khan, said that the death of Mr. Gandhi, who had "worked unceasingly to bring sanity to the people and to establish communal harmony," was an "irreparable loss to the people of both Dominions in the present strained state of Indian politics.

DEATH 'CHAGRINS' POPE

Vatican Uneasy Over Possible Reaction to Gandhi Slaying

Special to THE NEW YORK TIMES.

ROME, Jan. 30—Pope Pius XII was "deeply chagrined" at learning of the death of Mohandas K. Gandhi, a high-ranking prelate said today. The news was conveyed to the Pontiff early this afternoon after it had been received by the Secretariat of State.

Vatican circles said they were uneasy over the possible repercussions of Mr. Gandhi's disappearance from the Hindu political scene as they felt that the stabilizing influence of the slain leader had on countless occasions prevented bloodshed and widespread violence.

ALL BRITONS UNITE TO ACCLAIM GANDHI

Continued From Page 1

been full of admiration for Mr. Gandhi's successful efforts at Calcutta and recently at Delhi to bring about a better communal feeling through fasting.

That is why the tributes come first and they mean what they say. They are tributes to the character and career of Mr. Gandhi but almost all of them express the fervent hope that his death will lead to a sense of common Hindu-Moslem loss and will bring a reaction of a favorable nature to soothe communal feeling.

There was a frank sigh or relief when it was learned that the assassin was a Hindu, not a Moslem. It is realized that before the common people everywhere get to understand this fact there is going to be some trouble but it should die down soon, according to calculations here.

Prime Minister Attlee's message on behalf of the British Government, for instance, after a personal tribute to Mr. Gandhi, ended with these words:

"During the last months of his life he exerted with success his powerful influence to restrain communal bitterness and to promote the cooperation of all Indians for the common good. It is the earnest hope of the British Government in the United Kingdom that this example will be followed and that his moral influence will continue to guide men in the paths of peace."

Royalty Joins in Tribute

The message of the King, sent to Earl Mountbatten, Governor-General of India, said:

"The Queen and I are deeply shocked by the news of the death of Mr. Gandhi. Will you please convey to the people of India our sincere sympathy in the irreparable loss which they and indeed mankind suffered."

Winston Churchill, Opposition leader, said: "I am shocked at this wicked crime."

Sir Stafford Cripps, Chancellor of the Exchequer, was one of the many personal friends of Mr. Gandhi who pointed out that this loss will be deplored throughout the world.

The Earl of Halifax, who as Viceroy from 1926 to 1931, was closer to Mr. Gandhi and more respected by him than any Governor General of this century, also expressed the hope that the "effect of his tragic death may be to bring all his countrymen to understand and practice the principles he so constantly and faithfully preached."

Lord Pethick-Lawrence said: "I know there is one wish he would have made—that his death should not be revenged or made the occasion for further bloodshed but that it should lead to reconciliation among all the peoples of the subcontinent of Asia."

Communists Suggest Link

Aside from the government leaders, there were tributes from the Most Rev. Geoffrey F. Fisher, Archbishop of Canterbury and Anglican Primate, and from Bernard Cardinal Griffin, Archbishop of Westminster and Catholic Primate.

The Communist party's statement was not without its irony for it said that Mr. Gandhi was "in close association with all progressive democratic elements in India including the Communists." It is a matter of record that Mr. Gandhi at all times hated and feared communism because of its atheism.

A tribute that Mr. Gandhi would have appreciated came from his old political enemy (as he considered him) L. S. Amery, wartime Secretary of State for India. Mr. Amery expressed deep regret and conceded that "no one contributed more to the particular way in which the chapter of British rule in India has ended than Mr. Gandhi himself."

This statement points to old quarrels and it would, indeed, be hypocritical not to remember that many Britons over many years have had very low opinions of Mr. Gandhi. These men—rulers of India, civil servants and military men—considered him more or less of a charlatan. They felt that he was an unscrupulous politician, using his saintliness for political blackmail.

However, tonight it is recognized that final judgment can be left to history. No one denies that Mr. Gandhi was a very great man whose loss will be felt everywhere although especially in tortured India.

Canada Sends Message

OTTAWA, Jan. 30 (Canadian Press)—Prime Minister W. L. Mackenzie King was joined by other party leaders in the House of Commons today in expressing regret at the assassination of Mohandas K. Gandhi in India.

The Prime Minister read a message he sent the Prime Minister of India, expressing "profound regret" and adding that it "is particularly shocking that a life so selflessly devoted to the avoidance of violence should have been brought to its close by an act of violence."

"All the News That's Fit to Print"

The New York Times.

LATE CITY EDITION
Fair and warmer today and tomorrow.
Temperature Range Today—Max., 65; Min., 48
Temperatures Yesterday—Max., 53; Min., 46
Full U. S. Weather Bureau Report, Page 31

Copyright, 1948, by The New York Times Company.

VOL. XCVII..No. 32,984. Entered as Second-Class Matter, Postoffice, New York, N. Y. NEW YORK, SATURDAY, MAY 15, 1948. Times Square, New York 18, N. Y. Telephone Lackawanna 4-1000 THREE CENTS IN NEW YORK CITY

ZIONISTS PROCLAIM NEW STATE OF ISRAEL; TRUMAN RECOGNIZES IT AND HOPES FOR PEACE; TEL AVIV IS BOMBED, EGYPT ORDERS INVASION

NAVY PUSHES PLAN FOR CONSTRUCTION OF MISSILE VESSELS

Sullivan Asks House Committee to Approve Halting Work on Battleship, Destroyer Types

WANTS 65,000-TON CARRIER

Floating 'Submarine Killers' Are Also Stressed in Plea for Diverting $300,000,000 Fund

By C. P. TRUSSELL
Special to THE NEW YORK TIMES.

WASHINGTON, May 14—The Navy asked Congress today for authority to shift sharply its construction of fighting craft from battleship, cruiser and destroyer types to guided missile vessels, a 65,000-ton carrier able to base, far at sea, planes with an operating radius of 1,700 miles, better submarines and floating "enemy submarine killers."

Such new ships, John L. Sullivan, Secretary of the Navy, told the House Armed Services Committee, must have a higher priority "because of the more immediate need for them in the event of an emergency." The immediate reaction of the committee appeared to favor prompt action.

For such a shift in construction, Secretary Sullivan brought out, the Navy wanted to halt the building of thirteen naval vessels, including the battleship Kentucky, the large cruiser Hawaii, seven destroyers, two destroyer escorts and two submarines. To date about $197,000,000 has been spent on them.

However, this money was not to be abandoned, Mr. Sullivan emphasized. These craft could be converted now to the new program, he explained, or be put aside for a fitting-out later as new weapons were developed.

New Aims for $300,000,000 Fund

What the Navy wanted, Secretary Sullivan asserted, was Congressional permission to divert some $300,000,000 remaining in the present ship construction account to these purposes:

Starting the 65,000-ton aircraft carrier (the biggest ones now are the two of the Midway class, at 45,000 tons), which might cost around $124,000,000.

Building, for reproduction later, of a "submarine killer." (Hearings on the defense program have indicated that Russia has made great progress in the submarine field.) A "killer" machine, it is indicated, is developing in new work on the cruiser type of seacraft.

The construction of four submarines of types advanced beyond those now building.

In addition, there was under plan a conversion in an unidentified way of a carrier and two submarines.

Secretary Sullivan told the committee that the Kentucky and the Hawaii would not have to stand by for the development of new weapons. It is planned, he disclosed, that they be converted into guided missile ships. Apparently to allay fears in Congress that larger aircraft carriers make easier targets for enemy bombers, Mr. Sullivan drew upon experience in the second World War and the results of atom-bomb tests at Bikini.

Speed Held Bomb Defense

"The experiments at Bikini," Mr. Sullivan said, "have proved that a fast-moving fleet is an unprofitable target for an atomic bomb."

Members of the committee interpreted this as a Navy Department conclusion that even though a potential enemy might acquire the atomic bomb, the revised construction program proposed today promised a maximum of safety. Mr. Sullivan recalled that the Navy lost three large and two light carriers in the Pacific, but none was sunk by aircraft land-based. He indicated that mobility of a fleet, equipped to latest model, would discourage the spending of atomic bombs, even if an enemy had some.

Today, the Senate Republican

Continued on Page 7, Column 4

Heaviest Trading in 8 Years Marks Stock Market Spurt

3,840,000 Shares Change Hands as Wave of Bullish Enthusiasm Increases Securities 1 to 7 Points

The hectic days of the Nineteen Twenties were re-enacted yesterday on the floor of the New York Stock Exchange when the most turbulent session in recent years produced increases of 1 to 7 points in the share list. Accompanied by a burst of bullish enthusiasm not witnessed in almost a decade, the deluge of buying orders so taxed the facilities of the Exchange that the reporting ticker tape lagged behind floor transactions by five minutes.

The cracking of the 1947 high level at the approach of mid-day served as the signal for a buying rush. Public participation suddenly increased and buying orders pressed floor traders to the utmost. This condition existed for forty-five minutes in the final hour when 1,350,000 shares were traded.

Accompanied by the broadest market on record with a total of 1,151 issues dealt in, volume on the Stock Exchange spiraled to 3,840,000 shares, the largest since May 21, 1940, in contrast to the Thursday turnover of 2,030,000 shares.

Brokers termed it the "wildest" bull market in twenty years on the premise that at no time in the interval had the industrials and rails advanced with such a unity of force.

While the ground had been well laid for a movement of such scope earlier this week, it was the piercing of the 1947 resistance point that confirmed the presence of a bull market to those who act by the charts, or averages. Early in the day, telegrams were sent by several advisory services to their clients urging the purchase of securities. The response to this advice showed primarily in the late

Continued on Page 23, Column 4

AIR ATTACK OPENS

Planes Cause Fires at Port—Defense Fliers Go Into Action

BORDER IS BREACHED

Cairo Vanguard Takes Colony—Trans-Jordan Reports a Movement

By The Associated Press.

TEL AVIV, Palestine, Saturday, May 15—Air raiders bombed this all-Jewish city at about dawn today.

First reports said there were "some casualties" near the power and light station.

[Cairo reported that Egyptian armed forces had been ordered to enter Palestine. Arab armies moved from Trans-Jordan at 12:01 A. M. Saturday to "liberate the Holy Land from Zionism," said a Trans-Jordan communiqué reported by The United Press from Amman.]

Tel Aviv was under complete blackout all night but no sirens were sounded during the raid. Civil guards were alerted and fifteen to twenty ships in the port area moved out to sea.

The planes swooped over Tel Aviv little more than twelve hours after Jewish leaders proclaimed the existence of a new Hebrew state of Israel.

Some bombs fell in the vicinity of the power station along the Yarkum River near Tel Aviv.

Persons at the scene said there was one hit on or near the power station, causing "some casualties."

TEL AVIV, Saturday, May 15 (UP)—Some ten bombs were dropped on Tel Aviv by two aircraft described as bombers and accompanied by two small fighters. One Jew was killed and three were hospitalized. Jewish Army aircraft took to the skies a few minutes after the enemy planes whizzed over rooftops at an estimated altitude of 300 feet.

Several fires could be seen north

Continued on Page 2, Column 3

U. S. MOVES QUICKLY

President Acknowledges de Facto Authority of Israel Immediately

TRUCE AIM STRESSED

Soviet Gesture to New Nation Anticipated—Others Due to Act

By BERTRAM D. HULEN
Special to THE NEW YORK TIMES.

WASHINGTON, May 14—President Truman announced early tonight recognition by the United States of the new Jewish State of Israel. The President acted instantly upon being informed that the new nation had been proclaimed.

"This Government," he announced, "has been informed that a Jewish state has been proclaimed in Palestine and recognition has been requested by the provisional government thereof.

"The United States recognizes the provisional government as the de facto authority of the new State of Israel."

These two paragraphs constituted the text of the President's statement.

Coupled with the announcement was an expression of hope for peace in Palestine. This was made known through a separate White House statement issued by Charles G. Ross, Presidential press secretary.

"The desire of the United States to obtain a truce in Palestine," this said, "will in no way be lessened by the proclamation of a Jewish state.

"We hope that the new Jewish state will join with the Security Council Truce Commission in redoubled efforts to bring an end to the fighting—which has been throughout the United Nations' consideration of Palestine a principal objective of this Government."

[Pending stabilization of the Palestine situation and indications that the State of Israel

Continued on Page 3, Column 2

AT HELM OF THE JEWISH STATE

David Ben-Gurion
Premier

Moshe Shertok
Foreign Minister
The New York Times

THE JEWS REJOICE

Some Weep as Quest for Statehood Ends —White Paper Dies

HELP OF U. N. ASKED

New Regime Holds Out Hand to Arabs—U. S. Gesture Acclaimed

Text of declaration setting up new Jewish state, Page 2.

By GENE CURRIVAN
Special to THE NEW YORK TIMES.

TEL AVIV, Palestine, Saturday, May 15—The Jewish state, the world's newest sovereignty, to be known as the State of Israel, came into being in Palestine at midnight upon termination of the British mandate.

Recognition of the state by the United States, which had opposed its establishment at this time, came as a complete surprise to the people, who were tense and ready for the threatened invasion by Arab forces and appealed for help by the United Nations.

In one of the most hopeful periods of their troubled history the Jewish people here gave a sigh of relief and took a new hold on life when they learned that the greatest national power had accepted them into the international fraternity.

Ceremony Simple and Solemn

The declaration of the new state by David Ben-Gurion, chairman of the National Council and the first Premier of reborn Israel, was delivered during a simple and solemn ceremony at 4 P. M., and new life was instilled into his people, but from without there was the rumbling of guns, a flashback to other declarations of independence that had not been easily achieved.

The first action of the new Government was to revoke the Palestine White Paper of 1939, which restricted Jewish immigration and land purchase.

In the proclamation of the new state the Government appealed to the United Nations "to assist the Jewish people in the building of its state and to admit Israel into the family of nations."

The proclamation added:

"We offer peace and amity to all neighboring states and their peoples, and invite them to cooperate with the independent Jewish nation for the common good of all. The State of Israel is ready to contribute its full share to the peaceful progress and reconstitution of the Middle East."

World Jews Asked to Aid

The statement appealed to Jews throughout the world to assist in the task of immigration and development and in the "struggle for the fulfillment of the dream of generations—the redemption of Israel."

Plans for the ceremony had been laid with great secrecy. None but the hundred or more invited guests and journalists was aware of the meeting until it started, and even the guests learned of the site only ten minutes before. It was held in the Tel Aviv Museum of Art, a white, modern-design two-story building. Above it flew the Star of David, which is the state's flag, and below, on the sidewalk, was a guard of honor of the Haganah, the army of the Jewish Agency for Palestine.

As photographers' bulbs flashed and movie cameras ground out reels of the scene, great crowds gathered and cheered the Ministers and other members of the Government as they entered the building. The security arrangements were perfect. Sten guns were brandished in every direction and even the roofs bristled with them.

The setting for the reading of the proclamation was a dropped gallery whose hall held paintings by prominent Jewish artists. Many of them depicted the suffering and joys of the people of the Diaspora, the dispersal of the Jews.

The thirteen Ministers of the

Continued on Page 2, Column 6

Truman Sees His Election; Calls GOP 'Obstructionist'

By ANTHONY LEVIERO
Special to THE NEW YORK TIMES.

WASHINGTON, May 14—President Truman asserted tonight that there would be a Democrat in the White House during the next four years and that he would be the man. He made the statement to a cheering audience of 1,000 young Democrats at their meeting here.

The President's speech was a fighting one in the new Truman manner. He spoke extemporaneously, resorting to whimsy and irony and using forceful gestures of his arms to underscore his points.

Mr. Truman accused the Republican party of stealing Democratic platform planks. "You know," he said, "it has been their habit since 1936 of taking a few planks out of the old Democratic platforms and building a platform and then saying, 'Me, too.'"

[*The text of President Truman's speech is on Page 7.*]

"What have the Republicans done in the last fifteen and a half years?" Mr. Truman asked, then said:

"They have been obstructionists. They spent most of their time while I was in the Senate—and I was there for ten years—in obstructing progressive legislation that was for the welfare of the common man, and throwing bricks and mud at the greatest President that ever sat in the White House."

Mr. Truman was interrupted by applause at this obvious allusion to President Roosevelt.

"That has been their record," he continued, "and they haven't changed a bit. They were against Social Security. They were against TVA. They were against wages

Continued on Page 7, Column 2

MINNESOTA'S GUARD OUT IN MEAT STRIKE

Governor Acts After 200 Raid Cudahy Newport Plant, Attack 60 Workers and Abduct 25

Special to THE NEW YORK TIMES.

ST. PAUL, Minn., May 14—National Guard troops were ordered to South St. Paul and Newport, towns on opposite banks of the Mississippi River near here, by Governor Luther Youngdahl today following violent disorders at strike-bound packing plants in the area and the statement of the local sheriffs that their forces could not maintain law and order.

The Governor did not proclaim martial law but said the troops would take their orders from the civil authorities.

The Governor's action followed a serious outbreak at the Cudahy packing plant in Newport shortly before last midnight in which a group of about 200 men raided the plant with clubs, knives and hammers. In South St. Paul on Thursday strikers forced back police who tried to open a way through picket lines at the Swift & Co. plant at

Continued on Page 16, Column 3

Princess Elizabeth, in Paris Talk, Asks Common Effort of 2 Nations

By LANSING WARREN
Special to THE NEW YORK TIMES.

PARIS, May 14—Speaking in faultless French with just the touch of a British accent to delight French ears, Princess Elizabeth today asked France and Britain to make a common effort to lead Europe to moral and intellectual as well as economic reconstruction.

Her well-worded and discerning speech was cheered, but she went straight to the hearts of the Parisian throng when, with disarming frankness, she avowed her joy that her first foreign trip since her marriage had brought her here to Paris.

"For a long time," she said, "I have wanted to come to France. More fortunate than I, my husband already knew your admirable capital and he is all the happier to return. This trip is all the more important and agreeable for the warmth of your welcome which has touched us both."

From the time they stepped down from the train at the Gare du Nord early today, Princess Elizabeth and Prince Philip, Duke of Edinburgh, were the center of admiring attention from the throngs that lined the streets and from all the French officials who received them throughout the day.

President Vincent Auriol voiced the general feeling when in a statement issued tonight he said:

"I have been personally struck by her grace, her charm, her modesty and her nobility. I feel sure that the sentiments that she has expressed went straight to the hearts of all the French."

Elizabeth's address, broadcast to the French nation, was delivered from the top of the monumental entry to the Galliera Museum, where she came to open the British Government's exhibition of relics and souvenirs of famous Brit-

Continued on Page 6, Column 3

World News Summarized

SATURDAY, MAY 15, 1948

Several hours after the state of Israel, the first Hebrew nation in 2,000 years, had been proclaimed in a Zionist declaration of independence in Tel Aviv, [1:8.], President Truman announced that the United States recognized the "provisional government" of Israel as "the de facto authority of the new state." A second White House statement expressed the hope that the new regime would cooperate with United Nations efforts to bring about peace in Palestine. [1:5.] The British High Commissioner departed from Palestine and boarded a cruiser at Haifa as Britain's rule over the Holy Land formally ended. [1:7.]

The special session of the United Nations General Assembly ended last night after it had agreed to send a mediator to Palestine to try to arrange a truce. [1:6-7.] The trusteeship plan for Jerusalem sponsored by the United States was rejected by the Assembly, with the Arab states and the Soviet opposed to the measure. [1:6-7.]

Tel Aviv was bombed at dawn. Egypt ordered her troops to invade Palestine. Trans-Jordan reported her army on the move also. [1:4.] Haganah claimed that its forces captured Acre in the north. [2:8.]

Moscow the newspaper Pravda, in the first editorial comment on the recent exchange between Washington and Moscow, accused the United States of double-dealing. [4:8.]

Paris crowds gave an enthusiastic welcome to Princess Elizabeth and the Duke of Edinburgh when they arrived for a visit. [1:2-3.]

Congress received a request from the Navy for authority to shift the emphasis in its construction of fighting craft to guided-missile vessels. [1:1.]

President Truman predicted that he would be re-elected next November. [1:2-3.]

Minnesota National Guard troops were rushed to South St. Paul and Newport after 200 persons had raided the Cudahy meat packing plant at Newport, where a strike is in progress, attacking about sixty workers and abducting twenty-five of them. [1:2.]

The New York Stock Exchange enjoyed one of its biggest days in recent years as an avalanche of buying orders sent stocks up from 1 to 7 points. Trading reached a total of 3,840,000 shares, the largest since May 21, 1940. [1:2-3.]

Winston Churchill's War Memoirs

See Page 17 for today's installment, in which Mr. Churchill describes the invasion of Norway and the clash of the British and German fleets.

U. N. Votes for a Mediator; Special Assembly Is Ended

By THOMAS J. HAMILTON

After hearing both the Soviet Union and the Arab delegates denounce the United States for its sudden recognition of the new Jewish state in Palestine, the United Nations General Assembly decided last night to send a Mediator to the Holy Land to do what he could to arrange a truce and carry on public services.

The vote was 31 to 7, with sixteen abstentions and four delegates absent, and the General Assembly, which was called into special session at Flushing Meadow on April 16 at the request of the United States, adjourned for good at 8:32 P. M.

The failure of the General Assembly either to repeal the partition resolution of last November or to provide military force to keep the peace means that the fate of Palestine will be decided by the impending war between Jews and Arabs, not by any United Nations action.

The mediation resolution conforms substantially with a United States proposal announced last Wednesday, after it had become obvious that the General Assembly would not accept the original United States plan for a temporary trusteeship.

However, the General Assembly refused to accept a United States plan for a temporary trusteeship over Jerusalem, which was rejected earlier in the evening by a vote of 20 to 15, less than the necessary two-thirds majority.

Two other proposals regarding Jerusalem were rejected, but presumably the provisions of the partition resolution on Jerusalem, which was to have been established as an international enclave under the administration of the Trusteeship Council, still stand.

In addition, the Assembly de-

Continued on Page 4, Column 4

CUNNINGHAM GOES AS MANDATE ENDS

British Commissioner Boards Cruiser Off Haifa—Jews Take Down Union Jack

By The Associated Press.

HAIFA, Palestine, Saturday, May 15—Britain ended her mandate over the Holy Land last midnight. Lieut. Gen. Sir Alan Cunningham, the last British High Commissioner, sailed from Haifa port, finishing British mandate guidance.

Sir Alan's departure from Palestine's richest port caused little excitement among the Jews, who control most of the city.

The British fired a few rockets and searchlights spotlighted the cruiser as it steamed from the harbor.

Wearing the uniform of a British Army general, Sir Alan walked down a few steps of dock into a launch that took him to the cruiser Euryalus.

Upon getting into the launch, he turned and looked soberly up across the docks. There stood an honor guard of the King's Company of Grenadier Guards and Royal Marine commandos.

The launch pulled away amid the

Continued on Page 2, Column 7

U. N. Bars Jerusalem Trusteeship; Vote Follows Mandate Deadline

By MALLORY BROWNE

The United Nations General Assembly rejected yesterday the United States plan for a temporary trusteeship regime in Jerusalem.

Solidly opposed by the Arab States and the Russian bloc, the plan to set up a United Nations Commissioner authorized to protect the Holy City and its holy places failed to obtain the necessary two-thirds majority at the closing session at Flushing Meadow.

The vote, which came just after the bombshell of the United States recognition of the new Jewish State had burst in the Assembly, was 20 in favor, 15 against and 19 abstentions. The balance was turned by the hostility of Britain and most of the Dominions.

The United States fought hard all day, first in the Political and Security Committee of the Assembly, sitting at Lake Success, and then in the evening session of the Assembly, to get the trusteeship plan adopted before the end of the mandate at 6:01 P. M., New York time.

An Arab filibuster, aided by the Soviet bloc, defeated this effort. It was well past the zero hour when a roll-call vote showed that the Assembly preferred to leave Harold Evans, newly appointed Jerusalem municipal Commissioner, in sole charge of the Holy City and its treasures.

As one Arab after another filed up to the tribune and took up the maximum five-minute period allowed in repeating the arguments against a trusteeship plan, 6:01 o'clock went by.

At once Awni Khalidy of Iraq, who had led the Arab fight against the trusteeship plan, rushed up to the tribune and exultantly proclaimed that the time had passed; that the mandate was at an end, and that, since, as Francis B. Sayre, of the United States had said, the measure must

Continued on Page 3, Column 5

BRITAIN IS ALOOF TO THE NEW STATE

Recognition Awaits Stabilizing in Palestine—Payment on Sterling Balance Halted

By CLIFTON DANIEL

Special to THE NEW YORK TIMES.

LONDON, May 14—With obvious relief, Britain turned her back on Palestine today. From now until the final withdrawal of troops on Aug. 1, A. V. Alexander, Minister of Defense, told the House of Commons, Britain's main consideration in Palestine will be the safe and speedy evacuation of her troops.

Mr. Alexander assured the House that British forces in Palestine were sufficiently strong for the task and that if not they would be increased.

Only one hour was given by the House to the last Palestine debate during the British administration of the country. Not a word was said about Britain's attitude toward the new situation in the Holy Land.

Despite the United States' decision to recognize the Jewish state, there seemed to be no question of extending British recognition until the new country proved its authority and stabilized its frontiers. Britain was deterred partly by the attitude of the Arab states, with which she hopes to restore cordial relations.

The absence of any statement on Britain's intentions implied that nothing would be done to oppose the establishment of the Jewish state but that the British would not interfere with the Arab armies that proposed to invade Palestine.

Free Immigration Seen

So far as the British are concerned, Jewish immigration into Palestine will now be entirely free for the first time since General Allenby arrived in 1917 to open the gates. Mr. Alexander made only one proviso: that the immigrants should not pass through the British evacuation port of Haifa.

While falling back upon a policy of default, Britain has not yet extricated herself entirely from the Palestine problem. British arms are still flowing to three or four of the Arab states that are mounting an invasion of Palestine. British officers are still commanding Trans-Jordan's Arab Legion and training the Saudi Arabian Army.

Undisclosed thousands of British troops are still in the Holy Land, trying to rescue military supplies worth tens of millions of pounds. Major British commercial interests, the largest being the oil refinery in Haifa, must be salvaged. Britain owes Palestine money, about £100,000,000, [$400,000,000] in blocked sterling accounts in London that belong mainly to citizens of the new Jewish state.

Releases from blocked accounts have been made to finance food purchases for the next few weeks, but the British Treasury announced today that no further fixed amounts could be unblocked because there was no effective central exchange control in Palestine. The Treasury announcement added that permanent arrangements could be considered "as soon as circumstances render this practicable," in other words, when the Jewish state showed itself capable, responsible and stable.

Zionist Lauds Britain

The new state has made its first gesture of friendliness and gratitude to Britain. Berl Locker, a member of the Executive of the Jewish Agency for Palestine, said at a press conference, "the historic moment which has now arrived is due to historic names in the British Commonwealth, namely Lord Shaftesbury, Disraeli and Winston Churchill, and the Holy Land will never forget the good turns that have been done for it by Britain."

Arabs in London had no kind words for Britain. An Arab Office declaration charged that the Palestine tragedy had been created by the British mandate and "by Britain's obstinate attempts to carry out for thirty years the disastrous policy laid down in it."

The Times of London will say tomorrow that the British "share deeply in the sorrow and regret at this failure of a great mission."

Today ordinary Britons, who were enjoying the first holiday of the spring, the long Whitsun weekend, scarcely seemed to notice that the British sphere of dominion had been contracted by 10,429 more square miles and that British troops were withdrawing from a key base of the Eastern Mediterranean on the line of empire.

Newspaper headlines were devoted to matters of more general public interest. Only about thirty members appeared on the benches of the House of Commons. None of the great statesmen were there.

Aid to Trans-Jordan Goes On

LONDON, May 14 (Reuters)—Britain will continue her payments to the Arab Legion under the terms of the treaty with Trans-Jordan, a Foreign Office spokesman said today. The Legion receives an annual British subsidy of £2,000,000 [$8,000,000].

NEW CITIZENS TO HAVE DAY

Mayor, Broadway Stars, to Join in 'I Am An American' Fete

Mayor O'Dwyer will be the chief speaker at tomorrow's observance of "I Am An American Day," in Central Park, at which thousands of persons who became citizens during the year will take the oath of allegiance.

One thousand two hundred policemen have been assigned to the event, which is scheduled to start at 2:30 P. M. One hundred consular officials representing forty-three countries are expected to be present, in addition to United Nations representatives from twenty-three nations. Russia, although invited, will not be represented, the committee said.

Talent from Broadway hit shows will take part in the entertainment. The chairman for the day is John A. Coleman and the masters of ceremonies for the entertainment portion are Eddie Dowling and Harry Hershfield.

Proclamation of the New Jewish State

TEL AVIV, Palestine, May 14 (AP)—Following is the text of the Declaration of Independence of the Jewish state:

The land of Israel was the birthplace of the Jewish People.

Here their spiritual, religious and national identity was formed. Here they achieved independence and created a culture of national and universal significance. Here they wrote and gave the Bible to the world.

Exiled from Palestine, the Jewish people remained faithful to it in all the countries of their dispersion, never ceasing to pray and hope for their return and restoration of their national freedom.

Impelled by this historic association, Jews strove throughout the centuries to go back to the land of their fathers and regain statehood. In recent decades they returned in their masses. They reclaimed a wilderness, revived their language, built cities and villages and established a vigorous and ever growing community, with its own economic and cultural life. They sought peace, yet were ever prepared to defend themselves. They brought blessings of progress to all inhabitants of the country.

In the year 1897 the First Zionist Congress, inspired by Theodor Herzl's vision of a Jewish state, proclaimed the right of the Jewish people to a national revival in their own country.

Balfour Declaration Cited

This right was acknowledged by the Balfour Declaration of Nov. 2, 1917, and reaffirmed by the Mandate of the League of Nations, which gave explicit international recognition to the historic connection of the Jewish people with Palestine and their right to reconstitute their national home.

The Nazi holocaust which engulfed millions of Jews in Europe proved anew the urgency of the re-establishment of the Jewish state, which would solve the problem of Jewish homelessness by opening the gates to all Jews and lifting the Jewish people to equality in the family of nations.

Survivors of the European catastrophe, as well as Jews from other lands, claiming their right to a life of dignity, freedom and labor, and undeterred by hazards, hardships and obstacles, have tried unceasingly to enter Palestine.

In the second World War, the Jewish people in Palestine made a full contribution in the struggle of freedom-loving nations against the Nazi evil. The sacrifices of their soldiers and efforts of their workers gained them title to rank with the people who founded the United Nations. On Nov. 29, 1947, the General Assembly of the United Nations adopted a resolution for re-establishment of an independent Jewish state in Palestine and called upon inhabitants of the country to take such steps as may be necessary on their part to put the plan into effect.

This recognition by the United Nations of the right of the Jewish people to establish their independent state may not be revoked. It is, moreover, the self-evident right of the Jewish people to be a nation, as all other nations, in its own sovereign state.

Accordingly we, the members of the National Council, representing the Jewish people in Palestine and the Zionist movement of the world, met together in solemn assembly by virtue of the natural and historic right of Jewish people and of resolution of the General Assembly of the United Nations, hereby proclaim the establishment of the Jewish state in Palestine, to be called Israel.

We hereby declare that as from the termination of the mandate at midnight this night of the 14th to 15th of May, 1948, and until the setting up of duly elected bodies of the state in accordance with a Constitution to be drawn up by a Constituent Assembly not later than the first day of October, 1948, the present National Council shall act as the Provisional State Council and its executive organ, the National Administration, shall constitute the Provisional Government of the State of Israel.

Equality to All Promised

The State of Israel will promote the development of the country for the benefit of all its inhabitants; will be based on precepts of liberty, justice and peace taught by the Hebrew prophets; will uphold the full social and political equality of all its citizens without distinction of race, creed or sex; will guarantee full freedom of conscience, worship, education and culture; will safeguard the sanctity and inviolability of shrines and holy places of all religions; and will dedicate itself to the principles of the Charter of the United Nations.

The State of Israel will be ready to cooperate with the organs and representatives of the United Nations in the implementations of the resolution of Nov. 29, 1947, and will take steps to bring about an economic union over the whole of Palestine.

We appeal to the United Nations to assist the Jewish people in the building of its state and to admit Israel into the family of nations.

In the midst of wanton aggression we call upon the Arab inhabitants of the State of Israel to return to the ways of peace and play their part in the development of the state, with full and equal citizenship and due representation in all its bodies and institutions, provisional or permanent.

We offer peace and amity to all neighboring states and their peoples, and invite them to cooperate with the independent Jewish nation for the common good of all. The State of Israel is ready to contribute its full share to the peaceful progress and reconstitution of the Middle East.

Our call goes out to the Jewish people all over the world to rally to our side in the task of immigration and development and to stand by us in the great struggle for the fulfilment of the dream of generations—the redemption of Israel.

ZIONISTS PROCLAIM A SOVEREIGN STATE

Continued From Page 1

Government Council sat at a long dais beneath the photograph of Theodor Herzl, who in 1897 envisaged a Jewish state. Vertical pale blue and white flags of the state hung on both sides. To the left of the ministers and below them sat other members of the national administration. There are thirty-seven in all, but some were unable to get here from Jerusalem.

At 4 P. M. sharp the assemblage rose and sang the Hatikvah, the national anthem. The participants seemed to sing with unusual gusto and inspiration. The voices had hardly subsided when the squat, white-haired chairman, Mr. Ben-Gurion, started to read the proclamation, which in a few hours was to transform most of those present from persons without a country to proud nationals. When he pronounced the words "We hereby proclaim the establishment of the Jewish state in Palestine, to be called Israel," there was thunderous applause and not a few damp eyes.

After the proclamation had been read and the end of the White Paper and of its land laws pronounced, Mr. Ben-Gurion signed the document and was followed by all the other members of the administration, some by proxy. The last to sign was Moshe Shertok, the new Foreign Minister and the Jewish Agency's delegate to the United Nations. He was roundly applauded and almost mobbed by photographers.

The ceremony ended with everyone standing silently while the orchestral strains of the Hatikvah filled the room. Outside, the fever of nationalism was spreading with fond embraces, warm handshakes and kisses. Street vendors were selling flags, crowds gathered to read posted bulletins, and newspapers were being sold everywhere.

As the sabbath had started, there was not the degree of public rejoicing that there would have been any other day.

The proclamation was to have been read at 11 P. M. but was advanced to 4 because of the sabbath. Mr. Shertok explained that the proclamation had to be made yesterday because the mandate was to end at midnight and the Zionists did not want a split second to intervene between that time and the formal establishment of the state.

In the preamble to the declaration of independence the history of the Jewish people was traced briefly from its birth in the Land of Israel to this day. The preamble touched on the more modern highlights, including Herzl's vision of a state, acknowledgment of the Jewish national homeland by the Balfour Declaration in 1917 and its reaffirmation by the League of Nations mandate and by the United Nations General Assembly resolution of Nov. 29, 1947.

It asserted that this recognition by the United Nations of the right of the Jewish people to establish an independent state could not be revoked and added that it was the "self-evident right of the Jewish people to be a nation, as all other nations, in its own sovereign state."

The proclamation stated that as of midnight the National Council would act as a Provisional State Council and that its executive organ, the National Administration, would constitute a provisional government until elected bodies could be set up before Oct. 1.

Israel, the proclamation went on, will be open to immigration by Jews from all countries "of their dispersion." She will develop the country for the benefit of all its inhabitants, it added, and will be based on precepts of liberty, justice and peace taught by the Hebrew prophets.

The new state, according to the proclamation, will uphold the "social and political equality of all its citizens without distinction of race, creed or sex" and "will guarantee full freedom of conscience, worship, education and culture."

The statement pledged safeguarding of the sanctity and inviolability of shrines and holy places of all religions. It also contained a promise to uphold the principles of the United Nations.

There was great cheering and drinking of toasts in this blacked-out city when word was received that the United States had recognized the provincial Government. The effect on the people, especially those drinking late in Tel Aviv's coffee houses, was electric. They even ran into the blackness of the streets shouting, cheering and toasting the United States.

NEWS FROM TEL AVIV CENSORED FOR A DAY

TEL AVIV, Palestine, May 14 (AP)—A secret censorship was imposed for twenty-four hours, ending at noon today, on dispatches of foreign correspondents in Tel Aviv.

Correspondents were not notified in advance that officials of the Jewish state, which then was not officially in existence, had imposed security restrictions. They were not told that changes had been made in their copy or what the changes were.

After the censorship had been lifted, correspondents who investigated learned that all sentences in their dispatches referring to the date, time or place of declaration of Jewish independence had been deleted.

This was done on "orders of the National Council," the new Jewish Cabinet, by a censor in the Tel Aviv postoffice, who inked out the sentences.

At midnight last night, when censorship had been in effect for several hours, public relations officials told newsmen that they had no knowledge of it.

Public relations officers and the chief Jewish censor said today that their failure to notify correspondents of the censorship was an unintentional error and that they had no intention of censoring dispatches in the future.

Briton Assails Czech Action

LONDON, May 14 (UP)—A Foreign Office spokesman said tonight that Czechoslovakia's denial of entry permits to four British correspondents to cover the approaching "single list" elections showed an eclipse of civil liberties.

THE STATE OF ISRAEL

The New York Times May 15, 1948

Although no boundaries were set by the Zionist leaders in their proclamation of independence, they recently declared that they controlled all the towns and villages in the area assigned to them by the partition resolution of the United Nations General Assembly (shown by shading).

BRITISH CHIEFTAIN LEAVES PALESTINE

Continued From Page 1

slap of hands on rifle butts. Puffs of smoke and the small, hollow explosions of a 17-gun salute drifted in to shore from the cruiser outside a breakwater.

Preceding Sir Alan into Haifa was Lieut. Gen. G. H. A. Macmillan, British commander.

As he arrived earlier at Haifa airport, Sir Alan took the salute of a picked fifty-man company of the Palestine police. Then he walked over toward his car, stopping to chat quietly and shake hands with Jewish Mayor Shabatai Levi and Arab Vice-Mayor Haj Ta Er Haraman of Haifa.

His route to the dock was guarded carefully. No crowds were along the way. It lay mainly through Arab quarters, most of whose population had fled a few weeks ago after the Jews had seized control of the majority of Haifa.

The dock area was lined by Comet tanks. Near the dock gates, 200 or 300 curious watched Sir Alan pass. Work stopped inside the harbor and in near-by offices and warehouses so that employes might witness the brief ceremony of his embarkation. About 100 yards away dockers loaded and unloaded ships.

Britain has ruled Palestine since she took it from the Turks in 1917. She has held the mandate, granted by the League of Nations, since 1923.

The first fruits of the Jews' blood struggle—200 Jewish women and children refugees—arrived in Haifa from the Lebanese border about the time the mandate ended.

They huddled on the dark sidewalk outside the dock waiting for Jewish Welfare Committee buses to take them to shelter. They came from Chaneta, Mazuoa and Hilom. They were brought overland from those frontier settlements to Nahariya, a German-Jewish settlement on the coast, and then by tug and lighter into Haifa port.

They said the border was quiet now, but they had been under attack previously.

The end of the mandate also halted the British sea patrol against ships carrying unauthorized Jewish immigrants to Palestine. Jewish sources said it was expected immigration ships would begin to arrive soon. The Jewish Agency also is negotiating for the transfer of about 30,000 Jews, held in Cyprus detention camps since they were captured while trying to enter the Holy Land without visas.

Union Jack Is Taken Down

By DANA ADAMS SCHMIDT

Special to THE NEW YORK TIMES.

JERUSALEM, May 14—As Britain's last high commissioner in Palestine left Jerusalem today the Union Jack over Government House was hauled down and a Red Cross hoisted. A solitary bag-piper skirled the Highland lament as Sir Alan walked out of the official residence on Mount Zion for the last time.

Seventy-five minutes earlier the flag of the International Red Cross had replaced the Union Jack over the British Government's offices in King David Hotel, thereby making the building part of "neutral security area for refugees."

Sir Alan left behind "no successor authority" but an independent Jewish state whose army the Haganah had occupied Haifa, Jaffa, Tiberias, Safad, Beisan and countless villages. The Arab parts of Palestine are in chaos. Two hundred thousand Arabs have fled from their homes.

Sir Alan addressed the people of Palestine over the radio last night. "I have never believed that a seed of agreement between Jew and Arab does not exist," he said. "I am convinced that a solution to this problem is not to be reached through bullets or bombs * * * If unhappily conflict must come, there is yet time to insulate the Holy City from it. * * * Let peace for the Holy Land, which certainly must come, have its source in the Holy City to flow therefrom over the whole country."

Both Jews and Arabs agreed that Sir Alan was a man of good intent. But they also agreed that the British had failed in the function to which they devoted their greatest energy for twenty-eight years—that of police power. During the last five and one-half months of Sir Alan's administration about 3,000 Jews, Arabs and Britons have been killed and about 5,000 injured.

HAGANAH REPORTS CAPTURE OF ACRE

Takes Vital City Near Haifa—Wins Heart of Jerusalem, Battles for Bab el Wad

TEL AVIV, Palestine, May 14 (UP)—The Haganah said tonight that its forces had captured the strategic North Palestine port city of Acre.

A city of 8,000 inhabitants and one of the oldest in Palestine, Acre is the chief link between Haifa and the Lebanese border. It was earmarked for the Arabs under the United Nations partition plan.

Haganah said the port was taken almost without resistance. Jewish forces were said to have occupied a height east of the city, but a security blackout blanked details of the operation.

A United Press dispatch from Haifa and Arab sources in Beirut, Lebanon, reported the Jewish capture of Ez Zib and El Bassa, two small towns between Acre and the Lebanese border.

[Sumaria, in the same region, was also reported captured.]

The Irgun Zvai Leumi organization asserted today that it had taken five Arab villages in the northern triangle that the United Nations partition plan had earmarked for the Arabs.

Jews Gain in Jerusalem

Dispatch of The Times, London.

JERUSALEM, Saturday, May 15—As soon as the British Army and police left North Jerusalem firing started and increased steadily. The Jews began to take the central zone of the city, including police headquarters, as far as Barclay's Bank in Allenby Square. They also hoisted the Zionist flag on the tower of the old Italian hospital and the city is now cut in two along the road from Damascus Gate to Princess Mary Avenue.

Heavy firing also broke out between the Damascus gate and the Sheikh Jarrah quarter.

Bab el Wad Battle Rages

TEL AVIV, Palestine, May 14 (AP)—The Haganah, Zionist Army, was locked in a bitter battle today with the major strength of the Arab volunteer army at the Bab el Wad gorge, ten miles west of Jerusalem. Control of the Jerusalem-Tel Aviv Highway was at stake.

Other Haganah units were rushing to reinforce positions defending the Jewish state on the north, west and south. These Jewish troops, freed from siege duty by the surrender of the Arab port of Jaffa, were being transported to their new posts by buses withdrawn from normal runs.

The Arabs scored their first real victory in the Palestine fighting in the last hours preceding Jewish nationhood. Arab, Jewish and neutral sources said troops of Trans-Jordan's Arab Legion, supported by 2,000 tribesmen from the Hebron hills, had wiped out four Jewish colonies in the Kfar Etzion bloc, twenty miles south of Jerusalem. The colonies were athwart the Arab invasion route from the south.

According to the informants, 200 Jews died in the two-day battle that ended Thursday night. A number of prisoners were taken, including four physicians who were parachuted to aid the wounded. The Jewish Agency for Palestine declared the Arabs had killed prisoners of war despite promises of adherence to international law.

WEIZMANN APPEALED FOR TRUMAN ACTION

Dr. Chaim Weizmann, who is expected to be the first President of the State of Israel, appealed directly at noon yesterday to President Truman for recognition of the new Jewish nation.

In a letter delivered at the White House at that time, the elderly Zionist leader praised Mr. Truman's work on behalf of the Jewish state and asked the "greatest" democracy to be the first to welcome "the newest democracy" into the family of nations. The letter was made public at the United Nations session at Flushing Meadow after the announcement that the United States had recognized Israel.

Several times in his letter Dr. Weizmann paid tribute to the President's record in relation to the Zionist cause.

"The unhappy events of the last few months will not, I hope, obscure the very great contribution that you, Mr. President, have made toward a definitive and just settlement of the long and troublesome Palestine question," Dr. Weizmann said.

B'nai B'rith announced yesterday from Washington that the president of the organization, Frank Goldman, had urged President Truman to recognize the new Jewish state because "historic bonds of democratic ideals and traditions unite the new state to the United States."

RENTS STAY CONTROLLED

Westchester Plea for Higher Summer Rates Denied

WASHINGTON, May 14 (AP)—Housing Expediter Tighe E. Woods refused today to remove rent controls from furnished homes in Westchester County, N. Y., which are rented only on a seasonal basis during the summer.

Mr. Woods said he turned down the recommendation of the Westchester Rent Advisory Board because of lack of evidence that needs for such rental housing had been met.

Special to THE NEW YORK TIMES.

WHITE PLAINS, N. Y., May 14—Joseph E. Kelly, area rent director in Westchester County, said the Rent Advisory Board here had petitioned the Federal Housing Expediter in March to decontrol rents on Westchester homes offered for summer rental. He said the board believed such rentals fell in a luxury class, caused no displacements and that persons coming from New York City to rent houses could "take or leave" the rents asked without hardship.

TEL AVIV BOMBED; EGYPTIANS MARCH

Continued From Page 1

of Tel Aviv but damage was believed negligible.

Anti-aircraft guns opened up throughout the port area and in Sarona, the Tel Aviv suburb that is the new capital of Israel.

The bombing planes, which disappeared toward the sea after the raid, were believed too small for Egyptian aircraft.

Cairo Orders Invasion Action

Dispatch of The Times, London.

CAIRO, Saturday, May 15—Egyptian armed forces have been ordered to enter Palestine, the Egyptian Government announced in a communiqué issued last midnight.

The communiqué said that their object was the "restoring of security and order in that country and putting an end to the massacres perpetrated by terrorist gangs against the Arabs and against humanity."

[Immediately after the announcement of the communiqué over the official radio, Sheikh Mohamed Mamoun el-Shennawy, rector of Al Azhar University and chief of the Moslem Theological Institute, said, according to The United Press: "The hour for jihad (holy war) has struck."]

Martial law came into force in Egypt at midnight. Premier Mahmoud Fahmy Nokrashy Pasha was named military governor.

Censorship became effective immediately on mail, newspapers, photographs and parcels entering or leaving Egypt as well as on broadcasts, phonograph records and plays.

Captains of merchant ships were warned in a proclamation that their vessels were liable to be searched in Egyptian ports.

[On the fighting front the Haganah reported the capture of Acre, near Haifa.

[At the same time Jewish and Arab forces were locked in battle at Bab el Wad, vital point on the Jerusalem-Tel Aviv highway.]

Lewa [Brigadier] Ahmed Mohamed Aly el-Hawary Bey is Egyptian Commander in Chief on the southern front. According to the pro-government newspaper Al Assas, the order to advance into Palestine was given yesterday at dawn and Egyptian columns have occupied El Auja, which is inside the Palestine border about thirty miles south of Rafah. Brigadier el-Hawary is a 50-year-old staff officer who graduated from the Royal Military College in 1916. His staff consists of four officers.

Al Assas declares that Chief of Staff to King Abdullah of Trans-Jordan is the Egyptian officer Miralai [Colonel] Saad el-din Sabur Bey. His staff also includes Air Force officer Squadron Leader Mohamed Nazih Hashad, who studied flying and reconnaisance in Britain and the United States.

King Abdullah is to be supreme commander of the Arab forces on three fronts. The King will be advised by a war council on which the staffs of all the Arab armies will be represented. This staff will coordinate operations on all fronts.

The Arab Governments have come to an agreement that the Syrian and Lebanese Armies should operate under a unified command on the northern front. Iraqi and Trans-Jordan troops will be responsible for the eastern front, while Egyptian, Saudi Arabian and Yemenite forces will operate on the southern front. Saudi Arabian armored forces are also placed under Egyptian command, but the name of the Commander in Chief was not revealed.

Syrians, Lebanese Poised

CAIRO, Saturday, May 15 (AP)—Syrian and Lebanese troops also are poised on the northern border of the Holy Land apparently awaiting an invasion zero hour expected shortly after midnight, a Damascus dispatch said. A late report said Dan was under attack.

Earlier accounts from Syria said that troops of Iraq and Trans-Jordan were moving up to Palestine's western frontier. However, there was no sign of military preparation in Amman, the capital of Trans-Jordan's King Abdullah, who has announced his leadership of the threatened invasion of the Holy Land.

Irregular volunteers from the various Arab countries already are fighting inside Palestine.

Many units of Egypt's regular army have been reported massed in Sinai, on the southern frontier of Palestine, awaiting orders. Estimates of their number have ranged from 6,000 to 16,000.

A state of emergency has been declared in Syria. The Syrian Parliament is expected to declare martial law later and appoint Premier Jamil Mardam Bey as Military Governor.

Lebanon also declared a state of emergency and the Government said firm measures would be taken to safeguard security. Five hundred additional men were called up for police duty.

An official communiqué announced last night the imposition of martial law throughout Iraq.

Movements of the Egyptian Army were screened by a strict ban on civilian travel into the Sinai Peninsula.

Syrian armor and infantry moved southward from Saida on the Lebanese coast after traversing the outskirts of Beirut, Damascus dispatch said. Lebanese army units were deployed all along the Palestine frontier from Merjayoun to Naqura on the Mediterranean coast.

30,000 Trained Arabs Massed

CAIRO, Saturday, May 15 (UP)—Upwards of 30,000 trained Arab troops had massed on three frontiers of Palestine for an invasion, according to observers here.

It was expected that Egypt, Trans-Jordan and Iraq would provide nearly all the troops for the Palestine invasion. Syria was expected to send a modest force and Lebanon a token one. It was reported that little Yemen, and also Saudi-Arabia, would send some men to show Arab solidarity.

About 3,000 men of the Trans-Jordan Arab Legion had been on duty with the British Army in Palestine as police.

Some of these made what might be called a token withdrawal when British troops evacuated southern areas of Palestine. But they turned back again after crossing the Allenby Bridge over the Jordan. Many of them never even pretended to leave and those who had been in Trans-Jordan all along are reported in Palestine now.

A United Press Aman dispatch said that the bulk of the Legionnaires crossed the Jordan hills and disappeared into the Judean Hills with their artillery, armored cars and a few light tanks. They entered an Arab-earmarked area.

League Declares State of War

DAMASCUS, May 14 (AP)—The Arab League's General Secretariat proclaimed last night that a state of war exists between the Arab countries and Palestine Jewry.

Territorial Waters Closed

Navigation in Egyptian territorial waters in the area adjacent the Palestine border has been closed to navigation as of May 1, according to information received by the United States Navy Hydrographic Office from the United States Naval attaché in Cairo.

The prohibited area, which starts approximately 120 miles east of Port Said, Egypt, extends to the coastal town of Rafah on the Egypt-Palestine border.

ARAB ARMIES MOVE AGAINST JEWISH STATE

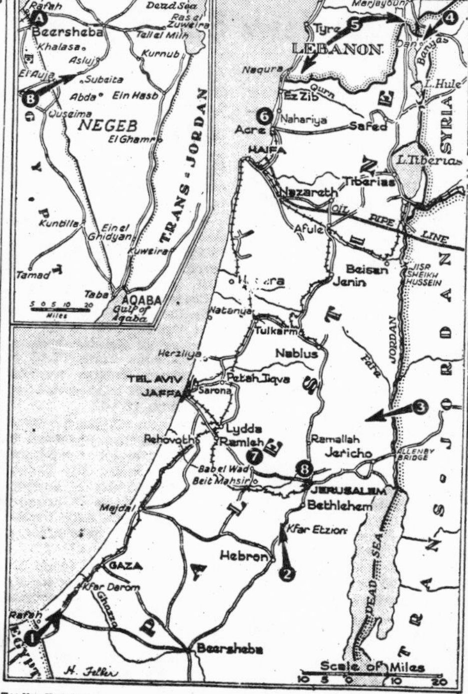

The New York Times May 15, 1948

Egypt ordered her forces to enter Palestine and columns were reported to have pushed through Rafah (1 and A on inset) and El Auja (B). Trans-Jordan's Arab Legion had captured Kfar Etzion (2); most of the Legion was said to have pushed into the Holy Land (3). Syrians were reported attacking Dan (4) and Lebanese troops were poised along the border from Marjayoun to Naqura (5). Haganah captured Acre (6). Arabs and Jews remained locked in battle for the Jerusalem-Tel Aviv highway at Bab el Wad (7). Haganah seized control of the center of Jerusalem (8).

"All the News That's Fit to Print"

The New York Times.

LATE CITY EDITION
Fair and quite cool today and tomorrow.
Temperature Range Today—Max.,62; Min.,49
Temperature Yesterday—Max.,66; Min.,50
Full U. S. Weather Bureau Report, Page 27

Copyright, 1949, by The New York Times Company.

VOL. XCIX..No. 33,481. Entered as Second-Class Matter, Postoffice, New York, N. Y. NEW YORK, SATURDAY, SEPTEMBER 24, 1949. Times Square, New York 18, N. Y. Telephone Lackawanna 4-1000 THREE CENTS IN NEW YORK CITY

ATOM BLAST IN RUSSIA DISCLOSED; TRUMAN AGAIN ASKS U.N. CONTROL; VISHINSKY PROPOSES A PEACE PACT

SMALL STEEL MILL SETS PENSION PLAN, A POSSIBLE PATTERN

Proposal by Employer of 1,200, With Workers Sharing Costs, Is Held Poser for Union

LIMITS CAUSE FOR STRIKE

Murray Is Firm for 'Package' Urged by Panel — Wildcat Walkout Hits Another Plant

By A. H. RASKIN

Special to THE NEW YORK TIMES.

PITTSBURGH, Sept. 23—The first hint at the strategy the steel industry may employ to head off a threatened strike of 500,000 steel workers Oct. 1 came today from one of the smallest companies in the industry.

While the United States Steel Corporation and other big companies marked time on the first day of their renewed negotiations with the United Steel Workers of America, CIO, the Follansbee Steel Corporation made a proposal to the union that was widely regarded here as the forerunner of similar offers to be made by the rest of the industry.

The company, which has 1,200 employes at plants in Follansbee, W. Va., and Toronto, Ohio, informed the union that it was prepared to commit itself to pay 6 cents an hour for pensions, provided its workers put up an additional 3 cents an hour.

Employes Pay for Insurance

The company already has a contributory program of social insurance, to which it gives about 4 cents an hour and the workers 2 cents.

The proposal would bring the company's outlay for pensions and welfare into line with the 10-cent "package" recommended by President Truman's fact-finding board. At the same time it would make an end run around the union's insistence that employers pay the whole cost of industrial social security.

The Truman panel endorsed the idea that employers should meet the bill for pensions and social insurance, but opened the door for supplementary payments by workers to increase the amount of protection that could be provided. The board said such arrangements could be effected through collective bargaining.

If other steel companies subscribe to the 6-cent figure for pensions and 4 cents for health, hospital and other forms of social insurance, on condition that their workers also contribute, the union would be maneuvered into the position of having to decide whether or not to strike solely for establishment of the non-contributory principle.

Philip Murray, president of the union, has stressed the union's belief that the most important element in the Truman board's report was its recommendation that care for the "human machine" should be as much a charge on industry as care of plant equipment. The union has barred any compromise on that issue.

Murray Again Threatening Strike

At a two-hour conference with representatives of United States Steel this afternoon, Mr. Murray reiterated the union's determination to strike unless the company agreed to shoulder the full cost of pensions and welfare on the 6-cent and 4-cent basis suggested by the fact-finders.

The company made no immediate reply. Subcommittees were set up by both sides to continue negotiations Monday, five days before the strike deadline.

There was nothing to indicate that "Big Steel" had abandoned the opposition it expressed in public statements last week to exemption of workers from any direct share of financial responsibility for their own pensions and insurance.

The company has committed itself to give 4 cents an hour for welfare, provided workers made an additional payment on their own, but it has declined to set any specific figure for pensions until a joint study of retirement benefits is completed next March 31.

Negotiations between the union and other large steel companies took place today in a dozen cities, but none of the companies gave any new indication of its position. In virtually all cases the talks were recessed until Monday without any sign of a break in the deadlock that has existed since the first negotiations got under way in June.

Union negotiators warned that the patience of the men in the steel mills was wearing thin at the lack of progress toward employer-

Continued on Page 22, Column 1

Cancer Patient Slain; Daughter Detained

Special to THE NEW YORK TIMES.

STAMFORD, Conn., Sept. 23—Carol Paight, 20 years old, was placed under police guard in Stamford Hospital tonight pending investigation of whether she shot her police-sergeant father in pity after learning that he had an inoperable cancer.

The father, Carl Paight, 52, died seven hours after he was shot with his own service pistol at 5:45 P. M. He had been in the hospital since Sept. 15, suffering from the effects of an operation that showed he had cancer.

The daughter, who had been alone with him, became hysterical. Sedatives were administered before she could be questioned by the police and a psychiatrist.

Father and daughter had been deeply attached, friends said. Police who knew both because of Sergeant Paight's twenty-eight years of service here, said that she had declared upon being told of the cancer that she did not want her father to suffer.

RED DEFENSE RESTS; REBUTTAL WAIVED

Jury in 9-Month Trial Excused Till Summaries Begin Oct. 4, May Get Case Week Later

By RUSSELL PORTER

The defense rested in the nine-month Communist trial yesterday, and the Government waived its right of rebuttal. Federal Judge Harold R. Medina gave counsel until 2 o'clock Tuesday afternoon to submit requests for instructions to be included in his charge to the jury and announced that arguments on closing motions would be heard at 10:30 o'clock Wednesday morning.

Judge Medina excused the jury until Tuesday morning, Oct. 4, when, if he denies the usual defense motions to throw out the case, summaries will begin. In the absence of unexpected developments, the case should go to the jury by the week beginning Monday, Oct. 10.

Eleven members of the Communist party's American Politburo or national board have been on trial since January 17, for criminal conspiracy to teach and advocate overthrow of the Government and destruction of American democracy by force and violence. Government witnesses have testified that the defendants reorganized the party for this purpose in 1945 on orders from Moscow.

The defense took roughly six months to present its case, including a two-month preliminary challenge to the Federal jury system. The Government introduced its evidence in two months.

The defense called thirty-five witnesses and the Government fifteen. The defense offered 429 exhibits, the Government 332.

Of the 158 trial days, the defense used 109—eighty-two in the trial proper and twenty-seven in the jury challenge. The Government spent thirty-seven days in the presentation of evidence. Ten days were devoted to picking the jury and two days to opening statements by opposing counsel.

The Government called its first witness on March 23 and rested on May 19. The defense began to present evidence on May 23, four months ago yesterday.

Nearly 20,000 pages of testimony

Continued on Page 7, Column 2

CIO SEES LEFTISTS QUITTING TO FORM OWN ORGANIZATION

High Officers Say Such Action Is Called for by New Line of Communist Party

FIGHT AT CONVENTION DUE

National Body Plans to Set Up Rival Right-Wing Unions if Pro-Red Groups Depart

By LOUIS STARK

Special to THE NEW YORK TIMES.

WASHINGTON, Sept. 23—High officers of the Congress of Industrial Organizations expressed the view today that the new Communist party line was to split all pro-Communist unions from the CIO and to form a new labor federation. This belief is supported by the following developments:

1. A factional struggle within the CIO Teachers Union in New York, in which the pro-Communists are demanding that the union leave the CIO, though their opponents proclaim loyalty to the parent body.

2. The decision of pro-Communist unions to carry the fight on autonomy and wage policies to the right wing, led by Philip Murray, president of the CIO.

3. The "impossible" demands decided on several days ago by the convention of the United Electrical Radio and Machine Workers that will be served on Mr. Murray.

4. Refusal of the Farm Equipment Workers Union to obey the CIO mandate to merge with the United Automobile Workers.

The Murray forces are prepared for a possible split. If it occurs, they will charter right-wing groups to form the nucleus of new organizations supplanting the dissidents.

Eleven Affiliates Involved

Eleven CIO affiliates may be affected by the possible schism. While they have been generally credited with a membership of 1,000,000 members, informed officials say that their total is more nearly 600,000.

The largest of the dissidents is the UE, which says it bargains for 600,000 members. This union, however, is reported by right-wing officers to be paying to the CIO on about 350,000 members. Some of the leftist-led unions have been in arrears in payments to the national organization for some months.

The largest nut that the CIO has to crack is the UE, its third largest affiliate. This union, well entrenched in General Electric, Westinghouse and other large radio and electrical manufacturing companies, is a strong, well-disciplined organization.

Despite its strength, CIO officials indicated that they would meet any challenge of the UE's re-elected officers. If the union should decide to leave the CIO, the latter's officers feel confident of winning adherence of the workers in the big General Electric and Westinghouse plants as the nucleus of a new electrical union.

Mr. Murray's associates are impatient for the battle because daily evidences of leftist dissidence convinces them that the latter have made up their minds to split the CIO and to put the blame on the right wing.

The latest aspect of the leftist attack on the CIO leadership is

Continued on Page 28, Column 7

Auto Crash Kills Publisher's Wife As He Reaches for Spilling Cup

Special to THE NEW YORK TIMES.

HARRISON, N. Y., Sept. 23—Marvin Pierce, president of the McCall Corporation, magazine and fashion publishers, at 230 Park Avenue, New York, was driving to the Rye railroad station this morning when he tried to prevent a cup of coffee from spilling on his wife's clothes. In an accident that followed, his wife, Mrs. Pauline Robinson Pierce, 53 years old, was killed and Mr. Pierce was injured.

The couple left their Purchase Street home, adjoining the Westchester Country Club, soon after 8 A. M. Mr. Pierce, who is 56, was at the wheel and his wife was beside him, ready to drive home from the station after her husband had boarded a commuters' train for New York.

Mrs. Pierce held in her hands a cup of coffee that she had carried from the breakfast table. After sipping the fluid, she placed the cup for a moment on the seat between her husband and herself. From a corner of his eye Mr. Pierce saw the cup tipping toward his wife.

As Mr. Pierce reached for the cup, the auto swerved to the left side of the road, hit a soft shoulder, plunged 100 feet down a moderate embankment, slid between a pole and a tree and crashed into a tree and a stone wall. Striking the windshield, Mrs. Pierce died of a fractured skull. The accident occurred on Highland Road near Purchase Street.

Taken to the United Hospital in Port Chester, Mr. Pierce told his story to the police. Detectives found the coffee cup, bone China of English manufacture, unbroken in the wreckage of the car and took it to police headquarters. Physicians listed Mr. Pierce's injuries as a cerebral concussion, fractured nose, four broken ribs and several bruises. His condition tonight was improving.

Besides her husband, Mrs. Pierce leaves two sons, James R. and Scott Pierce of Rye, and two daughters, Mrs. Walter G. Rafferty of West Hartford, Conn., and Mrs. G. H. W. Bush of Bakersfield, Calif.

ADDRESSING U. N.

Andrei Y. Vishinsky
The New York Times

VISHINSKY SAYS U.S. PLOTS ATOMIC WAR

Calls for Great Power Treaty to Strengthen World Peace in Assembly Speech

Text of Vishinsky address to U. N. Assembly is on Page 4.

By THOMAS J. HAMILTON

Andrei Y. Vishinsky, the Soviet Foreign Minister, accused the United States and Britain yesterday of planning an atomic war, and introduced a resolution at Flushing Meadow proposing that the United Nations General Assembly request the five Great Powers to conclude "a pact for the strengthening of peace."

The resolution also would call on all nations to settle their disputes without resorting to the use or threat of force, and would take note "of the unbending will and determination of peoples to ward

Continued on Page 4, Column 1

CAPITOL FOR ACCORD

Lucas Says 'Future of Civilization' May Rest on Atom Control

AIRING OF VIEWS URGED

McMahon Holds U. S. Should 'Demand Right' to Put Case Before Russians Via Radio

By WILLIAM S. WHITE

Special to THE NEW YORK TIMES.

WASHINGTON, Sept. 23—In a great anxiety that passed soon into a positive response—demands for fresh tries at international control of the atomic bomb—Congress heard today the news that an atomic explosion had occurred in the Soviet Union.

The atmosphere at the Capitol almost everywhere was consciously quiet and restrained. Some of the most responsible members of Congress issued statements saying that the American people could have confidence, in any possible crisis, in the military leadership and the military power of this country.

Beyond this, Administration Congressional spokesmen said in substance that the implications of the President's disclosure of what had happened in Russia were beyond the scope of any Congressional action. They looked toward the United Nations as the forum for this matter.

Senator Scott W. Lucas of Illinois, the Democratic leader of the Senate, and Senator Brien McMahon, Democrat, of Connecticut, the principal Congressional authority on atomic energy, came out almost at once for another attempt at bringing the bomb under the world's seal.

"I believe," said Senator Lucas, "that nothing could give the world greater confidence in survival than for the delegates at the United Nations to reconsider the question of atomic energy control, and arrive at an agreement acceptable to all.

"The world knows that our rep-

Continued on Page 3, Column 5

Truman Statement on Atom

By The United Press.

WASHINGTON, Sept. 23—The text of President Truman's statement today announcing a recent atomic explosion in the Soviet Union:

I believe the American people to the fullest extent consistent with the national security are entitled to be informed of all developments in the field of atomic energy. That is my reason for making public the following information.

We have evidence that within recent weeks an atomic explosion occurred in the U.S.S.R.

Ever since atomic energy was first released by man, the eventual development of this new force by other nations was to be expected. This probability has always been taken into account by us.

Nearly four years ago I pointed out that "scientific opinion appears to be practically unanimous that the essential theoretical knowledge upon which the discovery is based is already widely known. There is also substantial agreement that foreign research can come abreast of our present theoretical knowledge in time." And, in the three-nation declaration of the President of the United States and the Prime Ministers of the United Kingdom and of Canada, dated Nov. 15, 1945, it was emphasized that no single nation could, in fact, have a monopoly of atomic weapons.

This recent development emphasizes once again, if indeed such emphasis were needed, the necessity for that truly effective and enforceable international control of atomic energy which this Government and the large majority of the members of the United Nations support.

Soviet Achievement Ahead Of Predictions by 3 Years

By WILLIAM L. LAURENCE

President Truman's announcement that we have evidence of the occurrence of an "atomic explosion" in the Soviet Union within recent weeks ranks only next to his original announcement of the explosion of the first atomic bomb over Hiroshima on Aug. 6, 1945. It marks the end of the first period of the atomic age and the beginning of the second.

The momentous event is bound to have profound repercussions the world over. Though the scientists have predicted its coming, it came at least three years sooner than was expected. This was largely the result of an erroneous assumption that Russian scientists did nothing about developing an atomic bomb until after we informed them about it following Hiroshima. The fact of the matter is that scientists everywhere recognized the tremendous potentialities of atomic energy for war and peace as soon as the discovery of uranium fission was announced to the world in January, 1939.

While it is likely that Soviet scientists tested the first and only bomb they had, it would be dangerous to assume that they are four years behind us and that it would take them that long to catch up with us. It would be much more reasonable to assume that they have geared their plants to produce at the rate of one bomb a week, so that they will have a stockpile of at least fifty bombs a year from now, enough to destroy fifty of our cities with 40,000,000 of our population.

On the other hand, it is also likely that the latest event will make possible a better understanding between us and Russia, leading toward an agreement for the international control of atomic energy. Bargaining between equals is more likely to produce desirable results than bargaining between two principals, one of which holds

Continued on Page 2, Column 6

ACHESON RULES OUT SHIFT IN U. S. PLANS

Western Diplomats and Atomic Experts at U. N. Agree to Uphold Control Program

Text of Secretary Acheson's statement is printed on Page 2.

By A. M. ROSENTHAL

Secretary of State Dean Acheson said yesterday that he assumed the explosion in Russia reported by President Truman had been caused by an actual atomic weapon. He insisted, however, that the news had come as no shock and would not change the United States-sponsored plan for international control of atomic energy.

Other Western diplomats and atomic control specialists at the United Nations Assembly at Flushing Meadow took the same line. Unanimously, they said that the majority of the members of the United Nations would stick to the plan that had been fought by the Soviet Union for more than three years.

United Nations officials took it for granted that the President's announcement had pushed the world organization back into the center of the atomic picture despite the long deadlock on control negotiations. Secretary General Trygve Lie summed up the Secretariat attitude by saying that the

Continued on Page 2, Column 5

U. S. REACTION FIRM

President Does Not Say Soviet Union Has an Atomic Bomb

PICKS WORDS CAREFULLY

But He Implies Our Absolute Dominance in New Weapons Has Virtually Ended

By ANTHONY LEVIERO

Special to THE NEW YORK TIMES.

WASHINGTON, Sept. 23—President Truman announced this morning that an atomic explosion had occurred in Russia within recent weeks. This statement implied that the absolute dominance of the United States in atomic weapons had virtually ended.

"We have evidence that within recent weeks an atomic explosion occurred in the U.S.S.R.," President Truman said.

These words stood out in red-letter vividness in a brief undramatic statement in which the Chief Executive said that the United States always had taken into account the probability that other nations would develop "this new force."

He pleaded once again for adoption of the system of international control of atomic energy promulgated by the United States and supported by the large majority of countries now assembled in the United Nations General Assembly at Flushing Meadow.

McMahon Reveals News

Mr. Truman announced the discovery to the Cabinet, assembled in the White House at 11 A. M. for the usual Friday meeting. Simultaneously on Capitol Hill Senator Brien McMahon, Democrat, of Connecticut, stood before the members of the Joint Congressional Atomic Energy Committee and gave them the news, which Mr. Truman had passed on to him at 3:15 P. M. yesterday.

White House correspondents had their usual conference with Charles G. Ross, the President's secretary, at 10:30 A. M. It was routine, but as they filed out his secretary, Miss Myrtle Bergheim, advised them not to go away. A moment before 11 A. M. Miss Bergheim entered the press room and said: "Press!"

The news men filed into Mr. Ross' office. He said he wished the door closed, and a secret service man took his post there. Then Mr. Ross said that he would pass out statement and that nobody was to leave the room until everyone present had a copy. Then he began passing around the President's mimeographed statement.

Tass Correspondent Attends

One of the first reporters to scan his copy exclaimed, "Russia has the atomic bomb!" There was a wild rush through the door and to the telephones in the near-by press room. One of the news men who sprinted out was the correspondent of Tass, the official Soviet news agency.

"The President has just given it to the Cabinet," said Mr. Ross as they went.

Thus the President did not personally appear, and there was no opportunity then or later to put questions to him.

Secretary of Defense Louis Johnson came out of the Cabinet meeting soon afterward. He began shaking his head as the questions came. Reporters literally clutched his arms as he headed for his limousine.

"Have we made any change in the disposition of our forces since this happened?" This question was asked twice.

"No," Mr. Johnson finally said.

"Does the Cabinet know any more about this than is contained in the President's statement?"

"The Cabinet knows all about it," Mr. Johnson replied to this. "It was fully informed."

"Do you have reason to believe this was the first atomic explosion in Russia?" asked another reporter.

This time Mr. Johnson smilingly shook his head, negatively.

"Don't overplay it," remarked Mr. Johnson, departing. In the cir-

Continued on Page 2, Column 3

World News Summarized

SATURDAY, SEPTEMBER 24, 1949

President Truman issued yesterday a terse statement containing this dramatic disclosure: "We have evidence that within recent weeks an atomic explosion occurred in the U. S. S. R." His announcement, indicating that United States monopoly in atomic weapons had ended, added that "ever since atomic energy was first released by man, the eventual development of this new force by other nations was to be expected." He said this "probability" had always been "taken into account" by this nation, and he renewed his plea "for that truly effective and enforceable international control of atomic energy which the Government and the large majority of the members of the United Nations support." [1:8.]

Secretary of State Acheson said he assumed that it was an atomic weapon that had been exploded in the Soviet Union. He said the news would not lead to any shift in the United States position on international atomic control. [1:7.]

New efforts to achieve an acceptable plan for international control of atomic weapons were urged in Congress, where Mr. Truman's announcement was received with restrained anxiety. [1:5.] Reassuring statements were made by General Eisenhower and Maj. Gen. Leslie R. Groves, wartime chief of the atomic bomb project. General Eisenhower said he saw no reason why "a development that was anticipated years ago should cause any revolutionary change in our thinking or in our actions." [2:2.] One result expected by Washington observers was a spur to the North Atlantic defense program. Closer cooperation among the United States, Britain and Canada in atomic development was also seen. [2:3-4.]

Scientists who had generally predicted that the Russians would eventually succeed in discovering the secret of setting off an atomic explosion saw the Russian development as having come at least three years earlier than had been expected. [1:6-7.]

Soviet Foreign Minister Vishinsky said nothing about Russian possession of an atomic bomb in his eagerly awaited address to the United Nations General Assembly. He accused the United States and Britain of planning an atomic war. Mr. Vishinsky introduced a resolution calling for "the unconditional prohibition of atomic weapons" and another asking the five major powers to make "a pact for the strengthening of peace." [1:4.]

Renewed negotiations by the Big Four Foreign Ministers' deputies on an Austrian state treaty got off to a bad start. Russian refusal to reconsider the controversial issues forced an indefinite adjournment. [6:2.]

The British Labor Government will ask for a vote of confidence after Parliament convenes next week to debate the Government's devaluation of the pound. [6:3.]

In China the battle for the important seaport of Amoy reached new intensity. [5:1; with map.]

In a move that might set the pattern for the big companies in the steel industry to stave off a threatened strike by 500,000 steelworkers, the Follansbee Steel Corporation offered a pension plan under which the company would pay 6 cents an hour and its employes an additional 3 cents an hour. [1:1.]

High CIO officials were reported to believe that the new Communist party line was to try to split all pro-Communist unions from the CIO to organize a new labor federation. [1:3.]

Index to other news appears on Page 14.

Couple Held in Quebec Air Crash; Woman Said to Have Planted Bomb

By The Associated Press.

QUEBEC, Sept. 23—Police reported tonight that a drug-dazed woman confessed to carrying a package, believed to have contained dynamite, which was placed aboard an ill-fated Quebec Airways plane that blew up Sept. 9, killing all twenty-three persons aboard.

Police said the woman, identified as Mrs. Arthur Pitre, admitted taking the package to the Quebec Airport where it was placed aboard the plane, but she insisted that she did not know the contents of the package.

Royal Canadian Mounted Police said the woman was recovering from sleeping pills she took at the suggestion of her lover, whose wife was aboard the plane.

Provincial police detained as a material witness J. A. Guay, a young Quebec jeweler, whose 28-year-old wife was one of the passengers who lost their lives when the plane was ripped open by a blast in its luggage compartment. The plane smashed into a mountain near Sault au Cochon, forty miles northeast of Quebec.

Mrs. Pitre was also being held as a material witness.

Police also are reported to have questioned a third person in connection with the case.

Police described the third person as a 26-year-old "pretty waitress." They said she was a close acquaintance of Guay.

The crash took the lives of three New York executives of the Kennecott Copper Corporation. They were President E. T. Stannard, President-designate Arthur D. Storke and Vice President R. J. Parker.

Quebec Provincial police detained Mrs. Pitre at her home in Quebec. Persons living near by saw police enter the woman's Gauvreau Street home, an apartment. Crowds gathered outside and police were called to keep the curious on the move.

Police Inspector René Belec told newsmen:

"We have definite proof that explosives were aboard the plane to

Continued on Page 26, Column 3

ATOMIC LEADERS ARE REASSURING

Eisenhower and Groves Say President Merely Confirmed an Expected Development

By RICHARD H. PARKE

Gen. Dwight D. Eisenhower and Maj. Gen. Leslie R. Groves, retired, wartime atomic bomb chief, issued reassuring statements yesterday in commenting on the announcement that an atomic explosion had occurred recently in Russia.

General Eisenhower, who for a time relinquished his duties as president of Columbia University to serve as presiding officer of the Joint Chiefs of Staff, said he saw no reason why "a development that was anticipated years ago should cause any revolutionary change in our thinking or in our actions."

General Groves, who in World War II headed the Manhattan Project that produced the bomb, said he would not "lose any sleep over" the announcement because this country was "certainly in the lead" in any atomic race.

The statement by General Eisenhower read:

"Ever since the first atomic bomb was exploded, American scientists have predicted that others would, in a measurable space of time—perhaps within four or five years—solve the secret involved. Consequently, the news we have been given by the President merely confirms scientific predictions. I see no reason why a development that was anticipated years ago should cause any revolutionary change in our thinking or in our actions."

Groves Raises Questions

General Groves said the question was not whether Russia had built an atomic bomb "but how good that one is, and how many they have, and can they catch up with us?" He declared he could see no cause for "any disturbance or hysteria."

Interviewed at La Guardia Airport on his arrival from Washington, General Groves said he did not know whether the Russians had an atomic bomb "because I have never been in Russia—no one knows what goes on in Russia."

Bernard M. Baruch, author of the ill-fated plan for international control of atomic energy, would say only that he agreed with President Truman's assertion, in making the announcement, that the development emphasized the necessity for "truly effective, enforceable international control of atomic energy."

Mr. Baruch added that the President had "never wavered in his attitude" toward international control. He made his comment in the morning, saying he might have more to say after reading the President's statement. Later, however, he said he did not wish to elaborate on his first comment.

Dr. J. Robert Oppenheimer, director of the Institute for Advanced Study at Princeton, N. J., who was one of the fabricators of the first atomic bomb, said only, "I am very glad we know the facts."

Dr. Harold C. Urey, Nobel Prize winning chemist and a leader in atomic research, commented:

"There is only one thing worse than one nation having the atomic bomb—that's two nations having it."

He said he was "flattened, like everybody else," by the announcement but declared it was "inevitable" that Russia would produce the bomb. "Apparently," he went on, "they developed it faster than most people thought, but not much faster."

"Not a Surprise to Scientists"

Dr. John R. Dunning, Professor of Physics at Columiba University and one of the pioneer atomic scientists, said that the President's announcement "does not come as a surprise to scientists."

"It has been anticipated ever since the first bomb exploded in New Mexico," he asserted, "but it is an important reminder that scientific knowledge is universal and that in the end only international cooperation and good will can secure the peace.

"It should stimulate us to redouble our efforts to develop atomic energy for peacetime use on an international basis. At the same time, we should accelerate atomic weapon production so that we may continue to maintain peace through strength."

Dr. C. G. Suits, a vice president of the General Electric Company and director of the company's research operations, which include an Atomic Energy Commission laboratory, described the atomic explosion in Russia as "a most unhappy milestone in the history of human affairs." He said it demonstrated the "absolute necessity" for "complete international cooperation if civilization is to survive."

TIME LAG IS STRESSED

Scientists Note Period Needed by Russia to Stockpile Bombs

WASHINGTON, Sept. 23 (UP)—The Federation of American Scientists, which devotes its attention largely to matters of nuclear fission, said tonight that Russia's apparent development of an atomic bomb "probably will have no immediate effect on Russia's capacity to wage war."

"It should be kept in mind that it would take at least a couple of years, after making the first bomb, to build up a stockpile of military significance," the federation said in a statement issued here.

WASHINGTON, Sept. 23 (AP)—Dr. Arthur H. Compton, one of the scientists who helped develop the atomic bomb, said tonight:

"This does not mean that Russia is prepared now to match us in atomic war. Time is needed to accumulate enough atomic weapons. It does mean that within the next few years Russia will be able to wage effective atomic warfare. Unless firm agreements are reached to the contrary, the atomic weapons race is on."

Speed on Atlantic Defense Held Possible Result of News on Atom

By WALTER H. WAGGONER
Special to THE NEW YORK TIMES.

WASHINGTON, Sept. 23—Swift action on the North Atlantic defense program and closer relations among the United States, Canada and Britain in the field of atomic energy were seen in responsible quarters this evening as possible twin consequences of the reported atomic explosion in Russia.

While there was every effort made to discount in advance alarms that might be raised in response to President Truman's announcement, the probable and desirable outcome was set forth as follows:

1. The twelve member-nations of the North Atlantic Treaty would be spurred to prompt action on the defense organization created last week and announced at a meeting of the twelve Foreign Ministers last Saturday.
2. The three countries—the United States, Canada and Britain—discussing the "basic relationships" of their individual atomic energy programs here would be encouraged to accept ever closer cooperation on matters they might formely have regarded as separate and sovereign.

The desirability of speed in turning the defense organization of the North Atlantic Treaty nations, now simply a framework, into an actual security program is not based, according to reliable informants, on any suddenly-awakened fear of Soviet military abilities traceable to the reported explosion.

Rather, it is felt, the advance allegedly shown by the Soviet Union in the development of atomic energy, however partial and incomplete it may be, underlines the need for presenting an effective force behind a policy once described as "containment." This view was interpreted also as another way of expressing the United States position that military preparedness was the surest deterrent to aggression.

The Department of Defense seemed to bear out this afternoon the feeling that delays in military organization could not be tolerated. Louis Johnson, Secretary of Defense, named Gen. Omar N. Bradley, chairman of the Joint Chiefs of Staff, as United States representative on the North Atlantic Treaty's Military Committee and the important "standing group."

The latter unit, comprising the military representatives of the United States, Britain and France, is a key element in the larger organization. It is held responsible for providing, among other things, "specific policy guidance and information of a military nature" to the five regional defense groups.

In the field of atomic energy, the United States, Canada and Britain already are engaged in conversations to improve the basic understanding of the others' objectives. Currently, however, they exchange information of a very limited and nonmilitary nature under the provisions of the Atomic Energy (McMahon) Act of 1946.

Today's announcement by President Truman, in the view of some, may alter the present restricted working arrangement among the three countries.

TRUMAN DISCLOSES SOVIET ATOM BLAST

Continued from Page 1

cumstances this parting word was cryptic.

Privately as well as publicly, high civilian and military officials were calm and reassuring. In no quarter was there any hint of dismay. Tonight the soft-spoken Gen. Omar N. Bradley, chairman of the Joint Chiefs of Staff, expressed the official tone and demeanor in this statement:

"The calmer the American people take this the better. We have anticipated it for four years, and it calls for no change in our basic defense plan."

Acheson Mentions 'Weapon'

President Truman did not say that Russia had an atomic bomb. Only Secretary of State Dean Acheson, who was at the United Nations General Assembly in New York, went so far as to say he assumed that a "weapon" had caused the explosion. Other Cabinet members and lower officials neither privately nor publicly would go behind Mr. Truman's phrase—"an atomic explosion occurred"—to indicate precisely what had caused it.

Mr. Truman's use of that phrase was studied and premeditated, it was learned, and led certain officials to suggest that Russia might have been getting to the point of testing a bomb that might be neither so practicable nor so effective as that of the United States. There was also some doubt that Russia had been able to begin stockpiling numbers of the so-called absolute weapon, as the United States has been doing since the explosion over Hiroshima.

Nevertheless it was obvious that the force and the magnitude of the explosion had been comparable to the deadly effect of the United States atomic bombs, else its positive detection and evaluation by this country would not have been possible.

The Russian development, consequently, was bound to have a profound effect, ultimately, on international relations, and particularly on the balance of power between the democracies and Russia and her satellites. It appeared to have reduced this country's absolute dominance in atomic weapons to a relative superiority that would gradually diminish.

Four Years After

Today's announcement from President Truman came a little more than four years after the historic moment on Aug. 6, 1945, when he announced that one atomic bomb had erased one Japanese city.

President Truman, it was understood, will not alter his firm determination that the atomic bomb and its custody must remain in the hands of civilian officials — the Atomic Energy Commission. While the bombs are stored by the commission, it was said that the procedure for their immediate transfer to the military in case of emergency has been carefully worked out.

Congress received the news with demands that the United States should try once more in the United Nations to win approval of the atomic-control plan presented there by Bernard M. Baruch and obstructed by Russia and her allies. Other expressions on Capitol Hill reflected a confidence in the capability of United States military leaders to deal with the problem posed by probable Russian possession of atomic bombs.

Guarded, carefully considered views expressed privately by high, responsible officials in the Administration were to the effect that the development increased the insecurity of the United States "by a very small degree." Nevertheless they were concerned that the people in the United States should realize that there no longer was anything like total security, that it was better not to continue to take refuge in the false security that monopoly possession of the atomic bomb had created.

A military interpretation was that the explosion did not indicate a major improvement in Russian military potential. In support of this view, it was said that one experimental explosion did not mean that Russia had achieved mass production of the bomb. Also, while the United States has had a four-year head start in atomic bomb stockpiling, Russia will be hindered by her inferiority in know-how, raw materials, engineering facilities and electric power.

On the side of the United States, the discovery was expected to have a unifying effect—to bring about a keener appreciation of what should be done for national security without regard to partisanship. In the armed forces it was believed it would tend to diminish the fierce interservice rivalry currently dividing the Navy and the Air Force.

The news was expected to give added weight to Air Force strategists who contend that another war would be fought with massive, strategic air power, with the atomic bomb as the supreme weapon, and that the main avenues to the targets would be over the North Pole.

No Change in Policy

While airpower theories might get new stress, it was indicated there would be no change in the fundamental policy that there should be a balance of ground, air and naval power, employed as a unified team in their respective and traditional roles.

Discovery of the Russian explosion was a feat of United States intelligence operations. The achievement was credited both to scientific means — secret, delicate instruments able to detect atomic irradiation at great distances—and undercover activities.

Information about the time and the location of the explosion was carefully guarded. Inquiries indicated that it had occurred deep in Russia, perhaps nearer the Far East than Europe.

As to time, Mr. Truman said it had occurred within "recent weeks" and it was confirmed that this meant after the Blair House conference he had called in mid-July to consider whether there should be closed cooperation with Britain and Canada in the atomic field.

French Foreign Minister Robert Schumann told the Assembly yesterday that it would be useless to reopen the debate on international atomic control and disarmament until a "real spirit of confidence" had got the upper hand in international relations.

The United States delegation, it is understood, is in general agreement. Secretary Acheson, in his address to the Assembly Wednesday, said that the United States was ready to discuss any proposal advanced in good faith.

Detection of the explosion, in the achievement of which the Russians were said to have been aided by German physicists, was only the beginning of a momentous problem. Many experts—scientific, military, political—participated in analyzing and evaluating it, and then in deciding what should be said and done about it.

The task of evaluation took days. Painstaking work was done on the data collected, probably by high-flying aircraft with Geiger counters and other instruments, and also by far-flung detection ground bases equipped with seismographs and secret devices.

As often happened during wartime, the problem then arose: was it more important from an intelligence standpoint to make no disclosure so Russia could not measure how much we knew, or was it more important to tell the United States public? The decision was that the public should know.

How much should be told was a problem that had not been settled yet at 4 P. M. yesterday, when Mr. Truman held his weekly press conference.

Replacement of B-29's By B-50's Is Predicted

By The United Press.

LONDON, Sept. 23—A United States Air Force spokesman said today that it was "quite probable" that all United States B-29 bombers in Britain would be replaced "in the near future" by B-50's, which are designed to carry atomic bombs.

[Sources at Air Force headquarters in Washington described the London report as "optimistic." They declared that so far only one complete B-50 group and part of another had been organized.]

Informed sources said that the "atomic explosion" in Russia announced today might have occurred as early as July. These sources said the West European military authorities had been told that United States military circles had recorded an atomic blast—either a bomb or an experimental explosion—in Russia during that month.

ACHESON RULES OUT SHIFT IN U. S. PLANS

Continued from Page 1

United Nations was now "more indispensable" than ever.

The news from the White House came to Flushing Meadow while the Assembly was in session. Newspaper men sent word to the rostrum to Mr. Lie and to Brig. Gen. Carlos P. Momulo, Assembly President. In a few minutes the news was all over the hall and from then on there was talk of little else.

Acheson in Affable Mood

Secretary Acheson was in an affable mood when he faced a crowded conference of correspondents from all over the world—including the Soviet Union and other Eastern European countries. He said that he had known of President Truman's news as far back as Wednesday, when he had made his policy talk to the United Nations. The President, he went on, had no tricky plan of timing in mind when he broke the news but wanted to be on sure ground when he made the announcement.

Mr. Acheson refused to comment on exactly where or when the explosion in the Soviet Union had taken place or what its influence on the "cold war" would be. The next question was one that had been the subject of speculation at the Assembly all day: Did the Russians have a bomb or was their know-how still at an earlier stage?

For his purposes, Mr. Acheson told the press conference, he was assuming that the Russians had made a weapon that had exploded. Later he said he did not expect the Russians to confirm the President's announcement and did not expect the Council of Foreign Ministers to meet on the atomic controversy.

Throughout the question-and-answer session Mr. Acheson took pains to make the point that the news from the White House was no surprise to anyone. All discussions, he said, had been conducted on the assumption that other countries would some day begin to catch up to the atomic information of the United States.

Statement Was Foreshadowed

The President's announcement, he said, had been foreshadowed by repeated statements from United States and British leaders that others would be able to duplicate the knowledge in this country.

The Secretary of State repeatedly made another point: that the majority plan for atomic control was the only effective one and that it would be mere delusion to get an ineffective agreement down on paper. And several times he underscored the point that the United States had been working in the United Nations toward peace and would continue to do so.

The President's announcement came against this background in the United Nations atomic control situation: The United Nations Atomic Energy Commission, over the opposition of the Soviet Union, recently decided to suspend its activities until the Big Five and Canada, meeting in private, announced that some common ground had been reached that could break the deadlock.

Seven meetings have been held behind closed doors. Secrecy has been the rule, but reports have come out saying that there had been no bridging of the gap between majority and minority. The West is still solidly behind its plan for a vetoless control agency with wide powers of ownership and management. And Russia is said be clinging still to her own control outline, one that would put the international agency under the Security Council and would limit its powers of inspection.

To Meet Next Thursday

The next secret meeting—and Mr. Acheson came out in firm support of closed meetings—will be held next Thursday. Delegates agreed wryly that it would be an interesting one.

Frederick H. Osborn, United States delegate on the Atomic Commission, said the world would now see whether it was this country that had threatened the peace or whether "a totalitarian military dictatorship that is taking advantage of everybody to enlarge their own control is doing it."

Mr. Osborn added that it was "obvious" that the Russians never would have agreed to a system of international control that would have prevented them from developing an atomic weapon. One of his colleagues on the commission, François de Rose of France, said the news would not change the majority plan because it was based on technical rather than political or strategic considerations.

Gen. A. G. L. McNaughton of Canada underscored heavily his faith in the majority control plan. He said it was not only practical but the "only" plan that could work. The Canadian delegate said too that the news was no great surprise, that Russian ability to cause an atomic explosion had been forecast for some time next year.

French Foreign Minister Robert Schuman told reporters that Mr. Acheson had told him of the explosion early this morning.

"The fact that it was announced by President Truman shows that Americans have not lost their sang-froid," he said.

The Eastern European delegates generally shied away from comment. Dr. Ales Bebler of Yugoslavia and Soviet Foreign Minister Andrei Y. Vishinsky had nothing to say. Vladimir Houdek, Czechoslovakia's permanent delegate, said:

"Is that so? Okay."

U.N. Coca Study Fund Increased

Special to THE NEW YORK TIMES.

LAKE SUCCESS, Sept. 23—The General Assembly's Administrative and Budgetary committee today approved an additional $27,000 appropriation for the commission of inquiry to Peru to study the effects of the use of the coca leaf. The funds will enable the commission to extend its investigations to Bolivia. The commission began its work in Peru on Sept. 12, 1949, with only sufficient funds for it to remain in the field until Oct. 10.

SOVIET ACHIEVED THE BOMB QUICKLY

Continued from Page 1

a decided advantage over the other.

The best evidence of an "atomic explosion" anywhere in the world is obtained b ythe tell-tale Geiger counters, the highly sensitive instruments that not only detect the presence of radioactivity but measure its intensity.

The atmosphere always contains a certain definite amount of radioactivity, detectable by a Geiger counter. The detonation of an atomic bomb is equal to the radioactivity given off by hundreds, and possibly thousands, of tons of radium. This enormous amount of radiation registers on watchful Geiger counters thousands of miles away.

An atomic, or, more correctly, a nuclear explosion, gives off two types of radiations. The one type consists of super-X-rays. These partake of the nature of lightning; they flash for an instant and vanish. The second type of radioactivity comes from the split products of the uranium 235 or plutonium atoms used in the atomic bomb. These fission-products consist of more than a hundred radioactive elements that go up in the giant mushroom, following the explosion, to a height of some 50,000 to 60,000 feet.

Clouds Are Clue to Blast

This gigantic radioactive cloud is dispersed in the atmosphere and is carried by the winds around the earth. Within a few days, or a few weeks, the watchful Geiger countres pick up a vast increase of radioactivity in the atmosphere, an increase of a size that can be accounted for only by one phenomenon—an atomic explosion.

Even before the explosion of the first A-bomb on the New Mexico desert on July 16, 1945, this fact was expected by the scientists. Even before the secret became known three weeks later, scientists at the Eastman Kodak Company in Rochester, N. Y., were puzzled by the fact that films, packed in straw grown in Illinois, had somehow become spoiled. Tests revealed that the straw had somehow been exposed to radioactivity.

When the fact about the New Mexico test became known, it was realized at once that the radioactive cloud had traveled in the course of a few days to Illinois. This was soon proved by tests to be the case. While nothing was ever given out officially about what the Geiger counters revealed when the A-bombs devastated Hiroshima and Nagasaki, it is known that the explosions at Bikini in the summer of 1946 reached the Geigers on the Pacific coast, more than 4,000 miles away, within ten days. And while nothing was said about the explosions of the three new A-bomb models at Eniwetok in April, 1948, it is safe to assume that the opportunity was not lost to put the Geigers to the test in many strategic locations.

As a result of the explosion of seven atomic bombs of different types, it is practically certain that by now we have standardized the graphs shown by the Geiger counters, so that they could detect not only the fact that an atomic explosion had taken place anywhere in the world, but also the intensity of such an explosion. For example, the explosion at Hiroshima was equal to "more than 20,000 tons of TNT," while the explosion over Nagasaki was somewhere between 20,000 and 40,000 tons of TNT.

Blast Believed Measured

Obviously the greater the power of the explosion the greater the intensity of the radioactivity registered on the Geiger counters. By comparing the intensity of the radioactivity of any unknown bomb with the intensity of the bombs we know, an estimate may be obtained of the strength of the unknown explosion. In other words, it is quite likely that we know how good the Soviet explosion was as compared with ours.

The President's use of the term "atomic explosion," fits, in the true scientific sense, only the explosion of an atomic bomb, though the correct term is "nuclear explosion," since it is the breaking up of the nucleus of the atom that yields the enormous energy involved.

There are two types of nuclear reactions. One is a controlled chain reaction, with neutrons slowed down by means of a moderator to speeds of about one mile a second. This is the reaction used in our atomic piles (more correctly known as nuclear reactors) at Oak Ridge, Tenn., and at the plutonium-producing plants at Hanford, Wash.

The second type of nuclear chain reaction is an uncontrolled one with fast neutrons traveling at speeds of more than ten-thousand miles a second. This is the reaction that must be used in the explosion of an atomic bomb. A controlled chain reaction with slow neutrons can in no sense of the word be described as an "atomic explosion."

It is possible that an atomic pile, containing large amounts of radioactive fission products, might explode either through carelessness, inefficiency of design, or by internal or external sabotage. Such a nuclear reactor generates tremendous quantities of heat, which must be carried away by some cooling agent, such as water, air, or helium gas. If the heat is not properly carried off it may vaporize the graphite and uranium metal inside and cause terrific pressure that would lead to the explosion of the works and the scattering of radioactive material over a wide area.

Such an explosion, however, would not be an atomic explosion in the true sense of the word, but would rather resemble the explosion of a steam boiler or a gas tank as the result of excessive pressure. Furthermore, it is not very likely that the radioactivity thus let loose would carry over great distances, since the debris would be more likely to be deposited on the ground in the vicinity of the explosion.

It must also be borne in mind that the nuclear explosion requires what is known as a "critical mass," namely, a minimum amount of material below which no atomic explosion can take place. For example, if we take the critical mass to be somewhere between ten and thirty kilograms, as estimated by a British scientist, then no amount less than ten or thirty kilograms could be exploded.

This makes the explosion of an atomic bomb extremely difficult, since obviously the critical mass, once attained, starts the explosion automatically. On the other hand, as soon as the explosion takes place there is no longer a critical mass. The problem is to keep the mass from flying apart as long as possible, thus exploding enough atoms to equal about 20,000 tons of TNT, or a total of one kilogram.

This makes it unlikely for a nuclear explosion of any magnitude to take place accidentally. An accidental explosion, though it cannot be ruled out entirely, is likely to be what was known in atomic bomb circles as a "fizzler," not sufficient to carry very far.

Bomb Was Predicted for 1952

While it had been generally agreed among scientists that Russia was certain to develop an atomic bomb, the time estimate ranged as between three and ten years, and it had become customary to refer to 1952 as possibly the year when Russia was to reach the stage we were at in the summer of 1945.

These estimates were based on the incorrect assumption that Russia knew nothing about the possibilities of an atomic bomb until after we announced it following Hiroshima. This assumption was entirely unwarranted, since the discovery of fission was announced to the world in January, 1939, and the possibilities of an atomic bomb were openly discussed everywhere during 1939 and 1940, when American, British and scientists in some other countries agreed voluntarily to secrecy.

It would therefore be unwarranted to assume that Soviet scientists were completely unaware of the military potentialities of fission until 1945, and that they did nothing about it until then. It would be more reasonable to assume that they had been working on it in secrecy since January, 1939, and that it thus took them ten, rather than four years, to reach the stage of testing their first atom bomb.

It would also be dangerous to assume that we have a four-year head start on them, and that therefore they should not be able to catch up with us for at least four years. A nation possessing 10,000 atomic bombs is not 100 times more powerful than one possessing only 100 such bombs. A stockpile of fifty atom bombs may neutralize a much larger stockpile of much more powerful bombs.

Known Atomic Blasts In World Are Listed

By The United Press.

WASHINGTON, Sept. 23—Following is the calendar of known atomic explosions:

July 16, 1945—The world's first man-made atomic explosion is set off on the desert sands at Alamagordo, 120 miles south of Albuquerque, N. M.

Aug. 6, 1945—The first atom bomb to be used against man is dropped on Hiroshima, Japan.

Aug. 9, 1945—The Jananese city of Nagasaki is destroyed by the second and last atom bomb dropped in World War II.

July 1, 1946—The first atomic explosion since the war, an above-the-surface burst, is staged at Bikini.

July 25, 1946—A second test explosion is held at Bikini, this time "somewhere beneath the surface" of the ocean.

April and May, 1948—A new and improved atomic bomb is exploded in a series of three tests at Eniwetok in the Marshall Islands. The results were described as "highly satisfactory."

"Recently"—The Russians carry out an atomic explosion, shattering this country's atomic monopoly.

Acheson Comment on Atom News

Following is a statement by Secretary of State Dean Acheson to a news conference at the United Nations General Assembly yesterday:

I want to emphasize the four basic matters which were brought out in the President's release this morning. Those are: the President has stated the fact that there has been an atomic explosion in the Soviet Union. In the second place, the President has stated that we have been fully aware that sooner or later this development would occur and that in our thinking it has been taken into account. That is an important fact to remember. In the third place, the President has recalled what so many people have forgotten, that in every statement made by him and by the two Prime Ministers as well as by all the commissions and bodies which have studied this matter, it has always been clearly pointed out that this situation would develop. And finally, the President has stated that this event makes no change in our policy.

This nation, from the very beginning of the development of atomic power, has been determined to do everything in its power to proceed toward a truly effective international control of atomic energy. It would be deluding ourselves to get something on paper that is not really effective. The President's statement underlines the importance of having an effective method of control.

We are continuing our most earnest efforts in the organization of the world toward peace. That, of course, is the whole purpose and reason for the great efforts which we have made here in the United Nations, in the Rio Treaty, in the North Atlantic Treaty, in the Military Assistance Bill and in the Marshall Plan. The entire foreign policy of this Government is directed toward the organization and preservation of peace. It is only through the success of those efforts that we will avoid the increased hardships and perils of war.

BRITISH ALSO URGE EFFECTIVE CONTROL

London Atom Announcement Like Truman's—Parliament Expected to Discuss It

By CLIFTON DANIEL
Special to THE NEW YORK TIMES.

LONDON, Sept. 23—With an announcement today that an atomic explosion had occurred in the Soviet Union, the British Government re-emphasized, as did President Truman, the need for "truly effective and enforceable international control of atomic energy." The British Government used many of the same words as the President.

It was thought certain Foreign Secretary Ernest Bevin would refer to the problem when he addressed the United Nations General Assembly and that efforts to reach international agreement would be renewed in the wake of Secretary of State Dean Acheson's appeal to the Soviet Union to cooperate.

The Times of London said that while there might be "some slight improvement" in the prospects of attaining means of international control, "it would be unwise to hope for any immediate result."

Some members of the House of Commons are expected to ask for an extension of next week's special three-day sitting of Parliament to allow time for discussion of the means and prospects of control and other aspects of the atomic arms race.

The British Government's announcement was issued during the afternoon from 10 Downing Street, Prime Minister Attlee's residence. No responsible official would add one word to the statement. However, attention was called to the paragraph about control.

Major Topic of Conversation

The atomic bomb displaced devaluation of the pound as a chief topic of conversation.

Britons had been told often enough that it was only a matter of time before the Soviet Union would produce an atomic bomb, but the threat had receded from their minds.

Dr. J. H. Fremlin, one of Britain's team of nuclear scientists, said he was not surprised, but Dr. E. H. S. Burhop, who worked on the atomic bomb in the United States, said he had thought it would take the Russians at least five years after 1945.

The news reminded Britons that their island is extremely vulnerable to atomic attack, and that, although they have a unit of United States heavy bombers on their soil, Britain herself has no stock of atomic bombs for immediate retaliation.

The military correspondent of The Times of London says the United States appears to have a long start and to be in a strategic position superior to that of the Soviet Union; but there is scant comfort for Britain in such reflections. Yet there was little visible excitement in London.

The news was the first item on the 9 P. M. program of the British Broadcasting Corporation. It was presented in the usual dispassionate style of the BBC.

Still, as The Times of London says, it would be useless to pretend that the announcement was not a shock and that it would make no change in the balance of power.

Harry Pollitt, secretary of the British Communist party, weighing such a change, said the detonation in the U. S. S. R. represented a "tremendous gain for peace-loving forces of the world."

Speculation centered on whether possession of the means of atomic destruction would make the Soviet Union bolder and more aggressive in its foreign policy or more self-confident and therefore less touchy and frightened.

Ordinary people wondered whether "the bomb" would make war more probable or less probable.

Newspaper Comment

In early editions of tomorrow's London newspapers, there was no firm and unanimous opinion on the political and strategic effects of the Soviet Union's success.

While the Daily Herald called for renewal of efforts to attain international control of atomic energy, the Daily Mail said the Soviet Union would be less likely now to submit to control. The Daily Telegraph said that, "unless we can achieve genuine international control, we must keep ahead."

Britain's duty as an "aircraft carrier," The Daily Express said, was to strive for peace by making protective preparations. These preparations, the paper added, should be accompanied by diligent pursuit of reconciliation among the major powers.

No newspaper foresaw imminent war. Several remarked how terrible it would be.

NEW ATOMIC FURNACE

Commission Awards Contract to Pittsburgh Concern

WASHINGTON, Sept. 23 (UP)—The Atomic Energy Commission announced today the award of an engineering contract for the "hottest" atomic furnace ever designed.

The furnace or reactor will be built at the Commission's new testing station near Arco, Idaho, at a cost of about $20,000,000.

The contract was for architect-engineering work and went to the chemical division of the Blaw-Knox Construction Company of Pittsburgh.

The furnace will be used to test materials under the most intense atomic bombardment ever achieved. A big obstacle to harnessing atomic energy for industrial and other peacetime uses has been the fact that most materials break down under the high temperatures and heavy neutron bombardments generated by splitting atoms.

Robeson Urges U. N. Seek Peace

CHICAGO, Sept. 23 (UP)—Paul Robeson, leftist Negro singer, said today that "if it were true" that Russia had the atomic bomb, the United Nations should begin to use atomic energy as a basis for peace. Mr. Robeson made the statement at a press conference arranged to start a series of appearances in Chicago under the auspices of the Civil Rights Congress.

"All the News That's Fit to Print"

The New York Times.

LATE CITY EDITION
Sunny and mild today, cool tonight. Fair tomorrow.
Temperature Range Today—Max.,72; Min.,51
Temperature Yesterday—Max.,69; Min.,54
Full U. S. Weather Bureau Report, Page 29

VOL. XCIX...No. 33,488. Entered as Second-Class Matter. Postoffice, New York, N. Y. NEW YORK, SATURDAY, OCTOBER 1, 1949. Times Square, New York 18, N. Y. Telephone LAckawanna 4-1000 THREE CENTS NEW YORK CITY

STEEL STRIKE STARTS AS 500,000 QUIT; TRUMAN PLANS NO NEW INTERVENTION; LEWIS RECALLS 102,000 MINERS TO PITS

SOVIET IN U. N. ASKS INDEPENDENT LIBYA, BRITISH EVACUATION

Proposes Military Withdrawal Within Three Months as Colonies Debate Opens

DELEGATES ARE SURPRISED

U. S. Suggests Independence Within 3 to 4 Years, Britain Would Set Like Limit

By THOMAS J. HAMILTON
Special to THE NEW YORK TIMES.

LAKE SUCCESS, Sept. 30—In a surprise move the Soviet Union proposed today that the United Nations General Assembly grant Libya immediate independence, and that "within three months all foreign troops and all military personnel shall be withdrawn from Libyan territory."

The proposal was aimed directly at the Western powers, since Britain maintains air bases in Cyrenaica, which, it is generally understood, would be available to the United States in the event of war.

The Soviet proposal, made public just as the Assembly's Political and Security Committee began its debate on disposition of the former Italian colonies in Africa, was timed to anticipate the speeches later in the afternoon announcing United States and British support of independence for Libya.

Dr. Philip C. Jessup, United States Ambassador at Large, said the United States would favor independence for Libya within three to four years.

McNeil Seeks 3-Year Limit

Hector McNeil, British Minister of State, suggested a time limit of three to five years, but he confined his statement to Cyrenaica and Tripolitania, which are being administered by Britain pending a decision by the Assembly. Mr. McNeil said he would leave it to France to say what should be done with the Fezzan, which is under French administration. It is understood that France will propose that she continue to administer the area.

The Soviet resolution was introduced by Georgi N. Zarubin, after Mr. McNeil had spoken, with the comment that the Soviet delegation would explain at a later meeting of the committee the reasons that motivated its proposal.

Mr. McNeil, who was the first speaker, had been shown a copy of the Soviet resolution while he was speaking. He said it looked "distressingly familiar" and that he hoped no attempt would be made to make "propaganda warfare" of the situation.

Until a year ago, the Soviet Union had been trying to persuade the other members of the Big Four that Libya, together with the two other former Italian colonies, Italian Somaliland and Eritrea, should be administered by Italy under a United Nations trusteeship.

Soviet Switches Stand

In Paris, however, before the Big Four handed the question to the General Assembly, the Soviet Union proposed a collective or direct United Nations trusteeship, and it fought unsuccessfully for this solution at the continuation of the General Assembly session here last spring.

The new Soviet proposal still provides for a direct United Nations trusteeship over Eritrea and Italian Somaliland. At the end of five years they would become independent.

In each case, the Trusteeship Council (of which the five great powers are permanent members) would appoint an administrator, who would be assisted by an advisory council consisting of the Big Five, Italy, Ethiopia, and one European and two native residents, to be appointed by the other members. The resolution also provides that at an unspecified time a part of Eritrea needed to give Ethiopia "access to the sea through the port of Assab" would be ceded to Ethiopia.

U. S. Stand Unchanged

Dr. Jessup and Mr. McNeil advocated the same solutions for the two other colonies that they supported at the Assembly's spring session: Italian administration of Italian Somaliland, cession of the western province of Eritrea to the Anglo-Egyptian Sudan, and cession of the remainder to Ethiopia.

The only other speaker today was Abte-Wold Aklilou, the Ethiopian representative, who insisted that Eritrea was an integral part of Ethiopia, and urged the Assembly to allot all of Eritrea, except the western provinces, to Ethiopia. He made no recommendation regarding the western prov-

Continued on Page 4, Column 5

Mao Heads Peiping Regime; Program Supports Moscow

Red Government Launched —Chou's Name Is Linked to Office of Premier

By WALTER SULLIVAN
Special to THE NEW YORK TIMES.

Mao Tze-tung
The New York Times

SHANGHAI, Sept. 30—Mao Tze-tung, chairman of the Central Committee of the Chinese Communist party, was elected chairman of the new Central Government of the People's Republic of China today as the Chinese People's Political Consultative Council completed its job of launching the new government of Communist China.

Three other leading Communists and three non-Communists were named vice chairmen. The Communists are Gen. Chu Teh, Commander in Chief; Liu Shao-chi, a member of the Political Bureau and usually rated the highest ranking member of the party under Mr. Mao, and Kao Kang, chairman of the Northeast People's Government.

The three non-Communist vice chairmen are Mme. Sun Yat-sen, widow of the founder of the Chinese Republic; Chang Lan, aged chairman of the Democratic League, and Li Chi-shen, chairman of the Kuomintang Revolutionary Committee.

The organ headed by Mr. Mao

Continued on Page 4, Column 3

Yanks Lose, Trail Red Sox By One Game; Cards Beaten

As the major league pennant races enter upon their final two strides to the wire, Brooklyn's dauntless Dodgers today seemed to be sitting right handsomely in the National League scramble with a full game lead over the second place Cardinals and only two more encounters to play before the curtain rings down on the struggle tomorrow night. Though idle yesterday, they gained their advantage when the St. Louis Redbirds lost to the Cubs in Chicago, 6 to 5.

But not so the Yankees. The battered Bombers, season-long pace-setters in the American League until last Monday, fell out of their first place tie with the Red Sox yesterday by losing to the Athletics at the Stadium, 4 to 1, while Boston's Bosox downed the tail-end Senators, 11 to 9.

Thus, as the Yanks and Red Sox move into their final two games at the Stadium today and tomorrow, Joe McCarthy's Bosox, again leading by a full game, need only one victory to clinch the pennant. They could end the struggle by winning today. The Yanks, on the other hand, must win both games to capture the flag, with no chance left for even finishing the race in a deadlock, unless some circumstance, such as weather interference, should prevent one of the games from going to a decision.

At the moment the standing of the two American League contenders reads:

	Won	Lost	P.C.	G.B.	To Play
Boston	96	56	.632	..	2
New York	95	57	.625	1	2

Therefore, should the Red Sox win today, it would settle the race, for even were the Yankees to win the final game of the season tomorrow, the final standing would be:

	Won	Lost	P.C.
Boston	97	57	.630
New York	96	58	.623

Oddly, and perhaps for the first time in major league history, the National League goes into its final two days with the same figures prevailing as in the rival circuit.

However, there is a slight difference. For though the Dodgers lead the Cards by a full game and each club has two more games to play, they do not meet each other.

Continued on Page 17, Column 6

PAY RISE TO 1,355,000 CLEARED BY SENATE

Civil Service and Postal Bills Total $211,000,000—Fourth Spending Authority Ends

By C. P. TRUSSELL
Special to THE NEW YORK TIMES.

WASHINGTON, Sept. 30—The Senate today approved in rapid succession two bills to authorize an estimated $211,000,000 in annual pay increases for 1,355,000 classified and postal employes of the Government. About half a million of those slated for rises are in the Post Office Department.

This action raised the total of prospective increases voted by the Senate this week to more than $500,000,000 and affects 3,000,000 on the civilian and military payrolls. The House, in measures previously adopted, has approved rises of at least $120,000,000 more than the Senate's total.

The average increase for classified Civil Service workers is $124 a year. The increase for the post-office employes is $100. The House bill provides $150.

After the adjustment of differences in conference, appropriations must be authorized to cover the increases.

The pay rises are contained in four measures, these applying to the classified, or Civil Service, employes; to postmasters and postal workers; to top officials in the Executive Branch of the Government, and to military personnel in almost every rank or grade.

As the Senate acted today on the last of the major pay bills, Congress, as a whole, found itself under obligation to authorize, for a fifth time, the continued spending of funds by Federal establishments, even though formal appro-

Continued on Page 23, Column 4

Mrs. Patenotre Pays $2,000,000 In Tax Case; Fine, Term Suspended

By PAUL P. KENNEDY

Mrs. Eleanor Louise Patenotre, 80-year-old former owner of The Philadelphia Inquirer and widow of Jules Patenotre, one-time French Ambassador to the United States, pleaded guilty in Federal court yesterday to a charge of tax evasion and handed over a check for $2,000,000 in civil liability settlement.

The maximum penalty of $10,000 fine and a five-year jail sentence was suspended by Federal Judge Alfred C. Coxe, who placed the defendant on a one-day probation.

The Government has a lien on about $3,400,000 of the defendant's cash and securities in J. P. Morgan & Co., Inc., to satisfy additional tax claims amounting to about $3,000,000, it was announced after yesterday's hearing.

The Government's suit arose over the sale in 1930 of Mrs. Patenotre's 51 per cent interest in The Inquirer to the Curtis-Martin interests for $10,500,000. A few days before the sale, according to Thomas F. Murphy, assistant United States attorney, the stock had been transferred to her son, Raymond, a French citizen living in Montreal, where the sale was consummated.

The Government immediately began an investigation with a view to recovering taxes, at that time slightly less than $200,000 and which this year amounted to about $2,184,000. When it was learned, however, that the sale had been made by a French citizen outside the United States, the investigation was dropped.

In 1945, however, through a treaty with Canada, some bank

Continued on Page 25, Column 7

POLAND, HUNGARY RENOUNCE PACTS WITH YUGOSLAVIA

Two Countries Move Day After Similar Action by Russia—Warsaw Expels Diplomats

TITO HITS BACK AT SOVIET

Moscow Considers Agreements 'Scraps of Paper,' States Belgrade News Agency

By EDWARD A. MORROW
Special to THE NEW YORK TIMES.

WARSAW, Sept. 30—Poland joined Hungary today in formally denouncing a treaty of mutual aid and friendship with Marshal Tito's Yugoslavia. The two countries acted a day after the Soviet Union had similarly voided its treaty of friendship with Yugoslavia.

Following Hungary's lead of last week, Poland also ordered the expulsion of eight Yugoslav diplomats because of alleged spying and diversionary activities.

The friendship treaty was denounced on the ground that Yugoslav agents were sowing confusion in Poland.

[Hungary declared that she had denounced the treaty because Yugoslavia had "defamed" it by plotting to overthrow her Government. Tanyug, official Yugoslav news agency, said that the Soviet Union, in renouncing its treaty with Yugoslavia, had shown that it considered its solemn agreements as "scraps of paper."]

In a note delivered to the Yugoslav Ambassador today, the Polish Government underlined in the strongest possible terms the position it had taken earlier this month when on Sept. 8 it intimated that the friendship treaty was null and void.

Reminding Marshal Tito of that note, the Polish Government said "incontrovertible facts" had proved that the embassy had been engaged in spying and abetting a political diversion within this country. Such activities, the note continued, link Yugoslavia with the "Fascist underground and testify to its complete annexation with the imperialist camp."

Consequently, the note said, the immediate departure of eight Yugoslav officials was ordered. These included Ante Rukavina, counselor (who was mentioned in the recent Budapest spy trials as a diversionist planted in Poland); Lieut. Col. Janko Susnjar, the military attaché; Major Bogic Vlahovitch, his

Continued on Page 6, Column 3

COAL TIE-UP BREAKS

80,000 Anthracite Men and 22,000 Workers in West Return Monday

MAJOR WALKOUT PERSISTS

Big Shafts East of Mississippi Are Not Affected—UMW Calls Order Aid to Homes

Special to THE NEW YORK TIMES.

PITTSBURGH, Sept. 30—Orders for the 80,000 miners in the anthracite fields and for 22,000 in bituminous fields west of the Mississippi River to return to work Monday were issued by officials of the United Mine Workers today, but there was no indication of a break in the deadlocked negotiations with the major soft-coal producers of the country.

The UMW orders, which will return 102,000 of the union's estimated 480,000 members, or almost one-fifth of them, to the pits, were designed primarily to ease the fuel situation for domestic and public users, leaders indicated.

Unaffected will be the big bituminous fields in Pennsylvania, Kentucky, Alabama and other states east of the Mississippi from which heavy industry draws the bulk of its fuel.

Negotiations with the Northern and Southern groups of operators, employing about 378,000 miners in those fields, are stalemated at White Sulphur Springs and Bluefield, W. Va., where the groups have been meeting. The Western operators have been negotiating in conjunction with the Northerners.

In those two bituminous areas about 15,000 miners continued today to work in nonunion pits and strip operations in the face of continuing violence and mass picketing, which, however, was on a much smaller scale than in the preceding eleven days of the full work stoppage.

Another outburst of gunfire, in which a coal trucker's home and parked truck were "shot up," was reported in Pennsylvania but no

Continued on Page 3, Column 8

President 'Through' in Strike; Peace Hope Lies With Ching

Mediation Director Is Expected to Map Talks First With Major Operators Then With Union in Moves to Ease Deadlock

By FELIX BELAIR Jr.
Special to THE NEW YORK TIMES.

WASHINGTON, Sept. 30—President Truman will make no further attempt to intervene in the steel strike, the White House announced late today after the Chief Executive's return from Kansas City. A close associate of Mr. Truman, who would not be identified by name, said:

"The President is through—from now on they are on their own."

With the shutdown in steel at hand, one economist whose opinions go regularly to the White House compared the seriousness of the situation to the first hundred days of the New Deal. Federal agencies prepared to revise all forecasts of business conditions and employment to take account of a steel strike that would be felt throughout the industrial fabric.

The Presidential press secretary, Charles G. Ross, said the Government's effort to bring about a settlement of the pension dispute among 500,000 steel workers was in the hands of Cyrus S. Ching, director of the Federal Mediation and Conciliation Service.

When Mr. Ching left his office at 5 P. M. today he had just hung up the telephone after a conversation with the assistant mediation director, William N. Margolis, in Pittsburgh. He reported that Mr. Margolis had advised that there was no change in the situation as a result of all-day conferences. He received similar advices all day from his mediators in other steel centers.

Assuming that the strike is still under way early next week, Mr. Ching is reported to be determined to seek a way out of the continued deadlock by further conferences.

Continued on Page 3, Column 5

PARLEYS COLLAPSE

Murray Orders Men Out in Nation-Wide Tie-Up on Pensions Issue

SIDES ACCUSE EACH OTHER

CIO Chieftain Holds Industry 'Forced' Walkout—Fairless Blames Union Insistence

By A. H. RASKIN
Special to THE NEW YORK TIMES.

PITTSBURGH, Saturday, Oct. 1—The national steel strike began at 12:01 A. M. today. Telegraphic orders from Philip Murray, president of the United Steelworkers of America, CIO, ordered 500,000 workers from their jobs after Federal mediation efforts had collapsed.

All signs pointed to a long stoppage as President Truman, who had won three postponements of the walkout since last July 15, let it be known that he had no thought of again stepping into the dispute.

The bitterness of the conflict over whether employers should assume the full cost of pensions and social insurance for their workers was reflected in statements issued a few hours before the midnight strike deadline by leaders on both sides. Each blamed the other for a tie-up that meant the slow choking of the manufacturing industry.

The shutdown affected 401,216 workers in the plants of thirty-seven basic steel producers and their subsidiaries. It also halted mining of iron ore by 12,117 miners in the Mesabi range of northern Minnesota. The other workers involved were scattered over a score of allied industries.

No Hope for Week-End

Hope for bringing the strike to an end over the week-end vanished when Federal conciliators, who spent all day yesterday in conference with negotiators for Mr. Murray's union and the United States Steel Corporation, decided to return to Washington while both sides did "some soul-searching."

William N. Margolis, assistant director of the Federal Mediation and Conciliation Service, and Peter Seitz, its general counsel, reported that they had never encountered a situation in which the parties were "so adamant and yet so affable." They expressed the hope that the company and the union would se to work out their differences "in their own interest and in the interest of the nation."

Before the mediators withdrew Cyrus S. Ching, director of the service, talked by long-distance telephone with union and management representatives. He instructed members of his staff assigned to major steel companies to return to the capital for discussion of the Government's next moves.

The strike cut off virtually all the country's output of steel. Only a handful of plants—some nonunion and some having continuing contracts with the union—remain in production. The daily wage loss to the workers will run to $6,500,000 a day. No accurate estimate of the potential loss to industry was obtainable.

Each Accuses the Other

The gulf between the union and the companies was reflected in telegrams sent by Mr. Murray and in a comment issued immediately afterward by Benjamin F. Fairless, president of United States Steel.

Mr. Murray charged that the steel industry had "forced" the strike upon the union and the American people by "stubbornly and obstinately" refusing to accept the recommendations of President Truman's Steel Fact-Finding Board for employer-financed pensions and social insurance. He accused the companies of proceeding in "complete disregard of the national interest."

Mr. Fairless retorted that the strike call was attributable solely to the union's insistence that the recommendations of the Truman panel be considered "equivalent to those of a compulsory arbitration tribunal," despite the President's advance assurance that neither side would be bound by the board's findings. He accused the union of demanding that the comp

Continued on Page 3, Column 7

McMahon Clears Lilienthal; Proposed Report Stirs Row

By JOHN D. MORRIS
Special to THE NEW YORK TIMES.

WASHINGTON, Sept. 30—Circulation of a proposed report clearing David E. Lilienthal of accusations of "incredible mismanagement" as chairman of the Atomic Energy Commission stirred a harsh controversy today in the Joint Congressional Committee on Atomic Energy.

The confidential draft, distributed among committee members by the chairman, Senator Brien McMahon, Democrat, of Connecticut, stated that the country's atomic program was in good hands and in excellent shape despite some mistakes in administration. The importance of security by achievement, distinguished from security by concealment, was emphasized.

The proposed report was drawn up by the staff of the joint committee under the direction of Senator McMahon in consultation with Representative Carl T. Durham, Democrat, of North Carolina, the committee's vice chairman.

Its distribution, in printed galley-proof form, was immediately protested by Senator William F. Knowland, Republican, of California, in a letter to Mr. McMahon. The Californian said that it should have been first discussed with other committee members.

"It is my first experience in six years of service in the State Legislature and four years in the United States Senate when a report of this nature has been prepared and put into type without any prior consultation or discussion with the committee membership," he wrote. "The members of the joint committee and not the staff must make the decisions."

Mr. McMahon stated in reply that the proposed report was printed "not with any idea of finalizing it or to put it beyond your crit-

Continued on Page 4, Column 5

NAMED 'SCIENTIST X,' HE DENIES CHARGE

Dr. J. W. Weinberg of University of Minnesota Is Accused by House Committee

By The Associated Press.

WASHINGTON, Sept. 30—Ending a year-old mystery, the House Un-American Activities Committee today named a young Midwest university professor as the "Scientist X" it accused of giving war-time atomic secrets to a man it called a Communist spy.

The committee said that "Scientist X" was Dr. Joseph W. Weinberg of the University of Minnesota and formally recommended that the Justice Department prosecute him on perjury charges.

Dr. Weinberg promptly denied the accusation, saying it was a case of "mistaken identity."

The Justice Department said the Federal Bureau of Investigation had been investigating Dr. Weinberg "for a long period of time."

In Minneapolis, Dr. Weinberg, 32-year-old Assistant Professor of Physics, said:

"I am innocent. At no time have I participated in any way in disclosure of any secret or classified information or formula to any unauthorized person."

The young scientist also took a

Continued on Page 4, Column 6

Unemployment Cut Second Month; Sawyer Hails Sign of Trade Gains

Special to THE NEW YORK TIMES.

WASHINGTON, Sept. 30—Unemployment declined from 3,689,000 in August to 3,351,000 in September, according to the latest Census Bureau figures released today. This was the second successive decline in monthly unemployment figures.

Total civilian employment also dropped in the week ended Sept. 10, it was stated. The latest employment figure was placed at 59,411,000, about half a million lower than in August.

The simultaneous decline in employment and unemployment was attributed chiefly to the return to school of many summer workers and was smaller than that seasonally expected, said Charles Sawyer, the Secretary of Commerce.

Secretary Sawyer said that the September labor force report was gratifying as "it further bolsters accumulating evidence that general business conditions are improving."

While unemployment figures dropped appreciably in August they still remained nearly double the 1,899,000 reported in September, 1948.

The number of workers in civilian jobs in August was estimated at 59,947,000, against 60,312,000 in September, 1948.

Agricultural employment fell to 8,158,000 in the week ended Sept. 10 from 8,507,000 in the week ended Aug. 13. According to reports the cotton and tobacco crops were slow in maturing this year. As a result the usual heavy demand for workers for the harvest season had not as yet developed to the customary extent by the September survey week.

World News Summarized

SATURDAY, OCTOBER 1, 1949

The 500,000 members of the United Steelworkers of America, CIO, were ordered out on strike by their leaders last night. An eleventh-hour conference of union and company representatives called by Federal mediators in a desperate effort to avert a nation-wide steel strike collapsed. Union and company representatives blamed each other for the strike. [1:8.] The White House said President Truman did not plan further intervention in the dispute. [1:6-7.]

About 102,000 of the 480,000 coal miners now on strike were ordered back to work Monday by union officials. The orders will affect 80,000 miners in the anthracite fields and 22,000 in bituminous fields west of the Mississippi River. However, no break in the deadlocked negotiations with the soft-coal producers over pension and welfare funds was indicated. [1:5.]

The news of the steel strike broke as the nation's economy appeared to be taking a more hopeful turn with unemployment falling. The Census Bureau reported that unemployment dropped from 3,689,000 in August to 3,351,000 in September for the second successive monthly decline. [1:6-7.]

The Senate approved two bills that authorize an estimated $150,000,000 in annual pay increases to 855,000 classified Federal employes and an estimated $61,000,000 to 500,000 postal employes. [1:2.]

The House Un-American Activities Committee named a faculty member of the University of Minnesota as the "Scientist X" who allegedly had given atomic secrets to a man described as a Communist spy. The accused denied the charge. [1:7.]

The Joint Congressional Committee on Atomic Energy was stirred to controversy when it received a confidential draft of a proposed report to clear Chairman David E. Lilienthal of the United States Atomic Energy Commission of charges of "incredible mismanagement." [1:6-7.]

Immediate independence for Libya was urged in a resolution introduced by the Soviet Union before the Political and Security Committee of the United Nations General Assembly, which opened debate on disposition of the former Italian colonies. The Russian proposal also called for the evacuation from Libya within three months of all military personnel and equipment. The United States and Britain also favored Libyan independence, but not for at least three years. [1:1.]

Nationalist China's request for an early hearing on her charges that the Soviet Union had been aiding the Chinese Communists was also considered by the Political and Security Committee. The committee decided to defer the request to fifth place on its agenda. [4:1.]

In China, the Communists at the final session of the Political Consultative Conference in Peiping elected their leader, Mao Tze-tung, chairman of their new Central Government. [1:2-3.]

Washington rejected proposals for use of naval aid to free three United States freighters being detained off Shanghai by the Chinese Nationalists. [4:4.]

Quickly following Russia's example, Hungary and Poland denounced their treaties of friendship and mutual assistance with Yugoslavia. Poland ordered eight Yugoslav diplomats to leave Warsaw. [1:4.]

The historic airlift operations that began June 26, 1948, to supply blockaded Berlin ended with their 277,264th flight. [7:7.]

Index to other news appears on Page 14.

U.N. DEFERS HEARING OF CHINA'S CHARGE

Anti-Soviet Accusations Get Fifth Place on Agenda of Political Committee

TIE BALLOT DEFEATS PLEA

Delay of at Least One Month Is Now Foreseen—Jessup Backs Tsiang Motion

By DAVID ANDERSON
Special to THE NEW YORK TIMES.

LAKE SUCCESS, Sept. 30—China's hope for an early hearing of her charges against the Soviet Union received a setback today when the Political and Security Committee of the United Nations General Assembly assigned the case fifth place on its agenda. The action was interpreted as meaning a delay of at least one month.

Dr. T. F. Tsiang, the Chinese representative, asked consideration of his complaint immediately after the debate on the Italian colonies, which opened today. The United States delegation likewise favored speedy treatment of the Chinese question on the theory, it was said, that conditions there were deteriorating.

On the final vote, however, the United States, Britain and thirty-nine other nations supported placing the case fifth, defeating a Soviet-supported motion to relegate it to the sixth position.

As matters now stand, the committee will handle the business before it in this order: the Greek question (temporarily referred to a special committee), Italian colonies, the Soviet proposal for a "five-power pact strengthening peace," Palestine, China, Indonesia and the report of the Security Council.

Vote Is 22—22

When the committee's chairman, Lester B. Pearson of Canada, called for raised hands on the motion of Dr. Tsiang, the result was twenty-two votes supporting a high priority for China and twenty-two against it, with nine abstentions. The evenly split ballot, with the United States and the Soviet Union on opposite sides, was one of the most unusual seen in Assembly sessions. The motion, needing a majority, was thus defeated.

Another Soviet-backed motion to put the case near the end of the agenda was defeated, with 14 in favor and 30 against.

The relative urgency of the problems before the committee was debated at length with a majority of the delegates expressing the opinion that China had been in such a bad way for so long that there could be no object in suddenly focusing attention upon her. Dr. Philip C. Jessup, United States delegate, briefly endorsed the Chinese motion with the comment that he considered it "sound."

The only other speakers to back the Chinese plea of urgency were F. C. A. van Pallandt of the Netherlands, who said that a discussion "so highly controversial in nature should be thrashed out before the Soviet proposal," and Panayotis Pipinelis of Greece, who argued that anything affecting territorial integrity should be regarded as most urgent.

Some delegates echoed the estimate of Dr. Ales Bebler of Yugoslavia, who said that "the China debate will be the great ideological debate of our time and should be put off as late as possible." He added that to dislodge the Soviet proposal for a Big Five pact might perhaps have unfavorable political and psychological implications."

Even stronger were the words of Thor Thors of Iceland, who said: "We should be most careful before we change the little token of cooperation represented in the placement of the Soviet motion. Every small country is vitally interested in the prospect of great power harmony. The sooner it can be achieved, the better for this committee and the world."

The Proceedings In the U. N.

YESTERDAY (Sept. 30, 1949)

GENERAL ASSEMBLY

Committee 1 (Political and Security)—Opening debate on Italian colonies, received Soviet resolution calling for immediate independence for Libya and heard United States and British delegates back independence in three to five years.

Ad Hoc Political Committee—Received Soviet resolution calling for abolition of United Nations Commission on Korea.

Committee 3 (Social, Humanitarian and Cultural)—Began discussion of first article of draft convention on suppression of traffic in persons.

Committee 4 (Trusteeship)—Continued discussion of Trusteeship Council report.

Committee 5 (Administrative and Budgetary)—Adopted resolution on United Nations postal administration.

Committee 6 (Legal)—Continued consideration of rule dealing with discussion of main committee reports by plenary meetings of Assembly.

Advisory Committee on Administrative and Budgetary Questions—Held closed meetings.

SCHEDULED FOR TODAY (Oct. 1, 1949)

GENERAL ASSEMBLY

Committee 1 (Political and Security)—10:45 A. M. (Open.)

Ad Hoc Political Committee—10:45 A. M. (Open.)

Committee 2 (Economic and Financial)—10:45 A. M. (Open.)

Committee 6 (Legal)—10:45 A. M. (Open).

All meetings at Lake Success. Reservations may be made by telephoning FLushing 8-2000, extension 92, a day in advance.

Kremlin Gets the Lowdown: Baseball Is Anti-Atomic Plot

Pennant Excitement Merely a Capitalistic Opiate, Astigmatoff Tells Moscow

By JAMES RESTON
Special to THE NEW YORK TIMES.

LAKE SUCCESS, Sept. 30—If Arthur Krock's mythical Soviet diplomat, Comrade Astigmatoff, were to report from here on the present state of American opinion, his dispatch might very well read something like this:

To Comrades Stalin, Molotov, Gromyko, Beria:

I have to report various peculiar American reactions to the announcement of the Soviet atomic explosion. An elaborate attempt is being made in the United States to feign indifference. News of our great scientific accomplishment has disappeared from the front pages of the newspapers and has been replaced by an astonishing series of reports, statistics, charts, and photographs of a sport called base ball.

This is a form of the old Russian game, "beanballski," first played at Minsk in 1643. It has been popular here for some years. Like religion in other materialistic societies, it is a kind of opiate for the people. It blurs their worries over weightier things. It diverts them from the dreary monotony of their capitalist lives. It permits them, particularly in large American cities, to escape temporarily from their offices, their factories, their wives and their children. (Many ingenious devices are contrived to accomplish this objective.)

People's Mind Diverted

In the last week, an organized effort has been made to take advantage of the interest of the people in this game in order to turn their minds away from the failure of their government's policies at home and abroad. At home, 500,000 downtrodden American steel workers are on strike; abroad, Americans are worried about our atomic discoveries, the cuts in the imperialistic European Recovery Plan, and the difficulties of the British economy. Yet a fantastic attempt is being made to convince the diplomats at the United Nations General Assembly that what the American people are really interested in this week is base ball.

There is no doubt that the American press, officials of the American Government and even some of the capitalist delegates here at Lake Success are conniving at this conspiracy.

The American President (Truman) told a visitor this week that he was vitally interested in what are called the base ball "races." The Canadian Foreign Minister (Pearson), who is chairman of the Political Committee at the General Assembly, has been trying all week to postpone the debate on Greece so that he can attend the games. The British Minister of State (McNeil), a sporting fellow in his youth, is also indulging in this frivolity.

Gromyko Overshadowed

Today's copies of the New York newspapers carry reports of Comrade Gromyko's note to the Yugoslav diversionists, and they record Comrade Vishinsky's rebuff to the Chinese Kuomintang, but displayed above these important official pronouncements of our Government are various long dispatches on the peculiar athletic antics of some thirty-six young men representing New York, Boston, Brooklyn and St. Louis.

For example, THE NEW YORK TIMES, which of course is a tool of reactionary interests, etc., etc., devotes one of its most prominent headlines this morning to an interminable account of what it calls "the two sizzling pennant races." It reports that the nation's "fans," whatever they may be, are in a "turmoil of excitement," and The New York Herald Tribune—while insisting that the pennant races are "torrid" instead of "sizzling"—observes, accurately enough, that the Russians must think the Americans slightly "daft."

It is only when one probes into the structure, ownership and conduct of these American base ball corporations and their employes that the easy decadence and moral bankruptcy of this diversion become apparent. The players themselves are virtual slaves to the owners who hold their contracts. They cannot move from one corporation to another without the permission of their capitalistic bosses and managers. They are even lacking the fundamental protections of a union, and the slanderous things they shout in public at one another are equal to anything ever heard in the General Assembly or Security Council of the United Nations.

Authority Is Defied

Indolence, defiance of authority, and a snappish pugnacity are all encouraged by this corrosive pastime. One servant on the team representing the city of New York (Joseph Page) seldom works any longer than half an hour a day for six months of the year, yet receives more money per year than Comrade Vishinsky.

Moreover, it is a fascinating coincidence that teams representing the great centers of wealth or political power in America are most successful in this fabulous spectacle. The New York and Boston teams, both owned by millionaires, are leading in the American League. The leaders in the National League are the Brooklyn Dodgers, owned by a banking family, and the St. Louis Cardinals, a team from President Truman's home state, which was formerly owned by Robert Hannegan, Mr. Truman's first Postmaster General.

Without any authority from other nations, these teams are competing for what they call the world championship. They will perhaps continue to divert attention from our atomic discoveries for another ten days. Then, if Comrade Beria could produce another experimental explosion over there, I feel sure he would have a more attentive American audience.

ASTIGMATOFF.

INDIAN ATOM PLAN MEETS U. S. REBUFF

Proposal to Have the Question Settled by U. N. Law Group Rejected as Impractical

By A. M. ROSENTHAL
Special to THE NEW YORK TIMES.

LAKE SUCCESS, Sept. 30—The United States will not support India's plan to turn the tangled atomic control controversy over to the United Nations International Law Commission.

A decision that the Indian proposal was not practical was reached by the United States delegation after conversations with representatives of New Delhi, an authoritative United States source said.

The Indian recommendations were put forward informally by Sir Benegal N. Rau, chief of the delegation and one of the Law Commission's fifteen members. It was the first—and only—specific proposal made since President Truman's statement that an atomic explosion had taken place in the Soviet Union.

Sir Benegal's idea is to try to lift the atomic controversy out of the political arena by giving it to a group of jurists who serve as legal experts and not as official representatives of their governments.

An Indian delegation spokesman said that his country still was taking soundings on United Nations reaction to the plan. Some Western delegations, he said, indicated interest.

Atomic energy came up briefly in the Assembly's Political and Security Committee during a debate on priority for agenda items. Dmitri Z. Manuilsky of the Ukraine, pressing for a high place for the Soviet Union's resolution calling for prohibition of atomic weapons and signing of a Big Five peace pact, said that the motion had become all the more important after President Truman's announcement.

Mr. Manuilsky pointed out that the President's news had come the same day Foreign Minister Andrei Y. Vishinsky had made his proposals to the General Assembly. The Russian resolution, said Mr. Manuilsky, should now meet the "aspirations of millions of people" all over the world.

Russians Free Two GI's

VIENNA, Sept. 30 (UP)—United States Army officials announced tonight that the Russians had released two American soldiers held in the Soviet zone since Sept. 25. They are Cpl. John McGuire of Philadelphia and Pfc. Lawrence E. Viture of Hopedale, Ohio, both of Company G of the 350th Infantry.

RED CHINA'S FLAG

The New York Times Oct. 1, 1949

The national banner of the new regime has a red ground and the five stars are in gold.

U. N. Postal Service Pressed

Special to THE NEW YORK TIMES.

LAKE SUCCESS, Sept. 30 — The Administrative and Budgetary Committee of the United Nations General Assembly today approved a resolution asking Secretary General Trygve Lie to continue his efforts to establish a separate postal system for the world organization. By a vote of 34 to 0, with eight countries abstaining, the committee asked Mr. Lie to submit a new report describing his efforts and their results for study by the Assembly at its next regular session.

U. S. BARS NAVY AID TO SHIPS IN CHINA

Washington Cites 'Own Risk' Warning, but Asks Canton as to Shanghai Incident

By WALTER H. WAGGONER
Special to THE NEW YORK TIMES.

WASHINGTON, Sept. 30 — The United States Government turned down today a request for naval aid in freeing the three American merchant ships detained by Chinese Nationalist warships off Shanghai and referred their owner to an earlier warning that the vessels would run the "purported blockade" of Chinese ports at their own risk.

The State Department reported that the question of the "interception and detention" of the three freighters was being taken up with the Chinese Nationalist authorities in Canton by the United States Chargé d'Affaires there.

A telegram was sent by the State Department to the Isbrandtsen Company of New York, owners of the three ships intercepted yesterday, the Flying Trader, the Flying Clipper and the Flying Independent. Earlier, in reply to the specific request of the shipping line for aid by United States war ships near by, Admiral Louis E. Denfeld, Chief of Naval Operations, said that such "employment of United States naval force is not in accord with United States Government policy."

Nationalists' Intentions Asked

In this evening's telegram to the Isbrandtsen company, the State Department advised that the Embassy office in Canton had been instructed to get the facts from the Chinese Nationalists—evidently including their intentions regarding the ships. Thereafter, it continued, "the United States Government will decide what steps might appropriately be taken."

In its message of Sept. 16 to the Isbrandtsen company, replying to a request then for escort for one of the ships to enter Shanghai, the State Department said "the decision to move vessels into Chinese ports [rests] entirely with the shipping companies and masters." It added:

"It is not the policy of this Government to convoy commercial shipping into Shanghai or other Chinese ports. In consequence, you are advised that no naval escort will be provided for the projected movement of the Flying Independent into Shanghai. The Department of Navy concurs."

Isbrandtsen's decision to move its vessels into the blockaded waters, the telegram concluded, "was taken in full knowledge of Chinese Nationalist Government closure order and presumably in full knowledge of interception and detention of two British flag vessels departing Shanghai."

[The British ship Edith Moller reached Hong Kong Sept. 23 without her cargo, which the Chinese Nationalists had seized. The ship Leong Bee, said an Associated Press dispatch, was now on her way to Hong Kong under escort of a British warship, after having been freed by the Nationalists at Chusan Island.]

Ships Under "Threat of Fire"

Special to THE NEW YORK TIMES.

SHANGHAI, Sept. 30—The three American merchantmen were still being held off the mouth of the Yangtze under "continuous threat of fire," the Isbrandtsen Company's agent here reported tonight.

The Flying Clipper reported that she had been ordered to surrender all Chinese passengers. Her captain said he had protested the order. The Isbrandtsen agent, A. P. Pattison, said United States naval headquarters at Guam had been notified.

The agent said the latest message from the Flying Independent reported a warship, formerly a United States destroyer escort, had been alongside at battle stations for three hours.

"Guns loaded, the Chinese captain threatens continuously to fire on my crew and passengers," said the Flying Independent's master.

Mr. Pattison said the Chinese Nationalist naval commanders had ordered the two outbound ships, the Flying Independent and the Flying Clipper, to return to Shanghai, but their masters had refused pending instructions from the company. The Flying Trader was now anchored twelve miles north of Saddle Islands, also awaiting instructions.

M'MAHON'S REPORT CLEARS LILIENTHAL

Continued from Page 1

icism or that of any other member of the committee."

The text, he said, merely represented his and Mr. Durham's idea "of what should be said on the basis of the evidence that was presented to us."

Senator Bourke B. Hickenlooper, Republican, of Iowa, predicted that the report would not be adopted by the full committee. His accusation of "incredible mismanagement" led to a long investigation of the commission, public hearings on which ended last July.

With respect to the finding that the mismanagement charge was not supported by the evidence, Mr. Hickenlooper said:

"I haven't studied the report yet, but if it says that, it is an attempt at whitewash, and the facts won't sustain it."

Lack of Evidence Stressed

The draft report disposed of a number of Senator Hickenlooper's specific accusations with the assertion that the evidence failed to support them.

It was especially emphatic in denying the possibility, raised since the hearings by the Senator and others, that leaks of atomic energy information had aided Russia in developing atomic weapons.

Although Russia obtained them "considerably sooner than expected," the draft report said, any leaks that might have helped "occurred before the commission assumed responsibility." The commission took over the program in 1947 from the Army's Manhattan Project.

"The extensive testimony on security by concealment," the proposed report stated, "includes no evidence hinting that Russia obtained secrets from the commission which advanced by one day the date when she completed her first atomic bomb. Likewise, no evidence hints that Russia has acquired information from the commission which would enable her to improve by so much as mucilage and tissue-paper the current Soviet bomb designs."

Regarding Mr. Hickenlooper's accusations that a number of persons with "strong Communist leanings" were engaged in atomic energy work, the text said that there was "no foundation in the evidence."

"The only qualification," it added, "relates to the handful of 'calculated risk' cases where a combination of irreplaceable ability, an access to key secrets during the war and derogatory data limited mainly to associations may mean that a scientist gains clearance where normally it would be denied."

AEC Complimented on Losses

The proposed report complimented rather than criticized hte commission on the loss at a Chicago laboratory of some uranium-235 and the removal of uranium bars in a security test at the Hanford, Wash., atomic installation.

If the commission had not set up its system of accounting for materials, it said, "the incidents at Hanford and Chicago would have passed unnoticed and hence could hardly have been used as a basis for criticism."

Mr. Hickenlooper was accused of "a species of naïveté" in holding that the commission had been lax in security matters. His arguments reflected the hope "that by pyramiding fence upon fence, vault upon vault, FBI check upon FBI check, we could somehow prevent Russia from making her own atomic bombs," the draft report stated.

It also denied Senator Hickenlooper's contention that the commission had violated the Atomic Energy Act by shipping radioactive isotopes, atomic energy by-products, to the Norwegian military establishment.

The proposed report said that the committee's investigation, far from proving mismanagement, produced "strong and largely uncontested evidence that the commissioners have put our atomic project on its feet." The program had reached a "low point" when the commission took over, it held.

It was a paradox, the draft said, that Senator Hickenlooper conceded that the management of the program was bad while admitting that the results were good.

"A large body of uncontested evidence," it said, "shows that the commission is bringing to the people of the United States and to all freedom-loving people the most precious of defense commodities: security by achievement."

Criticizing the commission on some points, the McMahon-Durham draft found the development of reactors, or atomic piles, for military purposes to be "overslow, notwithstanding the many good reasons which account for it."

Doubt also was expressed whether the commission had moved with adequate aggressiveness to a point where it could withdraw from management of the towns at the Oak Ridge, Tenn., Los Alamos, N. M., and Hanford, Wash., installations.

The proposed report said, moreover, that "many kinks" still existed in relations between the commission and its contractors.

In an unrelated development in the atomic energy field, representatives of the United States, Great Britain and Canada completed today what an official statement called the "first stage" of their talks on the sharing of information and the distribution of uranium supplies.

The "results," it was stated, must now be studied by policy officials of the three Governments. The exploratory conversations began Sept. 20.

The statement authorized at today's meeting said that "good progress was registered." The combined committee, it added, will meet again in the "near future."

Gabrielson Accuses Truman

COLUMBUS, Ohio, Sept. 30 (UP)—The Republican national chairman, Guy George Gabrielson, asserted today that President Truman played politics in announcing an atomic explosion had occurred in Russia.

"The timing on Truman's publicity was political," Mr. Gabrielson said in an interview. "I am sure the timing of President Truman's release had something to do with the Administration's desire for increased appropriations to help Europe."

He further said that the President "was trying to grab the headlines from the GOP farm conference in Sioux City, which was meeting at the time."

Named 'Scientist X' by House Unit, Midwest Professor Denies Charge

Continued from Page 1

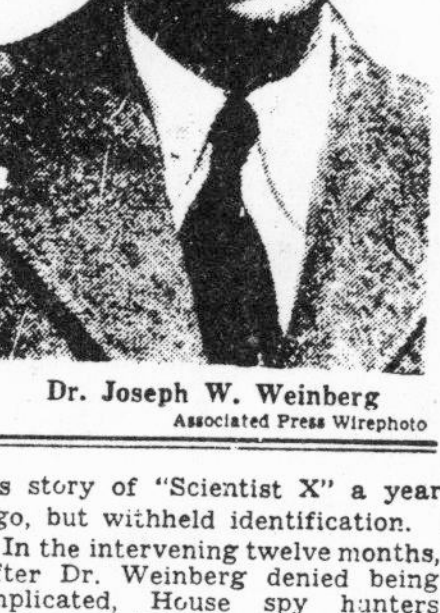

Dr. Joseph W. Weinberg
Associated Press Wirephoto

slap at the term "Scientist X," which he said was "a publicity-seeking phrase invented by the committee."

Dr. J. L. Morrill, president of the University of Minnesota, called for an immediate Government investigation to "establish the truth in this tragic situation for the security of the nation and with strict justice to Professor Weinberg."

Dr. Morrill said the university would not knowingly retain on its staff "any person guilty of perjury or traitorous Communist collaboration."

But he noted that no formal charges had yet been lodged against Dr. Weinberg and the university did not feel justified in taking any action "unless he has been indicted."

The House Committee said in its report today that the man it identified only under the pseudonym of "Scientist X" in a report issued in September, 1948, went to the home of Steve Nelson, Communist leader, in March, 1943, and gave Mr. Nelson highly confidential information. Mr. Nelson arranged a meeting with the Soviet Vice Consul in San Francisco several days later and gave him an envelope or package, the report said.

The committee accused Dr. Weinberg of lying under oath when the scientist appeared before the House group in a closed session last year. The committee said Dr. Weinberg perjured himself in denying:

1. That he was a Communist party member and attended "cell" meetings of the Young Communist League.
2. That he knew Steve Nelson. The committee also has called Mr. Nelson a Communist espionage agent.
3. That he knew Mr. Nelson's secretary, Bernadotte Doyle.

The committee also quoted testimony of James Sterling Murray, former atomic security officer, that he and two other Federal agents, posted on an apartment rooftop, witnessed a meeting Aug. 12, 1943, in the Weinberg home at Berkeley, Calif., allegedly attended by Mr. Nelson, his secretary and four other persons.

The four others were described in the report as Giovanni Rossi Lomanitz, until recently a professor at Fisk University, Nashville, Tenn.; David Bohm, now a physics professor at Princeton University; Irving David Fox, now a student at University of California; and Max Friedman, now Ken Max Manfred, who is studying for a doctor's degree at California.

Quotes From Report

The report said the committee had received testimony that Dr. Lomanitz was "the principal Communist party organizer" and that committee records "reflect" that Dr. Bohm was "also a member of this cell."

The House committee first told its story of "Scientist X" a year ago, but withheld identification.

In the intervening twelve months, after Dr. Weinberg denied being implicated, House spy hunters worked on their case against him.

In today's report, the committee quoted from what it described as a report by unidentified intelligence agents regarding orders Mr. Nelson purportedly gave to Dr. Weinberg. This report said, in part:

"The instructions were that Weinberg should furnish Nelson with information concerning the atomic bomb project so that Nelson could, in turn, deliver it to the proper officials of the Soviet Government.

"Nelson told Weinberg that all Communists engaged on the atomic bomb project should destroy their Communist party membership books, refrain from using liquor and use every precaution regarding their espionage activities."

The committee said that was in March, 1943, and that Dr. Weinberg then was employed in the radiation laboratory at the University of California, where experiments were going forward to perfect the atomic bomb.

Dr. Weinberg denied today that he was "connected with the radiation laboratory project or any other secret project relating to atomic energy or the atomic bomb in March, 1943."

At that time, he said, he had "no access to any such information or formulas."

Dr. Weinberg insisted that his employment as a part-time consultant in the Berkeley radiation laboratory "did not commence until a later time" and declared:

"I have always been loyal to my country and I love and respect the principles to which it is dedicated."

OFFICIAL HOUSE PLANNED

Canada to Provide a Permanent Residence for Premier

Special to THE NEW YORK TIMES.

OTTAWA, Sept. 30—The House of Commons approved today the provision of an official home in Ottawa for Prime Minister Louis St. Laurent and his successors in office.

All Canadian Prime Ministers since the confederation of the country in 1867 have lived in private houses, but because of the housing shortage Mr. St. Laurent, whose home was in Quebec, has had to be content with an apartment.

A house overlooking the Ottawa River recently bought by the Government and at present occupied by the Australian High Commissioner has been selected. Parliament will be asked to provide for its alterations, repairs and future maintenance so that the Prime Minister can be suitably housed and able to entertain distinguished visitors.

All party leaders agreed to the proposal.

SOVIET IN U. N. ASKS INDEPENDENT LIBYA

Continued from Page 1

ince, but said that the "troubled situation" would be "singularly aggravated" by the restoration of Italian administration over Somaliland.

The United States and British proposals regarding Libya differ from the plan based on an Anglo-Italian agreement that was defeated at the spring session of the General Assembly. This provided for the independence of Libya in 1959, unless the General Assembly at that time decided otherwise, and would have continued British administration of Cyrenaica and French administration of the Fezzan until that date, with Britain handing over the administration of Tripolitania to Italy in 1951.

The fixing of a date for the independence of Libya which would not be subject to further action by the Assembly and, in particular, the moving up of the date to 1955 at the latest, reflect the rising trend in the General Assembly against colonialism. The Libyan situation, in particular, has been complicated by the coolness between the British and Italian Governments on this issue which followed the rejection of their joint plan last spring.

Britain then proceeded to grant home rule to Cyrenaica, completing the process just before the General Assembly convened on Sept. 20, while Italy, having failed to get back the administration of either Tripolitania or Italian Somaliland, then came out in favor of immediate independence for all the former colonies.

Representatives of the Arab and Asiatic countries that have gained their independence only in recent years, are expected to press for the independence of Libya at an earlier date than those favored by the United States and Britain. However, it is believed that they will not support the Soviet proposal for withdrawal of troops from Libya in advance of its independence.

Jessup Favors Free Choice

Dr. Jessup told the committee that the people of Libya should be permitted to decide on their own form of government, which should not be "arbitrarily" imposed by any outside power nor by the United Nations, and suggested that representatives of the three Libyan areas should consult together at least a year before Libya became independent to decide what they wanted. He proposed that the General Assembly also set up a committee to advise the British and French administrations. It is understood that the United States wants to be a member of the advisory committee, together with Britain, France, Italy and some Arab country, probably Egypt.

Most of the Latin American delegates are expected to support the Anglo-American proposals regarding Libya and Italian Somaliland but would like eventually to restore Italian administration of Eritrea as well. Since the Arab countries are opposed to Italian administration of Eritrea, most delegates believe it will be impossible to reach a decision on Eritrea and Italian Somaliland at this session.

The decision of the General Assembly will be final because the Big Four pledged themselves in the Italian peace treaty to accept it. The committee decided unanimously today to give Italy, which is not a member of the United Nations, a place at the table, and Count Carlo Sforza, the Foreign Minister, will present Italy's claims tomorrow.

SPAIN TO REVALUE PESETA

Madrid Cabinet Decides to Alter Currency as Spur to Trade

MADRID, Saturday, Oct. 1 (AP)—Spain announced today that her currency would be revalued wherever necessary as a result of the recent devaluation of the British pound. This action was taken in order to maintain the "most active foreign commerce," a Government announcement said.

Education Minister Jose Ibanez Martin read the announcement to the press after an eight-hour Cabinet meeting last night.

Spain already has a variable exchange system based on preferential rates for the products Spain wants to export and import. Señor Martin said the peseta exchange rate would be "revalued with the dollar and the pound" for products the Government wanted to buy and sell abroad. He added that this would be done to "conform with the realities of the moment."

MAO HEADS REGIME OF REDS IN CHINA

Continued from Page 1

and the six vice chairmen is the Central People's Government Council which wields the supreme power of the Central Government.

The remaining fifty-six members of this Council were also elected today. Likewise 180 members of the National Committee were named.

Today's meeting, the first plenary session of the Chinese People's Political Consultative Council was adjourned. Normally it will meet henceforth only once every three years.

All the elections today were unanimous, according to a report of the official New China News Agency.

Notably absent from the list of those elected was Gen. Chou En-lai, leading Communist who played a major role in the formulation of the new government. However still unfilled is the post of Premier.

The latter will be head of the Administrative Council, which is one of the four organs that come directly under the Central People's Government Council, headed by Mr. Mao. The other three organs on this level are the People's Revolutionary Military Council, which will presumably still be headed by Gen. Chu Teh; the Supreme People's Court and the People's Office of Procurator General.

All the functions of government not covered by these three come under the Administrative Council, including the Foreign Affairs Ministry.

In a declaration passed today the Political Consultative Council repeated an earlier statement that the new regime would unite with "all peace and freedom loving countries, nations and people, first of all the Soviet Union and the new democratic countries, as allies to oppose jointly the imperialist plots for provoking war and to strive for lasting world peace."

Sunday has been named chief day for celebrating the formation of the new government and elaborate preparations are being made in Shanghai and, presumably elsewhere, for parades and other festivities on that date. A three-day holiday, beginning tomorrow has been proclaimed.

The text of the "common program" of China's new People's Democratic Republic was made public today detailing what are to be basic policies concerning the functioning of the Central Government, foreign relations, education, industrialization, the treatment of national minorities and many other fundamental issues.

Only an unofficial translation, issued by the New China News Agency is available so far.

The program guarantees that the people of the new republic have freedom of thought, speech, publication, assembly, association, correspondence, domicile, religion and the right to hold processions and demonstrations.

As indicated by earlier statements, these rights of the "people" will not apply to bureaucratic capitalists or "landlords."

The above freedoms are embodied in Article 5.

Article 49 adds that of "reporting true news." Utilization of the press for slander, the undermining of the state or inciting world war, will be prohibited, the program says.

The all-China People's Congress, which will be the supreme organ of the state over the continuing administrative structure when it is in session, will be elected by universal suffrage, according to the program. Likewise the "lower levels" of the People's Congress will be named by universal suffrage.

Jurisdiction Questions

Elections will not be held in any locality until the military government phase is terminated. The elections are also linked to the completion of agrarian reform.

Jurisdiction of the central and local governments will be determined by a decree of the central government so as to benefit "both national and local unification and expediency," says Article 16.

The convening of the all-China People's Congress will be some time hence in view of the conditions set for holding local elections. In the meanwhile the Chinese People's Political Consultative Council will exercise the functions of that body.

The foreign policy provisions of the program state that the new Central Government will examine the treaties and agreements concluded by the Kuomintang Government with other nations and "recognize, abrogate, or revise or renew them, according to their respective contents."

Previously announced conditions for the establishment of diplomatic relations are reiterated. One of these is that a foreign state that established relations with the new regime would have to sever relations with the Kuomintang. The sixtieth and last article of the program provides that foreign nationals will receive asylum in China if "they are oppressed by their own Governments for supporting the people's interests and taking part in the struggle for peace and 'democracy.'"

In education, "the scientific, historical viewpoint" shall be applied to the study and interpretation of history, economics, politics, culture and international affairs, it was said.

The method of education will be "unity of theory and practice," with emphasis on technical education.

"In the realm of military affairs there will be a system of people's militia to maintain local order, lay the foundation for national mobilization and prepare for the enforcement of an obligatory military service system at the appropriate moment."

It is also provided that in peace the armed forces will "systematically assist in agriculture and industry so far as does not hinder military tasks."

In the field of economy, the program state that the state shall "coordinate and regulate" state-owned enterprises, cooperatives, private capitalist enterprises and peasant and handicraft enterprises.

"All enterprises vital to the economic life of the country and to the people's livelihood shall come under unified operation by the state," Article 28 says.

Cooperatives are generally to receive preferential treatment. Private enterprises that are "beneficial to the national welfare will be fostered."

"All the News That's Fit to Print"

The New York Times.

LATE CITY EDITION
Cloudy, mild today and tomorrow, followed by clearing and colder.
Temperature Range Today—Max., 50; Min., 34
Temperatures Yesterday—Max., 40; Min., 24
Full U. S. Weather Bureau Report, Page 78

Section 1

NEWS INDEX, PAGE 79, THIS SECTION

VOL. XCIX..No. 33,601. Entered as Second-Class Matter. Postoffice, New York, N. Y. NEW YORK, SUNDAY, JANUARY 22, 1950. Including Magazine and Book Review. FIFTEEN CENTS New York City | 50 Mile Zone | Elsewhere Twenty Cents

HISS GUILTY ON BOTH PERJURY COUNTS; BETRAYAL OF U. S. SECRETS IS AFFIRMED; SENTENCE WEDNESDAY; LIMIT 10 YEARS

TRUMAN, ACHESON DEMAND CONGRESS VOTE AID TO KOREA

Rayburn Says Bill Will Come to Floor Again, and It Is 'Going to Be Passed'

SPEEDY ACTION IS SOUGHT

Secretary of State Expresses 'Concern and Dismay'—Sees Threat to U. S. Policy

By JOHN D. MORRIS
Special to The New York Times.

WASHINGTON, Jan. 21—President Truman today deplored the House of Representatives rejection of the Korean aid bill, and called for "speedy rectification."

In a statement released by the White House along with a letter in which Dean Acheson, Secretary of State, expressed "concern and dismay" over the development, the President said he would take up the matter with Congressional leaders and urge immediate action.

Even before he spoke out, however, Speaker Sam Rayburn told reporters that a bill would be brought to the floor again, and "the House is going to pass it."

The measure authorizing $60,000,000 of appropriations to continue the $120,000,000 economic aid program for the infant Korean Republic, was killed in the House Thursday by a surprise vote of 193 to 191. The Senate had passed a separate bill last year.

"Important Foreign Policy"

President Truman called for early reversal of the House action "in order that important foreign-policy interests of this country may be properly safeguarded."

He expressed his entire concurrence in the views expressed by Mr. Acheson in a letter to the President dated yesterday.

The Secretary said the House action, if not quickly repaired, would have "the most far-reaching adverse effects upon our foreign policy, not only in Korea but in many other areas of the world" where "our encouragement is a major element in the struggle for freedom."

Mr. Acheson said our conduct in Korea was regarded by the world "as a measure of the seriousness of our concern with the freedom and welfare of peoples maintaining their independence in the face of great obstacles."

He suggested that failure to provide further aid would imperil Korea's survival as a free nation and be "disastrous" for this country's foreign policy.

Dr. John Myun Chang, the Korean Ambassador, said tonight he was gratified and "very much encouraged" by the Truman and Acheson statements.

The envoy expressed "deep gratitude" for the statements and added the hope that the United States could find a way to continue aid to Korea, which, he said, is "absolutely essential to the recovery of its domestic economy."

Parley on Another Vote

Congressional leaders have already conferred with Mr. Acheson and other State Department officials on the question of obtaining another House vote on the question.

They are now seeking to determine the best way of doing so. To bring the defeated measure up for reconsideration would require a two-thirds majority vote. Consequently, it is believed that some other method must be found.

The prevailing view appeared to be that the quickest way would be to take the Senate-approved Korean aid bill to the House floor. It would have to be reported first by the Foreign Affairs Committee, after being amended there to conform with the House bill.

Speaker Rayburn, indicating that he favored this method, said an attempt could then be made to obtain Rules Committee clearance, and, if this failed, the measure could be called up under the "by-passing" procedure that the House retained yesterday.

Senator Tom Connally, Democrat, of Texas, chairman of the Senate Foreign Relations Committee, voiced his readiness to help with the problem, if necessary, by putting through a bill linking Korean aid with continuation of the authority to provide economic assistance to Nationalist China.

He said this might be done by revising a bill sponsored by Senators H. Alexander Smith of New Jersey and William F. Knowland of California, Republicans, now pending.

Continued on Page 4, Column 1

The New York Times Five Cents Tomorrow

Because of continued increasing costs in all phases of the operation of this newspaper, the newsstand price of THE NEW YORK TIMES *on weekdays in New York City will be five cents beginning tomorrow. The new price of* THE TIMES *will be the same as that of other standard-sized newspapers in New York and generally throughout the country.*

FULL ASIA VICTORY IS SEEN IN MOSCOW

Lenin Memorial Orator Says Capitalism Cannot Halt the Revolutionary Movement

By HARRISON E. SALISBURY
Special to The New York Times.

MOSCOW, Jan. 21—Top figures of the Soviet Government and the Communist party were told tonight that capitalism and imperialism were no longer capable of halting the mass revolutionary movement of millions of Asiatic peoples inspired by successes of communism in China and the Soviet Union.

This analysis of the contemporary situation in Asia was placed before leaders of the Soviet Union and Chinese Communist chiefs at the important annual memorial meeting held at the Bolshoi Theatre on the anniversary of Lenin's death twenty-six years ago.

The Lenin memorial oration is one of the year's most important Communist party declarations. Tonight as last year, it was given by P. N. Pospelov, editor of the party's newspaper Pravda.

[The Associated Press stated that among those reported present in the Bolshoi Theatre were Chinese Communist leader Mao Tze-tung and the regime's Premier and Foreign Minister, Chou En-lai. Mr. Mao received a special ovation at mention of his name by Mr. Pospelov.]

Chinese Leaders' Presence Cited

The leaders of the new Chinese Communist regime are in Moscow conferring upon the broadest kind of understandings with the Soviet leadership. Mr. Mao has been in Moscow for nearly five weeks. Last night he was joined by Mr. Chou, accompanied by a distinguished delegation including top figures in the new Northeast China Government established in Manchuria and most of the leading specialists of the new Chinese regime in trade, commerce and industry.

Mr. Pospelov's analysis of the revolutionary successes and possibilities in Asia was coupled with the sharpest denunciation of United States imperialists and a frank prediction that "capitalism will unavoidably be replaced by socialism."

The success of Communist construction in the Soviet Union, he declared, has become "an example for the people's democracies of Europe and Asia."

"The great victory of the Chinese people already has proved that imperialism is incapable of suppressing the forces of the people, that this struggle awakens and attracts into the struggle millions of toilers," he said. "The great teaching of Leninism shows the people of all countries the road of the fight against the unheard of calamities of imperialism, shows the road of liberation from the yoke of imperialism, the road to a new Socialist life."

He declared that the United

Continued on Page 5, Column 1

BERLIN RAIL OFFICE IS RETURNED BY U. S. TO EAST GERMANS

Commandant Says He Yielded to Avoid New Hardships in the Western Sectors

HITS SOVIET 'PROVOCATION'

Difficulties Following Seizure Outweighed the Gain of 600 Rooms, He Asserts

Special to The New York Times.

BERLIN, Jan. 21—Maj. Gen. Maxwell D. Taylor, United States Commandant in Berlin, this afternoon ordered the State Railway Administration building in the American sector restored to East German custody. Western sector police were withdrawn at 5 o'clock.

At a press conference called simultaneously with the release of the building, General Taylor made it clear that the basis of his action was the reprisals already taken against the population of the Western sectors and the threats of further hardships through nonpayment of wages to railway employes living in those sectors.

Confiscation of the Reichsbahn structure had been ordered, General Taylor said, as part of a program to obtain the maximum use of office and housing space in the United States sector of this badly damaged city; only forty of its 600 rooms had been used recently.

"Far from sympathizing with this purpose," his prepared statement read, "the Soviet authorities have seized upon the affair as an excuse to harass the residents of West Berlin, to threaten fresh reprisals against Reichsbahn workers and generally to disturb the peace of the city. They have not attempted to conceal their intention to discharge additional railway workers, and threaten to make further reductions in their West mark salary payments.

Claim Termed Absurd

"On Jan. 20, representatives of the Berlin press were given a tour of the Reichsbahndirektion building, where they verified the absurdity of the claim that the communications of the Reichsbahn were being interfered with. They found the usual communications personnel on the job, coming and going in the same way as during the Reichsbahn occupation. Furthermore, they verified the extent of the building space standing vacant.

"It was the American intention to put this space to use for the benefit of Berlin. Unfortunately, the unreasonable and provocative attitude of the Soviets and of the Reichsbahn makes it appear probable that the hardships which they intend to impose outweigh the benefits arising from the American plan.

"Having regretfully reached this conclusion, I am suspending the notice of custody and withdrawing the West sector police from the interior of the building.

"We now know the facts about it and shall watch to see whether the Reichsbahn puts it to a remunerative use in providing transportation service to the city.

"If our action accomplishes this, it will have served its purpose."

Obviously taken by surprise, Communist propaganda agencies were unprecedentedly brief in their comment tonight on General Taylor's move. The Soviet-controlled Radio Berlin said that the United States had succumbed to "thousands of protests by workers."

Continued on Page 12, Column 3

CHURCHILL WARNS OF SOCIALIST DRIFT, ASKS END TO CURBS

Defines Big Election Issue as More Regimentation or a Return to Freedom

LABOR CLAIMS FLOUTED

Conservative Leader Credits Full Employment to Loans From U. S. and Dominions

By RAYMOND DANIELL
Special to The New York Times.

LONDON, Jan. 21—Striking the first blow for the Conservatives in the election campaign, Winston Churchill called upon the nation's voters to set Britain free of Socialist controls and restrictions.

"The main reason why we are unable to earn our own living and make our way in the world is because we are not allowed to do so," he declared in a radio speech from his home at Westerham in Kent.

The former Prime Minister's radio address was described as a "political" but not an "election" speech. The fact is that the campaign does not officially begin until Feb. 3 when Parliament is dissolved.

As the first step toward its dissolution, taken in the orderly process of British electoral machinery, King George VI issued a proclamation today postponing the next meeting of Parliament until after Jan. 24, the date on which it had been called to reconvene. This means that this Parliament, elected in 1945, will not meet again.

It was a good Churchillian speech, which "pinked" the Laborites where it hurt, on spending, housing and the high cost of living, but possibly because of the high standard of oratorical leadership that the wartime leader has set, it fell a little flat on British ears.

The first five persons this correspondent talked to after its delivery found it "disappointing." But Mr. Churchill was under the handicap of sounding a keynote for his party before his party has made known its election program. That will be issued in the coming week.

It would have been a tactical blunder for him to anticipate any surprises that this Conservative manifesto will contain. So his address to the electorate tonight was necessarily primarily a critique rather than a statement of policy, but he did manage to get across the idea that between the Laborites and the Conservatives there is no dispute about the virtue of a country's whole labor force being usefully employed.

The choice before the people on

Continued on Page 30, Column 1

PRINCIPAL FIGURES IN THE HISS PERJURY TRIAL

Alger Hiss leaving Federal Building.

Mrs. Ada Condell, foreman of the jury.

Judge Henry W. Goddard, who presided. The New York Times

JURY OUT 24 HOURS

Verdict Follows a Call on Judge to Restate Rulings on Evidence

CHAMBERS STORY UPHELD

Defendant Is Impassive—His Counsel Announces That an Appeal Will Be Taken

By WILLIAM R. CONKLIN

Alger Hiss, a highly regarded State Department official for ten of his forty-five years, was found guilty on two counts of perjury by a Federal jury of eight women and four men yesterday.

Nearly twenty-four hours after receiving the case, the jury reported its verdict at 2:50 P. M. The middle-aged jurors had begun their deliberations at 3:10 P. M. on Friday after ten weeks of testimony in the second perjury trial.

By convicting Hiss on both counts, the jury found that he had betrayed his trust by passing secret State Department documents to Whittaker Chambers. The former courier for a Communist spy ring was the Government's key witness against the former official. The verdict meant that the jury believed Mr. Chambers and the corroborating evidence produced by the Government.

The convicted defendant faces maximum penalties of five years' imprisonment and a $2,000 fine on each count, a combined total of ten years and $4,000. Federal Judge Henry W. Goddard continued his bail at $5,000 and set Wednesday at 10:30 A. M. for sentencing. Sentence will be passed in the same thirteenth floor courtroom of the United States District Court where Hiss was tried.

Lapsing of Espionage Charge

The case of "The United States of America versus Alger Hiss" rested on a two-count perjury indictment. Thomas F. Murphy, Government prosecutor, had taxed Mr. Hiss with treason and espionage against his country. However any possible prosecution for espionage had been ruled out by a three-year statute of limitations which conferred immunity after March, 1941.

Hiss was thus brought to trial on one count of perjury for denying that he ever gave secret documents to Mr. Chambers. The second count charged perjury for denying that he had seen the ex-Communist after Jan. 1, 1937. The Government contended that the documents were passed in February and March, 1938.

By its verdict the jury upheld the Government's contention that Priscilla Hiss, 46-year-old wife of the defendant, had typed copies of the documents for Mr. Chambers on the Hisses' Woodstock typewriter.

Mr. Chambers had told the jury that he had been a paid functionary of the Communist party in Washington and had collected secret information for Russia from 1935 to April, 1938.

Basis Laid for Appeal

Claude B. Cross and Edward C. McLean, defense attorneys, would not say at first whether they would appeal the verdict. They had established a basis for an appeal by taking exception to a part of the charge of Judge Henry W. Goddard.

"There won't be any statement," Mr. McLean said. "I do not wish to discuss the possibility of an appeal now. There is just no statement." But later Mr. Cross said that "you can be sure the verdict will be appealed."

After the jury had convicted on both counts, Mr. Murphy asked that Hiss' bail of $5,000 be increased in conformity with the custom for "all convicted defendants." After Mr. Cross protested Judge Goddard permitted Hiss to remain at liberty under the same bail. Mr. Cross said he would make some motions on Wednesday, the day set for sentencing.

Should defense attorneys file an appeal, it would act as an automatic stay of sentence. If an appeal should reach the United Sta[illegible]

Continued on Page 50, Column [illegible]

EARLY 'RIGHTS' VOTE APPEARS UNLIKELY

Items of 'Unfinished Business' May Get Precedence Despite House Action on Rules

Special to The New York Times.

WASHINGTON, Jan. 21—Chances for consideration by the House of Representatives on Monday of the Administration's bill to establish a Federal Fair Employment Practices code were evaluated as practically nil at the Capitol today. Some proponents of the legislation had hoped a vote on it might be taken on that day.

Being the fourth Monday in the month, it will be in order for chairmen of committees that have favorably-reported bills pending before the Rules Committee for more than twenty-one days to move on the floor to proceed to their consideration. Such discharge motions

Continued on Page 37, Column 3

Senate to Sift R. F. C. Loans With View to Writing Curbs

By H. WALTON CLOKE
Special to The New York Times.

WASHINGTON, Jan. 21—The stage has been set for a full-scale Congressional investigation of the lending policy of the billion-dollar Reconstruction Finance Corporation. As a result of the inquiry, Congress is expected to set forth, once and for all, the terms on which it wants the RFC's lending operations to function.

Irritated by recent big loans that the RFC granted to several corporations, as well as some that were made in the earlier days of the agency, members on both sides of the aisle in Congress have been demanding a clarification of policy.

Leading this group is Senator J. William Fulbright, Democrat, of Arkansas, who recently lost a battle with the RFC over a loan to the Kaiser-Frazer Corporation.

The Senator, who has not forgotten the rather sharp rebuff, has started the wheels of Congressional investigation turning. On Tuesday he will ask the Senate Banking and Currency Committee, headed by Senator Burnet R. Maybank, Democrat, of South Carolina, to inquire into the RFC's action in granting the following loans:

Kaiser-Frazer Corporation	$44,000,000
Northwest Air Lines	12,000,000
Waltham Watch Co.	6,000,000
Texmass Petroleum Co.	15,100,000

Financial observers here foresee nothing that would block the Senator's request for action. As head of the Senate Banking and Currency subcommittee on the RFC, he conducted a three-day inquiry into the loan policy of the agency last summer. It was at that time that the Senator questioned the wisdom of advancing additional funds to the Lustron Corporation, Columbus, Ohio, which is now in default on $37,500,000 of RFC loans.

Once the full committee ap-

Continued on Page 42, Column 2

MAYOR RIDICULES IDEA OF RESIGNING

Telephones From Florida That He Is Getting Rid of Virus and Will Return to Job

By JAMES A. HAGERTY

In a telephone message to THE NEW YORK TIMES from Key Largo, Fla., Mayor O'Dwyer declared yesterday that he had no intention of resigning.

In his telephone conversation, the Mayor appeared to be hearty of voice and very cheerful. Questioned about a report that he contemplated retirement, he said:

"It is utterly ridiculous. It touches my sense of humor."

The Mayor then laughed heartily and continued:

"I am down here to get the virus out of my system. I am going to stay till I've got it licked and I think I am well on the way to doing that. I feel much better. I want to get completely well so that I can return to the city and stay at my desk in City Hall to work uninterruptedly on my program."

The Mayor said that Dr. Edward M. Bernecker, who left Newark Airport by plane on Friday, had not arrived but was expected to reach Key Largo today. It is understood that he will have a series of talks with the Mayor and that

Continued on Page 37, Column 4

Bonn Halts French Trade Talks After Clash Over Policy on Saar

By HAROLD CALLENDER
Special to The New York Times.

PARIS, Jan. 21—A diplomatic crisis between France and Western Germany developed suddenly today when the French learned that, after challenging France's policy in the Saar, the Bonn regime had suspended negotiations for the trade treaty with France that was to have been signed a week ago.

French officials were angered by these German actions, which they considered as endangering the faint beginnings of a French-German rapprochement in the field of economic relations.

[In Bonn, it was reported that Chancellor Konrad Adenauer, in a parting conference with High Commissioner John J. McCloy, had proposed the creation of an international statute for the Saar that would be similar to the Ruhr statute now in force.]

When asked by the French Foreign Office for an explanation of their suspension of the negotiations, Bonn officials replied that they did not mean to go back on the trade pact but they must postpone its signature because of internal difficulties raised by German farmers and because of "the positions taken on the Saar question."

French officials said this reply surprised them because they considered the treaty would contribute to development of intra-European trade and desired to sign it as soon as possible.

This move by Bonn was regarded here as a maneuver to force reconsideration of the status of the Saar. Such was considered the purpose likewise of the statement that Dr. Konrad Adenauer, Chancellor

Continued on Page 3, Column 5

World News Summarized

SUNDAY, JANUARY 22, 1950

The jury of eight women and four men in the Alger Hiss trial yesterday found the former State Department official guilty of perjury on two counts. The jury reached this verdict nearly twenty-four hours after receiving the case and its decision meant that it had accepted the testimony of Whittaker Chambers, confessed former spy, over the denials by Mr. Hiss of having passed secret documents to Mr. Chambers. Federal Judge Goddard will pass sentence Wednesday. [1:8.]

Mayor O'Dwyer characterized as "utterly ridiculous" rumors that he might resign his office because of ill health. [1:7.]

Although some supporters of the Truman Administration's Federal Fair Employment Practices code had hoped that the House might vote on it tomorrow, there was little likelihood the measure would get to the House floor by that time. [1:5.]

Congress planned a sweeping inquiry into the lending policy of the Reconstruction Finance Corporation as a preliminary to fixing the terms on which the organization's lending may operate in the future. [1:6-7.]

President Truman urged "speedy rectification" in the House of its rejection by a narrow margin of the bill providing $60,000,000 for aid to Korea. Secretary of State Acheson asserted that failure to assist Korea would jeopardize her survival as a free nation. [1:1.]

The journey to Moscow of Communist China's Foreign Minister, Chou En-lai, was seen as an indication that the negotiations between the Chinese Communists and the Soviet Union had reached the decisive stage. Peiping vigorously denied Russia was "detaching" four north China areas as charged by Mr. Acheson. [7:1.]

The annual Lenin memorial meeting in Moscow was told that the mass revolutionary movement in Asia could not be stopped by capitalism. [1:2.]

Winston Churchill set the keynote for the campaign of the Conservative party for next month's general election by telling British voters that the "main reason why we are unable to earn our own living and make our way in the world is because we are not allowed to do so." Mr. Churchill said the choice was to regain freedom or plunge the nation deeper into socialism. [1:4.]

General Taylor, the United States commander in Berlin, ordered the seized Railway Administration building in the United States sector restored to East German custody. [1:3.]

Franco-German rapprochement was seen jeopardized as the result of an announcement by the West German republic that it was suspending trade talks with France. German officials cited France's attitude over the Saar as a reason for the suspension [1:2-3] and proposed an international Saar statute similar to that in the Ruhr. [3:1.]

The Allied High Commission, in a move intended as a public censure of the Bonn regime for "impudent" behavior, will demand that the Germans withdraw their announcement that gas rationing would end the end of this month. [2:2.]

Finland virtually rejected Moscow's demand that she extradite 300 "war criminals" who are said by the Russians to have found refuge among the Finns. [24:2.]

350,000,000-Gallon Water Loss In 24 Hours Largest Since Dec. 12

By PAUL CROWELL

The city's water storage reservoirs suffered a loss of 350,000,000 gallons in the twenty-four hours ended at 8 A. M. yesterday.

It was the first storage loss since Dec. 26 and the largest since Dec. 12. Officials of the Department of Water Supply, Gas and Electricity attributed the loss to a slightly increased consumption of water, coupled with the absence of appreciable rain or snowfall in the up-state watershed areas.

The city's reservoirs lost 105,000,000 gallons in the twenty-four hours ended at 8 A. M. on Dec. 27. In the twenty-four hours ended at 8 A. M. on Dec. 13 the storage loss was 692,000,000 gallons.

The reversal of the upward trend of water storage gave city officials serious concern and boosted to 1,121,000,000 gallons the aver-

Continued on Page 47, Column 1

The Water Situation

The following figures as of 8 A. M. yesterday give the number of gallons of water in the city's reservoirs. The difference in the two days is the net after intake and the day's consumption:

Friday	106,662,000,000
Yesterday	106,312,000,000
Net loss	350,000,000
Average daily storage gain needed to fill reservoirs by June 1	1,121,000,000
Watershed snowfall:	
Schoharie	.0[illegible] inch
Esopus	.04 inch
Croton	.02 inch

At present consumption there remains about ninety days' supply before pressure fails.

Catskill and Croton reservoirs at capacity hold [illegible]53,136,000,000 gallons.

CHAMBERS STOLID OVER THE VERDICT

Pauses in Farm Chores to Say Americans Owe Gratitude to Jury and Prosecutor

Whittaker Chambers, accuser of Alger Hiss and chief prosecution witness, received yesterday the news of Hiss' conviction with the same lack of emotion that had characterized his conduct on the stand in two trials.

Reached by telephone at his 300-acre farm in Westminster, Md., where he had gone before the end of the trial, Mr. Chambers was ready with what appeared to be a prepared statement. He read it in a calm, matter-of-fact way as though he were dictating to a secretary. He said:

"I hope that the American people realize the debt of gratitude they owe to this jury, to Mr. [Thomas F.] Murphy [assistant United States Attorney] and to the tireless and splendid efforts of the FBI."

Then, as an afterthought, he added:

"Nor should they forget Congressman [Richard M.] Nixon [Republican, of California], who almost singlehanded forced the House Un-American Activities Committee to pursue the Hiss investigation."

His Disposal of Experts

"Do you have any comment on the testimony of Dr. Carl A. L. Binger, psychiatrist, and Dr. Henry A. Murray, psychologist?" he was asked. Both defense witnesses had described Mr. Chambers as a "psychopathic personality," given to chronic lying.

"I think that the testimony speaks for itself and the American people have enjoyed the fun," he replied.

Mr. Chambers had no opinion on these questions: "Do you plan to testify in any other cases?" "Do you think the outcome of the Hiss case will have repercussions, political or otherwise?" As for his own plans, he said:

"I intend to stay right here doing general farming."

Mr. Chambers summed up his feelings in these words:

"I don't see how any other verdict was possible."

Press service reports said that he had shown little interest while the jury was deliberating. He went about his chores at the farm, where he raises prize Guernseys.

Attitude at Hearing Recalled

His attitude was consistent with a statement he had given to the House Committee on Un-American Activities during the summer of 1948, when the Hiss case first came into the headlines. At that time he said:

"The story has spread that in testifying against Mr. Hiss I am working out some old grudge or motives of revenge or hatred. I do not hate Mr. Hiss. We were close friends but we are caught in a tragedy of history.

"Mr. Hiss represents the concealed enemy against which we are all fighting and I am fighting. I have testified against him with remorse and pity, but in a moment of history in which the nation now stands, so help me God, I could not do otherwise."

Mr. Chambers was born on April 1, 1901, in Philadelphia. He studied at Columbia University, from which after a brief and rebellious undergraduate career, he was expelled. Soon afterward he joined the Communist party and remained active in it from 1924 to 1937.

Break With Communists

In the latter year, according to testimony given to the House Committee, Mr. Chambers "repudiated Marx's doctrine and Lenin's tactics" and resolved to break with the party. For a year he lived in hiding in Connecticut and when he slept it was with a shotgun at his side, he said.

In 1938 Mr. Chambers tried to wean Hiss, who, he said, had been a fellow Communist inside the Government, away from the party, but without success.

"We talked," he said, "and I tried to break him away from the party. He cried when we separated, but he absolutely refused to break."

A year later Mr. Chambers went to work for Time Magazine. Before his resignation in 1948 he had become a senior editor at a salary of $30,000 a year. He also did writing of his own and translations of books from the German and Russian. He became a vigorous anti-Communist and tried to interest various public figures in his accounts of espionage but without success.

POST OFFICE METHODS HIT

Committee for Hoover Report Urges Early Congress Action

Special to THE NEW YORK TIMES.

WASHINGTON, Jan. 21—Congress was urged today by Dr. Robert L. Johnson, president of Temple University and chairman of the Citizens Committee for the Hoover Report, to proceed at once with the reorganization of the postoffice as recommended by the Commission on Organization of the Executive Branch of the Government. He said such a reorganization could reduce the postal deficit of $250,000,000 a year.

"Strong undercover opposition to the improvement of the post-office accounting methods is forming within the Government, Dr. Johnson said. "Citizens must encourage Congress to take the lead in carrying out the recommendations of President Truman and the Hoover Commission."

Dr. Johnson asserted that the postoffice was six months to a year behind in its financial accounts; that postmasters were hampered by detailed regulations, that it cost 2½ cents to print and deliver a penny postcard; that trucks and cars were so old it cost 20 per cent more to maintain them than modern cars, and that ambition, morale and efficiency in the postal service were undermined by the political selection of postmasters.

FOLLOWING DECISION HERE YESTERDAY IN LONG PERJURY TRIAL

Alger Hiss entering a car — The New York Times

Whittaker Chambers getting word of verdict at Westminster, Md. — Associated Press Wirephoto

HISS TURNS WHITE RECOVERS QUICKLY

Wife Hears Verdict Calmly—Foreman's Second 'Guilty' Is Almost Inaudible

By ALEXANDER FEINBERG

There was a stillness in the courtroom on the thirteenth floor of the United States Court House yesterday that made one conscious of one's own breathing as Joseph J. Toner, the court clerk, instructed attendants to "bring the jury in."

The second Hiss jury had filed into the courtroom many times in the nearly twenty-four hours that had elapsed since it first retired to deliberate the fate of Alger Hiss. This time, at 2:48 P. M., it was not to have testimony read or for guidance—it was for keeps.

Two minutes later the small voice of Mrs. Ada Condell, foreman, had given the jury's verdict, twice guilty. Eight women and four men had looked searchingly into the evidence and into their souls, and had branded the former assistant to the Assistant Secretary of State a perjuror.

Mrs. Condell's second "guilty" was almost inaudible. But there was no mistaking the verdict when Mr. Toner echoed the jury's findings.

"You find the defendant guilty on the first count and guilty on the second count, and so say you all," said he, in clipped, clear tones.

Hiss Quickly Recovers

Hiss, seated at the edge of the enclosure that partitions off the public benches, gave only a momentary sign that his fate had been sealed. He blanched visibly but recovered his composure in an instant. The half smile, half grin that he habitually has worn and that has made him appear almost boyish despite his 45 years, came to the surface again. His eyes—eyes that can be hard and penetrating—were fixed on the jury.

Mrs. Priscilla Hiss, his wife, took the verdict stoically. Seated at his left, she gave no outward sign of emotion.

She stared straight ahead, her hands crossed in her lap. After the jury had been dismissed, Hiss reached over and took one of her hands in his own. They walked slowly out to a room in one corner of the corridor. Hiss had lost some of his color but otherwise seemed composed. He gave his wife a comforting pat as they neared the door.

The jury had filed in with solemn countenance. When the crowd of reporters waiting in the corridor got word that it was coming back in, few expected a verdict. But once the jury had entered, it was sensed that a decision had been reached. There could be no mistaking the gravity of the moment.

Before dismissing the jurors, Federal Judge Henry W. Goddard advised them, as he had advised the two alternates on Friday, not to discuss the case with anyone.

"I want to caution you," he said, "against discussing the case when you leave here. You will be approached by some—shall I say likable reporters—who will ask you questions about matters you ladies and gentlemen considered during your deliberations.

"May I suggest to you that you may save yourselves considerable embarrassment if you refuse to comment on the case."

Jurors Refuse Comment

The jurors took this advice to heart and without exception later declined to comment. It was not learned how many ballots were taken before the agreement on conviction. Judge Goddard also said those jurors wishing it would be excused from Federal jury duty for four years in consideration of their labors on the case.

Outside, Foley Square was deserted on the raw, chilly Saturday afternoon as the jurors, still under the protecting wing of United States Marshals, filed out in a body. They posed willingly for the inevitable legion of photographers. The tension over, most of them appeared almost gay, but they were firm in refusing to discuss what had transpired in the jury room.

Once down the long flight of steps leading from the court house they broke up into groups. When a reporter suggested to a woman juror that he would buy her a drink, she remarked: "It won't do you a bit of good, bub."

Another one kept hurrying her companions. "Come on," she called out, "I need a drink." She was in a group of four women jurors who walked to a restaurant on Broadway near Reade Street, where, seated at a table, she had her drink.

Thirteen proved for Hiss an unlucky number, indeed. Indicted on Dec. 15, 1948, he was convicted thirteen months later on two counts of perjury in a courtroom on the thirteenth floor.

Thomas F. Murphy, Assistant U. S. Attorney, who prosecuted. — The New York Times

He appeared oblivious to these omens when he went to lunch after the jury had interrupted its deliberations at 1 P. M. Seemingly unworried, he had a martini at Andre's, a restaurant on Park Row, and ate half of a steak that he had ordered. There were fourteen persons in his luncheon party.

On the way back to the court house he, Mrs. Hiss and Defense Attorney Claude B. Cross stayed together. They walked leisurely and chatted, and from Hiss' easy manner one could not have guessed that he was the defendant in the trial.

The tall man strode easily through the door of the court house, the ever-present smile on his face. He wore a light coat despite the cold weather, and Mrs. Hiss a gray coat with black fur. Together they went up in the elevator just before the 2:15 P. M. resumption of the jury's deliberations.

"Keep Your Chin Up"

Hiss and his wife stayed in defense chambers until the courtroom and corridors had been cleared. Timothy Hobson, Mrs. Hiss' son by a former marriage, came out first. He nervously twirled a key chain.

With them were friends and Dr. Carl Binger, the psychiatrist who testified that Whittaker Chambers, Hiss' chief accuser, was a "psychopathic liar." According to witnesses, Hiss told his wife "keep your chin up" during the ride to the street floor.

Microphones were thrust in front of Hiss as he stepped out into the street and he kept saying: "No comment, no comment." Hiss and his wife finally got into a red sedan and were driven off.

The jurors apparently had made a compact among themselves that they would not discuss the case. All gave a variety of "no comments" and one called out, "no speak English." Another said she was too tired to talk, and still another said she was looking forward to forgetting about the trial as quickly as possible.

Some of the women jurors were heard to discuss passing the night away from their homes to avoid questioning and to obtain a full rest from the rigors of the ten-week trial.

TRUMAN TAX MESSAGE SET FOR TOMORROW

Special to THE NEW YORK TIMES.

WASHINGTON, Jan. 21—The White House announced today that President Truman's special tax message would be sent to Congress on Monday.

The President is expected to recommend reduction or repeal of excise taxes imposed during the war on items such as transportation, communications, furs and jewelry.

The President will propose also revision of other taxes to offset the cuts and produce a "moderate" increase in revenues as the net effect.

Congressional sources believe he will ask an increase of about $1,000,000,000, plus possibly $750,000,000 to compensate for the excise reductions. Higher gift, estate and corporation rates may be requested.

The House Ways and Means Committee is expected to begin hearings on the program later next week or early the following week. In the meantime, Senator Walter F. George, Democrat of Georgia, chairman of the Senate Finance Committee, will confer with the Ways and Means chairman, Representative Robert L. Doughton, Democrat of North Carolina, with a view of announcing which excises are to be affected.

MURPHY'S VICTORY LAUDED BY MUNDT

2 Justices Expected to Step Aside if Appeal Is Carried to the Supreme Court

WASHINGTON, Jan. 21 (UP)—Senator Karl E. Mundt, South Dakota Republican, telegraphed congratulations to Prosecutor Thomas F. Murphy today on his "magnificent victory" in the perjury conviction of Alger Hiss, former State Department official.

"Congratulations on a magnificent victory and long, difficult job, which was exceedingly well done and most successfully completed," Senator Mundt said.

He added in a statement that he had believed Hiss guilty ever since the defendant was confronted by his accuser, Whittaker Chambers, before the House Un-American Activities Committee in 1948. Mr. Mundt was a member of the committee at that time.

"The Hiss conviction demonstrates how an alert and energetic House Committee on Un-American Activities, supported by the investigative machinery of the FBI and the prosecution personnel of the Department of Justice, can cooperate in bringing to an end the methods by which Communists have been able to influence Government policies from within while at the same time relaying to their alien 'masters American secrets vital to our national security," Senator Mundt said.

Attorney General J. Howard McGrath and J. Edgar Hoover, director of the Federal Bureau of Investigation, refused comment on the conviction.

Two Justices Witnesses for Hiss

Other legal sources here, noting that Hiss' attorney plans an appeal, said that if the case ever reached the United States Supreme Court, Justice Stanley F. Reed and Justice Felix Frankfurter probably would disqualify themselves from sitting with the tribunal. They testified for Hiss as character witnesses in the first trial, which ended in failure of the jury to reach an agreement.

Representative Harold H. Velde, Illinois Republican, a member of the Un-American Activities Committee, said that Hiss' conviction "cooks President Truman's 'red herring' and I hope he enjoys eating it."

"Red herring" was the expression used by Mr. Truman to describe the committee's investigation involving Hiss and others in the Republican-controlled Eightieth Congress.

"The verdict speaks for itself," said Representative Francis Case, South Dakota Republican, a member of the committee. "It simply suggests that we be on guard. Frankly, it jolts me that people could be in a position of responsibility and be party to giving secrets or material to another country. It certainly does suggest that the committee has a real responsibility."

Bridges Urges Safeguards

Senator Styles Bridges, New Hampshire Republican, said:

"This man has taken advantage of every safeguard of the American judicial system and he has been found guilty. He is convicted as a liar. He lied when he said he was not in the service of the Soviet espionage system. We know that he worked for the Communists in 1938. The question is, how much longer was he a Communist stooge?

"Was he still rendering such service when he stood at Roosevelt's elbow at Yalta?

"He has many friends in high places. Only last January Dean Acheson, Secretary of State, listed Hiss as his good friend. He has many other friends in the State Department. What are we going to do about them?"

Representative Richard M. Nixon, California Republican, a member of the Un-American Activities Committee, said:

"I consider this verdict a vindication of the Congressional method of investigations when they are accompanied by adequate staff work and fair procedures. I also consider it another example of the reason why the people of the United States can have faith and pride in the American jury system."

In a radio interview he said that "high officials in two administrations" made a "definite, determined and deliberate effort" to keep the Alger Hiss "conspiracy" from the public. He added that he intended to place "information" before Congress next week that would bear out the charge.

Men, don't let water run continuously in the basin while shaving. Turn the water on and off as you need it.

OPPOSING LAWYERS CONTRAST SHARPLY

Murphy Is Big, Commanding, Serious—Cross Is Small, Quiet and a Strategist

Thomas F. Murphy, Assistant United States Attorney who headed the prosecution in the trials of Alger Hiss, is head of the criminal division of the Federal prosecutor's office here.

Mr. Murphy is 6 feet 4 inches tall and of massive build. He wears a mustache and his dark hair is graying prematurely—he is 43 years old. In his manner he is ponderous and determined, and this together with his height and bulk tend to make him a commanding courtroom figure, observers agree.

Mr. Murphy never even smiles in court. His only emotional changes in delivery have been from calm determination to satire when he wished to ridicule a defense claim, or ill-concealed anger when legal questions were in dispute. He burns the midnight oil in preparing for cross-examinations, his studies often carrying him far afield from the law.

Prior to the Hiss trials he prosecuted a succession of embezzlement, smuggling and other Federal criminal cases through the tenures of a series of United States attorneys in this district.

Mr. Murphy is a native of New York and was educated in Roman Catholic parochial schools here. He did his undergraduate work at Georgetown University in Washington, where he received his bachelor's degree. Afterward he entered Fordham Law School and was graduated with a law degree in 1930. He was in private practice until 1942, when he joined the criminal division of the United States Attorney's office. Soon afterward he was put in charge of the division.

Mr. Murphy's father, Thomas Murphy, was for many years chief clerk of the city Department of Water Supply, Gas and Electricity. His brother, "Fireman Johnny" Murphy, pitcher of the Boston Red Sox, formerly played with the New York Yankees.

Claude B. Cross of Boston, trial attorney for Hiss in the second trial, is Mr. Murphy's opposite in several respects. Mr. Cross, 56, gray-haired and 5 feet 6 in height, is quiet in manner, folksy in tone and shrewd in maneuver. He was deferential to his junior throughout the trial.

Mr. Cross is a member of the Boston law firm of Withington, Cross, Park & McCann. He replaced Lloyd Paul Stryker as the Hiss trial attorney.

Will Aid Long Beach Hospital

LONG BEACH, L. I., Jan. 21—A mass donation of blood for Long Beach Memorial Hospital will be held Tuesday. The hospital is in debt to the Blood Bank of Queens County, agency for Queens, Nassau and Suffolk hospitals. Under the chairmanship of Mrs. Jessica Sagor, members of B'nai B'rith, the American Legion, Knights of Pythias and the Long Beach Hospital Club will endeavor to contribute 100 pints of blood.

HISS IS CONVICTED ON PERJURY COUNTS

Continued from Page 1

Supreme Court, it was considered a foregone conclusion that Justices Felix Frankfurter and Stanley H. Reed would disqualify themselves. Both appeared at the first trial as character witnesses for Hiss, but were absent from his second trial.

In his first trial, which began on May 31 and ended on July 8, Hiss failed to win vindication from a jury. After hearing testimony for six weeks, the jury of ten men and two women deadlocked at eight to four for conviction. The second trial began on Nov. 17, took ten weeks and ended on its fortieth court day with the verdict.

United States Attorney Irving H. Saypol commended Mr. Murphy and his associates for the presentation of the Government's case.

"The verdict of the jury demonstrates that Mr. Murphy has vindicated justice," he said. "My personal and official commendations go to him and to the members of my staff, including Clarke S. Ryan, Assistant United States Attorney; Thomas J. Donegan, special assistant to the Attorney, General, and the Federal Bureau of Investigation."

Asked for his comment, Federal Prosecutor Murphy said:

"My job was to present the facts to an American jury, and it was their job to decide the facts. By their verdict this issue has now been permanently decided. I want to take the opportunity to thank sincerely all the men who have worked so hard and so long with me on this case."

Final Instruction of Jury

The jury, scheduled to resume deliberations at 10 o'clock yesterday morning, arrived at 9:20. At 10:31 the jurors asked Judge Goddard to reread parts of his charge on reasonable doubt, circumstantial evidence, corroborative evidence, and the relation of these factors to each other. They listened to the reading from 10:44 to 10:55 o'clock.

After luncheon, 12:55 to 2:08 P. M., the jury filed in with its verdict at 2:48. Two minutes later the verdict was on the record and Mr. Cross had polled the jury without changing the result. The jury was out a total of 23 hours 40 minutes, with 9 hours and 13 minutes spent in actual deliberations.

Hiss steadfastly refused comment on the outcome of the case, maintaining his silence until he left Foley Square with his wife in a friend's car at 3:23 o'clock. Like his wife, he had taken the verdict stolidly.

Hiss is the plaintiff in a $75,000 libel suit filed in November, 1948, in Baltimore against Mr. Chambers. The suit is based on the fact that Mr. Chambers called Hiss a Communist on a nation-wide broadcast.

Judge Goddard in his charge to the jury said the outcome of the perjury trial might well affect the decision in the libel suit. The Baltimore action has been deferred pending the outcome of the perjury trial here.

TRIAL JUDGE LONG ON FEDERAL BENCH

Goddard, Appointed by Harding in 1923, Has Presided Over Several Notable Cases

Federal Judge Henry Warren Goddard, who presided at the second trial of Alger Hiss, convicted yesterday of perjury, is one of the three Federal District Court Judges in the Southern District of New York with the longest service on the Federal bench. He was appointed by President Harding on Jan. 15, 1923. Judge William Bondy was appointed in the same year and Judge John Clark Knox was named by President Wilson in 1918.

Judge Samuel H. Kaufman, who presided at the first Hiss trial that ended in a jury disagreement, is the most recent appointee to the Federal bench in the Southern District. He was designated by President Truman in 1948.

Much of the early work done by Judge Goddard as a Federal judge was concerned with prohibition. Among such cases was that of Earl Carroll, theatrical producer, who was convicted of perjury after he had told a Federal Grand Jury that he had not seen a woman who had "stepped into, been pushed into or otherwise entered into a bathtub" on the stage of the Earl Carroll Theatre during the progress of an early morning party on Feb. 28, 1926. The tub had allegedly been filled with champagne.

On May 14, 1929, Judge Goddard dismissed a $3,000,000 suit filed by Anne Nichols against Universal Pictures Corporation and Carl Laemmle, its president. Miss Nichols alleged that the corporation and its president had pirated the material for their play, "The Cohens and the Kellys," from her successful Broadway comedy, "Abie's Irish Rose."

Judge Goddard also presided at the trial of Charles E. Mitchell, former chairman of the board of the National City Bank, who was acquitted of defrauding the Government out of $850,000 in income taxes. The verdict of acquittal was announced on July 22, 1933.

A trial requiring particular judicial skill came before Judge Goddard in 1942 when a former German Army major and five American citizens of German origin were brought into Federal court on charges of espionage on behalf of Nazi Germany. Public feeling ran high during the trial. The six persons were convicted on March 6, 1942.

Judge Goddard was born in New York City in 1876 and was a student in New York Law School in 1901. He was at one time a member of the law firm of Gay & Goddard and was for twelve years a member of Squadron A, New York National Guard. After enlisting for service in the first World War, he attended an artillery officers training school at Camp Taylor, Ky.

He is a member of several New York City organizations devoted to charity and to several bar associations. His clubs are the Union and the Racquet and Tennis. He was a director of the National Republican Club from 1912 to 1915 and is a Presbyterian.

Judge Goddard lives at 215 East Seventy-second Street.

STUYVESANT TENANTS TO FIGHT PARKING FEE

A mass meeting of residents to protest the charging of rental fees for parking under the viaduct of Franklin D. Roosevelt Drive in the Stuyvesant Town area has been planned for the evening of Feb. 6.

The meeting is part of a program formulated yesterday by the Town and Village Parking Committee at a two-hour session at the home of a member in Peter Cooper Village.

The committee's program calls for the distribution of literature urging the community's car owners to refrain if possible from taking space in the ramp area. It also demands an investigation of the legality of the city's plan to turn the area over to a private garage operator.

The Department of Marine and Aviation, which has jurisdiction over the marginal road, leased the area to New York Skyports, Inc. A charge of $10 a month for use of the sheltered parking area will be made as of Feb. 1. Previously residents had parked there without charge.

"All the News That's Fit to Print"

The New York Times.

LATE CITY EDITION
A little rain and cold today. Cloudy, continued cold tomorrow.
Temperature Range Today—Max., 38; Min., 31
Temperatures Yesterday—Max., 37; Min., 32
Full U. S. Weather Bureau Report, Page 53

VOL. XCIX...No. 33,611. Entered as Second-Class Matter. Postoffice, New York, N. Y. NEW YORK, WEDNESDAY, FEBRUARY 1, 1950. Times Square, New York 18, N. Y. Telephone LAckawanna 4-1000 RAG PAPER EDITION SEVENTY-FIVE CENTS

TRUMAN ORDERS HYDROGEN BOMB BUILT FOR SECURITY PENDING AN ATOMIC PACT; CONGRESS HAILS STEP; BOARD BEGINS JOB

PRESIDENT SEEKS 70-DAY COAL TRUCE, FACT-FINDING BOARD

He Ignores Taft Law in Asking 5-Day Week at Old Wages Pending Study of Dispute

AVOIDS WORD 'EMERGENCY'

Operator Acceptance Is Seen Likely, but the Plan Holds Disadvantages for Lewis

Text of announcement by White House on coal, Page 22.

By JOSEPH A. LOFTUS
Special to THE NEW YORK TIMES.

WASHINGTON, Jan. 31—President Truman moved into the soft coal dispute today with a proposal that John L. Lewis and the operators call a seventy-day truce and submit their arguments to a fact-finding board. He asked for an answer by 5 P. M. Saturday.

Under the truce "normal" production of coal would be resumed. This was understood to mean a return to the five-day work week by the members of the United Mine Workers, headed by Mr. Lewis. The wage scale of the expired union contract would be paid. A board of three would make recommendations in sixty days, but the recommendations would not be binding.

President Truman thus used the approach he used in the steel dispute last summer. This avoids use of the Taft-Hartley Law and its injunctive authority, although the President said in November that if he acted in the coal case he would use that law.

"Grave Concern" Voiced

The President's message to Mr. Lewis and the operators spoke of the "grave concern" about the dispute, but avoided Taft-Hartley words, such as "emergency" and "health and safety."

The dispute in the anthracite industry was omitted from the proposal.

The President said that in the final analysis the parties themselves must write their own agreement. "Voluntary action, not compulsion, in these matters is not only my personal conviction but the national policy," he declared.

Aware that the miners and operators were to meet at 2 P. M. tomorrow to try bargaining again, the President said he did not want to interfere with that. He told them that if they could reach an agreement to resume full production next Monday they should disregard his proposal and let him know about it by noon Saturday.

Mr. Lewis' attorneys are due in court at 10 A. M. tomorrow to answer a petition for an injunction filed by Robert N. Denham, general counsel of the National Labor Relations Board. Mr. Lewis and the other officers of the union filed affidavits in the case today. They denied violating the Taft-Hartley Law in the coal negotiations which began last May and accused the operators of refusing to bargain.

Surmise on Board Make-Up

The make-up of the fact-finding board, if the President's truce proposal goes into effect, is a matter of conjecture. When the proposal was under consideration at the White House in November the three men who had been asked if they were available were David L. Cole, who was a member of the fact-finding steel panel; John Dunlop, Harvard economics professor, and Willard Wirtz of Northwestern University, former chairman of the National Wage Stabilization Board.

Neither side would say tonight

Continued on Page 22, Column 2

Melchior Threatens To Quit Opera Here

Lauritz Melchior stepped into the Metropolitan Opera dispute last night by saying that he would not return next season "unless indicated plans change materially." He would make no comment on the possible return of Kirsten Flagstad, but, like Helen Traubel, he indicated resentment at not being approached sooner by Rudolf Bing, who will be the general manager for 1950-1951.

"I would have assumed," Mr. Melchior said, "that the natural courtesy of the management for the Metropolitan would dictate a call to any leading artist who had appeared regularly with the company for twenty-four years to determine his position with

Continued on Page 24, Column 2

By Winston Churchill: *The Second World War*

Volume III—The Grand Alliance

Book I—Germany Drives East

INSTALLMENT 6: THE JAPANESE ENVOY

THE New Year had brought disturbing news from the Far East. The Japanese Navy was increasingly active off the coasts of Southern Indo-China. Japanese warships were reported in Saigon harbour and the Gulf of Siam. On January 31 the Japanese Government negotiated an armistice between the Vichy French and Siam. Rumours spread that this settlement of a frontier dispute in South-east Asia was to be the prelude to the entry of Japan into the war. The Germans were at the same time bringing increased pressure to bear upon Japan to attack the British at Singapore.

• • •

About this time several telegrams arrived from our Commander-in-Chief in the Far East urging the reinforcement of Hong Kong. I did not agree with his views.

Prime Minister to General Ismay 7 Jan 41

This is all wrong. If Japan goes to war with us there is not the slightest chance of holding Hong Kong or relieving it. It is most unwise to increase the loss we shall suffer there. Instead of increasing the garrison it ought to be reduced to a symbolical scale. Any trouble arising there must be dealt with at the Peace Conference after the war. We must avoid frittering away our resources on untenable positions. Japan will think long before declaring war on the British Empire, and whether there are two or six battalions at Hong Kong will make no difference to her choice. I wish we had fewer troops there, but to move any would be noticeable and dangerous.

Later on it will be seen that I allowed myself to be drawn from this position, and that two Canadian battalions were sent as reinforcements.

• • •

IN the second week of February I became conscious of a stir and flutter in the Japanese Embassy and colony in London. They were evidently in a high state of excitement, and they chattered to one another with much indiscretion. In these days we kept our eyes and ears open. Various reports were laid before me which certainly gave the impression that they had received news from home which required them to pack up without a moment's delay. This agitation among people usually so reserved made me feel that a sudden act of war upon us by Japan might be imminent, and I thought it well to impart my misgivings to the President.

Former Naval Person to President Roosevelt 15 Feb 41

Many drifting straws seem to indicate Japanese intention to make war on us or do something that would force us to make war on them in the next few weeks or months. I am not myself convinced that this is not a war of nerves designed to cover Japanese encroachments in Siam and Indo-China. However, I think I ought to let you know that the weight of the Japanese Navy, if thrown against us, would confront us with situations beyond the scope of our naval resources. I do not myself think that the Japanese would be likely to send the large military expedition necessary to lay siege to Singapore. The Japanese would no doubt occupy whatever strategic points and oilfields in the Dutch East Indies and thereabouts they covet, and thus get into a far better position for a full-scale attack on Singapore later on. They would also raid Australian and New Zealand ports and coasts, causing deep anxiety in those Dominions, which have already sent all their best-trained fighting men to the Middle East. But the attack which I fear the most would be by raiders, including possibly battle-cruisers, upon our trade routes and communications across the Pacific and Indian Oceans. We could by courting disaster elsewhere send a few strong ships into these vast waters, but all the trade would have to go into convoy and escorts would be few and far between. Not only would this be a most grievous additional restriction and derangement of our whole war economy, but it would bring altogether to an end all reinforcements of the armies we had planned to build up in the Middle East from Australasian and Indian sources. Any threat of a major invasion of Australia or New Zealand would of course force us to withdraw our Fleet from the Eastern Mediterranean, with disastrous military possibilities there, and the certainty that Turkey would have to make some accommodation, for reopening of the German trade and oil supplies from the Black Sea. You will therefore see, Mr. President, the awful enfeeblement of our war effort that would result merely from the sending out by Japan of her battle-cruisers and her twelve 8-inch-gun cruisers into the Eastern oceans, and still more from any serious invasion threat against the two Australasian democracies in the Southern Pacific.

Some believe that Japan in her present mood would not hesitate to court or attempt to wage war both against Great Britain and the United States. Personally I think the odds are definitely against that, but no one can tell. Everything that you can do to inspire the Japanese with the fear of a double war may avert the danger. If however they come in against us and we are alone, the grave character of the consequences cannot easily be overstated.

The agitation among the Japanese in London subsided as quickly as it had begun. Silence and Oriental decorum reigned once more.

Former Naval Person to President Roosevelt 20 Feb 41

I have better news about Japan. Apparently Matsuoka is visiting Berlin, Rome, and Moscow in the near future. This may well be a diplomatic sop to cover absence of action against Great Britain. If Japanese attack which seemed imminent is now postponed, this is largely due to fear of United States. The more these fears can be played upon the better, but I understand thoroughly your difficulties pending passage of [Lend-Lease] Bill on which our hopes depend. Appreciation given in my last Personal and Secret of naval consequences following Japanese aggression against Great Britain holds good in all circumstances.

• • •

Behind the complex political scene in Japan three decisions seem to emerge at this time. The first was to send the Foreign Secretary, Matsuoka, to Europe to find out for himself about the German mastery of Europe, and especially when the invasion of Britain was really going to begin. Were the British forces so far tied up in naval defence that Britain could not afford to reinforce her Eastern possessions if Japan attacked them? Although he had been educated in the United States, Matsuoka was bitterly anti-American. He was deeply impressed by the Nazi movement and the might of embattled Germany. He was under the Hitler

Continued on Page 31.

FRANCE PROTESTS SOVIET RECOGNITION OF HO CHI MINH RULE

Note to Russia Asserts Action Could 'Gravely Impair' Paris-Moscow Ties

U. S. AND BRITAIN INFORMED

Government of North Korea Announces Acceptance of Viet Nam Rebel Regime

By LANSING WARREN
Special to THE NEW YORK TIMES.

PARIS, Jan. 31—France tonight delivered to the Soviet Embassy here a vigorous protest against Soviet recognition of Ho Chi Minh, the enemy of France in Indo-China. The note charged that the Soviet action was of a nature "gravely to impair French-Soviet relations."

In diplomatic circles here the Soviet Union's action was considered as a threat not only to the French position in Indo-China but as an effort to prevent the United States from building a policy of containment in Asia such as has been successful in Europe.

The text of the French note follows:

The French Government has learned through publication of a communiqué by the Tass Agency that the Government of the U.S.S.R. has taken the decision of recognizing as the Government of the Viet Nam the insurrectional government of Ho Chi Minh. Such a decision violates the principles of international law, since the only regular government of the Viet Nam is the government constituted by His Majesty Bao Dai, to whom the French Government has transferred the rights of sovereignty which it previously held.

In encouraging, as is the obvious intention of the Soviet Government, the insurrectional movement of Ho Chi Minh, this decision can only render more difficult the restoration of peace in Viet Nam. In taking the initiative which it has just announced, the Government of the U.S.S.R. is committing with regard to France an act whose character and consequences cannot be underestimated.

For all these reasons the French Government raises a solemn protest against a decision which is of a nature gravely to impair Franco-Soviet relations.

The note was delivered by Alexander Parodi, general secretary of the French Foreign Ministry, after Soviet Ambassador Alexandre Bogomolov, who was invited to the Quai d'Orsay, had replied he could not come today but would present himself tomorrow.

Copies of the French protest to

Continued on Page 11, Column 1

DISCUSSING PLANS FOR MAKING HYDROGEN BOMB

Members of the Joint Congressional Atomic Energy Committee talk with Sumner T. Pike, right, acting head of the Atomic Energy Commission, after President Truman gave his approval. Seated are Chairman Brien McMahon, Representatives Carl T. Durham, Chet Holifield and W. Sterling Cole. Standing are Senator John W. Bricker, Representatives Paul J. Kilday, Melvin Price, Carl Hinshaw and Charles H. Elston.

The New York Times (by George Tames)

HISTORIC DECISION

President Says He Must Defend Nation Against Possible Aggressor

SOVIET 'EXPLOSION' CITED

His Ruling Wins Bipartisan Support on Capitol Hill—No Fund Request Due Now

By ANTHONY LEVIERO
Special to THE NEW YORK TIMES.

WASHINGTON, Jan. 31—President Truman announced today that he had ordered the Atomic Energy Commission to produce the hydrogen bomb.

The Chief Executive acted in his role of Commander in Chief of the Armed forces, ordering an improved weapon for national security. Thus, from the domestic standpoint, he removed the question of producing the super-weapon as an issue that might be argued on moral grounds.

As for international statecraft, Mr. Truman, by treating the hydrogen bomb as an addition to the American armory, also removed it as an issue that might be interpreted as an advanced threat or inducement in seeking international control of atomic weapons.

Nevertheless, Mr. Truman said that his perseverance in providing for national defense would be matched by his efforts to seek international control of atomic weapons.

New Phase of Atomic Age

In his announcement, Mr. Truman regarded the hydrogen bomb as a progressive outgrowth of United States production of the uranium-plutonium atomic bomb. He put it this way: the commission was "to continue its work on all forms of atomic weapons, including the so-called hydrogen or super-bomb."

His use of the word "continue" was understood to imply that with national security the over-riding consideration, the chief factor guiding his decision was whether it was practicable to make the weapon. Scientists have said that it is.

In effect, the President's decision, which won wide acclaim in Congress, marked the advent of a new phase of the atomic age and a surge ahead of Russia in the race to retain military ascendancy:

The bombs that visited destruction on Hiroshima and Nagasaki split the atom. The new bomb would fuse atoms instead, but with a power 100 to 1,000 times greater than the improved fission bombs that have been developed since the Japanese cities were struck.

The President's Statement

The President made his decision known in the following brief statement:

"It is part of my responsibility as Commander in Chief of the armed forces to see to it that our country is able to defend itself against any possible aggressor. Accordingly, I have directed the Atomic Energy Commission to continue its work on all forms of atomic weapons, including the so-called hydrogen or super-bomb,

Continued on Page 3, Column 2

STIKKER IS NAMED E. R. P. CONCILIATOR

Council in Paris Accepts Dutch Leader Supported by Britain—E. C. A. Goals Unmet

By HAROLD CALLENDER
Special to THE NEW YORK TIMES.

PARIS, Jan. 31—Dr. Dirk U. Stikker, Foreign Minister of the Netherlands, was named today to the post of "political conciliator" of the European Marshall Plan Council instead of Paul-Henri Spaak, former Premier of Belgium, whose appointment was vetoed by the British Government. Paul G. Hoffman, Economic Cooperation Administrator, and W. Averell Harriman, ECA Ambassador in Europe, had desired that M. Spaak be chosen.

Dr. Stikker was elected by the Council. He was the candidate of the British who had first suggested Dr. Halvard M. Lange, Nor-

Continued on Page 14, Column 4

Truman Asks Utility Leader To Head Top Research Body

By JAMES RESTON
Special to THE NEW YORK TIMES

WASHINGTON, Jan. 31—President Truman has offered the Government's top scientific job—chairmanship of the Research and Development Board in the Department of Defense—to William Webster of Boston, a vice president of the New England Electric System, it was learned today.

Mr. Webster, 49 years old, a graduate of the United States Naval Academy and former chairman of the Defense Department's Military Liaison Committee with the Atomic Energy Commission, would be largely responsible for preparing an integrated military research and development program so that weapons such as the new hydrogen bomb would take their proper place in a well-balanced defense policy.

The chairmanship of the Research and Development Board was held by Dr. Vannevar Bush from 1947 to 1948 and by Dr. Karl T. Compton, former president of Massachusetts Institute of Technology, from 1948 until Nov. 3, 1949. Since then the work of the board has been supervised by Dr. Robert F. Rinehart as deputy chairman.

Coincidental with his offer of the Government's principal scientific position to Mr. Webster, President Truman was reported to be working actively on selection of a successor to David E. Lilienthal as chairman of the Atomic Energy Commission. One person said to be under consideration is Carroll Wilson, present general manager of the AEC.

Mr. Lilienthal is reliably reported to have proposed that control of

Continued on Page 5, Column 3

IT'S A TRITON BOMB, MIGHTIEST POSSIBLE

Would Release Energy More Than Seven Times '45 Type—No Critical-Mass Limit

By WILLIAM L. LAURENCE

What President Truman referred to yesterday as "the so-called hydrogen bomb" is not a hydrogen bomb at all in the true scientific meaning of the term.

This, the most powerful super-bomb that can be built on earth, it can now be revealed, actually is the triton bomb, in which the basic element used is tritium, a hydrogen isotope (twin) of atomic mass 3. It is an element hardly known to the public but well known to nuclear physicists. A triton is the nucleus of tritium, composed of one proton and two neutrons.

The term hydrogen, as used by scientists, refers strictly to the common form of hydrogen of atomic mass 1, a mass that cannot be made into a bomb.

While the process responsible for the vast amounts of energy released by the sun every second is

Continued on Page 4, Column 4

World News Summarized

WEDNESDAY, FEBRUARY 1, 1950

President Truman, acting in his capacity of Commander in Chief of the Armed Forces, yesterday directed the Atomic Energy Commission "to continue its work on all forms of atomic weapons, including the so-called hydrogen or super-bomb." The work, he said, would go forward "on a basis consistent with the over-all objectives of our program for peace and security" and "until a satisfactory plan for international control of atomic energy is achieved." [1:8.]

Congressional opinion heavily supported the President, and demands for speeding the work were made. The Atomic Energy Commission reported to Congress that atomic weapons now were being made by the "industrial type" of production and stockpiles were growing rapidly. [3:5.]

New defense safeguards were thrown about the atomic plants at Oak Ridge, Tenn.; Los Alamos, N. M., and Hanford, Wash. Any plane approaching within 100 miles of the plants without prior identification and clearance will be intercepted by Air Force fighters. [1:8.]

The hydrogen bomb, it was disclosed, is really a triton bomb, the basic element of which is tritium, a hydrogen isotope. [1:7.]

William Webster has been asked to head the Research and Development Board of the Department of Defense as successor to Dr. Karl T. Compton, who resigned. [1:6-7.]

Dealing with the major domestic problem of coal, President Truman asked John L. Lewis and the operators to call a seventy-day truce and to submit the issues to a nonstatutory fact-finding board such as he had named in the steel dispute. The President asked for a full five-day week in the soft-coal mines during the truce. [1:1.] Leaders of more than 100,000 striking miners were divided over urging the men to return. Operators indicated an inclination to accept the plan. [22:5.]

This state paid $357,000,000 in jobless benefits last year, nearly twice the 1948 total, Albany reported. [21:1.]

A House committee reported, 17 to 1, a bill for economic aid to Korea and Nationalist China. [13:2.] The brutality of South Korean police was seen as a major problem of the Seoul Government. [13:4.]

France, in a strong note of protest, told Moscow that Soviet recognition of Ho Chi Minh in Indo-China "gravely" impaired French-Soviet relations. Washington called Moscow's action proof that the Ho regime was Communist. [1:4.]

Senator Connally said Britain's policy of extending her embargo on dollar oil to the Commonwealth was "an act of hostility to our economy." [15:2.]

Britain won a victory in the European Marshall Plan Council when Foreign Minister Stikker of the Netherlands was elected "political conciliator." [1:5.]

French Premier Bidault won five close votes of confidence on the budget. [14:3.]

This city's tentative realty value for tax purposes was set at $18,493,559,079. [1:6-7.]

Index to other news appears on Page 30.

City Realty Values Up for 6th Year; Assessment Total $18,493,559,079

By LEE E. COOPER

New York's taxable realty wealth has increased on the city's books for the sixth consecutive year, with the result that property owners are due to pay levies on the highest aggregate valuation in seventeen years, according to official figures made public yesterday.

In a report to Mayor O'Dwyer's office, William E. Boyland, president of the Tax Commission, set the total tentative assessed valuation of real estate in the five boroughs for 1950-51 at $18,493,559,079. This is $381,327,900 above the final valuation for 1949-50, which was $18,112,231,179.

The high mark in realty valuations here, including utility property and special franchises, was reached in 1932, with $19,616,935,429.

The report showed a net rise for this year of $316,525,750 in "ordinary" real estate, to $16,120,113,875, and of $64,802,150 in the holdings of utility corporations, which were listed tentatively for the new tax year at $1,655,893,290.

Added to these sums was $717,531,914 for special franchises, the exact amount of which will not be set by the State Tax Commission for another month. The figure used by the city officials is based on the 1949-50 records.

Although no particular area was found by the field assessors to have increased generally in value—in contrast to last year when sharp gains were listed for the land around Stuyvesant Town and the United Nations site—there were three times as many rises as there were decreases in the city as a whole.

Largely for purposes of "equalization," to bring properties in line with neighboring valuations, in-

Continued on Page 20, Column 4

Air Defense Mapped For Atom Projects

By AUSTIN STEVENS
Special to THE NEW YORK TIMES.

WASHINGTON, Jan. 31—The Air Force disclosed tonight that it planned to throw a protective aerial "wall" around key atomic installations of the country.

Under a plan worked out today at the Pentagon, the Air Force will insist on the positive identification of any airplane flying within 100 miles of three atomic plants and, failing to be advised of an aircraft's identity will send fighter planes aloft to observe its character and course.

The plan in effect is a revival of a wartime measure whereby in combat zones any aircraft picked up by radar or other means of detection was consid-

Continued on Page 3, Column 6

THE MISSOURI BALKS; MAY REST ON ROCKS

Tide and Tugging Fail to Budge Battleship Hard Aground on Chesapeake Shoal

PUNCTURE OF HULL FEARED

Salvage Expert Says Combined Effort Yesterday Should Have Broken Vessel Free

By HANSON W. BALDWIN

Special to THE NEW YORK TIMES.

ON BOARD U.S.S. MISSOURI, Jan. 31—The great battleship Missouri was still high and dry on Thimble Shoals tonight, her sides still pocked with chafing gear, her decks cluttered with hawsers and lines. And the Navy saw a dark possibility that she was perched on a rock, with her bottom punctured.

Almost two weeks to the hour since the Missouri stranded in plain view of the famous old Army post at Fort Monroe, Old Point Comfort, Va., just off the busy shipping channel out of Norfolk, another Navy attempt to refloat the battle-wagon failed.

For almost two hours this morning, before and just after dawn thirteen tugs and two powerful salvage vessels huffed and puffed and beaching gear groaned and strained to drag the "Big Mo" off the ledge of compressed sand.

But fickle weather and bad luck—plus the ponderous bulk of the Missouri, perhaps the largest ship that ever has stranded—doomed the attempt. Dense fog, instead of the exceptionally high tide that last night's northeast winds seemed to indicate, greeted the morning's attempt and probably doomed it to failure. The fog, which lifted this afternoon, was the nemesis of two other vessels. A small Navy tug, used in the Missouri salvage work, ran aground and the United States Lines freighter Steel Navigator stranded off Willoughby Spit. The freighter was freed last night.

Another Attempt Today

Another attempt to refloat the Missouri, dubbed like today's a "coordination rehearsal," will be made tomorrow morning. If it does not succeed—and the odds seem to be against it—the main effort will be made on Thursday when the full moon is expected to bring the highest tide into Chesapeake Bay since the Missouri stranded.

This morning's failure emphasized the immensity of the job of refloating so large a ship. The salvage party, commanded by Rear Admiral Allan E. Smith, with Rear Admiral Homer N. Wallin as deputy, needed no such emphasis. Admiral Wallin, who commands the Naval Shipyard at Portsmouth, Va., is a veteran of the Pearl Harbor salvage, and many of the divers and specialists who work with him understand fully the problems of handling immense weights in water, of tunneling and diving, of rigging pontoons and handling heavy lines.

The Missouri's crew also appreciates, through rugged experience, the hard meaning of salvage work. Led by their skipper, Capt. William D. Brown, a tragic but gallant figure, they have worked day and night for two weeks, unloading stores and ammunition, handling great hawsers, transferring gear, loading and unloading anchors, shifting liquid ballast.

Essentially, the problem of refloating the Missouri is the same as that of refloating a rowboat stuck on a mud bank. Buoyancy must be increased by taking weight out of the rowboat, so the passengers get out. More water may be needed under the keel, so you wait for high tide. Then a pushing, pulling, levering or rocking motion may be necessary—usually in the case of the rowboat easily supplied by one or two persons—to "start" the boat out of its cradle of mud.

Same Principles Apply

Exactly these same principles apply in the case of the Missouri, but in her case such huge weights and tremendous horsepower and strain factors are involved that the mere mechanical difficulty of doing the right thing complicates and slows up the process.

Almost 12,000 tons of weight, for instance—fuel oil, water, stores, ammunition, anchors, chains, boats—have been removed. But the Missouri is almost as long as three football fields; even after lightening she displaces about 45,000 tons, and she rode up so high on Thimble Shoals 2,500 feet from the main ship channel that at low tide she presses down on her hummock of sand with a force of about 17,000 tons.

These gargantuan figures even the Navy seemed to have forgotten last night. The salvage experts felt that preparations for Feb. 2 were so well along and they were so beguiled by weather forecasts that indicated a flood tide six inches higher than normal, that they "stuck their necks out." Admiral Smith reported he was "almost" certain the Missouri would be refloated this morning, and Admiral Wallin backed this up in an even less qualified fashion.

Dredged Channel Narrow

After the failure this morning, Admiral Wallin reiterated that the "Big Mo" had had enough bouyancy plus enough pull and drag by the tugs and beaching gear to free her. There was some possibility, he said, that she was resting on a rock which had penetrated her outer skin and anchored her.

Anyway, the Missouri did not budge. The chief reason was the weather. The northeast wind—which tends to blow water into the bay, shifted to a gentle southwesterly breeze during the night. At 5:45 A. M., an hour before high water, the Missouri sat in heavy fog in a nearly normal tide, four to five inches lower than expected.

It was pehaps just as well the "Big Mo" was not freed, for the dredged channel astern of her through which she is to be dragged to deep water is in places only 120 feet wide, which would give the great ship a clearance of only six feet on either beam. Navigation so precise as this in weather like today's is almost impossible.

But there were causes besides the weather. Some of the tugs failed to pull in unison; others tended to veer away from the axis of the dredged channel; one of the heavy wire cables laid out to an anchor buried in the sand astern did not take the proper strain. One of the tugs parted a line; another line to a salvage ship was fouled by a small tug. Moreover, only four instead of the six pontoons originally planned had been affixed to the stern. Nevertheless, the "Big Mo," according to all the calculations, should have been dragged free. At the peak of the effort the battleship shook and quivered—but she did not budge.

Tomorrow more weight will be out of her; there may be eight lifting pontoons instead of four, and the tugs will be in a different position to give her a twisting and leverage movement. Destroyers at high speed may be used to create a wash along the Missouri's bottom, and other expedients to buoy her up and break her out may be tried.

The failure today was a double disappointment, for Admiral William H. P. Blandy, Commander in Chief of the Atlantic Fleet, is turning over command tomorrow in a formal ceremony to Admiral William Morrow Fechteler. Admiral Blandy, who will retire tomorrow, had hoped to turn over all his fleet afloat—but unless the "Big Mo" comes off at high tide tomorrow morning, this wish cannot be fulfilled.

ANOTHER UNSUCCESSFUL ATTEMPT TO FLOAT THE MISSOURI

Some of the tugs that early yesterday morning made a two-hour effort to slip the battleship from a sand shoal in Chesapeake Bay, where she was grounded on Jan. 17.

Associated Press Wirephoto

Truman Orders Hydrogen Bomb Built

Continued from Page 1

Like all other work in the field of atomic weapons, it is being and will be carried forward on a basis consistent with the over-all objectives of our program for peace and security.

"This we shall continue to do until a satisfactory plan for international control of atomic energy is achieved. We shall also continue to examine all those factors that affect our program for peace and this country's security."

On Capitol Hill when news of the Chief Executive's decision was received there, Republicans and Democrats joined in approving it. This bipartisanship boded well for Congressional backing of the new project, though it was said in informed quarters that Mr. Truman would not request funds for it at this time.

The Joint Congressional Committee on Atomic Energy held a previously scheduled meeting about an hour after the President's statement came out, and its chairman, Senator Brien McMahon, Democrat, of Connecticut, said that it had approved Mr. Truman's decision. He added that the committee would now proceed with meetings in which the implementation of the hydrogen bomb program would be studied.

Louis Johnson, Secretary of Defense, who had been in Mr. Truman's office today, would say no more than that "the President's statement speaks for itself." The view of the professional soldier was expressed by an anonymous but high-ranking officer speaking in the absence of Gen. Omar N. Bradley, Chairman of the Joint Chiefs of Staff. He said:

"This is one of the gravest decisions the United States has ever had to make, but it had to be done."

Mr. Truman was as undramatic in making his announcement as he was last Sept. 23 when he disclosed that Russia had achieved an atomic explosion — a development that clearly showed that our absolute dominance in atomic weapons was virtually ended. The President was not in his office when the historic statement came out. He was lunching at Blair House, the official residence.

It was 1:55 P. M. when Miss Genevieve Irish of the White House staff walked through the lobby of the Executive Offices and into the press room, crying "press."

White House reporters hurried into the office of Charles G. Ross, the press secretary. He requested that none should leave the room until each had a copy of the mimeographed statement that he held in his hands. He does not make such a request unless the subject is momentous.

Truman Preferred Secrecy

Mr. Truman's decision was a direct result of the discovery in September of the Russian explosion. After it was established beyond doubt that the Soviet Union had accomplished atomic fission, he called in David E. Lilienthal, chairman of the Atomic Energy Commission, and asked what should be done about holding this country's lead in atomic weapons.

Mr. Lilienthal, who is to resign about Feb. 15, was reported to have reminded the President of the possibility of producing the hydrogen super-bomb and asked if he wished to go head with it. Thereupon Mr. Truman sought the advice of Mr. Lilienthal as well as of the three other leading officials concerned—Mr. Johnson, General Bradley and Dean Acheson, Secretary of State.

It was learned that the President would have produced the hydrogen bomb in secrecy, as most military weapons have been in the past, except for the great debate over it that erupted last November and has continued since.

Mr. Truman was represented as feeling that while the new weapon was particularly destructive, this country should have kept its development secret so as to retain the element of surprise as an additional measure of security.

The President sought to discourage discussion of the new type of bomb after Senator Edwin C. Johnson, Democrat, of Colorado, said in a television broadcast that this country was making considerable progress in developing an atomic bomb 1,000 times deadlier than the one dropped on Nagasaki.

J. Howard McGrath, Attorney General, and Senator McMahon were called to the White House on Nov. 25 and urged by Mr. Truman to prevent leaks on data so vital to national security.

Informed sources characterized as ludicrous published estimates that it would take $2,000,000,000 to $4,000,000,000 to produce the hydrogen bomb. The figure would be nearer $200,000,000, it was said, since this country's vast, well-developed atomic plants and "know-how" would be used in its production. In this respect, it was added, the United States retained a great advantage over Russia.

Because the work could be undertaken by the Atomic Energy Commission with its present resources, officials said, no new funds would be needed immediately. The work could be carried on with present appropriations and plants until advanced stages were reached.

SANTIAGO BANKS STRUCK

Employes Go Out in Sympathy With Phone Workers

SANTIAGO, Chile, Jan. 31 (AP)—Banking activities in Santiago were at a standstill today as a result of a strike of 10,000 members of union of white collar workers.

Many business houses were unable to pay month-end wages. The strike was called in sympathy with 4,000 telephone and electric company workers who walked out Jan. 23 after demanding that Congress modify a Government plan for annual bonuses for employes of public utilities. The strikers ignored a plea by President Gabriel Gonzalez Videla to return to work.

The strike of white collar workers affected the Government savings institutions and social security services as well as banks. Some of the banks, such as the National City Bank of New York, and the Bank of London and South America, carried on skeleton operations with supervisory personnel and women clerks.

FINNS SEEK SOVIET AMITY

President Makes Special Plea in Closing Parliament

HELSINKI, Finland, Jan. 31 (AP)—President Juho Paasikivi, target of Moscow ire, closed Parliament's current session today with a plea for friendly relations with Finland's critical big neighbor—Russia.

The 78-year-old President, who recently won re-electioon despite strong Communist opposition, declared:

"The object of Finland's foreign policy has been to maintain and further develop good and confidential relations with all countries, but in particular with our eastern neighbor, the Soviet Union."

Russia has charged that Finland had broken a friendship and mutual assistance pact by harboring Russian war criminals. The Finnish Government rejected the accusation.

Soldier Receives Medal

Special to THE NEW YORK TIMES.

MITCHEL FIELD, L. I. Jan. 31—Master Sgt. John B. Wright received the soldiers' medal here today for heroism in rescuing an air force officer from the wreckage of a plane that crashed on take-off last May. A few hours after the ceremony, Sergeant Wright received his final papers for retirement after twenty-one years service, nineteen of which were with the Air Force.

CONGRESS TO SPEED HYDROGEN BOMBS

Reaction to Truman's Decision Is Overwhelmingly Favorable With Party Lines Dropped

By WILLIAM S. WHITE

Special to THE NEW YORK TIMES.

WASHINGTON, Jan. 31—The administrative and congressional controllers of atomic energy set out today within an hour of President Truman's announced determination to go on with the hydrogen bomb, to put the Government's unstinted resources into its swift development.

While Congress generally was responding in somber, overwhelming approval to the President's decision, its Joint Committee on Atomic Energy began discussing with the Atomic Energy Commission "ways and means and plans" to expedite the project.

Senator Brien McMahon, Democrat, of Connecticut, the committee's chairman, said that the "utmost speed" was necessary. He made it clear that a series of secret meetings could now be expected with the commission to "implement this program."

The commission during the morning sent to Congress a semi-annual report mentioning, among other things, that experiments in hydrogen had been going forward.

In a briefing on this report, which was given yesterday to reporters by commission members and held in confidence until the document reached Congress, all questions dealing with the practical prospects of this work in bomb production were answered by remarks that such information was secret.

Wide Support for Truman

The fact that a great majority of the Senate and House, Republicans as well as Democrats, was standing back of the President's decision was so plain as to require little inquiry among members There was a rush of statements in his support.

No Presidential announcement since Mr. Truman entered the White House seemed, in the opinion of many observers, to strike such an instant and general chord of nonpartisan congressional support.

The repeatedly expressed theme was that regardless of how dreadful the hydrogen weapon might be, Mr. Truman had no other course in view of the failure so far of negotiations for international control of atomic energy and of the "atomic explosion" some months ago in the Soviet Union.

There were, however, some sharp dissents. Representative W. Sterling Cole, Republican, of New York, asserted that the President had usurped Congressional authority and had acted against the recommendations of competent authorities. The security not simply of the United States but of "mankind" is at stake, he said.

Mr. Cole, as a member of the House Armed Services Committee as well as the Joint Committee on Atomic Energy, long since had indicated that he felt this country's defense policy was based too heavily on mass aerial bombardment.

Senator McMahon, apparently not then aware of Mr. Cole's statement, had told reporters that he believed it could be said that the joint committee was unanimous in approving the President's decision.

Some members of Congress made it clear that they now proposed to do all in their power to stimulate further efforts at reaching with the Russians an acceptable method for internationalizing atomic weapons.

No one in authority would discuss, in any specific way, the probable cost of developing the hydrogen bomb, but there was every indication that whatever was required would be provided by Congress.

Lilienthal Absent at Parley

The joint committee met about 3 P. M. with the Atomic Energy Commission. The only absentee on the commission's side was its retiring chairman David E. Lilienthal, who had strongly indicated at yesterday's press conference that he was troubled and undecided as to what should be done with the hydrogen bomb project.

"The joint committee," Senator McMahon said after the conference, "has discussed with the Atomic Energy Commission ways, means and plans for proceeding with the Presidential decision on the subject of the hydrogen bomb.

"It is my opinion, as it has been since I first made my recommendations to the President, that the utmost speed is necessary.

"I believe that this decision requires a nation-wide discussion in order that we may be sure that the decision to go ahead with hydrogen bombs for our defense will be made to promote world peace."

The Senator declined to elaborate on this latter remark, except to say that he entirely approved Mr. Truman's action, and to add:

"In other words, I believe we should have public discussion on the subject of armaments races; how they can be halted in the interest of the peace of the world, and the things we should think about and try to do.

"I was in favor of going ahead. I am in favor also of a political program to accompany it [the bomb.] I intend to discuss this later."

Report Somewhat Obscured

Somewhat obscured by the President's announcement was the seventh semi-annual report of the Atomic Energy Commission to Congress.

The report stated that production of the existing atomic weapons had progressed from a "custom-built" to "an industrial type of operation."

It also said that progress in exploration, in buying ore and in processing it had been so good that "it helped assure that future ore supplies, both from abroad and from sources in the United States, will be adequate for the operation of the atomic energy program."

Developing and stockpiling weapons had "moved on at a growing pace" during 1949, the report added, and the design of weapons had advanced. The production of materials to make weapons as well as for peaceable application also was declared to have "set new records."

On the subject of its experiments with three forms of hydrogen in seeking to produce atomic energy, the commission's report—and the accompanying comment of its members—was highly restrained.

It was said in substance only that in order "to study one of the simplest of all interactions," hydrogen—sometimes as pure gas, sometimes in a solid like paraffin—was being bombarded in two machines at the Berkeley, Calif., laboratory.

"One object of the experiments," it was added, "is to measure the force that holds the nucleus together and to try to get a better mathematical description of it.

"A tentative report on progress concludes that 'it is apparent that present theoretical concepts must be modified, and perhaps new concepts introduced, before a satisfactory mathematical description of the proton-proton force will be at hand.'"

This, and the briefing of reporters by the commission, left it an open question whether what was going on was wholly theoretical so far as a hydrogen bomb was concerned, or whether it might be considered practical progress in that program.

One of the questions asked on the point was whether this sort of work would aid the commission in producing hydrogen bombs.

Chairman Lilienthal replied only that information as to weapons development was "classified"; that is, secret.

Air Guard Is Mapped to Protect Three Key Atomic Installations

Continued from Page 1

ered to be an enemy craft until it was otherwise identified.

Aerial security cordons will be set around Oak Ridge, Tenn.; Los Alamos, N. M., and Hanford, Wash., all sites of atomic energy operations.

At the request of the Air Force, which is responsible for defending the nation against aerial attack and has recently been speeding the construction of its radar aircraft warning network (particularly in the most vulnerable area, the Northwest), all civil aircraft flying above a certain altitude must advise the military before flying through one of the designated high-security zones.

This will be done through the regular channels of the Civil Aeronautics Administration, which is responsible for civil air traffic control. The agency will soon send out instructions to all fliers to file a flight plan before entering the "air space" within 200 miles of the eastern coastal boundary of the United States at any point north of Norfolk, Va., or entering the 100-mile "defense areas" around the atomic energy sites.

With such flight plans before them operators of the military aircraft warning system will be able to plot the movements of all aircraft within the restricted zones.

Regular Schedules Not Affected

No interruption in the regular schedules of commercial airliners or private flying is contemplated under the new regulations. But should a pilot fail to advise the agency and the Air Force that he is entering one of the zones his plane will be "intercepted" by fighter aircraft at a distance close enough to establish visual recognition.

Representatives of civil aeronautical groups, the airlines, the airline pilots, non-scheduled operators, private fliers and state aviation officials attended today's meeting with military officials at the Pentagon.

The move was considered a logical step in the development of the aircraft warning system. Development of a radar "fence" about critical areas of the country and the acquisition of new "early warning" electronic equipment are among the Air Force's highest priority projects.

The Civil Aeronautics Administration will set the altitude above which an aircraft will be expected to file a flight plan. Unofficially, it was learned that it may be 2,000 feet.

The defensive radar screen now being expanded is designed to provide warning of approaching aircraft at a distance of between 150 and 300 miles. This "fence" can be extended from shore-based radar facilities through the use of offshore radar-equipped picket boats and by patrol aircraft. Last month the Air Force diverted $50,000,000 from other projects to strengthen the warning system, particularly in the vital Alaska area. Much of the radar in use is equipment left over from the second World War.

Defense Planners Concerned

Defense planners have expressed concern over the present aircraft warning structure. Where there is only what the Air Force calls a "one notch" ring of protection, or a reaching out by the "eyes" of radar for only 150 miles, fighters would have a very few minutes, it is pointed out, to take off and climb to high altitudes to intercept an enemy plane coming in at perhaps 300 miles an hour.

At present it is a violation of civil air regulations to fly directly over the three atomic plants listed today. The Civil Aeronautics Administration said that it would ask the voluntary cooperation of all aviation on the 100-mile zones and the East Coast boundary set by the Air Force.

The Defense Department announced after the meeting that the regulations formulated today were part of a long-range air defense plan and "were not related to any specific international developments." It was said that similar restrictions would be extended to other areas "as equipment and personnel are available at appropriate sites."

While it is planned to carry out the interception of unidentified planes on a 'round-the-clock basis, an Air Force spokesman said that sufficient equipment was not available at the moment to enforce the flight position rule on a full schedule.

PEIPING DROPS PLAN TO PAY AIDES SALARY

Special to THE NEW YORK TIMES.

HONG KONG, Jan. 21—The Peiping Government's plan to put state employes on a salaried basis this year have been dropped in view of the economic difficulties faced by the China mainland.

Reports in Communist publications from Shanghai say the Communist Government this year will continue in effect the system long enforced among Communists of paying the majority of party and Government workers by providing simple food, clothing and a small sum each month for minor personal expenses. The nonsalaried basis will continue in effect for 7,000,000 of 9,000,000 individuals now on official payrolls.

The reports say salaried personnel are mostly technical men or official employes taken over from the Nationalist Government. Technical personnel are said to get the highest pay with a few receiving as high as the equivalent of $25 a month.

Meanwhile, press reports from Communist China continue to give graphic indications of the march of starvation conditions in rural areas. A report in the Shanghai Liberation Daily from Taichow, a small town on the north bank of the Yangtze in Kiangsu states that 100,000 persons, 15 per cent of the total population of the county, are either starving, have fled their homes or have taken to begging.

This figure is said to have shown an increase of more than 20,000 in the ten days before the report was written.

Manila Objects to Marines

MANILA, Jan. 31 (UP)—The Philippine Government today rejected a request by the United States Embassy to station twenty-two marines in the embassy compound here as guards. Secretary of Justice Ricardo Nepomuceno said a marine guard would cause an "unsavory reflection upon the integrity of the Philippine Republic as a sovereign nation and its ability to maintain peace and order within its territory."

Dutch Seen Recognizing Peiping

THE HAGUE, the Netherlands, Jan. 31 (UP)—The Netherlands is ready to recognize the Chinese Communist Government, it was announced today. The Government will discuss the date with "some foreign powers," the announcement said.

"All the News That's Fit to Print"

The New York Times.

LATE CITY EDITION
Sunny with pleasant temperatures today. Fair tomorrow.
Temperature Range Today-Max.,80; Min.,60
Temperatures Yesterday-Max.,90.3; Min.,69
Full U. S. Weather Bureau Report, Page 55

VOL. XCIX..No. 33,758. | Entered as Second-Class Matter. Post Office, New York, N. Y. | NEW YORK, WEDNESDAY, JUNE 28, 1950. | Times Square, New York 18, N. Y. Telephone LAckawanna 4-1000 | FIVE CENTS

TRUMAN ORDERS U. S. AIR, NAVY UNITS TO FIGHT IN AID OF KOREA; U. N. COUNCIL SUPPORTS HIM; OUR FLIERS IN ACTION; FLEET GUARDS FORMOSA

114 RESCUED HERE AS LINER GROUNDS AFTER COLLISION

Excalibur, With Hole 15 Feet Wide in Side, Settles on Mud Flat Off Brooklyn

FIRES START ON FREIGHTER

One Person Slightly Injured—Responsibility for the Crash Still to Be Decided

By WILLIAM R. CONKLIN

Thirty-five minutes after a gay departure for a Mediterranean cruise, the American Export Line's Excalibur was disabled in a collision yesterday with a Danish freighter in the Narrows, but all her 114 passengers were taken off safely.

The confetti-speckled cruise ship left Pier 4, Jersey City, at noon for a forty-three-day voyage. At 12:35 P. M. the collision with the inbound Colombia occurred off Sixty-ninth Street, Brooklyn.

The impact crushed the bow of the freighter and tore a hole fifteen feet wide in the port side of the Excalibur forward of the bridge. Fire broke out in the Colombia's forepeak in a paint storeroom.

While passengers and both crews remained calm, water quickly flooded the forward holds of the cruise ship. The Excalibur settled with her bow on a midstream mud bank, with her screw lifted in the air.

Passengers Taken Off by Tugs

Passengers on the sinking ship donned bright orange life preservers and were taken off by two tugs of the Moran Towing Company. Except for one woman who bruised three fingers of her left hand, all passengers were uninjured. They were returned to Pier 4, and the ship line arranged for hotel accommodations for them.

No official on the scene would assess responsibility for the collision. The Coast Guard required both captains to file written reports on the crash today. Under usual procedure, a Coast Guard board of inquiry hears evidence and fixes blame. Unofficially, it was said that a misunderstanding of whistle signals was the probable cause of the accident.

Capt. S. N. Groves of Brooklyn, a veteran of twenty-five years at sea, commanded the Excalibur, a ship of 9,644 gross tons with a top speed of seventeen knots. The Colombia, owned by the United Steamship Lines of Denmark, was commanded by Capt. Christian Mikkelsen of Copenhagen. The freighter was operated by the Scandinavian-American Steamship Company of 25 Broadway. Carrying cotton, wool and lubricating oils, she was bound from Philadelphia to Pier 24 at Congress Street, Brooklyn.

When the collision occurred there was good visibility despite a light haze over the lower bay. Persons in Shore Road Park saw the collision clearly, half a mile off the Brooklyn waterfront.

As the Excalibur's forward holds filled, her nose dropped into a mudbank and she swung to face upstream on the incoming tide.

2 Fireboats Help Freighter

The fireboats William J. Gaynor and Firefighter put lines on the 5,146-ton freighter to fight the fire on board. With the help of the ship's forty-two crewmen they subdued a fire in the forward hold. A collision bulkhead between that point and the forecastle prevented them from tackling another fire in the peak.

With Army, Navy, Coast Guard and Moran tugs helping, the burning vessel was moved into the north side of the Sixty-ninth Street ferry pier. John L. Holian, Deputy Fire Chief commanding the Marine Division, summoned a hook and ladder company to pour streams into the burning peak from the pier. Within an hour, the fire was extinguished.

Joseph H. Boggs, senior assistant purser of the Excalibur, said it was fortunate that the collision had occurred in shoal water.

"Immediately after the crash we

Continued on Page 29, Column 2

SANCTIONS VOTED

Council Adopts Plan of U. S. for Armed Force in Korea, 7 to 1

THE SOVIET IS ABSENT

Yugoslavia Casts Lone Dissent—Egypt and India Abstain

Mr. Austin's statement to the United Nations is on Page 6.

By THOMAS J. HAMILTON
Special to THE NEW YORK TIMES.

LAKE SUCCESS, June 27—The Security Council adopted tonight a United States resolution recommending that members of the United Nations use armed force in repelling the invasion of southern Korea and restoring international peace and security.

The vote on the resolution, which amounted to Security Council authorization for President Truman's decision to send United States naval and air units to the defense of the Republic of Korea, was 7 to 1, with Yugoslavia voting against.

The representatives of India and Egypt did not vote because they had not received instructions from their Governments. The Soviet Union was absent.

Representatives of Britain, France, Nationalist China, Cuba, Ecuador and Norway announced this afternoon that they would vote for the United States resolution without change. However, the Council recessed at 5:12 P. M. to permit Sir Benegal Rau and Mahmoud Bey Fawzi, the representatives of India and Egypt, to try to reach their Governments by telephone.

The vote was finally taken at 10:45 P. M. after both said they had been unable to establish communication with responsible authorities. With Egypt and India again not participating, the Council then rejected, seven to one, a Yugoslav resolution proposing that the Council renew its appeal for compliance with the cease-fire resolution it adopted Sunday, and request the two sides to agree to United Nations mediation.

The Council then recessed again while Sir Benegal and Fawzi Bey again attempted to obtain instructions. Apparently Fawzi Bey did so, but neither he nor Sir Benegal made any further statement, and the Council adjourned at 11 P. M.

Both Security Council members and other delegates who crowded around their table showed their realization that a historic decision for the United Nations and the world was being taken tonight. Warren R. Austin, the United States representative, was determined to avoid postponing a decision until tomorrow, and the Indian and Egyptian representatives cooperated by not requesting a postponement because of their failure to receive instructions.

Mr. Austin said after the meeting that the immediate effect of the resolution "should be to stop

Continued on Page 7, Column 1

President Takes Chief Role In Determining U. S. Course

Truman's Leadership for Forceful Policy to Meet Threat to World Peace Draws Together Advisers on Vital Move

By ARTHUR KROCK
Special to THE NEW YORK TIMES.

WASHINGTON, June 27—Some of those who participated in the meetings Sunday and Monday nights, at which the momentous decisions were taken to resist further Communist aggressions, beginning in the Far East, with the combat air and naval power of the United States, described the President to associates today as determined from the outset to adopt the forceful policy which was announced this morning.

As soon as the first meeting assembled, they said, Mr. Truman made it plain that these were to be the bases of his decision:

1. The situation created by Communist tactics at various points of the world, culminating in the attack of North Korea on South Korea, had been allowed to drift too long.
2. The entire Far East was deteriorating in a manner to threaten the peace of the world, a line had to be drawn at once, and the United States had to draw it.
3. National security was the primary interest, but embedded in this were world peace and the prestige and future effectiveness of the United Nations, which was the architect of the South Korean Government.
4. It was a time for courage, even boldness, and calculated risk, which other members of the United Nations would be invited to share as they saw fit.
5. It was not a time to give the slightest consideration to previous policies or to individuals associated with those policies. If, for example, the fundamental change in the Far Eastern sit-

Continued on Page 4, Column 3

MAINLAND ATTACKS ENDED BY FORMOSA

Chinese Nationalists Halt Air, Navy Forays in Accordance With Request by Truman

By The Associated Press

TAPEI, Formosa, Wednesday, June 28—The Chinese Nationalists today ordered their Air Force and Navy to cease attacks on the Communist mainland in accordance with a United States request.

President Truman had ordered United States warships to protect Formosa against Communist attack and at the same time asked the Nationalists to cease offensive operations.

Nationalist Foreign Minister George Yeh hailed the President's order for warship protection as "a most welcome sign of comradeship in the fight against communism."

Generalissimo Chiang Kai-shek and his Cabinet had met after the United States note was delivered to the United States Embassy. It was understood the note carried with it instructions to see that it was brought personally to Generalissimo Chiang's attention.

Mr. Yeh translated the text to the Generalissimo last night in the presence of United States Charge d'Affaires Robert Strong.

Mr. Strong was with Generalissimo Chiang for about twenty minutes. After his departure the latter consulted with Mr. Yeh, Premier Chen Cheng and other officials.

The decision was announced after Generalissimo Chiang conferred with Gen. Chou Chih-jou, Chief of the Joint General Staff, and other top Nationalist commanders.

The Nationalists were believed to have agreed to Washington's re-

Continued on Page 8, Column 4

HOUSE VOTES 315-4 TO PROLONG DRAFT

Korea Crisis Breaks Deadlock—Bill Expected to Be Sent to White House Tonight

Special to THE NEW YORK TIMES.

WASHINGTON, June 27—The House of Representatives today passed, by a vote of 315 to 4, an extension of the draft for another year.

The bill added authority for President Truman to call to active duty members of the National Guard and the reserve forces for periods not exceeding twenty-one months.

The Senate agreed to vote on the bill tomorrow afternoon. Swift passage is expected there so that the bill may reach President Truman for his signature tomorrow night.

As recently as yesterday the Senate and the House appeared to be in a hopeless deadlock over the manner in which the selective service system could be kept alive without much leeway for the President to put it to use. Today when

Continued on Page 16, Column 5

U. S. FORCE FIGHTING

MacArthur Installs an Advanced Echelon in Southern Korea

FOE LOSES 4 PLANES

American Craft in Battle to Protect Evacuation—Seoul Is Quiet

By LINDESAY PARROTT
Special to THE NEW YORK TIMES.

TOKYO, Wednesday, June 28—The United States is now actively intervening in the Korean civil war, an announcement from Gen. Douglas MacArthur's headquarters here made clear this morning.

[Gen. Douglas MacArthur announced Wednesday that the forces of South Korea now were holding the Communist Korean invaders, a United Press dispatch from Tokyo said. At the same time he reported that United States fliers had begun bombing and strafing missions against North Korean forces. Seoul was reported quiet.]

General MacArthur revealed that a "small advanced echelon" from his headquarters had been established in Korea, presumably cooperating with the United States Military Advisory Group, which has been in Korea since the republic was established there under President Syngman Rhee two years ago.

The MacArthur announcement stated that Far East air forces and elements of the naval forces under the general's command were "conducting" combat missions south of the Thirty-eighth Parallel—the dividing line between Communist North Korea and the United States-recognized Korean Republic. These operations, it was officially stated, are "in support of the Korean Republic," whose Government has now been reinstalled in the capital, Seoul, after isolation of the Northern armored spearheads that had penetrated to the outskirts of the city yesterday.

The announcement said that United States planes, which were providing air cover for the evacuation of women and children dependents of various United States missions, had shot down four North Korean fighters that were interfering with the operation of

Continued on Page 17, Column 3

Statement on Korea

By The Associated Press.

WASHINGTON, June 27—The text of President Truman's statement today on Korea:

In Korea the Government forces, which were armed to prevent border raids and to preserve internal security, were attacked by invading forces from North Korea. The Security Council of the United Nations called upon the invading troops to cease hostilities and to withdraw to the Thirty-eighth Parallel. This they have not done, but on the contrary have pressed the attack. The Security Council called upon all members of the United Nations to render every assistance to the United Nations in the execution of this resolution.

In these circumstances I have ordered United States air and sea forces to give the Korean Government troops cover and support.

The attack upon Korea makes it plain beyond all doubt that communism has passed beyond the use of subversion to conquer independent nations and will now use armed invasion and war.

It has defied the orders of the Security Council of the United Nations issued to preserve international peace and security. In these circumstances the occupation of Formosa by Communist forces would be a direct threat to the security of the Pacific area and to United States forces performing their lawful and necessary functions in that area.

Accordingly I have ordered the Seventh Fleet to prevent any attack on Formosa. As a corollary of this action I am calling upon the Chinese Government on Formosa to cease all air and sea operations against the mainland. The Seventh Fleet will see that this is done. The determination of the future status of Formosa must await the restoration of security in the Pacific, a peace settlement with Japan, or consideration by the United Nations.

I have also directed that United States forces in the Philippines be strengthened and that military assistance to the Philippine Government be accelerated.

I have similarly directed acceleration in the furnishing of military assistance to the forces of France and the associated states in Indo-China and the dispatch of a military mission to provide close working relations with those forces.

I know that all members of the United Nations will consider carefully the consequences of this latest aggression in Korea in defiance of the Charter of the United Nations. A return to the rule of force in international affairs would have far-reaching effects. The United States will continue to uphold the rule of law.

I have instructed Ambassador Austin, as the representative of the United States to the Security Council, to report these steps to the Council.

NORTH KOREA CALLS U. N. ORDER ILLEGAL

Declares Security Council's 'Cease Fire' Invalid Without Assent of China and Russia

Special to THE NEW YORK TIMES

HONG KONG, June 27—The North Korean Government issued a statement today saying that it regarded the cease fire order of the United Nations Security Council illegal for two reasons. It said these were, one, because the Democratic Peoples Republic of North Korea was not represented when its affairs were discussed and, two, because the Soviet Union and (Communist) China did not participate.

On the latter point it cited the United Nations Charter, which requires unanimity of five permanent members of the Security Council on questions of substance. China and Russia are both permanent members. [But the Communist rulers of China have not been recognized by the United Nations as representing that country.]

Drastic measures were taken in North Korea yesterday to organize

Continued on Page 18, Column 5

LEGISLATORS HAIL ACTION BY TRUMAN

Almost Unanimous Approval Is Voiced in Congress by Both Sides—House Cheers

By HAROLD B. HINTON.
Special to THE NEW YORK TIMES.

WASHINGTON, June 27—President Truman's announcement today that United States air and sea power would be employed to expel the Communist invaders from South Korea evoked almost unanimous support in Congress. His statement was read by the majority floor leaders in both houses.

In the House of Representatives, the members rose to their feet and cheered as the reading was completed by Representative John W. McCormack, of Massachusetts. In the Senate, the reading by Senator Scott W. Lucas, of Illinois, brought immediate declarations of support from several Republican Senators.

Showing the same spirit of solidarity in the face of crisis, as the present situation was frequently described, Senate and House conferees agreed on legislation to ex-

Continued on Page 5, Column 1

BID MADE TO RUSSIA

President Asks Moscow to Act to Terminate Fighting in Korea

CHIANG TOLD TO HALT

U.S. Directs Him to Stop Blows at Reds—Will Reinforce Manila

By ANTHONY LEVIERO
Special to THE NEW YORK TIMES.

WASHINGTON, June 27—President Truman announced today that he had ordered United States air and naval forces to fight with South Korea's Army. He said this country took the action, as a member of the United Nations, to enforce the cease-fire order issued by the Security Council Sunday night.

Then acting independently of the United Nations, in a move to assure this country's security, the Chief Executive ordered Vice Admiral Arthur D. Struble to form a protective cordon around Formosa to prevent its invasion by Communist Chinese forces.

Along with these fateful decisions, Mr. Truman also ordered an increase of our forces based in the Philippine Republic, as well as more speedy military assistance to that country and to the French and Vietnam forces that are fighting Communist armies in Indo-China.

After he had started these moves that might mean a decided turn toward peace or a general war, the President sent Ambassador Alan G. Kirk to the Russian Foreign Office in Moscow to request the Soviet Union to use its good offices to end the hostilities. This was an obvious proffer of an opportunity for Russia to end the crisis before her own forces might get involved.

Door Opened for Russia

In the capital this was regarded as being at once a possible face-saving device for Russia in a showdown crisis and a feeler to determine her intentions.

The decisions amounted to a showdown in the "cold war" with Russia, in which this country had at last decided to begin shooting in a limited area. Yet all the decisions followed a carefully worked out formula of action within the framework of the United Nations as well as unilateral moves that avoided any direct provocation of the Soviet Union.

Mr. Truman based the decision to fight for the South Koreans entirely on the Security Council resolution which called upon all members of the United Nations to help carry it out. And at the Pentagon it was explained that our air and naval forces would fight only below the Thirty-eighth Parallel line that divides South Korea from the Russian-sponsored North Korea.

"The Security Council called upon all members of the United Nations to render every assistance to the United Nations in the execution of this resolution," Mr. Truman stated. "In these circumstances I have ordered United States air and sea forces to give the Korean Government troops cover and support."

Russia Is Not Mentioned

Mr. Truman carefully avoided mentioning Russia in his statement. He pivoted today's great shift in United States foreign policy on a conclusion that the "cold war" had passed from an uneasy passive stage to "armed invasion and war." He blamed "communism."

"The attack upon Korea makes it plain beyond all doubt that communism has passed beyond the use of subversion to conquer independent nations and will now use armed invasion and war," he said. "It has defied the orders of the Security Council of the United Nations issued to preserve international peace and security. In these circumstances the occupation of Formosa by Communist forces would be a direct threat to the security of the Pacific area and United States forces performi[ng]

Continued on Page 2, Column [illegible]

City, T.W.U. in 2-Year Peace Pact; Mayor Signs Fare Rise Resolution

Officials of the Transport Workers Union, C. I. O., the members of the Board of Transportation and Mayor O'Dwyer signed at City Hall yesterday a memorandum of understanding seeking to guarantee two years of peace in the city-owned rapid transit system.

The accord closely followed recommendations made on May 31 by the Mayor's Transit Fact-Finding Board, granting an 11-cent-an-hour increase to 35,929 operating employes, a third week of vacation after ten years and an additional holiday each year. The cost of the changes recommended by the fact-finders amounts to $13,188,515 a year.

The union bound itself not to engage in any strike or other interference with transit operations and not to seek any basic changes in the accord before July 1, 1952. It agreed to resolve all disputes in accordance with the grievance machinery set up in the pact. The union obligated itself also to recognize the board's managerial authority and to "cooperate in the attainment of efficient operations."

The Board of Transportation agreed to retain competent industrial engineers to report on a program for achieving a five-day, forty-hour week for all employes now having a scheduled work-week in excess of forty hours.

Mayor O'Dwyer also signed yesterday afternoon a resolution of the Board of Transportation, effective Saturday, increasing fares on the city-owned surface lines

Continued on Page 28, Column 4

World News Summarized

WEDNESDAY, JUNE 28, 1950

United States air and sea forces were ordered by President Truman yesterday to give Korean troops "cover and support." Moving directly to meet Communist "armed invasion and war" in Asia, the President instructed the Seventh Fleet to "prevent any attack on Formosa," called on the Chinese Nationalists to halt all attacks on the mainland, ordered United States forces in the Philippines strengthened and moved to speed military assistance to those islands and to Indo-China. He instructed Ambassador Kirk in Moscow to urge the Soviet Union to help end hostilities. [1:8; map P. 2.]

Naval and air elements are "conducting combat missions south of the Thirty-eighth Parallel of Korea in support" of the Seoul Government, General MacArthur announced. An advance echelon of his General Headquarters has been set up in Korea, he added. Conflicting reports of the fighting showed positions little changed during the day. [1:5; maps P. 17.] In Washington it was said that General MacArthur had sufficient forces to give the South Koreans air and sea preponderance. [13:3.]

This country's new Far East policy was set at conferences during which the President's positive program and leadership convinced his top aides that his decisions "were both inevitable and right." [1:3-4.] He brought unity to an Administration that had been split on many vital policy issues. [4:6-7.]

Governor Dewey, speaking as head of the Republican party, pledged full support to the President [4:3] and Congress was almost unanimous in its endorsement. [1:7.] The House, 315 to 4, passed a one-year extension of the draft with broad new powers for the President; the Senate will vote today. [1:4.] Senate Republicans, however, blocked a vote today on the foreign arms-aid bill. [14:3.] The National Security Resources Board has ready for introduction a sweeping bill authorizing the President to freeze prices, wages, manpower and materials. [15:2.]

The United Nations Security Council, with Russia absent and Yugoslavia voting no, approved a United States motion to permit member nations to send armed forces to help repel the Korean invasion. [1:2.]

British parties united in supporting President Truman's program. The Labor Government won confidence votes on its refusal to join talks on pooling Europe's heavy industry. [19:4.]

John S. Service, a key figure in Senator McCarthy's charges of communism in the State Department, has been cleared by the department's Loyalty Security Board. [22:3.]

Index to other news appears on Page 28.

Stocks Rally After Big New Losses In War Scare; Sales Near 5 Million

By ROBERT H. FETRIDGE

Securities markets the world over were subjected yesterday to wide fluctuations as the Korean situation approached a crisis of universal concern.

Calmer thinking emerged successful on the New York exchanges, but only after prices encountered terrific battering. Losses that at one time ranged to 5 points and even more in standard issues on the New York Stock Exchange were either trimmed or eliminated. Quotations were definitely on the recovery side at the close, with the final composite rate down only 0.75 point. As pictured by THE NEW YORK TIMES index, the market was midway between the highs and lows of the day at the final bell.

London was the worst sufferer among the major exchanges, while the Canadian markets followed the lead of New York.

It was a wild day on the trading floor of the Stock Exchange. Business almost reached the 5,000,000-share mark, the reporting ticker tape was constantly thrown behind actual transactions and at one time was twenty-seven minutes late. This necessitated "flash" prices on the ticker to keep brokerage offices at least abreast of the price changes in the key stocks.

The trend changed with such rapidity that selling orders were still being executed after the price direction changed for the better.

Continued on Page 41, Column 6

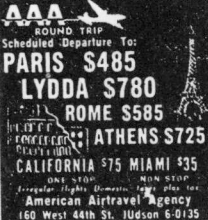

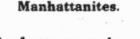

PRESIDENT ORDERS WAR AID TO KOREA

Continued From Page 1

their lawful and necessary functions in that area."

President Truman took the unusual action of virtually ordering the Chinese National Government to cease its air and sea operations against the Chinese mainland. He tersely stated that the Seventh Fleet "will see that this is done," adding that the future status of Formosa would have to await peace in the Pacific, or a peace settlement with Japan, or United Nations action.

In many major speeches Mr. Truman has not hesitated to name Russia as the country that had obstructed peace efforts in the United Nations through her use of the veto or the boycotting of its meetings.

In military parlance, the term "cover and support" used by Mr. Truman as missions for our forces means that they would seek to destroy any North Korea air, ground or sea forces, as well as their installations, that are encountered below the Thirty-eighth Parallel. They would do the same in support of any counter-offensive that the South Korea forces might be able to mount.

Thus the complexion of the Korean situation was changed overnight. Yesterday oficials were inclined to see South Korea, with her small, poorly equipped forces, as good as lost. It was acknowledged, as President Syngman Rhee of South Korea had complained, that aid in the form of munitions and supplies was "too little and too late."

Victory Is Seen for South

Today the view was that American air and naval forces could assure overwhelming superiority to South Korea and bring victory, unless, of course, Russia similarly aided North Korea.

The decisions were made last night in Blair House and before the night was over the coded action orders were being radioed to Gen. Douglas MacArthur in Tokyo and to other pertinent places. The formula encompassing all the action, it was learned authoritatively, began to take shape Sunday night in the first Blair House conference and it was custom-tailored for the resolution that the United States representative was directed to introduce in the Security Council meeting that night.

The correlated diplomatic action in Moscow was announced this afternoon by the State Department. Ambassador Kirk delivered a note, the text of which was not published.

Lincoln White, State Department press officer said:

"The Embassy asked that the Soviet Government use its influence with the North Korean authorities for the withdrawal of the invading forces and the cessation of hostilities."

President Truman was gratified with markedly good reaction that followed news of his decisions. There was typical bipartisan support as in other great emergencies that have faced the country, and Mr. Truman was particularly pleased with the message he received from Gov. Thomas E. Dewey of New York, his opponent in the Presidential race of 1948. He promptly sent a grateful reply. As one White House official expressed it, "there was a wonderful closing of ranks."

The unity on the political front was more than matched among the high civilian and military leaders of the nation who made the recommendations for action. Mr. Truman, before he even left his home in Independence, Mo., on Sunday to cope with the crisis, had formed a determination to do something drastic, something that would be neither appeasement nor merely passive. Both Defense and State Department officials, it was learned, worked with great harmony and easy agreement on the recommendations that were drawn up to meet his basic requirements.

Secretary of State Dean Acheson was said to have been a strong hand in working out the diplomatic requirements, both as to Moscow and the Security Council, and in urging the use of force. Those at the fateful council with the President in his home at Blair House last night were the same that met with him Sunday, after his hurried return from Independence.

They were Mr. Acheson, Philip C. Jessup, Ambassador at Large, John D. Hickerson, Assistant Secretary of State for United Nations Affairs, and Dean Rusk, Deputy Under Secretary of State; Louis Johnson, Secretary of Defense; Gen. Omar N. Bradley, chairman of the Joint Chiefs of Staff; Gen. J. Lawton Collins, Army Chief of Staff; Gen. Hoyt S. Vandenberg, Chief of Staff of the Air Force; Admiral Forrest P. Sherman, Chief of Naval Operations; Frank C. Pace Jr., Secretary of the Army; Thomas K. Finletter, Secretary of the Air Force; and Francis P. Matthews, Secretary of the Navy.

The proposed actions—air and naval support for South Korea to enforce the United Nations resolution and the decision on Formosa establishing unilaterally a line of United States defense in the Western Pacific—were already familiar. Mr. Truman canvassed the situation once again from every possible angle and then made his decisions. That, in brief, was the story of the meeting as told by one familiar with it.

This morning Secretary Johnson, Stephen T. Early, the Deputy Secretary of Defense, and Generals Bradley and Collins went to the President's office before 10 A. M. and apparently reported that the orders had gone out.

Then in mid-morning, before the announcement was made to the world, Mr. Truman summoned Congressional leaders and members of the committees dealing with foreign affairs in the Senate and the House. There were Republicans and Democrats, including Speaker Sam Rayburn, Senator W. Scott Lucas, the Senate Majority Leader, and Senator Tom Connally, chairman of the Senate Foreign Relations Committee, and John Kee, his opposite number in the House.

Secretary Johnson said, as the President's statement indicated, that none of our ground troops would be committee in the Korean conflict.

President Truman, as if to inspire confidence and calm in public, walked instead of drove to Blair House.

He lunched with his Cabinet. Eight were present, Maurice J. Tobin, Secretary of Labor, being out of town.

WHERE TRUMAN ORDERED ACTION IN FAR EAST

The New York Times June 28, 1950

The President has directed United States planes and warships to go to the assistance of South Korea (1) and ordered the Seventh Fleet to prevent any Communist attack on Formosa (2). Reinforcement of United States forces in the Philippines (3) and speedier military aid to that country and to Indo-China (4) were also set in motion by the President. The Seventh Fleet has been reported in the area south of Okinawa (cross).

100TH ANNIVERSARY
"All the News That's Fit to Print"
1851 1951

The New York Times.

Copyright, 1951, by The New York Times Company.

LATE CITY EDITION
Fair today, increasing cloudiness tomorrow and mild both days.
Temperature Range Today—Max., 60; Min., 45
Temperature Yesterday—Max., 65; Min., 48
Full U. S. Weather Bureau Report, Page 59

VOL. C..No. 34,045. Entered as Second-Class Matter. Post Office, New York, N. Y. NEW YORK, WEDNESDAY, APRIL 11, 1951. Times Square, New York 18, N. Y. Telephone Lackawanna 4-1000 FIVE CENTS

TRUMAN RELIEVES M'ARTHUR OF ALL HIS POSTS; FINDS HIM UNABLE TO BACK U. S.-U. N. POLICIES; RIDGWAY NAMED TO FAR EASTERN COMMANDS

HOUSE VOTES U. M. T. ONLY AS A PROGRAM; MARSHALL WORRIED

Chamber Accepts Compromise Setting Up Commission to Draft Details of Plan

FUTURE LAW IS REQUIRED

Congress' Approval Is Needed to Start Universal Training—General Sees Risk in This

By JOHN D. MORRIS
Special to The New York Times.

WASHINGTON, April 10—Concessions offered by advocates of Universal Military Training to save the program from outright rejection were approved today by the House of Representatives, but it remained to be seen whether the aim had been achieved.

General of the Army George C. Marshall, Secretary of Defense, meanwhile voiced the fear that current maneuvering in the House might "largely emasculate" the training features of the pending draft and training bill.

It was not clear, however, whether he was concerned over the main fight, expected later this week, over a proposal to eliminate all Universal Military Training provisions from the bill.

It was to head this off that the bill's managers headed by Representative Carl Vinson, Democrat of Georgia, offered the concessions that were approved today. The House accepted them on a voice vote.

Further Action Necessary

Consequently, as the bill now stands, little more than the principle of Universal Military Training is retained. A commission would be set up to draw up a detailed U. M. T. plan would be created. A "National Security Training Corps" would also be established, at least on paper.

But before anyone could be drafted to serve in the proposed corps, there would have to be another formal act of Congress, subject to Presidential approval or veto like any other bill, authorizing details of the training program.

At the same time, however, the revised bill retains safeguards against future pigeon-holing of U. M. T. in the House Rules Committee or elsewhere. The planning commission, which also would administer the program once Congress had authorized its institution, would be required to submit a detailed training plan to Congress within six months. The House and Senate Armed Services Committees would be required to report out a bill or resolution within forty-five days of receiving the plan. The measure then could be called up at any time.

Opponents Withhold Attack

In the House, bills ordinarily must be cleared by the Rules Committee before they can be considered on the floor. The Rules Committee bottled up a Universal Military Training Bill in the Eightieth Congress.

Opponents of any form of U.M.T. legislation did not fight the concessions approved in the House today, explaining that the proposals would make the bill less obnoxious although still unacceptable to them.

They were still hoping for approval of a substitute sponsored by Representative Graham A. Barden, Democrat of North Carolina, that would retain only what they regard as the "emergency" features of the pending draft measure. These include a three-year extension of authority to draft men 19 through 26 years of age for actual military service.

The Barden bill would eliminate authority to lower the draft age to 18½ as well as all long-range training features of the pending measure.

The Senate has already passed a draft and training bill adhering closely to the Administration's recommendations. It would authorise the drafting of men at the age of 18 and permit the President to put Universal Military Training

Continued on Page 15, Column 4

Tobey Asserts He Recorded R. F. C. Talks With Truman

President Said to Withdraw Fee Accusation—Niles Held Attempting to Aid Dawson

By C. P. TRUSSELL
Special to The New York Times.

WASHINGTON, April 10—Senator Charles W. Tobey, Republican of New Hampshire, was represented tonight as having told the Senate (Fulbright) subcommittee investigating the Reconstruction Finance Corporation that President Truman had charged in a telephone conversation with him that members of Congress had accepted fees for obtaining R. F. C. loans for constituents.

The Senator was said to have reported also that in a later telephonic communication the President had said that he had been mistaken.

Both telephonic conversations were said to have been recorded on disks in Mr. Tobey's possession. The date, or dates, were not made public. The Senator declined to discuss the matter and members of the investigating group also were silent.

In another development in the R. F. C. inquiry, former Senator Burton K. Wheeler, Democrat of

Burton K. Wheeler
Associated Press

Montana, said today that he had asked Senator Tobey to "go easy on" Donald S. Dawson, White House aide, during the Senate investigation of the agency. Mr. Wheeler asserted that he acted at

Continued on Page 25, Column 3

Sterling Hayden Was a Red; 'Stupidest Thing I Ever Did'

Special to The New York Times.

WASHINGTON, April 10—Sterling Hayden, motion picture actor and decorated former United States Marine, told the House Committee on Un-American Activities today that he had been a member of the Communist party from June to December of 1946.

"It was the stupidest and most ignorant thing I ever had done in my life," he said. "I went into it with an emotional and very unsound approach, but I don't mean to imply that I was dragged into it. I went in voluntarily."

Mr. Hayden, a native of Montclair, N. J., said there were thousands of others like him, who should come in and tell their stories.

He added that shortly after the invasion of South Korea his attorney had written to J. Edgar Hoover, director of the Federal Bureau of Investigation, giving his Communist case history and seeking a means of eliminating any prejudice against his recall to the service.

Under questioning for more than three hours, the former husband of Madeleine Carroll, screen star, told of a restless life that started with his quitting high school at the age of fifteen and going to sea, and winding up in Hollywood. A Capt. Warwich Tompkins, described by him as an "open and avowed Communist," ran through his story.

He identified Captain Tompkins as an employe of Amtorg, the of-

Continued on Page 14, Column 5

PRICE AIDE RESIGNS, CONDEMNS DI SALLE

M. E. Thompson, Ex-Governor of Georgia, Hits 'Kansas City Crowd' in Administration

Special to The New York Times.

WASHINGTON, April 10—With bitter words for Price Stabilizer Michael V. DiSalle, and for the "Kansas City crowd" he said was in the saddle in the national Administration, M. E. Thompson, former Governor of Georgia, resigned today as a consultant to the Office of Price Stabilization.

Mr. Thompson, once a power in Georgia politics, and who asserted that he battled successfully against the States Righters there who tried to keep President Truman's name off the ballot in 1948, declared that he would not support the Democratic party in 1952 if the "Kansas City crowd" still held control.

"If this be political treason,

Continued on Page 20, Column 1

RISE IN SALES TAX EXPECTED TO PASS CITY COUNCIL TODAY

Finance Committee Studies Bill at Length—Fight Against Measure Goes On

RUML A FISCAL ADVISER

Mayor Declines Challenge to Debate With Hoving—Joseph Suggests State-Wide Levy

The finance committee of the City Council spent an inconclusive three-hour executive session at City Hall yesterday afternoon weighing the merits of the proposed increase in the retail sales tax from 2 to 3 per cent, but when the meeting ended nothing had changed the prospect that the tax rise would be approved.

It was indicated that today the committee, after further behind-closed-doors deliberations, would favor the sales impost rise by a vote of 8 to 2, or possibly 7 to 3, and that later today the full City Council would adopt the measure by something like 19 to 6.

If the tax bill clears the Council hurdles today, as is indicated, it is expected that the Board of Estimate, whose members are committed to it, will give its approval at tomorrow's regular meeting.

Ruml to Advise Controller

Meanwhile, Controller Lazarus Joseph announced the appointment of Beardsley Ruml, business consultant, financier and economist, as a special deputy controller to advise Mr. Joseph on fiscal matters. Mr. Ruml, whose appointment was for an "indefinite" tenure, will serve without pay.

Mr. Ruml was at one time connected with the Federal Reserve Board and also with the New York Stock Exchange. He is a

Continued on Page 32, Column 4

U. S. PRODS NATIONS

Suggests U. N. Members Send More Troops to Fight in Korea

3 AVENUES ARE LISTED

Contributions Sought From Nations Not Yet Committed

By A. M. ROSENTHAL
Special to The New York Times.

UNITED NATIONS, N. Y., April 10—The United States has been quietly suggesting that members of the United Nations increase, or at least maintain, their contributions of troops for the Korean war effort.

Informed sources here report that for some time the United States has been keeping in touch with members of the world organization to see if non-United States representation in the international army could be increased.

[Chinese Communist troops in Korea clung to their positions along the Hwachon Reservoir in the face of daylong United Nations attacks. Eighth Army headquarters clamped a stringent security blackout on news from the front as a major battle seemed to impend in the reservoir area.]

So far there has been no general appeal to the United Nations members to contribute more troops; it has all been on a country-to-country basis. Diplomats said that there was no indication that a new general request for troops in Korea was in the making for the time being.

But on a longer-range basis, the question of more troops may be considered by the committee set up by the General Assembly on Feb. 1 to plan possible sanctions

Continued on Page 5, Column 3

World News Summarized

WEDNESDAY, APRIL 11, 1951

President Truman relieved General of the Army MacArthur of his command in the Pacific because the United Nations commander had been unable to give his "wholehearted support" to United States and United Nations policies. The Presidential ouster has forced the general from all his commands, including his role in the occupation of Japan. Lieut. Gen. Matthew B. Ridgway has been designated to take over all the Far Eastern commands. [1:8.]

The United States has been asking other United Nations members to increase, or at least maintain, their forces fighting in Korea and asking for troops from countries that have sent none. [1:5.]

Enemy resistance increased in the Hwachon Reservoir area of Korea. The Communists still held the dam although Hwachon itself appeared deserted. [2:1; map P. 2.] Mao Tse-tung was said to have been officially reported ill and Liu Shao-chi was said to be acting in his place at the head of the Chinese Communist regime. [9:2.]

Britain has suggested that the United States invite Communist China to the discussions on a Japanese peace treaty and send Peiping a draft of the proposed pact. The treaty, Britain holds, should include the return of Formosa to China. [1:6-7.]

The days of "easy and automatic" relations between the United States and Canada are over, Canada's External Affairs Minister declared. "There will be frictions" that can be settled easily, he said, if the United States recognizes that Canada's acceptance of Washington leadership does not mean she is "willing to be merely an echo of somebody else's voice." [1:6-7.]

A "severe, but not crippling" budget was presented to Britain by the Labor Government, which chose to increase taxes, already heavy, rather than cut social welfare funds. [1:7.]

The bill giving West German labor equal rights with management in the operation of the steel and coal industries was passed by the lower house. [14:2.]

The House passed and sent to the Senate a supplemental defense money bill 43 per cent below Administration requests [29:1] and cut from the draft bill a provision for Universal Military Training in favor of a Presidential commission to draw detailed plans. [1:1.] Defense Secretary Marshall ordered all three armed services to share equitably draftees of superior standing. [19:3.]

Mobilization Director Wilson called for an end to complacency, selfishness and partisanship if we are to beat down the "dreadful shadow" of history's most "absolute and ruthless" dictatorship. [23:1.] M. E. Thompson resigned as consultant to the Price Stabilizer in protest against "political" control and general wastefulness. [1:2.]

Organized baseball was ordered not to raise players' salaries above a club's 1950 highest. [33:2-3.] The Army halted certain pay rises for nonoperating rail workers until a special panel ruled in the case [33:1.]

Senator Tobey was said to have disclosed that he had recorded telephone talks with President Truman about the Senate R. F. C. inquiry. [1:2-3.]

The Navy suspended Dr. Stephen Brunauer, a scientist, as a "security risk," and the State Department dropped his wife, Esther, until the husband's case was settled. [1:2-3.]

NEWS BULLETINS FROM THE TIMES
Every hour on the hour
7 A.M. through Midnight
WQXR AM 1560
WQXR FM 96.3

Index to other news appears on last page of this section.

Navy Suspends Explosives Expert; State Department Then Bars Wife

Special to The New York Times.

WASHINGTON, April 10—The Navy Department suspended Dr. Stephen Brunauer today as a "security risk," giving the 47-year-old high explosives expert thirty days in which to answer the charges.

The State Department meanwhile, suspended Mrs. Esther Caukin Brunauer, wife of the Navy scientist, pending the outcome of the investigation of her husband. The State Department made it plain in a statement that the action against Mrs. Brunauer was based not on information about her, but only as a result of the Navy suspension.

Both of the Brunauers were named by Senator Joseph R. McCarthy, Republican of Wisconsin, in the course of his charges last year of Communist infiltration of the Government.

The announcement of Dr. Brunauer's suspension, effective immediately, was made while he was on a trip to New England for the Navy. Questioned by reporters at LaGuardia Field, on his way back to the capital, he said:

"I do not know for what reason I was suspended. I think some one made a mistake. I telephoned Washington and a Navy spokesman said he did not know the reason for the suspension. I do not want to comment further on anything."

Mrs. Brunauer issued a stout denial of the McCarthy charges on March 13, 1950, defending herself and her husband against the allegations they were Communists.

The Navy announcement of its suspension of Dr. Brunauer followed the disclosure by the State Department that the action had already taken place. The Navy gave no details of the charges, but said that Dr. Brunauer would have thirty days to answer the charges and request a hearing.

The decision of Francis P. Matthews, Secretary of the Navy will be final, it was said.

Asked whether the suspension of Mrs. Brunauer in response to charges against her husband was

Continued on Page 16, Column 3

DISMISSED BY THE PRESIDENT

General of the Army Douglas MacArthur

Britain Asks That Red China Have Role in Japanese Pact

By WALTER H. WAGGONER
Special to The New York Times.

WASHINGTON, April 10—Britain has suggested to the United States that Communist China be brought into the negotiations for a Japanese peace treaty. The British proposal also specifically asked that the United States send a copy of its treaty draft to the Peiping regime for its consideration, and, further, that the treaty provide for the ultimate if not immediate return of Formosa to "China."

By "China" the British mean the regime of Mao Tse-tung, since that is the China now recognized by London.

These suggestions have been made in the course of recent conversations between the two Governments. They represent another difference of opinion that has developed between London and Washington on both the procedure for negotiating a Japanese treaty and the form the settlement should have.

The basis for the British request that Peiping be given a look at the United States treaty draft is to enable the Chinese Communists to reject the proposal if they want to, as the Soviet Union is expected to do.

At the same time, it is vigorously denied here that Britain will refuse to sign any treaty draft that Communist China rejects. Reports that such an "or else" position has

Continued on Page 8, Column 5

BUDGET INCREASES BRITONS' TAX LOAD

Income, Profit, Purchase, Auto and Gasoline Imposts Rise—Social Services Uncut

By RAYMOND DANIELL
Special to The New York Times.

LONDON, April 10—The already heavily burdened British people were called upon today to pay even higher taxes to preserve their welfare state. Hugh Gaitskell, Chancellor of the Exchequer, introducing his first budget, told the House of Commons that there were only two ways of meeting the extra cost of rearmament. One, which brought cheers from the Conservative Opposition, was by reducing expenditures for social welfare.

The alternative he offered was a sharp rise in both direct and indirect taxes. This brought cheers

Continued on Page 10, Column 3

Canada Bars a 'Yes' Role to U. S.; Pearson Sees Unity Despite Friction

By The United Press

TORONTO, April 10—Lester B. Pearson, Canadian Secretary for External Affairs, said today that "easy and automatic" relations between Canada and the United States were a thing of the past.

In a speech apparently aimed at United States consumption, Mr. Pearson said that Canada was not willing to be "merely an echo of somebody else's voice" and reserved the right to criticize "our great friend, the United States."

Mr. Pearson said that Canada intended to prevent the United Nations from becoming "too much the instrument of any one country" and that it was time for the United States to stop telling Canada "that until we do one-twelfth or one-sixteenth, or some other fraction as much as they are doing, we are defaulting."

He said that there might be "angry waves which may weaken the foundation of our friendship" but that Canada would march forward with the United States "in the pursuit of objectives which we share."

"Nevertheless, the days of relatively easy and automatic relations with our neighbor are, I think, over," he added.

Mr. Pearson indicated that one of the "angry waves" that could weaken relations between Canada and the United States was the controversy over General of the Army Douglas MacArthur's statement on the war in Korea.

Later, in a second speech, Mr. Pearson made an indirect reference to General MacArthur when he said that a successful foreign policy must work toward goals accepted by the majority of the people, and it would have a better chance of "reaching these goals if we abandon what has been called 'hoop-la diplomacy' at Lake Success, at Ottawa, or, I hasten to add, at Tokyo."

He said that the free nations stood in danger of "nothing less

Continued on Page 6, Column 3

PRESIDENT MOVES

Van Fleet Is Named to Command 8th Army in Drastic Shift

VIOLATIONS ARE CITED

White House Statement Quotes Directives and Implies Breaches

Texts of statements and orders in MacArthur dispute, Page 8.

By W. H. LAWRENCE
Special to The New York Times.

WASHINGTON, Wednesday, April 11—President Truman early today relieved General of the Army Douglas MacArthur of all his commands in the Far East and appointed Lieut. Gen. Matthew B. Ridgway as his successor.

The President said he had relieved General MacArthur "with deep regret" because he had concluded that the Far Eastern Commander "is unable to give his wholehearted support to the policies of the United States Government and of the United Nations in matters pertaining to his official duties.

General MacArthur, in a message to House Minority Leader Joseph W. Martin Jr. of Massachusetts, made public by Mr. Martin last Thursday, had publicly challenged the President's foreign policy, urging that the United States concentrate on Asia instead of Europe and use Generalissimo Chiang Kai-shek's Formosa-based troops to open a second front on the mainland of China.

The change in command is effective at once. General Ridgway, who has been in command of the Eighth Army in Korea since the death in December of Gen. Walton H. Walker, assumes all of General MacArthur's titles—Supreme Commander, United Nations Forces in Korea, Supreme Commander for Allied Powers, Japan, Commander-in-Chief, Far East, and Commanding General U. S. Army, Far East.

Commanded in Greece

The Eighth Army command will pass to Lieut. Gen. James A. Van Fleet whose most recent important command was as head of the American military mission in Greece, when that country was repelling a Communist-directed guerrilla attack under the Truman doctrine.

In ousting General MacArthur for his public disagreement with American policy designed to localize the Asiatic war, the President said:

"Full and vigorous debate on matters of national policy is a vital element in the Constitutional system of our free democracy.

"It is fundamental, however, that military commanders must be governed by the policies and directives issued to them in the manner provided by our laws and Con-

Continued on Page 3, Column 1

News Stuns Tokyo; MacArthur Is Silent

By The Associated Press.

TOKYO, Wednesday, April 11—A small brown envelope with "flash" printed on it in red carried to General MacArthur today the news that he had been discharged from his commands by President Truman.

It was delivered by a senior aide, Col. Sid Huff, who said that the General received the news without comment. Colonel Huff indicated that the General had no forewarning that he was being relieved.

The General announced that he would have no statement immediately.

The message came as a Signal Corps communication about the time and Army radio announced the news.

General MacArthur got the word while at lunch with his wife, Senator Warren G. Mag-

Continued on Page 3, Column 4

TRUMAN RELIEVES M'ARTHUR OF POSTS

Continued From Page 1

stitution. In time of crisis this consideration is particularly compelling.

"General MacArthur's place in history as one of our greatest commanders is fully established. The nation owes him a debt of gratitude for the distinguished and exceptional service which he has rendered his country in posts of great responsibility. For that reason, I repeat my regret at the necessity for the action I feel compelled to take in his case."

The White House made the announcement of the relieving of General MacArthur at a hastily summoned press conference at 1 A. M. White House Press Secretary Joseph Short said that the announcement had been timed to coincide with delivery of the order to General MacArthur from the President which was dispatched over regular Army telecommunication. The hour in Tokyo was 3 P. M. Wednesday.

General MacArthur was told by the President to turn over all his commands at once to General Ridgway. The President added authority for General MacArthur "to have issued such orders as are necessary to complete desired travel to such place as you select." The General has not been in the United States for approximately fifteen years.

The order to General Ridgway to assume General MacArthur's commands was signed by Defense Secretary George C. Marshall, who added:

"It is realized that your presence is Korea in the immediate future is highly important, but we are sure you can make the proper distribution of your time until you can turn over active command of the Eighth Army to its new commander. For this purpose, Lieut. Gen. James A. Van Fleet is en route to report to you for such duties as you may direct."

Violations Indicated

In making public the order relieving General MacArthur the White House also released secret documents that had been sent as instructions to General MacArthur and that, it was indicated, the General had violated, leading to his dismissal.

The secret classification on these documents was removed by direction of the President in order that the public might be given the background leading to the President's action.

The first, under date of Dec. 6, 1950, and sent by the Joint Chiefs of Staff to General MacArthur and all other United States Army commanders, said that the President had directed, among other things, the following:

"No speech, press release or other public statement concerning foreign policy should be released until it has received clearance from the Department of State.

"No speech, press release or other public statement concerning military policy should be released until it has received clearance from the Department of Defense.

"In addition to the copies submitted to the Department of State or Defense for clearance, advance copies of speeches and press releases concerning foreign policy or military policy should be submitted to the White House for information.

"The purpose of this memorandum is not to curtail the flow of information to the American people, but rather to insure that the information made public is accurate and fully in accord with the policies of the United States Government."

Another Directive Cited

That same document included another Presidential directive to Defense Secretary Marshall and Secretary of State Dean Acheson. The President told them that all officials overseas, including both military commanders and diplomatic representatives, should exercise "extreme caution" in all their public statements, should clear all except routine statements with their departments and should "refrain from direct communication on military or foreign policy with newspapers, magazines, or other publicity media in the United States.

General MacArthur had, of course, violated this directive several times since it was issued.

The second document in the White House dossier dated March 20 and addressed to General MacArthur from the Joint Chiefs of Staff advised him that the State Department was planning a Presidential announcement in the near future that the United Nations was prepared to discuss condition of settlement in Korea now that the bulk of South Korea had been cleared of aggressors.

"Strong United Nations feeling persists that further diplomatic efforts toward settlement should be made before any advance with major forces north of the Thirty-eighth Parallel," the March 20 directive said.

"Time will be required to determine diplomatic reactions and permit new negotiations that may develop. Recognizing that [the Thirty-eighth] Parallel has no military significance, State [Department] has asked J. C. S. (Joint Chiefs of Staff) what authority you should have to permit sufficient freedom of action for next few weeks to provide security for United Nations forces and maintain contact with enemy. Your recommendations desired."

MacArthur Statement on Korea

The next document in the White House release was the text of General MacArthur's statement on Korea as it appeared in THE NEW YORK TIMES of March 25. The implication was obvious that the only source the White House had for this declaration was THE TIMES and that it had not arrived by cable from General MacArthur in advance as his military superiors had directed. It was in that statement that the general reported that South Korea had been substantially cleared of all organized Communist forces, that the enemy was suffering heavily from United Nations action and that General MacArthur announced his readiness to confer at any time with the enemy commander-in-chief in the field "in an earnest effort to find any military means whereby the realization of the political objectives of the United Nations in Korea, to which no nation may justly take exception, might be accomplished without further bloodshed."

On March 24 the Joint Chiefs of Staff in a message marked "Personal for MacArthur" told the Far Eastern Commander that Mr. Truman had again called his attention to the Dec. 6 directive for advance clearance of statements bearing on foreign or military policy. Referring to the general's most recent statement the Joint Chiefs of Staff added that "any further statements by you must be coordinated as prescribed" in the December instructions.

"The President has also directed that in the event 'Communist military leaders request an armistice in the field you immediately report that fact to the J. C. S. for instructions,'" the March 24 instruction said.

The next document dated Jan. 4 also addressed from the Joint Chiefs to General MacArthur said that the problem of arming additional Republic of Korea troops was under consideration. It detailed the problems of armament, supplies and shortages. The J. C. S. said that it appeared that the South Korean forces could be increased by from 200,000 to 300,000 men armed with rifles, automatic rifles, carbines and submachine guns.

The message added, however, that if these troops were organized into new divisions they would be relatively ineffecitve due to lack of artillery and other supporting weapons. The Joint Chiefs added, therefore, that it was probable that only about 75,000 more South Koreans can be effectively utilized immediately," with an ultimate build-up to 100,000.

General Asked for Comment

This message asked General MacArthur for his comments and recommendations as to how many additional South Korean troops could be employed profitably, how long it would take to organize and train them, whether they should be added to existing divisions or added to new ones and "other points in connection with current problems."

General MacArthur's answer dated Jan. 6 was interpreted by Mr. Short to reporters as a recommendation against the arming of additional South Koreans.

The White House press release gave the general's answer in full. Noting the shortages of available arms from the United States, General MacArthur suggested "it is possible that the over-all interests of the United States will be better served by making these weapons available to increase the security of Japan rather than arming additional R. O. K. forces."

"In view of the probable restricted size of the battlefield in which we may operate in the near future, and the high priority of N. P. R. J. (National Police Reserve of Japan) requirements the value of attempting to organize, train and arm additional R. O. K. forces in the immediate future appears questionable," said General MacArthur in his Jan. 6 message at a time when United Nations forces were in full retreat as a result of the unexpected intervention of Chinese Communist forces into the Korean war in late November.

"It is considered that the short-range requirements can best be met by utilizing available manpower to replace losses in existing R. O. K. units rather than creating new organizations. The long-range requirements for or desirability of arming additional R. O. K. pers. [personnel] appears to be dependent primarily upon determination of the future U. S. Mil. [military] position with respect to both the Korean campaign on the generally critical situation in the Far East."

The Final Document

The final document was General MacArthur's letter to Republican Leader Martin. In parentheses the White House noted that this statement of foreign and military policy had been obtained from the Congressional Record of April 5, 1951 although it was dated March 20, 1951 and had not come to the White House for review between the date of its writing and the time Representative Martin chose to make it public.

The implication was more than clear that this was the letter in which General MacArthur wrote himself out of a job.

There had been no indication when the White House closed up for the day at about 6 P. M. yesterday that any announcement was impending.

The only development that could be said to give a hint of the President's attitude was the abrupt cancelation of an appointment arranged by Erle Cocke Jr., American Legion commander, with Mr. Truman.

The interview was called off as soon as Mr. Cocke announced publicly his strong support of General MacArthur's proposal to use Generalissimo Chiang Kai-shek's Formosa-based troops to open a second front against the Chinese Communists on the mainland of China. Mr. Cocke also backed the Far Eastern commander's demand for authority to bomb Communist bases in Manchuria.

The White House stood on its dignity in discussing the Cocke incident. Joseph Short, Presidential Press Secretary, said that the Legion head had telephoned yesterday, reporting that he had just returned from Rome "and wanted to see the President before making any statement to the press."

"A couple of hours later there appeared on the news tickers interviews by Mr. Cocke in which he informed reporters what he was going to tell the President," Mr. Short added. "At that point, it seemed unnecessary for him to have the appointment. The appointment was canceled."

But Mr. Short's statement left an area of doubt as to whether Mr. Cocke was being left off the White House calling list because he had backed General MacArthur's policy or simply because he had offended the President by talking in advance of an appointment he had requested. He had accompanied the request with the voluntary statement that he wanted to see the President before he made any statements.

Request Made to Pace

TOKYO, April 10 (AP)—General MacArthur had asked Army Secretary Frank Pace Jr., for more troops and greater latitude in waging war against the Communists in Korea, informed sources said.

The requests reaffirm a MacArthur stand that has stirred up a widespread controversy in the United States and in Europe.

The controversy centers on General MacArthur's contention that the open war on communism in Asia should have priority over defensive plans against communism in Europe. Another factor is his forthright view on directives preventing air power in his command from attacking Red bases in Manchuria.

Pace With Eighth Army

Special to THE NEW YORK TIMES.

EIGHTH ARMY HEADQUARTERS, Korea, Wednesday, April 11—Frank Pace Jr., Secretary of the Army, arrived here this morning "to see the men and officers and to have an opportunity to know at first hand what the problems are" at the front lines in Korea.

Of his earlier conference with General MacArthur in Tokyo or reports—denied there—that he carried a Presidential reprimand to the United Nations commander, Mr. Pace said only that he had come to Korea because "I think I can do a better job" after gaining a personal knowledge of the country.

"There is a soft spot in my heart for the Army and the G. I. and also for my old friend General Ridgway," he said. "And, my gosh, it is good to see him looking so well." Mr. Pace will spend some time inspecting various types of Allied facilities in Korea but no detailed schedule was announced.

British Voice Stand Via Envoy

LONDON, April 10 (AP)—A Foreign Office spokesman said today Britain had expressed her concern over the MacArthur row to the United States through the "normal conversations" of Ambassador Sir Oliver Franks in Washington. The spokesman repeated at a news conference, however, his statement of yesterday that Britain's action did not constitute a "formal protest" over the United Nations Commander's recent statements about the Korean war.

Menzies Backs MacArthur

SYDNEY, Australia, April 10 (UP)—Prime Minister Robert Gordon Menzies defended General MacArthur's conduct of the Korean War today and said any negotiations in the present state of world affairs must be based on strength and "not weakness."

The Liberal Prime Minister addressed an Australian-American Association luncheon of 1,000 persons and took occasion to reply to former Labor Prime Minister Joseph B. Chifley, who said in an election speech last week that "the sooner we get out of Korea, the better." Mr. Menzies said: "We can't go out of Korea unless we are prepared to abandon the United Nations."

In defending General MacArthur, Mr. Menzies said:

"If you are fighting an enemy, you do not discontinue fighting him when he is fighting back. You do not just reach a line and say 'Here we stop!'"

Speaking again on General MacArthur, he said: "We do not propose to handicap him by giving him day-to-day instructions or advice as to the way he should measure his campaign."

Mr. Menzies said the Australian Government's policy regarding the Korean war was to resist aggression and maintain a strong position, to endeavor to limit the area of conflict and to continue to endeavor to negotiate a settlement.

246 Pass Pre-Induction Test

Army officials reported yesterday that 246 men passed pre-induction examinations here while 136 were rejected and twenty-one placed in an "undetermined" classification. There were seventy-six men inducted in addition to seventy-four who enlisted in the Army. Another forty-three joined the Air Force, seventy enlisted in the Navy and nineteen in the Marines.

President Truman's Statement of Regret In Announcing the Relieving of MacArthur

WASHINGTON, Wednesday, April 11 (AP)—Following is the text of President Truman's statement early today announcing his replacement of General MacArthur:

With deep regret I have concluded that General of the Army Douglas MacArthur is unable to give his wholehearted support to the policies of the United States Government and of the United Nations in matters pertaining to his official duties.

In view of the specific responsibilities imposed upon me by the Constitution of the United States and the added responsibility which has been entrusted to me by the United Nations I have decided that I must make a change of command in the Far East.

I have, therefore, relieved General MacArthur of his commands and have designated Lieut. Gen. Matthew B. Ridgway as his successor.

Full and vigorous debate on matters of national policy is a vital element in the constitutional system of our free democracy. It is fundamental, however, that military commanders must be governed by the policies and directives issued to them in the manner provided by our laws and Constitution. In time of crisis this consideration is particularly compelling.

General MacArthur's place in history as one of our greatest commanders is fully established. The nation owes him a debt of gratitude for the distinguished and exceptional service which he has rendered his country in posts of great responsibility. For that reason I repeat my regret at the necessity for the action I feel compelled to take in this case.

M'ARTHUR CAREER A STRENUOUS ONE

His Role in Japan and Korea Tops Brilliant Campaign in Pacific in World War II

At the age of 70 years, General of the Army Douglas MacArthur culminated a remarkable career by leading the United Nations forces in the Korean fighting, which marked his third war.

In the course of a strenuous military career, he was the first foreigner to govern Japan. As such, he received basic directives from the United States Government and the eleven-nation Far Eastern Commission in Washington, but practical policy was molded by General MacArthur himself.

One of the most decorated men in the world, he was named Supreme Allied Commander for Japan's surrender and occupation on Aug. 14, 1945, a goal for which he had fought and dreamed for almost four years. That appoinment marked his final redemption for the loss of the Philippines in 1942.

Took Command in Korea

He took command of United Nations' forces fighting the North Korean's Communists' invasion of South Korea. Besides his military duties, including personal visits to the fronts, the General continued as Supreme Commander for the Allied Powers in the Japanese Occupation.

President Harry S. Truman cabled MacArthur the nation's congratulations on his conduct of the Korean campaign, which he said was rivalled by "few operations in military history."

Mr. Truman flew more than 7,000 miles in mid-October of 1950 to hold a face-to-face conference with the General on Wake Island. It was the first time the two had met. On that occasion Mr. Truman pinned on MacArthur's open-neck shirt an Oak Leaf Cluster that was the equivalent of the fifth award of the Distinguished Service Medal.

In 1942, a few months after the United States entered the global conflict, MacArthur had been summoned from the hopeless defense of the Philippines to take supreme command of the Allied forces in the Southwest Pacific. He vowed that he would return—and he kept the faith with the heroes of Bataan and Corregidor.

It was a hard, uphill struggle, but a little more than three years later the Americans retook the Philippines. Shortly thereafter the Japanese surrendered unconditionally. MacArthur then became Supreme Allied Occupation Commander in Japan.

Boomed for President

A presidential boom was launched for General MacArthur in 1948 when he was put forward for the Republican nomination. He announced in Tokyo that he would accept the presidency if "called by the American people," but would not campaign.

He even turned down an invitation to testify before a Senate committee that would have given him an opportunity to return to the United States. His supporters believed a personal visit would greatly enhance his chances. He said it would be "repugnant" to him to return because the trip might be considered "politically inspired.

In making himself available as a candidate, MacArthur said he did not "actively seek or covet any office" and had no plans for leaving his post in Japan. He added, however, that "I would be recreant to all my concepts of good citizenship were I to shrink because of the hazards and responsibilities involved from accepting any public duty to which I might be called by the American people."

Among those active in his behalf was Gen. Jonathan M. Wainwright, who succeeded him in the defense of the Philippines.

At the Republican National Convention, MacArthur received 11 votes on the first ballot for the nomination and seven on the second. Gov. Thomas E. Dewey of New York was unanimously nominated on the third. MacArthur called Dewey "a splendid choice."

Because of the critical situation in the Far East, he declined several Congressional invitations to return home later for personal reports on developments.

M'ARTHUR OUSTER ASTOUNDS TOKYO

Continued From Page 1

nuson, Democrat of Washington, and William Sterns of Northwest Airlines. He was joined a few minutes later by his 13-year-old son, Arthur.

The news struck MacArthur headquarters like a thunderclap.

The American Embassy got the news and reporters relayed it to General MacArthur's honor guard. Guard members stood around their recreation room in stiff silence.

One captain remarked:

"I won't believe it until I see it on paper."

Sgt. Phillip Oberst, the guard at the gate, said:

"Boy, they sure made a big mistake."

The report of the announcement spread quickly throughout headquarters. Officers received it with evident bitterness and sadness.

"If the President does that," said one officer, "he will lose the next election—and then some."

Another asked:

"What grounds are there for his removal? Because he answered a personal letter from the Republican leader in Congress?"

The news astounded the Japanese. General MacArthur has been their unofficial emperor for more than five years.

The general's stature in this country has increased immeasurably with recent United Nations victories in Korea and, more particularly with the approach of a peace treaty, which most Japanese thinks General MacArthur engineered.

Series of Orders to MacArthur and His Command

WASHINGTON, April 11 (UP)—With the announcements of MacArthur's firing, the White House made public the following prior statements and orders relating to the Far Eastern situation:

6 Dec., 1950.

From joint chiefs of staff to commander-in-chiefs, Far East, Tokyo, Japan (and other commanders):

1. The President, as of 5 Dec., forwarded a memo to all Cabinet and to the Chmn N. S. R. B., Administrator E. C. A., Dir C. I. A., Administrator E. S. A. and Dir Selective Service, which reads as follows:

"In the light of the present critical international situation, and until further written notice from me, I wish that each one of you would take immediate steps to reduce the number of public speeches pertaining to foreign or military policy made by officials of the departments and agencies of the Executive Branch. This applies to officials in the field as well as those in Washington.

"No speech, press release, or other public statement concerning foreign policy should be released until it has received clearance from the Department of State.

"No speech, press release, or other public statement concerning military policy should be released until it has received clearance from the Department of Defense.

"In addition to the copies submitted to the Departments of State or Defense for clearance, advance copies of speeches and press releases concerning foreign policy or military policy should be submitted to the White House for information.

"The purpose of this memorandum is not to curtail the flow of information to the American people, but rather to insure that the information made public is accurate and fully in accord with the policies of the United States Government."

2. He also forwarded the following to the Secretary of State and Secretary of Defense:

"In addition to the policy expresesd in my memorandum of this date to the heads of departments, concerning the clearance of speeches and statements, I wish the following steps to be taken:

"Officials overseas, including military commanders and diplomatic representatives, should be ordered to exercise extreme caution in public statements, to clear all but routine statements with their departments, and to refrain from direct communication on military or foreign policy with newspapers, magazines, or other publicity media in the United States."

3. The above is transmitted to you for guidance and appropriate action.

20 March, 1951.

To: Commander in Chief, Far East, Tokyo, Japan, From Joint Chiefs of Staff:

State planning Presidential announcement shortly that, with clearing of bulk of South Korea of aggressors, United Nations now prepared to discuss conditions of settlement in Korea. Strong U. N. feeling persists that further diplomatic effort toward settlement should be made before any advance with major forces north of Thirty-eighth Parallel. Time will be required to determine diplomatic reactions and permit new negotiations that may develop. Recognizing that Parallel has no military significance, State has asked J. C. S. what authority you should have to permit sufficient freedom of action for next few weeks to provide security for U. N. forces and maintain contact with enemy. Your recommendations desired.

Text of General MacArthur's Korea statement, 25 March, 1951. Tokyo:

Operations continue according to schedule and plan. We have now substantially cleared South Korea of organized Communist forces. It is becoming increasingly evident that the heavy destruction along the enemy's lines of supply, caused by our 'round-the-clock massive air and naval bombardment, has left his troops in the forward battle area deficient in requirements to sustain his operations.

This weakness is being brilliantly exploited by our ground forces. The enemy's human wave tactics definitely failed him as our own forces become seasoned to this form of warfare; his tactics of infiltration are but contributing to his piecemeal losses, and he is showing less stamina than our own troops under rigors of climate, terrain and battle.

Of even greater significance than our tactical success has been the clear revelation that this new enemy, Red China, of such exaggerated and vaunted military power, lacks the industrial capacity to provide adequately many critical items essential to the conduct of modern war.

He lacks manufacturing bases and those raw materials needed to produce, maintain and operate even moderate air and naval power, and he cannot provide the essentials for successful ground operations, such as tanks, heavy artillery and other refinements science has introduced into the conduct of military campaigns.

Formerly his great numerical potential might well have filled this gap, but with the development of existing methods of mass destruction, numbers alone do not offset vulnerability inherent in such deficiencies. Control of the sea and air, which in turn means control over supplies, communications and transportation, are no less essential and decisive now than in the past.

When this control exists as in our case and is coupled with the inferiority of ground firepower, as in the enemy's case, the resulting disparity is such that it cannot be overcome by bravery, however fanatical, or the most gross indifference to human loss.

These military weaknesses have been clearly and definitely revealed since Red China entered upon its undeclared war in Korea. Even under inhibitions which now restrict activity of the United Nations forces and the corresponding military advantages which accrue to Red China, it has shown its complete inability to accomplish by force of arms the conquest of Korea.

The enemy therefore must by now be painfully aware that a decision of the United Nations to depart from its tolerant effort to contain the war to the area of Korea through expansion of our military operations to his coastal areas and interior bases would doom Red China to the risk of imminent military collapse.

These basic facts being established, there should be no insuperable difficulty arriving at decisions on the Korean problem if the issues are resolved on their own merits without being burdened by extraneous matters not directly related to Korea, such as Formosa and China's seat in the United Nations.

The Korean nation and people which have been so cruelly ravaged must not be sacrificed. That is the paramount concern. Apart from the military area of the problem where the issues are resolved in the course of combat, the fundamental questions continue to be political in nature and must find their answer in the diplomatic sphere.

Within the area of my authority as Military Commander, however, it should be needless to say I stand ready at any time to confer in the field with the Commander in Chief of the enemy forces in an earnest effort to find any military means whereby the realization of the political objectives of the United Nations in Korea, to which no nation may justly take exceptions, might be accomplished without further bloodshed.

24 March 1951.

To: Commander in Chief, Far East, Tokyo, Japan

From: Joint Chiefs of Staff, personal for MacArthur

The President has directed that your attention be called to his order as transmitted 6 December 1950. In view of the information given you 20 March 1951 any further statements by you must be coordinated as prescribed in the order of 6 December.

The President has also directed that in the event Communist military leaders request an armistice in the field, you immediately report that fact to the J. C. S. for instructions.

4 Jan., 51.

To: Commander in Chief, United Nations Command, Tokyo, Japan

From: Joint Chiefs of Staff

1. The problem of arming additional R. O. K. manpower is under consideration by J. C. S. Full info is furnished:

A. No machine guns, mortars, anti-tank guns or artillery can be made available from the Z. I.; however, the following can be made available in a reasonably short time:

(1) 160,000 model 1903 rifles, with a backup of spare parts for 50,000.

(2) 150,000 M1 carbines.

(3) 8,000 model 1918 Browning Automatic rifles.

B. Ammo supply for the M3 submachine guns, the Browning Auto rifles, 100,000 model 1903 rifles and 100,000 M1 carbines is feasible.

2. Based on availability of above weapons it appears that R. O. K. forces could be increased by from 200,000 to 300,000 men, armed with rifles, auto rifles, carbines and submachine guns. However, unless used in part to form new divisions, which would be relatively ineffective due to lack of infantry supporting weapons and artillery, it is probable that only on the order of 75,000 can be effectively utilized initially, with an ultimate build-up to approximately 100,000 in the following type organizations:

A. Augment the rifle strength of R. O. K. Div and other U. N forces.

B. Form special units for guarding lines of communication and for operations against Communist guerrillas.

C. Conduct guerrilla operations in Communist-held territory.

3. J. C. S. are of the opinion that recruitment for new units should include, but not be limited to, the membership of the Korean Youth Corps and or any other group in the R. O. K. Arms should be issued only to organized units under the control and discipline of the Mil authorities in Korea.

4. Request your comments and recommendations to include:

A. Total number of additional R. O. K. personnel that can be profitably employed.

B. Method of employment, namely, new divisions, additional strength in current divisions, etc.

C. Length of time required to organize and train additional manpower.

D. Other points in connection with current problem.

6 Jan. 51

From: Commander in Chief, Far East, Tokyo, Japan.

To: Department of the Army for the Joint Chiefs of Staff.

Considered here that influence of past and possible future events is of importance equal to or greater than matériel availability in analyzing problem of arming additional R. O. K. manpower.

Continued effort has been made since 25 June 1950 to effect the most practicable utilization of Korean pers. In addition to materially augmenting the R. O. K. Army, members of the youth corps and other qualified males have been supplied with significant quantities of small arms for the purpose of strengthening police units, anti-guerrilla security elements and creation of special organizations to operate in enemy held territory. Despite the relatively large number of non-army pers now under arms, enemy guerrilla units continue to operate effectively in many widely scattered regions of South Korea. Friendly guerrilla forces, however, have accomplished little in Communist rear areas—primarily due to lack of strong-willed leadership.

The type and quantity of weapons indicated by J.C.S. as being currently available would have equal application to equipping the National Police Reserve of Japan, the immediate requirements for which were stated. Unless the quantities listed in J.C.S. message are in excess of the current and foreseeable needs of the N.P.R.J., it is possible that the over-all interests of the U. S. will be better served by making these weapons available to increase the security of Japan rather than arming additional R.O.K. forces.

In view of the probable restricted size of the battle field in which we may operate in the near future, and the high priority of N.P.R.J. requirements, the value of attempting to organize, train and arm additional R.O.K. forces in the immediate future appears questionable. It is considered that the short-range requirement can best be met by utilizing available manpower to replace losses in existing R.O.K. units rather than creating new organizations. The long-range requirement for or desirability of arming additional R.O.K. pers appears to be dependent primarily upon determination of the future U. S. military position with respect to both the Korean campaign and the generally critical situation in the Far East.

Letter to Representative Martin of Massachusetts:

(From Congressional Record of April 5, 1951).

20 March, 1951

Dear Congressman Martin:

I am most grateful for your note of the eighth forwarding me a copy of your address of Feb. 12. The latter I have read with much interest, and find that with the passage of years you have certainly lost none of your old time punch.

My views and recommendations with respect to the situation created by Red China's entry into war against us in Korea have been submitted to Washington in most complete detail. Generally these views are well known and clearly understood, as they follow the conventional pattern of meeting force with maximum counter force as we have never failed to do in the past. Your view with respect to the utilization of the Chinese forces on Formosa is in conflict with neither logic nor this tradition.

It seems strangely difficult for some to realize that here in Asia is where the Communist conspirators have elected to make their play for global conquest, and that we have joined the issue thus raised on the battlefield; that here we fight Europe's war with arms while the diplomats there still fight it with words; that if we lose the war to communism in Asia the fall of Europe is inevitable, win it and Europe most probably would avoid war and yet preserve freedom. As you point out, we must win. There is no substitute for victory.

With renewed thanks and expressions of most cordial regard, I am,

Faithfully yours,

DOUGLAS MACARTHUR.

Texts of Orders to MacArthur and Ridgway For Change of Commanders in the Far East

WASHINGTON, Wednesday, April 11 (AP)—Texts of the orders by which General MacArthur was relieved of his commands and replaced by Lieutenant-General Ridgway:

ORDER TO GENERAL MACARTHUR FROM THE PRESIDENT:

I deeply regret that it becomes my duty as President and Commander in Chief of the United States military forces to replace you as Supreme Commander, Allied Powers; Commander in Chief, United Nations Command; Commander in Chief, Far East, and Commanding General, United States Army, Far East.

You will turn over your commands, effective at once, to Lieut. Gen. Matthew B. Ridgeway. You are authorized to have issued such orders as are necessary to complete desired travel to such place as you select.

My reasons for your replacement will be made public concurrently with the delivery to you of the foregoing order, and are contained in the next following message.

ORDER TO LIEUT. GEN. MATTHEW B. RIDGWAY; FROM GEN. GEORGE C. MARSHALL, SECRETARY OF DEFENSE.

The President has decided to relieve General MacArthur and appoint you as his successor as Supreme Commander, Allied Powers; Commander in Chief, United Nations Command; Commander in Chief, Far East; and Commanding General, United States Army, Far East.

It is realized that your presence in Korea in the immediate future is highly important, but we are sure you can make the proper distribution of your time until you can turn over active command of the Eighth Army to its new commander.

For this purpose, Lieut. Gen. James A. Van Fleet is en route to report to you for such duties as you may direct.

BRITISH FOR GIVING PEIPING PACT ROLE

Continued From Page 1

been taken by the British are thrown down as "completely wrong" here as well as in London.

The disposition of Formosa, according to the British line of reasoning, is determined by the three-power Cairo Declaration of Dec. 1, 1943, which provided that such territories as Formosa "shall be restored to the Republic of China."

Although the British do acknowledge the "Change of conditions and atmosphere" since that declaration was signed, London does in general respect the application of its principal terms.

It is indicated here that the British Government is willing to agree to a temporary arrangement for Formosa that does not immediately turn the island over to Communist China. Such an arrangement might be a trusteeship under the United Nations, as the United States has proposed for certain of the other islands.

In any event, the British would like the treaty to reaffirm the Cairo plan for the return of Formosa to "the Republic of China."

What is emphasized in this argument is the need for Britain and the United States to come to a working agreement on a definition of "China." Actually, this could mean only that the United States break relations with the Nationalist Government on Formosa, since London already recognizes Peiping and has no intention of re-establishing diplomatic intercourse with a force it regards as wholly unrepresentative, the Chiang Government.

The United States already has modified its original proposal for disposing of Formosa under the Japanese treaty. Initially, when it first circulated its "Seven principles" for a treaty to the members of the Far Eastern Commission last November, it suggested that the United States, Britain, China and the Soviet Union work out an arrangement for Formosa.

If those governments could not agree within a year, the question would be put to the United Nations General Assembly.

In the treaty draft that recently went to the other governments, the United States eliminated the Big Four possibility and suggested only that Formosa be taken up as future business when the treaty was signed.

"All the News That's Fit to Print"

The New York Times.

LATE CITY EDITION
Light snow this morning followed by clearing. Fair tomorrow.
Temperature Range Today—Max., 43; Min., 35
Temperature Yesterday—Max., 45; Min., 33
Full U. S. Weather Bureau Report, Page 55

VOL. CI..No. 34,347. Entered as Second-Class Matter, Post Office, New York, N. Y. NEW YORK, THURSDAY, FEBRUARY 7, 1952. Times Square, New York 36, N. Y. Telephone LAckawanna 4-1000 FIVE CENTS

KING GEORGE VI DIES IN SLEEP AT SANDRINGHAM; ELIZABETH, QUEEN AT 25, FLYING FROM AFRICA; PRESIDENT AMONG WORLD LEADERS IN TRIBUTE

2½% INTEREST RATE FOR SAVINGS BANKS APPROVED BY STATE

85% of Institutions Expected to Adopt 'Permissive' Rule Lifting 17-Year Ceiling

NEW U. S. TAXES A FACTOR

Board Adjusts Payments on Commercial Deposits, Acts to Clear Extra Dividends

By GEORGE A. MOONEY

New York's thrifty received a new incentive yesterday.

Terminating a policy that dates to 1935, the State Banking Board acted to raise its ceiling on interest-dividends paid on savings and thrift deposits from a 2 per cent maximum to 2½ per cent. Eighty-five per cent of the state's 130 savings banks are expected to put the increase in effect at an early date.

Last night the Dime Savings Bank of Brooklyn became the first in this area to announce it would pay 2½ per cent for the current quarter ending March 31.

Trustees of the Roosevelt Savings Bank announced they would meet today to increase the rate from 2 to 2½ per cent on account balances and deposits for the three-month period starting Jan. 1.

Other savings banks and competitive commercial banks, where possible, are likely to take similiar action soon.

Responding to the higher level of prevailing rates, and especially to Federal taxes imposed at the beginning of this year, several savings banks asked permission some weeks ago to pay larger dividends. Under the new tax law, savings institutions are made liable for income taxes at the regular corporate rate on all earnings after surplus and reserves total 12 per cent of deposits.

Regulation Is "Permissive"

William A. Lyon, Superintendent of Banks, in announcing the board's action yesterday said the new 2½ per cent rate was "permissive."

"Banks are permitted under the regulation to pay any rate up to that maximum which directors and trustees believe to be advisable in the light of the earning power and the capital or surplus position of their institutions," he explained.

Two other important amendments also were made in General Regulation No. 3, the dividend and interest rate regulation, Mr. Lyon said. In the first of these, relating to commercial banks' special interest and thrift deposits, the board approved a limit on interest payments at the maximum rate of 2½ per cent on the first $10,000 of any account and setting a ceiling rate of 1½ per cent on that portion of any special and thrift account in excess of $10,000.

The largest individual account that may be accepted by savings banks is $10,000, the maximum

Continued on Page 55, Column 6

Truman 'Shows Off' New White House

By W. H. LAWRENCE
Special to The New York Times.

WASHINGTON, Feb. 6—Ducking nimbly around and under scaffolding, President Truman today took a few correspondents on a conducted tour of the White House, which is being reconstructed. He said it was still his hope that the First Family would be able to move into it early in April after three and one-half years in Blair House.

Mixing history and comment about the tribulations of a tenant who decides to get a house done over, Mr. Truman led the reporters through the building for forty minutes, answering questions and volunteering observations about nearly every room.

The hum of power saws as workmen went ahead with their jobs sometimes drowned his

Continued on Page 33, Column 1

1-Way Traffic Signs Due Soon in Times Sq.

By JOSEPH C. INGRAHAM

Conversion of Seventh and Eighth Avenues to one-way operation has been decided upon by Acting Traffic Commissioner T. T. Wiley despite objections of the New York City Omnibus Corporation.

Preparations for the new traffic pattern were well under way yesterday, with new guideposts rising in Times Square and the fittings all set to hold the one-way arrows. Work on the other sections of the one-way routes, which extend from Columbus Circle to below Canal Street, also was progressing. Seventh Avenue-Varick Street will handle southbound flow and Hudson Street-Abingdon Square-Eighth

Continued on Page 17, Column 5

CHARGES OF WASTE IN DEFENSE DENIED

Pentagon Aides Tell Senators of Savings—Admiral Calls Himself 'Oyster Fork Fox'

By HAROLD B. HINTON
Special to The New York Times.

WASHINGTON, Feb. 6—Officials of the Department of Defense underwent a period of criticism before a Senate Appropriations subcommittee today and did not seem to like it. They were appearing in support of defense budget estimates of more than $52,000,000,000.

The principal witness was Vice Admiral Charles W. Fox, Chief of Naval Supplies, who told the Senators of the progress the Navy had made in simplifying the cataloguing of its supplies. When his presentation was interrupted by questions about allegations of waste and extravagance, the Pentagon contingent moved to the counter-offensive.

"I stand before you as Oyster Fork Fox," the admiral asserted, as the Senators and spectators laughed. "I am supposed to have bought 11,000,000 oyster forks for the Navy, and I had nothing more to do with it than you did."

He said that the Navy last

Continued on Page 4, Column 3

RED TRAPS FEARED IN FOE'S PROPOSAL FOR KOREA PARLEY

Communist Demand for Airing of Status of Formosa Viewed as Bar to U. N. Accord

TRUMAN CITED AS A GUIDE

Nam Il Argues Stand Taken by President on Blockading China Widens Issues

Text of Gen. Nam Il's statement is printed on Page 2.

By LINDESAY PARROTT
Special to The New York Times.

TOKYO, Thursday, Feb. 7—The United Nations Command began today a detailed study of the Communist proposal for a top-level political conference three months after the armistice in the Korean war to deal with related issues in the Far East.

This morning no hint of Allied reaction had come from the advance camp at Munsan, where the United Nations representatives took the Communist program after it had been delivered to them at a plenary session of the truce delegations at Panmunjom, or at the headquarters of the United Nations Commander, Gen. Matthew B. Ridgway, in Tokyo.

The enemy proposal was made by North Korean Gen. Nam Il, head of the Chinese and North Korean delegation, who drove to the meeting place in a big American limousine with whitewall tires. He nodded coldly to the senior United Nations representative, Vice Admiral Charles Turner Joy, and then launched into his prepared introductory remarks — considerably more extensive, it turned out, than the brief formal proposal for a governmental conference for "peaceful settlement of the Korean question and other questions related to peace in Korea."

Before the session adjourned it was agreed that a new plenary sitting should be held by the delegates of both sides after the United Nations study had been com-

Continued on Page 2, Column 6

World News Summarized

THURSDAY, FEBRUARY 7, 1952

King George VI died in his sleep at Sandringham Palace yesterday morning; his daughter was proclaimed Queen Elizabeth II. The King, who seemingly had recovered from an operation for the removal of a growth on his lung, had felt so well he had been out shooting the day before. [1:8.] The British people were stunned by their sudden loss. [1:7.]

King George became the British ruler in 1936 when his brother, King Edward VIII and later Duke of Windsor, abdicated. He saw little peace during his reign. Threats of war, armed conflict and the "cold war" marked his tenure. [10:1.] During the bombing of London he refused to take special precautions or leave Buckingham Palace. [13:7-8.]

The new Queen started for London by plane when she learned of her father's death. She had been touring East Africa with her consort, the Duke of Edinburgh. [1:6-7.] She is the first Queen to ascend Britain's throne since 115 years ago, when Queen Victoria was crowned. [1:5-6.] The Duke of Windsor sails from New York tonight, alone, to attend his brother's funeral. [14:8.]

President Truman, Secretary Acheson and others expressed the sorrow of the United States [1:5] as did former President Hoover, Mayor Impellitteri and others in this city. [14:5.] United Nations flags were flown at half-staff. [15:1.]

The Soviet Union, for the fifth time, vetoed Italy's membership in the United Nations. [1:4.] The Russians did not join forty-seven other countries in pledging funds for expanded technical assistance this year. [3:4.]

Allied officers studied the Communist proposal for a political conference three months after a Korean armistice. [1:3.]

West German leaders were unmoved by American and British pleas to cool their anger over French moves in the Saar and not to endanger plans for West Europe's defense. [6:3.]

A masked witness told a House committee he had seen Russians kill hundreds of Polish officers in Katyn Forest in 1939. [4:3.]

Defense Department heads, testifying on the military budget before a Senate group, vigorously defended their spending. [1:2.] Mobilization heads also were under attack for plans to spread defense contracts to unemployment areas. [39:4.]

The slow-down in the military aircraft production rate will have little immediate effect on consumer goods but will avoid more stringent curbs later, a survey showed. [3:1.]

Governor Byrnes of South Carolina blamed "Negro politicians of the North" for the Democratic party's shift from a State's Rights program. [21:1.]

This state authorized banks to pay up to 2½ per cent on savings and thrift accounts. [1:1.] Columbia University will increase tuition fees up to 25 per cent next fall and adjust faculty salaries upward. [29:1.]

NEWS BULLETINS FROM THE TIMES
Every hour on the hour 7 A.M. through Midnight
Except at 4 P.M. Today
WQXR AM 1560
WQXR FM 96.3

Index to other news appears on last page of this section.

THE NEW QUEEN AND THE LATE KING

ELIZABETH II — GEORGE VI — Associated Press

SOVIET AGAIN BALKS ITALY'S U. N. ENTRY

Russia for Fifth Time Vetoes Application—Is Beaten on En Bloc Admission Bid

By THOMAS J. HAMILTON
Special to The New York Times.

PARIS, Feb. 6—Italy's application for membership in the United Nation's was vetoed by the Soviet Union tonight for the fifth time. Ten of the eleven members of the Security Council voted for a French resolution recommending the admission of Italy.

Jacob A. Malik, the Soviet representative, based his action on the refusal of the United States and other Western powers to accept a Soviet proposal for en bloc admission of fourteen applicants, including five Communist governments.

The Soviet resolution afterward was rejected by a vote of six to two. The United States, Brazil, Nationalist China, Greece, the Netherlands and Turkey voted against the resolution, while Pakistan joined the Soviet Union in supporting it. Britain, France and Chile abstained.

Mr. Malik accused the United States of blocking Italy's admission. He declared that "the Italian people will note that it is the United States, with the help of the United Kingdom" that had "provoked" the Soviet veto. He added that if the Western powers had wanted to get Italy admitted, they would have agreed to the Soviet proposal.

Gross Protests "Horsetrade"

Ernest A. Gross, the United States delegate, retorted that on the contrary the Italian people would hardly be grateful for being made a part of the proposed "horse-trade." He asked whether Mr. Malik really believed that Italy should be "put in the same basket" with such "a shadow state" as Outer Mongolia, one of the Communist candidates included in the Soviet resolution.

Mr. Gross also expressed regret that the new state of Libya, which came into existence on Christmas Day, 1951, had been included in the Soviet en bloc proposal—which presumably meant that it likewise would encounter a Soviet veto unless the Western powers agree to the Soviet mass entry proposal.

Mr. Malik replied that Outer Mongolia deserved to be admitted. He said that its participation in the war against Japan "along with that of the Soviet Union" saved 1,000,000 American lives. He said he based his statement on statements by the United States high command.

Reconsideration today of Italy's long-standing application was the result of a General Assembly resolution last fall requesting the Security Council to reconsider it in the light of Italy's responsibilities

Continued on Page 3, Column 5

Ruler Becomes Elizabeth II; Her Son, 3, Is Crown Prince

By CLIFTON DANIEL
Special to The New York Times.

LONDON, Feb. 6—Britain entered a new Elizabethan era today. Upon the death of King George VI, Princess Elizabeth Alexandra Mary, his elder daughter, automatically became Queen of the United Kingdom and the Dominions Overseas at the age of 25.

Tonight at the first meeting of her Privy Council she was formally styled Queen Elizabeth II.

[Text of the Privy Council's proclamation is on Page 14.]

Thus, for the first time in 115 years, a woman ascended the world's most exalted and stable throne. At the Gloucester Assizes, as in other law courts of the land, the judges marshal closed the court with words not heard since the end of Queen Victoria's sixty-three-year reign in 1901: "God save the Queen and my lords the Queen's justices."

For the first time in British history the sovereign was abroad in the Empire at the moment of accession.

Already bearing the full responsibility of the crown, the new Queen will return here by air from Kenya in Africa tomorrow accompanied by her consort, the Duke of Edinburgh.

They were to have boarded the liner Gothic at Mombasa tomorrow to sail for Ceylon, Australia and New Zealand on a five-month ceremonial tour deputizing for the late King, whose illness prevented him from going.

With the accession of the Queen, her son Prince Charles, three years and two months old, became the Crown Prince and heir to the

Continued on Page 14, Column 3

TRUMAN EXPRESSES SORROW OF NATION

Voices Sympathy for British Over Loss of King—Acheson and Others Pay Tribute

Special to The New York Times.

WASHINGTON, Feb. 6—President Truman and the nation paid tribute to King George VI today in extending this country's sympathy to the British people on his death.

"He played his part nobly and with full understanding of the responsibility which was his," the President said in a formal statement.

All official Washington responded in kind following the surprise and shock at the news of the monarch's passing early this morning. Highest officials in the Government and leaders of both House of Congress joined in expressions of sympathy and praise for the man who had been a steadfast friend of the United States, and, indeed, had been the first British King to visit the country.

Secretary of State Dean Acheson commented on the courage with which King George had borne his physical suffering and noted: "It is a characteristic English spirit and the King possessed it in abundance."

Envoy Calls on Acheson

Sir Oliver Franks, British Ambassador, accompanied by seven representatives of the British Commonwealth, called on Secretary Acheson shortly after noon to inform him formally of the King's death.

"A world personage who maintained the highest tradition of the English constitutional monarchy passes in the death of His Majesty King George VI," President Truman said in his statement.

"From his accession to the throne through all the ills which beset the world throughout the years of his reign—including the most disastrous war in history—he played his part nobly and with full responsibility which was his. His heroic endurance of pain and suffering during these past few years is a true reflection of the bravery of the British people in adversity.

"The King was ever conscious of his obligations as sovereign of a nation which through centuries has been the champion of personal liberty and those free institu-

Continued on Page 14, Column 5

LONDON IS STILLED AS BRITONS MOURN

All Amusements Closed, Lights Dimmed, Streets Nearly Empty After News Stuns People

By FARNSWORTH FOWLE
Special to The New York Times.

LONDON, Feb. 6—This was a silent city tonight, with bright lights dimmed and all places of entertainment closed, as Londoners went home shocked by the death of their King.

The news reached most office workers at noon when they went out for lunch and found venders of early editions of afternoon papers shouting "The King is dead!"

"What King?" was a typical first reaction. It was hard to believe that it was indeed their own monarch, even though it had been generally realized since the King's operation last September that he might not have many years to live. Only a week ago tonight he attended a performance of "South Pacific" at the Drury Lane Theatre.

The suddenness of the news contrasted with the memory of how the public had been prepared during the final illness of the King's father, George V, with a broadcast communiqué saying, "The King's life is moving peacefully to its close."

Flags at half-staff appeared on public buildings and many private ones by noon. Theatres, cinemas and night clubs all shut down, as did the Stock Exchange and other markets.

The laughter of London's usually cheerful office girls was muted as

Continued on Page 13, Column 6

Elizabeth Weeps at News of Death, But Is Calm in African Take-Off

By The United Press.

NAIROBI, Kenya, Feb. 6—Young Queen Elizabeth II left hurriedly for home by plane tonight only a few hours after her husband had broken the news to her of her father's death.

The 25-year-old former Princess, after having broken down in tears, was composed when she departed early tonight on the long flight to London.

With Prince Philip she left the hunting lodge where the royal couple had been staying and drove in a closed automobile eight miles to a small airport near the East African town of Nunyuki. She took off in an East African Airways C-47 for Entebbe in Uganda, where the British Overseas Airways craft that had flown her to Africa waited to take her back to Britain.

The royal couple landed at Entebbe airport at 9:10 P. M. (1:10 P. M., Eastern standard time), but news of her arrival was kept from the local populace to spare the new Queen a further ordeal.

A tropical thunderstorm at Entebbe delayed the departure of the Queen's plane for more than two hours, but it finally took off at 11:47 P. M. for Libya as the weather cleared.

[The plane made a stop at the Royal Air Force base at El Adem, Libya, landing there at 1:15 A. M., Thursday, Eastern standard time, The United Press reported.]

At El Adem and Malta the Royal Air Force had planes standing by to escort the Queen's plane over the Mediterranean. It is scheduled to reach London at 4:30 P. M. Thursday, Greenwich time (11:30 A. M., E. S. T.)

Crowds of silent, sorrowful persons of all races lined the main street of Nunyuki as the Queen's party passed through. The Queen, her face showing the strain of the

Continued on Page 13, Column 5

15-YEAR REIGN ENDS

British Monarch's Death at 56 Follows a Lung Operation Last Fall

PARLIAMENT HALTED

Churchill Conveys News to Commons—Attlee Suspends Party Strife

By RAYMOND DANIELL
Special to The New York Times.

LONDON, Feb. 6—In the early hours of this morning George VI died peacefully in his sleep at the royal estate at Sandringham. As night fell upon this mourning capital of a still great family of nations, his elder daughter was proclaimed Queen of this realm and its dependencies, head of the British Commonwealth and the Defender of the Faith, with the title of Elizabeth II.

She is flying home tonight from her tragically interrupted visit to East Africa with her consort, the Duke of Edinburgh, and is expected back tomorrow to assume her royal duties as the wearer of the crown that somewhat mystically binds the British Commonwealth together.

Like the Elizabeth of England's golden age, she takes the throne at the age of 25.

Operated On 4 Months Ago

The King's death occurred just a little more than four months after an operation for the removal of a growth in his right lung. This operation resulted in the loss of the lung. His recovery seemed assured and in recent days he had been seen publicly at the theatre and at London Airport when he bade good-by to his daughter, now the Queen, as she set out with Prince Philip, her husband, on a journey that was to take her to East Africa, Australia and New Zealand. Only yesterday he was out shooting, his favorite sport.

It was assumed that the King had died as a result of a heart attack, probably caused by coronary thrombosis.

Tributes to the late monarch poured into London from leading world figures and from persons of humbler station.

His death came in his 57th year. It was the beginning of the sixteenth year of an unhappy reign. He never wanted or expected the throne of Britain, but he ascended to it when his brother Edward VIII abdicated to marry "the woman I love," Wallis Simpson.

Six years of his reign were war years when he and Elizabeth, his Queen, who now becomes Queen Mother, endeared themselves to their people by their bravery and devotion to their predestined role.

When he was crowned King on May 12, 1937, he was King Emperor but the title of Emperor went with the granting of independence to India. His reign marked the end of an era of British power.

Parliament Is Suspended

His death also brought to an end this session of Parliament in the midst of a bitter and acrimonious debate on how far this country should go in aligning itself with United States policy in the Far East lest it be dragged into war. That debate, which began yesterday, was left in mid-air as Parliament put aside its controversies to swear allegiance to the new Queen and deferred its partisan arguments on controversial issues until a more seemly time.

At Sandringham when the King died there were his two grandchildren, whom he adored, Prince Charles and Princess Anne; Sir Alan Lascelles, his private secretary; Sir Harold Campbell, his Equerry, and Lady Hyde, Lady-in-Waiting to his Queen. Soon after his death had been discovered by a servant bringing early morning tea, Dr. James Ansell, "Surgeon Apothecary" to the royal household at Sandringham, was called. He said that the King had died in his sleep without pain.

The news of the King's death went out over the news tickers at 10:45 A. M. At 11:15 it was broad-

Continued on Page 13, Column 2

King Known as 'Squire of Sandringham' Among Villagers in Favorite Hunting Grounds

TOWNSFOLK MOURN LOSS OF A 'FRIEND'

Companion on Hunting Trip on Day Before Death Says Monarch Appeared Fit

HE HAD SHOT NINE HARES

King Said to Have Remarked He Had a Most Pleasant Day at End of Long Outing

By TANIA LONG

Special to THE NEW YORK TIMES.

SANDRINGHAM, England, Feb. 6—This tiny hamlet of Sandringham mourned deeply tonight the loss of a beloved squire.

For to these simple folk in this and the neighboring villages, which form part of the late King's estate, George VI was so much more than a sovereign. He was something much closer, he was a part of their daily lives, he was the local squire.

Between them, there was the same friendly and human relationship that always has existed between the good English country squire and his tenants. George VI knew them all by name and spoke to them freely. He saw to it that they were well looked after. In times of trouble they knew they could count on him for help.

Many of the King's tenants saw him yesterday on his way to and from a hunt. He looked fit and cheerful. Thus, the shock to the villagers was all the greater when the news of his death was announced.

Lord Fermoy, a neighbor of the late King who was with yesterday's shooting party, said the King had been "on the top of his form" and had shot nine hares and one pigeon.

Exertion by King Doubted

Lord Fermoy said that there was no question of his having undergone any great exertion. The King's last words to him were "I will expect you here at 9 o'clock on Thursday," when the King was planning another hunting trip.

Sandringham, a collection of no more than a dozen brick cottages showed few outward signs of the King's death. The St. George's Cross of the Parish church flew at half-staff. Small groups of sorrowing villagers stood for a time at the gates to Sandringham House and then continued on their business.

There was no notice of the late King's death on the gates—only a small sign saying that the grounds would remain closed until further notice. Only those with passes were allowed in or out. By nighttime the big house appeared to be in darkness and the gates were opened only for the arrival of the Duchess of Kent.

Earlier in the day the Bishop of Norwich visited Sandringham House. The Rev. H. Anderson, rector of the Sandringham church where the King and the Royal Family attended Sunday morning services, also was at the house for part of the day. If the same procedure is followed as took place when King George V died here, the King's body will lie in Sandringham church for one night before being taken to Windsor Castle. However, it is understood that so far no instructions have been given for moving the King's body.

Out of respect to the Royal Family's sorrow and because of their own grief, the people of Sandringham and the neighboring villages canceled such entertainments as the weekly whist drive and a darts competition.

A few of the older inhabitants met at "the Feathers," a public house in the near-by village of Dersingham and sadly exchanged reminiscences of the late King.

Occasionally the tears would come to their eyes as they spoke of their contacts with him and realized all over again that these now had come to an end. "I still can't believe it," said one woman in her sixties.

Says King Had 'Good' Day

SANDRINGHAM, Feb. 6 (UP)—Lord Fermoy, the King's next-door neighbor who was out shooting with him yesterday, said today:

"Norfolk gave him a really wonderful last day. We were out shooting from 10 onward. I have seldom seen the King in better form. He was in good spirits and walking well.

"The King enjoyed himself in a day of beautiful winter sunshine. As we changed our boots at the end of the day he said, 'Now which of you will be coming with me again on Thursday?'

"The King was driven out to the area by car. He wore no coat or hat. He talked brightly all the time we were out and seemed to be thoroughly enjoying himself, plowing over the rough ground after the hares.

"At the end of the day he said, 'Well, it's been a very good day's sport, gentlemen.'"

PRINCESS ALICE MOURNS

New Queen's Mother-in-Law Is in Chicago on Fund Tour

Special to THE NEW YORK TIMES.

CHICAGO, Feb. 6—A royal Princess in the plain garb of a nun mourned the death of King George VI here tonight. She is Princess Alice of Greece, second cousin of the deceased King and mother-in-law of Queen Elizabeth. She is here on a tour to raise funds for the Sisterhood of Martha and Mary, a religious order of Greek Orthodox nuns, which she founded three years ago.

"The death of the King has greatly changed my plans for my visit here," she said. "This is a period of mourning for us of the royal family.

"The King's death was a great shock to me," she added. "I did not know about it for eight hours after he died. It is too late for me to change my plans in order to attend the funeral, but I shall cut short my visit and go to London."

AS LONDONERS HEARD THE NEWS OF KING GEORGE'S DEATH YESTERDAY

The grieving crowd that gathered around Wellington's Statue when word was spread that the monarch had passed. The flag atop the Royal Exchange building, center background, is at half staff.

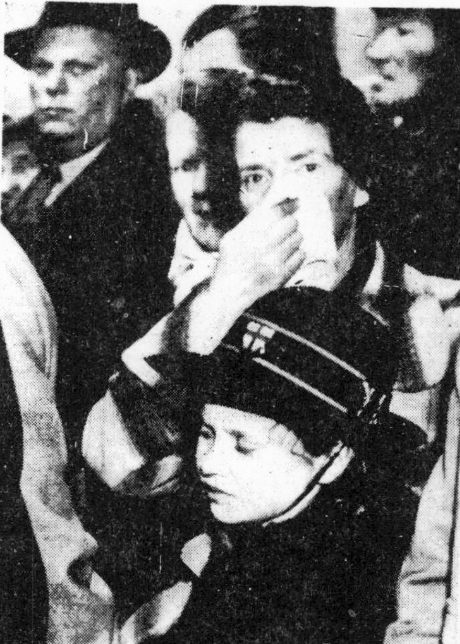

A tearful woman holding a handkerchief to her face as she stands with other mourners in Downing Street.

Associated Press Radiophotos

Prime Minister Winston Churchill, as he returned to his official residence at 10 Downing Street from the House of Commons.

BRITISH SURPRISED BY KING'S PASSING

Even His Doctors and Family Had No Intimation That End Might Be Imminent

Special to THE NEW YORK TIMES

LONDON, Feb. 6—From the medical point of view the death of King George VI today was a surprise to the nation and apparently to his family and his doctors as well.

The King himself seemed to have no intimation that the end was near. He did not live like a man who expected to die so soon. If he did anticipate his death he must have wanted his last days to be as normal and happy as possible, imposing no strain and anxiety on his family and friends.

Last June the King had influenza. In September he came to London from Balmoral for a medical examination, which disclosed "structural changes" in his right lung—possibly caused by cancer.

On Sept. 23 one of his lungs was removed and the King, showing good recuperative powers, gradually recovered from the impact of the operation.

He went outdoors for the first time on Armistice Day and last Dec. 21 went to his Sandringham estate for the usual family party at Christmas, the biggest in years. In a husky, strained voice he recorded his annual Christmas broadcast to the British peoples.

Last week he came back to London to say good-by to his daughter Elizabeth and the Duke of Edinburgh on their departure for Kenya.

On the eve of their departure he took his whole family to see the American musical comedy "South Pacific." At London Airport he walked about the field bareheaded and without a scarf. He sent away his elder daughter for a five-month tour and planned to take a spring cruise himself on the battleship Vanguard with his Queen and Princess Margaret. He, presumably, expected a family reunion in early summer.

When he was here his doctors examined him, found his condition satisfactory, noted that he was cheerful about his progress and readily allowed him to return to Sandringham.

Undoubtedly, the King was aware that an operation as serious as his might impose an unbearable strain on his constitution but aside from avoiding great exertion he appeared to make no concession to the possibility of death.

Then, alone and quietly, he died in bed. For lack of information it was assumed that he had had a heart attack, probably caused by coronary thrombosis (a blood clot forming in the coronary artery leading to the heart). It was the logical result of drastic surgery and a prolonged illness.

King George Refused to Quit Palace When Luftwaffe Tore at London

Expressed Wish to Share Danger With His People and Had Close Brush With Bombs —Tried to Join Normandy Invasion

The fury of the German air blitzkrieg over Britain in 1940-41 failed to shake King George's resolve to maintain his residence at Buckingham Palace, in the heart of London. The palace was bombed, yet he steadfastly refused to find a safer home, preferring instead to share danger with his people.

The first serious bombing occurred early in September, 1940, when a 500-pound delayed-action explosive fell in the palace grounds. It ticked for twenty-four hours before blasting out a wide crater and tearing at the walls. When the bomb went off the King and Queen were inspecting shattered dwellings in the East End of London during another air raid.

They were forced to duck into a shelter in the basement of a police station, where tea was served by air-raid wardens to the King and Queen and about thirty other persons from the neighborhood.

"It's 'im," they whispered. "Gor! I could collapse," murmured a woman, whose companion replied: "My, ain't 'e lovely!"

A few days later King George experienced what might well have been his closest brush with death during the war. Prime Minister Churchill, in his book, "Their Finest Hour," quoted a letter from the King recounting this event. It read:

"The Queen and I went upstairs to a small sitting room overlooking the Quadrangle (I could not use my usual sitting room owing to the broken windows by former bomb damage). All of a sudden we heard the zooming noise of a diving aircraft getting louder and louder, then we saw two bombs falling past the opposite side of Buckingham Palace into the Quadrangle.

Saw Bomb Flashes

"We saw the flashes and heard the detonations as they burst about eighty yards away. The blast blew in the windows opposite to us, and two great craters had appeared in the Quadrangle. From one of these craters, water from a burst main was pouring out and flowing into the passage through the broken windows.

"The whole thing happened in a matter of seconds, and we were very quickly out into the passage. There were six bombs; two in the Forecourt, two in the Quadrangle, one wrecked the Chapel, and one in the garden."

Mr. Churchill commented that the King "was exhilarated by all this, and pleased that he should be sharing the dangers of his subjects in the capital . . . had the windows been closed instead of open the whole of the glass would have splintered into the faces of the King and Queen, causing terrible injuries."

A palace spokesman was asked why the royal pair had been exposed in a raid. He explained: "They were supposed to be in their shelter, but it's so hard to get them there."

Mr. Churchill recalled that in the days when invasion threatened the King had a shooting range built in the palace garden, where he practiced with pistols and tommy-guns. Throughout the raids the King and Mr. Churchill held to a regular Tuesday luncheon date when they discussed state business.

Gave Awards in Shelter

Once, early in the "blitz," the King established the custom of holding investitures for awards for bravery in the tiny palace shelter, a former maid's room. All members of the royal family registered with the City of Westminster as fire watchers.

King George brought comfort to countless Britons by visiting the scenes of air attacks, often doing so while enemy planes still were over the island. Three warnings sounded in Liverpool when he was there.

A week later, at Coventry the King threaded his way past tottering walls and over mounds of smoking wreckage. When he inspected London's first deep shelter he was profoundly moved as thousands of men, women and children rose to cheer him and sang "God Save the King."

Danger of a different sort was courted by the King about three years after the last of the Nazi raiders had quit. He wanted to enter the battle zone for the invasion of Normandy. Mr. Churchill, writing in "Closing the Ring," said that his own wish to do the same thing resulted in refusal for both.

"He had not been under fire, except in air raids, since the Battle of Jutland, and eagerly welcomed the prospect of renewing the experiences of his youth," Mr. Churchill wrote. "But the King, it developed, slept on the matter and then informed the Prime Minister by letter:

"* * * a change of Sovereign at this moment would be a serious matter for the country and Empire. We should both, I know, love to be there, but in all seriousness I would ask you to reconsider your plan. Our presence, I feel, would be an embarrassment to those responsible for fighting the ship or ships in which we were, despite anyahing we might say to them.

"So, as I have said, I have very reluctantly come to the conclusion that the right thing to do is what normally falls to those to the top on such occasions, namely, to remain at home and wait."

KING GEORGE DIES PEACEFULLY IN BED

Continued From Page 1

cast by the British Broadcasting Corporation. By noon flags were flying at half-staff on almost every building in London with a flag-staff.

The exception was Marlborough House, the home of Queen Mary, that stanch old lady nearing 85 whose eldest son, the Duke of Windsor, renounced the throne; whose youngest son, the Duke of Kent, was killed in an airplane crash early in the war; whose husband, George V, died just over sixteen years ago on Jan. 21, 1936, and who now must bury the son who has been Britain's ruling sovereign for more than fifteen years. Over her home, alone in all London, her standard flew at the top of the staff, a dauntless symbol of the continuity of the British Crown and her own indomitable spirit.

The mood of London today was one of sorrow for the sovereign who had served his country so well and who was no more.

There is real love and affection for the new Queen Elizabeth which will show itself in the future. But today the nation's thoughts were devoted to the late King and his widow, Elizabeth, with the ready smile and the warm gesture of the uplifted hand. Today it was "The King is dead." Tomorrow it will be "Long live the Queen." But as yet tomorrow has not come and the Queen is not here.

Most newspapers presented the news in black bordered columns. The theatres shut down and restaurants and night clubs abandoned music and dancing. The B. B. C. gave up all its entertainment programs and stayed on the air only to give weather reports and gale warnings to ships at sea.

Prime Minister Churchill received the news at Downing Street and called a Cabinet meeting to discuss the constitutional issues involved. Clement R. Attlee left a meeting of the Parliamentary Labor party of the Opposition to take a telephone call and returned to tell his confreres in a hushed tone that for the moment there could be no thought of controversy over foreign policy or anything else because the sovereign was dead.

In the afternoon at the usual time Parliament met but only long enough to hear the grievous official news. In the House of Lords the Marquess of Salisbury announced it. In the House of Commons Mr. Churchill delivered the sad tidings to an already informed but attentive House. He said:

"We cannot at this moment do more than record the spontaneous expression of our grief."

The Prime Minister then asked the Speaker, W. S. Morrison, for guidance and the Speaker suspended the session of the House until 7 P. M. when, he said, he would resume the chair, after swearing allegiance to the new Queen, to receive the oaths of the other members. Thus ended a Parliament sworn to George VI, and opened was a new one with the same members sworn to serve as liege lords of Her Majesty the Queen.

At 5 o'clock members of the Privy Council met at St. James' Palace and drafted the proclamation that informed England that she had a second Queen Elizabeth. The proclamation of her sovereignty was signed by 150 Privy Councilors who attended the conclave in their colorful medieval costumes of scarlet and gold.

The proclamation they adopted will be read tomorrow by the Garter King at Arms, Sir George Rothe Bellew, from the rooftop of St. James' Palace and repeated throughout the realm by criers with drums and trumpets tomorrow or the next day.

The King died in the little hamlet where he was born and where his father George V had died. It is a little village that looked upon him as squire and whose inhabitants turned out each Sunday to see the royal family go to church.

Funeral plans are still somewhat indefinite. It is believed, however, that the King's body will be brought to London to lie in state in Westminster Hall in the Parliament Buildings for several days and that it will be taken to Windsor for burial at a private ceremony.

Tonight's Court Circular, issued from Buckingham Palace, was black bordered. It said:

"The King passed peacefully away in his sleep early this morning."

All day long while crowds gathered outside Buckingham Palace, Marlborough House and St. James's Palace, members of the diplomatic corps called to express their sympathy and leave their cards.

Walter S. Gifford, United States Ambassador, was one of the earliest arrivals at Buckingham Palace.

Valet Makes Discovery

WEST NEWTON, England, Feb. 6 (AP)—John Macdonald, the King's valet, made the tragic discovery of the monarch's death when he took the King his morning cup of tea at 7:30 A. M. today.

Mr. Macdonald immediately called an officer of the royal household. A lady-in-waiting rushed to awaken Queen Elizabeth and Princess Margaret. Radio messages were sent off to Princess Elizabeth and the Duke of Edinburgh in Africa.

Widowed Queen Withholds Tears

SANDRINGHAM, England, Feb. 6 (Reuters)—Court officials were called from their beds early this morning when the King died and the news was broken to the Queen. The Queen went immediately to his bedside, according to reports from the household.

She did not weep, according to these reports. Though her face was racked with misery, she kept control on her emotions.

She kissed the forehead of the dead King.

Then, straightening up, she said: "We must tell Elizabeth. We must tell * * *," she hesitated then added, "we must tell * * * the Queen."

Egypt's Court to Mourn 14 Days for British King

Special to THE NEW YORK TIMES.

CAIRO, Feb. 6—The Egyptian court will remain in mourning for fourteen days in tribute to King George VI of Britain, according to a royal decree issued tonight.

Abdel Latif Talaat, Grand Chamberlain, called at the British Embassy to express King Farouk's sympathy. It was also announced that Egypt would be represented at the funeral in London.

In the Canal zone, where British troops are stationed, all motion-picture theatres and dance halls were closed and a church service was held.

Prince Charles Outranks Father, but Not for Long

By The Associated Press.

LONDON, Feb. 6—Because he now is first in line for the throne, Prince Charles outranks his father in matters of precedence.

Three-year-old Charles thus may walk ahead of the Duke of Edinburgh in royal processions under present protocol. Queen Elizabeth—and only she—can change her husband's status on precedence.

She could, and is expected to, name the Duke "Prince Consort" by "letters patent" and rank him second to herself—ahead of little Charles.

IRELAND SORROWFUL OVER KING'S DEMISE

Special to THE NEW YORK TIMES.

DUBLIN, Feb. 6—The news of King George's death was received here today with unfeigned sorrow. Despite the Irish Republic's constitutional separation from the Crown, its people always had shown deep admiration for the King.

Flags were flown at half-staff atop public buildings, while all afternoon newspapers carried the fullest reports of the event together with tributes.

One of the earliest callers at the British Embassy was the Most Rev. John C. McQuaide, Roman Catholic Archbishop of Dublin. Prime Minister Eamon de Valera and Foreign Minister Frank Aiken also called on Sir Walter Frankinson, British Ambassador, to express their sympathy.

John A. Costello, Opposition leader and former Prime Minister, speaking at the annual convention of his party, recalled "the gracious message" sent by the King on the creation of the republic, and voiced deep regret on the ruler's death. The convention stood in a silent tribute to King George.

Messages of sympathy were sent to the Queen Mother and Queen Elizabeth II by President Sean T. O'Kelly.

LONDON IS STILLED AS BRITONS GRIEVE

Continued From Page 1

the news reached them. But older women seemed to take it more personally than other groups.

One of the first Londoners to learn of the death was Mrs. Alice Beaumont a news vender in the Strand near Fleet Street. Her mind immediately went back to a television view she had had of the King's farewell to his daughter at London airport on Thursday.

"I didn't think he looked at all well standing in that cold wind without a hat," she said. "Maybe he stayed so long because he had a presentiment that he wouldn't see her again. You could see the Queen tugging at his elbow."

Others who had seen that television program thought the King had looked quite himself again.

Housewives throughout Britain tuned to the mid-morning radio program, "Mrs. Dale's Diary," today and heard the news immediately afterward when it was first broadcast at 10:45. Except for regularly scheduled news programs and the weather report for shipping, broadcasting to home listeners then closed down for the rest of the day. So did television programs, which now reach more than 1,000,000 homes. The British Broadcasting Corporation's practice in this respect was established when King George V died.

Crowd Prays in St. Paul's

An unusually large congregation attended the regular noon service in St. Paul's Cathedral. The worshippers sang the 130th Psalm which begins, "Out of the deep have I called unto Thee, O Lord," and heard the Dean, the Rev. W. R. Matthews, pray for the new Queen.

A crowd of several hundred persons watching outside Buckingham Palace at noon saw United States Ambassador Walter S. Gifford arrive among the first members of the diplomatic corps to offer condolences by signing the visitors' book. Cars flying the flags of many other countries, including the Soviet Union, later drove in and out of the great gates past Coldstream Guards' sentries in bearskin hats and blue-gray great-coats.

But the crowds were not much larger than the conventional assembly of tourists from out of town. The same was true later outside St. James's Palace, where the Privy Council was meeting to approve the accession proclamation. Most Londoners feel that the proper time to turn out to show their feeling for the King and for his widow and children will come later, after their return from Sandringham and Africa.

Even before the Lord Chamberlain had ordered the closing of all theatres, most managers had arranged to do so. It was the same with cinemas, concert halls, hotels and restaurants, which canceled all music, dancing and floor shows.

Although bars remained open during the usual hours, they attracted only about half the usual number of customers. Travel on the subways was far below normal tonight.

A few United States soldiers who had gone to Piccadilly Circus on leave found bright signs turned out and the streets virtually empty. A hotel doorman with nearly three decades' experience said "I have never seen Piccadilly Circus so quiet—except after a heavy air raid."

A major soccer match was played after consultation with senior sporting officials, but before the start of play there was a ceremony with the two teams wearing black armbands. The crowd joined in singing "God Save the King" and the hymn "Abide With Me." One of the 40,000 spectators raised a cry soon to be heard all over Britain, "Long Live the Queen!"

Theatre, film and concert performances will be resumed tomorrow and will continue as usual except on the day of the funeral. Stores will remain open. However, some fashionable shops have already begun to remove brightly colored garments from their windows, leaving only blacks and grays.

Scotland Yard has instructed all officers of the metropolitan police force ranking as inspector or above to wear mourning armbands. The Navy, Army and Air Force—the King held an honorary top grade in all three—are expected to issue similar instructions. In many schools the pupils will be expected to wear black neckties.

Until after the funeral, flags will remain at half staff, except on Friday when the accession of the new Queen is publicly proclaimed.

King's Death May Bring Some Diplomatic Shifts

By The Associated Press

LONDON, Feb. 6—Important diplomatic changes may follow in the wake of the death of King George VI and the accession of Elizabeth II to the throne.

All foreign envoys in this country will have to present new letters of credence to Elizabeth.

British Ambassadors and Ministers abroad will need to be re-accredited as representatives of the Queen.

Because of Britain's rift with Egypt over their joint rule of the Sudan, it is possible that the Egyptian Government will refuse the new credentials of Sir Ralph Stevenson, the British Ambassador in Cairo. The Egyptian Government has proclaimed King Farouk as monarch of the Sudan.

Governments in the past have taken advantage of a shift in British monarchs to make diplomatic changes. Abdication of Edward VIII led to King George VI's name being deleted from the Irish constitution and consequent abolition of the post of Governor-General.

ELIZABETH FLYING HOME FROM AFRICA

Continued From Page 1

last hours, was dressed in a simple beige dress and white hat.

She and her husband talked with Lieut. Gen. Sir Alexander Cameron, British commander in East Africa, while their luggage was rushed aboard the plane and flares were lighted for the after-dark take-off. The new Queen mounted the ramp leading to the door of the craft, turned, and managed a smile for those who saw her off.

Only a few hours before, she had returned to the forest lodge presented to her by the people of Kenya as a wedding present, after a night spent in a tree-top bungalow watching jungle animals at a water hole. She and Philip were to have left by sea tomorrow on the next leg of their tour of Commonwealth countries.

Elizabeth first heard of her father's death at about 2 P. M. local time. The African Standard, the local newspaper, telephoned the news to the Princess' staff at the lodge, about eighty miles from Nairobi. The staff withheld the news from Elizabeth until a phone call could be put through to London. Almost simultaneously, London called, confirming the news.

The Duke was informed and he told his wife that she was the new Queen. At first, Elizabeth broke down in tears, but later, as a member of her staff said:

"She took it like a Queen."

The royal couple arrived in Kenya last Friday, and had spent most of the five days resting and walking in the sunshine. Their only big-game shooting was with cameras, but they frequently watched wild animals from specially prepared vantage points.

This afternoon, the ensign aboard the Gothic, the vessel that was to have taken the royal couple to Australia via Ceylon, was flown at half-mast.

EFFECT ON PARLIAMENT

Motion Critical of Churchill Is Put Off by King's Death

Special to THE NEW YORK TIMES.

LONDON, Feb. 6—When Parliament gets back to routine business there is a question whether it will resume where it left off—a Labor motion regretting that Prime Minister Churchill had not made British foreign policy clearer while in the United States.

The motion was to have been debated today, but the King's death led to a postponement until Feb. 18 at the earliest. Labor party leaders say they do not plan to revive the motion. However, the party's backbenchers, including some generally rated as moderates, believe strongly that the debate should be held.

If the Laborites permit the Government to move on to the next item on the agenda, they say, it will mean that Mr. Churchill has turned national mourning to his own political advantage.

"All the News That's Fit to Print"

The New York Times.

LATE CITY EDITION
Fair, little temperature change today. Mostly fair tomorrow.
Temperature Range Today—Max., 42; Min., 29
Temperatures Yesterday—Max., 44; Min., 33
Full U. S. Weather Bureau Report, Page 47

VOL. CII..No. 34,740. Entered as Second-Class Matter. Post Office, New York, N. Y. NEW YORK, FRIDAY, MARCH 6, 1953. Times Square, New York 36, N. Y. Telephone LAckawanna 4-1000 FIVE CENTS

STALIN DIES AFTER 29-YEAR RULE; HIS SUCCESSOR NOT ANNOUNCED; U.S. WATCHFUL, EISENHOWER SAYS

WORST CITY CRISIS SINCE 1933 IS SEEN IN STATE TAX PLAN

Moore and McGovern Demand Payroll Levy and Transit Unit Mandated to Raise Fares

MAYOR CALLS DEMOCRATS

Estimate Board to Get Report on Views of County Leaders —Bus Reduction Directed

By PAUL CROWELL

The city Government is facing the most serious financial and political crisis to confront any Administration since 1933, when leading banking houses rescued a Democratic regime from fiscal disaster.

This was the consensus last night of top city officials to whom Lieut. Gov. Frank C. Moore and State Controller J. Raymond McGovern had indicated earlier in the day that a sound fiscal program for 1953-54 and succeeding years should include both a city payroll tax and a transit authority with a duty to increase fares to meet operating deficits of the municipal lines.

That the city Administration realized the political dangers inherent in the adoption of the suggested fiscal program was indicated later in the day when Mayor Impellitteri, without consulting the Board of Estimate, asked the five Democratic county leaders to confer with him at noon today at City Hall. Among those invited was Tammany leader Carmine G. DeSapio, the only member of the group who is at loggerheads with the Mayor on matters of patronage.

Leaders' Views Important

After a two-hour conference with Mr. Moore and Mr. McGovern at Mr. McGovern's office, 270 Broadway, the Mayor and Board of Estimate held an even longer closed meeting at City Hall, which will be resumed at 3 o'clock this afternoon. At today's session an important factor will be the attitude of the five Democratic county leaders, as reported by the Mayor, toward the proposals upon which the two state officials apparently are insisting.

In another municipal development, the Mayor's Transit Advisory Commission demanded that the eight privately owned bus companies involved in the recent bus strike and Michael J. Quill's Transport Workers Union, C. I. O., take immediate steps to wipe out excess bus lines and to reduce the number of buses on lines that were needed. City tax relief was made dependent on such action.

The conference with Mr. Moore and Mr. McGovern was a continuation of last Monday's talks at Albany on the city's $218,700,000 fiscal program, which in effect already had been rejected by the two state officials in their joint memorandum of Feb. 22.

At the outset of the meeting the

Continued on Page 19, Column 1

F.B.I. Agents Depict Rebuff by Monaghan

By LUTHER A. HUSTON
Special to THE NEW YORK TIMES

WASHINGTON, March 5—Leland V. Boardman, special agent in charge of the New York office of the Federal Bureau of Investigation, asserted today that Police Commissioner George P. Monaghan had notified him that he would not make New York City policemen available to any Federal law enforcement agency for questioning and that they would respond only to summonses from a Federal grand jury.

This policy, Mr. Boardman said, was founded upon a purported agreement between the New York Police Department and the Criminal Division of the Department of Justice to "block out F. B. I. investigators from cases involving police brutality in civil rights cases.

Another agent quoted Commis-

Continued on Page 16, Column 3

Eisenhower Plans to Pare Policy-Level Civil Service

Directive Will Repeal 2 That Truman Issued Anchoring Some Democrats in Their Jobs —Organization of Administration Object

By PAUL P. KENNEDY
Special to THE NEW YORK TIMES.

WASHINGTON, March 5—Several hundred persons face the possibility of losing Civil Service status and probably their Government jobs under an Executive Order to be issued by President Eisenhower next week.

In announcing the forthcoming order, James C. Hagerty, White House press secretary, said that all those affected would not necessarily lose their jobs. The announcement was generally interpreted, however, to mean that the Administration was preparing to clear out holdover Democrats in high policy-making and administrative positions in order to replace them with personnel of the Administration's own choosing.

President Eisenhower's order, which he directed to be drafted immediately, will repeal two Executive Orders of former President Truman in 1947 and 1948 in which certain persons on Schedule A of Civil Service rules would receive Civil Service protection against separation from the Government.

The President's order will emphasize that the rights of veterans, specified in the Veterans Preference Act of 1944 would be respected.

Schedule A is a list of positions to which appointments may be made without reference to Civil Service rules or regulations. The appointees may assume their positions without Civil Service examinations and their classifications are not subject to review by Civil Service Boards.

Mr. Hagerty said the "several hundred" persons to be affected by the order were employed in all departments and agencies of the Government. The order, he said, applied to people who had been put under Civil Service in the last twenty years.

The new Administration, since coming into office Jan. 20, Mr.

Continued on Page 15, Column 2

President May Take a Hand If Inquiries Imperil Amity

By C. P. TRUSSELL
Special to THE NEW YORK TIMES.

WASHINGTON, March 5—President Eisenhower indicated today that if the Senate investigation into the Voice of America, being conducted by Senator Joseph R. McCarthy, or other Congressional inquiries, reached a point of inviting international misunderstandings and difficulties he might intervene.

This, he emphasized at a news conference, would mean that he would have to desert his long-held conviction that the Congress had an inherent right to investigate as it pleased. He was still hoping, he said, to avoid a situation in which a spokesman for the Executive Branch of the Government would have to take issue with actions of the coordinate Legislative Branch.

The question that prompted these responses was based upon the hearings being conducted, largely before television, by the Judiciary subcommittee headed by Senator McCarthy, Republican of Wisconsin.

The group is inquiring into the management and personnel of the Voice, the Government's radio program for telling the story of America. Broadcasts are beamed to eighty-seven countries in nearly forty languages.

At yesterday's hearing Reed Harris, deputy director of the State

Continued on Page 14, Column 6

EISENHOWER PRAISES RESTRAINT IN PRICES

Asserts There Has Been Little Evidence of Gouging—More Controls Are Removed

By CHARLES E. EGAN
Special to THE NEW YORK TIMES.

WASHINGTON, March 5—President Eisenhower today complimented business for what he termed the admirable restraint it had shown in pricing policies since the removal of most price controls.

General Eisenhower said at his news conference that since the program of removing major segments of the economy from price regulation got under way Feb. 6, there had been little discernible evidence of attempts to gouge consumers.

The President's observations came immediately before an announcement from the Office of Price Stabilization that it had removed price ceilings on another wide range of items, including bread and bakery products, new and used cars, major household appliances, dry cleaning and diaper services.

Hopes for a New Climate

Another development was a Senate committee hearing at which Charles R. Sligh Jr., president of the National Association of Manufacturers, attacked proposals to establish stand-by controls authority. With such authority, the President could declare a ninety-day "freeze" of all prices and wages in event of all-out war or other critical emergency.

About the only major price increase that has occurred since the Office of Price Stabilization began implementing his orders for relaxation of price ceilings, the President said, has been an expected rise of 6 to 7 cents a pound in copper.

The absence of price gouging, the President added, confirms his belief that the American people are ready to be considerate and moderate. He added that he hoped a climate might be established—in labor-management relations, for instance—that would minimize harmful pressures on the economy

Continued on Page 15, Column 3

VISHINSKY LEAVING

Foreign Minister Called to Moscow to Report —Will Sail Today

U. N. TO LOWER FLAG

Lie Praises Premier as Statesman—Pearson Hails Fight on Nazis

By THOMAS J. HAMILTON
Special to THE NEW YORK TIMES.

UNITED NATIONS, N. Y., March 5—Soviet Foreign Minister Andrei Y. Vishinsky, who was reported to have been informed of the death of Premier Stalin before the public announcement by the Moscow radio, plans to leave for Moscow tomorrow.

Mr. Vishinsky and a party of Soviet officials are scheduled to sail aboard the French liner Liberté tomorrow at 4 P. M. Plans for the sailing were disclosed at Police Headquarters. The police said they had been informed that the party would travel in seven automobiles from Glen Cove, L. I., where the Soviet delegation to the United Nations has headquarters, to Pier 88, Hudson River at Forty-eighth Street. The liner will call at Plymouth and Le Havre.

Mr. Vishinsky has a heart condition and therefore avoids air travel whenever possible.

Valerian A. Zorin, Soviet representative to the United Nations, revealed this afternoon Mr. Vishinsky's plans to leave tomorrow. Mr. Vishinsky's decision was taken after he had received a telephone call from Moscow earlier in the day.

Disclosure by Consulate

There was no indication whether this telephone call had given any indication of Mr. Stalin's death. The news that Mr. Vishinsky had been informed prior to the public announcement came from a telephone inquiry at the Soviet Consulate at 680 Park Avenue.

Earlier inquiries at the headquarters of the Soviet delegation to the United Nations had brought repeated denials that Mr. Vishinsky was there. The consulate revealed, however, not only that Mr. Vishinsky was actually at the delegation headquarters but also that he had been informed of the news earlier.

According to United Nations protocol, the only flag that will fly at the United Nations flagpole tomorrow is the banner of the United Nations itself, and it will be at half-staff. The same procedure will be followed during the day of the funeral of Premier Stalin.

Informed of the death of Mr.

Continued on Page 13, Column 2

CONDOLENCES SENT

President Orders Terse Formal Note on Stalin Dispatched to Soviet

TRIBUTE IS OMITTED

Eisenhower Still Ready to Confer on Peace With the Kremlin

By JAMES RESTON
Special to THE NEW YORK TIMES.

WASHINGTON, March 5—President Eisenhower authorized John Foster Dulles, Secretary of State, tonight to send the United States' "official condolences" to the Soviet Government on the death of Premier Stalin.

Earlier the President had told reporters at his press conference that he could not tell what effect the illness of the Premier would have on the "cold war." A definite watchfulness is our policy for the moment, the President added.

The President announced the statement of condolences less than an hour after he had been informed of Mr. Stalin's death by James C. Hagerty, press secretary, at 8:25 P. M. The statement was as follows:

The President authorized the Secretary of State to send the following message to the American Embassy in Moscow: The Government of the United States tenders its official condolences to the Government of the Union of Socialist Soviet Republics on the death of Generalissimo Joseph Stalin, Prime Minister of the Soviet Union.

Dulles Informed by Hagerty

Mr. Hagerty notified Mr. Dulles, who was a guest at the British Embassy, immediately after the President had been informed.

The press secretary said the President's message would be transmitted to the Soviet Government by Jacob D. Beam, Chargé d'Affaires in Moscow.

The terse wording of the message was noted here, especially the phrase "official condolences." Diplomatic circles suggested that the wording was about as brief and formal as possible under diplomatic protocol.

They recalled, however, that the President previously had expressed condolences. In the first White House statement issued after word had been received of the serious illness of Mr. Stalin, General Eisenhower directed his words to the Soviet people rather than the Premier or the Government.

Indications were that the President's official condolences would stand in so far as the Government

Continued on Page 12, Column 5

PREMIER JOSEPH STALIN
A portrait released by Sovfoto, Soviet picture agency

Soviet Fear of an Eruption Discerned in Call for Unity

By HARRY SCHWARTZ

The fact that appeals for "monolithic unity" and "vigilance" have now become the main theme of Soviet domestic propaganda appears to be a clear indication that the present Soviet rulers fear Premier Stalin's death may result in an explosive resolution of the major tensions now repressed in the Soviet Union.

The unity theme dominates the official announcement of Stalin's death. It was first voiced in the initial communiqué regarding Stalin's illness issued by the highest Government and Communist party authorities. Unity and vigilance were the central ideas in the long leading editorials that appeared yesterday morning on the front pages of both Pravda and Izvestia.

Yesterday's Pravda editorial may also have given the first hint that Georgi M. Malenkov is leading in the succession race, but this hint seemed far from conclusive. The editorial mentioned by name only Lenin, Premier Stalin, and Mr. Malenkov, quoting the latter's speech last October when he said, "The prospects and ways of our progress are based on the laws of the national economy, on the science of the Communist social structure which have been evolved by Comrade Stalin."

The fact that Moscow has announced that Nikita S. Khrushchev will head the committee preparing

Continued on Page 12, Column 2

AMMUNITION SHORT, VAN FLEET ASSERTS

He Affirms Scarcity in Korea and Byrd Writes to Wilson Demanding Explanation

By HAROLD B. HINTON
Special to THE NEW YORK TIMES.

WASHINGTON, March 5—Gen. James A. Van Fleet, former Commander of United Nations ground forces in Korea, told the Senate Armed Services Committee today that he had been handicapped during the entire twenty-two months he had had the command by shortages of ammunition and manpower. He specified hand grenades, and mentioned "other types" of ammunition as having been seriously short all the time and critically short on occasions.

The apparent contradiction of the General's testimony today with that of yesterday, in which he indicated there were no serious shortages of anything in Korea, was unexplained, except for the interpretation that yesterday he had been speaking for the present, whereas today he had been speaking for the past.

Praised by Symington

So much the general said before a public meeting of the committee. Senator Stuart Symington, Democrat of Missouri and former Secretary of the Air Force, praised General Van Fleet for his intelligence and courage in reporting these matters to the public. If other military figures would emulate the example, he declared, "we won't send our youth out to fight with these shortages, even if we have fewer television sets."

[In the Korean war action, Air Force Thunderjet fighter-bombers made a record 1,000-mile raid on a Communist industrial center on the northeast coast sixty miles from Siberia. Navy carrier bombers made heavy attacks in North Korea. Ground action was light.]

In a later closed session with the committee, General Van Fleet apparently amplified his discussion of the shortages. The amplification prompted Senator Harry F. Byrd, Democrat of Virginia, to write a letter to Charles E. Wil-

Continued on Page 3, Column 6

PREMIER ILL 4 DAYS

Announcement of Death Made by Top Soviet and Party Chiefs

STROKE PROVES FATAL

Leaders Issue an Appeal to People for Unity and Vigilance

Text of official announcement of Stalin's death, Page 8.

By HARRISON E. SALISBURY
Special to THE NEW YORK TIMES.

MOSCOW, Friday, March 6—Premier Joseph Stalin died at 9:50 P. M. yesterday [1:50 P. M. Thursday, Eastern standard time] in the Kremlin at the age of 73, it was announced officially this morning. He had been in power twenty-nine years.

The announcement was made in the name of the Central Committee of the Communist party, the Council of Ministers and the Presidium of the Supreme Soviet.

Calling on the Soviet people to rally firmly around the party and the Government, the announcement asked them to display unity and the highest political vigilance "in the struggle against internal and external foes." [No announcement was made of a successor to Premier Stalin.]

The Soviet leader's death from general circulatory and respiratory deficiency occurred just short of four days after he had been stricken with a brain hemorrhage in his Kremlin apartment.

Accompanying the death announcement was a final medical certificate issued by a group of ten physicians, headed by Health Minister A. F. Tretyakov, who cared for Mr. Stalin in his last illness under the direct and closest supervision of the Central Committee and the Council of Ministers.

Pulse Rate Was High

The medical certificate revealed that in the last hours Mr. Stalin's condition grew worse rapidly, with repeated heavy and sharp circulatory and heart collapses. His breathing grew superficial and sharply irregular. His pulse rate rose to 140 to 150 a minute and at 9:50 P. M., "because of a growing circulatory and respiratory insufficiency, J. V. Stalin died."

[The news of Mr. Stalin's death was withheld by Soviet officials for more than six hours.]

Pravda appeared this morning with broad black borders around its front page, which was devoted entirely to Mr. Stalin. The layout included a large photograph of the Premier, the announcement by the Government, the medical bulletins and the announcement of the formation of a funeral commission

Continued on Page 8, Column 2

Treaties Manifesto Shelved in Congress

By WILLIAM S. WHITE
Special to THE NEW YORK TIMES.

WASHINGTON, March 5—President Eisenhower's proposed United States declaration against "perversion" of the wartime Yalta and Potsdam agreements into instruments for enslaving peoples was put on the shelf in Congress today.

The announced Congressional reason was that the manifesto would be inopportune now in view of Premier Stalin's fatal illness, though the President himself indicated at his news conference that he thought this need not delay action. The Congressional developments came before the announcement of Mr. Stalin's death.

The Republican leaders in Congress could not take the resolution to the floor of either house

Continued on Page 6, Column 5

Pole Flies to Denmark in First Intact Russian MIG-15 to Reach West

Associated Press Radiophoto

A young Polish pilot seeking political asylum flew this Soviet-made MIG-15 into a Danish airport at Bornholm yesterday, making it the first fighter plane of its type acquired undamaged by the West. Name of pilot (center figure) was withheld.

Special to THE NEW YORK TIMES.

COPENHAGEN, Denmark, March 5—The first intact Russian-built MIG-15 jet fighter—the newest known type of Russian jet fighter—to land west of the Iron Curtain came down this morning at Roenne Airport on the Danish island of Bornholm. It came from a Polish Baltic base.

The 21-year-old Polish lieutenant who fled with the fighter gave himself up to Danish authorities as a political refugee and asked for asylum. Very little is known about his story. Danish authorities are keeping it secret for the time being.

The young Pole performed a fantastic maneuver in landing the jet fighter on the grass-covered airstrip at Roenne, only 1,200 meters (3,937 feet) long. Jet fighters normally require a 3,000-meter (9,843 feet) concrete runway to start and land.

At the farther end of the air-

Continued on Page 3, Column 2

CHURCHILL WARNS OF CRITICAL PERIOD

Describes Situation as 'Grave but Not Unhopeful'—House Backs 2-Year Conscription

By RAYMOND DANIELL
Special to THE NEW YORK TIMES.

LONDON, March 5—In a debate in the House of Commons today on Government defense policy Prime Minister Churchill described the period through which the world is passing as "critical but formative, grave but not unhopeful."

Neither he nor Clement R. Attlee, leader of the Opposition, who spoke after him, ever once referred to Premier Stalin though he was obviously in their minds. So much depends upon who succeeds the Russian leader that it is unlikely that they, any more than other Britons, could think of the future without considering that imponderable in their appraisal of the world situation.

"This is a testing time for the free world," said Mr. Churchill. "Any sign of weakening of purpose now would undermine what good has been done" in the post-war years toward strengthening Western Europe.

The Prime Minister was arguing against Opposition urgings that the period of national service, if not reduced from two years to eighteen months, should be reviewed by Parliament from year to year.

The Government's demand for authorization to continue the two-year term of service for a further five years was approved by 295 votes to 254, a majority of forty-one.

Home Defense Discussed

Mr. Churchill discussed at length the state of Britain's home defenses, saying that when he returned to power sixteen months ago the country was so defenseless that "I felt naked as I had not felt at any time in the recent war."

There is not even now a single combat division in the country and the Home Guard is still only about one-fourth of what is needed for safety. Nevertheless, Mr. Churchill said that in his term of office 450 mobile columns had been organized and were capable of concentrating swiftly at any point where paratroops of an enemy might land.

Since taking office, Mr. Churchill said, his Government has been pursuing the twin goals of solvency and security. Its defense program, he asserted, preserves a nice balance between the two but he declared that the rearmament program was the "absolute maximum of which we are capable."

"Solvency is valueless without security and security is impossible to achieve without solvency," he declared. He said that offshore purchases by the United States increased Britain's war potential and helped Britain in three ways. First, they help underwrite the cost of maintaining defense plants. Second, they increase this country's export earnings and, third, they add to the military strength of the whole free world.

Arms For Middle East

Discussing the sale of planes and munitions to Israel and the Arab states, Mr. Churchill said that Britain was merely carrying out agreements reached earlier, but he pointed out that great care must be exercised to make sure that the present balance between those countries, technically still at war, was not disturbed "in any appreciable way."

Mr. Attlee, replying, expressed regret that Mr. Churchill's speech did not give a broader survey of the world situation nor go into detail about the North Atlantic Treaty Organization. As Britain was making "great sacrifices" for common defense, Mr. Attlee said, he would have liked to hear what the Prime Minister thought about the progress that was being made toward the building up of Western defenses.

Mr. Attlee also deplored the attention that Mr. Churchill paid to matters of home defense. It could hardly fail to discourage continental faith in Britain's determination to help defend Europe from a line as far east as possible, he said. It is more important, he said, to prepare to deter an attack by an aggressor than to lay special stress on the defense of the islands after an aggressor's attack has succeeded to the point of threatening Britain's own shores.

BE CALM, BROADCASTS ASK

Radio Free Europe Cautions Satellite Populations

MUNICH, Germany, March 5 (AP)—Radio Free Europe turned on the full power of its twenty transmitters today to tell Iron Curtain listeners that Premier Stalin's death would not mean their immediate liberation. They were urged to "remain calm and act with caution."

The privately-financed American radio station said it had grouped its twenty transmitters in Germany and Portugal for the first time to concentrate full power on Poland, Hungary and Czechoslovakia. Engineers said the broadcasts were so powerful even crystal sets could receive them. Originally, the concentration of power to thwart Communist jamming had been planned for next month.

2 LETTERS TELL MEXICANS

Newspaper's 'Not Yet' on Stalin Becomes 'Ya' ('Finally')

MEXICO CITY, March 5 (AP)—The Mexico newspaper which yesterday told the Stalin story with a two-word headline reading "Not Yet" informed readers of the dictator's death today with just one two-letter word: "Ya," meaning "finally."

Ultimas Noticias, afternoon edition of Excelsior, had the five-inch-high type specially made for the extra on Stalin's death.

The dictionary definition of "Ya" is finally" or "now," but it is used as an expletive meaning "yes" and has something of the meaning of the American soldier's phrase, "This is it."

Moscow's Formal Announcement of Stalin's Death

LONDON, Friday, March 6 (AP)—Following is the text of Moscow's announcement of Premier Stalin's death:

From the Central Committee of the Communist party of the Soviet Union, the U. S. S. R. Council of Ministers and the U.S.S.R. Presidium of the Supreme Soviet—

To all members of the party, to all workers of the Soviet Union:

Dear comrades and friends: The Central Committee of the Communist party of the Soviet Union, the U.S.S.R. Council of Ministers and the Presidium of the U.S.S.R. Supreme Soviet announce with profound sorrow to the party and all workers of the Soviet Union that on the 5th of March, at 2150 hours (9:50 P. M., Moscow time, or 1:50 P. M., Eastern Standard Time), after a grave illness, the Chairman of the U.S.S.R. Council of Ministers and the Secretary of the Central Committee of the Communist party of the Soviet Union, Joseph Vissarionovitch Stalin, died.

Linked to Lenin

The heart of the comrade and inspired continuer of Lenin's will, the wise leader and teacher of the Communist Party and the Soviet people—Joseph Vissarionovitch Stalin—has stopped beating.

Stalin's name is boundlessly dear to our party, to the Soviet people, to the workers of the world.

Together with Lenin, Comrade Stalin created the mighty party of Communists, reared and forged that party.

Together with Lenin, Comrade Stalin was the inspirer and leader of the great October Socialist Revolution, founder of the world's first Socialist state.

Continuing Lenin's immortal cause, Comrade Stalin led the Soviet people to a world-historic victory of Socialism in our land.

Comrade Stalin led our country to victory over fascism in the second World War which wrought a radical change in the entire international scene.

Comrade Stalin's death—the man who devoted all his life to the unselfish service of the Communist cause—is a tremendous loss to the party, to the workers of the Soviet Union and to the whole world.

Comrade Stalin armed the party and all the people with a great and lucid program of building communism in the U. S. S. R.

Sorrow for People

The news of Comrade Stalin's death will bring profound pain to the hearts of the workers, the collective farmers, the intelligentsia, and all the workers of our Motherland, to the hearts of the warriors of our glorious Army and Navy, to the hearts of millions of workers in all countries of the world.

In these sorrowful days, all the peoples of our country are rallying even closer in a great fraternal family under the tested leadership of the Communist party, created and reared by Lenin and Stalin.

The Soviet people have boundless faith in and are permeated with deep love for their Communist party, for they know that the supreme law governing all the activity of the party is service in the interests of the people.

The workers, collective farmers, Soviet intelligentsia, and all workers of our country steadfastly pursue the policy mapped out by our party, which is in conformity with the vital interests of the workers and pursues the continued consolidation of the might of our Socialist Motherland.

The correctness of this policy of the Communist party has been proved by decades of struggle.

It has led the workers of the Soviet country to historic victories of socialism.

Inspired by this policy, the peoples of the Soviet Union under the leadership of the party advance confidently towards fresh successes of Communist construction in our land.

The workers of our country know that the further improvement of the material well-being of all sections of populace—the workers, the collective farmers, the intelligentsia—the maximum satisfaction of constantly growing material and cultural needs of the entire society, has always been and always is the subject of particular solicitude on the part of the Communist party and the Soviet Government.

The Soviet people know that the defense, capacity and might of the Soviet Sttae are growing and strengthening, that the party is in every way strengthening the Soviet Army, Navy and intelligence organs with a view to constantly raising our preparedness for decisive rebuff to any aggressor.

The foreign policy of the Comuist party and the Government of the Soviet Union has always been and always is a policy of maintaining peace, the struggle against the preparing and unleashing of another war, a policy of international collaboration, and development of businesslike relations with all countries.

The peoples of the Soviet Union, true to the banner of proletarian internationalism, strengthened and developed fraternal friendship with the great Chinese people, with the workers of all countries of the people's democracy; friendly relations with workers of capitalist and colonial countries fighting for the cause of peace, democracy and socialism.

Party Affirmation

Dear Comrades and Friends:

The great directing and guiding force of the Soviet people in the struggle for the building of Communism is to be found in our Communist party.

The steel-like unity and monolithic unity of the ranks of the party constitutes the main condition for its strength and might.

Our task is to guard like the apple of our eye the unity of the party, to educate Communists as active political fighters for the implementation of policy and decisions of the party, to strengthen even more the party's ties with all the workers, collective farmers, and intelligentsia—for in this indissoluble link with the people lies the strength and invincibility of our party.

The party regards as one its most essential tasks the education of all Communists and workers in a spirit of high political vigilance, irreconcilability and stalwartness in the struggle aginst internal and external foes.

The Central Committee of the Communist party of the Soviet Union, the U. S. S. R. Council of Ministers, and the Presidium of the U. S. S. R. Supreme Soviet, appealing in these sorrowful days to the party and the people, express their firm conviction that the party and all the workers of our Motherland will rally even closer around the Central Committee and the Soviet Government, will mobilize all their forces and creative energy in the great cause of building Communism in our land.

The immortal name of Stalin will live forever in the hearts of the Soviet people and all progressive mankind.

Long live the great and all-conquering teachings of Marx, Engels, Lenin and Stalin!

Long live our mighty Socialist Motherland!

Long live our heroic Soviet people!

Long live the great Communist party of Soviet Union!

THE CENTRAL COMMITTEE OF THE COMMUNIST PARTY OF THE U. S. S. R.

THE U. S. S. R. COUNCIL OF MINISTERS.

THE U. S. S. R. SUPREME SOVIET'S PRESIDIUM.

Sovfoto

POSSIBLE SUCCESSOR: Georgi M. Malenkov, a member of the Presidium of the Central Committee of the Communist party, is considered a leading contender for the Soviet Union's top position. He is shown here with Premier Joseph Stalin during 1949 May Day parade in Moscow.

STALIN SUCCUMBS; 29 YEARS IN POWER

Continued From Page 1

headed by Nikita S. Khruschchev, secretary of the Central Committee of the party.

Other members of the commission are Lazar M. Kaganovich, Premier Stalin's brother-in-law; Nikolai M. Shvernik, President of the Soviet Union; Alexander M. Vasilevsky, War Minister; N. U. Pegov, an alternate member of the Presidium; P. A. Artemyev, commander of the Moscow military district, and M. A. Yasnov, chairman of the city of Moscow.

Pravda's announcement said Mr. Stalin's body would lie in state in the Hall of Columns.

His death brought to an end the career of one of the great figures of modern times—a man whose name stands second to none as the organizer and builder of the great state structure the world knows as the Soviet Union.

[The United Press said members of Mr. Stalin's family and his closest associates in the Presidium and Central Committee were at his bedside.]

The Soviet leader began his life in the simple mountain village of Gori deep in poverty-stricken Georgia. He rose to head the greatest Russian state that has ever existed. For nearly thirty years, Mr. Stalin was at the helm of the country. No other statesman of modern times has led his nation for a longer period.

This morning's official announcement declared that the Government and party would strengthen "the defense, capacity and might of the Soviet state" in every manner, and in "every way" strengthen the Soviet Army, Navy and organs of intelligence "with a view to constantly raising our preparedness for a decisive rebuff to any aggressor."

The declaration comprised an important statement of policy, both external and internal. With regard to foreign relations, it declared that the party and Government stood by an inflexible policy of securing and strengthening peace, of struggle against the preparation and unleashing of a new war, and for a policy of "international collaboration and development of businesslike connections with all countries."

Friendship for China Cited

The second foreign policy point was the declaration of firm support for "proletarian internationalism," for the development of brotherly friendship with [Communist] China, with the workers of all countries of the "people's democracy" and with the workers of capitalist and colonial countries fighting "for peace, democracy and socialism."

The announcement of Mr. Stalin's death was made to the Soviet people by radio early this morning. The announcement was early enough so that persons going to work had heard the news before leaving their homes.

This correspondent circled the Kremlin several times during the evening and early morning. The great red flag flew as usual over the Supreme Soviet Presidium building behind Lenin's Tomb.

Lights blazed late as they always do in many Kremlin office buildings. Sentry guards paced their posts at the Great Kremlin Gate.

The city was quiet and sleeping, and in Red Square all was serene. The guards stood their duty at Lenin's Tomb, but otherwise the great central square was deserted, as it always is in the hours just before daylight.

The last medical bulletin before the announcement of Mr. Stalin's death was issued shortly before 9 o'clock last night, reporting his condition as of 4 P. M. yesterday. It said his condition had grown worse despite every method of therapy employed by Soviet physicians.

The bulletin revealed that, at 8 o'clock yesterday morning, there occurred a sharp heart circulatory collapse, which was corrected by "extraordinary curative measures."

A second "heavy collapse" occurred at 11:30 A. M., which "was eliminated with difficulty."

Pravda, organ of the Central Committee of the Communist party, and Izvestia, organ of the Soviet Government, called on the Soviet people yesterday to rally around the party and the Government in "these difficult days" and to display what Izvestia characterised as "heightened revolutionary vigilance." Pravda also demanded from all Soviet citizens "stanchness of spirit and vigilance."

Pravda's editorial appeal to the populace was read repeatedly over the radio. It was also read and discussed in factories, shops and offices throughout the country. Pravda had clearly sounded the theme of the day—vigilance and unity.

Last night's medical bulletin on the Premier's condition declared that an electrocardiogram taken at 11 A. M., showed "sharp disturbances in blood circulation in the coronary arteries of the heart with lesions in the back wall of the heart." An electrocardiogram taken on Monday had not established these changes, the bulletin said.

After measures taken to liquidate the 11:30 A. M. collapse, the condition was eased to some extent, although the "patient's general condition continued extremely grave," the bulletin asserted.

At 4 P. M., Mr. Stalin's blood pressure stood at 160 over 120, the bulletin said, with his pulse rate 120 a minute and his respiration 36 times a minute. His temperature stood at 37.6 centigrade (99.68 degrees Fahrenheit), slightly lower than in a 2 A. M. bulletin.

The bulletin noted that the white blood corpuscle count stood at 21,000. At 2 A. M. the white blood corpuscle count was 17,000.

The bulletin said the principal objective of the struggle now being waged with Mr. Stalin's illness was an effort to curb the interruptions in respiration and in blood circulation, particularly coronary circulation.

Every device and treatment known to modern medicine was employed by a team of ten top Soviet specialists, headed by the country's new Health Minister, A. F. Tretyakov, and directed closely by the highest bodies of the party and Government—the Central Committee and the Council of Ministers.

The medical bulletin issued at 7 o'clock yesterday morning, giving his condition as of 2 A. M., was the second issued since Mr. Stalin's stroke Sunday night. It carried a most detailed account of the progress of the illness and the measures taken to combat it. The communiqué showed that, despite every treatment thus far employed, Mr. Stalin's breathing and heart functions continued to be sharply impaired. He lay unconscious.

Penicillin had been administered to Mr. Stalin. Other treatments mentioned in the communiqué were directly concerned with the fight to maintain and regularize his breathing and heart functions. These included the use of oxygen to supplement his oxygen deficiency, and camphor and caffeine to stimulate the heart. Strophantine and glucose also were introduced, and medical leeches applied as a means of bringing down his blood pressure.

In its call to the people to rally in unity and in vigilance around the party and Government, Pravda declared that the qualities now needed were "unity and cohesion, stanchness of spirit and vigilance," and called on all citizens to stand firm behind Mr. Stalin's goal—"building communism in our country."

Pravda called its editorial "Great Unity of the Party and People." Izvestia called its editorial "Unity and Solidarity of the Soviet People."

Izvestia said that in these times "there is no doubt" that all citizens will "multiply their strength in the struggle for a successful fulfillment of the tasks of Communist construction and will ceaselessly raise their revolutionary vigilance and even more closely rally their ranks around the Central Committee of the party and the Soviet Government."

Throngs of Muscovites made their way to Red Square this morning and stood in silent tribute to their lost leader.

The Hall of Columns where Mr. Stalin's body will lie in state is one of the most beautiful buildings in Moscow and one of the architectural jewels of Europe.

The building is ordinarily used as the house of Soviet trade unions, but is often employed for important state functions. It was here that Lenin's body lay in state in January, 1924, and it is here that many great thinkers of the Soviet world have lain in the last hours before their burial.

The central hall of the building is dominated by twenty-four beautiful marble columns reaching three stories to the ceiling. The room is hung with great chrystal chandeliers.

The Hall of Columns was erected in the mid-nineteenth century as a club for Moscow noblemen.

The outside of the hall, which is located in the heart of the city only a few hundred yards from Red Square, was decorated just after dawn today with heavy black-bordered red Soviet flags, which are used here as a symbol of mourning.

A great forty-foot portrait of Mr. Stalin in his gray generalissimo's uniform was erected on the front of the building. It was framed in heavy gilt.

In this famous hall Mr. Stalin's body will lie in state so that millions of Soviet citizens can throng past the bier and pay their last respects.

Russian Exile Leaders in New York See Hope For Rebirth of Freedom Now Stalin Is Gone

Russian exiles in New York, who for thirty-five years have followed the news from their homeland with increasing anguish as the dictatorship of Joseph Stalin consolidated its power, read the Moscow dispatches eagerly yesterday. They viewed his passing from the Soviet political scene as offering hope for the future.

Raphael Abramovitch, veteran leader of the Russian democratic socialists, the Mensheviks, who has spent his adult life fighting Stalin from abroad, holds that Stalin's passing "is a turning point in the history of the Bolshevik dictatorship."

"It creates an authority vacuum," he explained. "In the modern totalitarian dictatorship, the personality of 'The Leader' is a political factor of tremendous importance. Take away the god-like authority of the Fuehrer and what remains? Various conflicting interests.

"Who will keep these interests together? The cohesive power of the tradition? But Stalin annihilated the Leninist tradition and installed his own. The enormous authority of one man, maintained by terror, coped with the complicated matter of keeping together a colossal empire; but his place has become void. Not immediately, but after a while, rivalries will begin, with the same old fights and struggles."

Alexander Kerensky, premier of the provisional government after the Russian Revolution that was overthrown in November, 1917, by the Bolshevik coup, said he was hopeful that "we are in the beginning of a new period of history."

He did not expect any immediate or sensational change, he said, but hoped that in the end freedom would be restored "to the Russian people, who were the first victims of the totalitarian Communist dictatorship, and to the other peoples now under the yoke of communism." He held that "to replace Stalin, with his extraordinary strategical and tactical capacity, is quite impossible."

Mrs. Oksana Kasenkina, the Russian school teacher who was held prisoner in the Soviet consulate here but gained freedom by leaping from a three-story window in 1948, said that the news was "the biggest happiness for my people."

YUGOSLAVS CONFER ON MOSCOW NEWS

Belgrade Chiefs Get Together to Assay Consequences of Soviet Premier's Death

By JACK RAYMOND
Special to THE NEW YORK TIMES.

BELGRADE, Yugoslavia, March 5—Yugoslavia's Communist leaders have met at least informally to discuss the consequences of the news from Moscow. It is not known whether any decisions were taken or contemplated, but it may be assumed that President Tito subscribes to the view prevalent here that a struggle for power is about to ensue among the heirs to Premier Stalin.

Moreover, after careful consideration of available material, some of which did not emanate exclusively from the official Soviet announcement, the Communist leaders here still are convinced Premier Stalin died prior to the first report on his illness Wednesday morning.

It was the immediate reaction here that Premier Stalin was dead despite the running descriptions of the state of his health. On second thought, the Communist leaders here who have reason to know intimately the techniques of Soviet leadership stood by their first analysis of the situation.

"We know those people," declared a high Yugoslav official. "We know them all personally and we know just what can be expected of them."

News Held Delayed

According to the Yugoslav Communist leadership, the Soviet dictator died but the Central Committee of the Communist party in Russia purposely delayed the news to protect the administrative machinery from disintegrating. The contention here is that Premier Stalin controlled this machinery to the very last.

Deputy Premier Georgi M. Malenkov was regarded here as the most powerful individual in the Soviet Government, but it was held possible—even likely—that if only one man were to be granted the title of leader it would be Deputy Premier Vyacheslav M. Molotov.

However, this would be a mere gesture, it was said and before long, on the basis of the existing political forces in the Soviet Communist party, Mr. Malenkov would come out on top—but that probably only temporarily.

A view strongly held among Communist authorities here and one that was discussed in their meeting was that Marshal Georgi K. Zhukov would be an important figure in the impending political maneuvering in Russia. It is said that Marshal Zhukov may be in a position to exert greater control over the army than even the new Chief of Staff Marshal Vassily D. Sokolovsky.

Yugoslavs Recall Experiences

Recalling their own experiences with some of the Soviet leaders, the Yugoslav Communist chiefs voiced, according to authoritative sources, their conviction that if Mr. Molotov assumed command of the Soviet Union's Communist apparatus for even a short time Foreign Minister Andrei Y. Vishinsky would be swiftly removed.

"Molotov hates Vishinsky," said a man who knew them both quite well.

This country's controlled press and radio gave continuous news reports and commentaries on the situation. The commentaries were violent in their denunciation of Premier Stalin, whose picture once ranked with President Tito's in displays throughout Yugoslavia.

Ivan Karainov, a member of the Central Committee of the Communist League of Yugoslavia, who lived in the Soviet Union from 1926 to 1944, said it was impossible to say anything favorable of Premier Stalin.

The newspaper Politika predicted "the beginning of the disintegration" of the "bureaucratic" system of government in Russia.

PRAYER URGED FOR STALIN

Vatican Holds the Premier's Soul Was 'Redeemed by Christ'

ROME, March 5 (UP)—The Vatican radio has urged Roman Catholics to pray for the soul of Soviet Premier Stalin.

The appeal was made in the course of a broadcast last night by the Rev. Antonio Ferri.

Father Ferri said Premier Stalin had personified the present-day phenomenon of world communism—"a phenomenon of no small responsibility and one whose attitude toward religion is known to all."

The Vatican broadcast added:

"For Catholics, this is the moment to regard the chief of the Soviet state as a soul, like all others, redeemed by Christ, and therefore in the sense of universal and supranatural Christian charity, object of the prayers that Catholics raise to infinitely merciful God."

JERUSALEM, March 5 (UP)—Orthodox Russian monks and nuns fasted and prayed today for Premier Stalin in the big green-domed Russian church here. Members of the Moscow Academy of Sciences with the Palestine Archaeological Society were taking part in religious services occasioned by Mr. Stalin's fatal illness.

Hurley Wary on Soviet Policy

SANTA FE, N. M., March 5 (AP)—Patrick J. Hurley, who as a roving Ambassador for President Roosevelt in World War II came to know Premier Stalin, said today it is futile to guess what would happen in Russia. "Stalin was unquestionably the leader of Russia and of world communism," Mr. Hurley said. "For all that is being said by statesmen and others, no one knows for certain what the future Soviet policy will be."

Vietnam Hopes for a Rest

SAIGON, Vietnam, March 5 (UP)—Premier Nguyen Van Tam said today that he hoped the efforts to find a successor to Premier Stalin would "lead Russia to take less interest in our country for a while." Vietnam and its associated Indo-Chinese states of Laos and Cambodia have been fighting against Communist-led Vietminh rebels for seven years.

Vishinsky Asserts Name Of Stalin Is Immortal

GLEN COVE, L. I., March 5 (AP)—Soviet Foreign Minister Andrei Y. Vishinsky said tonight that the death of Premier Stalin was a blow to all humanity.

Reached by telephone at his country retreat on Long Island, the Kremlin's diplomatic chief at the United Nations said:

"With great sorrow I confirm the death of Premier Stalin. It is a great blow to all of the Soviet people and to all humanity. The name of Stalin is immortal."

Rhee Regrets 'Human's' Death

SEOUL, Friday, March 6 (AP)—President Syngman Rhee, said today he was sorry that Premier Stalin had died. "I am sorry he, as a human, has died," Dr. Rhee said. "We are fighting against the attitude and principles of Communist leaders and not against one individual person."

"All the News That's Fit to Print"

The New York Times.

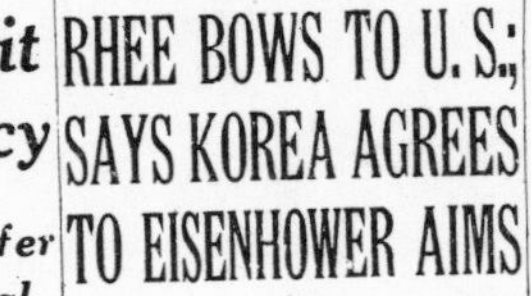

LATE CITY EDITION

Fair with little change in temperature today and tomorrow.
Temperature Range Today-Max., 72; Min., 52
Temperatures Yesterday—Max., 70; Min., 53
Full U. S. Weather Bureau Report, Page 59

Copyright, 1953, by The New York Times Company.

VOL. CII..No. 34,828. Entered as Second-Class Matter, Post Office, New York, N. Y. NEW YORK, TUESDAY, JUNE 2, 1953. Times Square, New York 36, N. Y. Telephone LAckawanna 4-1000 FIVE CENTS

2 OF BRITISH TEAM CONQUER EVEREST; QUEEN GETS NEWS AS CORONATION GIFT; THRONGS LINE HER PROCESSION ROUTE

AUTHORITY LEASES CITY TRANSIT LINES; FARE RISE IN SIGHT

Estimate Board Votes, 11-5, for 10-Year Pact Including Terms Asked by Joseph

EFFECTIVE DATE IS JUNE 15

New Agency Seeking Tokens From Mint, Indicating New Charge May Not Be 15c

Digest of lease signed by city and Transit Authority, Page 32.

By LEO EGAN

The Board of Estimate voted 11 to 5 yesterday to lease the city's $1,700,000,000 transit system to the newly created New York City Transit Authority for a period of ten years, during which the authority will be obligated to raise enough revenue from fares and incidental charges to meet operating costs.

By approving the lease, the board made it almost certain that the authority will raise transit fares by July 30 in an amount sufficient to overcome a prospective operating deficit of $47,000,000 for the fiscal year beginning July 1. A first step in this direction was taken by the authority within a few hours after the board acted when it decided to explore the possibility of obtaining from the United States Mint at Philadelphia an emergency supply of tokens, to be used on all three divisions of the rapid transit lines in the collection of a higher fare.

Casey Tells of Token Plans

The decision to request the Federal Government's help in obtaining enough tokens to put a fare change into effect by July 30, the statutory deadline, was announced by Maj. Gen. Hugh J. Casey, authority chairman, after a special authority meeting at the offices of the Board of Transportation, 370 Jay Street, Brooklyn.

Sidney H. Bingham, chairman of the Board of Transportation, will confer with the Director of the Mint at Philadelphia today on the possibility of obtaining 20,000,000 tokens, General Casey said. Subsequent additions to the supply would be obtained from private suppliers, he added.

To speed the negotiations with the Mint, the authority has requested Governor Dewey to intervene with the Secretary of the Treasury, General Casey said.

A design for the token was officially approved by the authority yesterday. It is a perforated coin, somewhat smaller than a dime.

By exploring the possibility of obtaining enough tokens for use on all three divisions, the authority indicated it might reject Mr. Bingham's recommendation for a 15-cent fare in favor of a smaller charge, perhaps 12 or 12½ cents a ride. The present fare is 10 cents.

A major justification for the Bingham recommendation was that it would involve use of tokens on only the I.R.T. division, which has electrically operated turnstiles. On the B.M.T. and IND divisions, which have mechanical turnstiles, two coins—a dime and a nickel—would be used to pay the fare.

General Casey emphasized in announcing the authority action that no decisions on a fare increase had been reached. It will not be possible to arrive at a conclusion, he said, until all pertinent facts are studied.

City Fiscal Problem Eased

The Board of Estimate's decision yesterday automatically relieved the city of the necessity of meeting the prospective operating deficit out of tax revenues in the new fiscal year that starts July 1. It likewise vested the city with power to collect $50,000,000 a year in additional taxes from real estate for general municipal purposes plus, for the next four years, enough to liquidate an accumulated deficit of $39,000,000 in the transit pension system.

Moreover, in accordance with special laws enacted by the Legislature earlier this year on the recommendation of Governor Dewey, transfer of the deficit-ridden transit system to the authority gives the city power at any time in the future to impose a one-half of 1 per cent payroll tax, payable in equal parts by employers and employes, estimated to raise $60,000,000 a year.

The city's budget for the new fiscal year, already approved by the Board of Estimate and City Council, contemplates full use of the additional real estate taxing powers, but no use of the payroll tax.

As had been forecast, Rudolph

Continued on Page 33, Column 2

Eisenhower Moves to Limit State Department to Policy

New Reorganization Plans Would Transfer Present Operating Functions to 2 Special Agencies, Information and Foreign Aid

By ANTHONY LEVIERO
Special to THE NEW YORK TIMES.

WASHINGTON, June 1—President Eisenhower proposed today to restore the State Department to its traditional pre-war policy-making role and to transfer virtually all its operating functions to new organizations — the United States Information Agency and the Foreign Operations Administration.

A far-reaching reorganization of the State Department was projected by the President in two plans submitted to Congress today, with a promise of further changes to be sought early next year.

Today he stressed two objectives:

1. To divest the department of the functional tasks that had involved it in political controversy during the post-war era.
2. To make the Secretary of State supreme, next to the President, in the policy supervision of all foreign information and aid programs.

The controversial Voice of America and other information programs would be swept out of the State Department, the Mutual Security Agency and other agencies and concentrated in the new Information Agency. The Mutual Security Agency itself would become the nucleus around which would be built the new Foreign Operations Administration to take over various other programs for technical, economic and military assistance.

Of operating programs, all that would be left in the State Department would be the programs for the educational exchange of persons.

The two new agencies would have administrative autonomy, just as the Mutual Security Agency has today. But a new idea in Government organization was introduced. The directors of the two agencies not only would be subject to close

Continued on Page 24, Column 4

Text of message on propaganda and aid plans, Page 24.

RHEE BOWS TO U.S.; SAYS KOREA AGREES TO EISENHOWER AIMS

Statement on Message From Washington Hint. Opposition to Truce Plans Is Easing

By The Associated Press.

SEOUL, Korea, June 2—President Syngman Rhee disclosed today he had received a three-point message from President Eisenhower, and added: "We must accept anything that the United States President wants."

"Common sense and wisdom require that we cooperate with the United States at any cost," Dr. Rhee said, without saying what President Eisenhower had told him.

The statement of the 78-year-old leader of the Republic of Korea indicated that South Korean opposition to the secret proposal by the United Nations Command for bringing an armistice in Korea was lessening.

Dr. Rhee also said he was looking for some one to take the place of Maj. Gen. Choi Duk Shin as the South Korean delegate on the United Nations armistice negotiation team.

Dr. Rhee declined to elaborate on his apparently conciliatory statement. He spoke to correspondents at a parade of the British Commonwealth Division honoring the Coronation of Elizabeth II.

Nor did he make it precisely clear whether he was ready now to accept the Allied truce proposal, to which he and his Government had expressed vigorous opposition.

South Korea's acting Premier, Pyun Yun Tae, threatened yesterday a break with the Allies and a go-it-alone policy for South Korea but deferred action until after next Thursday's critical truce session.

The Communists are expected to reply to the Allied proposal at Thursday's meeting.

Rhee Said to Seek Treaty

By JAY WALZ
Special to THE NEW YORK TIMES.

WASHINGTON, June 1—The Eisenhower Administration was reported today to have had a new request from President Syngman Rhee of South Korea for the pledge of a mutual defense pact and of military and economic help as a basis for the Seoul Government's support of present Allied truce proposals.

These conditions were said on good authority to be important features of a four-point program outlined in a letter forwarded to President Eisenhower through Ellis O. Briggs, United States Ambassador at Seoul.

The principal point in the still-secret United Nations proposal to the Communists for disposition of Korean war prisoners who refuse to return home was understood to be that final determination of the captives' fate would be up to the General Assembly of the United Nations.

Officially, the White House and State Department were silent on developments on Korea, and offered "no comment" even on reports that a letter from President Rhee might have been received.

Had Asked Pledge in Writing

The South Korean request for a mutual defense pact with the United States is not new. Dr. You Chan Yang, the Korean Ambassador here, has made repeated representations to the State Department for such a pledge of defense help in the event of future Communist aggression.

He has made the point that, while President Eisenhower has said publicly that the United States will never desert Korea, it would be more satisfying from the Korean standpoint to have "something down in black and white."

President Rhee's four points were reported to be (1) a pledge to sign a mutual defense pact with Korea; (2) a promise by the United States to provide military and financial help to Korea on a large scale; (3) withdrawal of all foreign troops on both sides as soon as a truce has started and prisoners have been exchanged, and (4) agreement that the United States would not stand in the way of South Korea in efforts to unite that country at some future time.

As far as the last point is concerned, sources felt South Korea did not have in mind the use of military force to bring together North and South Korea.

Meanwhile, some Capitol Hill leaders spoke out on recent Korean developments.

Senator William F. Knowland of California, who is chairman of the Senate Republican Policy Committee, said the United States should "risk" war with Russia to expand the fighting if truce negotiations with the Communists collapsed.

In another ... Senator H. Alexander ... Republican of New Jersey ... thought

Continued on Page ..., Column 5

MRS. HOBBY WARNS DOCTORS ON TASKS

Social-Economic Problems in the Field Must Be Solved by A.M.A. or Others, She Says

Mrs. Oveta Culp Hobby, Secretary of Health, Education and Welfare, declared at the annual meeting of the American Medical Association, which opened yesterday, that organized medicine must find solutions to the social-economic problems facing medicine today or the solution would be taken out of its hands. She expressed confidence that the American Medical Association "will meet this challenge."

Addressing the House of Delegates, policy-making body of the association, at the Waldorf-Astoria Hotel, Mrs. Hobby said the social and economic demands on the medical profession "are only the continuing challenge in this long history of constant adaptation to a changing society, but never have these problems been more onerous and critical than today."

The association opened its 102d annual meeting yesterday. For five days progress in all branches of medicine will be reviewed in 100 reports by leaders in their fields.

The sessions are being held in seven hotels and in Town Hall while 635 scientific and technical exhibits are being displayed on four floors of Grand Central Palace. The exhibits are open only to doctors and their guests.

Mrs. Hobby in her speech to the delegates said she agreed fully

Continued on Page 26, Column 5

HUMPHREY OPPOSES REVENUE LOSS NOW

He Calls Cut Gamble With U.S. Security—Asks House Unit to Extend Excess Profit Tax

By JOHN D. MORRIS
Special to THE NEW YORK TIMES.

WASHINGTON, June 1—George M. Humphrey, Secretary of the Treasury, told Congress today that only "full mobilization" would justify tax increases to produce any more revenue than the Administration was now seeking.

The Government's chief fiscal officer so testified in opening the Administration's case before the House Ways and Means Committee for a six-month extension of the excess profits tax and the cancellation of automatic cuts in regular corporation and excise (sales) levies slated for next April 1.

The Administration, he said, wants those three phases of its tax program carried out in a single bill this year, though the committee has limited its present deliberations to extension of the excess profits law, which is due to expire June 30.

The Secretary asserted that losses in Federal revenue now would be an unsafe gamble with the country's security.

Mr. Humphrey also made the following points:

¶ That he was "very strongly opposed" to any change in the excess profits tax during the extension period.

¶ That he would fight any continuation of the levy beyond Dec. 31.

¶ That tax relief starting next

Continued on Page 47, Column 2

Harvard Elects Dr. N. M. Pusey, Midwest Educator, as President

Lawrence College Head, 46, Has 3 Degrees From University—Favors Humanities Study

By JOHN H. FENTON
Special to THE NEW YORK TIMES.

CAMBRIDGE, Mass., June 1—Dr. Nathan Marsh Pusey, president of Lawrence College in Appleton, Wis., was elected the twenty-fourth president of Harvard by the Harvard Corporation today.

Dr. Pusey, who is a native of Council Bluffs, Iowa, and 46 years old, is a scholar in Greek history, and holds three degrees from Harvard: Bachelor of Arts, magna cum laude, 1928; Master of Arts, 1932, and Doctor of Philosophy, 1937. He prepared for college at Abraham Lincoln High School in Council Bluffs.

The Iowa educator will succeed Dr. James Bryant Conant, who will become president-emeritus of Harvard University on Sept. 1. Dr. Conant, now on leave, is serving as United States High Commissioner for Germany.

Dr. Pusey's election by the Harvard Corporation is subject to the confirmation of the Board of Overseers. This confirmation, customarily a formality, is scheduled to be voted on June 10, the day before the Harvard commencement. On only one occasion, in 1868, have the overseers refused the corporation permission to elect a president.

Associated Press
Dr. Nathan M. Pusey

The occasion of the only refusal was in the election of Dr. Charles W. Eliot, the original choice of the corporation, as the twenty-first president. The corporation prevailed after a delay of six months, and Dr. Eliot became president in 1869.

Dr. Pusey, reached by telephone at Appleton, said that he considered the corporation's action "a tremendous honor." But he de-

Continued on Page 27, Column 5

CROWDS DEFY RAIN

Face a Day of Showers After All-Night Vigil to Hail Their Sovereign

By RAYMOND DANIELL
Special to THE NEW YORK TIMES.

LONDON, Tuesday, June 2—This is the day that all London, all Britain, all the Commonwealth and half the world have been awaiting. It is the day on which the crown of her forefathers is placed upon the head of this old country's radiantly lovely young Queen Elizabeth II whose reign, it is hoped, will usher in another golden age.

The weather for the day was uncertain. By early morning the wind still blew, but rains that fell during the night had ceased, at least temporarily. The weather forecaster, however, was not optimistic about the prospects for the day, which was chosen originally because rain had not fallen on June 2 for many years. The forecast was for cool weather and showers, with sunny intervals.

Last night's gusts and rain discomfited the hundreds of thousands of persons who squatted the whole length of the royal way but if these hardships dislodged any it was unnoticeable because there were others waiting to take their places.

Some of these squatters, lacking reserved seats in the stands to accommodate 250,000 persons, began staking out their claims as early as midnight Sunday.

Squatters Sit on Curbs

By noon yesterday they were sitting on the curbs at Trafalgar Square and were packed two and three deep on the sidewalks along the Mall leading from Admiralty Arch to Buckingham Palace. By dinner time last night the East Carriage Drive in Hyde Park was filled with men, women and even young children with raincoats, blankets, lunch baskets and inflatable mattresses prepared to defend their little vantage points until the Queen's ornate gilded coach, with its eight gray horses, one named Eisenhower, had passed late in the afternoon.

During the day Queen Mother Elizabeth, accompanied by Princess Margaret, visited the palace to see the Queen on the eve of her coronation. By the time they left, an hour later, the crowd outside Buckingham Palace numbered nearly 50,000. The police, who had let the crowd swarm over the roadway, had to make strenuous efforts to clear a path for their car.

Later Princess Margaret made a visit to Westminster Abbey, where she was received by the Earl Marshal. Again the police had trouble clearing a way for her to return home.

Even Oxford Street, that busy shopping center, was taken over by sidewalk squatters almost as soon as the big stores closed. Trafalgar Square, through which the Queen will pass three times on her way from Buckingham Palace to Westminster Abbey, out again and back to the palace, was filled with curbstone sitters even at midday. Some of them had been there twelve hours then with an additional twenty-four in front of them. The litter they made of sodden

Continued on Page 8, Column 1

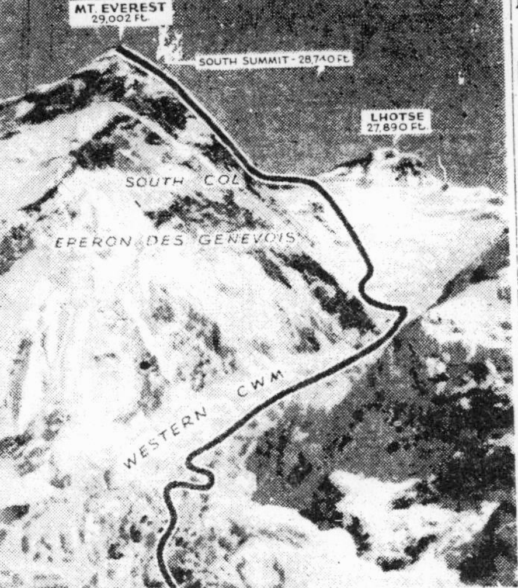

The New York Times June 2, 1953
AT THE TOP: Solid black line shows route of British expedition, the first to reach Mount Everest's summit.

Abbey, Bedecked and Aglow, Awaits the Coronation Hour

By TANIA LONG
Special to THE NEW YORK TIMES.

LONDON, Tuesday, June 2—As one enters Westminster Abbey, where Elizabeth II is to be crowned in a few hours, a magnificent scene greets the eye. The austere gray interior has been converted into a rich and glowing setting for the young Queen's coronation. Carpeting and hangings in warm tones of blue and gold, banners of white embroidered with the royal coats of arms, and the deep rose of the throne and the royal chairs blend into a splendid symphony of color.

In the pale light of early morning a hush lies over the Abbey. Only a few of the great assemblage of 7,000 guests have arrived, and there is little movement in the vast edifice.

From the great west door, where the Queen will enter, a thick carpet of deep azure blue reaches through the nave to the choir stalls. Hangings of blue silk with royal emblems embroidered in gold are draped over the edges of the stands and balconies, giving warmth to the gray fabric of the church.

From the choir to the altar in that area known as the Coronation Theatre the floor is covered in rich gold pile, against which the deep rose-covered throne and chairs, and the opulent blue hangings on the walls stand out in sharp contrast.

Under a huge chandelier in the center of the Coronation Theatre and raised on a dais stands the throne. Five steps lead up to it. It faces the altar, and because the Queen will be facing away from the majority of the guests, its back is low so that they too may see the Queen's crowned head during the latter part of the ceremony.

The throne chair is late seven-

Continued on Page 6, Column 3

Notables File Past Empty Thrones On Way to Offer Homage to Queen

By C. L. SULZBERGER
Special to THE NEW YORK TIMES.

LONDON, Tuesday, June 2—At 6 o'clock this morning the most distinguished men in Britain began filing past an empty throne. Within a few brief hours, seated upon it and wearing the heavy crown of St. Edward the Confessor, a young Queen will receive their homage.

For Britain and for her still vast empire, this is a significant moment. A new Elizabethan age of challenge and uncertainty has started.

Westminster Abbey, in its fullest splendor, with gold plate and regalia spread out on the altar, contains two thrones today. The first is that of King Edward I, a gnarled oaken chair having beneath it the Stone of Scone from the Scotland he had conquered.

Upon it the Queen is crowned. From it she will hear the acclaim of her subjects, the distant booming of her cannon and the solemn prayer of her primate, the Archbishop of Canterbury, exhorting:

"God crown you with a crown of glory and righteousness, that, having a right faith and manifold fruit of good works, you may obtain the crown of an everlasting kingdom by the gift of Him whose Kingdom endureth forever. Amen."

Only then, when she is fully consecrated and acclaimed, will the Queen, assisted by her lay and clerical peers, mount the royal throne on its dais.

Since the early dawn crept over the stirring city of London, pushing its light across gray Whitehall and through the soft rose and amber windows of this Holy Church of St. Peter, which is its rightful name, the Abbey has come to life for one of those great occasions when it nurtures monarchs.

Finely attired lords and ladies are sweeping to their places, bear-

Continued on Page 12, Column 3

DULLES SAYS U.S. AIM IS TO GAIN FRIENDS

Report on Near East-Asian Trip Urges 'Impartial' Approach to Arab-Israeli Dispute

Text of Secretary Dulles' talk about recent trip, Page 4.

Special to THE NEW YORK TIMES.

WASHINGTON, June 1—John Foster Dulles, Secretary of State, said tonight that it was the policy of the Eisenhower Administration to develop goodwill among the nations of the Near East and South Asia to thwart the Kremlin's desire to exploit their many differences.

To this end, he urged an "impartial" approach to Israeli-Arab disputes so as to win the support of both sides against the "common threat"—communism. He said the United States must make clear to all nations concerned with independence that the North Atlantic Treaty alliance was in no way related to a desire to help colonial powers keep or win back their colonies.

In a country-wide radio and television report on his twenty-day tour of the Middle East and South Asia, Mr. Dulles urged the strategic importance of the rich and populous area and said its problems could not be ignored without dangerous consequence.

'Primary Purpose' Stressed

The Secretary's half-hour address was carried over the radio and television networks of the American Broadcasting System and by the Du Mont television network, and the National Broadcasting Company radio network rebroadcast it. The Secretary gave a country-by-country account of the trip, on which he was accompanied by Harold E. Stassen, Director for Mutual Security. They made stops all the way from Egypt to Pakistan and India.

Mr. Dulles declared that the "primary purpose" of the trip "was to show friendliness and to develop understanding," and he added: "These people we visited are all proud peoples who have a great tradition and, I believe, a great future."

The Eisenhower Administration, he continued, plans to make "friendship—not fault-finding—the basis of its foreign policy."

Addressing himself to problems of the troubled Holy Land, Mr. Dulles said he had come back to Washington convinced that the Arabs were "more fearful of Zionism than of communism."

On the other hand, he added,

Continued on Page 5, Column 6

HIGHEST PEAK WON

New Zealander and a Guide Made the Final Climb to Top Friday

By Reuters.

KATMANDU, Nepal, Tuesday, June 2—The British expedition has conquered Mount Everest, a radio message flashed from Namche Bazar to the British Embassy here said today.

The message said Edmond Hillary, a New Zealand beekeeper and mountaineer, and Tensing Norkay, the famous Sherpa guide, had reached the hitherto unscaled summit from Camp Eight last Friday.

The news of this success had to be rushed by runner from the British expedition's base camp on Khumbu Glacier to the radio post at Namche Bazar.

It is understood here that this was the expedition's third attack on the last slopes leading to the summit, a first double attempt having failed.

Experts here said the success was largely due to the fine weather, combined with properly acclimatized climbers and the excellent organization and leadership of Col. H. C. J. Hunt.

Full details of the exploit are not expected to reach here for some days.

It is believed here that the news was transmitted specially to London by diplomatic channels so Queen Elizabeth could be told.

Queen Told at Palace

LONDON, Tuesday, June 2 (Reuters)—The Times of London reported the news of the scaling of Mount Everest in a copyrighted message today.

The news was published in a special edition of The Times on early sale among coronation crowds in London.

Queen Elizabeth, resting at Buckingham Palace, was told on the eve of her coronation that the British expedition had conquered the mountain. The news was brought to her as she spent a quiet evening "at home." The British climbers had succeeded in their plan to give her a world-shaking coronation present.

Mount Everest, the 29,002-foot giant, was the last main outpost of the world unknown to man.

The thirteen members of the expedition formed the eleventh team to try to conquer the mountain in the past thirty years. Many climbers have died in the high ice and snow of the Himalaya giant.

The Sherpa guide, Tensing Norkay, is a 42-year-old native veteran of more assaults on Mount Everest than any other man.

With 362 porters, twenty Sherpa guides and 10,000 pounds of baggage the expedition left the Nepalese base of Katmandu on March 10. Thus it took eighty days from start to finish.

The climbers carried three flags—the Union Jack, the United Nations flag and the Nepalese flag—to plant on the summit.

They made an approach to the "Goddess Mother of the Snows" from the south, or Nepalese, side.

It was the route reconnoitered by Sir Eric Shipton, who led a British

Continued on Page 14, Column 7

Tito Abolishes Rank Of Army Commissar

By JACK RAYMOND
Special to THE NEW YORK TIMES.

BELGRADE, Yugoslavia, June 1—President Tito abolished today the system of political commissars in the Yugoslav armed forces, asserting that present conditions no longer required them.

Not mentioned in Marshal Tito's order was the fact that this will undoubtedly make it easier for Yugoslavia to carry on with growing plans for integrating her military establishment with Western defense projects.

"It will be much easier to deal with Yugoslav military leaders now," said a Western military liaison expert here.

The political commissars, who wore uniforms and were equal in rank with military commanders in the Yugoslav Army, were introduced in imitation of Soviet military practice in the early days of partisan warfare against Germany.

Even after the break with the

Continued on Page 18, Column .

MT. EVEREST LONG DREAM OF CLIMBERS

Peak Thwarted 10 Previous Groups—Earth Movements Steadily Raising Height

The conquest of Mount Everest, highest charted mountain in the world, has been the burning dream of mountain climbers the world over for more than thirty years. But every previous attempt of men to clamber to its icy summit has been thrown back by the towering giant of the Himalayas.

In the hidden reaches of Central Asia there may be higher mountain peaks as yet uncharted and unconquered. But none of them has so challenged and fired the imagination of a generation bent on penetrating to the most inaccessible corners of the world on which it lives.

No one knows for sure how high Mount Everest is. A hundred years ago when it was first surveyed, a Bengali computer fixed its height at 29,002 feet. European scientists list its height at 29,141 feet, some American geographers put the height at 29,249 feet and members of the Swiss expedition in 1952 found the height to be 29,610 feet.

Actually, because of earthquakes and other geological movements in the Himalayas, which are the youngest mountains in the world, Mount Everest, the culminating peak of the range, is steadily being thrust higher and higher.

The mountain was named for Sir George Everest, the British Surveyor General of India, who in 1841 began the surveying project to map the Himalayan range. Its ancient Indian name was Gaurishanker, for the Hindue god Shiva.

Ten Earlier Expeditions

There have been ten previous expeditions in modern times that attempted without success to scale the mountain's heights. The Nepal Government allows no more than one country a year to make the attempt from the approaches it controls.

In 1921 George Leigh Mallory led a reconnaissance expedition to study the approaches to the peak and prepare for the first full-scale expedition the following year. The reconnaissance team reached a height of 23,000 feet, ascending from Lhapka Pass.

In the expedition in 1922 Mr. Mallory, Dr. T. H. Somervell and Maj. E. F. Norton were able to reach a height of 26,985 feet without oxygen. Brig. Gen. C. G. Bruce and Capt. G. I. Finch, with the aid of oxygen, reached 27,300 feet.

In 1924 the team made three more assaults on the mountain, and Major Norton, pushing ahead alone, reached an altitude of 28,306 feet. On June 8, 1924, Mr. Mallory and Andrew C. Irvine, an Oxford student, started out from a camp at 27,000 feet and were seen to have climbed to 28,230 feet. Then they were suddenly enveloped in a wind-whipped cloud of snow and were never seen again.

That accident, embroidered by time into a legend, added to the mystery and fancy that for years has attributed to supernatural forces on Mount Everest the power of repelling the men who dared trespass high on its slopes.

The Legendary 'Snowmen'

There were other, more fearsome tales, of the "abominable snowmen"—great white creatures, half animal and half human, that roamed the snow and ice at altitudes where no man could live unaided by oxygen. The snowmen were first reported in 1921, and some scientists listening to native tales of their appearance speculated that they might be a missing link between man and the apes. In 1951 a British expedition returned with photographs of footprints in the snow of the mountainside that some thought had been made by these beasts.

That expedition, the last to be made by Great Britain before the present one, was led by Sir Eric Shipton. Sir Eric had made his first climb on Mount Everest with the Hugh Ruttledge Expedition in 1933, the first to be made after the disappearance of Mallory and Levine.

The first airplane flight over the mountain peak was made in 1933 by a British plane, a feat not repeated until twelve years later when a United States military plane accidentally wandered off course over the mountain. In the intervening years three British expeditions tackled the mountain—in 1935, 1936 and 1938—all without success. Other attempts were made by French, German and Polish climbers.

The two last previous expeditions up the mountain were made by Swiss climbers in 1952. Their attempt in the spring came to within 900 feet of the summit before they were forced to turn back. In the fall the Swiss made the first attempt on record to scale the mountain at that time of year, when the mountain is doubly dangerous because of avalanches of snow and ice loosed by the sun.

Three men in that expedition reached a point 150 feet from the summit on Nov. 20.

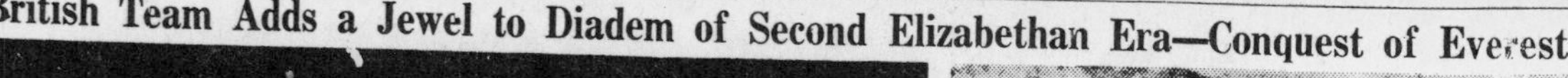

British Team Adds a Jewel to Diadem of Second Elizabethan Era—Conquest of Everest

Twenty thousand feet above sea level is this glacier on the side of Everest. At least fifteen men have died trying to conquer Everest, which, as one climber said, "taunts men from behind her armor of blizzard and avalanche and altitude." Why do men tackle such a formidable foe? George Leigh Mallory, who disappeared near the peak in 1924, put it simply: "Because it's there."

Until a British expedition accomplished feat, the attainment of Everest's peak had been one of the last great human exploits left unachieved. The porters, shown here climbing the North Col, were Sherpas from high southern slopes of the Himalayas.

GUIDE ON EVEREST A VETERAN CLIMBER

Tensing Norkay Is of Mountain Clan—New Zealand Alpinist Also a Keeper of Bees

Following are short biographies of members of the British Expedition, two of whose members reached the top of Mount Everest:

Tensing Norkay

Tensing Norkay, the 42-year-old "Tiger of the Snows," is a veteran Nepalese mountain climber who has served as guide for numerous European expeditions in the Himalayas, but never before has been a fullfledged member of a climbing party.

Last fall he climbed to within 150 feet of the summit of the mountain while serving as guide for the Swiss. But then he was forced by numbing winds and below-zero cold to turn back. If he reached the ton this time, he said, he would plant a Nepalese flag there beside the Union Jack.

A handsome, brown-skinned man with a ready smile, Tensing Norkay lives in Darjeeling, India, where his two daughters attend an English school. Although he is a member of the Sherpa clan of Tibetan invaders of ages ago, which now is native to the Mount Everest region, he is regarded by the Indian people as one of their own.

All told he has been on twenty Himalayan expeditions, starting his career as a porter and working up to sirdar, or commander. He was with the British expeditions of 1935, 1936 and 1938 and both Swiss expeditions of 1952.

Edmond P. Hillary

Edmond P. Hillary, a lean six-footer from Auckland, New Zealand, keeps bees for a living and climbs mountains for fun.

His mountain climbing started many years ago when as a schoolboy he spent his holidays climbing on the slopes of Mount Ruapehu, a New Zealand volcano. Ever since then, he says, Mount Everest has been his goal.

Now 34 years old, he is considered to be the originator of winter ski mountaineering in his native country, and is regarded by Col. H. C. J. Hunt, the Everest expedition leader, as an expert ice craftsman. In 1951 he took part in the New Zealand expedition to Garhwal in the Himalayas, conquering peaks well over 20,000 feet in height. The same year he went with the British reconnaissance expedition to Mount Everest, and the following year he was on the British expedition to Cho Oyu.

One of his major achievements was last April when he led a preliminary reconnaissance party that found a new and easier route from Camp One to Camp Two.

Col. H. C. J. Hunt

Col. H. C. J. Hunt was named to head the 1953 British expedition to Mount Everest last fall when Sir Eric Shipton, the leader of three previous British expeditions to the mountain, resigned over friendly differences of opinion with the sponsors.

Colonel Hunt, a veteran British mountaineer, has climbed many of the other peaks of the Himalayas and took part in expeditions in the area in 1933, 1937 and 1940.

He is 42 years old, relatively old as mountaineers go, and is a regular British Army officer who during the war was chief instructor of the Commando Mountain and Snow Warfare School. He was released from his army duties to make the attempt on Mount Everest.

A graduate of Marlborough and Sandhurst, he has also served in command of Indian infantry troops, and most recently was attached to the staff of SHAPE.

The New York Times June 2, 1953

EVEREST IS CONQUERED: British climbers reached top of mountain in Nepal Friday.

Maj. Charles G. Wylie

Maj. Charles G. Wylie, 33, a British Army officer who was most recently assigned to the War Office in London, was the organizing secretary for the expedition.

He was a prisoner of war in Malaya and Siam from 1942 to 1945, and then was assigned to Malaya guerrilla operations from 1948-1949.

A climber since his boyhood, he has attacked mountains in the United Kingdom, the Alps as well as other peaks in the Himalayas. In 1939 he was the British pentathlon champion.

C. Wilfred Noyce

C. Alfred Noyce, 35, is a schoolmaster and writer who pursues mountain climbing as a hobby. He was educated at Charterhouse, where he now teaches, and at Cambridge. During the war he served in a Friends Ambulance Unit and also as intelligence instructor at the Aircrew Mountain Center in Kashmir.

In the past he has organized expeditions to Garhwal and Sikkim, and led the ascent of 23,385-foot Mount Pauhunr.

George Low

George Low is a 28-year-old New Zealand schoolmaster, who has worked as a student guide in the New Zealand Alps.

George C. Band

George C. Band, 24, was the youngest member of the British expedition and has been described by its commander as "Britain's finest mountaineer." He is reported to have led one of the two unsuccessful attempts a few days ago.

His home is in Wirral, Cheshire, and he was educated at Eltham School. At Cambridge he is specializing in geology and postponed part of his university work to take part in the expedition.

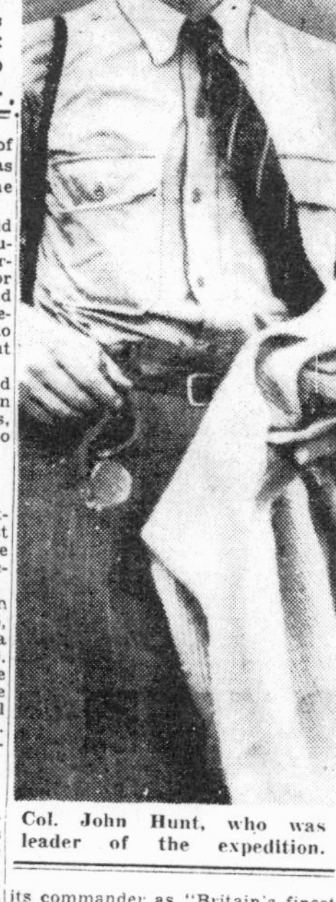

Col. John Hunt, who was leader of the expedition.

Michael Westmacott

Michael Westmacott, 28, is the president of the Oxford University Mountaineering Club and also works at the Rothamsted Experimental Station.

He began his climbing in the mountains of Great Britain and has spent the last four seasons climbing in the Swiss Alps. He was educated at Radley School before going to Oxford, and during the war served with the British of the British Isles and in the Alps.

Eastern Publishers

Sir George Everest, Surveyor General of India, for whom the height was named in 1852.

Thomas D. Bourdillon

Thomas D. Bourdillon is a rocket expert for the British Government and was taking part in his third Himalayan expedition.

A member of the Mount Everest reconnaissance expedition of 1951, led by Sir Eric Shipton, he also took part in the British Himalayan Expedition to Cho Oyu in 1952. At present he is employed as a physicist working on rocket motors for the British Ministry of Supply.

Alfred Gregory

Alfred Gregory is a 40-year-old travel agency executive from Blackpool. Most of his previous climbing has been in the Lake District Army in India and Burma.

Dr. R. Charles Evans

Dr. R. Charles Evans is a 34-year-old surgeon who lives in Wales, where he first started his mountain climbing. Together with Alfred Gregory he led the advance party of the expedition.

He was educated at Shrewsbury and, during the war, after having received his medical degree, served with the British forces in the Far East. Since then he has combined his medical wor' with mountain-climbing expeditions in the Alps and Himalayas. He took part in the 1952 British Himalayan expedition to Cho Oyu.

T. R. Stobart

T. R. Stobart, 35, served as the photographer of the expedition. He is a veteran mountaineer and has climbed in the Carpathians and the Alps, as well as the Himalayas.

He was graduated from Sheffield University with a degree in Zoology and from 1949 to 1952 served as photographer on the Norwegian-British-Swedish Expedition to the Antarctic.

Dr. Michael Ward

Dr. Michael Ward, 28, was the expedition's medical officer and served in the same capacity with the Everest reconnaissance mission in 1951.

He was educated at Marlborough, Cambridge University and the London Hospital and served with the Army Medical Corps in 1950 to 1952.

Dr. L. Griffith Pugh

Dr. L. Griffith Pugh, a well-known British long-distance skier, served as physiologist for the expedition.

He is 43 years old, and was educated at Harrow, Oxford and St. Thomas's. His skiing ability won him places on the Oxford, British Universities and the 1936 Olympic teams. In 1943 to 1944 he served as physiologist to the Mountain and Snow Warfare Training Center in Lebanon. In the fall of 1950 he joined the division of Human Physiology of the Medical Research Council as a physiologist.

U. S. Climbers in Pakistan

KARACHI, Pakistan, June 1 (AP)—An advance party of the United States mountaineering expedition seeking to conquer K2, the world's second-highest mountain, arrived today at the village of Skadu, in the Balistan Valley, to set up camp. The 28,250-foot peak's full name is Mt. Godwin Austen.

BRITISH EXPEDITION CONQUERS EVEREST

Continued From Page 1

expedition in 1951, and it was the approach by which the Swiss so nearly succeeded last year. All previous parties had started from the Tibetan side, now closed to explorers since the Chinese Communists have moved in.

Mount Everest is guarded by the treacherous glaciers and ice-falls of the western cwm (hollow), which forms a hugh punch-bowl between Everest itself and its southern sentinels: Lhotse (27,890 feet), to the southeast, and Nuptse (25,680) to the southwest.

The South col (face) is high above the western cwm, between Lhotse and the main mass of Everest. To reach it the party traversed stretches of dangerous ice and "bad" snow, under which crevasses are liable to open up suddenly into chasms of fearful depth.

On their way up these massifs of ice, rock and snow the Hunt party carried a new kind of "avalanche gun," resembling a two-inch mortar, to dislodge loose and dangerous snow which might start avalanches in their path.

Climber Is a Beekeeper

The victorious Hillary, who is a 34-year-old New Zealand beekeeper, joined the expedition in India. He has had wide climbing experience in the New Zealand Alps, where heavy snowfalls and peculiar ice-falls make conditions not unlike those in the Himlayas.

Tensing made an epic ascent last year with the Swiss climber, Raymond Lambert, reaching the previous record height of 28,215 feet.

George Band, the youngest of the party, at 24 years, was chosen with Tensing to make the first, unsuccessful, assault. He is a Cambridge geologist and president of the University Mountaineering Club. The expedition was his first Himalayan experience.

Here is the story of the expedition from the time it left Khatmandu March 10 to the day of final triumph:

In two separate parties they trekked the 170 miles to their headquarters at Namche Bazar. They arrived March 25, a day ahead of schedule. Then came a period of training and climbing from Namche Bazar at 13,000 feet to 19,000 feet.

The next stage was a twenty-mile advance to Camp One, 18,000 feet up on the Khumbu Glacier. Camp Two was pitched below the ice-fall at the head of it and Camp Three just above the ice-fall. Camp Three proved to be too exposed and the party pushed on to the Great Hollow known as the western cwm and established Camp Four at 23,000 feet. Camp Five was a stores depot at the head of the cwm, at the foot of the Lhotse face.

Colonel Hunt established Camp Six on the south col, within 4,000 feet of the top. Camp Seven was set up at the highest possible point for the final two-man assault—at about 26,000 feet.

Camp Eight, the last, was set up on the south col at 27,500 feet—1,500 feet from the top. It was to be a bivouac camp from which the picked pair of climbers would cover the last gruelling stretch.

The party planned on reaching the summit to look for traces of George Leigh Mallory and Andrew Irvine, who vanished near the top thirty years ago. It has never been known whether the two Britons ever conquered the mountain or fell to their deaths before they reached the summit.

It was expected the British achievement would help to solve at least one long-standing problem about Mount Everest: its actual height. Survey of India maps give it at 29,002 feet, but claims have been made that it is higher than that. The Swiss last year estimated it to be 29,610 feet. American and some other maps give it as 29,149 and 29,141 feet.

In any case it is said to be the highest mountain on the surface of the earth. It is situated on the Nepal-Tibet border in Latitude 27 degrees 59 minutes 16 seconds North, Longitude 86 degrees 55 minutes 40 seconds East. It was named after Sir George Everest, Surveyor-General of India just over 100 years ago.

Members of the expedition in addition to Mr. Hillary, Mr. Band and Colonel Hunt were:

Tom Bourdillon, Dr. Charles Evans, Alfred Gregory, G. Lowe, Wilfred Noyce, Dr. L. G. C. Pugh, T. R. Stobart, Dr. Michael Ward, M. H. Westmacott and Maj. C. G. Wylie. All are Britons except Mr. Lowe, who is from New Zealand.

The twenty Sherpa guides belong to a caste of mountain dwellers on the southern slopes of the Himalayas, with their capital at Namche Bazar. They have been an indispensable part of this, as of every preceding Mount Everest expedition.

Seven Sherpas died on the mountain in the 1922 expedition and many others have died since with later expeditions. But the supply of these good-humored, devoted and highly courageous men never fails.

CATHOLICS HONOR QUEEN

Cardinal Sings Mass for Her at Westminster Cathedral

Special to THE NEW YORK TIMES.

LONDON, June 1—As a climax to three days of prayer, the tribute of Britain's 4,000,000 Roman Catholics to their Protestant Queen, Bernard Cardinal Griffin, this country's Roman Catholic primate, sang the mass of Saint Augustine tonight at the high altar of Westminster Cathedral. Msgr. Fernando Cento, papal representative at the coronation and Apostolic Nuncio to Belgium, sang the mass with him.

It was the mass of Saint Augustine because today is the Feast of Augustine of Canterbury, who is believed to have brought Christianity to these islands in 595.

Three days of pre-coronation prayer "for the good estate of the Queen and her realms" had been ordered by the Roman Catholic hierarchy of England and Wales.

Representing the Queen at the mass was the Duke of Norfolk, England's chief Roman Catholic peer and hereditary Earl Marshal, stage manager of the coronation.

"All the News That's Fit to Print"

The New York Times.

LATE CITY EDITION
Fair and quite warm today. Hot and humid tomorrow.
Temperature Range Today—Max., 89; Min., 68
Temperature Yesterday—Max., 85; Min., 65
Full U. S. Weather Bureau Report, Page 31

Copyright, 1953, by The New York Times Company.

VOL. CII. No. 34,846. Entered as Second-Class Matter, Post Office, New York, N. Y.

NEW YORK, SATURDAY, JUNE 20, 1953.

Times Square, New York 36, N. Y. Telephone Lackawanna 4-1000

RAG PAPER EDITION SEVENTY-FIVE CENTS

REDS INSIST U.N. RECAPTURE ALL RELEASED PRISONERS; TRUCE TALKS RECESS AGAIN

FOE WRITES CLARK

Questions if Allies Can Control South Korean Leaders and Army

Text of the Communist note to General Clark is on Page 3.

By LINDESAY PARROTT
Special to The New York Times.

TOKYO, Saturday, June 20—Communist armistice delegates at Panmunjom demanded today that the United Nations recapture all 25,000 anti-Communist prisoners of the Korean war released by the order of Dr. Syngman Rhee, South Korean President.

The demand was made in the course of a twenty-five-minute meeting of the full truce delegations called for this morning by the senior Communist truce representative, Lieut Gen. Nam Il of North Korea.

The Communist high command sent a strong protest to Gen. Mark W. Clark, United Nations commander, asserting that the Allies, equally with Dr. Rhee, must bear "serious responsibility" for the incident. The message was signed by the top enemy commanders, Marshal Kim Il Sung, North Korean Premier, and Chinese Gen. Peng Teh-huai.

The Communist protest was an angry one, and it was significant that it was made directly to the Allied commander, not to the truce delegation. Yet it seemed to indicate that the enemy was not prepared to completely end the negotiations for an armistice.

The letter to General Clark repeated many of the old charges of American coercion and duplicity, but did not slam the door to further conversations.

[The Associated Press said that Pyun Yun Tae, Acting South Korean Premier, demanded Saturday in a letter to General Clark that all anti-Communist North Korean prisoners remaining in Allied stockades be turned over to the Republic for immediate release.

[Soon afterward, in Tokyo General Clark's United Nations headquarters made public a scorching letter to the South Korean President, saying General Clark could "not at this time estimate the ultimate consequences" of President Rhee's "precipitous and shocking" release of the 26,000 anti-Communist Korean war captives. General Clark accused Dr. Rhee of breaking a "personal commitment" not to take action.]

At the armistice conference, the Communists in effect demanded that the Allied command promise to control the fiery South Korean President from acting on his own. Pointedly, the Communists asked:

"Is the United Nations Command able to control the South Korean Government and Army? If not, does the armistice in Korea include the Syngman Rhee clique.

"If it is not included, what assurance is there for implementation of the armistice agreement on the part of South Korea?

"If it is included, then your side must be responsible for recovering immediately all the 25,952 prison-

Continued on Page 3, Column 4

Associated Press Wirephoto via Radio from Tokyo

HIS ATTEMPT TO ESCAPE FAILS: A U. S. Marine, right, escorts a wounded prisoner in the prisoner-of-war camp at Ascom City, near Inchon, where about 500 anti-Communists escaped. Marines and other troops prevented a larger break-out.

U. S. SEES POSITION IN KOREA AS GRAVE

Dulles Meets With Both Parties and Envoys of U. N. Allies in Atmosphere of Urgency

By WILLIAM S. WHITE
Special to The New York Times.

WASHINGTON, June 19—The United States Government worked in haste today to save a Korean truce that some responsible men regarded as all but lost through South Korea's angry defiance of the United Nations.

The position was described authoritatively as the gravest since June 25, 1950—the day the Communists invaded the Republic of Korea.

There was hope, however, that if the Communists genuinely wanted peace they would not make capital of the defiance shown by Dr. Syngman Rhee, President of South Korea, to the United States and to its allies in the United Nations force that went to the rescue of his country three years ago.

All the possibilities seemed in the end to narrow to this one, even though there was some speculation that it might be feasible to take some form of action to replace Dr. Rhee. Senator Walter F. George of Georgia, the senior Democratic member of the Senate Foreign Re-

Continued on Page 2, Column 5

U. N. OFFICERS FELT RHEE WAS BLUFFING

Warnings Unheeded, Prisoner Command Took No Steps to Prevent Mass Escape

By ROBERT ALDEN
Special to The New York Times.

SEOUL, Korea, June 19—The United Nations Command was not prepared for the precipitate action taken by Dr. Syngman Rhee, President of South Korea, in freeing non-Communist prisoners of war.

According to an authoritative source in the Prisoner-of-War Command at Pusan here, officials in Tokyo had been warned that such a measure might be taken by the Government of the Republic of Korea. However, the Prisoner-of-War Command was assured by higher headquarters that Dr. Rhee was "bluffing."

As a result, South Korean security guards were not replaced by American soldiers and other precautionary measures were insufficient.

However, the freeing of the prisoners came as no surprise to those who have been close to President Rhee these last few weeks. Nor was it a surprise to diplomatic circles in Pusan, the temporary South Korean capital.

They knew how defiant the President's attitude has been from the start, and they regard him as a rather unpredictable individual, apt to go off on a desperate tangent at almost any time.

Some Americans farther away from the scene, however, have had a tendency to underestimate what Dr. Rhee might do and to grasp at any straw that indicated that he was yielding ground in his fight. That was why the repeated threats to free the prisoners on the spot and the ample information available indicating that the South Korean Government was taking concrete steps along these lines were virtually ignored by those in a position to do something about it.

One reason for this reluctance to recognize the facts in the matter is that it is difficult for an American to understand Dr. Rhee's reasoning. The Korean leader feels that to accept a truce agreement as drawn is tantamount to inviting self-destruction.

He is not only worried about the question of complete unification of the country. He has a great fear, for example, of allowing into the country Communist representatives and "pro-Communist" Indian guards.

President Rhee and those close

Continued on Page 3, Column 2

AID BILL APPROVED AS DEMOCRATS SAVE MEASURE IN HOUSE

G.O.P. Split on Cutting Funds, but 280-108 Vote Prevails —4.9 Billion Authorized

By FELIX BELAIR Jr.
Special to The New York Times.

WASHINGTON, June 19—The House of Representatives authorized today an appropriation of $4,998,732,500 for military, economic and technical aid to fifty-six free governments and dependencies resisting communism. The vote sending the measure to the Senate was 280 to 108, with one Representative merely voting "present."

Throughout the afternoon, a smoothly functioning bipartisan majority shouted down repeated attempts to cut the authorization items below the recommendations of the Foreign Affairs Committee. But it was the Democrats under Representative Sam Rayburn of Texas, the minority leader, who provided the margin of victory.

Republicans by the score deserted the leadership of Speaker Joseph W. Martin Jr. to vote for economy amendments. There was no record vote on any of the attempts to slash the measure and, although the foreign policy prestige of President Eisenhower had been thrown into the debate by the Republican leadership, it was the Democrats who gave him his vote of confidence.

On the final vote, 160 Democrats joined with 119 Republicans and an Independent, Frazier Reams of Ohio, to provide the 280 majority for the bill. A total of eighty-one Republicans and twenty-seven Democrats voted against the measure. Representative Harold A. Patten, Democrat of Arizona, was the one who voted "present."

Members Rally to Vote

The high tide of opposition to the authorization—which is $476,000,000 less than the Administration had requested—came shortly before the final vote. Representative Hamer H. Budge, Republican of Idaho, offered an amendment to cut all the items by 10 per cent, but it was rejected by a standing vote of 152 to 101.

The same amendment had lost by a narrower margin a few minutes earlier when, on a count, the vote was put at 102 to 102. But when a vote by tellers was demanded, members burst from the cloakrooms on either side of the House to provide the extra votes.

An even earlier attempt to accomplish the same result and cut the authorization by $498,000,000 was made when Representative William M. Colmer, Democrat of Mississippi, sought to place a ceiling on the total authorization of $4,500,000,000. This move was rejected, 104 to 83.

The pattern of unrecorded voting on the amendments had been set shortly after the House met for business an hour before noon.

Representative Lawrence Smith, Republican of Wisconsin, proposed to cut $329,186,000 from the section providing military aid to Western Europe. The amendment would have eliminated military aid totaling $216,906,000 for Yugo-

Continued on Page 18, Column 4

ROSENBERGS EXECUTED AS ATOM SPIES AFTER SUPREME COURT VACATES STAY; LAST-MINUTE PLEA TO PRESIDENT FAILS

SIX JUSTICES AGREE

President Says Couple Increased 'Chances of Atomic War'

Texts of related documents in case are printed on Page 7.

By LUTHER A. HUSTON
Special to The New York Times.

WASHINGTON, June 19—President Eisenhower and the Supreme Court refused today to save Julius and Ethel Rosenberg from death in the electric chair.

The high court vacated the stay granted to the atomic spies on Wednesday by Justice William O. Douglas. It upheld the legality of the death sentence imposed by Federal Judge Irving R. Kaufman.

Less than an hour after the court had announced its verdict, President Eisenhower refused executive clemency for the second time. He had denied a similar petition on Feb. 11.

"I can only say that, by immeasurably increasing the chances of atomic war, the Rosenbergs may have condemned to death tens of millions of innocent people all over the world," the President said. "The execution of two human beings is a grave matter. But even graver is the thought of the millions of dead whose deaths may be directly attributable to what these spies have done."

He was convinced, the President said, that the Rosenbergs had received "the fullest measure of justice and due process of law."

"When in their most solemn judgment the tribunals of the United States have adjudged them guilty and the sentence just, I will not intervene in this matter," the President declared.

Vinson Reads Court's Ruling

The prevailing opinion setting aside Justice Douglas' stay of execution was read by Chief Justice Fred M. Vinson and was concurred in by Associate Justices Stanley F. Reed, Robert H. Jackson, Harold H. Burton, Sherman Minton and Tom C. Clark.

Justices Douglas and Hugo L. Black dissented. Justice Felix Frankfurter announced neither a concurrence nor a dissent. In a brief separate opinion he said the questions raised were "complicated and novel" and that he felt the application of the Attorney General for revocation of the stay should not be disposed of until more time had been afforded for study and argument. He promised to set forth more specifically in due course the ground for this position.

Also read from the bench were a concurring opinion by Justice Clark, in which he was joined by Justices Vinson, Reed, Jackson, Burton and Minton, and a concurring opinion by Justice Jackson.

Continued on Page 8, Column 5

Their Death Penalty Carried Out

Julius Rosenberg

Ethel Rosenberg

Associated Press

Eisenhower Is Denounced To 5,000 in Union Sq. Rally

Sympathizers of Julius and Ethel Rosenberg bombarded judges with new appeals last night and staged rallies in a desperate last-minute flurry of efforts to save the condemned atom spies from the electric chair.

As time ran out for the doomed couple, lawyers and sympathizers tried every avenue of appeal and protest in a feverish evening that included:

¶An order by Police Commissioner George P. Monaghan to all police commands to maintain a special city-wide vigil against any disorder or violence in connection with the execution.

¶Three separate appeals to Federal Judge Irving R. Kaufman, who sentenced the Rosenbergs, to stay their execution. He rejected all.

¶Two separate appeals to two Federal Circuit Court judges to grant a stay. These also were denied.

¶A rally by an estimated 5,000 persons in Seventeenth Street, west of the north end of Union Square, where members of the New York Clemency Committee of the National Committee to Secure Justice in the Rosenberg Case denounced President Eisenhower as "bloodthirsty."

Final Pleas to Kaufman

Judge Kaufman, for whom the police ordered a reinforced fifteen-man guard at his Park Avenue apartment, was importuned by attorneys making frantic new legal maneuvers to save the Rosenbergs.

Daniel C. Marshall, a Los Angeles lawyer who had pleaded with the Supreme Court for a stay, begged Judge Kaufman to telephone the prison and delay the execution for one hour so that Mr. Marshall could elaborate his argument. But Judge Kaufman refused about twenty minutes before the executions began.

Milton H. Friedman, a lawyer representing the Rosenberg defense counsel, asked Judge Kaufman to stay the scheduled executions on the ground that they would constitute "an outrageous insult to world Jewry" if they were carried out on the Jewish Sabbath. Judge Kaufman rejected the plea, saying he had been assured the executions would not be within the Sabbath period.

Frank Scheiner, another lawyer representing the defense, asked Judge Kaufman to throw out the convictions of the couple on the same grounds argued yesterday before the Supreme Court. Judge Kaufman rejected this motion without any opinion.

Another defense lawyer, Arthur Kinoy, went to New Haven, Conn., in an unsuccessful effort to induce Judges Jerome N. Frank and Thomas W. Swan of the Federal Court of Appeals to block the executions.

'Prayer Meeting' Denunciations

In Seventeenth Street, more than 5,000 persons assembled for "a prayer meeting" for the Rosenbergs heard President Eisenhower denounced as "bloodthirsty."

He was linked with Attorney General Herbert Brownell Jr., Senator Joseph R. McCarthy, Republican of Wisconsin, and Senator William E. Jenner, Republican of Indiana, in "a plot" to destroy the rights and liberties of the American people.

A premature announcement at 8 P. M. that the Rosenbergs had been put to death created such a wave of hysteria at the

Continued on Page 6, Column 6

PAIR SILENT TO END

Husband Is First to Die —Both Composed on Going to Chair

By WILLIAM R. CONKLIN
Special to The New York Times.

OSSINING, N. Y., June 19—Stoic and tight-lipped to the end, Julius and Ethel Rosenberg paid the death penalty tonight in the electric chair at Sing Sing Prison for their war-time atomic espionage for Soviet Russia.

The pair, first husband and wife to pay the supreme penalty here, and the first in the United States to die for espionage, went to their deaths with a composure that astonished the witnesses.

Julius, 35 years old, was first to enter the glaringly lighted, white-walled death chamber. He walked slowly behind Rabbi Irving Koslowe, a chaplain at Sing Sing, who was intoning the Twenty-third Psalm, "The Lord is my shepherd, I shall not want." As Rosenberg neared the brown-stained oak chair he seemed to sway from side to side.

Guards quickly placed him in the chair. He was clean-shaven, no longer wearing his mustache, and wore a white T-shirt. At 8:04 o'clock the first shock of 2,000 volts, with its ten amperes, coursed through his body. After two subsequent shocks his life ended at 8:06½ P. M.

Dr. H. W. Kipp and Dr. George McCracken applied stethoscopes to his chest, and Dr. Kipp said:

"I pronounce this man dead."

Wife Kisses Matron

Ethel Rosenberg, the 37-year-old wife, entered the death chamber a few minutes after the body of her husband had been removed. She wore a dark green print dress with white polka dots and, like her husband, was shod in loafer-type cloth slippers. Her hair was close-cropped on top to permit contact of an electrode.

Just before she reached the chair the five-foot, 100-pound woman held out her hand to Mrs. Helen Evans, a matron. As Mrs. Evans grasped her hand, Mrs. Rosenberg drew her close and kissed her lightly on the check. Rabbi Koslowe, standing about ten feet from the chair, was intoning the Fifteenth and Thirty-first Psalms.

Mrs. Evans choked up at the final farewell and left the room quickly. Mrs. Lucy Many, a former matron who is now a prison telephone operator, also shook hands with the doomed woman.

Mrs. Rosenberg sat in the electric chair "with the most composed look you ever saw," one witness said.

She winced a bit as the electrode came in contact with her head, but her arms remained relaxed under their binding straps. Silent, she waited while the guards dropped a leather mask over her face. To her right stood Joseph P. Francel, the state executioner, in an alcove.

The first of three successive shocks was applied at 8:11½ P. M. After the third shock the two doctors applied their stethoscopes and found she was still alive. After two more applications of the cur-

Continued on Page 6, Column 3

7 IN HAWAII GUILTY OF RED CONSPIRACY

Director of Bridges' Union and Six Others Convicted of Violating the Smith Act

Special to The New York Times.

HONOLULU, June 19—A Federal jury today found Jack W. Hall, regional director in Hawaii for the International Longshoremen's and Warehousemen's Union, and six other defendants guilty of a Communist conspiracy to teach and advocate the overthrow of the United States Government by force and violence.

[Immediately after the verdict, stevedores halted work on all island docks in the possible forerunner of a general protest strike. The United Press reported. Within two hours after the verdict was announced Hall's union suspended negotiations on a new contract and longshoremen began walking off the job at Castle and Cook Pier 32. By 3:30 P. M., Hawaii time, all Honolulu docks were abandoned and stevedores had walked off the only two ships in the port of Hilo on the island of Hawaii.]

The all-male, multi-racial jury returned its verdict shortly before 1 P. M. Hawaii standard time (7 P. M., Eastern daylight time) after having deliberated for sixteen hours. Six men defendants clad in sports or aloha shirts and one woman heard the verdict read without any show of emotion as they stood behind the defense counsel's table.

A defense request for a poll of the jury revealed that the verdict was unanimous in each case.

The defense attorney, Richard

Continued on Page 5, Column 3

West Asks Soviet to Bar Firearms In Keeping Order in East Berlin

By WALTER SULLIVAN
Special to The New York Times.

BERLIN, June 19—The three Western powers in Berlin urged the Soviet Union today to forbid the use of firearms by its troops and by the East German police in the Soviet sector of the city to prevent further bloodshed.

An announcement said Brig. Gen. Pierre Manceaux-Demiau, French Commandant in Berlin and this month's chairman of the Allied Kommandatura, had made repeated vain attempts to see high Soviet authorities to discuss the problem. It added that finally he had gone to Soviet headquarters in East Berlin to deliver in person a note stating the point of view of the Western Commandants.

Meanwhile, as the eastern part of the city continued to appear quiet, United States authorities delivered Otto Nuschke to Soviet officers. Herr Nuschke, East German Deputy Premier, was forced into the United States sector of Berlin by the rioters Wednesday.

Herr Nuschke, 70 years of age, was questioned thoroughly by both United States and West Berlin officials before being returned to the Soviet sector. According to an official announcement by the United States mission, he was asked whether he wanted political asylum in the West and said no.

The West Berlin police sought to determine whether he could be linked with "a kidnapping." Possibly this referred to the case of Dr. Walter Linse, anti-Communist leader, who was abducted from the United States sector last year.

East Germany's leading Communist newspaper, Neues Deutschland, conceded today that the work stoppages and disorders of the last few days had reached into the remote districts of that region. It expressed

Continued on Page 4, Column 4

4-Day Seamen's Strike Ends As Wage Demands Are Met

By GEORGE HORNE

The four-day-old seamen's strike, which immobilized 125 vessels and threatened to paralyze one-half of the nation's fleet of 1,500 ships, came to an end at 12:45 A. M. today.

National Maritime Union seamen, who struck on Tuesday when the operators refused to accede to wage demands, signed with the dry-cargo shipping employers at the headquarters of the Federal Mediation and Conciliation Service, winning wage rises ranging from 2 to 6 per cent. The settlement terms constituted a complete capitulation by the operators.

A few minutes earlier, the striking American Radio Association, also an affiliate of the Congress for Industrial Organizations, signed for a 6 per cent wage increase with a group of tanker operators.

Surrender of the employers in both cases had been foretold earlier in the day when a group of leading tanker operators submitted to the demands of the N. M. U. on the basis of similar wage rises that the dry-cargo group met. After this agreement was reached, it was a foregone conclusion that the rest of the industry would follow.

The mediators brought the N. M. U. into contact again with the Committee of Companies and Agents, Atlantic and Gulf Coasts, and it was apparent the costly hold-out of the companies was crumbling.

In its bargaining, the radio officer association also won its demands to gain full control over all radio telephones at sea, removing this equipment from the control of captains and other bridge officers. This was a major issue with the radio men.

All details of the fringe issues won by the seamen in their negotiations with the dry-cargo operators were not available, but mediators said they had matched those won earlier by the tanker men.

The new contract for the dry-cargo men will run for only a year, with a wage reopening in the fall. Union leaders called the wage terms "the best increases won by any industry this year." They were preparing to send out telegrams releasing the immobilized ships throughout the nation, including the superliner United States, tied up in New York.

Commissioners Harry Wanning and Sidney Sheiner, who have been serving under Frank Brown, regional director of the Federal Mediation and Conciliation Service, in seeking to settle the costly walk-

Continued on Page 35, Column 2

Professor Loses Fulbright Award After Wife Balks at Red Inquiry

By FREDERICK GRAHAM

A Fulbright award granted last April to Dr. Naphtali Lewis of Brooklyn College to study in Italy during the next academic year has been canceled by the State Department, Senator Joseph R. McCarthy, Republican of Wisconsin, said yesterday.

"I think it [the cancellation] is an excellent idea," the Senator asserted at the end of a thirty-seven-minute hearing of the Senate Permanent subcommittee on Investigations into the background of Dr. Lewis and his wife, Helen B. Lewis, who once held a teaching post at Brooklyn College.

The formal title of Fulbright award is the United States Educational Exchange Award. The awards are granted to educators and students for study abroad under the Fulbright Act, which is named for Senator J. William Fulbright, Democrat of Arkansas, who pioneered the program.

Senator McCarthy, who sat as a one-member subcommittee at the Federal Courthouse in Foley Square, said that the purpose of the inquiry was to learn whether Mrs. Lewis was now or ever had been a member of the Communist party.

Because she planned to go abroad with her husband for the study year at the expense of the Federal Government, Senator McCarthy declared that he believed it was very important to know if she was or had been a Communist. Unable to elicit an answer on that score from Mrs. Lewis, Senator McCarthy asserted that her record might tend to incriminate her was the same as saying that "I am a member of the party."

Mrs. Lewis steadfastly refused to answer questions as to whether she had held Communist cell meet-

Continued on Page 5, Column 4

SPY CASE A STORY OF LEGAL BATTLES

Rosenbergs' Death Sentences Signaled Court Maneuvers Exceeding Two Years

CLIMAX BY 'INTERLOPERS'

Plea to Douglas Raised Point That Kaufman Had Barred —Clemency Twice Denied

When Julius and Ethel Rosenberg were put to death last night two years, two months and fourteen days had passed since they were sentenced to die for betraying their country.

The death sentence was pronounced by Judge Irving R. Kaufman on April 5, 1951, and the next day the first notice of appeal was taken. Thus was signaled the beginning of a legal battle waged untiringly on behalf of the convicted atom spies. The arguments were taken from the District Court here to the Circuit Court of Appeals and to the United States Supreme Court.

In addition, the condemned couple appealed twice to the President of the United States for clemency, but both times, once in February and again yesterday, President Eisenhower refused.

Three times scheduled executions were stayed to permit the hearing of appeals and further argument. Even so, the Rosenbergs lived a day beyond the fourth date for the execution of their sentences.

"Interlopers" Gain a Stay

This extraordinary circumstance came about through the granting of a stay by Associate Justice William O. Douglas at the behest of two attorneys, Fyke Farmer of Nashville, Tenn., and Daniel G. Marshall of Los Angeles, who two days earlier had been termed "intruders" and "interlopers" by Judge Kaufman.

Newly entering the case, they presented to Justice Douglas, as they had attempted unsuccessfully to offer to Judge Kaufman, the contention that the General Espionage Act of 1917, under which the Rosenbergs were sentenced, had been superseded by the 1946 Atomic Energy Act. This latter act provides that the death penalty or imprisonment for life may be imposed in espionage cases only upon recommendation of the jury. The Rosenberg jury had not made such a recommendation.

The argument of the two attorneys was upheld by Justice Douglas at the special session of the recalled Supreme Court yesterday, but its applicability was rejected by a majority of the court 6 to 3. Justice Douglas' stay, under which the Rosenbergs had obtained an extra day of life, was vacated by this decision. A final appeal for executive clemency was denied by the President, and the doom of the Rosenbergs was sealed.

The couple became the first United States civilians to be put to death for espionage. Although the record of espionage in this country goes back to the British Major John André, put to death by the Continental Army for dealing with Benedict Arnold, the crime was not formally defined until the 1917 Act. It was under this act, as amended, that the Rosenbergs were tried and convicted.

Trial Opened in March, 1951

A jury of eleven men and a Bronx housewife in Federal Court here convicted the couple on March 29, 1951. The jury found that the 35-year-old electrical engineer and his 37-year-old wife had funneled vital information on the atomic bomb to the Soviet Union in the war years of 1944 and 1945.

The trial opened March 6, 1951, before Judge Kaufman. Irving H. Saypol, then United States Attorney for the Southern District of New York and now a Justice of the State Supreme Court, told the jury that the pair had conspired to steal and deliver to the Soviet Union "the one weapon that might well hold the key to the survival of this nation and the peace of the world—the atomic bomb." He branded the Rosenbergs as "traitorous Americans" worshipping and owing allegiance to the Soviet Union and to world communism.

Testimony at the trial disclosed that the Rosenbergs were part of an international spy apparatus that operated so effectively the Soviet Union obtained vital information enabling her to produce an atomic bomb years before her own scientists could have solved the secrets of nuclear fission. There is evidence that just a month after the bomb was dropped on Nagasaki a sketch and detailed description of the terrible weapon was in the hands of the Russians.

In passing sentence, Judge Kaufman said the crime of the Rosenbergs was "worse than murder." He expressed the belief that the placing of this weapon in the hands of the Russians had precipitated Communist aggression in Korea.

"By your betrayal," Judge Kaufman told the Rosenbergs, "you undoubtedly have altered the course of history to the disadvantage of your country. We have evidence of your treachery around us every day—for the civilian defense activities throughout the nation are aimed at preparing us for an atom bomb attack."

The Rosenbergs maintained their innocence to the end, but the evidence against them was damning. It was provided chiefly by David Greenglass, Mrs. Rosenberg's brother. He testified that his sister and his brother-in-law had recruited him to steal atomic bomb secrets, among them a rough sketch of the detonating device and other details of a bomb similar to that which was dropped on Nagasaki, Japan, in 1945, when he was an Army sergeant acting as foreman of an atomic assembly plant at Los Alamos, N. M.

Dr. Walter Koski, nuclear physicist, testified that the information revealed in sketches made by Greenglass was sufficient to disclose to any foreign-power expert the atomic research experiments then in progress at the atom bomb center.

The Rosenbergs, evidence showed, turned over the stolen atomic secrets to Anatoli A. Yakovlev, at that time the Soviet vice consul in New York. He was indicted with the Rosenbergs, but had left the country long before they were arrested.

The trial established links between the Rosenbergs and Harry Gold, a Philadelphia chemist, who confessed he was the contact man and courier for two Soviet agents. The agents were Alan Nunn May, British scientist, and Dr. Klaus Fuchs, German-born British-naturalized atomic physicist who was present at the birth of the atomic bomb at Los Alamos in 1945. Both scientists admitted their espionage activities and received prison terms. Gold is serving a thirty-year term in the United States, as is Morton Sobell, an electronics engineer convicted with the Rosenbergs. Greenglass was sentenced to fifteen years for his part in the conspiracy.

The Rosenbergs were natives of this city and were educated in New York schools. Both attended Seward Park High School, although they did not meet until several years after they had been graduated.

Rosenberg received a Bachelor of Science degree in Electrical Engineering at City College in February, 1939. He then worked for several engineering concerns and eventually was employed as a junior engineer in the signal service of the War Department's general depot in Brooklyn.

He transferred later to the Signal Corps, working his way up to the position of associated engineering inspector. He held that post until Feb. 9, 1945, when he was suspended on the recommandation of his commanding officer, who said he had received information that Rosenberg was a member of the Communist party.

From then until his arrest on July 17, 1950, Rosenberg was active as a partner in several private businesses dealing in surplus and engineering products.

Ethel Rosenberg, like her husband, grew up on New York's lower East Side. As a young girl she was interested in singing, the piano, dancing and dramatics. She was graduated from high school at the age of 15 and became the youngest member of the Schola Cantorum after having taken voice lessons.

She was employed at various times as a stenographer and typist. In 1940, she worked for three months as a temporary clerk in the Bureau of the Census in Washington.

Emotional Demonstration Held Here to Protest Rosenbergs' Execution

A crowd estimated by the police at 5,000 held a 'prayer meeting" last evening in behalf of Julius and Ethel Rosenberg in Seventeenth Street, west of Union Square. The rally was moved there after the police found no Park Department permit had been issued for the square, where it originally had been scheduled. Many signs quoted the Rosenbergs' "We are innocent."

Thin Crowds in Times Sq. Indifferent About Spies

Times Square received the news of the electric chair deaths of Ethel and Julius Rosenberg last night with an unusual quiet and an absence of any expressed reaction.

Only a thin crowd of several hundred persons stood on the corners at Seventh Avenue, Broadway and Forty-second Street as the lights carrying news around The Times Building reported the couple had gone to their deaths. The onlookers were devoid of comment.

The police had been prepared for a possible demonstration and had assigned fifty foot patrolmen, ten mounted police, and twenty-five detectives to the area with fifty more patrolmen on reserve at the West Forty-seventh and West Thirtieth Street stations.

Officers attributed the small crowd to the week-end exodus of residents and the heat.

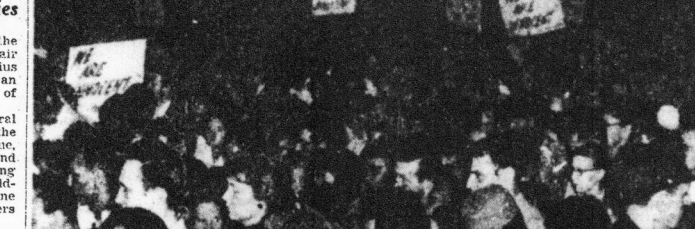

The New York Times (by Carl T. Gossett)

Some women wept and men bowed their heads when, at precisely 8 o'clock, a young woman called over the microphone: "In memory of the Rosenbergs." Actually, it was four minutes before Julius Rosenberg, the first of the couple to be executed, entered the death chamber at Sing Sing.

THE ROSENBERGS GO TO DEATH IN CHAIR

Continued From Page 1

rent Mrs. Rosenberg was pronounced dead at 8:16 P. M.

Both executions of the death sentence had been advanced from the usual Sing Sing hour of 11 P. M. so that they would not conflict with the Jewish Sabbath. The last rays of a red sun over the Hudson River were casting a faint light when the double execution was completed.

The couple heard early this afternoon that both the Supreme Court and President Eisenhower had rejected their final appeals. Prison officials allowed them to spend the afternoon and early evening together. At 7:20 P. M. they were separated and prepared for the execution. Because of the rapid developments in their case they did not get the special dinner normally granted to prisoners about to die.

For more than twenty-six months since they were sentenced to death on April 5, 1951, the Rosenbergs had fought their conviction through the courts. Their fifth appeal to the United States Supreme Court was decided adversely seven hours before they died.

They Do Not Look Their Parts

Small and plump, Ethel Rosenberg seemed more an East Side housewife than a key figure in an international spy plot. Her bespectacled, serious-looking husband, likewise seemed more like the electrical engineer he was than an American contact for a Soviet spy system.

Ethel Rosenberg's younger brother, David Greenglass, 31, had confessed his part in the spy plot and was a principal Government witness against his sister and her husband. He was sentenced in April, 1951, to fifteen years in prison. The trail led from Julius and Ethel Rosenberg to David Greenglass, through him to Soviet spy courier Harry Gold, and from Gold to Anatoli A. Yacovlev, Soviet vice consul at New York. Yakovlev, who fled to Russia with his wife and two children on Dec. 27, 1946, is still under indictment here as a principal in the conspiracy.

Gold also had a connection with Dr. Klaus Fuchs, a British atomic scientist who spied for Russia, and with Dr. Allan Nunn May in a Canadian espionage ring.

The Rosenbergs were put to death fourteen years and one day after their marriage in New York City in 1939. Their two sons, Michael, 10, and Robert, 6, are staying with relatives. The boys paid their last visit to their parents here several days ago.

Official witnesses to the double execution included United States Marshal William A. Carroll; his chief deputy, Thomas M. Farley; Warden Wilfred L. Denno of Sing Sing; the two doctors, and three wire service correspondents, Bob Considine of The International News Service, Relman Morin of The Associated Press and Jack Woliston of The United Press.

Under Federal law, not more than five persons, including members of the press, may witness Federal executions. Mr. Considine briefed thirty-two other correspondents in the prison administration building immediately after the death sentences had been executed.

The briefing was held in a stiflingly hot meeting room in which a large sign read: "No Smoking Eating Reading Writing." The electric clock on the tan-painted wall was eight minutes fast and the wall calendar already had been moved forward to Saturday, June 20.

Silent on Communist Ties

Throughout their trial both the Rosenbergs had refused to answer questions about Communist party membership and activities. They claimed the protection of the Fifth Amendment and were upheld by Judge Kaufman. Their political activity thus did not become a trial issue, although defense attorney Emanuel H. Bloch later charged they had been convicted "in an atmosphere of political hysteria."

Mr. Bloch, the Rosenbergs' most constant visitor during their Death House stay of more than two years was not present for the executions. David Rosenberg, older brother of Julius, arrived at the prison at 6:12 P. M., long after the 3 P. M. deadline for visiting on a day of execution. He entered the administration building but left after thirteen minutes without seeing either his brother or the latter's wife.

David Rosenberg, dressed in a blue suit and a gray fedora, ran a gantlet of newspaper, newsreel and radio men with a folded newspaper held before his face. On the way out he was supported by two prison guards, one on each side. No other relatives of the condemned pair sought to see them.

To the last, Marshal Carroll kept a telephone line open to Washington in case either husband or wife decided to make a full disclosure of their activities. Last week each had been informed by the Department of Justice that confessions could win them a reprieve from death. Both Julius and Ethel Rosenberg, however, maintained they were completely innocent and had nothing to confess.

Prison Guard Augmented

Outside Sing Sing's north gate sixty New York State troopers with night sticks augmented the prison guard force and Ossining police. Wooden barricades were placed across all roads leading to the prison, and only persons with approved credentials could pass. No signs of a demonstration were evident, however. Near the administration building gate newsreel camera men set up their equipment.

Local residents stood quietly outside their homes in the June heat, watching with interest as newsmen arrived in cars and on foot. After the death sentences had been executed they gathered around automobile radios in search of the answer to the question: "Did they talk?"

Many persons expressed the opinion that execution of the death sentences had been unduly delayed. Others voiced sympathy for the Rosenbergs' children and other relatives.

By 7 o'clock tonight all prisoners had been locked in their cells according to regular practice. They were permitted to listen to the prison radio up to 9 P. M., and to read or write letters until "Lights Out" at 11:15 o'clock.

In passing New York Central trains, passengers turned their eyes upward to the prison.

Judge Kaufman, who sentenced the Rosenbergs to death, is the youngest member of the Federal bench in Manhattan. He will be 43 on June 24. He had been under the constant pressure of adherents of the Rosenbergs to reduced the sentence he had imposed.

9 Women Put to Death In the Chair in New York

Mrs. Ethel Rosenberg was the ninth woman to be put to death in New York State since the electric chair was introduced in 1890. The eight who had preceded her had been convicted of murder.

The most recent to pay the full penalty at Sing Sing was Martha Beck of Valley Stream, L. I., called the "lonely hearts killer," who went to the death chair on March 8, 1951. Ruth Snyder, Queens Village housewife, died on Jan. 12, 1928, for the sash-weight murder of her husband.

The others who were put to death were: Helen Fowler of Buffalo, in 1944; Mary Frances Creighton of Baldwin, L. I., in 1936; Eva Coo of Maryland, N. Y., in 1935; Anna Antonio of Albany, in 1934; Mary Farmer of Watertown, in 1909; and Martha Place of Brooklyn, in 1899.

Records indicate that the only woman previously put to death by Federal authorities was Mrs. Mary E. Surratt, who was hanged in Washington for helping to plot the assassination of President Lincoln.

Albania Dooms 2 as Spies

LONDON, June 19 (UP)—Two Albanians were sentenced to death and five others were sentenced to prison terms of from three to twenty-five years as Yugoslav spies in Tropoje Province this week, the official news agency ATA said today. The agency, in a broadcast monitored here, said the accused were tried in the town of Mayram Tsourri Tuesday. The men were members of the local militia when Albania was occupied by the Italians, the broadcast said.

French and Chinese Reds Sign

TOKYO, June 19 (AP)—The official Communist New China News Agency said today the China Import and Export Company signed its first barter agreement contract Tuesday with the French trade mission for more than $882,000.

DEATHS PROTESTED AT UNION SQ. RALLY

Continued From Page 1

rally that the police ordered the loud speaker shut off and the meeting dispersed.

Long before 6 o'clock, when the meeting was scheduled to start, crowds began gathering in the police-barricaded street. But it was not until 6:30 P. M. that a sound truck arrived. From then on the crowd was whipped to fever pitch by speeches that alternately denounced the President and members of the Government and praised the Rosenbergs as "freedom-loving people who were to die for world peace and American democracy."

A few minutes before 8 o'clock a speaker climbed to the top of the sound truck to announce that the Rosenbergs were now 'in the death chamber." Precisely at 8, seemingly by carefully arranged pre-timing, a young woman's voice poured from the microphone above the sound of mass [illegible]ping.

"In memory of the Rosenbergs," she began, but the rest of her words were lost in a fresh outburst of lamentation.

The young woman began to sing, "Go Down, Moses." The wailing slowly subsided, but it was evident that the mood of the crowd was electric. It was then that Deputy Chief Inspector Patrick J. Kirley ordered the loud speaker cut off. But even as the woman's voice faded, the crowd picked up the words of the spiritual and finished the song in strength.

Earlier, a woman had fainted in the crowd. But the meeting was orderly, and the police were called upon only once to remove a heckler.

Eulogizing of Rosenbergs

In the crowd were placards proclaiming: "The Rosenbergs Are Innocent," with pictures of the condemned couple. This, too, was the theme of the speeches—that the Rosenbergs were being put to death because they had the courage to fight for peace and justice in a nation "whose sons were being killed in Korea while Korean children were being massacred."

They spoke of "the haste and brutality" of the executions and "the courage and fortitude" with which the Rosenbergs faced their fate. The crowd repeated after speakers pledges to carry on the work of the Rosenbergs until "we have created a world of peace and beauty."

The couple was portrayed as "little people who had become giants because they refused to crawl," whose names would remain "alive as a lesson in courage" long after those who had condemned them "faded into the scummy slime where they belong."

Even as the speeches continued, the illuminated clock hands in the Consolidated Edison Building across Union Square moved toward the hour of execution. Behind the crowd, the sun—a big red ball—sank slowly toward the horizon.

And when the singing of "Go Down Moses" ended and the dispersal began, the crowd turned and walked into Fifth Avenue toward the setting sun.

Police Alerted Over City

Police Commissioner Monaghan, in ordering a special alert, told all patrolmen in the city to be on guard against demonstrations, disorders, vandalism or other attempts to disturb peace or damage property.

He instructed them to pay special attention to places of worship, public buildings, power stations, homes of public officials and prominent persons and radio stations.

The alert for patrolmen, he said, would stand "until further notice" and precinct commanders and detectives were ordered to remain on duty until midnight.

14 YEARS AN EXECUTIONER

Electrician in State Post Is War Veteran, Has 2 Children

OSSINING, N. Y., June 19 (UP)—The Cairo, N. Y., electrician in charge of throwing the switch to end the lives of Julius and Ethel Rosenberg has put hundreds of criminals to death in his fourteen years as state executioner.

Joseph Francel, a father of two children, was appointed executioner on Oct. 13, 1939. A native of St. Cloud, Minn., he moved to Cairo in 1925. He served sixteen months overseas during World War I and was severely gassed.

A fee of $150 is paid Mr. Francel for each execution, making his fee for the deaths of the Rosenbergs $300.

Spies' Mothers Refuse to Talk to Newsmen; A Doctor Calls on Each in Apartments Here

Neither of the mothers of Julius and Ethel Rosenberg, convicted atom spies, would comment to newspaper men yesterday after their children had lost a last-minute legal fight before the Supreme Court and had died in the electric chair.

Mrs. Sophie Rosenberg, 71-year-old mother of Julius Rosenberg, arrived at her home at 36 Laurel Hill Terrace in Washington Heights shortly after 7 P. M. but went directly to her second-floor apartment without talking to reporters. She was accompanied by a young woman who would say only that she was "a member of the national committee."

Until 8 o'clock a radio could be heard from inside the apartment and a man and another woman arrived. The woman later came out to say that word of the execution had been received by telephone but added that Mrs. Rosenberg would not be told until her friends decided it was proper. An unidentified doctor joined the group caring for the elderly woman shortly before 10 P. M.

At the home of Mrs. Tessie Greenglass, the mother of Ethel Rosenberg, reporters had heard a radio playing music before the Supreme Court announced at noon its decision to permit the execution. After the decision was broadcast the radio was turned off and there was no answer to repeated inquiries from the hallway of the house at 64 Sheriff Street.

By 7 P. M. more than fifty persons had congregated in the lower East Side block. Many carried portable radios, and others began to peer from tenements across the street toward the windows in Mrs. Greenglass' apartment. The Rosenbergs had lived on Lewis Street, three blocks away, and Mrs. Greenglass has been a resident of the neighborhood for more than forty years.

At one point two young women appeared and knocked at the woman's door, shouting "Ruth" and "Mrs. Greenglass." They waited several minutes, explaining they had come to help and to urge her to appeal once again to President Eisenhower. They got no response.

The narrow street outside was noisy with chatter from the growing crowd and music from radios, but it became silent when announcement of the executions was made.

The lights in Mrs. Greenglass' ground-floor apartment were turned on shortly after 9 P. M., and a doctor visited her for twenty minutes. He said she had collapsed and he had given her a sedative. He said he felt she would need no further medical treatment at that time.

Jewish Sabbath Varies From Official Sundown

The Jewish Sabbath began last night at 8:13 o'clock, exactly eighteen minutes before official sundown as determined by the United States Weather Bureau for this latitude. The Sabbath will end at 9:13 o'clock tonight forty-two minutes after the formal hour of sunset.

The discrepancy in time, according to Jewish authorities, permits observant Jews to usher in the Sabbath with a few moments of "anticipation," and to relinquish it with a fitting period of "reluctance." The variations of eighteen minutes and forty-two minutes, they explained, are based on computations dictated by Jewish law.

Orthodox Jews conform strictly to the letter of the law in observing the Sabbath period, while the Reform and Conservative branches of Judaism permit varying degrees of elasticity.

The Sabbath Day becomes effective first in the home where candles are lighted in advance of the designated hour, for after the advent of the Sabbath not even a match may be struck. The lighting of a candle also marks the end of the Sabbath.

ROSENBERG SON GETS WORD OF FATE ON TV

TOMS RIVER, N. J., June 19 (UP)—Although friends tried to keep the news from him, Michael Rosenberg, 16-year-old son of Julius and Ethel Rosenberg, learned his parents were to be executed as he watched television today.

His brother, Robert, 6, still unaware of the fate of his mother and father, suggested sending a card to "my daddy" for Father's Day next Sunday.

The youngsters and Mr. and Mrs. Bernard Bach, with whom they have been staying for the last eighteen months, were in seclusion tonight when the Rosenbergs died in the electric chair at Sing Sing prison.

Mr. Bach, a salesman, heard the Supreme Court's decision on the radio and tried to keep word of it from the boys. He decided to keep them in the house this afternoon and urged them to watch the New York Yankees-Detroit Tigers baseball game on television.

Michael agreed, but Robert preferred to paint water-color pictures on a side porch of the Bach home at near-by Dover Township.

The ball game had just begun when it was interrupted with a news bulletin announcing that President Eisenhower would not intervene in the case.

Michael looked at Mrs. Bach and whispered: "My mommie and daddy. That was their last chance."

Later, the game again was interrupted with an announcement that the executions were to take place before the beginning of the Jewish Sabbath. He slumped in his chair and sobbed: "That's it. That's it," he said. "Goodbye, goodbye."

SPY CASE SENDS CALLS UP

Newspaper Offices Swamped by Inquiries by Telephone

The widespread interest in the Rosenberg case was indicated yesterday when newspaper offices were flooded with telephone calls after the Supreme Court gave its decision vacating the stay of execution granted by Justice William O. Douglas.

Most of the calls were for information on what the court vote was, which members of the court voted in the minority and what time the spies would go to the electric chair. One caller wanted to know if the execution of the death sentence would be televised.

Up to 5 P. M. THE NEW YORK TIMES had received 2,239 calls for information about the case.

'VOICE' RELAYS SPIES' FATE

Iron Curtain Countries Advised of Court Order and Execution

The State Department's Voice of America broadcasts to the Soviet Union and other Communist countries carried complete factual reports of developments in the Rosenberg case yesterday and last night.

News of the Supreme Court's decision to vacate the stay order and plans for the execution of sentence were incorporated into regularly scheduled broadcasts.

Persons in the Soviet Union did not learn of the deaths from Voice broadcasts until 10:15 P.M., E.D.T.

KAUFMAN REJECTS 11TH-HOUR APPEAL

Habeas Corpus Writ for 2 Spies Denied at 7:45 P. M.—Judge Refuses Prison Call for Stay

Federal Judge Irving R. Kaufman denied at 7:45 o'clock last night an application for a writ of habeas corpus on behalf of Julius and Ethel Rosenberg, the atom spies, made by an attorney who pleaded with the judge to call Sing Sing prison and stay the execution until he could present his entire argument. He indicated this would take an additional hour.

Judge Kaufman refused to call the prison, saying that the application had no merit. The application was brought by Daniel G. Marshall, Los Angeles attorney, who appeared on behalf of Irwin Edelman, who had described himself previously as a friend of the Rosenbergs in applying to Supreme Court Justice William O. Douglas for a stay of execution for the Rosenbergs.

Mr. Marshall rushed to New York from Washington by plane and arrived at La Guardia Airport at 5 P. M. He then went to the Federal Courthouse, Foley Square.

At 6:45 P. M. he went before Federal Judge Edward J. Dimock in an effort to get the jurist to hear his application. The jurist referred the application to Judge Kaufman, who began hearing argument in his chambers at 7:15 P. M.

Mr. Marshall told Judge Kaufman that the Supreme Court decision handed down earlier yesterday did not vacate the order of Supreme Court Justice Douglas to return the case to the district court to see if the Atomic Energy Act of 1946 was applicable in this case.

Urged to Hurry Argument

The attorney contended that the high court's decision only vacated the stay of execution. In opposing the motion, United States Attorney J. Edward Lumbard told Judge Kaufman that Supreme Court Justice Robert H. Jackson in his opinion said that Mr. Marshall had no standing in the Rosenberg case.

At 7:25 P. M. Judge Kaufman reminded Mr. Marshall that the execution was set for 8 P. M. and urged him to "get along with your argument." Mr. Marshall pleaded with the judge to call the prison and to stay the execution so he might complete his argument.

Mr. Marshall added that it would be "terrible if I could convince your honor that you should grant the application and it would be too late."

Judge Kaufman told the lawyer that he had read his papers carefully when they were "first presented to me a week ago." He added that he clearly understood all the points.

At 7:30 P. M. Mr. Marshall again pleaded with the judge to call the prison, saying that he needed an additional twenty minutes to complete his argument. Judge Kaufman answered: "I will not call Sing Sing prison unless you convince me that there is merit in your application. I am not inclined to issue a stay from what I have read in your papers and what you have said thus far."

Mr. Marshall said that this was the last chance that the judge had to correct the terrible miscarriage of justice, and the jurist replied:

"It is unfair to put that kind of a burden on a judge. It's difficult enough. I am aware of the tragedy involved."

2 Earlier Attempts for Stay

Earlier in the day there were two other attempts to stay the execution of the Rosenberg's, both denied by the judge.

One application was based on the plea that the two might be put to death on the Jewish Sabbath. Milton H. Friedman, an attorney representing defense counsel Emanuel H. Bloch, told Judge Kaufman it would be "an outrageous insult to world Jewry to permit the execution to go forward tonight" after the Sabbath had begun.

Mr. Friedman pointed out to the Court that there was some doubt as to when the Jewish Sabbath actually began, explaining that some held it started at sundown, others when the first star appeared.

In denying the application Judge Kaufman said:

"The matter of the execution of the Rosenbergs on the Sabbath has given me considerable concern. As a result, I have spoken with Attorney General Brownell, who also expressed similar concern.

"He assured this court that the execution would not be carried out during the Sabbath. Accordingly, there is no need for the stay urged here."

The second application denied by Judge Kaufman urged that he vacate the judgment of conviction on the same grounds as those presented yesterday before the United States Supreme Court. Frank Scheiner, another attorney representing Mr. Bloch, argued that the Rosenbergs could not be sentenced to death under the Atomic Energy Act of 1946, which, he contended, should have prevailed in this case.

Judge Kaufman denied the second motion without opinion. The defense had set up its machinery in the Federal Court in New Haven, Conn., in anticipation of the denials of the two applications.

Swan and Frank Say No

NEW HAVEN, Conn., June 19 (UP)—Two United States Circuit Court of Appeals judges rejected late today a last-minute motion for a stay of executoin of the death sentence on Julius and Ethel Rosenberg.

Judge Jerome N. Frank and Judge Thomas W. Swan based the denial on Chief Justice Fred M. Vinson's statement in the United States Supreme Court that "further proceedings to litigate were unwarranted."

Defense lawyer Arthur Kinoy asked the jurists to reverse a decision handed down earlier in the d[illegible] by Federal Judge Irving R. Kaufman in New York. Mr. Kinoy, who contended execution of the death sentence tonight would violate the Jewish Sabbath, demanded time to apply for a writ of habeas corpus.

The lawyer conferred first with Judge Swan, the court's senior judge, who accompanied him to Judge Frank's home.

"All the News That's Fit to Print"

The New York Times.

LATE CITY EDITION
Warm, humid, showers likely late today. Fair, not so warm tomorrow.
Temperature Range Today—Max., 88; Min., 68
Temperatures Yesterday—Max., 79; Min., 62
Full U. S. Weather Bureau Report, Page 35

Copyright, 1953, by The New York Times Company.

VOL. CII..No. 34,883. Entered as Second-Class Matter. Post Office, New York, N. Y. NEW YORK, MONDAY, JULY 27, 1953. Times Square, New York 36, N. Y. Telephone Lackawanna 4-1000 FIVE CENTS

TRUCE IS SIGNED, ENDING THE FIGHTING IN KOREA; P.O.W. EXCHANGE NEAR; RHEE GETS U. S. PLEDGE; EISENHOWER BIDS FREE WORLD STAY VIGILANT

GEROSA AND STARK PICKED BY WAGNER TO COMPLETE SLATE

Bronx Contractor to Run for Controller, Brooklyn Clothier for Council President

DESAPIO PRAISES CHOICE

Tammany Head Sees Approval This Week by Party Leaders Opposed to Impellitteri

By PAUL CROWELL

Lawrence E. Gerosa, a Bronx contractor, and Abe Stark, a Brooklyn merchant, were selected as running mates yesterday by Manhattan Borough President Robert F. Wagner Jr., who was chosen last week by the Democratic organizations of Bronx and New York Counties as their candidate for Mayor.

Mr. Gerosa was named as a candidate for Controller and Mr. Stark for President of the City Council. The slate headed by Mr. Wagner will wage a primary contest against the ticket headed by Mayor Impellitteri, whose running mates are City Councilman Charles E. Keegan of the Bronx for Controller and Julius Helfand, assistant district attorney of Kings County, for Council President.

The Impellitteri-Keegan-Helfand ticket has the backing of the Democratic organizations of Brooklyn, Queens and Staten Island.

At the Biltmore Hotel Mr. Wagner said that Mr. Gerosa and Mr. Stark were his personal choices but that he expected the Bronx and Tammany Hall executive committees to approve them without hesitation.

Wagner Voices Confidence

"I was given a free hand in picking my running mates," Mr. Wagner said. "I chose them after consulting with representatives of civic organizations, labor and business and the Bronx and Manhattan county leadership.

"I am confident that the Bronx and New York County executive committees will approve my choices. Speaking for myself and my running mates I am sure that we will win the primary contest next September and go on to win the November election."

Carmine G. DeSapio, the leader of Tammany Hall, expressed confidence that the executive committees of the Bronx and Manhattan organizations would approve Mr. Wagner's selections at a meeting to be held early this week. He described Mr. Gerosa and Mr. Stark as "outstanding representative business men who will make a great contribution to public service."

Mr. Gerosa, who was born in Milan, Italy, Aug. 10, 1894, lives at 615 West 252d Street in the Riverdale section. He is married and has three children.

He was designated in 1945 by four of the five Democratic county leaders as a candidate for Controller on a ticket headed by former Mayor William O'Dwyer, but withdrew in favor of Lazarus Jo-

Continued on Page 20, Column 4

Clark Ready to Start Release Of Red Captives in Few Days

But Allied Commander Says It May Be Two or Three Weeks Before Americans Freed by the Communists Arrive in U. S.

By JAMES RESTON

Special to THE NEW YORK TIMES.

SOMEWHERE IN KOREA, July 26—Gen. Mark W. Clark said tonight he was prepared to start shipping Communist prisoners of war to North Korea and Communist China within a "few days," but he thought it would be two or three weeks before American prisoners would reach the United States.

The United Nations commander told several reporters aboard his plane en route to the signing of the truce agreement at Munsan, Korea, that while the Communists had comparatively few prisoners to send back, United Nations procedures for handling captives were undoubtedly faster.

The United Nations Command now holds 68,000 North Koreans and 5,000 Chinese Communists who want to return to their native lands, and 8,000 North Koreans and about 15,000 Chinese Communists who have refused to return home.

In contrast, the Communists hold only 12,000 United Nations prisoners, of whom 3,000 are Americans.

Nevertheless, General Clark said, he thought it would be unwise for the Americans to expect that United States prisoners would be sent back as fast as the United Nations Command would return the Communists.

He said he expected the Communists to return the American captives at the rate of about fifty daily, while the Allies were in position to return as many as 1,500 Communists every day.

In accordance with plans that are now ready, General Clark asserted, the Communist captives would be put aboard small naval

Continued on Page 9, Column 2

Accord on plans for prisoners of war is on Page 7.

Eisenhower Accepts Aid Cut; Drive to Adjourn Advances

Special to THE NEW YORK TIMES.

WASHINGTON, July 26—The drive for adjournment of Congress by Saturday appeared more certain of success today as the Eisenhower Administration privately indicated it could operate under the $4,562,664,000 foreign aid fund bill approved yesterday by the Senate Appropriations Committee.

The Administration decision, already conveyed to Senate leaders, was said to represent an understanding, reluctantly reached, that little improvement could be hoped for on the committee action, which restored half the $1,115,050,000 reduction made last week in the House of Representatives.

The Administration leaders in the Senate are being asked to do no more than "hold the line" when the Mutual Security money bill comes to the floor for debate, and possibly a vote, on Wednesday.

For the record, the Administration still sought passage before adjournment of the postal rate increase bill, designed to produce an additional $240,500,000 in revenue, but the pressure for the proposal did not seem very great.

Summerfield Is Doubtful

Postmaster General Arthur E. Summerfield, guest on the National Broadcasting Company's "Meet the Press" television interview, said tonight he thought Congress should stay in session to pass the bill but conceded he did not know whether it would.

"I know they've had a busy six months," he said.

The House Post Office and Civil Service Committee, which has been conducting hearings for two weeks, has given no indication when a postal bill will be reported. The House leadership tentatively has scheduled the measure for midweek consideration on the floor. There have been no Senate hearings.

With debate beginning tomorrow, quick Senate approval was forecast for a compromise bill providing for the admission to this country over the next three years of 209,000 refugees, many of them from lands now behind the Iron Curtain. The Administration originally had proposed permitting the entry of 240,000 above-quota immigrants in two years.

The compromise figure, worked out with Senator Pat McCarran, Democrat of Nevada, who will continue to oppose the legislation but will not obstruct its passage, falls below the 220,000 admissions in three years approved by the Senate Judiciary Committee.

House Votes Wednesday

The House will vote Wednesday on its version of the bill in which 240,000 refugees would be admitted over a three-year period. Conferees later will agree to a median figure on entries.

Apart from conference reports, which will be coming up for votes daily, the refugee bill is the last major piece of legislation awaiting

Continued on Page 15, Column 3

55 REPORTED KILLED IN CUBAN REBELLION

Batista Voids Constitutional Guarantees, Hits Partisans of Ex-President Prio

By R. HART PHILLIPS

Special to THE NEW YORK TIMES.

HAVANA, July 26—Fifty-five persons were reported killed and many more wounded in a rebellion today at Santiago de Cuba and near-by Bayamo. Martial law was imposed in Santiago following the uprising and military authorities began to round up members of revolutionary groups.

President Fulgencio Batista and his Cabinet in a special session tonight suspended constitutional guarantees for a period of ninety days, according to an official note from the Presidential Palace. The action was taken to enable the Government to cope with revolutionary activities following the revolt earlier in the day.

"Mercenaries in the service of those who became rich during the regime of Prio [former President Carlos Prio Socarras], in conjunction with Communist elements" were accused of the attacks on the military posts at Santiago and Bayamo in a joint statement signed by the Ministers.

Continued on Page 11, Column 2

TALK CONDITION SET

U.S. to Boycott Political Parleys After 90 Days if It Finds Foe Stalls

By W. H. LAWRENCE

Special to THE NEW YORK TIMES

WASHINGTON, July 26—The United States has agreed to join South Korea in walking out of the projected Korean political conference ninety days after it begins if this Government is convinced that the Communists are not negotiating in good faith and that further sessions would be futile.

But this Government has not promised to resume hostilities in Korea at that time, nor has it promised to give South Korea any moral or material support if that Government carries out its threat to attempt to unify divided Korea by military force.

The conditional pledge to quit the Korean political conference after ninety days—if this Government believes it is futile—has been given to Dr. Syngman Rhee, South Korean President, who has already announced publicly that his agreement to cooperate in the armistice extends for only ninety days after the political conference convenes. Under the truce terms the conference will convene within ninety days after the signing of the armistice.

The Communists have not been told heretofore of this American intention to quit the political talks in any specified period if they seem to this Government to be fruitless. The United States contends that a walkout from the political talks would not violate the armistice.

U. S. to Make Decision

This Government is not committed to walk out of the peace talks simply if Dr. Rhee and the South Koreans walk out. The United States will make its own decisions as to whether the political negotiations are being carried on in good faith.

There is not, so far as is known, any agreement by the other principal members of the United Nations to walk out at the same time that the United States might decide to leave the conference.

Observers here did not feel that the assurances given to Dr. Rhee were necessarily in conflict with the guarantees given the Communists by Lieut. Gen. William K. Harrison Jr., chief United Nations negotiator, that there would be no time limit on the political conference.

It was pointed out that the armistice agreement included no time limitation for success or failure of the political conference—but it also imposed no requirement on either the Communists or the Allies to continue negotiations if it

Continued on Page 3, Column 2

PRESIDENT IS HAPPY

But Warns in Broadcast That Global Peace Is Yet to Be Achieved

Texts of Eisenhower and Dulles talks are on Page 4.

Special to THE NEW YORK TIMES.

WASHINGTON, July 26—President Eisenhower greeted the news of the Korean armistice tonight with prayers of thanksgiving but warned the nation that the Allies had won an armistice only on a single battleground and had not achieved peace in the world.

The President spoke over radio and television networks about an hour after the official cease-fire documents had been signed.

General Eisenhower said the United States and all the free world must not relax its guard, or fail to be vigilant against "the possibility of untoward developments."

After the President had spoken, Charles E. Wilson, Secretary of Defense, issued a statement warning against any relaxation in the country's defense program because of the truce. He advised, too, that it would be a "long time" before American troops could be withdrawn from Korea "with safety."

"We must not be misled into the same demobilization which followed World Wars I and II," he said. "Such a demobilization would inevitably again tempt an aggressor."

Dulles Sees U. N. Victory

John Foster Dulles, Secretary of State, described the armistice as a great victory for the United Nations because "for the first time in history an international organization had stood against an aggressor and has marshaled force to meet force."

President Eisenhower spoke from the White House, across Pennsylvania Avenue and about a block east from Blair House, where President Truman decided thirty-seven months ago to commit United States forces to the defense of South Korea, then being overrun by the Communist armies from the north.

The President said he hoped that the coming of peace to Korea would at last convince all nations of the wisdom of composing their differences by negotiation before—rather than after "various resorts to brutal and futile battle."

He closed his brief speech by quoting from the final paragraph of Lincoln's Second Inaugural Address, which he said expressed the resolution and dedication of all Americans, now as in 1865.

These were Lincoln's words: "With malice toward none, with

Continued on Page 4, Column 2

The New York Times (by Fred J. Sass)

REPORTS ON TRUCE: President Eisenhower making nation-wide television broadcast from the White House last night.

CEREMONY IS BRIEF

Halt in 3-Year Conflict for a Political Parley Due at 9 A. M. Today

Armistice text, on Pages 6, 7; Clark and Taylor statements, 9.

By LINDESAY PARROTT

Special to THE NEW YORK TIMES.

TOKYO, Monday, July 27—Communist and United Nations delegates in Panmunjom signed an armistice at 10:01 A. M. today [9:01 P. M., Sunday, Eastern daylight time]. Under the truce terms, hostilities in the three-year-old Korean war are to cease at 10 o'clock tonight [9 A. M., Monday, Eastern daylight time].

[President Syngman Rhee of South Korea promised in a statement at Seoul Monday to observe the armistice "for a limited time" while a political conference tried to unify Korea by peaceful means, The United Press said.]

The historic document was signed in a roadside hall the Communists built specially for the occasion. The ceremony, attended by representatives of sixteen members of the United Nations, took precisely eleven minutes. Then the respective delegations walked from the meeting place without a word or handshake between them.

The matter-of-fact procedure underlined what spokesmen of both sides emphasized: That though the shooting would cease within twelve hours after the signing, only an uneasy armed truce and political difficulties, perhaps even greater than those of the armistice negotiations, were ahead.

Signers Are Expressionless

The representatives of the two sides were expressionless as they put their names to a pile of documents, providing for an exchange of prisoners, establishment of a neutral zone for the cease-fire and a later political conference that would attempt to settle the tragic Korean questions, unsolved by three years of fighting that caused hundreds of thousands of casualties.

According to the latest figures, revealed July 21 by the Department of Defense, the United States has suffered a total of 139,272 casualties. This included 24,965 dead, 101,368 wounded, 2,938 captured, 8,476 missing and 1,525 previously reported captured or missing, but since returned to military control.

Early this afternoon the Allied part in conclusion of the armistice agreement was completed at advance headquarters near Munsan, where Gen. Mark W. Clark, United Nations commander, put his name to the documents previously signed at Panmunjom.

General Clark signed in the presence of some of his high-ranking officers, Vice Admiral Robert P. Briscoe, commander of the naval forces in the Far East; Gen. Otto P. Weyland, head of the Far East Air Forces; Gen. Maxwell D. Taylor, Eighth Army commander; Lieut. Gen. Samuel Anderson of the Fifth Air Force, and Vice Admiral J. J. Clark, heading the Seventh Fleet.

Also present at Munsan was

Continued on Page 2, Column 5

DEFENSE CHIEFS SEE BILLION CUT IN ARMS

Wilson Tells Quantico Parley Our Gain in Might Makes Any Attack on Us 'Foolhardy'

By AUSTIN STEVENS

Special to THE NEW YORK TIMES.

QUANTICO, Va., July 26—Defense officials attending the high-level defense conference at the Marine Corps base here predicted today that with any kind of "decent" Korean truce defense spending could be trimmed by as much as $1,000,000,000 in the next twelve months.

Secretary of Defense Charles E. Wilson told the conference that "we have attained a strength which should make any attack upon us foolhardy in the extreme, and we are increasing our strength daily."

The previously stated defense spending figure for the fiscal year that started July 1 was $43,200,000,000. Official announcement was made two days ago that W. J. McNeil, Assistant Secretary of Defense in charge of the budget, had told the conference, which included high military leaders, that cuts were expected in that figure. He did not indicate where the cuts were to be made.

In their prediction today the defense officials said that the post-truce reductions would not be greater than $1,000,000,000 in the year because so many fixed costs would continue.

The immediate economies would come in ammunition, trucks and other "consumption items" of war. Over-all military manpower gradually would be cut back from the present 3,500,000 by 200,000, perhaps more. One item mentioned today as an example was the immediate ending of combat pay, which is budgeted at $56,000,000.

However, defense officials stated, some other costs would rise. Assuming, for instance, that large numbers of United States troops would remain in Korea for some time, it was said, it would become necessary to build barracks and other semi-permanent structures.

The three-day highly secret conference called by Secretary Wilson to have the armed services present their situations and problems and also to get members of his new defense "team" to know

Continued on Page 9, Column 1

MARINES STOP REDS IN LAST-HOUR FIGHT

Chinese Foe's Dawn Attacks Hit U. S. Units on West and South Koreans in Center

By The United Press

TOKYO, Monday, July 27—Chinese Communist troops threw "last hour propaganda" attacks at Allied forces on the central and western fronts of the rain-swept Korean battle line today, only a few hours before the armistice was signed at Panmunjom.

An estimated two enemy companies smashed into United Nations lines at the bend of the Kumsong River on the central front. South Korean forces fought the Reds hand-to-hand for more than an hour.

Allied troops all along the 155-mile line across the peninsula were ordered to hold casualties to a minimum and not to pick fights with the Reds.

The Allied orders were issued as Chinese Red shock troops just before dawn attacked United States Marines on a western front outpost for the fourth consecutive day. The Reds hit the hillpost positions northeast of Panmunjom in forces up to 200 men.

First Marine Division officers said the first wave of the attack was turned off without casualty among the Americans. The marines

Continued on Page 2, Column 1

Arizona Raids Polygamous Cult; Seeks to Wipe Out Its Community

By GLADWIN HILL

Special to THE NEW YORK TIMES.

SHORT CREEK, Ariz., July 26—Arizona authorities, under an unusual proclamation of insurrection, raided this remote farming hamlet on the state's northern border at dawn today and placed virtually the entire adult population under arrest in an effort to wipe out the nation's last remaining center of organized polygamy.

The defendants, thirty-six men and eighty-six women, constituted the principal membership of a professed Fundamentalist sect — disowned by the Church of Jesus Christ of Latter Day Saints (Mormon) in 1939—that has continued to practice the plural marriage renounced by the Mormon church in 1890.

Separated from the outside world by the towering cliffs and arid gorges of Arizona's wild and inaccessible "Strip" between the Grand Canyon and the Utah border, members of the cult, organized on a communal economic basis, allegedly have been maintaining as many as a half-dozen wives and thirty children, and have fostered child marriages.

In addition to 122 adults and child brides named in warrants held by a raiding force of 120 peace officers, the colony included some 263 children.

The state's avowed objective is to wipe out the community, imprison the adult ringleaders, and find new homes and lives for the children and for the numerous

Continued on Page 36, Column 1

U.N. Assembly Meets Aug. 17 To Plan Post-Truce Parley

Special to THE NEW YORK TIMES.

UNITED NATIONS, N. Y., July 26—Promptly upon receiving formal notification of the signing of the Korean armistice, Lester B. Pearson of Canada, President of the General Assembly, issued a call tonight to member delegations for resumption on Aug. 17 of the suspended seventh Assembly session. The Assembly will decide details of the Far Eastern political conference scheduled to take place within ninety days of the signing of the truce agreement.

Official notification that the truce agreement had been signed was given orally to Secretary General Dag Hammarskjold and to Mr. Pearson by the permanent representative of the United States, former Senator Henry Cabot Lodge Jr., in the same committee room at headquarters here in which the Political and Security Committee held its lengthy debate on the Korean question some months ago.

Mr. Lodge then handed to Mr. Pearson a copy of the text of the communication, addressed to the Secretary General and signed by the United States Mission after word had been flashed from the Pentagon in Washington. It read:

"I have the honor to inform you that an armistice agreement has been entered into between the United Nations Command and the commanders of the Communist forces in Korea, i. e., the Korean People's Army and the Chinese People's Volunteers. The agreement was signed for the United Nations Command at 1000 hours [10 A. M.] on July 27, 1953, Korean time, and becomes effective at 2200 hours [10 P. M.], July 27, 1953, Korean time. [The actual signing was at 10:01 A. M., Korean time, or 9:01 P. M. Sunday, Eastern daylight time.]

"A report of the Unified Command transmitting the official text of the armistice agreement will be sent to you shortly."

Telegrams to the delegates, which had been prepared earlier, were dispatched to the delegations summoning them to report for the reconvened session in mid-August.

In a joint broadcast from the committee room, which followed that of President Eisenhower from Washington, all three of the United Nations principals repeated for radio and television audiences statements issued earlier.

"The whole world is thankful that the negotiations at Panmunjom have brought the fighting in Korea to an end by the signature of an armistice agreement," Mr.

Continued on Page 4, Column 5

Skeptical G. I.'s Finally Convinced; Most Take News With Little Elation

By GREG MacGREGOR

Special to THE NEW YORK TIMES.

SEOUL, Korea, July 26 — Tonight, on the eve of the armistice, front-line G. I.'s faced their last full night of fighting in the thirty-seven-month-old Korean war. Only a few minor clashes had taken place by early morning, and from all indications the war would be unofficially ended by dawn. No patrols were scheduled for tomorrow.

As news of the armistice filtered down to the men at the front, it left an atmosphere of mingled disbelief and temporary confusion in its wake. In many cases the soldiers flatly refused to accept the word of their own officers and noncommissioned officers. The men had had so many disappointments over cease-fire reports in the past that they were slow to accept the truth.

"It will never happen," a Marine private manning the line on the central front said with a laugh when his sergeant told him the war would end tomorrow.

Not until the Armed Forces Radio broadcast was picked up at 6 P. M. tonight by portable receivers along the front were the men willing to believe the news. Then the announcer's words struck like a bolt of lightning.

Some G. I.'s stared dumbly at each other and others broke out in howls.

"Didja hear that—didja hear that?" one man kept shouting over and over as he ran from his tent.

"Wait'll they sign it—who knows what's going to happen?" a skeptic

Continued on Page 2, Column 7

MARINES STOP REDS IN LAST-HOUR FIGHT

Continued From Page 1

had expected the attack; officers said they believed the Chinese were continuing their assaults for a propaganda effect.

Big guns and raiding parties probed across No Man's Land. Allied bombers dumped their loads on Communist targets through heavy cloud layers by radar controls.

The Air Force flew its final night B-29 mission against two Communist airfields in Northwest Korea, hitting at Samcham, near Sinanju, and at Taechon just before midnight. Only light antiaircraft fire and searchlights greeted the ten bombers.

The Navy, in the final full day of the war, set a record for carrier-launched sorties by putting 634 planes into the air from four United States carriers in the Sea of Japan. Planes from the Lake Champlain, Philippine Sea, Princeton and Boxer hit buildings, trains, troops and supply dumps in North Korea.

Throughout yesterday, United Nations F-86 Sabre jets roamed "MIG Alley" near the Manchurian border without finding any Communist jet fighter opponents.

Along the front, in the semi-tropic heat, artillery flares punctuated the velvet blackness of monsoon rains. Machine guns chattered nervously across mud-choked trenches. Mortar blasts echoed through outpost bunkers.

The Chinese Reds who hit the Marines on the outpost around the "Berlin" complex on the western front early today were beaten off by small-arms fire, artillery and mortars in twenty minutes.

All yesterday the Chinese foe made aimless and costly attacks against the Marines. The Leathernecks threw back three waves of Red shock troops before the enemy eased off on the forward position.

On the central front, men of the South Korean Eleventh Division had been reported advancing on an outpost seized from them by the Chinese Reds yesterday. The South Koreans were fighting in a cloudburst east of the bend in the Kumsong River.

'Sealed Orders' at the Front

ON EAST-CENTRAL FRONT, Korea, Monday, July 27 (AP)—All troop commanders along the Eighth Army front last night received field orders and swore on their honor "as officers and gentlemen" not to open them until today, a division spokesman said.

The orders presumably dealt with procedures and troop conduct after the armistice was signed, the officer said.

Yesterday, Eighth Army headquarters gave divisions at the front permission to use their own judgment on offensive action in the final hours of the war.

Iwo Flag Hero Freed From Jail

CHICAGO, July 26 (UP)—One of the marines who participated in the historic flag-raising on Iwo Jima's Mount Suribachi was released today after spending the week-end in jail on a drunk charge. Ira Hayes, 30-year-old Pima Indian, was found loitering in a park. He said it was his fifth arrest on the same charge since he had come to Chicago last May.

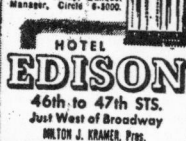

Official Reports of the Fighting in Korea

United Nations

TOKYO, Monday, July 27 (A. P.)—Eighth Army tactical summary 255, for Sunday to 6 P. M.:

Fighting across the 155-mile Eighth Army battle front decreased somewhat Sunday from the fighting of Saturday with the heaviest action occurring in the central sector of the Kumsong Bulge.

South of Kumsong the Eleventh R. O. K. Division outpost positions were attacked in a coordinated effort by a regiment of the Chinese prior to midnight. At 12:30 A. M. the enemy made slight advances into the central and western portions of the outpost, but at 1 A. M. the Chinese were forced to withdraw from the action.

In the western sector, the First Marine Division's front-line positions west of The Hook continued to be attacked by the enemy. At 1:50 A. M. a company of Chinese hit the Marines twice before withdrawing from the action at 3:15 A. M., when action ceased. Farther to the east, a Marine front-line position was engaged at 2:25 A. M. in a forty-nine-minute fire fight before the enemy broke contact.

South of Lookout Mountain in the Kumsong Bulge, Eighth R. O. K. Division front-line positions were hit by an estimated two companies of Chinese. After an intense thirty-five-minute fire fight, the Chinese withdrew.

Lighter enemy-initiated actions occurred near White House Mountain, in the vicinity of Boomerang and the Kumsong River bend in the central sector, and near Sandbag Castle in the eastern sector.

Eighth Army patrols clashed briefly to thirty-five minutes with enemy groups up to squad in size, with the contact most frequent in the central and eastern sectors.

Eighth Army communiqué, covering Saturday's activities:

Fighting across the Eighth Army battlefront increased somewhat Saturday over that of the day before, with the heaviest action centered in the western and central sectors of the 155-mile front. First United States Marine and First R. O. K. Divisions in the western sector reported continuing action, while the Third United States and Eleventh R. O. K. Divisions in the central sector reported new actions during the period of this communiqué. Elsewhere across the front, fighting was generally light.

The enemy fired 40,014 rounds of artillery and mortar on Allied positions during the twenty-four-hour period ended at 6 P. M.

Western sector: First Marine Division front-line positions southwest of The Hook in the western sector were attacked late Friday night by an estimated Chinese regiment, and at midnight the Chinese were reported as occupying the trenches on the northern slopes of the attacked positions. At 12:30 A. M. the enemy continued to hold the northern slope positions in the center of the attacked front, but had withdrawn from the right and left flanks. The enemy's strength at the center was estimated at two battalions. At 1 A. M. the Marines reinforced and counter-attacked, and by 5:30 A. M. had forced the enemy to withdraw.

At 8:30 A. M. an enemy company resumed the attack, but Marine small arms, artillery and mortar fire prevented the enemy from reaching the position. However, the intensity of the Marine artillery prevented the Chinese from withdrawing from the action, and at 12:30 P. M. the Marines were reported as cleaning up the area. Action remained sporadic until 9:30 P. M. when the Marine front line was hit briefly by two enemy squads. Sporadic action was continuing at the close of the period. The Marine Outpost Esther, to the southwest and near Bunker Hill, was hit by an estimated fifty Chinese Friday night, but at 1:50 A. M. the enemy was forced to withdraw and action ceased. The First R. O. K. Division's Outpost Betty, was hit by a company of Chinese at 12:10 A. M. At 3:45 A. M. the Chinese were forced to withdraw from the eastern flank of the outpost position, but continued their attack for the western and central positions. The R. O. K.'s reinforced their position and forced the Chinese to withdraw to the northern slope of Betty. At 8:30 A. M. an unknown number of Chinese renewed the attack and forced the R. O. K.'s to disengage to positions of the eastern flank of the outpost.

Action on Betty was sporadic until 1:30 P. M. when First R. O. K.'s counter-attacked the center of the position and engaged an unknown number of Chinese in a hand-grenade fight. Fighting continued sporadic until 5:45 P. M. when the enemy withdrew to the western end of Betty and action ceased, with the R. O. K.'s holding the central and eastern positions of the outpost. Outpost Snook, between Pork Chop and T-Bone, was hit at 9:15 P. M. by a platoon of Chinese. The enemy was forced to withdraw from the action after a seventeen-minute fire fight.

Central sector: Two outpost positions in the Third United States

The New York Times July 27, 1953

HAND TO HAND: Red and Allied forces fought bitter battles on central front (cross).

Division sector on the central front that had been retaken by Allied counter-attacking forces Friday evening, were retaken early Saturday by Chinese counter-attacking forces. The Allied troops on the westernmost outpost disengaged from the action at 12:08 A. M., while friendly troops on the other withdrew at 3:45 A. M., when attacked by two Chinese platoons. An estimated Chinese battalion, preceded by heavy concentrations of artillery, attacked a Third United States Division front-line position northeast of Sniper Ridge at 10:50 P. M.

An intense fire-fight, in which small arms, automatic weapons, hand grenades and mortar were employed by both sides, ensued until 11:30 P. M., when the fighting slackened and the enemy started to disengage. At 11:50 P. M. the enemy had withdrawn completely. Three Eleventh R. O. K. Division outpost positions were attacked in a coordinated effort by a regiment of Chinese at 10:35 P. M. At the close of the period, action was continuing. Lighter enemy-initiated actions occurred near Boomerang at 12:50 A. M. and 10:57 P. M., south of Sniper Ridge at 11:45, east of Sniper Ridge at 10:50 and 11:20 P. M., near White Horse Mountain at 9:45 P. M. and 9:55 P. M. Friendly initiated patrols engaged enemy groups ranging from squad to two platoons in size in eight brief to ten-minute skirmishes.

Eastern sector: Southeast of Anchor Hill, two Allied outpost positions were each probed by two North Korean platoons shortly after midnight, in thirty-minute and one-hour-and-fifty-five-minute fire-fights. Two North Korean platoons hit an Allied outpost position near Luke's Castle for ten minutes starting at 11:15 P. M. Lighter enemy-initiated actions occurred near Tankers Hill at 12:10 A. M. and near Sandbag Castle at 2 A. M.

There were twelve friendly initiated patrol contacts reported against enemy groups ranging from four men to platoon in size, in brief to twenty-minute fire-fights.

Far East Naval Forces summary of Sunday's operations:

Task Force 77 pyramided its record of daily sorties to an all-Korean high of 634 launchings during the period, while cruisers, destroyers and the battleship U. S. S. New Jersey raked the enemy coast line from seaward.

Pilots from the carriers U. S. S. Lake Champlain, Philippine Sea, Princeton and Boxer ranged from the battle lines north to Hungnam to strike buildings, trains, troops and supply concentrations.

One flight of aircraft bombed the airfield at Hoeryong and cratered it in thirty-two places. At Hungnam, the planes took a heavy toll of buildings and supply trucks while at Wonsan, caves, gun positions and rail cars bore the brunt of the heavy assault.

Damage totals for the record day were thirty-seven road cuts, ninety-two rail cuts and 100 yards of trench line destroyed; twenty-four highway bridges damaged, forty-six destroyed; five gun positions silenced and three destroyed; seventy-one buildings damaged, forty-six destroyed; ten trucks were destroyed, while another eight were damaged; sixty-eight railroad cars were heavily damaged, fifty-six completely destroyed; twenty-seven railroad bridges damaged, three destroyed; one locomotive damaged, one destroyed; eight supply shelters damaged, two transformers, six tunnels damaged; sixteen secondary explosions counted. In addition, the airfields at Hoeryong, Hoemun and Sondok were heavily damaged and cratered and eight enemy bunkers were knocked out.

Task Force 77 has launched a record 2,433 sorties in the past four days.

The battleship U. S. S. New Jersey aimed her 16-inch fire at the hub city of Wonsan, the ship's gunners concentrated on fortifications and harbor defense positions. New Jersey knocked out two 155-mm. gun positions, two 90-mm. guns and three 76-mm.'s in one sector. In addition, five bunkers and several automatic weapons positions were destroyed and the entire area heavily damaged with a score of direct hits. Rock slides started by New Jersey gunners covered one 155-mm. gun cave and caused heavy damage in a built-up area. Three gun caves were closed and another damaged while thirteen direct hits were scored on enemy trench lines.

Meanwhile, near Kosong, the cruiser U. S. S. Bremerton fired on automatic gun positions and bunkers. One bunker was destroyed and ninety yards of trench line cut. Three bunkers were heavily damaged by the ship's fire.

The heavy cruiser U. S. S. St. Paul with her escort destroyer U. S. S. Samuel N. Moore steamed north to Hungnam to fire on enemy targets. The ships bracketed a gun position causing heavy damage, scored two direct hits in a personnel cave and laid several rounds of accurate fire into a shelter area. In addition, spotter reported three camouflaged bunkers were well covered by the ship's fire.

Far East Air Forces summary of Saturday's operations:

Although rain and thick clouds covered most of North Korea for the fourth successive day, United Nations fighter and light bombers smashed more than 1,000,000 pounds of explosives into the enemy battle line and after dark light and medium bombers returned to the Red front line and also assaulted air fields deeper in enemy territory.

F. E. A. F. aircraft mounted 745 sorties during the period, with the close support day and night strikes highlighting the effort.

United States Air Force F-86 Sabre jet fighter-bombers during the day assaulted all sectors of the 155-mile battle line, sending their bombs into the Communist positions by electronic methods. Shore-based Marine Panther jets and carrier-based naval aircraft also participated in close-support attacks.

Results of all strikes were unobserved because of the cloud conditions.

In the late afternoon, weather deep in North Korea cleared partially and F-86 interceptors swept MIG Alley, but met no MIG-15's.

Saturday night, forty B-26 Invaders pounded the Communist front line, five B-26's hit a Communist airfield at Sinmak and six patrolled enemy supply lanes. Results were unobserved.

Seventeen B-29 Superforts from Japan hit the Pyongyang Main and East airfields, dividing into forces of nine and eight aircraft to pound the targets. Meager flak opposed them, as they bombed electronically through a solid undercast.

Two other B-29's hit Communist front-line positions, without opposition. Cargo transports of F. E. A. F.'s 315th Air Division airlifted 595 tons of personnel and supplies in continued logistical support of United Nations forces.

Far East Naval Forces summary of Saturday's operations:

Backing Friday's assembly-line schedule, Task Force 77 aircraft again ripped into Communist positions with a day's effort of 592 combat sorties for a total of over 1,100 strikes in the forty-eight-hour period. Pilots from the Boxer, Princeton, Philippine Sea and Lake Champlain pounded the bomb line in close air support, then returned to the carriers for refueling and rearming before swarming over the eastern half of North Korea on interdiction strikes and armed reconnaissance missions.

Bomb-line missions destroyed supply shelters, troop bunkers, gun positions, and two ammunition dumps, while target strikes netted thirty-four rail cuts and the destruction or damaging of seventy-four buildings, fourteen railroad bridges and three tunnels.

The day's biggest tally resulted from the Task Force's 203 reconnaissance missions. Banshees, Panther jets, Corsairs and Skyraiders teamed up to destroy or damage eighty-eight trucks, eighty-four boxcars, and two locomotives.

Standing off Hungnam, the New Jersey's guns started off the day by knocking out a gun cave, destroying two buildings and a marshaling yard and making five rail cuts. Switching her sights to industrial facilities, the battlewagon destroyed two factories, getting secondary explosions in the process and hit several oil storage tanks with resulting heavy fires.

In the afternoon's fire mission, the New Jersey dropped two spans of a highway bridge, damaged a rail bridge and filled a railroad tunnel.

Off Kosong, and firing on the Anchor Hill area, the heavy cruiser U. S. S. Bremerton and the destroyer Hamner averaged 75 per cent coverage in cutting 210 yards of enemy trenches, and destroying twenty troop bunkers, six observation posts, and damaging several supply areas.

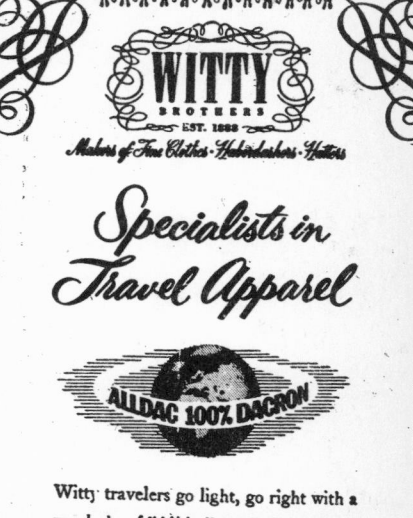

ADMIRAL JOY THANKFUL

But He Calls Korean War Only a Phase in Drive Against Reds

ANNAPOLIS, Md., July 26 (UP)—Vice Admiral Charles Turner Joy, commandant of the United States Naval Academy and first chief of the United Nations truce negotiators, expressed thankfulness tonight that the fighting in Korea was about to cease.

"But I hope every American will not forget that the Korean war is only a phase of the war that is being fought around the globe against communism in many ways and on many fronts," he said in a statement.

"We must not allow ourselves to be lulled into a false sense of security just because the most painful phase of that war appears to be over.

"We should always remember that the most effective way to discourage further acts of armed aggression by our Communist enemy will always be a strong defense establishment and the willingness to use our military strength whenever necessary."

Military Currency Off in Seoul

SEOUL, Korea, Monday, July 27 (AP) — The value of United States military payment certificates on the Korean black market fell nearly 30 per cent today with the signing of an armistice. The exchange rate for $1 in military pay dropped from 175 kwan to 125 in a few hours.

Gliding Contest Held in Germany

OERLINGHAUSEN, Germany, July 26 (AP)—Fifty thousand persons gathered at an airfield here today to witness the opening of Germany's first gliding competition in fourteen years. Twenty-eight teams, including two from Yugoslavia and one from France, will take part in the meeting, which ends Aug. 9.

Israeli Leftist Favors Coalition

TEL AVIV, Israel, July 26 (AP)—Mordechai Erem, one of the leaders of the Left-Wing Socialist Mapam party, announced today his party was ready to join a broad coalition Cabinet in Israel. Mapam has been one of the chief Opposition groups.

U. S. Forces' Casualtes in the Korean Fighting

WASHINGTON, July 26 (AP)—The Defense Department identified 295 Korean war casualties today in a list that included thirty-two killed, 215 wounded, fifteen missing and thirty-three injured. The following were from New York, New Jersey and Connecticut:

KILLED IN ACTION

COLLINS, Cpl. Thomas C., son of Mr. and Mrs. William Collins, Bridgeport.

THOMAS, A/1C James Clark, son of Mr. and Mrs. James R. Thomas, Paulsboro, N. J.

WOUNDED

ABBUHL, Pvt. Frederick A., son of Mr. and Mrs. Karl H. Abbuhl, Marathon, N. Y.

ALONZO, Pvt. Edward, son of Mr. and Mrs. Anthony Alonzo, 342 East Seventy-sixth Street, Manhattan.

ARNUM, Pvt. Gordon A., of Windsor Locks, Conn., husband of Mrs. Pauline M. Arnum, New Bedford, Mass.

BARNETT, 2d Lieut. Richard B., husband of Mrs. Elyse M. Barnett, 87-12 Thirty-second Avenue, Jackson Heights, Queens, c/o Louis Light, 37-[illegible] Seventy-fifth Street, Jackson Heights.

BLACKBURN, Pvt. George L., son of George L. Blackburn, North Syracuse.

BRAINARD, Pfc. John R., son of Mrs. Dorothy F. Brainard, Jersey City.

BROWN, Pvt. Alvin E., Bloomsbury, N. J., brother of Mrs. Alice M. Schaffer, Easton, Pa.

CHAMBERLAIN, Pvt. James H., husband of Mrs. Mildred E. Chamberlain, Camden.

CHRISTIE, Pvt. James C., husband of Mrs. Ruth A. Christie, Troy.

CUTRUFELLO, Cpl. John W., son of Mr. and Mrs. Joseph Cutrufello, Roselle Park, N. J.

DAMIANO, Pfc. Albert L., son of Mrs. Angelina M. Damiano, Colonia, N. J.

DEARBORN, Pvt. James E., brother of Mrs. Florence Henny, 746 Columbus Avenue, Manhattan.

DeLUCA, Cpl. George G., son of Mr. and Mrs. George G. De Leon, New Haven.

DELUCA, Pfc. Ralph A., Jr., husband of Mrs. Therese M. Deluca, Bridgeport.

ELLIOTT, Pfc. Frank E., son of Mr. and Mrs. Clifford Elliott, Pavilion, N. Y.

FIORELLO, Pvt. Joseph P., son of Mr. and Mrs. Anthony Fiorello, Bridgeport.

FITZGERALD, Pvt. John P., son of Mr. and Mrs. Michael Fitzgerald, 434 East Sixty-seventh Street, Manhattan.

GEHM, Pvt. George E., husband of Mrs. Virginia M. Gehm, Syracuse.

GONZALES, Pvt. Ralph A., son of Mrs. Frances Anderson, 334 Atlantic Avenue, Brooklyn.

GOUGH, Pvt. Thomas A., husband of Mrs. Elvera M. Gough, c/o James Pipia, Skillman, N. J.

HAZELL, Pvt. Newton L., son of Mr. and Mrs. Claremont Hazell, Perth Amboy.

HEGEMAN, Pvt. Arthur M., son of Mr. and Mrs. Augustine Hegeman, 1455 East Fifty-fourth Street, Brooklyn.

JACKSON, Pvt. Royce D., son of Mr. and Mrs. Millard D. Jackson, Wellsville, N. Y.

JOST, Pvt. Edward, son of Mrs. Emma Semler, 1716 Gates Avenue, Brooklyn.

KESLING, Pvt. Ronald A., son of Mr. and Mrs. Joseph Kesling, Bloomfield, N. J.

LAPOINT, Cpl. Rupert H., ward of Harry G. Campbell, Fort Dix, N. J., c/o Office of Army Chaplain, Governors Island.

McGINLEY, Pvt. Paul W., son of Mr. and Mrs. Patrick McGinley, Newark.

RIBBECK, Cpl. James T., son of Mr. and Mrs. Arthur Ribbeck, Clarence, N. Y.

RICE, Pvt. Walter F., son of Mr. and Mrs. William D. Rice, Newark.

ROGERS, Pvt. Charles W. son of Mrs. Hilda L. Griswold, Wellsville, N. Y.

ROSADO-RODRIGUEZ, Cpl. Eugenio, husband of Mrs. Marina Rosado-Rodriguez, 860 East 161st Street, the Bronx.

SABATINO, Pvt. Anthony, son of Mrs. Anna Sabatino, Bridgeport.

SAUER, Pvt. Henry J., husband of Mrs. Kathleen Sauer, Elmont, L. I.

SCHECHTMAN, Pvt. Jack, son of Mr. and Mrs. James Schechtman, 1836 Forty-fifth Street, Brooklyn.

SCHNELLE, Sgt. John W., son of Mr. and Mrs. Charles J. Schnelle, Hamden, Conn.

SCOTT, Sgt. William A., of Camden, husband of Mrs. Odessa L. Scott, [illegible], N. C.

SECATELLO, Pvt. Dominick S., son of Mrs. Lena Secatello, Hoboken.

STOWELL, Pfc. Arnold E., son of Mr. and Mrs. Leon D. Stowell, Geneva, N. Y.

WARENIK, Cpl. Raymond J., son of Mr. and Mrs. Felix Warenik, Westbury, L. I.

WUSSLER, Pfc. Donald E., son of Mrs. Margaret Wussler, Scotch Plain, N. J.

ZERBARINI, Pfc. Robert H., son of Mr. and Mrs. Henry Zerbarini, 169-42 Twenty-third Avenue, Whitestone, Queens.

INJURED

ATTERBERRY, Pvt. Richard, son of Mrs. Anna L. Atterbury, Stamford.

BEIMS, Cpl. Arthur C., nephew of Charles Beims, 114-03 Ninety-fifth Avenue, Richmond Hill, Queens.

BUCKNER, Pfc. William J., son of Mrs. Elizabeth Buckner, Mullbrook, N. Y.

FIDEN, Pfc. Bernard, son of Mr. and Mrs. Harry Fiden, 1819 Seventy-ninth Street, Brooklyn.

HENDRICKSON, Pvt. John B., son of Mr. and Mrs. Frank Hendrickson, 3009 Kingsbridge Terrace, the Bronx.

HOFFMANN, Sgt. 1/C Arthur W., son of Mrs. Florence Lane, Middletown.

JACOBER, Pfc. John, husband of Mrs. Carmella Jacober, 1327 Peteley Avenue, the Bronx.

LeDONNE, Pfc. Philip G., son of Mr. and Mrs. Philip LeDonne, 29 Conselyea Street, Brooklyn.

LOURENCO, Pvt. Carlos, nephew of Mrs. Gloria Figueiredo, Danbury.

TRAVLINE, Pfc. Frank H., husband of Mrs. Shirley Travline, Bridgeton, N. J.

YACOVELLI, Pvt. Anthony J., son of Mr. and Mrs. Joseph Yacovelli, Pleasantville.

MISSING IN ACTION

COLELLO, Pvt. Daniel, son of Mr. and Mrs. Frank Colello, 59 Oswego Street, Staten Island.

DANKOWSKI, 1st Lieut. Stanley R., son of Mrs. Marie A. Dankowski, East Orange.

MALETTA, Pfc. Daniel D., son of Mr. and Mrs. Louis Maletta, 109-10 119th Street, Ozone Park, Queens.

RING, Pvt. Emmett W., husband of Mrs. Lila Ring, Stratford, Conn.

CEASE-FIRE SIGNED IN THE KOREAN WAR

Continued From Page 1

Maj. Gen. Choi Duk Shin, former South Korean representative on General Choi, who walked out of the United Nations armistice team. the meetings at Panmunjom last May, also had boycotted the ceremony there this morning. As a result, no South Korean representative signed the truce, which South Korea will observe, at least temporarily, but did not approve.

Almost simultaneously, General Clark's headquarters in Tokyo released a message the general had written in advance of the armistice—a grim warning that the mere military armistice would not permit the United Nations to relax its vigilance against communism.

"I must tell you as emphatically as I can," said the statement, addressed to all members of the United Nations Command, "that this does not mean immediate or even early withdrawal from Korea. The conflict will not be over until the Governments concerned have reached a firm political settlement."

General Taylor, at Eighth Army heaquarters in Korea, echoed General Clark's views and warning.

"There is no strong feeling that our problems here are [illegible]er, nor that the armistice is an occasion for unrestrained rejoicing," he said.

For the United Nations, the documents were signed at Panmunjom by Lieut. Gen. William K. Harrison Jr. For the Communists, the signer was Lieut. Gen. Nam Il of North Korea, a Russian-trained school teacher who donned a military uniform after the outbreak of the Korean war.

Each Signs Nine Times

Seated at separate tables, each put his name nine times to nine copies of the armistice agreement in English, Korean and Chinese.

On General Harrison's table stood a miniature flag of the United Nations. The North Korean flag decorated the Communists' place in the meeting house. On a central table lay piled copies of the agreement, bound in stiff blue cardboard covers. Aides passed them in turn to the two signers.

Pooled dispatches over Army communications from Panmunjom said General Harrison signed the first copy of the agreement at 10:01 A. M. General Nam put his signature to the final copy at 10:11 o'clock, ending the brief ceremony.

Because of what General Clark called unreasonable restrictions demanded by the Communists, the top military leaders of the opposing armies did not appear at the session. The enemy, it was revealed, had demanded that if Marshal Kim Il Sung, North Korean Premier and Commander in Chief, and Gen. Peng. Teh-huai, commander of the Chinese Communist troops in Korea, came to Panmunjom, all correspondents and all representatives of South Korea would be barred from the neutral zone. General Clark refused.

Following signing of the truce documents by General Clark, the agreement was scheduled to be sent to Marshal Kim and General Peng. Their names probably will be affixed in their secret headquarters near the bombed out North Korean capital of Pyongyang.

The United Nations delegation appeared on the scene at 9:30 o'clock this morning, alighting from helicopters that had brought them from Munsan, and filing past a guard of honor representing all units and services fighting on the peninsula.

Allied Observers Present

General Harrison was accompanied by his fellow American delegates, Rear Admiral John C. Daniel, Brig. Gen. R. N. Osborne and aides. The observers from the United Nations members lined the Allied section of the hall.

There were representatives of Turkey, Thailand, the Netherlands, France, the United Kingdom and the Commonwealth countries, Colombia, Belgium, Denmark, Luxembourg, Ethiopia, Philippines and Norway.

The Communists came to Panmunjom in a fleet of jeeps, thirty-five correspondents of Iron Curtain countries accompanying them. Altogether, it was calculated that there were 130 press and radio correspondents and photographers of many nations in the hall.

Outside the thin wooden walls there was the mutter of artillery fire—a grim reminder that even as the truce was being signed men were still dying on near-by hills and the fight would continue for twelve more hours.

As the delegates settled in seats, aides took the bound copies of the armistice agreement from the central table and passed them to their chiefs. Marine Col. James C. Murray, one of the few Americans present today who saw the start of the truce negotiations two years ago, handed the documents to General Harrison and pointed out to him the place where he should sign. Both General Harrison and General Nam used a single fountain pen.

Lieut. Col. H. M. Orden of the liaison officers group blotted General Harrison's signatures and returned the documents, one by one, to the central table, from where they were passed to General Nam by a North Korean colonel, You Ju.

At no point in the armistice negotiations have the delegates given each other greetings beyond a possible silent nod. The procedure was the same today.

At one point General Harrison whispered briefly to Colonel Orden and an interpreter, Lieut. Kenneth Wu. There was a click of cameras and the grinding of newsreels. Otherwise, only the distant artillery broke the silence.

At 10:10 A. M. General Harrison finished, and General Nam one minute later. The North Korean general glanced at his watch, rose and strode quickly from the hall, without a glance at the United Nations table.

General Harrison strolled out in more leisurely fashion. To correspondents who asked him for comment, he replied: "You know I don't do that."

But he smiled and posed for pictures, saluted the honor guard and greeted some United Nations representatives before he climbed into a helicopter to fly back to Munsan at 10:27 A. M.

Inside the hall, the signed documents remained on the central table, watched by security guards and liaison officers, who remained for a brief meeting with interpreters. Presumably they were arranging the later signing of the armistice by the high commanders.

Seventy-two hours after the signature of the armistice, the troops will withdraw one and a quarter miles from the fighting line, and a neutral zone will be established between the armies.

Within a few days the first of returning United Nations war prisoners might be expected to trickle in. They are expected to reach their homes probably next month.

General Clark flew to Korea late yesterday afternoon to play his part in the revamped signing ceremonies.

The armistice negotiations were closing on the same note of scarcely veiled hostility and accusations of bad faith with which they began more than two years ago. General Clark, landing in Korea made it clear he also had scant hope the truce would go far to solve the tangled problems of a divided Korea.

"A long and difficult road still lies ahead," he warned. "There are no short cuts. If we are to honor the great sacrifices which have been made in the name of freedom, if we are to achieve peace, if we are to uphold the principles of freedom justice and human dignity we must continue our efforts toward peace and we must be ready to defend these principles whenever and wherever they are challenged."

Persons close to Dr. Rhee said his major interest today centered on a political conference that is to follow the truce, with the armistice for the time being regarded as an accomplished fact despite his former stubborn opposition to the cease-fire.

Thus far, there was little knowledge here just what the conference will do, and even how it will be constituted. The armistice agreement itself states only that the commanders in the field "recommend to the Governments concerned" that the meeting be held to negotiate a withdrawal of foreign troops from Korea, a peaceful settlement of the Korean question, "etcetera."

No mention was made of what Governments would be included or of the question of unification of Korea, which Dr. Rhee demands. Neither is the word "etcetera," on which the Communists insisted during the truce negotiations, further defined.

The Communists, it has been suggested, meant to bring in under that word such questions as Chinese Communist admission to the United Nations and the status of the Chinese Nationalist regime on Formosa.

Dr. Rhee, on the other hand, has stated that unification of Korea will be the conference's immediate task, and he is understood to have been disappointed over the supposed failure of the United States to clarify further conversations to that effect he held with Walter S. Robertson, Asssistant Secretary of State for Far Eastern Affairs.

Truman Expresses Hope That Truce Means Peace

INDEPENDENCE, Mo., July 26 (UP)—Former President Harry S. Truman said he was "certainly glad" a truce in Korea had been signed.

"I sincerely hope—and I want to underline that word hope—that it means peace," he said.

Mr. Truman, who received the news at his home with relatives here tonight, issued a brief statement to the press and refused to elaborate.

He declined to answer any other questions, and said only the statement "is exactly the way I feel about it."

DISBELIEVING G. I.'S FINALLY CONVINCED

Continued From Page 1

said. "I ain't buying nothin' yet."

There was no single pattern of reaction. Generally speaking, however, there was little elation or emotion displayed. That may come later, when the impact of the news has had time to sink in.

Possibly the first hint that something important was afoot came to enlisted men in the forward areas early in the afternoon, when various company commanders called them together and warned against the haphazard firing of ammunition. The object was to prevent displays of "fireworks" or other celebrations that might lead to incidents.

Some officers chose, however, to withhold the news as long as possible, and had it not been for the broadcast, would not have revealed it until the last minute.

"I have sent men out on patrol tonight," a platoon leader said. "You just don't tell a man the war is over tomorrow and then send him out to get killed tonight. This is a helluva thing."

But at most locations along the front, the G. I.'s were told unofficially to "take it easy unless somebody starts hitting you."

Ready to Vacate Posts

Although no official order has been given, the units manning the front now could be ready to vacate their present positions within a few hours. Shortly after the broadcast many men announced loudly that they were ready to move anywhere immediately just so it was away from the front.

Within seventy-two hours after the truce becomes effective at 10 P. M. tomorrow, all units on the front—both Allied and Communist—must retire approximately one and a quarter miles. Tonight some units knew exactly where they would go but others had only a hazy idea.

Though the men were not demonstrative, there was little sleep tonight. Many chatted while piecing their belongings together. The talk centered on rotation points.

"Now how long do they keep us here?" one stubble-bearded soldier asked after the first flush of excitement had worn off. "I'm due home in October. Now maybe they will cut the points in half."

However, there was no evidence that the men interpreted the ending of the war as a ticket home in the near future. They seemed resigned to serving out their full time on the peninsula.

Special to THE NEW YORK TIMES.

MUNSAN, Korea, Monday, July 27—The news that the truce was to be signed today did not touch off and wild celebration here. For the most part United Nations soldiers listened to the good word in solemn fashion. Then many shook their heads quietly and said, "Thank God!"

There were those who were exceptionally moved by the news. One soldier's hand began to tremble when he was told and he said, almost shamefacedly, "I just can't help shaking."

A swarthy French soldier of fortune exclaimed "Oh boy!" then added: "Wait till I tell the men of my battalion. We will drink much wine tonight!"

A youth from mid-Manhattan, Cpl. Angel Aponte Ortiz of 44 West Forty-fourth Street and Headquarters Company, Second Division, said: "If they gave me the word I'd leave everything behind but these"—pointing to his grimy fatigue clothes—"and head straight for Times Square."

A military policeman at the Han River bridge in Seoul said: "I just bet those guys up there are sure glad to hear about it. It sure will mean a lot to them."

There was bitterness, too. A burly marine shook his head and said: "It should have come a month ago. There were a lot of men killed in that month. One of them was my best buddy."

World Farm Fair Opens in Italy

ROME, July 26 (AP) — Italy opened a huge international agricultural exposition on the outskirts of Rome today in buildings started by Mussolini for a 1942 world's fair. The modern, marble buildings, covering hundreds of acres, were finished recently.

"All the News That's Fit to Print"

The New York Times.

LATE CITY EDITION
Considerable cloudiness today.
Partly cloudy, cold tomorrow.
Temperature Range Today-Max., 40; Min., 35
Temperatures Yesterday-Max., 56.4; Min., 47.7
Full U. S. Weather Bureau Report, Page 19

VOL. CIII..No. 35,101. Entered as Second-Class Matter. Post Office, New York, N. Y. NEW YORK, TUESDAY, MARCH 2, 1954. Times Square, New York 36, N. Y. Telephone Lackawanna 4-1000 FIVE CENTS

FIVE CONGRESSMEN SHOT IN HOUSE BY 3 PUERTO RICAN NATIONALISTS; BULLETS SPRAY FROM GALLERY

Associated Press Wirephoto

SEIZED IN SHOOTING: Capitol police hold three Puerto Rican Nationalists after they fired from gallery seats into House chamber, wounding five Representatives. Prisoners, left to right, are Lolita Lebron, Rafael C. Miranda and Andres Cordero.

HIDDEN OWNERSHIP OF RACEWAY STOCK BARED AT HEARING

Former Legislator, Intimate of O'Dwyer, Erickson Kin and Ex-Convict Are Identified

HOLDINGS PUT AT MILLION

Moreland Inquiry Opens Public Sessions, Gets Details of Yonkers Track Purchase

By EMANUEL PERLMUTTER

Politicians and persons with underworld backgrounds or friendships were found yesterday to have been the hidden owners of close to a million dollars' worth of stock in several New York harness racing tracks.

These disclosures were made as the Moreland Act Commission opened public hearings here on the scandal-ridden raceways. The proceedings are being held in the Criminal Court Building, 100 Centre Street.

Among those who were shown to have struck it rich secretly on the trotting tracks were former Assemblyman Elmer J. Kellam of Hancock, N. Y.; Irving Sherman, political intimate of former Mayor William O'Dwyer and admitted friend of gangsters; Frank J. Erickson, son of the convicted gambler, and Samuel J. Stirratt, an ex-convict with a long police record.

Additional testimony was introduced indicating that loans from racketeers had helped the original incorporators of the Algam Corporation to purchase Yonkers Empire City Race Track—now Yonkers Raceway—for $2,400,000 in 1949.

Named a Racing Steward

Mr. Kellam, who served in the Assembly from Delaware County between 1943 and 1950, admitted on the witness stand that he had transferred 10,000 shares in Mid-State Raceway, near Syracuse, to a "dummy" owner after he had been appointed as a state racing steward last year.

The former Republican legislator said that he became the beneficiary of the stock, which was listed in the name of Marvin Wynkoop of Downesville, N. Y., and that he intended to sell it but had been unable to do so because of the pressure of his duties as a steward at Roosevelt Raceway, Westbury, L. I. He described the duties of a steward as "protecting the public, to see if the races are on the level."

"Did you think it was proper for a steward to own stock in a track?" Bruce Bromley, the commission chairman, asked him.

Mr. Kellam, a sandy-haired, florid-faced man, shook his head apologetically. "I don't think it's good judgment," he conceded. "But I never performed any duties at a track where I was a stockholder."

Still Owns Track Stock

The witness said he now owned 9,500 shares in the upstate track. He said he assumed he still held the job as racing steward.

At this point, Harness Racing Commissioner George P. Monaghan, sitting as a member of the Moreland Commission, interrupted to point out that stewards served for one year and that they had to be reappointed each racing season.

The testimony involving Irving Sherman, who was referred to as the contact man for Frank Costello during Mayor O'Dwyer's administration, was given by Sam Sherman, a raincoat manufacturer, of 30 West Fifty-fourth Street. He is not related to Irving Sherman.

Sam Sherman testified that although he was the listed owner of 22,500 shares of stock and $50,000 worth of bonds in the Algam Corporation, holding company for the Yonkers track, Irving Sherman actually owned 80 per cent of the investment.

In October, 1953, soon after the Moreland Commission was appointed, Algam purchased 20,000 shares from him, Mr. Sherman said. He said the purchase price was $296,000, a total of $30 a share. Of this sum, he testified, he gave $145,000 to Irving Sherman, the remainder of the latter's share being tied up in litigation.

In addition, Mr. Sherman said, the 2,500 shares of voting stock that he and his secret partner owned were sold at the same time for $75,000 to M. Duke Manacher, a stockholder in Algam. He said he gave $60,000 of this sum to Irving Sherman. The $50,000 worth of bonds

Continued on Page 12, Column 3

Jarka, Big Stevedore, Quits Port Under Fire

By A. H. RASKIN

The Jarka Corporation, one of the world's largest stevedoring enterprises, decided yesterday to stop operating in the Port of New York.

The company and its president, Frank W. Nolan, are awaiting trial in Special Sessions on charges of having paid out $119,859 in bribes to shipping executives for steering contracts to Jarka. The Waterfront Commission has been conducting an investigation to determine whether the company should be barred from doing business here.

The Jarka decision to withdraw its application for a stevedoring license was the highlight of another hectic day on the strife-swept waterfront. Other developments included:

¶A request by Charles T.

Continued on Page 11, Column 1

UNITY PLEA OPENS CARACAS MEETING

Hemisphere Accord Founded on Sovereignty and Equality Is Urged on Delegates

By SAM POPE BREWER

Special to The New York Times.

CARACAS, Venezuela, March 1—President Marcos Perez Jimenez of Venezuela opened the tenth Inter-American Conference today with a plea for closer unity among the American States on the basis of sovereignty and equality.

There is explosive material on the agenda in questions such as Communist infiltration in Latin America and rules for granting political asylum. Yet all indications today were that most of the delegates were in a conciliatory mood and that means would be sought to avoid heated clashes.

The elaborate security precautions taken for the conference seemed to grow in importance when word of the shooting in the United States Congress was received.

[Guatemala lost her first test at the parley on a procedural question, while at home President Jacobo Arbenz Guzman denied any Soviet intervention in the country's internal affairs.]

Speaking at the first session in the great modernistic assembly hall of University City, President Perez emphasized that the idea of continental unity had existed from the day the American nations won their independence.

"The existence of basic factors of a type common to all the continent, and the desire to obtain and preserve independence were the fundamental reasons for which there appeared almost simultaneously in the greater part of the peoples of America the idea of unity among them," he said.

He added, however, that "the unity of our peoples should be based on comprehension, the feeling of reciprocal assistance and mutual respect."

"We shall understand each

Continued on Page 9, Column 1

31 KILLED IN SUDAN IN NATIVES' CLASH AS NAGUIB ARRIVES

117 Hurt in Battle at Khartum Palace Between Tribesmen and Pro-Egyptian Group

Dispatch of The Times, London.

KHARTUM, the Sudan, March 1—The arrival in the Sudan today of Maj. Gen. Mohammed Naguib, Egyptian President, revived factional passions of this nascent state in a clash in which at least twenty-two persons were killed. [The Associated Press placed the toll at thirty-one.]

Among the dead were eight of the police force, including the British police commandant of Khartum, H. S. McGuigan, and the superintendent, Mustapha el Mahdi. One hundred seventeen were wounded, of whom thirty-two were seriously injured.

The factional struggle was of a primitive nature. The dead and wounded were seen to bear the marks of clubs and spears, not gunshot wounds.

[Meanwhile, a spokesman for the ruling junta in Egypt said in Cairo Monday that General Naguib owed his reinstatement as President to agitation begun by eight Communist army officers.]

The tragedy here was enacted outside the Governor General's palace, which stands on the site of the residency where Gen. Charles G. Gordon, then Governor General, died from the thrusts of tribesmen's spears during the historic Khartum siege in 1885. Inside the residency, General Naguib, Sir Robert Howe, Governor General, and Selwyn Lloyd, Minister of State of the British Foreign Office, were at lunch during today's events.

Parliament Opening Put Off

In view of the passions aroused by the rioting, the Governor General postponed a meeting of the Sudanese Parliament, scheduled for this afternoon, until March 10.

It seemed today as though the army of Mohammed Ahmed, the Mahdi, or Moslem leader who defeated General Gordon, were on the march again. The rioters massed outside the Khartum airport, turbaned and robed in shining white, with their hundreds of banners waving above the throng. They were supporters of the patron of the Sudanese independence movement, Sir Abdel Rahman el Mahdi, mainly Baggara tribesmen from the provinces who gathered to greet General Naguib with chanted slogans demanding independence for the Sudan.

"No Egypt, No Britain!" they cried as they surged up to Sudanese Defense Force troops who barred their way to the airport. This was no unkempt rabble; their banners were of trim red, green and black stripes, superimposed with a white spear cutting a white crescent.

General Naguib left his aircraft at Khartum airport at 10 A. M. He was accompanied by Maj. Salah Salem, Egyptian Minister of National Guidance and Minister of State for Sudanese Affairs. Sir Robert, Ismail el Azhary, Prime Minister of the

Continued on Page 2, Column 2

Nehru Decries U. S. Policy On Asia and the 'Cold War'

By ROBERT TRUMBULL

Special to The New York Times.

NEW DELHI, India, March 1—Prime Minister Jawaharlal Nehru scathingly condemned virtually the entire United States policy in Asia and in the "cold war" today.

His most outspoken speech delivered to the House of the People, the lower chamber of Parliament, was repeatedly interrupted by thunderous applause. He was given a prolonged ovation at its end.

Mr. Nehru was commenting on President Eisenhower's personal letter last week informing the Indian leader of Washington's intention to furnish military aid to Pakistan and simultaneously offering the same assistance to India.

Mr. Nehru scorned General Eisenhower's tender with the statement that "in making this suggestion, the President has done less than justice to us or to himself."

"If we object to military aid being given to Pakistan, we would be hypocrites and unprincipled opportunists to accept such aid ourselves," he added.

The Prime Minister told the cheering House that United States members of the United Nations cease-fire observer team in Kashmir should be removed. He said that "these American observers can no longer be treated by us as neutrals" in India's dispute with Pakistan over possession of the strategic northern state.

[At United Nations Headquarters a spokesman said no action would be taken pending an official communication from India. In Washington a State Department spokesman said India would have to complain to the United Nations if she wanted the United States members withdrawn.]

In his tersely formal reply to General Eisenhower, which he read out, Mr. Nehru coldly thanked the President for his "assurances," but dismissed them with this curt statement: "You are, however, aware of the views of my Government and our people in regard to this matter. We shall continue to pursue that policy."

The Indian note ignored the offer of arms.

Mr. Nehru, in his speech, took especially heated exception to the version of United States policy in Asia as quoted from testimony by Walter S. Robertson, Assistant Secretary of State, before a

Continued on Page 5, Column 2

M'LEOD AUTHORITY IS CUT BY DULLES

Friend of McCarthy Loses Personnel Duties, Keeps His Security Office

Special to The New York Times.

WASHINGTON, March 1—The Eisenhower Administration stripped Scott McLeod today of his authority over State Department personnel. It left him in charge of security matters.

This action, which was announced on the authority of John Foster Dulles, the Secretary of State, was widely interpreted as a thrust by the Administration at the McCarthy wing of the Republican party.

Mr. McLeod is a close friend of Senator Joseph R. McCarthy, Republican of Wisconsin. He went to the State Department last January from the office of Senator Styles Bridges, Republican of New Hampshire.

He had served as administrative assistant to Senator Bridges and at one time was an agent of the Federal Bureau of Investigation.

Mr. McLeod made five speeches for the Republican party in the recent Lincoln Week series of partisan addresses, and there were Democratic protests that he was improperly using his office. A Republican member of the Civil Service Commission, George Moore, held informally that such political activity was forbidden by the Hatch Act, which limits the partisanship of certain Federal officials and employes.

However, the counsel of the State Department ruled that Mr. McLeod was not under the Hatch Act.

Policies Criticized

On Jan. 16, five former United States Ambassadors charged in an open letter that State Department personnel and security policies might be "laying the foundations for a Foreign Service competent to serve a totalitarian government rather than the Government of the United States as we have heretofore known it."

They did not mention Mr. McLeod by name, but both the personnel and security policies were under his direction.

In a speech on Feb. 18 in Larchmont, N. Y., Mr. McLeod described as "scandalous libel" any suggestion that he was attempting to destroy the diplomatic service by spreading fear among its people.

The State Department an-

Continued on Page 15, Column 1

McCarthy, Dirksen Suggest Labor Camps for Army Reds

By W. H. LAWRENCE

Special to The New York Times.

WASHINGTON, March 1—Senators Joseph R. McCarthy and Everett M. Dirksen suggested today "disagreeable" labor camps for armed services personnel who were Communists or who invoked the Fifth Amendment when asked about Communist associations.

Their suggestion grew out of new disclosures by the Senate Permanent Subcommittee on Investigations of "contradictions" in the Army system of handling officers and enlisted men who are alleged Communists or admitted former Communists.

Senator McCarthy, Republican of Wisconsin, is chairman of the subcommittee, and Senator Dirksen, an Illinois Republican, is a member.

The subcommittee accepted an Army suggestion that it question Robert T. Stevens, Secretary of the Army, at a closed session on Thursday or next Monday. All advance indications on both sides were that it would be a "friendly" hearing and not a controversial showdown such as was threatened but called off last week.

With four Republicans and one Democrat present, the subcommittee today questioned in secret an Army private and a former private in considering a problem of fundamental importance to all the armed forces. Stated broadly, the subcommittee raised these questions:

¶Should admitted Communists,

Continued on Page 14, Column 2

U. S. Dismissed 355 In Subversive Cases

Special to The New York Times.

WASHINGTON, March 1—The Civil Service Commission reported today that 355 Federal employes whose personnel files contained some allegations of subversive associations had been separated from the Government payroll between May 28 and Dec. 31, 1953.

The report was the first overall breakdown provided by the Administration to Congress since the controversy over the 2,200 persons said by President Eisenhower to have been separated as "security risks."

Philip Young, commission chairman, said the "security" separation totaled 2,224, of whom 983 were dismissed and 1,241 resigned. These figures included 211 dismissals and 231 resigna-

Continued on Page 13, Column 2

WITNESS DESCRIBES SHOOTING, CAPTURE

Reporter Sees Firing in House —Struck on Cheek by Chip Torn Loose by Bullet

By C. P. TRUSSELL

Special to The New York Times.

WASHINGTON, March 1—Until the shooting in the House of Representatives today things were somewhat dull.

So dull, in fact, that a short time before members had been summoned by bells to the floor to listen to the issue at hand, whether they wanted to or not. It concerned admittance of Mexican farm laborers.

The quorum bell was answered by 243 members, most of whom were still on the floor when the shooting started in what is called the Ladies' Gallery.

As a police reporter many years ago I was irked by eyewitnesses who had heard shots only as "backfiring automobiles," "blowouts" and "firecrackers." But this time I too thought that firecrackers were going off, and I thought it was a Latin demonstration.

But only for a moment. I saw two men and a woman, in the second row of the Ladies Gallery, pumping at pistols. The two men appeared to be aiming at the desk of Representative Charles A. Halleck of Indiana, the Republican Floor Leader.

The woman had her pistol high,

Continued on Page 16, Column 7

EISENHOWER TARGET FOR FANATICS ALSO

Secret Service Men Detected Puerto Rican Plot Against President in November

Special to The New York Times.

WASHINGTON, March 1—Puerto Rican extremists have been conspiring to harm President Eisenhower if they got the opportunity, according to the Federal Secret Service.

Henry Cabot Lodge Jr., chief of the United States delegation to the United Nations, was put under twenty-four-hour guard last November for the same reason.

U. E. Baughman, chief of the Secret Service, was asked tonight about the reports of a conspiracy against the President.

"Three or four months ago," he replied, "the Secret Service obtained information indicating the Puerto Rican Nationalists were still possibly interested in harming the President in their fight for independence."

This statement from the head of the agency charged with protecting the President reflected the close watch that the Secret Service had kept on the Nationalist movement ever since two of its members tried to kill President Truman on Nov. 1, 1950.

Truman Case Still 'Open'

Although one assassin was killed in the gun battle in front of Blair House and Oscar Collazo, his companion, is serving a life sentence, the Secret Service still carries the attempted assassination of Mr. Truman as an "open case." It does this because it has not given up the possibility of rounding up the conspirators who directed the assassins.

Mr. Baughman said that the Secret Service had obtained information about designs on President Eisenhower last November. That coincided with the threats on Mr. Lodge. It was indicated tonight that there was an apparent link between the threats to Mr. Lodge and the designs on the President.

A police guard was put around

Continued on Page 17, Column 2

CAPITOL IN UPROAR

Woman, Accomplices Quickly Overpowered —High Bonds Set

By CLAYTON KNOWLES

Special to The New York Times.

WASHINGTON, March 1—Five members of the Congress of The United States were shot down on the floor of the House of Representatives today.

Their assailants, at least three Puerto Rican Nationalists, shouted for freedom of their homeland as they fired murderously although at random from a spectators' gallery just above the House floor. Possibly twenty-five shots were fired.

Bullets rained down from two German Lugers and other pistols of lesser caliber. They crashed through the table of the majority leader and chairs around it, and struck near the table of the Minority Leader beyond. The time was 2:32 P. M.

House members at first thought the sounds were those of firecrackers. But as their colleagues fell or took cover as they heard the slugs hit around them, all realized what was happening.

The wounded House members:

ALVIN M. BENTLEY, 35 years old, multimillionaire Michigan Republican, shot through lung, liver and intestine. Condition critical.

BEN F. JENSEN, 61, Republican of Iowa, shot in back. Condition serious.

CLIFFORD DAVIS, 56, Democrat of Tennessee, shot in the leg. Condition good.

GEORGE H. FALLON, 51, Democrat of Maryland, leg wound. Condition good.

KENNETH A. ROBERTS, 41, Democrat of Alabama, leg wound. Condition good.

Assailants Subdued

Within a matter of minutes, the episode, which threw the Capitol and most of official Washington into an uproar, was at an end. Gallery attendants, aided by spectators, Capitol police and even one House member, quickly overcame and disarmed the three gun wielders.

The three Puerto Ricans, all residents of New York, were booked at police headquarters on charges of assault with intent to kill. They gave their names and addresses as:

LOLITA LEBRON, 34, 315 West Ninety-fourth Street.

RAFAEL C. MIRANDA, 25, 120 South First Street, Brooklyn.

ANDRES CORDERO, or FIGUEROA, 29, of 108 East 103d Street.

A fourth Puerto Rican, also resident in New York, was arrested at a downtown bus station and booked on the same charge. He was booked as Irving Flores, 27, also of 108 East 103d Street. He was described by Police Chief Robert Murray as a fourth member of the shooting party who had fled the Capitol successfully. When arrested, Flores still had a .45 caliber pistol.

Later, United States Commissioner Cyril S. Lawrence ordered all four held under $100,000 bonds each. He put off a preliminary hearing until March 10 to give them time to get counsel. Five counts of assault with intent to

Continued on Page 16, Column 1

Atom Blast Opens Test in Pacific; No Hint of Hydrogen Plans Given

Special to The New York Times.

WASHINGTON, March 1—The Atomic Energy Commission today announced the first in a new series of test explosions at its Pacific proving ground in the Marshall Islands.

No further announcement was expected until the series ended. A forty-two word statement told as much of the story as the commission wanted the public to know at this stage. It read:

"[Rear Admiral] Lewis L. Strauss, chairman of the United States Atomic Energy Commission, announced today that Joint Task Force Seven has detonated an atomic device at the A. E. C.'s Pacific proving ground in the Marshall Islands. This detonation was the first in a series of tests."

The language of Admiral Strauss' statement did not make clear whether the "atomic device" was of the fission or thermonuclear (hydrogen) type. There have been unofficial indications, however, that a variety of hydrogen weapons or devices will be tested during the next several weeks.

The most powerful of these is expected to be an actual hydrogen bomb with perhaps twice the explosive power of the experimental device that obliterated an island of Eniwetok atoll on Nov. 1, 1952.

Representative W. Sterling Cole of upstate New York, the chairman of the Joint Congressional Committee on Atomic Energy, disclosed only two weeks ago that the first device had "completely obliterated" the island

Continued on Page 6, Column 5

Aftermath of Attack in Which Five House Members Were Shot by Puerto Rican Nationalists

Representative Clifford Davis of Tennessee is carried to ambulance after demonstration in which three Puerto Rican Nationalists, screaming hysterically for freedom for their homeland, fired pistol shots into the House chamber from the visitors' gallery. Services of the Washington police, hospitals and emergency units were mobilized to meet situation.

One of the assailants is obscured as guards subdue him in a corridor after his attempt to reload pistol. Holding him down are Doorkeepers Charles Santoro, left, and Mathew Fardella, right, and a Capitol policeman. Altogether, between 20 and 25 shots were fired.

Representative Kenneth A. Roberts of Alabama is carried on stretcher down the steps of the Capitol. Some members of the House, taken completely unaware, thought someone had set off a string of firecrackers until they saw their colleagues falling among them. In the fascination of their horror, visitors and Representatives, even after they had thrown themselves to the floor, watched the galleries as the demonstrators were firing their shots.

Associated Press Wirephotos

Patrolman Jack Brunner of the Capitol police shows correspondents the Puerto Rican flag taken from Mrs. Lolita Lebron, one of the demonstrators. After she had emptied her pistol, Mrs. Lebron cried, "Viva Puerto Rico!" and waved the flag, though she never did manage to unfurl it fully.

FIVE CONGRESSMEN SHOT IN CAPITOL

Continued From Page 1

kill were brought against each of the four, one count for each of the legislators wounded.

Chief Murray reported tonight that all, except Flores, had confessed to the shootings. Edgar E. Scott, deputy chief of detectives, said that Flores, though identified by Mrs. Lebron as one of the party, would not admit being present at the scene.

At police headquarters Mrs. Lebron said none of the four had intended to kill anyone.

She said the shooting date had been picked to coincide with the opening of the Inter-American Conference at Caracas.

Three other Puerto Ricans, all residents of Florida, were picked up as the police threw a dragnet around the whole Capitol area. They were not booked immediately and appeared to have no connection with the shooting.

Mrs. Lebron was identified as an associate of the wife of one of the Puerto Rican Nationalists who made an attempt on the life of President Truman outside Blair House on Nov. 1, 1950.

A note found in her purse by the police read:

"Before God and the world my blood claims for the independence of Puerto Rico. My life I give for the freedom of my country. This is a cry for victory in our struggle for independence. Which for more than a half century has tried to conquer that land that belongs to Puerto Rico.

"I state that the United States of America are betraying the sacred principles of mankinf in their continuous subjugation of my country, violating their rights to be a free nation and a free people in their barbarous torture of our apostle of independence, Don Pedro Albizu Campos."

Across the back of the note was scrawled "I take responsible for all."

Strike Without Warning

The two men who stormed Blair House steps seeking to kill President Truman also were followers of Albizu Campos. Today as then, there was no warning as the assailants struck.

The House members—at least 243 of them in the chamber at the time—were set up like sitting ducks for their assailants. The Puerto Ricans literally sprayed the House floor with their fire.

As they shot, they screamed: "Viva Puerto Rico."

Most of the members said later that they thought a string of firecrackers had been set off in the gallery when the guns began to fire. It was only as they saw their colleagues falling about them that they realized what was going on.

"Hit the deck," shouted Representative James E. Van Zandt, Republican of Pennsylvania. He then dashed from the chamber and up one flight to the gallery to help disarm one of the gunmen.

Similar outcries went up from all over the House floor and from the galleries. Piercing the confusion were the screams of the Puerto Rican woman: "Viva Puerto Rico!" She emptied the chambers of a big Luger pistol, holding it in her two hands, and waving it wildly.

Then, she threw down the pistol and whipped out a Puerto Rican flag, which she waved but never did manage to unfurl fully. As she screamed, her companions trained their weapons on the House floor.

Five of the bullets hit Congressmen. Four shots shattered the wood paneling behind the Democrats. Four more pierced or splintered chairs. Two others struck the big mahogany table behind which sat Majority Leader Charles A. Halleck of Indiana and Leslie C. Arends of Illinois, the Republican whip.

A splinter from the desk hit Mr. Arends in the face, piercing the left eyelid. It was only then that he realized that it was "business, not a misguided prank," as he said later.

Jensen Keeps His Feet

Beside the majority table, Mr. Bentley keeled over. Representative Jensen, standing near the door, was struck, but kept his feet to stagger to the cloakroom where he collapsed.

Across the aisle, a bullet pierced a chair and lodged in Representative Roberts' leg. Other bullets got Mr. Davis and Mr. Fallon in their legs.

After an exploratory operation at Casualty Hospital about five hours after the shooting, Mr. Bentley tonight was given a "50-50 chance" to live by the surgeon who performed the operation.

Dr. Joseph R. Young, Chief of Staff at Casualty Hospital, said there would be a critical period of "about seventy-two hours," and disclosed that the operation had shown "extensive visceral damage," including damage to the liver.

He reported that the bullet had apparently torn through the liver with "explosive force," so that there was danger of infection. He also described the danger of peritonitis as "very great."

As realization of what was happening spread, members threw themselves to the floor or behind chairs. Others seemed frozen as they looked up to watch the Puerto Ricans shooting.

Representative Pat Hillings, Republican of California, a veteran of fighting in the South Pacific, said:

"I'd been shot at before but never saw who was firing at me."

Speaker Joseph W. Martin Jr. of Massachusetts, presiding at the time, whirled behind a marble pillar for protection. He later said, "I think the shot that got Jensen was meant for me."

Two Dozen Shots Fired

"I think I got hit before I heard the shooting," said Mr. Fallon at the hospital tonight. His reaction was typical. While the force of the shot threw him to the floor, Mr. Fallon did not actually realize he had been shot until he noticed blood on his hip.

Even when some saw the guns smoking, their first reaction was that demonstrators were shooting blank cartridges.

Representative Louis P. Graham, a Pennsylvania Republican, stood watching as did many others on the floor, participating in a vote when the bullets began to rain down.

"Get down, you damn fool! Those are bullets," shouted Representative Benjamin James, a Republican colleague from Pennsylvania.

It was over in a matter of seconds. A full count on the number of shots fired has yet to be announced but the number probably was somewhere between twenty and twenty-five. Two shots, apparently fired by the woman, buried themselves in the House ceiling.

Immediately after the firing ceased, the paralysis that gripped the members and the galleries ended.

There was a rush to the Visitors' Gallery adjacent to the press section, where the Puerto Ricans were fighting their way toward the exit, smoking pistols still in hand.

First out was the woman, still clutching the Puerto Rican flag. She was quickly collared. Then came one of her male companions who was hit from at least four quarters and knocked to the ground.

In the group that struck him down was Boyd Crawford, clerk of the House Foreign Affairs Committee. Mr. Crawford, an excellent pistol shot himself, thrust his finger under the trigger guard of the gun the Puerto Rican carried. It kept him from shooting.

"Then we sat on him until the police arrived," said the 190-pound clerk.

Helping disarm this gunman was Representative Van Zandt, a veteran of both World Wars and former national chairman of the Veterans of Foreign Wars. Also in on the team play was Frank Wise, a suburbanite recuperating from illness and visiting in the gallery to get some of the relaxation his doctor had ordered.

"I didn't know whether to take cover or do my duty," he said. "I closed with him and grabbed his arm."

Another spectator, whose identity was undisclosed, threw a headlock around a second gunman. As they wrestled out the door, the spectator cried: "Look out! He's got a gun."

Doorman Wades In

Closing in to help was another group of willing hands, including those of William Belcher, a doorman, who suffered a heart attack afterward and was hospitalized.

The final subduing was administered by a 71-year-old Capitol policeman. Despite his years, Patrolman A. S. (Buck) Rodgers, a former Texas farmer, grabbed the Puerto Rican by the coat collar and brought his own hand down sharply edgewise on the wrist of his victim's gun hand.

A big Luger clattered to the tile floor, close by the other Puerto Rican, head bleeding and still lying on the floor with Mr. Crawford sitting on him.

The actual arrests were made by Capt. Carl Schramp, a city detective heading the city police detail on the House side of the Capitol.

On the floor, meanwhile, hasty first aid was being administered. Representatives A. L. Miller of Nebraska and Walter H. Judd of Minnesota, both medical doctors, gave orders for emergency care of the wounded. Both gave particular attention to Mr. Bentley, who bled profusely.

Dr. Judd, a former medical missionary in China, diagnosed Mr. Bentley's condition as serious.

Representative Percy Priest, sitting beside Mr. Roberts, whipped off his own necktie for use as a tourniquet.

Out in the cloakroom, Mr. Jensen gritted through clenched teeth: "They got me, they got me. Did they hit me in the spine?" Anxious members sought to reassure him.

Many of those in the gallery thought the Puerto Ricans were shouting "Viva Mexico" but some later confessed that they probably made this out of the jumble of Spanish because of the fact that the "wetback bill," governing the flow of Mexican farm labor to the United States, was the business before the House.

At 2:27, shortly before the shooting began, a member had demanded a quorum count. Speaker Martin stated there were 243 members present.

With the quorum established, the resolution before the House for a rule, officially bringing the bill to the floor, was called up for a vote. It appeared to pass on a voice vote but the Democrats demanded a division.

The Speaker asked for all those supporting the rule to rise. He went through his count and just was about to call for the "nays" when the shooting began. He later said he had counted 168 members for the rule.

After the confusion died down somewhat, Mr. Martin returned to the chair, ordered the House floor cleared of nonmembers and proceeded, upon motion, to adjourn the House.

President Eisenhower, informed of the shootings, put through a quick call to Mr. Martin to offer any help he could. Later in the evening, the White House canceled the Congressional reception scheduled for tomorrow night.

Security provisions at the Capitol, White House, Interior and Justice departments were tightened immediately. The Capitol was cleared as both houses quickly quit for the day. Admission to the galleries henceforth will be by card only.

Thousands of persons rushed to the Capitol Plaza within minutes of the shooting. Not since the British burned the Capitol in August, 1814, had there been such an incident there.

Squad cars of the Metropolitan police force sped to join the Capitol police, who guard the building day and night. The entire area was barricaded in fifteen minutes, so quickly that 2,000 persons were caught inside the cordon. Several news photographers were whacked and a few received painful bruises when the police started to swing clubs to disperse the cameramen.

The Plaza, a broad space on the east side of the Capitol, is at the rear of the building. However, most persons enter the national legislative halls there and it has been the scene of inaugurations and historic visits for years.

GUNPLAY INCIDENTS RARE IN THE CAPITOL

Special to The New York Times.

WASHINGTON, March 1—The shooting at the Capitol today has no recent parallel.

A check of Congressional records showed that no Senator or Representative had been killed on the floor since the last century.

On Dec. 13, 1932, however, Representative Melvin J. Maas, Republican of Minnesota, earned a Carnegie Medal for disarming a young man who had demanded at gunpoint the right to address the House of Representatives for twenty minutes.

As the youth leaned over the rail waving a revolver, the gallery and the floor of the House emptied rapidly. The late Fiorello H. LaGuardia, then a Representative and later Mayor of New York, sprinted from the floor to the gallery and moved in behind the youth in the hope of grabbing him.

However, Representative Maas talked the young man into dropping his revolver and Mr. Maas, a former Marine, caught it.

On Feb. 28, 1890, the House was horrified by a shooting that ended in the death of William Preston Taulbee, a former Democratic Representative from Kentucky. Mr. Taulbee died eleven days after he was shot on a staircase in the Capitol by Charles E. Mincaid, a newspaper man.

Senator John W. Bricker, Republican of Ohio, escaped an assassin's bullet in the Senate subway July 12, 1947. His assailant was William L. Kaiser, a former Capitol policeman who had lost money in an Ohio building venture.

EYEWITNESS TELLS OF HOUSE SHOOTING

Continued From Page 1

working it with both hands, and was apparently shooting at the ceiling or at areas along gallery rails. When she had emptied it, she handed it to a companion, apparently for reloading, and waved a Puerto Rican flag, shrieking "freedom for my country."

My next thought was that they were shooting blanks. But a chip from the ceiling or a press gallery rail struck my cheek—and I knew they were not firing blanks.

A glance at the floor, at which the bullets had poured at almost machine-gun rapidity, showed most members feeling themselves to see if they had been hit. The number who threw themselves to the floor was astonishingly small. But several could not get up and other House members hovered over them.

A bullet crashed through Representative Halleck's desk, missing him by less than a foot. Another ricochetted about three feet from him.

The bullets aimed higher reached the Democratic side, hitting members there. One passed through a chair close to the Minority Leader, Representative John W. McCormack of Massachusetts.

In the Ladies' Gallery the attackers sought to escape. One of the men apparently was reloading his automatic pistol. It developed later that his pistol had jammed. He ran up a stairway to an exit.

The woman, crying out about "freedom." again waved her flag, then threw it into the gallery row in front of her.

I ran to Door No. 11. Already the woman stood there, with her arms pinned to her sides. She still cried shrilly for "freedom."

Outside the gallery door a man was prone, held down by so many persons that news photographers had to fight their way through to get a picture. A second man had been pinned against a wall.

The man on the floor still had a pistol in his hand and was defying attempts to make him let go.

Finally Representative James E. Van Zandt, Republican of Pennsylvania, a Naval Reserve captain with a long South Pacific war record, and others broke the man's hold on the pistol. Mr. Van Zandt had run to the gallery when the firing started and had helped capture the gunmen.

Boyd Crawford, staff administrator of the House Foreign Affairs Committee, was among those who helped disarm one of the assailants.

The man on the floor was picked up and hauled to a back elevator. More bullets were found in his overcoat pockets. As the crowd followed, one man talked of lynching.

Frank Wise, a Washington suburbanite, said he was sitting in the gallery about five feet from the Puerto Rican group when the shooting started.

Mr. Wise said he jumped at one man who was firing and pinned his arms to his side after the first fusillade. Others jumped up to help. Then, Mr. Wise said, he saw another still shooting and rushed him, managing to hold him until others took part.

W. S. Elgin of Clifton, Va., the doorkeeper at No. 11, was upset over the easy admittance of the Puerto Rican group to his gallery. No. 11 is one of two galleries in the House that require no cards for admission. The other is No. 1, almost directly across the chamber.

It was Mr. Elgin's impression that there were only three members of the party, although numerous eyewitness accounts indicated that there might have been more.

The group of three, two men and a woman, Mr. Elgin said, were neat in appearance, spoke English well and asked politely whether they could enter the gallery.

Mr. Elgin said he asked whether they had cameras. They said they did not, and they went in.

Puerto Rican Accused Of Threat to President

HARTFORD, March 1 (AP)—A 24-year-old Puerto Rican was held for a Federal grand jury tonight on a charge of threatening to kill President Eisenhower.

Police Capt. Joseph P. MacDonald said Pedro Orozco made repeated threats today that he was "going to kill the President" while objecting to being finger-printed in connection with a nonsupport charge.

Orozco was held for a Federal grand jury tomorrow in New Haven. Bail was set at $15,000.

At the hearing Orozco denied he made the threats.

"I never carried a gun or a pistol. I no kill anyone," he testified.

The arrest occurred about the same time that gunfire from three Puerto Ricans wounded five Representatives in the House of Representatives in Washington.

ISLAND VISIT CANCELED

McKay and Benson Advised Not to Go to Puerto Rico

WASHINGTON, March 1 (AP)—Ezra Taft Benson, secretary of Agriculture, and Douglas McKay, Secretary of the Interior, on police advice, canceled a visit to Puerto Rico tomorrow as a result of the wounding of five House members here today.

The two Cabinet officers were told that their arrival on the island might set off demonstrations, an Interior Department official said.

Secretaries Benson and McKay had planned to stop in Puerto Rico on a flight to the Virgin Islands for a meeting of the Virgin Islands Corporation, of which they are members. The Interior official said that they would leave tomorrow, but with a changed itinerary.

The Five Representatives Who Were Wounded in House Shooting Yesterday

Alvin M. Bentley
Republican of Michigan

Clifford Davis
Democrat of Tennessee

Ben F. Jensen
Republican of Iowa

Kenneth A. Roberts
Democrat of Alabama

George H. Fallon
Democrat of Maryland

Associated Press

"All the News That's Fit to Print"

The New York Times.

LATE CITY EDITION

Fair and cool today. Mostly sunny, continued cool tomorrow.

Temperature Range Today-Max., 68; Min., 52

Temperature Yesterday—Max., 69; Min., 61

Full U. S. Weather Bureau Report, Page 51

VOL. CIII... No. 35,178. Entered as Second-Class Matter. Post Office, New York, N. Y. NEW YORK, TUESDAY, MAY 18, 1954. Times Square, New York 36, N. Y. Telephone LAckawanna 4-1000 FIVE CENTS

HIGH COURT BANS SCHOOL SEGREGATION; 9-TO-0 DECISION GRANTS TIME TO COMPLY

McCarthy Hearing Off a Week as Eisenhower Bars Report

SENATOR IS IRATE

President Orders Aides Not to Disclose Details of Top-Level Meeting

President's letter and excerpts from transcript, Pages 24, 25, 26.

By W. H. LAWRENCE

Special to The New York Times.

WASHINGTON, May 17—A secrecy directive by President Eisenhower resulted today in an abrupt recess for at least a week of the Senate's Army-McCarthy hearings.

Democratic and Republican Senators, some publicly and some privately, predicted that the investigation might never resume in earnest. However, there were other Senators who insisted that the investigation would go on to completion.

The recess was voted after Herbert Brownell Jr., the Attorney General, disclosed formally that criminal prosecutions might be instituted against those involved in the "preparation and dissemination" of an altered, condensed but still confidential Federal Bureau of Investigation report. This was offered in evidence last week by Senator Joseph R. McCarthy, Republican of Wisconsin.

Republicans outvoted Democrats 4 to 3 on the Senate Permanent Subcommittee of Investigation to recess the hearings until 10 o'clock next Monday morning. They acted amid charges and denials that the way was being prepared for a "whitewash."

Constitutional Division Cited

President Eisenhower cited the constitutional separation of powers between the Executive and Legislative branches in directing that details and conversations at a "high level" Administration meeting on Jan. 21 must be withheld from the committee.

Testimony already has been given that top White House, Justice and Defense officials had made plans at that conference to deal with Senator McCarthy.

The Presidential order served effectively to seal the lips of John G. Adams, the Army's regular counselor, about what Sherman Adams, the chief Presidential assistant, said to him in advising that a written report be prepared on how Senator McCarthy and his chief counsel, Roy M. Cohn, persistenly sought preferential treatment for Pvt. G. David Schine.

Before his induction, Mr. Schine was an unpaid consultant to the McCarthy subcommittee, the same group that is now conducting the hearings under the temporary chairmanship of Senator Karl E. Mundt, Republican of South Dakota.

Senator McCarthy angrily denounced today's Eisenhower order as "an Iron Curtain." His ire was shared, but in more restrained terms, by all the Republican and Democratic members of the investigating committee.

The week's postponement of

Continued on Page 24, Column 1

Communist Arms Unloaded in Guatemala By Vessel From Polish Port, U. S. Learns

State Department Views News Gravely Because of Red Infiltration

Special to The New York Times.

WASHINGTON, May 17—The State Department said today that it had reliable information that "an important shipment of arms" had been sent from Communist-controlled territory to Guatemala.

It said the arms, now being unloaded at Puerto Barrios, Guatemala, had been shipped from Stettin, a former German Baltic seaport, which has been occupied by Communist Poland since World War II. The Guatemalan regime has been frequently accused of being influenced by Communists.

"Because of the origin of these arms, the point of their embarkation, their destination and the quantity of arms involved, the Department of State considers that this is a development of gravity," the announcement said.

A freighter arrived at Puerto

Gulf of Mexico · MILES 0 150 · Caribbean Sea · MEXICO · BRITISH HONDURAS · GUATEMALA · Puerto Barrios · Puerto Cortes · DISPUTED AREA · HONDURAS · Guatemala · Pacific Ocean · EL SALVADOR · NICAR.

The New York Times May 18, 1954

Site of arms arrival (cross)

Embassy Says Nation of Central America May Buy Munitions Anywhere

Barrios last Saturday, the State Department reported, carrying a large shipment of armament consigned to the Guatemalan Government.

The State Department did not divulge the exact quantity of the arms, their nature or where they had been manufactured.

Reliable sources told The New York Times, however, that ten freight car loads of goods listed in the manifest as "hardware" had been unloaded from this ship and sent to the city of Guatemala since Sunday. Guatemala is 150 miles from Puerto Barrios. The

Continued on Page 10, Column 5

REACTION OF SOUTH

'Breathing Spell' for Adjustment Tempers Region's Feelings

By JOHN N. POPHAM

Special to The New York Times.

CHATTANOOGA, Tenn., May 17—The South's reaction to the Supreme Court's decision outlawing racial segregation in public schools appeared to be tempered considerably today.

The time lag allowed for carrying out the required transitions seemed to be the major factor in that reaction.

Southern leaders of both races in political, educational and community service fields expressed comment that covered a wide range. Some spoke bitter words that verged on defiance. Others ranged from sharp disagreement to predictions of peaceful and successful adjustment in accord with the ruling.

But underneath the surface of much of the comment, it was evident that many Southerners recognized that the decision had laid down the legal principle rejecting segregation in public education facilities.

They also noted that it had left open a challenge to the region to join in working out a program of necessary changes in the present bi-racial school systems.

Three of the most illustrative viewpoints were those expressed by Govs. James F. Byrnes of South Carolina and Herman Talmadge of Georgia, and Harold Fleming, a spokesman for the Southern Regional Council, the most effective interracial organization in the South.

Byrnes Sees Reversal

Governor Byrnes, who has vigorously defended the doctrine of separate but equal facilities in education, said that he was "shocked to learn that the court has reversed itself" with regard to past rulings on that doctrine.

However, Governor Byrnes, a former Associate Justice of the Supreme Court, noted that the tribunal had not yet delivered its final decree setting forth the time and terms for ending segregation in the schools.

Pointing out that South Carolina, a party in the litigation before the court, had until October to present arguments on how the Supreme Court should order the implementation of the decision, Governor Byrnes declared "I urge all of our people, white and colored, to exercise restraint and preserve order."

Governor Talmadge repeatedly has vowed there "will never be mixed schools while I am Governor" and has warned that school integration would lead to "blood-

Continued on Page 20, Column 1

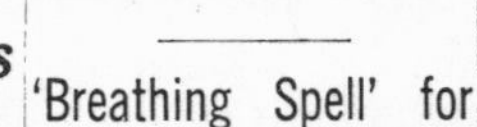

Associated Press Wirephoto

LEADERS IN SEGREGATION FIGHT: Lawyers who led battle before U. S. Supreme Court for abolition of segregation in public schools congratulate one another as they leave court after announcement of decision. Left to right: George E. C. Hayes, Thurgood Marshall and James M. Nabrit.

1896 RULING UPSET

'Separate but Equal' Doctrine Held Out of Place in Education

Text of Supreme Court decision is printed on Page 15.

By LUTHER A. HUSTON

Special to The New York Times.

WASHINGTON, May 17—The Supreme Court unanimously outlawed today racial segregation in public schools.

Chief Justice Earl Warren read two opinions that put the stamp of unconstitutionality on school systems in twenty-one states and the District of Columbia where segregation is permissive or mandatory.

The court, taking cognizance of the problems involved in the integration of the school systems concerned, put over until the next term, beginning in October, the formulation of decrees to effectuate its 9-to-0 decision.

The opinions set aside the "separate but equal" doctrine laid down by the Supreme Court in 1896.

"In the field of public education," Chief Justice Warren said, "the doctrine of 'separate but equal' has no place. Separate educational facilities are inherently unequal."

He stated the question and supplied the answer as follows:

"We come then to the question presented: Does segregation of children in public schools solely on the basis of race, even though physical facilities and other 'tangible' factors may be equal, deprive the children of the minority group of equal educational opportunities? We believe that it does."

States Stressed Rights

The court's opinion does not apply to private schools. It is directed entirely at public schools. It does not affect the "separate but equal doctrine" as applied on railroads and other public carriers entirely within states that have such restrictions.

The principal ruling of the court was in four cases involving state laws. The states' right to operate separated schools had been argued before the court on two occasions by representatives of South Carolina, Virginia, Kansas and Delaware.

In these cases, consolidated in one opinion, the high court held that school segregation deprived Negroes of "the equal protection of the laws guaranteed by the Fourteenth Amendment."

The other opinion involved the District of Columbia. Here schools have been segregated since Civil War days under laws passed by Congress.

"In view of our decision that the Constitution prohibits the states from maintaining racially segregated public schools," the Chief Justice said, "it would be unthinkable that the same Constitution would impose a lesser duty on the Federal Government.

"We hold that racial segregation in the public schools of the District of Columbia is a denial

Continued on Page 14, Column 6

SOVIET BIDS VIENNA CEASE 'INTRIGUES'

Envoy Warns Austrian Chief on Inciting East Zone—Raab Denies Charges

By JOHN MacCORMAC

Special to The New York Times.

VIENNA, May 17—The Soviet Union warned Austria today to put an end to "hostile and subversive intrigues" against the Soviet occupation forces, or Soviet authorities would do it themselves.

Ivan I. Ilyichev, Soviet High Commissioner, reverted to a practice of early post-war days by summoning Chancellor Julius Raab and Vice Chancellor Adolf Schaerf to give them this warning. The Chancellor denied the Soviet charges.

Mr. Ilyichev said the Austrian Government had been guilty of staging actions hostile to the Soviet while the Austrian press had published daily slanderous and inciting announcements about the Soviet Union and Soviet occupation troops.

The cessation of Soviet control over the movement of freight, said the High Commissioner, was abused to smuggle militarist literature and provocative incitements into the Soviet zone with the connivance of the Austrian Minister of Interior.

When Soviet authorities ordered the removal of anti-Soviet placards in their zone, the minister instructed his subordinates to disregard the order and the Government approved his action, said Mr. Ilyichev.

He added that the Government, and particularly the Minister of Interior, had tolerated militarist propaganda by former soldiers' organizations and dissemination of propaganda for another Anschluss (union) with Germany.

The High Commissioner reminded the Government leaders that since Austria had not ob-

Continued on Page 9, Column 3

City Colleges' Board Can't Pick Chairman

The Board of Higher Education was unable to elect a chairman at its annual meeting last night at Hunter College.

A spokesman said it was the first time "within memory of board officials" that such a situation had occurred.

Nineteen of the twenty-one members of the board, which governs the four municipal colleges, attended.

Two members nominated for the one-year-term were unable to attain the required majority of eleven votes. They were Joseph B. Cavallaro, who was up for re-election as chairman, and Dr. Harry J. Carman, who was restored to the board on March 2 by Mayor Wagner.

The election was laid over until June 15.

INDO-CHINA PARLEY WEIGHS TWO PLANS

French and Rebel Peace Bids Will Be Studied Jointly as a Basis for Settlement

By THOMAS J. HAMILTON

Special to The New York Times.

GENEVA, May 17—The Far East conference decided today to take up French and Vietminh proposals jointly as a basis for settlement of the war in Indo-China.

The secret session, which lasted three and a half hours, was generally recognized as the opening round in what may turn out to be a long process of negotiation. Another secret meeting will be held tomorrow.

Western delegates felt that Vyacheslav M. Molotov, Soviet Foreign Minister, was continuing to give the impression that in the end he might throw Moscow's influence on the side of an agreed settlement.

However, the West failed to obtain answers to the two fundamental questions that are expected to determine whether the negotiations here will have any chance of success: Will the Communists agree to a separate settlement for Laos and Cambodia, and will they agree to an armistice in Vietnam without at the same time requiring a political settlement?

The conference will address itself tomorrow to the issue of Laos and Cambodia. The two Indo-Chinese states are relatively free from Communist infiltration, and their leaders contend, with the support of the French, that the only thing that needs to be done is the withdrawal of the Communists.

The Laos-Cambodia and Vietnam issues were discussed inconclusively today after the delegates had devoted the first part of their meeting to the intricate dispute over evacuation of French Union wounded from Dienbienphu, seized by the Communist-

Continued on Page 2, Column 2

2 TAX PROJECTS DIE IN ESTIMATE BOARD

Beer Levy and More Parking Collections Killed—Payroll Impost Still Weighed

By CHARLES G. BENNETT

Two possible new revenue sources were definitely eliminated yesterday by the Board of Estimate in executive session. They were the proposed 1-cent-a-glass tax on beer and the suggestion to extend metered parking into hours now "free."

In a three-hour City Hall parley the board failed once more to decide on a new impost or imposts to balance the 1954-55 budget of $1,639,438,325. Mayor Wagner said after the meeting that the highly controversial 3 per cent sales tax on commercial services was "still one of the taxes at the top of the list."

Saying he felt the Board of Estimate was close to a decision on the knotty tax question, the Mayor added that "there's no decision to discard any tax" except the two mentioned above, and that at the same time "no tax is inevitable."

The board will wrestle with the tax question again in executive session on Thursday at 2:30 P. M. The Mayor said the City Council, which is holding up a bill to impose the sales tax extension, would be invited to send a delegation to the Thursday session.

Mr. Wagner asserted that he would like to see the Board of Estimate decide the tax question

Continued on Page 32, Column 5

MORETTIS' LAWYER MUST BARE TALKS

Jersey Court Orders Counsel to Racketeers in Bergen to Divulge Data to Grand Jury

By GEORGE CABLE WRIGHT

Special to The New York Times.

TRENTON, May 17—The New Jersey Supreme Court today ordered a lawyer who once had represented top Bergen County racketeers to divulge to a grand jury the substance of confidential talks with those clients.

The four-to-three decision reversed the rulings of two lower courts. Involved was the refusal more than a year ago of John E. Selser, Hackensack attorney, to answer four questions put to him by the Bergen County grand jury.

Mr. Selser told the jury that one of his clients, Willie Moretti, slain gambler, had given him the names of persons connected with Walter G. Winne who had received protection money from syndicate gamblers. Mr. Winne, superseded prosecutor of Bergen County, was acquitted last week of nonfeasance in office.

But the attorney balked when asked to reveal these and the names of other persons who, his clients alleged, had been paid protection money or who had received political contributions on the state and county level. He pleaded that his lips were sealed by the duty of "nondisclosure of confidential communications between client and attorney."

Represented Morettis, Others

Mr. Selser had represented Moretti, who was murdered in Cliffside Park in October, 1951, and his brother, the late Salvatore Moretti, for many years. He also was the attorney of record for Joe Adonis, Arthur Longano and James (Piggy) Lynch. The last four were among five men convicted and sent to prison in May, 1952, as the leaders of the Bergen gambling syndicate.

Mr. Selser appeared before the grand jury in February, 1953. The present court action was brought by the state after his refusal to answer the above questions on that occasion and two other questions. The latter pertained to testimony by John J. Dickerson, former Republican state chairman, before the same grand jury.

Mr. Dickerson had testified that Adonis and the two Morettis visited his home in November, 1950, and that Willie told him then that $225,000 in protection money had been paid to Harold

Continued on Page 36, Column 2

RULING TO FIGURE IN '54 CAMPAIGN

Decision Tied to Eisenhower—Russell Leads Southerners in Criticism of Court

By WILLIAM S. WHITE

Special to The New York Times.

WASHINGTON, May 17—Congress as a whole grappled gingerly today with the profound political implications of the Supreme Court's anti-segregation decision.

It became clear at once—and by both parties was accepted in private as inevitable—that the court's action would figure importantly in the coming Congressional election campaigns.

Publicly, however, the Republicans and the non-Southern Democrats, on the whole maintained silence. The Southerners, all angry or sorrowing in one degree or another, were quickly articulate and split among themselves into at least three factions.

¶One Southern group, by all the indications not a large one, was openly defiant of the court, as typified by the comment of Senator James O. Eastland of Mississippi.

"The South," Mr. Eastland said, "will not abide by nor obey this legislative decision by a political court."

¶A second Southern group, while not openly challenging the court, began to threaten efforts to force an alteration of its view, as illustrated by the comment of

Continued on Page 20, Column 2

Churchill Asks Negotiated Peace With Guarantees for Indo-China

By DREW MIDDLETON

Special to The New York Times.

LONDON, May 17—Britain will seek effective international guarantees for any peace settlement in Indo-China, Prime Minister Churchill declared today.

Negotiation of an "acceptable" settlement at the Geneva conference remains the immediate task of the British Government, Sir Winston emphasized in a statement to the House of Commons.

Until the outcome of that conference is known, he added, "final decisions" cannot be taken by the Government about the establishment of a collective defense system in Southeast Asia and the Western Pacific.

Peace by negotiation emerged from Sir Winston's cautious statement as the only policy that the Cabinet was ready to apply to the problem of Indo-China. Observers were struck by the fact that, aside from the Prime Minister's reference to the necessity of backing a settlement there with guarantees, the British position was substantially the same as when the Geneva conference began.

[Indonesia is considering asking India and Burma to join her in a nonaggression treaty with Communist China as a means of offsetting United States plans for a Southeast Asian alliance.]

Sir Winston's adherence to negotiation is acceptable to both major parties in the Commons.

Continued on Page 4, Column 3

Costello Is Sentenced to 5 Years, Fined $30,000 in U. S. Tax Case

By EDWARD RANZAL

Frank Costello was sentenced yesterday by Federal Judge John F. X. McGohey to five years in jail and fined $30,000 for income tax evasion.

The dapper, 61-year-old gambler was remanded immediately. Later Judge Harold R. Medina in the United States Court of Appeals refused to set bail pending appeal. Costello, who listened to the sentencing in icy-calm manner, was taken to the Federal House of Detention, 427 West Street.

Besides the jail sentence and the fines, Judge McGohey also assessed Costello for court costs. Lloyd F. MacMahon, chief assistant United States Attorney, said the costs would be about $5,000, only a fraction of what it cost the Government in its investigation, which began in earnest in 1952.

Costello was convicted Thursday night by a Federal court jury of five women and seven men of three counts of a four-count indictment. They found the gambler guilty of evading a total of $51,095 in taxes from 1947 through 1949.

In 1947 Costello evaded $22,563; in 1948, $13,786, and in 1949, $14,746. He was acquitted of the charge of evading taxes in 1946. Costello's attorney, Leo C. Fennelly, told Judge McGohey that the acquittal on this count meant that the gambler was entitled to a refund for that year.

Before the sentencing Mr. MacMahon said that for years Costello had schemed to cheat the Government out of taxes. He added that the gambler had concealed at least $140,000 of his income from 1947 through 1949, more than half his income.

Mr. MacMahon contended that Costello, by devious means, had concealed the receipt of his income as well as the source by using cash in every transaction where it was possible.

Evidence at the six-week trial, the prosecutor said, showed that from 1937 through 1945 Costello deliberately underestimated his income by at least $202,000. The statute of limitations, he added, bars prosecution for the earlier tax evasions.

"Costello has spent a lifetime making money on the shady side

Continued on Page 36, Column 4

'Voice' Speaks in 34 Languages To Flash Court Ruling to World

Within an hour after the Supreme Court decision on school segregation yesterday afternoon, the Voice of America sent a news broadcast by shortwave to Eastern Europe.

The decision came in time for the regularly scheduled "World-wide English Broadcast" at 2 o'clock. The broadcast was written in English on the Voice's central desk and was sent by teletype to the thirty-four language desks.

There it was translated and sent out in various foreign tongues all over the world as broadcast time arrived for each.

"The Supreme Court has ruled unanimously," the Voice said in its broadcast, "that racial segregation has no place in American public education. It held that separation of students on a racial basis denies equal educational opportunities.

"Chief Justice [Earl] Warren, reading the court's findings, said that the doctrine of providing separate but equal facilities has no place in public education. Separation of children solely because of race, he said, generates feelings in their hearts and minds which might never be undone. * * *

"The ruling in effect outlaws all segregation in public schools throughout the United States. The court held that to separate students is a denial of the due process of law guaranteed by the Fifth Amendment to the Constitution and equal opportunity

Continued on Page 15, Column 4

SCHOOL LEADERS APPLAUD DECISION

Foresee Few Difficulties — Southerners Say Time Will Be Needed for Adjustments

By BENJAMIN FINE

Leading American educators yesterday applauded the decision of the Supreme Court outlawing segregation in the public schools of the South.

In general, the school and college spokesmen asserted that the decision would benefit both Negro and white children in the twenty-one states where the dual system of education is mandatory or permissive.

They did not believe there would be great difficulty in putting the ruling into effect. They did not think that the threats to abandon the public school system would be carried out.

Several Southern educators, however, foresaw some difficulty in an immediate application of the anti-segregation policy. They felt that time would be needed to bring about the historic change from all-white to mixed public schools. But they did not believe that the long-range program could be thwarted for any considerable period.

Most of the educators indicated that they had expected the decision, and that the South, too, had known that the segregation laws probably would be overthrown. No one expected any violence nor any real crisis to develop. A gradual changeover from the present system to a nonsegregated policy was predicted.

In the opinion of Dr. Harold Taylor, president of Sarah Lawrence College, this is one of the most important decisions ever made by the Supreme Court in the history of the United States.

The fact that the decision was reached unanimously, and that it was stated unequivocably, he added, declared to the world "the United States means what it says about human rights."

Decision Called Logical

Dr. Taylor said: "Because the educational system of this country is the basic means by which the mind values of democracy are projected into society, this will mean that in the long run segregation of Negro and whites in the United States will come to an end. The matter now rests with men and women of goodwill working together to achieve that goal."

The decision was cited as "excellent and logical" by Dr. Henry T. Heald, Chancellor of New York University. Expressing the hope that it would be looked upon constructively by both sides, Dr. Heald declared that the ruling would be an answer to those Communist countries that belittled our democratic way of life.

"I think this is an excellent decision," Dr. Heald said. "It is certainly a logical outcome of the way segregation has developed in recent years. In the long run it will strengthen education, although in certain areas it will take time to put into effect properly. I would hope that the decision would be acted upon constructively by persons on both sides of this issue."

Dr. Heald said he did not believe that the public schools would be abolished. Even though threats have been heard, suggesting that these schools will be tossed aside if segregation is enforced, the good judgment of the American people will not permit that to happen, he asserted.

"This is further evidence that we do what we say we do concerning the democratic principles," Dr. Heald observed. "Segregation has been a weak point in our democracy. By getting rid of it in a peaceful manner we will strengthen the cause of democracy. I'm certain that the Supreme Court decision is an extremely significant move, far-reaching in its implications."

Dr. Arthur S. Adams, president of the American Council on Education, the most influential educational group in the country, said that the events of the last quarter century clearly indicated that the decision was not unexpected. He asserted that responsible persons in the South have long recognized that segregation could not continue indefinitely.

"An important question that must be answered," said Dr. Adams, "is how will the areas affected accept the decision? Many leaders in the South are concerned with the problem. Of course there will be many practical problems that will have to be resolved. Now is the time for patience on the part of all of us. The anti-segregation policy will represent a substantial change in social habits."

"Normal" Segregation Foreseen

Dr. Adams added that because of the importance of the decision, "all hands will rally around to find the best solution that can be devised."

Southern educators did not expect undue difficulty or violence in bringing the new policy into action. Dr. Henry E. Hill, president of George Peabody College for Teachers, Nashville, Tenn., suggested that in effect the South would have "normal" rather than legal segregation.

This will come about through segregated living conditions. He noted that in such communities as Pittsburgh or Cincinnati many schools were in effect under a segregated program. Not legal segregation, to be sure, but segregation through "natural" conditions, he said.

The Supreme Court ruling, he declared, will mean better treatment of all minority groups. There have been advances made toward a better school system for Negroes. The South, he said, now is spending millions of dollars to improve Negro education.

"I don't anticipate any particular violence or outbreak," said Dr. Hill. "We must expect a long-term adjustment, perhaps to take the best part of a generation. However, if we insist upon complete adjustment by next fall we will have unusual difficulties. The key is to give the South enough time to make normal adjustments."

Dr. William A. Early, superintendent of schools in Savannah, Ga., and president of the National Education Association, expected that the public schools would continue, regardless of the threats against them made by political leaders of the state.

Stressing that he was talking personally and not for the N. E. A., Dr. Early said that Savannah schools would continue to operate under the dual system until they received specific instructions from the State Attorney General's office.

The voters will have an opportunity, according to present plans, to ballot on the abolition of the public school system at the November election. Many influential individuals and groups have taken a stand in favor of the continuance of the public schools, even though segregation is ended, Dr. Early said.

Another Southern school leader, Dr. John E. Ivey Jr., director of the Southern Regional Education Board at Atlanta, Ga., did not expect undue trouble.

The fact that the Supreme Court, while outlawing segregation, did not provide specific directives as to the time and methods of putting the ruling into force, will prove immeasurably helpful to the South, Dr. Ivey said.

This will permit the statesmen of the South, who have no sympathy with either extreme, to develop a workable plan, Dr. Ivey asserted.

"I believe that the system of public schools that the American people have built up over the last 150 years as an essential part of our way of life will continue," Dr. Ivey declared.

That appeared the general sentiment of most educators.

Negro Gets Church Office

Special to The New York Times.

QUINCY, Mass., May 17 — Julian D. Steele of West Newbury was elected moderator today of the Massachusetts Congregational Christian Conference. He is the first Negro to hold the highest lay office in the conference, which held its annual meeting here. Mr. Steele was vice moderator last year.

A Sociological Decision

Court Founded Its Segregation Ruling On Hearts and Minds Rather Than Laws

By JAMES RESTON
Special to The New York Times.

WASHINGTON, May 17—The Supreme Court not only upheld Justice John M. Harlan's famous dictum that "the Constitution is colorblind" today but also based its decision on the primacy of the general welfare.

At a time when the Executive and Legislative Branches of the Government were involved in a major conflict over their respective powers, the principal court of the land managed to agree unanimously on what heretofore had been one of the most controversial questions of the century.

In ruling out racial segregation in the nation's public schools, it rejected history, philosophy and custom as the major basis for its decision and accepted instead Justice Benjamin N. Cardoza's test of contemporary social justice.

Relying more on the social scientists than on legal precedents—a procedure often in controversy in the past—the court insisted on equality of the mind and heart rather than on equal school facilities:

"To separate them [Negro children] from others of similar age and qualifications solely because of their race," Chief Justice Earl Warren said for the court, "generates a feeling of inferiority as to their status in the community that may affect their hearts and minds in a way unlikely ever to be undone."

The court's opinion read more like an expert paper on sociology than a Supreme Court opinion. It sustained the argument of experts in education, sociology, psychology, psychiatry and anthropology in the Gebhart case, namely, that even with equal school buildings, segregated Negro children received a substantially inferior education.

Two arguments seemed to impress the court: the testimony in the South Carolina, Kansas and Delaware cases on the effects of segregation on the Negro students in those states; and the testimony of social scientists on the effects of discrimination on personality development.

In the South Carolina case, witnesses testified that compulsory racial segregation in the public schools of that state injured Negro students by:

¶Impairing their ability to learn.

¶Deterring the development of their personalities.

¶Depriving them of equal status in the school community.

¶Destroying their self-respect.

¶Denying them full opportunity for democratic social development.

¶Subjecting them to the prejudices of others.

¶Stamping them with a badge of inferiority.

The South Carolina Argument

The argument in the South Carolina case, which the court sustained, was this:

In a democracy, citizens from every group, no matter what their social or economic status or their religious or ethnic origins, are expected to participate widely in the making of important public decisions.

The public school, even more than the family, the church, business institutions, political and social groups and other institutions, has become an effective agency for giving to all people that broad background of attitudes and skills required to function effectively as participants in a democracy.

Thus, this argument continues, "education" comprehends the entire process of developing and training the mental, physical and moral powers and capacities of human beings, and these capacities cannot be developed properly, even in the finest of school buildings, if the students are segregated from the majority by law.

The appellants in the case presented to the court a brief by what they described as a "consensus of social scientists with respect to the issue * * *." This "Brandeis-type" brief seems to contain the major arguments on this key question of the detrimental effects of segregation in the schools.

The report argued that segregation damaged not only the minority Negro students in the segregated schools but the majority group students as well. It made these points about the effects on Negro children:

¶Negro children, observing that they are kept apart from the white children who are better treated, "often react with feelings of inferiority and a sense of personal humiliation."

¶Some Negro children—usually of the lower socio-economic classes—"may react by overt aggressions and hostility directed toward their own group or members of the dominant group."

¶Middle-class and upper-class minority group children are "likely to react to their racial frustrations and conflicts by withdrawal and submissive behavior."

Defeatist Attitude Seen

"Minority group children of all social and economic classes," the report said, "often react with a generally defeatist attitude and a lowering of personal ambitions.

"This, for example, is reflected in a lowering of pupil morale and a depression of the educational aspiration level among minority group children in segregated schools.

"In producing such effects, segregated schools impair the ability of the child to profit from the educational opportunities provided him."

The report to the court also noted that white children, under these circumstances, were hurt because they were encouraged to think of whole groups of people as inferior. This, it was contended, set up conflicts in the white child's mind because he was taught principles of equality that were not applied to the Negro children.

The report also made these points:

¶The child who is compelled to attend a segregated school may be able to cope with ordinary expressions of prejudice by regarding the prejudiced person as evil or misguided; but he cannot readily cope with symbols of authority, the full force of the authority of the state—the school or the school board, in this instance—in the same manner.

¶Segregation leads to a blockage in the communications and interaction between the two groups. Such blockages tend to increase mutual suspicion, distrust and hostility.

¶Segregation not only perpetuates rigid stereotypes and reinforces negative attitudes toward members of the other group, but also leads to the development of a social climate within which violent breaks of racial tensions are likely to occur.

Thus the court today added one more illustration to Justice Cardoza's power of prophecy:

"When the social needs demand one settlement rather than another," he said, "there are times when we must bend symmetry, ignore history and sacrifice custom in the pursuit of other and larger ends.

"From history and philosophy and custom, we pass, therefore, to the force which in our day and generation is becoming the greatest of them all, the power of social justice which finds its outlet and expression in the method of sociology * * *.

"The final cause of law is the welfare of society * * *."

Decision Is Applauded By Savannah Rotarians

Special to The New York Times.

SAVANNAH, Ga., May 17—The Rotarians were holding a luncheon meeting when word of the Supreme Court decision came through today. One of the members rose and announced the segregation in schools in the South had been outlawed.

The announcement was greeted with some applause. Few of the members seemed much concerned.

"Well it's just what I expected," one Rotarian said.

"It a good thing," another said to his neighbor. "We can now practice the true Christian principles of brotherhood."

PAY SCALES COMPARED

3 States in South Give More to Negro Teachers

In three of twelve Southern states, which reported teachers salaries in a recent study, Negro teachers received higher pay than white teachers. Salaries are geared to the amount of college training received.

North Carolina, Oklahoma and Tennessee gave the higher amounts, although the differences were slight. For white and Negro respectively the figures were: North Carolina — $2,895 and $2,935; Oklahoma — $2,978 and $2,985; Tennessee — $2,141 and $2,244. The highest salaries reported were in Texas, where white teachers receive $3,204 and Negro teachers $3,078. The lowest average was in Mississippi—white $1,991, Negro $1,019.

Negro Pupils Fourth of Total

On the basis of average daily attendance, Negro children represented one-fourth of the public school population in the Southern states in 1952. The proportion among the states varied radically with one out of sixteen pupils in Kentucky schools being a Negro while in Mississippi schools almost half the students were Negrose.

HIGH COURT BANS PUBLIC PUPIL BIAS

Continued From Page 1

of the due process of law guaranteed by the Fifth Amendment to the Constitution."

The Fourteenth Amendment provides that no state shall "deny to any person within its jurisdiction the equal protection of the laws." The Fifth Amendment says that no person shall be "deprived of life, liberty or property without due process of law."

The seventeen states having mandatory segregation are Alabama, Arkansas, Delaware, Florida, Mississippi, Missouri, North Carolina, Oklahoma, Georgia, Kentucky, Louisiana, Maryland, South Carolina Tennessee, Texas, Virginia and West Virginia.

Kansas, New Mexico, Arizona and Wyoming have permissive statutes, although Wyoming never has exercised it.

South Carolina and Georgia have announced plans to abolish public schools if segregation were banned.

Although the decision with regard to the constitutionality of school segregation was unequivocal, the court set the cases down for reargument in the fall on questions that previously were argued last December. These deal with the power of the court to permit an effective gradual readjustment to school systems not based on color distinctions.

Other questions include whether the court itself should formulate detailed decrees and what issues should be dealt with. Also, whether the cases should be remanded to the lower courts to frame decrees, and what general directions the Supreme Court should give the lesser tribunals if this were done.

Cases Argued Twice

The cases first came to the high court in 1952 on appeal from rulings of lower Federal courts, handed down in 1951 and 1952. Arguments were heard on Dec. 9-10, 1952.

Unable to reach a decision, the Supreme Court ordered rearguments in the present term and heard the cases for the second time on Dec. 7-8 last year.

Since then, each decision day has seen the courtroom packed with spectators awaiting the ruling. That was true today, though none except the justices themselves knew it was coming down. Reporters were told before the court convened that it "looked like a quiet day."

Three minor opinions had been announced, and those in the press room had begun to believe the prophesy when Banning E. Whittington, the court's press information officer, started putting on his coat.

"Reading of the segregation decisions is about to begin in the court room," he said. "You will get the opinions up there."

The courtroom is one floor up, reached by a long flight of marble steps. Mr. Whittington led a fast moving exodus. In the courtroom, Chief Justice Warren had just begun reading.

Each of the Associate Justices listened intently. They obviously were aware that no court since the Dred Scott decision of March 6, 1857, had ruled on so vital an issue in the field of racial relations.

Dred Scott was a slave who sued for his freedom on the ground that he had lived in a territory where slavery was forbidden. The territory was the northern part of the Louisiana Purchase, from which slavery was excluded under the terms of the Missouri Compromise.

The Supreme Court ruled that Dred Scott was not a citizen who had a right to sue in the Federal courts, and that Congress had no constitutional power to pass the Missouri Compromise.

Thurgood Marshall, the lawyer who led the fight for racial equality in the public schools, predicted that there would be no disorder and no organized resistance to the Supreme Court's dictum.

He said that the people of the South, the region most heavily affected, were law-abiding and would not "resist the Supreme Court."

Association Calls Meetings

Mr. Marshall said that the state presidents of the National Association for the Advancement of the Colored People would meet next week-end in Atlanta to discuss further procedures.

The Supreme Court adopted two of the major premises advanced by the Negroes in briefs and arguments presented in support of their cases.

Their main thesis was that segregation, of itself, was unconstitutional. The Fourteenth Amendment, which was adopted July 28, 1868, was intended to wipe out the last vestige of inequality between the races, the Negro side argued.

Against this, lawyers representing the states argued that since there was no specific constitutional prohibition against segregation in the schools, it was a matter for the states, under their police powers, to decide.

The Supreme Court rejected the "states rights" doctrine, however, and found all laws ordering or permitting segregation in the schools to be in conflict with the Federal Constitution.

The Negroes also asserted that segregation had a psychological effect on pupils of the Negro race and was detrimental to the educational system as a whole. The court agreed.

"Today, education is perhaps the most important function of state and local governments," Chief Justice Warren wrote. "Compulsory school attendance laws and the great expenditures for education both demonstrate our recognition of the importance of education in our democratic society. It is the very foundation of good citizenship.

"In these days it is doubtful that any child may reasonably be expected to succeed in life if he is denied the opportunity of an education. Such an opportunity, where the state has undertaken to provide it, must be made available to all on equal terms."

As to the psychological factor, the high court adopted the language of a Kansas court in which the lower bench held:

"Segregation with the sanction of the law, therefore, has a tendency to retard the educational and mental development of Negro children and to deprive them of some of the benefits they would receive in a racially integrated school system."

1896 Doctrine Demolished

The "separate but equal" doctrine, demolished by the Supreme Court today, involved transportation, not education. It was the case of Plessy vs. Ferguson, decided in 1896. The court then held that segregation was not unconstitutional if equal facilities were provided for each race.

Since that ruling six cases have been before the Supreme Court, applying the doctrine to public education. In several cases, the court has ordered the admission to colleges and universities of Negro students on the ground that equal facilities were not available in segregated institutions.

Today, however, the court held the doctrine inapplicable under any circumstances to public education.

This means that the court may extend its ruling from primary and secondary schools to include state-supported colleges and universities. Two cases involving Negroes who wish to enter white colleges in Texas and Florida are pending before the court.

The question of "due process," also a clause in the Fourteenth Amendment, had been raised in connection with the state cases as well as the District of Columbia.

The High Court held, however, that since it had ruled in the state cases that segregation was unconstitutional under the "equal protection" clause, it was unnecessary to discuss "whether such segregation also violates the due process clause of the Fourteenth Amendment."

However, the "due process" clause of the Fifth Amendment was the core of the ruling in the District of Columbia case. "Equal protection" and "due process," the court noted, were not always interchangeable phrases.

Liberty Held Deprived

"Liberty under law extends to the full range of conduct which an individual is free to pursue, and it cannot be restricted except for a proper governmental objective," Chief Justice Warren asserted.

"Segregation in public education is not reasonably related to any proper governmental objective, and thus it imposes on Negro children of the District of Columbia a burden that constitutes an arbitrary deprivation of their liberty in violation of the due process clause."

Two principal surprises attended the announcement of the decision. One was its unanimity. There had been reports that the court was sharply divided and might not be able to get an agreement this term. Very few major rulings of the court have been unanimous.

The second was the appearance with his colleagues of Justice Robert H. Jackson. He suffered a mild heart attack on March 30. He left the hospital last week-end and had not been expected to return to the bench this term, which will end on June 7.

Perhaps to emphasize the unanimity of the court, perhaps from a desire to be present when the history-making verdict was announced, Justice Jackson was in his accustomed seat when the court convened.

Bunche Nearly Loses $35 After News of Decision

Special to The New York Times.

UNITED NATIONS, N. Y., May 17—The Supreme Court's anti-segregation ruling today made Dr. Ralph J. Bunche a happy man but it almost cost him $35.

Dr. Bunche, director of the United Nations Trusteeship Division and a Nobel Peace Prize winner for his mediation work in Palestine, often has spoken out against segregation.

He was in his office when Walter White, of the National Association for the Advancement of Colored People, telephoned to say that the reading of the court ruling had begun.

Dr. Bunche rushed down to the Associated Press office to read the bulletins. Then he went to the near-by Chemical Bank and Trust Company branch in the building to cash a check. He turned in the check, returned to the news agency office.

Ralph Gardell, a guard, rushed down to say that the check was all right, but Dr. Bunche in the excitement had left the money on the counter.

Dr. Bunche had one comment on the ruling:

"On the basis of early bulletins, this decision appears to be an historic event in the annals of American democracy."

A.F.L. CHIEF HAILS COURT

Decision Will Stir Confidence in Us Abroad, Meany Says

Special to The New York Times.

CHICAGO, May 17—George Meany, president of the American Federation of Labor, today hailed the Supreme Court decision outlawing racial segregation in the public schools.

"This decision," he said, "squares with the A. F. L. policy of nondiscrimination throughout its entire history. It is a matter of simple justice, and what the Supreme Court has done is to state a policy that is essential in a country where all people are equal and there is no place for distinction as to race, creed or color.

"It is a history-making decision in keeping with what we believe is the American way of life. It will stir new confidence in us on the part of millions of persons in Europe, Asia and Africa, and will prove of tremendous benefit in the fight against communism."

'HOW' AND 'WHEN' REMAIN AS ISSUES

Court to Hear Rearguments on Bias Case in October Before Decreeing Action

Special to The New York Times.

WASHINGTON, May 17—Although it settled the main problem of constitutionality today, the Supreme Court will have another round in the issue of school segregation when it returns in October for the 1954-1955 term.

It will hear rearguments then on the question of how and when the practice it outlawed today may finally be ended. No date was set for these arguments, but they are expected early in the next term.

The effect of the court's action in this regard was to give the states and the District of Columbia a period of time in which to integrate their schools. It does not eliminate the requirement of eventual integration.

Two questions will be reargued. They were included in a list of five asked by the court last June, when it set the cases for reargument in the present term. They deal with the decrees that are to be issued.

These are the questions:

IV

Assuming it is decided that segregation in public schools violates the Fourteenth Amendment:

A. Would a decree necessarily follow providing that, within the limits set by normal geographic school districting, Negro children should forthwith be admitted to schools of their choice, or

B. May this court, in the exercise of its equity powers, permit an effective gradual adjustment to be brought about from existing segregated systems to a system not based on color distinctions?

V

On the assumption on which Questions 4-A and B are based, and assuming further that this court will exercise its equity powers to the end described in Question 4-B:

A. Should this court formulate detailed decrees in these cases?

B. If so, what specific issues should the decrees reach?

C. Should this court appoint a special master to hear evidence with a view to recommending specific terms for such decrees?

D. Should this court remand to the courts of first instance with directions to frame decrees in these cases, and if so what general directions should decrees of this court include and what procedures should the courts of first instance follow in arriving at the specific terms of more detailed decrees?

The first three questions on the list submitted nearly a year ago dealt with whether it had been the understanding of Congress and the states that ratified the Fourteenth Amendment that it would abolish segregation in the public schools.

They also included whether Congress and the states understood that future Congresses might abolish segregation or the courts might construe the amendment as abolishing it, and whether it was within the judicial power to construe the amendment that way.

The court answered these questions in its decisions today.

But Chief Justice Earl Warren said that the formulation of decrees "presents problems of considerable complexity" because of the great variety of local conditions and other factors. The cases will be restored to the docket, he said, "in order that we may have the full assistance of the parties in formulating decrees."

In addition to lawyers for the states, the District of Columbia and the Negro plaintiffs, the Attorney General was "invited to participate" as he did in the arguments at the present term.

If the Attorneys General of the states that require or permit segregation wish to appear as amicus curiae "friend of the court), they must so request by Sept. 15 and file their briefs by Oct. 1.

The position of John W. Davis, the noted constitutional lawyer who argued for South Carolina, was that the court had no power to formulate a decree that would alter state laws. The state of South Carolina, he said, must "devise the remedies" if its present school system is unconstitutional.

Other lawyers argued that the cases should be remanded to the lower courts for formulation of decrees consistent with the Supreme Court's ruling.

Thurgood Marshall, principal lawyer for the Negro side, said that the high court could instruct the lower courts to give the states time to integrate their schools but should not take over the administrative functions of the states. He thought a year would be long enough.

TRAINING OF TEACHERS

Gap Between Negro and White Is Closing in South

The number of years of college training received by Negro and white teachers in the Southern states is almost the same, although the gap was wide up to 1940.

An average for twelve of the states showed that white teachers received 3.8 years of training while the Negro teachers had 3.5 years. Texas led with 4.2 and 4.1 years respectively. In 1940 Georgia, white teachers had an average of three years against 1.7 years for Negroes but last year the gap closed and the Negroes had 3.7 compared with 3.6 years for white teachers.

Ruling Called No Surprise

LONDON, May 17 (UP)—Ralph McGill, editor of The Atlanta (Ga.) Constitution, said tonight the Supreme Court ruling against segregation in the public schools was "not too surprising" except for the unanimity of the decision. Mr. McGill, who is visiting England with a group of United States editors, said he would like to read the court's decision before making any further comment.

"All the News That's Fit to Print"

The New York Times.

LATE CITY EDITION
Fair and cold today and tonight.
Fair and milder tomorrow.
Temperature Range Today-Max., 40; Min., 25
Temperature Yesterday-Max., 37.4; Min., 28.5
Full U. S. Weather Bureau Report, Page 51

VOL. CIV..No. 35,377. Entered as Second-Class Matter, Post Office, New York, N. Y. NEW YORK, FRIDAY, DECEMBER 3, 1954. Times Square, New York 36, N. Y. Telephone LAckawanna 4-1000 FIVE CENTS

FINAL VOTE CONDEMNS M'CARTHY, 67-22, FOR ABUSING SENATE AND COMMITTEE; ZWICKER COUNT ELIMINATED IN DEBATE

POPE IN COLLAPSE, BUT REST FOLLOWS A DIFFICULT NIGHT

Morning Announcement Tells of the 78-Year-old Pontiff's Battle Against Illness

KIN CALLED TO BEDSIDE

Trouble Laid to a Perforated Ulcer and Physicians Study Possibilities of Operation

By The Associated Press.

ROME, Friday, Dec. 3—The Vatican announced this morning that Pope Pius XII, gravely stricken, had survived the night. A spokesman said a more detailed bulletin would be issued later today.

The Pope suffered a severe collapse yesterday.

The first word this morning on his condition was given by Dr. Luciano Casimiri, spokesman for the Vatican press office, at 8:05 o'clock [2:05 A. M., Eastern standard time.]

"After a difficult night, the Holy Father is now resting," the spokesman said.

There were unconfirmed reports that the Pope had suffered a heart attack in the night, accompanied by more of the intense gastritis, nausea and hiccups for which he has been under treatment. There were indications also that the Pope's condition may be aggravated by a gastric ulcer.

His personal physician, Dr. Riccardo Galeazzi-Lisi, spent the entire night at his bedside, after making emergency X-rays yesterday and calling in a surgeon for consultation.

Grave Fears Felt

By ARNALDO CORTESI
Special to The New York Times.

ROME, Friday, Dec. 3—Pope Pius XII suffered a collapse at 3:30 o'clock yesterday afternoon due, it is believed, to a perforated ulcer.

The Pope fell into a coma and the gravest fears for his life were felt. He is 78 years old and has been weakened because for the last four days his feeding has been by artificial means.

Extreme unction was administered and Pius' nearest relatives—three nephews—were called to his bedside.

Five hours later, the Pope had overcome the crisis and his archiater, or chief physician, Prof. Riccardo Galeazzi-Lisi, said there was no immediate cause for alarm.

The Pope was stated to be resting as easily as could be expected under the circumstances, although breathing heavily and reduced to exhaustion.

It was learned that the possibility of an abdominal operation sometime today or in the next few days was being considered. The exact nature of the operation under consideration was not stated but it is understood that a noticeable swelling of the Pope's abdomen developed yesterday afternoon, accompanied by cramps and excruciating pain. Radioscopic and clinical tests were made late in the evening to ascertain both the exact nature of the Pope's ailment and whether he is in condition to undergo surgery.

From the time he fell seriously ill in January of this year, Pope Pius had refused to take the barium meal necessary if full X-ray examination of his stomach

Continued on Page 4, Column 1

Rio Conference Ends With Major Accords

By SAM POPE BREWER
Special to The New York Times.

PETROPOLIS, Brazil, Dec. 2—The twenty-one American republics ended tonight their first general economic conference with agreements on many major points and plans to hold another such meeting within two years.

Antonio Carrillo Flores, Minister of Finance of Mexico, said in the principal address at the closing session that public opinion of this hemisphere would find on studying results of the conference that its work "was not sterile."

Carlos Lleras Restrepo of Colombia introduced a dissenting note into the general air of agreement. He said at this final session that his country did not feel the conference had gone far enough toward increasing international banking facilities and stabilizing commodity prices. An

Continued on Page 10, Column 5

President Rejects Blockade Of China Now as Act of War

But He Pledges No Let-Up in Efforts to Free 13 Americans Jailed by Peiping—Holds Truce Obligates U. N. to Act

By JOSEPH A. LOFTUS
Special to The New York Times

WASHINGTON, Dec. 2—President Eisenhower asserted today he was not going to be pushed emotionally into an act of war—such as a naval blockade of Communist China.

Neither, he said, is he going to let Peiping get away with the imprisonment of thirteen Americans on spy charges.

He insisted that the United Nations act for the release of at least eleven of the Americans because they were uniformed veterans of the Korean war and as such the United Nations was obligated to act in their behalf.

[At the United Nations, the United States said it wanted the world body to condemn the imprisonment by Red China of eleven American airmen shot down during the Korean war.]

"We are yet far from exhausting all of our resources" to liberate these men, the President said at his news conference: "I mention only one of those that is available to us."

He asserted that Red China deliberately timed its announcement of the imprisonment to divide the people of the United States as well as the United States from its allies. He added that the United States must be forever on its guard against this divide-and-conquer technique.

His personal feelings of anger, resentment and frustration were as great as any American's, he said, but he believed that restraint in public expression was the wiser course. To respond with patience rather than with truculence does not mean appeasement, he declared.

The President was clearly reading a lesson in the behavior of public officials to Senator Wi-

Continued on Page 2, Column 4

East Bloc Says Joint Army Will Counter Bonn in NATO

By CLIFTON DANIEL
Special to The New York Times.

MOSCOW, Dec. 2—In a declaration signed in the Kremlin tonight, eight European Communist regimes gave notice that if the Atlantic powers enlisted West Germany in their alliance, an East European defense organization would be created.

Representatives of eight governments concluding a four-day conference here said another meeting would be called to plan defense measures should the London and Paris agreements for West German armament and sovereignty be finally ratified.

The envisioned defense organization would have combined military forces under a joint command like that of the North Atlantic Treaty Organization. It would be in addition to the existing framework of treaties concluded long ago among the eight powers.

Communist China's complete approval of the declaration and the measures envisioned in it was signified at the final meeting of the representatives of the eight European powers today. China's endorsement was given by Chang Wen-tien, Peiping's Deputy Foreign Minister and Ambassador to Moscow.

Having in mind the combined strength of Communist China, the Soviet Union and seven other units in the East bloc conference, the delegates declared:

"Never before have the forces of peace and socialism been so mighty and so consolidated as now. Any attempts to attack, launch a war and interfere with the peaceful life of our peoples will meet with a shattering rebuff."

The declaration, bound in a red Morocco folder with ribbons

Continued on Page 5, Column 5

ATOM POWER SEEN AS COMMON IN 1976

Half of All Electric Plants Then Building Will Use It, G. E. Head Tells N.A.M.

By A. H. RASKIN

By 1976 atomic energy will be used to fuel half of all the electric generating plants then being built, it was predicted yesterday. This forecast was put before the National Association of Manufacturers by Ralph J. Cordiner, president of General Electric.

His estimate of the speed with which nuclear power would come into widespread use as a source of electric power was considerably more optimistic than most official calculations. Mr. Cordiner made his prediction as part of a plea to industrialists to shun "creeping conservatism" in their approach to business planning.

The head of the country's biggest electrical manufacturing company advised his fellow-executives to make their plans on a twenty-year basis, instead of limiting themselves to the ups and downs of the immediate sales market.

West Called Stronger

Other highlights at the second session of the association's fifty-ninth annual Congress of American Industry in the Waldorf-Astoria Hotel included:

¶An assertion by Gen. Walter Bedell Smith that the United States and its allies had built up a sufficient superiority over the Communist countries to "deter aggression and maintain peace." The former Under Secretary of State emphasized, however, that the balance of power was still "rather tenuous."

¶A report by a Dutch industrialist that five of his employes, who spent three months working in a Pennsylvania linoleum factory, had come home convinced that "America is a working man's world."

¶An attack by Charles R. Sligh Jr., N. A. M. board chairman, on union proposals for a guaranteed annual wage. He contended that wage guarantees would destroy business, rather than stabilize employment.

¶An assertion by Prof. Leo Wolman of Columbia University that the Taft-Hartley Act represented no substantial improvement over the old Wagner Act in curbing union power and preventing encroachment on management rights.

¶Election as N. A. M. president of Henry G. Riter 3d of Montclair, N. J., president of Thomas A. Edison, Inc., and chairman of the board of Copperweld Steel. Mr. Riter, who was an investment banker before he became an industrialist, succeeds H. C. McClellan of Los Angeles.

General Smith, who quit the State Department two months

Continued on Page 24, Column 3

EISENHOWER WARNS G. O. P. RIGHT WING; CHIDES KNOWLAND

Insists Party Must Follow a Progressive Course or Face Loss of Influence

Transcript and summary of the news conference, Page 18.

By WILLIAM S. WHITE
Special to The New York Times.

WASHINGTON, Dec. 2—President Eisenhower, reasserting leadership for his concept of a progressive Republican party, rebuked today the Senate Republican floor leader, William F. Knowland of California, and the party's right wing generally.

The President did not seek to disclaim the existence of a split in the party. He said instead that the party would not long be a force in American life unless it followed a course of progressivism.

As before, he defined this progressivism as a liberal attitude in the Government's relationship with the individual and a conservative attitude concerning the national economy and the individual's pocketbook.

It was the first time since he entered the White House two years ago that General Eisenhower publicly and without apology had criticized a leading member of his party in Congress. Always before, he had avoided such criticisms, relying frequently on the fact that the Constitution made Congress an independent branch of Government.

Even this time, the President somewhat softened his language toward the end, with the comments that while Senator Knowland sometimes made statements that certainly did not conform with the Administration's approach these normally affected method rather than principle.

China Blockade Urged

He made it clear, nevertheless, that distinctions in methods were important, suggesting that the methods of Senator Knowland might mean the difference between peace and war in Asia.

Senator Knowland, in the face of rejections from John Foster Dulles, Secretary of State, and the President himself, has been calling for a blockade of Communist China to force the liberation of United States citizens in Communist prisons.

Yesterday, moreover, Mr. Knowland broke with the Administration on another sensitive issue, coming out against a Senate censure of Senator Joseph R. McCarthy, Republican of Wisconsin.

The President said little about his differences with Senator Knowland over the McCarthy issue, observing only that it was up to the Senate to determine what was required for the preservation of its dignity.

On the point of the profound division within the Republican party over policy toward Red China, however, the President spoke extensively and voluntarily.

He took up Senator Knowland's

Continued on Page 18, Column 5

'Copter Saves 5 Plane Survivors Down 45 Hours on Mountainside

Two Perish in Crash of DC-3 in New Hampshire—Work of Stewardess Praised

By JOHN H. FENTON
Special to The New York Times.

BOSTON, Dec. 2—Five survivors of the crash of a Northeast Airlines plane were plucked by helicopter today from a bleak mountainside near the Maine-New Hampshire border. They had spent forty-five hours on the snow-covered spot in bitter cold.

The two others aboard the DC-3 died of injuries a few hours after the plane had fallen into a stretch of pine woods.

The dead were George McCormick, 37 years old, of Kingston, N. Y., co-pilot, and John McNulty, 39, of Boston, flight supervisor.

First to be rescued was the pilot, Capt. W. Peter Carey, 37, of Swampscott, Mass. He suffered severe head injuries. He and Miss Mary McEttrick, 23, of Boston, the stewardess, were flown here for medical treatment. Miss McEttrick suffered from shock and exposure.

The survivors praised Miss McEttrick for her coolness throughout the ordeal during which they huddled in the wrecked plane for nearly two days. Her cheerful attempts to make them comfortable and her care of the injured prompted them to agree that "she's quite a girl."

Seventy-five Northeast employes, who were flown to Berlin,

Continued on Page 29, Column 4

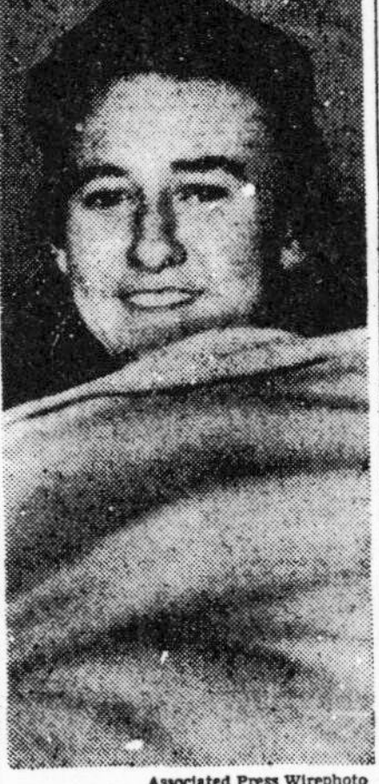

Associated Press Wirephoto
Stewardess Mary McEttrick in Berlin (N. H.) hospital.

RANCOR CONTINUES

Welker Refuses to Let Flanders Apology Go Into the Record

By JAMES RESTON
Special to The New York Times.

WASHINGTON, Dec. 2—The McCarthy debate ended as it began in a spasm of rancor and vindictiveness that will divide the Senate and the country for a long time to come.

Though there were some light-hearted semantics at the close over whether Senator Joseph R. McCarthy was "censured" or "condemned," the underlying feeling among the principals ranged from uneasiness to sullen anger.

The junior Senator from Wisconsin himself produced almost the only hint of humor all day. Asked whether he thought the Senate had passed a resolution of "censure" or "condemnation," he replied:

"I wouldn't say it was a vote of confidence."

He then announced that he was "very happy to get this circus over" and would get back to "the job of digging Communists out of the Government" on Monday.

Controversy Continues

Even after the vote was over, the controversy went on.

Senator Ralph E. Flanders, Republican of Vermont, arose and said he wanted to apologize to the Senate for some remarks he had made about Senator McCarthy some months ago. He added that he had told the Wisconsin Senator that he proposed to do so and had asked him to remain in the chamber, but Senator McCarthy had declined.

Then Senator Flanders asked for unanimous consent to have the Congressional Record amended to show that he had apologized for some of his remarks. This was blocked by Senator Herman Welker, Republican of Idaho, who angrily refused to give consent.

The usual lavish courtesy of the upper chamber gave way to biting sarcasm at the close. When Senator J. William Fulbright, Democrat of Arkansas, said he would try to answer a question by Senator Welker, the latter remarked that he would be "very surprised if a distinguished Rhodes scholar could not answer any question."

The End of a Phase

The main significance of the special session was that it ended that phase of the McCarthy controversy in which the Senate of the United States was hesitant to take action against the Wisconsin Senator.

For most of the five years since Senator McCarthy launched his anti-Communist crusade, the Senate of the United States has led a double life—critical of the Senator in private, and afraid of his political power in public.

During most of this period there has been a kind of political paralysis among the anti-McCarthy faction, and it was never entirely clear who was for him and who was against him. This doubt has now been removed.

The Senator from Wisconsin will remain for a month as chairman of the Government Operations Committee. He will lose none of his rights. He will have the power of subpoena and he will wield his gavel.

What has changed is not Mr. McCarthy but his opponents. They are in the open now, willing and in some cases eager to match his criticisms with their own. In short, the balance of criticism, dominated for so long by Senator McCarthy, has been restored.

Behind this, too, is a decision by the Executive Branch of the Government to take a firmer position against his efforts to persuade Federal employes to give him documents they are not authorized to disclose.

So long as Congress hesitated to take action against Mr. McCarthy, the Executive itself was divided about how to defend its own classified files, but today's vote—regardless of what it is called—has stiffened the anti-McCarthy element in the Administration.

Thus, while he can exercise all

Continued on Page 16, Column 7

Associated Press Wirephoto
CONDEMNED ON TWO COUNTS: Senator McCarthy as he left the Senate floor last night after members adopted a resolution condemning his conduct. The vote was 67-22.

PRESIDENT ALERTS MAYORS ON ATTACK

Cities Are Front-Line Targets, He Warns—Asks Teamwork in Federal-Local Defense

By ELIE ABEL
Special to The New York Times.

WASHINGTON, Dec. 2—President Eisenhower warned today that United States cities were front-line targets for modern weapons "capable of such destruction as to appall the imagination."

The President called for closer municipal-Federal cooperation in civil-defense planning as he welcomed about 240 mayors, city manager and other local officials to a two-day conference in the State Department auditorium.

Val Peterson, Federal Civil Defense Administrator, expanded on the President's warning in a guarded discussion of radioactive "fall-out," a phenomenon that adds a new dimension to the terror of thermonuclear (hydrogen) bombs.

The idea that only city dwellers need to worry about bombing is obsolete today, Mr. Peterson said. If a hydrogen bomb is detonated on or close to the ground, he explained, tremendous amounts of earth and debris are sucked up into the fireball and made radioactive.

Although the heavy particles will not travel far, he said, the lighter ones may be swept along by winds of the upper air, at alti-

Continued on Page 19, Column 1

SENATORS CLEARED ON M'CARTHY MAIL

Inquiry Indicates Request for Check Was Handled by Staff as Routine Matter

By WILLIAM M. BLAIR
Special to The New York Times.

WASHINGTON, Dec. 2—A special Senate committee apparently will report to the Senate that a check of Senator Joseph R. McCarthy's mail in 1952 was handled as a routine matter by a subcommittee's staff members.

Senator Walter F. George, Democrat of Georgia, indicated as much to Senator McCarthy this afternoon as the special two-member committee completed its overnight inquiry into how the mail check was authorized.

"There's nothing to be gained from pursuing the matter further," Senator McCarthy told Senator George, who replied, "I don't think so."

Senator George and Senator Homer Ferguson, Republican of Michigan, spent the day in closed session to hear testimony from persons on the staff of the Senate subcommittee on Privileges and Elections, which had inquired into Senator McCarthy's finances in 1952.

Mr. Ferguson said that a written report would be filed with the Senate. The report is expected to be filed with the secretary of the Senate tomorrow.

The two Senators were named by the Senate last night to in-

Continued on Page 15, Column 3

G.O.P. Weighs End of Rent Curb Outside of the Metropolitan Area

By LEO EGAN

Republican legislative leaders are giving serious consideration to relaxing state rent controls outside of the New York metropolitan area, which includes Nassau and Westchester counties as well as New York City.

Such a proposal could set the stage for a major clash between Governor-elect Averell Harriman, Democrat-Liberal, and Republican majorities in the Senate and Assembly.

The Democratic platform on which Mr. Harriman was elected favors tightening rather than relaxing rent control. Moreover, Mr. Harriman affirmed his full support of this position on several occasions during the campaign.

One proposal favored by some Republicans calls for decontrolling all rents outside of the New York metropolitan area. If this is politically impossible or unacceptable they favor decontrolling all one and two-family houses outside of the metropolitan area, leaving controls in effect only on apartments and tenements.

Both suggestions were formally advanced at a recent closed-door meeting of the Temporary State Commission on Rents and Rental Conditions, headed by Assemblyman Joseph F. Carlino of Long Beach, L. I.

As a result, Joseph D. McGoldrick, State Rent Administrator, was instructed by the commission to prepare a report and recommendations on both proposals covering the probable effect of such a relaxation of controls, the number of dwelling units involved, and the ratio of vacancies to dwelling units affected at present.

Major up-state cities that would be affected by such a

Continued on Page 24, Column 5

REPUBLICANS SPLIT

Democrats Act Solidly in Support of Motion Against Senator

Excerpts from transcript of Senate debate, Pages 12, 13

By ANTHONY LEVIERO
Special to The New York Times.

WASHINGTON, Dec. 2—The Senate voted 67 to 22 tonight to condemn Joseph R. McCarthy, Republican Senator from Wisconsin.

Every one of the forty-four Democrats present voted against Mr. McCarthy. The Republicans were evenly divided—twenty-two for condemnation and twenty-two against. The one independent, Senator Wayne Morse of Oregon, also voted against Mr. McCarthy.

In the ultimate action the Senate voted to condemn Senator McCarthy for contempt of a Senate Elections subcommittee that investigated his conduct and financial affairs, for abuse of its members, and for his insults to the Senate itself during the censure proceeding.

Lost in a day of complex and often confused parliamentary maneuvering was the proposal to censure Senator McCarthy for his denunciation of Brig. Gen. Ralph W. Zwicker as unfit to wear his uniform.

This proposal was defeated by a parliamentary device that avoided a direct vote on the merits of the issue. Inquiry among influential Senators indicated they considered the Zwicker proposal a dilemma they wished to avoid.

Amendment Substituted

They said they wished to censure because the facts warranted it. If they failed to do so, they believed large elements of the public would feel the Senate took notice of offenses only against itself and not against ordinary citizens.

But also if they did censure for this, then Senator McCarthy could exploit the decision, contending he was being punished for his effort to expose former Maj. Irving Peress, the Army dentist who was promoted and honorably discharged, and who was denounced by Mr. McCarthy as a "Fifth Amendment Communist."

Mr. McCarthy's denunciation of General Zwicker, who was commanding officer at Camp Kilmer, N. J., when Dr. Peress was discharged, occurred when the Senator interrogated General Zwicker on the question of who had promoted Dr. Peress.

The direct test on the Zwicker issue was avoided by the substitution of the amendment to condemn Senator McCarthy for having insulted the Senate during the censure trial.

McCarthy Loses Three Tests

Thus in its final form the resolution of condemnation was in two parts, covering the offenses against the Elections subcommittee and its members in the first part, and against the Senate in the second. Three test votes were all lost by Mr. McCarthy before the final condemnation.

First was a motion to table the Zwicker proposal, made by Senator Styles Bridges, Republican of New Hampshire, the president pro tem of the Senate, who assumed the leadership of the effort to save Mr. McCarthy yesterday.

Such a motion, if it had succeeded, might have led to a situation that would have prolonged the debate.

But amid signs that the Zwicker issue would have tough sledding, Senator Wallace F. Bennett, Republican of Utah, served notice that if Mr. Bridges' move were defeated he would attempt to substitute for the Zwicker issue his amendment for abuse of the Senate. The significance of this was that an amendment by substitution would require no time out for debate.

Then the voting proceeded. The motion to table was defeated 55 to 33. Mr. Bennett's motion to substitute passed by 64 to 23 and in the next vote his amendment was adopted by the same tally.

The final vote placing Mr. Mc-

Continued on Page 14, Column 3

SENATE CONDEMNS M'CARTHY, 67 TO 22

Continued From Page 1

Carthy under moral condemnation by the Senate came at 5:03 P. M.

The moment of decision was something of an anti-climax after days of emotional and bitter debate. It was punctuated by mocking laughter from the hard core of Mr. McCarthy's adherents.

The accused Senator was present, but he was not led to the bar of the Senate to hear any punishment. Instead Mr. Bridges arose from the coterie in the vicinity of Mr. McCarthy and asked Vice President Richard M. Nixon if the word "censure" appeared anywhere in the resolution in its final form.

Laughter from Senator William E. Jenner, Republican of Indiana, and one of Mr. McCarthy's most vociferous supporters, resounded through the chamber. Senator McCarthy was grinning. Senator George W. Malone, Republican of Nevada, standing by Senator Jenner, was laughing, and so was Senator Herman Welker, Republican of Idaho, sitting beside Mr. Jenner, who all through the debate made the running defense for Mr. McCarthy.

Mr. Jenner guffawed loudly again as Mr. Nixon, after examining the text with a clerk, announced the word "censure" was absent. The document used the word "condemned" in each of its two parts, it was explained.

"Then it is not a censure resolution," said Mr. Bridges, who by virtue of his office presides over the Senate when Mr. Nixon is absent. He also asked if condemnation was censure.

Fulbright Reads Definitions

"The resolutoin does concern the conduct of the junior Senator from Wisconsin," replied the Vice President. "The interpretation must be that of the Senator or any other Senator."

Then Senator J. William Fulbright, Democrat of Arkansas, rose with Webster's International Dictionary before him and read definitions of condemn and censure amid general laughter. Senator Jenner, without asking for the floor said, "Let's do it over again. Let's do a retake."

Senator Bridges then remarked that this was "peculiar censure" to discover after all the time and expense of a special Senate session that the resolution did not contain the word "censure."

Senator Fulbright asserted that Senator Welker had attached a more serious meaning to "condemn" than to "censure." Earlier today in one of his impassioned speeches Mr. Welker had said, "You don't censure a man to death, you condemn him to death."

Senator Arthur V. Watkins, Republican of Utah, who was chairman of the special committee that recommended censure, then said that in the last censure proceeding, twenty-five years ago, the word "censure" was not used but that the resolution had stated that "such conduct is hereby condemned."

"The point I wanted to make," said Senator Watkins, "is that it is the historical word used in censure resolutions."

Then Mr. Jenner asked for the floor in the usual parliamentary way, this time, to remark, grinning, there was some confusion and "do you suppose we could do it all over again?"

Senator Welker rose to comment on definitions and referred to the censure proceedings as a "mock court."

Shortly afterward Senator McCarthy left. He had been in the Senate chamber only briefly, coming in after the final roll-call on the ultimate vote had started. He said "present" instead of voting on the issue that is bound to have a marked effect on his political career.

Later, outside the chamber, reporters asked him if he felt he had been censured.

"Well, it wasn't exactly a vote of confidence," replied Mr. McCarthy, who was still wearing his right arm in a bandage for the bursitis that had interrupted the censure proceedings for ten days.

"I'm happy to have this circus ended so I can get back to the real work of digging out communism, crime and corruption," he continued. "That job will start officially Monday morning, after ten months of inaction." He was referring to a coming inquiry into alleged Communists in defense plants.

He had referred to the session as a "lynch party"—one of the remarks for which he was condemned in the Bennett amendment—and was asked if he felt he had been "lynched."

"I don't feel I have been lynched," he replied.

He expressed his disappointment that the Democrats had voted "straight down the party line, even though they had declared before it started that this was to be a judicial proceeding."

Among Democrats the view was that he might have received a number of their votes if he had not condemned the whole Democratic party some months ago as "the party of treason."

Mr. McCarthy said after referring to the "circus" that he felt no different than he had last night. That is when he had referred to the censure proceeding as a "farce" and a "foul job."

Shouting objections, Senator Jenner opposed an amendment by Senator Edwin C. Johnson, Democrat of Colorado, and vice chairman of the censure committee, that would have placed the Senate on record in the censure resolution as being against communism and determined to investigate subversion relentlessly.

"You're not going to gild the lily now," shouted Senator Jenner. "The record has been made and you are going to stay with it."

He declared that the Democrats had permitted Communists to steal Government secrets through infiltration of the Government.

Senator Price Daniels, Democrat of Texas, then made an eloquent plea, proposing that the resolution be amended to state that the resolution should not be construed to limit the investigative powers of the Senate, especially as to any Communist conspiracy.

He said he wanted to do this to counter the McCarthy charge that the Communist party had reached into the Senate to make a censure committee "do the work of the Communist party.

"I want to make them [the Communists] unhappy and they will be unhappy if you will permit this amendement to be adopted," said Mr. Daniels to Mr. Jenner. "We will be able to say to the world that the allegation is untrue that the Communist party instigated this."

Vice President Nixon ruled that under a consent agreement between the two parties neither the Johnson nor the Daniel amendment could be accepted because it was not germane to the issue of censure.

Flanders Retracts One Point

Toward the end of the Senate session, which adjourned sine die for this year at 7:10 P. M., Senator Ralph E. Flanders, Republican of Vermont, who had sponsored the original censure resolution, said he would stand by all the speeches he had made against Senator McCarthy except that he would like to apologize for a passage in a speech of last March, when he had likened Mr. McCarthy to Hitler.

He also asked unanimous consent to strike the passage from whatever volumes of The Congressional Record remained unbound, but Senator Welker made the single objection that prevented this.

Senators McCarthy, Welker and Jenner have threatened to file counter censure resolutions against Senators Flanders, Fulbright and Morse, who had filed the specifications for the McCarthy censure action. They gave no indication of their plans, and adjournment of the Senate tonight would compel them to wait until the next session.

But Senator Jenner threatened Mr. Flanders with a subpoena if he did not appear before some committee to testify about any relations he might have had with Owen Lattimore.

Mr. Lattimore is a former State Department consultant and professor at Johns Hopkins University who is under indictment on a charge of perjury in a Congressional hearing on his alleged Communist associations.

General Zwicker, now with combat troops in Japan, was criticized by a few McCarthy adherents today as an arrogant and evasive witness against the contrary evidence of the censure committee, which had called him as a witness.

He had a great many champions, though, even among some Senators who said they would not vote for censure in his case, though they deplored the treatment he had received.

Senator Herbert H. Lehman, Democrat of New York, was among those urging censure in the Zwicker incident. The view of this group was that it would be notice to the country that the Senate was interested only in the offenses against itself but cared nothing of abusive treatment of ordinary citizens.

Senator A. S. Mike Monroney, Democrat of Oklahoma, declared that failure to censure on this count would be notice to the public that the Senate was "a privileged class." He asserted the Zwicker incident was a prime example of how Senator McCarthy indiscriminately abused heroes of the United States and Communists.

Senator Monroney also said failure to censure on this count would be notice that it was all right to place wire taps and intercept mail and telephone calls of teachers, professors, private citizens, whether it was constitutional or not, but that it was not all right to do so in the case of the ninety-six Senators.

It would also amount to saying, he added, that "We are sacrosanct, we are going to disregard the constitutional guarantees."

His allusion here was to the charge by Senator McCarthy that the Elections subcommittee that had investigated his conduct and finances in 1952 had kept a undercover watch on his mail and telephone calls.

Mr. McCarthy contended this was illegal, but the debate brought out yesterday that the subcommittee had been investigating the charge that Senator McCarthy was using money sent him by the public to fight communism to speculate on a commodity exchange.

Senator Charles E. Potter, Republican of Michigan, a Silver Star Army veteran who lost both legs in combat, said he also favored censure in the Zwicker case.

Senator Irving M. Ives, Republican of New York, defeated in the race for Governor in the recent election, kept silent on the McCarthy issue all through the debate, but voted against Mr. McCarthy.

However, whenever Senator Watkins made the pro forma motions to reconsider each vote—a technicality needed to make it final—Senator Ives each time made the necessary motion to table.

New Senate Democrat Gives Party Majority

Special to The New York Times.

WASHINGTON, Dec. 2—The Democrats gained a majority in the Senate today.

Alan Bible, Democrat, who was elected in Nevada on Nov. 2, was sworn in to give the Democrats a one-seat margin. The line-up now is forty-eight Democrats, forty-seven Republicans and one Independent, Senator Wayne Morse of Oregon. This same division will prevail when the Eighty-fourth Congress convenes in January.

The change occurred before the final vote to condemn Senator Joseph R. McCarthy, Republican of Wisconsin. Control of the Senate, however, was not transferred to the Democrats.

Senator Bible succeeded Senator Ernest P. Brown, Republican. Senator Brown was named to fill the vacancy created by the death of Senator Pat McCarran before the election.

"All the News That's Fit to Print"

The New York Times.

LATE CITY EDITION
Cloudy with some rain today. Chance of showers tomorrow.

Copyright, 1955, by The New York Times Company.

VOL. CIV..No. 35,508. Entered as Second-Class Matter, Post Office, New York, N. Y. NEW YORK, WEDNESDAY, APRIL 13, 1955. FIVE CENTS

SALK POLIO VACCINE PROVES SUCCESS; MILLIONS WILL BE IMMUNIZED SOON; CITY SCHOOLS BEGIN SHOTS APRIL 25

WORDS OF HOPE: Dr. Thomas Francis Jr., left, and Dr. Jonas E. Salk on speakers' platform at Ann Arbor, Mich., where they addressed scientists on effects of polio vaccine. Associated Press Wirephoto

TRIAL DATA GIVEN

Efficacy of 80 to 90% Shown—Salk Sees Further Advance

Abstract of report, summary of data on tests, Page 22.

By WILLIAM L. LAURENCE

Special to The New York Times.

ANN ARBOR, Mich., April 12—The world learned today that its hopes for finding an effective weapon against paralytic polio had been realized.

The triple anti-polio vaccine originated by Dr. Jonas E. Salk works. This was revealed in the long-awaited report on the mass field trials of 1954, largest of their kind in medical history.

In these tests the vaccine, designed to protect against the crippling effects of all the three types of virus known to produce paralytic polio, was administered to 440,000 children in forty-four states.

The report, a medical classic, was presented at a special scientific meeting at the University of Michigan by Dr. Thomas Francis Jr. It was he who had directed the evaluation of the vast mass of data provided by the tests, involving the correlation of 144,000,000 separate items of information.

Half Get Dummy Shot

Dr. Francis reported the vaccinations had been 80 to 90 per cent effective on the basis of results in eleven states.

In these states, which included New York, half of the children vaccinated got the Salk vaccine. The other half received a placebo, or dummy shot.

These results, Dr. Francis reported, were looked upon with "greater confidence" than the figures in other areas. In these the results indicated an effectiveness of 60 to 80 per cent against paralysis by any polio virus.

Dr. Salk reported at the meeting that new and more potent vaccines and more effective methods of administering them, were ready for the 1955 vaccinations.

Dr. Salk, who is a member of the faculty at the University of Pittsburgh's School of Medicine, said:

"Theoretically, the new 1955 vaccines and vaccination procedures may lead to 100 per cent protection from paralysis of all those vaccinated."

The new procedures he out-

Continued on Page 20, Column 2

STEVENSON COPIED PLAN ON FORMOSA, DULLES CHARGES

He Says Democrat Proposed as His 'Original' Ideas the Administration's Policy

SOME DIPLOMATS DIFFER

Know of No U.S. Moves in U.N. or With Allies Paralleling Views of 1952 Candidate

Special to The New York Times.

WASHINGTON, April 12—Secretary of State Dulles said today Adlai E. Stevenson advocated "as original ideas" the same steps toward peace in the Formosa Strait that the Administration was exploring.

The only major point of difference between the proposals made by the 1952 Democratic Presidential candidate in a Chicago speech last night and his own idea, Mr. Dulles said, lay in the degree of solicitude the United States should show toward Nationalist China.

"Mr. Stevenson speaks feelingly about our 'allies'," the Secretary of State said at his news conference this morning. "However, he forgets one ally, namely, the Republic of China.

"It is upon the loyalty and resources of that ally that the free world must primarily depend for the defense of Formosa. Yet Mr. Stevenson seems to assume that that ally can be ignored and rebuffed.

"Aside from this, Mr. Stevenson has in fact endorsed the main features of this Administration's program in relation to Formosa."

News to Some Diplomats

Mr. Stevenson's speech was on the whole more warmly received in the embassies of the major powers allied with the United States in Europe and Asia.

In these quarters, however, there was some puzzlement among some diplomats over Mr. Dulles' statement that the ideas advanced by Mr. Stevenson in his Chicago speech were "the very approaches which the Government has been and is actively exploring."

If the State Department was exploring with its allies a joint pledge for the united defense of Formosa combined with an effort to extricate the Chinese Nationalists from the Matsu and Quemoy Island groups, that was news to several senior diplomats today. Mr. Stevenson had urged such steps.

These diplomats did not know, either, of any active move by the United States and its allies calling on the United Nations General Assembly to "condemn any effort to alter the present status

Continued on Page 4, Column 3

Dulles Doubts Corsi Ability; Ex-Aide Charges Untruths

Associated Press Wirephoto

Edward Corsi at his Arlington, Va., home yesterday as he replied to charges made by Secretary of State Dulles.

Special to The New York Times.

WASHINGTON, April 12—It was open war today between John Foster Dulles, Secretary of State, and his former "old friend," Edward Corsi.

Mr. Dulles accused the New Yorker of making reckless charges, of trying to circumvent the law and of not being qualified to run the refugee relief program. Mr. Corsi charged the Secretary of State with "a whole string of falsehoods," adding that he was "terribly shocked and astounded that a man like Dulles for whom I had such respect could stoop so low."

Only four months ago Mr. Dulles had appointed Mr. Corsi his special assistant on refugee

Continued on Page 16, Column 6

HIGH COURT HEARS SOUTH WILL DEFY QUICK END TO BIAS

Gradual Approaches Urged for Integration of Schools—Negro Lawyers Opposed

By LUTHER A. HUSTON

Special to The New York Times.

WASHINGTON, April 12—Spokesmen for South Carolina and Virginia told the Supreme Court today that their people would not obey a decree ordering an immediate end to racial segregation in the public schools.

When Chief Justice Earl Warren asked S. E. Rogers, representing Clarendon County, S. C., if he were willing to say that an "honest attempt" would be made to conform to whatever decree the court might issue, Mr. Rogers said:

"Let's get that word 'honest' out of there. It would depend upon the kind of decree. The white people would not send their children to school with Negroes."

Archibald O. Robertson, who represented Virginia, said that Virginia would not defy the court; but that there were "subtle ways" of not complying with an order for an abrupt end to segregation. One would be for the voters to refuse to approve funds for an immediate integration of a school system.

Time Asked for South

J. Lindsay Almond Jr., Attorney General of Virginia, said that "forthwith enforcement of integration would be pre-emptive of the rights of a sovereign people." He asserted that the schools of his state "might have to close" if an abrupt end to segregation were ordered.

Throughout the second day of arguments on the type of decrees the court should issue to carry out its decision of last May 17 that public school segregation was unconstitutional, the Southern states pleaded for time to adjust their educational systems to the new order.

The states were not specific, however, as to the length of time they would need. Estimates ranged from a tentative five years to as high as the year 2045.

The lawyers for the Negro side, however, were specific. Thurgood Marshall, counsel for the National Association for the Advancement of the Colored People, submitted two proposed decrees. One would end all school segregation everywhere next September.

An alternate decree, which Mr. Marshall said was the least the Negroes should be asked to accept, would terminate separate schools for white and Negro pupils by September, 1956.

Mr. Marshall asserted that there could not be a "moratorium on the Fourteenth Amendment or local option" to enforce a constitutional decision of the court. The Fourteenth Amendment to the Constitution prohibits a state from denying to

Continued on Page 18, Column 5

SOVIET ARMED AID OFFERED AFGHANS

Moscow Said to Back Kabul in Dispute With Pakistan on North-West Frontier

By JOHN P. CALLAHAN

Special to The New York Times.

KABUL, Afghanistan (via Peshawar, Pakistan), April 11—The Soviet Ambassador was reported today to have offered help to Afghanistan's Premier. The aid was to be military support if Pakistan or her Western allies "threaten aggressive interference" in Afghanistan's demand for a plebiscite in the adjoining North-West Frontier Province.

The Soviet Union borders on Afghanistan.

The report of the Soviet offer was made by an Afghan Government officer who has been observing the almost daily meetings since March 30 between Soviet Ambassador Mikhail V. Degtyar and Premier Sardar Mohammed Daud of Afghanistan.

It followed by a few hours a report, confirmed by foreign envoys, that King Mohammed Zahir Shah had informed the Ambassadors of the United States, Britain and Turkey that he was prepared to replace Premier Daud with his predecessor, Mahmood Zahir if their Governments would assure Afghanistan of "full" support in event of attacks by "unfriendly powers."

Embassy spokesmen said Washington and London had been informed of the King's request and that they were awaiting replies. The Ambassadors of

Continued on Page 2, Column 3

YONKERS IS FACING LOSS OF STATE AID

Albany Threatens to Cut Off Grants Unless Schools Are Improved by Jan. 1

By LEONARD BUDER

The State Education Commissioner warned the City of Yonkers yesterday that it would lose its state grants to aid education unless it improved its public school system.

The Commissioner, Dr. Lewis A. Wilson, acted in response to an appeal made last year by a group of Yonkers residents who charged that the city's "starvation" budgetary allowances had produced "shocking" school conditions. He set Jan. 1 as the deadline for the Yonkers Board of Education to submit "sufficient evidence of an adequate program, both in respect to its educational offerings and its building needs for the ensuing year."

Commenting upon his action, Dr. Wilson said that his threat to withhold state aid to Yonkers was an "uncommon" but not an unprecedented move.

Yonkers this year is receiving $2,046,000 in regular state aid

Continued on Page 32, Column 5

281,853 ELIGIBLE FOR VACCINE HERE

City to Vote Fund Quickly for Equipment—Experts to Set Number of Shots

Mayor Wagner announced yesterday that a special appropriation of $100,000 would be made to speed the city's polio vaccination program.

Elated by the success of the Salk vaccine, city officials said they were ready to begin vaccination on April 25. Those eligible to receive free inoculations from the city are 281,853 school children. These include all first and second graders and those third and fourth graders who received dummy shots in last year's field trials.

In New York State, 725,000 children between 5 and 14 years of age will be vaccinated by June 1. In making this announcement, Dr. Herman E. Hilleboe, State Health Commissioner, said that if the dosage was reduced from three shots to two, the number of children immunized could be increased to 1,100,000.

In New Jersey, the inoculation of nearly 300,000 school children will begin on Monday, when the

Continued on Page 23, Column 3

Supply to Be Low for Time, But Output Will Be Rushed

By DAMON STETSON

Special to The New York Times.

ANN ARBOR, Mich., April 12—The Salk vaccine for poliomyelitis will be made available for the immunization of children as rapidly as possible, but it is expected to be in short supply temporarily. The National Foundation for Infantile Paralysis announced today that vaccine already purchased for 9,000,000 immunizations (three inoculations a child) would be turned over to state and territorial health officers.

This amount will be offered to all children who participated in last year's field trials but who did not actually receive vaccine. Children enrolled in the first and second grades of all public, private and parochial schools in the United States, Hawaii and Alaska also will be offered the vaccine.

Dr. Jonas E. Salk, who originated the vaccine, reported his belief that the maximum effect of the third (booster) inoculation could be achieved only if administered at least seven months after the primary inoculation of two shots.

Such a procedure would make it possible to give 13,500,000 children primary inoculations immediately upon approval of the vaccine by the National Institutes of Health. When the seven-month period had elapsed, additional vaccine would have been produced.

Dr. Salk also urged that all children who received inoculations during the 1954 field trials be given an additional booster dose in 1955. This is necessary, he said, because the three doses

Continued on Page 22, Column 6

6 VACCINE MAKERS GET U. S. LICENSES

Government Clears the Way for Quantity Production of Salk Preventive

By BESS FURMAN

Special to The New York Times.

WASHINGTON, April 12—The Federal Government today quickly gave a clear track to Salk polio vaccine.

It licensed six concerns to manufacture and distribute throughout the country the protective substance developed by Dr. Jonas E. Salk of the University of Pittsburgh.

The key action in the licensing was the signature of Oveta Culp Hobby, the Secretary of Health, Education and Welfare. Federal approval is required by the National Biologics Control Act. As she signed Mrs. Hobby said:

"It's a great day. It's a wonderful day for the whole world. It's a history-making day."

Licensed Concerns Named

The concerns approved to make and sell the product are:

Cutter Laboratories, Berkeley, Calif.; Eli Lilly Company, Indianapolis; Parke, Davis & Co., Detroit; Pittman-Moore Company, Zionsville, Ind.; Sharp & Dohme, Philadelphia, and Wyeth Laboratories, Inc., Marietta, Pa.

Mrs. Hobby affixed her signature at 5:15 P. M. Had it been possible for her to sign at 4 P. M., the signing would have been what Washington calls a "full dress" ceremony for photographers and the press.

This press meeting was canceled because Mrs. Hobby had to wait for the final judgment of the Public Health Service on the vaccine evaluation study made public today by Dr. Thomas Francis Jr.

Thus it happened that only Surgeon General Leonard A. Scheele of the Public Health Service and a few other members of the departmental staff were present when Mrs. Hobby signed.

Earlier Dr. Scheele had said the delay had been because of "things running late out in Ann Arbor." He reminded that before licensing a new drug the Public Health Service must approve both safety and potency.

"The data on safety had all

Continued on Page 24, Column 4

CENSORSHIP MOVE DENIED BY WILSON

Secretary Defends His Curb on Giving Information

By ANTHONY LEVIERO

Special to The New York Times.

WASHINGTON, April 12—Charles E. Wilson, Secretary of Defense, defended today his directive for control of defense information, denying that it was "censorship."

He said in a news conference that the widespread publication of technical information in the hydrogen bomb age made national security a "greater problem than ever before in history."

He declared he would be willing to pay hundreds of millions of dollars to get the same kind of information about the Soviet Union as that country gets about the United States in its newspapers and periodicals.

The Secretary outlined a dilemma created by the great outpouring of technical information in a free and highly industrialized society. He said "our top folks" felt too much was being published as a result of rivalries between corporations with defense contracts and between the armed forces, and of the enterprise of a free press and the historical tendency of scientists to report all the latest developments.

Mr. Wilson said the Administration was grappling with a complex problem the solution

Continued on Page 11, Column 1

Austro-Soviet Talk Toasted by Bohlen

By CLIFTON DANIEL

Special to The New York Times.

MOSCOW, April 12—In the presence of senior leaders of the Soviet state, Charles E. Bohlen, United States Ambassador, offered a toast this evening to the speedy restoration of Austria's independence and freedom.

Vyacheslav M Molotov, Soviet Foreign Minister, said it was a good toast and raised his glass. So did Premier Nikolai A. Bulganin and Deputy Premiers Lazar M. Kaganovich, Anastas I. Mikoyan and Mikhail G. Pervukhin.

Drinking with them were Julius Raab, Chancellor of Austria, and other members of the Austrian delegation that arrived here yesterday. The Austrians opened negotiations with Mr. Molotov during the afternoon on the terms of a treaty intended to achieve

Continued on Page 5, Column 3

Eisenhower Gets Degree From Clark at The Citadel

Associated Press Wirephoto

President Eisenhower and Gen. Mark W. Clark, retired, review honor guard at The Citadel

By W. H. LAWRENCE

Special to The New York Times.

AUGUSTA, Ga., April 12—President Eisenhower declared today that military men of the present and future must be "apostles of peace" working to understand what makes humans and nations "tick." This was his advice to the corps of cadets at The Citadel, the military college of South Carolina, in Charleston. He received an honorary Doctor of Laws degree from retired Gen. Mark W. Clark, president of The Citadel, and reviewed the cadets en route here for an eight-day golfing vacation. Greeting the cadets and applauding thousands who lined Charleston's streets, the Presi-

Continued on Page 12, Column 4

T. V. A. Detractors Scored by Lilienthal

By JOHN N. POPHAM

Special to The New York Times.

CHATTANOOGA, Tenn., April 12—David E. Lilienthal made a blistering attack tonight on the economic and political detractors of the Tennessee Valley Authority, "from the White House down."

The former chairman of the authority said that as a onetime neighbor he felt impelled to return to the valley region to help warn its residents concerning the tactics of the enemies currently waging a "cold war" against the famous river resources agency.

Mr. Lilienthal guided the development of T. V. A. through a succession of national controversies from 1933 to 1946. Then he spoke for public power philosophies espoused by the Federal Government, in contrast with his role of accusing the present Administration of

Continued on Page 15, Column 3

FANFARE USHERS VERDICT ON TESTS

Medical History Is Written in Hollywood Atmosphere

Special to The New York Times.

ANN ARBOR, Mich., April 12—The formal verdict on the Salk vaccine was disclosed today amid fanfare and drama far more typical of a Hollywood premiere than a medical meeting.

The event that made medical history took place in one of the University of Michigan's most glamorous structures—Rackham Building. Television cameras and radio microphones were set up outside the huge lecture hall. Inside the salmon-colored hall a battery of sixteen television and newsreel cameras were lined up across a long wooden platform especially built at the rear.

At 10:20 A. M. Dr. Thomas Francis Jr., director of the Poliomyelitis Vaccine Evaluation Center and the man of the hour, was introduced. A short, chunky man with a close-cropped mustache, he was wearing a black suit, white shirt and striped gray tie.

He stepped behind a lectern decorated with a blue and gold banner bearing the seal of the university. He appeared small, hidden up to his breast pocket by the lectern, as he looked out toward his audience of 500 scientists and physicians. Cameras ground and spotlights played

Continued on Page 30, Column 6

U. N. Health Agency Welcomes Vaccine, but Stresses Need of Further Research

QUESTIONS VALUE IN OTHER NATIONS

Geneva Official Urges Study to Determine Efficacy Against Alien Strains

REPORT IS 'ENCOURAGING'

Canada Plans to Inoculate One Million This Summer—Britain Maps Tests

Special to The New York Times.

UNITED NATIONS, N. Y., April 12—Officials of the World Health Organization hailed the report on the Salk poliomyelitis vaccine today as "extremely encouraging."

They cautioned, however, that more remained to be learned about the development.

The reaction from the United Nations medical agency was received by telephone from its Geneva headquarters. The caution expressed resembled other warnings that the vaccine may not be effective against strains of polio elsewhere.

An official of the health organization said at Geneva that further research must determine the duration of the protection conferred by the Salk vaccine and how it can be used.

For months the health organization has been planning a network of regional polio laboratories. One research center has been set up at the Yale University School of Medicine under Prof. John Rodman Paul.

A second center to cover the eastern Mediterranean has been established at the Hadassah Medical School in Jerusalem. Other regional centers are planned for Africa, Europe, the Western Pacific and Southeast Asia.

Ottawa to Aid Provinces

Special to The New York Times.

OTTAWA, April 12—Canada prepared today to inoculate about 1,000,000 children with the Salk vaccine this summer.

The Government offered the provinces additional Federal aid to increase their supplies. The vaccine at present is sufficient for 500,000 children. It licensed two United States drug manufacturers to produce and distribute the vaccine throughout Canada. They are Parke, Davis & Co., and the Eli Lilly Corporation. Both have branches in Canada.

It also announced that the Connaught Medical Research Laboratories of Toronto University, which made important contributions to the success of the vaccine, and the Institute of Microbiology of Montreal would step up their production.

British Plan Own Tests

Special to The New York Times.

LONDON, April 12—British medical authorities intend to test the Salk vaccine on a "limited scale."

Samples made in Britain and in the United States are available here. They will not be used until the British Medical Research Council has examined the latest reports in "detail," an official spokesman said tonight.

British reaction to reports of the trials in the United States have been summed up by the National Fund for Poliomyelitis Research thus:

"It does not necessarily follow that the strains of polio virus in the United States and the United Kingdom are sufficiently alike for a vaccine made in one country to be effective in the other. A number of very important questions remain to be answered."

A spokesman for the Ministry of Health said, "The Ministry will be ready with plans for wider use of polio vaccines just as soon as vaccines which have been proved safe and effective in this country are available. This stage has not yet been reached."

French Have Own Vaccine

Special to The New York Times.

PARIS, April 12—France is able to produce a "Salk-type" vaccine, Bernard LaFay, Minister of Public Health and Population, announced today.

The vaccine was perfected by Prof. Pierre LePine of the Pasteur Institute. It will not be widely tested on humans, but will be manufactured by the institute and held for emergencies.

Vaccination Planned in Europe

PARIS, April 12 (Reuters)—The United States report on a successful anti-polio vaccine stimulated mass vaccination plans throughout Europe.

In Copenhagen, the Folketing (Parliament) will debate tomorrow a bill to spend $280,000 on an anti-polio vaccination plan.

At Stockholm, the Swedish Board of Medicine has ordered enough of the United States vaccine for 100,000 persons.

All Oslo's 40,000 school children are expected to be vaccinated before they start their summer holidays.

Swiss private concerns have ordered supplies of the vaccine.

At Brussels, a special committee appointed by Edmond Leburton, Belgian health minister, already is studying Dr. Salk's methods of fighting polio, a Health Ministry spokesman said here tonight.

The Netherlands Health Ministry has been in touch with Dr. Thomas Francis, who evaluated the results, with a view to applying the discovery here.

At Bonn, the Health Section of the West German Interior Ministry said the ordering of supplies would not be considered until the Salk report had been studied further.

All Italian papers reported on the Salk test.

AT ANN ARBOR: Scientists listen to Dr. Thomas Francis Jr. speak on the effectiveness of the Salk polio vaccine

SALK'S VACCINE PROVES SUCCESS

Continued From Page 1

lined require two inoculations spaced two to four weeks apart, with a third "booster" shot seven months later.

This means that the amount of vaccine immediately available this season is automatically increased by 50 per cent, because in last year's trials the first two inoculations were given a week apart, and the third only one month after the second.

Comparisons Made Possible

There are three distinct types of polio virus, known respectively as Type I, II and III, or Brunhilde, Lansing and Leon. Each is able to produce paralytic polio.

The Salk vaccine is made of the three types of virus, killed by formaldehyde, so that they no longer can produce the disease, but retain their ability to stimulate the production of antibodies (immunity factors) in the recipient's blood stream.

In thirty-three states the vaccine was administered only to children in the second grade. Children in the first and third grades received no injections. The latter served as controls. That is, they were watched for the incidence of paralytic polio among them as compared with the vaccinated second graders.

The areas in these thirty-three states were known as the observed areas, as contrasted with the areas in the eleven states, in which all children in the first three grades were vaccinated. In these latter areas half of those injected were given the placebo. Hence they were known as the placebo areas.

The placebos and the real vaccines looked exactly alike. No one knew which was which until they were decoded by Dr. Francis. The placebos were used to eliminate any possible subjective influence, to make sure of 100 per cent objectivity in the tests.

Results Found to Differ

Dr. Francis' report states, however, that the data show that the vaccine was not equally effective against all the three types of the polio virus, either in the observed or in the placebo areas.

The report adds, "from these data it is not possible to select a single value giving numerical expression in a complete sense to the effectiveness of the vaccine as a total experience."

The results from the observed areas in the thirty-three states, the report states, suggest a lower effectiveness than those in the placebo areas.

"If the results from the observed study are employed," the Francis report declares, "the vaccine could be considered to have been 60 to 80 per cent effective against paralytic poliomyelitis, 60 per cent against Type I poliomyelitis, and 70 to 80 per cent effective against disease caused by Types II and III.

"There is, however, greater confidence in the results obtained from the strictly controlled and almost identical test populations in the placebo study area.

Effectiveness Calculated

"On this basis it may be suggested that vaccination was 80 to 90 per cent effective against paralytic poliomyelitis; that it was 60 to 70 per cent effective against disease caused by Type I virus and 90 per cent or more effective against that of Type II and Type III virus.

"The estimate would be more secure had a larger number of cases been available."

Type I polio is the most prevalent type of the disease. It accounts for about 65 per cent of all cases of clinical polio. Type II accounts for about 5 per cent of the clinical cases. Type III causes about 30 per cent.

Dr. Salk, talking further about the prospects for the current 1955 tests, said it had been found that a certain chemical that had been used as a preservative for the vaccine had destroyed a great deal of the vaccine potency. This may account for the lack of consistency in the results, the lower figures possibly being due to batches of vaccine that had lost their potency because of the preservative.

The field trails were made possible by $7,500,000 in March of Dimes funds provided by the National Foundation for Infantile Paralysis. The evaluation was carried out at a special center at the University of Michigan by a large staff directed by Dr. Francis, one of the world's outstanding epidemiologists.

Comparable Efficacies Cited

While no official figures are available, authorities here said that the effectiveness of most vaccines was in the neighborhood of 90 to 95 per cent. However, it was pointed out, none of them was 90 per cent efficient the first year it was given.

The two most effective vaccines now known are those against smallpox and yellow fever. Both are made of live attenuated virus. Their effectiveness is in the range of 95 per cent. This means that ninety-five out of every 100 vaccinated are protected against the disease if exposed to it. Effective vaccines, in the form known as toxoids, also exist against diphtheria, about 90 per cent effective, and tetanus, about 95 per cent effective.

Potent vaccines also exist against whooping cough, typhoid fever, typhus fever, Rocky Mountain spotted fever, rabies and influenza. The vaccine against typhus reduces mortality from the disease to zero, but that does not mean it also completely eliminates the sickness. The vaccine against influenza is effective against only the same strain of virus.

The vaccine last year was given in three separate inoculations, of one cubic centimeter each. The first two were given one week apart, while the third, known as the "booster" shot was given one month after the second.

The first two inoculations are the conditioning shots, creating in the blood stream a "memory" that mobilizes the body's defensive forces quickly as it is invaded by the specific microbe against which the vaccine has been designed.

The third "booster" shot is thus the one, aided by the "memory," that produces in the blood stream the largest amount of anti-bodies.

The effectiveness of the "booster" shot depends on the time interval between it and the conditioning shots, as it takes a definite amount of time for the "memory" to be fully developed. Dr. Salk's latest studies have revealed, he reported today, that the "booster" shot should properly be given some seven months after the first conditioning shots, as it takes that long for the anti-polio "memory" to be fully developed.

These findings, therefore, indicate that the percentage of effectiveness on the mass trials last year would have been considerably greater had the "booster" shot been given seven months after the first two, instead of only one month later.

Would Cut Inoculations

Only two inoculations, spaced two to four weeks apart, should be given in 1955, instead of three over a five-week period, Dr. Salk reported today.

The third shot, should not be given before at least seven months have elapsed, but certainly before the onset of the 1956 polio season, he said.

At present it is known that the National Foundation for Infantile Paralysis has ordered a total of 27,000,000 cubic centimers of the vaccine on the basis of three shots of one cubic centimer each. This quantity is enough for the immunization of 9,000,000 children.

However, if only two shots of one cubic centimer each are to be given this year, with the third shot to be postponed for seven months, the 27,000,000 cubic centimers would provide immunization for 13,500,000 individuals.

Basil O'Connor, president of the National Foundation, said no decision had as yet been made as to what course of distribution to follow in the light of Dr. Salk's latest findings.

Reactions to the vaccine were nearly negligible, the Francis report showed. Only 0.4 per cent of the vaccinated children suffered minor reactions. An even smaller percentage suffered more severe reactions.

The persistence of protection appears reasonably good. When good anti-body responses were obtained from vaccination, the report said, "the effect was maintained with but moderate decline after five months."

Distribution of anti-body levels among vaccinated persons was much higher than that in the control population from the same areas.

Out of a total population of 1,829,916 children a total of 1,013 cases of polio developed during the study period and were reported to the center.

In places of control areas, where vaccine was interchanged with an inert substance, 428 out of 749,236 children contracted the disease.

In the observed control areas where only second graders were inoculated, 585 cases developed among 1,080,680 children.

Only One Death Reported

Specifically, thirty-three inoculated children in the placebo areas receiving the complete vaccination series became paralyzed. This is opposed to 115 uninoculated children who contracted the disease.

Similarly, in the observed areas there were thirty-eight such children who became paralyzed, as opposed to 330 uninoculated children.

There were four deaths among children who received placebo; none among the vaccinated. In observed areas there were eleven fatalities; none among children receiving the vaccine.

Only one child who had been inoculated with the vaccine died of polio, and this death followed a tonsillectomy two days after the second injection of the vaccine in an area where polio was already prevalent.

Other findings were:

¶The vaccine's effectiveness was more clearly seen when measured against the more severe cases of the disease.

¶Although data were limited, findings in Canada and Finland support the report in showing a significant effect of the vaccine among cases from whom virus was isolated.

¶Vaccination protected against family exposure. One out of 233 inoculated children developed the disease, while eight out of 244 children receiving placebo contracted the disease from family contact.

Dr. Salk further urged that all children who had received polio inoculations during the 1954 field trials should be given an additional dose in 1955. This is necessary, he said, because the three doses given in 1954 could not have been expected to produce more than a primary effect.

Dr. Salk explained that the first two inoculations in the three-inoculation series were sufficient to induce a primary stimulation of disease fighters in the blood. Over a period of months, a hyper-reactive state develops. This is simply a state of readiness, somewhat like a revolver that is cocked and ready to fire at a slight pressure on the trigger.

While the amount of measureable anti-body in the blood serum may not be large during this state of readiness, a "booster" shot administered after the required seven months serves as a trigger to explode the anti-body formation to remarkably high levels.

He added that exposure to a natural polio infection also served to induce the rapid production of anti-body once the hyper-reactive state has been developed in the anti-body cells.

In other words, even though anti-body may not be demonstrable in the blood serum at the time of invasion by polio virus, previous vaccination will have so primed the immunologic mechanism that anti-body in good concentration would appear in the serum shortly after the initiation of virus multiplication at the portal of entry.

If such anti-body development occurs prior to invasion of the blood stream and is present in sufficient concentration, access of virus to the central nervous system would be intercepted.

Dr. Salk said that use of vaccine for the first time during the polio season, or even in epidemic areas, might be expected to have a beneficial effect so long as certain time limitations are kept in mind.

He said that measurable anti-body was almost always induced by the fourteenth day after first vaccination. It is conceivable, then, that the probability of contracting paralytic polio would be less if exposure occurred after anti-body was present in the serum in concentration.

Hollywood Atmosphere Ushers Event Making Medical History

Continued From Page 1

upon him. Then Dr. Francis adjusted his horn-rimmed glasses and began to read his long-awaited report in a slow, conversational tone. It was the report of a meticulous and dedicated scientist, presented without dramatics.

Nevertheless, the moment was a dramatic one, no matter how hard the Professor of Epidemiology tried to make it otherwise with his charts and statistics and careful qualifications. The nation and the world had been waiting for this report, a report that could mean hope for millions of parents and a great step forward in the control of paralytic polio.

Dr. Francis talked for an hour and forty minutes. Occasionally he would step back from the lectern. The lights would dim out and a slide would be flashed on a screen behind the lectern. Dr. Francis would call attention to various statistics and chart illustrations by pointing a flashlight on the screen.

The audience was quiet and respectful. There were no bursts of applause. Even at the end of Dr. Francis' address, after he had made it clear that the Salk vaccine had been proved an effective weapon, the applause seemed restrained.

Outside the hall, however, the Hollywood atmosphere prevailed. Students and the curious crowded close behind television cameras set up for interviews with medical celebrities. In a press room three floors above, more than 150 newspaper, radio and television reporters were sending out details.

Actually word of the findings had been sent out before Dr. Francis began to talk. University public-relations officials brought 300 copies of the report to the pressroom at 9:15 A. M.

Although there had been purported leaks regarding the report, university officials had denied they were authentic and had put up a well-nigh impenetrable barrier around the evaluation center.

It was disclosed today that Dr. Francis did not finish writing his report until 3 A. M. last Friday. It was not until late Thursday evening, according to Robert B. Voight, statistician for the center, that Dr. Francis and his staff reached the point where they could set down accurate estimates.

There was other evidence of the tight security. Dr. Jonas E. Salk, who developed the vaccine, acknowledged that he had not had an opportunity to read the report. Basil O'Connor, president of the National Foundation for Infantile Paralysis, indicated that he had not seen it in advance either.

With Dr. Salk today in his hour of triumph were his wife, Mrs. Donna Salk, and three sons, Peter, 11 years old; Darrell, 8 and Jonathan, 5. The two older boys were among the first to be inoculated with the vaccine developed by their father.

Much attention was focused throughout the day on Dr. Salk, who had spend long hours in the laboratory to make this day possible.

Mrs. Salk seemed somewhat embarrassed by all the attention. She said that she and her family would be glad when things calmed down again and they could return to normal life.

LEADERS OF A.M.A. HAIL VACCINE TEST

Chairman of Trustees Terms Announcement a Great Event in Medicine

Special to The New York Times.

ANN ARBOR, Mich., April 12—Dr. Dwight H. Murray of Napa, Calif., termed the announcement here today that the Salk anti-polio vaccine had been proved effective in preventing paralytic polio "one of the greatest events in the history of medicine."

"Up to this time," Dr. Murray, chairman of the board of trustees of the American Medical Association, said, "Dr. Salk's work has made available for the public the most encouraging new weapon in the history of poliomyelitis control.

"While further study is necessary to determine the long-term effectiveness of the vaccine, today's historic announcement signals the launching of vaccination programs, involving millions of children, all over the country.

"The American people can be assured that the thousands of practicing physicians in cities, towns and hamlets will give their wholehearted cooperation to get the programs under way as effectively and safely as is humanly possible."

He urged adults to have patience and not rush to doctors' offices immediately because probably most parents already have immunity to the disease. "Give the children priority," he said.

He said many medical societies throughout the country had, with aid of state and local health officers, worked out orderly plans for the administration of the vaccine.

Dr. Murray said he understood that far more vaccine than was originally planned was expected to be available by early summer.

Other Leaders Comment

Dr. Murray was one of four A. M. A. officials who heard Dr. Thomas Francis Jr., director of the Independent Poliomyelitis Vaccine Evaluation Center of the University of Michigan, make his official report on the effectiveness of the vaccine developed by Dr. Jonas E. Salk.

The other three officials were Dr. Elmer Hess of Erie, Pa., president-elect of the association; Dr. Ernest B. Howard of Chicago, assistant secretary, and Dr. Austin Smith, editor of the Journal of the American Medical Association.

"While our knowledge of the mechanism of poliomyelitis still has great gaps waiting to be filled in, Dr. Hess said, the Francis report is scientific proof that we now hold the key pieces to a jigsaw puzzle which has held the attention of scientific minds for many years."

Dr. Hess termed today's report "more thrilling than any detective story."

Other prominent medical authorities at the scientific meeting also commented on the vaccine.

Dr. Alan Gregg, vice president of the Rockefeller Foundation: "It is possible that the degree of protection offered by the Salk vaccine will be such as to give a control of infantile paralysis comparable to the control we have over smallpox, yellow fever, diphtheria and typhoid.

"This does not mean or imply complete eradication, though it does not exclude it * * * Measures that give protection to every one individual protect others from exposure and vice versa. This first possible is one of immeasurable importance.

"A second possible derives from the first. The remarkable successes of last year's controlled experiment * * * may pave the way for comparably intelligent and courageous mass experiments in point of other diseases. Even that ever-present and menacing uncertainty among diseases, the common cold, may prove susceptible of control."

Dr. Thomas M. Rivers, director of the Rockefeller Institute for Medical Research, New York, and chairman of the Vaccine Advisory Committee, National Foundation for Infantile Paralysis, who accepted the Francis report on behalf of the Foundation:

"Whoever accepts your report does so not for a committee, a foundation, a sector of the world of science. He accepts it for America. He must acknowledge it on behalf of millions of children and young people and their mothers and fathers. He must at this moment speak for untold and yet unborn generations, in this country and the world over, whose lives and usefulness will have been saved by the achievement to which you have contributed.

"That contribution is very large indeed. I do not know whether all of us here realize how very exacting was the assignment of evaluating the greatest field trial and one of the greatest endeavors in the history of preventive medicine."

Dr. David Bodian, Associate Professor of Epidemiology, the Johns Hopkins University:

"As I see it, the meaning of the field trial as a step in the eradication of poliomyelitis is that it proves that small amounts of antibody in the serum produced by three viruses in the vaccine will prevent the paralytic effects of most of the viruses active in this country last summer.

"Without the strong probability of this effect, deduced from laboratory experiment, the trial would have been only a vain flexing of muscles.

"In addition, the field trial gives us the first complete assurance that poliomyelitis vaccines now and in the future can be adequately tested for safety in the laboratory before release for human use."

Dr. William G. Workman, director of the Laboratory of Biologics Control, the National Institutes of Health, United States Public Health Service:

"Although an important milestone has been reached it is important to realize that it is just that and an arduous task lies ahead to gain the benefits of the knowledge which has been developed.

"An immediate problem for which there is no obvious solution is a means for determining by a quick reliable method the immune status of the individual. Such a test would permit the selection for immunization of those persons who need it most and the most effective use of the available supply of vaccine.

"Another important question is that of the durability of immunity. It is a reasonable hope that, as in diphtheria, natural exposure to the poliomyelitis viruse will continue to reinforce the immunity established by vaccination, but experience possibly of some years will be required to establish this hypothesis."

Mrs. Roosevelt Pleased By Salk Test Outcome

HYDE PARK, N. Y., April 12 (AP)—Mrs. Franklin D. Roosevelt, whose husband suffered from poliomyelitis, said today that she was "delighted" with the outcome of the Salk vaccine tests.

"Of course, we will have to go on with the March of Dimes for a long time, because we still have people who have had the disease who must be cared for," she declared.

Mrs. Roosevelt made her comments soon after putting a wreath of lilies on her husband's grave. He died ten years ago today.

AGE OF SALK'S AIDES AVERAGES UNDER 40

PITTSBURGH, April 12 (UP)—The assistants whom Dr. Jonas E. Salk credits with major roles in the development of his poliomyelitis vaccine average less than 40 years of age.

The key members were gathered from points as distant as Australia and Germany. About fifty persons work in the laboratory, which occupies three floors in the Pittsburgh Municipal Hospital for Contagious Disease.

Included on Salk's "team" are: Maj. Byron L. Bennett, 47 years old, a Texas-born ex-sailor who switched to the Army Medical Service in World War II and was cited for his work against typhus in Egypt and Italy.

Dr. Julius S. Youngner, 34, a former New York resident who worked on the Manhattan project but did not know the goal was the atom bomb until after one was dropped on Hiroshima.

Dr. Percival L. Bazeley, 44, whose earnings as a veterinarian financed his way through medical school with four and one-half years out as a combat officer in an Australian tank corps in the southern Pacific.

Dr. Ulrich Krech, 35, a German who was drafted into the Nazi air force and assigned to a field hospital as a physician although he had not yet received his medical degree.

Dr. L. James Lewis, 34, an antibiotic and vaccine expert who, although a Doctor of Philosophy, has performed surgery on an estimated 15,000 monkeys during the polio research.

Robert Rotunda, 35, research assistant.

Philadelphia to Act

Special to The New York Times.

PHILADELPHIA, April 12—This city will start to inoculate 78,850 first and second grade pupils with the Salk anti-polio vaccine on April 25.

SCIENCE QUELLING ANCIENT PLAGUES

In Half a Century, Scourges of Mankind Have Yielded to Medical Advances

In half a century, medical science has virtually eliminated in some parts of the world afflictions that had plagued mankind through the ages.

These accomplishments are marked in the United States by a comparison of the life expectancy at the time of birth. In 1900, according to the best estimates, the average was an expectancy of about fifty years. This year, the expectancy is nearing the Biblical three score and ten years. Half a century ago, three out of five infants reached seventy years. Now, about half of all infants attain this age.

Most of this progress in the United States has come through control of infectious diseases, particularly those that afflict children. Vaccines to prevent diseases and new germ-killing drugs to prevent lethal complications following benign infections have caused part of the reduction in death due to infection.

Other Factors Credited

Part also has come through scientific supervision of food and water supplies, provision of adequate sanitary facilities and wide dissemination of scientific health information. Social and economic changes have played a part, too, as has control of insects and rodents.

The four principal communicable diseases of children were once measles, scarlet fever, whooping cough and diphtheria. Diphtheria and smallpox have largely been controlled by immunizations. A combination of immunization and antibiotic drugs has taken much of the peril out of whooping cough.

Measles is mitigated by gamma globulin injections. A combination of immunization and chemotherapy has lowered the death rates from scarlet fever.

In large areas of the world, typhoid fever and dysenteries have almost disappeared. Malaria has been reduced by the use of the insecticide DDT, and by sanitation. Vaccination has been effective in reducing cholera, rabies and typhus.

Tuberculosis was the second leading cause of death in 1900, following pneumonia and influenza. Tuberculosis is now partly controlled by a combination of drug therapy, public health prevention, surgery and vaccination. The anti-TB vaccine BCG is widely used in Europe. At this time, tuberculosis ranks much lower as a cause of death, although it is still important.

Pneumonia Toll Lower

Pneumonia and influenza were the leading cause of death in 1900. Now they rank lower, near tuberculosis, following the institution of antibiotic therapy that helps prevent complications that used to be fatal. Infantile diarrhea, which used to rank high, has been virtually eliminated.

Despite these successes, modern medical science has some areas in which death rates appear to have gone up. In large part, they may have gone up because the increasing life expectancy has put more people into the age groups where the degenerative diseases usually strike. The degenerative diseases include heart disease and cancer. They now rank in that order as leading causes of death. Excepted are accidents, which kill and maim more people in the United States each year than any other single factor.

New attacks on heart disease and cancer are being made now in laboratories across the nation. Some such studies are supported partly by public fund drives like those of the National Foundation for Infantile Paralysis, and partly by the Federal Government. Leading fund-raising organizations are the American Cancer Society and the American Heart Association.

CANADIANS HELPED BY PRODUCING VIRUS

Special to The New York Times.

TORONTO, April 12—One of the important roles in the mass assault on polio was played by the Connaught Medical Research Laboratories of the University of Toronto.

It was here that two teams of scientists headed by Drs. R. C. Parker and Andrew Rhodes made the discoveries that led to mass culture of the virus from which the Salk vaccine was produced.

Connaught manufactured more than 90 per cent of the virus used to obtain the vaccine for the mass testing of United States and Canadian school children. The laboratories are now turning out their own vaccine for Canadian use.

At Harvard University in 1949 Dr. John Enders had shown that polio virus could be kept alive on animal nerve tissues but the tissues were expensive and difficult to obtain.

Connaught Dr. Rhodes and Miss L. N. Farrell, a researcher, sought a new method, testing scores of tissues suspended in a wide variety of liquids.

Finally they came up with the combination of monkey kidney tissue and a nutrient fluid called Medium 199, developed at Connaught years before for cancer studies.

The fluid, formulated by Dr. Parker, Dr. J. F. Morgan and Miss H. J. Morton, was composed of sixty-two ingredients, many of them costly. But when the monkey kidneys were immersed in it it provided a fast efficient breeding ground for the virus.

300,000 Pupils in Jersey to Get Vaccine; Bergen to Start the Injections Monday

Special to The New York Times.

TRENTON, April 12—The inoculation of nearly 300,000 school children with the Salk polio vaccine will begin Monday in New Jersey. The program will be started in Bergen County.

The mass immunization in the lower grades was planned several months ago. It will be financed and directed by the National Foundation for Infantile Paralysis.

State health authorities explained that the time it would take for the vaccine to become available for other children throughout the state would depend primarily on its availability and on the costs of the vaccine to be purchased for it.

Dr. Carl E. Weigele, assistant State Commissioner of Health, said that vaccine to immunize one child would cost $3 to $4.

Under the present program, he explained, first and second grade pupils in public, parochial and private schools in sixteen counties would be eligible to receive the Salk inoculations without charge. It will also be administered to first, second, third and fourth grade pupils in the state's five other counties.

The latter are Bergen, Morris, Monmouth, Cape May and Warren. The vaccine was tested in those counties last year among second grade pupils. The 15,000 children who received it at that time will not be eligible for the forthcoming injections.

Scores of physicians throughout the state have volunteered their services without charge to help give the injections in schools.

The City of Trenton is considering making the vaccine available to children whose parents are unable to pay for the required three inoculations.

"All the News That's Fit to Print"

The New York Times.

LATE CITY EDITION

Heavy rain and high winds today; clearing tonight. Fair tomorrow.

Temperature Range Today—Max., 79; Min., 71

Temperatures Yesterday—Max., 78.6; Min., 67

Full U. S. Weather Bureau Report, Page 61

VOL. CV. No. 35,668. Entered as Second-Class Matter. Post Office, New York, N. Y. NEW YORK, TUESDAY, SEPTEMBER 20, 1955. Times Square, New York 36, N. Y. Telephone Lackawanna 4-1000 FIVE CENTS

PERON'S REGIME IS OVERTHROWN; JUNTA WILL MEET WITH REBELS; CROWDS HAIL FALL OF DICTATOR

GALES MOVE ON THE CITY; SOUTH IS HIT

DAMAGE IS SEVERE

New York Area Due to Feel the Effects of Hurricane Today

By PETER KIHSS

Hurricane Ione tore wide destruction in coastal North Carolina when it roared in from the Atlantic Ocean yesterday morning.

Then it slowed down and became a tricky problem that kept the entire Eastern Seaboard worried.

In Washington the United States Weather Bureau said at 3 o'clock this morning that the tropical twister was centered about twenty miles southeast of Norfolk, Va., with winds of over thirty-five miles an hour swirling outward 200 miles to the north and east.

Swirling northeastward at eight to ten miles an hour, it is expected to pick up speed and intensity as it swings out to sea. It was expected to be off the Delaware coast this morning and southeast of Long Island in the afternoon.

Ernest J. Christie, in charge of the Weather Bureau here, said at 3 o'clock this morning that New York City would feel the worst effects of the storm later today.

The center of the storm, he said, would pass southeast of the city during the day. New York City, on the northern fringe of the storm, would have heavy rain at times with wind velocities of forty to fifty miles an hour and gusts possibly up to sixty miles an hour. Clearing weather was forecast for tonight.

Forecasts Are Qualified

Hurricane force is seventy-five miles an hour or more, according to the Weather Bureau scale.

But meteorologists were qualifying all their forecasts, warning that Ione—whose name comes from the Greek word meaning "go"—was an erratic personality.

Ione, hatched last Wednesday east of Puerto Rico, did millions of dollars worth of damage as it roared overland across the coastal areas of North Carolina with winds up to 107 miles an hour.

Communications lines were down, roads and bridges washed out, crops destroyed, large areas of cities flooded and hundreds made homeless.

Reports of the damage were fragmentary, but mounting rapidly as communications were restored. Four persons were reported dead at New Bern, N. C., and three at Beaufort, N. C. The Red Cross said it was providing shelter for 1,800 persons in the state.

New Bern, a city of 15,000 persons, was jammed before the hurricane with hundreds of refugees from tidal river lowlands. Forty blocks of the city were flooded and for fifteen hours the community was without power, communications and drinking

Continued on Page 24, Column 1

Hilda Rips Tampico In 'Worst Disaster'

By The United Press.

MEXICO CITY, Sept. 19—President Adolfo Ruiz Cortines tonight ordered unlimited Government aid for storm-lashed Tampico as Hurricane Hilda sent a flood of "catastrophic proportions" over three-quarters of the port city.

The President said Tampico, cut off by winds and water from the outside world, was confronted with "the worst disaster in its history."

[The Associated Press said Monday that Gov. Horacio Teran reported the hurricane had killed twelve persons and injured 350 in Tampico. The Governor of Tamaulipas State said 90 per cent of the buildings in the city had been damaged and 15,000 were homeless. A state of emergency was ordered.]

A medical brigade of 200

Continued on Page 24, Column 7

CITY IS PREPARED FOR STORM'S FURY

Lines Kept Open From Center at Police Headquarters to Waiting Emergency Men

Residents of the metropolitan area battened down for Hurricane Ione yesterday while Government and welfare agencies made elaborate plans to mitigate the fury of wind, rain and high tides.

New York and surrounding communities, long forewarned, appeared to be prepared as never before to weather a big storm.

The focal point of relief, rescue and damage control activities was Mayor Wagner's board of planning and operations sitting at Police Headquarters.

A communications center in the line-up room, staffed by 114 policemen, maintained open lines to all city departments and welfare agencies. Representatives of each organization were posted there at nightfall ready to flash orders to emergency crews on stand-by throughout the city.

Police Commissioner Stephen P. Kennedy urged the public, in event of emergency, to telephone available information to the Police Department.

The Civil Defense Administration, on alert since Sunday night, had its 149 fire and rescue units ready for instant action. At 5 P. M. Robert E. Condon, City Director of Civil Defense, ordered his top personnel to remain on duty until further notice.

Two thousand Red Cross workers were standing by in the city and neighboring communities. The city's Department of Welfare was similarly prepared to staff 100 relief centers in the five boroughs.

In Albany three units of the New York National Guard, including the Forty-second Division stationed here, were alerted

Continued on Page 24, Column 8

HARRIMAN READY TO COMPETE IN '56, ADVISER DECLARES

Prendergast Says Governor Would Oppose Stevenson if Party Wanted Him

By WARREN WEAVER Jr.

Special to The New York Times.

ALBANY, Sept. 19—Governor Harriman will seek the Presidential nomination next year if "convinced the convention wanted him," the Democratic State Chairman said today.

The chairman asserted the Governor would do this even in the event of a floor fight with Adlai E. Stevenson.

Michael H. Prendergast, the Governor's chief political lieutenant, declared that under such conditions Mr. Harriman would take the nomination "regardless of whether Stevenson stepped aside or not."

This was the first public indication from within his official political family that Mr. Harriman's repeated expressions of support for Mr. Stevenson might be weakening in the face of insistence that he seek the nomination.

Charles Van Devander, the Governor's press secretary, said tonight there would be no comment from his office on the Prendergast statement. He said the Governor was in New York City. The Governor's aides in New York likewise said there would be no comment.

For the last year whenever Presidential politics were discussed, Mr. Harriman has said "I'm for Stevenson," smiled broadly and declined to discuss any other possibilities.

Says Democrats Can Win

Mr. Prendergast was the Governor's personal choice to succeed Richard H. Balch as head of the Democratic State Committee last July.

The Democratic chairman characterized as "a lot of nonsense" Republican assertions that no opponent could beat President Eisenhower.

"I don't give a damn who they run," Mr. Prendergast declared. "We can win next year with the right man, and I think Harriman is the right man. Regardless of who he says he's for, I'm representing the Democratic party—the rank and file of it—when I say I'm for Harriman."

Although Mr. Prendergast said he could not speak for the Governor, he described Mr. Harriman indirectly as a man who was thinking now in terms of his own candidacy, rather than Mr. Stevenson's or anyone else's.

"I know Mr. Harriman well enough to know that he is so definitely interested in a Democratic victory in 1956 that if he felt someone else, other than himself, were stronger and had a better chance of winning, he would be for him regardless," the state chairman declared.

Mr. Prendergast's analysis of the situation was made at a press conference. He called the session to announce that former President Harry S. Truman would speak at the state-wide Democratic candidate's rally here on Oct. 7.

The state chairman was generally deprecatory of Mr. Stevenson's chances. He said that the former Illinois Governor's announcement of his plans in November "isn't going to stampede anybody." He predicted that getting the nomination would be "no walkover for Stevenson."

Sees Swing to Harriman

On the contrary, Mr. Prendergast said, prospects that the national convention might look favorably on Mr. Harriman appear to be increasing daily.

"I think we're going into the convention with a lot of sentiment in our favor," he asserted. "Unless something unforeseen happens, I don't see how we can miss."

He later amended this to say he believed that the Governor has "a better than even chance of getting the nomination."

Mr. Prendergast was asked if the Governor had requested him to "soft-pedal" his Harriman-for-President campaign, inasmuch as Mr. Harriman was on record for Mr. Stevenson.

"No, he's said nothing about that," the chairman replied.

Mr. Prendergast also announced that he would open an upstate office for the State Committee in the Sheraton Ten Eyck Hotel here on Oct. 1. It will include offices for Miss Mary Louise Nice of Tonawanda, state committee vice chairman, and Carmine G. DeSapio, the party's national committeeman.

The Democratic leader said he was particularly glad to have

Continued on Page 22, Column 5

U. S. TIES HINTED

Will Grant Recognition to Insurgents as They Take Over Nation

By DANA ADAMS SCHMIDT

Special to The New York Times.

WASHINGTON, Sept. 19—Administration officials said tonight that the United States would undoubtedly recognize any new Argentine Government that showed it was in control of the country.

The State Department, insisting that any comment at this time would be a form of interference, declined to discuss the attitude the United States might take toward a new Argentine Government.

However, other officials of the Administration pointed out that the United States had followed the practice of recognizing Latin-American revolutionary governments as soon as they exercised full authority. In some cases there has been preliminary discussion with other Latin-American governments.

But the fact that relations between the United States and President Juan D. Perón were frequently strained during his nine years as President made it unlikely the United States would hesitate, these officials said.

Hostile Attitude Cited

For several years after President Perón had taken power his attitude toward the United States was hostile, thus playing upon popular antipathies toward the "Yankee imperialists." However, in recent years relations between Washington and Buenos Aires have been correct, although "hardly warm," in the view of one diplomatic student of Latin-American affairs.

President Perón has sought and obtained from the United States a number of loans that have helped his Government through the difficulties that followed the application of "Perónist economics." This consisted of building up industry at the expense of agriculture.

As to whether the United States has ever "supported" the Peronist regime, there are strong differences of opinion among officials. The prevailing view is that the United States Government's attitude has been carefully "objective."

While avoiding anything that would look like official interference, State Department officials told a Congressional committee after the unsuccessful June 16 rising in Argentina that they were seeking to use United States influence quietly to prevent persecution of the Roman Catholic Church.

Catholic groups in the United States at that time demanded that the United States openly

Continued on Page 2, Column 6

COMMAND VAGUE

Rebels Believed to Be in 3 Groups, With No Over-All Chief

By TAD SZULC

Special to The New York Times.

SANTIAGO, Chile, Sept. 19—Broadcasts from Argentina indicated today that the rebel forces were operating with at least three separate commands and that no over-all chief of the movement had yet emerged.

Admiral Issac Rojas was in charge of the naval operation along the Argentine coast and of the marine units ashore. There were contradictory reports as to the identity of the leaders of the insurgent army forces operating inland.

In a telephone interview from the headquarters of the rebel-directed Second Army in Mendoza, in the foothills of the Andes, a general who identified himself as the chief of staff of the revolutionary command said that Gen. Eduardo Leonardi was the top military leader of the movement.

He said that General Leonardi was in Cordoba, where attacks of the Government forces had been fought off for several days.

General About 52 Years Old

He described General Leonardi as a "respected" officer who had served at one time as an Argentine military attaché abroad. He said General Leonardi was about 52 years old. No other data about General Leonardi were available here.

A virtually independent command in Mendoza, embracing the provinces of Mendoza, San Juan and San Luis, was held by Gen. Julio Alberto Lagos.

In an earlier telephone interview General Lagos identified himself as the chief of the revolution. But his chief of staff said later that General Lagos meant he was merely in charge of the three western provinces.

The chief of staff said that the coordination among the various commands was still deficient and he refused to say what plans the rebels had to take over the Government of Argentina. He declined to say what form of revolutionary government was being contemplated.

He declared that communication among the various commanders was by radio and courier planes.

Broadcasts picked up in Santiago told the series of dramatic events that culminated today in the virtual surrender of the man who for twelve years had ruled Argentina as a dictator.

It came on the fourth day of the bloody rebellion against President Juan D. Perón by the Navy and sections of the Army as the insurgent fleet stood off

Continued on Page 2, Column 3

GEN. JUAN D. PERON

PEACE IS SOUGHT

Government Orders Its Forces to End Fight —Port Is Shelled

Texts of the Government and Perón statements, Page 3.

By EDWARD A. MORROW

Special to The New York Times.

BUENOS AIRES, Tuesday, Sept. 20.—The Government of President Juan D. Perón fell last night.

A four-man junta of army generals assumed command of the forces that had fought unsuccessfully to keep General Perón in power. He had been master of Argentina since Oct. 17, 1945, and its President for nine years.

[A loyalist military junta told the rebels that General Perón had officially resigned the Presidency, The Associated Press reported.]

The junta quickly entered into negotiations to end the four-day civil war. Army and Navy units had joined in the rebellion and forced the resignation of the President, the Cabinet and other authorities.

Among those who tended their "irrevocable" resignations was the Minister of the Army, Gen. Franklin Lucero. On June 16 he had quelled a navy-led revolt.

There was no news about the whereabouts of President Perón tonight. Some reports had him in asylum at the Paraguayan Embassy in Buenos Aires. The embassy denied these.

Perón Statement Read

The low ceiling prevented any planes from leaving the city's army airport and seemed to cast doubt on other reports that the President had fled to Paraguay.

General Perón offered his resignation yesterday afternoon in a statement read for him over the state radio. He suggested that the Army take charge. He had made a somewhat similar offer to resign Aug. 31 but withdrew it after "protests" from his followers.

It was widely rumored that General Perón had committed suicide. There was no official announcement to this effect, and well-informed diplomats doubted the report.

[A rebel radio broadcast from Bahia Blanca said the Argentine Confederation of Labor was planning a general strike for dawn Tuesday in an effort to restore General Perón to power, The Associated Press reported.]

The Government ordered troops that still remained loyal to it to cease fighting. It asked the rebels to do likewise to prevent further bloodshed after the Navy had shelled the seaside city of Mar del Plata and the rebels had shown other signs of strength throughout the country.

Large sections of the Buenos Aires population braved a light rain this afternoon to stage joyful demonstrations in the city's streets. The Plaza de Mayo, scene of many mass Peronist demonstrations in the past, had a small number of the Presi-

Continued on Page 3, Column 5

MOSCOW TO INSIST ON BONN-RED TALK

Soviet Will Shun Any Voice in German Domestic Rifts in Treaty Due Today

By CLIFTON DANIEL

Special to The New York Times.

MOSCOW, Sept. 19—Measures to force West Germany to deal directly with the East German Communist Government were being planned today in Moscow.

Walter Ulbricht, East German Deputy Premier and Communist party chief, declared that in the future there would be no other way of settling questions in dispute between the two parts of Germany.

He said that under the treaty to be concluded with the Soviet Union here tomorrow the East German Government would control the border with West Germany and communications between West Germany and West Berlin.

"The sooner the politicians of Bonn and West Berlin realize that they cannot undermine the East German regime, the better it will be for the populace of West Berlin," Herr Ulbricht said ominously.

His implication seemed to be that the East German Government would be in a position to impose a new blockade on Berlin and that on such matters the Bonn Government would have to negotiate not with mere officials or technicians but with the East German Government itself.

Sovereign Status Due

Herr Ulbricht spoke during the negotiations with Soviet leaders on a treaty that will give to the East German regime the same sovereign status the Western Allies gave West Germany.

Upon conclusion of the treaty the Soviet Government will abolish the office of High Commissioner in Germany, Marshal Nikolai A. Bulganin, Soviet Premier, disclosed in a speech.

Henceforth, the Soviet Ambassador to East Germany will deal with United States, British and French representatives in West Germany on questions concerning Germany as a whole and on questions arising from four-power agreements, the Soviet Premier declared.

In addition, Marshal Bulganin said all laws, decrees and directives promulgated by the four-power Allied Control Council for Germany would be annulled on the territory of East Germany. Those regulations were enacted between 1945 and 1948, when the Soviet representative, Marshal Vassily D. Sokolovsky, withdrew and the Allied Control Council ceased to function.

The treaty between the Soviet Union and East Germany will provide that East Germany is free in all internal and foreign affairs, including relations with West Germany, Herr Ulbricht

Continued on Page 8, Column 3

FINNS AND SOVIET RENEW ALLIANCE

Moscow Agrees to Withdraw Its Military and Naval Forces Within 3 Months

Special to The New York Times.

MOSCOW, Sept. 19—Finland and the Soviet Union renewed their mutual defense alliance today for a period of twenty years.

At the same time the Soviet Government formally agreed to withdraw its military and naval forces from their base on Finnish territory within three months.

Those were the results of the Soviet-Finnish negotiations concluded here today and they gave "great joy" to the witty and lively old man who is President of Finland, Juho K. Paasikivi.

"I am here in Moscow for the seventh time for negotiations on affairs of state concerning Finland and the Soviet Union," the President said this evening at a party held in the Kremlin to celebrate the signing of the two agreements.

"But this is the first time that I return to our capital satisfied," he said. "Usually I have returned unsatisfied."

His audience laughed and applauded.

Exactly eight years ago today President Paasikivi was here on one of those unsatisfying missions. He signed a fifty-year lease that gave to the Soviet Union a naval and military base on the Porkkala Peninsula as provided by the truce agreement that ended the war between the two countries in 1944.

Tonight President Paasikivi observed that the Porkkala base now to be handed back to Finland was situated only twelve

Continued on Page 6, Column 3

Governor Calls for Federal Aid To Save Nation's Ailing Schools

But Royall Tells Conference That the Education System Should Be Contracted

By BENJAMIN FINE

A sweeping program of Federal aid to education, on both school and college levels, was advocated yesterday by Governor Harriman.

Speaking before 800 community, labor, business and school leaders at the New York State Conference on Education, the Governor said that nothing but Federal support could solve the critical problem in American education.

The two-day meeting at the Biltmore Hotel is a preliminary to the White House Conference on Education in Washington from Nov. 28 to Dec. 1. Major school issues are on the agenda, for both the New York and the Washington sessions.

Unexpectedly, the conference opened on a controversial note. The chairman of the New York State committee, Kenneth C. Royall, who was the keynote speaker, told the delegates they should be thinking of ways to contract, not expand, the educational system. Mr. Royall, who was Secretary of War under

Kenneth C. Royall

President Truman, said that too many young people were attending college who should not be there.

He deplored the "widespread feeling" among educators that every high school boy and girl should go to college. He urged

Continued on Page 25, Column 6

Democratic Farm Experts Call Republicans' Program Ruinous

By RICHARD J. H. JOHNSTON

Special to The New York Times.

CHICAGO, Sept. 19—The nation's farmers face a grim future unless action is taken immediately to relieve them of economic stress, a Democratic agricultural advisory committee said today.

Under the chairmanship of Claude R. Wickard, former Secretary of Agriculture, the fourteen-man committee met here in the Conrad Hilton Hotel to "explore all aspects of our agricultural problems."

This was the first meeting of the group that was formed to guide the Democratic farm policy fight. It was created on Aug. 31 at the behest of Paul M. Butler, chairman of the Democratic National Committee.

[Meanwhile, Democrats in Washington opened a drive to goad the Administration into unveiling its farm plans before Congress reconvenes in January. This was part of a Democratic effort to keep the offensive in building sagging farm prices and income into a major issue of the 1956 Presidential election.]

The advisory committee, which included another former Agriculture Secretary, Charles F. Brannan, as well as former Agriculture Department aides and five farmers, according to Mr. Wickard, had reached the conclusion that the Eisenhower Administration was neglecting the farmers' plight and ignoring distress.

While the committee went into executive session, Mr. Butler issued a statement on its aims and purposes. The statement bore down hard on the Republican Administration, which, he said, was both "ill-tempered and

Continued on Page 23, Column 4

U.N. Opening in Harmony Today; Chilean Next Head of Assembly

By THOMAS J. HAMILTON

Special to The New York Times.

UNITED NATIONS, N. Y., Sept. 19—A noncontroversial start is assured for the 1955 session of the United Nations General Assembly, which will convene tomorrow afternoon. The only important business scheduled for tomorrow is the election of José Maza, a veteran Chilean diplomat, as President of the Assembly.

Some delegates believe that Vyacheslav M. Molotov, the Soviet Foreign Minister, will immediately put forward the standard Soviet demand for the seating of Chinese Communist representatives.

If he should do so, it would not cause more than a short flurry, since the United States is ready with its equally standard counter-proposal that the question of Chinese representation should not be taken up at the current session. The United States is known to have enough votes to assure the adoption of its resolution.

Dr. Joseph M. A. H. Luns, co-Foreign Minister of the Netherlands, will call the Assembly to order in the absence of the President of the 1954 session, Dr. Eelco N. van Kleffens, Dutch Minister to Portugal. The election of vice presidents and committee chairmen will take place Wednesday and the opening debate will begin Thursday.

Secretary of State Dulles will speak Thursday morning and Mr. Molotov on Friday. The two other Big Four Foreign Ministers, Harold Macmillan of Britain and Antoine Pinay of France, will not speak until next week.

In any event, the speeches by Mr. Dulles and Mr. Molotov are expected to set the keynote for

Continued on Page 12, Column 1

GAINZA PAZ HOPES TO REGAIN PRENSA

Former Publisher Wants New Argentine Regime to Give Back 'Stolen' Paper

The former publisher of the Buenos Aires newspaper La Prensa, which was confiscated by the Perón Government four years ago, said last night that he hoped soon to return to Argentina and put his 86-year-old publication back into public service.

Dr. Alberto Gainza Paz, who escaped arrest by Gen. Juan D. Perón's regime by fleeing to Uruguay, expressed the belief that the new regime in Argentina would move quickly to restore "all stolen property" to former owners. He emphasized that La Prensa had not been "expropriated," as some accounts had said, but had been seized without any compensation.

Dr. Gainza Paz said that the Perón authorities had simply seized the paper and turned it over to labor unions to operate under firm Government control.

La Prensa had been famous throughout the world as one of the great democratic journals. It was founded on Oct. 18, 1869 by Dr. Gainza Paz's grandfather and, except for the last four years, has been operated by the same family.

Desire for Freedom Cited

The publisher said that the revolution in Argentina was inspired "by a desire to regain freedom for all the Argentines." He said that General Perón had wiped out ninety years of democratic government in Argentina. But the people did not forget, he added.

It took a world war, Dr. Gainza Paz declared, for the Germans and Italians to get rid of Hitler and Mussolini. The Argentines ousted General Perón by themselves, he said, "and every one of them may feel proud of it."

Dr. Gainza Paz asserted that the Argentines did not willingly accept life under "Peron's unconstitutional regime, copied from the totalitarian states."

"They hated the rule of a man who was, as Churchill said of Hitler, 'a monstrous product of wrong and shame,'" he declared.

The publisher said that during the ten years that General Perón had been in power, including the period before he took over the Presidency, the Argentines were "shamed and humiliated, their legislature and courts and schools were corrupted, their labor unions were taken over by Perón, the country's resources were squandered in graft." Their free press, he asserted, was murdered.

Dr. Gáinza Paz repeated what he said in 1951, after La Prensa had been confiscated: "I believe that freedom always wins the last battle."

CELLER CRITICIZES STAND ON REFUGEES

Special to The New York Times.

LONDON, Sept. 19—Representative Emanuel Celler denied today that relaxation of immigration requirements would have a deleterious effect on United States security.

The Brooklyn Democrat, in an interview, criticized a statement to that effect by Senator James O. Eastland, Demócrat of Mississippi and chairman of the Senate Internal Security subcommittee.

Last Friday, the Senator said in Washington that such a relaxation would flood the United States with "criminals and Communist agents." He cited an investigation that he said had produced estimates that 30 to 40 per cent of adults admitted to West Germany up to nine months ago were Communist agents.

Among them were agents seeking entry to the Western Hemisphere, Senator Eastland held. His conclusions were based largely on testimony given in June by William F. Heimlich, former Army intelligence chief in Berlin.

Mr. Celler said it was "rather anomalous" that Senator Eastland's conclusions had not been based on his own recent trip to Europe but on Mr. Heimlich's statements.

CAMBODIA TO BREAK ALL TIES TO FRANCE

PNOMPENH, Cambodia, Sept. 19 (UP)—Former King Norodom Sihanouk announced today that Cambodia soon would break all her remaining ties with France.

Prince Norodom said the newly elected Congress under his control would re-draft Cambodia's Constitution and drop any reference to her participation in the French Union, the post-war name for France's overseas mpire..

The 33-year-old Prince, who relinquished his throne early this year, said there was no longer any need for associating with France. Cambodia now is a sovereign and independent country, free to decide her own alliances, he said.

The Prince's People's Socialist Community party won all ninety-one seats in the new Cambodian Congress.

In a communiqué he said the Congress and the Cambodian people also must decide on the problem of United States aid to the key Indochina state.

In a press conference last week, Norodom said he believed popular pressure would force the new Congress to vote against a direct military pact with the United States and refuse to permit United States bases on Cambodian soil.

Cuban Congress Opens Session

Special to The New York Times.

HAVANA, Sept. 19—The second legislative period of the twenty-fourth Cuban Congress opened at the capitol this afternoon. In a message read to the legislators, President Fulgencio Batista reviewed the accomplishments of his administration and recommended various legislative measures.

Associated Press Radiophoto

CHEER FALL OF PERON: Rain-soaked demonstrators express their approval in front of Foreign Ministry Building in Buenos Aires after hearing that regime was overthrown.

Texts of Statements by Peron Regime

BUENOS AIRES, Sept. 19 (AP)—Following are translated texts of the Argentine Government's offer to confer with the rebels, as broadcast by the Argentine state radio today, and of President Juan D. Perón's statement, as read by Gen. Franklin Lucero:

Offer to Negotiate

From Gen. Franklin Lucero, Commander in Chief of the Forces of Repression, in the name of His Excellency the President of the nation and Commander in Chief of the armed forces:

In the face of the ultimatum to bombard the city of Buenos Aires and the Eva Perón petroleum refineries, and to avoid further bloodshed, he [General Lucero] invites the revolutionary commanders to join him in his command headquarters in the Army Ministry to begin immediately discussions to settle the conflict.

He also invites these [rebel] commands to cease their activities immediately.

Peron's Statement

To the Army and the people of the nation:

We have reached present events guided only by the fulfillment of our duty. We have tried by every means to respect the Constitution and the law and to have them respected. We have obeyed only the interests of the people and their benefit.

Nevertheless, neither the Constitution nor the law can be above the very nation itself and its sacred interests.

If we have had to face a fight it has been contrary to our desire, and obliged by [the forces of] reaction which prepared it and unleashed it.

The responsibility falls exclusively upon them because we have only complied with the mandate of our irrenounceable duty.

A few days ago I tried to leave the Government if that would be a solution to the present political problems.

Circumstances known to the public prevented me from doing this.

Now as before I continue to think that I [should] insist in my attitude in offering this solution.

The decision of the Vice President [Alberto Teisaire] and the legislators to follow my example with theirs [resignations] impedes, in a certain manner, a constitutional solution.

On the other hand, I think that a dispassionate intervention to face the problem and resolve it is necessary.

I do not believe there exists a man in this country with enough stature to attain this, which impels me to think that an institution which has been, is, and always will be a guarantee of honor and patriotism might realize it.

The army could take charge of the situation, preserve order and take charge of the Government so as to seek pacification among the Argentines before it might be too late—using for this the most adequate and equanimous methods.

I believe this is imperative to defend the highest interests of the nation.

I am convinced that the people and the army will crush the uprising but, then, that would be too bloody and harmful to the country's permanent interests.

I, who love the people profoundly, am suffering a deep wound in my soul for their fight and their martyrdom.

I should not wish to die without having made a last effort for their peace, their tranquillity and their happiness.

If my spirit as a fighter impels me to the fight, my patriotism and my love for the people induces me toward every personal resignation.

In the face of threatened bombardments of the invaluable wealth of the nation and its innocent people, I think nobody can fail to put aside his other interests and his passions.

I believe blindly that this should be my conduct.

I am not afraid to follow that road.

NEWS BAN ON KASHMIR

India to Bar Correspondents if Pakistanis Invade Area

Special to The New York Times.

NEW DELHI, India, Sept. 19—The Indian Government indicated today it would not allow correspondents to cover on the spot any "peaceful invasion" of Kashmir by Pakistanis.

There has been talk in Pakistan of a march into the disputed Himalayan state along the lines of India's Aug. 15 march into Portuguese Gao. Indian officials do not think an "invasion" will materialize.

A Government spokesman said the cease-fire area on the borders had been out of bounds to correspondents and would remain so. He indicated that in case of trouble correspondents, Indian and foreign, might not even be allowed to go to Srinagar, the summer capital of Indian Kashmir.

SOVIET REPLY REJECTED

Answer to U. S. Protest Over Abuse of Holt Criticized

MOSCOW, Sept. 19 (AP)—The United States Embassy said today it had received an unsatisfactory reply to its protest against the treatment of Representative Joseph Holt, Republican of California, during his visit to Moscow last month.

Mr. Holt said he was held at pistol point by a Russian officer for more than on hour Aug. 31 although accompanied by an embassy official and had all proper credentials on a sight-seeing tour of the Soviet capital's suburbs.

An embassy spokesman declined to disclose the contents of the Soviet reply to the protest delivered Sept. 1, but said: "We consider this reply unsatisfactory."

Eden Continues Recovery

CHEQUERS, England, Sept. 19 (AP)—Prime Minister Eden was up and about today after an attack of influenza which confined him to bed for several days. On doctor's orders he remained at his country residence here, but is expected to preside over a Cabinet meeting in London Wednesday or Thursday.

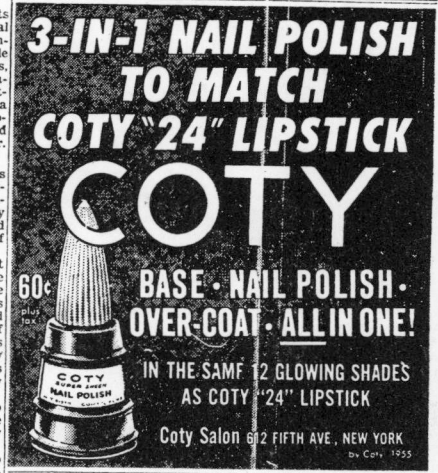

REVOLT TOPPLES PERON'S REGIME

Continued From Page 1

dent's supporters waiting for others to join them.

The occasional shouts of some supporters asserting that the Perón defeat was nothing but a lie were answered by jeers of other onlookers.

Two statues of Eva Perón, the President's late wife, at the city's railway station were toppled, roped to automobiles and dragged through the city's main street.

The Government's junta consisted of the Army Chief of Staff, Gen. Carlos Adolfo Wirth; Gen. Emilio Forcher, commander of the Forces of the Interior, and Gen. Angel Juan Manni, Chief of the Coordination Staff.

The junta became a four-man group when Gen. Jose Domingo Molina, Commander in Chief of the Army, was made its president.

A message reportedly read by Hugo de Prieto, secretary general of the Confederation of Labor, advised all its members "to maintain order and to follow the confederation's instructions."

In his statement, read for him by General Lucero, President Perón said, "I should not wish to die without having made a last effort for their [the people's] peace, their tranquility and their happiness."

He added that although his fighting spirit urged him to struggle, "my patriotism and my love for the people induces me toward every personal resignation" before the threat of bombing the nation's property "and its innocent people."

The Government junta offered to meet the rebel command last night at either the Cabildo, the capital's old City Hall, which is now a museum, or in the Palace of Justice. However, the rebels announced they were ready to meet only on the flagship of General Issac Rojas and on the understanding that the Government was ready to "surrender unconditionally."

The rebels' second demand was the recognition of a de facto Government of the Revolution "to be named by the triumphant forces."

Just before midnight it was announced that Admiral Rojas had asked the leader of the opposition forces in Cordoba, Gen. Eduardo Leonardi, to fly to the port and to join in any discussions aboard the cruiser.

Wording Unclear

General Lucero issued a statement offering to negotiate with the rebels, but the wording of his and General Perón's statements was unclear. President Perón referred to the fact that he had attempted to resign on Aug. 31. The next day the General Confederation of Labor staged a mass demonstration asking him to retract his offer and he did.

The President also said that he did not believe there was one man capable enough to rule the country, and this led him to think that it should be ruled by the army. If the army decided he should leave the Government, he would do so, the statement implied.

These events were the climax of four days of fighting. This city and other areas dominated by loyal troops thus fell under the rule of the junta, which immediately confirmed Gen. Felix Robles as Chief of the Forces of Security. These forces were taking drastic steps to enforce order after curfew regulations became effective at 8 o'clock tonight.

The sudden turn in events was largely caused by the navy's shelling of Mar del Plata yesterday and its threat to take similar action against this capital.

Aided by the low ceiling, which protected them from any important attack by planes, elements of the fleet lay a half-mile off the seaside resort and at 7:30 A. M. opened fire against the port and its installations.

Some of the shells struck the huge tanks of the Government's oil refinery and started large fires.

Although reports said that the damage caused was extensive, there were no details. Nor were there any casualty estimates.

Reports from Tres Arroyos in the northern part of Buenos Aires showed that the rebels had considerable air strength despite the Government's contention to the contrary. Loyal forces moving against a rebel force half way between that city and the town of Colonel Pringles were attacked by three bombers and four fighters Sunday.

Casualties among the Government troops were reported high.

In the Province of Mendoza the Commander in Chief of the revolutionary command, Gen. Julio Alberto Lagos, named Gen. Roberto Valentin Nazar the province's governor.

There were widespread reports that the provisional national government the rebels were planning to set up would include General Lagos, Admiral Rojas, Gen. Dalmiro Felix Videla Balaguer and three civilians. The latter were Maurico Yabarola, a Radical Deputy, Enrique Corominas Seguro, a Democrat, and Alfredo Paladios, a party leader.

Shops Close Quickly

Meanwhile, in Buenos Aires after word filtered to the population about the possible imminent bombardment, shops quickly closed. Most persons gathered around radios to keep abreast of developments.

President Perón's most ardent supporters, members of the Alianza Nacionalista, were armed with submachine guns and requisitioned trucks to add to their mobility. For a brief time they commanded the city's downtown streets, menacingly waving their guns at persons who failed to respond favorably to their cries of "Viva Perón!"

Late in the afternoon a group of demonstrators cheering the rebel victory were fired upon by a group of Perón supporters.

Two tanks were brought up in front of the Alianza headquarters. Those inside were ordered to surrender. They left the building, were disarmed and got into waiting trucks. Not a shot was fired.

However, in other sections of the city and particularly the fashionable northern districts and suburbs, many shooting incidents occurred between unidentifiable civilian groups.

The Confederation's headquarters were abandoned.

For the first time in more than a year the official radio carried a message by the Archbishop of Buenos Aires, Santiago Cardinal Luis Copello. He called upon all Argentines to adopt an attitude that would bring peace back to a nation that "once again has been sown with sorrow and death where there should only be happiness and concord."

General Strike Reported Set

BUENOS AIRES, Tuesday, Sept. 20 (AP)—Argentina's labor federation was reported preparing a general strike for dawn today in an effort to put General Perón back into power.

A rebel radio broadcast from Bahia Blanca said leaders of the 6,000,000-member General Federation of Labor, backbone of the ousted President's popular following, had decided secretly on the strike under General Perón's inspiration.

The federation used the same sactic successfully in 1945 to return General Perón to power after a military clique jailed him.

Warning for Rebel Leader

MONTEVIDEO, Uruguay, Tuesday, Sept. 20—A broadcast from the self-styled "Civilian Command of Buenos Aires," heard here, asked Admiral Rojas not to come into the capital but to let the junta "go to you." The broadcast said "another Oct. 17 is being prepared," a reference to the date on which General Perón was reinstated in 1945.

In another broadcast, the "Civilian Command" told Admiral Rojas that a colunm of tanks loyal to General Perón had reached Buenos Aires Province from Corrientes Province and was advancing on the Argentine capital.

BONN CABINET BACKS MOSCOW RELATIONS

Special to The New York Times.

BONN, Germany, Sept. 19—The West German Cabinet unanimously approved tonight the agreement to establish diplomatic relations with Moscow. Chancellor Konrad Adenauer was congratulated for having obtained a Soviet promise to release 9,626 prisoners of war.

The Chancellor will go before the Bundestag, the lower house of Parliament, Thursday and request legislative approval of the agreement. He will make a long policy declaration explaining his decision to accept the Soviet formula for relations.

Debate on two resolutions, one approving diplomatic relations and the second congratulating the Chancellor for obtaining the Soviet promise is to begin Friday.

In his policy statement Dr. Adenauer will review his reasons for changing his mind at the last minute and agreeing to establish relations. Before going to Moscow, he had insisted that no firm decisions would be made, and that the purpose of the visit was to explore intentions of the Soviet Government on the problem of Germany's reunification.

Efforts of the Soviet Government to fortify the east-zone Communist regime in the current Moscow negotiations with Premier Otto Grotewohl are being watched in Bonn with misgivings.

"All the News That's Fit to Print"

The New York Times.

7:30 A. M. EXTRA
Condensation of U. S. Weather Bureau forecast: Mostly sunny and warm today. Mostly fair and warm tomorrow.
Temperature range today: 84—69.
Temperature range yesterday: 85.2—67.
Full U. S. Weather Bureau Report, Page 54.

VOL. CV No. 35,978. Entered as Second-Class Matter, Post Office, New York, N. Y. NEW YORK, THURSDAY, JULY 26, 1956. Times Square, New York 36, N. Y. Telephone LAckawanna 4-1000 FIVE CENTS

ANDREA DORIA AND STOCKHOLM COLLIDE; 1,134 PASSENGERS ABANDON ITALIAN SHIP IN FOG AT SEA; ALL SAVED, MANY INJURED

STASSEN SUGGESTS EISENHOWER STATE IF HE IS FOR NIXON

Aide to End Pro-Herter Drive If the President Gives Nod to the Vice President

GETS NO G.O.P. BACKING

Says Hall Tries to Foreclose Choice of Delegates at Convention

By JAMES RESTON
Special to The New York Times.

WASHINGTON, July 25 — Harold E. Stassen, the loneliest man in Washington, said today he would abandon his anti-Nixon campaign if President Eisenhower personally expressed a preference for Vice President Richard M. Nixon on the 1956 election ticket.

In the absence of such a statement from the President, the White House disarmament aide made it clear that he would continue to advocate the Vice-Presidential nomination of Gov. Christian A. Herter of Massachusetts.

The President has let it be known he was "delighted" that Mr. Nixon was available for the Vice - Presidential nomination. But he has not expressed a clear preference for him over other possible candidates.

Takes Aim at Hall

However, a reliable source informed The New York Times today that Governor Herter agreed to nominate Mr. Nixon for the Vice Presidency yesterday after a telephoned message from the White House saying that it was the President's wish that he do so.

Mr. Stassen was left today without the cooperation of Governor Herter or the public support of a single influential Republican politician.

Nevertheless, he took dead aim both at Mr. Nixon and the chairman of the Republican National Committee, Leonard W. Hall.

The 43-year-old Vice President, Mr. Stassen said, ran last in a private poll he (Stassen) conducted on eight potential Republican Vice - Presidential candidates. He did not say who was polled, or who did the polling, or what questions were asked—only that Mr. Nixon, Governor Herter and Mr. Stassen himself were among the eight.

He also wrote a letter in the middle of last night to Repre-

Continued on Page 8, Column 5

Jordanian Group Attacks U. N. Palestine Truce Unit

Villagers' Fire Wounds One Observer —Burns Scores Incident — Amman Puts the Blame on Israelis

By HOMER BIGART
Special to The New York Times.

JERUSALEM, July 25—Jordanian villagers attacked a team of United Nations military observers today near Jerusalem. Lieut. Col. E. H. Thalin of Sweden was seriously wounded by the Jordanian fire, United Nations sources said.

They reported that the villagers "went berserk" after an exchange of fire with Israelis in which several Jordanians were wounded. During the engagement the Israelis employed mortar fire. There were no Israeli casualties.

[Jordanian sources in Amman said Israeli fire had been responsible. The Amman reports said ten Jordanians were wounded.]

Colonel Thalin was the third United Nations casualty in two days. Yesterday two Canadian officers were seriously wounded in a mine explosion on Mount Scopus.

Maj. Gen. E. L. M. Burns of Canada, United Nations truce supervisor, said tonight that he was "astonished and deeply concerned by the attack by the Jordanian villagers."

He had already made arrangements to confer tomorrow with Maj. Gen. Ali Abu Nuwar, Chief of Staff of the Jordanian Army, on measures to be taken by Jordan to reduce the number of provocative incidents along the Israeli frontier. Israel's Premier, David Ben-Gurion, has threatened punitive action unless the provocations cease.

The current trouble spot on the frontier is in the Judean hills only five miles from Jerusalem where raw, new houses

Continued on Page 2, Column 3

CRAFT RUSH TO AID

Terse Radio Messages of the Rescue Vessels Depict Operations

Help for the stricken liners Andrea Doria and Stockholm flowed almost instantly from all points of the compass to the spot at which they collided last night.

Ships large and small, Coast Guard vessels, luxury liners, Gloucester fishing boats, coastal steamers, all headed for the spot off Nantucket Lightship where the lives of some 2,500 persons were in danger.

It was 11:22 last night when the ships collided in a dense fog. The Andrea Doria, luxury liner of the Italian Line, shaken dangerously despite a double hull and other special safety features, sent out the first SOS less than a minute later.

The Coast Guard, with stations at Cape Ann, Cape Cod, Boston and other near-by points, sent out every available craft as soon as the position of the crash had been determined. Then came reassuring promises of help from the Ile de France and other craft within quick reach of the spot.

The Search and Rescue Division of the Coast Guard in New York received its first alert at 11:25 last night. It was then that the Coast Guard radio station at East Moriches, L. I. notified New York headquarters: "Andrea Doria and Stockholm collided 11:22 local time Lat. 40:30 N., Long. 69:53 W."

Coast Guard Cutters Aid

The East Moriches radio had picked up simultaneous SOS messages from the ships a minute or two before. The next hour was spent verifying positions and notifying all Coast Guard and merchant ships of the disaster and calling on them for help. The Coast Guard sent out ten cutters from New York, Boston and New London, Conn., and diverted three other ships cruising in that area.

The stark drama being played on the open ocean in darkness and fog was pictured in tense, taut radio messages recorded by the wireless room of The New York Times. They read:

12:21 A. M.—S. S. Stockholm says: Badly damaged. The whole bow crushed and No. 1 hold filled with water. Have to stay in our position. If you [Andrea Doria] can lower your lifeboats we can pick them up.

12:21 A. M.—S. S. Andrea Doria replied: You have to row to us.

12:38 A. M.—S. S. Cape Ann reports: Now between the two ships and her boats are ready. Has two lifeboats.

12:45 A. M. Coast Guard boat says: Ten miles away; have eighteen boats.

1:12 A. M. Andrea Doria says: Needs more lifeboats still.

1:13 A. M. Unidentified ship, when queried, says: We have twelve lifeboats.

Stricken Ship's Boats Useless

1:21 A. M. Cape Ann asks Doria: How close do you want our ship to come to you?

1:24 A. M. Cape Ann reports: We have two boats for Andrea. Now proceeding to get close to her.

1:26 A. M. Andrea Doria reports: Danger immediate, need lifeboats, as many as possible. Can't use our lifeboats.

1:30 A. M. Stockholm gives position: Lat. 40:34 N; Long. 69:45 W.

1:33 A. M. Cape Ann asks Andrea: Want Cape Ann to move in any closer than Cape Ann is now?

1:34 A. M. Ile de France says: We are nine miles from you. Will launch as many boats as possible.

1:43 A. M. Doria repeats earlier message: Here danger immediate. Need lifeboats, as many as possible. Can't use our lifeboats.

1:46 A. M. Unidentified ship radios Andrea: Two lifeboats on way over to you.

1:53 A. M. S. S. Manaqui radios both ships: Will arrive yours 0900 G. M. T. (5 A. M., E. D. T.) Have two lifeboats.

1:54 A. M. Andrea replies: O. K. Thanks.

1:56 A. M. Unidentified Nor-

Continued on Page 15, Column 1

The 29,000-ton Italian Line vessel, the Andrea Doria, which carried 1,134 passengers

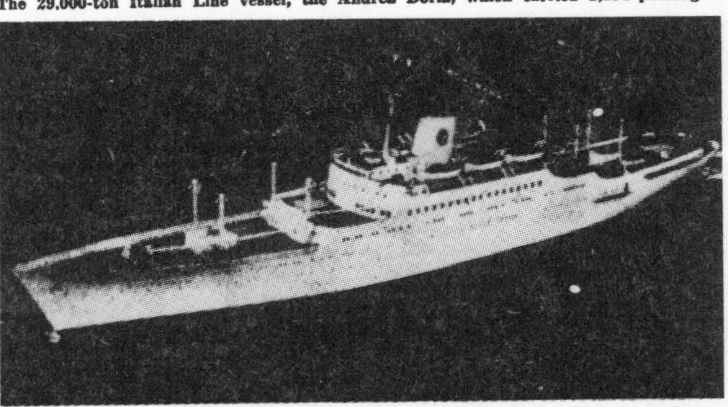

The 12,644-ton Swedish American liner Stockholm, largest liner ever built in Sweden

2D VESSEL IS SAFE

Ile de France In Today With Survivors From Crash Off Nantucket

By MAX FRANKEL

The trans-Atlantic liners Andrea Doria and Stockholm collided in a heavy Atlantic fog at 11:22 o'clock last night, forty-five miles south of Nantucket Island.

The Andrea Doria ordered her 1,134 passengers aboard to abandon ship. All were reported to have been rescued at 4:58 A. M. There was no immediate word, however, on the fate of her crew of 575.

At 5:15 A. M. today, however, the Ile de France reported from the scene that no more help was needed.

The French Liner estimated at 7 A. M. that she would arrive in New York shortly after 6 o'clock this afternoon with 1,000 survivors from the Andrea Doria. It was not clear to which ports the other survivors would be taken.

The Stockholm, although it had taken water through a crushed bow, was able to keep her 550 passengers and crew of 200 aboard. She was waiting for an escort to attempt to return to New York at a slow speed.

Many survivors of the Italian ship were said to have been seriously injured. The Stockholm said she had five "critical" cases aboard. Desperate and repeated calls for medical assistance were radioed from the score of rescue vessels in the area.

Deck Dips into Water

The Andrea Doria lay helpless in the thick fog. The black-and-white ship reported she was listing "very badly." She gave no other indication of the extent or nature of her damage nor was there word whether she could remain afloat.

The Stockholm reported at 6 A. M. that the Andrea Doria's main deck was dipping to the surface of the water.

The 29,000-ton Italian Line vessel apparently was listing so severely that she could launch no more than two of her lifeboats. Her lifeboats can carry 2,000 persons.

The French Ile de France, largest of the rescue vessels on hand, and the Stockholm apparently recovered the bulk of the Andrea Doria's passengers. At one time as many as 100 lifeboats probably were in the area. It was not clear how the passengers were loaded into the lifeboats.

At 4:58, the master of the Ile de France told the Stockholm: "All passengers rescued. "Proceeding to New York full speed."

The Ile de France left New York yesterday bound for Le Havre.

Since shortly after the collision, the Andrea Doria had run her lights and radio on emergency power and said she did not know how much longer she could keep in touch with rescue craft. Her radio was so weak the Stock-

Continued on Page 14, Column 5

DOWNTOWN TO GET 4TH NEW BUILDING

25-Story Structure Is Slated on Broad Street Site of R. C. A. Communications

By GLENN FOWLER

Another large office building is soon to rise in the downtown Manhattan financial district.

The building, the fourth large structure to be planned in the area within the last two years, will be twenty-five stories high. It will cover the block front on Beaver Street between Broad and New Streets, near Bowling Green.

It will stand on a plot of 48,000 square feet, running back 215 feet along Broad Street and 200 feet along New Street.

To be known as 60 Broad Street, the building will have an aluminum facade and a beacon light atop the roof. It will be fully air-conditioned, will have acoustic ceilings and will be equipped with operatorless elevators. Garage space will be provided in the basement. There will be 650,000 square feet of floor space above the ground floor.

The property on which the structure will be built is owned by R. C. A. Communications,

Continued on Page 41, Column 2

CONFEREES VOTE 3.7 BILLION IN AID

Reappropriated Fund Lifts Total to $4,006,570,000—Curb on Tito Supported

Special to The New York Times.

WASHINGTON, July 25—Conferees from the Senate and House of Representatives agreed today on a compromise foreign aid appropriation of $3,766,570,000.

This sum to carry the Mutual Security Program for another year would be increased by $240,000,000 of reappropriated money to a total of $4,006,570,000.

The bargain struck by the conferees amounted to a substantially even split between the $4,110,920,000 in new money originally allocated by the Senate and the $3,425,120,000 provided originally by the House.

President Eisenhower initially had asked for $4,900,000,000 for the fiscal year that opened July 1, although the appropriation for the fiscal year just ended was only $2,700,000,000.

Retained by the conferees was a rider in the Senate bill directing President Eisenhower not to give new military assistance funds to Communist Yugoslavia except for spare parts and replacements.

This stipulation was primarily the work of the Senate Republican leader, William F. Knowland of California. It did not affect $100,000,000 in military aid to Yugoslavia that already is "in the pipeline," nor did it

Continued on Page 12, Column 3

SHIPS' PIERS QUIET IN NEW YORK PORT

Crowds Expected at Andrea Doria's Docks—Relatives Begin Calling Lines

The sea diaster had not early today awakened the pier at West Forty-fourth Street where the Andrea Doria had been scheduled to dock later in the morning.

This pier, as well as the terminal at West Fifty-seventh Street, where the Stockholm had left just before noon yesterday in a gala sailing, remained dark and quiet.

However, unaccustomed night lights began blinking on at the Italian Line's office at 24 State Street before 4 o'clock when members of the company's staff began arriving.

They had been rounded up from their scattered homes around the Metropolitan area by officials of the line under Rosmino Pernigotti, assistant general manager of the company here.

The company officials were making plans to handle expected crowds at West Forty-fourth Street during the morning. Several thousand visitors were expected to begin gathering there by 8 o'clock, some not knowing about the collision.

It is an axiom in the harbor that every arriving passenger attracts five or more relatives and friends as welcomers, and the Italian Line officials were preparing to give them the tragic news and to forestall a rush by worried relatives on the line's downtown office.

Many of the relatives already knew of the crash at sea, and the office and pier of the com-

Continued on Page 14, Column 3

Many Notables Are Listed Aboard the Andrea Doria

Persons prominent in business, the theatre, politics, journalism and government were among the passengers aboard the Andrea Doria when she collided last night with the Stockholm. Two directors of the Standard Oil Company (New Jersey) were on the passenger list. They were Stewart Coleman, traveling with his family, and Marion W. Boyer, accompanied by his wife. Mr. Coleman, 57 years old, lives at 365 Barrett Road, Cedarhurst, L. I. Mr. Boyer, 54, lives in Greenwich, Conn.

Another passenger was Richardson Dilworth, Mayor of Philadelphia, and his wife. Mr. Dilworth, a lawyer by profession, is 57. He served as a Marine in both World Wars, and received the Purple Heart in World War I and the Silver Star in World War II.

Ruth Roman, Hollywood motion picture star, and her son, Richard Hall, were on the Andrea Doria. Miss Roman recently divorced Mortimer Hall, owner of a Los Angeles radio station.

Two refugees from behind the Iron Curtain, the dancers Istvan Rabovsky and his wife Nora Kovach, also were passengers. They are natives of Hungary. In May, 1953, they fled to the West from East Berlin, where they had gone for a dancing engagement. In 1954, they came to this country.

Also on board were Camille M. Cianfarra, Madrid correspondent of The New York Times, and his family. A native of New York, Mr. Cianfarra joined The Times in 1935 in Rome. He became a specialist in Vatican affairs, and has written two books about the Vatican. He became Madrid correspondent in 1951.

Others on board included Ferdinand M. Thieriot, circulation manager of The San Francisco

Continued on Page 15, Column 5

SHIP BUILT TO TAKE COLLISION SAFELY

Andrea Doria Hull Divided to Give Stability—Lifeboats Could Carry 2,000

The Andrea Doria was specially built to give her more stability in case of just such a collision as she had last night with the Stockholm.

The hull was subdivided into eleven watertight compartments extending the entire length of the ship. Bulkheads parallel with her engine rooms were designed to lessen the effect of a collision.

The ship carried lifeboats with a capacity of 2,000 persons. Some of these boats were made of light metal alloy and were hung from davits operated by motor-driven winches. Two of the boats were motor-driven and fitted with radios.

Luxurious to the last detail, the ship was completely fire-proofed and radar-equipped.

The ship has two groups of turbines capable of generating 50,000 horsepower to turn its three blade propellors, each weighing sixteen tons. They are nineteen feet in diameter and turn 143 revolutions a minute.

The Andrea Doria and the Stockholm had been the prides of the Italian and Swedish merchant marines.

The Stockholm, when launched in 1948, was the largest passenger vessel ever to have been built in Swedish yards. The Andrea Doria, when launched in 1951, was the last word in modern design and comfort. Each was flagship of its line until supplanted by new vessels a few years later.

When she went into service as flagship of the Swedish American Line, the Stockholm had a capacity of 364 passengers and 150 officers and crew. Alterations in 1953 increased the capacity to nearly 600 passengers with a proportionate increase in the size of the crew.

The Stockholm had an over-all length of 510 feet and a beam of

Continued on Page 15, Column 6

SCENE OF THE COLLISION: The liners Andrea Doria and the Stockholm stricken off Nantucket Island (cross).

Eisenhower's Four Years

An Analysis of Agriculture Policy And Steps Taken to Meet Problems

This is the fifth of a series of articles analyzing the record of the Eisenhower Administration at the start of the Presidential election campaign.

By WILLIAM M. BLAIR
Special to The New York Times.

WASHINGTON, July 25—President Eisenhower has faced a number of stubborn dilemmas in the last four years but no other problem on the home front has been comparable to the one on farms.

Like the Communist problem overseas, it has absorbed his attention. From time to time it has been mitigated by his policies. Always, however, it has returned to plague him in one form or another.

In his home town of Abilene, Kan., in mid-1952 the President began formulating his program to reconcile freedom and prosperity for the American farmer. As he put it later, "full parity in the market place" and a minimum of Government regulation were his aims.

It has been a long, perplexing struggle for the President. But despite a notable effort, success has eluded him. The farmer still is tied up in Government controls and has considerably less cash in his pockets.

Every new Administration inherits the past. Thus twenty years of Democratic and often bipartisan farm policies have failed, despite high Federal subsidies, to solve the boom and bust ills that have beset agriculture in the midst of an expanding industrial economy and national prosperity.

Indeed, President Eisenhower and his embattled Secretary of Agriculture, Ezra Taft Benson, have blamed these policies and the last two wars for the surpluses that have resisted their remedies and have depressed farm prices.

From a peak of $15,943,000,000 in 1948, farm income fell to $12,851,000,000 in 1950, before the Korean war. It climbed to $14,801,000,000 in 1951, slipped to $14,051,000,000 in the Presiden-

Continued on Page 12, Column 1

Ailing Millikin Plans To Leave the Senate

By WILLIAM S. WHITE
Special to The New York Times.

WASHINGTON, July 25—Senator Eugene D. Millikin of Colorado, a powerful member of the Republican leadership, said a farewell today in the Senate.

He was compelled by long and agonizing illness to announce that he would not seek re-election in the fall.

The decision was a heavy blow to the Republican party generally, and to its conservative wing in particular.

Mr. Millikin as a well campaigner would have been a formidable favorite to keep his seat safe for the Republicans. Even as an ailing prospective campaigner he had been greatly feared by the Democrats.

His retirement seemed plainly to forward Democratic prospects for retaining control

Continued on Page 10, Column 3

Cause of the Crash Puzzles Radar Men

Experts on radar said today they could not explain how the collision between the Andrea Doria and the Stockholm could have taken place because both vessels were equipped with radar equipment.

They said that even with the "visibility nil" conditions reported in the vicinity each ship should have been able to observe the other for distances up to fifty miles.

The experts declared that, even without knowing precisely what systems the vessels carried, they almost certainly were flexible installations such as are standard on large passenger vessels. They should have been capable of two types of operation—generalized scanning all about the vessel, and a narrower type of observation of a restricted sector of the horizon.

They should also have been

Continued on Page 14, Column 4

M'KEON'S STORY IS TOLD AT TRIAL

Marine Statement Recounts Drinking and Decision to Hold Night March

By WAYNE PHILLIPS

Special to The New York Times.

PARRIS ISLAND, S. C., July 25—According to evidence introduced today at his court-martial, S/Sgt. Matthew C. McKeon spent the afternoon of April 8 drinking vodka and mulling over the idea of taking his platoon into the swamps to teach it discipline.

This admission was said to be part of a statement he dictated to an investigator for the Provost Marshal's office here the morning after six of his men were drowned in the rushing tidal waters of Ribbon Creek.

The statement was introduced in evidence this afternoon as the Government neared the end of its case against him in a general court-martial. He is charged with drinking on duty, oppression of troops and involuntary manslaughter.

The statement, signed by Sergeant McKeon, contradicts testimony given by Cpl. Richard J. King, who had been assigned to Platoon 71 as a junior drill instructor with Sergeant McKeon.

Corporal King testified that he and Sergeant McKeon and T/Sgt. Elwyn B. Scarborough had been drinking vodka in a drill instructor's room of the barracks where the platoon was assigned during the morning of April 8.

Sergeant McKeon spent most of that afternoon—from about 2 to 5 P. M.—sleeping in his bunk, the corporal testified. Another witness, a member of the platoon, has testified that he saw the sergeant take a drink of vodka shortly before the march was ordered.

Maj. Charles B. Sevier, trial counsel and, in effect, prosecutor, also introduced into evidence the record of a blood test taken at midnight that night, four hours after the march.

Objection by Berman

The score of the test given in the record was 1.5. This meant, it was explained outside court, 1.5 miligrams of alcohol per cubic centimeter of whole blood. This is a level, according to Emile Zola Berman, defense counsel, between possible intoxication and intoxication.

Mr. Berman strenuously objected to the introduction of the record of the test on the ground that it was one for determining intoxication, and intoxication had not been charged by the Government.

Any evidence relating to intoxication, he argued, would prejudice the seven officers sitting on the court-martial in their decision on the charges before them.

"Intoxication is a moral offense and of its nature creates prejudice," he said.

Navy Capt. Irving N. Klein, law officer of the court and in effect judge, ruled that the evidence of the test could be admitted as corroborative evidence that Sergeant McKeon had been drinking, as charged — without relation to intoxication.

The Government presented eleven witnesses today, including five of the sixty-eight members of the platoon who survived the night march. Major Sevier expects to rest his case tomorrow.

After recounting how the recruits had incurred Sergeant McKeon's displeasure when some of them failed to wash their clothes as ordered in the morning, the statement said:

"At about 1300 (1 P. M.) I went to get the mail and while getting same I got the idea to take them out into the swamps that night, thinking I could teach them a little discipline.

"Sometime during the previous night someone had brought a fifth of vodka to my room and all during the afternoon I had some drinks from the bottle. I believe at the most I had three or four drinks."

The sergeant's statement described how he had called in the recruit platoon leaders at about 6:30 P. M. and told them of his intention to hold the march.

Then he described how the march through the waters had turned to panic:

"When we had gotten past the point where we had initially entered the stream still in somewhat of a formation, I heard some men to my right, out toward the center of the stream, yelling for help.

"I would say that there were about six or seven men out there. At this point I told the men to keep cool and to go onto the beach. I at this point swam out to the men in the middle of the stream.

"I grabbed one man and took him to the beach to a point where he could stand up. I asked him if he could touch ground and stand up. When he gave me an affirmative reply I headed back into the stream to help the others.

"I swam out and as I passed one of the men a colored boy who I thought was OK, grabbed me and we both went down under the surface of the water. And then came back up to the surface. We went down a second time and at this point he let go of me and I could not find him after that.

"After several attempts to locate the boy and had had no success I headed for the beach as I could see no one else in the area."

Captain of the Doria, a Veteran of 2 Wars, Descendant of Genoese Seafaring Family

Capt. Piero Calamai was appointed master of the Andrea Doria in December, 1952, when the luxury liner was ready to enter the Italy-North American service. Then 54 years old, he was one of the youngest officers to command a major Italian Line passenger vessel.

The captain is a descendant of an old Genoese seafaring family and makes his home there. One of his brothers attained the rank of admiral in the Italian Navy.

A graduate of the Nautical Institute in Genoa, Captain Calamai served as a junior officer in the Italian Navy during World War I. After that he became third mate on the Moncalieri of the Lloyd Sabaudo Line. In 1931 he was promoted to master of the 16,000-ton Toscana of the Lloyd Triestino Line. Later he served as staff captain on the Conte Grande, Augustus and Conte De Savoie, trans-Atlantic ships of the Italian Line.

In World War II, Captain Calamai served as a lieutenant commander and commander of escort ships. After the war, he commanded three new Italian Line vessels in the Italy-South American service. Early in 1951 he took command of the line's motor vessel Saturnia, going from that ship to the Andrea Doria.

He is married and has two daughters.

Capt. Piero Calamai
Skipper of the Andrea Doria

SHIPS' PIERS QUIET IN NEW YORK PORT

Continued From Page 1

pany were beginning to get telephone calls at 5 A. M.

James Newell, a gateman at the Stockholm's pier said he had had a few calls, and could only tell the callers that he had no official news.

"One man called and said he had heard on the radio that the Stockholm was sinking," Mr. Newell said, "But I could not tell him anything because I did not know."

G. Hilmer Lundbeck, director of the Swedish American Line here said a few hours after the first report came in that he had received no offical information, and knew only what he had heard in broadcasts.

Many telephone calls were placed to newspapers early in the morning by people alerted by radio and television broadcasts, which interrupted programs with frequent reports on the crash.

By 5 A. M. The New York Times had received nearly a hundred calls.

One was from Joseph Vulpis, an owner of a fuel oil company in Sea Cliff, L. I.

He said that his father, Gaetano, was returning on the Andrea Doria after a five month vacation trip to Bari, Italy, where he was born seventy-one years ago. Mr. Vulpis said he had spoken with his father yesterday afternoon and that the olderman had said the trip had been very pleasant on the liner. He embarked on the ship at Naples. His father lives at 80 Roslyn Avenue, Sea Cliff, with his wife and two daughters. But he was unaccompanied on his Andrea Doria voyage.

At Police Headquarters, Patrolman Paul Morgan, assigned to the correspondence bureau, said that a call had been received from Philadelphia police inquiring about Mayor Richardson Dilworth. Mr. Dilworth is listed as a passenger on the Andrea Doria.

Mr. Morgan said that he had referred the call to the Harbor police at the Battery but that the latter said they had no information other than that the collision had occurred. It was said at headquarters that no police action would be taken here unless a report was received that passengers from the two ships were to be brought to New York.

Rescue Data on WQXR

Bulletins giving latest details of the rescue operations following the collision at sea between the Andrea Doria and the Stockholm will be broadcast as frequently as available today by WQXR, The New York Times radio station, 1560 on AM dials, 96.3 on FM sets.

CAUSE OF CRASH PUZZLES EXPERTS

Continued From Page 1

capable of being instantly switched from the fifty-mile scale to a scale encompassing only a few miles' radius about the vessel, but in far greater detail.

The radar experts declared that the fog would not have impaired the penetrating power of the electronic waves. The waves are emitted from the radar equipment and are reflected back from such obstacles as other vessels, land and aircraft.

The experts also discounted the possibility that either ship's outline might have been masked by the land masses on either side. They said that radar readings normally give a precise record of distance on the screen before the observer on the ship's bridge. The "blips" that represented the two ships should have been clearly distinct from any land.

Human Failures Cited

Nevertheless, Coast Guard observers said, accidents do continue to happen, even with the postwar radar installations on virtually all ocean-going vessels that carry passengers. They cited human failure as the general cause of accidents. They also pointed out the trying conditions that put a premium on master seamanship.

In July, 1953, the freighter Jacob Luckenbach went to the bottom after a crash with the Hawaiian Pilot outside San Francisco's Golden Gate. Each skipper testified at the Coast Guard inquiry that he saw the other vessel on his radar screen and tracked it for several miles before the collision. One mistook the other ship for a stationary lightship; the other recognized the object as a moving vessel, but thought he would clear it safely.

The waters where the collision took place were described by John A. Brown, meteorologist on night duty at the Weather Bureau, as one of the foggiest areas along the East Coast.

Last night's conditions, he said, were ideal for the production of a close, lasting fog blanket. Water temperature was about 64 degrees Fahrenheit, while warm, moist air masses above were ten degrees warmer, according to a balloon observation taken at midnight.

The moist air was held down over the cooler sea by a condition known to meteorologists as "inversion." The air, circulating and swirling, was cooled on contact with the surface and fog masses were precipitated.

2 LINERS COLLIDE NEAR NANTUCKET

Continued From Page 1

holm had to relay all messages after 1:30 A. M.

In the first two confusing hours after the accident, the messages from Capt. Piero Calamai of the Andrea Doria were urgent and terse.

"Here danger immediate—need lifeboats—as many as possible—can't use our lifeboats," he said at 1:26 A. M. and again at 1:43 A. M.

Many of the survivors of the Italian ship were said to have been seriously injured. Desperate and repeated calls for medical assistance were radioed from the score of rescue vessels in the area.

Italian Ship Helpless

The Andrea Doria lay helpless in the thick fog. The black-and-white ship reported she was listing "very badly." There was no other indication of the extent or nature of her damage nor was there word whether she could remain afloat.

The French Line's Ile de France, largest of the rescue vessels on hand, apparently recovered the largest number of the Andrea Doria's passengers. At one time as many as 100 lifeboats probably were in the area.

The response from all parts of the Middle Atlantic was immediate. Large and small ships, Coast Guard and Navy vessels, luxury liners, fishing boats and steamers headed for the spot—identified by the Coast Guard as Latitude 40 degrees 30 minutes North, Longitude 69 degrees 53 minutes West.

Freighter First There

The United Fruit Line's freighter Cape Ann was three miles away and the first to edge between the stricken ships. She lowered her eight lifeboats and was the first to take survivors aboard—at 2:24 A. M.

The Coast Guard said seas at the scene were "not rough." The Weather Bureau estimated, however, that visibility there at the time of the collision was "probably less than a mile."

The Cape Ann radioed at 3:55 A. M. that any attempt at searching the area by plane would be "suicidal," the fog was so dense.

The Stockholm, as soon as she had looked over her damage and decided that she could remain afloat, sent her lifeboats to the Andrea Doria.

At one point the rescue vessels pleaded for the Italian ship to focus whatever lights it could muster on the milling lifeboats and to send flares into the air so that the helpless vessel could be easily identified.

The 12,644-ton Stockholm, the largest passenger ship ever built in Sweden, is owned and operated by the Swedish-American line. She left New York yesterday at 11:30 A. M. bound for Copenhagen, where she was expected on Aug. 3.

The Andrea Doria, left Genoa, Italy, July 17 and made stops at Naples, Cannes and Gibraltar. She was expected here at 9:30 A. M. today at the Forty-fourth Street Hudson River pier.

Built for Safety

The Italian liner was launched in 1951, three years after the Stockholm. Italian Line officials were especially proud of her safety features. The hull was subdivided into eleven watertight compartments and had a double bottom extending the entire length of the ship. The latter feature was designed for greater stability in the event of collision.

Among many prominent persons aboard the Andrea Doria on her fifty-first Atlantic crossing were Mayor Richardson Dilworth of Philadelphia and Mrs. Dilworth, who embarked at Cannes.

Also aboard were Stewart Coleman and Marion W. Boyer, directors of the Standard Oil Company of New Jersey; Camille Cianfarra, The New York Times correspondent in Madrid, and F. M. Thieriot, circulation manager of The San Francisco Chronicle.

The Andrea Doria sent the first S. O. S. immediately after the collision. From the desperate calls among ships at sea that followed almost immediately, it became clear that prompt rescue work would be required to prevent a major disaster.

For a few minutes, there was calm talk from the stricken vessels of "inspecting" and "surveying" damage. Soon, however, all the valuable radio time was devoted to the dire need for lifeboats and medical help.

Offers Accepted

The messages, as monitored by The New York Times, indicated that no offer of help, no matter how small, was being discouraged. Ships that at 1 A. M. promised to arrive at 5 A. M. with two or three lifeboats received a terse:

"Okay. Thanks."

At first there was word of survivors being picked up, then apparently contradictory messages that amounted to pleas of ships asking where their lifeboats were.

Finally, at 3:45 A. M. the Cape Ann said she had 175 passengers from the Andrea Doria and was standing by for more. The Private William Thomas, an Army transport, said she had fifty an dwas remaining at the side of the Andrea Doria. The Ile de France said she had 200 passengers, then added more. The Stockholm reported she had 425.

The climax was the French liner's message: No more help needed.

"All the News That's Fit to Print"

The New York Times.

LATE CITY EDITION
Condensation of U. S. Weather Bureau forecast: Partly cloudy, little temperature change today and tomorrow.
Temperature range today: 65—51. Temperature range yesterday: 68.3—53. Full U.S. Weather Bureau Report, Page 44.

VOL. CVI—No. 36,078. Entered as Second-Class Matter, Post Office, New York, N. Y. NEW YORK, SATURDAY, NOVEMBER 3, 1956. Times Square, New York 36, N. Y. Telephone LAckawanna 4-1000 FIVE CENTS

BRITISH AND FRENCH PUSH TOWARD LANDING; ISRAELIS CAPTURE GAZA AND CONTROL SINAI

Hungary Protests to Soviet Against New Troop Moves; West Urges Action by U. N.; Tension Is Rising in Poland

STEVENSON OFFERS A PROGRAM TO END STRIFE IN MIDEAST

Calls for a Cease-Fire and Israel's Security—Detroit Crowd Boos President

Speech at Detroit and remarks at Cleveland, Page 20.

By HARRISON E. SALISBURY
Special to The New York Times.

DETROIT, Nov. 2—Adlai E. Stevenson offered tonight a program to restore peace in the Middle East, based on the security of Israel and restoration of the Western Alliance.

Mr. Stevenson submitted his program to an enthusiastic overflow audience at the Fox Theatre.

He charged that President Eisenhower did not know what had been happening in the Middle East and that "someone had misled him."

Mr. Stevenson's program called for these steps:

¶A cease-fire in the Middle East.

¶Restoration of the Western grand alliance of the United States, France and Britain.

¶Security for Israel against Arab attack.

¶Establishment of the principle of international concern for the Suez Canal and an end of one-man or one-country control.

¶An all-out attack on resettlement of 900,000 Arab refugees in Middle Eastern lands.

¶A joint program for improvement of economic conditions in the Middle East.

Mr. Stevenson's address was carried on a state TV network. Several thousand persons were unable to gain admission to the theatre.

Earlier today, Mr. Stevenson spoke in Cleveland's Public Square. A huge throng heard him demand United Nations action in behalf of the new Hungarian regime.

Democratic officials put the crowd at 65,000. Newspaper reporters estimated it at closer to 30.000. There was agreement, however, that it was larger than General Eisenhower drew in the same place and time three weeks ago.

Tonight Mr. Stevenson asserted that the first task in the

Continued on Page 20, Column 5

COUNCIL HEARING ON QUINN SLATED

Mayor Backs Tenney Report on Official's Carting Job

By CHARLES G. BENNETT

The City Council will hold hearings soon to consider charges against Councilman Hugh Quinn, Queens Democrat.

In a report to Mayor Wagner on Thursday, Investigation Commissioner Charles H. Tenney found that Mr. Quinn had committed an "apparent" violation of the City Charter and had given grounds for his removal from office.

Yesterday Mayor Wagner said he agreed with the Investigation Commissioner's conclusions.

Council Majority Leader Joseph T. Sharkey, Brooklyn Democrat, said he would call the Councilmen together next week, probably Wednesday, to arrange for hearings in the Quinn case. A question for the Councilmen to determine, Mr. Sharkey said, is whether the hearings will be public or private.

The Council, under the Charter, is the judge of the qualifications of its members. It may expel a member by a two-thirds vote.

Mr. Sharkey said he thought

Continued on Page 48, Column 3

Associated Press Radiophoto

HUNGARIAN PREMIER Imre Nagy, Communist who took office during national anti-Soviet uprising, addressing nation by radio. Date when photograph was taken was not given.

Eisenhower Sees Victory, Leaves Campaign to Nixon

By RUSSELL BAKER
Special to The New York Times.

WASHINGTON, Nov. 2—President Eisenhower now is so confident of re-election Tuesday that he is treating Adlai E. Stevenson's driving campaign finish with a show of indifference. This was emphasized last night in Philadelphia when he indicated that, from his point of view, the campaign was over and that henceforth he would address the nation only in the nonpartisan role of President.

It was pointedly driven home today when the White House noted that Vice President Richard M. Nixon, rather than the President, had been selected to reply tonight to the Democratic nominee's attack on foreign policy.

James C. Hagerty, White House press secretary, said the President's discussion of the Middle Eastern and Central European crises Wednesday had been "nonpolitical." Mr. Stevenson's reply last night, he added, "was strictly political."

Mr. Hagerty's implication was that the President no longer intended to trouble with replies to Mr. Stevenson's "political" charges and that this chore now could be handled adequately by Mr. Nixon.

The President, he added, knew in advance the substance of the Vice President's speech. The White House staff had helped Mr. Nixon get "the facts to refute a lot of misstatements that Mr. Stevenson made last night," Mr. Hagerty said.

The White House also an-

Continued on Page 19, Column 6

PRESIDENT LEADS IN PENNSYLVANIA

Slim Edge Not Widened Yet by Crises Abroad—Clark's Margin for Senate Cut

A Times Team Report

Teams of New York Times reporters have now completed a survey of political trends in twenty-seven closely contested states. They have rechecked eight of those states—the most doubtful ones. Following is a final resurvey report by Leonard Buder, Donald Janson and Wayne Phillips.

By WAYNE PHILLIPS
Special to The New York Times.

PHILADELPHIA, Nov. 2—President Eisenhower is clinging to a lead in this state so insubstantial that it could be washed away by a heavy rain on election day.

Depending upon developments in the Middle East crisis, he may be able to increase that lead in the four days remaining before the election. But at the moment the world crisis has served only to create doubts in the minds of voters on both sides of the fence. Those doubts have not yet crystallized in favor of either candidate.

Two weeks ago a New York Times team found the Pennsylvania Democrats well organized and confident. They were fighting an uphill battle against the appeal of the President's personality, but the odds were on their side in a state that once was a bastion of Republicanism.

They appeared to have won the public—and some Republican newspapers, too—to their Senatorial candidate, Joseph S. Clark Jr. They had created a substantial indecision among the 1952 supporters of President Eisenhower, and had won over enough of them to give some hope of carrying the state for Adlai E. Stevenson.

For Mr. Stevenson this state is the keystone in any arch of triumph he may hope to build. Its thirty-two electoral votes, with various combinations of states, could carry him to a

Continued on Page 18, Column 2

Nixon Hails Break With Allies' Policies

By WILLIAM M. BLAIR
Special to The New York Times.

HERSHEY, Pa., Nov. 2—Vice President Richard M. Nixon hailed tonight this country's break with Anglo-French policies as a "declaration of independence that has had an electrifying effect throughout the world."

Speaking with the full backing of President Eisenhower, he assailed Adlai E. Stevenson for charging that the Administration's foreign policy was a failure and that the President should have averted the Middle East crisis.

He said that the United Nations General Assembly vote gave "the lie to [Mr. Stevenson's] preposterous charge" that the United States stood alone "in an unfriendly world."

The General Assembly early

Continued on Page 19, Column 1

TROOPS REPORTED CROSSING POLAND

Soviet Movement Is Said to Be to East Germany—Panic Buying in Warsaw

By SYDNEY GRUSON
Special to The New York Times.

WARSAW, Nov. 2—Reports reached Warsaw tonight of large-scale Soviet troop movements across Poland from Russia to East Germany. No details were available.

The purpose and the meaning of the troop movements were not disclosed. But even before they had been reported the situation in Poland had reached a point of extreme tension.

All through the day the Polish radio repeated its broadcast of an appeal by the Communist party's new leadership for "calm, discipline and a sense of responsibility" within the nation.

In Warsaw panic buying began. People bought up all the foodstuffs in the stores and then after withdrawing their money from the banks began to buy jewelry and valuables.

Word came from various parts

Continued on Page 14, Column 4

U. S. Protests Refusal by Soviet To Let Americans Quit Hungary

Special to The New York Times.

WASHINGTON, Nov. 2—The United States protested tonight to the Soviet Union against the action of Soviet troops who prevented a convoy of Americans from leaving Hungary.

A report of the incident from the United States Legation in Budapest reached the State Department in early evening. Deputy Under Secretary of State Robert Murphy called in Georgi N. Zaroubin, the Soviet Ambassador, at once.

Mr. Zaroubin told Mr. Murphy he would get in touch with his Government in Moscow about the matter.

A State Department spokesman said Mr. Murphy spoke "energetically" to the Soviet Ambassador against the "interference with American official personnel."

According to the official report, the convoy consisted of dependents—wives and children—of diplomatic personnel at the American Legation. Lincoln White, State Department press officer, said the convoy returned safely to Budapest and would attempt to leave the city again tomorrow.

"We had a report from Budapest that a convoy of our legation dependents was turned back near the Austrian border this afternoon by Soviet tank blocks," said Mr. White. "They returned to Budapest safely."

According to Mr. White, Mr. Murphy told the Soviet envoy he "assumed the incident must be due to an error on the part of the Soviet military commander, although he could not imagine why Soviet forces were in that area."

The Ambassador said he had no information on this, Mr. White told reporters, but added "he would immediately communicate with his Government and that he assumed the matter would be straightened out."

Special to The New York Times.

BUDAPEST, Hungary, Nov. 2—A diplomatic convoy carrying out the wives and children of a United State legation staff in Budapest as well as French, British and American correspondents was turned back from the Austrian border by Soviet troops at 4:30 P. M. today.

"Polemics are useless," a Soviet officer told them. "It is requested that you turn around

Continued on Page 16, Column 8

NEW PLEA BY NAGY

Premier Asks That U.N. Defend Neutrality of Hungary

By JOHN MacCORMAC
Special to The New York Times.

BUDAPEST, Hungary, Saturday, Nov. 3—The Hungarian Government made three oral protests yesterday to the Soviet Ambassador in Budapest, complaining that Russian reinforcements were still pouring across the frontier.

[Soviet tanks sealed the main crossings of the Austrian-Hungarian border Friday. This was regarded as a preliminary to dealing sternly with the insurgents.]

Premier Imre Nagy also sent a new appeal to the Secretary General of the United Nations to guarantee Hungary's neutrality and to bring her case before the General Assembly.

Similarly Joseph Cardinal Mindszenty, primate of Hungary, appealed to the West for political support of the revolutionaries and relief for the needy.

Soviet Forces Approaching

Early today, forces at the command of the Revolutionary Council of the Hungarian Army occupied the Foreign Ministry. Other Army units cordoned off the Parliament Building and took up posts on and near all bridges spanning the Danube.

These measures were prompted by information that Soviet forces were approaching the capital.

In his plea to the Secretary General of the United Nations, Premier Nagy said that Hungary's first demand for the withdrawal of Soviet troops had been received favorably by Moscow. In spite of this, he went on, fresh Soviet troops were brought in to Hungary on Tuesday and Wednesday.

The Hungarian Government then denounced the Warsaw Pact, proclaimed Hungary a neutral state and demanded the withdrawal of all Soviet troops. Budapest also proposed the appointment of two joint Hungarian-Soviet committees, one political and one military, to discuss the terms and set the timetable for this withdrawal.

The Premier said that he had protested against any further influx of Soviet soldiers, pointing out to the United Nations that new Soviet units had entered

Continued on Page 15, Column 1

Israelis Are Mopping Up; Egypt Braces for Landing

12,000 Prisoners Taken

By HOMER BIGART
Special to The New York Times.

TEL AVIV, Israel, Saturday, Nov. 3—Israel's lightning conquest of Egypt's Sinai Peninsula and the Gaza Strip is complete except for minor mopping-up operations. The ancient Philistine capital of Gaza was the last town to fall.

In its drive, Maj. Gen. Moshe Dayan's tough Army had killed, captured or put to flight 30,000 Egyptian troops east of the Suez Canal.

With Israel's southern flank secure after only four days of operations, the Government faced with calm confidence reports that Jordan was being reinforced by Syrian troops and that the Syrian-Jordanian-Egyptian defense pact was about to become operative.

Gaza collapsed after a three-hour fight yesterday morning. A United Nations truce aide,

Continued on Page 3, Column 5

Cairo Defense Held Ready

By The United Press.

CAIRO, Nov. 2—Waves of British and French bombers and fighters blasted Cairo and outlying villages today. An Egyptian communiqué said 100 persons had been killed in one town alone.

Simultaneously, President Gamal Abdel Nasser announced that Egyptian forces in the Sinai desert had "completed their withdrawal safely."

"Now we are waiting for the British and French in the delta," he said. Only "suicide commandos" had been left in Sinai to harass the advancing Israeli forces, he added.

The communiqué asserted that fourteen British and French planes had been shot down in today's raids. An earlier communiqué had claimed three kills in the last twenty-four hours in addition to six reported downed yesterday morning. This would

Continued on Page 3, Column 2

U. N. SPEAKERS ASK HELP FOR HUNGARY

Override Soviet Objections as Security Council Argues International Action

Excerpts from Security Council debate are on Page 16.

By LINDESAY PARROTT
Special to The New York Times.

UNITED NATIONS, N. Y., Nov. 2—The Western powers overrode Soviet objections today and called on the United Nations to take measures against Soviet military action in Hungary.

An emergency meeting of the Security Council heard all nations that spoke, except the Soviet Union, appeal for international action against the reinforcement of Soviet troops in Hungary, where rebel nationalists appear to have taken control. Imre Nagy, Hungarian Premier, asked the United Nations yesterday to guarantee the country's neutralism.

No decision was reached at the two-hour session of the Council tonight. The members will meet again tomorrow afternoon in an attempt to decide on a course of action.

The meeting was sparked by a new message from Mr. Nagy distributed to Council members tonight.

The letter, couched in terms similar to the one Mr. Nagy sent to the United Nations yesterday, charged that "large" Soviet military units had crossed the Hungarian border. Moving toward

Continued on Page 16, Column 5

Eisenhower Offers Relief to Hungary

Special to The New York Times.

WASHINGTON, Nov. 2—President Eisenhower late today offered $20,000,000 worth of food and medical supplies to relieve the suffering in Hungary resulting from the revolt against Soviet domination.

The White House announcement of this offer followed a conference between the President, Secretary of State Dulles, and Under Secretary of State Herbert Hoover Jr.

The aid would consist of $15,000,000 in surplus foodstuffs and $5,000,000 in specially purchased meats, oils, fats, and medical supplies.

The President urged the American people to continue sending their contributions to the American Red Cross, which is pouring relief supplies into

Continued on Page 16, Column 7

PARIS ACTS TO BAR CEASE-FIRE NOW

Fears That Immediate Halt in Military Operations Would Save Nasser

By HAROLD CALLENDER
Special to The New York Times.

PARIS, Nov. 2—The French Government moved fast today to prevent a United Nations cease-fire in the Suez Canal Zone.

It feared a halt in military operation now would save Gamal Abdel Nasser, President of Egypt, whose regime the French and British seek to liquidate. In that case the French would feel deprived of a victory they regard as already within their grasp.

This was the explanation of the hurried trip to London during the day by Christian Pineau, French Foreign Minister, that was given by high political authorities here tonight.

In London, M. Pineau, Prime Minister Eden and Selwyn Lloyd, British Foreign Secretary, were reported to have agreed they would not accept a cease-fire at least until British-French troops had landed. They were expected to land tomorrow.

Action by U. N. Noted

The United Nations General Assembly voted early today for a cease-fire in the Middle East but the question was how it could be carried out.

[Prime Minister Eden rejected a Laborite demand that he order an immediate end to British attacks on Egypt. This was in response to Laborite pressure that he comply with the resolution of the United Nations General Assembly calling for a cease-fire.]

The fear that took posession of French officials was that Prime Minister Eden might agree to a premature cease-fire.

If so, he would do it, according to these officials, because he is harried by the British Labor party to call off the French-British military expedition to Egypt, and because he is pressed by Secretary of State Dulles, who is credited here with desiring a cease-fire before the United States election Tuesday.

It was even suggested that the United States Sixth Fleet, now in the Mediterranean, might be mandated by the General Assembly to occupy the Suez Canal zone, instead of the French-British forces now preparing to occupy it.

This fear arose because Lester B. Pearson, Canadian Secretary of State for External Affairs, proposed yesterday in New York that the General Assembly should authorize the immediate

Continued on Page 6, Column 4

BOMBING PRESSED

Planes Center Attacks on Army After Cairo Loses Airpower

By DREW MIDDLETON
Special to The New York Times.

LONDON, Nov. 2—The neutralization of the Egyptian Air Force, a primary condition to successful landing operations, was claimed tonight by British and French airpower.

More than a hundred Egyptian planes have been destroyed or damaged at airfields by bombers and fighters of Royal Air Force and French Air Force. A high proportion of these were Soviet-built MIG-15 jet fighter planes and Ilyushin-28 twin-jet bombers, R. A. F. sources said.

At the outset of the operations the Egyptian Air Force had ninety MIG's and fifty Ilyushins. Since not all of them were airworthy Wednesday when the attack began, the allies' claim to have neutralized Egypt's airpower appears valid.

Transit Camp Bombed

The British-French air attack is shifting away from air bases onto the Egyptian Army's central forces, now known to be moving slowly northward and northeastward away from the Cairo area.

British air reconnaissance reported the movement of tanks and infantry into the area around Port Said, one of the three sites chosen by the allies for occupation.

One target successfully attacked was a military transit camp, around which tanks and guns were concentrated, about fifteen miles northeast of Cairo in the El Khanka area.

[The British reported that the Egyptians had sunk seven ships in an effort to block the Suez Canal. It was not known in London whether the Egyptian effort had succeeded. No word of an allied landing in Egypt had been received up to 4 A. M., New York time.]

Information that the Syrian Government was placing its armed forces under the commander in chief of the Egyptian forces has not altered British or French planning for forthcoming operations.

As part of the psychological preparation for the allied landing operations the Cairo Radio, the Voice of Arabia, was silenced

Continued on Page 2. Column 3

ARABS SAID TO PUT TROOPS IN JORDAN

Syrian and Iraqi Forces Are Reported on March

By DANA ADAMS SCHMIDT
Special to The New York Times.

WASHINGTON, Nov. 2—Syrian and Iraqi troops are marching into Jordan, according to information telephoned from Cairo, the Egyptian Embassy press counselor announced tonight.

The official, Mohammed Habib, reported also that Lebanese workers had cut one of the pipelines that carry Arabian oil to the Mediterranean.

The report of the troop movements followed announcement by Syria, in a formal note to the State Department, that she had placed her armed forces under Egyptian command. This was done under terms of the Syrian-Egyptian defense pact, the Syrian Chargé d'Affaires, Mamun Jamui, informed the State Department.

"The Syrian armed forces are now taking orders from the Egyptian Commander in Chief, Gen. Abdel Hakim Amer," Mr. Jamui said, continuing, "Syria

Continued on Page 3, Column 3

News Summary & Index

THE NEW YORK TIMES, SATURDAY, NOV. 3, 1956

International

London reported that Allied air power had neutralized the Egyptian Air Force, thus setting the stage for successful landing operations. It said British and French bombers and fighters had put more than 100 Egyptian planes out of commission. The bombers turned their attention to Egyptian troops. [Page 1, Column 8.]

Israeli forces completed their conquest of the Sinai Peninsula and the Gaza strip, except for minor mopping-up operations. The ancient Philistine city of Gaza fell after a three-hour battle and Israeli troops moved in. [1:6.]

Cairo reported that more than 100 persons had been killed in one town alone as British and French planes bombed the Egyptian capital and outlying villages. President Nasser announced that Egyptian forces had completed their withdrawal from Sinai and had regrouped to meet the expected British and French invasion. [1:7.]

Syrian and Iraqi troops are moving into Jordan, which borders Israel on the east, the Egyptian Embassy in Washington reported. [1:8.]

Washington banned shipments of military supplies to Israel. [4:3.]

The French Government moved swiftly to bar a United Nations cease-fire in Egypt before President Nasser could be ousted from power with the success of Allied military operations. [1:7.]

Prime Minister Eden rejected a Labor party demand that he comply with the United Nations resolution for a cease-fire by halting immediately British attacks on Egypt. [6:1.]

Secretary General Hammarskjold was urged by the twenty-three member bloc of Asian and African nations to take "appropriate measures" to meet the Egyptian crisis. [5:1.]

Premier Nagy protested to the Soviet Ambassador in Budapest that Soviet troops continued to enter Hungary. He also appealed to the United Nations for help to guarantee Hungary's neutrality. [1:5.]

Cardinal Mindszenty supported this appeal with his own plea to the Western powers for aid in his country's fight against Soviet domination. [17:1.]

An emergency session of the Security Council heard the Western powers urge, over Soviet objections, that the United Nations act against Russian military moves in Hungary. [1:6.]

Washington protested to Moscow the refusal of Soviet troops in Hungary to allow a convoy of families of United States diplomats to cross the border into Austria. [1:4-5.]

President Eisenhower offered $15,000,000 in surplus food-stuffs and $5,000,000 worth of special foods and medical supplies to relieve suffering in Hungary. [1:6.]

Large-scale Russian forces were moving across Poland from the Soviet Union to East Germany, according to Warsaw dispatches. [1:4.]

Flier describes attack on radio station near Cairo. Page 2
Tunisia sides with Egypt against Britain, France. Page 3
Canadian Cabinet meets today on Middle East stand. Page 4
British and French criticized by 13 NATO allies. Page 4
Navy evacuates 1,500 Americans from Alexandria. Page 5
Londoner's, Parisians voice support on Mid East. Page 6
Israeli envoy sets condition for exit from Egypt. Page 6
U. N. proceedings yesterday and today's schedule. Page 6
World shipping feels impact of Suez crisis. Page 8
British report Cairo bid to block Suez Canal. Page 8
Red Vietnam announces reforms in regime. Page 10
Pope renews appeal for a crusade of prayer. Page 10
U. S. hesitation on Hungarians disturbs Bonn. Page 13
Strong security measures enforced in Bulgaria. Page 14
Yugoslavs weigh attitude in relation to Hungary. Page 16
El Salvador's President maps fight on crime. Page 17
Colombia relaxing censorship during assembly. Page 23
113 miners trapped in Nova Scotia believed dead. Page 48

Government and Politics

Adlai E. Stevenson charged that the Eisenhower foreign policy had failed and offered a program to restore peace in the Middle East. The program included security for Israel from attack and the restoration of this country's alliance with Britain and France. [1:1.]

President Eisenhower was pictured as so confident of victory next Tuesday that he was treating Mr. Stevenson's bid for election with indifference. He was said to believe that the campaign was over, and that Vice President Nixon could make whatever reply that might be needed to Mr. Stevenson's criticisms. [1:2-3.]

Mr. Nixon denied Mr. Stevenson's charge that the Administration foreign policy had failed, particularly in the Middle East, and hailed this country's break with Anglo-French policies toward Asia and Africa as a "declaration of independence that has had an electrifying effect throughout the world." [1:3.]

A survey of Pennsylvania by a team of New York Times reporters indicated that the contest for that state's thirty-two electoral votes was very close, with President Eisenhower holding a narrow lead. [1:2.]

Council to weigh charges against Quinn. Page 1
Fur workers at Liberal rally hear Democrats. Page 18
House seat race in 20th District a lively one. Page 19
Official denies discussing H-bomb tests. Page 20
Stevenson sees "cover-up" on strontium effects. Page 20
Javits pictures Wagner as "party-line hack." Page 24
Wagner lays Mideast strife to betrayal of allies. Page 24
Russians are guests of "typical" U. S. town. Page 26
Dewey confident of lasting peace in Mideast. Page 28
Kefauver presses drive in Pennsylvania. Page 28
5,284 face vote challenge as frauds set records. Page 48

General

Blizzard sweeps six states in the West. Page 23
Kennedy intensifies drive against gamblers here. Page 25
League says Brooklyn school can be integrated. Page 25
Central's bid for fare rise is sharply protested. Page 25
Smith College president criticizes Ph. D. program. Page 25
South Pole still too cold for U. S. work there. Page 29
Gunman escapes with $2,400 from midtown bank. Page 48
Government asks two trials in Riesel case. Page 48
Indicted police inspector retires on $5,225 pension. Page 48

Industry and Labor

Heavy labor vote for Eisenhower seen in survey. Page 18
Bethlehem and 8 shipyards reach settlement. Page 46
Delta Air Lines disputes route award to Northeast. Page 46

Amusements and the Arts

Networks refuse Republicans time for TV reply. Page 19
Walter White's biography by his wife reviewed. Page 21
Debut of lawyer's opera fulfills 4-year ambition. Page 25
Charles Goren is victor in Las Vegas bridge. Page 26
Rolando Valdes-Blain heard in guitar program. Page 27
Eric Friedman, 17, offers debut violin recital. Page 27
"Don Pasqual" sung first time this "Met" season. Page 27
Globe offers the screen debut of "Port Afrique." Page 27
"Soiree" ballet offered anew at the "Met." Page 27
Anita Weschler shows paintings at Wellons. Page 29
Girls take over the "Chevy Show" on Channel 4. Page 47

Obituaries

Dr. Leo Baeck, 83, head of Judaism union. Page 23
Dr. Jacob Weinberg, Jewish composer, was 77. Page 23

Financial and Business

The stock market continued Thursday's upward move, with yesterday's gain of the combined average of the New York Times index of fifty leading stocks registering 1.23 points. The gain for the week was 2.32 points to 334.05. Sales totaled 2,178,200 shares as compared with 1,890,000 on Thursday. [33:8.]

New patents: fire alarm jails its user. Page 33
U. S. criticized on farm import curb at GATT meeting. Page 33
Sterling area's gold and dollar reserves fall. Page 33
Sterling Drug declares a 100 per cent stock dividend. Page 33
Steel mill to be operated by "memory" machine. Page 33
Chrysler reports $12,339,119 loss in quarter. Page 33

Sports

Boston College nips Villanova on conversion, 7—6. Page 30
Miami reserves down Florida State eleven, 20—7. Page 30
Poly Prep tops Horace Mann on gridiron, 27—13. Page 30
Dodgers hit 8 homers to win at Osaka, 14—0. Page 30
Rosi knocks out Brown in 8th round at Washington. Page 30
Connolly beats world record for hammer throw. Page 31
Irish, Canadian and Mexican horse show riders win. Page 32
Hirsch saddles 3 winners in row at Jamaica. Page 32
Adios Harry, 7-20, captures pace at Yonkers. Page 32

ADVERTISING INDEX

Classified pages are published in metropolitan New York and adjacent territory.

Three-Power Drive Against Egypt Pushed by Land, Sea and Air Forces

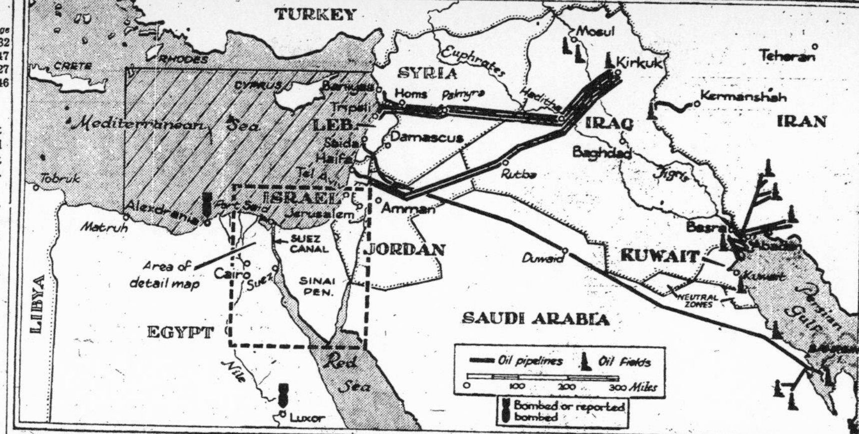

The British warned shipping to avoid a large sector of the eastern Mediterranean (diagonal shading). Arab quarters reported the sabotaging of pipelines. The line running through Israel has not been in operation.

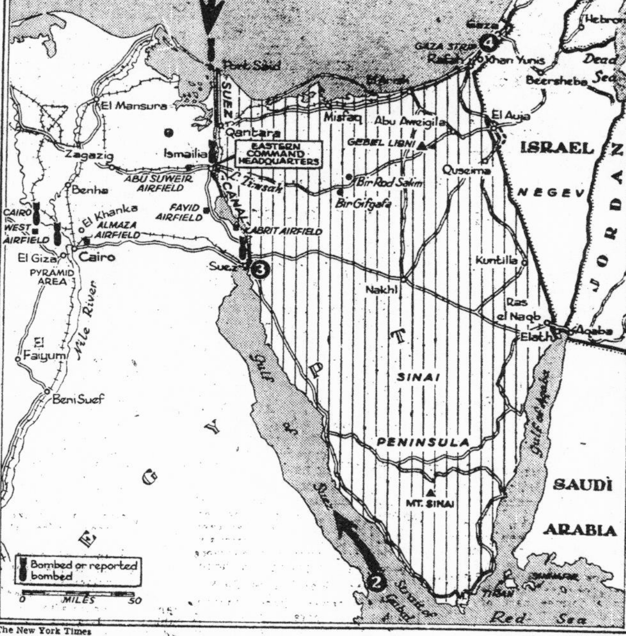

The New York Times Nov. 3, 1956

British and French amphibious forces were said to be approaching the Suez area from the north (1) and south (2). The canal was blocked at its southern end (3). The Israelis captured Gaza (4) as well as virtually all of the Sinai Peninsula (vertical shading).

ALLIES PRESSING TOWARD LANDING

Continued From Page 1

by 500-pound bombs dropped by British Canberra light bombers.

This gave a clear field to a Cyprus station calling itself "Radio Free Egypt" broadcasting in Arabic near the Cairo radio's frequency. It told its listeners that the allies' landing was a "matter of hours" away. The British-French forces only want to help the Egyptians rid the nation of "that traitor (President Gamal Abdel) Nasser who "had almost delivered our country into Moscow's clutches" the station said.

The radio said "we will do all in our power to spare your lives but you must do your part."

"Seek shelter from air attacks and keep away from military installations so that you may escape death and injury," the radio added.

British and French pilots returning from sorties over Egypt reported the absence of any sort of defensive action on ground or interception in the air in their attacks. At least one airfield appeared to have been abandoned.

With the Egyptian Air Force disorganized and the Cairo radio out of action, the British Admiralty added another indication that the invasion was on its way. Amplifying a previous warning for merchant shipping to keep clear of the Eastern Mediterranean, the Admiralty defined the area more specifically. The area is an oblong box bounded in the north by Cyprus, in the east by Lebanon and Israel and in the south by the coast of Egypt as far west as Matruh.

Considering the difficulties of collecting the seaborne invasion force from Malta, Oran in Algeria and Nicosia in Cyprus these developments indicate landing operations are feasible this week-end. When the landings are made the allies' command intends to put maximum emphasis on speed.

Battle of Movement Set

The military reason is that the Egyptian forces, whose standard of training and discipline is not considered high, will be less effective in battles of movement than in positional warfare. The allies' High Command also would get greater dividends from its air superiority if the Egyptians were kept moving in the open.

Both the British and French Governments seek early completion of their self-appointed task of taking control of the Suez canal by occupying Port Said, Ismailia and Suez. Only then can they appeal to the United Nations to assume physical control of the area they have stabilized.

Thus the expectation is that the initial landing operations will be delivered with the maximum force available. Commandos landing by sea and parachutists dropping from the air will be used to divert the main Egyptian forces from the main seaborne landing.

This will be pushed as rapidly as possible with armored forces in the van. Israeli experience in the present campaign has been that the anti-tank artillery in the Egyptian Army, although of good quality, is poorly served.

The British are continuing to build up their forces in the Eastern Mediterranean. Three troopships, the New Australia, Asturias and Dilwara, have left Southampton. Battalions of four line regiments embarked on them. The regiments were Argyll and Sutherland Highlanders, the Royal West Kents, the Royal Fusiliers and the Yorkshire and Lancashire Regiment.

A unit of the Royal Engineers was also embarked.

Syrian Moves Discounted

Reports that Syrain forces would join the Egyptian army will not alter the British and French plans to occupy the canal zone, informed sources said. The Syrian Army is said to consist of only about 25,000 men.

Troop movements by potential allies will not affect the redistribution of the Egyptian Army to positions to defend the Suez Canal. From the standpoint of Egypt's military fortunes this is the most important land operation of the moment.

According to a French spokesman, air and sea operations henceforth will seek to establish conditions necessary for occupation of the Suez Canal Zone.

This is interprted as heralding prolonged air attacks on the Egyptian forces as they move to new positions. Egyptian civilians have been warned by the Cyprus radio to stay away from transit camps and other troop concentrations.

The fighting at sea has died down for the present. The French announced their Corsair bombers had set fire to an Egyptian frigate during the action that sank a Soviet-built Egyptian destroyer off Alexandria. Two other frigates escorting the destroyer escaped.

According to British intelligence sources, President Nasser last night told the Egyptians by radio that his forces had taken over British installations in the Suez Canal Zone. He said the stores were worth £300,000,000 (about $840,000,000) and included tanks and other weapons that would be distributed to the Egyptian forces.

The British contradicted this. They said stores were worth about £40,000,000 and contained no serviceable tanks or weapons.

The names of the commanders of the allies' task forces of the three services to be employed in the invasion have been made known today They are:

Navy Vice Admiral Leonard Durnford-Slater; Deputy, Rear Admiral Pierre Lancelot.

Army Lieut. Gen. Sir Hugh Stockwell; deputy, General de Division (general of division or equivalent of American major general) Charles Beaufre.

Air Force—Air Marshal Denis Barnett; deputy, General de Brigade Aerienne (general of air brigade, equivalent to American brigadier general Brohon.

Associated Press Radiophoto

DESTINATION EGYPT: At a British airfield on Cyprus ground crewmen arm bombs under the wing of a Canberra jet. The aircraft took part in a bombing mission yesterday.

OIL SUPPLY ASSURED

Canada Said to Have No Cause for Alarm in Mideast Crisis

TORONTO, Nov 2 (Canadian Press) — Canada, consuming some 700,000 barrels of oil a day, seems to have no immediate cause for alarm about her supply, regardless of what happens in the Middle East, according to opinion here.

This is because she gets only about 30,000 barrels a day from Middle-East sources and present indications are that this could easily be made up from Western Hemisphere suppliers.

Nevertheless, the Middle East supplies about 21 per cent of world demand, and if it were removed it would set up world-supply strains.

Nu Conciliatory to Chou

Special to The New York Times.

HONG KONG, Nov. 2—Former Prime Minister Nu of Burma has told a Chinese Communist committee attended by Premier Chou En-lai that China and Burma have not the time "to quarrel or to fight or to commit aggression on each other's land," the Peiping radio reported tonight.

FLIER DESCRIBES CAIRO RADIO BLOW

Says Cyprus-Based Bombers Met No Foes in Attack on Voice of the Arabs Station

By HANSON W. BALDWIN

Special to The New York Times.

NICOSIA, Cyprus, Nov. 2—The air attack that silenced the Egyptian propaganda radio station near Cairo was described today by the pilot of one of the raiding Canberra jet bombers.

Wing Comdr. P. W. Helmore, 35-year-old veteran of World War II, spoke of the attack on the Voice of the Arabs station in a brief appearance just after his sleek twin-jet bomber had returned to an airfield in Cyprus.

He said the Canberras encountered no "enemy opposition" except some "very sporadic and inaccurate tracer fire" from light anti-aircraft guns.

Wing Commander Helmore was on his third mission against Egyptian targets since the air attacks started about 6 P. M. Wednesday. En route to today's objective his plane passed over yesterday's target airfield at Inchas and "we observed some very satisfactory cratering," he said. He added that he saw one of two peasants going about their daily tasks. "One looked up and seemed quite surprised," he said.

Deny Hitting Cairo

Both Wing Commander Helmore and his navigator, apprised of the Egyptian assertion that Cairo had been bombed, said none of their bombs had fallen anywhere near Cairo in any of their attacks.

The flier said he had been given very competent top cover by French Thunderstreak fighters based on Cyprus. He also said he had passed over what he believed to be units of the United States Sixth Fleet, which, he assumed, were covering the evacuation of United States nationals from Alexandria.

At an airport visited this morning long parked lines of Meteors, Canberras, Hastings and Valetta transports, Shackleton maritime reconnaissance planes and awkward-looking Beverley transports and naval Gannets were parked.

The field was crammed with planes and the whine of jets or the roar of prop-driven planes punctuated each conversation. Royal Air Force men in shorts and shirtless in the hot sun were "bombing up" planes for future missions or were guarding parked aircraft with rifles against sabotage.

The British have not forgotten that Cyprus is still not rid of the National Organization of Cypriotic Fighters, otherwise known as E. O. K. A. Barbed wire, gun emplacements and armed patrols are everywhere. Even newsmen are searched for bombs or weapons before they are allowed to enter airfields or headquarters.

Markings Look Alike

The Royal Air Force and French air markings look much alike and the Egyptians in any case had at the start of the conflict some British Meteors and Vampires.

The airmen were quietly doing their job this morning with efficiency and good morale but none of the obvious zest that marked World War II. There were two messages for President Gamal Abdel Nasser of Egypt lettered with chalk on the bombs. One read "Nasser's Rock 'n' Roll."

The other read "Love to Nasser." The last three letters of Nasser's name were crossed out and the letters t and y substituted, making the sign read "Love to Nasty." But these signs were not spontaneous; both were lettered on bombs for the benefit of a group of visiting photographers.

PRO-ISRAELI RALLY IS HELD ON 7TH AVE.

Two thousand persons attended an outdoor rally at noon yesterday at Seventh Avenue and Thirty-eighth Street at which speakers called for support of Israel in its conflict with Egypt.

The demonstration, held under the auspices of Brit Trumpedlor of America, a Zionist youth group, was marked by the collection of funds and the display of placards reading, "Gaza belongs to Israel, Suez to the world," and "Boycott Egyptian cotton."

Members of the group staged a demonstration several months ago in the offices of the Egyptian consulate in protest against Egyptian attacks against Israel.

Rabbi Louis I. Newman, spiritual leader of Congregation Rodeph Sholom, 7 West Eighty-third Street, opened the meeting with a prayer.

Mitchell S. Fisher, a lawyer; Yaakov Liberman, a member of the Herut political party in Israel, and Yitzchak Heimowitz, president of the organization, also addressed the meeting.

"All the News That's Fit to Print"

The New York Times.

LATE CITY EDITION
Condensation of U. S. Weather Bureau forecast: Considerable cloudiness, seasonably cool today and tomorrow.
Temperature range today: 58—49. Temperature range yesterday: 53.8—48.2.
Full U. S. Weather Bureau Report, Page 95.

SECTION ONE

NEWS SUMMARY AND INDEX, PAGE 95

VOL. CVI.. No. 36,079. Entered as Second-Class Matter, Post Office, New York, N. Y. NEW YORK, SUNDAY, NOVEMBER 4, 1956. Including Magazine and Book Review. TWENTY-FIVE CENTS

SOVIET ATTACKS HUNGARY, SEIZES NAGY; U. S. LEGATION IN BUDAPEST UNDER FIRE; MINDSZENTY IN REFUGE WITH AMERICANS

U. N. Assembly Backs Call to Set Up Mideast Truce Force

STEVENSON HOLDS PRESIDENT LACKS 'ENERGY' FOR JOB

In Last Big Address, He Asks if Nation Is Prepared to Accept Nixon as Leader

Stevenson statement, Page 72; text of speech, Page 73.

By HARRISON E. SALISBURY
Special to The New York Times.

CHICAGO, Nov. 3—Adlai E. Stevenson charged tonight that President Eisenhower "now lacks the energy" to cope with world problems such as the present crisis in the Middle East.

He asked the nation whether it was prepared to accept Richard M. Nixon "as Commander in Chief to exercise power over peace and war."

"Every consideration," Mr. Stevenson said, "the President's age, his health and the fact that he cannot succeed himself make it inevitable that the dominant figure in the Republican party under a second Eisenhower term would be Richard Nixon."

This was the first time that Mr. Stevenson in direct fashion had raised the question of General Eisenhower's health, his physical strength and his ability to survive his full term if re-elected.

It placed—on the eve of the election—the question of General Eisenhower's age and his health directly in the forefront of the campaign.

Nixon Draws Boos

Mr. Stevenson's every reference to Mr. Nixon brought forth a hurricane of boos that was equaled only by several waves of boos for General Eisenhower's foreign policy and references to the asserted errors of John Foster Dulles, Secretary of State.

Mr. Stevenson's remarks, which were carried to the nation by television, were cut off the air on a chorus of boos for Mr. Nixon. The conclusion of his address ran over the allotted air time.

General Eisenhower is 66 years old. Mr. Stevenson had foresworn any discussion of the President's health, insisting that this was a matter for each individual voter.

However, in charging tonight that the crisis in world affairs had stemmed directly from the President's "part-time conduct" of his office, Mr. Stevenson took a look into the future.

The fact is, he asserted, General Eisenhower "in the next years would inevitably recede more and more from the picture."

The President, Mr. Stevenson

Continued on Page 73, Column 2

London, Paris Bar Truce; Eden Pledges Israeli Exit

U. N. Occupation Offered

By HAROLD CALLENDER
Special to The New York Times.

PARIS, Nov. 3—Britain and France rejected today the United Nations call for a cease-fire in the Suez area.

At the same time they made a counter-proposal designed to bring their independent military action under the authority of the United Nations. They thus sought to heal the breach between the two powers on the one hand and the United Nations and the United States on the other.

The United Nations General Assembly recommended the cease-fire Thursday by adopting a resolution introduced by the United States.

The two European powers de-

Continued on Page 18, Column 1

Prime Minister Speaks

By DREW MIDDLETON
Special to The New York Times.

LONDON, Nov. 3—The British Government will insure the withdrawal of Israeli forces from Egyptian territory once British and French troops have occupied

Eden's text and Gaitskell excerpts are on Page 28.

key points on the Suez Canal, Sir Anthony Eden declared tonight.

The objective of his policy of intervention in the Middle East is a lasting settlement in the area and a stronger United Nations, able "to act as well as to talk," the Prime Minister told

Continued on Page 28, Column 6

BID TO U. N. CHIEF

Canada's Motion That He Plan Suez Unit Adopted, 59 to 0

Texts of draft resolutions and debate excerpts, Page 29.

By KATHLEEN TELTSCH
Special to The New York Times.

UNITED NATIONS, N. Y., Sunday, Nov. 4—The General Assembly voted early today to ask the Secretary General to submit a plan for creation of a United Nations police force to obtain and supervise a cease-fire in the Middle East.

The policing proposal, sponsored by Canada, was adopted 57 to 0, at 2:17 A. M. at an emergency session of the Assembly.

Nineteen states abstained, among them Israel, France and Britain. The latter two earlier had rejected an Assembly call for a cease-fire and said they would keep on with their "police action" in Egypt to safeguard the Suez Canal.

The proposal, made by Lester B. Pearson, Canada's Secretary for External Affairs, calls on Secretary General Dag Hammarskjold to submit blueprints within forty-eight hours for an "emergency international United Nations force."

New Truce Plan Adopted

No details were suggested by Mr. Pearson, but such a police force presumably would have to include several thousand men. The Canadian spokesman has said he would recommend Canada's participation. His proposal, however, left all arrangements to the Secretary General.

Within minutes, the emergency session adopted a second resolution, co-sponsored by nineteen Asian and African countries. This renewed the cease-fire appeal made two days ago and asked Mr. Hammarskjold to report within twelve hours on whether the states had complied.

The second resolution was approved, 59 to 5, with twelve abstentions. Among the abstainers were France, Britain, Israel, Autralia and New Zealand.

[Washington indicated that the Administration, after initial anger at the British-French and Israeli moves, was taking a more moderate, hopeful and understanding attitude.]

Weary United Nations delegates approved the new proposals at an event-filled emergency session, at which the United States presented a new Middle East plan. This seeks a long-range settlement of the Palestine problem and also of the current Suez Canal dispute.

In warmly supporting the Ca-

Continued on Page 29, Column 8

SOVIET ROAD BLOCK IN HUNGARY: Soviet tank obstructs road near Magyarovar
Associated Press Radiophoto

CAPITAL STORMED

Freedom Radios Fade From Air as Russians Shell Key Centers

By PAUL HOFMANN
Special to The New York Times.

VIENNA, Sunday, Nov. 4—Soviet troops started attacking Budapest and other Hungarian cities, towns and key military installations at dawn today.

At 9 A. M., local time (3 A. M. Eastern standard time) four hours after Budapest had been awakened by Russian artillery fire, overpowering Soviet tanks and infantry forces had stormed the Parliament Building and made Premier Imre Nagy and most members of his government prisoners.

Fighting in Budapest and many other parts of the country was continuing, but the prospects for the free Hungarian Government forces were nearly hopeless in the face of crushing Soviet superiority.

The Budapest radio and other Hungarian freedom stations went off the air one after another.

Before going silent, they directed desperate pleas to the West, especially to the United States, and to the United Nations for help to save the Hungarian people from "annihilation."

Mindszenty in U. S. Legation

Joseph Cardinal Mindszenty, Roman Catholic primate of Hungary, who had been freed from detention last week, and his secretary had taken refuge in the building of the United States Legation.

The United States legation, near the Parliament Building, was under fire at 9:30 A. M.

A fierce battle was raging in the immediate surroundings.

At 7 A. M. "several hundred" Soviet heavy tanks were reported attacking key Hungarian Army positions on the outskirts of Budapest and attempting to penetrate the city. The main thrust of the Soviet forces came apparently from the southeast.

Shortly before 7 A. M. the Budapest radio repeated Premier Nagy's announcement of the Soviet attack. It directed an appeal to Dag Hammarskjold, Secretary General of the United Nations. At the same time the M. T. I. Hungarian news agency reported:

"Russian troops have suddenly attacked Budapest and the entire country. They have opened fire on everyone in Hungary. It is a general attack.

"Janos Kadar [since Oct. 24 secretary of the Hungarian Communist party], Gyorgy Marosan and Sandor Ronai have formed a new Government and started crushing the counter-

Continued on Page 34, Column 5

EISENHOWER PLANS TALKS TOMORROW

To Make 2 Short Speeches on TV—Mitchell Reports Advances by Labor

By CHARLES E. EGAN
Special to The New York Times.

WASHINGTON, Nov. 3—Politics held an active, if subordinate, role in White House operations on this Saturday before election.

While the President was closeted with advisers in discussions of events in the Middle East and Europe, his top aides found time:

¶To consult with Leonard W. Hall, chairman of the Republican National Committee, on campaign strategy.

¶To issue a special report by James P. Mitchell, Secretary of Labor, detailing aid given to workers by his department under the present Administration.

¶To give a preliminary outline of the President's two Election Eve television appearances on Monday.

Mr. Hall arrived at the White House at 11:30 this morning. He spent more than an hour there first with Sherman Adams, the Assistant to the President, and later with James C. Hagerty, White House press secretary.

Continued on Page 78, Column 4

DULLES IS GAINING AFTER OPERATION

Part of His Large Intestine Is Removed—He Will Stay in Hospital 2 Weeks

By EDWIN L. DALE Jr.
Special to The New York Times.

WASHINGTON, Nov. 3—John Foster Dulles, Secretary of State, underwent successful surgery today for removal of a perforated portion of his large intestine.

It was announced after the two-and-one-half-hour operation that Mr. Dulles had "left the operating table in good condition" and that he was "resting comfortably."

The announcement was made by a State Department spokesman, Lincoln White, at Walter Reed Army Hospital. It said Mr. Dulles, 68 years old, probably would be in the hospital for two to three weeks and that he "should be able to return to his desk in approximately six weeks." Mr. Dulles' pulse was reported to be 76, his blood pressure 126/75.

The surgery was performed by Maj. Gen. Leonard D. Heaton, commanding officer of Walter Reed, who had operated on President Eisenhower in June for ileitis. He was assisted today by

Continued on Page 78, Column 3

ISRAELI PATROLS REACH SUEZ BANK

Penetrate Zone at 3 Points as Delay in British-French Landings Irks Regime

By HOMER BIGART
Special to The New York Times.

TEL AVIV, Israel, Sunday, Nov. 4—Israeli patrols reached the east bank of the Suez Canal yesterday.

A Government spokesman said Israeli columns had penetrated at three places the ten-mile buffer zone east of the canal that Britain and France wanted kept clear of warring Israeli and Egyptian forces.

Meanwhile, the Cabinet of Premier David Ben-Gurion studied reports that Syrian and Iraqi troops had entered Jordan. These developments in Jordan were being followed with "concern and alertness," according to a Foreign Ministry source.

[In Moscow, Marshal Kliment Y. Vorshilov, Soviet chief of state, told President Shukry al-Kuwatly of Syria at a farewell reception that the Soviet Union was prepared to give Syria the "necessary assistance" "to reinforce her independence against foreign threats."]

2-Nation Plan Criticized

The Government spokesman offered no reason why the Israelis had entered the proscribed zone. But the Israelis are increasingly disturbed over the slowness of British and French forces in occupying the canal.

The announcement that Israelis were within ten miles of the canal at three points—opposite El Qantara in the north, Ismailia in the center and Suez at the southern terminus—may have been timed to coincide with reports here that the British-French invasion had been put off because of United States pressure.

The British-French proposals for an international police force to occupy the canal zone were regarded here as "unrealistic."

Until its announcement, the Israeli Government had indicated compliance with the British-French ultimatum.

But Israel has insisted that no firm deal was made with the French on where the advance would be halted.

Meanwhile, the Israelis reported, they were rapidly occupying all key points on the conquered Sinai Peninsula.

Lieut. Col. Moshe Pearlman, Government and Army spokesman, said that the whole area was "relatively quiet" and that the "entire peninsula in very short time will be in Israeli hands."

British Embassy sources said

Continued on Page 30, Column 4

British Bomb Raids On Egypt Continued In Landing Prelude

Texts of the communiqués are printed on Page 26.

By LEONARD INGALLS
Special to The New York Times.

LONDON, Nov. 3—British bombers turned their heaviest attack today from airfields in Egypt to ammunition dumps, barracks and armored weapons depots of the Egyptian Army.

There were indications that the landing by British and French forces in the Suez Canal Zone would be made by paratroopers and seaborne invasion units within the next forty-eight hours.

The Beirut radio, quoting an Egyptian communiqué, reported that a British-French force attempted to land at the southern entrance to the canal, but was driven off with heavy losses.

The Egyptians said they had sunk four British naval vessels and captured three troop landing craft at Suez with fire from shore batteries and torpedo boats. One British ship was said by the Egyptians to have been sunk by gunfire, and a British destroyer, a troop carrier and another British naval unit were said to have been sunk by torpedoes.

The Egyptians also reported they had shot down seventeen British-French planes over the Suez Canal area.

[There was little additional information on the military situation in announcements or dispatches from Cairo.]

An Admiralty spokesman said "there is no information in London to support the Egyptian

Continued on Page 17, Column 1

SOVIET VETO BARS ACTION IN COUNCIL

Censure Move in U. N. Over New Attack on Hungary Carried to Assembly

Excerpts from statements in Security Council, Page 35.

By LINDESAY PARROTT
Special to The New York Times.

UNITED NATIONS, N. Y., Sunday, Nov. 4—The Soviet Union early today vetoed a United States resolution proposing Security Council censure of the Russian military attack on Hungary.

Nine nations favored the United States proposal and one abstained, Yugoslavia.

The veto was at 5:15 A. M.

Henry Cabot Lodge Jr., United States representative, immediately moved for an emergency session of the General Assembly to take up the Hungarian crisis. The Assembly already was in permanent special session over the French-British intervention in the Suez Canal area.

Council's Will 'Thwarted'

Angrily, Mr Lodge told the Council that the will of the world organization had been "thwarted" by the Soviet veto and that the eleven-nation body had been prevented from fulfilling its responsibilities. In this "grave situation," he said, Assembly action was required.

The Council adopted the United States resolution for reference to the Assembly by a vote of 10 to 1. This ballot came at 5:21 A. M.

The Assembly meeting was set for 8 o'clock tonight.

The Council adjourned at 5:24 A. M.

The Council's action, marking the Soviet Union's seventy-ninth veto, was taken after the United States had called the group together at 3 A. M. to protest against the reoccupation of Budapest by Soviet troops. According to the latest reports here early today, the Hungarian capital was in the hands of Soviet troops after Russian tanks earlier had ringed the city.

The United States legation was understood to have been under fire. Mr. Lodge also reported that Joseph Cardinal Mindszenty and his staff had taken refuge in the legation.

The Security Council had adjourned shortly after midnight

Continued on Page 35, Column 6

President Expected to Win; Democratic Congress Seen

New York Times Team Reports

Following are summaries of the apparent voting trends for President and the United States Senate and House of Representatives. They are based on the reports of New York Times teams that have surveyed twenty-seven closely contested states and of correspondents in twenty-one other states.

Presidential Race

By W. H. LAWRENCE

Surveys indicate that President Eisenhower and Vice President Richard M. Nixon will be re-elected on Tuesday by comfortable majorities of both the popular and electoral votes.

Reports from New York Times correspondents who have investigated political sentiment in the forty-eight states indicate these probable results:

For President Eisenhower—A minimum of twenty-seven states with 285 electoral votes, or nineteen votes more than required for a majority of the 531-member Electoral College.

For Adlai E. Stevenson—A minimum of seven states with seventy-six electoral votes.

Leaning toward President Eisenhower—Eight states with ninety-nine electoral votes.

Leaning toward Mr. Steven-

Continued on Page 66, Column 5

Congressional Races

By WILLIAM S. WHITE

The Democrats appear likely to hold Congress in Tuesday's national elections in spite of the prospect that President Eisenhower will retain the White House for the Republicans.

The outlook thus is for a continuation of the divided form of government that has guided the country since 1954.

A landslide for President Eisenhower would, of course, alter every present prospect. The weight of all current evidence suggests clearly, however, these approximate results:

¶The Democrats should at least retain their present thin margin of control in the Senate—49 Democrats to 47 Republicans.

¶There should be a Democratic House of Representatives again with no less than the

Continued on Page 66, Column 3

Major Sports News

FOOTBALL

Yale, Navy, Syracuse, Columbia and Army won major Eastern contests yesterday. Scores of leading games:

Amherst	6	Tufts	0
Army	55	Colgate	46
Columbia	25	Cornell	19
Georgia Tech	7	Duke	0
Illinois	7	Purdue	7
Michigan	17	Iowa	14
Michigan St.	33	Wisconsin	0
Minnesota	9	Pitt	6
Navy	33	Notre Dame	7
Ohio State	6	Northwest'n	2
Oklahoma	27	Colorado	19
Penn	28	Harvard	14
Princeton	21	Brown	7
Rutgers	20	Lafayette	19
Syracuse	20	Penn State	9
Tennessee	20	N. Carolina	0
T. C. U.	7	Baylor	6
U. C. L. A.	14	Stanford	13
W. Virginia	14	G. Wash'gton	0
Yale	19	Dartmouth	0

HORSE RACING

Summer Tan took the Gallant Fox Handicap in track record time at Jamaica.

Details in Section 5.

Mideast Oil Lines Reported Blown Up

By SAM POPE BREWER
Special to The New York Times.

BEIRUT, Lebanon, Nov. 3—Pipelines carrying more than half a million barrels of oil daily from Iraq to the Mediterranean coast have stopped operating as a result of the fighting in Egypt.

Reports circulating here were that the Iraq Petroleum Company's three pumping stations in Syria known as T-2, T-3 and T-4 had been blown up and burned.

[At the United Nations an Egyptian spokesman was quoted by The United Press as having said all oil pipelines in every Middle East country except Saudi Arabia had been blown up or shut down.]

No oil installations in Lebanon were damaged up to tonight. Reports abroad to that effect are incorrect, according

Continued on Page 30, Column 3

Nutting Quits Post; Churchill For Eden

The text of Churchill letter will be found on Page 24.

Special to The New York Times.

LONDON, Nov. 3—Anthony Nutting, Minister of State in the Foreign Office, resigned from the Government tonight because he strongly disagreed with its policy of armed intervention in Egypt.

The blow to the Government represented by the defection of one of its best-known and most effective young ministers at a critical juncture was balanced by a resounding declaration of support from Sir Winston Churchill.

Writing from his lair at Chartwell, the old lion of British politics blamed Egypt for provoking war with Israel, criticized the United States for failing to cooperate fully and

Continued on Page 24, Column 3

This section consists of 140 pages divided into three parts. The news summary and index will be found on Page 95. Society news begins on Page 90 and obituary articles will be found on Pages 86 and 87.

Pravda Denounces Nagy for 'Reaction

By Reuters.

LONDON, Sunday, Nov. 4—The Soviet Communist party newspaper Pravda attacked Premier Imre Nagy of Hungary today "in strong terms," according to the Moscow radio.

Pravda said: "The task of barring the way to reaction in Hungary has to be carried out without the slightest delay—such is the course dictated by events."

The broadcast quoted Pravda as saying: "Imre Nagy turned out to be, objectively speaking, an accomplice of the reactionary forces. Imre Nagy cannot and does not want to fight the dark forces of reaction."

Pravda asserted that it was Mr. Nagy who had requested bringing Soviet troops into Budapest, "as it was vital for the interests of the Socialist regime."

Continued on Page 15, Column 2

U. S. AND RUMANIA BREAK OFF TALKS

Bucharest Held Evasive in Parleys—An Uneasy Calm Pervades the Country

By WELLES HANGEN

Special to The New York Times.

BUCHAREST, Nov. 3 — The first formal United States-Rumanian negotiations since World War II were broken off today after three weeks of abortive discussions.

The Bucharest satellite regime refused to permit the United States to reopen its reading room here. It also was evasive on questions of consular privileges and the rights of Rumanian-Americans to leave this country.

Rumania fought to make these matters bargaining points in driving a deal with Washington on expanded trade and outstanding claims for former United States property in this country.

The Government here is unwilling or unable to commit itself to agreement on any of the issues raised by the United States. It is clear that Bucharest Communists are continuing to adhere closely to the Moscow line in all essentials.

The traditional Soviet style orthodoxy of Rumanian foreign and domestic policy has been reemphasized since Gheorghiu-Dej and other top leaders returned Sunday from Yugoslavia. This cautious attitude is apparently dictated by the regime's complete dependence on Moscow and this year's deficit harvest that is already causing notable food shortages.

Her lack of foreign exchange, coupled with prestige considerations, made Rumania eager to enter bilateral talks with the United States. Rumania hoped to arrange a trade credit equal to $22,500,000 in Rumanian Government and corporate assets seized by Washington against unpaid claims.

These hopes have now vanished, at least for time being. Washington told the Rumanians that claims against war-damaged or nationalized United States property in this country would have to be sifted for several months before there could be any discussion of the future disposition of seized Rumanian assets.

U. S. Ready to Resume

The United States is ready to resume talks at any "appropriate time." However, it insists that each question be settled separately on its merits rather than as part of a package deal.

Meanwhile, there is an uneasy surface calm in Rumania as wer continues in Hungary. The Rumanian Workers (Communist) party again appealed today for "increased vigilance" in the light of the Hungarian upheaval and what it termed "the machinations of international reactionaries."

In a long editorial in its newspaper Scintela, the party praised "the growing friendship" among Rumanians and minority nationalities. This theme has been sounded frequently of late to counteract unrest among the Hungarian-speaking Magyars of Transylvania who sympathize with their kinsmen in Hungary.

All Bucharest papers reported today that meetings had been organized recently in Targu Mures, the capital of the Magyar autonomous region. Meetings were said to have been attended by both Rumanian and Hungarian-speaking workers who came "to protest against illegal deeds committed by counter-revolutionaries in Hungary."

Other workers in Targu Mures were reported to have thanked the Government for raising minimum wages and to have assured it of their "loyalty to the present rulers of Rumania."

Union Leader's Speech

All papers also published an unusual speech by Gheorghe Apostol, the Rumanian trade union boss, to Bucharest railway workers, giving the party line on the Hungarian situation. He appealed to railwaymen to show discipline in "crushing any endeavor to strike at the peoples' democratic regime by anyone inside or outside the country."

M. Apostol promised that Government leaders would take a closer interest in the railwaymen's problems and implored them to "stand by the party and the present rulers of the country."

These remarks uttered by one of Rumania's most important leaders coincide with reliable reports of recent anti-Government demonstrations by railway workers, apparently set off by events in Hungary.

Simultaneously, Rumanian propaganda continued to denounce the "black terror" allegedly unleashed by Hungarian nationalists in an effort to split their country from the Communist bloc. Scinteia charged that Fascists and mercenaries in the service of Radio Free Europe and American billionaires were plotting the destruction of Hungary's independence.

This new violent anti-American campaign may presage open Rumanian participation in Moscow's struggle to crush the Hungarian rebellion.

Meanwhile, travel restrictions on foreigners were further tightened. For the first time, members of the United States legation have been refused permission to visit the legations' villa at Sinai in the mountains north of here. In Bucharest foreigners' movements are closely watched.

Rumors also are circulating that the Government has decided to cancel its usual Nov. 7 celebrations in honor of the Russian Revolution because of the unsettled condition of the country.

2 in Hawaii Helicopter Killed

HONOLULU, Nov. 3 (AP)—A Hawaii National Guard Helicopter crashed yesterday afternoon on Diamond Head, killing Capt. Frederick Cheney of Honolulu, the pilot, and Carlton Merrell, a civilian employe of the National Guard Bureau in Washington.

Hungarians Charged With Going Over to Russians

Gyorgy Marosan

Sandor Ronai

Janos Kadar

MOSCOW WEIGHED STEPS IN HUNGARY

Soviet Leaders Conferred on Method of Handling Budapest Situation

Special to The New York Times.

MOSCOW, Nov. 3—Soviet leaders were believed tonight to be taking a much more serious view of events in Hungary than they had a few days ago. They were reported to be in almost continuous conference on now best to handle the increasingly involved situation.

During the last thirty-six hours there has been a noticeable hardening in the Soviet press treatment of affairs in Budapest. No very firm position has been adopted as yet, but the way was clear for the strongest kind of action if that should be deemed necessary.

Reports from Budapest that a joint Soviet-Hungarian commission had been set up to work out a procedure for handling the evacuation of Soviet forces and families showed that negotiations between the two governments still were possible and that the Soviet was not ready now to use all-out force.

The Soviet leadership clearly has been upset by the recent Hungarian declaration of intention to withdraw from the Warsaw pact, a military grouping of the Soviet Union and nations in central Europe.

'Deteriorating' Events Reported

Nor are the Russians pleased by Premier Imre Nagy's appeal to the United Nations to arrange for a big-power guarantee of Hungary's neutrality. The Soviet Union sees in these moves the possibility of a significant opening in the elaborate bufferzone defense system.

Hungary alone would not be too significant in that defense system, though she would complicate communications and transport problems. The main danger, in the Soviet view clearly reflected in recent press comment, is that Hungarian independence and neutrality would spread through Eastern Europe a dangerous virus that might eventually infect more strategically important areas like Poland, East Germany and Czechoslovakia.

Signs of the hardening Soviet position appeared in Pravda today and yesterday. The Communist party paper has carried only brief reports of developments in Hungary, but all told of conditions deteriorating with "counter-revolutionary bands" committing "outrages."

Today a Soviet news agency report from Hungary said there had been "mass vengeance" and "murders of public officials"—presumably of officials of the former Communist regime.

The Soviet press also has reported that former "fascist officers" who had served in the Hungarian forces when that country sided with Germany in World War II now were being flown into Hungary. An article prominently displayed said there was an operations center in Salzburg, Germany, where "American and Hungarian reactionaries are directing the counter-revolutionary outbursts in Hungary."

Both these reports might well be used to bolster any future Soviet contention that it was preventing foreign interference.

Belgrade, Peiping Alarmed

These reports pointed up another matter of concern for the Soviet leadership. That is the pace at which non-Communist influences are being introduced into the administrative machinery of the Hungarian state.

Announcement today of a new Cabinet in Hungary, which includes Social Democrats, Freeholders and Peasant party representatives must have shaken the belief here that Hungary would emerge at least as a Communist state, even if not under Moscow's direct control.

Unlike the situation in Poland, where quick-thinking on both sides kept Communist control intact, the Hungarian situation faced the Soviet Union with the prospect of a country on its borders that might soon become "capitalist" and "bourgeois."

Almost as interesting as the Soviet reaction to that possibility has been that of Yugoslavia and Communist China. Both those countries have existed outside Moscow's firm control. Both praised the Soviet statement earlier this week that the Kremlin had made serious mistakes in dealing with other Communist states and was prepared to work for a "commonwealth of Socialist states."

But both Red China and Yugoslavia now have taken alarm similar to that felt because of the Hungarian developments. Both have expressed shock that Hungary seemed to be moving away from communism and that the "victories of revolution" were in danger.

U. S. Sells to Yugoslavia More Farm Surpluses

WASHINGTON, Nov. 3 (AP)—The United States has agreed to sell Yugoslavia $98,300,000 in surplus farm commodities, the Agriculture Department announced today.

The action came little more than two weeks after President Eisenhower had ruled that United States economic aid to Yugoslavia could continue.

In announcing the agreement, the department said it was the third to be reached with Yugoslavia, bringing the total value of such aid to $221,300,000. Yugoslavia will pay for the new shipments in dinars, its national currency.

Secretary of Agriculture Ezra Taft Benson said an immediate authorization for the purchase of 100,000 tons of wheat would be issued.

U. S. AIDES STUDY BUDAPEST NEWS

High Officials Rush to Their Offices in Early Hours—Legation Sends Report

Special to The New York Times.

WASHINGTON, Sunday, Nov. 4—First bulletins of the Soviet bombardment on Budapest brought top officials of the State Department to their offices early this morning.

They were alerted as soon as the communications center in the department received flashes from the United States Embassy in the Hungarian capital. The legation said that jets were overhead and that tanks were closing in on the city but that there had been no street fighting so far.

Herbert Hoover Jr., Acting Secretary of State, was kept in constant touch with developments as they were reported to the department through the official channels. Officials, many of whom had received first word of the disturbance while listening to radio broadcasts of the General Assembly at the United Nations, rushed to their offices and made a first order of business the relaying of dispatches to Ambassador Henry Cabot Lodge Jr. at the United Nations.

Department spokesmen said that for the time being the matter would be left in the hands of Mr. Lodge, who immediately called for a special session of the Security Council. Pending developments at the United Nations there was no official comment from the department.

Early reports from Budapest contained no information on the convoys taking legation dependents out of Budapest.

Washington Is Alerted

Special to The New York Times.

WASHINGTON, Sunday, Nov. 4—The State Department in Washington was alerted shortly after midnight that there had been new outbreaks in Budapest.

Luther J. Reid, acting press officer for the department, who went to the department on a phone call from the communications center, said:

"We are alerted by our Legation."

Mr. Reid said the department had been in touch with the United States legation in Budapest "intermittently" and had been told that Hungarian Premier Imre Nagy had gone on the air to "warn the world" that the Russians were attacking all over.

Iraqi Premier in Teheran

TEHERAN, Iran, Nov. 3 (AP)—Premier Nuri as-Said of Iraq flew here today to discuss the Middle East crisis with Iranian officials and representatives of Turkey and Pakistan. These four countries — plus Britain — make up the Baghdad Pact Alliance. Teheran is continuing under martial law.

REDS AGAIN STOP U. S. AUTO CONVOY

Families of Legation's Staff in Budapest Are Barred at Austrian Border

By ELIE ABEL

Special to The New York Times.

VIENNA, Nov. 3—Soviet tanks halted a convoy of United States legation cars coming from Budapest for the second time this afternoon as it approached the Austrian frontier.

Having been turned back yesterday, the convoy had set out from the Hungarian capital again this morning in hope that a United States protest to the Soviet Union would have had an effect. But the automobiles got no farther than Hegyeshalom on the Hungarian side of the border, where Russians barred the main highway into neutral Austria.

According to reports reaching Vienna by telephone, four wives and ten children of United States legation staff members were camping overnight in a school building at Magyarovar, 10 miles from the frontier, which was being used as a hostel by the Swiss Red Cross.

2 Cars Do It on Own

Two privately owned automobiles left the convoy and managed to follow back roads into Austria. In this group were Mrs. Ernest Leiser, wife of a Columbia Broadcasting System correspondent, and Herman Blumenthal of Fox Movietone News. They were accompanied by a German photographer, two Austrian cameramen and an elderly Swiss woman.

Mrs. Leiser said they had decided to disregard warnings of Red Cross officials about encountering Soviet soldiers and had reached Vienna unchallenged.

The incident of the day before, not in accordance with diplomatic practice, evolved prompt action by the State Department in Washington. Robert Murphy, Deputy Under Secretary of State, called in the Soviet Ambassador and delivered a formal protest.

If this had any effect in Moscow, it had not trickled down to the troop commanders along the Austro-Hungarian frontier. It was rumored along the border that the Russians were planning to set up their own military government in the area within a day or two. Once this was functioning, detained foreigners would be allowed to leave Hungary by rail with their automobiles following on flat cars according to the rumors.

Soviet Assures Washington

WASHINGTON, Nov. 3 (UP)—The Soviet Union assured the United States today that wives and children of United States diplomats twice turned back by Soviet troops, would be allowed to leave Hungary.

Soviet Ambassador Georgi N. Zaroubin informed the State Department that the matter had been "settled." A State Department spokesman said Mr. Zaroubin had agreed to take up the question with his government "immediately with a view of having the convoy let through."

Chile Affirms Economic Plan

Special to The New York Times.

SANTIAGO, Chile, Nov. 3—Gen. Carlos Ibanez, now 79 years old, started today the fifth year of his six-year term as President of Chile. Newspapers headlined his open letter indicating that his anti-inflation campaign, which started last January, will continue. The President's letter outlines the accomplishments of almost a year's application of the plan, conceived by the Kleins Saks financial mission of experts, and it reaffirms his faith in what is termed a last stand to save Chile from economic chaos.

Adenauer Condemns Soviet's Renewal Of Its Military Intervention in Hungary

Special to The New York Times.

BONN, Germany, Nov. 3—Chancellor Konrad Adenauer tonight sharply condemned renewed Soviet military intervention in Hungary. The Soviet Union should realize that "the well being of peoples cannot be built upon tanks and airplanes but solely on respect of the will of each individual people," he said.

In a radio address Dr. Adenauer asserted that events in Poland and Hungary proved that the internal and external security of the West German Federal Republic could not be adequately safeguarded without forces of its own. He said he hoped developments in eastern Europe would convince the opponents of armament of its necessity.

Dr. Adenauer assured the Hungarian people of the admiration of the entire German people in their struggle for freedom. West Germany, he said, could help only with medical supplies and food "but our hearts accompany these gifts."

The Chancellor, in line with the neutral position adopted by the West German Government on the Franco-British actions in the Middle East, confined his reference to the Suez crisis to a statement that the German Government would do everything to help eliminate "this danger" if called upon to do so.

ULBRICHT APPEALS TO WEST GERMANS

Red Leader Bids Socialists Fight Militarism—Rejects Students' Free Press Plea

Special to The New York Times.

BERLIN, Nov. 3—Walter Ulbricht, Communist leader of East Germany, appealed to West German Socialists today to combat the "revival of German militarism." He cited the events in Egypt as his chief argument.

The British-French "aggression," he said, has shown every worker the "character of the North Atlantic Treaty Organization." He urged the Social Democratic party of West Germany to establish a united front of workers to "counterattack" rearmament.

There should be established a "zone of limited armament" to which Germany would belong and this should fit in with a new European security pact, he said.

Herr Ulbricht's advice to the West German workers was delivered during a speech this morning before the Volkskammer, East Germany's lower parliamentary body. Herr Ulbricht is a Deputy Premier.

An idea of the shrewdness of this argument at the moment could be gathered from today's West Berlin newspapers. Regardless of politics, most of them were saying that the British-French action had given the Soviet Union the semblance of a defense for its actions in Hungary.

Soviet Troops Remain

Herr Ulbricht made it plain that the Soviet troops would remain in East Germany. They will "fulfill their task on the peace watch until the peaceful solution of the German problem becomes possible," he declared.

The Communist leader devoted another section of his hour-long speech to students whose feelings are obviously worrying the East German regime. He rejected outright a demand that he said, came from West Berlin students for "absolute freedom of the press." This demand, he said, was directed to the wrong address. He said the press in West Germany was in the hands of capitalists and the Communist press was barred.

Herr Ulbricht said he addressed the students not as minister, "but as an old worker." He asserted that the state gave the students "more than corresponded to the economic situation of our country."

These comments, in the view some West Berlin observers, constituted a reminder to the students that most of them received higher education on the basis of financial aid from the state, which could also cut it off.

Herr Ulbricht, like Premier Otto Grotewohl in a speech yesterday, told the Volkskammer that a cut in the working week, an increase in old age pensions and other improvements in living conditions were in the offing.

The situation in Hungary, he said, "teaches us that the people must be on their guard."

Criticism at University

Articles in two East Berlin newspapers today gave additional indications that the regime was under criticism from the students at Humboldt University. Junge Welt, the newspaper of the Free German (Communist) Youth, devoted almost a page to the subject.

It appeared that Karl Schirdewan, a member of the Politburo of the Socialist Unity (Communist) party, had a long discussion with the students of the medical and veterinary medical faculty. He said there were students in East Germany who, "without exact knowledge of the situation, identify themselves with certain tendencies among the students in Poland and, in another manner, in Hungary."

Herr Schirdewan said "there were, and still are, movements of an anti-Soviet character in Poland." Anti-Soviet movements are always of an anti-Socialist character, he said, "and the Socialist Unity party is not willing to tolerate them."

He said it would be wise to expand the "co-determination rights" of the students at the universities "under the leadership of the Free German Youth."

However, he said, it could not be tolerated that the students "should now determine how and what is to be taught and learned."

This comment, it developed, bore on the complaints of students about learning Russian.

The National Defense Minister, Willi Stoph, told the students that the Government would improve educational methods at the university but would not "permit enemies" to interfere.

WIDOW WINS AWARD

Court Orders the Payment of Florida Rents

PHILADELPHIA, Nov. 3 (AP)—A Tampa, Fla., Rabbi was ordered today to return $12,100 to a widow who said the money was owed her in rents collected by his father-in-law.

Judge Charles L. Guerin made the award to Mrs. Lena Shainerman, 65 years old, of Philadelphia.

Mrs. Shainerman filed suit against Rabbi Theodore Brod: his wife, Freda, daughter of the late Rabbi Morris Warhaftig, and Tillie Warhaftig, his widow, also of Tampa. All were Philadelphians.

Mrs. Shainerman maintained that the money was owed her in rents Rabbi Warhaftig, who was in the real estate business, collected on her property prior to his death on Oct. 16, 1954.

Ceylon Acts to Conserve Food

COLOMBO, Ceylon, Nov. 3 (Reuters)—The Government put into effect today emergency regulations to maintain reserve stocks of rice, sugar and flour. Special regulations will empower the Government to requisition food stocks without payment of compensation to hoarders.

The New York Times Nov. 4, 1956

NEW SOVIET OFFENSIVE: Russian forces began a new attack on Budapest (1), took over control of airfields at Szolnok (2) and Kalocsa (3) and assaulted Pecs (4).

RUSSIANS ATTACK HUNGARIAN CITIES

Continued From Page 1

revolution. They are on the side of the Russians."

Other reports said the three men had proclaimed a pro-Soviet regime in opposition to the Nagy Government.

This report indicated that the Soviet authorities had carefully prepared today's all-out assault politically, as well as militarily. They had apparent assurance about Kadar, who has the reputation of being an old tough Communist, as head of the counter-government challenging the Nagy cabinet.

During the early morning Premier Nagy again went on the air and called dramatically for Maj. Gen. Pal Maleter and Maj. Gen. Istvan Kovacs to return to their posts. General Maleter was the Nagy regime's Defense Minister and General Kovacs was Chief of Staff.

Generals Maleter and Kovacs and other members of a Hungarian military mission had left Budapest last night to meet Soviet officers for preliminary discussion of the withdrawal of Russian troops from Hungary. This meeting appears to have been a trap for the Hungarians. The indication here is that Generals Maleter and Kovacs and their companions were made prisoners by Russians.

Blow Struck from South

Information reaching Vienna confirmed that the main attack of the Soviet forces on Budapest came from the South. The thunder of artillery from the hillside south of the Danube stirred the city at 5 A. M.

Immediately afterward Hungarian armored detachments and troop transports raced into the suburbs and reinforced the roadblocks on the approaches to the Danube bridges.

Other reports from the Hungarian provinces showed that the Russians had started attacking everywhere at dawn.

The M. T. I. agency said that Gyor, a town half way between Vienna and Budapest, was completely encircled by the Soviet forces. Communications between Budapest and Szekesfehervar, the old coronation city southwest of Budapest, had been cut.

Farther to the south Pecs near the Yugoslav border was believed to be the scene of heavy fights between Soviet and Hungarian troops.

Soviet forces had started attacking the uranium mines and airfields near Pecs as early as 2 A. M. After several hours of fierce combat the Russians were said to have taken Pecs while the Hungarians claimed to be holding highways that lead out of that city.

Later, Soviet aircraft including MIG jet fighters were reported to participate in operations at Budapest. After thorough artillery preparation had attempted to soften Hungarian resistance, the Russian tanks and infantry advanced on the center of Budapest and stormed public buildings.

Radio Budapest went silent shortly after 8 A.M.

Afterward only the faint voice of the Freedom Radio at Eger in Northeast Hungary was heard. It implored the West to give immediate help.

"UN comes too late," the Eger station said. "Only an American ultimatum could halt the Russians from annihilating our whole people."

Nagy's Broadcast

Following is the text of Mr. Nagy's announcement made over the Free Budapest Radio Kossuth shortly after 5 A. M. (11 P. M. Saturday, Eastern standard time):

"Early this morning Soviet troops attacked the Hungarian capital with the open purpose to overthrow the legal Government.

"The Hungarian troops are in combat and the Hungarian Government is on its post.

"This I announce to our people and to the world."

The announcement was repeated in English, French and German by excited-sounding speakers on the Budapest radio every five minutes. Between announcements the Hungarian National Anthem and other patriotic musical pieces was played.

The Russians seized the military delegation commissioned by Mr. Nagy to negotiate for the withdrawal of all Soviet troops from Hungary.

A late message from M.T.I. ended with the words: "Long live Hungary and Europe! We shall die for Hungary and Europe!"

A Budapest broadcast in the Russian language to Soviet troops was heard about 7:20. It said, "Russian soldiers, do not shoot at Hungarians. Avoid bloodshed. The Hungarians are your friends."

Nagy's Ousting Reported

VIENNA, Sunday, Nov. 4 (AP)—The Russians launched a massive early morning attack against Hungary today and apparently succeeded in ousting the Government of Premier Imre Nagy.

An informant in the Szabad Nep newspaper office in Budapest reported shortly before 9 A.M. that the Government had been taken over by Janos Kadar, first secretary of the Hungarian Communist party. This had been announced on the radio, said the informant.

Heavy firing had been reported at the parliment building in Budapest where the Nagy Government had been installed. Mr. Nagy's fate was not known immediately, although it had been reported earlier that he had been taken to safety.

The Austrian press agency said, without stating its source of information, that the Parliament Building had been occupied and Mr. Nagy taken prisoner along with other members of his Government. Many of the Government ministers had been living in the building.

Bela Kovacs, leader of the Small Landholders party, who had joined in attempting to set up a coalition Government with Premier Nagy, also was reported to have disappeared.

The first Russian bombers were reported over Budapest at about 9:15 A. M. There were about fifteen planes accompanied by fighters.

Kadar's Red Move

VIENNA, Sunday, Nov. 4 (UP)—The proclamation by Janos Kadar, Hungarian Red who went over to the Russians during the night, was broadcast in Szolnok, a city sixty miles east of Budapest. Mr. Kadar said he had asked the Russian troops for help.

Word of the Soviet attack in Budapest and the proclamation from Szolnok apparently heralded a new bloodbath for Hungary.

As many as 15,000 persons were estimated to have died in the revolution that erupted the night of Tuesday, Oct. 23, and as late as yesterday had seemed to be leading the way to a free Hungary.

Early today the Soviet troops that had been pouring into the country from Russia, Czechoslovakia and Rumania began their new drive.

The M. T. I. Hungarian news agency said fighting was under way at Veszprem, fifty miles southwest of Budapest, and in Jutas and Hajmasker. It said the "biggest and heaviest fight" was near Hajmasker.

The Szolnok radio reporting on the Kadar announcement of a new pro-Soviet regime, said four persons dismissed from Premier Nagy's cabinet last Thursday when Mr. Nagy was liberalizing his government, had been installed as ministers in the Kadar Government.

They included former Interior Minister Ferenc Munich, who had been considered a Titoist; Imre Dogei, who had been a National Assembly President; Istvan Kossa, former Finance Minister, and Gyorgy Marosan, a Social Democrat who helped put his party under Communist control.

Nagy Regime Balked

By JOHN MacCORMAC

Special to The New York Times.

BUDAPEST, Hungary, Nov. 3—Zoltan Tildy announced on behalf of the Hungarian Government at a news conference today that a joint Hungarian-Soviet military commission now was discussing how Soviet troops could be withdrawn from the country.

Mr. Tildy, a non-Communist and leader of the Smallholders party, said the Russians had agreed "in principle" to the appointment of a political committee to discuss the same subject.

Any aptimism was dissipated, however, when Mr. Tildy, after absenting himself some minutes, declared on his return:

"The answers to our protests against the influx of Soviet reinforcements have been unsatisfactory. This Government from its first days had demanded the withdrawal of Soviet troops. With this any legal or political basis for their presence disappeared. We demanded their withdrawal in innumerable notes. We have never received a satisfactory reply.

"Neither the Soviet Government nor the military commanders have ever informed us what roads they want to use, what points they want to occupy, or the direction or purpose of their military movements."

His replies strengthened a belief widely entertained here that the Russians, in their customary fashion, were dragging out the negotiations for the withdrawal of their troops to gain time to widen their occupation.

HUNGARIANS HELD TO WANT UNION

U. S. Relief Worker Says After Mission 99 Per Cent Would Join Austria

Leo Cherne, chairman of the International Rescue Committee, said here yesterday that if free elections were held in Hungary now, 99 per cent of the people would vote for union with Austria.

Mr. Cherne returned yesterday from a visit to Hungary to arrange for the shipment and distribution of aid by his organization. He was in Budapest on Nov. 1.

In an adventurous two-day trip by automobile into Hungary and back to Austria, Mr. Cherne said that he was struck by the enormous gratitude the Hungarians held for the Austrians for the aid they had given the revolutionaries. He also spoke to Joseph Cardinal Mindszenty, who expressed the hope that the revolutionary victory would be permanent.

In a new conference at International Rescue Committee headquarters, 60 West Forty-fifth Street, Mr. Cherne said that he and Angier Biddle Duke, president of the organization, left New York by air last Monday to set up full-scale operations to aid the Hungarian rebels.

Immediately after their arrival in Vienna Tuesday evening, he said, Mr. Biddle began to make preparations for the receipt and purchase of goods in Austria, and for the arrangement of "pipelines" into Hungary.

Antibiotic Distributed

Accompanied by Marcel Faust, director of I. R. C. in Vienna, Mr. Cherne set off for Hungary in a 1952 Chevrolet loaded with "token" gifts of 15,000 vials of Terramycin, an antibiotic donated by Charles Pfizer & Co., the manufacturer, and some rolls of bandage gauze, a few clothing parcels and thirty loaves of bread.

Mr. Cherne said that the pair had no papers of any kind, and that they got all the way to Budapest, thanks to a Red Cross flag hastily sewn together before their departure. They were stopped thirty times en route, and neither of them spoke Hungarian but they were allowed to proceed when they shouted "medicine" and could prove they were carrying no arms. One of the road blocks was Russian, the rest Hungarian.

Once in the Hungarian capital Mr. Cherne and Mr. Faust managed to find the United States embassy and later a hotel, although the city looked like a "ghost town" populated only by occasional groups of youthful Freedom Fighters looking for members of the hated A.V.H., or Hungarian secret police.

The Most Hated People

"The Russians are not the most hated people in Hungary," Mr. Cherne said. "The most hated are the members of the secret police. Every nook and cranny is searched for them and when they are found they are destroyed."

Mr. Cherne reported that the streets of Budapest were littered with debris and bodies. At one point his automobile became entangled with downed trolley cables. The Astoria Hotel, where they found rooms, he said, was "well ventilated," as it had been shelled by Soviet troops an hour earlier. The Soviet, he said, had committed "barbarous butchery" in the city and "conservative" estimates were that there had been between 7,000 and 10,000 Hungarian dead, and between 30,000 and 40,000 wounded.

Guided by two English-speaking college students on the morning after their arrival, Mr. Cherne explained, he managed to see Cardinal Mindszenty at his residence overlooking the Danube. Mr. Cherne presented the Terramycin to the prelate who said that "he was moved as he always had been by the quick generosity of the American people."

Cardinal Mindszenty, Mr. Cherne added, sent his thanks to the American people and to President Eisenhower, and expressed the hope that "the victory will be a permanent one."

After his meeting with Cardinal Mindszenty, Mr. Cherne said, he met "two valid anti-Communists, one of them a leader of the Social Democratic party and the other a leader of the Christian Democrat party who I prefer not to name for obvious reasons," to arrange for future distribution of I. R. C. aid. He said that he was also taken to visit the heaquarters of the Freedom Fighters. The backbone of the fighters, he said, were youths, and mainly college students. The bottom age for the revolutionaries, he was told, was 10 years.

HASS DISCUSSES WAR

Socialist Sees No Solution in Capitalist System

Eric Hass, Socialist Labor party candidate for President, declared yesterday that no solution to war was possible within the capitalist system.

"Our only hope of stopping the expansion of Russian imperialism," he said, "is to win over the oppressed masses of the world and a capitalist America can't do that. A socialist America could."

In a speech telecast on three channels and broadcast over two radio networks, Mr. Hass said Russian imperialism had made headway by trading on the hatred of capitalism by oppressed people.

"But now the Russian bureaucrats stand unmasked," he said. "In Eastern Europe they are quite obviously losing not merely their dictatorial control, but their ideological influence. This is an hour when a socialist America could once again make this nation the shining example and hope of freedom that it was after 1776."

"All the News That's Fit to Print"

The New York Times.

LATE CITY EDITION
U. S. Weather Bureau Report (Page 59) forecasts: Mostly fair and seasonable today and tomorrow.
Temp. range: 70—57. Yesterday: 67.7—55.9.

VOL. CVII..No. 36,404. NEW YORK, WEDNESDAY, SEPTEMBER 25, 1957. 10c beyond 100-mile zone from New York City FIVE CENTS

PRESIDENT SENDS TROOPS TO LITTLE ROCK, FEDERALIZES ARKANSAS NATIONAL GUARD; TELLS NATION HE ACTED TO AVOID ANARCHY

WEST AGAIN BARS SOVIET PROPOSAL ON MIDEAST TALK

U. S. Says Latest Moscow Note 'Cynically Distorts' American Actions

Text of U. S. note to Soviet will be found on Page 5.

By DANA ADAMS SCHMIDT
Special to The New York Times.

WASHINGTON, Sept. 24—The United States, Britain and France rejected today the latest in a series of Soviet bids for recognition of the Soviet Union's role in the Middle East.

A brief United States reply delivered in Moscow today said a Soviet note of Sept. 3 was "offensive in tone and cynically distorts United States objectives and actions in the Middle East."

It accused the Soviet Union of setting in motion "a chain of events leading to the present dangerous situation" by shipping large quantities of arms into the area.

U. S. Affirms Doctrine

The note warned the Soviet Union that the United States Government intended to carry out the national policy laid down in the Eisenhower Doctrine, which "regards the preservation of the independence and integrity of the nations of that region as vital to world peace and as vital, therefore, to its own national interests."

The doctrine, proclaimed in a Joint Resolution of the House of Representatives and the Senate on March 9, 1957, also affirmed the President's authority to use United States forces to aid any Middle East state that asked for help against aggression by a power controlled by international communism.

The Soviet Union's note had accused the United States of seeking to overthrow the Syrian Government and of generally fomenting trouble in the Middle East.

3d Rejection of Soviet Bid

It had proposed, for the third time, a four-power declaration renouncing the use of force in the area. Earlier Soviet proposals for such a declaration, all rejected by the West, were made Feb. 11 and April 19.

As interpreted by United States experts on the Middle East, these notes were meant to convey the idea that the four powers should meet to negotiate a settlement of their rivalries in the Middle East. The first of the notes even went into detail with a proposal for an embargo on shipment of arms to the area.

Because the Soviet Union has asserted its presence in Syria, and because there seems to be little the Western powers can do to reverse developments in

Continued on Page 5, Column 3

London and Bonn Rule Out Any Currency Revaluation

Britain Tells Monetary Fund Session She Will Draw $500,000,000 in Stand-By Credit From Export-Import Bank

By EDWIN L. DALE JR.
Special to The New York Times.

WASHINGTON, Sept. 24—British and West German spokesmen and the Managing Director of the International Monetary Fund said today that the question of exchange rates for the pound and the mark was "definitely settled." There will be no change.

At the same time, Britain, through Peter Thorneycroft, Chancellor of the Exchequer, announced she would draw "over the coming weeks" the $500,000,000 stand-by credit she arranged last winter with the United States Export-Import Bank.

In his speech at the annual meeting of the fund, Mr. Thorneycroft indicated that Britain was drawing the money to demonstrate to speculators that she had the resources to defend the pound.

Both the British and the West Germans emphasized that the recent huge flow of gold and dollars out of Britain and into West Germany had been based solely on speculation, not on basic factors in their foreign trading accounts.

Per Jacobsson, the Fund's Managing Director, said: "The growing knowledge that there will be no alteration in the value of either the Deutsche

Continued on Page 8, Column 5

SOLDIERS FLY IN

1,000 Go to Little Rock —9,936 in Guard Told to Report

The texts of Executive orders on troops are on Page 16.

By JACK RAYMOND
Special to The New York Times.

WASHINGTON, Sept. 24—The Army ordered all Arkansas National Guardsmen to report for Federal duty tonight and rushed 1,000 airborne troops of the Regular Army into Little Rock to preserve order.

The Regulars were members of the 101st Airborne Division, which won fame in World War II under the command of Gen. Maxwell D. Taylor, now Chief of Staff of the Army.

Maj. Gen. Edwin A. Walker, a much-decorated combat commander with a reputation for toughness, was put in command of the Regular Army contingent and the federalized Guardsmen in Arkansas. He is the commander of the Arkansas Military District.

General Walker's mission is to make sure that no one frustrates Federal Court orders that nine Negro pupils be admitted to Central High School.

Wilson Carries Out Order

Charles E. Wilson, Secretary of Defense, carrying out President Eisenhower's mandate, earlier had called the entire Arkansas Army and Air National Guard, totaling 9,936 men, into Federal service.

The Secretary of Defense and Wilber M. Brucker, Secretary of the Army, acted two hours after President Eisenhower's executive order authorizing "all appropriate steps" to make school attendance possible for the Negroes who had been admitted to the high school.

However, an Army spokesman said that it was planned to make "the absolute minimum demonstration of force necessary."

Immediately after Secretary Wilson signed the federalization call to the Arkansas Guard at 2:25 P. M., Secretary Brucker telephoned the office of Gov. Orval E. Faubus in Little Rock.

At the same time he sent a telegram to the Governor, explaining that President Eisenhower "desires" the personnel of the Arkansas Army and Air National Guard organizations

Continued on Page 14, Column 2

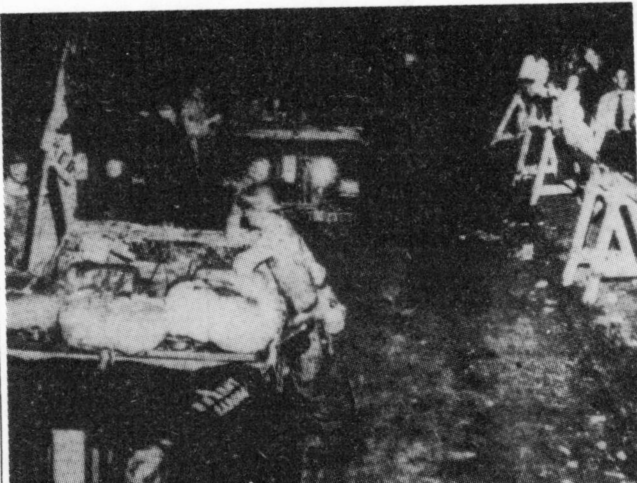

Associated Press Wirephoto

SOLDIERS IN LITTLE ROCK: Residents of Arkansas capital looking on last night as men of the 101st Airborne Division took positions outside the Central High School.

EISENHOWER ON AIR

Says School Defiance Has Gravely Harmed Prestige of U. S.

Text of President's address appears on Page 14.

By ANTHONY LEWIS
Special to The New York Times.

WASHINGTON, Sept. 24—President Eisenhower sent Federal troops to Little Rock, Ark., today to open the way for the admission of nine Negro pupils to Central High School.

Earlier, the President federalized the Arkansas National Guard and authorized calling the Guard and regular Federal forces to remove obstructions to justice in Little Rock school integration.

His history-making action was based on a formal finding that his "cease and desist" proclamation, issued last night, had not been obeyed. Mobs of pro-segregationists still gathered in the vicinity of Central High School this morning.

Tonight, from the White House, President Eisenhower told the nation in a speech for radio and television that he had acted to prevent "mob rule" and "anarchy."

Historic Decision

The President's decision to send troops to Little Rock was reached at his vacation headquarters in Newport, R. I. It was one of historic importance politically, socially, constitutionally. For the first time since the Reconstruction days that followed the Civil War, the Federal Government was using its ultimate power to compel equal treatment of the Negro in the South.

He said violent defiance of Federal Court orders in Little Rock had done grave harm to "the prestige and influence, and indeed to the safety, of our nation and the world." He called on the people of Arkansas and the South to "preserve and respect the law even when they disagree with it."

Guardsmen Withdrawn

Action quickly followed the President's orders. During the day and night 1,000 members of the 101st Airborne Division were flown to Little Rock. Charles E. Wilson, Secretary of the Defense, ordered into Federal service all 10,000 members of the Arkansas National Guard.

Today's events were the climax of three weeks of skirmishing between the Federal Government and Gov. Orval E. Faubus of Arkansas. It was three weeks ago this morning that the Governor first ordered National Guard troops to Central High School to preserve order. The nine Negro students were prevented from entering the school.

The Guardsmen were gone yesterday, withdrawn by Governor Faubus as the result of a

Continued on Page 14, Column 6

SOVIET ASSAILED BY LLOYD AT U. N.

Briton Suggests Arms Sent Arabs May Be Stocks for Future Bases

Excerpts from Lloyd's speech are printed on Page 4.

By THOMAS J. HAMILTON
Special to The New York Times.

UNITED NATIONS, N. Y., Sept. 24—Britain denounced today Soviet arms shipments to Arab countries. Selwyn Lloyd, British Foreign Secretary, suggested that the purpose might be to "pre-stock forward bases for the Soviet Union itself."

Mr. Lloyd told the General Assembly that Soviet arms had been delivered "on such a scale as to give some color to this suggestion." He added that Britain viewed the Syrian situation "with grave concern." In addition, he criticized Soviet policy throughout the area.

Mr. Lloyd devoted most of his speech to the Middle East and to disarmament. He did not say what action the Assembly should take on either subject.

However, he declared that Secretary of State Dulles, in

Continued on Page 4, Column 3

City Approves Plan By Wiley to Build Midtown Garages

By JOSEPH C. INGRAHAM

The Board of Estimate has approved in principle the program of Traffic Commissioner T. T. Wiley for garage construction in the heart of lower and mid-Manhattan.

The decision clears the way for a start on $24,000,000 of garages. It also settles a three-year dispute between Mr. Wiley and other city executives that has stymied off-street parking relief.

As a result, the first of the projects—a garage in the Herald Square area—will be on the board's calendar on Oct. 9. Eight other garages are to be centrally located in Manhattan and two in the busiest parts of the Bronx.

The Herald Square garage will be east of the Avenue of the Americas between West Thirty-fifth and Thirty-sixth Streets with entrances and exits on both streets. There will be space for 610 cars on eight levels accessible by ramps. Rates will be geared to "meet the heavy unsatisfied demand for short-time parking," Mr. Wiley said.

Rates proposed by the Commissioner would be 25 cents a

Continued on Page 25, Column 1

GOVERNORS URGE WHITE HOUSE TALK

Southerners Move to Set Up Mediation Machinery in Use of Federal Troops

By JOHN N. POPHAM
Special to The New York Times.

SEA ISLAND, Ga., Sept. 24—Southern Governors moved tonight to establish mediation machinery that would remove Federal troops from the South. The Governors acted a few hours after the President had federalized the Arkansas National Guard.

Gov. Luther Hodges of North Carolina, chairman of the Southern Governors Conference in session here, announced that two proposals would be submitted to the resolutions committee of the conference for formal consideration tomorrow.

One is a proposal of Gov. Frank G. Clement of Tennessee to establish an informal committee of Southern Governors to seek a meeting with President Eisenhower in a search for a solution to the Little Rock school integration crisis.

The other is a request to the President to hold off the use of Federal troops and to agree

Continued on Page 16, Column 2

Troops on Guard at School; Negroes Ready to Return

By BENJAMIN FINE
Special to The New York Times.

LITTLE ROCK, Ark., Sept. 24—Troops from the Army's crack 101st Airborne Division, carrying carbines and billy clubs, took posts around Central High School tonight. They were here to see that court-ordered integration is carried out.

With police sirens wailing and headlights flashing, Army trucks loaded with soldiers roared into position. The soldiers represented about a quarter of the contingent of 1,000 crack troops of the division that was ordered to Little Rock by President Eisenhower to prevent mob riots and violence.

The first group of 500 airborne soldiers came to the city this afternoon from Fort Campbell, Ky., and a second group of 500 arrived by plane this evening. The bulk of the two groups bivouacked for the night in areas away from the school.

General Issues Order

Maj. Gen. Edwin A. Walker, commander of the Arkansas Military District, issued a formal order to the people of Little Rock not to collect in crowds and to let Central High School be integrated peaceably.

With the arrival of Federal troops, including some Negro soldiers who were not expected to be on duty at the school, Negro students were ready to try again to enter the high school.

A mob of 1,000 persons yesterday forced the city and school authorities to withdraw nine Negro students who had attended integrated classes for 3 hours and 13 minutes. The students did not try to enter the school today.

Mrs. L. C. Bates, president

Continued on Page 15, Column 1

CONGRESS IS SPLIT ON USE OF TROOPS

Johnston Calls for Faubus to Resist President but Others Hail His Move

By JOHN W. FINNEY
Special to The New York Times.

WASHINGTON, Sept. 24—Congressional reaction to President Eisenhower's decision to use troops in the Little Rock integration crisis ranged from angry denunciation to outright praise today.

Southern Senators sharply criticized the President and suggested he had exceeded his legal authority. Northern Senators supported the President, but some of them expressed reservations that the action was rather belated.

Expects Faubus to Act

Senator Olin D. Johnston, Democrat of South Carolina, suggested that Gov. Orval E. Faubus of Arkansas "stand up for states' rights" and force a showdown with the President by calling out the Arkansas National Guard on his own.

Senator Johnston, a former Governor of South Carolina, said if he were Governor Faubus, "I'd proclaim a state of insurrection down there, and I'd call out the National Guard, and I'd then find out who's going to run things in my state."

Asked by reporters whether he believed Governor Faubus would take such steps, Senator Johnston said, "I think he will and I hope he will."

Aiken Defends Move

Senator John L. McClellan, Democrat of Arkansas, said he believed such use of military force by the Federal Government was "without authority of law."

He said he was "very apprehensive that such action may precipitate more trouble than it will prevent."

Senator Richard B. Russell, Democrat of Georgia and leader of Southern opposition to the Civil Rights Bill in the last session, said that President Eisenhower's use of troops might "put Negro children in the white schools," but that it would "have a calamitous effect on race relations and on the cause of national unity."

On the other side of the issue, Senator George D. Aiken, Republican of Vermont, said the President "is undoubtedly within

Continued on Page 17, Column 3

U. S. Cutters Conquer Northwest Passage

3 Coast Guard Craft First of the Nation to Make Transit

By JOHN H. FENTON
Special to The New York Times.

BOSTON, Sept. 24 — Two Coast Guard cutters were saluted in Boston Harbor today at the end of a successful mission to find a practical Northwest Passage—a route around the top of the North American Continent.

A third cutter, the Spar, proceeded directly to her home port at Bristol, R. I., to be welcomed there as the first United States vessel to circumnavigate the continent.

The cutters Storis, from Juneau, Alaska, and the Bramble, from Miami, Fla., put in here for their welcoming. They will continue their homeward voyages later in the week.

The three cutters were the first United States vessels to make the passage.

The shrill sirens of water-spouting fireboats and the deeper-throated whistles of other craft sounded a "well done" as the two bulky cutters made their way up the harbor.

Ranking Coast Guard officers and civil officials joined with members of families of the crews in a dockside welcome as the cutters tied up at

Continued on Page 19, Column 1

U. S. Coast Guard

Coast Guardsmen on the stern of the Spar view her sister cutters, Bramble, left, and Storis, during the transit of Simpson Strait. This was a difficult part of the voyage.

Rebel Chief Seized In Algiers Gunfight

By THOMAS F. BRADY
Special to The New York Times.

ALGIERS, Algeria, Sept. 24—The chief of the nationalist terrorist organization in Algiers was in the hands of French parachute troops today. The rebel leader, Saadi Yacef, 29 years old, had eluded capture in the crowded Casbah for more than two years.

With him was 24-year-old Miss Zorah Drif, an Algerian revolutionary, who was condemned to death in absentia by a French military tribunal.

A parachute colonel told reporters this evening that Mr. Yacef and Miss Drif had surrendered at 5:30 A. M. after the terrorist chief had wounded a lieutenant colonel and a master sergeant of a Foreign Legion parachute regiment. The colonel then took reporters to a hideout high in the Casbah where he described how the

Continued on Page 4, Column 3

Price Index Up .2%; Sets Another High

By RICHARD E. MOONEY
Special to The New York Times.

WASHINGTON, Sept. 24—The United States Consumers' Price Index rose two-tenths of a per cent in August, setting another record. It was the twelfth consecutive monthly increase, but among the smallest of the twelve.

The Labor Department's Bureau of Labor Statistics reported today that the index rose in August to 121, using the price average in the 1947-49 period as a comparison base of 100. All the major categories of prices increased, but food and housing were the strongest factors.

The August index was 3.6 per cent higher than that of a year earlier. This meant that a typical city family paid $1.03 3/5 in August of 1957 for the goods and services that cost $1 in August of 1956.

The Commerce Department

Continued on Page 24, Column 3

Textile Union Gets 30 Days to Reform

By A. H. RASKIN

A scandal-tainted textile union was ordered yesterday to oust its two chief officers within thirty days or face possible suspension from the merged labor federation.

The ultimatum was given to the 40,000-member United Textile Workers by the executive council of the American Federation of Labor and Congress of Industrial Organizations.

It foreshadowed the fixing of a similar clean-up deadline today for the 1,400,000-member International Brotherhood of Teamsters and the 140,000-member Bakery and Confectionery Workers International Union.

The federation's Ethical Practices Committee has found all three unions guilty of violating the anti-racketeering provisions of the A. F. L.-C. I. O. constitution. The findings were based

Continued on Page 13, Column 3

TROOP PRECEDENT GOES BACK TO 1792

Washington Signed Law Then—Used Powers in Whisky Rebellion

Special to The New York Times.

WASHINGTON, Sept. 24 — The President's power to use troops for the enforcement of Federal law has had specific statutory support since May 2, 1792.

On that day President Washington signed a law whose essence is still on the statute books. The key sections read:

"Whenever the laws of the United States shall be opposed, or the execution thereof obstructed, in any state, by combinations too powerful to be suppressed by the ordinary course of judicial proceedings, it shall be lawful for the President to call forth the militia of such state to suppress such combinations, and to cause the laws to be duly executed * * *

"[The President] shall forthwith, and previous thereto, by proclamation, command such insurgents to disperse, and retire peaceably to their respective abodes, within a limited time."

Some of the exact phraseology of that statute still is in the United States Code. President Eisenhower's proclamation yesterday followed the form required by the 1792 act precisely, and used the phrases "ordinary course of judicial proceedings" and commanding the insurgents "to disperse."

Washington Used Powers

President Washington used the powers of the act, in 1794, to suppress the Whisky Rebellion in western Pennsylvania. Whisky-makers there were rioting against a Federal excise tax. Troops called out by Washington suppressed the rebellion.

The act was to expire after two years. But in 1795 Congress repassed it in permanent form, with some revisions.

The 1795 act made plain that the President could federalize the militia of "any other state or states as may be necessary." It removed a requirement of the 1792 act that, before moving, the President be "notified" by a Federal judge of the need for troops.

These early statutes spoke only of the President's using state militia, the equivalent of today's National Guard, and not of employing Federal troops.

uBt Edward S. Corwin, the noted authority on constitutional history, has said this was "probably without interpretative significance, inasmuch as the regular army of that day was fully employed in manning the seacoast and frontier fortifications."

Power Is Extended

In any case, Congress in 1807 extended the same Presidential power to the regular United States forces. It authorized him to use the troops for the same purposes detailed in the act providing for calling-up of the state militia.

This statutory history is the reason for the general bewilderment among lawyers here over the contention by Gov. Orval E. Faubus of Arkansas that President Eisenhower cannot properly use Federal troops in Little Rock unless he, the Governor, first requests the move.

Another statute of early origin, and still on the books, authorizes the President to send troops at the request of a state Legislature or Governor to help put down an "insurrection in any state against its government."

But the problem in Little Rock, rather than one of an insurrection against the state government, is the very obstruction of Federal law that the President is authorized to remove with troops—regardless of the views of the state Governor or Legislature.

In 1827, in the case of Martin v. Mott, the Supreme Court held that the President was "the sole and exclusive judge" of the facts as to whether use of troops was necessary. The court's opinion, by Justice Story, continued:

"It is no answer that such a power may be abused, for there is no power which is not susceptible of abuse. The remedy for this, as well as for other official misconduct, if it should occur, is to be found in the Constitution itself.

"In a free government the danger must be remote, since in addition to the high qualities which the Executive must be presumed to possess, of public virtue and honest devotion to the public interests, the frequency of elections, and the watchfulness of the representatives of the nation, carry with them all the checks which can be useful to guard against usurpation or wanton tyranny."

Rests With President

Mr. Corwin thus sums up the President's power:

"In short, it still rests with the President, as it has ever since the Act of 1807, to say when the national forces shall be employed against "combinations too powerful to be dealt with in the ordinary course of judicial proceedings."

One example of the use of Federal troops against a state Governor's wishes came in Illinois in the great Pullman strike of 1894.

President Grover Cleveland, a Democrat, used troops to enforce a sweeping Federal injunction against the strike. Hundreds of persons were arrested, among them Eugene V. Debs, the Socialist and labor leader.

The Democratic Governor of Illinois, John P. Altgeld, had opposed crushing of the strike and had opposed the use of Federal troops. He told his Legislature in 1895 that President Cleveland had sent the troops "without calling on the local authorities to enforce the law or making any inquiry as to whether any assistance was needed, and at a time when the local authorities felt they could easily control the situation."

Eisenhower Address on Little Rock Crisis

Following is the text of President Eisenhower's radio-television talk from Washington last night to the country on his moves in the Little Rock school integration problem as recorded by The New York Times:

Good evening, my fellow citizens.

For a few minutes this evening, I should like to speak to you about the serious situation that has arisen in Little Rock. To make this talk I have come to the President's Office in the White House.

I could have spoken from Rhode Island where I have been staying recently. But I felt that, in speaking from the house of Lincoln, of Jackson and of Wilson, my words would better convey both the sadness I feel in the action I was compelled today to make, and the firmness with which I intend to pursue this course until the orders of the Federal Court at Little Rock can be executed without unlawful interference.

In that city, under the leadership of demagogic extremists, disorderly mobs have deliberately prevented the carrying-out of proper orders from a Federal Court. Local authorities have not eliminated that violent opposition. And under the law I yesterday issued a proclamation calling upon the mob to disperse.

This morning the mob again gathered in front of the Central High School of Little Rock, obviously for the purpose of again preventing the carrying-out of the court's order relating to the admission of Negro children to that school.

Inescapable Duty

Whenever normal agencies prove inadequate to the task and it becomes necessary for the Executive Branch of the Federal Government to use its powers and authority to uphold Federal Courts, the President's responsibility is inescapable.

In accordance with that responsibility I have today issued an Executive Order directing the use of troops under Federal authority to aid in the execution of Federal law at Little Rock, Ark. This became necessary when my proclamation of yesterday was not observed and the obstruction of justice still continues.

It is important that the reasons for my action be understood by all our citizens. As you know the Supreme Court of the United States has decided that separate public educational facilities for the races are inherently unequal and therefore compulsory school segregation laws are unconstitutional.

Our personal opinions about the decision have no bearing on the matter of enforcement; the responsibility and authority of the Supreme Court to interpret the Constitution are very clear. Local Federal courts were instructed by the Supreme Court to issue such orders and decrees as might be necessary to achieve admission to public schools without regard to race—and with all deliberate speed.

During the past several years, many communities in our Southern states have instituted public school plans for gradual progress in the enrollment and attendance of school children of all races in order to bring themselves into compliance with the law of the land.

Thus they demonstrated to the world that we are a nation in which laws, not men, are supreme.

I regret to say that this truth—the cornerstone of our liberties—was not observed in this instance.

It was my hope that this localized situation would be brought under control by city and state authorities. If the use of local police powers had been sufficient, our traditional method of leaving the problem in those hands would have been pursued. But when large gatherings of obstructionists made it impossible for the decrees of the court to be carried out, both the law and the national interest demanded that the President take action.

Events Are Reviewed

Here is the sequence of events in the development of the Little Rock school case.

In May of 1955, the Little Rock school board approved a moderate plan for the gradual desegregation of the public schools in that city. It provided that a start toward integration would be made at the present term in the high school, and that the plan would be in full operation by 1963.

Here I might say that in a number of communities in Arkansas integration in the schools has already started and without violence of any kind. Now this Little Rock plan was challenged in the courts by some who believe that the period of time as proposed in the plan was too long.

The United States Court at Little Rock, which has supervisory responsibility under the law for the plan of desegregation in the public schools, dismissed the challenge, thus approving a gradual rather than an abrupt change from the existing system. The court found that the school board had acted in good faith in planning for a public school system free from racial discrimination.

Since that time the court has on three separate occasions issued orders directing that the plan be carried out. All persons were instructed to refrain from interfering with the efforts of the school board to comply with the law.

Proper and sensible observance of the law then demanded the respectful obedience which the nation has a right to expect from all its people. This, unfortunately, has not been the case at Little Rock. Certain misguided persons, many of them imported into Little Rock by agitators, have insisted upon defying the law and have sought to bring it into disrepute. The orders of the court have thus been frustrated.

The very basis of our individual rights and freedoms rests upon the certainty that the President and the Executive Branch of Government will support and insure the carrying out of the decisions of the Federal Courts, even, when necessary, with all the means at the President's command.

President Fears Anarchy

Unless the President did so, anarchy would result. There would be no security for any except that which each one of us could provide for himself.

The interest of the nation in the proper fulfillment of the law's requirements cannot yield to opposition and demonstrations by some few persons.

Now let me make it very clear that Federal troops are not being used to relieve local and state authorities of their primary duty to preserve the peace and order of the community. Nor are the troops there for the purpose of taking over the responsibility of the school board and other responsible local officials in running Central High School.

The running of our school system and the maintenance of peace and order in each of our states are strictly local affairs and the Federal Government does not interfere except in very special cases and when requested by one of the several states. In the present case the troops are there, pursuant to law, solely for the purpose of preventing interference with the orders of the court.

The proper use of the powers of the Executive Branch to enforce the orders of a Federal Court is limited to extraordinary and compelling circumstances. Manifestly, such an extreme situation has been created in Little Rock. This challenge must be met and with such measures as will preserve to the people as a whole their lawfully protected rights in a climate permitting their free and fair exercise.

The overwhelming majority of our peopple in every section of the country are united in their respect for observance of the law—even in those cases where they may disagree with that law.

They deplore the call of extremists to violence.

The decision of the Supreme Court concerning school integration of course affects the South more seriously than it does other sections of the country. In that region I have many warm friends, some of them in the city of Little Rock. I have deemed it a great personal privilege to spend in our southland tours of duty while in the military service and enjoyable recreational periods since that time.

Voices Faith in People

So from intimate personal knowledge I know that the overwhelming majority of the people in the South—including those of Arkansas and of Little Rock—are of goodwill, united in their efforts to preserve and respect the law even when they disagree with it.

They do not sympathize with mob rule. They, like the rest of our nation, have proved in two great wars their readiness to sacrifice for America.

And the foundation of the American way of life is our national respect for law.

In the South, as elsewhere, citizens are keenly aware of the tremendous disservice that has been done to the people of Arkansas in the eyes of the nation, and that has been done to the nation in the eyes of the world.

At a time when we face grave situations abroad because of the hatred that communism bears toward a system of government based on human rights, it would be difficult to exaggerate the harm that is being done to the prestige and influence, and indeed to the safety, of our nation and the world.

Our enemies are gloating over this incident and using it everywhere to misrepresent our whole nation. We are portrayed as a violator of those standards of conduct which the peoples of the world united to proclaim in the Charter of the United Nations. There they affirmed "faith in fundamental human rights and in the dignity and worth of the human person" and they did so "without distinction as to race, sex, language or religion."

And so, with deep confidence, I call upon the citizens of the State of Arkansas to assist in bringing to an immediate end all interference with the law and its processes. If resistance to the Federal court orders ceases at once, the further presence of Federal troops will be unnecessary and the City of Little Rock will return to its normal habits of peace and order and a blot upon the fair name and high honor of our nation in the world will be removed.

Thus will be restored the image of America and of all its parts as one nation, indivisible, with liberty and justice for all.

Good night, and thank you very much.

Associated Press Wirephoto

TROOP CONVOY, carrying men assigned to cope with the disorders in Little Rock, Ark., moves into the city from near-by air base. The troops had flown in from Kentucky.

PRESIDENT WARNS OF ANARCHY PERIL

Continued From Page 1

Federal Court order. But a shrieking mob compelled the nine children to withdraw from the school.

President Eisenhower yesterday cleared the way for full use of his powers with a proclamation commanding the mob in Little Rock to "disperse."

At 12:22 P. M. today in Newport the President signed a second proclamation. It said first that yesterday's command had "not been obeyed and willful obstruction of said court orders exists and threatens to continue."

The proclamation then directed Charles E. Wilson, Secretary of Defense, to take all necessary steps to enforce the court orders for admission of the Negro children, including the call of any or all Arkansas Guardsmen under Federal command and the use of the armed forces of the United States.

Later in the afternoon the President flew from Newport to Washington, arriving at the National Airport at 4:50 o'clock.

He began his broadcast speech with this explanation of the flight:

"I could have spoken from Rhode Island, but I felt that, in speaking from the house of Lincoln, of Jackson and of Wilson, my words would more clearly convey both the sadness I feel in the action I was compelled to take and the firmness with which I intend to pursue this course. * * *"

It was a firm address, with some language unusually strong for President Eisenhower.

President Traces Dispute

"Under the leadership of demagogic extremists," the President said, "disorderly mobs have deliberately prevented the carrying out of proper orders from a Federal court. Local authorities have not eliminated that violent opposition."

The President traced the course of the integration dispute in Little Rock. He noted especially that the Federal Court there had rejected what he called an "abrupt change" in segregated schooling and had adopted a "gradual" plan.

"Proper and sensible observance of the law," the President said, "then demanded the respectful obedience which the nation has a right to expect from all the people. This, unfortunately, has not been the case at Little Rock.

"Certain misguided persons, many of them imported into Little Rock by agitators, have insisted upon defying the law and have sought to bring it into disrepute. The orders of the court have thus been frustrated."

The reference to "imported" members of the mob was seen as a sign that the Federal Bureau of Investigation had information, obtained through agents in Little Rock, on the organization of yesterday's violence.

The President tried to make it plain that he had not sought the use of Federal power in Little Rock, nor welcomed it. Rather he suggested that as Chief Executive he had no choice.

"The President's responsibility is inescapable," he said at one point. At another he said that when the decrees of a Federal court were obstructed, "the law and the national interest demanded that the President take action."

"The very basis of our individual rights and freedoms," he said, "is the certainty that the President and the Executive Branch of Government will support and insure the carrying out of the decisions of the Federal Courts, even, when necessary with all the means at the President's command.

"Unless the President did so, anarchy would result.

"There would be no security for any except that which each one of us could provide for himself.

"The interest of the nation in the proper fulfillment of the law's requirements cannot yield to opposition and demonstrations by some few persons.

"Mob rule cannot be allowed to override the decisions of the courts."

The President appeared fit and vigorous when he stepped into his White House office tonight to face a battery of news and television cameras.

His face showed the ruddiness of the outdoors exercise he has been enjoying on the golf links.

The President, who wore a gray single-breasted suit with blue shirt and tie, spoke calmly and his voice, after setting a steady deliberate pace, rose only occasionally as he sought emphasis for certain words and phrases.

It rose on the word "firmness" when he spoke of his course in this grave situation, and "mob" when he referred to the perpetrators of the Little Rock violence, and "agitators" he said were brought in from the outside.

At either side on the wall on either side of him as he spoke hung portraits of the four leaders whom the President has stated he regards as the greatest American heroes—Benjamin Franklin, George Washington, Abraham Lincoln and Robert E. Lee.

But in his thirteen-minute address tonight, General Eisenhower mentioned only Lincoln.

President Fails to Put 'Under God' in Pledge

President Eisenhower omitted the phrase "under God" at the conclusion of his address last night, when he quoted part of the Pledge of Allegiance.

"Thus will be restored the image of America and of all its parts as one nation, indivisible, with liberty and justice for all," the President said.

By law, the phrase "under God" has been made part of the pledge, coming after "one nation."

The law was signed by President Eisenhower on June 14, 1954, after Congressional approval.

The late Rev. Francis Bellamy of Rome, N. Y., wrote the pledge in 1892, when he was an editor of the magazine, the Youth's Companion. The pledge was made official by Congress in 1945.

President Gets Reports

By W. H. LAWRENCE

Special to The New York Times.

NEWPORT, R. I., Sept. 24—All during the morning President Eisenhower had kept in close touch with the White House, the Justice Department and high defense officials on the developing situation in Little Rock.

The reports relayed to him advised him that his command to persons obstructing justice in the school area to cease and desist from such activities and to disperse had not been obeyed. He made a formal finding that "wilful obstruction of enforcement" of the court-ordered school integration "still exists and threatens to continue."

Then followed the direction to the Secretary of Defense to order the Arkansas Guard into the Federal service for an indefinite period, and to use it to enforce any orders of the Federal court for the integration of the schools at Little Rock.

By this action, the President, as commander-in-chief, assumed command of the National Guard that previously had been vested in Governor Faubus.

A further section authorized Secretary Wilson to use any other of the regular armed forces "as he may deem necessary" to keep order and prevent the continuing obstructions to justice.

Governor Faubus and others had challenged the President's right to use Federal troops in the Little Rock controversy without a formal request from state authorities and a declaration that state authorities themselves were unable to preserve order.

Federal Laws Cited

But the White House said there was no doubt of the President's authority to act. It distributed to the press mimeographed copies of three sections of Federal law on which the President's action was based.

One of them specifically provided that "whenever the President considers that unlawful obstructions, combinations or assemblages, or rebellion against the authority of the United States, makes it impracticable to enforce the laws of the United States in any state or territory by the ordinary course of judicial proceedings, he may call into federal service such of the militia of any state, and use such of the armed forces, as he considers necessary to enforce those laws or to suppress the rebellion."

The President's proclamation last night had described the unlawful assemblages that obstructed justice and made law enforcement impracticable by the ordinary course of judicial proceedings.

"It would seem to me," said James C. Hagerty, the press secretary, "that other people quoting laws on the President's action do not know what they are talking about."

Mr. Hagerty said the legal opinion had come to him from Herbert Brownell Jr. The President talked several times this morning with the Attorney General, with Secretary Wilson, with Gen. Maxwell D. Taylor, the Army Chief of Staff, and with Sherman Adams, the President's principal deputy in the White House.

SOLDIERS FLOWN TO LITTLE ROCK

Continued From Page 1

to proceed "forthwith" to points of assembly.

In a separate statement, Secretary Brucker announced that "all units of the Arkansas Army and Air National Guard are now in Federal service and are ordered to report to their armories."

On Sept. 2 Governor Faubus ordered the Arkansas National Guard to the high school. The troops barred the Negro students on the instructions of the Governor, who said he was acting to prevent disorder.

The Governor withdrew the Guard last Saturday night in compliance with a temporary injunction order issued by Federal Judge Ronald N. Davies.

Secretary Brucker pointed out in his statement that "only selected units" of the Guard would be needed for "immediate duty" in the vicinity of the school.

Brig. Gen. Chester V. Clifton, acting information chief of the Army, said that General Walker would decide which troops he wanted to use.

General Walker will assign some National Guard troops to specific tasks and will ask others to "stand fast" or allow them to go home, General Clifton said.

However, until General Walker has issued his instructions, it was pointed out, all Guardsmen are regarded as being in Federal service. They were placed on the Federal payroll at 2:50 P. M., the Army announced.

General Walker is commander of the Arkansas Military District.

General Clifton revealed that the 101st Airborne had been designated for the emergency by General Taylor. No reason was offered, and the role of sentiment was as much a speculation as the division's special training.

General Clifton said the troops were to be used only in the Little Rock School District.

The 101st Airborne was under General Taylor's command in the Battle of the Bulge at Bastogne, Belgium, during World War II. After being deactivated, it was reorganized two years ago to become the Army's first modern-style pentomic division.

Pentomic troops are trained to use atomic or conventional weapons and are organized in five battle groups for mobile warfare. Their forte is supposed to be small "brush fire" wars.

There are 8,605 officers and men in the Army National Guard and 1,331 officers and men in the Air National Guard in Arkansas, a total of 9,936. The biggest unit is the Thirty-Ninth National Guard Division, a unit, however, that includes guardsmen of Louisiana who are not affected by today's orders.

Brig. Gen. John W. Webb is commander of the division, with headquarters in Little Rock.

National Guardsmen are volunteer members of the Reserve who normally drill once a week and participate in two weeks of field maneuvers each year. They are paid from Federal funds when in "drill status."

General Clifton was asked whether members of the Arkansas Guard had the right to quit in view of the federalization order. He replied that they now were subject to the same rules as Regular Army troops and "it is a little difficult" to leave the Army.

Guardsmen in Federal service, he said, are "subject to the same rules as anyone else who fails to heed an order to appear at a military station."

This was a reference to the orders to guardsmen to report to their armories "forthwith."

Although General Walker, a veteran of the Special Service Force in World War II and of the fighting in Korea, was given full command, General Clifton made it clear that he had received "detailed instructions."

The orders by Secretaries Wilson and Brucker were issued after consultations in Mr. Wilson's office. The two secretaries met with Robert Dechert, the Defense Department Counsellor, and were in frequent contact by telephone with President Eisenhower's office in Newport, R. I.

A Pentagon official explained that the long deliberations were necessary "because this is the first time we have ever done anything like this."

Mr. Dechert said that he could think of no precedent off-hand in which the federalization of a state's National Guard was brought about despite the obvious lack of enthusiasm of the Governor involved.

However, Mr. Dechert emphasized that the Governor's approval or attitude was not concerned. Under the statutes cited by President Eisenhower in his executive order, the Governor has no role, Mr. Dechert said.

In his order, Secretary Wilson called attention to the directions by President Eisenhower to federalize National Guardsmen and to use Regular Army troops as he (Mr. Wilson) deemed appropriate.

The phraseology of Mr. Wilson's order was considered important. He said "* * * hereby call into the Federal service all of the units and the members thereof of the Army National Guard and the Air National Guard of the State of Arkansas to serve in the active military service of the United States for an indefinite period and until relieved by appropriate orders."

The "call" into service, as distinct from direct federalization, was meant to distinguish it from situations of national emergency, as in wartime, when the Congress has authority to act on the number of Guard troops involved.

Throughout the day the role of the civilian officials rather than the military commanders was stressed in the issuance of orders and instructions.

"All the News That's Fit to Print"

The New York Times.

LATE CITY EDITION

U. S. Weather Bureau Report (Page 33) forecasts: Cloudy and cool today and tonight. Mostly fair tomorrow. Temp. range: 65—53. Yesterday: 62.4—49.2.

VOL. CVII..No. 36,414.

NEW YORK, SATURDAY, OCTOBER 5, 1957.

10c beyond 100-mile zone from New York City

FIVE CENTS

SOVIET FIRES EARTH SATELLITE INTO SPACE; IT IS CIRCLING THE GLOBE AT 18,000 M. P. H.; SPHERE TRACKED IN 4 CROSSINGS OVER U. S.

HOFFA IS ELECTED TEAMSTERS' HEAD; WARNS OF BATTLE

Defeats Two Foes 3 to 1 —Says Union Will Fight 'With Every Ounce'

Text of the Hoffa address is printed on Page 6.

By A. H. RASKIN

Special to The New York Times.

MIAMI BEACH, Oct. 4—The scandal-scarred International Brotherhood of Teamsters elected James R. Hoffa as its president today.

He won by a margin of nearly 3 to 1 over the combined vote of two rivals who campaigned on pledges to clean up the nation's biggest union.

Senate rackets investigators and Hoffa critics in the union rank-and-file immediately opened actions to strip the 44-year-old former warehouseman from Detroit of his election victory.

A jubilant Hoffa exhibited, however, greater concern over the possibility that his union might be ousted from the American Federation of Labor and Congress of Industrial Organizations. He appealed for time to prove that he could make the teamsters "a model of trade unionism."

The parent organization has ordered the 1,400,000-member Teamsters Union to get rid of corrupt leadership by Oct. 24 or face suspension. Hoffa said he felt actions by the union at its week-long convention here should satisfy the federation.

Warns Union Will Fight

He made it plain to the 1,700 cheering delegates that he did not intend to go before the convention in the role of suppliant. He said expulsion would not destroy the teamsters. He warned that the union would fight "with every ounce of strength we possess" if it found itself outside.

In such a civil war the teamsters would start with a war-chest of $38,000,000 in the hands of the international union and much more at the disposal of its locals. The teamsters also could count on their strategic power over other unions through their control of trucks and warehouses.

The Hoffa victory brought warnings of repressive legislation from James P. Mitchell, Secretary of Labor, and Senator John L. McClellan, Democrat of Arkansas. The Senator heads the Select Committee on Improper Activities in the Labor or Management Field, which has accused Hoffa of gangster associations and questionable financial practices.

Winner on First Ballot

A three-hour roll-call gave Hoffa the $50,000-a-year union presidency on the first ballot. His machine, in full command of the convention since it opened Monday, registered 1,208 votes for Hoffa.

William A. Lee of Chicago, the union's seventh vice president, was second with 313 votes. Thomas J. Haggerty of Chicago, secretary-treasurer of Milk Wagon Drivers Union, Local 753, trailed with 140 votes.

The Hoffa forces then began providing the new leader a rubber stamp board. It elected five of thirteen vice presidents and would have elected the rest today if time had permitted completion of the cumbersome balloting procedure.

Hoffa repeatedly indicated his irritation that some of the old vice presidents marked for elimination had refused to give up without the formality of a roll-call.

Even before the voting, the McClellan committee subpoenaed the full records of the convention's credentials committee. A United States marshal served the subpoena this morning on Joseph Konowe of New York, the committee secretary. He was directed to turn over all

Continued on Page 6, Column 7

Associated Press Wirephoto

IN TOKEN OF VICTORY: Dave Beck, retiring head of the Teamsters Union, raises hand of James R. Hoffa upon his election as union's president. At right is Mrs. Hoffa.

FAUBUS COMPARES HIS STAND TO LEE'S

Says He Will Remain Loyal to People of Arkansas— All Is Quiet at School

By HOMER BIGART

Special to The New York Times.

LITTLE ROCK, Ark., Oct. 4—Gov. Orval E. Faubus said today that he had made a decision as painfully difficult as the one that had confronted Robert E. Lee at the outset of the Civil War.

"Lee was offered command of the Federal Army in 1861," Governor Faubus recalled. "Lee decided to remain loyal to the people of his state.

"The Democratic party of the North wants me to go along with them on the integration issue. I will remain with the people of Arkansas."

Governor Faubus said he had come under no local pressure to change his stand on integration at Little Rock Central High School. It was a stand that forced President Eisenhower to send Federal troops into this city to uphold Federal Court decisions and to safeguard the nine Negro students registered at Central High.

Winthrop Rockefeller, chairman of the Arkansas Industrial Development Commission, broke silence today on the Little Rock integration crisis, declaring it had "damaged" the state's prospects for economic progress. He called events of the past month "tragic."

It was a quiet day in Little Rock. The nine Negro boys and girls attended school without incident. But no early solution to the crisis seemed likely.

There was no break in the impasse reached Tuesday night when a compromise plan for the

Continued on Page 18, Column 2

Flu Widens in City; 10% Rate Predicted; 200,000 Pupils Out

By ROBERT ALDEN

Asian influenza continued to spread through the city yesterday.

Commissioner of Hospitals Morris A. Jacobs reported that there were ten times more respiratory infections than during the comparable period a year ago.

Attendance in the city's schools fell again. The Board of Education said that close to 200,000 of the city's 941,000 pupils were not in their classrooms yesterday. On Thursday 160,000 pupils were absent.

The attendance estimates were based on a sampling of the schools by the board. The sampling showed that in some schools in the Harlem area—the section hardest hit by the epidemic—more than 50 per cent of the pupils were absent. The board estimated that the over-all city absence rate was 20 per cent.

3,000 Teachers Absent

About 3,000 teachers out of about 39,000 were not in their classrooms yesterday, compared with 2,700 absent on Thursday.

The city's acting Health Commissioner Dr. Roscoe P. Kandle, said he expected that the total number of people affected by the highly infectious disease would run closer to 800,000 rather than 1,600,000 as predicted in some quarters.

It was estimated Thursday that 200,000 persons in New York had contracted the respiratory infection, and the total yesterday was believed to be somewhat higher.

Commissioner Kandle explained that any attempt to project the ultimate number of cases would involve conjecture

Continued on Page 8, Column 1

ARGENTINA TAKES EMERGENCY STEPS

State of Siege Proclaimed in Buenos Aires Region —Arrests Reported

By Reuters.

BUENOS AIRES, Oct. 4—A state of siege, suspending constitutional guarantees, was proclaimed tonight in Buenos Aires city and Province.

The Under Secretary of the Ministry of Interior, Garcia Puente, announced the state of siege at a news conference.

He said the emergency move suspended for thirty days the constitutional guarantees in the capital and the Province of Buenos Aires, but not in the remainder of the nation.

He said the measure was aimed exclusively "at defending the normal development of the Government's political plan, jeopardized through sabotage and social unrest."

The proclamation of the state of siege followed the arrest of scores of labor leaders during the day. The number arrested was estimated by observers as 100 to 300.

Bankers, telephone workers, oilworkers, seamstresses and other unions reported tonight that their leaders had been detained and were taken aboard

Continued on Page 4, Column 5

City Sifts Charge That Schupler, Brooklyn Councilman, Sold a Job

By PAUL CROWELL

The city is investigating a complaint that Councilman Philip J. Schupler accepted a $500 fee last year in exchange for a promise to get a job for a Brooklyn business man.

William R. Peer, executive secretary to Mayor Wagner, said yesterday that the inquiry was started several weeks ago after the complaint had been made by Sol L. Hoffman of 1934 Sixty-third Street, Brooklyn.

At the office of Investigation Commissioner Charles H. Tenney, who is making the investigation, it was said that no findings or conclusions had been reached.

The charge was denied by Mr. Schupler, a Democrat-Liberal, in a telephone interview. He said that he had received a $500 check from Mr. Hoffman in May, 1956, but that it was given to him as a campaign contribution. Mr. Schupler was then a candidate for re-election as a Democratic district leader. He was defeated in the primary election a month later.

Disclosure of the investigation brought from Robert K. Christenberry, the Republican candidate for Mayor, the charge that "corruption and scandal in our City Council is symptomatic of the Wagner administration."

In a formal statement commenting on the Schupler case Mr. Christenberry called upon the city's voters to support his

Continued on Page 15, Column 2

COURSE RECORDED

Navy Picks Up Radio Signals—4 Report Sighting Device

By WALTER SULLIVAN

Special to The New York Times

WASHINGTON, Saturday, Oct. 5—The Naval Research Laboratory announced early today that it had recorded four crossings of the Soviet earth satellite over the United States.

It said that one had passed near Washington. Two crossings were farther to the west. The location of the fourth was not made available immediately.

It added that tracking would be continued in an attempt to pin down the orbit sufficiently to obtain scientific information of the type sought in the International Geophysical Year.

[Four visual sightings, one of which was in conjunction with a radio contact, were reported by early Saturday morning. Two sightings were made at Columbus, Ohio, and one each from Terre Haute, Ind., and Whittier, Calif.]

Press Reports Noted

Soviet newspapers reported several weeks ago that the Soviet satellites would broadcast on frequencies in the neighborhood of twenty and forty megacycles. More exact frequencies were given by Soviet scientists at a conference on rockets and satellites that took place here this week.

Presumably the Naval Research Laboratory, which is responsible for the United States satellite program under the National Academy of Sciences, immediately set up receivers on those frequencies.

The tracking system established in this country to monitor its own satellites uses 108 megacycles, since much more accurate positions can be obtained with the higher frequencies. The Russians at first agreed to use equipment "compatible" with that of the United States, but then announced the lower frequencies.

Deception Ruled Out

American scientists believe this was because of a shortage of Soviet receivers capable of handling the higher frequency. It was not thought to be designed to hide the satellite since the Soviet signals are within easy reach of American listeners.

This was demonstrated last night as amateur and commercial radio stations, as well as the Naval Research Laboratory, reported hearing them.

Teams of visual observers at 150 stations in the United States and other Western nations were alerted during the

Continued on Page 3, Column 6

Ex-Premier Mollet Accepts Bid To Form a New French Cabinet

Socialist Leader Agrees With Reluctance and Without Giving Much Hope

By ROBERT C. DOTY

Special to The New York Times.

PARIS, Oct. 4—Former Premier Guy Mollet agreed reluctantly and without much hope today to try to form a new French Cabinet.

M. Mollet's pessimism, shared by many observers here, was based on the fact that both he and his party, the Socialists, still hold strongly to the policies that caused the defeat of the last two Cabinets, M. Mollet's own and that of Premier Maurice Bourgès-Maunoury, a Radical.

Thus the Socialists still support the views on economic and social questions, including the demand for extensive governmental decree powers in those domains, that brought M. Mollet's Government down last May after a record-breaking sixty-eight weeks in office. The average Cabinet's life span has been twenty-nine weeks.

At the same time the Socialists regard as a minimum of reform the program for limited

Associated Press

Guy Mollet

Algerian home rule outlined in the framework law that was defeated in the Assembly Monday.

In both cases, opposition from the Right-wing Independents constituted the margin of defeat.

If M. Mollet should find it impossible to muster a new major-

Continued on Page 5, Column 4

The New York Times Oct. 5, 1957

The approximate orbit of the Russian earth satellite is shown by black line. The rotation of the earth will bring the United States under the orbit of Soviet-made moon.

Device Is 8 Times Heavier Than One Planned by U.S.

Special to The New York Times.

WASHINGTON, Oct. 4—Leaders of the United States earth satellite program were astonished tonight to learn that the Soviet Union had launched a satellite eight times heavier than that contemplated by this country.

Dr. Joseph Kaplan, chairman of the United States program for the International Geophysical Year, described the 184-pound weight as "fantastic." The heaviest American satellites are to weigh twenty-one and a half pounds.

The actual launching, nevertheless, did not take the American scientists by surprise. At the end of working sessions on the International Conference on Rockets and Satellites, which has been taking place here, some said they thought the pitching of a Soviet satellite into the sky was imminent.

The satellite must fly at a speed of about 18,000 miles an hour to counteract the force of gravity at an altitude of 560 miles. The initial announcement in Moscow did not make it clear whether or not the rocket that placed it in orbit was aimed north or south.

Its Direction in Doubt

This would determine whether or not the satellite's initial crossing of the United States was northbound or southbound. Since the earth rotates within the orbit the satellite should in one day traverse almost all nations of the world.

With an orbit inclined 65 degrees to the equator, its sweep would cover virtually the entire region between the Arctic circle and the Antarctic circle.

William A. Holaday, special assistant to the Secretary of Defense for guided missiles, said the launching was not evidence of Soviet technological superiority in missile and rocket developments.

Mr. Holaday noted that Project Vanguard, the United States satellite program, had been an "open" project as part of the International Geophysical year and there has been no

Continued on Page 3, Column 7

SATELLITE SIGNAL BROADCAST HERE

Impulse Carried on Radio and TV—First Reported by Long Island Station

By ROY SILVER

Radio signals from the first satellite launched yesterday by the Russians were broadcast to radio and television audiences here last night.

The first word that the signals had been received in this country was reported by RCA Communication, Inc. It said that its receiving station at Riverhead, L. I., had picked up what it believed to be impulse signals from the Soviet satellite.

The National Broadcasting Company and the Columbia Broadcasting System broke into their radio and television programs to enable their audiences to hear the pinging sound of the "moon's" signal. The British Broadcasting Corporation in London said it had tuned powerful receivers to the Soviet earth satellite frequencies. Reuter's radio station north of London reported hearing the signals.

RCA Communications, a subsidiary of Radio Corporation of America, said the first signal had been received at 8:07 P. M. on a frequency of 20.005 megacycles on the 15-meter wave length.

One hour and twenty-nine minutes later, at 9:36 P. M., the receiving station, situated about eighty miles from the city, reported that the satellite was making another round of the earth. Other approaches by

Continued on Page 2, Column 4

Warsaw Crushes New Protest; Clubs, Tear Gas Rout Students

By SYDNEY GRUSON

Special to The New York Times.

WARSAW, Oct. 4—Policemen and students clashed again in the streets of Warsaw tonight.

Security chiefs, seemingly nervous, threw a guard of several hundred workers' militia around the downtown headquarters of the ruling United Workers (Communist) party.

For the second successive night the police broke up demonstrations by firing tear gas and beating students and others with rubber truncheons.

What began last night as a protest against the closing of one newspaper was turning tonight into a general clamor against police brutality and the suppression of free speech. By midnight the city had calmed down and the people had left the streets.

Among those clubbed tonight was Franco Fabiani, permanent correspondent here of the Italian Communist paper L'Unita. He suffered two minor head wounds.

Signor Fabiani was caught in crowds charged by the police after about 3,000 students had met in the Polytechnic and adopted a resolution protesting both the closing of the newspaper Po Prostu and the "brutal interference" of the police at last night's meeting.

Tonight's trouble centered on the Polytechnic, the huge advanced technical school near the heart of Warsaw. It was

Continued on Page 5, Column 2

560 MILES HIGH

Visible With Simple Binoculars, Moscow Statement Says

Text of Tass announcement appears on Page 3.

By WILLIAM J. JORDEN

Special to The New York Times.

MOSCOW, Saturday, Oct. 5—The Soviet Union announced this morning that it successfully launched a man-made earth satellite into space yesterday.

The Russians calculated the satellite's orbit at a maximum of 560 miles above the earth and its speed at 18,000 miles an hour.

The official Soviet news agency Tass said the artificial moon, with a diameter of twenty-two inches and a weight of 184 pounds, was circling the earth once every hour and thirty-five minutes. This means more than fifteen times a day.

Two radio transmitters, Tass said, are sending signals continuously on frequencies of 20.005 and 40.002 megacycles. These signals were said to be strong enough to be picked up by amateur radio operators. The trajectory of the satellite is being tracked by numerous scientific stations.

Due Over Moscow Today

Tass said the satellite was moving at an angle of 65 degrees to the equatorial plane and would pass over the Moscow area twice today.

"Its flight," the announcement added, "will be observed in the rays of the rising and setting sun with the aid of the simplest optical instruments, such as binoculars and spy-glasses."

The Soviet Union said the world's first satellite was "successfully launched" yesterday. Thus it asserted that it had put a scientific instrument into space before the United States. Washington has disclosed plans to launch a satellite next spring. Oct. 4."

The Moscow announcement said the Soviet Union planned to send up more and bigger and heavier artificial satellites during the current International Geophysical Year, an eighteen-month period of study of the earth, its crust and the space surrounding it.

Five Miles a Second

The rocket that carried the satellite into space left the earth at a rate of five miles a second, the Tass announcement said. Nothing was revealed, however, concerning the material of which the man-made moon was constructed or the site in the Soviet Union where the sphere was launched.

The Soviet Union said its sphere circling the earth had opened the way to interplanetary travel.

It did not pass up the opportunity to use the launching for propaganda purposes. It said in its announcement that people now could see how "the new socialist society" had turned the boldest dreams of mankind into reality.

Moscow said the satellite was the result of years of study and research on the part of Soviet scientists.

Several Years of Study

Tass said:

"For several years the research and experimental designing work has been under way in the Soviet Union to create artificial satellites of the earth. It has already been reported in the press that the launching of the earth satellites in the U. S. S. R. had been planned in accordance with the program of International Geophysical Year research.

"As a result of intensive work by the research institutes and design bureaus, the first artificial earth satellite in the world has now been created. This first satellite was successfully launched in the U. S. S. R. October four."

The Soviet announcement said that as a result of the tremendous speed at which the satellite was moving it would

Continued on Page 3, Column 5

SATELLITE FLIGHT IS STEP INTO SPACE

Soviet Project Appears to Go Beyond Plans Made by U. S. Scientists

By ROBERT K. PLUMB

If details given by Russians about man's first artificial moon are correct, the Soviet has taken a giant step into space, a step beyond that contemplated by scientists in this country.

Soviet reports placed the weight of the successfully launched satellite at about 184 pounds. The diameter of the sphere was said to be about twenty-two inches. The Soviet "moon" was said to be up in an orbit 560 miles above the surface of the earth, where it is speeding around the world at about 18,000 miles an hour.

In contrast to this large satellite American scientists told Congress last spring that they hoped for a twenty-inch sphere weighing 21.5 pounds up 300 miles. These plans have since been dropped—an American September launching was at one time envisioned—in favor of plans to launch the twenty-pound satellite some time in 1958. Perhaps a tiny test satellite scarcely six inches in diameter could be achieved this fall, American scientists said recently.

The difference between twenty pounds planned to be in space in 1958 and 184 pounds already in place is far greater in terms of rocket technique than the bare figures suggest.

The weight lifted beyond the strong pull of gravity by the Soviet must be multiplied by the altitude achieved. As far as is known, no nonmilitary rocket combinations in this country have soared as high as 300 miles from the earth's surface.

Recently Soviet scientists have said that they might make some sun photographs from a satellite. The weight and size of the satellite suggests that a recoverable photograph of the sun—or of the earth's surface—might be made.

TV System Discussed

Perhaps it could even be transmitted to earth by a television system. This thought has been a favorite speculation but a remote possibility in planning of satellite designers here and elsewhere.

In Washington last week, Soviet scientists attending a conference on the International Geophysical Year dodged precise questions about their satellite plans. But they suggested that their satellite—only a few days away then, unknown to American scientists—might contain a tiny flashing light to mark its path across the night sky.

The Russians recently indicated their satellite would be fired from somewhere along a line of sites on the meridian 56 degrees East.

The reported speed of the Soviet satellite—18,000 miles an hour—is considerably below the so-called "escape" velocity of about 25,000 miles an hour. At this speed, a body could leave the earth never to return, perhaps arriving at the moon or nearer planets. But if a speed of 18,000 miles has been achieved with a 184 pound object at an altitude of 560 miles, then travel into space is not far away.

Not Solely Academic

The usefulness of an earth satellite carrying only radio equipment—as the first Russian reports had it—is not so great as some of the dream projects high altitude flight engineers have had in mind. But it is nevertheless of striking scientific importance, if it is only a minimum sphere.

As the satellite speeds around the earth, it will assume an elliptical orbit with a near point of approach (perigee) and a point (apogee) where it travels farthest from earth. The shape of the elliptical path will be determined by the gravitational pull of the earth.

This, in turn, will depend upon the shape of the part of the earth over which the satellite is traveling at the time. Thus the earth, which is not truly round, will cause perturbations in the motion of the sphere. Precise measure of the perturbations by optical tracking and by radio signals recorded on tape and fed into electronic calculators will reveal for the first time precisely how much the earth bulges at the equator and flattens at the poles.

This information might be regarded as being of academic interest alone—except that in a world with intercontinental ballistic missiles, precise information about how the earth is shaped could help speed missiles to their marks half a world away.

First Aid Trophy Awarded

LOUISVILLE, Oct. 4 (AP)—A team from West Virginia tonight was awarded first place in first-aid competition in the seventeenth national first-aid and mine-rescue contest. The team, representing the Island Creek Coal Company's Wyoming Mine at Holden, W. Va., was awarded a trophy. The Lynch, Ky., district of the United States Steel Corporation won the mine rescue competition.

Ordinary Radio Sets Can't Monitor 'Moon'

Owners of ordinary radio sets who attempt to monitor the signals from the Soviet satellite will be unable to do so because of the limited frequency range of their sets.

The regular broadcasting frequency range runs from 550 to 1,600 kilocycles.

Those who have short wave receivers that will cover the 20 megacycle (20,0000 kilocycle) and 40 megacycle ranges may be able to pick up the signals. It will also be necessary to have a beat frequency oscillator, however.

Associated Press Wirephoto

DISCUSS LAUNCHING OF EARTH SATELLITE: United States and Soviet scientists who are leaders in the nation's respective satellite programs conferring last night in Washington. From left: Dr. Richard W. Porter of General Electric; Prof V. V. Belousov and A. A. Blagonravov of the Soviet committee for the International Geophysical Year, and Prof. Joseph Kaplan, head of United States I. G. Y. program. They met at Soviet Embassy.

'MOON' HOLDS KEY TO EARTH'S SHAPE

Secrets of Interior's Density May Also Be Revealed—Current Data Inexact

Special to The New York Times.

WASHINGTON, Oct. 4—The artificial moon now in orbit and those to follow should give man his first information on the precise shape of his planet and the lumpiness of its interior.

These are among the chief objectives in the costly Soviet and United States satellite programs. If the earth were a perfect sphere with an interior of uniform density the satellite orbits would be symmetrical.

The earth, however, flattens toward the poles. Its interior, at least in the region immediately below the surface, is irregular in density. Hence surveyors plumb bobs and bubble levels do not indicate the true vertical. They are oriented by gravity, whose direction of pull varies with the varying density of the earth below.

Precise observation of the satellite orbit will provide a world-wide picture of these anomalies.

Data on Electrons

By watching the rate at which the satellite slows down scientists will also be able to determine how much air there is on the fringes of space. Study of its radio signals should show the average number of electrons in the region between the satellite and the earth.

The radio signal from the satellite is bent as it passes through the electron-charged ionized layers of the atmosphere. The lower the frequency the more it bends. By using two frequencies, one double the other, the Russians hope to determine the difference in bending and thus the electron density.

The United States satellite program calls for a similar experiment, but with the use of high-precision observation of the satellites with a special camera as a basis of comparison with the radio beam.

Only one of these American cameras is currently in operation and the eleven others scheduled for study of satellite orbits may not all be working until next summer. The Soviet Union apparently does not have any such cameras and has expressed an interest in those being made here.

It would probably be impossible to deliver any to the Russians before the end of the International Geophysical Year. The satellite programs are part of that world-wide study of the earth and its environment.

Peak at 560 Miles

The lifetime of the Soviet satellite will presumably depend on its altitude at the lowest point of its elliptical orbit. The Moscow announcement merely said that the highest point of the orbit was 560 miles.

Two days ago a Soviet scientist, reputed to be one of Moscow's leading missile specialists, told the satellite conference here that a satellite with maximum elevation of 500 miles and a minimum elevation of 125 miles would last only three days.

He was Academician A. A. Blagonravov, chief of the Soviet delegation to the conference.

There is enough air at an elevation of 125 miles to slow the satellite appreciably every time around. Once it loses the speed necessary to counteract gravity it will plunge downward as a fireball or break into smaller pieces. Each of the pieces presumably will be consumed like a meteor or reach the earth like a flaming meteorite.

If the top elevation of the orbit were 1,500 miles and the bottom elevation 500 miles, Dr. Blagonravov said, it would circle the earth for about thirty years. He admitted that this was only a guess, since the density of air on the fringes of space is much disputed.

United States satellite experts believe that 200 miles is the minimum altitude at which an artificial moon can be expected to survive more than a few hours.

Text of Satellite Report

LONDON, Oct. 4 (Reuters)—Following is the text in translation of the announcement by the Soviet news agency Tass of Russia's launching of an earth satellite:

For several years research and experimental designing work has been under way in the Soviet Union to create artificial satellites of the earth. It has already been reported in the press that the launching of the earth satellites in the U. S. S. R. was planned in accordance with the program of the International Geophysical Year research.

As a result of the intensive work by research institutes and designing bureaus the first artificial earth satellite in the world has now been created. This first satellite was successfully launched in the U. S. S. R. on Oct. 4.

According to preliminary information the carrier rocket has imparted to the satellite the required orbital velocity of about 8,000 meters (26,000 feet) a second. At the present time the satellite is describing elliptical trajectories around the earth. Its flight will be observed in the rays of the rising and setting sun with the aid of the simplest optical instruments such as binoculars and spy-glasses.

Will Pass Over Moscow

According to calculations which are being supplemented by direct observation the satellite will travel at altitudes of up to 900 kilometers 560 miles) above the surface of the earth. A complete revolution of the satellite will take one hour and thirty-five minutes. Its orbit is inclined at an angle of 65 degrees to the equatorial plane. Tomorrow the satellite will pass twice over the Moscow area, at 1:46 A. M. and at 6:42 A. M. Moscow time.

Reports about the subsequent movement of the first artificial satellite launched in the U. S. S. R. on the 4th of October will be issued regularly by Soviet broadcasting stations.

The satellite is of spherical shape, fifty-eight centimeters (about twenty-two inches) in diameter and weighs 83.6 kilograms (about 184 pounds). It is fitted with steel radio transmitters continuously emitting signals at a frequency of 20.005 and 40.002 megacycles or 15 and 7.5 meters wavelengths respectively.

The power of the transmitter is such as to ensure reliable reception by a broad range of amateurs. The signals are of the nature of telegraph signals at about zero point three seconds duration with a pause of the same duration. The signals of one frequency are sent during the pauses in the signals of the other frequency.

Scientific stations at various points in the Soviet Union are conducting observations of the satellite and determining elements of its trajectory. Since the density of the rarified upper layers of the atmosphere is not accurately known there are no data available at present for determining the exact period of the satellite's existence or the point of its entry into the denser layers of the atmosphere.

Burn-Up Point Cited

Calculations have shown that owing to the tremendous velocity of the satellite at the end of its existence it will burn up on reaching the denser layers of the atmosphere at an altitude of several scores of kilometers.

The possibility of cosmic flight with the help of rockets was first scientifically substantiated in Russia, as early as the end of the nineteenth century, in the works of the outstanding Russian scientist Konstantin Tsiolkovsky.

The successful launching of the first man-made earth satellite makes a tremendous contribution to the treasure house of world science and culture. The scientific experiment staged at such a great height is of great importance for fathoming the properties of cosmic space and for studying earth as part of our solar system.

The Soviet Union proposes to send up several more artificial satellites during the International Geophysical Year. These will be bigger and heavier and will help to carry out an extensive program of scientific research.

Artificial earth satellites will pave the way for space travel and it seems that the present generation will witness how the freed and conscious labor of the people of the new socialist society turns even the most daring of man's dreams into a reality.

AIR FORCE COLONEL MAY BE DISMISSED

SAN ANTONIO, Tex., Oct. 4 (AP)—Col. James A. Smyrl faces dismissal from the Air Force if a Pentagon board upholds a verdict announced yesterday at Lackland Air Force Base. Three generals reached the decision after a nine-day hearing.

The hearing board, headed by Maj. Gen. Eugene P. Mussett, found Colonel Smyrl had failed to demonstrate acceptable qualities of leadership required of a colonel and was temperamentally unsuitable.

Colonel Smyrl had testified he wanted to remain in the Air Force "more than anything else."

Maj. Gen. Herbert Grills, Lackland commandant, ousted Colonel Smyrl March 22 as training commander. General Grills said the colonel had disregarded an order to allow recruits three hours of free time weekly.

Colonel Smyrl testified that he had been ordered to make enough basic trainees available to provide $300 a day in patronage for a civilian-operated skating-rink concession at the base. He said he had been relieved as training commander after telling General Grills he knew of no way to carry out the directive.

The board held Colonel Smyrl had not failed in proper discharge of assignments commensurate with his rank, as was charged.

Burgess Off for NATO Post

W. Randolph Burgess, former Under Secretary of the Treasury, left for Europe aboard the superliner United States yesterday to take over his new post as Ambassador to the North Atlantic Treaty Organization.

ZHUKOV OFF ON TRIP

Visit to Crimea to Precede Journey to Yugoslavia

Special to The New York Times.

MOSCOW, Oct. 4—Marshal Georgi K. Zhukov, Soviet Defense Minister, left Moscow tonight on the first leg of his journey to Yugoslavia.

The evening papers reported that he was going first to the Crimea but did not state the purpose of the preliminary trip. Nikita S. Khrushchev, Communist party chief, has been vacationing at Yalta in the Crimea for the last six weeks.

Soviet Embassy Guests Hear of Satellite From an American as Russians Beam

Special to The New York Times.

WASHINGTON, Oct. 4—Guests at a Soviet Embassy reception for rocket and satellite specialists tonight heard the news of the Soviet moon launching from an American.

Dr. Lloyd Berkner, president of the International Council of Scientific Unions, an originator of the idea for the International Geophysical Year, beat on a glass at the reception for silence.

"I wish to make an announcement," he said. "I am informed by The New York Times that a satellite is in orbit at an elevation of 900 kilometers. I wish to congratulate our Soviet colleagues on their achievement."

Soviet scientists beamed as he made the announcement. The reception was being given for participants in a conference to coordinate plans for satellite and rocket firings during the I. G. Y., at the conference, which ends tomorrow, the Russians had assiduously dodged all questions as to when they would attempt a satellite launching.

Feat Called 'Remarkable'

WASHINGTON, Oct. 4 (AP)—Dr. Joseph Kaplan, chairman of the United States National Committee for the I. G. Y. said:

"I am amazed that in the short time which they had to plan—obviously not any longer than we had—I think it was a remarkable achievement on their part."

"From the point of view of international cooperation the important thing is that a satellite has been launched. They did it and did it first.

"I hope they give us enough information so that our Moonwatch teams can help learn the scientific benefits."

Noting reports that the satellite was twenty-two inches across and weighed 184 pounds, Mr. Kaplan said: "This is really fantastic and if they can launch that they can launch much heavier ones."

SOVIET LAUNCHES EARTH SATELLITE

Continued From Page 1

burn up as soon as it reached the denser layers of the atmosphere. It gave no indication how soon that would be.

Military experts have said that the satellites would have no practicable military application in the foreseeable future. They said, however, that study of such satellites could provide valuable information that might be applied to flight studies for intercontinental ballistic missiles.

The satellites could not be used to drop atomic or hydrogen bombs or anything else on the earth, scientists have said. Nor could they be used in connection with the proposed plan for aerial inspection of military forces around the world.

An Aid to Scientists

Their real significance would be in providing scientists with important new information concerning the nature of the sun, cosmic radiation, solar radio interference and static-producing phenomena radiating from the north and south magnetic poles. All this information would be of inestimable value for those who are working on the problem of sending missiles and eventually men into the vast reaches of the solar system.

Publicly, Soviet scientists have approached the launching of the satellite with modesty and caution. On the advent of the International Geophysical Year last June they specifically disclaimed a desire to "race" the United States into the atmosphere with the little sphere.

The scientists spoke understandingly of "difficulties" they had heard described by their American counterparts. They refused several invitations to give any details about their own problems in designing the satellite and gave even less information than had been generally published about their work in the Soviet press.

Hinted of Launching

Concerning the launching of their first satellite, they said only that it would come "before the end of the geophysical year"—by the end of 1958.

Several weeks earlier, however, in a guarded interview given only to the Soviet press, Alexander N. Nesmeyanov, head of the Soviet Academy of Science, dropped a hint that the first launching would occur "within the next few months."

But generally Soviet scientists consistently refused to boast about their project or to give the public or other scientists much information about their progress. Key essentials concerning the design of their satellites, their planned altitude, speed and instruments to be carried in the small sphere, were carefully guarded secrets.

'MOON' TRACKED GOING OVER U. S.

Continued From Page 1

night to watch for the Soviet sphere at dawn and evening twilight. They have been organized in "Project Moonwatch" to sight the satellite through binoculars or telescopes as it passes overhead.

At a typical station, each watcher wears a lapel microphone that is wired into a tape recorder that also receives radio time signals.

When the satellite is seen by someone to cross the section of the meridian he is responsible for, he shouts "mark" and notes which stars lay behind its path, to establish its exact elevation. This information is then phoned to Cambridge, Mass., for analysis.

Ultimately, the United States is to have special cameras installed at a dozen points around the world to take high precision photographs of the satellites against a star-studded background. These can be used for detailed studies of the sellite orbits.

Only one of these cameras has been set up so far and the last will probably not be in operation until next summer. The Soviet Union does not appear to have any such precision cameras and has expressed an interest in those being made here.

Soviet radio tracking of the satellite differs from that of the United States system, which is dependent on radio phasing devices. Such equipment is of limited value at the Soviet frequencies. Hence the Russians are using a procedure that in the American view, is of low accuracy.

The Soviet tracking depends on radio doppler, a phenomenon comparable to the change in pitch of a whistle on a passing locomotive. While approaching it is shriller because the speed of sound is augmented by the train's motion. Once the train has passed the movement is subtracted from the sound, making the pitch lower.

The Soviet Union has asked radio amateurs and commercial stations to record the sound of the satellite on magnetic tape. The turning point of the frequency change will mark the instant of satellite passage and the degree of change will show how close it passed.

4 Sightings Reported

Special to The New York Times.

CAMBRIDGE, Mass., Saturday, Oct. 5—The visual tracking center of the Smithsonian Astro-physical Observatory here early today had reported four unconfirmed sightings of the Soviet satellite. One of the sightings was made simultaneously with a radio contact.

The sightings were made at Columbus, Ohio, Terra Haute, Ind., and Whittier, Calif. Dr. J. Allen Hynek, who is in charge of the optical-charting program for the International Geophysical Year at the observatory, said the reports were unconfirmed because of descrepancies in direction and time.

The simultaneous sighting and radio contact gave more credence to the theory that the object seen was the satellite, he said.

All four sightings were made at Moonwatch stations. Two sightings were made at Columbus and one each from Terre Haute and Whittier. The first sighting was reported last night at 10:28, Eastern standard time, from Columbus. Larry Ochs said the object was traveling very quickly in a west-to-east direction.

The second report came from Terre Haute at 7:50, Central standard time. Munz Addabbo said he saw a bright object high in the sky moving from west to east. The third report was from Whittier at 7:46, Pacific time. Gary A. McCue said an object with a brightness in the six or seven magnitude passed from east to west.

Second Sighting for Ohio

Columbus reported its second sighting at 12:06 A. M., Eastern standard time, this time in conjunction with a radio contact. Miss Jane Gann said the object went from west to east with a steady light of the same magnitude as the first sighting. The sightings here were one hour and thirty-seven minutes apart.

Dr. Fred L. Whipple, Smithsonian Institution director, said. "We have not enough specific information yet to orient the satellite. Such data as we have indicate that the orbit has 65 degrees."

Moonwatch teams all over the country were alerted to watch for the satellite after its launching had been reported by Moscow. The alert went out to ninety teams.

"We were somewhat surprised by the Russian announcement," Dr. Hynek said. "But we were more or less prepared for it on a contingency basis."

Dr. Hynek said that his staff received the news about 7 P. M. and began a frantic job of rousing the satellite observation groups. He declared that if an artificial moon were sighted, he would announce the information promptly.

Within forty-five minutes after receiving the Soviet news, Dr. Hynek had all forty I. G. Y. teams west of the Mississippi alerted.

"The Russian announcement came without warning," Dr. Hynek said, "but we always knew there was a real possibility that they would launch one. We just didn't expect it quite so soon."

An alert was cabled to the I. G. Y.'s thirty satellite tracking stations in Japan.

Because the satellite is most easily seen in twilight, the watchers will be instructed to man their stations in the twilight before sunrise and sunset for several days, Dr. Hynek said.

Headquarters here also tuned in to short wave broadcasts from Moscow to obtain additional information on the launching.

Great Soviet Encyclopedia

RUSSIAN PIONEER: The late Konstantin E. Tsiolkovsky, a leader in developing modern theory of interplanetary travel. Mr. Tsiolkovsky died in 1935.

WEIGHT OF 'MOON' A SURPRISE TO U.S.

Continued From Page 1

"crash" program to rush a satellite into orbit.

Mr. Holaday suggested that the Russians deliberately may have placed great emphasis, time and money in getting a satellite into orbit first in order to embarrass the United States.

Rear Admiral Rawson Bennett, whose Office of Naval Research is in charge of launching the United States satellites, said the United States had never envisaged the satellite launching program as "a race." He said that Project Vanguard, the United States satellite program, would "proceed as presently scheduled."

The long-delayed firing of Test Vehicle No. 2 of the American satellite program is now scheduled at Cape Carnaveral, Fla., within five days. Its purpose is to test the first-stage rocket. The rest of the bullet-shaped vehicle will be a dummy.

The firing of a three-stage test vehicle is planned this fall and may place a miniature satellite, six inches in diameter, in an orbit.

Assumptions on 'Moon'

The impression gained by American delegates from five days of meetings with Soviet scientists this week was that the Russians planned to send up a simple-instrumented first satellite before attempting more elaborate observations. It was assumed that one of the Soviet military missiles would be used to lift it into the sky.

This was thought to account in part for the secrecy surrounding Soviet satellite plans.

Presumably the satellite is giving a workout to any warning system established by the Russians against guided missiles soaring over the Arctic. Those who know to what extent the United States is prepared to track such high-flying targets would not discuss the matter.

The United States has said it had a newly developed radar with a range of 3,000 miles, but specialists noted today that it was still at an early stage of operational development.

In particular they cited the false and often fast-moving "targets" that are produced by invisible bubbles of humid air. It may be some time before these can be distinguished from missiles and satellites, they said.

The first full-sized United States moon, comparable in girth to that sent up by the Soviet Union, is to be launched in early spring. It will make delicate observations of virgin ultra-violet light above the earth's atmosphere. Information from this and other experiments will be radioed to stations on the earth.

American scientists at a Soviet Embassy reception, while disappointed that the Russians had beaten them into space, breathed a sigh of relief. "The pressure is off," they said. "Now we can concentrate on doing a good job."

LAUNCHING TIMED AS IF FOR TRIBUTE

Satellite Success Follows Anniversary of Birth of Soviet Space Pioneer

By THEODORE SHABAD

The launching of the Soviet earth satellite has been timed as if in tribute to the man the Russians say is the grandfather of space travel.

Less than three weeks ago the Soviet press celebrated with considerable fanfare the 100th anniversary of the birth of Konstantin E. Tsiolkovsky, who died in 1935 at the age of 78.

Tsiolkovsky is regarded by the Russians as the founder of the science and technology of rockets and as the first to formulate the modern theory of interplanetary travel.

Both Pravda and Izvestia, the principal Soviet newspapers, devoted a page to the anniversary Sept. 17, acclaiming the pioneering work of the Russian scientist in glowing terms.

A. A. Blagonravov, Soviet academician, who is attending the earth satellite meetings in Washington, eulogized Tsiolkovsky before a crowd in the city of Kaluga, southwest of Moscow, where the rocket pioneer is buried. A memorial on his grave will show the figure of Tsiolkovsky standing in front of a rocket pointed skyward.

Credited on Rocket

Tsiolkovsky is credited by the Russians with having developed the theory of the multi-stage rocket, an essential feature of all long-distance rockets. It made possible not only the launching of the earth satellite but also the flight of the intercontinental missile recently announced by the Russians.

The Soviet press reports that Tsiolkovsky predicted fifty years ago that earth satellites would be launched in the "not-too-distant future." He suggested the idea of establishing manned landing platforms in space that would make possible interplanetary travel.

S. Korolev, writing in Pravda, says that Tsiolkovsky envisaged the landing platforms as way-stations for interplanetary rockets. The platforms would make it possible to refuel rockets on their long journeys.

Saw Use of Solar Energy

Tsiolkovsky assumed that the utilization of solar energy would enable man to exist on these space stations and even to grow food.

V. Glushko said in Izvestia that the launching of the Soviet satellite in the International Geophysical Year would constitute the "best memorial" to Tsiolkovsky on his anniversary.

Mr. Glushko, a corresponding member of the Soviet Academy of Sciences, wrote that the first test satellites of the Soviet Union would be heavier than the models being prepared in the United States.

He said the Soviet satellite would contain a powerful radio transmitter, whose signals could be intercepted not only by the authorities but by a wide circle of radio amateurs.

BRAZILIAN LABORITE CALLS FOR REALISM

Special to The New York Times.

RIO DE JANEIRO, Oct. 4—Vice President João Goulart has declared "pragmatic nationalism" to be the guiding line of his Brazilian Labor party.

Speaking last night at the closing session of the fourth national convention of the party, Senhor Goulart attacked the "demagogic attitudes" of other Brazilian nationalists, saying that nationalism must be rooted in the reality of Brazil's development problems.

This sounded like a voice of relative moderation in the midst of an intense ultranationalistic campaign, usually and indiscriminately directed at the United States, that has been developing here for more than a year. Prominent members of the Labor party have been taking an active part in it.

But even Senhor Goulart's definition of "pragmatic nationalism" seemed vague. The Vice President spoke of "economic emancipation" and said the party would not "give an inch" in its defense of nationalist principles.

"All the News That's Fit to Print"

The New York Times.

LATE CITY EDITION
U.S. Weather Bureau Report (Page 38) forecasts: Fair and pleasant today; fair tonight and tomorrow.
Temp. range: 83—67. Yesterday: 83.0—70.0.

VOL. CVII. No. 36,722. NEW YORK, SATURDAY, AUGUST 9, 1958. 10c beyond 100-mile zone from New York City. Higher in air delivery cities. FIVE CENTS

NAUTILUS SAILS UNDER THE POLE AND 1,830 MILES OF ARCTIC ICECAP IN PACIFIC-TO-ATLANTIC PASSAGE

U. S. Navy, from Associated Press

TIME OF DECISION: Officers of the Nautilus choose a place to submerge below ice for undersea voyage across Arctic regions. Standing at the right in the conning tower of the submarine is her skipper, Comdr. W. R. Anderson.

The New York Times — Aug. 9, 1958

NEW PASSAGE: Heavy line traces the Nautilus' route from Pacific to Atlantic Oceans

FOUR-DAY VOYAGE

New Route to Europe Pioneered—Skipper and Crew Cited

Text of Navy fact sheet, Page 6. The Citation, Page 7.

By FELIX BELAIR Jr.
Special to The New York Times.

WASHINGTON, Aug. 8 — History's first undersea voyage across the top of the world, a distance of 1,830 miles under the polar icecap, was disclosed at the White House today.

The trip was made in four days by the Nautilus, the world's first atomic submarine. The voyage pioneered a new and shorter route from the Pacific to the Atlantic and Europe — a route that might be used by cargo submarines. It also added to man's knowledge of the subsurface of the Arctic basin.

The voyage took the Nautilus under the North Pole. The overall trip began at Pearl Harbor July 23 and ended at Iceland Aug. 7.

Dives at Point Barrow

The Nautilus went under the icecap at Point Barrow, Alaska, and surfaced four days later at a point in the Atlantic between Spitzbergen and Greenland. She is now on her way to Western Europe.

The feat of the Nautilus, with 116 crewmen and scientific observers aboard, was revealed as President Eisenhower decorated the submarine's skipper, Comdr. W. R. Anderson, with the Legion of Merit. A Presidential Unit Citation—the first ever conferred in peacetime—went to the submarine, with a ribbon and special clasp in the form of a golden "N" to all who participated in the cruise.

The Presidential citation to Commander Anderson said that the Nautilus under his leadership had pioneered a submerged sea lane between the Eastern and Western Hemispheres. It added:

"This points the way for further exploration and possible use of this route by nuclear powered cargo submarines as a new commercial seaway between the major oceans of the world."

Skipper Tells Story

A few minutes after the award, Commander Anderson, admittedly "a little dazed" by the speed of events that brought him here overnight by helicopter and jet plane from Arctic waters, was telling his story of "Operation Northwest Passage."

News of the voyage reached the Capitol with electrifying effect. William F. Knowland of California, the Senate Republican leader, read a brief dispatch to the Senate and remarked:

"This should give us courage and remind us to have faith. It shows that this is no time to sell America short."

Senator Mike Mansfield of Montana, the Democratic acting

Continued on Page 6, Column 1

CHIEF OF U.N. GIVES A PLAN FOR MIDEAST

ASSEMBLY MEETS

Hears Call for Step-Up of Its Economic and Political Efforts

Hammarskjold and Munro statements are on Page 2.

By THOMAS J. HAMILTON
Special to The New York Times.

UNITED NATIONS, N. Y., Aug. 8—Secretary General Dag Hammarskjold proposed today that the United Nations step up its political and economic activities in the Middle East to stabilize the area.

Mr. Hammarskjold took the floor at the opening of the General Assembly's emergency special session on the Middle East to put forward his program. He had intended to present this proposal if there was a meeting of heads of government within the framework of the United Nations Security Council.

The principal provisions of his plan are:

¶A declaration by the Arab states reaffirming their adherence to the principles of mutual respect for each other's territory, non-aggression and non-interference in each other's internal affairs.

¶The continuation and extension of present United Nations activities in Lebanon and Jordan.

¶Joint action by the Arab states, with the support of the United Nations, in economic development. This would include arrangements for cooperation between "oil-producing and oil-transiting countries" and joint utilization of water resources.

Session Is Adjourned

Mr. Hammarskjold's statement was the outstanding development of the opening session, which lasted thirty-five minutes. The Assembly adjourned until 10:30 A. M. Wednesday to give foreign ministers of some of the eighty-one member nations time to get here.

Contrary to the general expectation, Arkady A. Sobolev, Soviet delegate, did not demand the admission of Chinese Communist representatives. However, he took the floor to repeat his denunciation of the presence of United States forces in Lebanon and British forces in Jordan, and again demanded their immediate withdrawal.

Henry Cabot Lodge of the

Continued on Page 2, Column 3

The New York Times

CALL TO ACTION: Dag Hammarskjold addressing the General Assembly.

U.S. LEADERS SPLIT ON MIDEAST AIMS

Eisenhower Action May Be Needed to Fix Policy for Assembly Debate

By E. W. KENWORTHY
Special to The New York Times.

WASHINGTON, Aug. 8—High-level differences of opinion have developed within the Administration over the strategy and tactics to be used in the United Nations debate on the Middle East crisis, officials indicated today.

The differences are being argued out thoroughly and amicably, and a concerted position will almost certainly be arrived at during the week-end, these officials said. Nevertheless, it was considered possible that President Eisenhower might have to make the final decision on the United States approach.

Dulles Remark Recalled

The differences were said to have become apparent soon after Secretary of State Dulles' news conference a week ago Thursday. At that conference he made it clear that the United States intended to meet the Soviet charge of United States and British aggression in Lebanon and Jordan with a counter-arraignment against the Soviet Union and the United Arab Republic on "indirect aggression."

Until the problems of indirect aggression are met directly and dealt with it will not be possible to create the atmosphere of political stability in the Middle East necessary for any attack on economic problems, Mr. Dulles said.

Almost immediately some

Continued on Page 3, Column 3

U. S. MAY REDUCE FORCE IN LEBANON

Token Removal of Marine Battalion Planned

By W. H. LAWRENCE
Special to The New York Times.

BEIRUT, Lebanon, Aug. 8—The United States tentatively plans to reload a marine battalion on ships next week in a "symbolic" gesture of withdrawal from Lebanon.

A responsible source said the decision to reduce the force on shore by about 2,000 men had been communicated to the Lebanese Government and to Gen. Fouad Chehab, armed forces commander and President-elect.

Before the marine unit is pulled out, a small detachment of Army engineers and truck personnel will be moved from Lebanon to the Turkish port of Iskenderun to improve facilities at the Atlantic alliance base at Adana, an important center of air striking power and supply for the United States operation in Lebanon.

The moves will have both political and military effects, it is believed. The political aims are both local and international.

Locally, leaders of the continuing insurrection against the Government of President Camille Chamoun have been insisting on speedy removal of United States troops as a condition for a cease-fire now that General Chehab has been elected. He will succeed Mr. Chamoun Sept.

Continued on Page 3, Column 2

HOUSE VOTES BILL TO AID EDUCATION IN SCIENCE FIELD

Student Loans Raised in Place of Scholarships by 900 Million Measure

By BESS FURMAN
Special to The New York Times.

WASHINGTON, Aug. 8 — The House of Representatives adopted today a four-year, $900,000,000 bill to aid science education.

No money was shorn from the bill. But the scholarship provision, on which a compromise had already been made with President Eisenhower, was deleted.

The scholarship funds were shifted to the bill's loan provisions. This was accomplished in a standing vote of 109 to 78, on a motion offered by Representative Walter H. Judd, Republican of Minnesota.

The loan provisions of the bill were increased from $40,000,000 in the first year to $60,000,000 and from $60,000,000 in each of the three succeeding years to $80,000,000.

The final adoption was by voice vote, after a motion to kill the bill by sending it back to committee had been defeated in a roll-call vote of 233 to 139. The motion was offered by Representative Ralph W. Gwinn, Republican of Westchester.

The legislation now goes to the Senate, which has already scheduled to consider on Monday its own broader science-aid bill, sponsored by Senator Lister Hill, Democrat of Alabama.

Scholarships in Senate Bill

The Senate bill includes a four-year program totaling $70,000,000 for college scholarships. If that survives on the Senate floor, some compromise on scholarships will have to be worked out by House and Senate conferees.

As adopted, the House bill would cost an estimated total of $147,000,000 in the first year of operation.

It would provide:

¶Loans averaging $600 to more than 90,000 needy students, of which the Federal Government would pay a total of $60,000,000.

¶One thousand fellowships of $2,000 each to train college teachers, with reimbursement to universities for additional costs to expand graduate schools.

¶Grants to the states for scientific teaching equipment and laboratory improvement, totaling $60,000,000.

¶Grants to states to improve testing and guidance programs, $15,000,000, and $6,000,000 to set up teacher-training institutes in this field.

¶Grants to institutions to set up short-term institutes for foreign language teachers, to pay half the cost of permanent foreign language centers and stipends for those attending. This was estimated at a total of $4,500,000.

¶For research under the United States Office of Education on better educational use

Continued on Page 5, Column 3

VETO THREATENED ON PENSIONS BILL

Social Security Rate Rise Backed by White House but State Plan Is Fought

By JOHN D. MORRIS
Special to The New York Times.

WASHINGTON, Aug. 8—The Eisenhower Administration raised the threat of a veto today against a bill to increase Social Security benefits.

The measure, approved by the House, calls for a 7 per cent increase in Old Age and Survivors Insurance benefits and higher Social Security taxes to finance it. Those provisions were endorsed by Arthur S. Flemming, Secretary of Health, Education and Welfare.

But the Administration is "strongly opposed," Mr. Flemming told the Senate Finance Committee, to provisions that would increase the Federal Government's share in the cost of state relief programs.

Would Recommend Veto

"Suppose we passed the House bill, would you recommend a veto?" asked Senator Paul H. Douglas, Democrat of Illinois.

"I would," Mr. Flemming replied.

Mr. Flemming was the first witness at the opening of two days of hearings on the measure, which is scheduled for Senate action before Congress adjourns. He told the Senators that his views were those of the Administration.

The bill calls for increases in monthly cash benefits under the insurance program starting

Continued on Page 5, Column 2

Peronists Win Rule Of Argentine Labor

By JUAN de ONIS
Special to The New York Times.

BUENOS AIRES, Aug. 8—The Argentine Senate adopted today a controversial union organization law that virtually hands the labor movement back to Peronist control.

President Arturo Frondizi's Senate majority approved the text of a bill, passed by the Chamber of Deputies, without changing a word. It did so despite formal opposition to the measure by the Roman Catholic Church, business and professional organizations, nearly all of the press and the anti-Peronist labor unions.

The bill, which re-establishes the single General Labor Confederation, with the official right to speak for labor, awaits the President's signature only.

In eighteen of the bill's fifty-

Continued on Page 4, Column 7

Glennan, Ohio Educator, Named To Direct New U.S. Space Unit

Case Tech President Served on A.E.C. Under Truman—Dryden Picked as Aide

Special to The New York Times.

WASHINGTON, Aug. 8—T. Keith Glennan, a Cleveland educator and former member of the Atomic Energy Commission, is President Eisenhower's choice to head the new civilian space agency.

The President sent Mr. Glennan's nomination to the Senate today along with that of Dr. Hugh L. Dryden as Deputy Administrator of the agency.

Mr. Glennan is president of the Case Institute of Technology. Dr. Dryden is director of the National Advisory Committee for Aeronautics.

The National Aeronautics and Space Administration was created by an Act of Congress signed by the President ten days ago.

Mr. Glennan's appointment is believed to be noncontroversial. There may be some objection to the choice of Dr. Dryden, however, and this could delay Senate confirmation of the nominees.

If the Senate does not act

Associated Press

T. Keith Glennan

before Congress adjourns, both can be installed under recess appointments.

Members of the House Space Committee have criticized Dr. Dryden as presenting a program for the conquest of space that lacked "boldness, imagina-

Continued on Page 4, Column 3

Hogan Is Expected To Enter the Race For Senate Monday

By DOUGLAS DALES

A statement circulated yesterday by the New York Young Democratic Club indicated that District Attorney Frank S. Hogan had made up his mind to enter the race for the Democratic Senate nomination nearly a month ago.

Mr. Hogan yesterday scheduled a news conference for Monday noon to "issue a statement."

If, as expected, he then announces his entry, he will become the fifth declared candidate in the field.

Mr. Hogan's intentions were forecast in a summary of an interview conducted by a committee of the Young Democratic Club with Mr. Hogan on July 17. The summary was submitted to Mr. Hogan for revisions before its circulation among club members.

The summary indicated that Mr. Hogan was already making plans for the future operation of his office and that he expected to have a say in the selection of a successor.

His views on this were given as follows:

"When queried as to the

Continued on Page 14, Column 5

Rackets Unit Asks Prosecution for 13

By ALLEN DRURY
Special to The New York Times.

WASHINGTON, Aug. 8—Senate rackets investigators voted unanimously today to ask the Senate to approve contempt-of-Congress citations against thirteen witnesses.

They include the president of the Carpenters Union and the reputed heir to Al Capone's gangland empire.

The action was taken by the Select Committee on Improper Activities in the Labor or Management Field. It acted in a closed meeting between morning and afternoon public sessions at which it heard witnesses give further testimony on associates of James R. Hoffa, president of the International Brotherhood of Teamsters.

Senator John L. McClellan, Democrat of Arkansas, the committee

Continued on Page 5, Column 6

POLAR TRIP OPENS DEFENSE FRONTIER

U.S. Strategic Advantage Is Seen as Temporary—Soviet Effort Expected

By HANSON W. BALDWIN

A new ocean — the frozen wastes of the Arctic — has been opened to navigation and hence to naval utilization.

This is the meaning of the transpolar, under-ice voyage from Alaska to the Greenland Sea of the nuclear-powered submarine Nautilus.

The newest achievement of the Nautilus, which had already broken all records in submarine history, has immense strategic implications.

Last year the Nautilus made a five-and-one-half-day, 1,000-mile trip under the Arctic ice pack and clearly foreshadowed the shape of things to come.

The Arctic ice pack has hitherto prevented penetration of the Arctic Ocean except, with great difficulty, by foot or by air.

Ships Skirt Land

In certain seasons of the year when the ice pack recedes from the land, or thins out, surface ships have skirted the land masses bordering the Arctic, but their cruises have been short and difficult and they have never penetrated deep into the pack.

The submerged navigation of the Nautilus under the Pole and from Pacific to Atlantic means that utilization of the Arctic Ocean for military purposes is now possible for the first time in history.

Three military capabilities for Arctic submarine operations are immediately foreseeable.

Potentially the most important—in a strategic sense—is the utilization of the Arctic for the launching of guided missiles from submarines. The fleet ballistic missile, Polaris, a two-stage, solid-fuel rocket with a range of 500 to 1,500 miles, and a powerful thermonuclear warhead, is now under development. It has been designed for launching from a submerged submarine at considerable depths.

Nine nuclear-powered submarines, each much larger than the Nautilus and each capable

Continued on Page 6, Column 5

Nautilus' Skipper Helps to Mitigate A Snub to Rickover

By ANTHONY LEWIS
Special to The New York Times.

WASHINGTON, Aug. 8—The man largely responsible for construction of the world's first nuclear-powered submarine was not asked to the White House today to share her moment of triumph.

Some thought was given to inviting Rear Admiral Hyman G. Rickover to the ceremony for the Nautilus, White House officials said. But only "top brass" had been asked and it was decided no exception could be made for him.

The skipper of the Nautilus, Comdr. W. R. Anderson, proved in the circumstances to be as bold a navigator in Navy politics as in the waters under polar ice.

Commander Anderson went directly from the White House to Admiral Rickover's office in the Navy Building, a few blocks away. There he paid his personal respects on the slight, frail figure whose tough-minded drive made the Nautilus a reality.

For Admiral Rickover the of-

Continued on Page 7, Column 3

479 Get Jaywalking Summonses But Public Is Hailed on Response

By BERNARD STENGREN

Pedestrians waited for traffic lights and motorists waited for pedestrians yesterday as the police began enforcing New York's new safety law.

High officials of the Traffic and Police Departments said they were gratified at the extent of compliance by drivers and walkers.

Traffic Commissioner T. T. Wiley said:

"My hat is off to New York. The reaction is wonderful."

He spoke after a tour of midtown Manhattan during which turning trucks waited for pedestrians and cab drivers not only waited but also shouted warnings to pedestrians starting to cross against lights.

John J. King, assistant Chief Inspector and head of the Safety Division, said that although some persons had argued, most had stopped when patrolmen admonished them about jaywalking.

There were, however, exceptions. Between 8 A. M., when enforcement began, and 4 P. M., when the police day shift ended, 479 summonses returnable for $2 were issued to pedestrians.

These included 255 in Manhattan, ninety-three in Brooklyn, ninety-eight in Queens, thirty-one in the Bronx and two in Richmond—where there is only one "Don't Walk" signal.

Twenty-two motorists who failed to give the right of way to pedestrians received summonses for that infraction, which was added Thursday to violations subject to "rigid enforcement."

In Manhattan, five were is-

Continued on Page 15, Column 5

Submarine Nautilus Sails Under the North Pole and 1,830 Miles of Arctic Icecap

VOYAGE PIONEERS A NEW SEA LANE

Cargo Craft Expected to Go Under the Water Between Pacific and Atlantic

Continued From Page 1, Col. 8

leader, congratulated Commander Anderson and his crew.

President Eisenhower had already extended the Nautilus skipper his own "very, very best congratulations" after pinning the decoration on the commander's tunic. He also asked the commander to act for him in conveying his personal "well done" to the submarine's officers and crew.

With an occasional glance at his wife who was flown here by Navy plane earlier today from New London, Conn., without being told why, the 37-year-old Navy officer sat for about half an hour under floodlights telling reporters of the voyage. Newsreel and television cameras recorded the ceremony as did tape recorders for radio broadcasting.

A circular flat map—based on a polar stereographic projection—of the Pacific and Arctic areas from Pearl Harbor to Greenland was in place in a conference room near the President's office when James C. Hagerty, White House press secretary, broke the secrecy surrounding the "very good story" he told reporters would be coming at 1:30 P. M.

The press secretary pointed out that the distance from London to Tokyo at the present time was about 11,200 nautical miles—by the Panama Canal. By traversing the Arctic under the icecap the distance was only 6,300 miles—a saving of 4,900 miles, he said.

Mr. Hagerty told how the nautical mileage from Honolulu to London would be cut from the conventional surface route of 9,500 miles to 6,700 miles by the polar route.

After the citations had been read by the President's naval aide, Capt. E. P. Aurand, and the President had talked, Thomas S. Gates Jr., Secretary of the Navy, remarked in an aside to Commander Anderson that "this is the first time a Presidential Citation has been given in peacetime."

On hearing the observation, the President remarked: "I couldn't think of a better time to do it."

Beaming in the background as the President presented the decoration were Vice Admiral James A. Russell, acting Chief of Naval Operations; Admiral Frederick B. Warder, Commander of the Atlantic Fleet Submarine Force; Admiral Jerauld Wright, Supreme Commander Atlantic Forces of the North Atlantic Treaty Organization; John A. McCone, chairman of the Atomic Energy Commission, and Lewis Strauss, Administrative Assistant to the President on Peaceful Purposes of Atomic Energy.

Anderson Tells Story

The group having withdrawn, Commander Anderson began the story of Operation Northwest Passage as it got under way from Pearl Harbor in the predawn hours of July 23 under highest secrecy. He recounted briefly how the Nautilus had cruised submerged on a northerly course past the Aleutian Islands and through the Bering Strait between Alaska and Siberia toward the brittle fringe of the ice pack and then beneath it.

From Pearl Harbor to the Bering Strait, some 2,900 miles, the Nautilus maintained an average speed of "almost 20 knots." Commander Anderson said it was his original plan to make "a straight shot" for the polar crossing from the Bering Sea. However, observations showed a stiff northerly wind had pushed the ice pack farther south than anticipated.

Looking back, Commander Anderson said that the Nautilus probably could have gotten through on that route, but that he wanted to find the best possible "highway" and the search for it took him from the vicinity north of the Bering Strait over to the coast of Northern Alaska and Point Barrow.

At this point Commander Anderson said that he had discovered the "lead" that normally opens into deep water at this time of year was easily accessible. The Barrow Sea Valley, a deep canyon in the ocean floor, was located and followed from a point just north of Point Barrow to its entry into the true Arctic Basin.

Once in the Barrow Sea Valley, the skipper explained, "we were in our true element and able to cruise fast and deep—we were on our way."

The Nautilus surfaced only in the Point Barrow area to photograph the area and to track the ocean floor for the sea valley. It periscoped off the Diomedes Islands between Alaska and Siberia and for about thirty seconds sent up its radar for checking bearings.

"If the Russians detected us they are awfully good," Commander Anderson said in answering a question. He explained that the submarine had been in international waters throughout the trip and well on the American side of Bering Strait while traversing that waterway.

Above the Nautilus the covering icecap was plainly visible over the vessel's closed-circuit television, the six months period of Arctic daylight making visibility no problem. Now and then great holes appeared in the icecap but the Nautilus sped on.

"We were in a hurry," Commander Anderson explained.

"Why were you in hurry?" he was asked.

"Navigating under these conditions up close to the pole, making the voyage with the minimum number of turns, speed changes, depth changes, angle changes, facilitates the accuracy of navigation by a very marked degree," Commander Anderson went on.

"It is possible to get yourself considerably confused by subjecting the ship to a number of turns, and so on, knowing what we know now, we would make the crossing in a much more relaxed fashion. We wouldn't hesitate to charge course, or probe openings. However, we were anxious on this trip to show the possibility of utilizing this route some day as a fast commercial route."

Commander Anderson was casual but careful in describing the performance characteristics of his submarine. Its cruising depth and average speed were only generally described because of security reasons.

"I am able to tell you," the skipper said at one point, "that the Nautilus cruises at lower than 400 feet. I am able to tell you that we made better than 20 knots. The speed is somewhat faster in cold water."

The Nautilus skipper was interrupted repeatedly with questions. His answers disclosed among other things that the Arctic Sea at the North Pole was considerably deeper than had been supposed. Precision measurements placed the true depth at 13,410 or 1,927 feet greater than earlier estimates.

Commander Anderson indicated a distinct lack of curiosity about the precise make up and penetration of the icecap below the surface of the sea. It ranged in thickness from ten to fifteen feet and loses about three feet of its winter depth in summer. But pressures caused by wind and tide sent it to a depth of fifty feet in uncharted places and these were well above the submarine, he explained.

Hitherto unknown underwater mountain ranges were found to crisscross the Barrow Sea Valley from its beginning near Point Barrow to a point where it enters the Arctic Basin. These ranges were apart from the previously known Lomonosov Ridge extending from Canada almost directly across the Pole into the Soviet Union.

It was exactly at 11:15 P. M. Eastern standard time last Sunday that the atomic-driven submarine passed directly beneath the North Pole with a larger company than ever had been on the spot before. It neither paused nor notified Washington until the Nautilus surfaced some thirty-six hours later in the Greenland Sea.

No Mishaps

The entire voyage under the icecap—a distance equivalent to that from Chicago to San Francisco—was without a close call or mishap of any kind and without casualty or illness.

As he told his story Commander Anderson said that he wanted to "brag a little about our navigators."

"I really think that this is the most remarkable job in ship navigation that has even been done," he added.

A humorous note crept into the recitation as Commander Anderson gave the first public definition of what he called "longitudinal roulette," a pass-time not to be induiged in while traversing the arctic sea for the first time in a submarine.

"A trip across the North Pole, where there is no opportunity to observe anything outside of the ship, no opportunity to observe stars or do any type of electronic navigation, presents a very formidable problem—or what has been up to now a very formidable problem," the skipper explained.

"For example, it would be possible for a ship equipped with conventional navigation equipment to become so confused at the North Pole that they might actually work themselves around in a slow circle, thinking that they were going in a straight line, and end up coming intb perhaps the ice-locked coast off Greenland, or even more disappointing, back where they came from."

How did he manage to avoid this confustion?

"By having superb navigation equipment—superb compasses—by having this advanced inertial type navigation system, and by having such a complex of navigation equipment to check one thing against the other, and the other thing against something else—repeated over and over again, that we knew we were in business," Commander Anderson replied.

An inertial guidance system is made up of gyroscopes and other devices that automatically determine a submarine's position even on long submerged cruises.

The Nautilus skipper said that no contacts of a hostile nature had been made throughout the nineteen days and 8,146 miles covered from Pearl Harbor. Contacts not of a hostile nature were made, but Commander Anderson did not explain what these might have been.

Associated Press Wirephoto

ROUTE OF THE NAUTILUS is shown by Comdr. W. R. Anderson on stereographic projection of Northern Hemisphere. White lines depict ordinary sea routes from Hawaii to the British Isles. Black line denotes the Nautilus' route, which was changed when it was decided to go to Iceland. The change is indicated by broken line, partly hidden.

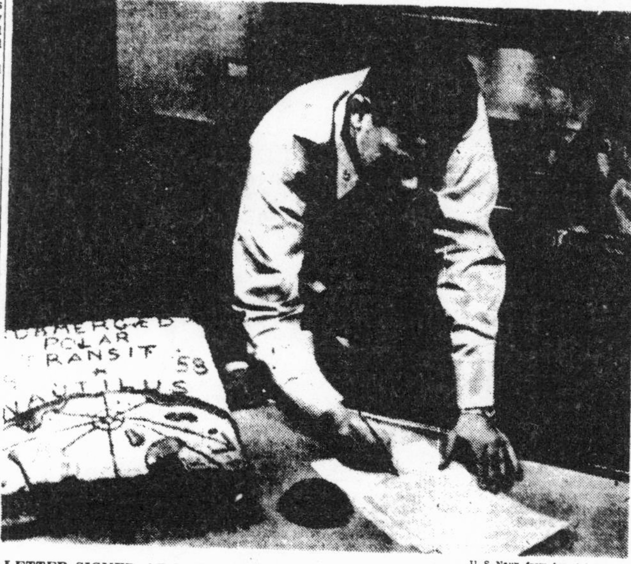

U. S. Navy, from Associated Press

LETTER SIGNED AT NORTH POLE: Message to President and Mrs. Eisenhower is signed by Commander Anderson, the master of the Nautilus, as vessel passes under the Pole. The cake was made for celebration of the event during the undersea voyage.

Anderson Sent a Letter To President From Pole

WASHINGTON, Aug. 8 (UPI)—The White House made public today a letter written to President Eisenhower by Comdr. William R. Anderson while his submarine Nautilus was traveling under sea beneath the North Pole.

The text follows:

Sunday, 3 August, 1958.

Dear Mr. President:

It is an honor and a privilege to report to you that the U. S. S. Nautilus will, in a few minutes, reach the North Pole while making the world's first transpolar voyage.

We submerged under the Arctic ice pack off Point Barrow, Alaska, on 1 August and expect to emerge in the Greenland Sea on 5 August.

I hope, sir, that you will accept this letter as a memento of a voyage of importance to the United States. It would not have been possible had it not been for your personal interest, approval and support. All of the men of the Nautilus join me in wishing you Godspeed in your continuing fight for world peace.

Very Respectfully,
W. R. Anderson,
Commander, U. S. Navy
Commanding Officer

(Signed at the North Pole at 11:15 P. M. Eastern daylight time.)

NAUTILUS SKIPPER TELLS OF HIS TRIP

'A Little Dazed Now,' He Says After Receiving a Medal From Eisenhower

Special to The New York Times.

WASHINGTON, Aug. 8—"I'm a little bit dazed right now, because fourteen hours ago I was submerged, seventy-two hours ago under ice, and only five days ago at the North Pole. Things are moving too fast."

Thus, Comdr. W. R. Anderson gave a roomful of reporters a quick summation of an exciting week.

The summation took place in a conference room at the White House, just off the lobby in the President's office wing. A few minutes before, President Eisenhower had pinned the Legion of Merit on the much-decorated skipper.

Reporters were there in greater numbers than the room would hold, curiosity aroused by a mysterious morning announcement that there would be "a very good story" at approximately 1:30 P. M.

The mystery was such that even one of the invited "V. I. P.'s" said in advance that he did not know what the announcement would be. The city was alive with speculation all of it wrong.

Some Reporters Lose Out

Almost one hundred reporters turned out. Approximately seventy-five got in. There were chairs for about sixty. The rest squeezed in along the wall and in front of the bank of television cameras at the back of the room. The ones who did not make it did not even get a peak. The door was closed on them.

James C. Hagerty, White House news secretary, broke the news in a most matter of fact fashion, and not loud enough for the boys in back.

"Several things before we start," he said. "Since July 22 the Nautilus has been engaged in an exercise known as Northwest Passage."

Mr. Hagerty gave brief details on the voyage, said that Commander Anderson was at that moment across the hall with the President, and added with a smile that Mrs. Anderson was among those present.

"She was flown down from New London last night," he said. "She did not know why." (It turns out that she thought her husband was in Panama.)

In came the invited guests: the Secretary of the Navy, the Acting Chief of Naval Operations, the present and immediate past chairman of the Atomic Energy Commission, Mrs. Anderson—bright-eyed and smiling—a handful of admirals and captains, and an enlisted man in summer whites. They were squeezed, too.

And then the President and the commander, a man of medium build with a tan that he did not get under the ice. The ceremony was quick. The president's Naval Aide read the citation and then stepped out of camera range. The President spoke a few words of congratulation and left the room, followed by the honor guests.

Center of TV Floodlights

Commander Anderson took a seat at a table that was brought in for him, hot in the focus of television floodlights. Mr. Hagerty sat at his elbow. Mrs. Anderson moved to a chair close by.

The commander told first about his daze, and quickly revealed that he is a security-conscious man with a light touch of humor.

The Nautilus, he said, was now headed to a "West European port" without him, and he was a little worried that his men might find him "not so indispensable."

When reporters wanted to know how deep she went below the ice, he replied: "We are permitted to say that we can submerge more than four hundred feet."

"How deep did you go?"

"More than four hundred feet," he replied, smiling.

What does it feel like to take a 1,830 mile sail under ice? Apparently just what you'd expect—a little scary.

The Nautilus had two peepholes to the icy sky above—the periscope and a closed circuit television arrangement. To Commander Anderson, the ice looked "like clouds going by extremely rapidly."

The commander was clearly an expert. He described mountains and valleys in the deep, talked about the ship's complicated inertial navigations system, and reeled off fact and figures from his head and a small scratch pad of notes.

Thirty-eight movies were shown during the trip and chess, cribbage and acey-deucey tournaments were held, he said. The jukebox played almost all the time.

Modern Captain Nemo

William Robert Anderson

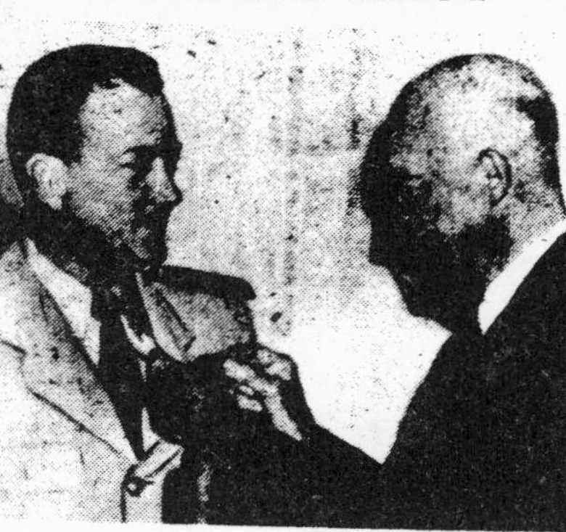

Associated Press Wirephoto

"A star from the very start"
(Comdr. Anderson receives Legion of Merit from President)

A SUCCESSFUL skipper is usually credited with having two special qualities. One is that he run "a taut ship." The other is that his vessel must nevertheless be "a happy ship." Shipmates and superior officers of Comdr. William Robert Anderson, who just made a trans-polar voyage in the Nautilus from the Pacific to the Atlantic, say he has these two assets.

Man in the News

The Navy obviously was very proud of him yesterday when announcement of the Nautilus achievement was made. An admiral, who knew him as a plebe at the Naval Academy, said he was "a star from the very start."

"He can even write wonderful reports," the admiral said as an afterthought.

A colleague at the Submarine Base in Groton, Conn., described him as "a quiet genius, almost taciturn." An officer who has sailed with him placed him "at the top of the list," and a man who had his crew behind him despite being a spit-and-polish commanding officer.

"And he is always cool," he added. "They picked the right man for this assignment."

The modern Captain Nemo was an inland boy who decided to go to sea without ever having seen it.

He was born and raised in Waverly, Tenn., which had a population of 1,892 and is situated in central Tennessee fifty-five miles west of Nashville.

The commander and his attractive wife, the former Yvonne Etzel of Newark, Del., disappeared shortly after President Eisenhower awarded him the Legion of Merit for the Nautilus voyage.

Wife Flown to Ceremony

Mrs. Anderson, a former airline stewardess, was flown to Washington for the ceremony from the Anderson home in Mystic, Conn., a short distance from the submarine base. Commander Anderson calls her "Bonnie."

Her hobby is restoring fine old houses, like the one they bought in Mystic several years ago and live in now. She likes oriental touches in her interior decorating.

Commander Anderson's main hobby is woodworking, helping Mrs. Anderson at restoration. He also makes small boats and ship models for their two sons, Michael D., 13, and William R. Jr., 3.

The Andersons have a poodle, Jacques, which they have entered in shows with success.

"But," as a fellow officer said, "there is not much time for hobbies when you have sea duty."

Commander Anderson, now 37 years old, attended Columbia (Tenn.) Military Academy; entered the Naval Academy in 1939 and was graduated in 1942 in an accelerated three-year wartime class.

He went immediately to the Navy's submarine school in New London, Conn., was qualified in September of the same year and put to sea a month later. All his service in wartime has been on submarines. They were the Tarpon, the Narwhal, and the Trutta. He made eleven war patrols.

Taught R. O. T. C. Unit

He served on the Sarda from 1946 to 1949 and then was assigned to the Naval Reserve Officers Training Corps at the University of Idaho.

In 1951 he went back to sea, first on the Trutta and then on another submarine, the Tang. In May, 1953, he became commanding officer of the Wahoo, which saw action in Korea from January to May, 1954.

In July, 1955, he became head of the tactical department of the submarine school, and afterward served in the Division of Reactor of Development under the Atomic Energy Commission in Washington.

He took command of the Nautilus on June 19, 1957.

Commander Anderson next appeared in the news last October after he had made an under-ice exploration of the Arctic Ocean, going within 180 miles of the pole.

POLAR TRIP OPENS DEFENSE FRONTIER

Continued From Page 1, Col. 6

of launching sixteen of the Polaris-type missiles, have been appropriated for by Congress. The first, complete with missiles, is expected to be ready in late 1960 or early 1961.

Each of these submarines will be equipped with Ships' Inertial Navigation System (designated SINS by the Navy, a complex of gyroscopes, accelerometers, integrators, star trackers, depth finder sand other instruments, which automatically enables an accurate determination of the ship's position even on long submerged cruises.

It is possible that the Nautilus utilized a modification of this system for her long trans-polar passage.

SINS is essentially a computer of great accuracy that provides precise ship's position in latitude and longitude, true heading or course, ground speed, and pitch and roll information. An occasional star sight through the submarine periscope monitors and corrects the computer.

Ice Not a Solid Mass

Contrary to popular impression the Arctic ice pack is not a solid, impenetrable mass, through which no submarine could surface.

Comdr. Robert D. McWethy, U. S. N., pointed out in an article in The U. S. Naval Institute Proceedings recently that "at any time of the year a submarine maneuvering under the polar ice pack could expect to find either open water or ice thin enough for the submarine to break through on the surface, provided the submarine is designed with sufficient topside strength to permit contact with the ice."

Some of the topside superstructure of the Nautilus was specially "toughened" for her recent cruise.

Utilizing these open or thin spots in the ice pack to put up a periscope occasionally, a missile-firing submarine could range pretty much at will across the Arctic, virtually secure from detection.

She could fire her missiles at points of her own choosing and, as Commander McWethy pointed out, from "the ice pack east of Spitsbergen" the distance to Murmansk is about 400 miles and it is 1,180 miles to Leningrad and 1,420 to Moscow, both well within the range of the Polaris.

Thus the missile-firing submarine, maneuvering in the Arctic, opens a new strategic frontier. The whole vast Arctic coastline of the Soviet Union, which extends virtually halfway around the world, is potentially open to assault. This fact greatly complicates and burdens the tremendous defense problem of the Soviet.

But in the same way it will eventually complicate our own defense problem. Russia is not believed as yet to have any nuclear powered submarines, which are more suitable because of their long submerged endurance for under-ice cruising. But it will have them in time, and the ballistic missiles to launch from them.

Hudson Bay forms a deep enclave into the continent of North America and flanks many of our Arctic defenses.

Canadian and American military men already have worried about the possibility of Soviet submarine operations in Hudson Bay. This worry will deepen when the Soviet acquires nuclear-powered submersibles.

In the short-term view, therefore, the United States gains a definite strategic advantage but in the long-term view this is neutralized by a similar Soviet capability.

Difficult to Detect

But submarines operating under Arctic ice would be almost impossible to detect by either side. In balance therefore the advent of the missile-firing, ice-navigating submarine would seem to mean that neither side could hope by an initial nuclear surprise attack to wipe out the other side's capability for massive retaliation.

More and more as new mobile weapons systems come into service the fear of nuclear retaliation may tend to restrain nuclear attack.

The second potential capability of the submarine in the Arctic is as a conventional commerce destroyer. Here the strategic balance heavily favors the United States.

The Russians have developed and are dependent upon a Northern sea route between Murmansk and the Bering Strait area. For a few weeks each summer Soviet convoys, escorted by ice breakers and with helicopters and planes to spot ice leads, have skirted the Arctic coast.

Supply Arctic Bases

They resupply Russia's Arctic settlements, take out raw materials and supply and reinforce the extensive series of air, missle and naval bases in being or under development in Siberia.

Sizable naval reinforcements for the Soviet Pacific fleets have taken this northern route in the last three years. The Nautilus cruise proves that this route, both militarily and commercially of high importance, would no longer be secure in war against submarine attack.

The third capability demonstrated by the Nautilus is a multipurpose one. Weather reconnaissance in the Arctic's air-sea rescue for the crews of planes forced to crash-land on the Polar ice, radar warnings, scouting and patrol missions, particularly for the observation of Soviet missile impact areas in the Arctic and limited raiding or amphibious operations against potential enemy bases or radar sites or to establish advanced bases, are all now possible in the Arctic Ocean area

Navy's Fact Sheet on Transpolar Trip by Nautilus

WASHINGTON, Aug. 8 (UPI)—Following is a fact sheet issued by the Navy on the nineteen-day 8,146-mile trip by the atomic submarine Nautilus, which made the first voyage under the Arctic icecap:

1.—Schedule:

Departed Honolulu, 2 A. M., July 21.

Transted Bering Strait, July 29.

West under Arctic pack off Point Barrow, Alaska, 8:37 A. M., Aug. 1.

North Pole, 11:15 P. M., Aug. 3.

Emerged from pack on Greenwich Meridian at Lat. 79 degrees N., 9:54 A. M., Aug. 5.

Arrived off Iceland, 11 P. M., Aug. 7.

2.—The first transpolar voyage of a ship in history, Honolulu to Europe, will take the Nautilus nineteen days and cover 8,146 miles at an average speed of over seventeen knots.

3.—When Nautilus reached the North Pole at 11:15 P. M., Aug. 3, more men—116—were assembled at the Pole at one time than ever before.

4.—Nautilus is equipped with a closed television network with the camera pointing up for observing ice.

5.—Nautilus traveled 1,830 miles in ninety-six hours from Point Barrow, Alaska, to the Atlantic Ocean between Greenland and Spitzbergen.

6.—Nautilus is equipped with ten separate sound equipments for detecting ice above and three for measuring the distance to the ocean floor below.

7.—One Nautilus crew member, James R. Sordelet, electrician's mate first class, became the first Navy man in history to re-enlist at the North Pole.

8.—In 1957, Nautilus traveled 1,383 miles under ice in three separate trips totaling 5.5 days and reached Lat. 87 degrees N., 180 miles from the North Pole.

9.—Polar ice is on the average twelve feet thick, although some ridges extend down fifty feet and even farther.

10.—Nautilus is equipped with four compasses of various types.

11.—The water at the North Pole was measured with a precision fathometer to be 13,410 feet deep. This is 1,927 feet deeper than the maximum measured by others who have reached the Pole.

12.—Prior to Nautilus' 1957 Arctic trip, no ship had ever been north of Lat. 83 degrees 21 minutes N under its own power (reached by) a Russian icebreaker in 1955. The Fram Under Nansen had drifted locked in the ice pack to 85 degrees 57 minutes N. in 1895.

13.—Nautilus on arrival in Europe will have traveled 129,000 miles on nuclear power—62,560 on the first charge of nuclear fuel and over 66,000 so far on the second charge.

Water 32 to 40 Degrees

14.—The water deep in the Arctic Ocean is about 32 degrees Fahrenheit although north of Spitzbergen a branch of the Gulf Stream brings it up to about 40 degrees Fahrenheit.

15.—Nautilus' nuclear power plant performed perfectly with no casualties on the transpolar voyage. It operated more efficiently in the cold water. The power plant in the past has operated continuously for as long as 47.5 days.

16.—Nautilus obtained a continuous record of water depth and ice thickness all the way across the Arctic Ocean. This record will provide our scientists and hydrographers with much information not previously known. Over 11,000 individual soundings were obtained in the relatively unchartered Arctic Basin.

17.—A contest was held to design a suitable flag for the ship commemorating the transpolar voyage with the prize a three-day liberty in Europe.

18.—Nautilus has now steamed 91,049 miles submerged, 72 per cent of her time under way. 36,498 miles of these miles were on the first nuclear charge, 57.5 per cent of the total mileage, and 54,551 miles on the second charge, 85 per cent of the total mileage.

19.—Nautilus is equipped with automatic control gear for holding her exactly on course and depth.

20.—Nautilus traveled within thirty miles of the so-called Pole of Inaccessibility, geographic center of the arctic ice pack.

21.—The Arctic Ocean is bisected by a 9,000-foot submerged mountain range, the Lomonosov Ridge, running from Canada to Russia. This ridge comes within 2,500 feet of the surface. Many uncharted bottom features were discovered.

22.—Prior to Nautilus' operations in 1957 the most total mileage for a United States submarine under ice was fifty miles by the Redfish in 1955.

23.—Nautilus is the first combatant ship with an inertial navigational system. Such a system works as well at the North Pole as any where else, unlike an ordinary gyro compass.

24.—The temperature inside Nautilus during the entire trip was 72 degrees. The relative humidity was 40-50 per cent.

25.—Ninety-three per cent of the trip from Pearl Harbor to Iceland was made submerged. The small time on the surface was used in surveying the ice pack edge.

Ice Constantly in Motion

26.—Ice in the Arctic Ocean is constantly in motion due to the ocean currents and the wind. Water openings are always present even in the dead of winter although unbroken ice sometimes stretches for ten or more miles.

27.—People on board Nautilus during her transpolar trip will have the title of Panopo—Pacific to Atlantic via the North Pole.

28.—Nautilus carried seventy-five days of food for 116 men. The meal served after the North Pole crossing was steak, french fries, and creamed peas and carrots, fresh fruit salad, fresh bread and North Pole cake.

29.—Thirty-eight movies were shown during the trip. Chess, cribbage and acey-deucey tournaments were held. The juke box (free) played almost continuously.

30.—Eleven Nautilus crew members were qualified in nuclear submarines at the North Pole.

31.—The submerged voyage from Honolulu to Bering Strait (2,901 miles) was made at an average speed of almost twenty knots. This is a record for a long submerged voyage.

"All the News That's Fit to Print"

The New York Times.

LATE CITY EDITION

U. S. Weather Bureau Report (Page 53) forecasts: Mostly fair and cold today, tonight and tomorrow. Temp. range: 30—19. Yesterday: 36.2—21.

VOL. CVIII..No. 36,875. NEW YORK, FRIDAY, JANUARY 9, 1959 — 10c beyond 100-mile zone from New York City. Higher in air delivery cities. — FIVE CENTS

DE GAULLE TAKES THE PRESIDENCY; DEBRE IS PREMIER

General's Entry Into Office Marks Start of Fifth French Republic

SOUSTELLE IS SELECTED

Post of Minister-Delegate Indicates He Has Second Top Spot in Cabinet

De Gaulle's statement will be found on Page 3.

By ROBERT C. DOTY

Special to The New York Times.

PARIS, Jan. 8—Gen. Charles de Gaulle was proclaimed today the first President of the new Fifth Republic and the French overseas community.

His first official act as President was to name former Minister of Justice Michel Debré, a loyal Gaullist certain to accept Presidential leadership, as his successor as Premier.

M. Debré's Government, announced tonight, includes most of the ministers who have served General de Gaulle since his return to power June 1, with the exception of the Socialists who withdrew in disagreement over policies of economic austerity.

Soustelle Gets High Post

Named Minister-Delegate with functions suggesting the role of Vice Premier was Jacques Soustelle, former Information Minister and architect of the victory of the neo-Gaullist party in the November legislative elections.

Stately ceremonies of transfer of power from the outgoing President, René Coty, marked the end of the eight-month transitional period opened by the May 13 revolt by Frenchmen in Algeria, which shook and finally brought down the Fourth Republic. The ceremonies signified the final launching of the Fifth Republic with what is in many respects a Presidential regime within parliamentary forms.

President de Gaulle reasserted in unmistakable terms his concept of his Presidential role as that of 'supreme guide and arbiter, rather than of the largely ceremonial figure French Presidents have been in the past.

His duty, he told 200 of France's dignitaries in the Grand Hall of the Elysée Palace at the inaugural ceremonies, is to assert, "even to impose" if necessary, the interests of the

Continued on Page 3, Column 3

TRIUMPHANT ENTRY: Fidel Castro, Cuban revolutionary leader, waves to crowds as he rides down Havana's Malecón sea drive in a jeep at head of an armored column. Parade proceeded to Camp Columbia, Army Headquarters.

Associated Press Wirephoto

MIKOYAN APPEALS FOR A 'HOT PEACE'

Tells Detroit Dinner 'We're All Tired of Cold War'—President Asks Courtesy

By HARRISON E. SALISBURY

Special to The New York Times.

DETROIT, Jan. 8—Anastas I. Mikoyan told Detroit's top industrial leaders tonight that "we are all tired of the cold war and would very much like to have a hot peace."

Mr. Mikoyan made his plea for a new and friendly relationship between the United States and the Soviet Union before a group of Detroit business men including the chiefs of the Ford, General Motors and Chrysler automotive empires.

Those who heard the Soviet First Deputy Premier at the swank Detroit Club said they had been impressed by his frank talk and the straightforward way in which he discussed Soviet-American differences.

Mr. Mikoyan had entered the club through a shouting crowd of about 300 Hungarian and Ukrainian demonstrators, who threw eggs and snowballs.

Three of the crowd were arrested. Mr. Mikoyan was not touched by any of the missiles.

[President Eisenhower, having been told of the demonstrations, called on Americans to show courtesy to take home an "accurate" picture of the United States.]

Visits Auto Plants

Mr. Mikoyan's address capped a day spent inspecting auto plants and speaking plainly on every occasion. At a luncheon at the Ford Administration Building, Mr. Mikoyan engaged in a no-holds-barred talk about Soviet-American conflicts with Henry Ford 2d and other auto executives.

It was apparent from comments by the auto executives that Mr. Mikoyan's campaign had made a positive impact.

Mr. Mikoyan said tonight that Soviet-American relations had passed through many stages: they had been good, they had been bad, they had been very, very bad. Now, he said, they are moving in the right direction.

"The wind is still cold but it is the wind of spring," he said.

Praises U. S. Aid in War

He recalled that Detroit sent the Soviet Union many trucks during World War II. He said this contribution was well remembered in the Soviet Union. The trucks gave great satisfaction. If they could speak, he said, they would express satisfaction with the people who had driven them.

"Gentlemen," Mr. Mikoyan said, "let us leave to the historians the question of who is to blame for the deterioration of our good wartime relations, and do all we can to improve our relationship now."

Mr. Mikoyan said he had great faith in the common sense of the American people. He said many barriers between the Soviet and the United States were "nonsense." He cited restrictions on trade and particularly the list of commodities of which ex-

Continued on Page 4, Column 2

Havana Welcomes Castro At End of Triumphal Trip

By R. HART PHILLIPS

Special to The New York Times.

HAVANA, Jan. 8—Fidel Castro rolled into Havana this afternoon with 5,000 of his victorious rebels to receive a delirious welcome from the city's populace.

Riding in a jeep, the tall, 32-year-old leader received the cheers of thousands who jammed the streets. Looking exhausted but happy, he still wore the beard that has become a symbol of the revolution.

Señor Castro and his young rebels seemed to enjoy their triumphant entry into this capital city of 1,000,000 inhabitants after two long years of fighting in eastern Cuba against the military rule of Fulgencio Batista, who fled to the Dominican Republic New Year's Day.

Later, addressing 40,000 people at Camp Columbia, the army headquarters, Señor Castro appealed for unity among the various revolutionary groups and called for all rebel fighters to lay aside their arms. "No private armies will be tolerated," he warned.

Warships Fire Salute

Two Cuban warships steamed past the flag-decorated Morro Castle into the harbor and fired a salute as the Castro column passed along the Malecón sea drive on its way to Camp Columbia. Exuberant young rebels on guard duty throughout the city fired their weapons into the air.

The rebels rode in jeeps, trucks, automobiles and armored trucks and perched on Sherman tanks purchased by the Cuban Army for use against them.

The crowds showered them with confetti, waved the Cuban flag and the black and red flag of the Castro movement, and shouted greetings and cheers for Fidel, as the young leader is known throughout the island.

Some of the youthful fighters had already shaved off the beards they had vowed to keep until the dictatorship was overthrown, but others kept their hair and whiskers long.

Overhead flew army planes and the helicopter that had hovered over the vehicle of the rebel leader on his victory march to Havana from Santiago de Cuba, center of the revolution, where

Continued on Page 9, Column 5

U.S. BARS INCREASE IN MISSILE FORCES

Rejects Air Force Request for More ICBM Groups Despite 'Gap' Warning

By RICHARD WITKIN

In the face of warnings of a fast-developing "missile gap," the Administration has rejected Air Force recommendations for increasing the planned force of intercontinental ballistic missiles, informed sources revealed yesterday.

The proposed budget for the 1960 fiscal year is said to contain no money to expand the ICBM force beyond the thirteen squadrons previously authorized.

The Administration's over-all defense proposals have already provoked strong criticism from influential members of Congress in both parties.

Ammunition for Debate

The issue of the ICBM force promises to provide much of the ammunition in the defense debate now getting under way in Congress.

The proposed defense budget figure for 1960 has been held, in the interests of budget balancing, to $40,900,000,000. This is about $100,000,000 more than the expected total for the fiscal year that ends June 30.

Administration critics argue that, if inflation and military paybills are considered, the 1960 proposal may provide less than the 1959 budget for military hardware.

The thirteen ICBM squadrons now authorized include nine Atlas and four Titan units.

The Atlas is a one-and-a-half stage missile expected to reach initial combat status this summer. All three rocket engines fire at take-off. Two of them drop away after expending their fuel.

Duty in Mid-1961

The Titan is a two-stage ICBM slated for operational duty about mid-1961.

Both missiles are designed to carry large thermonuclear warheads a distance of 6,325 miles in less than thirty minutes.

At about ten missiles a squadron, thirteen squadrons would give the nation a total ICBM force of 130 by 1962. A number of observers with limited access to intelligence data have warned repeatedly that the Soviet Union would, or at least could, have an ICBM force totalling 500 by 1961 and perhaps 1,000 by 1962.

These observers fear that the huge disparity between such a force and that planned by this country might tempt the Soviet Union either to launch an all-out attack or blackmail the

Continued on Page 10, Column 5

CENTRAL SPURNS PENNSY MERGER

Drops Studies to Determine Feasibility of Rail Plan—Symes 'Disappointed'

By ROBERT E. BEDINGFIELD

Directors of the New York Central Railroad called a halt yesterday to joint studies that had been under way thirteen months with the Pennsylvania Railroad as to the feasibility of a merger.

On learning of the Central's decision, James M. Symes, president of the Pennsylvania, issued the following statement:

"Quite frankly I am disappointed at the New York Central's announcement."

The two big rail systems first announced that they were embarking on the study on Nov. 1, 1957. Executives of both carriers have been guarded in all statements since then as to the progress being made.

Last fall, Alfred E. Perlman, Central's president, said that all stages of the study had been completed except those to be conducted in their special fields by the financial vice presidents of the roads. Late last month David Bevan, financial vice president of the Pennsylvania, said the financial stage, too, was near completion.

Central's directors announced their decision to break off the merger study following their regular monthly board meeting, which was held in Palm Beach, Fla. In a statement issued from the company's executive headquarters here, the directors indicated that rather than a

Continued on Page 33, Column 6

OFFICIAL AGENCY TO PLAN GROWTH OF REGION URGED

Report Asks Legal Status for Metropolitan Council as Government Adviser

Text of committee report is printed on Page 16.

By CLAYTON KNOWLES

A proposal that the Metropolitan Regional Council receive "full and effective" legal status was put before the Regional Plan Association yesterday.

The association's special committee on metropolitan government affairs urged in essence that the council, now a voluntary group, be transformed into the official planning and steering agency for all government in the region.

It warned that the future of the region hinged on the development of such an "official leadership institution with the capacity to foresee the region's difficulties, to develop alternative solutions and to lead the way for the region, step by step, from specific recommendations to official action to firm accomplishment."

The region embraces twenty-two counties in New York, New Jersey and Connecticut.

Congress Charter Urged

The report was produced after a three-month study by a committee of eight community leaders, headed by Prof. Wallace S. Sayre of Columbia. It found that no local or state government or ad hoc commission was equipped to provide the leadership the council could give.

But it stressed that the council, in which top elected officials of the area now cooperate informally, must be chartered by Congress and the respective state Legislatures "to make its proposals both authoritative and acceptable to the regional community."

In urging an official dual planning-steering role for the council, the Sayre Committee visualized recommendations emerging that would carry added weight at the national, state, regional and local levels.

Meeting Set for Today

It said that difficulties confronting the region were "already visible to many of its leaders, but the future dimensions of these problems, even within the coming decade, will be much greater, more complex and more critical than the present crisis in transportation."

Harold S. Osborne, president of the Regional Plan Association, has called a meeting of his board for noon today at the Century Club, 7 West Forty-third Street, to consider the report. The association is a voluntary citizen group.

If approved, the report will be presented by the association as its official position to the Metropolitan Regional Council

Continued on Page 16, Column 6

G.O.P. Aims to End 'Big Business' Label

By W. H. LAWRENCE

Special to The New York Times.

WASHINGTON, Jan. 8—Republican leaders are discussing plans for an extensive party face-lifting operation before the 1960 election. The principal aim would be to change the public's conception of the G. O. P. as the party of big business.

The Republican leaders are counting on President Eisenhower for a great deal of help, expecting more partisanship from him in his final months in office than he has shown since he has been in the White House.

Plans for the Republican come-back drive will be laid before the party's national committee at its meetings in Des Moines, Iowa, Jan. 22-23.

In analyses of the 1958 election reversals prepared for President Eisenhower, some

Continued on Page 14, Column 7

FILIBUSTER FOES FACE A SETBACK IN VOTING TODAY

Johnson Sets Up Showdown on Issue of Senate's Right to Adopt New Rules

HE ACTS TO KILL PLAN

Liberals Call Test Crucial for Success of Tighter Limitation on Debate

By RUSSELL BAKER

Special to The New York Times.

WASHINGTON, Jan. 8—Senator Lyndon B. Johnson forced the filibuster battle toward a decisive stage today and confronted Senate liberals with the prospect of a major defeat in the first showdown vote.

The Senate Democratic leader, apparently commanding the votes to beat the liberals on the point they want most to win, scheduled this first test for 11:30 o'clock tomorrow morning.

The vote is scheduled to begin just one hour before President Eisenhower's State of the Union Message to a joint session of Congress.

Moving with surprising speed, Mr. Johnson cut through a parliamentary morass this morning, set up the showdown in relatively clear-cut outline and was confidently prepared to take on the liberals in a late-afternoon vote.

Vote Delayed for Morse Talks

The vote was postponed until tomorrow after Senator Wayne Morse, Democrat of Oregon, announced that he wanted to talk far into the evening on behalf of the liberal position.

Senator Morse did just that, speaking from 6:04 P. M. until 10:10 P. M., when the Senate recessed until 10 o'clock tomorrow morning. During his talk Senator Morse introduced his anti-filibuster proposal providing for limitation of debate by a majority vote of those present. Under it, with just a quorum of fifty Senators on hand, twenty-six votes could force closure.

Basically this is a three-way struggle over the fate of the old filibuster rule, which empowers a determined minority to block passage of controversial legislation through dilatory debate.

It was touched off by a group of Eastern and Northern liberals who want the rule drastically changed. The Southern bloc opposes any change. The leadership of both parties, behind Senator Johnson of Texas, is

Continued on Page 14, Column 4

REPUBLICANS BACK MORE STATE TAXES

Leaders Predict Legislature Will Adopt Higher Levies and Withholding Plan

By LEO EGAN

Special to The New York Times.

ALBANY, Jan. 8—Republican leaders, following a canvass of their members in the Senate and Assembly, were confident tonight that they could muster the votes needed for Governor Rockefeller's tax-increase program.

The exact dimensions of this program remain to be determined. But it is expected to include putting state income taxes on a withholding basis, raising the gasoline tax from 4 to 6 cents a gallon and increasing the cigarette tax from 3 to 4 cents a package.

Senator Walter J. Mahoney of Buffalo, the Republican leader of the Senate, went on record today in favor of the change in the income-tax payment system. "I would certainly be in favor of it if a feasible plan is worked out," he said.

Plan to Blame Harriman

Republican leaders are planning to blame former Gov. Averell Harriman's Democratic administration for the tax increases. In this way they hope to make it easier, politically, for Republicans to muster the necessary strength to obtain approval of the program.

Well aware of the Republican strategy, Democrats are preparing to fight back. They are prepared to emphasize that all the expenditures made under Governor Harriman were authorized by the Republican-controlled Legislature.

They are likewise ready to demonstrate that Republicans, in many instances, went beyond Mr. Harriman's recommendations in voting appropriations.

But Controller Arthur Levitt, the only Democratic official holding elective office in the administration, has indicated that he will cooperate with Mr. Rockefeller in introducing the withholding system for income taxes.

Deficiency Funds Sought

The state's need for further revenues in the fiscal year starting April 1 was further emphasized today with the submission to the Legislature of an administration deficiency appropriation bill.

This measure would authorize the spending of $28,100,000 more than had been appropriated in Governor Harriman's last budget in the time remaining before March 31. It would likewise authorize loans amounting to $41,200,000 during the same period.

The bulk of the loans would be used to meet the Federal Government's share of state highway costs. These would be repaid as Federal funds become available.

A statement issued in connection with the bill said that $10,700,000 more than had been appropriated would be needed to meet the state's share of welfare costs. Caseloads since April 1 have been higher than anticipated and allowances to families have been raised.

A program for combating the legislative payroll abuses disclosed last year was also officially announced today. It involves making public the names, addresses, compensation and party sponsorship of all legis-

Continued on Page 17, Column 6

16 NEW CITY TAXES BEING CONSIDERED

A Big One and Several Little Ones Likely to Be Picked

By PAUL CROWELL

The Board of Estimate is wrestling with the problem of picking one large nuisance tax and a combination of small ones to raise $145,000,000 for the next expense budget.

It considers that amount necessary to balance the budget, which is certain to go substantially above $2,000,000,000 for the fiscal year beginning July 1.

Informed City Hall sources let it be known yesterday that sixteen special taxes, including the proposed levy on legalized off-track betting on horse races, were under consideration.

Six of these are taxes the city already has authority to impose without action by the Legislature. The remaining ten would require action at Albany, either to permit the city to increase rates now in force or to impose entirely new levies, such as a tax of 5 or 10 cents on taxicab rides or an off-track betting levy.

Although it was expected that the Board of Estimate would not make even a tentative choice before the end of this month, it was strongly indicated that at least three of the revenue-producing steps under consideration would be included in the final program.

These are a proposed tax on draught beer sales; a proposed 10-cent toll on the East River bridges and reimposition of the

Continued on Page 13, Column 1

BREAK WITH CAIRO IS HINTED BY BONN

Nasser Is Asked to Clarify Tie With East Germany

By SYDNEY GRUSON

Special to The New York Times.

BONN, Germany, Jan. 8—West Germany instructed its Ambassador in Cairo today to ask President Gamal Abdel Nasser for immediate clarification of the United Arab Republic's decision to establish consular relations with East Germany.

Spokesmen for the Bonn Government dropped strong hints that West Germany would consider breaking diplomatic relations with the United Arab Republic unless a satisfactory explanation was received from the Arab leader.

In the meantime the Foreign Ministry declared that there was no question of the Government's proceeding with its plans to send a delegation to Cairo to discuss West German participation in the building of the Aswan High Dam project on the Nile River. The Government has been considering guaranteeing a $50,000,000 investment in the project by private companies.

Government spokesmen used strong language to underline Bonn's displeasure with the agreement announced by Premier Otto Grotewohl of East Germany at the conclusion of his visit to Cairo yesterday. At the Foreign Ministry here it was said the agreement had "surprised and alienated" the West German Government. From

Continued on Page 6, Column 4

Reds Here Suspend Touring Party Aide

By PETER KIHSS

One of the Communist party's top leaders, Charles Loman, has been suspended from his state party posts by New York State Communist leaders.

Mr. Loman, a member of the party's national committee and its Kings County chairman, is understood to have gone abroad last month. There are reports that he left without party permission and without rendering a required accounting.

There is an unconfirmed report that his Brooklyn organization refused to support the state board's suspension by sixteen votes to twelve.

Party leaders declined to confirm or deny that the Brooklyn group has had major party funds under its control. One estimate is that perhaps as much as $250,000 may have been built up in the last seven

Continued on Page 8, Column 5

De Valera to Quit as Premier And Seek Ireland's Presidency

His Government Party Seeks to Abolish the Proportional Representation System

Special to The New York Times.

DUBLIN, Jan. 8—Eamon de Valera intends to resign as Premier of Ireland in the next few weeks and seek election as President. He made the decision known to close associates within the last few days.

The New York-born Premier, 76 years old, has been an Irish leader for more than half a century. He is expected to announce his decision to his party formally at the end of this month.

Already the machinery of his party, Fianna Fail, is being geared for the twin electoral battle of making him President and of abolishing the proportional representation system of parliamentary election.

John A. Costello's United Ireland party has chosen Gen. Sean MacEoin as its Presidential nominee.

In the early days of the war against the British the general was, known as the doughty fighting "Blacksmith of Ballinalee." Between shoeing horses in the village of Ballinalee in County Longford, he led a column of the Irish Republican Army against the British troops.

It is generally conceded, however, that no candidate has much chance against Mr. de Valera. His election as the next President, if he is nominated, is taken for granted here.

The New York Times

Eamon de Valera

Fourteen years ago General MacEoin ran against President Sean T. O'Kelly, who is retiring in June, but was defeated.

Mr. de Valera has indicated that he would like Sean F. Lemass to succeed him. He is Deputy Prime Minister and Minister for Industry and Commerce. In the last year his po-

Continued on Page 2, Column 6

EDUCATORS SCORE STUDENT-AID OATH

Cite Challenge to Freedom —Association to Vote on Urging Repeal of Law

KANSAS CITY, Jan. 8 (AP) —A Federal law requiring students receiving loan assistance to sign a Communist-disclaimer affidavit and take an oath of allegiance was assailed today at the closing session of the Association of American Colleges.

Delegates attending the annual meeting agreed to take a mail ballot by Feb. 1 on whether to urge Congress to repeal that part of the National Defense Education Act of 1958. The association has 750 member schools.

Some delegates urged a convention vote on what was termed a challenge to academic freedom. The mail-ballot system was adopted after it had been noted that only one-third of the membership was represented at the session.

Hamilton A. Mathes of the United States Information Agency reported that Arthur S. Flemming, Secretary of Health, Education and Welfare, was considering asking Congress to amend the controversial law.

Humphrey Eelected

Dr. George D. Humphrey, president of the University of Wyoming, was elected association president, succeeding William W. Whitehouse, head of Albion College.

A philosopher recommended last night that room be made in education for the troublemaker, for he was the one with the inquiring mind.

Dr. George Boas of the Johns Hopkins University held that American education had failed to provide for inquiring and inventive minds.

"You will not have excellence if a man does not feel free to ask any question whatsoever, whether it impinge upon vested scientific authority or on theology or politics," Dr. Boas said. "You will not have excellence if a student is made to feel that he no longer belongs to the group, once he spends more time in the library than on the football field."

Scores Tradition

Dr. Boas, a professor emeritus, was the main speaker at the convention. He said the inquiring student was bound to be regarded as a troublemaker by his high school or college teacher. However, he observed, through history it has been the troublemakers who think, do and achieve.

"It is a tradition, not only in our schools but in our culture as a whole, that the common man, the average citizen, the good mixer, the anti-intellectual, the middle brow, is our ideal," he said.

Associated Press Wirephoto

CASTRO'S SON IN PARADE: Fidel Castro Jr., 9-year-old son of the rebel chief, with members of the 26th of July Movement atop a tank in Havana. The boy returned this week to Cuba, after living with relatives and attending Public School 20 in Queens.

GANG SEIZES TRUCK, LEAVES IT BURNING

A dozen men commandeered a truck carrying paper napkins yesterday and kidnapped the driver and his son for a short time. Later, the truck and its cargo were found, almost destroyed by fire.

At 5:30 P. M., according to the police, three cars forced the thirty-two-foot trailer truck to the curb at Amsterdam Avenue at Sixty-third Street. The men ordered the driver and his son to get into one of the cars, while others drove off with the truck.

The victims were taken to Eighth Avenue and Fourteenth Street and told to take a subway home. About an hour later, the police found the truck, worth about $5,000, and the paper napkin cargo afire at Christopher and West Streets.

Matthew McGrath, the driver, 50 years old, of 43 School Street, Yonkers and his 17-year-old son Neil, were questioned. Mr. McGrath said that he had picked up the cargo at the Royal Lace Company, 59 Gold Street, Brooklyn, and was headed for Yonkers.

The police said they believed that labor difficulties at the Royal Lace Company might have led to the hijacking.

Power Aide to Hold 2 Posts

William S. Chapin, general manager of the State Power Authority, also will serve as chief engineer, the agency announced yesterday.

HAVANA THRONGS WELCOME CASTRO

Continued From Page 1, Col. 8

he had named Dr. Manuel Urrutia Lleo Provisional President.

Señor Castro halted his jeep on the Avenida del Puerto and walked up through Misiones Park to the Presidential Palace to greet Dr. Urrutia, his Cabinet and other supporters of the revolution.

Near by was slim, uniformed Celia Sanchez, the best known woman figure of the revolution. She was Señor Castro's aide during the two years of fighting.

Speaks From Balcony

The rebel chief, wearing a peaked fatigue cap, held a rifle beside him as he talked. He looked exhausted. He had slept little during the march through the island, with huge celebrations in each big town.

A few minutes later Señor Castro, his rifle slung over his shoulder, spoke briefly from the palace balcony to a crowd that filled the park and the adjoining streets.

He remarked that he had never been in the palace before. He said he did not like the palace, and knew that the people did not, but he hoped that the actions of the revolutionary Government would cause the people to regard the building with affection.

On his plea, the crowd separated to form a lane and the rebel chief walked through the park to resume the slow procession to Camp Columbia.

He reached his destination at 8 P. M., five hours after he had entered the city. His jeep had moved at a snail's pace, often being halted by the enthusiastic crowds.

In Camp Columbia, thrown open to the people for the first time in memory, thousands of civilians gathered on the parade ground.

Men entering the camp were searched for weapons by bearded rebels. Women were asked to open their purses for inspection. The rebels were trying to protect their leader from possible assassination.

Speaking at Camp Columbia tonight, Señor Castro held the huge throng in his spell for fully two hours. He spoke easily and with force.

He said that a certain revolutionary group—observers took it to be the Revolutionary Directorate—was storing arms. He demanded to know what they intended to do with them, since "there is no longer an enemy."

The directorate rebels fought in Las Villas Province. They have publicly voiced discontent at not having been consulted by Señor Castro's Twenty-sixth of July movement in the establishment of the Government.

Señor Castro said that there should have been only one revolutionary organization. He invited all rebels to join the armed forces headed by him.

He said regular army soldiers would be kept in their posts if they had committed no crimes, but warned that "those who have committed crimes will face a firing squad."

Señor Castro assured the people that he would command the armed forces only "a minimum time." He did not indicate how long that might be.

"An attempt to break the peace is the greatest crime that can be committed now," he said.

Early in the speech, someone in the crowd released three white doves. One of these flew directly to Señor Castro's shoulder, where it perched as he spoke.

Commerce and industry closed at noon today for the Castro welcome. The sale of alcoholic beverages was prohibited.

The Government early this morning banned all subsidies to publications and their employes. The President also decreed a thirty-day suspension of legislation that provides that judges may not be removed by the Executive.

Dr. Juan Menocal Barreras was named director of the Monetary Stabilization Fund.

Alberto Fernandez was appointed to head the Sugar Stabilization Institute, which together with the Government, controls the sugar industry.

Mexico Demands an Apology

MEXICO CITY, Jan. 8 (UPI) —The Mexican Government has demanded an immediate apology from the Guatemalan Government for the strafing of three Mexican fishing boats by Guatemalan planes Dec. 31.

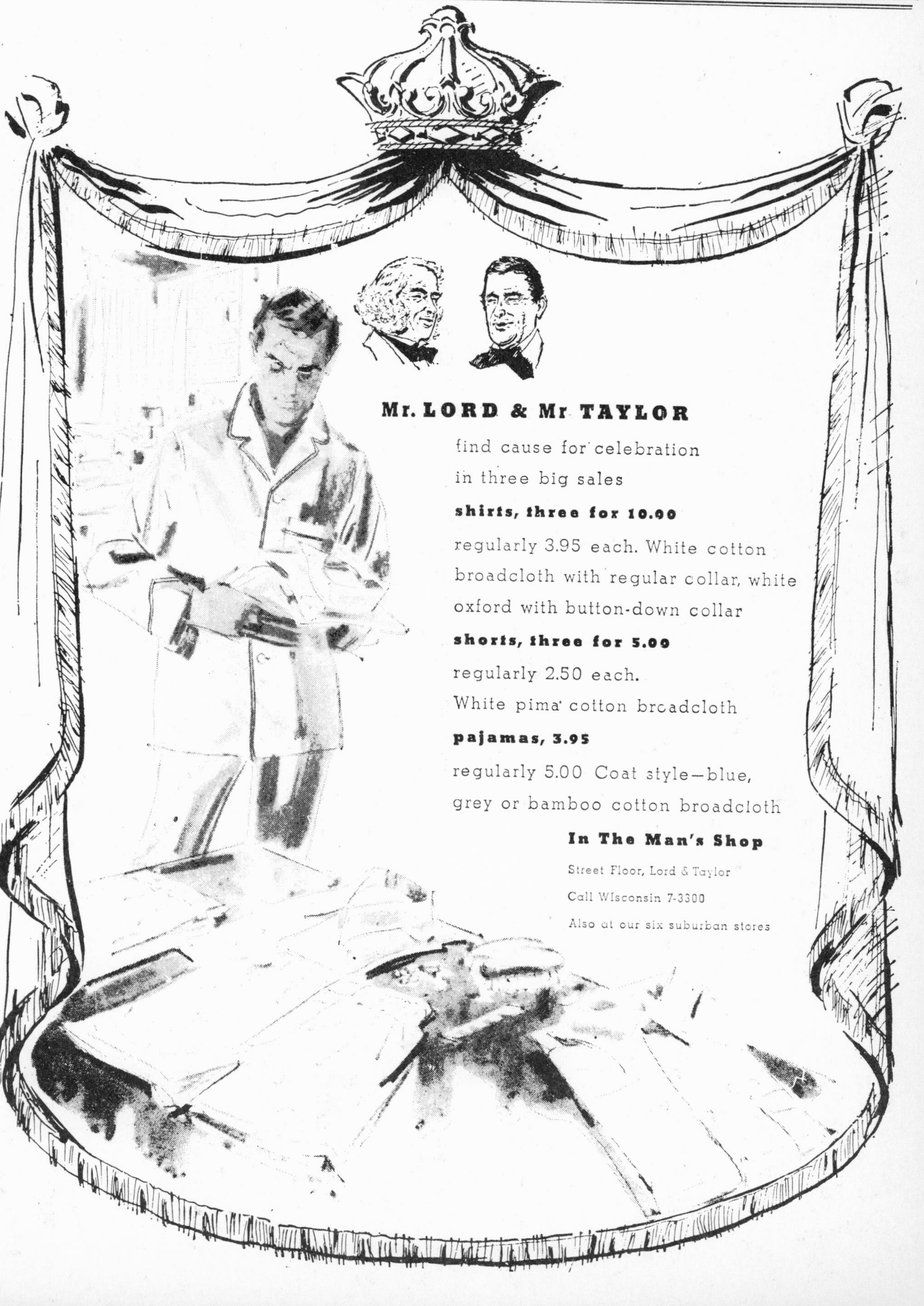

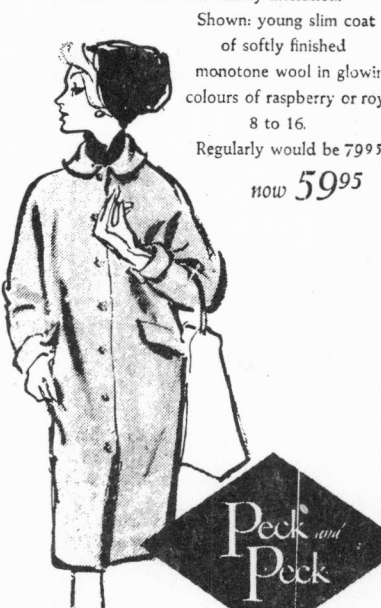

"All the News That's Fit to Print"

The New York Times.

LATE CITY EDITION
U.S. Weather Bureau Report (Page 57) forecasts: Partly cloudy, warmer today; cloudy milder, chance of rain tomorrow.
Temp. range: 42—25. Yesterday: 35.3—27.9.

VOL. CVIII . . No. 36,938. NEW YORK, FRIDAY, MARCH 13, 1959. 10 cents beyond 50-mile zone from New York City except on Long Island. Higher in air delivery cities. FIVE CENTS

HAWAII IS VOTED INTO UNION AS 50TH STATE; HOUSE GRANTS FINAL APPROVAL, 323 TO 89; EISENHOWER'S SIGNATURE OF BILL ASSURED

ADENAUER IS FIRM AGAINST TROOP CUT IN MIDDLE EUROPE

Gets Assurance in Talks With Macmillan That the British Seek No Disengagement

By SYDNEY GRUSON
Special to The New York Times.

BONN, Germany, March 12—Chancellor Konrad Adenauer restated to Prime Minister Harold Macmillan today West Germany's opposition to any reduction of Allied forces in Central Europe except within a general disarmament agreement.

The British leader came to Bonn today to give the Chancellor a personal report on his recent conversations in Moscow and to reassure the West Germans that Britain was not seeking the disengagement of Eastern and Western forces in Germany.

Nor, said a British Foreign Office spokesman, does London favor even a controlled limitation of forces if this would result in disequilibrium between the troops and armaments of East and West in Central Europe.

Trip Is Second of Three

Mr. Macmillan's trip here was the second of his three planned journeys to brief other Western leaders about his talks with Premier Nikita S. Khrushchev of the Soviet Union. Mr. Macmillan was in Paris earlier this week and he will cross the Atlantic for separate meetings with President Eisenhower and Prime Minister John Diefenbaker of Canada next week.

The first session between Mr. Macmillan and Dr. Adenauer, who were accompanied by their foreign ministers and two advisers each, lasted three hours. The talks were resumed tonight after a dinner in Mr. Macmillan's honor. They will continue tomorrow in the Chancellor's Palais Schaumburg offices.

The differences in outlook between the Prime Minister and the Chancellor were evident in their remarks at the airport on Mr. Macmillan's arrival.

Mr. Macmillan said the West was firm and united on the prin-

Continued on Page 3, Column 4

ROCKEFELLER ASKS A DRIVE ON CRIME

In Message to Legislature, He Urges Tighter Laws

By WARREN WEAVER Jr.
Special to The New York Times.

ALBANY, March 12—Governor Rockefeller called on the Legislature today to join him in prosecuting a war against organized crime "more vigorously than ever before."

The Governor sent a special message to the lawmakers, with a dozen recommendations for tightening the existing criminal law and making law-enforcement organizations more powerful and better trained.

In his election campaign last fall, Mr. Rockefeller was outspoken in his criticism of the increase in criminal activity during the Harriman Administration. He pledged swift action against racketeers and law violators if he should be elected.

Mr. Rockefeller urged today that the Legislature:

¶Make it a misdemeanor to defy a subpoena from the State Commission of Investigation or engage in obstructive or contemptuous conduct before the crime panel.

¶Set up a municipal police training council that would establish minimum training standards for all members of police forces.

¶Increase the statute of limitations for prosecution for tax evasion from two to six years, thus giving the state more time

Continued on Page 16, Column 2

Governor Taking Charge Of Meeting City Tax Needs

Orders Report on Costs and Resources for Conference With Mayor Tomorrow —Wants an Agreement Next Week

By DOUGLAS DALES
Special to The New York Times.

ALBANY, March 12,—With his own program for higher state taxes out of the way, Governor Rockefeller has decided to take personal command of the Albany action needed to help New York City balance its budget for the fiscal year starting July 1.

The decision was made at a meeting with Republican legislative leaders today, called to discuss the conference to be held with Mayor Wagner Saturday morning on the city's budget problem.

The meeting will be held at the Executive Mansion and will be attended by Republican and Democratic legislative leaders

In preparation for the meeting, Governor Rockefeller hastily named a task force to examine New York City's needs and the resources that might be tapped to meet them. A report has been asked by tomorrow night in time to be digested before the meeting with the Mayor.

The task force was designated at a meeting attended by Mr. Rockefeller, Tax Commissioner Joseph H. Murphy, Budget Director T. Norman Hurd, Majority Leader Walter J. Mahoney of the Senate and Majority Leader Joseph F. Carlino of

Continued on Page 16, Column 4

Snowfall of 5 to 10 Inches Delays All Transit in Area

By PETER KIHSS

With spring only nine days away, the city got its heaviest snowfall of the season yesterday—5.3 inches. It was perhaps nature's way of marking the seventy-first anniversary of the famous blizzard of '88.

On March 12, 1888, that storm hurled 16.5 inches of snow on the city, and in two more days brought the total to 20.9 inches.

Rockland and Fairfield Counties reported ten inches of snow yesterday; Westchester, seven to nine; Bergen, six to seven; Long Island, five to six; Elizabeth, N. J., 5.4, and New Brunswick, N. J., two to three.

Rain and warming temperatures turned the snow into slush in the city. Temperatures dropped during the night, however, and turned the slush to ice on some roadways. The less heavily traveled roads in the suburbs and upstate were reported especially dangerous.

The forecast for today was for partly cloudy and warmer. The temperature may reach the low forties and cause the ice and snow to melt.

Yesterday's storm was caused by two low-pressure areas moving in from the Midwest and from the Virginia coast. Snow fell throughout the Northeast. Depths ranged up to fourteen inches in Chautauqua County on Lake Erie, the Schoharie Valley west of Albany and in western Maryland.

Seven deaths were attributed to the storm in New York, New Jersey and Ohio.

The city's public schools had only 70 per cent attendance. Radio station WOR, which gathers and broadcasts news of

Continued on Page 22, Column 1

GOVERNOR NAMES COMMERCE HEAD

Appoints McHugh, President of New York Telephone—Utility Picks Successor

Governor Rockefeller completed his Cabinet in Albany yesterday with the appointment of Keith S. McHugh to head the Department of Commerce.

Mr. McHugh, who is 64 years old, will retire as president of the New York Telephone Company on April 30 to accept the appointment.

Governor Rockefeller said he was looking to Mr. McHugh to "invigorate" the department so that its full potential to stimulate business in the state would be realized.

Mr. McHugh is leaving a $150,000-a-year job for one that pays $18,500. However, within a year, he will qualify for a company pension as a forty-year man. A company spokesman said a pension arrangement would be worked out by the board of directors.

Meanwhile, the directors of the telephone company elected Clifton W. Phalen to succeed

Continued on Page 16, Column 2

CITY VOTES DEAL ON POWER PLANTS WITH CON EDISON

But Contract Is Changed to Permit New Bids When Final Auction Is Held

By PAUL CROWELL

Contracts for the sale of the city's three rapid-transit power plants to the Consolidated Edison Company at a gross price of $125,840,000 were approved unanimously by the Board of Estimate last night.

The vote was taken after the language of the contracts had been changed slightly to make certain that bidders other than Consolidated Edison could submit offers when the power plants were disposed of at public auction, as required by the City Charter.

The changes were made after Harvey M. Spear, counsel for unidentified "substantial New York interests," had complained that his clients might not be able to submit bids technically admissible under the terms of the agreements.

Clients Not Identified

Mr. Spear declined to tell the board the names of his clients, saying that they would be disclosed when bids were received.

Mr. Spear said his clients, while preferring to submit an offer to purchase the power plants for lease back to the Transit Authority, would also be prepared to submit a bid for purchase and operation.

The contracts approved by the board paved the way for transfer of the plants to Consolidated Edison by July 1, assuming that the company was the successful bidder.

The company's bid was for at least $99,382,871 in cash in addition to concessions that would bring the total minimum purchase price up to $125,840,000. The company also offered to supply the three divisions of the city subway system with power under a ten-year contract at uniform rates.

Company Supplies IND

The company now supplies all power for the IND division. The IRT and BMT divisions obtain power from the three city plants that are on Kent Avenue, Brooklyn, and West Fifty-ninth Street and East Forty-seventh Street in Manhattan.

By its vote the Board of Estimate authorized the Mayor to execute, subject to specified conditions, a contract for selling the three plants and one for purchasing power for the three divisions of the city subway system now operated by the Transit Authority.

The board also authorized the Commissioner of Marine and Aviation, Vincent A. G. O'Connor, to execute waterfront leases in connection with the transfer

Continued on Page 15, Column 2

Associated Press Wirephoto

THE BIG NEWS: Chester Kahapea, 13, offering copies of The Honolulu Star-Bulletin yesterday in the Hawaiian capital. The flag on the front page contains fifty stars.

3 OF JOINT CHIEFS WILL BE RENAMED

Twining, Burke and White Slated for New Terms—Lemnitzer to Get Post

By HANSON W. BALDWIN
Special to The New York Times.

WASHINGTON, March 12—The reappointments of three members of the Joint Chiefs of Staff will be announced soon.

Those who will be reappointed to new two-year terms starting this summer are Gen. Nathan F. Twining, chairman of the Joint Chiefs of Staff; Gen. Thomas D. White, Chief of Staff of the Air Force, and Admiral Arleigh A. Burke, Chief of Naval Operations.

Gen. Lyman L. Lemnitzer, Vice Chief of Staff of the Army, will succeed Gen. Maxwell D. Taylor, present Army Chief of Staff, whose second two-year term ends June 30. General Taylor is expected to retire.

The second two-year term of Gen. Randolph McC. Pate, as Commandant of the Marine Corps, does not expire until next Dec. 31, and as far as is known his successor has not yet been selected. General Pate also expects to retire.

The names of Lieut. Gen. Merrill B. Twining, a brother of the chairman of the Joint Chiefs, and of Lieut. Gen. Edwin A. Pollock have been men-

Continued on Page 4, Column 2

U. S. and Canada List Seaway Tolls, Effective on April 1

By RICHARD E. MOONEY
Special to The New York Times.

WASHINGTON, March 12—The United States and Canada announced St. Lawrence Seaway tolls today, to take effect April 1.

They are identical to those proposed last June after negotiations by committees of both nations. The differences are primarily in definitions, mostly for the types of cargo that would qualify for the low rate applying, to "bulk" shipments.

[Opposition to the toll setup came from port, rail, shipping and civic interests. They called the rates unrealistically low and the estimated revenue too high. The Port of New York Authority feared a loss of 3,500 waterfront jobs because of "unfair competition" resulting from the tolls.]

Railroads Competing

The Seaway links the Great Lakes and the Atlantic for deepwater ships. Part of it was opened last summer, and the full length is scheduled to be working soon.

Interests that would benefit from the new water route and those against whom it would compete had been fighting over the toll issue.

The fight was moving into a new phase. Major railroads are considering a 20 to 25 per cent reduction of rates they charge for transporting grain for export. This would enable them better to compete with the price for shipping via the waterway.

Seaway tolls are intended to

Continued on Page 10, Column 2

HOUSE UNIT CUTS JOBLESS AID BILL

Restricts Extension of U. S. Assistance to 3 Months Instead of One Year

Special to The New York Times.

WASHINGTON, March 12—The House Ways and Means Committee approved today a bill for a three-month tapering-off of emergency Federal aid to the unemployed.

The measure falls far short of earlier plans by Democratic leaders for a year's extension of the program beyond its present expiration date of March 31.

The effect would be to prevent an abrupt cut-off of payments to about 300,000 jobless workers expected to be drawing the emergency benefits at the end of this month.

Instead, these workers would stay on the rolls until they had exhausted the benefits to which they would have been entitled in the absence of a March 31 termination date.

The committee acted in closed session by what was reported as a one-sided voice vote. The House is expected to pass the bill early next week.

Democratic sources reported that the one-year extension plan had been set aside in the interest of assuring quick enactment of a bill. President Eisenhower and House Republican leaders had voiced strong opposition to the earlier Democratic proposal.

Another factor was the apparent lack of enthusiasm with which the proposed one-year

Continued on Page 18, Column 4

MEASURE SPEEDED

A Short-Cut Sends It Direct to President, Who Is 'Delighted'

By C. P. TRUSSELL
Special to The New York Times

WASHINGTON, March 12—The Territory of Hawaii was voted into the Union today as its fiftieth state.

The House of Representatives gave its approval by a vote of 323 to 89. Yesterday the Senate approved the Hawaii bill, 76 to 15.

President Eisenhower's approval is assured. The White House said today he was "delighted" and noted that "he has been urging it for some time."

Thus, after one of the fastest actions by Congress in years, only the mechanics of admitting a new state remain before Hawaii joins the Union.

The question arose as to whether the island territory some 2,000 miles from continental United States would seek to put its fiftieth star into the flag July 4 of this year when Alaska adds its forty-ninth. There is barely enough time to do so and island leaders doubted that it would be done.

Governor Gives Word

With the galleries filled, the House started its long roll-call in midafternoon. Among the spectators was the Governor of Hawaii, William F. Quinn. When the roll-call began he quietly left the gallery and went to the office of Sam Rayburn, Speaker of the House.

At the Speaker's office Governor Quinn telephoned Acting Gov. Edward E. Johnston at Honolulu and asked him to hold the line. When he was notified that the roll-call had recorded 219 ayes—a majority of the House—Governor Quinn set off a celebration in the islands by shouting:

"Sound the sirens, close the schools and get going."

A little later he added a note of caution:

"Keep the lid on a little, Ed."

Before Hawaii can attain statehood it must hold a referendum on whether it wants to assume the burdens at this time. Besides agreeing at the polls with provisions of the new law,

Continued on Page 13, Column 2

HAWAIIANS START 2 DAYS' FESTIVITY

Alaska Sends First 'Aloha' to Celebrating Islanders

By LAWRENCE E. DAVIES
Special to The New York Times.

HONOLULU, March 12—The kamaaina and the malihini celebrated today Congressional assurance that the nation was ready to welcome Hawaii as the fiftieth state.

That is to say, the oldtimer—the Hawaiian version of the Alaskan sourdough—joined with the newcomer—the Hawaiian counterpart of the Alaskan cheechako—in opening a two-day demonstration of gratitude over the prospective ending of territorial status for the islands.

The celebration got off to a restrained start. It picked up momentum as the day wore on toward a climax here on the island of Oahu with huge bonfire, aerial and offshore military pyrotechnics and hula dancing.

At the beginning everyone seemed to be waiting for someone else to show the way. Within a half-hour after word came from Washington of the action in the House of Representatives, however, the Waikiki area was clogged with horn-tooting automobiles. Bands and colorfully clad marchers took over at midafternoon.

Colored paper streamers were flung from downtown office buildings along King and Merchant Streets. Hands were thrust forward with a "happy statehood" salutation. Mayor Neal Blaisdell of Honolulu was so

Continued on Page 13, Column 1

There Are Times When Bad Weather Brings Out the Best in a Man

It was such a time yesterday at Vesey St. and Broadway

The New York Times (by Neal Boenzi)

And a man came forward to lend a gallant, helping hand

Fulton Street Widening Dropped By Jack on Protest of Merchants

The highly controversial proposal to widen part of Fulton Street in lower Manhattan was withdrawn from further consideration yesterday by Borough President Hulan E. Jack of Manhattan.

The action by the Board of Estimate permitting Mr. Jack to drop the project constituted a victory for a group of Fulton Street merchants.

Opponents have fought the proposal as threatening hardship to "hundreds of business men and thousands of their employes." They have also argued that the widening would not materially relieve the area's traffic situation.

Mr. Jack said he favored studies of the possibility of both an eastbound and a westbound artery in lower Manhattan.

Pending such studies, he said, it would be better to withdraw the Fulton Street proposal. In the meantime, he added, he hoped all of those who have been involved in the widening dispute would have a better understanding of the problem.

The proposal that Mr. Jack withdrew called for widening Fulton Street on its south side from Broadway to Water Street. The project was intended as the first stage of an ultimate widening of Fulton Street from South Street to West Street.

Two major slum clearance cooperative housing projects totaling $61,000,000 in cost in the Rockaways, Queens, were approved by the board.

One was Hammels-Rockaway,

Continued on Page 22, Column 6

Islanders Start Two-Day Celebration and Show of Gratitude on Statehood Vote

ALASKA EXTENDS THE FIRST 'ALOHA'

Wire Comes as Quinn Phones the Result to Honolulu—Rain Falls Symbolically

Continued From Page 1, Col. 8

choked with emotion that he found it hard to speak.

Acting Gov. Edward E. Johnston had an open telephone line from Iolani Palace here to Gov. William F. Quinn in Washington. As Governor Quinn shouted the vote over the phone, at about 9:42 A. M. Hawaii time, a telegram of congratulation was laid before Mr. Johnston.

"We in Alaska," it said, "are overjoyed that Hawaii joins the U. S. A. and fills out the fifty-star flag. Aloha to the Cheechako State."

The message was signed by Col. M. R. Marston, president of the Alaska Committee for Hawaiian Statehood. Colonel Marston headed the major Alaskan celebration at Anchorage last June 30, when the Senate voted statehood to that territory. Mr. Marston was here for several weeks earlier this year to advise Hawaiians.

In other parts of the palace what presumably will be the last territorial House and Senate were in session when the word came from Washington. The two bodies were to join in an official statehood celebration tomorrow.

At the near-by City Hall, Mayor Blaisdell described himself as "sort of weepy." He vigorously rang the Honolulu bell presented to the city from a decommissioned cruiser of that name.

The Royal Hawaiian Band, seated in the City Hall patio, struck up the Hawaiian anthem, "Hawaii Ponoi," while drops of rain drifted through the open roof to the acclaim of the applauding audience. To the Hawaiian, rain is a heaven-sent blessing if it falls on an auspicious occasion.

'Part of States System'

"This is the most momentous event ever to come to pass for Hawaii, as the way is open for us to be a part of the system of states," the Mayor said.

He asked his hearers to step across the street a little later to Kawaiahao Church "to thank God for the wonderful thing that has happened and ask his guidance as we become first-class citizens in a new state—first-class American citizens to further the concept of the American way of life." The Mayor said:

"God bless you and God bless the Congress of the United States. Aloha."

The church to which the Mayor referred is a Congregational body presided over by a Hawaiian, the Rev. Abraham Akaka. He preaches in both Hawaiian and English.

Meanwhile, a helicopter landed at the hall to pick up statehood messages to be carried to the other islands in this Pacific melting pot of races and nationalities.

In office buildings within a few hundred yards, private and semi-public celebrations were under way at the same time.

Business and labor alike applauded. Alexander G. Budge, president of Castle and Cooke, one of the "big five" companies influential in the islands' economy, noted that his company long had advocated statehood. Even Walter F. Dillingham, a leading industrialist who had preached delay in statehood, said he was ready to accept it now that it was the will of the majority under the "American rules of the game."

A thousand or so of Harry Bridges' longshoremen got two days off to help celebrate as work on ships was called off by management. Jack W. Hall, controversial left-wing union organizer—Mr. Bridges' right-hand man in the islands—confided:

"I'm having a drink or two to end an era."

50 STATES, 48 STEPS

Louisiana Must Rearrange Its Marble Staircase

BATON ROUGE, La., March 12 (UPI)—Emile J. Bourg, Supervisor of State Buildings for Louisiana, said today that "we're going to have some trouble finding room for Hawaii."

Mr. Bourg was talking about the marble steps to the Louisiana Capitol, each of which is engraved with the name of a state.

The top step is inscribed "E Pluribus Unum."

Mr. Bourg said the E Pluribus Unum step would be moved higher to make room for Hawaii and Alaska.

Statehood's Tax Cost 68 Cents a Year a Man

HONOLULU, March 12 (AP)—Fiscal experts say Hawaii's change from a territory to a state will cost each taxpayer here an additional 68 cents a year.

The Tax Foundation of Hawaii, a research organization, estimates that it will cost the people about $400,000 more a year to run their government as a state.

But, the foundation says, in the end Hawaii may be better off financially as a state.

With voting representatives in Congress for the first time, the foundation expects increased Federal appropriations for public improvements, harbor development, flood control, highway funds, buildings, slum clearance and the like.

Associated Press Wirephoto

50 IS THEIR FAVORITE NUMBER: Hawaii's Gov. William F. Quinn and Dolores Martin, a Democratic leader of the prospective fiftieth state, celebrating yesterday in Washington over House action on the statehood bill.

Appointed Governor of Hawaii Aims to Become an Elected One

HONOLULU, March 12 (AP)—To William F. Quinn statehood for Hawaii means "equality with fellow Americans."

"It means," he says, "we will have an opportunity to share fully in the national political life. Particularly significant is the added prestige for Hawaii in carrying out our mission as the hub of the Pacific in promoting greater East-West understanding."

Mr. Quinn, 39 years old, is personable and popular. He is Hawaii's twelfth and last appointed Governor and he wants to be its first elected one.

Early last February, Mr. Quinn announced that he would seek the office when Hawaii gained statehood. He startled local politicians, not by his intention, but by the early announcement.

Although a Republican in a place where the majority has lately voted heavily Democratic, Mr. Quinn is rated at least an even chance of making it.

The cause of statehood propelled him into the governorship.

As a member of the Hawaii Statehood Commission in 1957, he went to Washington to testify for statehood before Congressional committees. Apparently, he made a good impression in the Capitol.

In August, 1957, President Eisenhower selected Mr. Quinn from relative political obscurity to be Governor. It was a surprise choice.

He took office in early September, the second youngest Governor of the islands. He was then 38.

Mr. Quinn was keenly aware that he had been appointed to the job and was therefore not necessarily the popular choice. In his inaugural address, he said

"I shall meet all the people of our islands, and I shall, in fact, be their Governor to the best of my ability."

Since then, he has worked a fourteen-hour day, meeting "all the people of our islands." He has hopped up and down the island chain by plane, speaking at political and community functions—singing at public affairs at the slightest request.

A six-footer with a better-than-average Irish tenor voice, Mr. Quinn loves to join in community singing. He was active in amateur theatricals before he became Governor.

For a decade before he was appointed, Mr. Quinn practiced law in Honolulu, served on Republican party committees and devoted a lot of time to the Roman Catholic Church and to civic affairs.

In his only bid for elective office, Mr. Quinn ran for the Territorial Senate in 1956. He lost by 3,000 votes.

Mr. Quinn came to the islands in 1947 from St. Louis, where he spent much of his life. He was born in Rochester, N. Y. He was graduated, summa cum laude, from St. Louis University and received a law degree from Harvard, with cum laude honors.

He was married in 1942 to the former Nancy Witbeck. They have four sons and two daughters.

Even Democrats admit that Mr. Quinn has grown in stature in his year and a half as Hawaii's Governor. He was helped in this by the fact that he took office at a moment when Hawaii was surging ahead politically and economically.

During his tenure, he never stopped working for statehood, and it helped his popularity both at home and in making a name on the mainland.

HAWAII IS VOTED THE 50TH STATE

Continued From Page 1, Col. 8

a majority of voters must vote "yes" on this question:

"Shall Hawaii immediately be admitted into the Union as a state?"

The President has ten days, not counting Sundays, to sign the bill once it reaches him.

After the President signs it the Governor must wait for thirty days before issuing an election proclamation. State officials, two Senators and a Representative would be chosen.

The primary for this election can be set for not less than sixty days or more than ninety days after the proclamation. The election cannot be held until forty days after the primary results are known. Then the President has to issue a proclamation.

The referendum would be held with either the primary or the election.

By keeping strictly to this schedule, it would be possible to add the fiftieth star to the flag by July 4. But Governor Quinn observed that this would be "very difficult."

The House action ended a long struggle by the Pacific islands. On three previous occasions, in 1947, 1950 and 1953, the House approved statehood.

Tributes were paid to Representative Leo W. O'Brien, Democrat of upstate New York, who handled both the Alaskan and Hawaiian statehood measures in the House, and to Senator Henry M. Jackson, Democrat of Washington, who handled the Hawaii bill in the Senate.

Hawaii's supporters brought out crates of leis, the islands' floral necklaces, when the measure passed.

Today's opposition in the House, as it was in the Senate yesterday, came largely but not wholly from the South. Members from Ohio, Missouri, Illinois and elsewhere in the North objected.

A short-cut to the White House for the bill was maneuvered early in today's proceedings. Representative John W. McCormack of Massachusetts, the Democratic leader, obtained consent to put the Senate-approved measure before the House. This meant that the bill would not have to go to a House-Senate conference for adjustments of differences as would be the case if the House passed a separate measure.

Representative W. R. Poage, Democrat of Texas, apparently expecting other Pacific areas to attain statehood later, proposed that any other Pacific islands admitted be made a part of the state of Hawaii. His amendment was shouted down. Mr. Poage later voted for the bill.

CONGRESS DEFINES NEW STATE'S AREA

All Islands of Territory Are Included Except Palmyra—Digest of Provisions

Special to The New York Times.

WASHINGTON, March 12—Congressional approval of the admission of the Territory of Hawaii as the fiftieth state of the Union provides as follows:

It recognizes the State Constitution adopted by Hawaiian referendum to be republican in form and in conformity with the Constitution of the United States. It demands that this always be the case.

It sets the boundaries of the new state in this way:

The State of Hawaii shall consist of all the islands, together with their appurtenant reefs and territorial waters, included within the Territory, except the atoll known as Palmyra Island. This island, far away from Hawaii proper, is owned by a single family and thus was not included in the full statehood set-up.

The new state would not include the Midway Islands, Johnston Island, Sand Island (offshore from Johnston Island), or Kingman Reef and other islands outlying.

Islands in the new state include Hawaii, Maui, Kahoolawe, Lanai, Oahu, Molokai, Kauai, Niihau, Kaula, Nihoa, Necker, French Frigate Shoals, Gardner Pinnacles, Maro Reef, Lisianski I., Laysan I., Pearl and Hermes Reef and Kure.

Homes Act Retained

As to the original acquisition by the United States of the Hawaiian Islands, land would be retained to provide benefits for native-born Hawaiians. These would be included in the retention of the Hawaiian Homes Act of 1920, in which home-owning opportunities and educational facilities would be preserved.

Hawaii would succeed generally to the land titles held by the territory. However, during a five-year period any public lands now controlled by the United States might be set aside for the permanent use of the United States by an act of Congress or by Presidential order. At all times the Federal Government could take over lands required for military purposes.

Hawaiian statehood would not be effected until it had elected its principal officials. Upon the President's approval of a statehood bill, the Governor of Hawaii would issue a proclamation of elections. This proclamation would provide that a primary election be held no less than sixty or more than ninety days later. A general election would be held within forty days after the primary.

'Yes' Vote Needed

At this election the people of Hawaii, by a majority vote, would have to ask specifically for statehood. If the "yes" vote fell below a majority the matter would drop.

At the general election the citizens would elect a Governor, a Lieutenant Governor and a State Legislature. It also would elect two United States Senators and one Representative. When these elections were certified to the President, he could proclaim the entry of the new state.

The Federal court would be maintained, and the territorial courts would transfer to statehood status. The laws passed by Congress in the interests of the Territory of Hawaii would be cut off after two years unless the new state re-enacted them.

The Federal Government would have exclusive jurisdiction over any military installations determined to be critical areas by the President or the Secretary of Defense.

Maritime matters are dealt with extensively, leaving with the Federal Maritime Board the present jurisdiction over water transportation to and from the new state.

The New York Times — March 13, 1959

THE FIFTIETH: The eight largest islands that will make up new state of Hawaii

NO OTHER AREAS NEAR STATEHOOD

Hawaii Is Last of Organized Territories, Status That Precedes Admission

With the admission of Hawaii as a state the United States has no more organized territories—that is, possessions on the road to becoming states.

What is left are the Virgin Islands, the Canal Zone and clusters of islands in the Pacific. Puerto Rico is a free commonwealth in association with the United States.

VIRGIN ISLANDS

The Virgin Islands are an unorganized territory lying east of Puerto Rico in the Caribbean Sea, 1,500 miles southeast of New York. They were purchased from Denmark in 1917 for $25,000,000. Of fifty-odd islands making up the Virgins, the largest are St. Thomas, St. John and St. Croix.

The popul tion is estimated to be 30,061. About 80 per cent of Virgin Islanders are Negroes. Since 1927 the residents have been citizens of the United States. The Government is at St. Thomas and consists of a Governor appointed by the President and a unicameral elected legislature composed of eleven Senators. The islands are under the control of the Department of the Interior. The area of the three main islands is 132 square miles.

The Virgin Islands have beautiful beaches and very little rainfall. Most of their potable water is imported from Puerto Rico. Rum and bay rum are the chief exports.

CANAL ZONE

The Canal Zone is a strategic United States military reservation on the Isthmus of Panama, which is cut across by the Panama Canal. The canal connects the Caribbean with the Gulf of Panama on the Pacific.

The zone is under United States jurisdiction by treaty with the Republic of Panama.

The treaty was signed in 1904 after the United States had helped Panama maintain her newly won independence from Colombia.

The zone is administered by the Canal Zone Government and the Panama Canal Company. The Governor of the zone and the president of the company are the same person. He reports to the Secretary of the Army.

Exclusive of military personnel, the population is about 39,000, mostly employes and dependents of armed forces personnel.

GUAM

Guam is the largest of the Mariana Islands in the Pacific. An unincorporated territory, it was ceded to the United States by Spain in 1898, after the Spanish-American War.

Guam is the chief Pacific base of the Strategic Air Command. It is a little more than 5,000 miles from San Francisco. It is about thirty miles long and from four to eight miles wide.

The island is under the jurisdiction of the Interior Department and has a governor, appointed by the President, and a twenty-one-member elected unicameral legislature. Guamanians are American citizens but do not vote for President. The native population (otal population 37,568) are of Malay stock and are called Chamorros.

AMERICAN SAMOA

American Samoa is composed of the seven eastern islands of the Samoan group, 2,300 miles southwest of Hawaii. The islands became a United States possession under a convention with Britain and Germany in 1899. Pago Pago, the capital city on the island of Tutuila, had been ceded to the United States in 1872 by the native king.

American Samoa is administered by the Interior Department, which appoints the gover- ture. The Population is about nor. It has a bicameral legisla- 20,000. The residents are mostly Polynesians, and are nationals of the United States. Nationals owe allegiance to the United States but do not enjoy all the privileges of citizenship.

WAKE ISLAND

Wake Island, lying on the Hawaii-Hong Kong route 2,000 miles west of Hawaii, was annexed from Spain in 1899. With the sister islands, Wilkes and Peale, the group covers about 2,000 acres.

MIDWAY ISLANDS

The Midways, 1,200 miles northeast of Hawaii, were discovered by Americans in 1859 and acquired in 1867. They were the scene of one of the great naval engagements of World War II, in which the United States Navy defeated the Japanese.

OTHER ISLANDS

Johnston Island, Sand Island and Kingman Reef are south of the Hawaiian group. They are under Navy control. Howland, Jarvis and Baker Islands, also south of Hawaii, are under the jurisdiction of the Interior Department. The latter three have been uninhabited since World War II.

Canton and Enderbury Islands, in the Phoenix Group in the Pacific, are under joint control and administration of the United States and Britain. Canton is an airstop between Hawaii and Australia-New Zealand. Enderbury is uninhabited.

The Caroline, Marshall and Mariana Islands (except for Guam), formerly under Japanese mandate, are administered by the United States under a United Nations trusteeship.

PUERTO RICO

Puerto Rico achieved commonwealth status in 1952 by Congressional resolution.

The island was ceded by Spain after the Spanish-American War. Puerto Ricans were granted American citizeznship in 1917 but do not vote for President unless they move to the mainland.

Puerto Rico's chief executive is a governor elected by direct vote. The country has a bicameral Legislative Assembly, consisting of a Senate and a House of Representatives.

The population is 2,258,000. The prevailing language is Spanish.

Pure Hawaiians Vanishing Race; Japanese Now Dominate Islands

By MURRAY SCHUMACH

Pure-bred Hawaiians, the descendants of the Polynesians, have become almost a novelty in Hawaii and may be extinct within a century.

But numerous other racial varieties, all unknown in Hawaii when Capt. James Cook landed there in 1778, live in a profusion as dramatic as the contrast between the island chain's lush foliage and its neon lights.

"In few places," according to Dr. Harry L. Shapiro, chairman of the anthropology department at the American Museum of Natural History, "has so relatively great a revolution in population taken place as in the Hawiian Islands within the brief span of a century and a half."

When Captain Cook arrived in Hawaii, he found a healthy population of about 400,000 living in easily constructed thatch huts, making clothes of the bark of mulberry trees, feeding on pork, fish, vegetables and fruit.

By 1860, the population was down to less than 70,000. Today, about 640,000 persons, including 60,000 military personnel, probably the most in its history, live in the islands.

The story of the vanishing Hawaiian and the rising population is rooted in economics, disease, war and social custom. These are the forces that have made the population about 38 per cent Japanese; 20 per cent European and American; 15 per cent Hawaiian of mixed descent; 13 per cent Filipino; 7 per cent Chinese; 3 per cent Puerto Rican and Korean and the remaining 3 per cent Hawaiian.

Up to 1820, there was little mixing between Europeans and Hawaiians. Those who followed the early explorers were mainly whalers and sandalwood traders.

However, the comparatively small number of Caucasians brought to Hawaii a collection of European diseases, such as cholera, measles, smallpox, syphilis and alcoholism that almost ravaged the population. By 1823, according to one estimate, the population was down to 142,000.

To make matters worse, war broke out as Kamehameha I began his conquest of the islands. This added scourge brought the population down to 69,000 by 1860, of whom more than 2,500 were European.

The first strong influence from the United States came early in this decline in the form of missionaries. In 1820 the first missionaries came from Boston, the vanguard of more than a dozen parties of missionaries in the next twenty years.

"Very early," according to Dr. Shapiro, "the affairs of the islands fell into the hands of the missionaries who attempted to re-create another New England in this tropical setting."

By the middle of the nineteenth century the Americans were the largest of the foreign groups. But the growth of the sugar industry changed this quickly.

Cheap, hard-working labor was needed in large numbers to work in the cane fields. From 1870 to 1880 thousands of Chinese were imported. And, in search of the profits of sugar, came Portuguese and Scandinavians.

Toward the end of the century, the Japanese wave of sugar workers began arriving in force so that by 1900 they had become the dominant group.

Then, in this century, labor was imported from Korea, Puerto Rico and, more recently, from the Philippines.

Since most of the imported workers were young, single men and the Hawaiian women were not prejudiced against marriage to foreigners, the pure Hawaiians began disappearing rapidly.

One consistent pattern that forced new sources for labor was the tendency to leave manual work after a generation on the land. First the Chinese became merchants and professional men. Then the Japanese began to regard agricultural work as an inferior pursuit.

Despite the widespread intermarriage and the variety of racial stocks, integration is far from complete. Thus, though schools are integrated, some residential areas are restricted and so are some clubs.

HAWAII MAY BUOY KEY SENATE BLOC

New State Expected to Join Western Group and Hasten Decline of Southerners

By RUSSELL BAKER

Special to The New York Times.

WASHINGTON, Mar. 12—One of the immediate implications of Hawaii's prospective admission as the fiftieth state is a hastening of the decline of Southern power in the Senate and a strengthening of the Senate's new power bloc, the West.

This has been a gradual shifting of the traditional centers of Senate power that has been proceeding almost unnoticed for the last five years.

Now, with Hawaii's admission due to bring the Senate membership to 100, the South, which has historically looked to the Senate as its chief stronghold in the American system, sees its forces cut to a mere 20 per cent of the membership. And even this group can no longer be relied upon to vote as a unit on such fundamental issues as civil rights.

While this has been happening, the Western states, with their own distinctive interests and problems, have been emerging as a power now equal to the old Southern group in size and cohesion.

Can Swing Both Ways

Although the seniority system still gives the Southern bloc authority out of proportion to its size, the Western states, now camped en masse within the Democratic party, wield a comparable influence because of their position at the fulcrum of the Senate.

On issues that divide the Southern bloc and the men from the industrial states the Westerners are for the most part indifferent. Their interests—reclamation, irrigation, development, power—can be served by entering into coalition with either the liberal or conservative wing of the party.

Thus, they form a Senate balance wheel whose movements can determine the outcome of most sensitive issues. Inevitably, this puts them in an enviable bargaining position.

In its heyday, the Southern bloc was a hard core of twenty-two votes from the eleven states of the old Confederacy.

Twenty-two votes in a body of ninety-six men was still less than a quarter of the troops, but when they were skilled veterans and could easily make common cause with the economic conservatives, they spoke with a mighty voice. By adding four non-Southerners to the total membership, their voice is diminished.

Defections Arise

This loss has been compounded by an erosion from within. The first overt sign of the break came with the Southern Manifesto of 1956 attacking the Supreme Court. The two Tennesseeans—Estes Kefauver and Albert Gore—and Lyndon B. Johnson of Texas, the Senate leader, refused to sign it.

The second significant crack appeared during the fight on the Civil Rights Act of 1957. Five men from the old Confederacy voted for the bill, although one—George A. Smathers of Florida—reversed himself when the conference report finally came before the Senate. The four others were Senators Gore, Kefauver, Johnson and Ralph W. Yarborough, also of Texas.

The third break occurred during the fight to curb unlimited debate in the Senate in January of this year. Eight men from the old Confederacy broke from the Southern position and voted for a slight tightening.

Again they included the two Tennesseeans, the two Texans and Senator Smathers. This time, however, their ranks were swelled by Senator Spessard L. Holland of Florida and Senators Sam J. Ervin Jr. and B. Everett Jordan, both of North Carolina.

Thus, within the last few years the once-solid South with its twenty-two votes has shrunk to a hard core of fourteen militants with six or eight fringe adherents. The filibuster is now virtually useless to them. And with Hawaii about to swell the ranks of their civil rights opposition, they find themselves increasingly beleaguered.

Don't Say Uke, Say Ook When You Go to Hawaii

HONOLULU, March 12 (AP)—To pronounce Hawaiian words, just sound the consonants as they sound in English and the vowels as they sound in Latin.

The vowel sounds are A as in army, E as in they, I as in machine, O as in no and U as in too. Hawaiian has only seven consanants—H, K, L, M, N, P and W.

Here is the way to pronounce the names of the main islands and some other words:

HAWAII—Hah-wy-ee.
MAUI—Mow-ee.
KAUAI—Cow-eye.
OAHU—Oah-hoo.
MOLOKAI—Mo-lo-kye.
ALOHA—(welcome)—A-lo-hah.
MAHALO (thank you)—Ma-hah-lo.
LUAU (feast)—Lu-ow.
PAU (finished)—Pow.
WAIKIKI (a beach)—Wy-kee-kee.
WAHINE (woman)—Wah-heeney.
UKELELE—Oo-kuh-lay-lee.
MALIHINI (newcomer)—Mah-luh-hee-nee.
KAMAAINA (oldtimer)—Kah-mah-eye-nah.
MAUNA LOA (a volcano)—Moan-ah-lo-ah.
KAMEHAMEHA, (Hawaiian king)—Kah-may-hah-may-hah.
KALAKAUA (main street in Waikiki)—Cal-ah-cow-ah.

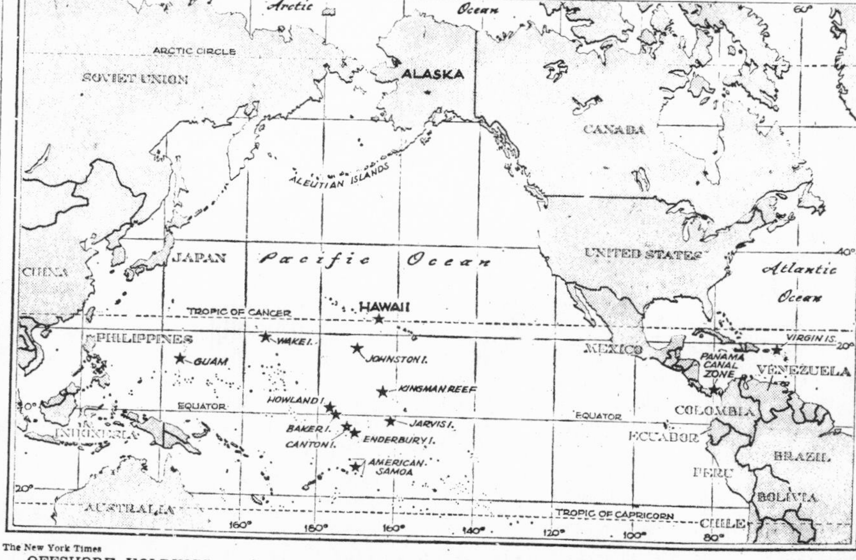

The New York Times — March 13, 1959

OFFSHORE HOLDINGS: The United States' outlying possessions including Hawaii are shown by stars

"All the News That's Fit to Print"

The New York Times.

LATE CITY EDITION

U. S. Weather Bureau Report (Page 66) forecasts: Mostly fair, seasonably cold today and tonight. Fair, warmer tomorrow. Temp. range 38—25; yesterday: 35—31.

VOL. CX . No. 37,601. NEW YORK, WEDNESDAY, JANUARY 4, 1961. 10 cents beyond 50-mile zone from New York City except on Long Island. Higher in air delivery cities. FIVE CENTS

U. S. BREAKS ITS DIPLOMATIC TIES WITH CUBA AND ADVISES AMERICANS TO LEAVE ISLAND; EISENHOWER CITES 'VILIFICATION' BY CASTRO

CONGRESS OPENS WITH CONFLICTS ON PROCEDURES

Filibuster Curbs Sought in Senate—Colmer's Purge Is Believed Certain

By RUSSELL BAKER

Special to The New York Times.

WASHINGTON, Jan. 3—The Eighty-seventh Congress convened today amid clashes in both houses over rules of procedure.

In the Senate, proponents of tighter curbs on the rules of debate opened a battle to make it easier to cut off filibusters. The skirmishes ended inconclusively with a decision to postpone further action until tomorrow.

In the House of Representatives, Speaker Sam Rayburn was reported to have completed arrangements for removing Representative William M. Colmer, Democrat of Mississippi, from the Rules Committee and replacing him with a member who would reinforce the Texas Democrat's leadership.

Pledges by Leaders

The Senate session was marked by a clash between Vice President Nixon and Richard B. Russell. The Georgia Democrat, leader of the Southern bloc, normally gets deference from the chair. Twice, however, Mr. Nixon used his gavel against him with authority.

In the House's traditional opening procedures, Mr. Rayburn and Charles A. Halleck of Indiana, the Republican minority leader, made pledges to work for responsible government.

Behind the scenes, however, a liberal-conservative fight for control of the Rules Committee continued unabated. Mr. Rayburn was assured of the necessary votes in the Democratic Committee on Committees to help purge Mr. Colmer.

This presumably would create a Rules Committee majority favoring critical parts of President-elect John F. Kennedy's program. Capitol observers described the Rayburn plan as "replacing a 'no' man with a 'yes' man."

Friction in Caucus

Meanwhile, Senate Republicans joined Democrats in a standing ovation for the new and only woman member on the Democratic side, Mrs. Maurine Neuberger of Oregon.

Mr. Nixon's duty on the rostrum was to administer the oath to each Senator elected in November.

A Senate Democratic caucus this morning brought more friction. As expected, Mike Mansfield of Montana was elected to succeed Vice President-elect Lyndon B. Johnson as majority leader, and Hubert H. Humphrey of Minnesota was named assistant leader.

Mr. Mansfield, however, created a surprise when he announced that he wanted the

Continued on Page 24, Column 3

Legislators Choose Mahoney, Carlino

By WARREN WEAVER Jr.

Special to The New York Times.

ALBANY, Jan. 3—Senators and Assemblymen descended on the capital tonight to prepare for the opening of the 1961 legislative session here tomorrow.

The Republican majorities in the Senate and Assembly held separate caucuses to choose their leaders and housekeeping officers for the next two years.

The Democrats chose their own nominees at separate sessions, but since the Republicans control both houses their nominations were equivalent to election.

There were no surprises. Senator Walter J. Mahoney of Buffalo was chosen temporary President of the Senate, the official title of the majority leader, a post he has held for the last seven years. In the Assembly, Joseph F.

Continued on Page 14, Column 1

L.I.R.R. SEEKS AID TO AVERT 'CRISIS'

Says It Will Be Unable to Meet April Payroll—Two Rail Walkouts Cited

By CLARENCE DEAN

The Long Island Rail Road appealed yesterday for financial help to avert what it said was an impending crisis.

A statement by Thomas M. Goodfellow, president of the line, declared that unless the help was forthcoming the railroad would be unable to meet its payroll by the last week in April.

The present indications, Mr. Goodfellow said, are that the carrier's deficit by the end of this year will exceed $4,000,000.

If there is no financial help, Mr. Goodfellow said, three alternatives will arise: "a whopping fare increase," a cut in maintenance "to rock bottom" or "an arbitrary 12 per cent slash in the number of commuter trains." He declined to suggest specifically what kind of financial help the road wanted.

He attributed the railroad's predicament to unforeseen emergencies, chiefly a twenty-six-day strike on the Long Island last summer and a subsequent twelve-day shutdown of Pennsylvania Station as a result of a strike against the Pennsylvania Railroad.

For last October and Novem-

Continued on Page 67, Column 2

U. S. SAYS SOVIET AND RED VIETNAM AID LAOS REBELS

Asserts 180 Air Drops Were Made in Nineteen Days—President Sees Advisers

Text of the State Department statement is on Page 8.

By WILLIAM J. JORDEN

Special to The New York Times.

WASHINGTON, Jan. 3—The United States Government charged today that the Soviet Union and North Vietnam were guilty of "extensive participation" in military operations against the Government of Laos.

To bolster its charge, the State Department released a listing of Communist supply flights over Laos, serial numbers of Soviet planes engaged in the airlift, dates and places of air drops to the anti-Government rebels and other details.

The department said the two Communist powers had carried out more than 180 air sorties into Laos in the nineteen days from Dec. 15 through Jan. 2 to drop supplies and personnel to pro-Communist forces. It said that "substantial numbers" of North Vietnamese had been parachuted into Laos to help the rebels.

Elaboration Is Declined

A department spokesman would not elaborate on the numbers. Nor would he use the term "aggression" to describe the Communists' activities.

The charges against the Communist states were attributed to "hard evidence," however. Today's bill of particulars detailed earlier general charges of Communist intervention in Laos.

The catalogue of Communist involvement should be read, officials said, with the strong statement issued by the United States Government three days ago in mind. On Saturday the State Department warned that the Government would take "the most serious view" of intervention in Laos by the Chinese Communists, North Vietnamese "or others" in support of the anti-Government rebels.

Today's Government statement on Laos was issued soon after a special briefing on the Laos situation for President Eisenhower by his top diplomatic, military and intelligence advisers. It was the third White House conference on Laos in four days.

On Capitol Hill a group of House members also received an up-to-date report on developments in Laos. John M.

Continued on Page 8, Column 5

Associated Press Radiophoto

NO ENTRY: Portion of the crowd in front of the U. S. Embassy in Havana as Cubans sought visas yesterday. When they discovered that the visa section of the embassy had been closed, there were cries of protest and dismay.

Belgian Assembly Defeats Socalists; Violence Continues

By HARRY GILROY

Special to The New York Times.

BRUSSELS, Belgium, Jan. 3—The Belgian House of Representatives rejected today a motion to withdraw the proposed new law to raise taxes and tighten up the social security administration, against which 500,000 Socialist workers are striking.

Leo Collard, president of the Socialist party, and Achille van Acker, a former Premier, presented the motion. It was defeated by a vote of 121 to 83 with 1 abstention.

The House gave the Government three votes of confidence before adjourning at 8 P. M. until 2 P. M. tomorrow. The votes followed three critical speeches by Socialists and one by a Communist member on the conduct of public affairs and on the treatment of strikers.

The votes were taken in a calm parliamentary atmosphere that contrasted with an unruly session in which the measure was last discussed Dec. 23, and even more with the street demonstrations that turned up new

Continued on Page 12, Column 3

CASTRO'S CABINET DRAFTING A REPLY

Emergency Session Called After U. S. Acts—Premier Says 'Cuba Is Alert'

By R. HART PHILLIPS

Special to The New York Times.

HAVANA, Jan. 3—Premier Fidel Castro, President Osvaldo Dorticós Torrado and members of the Cuban Cabinet met in the Presidential Palace tonight at 10:30 to draft a reply to the United States' break in diplomatic relations with Cuba.

The reply will be delivered to the United States Embassy here soon, according to a statement by Dr. Carlos Olivares, Cuba's Foreign Under Secretary.

The Cabinet meeting ended without any announcement.

The Cuban people learned of the United States move tonight when the announcement was made over all radio stations.

The announcer said that "according to cables received President Eisenhower had broken off diplomatic relations with Cuba on the pretext of the order of the Revolutionary Government that he withdraw his 300 spies in the embassy from Cuba."

"Being discovered in his criminal plans of terrorism Eisenhower has responded with the habitual shamelessness of imperialism," the announcer declared.

The announcer said the radio would keep the people informed

Continued on Page 3, Column 5

U. S. Will Help Evacuate Its Citizens Living in Cuba

Special to The New York Times.

HAVANA, Wednesday, Jan. 4—The United States Embassy last night urged all Americans in Cuba to leave the island. A statement issued by the press attaché said that "all American citizens are urged to depart from Cuba immediately unless compelling reasons oblige them to remain."

The embassy has arranged for a ferry of the West Indies Fruit and Steamship Company to sail from Havana to West Palm Beach today and Friday to evacuate the Americans.

Additional extra flights to Miami from the José Marti International Airport will augment the facilities for departure today and tomorrow.

Cuba Guarantees Safety

The Castro regime, in a note delivered this morning to the United States Chargé d' Affaires, Daniel M. Braddock, pledged the "most absolute guarantees" for the safety of all American citizens in Cuba, including diplomatic or consular officials "as well as residents or tourists."

Meanwhile, thousands of Cubans who for months have been seeking visas to the United States were dismayed yesterday by the Cuban-United States crisis.

A long line of Cubans appeared as usual at the United States Embassy early in the morning after Premier Fidel Castro had ordered a cut in the embassy staff. They found the

Continued on Page 3, Column 6

KENNEDY AVOIDS ROLE IN DECISION

Rusk Turns Down Herter Move to Link Democrats to Break With Cuba

By JAMES RESTON

Special to The New York Times.

WASHINGTON, Jan. 3—The Eisenhower Administration took full responsibility tonight for the diplomatic break with Cuba.

Secretary of State Christian A. Herter yesterday informed Dean Rusk, who will succeed him in less than three weeks, of the President's decision, but he did not seek the advice of the leaders of the incoming Administration on what should be done.

Mr. Herter asked Mr. Rusk whether the incoming Democratic Administration wished to associate itself with the break. Mr. Rusk replied after consultations with President-elect John F. Kennedy that in the absence of complete information on all the relevant factors the new Administration did not feel that it could participate in the decision.

Both parties thus found themselves in an extremely delicate position. The Republicans were well aware of the fact that they were taking a decision that would greatly complicate the problems of the Kennedy Administration in the early days of its responsibility after the inauguration Jan. 20.

At the same time, they did not feel that they could avoid responsibility for reacting quickly to Premier Fidel Castro's demand that the United States diplomatic mission in Cuba should be reduced to eleven persons.

The Democrats were equally

Continued on Page 4, Column 3

REGIME IS SCORED

People Suffer Under 'Yoke of Dictator,' President Says

Texts of President's statement and notes are on Page 3.

By E. W. KENWORTHY

Special to The New York Times.

WASHINGTON, Jan. 3—The United States formally terminated diplomatic and consular relations with Cuba tonight.

President Eisenhower announced the break with the Government of Premier Fidel Castro in a statement issued at the White House at 8:30 o'clock.

The break came a day and a half after the Cuban Government had delivered a note to the United States Embassy in Havana demanding that the staff of the embassy and the consulate there be reduced to eleven persons within forty-eight hours.

The President said in his statement:

"There is a limit to what the United States in self-respect can endure. That limit has now been reached."

Normal Situation 'Impossible'

The action of the Castro Government, the President said, "can have no other purpose than to render impossible the conduct of normal diplomatic relations with that Government."

Therefore, the President said, he had instructed the Secretary of State to deliver a note to the Cuban Embassy here announcing the formal ending of relations.

The President added that "this calculated action on the part of the Castro Government is only the latest of a long series of harassments, baseless accusations and vilification."

President Eisenhower said in his statement that the friendship of the United States for the Cuban people "is not affected" by the breaking of diplomatic relations with the Castro regime.

Sympathy Expressed

"It is my hope and my conviction," the President said, "that in the not too distant future it will be possible for the historic friendship between us once again to find its reflection in normal relations of every sort."

"Meanwhile," the President said, "our sympathy goes out to the people of Cuba now suffering under the yoke of a dictator."

The United States requested the Government of Cuba, in turn, to withdraw "as soon as possible" the entire Cuban personnel in the Cuban Embassy in Washington and in all Cuban consular offices in the United States.

In a note to the Cuban Government, Secretary of State Christian A. Herter stated that it was requesting the Government of Switzerland to assume

Continued on Page 3, Column 1

I.T.T. Voices Hopes On H-Bomb Power

By GENE SMITH

Experiments that might lead to a "low-cost nuclear fusion process" were announced here yesterday by the International Telephone and Telegraph Corporation.

No details were given, but the experiments apparently deal with a concept that many nuclear experts have not considered promising. The company said the experiments had been conducted "for a number of years" but made no claim of success.

The problem of producing a controlled and sustained nuclear fusion, and thus harnessing the reaction of the hydrogen bomb, is the goal of many experiments being conducted both here and abroad.

Temperatures of millions of degrees Centigrade are neces-

Continued on Page 10, Column [illegible]

Associated Press Wirephoto

WELCOME TO WASHINGTON: Lyndon B. Johnson, right, Vice President-elect, re- [illegible] A. Blakey, successor as [illegible] Senate. With them at [illegible] A. Smith 2d of [illegible] Kennedy's successor.

Hammarskjold Flying to Congo To Try to End Factional Strife

By JAMES FERON

Special to The New York Times.

UNITED NATIONS, N. Y., Jan. 3—Secretary General Dag Hammarskjold left for the Congo today in an attempt to end the civil disorders threatening the work of the United Nations force there.

His departure, which had been delayed a day to study disorders in Kivu Province, remained uncertain until two hours before he left because of the changing situation in Laos.

At New York International Airport, Mr. Hammarskjold said he did not intend to visit Laos on this trip but that he might return to the United Nations earlier than he had planned if the Laotian situation required his presence here.

The Secretary General was warmly applauded by a large crowd in the main lobby of the airline terminal. His plane left for Leopoldville at 5:55 P. M.

He will spend two days in the Congo and will talk with members of the eleven-nation United Nations Conciliation Commission, the Congo Government and United Nations force leaders. Technically, the visit is only a side trip on the way to South Africa, where the Secretary General will spend eight days studying racial segregation.

However, United Nations sources suggested that Mr. Hammarskjold's principal concern now was the "developing civil war" in the Congo. They felt that continuing strife between opposing Congolese factions could put the United Nations force in an untenable

Continued on Page 12, Column 5

Cuban U.N. Charge To Get Stern Reply

By LINDESAY PARROTT

Special to The New York Times.

UNITED NATIONS, N. Y., Jan. 3—The United States will follow up its break in relations with Cuba by sharply rejecting in the Security Council tomorrow Cuban charges of American "aggressive intentions."

Representatives of Western delegations here tonight expressed some surprise at the United States severance of relations. The American delegation, during the day, had been in contact with allied nations over the Cuban charges. It was understood, however, that the question discussed was largely whether opposition should be offered to Cuba's request to put the issue on the agenda.

The Council is to meet at 10:30 A. M. at the request of Foreign Minister Raul Roa of

Continued on Page 4, Column 4

NEWS INDEX

U. S. Severs Diplomatic Relations With Cuba and Cites 'Vilification' by Castro

PRESIDENT SCORES REGIME IN HAVANA

Eisenhower Asserts Limits of Nation's Endurance Have Been Reached

Continued From Page 1, Col. 8

diplomatic and consular representation in Cuba on behalf of the United States.

[In Havana the Cuban Government announced it had asked Communist Czechoslovakia to take charge of Cuban affairs in Washington, according to United Press International.]

The note formally breaking relations was addressed to Dr. Armando Florez-Ibarra, chargé d' affaires of the Cuban Embassy here.

In a speech last night, Premier Castro declare that Cuba was reducing its Embassy staff in Washington to eleven, and that the United States had forty-eight hours to do likewise in Havana.

At the outset the Eisenhower Administration hoped that the Castro regime would bring about long-needed reforms in Cuba. On Jan. 21, 1959, it named as Ambassador Philip W. Bonsal, a man of long experience in the hemisphere and with wide sympathies for the social and economic aspirations of Latin Americans.

However, it was less than nine months before the seizure of United States property and anti-American attacks by Premier Castro resulted in the recall of Ambassador Bonsal for consultations.

He returned to Havana, but was summoned home again last January after Premier Castro had charged that he had conspired to bring about the downfall of the regime. Two months later Mr. Bonsal went back to Havana. Finally he was recalled last Oct. 29.

As he arrived in West Palm Beach by boat, Mr. Bonsal said he had returned "for what will apparently be a long stay." He has never gone back.

Cuba has not had an Ambassador in Washington since December, 1959.

In his speech, Premier Castro charged that the Embassy had 300 officials, of whom 80 per cent were spies for the Federal Bureau of Investigation and the Pentagon.

James C. Hagerty, White House press secretary who read the President's statement, refused to answer questions on whether the United States would defend its naval base at Guantanamo Bay if it were attacked.

"I am not going to answer any hypothetical questions," Mr. Hagerty said.

Base Decision Given

However, Joseph W. Reap, State Department press officer, said, "this has no effect at all on the base."

Other State Department officials asserted that the United States had repeatedly stated that it would not consent to unilateral abrogation of the 1903 treaty under which the United States maintains the base. They also emphasized that President Eisenhower had firmly stated the United States would defend the base if it were attacked.

About 3,000 Cubans are employed at the Guantanamo Naval Base. How these Cuban employes will be affected by the break in diplomatic relations could not be ascertained.

The base and its about 5,000 Americans plus bluejackets and officers on visiting vessels of the fleet are dependent upon a water supply that is outside its boundaries. However, the Navy is confident that water could be supplied by tanker should the regular supply be cut off.

Normally, Cuba has had twenty-eight consular offices in seventeen states in the United States. At present, however, there are only thirteen offices operating. These include the consulate at New York.

The United States consular office in Cuba is located at Santiago de Cuba. There is also a consular office connected with the embassy at Havana. There are five employes at Santiago. The consular officers at Havana were included in the seventy-six persons listed at the embassy.

The bulk of the embassy staff made plans to leave Havana by ferry. The personnel will travel to the Florida mainland tomorrow. Their property and belongings will be ferried across later.

Six Latin-American nations have broken relations with the Castro Government. They are the Dominican Republic, Paraguay, Nicaragua, Haiti, Guatemala and Peru.

There have been reports that Uruguay, Venezuela, Argentina and Chile have been considering whether to sever relations.

At the conference of American Foreign Ministers in San Jose, Costa Rica, last August, the United States sought unavailingly to get a condemnation of Cuba. But it succeeded only in getting a resolution against the solicitation and acceptance by any American nation of support from the Chinese-Soviet bloc. This was a reference to Cuba, who had welcomed the offer of Soviet aid "if attacked."

The United States also succeeded in having a special committee named to examine the factual basis of the charges made by the United States and Cuba against each other. The Castro regime has refused to cooperate with this committee.

This refusal has angered several Latin-American countries, the more so since Cuban diplomatic officials in their capitals have been giving money and counsel to Communist and left-wing groups seeking the overthrow of elected governments.

It was noticeable today that the United States chose Switzerland, rather than any Latin-American country to represent its interests in Cuba.

United States relations with the Castro regime have been stormy almost from the time he took power on Jan. 1, 1959. Before the first year was out, he began confiscating the property of United States firms and citizens.

The total value of United States-owned holdings in Cuba was nearly $1,000,000,000. Virtually all of this has been seized. Although the Castro Government promised to pay for this property in 4½ per cent bonds maturing in twenty-five years, no bond has ever been delivered, or even seen.

Negotiations Not Scheduled

Repeatedly the United States sent notes to Havana, affirming its support of real agrarian reform and asking only that compensation be made for the seizures. The Castro Government finally agreed to negotiations, but has steadily refused to name a time.

Last July, the United States cut off further purchases of Cuban sugar. Under the Sugar Act, Cuba had received a privileged position in the United States market. She supplied roughly one-third of United States consumption.

Cuba not only benefited by the 2 cent a pound premium all producers receive in the United States market, but she also enjoyed a lower import tax than other foreign suppliers.

The United States finally cut off Cuban sugar after Cuba had negotiated large barter sales to the Soviet Union and Communist China. The Soviet Union has agreed to buy 1,000,000 tons a year for five years, plus 700,000 tons cut from this year's quota in the United States. Communist China has agreed to buy 1,000,000 tons next year, and 500,000 tons a year for the following four years.

Last October the United States embargoed all exports to Cuba except food and medical supplies in retaliation for the uncompensated seizures.

The breaking of relations was received uncritically for the most part on Capitol Hill.

Senator J. W. Fulbright, Democrat of Arkansas, Chairman of the Senate Foreign Relations Committee, said, "we certainly had sufficient provocation."

Senator Mike Mansfield, Democrat of Montana, new majority leader, said, "I'm not surprised. We've been building up to it for a long time."

Senator Henry M. Jackson, Democrat of Washington, chairman of the Democratic National Committee, said, "it was only a question of time."

However, there was a feeling among some Western diplomats here that the decision was a mistake. It was their view that Premier Castro's order last night was designed to provoke the United States into breaking relations, and that the Administration had accommodated him.

There was also some feeling in Western diplomatic circles that the United States might have put itself in an awkward position just before tomorrow's consideration by the United Nations Security Council of Cuba's charges that the United States planned to intervene militarily in Cuba.

The United States action, some diplomats thought, might lead some newly emerging nations to believe there was some basis for the Cuban charges.

State Department officials did not share these views however. It was their opinion that the Cuban Foreign Minister Dr. Raul Roa, had nothing to back up his charges and that he would merely rehash "old stuff" about United States "imperialism."

High State Department officials deliberated most of the day on whether to recommend to Secretary Herter and President Eisenhower a break in relations.

They considered, it was said, whether it was not better to endure the insults to have some diplomatic observers on the scene.

They also considered whether Premier Castro might follow a break in relations by ordering the surrender of Guantanamo.

Finally, it was said, they considered the humanitarian question of Cuban refugees who have been queuing up before the United States consulate to obtain visas to the United States. In the last five months 34,502 have received visas.

Bossi to Represent U. S.

WASHINGTON, Jan. 3 (AP)—The Swiss Ambassador in Havana, Walter Bossi, will handle United States business under the arrangement announced today in the wake of the end of diplomatic relations between the United States and Cuba.

United Press International Telephoto

LIGHTS BURN LATE at the Cuban Embassy in Washington after announcement that the U. S. was breaking diplomatic relations with Cuba. Policeman is on duty at entrance.

CASTRO'S CABINET DRAFTING A REPLY

Continued From Page 1, Col. 5

and alert. The national anthem was played over all stations and employes of all radio stations pledged "to defend with our lives the national sovereignty of Cuba."

The Castro order reducing the staff of the United States Embassy and Consulate in Havana was received at the embassy at 1:20 A. M.

The note said the Cuban Government had decided that only eleven persons could remain at the Cuban Embassy in Washington and that only eleven could stay on at the United States Embassy in Havana.

A forty-eight-hour period was set to "facilitate the departure of the persons who for this reason must abandon the national territory."

The note followed a speech by Premier Fidel Castro last night in which he charged that the United States Embassy was a center of counter-revolutionary activities.

A seven-hour parade yesterday celebrating the second anniversary of the Castro regime was highlighted by a display of new arms from the Soviet Union. The Premier asserted that a United States invasion was "imminent."

Castro Says 'Cuba Is Alert'

HAVANA, Jan. 3 (AP)—The break in diplomatic relations brought this terse comment tonight from Premier Fidel Castro: "Cuba is Alert."

The Premier made the comment as he emerged from the Presidential Palace where he attended a reception for visiting foreign delegations.

Asked if he knew that the United States had broken diplomatic relations with Cuba, he replied, "yes."

Asked for comment, he said: "I don't have to comment. Cuba is alert." Then he sped off to an undisclosed destination with Capt. Antonio Nunez Jimenez, chief of the Cuban Agrarian Reform Institute.

In another development, three Americans, two of them employes of the United States Embassy, were held in jail tonight after an argument with the Cuban police over a theft accusation against a Cuban.

The Americans were Stewart H. Adams of Bisbee, Ariz., a United States Treasury agent at the embassy; Miss Frances Simopolous of Boston, Mass., an embassy secretary, and Tony Ferrante of Los Angeles, Calif., whose dairy property in Cuba was recently seized.

The arrests appeared to have no connection with the break in diplomatic relations. It was expected the trio would be released soon.

An embassy spokesman said the three went to police headquarters to lodge a complaint about a theft of furniture from Mr. Adam's home.

The spokesman said an argument developed and military investigators lodged the trio in jail.

COLOMBIA IS ALARMED

Stirred By U. S.-Cuban Break —Naming of Envoy Put Off

BOGOTA, Colombia, Jan. 3 (AP)—Colombian officials said tonight their Government had received with alarm the United States break of diplomatic relations with Cuba.

It was learned, meanwhile, that Colombia would not appoint a new ambassador to Cuba for the time being.

The Foreign Minister, Julio César Turbay Ayala, declined to comment on a proposal made by some newspapers to break relations with Cuba.

AMERICANS URGED TO EVACUATE CUBA

Continued From Page 1, Col. 6

visa section closed. There were cries of protest and dismay and some wept.

Appointments had been made by the embassy for as far ahead as March of 1962, it was said.

All the consuls were said to be preparing to leave today.

The note to the United States early today was signed by Dr. Carlos Olivares, Cuba's Acting Foreign Minister. It said that Cuba would, if requested, grant a "reasonable period" for officials of the United States Embassy to leave the island.

On Monday night, Cuba told the embassy to send home most of its staff within forty-eight hours. This provoked the United States to break relations completely.

United States officials will be stationed at the ferryboat dock and airport here to facilitate the evacuation of American citizens. The officials will provide any special documents required by the travelers.

All United States citizens wishing to return to their homeland were told to be prepared to present embassy officials with evidence of their United States citizenship.

3,000 American Residents

WASHINGTON, Jan. 3 (AP)—The State Department estimated today that 3,000 to 3,500 United States civilians still resided in Cuba.

The department disclosed its request to those Americans to return home shortly after the White House had announced the severing of diplomatic relations with the Government of Premier Fidel Castro.

The remaining American residents of the island are largely business men, missionaries, engineers and technicians.

A department spokesman explained that the severing of diplomatic relations did not mean that United States citizens must leave Cuba, where many have lived for several decades. But they are being urged to leave, and the United States Government might assist in the evacuation if necessary.

The break in diplomatic relations does not automatically stop all travel between the countries. There were very few restrictions on such travel by Americans to and from Cuba until recently, when the Cuban Government began requiring a United States passport and a Cuban visa for visitors from the United States.

The closing of the United States Embassy in Cuba, which will be an immediate result of the severence of diplomatic relations, will leave American civilians with no direct source of help to get out of Cuba.

Status of Base at Guantanamo Is Not Expected to Be Altered

Defense officials in Washington indicated last night that there was no immediate likelihood of a change in the status of the United States' naval base at Guantanamo Bay, despite the severing of relations with Cuba.

The big naval installation, at the eastern tip of Cuba, has been in United States hands since 1903.

Rear Admiral Allen Smith Jr., commander of the Caribbean Sea Frontier, speaking by telephone from his headquarters at San Juan, Puerto Rico, said that there had been no reports of Cuban demonstrations near the base and that he expected none.

The United States' possession of the 28,000-acre base—whose area is about one third larger than Manhattan Island—is guaranteed by a treaty with the Cuban Republic signed in 1903 and renewed in 1934.

The consent of both Governments is required to change the agreement. President Eisenhower announced on Nov. 1 that this country would not waive its rights and would defend the base in the event of an attack.

The Cuban President, Osvaldo Dorticos Torrado, replied that his nation would never order such an attack, since it might serve as a pretext for a United States invasion of Cuba, but would attempt to take over Guantanamo legally.

The original treaty set an annual rental of $2,000 in gold. The low figure was a gesture of Cuban gratitude to this country for its having helped the Cubans to gain independence from Spain. Last year, for the first time, the rental payment was refused by the Cuban Government.

3,000 Cubans Work at Base

Despite many angry official exchanges, about 3,000 Cuban workers continue to report daily for their jobs in the naval base. They are covered by United States Civil Service regulations and some have been employed there for as long as thirty-five years.

Their total weekly payroll of $125,000 has already attracted the attention of Premier Fidel Castro. He has been trying, with small success, to persuade them to convert their dollars into pesos at the official one-for-one rate. On the black market the peso is worth about 28 cents.

Admiral Smith indicated that he thought the diplomatic break would not close the base to the workers and that the Cuban Government would not force them to leave their jobs.

However, since last summer none of the United States servicemen or their dependents stationed at Guantanamo has been permitted to go beyond the seven-foot, double fence that bounds the base. The Navy action followed a series of incidents in near-by towns that had for decades been happy "liberty" ports.

Nevertheless, Admiral Smith reported that morale on the base was high. Navy wives hold picnics amid tropical foliage and their children attend primary and high school. The men participate in an extensive sports program.

The Defense Department reported last night that about 1,550 sailors and Marines and 3,200 dependents lived on the base. Several months ago the United States formed a reinforced Marine battalion of 1,800 men that has been operating with the fleet in Caribbean waters.

When 1,450 members of the unit were landed at Guantanamo for week-end shore leave last November, the Cuban Government raised the cry of "invasion." However, the men returned to their ships on schedule.

Defensive drills are held constantly at the base and although its armed strength would be thinly spread around a twenty-seven mile perimeter in the event of attack, Rear Admiral Edward J. O'Donnell, the commander there, has estimated that it could hold out for seventy-two hours—long enough for reinforcements to arrive.

The base, which includes an excellent deep water harbor, had strategic importance early in this century as a guardian of the Windward Passage, one of the approaches to the Panama Canal. During the World War II anti-submarine forces were stationed there.

In recent years the Guantanamo base has become valuable chiefly as a training and refitting area for the Atlantic Fleet. It also has two airstrips from which Navy jet fighters operate. These planes, no longer permitted to fly over Cuban territory, must approach and leave these fields over water.

The Navy values the Guantanamo base at more than $70,000,000, but in terms of the power struggle taking place its worth is regarded as infinitely greater.

Statement and Notes in Cuba Break

Special to The New York Times.

WASHINGTON, Jan. 3—Following are the texts of President Eisenhower's statement tonight announcing a break in diplomatic relations with Cuba, of a Cuban note to the United States and of a United States note to Dr. Armando Florez-Ibarra of the Cuban Embassy:

Eisenhower Statement

Between 1 and 2 o'clock this morning, the Government of Cuba delivered to the United States Chargé d'Affaires ad interim of the United States Embassy in Havana a note stating that the Government of Cuba had decided to limit the personnel of our embassy and consulate in Havana to eleven persons. Forty-eight hours was granted for the departure of our entire staff with the exception of eleven. This unusual action on the part of the Castro Government can have no other purpose than to render impossible the conduct of normal diplomatic relations with that Government.

Accordingly, I have instructed the Secretary of State to deliver a note to the Charge d'Affaires ad interim of Cuba in Washington which refers to the demand of his Government and states that the Government of the United States is hereby formally terminating diplomatic and consular relations with the Government of Cuba. Copies of both notes are being made available to the press.

This calculated action on the part of the Castro Government is only the latest of a long series of harassments, baseless accusations, and vilification. There is a limit to what the United States in self respect can endure. That limit has now been reached. Our friendship for the Cuban people is not affected. It is my hope and my conviction that in the not-too-distant future it will be possible for the historic friendship between us once again to find its reflection in normal relations of every sort. Meanwhile, our sympathy goes out to the people of Cuba now suffering under the yoke of a dictator.

Cuban Note

Havana, Jan. 2, 1961, Year of Education

Mr. Chargé d'Affaires:

I have the honor to inform you that the revolutionary Government has decided that under present circumstances the personnel of the embassy and consulate of Cuba in the city of Washington, whether diplomatic, consular or of other character, whatever their nationality, should not exceed eleven persons. Likewise it has decided that the personnel of the embassy and consulate of the United States in the city of Havana, whether diplomatic, consular or of other character, whatever their nationality, should likewise be limited to eleven persons.

For the purpose of facilitating the departure of the persons who for this reason must abandon the national territory, a period of forty-eight hours has been fixed from the time of receipt of this note.

I take the opportunity, Mr. Chargé d'Affaires, to reiterate to you the assurance of my reciprocity of your considerations.

CARLOS OLIVARES,
Under Secretary-Minister of Foreign Office.

United States Note

Sir:

I have the honor to refer to a note dated Jan. 2, 1961, from the Government of Cuba to the Chargé d'Affaires of the United States Embassy in Havana stating that the Government of Cuba has decided that personnel of the embassy and consulate of the United States in the city of Havana, regardless of nationality, shall not exceed eleven persons.

This unwarranted action by the Government of Cuba places crippling limitations on the ability of the United States mission to carry on its normal diplomatic and consular functions. It would consequently appear that it is designed to achieve an effective termination of diplomatic and consular relations between the Government of Cuba and the Government of the United States. Accordingly, the Government of the United States hereby formally notifies the Government of Cuba of the termination of such relations.

The Government of the United States intends to comply with the requirement of the Government of Cuba concerning the withdrawal of all but eleven persons within the period of forty-eight hours from 1:20 A. M. on Jan. 3, the time of the delivery of the note under reference. In addition, the Government of the United States will withdraw its remaining diplomatic and consular personnel in Cuba as soon as possible thereafter.

The Government of Cuba is requested to withdraw from the United States as soon as possible all Cuban nationals employed in the Cuban Embassy in Washington and in all Cuban consular establishments in the United States.

The Government of the United States is requesting the Government of Switzerland to assume diplomatic and consular representation in Cuba on behalf of the Government of the United States.

I take this opportunity to reiterate to you the assurances of my reciprocity of your considerations.

CHRISTIAN A. HERTER.

"All the News That's Fit to Print"

The New York Times.

LATE CITY EDITION

U.S. Weather Bureau Report (Page 81) forecasts: Increasing cloudiness today; chance of rain tonight and tomorrow. Temp. range: 54—40; yesterday: 52—43.

VOL. CX..No. 37,699.

NEW YORK, WEDNESDAY, APRIL 12, 1961.

10 cents beyond 50-mile zone from New York City except on Long Island. Higher in air delivery cities.

FIVE CENTS

SOVIET ORBITS MAN AND RECOVERS HIM; SPACE PIONEER REPORTS: 'I FEEL WELL'; SENT MESSAGES WHILE CIRCLING EARTH

HEAD OF RESERVE URGES PRICE CUTS TO RELIEVE SLUMP

Martin Asserts Reductions Would Mean More Jobs and Demand for Goods

By RICHARD E. MOONEY

Special to The New York Times.

WASHINGTON, April 11—The chairman of the Federal Reserve Board made a strong appeal today for price reductions as a means of solving the nation's economic problems.

"Throughout our country, we must not only increase our productivity but also pass some of the gains on to the consumer in the form of lower prices, rather than having all of it go exclusively to labor in higher wages or to management in higher profits," he said.

The chairman, William McC. Martin Jr., said that price cuts could stimulate buying demand that would "provide more jobs for those who are now unemployed, keep the economy moving to higher levels, and [provide] still greater job opportunities in the future."

Some Gains Reported

The Labor Department reported, meanwhile, a modest increase in the factory work week and factory pay for March.

Mr. Martin spoke at the annual meeting of the Association of Reserve City Bankers at Boca Raton, Fla. Copies of his talk were made available here.

It was not the first time that a voice from Washington had been raised in favor of price cuts. It is a point that gets lost, however, in the debates most often heard here, over what the Government should or should not do. In the form presented, it is simply an exhortation. Neither Mr. Martin nor the Kennedy Administration advocates price or wage controls.

Addressing himself to the domestic economy, Mr. Martin said that "at the moment we have pressing need to reduce unemployment and to promote economic growth at the maximum sustainable speed." The way to meet the need, he said, is "a judicious blend" of specific actions, monetary and fiscal policies, and wage-price policies.

Answers Critics of Policy

In such a setting, he said, interest rates need not rise so high nor fall so low as they have in past business cycles.

Mr. Martin used his speech to answer critics who have said that recent Federal Reserve strategy cannot work and has already failed. Seven weeks ago the reserve system abandoned its established policy of buying and selling only the shortest-term securities—Treasury bills—when it sought to impose its influence on credit conditions

Continued on Page 25, Column 5

Wide College Aid Is Adopted by State

By WARREN WEAVER Jr.

Special to The New York Times.

ALBANY, April 11—A higher-education program that will make $12,300,000 in new financial assistance available to college and university students in New York State this year was approved by Governor Rockefeller today.

He said the program gave assurance that "no young man or woman with the ability and desire for a higher education need be deprived of that opportunity for lack of funds."

The seven higher education measures that were signed included a bill that gave New York City permission to establish a city university to consist of the four municipal colleges and the community colleges in the five boroughs.

One of the bills provides

Continued on Page 48, Column 3

COUNCIL APPROVES OWN CHARTER BILL

Rebuffs Mayor by Spurning State Law Under Which He Named Commission

By CHARLES G. BENNETT

The City Council passed its own bill yesterday calling for the appointment of a commission to draft a new City Charter. The vote was 21 to 3.

Council officers immediately prepared to send the measure directly to Mayor Wagner for his signature or veto. This would be based on a contention by the Council's high command that since the bill merely calls for the appointment of a commission, it does not require Board of Estimate action.

The Council's stand constituted a challenge to the new state law under which Mayor Wagner already has appointed an eleven-member commission to revise the Charter.

Majority Leader Joseph T. Sharkey, who is also Democratic leader of Kings County, repeated his charge that Governor Rockefeller and Mayor Wagner had been "playing together" on Charter revision. Mayor Wagner supported the state bill.

Mr. Sharkey also said he "hoped and expected" that there

Continued on Page 26, Column 3

ISRAEL DEFENDS TRIBUNAL'S RIGHT TO TRY EICHMANN

Ex-Nazi Is More Confident as Jerusalem Hearing Enters Its 2d Day

By HOMER BIGART

Special to The New York Times.

JERUSALEM (Israeli Sector), Wednesday, April 12—The Attorney General of Israel, Gideon Hausner, resumed this morning his defense of the right of his country to try Adolf Eichmann for the murder of millions of Jews.

The defendant, as he entered his bulletproof glass cage on the second day of his trial seemed more confident. For the first time, he looked out at the audience. Then he sat down and engaged in an animated conversation with his German lawyer, Dr. Robert Servatius through a microphone in the glass cage. Eichmann smiled at his lawyer and seemed at ease.

On the first day of the trial, Eichmann, stonily impassive, heard his lawyer challenge the court's right to try the former Nazi leader on charges of delivering millions of Jews to Nazi annihilation camps.

The debate over Israel's right to try Eichmann was expected to continue through today's session. The court will not meet tomorrow, Holocaust Day, a day of mourning in Israel for the victims of Nazi terror.

Indictment Is Read

For seventy minutes Eichmann remained standing while the presiding judge, Justice Moshe Landau of the Israeli Supreme Court, read in Hebrew a fifteen-count indictment charging him with crimes against the Jewish people and crimes against humanity. The indictment was translated into German for Eichmann's benefit.

Rigidly erect, his head tilted back and his thin lips tightly compressed, the one-time chief of the Gestapo's Jewish Affairs Section betrayed no emotion during the opening day of trial.

His thin, hawklike visage with its large, sharply pointed nose was fixed intently on the proceedings. Not once did Eichmann turn to gaze on the throng of newsmen, foreign observers and Israeli citizens in the 750 seats in the Beit Haam (House of the People), the converted

Continued on Page 16, Column 1

Former Nazi Hears Indictment Read as Trial Begins in Jerusalem

Adolf Eichmann, charged with crimes against the Jewish people and against humanity, standing in special booth in Beit Haam courtroom yesterday. Justices at bench are, from left, Benyamin Halevi, Moshe Landau, Yitzhak Raveh.

Associated Press Radiophotos

Eichmann peers intently at tribunal during proceedings

U. S. IS DISTURBED BY DELAY ON LAOS

Soviet Lag on Cease-Fire and Increase in Supplies Regarded as Ominous

By WILLIAM J. JORDEN

Special to The New York Times.

WASHINGTON, April 11—Officials said today the United States Government was disturbed by Moscow's delay in accepting a Western plan for an immediate cease-fire in Laos.

A spokesman for the State Department said that continued delay would be regarded here as "a matter of very serious concern."

Adding to the worries of Administration leaders were intelligence reports of a general increase in the flow of Soviet-bloc military supplies to the Pathet Lao movement in recent days. This was regarded as an ominous sign of Soviet intentions in Laos.

Rusk Voices Hope

High officials continued to be hopeful, however, that Moscow would soon give a favorable answer to the cease-fire plan advanced by the British several weeks ago.

That hope was voiced on Capitol Hill today by Secretary of State Dean Rusk. The Secretary told Senators that he expected a Soviet answer "within a very few days."

The presumption here is that continued fighting in Laos contains the seeds of a possibly enlarged conflict and that the Soviet bloc does not want to

Continued on Page 12, Column 4

BRITISH CONSIDER TRADE UNITY STEP

Kennedy Hopes London Will Enter Common Market

By JAMES RESTON

Special to The New York Times.

WASHINGTON, April 11—President Kennedy now has the impression that the British Government is seriously thinking about joining the European Economic Community, or Common Market.

This impression is based on the fact that during the President's conversations with Prime Minister Macmillan here last week the British leader asked what the United States Government would think if Britain decided to reverse her policy and join the Western European nations now working toward economic and political integration.

Administration to Cooperate

President Kennedy's reply was that the United States would regard this as a major advance toward the unity of the West.

The President did not in any way imply that the United States was thinking of joining the Common Market itself, but he did stress his Government's determination to cooperate fully with its allies in the Organization for Economic Cooperation and Development.

On a recent trip to London it is known that George Ball, United States Under Secretary of State for Economic Affairs, urged upon Viscount Hailsham, the British Lord President of the Council, that Britain give the most serious consideration

Continued on Page 2, Column 3

ADENAUER IN U. S. TO SEE KENNEDY

Arrives for First Talks With President—Stresses Unity

Special to The New York Times.

WASHINGTON, April 11—Chancellor Adenauer of West Germany arrived here tonight for his first meetings with President Kennedy.

He alighted at Andrews Air Force Base from the Lufthansa jet airliner that brought him without stop from Bonn.

In an arrival statement the 85-year-old Chancellor said the German people had already developed "great confidence" in the new President of the United States. He said he was looking forward to establishing personal contact with Mr. Kennedy.

Dr. Adenauer pledged that his country's considerable energy and ability would be devoted to the cause of peace and freedom. He said that his Government realized that its share of responsibility for the future of the world grew "in proportion with our efficiency and capacity."

"Our times are filled with threats and dangers," the Chancellor said, "but I feel sure that the free people of the world will overcome those dangers if they are united and resolute."

The West German leader and his party, including his daughter, Frau Libeth Werhahn, were

Continued on Page 4, Column 5

FRANCE DECLARES ANTI-U.N. 'STRIKE'

De Gaulle Bars Any Role in Armed Ventures—Warns Algerians on Partition

By HENRY GINIGER

Special to The New York Times.

PARIS, April 11—France proclaimed today a virtual strike against the United Nations.

In one of the harshest indictments he has ever made against the organization, President de Gaulle said France "did not wish to participate either by her men or her money in any present or possible enterprise of this organization—or of this disorganization."

The President, in response to a question, confirmed his country's refusal to contribute to the costs of the United Nations force in the Congo. A Foreign Ministry spokesman said that in this context the President's statement referred to present or future military enterprises, although the word "military" did not occur in the text of the news conference.

On another issue, President de Gaulle offered a mixture of incentives for Algerian rebel cooperation with France. He warned anew that a "rupture" might result in the partitioning of Algeria to protect those Algerians who wished to remain under French control.

The President called for reform of the United Nations as well as of the Atlantic Alliance. He made it clear that the future of the alliance would be a major

Continued on Page 3, Column 5

187-MILE HEIGHT

Yuri Gagarin, a Major Makes the Flight in 5-Ton Vehicle

Text of the Tass statement is printed on Page 22.

By United Press International.

MOSCOW, Wednesday, April 12—The Soviet Union announced today it had won the race to put a man into space. The official press agency, Tass, said a man had orbited the earth in a spaceship and had been brought back alive and safe.

A brief announcement said the first reported space man had landed in what was described as the "prescribed area" of the Soviet Union after a historic flight.

A Moscow radio announcer broke into a program and said in emotional tones:

"Russia has successfully launched a man into space. His name is Yuri Gagarin. He was launched in a sputnik named Vostok, which means "East."

Reports on Landing

Tass said that, on landing, Major Gagarin said: "Please report to the party and Government, and personally to Nikita Sergyevich Khrushchev, that the landing was normal, I feel well, have no injuries or bruises."

He landed at 10:55 A. M. Moscow time [2:55 A. M. New York time].

Earlier, the major reported: "Flight is proceeding normally, I feel well."

After orbiting the earth the major applied a braking device and the vehicle space landed in the Soviet Union, Tass said.

Major Gagarin, 27 years old is an industrial technician, and married. He was reported to have received pre-flight training similar to that of the astronauts who will man the United States first space ships.

Soared to 187 Miles

The announcer said the Sputnik reached a minimum altitude of 175 kilometers (109½ miles) and a maximum altitude of 302 kilometers (187¾ miles).

He said the weight of the Sputnik was 10,395 pounds, or slightly over five tons.

The announcement of the launching came at 2 A. M. New York time.

It said everything functioned normally during the flight.

Constant radio contact was maintained between earth and the sputnik, the Moscow radio said.

The announcer said the duration of each revolution around the earth was 89.1 minutes.

The title of the announcement was "The First Human Flight into the Cosmos."

The radio, which was quoting a Tass press agency statement on the launching said that Maj.

Continued on Page 22, Column 1

Population Center Moves West; Census Puts It at Centralia, Ill.

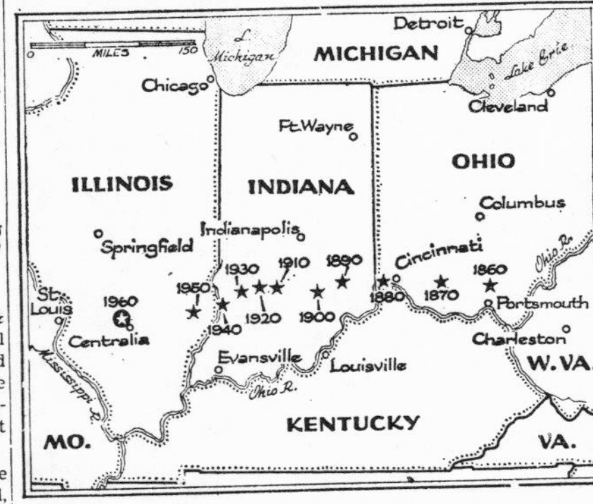

The New York Times April 12, 1961

United States center of population, which was near Portsmouth, Ohio, a hundred years ago, has continued moving west and by 1960 was just northwest of Centralia, Ill.

By The Associated Press.

WASHINGTON, April 11—The population center of the United States has moved again.

Secretary of Commerce Luther H. Hodges announced today that the new center, based on the 1960 census, was near Centralia, Ill., fifty-seven miles west of its 1950 location.

In general, the population center is the point through which a straight line can be drawn in any direction dividing the country's population in half. As many people would live on one side of the line as on the other.

Mr. Hodges had another def-

Continued on Page 27, Column 3

Realtor Is Indicted In Expense Padding

By EDWARD RANZAL

The president of Pease & Elliman, Inc., a leading real estate concern here, was indicted yesterday on charges of income tax evasion through fraudulent claims for entertainment and travel expenses.

The indictment against the executive, Robert Neaderland, by a Federal grand jury was said to be the first of its kind in the Southern District of New York. It was expected to break ground for future prosecutions for overstatement of business expenses.

Mr. Neaderland, 53 years old, lives at 160 Central Park South. His company is one of the leading developers of apartments on the East Side. He is charged with attempting to evade $27,550 in income taxes in 1954 and 1955, according to

Continued on Page 30, Column 3

Centennial of War Rocked by Dispute

By The Associated Press.

CHARLESTON, S. C., April 11—New Jersey accused the National Civil War Centennial Commission of "pathetic mismanagement" tonight and asked that President Kennedy remove Maj. Gen. Ulysses S. Grant 3d as chairman.

Joseph Dempsey, vice chairman of the Jersey Centennial Commission, made the charge at a news conference after General Grant had turned down the state's request for time to rebut a dinner speaker who had criticized its civil rights practices.

General Grant and Donald Flamm, Jersey chairman, engaged in an unscheduled standing debate at the crowded dinner at the Charleston Naval Base. General Grant, to loud applause, insisted that New

Continued on Page 36, Column 3

White House Confirms Firing; Feat Hailed by U. S. Scientists

By JOHN W. FINNEY

Special to The New York Times.

WASHINGTON, Wednesday, April 12—Pierre Salinger, White House press secretary, announced early today that "American tracking stations have confirmed the fact that the Soviet Union has launched a satellite today."

"We are keeping in close touch with the situation but have no additional comment at this time," he said.

The Soviet success in sending the first man into space left United States officials in a resigned mood of congratulations.

The United States has no chance of equaling the Soviet feat until perhaps late this year.

The Soviet announcement did not take them by surprise, since there had been advance information from United States tracking stations that a satellite had been launched.

James E. Webb, head of the National Aeronautics and Space Administration, described the feat as "a significant accomplishment" that "demonstrates great technical capacity."

"I hope that they can find it possible to make the benefits of this event available to the rest of the world," he said.

Dr. Hugh L. Dryden, deputy administrator of the space agency, commented, "This is something we have been expecting for some time."

"It is only the beginning of man's continued effort of manned exploration of space," he said, "and I think we should continue as rapidly as we can with our own program."

In appraising the achieve-

Continued on Page 24, Column 1

NEWS INDEX

Russians Succeed in Orbiting an Astronaut and Returning Him Safely to Earth

SOVIET IN TOUCH WITH SPACE MAN

Successful Launching of Yuri Gagarin in 'East' Sputnik Is Announced in Moscow

Continued From Page 1, Col. 8

Gagarin "is feeling well" and that "conditions in the cabin are normal."

As soon as the Moscow announcement was made, Russians began to telephone congratulations to each other.

The first astronaut is a major in the Soviet Air Force and is believed to be a test pilot.

The Tass announcement said that the launching of the multi-stage space rocket, which carried the Sputnik into orbit, was successful.

After attaining the first escape velocity, it said, and the separation of the last stage of the carrier rocket, the space ship went into free flight on a round-the-earth orbit.

Reports of the launching of a Soviet space man had been reported repeatedly in Moscow for the last twenty-four hours. The London Daily Worker and other sources had said the Soviet Union had sent a man into space last Friday and had brought him back alive.

Many persons in Moscow were convinced after today's announcement that another flight into space was attempted on Friday and there was speculation that something might have gone wrong.

The announcement of the first flight into space was repeated three times, after which the normal radio program of music was resumed.

The radio also broadcast patriotic songs.

The announcement said the condition of the navigator was being observed by means of radio telemetering devices and television.

Major Gagarin, the announcement went on, withstood satisfactorily the placing of the satellite ship into orbit.

He's 'You-Ree Gah-GAH-Rin'

The Soviet Union's man in space is Maj. Yuri Gagarin—pronounced 'You' ree Gah-GAH-rin with the acent on the second syllable of his last name. The New York office of Tass, official Soviet news agency, gave the pronunciation of his name.

BROOKS UNSATISFIED WITH SPACE BUDGET

WASHINGTON, April 11 (UPI) — Representative Overton Brooks, chairman of the House Space Committee, said today he was "not entirely satisfied" with the space budget proposed by President Kennedy.

The Louisiana Democrat said he did not propose to force the Administration to take more money than it wanted, but that there were a number of projects that he felt should be given more support.

Chief among these projects, he said, was increased research and development for solid fuel technology.

Mr. Brooks made his comments as the Space Committee called officials of the National Aeronautics and Space Administration for the second day of hearings on the agency's $1,200,000,000 request for the fiscal year beginning July 1.

He said the agency should have asked Congress for $1,500,000,000 and said there were critical space projects that needed additional funds.

He pointed to testimony given yesterday by James E. Webb, head of the agency, that the Budget Bureau had turned down a $5,000,000 request for increasing solid propellant research.

Mr. Brooks also said the program to develop nuclear rockets should be speeded up with additional funds.

SUN HELPS TO KEEP ECHO SATELLITE UP

CAMBRIDGE, Mass., April 11 (AP)—The satellite Echo I is proving more durable than scientists expected it would. In recent weeks the 100-foot balloon of thin plastic has actually been going up instead of down. Launched from Cape Canaveral on Aug. 12, the satellite was expected to last only a few weeks. Its great size and weight of less than 100 pounds was expected to make it very vulnerable to the atmospheric drag it was designed to measure.

Now, scientists say Echo's great bulk and light weight have helped to keep it aloft because of slight pressure from sunlight.

Previously, solar pressure had been blamed for nudging Echo toward the earth. In recent weeks the balloon's orbit has changed in relations to the sun and now solar pressure is causing Echo to have a more circular path around the earth.

Dr. Pedro Zadunaisky, a Smithsonian Astrophysical Observatory astronomer, estimates that probably a pound of matter, including microscopic meteorites and air molecules, has collided with the balloon in the nearly 100,000,000 miles it has traveled.

Officials to Hear Poet Frost

WASHINGTON, April 11 (AP)—"An Evening with Robert Frost" will be presented by members of President Kennedy's Cabinet on May 1 in the State Department Auditorium. The 87-year-old poet will read from his poetry. He will also lecture.

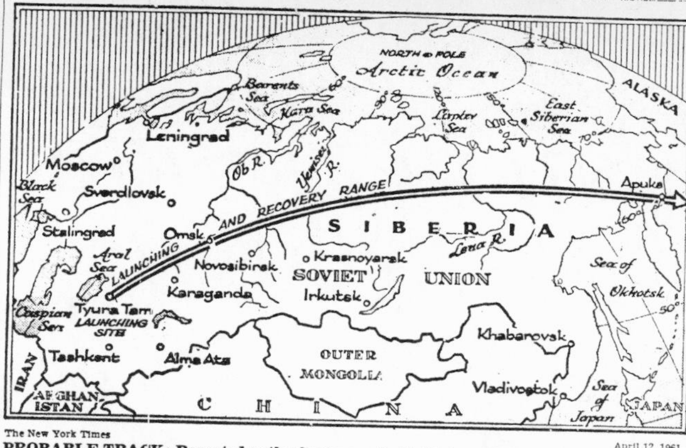

The New York Times April 12, 1961

PROBABLE TRACK: Reported path of astronaut's flight from launch site at Tyura Tam.

ASTRONAUT'S TRIP A CONSTANT PERIL

Training Prepared Him for Some Dangers, but Real Flight Brought New Ones

By JOHN A. OSMUNDSEN

Most of the features of flight into space that the Soviet astronaut experienced in orbit for the first time had been sampled by him and several other men in tests on earth.

This familiarity with the hazards of space flight did not, however, diminish the constant threat that the experience posed to the Soviet flier's life.

For one thing, there were certain hazards that could not have been simulated on earth and that might have been crucial to the outcome of the flight.

Also, the hazards the astronaut experienced, one or a few at a time, over a training period of several months were crammed into a few hours—thus an enormous strain was set up.

And today, it was for keeps. There would be no one to shut down the centrifuge if the flier blacked out from G-forces nor anyone to pull him out of the high temperature chamber if he neared the border of heat stroke.

These factors may have crossed the Russian astronaut's mind in the hour or two before the launching. For that time he lay strapped to his contour couch in the sealed chamber above the rocket that eventually boosted his space ship into orbit around the earth.

Just after the countdown on the rocket reached zero, the man inside the capsule began to experience the first of the hazards of the flight, G-force.

This is the force that the acceleration of the rocket produces on the body. It is measured in multiples of the force of gravity, or G's. A man standing motionless at sea level, for example, experiences a force of one G.

Force Rises After Drop

It might be assumed that the Soviet astronaut experienced what Americans in the manned space flight effort named Project Mercury will. If such were the case, the Russian was pressed against his form-fitting couch with a force of about eight G's within the first few minutes. Then, the flier weighed eight times his normal weight.

When the first-stage rocket burned out, the force dropped abruptly to zero G. Then it rose again to between eight and ten G's under the acceleration of the second stage.

The first novel experience was encountered when the final stage rocket burned out, injecting the capsule into orbit. At that moment, the G-force dropped abruptly from around ten G's to zero. This left the flier in a state of complete weightlessness, which he endured for the next several hours.

Before today, it was uncertain how man would react to such a drastic change in G-force or to a prolonged state of weightlessness.

On the way to its orbit, the space capsule left behind the protective comforts of the atmosphere. It became increasingly exposed to the full fury of the space environment, but protected the man inside against most of these.

Air Pressure Falls

At an altitude of ten miles, the air pressure dropped to a value lower than that inside a man's lungs. Two miles higher it was lower than the vapor pressure of body fluids.

The sealed, pressurized capsule gave protection against these hazards. It permitted the man to breathe in oxygen and prevented his body fluids from boiling.

At twenty-four miles, the air was no longer dense enough to provide the shield against primary cosmic rays that protects life on earth from the rays' harmful effects.

However, the danger of cosmic-ray exposure to the space cabin's occupant had been calculated as not great at the altitude and for the duration of the manned satellite's flight—unless showers of particles from an unpredictable solar flare were encountered.

Above the ozone layer of the atmosphere, about twenty-eight miles up, absorption of the burning rays of ultra-violet radiation from the sun ceased. However, the space capsule protected the astronaut against their effects.

The vehicle also shielded its occupant from micrometeorites and cosmic dust, which became a hazard at about seven y-five miles. Only the larger meteorites still posed a serious threat, but the chances of colliding with one were small.

When the vehicle reached its orbital altitude, another hazard came into play, one that had been completely unevaluated until today. That hazard was remoteness and the unknown effects that removal from a familiar sphere of human experience might have on a man's mind.

There was still one more hazard that the Soviet space flier had to face after enduring multiple and complex G-forces and heating of re-entry into the atmosphere and the dangers of landing on earth again. He had to steel himself for the prospect of being the subject of scientific study and scrutiny for **the rest of his life.**

Sovfoto

FIRST CREATURE TO ORBIT EARTH was Laika, sent up by Soviet Union on Nov. 3, 1957. She lived about a week. The satellite disintegrated after five months.

ONLY JUST THE U.S.

Daily Worker

CANDID ON POLARIS

Soviet astronaut circles the earth three times

THE FIRST MAN IN SPACE

Back alive—but suffering from effects of his flight

EDITORIAL Big Business butts in

De Gaulle threat to Algerian talks

Six million dead accuse Eichmann

United Press International Radiophoto

AN EARLY STORY: Part of the front page of today's Daily Worker of London. The Communist paper appeared hours before the official announcement from Moscow.

United Press International

SOVIET SPACE SUIT: This official photograph, released in 1958, shows a Soviet astronaut testing equipment designed to be used on rocket flights beyond the atmosphere.

Tass Statement on Shot

Following is the text of a statement by Tass, Soviet press agency issued here on the man in space:

The world's first satellite space ship Vostok, with a man on board, was placed in an around-the-earth orbit in the Soviet Union on April 12, 1961.

The pilot space navigator of the Vostok is a citizen of the U. S. S. R., Flight Maj. Yuri Alekseyevich Gagarin.

The launching of the multi-stage space rocket was successful, and after attaining the first escape velocity and the separation of the last stage of the carrier-rocket, the space ship went into free flight on an around-the-earth orbit.

According to preliminary data, the period of the revolution of the satellite space ship around the earth is 89.1 minutes. The minimum distance from the earth (at perigee) is 175 kilometers [109½ miles] and the maximum (at apogee) is 302 kilometers [187⅝ miles]. The angle of inclination of the orbit plane to the equator is 65 degrees 4 minutes.

The space ship with the navigator weighs 4,725 kilograms [about five tons], excluding the weight of the final stage of the carrier.

Bilateral radio communications have been established and are maintained with Space Navigator Gagarin. The frequency of the short-wave transmitters on board are 9,019 megacycles and 20,006 megacycles, and in the ultra-short-wave range 143.625 megacycles.

The condition of the navigator in flight is observed by means of radio telemetric and television systems.

Space Navigator Gagarin withstood satisfactorily the placing of the satellite ship Vostok into orbit, and at present feels well. The systems insuring the necessary vital conditions in the cabin of the spaceship are functioning normally.

The spaceship, with Navigator Gagarin on board, is continuing its flight in orbit.

HIRSCH GOES FREE

U.S. Drops Spying Indictment Because Melekh Left

Special to The New York Times.

CHICAGO, April 11—A man charged with spying for the Soviet Union went free today in Federal Court here as the Government kept its word not to prosecute him if a Russian, accused of being a co-conspirator, left the country.

Willie Hirsch, 52 years old, a German-born medical illustrator from New York City, was released after Judge Julius J. Hoffman dismissed an indictment charging he had conspired with Igor Melekh, a United Nations employe, to steal American defense secrets.

James P. O'Brien, new United States Attorney for Northern Illinois, told the judge he had received a telegram from Robert F. Kennedy, the Attorney General, authorizing him to dismiss the indictments.

Melekh left the country Saturday, sailing from New York for France.

U. N. COMMISSION MEETS

Economic Group for Europe Faces Soviet Pressures

Special to The New York Times.

GENEVA, April 11—The United Nations Economic Commission for Europe began its sixteenth session here today with Cyprus present as a member for the first time.

The Soviet Union is expected to press during the nearly three-week session for the admission of Communist East Germany and increased representation on the commission's international staff.

Vladimir Velebit, the commission's new executive secretary, told the delegates he thought the organization had a major role to play in meeting the "problems arising from the co-existence of countries with different economic systems."

M. Velebit, a Yugoslav, is the thirty-nation commission's first executive secretary from a non-Scandinavian country.

EX-NAZI SENTENCED

Bonn Court Gives Former Camp Chief Life Terms

Special to The New York Times.

BONN, Germany, April 11—The only current major war crimes trial in West Germany ended today with the sentencing of the former commandant of the Gusen concentration camp in Austria to life at hard labor.

The former commandant, Karl Chmielewskim, was found guilty of murder in 282 cases. The Gusen camp was an adjunct of the Mauthausen concentration camp.

SOVIET FEAT CAPS INTENSE EFFORTS

Russian Plan, Unlike U. S., Brings Astronaut Back to Home Territory

By WALTER SULLIVAN

The Soviet launching of a man into space was the culmination of many preliminary firings, virtually all of which appear to have been made down the same missile range.

Orbital tests of the vehicle designed for carrying a passenger did not begin until last May 15. Since then, and prior to the most recent shot, only five were launched.

In contrast to the American man-in-space program, whose timetable lags behind that of the Russians, the Soviet recovery scheme called for parachuting of its space traveler onto the home territory of the Soviet Union.

In fact, it is widely believed that the range allocated for recovery of the space cabin was identical to that down which the vehicle was launched. In a normal firing this would mean that the vehicle would have to remain in orbit roughly one day. This would enable the earth to rotate within the satellite orbit and bring the vehicle's flight back over the launching range.

Location Is Secret

Moscow has never disclosed the location of its missile ranges, but analyses of earlier trajectories have suggested that the long-range launching site is east of the Aral Sea, 175 miles east of the Caspian.

Some rockets have also been launched from the vicinity of Kapustin Yar, southeast of Stalingrad, but the nearness of populated areas is said to have limited the extent of firings from there.

From the start, the heavy rockets developed for the Soviet intercontinental ballistic missiles have given the Russians a large margin in lifting power over their American competitors.

Early last year the Soviet Union began firing what it said was a new and larger booster along an extension of its standard missile range that reached far across the Pacific Ocean.

There was speculation that this booster might be used for the man-in-space program and in May Russia launched a five-ton vehicle in the initial test of its man-carrying capsule. It was not recovered, failed and a new series of test shots into the Pacific was carried out in July.

Success for U. S.

On August 19 the United States space program took the center of the stage briefly when a capsule from Discoverer XIV was recovered by parachute-snatching aircraft over the Pacific. The capsule was small, however, and not related to the American man-in-space program.

Only a few hours later the cabin aboard the Soviet Union's Spacecraft II, with two dogs aboard, was recovered on the range spanning that country.

By the completion of the last shot in that nation's man-in-space rehearsals, on March 25, three of the five recovery attempts had been successful. The other two had failed, in one case with the loss of two dogs and several smaller animals.

Because of the geographical location of the Soviet Union, a recovery of the manned capsule from water appeared impracticable. On the other hand, the vast reaches of the Atlantic Ocean offer an ideal recovery area for the American program, based at Cape Canaveral, Fla.

Having decided to bring their man down on land, the Russians are said to have decided to use their launching range, with its elaborate optical and radar tracking gear, to follow his return to earth. Because of the fixed nature of this range, virtually all Soviet space vehicles have followed the same path into the heavens.

This has placed them in orbits inclined roughly 65 degrees to the Equator.

New Era in War May Be Opened, With Space Ship Used in Battle

Special to The New York Times.

WASHINGTON, April 11—Like the Wright brothers' first flight a half century ago, the Soviet feat of placing the first man in space may ultimately add a new dimension to warfare in which space craft are used to win wars on earth.

For the moment, however, the Soviet accomplishment was being viewed by United States officials as of more psychological importance in giving the Soviet Union once again the "high ground" in world prestige than of immediate military significance.

If officials tended to minimize the military significance of the Soviet space flight, it was because the potential military uses of manned space craft are still unclear.

It is still not certain—at least as far as United States policy-makers are concerned—that man, under the rigors of space travel, can perform useful military functions in the hostile environment of space. And even if he can, it is yet to be established that he can do them better or cheaper than unmanned, instrumented space craft or by weapons based on earth.

The Soviet flight should help answer the first question of whether man can exist and function under the stresses of space flight. This, in fact, is probably its main objective, just as it is for Project Mercury, the man-in-space program of the National Aeronautics and Space Administration.

Ever since the start of the space age, an unresolved debate has been going on within the Defense Department and among scientists over the military usefulness of manned spacecraft.

Space enthusiasts, thus far a minority concentrated within the Air Force, have foreseen all sorts of military functions for man in space, ranging from flying satellite bombers to manning bases on the moon from which it would be possible to carry out reconnaissance or bombard the earth.

The skeptical attitude toward these futuristic visions of space war was typified in a report by the President's Science Advisory Committee in 1958 that said that "most of these schemes * * * appear to be the clumsy and ineffecive way of doing a job."

Noting the inherent technical difficulties of accurately firing a rocket from a space ship or from the moon to a target on earth, the report observed that "the earth would appear to be, after all, the best weapons carrier."

As seen by military enthusiasts, these factors dictate the inevitability of man one day flying off into space to conduct war:

—The historic military advantage that goes to the adversary who obtains the "high ground." And in the space age, the "high ground" has become the 240,000-mile distance between the earth and the moon.

—With his brain, man is one of the world's best computers with a sense of judgment and decision-making power that can never be equaled by an electronic gadget.

—Warfare historically has taken on a new dimension with each technological development, from the invention of the bow and arrow to the splitting of the atom. The same progression inevitably will occur now that man has developed rockets that can carry him into space.

At first, it seems apparent that manned space craft will be developed for carrying out primarily defensive duties, such as servicing instrumented satellites or performing reconnaissance.

But following the course of technological development, some military space enthusiasts foresee the day when manned interceptors are built to go up and knock apart enemy satellites. And the next step, of course, would be development of manned space fighters to go up and knock down the adversary's interceptors.

SPACE FLIGHT TIED TO MAN'S ADVANCE

Some Doubt Project's Value, but It May Help to Solve Mysteries of Universe

By ROBERT K. PLUMB

A few land-bound souls have questioned the whole idea behind man-in-space programs. Why send a man into space?

A few scientists have even suggested that for man's first ventures away from the earth an instrumented package could make more accurate and valuable measurements than a human observer. A man is too valuable and fragile a package to make an exploratory space trip, they say.

While there seems little doubt that propaganda considerations have stimulated both the Soviet and American man-in-space programs, there is also scientific backing for such efforts. It is reasoned that, sooner or later, an investigator will have to be on the scene. Remote control of the experiments will not be enough.

Thus, while there is talk of television-bearing tankettes for exploration of the moon's surface, it seems doubtful that scientists could long resist the temptation to go along themselves. Many people probably view manned travel into space as the greatest adventure the human race has undertaken.

In a real sense, space travel is an adventure in which all can participate. It is a costly and complicated affair. Every one who supports a Governmental space project, even as a taxpayer, is along on the ride and shares in the discovery.

Deep Meaning in Studies

There is a deep meaning for all in studies beyond the earth. The studies underly man's view of himself and they may impinge upon deep convictions that many persons hold.

In the beginning, when the first man looked about and pondered, it must have seemed that man was the center of everything, the favored creature of all.

Then began early feeble exploration of the planet. Man found he had neighbors other than those in the animal kingdom. He found other communities and other men like himself.

For centuries thinking man clung to the belief that the earth itself, if not his species, was the center of all creation. The stars and the sun were seen as remote and unimportant objects. The earth was the center of all and surely so grand a creature as man must inhabit the grandest body in the universe.

Man Dwindles

This view died with the scientific studies of Copernicus, Kepler and finally Newton. Man was reduced again in scale by the knowledge that the sun is the center of our solar system and that the nearest stars are far away from our own local star, the sun. The earth became one of a number of planets orbiting the sun and not a big one at that.

There followed studies that have dealt another great blow to man's concept in the scheme of things.

Even our great neighbor the sun came to be recognized as a minor body in a universe that might be boundless. Our own galaxy, the Milky Way, is believed to be a great round disk so big that it takes light 80,000 years to travel across it. The galaxy weighs some 200,000,000,000 times more than our sun.

Now it is held that our galaxy is probably nothing spectacular or unusual. Other, bigger galaxies are seen as far away as the most powerful instruments of man can probe. Out as far as we can see there are galaxies and even clusters of galaxies. We cannot see an edge to the universe that surrounds us in space.

Life In Other Worlds

The space-travel age is a time in which scientists are experimenting with the possibility that there may be other worlds around us and that we might communicate with them when we learn how.

Surely there must be other worlds with temperature and chemical conditions like those of earth in all the matter that surrounds us. If life arose as a result of natural events, then the other worlds must be populated.

Perhaps other worlds are inhabited by more advanced creatures than we, some suggest. It might even be that something practical could be achieved if we could ask questions of a more mature civilization. How do you cure cancer, for example, or how do you prevent wars?

During human history man has steadily seen the universe of which he is a part grow larger. Man himself has become smaller. But knowledge has grown.

Man now knows that other species have become extinct. He knows that evolution will proceed: the evolution of stars, of earths and of species including the human species. It may be that the accumulation of book knowledge is part of the evolutionary pattern for the human species. With knowledge, perhaps man can control his own evolution and prevent his extinction.

Looking at things that way it is possible to think that space travel is the next and the inevitable step in human evolution. The pressure of evolution is more than a mere urge to travel into space because "it is there." It is a necessary new step for man.

"All the News That's Fit to Print"

The New York Times.

LATE CITY EDITION
U. S. Weather Bureau Report (Page 74) forecasts: Mostly fair today. Fair tonight and tomorrow.
Temp. range: 56—42; yesterday: 55—42.

VOL. CX. No. 37,705.

NEW YORK, TUESDAY, APRIL 18, 1961.

10 cents beyond 50-mile zone from New York City except on Long Island. Higher in air delivery cities.

FIVE CENTS

ANTI-CASTRO UNITS LAND IN CUBA; REPORT FIGHTING AT BEACHHEAD; RUSK SAYS U. S. WON'T INTERVENE

SUPREME COURT UPHOLDS UNIONS AGAINST N. L. R. B.

It Upsets Board's Ruling That Contracts Illegally Force Membership

MAILERS' PACTS BACKED

New York Printers' Local and California Teamsters Win on Agreements

By ANTHONY LEWIS
Special to The New York Times

WASHINGTON, April 17—A series of decisions by the National Labor Relations Board designed to prevent the compelling of union membership was struck down today by the Supreme Court.

The court disposed of a group of major labor cases that will affect dozens of others pending in the lower courts and before the labor relations board. The court did the following things in its principal rulings:

¶It upheld, 6 to 2, contracts of the International Typographical Union with newspapers that provided that the foreman of the composing room or mail room must be an I. T. U. member and must handle all hiring in his operation.

¶By the same vote, it upheld a provision in I. T. U. contracts that made the I. T. U. "general laws" applicable unless in conflict with Federal or state laws.

¶By the same vote, it held there was nothing illegal in bargaining agreements that provided that casual workers, both union and nonunion, be hired through a union-operated hiring hall.

¶It killed, 7 to 1, an N. L. R. B. ruling making labor and management refund to employes all union dues collected under an agreement found to constitute an illegal closed shop.

Douglas Writes Opinion

Justice William O. Douglas wrote the opinion of the court in all the cases. There was an eight-man court because Justice Felix Frankfurter took no part in the decisions.

Two cases settled long disputes over standard contracts sought by the typographical union. The first of these involved the New York Mailers' Union 6, which is affiliated with the I. T. U., and The New York Daily News and The Wall Street Journal.

The contract specified that mail room foremen must be members of the I. T. U. and must do the hiring. The N. L. R. B. had ruled that the foremen clause was a coercive device to make sure that only union members were hired and that it was thus a violation of the Taft-Hartley Law.

Justice Douglas wrote today that first, the contract said no foreman should be disciplined by the union for carrying out the publisher's instructions, and he concluded that the foreman remained the employer's agent despite his union membership.

Second, Justice Douglas said, the court would "not assume" that the foremen clause would produce discrimination in favor of union members in the absence of actual proof of discrimination.

The N. L. R. B. was thus left free to bring a case to show that

Continued on Page 27, Column 3

Jersey Votes Today In Primary Election

By GEORGE CABLE WRIGHT
Special to The New York Times.

TRENTON, April 17 — New Jersey residents will nominate major party candidates for Governor tomorrow, along with candidates for ten of twenty-one State Senate seats and for all sixty seats in the Assembly.

Also at stake will be the nominations for a number of county and local posts.

The polls will open at 7 A. M. and close at 8 P. M.

Interest will center on the balloting for the Republican nomination for Governor. A bitter three-way contest for the nomination came to a close tonight with television and radio appeals by the participants.

They are James P. Mitchell, the former Secretary of Labor, and State Senators Walter H. Jones of Bergen County and

Continued on Page 38, Column 1

U. S. Finds Soviet's Reply On Laos Is Unsatisfactory

Rusk Says Note Is Unclear on Timing and Verification of Cease-Fire—Calls Issue 'Very Critical'

By E. W. KENWORTHY
Special to The New York Times.

WASHINGTON, April 17—Secretary of State Dean Rusk said today that the new Soviet note on Laos did not satisfy the United States on the timing and verification of a cease-fire.

This, Mr. Rusk said at his news conference, is a "very critical matter" in any attempt to bring "the situation to a peaceful and satisfactory conclusion." [Introductory statement, Page 18.]

The Soviet note "clarifying" Moscow's first reply to the British proposals of March 23 was delivered to Sir Frank Roberts, the British Ambassador, yesterday. The British Embassy informed Mr. Rusk of the contents of the reply last night.

The British had proposed a three-step procedure—a call for a cease-fire by Britain and the Soviet Union, the co-chairmen of the 1954 Geneva Conference that brought the Indochinese war to an end; verification of the cease-fire by the three-nation International Control Commission, which observed the carrying out of the Geneva accord in Laos, and a fourteen-nation conference to set up a neutral, independent Laotian Government.

It was the British intention that these steps should take place in quick order. But Britain and the United States had made clear that there could be no conference until a cease-fire was in effect.

In one respect the Soviet note represented an advance over the earlier response, according to informed sources here. Previously Moscow had indicated that the cease-fire and the conference must take place simultaneously—or very nearly so.

In yesterday's note, these

Continued on Page 2, Column 3

GIZENGA OFFICERS ACCEPT MOBUTU AS ARMY'S CHIEF

Kasavubu Agrees to Reform Troops—Signs Accord on Congo-U.N. Cooperation

By HENRY TANNER
Special to The New York Times.

LEOPOLDVILLE, the Congo, April 17—Congolese Army headquarters announced tonight that field commanders operating under the control of the Leftist regime of Antoine Gizenga had recognized the authority of Maj. Gen. Joseph D. Mobutu as military commander in chief.

General Mobutu is the commander of the Central Government's forces.

The announcement said officers of the Gizenga regime had recognized General Mobutu during a conference at Bundoki, on the border of Eastern Province. The province is controlled by Mr. Gizenga.

The announcement also said a cease-fire had been ordered all along the border of Eastern and Equator Provinces.

Here in Leopoldville President Joseph Kasavubu and representatives of Secretary General Dag Hammarskjold signed an agreement on reorganization of the Congolese Army and the withdrawal of some foreign advisers.

Resolution 'Accepted'

The Congolese President and his Government "accepted" the Security Council resolution of Feb. 21 with the "understanding" that the United Nations, in implementing the resolution, respected the sovereignty of the Congo Republic.

The announcement on the military agreement did not say whether Gen. Victor Lundula, who has been commanding Mr. Gizenga's forces, took part in the conference.

Despite rumors of rivalry between him and Mr. Gizenga, General Lundula has consistently stressed his loyalty to his civilian superiors in Stanleyville, capital of Eastern Province.

General Mobutu left Leopoldville a week ago for the border area where the military conference took place. Talks between the two sides had continued intermittently for several weeks with and without his participation.

Kasavubu Plan Backed

In accepting the Security Council resolution the Leopoldville Government "recognized" the necessity for reorganizing the Congolese National Army. It reaffirmed President Kasavubu's earlier proposal that the reorganization take place with United Nations assistance, but under his personal authority as chief of state.

The agreement called for the United Nations to give assistance to the President so that "all foreign civil officials, military and paramilitary mercenaries and political advisers who have not been engaged under his authority" will be re-

Continued on Page 4, Column 3

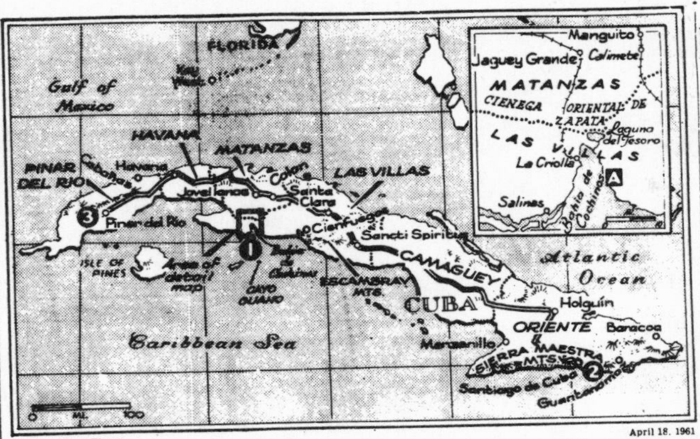

The New York Times — April 18, 1961

CARIBBEAN STRIFE: Rebel forces attacking Cuba landed in Las Villas Province in the area of Bahia de Cochinos (1, and A on the inset map). Other anti-Castro landings were said to have taken place in area of Santiago de Cuba (2) and in Pinar del Rio (3).

PREMIER DEFIANT

Says His Troops Battle Heroically to Repel Attacking Force

The texts of Castro appeals are printed on Page 14.

By TAD SZULC
Special to The New York Times.

MIAMI, Tuesday, April 18—Rebel troops opposed to Premier Fidel Castro landed before dawn yesterday on the swampy southern coast of Cuba in Las Villas Province.

The attack, which was supported from the air, was announced by the rebels and confirmed by the Cuban Government.

After fourteen hours of silence on the progress of the assault, the Government radio in Havana broadcast early today a terse communiqué signed by Premier Castro announcing only that "our armed forces are continuing to fight the enemy heroically."

The announcement, made shortly before 1 A. M., said that within the next few hours details of "our successes" would be given.

The communiqué came amid a wave of rebel assertions of victories, new landings and internal uprisings. The rebel spokesmen were acclaiming important progress in new landings in Oriente and Pinar del Rio Provinces, but none of these reports could be confirmed.

Government Reports Battle

The Government communiqué said a battle had been fought in the southeastern part of Las Villas Province, where yesterday morning's landings occurred.

Although the communiqué was signed by Premier Castro, the Cuban leader has not spoken to his nation since the attack began. An earlier communiqué, issued yesterday, reported the rebel landings.

In a communiqué issued last night, the Revolutionary Council, the top command of the rebel forces, said merely that military supplies and equipment were landed successfully on the marshy beachhead. The communiqué added that "some armed resistance" by supporters of Premier Castro had been overcome.

Premier Castro was reported to have escaped injury in an early-morning air raid yesterday near the beachhead.

The Revolutionary Council's announcement spoke of action in Matanzas Province, indicating that the rebels might have

Continued on Page 14, Column 1

HIGH COURT VOIDS CAFE'S NEGRO BAN

Holds Private Restaurant on State Land in Delaware Cannot Refuse Service

Special to The New York Times.

WASHINGTON, April 17—The Supreme Court held today that a privately operated restaurant situated in a publicly owned parking garage in Wilmington, Del., could not refuse to serve Negroes.

Six justices agreed on that result. The three others thought the case should have been sent back to the Delaware Supreme Court for clarification of its views on state law.

The decision is a significant one because of the light it throws on the established doctrine that only "official action" is covered by the Fourteenth Amendment. The Constitution does not prohibit racial discrimination by private persons or enterprises.

The court concluded that the Government of Delaware was sufficiently involved in this private enterprise, the restaurant, to bring it under the Constitution. In the view of observers here, the court broke at least some new ground in reaching that conclusion.

Justice Tom C. Clark wrote the opinion of the court. He was joined by Chief Justice Earl Warren and Justices Hugo L. Black, William O. Douglas and William J. Brennan Jr.

A separate concurring opinion, resting on quite different grounds, was filed by Justice Potter Stewart. Dissents suggesting that the court should

Continued on Page 26, Column 1

HAUSNER ATTACKS EICHMANN'S PLEA

Israeli Prosecutor Details His Charges After Ex-Nazi Says He Is Not Guilty

Text of decision and Hausner excerpts are on Page 23.

By HOMER BIGART
Special to The New York Times.

JERUSALEM (Israeli Sector), April 17 — Attorney General Gideon Hausner began an attack today on Adolf Eichmann's plea of innocence at his trial for responsibility in the killing of millions of Jews.

Earlier in the day Eichmann lost a challenge to the court's jurisdiction and entered his not-guilty plea when the trial was resumed after the week-end recess. Eichmann's plea for a hearing on his kidnapping from Argentina was rejected by the court.

"In the sense of the indictment I am not guilty," Eichmann had told the three Israeli judges.

He made his statement of innocence in a precise but toneless voice in reply to charges that he had planned the annihilation of 6,000,000 European Jews for the Nazis during World War II.

From the qualified nature of his plea, it was clear that Eichmann's defense would be based on the contention that he was a mere cog in the machinery of genocide and that he was bound by higher orders when he delivered the Jews to death camps.

Standing rigidly erect and

Continued on Page 23, Column 7

ROA CHARGES U.S. ARMED INVADERS

Tells U.N. That C.I.A. Aided Attacks—'Aggression' Is Denied by Stevenson

Excerpts from Stevenson and Roa statements, Page 16.

By THOMAS J. HAMILTON
Special to The New York Times.

UNITED NATIONS, N. Y., April 17—Dr. Raul Roa, Foreign Minister of Cuba, charged today that his country had been invaded this morning "by a force of mercenaries, organized, financed and armed by the Government of the United States."

Dr. Roa told the General Assembly's Political Committee that "the attack had been launched from points in Florida and Guatemala under the direction of the Central Intelligence Agency, which he called the "Gestapo." The Gestapo was the Nazi security police force.

He continued to use terms made familiar to nazism by calling Dr. José Miró Cardona, head of the anti-Castro Cuban Revolutionary Council, the "gauleiter." Gauleiters were regional party leaders under the Nazis.

Florida Launching Denied

Adlai E. Stevenson, chief United States delegate, said in reply that "the United States has committed no aggression against Cuba and no offensive has been launched from Florida or from any other part of the United States."

[In Guatemala, the Government denied that it had participated in any attack on Cuba.]

Just before the debate ended late this evening Dr. Roa charged that two jet planes from a United States carrier had escorted a Cuban rebel plane to safety this afternoon. He also alleged that forces from the United States Naval Base at Guantanamo had entered Oriente Province, where

Continued on Page 17, Column 1

Rusk Declares Sympathy Of Nation for Castro Foes

By JAMES RESTON
Special to The New York Times.

WASHINGTON, April 17—Secretary of State Dean Rusk expressed today the sympathy of the American people for those who struck against Castroism in Cuba, but emphasized "there is not and will not be any intervention there by United States forces."

The Administration did not deny that it was giving material support to the raiding parties, but this aid was undoubtedly on a much smaller

Transcript of Rusk's news conference is on Page 18.

scale than originally planned here and the landings in Cuba were much smaller than excited reports of "invasion" suggested.

No more than 200 to 300 men were involved in the week-end landings on the vast coastline of Cuba, according to reliable information reaching here.

In fact, the landings of the last forty-eight hours were not designed to get a lot of fighting men on the ground, but to provide supplies for the anti-Castro underground already operating there as a result of at least six other landings that have taken place over the last few months.

Refugees Assume Control

In the last ten days, the Cuban refugees have assumed control of the operations against Premier Fidel Castro. Accordingly, official Washington could not be sure of the fate of all the small parties that went ashore.

Secretary Rusk was extremely cautious in his remarks on the situation at his news conference this morning. What happens in Cuba, he said, is for the Cuban people to decide. He added, however, that the Administration was "not indifferent" to the intrusion of the "Communist conspiracy" into this hemisphere and promised to "work together with other governments of this hemisphere to meet efforts by this conspiracy to extend its penetration." [Opening statement, Page 18.]

On this point, considerable attention was being paid here

Continued on Page 18, Column 1

MOSCOW BLAMES U. S. FOR ATTACK

Izvestia Asserts 'American Hirelings' Invade Cuba—Khrushchev Confers

By SEYMOUR TOPPING
Special to The New York Times.

MOSCOW, April 17—The Soviet Union charged tonight that the United States is responsible for the landing in Cuba of what it described as "American hirelings."

Izvestia, the Soviet Government newspaper, contended that plans for landing anti-Castro forces in Cuba had been worked out and inspired by "American imperialists."

"On all continents voices now are crying out determinedly for an end to the armed aggression against Cuba and for the defense of the freedom and independence of the Cuban people," Izvestia said.

At his vacation retreat in Sochi on the Black Sea, Premier Khrushchev conferred on the Cuban crisis with Foreign Minister Andrei A. Gromyko. A formal Government statement is expected tomorrow.

Atmosphere Is Tense

An atmosphere of tension gripped the Soviet capital after the announcement at 4 P. M. by the Moscow radio that "an armed intervention against Cuba had begun."

It was felt by most Western experts that the Soviet reaction would be confined to strong diplomatic representations, complaints in the United Nations and a propaganda onslaught against the United States.

Some observers recalled that in a speech here July 10, Mr. Khrushchev had declared: "Figuratively speaking, if need be, Soviet artillerymen can support the Cuban people with their rocket fire, should the aggressive forces in the Pentagon dare to start intervention against Cuba."

The Soviet leader also had noted that the United States was no longer out of range of Soviet missiles.

Western experts said that Mr. Khrushchev's statement seemed to have more applicability to an invasion of Cuba by United States forces than to an attack of the type being under-

Continued on Page 17, Column 2

CHANTING CUBANS BACK CASTRO HERE

1,000 in Midtown March Dispersed by Police

Nearly 1,000 chanting, sign-bearing pro-Castro Cubans demonstrated last night outside the United Nations and the United States Mission to the United Nations and in the Times Square area.

Heavy police details had kept the crowds behind barriers most of the day and no violence erupted until a smaller group of pro-Castro Cubans blocked pedestrian traffic in Times Square. The police made two arrests and two policemen were injured during a brief scuffle with the demonstrators.

Many of the demonstrators carried Cuban flags and pictures of Dr. Castro as they marched from the United Nations Plaza along Forty-second Street to the corner of Eighth Avenue and Forty-third Street.

An emergency police signal brought ten radio cars and ten mounted policemen to that area. The crowd then broke up into four factions and departed in different directions.

A few minutes later, at 8 P. M., a smaller group of demonstrators formed on the sidewalk on Broadway between

Continued on Page 14, Column 5

Eisenhowers Are Welcomed Home to Pennsylvania

United Press International Telephoto

General and Mrs. Eisenhower in Harrisburg with Gov. David L. Lawrence of Pennsylvania

By The Associated Press.

HARRISBURG, Pa., April 17—Thousands of persons welcomed former President Dwight D. Eisenhower and Mrs. Eisenhower home to Pennsylvania today. The gathering was the state's official welcome for General Eisenhower, who left the White House Jan. 20. The former President, looking tanned and rested after a six-week vacation in California, was obviously touched. Gov. David L. Lawrence, a Democrat, headed the state and city officials on the platform. The Eisenhowers have a farm home in Gettysburg, thirty-five miles southwest of this capital city. It is the only home they have ever owned. They left for home by car after the ceremonies.

Walker Is Relieved of Command While Army Checks Birch Ties

Special to The New York Times.

WASHINGTON, April 17—The Army said today that Maj. Gen. Edwin A. Walker had been relieved of his command in Germany while an investigation was made into reports that he had been indoctrinating his troops with the views of the John Birch Society.

The announcement said that Secretary of the Army Elvis J. Stahr Jr. had ordered General Walker transferred immediately from command of the front-line Twenty-fourth Division "pending the outcome of an official investigation."

The investigation will involve "certain published statements and actions of General Walker," the Army said.

General Walker was ordered transferred to the headquarters of the United States Army in Europe at Heidelberg, Germany, the Army said.

The announcement did not mention the Birch Society. However, officials acknowledged that the transfer and investigation had been prompted by allegations that the 51-year-old general had been urging the views of the Right-Wing group upon his troops for the last six months.

The Overseas Weekly, a privately owned newspaper distributed among American troops in Europe, reported last week that General Walker had instituted a special troop-indoctrination program using materials and publications of the society.

General Walker accused the newspaper yesterday of being "immoral, unscrupulous, corrupt and destructive." The newspaper stood by its original report and said that his charges

Continued on Page 24, Column 6

NEWS INDEX

News Summary and Index, Page 39

Anti-Castro Military Units Land in Southern Cuba and Battle Government Forces

PREMIER DIRECTS ISLAND DEFENSES

Escapes Injury in Bombing Raid—Aircraft Support Rebels at Beachhead

Continued From Page 1, Col. 8

crossed the provincial border from Las Villas. The border is about ten miles north of the presumed landing spot.

The communiqué also said that "substantial amounts of food and ammunition" had reached the underground units in that region.

The Government accused the United States of having organized the attack.

Late last night unconfirmed reports from rebel leaders asserted that the attacking force had penetrated deep into Matanzas Province, reaching the central highway near the town of Colón.

An insistent spate of reports said that numerous landings also had occurred in Oriente Province, in the eastern part of Cuba, in the vicinity of Santiago de Cuba. But a complete blackout of direct news from Cuba made it impossible to assess the situation accurately.

In New York, the Revolutionary Council announced that "much of the militia in the countryside has already defected from Castro." The council predicted that "the principal battle" of the revolt would be fought along with a coordinated wave of sabotage before dawn.

President José Miró Cardona of the council in an earlier statement had called for Western Hemisphere peoples to support the revolt "morally and materially." The council has announced its aim to set up a "government in arms" as soon as it can get territory in Cuba and then to ask for foreign recognition and help.

[A dispatch said that the Cuban naval station at Veradero had reported a fleet of eight strange ships off Cardenas, north coast seaport about eighty-five miles east of Havana.]

National Alert Declared

The invaders, in undetermined numbers, are under the orders of the Revolutionary Council. In the words of its declaration, the Council seeks the overthrow of the Castro regime and the freeing of Cuba from "international communism's cruel oppression."

Premier Castro declared shortly before noon a state of national alert and called all his militia forces to their posts.

The Cuban official radio devoted most of its time yesterday to broadcasts of Dr. Castro's three proclamations and to vituperation against United States "imperialists."

The official Cuban radio announced last night the arrest of Havana's Auxiliary Bishop, Msgr. Eduardo Boza Masvidal, on charges of hiding United States currency and medicine for anti-Castro rebels.

The Government-controlled radio stations offered their normal music programs and soap operas. There were no further references to the landings.

An occasional announcement spoke of foreign support for Cuba, including a mention of volunteers from Czechoslovakia seeking to enlist to fight in Cuba.

According to official statements by both sides, the rebel forces went ashore during the night near the Bay of Cochinos as paratroop units were dropped farther inland to link up with underground fighters.

It was believed that the rebels landed near Playa Larga, on the eastern bank of the Cochinos Bay, which means the Bay of Pigs. This bay is wedged into the vast swamp of the Cienega de Zapata.

Report of Capture Unconfirmed

Persistent reports in exile circles that Raul Castro, Fidel's brother and Minister of the Revolutionary armed forces, had been captured somewhere near Santiago could not be confirmed.

One Cuban in close touch with Democratic Revolutionary Front activities here said the report was given credence by the fact that Dr. Castro had assumed the military role that for recent months he had turned over to his brother.

Dr. Castro charged that the invaders were "mercenaries" in the service of United States "imperialism." He pledged the Cubans to fight until death for the preservation of their "democratic and Socialist revolution."

The Revolutionary Council members were standing by, ready to move into Cuba and proclaim a "government in arms" as soon as the beachhead is firmly secured.

It was not known early last night how many troops had participated in the Las Villas landing. Whether this was to be the principal thrust against the Castro forces or the first of several such attacks also was not known.

The total strength of forces available to the rebels is estimated at somewhat over 5,000 men. Opposed to them is a military establishment of 400,000 of the regular army and the militia armed with the most modern Soviet bloc weapons.

The rebel command is known to believe that one or more major landings would set off internal uprisings and many desertions by soldiers and the militia.

Today it was too early to tell whether this optimism was justified.

The use by the rebels yesterday of planes and gunboats covering the landing indicated that it was an operation of major scope and not just another guerrilla foray of the type that has been occurring in the past.

It was believed here that the attacking forces came from the camps in Guatemala, where they have been trained for the last nine months. Some of the units may have come from a rebel camp in Louisiana.

Battle Area Strafed

It was believed, however, that the rebel troops left their camps a day or so ago and were staged for the jump-off at Caribbean islands somewhere between Central America and the Cienega de Zapata Peninsula of Las Villas Province.

A possible location of the staging area is the Swan Islands, where there is an anti-Castro radio station.

Capt. Manuel Artime, a 29-year-old former Castro officer, is reported to be the field commander of the operation. He was appointed last week by the Revolutionary Council as its "delegate to the armed forces."

Rebel aircraft bombed and strafed the battle area that extends into Matanzas Province.

About 7 o'clock in the morning, Premier Castro, personally leading the defense operations, was reported to have found himself under an aerial bombardment in the small town of Boca de Laguna de Tesoro, about ten miles to the northeast of Cochinos Bay.

Cuban radio stations broadcast at 11:07 A. M. proclamations by Dr. Castro and President Osvaldo Dorticos Torrado acknowledging that Cuba had been attacked and declaring a state of national alert.

Up to then, radio stations had kept up normal musical programs, which beginning at 8 A. M. were interrupted by constant "urgent" calls from the general staff of the army ordering militiamen to report immediately to their battle stations.

The only report issued during the day by the Castro regime on the progress of the fighting came in the Premier's proclamation. He declared that "our troops are advancing against the enemy * * * in the certainty of victory."

Radio messages on the Government microwave network monitored here—which gave a dramatic minute-by-minute account of the first hours of the landing—included appeals for reinforcements from additional militia battalions and a request for ambulances for the "many wounded."

It was a frantic conversation between Government radio operators in the invasion area that provided the news that Premier Castro was in the town being bombed.

The network ceased transmitting at 7:20 A. M.—except for the sudden call for the ambulances that came at 11 A. M.

Varona's Visit Cited

There were many indications that the mechanism of the invasion was set finally into motion Sunday when Dr. Manuel Antonio de Varona, a member of the Revolutionary Council and Minister of Defense in the Provisional Government, made a quick flight and visit to Miami.

Simultaneously, a large number of exile leaders here, including military figures, vanished early Sunday. They have not been seen since.

The climate for the invasion—anticipated and promised by the Cuban rebels for many weeks—was created to a large extent by events of last week.

Since last Thursday a major wave of sabotage swept Cuba. Saturday three B-26 aircraft bombed three air bases on the island. Beginning in the middle of last week informants in Cuban groups made it known confidentially that "important events" were to be expected over the week-end.

Final preparations for the move against the Castro regime started in earnest about three weeks ago after the Revolutionary Council was formed and a secret mobilization order went out to rebel volunteers.

For the last three weeks hundreds of volunteers had been leaving the Miami and New York areas for the camps in the training grounds in Guatamala.

Yesterday as word of the attack spread in Miami, additional hundreds of volunteers began appearing at the recruiting offices of several of the movements that make up the Revolutionary Council.

At least one sizable group of highly trained officers and men were still held back at a ranch on the outskirts of Miami.

In his proclamations, Dr. Castro appealed repeatedly for support by Latin-American nations. The Havana radio broadcast reports of Latin-American solidarity for the Cuban cause.

The Revolutionary Council also addressed itself to Latin America. Its dawn declaration stated that the rebels were convinced that "the freedom loving people of this hemisphere will make common cause with them and support them."

Rebel Gains Reported

MIAMI, April 17 (AP) A Cuban rebel spokesman said tonight an invading force had penetrated to Cuba's main east-west highway in a drive from the south into Matanzas Province.

There have been two confirmed landings on the island by invading forces and a possible third landing, the spokesman said.

The confirmed landings are in Oriente Province, probably somewhere in the area of Santiago de Cuba, and on the southern coast of Las Villas Province, a rugged, swampy and sparsely populated area in the vicinity of the Bahia de Cochinos. It is possible a third landing took place in the westernmost province, Pinar del Rio.

10,000 Reported Freed

MEXICO CITY, April 17 (AP) —The Mexico City agency of the Cuban Revolutionary Council said today anti-Castro rebels had taken the Isle of Pines and freed 10,000 political prisoners, who joined the rebellion. The agency said its information came in radio broadcasts from the Isle of Pines.

The New York Times April 18, 1961

CASTRO UNDER ATTACK: Cuba said the forces landing on her south coast (1) had originated in Guatemala (2) and Florida (4). It was speculated that another base for the anti-Government units was the Swan Islands (3).

MESSAGES DEPICT CUBAN CONFUSION

Radio Listeners Hear Report of Bombs Near Castro

Special to The New York Times.

MIAMI, April 17—Intercepted military messages by radio were the first source today of direct information from Cuba on the invasion by anti-Castro rebels.

They gave a vivid if fragmentary picture of violence and confusion. Fidel Castro's officers shouted urgently back and forth to each other.

The messages were interrupted by static. Much of the time only one side of an exchange could be heard. However, pieced together, the fragments were informative.

The radio network was shut down abruptly at 7:20 A. M. on the ground that too many Cubans were hearing the messages and "they are alarming the public a little."

Further use of the station was reserved for serious emergencies, at the discretion of the field commanders. At 11 A. M., for instance, one was used to call for ambulances.

Castro Under Fire

Meanwhile, they had revealed that Dr. Castro had been under bombardment near the scene of a landing.

Messages that were understandable gave the following series of developments:

(A dash at the beginning of a paragraph indicates a change of speakers. In many cases there is no way of identifying the station or the speaker. The exchanges were over the island-wide net of microwave stations generally relied on for official communication.)

(6:40 A. M.): A Sea Fury has pursued a B-26. Orders have been given to post lookouts on hilltops to know what planes are coming and going. [The Cuban Air Force has some British Sea Fury planes. The anti-Castro forces are not believed to have any.]

—(6:43): The aircraft are asking for reinforcements. They are firing on the boats.

—(6:45): (Havana central to Laguna) Please repeat the message from the boat in the inlet that picked up the call from the planes asking for help.

—(6:47): (From Laguna) According to the boat, they are asking for help.

—(6:50): (From Havana) The chief of operations wants to know who is authorizing the information bulletins.

—They are being authorized by Osmani Cienfuegos and by Sergio. [Osmani Cienfuegos is Minister of Communications in the Castro Government. Maj. Sergio del Valle is the air force commander.]

'Alarming the Public'

—Listen, Osmani, this is Captain Ruiz of the detachment at Jovellanos. The problem is this: You know that the army bulletins can't be transmitted by the microwave stations of the various departments. The adjutant says it must be done exclusively through official channels because all the departments are picking them up and they are alarming the public a little.

—(From Cienfuegos) Listen, this is the problem: We here are in direct communication with Fidel and we are using a part of this information to keep up to date on what is happening.

—(Havana, apparently in answer to a question) Osmani and Sergio are at the headquarters of the militia. They are still using the station at Jaguey.

—(After an unintelligible period) Ask if our people also are dropping parachutes.

—Tell him no.

—What are they dropping? Men or cases?

—They are dropping parachutes and bombs. In the Boca de la Zanja they are dropping bombs. The lieutenant says the enemy is among the works [apparently referring to the construction work in progress] on Playa Larga [Long Beach]. Our people are passing through Palpite.

—(After another interruption) The four planes are already over the beach. Message signed Evelio Rodriguez.

Bombs 'Where Fidel Is'

—(Havana calling) Tell me, Laguna, how many parachutes? La Boca is still calling. A bomb fell near La Boca.

—(Jaguey to Havana headquarters) They bombed here where Fidel is.

—(Havana) If they bombed where Fidel was, how is it you did not know about it when you have him there almost in front of you?

—Tell me if they are men or bundles being dropped. It is very far from here and we cannot tell. There are about thirty parachutes and bombs can be heard. Explosions can be heard and the walls are shaking.

—(Apparently Jaguey to Havana) Czech truck passed through here with about thirty militiamen of Battalion 225, Company 1.

The network was heard again at 11 A. M. in an urgent call from Jaguey to the Red Cross in Havana, asking that all possible ambulances be sent to pick up "many wounded."

All the places mentioned in the messages are in the area north of Bahia Cochinos, where a landing was reported under way. Jaguey is about twenty-five miles north of the inner tip of the bay. Jovellanos is about the same distance north of Jaguey. They are mostly in Matanzas Province, though the landing point was in Las Villas Province.

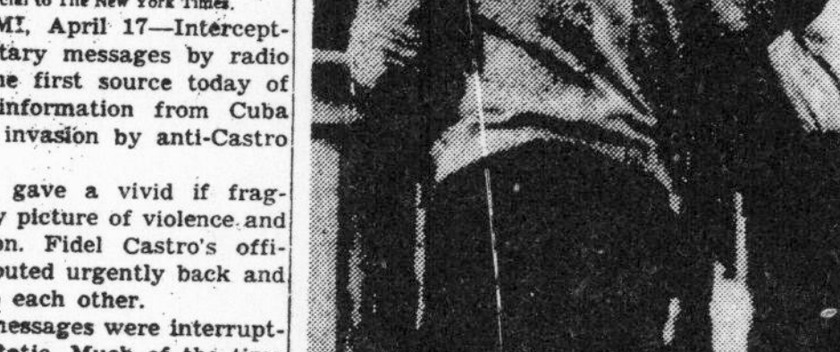

Associated Press Wirephoto

PRAY FOR COMBATANTS: Cuban women kneeling at altar yesterday in Gesu Roman Catholic Church, Miami.

Castro Hailed by Cubans Here; Police Break Up Midtown Rally

Continued From Page 1, Col. 8

Forty-second and Forty-third Streets to cheer and boo the sign bulletins revolving around the building in Times Square.

They shouted, "Yellow press," "Hands off Cuba" and "Yankee no, Cuba si."

At this point ten mounted policemen arrived, drove their horses on the sidewalk, dispersed the crowd and made two arrests. The demonstrators shouted angry epithets at the police, but then dispersed.

The demonstrations began at the United Nations and the United States Mission at 2 Park Avenue about 5 P. M. Each group numbered about 500.

An hour later, the group demonstrating at the mission offices marched to the United Nations Plaza and was assigned to a separate picketing area. In general, the demonstration was noisy but orderly.

Many carried placards bearing such hand-written inscriptions as "End U. S. intervention in Cuba," "Hands off Cuba," "Socialism si, Imperialism no," and "Cuba si, Yankee no."

Shortly after 7 P. M. the two groups left the United Nations Plaza and were allowed to march west along Forty-second Street on both sidewalks.

The police, including about twenty-five mounted patrolmen, held back traffic at the lights but restrained the demonstrators from crossing from one side of the street to the other.

Pedestrians along the route paid little attention to the marchers. The parade was orderly until it reached Eighth Avenue.

When the police dispersed the crowds there, it appeared that the demonstration was over, but a few minutes later the smaller, disorderly group appeared in Times Square.

South African Assails U. N.

CAPETOWN, South Africa, April 17 (Reuters)—Eric Louw, Minister of External Affairs, charged today that there was more racial discrimination in the United States than in this country. He told the House of Assembly there was discrimination also in Canada, India, Norway and Sweden. He said he was referring to those countries to show what he called the hypocrisy of the United Nations.

LATIN AID MEASURE SCORED IN CONGRESS

WASHINGTON, April 17 (AP)—President Kennedy's request for a Latin-American aid appropriation of $500,000,000 received a sour reception in Congress, according to testimony that was disclosed today.

But Administration spokesmen, fighting for the measure, warned that if the money was not granted "it would be a disaster for the United States," with "an exceedingly bad reaction in Latin America."

The proposals were criticized by Representative Otto Passman, Democrat of Louisiana, as "slipshod" and "a blank check." Other members of his Appropriations subcommittee agreed that additional details were needed.

Mr. Passman said that in regard to the need for the full $500,000,000, "there is some difference of opinion among officials in Government at a very high level." The difference had been at Cabinet level, he indicated.

The hearings on the President's request, an integral part of his "alliance for progress" program, were held the week of March 20. The full Appropriations Committee has yet to vote on the measure.

Lincoln Gordon, a member of the State Department's Inter-American task force and the principal spokesman for the bill, indicated that the $500,000,000 might be the first installment of a program that would cost $2,500,000,000 over the next ten years. Additional money might be sought in 1963, he said.

REBEL AID DENIED BY GUATEMALANS

Regime Says Country Was Not Base for Cuban Raid

By PAUL P. KENNEDY

Special to The New York Times.

GUATEMALA, April 17—The Guatemalan Government categorically denied today that it was participating in the attack on Cuba.

An official statement published at noon in the Government newspaper Diario de Centro America dealt principally with a charge that part of the invasion of Cuba had been launched from Guatemalan bases. The statement denied this charge.

The Government statement concluded with the declaration, "Guatemala, faithful to her international obligations and invariable policy, has not intervened and will not intervene in the internal affairs of other countries, including Cuba."

Referring to the charge that the invasion had been launched from Guatemala, the Government statement declared, "Anyone interested in proving the inaccuracy of those accusations may inspect the seventy kilometers (about forty-four miles) of Guatemalan Atlantic coastline and the cities of this shore, including Puerto Barrios, Matias de Galvez, Livingston, etc."

Peten Base Mentioned

Meanwhile, there have been persistent reports here that part of the military strike against Cuba originated at a training camp in the Guatemalan Department of Peten, which lies between Mexico and British Honduras.

The Government, before today's statement, has repeatedly denied that Guatemala has been involved in the action against Cuba. President Miguel Ydigoras Fuentes declared in an interview that Guatemala was not going to send "anything or anybody" against Cuba from Guatemala.

The reports on the training camp, wholly unconfirmed, maintain the camp is in southeastern Peten, the largest and most isolated of Guatemala's twenty-two departments. The reports maintain that the camp is near the town of Sayaxché. This town is on the Pasión River, about thirty miles west of the Mexican border, between Honduras and the Mexican State of Chiapas.

Flights of private planes recently have been forbidden over this area. Last week an anthropological expedition from the National University of Guatemala had to postpone flights over the area on the orders of Government authorities.

Students Score Government

Reports that the airfield at the Caribbean port of Puerto Barrios had been closed to all except military traffic were confirmed here this morning. There is no other Guatemalan airport on the Caribbean coast. All traffic for the port, about 200 miles from Guatemala City, now must go by highway or rail.

The Association of Engineering Students at the Guatemala National University issued a statement last night criticizing the Government for what it alleged was the toleration of foreign military bases on Guatemalan territory. The statement declared that the association was "greatly preoccupied by the gravity of the existence of foreign military contingents on our soil."

The statement also "repudiated whatever type of aggression operated against the Cuban Government from our territory." It demanded that the national army "maintain national sovereignty, avoid the installation of foreign military bases on Guatemalan territory and repel any type of aggression against this country."

A statement charging the United States with an "offensive" against Latin-American sovereignty in the Cuban invasion has been issued by the Association of Students in Economics Sciences at the National University. This statement declared that the attack on Cuba was "by North American imperialism at a time when the wounds of aggression by these same forces against the Guatemalan people in 1954 has still not healed."

The Cuban invasion was the chief topic of conversation in the streets and in stores and cafes here. The morning papers and radio news broadcasters devoted many words to the event. The morning newspapers, however, did not react editorially to the situation.

Guatemala Opens Maneuvers

GUATEMALA, April 17 (Reuters) — The Guatemalan Army announced today the immediate opening of week-long military maneuvers. However the Defense Ministry said the maneuvers were not connected with the Cuban situation.

The Ministry said army guards surrounding the United States embassy and residence were also a routine preventative measure.

PHONE LINK TO U. S. IS CLOSED BY CUBA

Cuba shut down yesterday all telephone and commercial cable and wireless service to the United States.

According to a spokesman for the Bell System all calls were being blocked. Long-distance operators informed callers that service would be out indefinitely.

Radiograms were being accepted in Havana, but there was no word on whether they were being delivered.

Two airlines at New York International Airport reported this afternoon that as a precautionary measure they have ordered all flights that normally fly over Cuba to take routes that would skirt the island.

The airlines were the British Overseas Airways Corporation and Avianca.

WASHINGTON, April 17 (AP) — The Federal Aviation Agency today ordered cancellation until further notice of all flights by United States civilian aircraft over Cuban territory or the vicinity of Cuba.

Statements Broadcast by Castro Regime

Special to The New York Times.

MIAMI, April 17—Following, in unofficial translation, are the texts of an "exhortation to the peoples of the Americas" signed by Premier Fidel Castro and President Osvaldo Dorticos Torrado and broadcast today by Cuban stations, and of a "declaration of alert" and a statement to the Cubans issued by Premier Castro and broadcast also:

Plea to Americas

The United States imperialism has launched its announced and cowardly aggression against Cuba. Mercenaries and adventurers have landed at a point of our country. The peoples of Cuba, with valor and heroism, are already certain of smashing it.

The solidarity of the peoples of Latin America and of the world is against the North American imperialists.

The world has become aware that the students, the intellectuals of Latin America, are with Cuba and her revolution that redeems the humble.

In strengthening the struggle against its principal enemy, the Yankee imperialism, all Cuba rises with the password of "Fatherland or Death," because our battle is your battle. Cuba shall win.

Declaration of Alert

The commander in chief and Premier of the Government declares the country in a state of alert and orders the Rebel Army, the militias and all the security forces to increase the vigilance and to act without hesitation against those who are caught committing acts of sabotage, shooting or crimes.

To double the vigilance, to denounce the counter-revolutionaries and their activities.

To exhort the workers to remain in their posts and redouble their efforts of production and vigilance.

To the entire population, to maintain order and the strictest discipline against mercenaries, fifth columnists, saboteurs and counter-revolutionaries in general.

All to action for a free and sovereign Cuba. All for the revolution that redeems the humble—the patriotic, democratic and socialist revolution of Cuba. With the password of "Fatherland or Death"—We shall win.

Statement to Cubans

Troops landed by sea and air are attacking the south of Las Villas, supported by aircraft and warships. Rebel troops [Dr. Castro's Army] are fighting the enemy. We are fighting in the defense of our sacred fatherland against the mercenaries organized by the imperialistic Government of the United States.

Our troops are already advancing against the enemy, certain of victory. The people are mobilizing already.

Forward, Cubans, to answer with fire and iron the barbarians who pretend to take away our liberties.

The people are mobilizing against a Government that wants a return to slavery. They come to take away the land that the revolution handed to the peasants and the cooperatives. We are fighting to defend the lands of the peasant and the cooperatives.

They want to take away the factories from the people, the sugar mills from the people, the mines from the people.

We fight to defend our factories, our sugar mills and our mines.

They come to take away from our sons and our peasant girls our schools that the revolution had given to them. They come to take away from the Negro man and woman the dignity that the revolution had returned to them.

We shall fight to maintain in all the people this supreme dignity of the Cuban nation. They come to take away our workers from their new jobs. We shall fight for a free Cuba. They come to destroy our fatherland and we shall defend the fatherland.

Forward, Cubans! All to your posts and to your work. Forward, Cubans! Because revolution is invincible, and against her and against the heroic people that defends her, all the enemies will be smashed. Let us shout now with more ardor and firmness now that the Cuban is suffering in combat—"Long live Free Cuba! We shall win!"

"All the News That's Fit to Print"

The New York Times.

LATE CITY EDITION

U. S. Weather Bureau Report (Page 62) forecasts: Cloudy, warm, chance of rain late today or tonight and tomorrow. Temp. range: 61—48; yesterday: 70—47.

VOL. CX..No. 37,723.

NEW YORK, SATURDAY, MAY 6, 1961.

10 cents beyond 50-mile zone from New York City except on Long Island. Higher in air delivery cities.

FIVE CENTS

U. S. HURLS MAN 115 MILES INTO SPACE; SHEPARD WORKS CONTROLS IN CAPSULE, REPORTS BY RADIO IN 15-MINUTE FLIGHT

JOHNSON TO MEET LEADERS IN ASIA ON U. S. TROOP USE

President Says Decision on South Vietnam Action Will Await Report

TALKS SET IN CAPITALS

Ngo Dinh Diem Is Expected to Seek American Units to Deter Red Attack

Transcript of news conference and summary, Page 14.

By WILLIAM J. JORDEN

Special to The New York Times.

WASHINGTON, May 5—President Kennedy said today that the assignment of United States armed forces to South Vietnam would be one of several important matters Vice President Lyndon B. Johnson would discuss on his coming trip to Asia. [Opening statement and Question 4, Page 14.]

The President confirmed that the possibility of sending United States troops to Southeast Asia was under study. He indicated that the final decision would depend on the results of Mr. Johnson's talks in Saigon with President Ngo Dinh Diem and others.

Mr. Kennedy said at a news conference that a special task force in the Government was working on problems related to helping South Vietnam maintain its independence. The question has been considered by the National Security Council as well, he said.

Vital Assignment

Mr. Johnson is expected to leave next Tuesday for the Far East. He also will meet with top Government officials in Bangkok, Thailand; Manila, and other capitals.

The President today described the Johnson mission as "an extremely important assignment."

It is widely assumed here that President Ngo will ask for the assignment of at least a token force of United States troops and regard it as a guarantee of United States' involvement should his country be attacked in force by the Communist North.

Mr. Kennedy did not touch on the matter today, but it is known that the Government is also considering the possibility of sending a similar token force to Thailand. The latter is allied to the United States in the

Continued on Page 3, Column 4

Talks Open in Laos On Truce Details; Meeting 'Friendly'

By JACQUES NEVARD

Special to The New York Times.

HIN HEUP, Laos, May 5—Military representatives of the pro-Western Laotian Government and the pro-Communist Pathet Lao rebels held a preliminary conference here today on machinery for continuing the cease-fire that became effective Wednesday.

The conference lasted one hour and five minutes and was described as "friendly."

According to a Laotian Army spokesman, Col. Oudom Sananikone, the meeting did not take up any political questions.

There appeared to be few tangible results of the talks, but Colonel Oudom Sananikone stressed that the meeting was a preliminary one.

He said that the first Pathet Lao request was that the next meeting take place at Namone, thirty-five miles north of here

Continued on Page 3, Column 2

2 BILLION AID PLAN FOR BRAZIL IS NEAR

U. S. Presses World-Wide Program of New Loans and Debt Deferments

By TAD SZULC

Special to The New York Times.

WASHINGTON, May 5—An international financial rescue package worth more than $2,000,000,000 is being prepared for Brazil. Negotiations, already well advanced, involve the United States, six Western European countries, Japan and the International Monetary Fund.

The agreements, which may be announced late next week, call for new loans totaling nearly $630,000,000. About $340,000,000 of this is to be provided by the United States. The remainder will take the form of a postponement in the repayment of much of Brazil's huge foreign debt.

This international financial operation, the largest ever involving a Latin-American country and one of the largest anywhere in postwar years, is designed to provide President Janio Quadros with extra time and resources to reorganize his economy.

Broad Effort in View

The United States is playing a key role in putting together the Brazilian package. It will also supply separate smaller loans to bolster the economies of Venezuela and Bolivia. Venezuela, which is facing serious budget difficulties, expects to receive soon an initial loan of $50,000,000.

Besides these emergency measures to assist the economies of individual Latin-American republics, the United States moved today to call a special inter-American conference to blueprint long-range economic and social development programs.

President Kennedy announced at his news conference that the United States' delegation to the Council of the Organization of American States had been in-

Continued on Page 17, Column 1

NIXON ASKS DRIVE TO OFFSET SOVIET

Bids Kennedy Rally America to a Fresh Foreign Policy

Excerpts from Nixon speech are printed on Page 2.

By AUSTIN C. WEHRWEIN

Special to The New York Times.

CHICAGO, May 5—Former Vice President Richard M. Nixon urged President Kennedy today to rally the American people for a new start in American foreign policy.

Mr. Nixon called for a "searching reappraisal of the free world's ability, particularly America's ability, to deal with the kind of aggression in which Communists are now engaging."

He further revealed that he had given President Kennedy the "assurance that I will support him to the hilt in backing positive action he may decide is necessary to resist Communist aggression."

[President Kennedy, meanwhile, sent his nuclear test-ban negotiator back to Geneva with an implied warning that the United States might not continue the talks much longer without some prospect of a safeguarded treaty.]

To meet such threats, the former Vice President said that the United States should be prepared to act alone if swift action were needed while machinery for collective action was being set up.

The lesson of Cuba and Laos, he said, is this:

"We must never talk bigger than we are prepared to act.

"When our words are strong and our actions are timid, we

Continued on Page 2, Column 3

LAUNCHING: Rocket lifts the capsule

RETURN: Astronaut rides in one of helicopters carrying his Mercury capsule to the Lake Champlain

Associated Press Wirephotos

SAFE ABOARD: On the Lake Champlain's deck, Comdr. Alan B. Shepard Jr. views capsule he occupied

ASTRONAUT: Commander Shepard removes space suit.

IN FINE CONDITION

Astronaut Drops Into the Sea Four Miles From Carrier

Excerpts from radioed reports by Shepard, Page 8

By RICHARD WITKIN

Special to The New York Times.

CAPE CANAVERAL, Fla., May 5—A slim, cool Navy test pilot was rocketed 115 miles into space today.

Thirty-seven-year-old Comdr. Alan B. Shepard Jr. thus became the first American space explorer.

Commander Shepard landed safely 302 miles out at sea fifteen minutes after the launching. He was quickly lifted aboard a Marine Corps helicopter.

"Boy, what a ride!" he said, as he was flown to the aircraft carrier Lake Champlain four miles away.

Extensive physical examinations were begun immediately.

Tonight doctors reported Commander Shepard in "excellent" condition, suffering no ill effects.

Major U. S. Step

The near-perfect flight represented the United States' first major step in the race to explore space with manned space craft.

True, it was only a modest leap compared with the once-around-the-earth orbital flight of Maj. Yuri A. Gagarin of the Soviet Union.

The Russian's speed of more than 17,000 miles an hour was almost four times Commander Shepard's 4,500. The distance the Russian traveled was almost 100 times as great.

But Commander Shepard maneuvered his craft in space—something the Russians have not claimed for Major Gagarin.

All in all, the Shepard flight was welcomed almost rapturous-

Continued on Page 8, Column 1

Kennedy Plans Aid To Retrain Jobless And Spur Recovery

By PETER BRAESTRUP

Special to The New York Times.

WASHINGTON, May 5—The Kennedy Administration expects to ask Congress for at least $75,000,000 to provide retraining for the long-term unemployed. Other new anti-recession measures also are being considered.

The key question that President Kennedy has yet to decide is whether to break the Administration's self-imposed limit on Federal spending in an effort to stimulate the economy and spur employment.

The $75,000,000 program for retraining workers who have been laid off by technological change and by the decay of their own industries will not materially affect the budget. Nor will the President's orders to the Pentagon to channel more defense contracts to small

Continued on Page 19, Column 2

MAYOR IS UPHELD ON CHARTER LAW

But Court Reverses Ban on Action by Council, Opening Way to Rival Proposals

By RONALD MAIORANA

Mayor Wagner's right to appoint a Charter Revision Commission was upheld by Justice Irving Saypol yesterday in State Supreme Court.

However, Justice Saypol ruled invalid part of the law under which the Mayor had acted. This part excluded the City Council from Charter-revision activity.

Lawyers said the ruling appeared to make possible the enactment of the City Council's own plan for a Charter Revision Commission. Thus, it is conceivable, they said, that two competing Charters—one drawn by the Mayor's commission and the other by a commission created by the Council—could be submitted to the voters Nov. 7.

In a twenty-two-page decision that caused confusion at City Hall Justice Saypol ruled that the section of the state law that had the effect of bypassing the City Council was invalid because it was an improper delegation of legislative power. He said: "The newly enacted au-

Continued on Page 32, Column 1

Shepard Had Periscope: 'What a Beautiful View'

By JOHN W. FINNEY

Special to The New York Times.

CAPE CANAVERAL, Fla., May 5—"All systems go * * * Everything A-O.K. * * * Mission very smooth * * * What a beautiful view! * * * Coming in for a landing."

These were the reports of Comdr. Alan B. Shepard Jr. as he rode the capsule Freedom 7 115 miles up into space today in the United States' first step toward manned exploration of space. His "A-O.K," is a rocket engineer term meaning double O.K. or perfect.

In a calm, methodical way he reported back by radio on every detail of his fifteen-minute flight, even during the moments of greatest stress as his capsule accelerated from the launching pad and then quickly decelerated upon re-entering the earth's atmosphere.

And there were moments of excitement in his voice, such as when he viewed much of the Eastern Coast of the United States through a periscope from 115 miles up in space.

"What a beautiful view!" he exclaimed into a microphone inside his visored space helmet and then, according to instructions, he returned to scientific observations to report that the cloud cover was three- to four-tenths and was obscuring much of the coast up through Cape Hatteras.

Three-to-four-teenths cloud cover is a description used by

Continued on Page 10, Column 1

PRESIDENT TO ASK INCOME TAX CUTS

Drop Next Year Is Planned, Dillon Tells House Unit

By JOHN D. MORRIS

Special to The New York Times.

WASHINGTON, May 5—The Kennedy Administration plans to lay before Congress next year a tax reform program that will include reduction of individual income taxes.

Secretary of the Treasury Douglas Dillon told the House Ways and Means Committee of the plan today but gave no details. He made it clear, however, that taxpayers with high incomes would probably be among the chief beneficiaries of a proposed reduction in rates.

"I think those in high brackets deserve relief," he said.

Mr. Dillon was questioned for nearly three hours, mainly by Republican committee members, as he completed three days of testimony on tax-revision legislation being sought now by the Administration.

The pending proposals include $1,700,000,000 a year in special tax credits for business enterprises to encourage modernization and expansion of plant and equipment. Tax laws on foreign income, business expense accounts and stock dividends

Continued on Page 22, Column 3

NATION TO WIDEN ITS SPACE EFFORTS

Kennedy Wants More Funds—He Telephones Shepard to Offer Congratulations

Texts of Kennedy statement and call to Shepard, Page 11

By DAVID HALBERSTAM

Special to The New York Times.

WASHINGTON, May 5—An even greater effort in the exploration of space was promised today by President Kennedy.

On the day of this country's first manned space flight, he told a news conference he would make an additional request for appropriations for its space program this year.

"We are going to make a substantially larger effort in space," he declared. [Question 1, Page 14.]

Earlier in the day the President telephoned his personal congratulations to Comdr. Alan B. Shepard Jr., the nation's first space traveler, in a call from the White House to the aircraft carrier Lake Champlain.

The President also congratulated the commander's wife and his six fellow-astronauts.

Commander Shepard will visit Washington Monday. There will be a ceremony at noon on

Continued on Page 11, Column 7

Elizabeth Visits Pope in Vatican

Associated Press Wirephoto

Pope John XXIII in private audience with Queen Elizabeth

By ARNALDO CORTESI

Special to The New York Times.

ROME, May 5—Pope John XXIII received Queen Elizabeth II and Prince Philip in a private audience today with traditional pomp and ceremony. The meeting was marked by extreme cordiality. Addressing the Queen in French, the Pope said that relations between Britain and

Continued on Page 19, Column 4

14 Dead, 57 Hurt by Tornado; 2 Towns in Oklahoma Hard Hit

By The Associated Press.

POTEAU, Okla., May 5—A vicious tornado tore through two tiny eastern Oklahoma communities near here tonight, killing at least fourteen persons and injuring fifty-seven.

Ten were reported dead at Howe and four at Reichert. The death toll could go higher as rescue workers dug into the debris.

There was a report that a light plane—trying to avoid the massive storm cloud—crashed after a wing tore off. The highway patrol said that a woman who lived in the area reported she saw the plane go down west of Heavener near Summerfield.

It was a grim anniversary for this rolling, wooded area some 200 miles southeast of Oklahoma City. Just one year ago twelve were killed when a twister destroyed most of the downtown area of Wilburton.

Tornadoes had plagued Oklahoma for two days, but until tonight there had been only one fatality from the scores of funnels sighted.

Two of the dead were babies. One father died with his 3-month-old son and a mother with her 14-month-old boy.

Tiny farms are scattered throughout the twister-pounded

Continued on Page 62, Column 6

NEWS INDEX

Nation Exults Over Space Feat; City Plans to Honor Astronaut

By ROBERT CONLEY

The successful flight of America's first astronaut, Comdr. Alan B. Shepard Jr., roused the country yesterday to one of its highest peaks of exultation since the end of World War II.

The achievement brought relief from the strain of hearing about the Soviet Union's success in orbiting a man, feelings of new hope for the future from Maine to Hawaii and dancing in the streets at New York's Columbus Circle.

"Wonderful," "Tremendous," "The greatest thing that ever happened," thousands of persons said as the reaction took hold across the country.

Knots of people crowded sidewalks to watch television screens in store windows. Others jumped up to cheer, pounded friends on the back, ran into neighbors' houses or fell silent.

"He made it," a woman gasped in Chicago, then broke into tears. "He made it."

New York City laid plans for the "most fabulous" ticker tape welcome ever given—one that a city official said would be "even bigger than the one for Charles Lindbergh."

In Washington, Congressmen moved to bestow the nation's

Continued on Page 11, Column 5

U. S. Hurls Man 115 Miles Into Space; He Works Controls in Capsule During Flight

ASTRONAUT SENDS DATA FROM CRAFT

Shepard's Condition Is Fine After 15-Minute Trip From Cape Canaveral

Continued From Page 1, Col. 8

ly here and in much of the non-communist world as proof that the United States, though several years behind in the space race, had the potential to offer imposing competition.

Commander Shepard, a native of East Derry, N. H., was a long time starting his journey.

He lay on his contoured Fiberglas couch atop the Redstone missile—"the least nervous man of the bunch," the flight surgeon reported—for three an a half hours while the launching crew delayed the countdown because of weather and a few technical troubles.

Finally, at 10:34 A. M. Eastern daylight time, the count reached zero. A jet of yellow flame lifted the slender rocket off its pad as thousands watched anxiously from the Cape and along the public beaches south of here.

Hundreds of missiles had been launched here, but never before with a human being aboard. Only once before, so far as is known, had a human ridden a missile into space anywhere—and that was from the Soviet base at Tyura Tam, near the Aral Sea last month.

The rocket, and the pilot in the Project Mercury capsule on top, performed flawlessly.

Commander Shepard kept up a running commentary with the command center during the flight. He experienced six times the force of gravity during the rocket's climb, then there were five minutes during which gravity seemed to have vanished. The abrupt re-entry into the atmosphere pressed him into his couch with a force of more than ten times gravity.

At 7,000 feet, his capsule descending by a red and white parachute, Commander Shepard radioed, as if returning from a routine flight by plane:

"Coming in for a landing."

Drops Gently to Water

The capsule, dropping then at a fairly gentle thirty feet a second, hit the water at 10:49 A. M. The commander, apparently as sound and healthy as when he had entered the capsule at 6:20 A. M., radioed that he would climb out immediately rather than ride inside it to the carrier.

A horse-collar-like sling was lowered from Marine helicopter 44 and he was pulled aboard, less than five minutes after hitting the gently rolling waves. His first words were:

"Thank you very much. It's a beautiful day."

A minute later, the capsule was hooked and flown, dangling below the helicopter, to a mattress-covered platform on the carrier. Moments later, as hundreds of sailors cheered, the astronaut, his silver space suit gleaming, debarked from the helicopter.

Instead of going directly to the admiral's quarters below, where he was to receive a thorough physical examination and pour out his fresh impressions of his journey, he jogged to the capsule to retrieve his space helmet.

The formalities below were interrupted when a call came into the carrier bridge from the White House. It was President Kennedy.

'Very Thrilling Ride'

A naval officer who overheard the conversation quoted the astronaut as saying:

"Thank you very much, Mr. President. It was certainly a very thrilling ride. I'd like to thank everyone who made it possible."

While being checked by the doctors, Commander Shepard told one:

"I don't think there's much you'll have to do to me, doc."

In the twenty-four to forty-eight hours following the flight, Commander Shepard is to undergo the physical check-ups and interviews. He is resting tonight at Grand Bahamas Island.

All aboard the carrier, except for two physicians, were under strict orders not to speak to the astronaut unless he asked a question.

The precaution was taken so that the astronaut's reactions could be recorded with the meagerest possible distortion by intervening discussions.

The chief physican on the carrier, Comdr. Robert C. Laning, reported the astronaut in "excellent physical condition."

Commander Shepard's first refreshment was a glass of orange juice. He told the dactor that he was "thrilled and experienced a great sense of humility."

To Go to Washington

The astronaut spent two hours and twenty-five minutes on the carrier, then was flown to a special clinic on Grand Bahama, where the examinations and questioning continued.

There, after an extensive examination, Col. William Douglas, personal physician for the seven astronauts, found Mr. Shepard in "excellent shape and health." He doubted that the further tests to be made would show any ill effects.

Plans are to fly Commander Shepard to Washington Monday for a hero's welcome and a meeting with President Kennedy.

What were the scientific contributions made by the fifteen-minute Mercury flight?

Chief among them, according to Dr. Hugh A. Dryden, Deputy Administrator of the National Aeronautics and Space Administration, was information on the reactions of the astronaut under the stresses of space flight.

Commander Shepard was reported to have performed no differently during the actual rocket flight than he had in dozens of practice flights in ground simulators and whirling centrifuges.

He was able to click off moment-by-moment reports on the operations of the complex array of mechanisms, without missing a beat. His voice remained normal except during the exposure to the maximum gravity force. Then it became strained, as had the voices of all astronauts during training.

In addition, Mr. Shepard was able to control the attitude, or position, of the capsule in space by operation of a control stick that sent squirts of hydrogen peroxide rushing from sixteen strategically located jets.

In this way, Commander Shepard was able to change not the path of the capsule, which was determined by the ballistic trajectory established by the rocket, but the angle at which the capsule flew through space. Turning levers [illegible] the capsule he was able to control the pitch (nose up or down), yaw (right or left motion) and roll of the capsule.

The astronaut also regulated the attitude of the capsule for the firing of the retro or backward-firing rockets and fired the rockets as the capsule started descending toward earth. For the sub-orbital flight the firing of the three retro rockets on the blunt nose of the capsule was only practiced. But in orbital flight, the retro rockets are necessary to slow down the capsule and start it returning to earth.

Commander Shepard talked about his experiences "flying" the capsule to Capt. Ralph Weymouth, skipper of the Lake Champlain.

"He told me," the captain said, "that four or five years from now, we may look back at this as a pretty crude thing, but a this moment it seemed a tremendous event."

Dr. Stanley C. White of the Air Force said there had been very little change in the astronaut's pulse or respiration throughout the flight.

Temperatures both in the capsule and in the astronaut's air-tight air-conditioned double layer space suit rose only slightly during the friction-generating descent into the atmosphere.

According to Dr. White, the suit temperature rose from 75 to 78 Fahrenheit during reentry and the cabin air temperature rose from 99 degrees to 102.

To indicate the decelerating impact of the atmosphere, it was calculated that the capsule, in one minute, slowed from a speed of 4,227 miles an hour at forty miles altitude to 341 miles an hour at twelve miles altitude.

The Mercury capsule was a compact, 2,300 pound steel and titanium craft shaped something like a television tube. The astronaut, lying on his couch against the blunt "picture" end of the tube, had about as much space he he would in the cockpit of a jet fighter plane.

Before him were panels containing more than 100 switches, buttons, and levers for performing such functions as firing retro rockets; switching radio channels; turning on and off the manual control jets; blowing out the escape hatch at the side; and extending or retracting a periscope with which he could monitor operations of devices not visible to the direct-view porthole down through his legs.

The barrel-shaped capsule bore the name of "Freedom 7" painted in white letters on the black side of the capsule. The name was thought up by the seven Mercury astronauts.

There were many emergency measures that the astronaut himself could initiate in case the automatic and ground-controlled systems both malfunctioned.

Perhaps most important was triggering of the escape tower, a rocket powered pylon atop the capsule that would carry the capsule up and away from the Redstone booster if trouble developed anywhere from launch pad to burnout and separation of the booster.

Commander Shepard did report that he encountered several "unexpected sensations."

One was what he termed "a bit of roughness" during the early part of the flight, apparently when the Redstone nosed its way upward through the sonic barrier.

There also was a bit of wobbling when one of the retro-rockets was fired.

Otherwise, the commander said, "everything went like clock work."

Space agency officials were asked whether any special insurance policies had been taken out to cover the astronaut in case he had been killed or injured.

The officials did not know of any.

DRAWING of capsule's interior by National Aeronautics and Space Administration

Transcript of Space Flight Messages

Special to The New York Times.

CAPE CANAVERAL, Fla., May 5—Following is a partial transcript of the radio conversation between Comdr. Alan B. Shepard Jr. and the Mercury control center during the space flight today:

VOICE—One minute and counting, mark. Forty-five and counting, mark.

SHEPARD—Roger.

VOICE—Firing command, thirty, mark.

SHEPARD—Roger. Periscope has retracted.

VOICE—That is the best periscope we've got.

SHEPARD—Main buss 24 volts, 26 amps.

VOICE—Fifteen, ten, nine, eight, seven, six, five, four, three, two, one, zero. Lift off.

SHEPARD—Roger, lift off and the clock is started.

SHEPARD—Roger, reading you loud and clear.

SHEPARD—This is Freedom 7, the fuel is go, 1.2 G, cabin at 14 p.s.i. [pressure per square inch] oxygen is go.

SHEPARD—Freedom 7, it is still go.

SHEPARD—This is 7, fuel is go, 1.8 G, 8 p.s.i. cabin, and the oxygen is go.

SHEPARD—Cabin pressure is holding at 5.5, cabin holding at 5.5.

VOICE—I can understand; cabin holding at 5.5.

SHEPARD—Fuel is go, 2.5 G, cabin 5.5. Oxygen is go. The main buss is 24 and the isolated battery is 29.

SHEPARD—Okay it is a lot smoother now. A lot smoother.

VOICE—Roger.

SHEPARD—Fuel is go, 4 G, 5.5 cabin. Oxygen. All systems are go.

VOICE—All systems go. Trajectory okay.

SHEPARD—5 G Cap sep [capsule separation] green.

VOICE—Roger.

SHEPARD—Disarm. Auto retro jettison circuit. Cap sep is green.

VOICE—Periscope is coming out.

SHEPARD—Periscope is coming out; and the turnaround has started.

VOICE—Roger.

SHEPARD—A.S.C.S. (automatic control stabilization control system). Control movements.

VOICE—Roger.

SHEPARD—Okay. Switching to manual pitch.

VOICE—Manual pitch.

SHEPARD—Pitch is okay. Switching to manual yaw.

VOICE—I understand. Manual yaw.

SHEPARD—Yaw is okay. Switching manual roll.

VOICE—Manual roll.

SHEPARD—Roll is okay.

VOICE—Roll okay. Looks good here.

SHEPARD—On periscope. What a beautiful view.

VOICE—I'll bet it is.

SHEPARD—Cloud cover over Florida three to four-tenths in the upper east coast, obscured up through Hatteras. Can see Okeechobee, identified Andrus Island, identified the reefs.

VOICE—Roger. Countdown to retro, five, four, three, two, one, retro angle.

SHEPARD—Start retro sequence and retro attitude green.

VOICE—Roger.

SHEPARD—Control is smooth.

VOICE—Roger, understand, all going smooth.

SHEPARD—Retro one fired, very smooth.

VOICE—Roger, Roger.

SHEPARD—Retro two.

SHEPARD—Retro 3. All three retros are fired.

VOICE—All fired on the button.

SHEPARD—OK, three retros fired. Retro jettison on.

VOICE—Roger. Do you see the booster?

SHEPARD—Negative.

VOICE—Roger, switching fly by wire (manual control by instrument). Understand.

SHEPARD—All is OK.

VOICE—Roger . .

SHEPARD—Roger. I do not have a light.

VOICE—Understand you do not have a light.

SHEPARD—I do not have a light. I see the straps falling away. I heard a noise. I will use override (use manual controls in place of automatic controls.)

VOICE—Roger.

SHEPARD—Override used. The light is green.

VOICE—* * * Retrojet?

SHEPARD—Roger. Periscope is retracting.

VOICE—Periscope retracting.

SHEPARD—* * * Going into re-entry attitude.

VOICE—Re-entry attitude. Roger. Trajectory is right on the button.

SHEPARD—O. K., buster. Re-entry attitude pitching to A. S. C. S. normal.

VOICE—Roger.

SHEPARD—A.S.C.S. is okay.

VOICE—Understand.

SHEPARD—Switching to HF (high frequency) for radio check.

VOICE— . . . On UHF (ultra high frequency). Back to UHF.

SHEPARD—All clear. This is Freedom 7.

SHEPARD—Three, six, nine (counting G's). Okay. Okay. Okay.

VOICE—Coming through loud and clear.

SHEPARD—Okay. Okay.

VOICE— . . . Cap Com [capsule communicator], your impact will be right on the button.

SHEPARD—30,000 feet.

VOICE—Cap Com, I can read now.

SHEPARD—Roger D.E. A.C. [Astronaut Donald A. Slayton]. Loud and clear how me? 25,000.

VOICE—Switching over to G.B.I. (Grand Bahama Island).

SHEPARD—Roger. The drogue [parachute] green, 21,000, the periscope is out. Good drogue—the drogue good—the drogue is blowing at 70 per cent auto, 90 per cent manual, oxygen is still okay.

VOICE—Cap Com, can you read?

SHEPARD—thirty-five feet per second.

VOICE—Cap Com can you read?

SHEPARD—I read.

VOICE—Cap Com. How do you read now?

SHEPARD—Cap Com, glad to be heard aboard. I am at 7,000 feet. The . . . is good . . . my condition is good. Landing bag green. Descent good.

VOIVE—Roger . . .

SHEPARD—altitude 4,000 feet. Condition as before . . . feel good, will land . . .

VOICE—Cap Com. This is card file [check list] 23.

SHEPARD—This is . . . Cap com.

VOICE—This is 23, over.

SHEPARD—Will you please relay? Need information.

VOICE—Freedom 7 reports good drogue . . . deployed, 7,000 feet.

SHEPARD—All OK. Card file 23 from Freedom 7 4,000 feet. Condition as before. Main chute good. Landing bag deployed. Peroxide dump.

SHEPARD—Cap Com . . . everything A-OK. Over . . . dye marker out.

VOICE—Coming alongside . . . now. Over.

VOICE—Astronaut now on board.

The New York Times May 6, 1961

FLIGHTS COMPARED: The summit, or apogee, of American astronaut's flight path lay between the high and low points (apogee and perigee) of Soviet orbit.

SEVEN SPACE MEN TRAINED 2 YEARS

All Underwent Simulated Rigors of Shepard Shot

By BERNARD STENGREN

Special to The New York Times.

CAPE CANAVERAL, Fla., May 5—Almost every sensation of twist and turn, acceleration and weightlessness that Comdr. Alan B. Shepard Jr. went through today was something that he had been through in make-believe several times while in training.

The care, intensity, thoroughness and vigor under which all seven astronaut candidates were trained for twenty-four months exceeded if possible the preparation that went into the first United States space vehicle.

Beginning in May of 1959, the astronauts were crammed with more information than most people could acquire in a lifetime about the natural sciences. Their bodies were subjected to almost inconceivable stresses, and they were tested physically and psychologically so often that they lost track of the times.

Endless Rehearsals

They were rehearsed endlessly in simulators until their responses were almost fully conditioned. They were interviewed repeatedly—some say this was the worst ordeal of all—and yet they were encouraged to relax with their families for the last several days at the swimming pool of the Holiday Inn motel in near-by Cocoa Beach, where all seven have been lodged.

The extent of their training can be judged by the following incomplete list of the subjects covered:

¶At Langley Field, Va., they completed a fifty-hour course in astronautics given by the National Astronautics and Space Administration.

¶The McDonnell Engineering Corporation conducted lectures on the Project Mercury subsystems and on code training.

¶Dr. William K. Douglas taught them about the aeromedical problems of space flight.

¶At the Morehead Planetarium of Chapel Hill, N. C., they took a concentrated course on star recognition and celestial navigation, including laboratory work in a space capsule simulator to navigate by the stars.

¶At Stead Air Force Base in Nevada they took a five-and-a-half-day course in desert survival, on the less than 1-in-10 chance that they might land on an island.

As launch time approached, rehearsals using actual flight hardware under realistic conditions were conducted first at the Navy's centrifuge at Johnsville, Pa., and later in a specially designed altitude chamber in Hangar S here.

In addition, there were the numerous fittings for the custom-designed space suits and the contour couches made to fit literally every inch of the feet, legs, backs, necks and heads of the seven astronauts.

And because research into the human reaction to space flight was a prime object of today's test, each of the men was tattooed at four places on his torso to facilitate the placement of suction cups attached to electrocardiographic recording equipment.

During this period, the men "relaxed" by making regular flights in one of the two F-106 jet fighters, set aside for their use, or by making regular proficiency and instrument check flights in T-33 jet trainers. Each of them is an experienced test pilot.

Learned to Use Controls

The most extreme training device used during the period was the M. A. S. T. I. F., at the space agency's Lewis Research Center at Cleveland. The initials stand for Multiple Axes Space Test Inertia Facility—a combination loop-the-loop, roller coaster and spinning top that can rotate every two seconds on any of its three axes.

According to the space agency M. A. S. T. I. F. aided the astronauts in learning to use their controls to correct for roll, pitch and yaw and thus right their simulated space capsule.

In their training, the seven also accumulated forty minutes of "weightless flying time" each over a number of flights in which C-131, C-135 and F-100 type aircraft were flown in parabolic trajectories to give as much as a minute of weightlessness at each peak of the parabolic arc.

Another method of simulating the experiences that Commander Shepard went through today was the Johnsville centrifuge. In that device, the astronauts were subjected to "G" or gravity forces greater than normal and were trained in performing the tasks included in today's test.

Today Commander Shepard kept in voice contact by radio and operated the controls of his space capsule during portions of the flight—all of which were recorded by sensitive measuring instruments. In addition, his movements were recorded by a control panel camera during his period of weightlessness as he identified by touch 127 switches, dials, buttons and fuses in the cabin as a test of his psychomotor ability.

When he landed, Commander Shepard put to use the last item of training he had undergone, crawling out of the capsule as it bobbed in the swells of the open sea.

Union Scores Holy Loch Pact

Special to The New York Times.

LONDON, May 5—The National Executive Committe of the Amalgamated Engineering Union unanimously approved today a resolution demanding the cancellation of the agreement between the United States and Britain permitting a Polaris submarine base at Holy Loch, Scotland.

First U. S. Space Man

Alan Bartlett Shepard Jr.

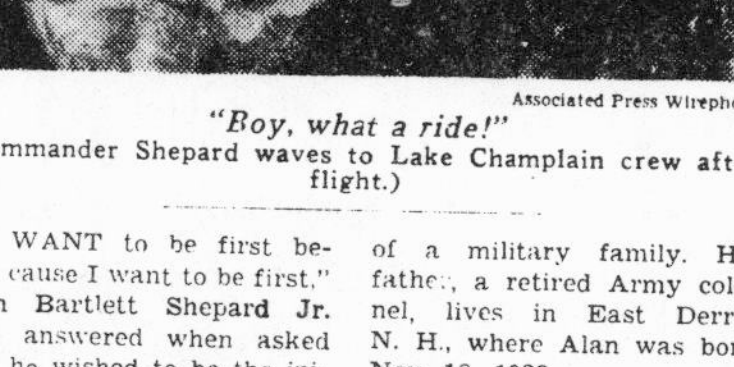

Associated Press Wirephoto

"Boy, what a ride!"
(Commander Shepard waves to Lake Champlain crew after flight.)

"I WANT to be first because I want to be first," Alan Bartlett Shepard Jr. once answered when asked why he wished to be the initial American in space. And it was as if this cool, aloof Naval commander was just hard-nosed enough to drive himself to be first. Commander Shepard has been a competitor all his life, "closing out the fear and concentrating on my job." He spent two brutal years cudgeling his mind with complex problems and allowing his body to be jolted, spun, chilled, roasted, crushed and floated in air in preparation for yesterday's flight.

Man in the News

But Commander Shepard has faced danger before.

"There's no real point in worrying anyhow," he once said. "It just messes you up.

"I've had engine flameouts at extremely high altitudes. I've had canopies blown off suddenly and I've had to land on carriers in the black night. The only way to make it is to work at it."

'Never Feared Anything'

His mother has said of her son:

"Alan has never feared anything."

His wife, Louise, has said:

"It is characteristic of him always to find a challenge."

His prep school coach said:

"He was a hard-nosed kid, always accepted a challenge. He always had a lot of courage."

A crewmate on the varsity rowing team at Annapolis said:

"He amazed the coaches and everybody else, beating out bigger guys for a seat" in the boat.

A flight surgeon described him and the six other astronauts as "supernormal"—relaxed, mature, stable, dedicated.

His I. Q. is high, between 135 and 147. But physically, he would not stand out in a crowd. He stands 5 feet 11 inches tall, weighs 160 pounds, has blue eyes and brown, crew-cut hair.

Commander Shepard's outstanding characteristic is his fierce desire to leap any hurdle.

His wife says that when he was a cadet dating her at Annapolis, he joined the crew to win his "N" just so he could take her to the Navy lettermen's ball.

He became so impatient to get his wings and pilot's license during Navy flight training that he got a license at a civilian flight school in his spare time.

And when he discovered the thrills of water skiing, it was first on two skis and then on one.

Commander Shepard comes of a military family. His father, a retired Army colonel, lives in East Derry, N. H., where Alan was born Nov. 18, 1923.

A teacher in East Derry recalls that Alan was a "good student, a good athlete and a boy extremely well liked."

In 1944, he was graduated from the Naval Academy, placing 462d in a class of 913. He served on a destroyer during World War II and turned to the air later.

As a test pilot flying high altitude research missions he built up 3,600 flight hours, 1,700 of them in jets. He was then placed in the key job of aircraft readiness officer for the Atlantic Fleet.

Commander Shepard was an unhappy man when he learned that the National Aeronautics and Space Administration had sent orders to 110 test pilots asking if they would volunteer for space flight. He had not received the orders, but it turned out they had been mislaid and he was on the list after all.

Secure in Navy

The night he got his orders for Project Mercury, he had a long talk with his wife.

"We talked about what might happen if I became an astronaut and what we might be giving up," he recalled. "I had a good, responsible billet in the Navy and could look forward to the possibility of getting a squadron command."

They discussed how comfortable and secure they were with their two daughters, Laura, then 12 years old, and Juliana, then 8.

Commander Shepard's wife said little. Finally she remarked:

"What are you bothering to ask me for? You know you'll do it anyway."

As an astronaut, he did not bring home the day-to-day crises.

"It's hard to hide a blow-up on the pad, but life goes on normally," he said recently. "The kids exhibit their mother's calm, rational approach."

Service to Country

Both Mrs. Shepard and her husband are Christian Scientists and she has spoken feelingly of her "strong spiritual faith."

"If the brakes don't work, I know that something else will," she has said.

As for Commander Shepard, he once expressed high purpose about his role in Project Mercury.

"Without being too Navy blue and gold, I'm here because it's a chance to serve the country," he said. "I'm here too, because it's a great personal challenge: I know it can be done, that it's important for it to be done, and I want to do it."

He has done it.

CAPSULE TOOK ALOFT FLAG SCHOOL GAVE

Special to The New York Times.

CAPE CANAVERAL, Fla., May 5—Comdr. Alan B. Shepard Jr. carried with him into space today an American flag donated by the students of the Cocoa Beach Elementary School.

No advance notice was given that the flag, 2 feet by 3 feet in size, was tucked inside the capsule, "Freedom 7." The only national designation carried by the capsule were the words "United States" painted on the black exterior.

The idea of putting an American flag aboard originated with Douglas M. Dederer, a reporter for The Cocoa Tribune. Robert R. Gilruth, director of Project Mercury, approved the idea and arranged for the flag to be placed in the capsule.

The flag weighed only two ounces and, therefore, presented no weight problem.

The flag was presented to Mr. Dederer by Robert J. Fritz, principal of the Cocoa Beach Elementary School, and Danny F. Woodell, the 11-year-old president of the school's Student Council. Mr. Dederer gave it to Mr. Gilruth.

"Voice" Tells the World Of U. S. Space Flight

Special to The New York Times.

WASHINGTON, May 5—The Voice of America told the world in thirty-five languages today of the space flight by Comdr. Alan B. Shepard Jr.

At 10:35 A. M. it interrupted its broadcasts with a bulletin announcing that "America's first man in space has just been launched." Later the Voice interrupted broadcasts with bulletins on the landing of the space capsule and other reports.

At noon a special half-hour program was beamed in English to South Asia, the Middle East, Europe and the Far East. O[illegible] went to other areas.

Details of the space flight were heard by listeners behind the Iron Curtain through broadcasts made yesterday by Radio Free Europe.

News bulletins and eyewitness accounts were broadcast over the system's transmitters to Czechoslovakia, Hungary, Poland, Bulgaria and Rumania immediately after the flight's completion.

CHEERING SAILORS GREET ASTRONAUT

Lake Champlain Crew Sees Him Picked Up by 'Copter

ABOARD U. S. S. LAKE CHAMPLAIN, May 5 (UPI)—The cherry red glow of a capsule appeared suddenly in the bright blue Bahamas sky today. Just as suddenly, a red and white parachute opened. Alan Shepard was right on target.

A tremendous cheer went up from the Lake Champlain as the capsule descended slowly. Marine helicopters hovered protectively near-by.

At 10:49 P. M. the capsule hit the water. The splash could be seen clearly from the carrier's deck. The olive drab helicopter, piloted by Lieut. Wayne Koons of Lyons, Kans., was only about 700 feet from the impact point.

By radio, Lieutenant Koons and Lieut. George Cox of Eustis, Fla., the co-pilot, asked Cmdr. Alan B. Shepard if he wanted to be picked up.

"Roger. Come after me," was the reply from the 37-year-old astronaut, who survived, healthy and happy, one of the most dangerous journeys ever undertaken by man.

Lieut. Cox, who last January recovered Ham, the rocket-riding chimpanzee, lowered the pickup gear and Commander Shepard was hoisted up. Then the capsule was picked up and the helicopter headed back to the Champlain.

The 1,200 cheering and whistling sailors, who had followed the countdown and the zoom through space, saw Commander Shepard wave. On the fifteen-minute ride, he looked out the window of the helicopter and said: "What a beautiful day."

Lieut. Koons gently set the capsule down on a pad. Then he dropped his helicopter to the flight deck. The door opened and Commander Shepard leaped quickly and jauntily to the deck. If there had been any doubt that he had survived his flight intact, the crew-cut commander dispelled it immediately.

Two physicians, Dr. Robert Laning and Dr. Jerome Strong, approached the helicopter. Still in his flight suit, Commander Shepard turned to Lieut. Cox and said "thank you very much."

Dr. Strong, an Army captain, began to show Commander Shepard the way to the catwalk leading to the cabin of Admiral K. P. Koch, commander of the recovery task force, consisting of the Lake Champlain and six destroyers. "Just a minute," the astronaut said.

Leaps Onto Platform

Briskly, he walked to the twelve-foot, mattress-covered platform on which the capsule had been set. He leaped onto the platform and peered into the open hatch of the vehicle that for fifteen minutes had been his home in space. He looked like a man who had forgotten something.

He fished inside, took out his white helmet and put it cockily under his arm. Then, with the doctors at his side, he strode to the admiral's suite for a medical examination.

"I don't think you're going to have much to do," he told Dr. Laning. He was in fine spirits and showed a sense of humor.

The examination was brief.

"There is nothing we can determine that is in any way abnormal," Dr. Strong said.

A superb physical specimen before the flight, Commander Shepard was the same after it.

The only apparent symptoms of excitement were noticeable perspiration and a high pulse. But the pulse returned to normal right after Commander Shepard entered the captain's cabin to relax.

Less than an hour after coming aboard, he donned an orange Navy flight suit belonging to Admiral Koch. Then he went to the flight bridge and told President Kennedy by radiophone what it had been like to hurtle through space.

Meanwhile, on the deck below, the capsule was undergoing its own physical examination. Charles Tynan, a representative of the National Aeronautics and Space Administration, said it was in perfect condition. The exit hatch had dropped into the water when Commander Shepard opened it.

Mr. Tynan said instruments showed Commander Shepard had withstood a force ten to eleven times that of gravity. The capsule was dry inside, he said, and it did not appear that Commander Shepard had had to use any emergency controls.

Astronaut Toasted

GRAND BAHAMA ISLAND, May 5 (AP)—Commander Alan B. Shepard's "perfect flight" was toasted in champagne when he arrived here today, but doctors waiting to check him over did not allow him to participate.

Flashing a hearty grin, the hungry astronaut enjoyed a huge shrimp cocktail, roast beef sandwich and iced tea.

Hurried into isolation at a hospital guarded by a sentry, the young astronaut then began at least twenty-four hours of comprehensive medical and psychological tests. He also started giving detailed reports on technicalities of his historic mission.

"He looks great, feels great. He is jolly and joking as Al always is," said Capt. Virgil Grissom, a fellow astronaut who admits he was a bit envious and who said he hoped he would be chosen for the next rocket ride.

Gourmets Salute Space Men

LONDON, May 5 (Reuters)—British business men at a Gourmet Club luncheon today toasted the United States space achievement with vodka while eating a special horsd'oeuvre dedicated to the Soviet Union's space man, Yuri A. Gagarin.

"All the News That's Fit to Print"

The New York Times.

LATE CITY EDITION
U. S. Weather Bureau Report (Page 90) forecasts:
Increasing cloudiness today.
Snow, rain tonight. Rain tomorrow.
Temp. range: 38—26; yesterday: 37—30.

VOL. CXI..No. 38,014. | NEW YORK, WEDNESDAY, FEBRUARY 21, 1962. | FIVE CENTS

10 cents beyond 50-mile zone from New York City except on Long Island. Higher in air delivery cities.

GLENN ORBITS EARTH 3 TIMES SAFELY; PICKED UP IN CAPSULE BY DESTROYER; PRESIDENT WILL GREET HIM IN FLORIDA

N.A.S.A. via Associated Press Wirephoto

READY: Lieut. Col. John H. Glenn Jr. walks to the van to take him to the launching site at Cape Canaveral, Fla.

N.A.S.A. via United Press International Telephoto

LIFT-OFF: The Atlas rocket booster bearing the Project Mercury spacecraft roars aloft with 360,000-pound thrust.

N.A.S.A. via Associated Press Wirephoto

RECOVERY: Crewmen of destroyer Noa secure capsule carrying astronaut before lifting it out of the Atlantic.

CARLINO CLEARED IN SHELTER CASE BY ETHICS PANEL

Lane Scored in Unanimous Report, Which He Calls 'Cynical and Callous'

Text of concluding sections of report is on Page 50.

By WARREN WEAVER Jr.
Special to The New York Times.

ALBANY, Feb. 20—The Assembly Committee on Ethics and Guidance exonerated Speaker Joseph F. Carlino today of charges of conflict of interest made by Assemblyman Mark Lane.

In a unanimous report submitted to the Legislature, the bipartisan committee said:

¶Mr. Carlino did not "betray the public trust" by serving as a director of a company manufacturing home fall-out shelters while helping to pass school-shelter legislation last November.

¶He did not draft or support the shelter legislation "in any improper manner" for the benefit of the company, Lancer Industries, Inc.

¶The Speaker was not influenced in his official actions in behalf of the bill by the fact that he was a member of the board of directors of Lancer.

¶He did not receive any special benefit from the passage of the legislation.

Charges Unsubstantiated

"The committee concludes with respect to each and every accusation contained in the charges filed," the report said, "that Assemblyman Lane and those who testified in their support failed to submit credible evidence to substantiate them."

In submitting the report, the Ethics Committee requested that the full 150-member lower house vote "with respect to the conclusions reached herein" in the light of the fact that "the charges were directed against its [the Assembly's] highest ranking official."

Assemblyman Donald A. Campbell, Republican of Amsterdam, who is chairman of the committee, said he would move in the Assembly tomorrow for acceptance of the report. Mr. Carlino is expected to be absent during the debate and vote.

Assemblyman Lane, a Democrat of Manhattan, had charged that the Speaker was guilty of

Continued on Page 50, Column 1

ROCKEFELLER BARS KOREA WAR BONUS

Voices Opposition in Face of Legislators' Backing

By LAYHMOND ROBINSON
Special to The New York Times.

ALBANY, Feb. 20—Governor Rockefeller expressed strong opposition tonight to a state bonus for veterans of the Korean war.

Mr. Rockefeller told the New York State Department of the American Legion that he could not "as a responsible leader of government" support the demand for a bonus. The veterans' group had been campaigning for a $100,000,000 bonus for the 482,000 Korean war veterans or their next-of-kin in the state.

The Governor said his stand was backed "unanimously" by the "Republican leadership of the state." This was a reference to the leaders of the Republican-controlled Legislature.

He said that demands for funds for education, mental health, narcotics control and other state services were too great to permit a diversion of money for a veterans' bonus.

Mr. Rockefeller thus took a position in direct opposition to that of most of the Republican and Democratic members of the Legislature, who have been pushing for the bonus. The issue

Continued on Page 51, Column 1

Jersey Bus Strike Settled; Service Is Due Tomorrow

By PETER KIHSS

An agreement to end the New Jersey bus strike was reached last night. The agreement, subject to ratification by the striking employes, was announced by Gov. Richard J. Hughes. The pact will be submitted to the union members at their garages starting at 7 A. M. today.

Union and management men expressed hope that buses could begin operating tomorrow at 4:30 A. M.

The strike against Public Service Coordinated Transport started at 12:01 A. M. Monday and halted 2,511 buses providing 1,000,000 rides a day. The company's 200 routes serve all of New Jersey's twenty-one counties except Warren and Hunterdon and go into New York City and Philadelphia. The Newark subway system was also shut.

Carlin Gets Credit

Governor Hughes credited Mayor Leo P. Carlin of Newark with having "sparkplugged" the successful negotiations. Mayor Carlin flew back from a Miami Beach vacation yesterday and arranged the talks with both sides and with Daniel F. Fitzpatrick, a Federal mediator, and the Governor and himself. The meeting started in Newark at 8:30 P. M., and the agreement was announced at 11:28 P. M.

Earlier, David L. Yunich, president of Bamberger's New Jersey, had asserted that the strike was having a "devastating * * * almost catastrophic" effect on retail business in Newark and elsewhere in the state. A Camden department store reported sales had fallen nearly 50 per cent on Monday, although not that far yesterday.

Despite the drop in shopping, most commuters managed to get to work by alternate means and with a minimum of confusion.

The agreement reached last night provides for a wage increase of 10 cents an hour retroactive to Feb. 1 and extending to next Feb. 1; 4 cents more an hour from then until Aug. 1, 1963, and another 4 cents an hour from then until

Continued on Page 39, Column 3

ROSENTHAL WINS QUEENS ELECTION

But Democrat-Liberal Has Margin of Only 193 Votes —Machines Guarded

By CLAYTON KNOWLES

Benjamin S. Rosenthal, a Democrat-Liberal backed by President Kennedy, squeaked through to victory last night in a special Congressional election in Queens' Sixth District.

By the slim margin of 193 votes, Mr. Rosenthal, a lanky 38-year-old Elmhurst lawyer, edged past Thomas F. Galvin of Flushing, the Republican candidate, to win a three-way race. Emil Levin of Flushing, a Democrat running as an independent, finished far behind.

The unofficial final tally, delayed as the early vote was hastily rechecked for errors, was: Rosenthal, 16,032; Galvin, 15,839, and Levin, 4,216.

Republicans immediately challenged the result and, while Mr. Galvin did not immediately ask for a recount, he sent a telegram demanding that the voting machines be impounded. All voting machines, normally just

Continued on Page 48, Column 3

McNamara Reports Gains by Vietnamese

By JACK RAYMOND
Special to The New York Times.

WASHINGTON, Feb. 20—Secretary of Defense Robert S. McNamara returned to the capital today and reported improvement in the South Vietnamese effort against Communist insurgents.

He had presided at a meeting of United States military and civilian officials yesterday at the headquarters in Hawaii of Admiral Harry S. Felt, commander of United States forces in the Pacific. The meeting was the third in a series of monthly talks on the hostilities in South Vietnam.

A spokesman for Mr. McNamara said that the forces of South Vietnam, supported by the United States, "are hitting

Continued on Page 5, Column 5

KENNEDY PRAISES 'WONDERFUL JOB'

Tells Glenn Nation Is 'Really Proud of You'—Welcome at White House Planned

By TOM WICKER
Special to The New York Times.

WASHINGTON, Feb. 20 — President Kennedy phoned Lieut. Col. John H. Glenn Jr. today immediately after the astronaut's successful orbital flight and arranged to meet him at Cape Canaveral Friday morning.

The President also set in motion plans for bringing Colonel Glenn to Washington on Monday or Tuesday, for receptions at the White House and the Capitol and a parade down Pennsylvania Avenue.

A television set in his office and an open telephone line to Cape Canaveral had kept Mr. Kennedy informed of Colonel Glenn's progress all through the day.

The astronaut's three orbits around the earth, Mr. Kennedy said in a statement, have embarked the United States on a "new ocean"—that of space.

"I believe the United States must sail on it and be in a position second to none," the President said within minutes of Colonel Glenn's safe emergence from his Mercury capsule.

Colonel Glenn, he said, is the "kind of American of whom we are most proud." Mr. Kennedy also praised "all those who participated" in making the astronaut's flight successful.

Then, at 4:10 P. M., Mr. Ken-

Continued on Page 23, Column 7

Leaders of Algeria Back Peace Terms

By THOMAS F. BRADY
Special to The New York Times.

TUNIS, Feb. 20—The Algerian nationalist Provisional Government met today and gave full approval to peace accords negotiated with the French by four members of the rebel regime.

One Algerian said afterward: "All twelve members of the Government are in unanimous agreement." This was a reference to five ministers who are prisoners in France, the four negotiators and three ministers who remained in Tunis during the secret talks last week on the French-Swiss border.

The negotiators were Belkacem Krim, M'Hammed Yazid, Saad Dahlab and Lakhdar Ben Tobbal. They met here today

Continued on Page 11, Column 1

NEWS INDEX

The President's Statement

Special to The New York Times.

WASHINGTON, Feb. 20—Following is the text of President Kennedy's statement on Colonel Glenn's flight:

I know that I express the great happiness and thanksgiving of all of us that Colonel Glenn has completed his trip, and I know that this is particularly felt by Mrs. Glenn and his two children.

A few days ago Colonel Glenn came to the White House and visited me, and he is—as are the other astronauts—the kind of American of whom we are most proud.

Some years ago, as a Marine pilot, he raced the sun across this country—and lost. And today he won.

I also want to say a word for all those who participated with Colonel Glenn in Canaveral. They faced many disappointments and delays—the burdens upon them were great—but they kept their heads and they made a judgment, and I think their judgment has been vindicated.

We have a long way to go in this space race. We started late. But this is the new ocean, and I believe the United States must sail on it and be in a position second to none.

Some months ago I said that I hoped every American would serve his country. Today Colonel Glenn served his, and we all express our thanks to him.

ADENAUER WANTS PARLEY ON BERLIN

Suggests Foreign Ministers of Big Four Meet 'Soon'

By SYDNEY GRUSON
Special to The New York Times.

BONN, Germany, Feb. 20—Chancellor Adenauer suggested today that a Big Four foreign ministers' conference on Berlin should be convened "soon." He was speaking to the Parliamentary group of the Christian Democratic Union.

He said that it might be "expedient" to "take a pause" in the Berlin talks now going on between Andrei A. Gromyko, the Soviet Foreign Minister, and Llewellyn E. Thompson Jr., the United States Ambassador to Moscow.

Ambassador Thompson should not continue "negotiating" endlessly, Dr. Adenauer added. There have been four meetings in the last seven weeks between Mr. Gromyko and Mr. Thompson without any advance toward a Berlin settlement.

[A warning by Izvestia, the Soviet Government newspaper, that Moscow was ready to push through a separate peace treaty with East Germany if the United States did not alter its position in the talks raised the possibility of a renewal of the Soviet deadline on a peace pact.]

Dr. Adenauer's advocacy of a new conference of the United States, British, French and Soviet foreign ministers reflected his unhappiness with the course of the Gromyko-Thompson talks.

He is known to believe that Mr. Thompson has made what

Continued on Page 2, Column 2

URBAN PLAN VOTE PUT OFF IN SENATE

Administration Rebuffed on Forcing Issue to Floor

By RUSSELL BAKER
Special to The New York Times.

WASHINGTON, Feb. 20 — President Kennedy affronted the Senate's dignity today and got a political rebuff for it.

In a surprising repudiation of the Administration's voting form sheets, the elders turned on the White House and rejected a leadership move to get a quick floor test of the President's urban affairs proposal. The vote was 58 to 42.

Thus, the White House lost its chance to get a favorable Senate vote on the plan before the House could vote to kill it. The Democrats also lost their chance to get the Senate's Republicans clearly on record for or against the plan to create a Cabinet-level Department of Urban Affairs and Housing.

Today's test came on the dusty parliamentary question whether the Senate should take the plan away from the Government Operations Committee and bring it to an immediate floor vote. This is known as "discharging" the committee. It is an extraordinary procedure that is rarely used because it is repugnant to Senate traditions.

Today it became the instrument of the President's defeat.

The move to discharge the Government Operations Committee was undertaken with misgivings yesterday by Mike Mansfield of Montana, Senate Democratic leader. The reason was a sudden threat by the

Continued on Page 16, Column 4

COL. GLENN FLOWN TO ISLE FOR CHECK

He Feels Tired but Elated —Goes to Grand Turk for Report and Examination

By JOHN W. FINNEY
Special to The New York Times.

GRAND TURK ISLAND, Feb. 20—An elated but tired John H. Glenn Jr. returned to earth tonight and reported that he "couldn't feel better."

The 40-year-old astronaut also reported that he had felt no sickness or discomfort during his five-hour, three-orbit flight around the earth, even during the extended period of weightlessness.

Colonel Glenn landed at this small British possession at 9:11 P. M. in a Navy S-2-F submarine patrol plane. He was clad in light blue coveralls. He had co-piloted the plane from the carrier Randolph, where he spent several hours after being retrieved from the Atlantic ocean.

Around his ears were the marks of the earphones that he had worn while piloting a plane that traveled at about one-hundredth the speed of his Friendship 7 space capsule. And on his face was an excited enthusiastic smile.

Asked how he felt, the red-headed marine replied: "Fine, wonderful, I couldn't feel better."

And he was also hungry. His first comment on stepping into the small hospital arranged for him was: "First I want something to eat—I am hungry." A steak dinner was promptly or-

Continued on Page 22, Column 2

Moscow, Unmoved, Gives News of Orbit

By THEODORE SHABAD

MOSCOW, Feb. 20 — The Russians voiced congratulations tonight on hearing of Lieut. Col. John H. Glenn Jr.'s orbital space flight.

But they showed no enthusiasm on the successful launching and landing of the spacecraft Friendship 7.

These reactions were reported from Moscow University by United States exchange students who had been listening with Russians to radio reports of Colonel Glenn's progress.

"They congratulated us in friendly fashion but were oddly reserved," an American said.

Soviet radio and television were unusually prompt in reporting the flight. The first bul-

Continued on Page 22, Column 5

81,000-MILE TRIP

Flight Aides Feared for the Capsule as It Began Its Re-Entry

Transcript of conversations with Glenn, Pages 25 and 26.

By RICHARD WITKIN
Special to The New York Times.

CAPE CANAVERAL, Fla., Feb. 20—John H. Glenn Jr. orbited three times around the earth today and landed safely to become the first American to make such a flight.

The 40-year-old Marine Corps lieutenant colonel traveled about 81,000 miles in 4 hours 56 minutes before splashing into the Atlantic at 2:43 P. M. Eastern Standard Time.

He had been launched from here at 9:47 A. M.

The astronaut's safe return was no less a relief than a thrill to the Project Mercury team, because there had been real concern that the Friendship 7 capsule might disintegrate as it rammed back into the atmosphere.

There had also been a serious question whether Colonel Glenn could complete three orbits as planned. But despite persistent control problems, he managed to complete the entire flight plan.

Lands in Bahamas Area

The astronaut's landing place was near Grand Turk Island in the Bahamas, about 700 miles southeast of here.

Still in his capsule, he was plucked from the water at 3:01 P. M. with a boom and block and tackle by the destroyer Noa. The capsule was deposited on deck at 3:04.

Colonel Glenn's first words as he stepped out onto the Noa's deck were: "It was hot in there."

He quickly obtained a glass of iced tea.

He was in fine condition except for two skinned knuckles hurt in the process of blowing out the side hatch of the capsule.

The colonel was transferred by helicopter to the carrier Randolph, whose recovery helicopters had raced the Noa for the honor of making the pick-up. After a meal and extensive "de-briefing" aboard the carrier, he was flown to Grand Turk by submarine patrol plane for two days of rest and interviews on technical, medical and other aspects of his flight.

The Noa, nearest ship to the

Continued on Page 20, Column 1

NEW YORK PAUSES TO 'WATCH' GLENN

Millions Rivet Attention on Astronaut in Flight

By NAN ROBERTSON

The thoughts of millions of New Yorkers were riveted for hours yesterday on one man alone in space.

Minute by minute, they followed the orbital flight of Lieut. Col. John H. Glenn Jr. three times around the earth, waiting in agonizing suspense for his safe return. The life of New York almost stood still during the dramatic countdown.

From then on until Colonel Glenn scrambled "hale and hearty" out of his capsule on the destroyer Noa, people carried on absent-mindedly and in spurts. Millions of working hours were lost during the day, but no one could have begrudged this. Employers and the employed alike were drawn irresistibly to radio and television sets.

The most spectacular display of interest occurred in Grand Central Terminal, where throngs of up to 9,000 persons massed before a huge television screen. The police described it as the largest static crowd in the station's history. The terminal manager said those who

Continued on Page 21, Column 6

Glenn Orbits Earth 3 Times and Is Picked Up in His Capsule by a U. S. Destroyer

ASTRONAUT SAYS CONDITION IS FINE

Mechanical Trouble Almost Shortened Flight—Craft Yawed on First Trip

Continued From Page 1, Col. 8

capsule as it parachuted into the ocean, took just twenty-one minutes to close the six-mile gap, lift the capsule aboard with a boom-block-and-tackle rig and place it gently on the deck.

Colonel Glenn first was set to wriggle out of the narrow top. But when difficulty was encountered in getting one of the bulkheads loose, the explosive side hatch was blown off, and the man from space stepped out on deck, apparently in excellent shape. He was soon afterward transferred to the carrier Randolph.

In the course of his three orbits, Colonel Glenn reported frequently to tracking stations at various points on earth and to the control center here. Invariably, he said that his condition was fine.

Shortly after Colonel Glenn was picked up by the Noa, he received congratulations on his feat from President Kennedy by radio telephone.

A situation that seemed at the moment to pose the greatest danger developed near the end of the flight.

A signal radioed from the capsule indicated that the heat shield—the blunt forward end made of ceramic-like material that dispels the friction heat of re-entry and chars in the process—might be torn away before it could do its job.

If it had, the flight would have had a tragic end.

Signal Is Received

The signal, received as the capsule was traveling between Hawaii and the West Coast, indicated that the heat shield had become unlatched from the main capsule body. This action was not intended to happen until the final stage of the parachute descent.

At that point, it would fall a few feet, and deploy, between it and the capsule base, a cloth landing bag to cushion the impact on the water.

Colonel Glenn was asked by radio to flip a switch to check whether the shield had, in fact, become unlatched. When the light did not go on, it appeared that the "unlatch" signal had been spurious.

But the Mercury team was taking no chances. It changed the sequence of re-entry events to try to insure that, even if unlatched, the heat shield would not fall away prematurely.

Colonel Glenn, apparently sensing possible serious trouble, asked: "What are the reasons for this? Do you have any reasons?"

"Not at this time," came the reply from the control center.

Normally, after the firing of the three braking rockets to bring the capsule out of orbit, the empty braking-rocket package is jettisoned.

Jettisoning was delayed today so that, in case the heat shield had become unlatched, the rocket-packet straps would hold the shield in place until this function was taken over by the force of re-entry into the atmosphere.

The package burned on re-entry. The heat shield did not drop away until it was supposed to. This indicated that the signal that had caused so much anxiety had, in fact, been a false one.

100,000 See Launching

The whole continent watched on television as Colonel Glenn's capsule was launched. The world listened by radio. And almost 100,000 persons had a direct view from here and the beaches around as the Atlas rocket booster bore the Project Mercury capsule upward with a thrust of 360,000 pounds.

The Friendship 7 was lofted into a trajectory that varied between a low point, or perigee, of about ninety-nine miles, and a high point, or apogee, of 162 miles.

It traveled at a speed of about 17,530 miles an hour and went from day to night three times before whirling east across the Pacific on the final leg of the flight.

Some 300 miles west of the California coast, three retro, or braking, rockets slowed the capsule enough to bring it out of orbit.

The elated astronaut on board radioed, "Boy, that was a real fireball of a ride!" as the capsule rammed back into the atmosphere.

Besides generating heat that gave him a spectacular moment of fireworks outside his capsule window, the re-entry ended Colonel Glenn' long hours of weightlessness and shoved him forcefully back against his contoured couch.

At 2:43 P. M., a sixty-three-foot red-and-white parachute deposited the Friendship 7 on gentle Caribbean waters.

After the capsule had been picked up by the Noa and safely placed on her deck, Colonel Glenn emerged triumphant in his gleaming silver space suit.

Sends Word of Trouble

It was on his first turn around the globe that Colonel Glenn sent word of erratic behavior by the attitude control system. This caused some concern almost to the end of the flight.

The system is designed to control the capsule's attitude in space.

This does not mean that it in any way alters the course of the capsule over the ground. The course is set once the Air Force Atlas booster has imparted to the capsule its speed and direction, and has been dropped away.

The astronaut exercises no control over the capsule attitude until after the Atlas booster rocket has finished burning and dropped away. During the climb to space, the Atlas provides the guidance and attitude control. Its engines swivel like a juggler's palm under a broomstick.

The attitude system, rather, controls the orientation of the capsule—whether the forward end tilts up or down; whether it yaws right or left; or whether the capsule rolls one way or the other.

If the capsule moves out of proper line on any of the three axes, it can be realigned by squirting hydrogen peroxide through tiny jets.

There are two completely independent systems for making these corrections. One is called automatic; the other manual. There are different ways to operate each system.

Used Automatic System

When the trouble developed, Colonel Glenn was flying by the completely automatic method. Gyroscopes were set to the desired attitudes. And when the capsule strayed too far, squirts of hydrogen peroxide were to be automatically ejected through the proper jets.

On this system, there are four jets for roll; four for pitch up and down; and four for yaw right and left. Two of the four jets in each set have a thrust of only one pound, while the other two have much larger thrusts.

Only the small jets are supposed to be brought into play during the main portion of the orbital journey. The large ones are mainly for more radical corrections necessary when attitude changes are likely to be most violent—coming back from orbit.

What happened to Colonel Glenn's capsule was that the small jets did not do their job. When the capsule drifted beyond the proper limits, and the small jets did not respond, the larger jets, with twenty-four pounds of thrust, automatically cut in.

Dangers Are Described

A similar malfunction occurred on the roll jets during the second orbit of the flight made by Enos the chimpanzee last year. Because there was no human aboard to analyze the trouble and make corrections, Enos's mission had to be ended one orbit ahead of schedule.

The danger today was that the large jets would consume the hydrogen peroxide too fast and that, when it came time to perform the important return-from-orbit maneuver, there would be none left to orient the capsule properly for re-entry.

Colonel Glenn initially met the problem by switching to a technique called fly-by-wire. He controlled the vehicle by manually moving the control stick.

This was not the regular "manual" system. The stick was electronically connected to the same jets used in the completely automatic system. But it had the result of making very finely calculated corrections that did not waste hydrogen peroxide.

At later stages of the flight, Colonel Glenn switched to the completely independent "manual" system that used six different jets, two for each axis. The amount of squirt ejected through these jets was also determined by how far the control stick moved, and it wasted no hydrogen peroxide.

The original trouble seemed to have disappeared by the time the colonel was ready to return from orbit.

He successfully used the automatic system for the difficult re-entry maneuver, while keeping himself ready to switch immediately to manual controls if the trouble recurred. It did not.

10 Previous Attempts

Today's orbital flight had been scheduled for just before Christmas There had been ten attempts to send Colonel Glenn on his trip, and ten frustrating postponements, either because of weather or technical problems.

Last night, the weather men talked about being "cautiously optimistic." But few observers agreed with them. It did not seem possible that the mess of weather bearing down on Florida could clear away in time, and that is the way it still looked when the swarm of official observers arrived here about 4 A.M.

Colonel Glenn had been awakened at 2:20 A.M. The countdown ritual was not much different from what had been witnessed on the suborbital 300-mile trips made last year by Comdr. Alan B. Shepard Jr., and on the attempt Jan. 27 to orbit Colonel Glenn.

A number of changes had been made in the mission plan since the short-range flights. The recovery system had been revised to minimize chances of another after-landing mishap that caused loss of Capt. Virgil I. Grissom's capsule and almost cost that astronaut his life.

Colonel Glenn was given a special camera with which to try to take various types of pictures of cloud cover and other phenomena.

He had a "bungee" chord—a "king size rubberband" — on which he was to pull, like an oarsman pulling oars, to see how his blood pressure was affected by exercise when he was in a weightless state.

He had a medical kit of spring-loaded needles with which he could give himself various injections. One was to suppress nausea or other symptoms of motion sickness. (Colonel Glenn reported frequently that weightlessness bothered him not at all.)

He had also a pain-killer, morphine; a stimulant, benzadrine; and a drug to counter shock.

Under his flying suit Colonel Glenn wore a plastic tube and container for bladder relief.

As the sun rose, the low-hanging clouds disappeared, and left conditions here as ideal as anyone ever had seen them. The weather in key recovery areas at sea was equally perfect.

While waiting for the count to proceed, Colonel Glenn had a chance to talk by phone with wife Anna, his 16-year-old son David, and his 15-year-old daughter Lynn. They watched the proceedings on TV from their home in Arlington, Va.

Visually, there was nothing particularly memorable about the take-off, at 9:47. Emotionally, the atmosphere was charged, because a man was going into orbit.

There were the usual cries of "Go! go!" at take-off. Tears came to the eyes of some viewers, in the blockhouse, at the observer's stand two miles from the launching pad, and on the beaches. But, generally, the emotions were held in. Everyone waited.

Colonel Glenn apparently had a fine, exhilarating time, right from the start. He experienced some vibration along with acceleration force, as he climbed through the atmosphere.

Then it smoothed out; the rocket burning stopped; the acceleration switched abruptly to weightlessness; and the capsule automatically turned its blunt end forward for the almost five hours he was to be in orbit.

"Capsule is turning around," he radioed. "Oh, that view is tremendous."

He was the professional test pilot, and at the same time a human being experiencing pure joy. The tone was full of enthusiasm.

On the first orbit, over the Canary Islands, Colonel Glenn reported that "the horizon is a brilliant blue."

One after another of the stations in the eighteen-station world-wide tracking net locked its radar on the Friendship 7, and most of them established voice communications with the astronaut on board.

Colonel Glenn received a special greeting from the citizens of Perth, Australia, who turned on the lights all over town.

"Thank everybody for turning them on," he radioed. About there, too, he tried the first of the special foods prepared for consumption in orbit, where there is no gravity to let liquids pour or meats stay on a dish. He ate tubes of food and meat, and malted milk tablets.

An odd phenomenon occurred when he was within range of Guaymas, Mexico. He reported "luminous particles around the capsule — just thousands of them—right at sunrise over the Pacific."

Maj. Gen. Leighton Davis, a Project Mercury officer here, suggested later that they might have been dust particles, or chips of paint from the capsule.

Moment of Decision

Then started the troubles with the attitude controls system—troubles that were to occupy the pilot the rest of the flight.

The moment of decision came near the end of the second orbit. Colonel Glenn was reporting continued erratic behavior of the controls, apparently even with the manual system—the alternative to the one that originally malfunctioned.

He also was reporting a warning light indicating that hydrogen peroxide fuel for at least one of the systems was getting low.

To many experts listening to these events unfold, there seemed no alternative to bringing Colonel Glenn back at the end of the second orbit rather than risking another circuit.

But the astronaut thought he could handle the situation without excessive trouble.

Between the technical talk, there was time for joking—the exuberance of a man who, no matter how experienced in combat and test flying, had never done anything quite like this.

Then he got down to the business of preparing himself for the critical firing of the braking rockets and the re-entry into the atmosphere.

Greatest Day in Space

Today's flight gave the United States, by any standards, its greatest day in space.

The achievement, however, could still not be considered quite up to what the Russians had done.

Colonel Glenn's flight was two orbits more than were flown by Maj. Yuri A. Gagarin, the Soviet space man, last April 12 but fourteen less than another Russian, Maj. Gherman S. Titov, flew on Aug. 6.

In addition, there were some technical respects in which both Soviet orbital flights appeared to observers here to have an advantage: the size of the capsule orbited (five tons as against a ton and a half); the reliability of automatic controls; and the cabin atmosphere in which the pilot had to work.

But Colonel Glenn's trip was considered by most observers here to have gone a long way toward erasing this nation's "second-best" look in space.

Associated Press Wirephoto

THE HOPES: Spectators on the sands of Cocoa Beach, Fla., follow spacecraft launching at Cape Canaveral near-by

United Press International Telephoto

AND FEARS: A prayerful attitude is struck by a viewer

50,000 on Beach Strangely Calm As Rocket Streaks Out of Sight

'He's in Hands of the Lord Now,' Woman Says—Hilarity Erupts at Word of Recovery—900-Pound Cake Is Cut

By GAY TALESE

Special to The New York Times.

COCOA BEACH, Feb. 20—At 9:47 A. M. today the rocket rose slowly over the beach like a high infield fly, but moments later it was streaking out of sight, leaving a thin, white and fluffy vapor trail.

Fifty thousand spectators stood along the beach watching the climbing Atlas carrying Lieut. Col. John H. Glenn Jr. into orbit. Some cheered, some clapped. An elderly woman said solemnly: "He's in the hands of the Lord now." Most remained silent.

They watched the sky until there was nothing left to see except pelicans and sea gulls, and until the rocket's vapor trail had lost its shape and become a floating, upside-down question mark.

Then they slumped on the beach to hear the rest by radio, or returned to homes, motels or taverns to watch on television, as millions were doing around the country.

Not until 3:01 P. M., when the astronaut had gone thrice around the earth and had been safely retrieved from the Atlantic by the destroyer Noa, did the hilarity begin. Faces lost their looks of concern.

Cheers Go Up

A 900-pound cake, the size and shape of the Mercury capsule, was sliced. And a huge movie-type marquee along the main road lighted up to say: "Our Prayers Were Answered."

There were cheers around poolsides when it was reported that President Kennedy would come here Friday to honor Colonel Glenn. By twilight, Cocoa Beach's jazz bands and cash registers were swinging and ringing in merry syncopation.

"Oh, he done it buddy, he done it, so let's have a drink," John Godbee of Deland called to the crowd around him at the Vanguard Bar.

"I said 'go, go, go,' and seeing it go gave me a glorious feeling," John Pellegrino, the Vanguard's bass player, said.

"It was just undescribable," said Mrs. Thomas J. Knight of Baltimore, relaxing on the beach.

"Undescribable is right." Mrs. Howard Balliet of Orlando agreed with a nod.

Though the countdown was halted a few times, there was an undefinable feeling of optimism. People seemed to sense that this was finally the big day, that after ten postponements the orbital shot would leave the launching pad.

At 9:23, radios in cars, on people's shoulders and in their pockets could be heard everywhere saying, "T minus 22, and counting . . . T minus 20 minutes, and counting . . . T minus 17 minutes . . . T minus 13 minutes."

Now there was a vast quiet along the beach. People stood on sand dunes, motel porches, trucks and trailers, all with eyes fixed on the missile gantries, towering like a mirage eight miles north over the waves.

"Rosemary!" screamed a mother, almost hysterically, grabbing her fleeing child. "Get over here."

"T minus 3 minutes," went the radio. "T minus 30 seconds * * * 20 seconds * * * 10 seconds * * * 5 * * * 4 * * * 3 * * * 2 * * *."

"Lift-off!" somebody yelled.

"Look, it's up!"

"Go, baby, go!" a man cried, clenching his fist.

But the great majority watched silently as the missile moved slowly skyward. There was a red flame behind it as it began to climb. Then it was just a blazing speck, rising higher and higher, with only the vapor trail marking the ascent for those without binoculars.

Pensiveness Noted

The lack of delirium, the pensiveness of the thousands who stared toward the sky were hard to interpret. The flights of Comdr. Alan B. Shepard and Capt. Virgil I. Grissom here had brought rousing demonstrations. Each had evoked cheers usually heard after a game-winning world series home run.

Perhaps the crowd was quieter because it had been let down by the postponements, or maybe it thought there was no cause for cheering until Colonel Glenn had safely returned.

There was noticeable excitement at 2:30 P. M., when somebody at the Holiday Inn's television set shouted, "He's coming down, he's on his way down!"

Nine-year-old Michael von Fremd of Bethesda, Md., jumped up and down.

"I knew things would go right today," said Mrs. Marion Fega of Los Angeles.

A few hours later, the happy trailer caravans began to leave the beach, where some had been entrenched more than a week. The drivers shook hands and promised to write.

"Today was the highlight of my life," said Ernest Perkins, gunning his motor and heading back to Toledo.

First American in Orbit

John Herschel Glenn Jr.

THE sturdy, sandy-haired man who squirmed his way into the crowded capsule atop the giant Atlas missile and was shot into space yesterday on one of the most dangerous trips ever taken by a human expressed a feeling not long ago.

Man in the News

"You fear the least what you know the most about," said Lieut. Col. John Herschel Glenn Jr., a remarkably uncomplicated man in a markedly complicated job. He made that simple statement recently after discussing some of his intensive preparations for his historic flight.

He spoke then as the "premier mission pilot" for Project Mercury. And the statement was characteristic of the 40-year-old Marine Corps officer, the "old man" of the team of seven astronauts who for two and a half years had trained for the space-penetrating venture.

Pilot in Pacific War

A former combat and test pilot, Colonel Glenn flew fifty-nine fighter-bomber missions in the Pacific in World War II and ninety missions in Korea. His awards include five Distinguished Flying Crosses and the Air Medal with eighteen clusters.

To an interviewer wondering what the values of combat and test-piloting experiences were to anyone preparing for a journey into space, Colonel Glenn had this to say:

"Experience in dangerous and unexpected situations is even more valuable than good conditioning. If you have successfully controlled your airplane in an emergency, or dealt with an enemy pilot whose prime object is to destroy you, your chances of making the proper decision next time are increased.

"The space traveler, alone where no one has been before, will need a confidence only experience can give him."

Like the other astronauts, Colonel Glenn went through dozens of physical tests. They included occupying a high-heat chamber that simulated conditions that would prevail inside the Mercury capsule if overheating occurred during its re-entry to the earth's atmosphere. Other rigors included spinning on a centrifuge and in isolation in a blacked-out room.

Exercise Before Breakfast

As part of his personal regimen, he took a two-mile run every morning before breakfast.

Most of Colonel Glenn's technical experiences in training for the Project Mercury flight have been likened to those of a man sitting inside a computer. The small capsule, crowded with instruments and safety gear, barely allows room for the astronaut in his "custom-made" contour couch.

The 180-pound, five-foot, ten-inch officer is ruggedly handsome, with close-cropped hair, green eyes and a ready grin. He emits quiet confidence and appears to be in command of himself at all times.

Colonel Glenn was the back-up pilot for the suborbital space rides made last year by Comdr. Alan B. Shepard Jr. and Capt. Virgil I. Grissom.

Ready for 'The Big One'

A Marine Corps officer who served at Colonel Glenn's side for four years was quoted recently as having said that he knew all along that the space officials were "holding Glenn back to ride the big one."

"He could ride a cookstove back if they could find a way to throw it up there," the officer said.

The newest United States space hero is a Presbyterian who once said that religion should not be a sometime thing, handy only for emergencies. He was born in Cambridge, Ohio, and went to Muskingum College, leaving in his junior year to become a naval air cadet. As a Navy test pilot, he made headlines in 1957 when he was the first man to fly at supersonic speed from Los Angeles to New York.

He is married to the former Anna Margaret Castor of New Concord, Ohio, which he calls his home town. They have two teen-age children, David and Carolyn Ann. Boating and water skiing are the family sports.

United Press International Telephoto

"You fear the least what you know the most about."

GLENN'S TRIP PUTS MAN NEARER MOON

Provides Data Needed for Flight to Satellite

Special to The New York Times.

CAPE CANAVERAL, Fla., Feb. 20—The three-orbit flight around the world by Lieut. Col. John H. Glenn Jr. today was a dramatic probe that puts man closer to the moon.

It will probably take something like eight years, with continued missile successes in the interim, before an astronaut steps from his planetary craft onto the surface of the moon. But the successful flight of Colonel Glenn today is certain to provide valuable information for the next exploratory probes.

The next step toward the moon will be a "repeat performance" of the triple orbit, this one by another astronaut, some time within the next eight weeks, under the present timetable. And before the end of 1962, plans call for a series of three more triple orbits as well as one flight that will attempt to surpass the trip taken by Russia's Maj. Gherman S. Titov on Aug. 6 last year, when the Soviet astronaut circled the globe seventeen times in a little more than twenty-five hours.

For next year, the plans include an undetermined number of orbital flights, each one of them constituting eighteen trips around the earth, that is, one more than Major Titov made. But the emphasis will be not so much on the competitive aspect as on the need to find out if longer trips will make the human pilots sick.

Glenn's Contribution

When Major Titov landed after his historic flight he reported that he had suffered illness, and one of the main purposes of longer flights around the earth will be to determine if other astronauts also fall victim to nausea on extended trips and if they do what can be done about it.

It is hoped that in 1964 two men can be assigned to a space capsule for a flight lasting from seven to fourteen days. This flight is expected to be the penultimate trip that will lead directly — if not necessarily quickly—to the historic moment when man sets foot on the moon.

While the Russian space flight with Major Titov was particularly impressive for the fact that he was taken aloft in a five-ton capsule — the capsule that carried Colonel Glenn weighed a ton and a half—the American's contribution is expected to be extremely valuable in terms of showing in much greater dimension what a human pilot can do in terms of rider-control.

There will be many dramatic and daring flights in the next couple of years, but probably the next major advance will be the Gemini 1964 mission, the flight involving two men riding a capsule shot into orbit by a Titan II rocket.

At the same time, research continues on the 1,500,000-pound-thrust Saturn booster that is scheduled to take three men in a capsule around the globe in 1966.

This flight will be one of the phases of the Apollo project, which includes, later, the man-on-the-moon trip.

Space Shot Halts Crime

CHICAGO, Feb. 20 (UPI)—The police said Lieut. Col. John H. Glenn Jr.'s space venture apparently interrupted crime today. They said that during the period from fifteen minutes before blast-off and fifteen minutes afterward, "only one or two calls were received by the Police Department."

Glenn Sees Lights Of Perth and Says: 'Thank Everybody'

PERTH, Australia, Feb. 20 (UPI)—Australians turned their cities into saucers of light tonight to give Lieut. Col. John H. Glenn Jr. some visual contact with the dark side of the earth he was orbiting.

But apparently only the city of Perth, where residents switched on every street light and neon sign and even rigged special lights and homemade reflectors, got through to the orbiting American.

Colonel Glenn reported in a talk with Leroy G. Cooper, another American astronaut, at Australia's Muchea tracking station that he had seen bright lights while passing over western Australia—apparently those of Perth.

"Thank everybody for turning them on," he said.

When this word was relayed by the Voice of America, Perth was delighted.

Colonel Glenn told the Muchea station that he could not see the lights of Woomera or Adelaide because of clouds.

Consultations with Muchea had brought about the idea of turning Perth and its suburban area into a blaze of light. Some residents even used bedsheets to reflect light.

Perth has about 100,000 residents. The metropolitan area has about 275,000.

As the capsule blasted off at Cape Canaveral, Fla., the description of the scene was relayed by the Voice of America by radio into tens of thousands of homes. In the streets, people craned their necks, gazing skyward in hopes of glimpsing the capsule as it passed over during the first orbit.

However, at 11:37 P. M. (10:37 A. M. Eastern Standard Time), the west coast of Australia was on the dark side of the earth.

Comparison of Statistics on the Five Space Flights

Following is a comparison of the five space flights made so far, by Lieut. Col. John H. Glenn Jr. of the United States, Maj. Gherman S. Titov of the Soviet Union, Capt. Virgil I. Grissom and Comdr. Alan B. Shepard Jr. of the United States, and Maj. Yuri A. Gagarin of the Soviet Union: (all distances are given in statute miles):

	Glenn	Titov	Grissom	Shepard	Gagarin
Date	Feb. 20, 1962	Aug. 6, 1961	July 21, 1961	May 5, 1961	April 12, 1961
Nature of flight	Earth orbit	Earth orbit	Suborbital	Suborbital	Earth orbit
Number of orbits	3	17	0	0	1
Altitude (miles)	99 to 162	111 to 160	118	116.5	109-188
Distance (miles)	About 81,000	437,500	302	303	About 25,000
Top speed (est., in m. p. h.)	17,545	17,750	5,280	5,100	17,400
Flight time	4 hrs. 56 min.	25 hrs. 18 min.	16 min.	15 min.	108 min.
Weight of craft (lbs.)	4,200	10,430	4,040	4,040	10,460
Craft name	Friendship 7	Vostok II	Liberty Bell 7	Freedom 7	Vostok I
Rocket thrust (est., in lbs.)	360,000	800,000	78,000	78,000	800,000
Weightlessness	About 4 hrs. 40 minutes.	About 25 hrs.	5 min.	5 min.	89.1 min.

"All the News That's Fit to Print"

The New York Times.

LATE CITY EDITION
U. S. Weather Bureau Report (Page 77) forecasts: Mostly sunny today. Fair tonight and tomorrow.
Temp. range: 75—54; yesterday: 74—52.

VOL. CXII . No. 38,237.

NEW YORK, TUESDAY, OCTOBER 2, 1962.

10 cents beyond 50-mile zone from New York City except on Long Island. Higher in air delivery cities.

FIVE CENTS

3,000 TROOPS PUT DOWN MISSISSIPPI RIOTING AND SEIZE 200 AS NEGRO ATTENDS CLASSES; EX-GEN. WALKER IS HELD FOR INSURRECTION

SENATE REJECTS AID CUTS AND BAN ON HELP FOR REDS

Upholds Kennedy's Authority to Assist Nations That Do Business With Cuba

By FELIX BELAIR Jr.
Special to The New York Times.

WASHINGTON, Oct. 1—The Senate decided for the Administration today in preliminary votes on the foreign aid appropriation bill, due for passage tomorrow.

It voted, 47 to 28, against cutting $785,000,000 from the $792,400,000 of military and economic aid funds that its Appropriations Committee restored to the bill the House had cut heavily.

The effect of the vote was to hold the appropriation at $4,422,800,000, as recommended by its Appropriations Committee. The Administration had requested the full amount of the authorized ceiling of $4,754,800,000 but the House cut this back to $3,630,400,000.

On a later vote, the Senate confirmed this action by rejecting a proposal by Senator Allen J. Ellender, Democrat of Louisiana, to adopt the House cut of $150,000,000 for military aid.

Votes Become Narrow

By increasingly narrow margins, however, it supported other Administration goals. For instance, it voted, 39-36 to continue the President's discretion to aid countries doing business with Cuba. Then it decided, 39-37, to give the President similar discretion to waive the ban on aiding Communist nations such as Yugoslavia and Poland.

All three proposals were sponsored by Senator William Proxmire, Democrat of Wisconsin.

They were intended, first, to cut back the separate money items in the bill to the low levels voted by the House. Second, they would have approved the House's ban on aiding any Communist countries or free nations that help the Castro regime or allow their ships to deliver cargo to Cuba.

Only with the help of Republican members was the Democratic leadership able to turn back the Proxmire attack on the President's discretionary powers. On the proposal to ban aid to nations shipping to Cuba, 12 Republicans voted with 27 Democrats to defeat the move, while 22 Democrats and 14 Re-

Continued on Page 16, Column 4

Associated Press Wirephoto
PRISONERS ARE MARCHED TO ARMORY IN OXFORD: Army men escort a group of prisoners to National Guard Armory. The group had participated in a disturbance and was apprehended after the soldiers were ordered to fire at the feet of the rioters.

United Press International Telephoto
WALKER IS STOPPED BY TROOPS: Former Maj. Gen. Edwin A. Walker is detained by soldiers near the courthouse in Oxford. He was turned over to U.S. marshals and is being held in $100,000 bail on charges stemming from his role in Sunday's campus riots.

SHOTS QUELL MOB

Enrolling of Meredith Ends Segregation in State Schools

By CLAUDE SITTON
Special to The New York Times

OXFORD, Miss., Oct. 1—James H. Meredith, a Negro, enrolled in the University of Mississippi today and began classes as Federal troops and federalized units of the Mississippi National Guard quelled a 15-hour riot.

A force of more than 3,000 soldiers and guardsmen and 400 deputy United States marshals fired rifles and hurled tear-gas grenades to stop the violent demonstrations.

Throughout the day more troops streamed into Oxford. Tonight a force approaching 5,000 soldiers and guardsmen, along with the Federal marshals, maintained an uneasy peace in this town of 6,500 in the northern Mississippi hills.

[There were two flareups tonight in which tear gas had to be used, United Press International reported. A small crowd of students began throwing bottles at marshals outside Baxter Hall where Mr. Meredith was housed. They were quickly dispersed by tear gas. Soldiers also broke up a minor demonstration at a downtown intersection.]

200 Are Seized

The troops seized approximately 200 persons.

They were seized in the mobs of students and adults that besieged the university administration building last night and attacked troops on the town square this morning.

Among those arrested was former Maj. Gen. Edwin A. Walker, who resigned his commission after having been reprimanded for his ultra-right-wing political activity. He was charged with insurrection.

The university's acceptance of Mr. Meredith, a 29-year-old Air Force veteran, followed Gov. Ross R. Barnett's retreat from his defiance of Federal court orders that the Negro be enrolled.

The 64-year-old official, a member of the militantly segregationist Citizens Councils, had vowed he would go to jail if necessary to prevent university desegregation.

Mr. Meredith's admission marked the first desegregation of a public educational institution in Mississippi. It reduced the Deep South bloc of massive-resistance states to two—

Continued on Page 24, Column 6

Home Urges West to Help East's Coexistence Moves

By ARNOLD H. LUBASCH

The Earl of Home, Britain's Foreign Secretary, urged last night that the West pursue policies designed to help the Soviet bloc move toward genuine coexistence. He suggested that nuclear war was no longer a useful instrument of policy, that Communist doctrine was changing because of this and that Soviet society was changing even faster.

The West should recognize these facts, he said, and adapt its policies to them.

Lord Home's remarks were made at a dinner in the Waldorf - Astoria Hotel. The dinner was given by the Pilgrims of the United States, a friendship society devoted to cultivating understanding between this country and the nations of the British Commonwealth.

The organization, composed of 1,000 prominent persons, was founded in 1903. A sister organization across the Atlantic is known as the Pilgrims of Great Britain. The groups give dinners in honor of leading statesmen to promote understanding and brotherhood among nations.

Cites Soviet Ingenuity

Lord Home observed that the Russians exercise great ingenuity to reconcile their propaganda about peaceful coexistence with a program that permits limited force in certain regions to further the cause of Communist domination.

The West must be on guard against this technique, he said, and against the force that backs it up. He mentioned Berlin and South Vietnam as two areas of particular concern.

"I pray," he added, "that Cuba may never become a third."

Communist doctrine has begun to change, Lord Home

Continued on Page 2, Column 3

SPAAK REASSURES AFRICA ON TRADE

Tells Newer U.N. Members That Common Market Will Aid Their Development

By THOMAS J. HAMILTON
Special to The New York Times.

UNITED NATIONS, N. Y., Oct. 1—Paul-Henri Spaak, the Foreign Minister of Belgium, assured underdeveloped countries today that they could count on the cooperation of the members of the European Economic Community in the fight for economic advancement.

In addition, Mr. Spaak appealed to the entire world to understand the "new Europe" and its goal of "world cooperation."

Mr. Spaak's policy statement in the General Assembly was addressed in the first instance to 18 newly independent African states, all former possessions of France, Belgium or Italy.

Some of the states have asked the European Economic Community, or Common Market, for status as associates. The six members of the market — Belgium, France, West Germany, Italy, the Netherlands and Luxembourg—are negotiating with the African states in Brussels.

Success Is Predicted

Mr. Spaak predicted that these talks would be concluded successfully by the end of 1962.

He also predicted that the negotiations with Britain for her admission to the market would be successful. He said the market would then have about the same productive capacity as the United States, and more than the Soviet Union.

The Belgian Foreign Minister, who was one of the leaders in the formation of the Common Market, defended it against two charges: that it is a manifestation of "neo-colonialism," and that it is merely intended to provide economic support for the North Atlantic Treaty Organization.

Mr. Spaak devoted almost his entire speech to his explanation of the market's program. He received an ovation at the end, with African and Asian members joining.

The Belgian Foreign Minister emphasized that the exports of African associate members would be admitted duty-free to the Common Market countries, while the Africans would retain

Continued on Page 5, Column 2

KENNEDY MOVING TO END PIER TIE-UP

He Names Board of Inquiry as First Step in Obtaining Taft-Hartley Injunction

By JOHN D. POMFRET
Special to The New York Times

WASHINGTON, Oct. 1—President Kennedy took the first step today toward getting an injunction to end the Atlantic and Gulf Coast longshoremen's strike for 80 days.

Declaring that continuation of the strike would imperil the national health and safety, the President issued an Executive order naming a three-man board of inquiry to investigate the dispute and to report to him by Thursday.

[Meanwhile in New York, leaders of the nation's seven major maritime unions abandoned inter-union battling to plan support for the striking longshoremen. American seamen and officers started leaving their ships, while other unions made plans to avoid servicing foreign-flag ships entering Atlantic and Gulf ports.]

The strike, which began at 12:01 A.M. today, has tied up all ports from Searsport, Me., to Brownsville, Tex. About 75,000 members of the Internation-

Continued on Page 78, Column 5

WALKER IS FACING 4 FEDERAL COUNTS

Flown to Medical Center in Missouri to Await Trial—Bail Put at $100,000

Special to The New York Times

OXFORD, Miss., Oct. 1 — Former Maj. Gen. Edwin A. Walker was arrested today on four charges, including insurrection, for his role in last night's rioting at the University of Mississippi.

The man who commanded Federal forces during the school integration crisis at Little Rock in 1957 was held in $100,000 bail.

Unable to put up the bail, he was flown to the United States Medical Center for Federal Prisoners in Springfield, Mo., to await his trial.

[Mr. Walker, accompanied by marshals, arrived at the medical center Monday night, The Associated Press said.]

"They don't have a thing on me," Mr. Walker said after his arrest. He dictated a message to Gov. Ross R. Barnett, which said:

"Mr. Walker hopes his efforts were in your behalf and in behalf of the stand for freedom everywhere. Do nothing based on my status that is not in support of your own objectives.

Continued on Page 27, Column 3

Mississippi Aides Blamed By U.S. Officials for Riot

By ANTHONY LEWIS
Special to The New York Times.

WASHINGTON, Oct. 1 — The Federal Government asserted today that the failure of Mississippi officials to keep their word led to the bloody rioting in Oxford, Miss., last night. Attorney General Robert F. Kennedy and other spokesmen said that Gov. Ross R. Barnett and his aides had repeatedly given as-

Statements by Robert Kennedy and Eastland, Page 25.

surances that they could and would maintain order when James H. Meredith, a Negro, entered the University of Mississippi last night.

Instead, the Federal spokesmen said, the state police were withdrawn at the crucial moment of the developing mob scene. Federal troops were then called in, but two men were dead and many were injured by the time they arrived.

Senator James O. Eastland, Democrat of Mississippi, read on the Senate floor this morning a report on the rioting. He said the report had been prepared by officials of the University of Mississippi.

Eastland Orders Inquiry

Tonight, Senator Eastland directed the Senate Judiciary Committee, which he heads, to make an investigation "of all events at the University of Mississippi since U.S. marshals and Army troops moved in."

The report read by Mr. Eastland this morning sought to put the blame for the rioting on "amateurism by untrained marshals." It said that the 300 marshals at the university last night had "provoked" the crowd of 2,500 persons gathered on the campus.

The university officials also

Continued on Page 25, Column 1

BARNETT CHARGES MARSHALS ERRED

Says 'Trigger-Happy' U. S. Officers Are Responsible for Campus Bloodshed

Text of Barnett statement appears on Page 25.

By HEDRICK SMITH
Special to The New York Times

JACKSON, Miss., Oct. 1—Gov. Ross R. Barnett tonight attributed the fatal rioting at the University of Mississippi last night to "inexperienced, nervous and trigger-happy Federal marshals."

The Governor made the statement in a recorded broadcast carried by the National Broadcasting Company, in a later recorded broadcast, carried by the Columbia Broadcasting System, Mr. Barnett directly assailed President Kennedy.

"The responsibility for this unwarranted breach of the peace and violence in Mississippi rests directly with the President of the United States," he said. "He ordered armed forces to invade Mississippi and their actions were directly responsible for violence, bloodshed and death.

People Are "Enraged"

In his earlier statement, the Governor said that the people of Mississippi "are enraged, incensed—and rightly so."

"Free men do not submit meekly to the kind of treatment Mississippians received," he said.

The Governor also said that the only solution to the Mississippi integration crisis was for the Federal Government to remove James H. Meredith, a 29-year-old Negro student, from the university.

"The Federal authorities alone have the power to stop bloodshed in Mississippi," he said.

Continued on Page 25, Column 5

MOSCOW FOCUSING ON BLOC IN EUROPE

Rift With Chinese Believed Behind New Emphasis

By SEYMOUR TOPPING
Special to The New York Times

MOSCOW, Oct. 1—The Soviet Union has decided to pursue its program of rapprochement with Yugoslavia even at the risk of a further deterioration in relations with Communist China.

Diplomatic officials here have found evidence of this development in a comparative study of Soviet and Chinese Communist documents.

These officials believe that the ideological quarrel with Peking has caused Moscow to resolve to concentrate its resources on the consolidation of the European Communist economic bloc.

Pravda, the Communist party newspaper, published today an edited version of the communiqué issued by the Central Committee of the Chinese Communist party at the conclusion of its plenary session Friday.

The Soviet summary, which covered half a page in Pravda, omitted the strong attacks on President Tito of Yugoslavia for his so-called "modern revision-

Continued on Page 3, Column 1

Columbia Study Scores Doctors; Says Quality of Care Lags Here

Financial Sanctions Under Blue Shield Suggested in Trussell Report

By FARNSWORTH FOWLE

The medical profession is "doing little" about the quality of medical care in the metropolitan area, the state was told yesterday in an experts' report.

The report warned that the first reaction of many laymen to poor medical care "is to demand firm and drastic government action—and indeed this may occur." It said that "strong medical, hospital, community and government leadership must be asserted in the public interest."

The conclusions were contained in the final volume of the Trussell-van Dyke Report, an independent study for the state by the Columbia University School of Public Health and Administrative Medicine. It was directed by Dr. Ray E. Trussell, chairman of the school, now on leave from the school while serving as New York City's Commissioner of Hospitals, and Frank van Dyke, an associate professor at the school.

The report called on the medical profession to welcome current efforts of management and labor toward improving medical care.

The New York Times
Dr. Ray E. Trussell

"The organized purchasers of medical and hospital care can be the strongest arm of the community in upgrading standards, and it is to the best interest of organized medicine and hospitals to work with them,"

Continued on Page 42, Column 1

Congo Flies Troops To End Kasai Revolt

By Reuters

LEOPOLDVILLE, the Congo, Oct. 1—Reliable sources said today that the central Congolese Government was flying troops to Luluabourg to put down a new revolt by supporters of Albert Kalonji in South Kasai. Luluabourg is the Government army base nearest to the diamond-rich province.

The troop movement followed the declaration by the Government of a state of emergency in South Kasai. No immediate action was planned by the United Nations.

Mr. Kalonji, self-styled "king," virtually seceded from the central Government shortly after the Congo became independent two years ago. He escaped recently from a prison near Leopoldville and returned to his capital of Bakwanga.

A United Nations spokesman

Continued on Page 9, Column 3

Bidwell's Tax Trial Ends in Hung Jury

By DAVID ANDERSON

The tax-evasion trial of J. Truman Bidwell, former chairman of the New York Stock Exchange, ended early today with a hung jury.

The jury, which had been deliberating since 1 P.M., filed into the courtroom shortly after midnight and told Federal Judge Thomas F. Murphy that it was "hopelessly deadlocked."

Judge Murphy, who two hours earlier had rejected a similar report and had instructed the jurors to try once more, now said:

"I declare a mistrial. Unhappy as I am, I guess there is nothing else we can do."

The prosecutor, Assistant United States Attorney Stephen E. Kaufman, said the Government would now consider

Continued on Page 18, Column 3

CAMPUS A BIVOUAC AS NEGRO ENTERS

2,000 Troops Stand Guard —Meredith Eats Alone

By McCANDLISH PHILLIPS
Special to The New York Times

OXFORD, Miss., Oct. 1—The University of Mississippi campus was under military occupation today as James H. Meredith, its first Negro student, registered and attended two classes.

Two thousand of the more than 3,000 Army and National Guard troops here made the tree-studded, rolling campus look like a cross between a bivouac and a prisoner-of-war camp. More olive drab uniforms were evident on campus than student casual dress.

Mr. Meredith, who did not get his first meal on campus until supper was served to him privately tonight, was housed in an end room in Baxter Hall, a male residence dormitory. The room next door was occupied by Federal marshals.

The 29-year-old Negro was taken from his dormitory quarters at 7:45 A. M. and marched to the Lyceum, the administration building. There he was registered in 45 minutes—

Continued on Page 26, Column 1

NEWS INDEX

Mobs Armed With Bottles and Bricks Terrorized Oxford From Dawn Until Noon

SOLDIERS BEATEN; HOMES DAMAGED

Broken Glass Covers Streets —Troops Fire High and Low to Subdue Rioters

By THOMAS BUCKLEY
Special to The New York Times

OXFORD, Miss., Oct. 1 — From dawn until noon today mobs of bottle and brick-throwing marauders terrorized this city.

Soldiers, Negroes and newsmen were beaten. Homes and automobiles were damaged.

When a measure of peace had been restored by regular Army and federalized Mississippi Guard units, troops ringed the courthouse square. Other detachments were posted at intersections.

Military police units remained on duty at roadblocks set up about a half-mile from town. All cars entering and leaving the city were searched.

Well over 100 persons were in military custody at the Guard Armory on University Avenue.

A particularly dangerous group of about 75 collected at Lamar Street and University Avenue, a block from the town square. Gas stations are situated on each corner, and traffic is controlled by a stoplight.

Outsiders Noticed

Many students of Mississippi State University at Starkville were among them. A Confederate flag flew from a lamppost.

These rioters threw empty soft-drink bottles and rocks at military vehicles and Negro motorists. When they had exhausted the supply of bottles from the racks at the gas station, they obtained full bottles from vending machines. They emptied these, broke off the necks and threw again. As the sun rose the intersection was carpeted with glass fragments.

Meanwhile, Mayor Richard W. Elliott absolved townspeople from blame for the riots.

"I'd say it was caused by outside agitation," he said.

Hundreds of rioters were believed still in the city, making the troops wary. Their frenzy, spent in hours of destruction at the campus of the University of Mississippi, was renewed by the news that James H. Meredith, 29-year-old Negro had been registered as a student and was attending classes.

Further outbreaks after nightfall had been feared, but none was reported so far.

At 5:30 A.M., after having been driven off the campus, the mob began collecting at intersections of the tree-lined streets. It consisted mostly of backcountry youths with sideburns, wearing leather jackets. Older men wore dungarees and overalls. Many were drunk.

Guardsman Retaliates

On a back road nearby, a Guardsman halted a group of hooligans at rifle point. He took a Confederate flag from one and ground it into the dirt.

"I'm from Marks, Miss.," he said, "but when they start throwing rocks I don't care a damn about anything else."

Several youths invaded the yard of the home occupied until her death by Mrs. Maud Falkner, mother of William Faulkner, the late novelist. They tore bricks from the borders of flower beds and trampled the shrubbery. The residents appealed to the police in vain, but Guardsmen finally routed the vandals.

A Negro woman, head held high, walked in the midst of the demonstrators on her way into town. She was not molested. Few other pedestrians, and almost no Negroes, were on the street.

By 9 A. M. the Guardsmen had become the main targets of missiles. Leaving their jeeps, they moved repeatedly forward with bayonets leveled. The crowd would retreat, then advance again.

A little later seven troop-carrying Marine helicopters circled low over the center of town.

Finally, at 10:15, the command was given to fire over their heads and at their feet. A volley ripped through the trees and ricocheted off the sidewalk. Nobody apparently was hit.

Then the Guardsmen surrounded the group and took them into custody. Ringed by bayonets and with hands clasped behind their heads, the prisoners were removed on the trot to the armory.

Douglas Downs of New York, a National Broadcasting Company cameraman, took pictures of the guards and their prisoners. He was rushed by four Guardsmen, led by an unidentified captain, who had drawn and cocked his pistol.

Thrusting the pistol at Mr. Downs, the officer ordered him to give up the film. Mr. Downs convinced him that he had merely been sighting the camera.

The armory is the headquarters for Troop E of the Second Reconnaissance Squadron, which is commanded by Capt. Murry C. Falkner, 33 years old, a nephew of the novelist.

His unit was the first to go into action at the university. Captain Falkner's left arm was broken when he was struck by a brick in front of the Lyceum, the administration building. He was still on duty.

In three small, shabby houses overlooking the road within 50 yards of the armory encampment, Negro families sat on porches and quietly watched the parade of prisoners. There were no reports that Negroes had been mistreated in their homes, but only a few went to work today.

Associated Press Wirephoto

UNDER ARREST: Men taken into custody during the rioting at the University of Mississippi stand against wall

MISSISSIPPI LOSES NEW COURT TEST

Motion Taken Under Study, but All Rulings Stand

By FOSTER HAILEY
Special to The New York Times

NEW ORLEANS, Oct 1 — The State of Mississippi failed today in an effort to get a Federal Court to vacate its decisions ordering enrollment of James H. Meredith in the University of Mississippi.

Three judges of the United States Court of Appeals for the Fifth Circuit took the state's motion under advisement and called for briefs.

The court's action left standing the contempt rulings against Gov. Ross R. Barnett and Lieut. Gov. Paul H. Johnson, which are to take effect tomorrow morning at 11 o'clock.

Federal marshals are under orders to take both men into custody at that hour. At the same time fines of $10,000 a day against the Governor and $5,000 a day against Mr. Johnson would also take effect.

"The orders of this court remain," said Judge Richard T. Rives of Montgomery, Ala., who presided at today's hearing.

"This delay does not delay any other orders of this court."

Later Judge Rives declared, "This court is not prepared at this time to set aside its previous order. It now stands adjourned, subject to further call."

Briefs Set for Friday

The court gave the state's lawyers until Friday to file briefs and said it would allow the Federal Government's and Mr. Meredith's attorneys until the following Tuesday, Oct. 9, to file answers.

Judge Rives and his two fellow judges, John Minor Wisdom of New Orleans and Walter Gewin of Jacksonville, Fla., heard arguments for three hours.

John C. Satterfield of Yazoo City, Miss., a former president of the American Bar Association, made the principal argument for Mississippi.

He contended that the Appeals Court lacked jurisdiction because the matter already was before the Southern District Court in Mississippi. He also argued that the Appeals Court lacked territorial jurisdiction, that the hearings on the Meredith case should have been held in Hattiesburg and not in New Orleans.

In contrast to events of the last few days in Jackson and Oxford, Miss., the court session was quiet. Federal marshals were in the corridors of the Federal Court Building, but they had nothing to do.

There were only half a dozen spectators in the courtroom and both the judges and the lawyers spoke in low tones. There were no histrionics.

Appearing for the Government were St. John Barrett and Harold Green, Justice Department lawyers who were sent down from Washington several weeks ago to represent the Government when it intervened in the case as a friend of the court.

Appearing for Mr. Meredith, who was not in court but attending classes in Oxford, were Mrs. Constance Baker Motley and Jack Greenberg, both of New York, attorneys for the National Association for the Advancement of Colored People.

The next scheduled session of the Appeals Court is at 10 A. M. Friday, when it will hear further arguments on a Federal motion for a preliminary injunction forbidding the University of Mississippi or any officials of the state from interfering with not only the registration of Mr. Meredith but also with his peaceful attendance at classes.

At the start of the hearing Judge Rives asked Mr. Satterfield if he represented the Governor and Lieutenant Governor as well as the state. Mr. Satterfield said, he did not. He argued that only the "sovereign state of Mississippi" was involved and not any individual.

The registrar and the trustees of the university, by previous statements to the court and by registering Mr. Meredith today, have purged themselves of contempt. The Governor and Lieutenant Governor have not.

Mr. Barnett and Mr. Johnson have failed to appear in court to show why they should not be held in contempt. Nor has Mr. Barnett withdrawn his declaration of "interposition" by which he asserted he was placing his authority between the Federal courts and state officials.

United Press International Telephoto

DISORDER IN THE STREETS OF OXFORD: Youths gather at courthouse in college town and hurl bottles at Federal troops, who later dispersed unruly group with tear gas.

BRANDT PRAISES U.S. ON MISSISSIPPI ROLE

Mayor Willy Brandt of West Berlin said here yesterday that this country's integration problems in Mississippi would be cause for some concern in Europe.

But, he added, "Many in Europe will be impressed by the great energy the Government has exerted to support a principle for one citizen—it shows how serious the Americans consider the rule of law."

Mayor Brandt expressed his opinion when interviewed at the Carlyle Hotel after a luncheon at which he was a guest of Mayor Wagner and civic leaders. Mr. Brandt has been visiting the city since last week. He is flying today to Boston and will speak at Harvard University.

Mayor Brandt, who received a key to the city from Mayor Wagner, talked informally at the luncheon about West Berlin's problems, assets and liabilities.

He pictured his city as confident. He suggested, however, that groups interested in human rights should visit West Berlin and study the human, rather than the economic, problems presented by the Communist wall that separates East and West Berlin.

Leader in Jackson Asks Barnett to Halt Violence

Special to The New York Times

JACKSON, Miss., Oct. 1 — William H. Mounger, a prominent Jackson businessman, called upon Gov. Ross R. Barnett today to go to the University of Mississippi and bring an end to the violence there.

Mr. Mounger, president of the Lamar Life Insurance Company, made his plea in a brief, personal radio and television statement at 8 o'clock this morning.

"I am not in conflict with the Governor's purpose of trying to test the legal and sovereign rights of our state," he said, "but I think it should be done legally, not by violence. And the Governor is the only man who can stop the violence."

Communist Party Supports U. S. Action in Mississippi

The Communist party of America yesterday gave its full support to President Kennedy in the Mississippe racial crisis. But it criticized him for what it called tardiness in acting.

In a statement issued from its headquarters nere, it said:

"We support all acts of Federal intervention to uphold the Constitution and to supress this rebellion.

"We fully support moves by President Kennedy in this direction. It is regrettable that the tardiness and indecisiveness of Administration in this crisis resulted in dangerous delay in taking necessary measures."

The statement called on Mr. Dennedy to place Mississippi under martial law.

CALL-UP INCIDENTS DENIED IN JACKSON

Special to The New York Times

JACKSON, Miss., Oct. 1— Mississippi's 11,000-man National Guard has responded to its latest Federal call-up in "completely satisfactory" fashion, the State Adjutant General said today.

Maj. Gen. William P. Wilson, who is politically appointed and was himself not federalized, was asked about reports that there might have been some incidents and that at least one guardsman might have been court-martialed for refusing to report.

"The National Guard," he replied, "was mobilized in accordance with a mobilization plan which has been practiced on many occasions. The response on this occasion was completely satisfactory.

"There have been absolutely no incidents of any individual willfully refusing to report for mobilization.

"When the call went to the National Guard units, they did not know the purpose for which they were being called, and therefore responded in the same manner as though they were being mobilized for a real—and I say again a real—national emergency."

Man Seized With Arsenal

DALLAS, Oct. 1 (AP) — A 22-year-old man has been arrested for trying to transport a small arsenal to Mississippi, the police said today. They said the man, Ashland Burchwell of Dallas, told them he had worked for Edwin A. Walker in the latter's unsuccessful campaign for Governor. Four pistols, a rifle and more than 3,000 rounds of ammunition were seized.

United Press International Telephoto

FIRST AID: One Negro soldier assists another, injured in rioting at Oxford, Miss.

TROOPS PUT DOWN RIOTING IN OXFORD

Continued From Page 1, Col. 8

Alabama and South Carolina.

Although the step brought an apparent end to the most serious Federal-state conflict since the Civil War, its cost in human lives and bitterness was the greatest in any dispute over desegregation directives of the Federal courts.

Two men were killed in the rioting, which broke out about 8 o'clock last night after Mr. Meredith had been escorted onto the campus by the marshals.

The victims were Paul Guihard, 30 years old, a correspondent for Agence France Presse, and Ray Gunter, 23, a jukebox repairman from nearby Abbeville, Miss.

The number of injured could not be determined definitely. But Mr. Guthman told newsmen 25 marshals had required medical treatment. One of them, shot through the neck, was reported in critical condition.

A military spokesman said 20 soldiers and guardsmen had been injured, none of them seriously.

Dr. Vernon B. Harrison, director of the Student Health Service, said between 60 and 70 persons, including some marshals, had been treated at the university infirmary.

Others who were wounded or were burned by exploding tear-gas grenades obtained aid from local physicians or from Army doctors who moved into the infirmary last night.

Corps Chief in Command

Lieut. Gen. Hamilton Howze, commander of the 18th Airborne Corps, arrived here from Fort Bragg, in North Carolina, to take over the field command. The corps includes the 82d and the 101st Airborne Divisions.

Lieut. Col. Gordon Hill, Army public information officer here, said General Howze was accompanied by his corps command. There were reports that other units of the two famed airborne divisions were moving into the area.

The general's presence indicated that a major build-up of Army troops was under way here, in Columbus, Miss., and at Memphis.

General Howze took over command from Brig. Gen. Charles Billingslea, assistant commander of the Second Infantry Division, Fort Benning, Ga.

Mr. Guthman said Federal forces were prepared to remain as long as necessary.

"Our mission is to see that the orders of the courts are enforced," he said.

Asked if the mission included the preservation of order in the town, he replied:

"I think we have a duty to maintain law and order."

The toll of property damaged included five automobiles and a mobile television unit that were burned.

Garden Ripped Up

Bricks, lumber and other building materials were stolen from a construction site and used as missiles or roadblocks. The rioters ripped up the garden of a home in their search for brickbats and commandeered a fire engine and a bulldozer.

A hard core of 70 to 100 youths, most of whom appeared to be Ole Miss students, touched off the riot. They were soon joined by students from other universities and colleges in this area.

Youths and men from Lafayette County, of which Oxford is the seat, and from surrounding counties joined the fray.

Some members of the mob wore jackets from Mississippi State University, at Starkeville, and Memphis State College, in Memphis.

Members of the Ku Klux Klan and similar racist groups in Alabama and northern Louisiana reportedly had threatened to join the opposition against Mr. Meredith's enrollment.

State Charge Denied

In briefing newsmen, Mr. Guthman flatly denied assertions by state officials that Chief United States Marshal James J. P. McShane had precipitated the riot by ordering use of tear gas prematurely.

The Justice Department spokesman said tear gas had been used only after the students had showered the marshals with rocks and one deputy had been struck with an iron pipe, which left a deep dent in his helmet.

A force of 200 state troopers, used by Governor Barnett to block one of Mr. Meredith's three previous attempts to register, stood by on and around the campus last night. The troopers made no effort to break up the mob at the administration building, called the Lyceum. Some made it plain they sided with the students.

The troopers pulled back from the riot scene shortly after 9 o'clock, leaving the marshals to defend themselves.

The action was authorized by State Senator George Yarborough of Red Banks, the President pro tem of the Senate and Governor Barnett's official representative on the campus.

"We had been assured by the Governor that the state police would assist us in maintaining law and order," Mr. Guthman said.

The besieged marshals, commanded by Chief Marshal McShane and Nicholas deB. Katzenbach, Deputy United States Attorney General, held their redoubt at the Lyceum until shortly after midnight.

They got reinforcement then from Troop E, Second Reconnaissance Squadron, 108th Armored Cavalry, of the Mississippi National Guard.

The first unit of combat military policemen called up by the President did not arrive until 4:30 this morning. This was Company A of the 503d Military Police Battalion, from Fort Bragg, N. C.

Other troops poured into Oxford by truck and by plane. They included the 716th Military Police Battalion, which came overland from Fort Dix, N. J.; the 720th Military Police Battalion from Fort Hood, Tex.; the Second Battle Group, Second Infantry Division, from Fort Benning, Ga., and the 31st Helicopter Company from Jacksonville, N. C.

The Mississippi National Guard units sent here included the 108th Armored Cavalry Regiment from Tupelo and the Second Battle Group, 155th Infantry, from Amory.

A detachment of the 70th Engineering Battalion from Fort Campbell, Kentucky, operated a "tent city" for the marshals 15 miles north of here, in the Holly Springs National Forest.

The unit included medical and communications specialists from the 101st Airborne Division.

The 101st had been ordered to Little Rock, Ark., in September of 1957 by President Eisenhower to put down rioting and to enforce Federal court desegregation orders directing the admission of nine Negroes to Central High School.

The first military policemen to arrive helped the marshals and National Guardsmen repel a final assault on the Lyceum at 5 A. M. Barrage after barrage of tear gas and smoke grenades drove back the howling mob, whose strength had dwindled from a peak of 2,500 to 100.

It was difficult to estimate the number of persons who actually took part in the riot. Acrid clouds of smoke and tear gas billowed across the front of a campus area called the Grove, a tree-shaded oval in front of the Lyceum.

Virtually all the street lights were shot out or broken by rocks early in the evening. Observers edging as close to the action as the tear gas and prudence would permit got a view of shadowy forms racing back and forth behind Confederate battle flags.

The rioters cranked up the bulldozer twice and sent it crashing driverless toward the marshals. Both times it hit trees and other obstructions that stopped it before it reached their ranks.

Shouting members of the mob raced the fire engine back and forth through the trees and strewed links of hose across the Grove. At one point the engine careened down the asphalt drive only a few feet from the marshals, who peppered it with blasts from their tear-gas guns.

Several persons were burned as canisters of tear gas struck them or exploded near them.

Snipers Fire in Darkness

Snipers operated under the cover of darkness, aiming blasts of birdshot and pistol and rifle fire at the marshals and others.

Mr. Guihard received a bullet wound in the back. Mr. Gunter was shot in the forehead.

A sniper fired three quick shots at Karl Fleming, a reporter in the Atlanta bureau of Newsweek magazine, but the bullet struck the doorway of the Lyceum.

Other newsmen were attacked and beaten. Gordon Yoder, a Telenews cameraman from Dallas, and Mrs. Yoder were set upon by the mob. State troopers rescued them.

A group of teen-agers and a few men massed on the town square before the three-story Lafayette County Courthouse about 9:30 A. M. today. Many of them wore gray caps bearing Confederate battle flags.

They took up positions on the southeast corner of the square, facing two platoons of military policemen on the southwest corner. About a third of the M.P.'s were Negroes.

The youths began hurling bottles at the soldiers, drawing lusty cheers from adult bystanders when they scored a hit. The soldiers remained in ranks.

The platoons fixed bayonets, formed two wedges and scattered the assailants. But the mob returned and began tossing bottles and rocks at the soldiers again.

The M.P.'s donned their gas masks, formed in a line and moved across the square, throwing tear-gas grenades. The youths retreated.

The mob returned again, and squads of eight to ten soldiers chased them back along the streets, firing rifles over their heads. This broke up the mob.

Business establishments that had opened this morning closed their doors hurriedly. Except for the troops, the square was deserted at noon.

Associated Press

ASSUMES COMMAND: Lieut. Gen. Hamilton Howze.

Combat-Tested General

Charles Billingslea

Man in the News

BRIG. GEN. CHARLES BILLINGSLEA, a 6-foot-4 former paratrooper who was the original commander of military units in the University of Mississippi crisis, had a wartime habit of jumping into hot spots from the Mediterranean to Central Europe. He has an impressive military background, studded with positions such as executive officer, operations planner and field commander in combat. Last Tuesday, after five months with a publicity-shy Army aviations study group called the Howze Board at Fort Bragg, N. C., he took command of the Second Infantry Division at Fort Benning, Ga. The board is named for Lieut. Gen. Hamilton Howze, who took command from General Billingslea last night.

A junior officer working with General Billingslea describes him as looking "the way a general ought to look."

He stands saber-straight, carrying his height well on medium build.

General Billingslea was born in Chicago on May 16, 1914, and was graduated from West Point in 1936. Five years later he was graduated from the Parachute School at Fort Benning.

On Staff in Britain

He went to Britain in 1942 to join the staff of II Corps in the headquarters of Allied Forces, then planning the invasion of North Africa. He took part in assault landings against Algiers with United States forces and, with British forces, in airborne operations in Tunisia.

When the 82d Airborne Division left Africa for some of the fiercest fighting in Europe, he went with it. He was executive officer of a parachute brigade that jumped into Sicily and then was chief of a Pathfinders unit that parachuted into Salerno. As executive officer of the 504th Parachute Regiment, he was in the fighting at Naples, Volturno, Cassino and Anzio.

His next combat was as commander of the 325th Parachute Regiment, which he led from Arnheim-Nijmegen operations in the Netherlands through the Central European command and the occupation of Berlin.

His duty with the 82d Airborne continued after the war. In 1949 he became a faculty member at the command and General Staff School at Fort Leavenworth, Kan. That year he married the former Bettina Hill in Boston.

A more peaceful assignment in Europe came in November, 1953, when he became Chief of Plans for Supreme Headquarters, Allied Powers in Europe (SHAPE) in Paris. In December 1956, he enrolled for a program of advanced management courses at Harvard University and in 1957-58 he attended the National War College. He won the Star of a brigadier general Oct. 1, 1960.

A Pentagon assignment was followed by transfer, in January, 1961, to Korea, where he was deputy chief and later chief of staff of the Eighth Army. He returned to the United States in May, 1962, and was assigned to the Howze Board at Fort Bragg, a group of senior officers studying Army aviation.

General Billingslea has been described by an associate as a tall lumbering man whose ears stick out under sandy gray hair. He has rugged features, rugged frame, but despite his height, he keeps his weight below 200 pounds.

He has an urge for buying houses, fixing them, then selling them. He does not engage in sports very often. However, he likes to sail, ride horses.

He married late, after the war. His son, Charles Billingslea Jr., now 5 years old, is the apple of his eye, a colleague says.

Two years ago, when the general went to Korea, he bought his son an English bulldog "so they can learn about life from each other."

The general has owned Irish wolfhounds and English bulldogs. He likes them because they are big.

As a combat man, he has earned two Distinguished Service Crosses. But his friends say he is not given much to military reminiscing. He reads military histories and books on broad military and diplomatic strategy.

U. S. Army via Associated Press Wirephoto

Combat leader and planner

"All the News That's Fit to Print"

The New York Times.

LATE CITY EDITION

U. S. Weather Bureau Report (Page 91) forecasts: Partly cloudy, breezy, cool today. Fair and cool tonight and tomorrow. Temp. range: 54—45; yesterday: 66—44.

VOL. CXII..No. 38,258. NEW YORK, TUESDAY, OCTOBER 23, 1962.

10 cents beyond 50-mile zone from New York City except on Long Island. Higher in air delivery cities.

FIVE CENTS

U.S. IMPOSES ARMS BLOCKADE ON CUBA ON FINDING OFFENSIVE-MISSILE SITES; KENNEDY READY FOR SOVIET SHOWDOWN

U. S. JUDGES GIVEN POWER TO REQUIRE VOTE FOR NEGROES

High Court Upholds Order Forcing the Registration of 54 in Alabama County

Special to The New York Times

WASHINGTON, Oct. 22 — The Supreme Court held today that Federal judges have the power to make state registrars put specific Negroes on the voting rolls.

Alabama had challenged an order by Federal District Judge Frank M. Johnson Jr. requiring the registration of 54 specific Negroes in Macon County, Ala. The order was upheld by the United States Court of Appeals for the Fifth Circuit.

Today the Supreme Court unanimously affirmed the disputed order. And it did so in a way that indicated once again its mood of impatience with Southern efforts to maintain denials of Negro rights.

One-Sentence Ruling

All that was before the court was an application for review of the Fifth Circuit decision. The usual alternatives would have been to deny the petition or to grant it and hear oral argument later.

Instead, the court granted review and then, summarily, affirmed the lower courts. It did so in a single sentence, with just one citation in the way of explanation.

The citation was to a decision in 1960 upholding a Federal Court order in a Louisiana voting case. There, a district judge had told Louisiana registrars to put back on their books 1,377 Negroes whose names had been removed in a purge by the segregationist Citizens Council.

Action by Congress

The Macon County case was one of the first brought by the Department of Justice under the Civil Rights Act of 1957. It is especially significant because the county is in the so-called Black Belt, with a predominantly Negro population.

In 1958, when the suit was started, virtually all of the 3,000 white persons of voting age in the county were registered. But only about 1,000 of the 12,000 potential Negro voters were actually eligible.

In a further move, the registrars resigned, and this was held to leave no defendants to be sued. Congress in 1960 handled this problem by providing

Continued on Page 24, Column 4

Chinese Open New Front; Use Tanks Against Indians

Nehru Warns of Peril to Independence —Reds Attack Near Burmese Border and Press Two Other Drives

Special to The New York Times

NEW DELHI, Oct. 22—Prime Minister Jawaharlal Nehru told the people of India tonight that the Chinese Communist attack was a threat to their liberty.

His grave warning followed word that the advancing Chinese had opened a third front in

Excerpts from Nehru's speech will be found on Page 2.

the Himalayas, near the Burmese border, and had used tanks for the first time. Five more Indian posts fell to the Chinese on the third day of savage fighting.

[A bid for negotiations for a peace accord was broadcast by the Chinese Communist radio early Tuesday, The Associated Press reported from Tokyo.]

In a broadcast, Mr. Nehru denounced the Peking regime as "a powerful and unscrupulous opponent, not caring for peace or peaceful methods."

"The time has come," he said, "for us to realize fully this menace that threatens the freedom of our people and the independence of our country."

Prime Minister Nehru said India would not abandon her economic development program and policy of nonalignment with international blocs, but called on the nation to switch "from the slow-moving methods of peacetime to those which produce results quickly."

"We must build up our military strength by all means at our disposal," he said.

The third front in the Himalayan fighting was opened early today when the Chinese attacked an Indian post at Kibitoo, on the border between

Continued on Page 2, Column 1

U.S. Bids U.N. Bar China; Denounces Attack on India

By SAM POPE BREWER

Special to The New York Times

UNITED NATIONS, N. Y., Oct. 22—Adlai E. Stevenson told the General Assembly today that Communist China's "naked aggression" against India was new proof that it was unfit for membership in the United Nations.

The chief United States representative at the United Nations spoke as the Assembly took up the perennial question of admitting Peking.

Mr. Stevenson told the members that by their actions on the Indian frontier the Chinese Communists "again show their scorn for the Charter of this organization."

The Vice President of the Philippines, Emmanuel Pelaez, told the Assembly that there were more than 40,000,000 Chinese living outside China who would become "a Trojan horse" if the United Nations accepted the Communist Government.

Mr. Pelaez said that the Chinese abroad, 1,000,000 of them in the Philippines, would be used for subversion by the Peking Government. He said they could now be controlled because the Communist Government did not have the means to get at them.

On the fighting in India, Mr. Stevenson declared: "Should there be some among us who think that perhaps the whole thing is a mistake that will right itself before long, let me point out that when a nation moves its troops with tanks and armor, it is no mistake. It is a premeditated act. It is naked aggression. And it has been going on with gathering momentum for some three years."

He quoted Prime Minister

Continued on Page 5, Column 3

U. S. SAID TO EASE KATANGA POLICY

Reported Willing to Put Off Any Economic Sanctions —Congolese Disturbed

By LLOYD GARRISON

Special to The New York Times

LEOPOLDVILLE, the Congo, Oct. 22 — Authoritative sources said today that the United States was no longer insisting that Katanga Province strictly meet the deadlines of the United Nations plan to end its secession from the Congo.

This has alarmed Congolese officials. They say that the United States shift is reflected in United Nations policy.

The United Nations plan, introduced Aug. 2 by U Thant, Acting Secretary General, was said to have been conceived largely by the United States.

As outlined by Mr. Thant, the plan's first stage called for the following timetable:

Within thirty days a program was to be decided on for the reintegration of Katanga's army into the Congolese National Army. Sixty days were to be allowed for the program to be carried out.

Recall of Missions

All Katangese foreign missions were to be recalled immediately, and all Katanga's foreign currency reserves were to be put under the control of the central Government, with 50 per cent of these reserves rebated to Katanga.

Unification of the Congo's currency was to have begun within 10 days.

Katanga was to have started immediately to share 50 per cent of her tax revenues with the central Government.

Not one of these conditions has been met.

Last week Cyrille Adoula, Premier of the central Government, declared that "the deadline for the first stage has passed." He said that it was now time for the United Nations to consider the second stage — economic sanctions.

A shift in United States policy became apparent over the weekend after the departure of George C. McGhee, Under Secretary of State for Political Af-

Continued on Page 3, Column 6

102 SAVED AT SEA AS PLANE DITCHES

Rescue Is Made off Alaska Minutes After Accident

By The Associated Press.

SITKA, Alaska, Oct. 22—A military-charter airliner ditched in the ocean near here today, but all 102 persons aboard were saved in a quick rescue operation.

The plane, a DC-7C of Northwest Airlines, was going from McChord Air Force Base in Washington to Anchorage, Alaska. It carried 95 passengers and a crew of seven.

The rescue was reported by Northwest and the Alaska Coastal-Ellis Airline at Sitka, which also reported that there apparently were no serious injuries.

The plane went down shortly after the Federal Aviation Agency at Anchorage got word that it was being ditched because of propeller trouble.

A Coast Guard plane alighted on the water nearby; the Air Force sent two rescue planes, and small boats from Sitka, about seven miles north of the

Continued on Page 8, Column 3

Stocks Plunge Early On Crisis, but Rally

By RICHARD RUTTER

An already badly battered stock market was hit by massive selling yesterday as talk of a new international crisis spread in Wall Street.

The selling was of dimensions reminiscent of late May when the market experienced its worst break in a generation. Yesterday, the tape ran as much as 19 minutes late before a half-hearted recovery set in that cut losses by about one-third.

Both tape lateness and volume were the greatest since July 10. Two million shares were traded in the first two hours.

Stock markets in London, Frankfurt and Brussels, following Wall Street's lead, also took large losses.

The selling was directly ascribed to news in the morning about an air of crisis in Wash-

Continued on Page 49, Column 6

SHIPS MUST STOP

Other Action Planned If Big Rockets Are Not Dismantled

By JAMES RESTON

Special to The New York Times

WASHINGTON, Oct. 22—President Kennedy drew the line tonight, not with Cuba, but with the Soviet Union. After almost a generation of trying to keep the "cold war" from reaching a direct confrontation between United States and Soviet power, a decision has been made to force Soviet missile bases from this hemisphere at the risk of war.

This is the official interpretation of President Kennedy's speech tonight, and the orders to American forces bear it out. On the highest authority, it can be said that these orders include the following:

¶Ships carrying to Cuba weapons capable of striking the continental United States must either turn back or submit to search and seizure, or fight. If they try to run the blockade, a warning shot will be fired across their bows; if they still do not submit, they will be attacked.

¶This applies not only to ships but to any planes suspected of carrying additional offensive weapons to Cuba. There is no evidence that there are nuclear warheads in Cuba, but long-range aircraft suspected of carrying these or any other offensive weapons, will be intercepted, and instructions have been issued to do everything possible to check all Communist-bloc planes en route to Cuba via Newfoundland or Africa.

Prepared to Risk War

Even this will not satisfy the new policy announced by President Kennedy. Not only must new offensive weapons be stopped, under the President's orders, but those already in Cuba must be dismantled, or the United States will take whatever additional action is necessary, beginning with a much more rigorous blockade of such things as Cuba's essential oil supplies, to force compliance.

If this leads to Soviet retaliation, such as a counter-blockade of Berlin, the United States is prepared to risk a major war to defend its present position in the former German capital. Accordingly, American forces, not only in Berlin and West Germany but all over the world, have been placed on emergency alert. The new policy has been defined in a private communi-

Continued on Page 19, Column 1

Associated Press Wirephoto

ANNOUNCES HIS ACTION: President Kennedy speaking to the nation last night on radio and television. He told of moves to keep offensive equipment away from Cuba.

TRAFFIC DELAYED AT BERLIN BORDER

Reds Start Intensive Check of Civilian Trucks an Hour Before Kennedy Speech

By SYDNEY GRUSON

Special to The New York Times

BONN, Oct. 22—The East German police began to slow down civilian traffic between West Berlin and West Germany late tonight.

About an hour before President Kennedy announced the United States countermeasures against the Soviet build-up in Cuba, the police started intensive examination of the papers of trucks moving into East German territory.

The connection, if any, between the two actions was not immediately clear. Similar harassment of civilian traffic has occurred periodically over the years. The immediate reaction in West Berlin was to consider tonight's harassment as part of the regular order of things, rather than as an advance countermeasure to the American moves against Cuba.

Nevertheless, there was deep anxiety that the Soviet Union would retaliate by causing trouble on the West's access lines to the city.

The outcome of tomorrow's meetings between Andrei A. Gromyko, the Soviet Foreign Minister, and East German Communist leaders was awaited with concern. Mr. Gromyko

Continued on Page 17, Column 3

Canada Asks Inspection of Cuba; Britain Supporting Quarantine

Diefenbaker Comments

By RAYMOND DANIELL

Special to The New York Times

OTTAWA, Oct. 22 — Prime Minister John Diefenbaker of Canada declared tonight the time had come for an impartial inspection of what is happening in Cuba by eight of the "nonaligned nations."

Interrupting debate of the Canadian economic crisis in the House of Commons, Mr. Diefenbaker described President Kennedy's speech on Cuba as "somber and challenging."

"Naturally," he said, "there has been little time to give consideration to positive action that might be taken. But I suggest that if there is a desire—and I am sure there is on the part of the U.S.S.R.—to have the facts, if a group of nations, perhaps the eight comprising the unaligned members of the 18-nation disarmament committee, were given the opportunity of making an on-site inspection of Cuba to ascertain what the facts are, a major step forward would be taken."

Meanwhile it was disclosed that Canada has barred the use of her airfields, including that

Continued on Page 21, Column 2

British Note Peril

By DREW MIDDLETON

Special to The New York Times

LONDON, Oct. 22—Qualified sources said today that approval for President Kennedy's military quarantine of Cuba could be expected from the British government.

A Foreign Office spokesman declared, "Revelation of the Soviet build-up in Cuba will come as a shock to the whole civilized world."

Official comment cannot be given until after Prime Minister Macmillan and his Cabinet have discussed the President's statement.

Initial reaction among diplomats was that the President had taken the most reasonable course to frustrate what military circles regard as evident danger to the United States: a buildup of Soviet nuclear capacity in Cuba.

The danger that war might result from a Soviet attempt to break what amounts to a military blockade of Cuba is accepted. But one experienced airman expressed the general feeling this way: "War can come from any one of a number of causes,

Continued on Page 21, Column 1

Moscow Says U.S. Holds 'Armed Fist' Over Cuba

By SEYMOUR TOPPING

Special to The New York Times

MOSCOW, Tuesday, Oct. 23—In a broadcast before President Kennedy's speech on the missile build-up in Cuba, the Moscow radio said that the unusual activity in Washington indicated that the United States "once again was raising its armed fist over Cuba." The broadcast said there was "real hysteria" in Washington.

A Soviet reply to the United States note on Cuba that was given last night to Anatoly F. Dobrynin, the Soviet Ambassador to Washington, was expected to be delivered in 24 hours. It was expected that the reply would take the form either of a diplomatic communication or a message to President Kennedy from Premier Khrushchev.

Western observers said it appeared inevitable in view of recent Soviet statements that the reply would be a denial of any offensive Soviet intent and a charge of United States aggression against Cuba.

Veracity Questioned

The veracity of the Soviet Government was directly questioned in President Kennedy's speech, which was given after delivery of the note. The President said evidence had been obtained that Moscow was constructing offensive missile bases on Cuban territory.

The Soviet Government statement of Sept. 11, which warned the United States that an attack on Cuba would mean war, contended that the Soviet weapons supplied to Cuba were of a defensive nature.

Western observers said the crisis over Cuba would enter a critical phase when and if United States war vessels sought to halt and search a Soviet ship bound for Cuba.

A number of Soviet vessels carrying civilian goods and pos-

Continued on Page 18, Column 3

BIG FORCE MASSES TO BLOCKADE CUBA

Armada Is Under Orders to Open Fire if Necessary— All Troops Are Alerted

By JACK RAYMOND

Special to The New York Times

WASHINGTON, Oct. 22—American ships and planes began preparing tonight to impose a blockade of Cuba. United States forces are under orders to thwart any attempt to deliver offensive weapons to Havana.

A Defense Department spokesman said that a large force of ships and planes concentrating in the Caribbean area had instructions to use force if necessary, including sinking of ships, to carry out President Kennedy's orders for a "quarantine" of Cuba.

The Pentagon said also that United States military units throughout the world, including the garrison in Berlin and the nuclear-armed Strategic Air Command, had been placed "on alert."

Dependents of servicemen at the Guantanamo Bay Naval Base in Cuba have been evacuated, the department said.

Forces at Base Doubled

It added that the military forces there, which were previously put at 3,300 naval officers and men and several hundred Marines, have been doubled.

Air defense units in the United States, particularly radar warning stations, interceptor aircraft and ground-to-air missiles, "have been redeployed," the department spokesman said.

The orders for additional defense precautions were taken the spokesman continued, on the basis of aerial photographic evidence of long-range ballistic missile bases and the arrival of Soviet Ilyushin-28 bombers in Cuba.

The spokesman displayed some of the aerial photographs and pointed to some missiles sites that, he said, had been established only in the last 10 or 15 days.

He said some of the missile

Continued on Page 20 Column 1

All Military Forces Mobilized by Castro

By The Associated Press

KEY WEST, Tuesday, Oct. 23—All of Cuba's military forces have been mobilized as a result "of the news from the United States," the Havana radio said today.

The broadcast said the order was issued by Premier Fidel Castro, who will address the nation later today.

"Our combat units rapidly placed themselves on a fighting basis," said the Havana broadcast.

"Hundreds of thousands of men were mobilized in the course of a few hours," added the broadcast, which followed by some hours President Kennedy's announcement of a naval blockade against Cuba.

During the evening, Havana appeared slow to react to President Kennedy's broadcast and

Continued on Page 20 Column 5

NEWS INDEX

PRESIDENT GRAVE

Asserts Russians Lied and Put Hemisphere in Great Danger

Text of the President's address is printed on Page 18.

By ANTHONY LEWIS

Special to The New York Times

WASHINGTON, Oct. 22 — President Kennedy imposed a naval and air "quarantine" tonight on the shipment of offensive military equipment to Cuba.

In a speech of extraordinary gravity, he told the American people that the Soviet Union, contrary to promises, was building offensive missile and bomber bases in Cuba. He said the bases could handle missiles carrying nuclear warheads up to 2,000 miles.

Thus a critical moment in the cold war was at hand tonight. The President had decided on a direct confrontation with — and challenge to — the power of the Soviet Union.

Direct Thrust at Soviet

Two aspects of the speech were notable. One was its direct thrust at the Soviet Union as the party responsible for the crisis. Mr. Kennedy treated Cuba and the Government of Premier Fidel Castro as a mere pawn in Moscow's hands and drew the issue as one with the Soviet Government.

The President, in language of unusual bluntness, accused the Soviet leaders of deliberately "false statements about their intentions in Cuba."

The other aspect of the speech particularly noted by observers here was its flat commitment by the United States to act alone against the missile threat in Cuba.

Nation Ready to Act

The President made it clear that this country would not stop short of military action to end what he called a "clandestine, reckless and provocative threat to world peace."

Mr. Kennedy said the United States was asking for an emergency meeting of the United Nations Security Council to consider a resolution for "dismantling and withdrawal of all offensive weapons in Cuba."

He said the launching of a nuclear missile from Cuba against any nation in the Western Hemisphere would be regarded as an attack by the Soviet Union against the United States. It would be met, he said, by retaliation against the Soviet Union.

He called on Premier Khrushchev to withdraw the missiles from Cuba and so "move the

Continued on Page 18, Column 1

KENNEDY CANCELS CAMPAIGN TALKS

He and Johnson Take Step to Concentrate on Crisis

By CABELL PHILLIPS

Special to The New York Times

WASHINGTON, Oct. 22—The White House announced tonight that President Kennedy and Vice President Johnson would make no further political appearances in the Congressional campaign because of the Cuban crisis.

The move by the Administration was considered evidence not only of the seriousness of the situation but also of the desire of the President to unify the country behind his blockade order and keep the issue out of partisan politics.

In this connection, the White House said the President personally informed former Republican Presidents Dwight D. Eisenhower and Herbert Hoover, as well as former Democratic President Harry S. Truman, of his decision.

And the White House announced that John J. McCloy, former disarmament adviser to the Kennedy Administration and a Republican, had been as-

Continued on Page 18, Column 7

U. S. Imposes Arms Blockade on Cuba Because of the New Offensive-Missile Sites

KENNEDY WARNS NATION OF PERIL

Says in Radio-TV Address That Soviet Broke Its Promises on Bases

Continued From Page 1, Col. 8

world back from the abyss of destruction."

All this the President recited in an 18-minute radio and television address of a grimness unparalleled in recent times. He read the words rapidly, with little emotion, until he came to the peroration—a warning to Americans of the dangers ahead.

"Let no one doubt that this is a difficult and dangerous effort on which we have set out," the President said. "No one can foresee precisely what course it will take or what costs or casualties will be incurred."

"The path we have chosen for the present is full of hazards, as all paths are—but it is the one most consistent with our character and courage as a nation and our commitments around the world," he added.

"The cost of freedom is always high—but Americans have always paid it. And one path we shall never choose is the path of surrender or submission.

"Our goal is not the victory of might but the vindication of right—not peace at the expense of freedom, but both peace and freedom, here in this hemisphere and, we hope, around the world. God willing, that goal will be achieved."

The President's speech did not actually start the naval blockade tonight. To meet the requirements of international law, the State Department will issue a formal proclamation late tomorrow, and that may delay the effectiveness of the action as long as another 24 hours.

Crisis Before Public

The speech laid before the American people a crisis that had gripped the highest officials here since last Tuesday, but had only begun to leak out to the public over the weekend. The President said it was at 9 A.M. Tuesday that he got the first firm intelligence report about the missile sites on Cuba.

Last month, he said, the Soviet Government publicly stated that its military equipment for Cuba was "exclusively for defensive purposes" and that the Soviet did not need retaliatory missile bases outside its own territory.

"That statement was false," Mr. Kennedy said.

Just last Thursday, he continued, the Soviet foreign minister, Andrei A. Gromyko, told him in a call at the White House that the Soviet Union "would never become involved" in building any offensive military capacity in Cuba.

"That statement was also false," the President said.

Appeal to Khrushchev

He made a direct appeal to Premier Khrushchev to abandon the Communist "course of world domination." An hour before the President spoke, a personal letter from him to Mr. Khrushchev was delivered to the Soviet government in Moscow.

Mr. Kennedy disclosed that he was calling for an immediate meeting of the Organ of Consultation of the Organization of American States to consider the crisis.

The O.A.S. promptly scheduled an emergency session for 9 A.M. tomorrow. State Department officials said they were confident of receiving the necessary 14 votes out of the 20 nations represented.

The President said the United States was prepared also to discuss the situation "in any other meeting that could be useful." This was taken as an allusion to a possible summit conference with Mr. Khrushchev.

But the President emphasized that discussion in any of these forums would be undertaken "without limiting our freedom of action." This meant that the United States was determined on this course no matter what any international organization—or even the United States' allies—might say.

Support From Congress

Congressional leaders of both parties, who were summoned to Washington today to be advised by the President of the crisis and his decision, gave him unanimous backing.

Mr. Kennedy went into considerable detail in his speech in outlining the nature of the military threat in Cuba, and this country's response.

He said "confirmed" intelligence indicates that the Cuban missile sites are of two types.

One kind, which his words implied were already or nearly completed, would be capable of handling medium-range ballistic missiles. The President said such missiles could carry nuclear weapons more than 1,000 nautical miles — to Washington, the Panama Canal, Cape Canaveral or Mexico City.

The second category of sites would be for intermediate range ballistics missiles, with a range of more than 2,000 miles. The President said they could hit "most of the major cities in the Western hemisphere" from Lima, Peru, to Hudson's Bay in Canada.

Mr. Kennedy declared:

"This urgent transformation of Cuba into an important strategic base by the presence of these large, long-range and clearly offensive weapons of sudden mass destruction constitutes an explicit threat to the peace and security of all the Americas."

He said the Soviet Union's action was "in flagrant and deliberate defiance" of the Rio (Inter-American) Pact of 1947, the United Nations Charter, Congressional resolution and his own public warnings to the Soviet Union.

O.A.S. Chiefs Back Kennedy

HOUSTON, Tex., Oct. 22 (AP)—Three high-ranking officials of the Organization of American States said here tonight that the O.A.S. would fully support President Kennedy's blockade of Cuba, even to the point of using arms.

The officials were Dr. José A. Mora, secretary general, Dr. Alberto Zuleta Angel, President and Gonzalo J. Facio, Costa Rican ambassador to the organization and to the United States.

Text of Kennedy's Address on Moves to Meet the Soviet Build-Up in Cuba

Following is the text of President Kennedy's address last night on the Soviet build-up in Cuba, as recorded by The New York Times:

This Government as promised has maintained the closest surveillance of the Soviet military build-up on the island of Cuba.

Within the past week unmistakable evidence has established the fact that a series of offensive missile sites is now in preparation on that imprisoned island.

The purpose of these bases can be none other than to provide a nuclear strike capability against the Western Hemisphere.

Upon receiving the first preliminary hard information of this nature last Tuesday morning at 9 A.M., I directed that our surveillance be stepped up. And having now confirmed and completed our evalation of the evidence and our decision on a course of action, this Government feels obliged to report this new crisis to you in fullest detail.

The characteristics of these new missile sites indicate two distinct types of installations. Several of them include medium-range ballistic missiles capable of carrying a nuclear warhead for a distance of more than 1,000 nautical miles.

Range Is Described

Each of these missiles, in short, is capable of striking Washington, D. C., the Panama Canal, Cape Canaveral, Mexico City or any other city in the southeastern part of the United States, in Central America or in the Caribbean area.

Additional sites not yet completed appear to be designed for intermediate-range ballistic missiles capable of traveling more than twice as far, and thus capable of striking most of the major cities in the Western Hemisphere ranging as far north as Hudson's Bay, Canada, and as far south as Lima, Peru.

In addition, jet bombers, capable of carrying nuclear weapons, are now being uncrated and assembled in Cuba while the necessary air bases are being prepared.

This urgent transformation of Cuba into an important strategic base by the presence of these large long-range and clearly offensive weapons of sudden mass destruction constitutes an explicit threat to the peace and security of all the Americas in flagrant and deliberate defiance of the Rio Pact of 1947, the traditions of this nation and hemisphere, the joint resolution of the 87th Congress, the Charter of the United Nations and my own public warnings to the Soviets on Sept. 4 and 13.

Contradiction Cited

This action also contradicts the repeated assurances of Soviet spokesmen both publicly and privately delivered that the arms build-up in Cuba would retain its original defensive character and that the Soviet Union had no need or desire to station strategic missiles on the territory of any other nation.

The size of this undertaking makes clear that it had been planned for some months.

Yet only last month after I had made clear the distinction between any introduction of ground-to-ground missiles and the existence of defensive antiaircraft missiles, the Soviet Government publicly stated on Sept. 11 that, and I quote, the armaments and military equipment sent to Cuba are designed exclusively for defensive purposes, unquote, that there is—and I quote the Soviet Government—there is no need for the Soviet Government to shift its weapons for a retaliatory blow to any other country, for instance, Cuba, unquote, and that — and I quote the Government—the Soviet Union has so powerful rockets to carry these nuclear warheads that there is no need to search for sites for them beyond the boundaries of the Soviet Union, unquote.

That statement was false.

Gromyko Stand Quoted

Only last Thursday, as evidence of this rapid offensive build-up was already in my hand, Soviet Foreign Minister Gromyko told me in my office that he was instructed to made it clear once again, as he said his Government had already done, that Soviet assistance to Cuba, and I quote, pursued solely the purpose of contributing to the defense capabilities of Cuba, unquote.

That, and I quote him, "training by Soviet specialists of Cuban nationals in handling defensive armaments

Associated Press

CONFERENCE CITED BY KENNEDY: Andrei A. Gromyko, Soviet Foreign Minister, with the President last Thursday at the White House. At this meeting, Mr. Kennedy said, Mr. Gromyko told him "the Soviet assistance to Cuba 'pursued solely the purpose of contributing to the defense capabilities of Cuba.'" This, Mr. Kennedy said, was false.

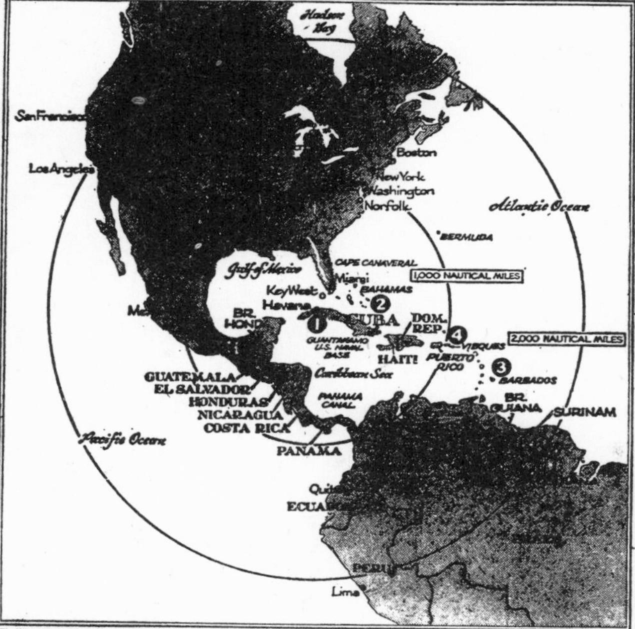

The New York Times Oct. 23, 1962

CUBAN EMERGENCY: Major points in the blockade of Cuba will be the harbor at Havana (1), the sea lanes that run through the Bahamas (2) and an arc extending from the Bahamas to Barbados (3). A landing at Vieques (4), which was to have been the climax of a United States training exercise, has been canceled. The inner circle, centered on Havana, indicates the range of medium-range ballistic missiles and the outer circle shows the range for intermediate range ballistic missiles. President Kennedy declared in his speech to the nation that sites for both types of missiles were being built in Cuba.

was by no means offensive," and that if it were otherwise, Mr. Gromyko went on, "the Soviet Government would never become involved in rendering such assistance."

That statement also was false.

Neither the United States of America nor the world community of nations can tolerate deliberate deception and offensive threats on the part of any nation, large or small. We no longer live in a world where only the actual firing of weapons represents a sufficient challenge to a nation's security to constitute maximum peril.

Definite Threat

Nuclear weapons are so destructive and ballistic missiles are so swift that any substantially increased possibility of their use or any sudden change in their deployment may well be regarded as a definite threat to peace.

For many years both the Soviet Union and the United States, recognizing this fact, have deployed strategic nuclear weapons with great care, never upsetting the precarious status quo which insured that these weapons would not be used in the absence of some vital challenge.

Our own strategic missiles have never been transferred to the territory of any other nation under a cloak of secrecy and deception and our history, unlike that of the Soviets since the end of World War II, demonstrates that we have no desire to dominate or conquer any other nation or impose our system upon its people.

Nevertheless, American citizens have become adjusted to living daily on the bull's-eye of Soviet missiles located inside the U.S.S.R. or in submarines.

In that sense missiles in Cuba add to an already clear and present danger—although it should be noted the nations of Latin America have never previously been subjected to a potential nuclear threat.

But this secret, swift, extraordinary build-up of Communist missiles in an area well-known to have a special and historical relationship to the United States and the nations of the Western Hemisphere, in violation of Soviet assurances and in defiance of American and hemispheric policy—this sudden, clandestine decision to station stategic weapons for the first time outside of Soviet soil—is a deliberately provocative and unjustified change in the status quo which cannot be accepted by this country if our courage and our commitments are ever to be trusted again, by either friend or foe.

The nineteen thirties taught us a clear lesson. Aggressive conduct, if allowed to go unchecked and unchallenged, ultimately leads to war.

This nation is opposed to war. We are also true to our word.

Our unswerving objective, therefore, must be to prevent the use of these missiles against this or any other country; and to secure their withdrawal or elimination from the Western Hemisphere.

Our policy has been one of patience and restraint, as befits a peaceful and powerful nation which leads a worldwide alliance.

'Only the Beginning'

We have been determined not to be diverted from our central concerns by mere irritants and fanatics. But now further action is required. And it is under way. And these actions may only be the beginning.

We will not prematurely or unnecessarily risk the course of worldwide nuclear war in which even the fruits of victory would be ashes in our mouth, but neither will we shrink from that risk at any time it must be faced.

Acting, therefore, in the defense of our own security and of the entire Western Hemisphere and under the authority entrusted to me by the Constitution as endorsed by the resolution of the Congress, I have directed that the following initial steps be taken immediately:

First, to halt this offensive build-up, a strict quarantine on all offensive military equipment under shipment to Cuba is being initiated. All ships of any kind bound for Cuba from whatever nation or port will, where they are found to contain cargoes of offensive weapons, be turned back. This quarantine will be extended if needed to other types of cargo and carriers.

We are not at this time, however, denying the necessities of life as the Soviets attempted to do in their Berlin blockade of 1948.

Second, I have directed the continued and increased close surveillance of Cuba and its military build-up.

The foreign ministers of the O.A.S. in their communiqué of Oct. 6 rejected secrecy on such matters in this hemisphere. Should these offensive military preparations continue, thus increasing the threat to the hemisphere, further action will be justified.

Knowledge of Hazards Urged

I have directed the armed forces to prepare for any eventualities, and I trust that in the interests of both the Cuban people and the Soviet technicians at the sites, the hazards to all concerned of continuing this threat will be recognized.

Third, it shall be the policy of this nation to regard any nuclear missile launched from Cuba against any nation in the Western Hemisphere as an attack by the Soviet Union on the United States requiring a full retaliatory response upon the Soviet Union.

Fourth, as a necessary military precaution, I have reinforced our base at Guantanamo, evacuated today the dependents of our personnel there and ordered additional military units to be on a stand-by alert basis.

Fifth, we are calling tonight for an immediate meeting of the organization of consultation under the Organization of American States to consider this threat to hemispheric security and to invoke Articles 6 and 8 of the Rio Treaty in support of all necessary action.

The United Nations Charter allows for regional security arrangements and the nations of this hemisphere decided long ago against the military presence of outside powers.

Our other allies around the world have also been alerted.

U. N. Meeting Requested

Sixth, under the Charter of the United Nations we are asking tonight that an emergency meeting of the Security Council be convoked without delay to take action against this latest Soviet threat to world peace.

Our resolution will call for the prompt dismantling and withdrawal of all offensive weapons in Cuba under the supervision of U. N. observers before the quarantine can be lifted.

Seventh, and finally, I call upon Chairman Khrushchev to halt and eliminate this clandestine, reckless and provocative threat to world peace and to stable relations between our two nations.

I call upon him further to abandon this course of world domination and to join in an historic effort to end the perilous arms race and to transform the history of man.

He has an opportunity now to move the world back from the abyss of destruction by returning to his Government's own words that it had no need to station missiles outside its own territory, and withdrawing these weapons from Cuba; by refraining from any action which will widen or deepen the present crisis, and then by participating in a search for peaceful and permanent solutions.

This nation is prepared to present its case against the Soviet threat to peace and our own proposals for a peaceful world at any time and in any forum—in the O.A.S., in the United Nations, or in any other meeting that could be useful without limiting our freedom of action.

We have, in the past, made strenuous efforts to limit the spread of nuclear weapons. We have proposed the elimination of all arms and military bases in a fair and effective disarmament treaty. We are prepared to discuss new proposals for the removal of tensions on both sides including the possibilities of a genuinely independent Cuba free to determine its own destiny.

We have no wish to war with the Soviet Union, for we are a peaceful people who desire to live in peace with all other peoples.

But it is difficult to settle or even discuss these problems in an atmosphere of intimidation.

That is why this latest Soviet threat or any other threat which is made either independently or in response to our actions this week must and will be met with determination.

Any hostile move anywhere in the world against the safety and freedom of peoples to whom we are committed including in particular the brave people of West Berlin will be met by whatever action is needed.

Finally, I want to say a few words to the captive people of Cuba to whom this speech is being directly carried by special radio facilities.

I speak to you as a friend as one who knows of your deep attachment to your fatherland, as one who shares your aspirations for liberty and justice for all.

And I have watched and the American people have watched with deep sorrow how your nationalist revolution was betrayed and how your fatherland fell under foreign domination.

Calls Leaders Puppets

Now your leaders are no longer Cuban leaders inspired by Cuban ideals. They are puppets and agents of an international conspiracy which has turned Cuba against your friends and neighbors in the Americas and turned it into the first Latin-American country to become a target for nuclear war, the first Latin-American country to have these weapons on its soil.

These new weapons are not in your interests. They contribute nothing to your peace and well being; they can only undermine it.

But this country has no wish to cause you to suffer or to impose any system upon you. We know that your lives and land are being used as pawns by those who deny your freedom. Many times in the past the Cuban people have risen to throw out tyrants who destroyed their liberty.

And I have no doubt that most Cubans today look forward to the time when they will be truly free, free from foreign domination, free to choose their own leaders, free to select their own system, free to own their own land free to speak and write and worship without fear or degradation.

He Envisions Welcome

And then shall Cuba be welcomed back to the society of free nations and to the associations of this hemisphere.

My fellow citizens, let no one doubt that this is a difficult and dangerous effort on which we have set out. No one can foresee precisely what course it will take, or what course or casualties will be incurred.

Many months of sacrifice and self-discipline lie ahead, months in which both our patience and our will will be tested. Months in which many threats and denunciations will keep us aware of our dangers. But the greatest danger of all would be to do nothing.

The path we have chosen for the present is full of hazards, as all paths are. But it is the one most consistent with our character and courage as a nation and our commitments around the world.

The cost of freedom is always high, but Americans have always paid it.

And one path we shall never choose, and that is the path of surrender, or submission.

Our goal is not the victory of might, but the vindication of right; not peace at the expense of freedom, but both peace and freedom here in this hemisphere, and, we hope around the world.

God willing, that goal will be achieved.

Roosevelt Suggested A Quarantine in 1937

Special to The New York Times

WASHINGTON, Oct. 22—The word quarantine, used tonight by President Kennedy in the sense of a blockade, was also used by President Franklin D. Roosevelt to suggest a world cooperative effort to halt aggression.

Speaking in Chicago, Oct. 5, 1937, when Japanese forces were invading China, Mr. Roosevelt said:

"When an epidemic of physical disease starts to spread, the community approves, then joins in a quarantine of the patients in order to protect the health of the community against the spread of the disease."

"War is a contagion," he went on, "whether it is declared or undeclared."

KENNEDY CANCELS CAMPAIGN TALKS

Continued From Page 1, Col. 8

signed as a special adviser to Adlai E. Stevenson, the United States's chief delegate to the United Nations.

A score of Congressional leaders were summoned to Washington today for a White House meeting on the Cuban situation.

Move Counters G.O.P.

The President's action tonight in ordering the blockade is expected to have the effect, at least momentarily, of countering the most telling political attack Republicans have been making against his Administration.

In effect, the President has moved to provide an answer to Republican demands that he "do something" about Cuba and the build-up there of Soviet arms and technicians.

This has evolved as the nearest thing to an over-riding national issue in the current Congressional campaign. The Republican National Committee so designated it in a recent official statement, and numerous polls and reports by political correspondents say that it is the national issue of most concern to candidates and voters alike.

Republican spokesmen have been using the Cuban issue to depict the Kennedy Administration as timid and indecisive, not only in respect to Cuba, but in other international trouble spots as well.

The Democratic candidates have been at a sharp disadvantage in countering these attacks. The defeat of the invasion of Cuba in April, 1961, and the many subsequent pro-Communist activities by the Cuban Government have been well publicized and widely discussed.

Issue Stirs Emotions

The Cuban question has generated, as a result, a highly emotional reaction in many people that the Democrats have found difficult to dispel.

Republican leaders in the past, however, have taken the position that while foreign policy in the formative stage is a legitimate target for partisan criticism, a major policy should be immune once activated.

There has been nothing binding about this rule as far as individual candidates or spokesmen are involved, and, last Thursday, the National Republican Chairman, William E. Miller proclaimed Cuba "the dominant issue of this campaign."

Yesterday, however, former President Dwight D. Eisenhower, in a television interview, took a firm stand against "badgering" the President about the Cuban situation at this time. Moreover, with the country now committed to a firm and possibly dangerous course of action toward Cuba, the Republican attacks are expected to be more restrained.

Republican leaders who attended the White House meeting on the blockade said tonight that "Americans will support the President on the decision or decisions he makes for the security of our country."

There was some acceptance here of the contention that political considerations had played more than a minor part in the blockade decision.

The President, and many of those closest to him in the White House, are known to have been smarting under Republican jibes at his "indecisiveness" in dealing with Premier Fidel Castro and his Soviet ally.

Whether or not the Cuban issue will directly affect the election prospects of any Democratic candidates this year, it apparently has hurt the President's personal popularity and that of the Democratic party as a whole.

This could prove harmful both to the President's influence with Congress next year, and to his re-election prospects in 1964. One of Mr. Kennedy's most effective tactics in the campaign of 1960 was his criticism of President Eisenhower's "indecisiveness" in executing foreign policy. It is galling to now have the same criticism turned upon himself.

If the Cuban crisis should be removed from the arena of partisan debate, however, it is unlikely that the subject as a whole will be ignored.

In addition to the charge of "indecisiveness," Mr. Kennedy has come under sharp attack from some Republican spokesmen for failing to take the public more fully into his confidence on the developing crisis in Cuba.

Senator Kenneth B. Keating, Republican of New York, has been particularly aggressive in pressing this viewpoint. He has insisted frequently that his own intelligence sources have shown a far more serious build-up of Soviet offensive weapons in Cuba than Administration spokesmen had acknowledged. Speaking to the Senate on Oct. 10, he said:

"When are the American people going to be given all the facts about the military build-up in Cuba? We are not getting the whole story. .

"The fact of the matter is, according to my reliable sources, that six [missile] launching sites are now under construction—pads which will have the power to hurl rockets into the American heartland and as far as the Panama Canal Zone."

The President and other Administartion spokesmen had insisted until today that the arms build-up did not constitute an offensive threat.

MOSCOW CHARGES U.S. 'ARMED FIST'

Continued From Page 1, Col. 6

sibly military equipment are now believed to be at sea or ready to depart for the Caribbean.

Western observers said Moscow would as a mater of international prestige regard such a search as intolerable. However, the Soviet Union lacks the naval and air units and bases to support a military operation in the Caribbean to breach the quarantine.

The observers speculated that the Soviet Union would be more likely to withhold its shipping from the Caribbean while attempting in the debate in the Security Council to obtain some breach in the quaratine.

The loophole might take the form of an acceptance of some kind of inspection by a neutral party.

The sudden increase in tension over Cuba appeared to threaten a round of exploratory talks on a Berlin settlement. New talks, after the United States Congressional elections, had been urged by Premier Khrushchev last Tuesday.

It was considered unlikely that the Soviet Union would make any overt move in Berlin unless the conflict over Cuba erupted.

President Kennedy delivered his message at 2 A.M., Moscow time and in the early morning hours there was no apparent official Soviet reaction.

No Polish Shipments Due

Special to The New York Times

WARSAW, Tuesday, Oct, 23—The Polish Government told the United States Embassy yesterday that it did not expect Polish ships to attempt to deliver military equipment to Cuba.

The declaration was made before President Kennedy's speech. It was made to a United States Embassy official who was summoned to the Foreign Ministry to hear a complaint about remarks made by President Kennedy regarding Poland.

No official comment was available early today on the import of President Kennedy's speech.

Police Here Act to Prevent Disturbances Over Cuba

The police took security precautions last night to aver disturbances over President Kennedy's moves on Cuba.

Police Commissioner Michael J. Murphy met with his top aides to decide on the measures.

Details were not announced, but units assigned to the United Nations were reinforced and additional patrolmen were sent to "strategic" spots in the city.

Guards at police headquarters, 240 Centre Street, required all persons seeking admission to show identification cards.

The night guards at City Hall and Gracie Mansion were increased, and guards were assigned to radio and television stations.

State Liberal Party Says 'Appeal Will Be Approved'

The Liberal party endorsed President Kennedy's action on Cuba last night. Dr. Timothy W. Costello, state chairman, sent a telegram to the President that said, in part:

"We feel your appeal will be approved by the American people and free people all over the world with renewed dedication to maintain the peace and prevent Soviet aggression and imperialism from spreading into our hemisphere or elsewhere."

Democratic Representative Leonard Farbstein of New York said:

"As a member of the Committee on Foreign Affairs of the House of Representtives I am in full accord with the position taken by him, and I pledge him my full support."

Kennedy Ready for Showdown With Soviet Union on Issue of Missiles in Cuba

SHIPS MUST STOP OR BE ATTACKED

If Offensive Rockets Are Not Dismantled, U.S. Intends to Broaden Blockade

Continued From Page 1, Col. 4

cation from President Kennedy to Premier Khrushchev.

The President's pronouncement surprised the Washington diplomatic corps. Only a few short weeks ago, the Administration was insisting, despite assertions on the Senate floor to the contrary, that there were no offensive missile bases in Cuba, and condemning "loose talk" about the possibility of an American blockade of Cuba.

At the same time, the Administration expressed confidence that its surveillance of Cuba was so complete that there was little chance of any surprise revelations.

Yet within a few days, according to the official report tonight, a new and alarming Soviet offensive missile and bomber capacity was discovered, leading to a fundamental change in the Administration's policy.

The test of the President's speech will come fairly soon. A number of ships under the control of the Soviet bloc are now en route to Cuba. Intelligence reports say that the captains of these ships are under orders not to permit any surveillance of their cargoes by the United States.

Accordingly, it is the hope of the Administration that, after Ambassador Anatoly F. Dobrynin's call at the State Department tonight, during which the new United States policy was defined, the Soviet Union will issue new orders to those captains.

If no new orders are issued, then the ships will be intercepted by vessels of the growing United States Naval forces around Cuba.

President Kennedy's talk with the Soviet Foreign Minister, Andrei A. Gromyko, last Thursday had an important bearing on the President's decision that the Soviet Union was acting in bad faith and therefore had to be confronted with a stern policy.

At the end of the previous week, United States reconnaissance planes had not been able to carry out their observation missions over Cuba because of Hurricane Ella. However, reports from other United States sources had been coming in about the arrival not only of medium-range missiles (range 1,020 to 1,100 miles) but of intermediate range missiles (2,200 miles).

Missiles Detected

By Sunday, Oct. 14, however, Air Force planes were able to survey Cuba again. They brought back confirmation of the reports of the medium and intermediate missiles.

They are understood to have spotted at a site in west Cuba medium-range missiles of what are described as the "field type," which do not require concrete emplacements but which can be moved from one position to another.

These were not, as had previously been reported by Senator Kenneth B. Keating, Republican of New York, merely the sites for missiles but the actual missiles themselves. They also photographed Ilyushin-28 bombers and several MIG-21 fighters. Previous intelligence reports had merely noted the presence of older MIG 15's and MIG 17's.

These reports were verified, according to official sources, and the photographs developed on Monday night and presented to President Kennedy for the first time on the morning of Tuesday.

Yet when Mr. Gromyko came to the White House two days later, as the President said in his speech tonight, he (Mr. Gromyko) insisted that the weapons in Cuba were purely defensive and the Soviet technicians there "would never become involved in rendering assistance" in offensive weapons.

The information on which the Government is acting is not only different from this, but United States intelligence indicates that all Cubans have been removed from the missile sites and replaced by Russians and that all the Ilyushin-28 Soviet bombers are under the command of Soviet flyers.

There is no inclination here to minimize the seriousness of the situation that may now follow the policy announced by the President. It is realized that the President has in effect asked the Soviet Union to abandon its offensive support of the Castro regime, and that this, if accepted by Moscow, will be a serious challenge to the Soviet Union's prestige and a disastrous blow to Premier Castro.

Accordingly, in the last few days, every conceivable retaliatory measure by the Soviet Union has been analyzed. These have included a possible attack on the United States base at Guantanamo Bay. Accordingly, its civilian personnel have been evacuated and its military personnel strengthened.

Meanwhile, all United States forces throughout the world, including those in Berlin and West Germany, have been put in a state of alert.

A counterblockade by the Soviet Union on United States supplies to the NATO bases in Italy and Turkey has also been considered, but the feeling here is that they are now self-sufficient to a point where they will not need supplies for a considerable period.

The prospect that the new Cuban policy may lead to an early Soviet peace treaty with the East German regime has also been taken into account, but it has been taken for granted that this would probably come before the end of the year anyway.

This by no means disposes of all the other places where the Soviet Union could open up a new front—Iran, Thailland and South Vietnam, to mention only three, but the decision here was that the risk of permitting the Soviet build-up to continue in Cuba was greater than the risk of retaliation elsewhere.

Tough as is the Kennedy response to the Soviet offensive missiles, the Administration is still hoping to avoid a military clash. An invasion of Cuba was considered and rejected. This, it is said, is at least partly because the build-up of Soviet military technicians is now so great that it could not be carried out without a direct clash between United States and Soviet troops in Cuba.

The same thing applies to another possible course of action—direct bombing of the Soviet missiles, supply dumps, and planes in Cuba.

Accordingly, what the Administration calls a quarantine and what everybody else here calls a blockade was chosen, beginning with a decision, not to halt the supply of oil, foodstuffs and other things necessary to the civilian life of the island, but only offensive weapons.

The really hard question, however, is how those missiles and missile sites now in place and in construction are to be dismantled if the Cubans and the Russians do not submit to the President's demands?

The Administration is confident that two-thirds of the members of the Organization of American States will approve the United States decision. There is confidence here that the evidence of those longer-range Soviet missiles in Cuba, capable of hitting a large part of South America, will pull the republics of the hemisphere together and provide the support of the Rio Treaty for Mr. Kennedy's policy.

U. N. Reaction Uncertain

There is less confidence that the United Nations General Assembly will go along with the United States resolution, which will call on the United Nations to supervise the dismantling of the Soviet missiles and bases.

However, with or without the support of the United Nations and the O.A.S., this is not likely to get the Castro regime and the Russians to submit. Then the question will arise whether an extended blockade of the civilian commerce of Cuba can achieve the American objective.

If not, Washington will still be confronted by the prospect of taking direct military action against these missiles, and this could eventually raise the dangerous prospect Washington has tried since the beginning of the "cold war" to avoid, namely attacking bases manned by Soviet forces.

President Kennedy's decision to cancel all remaining political engagements for the rest of the Congressional election campaign indicates the swift change of mood in the Administration.

From now on the focus will be on the international scene, for it is realized here that the Soviet Government has committed itself to support Cuba, and while the United States does not regard its "quarantine" as an "act of war," there is the chance that the Soviet Union and Cuba may so regard it.

The issue has been drawn so far as this hemisphere is concerned. In the 17 years of the "cold war," Moscow has not committed itself to action to get the American missiles out of Turkey. It has protested bitterly about these bases close to the Soviet border, but it has held back from the ultimate commitment now taken by the United States against the Soviet bases in Cuba.

United Press International Telephoto

CALLED TO WASHINGTON: Senator Leverett Saltonstall, left, Massachusetts Republican, and Representative John W. McCormack, House Speaker, prepare to board a Military Air Transport plane for flight to the capital.

Associated Press Wirephoto

TRAVELS BY JET: Senator Thomas H. Kuchel, Republican of California, dons Navy flying gear in San Diego for trip to Washington. The Senator was among twenty Congressional leaders summoned to capital by President.

Capital's Discussions on Crisis Kept a Tight Secret for a Week

Special to The New York Times

WASHINGTON, Oct. 22—A week of official tension and public mystery lay behind the Presidential decision to broadcast to the country tonight.

It was last Tuesday morning that officials heard the chilling news that there were Soviet offensive missiles in Cuba. It came in the form of a hard, detailed intelligence report.

For a small group of the highest officials in the Government the next six days were a continuous round of meetings—and of private soul-searching that one man called the most terrible he had ever undergone.

But until last Friday night or Saturday morning no one outside that group knew a crisis was brewing, much less what courses were under consideration. One official said today:

"It was the best-kept secret I have ever known in Washington, especially considering its importance."

Saturday night all of Washington was gripped by the awareness that a critical turn in world affairs was at hand. But even then only a few knew exactly what was involved.

Press Observes Secrecy

Yesterday several newspapers learned the nature of the threat that was seen by the Government. At the request of the White House the story was not carried in this morning's editions.

Allies of the United States were not informed until late today of the course chosen by the President, although some had known somewhat earlier of the new intelligence estimates.

The basic reason for the secrecy was the fear that the Soviet Union, if it knew the plans in advance, would make some move to anticipate and undercut the President's course. For example one such action might have been a resolution introduced in the United Nations.

The week's activities involved not only the top officials of the State and Defense Departments, but others with special skills or with the President's special confidence.

The President's brother, Attorney General Robert F. Kennedy, was in on the planning from the first morning. An aide said he had spent "pretty near full time" on the Cuban crisis.

Dean Acheson, the former Secretary of State, was called in from his country home in Sandy Springs, Md., where he was working on a lecture to be given at the University of California on Wednesday. This morning he flew to Paris to take the news of the President's decision to the Council of the North Atlantic Treaty Organization.

Key Figures at Talks

Secretary of State Dean Rusk, Secretary of Defense Robert S. McNamara and John A. McCone, director of the Central Intelligence Agency, were all key figures in the discussions. So was McGeorge Bundy, the President's Special Assistant for National Security Affairs.

Some of Attorney General Kennedy's assistants worked with State Department lawyers, and at the White House, on the legal underpinning of the "quarantine" and other steps.

There were clues during the week that the few insiders recognized. But it was not until these clues began accumulating during the weekend that general awareness of a crisis arose.

Last Thursday morning's papers carried a report that the Defense Department had quietly begun a build-up of air power in the southeastern United States. A Pentagon spokesman termed this "an ordinary thing to do" in the light of Cuban possession of Soviet jet fighters.

On Friday it was disclosed that Secretary McNamara had asked the Joint Chiefs of Staff and the service Secretaries to stay in Washington for the next six weeks. This was explained as necessary for consultations on defense budget planning.

Friday night Secretary Rusk cancelled a speech in Virginia because of "the press of business."

Then, on Saturday, President Kennedy abruptly cut short a campaign trip to the West and Middle West. He flew home from Chicago, and the official explanation was that he had a cold.

One question asked today was why, in the light of the situation, the President had left Washington Friday for the campaign trip.

Officials answered that the decision to go ahead with the trip was deliberate, to avoid arousing suspicions.

When the President broke off the trip Saturday, questions about the possibility of an emergency were put to his press secretary, Pierre Salinger. Mr. Salinger insisted the President had a "heavy cold" and that he knew of no emergency.

It was explained today that the cold was of a kind that Mr. Kennedy ordinarily would have ridden out. What he returned for was final consultations on the Cuban crisis.

From the point of view of history, the commitment that led to tonight's action can be traced to the President's last press conference, on Sept. 13.

He said then that "unilateral military intervention" in Cuba "on the part of the United States cannot currently be either required or justified," and he added that "loose talk about such action" was "regrettable."

He Adds a Condition

But, Mr. Kennedy added, if the Communist build-up in Cuba were ever to "endanger our security in any way" or "become an offensive military base of significant capacity for the Soviet Union," then the United States would do "whatever must be done to protect its own security and that of its allies."

On Oct. 10 Senator Kenneth B. Keating, Republican of New York, said in a floor speech that he had substantiated reports of half a dozen intermediate range ballistic missile sites under construction in Cuba.

Administration sources vigorously denied this report. As late as last Tuesday—after the President had the intelligence report—State Department officials were saying that no offensive weapons were in Cuba.

It was explained today that the news, tightly controlled, had not at the time filtered down the line in the State Department. Officials also said that Senator Keating's statement, when made, was premature and, at the time, inaccurate.

DONOVAN CONCERNED ON PRISONERS' DEAL

James B. Donovan, chief negotiator in the barter deal to release 1,113 invasion prisoners held in Cuba, was shaken by President Kennedy's blockade announcement last night.

Mr. Donovan, who is the Democratic-Liberal candidate for United States Senator, said:

"Obviously I'm going to have to face up to this in the next day or two, but please remember I'm only general counsel for a committee."

Mr. Donovan decided against going on with a speech at the State Teachers College in Oneonta, N. Y., after having seen the President's telecast. Later, he issued this statement:

"The President's statement exhibited his characteristic combination of firm courage and statesmanlike restraint. Pending further study and consultation with the Cuban Families Committee for Liberation of Prisoners of War, I must decline to comment on the statement's possible effect upon my mission."

President Calm Despite Tension Throughout Day in White House

Special to The New York Times

WASHINGTON, Oct. 22—Outwardly, President Kennedy was the calmest man around the White House today.

In White House offices and the press lobby, tension mounted throughout the day as the time approached for the President's scheduled speech to the nation.

However, the President did not appear flustered by the day's events. He awoke early, was in his office early, and he took time out for a swim in the White House pool. He lunched quietly in the family quarters.

Quiet Moments Deceptive

Despite these quiet moments, this was one of the busiest, most crucial days, President Kennedy has spent in the White House.

His day was supposed to be a light one. His schedule called for just two appointments: A 10:30 A.M. meeting with Under Secretary of State George C. McGhee and a 4 P.M. conference with Prime Minister Milton Obote of Uganda.

Before the day was over, Mr. Kennedy had met at the White House with most of the top officials of Government.

During the morning, he held conferences with Secretary of State Dean Rusk, Secretary of Defense Robert S. McNamara, Attorney General Robert F. Kennedy, Martin Hillenbrand, head of the State Department's Berlin task force, Llewellyn E. Thompson Jr., until recently Ambassador to Moscow and now Special Adviser on Soviet Affairs, and others.

At 1 P. M., the President slipped away for a swim in his private pool, near his office. He ate lunch in the family dining room, then returned to the west wing for another series of conferences.

Members of the National Security Council began arriving for a meeting with the President shortly before 3 P. M., 15 minutes earlier than scheduled. They met for an hour in the Cabinet room, next door to the President's office.

The National Security Council was still in session when G. Mennen Williams, Assistant Secretary of State for African Affairs, arrived in the west wing lobby with Prime Minister Obote.

Minutes later, the National Security Council members slipped out a side door and the President kept his appointment with the Uganda Prime Minister. They too, met in the Cabinet room.

At 4:45 P.M., the President and Prime Minister Obote walked into the west wing lobby. He escorted Prime Minister Obote to a limousine outside shook hands and walked briskly back into the White House.

Cabinet Sees President

Waiting for him in the Cabinet room were members of his Cabinet. Some had arrived by a side door in the west wing basement, others through a west gate.

There had been indications earlier in the day that the President might make a speech or that some other official might have something to say before the scheduled telecast tonight.

After the Cabinet meeting, the President had one final session—this one with Congressional leaders—before walking back into his office for the broadcast to the nation.

Automobile Industry Backs Kennedy Action

Special to The New York Times

DETROIT, Oct. 22—The automobile industry pledged its support to President Kennedy tonight.

Henry Ford 2d, president of the Automobile Manufacturers Association and chairman of the Ford Motor Company, made public a telegram to the President preceding the industry's banquet at the National Automobile Show.

The telegram said:

"At a meeting of the board of directors of the automobile manufacturers association held immediately following your address to the nation tonight and just before the banquet of the 44th National Automobile Show, there was a spontaneous and unanimous expression of confidence and support for you in the action you have just taken to insure that peace and justice shall be maintained in this hemisphere and elsewhere in the free world.

"My associates and I—the principal officers of the companies in the American automotive industry — pledge to you aid and assistance in full measure in the critical days now beginning. Our first interest is the National interest and we believe it is our privilege and duty to serve this interest in any manner you may direct."

The telegram was signed by Henry Ford 2d, president of Automobile Manufacturers Association.

CONGRESS CHIEFS FLOWN TO CAPITAL

Armed Forces Planes Pick Them Up in Many States

By C. P. TRUSSELL

Special to The New York Times

WASHINGTON, Oct. 22 — A score of Congressional leaders were summoned to Washington today by President Kennedy from all quarters of the country.

The summons took them by surprise. They did not learn of the decision to blockade Cuba until a meeting at the White House late in the afternoon. The meeting was preceded by sessions of the National Security Council and the Cabinet.

The leaders will meet with the President again Wednesday, if not sooner, one source reported. Mr. Kennedy requested that they remain in Washington indefinitely, the White House said.

Republicans Back Kennedy

Republican leaders who attended the White House meeting issued the following statement:

"We Republican leaders met today at the White House at the urgent request of the President. We listened to a report of the Central Intelligence Agency, the Secretary of State, and Secretary of Defense; we were told of the unanimous report of the [National] Security Council and the Joint Chiefs of Staff; were informed by the President of his already determined course of action which he later stated in his broadcast for all the world to hear.

"Americans will support the President on the decision or decisions he makes for the security of our country.,

"The President has asked the leadership to stay in Washington for further consultation and we will do so."

Senator Mike Mansfield, the Senate's Democratic leader, made this comment tonight:

"The leadership expressed full support for the President and recognized that he and he alone had to make the decisions in the light of all the information available."

Senator Thomas H. Kuchel of California, the Senate minority whip, said: "So far as American foreign policy is concerned, politics has adjourned. This is a deadly serious situation and the American people are going to rally behind the President."

Hodges Gets a Lift

Secretary of Commerce Luther H. Hodges was aboard a commercial jet liner to keep a speaking engagement in Las Vegas. Secretary of the Treasury Douglas Dillon was in Mexico City, attending sessions of the Economic and Social Council of the Organization of American States. Neither was called back for the Cabinet session.

Air Force, Navy and National Guard planes picked up those summoned. The urgency of the call prompted some Republicans to pledge support for the President even in advance of enlightenment about the cause for the summons.

Vice President Lyndon B. Johnson, President of the Senate, remained in Washington. He canceled a trip to Detroit, where he was to have been the principal speaker at the National Automobile Show dinner tonight.

He also had been scheduled to make a major political speech there tomorrow morning and to go to Grand Rapids for an afternoon rally there.

Senator Everett McKinley Dirksen of Illinois, the minority leader, was about to board a commercial plane in answer to the summons to the White House. He was intercepted and flown to Washington by an Air Force jet. The same jet picked up Representative Leslie C. Arends of Illinois, the House Republican whip.

Kuchel Interrupts Tour

Senator Kuchel was campaigning at San Diego, Calif. He was picked up by a Navy jet plane coming in from Guam. A helicopter met him in Washington and set him down on the White House lawn.

The House Speaker, John W. McCormack of Massachusetts, was picked up in Boston. He was accompanied by a Republican colleague, Senator Leverett Saltonstall, an assistant leader and ranking minority member of the Armed Services Committee.

Representative Charles A. Halleck of Indiana, the House minority leader, had been campaigning in South Dakota for the two incumbents, Ben Reifel and E. Y. Berry.

A military plane picked him up at Sioux City and on the way it stopped off at Cedar Rapids for Senator Bourke B. Hickenlooper of Iowa, chairman of the Senate Republican Policy Committee and member of the foreign legations panel. The plane stopped in Minneapolis for Senator Hubert H. Humphrey of Minnesota, deputy Senate majority leader.

Representative Carl Albert of Oklahoma, the House Majority leader, boarded a plane at Indianapolis. He had gone into Indiana to campaign for the Fifth District incumbent, J. Edward Roush.

Other planes brought in Senator J. W. Fulbright, of Arkansas, chairman of the Senate Foreign Relations Committee; Senator Alexander Wiley of Wisconsin, that panel's ranking Republican member; Representative Thomas E. Morgan of Pennsylvania, chairman of the House Foreign Affairs Committee, and Representative Robert B. Chiperfield of Illinois, ranking minority member of that committee.

U.S. Is Prepared for Any Moves Against Its Bases by Russians

By MAX FRANKEL

Special to The New York Times

WASHINGTON, Oct. 22—The quarantine or blockade of Cuba was a unilateral decision by the United States. It was ordered despite an awareness here that it might invite some Soviet retaliation and threats against Western allies around the world.

President Kennedy, in his radio-television speech to the nation, made it plain that nothing would be allowed to limit his "freedom of action."

The President warned the Soviet Union against interfering with the vulnerable Western access routes to Berlin, which are regarded here as a likely target of Communist countermeasures.

Hostile moves against Berlin or any other positions to which the United States is committed, he said, will be met "by whatever action is needed."

The major Western powers were informed of the President's decision, but they were not consulted. The Administration will seek support for its action tomorrow both in the Organization of American States and in the United Nations, but high officials said the blockade would not be delayed.

Soviet officials were not forewarned either, except by the indications of crisis in the capital this weekend. It was not until 6 P.M., one hour before the President went on the air, that Secretary of State Dean Rusk received the Soviet Ambassador, Anatoly F. Dobrynin, to announce the blockade.

The elaborate secrecy here in the last few days and the lack of consultation with its allies was an important ingredient of United States strategy.

Every precaution was taken to prevent premature disclosure so that Moscow would not be able to intercede with an ultimatum or new commitment to Cuba before the President spoke.

Policy of Soviet

The Soviet Union is on record with a series of tough-sounding but vague commitments to defend Cuba against aggression. It has repeatedly proclaimed the right to construct bases in Cuba for "defensive purposes."

Moscow has equated this with Western rights to maintain bases in Turkey, Italy and Japan, among other places.

Mr. Kennedy's intention was to present the Russians with the blockade as an accomplished fact before Moscow and Washington became engaged in an exchange of commitments that might have made a direct clash a certainty.

The President had been prepared to advance the time of his announcement if there had been any sign of a Soviet move.

Former Secretary of State Dean Rusk and other top planners of the Administration move, flew to Paris today to report the action to the Council of the North Atlantic Treaty Organization.

In London, Ambassador David K. E. Bruce informed Prime Minister Macmillan. Ambassador Walter C. Dowling called on Chancellor Adenauer in Bonn.

When it appeared this afternoon that sufficient secrecy had been maintained long enough to prevent a Soviet intercession, Ambassador Dobrynin was requested to call upon Mr. Rusk.

The Soviet diplomat had to rush back from New York, where he had gone to see off Andrei A. Gromyko, the Soviet Foreign Minister, who took off for East Berlin and Moscow.

Dobrynin Sees Rusk

Mr. Dobrynin spent 25 minutes with Secretary Rusk; Edwin M. Martin, Assistant Secretary of State for Inter-American Affairs; John C. Guthrie, director of the Soviet Affairs Office, and Helmut Sonnenfeldt, a specialist on Soviet affairs.

Officials said the Ambassador was given a copy of the President's speech and a copy of a letter from the President to Premier Khrushchev, covering essentially the same points. The original of the letter was delivered at the same time to Soviet authorities in Moscow.

Mr. Kennedy's letter, like his speech, left the way open for direct discussion of the blockade and the Soviet build-up in Cuba, possibly in a Kennedy-Khrushchev meeting.

The usually amiable and cheerful Soviet Ambassador managed only a few forced smiles when he encountered newsmen outside Mr. Rusk's office. Then his face froze and he appeared shaken.

Asked whether he had received a document, Mr. Dobrynin nodded grimly and held up a manila envelope. When asked whether there was a crisis, he replied: "Ask the Secretary." When asked to appraise the situation, he replied: "You can judge for yourself."

Before Mr. Dobrynin left the Secretary's office the Ambassadors of 46 pro-Western nations were assembled in a ground-floor auditorium to hear a report from Under Secretary of State George W. Ball, Roger Hilsman, the State Department's director of intelligence and research, and several assistant secretaries. At the end of the briefing the group watched the President's address on a giant television screen.

For most of the ambassadors, the unusual mass briefing brought the first news of the blockade. They appeared grim as they left the conference room and could be heard to remark: "This is very serious."

Some Were Reluctant

Both in Latin America and among the United States' allies in Europe and Asia, a number of governments have been reluctant to accept Washington's view that Cuba is a threat to the West.

Although many of the allies have cooperated in efforts to prevent Western ships from conveying arms to Cuba, some had insisted on the right of continued peaceful trade. Public opinion in Britain and elsewhere has generally been unreceptive to United States' demands for action against the Government of Premier Fidel Castro.

With this in mind, the State Department invited newsmen of allied nations as well as Americans to the special news briefings held after the President's speech. Simultaneously, a report was also made to the ambassadors of nonaligned countries.

The realization that a United States move against Cuba might quickly provoke retaliation elsewhere has long been evident in the comments of high Administration officials.

They have always denied, for instance, that there is a negotiable link between Cuba and West Berlin. But they have persistently warned that there was a "factual connection" in the sense that action in one place might become the signal for conteraction in the other.

Countermeasures Set

Countermeasures to cope with Soviet moves against West Berlin had been prepared even before there was talk of a threat from Cuba.

Possible targets of Soviet retaliation might be any of the 127 United States bases that the Defense Department says are maintained in 18 foreign countries.

These bases were described here today as not particularly vulnerable to a Soviet naval blockade. But the nations that tolerate the bases could become the objects of Soviet diplomatic and propaganda attacks.

The United States' request for support from the Organization of American States and the United Nations, officials pointed out, is intended to strengthen the country's moral position.

The O.A.S. will be called together tomorrow afternoon to approve the blockade and further measures, if necessary, under Articles 6 and 8 of the Rio pact of 1947. These articles sanction measures to defend the hemisphere against any "fact or situation that might endanger the peace of America."

A two-thirds vote of at least 14 American nations will be needed in the O.A.S. Council and Administration officials are confident of these votes.

The move in the United Nations promises to be more difficult. The Soviet Union is expected to veto the United States resolution in the Security Council but it will then be referred to the General Assembly, where each of the world organization's 109 members has one vote and none has a veto.

KHRUSHCHEV TRIP NOW QUESTIONED

Cuba Situation Recalls the Upset of 1960 Summit

Speculation was rife last night whether Premier Khrushchev would go through with an expected visit here to meet President Kennedy, after the President had accused Soviet officials of having lied on the Cuban question.

The situation recalled how Mr. Khrushchev broke up the scheduled Big Four summit meeting of May, 1960, in Paris which he had been seeking with President Eisenhower, Prime Minister Macmillan and President de Gaulle. He made his reason then the flight of the U-2 reconnaissance plane that was down in the Soviet Union.

This fall Mr. Khrushschev has been permitting hints that he might come in November to the United Nations General Assembly and might meet with President Kennedy at that time. As in 1960, the Soviet Premier has been building up a critical atmosphere over Berlin.

Last night, President Kennedy was accusing the Soviet Union of an offensive military build-up in Cuba. Mr. Kennedy charged that a Soviet "Government" statement Sept. 11 to the contrary and a private assurance to him by Foreign Minister Andrei A. Gromyko last Thursday were both "false."

Mr. Kennedy did call on Premier Khrushchev to abandon his present course and to "join in an historic effort" to end the arms race and achieve peaceful solutions of world problems. But he added that it was "difficult to settle or even discuss these problems in an atmosphere of intimidation."

One interpretation was that the President was suggesting that a visit from Mr. Khrushchev would be unwelcome unless preceded by a change in policy. Another, however, was that the President had not said discussions were impossible. This would leave the next move—and perhaps the choice—to Mr. Khrushchev.

Meany Promises Unionists Will Back Kennedy on Cuba

Special to The New York Times

WASHINGTON, Oct. 22 — George Meany promised the backing of America's organized workers for President Kennedy's Cuban policy tonight.

The president of the American Federation of Labor and Congress of Industrial Organizations watched Mr. Kennedy's television address in his home in Bethesda, Md.

U.S. Assembles Massive Military Force in the Caribbean to Impose the Blockade

MORE NAVAL UNITS JOIN PATROL SHIPS

Pentagon Confident It Can Carry Out Order—Families to Leave Base in Cuba

Continued From Page 1, Col. 7

bases apparently were ready for combat operations that could launch weapons 1,200 miles and appeared to be aimed at targets deep in the United States. He added also, in response to a qustion, that the United States had no specific defense against such ballistic missiles.

In the meantime, naval units including destroyers, aircraft carriers and submarines put to sea to join ships already on station in the heightened surveillance of Cuban waters that was ordered last week.

More than 40 ships and 20,000 men, including 6,000 Marines originally scheduled to carry out training maneuvers southeast of Puerto Rico, have been diverted to join the blockade, Navy sources said.

'More Than Enough' Units

The defense spokesman, asked how many military units were engaged in the blockade, replied "more than enough."

Asked then whether the planes had orders to sink Soviet ships that might attempt to run the blockade, he answered tersely: "Yes."

The spokesman added, however, that the blockade was being imposed against all ships, not only those of the Soviet bloc, that attempted to deliver offensive weapons to Cuba.

Adm. Robert L. Dennison, commander of the Atlantic Fleet, was said to be the commanding officer in charge of the widespread operation, including the Air Force units that were taking part.

The defense spokesman would not give exact areas of surveillance. It appeared from other sources that planes would signal the appearance of ships anywhere in the Atlantic that appeared to be bound for Cuba.

Critical Search Area

Military sources said that the critical area of possible search and seizure probably would embrace about 5,000 miles of ocean around the island whose western extremity is only 90 miles off the Florida shore.

North of Cuba, the blockade would call for barring free access to the main harbors, including Havana, by air and sea patrols from the Grand Bahamas to Barbados, east of the Leeward islands, it was indicated.

South of Cuba, the blockade patrols were expected to concentrate their attention on the sea regions beginning at the Yucatan channel just south of the Tropic of Cancer, eastward past Jamaica and possibly a relatively short distance beyond that.

The most important segment of the blockade, it was believed, would be the well traveled sea lanes that run through the shoals and reefs of the Bahama islands as well as the famous windward passage between the eastern tip of Cuba and Haiti.

Invasion Plan Denied

Military sources continued to insist that no invasion of Cuba was being contemplated at present. The same sources said that the forces involved in the amphibious exercised that were planned at Vieques near Puerto Rico but suddenly called off would be insufficient to mount such an invasion.

Outlining how the blookade would be enforced, the spokesman said that planes would be sent on surveillance missions with orders to signal to "control centers" the identification of ships that might be bearing arms to Cuba.

For the time being the Defense spokesman said, the Administration did not intend to make use of the special authority Congress granted President Kennedy to call up to 150,000 reservists and extend the tours of men in service.

The situation, the spokesman added, however, did fit into the kind that was contemplated when the President asked for the standby powers.

Navy sea and air patrols have been conducting a tight surveillance of Cuban shipping for many weeks.

Military sources stressed unofficially that the effectiveness of any blockade, as distinguished from surveillance, depended upon the reaction of ships subjected to search and seizure.

A sea blockade, they said, would require United States naval vessels to halt and search those ships that attempt to reach Cuban ports in disregard of a warning.

If arms or other military goods were found, the navy patrols would escort the boarded ship to an American-controlled port.

Key West Base Active

Special to The New York Times

KEY WEST, Fla., Oct. 22—This southernmost military establishment of the United States was in the midst of the biggest military buildup tonight since World War II days.

At periodic intervals jet fighters could be heard roaring off the runways of the Boca Chica Naval Air Base.

A squadron of the Navy's most modern supersonic fighters flew in last week and was said to be on 24-hour patrol.

Air Force Moves Fighters

COLORADO SPRINGS, Colo., Oct. 22 (AP)—Air Force fighter interceptors have been redeployed and placed on increased alert status as a result of President Kennedy's declaration of a quarantine against Cuba tonight.

This announcement was made by the Continental Air Defense Command. The command, representing the Army, Navy and Air Force units of the over-all North American Air Defense Command. A spokesman said the increased alert status was ordered for all its tactical forces, and that some of these units have been redeployed to bases in the southeastern United States.

Amphibious Action Off

Special to The New York Times

CHARLOTTE AMALIE, Virgin Islands, Oct. 22—The scheduled amphibious landing on Vieques Island, east of Puerto Rico, was canceled today. It was to have been the high point of the United States naval maneuvers in the Caribbean.

The landing was to have involved 40 ships and 20,000 men, including 6,000 Marines.

Rear Admiral Allen Smith Jr., commander of the Caribbean Sea Frontier, made the announcement at the Naval Air Station in San Juan.

"According to word received from Admiral Dennison's headquarters," he said, "the exercise has not been canceled but the landing has, at least as far as its originally scheduled date of Tuesday [tomorrow] is concerned.

"The reason for this is due to the dispersal of ships caused by Hurricane Ella."

Admiral Dennison is chief of the Atlantic Fleet. The training operation, which began Oct. 15 and was to continue until Oct. 30, is under Vice Admiral Horacio Rivero.

Several hours before the cancellation, it had been announced at the Roosevelt Roads naval station east of San Juan that the "rehearsal" for the landing had ben called off but that the landing would take place tomorrow, as scheduled.

Admiral Smith disavowed a direct connection with the training maneuver and said he would leave all questions on Cuba to a "higher level."

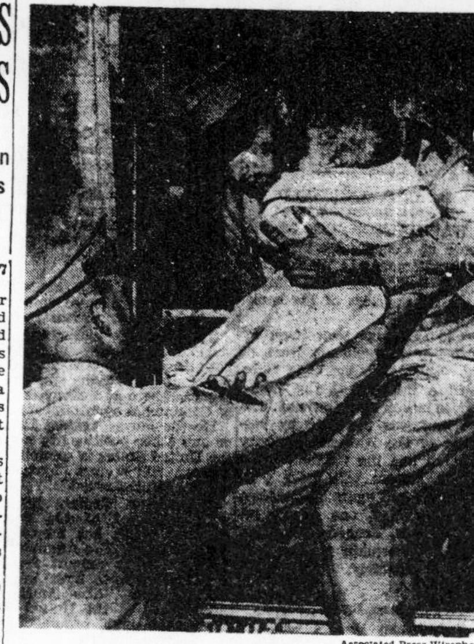

Associated Press Wirephoto

EVACUATED FROM U. S. BASE IN CUBA: Marines lift infant from plane at Norfolk, Va., air base last night. Several hundred dependents of servicemen stationed at Guantanamo Bay Naval Base were flown from Cuba.

Cuban Missile Puzzle

When Are 'Defensive' Arms Offensive? U.S. Intelligence Weighs Potential Peril

By HANSON W. BALDWIN

The problem of differentiating between a defensive missile site and an offensive one is one of the factors influencing the Administration's judgment in the Cuban situation.

Weeks ago President Kennedy described the Soviet arms buildup in Cuba as essentially "defensive," but he implied the United States might react quickly if it determined that missiles of a range sufficient to reach the United States were being emplaced at Cuban bases.

News Analysis

Senator Kenneth B. Keating, Republican of New York, said recently that a number of sites for intermediate range ballistic missiles had been identified in Cuba, and a few press reports supported him. These reports were denied by Government sources. The rumors nevertheless have persisted.

U.S. Within Range

An intermediate range ballistic missile, as differentiated from an intercontinental ballistic missile, is one incapable of spanning oceans but, from Soviet bases, with sufficient range—generally 500 to 1,500 miles—to reach most of the periphery of the Eurasian continent and some off-lying islands.

Cuba is only about 90 miles from Florida at her closest point. Intermediate range ballistic missiles based in Cuba could reach much of the eastern United States. Missiles of this type have sufficent thrust to lift megaton thermonuclear warheads.

The Russian missile inventory includes rockets of many types and designs with ranges varying from 50 miles to 9,000 or more. There are several types of missiles in the 90-to-600-mile category that could reach Florida but that are considerably smaller and therefore more easily concealed than the longer-range missiles.

So far the missiles publicly identified as in Cuba are short-range antiaircraft missiles, short-range coast defense missiles and short-range, ship-based bombardment missiles. None of these have adequate range to reach Florida; all could be classified as defensive, although the manner in which a weapon is used rather than the weapon itself is the best yardstick for classification.

Missile sites — particularly sites for large, long-range missiles—are difficult to conceal. This is especially true in Cuba, where the United States has been maintaining for a long time a very close surveillance and intelligence operation. The island is photographed almost daily, and planes and ships maintain a close coastal watch.

Cuban workers at the United States Naval Base at Guantanamo, Cuban refugees, anti-Castro underground units in Cuba, and Central Intelligence Agency and other intelligence agents gather a great mass of information. Electronic eavesdropping—the interception of radio messages and the detection of radar pulses—adds to the mass of undigested intelligence available.

All of this is pieced together and interpreted to present a refined picture of the military strength of today's Cuba.

It has been rather generally agreed among intelligence experts that it would be entirely possible without prior detection by the American surveillance and intelligence gathering system to bring into Cuba in crates disassembled missiles of sufficient range to reach the United States. There is no good way to tell exactly what is in each crate when it is unloaded from the hold of a freighter.

It is also agreed however that the construction of an intermediate range missile launching site cannot be long concealed; that it will probably be detected by aerial photographs and other means before the site is fully operational. However, if the missile were small and with a range of about 100 to 500 miles, its detection might be delayed.

Delay Inevitable

Intelligence information, if accurately assayed, nearly always involves some time lag; it may be hours, days or weeks after a photograph is taken or information is received before it is fully interpreted.

Nevertheless there is not much doubt that large missile sites in Cuba should be easily distinguishable from the far smaller short-range sites so far publicly identified, and the time lag should not be very great. The sheer size of an IRBM complex, the bulk of the missile, the radar installations, the pattern of the layout, the extensive support and supply network necessary and the security arrangements are all telltale signs to the expert photo and image interpreter.

But the MIG jet fighters now in Cuban hands emphasize even more than missiles the danger of classifying any weapon as "defensive" or "offensive." The Cubans have probably 70 to 100 jet fighters—most of them apparently MIG-17's, some MIG-19's and one or more of the supersonic MIG-21's. All of these types are useful as fighter interceptors. But all can easily fly over Florida and other parts of the southeastern United States, and like our own fighter interceptors many of them could be armed with various types of conventional or nuclear arms, including rockets and bombs.

As weapons technology alters, the problem of how to determine weapons use—whether offensive or defensive—as well as weapons capabilities becomes more and more complex.

CUBA'S ECONOMY TIED TO IMPORTS

Soviet Tried to Fill the Gap Caused by U.S. Embargo

By HARRY SCHWARTZ

Cuba's normal economic life depends heavily upon many different imports. The country is extremely vulnerable to any interruption of the flow of its foreign trade.

One indication of that vulnerability is the disruption caused by an embargo by the United States on most shipments to Cuba. The many difficulties in the Cuban economy recently have arisen despite the major effort of the Soviet Union and other Communist bloc countries to supply many essential goods that once came from the United States.

Petroleum and petroleum products make up probably the most essentail single group of imports in the short run since all Cuban motor transport, much of its power supply and all Cuban machinery require gasoline, fuel oil, lubricants, and the like. All must be imported or refined from imported crude oil.

Last year the Soviet Union shipped more than 4,000,000 metric tons of crude oil and refined oil products to Cuba to meet these needs. Maj. Ernesto Guevara, Cuban Minister of the Economy, has said that, without Soviet petroleum the Cuban economy would have been paralyzed.

Cuba Also Needs Food

Food is another major import item in the Cuban economy since that country does not produce enough. Cuba has abundant land, much of it still little used, and an excellent climate for farming, but most of its commercial agriculture up to now has been concentrated on a few export crops, sugar.

The Soviet Union last year sent Cuba more than 200,000 tons of grains, while significant quantities of rice were said to have been from other countries, notably Communist. These food imports have continued this year, but the food shortage became so extreme earlier this year that stringent rationing had to be instituted last March.

Efforts to increase domestic food production have been made by the regime of Premier Fidel Castro, but these have made relatively little progress. The Castro regime could presume to expand food production over several years meeting all the country's domestic needs. Part of this might have to be done by cutting back sugar acreage and that of other export crops. Most of Cuba's ability to buy abroad rests on these products.

Cuban agriculture also depends heavily upon imports of fertilizers. More than 400,000 tons of artificial fertilizer were shipped to Cuba from the Soviet Union last year. Cuban sugar yields, which were reduced by drought this past year, would presumably be seriously affected by any cutting off of fertilizers.

Much of the raw material used in many different types of Cuban production comes from abroad—including metals, rubber, paper, and many chemicals and the like. Cuba has also been heavily dependent upon imports for spare parts to keep its machinery going, although efforts have been made under the Castro regime to organize the domestic production of essential spare parts.

Any interruption of Cuba's foreign trade would force a quick halt to the ambitious program of industrialization now in its early stages with help from the Soviet Union and other Communist nations. Almost a quarter of the more than $270,000,000 Soviet exports to Cuba last year was in machinery and equipment of many kinds, most for the industrialization program.

In the short run the impact of an interruption of Cuban foreign trade would presumably depend upon the reserves built up in the island and the success of the Castro regime in cutting consumption of imported goods.

Observers have long speculated about whether a blockade alone could bring the Castro regime's downfall. Skeptics have pointed out that many Cubans are accustomed to a low standard of living. An intensive effort by the Castro regime might possibly permit domestic agriculture to produce a subsistence diet for the country's roughly 7,000,000 people.

REDS IN U.S. WARN AGAINST ATOM WAR

The Communist party of the U. S. A. issued a warning yesterday that "a nuclear world war" could result if "grave new acts of aggression against Cuba . . . being prepared in Washington" were carried through.

The statement was put out in the name of Gus Hall, identified as "leading Communist spokesman." It was distributed before President Kennedy's broadcast last night announced a blockade of shipments of offensive weapons to Cuba.

Mr. Hall demanded that "naval vessels now ringing Cuba's territory be withdrawn" and that "aircraft and potential invasion troops" be recalled from "advanced staging areas."

His "answer to the so-called Cuba question" proposed that the great powers, first of all the United States and the Soviet Union, pledge to "respect and guarantee the sovereign independence of Cuba" and "agree to normalize trade with Cuba on the basis of equality and mutual interest." This, he said, would allow for the solving of all disputed questions through negotiations.

Admiral With 2 Hats

Robert Lee Dennison

At the Pentagon, Admiral Robert Lee Dennison's designation is Commander in Chief, Atlantic Fleet. At NATO headquarters in Paris it is Supreme Allied Commander, Atlantic. But the sign on his desk at fleet headquarters in Norfolk proclaims simply, "Bob Dennison, Sailor." Among his staff there was no expectation yesterday that heightened responsibilities growing from the Cuban crisis would in any way diminish this unpretentiousness. The duty will be his to enforce President Kennedy's directive that any ships carrying offensive weapons to Cuba be turned back.

Man in the News

"A real fine guy with a host of friends, both civilian and military," was the description offered by a captain assigned as Admiral Dennison's aide three months ago.

Admiral Dennison still lists his official home address as Warren, Pa., where he was born April 13, 1901. He studied at the Kiskiminetas School in Saltsburg, Pa., before his appointment to the United States Naval Academy.

Graduated in 1923

He was graduated from the Academy in 1923, ranking 83d in a class of 411, and assigned to his first sea duty aboard the battleship Arkansas. Two years later, after training at the submarine base at Groton, Conn., he joined the crew of the submarine S-8.

Then, back to academia: a postgraduate course in diesel engineering at Annapolis; a master's degree in engineering from Pennsylvania State College; a doctorate in engineering from Johns Hokpins University.

His first command was the rescue vessel Ortolan, from 1935 to 1937; his second, the submarine Cuttlefish; next, the destroyer John D. Ford.

By the time the Japanese attacked Pearl Harbor, he had been assigned to the staff of the Commander in Chief, Asiatic Fleet. He participated in the defense of the Philippines and in the early fighting with the Japanese in the East Indies.

A White House Aide

He emerged from World War II with the rank of captain and his first postwar assignment was as assistant chief of naval operations for politico-military affairs.

It was his understanding of international politics that took him to the White House in 1948 as naval aide to President Harry S. Truman. Before this assignment, he had been commander of what Mr. Truman regarded as the pride of the Navy, the battleship Missouri.

Associated Press

"Bob Dennison, Sailor"

President Truman promoted him to rear admiral, making him an adviser with far greater responsibilities than the customary ceremonial duties of the post.

With the change of administration in 1953, Admiral Dennison returned to sea duty for a year as commander of Cruiser Division Four in the Atlantic. In January, 1954, he was detached to serve again in Washington, this time as director of the strategic plans division under the Chief of Naval Operations.

Golf for Relaxation

On February 29, 1960, now a full admiral after various assignments at home and abroad, he donned both the hats he now wears, as United States Atlantic Fleet commander and NATO's Supreme Allied Commander, Atlantic.

On the rare ocasions when he can take off both hats at once, Admiral Dennison enjoys a round of golf (his aides say his score is classified). Recently he has been seen on the course at Norfolk giving pointers to his 13-year-old son, Robert Lee, Jr. His daughter, Lee, 17, is attending the Stone Ridge Academy in Washington.

Denny or Bob—close friends use both nicknames—is a moderate cigarette smoker and enjoys a drink at the end of a day at his desk, though an aide reports he hasn't noted a particular favorite brand of beverage.

When time permits, Admiral Dennison also enjoys photography. He owns several cameras and can do his own darkroom work. His preferences in reading are mysteries and current affairs.

CASTRO MOBILIZES ALL ARMED FORCES

Continued From Page 1, Col. 6

his accusations against Cuba and the Soviet Union.

More than an hour after the President had completed his address, a news commentator reported briefly on it.

He said that President Kennedy had issued a declaration that could lead to a world atomic war, and promised that the Cuban people would fight to the end.

Act of War, Havana Says

HAVANA, Oct. 22 (AP)—A Havana television commentator told the Cuban people tonight of the United States arms blockade and called it an act of war that could provoke "tragic world events."

The commentator, Luis Gomez Wanguemert, said the United States appeared not to be heeding the Soviet Union's guarantees to defend Cuba.

In his statement, Mr. Wanguemert said the Cuban people must "prepare us even more and better against any direct aggression" without overlooking everyday tasks.

He scoffed at President Kennedy's assertions that Soviet intermediate range ballistic missiles are stationed in Cuba. He accused President Kennedy of "a whole series of falsehoods on Cuba" and said the President's words were "not worthy of credit."

Mr. Wanguemert is editor of the newspaper El Mundo and Director of European Affairs at the Cuban Foreign Ministry.

There was no marked reaction from the Cuban man in the street to the American action and no sign of public apprehension. It was doubtful that Mr. Kennedy's speech was heard by many Cubans, since most—in Havana at least—were en route home from work at the time of his broadcast.

Well - informed neutralist sources in Havana predicted that the United States blockade would cause serious repercussions.

They predicted a new Soviet blockade of Berlin and other strong Soviet countermeasures—perhaps at such points as Laos and South Vietnam and on Taiwan.

'Aggression' Predicted

The newspaper Revolucion gave front-page space under a banner headline today to Washington dispatches reporting a crisis atmosphere in Washington and accused the United States of preparing aggression" against Cuba.

The newspaper, the only one published here on Monday mornings, made no other comment on the massive United States naval maneuvers in the eastern Caribbean.

The headline said: "More war planes and ships Florida-wards, warlike hysterics grip U. S. capital."

Envoy's Death Explained

RIO DE JANEIRO, Oct. 22 (AP) — The Soviet Embassy said today that Ambassador Ilya Chenyshev, who died while swimming yesterday at Rio's Tijuca Beach, had suffered a heart attack.

Pacifists Refused Visa After Sailing to Soviet

Special to The New York Times

MOSCOW, Oct. 22 — Twelve pacifists of various nationalities who arrived Saturday in Leningrad aboard the ketch Everyman III have been refused admittance to the Soviet Union.

Members of the Soviet Peace Committee who met the group said the visitors had sought a visa to distribute anti-war literature at Soviet military installations. The visa was refused.

The pacifist group, headed by Dr. Earle Reynolds, an American resident of Japan, reached Leningrad from London after stops at Hamburg, Copenhagen and Stockholm.

Delegations of the Soviet Peace Committee from Moscow and Leningrad met with the pacifists Saturday evening on a ship in Leningrad harbor for an eight-hour discussion of problems of disarmament and nuclear testing.

DILLON LEAVING LATIN AID TALKS

Cuts Stay at Mexican Parley on Alliance for Progress

By PAUL P. KENNEDY

Special to The New York Times

MEXICO CITY, Oct. 22 — Secretary of the Treasury Douglas Dillon will leave for Washington tomorrow, cutting short by four days his stay at a conference on the Alliance for Progress.

Mr. Dillon, United States delegate to the conference, said he would leave after his speech to the assembled Ministers of Finance of the 20 countries participating in the Latin-American aid program.

The Treasury Secretary, along with Teodoro Moscoso, United States coordinator of the alliance program, and deLesseps S. Morrison, United States representative in the Organization of American States, left the first plenary session of the conference today shortly before President Kennedy's speech was heard here.

In meetings throughout the week the ministers will consider resolutions aimed at raising the effectiveness of the program of United States aid to Latin America, now in its second year.

There was considerable conjecture over the impact of Mr. Dillon's early departure on the conference. Few appeared to doubt that the effect would be harmful.

The new United States moves on Cuba will inevitably distract attention in the United States and in Latin America from the efforts undertaken in Mexico City to bolster the lagging alliance.

Until now the Kennedy Administration had insisted that United States concern over Cuba should not divert attention from the Alliance for Progress effort.

Impact Will Weaken

Though this view has presumably not changed, the Cuban developments inevitably will weaken what it had been hoped would be the great political impact of the Mexico City conference.

Among the key reasons cited at the meeting for the disappointingly slow progress of the alliance in its first year was that the Latin-American public had not been properly acquainted with the program's broad concepts and goals.

The conclusion that the alliance has failed so far to make a political and psychological impact on Latin America is contained in the report serving as a basis for the ministers' deliberations.

One of the objectives of the gathering here, therefore, was to evolve means for spreading the alliance gospel in the hemisphere. But the events concerning Cuba threatened to complicate this effort.

It is believed that one of Secretary Dillon's main assignments here may be to explain the new United States policies on Cuba to the Latin-American ministers present.

DR. PAULING TERMS SPEECH 'HORRIFYING'

Special to The New York Times

PASADENA, Calif., Oct. 22—Dr. Linus Pauling, the Nobel Prize winning biochemist and a leading advocate of nuclear disarmament, tonight called President Kennedy's speech "horrifying."

In a telegram to the White House, Dr. Pauling and his wife said the President's threat of military action placed "all the American people, as well as people of many other countries in grave danger of death through nuclear war."

The telegram said the President's action was "warlike" and "labels our nation recklessly militaristic." It urged the President to rescind his "orders and threats" and devote his energies and powers to achieving solutions to world problems through the United Nations.

The National Committee for a Sane Nuclear Policy commended President Kennedy last night for taking the Cuban issue to the Organization of American States and to the United Nations.

The committee's national board urged the President to ask the United Nations Security Council "to form a commission to visit Cuba immediately for confirmation of the exact military situation." It also urged him to "adhere to your previous vow not to take military action against Cuba."

Text of the 1947 Rio Pact

Special to The New York Times

WASHINGTON, Oct. 22—Following is the text of the provisions of the 1947 Rio pact on which the Administration bases its actions announced tonight against Cuba:

ARTICLE 6

If the inviolability or the integrity of the territory or the sovereignty or political independence of any American state should be affected by an aggression which is not an armed attack or by an extra-continental or intra-continental conflict, or by any other fact or situation that might endanger the peace of America, the organ of consultation shall meet immediately in order to agree on the measures which must be taken in case of aggression to assist the victim of the aggression or, in any case, the measures which should be taken for the common defense and for the maintenance of the peace and security of the continent.

For the purposes of this treaty, the measures on which the organ of consultation may agree will comprise one or more of the following: recall of chiefs of diplomatic missions; breaking of diplomatic relations; breaking of consular relations; partial or complete interruption of economic relations or of rail, sea, air, postal, telegraphic, telephonic and radiotelephonic or radiotelegraphic communications; and use of armed force.

ARTICLE 8

For the purposes of this treaty, the measures on which the organ of consultation may agree will comprise one or more of the following: recall of chiefs of diplomatic missions; breaking of diplomatic relations; breaking of consular relations; partial or complete interruption of economic relations or of rail, sea, air, postal, telegraphic, telephonic and radiotelephonic or radiotelegraphic communications; and use of armed force.

ACTION IS BASED ON '47 RIO PACT

19th-Century Legal Concept of Blockade Superseded

By E. W. KENWORTHY

Special to The New York Times

WASHINGTON, Oct. 22—The "legality" of a blockade and the form it takes are determined by what steps the imposing nation believes it can enforce.

President Kennedy did not use the word "blockade" tonight to describe the action he had ordered against ships carrying offensive weapons to Cuba.

He used the word "quarantine." Furthermore, officials here emphasized that the United States was not basing its action on nineteenth-century legal concepts supposedly governing the imposition of a blockade.

They insisted that the action was based on two articles in the Inter-American Treaty of Reciprocal Assistance of 1947, the so-called Rio Treaty.

Parley Provided

The first provides that the American states shall consult when the independence of one is threatened by an aggression that is not an armed attack, or by any situation endangering hemisphere peace.

The second provides that among the measures that can be taken to meet such a situation is armed force. In this case the armed force would be used by naval blockading ships if vessels carrying offensive weapons did not turn back.

International law recognizes two kinds of blockade, but international lawyers have never agreed on the rules that should govern them.

The oldest and most common form is the "belligerent" blockade. This is an act of war carried out by warships and planes of a belligerent power. They are assigned the task of preventing access to, or departure from, a defined part of the enemy's coast.

The blockade is directed not only against enemy ships but also against those of any neutral nation that may be carrying contraband.

The nation imposing the blockade reserves the right to declare what is contraband. Formerly contraband was limited largely to weapons of war. However, under conditions of modern war, contraband has been extended to cover virtually everything that enables the enemy to carry on his war effort.

A belligerent blockade is designed to make an enemy surrender or come to terms.

Then there is the "pacific" blockade, which dates only to the second quarter of the nineteenth century. This is not an act of war, at least not in the lexicon of international law, but an "act short of war."

Technically the lawyers regard a pacific blockade as an "intervention" or a "reprisal." By this act a state undertakes to blockade the ports of another to compel it to make amends for an alleged injustice or injury, or alter conduct that the blockading country regards as threatening its interests or security.

Not in Either Category

The action ordered by President Kennedy was not in either category.

The United States is not at war with Cuba, nor with the Soviet Union, and the President did not ask Congress to declare a state of war. Therefore the normal condition for a belligerent blockade is absent.

But the quarantine is hardly a pacific blockade. For one thing, it is understood, United States ships will fire if necessary to prevent the delivery of offensive weapons.

For another, the blockade also applies to ships of third nations. International lawyers are agreed that under a pacific blockade, the blockading state has "no right to seize the sequestrate" ships of third states trying to run the blockade.

Apart from "right," however, blockading nations have seized third-power ships when they were able to, and have later returned them.

The United States has adapted the instrument of the blockade to the situation and to changing conditions imposed by the cold war and new weapons.

International law with respect to blockades, officials insist, has always been fuzzy, and nations have interpreted it to meet their needs.

The devices by which nations have expanded the scope of blockades are numerous.

For example, during the Napoleonic wars, United States shipowners tried to circumvent a British blockade by taking cargo from the French West Indies to American ports before transhipping to France.

But the British enforced the doctrine of "continuous voyage" to stop this. British courts held that regardless of the stop at American ports, such voyages were continuous and the traffic could not be considered neutral commerce.

In the Civil War the positions were reversed. British shippers tried to run the Northern blockade of Southern ports by resort to intermediate stops. The Federal Government applied, and the Supreme Court upheld, the doctrine of continuous voyage.

Nations have also expanded the scope of blockades under the justification of "retaliation" for actions taken by an enemy.

They have achieved the same result by resorting to "sovereign rights." In World War I, for example, Britain used that doctrine to forbid British-owned coaling stations to bunker ships of neutral powers presumed to be carrying cargo to Germany or to neutral nations with inland communications to Germany.

"All the News That's Fit to Print"

The New York Times.

LATE CITY EDITION

U. S. Weather Bureau Report (Page 58) forecasts: Cloudy with scattered showers today; partly cloudy tonight and tomorrow. Temp. range: 77—62; yesterday: 81—61. Temp.-Hum. Index: 70 to 75; yesterday: 72.

VOL. CXII . No. 38,568.

NEW YORK, THURSDAY, AUGUST 29, 1963.

TEN CENTS

200,000 MARCH FOR CIVIL RIGHTS IN ORDERLY WASHINGTON RALLY; PRESIDENT SEES GAIN FOR NEGRO

ACTION ASKED NOW

10 Leaders of Protest Urge Laws to End Racial Inequity

Excerpts from talks at rally are printed on Page 21.

By E. W. KENWORTHY

Special to The New York Times

WASHINGTON, Aug. 28—More than 200,000 Americans, most of them black but many of them white, demonstrated here today for a full and speedy program of civil rights and equal job opportunities.

It was the greatest assembly for a redress of grievances that this capital has ever seen.

One hundred years and 240 days after Abraham Lincoln enjoined the emancipated slaves to "abstain from all violence" and "labor faithfully for reasonable wages," this vast throng proclaimed in march and song and through the speeches of their leaders that they were still waiting for the freedom and the jobs.

Children Clap and Sing

There was no violence to mar the demonstration. In fact, at times there was an air of hootenanny about it as groups of schoolchildren clapped hands and swung into the familiar freedom songs.

But if the crowd was good-natured, the underlying tone was one of dead seriousness. The emphasis was on "freedom" and "now." At the same time the leaders emphasized, paradoxically but realistically, that the struggle was just beginning.

On Capitol Hill, opinion was divided about the impact of the demonstration in stimulating Congressional action on civil rights legislation. But at the White House, President Kennedy declared that the cause of 20,000,000 Negroes had been advanced by the march.

The march leaders went from the shadows of the Lincoln Memorial to the White House to meet with the President for 75 minutes. Afterward, Mr. Kennedy issued a 400-word statement praising the marchers for the "deep fervor and the quiet dignity" that had characterized the demonstration.

Says Nation Can Be Proud

The nation, the President said, "can properly be proud of the demonstration that has occurred here today."

The main target of the demonstration was Congress, where committees are now considering the Administration's civil rights bill.

At the Lincoln Memorial this afternoon, some speakers, knowing little of the ways of Congress, assumed that the passage of a strengthened civil rights bill had been assured by the moving events of the day.

But from statements by Congressional leaders, after they had met with the march committee this morning, this did not seem certain at all. These statements came before the demonstration.

Senator Mike Mansfield of Montana, the Senate Democratic leader, said he could not say whether the mass protest

Continued on Page 16, Column 1

VIEW FROM THE LINCOLN MEMORIAL: The scene during the march looking toward the Washington Monument

Associated Press

United Press International Telephoto

VIEW FROM THE WASHINGTON MONUMENT: Marchers assembling around Reflecting Pool at the Lincoln Memorial

KENNEDY SIGNS BILL AVERTING A RAIL STRIKE

PRECEDENT IS SET

Arbitration Imposed by Congress—Vote in House 286-66

Text of Kennedy's statement will be found on Page 13.

By JOHN D. POMFRET

Special to The New York Times

WASHINGTON, Aug. 28 — Congress passed today a bill that prevented a national railroad strike scheduled for midnight. President Kennedy signed it immediately.

The House completed the Congressional action. It adopted by a standing vote of 286 to 66 the same joint resolution passed yesterday by the Senate. The measure provides for arbitration of the two principal issues in the railroad work rules dispute and bars a strike for 180 days.

The action was without Federal precedent. Never before in the history of peacetime labor relations has Congress imposed arbitration in a labor-management dispute.

The failure of the railroads and the five train operating unions to resolve their dispute, and the Congressional action this made necessary, is considered by many to represent a major failure for the collective bargaining system.

Many Are Reluctant

Even many Congressmen who voted for the measure, convinced that the economic consequences of a national railroad strike made action to head it off essential, did so with great reluctance. They said they feared that their action might set a precedent detrimental to collective bargaining.

An arbitration board was created by Congress to consider the two key issues. These are whether diesel locomotive firemen are necessary in freight and yard service and the size of train-service crews.

Congress ordered negotiations on the remaining issues on the theory that with the two main issues disposed of, the presumably less important matters could be settled by traditional collective bargaining.

But some well-informed Government sources do not believe the remaining issues will be

Continued on Page 13, Column 1

8 Dead in Utah Mine; Fate of 15 Unknown

Special to The New York Times

MOAB, Utah, Aug. 28 — Eight men were known dead today and 15 were trapped a half-mile underground in a potash mine rocked yesterday by a severe explosion.

Two survivors hoisted to the surface today reported that three men were dead, at least five were alive and the fate of 15 was unknown. Later, however, rescue workers deep in the mine spotted five more bodies that officials said might be the men whom the survivors first believed alive.

Rescuers were being hampered by deadly gas, extreme heat, water and mechanical failures. A communications breakdown added to their frustrations.

Donald Hanna, 27 years old, of Price and Paul McKinney,

Continued on Page 14, Column 3

U.S. SPURNS DENIAL BY DIEM ON CRISIS

Absolves the Army Again in Vietnam Pagoda Raids and Points Toward Nhu

By TAD SZULC

Special to The New York Times

WASHINGTON, Aug. 28.—The United States reaffirmed today its belief that the South Vietnamese Government had violated pledges on the Buddhist crisis and that Vietnamese military chiefs were innocent of responsibility for assaults on pagodas.

This was the reaction of the Administration to communiqués issued in Saigon in the last 24 hours by the Government of President Ngo Dinh Diem in the name of the Vietnamese Joint General Staff.

The communiqués charged that Washington's public statements on the crisis reflected "totally erroneous information."

[In Saigon, youths loyal to the secret police were reported to be warning the population against anti-Government demonstrations.].

Change Is Held Vital

With the Vietnam crisis already regarded by the United States as extremely grave, this public dispute seemed to push it toward an unpredictable showdown.

The quarrel over who smashed pagodas and who arrested leaders of the Buddhist protest movement is understood to affect deeply the Kennedy Administration's evolving policy of encouraging Vietnamese military chiefs to reach for power.

This policy, still tentative, is that a fundamental change is required in the structure of the Saigon Government, Washington sources explain. They say the goal is national harmony that would let Vietnam concentrate again on the war against the Communist guerrillas of the Vietcong.

Specifically, Washington is said to deem internal peace out of the question as long as Ngo Dinh Nhu, chief of secret police and brother of the President, retains his vast power.

Mr. Nhu is considered almost a symbol of the friction between Vietnam's Buddhists and the Roman Catholic Ngo family, which dominates the Government.

It is reported that in searching for an alternative to the regime—a course that was unthinkable here before the Buddhist crisis—the United States has almost openly been ad-

Continued on Page 3, Column 4

U.S. PRESSES U.N. TO CONDEMN SYRIA ON ISRAELI DEATHS

Stevenson Deplores Killing of Youths—Thant Assures Council on Cease-Fire

Text of Stevenson statement appears on Page 2.

By KATHLEEN TELTSCH

Special to The New York Times

UNITED NATIONS, N. Y., Aug. 28 — Adlai E. Stevenson declared today that the recent slaying of two Israeli farmers by Syrians was "wanton murder" deserving the strongest condemnation by the Security Council.

The United States delegate, followed by the British representative, gave forceful support to Israel's charges arising from the Aug. 20 ambush killing of two 19-year-old Israelis at the Almagor farm settlement.

Mr. Stevenson rejected Syria's countercharges against Israel as "not corroborated" by United Nations investigations.

The United States policy statement drew a favorable reaction from Michael S. Comay of Israel, who said it encouraged him to expect the Council to take "firm and vigorous action."

Syrian Disapproves

However, there was disapproval from Dr. Salah el-Tarazi of Syria, who criticized Mr. Stevenson as "not particularly objective." He added that Mr. Stevenson in past years had not deplored Syrian losses with equal feeling.

The Council, resuming its airing of the new crisis, was told by the Secretary General, U Thant, that United Nations inspection showed "no evidence of a military build-up on either side" of the armistice line.

Mr. Thant reported that both parties were heeding the United Nations cease-fire achieved last Friday after the ambush and subsequent exchanges of shooting greatly increased tension in the area. Bullets collected at one shooting site were on exhibit in the Council chamber.

Both Mr. Stevenson and Roger W. Jackling of Britain urged Syria and Israel to accept the suggestion by the United Nations truce chief, Lieut. Gen. Odd Bull, for avoiding new eruptions along their border, including an exchange of prisoners. Mr. Comay indicated a favorable Israeli reaction.

Evidence Questioned

Dr. Tarazi, in his turn, insisted that Israel's allegations remained unproved and that some evidence could have been faked. He noted photographs of footgear found at the ambush scene and said Syrian soldiers did not wear such shoes.

He was supported by Sidi Baba of Morocco, who accused Israel of making a "great superficial fuss" over the Almagor incident to create a climate for pressuring the Arabs into signing a peace treaty.

The United States and Britain are understood to be drafting a resolution that would condemn the killings and rebuke Syria by implication, rather than by outright condemnation, as Israel has been asking. Similar formulas have been used in the past.

Such an indirect condemnation might be blocked by a veto from the Soviet Union, however, which in the past has rejected resolutions opposed by the Arabs.

Mr. Stevenson told the 11-nation Council that General Bull's information was admit-

Continued on Page 2, Column 3

LODI KILLER SLAIN; 2D MAN GIVES UP

Ex-Convict Is Shot 7 Times in a Midtown Hotel

One of the killers of two New Jersey policemen was shot to death early yesterday by New York detectives during a violent struggle in his midtown hotel room. Sixteen hours later, the second man wanted in the slayings quietly surrendered.

The slain killer, 25-year-old Frank Falco, was asleep in his underwear when the police, using a passkey, entered his room at the Manhattan Hotel, Eighth Avenue and 44th Street. Although awakened with a revolver pressed to his throat, he fought desperately before being killed by seven bullets. He died snarling at the police and cursing them.

Thomas (Rabbi Tom) Trantino, 27, the second man, walked into the East 22d Street station house at 9:10 P.M., accompanied by a lawyer. He was neatly dressed and clean-shaven.

The men, both ex-convicts, had been the object of a grim police hunt since Detective Sgt. Peter Voto and Gary Tedesco, a police appointee, were gunned down early Monday morning in the Angel Lounge on Route 46 in Lodi, N. J. Mr. Tedesco was to have officially joined the Lodi force today.

A tip led the New York detectives to the hotel, where Falco had checked in at 8 P.M. Tuesday under the name of J. Rello of Newport, R. I.

Lieut. Thomas Quinn, a 53-year-old police veteran with 16 citations for bravery, entered Falco's 23d-floor room first, his

Continued on Page 35, Column 2

NEWS INDEX

2 Girls Murdered In E. 88th St. Flat

Two young women, one the daughter of a writer and the other of a prominent surgeon, were bound and stabbed to death yesterday in their apartment at 57 East 88th Street.

The victims, Janice Wylie, 21 years old, and Emily Hoffert, 23, had been slashed repeatedly. Three bloodstained kitchen knives were found in the five-room apartment, which the girls shared with another young woman. The suite had been ransacked.

The bodies were found on a bedroom floor by Janice's father, the writer Max Wylie, and by Patricia Tolles, 23, the third roommate.

Mr. Wylie, who lives nearby, at 55 East 86th Street, is a

Continued on Page 35, Column 5

CONGRESS CORDIAL BUT NOT SWAYED

Leaders of March Pay Calls of Courtesy at Capitol

By WARREN WEAVER Jr.

Special to The New York Times

WASHINGTON, Aug. 28—The civil rights demonstration that swept more than 200,000 people through the capital today appeared to have left much of Congress untouched — physically, emotionally and politically.

In the morning, 13 demonstration leaders drove quietly up Capitol Hill and paid courtesy calls on Congressional leaders of both parties. The atmosphere was cordial, but there were no conversions.

In the afternoon, about 75 Senators and Representatives went from Capitol Hill to the Lincoln Memorial to be introduced, sit on the steps and listen to Gospel singing and speeches on civil rights.

A few demonstrators violated marching orders and went up to the Capitol to visit legislators in their offices. A few Senators welcomed trainloads and busfuls of constituents in person.

Otherwise, there was really very little contact between the marchers and the group they were working hardest to impress. And there was very little evidence that the demonstration, however large and fervent, would play a material role in advancing civil rights legislation.

Senator Hubert H. Humphrey, one of the most enthusiastic of

Continued on Page 17, Column 1

'I Have a Dream . . .'

Peroration by Dr. King Sums Up A Day the Capital Will Remember

By JAMES RESTON

Special to The New York Times

WASHINGTON, Aug. 28—Abraham Lincoln, who presided in his stone temple today above the children of the slaves he emancipated, may have used just the right words to sum up the general reaction to the Negro's massive march on Washington. "I think," he wrote to Gov. Andrew G. Curtin of Pennsylvania in 1861, "the necessity of being ready increases. Look to it." Washington may not have changed a vote today, but it is a little more conscious tonight of the necessity of being ready for freedom. It may not "look to it" at once, since it is looking to so many things, but it will be a long time before it forgets the melodious and melancholy voice of the Rev. Dr. Martin Luther King Jr. crying out his dreams to the multitude.

News Analysis

It was Dr. King who, near the end of the day, touched the vast audience. Until then the pilgrimage was merely a great spectacle. Only those marchers from the embattled towns in the Old Confederacy had anything like the old crusading zeal. For many the day seemed an adventure, a long outing in the late summer sun—part liberation from home, part Sunday School picnic, part political convention, and part fish-fry.

But Dr. King brought them alive in the late afternoon with a peroration that was an anguished echo from all the old American reformers. Roger Williams calling for religious liberty, Sam Adams calling for political liberty, old man Thoreau denouncing coercion, William Lloyd Garrison demanding emancipation, and Eugene V. Debs crying for economic equality—Dr. King echoed them all.

"I have a dream," he cried again and again. And each time the dream was a promise out of our ancient articles of faith: phrases from the Constitution, lines from the great anthem of the nation, guarantees from the Bill of Rights, all ending with a vision that they might one day all come true.

Find Journey Worthwhile

Dr. King touched all the themes of the day, only better than anybody else. He was full of the symbolism of Lincoln and Gandhi, and the cadences of the Bible. He was both militant and sad, and he sent the crowd away feeling that the long journey had been worthwhile.

This demonstration impressed political Washington because it combined a number of things no politician can ignore. It had the force of numbers. It had the melodies of both the church and the theater. And it was able to invoke the principles of the founding fathers to rebuke the inequalities and hypocrisies of modern American life.

There was a paradox in the day's performance. The Ne-

Continued on Page 17, Column 6

PRESIDENT MEETS MARCH LEADERS

Says Bipartisan Support Is Needed for Rights Bill

Rights statement and Labor Day proclamation, Page 16.

By TOM WICKER

Special to The New York Times

WASHINGTON, Aug. 28—President Kennedy served tea and sympathy and blunt political advice late today to the tired but proud leaders of the march on Washington.

In an hour-long conference, the President told the 10 leaders that "very strong bipartisan support" would be needed to get civil rights legislation enacted this year.

In a statement issued immediately after the conference, Mr. Kennedy said that "the cause of 20,000,000 Negroes has been advanced" by the orderly demonstration, "conducted so appropriately before the nation's shrine to the Great Emancipator."

Earlier, in a Labor Day statement released in advance of the holiday, the President called on the nation to speed up its efforts to achieve equal rights for all in jobs, education and voting.

The main discussion between the march leaders and the President concerned prospects for civil rights legislation, the leaders said after the White House meeting. They talked with Mr. Kennedy around the long table in the Cabinet Room, where the leaders were served tea, coffee,

Continued on Page 16, Column 7

Capital Is Occupied By a Gentle Army

By RUSSELL BAKER

Special to The New York Times

WASHINGTON, Aug. 28 — No one could remember an invading army quite as gentle as the 200,000 civil rights marchers who occupied Washington today.

For the most part, they came silently during the night and early morning, occupied the great shaded boulevards along the Mall, and spread through the parklands between the Washington Monument and the Potomac.

But instead of the emotional horde of angry militants that many had feared, what Washington saw was a vast army of quiet, middle-class Americans

Continued on Page 17, Column 7

200,000 Join Orderly March in Capital for Civil Rights; Kennedy Sees Negro Gain

Associated Press

LEADERS MEET WITH KENNEDY: From left Whitney M. Young Jr., of National Urban League; the Rev. Dr. Martin Luther King Jr., Southern Christian Leadership Conference; John Lewis, partly hidden, Student Nonviolent Coordinating Committee; Rabbi Joachim Prinz, American Jewish Congress; the Rev. Dr. Eugene Carson Blake, United Presbyterian Church in U.S.A.; A. Philip Randolph, Negro American Labor Council; the President; Walter P. Reuther, the United Automobile Workers; Vice President Johnson, almost hidden, and Roy Wilkins, N.A.A.C.P. Mr. Kennedy and Mr. Johnson met with leaders of the civil rights march at the White House after the ceremonies at the Lincoln Memorial.

LEADERS OF RALLY URGE ACTION 'NOW'

Ask Laws Against Inequity —Picnic Air Prevails as Crowds Clap and Sing

Continued From Page 1, Col. 8

would speed the legislation, which faces a filibuster by Southerners.

Senator Everett McKinley Dirksen of Illinois, the Republican leader, said he thought the demonstration would be neither an advantage nor a disadvantage to the prospects for the civil rights bill.

The human tide that swept over the Mall between the shrines of Washington and Lincoln fell back faster than it came on. As soon as the ceremony broke up this afternoon, the exodus began. With astounding speed, the last buses and trains cleared the city by mid-evening.

At 9 P.M. the city was as calm as the waters of the Reflecting Pool between the two memorials.

At the Lincoln Memorial early in the afternoon, in the midst of a songfest before the addresses, Josephine Baker, the singer, who had flown from her home in Paris, said to the thousands stretching down both sides of the Reflecting Pool:

"You are on the eve of a complete victory. You can't go wrong. The world is behind you."

Miss Baker said, as if she saw a dream coming true before her eyes, that "this is the happiest day of my life."

But of all the 10 leaders of the march on Washington who followed her, only the Rev. Dr. Martin Luther King Jr., president of the Southern Christian Leadership Conference, saw that dream so hopefully.

The other leaders, except for the three clergymen among the 10, concentrated on the struggle ahead and spoke in tough, even harsh, language.

But paradoxically it was Dr. King—who had suffered perhaps most of all—who ignited the crowd with words that might have been written by the sad, brooding man enshrined within.

As he arose, a great roar welled up from the crowd. When he started to speak, a hush fell.

"Even though we face the difficulties of today and tomorrow, I still have a dream," he said.

"It is a dream chiefly rooted in the American dream," he went on.

"I have a dream that one day this nation will rise up and live out the true meaning of its creed: 'We hold these truths to be self-evident, that all men are created equal.'

Dream of Brotherhood

"I have a dream . . ." The vast throng listening intently to him roared.

". . . that one day on the red hills of Georgia, the sons of former slaves and the sons of former slave-owners will be able to sit together at the table of brotherhood.

"I have a dream . . ." The crowd roared.

". . . that one day even the State of Mississippi, a state sweltering with the heat of injustice, sweltering with the heat of oppression, will be transformed into an oas s of freedom and justice.

"I have a dream . . ." The crowd roared.

". . . that my four little children will one day live in a nation where they will not be judged by the color of their skin but by the content of their character.

"I have a dream . . ." The crowd roared.

". . . that one day every valley shall be exalted, every hill and mountain shall be made low, the rough places will be made plain, and the crooked places will be made straight, and the glory of the Lord shall be revealed and all flesh shall see it together."

As Dr. King concluded with a quotation from a Negro hymn —"Free at last, free at last, thank God almighty"—the crowd, recognizing that he was finishing, roared once again and waved their signs and pennants.

But the civil rights leaders, who knew the strength of the forces arrayed against them from past battles, knew also that a hard struggle lay ahead. The tone of their speeches was frequently militant.

Roy Wilkins, executive secretary of the National Association for the Advancement of Colored People, made plain that he and his colleagues thought the President's civil rights bill did not go nearly far enough. He said:

"The President's proposals represent so moderate an approach that if any one is weakened or eliminated, the remainder will be little more than sugar water. Indeed, the package needs strengthening."

Harshest of all the speakers was John Lewis, chairman of the Student Nonviolent Coordinating Committee.

"My friends," he said, "let us not forget that we are involved in a serious social revolution. But by and large American politics is dominated by politicians who build their career on immoral compromising and ally themselves with open forums of political, economic and social exploitation."

He concluded:

"They're talking about slowdown and stop. We will not stop.

"If we do not get meaningful legislation out of this Congress, the time will come when we will not confine our marching to Washington. We will march through the South, through the streets of Jackson, through the streets of Danville, through the streets of Cambridge, through the streets of Birmingham.

"But we will march with the spirit of love and the spirit of dignity that we have shown here today."

In the original text of the speech, distributed last night, Mr. Lewis had said:

"We will not wait for the President, the Justice Department, nor the Congress, but we will take matters into our own hands and create a source of power, outside of any national structure, that could and would assure us a victory."

He also said in the original text that "we will march through the South, through the heart of Dixie, the way Sherman did."

It was understood that at least the last of these statements was changed as the result of a protest by the Most Rev. Patrick J. O'Boyle, Roman Catholic Archbishop of Washington, who refused to give the invocation if the offending words were spoken by Mr. Lewis.

The great day really began the night before. As a half moon rose over the lagoon by the Jefferson Memorial and the tall, lighted shaft of the Washington Monument gleamed in the reflecting pool, a file of Negroes from out of town began climbing the steps of the Lincoln Memorial.

There, while the carpenters nailed the last planks on the television platforms for the next day and the TV technicians called through the loudspeakers, "Final audio, one, two, three, four," a middle-aged Negro couple, the man's arm around the shoulders of his plump wife, stood and read with their lips:

"If we shall suppose that American slavery is one of the offenses which in the providence of God must needs come but which having continued through His appointed time, He now wills to remove. . . ."

The day dawned clear and cool. At 7 A. M. the town had a Sunday appearance, except for the shuttle buses drawn up in front of Union Station, waiting.

By 10 A. M. there were 40,000 on the slopes around the Washington Monument. An hour later the police estimated the crowd at 90,000. And still they poured in.

Because some things went wrong at the monument, everything was right. Most of the stage and screen celebrities from New York and Hollywood who were scheduled to begin entertaining the crowd at 10 did not arrive at the airport until 11:15.

As a result the whole affair at the monument grounds began to take on the spontaneity of a church picnic. Even before the entertainment was to begin, groups of high school students were singing with wonderful improvisations and hand-clapping all over the monument slope.

Civil rights demonstrators who had been released from jail in Danville, Va., were singing:

Move on, move on,
Till all the world is free.

And members of Local 144 of the Hotel and Allied Service Employes Union from New York City, an integrated local since 1950, were stomping:

Oh, freedom, we shall not,
we shall not be moved,
Just like a tree that's
planted by the water.

Then the pros took over, starting with the folk singers. The crowd joined in with them.

Joan Baez started things rolling with "the song"—"We Shall Overcome."

Oh deep in my heart I do
believe
We shall overcome some
day.

And Peter, Paul and Mary sang "How many times must a man look up before he can see the sky."

And Odetta's great, full-throated voice carried almost to Capitol Hill: "If they ask you who you are, tell them you're a child of God."

Jackie Robinson told the crowd that "we cannot be turned back," and Norman Thomas, the venerable Socialist, said: "I'm glad I lived long enough to see this day."

The march to the Lincoln Memorial was supposed to start at 11:30, behind the leaders. But at 11:20 it set off spontaneously down Constitution Avenue behind the Kenilworth Knights, a local drum and bugle corps dazzling in yellow silk blazers, green trousers and green berets.

Apparently forgotten was the intention to make the march to the Lincoln Memorial a solemn tribute to Medgar W. Evers, N.A.A.C.P. official murdered in Jackson, Miss., last June 12, and others who had died for the cause of civil rights.

The leaders were lost, and they never did get to the head of the parade.

The leaders included also Walter P. Reuther, head of the United Automobile Workers; A. Philip Randolph, head of the American Negro Labor Council; the Rev. Dr. Eugene Carson Blake, vice chairman of the Commission on Religion and Race of the National Council of Churches; Mathew Ahmann, executive director of the National Catholic Conference for Interracial Justice; Rabbi Joachim Prinz, president of the American Jewish Congress; Whitney M. Young Jr., executive director of the National Urban League, and James Farmer, president of the Congress of Racial Equality.

All spoke at the memorial except Mr. Farmer, who is in jail in Louisiana following his arrest as a result of a civil rights demonstration. His speech was read by Floyd B. McKissick, CORE national chairman.

At the close of the ceremonies at the Lincoln Memorial, Bayard Rustin, the organizer of the march, asked Mr. Randolph, who conceived it, to lead the vast throng in a pledge.

Repeating after Mr. Randolph, the marchers pledged "complete personal commitment to the struggle for jobs and freedom for Americans" and "to carry the message of the march to my friends and neighbors back home and arouse them to an equal commitment and an equal effort."

Texts of the President's Statements on Rights and on Labor Day

Special to The New York Times

WASHINGTON, Aug. 28 — Following are the texts of President Kennedy's statement on the civil rights demonstration and his Labor Day statement:

Rights Statement

We have witnessed today in Washington tens of thousands of Americans —both Negro and white — exercising their right to assemble peaceably and direct the widest possible attention to a great national issue. Efforts to secure equal treatment and equal opportunity for all without regard to race, color, creed or nationality are neither novel nor difficult to understand. What is different today is the intensified and widespread public awareness of the need to move forward in achieving these objectives — objectives which are older than this nation.

Although this summer has seen remarkable progress in translating civil rights from principles into practices, we have a very long way yet to travel. One cannot help but be impressed with the deep fervor and the quiet dignity that characterizes the thousands who have gathered in the nation's capital from across the country to demonstrate their faith and confidence in our democratic form of government. History has seen many demonstrations— of widely varying character and for a whole host of reasons. As our thoughts travel to other demonstrations that have occurred in different parts of the world, this nation can properly be proud of the demonstration that has occurred here today. The leaders of the organizations sponsoring the march and all who have participated in it deserve our appreciation for the detailed preparations that made it possible and for the orderly manner in which it has been conducted.

The executive branch of the Federal Government will continue its efforts to obtain increased employment and to eliminate discrimination in employment practices, two of the prime goals of the march. In addition, our efforts to secure enactment of the legislative proposals made to the Congress will be maintained, including not only the civil rights bill, but also proposals to broaden and strengthen the manpower development and training program, the youth employment bill, amendments to the vocational education program, the establishment of a work-study program for high-school-age youth, strengthening of the adult basic education provisions in the Administration's education program and the amendments proposed to the public welfare work-relief and training program. This nation can afford to achieve the goals of a full employment policy—it cannot afford to permit the potential skills and educational capacity of its citizens to be unrealized.

The cause of 20,000,000 Negroes has been advanced by the program conducted so appropriately before the nation's shrine to the Great Emancipator, but even more significant is the contribution to all mankind.

Labor Day Statement

On this Labor Day of 1963 —the third within the period of my Administration—this nation once again salutes the role of labor in our national life.

The history of the United States is in vital respect the history of labor. Free men and women, working for a better life for themselves and their children, settled a continent, built a society and created and diffused an abundance hitherto unknown to history. Free men and women, affirming their dignity as individuals and asserting their rights as human beings, developed a philosophy of democratic liberty which holds out hope for oppressed peoples across the world. In commemorating the role of labor, we honor the most essential traditions in American life.

We honor, too, the contributions of labor to the strength and safety of our nation. America's capacity for leadership in the world depends on the character of our society at home; and, in a turbulent and uncertain world, our leadership would falter unless our domestic society is robust and progressive. The labor movement in the United States has made an indispensable contribution both to the vigor of our democracy and to the advancement of the ideals of freedom around the earth.

We can take satisfaction on this Labor Day in the health and energy of our national society. The events of this year have shown a quickening of democratic spirit and vitality among our people. We can take satisfaction, too, in the continued steady gain in living standards. The nation's income, output and employment have reached new heights. More than 70,000,000 men and women are working in our factories, on our farms and in our shops and services. The average factory wage is at an all-time high of more than $100 a week. Prices have remained relatively stable, so the larger pay check means a real increase in purchasing power for the average American family.

Bids Nation Move Fast

Yet our achievements, notable as they are, must not distract us from the things we have yet to achieve. If satisfaction with the status quo had been the American way, we would still be 13 small colonies straggling along the Atlantic Coast. I urge all Americans, on this Labor Day, to consider what we can do as individuals and as a nation to move speedily ahead on four major fronts.

First, we must accelerate our effort against unemployment and for the expansion of jobs and opportunity. In spite of our prevailing prosperity, 4,250,000 of our fellow citizens cannot find useful employment. While automation increases productivity and output, it also renders jobs and skills obsolete. While new industries emerge, old industries decline. While most of the country shows a high degree of economic activity, some areas have failed to share in the general recovery. And, while our economy continues to grow, it must grow even faster in the future if it is to provide for the 2,500,000 new persons entering the labor market every year. To combat unemployment, we need to pass the tax bill recently approved by the House Ways and Means Committee and thereby provide general stimulus to the economy. This bill will benefit every family, every business and every area of our country. We need, in addition, to continue and enlarge the measures designed to help the communities, industries and individuals bypassed by prosperity to help themselves and to increase their contributions to our society.

Second, we must accelerate our effort to strengthen our educational system. As our economy becomes increasingly complex, education becomes increasingly the key to employment. The fewer grades our boys and girls complete, the greater the probability that they will not find jobs. Inadequate schooling, inadequate training, inadequate skills — these are major obstacles to employment and a fruitful life. Dropping out of school today may well destroy a person's entire future. I hope that the Congress will enact legislation to strengthen the nation's educational system; and I ask all parents, for the sake of the future, their children's and the nation's, to have their children return to school this fall.

Calls for Opportunities

Third, we must accelerate our effort to offer constructive opportunities to our young people. Our youth are our national future. Today one out of every four persons in the labor force between 16 and 21 is out of school and out of work. The persistence of unemployment and of juvenile delinquency is a sign of our society's failure to enlist the full energy and talent of our young men and women in positive tasks and purposes. The Youth Conservation Corps and the Home Town Youth Corps seem to me especially promising ways of improving both the skills of our young people and their contribution to the general welfare.

Fourth, we must accelerate our effort to achieve equal rights for all our citizens— in employment, in education, in voting and in all sectors or our national activity. This year, I believe, will go down as one of the turning points in the history of American labor. Foremost among the rights of labor is the right to equality of opportunity; and these recent months, 100 years after the Emancipation Proclamation, have seen the decisive recognition by the major part of our society that all our citizens are entitled to full membership in the national community. The gains of 1963 will never be reversed. They lay a solid foundation for the progress we must continue to make in the months and years to come. We can take satisfaction on this Labor Day that 1963 marks a long step forward toward assuring all Americans the opportunities for life, liberty and the pursuit of happiness pledged by our forefathers in the Declaration of Independence.

As we make progress in these four areas, we make progress toward improving both the strength of our national society and the quality of our national life. We demonstrate to the world that a free society provides men and women the best chance for decent and fulfilled lives. Most of all, we demonstrate to ourselves that our society is vital, that our purpose is steadfast, and that our determination to fulfill the promise of American life for all Americans is unconquerable. Let this be our solemn resolve on Labor Day, 1963.

President Meets March Chiefs; Urges Bipartisan Aid on Rights

Continued From Page 1, Col. 7

canapes and sandwiches by Filipino mess boys.

Several of the march leaders had not eaten during a long, exhausting day.

The leaders, a mixed Negro and white group for whom A. Philip Randolph served as spokesman, made it plain in a news conference after their meeting with the President that they were exhilarated and encouraged by the day's events.

Mr. Randolph, president of the Brotherhood of Sleeping Car Porters, called the march "one of the biggest, most creative and constructive demonstrations ever held in the history of our nation" and one of which "every American could be proud."

President Kennedy concurred. "One cannot help but be impressed," he said, "with the deep fervor and the quiet dignity that characterizes the thousands who have gathered in the nation's capital from across the country to demonstrate their faith and confidence in our democratic form of Government."

The leaders of the march, most of whom spoke briefly at the White House news conference, emphasized their intention to seek strong bipartisan support for the civil rights legislation now pending in Congress.

Voices 'Grim Determination'

The Rev. Dr. Martin Luther King Jr., president of the Southern Christian Leadership Conference, said that the President had "made it very clear that we would need very strong bipartisan support to get civil rights legislation this year."

He urged those in Congress who "are still on the fence" to come down on the side of civil rights. Those who had made the march on Washington, he said, "will go back to their communities and work with bold and grim determination" for Congressional support.

In effect, he said, the march had "subpoenaed the conscience of the nation to appear before the judgment seat of morality."

Mr. Kennedy apparently made a strong impression on the march leaders with his comments about the need for bipartisan support. All pledged themselves to an effort to arouse such support.

Mr. Randolph said the group was "looking forward" to bipartisan support, not only for pending legislation but also for fair employment practices legislation and for "Part three."

"Part Three" refers to a section deleted from a civil rights bill passed in 1957. It would permit the Federal Government to institute legal action on behalf of aggrieved citizens in a variety of civil rights fields.

"It is our belief that it is possible to get civil rights legislation enacted in this Congress," Mr. Randolph said. But he acknowledged the task would not be easy.

Will Increase Efforts

Roy Wilkins, executive secretary of the National Association for the Advancement of Colored People, said Mr. Kennedy had told the group "we could help a little more than we have been" in getting civil rights legislation enacted. He said that efforts would be stepped up.

"We invite Democrats and Republicans to come together in this great civil rights crisis," Mr. Wilkins said. He added that, in conferences today with leaders of both parties, the march leaders had received assurances of support.

Whitney M. Young Jr., executive director of the National Urban League, said the demonstration should have dispelled the notion that Negroes appealed to one party or the other for help. "Our clear aim is bipartisanship," he said.

In future, the only distinction will be between "those who are calloused and those who care," he said.

Walter P. Reuther, president of the United Automobile Workers, noted the task lying beyond legislation—"to take the new tools" a civil rights bill would provide and to find ways to apply them to the "day-to-day job of fighting discrimination."

Thus, Mr. Reuther said, the true significance of the march on Washington was that it "laid the groundwork for building a functioning, broad coalition of conscience."

The Rev. Eugene Carson Blake of the National Council of Churches said the purpose of participating church groups had been achieved in that they "did produce an integrated march." He said he hoped there need be no more all-Negro protest marches or demonstrations.

Mr. Randolph said the march also demonstrated "unity among leadership of the Negroes." But at the White House news conference there was what appeared to be some subtle jockeying for position among them.

Mr. Blake referred, for instance, to Dr. King as "clearly the religious leader of this demonstration."

Randolph Lauds Wilkins

Almost immediately, Mr. Randolph introduced Mr. Wilkins as "the acknowledged leader of the civil rights movement in America."

When it came time to introduce Dr. King, Mr. Randolph termed him "the moral leader of the nation."

Rabbi Joachim Prinz, chairman of the American Jewish Congress, said, however, that "the hero of this day was the people" who came from all over the nation for the demonstration.

Other march leaders meeting with the President were John Lewis of the Student Nonviolent Coordinating Committee; Mathew Ahmann of the National Catholic Conference for Interracial Justice, and Floyd B. McKissick of the Congress of Racial Equality, who was replacing James Farmer of that organization. Mr. Farmer is in jail in Plaquemine, La., a recent scene of civil rights demonstrations.

Greeting these leaders with Mr. Kennedy were Vice President Johnson, Secretary of Labor W. Willard Wirtz, and Burke Marshall, head of the Civil Rights Division of the Justice Department.

The meeting was cordial, even jovial in tone. Mr. Kennedy told Dr. King that he had heard and seen several of the day's speeches on television.

Had he heard Mr. Reuther? Mr. King inquired.

"I didn't hear Walter," the President said, "but I've heard Walter before."

"I had a couple of new punchlines today," Mr. Reuther, a renowned orator, said.

As tens of thousands gathered on the Washington Monument grounds this morning, the sound of their songs drifted across the South Grounds of the White House to the Rose Garden outside the President's office.

Tourist traffic through the central corridor and the public rooms of the White House was light. Usually 9,000 to 10,000 tourists troop through daily; only 1,612 went in the east gate today.

There was no official White House delegation in the march or at the Lincoln Memorial, but a number of staff members walked down to Constitution Avenue, two blocks away, to see the marchers go past. Television sets were turned on and the President watched part of the ceremonies.

There was no picketing or demonstrating in front of the White House, where the broad sidewalk of Pennsylvania Avenue almost daily attracts someone with a placard.

Precautions Are Taken

Discreet security precautions had been taken, however, and an unusual number of uniformed White House guards were in evidence around the perimeter of the grounds.

Even before the demonstration began, Mr. Kennedy recognized it in an unusually early Labor Day message.

"We must accelerate our effort to achieve equal rights for all our citizens—in employment, in education, in voting and in all sectors of our national activity," the statement said. It went on:

"This year, I believe, will go down as one of the turning points in the history of American labor. Foremost among the rights of labor is the right to equality of opportunity and these recent months, 100 years after the Emancipation Proclamation, have seen the decisive recognition by the major part of our society that all our citizens are entitled to full membership in the national community.

"The gains of 1963 will never be reversed."

Marcher Falls Into Pool

WASHINGTON, Aug. 28 (AP)—Mrs. Kathleen Johnson of Newark fell into the reflecting pool between the Washington Monument and the Lincoln Memorial while taking pictures of the civil rights rally. She was helped from the water by other demonstrators. The maximum depth of the pool is two and one-half feet.

Tour of the White House Has Only a Few Patrons

WASHINGTON, Aug. 28— (UPI)—The civil rights march from the Washington Monument to the Lincoln Memorial left the White House tour, only a few blocks away, begging for tourists.

White House officials said the tour was so lightly patronized that plans to extend the hours today were dropped.

Only 1,612 people took the public tour today, compared with up to 10,000 on a normal day, the White House said.

Many of those who did take the tour wore buttons identifying themselves as marchers, the White House said, and they went directly to the monument grounds after the tour.

Rights Marchers' Pledge

WASHINGTON, Aug. 28 (AP)—Civil rights marchers checking in for today's demonstration were given this pledge to sign at the headquarters tent:

Standing before the Lincoln Memorial on the 28th of August, in the centennial year of emancipation, I affirm my complete personal commitment for the struggle for jobs and freedom for all Americans.

To fulfill that commitment, I pledge that I will not relax until victory is won.

I pledge that I will join and support all actions undertaken in good faith in accord with time-honored democratic traditions of nonviolent protest, or peaceful assembly and petition, and of redress through the courts and the legislative process.

I pledge to carry the message of the March to my friends and neighbors back home and to arouse them to an equal commitment and an equal effort. I will march and I will write letters. I will demonstrate and I will vote. I will work and make sure that my voice and those of my brothers ring clear and determined from every corner of our land.

I will pledge my heart and my mind and my body, unequivocally and without regard to personal sacrifice, to the achievement of social peace through social justice.

Goals of Rights March

Special to The New York Times

WASHINGTON, Aug. 28—Following are the major goals of today's March on Washington for Jobs and Freedom:

¶A comprehensive civil rights bill from the present Congress, including provisions guaranteeing access to public accommodations, adequate and integrated education, protection of the right to vote, better housing, and authority for the Attorney General to seek injunctive relief when individuals' constitutional rights are violated.

¶Withholding of Federal funds from all programs in which discrimination exists.

¶Desegregation of all public schools in 1963.

¶A reduction in Congressional seats in states where citizens are disenfranchised.

¶A stronger Executive order prohibiting discrimination in all housing programs supported by Federal funds.

¶A massive Federal program to train and place unemployed workers.

¶An increase in the minimum wage to $2 an hour. The Federal minimum, covering workers in interstate industry, is now $1.15 an hour and will rise to $1.25 next Tuesday.

¶Extension of the Fair Labor Standards Act to include exempted fields of employment.

¶A Federal Fair Employment Practices Act barring discrimination in all employment.

Rights Chiefs See Leaders at Capitol, but Demonstration Fails to Sway Congress

75 LEGISLATORS AT MARCH SCENE

McCormack Says Rally May Bring Support—Others Are Doubtful of Effect

Continued From Page 1, Col. 4

the 15 or more Senators who participated, summed it up as he stood on the steps of the memorial and looked down the jammed Mall.

"All this probably hasn't changed any votes on the civil rights bill," the Minnesota Democrat said, "but it's a good thing for Washington and the nation and the world."

Demonstration leaders had said they would announce the names of all members of Congress who attended the rally, or of all those who did not. But this plan to spotlight their friends and enemies was abandoned.

Apparently because Congressional attendance was relatively sparse, the Senators and Representatives were introduced as a group, with a claimed membership of 150 that was clearly generous.

As the legislators rose on the Memorial steps and waved at the demonstrators, those in the front began to chant "pass the bill." The rhythmic cry rolled back, rank by rank, through the massed thousands.

House Debates Rail Bill

House members had a valid excuse to be elsewhere. They were debating the railroad strike bill while the rally was under way. However, about 60 of them left the floor for an hour to take buses to the rally. The Senate had recessed at 1:15 P.M., 45 minutes before the formal program opened.

The morning visit to Capitol Hill by the demonstration leaders did not produce evidence that the politicians were prepared to be impressed.

The leaders of the Senate predicted that the demonstration would neither improve nor diminish the prospects for Congressional approval of civil rights legislation this year.

After a half-hour morning meeting with the leaders of the march, Senator Mike Mansfield of Montana, the Democratic leader, was asked if he thought the mass protest would help speed Senate action on civil rights.

Dirksen Doubts Effect

"I couldn't say," he replied. "These things are either right or wrong. That's the way you have to face up to these problems, whatever else is involved."

An hour later, after he saw the same group in his office, Senator Everett McKinley Dirksen of Illinois, the Republican leader, said he did not believe the demonstration would prove to be an advantage or disadvantage to the Administration's civil rights proposals.

"I go on feeling," Senator Dirksen declared, "that the members of the national legislature have a responsibility to render an independent judgment on these matters, to get all the facts and, mindful always of their constitutional responsibilities, proceed from that broad base."

Speaker John W. McCormack was the only Congressional leader to voice the belief that the demonstration might stimulate more activity and support in Congress. The Massachusetts Democrat said "an orderly march would be helpful" in getting the Administration bill through the House.

Privately, the Congressional leaders agreed that a disorderly demonstration, culminating in violence would have cost civil rights legislation considerable support among uncommitted members of both parties.

A Courteous Atmosphere

Throughout the two hours that the march leaders spent on Capitol Hill this morning, the atmosphere was one of courtesy and restraint, by both the civil rights advocates and the Congressmen.

The demonstration leaders were obviously anxious to avoid any impression that they were attempting to put pressure on the Congressional leaders to adopt their cause. They did not discuss the demonstration itself, the prospect of a Senate filibuster or any ensuing attempt to close off debate.

"There was no pressure, there was no insistence," Mr. Dirksen reported afterward. "It was rather that they were expressing the hope that we could see the picture as they see the picture."

By and large, the Congressional leaders told the march leaders just what they had been saying publicly about civil rights for some time.

Dirksen Reaffirms Stand

Senator Mansfield said he hoped to receive from the House "early in October" an omnibus civil rights bill, including a section barring discrimination in places of public accommodation.

Senator Dirksen reaffirmed his opposition to the public accommodations proposal but promised to support all other provisions in the Administration bill.

The march leaders paid three separate calls on Capitol Hill. First, they saw Mr. Mansfield in the Old Senate Office Building. Then they joined Senator Dirksen and Representative Charles A. Halleck of Indiana, the House Republican leader, in Mr. Dirksen's Capitol office. Finally they spent nearly an hour with Speaker McCormack and Representative Carl Albert of Oklahoma, the House Democratic leader, in the Speaker's office.

A. Philip Randolph, national chairman of the march, summed up the group's reaction to its Capitol visit as "very encouraging."

The civil rights leaders were particularly encouraged by Speaker McCormack's prediction that the House would approve a fair employment practices commission and broad civil rights injunctive power for the Attorney General if these provisions were made part of the Administration's legislative package.

Both these proposals represent goals of the march demonstrators, but the President's reluctance to include them in his bill has made their adoption doubtful.

Besides Mr. Randolph, the demonstration leaders making the Congressional calls were Matthew Ahmann, executive director of the National Catholic Conference for Interracial Justice; Arnold Aronson, secretary of the Leadership Conference on Civil Rights; the Rev. Eugene Carson Blake, vice chairman of National Council of Churches' Commission on Race Relations; John Lewis of the Student Nonviolent Coordinating Committee.

Also, Clarence Mitchell, director of the Washington Bureau of the National Association for the Advancement of Colored People; Rabbi Joachim Prinz, chairman of the American Jewish Congress; Joseph Rauh, vice president for civil rights of Americans for Democratic Action; Walter P. Reuther, president of the United Automobile Workers; Roy Wilkens, executive secretary of the N.A.A.C.P. and Whitney M. Young, Jr., executive director of the National Urban League.

Also, the Rev. Dr. Martin Luther King Jr., president of Southern Christian Leadership Conference, and Floyd B. McKissick, national chairman of the Congress of Racial Equality.

Legislation Is Delayed

It developed at midday that the lagging legislative schedule on civil rights was due for a further delay. Representative Emanuel Celler, chairman of the House Judiciary Committee, reported that the subcommittee considering the Administration bill would not meet again until Sept. 9.

The reason, the Brooklyn Democrat said, was that the House was taking a Labor Day recess until then. The comparable Senate recess began this afternoon and will end next Tuesday morning.

Despite the lack of contact between Congress and the demonstration, many of those who participated were hopeful about the march's long-range effects. These were some of the comments:

Senator Kenneth B. Keating, Republican of New York: "It was an amazing demonstration of the feeling of Negroes and non-Negroes for civil rights legislation. It may have its effect on the waverers."

Javits Applauds Discipline

Senator Jacob K. Javits, Republican of New York: "An unforgettable demonstration, dignified, extraordinarily disciplined and intensely patriotic. It may or may not change the votes of any member of Congress, but it will certainly establish a mood for the coming civil rights Congressional battles."

Senator Humphrey: "The American people will speak to their representatives in Congress about what they saw and heard."

Senator Harrison A. Williams Jr., Democrat of New Jrsey: "A deeply moving experience that combined the happiness and goodwill of a picnic with the solemnity of a church service."

Marcher Urges Ban on Bomb

WASHINGTON, Aug. 28 (AP)—Marchers in today's civil rights demonstration carried placards demanding equality for Negroes and home rule for Washington. One showed up at the Lincoln Memorial with a sign supporting another cause. It read: "Ban the Bomb."

Marcher From Alabama

Hazel Mangle Rivers

Special to The New York Times

WASHINGTON, Aug. 28—Hazel Mangle Rivers has not seen much of this world, and until today most of life's excitements were denied to her. But today Mrs. Rivers marched on Washington. She said that her life would never be the same.

Woman in the News

Mrs. Rivers was born some years ago—she declines to tell just how many—to George and Savannah Mangle, farmers near Athens, Ga. As a Negro, Hazel Mangle learned early in life not to expect too much from the world.

She went to Birmingham and was married to James Rivers. Together they brought six girls and two boys into the world. She recalled all their names, after a little hesitation, today. They are Hazel, Shirley, Carolyn, Elaine, Shelly May, Bonita, Johnny and Alvin. They all live in Birmingham, Ala., where Mr. Rivers is a truck driver.

About two years ago, Mrs. Rivers said, she felt the passion of the civil rights movement. She had always been a believer in integration, she said, but one day she realized that the natinal movement concerned her as an individual.

She started attending mass meetings in Birmingham. She agreed to picket and boycott. In May she picketed in downtown Birmingham. She was arrested twice.

Signed Up for March

And when the word went out that there would be a civil rights march on Washington, Mr. Rivers was one of the first to sign up.

The $8 bus ticket represented more than one-tenth of her husband's weekly salary, and there were other sacrifices. But Mrs. Rivers was determined to march on Washington.

So yesterday morning she boarded a bus in Birmingham and rode all night. Today at noon she alighted—farther north than she has ever been before, picked up a flag, and marched from the Washington Monument to the Lincoln Memorial.

Afterward, sitting on the wall of a Government building and waiting for her bus to start the long trip back home, Mrs. Rivers was more fervent than ever about civil rights.

Her Doubts Resolved

"If I ever had any doubts before," she said, "they're gone now. When I get back home I'm going to follow this on out. I've followed it this far. When I get back there tomorrow I'm going to do whatever needs to be done. I don't care if it's picketing or marching or sitting-in or what. I'm ready to do it.

"I'm ready to march on Montgomery or even march in Birmingham again. When they march I'm going to march."

Mrs. Rivers was equally fervent in her praise of Washington, praise that might bring disagreement from Northern civil rights workers. But to the Southern housewife who had been jailed twice in Alabama, this city today was the acme of freedom.

"The people are lots better up here than they are down South," Mrs. Rivers said. "They treat you much nicer. Why, when I was out there at the march a white man stepped on my foot, and he said 'Excuse me,' and I said 'Certainly'.

"That's the first time that has ever happened to me. I believe that was the first time a white person has ever really been nice to me."

Mrs. Rivers thought a moment, as hundreds of tired marchers walked past on their way back to their buses, and as the clear, almost crisp day neared its end, and she said:

"As a matter of fact, I think I'd like to stay here. I'd like to live here. I think maybe someday we'll move here to live."

Tired New Yorkers Head Home Full of Praise for Capital Rally

By THEODORE JONES

Special to The New York Times

WASHINGTON, Aug. 28—New Yorkers left no doubt today in their appraisal of the March on Washington rally.

Although tired and exhausted from the long day's activities, they found only praise for the rally, its leaders and the decorum of the marchers.

"It was wonderful," declared Mrs. Icelle Coleman, a Manhattan garment worker, "I've never been so proud of my people. Everything went so well. It was just amazing."

Mrs. Coleman, who lives at 29 Putnam Avenue, Brooklyn, described the program from start to finish as "excellent." However, she singled out the Rev. Dr. Martin Luther Jr. and said he "stole the show."

"He said so much," she said, "it was just uplifting. And so were the others and so were the people."

Harvey Swados, a freelance writer, admitted that he had been "uneasy" about how the Negro and white residents of Washington would behave at the rally.

"They conducted themselves in an orderly fashion just like everybody else," he said. "I was impressed and relieved."

Mr. Swados described the march as "magnificent," declaring that it could not help but exert "a great influence" on Congress to pass the President's civil rights bill.

His views were seconded by his 15-year-old son, Marco, who attends Nyack High School. The youth observed that both the march and Dr. King "had come off very successfully."

"It was a tremendous event as far as the Negro's fight for his rights is concerned," Mrs. Doris Offley, a Manhattan nurse, said. "Dr. King talked about racial harmony, and there it was for all to see."

Another person interviewed as he prepared to board the six o'clock train for home at Union Station was Milton Master, who works in the City's Department of Real Estate and resides in Whitestone, Queens.

"It was thrilling," he said. "But more than that they accomplished their point."

One particular group who also established their point were the 15 New York and Brooklyn members of the Congress of Racial Equality, who started a walk to Washington on Aug. 15.

They arrived in the capital on Tuesday night with five other members, who joined the march in Philadelphia. Today, they were all honored with seats on the guest's platform during the Lincoln Memorial program.

The march also served to renew the faith of a Hungarian Freedom Fighter, who now makes his home in New York and is a computer programmer with International Business Machines.

Thomas Mandey said during an early morning conversation on a bus coming to Washington that he had wanted "to do something in the civil rights fight."

"I wrote a letter to C.O.R.E.," he explained, "asking what I could do. But I guess they were so busy that they couldn't answer. So the rally was the obvious thing."

After the rally, Mr. Mandey, who came to this country in December, 1956, following the Hungarian uprising, smiled and simply said, "Tremendous."

Another marcher, Mrs. Rosa Arnold, a nurse's aide who lives at 525 West 138th Street, was more verbose. The rally, she declared, "has given us real recognition as a group."

"It shows that we are together and that we want freedom now!" she said.

3 Rights Buses Are Stoned

BALTIMORE, Aug. 28 (AP)—Three buses, homeward-bound for Connecticut with demonstrators from the civil rights march on Washington today, were pelted with stones near the entrance to the Baltimore Harbor tunnel. The police said no one was injured although a stone crashed through the windshield of one bus.

MOST OF CAPITAL DESERTED FOR DAY

Many Businesses Shut Down—Thousands Stay Home

By EDWIN L. DALE Jr.

Special to The New York Times

WASHINGTON, Aug. 28—The city of Washington all but closed down today because of the civil rights march, though no one exactly planned it that way.

People stayed home in droves. As a result, the downtown area, except for the section occupied by the marchers, had the appearance of a normal Sunday. Traffic was exceptionally light.

At least half the retail stores remained open, but their proprietors grumbled that business was awful. Leading department stores resembled a railroad station at 3 A.M. They reported business well under 50 per cent of normal.

"Every store in the downtown section had a bad day," said William Press, executive vice president of the Washington Board of Trade.

He put the loss of business at "hundreds of thousands of dollars."

While thousands of Washingtonians kept to their homes, the normal inflow of tourists and other visitors also was much reduced. The Washington Hotel Association reported double the normal number of vacant rooms, with 5,000 available last night and 6,000 tonight.

Holidays Encouraged

Both the Government and private employers encouraged their employes to stay home if they wanted to. Some private concerns closed down. The Government left the matter to its employes, encouraging them to take a day off at the expense of one day of annual leave.

The effects differed widely among the agencies, but an early estimate was that about half of the 160,000 Federal and District of Columbia employes who work downtown stayed home.

The policy was designed primarily to avoid a massive traffic jam, while an important part of the downtown area was closed off for the march. The policy seemed to work better than had been expected.

Liquor Sales Forbidden

All bars and liquor stores were closed and restaurants and hotels forbidden to serve alcoholic beverages by order of the District Commissioners. Many normally jammed restaurants were only half or two-thirds full. Some closed for the day.

It was clear that business Washington was unhappy about the situation, regardless of the individual's views on racial issues.

"You can hardly expect me to jump with joy," said one store proprietor, who had had only three customers in the morning.

Penalty Urged for States With Voting Discrimination

WASHINGTON, Aug. 28 (AP)—Reapportionment of the House by reducing the number of Representatives from states that deny the franchise to qualified voters has been proposed by Representative Abraham J. Multer, Democrat of Brooklyn.

He introduced a resolution yesterday calling for creation of a committee to determine the number of Representatives each state should have under the 14th Amendment to the Constitution.

This amendment provides that a state's representation shall be reduced in the proportion that the number of citizens denied the right to vote shall bear to the whole number of citizens over 21 years of age.

DR. KING ECHOES NEGROES' DREAM

Continued From Page 1, Col. 6

gro leaders demanded equality "now," while insisting that this was only the "beginning" of the struggle. Yet it was clear that the "now," which appeared on almost every placard on Constitution Avenue, was merely an opening demand, while the exhortation to increase the struggle was what was really on the leaders' minds.

The question of the day, of course, was raised by Dr. King's theme: Was this all a dream or will it help the dream come true?

No doubt this vast effort helped the Negro drive against discrimination. It was better covered by television and the press than any event here since President Kennedy's inauguration, and, since indifference is almost as great a problem to the Negro as hostility, this was a plus.

None of the dreadful things Washington feared came about. The racial hooligans were scarce. Even the local Nazi, George Lincoln Rockwell, minded his manners, which is an extraordinary innovation for him. And there were fewer arrests than any normal day for Washington, probably because all the saloons and hootch peddlers were closed.

Politicians Are Impressed

The crowd obviously impressed the politicians. The presence of nearly a quarter of a million petitioners anywhere always makes a Senator think. He seldom ignores that many potential votes, and it did not escape the notice of Congressmen that these Negro organizations, some of which had almost as much trouble getting out a crowd as the Washington Senators several years ago, were now capable of organizing the largest demonstrating throng ever gathered at one spot in the District of Columbia.

It is a question whether this rally raised too many hopes among the Negroes or inspired the Negroes here to work harder for equality when they got back home. Most observers here think the latter is true, even though all the talk of "Freedom NOW" and instant integration is bound to lead to some disappointment.

The meetings between the Negro leaders on the one hand and President Kennedy and the Congressional leaders on the other also went well and probably helped the Negro cause. The Negro leaders were careful not to seem to be putting improper pressure on Congress. They made no specific requests or threats, but they argued their case in small groups and kept the crowd off Capitol Hill.

Whether this will win any new votes for the civil rights and economic legislation will probably depend on the over-all effect of the day's events on the television audience.

The Major Imponderable

This is the major imponderable of the day. The speeches were varied and spotty. Like their white political brethren, the Negroes cannot run a political meeting without letting everybody talk. Also, the platform was a bedlam of moving figures who seemed to be interested in everything except listening to the speaker. This distracted the audience.

Nevertheless, Dr. King and Roy Wilkins, head of the National Association for the Advancement of Colored People, and one or two others got the message across. James Baldwin, the author, summed up the day succinctly. The day was important in itself, he said, and "what we do with this day is even more important."

He was convinced that the country has finally grappling with the Negro problem instead of evading it; that the Negro himself was "for the first time" aware of his value as a human being and was "no longer at the mercy of what the white people imagine the Negro to be."

Merely the Beginning

On the whole, the speeches were not calculated to make Republican politicians very happy with the Negro. This may hurt, for, without substantial Republican support, the Kennedy program on civil rights and jobs is not going through.

Apparently this point impressed President Kennedy, who listened to some of the speeches on television. When the Negro leaders came out of the White House, Dr. King emphasized that bipartisan support was essential for passage of the Kennedy civil rights program.

Aside from this, the advantages of the day for the Negro cause outran the disadvantages.

Above all, they got over Lincoln's point that "the necessity of being ready increases." For they left no doubt that this was not the climax of their campaign for equality but merely the beginning, that they were going to stay in the streets until they could get equality in the schools, restaurants, houses and employment agencies of the nation, and that, as they demonstrated here today, they had found an effective way to demonstrate for changes in the laws without breaking the law themselves.

Lost Boy Quickly Found

WASHINGTON, Aug. 28 (AP)—The first youngster who strayed at the Washington Monument today was 9-year-old Larry Johnson of East Orange, N. J. Larry was quickly reunited with his father, Roosevelt Johnson, a few hundred yards from the speaker's stand at the mammoth civil rights rally.

Gentle Army Occupies Capital; Politeness Is Order of the Day

Continued From Page 1, Col. 8

who had come in the spirit of the church outing.

And instead of the tensions that had been expected, they gave this city a day of sun, music, strange silences and good feeling in the streets.

It was apparent from early morning that this would be an extraordinary day. At 8 A.M. when rush-hour traffic is normally creeping bumper-to-bumper across the Virginia bridges and down the main boulevards from Maryland, the streets had the abandoned look of Sunday morning.

From a helicopter over the city, it was possible to see caravans of chartered buses streaming down New York Avenue from Baltimore and points North, but the downtown streets were empty. Nothing moved in front of the White House, nor on Pennsylvania Avenue.

A Day of Siege

For the natives, this was obviously a day of siege and the streets were being left to the marchers.

By 9:30, the number of marchers at the assembly point by the Washington Monument had reached about 40,000, but it was a crowd without fire. Mostly, people who had traveled together sat on the grass or posed for group portraits against the monument, like tourists on a rare visit to the capital.

Here and there, little groups stood in the sunlight and sang. A group of 75 young people from Danville, Va., came dressed in white sweatshirts with crudely cut black mourning bands on their sleeves.

"We're mourning injustice in Danville," explained James Bruce, a 15-year-old who said he has been arrested three times for participating in demonstrations there.

Standing together, the group sang of the freedom fight in a sad melody with words that went, "Move on, move on, move on with the freedom fight; move on, move on, we're fighting for equal rights."

Other hymns came from groups scattered over the grounds, but there was no cohesion in the crowd.

Instead, a fair grounds atmosphere prevailed. Marchers kept straggling off to ride the elevators to the top of the monument. Women sat on the grass and concentrated on feeding babies.

Among the younger members of the crowd, beards were in high vogue. "It's just that we're so busy saving the world that we don't have time to shave," Kyle Valkar, 19-year-old Washingtonian, explained.

Up on the slope near the monument's base, Peter Ottley, president of the Building Services International Union, Local 144, in New York City, was ignoring the loudspeaker and holding a press conference before about 100 of his delegates.

He thought the march would "convince the legislators that something must be done, because it is the will of the people to give equality to all."

In the background, the amplifier was presenting Joan Baez, the folk singer.

One Note of Bitterness

In one section of the ground, a group from Americus and Albany, Ga., was gathered under its own placards singing its own hymn. The placards conveyed an uncharacteristic note of bitterness.

"What is a state without justice but a robber band enlarged?" asked one. Another bore the following inscription: "Milton Wilkerson 20 stitches Emanuel McClendon—3 stitches (Age 67). James Williams—broken leg."

Charles Macken, 15, of Albany, explained the placard in a deep Georgia accent.

"That's where the police beat these people up," he said.

Over the loudspeaker, Roosevelt Johnson was urged to come claim his lost son, Lawrence.

From the monument grounds the loudspeaker boomed an announcement that the police had estimated that 90,000 marchers were already on the scene.

At 10:56 the loudspeaker announced desperately that "we are trying to locate Miss Lena Horne," and a group from Cambridge, Md., was kneeling while the Rev. Charles M. Bowen of Bethel A.M.E. Church prayed.

"We know truely that we will—we shall—overcome—some day," he was saying.

The Cambridge group rose and began a gospel hymn and clapped and swayed. The loudspeaker was saying, "Lena—wherever you are—."

Many were simply picnicking. They had brought picnic baskets and thermos jugs and camp stools, and lunched leisurely in the soft August sunshine. Some stretched out to doze on the grass.

Singer Introduced

At 11:10 Bobby Darin, the teen-age pop singer, was being introduced over the amplifier. He was, he announced, "Here as a singer, and I'm proud and kind of choked up."

The marchers by this time, however, had had enought of the Monument grounds. Spontaneously, without advice from the platform, they began to flow away, moving toward the Lincoln Memorial, where the official program was to begin at noon.

Thousands simply began to move out into Constitution Avenue, and in a few minutes it was tens of thousands. They trooped leisurely out into the boulevard and moved happily along in a strange mood of quiet contentment.

By 11:55, much of the crowd had regrouped at the Lincoln Memorial, where the speaker's platform was set on the top step under the Lincoln statue.

This made an impressive stage for the star performers, but it was a bad theater for most of the audience, which was dispersed down the sides of the reflecting pool for a third of a mile.

Still the crowd remained in good temper, and many who could not find comfortable space in the open with a clear view up to the Memorial steps filtered back under the trees and sat down on their placards.

On the platform, Roy Wilkins, executive secretary of the National Association for the Advancement of Colored People, surveyed the sea of people and said, "I'm very satisfied. It looks like a Yankee game."

Photographers Busy

Inside, under the Lincoln statue, the photographers were deployed five deep around Burt Lancaster, Harry Belafonte and Charlton Heston. On metal chairs in the guest sections, Marlon Brando and Paul Newman were submitting to microphone interviewers.

As the crowd on the steps thickened and gradually became an impassable mass, the extraordinary politeness that characterized the day was dramatized every time an elbow was crooked.

People excused themselves for momentarily obstructing a view, excused themselves for dropping cigarette ashes on shoeshines.

When the marshals called for a clear path, hundreds hastened to fall aside with a goodwill rarely seen in the typical urban crowd. The sweetness and patience of the crowd may have set some sort of national high-water mark in mass decency.

The program at the Memorial began with more music. Peter, Paul and Mary, a folk-singing trio, were there "to express in song what this meeting is all about," as Ossie Davis, the master of ceremonies, put it.

Then there was Josh White, in a gray short-sleeved sports shirt, singing "ain't nobody gonna stop me, nobody gonna keep me, from marchin' down freedom's road."

And the Freedom Singers from Mississippi, a hand-clapping group of hot gospel shouters whom Mr. Davis introduced as "straight from one of the prisons of the South."

"They've been in so many, I forget which one it is," he added.

At 1:19 P.M. there was the Rev. Fred L. Shuttlesworth, president of the Alabama Christian Movement for Human Rights and a leader of the Birmingham demonstrations.

A 1:28 P.M. Miss Baez was singing "Little baby, don't you cry, you know your mama won't die, all your trials will soon be over."

As she sang, Mayor Wagner of New York made his appearance, walking down the Memorial steps.

Bunche Speaks

Miss Baez was followed by Dr. Ralph Bunche.

"Anyone who cannot understand the significance of your presence here today," he said, "is blind and deaf." The crowd roared approval.

Then came Dick Gregory, the comedian.

"The last time I saw this many of us," he said, "Bull Connor was doing all the talking." The reference was to Eugene (Bull) Connor, who was police commissioner of Birmingham during the spring demonstrations there.

To many of the marchers, the program must have begun to seem like eternity, and the great crowd slowly began dissolving from the edges. Mr. Lancaster read a lengthy statement from 1,500 Americans in Europe. They were in favor of the march. Mr. Belafonte read a statement endorsed by a large group of actors, writers and entertainers. They also favored the march.

Bob Dylan, a young folk singer, rendered a lugubrious mountain song about "The day Medgar Evers was buried from a bullet that he caught." Mr. Lancaster, Mr. Belafonte and Mr. Heston found time dragging, stood up to stretch and chat, and set off pandemonium among the photographers. Mr. Brando submitted to another microphone interviewer.

Speaking Begins

At 1:59 the official speaking began. For those who listened it was full of noble statement about democracy and religious sincerity, but the crowd was dissolving fast now. Tens of dissolving fast now.

These missed two of the emotional high points of the day. One was Mahalia Jackson's singing, which seemed to bounce off the Capitol far up the mall. The other was the speech of the Rev. Dr. Martin Luther King Jr., president of the Southern Christian Leadership Conference.

Long before that, however, huge portions of the crowd had drifted out of earshot. Thousands had moved back into Constitution Avenue to walk dreamily in the sun. The grass for blocks around was covered with sleepers. Here and there, a man sat under a tree and sang to a guitar.

Mostly though, the "marchers" just strolled in the sunshine. Most looked contented and tired and rather pleased with what they had done.

Mississippians Do Extra Duty

WASHINGTON, Aug. 28 (UPI)—About 25 demonstrators from Clarksdale, Miss., marched back to the Washington Monument grounds today, while some groups were still headed for the civil rights rally at the Lincoln Memorial. Members of the group felt Mississippi had a peculiar problem and they wanted to do extra marching to demonstrate that, a spokesman said.

Excerpts From Addresses at Lincoln Memorial During Capital Civil Rights March

Following are excerpts from addresses delivered yesterday at ceremonies at the Lincoln Memorial during the civil rights march on Washington, as recorded by The New York Times:

Sketches of the 10 Leaders of Civil Rights March on Washington

Mathew Ahmann

EXECUTIVE director of the National Catholic Conference for Interracial Justice . . . Was organizer and executive secretary of the National Conference on Religion and Race in Chicago a year ago . . . Graduate of St. John's University in Minnesota . . . Author of "The New Negro" and "Race: Challenge to Religion" . . . Married, father of four children . . . 31 years old . . . Did Graduate work in sociology at the University of Chicago . . . Was social worker for the Chicago Department of Welfare . . . Acted as business and circulation manager of Today magazine . . . Field representative of the Catholic Interracial Council of Chicago . . . Later, its assistant direcaor and action director.

Dr. Eugene Carson Blake

CHIEF executive officer of the United Presbyterian Church in the U.S.A. . . . President of the National Council of Churches of Christ until 1957, now serves as vice chairman of the council's Commission on Religion and Race . . . Urbane, tough-minded liberal . . . Attended Lawrenceville School, Princeton and Princeton Theological Seminary . . . Taught school in India, taught religion at Williams College and has held pulpits in Pasadena, Calif.; Albany, N. Y., and New York City . . . Was an opponent of McCarthyism in the nineteen-fifties . . . Arrested in a Baltimore civil rights demonstration this summer . . . 56 years old . . . Is married to the former Valina Gillespie . . . No children.

Martin Luther King Jr.

FOUNDER and president of the Southern Christian Leadership Conference . . . Helped direct the Negro bus boycott in Montgomery, Ala., in 1956 and the Birmingham demonstrations last May that preceded the summer's national wave of protests . . . Has been in jail at least 12 times . . . Travels 200,000 miles a year on civil rights business . . . Son of a clergyman, is co-pastor of Ebenezer Baptist Church in Atlanta . . . Left Morehouse College in Atlanta in 1948 to attend Crozer Theological Seminary, Chester, Pa., where he was voted outstanding student in his class . . . Received Ph.D. from Boston College in 1955 . . . Married to the former Coretta Scott . . . Is 34 years old . . . Has three children.

John Lewis

CHAIRMAN of the Student Nonviolent Coordinating Committee . . . At 25, youngest of civil rights leaders . . . Former philosophy student at Fisk University, Nashville . . . Graduate of American Baptist Seminary . . . Took part in Freedom Ride from Washington to Birmingham, Ala., in 1961 . . . Beaten by white mob when riders arrived at Montgomery, Ala. . . . Arrested 24 times in civil rights demonstrations . . . Was also attacked by a white during a Freedom Ride stop in South Carolina . . . Succeeded Charles McDew, becoming the third chairman of the Student Committee, known popularly as Snick . . . Is a member of the militant Nashville Group, which has provided a number of leaders to the civil rights struggle . . . Is unmarried.

Floyd B. McKissick

NATIONAL chairman of the Congress of Racial Equality . . . marching in place of CORE president, James Farmer, who chose to remain in jail in Louisiana rather than come to Washington . . . Joined civil rights movement at age of 12 when pickets from his home town of Asheville, N. C., demonstrated at the State capital in Raleigh against lack of accreditation for the Negro law school at North Carolina College . . . Graduate of University of North Carolina Law School, where he became the first Negro to attend after winning a suit to force his admission . . . Largely authored the Durham Plan, successful negotiating formula used in Durham and other North Carolina cities . . . Married to the former Evelyn Williams . . . Has four children.

Rabbi Joachim Prinz

PRESIDENT of the American Jewish Congress . . . Expelled from Germany by Adolf Eichmann in 1937, when he was rabbi of the Berlin Jewish Community . . . Rabbi of Temple B'nai Abraham in Newark, N. J. in 1939 . . . A lifelong Zionist, he quit the active Zionist movement when Israel became a nation in 1948, a step that brought him much criticism . . . Has been in frequent civil rights controversies . . . Won a libel suit against a right-wing magazine that called him a Communist . . . Has been a United States citizen since 1944 . . . Married to the former Hilde Goldschmidt . . . Has four children, one by adoption . . . Is 61 years old.

A. Philip Randolph

DIRECTOR of the March on Washington for jobs and freedom . . . Founder and president of the Brotherhood of Sleeping Car Porters . . . Only Negro vice president of the A.F.L.-C.I.O. . . . Organizer of two previous mass movements on the capital, including the nineteen forty-one March on Washington Movement in 1941, the antecedent of today's march, which prompted President Franklin D. Roosevelt to establish the Fair Employment Practices Commission . . . Born in Crescent City, Fla., son of a preacher . . . worked his way through the City College . . . Arrested in 1917 but soon released for opposition to entry in World War I . . . Is 74 and married to the former Lucille Campbell—and to the works of Shaw and Shakespeare.

Walter P. Reuther

PRESIDENT of the United Automobile Workers Union, vice president and head of the Industrial Union Department of the A.F.L.-C.I.O. . . . An old-timer at picketing and labor demonstrations . . . One of three members of the A.F.L.-C.I.O. Executive Council who strongly criticized that group's failure earlier this month to endorse today's march . . . Is married to the former May Wolf . . . Has two children . . . Is 55 years old . . . Father and grandfather were active union officials . . . Completed high school through night courses . . . Active tennis player, swimmer and hiker . . . Received C.I.O.'s award for furthering fight against racial discrimination in late nineteen-forties.

Roy Wilkins

EXECUTIVE secretary of the National Association for the Advancement of Colored People . . . Chairman of the Leadership Conference on Civil Rights . . . Joined the N.A.A.C.P. in 1931, after resigning the managing editorship of The Kansas City Call . . . Served as assistant secretary, under the late Walter White . . . Elected to succeed Mr. White in 1955 . . . Native of St. Louis, was graduated from University of Minnesota in 1923 . . . Married the former Aminda Badeau in 1929 . . . Is 62 years old . . . Succeeded Dr. W. E. B. DuBois in 1934 as editor of The Crisis, official organ of the N.A.A.C.P. . . . Avid reader and author in his own right . . . Received elementary and secondary education in St. Paul

Whitney M. Young Jr.

EXECUTIVE director of the National Urban League . . . 42 years old . . . Former dean of Atlanta University's School of Social Work . . . Abandoned premedical studies for social work after combat engineer duty in the Army in Europe in World War II . . . Joined staff of St. Paul Urban League in 1947 . . . Became director of Omaha Urban League in 1950 . . . Quit in 1954 to accept the Atlanta University post . . . Served on the President's Committee on Youth Employment and the President's Committee on Equal Opportunity in the Armed Forces . . . Received the Florina Lasker Award in 1959 for outstanding achievement in the field of social work . . . Elected head of National Urban League in 1961

Most Rev. Patrick O'Boyle, Archbishop of Washington

INVOCATION

In the name of the Father and of the Son and of the Holy Ghost, amen.

Our Father, who art in heaven, we who are assembled here in a spirit of peace and in good faith dedicate ourselves and our hopes to You. We ask the fullness of Your blessing upon those who have gathered with us today, and upon all men and women of good will to whom the cause of justice and equality is sacred. We ask this blessing because we are convinced that in honoring all Your children, we show forth in our lives the love that You have given us.

Bless this nation and all its people. May the warmth of Your love replace the coldness that springs from prejudice and bitterness. Send in our midst the Holy Spirit to open the eyes of all to the great truth that all men are equal in Your sight. Let us understand that simple justice demands that the rights of all be honored by every man.

Give strength and wisdom to our President and Vice President. Enlighten and guide the Congress of these United States. May our judges in every court be heralds of justice and equity. Let just laws be administered without discrimination. See to it, we implore, that no man be so powerful as to be above the law, or so weak as to be deprived of its full protection.

We ask special blessing for those men and women who in sincerity and honesty have been leaders in the struggle for justice and harmony among races. As Moses of old, they have gone before their people to a land of promise. Let that promise quickly become a reality, so that the ideals of freedom, blessed alike by our religious faith and our heritage of democracy, will prevail in our land.

Finally, we ask that You consecrate to Your service all in this crusade who are dedicated to the principles of the Constitution of these United States. May we be sensitive to our duties toward others as we demand from them our rights. May we move forward without bitterness, even when confronted with prejudice and discrimination.

May we shun violence, knowing that the meek shall inherit the earth. But may this meekness of manner be joined with courage and strength so that with Your help, O heavenly Father, and following the teaching of Christ, Your Son, we shall now and in the days to come live together as brothers in dignity, justice, charity and peace. Amen.

Rev. Dr. Eugene Carson Blake, National Council of Churches

I wish indeed that I were able to speak for all Protestant, Anglican and Orthodox Christians as I speak in behalf of full justice and freedom for all, born or living under the American flag.

But that is precisely the point. If all the members and all the ministers of the constituency I represent here today were ready to stand and march with you for jobs and freedom for the Negro community together with all the Roman Catholic Church and all of the synagogues in America, then the battle for full civil rights and dignity would be already won.

I do, however, in fact, officially represent the Commission on Religion and Race of the National Council of Churches.

For many years now the National Council of Churches and most of its constituent communions have said all the right things about civil rights. Our official pronouncements for years have clearly called for "a nonsegregated church in a nonsegregated society." But as of Aug. 28, 1963, we have achieved neither a nonsegregated church nor a nonsegregated society.

And it is partially because the churches of America have failed to put their own houses in order that 100 years after the Emancipation Proclamation, 175 years after the adoption of the Constitution, 173 years after the adoption of the Bill of Rights, the United States of America still faces a racial crisis.

We do not, therefore, come to this Lincoln Memorial in any arrogant spirit of moral or spiritual superiority to "set the nation straight" or to judge or to denounce the American people in whole or in part.

Rather we come—late, late we come—in the reconciling and repentant spirit in which Abraham Lincoln of Illinois once replied to a delegation of morally arrogant churchmen. He said "Never say God is on our side, rather pray that we may be found on God's side."

We come in the fear of God that moved Thomas Jefferson of Virginia, whose memorial stands across the Lagoon, once to say:

"Indeed, I tremble for my country, when I reflect that God is just."

Rabbi Joachim Prinz, President of American Jewish Congress

I speak to you as an American Jew.

As Americans we share the profound concern of millions of people about the shame and disgrace of inequality and injustice which make a mockery of the great American idea.

As Jews we bring to the great demonstration, in which thousands of us proudly participate, a two-fold experience—one of the spirit and one of our history.

In the realm of the spirit, our fathers taught us thousands of years ago that when God created man, he created him as everybody's neighbor. Neighbor is not a geographic term. It is a moral concept. It means our collective responsibility for the preservation of man's dignity and integrity.

From our Jewish historic experience of three and a half thousand years we say:

Our ancient history began with slavery and the yearning for freedom.

During the Middle Ages my people lived for a thousand years in the ghettos of Europe.

Our modern history begins with a proclamation of emancipation.

It is for these reasons that it is not merely sympathy and compassion for the black people of America that motivates us, it is above all and beyond all such sympathies and emotions a sense of complete identification and solidarity born of our own painful historic experience.

When I was the rabbi of the Jewish community in Berlin under the Hitler regime, I learned many things. The most important thing that I learned in my life and under those tragic circumstances is that bigotry and hatred are not the most urgent problem. The most urgent, the most disgraceful, the most shameful and the most tragic problem is silence.

A great people which had created a great civilization had become a nation of silent onlookers. They remained silent in the face of hate, in the face of brutality and in the face of mass murder.

America must not become a nation of onlookers. America must not remain silent. Not merely black America, but all of America. It must speak up and act, from the President down to the humblest of us, and not for the sake of the Negro, not for the sake of the black community but for the sake of the image, the idea and the aspiration of America itself.

Our children, yours and mine in every school across the land, every morning pledge allegiance to the flag of the United States and to the republic for which it stands and then they, the children, speak fervently and innocently of this land as the land of "liberty and justice for all."

The time, I believe, has come to work together—for it is not enough to hope together, and it is not enough to pray together—to work together that this children's oath — pronounced every morning from Maine to California, from North to South — that this oath will become a glorious, unshakable reality in a morally renewed and united America.

A. Philip Randolph, Sleeping Car Porters

We are gathered here in the largest demonstration in the history of this nation. Let the nation and the world know the meaning of our numbers. We are not a pressure group, we are not an organization or a group of organizations, we are not a mob. We are the advance guard of a massive moral revolution for jobs and freedom.

This revolution reverberates throughout the land touching every city, every town, every village where black men are segregated, oppressed and exploited.

But this civil rights revolution is not confined to the Negroes, nor is it confined to civil rights. Our white allies know that they cannot be free while we are not. And we know that we have no interest in a society in which 6,000,000 black and white people are unemployed, and millions more live in poverty.

Nor is the goal of our civil rights revolution merely the passage of civil rights legislation.

Yes, we want all public accommodations open to all citizens, but those accommodations will mean little to those who cannot afford to use them.

Backs School Aid

Yes, we want a Fair Employment Practice Act, but what good will it do if profits geared to automation destroy the jobs of millions of workers, black and white?

We want integrated public schools, but that means we also want Federal aid to education, all forms of education.

Now, we know that real freedom will require many changes in the nation's political and social philosophies and institutions. For one thing we must destroy the notion that Mrs. Murphy's property rights include the right to humiliate me because of the color of my skin.

The sanctity of private property takes second place to the sanctity of a human personality.

The months and years ahead will bring new evidence of masses in motion for freedom. The march on Washington is not the climax to our struggle but a new beginning, not only for the Negro but for all Americans, for personal freedoms and a better life.

Look for the enemies of Medicare, of higher minimum wages, of Social Security, of Federal aid to education, and there you will find the enemy of the Negro, the coalition of Dixiecrats and reactionary Republicans that seek to dominate the Congress.

We must develop strength in order that we may be able to back and support the civil rights program of President Kennedy.

We here, today, are only the first wave. When we leave it will be to carry on the civil rights revolution home with us, into every nook and cranny of the land. And we shall return again, and again, to Washington in ever-growing numbers until total freedom is ours.

Dr. Martin Luther King Jr., Southern Christian Leadership Conference

Now is the time to make real the promises of democracy. Now is the time to rise from the dark and desolate valley of segregation to the sunlit path of racial justice. Now is the time to lift our nation from the quicksands of racial injustice to the solid rock of brotherhood. Now is the time to make justice a reality for all of God's children.

There will be neither rest nor tranquility in America until the Negro is granted his citizenship rights. The whirlwinds of revolt will continue to shake the foundations of our nation until the bright day of justice emerges.

And that is something that I must say to my people who stand on the threshold which leads to the palace of justice. In the process of gaining our rightful place we must not be guilty of wrongful deeds.

Again and again, we must rise to the majestic heights of meeting physical force with soul force. The marvelous new militancy which has engulfed the Negro community must not lead us to a distrust of all white people, for many of our white brothers as evidenced by their presence here today have come to realize that their destiny is tied up with our destiny.

'Never Be Satisfied'

There are those who are asking the devotees of civil rights, "When will you be satisfied?" We can never be satisfied as long as the Negro is the victim of the unspeakable horrors of police brutality. We can never be satisfied as long as our bodies, heavy with the fatigue of travel, cannot gain lodging in the motels of the highways and the hotels of the cities.

We can never be satisfied as long as our children are stripped of their selfhood and robbed of their dignity by signs stating "for whites only." We cannot be satisfied as long as the Negro in Mississippi cannot vote and the Negro in New York believes he has nothing for which to vote.

No, we are not satisfied and we will not be satisfied until justice rolls down like water and righteousness like a mighty stream.

Now, I am not unmindful that some of you have come here out of great trials and tribulations. Some of you have come fresh from narrow jail cells.

Continue to work with the faith that honor in suffering is redemptive. Go back to Mississippi, go back to Alabama, go back to South Carolina, go back to Georgia, go back to Louisiana, go back to the slums and ghettos of our Northern cities, knowing that somehow this situation can and will be changed. Let us not wallow in the valley of despair.

Now, I say to you today, my friends, so even though we face the difficulties of today and tomorrow, I still have a dream. It is a dream deeply rooted in the American dream. I have a dream that one day this nation will rise up and live out the true meaning of its creed: "We hold these truths to be self-evident, that all men are created equal."

I have a dream that one day on the red hills of Georgia the sons of former slaves and the sons of former slave-owners will be able to sit down together at the table of brotherhood.

I have a dream that one day even the state of Mississippi, a state sweltering with the people's injustice, sweltering with the heat of oppression, will be transformed into an oasis of freedom and justice.

I have a dream that my four little children will one day live in a nation where they will not be judged by the color of their skin, but by the content of their character.

This is our hope. This is the faith that I go back to the South with—with this faith we will be able to hew out of the mountain of despair a stone of hope.

Roy Wilkins, Executive Secretary, N.A.A.C.P.

We came to speak here to our Congress, to those men and women who speak here for us in that marble forum over yonder on the hill.

They know, from their vantage point here, of the greatness of this whole nation, of its reservoirs of strength, and of the sicknesses which threaten always to sap its strength and to erode, in one or another selfish and stealthy and specious fashion, the precious liberty of the individual which is the hallmark of our country among the nations of the earth.

We want employment and with it we want the pride and responsibility and self-respect that goes with equal access to jobs. Therefore we want an F. E. P. C. bill as a part of the legislative package.

Now for nine years our parents and their children have been met with either a flat refusal or token action in school desegregation. Every added year of such treatment is a leg iron upon our men and women of 1980. The civil rights bill now under consideration in the Congress must give new powers to the Justice Department to enable it to speed the end of Jim Crow schools, South and North.

Now, my friends, all over this land, and especially in parts of the Deep South, we are beaten and kicked and maltreated and shot and killed by local and state law enforcement officers.

It is simply incomprehensible to us here today and to millions of others far from this spot that the United States Government, which can regulate the contents of a pill, apparently is powerless to prevent the physical abuse of citizens within its own borders.

Now, the President's proposals represent so moderate an approach that if it is weakened or eliminated, the remainder will be little more than sugar water.

Now, we expect the passage of an effective civil rights bill. We commend those Republicans in both houses who are working for it. We salute those Democrats in both houses who are working for it.

In fact, we even salute those from the South who want to vote for it but don't dare to do so. And we say to those people, just give us a little time, and one of these days we'll emancipate you.

James Farmer, National Director of CORE

Delivered by Floyd B. McKissick, national chairman of the Congress of Racial Equality, for Mr. Farmer, who is in jail in Louisiana on charges stemming from civil rights demonstrations.

From a south Louisiana parish jail, I salute the march on Washington for jobs and freedom. Two hundred and thirty-two freedom fighters jailed with me in Plaquemine, La., also send their greetings.

I wanted to be with you with all my heart on this great day. My imprisoned brothers and sisters wanted to be there too. I cannot come out of jail while they are still in; for their crime was the same as mine—demanding freedom now. And most of them will not come out of jail until the charges are dropped or their sentences reversed.

I know that you will understand my absence. So we cannot be with you today in body, but we are with you in spirit. By marching on Washington your tramping feet have spoken the message—the message of our trouble in Louisiana.

You have come from all over the nation and in one mighty voice you have spoken to the nation. You have also spoken to the world. You have said to the world by your presence here as our successful direct action in numberless cities has said, that in the days of thermonuclear bombs, violence is outmoded to the solution of the problems of men.

It is a truth that needs to be shouted loudly. And no one else anywhere in the world is saying it as well as the American Negro through their nonviolent direct action.

The tear gas and the electric cattle prod of Plaquemine, La., like the fire hoses and dogs of Birmingham are giving to the world a tired and ugly message of terror and brutality and hate.

If we can solve our probnems and remove the heavy heel of oppression from our necks with our methods, then man has no problem anywhere in the world which cannot be solved without death.

We will not slow down; we will not stop our militant, peaceful demonstrations; we will not come off of the streets until we can work at a job befitting of our skills in any place in the land.

We will not stop our marching people until our kids have enough to eat and their minds can study a wide range without being cramped in Jim Crow schools.

We will not stop until the heavy weight of oppression is removed from our back, and like proud men everywhere, when we can stand tall together again.

Whitney M. Young Jr., National Urban League

One should not seek here to atone for his past failures as a responsible citizen of the majority group. The evils of the past, and the guilt about it, cannot be erased by a one-day pilgrimage, however magnificent. Nor can this pilgrimage substitute for an obligation to tomorrow by these same citizens.

And so, this march must go beyond this historic moment. For the true test of the rededication and the commitment which should flow from this meeting will be in our recognition that, however impressed or however incensed our Congressional representatives are by this demonstration, they will not act because of it alone.

We must support the strong, we must give courage to the timid, we must remind the indifferent, and warn the opposed. Civil rights, which are God-given and constitutionally guaranteed, are not negotiable in 1963.

Furthermore, we must work together even more closely back home where the job must be done to see that Negro Americans are accepted as first-class citizens and that they are enabled to do some more marching.

They must march from the rat-infested, overcrowded ghettos to decent, wholesome, unrestricted residential areas dispersed throughout our cities.

They must march from the cemeteries, where our young, our newborn die three times sooner and our parents die seven years earlier. They must march from there to nearby established health and welfare centers.

They must march from the congested, ill-equipped schools which breed dropouts and which smother motivation to the well-equipped, integrated facilities throughout the cities.

And finally they must march from a present feeling of hopelessness, despair and frustration to a renewed faith and confidence due to tangible programs and visible changes made possible only by walking together.

Mathew Ahmann, Catholic Conference for Interracial Justice

Who can call himself a man, say he is created by God, and at the same time take part in a system of segregation which destroys the livelihood, the citizenship, family life and the very heart of the Negro citizens of the United States?

Who can call himself a man, and take part in a system of segregation which frightens the white man into denying what he knows to be right, into denying the law of his God?

We dedicate ourselves today to secure Federal civil rights legislation which will guarantee every man a job based on his talents and training; legislation which will do away with the myth that the ownership of a public place of business carries the moral or legal right to reject a customer because of the color of his hair or of his skin.

But, we are gathered too to dedicate ourselves to building a people, a nation, a world which is free of the sin of discrimination based on race, creed, color or national origin, a world of the sons of God, equal in all important respects; a world dedicated to justice, and to fraternal bonds between men.

Walter P. Reuther, Auto Workers President

It is the responsibility of every American to share the impatience of the Negro Americans. And we need to join together, to march together and to work together until we've bridged the moral gap between American democracy's noble promises and its ugly practices in the field of civil rights.

There is a lot of noble talk about brotherhood and then some Americans drop the brother and keep the hood.

To me, the civil rights question is a moral question which transcends partisan politics, and this rally today should be the first step in a total effort to mobilize the moral conscience of America and to ask the people in Congress of both parties to rise above their partisan differences and enact civil rights legislation now.

Now the President—President Kennedy—has offered a comprehensive and moderate bill. That bill is the first meaningful step. It needs to be strengthened. It needs F.E.P.C. and other stronger provisions. And the job question is crucial; because we will not solve education or housing or public accommodations as long as millions of American Negroes are treated as second-class economic citizens and denied jobs.

I am for civil rights, as a matter of human decency, as a matter of common morality. But I am also for civil rights because I believe that freedom is an indivisible value. That no one can be free unto himself, and when Bull [former Safety Commissioner Eugene] Connor with his police dogs and firehoses destroys freedom in Birmingham he is destroying my freedom in Detroit.

This rally is not the end, it's the beginning. It's the beginning of a great moral crusade to arouse America to the unfinished work of American democracy. The Congress has to act. And after they act, we have much work to do.

Mrs. Daisy Bates, N.A.A.C.P. Director

The women of this country, Mr. Randolph, pledge to you, to Martin Luther King, Roy Wilkins and all of you fighting for civil liberties, that we will join hands with you as women of this country.

We will kneel-in, we will sit-in, until we can eat in any counter in the United States. We will walk until we are free, until we can walk to any school and take our children to any school in the United States. And we will sit-in and we will kneel-in and we will lie in if necessary until every Negro in America can vote. This we pledge you, the women of America.

"All the News That's Fit to Print"

The New York Times.

LATE CITY EDITION
U. S. Weather Bureau Report (Page 56) forecasts: Cloudy, windy, chance of showers today and tonight. Cold tomorrow.
Temp. Range: 62—54; yesterday: 64—51.

VOL. CXIII... No. 38,654. NEW YORK, SATURDAY, NOVEMBER 23, 1963. TEN CENTS

KENNEDY IS KILLED BY SNIPER AS HE RIDES IN CAR IN DALLAS; JOHNSON SWORN IN ON PLANE

TEXAN ASKS UNITY

Congressional Chiefs of Both Parties Promise Aid

By FELIX BELAIR Jr.
Special to The New York Times

WASHINGTON, Nov. 22—Lyndon B. Johnson returned to a stunned capital shortly after 6 P.M. today to assume the duties of the Presidency.

The new President asked for and received from Congressional leaders of both parties their "united support in the face of the tragedy which has befallen our country." He said it was "more essential that ever before that this country be united."

Partisan differences disappeared in the chorus of assurances with which the Congressional leaders responded.

Mr. Johnson was described by those who talked with him as "stunned and shaken" by the assassination of President Kennedy.

Discusses U.S. Security

But he moved quickly from problems of national security and foreign policy to funeral arrangements for Mr. Kennedy.

Across the street from the West Wing of the White House, the President conferred with officials in his old Vice-Presidential offices in the Executive Office Building.

Senator George A. Smathers, Democrat of Florida, a personal friend of the dead President, was one of those who described Mr. Johnson as shaken.

"Everyone is," he added. "But the President is the more so because he was right there when the tragedy occurred."

While flying to Washington aboard the Presidential plane, Mr. Johnson arranged for a meeting with Cabinet members to ask that they remain at their posts. He made the same request of staff members in the executive office.

Meets With Harriman

"Calm and contained" was the way Senator J. W. Fulbright described the President's manner during a discussion of foreign-policy matters with Under Secretary of State W. Averell Harriman. The Arkansas Senator said the President had been working on "what looked like a statement"—presumably an assurance of continuity of the nation's foreign policy.

The new President's first conference was aboard the helicopter that flew him the 15 miles from Andrews Air Force Base

Continued on Page 11, Column 3

Henry Grossman

"This is a sad time for all people. We have suffered a loss that cannot be weighed. For me it is a deep personal tragedy. I know the world shares the sorrow that Mrs. Kennedy and her family bear. I will do my best. That is all I can do. I ask for your help—and God's."—President Lyndon Baines Johnson.

PRESIDENT'S BODY WILL LIE IN STATE

Funeral Mass to Be Monday in Capital After Homage Is Paid by Public

By JACK RAYMOND
Special to The New York Times

WASHINGTON, Nov. 22—The body of John F. Kennedy will lie in state in the rotunda of the Capitol Sunday and then will be borne to St. Matthew's Roman Catholic Cathedral for a pontifical requiem mass at noon Monday.

The President's body was returned to Washington today in the same Air Force jet that carried him to Texas. The airliner, with Mrs. Kennedy, the new President, Lyndon B. Johnson, and Mrs. Johnson aboard, arrived at Andrews Air Force Base at 5:58 P.M.

It was announced later that Mr. Kennedy's body would lie in the White House tomorrow from 10 A.M. to 6 P.M., during which time Government and diplomatic officials will pay their respects.

The coffin will be taken from the White House to the Capitol rotunda Sunday morning, where

Continued on Page 9, Column 3

PARTIES' OUTLOOK FOR '64 CONFUSED

Republican Prospects Rise—Johnson Faces Possible Fight Against Liberals

By WARREN WEAVER Jr.
Special to The New York Times

WASHINGTON, Nov. 22—President Kennedy's assassination threw the American political scene into turmoil today.

It removed at a single blow the man who would have been renominated for a second term in the White House by acclamation nine months from now.

It elevated into the Presidency and the leadership of the Democratic party an older, more conservative man still emerging from his Southern heritage.

It increased immeasurably for the leaders of the Republican party prospects of electing a President next November.

The shock of the President's death stilled the official voices of politics in the capital. But so profound was the potential effect on the government and leadership that private consideration could not be silenced.

Before, there had been facts and strong probabilities on the

Continued on Page 6, Column 3

LEFTIST ACCUSED

Figure in a Pro-Castro Group Is Charged—Policeman Slain

By GLADWIN HILL
Special to The New York Times

DALLAS, Tex., Nov. 22—The Dallas police and Federal officers issued a charge of murder late tonight in the assassination of President Kennedy.

The accused is Lee Harvey Oswald, a 24-year-old former marine, who went to live in the Soviet Union in 1959 and returned to Texas last year.

Capt. Will Fritz, head of the Dallas police homicide bureau, identified Oswald as an adherent of the left-wing Fair Play for Cuba Committee.

Oswald was arrested about two hours after the shooting, in a movie theater three miles away, shortly after he allegedly shot and killed a policeman on a street nearby.

He was arraigned tonight on a charge of murdering the police officer. The charge related to the Kennedy killing was made later.

Appears in Line-Up

After the arraignment, the suspect, a slight, dark-haired man, was taken downstairs to appear in a line-up, presumably before witnesses of the Kennedy assassination.

While being escorted, handcuffed, through a police building corridor, he shouted: "I haven't shot anybody."

Captain Fritz said Oswald was employed—the exact job was unknown—at the Texas School Book Depository, a warehouse from which the assassin's bullets came. The captain said some witnesses had placed Oswald in the building at the time of the assassination.

The sequence of events leading to his arrest was as follows:

As a citywide manhunt began during the hour following the assassination, an unidentified man notified police headquarters, over a police-car radio, that the car's officer had been

Continued on Page 4, Column 1

NEWS INDEX

Henry Grossman

John Fitzgerald Kennedy
1917-1963

Why America Weeps

Kennedy Victim of Violent Streak He Sought to Curb in the Nation

By JAMES RESTON
Special to The New York Times

WASHINGTON, Nov. 22—America wept tonight, not alone for its dead young President, but for itself. The grief was general, for somehow the worst in the nation had prevailed over the best. The indictment extended beyond the assassin, for something in the nation itself, some strain of madness and violence, had destroyed the highest symbol of law and order.

Speaker John McCormack, now 71 and, by the peculiarities of our politics, next in line of succession after the Vice President, expressed this sense of national dismay and self-criticism:

"My God! My God! What are we coming to?"

The irony of the President's death is that his short Administration was devoted almost entirely to various attempts to curb this very streak of violence in the American character.

When the historians get around to assessing his three years in office, it is very likely that they will be impressed with just this: his efforts to restrain those who wanted to be more violent in the cold war overseas and those who wanted to be

Continued on Page 7, Column 6

The City Goes Dark

By ROBERT C. DOTY

The center of New York, the restless night city, wore darkness and went in near silence after the murder of President Kennedy last night.

In and around Times Square, the normal, frenetic Friday night pulse slowed as near to a halt as it ever comes. Most legitimate and movie theaters, night clubs and dance halls closed their doors and darkened their marquees.

As dusk came, automatic devices turned on the huge, gaudy display signs that normally blot out the night. Then, one by one, the lights blinked out, turning the great carnival strip into what was almost a mourning band.

There were exceptions, of course. Restaurants, by decision of their trade associations, remained lighted and open as a

Continued on Page 5, Column 2

Gov. Connally Shot; Mrs. Kennedy Safe

President Is Struck Down by a Rifle Shot From Building on Motorcade Route—Johnson, Riding Behind, Is Unhurt

By TOM WICKER
Special to The New York Times

DALLAS, Nov. 22—President John Fitzgerald Kennedy was shot and killed by an assassin today.

He died of a wound in the brain caused by a rifle bullet that was fired at him as he was riding through downtown Dallas in a motorcade.

Vice President Lyndon Baines Johnson, who was riding in the third car behind Mr. Kennedy's, was sworn in as the 36th President of the United States 99 minutes after Mr. Kennedy's death.

Mr. Johnson is 55 years old; Mr. Kennedy was 46.

Shortly after the assassination, Lee H. Oswald, described as a one-time defector to the Soviet Union, active in the Fair Play for Cuba Committee, was arrested by the Dallas police. Tonight he was accused of the killing.

Suspect Captured After Scuffle

Oswald, 24 years old, was also accused of slaying a policeman who had approached him in the street. Oswald was subdued after a scuffle with a second policeman in a nearby theater.

The shooting took place at 12:30 P.M., Central standard time (1:30 P.M., New York time). Mr. Kennedy was pronounced dead at 1 P.M. and Mr. Johnson was sworn in at 2:39 P.M.

Mr. Johnson, who was uninjured in the shooting, took his oath in the Presidential jet plane as it stood on the runway at Love Field. The body of the President was aboard. Immediately after the oath-taking, the plane took off for Washington.

Standing beside the new President as Mr. Johnson took the oath of office was Mrs. John F. Kennedy. Her stocking was saturated with her husband's blood.

Gov. John B. Connally Jr. of Texas, who was riding in the same car with Mr. Kennedy, was severely wounded in the chest, ribs and arm. His condition was serious, but not critical.

The killer fired the rifle from a building just off the motorcade route. Mr. Kennedy,

Continued on Page 2,

Capt. Cecil Stoughton via United Press International

THE NEW PRESIDENT: Lyndon B. Johnson takes oath before Judge Sarah T. Hughes in plane at Dallas. Mrs. Kennedy and Representative Jack Brooks are at right. To left are Mrs. Johnson and Representative Albert Thomas.

Associated Press

WHEN THE BULLETS STRUCK: Mrs. Kennedy moving to the aid of the President after he was hit by a sniper yesterday in Dallas. A guard mounts rear bumper. Gov. John B. Connally Jr. of Texas, also in the car, was wounded.

Kennedy Killed by Sniper as He Rides in Car in Dallas; Johnson Sworn In on Plane

Continued From Page 1

Governor Connally and Mr. Johnson had just received an enthusiastic welcome from a large crowd in downtown Dallas.

Mr. Kennedy apparently was hit by the first of what witnesses believed were three shots. He was driven at high speed to Dallas's Parkland Hospital. There, in an emergency operating room, with only physicians and nurses in attendance, he died without regaining consciousness.

Mrs. Kennedy, Mrs. Connally and a Secret Service agent were in the car with Mrs. Kennedy and Governor Connally. Two Secret Service agents flanked the car. Other than Mr. Connally, none of this group was injured in the shooting. Mrs. Kennedy cried, "Oh no!" immediately after her husband was struck.

Mrs. Kennedy was in the hospital near her husband when he died, but not in the operating room. When the body was taken from the hospital in a bronze coffin about 2 P.M., Mrs. Kennedy walked beside it.

Her face was sorrowful. She looked steadily at the floor. She still wore the raspberry-colored suit in which she had greeted welcoming crowds in Fort Worth and Dallas. But she had taken off the matching pillbox hat she wore earlier in the day, and her dark hair was windblown and tangled. Her hand rested lightly on her husband's coffin as it was taken to a waiting hearse.

Mrs. Kennedy climbed in beside the coffin. Then the ambulance drove to Love Field, and Mr. Kennedy's body was placed aboard the Presidential jet. Mrs. Kennedy then attended the swearing-in ceremony for Mr. Johnson.

As Mr. Kennedy's body left Parkland Hospital, a few stunned persons stood outside. Nurses and doctors, whispering among themselves, looked from the window. A larger crowd that had gathered earlier, before it was known that the President was dead, had been dispersed by Secret Service men and policemen.

Priests Administer Last Rites

Two priests administered last rites to Mr. Kennedy, a Roman Catholic. They were the Very Rev. Oscar Huber, the pastor of Holy Trinity Church in Dallas, and the Rev. James Thompson.

Mr. Johnson was sworn in as President by Federal Judge Sarah T. Hughes of the Northern District of Texas. She was appointed to the judgeship by Mr. Kennedy in October, 1961.

The ceremony, delayed about five minutes for Mrs. Kennedy's arrival, took place in the private Presidential cabin in the rear of the plane.

About 25 to 30 persons—members of the late President's staff, members of Congress who had been accompanying the President on a two-day tour of Texas cities and a few reporters—crowded into the little room.

No accurate listing of those present could be obtained. Mrs. Kennedy stood at the left of Mr. Johnson, her eyes and face showing the signs of weeping that had apparently shaken her since she left the hospital not long before.

Mrs. Johnson, wearing a beige dress, stood at her husband's right.

As Judge Hughes read the brief oath of office, her eyes, too, were red from weeping. Mr. Johnson's hands rested on a black, leather-bound Bible as Judge Hughes read and he repeated:

"I do solemnly swear that I will perform the duties of the President of the United States to the best of my ability and defend, protect and preserve the Constitution of the United States."

Those 34 words made Lyndon Baines Johnson, one-time farmboy and schoolteacher of Johnson City, the President.

Johnson Embraces Mrs. Kennedy

Mr. Johnson made no statement. He embraced Mrs. Kennedy and she held his hand for a long moment. He also embraced Mrs. Johnson and Mrs. Evelyn Lincoln, Mr. Kennedy's private secretary.

"O.K.," Mr. Johnson said. "Lets get this plane back to Washington."

At 2:46 P.M., seven minutes after he had become President, 106 minutes after Mr. Kennedy had become the fourth American President to succumb to an assassin's wounds, the white and red jet took off for Washington.

In the cabin when Mr. Johnson took the oath was Cecil Stoughton, an armed forces photographer assigned to the White House.

Mr. Kennedy's staff members appeared stunned and bewildered. Lawrence F. O'Brien, the Congressional liaison officer, and P. Kenneth O'Donnell, the appointment secretary, both long associates of Mr. Kennedy, showed evidences of weeping. None had anything to say.

Other staff members believed to be in the cabin for the swearing-in included David F. Powers, the White House receptionist; Miss Pamela Turnure, Mrs. Kennedy's press secretary, and Malcolm Kilduff, the assistant White House press secretary.

Mr. Kilduff announced the President's death, with choked voice and red-rimmed eyes, at about 1:36 P.M.

"President John F. Kennedy died at approximately 1 o'clock Central standard time today here in Dallas," Mr. Kilduff said at the hospital. "He died of a gunshot wound in the brain. I have no other details regarding the assassination of the President."

Mr. Kilduff also announced that Governor Connally had been hit by a bullet or bullets and that Mr. Johnson, who had not yet been sworn in, was safe in the protective custody of the Secret Service at an unannounced place, presumably the airplane at Love Field.

Mr. Kilduff indicated that the President had been shot once. Later medical reports raised the possibility that there had been two wounds. But the death was caused, as far as could be learned, by a massive wound in the brain.

Later in the afternoon, Dr. Malcolm Perry, an attending surgeon, and Dr. Kemp Clark, chief of neurosurgery at Parkland Hospital, gave more details.

Mr. Kennedy was hit by a bullet in the throat, just below the Adam's apple, they said. This wound had the appearance of a bullet's entry.

Mr. Kennedy also had a massive, gaping wound in the back and one on the right side of the head. However, the doctors said it was impossible to determine immediately whether the wounds had been caused by on bullet or two.

Resuscitation Attempted

Dr. Perry, the first physician to treat the President, said a number of resuscitative measures had been attempted, including oxygen, anesthesia, an indotracheal tube, a tracheotomy, blood and fluids. An electrocardiogram monitor was attached to measure Mr. Kennedy's heart beats.

Dr. Clark was summoned and arrived in a minute or two. By then, Dr. Perry said, Mr. Kennedy was "critically ill and moribund," or near death.

Dr. Clark said that on his first sight of the President, he had concluded immediately that Mr. Kennedy could not live.

"It was apparent that the President had sustained a lethal wound," he said. "A missile had gone in and out of the back of his head causing external lacerations and loss of brain tissue."

Shortly after he arrived, Dr. Clark said, "the President lost his heart action by the electrocardiogram." A closed-chest cardiograph massage was attempted, as were other emergency resuscitation measures.

Dr. Clark said these had produced "palpable pulses" for a short time, but all were "to no avail."

In Operating Room 40 Minutes

The President was on the emergency table at the hospital for about 40 minutes, the doctors said. At the end, perhaps eight physicians were in Operating Room No. 1, where Mr. Kennedy remained until his death. Dr. Clark said it was difficult to determine the exact moment of death, but the doctors said officially that it occurred at 1 P.M.

Later, there were unofficial reports that Mr. Kennedy had been killed instantly. The source of these reports, Dr. Tom Shires, chief surgeon at the hospital and professor of surgery at the University of Texas Southwest Medical School, issued this statement tonight:

"Medically, it was apparent the President was not alive when he was brought in. There was no spontaneous respiration. He had dilated, fixed pupils. It was obvious he had a lethal head wound.

"Technically, however, by using vigorous resuscitation, intravenous tubes and all the usual supportive measures, we were able to raise a semblance of a heartbeat."

Dr. Shires said he was "positive it was impossible" that President Kennedy could have spoken after being shot. "I am absolutely sure he never knew what hit him," Dr. Shires said.

Dr. Shires was not present when Mr. Kennedy was being treated at Parkland Hospital. He issued his statement, however, after lengthy conferences with the doctors who had attended the President.

Mr. Johnson remained in the hospital about 30 minutes after Mr. Kennedy died.

The details of what happened when shots first rang out, as the President's car moved along at about 25 miles an hour, were sketchy. Secret Service agents, who might have given more details, were unavailable to the press at first, and then returned to Washington with President Johnson.

Kennedys Hailed at Breakfast

Mr. Kennedy had opened his day in Fort Worth, first with a speech in a parking lot and then at a Chamber of Commerce breakfast. The breakfast appearance was a particular triumph for Mrs. Kennedy, who entered late and was given an ovation.

Then the Presidential party, including Governor and Mrs. Connally, flew on to Dallas, an eight-minute flight. Mr. Johnson, as is customary, flew in a separate plane. The President and the Vice President do not travel together, out of fear of a double tragedy.

At Love Field, Mr. and Mrs. Kennedy lingered for 10 minutes, shaking hands with an enthusiastic group lining the fence. The group called itself "Grassroots Democrats."

Mr. Kennedy then entered his open Lincoln convertible at the head of the motorcade. He sat in the rear seat on the right-hand side. Mrs. Kennedy, who appeared to be enjoying one of the first political outings she had ever made with her husband, sat at his left.

In the "jump" seat, directly ahead of Mr. Kennedy, sat Governor Connally, with Mrs. Connally at his left in another "jump" seat. A Secret Service agent was driving and the two others ran alongside.

Behind the President's limousine was an open sedan carrying a number of Secret Service agents. Behind them, in an open convertible, rode Mr. and Mrs. Johnson and Texas's senior Senator, Ralph W. Yarborough, a Democrat.

The motorcade proceeded uneventfully along a 10-mile route through downtown Dallas, aiming for the Merchandise Mart. Mr. Kennedy was to address a group of the city's leading citizens at a luncheon in his honor.

In downtown Dallas, crowds were thick, enthusiastic and cheering. The turnout was somewhat unusual for this center of conservatism, where only a month ago Adlai E. Stevenson was attacked by a rightist crowd. It was also in Dallas, during the 1960 campaign, that Senator Lyndon B. Johnson and his wife were nearly mobbed in the lobby of the Baker Hotel.

As the motorcade neared its end and the President's car moved out of the thick crowds onto Stennonds Freeway near the Merchandise Mart, Mrs. Connally recalled later, "we were all very pleased with the reception in downtown Dallas."

Approaching 3-Street Underpass

Behind the three leading cars were a string of others carrying Texas and Dallas dignitaries, two buses of reporters, several open cars carrying photographers and other reporters, and a bus for White House staff members.

As Mrs. Connally recalled later, the President's car was almost ready to go underneath a "triple underpass" beneath three streets—Elm, Commerce and Main—when the first shot was fired.

That shot apparently struck Mr. Kennedy. Governor Connally turned in his seat at the sound and appeared immediately to be hit in the chest.

Mrs. Mary Norman of Dallas was standing at the curb and at that moment was aiming her camera at the President. She saw him slump forward, then slide down in the seat.

"My God," Mrs. Norman screamed, as she recalled it later, "he's shot!"

Mrs. Connally said that Mrs. Kennedy had reached and "grabbed" her husband. Mrs. Connally put her arms around the Governor. Mrs. Connally said that she and Mrs. Kennedy had then ducked low in the car as it sped off.

Mrs. Connally's recollections were reported by Julian Reade, an aide to the Governor.

Most reporters in the press buses were too far back to see the shootings, but they observed some quick scurrying by motor policemen accompanying the motorcade. It was noted that the President's car had picked up speed and raced away, but reporters were not aware that anything serious had occurred until they reached the Merchandise Mart two or three minutes later.

Rumors Spread at Trade Mart

Rumors of the shooting already were spreading through the luncheon crowd of hundreds, which was having the first course. No White House officials or Secret Service agents were present, but the reporters were taken quickly to Parkland Hospital on the strength of the rumors.

There they encountered Senator Yarborough, white, shaken and horrified.

The shots, he said, seemed to have come from the right and the rear of the car in which he was riding, the third in the motorcade. Another eyewitness, Mel Crouch, a Dallas television reporter, reported that as the shots rang out he saw a rifle extended and then withdrawn from a window on the "fifth or sixth floor" of the Texas Public School Book Depository. This is a leased state building on Elm Street, to the right of the motorcade route.

Senator Yarborough said there had been a slight pause between the first two shots and a longer pause between the second and third. A Secret Service man riding in the Senator's car, the Senator said, immediately ordered Mr. and Mrs. Johnson to get down below the level of the doors. They did so, and Senator Yarborough also got down.

The leading cars of the motorcade then pulled away at high speed toward Parkland Hospital, which was not far away, by the fast highway.

"We knew by the speed that something was terribly wrong," Senator Yarborough reported. When he put his head up, he said, he saw a Secret Service man in the car ahead beating his fists against the trunk deck of the car in which he was riding, apparently in frustration and anguish.

Mrs. Kennedy's Reaction

Only White House staff members spoke with Mrs. Kennedy. A Dallas medical student, David Edwards, saw her in Parkland Hospital while she was waiting for news of her husband. He gave this description:

"The look in her eyes was like an animal that had been trapped, like a little rabbit—brave, but fear was in the eyes."

Dr. Clark was reported to have informed Mrs. Kennedy of her husband's death.

No witnesses reported seeing or hearing any of the Secret Service agents or policemen fire back. One agent was seen to brandish a machine gun as the cars sped away. Mr. Crouch observed a policeman falling to the ground and pulling a weapon. But the events had occurred so quickly that there was apparently nothing for the men to shoot at.

Mr. Crouch said he saw two women, standing at a curb to watch the motorcade pass, fall to the ground when the shots rang out. He also saw a man snatch up his little girl and run along the road. Policemen, he said, immediately chased this man under the impression he had been involved in the shooting, but Mr. Crouch said he had been a fleeing spectator.

Mr. Kennedy's limousine—license No. GG300 under District of Columbia registry—pulled up at the emergency entrance of Parkland Hospital. Senator Yarborough said the President had been carried inside on a stretcher.

By the time reporters arrived at the hospital, the police were guarding the Presidential car closely. They would allow no one to approach it. A bucket of water stood by the car, suggesting that the back seat had been scrubbed out.

Robert Clark of the American Broadcasting Company, who had been riding near the front of the motorcade, said Mr. Kennedy was motionless when he was carried inside. There was a great amount of blood on Mr. Kennedy's suit and shirtfront and the front of his body, Mr. Clark said.

Mrs. Kennedy was leaning over her husband when the car stopped, Mr. Clark said, and walked beside the wheeled stretcher into the hospital. Mr. Connally sat with his hands holding his stomach, his head bent over. He, too, was moved into the hospital in a stretcher, with Mrs. Connally at his side.

Robert McNeill of the National Broadcasting Company, who also was in the reporters' pool car, jumped out at the scene of the shooting. He said the police had taken two eyewitnesses into custody—an 8-year-old Negro boy and a white man—for informational purposes.

Many of these reports could not be verified immediately.

Eyewitness Describes Shooting

An unidentified Dallas man, interviewed on television here, said he had been waving at the President when the shots were fired. His belief was that Mr. Kennedy had been struck twice—once, as Mrs. Norman recalled, when he slumped in his seat; again when he slid down in it.

"It seemed to just knock him down," the man said.

Governor Connally's condition was reported as "satisfactory" tonight after four hours in surgery at Parkland Hospital.

Dr. Robert R. Shaw, a thoracic surgeon, operated on the Governor to repair damage to his left chest.

Later, Dr. Shaw said Governor Connally had been hit in the back just below the shoulder blade, and that the bullet had gone completely through the Governor's chest, taking out part of the fifth rib.

After leaving the body, he said, the bullet struck the Governor's right wrist, causing a compound fracture. It then lodged in the left thigh.

The thigh wound, Dr. Shaw said, was trivial. He said the compound fracture would heal.

Dr. Shaw said it would be unwise for Governor Connally to be moved in the next 10 to 14 days. Mrs. Connally was remaining at his side tonight.

Tour by Mrs. Kennedy Unusual

Mrs. Kennedy's presence near her husband's bedside at his death resulted from somewhat unusual circumstances. She had rarely accompanied him on his trips about the country and had almost never made political trips with him.

The tour on which Mr. Kennedy was engaged yesterday and today was only quasi-political; the only open political activity was to have been a speech tonight to a fund-raising dinner at the state capitol in Austin.

In visiting Texas, Mr. Kennedy was seeking to improve his political fortunes in a pivotal state that he barely won in 1960. He was also hoping to patch a bitter internal dispute among Texas's Democrats.

At 8:45 A.M., when Mr. Kennedy left the Texas Hotel in Fort Worth, where he spent his last night, to address the parking lot crowd across the street, Mrs. Kennedy was not with him. There appeared to be some disappointment.

"Mrs. Kennedy is organizing herself," the President said good-naturedly. "It takes longer, but, of course, she looks better than we do when she does it."

Later, Mrs. Kennedy appeared late at the Chamber of Commerce breakfast in Fort Worth.

Again, Mr. Kennedy took note of her presence. "Two years ago," he said, "I introduced myself in Paris by saying that I was the man who had accompanied Mrs. Kennedy to Paris. I am getting somewhat that same sensation as I travel around Texas. Nobody wonders what Lyndon and I wear."

The speech Mr. Kennedy never delivered at the Merchandise Mart luncheon contained a passage commenting on a recent preoccupation of his, and a subject of much interest in this city, where right-wing conservatism is the rule rather than the exception.

Voices are being heard in the land, he said, "voices preaching doctrines wholly unrelated to reality, wholly unsuited to the sixties, doctrines which apparently assume that words will suffice without weapons, that vituperation is as good as victory and that peace is a sign of weakness."

The speech went on: "At a time when the national debt is steadily being reduced in terms of its burden on our economy, they see that debt as the greatest threat to our security. At a time when we are steadily reducing the number of Federal employes serving every thousand citizens, they fear those supposed hordes of civil servants far more than the actual hordes of opposing armies.

"We cannot expect that everyone, to use the phrase of a decade ago, will 'talk sense to the American people.' But we can hope that fewer people will listen to nonsense. And the notion that this nation is headed for defeat through deficit, or that strength is but a matter of slogans, is nothing but just plain nonsense."

The President's Death: The Scene, Return to Washington, a Stunned New York

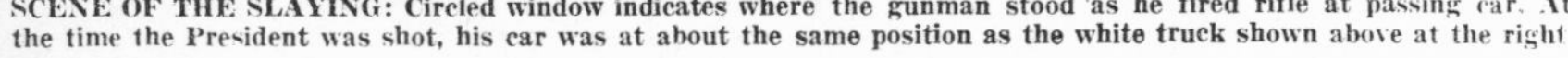

SCENE OF THE SLAYING: Circled window indicates where the gunman stood as he fired rifle at passing car. At the time the President was shot, his car was at about the same position as the white truck shown above at the right.

ASSASSIN'S VIEW: This photograph was taken through the window from which President Kennedy was shot. The arrow points to a car in approximately the same position as the President's limousine was at the time of shooting.

EXPRESSIONS OF SORROW: President Johnson and Mrs. Johnson with Mrs. John F. Kennedy in Presidential plane at Dallas airport. Mr. Johnson took oath aboard plane.

ARRIVAL IN WASHINGTON: The coffin containing the body of the slain President is moved into Navy ambulance at Andrews Air Force Base

A SADDENED MEETING: Attorney General Robert F. Kennedy greets his sister-in-law

ESCORTED BY WIDOW: Mrs. Kennedy, her stockings still stained with her husband's blood, enters vehicle for trip to Bethesda Naval Hospital

Associated Press, United Press International, The New York Times

THE CITY MOURNS: The darkened marquees of theaters in the Times Square area reflected the stillness that descended on the city. Performances were canceled, sports events were called off, as were classes at the universities.

Leftist Charged With Murder in Assassination of Kennedy and Policeman's Death

PRISONER LINKED TO CASTRO GROUP

He Is Subdued in Theater —Ex-Marine Defected to Soviet and Returned

Continued From Page 1, Col. 4

fessed," Chief Curry said. "Physical evidence is the main thing we have."

He murmured seeming assent to a suggestion that such evidence included the assassination gun.

Fingerprint experts had been conspicuous in the procession of officers into and out of the homicide bureau during the afternoon and evening. They included agents of the Secret Service and the Federal Bureau of Investigation, who collaborated with city, county and state law enforcement officers in investigating the crime.

Three and a half hours before Chief Curry's announcement, Oswald had been arraigned on a charge of murder in the death of the policeman, J. D. Tippitt.

Dallas County District Attorney Henry Wade said there were "a few loose ends" in the case to be wrapped up, and he expected that the case would not go to the grand jury before next week.

Oswald faces a death sentence if convicted.

Appears in Line-Up

After the arraignment, the suspect, a slight, dark-haired man, was taken downstairs to appear in a line-up, presumably before witnesses of the Kennedy assassination.

The sequence of events leading to his arrest was as follows:

As a citywide manhunt began during the hour following the assassination, an unidentified man notified police headquarters, over a police-car radio, that the car's officer had been shot and killed. The car was in the 400 block of East Jefferson Boulevard in the Oak Cliff section, on the edge of the downtown area.

The car's driver, Patrolman Tippitt, had not made any call that he was going to question anyone.

Eight other officers converged on the spot. They found Patrolman Tippitt lying on the sidewalk, dead from two .38-caliber bullet wounds.

They began a search of nearby buildings for the killer.

Then another call came to police headquarters from Julie Postal, cashier of the Texas Theatre at 231 West Jefferson Boulevard, six blocks from the scene of the policeman's slaying.

She said an usher had told her that a man who had just entered the theater was acting peculiarly.

The investigating police officers were dispatched to the theater. They began checking patrons, starting at the front of the house.

One of the officers, Sgt. Jerry Hill, said that when they came to Oswald, sitting in the rear four seats in from the aisle, the suspect jumped up and exclaimed: "This is it!"

The Dallas Police Department appeared to be the nerve center of the overall investigation of the President's death, although the various lines this might be taking were not defined.

State Has Jurisdiction

The Justice of the Peace before whom Oswald was arraigned, David Johnston, said the assassination was a matter of state jurisdiction so far.

Little was known here about Oswald, except reports published locally in 1959 when he went to the Soviet Union after his discharge from the Marine Corps.

He was said to have tried to renounce his United States citizenship by turning in his passport to the United States Embassy in Moscow. The Embassy, it was reported then, advised him to hold on to it until he had some assurance of Soviet citizenship. He was reported to have worked in factories in the Soviet and to have married a Russian girl.

At the time of his quasi-defection, his mother and his brother, a milkman in nearby Fort Worth, sent messages vainly trying to dissuade him.

Shortly after he was escorted from his araignment last night, a tall, slender women with a little girl about 2 years old and a baby in her arms left the homicide bureau. An officer said they were the suspect's wife and daughter.

A housekeeper at Oswald's rooming house said the young man entered his room shortly after the shooting of the President, got a coat, and went back out.

The housekeeper, Mrs. Earlene Roberts, said:

"He came in in a hurry in his shirt sleeves and I said, 'Oh, you're in a hurry,' and he didn't say anything. He went on in his room and got a coat and put it on. He went out to the bus stop and that's the last I saw of him."

Mrs. Roberts said Oswald rushed into the rooming house, at 1026 North Beckley Road in suburban Oak Cliff. This was shortly after Mrs. Roberts had learned, in a telephone call from a friend, that the President had been shot. She said she had not connected Oswald's appearance with the shooting.

She described Oswald, who had lived in the house since the end of October, as quiet.

Justice of the Peace Johnston said he was one of four from outlying communities, assembled for the Kennedy visit, who had been recruited to assist law enforcement officers with the inquiry.

Judge Johnston said Judge Theron Ward had been assigned to the President's death and Judge Joe B. Brown Jr. to the death of the policeman. Judge Johnston and Judge Lloyd Russell were assisting in such matters as the issuance of search warrants and handling the arraignment.

The arraignment involved no plea. Oswald was held without bail for grand jury action and was advised of his rights to counsel.

Captain Fritz emerged from the homicide bureau after the arraignment and said: "We've charged this man with the killing of the officer."

Asked whether Oswald had been linked with the assassination, the officer replied: "He doesn't admit it—we have some more work to do on that case."

The revolver carried by Oswald in the theater was not suspected of having figured in President Kennedy's death.

Police ballistics experts were still studying, with apparently no conclusive findings, the rifle found in the book warehouse.

Captain Fritz said it was of obscure foreign origin, possibly Italian, of about 1940 vintage, and of an unusual, undetermined caliber. He displayed a bullet he said fitted the gun. It was about .30 caliber and about two and one-half inches long, with a narrow tapered nose.

Sergeant Hill said Oswald had a .38-caliber revolver under his shirt, and that in a scuffle that ensued, it was fired once, harmlessly. The time was 2:15 P.M. yersterday.

Oswald was subdued, handcuffed, rushed to downtown police headquarters and put in a fifth-floor cell.

At 6:35 P.M. he was taken down to the third-floor homicide bureau. He wore black slacks, black loafer shoes, a white undershirt and an olive plaid sport shirt, unbuttoned.

His left eye was slightly blackened, and there was a contusion on his right cheekbone.

CHARGED WITH ASSASSINATION: Lee H. Oswald, in handcuffs, at police headquarters in Dallas. He was charged by police last night with the murder of President Kennedy.

Truman Calls Slaying A Tragedy for Country

INDEPENDENCE, Mo., Nov. 22 (UPI)—Former President Harry S. Truman, who himself was an intended victim of assassins' bullets 13 years ago this month, said today the assassination of President Kennedy was a tragedy for the nation.

"I am shocked beyond words at the tragedy that has happened to our country and to President Kennedy's family today," Mr. Truman said in a statement. "The President's death is a great personal loss to the country and to me.

"He was an able President, one the people loved and trusted. Mrs. Truman and I send our deepest sympathy to Mrs. Kennedy and the family."

Mr. Truman said he planned to attend the funeral and burial services for Mr. Kennedy in Boston.

Mrs. Truman said the 79-year-old former President had suffered "quite a shock" when he heard the news of the assassination, and was "too upset" to make the statement until four hours later.

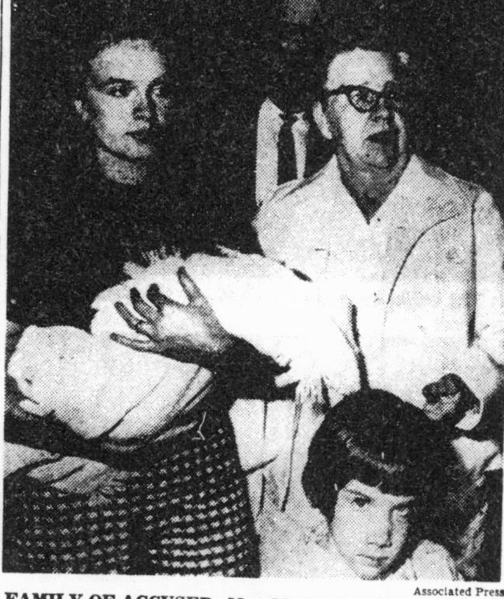

Associated Press

FAMILY OF ACCUSED: Mrs. Marina Oswald, wife of Lee H. Oswald, carrying one of her children as she left police headquarters in Dallas where she had attempted to visit her husband. With her was her daughter, in foreground, and Mrs. Marguerite Oswald, mother of accused.

NASSER SAYS DEATH IS HUMANITY'S LOSS

Special to The New York Times

CAIRO, Nov. 22—President Gamal Abdel Nasser, in a condolence message to Mrs. Kennedy today, said that humanity, progress and peace had suffered a loss in President Kennedy's death.

Special to The New York Times

ALGIERS, Nov. 22 — President Ahmed Ben Bella accused "partisans of racial segregation" tonight of having carried out the assassination of President Kennedy.

In a declaration issued after the United States Ambassador, William J. Porter, had informed him of Mr. Kennedy's death, the Algerian leaders said:

"We denounce with venemence this absolutely infamous act which through President Kennedy sought to brake his humane actions in favor of desegregation."

Kennedy Photo Requests Flood Party Office Here

Requests for photographs of the late President Kennedy were so heavy at the Democratic state committee headquarters in Manhattan last night that a special desk was set up in the Hotel Commodore to accommodate them.

The committee said it had received as many requests late yesterday afternoon after the President was killed as it had since his election.

Hundreds of citizens telephoned, saying they wished to place floral memorial displays in their homes

Border Closed and Reopened

MEXICO CITY, Nov. 22 (AP) — The Mexico-United States border was reopened tonight after being closed for several hours in a joint move by both governments. A Mexican Government spokesman said the border had been closed as a security measure following the slaying of President Kennedy. He said the governments had decided to reopen the border so as not to obstruct further the heavy flow of travelers.

The New York Times Nov. 23, 1963

TRIP: President Kennedy flew to San Antonio (1) Thursday, speaking there and at Houston (2). Yesterday, he continued his trip to Fort Worth (3) and Dallas (4). Mexicans briefly sealed their border with U.S. (dotted line).

CAREER OF SUSPECT HAS BEEN BIZARRE

U.S. Loan Enabled Oswald to Return From Soviet

By PETER KIHSS

It was a $435.71 United States Government loan that enabled Lee Harvey Oswald to return to this country 18 months ago after living two and a half years in the Soviet Union.

The 24-year-old Texan who was charged last night with the murder of President Kennedy has had a bizarre career.

An ex-marine, he applied for Soviet citizenship in Moscow in 1959, only to appeal later to a United States Senator for help in getting back home no the ground that the Soviets were holding him and his Russian wife against his will.

Last July, he tried to infiltrate the Cuban Student Directorate, seeking to overthrow Cuban Premier Fidel Castro, according to Cuban exiles in New Orleans and Miami.

Turned down, he appeared later as asserted chairman of a New Orleans chapter of the Fair Play for Cuba Committee, propagandizing in favor of the Castro regime.

Passport for 'Photographer'

Currently he has been holding a passport obtained on his contention that he was a photographer and wanted to go abroad during October, November and December of this year to visit the Soviet Union, Britain, France, Germany, the Netherlands, Finland, Italy and Poland.

In Buffalo yesterday, a man who said he served in the same Marine Corps unit at El Toro, Calif., that Oswald in 1954-55, said was a "lonely, introverted aloof boy" during that time.

The Buffalo man, Allen D. Graf, of 31 West Utica Street, said Oswald "always said he hated the outfit," and was bitter about the "tough time his mother had during the depression."

"We all thought it was the usual gripes of a guy in service," Mr. Graf said, according to The Associated Press. Mr. Graf said Oswald stayed by himself much of the time, and was "somewhat of a problem boy then."

Teacher Recalls Him

It is also as "an introvert" that Oswald is remembered by Mrs. Howard Green, wife of a Texas State Representative from Fort Worth.

Mrs. Green said yesterday in Austin that she had taught him in the sixth grade at Ridgelea Elementary School in Fort Worth.

He was a loner who sought escape in books, but did not apply himself in school and wound up with below-average grades, Mrs. Green said, according to United Press International.

Recently Oswald has described himself as a "Marxist." The Dallas police said he had been working in the Texas Schoolbook Depository Building, from which, it is believed, the rifle bullet that killed President Kennedy was fired.

Newsmen called him arrogant when they saw him yesterday in the custody of the Dallas police. A sharp-featured man with dark, intent eyes, he raised his handcuffed hands in a clenched fist.

Born in New Orleans

As pieced together from various quarters, including reports of The Associated Press and United Press International from various points, Oswald's career has gone like this:

He was born in New Orleans, Oct. 18, 1939, after his father had died. He lived two years in New York. He attended two Fort Worth elementary schools and then enrolled in a high school in September, 1956. But he withdrew from high school only 23 days after starting classes, and joined the Marines.

He served three years in the Marines, including service in Japan, and was discharged Sept. 11, 1959, as a radar operator. The discharge was granted on a plea of hardship.

When he was discharged, he visited a sister-in-law, Mrs. Robert L. Oswald, in Fort Worth. She recalled later that "he said he wanted to travel a lot and talked about going to Cuba."

Instead, he turned up in Moscow as a tourist on Oct. 13, 1959. His occupation was then listed as shipping export agent, his permanent address as 3124 West Fifth Street, Fort Worth.

On Oct. 31, 1959, the former marine, then 20 years old, walked into the United States Embassy and slapped his passport down on a desk. He said he had applied for Soviet citizenship. The embassy suggested that he refrain from signing any papers until he was sure the Soviet Union would accept him.

His brother, Robert L. Oswald, a Fort Worth milk route carrier, cabled him a plea to change his mind, and also telegraphed Secretary of State Christian A. Herter asking for help in making contact with the would-be defector.

"Lee, through any means possible, contact me," Robert's cable read. "Mistake. Keep your nose clean."

But on Nov. 2, 1959, Lee Oswald swore out an affidavit: "I affirm that my allegiance is to the Soviet Socialist Republic."

His passport was accepted by embassy officials and sent to the Justice Department in Washington.

Aline Mosby, a United Press International correspondent who interviewed him in Moscow then, wrote from Paris last night that she had "judged him as a person very determined but unsure of himself, naive and emotionally unbalanced."

"I'm a Marxist," she quoted him as saying. "I became interested about the age of 15. An old lady handed me a pamphlet about saving the Rosenbergs. I still remember that pamphlet about the Rosenbergs. I don't know why.

"Then we moved to North Dakota and I discovered one book in the library, 'Das Kapital.' It was what I'd been looking for. It was like a very religious man opening the Bible for the first time.

"I started to study Marxist economic theories. I could see the impoverishment of the masses before my eyes in my own mother. I thought the worker's life could be better. I found some Marxist books on dusty shelves in the New Orleans library and continued to indoctrinate myself for five years."

He said he had been waiting to get out of the Marine Corps "like waiting to get out of prison."

Dispatches at the time had also quoted him as saying he considered the occupation of Japan "imperialistic."

Oswald was said to have told embassy officials he planned to inform the Soviets about everything he learned while he had been a radar operator during his three-year enlistment in the Marines.

On Nov. 14, 1959, he said Soviet officials had refused to grant him citizenship, but had told him he could live in the Soviet Union as an alien resident.

In the Soviet Union he was understood to have worked in a factory at Minsk, where he ostensibly became disillusioned with life under Communist rule. He married a Minsk hospital employe, Marina Nikoloyevna, now about 22 years old.

The United States Embassy in Moscow said yesterday that a daughter was born to the couple last year.

In Washington, Senator John G. Tower, Republican of Texas, made public yesterday a letter he had received from Oswald from Minsk in January, 1962: With misspellings, it read:

"Dear Senator Tower,

"My name is Lee Harvey Oswald, 22, of Ft. Worth up till Oct. 1959, when I came to the Soviet Union for a residenual stay. I took a residenual document for a non-Soviet person living for a time in the U.S.S.R. The American Embassy in Moscow is familiar with my case.

"Since July 20th, 1960, I have unsuccessfully applied for a Soviet exit visa to leave this country, the Soviets refuse to permit me and my Soviet wife, (who applied at the U.S. Embassy Moscow, July 8, 1960 for immigration status to the U.S.A.) to leave the Soviet Union. I am a citizen of the United States of America (Passport Number 1733242, 1959) and I beseech you, Senator Tower, to rise the question of holding by the Soviet Union of a citizen of the U.S., against his will and expressed desires.

"Yours very truly,

"Lee H. Oswald."

Request Relayed

Senator Tower passed on this word by a letter Jan. 26, 1962, to Frederick G. Dutton, Assistant Secretary of State for Congressional Relations. The Senator said he did not know Oswald or any of the facts, or what action, if any, this Government should take.

A memorandum by one of the Senator's aides, Miss Linda Lovelady, said the State Department reported on Feb. 1, 1962, that Oswald "now wishes to return to U. S. with his Soviet wife, who is pregnant."

The memorandum said his mother was living in Vernon, Tex., and "unable to pay for his return—State Department will probably finance this on a loan basis."

The State Department decided Oswald had not expatriated himself, and still held United States citizenship. As it does for United States citizens stranded abroad, it provided for a loan—listed at $435.71—to pay for the transportation of Oswald, his wife and newborn child.

Government records indicate he left Moscow at the end of May, 1962. It is not clear whether he ever repaid the loan.

The Soviet authorities had granted exit permits for him and his family, not always the easiest problem for foreigners with Russian wives.

In Miami, José Antonio Lanuza, spokesman for the Cuban Student Directorrate, said yesterday that Oswald had approached that anti-Castro group's New Orleans delegate, Carlos Bringuier, last July. Mr. Lanuza said Oswald asserted he wanted to help Cubans in a fight against Communism, and offered a $10 contribution and his aid in military training for an invasion.

"I was suspicious of him from the start," said Mr. Bringuier, 29, who has lived in New Orleans since February, 1961, and who operates a retail clothing store. "But frankly I thought he might be an agent from the F.B.I. or the C.I.A. trying to find out what we might be up to."

Mr. Bringuier said in New Orleans that Oswald had given him a blue paperback, "Guidebook for Marines," with his name penciled on the first page, "Pvt. Lee H. Oswald."

According to Mr. Lanuza, Oswald showed up with some pickets on Canal Street, New Orleans, some days later. Their signs read: "Hands Off Cuba," "Viva Castro!" and "Let's Send Medicine and Food to Cuba Instead of Cuban Raiders."

Mr. Bringuier and some other anti-Castro Cubans grabbed his literature away, and Mr. Bringuier and Oswald and some others were arrested. The New Orleans police reported that Oswald was fined $10 in City Court last August for disturbing the peace.

Discussion on Radio

On Aug. 21, Oswald took part in a panel discussion on radio station WDSU in New Orleans. He had identified himself as secretary of the New Orleans Chapter of the Fair Play for Cuba Committee—although last night that national organization's director, Vincent Theodore Lee, said there was no such chapter and denied knowing Oswald.

In the discussion, Oswald said he was a Marxist but denied he was a Communist, and said there was "a very great difference." He noted that many diverse parties were "based on Marxism."

Oswald said his three-year residence in the Soviet Union "gives me excellent qualifications to repudiate charges that Cuba and the Fair Play for Cuba Committee's Communist controlled." He said the committee had been investigated and "the total result was zero."

'Ideals Are Very Clear'

"The principles of the Fair Play for Cuba," he went on, "consist of restoration of diplomatic trade and tourist relations with Cuba. We are striving to get the United States to adopt measures which would be more friendly toward the Cuban people and the new Cuban regime in this country. . . .

"Our aims and our ideals are very clear, and in the best keeping with American traditions of democracy."

A participant asked if Oswald agreed with a Castro statement describing President Kennedy as a ruffian and a thief.

"I would not agree with that particular wording," Oswald said.

The panel program "so discredited" Oswald, Mr. Lanuza asserted in Miami, that "the Fair Play for Cuba Committee transferred him to Dallas." Mr. Lee denied last night that there were any Fair Play chapters in Texas.

Recently he and his wife have been living in Irving, a suburb of Dallas. The Dallas police said they now have two children. His wife does not speak English.

His mother, Mrs. Marguerite Oswald, lives in Fort Worth. When told yesterday her son had been arrested, she said:

"I am heartbroken about this. He is really a good boy."

Associated Press

ROOM FROM WHICH SHOTS WERE FIRED: Police officials and newsmen examining the store room at the Texas School Book Depository which was used in fatal shooting.

United Press International

WEAPON FOUND: A rifle, found on a fifth-floor landing of the building overlooking the place where President Kennedy was shot, is carried by a Dallas detective.

Oswald, When a Marine, Was Not a Crack Shot

As marines go, Lee Harvey Oswald was not highly regarded as a rifleman.

When he first entered the Marine Corps in 1956, he qualified as a sharpshooter with a score of 212 out of a possible 250. On his second proficiency test two years later, he fell back to marksman category with a score of 191.

The Marine rifle ratings are: marksman, 190 to 209; sharpshooter, 210 to 219, and expert, 220 to 250.

First, 'Is It True?' Then Anger and Anguish Among New Yorkers and Visitors

NEWS OF TRAGEDY SPREADS QUICKLY

Men Say 'My God!' and Cry, Shoppers Stop to Pray and Many Businesses Close

By GEORGE BARRETT

The cry rang across the city, echoing again and again: "Is it true?" Another cry quickly took its place as the news of the death of President Kennedy swept with stunning impact: "My God!"

Women wept, and men wept. A refusal to believe the report of the assassination was the immediate reaction, but swiftly came horror, then anguish, and then, among many, both city residents and visitors, deep anger.

The news spread quickly, and the shocked hundreds of thousands reached for so many telephones that the system blacked out and operators had to refuse calls. Shoppers in department stores clustered instinctively, and in at least one store they stopped buying and prayed together, some of them silently, some aloud.

In all parts of the five boroughs motorists pulled up their cars and sat hunched up over their dashboard radios. At red traffic lights the cry cascaded from car to car, from pedestrian to motorist: "Is it true?"

Many companies canceled newspaper advertisements as they carried out plans to curtail operations in mourning.

In many respects the biggest city in the nation turned into something of a ghost town. All Broadway theaters and all musical events closed last night in mourning for the President. Almost every major event — social, political, athletic—was canceled.

Hotel Ballrooms Closed

A number of the city's colleges and universities called off their classes yesterday afternoon. In some cases Saturday classes were also canceled.

The city's hotels closed their ballrooms and suites where social events had been scheduled.

In some hospitals physicians and nurses went on emergency rounds to give sedatives to patients who were agitated by the news.

Uptown, midtown, downtown, work in offices came to an abrupt halt as employes hovered over transistor radios. Some people went home at once, and many managements shut up shop for the day.

The grief, shock and incredulity were a terrible mirror of April 12, 1945, when the news of President Franklin D. Roosevelt's death toward the end of World War II hit the city and the world. But there was another dominant emotion yesterday—anger.

Bitterness and even savagery were expressed. A question repeated time and again was: "Where was his protection?"

It was a truck driver, Griff Clarke of Huntington Beach, L.I., who caught the sentiment that so many shared with this outburst: "This is a disgrace to the country!"

It was Michael Baruth of Yonkers who reflected the feeling of horror with the query: "What kind of madmen would do a thing like that?"

Flags at Half-Staff

All flags on municipal buildings were ordered to half-staff by Mayor Wagner, and throughout the city businesses, theaters and apartment houses lowered their flags without waiting for instructions.

Typical of the business community's reaction to Mr. Kennedy's death was the order that went out from the Fifth Avenue Association to all member stores. They were asked to fly flags at half-staff and to turn off all Christmas lighting, including the annual spectaculars in Fifth Avenue windows, until further notice.

Saks Fifth Avenue and Best & Company changed Fifth Avenue windows late in the afternoon to pay homage to Mr. Kennedy. At Saks a photograph of President Kennedy was placed on a chair and flanked by urns of red roses. At Best's the window contained an American flag with a black crepe on its staff and a watercolor of Mr. Kennedy.

Crowds gathered in front of the displays, and tears were openly shed.

At hundreds of places all flags were taken down — the flags of members of the United Nations, the city flag, the state flag, house and club flags — to express full homage with the United States flag alone.

Texas was the target of wrath for scores of persons, who used phrases like "damned Texans" and other profanities.

A number of persons said that they did not take subways or buses on short trips after the news, but decided to walk just to be alone with their thoughts. One common scene was the tight grasp of one man's hand on another's arm as they discussed the assassination.

In the Bronx, at the corner of Fordham Road and Grand Concourse, a predominantly Jewish and Irish area where the President had been popular, immediate reaction was as much anger as shock.

Max Schechter, a newsstand dealer, said: "Our President traveled to practically every country in the world and was safe. In his own country he had to be assassinated. It's a disgrace."

Mrs. Anne Nightingale, a department store saleswoman who lives at 966 East 181st Street, declared: "He didn't deserve it. I would do anything to bring him back."

The grief and the acts of mourning knew no special group, no particular section of the city and no political convictions. The sorrow and the shock were unfolded in the human vignette, the collection of individuals who stared as though in a trance from their subway seats, their stools at luncheon counters, their chairs near television sets.

At the intersection of Court and Centre Streets, one motorist stopped his car in the middle of traffic and walked over to a sidewalk luncheonette. He asked the counterman: "Is it true?" The counterman didn't look up. "Yes, he's dead," he said.

The motorist returned to his car, slipped under the wheel and sat, motionless and staring. Horns blared, then went soundless as word of the President's death filtered from driver to driver.

Strangers talked to each other in the subway, mostly in soft voices or whispers. Again the awful question, "Is it true?" One man, eyes watering as he heard the answer, spoke as though to himself: "Another Lincoln; he's another Lincoln."

For some hours there was an almost eerie quality as numbers of men and women seemed totally unable to grasp the reality. They ate their lunches automatically; they typed letters without really seeing the unwinding sentences; they reached for the telephone to call home, to talk to someone they know. Those who had no one familiar at hand walked up to strangers and talked about President Kennedy.

The bells of St. Patrick's Cathedral tolled solemnly, and thousands of Roman Catholics went to churches to pray for the nation's first Catholic President.

Msgr. Timothy Flynn of the New York Archdiocese spoke for Catholics and non-Catholics alike when he described the reaction at the archdiocese: "Stupefied horror."

Four servicemen sat in the recruiting booth in Times Square dazed at the news of the loss of their Commander in Chief. Recruiting was halted for the day.

The Astor Bar was grim and silent. One bartender said: "Everybody feels dead, real dead. Everybody feels like crying."

The death of the President was tied in by many Harlem mourners with the fight for civil rights.

Miss Dorothy Cooper of 85 West 119th Street said she was convinced that the assassination "would put quite a damper on the civil-rights fight."

"I think it's going to be terrible, as far as civil rights are concerned," Mrs. Anna Thomas of 226 Edgecombe Avenue said.

However, an attorney, Ivan Michael, said he felt the drive for civil rights would now have greater impetus. "I think we are going to witness a more vigilant drive toward the individual liberty of man," Mr. Michael declared.

Many in the suburbs heard the news quickly because television programs were interrupted. Fred Tracz, a postman in Greenwich, Conn., encountered many housewives who wept as they told him the news.

"They talked about it just as if they lost their son or daughter," he said.

Like hundreds of motorists, James Falabella of Pleasantville, N. Y., had to pull his car to the side of the road and try to absorb the tragedy. "I couldn't drive for a half-hour after I heard the news on my car radio," he said.

Mrs. John Andrews, a housewife in Greenwich, said: "We all have our ideas about this and that in politics. But when the President dies, we are all one family."

"This is an indictment of the American people," Robert L. Tooker, a lawyer in Riverhead, commented. "We have allowed certain factions to work up such furor throughout the South with fanatic criticism of the office of President that a demented person can feel confident that such atrocious action is justifiable."

A farmer in a clothing store said: "I feel sick to my stomach. Maybe in Europe or Asia, but not in the United States in 1963."

Mrs. Edith Bouvier Beale of Apaquoque Road, East Hampton, an aunt of Mrs. Kennedy, said: "My heart is broken."

Here, 'in Our Country'

Misthopoulos Georges, a Greek-born barber who came to the United States 10 years ago, sat in his shop, hunched over, and wept.

"I feel he was a very good boy," he said. "I cry."

For many of the grief-stricken there was special bitterness that such brutality was still possible in the United States. A counter girl commented that the President had traveled over so much of the world and "yet here, in our own country, a savage kills him."

At the intersection of Flatbush Avenue and Sixth Avenue, in the Park Slope area of Brooklyn, pedestrians and office workers out for lunch groped to describe their emotions, and often just shook their heads and refused to speak.

"Oh, my God, oh, my God, oh, my God," were the only words that Mrs. Louis Greenberg could say. She did not buy the lamp that she and her husband had decided to get yesterday.

In Trenton grief spread through the corridors of the New Jersey State House, and at 3 P.M. Gov. Richard J. Hughes ordered all state offices closed for the day.

Dr. Edward Brailove, a dentist, weeping said: "Wasn't it horrible? I can't work. I've sent two patients home and I've closed my office."

THE NEWS TRAVELED FAST: One of the crowds that gathered yesterday as word of the attack on the President was given on the radio. This was a Times Square scene. Many telephoned friends of shooting, after hearing radio.

AT ST. PATRICK'S: Passers-by stop to worship at the cathedral after hearing of the President's death

The New York Times

SILENT MOURNER: A woman pauses on hearing the news

Eyewitnesses Describe Scene of Assassination

Sounds of Shooting Brought Cars to Halt — Motorcade Sped Kennedy to Hospital

Following is a description of the assassination of President Kennedy yesterday, written by Jack Bell of The Associated Press, who witnessed the shooting from the fourth car behind the President:

DALLAS, Nov. 22 (AP)—There was a loud bang as though a giant firecracker had exploded in the caverns between the tall buildings we were just leaving behind us.

In quick succession there were two other loud reports.

The ominous sound of these dismissed from the minds of us riding in the reporters' "pool" car the fleeting idea that some Texan was adding a bit of noise to the cheering welcome Dallas had given John F. Kennedy.

The reports sounded like rifle shots.

The man in front of me screamed, "My God, they're shooting at the President!"

Our driver braked the car sharply and we swung the doors open to leap out. Suddenly the procession, which had halted, shot forward again.

In the flash of that instant, a little tableau was enacted in front of a colonnade toward which the velvetly green grass swelled upward to a small park near the top of an underpass for which we had been headed.

Cars Speed Ahead

A man was pushing a woman dressed in a bright orange to the ground and seemed to be falling protectively over her. A photographer, scrambling on all fours toward the crest of the rise, held a camera trained in their direction.

As my eye swept the buildings to the right, where the shots—if they really were shots; and it seemed unbelievable—might have come, I saw no significant sign of activity.

Four cars ahead, in the President's Continental limousine, a man in the front seat rose for a moment. He seemed to have a telephone in hand as he waved to a police cruiser ahead to go on.

The Presidential car leaped ahead and those following it attained breakneck speed as the caravan roared through the underpass and on to a broad freeway, police sirens whining shrilly. These sirens had been silenced by Presidential order throughout Mr. Kennedy's Texas trip.

Up to the highway we thundered, careening around a turn into the Parkland Hospital and screeching to a stop at the emergency entrance.

As we piled out of our car, I saw Mrs. Kennedy, weeping, trying to hold her husband's head up. Mrs. John Connally was helping hold up the Governor of Texas.

President in Back Seat

Mr. Connally's suit front was splattered with blood, his head rolling backward.

By the time I had covered the distance to the Presidential car, Secret Service men were helping Mrs. Kennedy away. Hospital attendants were aiding Mr. and Mrs. Connally.

For an instant I stopped and stared into the back seat. There, face down, stretched out at full length, lay the President, motionless.

His natty business suit seemed hardly rumpled. But there was blood on the floor.

"Is he dead?" I asked a Secret Service man.

"I don't know," he said, "but I don't think so."

I ran for a telephone.

A few minutes later I was back for more information.

The President and Mr. Connally had been moved into an emergency operating room. Vice President Johnson, Mrs. Johnson and Mrs. Kennedy had been escorted into the hospital.

The shiny White House automobile, a manufacturers' dream, stood untouched. It had been flown 1,500 miles from Washington only to become the death vehicle of the President, to whom it was designed to give maximum protection.

Two Hats on Seat

On the front seat floor lay the soft felt hat the President often carried but seldom wore. Beside it in mute comradeship was the wide-brimmed, light-colored Texas-style hat that Mr. Connally wore.

In the wide area between the seats, now cleared of its jump seats, three twisted and torn roses lay in a pool of blood on the floor. Beside them was a tattered bouquet of asters.

It all seemed so unreal. This was the conveyance for what had been in the nature of triumph for Mr. Kennedy and the First Lady, who had been smiling, shaking hands and filled with happiness at a day of meeting the folks in the streets, the airports and the hotels.

Ironically, if their reception in Texas had not been so warm, precautions might have been taken to raise the shatter-proof side glasses, even though the top of the convertible was down. Such protection might have saved the President.

But Dallas, where the President's policies had raised a storm of conservative protests, had been warm in its welcome to the handsome, bronzed President and his pretty, chic wife.

The Presidential party appeared to be chatting gaily among themselves after they had left the crowds of downtown Dallas behind and their caravan had swung into a quiet area where admirers had not chosen to stand.

But there the assassin took his stand.

His three well-aimed shots plunged America and the world into grief.

10 Feet From President

TORONTO, Nov. 22 (Canadian Press)—A man from suburban Willowdale who was only 10 feet away when President Kennedy was assassinated today said he first thought the gunfire was the sound of firecrackers.

Norman Similas, 34 years old, told The Star in a telephone conversation that he had been in Dallas on business. He was taking pictures of the motorcade when he saw the President slump to the floor, he said.

Here is his story:

"I was in Dallas on a convention and I decided to snap a picture of the President as the motorcade rolled by.

"The crowds had thinned out just past an overpass near the Trade Mart, so I had a good position when the motorcade came by at about 8 miles an hour.

"Then I suddenly heard a sharp crack. The first thing that came to my mind was that someone was setting off firecrackers. I turned away from the President's car and looked back to where the noise seemed to come from.

Agent Draws Gun

"Then somebody — I don't know who it was—yelled: 'The President's been shot.'

"I swung back to look at the car. A Secret Service man ran up with his gun drawn. A policeman beside me drew his revolver and his eyes searched the crowd.

"Then another shot rang out and a third almost immediately on top of it.

"I was still staring at the car. The Secret Service man opened the car door and I saw the President slumped down to the floor and falling toward the pavement.

"Jackie Kennedy was sitting on the left side of the car and Governor Connally on the President's right.

"I could see a hole in the President's left temple and his head and hair were bathed in blood.

"The agent looked in and gasped: 'Oh, my God, he's dead.'"

Boy Describes Shooting

Special to The New York Times

CHICAGO, Nov. 22—The Chicago Tribune published today an eyewitness report by a 14-year-old boy who was standing 10 feet away and looking directly at President Kennedy at the time of the assassination. The boy, Alan Smith, a Boy Scout and a ninth-grade pupil at the Stockyard Junior High School, giving the following description:

"It made me weak. I felt like sitting down. It was horrible.

"I was standing on the curb watching the parade along Main Street. We were permitted to skip school, if we had a note from our parents, to watch it.

"The crowds were cheering, but all at once they changed to screaming. The car was about 10 feet from me when a bullet hit the President in his forehead. The bullets came from a window right over my head in the building in front of which my friends and I were standing.

"Mr. Kennedy had a big wide smile. But when he was hit, his face turned blank. There was no smile no frown—nothing. He fell down over Jackie's knees and didn't say anything.

"She stood up screaming, 'God, oh God, no.' There was blood all over her and everything. She tried to raise him up but he fell back over her."

The New York Times Nov. 23, 1963

ASSASSINATION: President Kennedy was shot at triple underpass (1) in Dallas. He was en route to Merchandise Mart (2) where he was scheduled to speak. He was taken to Parkland Hospital (3), where he was pronounced dead. At Love Field (4), his body was flown back to Washington and Lyndon Johnson took oath of office as President.

MEMORIES OF VISIT ADD TO IRISH GRIEF

Special to The New York Times

DUBLIN, Nov. 22—All Ireland was stunned by the President's assassination.

With the memory of his triumphal visit last summer to the land of his forefathers still fresh, people felt a sense of terrible shock and personal loss.

Many people wept in the streets. Others went into churches to pray.

Crowds gathered around radio and television stores.

The state radio and the Irish television station canceled all previously scheduled programs.

Extracts from the film of the President's visit to Ireland were shown on television.

United States Ambassador Matthew H. McCloskey, an old friend of the Kennedy family, spoke on the radio.

President DeValera said in a message to Mrs. Kennedy: "The whole Irish people mourn in sympathy with you. Their hearts go out to you in this hour of terrible sorrow for you."

Prime Minister Sean Lemass also sent a message of sympathy.

DUBLIN, Nov. 22 (Reuters) — President de Valera twice broke down from emotion as he addressed the nation over television in a tribute to President Kennedy.

Jagan Sends Condolences To Mrs. Kennedy and Nation

Special to The New York Times

GEORGETOWN, British Guiana, Nov. 22—Premier Cheddi B. Jagan conveyed the sympathy of his Government and the people of British Guiana in a message to Mrs. Kennedy, members of the Kennedy family and the United States.

Flags on the Parliament house and other government buildings were ordered flown at half-staff.

Sir Ralph Grey, the colony's Governor, called Mr. Kennedy "one of the greatest advocates of fair play and justice in the 20th century."

The Most Rev. Dr. Alan Knight, Anglican Archbishop of the West Indies, said "he was beloved by true Christians everywhere on earth."

The City Goes Dark and Cancels Activities as the President Is Mourned

Continued From Page 1, Col. 5

their doors and darkened their marquees. Television chains canceled all entertainment programs and commercials.

As dusk came, automatic devices turned on the huge, gaudy signs that normally blot out the night in the Times Square area. Then, one by one, the lights blinked out, turning the great carnival strip into what was almost a mourning band on the city's sleeve.

The Harvard-Yale and Princeton-Dartmouth football games and scores of other contests at colleges and schools were canceled for Saturday.

Dinner dances, cocktail parties, banquets and other social events were called off throughout the metropolitan area. All the city's major hotels canceled entertainment in their public rooms.

There were exceptions, of course. In outlying Manhattan neighborhoods and in the other boroughs, the visible evidence of shock and sorrow was less spectacular. Movie theaters and shops remained lighted and open, but crowds were sparse and subdued.

Restaurants, by decision of their trade associations, operated as usual for public convenience and necessity. Bars were open, often with customers three deep, talking in hushed tones, eyes glued to television sets that repeated the news over and over again.

Twelve all-night movie houses on 42d Street between the Avenue of the Americas and Eighth Avenue darkened their main display signs but were open for business. One of them expressed the street's attitude with a picture called "Carry On, Regardless."

In the same area, in a penny arcade, rifle shots snapped against moving targets and none of half a dozen marksmen seemed to think it was an odd way to pass the time. Two record stores blared music into the otherwise subdued street.

Crowd Below Normal

Elsewhere in the city's five boroughs, stores and most theaters remained open as usual, but in many centers crowds were well below normal for Friday night.

Most neighborhood movie theaters remained open, but they had nearly empty houses. In Greenwich Village most of the major night spots that offer entertainment were closed and the majority of off-Broadway legitimate houses also canceled performances.

In Brooklyn, only the young seemed to be out in normal force and spirits.

In the King's Highway area, the police and store-keepers found activity off by at least 60 per cent. There was a similar relative hush at Flatbush and Church Avenues, where a taxi driver commented, "It looks like a different town."

Most Brooklyn movie houses were open, but the Albemarle Theater on Flatbush Avenue turned away would-be patrons with a sign: "Out of respect for the late President John F. Kennedy this theater will be closed for the rest of the day."

Along Jamaica Avenue in Queens, the three big department stores that dominate most busy Friday nights — Macy's, May's and Gertz—had closed their doors. Many smaller stores also closed, and those that remained open had little or no business.

The early evening pattern was less distinct in Harlem, where night life normally gets under way at a later hour. Crowds appeared nearly normal and the only notable closing reported was that of the Apollo Theater, a vaudeville house on 125th Street.

Rights Drive Questioned

Harlem bar conversation centered nervously and with some hostility on the new President, Lyndon B. Johnson, and speculation that the drive for integration and a major civil rights bill would be slowed or halted with a Texan in the White House.

"Let's see what your cracker President is going to do for you now," a Harlem bartender said to his customers.

At the Chinese Public School, supported by Chinatown residents, Kenneth Chan, the principal, called 700 students together for a special memorial service at nightfall.

Earlier in the day, hundreds of public and private events—school and university classes, receptions, formal dinners, dances—were halted in mid-course or canceled.

All city, state and Federal courts closed as soon as word of the assassination spread.

George Szell, conducting the New York Philharmonic at Philharmonic Hall, ended the concert abruptly after completing Beethoven's "Leonore" Overture No. 3.

Among scores of social events abruptly canceled was the Annual Freedom Award Dinner of the Order of Lafayette at which former President Dwight D. Eisenhower and Gen. Lucius D. Clay were to have received awards.

Senate, Stunned and Confused by Word of the Shooting, Adjourns Until Monday

BROTHER IN CHAIR AS NEWS ARRIVES

Edward Kennedy Leaves the Dais Quickly — Party Leaders Voice Grief

By CABELL PHILLIPS
Special to The New York Times

WASHINGTON, Nov. 22—The Senate was stunned into somber confusion today with news that President Kennedy had been shot.

Majority Leader Mike Mansfield was too overcome to offer a motion for adjournment. The task fell to Minority Leader Everett McKinley Dirksen.

Nowhere does the official record show the reason for the sudden cessation of the day's activities. In the confusion, the shooting was not mentioned.

By ironic coincidence, the Presidents' brother Senator Edward M. Kennedy of Massachusetts, was occuping the presiding officer's chair when a Senate aide whispered the news in his ear. He gathered his papers and quickly left the dais.

About 50 visitors were scattered about the galleries. They apparently had no intimation of the tragedy until Senate Chaplain Frederick Brown Harris invoked God's assistance "as the President of the Republic goes down like a giant cedar." Suddenly, they stirred in consternation.

The word spread quickly, however, after the first bulletins arrived over the news wires. Expressions of shock, sympathy and anger against the assassination poured forth as the news spread over Capitol Hill. The familiar roles of partisan and ideological difference dissolved in a common wave of grief and dismay.

Senate Leaders Comment

Senator Mansfield, in a statement issued later in the afternoon, said: "I will miss him as a friend, the nation will miss him as a President and the world will miss him as a leader."

Senator Dirksen told reporters: "Only someone suffering from aberrations of personality and motivated insane passion would be guilty of the assassination of the great leader of the greatest country on earth."

The House of Representatives was not in session today and many of its members were out of the city.

First word of the attack on the President was taken to the Senate floor by Richard Riedel, press liaison officer. He spotted the bulletins on the Associated Press news ticker in the Senators' lobby at 1:42 o'clock.

He darted onto the floor, where a handful of members were in desultory debate over a bill on Federal library services. Senator Winston Prouty, Republican of Vermont, was speaking. Neither the Republican nor Democratic leader was present. The leader's seat was occupied by Senator Wayne Morse, Democrat of Oregon, manager of the library bill.

Mr. Reidel gave his message to the first Senator he encountered, Spessard Holland, Democrat of Florida.

"The President has just been shot," he whispered. He went next to Senator Morse and repeated the message.

Then he spotted Senator Kennedy on the dais and went to him.

"Senator," he said, "your brother has just been shot."

Mr. Reidel said that Senator Kennedy gasped: "No!," quickly left his seat and went into the lobby. There he put through a telephone call to the White House and another to Attorney General Robert F. Kennedy, his brother. He then departed hastily for his office in the Old Senate Office Building.

Senator Holland quietly replaced Senator Kennedy in the presiding officer's chair.

Meanwhile, Senator Morse had interrupted debate to ask for a quorum call. This most familiar of delaying tactics, he said later, was used to gain time until he could get the two Senate leaders on the floor.

Senators Mansfield and Dirksen had already been appraised of the news in their offices by a call from a reporter in the press gallery. They hurried to the floor.

Mr. Mansfield withdrew the quorum call and announced that the Senate would be in recess "pending further developments."

As a dozen or more Senators gathered in knots to discuss the news, the two leaders withdrew to the majority leader's office. Mr. Mansfield talked briefly by telephone with a Presidential assistant, Ralph Dungan. It was not certain at that time whether the President had succumbed.

The two leaders returned to the Senate and the session was reconvened at 2:10. About 50 Senators, anxiety marking their faces, had assembled. In a voice that occasionally quavered with emotion, Mr. Mansfield rose to address the chair.

"Mr. President," he said, "after discussing the tragic situation which now confronts the nation and the free world, the distinguished minority leader and I feel that it is only appropriate and proper, in view of the tragic circumstances which have arisen, and the extreme danger which confronts a good, decent and a kindly man, that it would not be inappropriate for the chaplain of the Senate to deliver a prayer at this time of hope that he and the Governor of Texas [John B. Connally Jr.] will recover."

"On the completion of that prayer, we shall move to adjourn until 12 o'clock noon Monday next."

The chaplain asked the Senate to stand for a moment of silent prayer. Then, with deep gravity, he said:

"Our Father, Thou knoweth that this sudden almost unbelievable news has stunned our minds and hearts. We gaze at a vacant place against the sky, as the President of the Republic goes down like a giant cedar, green with boughs. We pray that in Thy will his life may still be spared.

"In this hour we cry out in words that were uttered in another hour of deep loss and bereavement: 'God lives and the Government at Washington still stands.'

"Hold us, we pray, and the people of America, calm and steady and full of faith for the Republic this tragic hour of our history.

"God save the state and empower her for whatever awaits the great world role she has been called upon to fill in this time of destiny. Amen."

The Senate Republican conference formally adopted a resolution describing President Kennedy as a "friend" and a "distinguished Chief Executive."

The resolution was approved at a midafternoon meeting in the office of Senator Dirksen of Illinois, after news of the President's death had been received. It expressed "profound regret and sorrow over his untimely and tragic passing" on behalf of the Senate's 33 Republicans.

As a former Senate colleague, it said, the President "maintained with the Republican members a cordial and understanding relationship which endeared him as a friend and a fellow public servant."

The resolution will be sent to the Kennedy family.

Other Congressional Comment

WASHINGTON, Nov. 22 (UPI)—"My God . . . My God . . . what are we coming to," were the only words that John McCormack, Speaker of the House of Representatives, could utter when told that President Kennedy had been shot down in Dallas.

Mr. McCormack's dazed response was echoed throughout the tragic afternoon by other Senators and Representatives who had served with the slain Chief Executive before he entered the White House.

Senator Margaret Chase Smith, Republican of Maine, burst into tears when she was told the news while eating lunch.

Senator Richard B. Russell, Democrat of Georgia, leader of the Senate's Southern bloc, spoke of "this dastardly crime." He said: "The assassin's bullet has stricken a brilliant and dedicated statesman at the very height of his powers."

The House Republican leader, Charles A. Halleck of Indiana, branded the assassination "an unspeakable crime against all the people of this country."

"The world should know," he eulogized, "that in this hour of national tragedy, Americans stand together as one—shocked and grieved at this unbelievable news."

The Senate Democratic whip, Hubert H. Humphrey of Minnesota, who contested the Presidential primaries with Mr. Kennedy in 1960, said: "America has lost a great President. The world has lost a great leader. I have lost a good friend. What an incredible tragedy."

Representative Adam Clayton Powell, Democrat of New York, said every Federal and state effort should be made to punish the guilty. He also said that "all Americans who have any sanity, any character, any religious beliefs, irrespective of color, political creed or religion, should now rally around Lyndon Johnson to try to lift America back to the level of prestige that has now been destroyed."

United Press International Telephoto

SYMBOL OF THE NATION'S MOURNING: Flag on White House flies at half-staff

PARTIES' OUTLOOK FOR 1964 ALTERED

Continued From Page 1, Col. 3

national political scene: The President would run again. He would be stronger in some states, weaker in the South. He would run with Lyndon B. Johnson again. He would debate his opponent. He would be favored to win.

Now, following the tragedy in Texas, there seemed to be only questions, thrust so suddenly on the minds of political leaders of both parties that there were few answers. These were some of the questions:

Questions Raised

¶Will President Johnson be able to insure his own nomination next August, on the basis of an inherited nine months in the White House?

¶Will liberal elements in the Democratic party make any attempt to dislodge Mr. Johnson in favor of a candidate more to their liking?

¶Could Mr. Johnson, running as the first Southern Presidential candidate of this century, win support in the South despite his espousal of the civil rights cause?

¶What influence will the political motivation of the assassin, if any, have on the great wave of public revulsion against the act? Will the people turn against left-wing or right-wing extremists — or both?

¶How will the immediate prospect of fierce two-party competition in next year's Presidential election influence Republican leaders in their choice of a candidate?

Despite the many questions raised, one political consequence seemed clear in the hushed, almost ashamed, assessments that observers undertook this evening: The death of the President gave new life to Republican hopes.

Whatever political liabilities might have encumbered him, John F. Kennedy was an incumbent President, one whose person and personality had been impressed on the American electorate.

All Changed Now

Republican leaders knew this. While they loudly scored what they saw as his weaknesses, they saw Mr. Kennedy as a figure to be reckoned with politically. Their candidate would almost surely be the underdog.

Now, in the flash of a gunshot, all that is changed. The Republican Presidential candidate, whoever he may be, will be running against a man with nine months in the White House—or none at all—instead of nearly four years of unremitting public exposure.

When the first shock of the tragedy has subsided and politicians talk again, they are sure to feel that the Republicans face a new, more favorable course next year. And this is likely to affect their choice of a candidate considerably.

Republican leaders have been saying for months that one of the powerful factors favoring the nomination of Senator Barry Goldwater of Arizona was the prevailing belief that President Kennedy would win anyway. Next year, they said, could be the one to gamble with a controversial candidate.

But now, they may reason, it may not be a time for Republican gambling. It may instead be a time to put a Republican candidate of the broadest possible appeal into the lists to challenge President Johnson or another Democratic nominee.

This conviction, if it became strong enough, could move Republican leaders strongly toward a candidate like Richard M. Nixon, or even Thomas E. Dewey.

Rockefeller's Chances

It might assist Nelson A. Rockefeller by removing his chief current rival, Senator Goldwater, from the scene, but it might also find the New York Governor too narrow in appeal for a real Presidential candidate.

The prospect of President Johnson's candidacy next year appeared also to have raised serious, if not fatal, questions about the Southern strategy on which Senator Goldwater's supporters have been relying heavily.

While Mr. Goldwater might have carried the states of the Old Confederacy against President Kennedy, there is not the same assurance that he could do so against Mr. Johnson, even with the President firmly dedicated to civil rights. Goldwater supporters may have to tally their possible electoral votes again.

Among the Democrats, the passing of the President seems sure to focus increased political attention on his brother, Attorney General Robert F. Kennedy, and the role he may play in the new administration.

If the great national wave of sadness and sympathy is still perceptible a year from now, it is the Attorney General rather than the President to whom it is more likely to attach.

Widespread Effect

Like all major political catastrophes at the highest level, the passing of President Kennedy will be measurable down through the ranks of the Democratic party among many if not all of those whose names would have shared the ballot with him next November.

Where Mr. Kennedy appeared strong, in the urban industrial states of the nation, Democratic candidates for the Senate and House must reassess their prospects. Now they must try to measure what it will mean to them to run with President Johnson, or another Democrat as yet unknown.

In these same states, Republican Congressional nominations may become more attractive to candidates who have been avoiding such a challenge in a Presidential year.

In politics, the day's appalling events demonstrated, there is only change.

All New York Police Are Placed on Alert

All New York City policemen were held in reserve last night, should there be "any unexpected reaction" to the assassination of President Kennedy, Police Commissioner Michael J. Murphy said.

A message sent to all police commands ordered patrolmen normally off duty at 4 P.M. stay at their posts until 8 P.M.

Those patrolmen who had been scheduled to report at midnight were told to report to their precincts at 8 P.M.

THRONG GATHERS AT WHITE HOUSE

Capital Church Bells Toll—Embassy Flags Lowered

By NAN ROBERTSON
Special to The New York Times

WASHINGTON, Nov. 22—The sound of Washington today was the sound of church bells endlessly tolling and transistor radios conveying the unbelievable horror that the President of the United States was dead from an assassin's bullet.

A thousand people gathered along Pennsylvania Avenue opposite the White House as dusk settled, drawn irresistibly to stand and wait—for what they did not quite know.

A car with a poster on the roof rolled around and around the square. "The wrath of God is upon us," it said. "Jesus Christ saves from all sin."

On Massachusetts Avenue's embassy row, flags of every hue and nation hung at half-staff in the muggy, breathless atmosphere.

In a Washington supermarket, men and women wept unashamedly as the news blared from the radio. Check-out clerks fled their stations in tears.

Strangers stopped one another on the streets. "My God, my God!" they said. "Did you hear?"

Birchers Accused

In a Washington office, a man ranted against the assassin. "Look what the Birchers have done!" he cried. Neither he nor fellow workers who listened to him knew then that a prime suspect had been picked up in Dallas — a left-winger.

The first word of the shooting, coming during the lunch hour, nearly emptied restaurants.

Robert Auburn of Pasadena, a travelogue producer, was at a restaurant with his wife when he heard a waitress say: "Assassinated!"

"I knew it was somebody important, he said. "Ordinary people get killed. Important people are assassinated The last thought in my mind was that our President was the one."

A woman tourist, impelled like so many others to wait near the White House, said: "It seems unpardonable in a country that is so blessed with all the good things. I wouldn't have thought the man would have any enemies that felt that wickedly."

Those who refused to believe it was true — and there were many disbelievers in Lafayette Square facing the White House — finally accepted it when the flag above the Executive Mansion was lowered to half staff at 2:45 P.M.

Civil-Rights Issue Blamed

David S. Urey, a law student, watched the flag flutter down the staff.

"I certainly wasn't pro-Kennedy," he said. "As a matter of fact, I was supporting Goldwater. But the thought that comes to me is that this is the second President we've lost now on the civil-rights issue—Lincoln and Kennedy. I don't know how anyone could have strong enough sentiment on another issue to assassinate him."

A strapping man standing nearby did not bother to wipe away the tears that streamed down his cheeks. Haltingly, he said: "I was driving to pick up my little girl at school. I heard it over my radio. I don't know why I came here. I had a feeling."

A retired civil servant heard the "unbelievable news that he was dead" on her radio at home. "I felt as if I couldn't stay at home alone and endure it," she said, so she walked more than a mile to join the throng at the White House.

Before policemen asked the crowd to leave the fence in front of the Executive Mansion and step behind ropes across the street, a young girl thrust a bunch of crysanthemums through the bars. It hung there, flowers for the dead, until White House policemen took it away.

Blaring Headlines

On street corners all over the city, people huddled close around anyone who carried a transistor radio. Others walked or stood gazing at newspaper extras with large headlines reading, "JFK Is Slain!" or "President Is Killed by Sniper in Texas!"

Worshipers knelt or sat with bowed heads and brimming eyes in St. John's Episcopal Church, known as the "Church of the Presidents," a block from the White House. Every President from Madison to Eisenhower attended services there occasionally. In the gold-topped spire above, the bell tolled through the long afternoon.

A 20-year-old busboy was standing in front of the White House clutching four color postcards of Mr. Kennedy. "When I heard the news, I was so shocked I just went out and bought these for my own personal use," he said.

"This is a black day," said Philip Warren, an employe of the National Association of Counties. "This doesn't make sense at all. I thought this country was beyond that."

A bearded student from George Washington University felt "as if the end of the world had come along and you're not prepared for it." When he first heard the news, he said, "I went for a drive to calm myself down; when that didn't work, I finally came to the White House."

Few of those clustered in the area could give a reason for their presence. No one could understand why the president had been assassinated.

"It must have been a maniac," one said. "What will happen to us now?"

Foreign Policy Role

As Kennedy Grew in the Presidency Effective Diplomacy Was His Forte

By MAX FRANKEL

The death of President Kennedy was evaluated in the gravest terms yesterday by foreign diplomatic circles. Mr. Kennedy, by the testimony of all who watched him, had learned in three years to become an effective diplomat.

News Analysis

He managed to assemble and hold together a knowledgeable team of foreign-affairs specialists. He developed an awareness of the nuclear power at his command and persistently sought a working relationship with his principal adversary, Premier Khrushchev.

Even those who have disagreed at times with Mr. Kennedy's policy came to value his grasp of international issues and his simultaneous firmness toward and prudence in dealing with the Soviet Union.

Mr. Kennedy acquired most of his knowledge and skill in office, and it is doubtful that his successor, though widely traveled and reasonably well-briefed, can quickly display comparable talent.

President Kennedy learned from the early mistakes at the Bay of Pigs in Cuba and in complex diplomacy with Europe, and he was soon praised as a man determined to become a forceful leader of the non-communist world.

President Johnson will have to work to match that reputation, which in itself is an indispensable tool of American diplomacy.

Premier Khrushchev had come to have a measure of respect for and understanding of Mr. Kennedy. He valued the American leader's lack of belligerence even as he came to appreciate his agility and toughness in a crisis — as in the Cuban missile affair a year ago.

Soviet propaganda always pulled its punches when it came to Mr. Kennedy's person. Though the first and only Khrushchev-Kennedy meeting in Vienna in 1961 did not go well for the American side, the two men learned each other's habits later on, and depended even in the worst of times on their private channels of communication, on which they realized the peace of the world would hang.

Effect of a Phone Call

When Mr. Kennedy demanded the release of Prof. Frederick C. Barghoorn last week, Mr. Khrushchev readily yielded, with a bow to the personal interest of the President.

Among the Western allies, although diplomacy will remain turbulent, Mr. Kennedy's personality, his grasp of economic issues and his devotion to unity were widely appreciated.

Repeatedly, where diplomats failed, it was the President himself—by letter to Rome or Bonn or, more often, by telephone call to Paris or London—who kept negotiations on the rails and who restored a confidence bruised by events.

The fear of another wave of American isolationism began to spread through Western Europe in recent years. Everywhere, however, there was confidence that as long as John F. Kennedy held office, the United States would remain true to its commitments and forceful in its leadership.

In other nations, especially the smaller nations that themselves are held together often by a single personality, the loss will be even more manifest. Dozens of those leaders have been to Washington in the Kennedy years, and they have gone away impressed by the President's interest in their problems and dedication to their independence.

None of the more important foreign-policy projects of the Kennedy Administration has come anywhere near completion.

The test ban treaty with the Soviet Union, by the President's own definition, was a first step toward relaxing East-West tensions.

The Alliance for Progress, a 10-year project of social reform and economic development in Latin America, was noticeably in trouble.

The grand design of partnership between North America and Western Europe was wracked by dissension, by new nationalism in Europe and by the complexities of economic relations.

But the broad themes of policy behind these projects were beginning to be felt around the world. Mr. Kennedy, it was recognized, stood for toughness against the Russians, but only to achieve more lasting settlements and never at the risk of destroying essential confidence between Moscow and Washington.

Stress on Independence

In a world increasingly preoccupied by nationalist struggles, it was also becoming plain that Mr. Kennedy stood for the gradual erosion of national sovereignty, for the institutional as well as philosophic unity of the Western world.

His central theme in relations with all countries was that the United States wished nothing more than the right of every people to be independent. Leaders in the newer countries—in Ghana and Guinea and Indonesia—came to understand and value that concept.

The President also found that the range of new policies that any Administration can introduce is severely limited by history, by economic forces beyond a nation's control and by the swirl of events. He had hoped, for instance, to move much further toward cooperation with the Russians, and even, one day, to take a new look at policy on Communist China.

Charm, Wit and Grace

These limitations are certain to be felt by President Johnson. The chances are that, like Presidents Truman, Eisenhower and Kennedy, the new leader will preserve, and in any case will usually find himself forced to preserve, the essential lines of international policy.

Mr. Kennedy had a temperament that kept his passions out of world affairs most of the time. He had personal charm, wit and grace that often made the difference in relations with other leaders.

His traits of personality and intelligence were thought to be solely responsible for keeping together the varied personalities of his foreign-policy staff—men like Secretary of State Dean Rusk; Secretary of Defense Robert S. McNamara; the President's special assistant, McGeorge Bundy; Under Secretaries of State George W. Ball and his deputy, Averell Harriman, and Adlai E. Stevenson, representative at the United Nations.

Behind them served other admirers of Mr. Kennedy, men from the universities and foundations and law offices who answered the call of the New Frontier and allowed the Kennedy charm and intelligence to hold them in Washington and in embassies around the world much longer than they wished to serve.

6 Cabinet Members Turn Back After Getting News Over Pacific

By HENRY RAYMONT
Special to The New York Times

WASHINGTON, Nov. 22—A plane carrying six members of the Cabinet turned back over the Pacific today at the news of President Kennedy's death. The officials were bound for Japan for political and economic talks.

Secretary of State Dean Rusk was first to receive word of the assassination, an hour after a special Air Force jet carrying the party had left Hickam Air Force Base in Honolulu for Tokyo.

The news was radioed to the pilot of the aircraft, who notified Mr. Rusk The Secretary of State is fourth in line of succession to the Presidency after the Vice President, the Speaker of the House, and the President Pro Tempore of the Senate.

Mr. Rusk, after consulting with the other Cabinet officers, ordered the pilot to turn around and fly to Washington, where the party is expected at 1 A.M. tomorrow.

The officials, most of whom had had close personal bonds with the late President, were reported to have been stunned at the news.

The other Cabinet members were Douglas Dillon, Secretary of the Treasury; Stewart L. Udall, Secretary of the Interior; Orville L. Freeman, Secretary of Agriculture; W. Willard Wirtz, Secretary of Labor and Luther H. Hodges, Secretary of Commerce. They were accompanied by their wives.

Also on the aircraft were Pierre Salinger, the White House press secretary, and Robert Manning, Assistant Secretary of State for Public Affairs.

Richard I. Phillips, press officer of the State Department, said that Acting Secretary George Ball had had a brief radio conversation with Mr. Rusk after the Secretary had decided to turn back.

The talks in Japan, which had become an annual event for the review of diplomatic and trade relations, were canceled.

Diplomats Shocked

The slaying came as a shock to the diplomatic corps here.

West German Ambassador Heinrich Knappstein said that "the people of Germany and Berlin, who recall so vividly President Kennedy's recent visit, mourn together with the free world the tragic loss of a very good friend and most able statesman."

British Ambassador Sir David Ormsby Gore, a close personal friend of the Kennedys, called the assassination a "horrible, wicked and senseless act."

"Jack Kennedy was the best and the most loyal friend one could ever hope to have and I feel a sense of loss beyond description," he said.

Herve Alphand, the French ambassador, said President Kennedy "died as a soldier and we shall never forget his example or his memory."

West Point in Mourning

WEST POINT, N. Y., Nov. 22 (AP)—The corps of cadets, staff and faculty at the United States Military Academy mourned today the death of their commander-in-chief, John F. Kennedy. Maj. Gen. James B. Lampbert, Academy superintendent, said the whole Academy joined in "heartfelt sympathy for the Kennedy family and in sorrow at the untimely loss to the nation and free world."

RACIAL HOSTILITY IGNORED BY SOUTH

Many Who Fought Policies of Kennedy Voice Grief

By CLAUDE SITTON
Special to The New York Times

BIRMINGHAM, Ala., Nov. 22—Many of this city's residents expressed grief today over the assassination of President Kennedy. Among them were whites who had bitterly opposed Federal policies in a series of racial crises here.

T. Eugene Connor, the former police commissioner, known as "Bull," said Mr. Kennedy's slaying "was one of the most terrible things that have happened in my lifetime." "I regret it very much. My sympathy goes out to his wife and his whole family."

David Vann, a lawyer who has attempted to steer Birmingham toward moderation on racial issues, said the city had lost a friend.

"While many disagreed with him, in depth of concern he was one of the city's closest friends," Mr. Vann said. "Emotion often prevented our seeing this, but Birmingham has a big share in the world's tragic loss."

A Symbol of Hate

He continued:

"I cannot help but feel that this tragedy is in many ways symbolic of . . . professionally promoted hate into what is always its natural and ultimate consequences. The Scriptures say that 'he who hates his brother kills him.'

"Often we fail to realize that in every community, there are some emotionally disturbed people who need but little encouragement to carry out the faultlessly unintended consequences of the type of deliberate, organized heckling that met the President yesterday in Texas, which met Adlai Stevenson on his last visit to Texas and which we have seen in this city and other cities around the country. I can only hope that the nation's sorrow will be a sobering sorrow."

Frances Green, a student at Phillips High School, said, "I think it was the most horrible thing that has happened since I've been living." "Anyone that would do something like that would have to be insane. The President was a great person, despite the racial trouble."

"A girl came through the halls at school screaming about it when it happened," she said. "When my teacher found out about it, she laid her head down and cried."

Some in Birmingham, while expressing sorrow, saw in the President's assassination further evidence of the "Communist plot" they hold responsible for racial troubles here. Among them was former Mayor Arthur J. Hanes.

"I, like all Americans, am grieved and shocked over the tragic, cowardly and dastardly assassination of the highest elected oficial of our beloved country," Mr. Hanes, a caustic critic of the late President, said.

"In the untimely death of President Kennedy is apparently another episode in the long and sordid history of Communistic-left wing policy—of control by revolution and assassination," he declared, adding:

"How much longer will this great and proud nation permit the deadly Cuban-Communist cancer to eat away at the unity and vitality of this nation?"

Not even death could remove the bitterness felt by some whites. A youth who identified himself as Rusty Wesson of Birmingham telephoned radio station WQXI in Atlanta tonight and voiced these sentiments over its "Open Mike" show before the announcer cut him off:

"I feel sure, and I'm sure that the majority of the people of Alabama feel that Mr. Kennedy got exactly what he deserved. I'm sorry for his family. But I want to say that any man, any white man who did what he did for niggers should be shot."

Special to The New York Times

ATLANTA, Nov. 22—The news of President Kennedy's assassination came to many people here as they walked or drove along downtown streets under sunny, clear skies.

Although the President carried Georgia by a greater margin than any other state in 1960, his popularity had waned with the civil righs bill.

There was little evidence of this, however, in the reactions to the news.

Almost invariably people spoke of the broader meaning for the country and of the tragedy for the President's family.

Word Passed Quietly

Word was quietly passed between friends, sometimes from car to sidewalk.

Bobby Jones, famous golfer of three decades ago and an early leader of the Eisenhower for President movement, drove past Jack Spalding, editor of The Atlanta Journal, on a downtown street.

"Did you hear about it?" he asked. "Did you hear about it?"

Many people heard the news from a radio-television station news ticker over a downtown building. "President Kennedy has been shot. . . . Bulletin. . . . President Kennedy has been shot. . . ." The message left people in clusters, asking, "Is he alive?"

"It's sickening," a young businessman said.

At the Atlanta City Hall, members of the Mayor's staff hovered over a radio. A secretary, Mrs. Betty Robinson, sobbed openly and uncontrollably.

Priest Describes How He Administered Last Rites After the President's Death

ABSOLUTION GIVEN AT THE HOSPITAL

Mrs. Kennedy Takes Part in 15-Minute Ceremony but Appears to Be in Shock

By RONALD SULLIVAN

The priest who administered the last rites of the Roman Catholic Church to President Kennedy said last night that when he arrived at the hospital the President was dead.

The priest, the Very Rev. Oscar L. Huber, said he had to draw back a sheet that was covering the President's face so that he could anoint his forehead with oil.

Father Huber said the President's body was on a portable treatment table in an emergency room on the first floor of Parkland Hospital in Dallas. In the room, he said, were the President's wife, a few aides and a number of Secret Service agents.

Father Huber, who is 70 years old, was accompanied by another priest, the Rev. James Thompson, who drove their car to the hospital.

Because the President was dead, Father Huber said, a "short form" of conditional absolution was administered. Then the last sacrament of the Church, Extreme Unction, or The Anointing of the Sick, was administered.

All Stood for Ceremony

Father Huber answered questions in a telephone interview from Dallas. He said that everyone in the President's room stood during the ceremony. He said a few, but he was not certain, might have blessed themselves with the Sign of the Cross.

The ceremony took about 15 minutes, Father Huber said. Afterward, he added, he and Father Thompson left the room and remained in a hospital corridor for a half an hour.

Father Huber was the first to report that the President was dead.

He and the other priests at Holy Trinity Church in Dallas were in the rectory when they heard that the President had been shot.

Almost immediately, since the hospital was in his parish, Father Huber, the pastor, went upstairs for his small black prayer books. Father Thompson, a curate, met Father Huber coming downstairs and they both got into Father Thompson's car.

The drive to the hospital normally would take just a few minutes. But the shooting had drawn swarms of cars and pedestrians. Traffic was jammed.

'Just Couldn't Happen'

Father Huber said they felt shocked as their car inched through the crowds, and Father Thompson kept repeating.:

"It just couldn't happen. It just couldn't happen."

The two priests were met by members of a police emergency squad when they arrived at the hospital. They were quickly ushered inside the room where the President had been taken.

Father Huber said he thought he had arrived at nearly 1 P. M. (2 P. M. New York time). But, he said that because of his shock, he was not certain.

Father Huber administered conditional absolution. This is given when a priest has no way of knowing the mind of the recipient and whether the soul has left the body. In doing this, he said in Latin:

"I absolve you from all censures and sins in the Name of the Father, and of the Son, and the Holy Spirit. Amen."

Father Huber then said:

"If you are living, may the Lord by this Holy Anointing forgive whatever you have sinned. Amen."

As Father Huber spoke these words, he anointed the President on the forehead, making a small Sign of the Cross with his thumb, which had been dipped in the oils.

Gives Apostolic Blessing

Father Huber then gave the Apostolic Blessing:

"I by the faculty given to me by the Apostolic See grant to you a plenary indulgence and remission of all sins and I bless you. In the Name of the Father, and of the Son, and of the Holy Spirit. Amen."

With that, Father Huber replaced the sheet over the President's face.

He went on in English with the Prayers for the Dying and for the Departed Soul:

"May the most clement Virgin Mary, Mother of God, the most loving consoler of the afflicted, commend to her Son the soul of this servant, John, so that through her maternal intercession he may not fear the terror of death, but in her company may he joyfully enter the desired heavenly home. Amen.

"Into Thy hands I commend my spirit O Lord Jesus Christ. Receive my spirit. Holy Mary pray for me. O Mary Mother of Grace, Mother of Mercy, do thou protect me from the enemy and receive me at the hour of death. St. Joseph pray for me. St. Joseph in the company with the Blessed Virgin, thy spouse, open to me the bosom of divine mercy. Jesus, Mary and Joseph I give my heart and my soul. Jesus, Mary and Joseph assist me in my last agony. Jesus, Mary and Joseph may I sleep and rest in peace in Your holy company.

"Let us pray.

"To Thee O Lord we commend the soul of Thy servant, John, that being dead to the world he may live unto Thee and whatever sins he has committed through the frailty of his mortal nature do Thou in Thy most merciful goodness forgive and wash away through Christ our Lord. Amen.

"Grant O Lord that while we here lament the departure of your servant, we may ever remember that we are most certainly to follow him. Give us grace to prepare for that last hour by a good life, that we may not be surprised by a sudden death but be ever watching, for when Thou shalt call that soul we may enter eternal glory through Christ our Lord. Amen.

"Eternal rest grant him O Lord and let perpetual Light shine upon him."

After this Mrs. Kennedy took a place beside Father Huber near the President's body. Father Huber led a recitation of the Lord's Prayer and Hail Marys. Mrs. Kennedy, with a clear and audible voice, responded as did others in the room who knew the endings of the prayers.

Before leaving the room, Father Huber consoled the President's wife. He said she appeared to be in a state of shock, even though she was erect, clear-eyed and coherent.

Mrs. Kennedy followed Father Huber out of the room. In the corridor, she thanked the priest for his expressions of sympathy and for praying for her husband.

THE KENNEDY FAMILY: Presidential family during vacation last Easter Sunday at Palm Beach, Fla. With Mr. and Mrs. Kennedy are their children, John F. Jr., and Caroline.

Hagerty Tells of Plots To Slay Eisenhower

James C. Hagerty, former press secretary to President Dwight D. Eisenhower and now an American Broadcasting Company executive, said last night there were two plots against Mr. Eisenhower's life during his term of office.

Interviewed on the ABC network, Mr. Hagerty said that both plots had been traced to the Nationalist party of Puerto Rico. That same group was accused of an earlier attempt on the life of President Harry S. Truman.

Mr. Hagerty explained that in 1958 Secret Service agents learned that an attempt would be made to toss grenades into President Eisenhower's car. He said two grenades were found in the mail, sent from outside the country.

The second assassination plot, he said, was reported to the Secret Service in the spring of 1959 on word that Puerto Rican nationalists had decided to kill the President. Security measures were tightened and the reported attempt failed.

James Roosevelt to Urge Medal of Honor for Kennedy

LOS ANGELES, Nov. 22 (AP)—Representative James Roosevelt said today that he would propose that the Medal of Honor be awarded posthumously to President Kennedy.

The California Democrat, son of another President who died in office, told Kenneth Hahn, Los Angeles County supervisor, by telephone from Washington that he would introduce a joint resolution "in the name of the people of the United States."

Mr. Hahn had suggested the action, saying: "certainly, in the battle of peace and human understanding, President John F. Kennedy earned his medal."

The Medal of Honor is the nation's highest award for heroism.

Grandmother Not Told

BOSTON, Nov. 22 (UPI)—Mrs. John F. Fitzgerald, 98 years old, President Kennedy's maternal grandmother, was not told immediately of the assassination because of her age, her son, Thomas A. Fitzgerald, said.

PRESIDENT'S BODY WILL LIE IN STATE

Continued From Page 1, Col. 2

when it will be placed under honor guard in ceremonies to be attended by the President's family, United States officials and foreign representatives.

The public will be allowed to file past all day tomorrow until 9 P.M.

The body was taken to the White House on a catafalque similar to the one used for a martyred predecessor, Abraham Lincoln.

Lighted candles burned on both sides of the dark mahogany coffin. Two Roman Catholic priests were in attendance, kneeling in constant prayer beside the bier. A military guard of honor stood watch.

Richard Cardinal Cushing, Archbishop of Boston, a longtime friend of the Kennedy family, will officiate at the mass.

Former Presidents Harry S. Truman and Dwight D. Eisenhower were expected to appear but former President Herbert Hoover, who is 89 years old, will be unable to come to Washington.

The President was expected to be buried at the Kennedy family plot in Holyhood Cemetery, near Brookline, Mass. He is a native of Boston.

The Presidential plane was met by an honor cordon of airmen in dress uniform, with rifles and bayonets, and by high-ranking officials.

Carried in Navy Vehicle

The coffin containing the President's body was placed in a Navy ambulance and taken to the naval hospital at Bethesda, Md. Mrs. Kennedy and the President's brother, Attorney General Robert F. Kennedy, rode in the ambulance after making their way to it through the crowd.

Cabinet and Congressional officials had stayed apart from the crowd near the ambulance, waiting to greet the new President formally when he alighted moments later from the plane.

By the time the ambulance arrived at Bethesda shortly after 7 P.M., a crowd of several hundred people had gathered at the front entrance. They stood back in silence.

An honor guard of 200 sailors that had waited marched to the front entrance.

Mrs. Kennedy, tearless but looking dazed, and Attorney General Kennedy conferred with the commanding officer of the hospital, Admiral C. B. Galloway. They were joined by Secretary of Defense Robert S. McNamara.

Later a White House chauffeur appeared at the hospital with two suitcases for Mrs. Kennedy. She spent the night in the special 17th-floor suite for high officials.

Four Roman Catholic priests arrived to offer their services and the Roman Catholic chaplain at the hospital, Comdr. Robert B. Brengartner, consoled Mrs. Kennedy.

Others who joined her were the President's aides and close friends, Lawrence F. O'Brien, P. Kenneth O'Donnell and David J. Powers, and Pamala Turnure, her secretary.

'A Lot of Doctors Here'

Charles Bartlett, a newspaper columnist and close friend of the Kennedys, also arrived at the hospital.

A spokesman for Mrs. Kennedy, asked whether she was under doctors' care, replied: "I wouldn't say she is under the care of a doctor in the usual sense, but obviously there are a lot of doctors here."

At Andrews Air Force Base tension had prevailed as the great blue and white jet, known as Air Force 1, and with the words "United States of America" on its fuselage, ended its journey from Dallas.

Slowly the plane turned at the end of the runway, its landing lights piercing the darkness in the unusually warm November evening. Heading directly for the terminal building where the Cabinet and other officials waited, it came to a halt with its rear door slightly open.

A yellow lift ramp was rolled to it, with four Navy men, two officers and two sailors aboard.

Aides Lend a Hand

Some difficulty developed in moving the heavy bronze coffin, and aides of the President.

Finally they succeeded in turning the coffin so it could be placed on the lift and lowered to the ground. There was more hauling as military men and civilians sought to lend a hand, as though by this act they could help the President.

At last they managed to get the coffin into the ambulance. Then Mrs. Kennedy and the Attorney General came down on the lift. A Navy officer reached up and caught Mrs. Kennedy under the arms to help her to the ground.

Kennedy Denied Talk Of Dropping Johnson

President Kennedy reaffirmed his confidence in Lyndon B. Johnson 24 days ago. He said at a news conference that he wanted the Texan as his running mate for Vice President again in 1964.

A reporter, referring to "talk that Lyndon B. Johnson would be dumped next year," asked Mr. Kennedy at his Oct. 31 conference if he wanted Mr. Johnson on the ticket and if he expected that he would be put on the ticket.

"Yes to both those questions," the President said. "That's correct."

Pearson to Attend Rites

OTTAWA, Nov. 22 (AP)—Prime Minister Lester B. Pearson of Canada said tonight that he planned to attend the funeral of President Kennedy Monday.

Fort to Pay Tribute to Kennedy

BOSTON, Nov. 22 (UPI)—Fort Banks will hold reveille-to-retreat gun salute ceremonies tomorrow in tribute to President Kennedy. A salute will be fired every hour from 4:30 A.M. through 4:30 P.M.

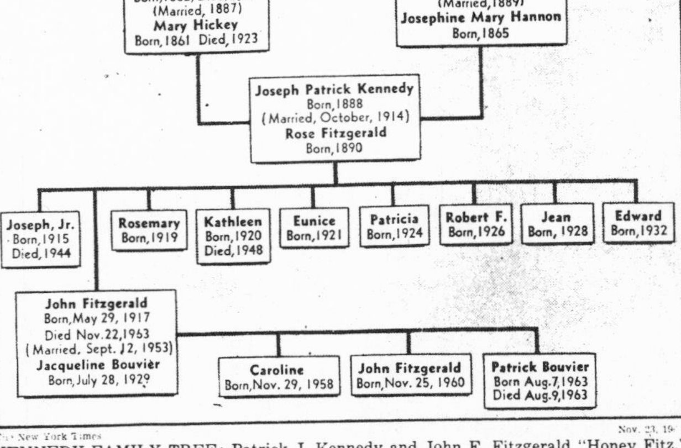

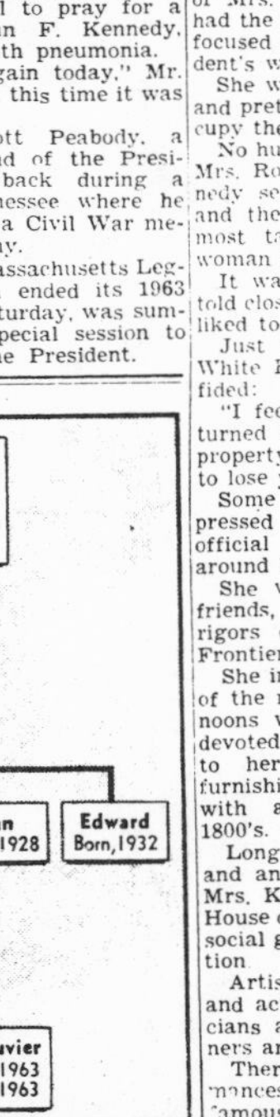

The New York Times Nov. 23, 1963

KENNEDY FAMILY TREE: Patrick J. Kennedy and John F. Fitzgerald "Honey Fitz," laid the foundations in Boston for the family's national political activities. The fortune of Joseph P. Kennedy has helped the next generation, which included the President.

NEWS WITHHELD FROM 2 CHILDREN

They Leave the White House Without Seeing Mother

By EILEEN SHANAHAN

Special to The New York Times

WASHINGTON, Nov. 22—President Kennedy's children, Caroline and John Jr., went to bed tonight without having been told of their father's death.

Mrs. Kennedy apparently wished to tell them herself and they were shielded from the news throughout this afternoon and evening.

The children, after following their regular schedules until late afternoon, under the custody of their nurse, Maude Shaw, were taken from the White House to an unknown destination shortly before Mrs. Kennedy arrived back in Washington with the body of the President.

It was thought that Caroline and John Jr. had probably been taken to the home of their uncle, Attorney General Robert F. Kennedy, in nearby McClean, Va. White House assistants would not say, however, where the children were.

Mrs. Kennedy at Hospital

Mrs. Kennedy, who at first had been expected to join the children before their bedtime and tell them that their father was dead, decided instead to spend the night at the Bethesda Naval Hospital, just outside Washington. The President's body was taken there before being returned to the White House.

Caroline, whose sixth birthday is next Wednesday, went to school as usual this morning in the private schoolroom on the third floor of the White House.

She returned to the family living quarters on the second floor about 1:15 P. M., before the assassination of the President. John spent the day in the family living quarters.

The only break in their routine before they left the White House around 5:30 P.M. was a brief visit from their uncle, Senator Edward M. Kennedy, and their aunt, Mrs. Eunice Shriver, the President's sister. They saw the children before leaving Washington for Hyannis Port, Mass., to be with President Kennedy's father and mother, Mr. and Mrs. Joseph P. Kennedy.

White House staff assistants assumed that Mrs. Shaw, Senator Kennedy and Mrs. Shriver had all agreed that the children should not be told of their father's death until Mrs. Kenedy returned to Washington.

She had not been in touch with the White House prior to her take-off from Dallas on the airplane carrying the President's body back to Washington.

Third Child to Die

The assassination was the second tragedy to befall the family in four months. Patrick Bouvier Kennedy, the President's third child, born prematurely Aug. 7, died in Boston two days later of a lung ailment.

For the President's parents, this was the third of their nine children to die. The President's oldest brother, Joseph P., Jr., was killed in the explosion of a Navy plane over the English Channel in World War II. A sister, Kathleen, also perished in an airplane crash. She was the widow of the Marquess of Hartington.

The President's brother, Senator Kennedy, was presiding over the Senate when he received word that the President had been shot in Dallas. He left the Senate chamber immediately and went to the White House.

The Attorney General was lunching at his home in near-by McLean, Va., when the assassination occurred. He apparently remained there through the afternoon.

Mrs. Shriver and her husband, the Peace Corps director, were reportedly in the White House at the time of the shooting. Mr. Shriver remained in Washington to help make the funeral arrangements.

The Kennedy family had been planning a traditional gathering for Thanksgiving next week at the home of the President's father on Cape Cod, Mass Mrs. Kennedy and Caroline and John, with most of the children's cousins, were scheduled to attend.

Kennedy Car Built for Security

CINCINNATI, Nov. 22 (UPI) — The automobile in which President Kennedy was fatally shot today was custom built here in 1961 to rigid Secret Service specifications.

Delivered to the White House in June, 1961, the car, called the Presidential Continental, had more specially designed features than any car ever before used for Government duties.

The metallic navy blue vehicle is owned by the Ford Motor Company and was leased to the White House.

Hess & Eisenhardt, which outfitted the auto, said today it had a protective "bubble top" but declined to specify whether the cover was bullet-proof.

The vehicle was equipped with radiotelephones to keep the President and his guards in communication with staff members along any parade route.

Vytas Valaitis

President Kennedy riding in his special limousine on a recent visit to U.N.

KENNEDYS GATHER AT HYANNIS PORT

Senator and Sister Join President's Parents

By JOHN H. FENTON

Special to The New York Times

HYANNIS PORT, Mass., Nov. 22—Senator Edward M. Kennedy and his sister, Mrs. Eunice Schriver, flew from Washington today to join their sorrowing parents, Mr. and Mrs. Joseph P. Kennedy, at the family compound here where President Kennedy had spent many summers.

The town was shocked by the news of the President's assassination. A cordon of grim state and local policemen stood guard at the gate of the compound to assure the family complete seclusion.

Newsmen and photographers, who were at the Hyannis Airport in Barnstable when the Senator and his sister arrived shortly before 5 P.M., apologized for having to be on hand.

The Senator said, "I understand, gentlemen," and entered a car to be driven here.

The President's mother, Mrs. Rose Kennedy, was playing golf at the Hyannis Port Golf Club when she learned of the tragedy. Her chauffeur was reported to have told her the news after hearing it on a Secret Service radio in the car.

Attorney General Due

Mrs. Kennedy left immediately to join her husband, who is convalescing here from a stroke suffered a year ago. Attorney General Robert F. Kennedy was expected later.

In Boston, the Most Rev. Richard Cardinal Cushing, a close friend of the President and his family, spent more than an hour in his private chapel praying. Later, he issued a statement expressing his deep grief. He then left for Hyannis Port to join the Kennedy family.

The cardinal married the President and his wife, Jacqueline, and baptized their two children, Caroline and John Jr. He also presided at a Mass for a third Kennedy child, Patrick Bouvier Kennedy, who died shortly after birth last summer.

Much of the area where the Kennedy summer homes is situated is quiet at this time of year. Many homes, motels and other summer resorts have been boarded up for the winter.

Radio stations throughout the area immediately canceled regular programs to broadcast a continuing report of developments.

State Representative Paul D. Reed, a Republican, recalled that on the first day he had attended Choate School, a private secondary school in Connecticut, the student body was called into the chapel to pray for a classmate, John F. Kennedy, who was ill with pneumonia.

"I prayed again today," Mr. Reed said, "but this time it was too late."

Gov. Endicott Peabody, a long-time friend of the President, turned back during a flight to Tennessee where he was to attend a Civil War memorial ceremony.

Later, the Massachusetts Legislature, which ended its 1963 session last Saturday, was summoned to a special session to memorialize the President.

KENNEDY'S WIFE KEPT COMPOSURE

Accompanied His Body to Bethesda Naval Hospital

By MARJORIE HUNTER

Special to The New York Times

WASHINGTON, Nov. 22—Mrs. John F. Kennedy returned tonight to a city she had left 31 hours earlier as the wife of the President of the United States.

Clutching the hand of her brother-in-law, Attorney General Robert F. Kennedy, she watched the coffin bearing the body of her husband as it was lowered to the ground by a yellow lift drawn up beside the Presidential jet and loaded onto an ambulance.

She then climbed into the ambulance beside the coffin for the ride to Bethesda Naval Hospital.

She wore the pink wool suit she had been wearing, hours earlier, when her husband collapsed by her side, the victim of an assassin's bullet, on the streets of Dallas.

Mrs. Kennedy spent the night on the 17th floor of the Naval Hospital. She is expected to go to the White House tomorrow morning.

There was no indication where her two children, Caroline and John Jr., slept. They were taken from the White House about 5:30 P.M., but aides would not say where they went or who had accompanied them.

The children had been left in the care of their nurse, Miss Maude Shaw, when the Kennedys left yesterday morning for a two-day swing through Texas.

The Texas trip, plainly a political one, was to have been the first of many such trips in which Mrs. Kennedy planned to campaign with her husband for 1964.

It was the first political appearance she had made with him in the United States, outside of Washington, since the early Presidential primaries in the spring of 1960.

While generally shunning politics, Mrs. Kennedy proved to be a sparkling addition to the Presidential party on several trips abroad.

She was such a hit in Paris in the summer of 1961 that President Kennedy referred to himself as "the man who accompanied Jacqueline Kennedy to Paris."

On another occasion, President Kennedy jokingly said that Mrs. Kennedy and Caroline "are the only things keeping the Democratic party going."

In Publicity Spotlight

Certainly, not since the days of Mrs. Franklin D. Roosevelt had the publicity spotlight been focused so steadily on a President's wife.

She was one of the youngest and prettiest women ever to occupy the White House.

No humanitarian crusader, as Mrs. Roosevelt was, Mrs. Kennedy set the pace in fashions and the arts. She became the most talked-about and copied woman in the nation.

It was a role that she once told close friends that she would liked to have avoided.

Just before moving into the White House in 1961, she confided:

"I feel as though I had just turned into a piece of public property. It's really frightening to lose your anonymity at 31."

Some months later, she expressed misgivings about the official life that was closing around her and her family.

She was not sure, she told friends, that she was up to the rigors of her husband's New Frontier, but she kept trying.

She insisted on spending part of the mornings and the afternoons with her children. She devoted several hours each day to her favorite project—refurnishing the White House with antiques of the early 1800's.

Long interested in the arts, and an amateur artist herself, Mrs. Kennedy made the White House one of the most glittering social gathering spots in the nation.

Artists and writers, musicians and actors mingled with politicians at the White House dinners and other socials.

There were command performances by many of the most famous names of the age — for example the cellist, Pablo Casals, and the violinist, Isaac Stern. White House performers ranged from ballet stars to readers of Elizabeth poetry.

AGENTS CHECKED KENNEDY'S ROUTE

Dallas Police Also Helped in Security Precautions

By JOHN HERBERS

Special to The New York Times

DALLAS, Nov. 22 — The Secret Service made elaborate and painstaking security preparations for President Kennedy's visit here.

Agents made a minute check of the parade route he was to follow, the food he was to eat, the flowers that were to decorate the platform and potential trouble-makers.

Secret Service men who were all around the President when he was shot, looking into the crowds and the buildings, were ready for any eventuality. In addition, 350 uniformed officers of the Dallas police provided additional security for the President.

It was impossible, however, for agents to make sure that every room, every window and every alleyway and rooftop along the six-mile route from the airport to the Trade Mart did not contain a sniper.

Secret Service agents had been in Dallas for several days making security preparations.

At first, agents were reluctant to approve the Trade Mart for the scheduled luncheon. It is a huge modern building for showing merchandise and holding meetings. They said a number of balconies overlooking the speaking stand might pose a problem, but after further study they approved the site.

The Dallas police provided agents with a list of known agitators who might cause trouble. The agents studied their pictures and habits.

Buildings along the route were checked.

Detailed security was arranged for the 14 entrances to the Trade Mart. Agents secured a guest list and planned to check the tickets of everyone attending.

Agents poked through 5,000 yellow roses that were arranged in the Trade Mart to make sure they contained no explosive or weapons.

It was decided that the President and his party would receive the same kind of steak at the luncheon as everyone else. The President's steak was to be selected at random in the belief that nobody would attempt to poison the entire lot.

Employes of the Trade Mart and those persons in the official greeting party at the airport were thoroughly looked over by agents.

Before the President arrived, agents gave the airport a thorough check. Balconies, windows and other vantage points were covered.

The Dallas police said the preparations were as thorough as could have been made.

Tighter Security Seen

By BEN A. FRANKLIN

Special to The New York Times

WASHINGTON, Nov. 22 — The assassination of President Kennedy is likely to have profound and lasting effects on the Presidency itself.

It is considered certain, for example, that the informality of the office under recent Presidents, especially President Kennedy, will be sharply curtailed.

President Johnson is expected to be less publicly accessible, less in the public view.

Mr. Kennedy persisted in a relatively carefree attitude toward the security problems inherent in his office, even with a steep rise in threats made against him.

In 1961, the Secret Service reported that it had investigated 870 threatening letters addressed to the President. The White House police, a separate, uniformed force, turned back 643 callers at the gates, including many seeking to see the President about various grievances.

50 Per Cent Increase

These figures were about 50 per cent higher than those for the final year of President Eisenhower's Administration. In addition, there was an increase in the number of known plots against the President's life, in Washington and at other Kennedy family gathering points, including Palm Beach, Fla. and Hyannis Port, Mass.

Mr. Kennedy's habit of easy-going familiarity with crowds—at airports, on a California beach and at receptions in the White House Rose Garden—made him an easy mark for potential assassins and gave the Secret Service some of its worst hours.

Presidential travel by jet aircraft has greatly increased the President's mobility and mobility has increased the chances for assassins.

Presidents have had to live with the thought that at every public appearance there was a chance that someone would try to kill them.

Since the turn of the century, protection of the President had grown from an informal, three-man bodyguard to the present highly organized detail of 58 special agents.

When the President travels, at home or abroad, the 58-man complement on full-time White House duty is augmented — often doubled—by the temporary assignment of other Secret Service agents normally engaged in the other chief duty of the service, the detection, capture and prosecution of counterfeiters, forgers, and others who would debase the United States currency.

McCormack, Next in Line of Succession to the Presidency, Is Given Security Guard

SPEAKER SHAKEN BY NEWS OF DEATH

He and Other House Officials Meet Plane as Coffin Is Taken to Washington

By JOHN D. MORRIS
Special to The New York Times

WASHINGTON, Nov. 22 — House Speaker John W. McCormack became first in line of succession to the Presidency today and was immediately made acutely aware of it.

Within minutes after President Kennedy's death had been announced a Secret Service detail arrived at the Capitol to begin an around-the-clock guard of the Massachusetts Democrat. Secret Service agents were also assigned to the Washington Hotel, where Mr. and Mrs. McCormack maintain a suite.

The guard is required under a 1962 law designed to insure the safety of the person next in line to the Presidency.

Such protection had been available to Mr. McCormack on request, but the Speaker valued his privacy to a greater extent than he feared for his safety. When he became Speaker in 1961, he was understood to have turned down suggestions that he ask for a guard.

Mr. McCormack's official role in the Government is not changed by Mr. Kennedy's death. However, it seemed likely that President Johnson would bring him into continuously close consultation and keep him fully informed of the Administration's affairs in view of his position as first in line of succession.

After Mr. McCormack, those next in the line of succession are the President Pro Tempore of the Senate, Senator Carl Hayden, Democrat of Arizona, and the Secretary of State, Dean Rusk.

Will Be 72 Next Month

The Speaker, who will be 72 years old on Dec. 21, was visibly shaken on receiving word of the shooting of Mr. Kennedy. He was having lunch in the House restaurant with Dr. Martin Sweig, an aide, and Edward Fitzgerald, administrative assistant to the Clerk of the House.

Two news correspondents went to the table and told the three men President Kennedy had been shot.

"My God! My God! What are we coming to?" Mr. McCormack exclaimed.

He finished his lunch and went to his office just off the House floor. He was joined by Representatives Carl Albert, the House Democratic leader, and Carl Vinson, Democrat of Georgia.

A short vigil there was ended by a call from the White House. Theodore C. Sorensen, special counsel to the President, was on the telephone. He reported that President Kennedy was dead.

"I was stunned," the Speaker told reporters later. "I just simply said, 'My God, it's tragic.'"

A three-man Washington police detail of plainclothes men regularly assigned to the Capitol went immediately to the Speaker's office at the request of the Secret Service to provide an interim guard. Within minutes, a Secret Service detail commanded by Inspector Burrill A. Peterson arrived and went to the corridor and anteroom of the Speaker's private office.

Inspector Peterson declined to say how many agents were assigned to the detail. There were at least four at the Speaker's office.

Mrs. McCormack remained at the Washington Hotel suite, where other agents were sent. The guard is expected to operate in three shifts, 24 hours a day, as has been the custom in providing protection for Mr. Johnson as Vice President.

Mr. Fitzgerald, Mr. McCormack's luncheon companion, is not related to the Fitzgerald family to which President Kennedy's mother, Rose, belongs. But Mr. Fitzgerald said the President, whom he knew well, always called him "Cousin."

Orders Flags Lowered

Speaker McCormack's first official act on being informed of Mr. Kennedy's death was to order flags on Capitol Hill lowered to half-staff. Then he prepared a public statement, called reporters into his office and read it to them.

He sat at his desk, looking pale and tense. Representative Albert, in a nearby chair, was red-faced, and his eyes were bloodshot. Representative Vinson sat staring at the floor, an unlighted cigar in his mouth.

"This is a tragic event," Mr. McCormack began. "I feel very inadequate in expressing my thoughts. The nation has sustained a staggering loss. . ."

He choked momentarily.

". . . the significance of which," he continued, "is stupendous. Our country and the entire world will never forget President Kennedy. His leadership was superb in meeting the challenges of this period of world history. The warmth of his personality will never be forgotten."

Again the Speaker paused, fighting back tears.

"The relationship that existed between the President and myself throughout the years has been close and most friendly," he went on. "In his tragic passing I have lost a dear and personal friend. The nation has lost a great leader. I mourn for his family, for the nation, for Mrs. McCormack and myself."

The group in the Speaker's office was joined a few minutes later by Representative Hale Boggs of Louisiana, the House majority whip, or assistant Democratic leader.

The four House leaders, Representatives McCormack, Albert, Boggs and Vinson, went to Andrews Air Force Base in the Speaker's limousine. There they joined other Congressional and Administration leaders who met the plane bearing Mr. Kennedy's body.

Speaker McCormack and Congressional leaders of both parties then went to the White House for a conference with President Johnson.

The white-haired Mr. McCormack, tall, erect and vigorous, will continue his duties as presiding officer of the House and principal leader of its Democratic majority. He declined to discuss his new status as first in line of Presidential succession.

There was speculation at the Capitol that no functions of an executive nature, such as Mr. Johnson had as Vice President, were likely to be assigned to Mr. McCormack by the President, since the Speaker is an elected member of the House and his office is distinctly different from that of the Vice President.

The Speaker's office is wholly one of the legislative branch, while the Vice-Presidency is a parliamentary office only to the extent that its occupant presides over the Senate.

The concept of separation of powers between executive and legislative branches of the Government apparently makes it unlikely that Speaker McCormack's role in the Administration will be almost entirely one of consultation and information.

The late Speaker Sam Rayburn of Texas was first in line of succession to the Presidency from July 18, 1947, when the present succession law was enacted, until Jan. 20, 1949, when Harry S. Truman was inaugurated for a full term as President. With Mr. Truman's inauguration, the late Alben W. Barkley became Vice President and Mr. Rayburn reverted to second in the line of succession.

Mr. Rayburn performed no executive duties during the 1947-49 period when there was no Vice President. However, President Truman consulted with him almost daily, in person or by telephone. He was kept fully informed of Administration affairs.

Spellman Gets News in Rome

ROME, Nov. 22 (Reuters)—Cardinal Spellman of New York said here tonight he was "shocked and grief-stricken to hear of the President's death.

Associated Press

RETURN TO THE CAPITAL: President Johnson speaks at Andrews Air Force Base on arrival from Dallas. With him is Mrs. Johnson. Plane carried President Kennedy's body.

Kennedy Was Called Man Subject to Moods

President Kennedy was described by a close associate as a man "subject to moods" and sometimes discouraged by his inability "to get everything done as quickly as he would like to get it done."

Theodore C. Sorensen, President Kennedy's special counsel, once described Mr. Kennedy's moods in a television interview.

"He's exuberant at times," Mr. Sorensen said. "He's discouraged at times. There are events which interest and those which bore him. There are those which make him laugh and there are those which make him sad. And nothing is done by anyone else to dispel them, I suppose."

JOHNSON IS GIVEN PLEDGES OF UNITY

Continued From Page 1, Col. 1

to the south lawn of the White House. He was briefed during the flight by Secretary of Defense Robert S. McNamara and the White House assistant for national security affairs, McGeorge Bundy. Under Secretary of State George W. Ball also took part.

During the afternoon two Johnson aides moved into the White House. They were Walter Jenkins, his administrative assistant as Vice President, and George Reedy, his press secretary.

Bill D. Moyers, top aide to Mr. Johnson during the 1960 campaign, went out to the Johnson home this evening to spend the night. Mr. Moyers, who is 29 years old, is now deputy director of the Peace Corps.

Before leaving his old offices in the Executive Offices Building for his Spring Valley residence, President Johnson discussed with J. Edgar Hoover, Director of the Federal Bureau of Investigation, the progress of the investigation into the assassination.

He talked by telephone with the physician of Gov. John B. Connally of Texas, who was wounded while sitting across from President Kennedy, and was relieved to learn that the Governor's condition was satisfactory.

He arranged to meet with Secretary of State Dean Rusk at 9 A.M. tomorrow and with former President Eisenhower at 11:30 A.M. tomorrow. He had already talked by telephone with General Eisenhower as well as with former Presidents Herbert Hoover and Harry S. Truman.

One of the first acts of the President tomorrow will be to issue a proclamation fixing Monday, the day of Mr. Kennedy's funeral, as a day of national prayer and mourning.

Lands at Air Base

The Presidential jet landed at Andrews Air Force Base in nearby Maryland after the flight from Dallas.

Both President Johnson and his wife, Lady Bird, remained aboard the jet aircraft until the coffin bearing the body of the slain President had been removed from a forward compartment in an enclosed ramp and then to a waiting Navy ambulance.

A large delegation of Administration officials was on hand as the plane taxied to a stop. President Johnson solemnly shook hands with a few persons and then walked toward a large Congressional delegation.

The President was somberly attired in a black three-button suit and stood hatless in a breeze as he spoke a terse message to the country. Mrs. Johnson was at his side. A thin silver stripe across his black four-in-hand necktie was the only deviation in his somber appearance.

It was 6:23 P.M. when the Army helicopter with the President and Mrs. Johnson aboard skirted the illuminated Washington Monument and descended to the White House lawn.

Two more helicopters came roaring in moments later. The first carried the Presidential assistants, Lawrence O'Brien, Kenneth O'Donnell and Malcolm Kilduff, who was acting press secretary on the trip to Dallas. Other staff members and Secret Service agents were aboard the second craft.

Several staff members wept. It had been the same at Andrews Air Force Base. Several among the diplomatic corps made no attempt to hide their grief as the new President passed among them.

President Johnson seemed to move with confidence into his new responsibilities.

Compared with former President Harry S. Truman's lack of preparation for the White House, it was as though Lyndon B. Johnson had been tutored every step of the way by President Kennedy himself.

It was at the insistence of the late President that Mr. Johnson attended all Cabinet meetings as a matter of a Vice President's right. It was President Kennedy's idea that his second in command should participate actively in the administration of the Executive Branch as well as in the formulation of policy.

As Vice President, he was named chairman of the National Aeronautics and Space Council and made responsible for setting up the President's Committee on Equal Employment Opportunity.

Mr. Johnson had viewed the Vice Presidency in a more traditional sense—that of presiding over the Senate and furthering the Administration's legislative program while increasing his knowledge of Federal affairs at the highest level.

Toured Foreign Capitals

It was also President Kennedy's idea that his Vice President should become better known abroad as well as at home. Thus Mr. Johnson became the President's special emissary. He went around the world on a goodwill tour in 1961 on an itinerary that included battle-scarred South Vietnam.

Later he visited the Middle East on a fact-finding mission for the President. More recently he visited the Scandinavian countries on a tour that ended with a whirlwind visit to the capitals of the European Economic Community.

Returning from the tour he acknowledged being tired. But he was off again the next day to make a speech in West Virginia.

Mr. Truman had been excluded so completely as Vice President from affairs of the Presidency and his official family that he remarked a few years after assuming the highest office that he was the worst prepared man for the responsibilities since Andrew Johnson succeeded Abraham Lincoln.

In this sense Mr. Johnson may be the best prepared Vice Presidential successor in American history. He has had access, as a member of the National Security Council, to the nation's most closely held military and diplomatic secrets.

No Heart Attack

DALLAS, Nov. 22 (UPI)—Rumors that Mr. Johnson had suffered another heart attack circulated after Mr. Kennedy was shot. The rumors were denied.

After the assassination Mr. Johnson went to Parkland Hospital, where Mr. Kennedy had been taken. Mr. Johnson walked in, with his hand on his chest. Apparently this is what gave rise to the rumors.

In 1955 Mr. Johnson suffered a serious heart seizure while a Senator. After six months he returned to his 16-hour a day work schedule and has suffered no recurrence.

SETBACK TO UNITY OF EUROPE FEARED

Allied Diplomats See Peril of Weakened U.S. Backing

By DREW MIDDLETON
Special to The New York Times

PARIS, Nov. 22—The United States' leadership of the Atlantic community, desperately needed in a time of change, has been dealt a grievous blow by the assassination of President Kennedy.

Diplomats here and in other capitals of Western Europe emphasized tonight that the conflict between the President's view on the organization of the Atlantic community and those of General de Gaulle and his followers was nearing a climax.

The President's death, they said, has left General de Gaulle as the senior Western leader. Within three months Chancellor Konrad Adenauer of West Germany and Prime Minister Harold Macmillan of Britain have retired and Mr. Kennedy has been killed.

General de Gaulle, himself a target for at least four known assassination attempts, survives able to continue preaching his policies of European independence to a Continent temporarily bereft of United States leadership and uncertain about the new masters of the great powers.

Johnson's Voice Awaited

The immediate need, diplomats agreed, is for an early and authoritative reassertion by President Johnson of continued United States interest in two cardinal policies laid down by Mr. Kennedy. These were specified as:

¶The American belief that integration of conventional and nuclear forces provides a better defense for Europe than the national military organizations advocated by General de Gaulle.

¶The conviction that, whatever difficulties arise in dealing with the Soviet Union, discussions should continue over the future of Germany, Berlin and Central Europe generally.

Implicit in this assessment, the sources declared, is the fear that the new Administration may veer away from internationalism toward the political philosophy of "fortress America."

President Kennedy's assassination came at a moment when many European governments were hoping for a firm reassertion of United States policy toward Europe. Diplomats conceded regretfully that they had been critical of the late President for not making his policies better known.

One Scandinavian minister remarked that avowals of European dependence on the United States, such as that made today by Chancellor Ludwig Erhard of West Germany, while welcome, were no substitute for equally firm assertions of American inter-dependence with Europe.

The first duty of the new Administration toward Europe, most sources believed, would be a statement that the United States, in this troubled time, has no intention of discarding its responsibilities overseas.

U. S. Withdrawal Feared

Reports from The Hague, Brussels, Bonn and Copenhagen indicated a deep-seated fear that the United States was planning a sizable withdrawal of military forces from Europe.

This fear has been strengthened by former President Dwight D. Eisenhower's suggestion that five American divisions could be recalled and by Secretary of Defense Robert S. McNamara's statement discounting the strength of the Soviet army in Eastern Europe.

In these circumstances, General de Gaulle's warnings that the United States would not forever protect Europe have gained credibility in Western Europe.

This mood inevitably will gain new importance in Western Europe in the aftermath of President Kennedy's death. But even before that, a Belgian source said, Europeans had begun to question the long-term intentions of the United States.

Europe, a West German source said, is now at a halfway house between independence and interdependence. The path it takes, he said, will be indicated by the force and clarity with which the new Administration reasserts United States policy toward this questioning Continent.

People Across U.S. Voice Grief and Revulsion

CHICAGO

Special to The New York Times

CHICAGO, Nov. 22—The President's assassination left people here in a state of stunned outrage. Women wept in the streets. Flags throughout the city dropped to half-staff as though a single hand had pulled the halyards.

"I wanted to do something. But there was nothing to do but pray for him and his family," Mrs. T. S. Rivera, a housewife said.

In a crowded bar-lunch room at State and Kinzie Streets, laborers from a nearby construction project gasped as the announcement of the death came over a radio.

A husky Negro workman knocked a glass of whiskey from the bar, said "for God's sake" and rushed out the door.

Women at a table burst into tears. All was silent except for the radio announcer's voice.

"I thought we were living in a civilized country," a man finally said.

In a luxurious restaurant on Michigan Avenue, the crowd melted away, customers leaving large sums of money on the tables rather than waiting for the waitresses to present a bill.

Down the avenue, in front of a television store where sound was piped to the street from sets behind the show window, women in a crowd of spectators wiped away tears.

Farther along, Tom Buskerus, a student who had a transistor radio held to his ear, could hardly speak. "There is nothing I can say, it's thoughtless," he said at last.

Mrs. Elizabeth Carter, a housewife, said: "They must be crazy—they'd have to be crazy."

A meatcutter said, "It's a pathetic thing." William A. Lee, president of the Chicago Federation of Labor, said: "It is the most terrible moment in our history."

Mayor Daley Weeps

Mayor Richard J. Daley, who was close to Mr. Kennedy, burst into tears when he learned the news during a luncheon with several associates.

Many city and private business offices, as well as the Federal courts, closed for the day.

The bells of Holy Name Cathedral tolled as 700 school children and hundreds of adults filed into the sanctuary for a special recitation of the rosary "for the repose of the soul of the President. Religious leaders of all faiths asked for prayers for the President's family.

Edwin C. Berry, executive director of the Chicago Urban League, said the President's civil-rights program was the most forward looking ever advanced by a President, and his death was a setback for those who believed in equality for all.

Many Weep as Bells Toll and Flags Are Lowered at Word of the President's Death

The commercial center almost came to a standstill. Shoppers moved toward television departments. In some stores the soft music played over loudspeakers stopped and radio bulletins were cut in.

Prices plunged on the Board of Trade, which stayed open beyond its customary closing hour of 1:15 P.M.

Wheat closed 1 to 4¼ cents a bushel lower, soybeans 2½ to 4¾ lower, corn ¾ to 1¼ lower, oats 1 to 1½ lower, and rye 1½ to 3¾ lower.

The Illinois Bell Telephone Company had a surge of traffic immediately after the announcement of the shooting. "We haven't seen anything like this since the death of President Roosevelt and the end of World War II," a company official said.

A Negro civil rights demonstration, scheduled at City Hall to protest segregation, evaporated. A National Association for the Advancement of Colored People membership meeting was turned into a memorial service.

Dark clouds covered the city during an unseasonable warm rain.

LOS ANGELES

Special to The New York Times

LOS ANGELES, Nov. 22—Grief and revulsion was the reaction here to Mr. Kennedy's assassination.

From Mayor to bootblack, from executive to laborer, the general response mixed a sense of deep loss with a welling up of indignation.

Even those who admitted little personal involvement appeared shocked.

"It would appear we're going back to the days of the jungle," said one young real estate dealer. "I didn't agree with the man, but this sort of thing can't be condoned."

A group of executives, strongly opposed to Mr. Kennedy's policies, expressed shock and disgust. Most of the women and many of the men in an elevator wept as the news of the death was confirmed.

Downtown banks, stores and streets were alive with people carrying transistor radios and wearing dazed expressions for at least an hour after the news.

"I have the kind of feeling that I had the morning of Pearl Harbor," said Melvyn Rivkind, a public relations man. "This is a legacy of the hate that has arisen. Frankly, I feel pretty sick."

Mayor Sam Yorty called the assassination "an awful black mark" on the nation's history and added: "Maybe the American people will stop and think about the hate groups who encourage this type of thing."

A salesman in a hotel bar said it more pungently:

"It's those flag-waving screwballs, they're only about 10 per cent of the people, but it's people like them that cause this kind of thing. I'm a conservative and I didn't agree with him. But, my God, he was our President."

"I feel like I've lost a real friend," a shoeshine man said.

At various levels, from a hotel chef up to a City Councilman and clergymen, Negroes seemed to be in general agreement.

The Rev. Maurice E. Dawkins, pastor of the Peoples' Independent Church, called President Kennedy "the new Lincoln" and said he died "for the freedom of all people of all races and creeds."

A Negro assemblyman in the California legislature, Mervin Dymelly, expressed the fear "that this uncivilized act" might set the Negroes' civil rights cause "back to Civil War days."

Flags were at half-staff minutes after the President's death was verified.

Many families felt a sense of personal bereavement. One mother, crying despite her daughter's efforts to comfort her, said: "Why do people have to be cavemen? Why can't people progress at all?"

PHILADELPHIA

PHILADELPHIA, Nov. 22—News of President Kennedy's assassination stunned the people of Philadelphia this afternoon. Mayor James H. J. Tate called the murder "a sin against humanity" and likened Mr. Kennedy to Abraham Lincoln.

At the Academy of Music, Eugene Ormandy abruptly halted the regular Friday afternoon concert of the Philadelphia Orchestra. The Pennsylvania Supreme Court, the United States District Court and the county courts all adjourned until Monday.

Mr. Tate, his eyes red and his face flushed, recalled that President Kennedy visited Philadelphia three weeks ago in support of Mr. Tate's successful candidacy. The Mayor said:

"He told me how he looked forward to coming here for the Army-Navy game next week and to the Democratic National Convention in Atlantic City next year.

"He told me he looked forward to bathing in the surf and spending some time on the beach in Atlantic City.

"President Kennedy was the world's leading spokesman of goodwill and tolerance for all men and all nations. I pray that Vice President Johnson will be able to lead us in the path that was laid out by President Kennedy."

Churches Fill Up on News of Death

By PAUL L. MONTGOMERY

Many New Yorkers filed solemnly to their houses of worship yesterday to pay homage to the dead President.

In the hour when no one here knew whether President Kennedy was alive, they went to pray for his life. When the news of his death came, they prayed for his soul.

At Roman Catholic and Protestant churches and Jewish synagogues alike weeping men and women went to seek comfort in their grief.

During the afternoon more than 20,000 people passed in and out of St. Patrick's Cathedral to pay their respects. At 5 P.M. Bishop John Maguire, vicar general of the archdiocese, presided at a memorial service. A catafalque covered with an American flag rested before the altar.

Bishop Maguire sprinkled holy water on the catafalque as 15 priests joined with the crowd of 7,000 in repeating prayers.

The scene was repeated over the city in Catholic churches. In the churches and synagogues of other faiths memorial and remembrance services were held. The nation's religious leaders, numbed by the President's death, paid tribute to him and prayed for guidance in the time ahead.

By 2 P.M. St. Patrick's Cathedral was filling up. Six priests of the cathedral knelt in a row before the white altar and prayed for the President. Girls in bright scarves and businessmen with attaché cases knelt at the altar rail, their heads bowed.

In the aisles the votive candles flickered as auxiliary Bishop Joseph Flannelly, administrator of the cathedral, intoned the prayers. Many of the congregation anxiously fingered their rosaries.

At 2:30 Bishop Flannelly broke off the prayer and turned to face the growing crowd.

"We have just been informed that President Kennedy is dead," he said softly. And then, softer still, "May God have mercy on his soul."

For a moment, there was not a whisper in the huge cathedral. Then a muffled wail, subtle as smoke, crept over the crowd. Women bowed down sobbing and men cradled their heads in their arms.

Bishop Flannelly began the ancient litany for the dead:

"O God the creator and redeemer of all the faithful, hear our supplication, and through Thy infinite mercy graciously grant to the soul of Thy servant departed the remission of all his sins."

Five minutes later, the great bells of the cathedral began to toll solemnly. The crowd passing on Fifth Avenue looked up and knew. "Oh my God," a woman said. "He's dead."

Two blocks up Fifth Avenue, at St. Thomas Protestant Episcopal Church, the carillon took up the toll. A sidewalk Santa Claus slowed his vigorous bell-ringing to keep time.

Inside St. Patrick's, the prayers continued. Many who seemed never to have been there before stopped for a moment in the back and bowed their heads. Women used improvised ways to cover their heads—paper napkins, envelopes and pocketbooks.

The altars at the sides were bright with the candles lit for the President.

Services at the cathedral continued through the evening. A solemn pontifical mass for the President will be sung at 10 A.M. today.

Elsewhere in the city, people began filing into churches and synagogues soon after the announcement that the President had been shot.

In the Cathedral Church of St. John the Divine a prayer service was held in front of the great choir. In old Trinity Church, at Broadway and Wall Street, the Rev. Thorley Bridgeman led a memorial prayer service.

At many of the services, the sincerity of the worshipers' grief overrode the impromptu nature of the gatherings. Bishop Maguire led the congregation at St. Patrick's in singing the national anthem, something that is rarely done in a Catholic church. At St. Thomas church the carillon played "My Country, 'Tis of Thee."

Jewish men, women and children went to their houses of worship to pray and intone the Kaddish, the traditional prayer for the dead, in homage to the President.

At the same time, the Synagogue Council of America, the representative body of the Orthodox, Conservative and Reform branches of Judaism, called on spiritual leaders to lead their congregations in special prayers at the beginning of the Sabbath last night and through today.

The churches of the city planned memorial services for the late President. At the Cathedral of St. John the Divine there will be a service at 4 P.M. tomorrow. There will also be a service at the time of the President's funeral.

Three other Episcopal churches in the city also announced services—St. Bartholomew's at Parke Avenue and 51st Street, St. George's at 207 East 16th Street and the Church of the Resurrection at 115 East 74th Street—for tomorrow morning. The one at St. George's will be at 10:30, the others at 11.

Christ Church Methodist, Park Avenue and 60th Street, will also have a service tomorrow at 11 A.M.

The Rev. Dr. Adam Clayton Powell Jr. will lead the memorial service at 3 P.M. tomorrow at the Abyssinian Baptist Church, 132 West 138th Street.

Archbishop Iakovos of the Greek Orthodox Church of North and South America instructed the 400 churches in this country to hold services for the President Sunday morning.

The archbishop will preside at a memorial observance at Holy Trinity Cathedral, 319 East 74th Street, tomorrow at 10 A.M.

The Protestant Council of the City of New York urged all church and synagogue members to offer prayers for "President Johnson, our nation and the entire free world in this most tragic crisis."

Harold E. Stassen, president of the American Baptist Convention, requested the churches of the denomination to join in mourning for "the tragic loss of our President."

The Rev. Oliver R. Harms, president of the Lutheran Church-Missouri Synod, said that tomorrow would be observed as "a day of penitence and prayer" in the 6,000 churches of the denomination.

The Rev. Theodore M. Hesburgh, president of the University of Notre Dame in South Bend, Ind., pledged in messages to the Kennedy family that 100 masses would be offered at Notre Dame for the late President.

Kennedy Quoted Psalm In Talk He Never Gave

The speech that President Kennedy was to have delivered in Dallas yesterday ended with these words: ". . . and the righteousness of our cause must always underlie our strength. For as was written long ago: 'Except the Lord keep the city, the watchman waketh but in vain.'"

The quotation, ironic in the light of events, is from Psalm 124 in the Bible.

The complete verse reads:

Except the Lord build the house,
They labor in vain that build it:
Except the Lord keep the city,
The watchman waketh but in vain.

ESHKOL CONDEMNS 'DASTARDLY' CRIME

Special to The New York Times

JERUSALEM (Israeli Sector), Nov. 22—Premier Levi Eshkol said today that Israel was deeply grieved by the "dastardly assassination" of President Kennedy.

In a message to President Johnson, the Premier called Mr. Kennedy a "great and dynamic President of the United States and a courageous leader of the free world."

President Shneor Zalman Shazar also sent a message to President Johnson. He said he was "stunned with grief at the tragic blow which has afflicted the United States and all humanity."

The acting Foreign Minister, Abba Eban, a former Ambassador in Washington, said that he recalled Mr. Kennedy as a man of "restless and vivid energy constantly seeking new areas of expression."

"He was Israel's friend and he was the champion of all causes of which freedom was the central theme," Mr. Eban said. "We, the men of his generation, have lost our proudest standard bearer."

Mississippian Resigns Post

PASCAGOULA, Miss., Nov. 22 (UPI)—Robert Oswald, a lawyer, resigned tonight as president of the Mississippi Young Democrats. "The tragic event in Dallas, in the light of the 'hate the Kennedys' attitude of the leadership of the Mississippi Democratic party and its present administration should require no further explanation for my action," he said.

"All the News That's Fit to Print"

The New York Times.

LATE CITY EDITION

U. S. Weather Bureau Report (Page 35) forecasts: Sunny and cool today; fair, milder tonight. Cloudy, milder tomorrow.

Temp. Range: 46—32; yesterday: 53—37.

VOL. CXIII..No. 38,656.

NEW YORK, MONDAY, NOVEMBER 25, 1963.

TEN CENTS

PRESIDENT'S ASSASSIN SHOT TO DEATH IN JAIL CORRIDOR BY A DALLAS CITIZEN; GRIEVING THRONGS VIEW KENNEDY BIER

Associated Press Wirephoto

FAREWELL: Kneeling with her mother at John Fitzgerald Kennedy's coffin in the Capitol, Caroline touches the flag

Mrs. Kennedy Leads Public Mourning

By MARJORIE HUNTER

Special to The New York Times

WASHINGTON, Nov. 24 — Mrs. John F. Kennedy, firmly holding the hands of her two children, followed the coffin bearing the body of her husband as it left the White House today for the last time.

Her eyes swollen, she moved quietly to the edge of the steps of the North Portico and paused to watch the coffin placed in the caisson by military bearers.

Her son, John Jr., tugged at her hand and pointed to a black, riderless horse, part of the ceremonial procession. She leaned down and spoke to him.

Mrs. Kennedy wore a simple black suit and black lace mantilla. John Jr., who will be 3 years old tomorrow, and Caroline, who will be 6 on Wednesday, wore similar pale blue coats, white anklets and red shoes.

As the three stood there, framed against the black-draped doorway, there was an eerie silence. It was broken only by the occasional sound of hoofs of the restless gray horses that were to pull the caisson up Pennsylvania Avenue to the Capitol.

Mrs. Kennedy was composed, but appeared to be on the verge of tears as she and the children stepped into a black limousine for the slow ride to the Capitol. In the car, too, were President and Mrs. Johnson and Attorney General Robert F. Kennedy.

Still holding the hands of her children, Mrs. Kennedy followed the flag-draped coffin into the Capitol Rotunda. She stared straight ahead as the coffin was placed on the catafalque, a simple funeral bier draped in black broadcloth.

John Jr., wide-eyed and bewildered, was restless. Clutching a tiny flag, he was led away by a military aide.

Later, after the tributes had been spoken, Mrs. Kennedy walked slowly to the coffin, touched it with her fingertips, knelt and kissed it. Caroline was by her side. They were rejoined by John Jr. at the door.

Shortly after 9 o'clock tonight Mrs. Kennedy returned to the Capitol and again kneeled before the coffin and kissed it.

Mrs. Kennedy walked into the Rotunda on the arm of her husband's brother, Robert, who stopped at the rope holding

Continued on Page 2, Column 8

JOHNSON AFFIRMS AIMS IN VIETNAM

Retains Kennedy's Policy of Aiding War on Reds—Lodge Briefs President

By E. W. KENWORTHY

Special to The New York Times

WASHINGTON, Nov. 24 — President Johnson reaffirmed today the policy objectives of his predecessor regarding South Vietnam. He called upon all Government agencies to support that policy with full unity of purpose.

This was disclosed by White House sources after a meeting between President Johnson and Henry Cabot Lodge, United States Ambassador to South Vietnam.

The meeting lasted nearly an hour. It was described as being devoted to a full review of the conclusions reached by participants in a strategy conference on South Vietnam held in Honolulu last Wednesday.

In another move today that emphasized the President's desire to convey at home and abroad the impression of continuity, Mr. Johnson asked all members of the White House staff to remain at their jobs. This was announced by Pierre Salinger, White House press secretary.

Some Expected to Leave

Mr. Salinger said the President would leave up to the officials involved how long they wished to serve him.

Inevitably some of these officials especially those from the universities and foundations will decide to leave their posts after an interval.

But the President's request today would seem to insure that during the difficult days of adjustment and transition he would continue to have the benefit of the experience of key policy figures.

Attending the meeting between the President and Ambassador Lodge today were Secretary of State Dean Rusk, Secretary of Defense Robert S. McNamara, Under Secretary of State George W. Ball, John A. McCone, director of the Central Intelligence Agency, and McGeorge Bundy, special assistant to the President for national security affairs.

Secretaries Rusk and McNamara, Ambassador Lodge and Mr. Bundy all took part in the Honolulu conference.

As a result of the meeting, White House informants said, President Johnson laid down a

Continued on Page 5, Column 1

CROWD IS HUSHED

Mourners at Capitol File Past the Coffin Far Into the Night

Texts of eulogies spoken in Washington, Page 4.

By TOM WICKER

Special to The New York Times

WASHINGTON, Monday, Nov. 25—Thousands of sorrowing Americans filed past John Fitzgerald Kennedy's bier in the Great Rotunda of the United States Capitol yesterday and early today.

Mr. Kennedy's body lay in state in the center of the vast, stone-floored chamber. Long after midnight the silent procession of mourners continued.

Some wept. All were hushed. As the two lines moved in a large circle around either side of the flag-covered coffin, almost the only sounds were the shuffle of feet and the quiet voices of policemen urging the people to "keep moving, keep moving right along."

By 2:45 A. M. today 115,000 persons had passed the bier.

Yesterday afternoon a crowd estimated at 300,000 lined Pennsylvania and Constitution Avenues to watch the passage of the caisson bearing the body of the 35th President of the United States, slain in the 47th year of his life by an assassin's bullet.

A Riderless Horse

Behind the caisson, following military tradition, came a riderless bay gelding, with a pair of military boots reversed in the silver stirrups.

The horse was Sardar, the thoroughbred that belongs to Mrs. John F. Kennedy.

Mrs. Kennedy, her two children, President and Mrs. Johnson and Mr. Kennedy's brother, Attorney General Robert F. Kennedy, rode in the first car of a 10-car procession that followed the caisson.

The procession moved at a funeral pace, to the sound of muffled drums, from the White House to Pennsylvania Avenue. It was a journey Mr. Kennedy had made formally four times.

At the Capitol, brief ceremonies of eulogy were held in the Rotunda before the admission of the waiting thousands who swarmed over the plaza and stretched in a long line up East Capitol Street.

At the conclusion of the cere-

Continued on Page 2, Column 1

World's Leaders to Attend Requiem Today in Capital

Mrs. Kennedy Will Walk Behind the Caisson to Mass at Cathedral

By JACK RAYMOND

Special to The New York Times

WASHINGTON, Nov. 24 — Mrs. John F. Kennedy, joined by world and national leaders, will walk behind the horse-drawn caisson that bears her husband's body from the White House to St. Matthew's Roman Catholic Cathedral tomorrow.

Following a requiem mass, John Fitzgerald Kennedy, the 35th President of the United States, will be escorted in a solemn state procession to Arlington National Cemetery to be buried with military honors.

The gravesite, on a beautiful grassy knoll, provides a sweeping view of the capital city and it is itself easily in view from the Memorial Bridge approach to the national burial ground.

The state funeral procession will begin at 10:30 A.M. at the Capitol, where the closed, flag-draped coffin of the President

Continued on Page 6, Column 8

Officials of Nearly 100 Lands in U.S.—They Will Meet Johnson

By MAX FRANKEL

Special to The New York Times

WASHINGTON, Nov. 24 — An emperor, a king, a queen, princes, presidents, premiers and ministers from every continent converged on Washington this evening to pay final tribute to

List of leaders expected at the funeral, Page 6.

President Kennedy and to make the acquaintance of President Johnson.

Representing nearly 100 nations, the foreign dignitaries will include the largest assembly of ruling statesmen ever gathered in the United States for any event.

Their arrival here, through the night, virtually overwhelmed an already tense and overburdened capital. Nonetheless, each visitor received the protocol deference and police protection of more normal

Continued on Page 6, Column 1

ONE BULLET FIRED

Night-Club Man Who Admired Kennedy Is Oswald's Slayer

By GLADWIN HILL

Special to The New York Times

DALLAS, Nov. 24 — President Kennedy's assassin, Lee Harvey Oswald, was fatally shot by a Dallas night-club operator today as the police started to move him from the city jail to the county jail.

The shooting occurred in the basement of the municipal building at about 11:20 A.M. central standard time (12:20 P.M. New York time).

The assailant, Jack Rubenstein, known as Jack Ruby, lunged from a cluster of newsmen observing the transfer of Oswald from the jail to an armored truck.

Millions of viewers saw the shooting on television.

As the shot rang out, a police detective suddenly recognized Ruby and exclaimed: "Jack, you son of a bitch!"

A murder charge was filed against Ruby by Assistant District Attorney William F. Alexander. Justice of the Peace Pierce McBride ordered him held without bail.

Detectives Flank Him

Oswald was arrested Friday after Mr. Kennedy was shot dead while riding through Dallas in an open car. He was charged with murdering the President and a policeman who was shot a short time later while trying to question Oswald.

As the 24-year-old prisoner, flanked by two detectives, stepped onto a basement garage ramp, Ruby thrust a .38-caliber, snub-nose revolver into Oswald's left side and fired a single shot.

The 52-year-old night-club operator, an ardent admirer of President Kennedy and his family, was described as having been distraught.

[District Attorney Henry Wade said he understood that the police were looking into the possibility that Oswald had been slain to prevent him from talking, The Associated Press reported. Mr. Wade said that so far no connection between Oswald and Ruby had been established.]

Oswald slumped to the concrete paving, wordlessly clutching his side and writhing with pain.

Oswald apparently lost con-

Continued on Page 10, Column 1

Millions of Viewers See Oswald Killing On 2 TV Networks

By JACK GOULD

The fatal shooting of Lee H. Oswald, who was held as the assassin of President Kennedy, was seen as it occurred yesterday by millions of television viewers.

The National Broadcasting Company telecast the dramatic happening live. Less than a minute later the Columbia Broadcasting System telecast it by means of tape, made as the shooting occurred.

C. B. S. headquarters recorded the pictures from Dallas as they were received here over a closed circuit. Officials, upon seeing the contents of the Dallas relay, put the tape out over the network instantly.

The incident marked the first time in 15 years of television around the globe that a real-life homicide had occurred in front of live cameras. The closest parallel occurred in October, 1960, when Inejiro Asanuma, Japanese political leader, was knifed on a public stage in

Continued on Page 10, Column 8

JOHNSON SPURS OSWALD INQUIRY

President Orders F. B. I. to Check Death—Handling of Case Worries Capital

By ANTHONY LEWIS

Special to The New York Times

WASHINGTON, Nov. 24—President Johnson directed the Federal Bureau of Investigation tonight to look into "every aspect" of the murder of Lee H. Oswald.

He spoke with the director of the F.B.I., J. Edgar Hoover, and ordered the redoubled investigation.

The action came as official Washington was showing increasing concern about the entire handling of the aftermath of President Kennedy's assassination.

Officials were convinced that Oswald was the assassin. But their concern was over the public impression of the criminal proceedings.

Tonight they were consider-

Continued on Page 11, Column 3

BUSINESS OF CITY WILL HALT TODAY

Mayor Says Only Essential Services Will Be Provided

Changes in events here are listed on Page 9.

By LEONARD INGALLS

Normal public, business and social activity in the city will be almost completely suspended today out of respect for President Kennedy.

Mayor Wagner announced yesterday that the city would continue in full mourning throughout the day. Only essential city services will be maintained, he said.

"Those city employes not engaged in activities imperative to the health, safety and welfare of our citizens are to be released from duty and their offices closed through Monday," Mr. Wagner said at City Hall.

Proclamation of the day as a legal holiday by Governor Rockefeller in observance of Mr. Kennedy's funeral permits banks and other institutions to close.

Classes at schools and colleges will be suspended. Department stores and specialty shops will be shut. Securities exchanges and commodity markets will not operate. Most places of entertainment will be closed. There will be no deliveries of mail and post offices will be shut.

Special memorial services for the murdered President have been scheduled at churches and synagogues.

At St. Patrick's Cathedral

Continued on Page 9, Column 1

Pope Paul Warns That Hate and Evil Imperil Civil Order

Special to The New York Times

ROME, Nov. 24 — Pope Paul VI, alluding to the assassination of President Kennedy, said today that it showed how much "capacity for hatred and evil still remains in the world."

Without mentioning Mr. Kennedy by name, the Pontiff spoke of "the crime that has aroused in these days the deploration of the whole world." He said it illustrated "how great the threat to civil order and peace still is."

The Pope was addressing thousands of people gathered in St. Peter's Square for his usual Sunday-noon benediction.

"We cannot, at this moment of prayer together, take our thoughts from the crime that has aroused in these days the deploration of the whole world," he said.

"After dwelling upon the man who is no longer with us and after comforting those who still live in mourning and grief, our thoughts show us how much the capacity for hatred and evil yet remains in the world, how great the threat to civil order and peace still is, and how great is the need for the grace

Continued on Page 4, Column 7

NEWS INDEX

JOHNSON SCORED BY CHINESE REDS

Views Called 'Reactionary' —Taiwan Aid Attacked

By United Press International

TOKYO, Nov. 24 — Communist China bitterly criticized President Johnson today and termed him a supporter of the late President Kennedy's "trickery policy."

"Since the emergence of the Kennedy regime," the Chinese Communist press agency Hsinhua said, "Johnson has positively supported various reactionary policies of the Kennedy Administration and participated in formulating and promoting such policies.

"Johnson has supported Kennedy's trickery policy and has called for the maintenance of such a policy in a series of his speeches."

The Chinese Communists reported the assassination of President Kennedy in a four-paragraph dispatch eight hours after it occurred. But they made no comment.

Hsinhua said Mr. Johnson "was one of the central figures in the Kennedy Government and has made frequent trips abroad."

The Chinese statement added that Mr. Johnson believed "the United States, in making two-faced antirevolutionary plots, must maintain a strong position on the basis of strong force."

"He also looks toward Cuba with animosity and has called for the elimination of the Cuban revolutionary Government,"

Continued on Page 7, Column 6

Copyright 1963—Dallas Times-Herald and Photographer Bob Jackson, from United Press International Telephoto

OSWALD IS SHOT: Lee Harvey Oswald cringes as Jack Ruby attacks him at Dallas jail. Policeman is J. R. Leavelle.

Grieving Thousands File Past Kennedy's Bier in the Great Rotunda of the Capitol

CROWD IS HUSHED AS IT MOVES BY

Line of Mourners Continues Into Night—300,000 See Caisson Procession

Continued From Page 1, Col. 5

monies, Mrs. Kennedy and her daughter, Caroline, stepped a few feet forward. Each reached out and touched the flag and the coffin it covered.

Mrs. Kennedy knelt, kissed the coffin, then rose and led her daughter away.

President Johnson had already come forward, following a soldier who walked backward carrying a wreath of red and white carnations. As the soldier placed the wreath at the foot of the coffin, the man who had taken Mr. Kennedy's place in office stood with his head bowed, then withdrew.

The wreath was marked "From President Johnson and the Nation." Numbers of other wreaths and sprays, sent despite a White House request that flowers be omitted, were arranged in nearby rooms.

After a short interval, during which staff workers of the Senate and the House of Representatives and their guests were admitted to the Rotunda from the North and South Wings of the Capitol, the great central doors of the Capitol were thrown open to the people.

Across the East Plaza, in long, silent lines, they came—patient, quiet, thousands upon thousands of them. They moved slowly up the towering marble steps, above which, on Jan. 20, 1961, a platform had been built for the Inaugural of John F. Kennedy as President of the United States.

As they entered the Rotunda, they formed two lines, each moving in a great semi-circle around the Rotunda. Only red velvet ropes and 25 feet of stone floor separated them from the catafalque upon which rested Mr. Kennedy's coffin.

Enlisted men from each of the armed services stood motionless at the four corners of the catafalque. As the guard changed every half hour, first an Army officer, than a Marine Corps officer, then an officer from the Navy and the Air Force took up his position at the head of the coffin. They rotated command of the guard through the night.

Behind the commander, a sailor held the flag of the President. To the sailor's right stood an unattended American flag.

Footprints on Catafalque

Yesterday afternoon the dusty footprints of the military men who had placed the coffin upon the catafalque were still visible on the catafalque's black velvet drapings. At each side of the coffin were sprays of chrysanthemums and white lilies.

That simple scene was all the people saw as they filed past—the coffin covered with its flag, the motionless guards, the two listless flags upon their standards, the traditional flowers of death.

The police were nearly overwhelmed by a crowd far beyond their expectations. Within the Rotunda, however, all was order and silence. The lines moved rapidly around the circle—about 35 persons a minute in each line—and were directed out the west door to the wide porch that overlooks the Mall and the Washington Monument.

Outside, virtually the whole Metropolitan police force was on duty. At 4:30 P.M., the lines of those waiting to get in the Capitol stretched across the East Plaza back and six blocks, past the Supreme Court building on East Capitol Street.

At 9 P.M. the waiting line stretched for 30 blocks, with four to six persons abreast. And the line was growing, as people joined it faster than it moved through the Rotunda.

Thousands Turn Back

Originally, it had been planned to close the Capitol's doors at 9 P.M., reopening the Rotunda for an hour this morning. When the size of the crowds became apparent, it was decided to keep it open as long as people came.

Thousands were giving up late yesterday, however, under the impression that the doors would be closed by the time they reached the Rotunda. Families from as far away as Baltimore and Richmond left without having gotten near the Capitol.

However, millions throughout the county were watching on television. The brilliant lights needed for the cameras played steadily on the Rotunda and broadcasters spoke constantly in low monotones into their microphones.

Across the wide lawns and the paved drives of the Capitol Plaza, the people coming and going swarmed like ants. Most were good-natured. There was little pushing and shoving, and no fighting was observed. But confusion was constant as people tried to find out where to get into line, how long it was and how to get out of the jammed plaza.

Even Mrs. Kennedy was inconvenienced by the crowds in the plaza. When she left the Capitol, in a limousine with her children and Attorney General Kennedy, her planned route along Independence Avenue was impassable. She was rerouted over other streets, led by a motorcycle escort.

Throughout yesterday among the throngs that watched the procession and those that jammed around the Capitol, there were few evidences of open emotionalism. Not many people wept, or cried out. The mood was rather one of sorrow and respect.

Even among teen-agers, of whom thousands and thousands seemed to be present, there was quiet. People passing through the Rotunda were told that no photographs were to be taken; only a few, looking somewhat furtive, broke the restriction.

The police said some persons began lining up at midnight Saturday. Yesterday morning, hours before the procession began, crowds began to form along the streets and in Lafayette Square across Pennsylvania Avenue from the White House.

A half-hour before the procession began, the news reached the White House that Lee H. Oswald, charged with the murder of Mr. Kennedy in Dallas on Friday, had been shot down in that city.

Among the crowds many had transistor radios, and the news from Dallas swept rapidly. It was a constant subject of conversation in the crowd, and one gray-haired woman, seated on a bench in Lafayette Square, told her husband:

"I told you last night, Henry, I had a feeling something like this would happen. That man held so many secrets, some one had to kill him."

Another woman exclaimed: "My God, how long will this go on?"

On the lawn before the north portico of the White House, a small crowd of White House employes and workers in the Executive Office Building was permitted to assemble. The circular drive in front of the mansion was lined, shortly after noon, with black limousines. Near the northeast gate, an honor guard and the bearers of flags of all the states were lined up.

At 12:40 P.M., President and Mrs. Johnson arrived at the north portico and entered the black-draped doors of the building that will now be their home. Shortly thereafter, the empty caisson, draped in black and drawn by six gray horses, came up the drive and stopped under the portico.

It was the same caisson upon which the body of Franklin D. Roosevelt was carried from the White House to the Capitol in 1945.

Behind it was Sardar. The horse was given to Mrs. Kennedy in March, 1962, by President Ayub Khan of Pakistan when she visited that country. The White House said Mrs. Kennedy had requested that the horse be used as the traditional symbol of a fallen warrior. A black-handled sword hung in a silver scabbard from the saddle.

Mrs. Kennedy has ridden the horse in the hunt country around nearby Atoka, Va., where the late President built a new home.

The other horses were Army stock from Fort Myer in Virginia.

Then Mr. Kennedy's military aides, Maj. Gen. Chester V. Clifton of the Army, Brig. Gen. Godfrey McHugh of the Air Force and Capt. Tazewell T. Shepard Jr. of the Navy, lined up at attention behind the caisson.

Eight enlisted men of the various armed services carried the coffin out onto the north portico, down the few steps and placed it on the caisson. The military aides moved to the front. The caisson pulled slowly away, followed by the black horse. And a limousine slid into place at the foot of the steps.

Mrs. Kennedy, in black and wearing a black mantilla, came out, holding Caroline and John Jr. by the hand. The children were dressed in identical shades of blue. The three entered the car and 2-year-old John Jr., apparently unaware of the nature of the occasion, bounced up on the seat and peered out the rear window.

Attorney General Kennedy followed them into the car. President and Mrs. Johnson took the jump seats, and the limousine pulled away.

In rapid order, other limousines drove up to the steps and were filled. In the second car were Mr. Kennedy's sisters Patricia and Jean, and their husbands, Peter Lawford and Stephen E. Smith. In the third were Mrs. Kennedy's stepfather and mother, Mr. and Mrs. Hugh D. Auchincloss, and others of the Auchincloss family.

Mrs. Robert Kennedy, several of her children, and Sargent Shriver, the husband of the former Eunice Kennedy, were in the next car. Mrs. Shriver, her mother, Mrs. Rose Kennedy, and Senator Edward M. Kennedy, the youngest brother, were flying to Washington from Hyannis Port, Mass., and were not in the procession.

A number of employes of the Kennedy family and the White House rode in another car.

Other cars with officials, security agents and policemen joined the line. As the procession moved slowly onto Pennsylvania Avenue, turned briefly on 15th Street, and then rounded on to the long straight stretch of Pennsylvania that reaches from the Treasury Building to the Capitol, the line was about two city blocks long.

Joint Chiefs March

In advance of the caisson, on foot, were policemen, the escort commander — Maj. Gen. Philip C. Wehle of the Military District of Washington — five military drummers, a drum major and a company of Navy enlisted men. They walked at funeral pace, 100 paces a minute.

Behind them was a special honor guard, composed of the Joint Chiefs of Staff led by their chairman, Gen. Maxwell D. Taylor, and followed by Mr. Kennedy's military aides.

The national colors immediately preceded the caisson. Between it and the car carrying Mrs. Kennedy and President Johnson, there were personal flags, the marching body bearers, and the riderless Sardar.

Three clergymen also marched in the procession. They were the Very Rev. Francis Bowes Sayre Jr., dean of the Cathedral of Saints Peter and Paul (Washington Cathedral), Protestant Episcopal; the Right Rev. John S. Spencer of Sacred Heart Shrine (Roman Catholic), and the Very Rev. K. V. Kazanjian, rector of St. Mary's Armenian Apostolic Church.

Dean Sayre was born in the White House on Jan. 17, 1915. His mother was the daughter of President Woodrow Wilson, the late Mrs. Jessie Woodrow Wilson Sayre.

Crowds lined the entire route at least 10 deep, and twice that thick at some places. Others stretched up the side streets, hung from windows of buildings along the street, lined open-tiered parking buildings and mounted the pedestals of the street's numerous statues.

At 25-foot intervals, soldiers with fixed bayonets lined the street on each side, standing at parade rest.

The Secret Service and the police, nervous after the Dallas motorcade that ended in death for Mr. Kennedy, took unusually stringent security precautions for Mr. Johnson.

As the President's car passed 14th Street, for instance, a police official was designating an officer to watch each building on the street. It was from a building beside a Dallas street that Mr. Kennedy was shot through the head by a sniper with a high-powered rifle.

For the first few blocks, the crowds stood silently, almost unmoving, as each element of the procession passed. As at the Capitol later, there were few evidences of emotionalism—very little, for instance, of the weeping, screaming and kneeling in the street that was observed at the last such occasion, the funeral procession for President Franklin Roosevelt 18 years ago.

A sizable group of reporters and photographers were allowed to walk in the street at the rear of the procession. Many of them had followed Mr. Kennedy in happier times when he drove to the Capitol along the same route for his inauguration, for two addresses to Congress in 1961, and for his State of the Union Messages in 1962 and 1963.

But their presence at the rear of the procession had been apparently mistaken by the crowd as an invitation for others to join. By the time the rear of the procession passed 11th Street, hundreds were seeping out from the curbs to walk behind Mr. Kennedy's coffin. Many were teen-agers, and some surged past the reporters as if to walk beside the cars ahead.

At Ninth Street, apparently on orders from a Secret Service car that pulled out of the procession, the police formed a cordon across the avenue and stopped the crowd, which was massed from curb to curb and extended back for more than a block.

The reporters were let through the line at that point and continued along the avenue. Again, however, the crowds began coming from the curbside to join in. Finally, at John Marshall Place, a few blocks from the point where the procession slanted off onto Constitution Avenue, a line of marines with fixed bayonets halted everyone, including the reporters.

As the procession moved slowly up Capitol Hill on Constitution Avenue, and turned into the East Plaza, the restrictions were relaxed.

As seen from below, the sloping hillsides around the building were almost solidly covered with moving figures — many with children in their arms, some running, some leaping stone walls, all swarming up the hillside and the steps toward the West Front of the Capitol.

The police estimated that on the other side of the building, 35,000 persons were in the East Plaza to see the procession arrive.

The caisson and the cars following reached the east steps of the Capitol at 1:50 P.M., 45 minutes after the coffin had been borne from the White House. A 21-gun salute boomed across the crowd and echoed across the vast plaza stretching north to Union Station.

A military band played "Hail to the Chief." As the eight bearers removed the coffin from the caisson and bore it slowly up the marble steps, the band softly played — perhaps in honor of the service during which Mr. Kennedy nearly gave his life in World War II — the Navy hymn, "Eternal Father, Strong to Save."

The various parties from the limousines followed the coffin in the order they had arrived. Inside the Rotunda, members of the Senate, House and Cabinet and other dignitaries stood in a semicircle. Mrs. Kennedy, President and Mrs. Johnson and others who had come in the procession stood in the northeast quadrant of the hushed chamber, near a temporary lectern.

The members of the Kennedy family gathered near them. Caroline and John Jr. stood holding their mother's hands, Caroline sedately, John occasionally capering about.

Among those in the Rotunda was former President Harry S. Truman. He was accompanied by his daughter, Mrs. E. C. Daniel of New York.

Senator Mike Mansfield of Montana, the Democratic leader of the Senate, was the first eulogist.

Mansfield's Eulogy

As television lights washed the Rotunda in a harsh, artificial glare, Senator Mansfield spoke in tones that grew ever more ringing.

Four times, in praising the man who was dead, and the life he had lived for his country and with his wife, Senator Mansfield repeated:

"In a moment, it was no more. And so she took a ring from her finger and placed it in his hands."

A fifth time he said it and added -- "and kissed him, and closed the lid of a coffin."

The Senator referred to Mrs. Kennedy's having put her ring on a finger of the President and and having kissed him as the body was about to be taken to the plane for its return to Washington.

At that moment, the Senator said, "a piece of each of us died."

Mr. Kennedy, he said, "gave us of his love that we, too, in turn, might give. He gave that we might give of ourselves, that we might give to one another until there would be no room, no room at all, for the bigotry, the hatred, the prejudice and the arrogance which converged in that moment of horror to strike him down."

Chief Justice Earl Warren struck much the same note in the eulogy that followed.

"What moved some misguided wretch to do this horrible deed may never be known to us," he said, "but we do know that such acts are commonly stimulated by forces of hatred and malevolence, such as today, and are eating their way into the bloodstream of American life."

"What a price we pay for this fanaticism!" he declared.

Then the Chief Justice said: "If we really love this country, if we truly love justice and mercy, if we fervently want to make this nation better for those who are to follow us, we can at least abjure the hatred that consumes people, the false accusations that divide us and the bitterness that begets violence.

"Is it too much to hope that the martyrdom of our beloved President might even soften the hearts of those who would themselves recoil from assassination, but who do not shrink from spreading the venom which kindles thoughts of it in others?"

Speaker of the House John W. McCormack was more personal.

"As we gather here today, bowed in grief," he said, "the heartfelt sympathy of the members of the Congress and of our people are extended to Mrs. Jacqueline and to Ambassador and Mrs. Joseph P. Kennedy and their loved ones."

"Their deep grief," he went on, "is also self-shared by countless millions of person throughout the world; considered a personal tragedy, as if one had lost a loved memebr of his own immediate family."

Most of these remarks were inaudible to many in the chamber, which was not designed for speeches. Even strong voices are lost in the vast open space that rises above the stone floor to the top of the Capitol Dome.

During the eulogies, Mrs. Kennedy stood with regal bearing, seeming to listen intently. Tears rolled down the face of Robert F. Kennedy. At the moment that Mrs. Kennedy walked forward and knelt by her husband's coffin, all who saw her were profoundly moved.

Then it was over. Mrs. Kennedy and her children walked slowly down the steps of the Capitol. President and Mrs. Johnson followed. At the foot of the steps, in the softer light of the afternoon, they talked for a few moments.

Mrs. Johnson held Mrs. Kennedy's hands as they spoke; once she leaned forward and placed her head near Mrs. Kennedy's. Then the President took Mrs. Kennedy's hand in one of his, patted it with the other. Mrs. Kennedy, her children and Robert Kennedy entered a car and sped away.

Mr. Johnson, headed for one of the important meetings that will constantly occupy him in coming days, entered another car with Secret Service men and a military aide. After him, alone with her driver and a security guard, rode the new First Lady.

Behind them, in the stillness of the Rotunda, they left the body of John Fitzgerald Kennedy upon the same catafalque on which had rested—98 years ago—the body of Abraham Lincoln, the first American President to be murdered. Gazing on the scene with silent stone eyes from beside the north entrance was a statue of James A. Garfield, the second President to fall before an assassin.

It was time, then, for the doors to be opened to those waiting outside.

Associated Press Wirephoto

AFTER EULOGY: Mrs. John Fitzgerald Kennedy and her children, Caroline and John Jr., leave Capitol, followed by other members of the Kennedy family and, at top, President and Mrs. Johnson. Behind Caroline is Robert F. Kennedy, who is followed by Sydney Lawford and Mr. and Mrs. Peter Lawford. Behind Mrs. Kennedy are Mrs. Stephen Smith and her husband. Mrs. Lawford and Mrs. Smith are sisters-in-law of Mrs. Kennedy.

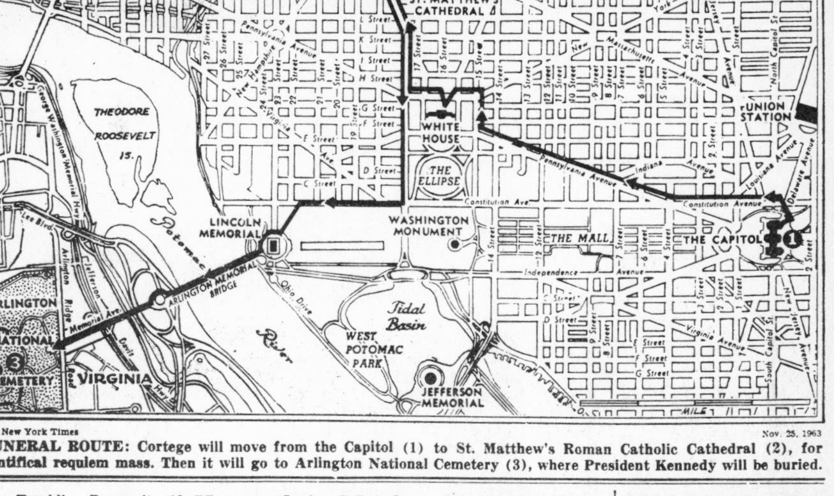

The New York Times — Nov. 25, 1963

FUNERAL ROUTE: Cortege will move from the Capitol (1) to St. Matthew's Roman Catholic Cathedral (2), for pontifical requiem mass. Then it will go to Arlington National Cemetery (3), where President Kennedy will be buried.

Kennedy's Mother Visits Altar Dedicated to Son Killed in War

HYANNIS PORT, Mass., Nov. 24 (UPI)—The mother of President Kennedy worshiped today before an altar dedicated to another son—Joseph P. Kennedy Jr., who was killed in World War II.

Mrs. Joseph P. Kennedy, 72 years old, attended two masses in the white clapboard Roman Catholic Church at this Cape Cod community. One son, Senator Edward M. Kennedy, Democrat of Massachusetts, and a daughter, Mrs. Sargent Shriver, also attended the church a few hours before all three flew to Washington for the President's funeral tomorrow.

Today, in church, one seat was empty.

At the 11 A.M. mass, the priest, Msgr. Leonard J. Daley, noted that the empty seat in a side chapel of St. Francis Xavier Church was the one occupied by President Kennedy when he attended church while home from Washington.

"It is empty," Msgr. Daley said.

"We like to think of him in the days before he became President when he worshiped at this altar," the priest went on.

Sobs were audible among the congregation that included a 150-member uniformed veterans group.

The President's mother, his brother, and married sister had attended church earlier. The mother prayed through two masses starting at 7 A.M.

Mrs. Kennedy sat in the vestry. She emerged only to receive communion with the other parishioners. Senator Kennedy and Mrs. Shriver sat in a pew.

The President's 75-year-old father, left virtually speechless from a stroke in December, 1960, was reported bearing the strain bravely.

Family Is Appreciative

HYANNIS, Mass., Nov. 24—Senator Kennedy made a statement today expressing appreciation for the sympathy shown to him and his family in the death of President Kennedy. His statement, made before boarding a plane for Washington, follows:

"I would just like to say a word. I'm going down to Washington now with my mother and my sister, Eunice.

"I do want to say how appreciative that both my parents have been for the tremendous outpouring of thoughtfulness and prayers that have come from all Americans in all parts of the country, from every religious group.

"This has been a matter which has been a source of tremendous consolation to both my parents and they certainly wanted me to express their great thanks to all of the peo-people who've been so kind in remembering them now."

Grandmother Not Told

Special to The New York Times

BOSTON, Nov. 24—Mrs. John F. Fitzgerald has not been told and probably will not be told that her grandson, John F. Kennedy, was assassinated on Friday. She is 98 years old.

Thousands Pass Bier at Night Despite the Cold and Long Wait

WASHINGTON, Monday, Nov. 25 (AP)—People by the thousands who had endured the cold and hours of patient waiting passed in homage last night and early this morning past the bier of President Kennedy in the Capitol.

At least 115,000 had moved up the Capitol steps, and passed the coffin by 2:45 A.M. The line of those waiting to pay a final tribute extended for miles in a chill wind.

Representative William J. Randall, Democrat of Missouri, drove the length of the line of waiting people at 11 P.M. He said the line was nine miles long.

Original plans had called for the viewing of the flag-draped coffin to continue until 10 A.M. but military authorities announced at a late hour that all viewing would cease by 9 A.M.

The people were filing swiftly through the rotunda and moving on into the night with their memories.

They came alone, they came with children. Some were the mighty, most were the meek.

Among them was the grieving widow, back for a second brief visit to the bier of her husband.

An hour later the late President's mother, Mrs. Joseph P. Kennedy, moved through the line and kneeled in silent prayer alongside the coffin of her son.

Another mourner was Eamon de Valera, aging President of Ireland, from which Mr. Kennedy's forefathers had come.

But mostly they were just people, shuffling in awed silence, two abreast, in two semi-circles around the bier guarded by military men.

As midnight approached, and the temperature dropped to 39 degrees, newsmen estimated that some 75,600 persons had passed through the Rotunda.

Many on the line said they had been waiting nine hours to view the bier. Almost unanimously they said they would do it again.

Earlier the police had doubled the pace by ordering viewers to go two-abreast instead of single file, increasing the rate to about 14,400 an hour. But they feared that even the all-night vigil would not accommodate the waiting thousands.

U.N. Will Be Closed Today

In mourning for President Kennedy, all United Nations meetings have been canceled the Secretariat is closed for the day and the public tour service will not operate.

MOURNING IS LED BY MRS. KENNEDY

Continued From Page 1, Col. 8

back the crowd while she went on through.

She walked slowly to the side of the coffin, knelt beside it and then, with her hand on the flag again, kissed the coffin.

Standing, she turned, looked long at the crowd and then rejoined the Attorney General. They walked slowly out of the front entrance, passing the crowd, seeming to look at its faces.

After walking down the steps beside the line filing up, Mrs. Kennedy was heard to say, "Let's walk a bit."

They walked west to the bottom of Capitol Hill, stopped to chat with some nuns they met, and finally got in a limousine when a crowd began to gather.

The limousine carrying Mrs. Kennedy and the children back to the White House this afternoon had to be rerouted over side streets because of crowds.

Another Sad Journey

Tomorrow, Mrs. Kennedy will again follow the caisson by car from the Capitol to the White House. There, she will alight to follow the coffin by foot for five blocks to St. Matthew's Cathedral for the funeral mass.

White House aides declined tonight to say if the children would attend the service or the burial, which will be held in Arlington National Cemetery.

Mrs. Kennedy will meet with foreign heads of state at the White House at 3:30 tomorrow afternoon, shortly after the burial, it was announced tonight. The State Department was flooded all day with requests of foreign dignitaries to meet her.

The solemn ceremonies of the day began in late morning for Mrs. Kennedy and her children when they attended a private mass in the East Room, where the coffin rested under a crystal chandellier.

The mass was celebrated by the Rev. M. Frank Ruppert of St. Matthews Cathedral. Present were members of the family and close friends, including Under Secretary of the Navy Paul Fay and Charles Spaulding of New York.

Joining Mrs. Kennedy at the White House before the procession to the Capitol were her stepfather and mother, Mr. and Mrs. Hugh D. Auchincloss of Washington and Newport, and her stepsister and stepbrother, Miss Janet Auchincloss and Jamie Auchincloss.

Sister Is Visiting

Mrs. Kennedy's sister, Princess Stanislas Radziwill of London, arrived yesterday to stay with her sister until after the funeral. Attorney General and Mrs. Kennedy also are staying with her much of the time.

Other members of the family at the White House during the mourning were two of President Kennedy's sisters and their husbands, Mr. and Mrs. Stephen Smith and Mr. and Mrs. Peter Lawford.

Arriving from Hyannis Port, Mass., aboard the family plane, the Caroline, late today were Mr. Kennedy's mother, Mrs. Joseph P. Kennedy, a sister, Mrs. Sargent Shriver; and a brother, Senator Edward M. Kennedy.

President Kennedy's mother, one of her daughters, two daughters-in-law and one son-in-law visited the catafalque in the Rotunda just after 10 P.M.

Kneeling and praying beside the coffin for several minutes were the senior Mrs. Kennedy, Joan Kennedy, wife of Senator Kennedy; Mrs. Robert Kennedy, and Mrs. Shriver, who is the Presidents sister Eunice.

Standing by was Mr. Lawford, the actor, husband of the President's sister Patricia, who was not present.

White House aides said that Mrs. Kennedy is holding off on plans for her future until after the funeral. They said that only the files from President Kennedy's office had been moved out.

It is possible that, after leaving the White House, Mrs Kennedy will go to her country home on Rattlesnake Mountain, near Atoka, Va.

Or she may go to the Kennedy summer home at Hyannis Port, to the Auchincloss estate, Hammersmith Farm, at Newport, R.I., or the Auchincloss home in Georgetown.

A Widow's Courage Catches at the Heart of a Nation as Kennedy Lies in State

Mrs. Kennedy, Caroline and John Kennedy Jr. wait as the President's coffin is placed on the caisson. In the rear are the President's brother Robert, and sister Mrs. Jean Smith.

Procession, moving at funeral pace, leaves the Capitol. Clergymen are, from left: Dean Francis Bowes Sayre Jr. of Washington Protestant Episcopal Cathedral, Msgr. John S. Spence of Sacred Heart Roman Catholic Shrine, and Very Rev. K. V. Kazanjian, St. Mary's Armenian Apostolic Church.

The solemn cortege proceeds along Pennsylvania Avenue toward the Capitol. The crowds that were massed on Pennsylvania and Constitution Avenues were estimated at 300,000.

Mrs. Kennedy and her children follow as the President's coffin is carried into the Capitol. Behind them are Attorney General Robert Kennedy and other members of the family.

The coffin is in place in the Rotunda of the Capitol for the brief ceremony of eulogy

Associated Press and United Press International

As the sun streams through the windows of the Rotunda Mrs. Kennedy and Caroline kneel to pray. Both touched flag, Mrs. Kennedy kissed the coffin.

Cushing Eulogizes Kennedy as Both a Great Leader and a Family Man of Warmth

EXTOLS PRESIDENT IN MEMORIAL MASS

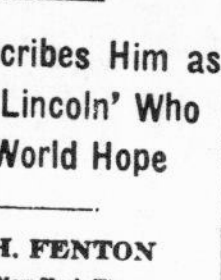

Cardinal Describes Him as a 'Youthful Lincoln' Who Gave the World Hope

By JOHN H. FENTON

Special to The New York Times

BOSTON, Nov. 24 — Richard Cardinal Cushing, who served the spiritual needs of John F. Kennedy in joy and in sorrow, celebrated a memorial mass for the slain President today.

The mass was televised nationally from the archdiocesan television center here.

The Roman Catholic Archbishop of Boston eulogized Mr. Kennedy as a husband and a father who made the most of the few moments he could share with his family. The Cardinal continued:

"What comfort can I extend to their heavy hearts today — mother, father, sisters, brothers — what beyond the knowledge that they have given history a youthful Lincoln, who in his time and in his sacrifice has made more sturdy the hopes of this nation and its people."

Like Cardinal Cushing, two priests who also had played roles in Mr. Kennedy's spiritual life noted the sacrifice that the demands of public office required of his private life.

The priests were attached to churches in Boston, where the President maintained a residence in the early years of his political career.

Cardinal Cushing married Mr. Kennedy and Jacqueline Bouvier at Newport, R.I., in 1953. He baptized their two children, Caroline, 6 years old next week, and John Jr., 3 tomorrow.

Three months ago, the prelate celebrated a mass for a third child, Patrick Bouvier Kennedy, who died two days after his birth.

Offered Invocation

When Mr. Kennedy was inaugurated as 35th President of the United States, Jan. 20, 1961, Cardinal Cushing offered the invocation.

This afternoon, the Cardinal flew to Washington, where tomorrow he will preside at noon at a pontifical funeral mass in St. Matthew's Cathedral.

After the televised mass, Cardinal Cushing recalled that he had watched Mr. Kennedy "mature with ever expanding responsibility." The Cardinal went on:

"I have been with him in joy and sorrow, in decision and in crisis, among friends and with strangers, and I know of no one who has combined in more noble perfection the qualities of greatness that mark his cool intelligence and his brave heart."

While others may pay tribute to Mr. Kennedy's virtues as a world leader, Cardinal Cushing said, "for me, it will be proper to recall him on this day of mourning as a husband and father, surrounded by his young and beloved family."

"Although the demands of office carried him often on long journeys and filled even his days at home with endless labors," the prelate said, "how often he would make time to share with his son and daughter those few minutes that could be his."

The Cardinal notified all pastors in the archdiocese yesterday that, by permission of the Holy See, one Sunday mass in each parish might be a mass of requiem, offered for the repose of the soul of the President. Normally, masses of requiem are not permitted on Sundays or feast days of major rank.

Masses Are Offered

Such requiem masses were offered at 10 A.M. at St. Joseph's Church, in the West End, and at Holy Ghost Chapel, at the Paulist Information Center, on Park Street, overlooking the Boston Common.

The Rev. Francis X. Quinn, pastor of St. Joseph's, recalled times when Mr. Kennedy had attended services there. During Mr. Kennedy's residency at 122 Bowdoin Street, near the Massachusetts State House, St. Joseph's was his parish.

In those days, Mr. Kennedy was embarking on his political career and was away much of the time.

Father Quinn said that the Paulist Fathers headquarters, just below the State House, was more convenient for Mr. Kennedy.

A priest there, who asked not to be identified, recalled that Mr. Kennedy had once taken up the collection at a mass while one of the ushers was in the sacristy, protesting that "that guy is using our vestibule as a rallying place." The priest identified the protesting usher as a Republican.

He said that Mr. Kennedy, then campaigning for the Senate, had dropped by to attend mass. Wherever he appeared in Boston, Mr. Kennedy always founds outstretched hands seeking to shake his.

Will Shorten Family Grief

BOSTON, Nov. 24 (AP) — The decision to bury President Kennedy in Arlington National Cemetery was taken to avoid prolonging the family's grief, Cardinal Cushing said tonight.

In a local television interview, the prelate explained that, if the body had been brought to Brookline for burial beside the body of the Kennedy's infant son who died in August, it would have extended the funeral period into Tuesday.

Cardinal Cushing added that a similar reason was behind the decision to have a low mass at St. Matthew's Cathedral instead of a high mass.

THE PEOPLE MOURN: Men, women and children wait quietly outside the Capitol for their turns to pass John F. Kennedy's coffin in the Rotunda. Associated Press Wirephoto

The Transcript of Cushing's Eulogy

Following is the text of Richard Cardinal Cushing's eulogy of President Kennedy on a nationally televised mass from Boston as recorded by The New York Times through the facilities of WOR Radio:

In the name of the Father and of the Son and of the Holy Ghost, amen.

My dearly beloved, friends in Christ and guests:

A shocked and stricken world stands helpless before the fact of death, that death brought to us through a tragically successful assault upon the life of the President of the United States.

Our earliest disbelief has slowly given way to unprecedented sorrow as millions all over the earth join us in lamenting a silence that can never again be broken and the absence of a smile that can never again be seen.

For those of us who knew the President as friend as well as statesman, words mock our attempts to express the anguish of our hearts.

It was my privilege to have been associated with John F. Kennedy from the earliest days of his public life, and even prior to that time, my privilege to have watched him mature with ever-expanding responsibility, to have known some of the warmth of his hearty friendship, to see tested under pain and loss the steely strength of his character.

I have been with him in joy and in sorrow, in decision and in crisis, among friends and with strangers and I know of no one who has combined in more noble perfection the qualities of greatness that marked his cool, calculating intelligence and his big, brave bountiful heart.

Tribute as World Leader

Now all of a sudden, he has been taken from us and I dare say we shall never see his like again.

Many there are who will appropriately pay tribute to the President as a world figure, a tribute due him for his skill in political life and his devotion to public service.

Many others will measure the wide interests of his mind, the swiftness of his resolution, the power of his persuasion, the efficiency of his action and the courage of his conviction.

For me, however, it is more fitting and proper to recall him during these days of mourning as husband and father, surrounded by his young and beloved family.

Although the demands of his exhalted position carried him often on long journeys and filled even his days at home with endless labors, how often he would make time to share with his little son and sweet daughter whatever time would be his own.

What a precious treasure it is now and will be forever in the memories of two fatherless children? Who among us can forget those childish ways which from time to time enhance the elegance of the Executive mansion with the touching scenes of a happy family life?

Charming Caroline stealing the publicity, jovial John-John on all fours ascending the stairs of an airplane to greet his daddy and a loving mother like all mothers joyfully watching the two children of her flesh and blood, mindful always of three others in the nurseries the Kingdom of Heaven.

At the side of the President in understanding devotion and affection behold his gracious and beautiful Jacqueline. True always to the obligations of her role as mother, she has given new dimensions to the trying demands of being America's First Lady.

The pride in her husband which he so eminently justified, was plainly reciprocated in his pride of her. The bonds of love that made them one in marriage became like hoops of steel binding them together.

From whatever men may look out from eternity to see the workings of our world, Jack Kennedy must beam with new pride in that valiant woman who shared his life, especially to the moment of its early and bitter end.

It will never be forgotten by her for her clothes are now stained with the blood of her assassinated husband.

These days of sorrow must be difficult for her — more difficult than for any others. A Divine Providence has blessed her as few such women in history by allowing her hero husband to have the dying comfort of her arms.

When men speak of this sad hour in times to come, they will ever recall how well her frail beauty matched in courage the stalwart warrior who was her husband. We who had so many reasons for holding her person in a most profound respect must now find an even wider claim for the nobility of her spirit.

One cannot think, my dearly beloved, especially one such as myself, of the late President without thinking also of the legacy of public service which was bequeathed to him by his name and his family.

Family Dedication

For several generations in a variety of tasks, this republic on one level or another has been enriched by the blood that was so wantonly shed on Friday last. Jack Kennedy fulfilled in the highest office available to him the long dedication of his family.

It is a consolation for us all to know that his tragic death does not spell the end of this public service but commits to new responsibilities the energies and the abilities of one of the truly great families of America.

What comfort can I extend to their heavy hearts today — mother, father, sisters, brothers — what beyond the knowledge that they have given history a youthful Lincoln, who in his time and in his sacrifice, had made more sturdy the hopes of this nation and its people.

The late President was even in death, a young man—and he was proud of his youth. We can never forget the words with which he began his short term as President of the United States:

Let the word go forth, he said, from this time and place, to friend and foe alike, that the torch has been passed to a new generation of Americans—born in this century, tempered by war, disciplined by a hard and bitter peace, proud of our ancient heritage . . . .

No words could describe better the man himself who spoke, one whose youth supplied an almost boundless energy, despite illness and physical handicap, whose record in war touched heroic proportions, whose service in Congress was positive and progressive.

It was against this personal background that he continued by saying:

"Let every nation know . . . that we shall pay any price, bear any burden, meet any hardship, support any friend, oppose any foe to assure the survival and success of liberty. This much we pledge and more."

All that the young President promised in these words, he delivered before his assassination. He has written in unforgetable language his own epitaph.

A Fully Human Life

Two days ago, he was the leader of the free world, full of youth, vigor and promise, his was a role of action, full of conflict, excitement, pressure and change, his was a fully human life, one in which he lived, felt dawn, saw sunset glow, loved and was loved.

Now in the inscrutable ways of God, he has been summoned to an eternal life beyond all striving, where everywhere is peace.

All of us who knew personally and loved Jack Kennedy his youth, his drive, his ideals, his heart, generosity and his hopes mourn now more for ourselves and each other than for him.

We will miss him; he only waits for us in another place. He speaks to us today from there in the words of Paul to Timothy:

"As for me, my blood has already flown in sacrifice. I have fought the good fight; I redeemed the pledge; I look forward to the prize that awaits me, the prize I have earned. The Lord whose award never goes amiss will grant it to me to me, yes, and to all those who have learned to welcome His coming."

John F. Kennedy, 35th President of the United States of America, has fought the good fight for the God-given rights of his fellow man and for a world where peace and freedom shall prevail.

He has finished the race at home and in foreign lands alerting all men to the dangers and the hopes of the future, pledging aid in every form to those who attempted to misinterpret his words, to misunderstand his country, to become discouraged and to abandon themselves to false prophets.

He has fulfilled unto death a privilege he made on the day of his inauguration — a privilege in the form of a pledge — I shall not shrink from my responsibilities.

Far more would he have accomplished for America and the world if it were not for his assassination here in the land that he loved and for which he dedicated and gave his life.

May his noble soul rest in peace. May his memory be perpetuated in our hearts as a symbol of love for God, country and all mankind, the foundation upon which a new world must be built if our civilization is to survive.

Eternal peace grant unto him, O Lord, and let perpetual light shine upon him.

In the name of the Father and the Son and the Holy Ghost, amen.

Britons to See Funeral on TV

LONDON, Nov. 24 (Reuters) British television viewers will see part of President Kennedy's funeral procession tomorrow in live transmissions from Washington by the communications satellite Telstar, it was announced today.

CUSHING TO OFFER PONTIFICAL MASS

Cardinal to Be Celebrant at Simple Requiem Service

By PAUL L. MONTGOMERY

The pontifical requiem mass to be said for President Kennedy today in Washington will differ only in particulars from the masses offered in all the Roman Catholic churches of the world on each day of the year.

The form "pontifical requiem mass" contains three concepts.

"Pontifical" means that the celebrant will be a bishop—in this case Richard Cardinal Cushing, Archbishop of Boston. By the doctrine of apostolic succession, which holds that bishops are the direct inheritors of the duties of the apostles of Jesus, the bishops are created by the Pope. Thus a bishop is acting for the Pope and is performing a "pontifical" service.

"Requiem," from the Latin word for "rest," means that some parts of the mass, which are joyous in nature, are omitted because the mass is not being offered for a joyous occasion. Certain funeral elements are added in the requiem mass.

Central Act of Worship

"Mass" is the central act of worship of the Roman Catholic church. It is a recreation, in words and symbolic actions, of the crucifixion and sacrifice of Jesus

The mass contains prayers and recitations of two kinds, the proper and the ordinary. The ordinary of the mass is invariable in wording but some sections can be omitted. In the requiem mass, for example, the psalm "Judica me" (Give judgment for me) at the beginning is not said.

The texts of the proper of the mass vary with the occasion and day of the year. It is in the proper that the solemn elements of the requiem are introduced.

The mass for President Kennedy today will be a low mass that is, it will be said, rather than sung as in a high mass.

Not A 'Solemn' Mass

Because it will be celebrated by only one priest, it will not be a solemn mass in the Catholic sense of the term. A solemn mass is celebrated by three men the celebrant, the deacon and the sub-deacon.

The mass is always offered to God. However, it can be offered for a specific person. The church and all the faithful are considered to partake of the benefits of all masses offered.

The funeral service preceding requiem mass begins with a ceremony at the church door when the coffin is brought in. The celebrant sprinkles the coffin with holy water and recites, in Latin, the 129th Psalm and other prayers.

The mass begins with the words "In nomine Patris, et Filii, et Spiritus Sancti. Amen" (In the name of the Father, the Son and the Holy Ghost, Amen).

Prayer for Mercy

After several prayers, both ordinary and proper, the Gradual, Tract and Sequence are said. In the requiem, the Sequence is the famed Dies Irae (Day of Wrath), a description of the Last Judgment and a prayer to Jesus for mercy.

Other prayers in the proper of a requiem mass also dwell on the immortality of the soul. They include, in Latin, the words of St. Paul—"We would not have you ignorant concerning those who are asleep, lest you should grieve even as others who have no hope"—and part of Jesus' message in the Gospel of St. John—"I am the resurrection and the life; he who believes in Me, even if he die, shall live.'"

The canon, or the central part of the mass, consists of the consecration—the essence of the sacrificial act—and the communion. These parts are invariable.

When this part is concluded, the celebrant pronounces absolution at the bier, sprinkling the coffin with holy water and wafting incense over it.

The mass will end with this prayer: "O God, Who alone art ever merciful and sparing of punishment, humbly we pray Thee in behalf of the soul of Thy servant John, whom Thou hast commanded to go forth from this world."

During the absolution and prayers the words are English. In the rest of the mass they are Latin.

Tokyo Stocks Drop Sharply

TOKYO, Monday, Nov. 25 (UPI)—The Tokyo Stock Exchange opened today with heavy selling on a wide range of issues and a sharp drop in prices, generated by the assassination of President Kennedy. Heiwa Real Estate, a barometer stock, which closed at 224 yen on Friday, dropped by 17 yen early in today's session.

MASS IN BOSTON: Richard Cardinal Cushing officiates at Archdiocesan TV center

Eulogies Given by Leaders

Following are the texts of eulogies to President Kennedy made yesterday as recorded by The New York Times or transmitted by The Associated Press or United Press International:

By Speaker McCormack

As we gather here today bowed in grief, the heartfelt sympathy of members of the Congress and of our people are extended to Mrs. Jacqueline Kennedy and to Ambassador and Mrs. Joseph P. Kennedy and their loved ones. Their deep grief is also self-shared by countless millions of persons throughout the world, considered a personal tragedy, as if one had lost a loved member of his own immediate family.

Any citizen of our beloved country who looks back over its history cannot fail to see that we have been blessed with God's favor beyond most other peoples. At each great crisis in our history we have found a leader able to grasp the helm of state and guide the country through the troubles which beset it. In our earliest days, when our strength and wealth were so limited and our problems so great, Washington and Jefferson appeared to lead our people. Two generations later, when our country was torn in two by a fratricidal war, Abraham Lincoln appeared from the mass of the people as a leader able to reunite the nation.

In more recent times, in the critical days of the Depression and the great war forced upon us by Fascist aggression, Franklin Delano Roosevelt, later Harry S. Truman appeared on the scene to reorganize the country and lead its revived citizens to victory. Finally, only recently, when the cold war was building up the supreme crisis of a threatened nuclear war capable of destroying everything—and everybody—that our predecessors had so carefully built, and which a liberty-loving world wanted, once again a strong and courageous man appeared ready to lead us.

No country need despair so long as God, in His infinite goodness, continues to provide the nation with leaders able to guide it through the successive crises which seem to be the inevitable fate of any great nation.

Surely no country ever faced more gigantic problems than ours in the last few years, and surely no country could have obtained a more able leader in a time of such crisis. President John Fitzgerald Kennedy possessed all the qualities of greatness. He had deep faith, complete confidence, human sympathy and broad vision which recognized the true values of freedom, equality and the brotherhood which have always been the marks of the American political dreams.

He had the bravery and a sense of personal duty which made him willing to face up to the great task of being President in these trying times. He had the warmth and the sense of humanity which made the burden of the task bearable for himself and for his associates, and which made all kinds of diverse peoples and races eager to be associated with him in his task. He had the tenacity and determination to carry each stage of his great work through to its successful conclusion.

Now that our great leader has been taken from us in a cruel death, we are bound to feel shattered and helpless in the face of our loss. This is but natural, but as the first bitter pangs of our incredulous grief begins to pass we must thank God that we were privileged, however briefly, to have had this great man for our President. For he has now taken his place among the great figures of world history.

While this is an occasion of deep sorrow it should be also one of dedication. We must have the determination to unite and carry on the spirit of John Fitzgerald Kennedy for a strengthened America and a future world of peace.

By Senator Mansfield

There was a sound of laughter; in a moment, it was no more. And so she took a ring from her finger and placed it in his hands.

There was a wit in a man neither young nor old, but a wit full of an old man's wisdom and of a child's wisdom, and then, in a moment it was no more. And so she took a ring from her finger and placed it in his hands.

There was a man marked with the scars of his love of country, a body active with the surge of a life far, far from spent and, in a moment, it was no more. And so she took a ring from her finger and placed it in his hands.

There was a father with a little boy, a little girl and a joy of each in the other. In a moment it was no more, and so she took a ring from her finger and placed it in his hands.

There was a husband who asked much and gave much, and out of the giving and the asking wove with a woman what could not be broken in life, and in a moment it was no more. And so she took a ring from her finger and placed it in his hands, and kissed him and closed the lid of a coffin.

A piece of each of us died at that moment. Yet, in death he gave of himself to us. He gave us of a good heart from which the laughter came. He gave us of a profound wit, from which a great leadership emerged. He gave us of a kindness and a strength fused into a human courage to seek peace without fear.

He gave us of his love that we, too, in turn, might give. He gave that we might give of ourseleves, what we might give to one another until there would be no room, no room at all, for the bigotry, the hatred, prejudice and the arrogance which converged in that moment of horror to strike him down.

In leaving us—these gifts, John Fitzgerald Kennedy, President of the United States, leaves with us. Will we take them, Mr. President? Will we have, now, the sense and the responsibility and the courage to take them?

By Chief Justice Warren

There are few events in our national life that unite Americans and so touch the heart of all of us as the passing of a President of the United States.

There is nothing that adds shock to our sadness as the assassination of our leader, chosen as he is to embody the ideals of our people, the faith we have in our institutions and our belief in the fatherhood of God and the brotherhood of man.

Such misfortunes have befallen the nation on other occasions, but never more shockingly than two days ago.

We are saddened; we are stunned; we are perplexed.

John Fitzgerald Kennedy, a great and good President, the friend of all men of goodwill, a believer in the dignity and equality of all human beings, a fighter for justice and apostle of peace, has been snatched from our midst by the bullet of an assassin.

What moved some misguided wretch to do this horrible deed may never be known to us, but we do know that such acts are commonly stimulated by forces of hatred and malevolence, such as today are eating their way into the bloodstream of American life.

What a price we pay for this fanaticism!

It has been said that the only thing we learn from history is that we do not learn. But surely we can learn if we have the will to do so. Surely there is a lesson to be learned from this tragic event.

If we really love this country, if we truly love justice and mercy, if we fervently want to make this nation better for those who are to follow us, we can at least abjure the hatred that consumes people, the false accusations that divide us and the bitterness that begets violence.

Is it too much to hope that the martyrdom of our beloved President might even soften the hearts of those who would themselves recoil from assassination, but who do not shrink from spreading the venom which kindles thoughts of it in others?

Our nation is bereaved. The whole world is poorer because of his loss. But we can all be better Americans because John Fitzgerald Kennedy has passed our way, because he has been our chosen leader at a time in history when his character, his vision and his quiet courage have enabled him to chart for us a safe course through the shoals of treacherous seas that encompass the world.

And now that he is relieved of the almost superhuman burdens we imposed on him, may he rest in peace.

POPE PAUL WARNS ON HATE AND EVIL

Continued From Page 1, Col. 2

of God, for His mercy and for His pardon."

The Pontiff spoke from a window of his apartment in the Apostolic Palace. Before reciting the Angelus, a prayer commemorating the Incarnation, and imparting his benediction, he said:

"Now, let us pray as Jesus has taught us: 'Lead us not into temptation and deliver us from evil' through the maternal and most humane intercession of the Virgin Mary."

The phrase he quoted is from the Lord's Prayer.

As the Pope spoke, hundreds of people went to the United States Embassy to express their sympathy and to sign the register. By late this afternoon more than 35,000 had signed.

Memorial services for the President were held in many cities in Italy and at military posts.

In Rome, Protestant Episcopal memorial services were conducted by the Rev. Wilbur C. Woodhams in St. Paul's American Church. Hundreds of Americans attended the services, and the United States was represented by the Ambassador, G. Frederick Reinhardt.

A memorial was also held at the Rome Synagogue, with Chief Rabbi Elio Toaff officiating. The United States was represented by embassy officers.

Tomorrow, the day of the President's funeral, the Basilica of St. John Lateran, the Pope's church as Bishop of Rome, will be the scene of official memorial services, with diplomats and Government representatives attending. Cardinal Spellman, Archbishop of New York, will say the mass, at which many American prelates and prelates from other countries will be present. They are here for the Ecumenical Council.

Other services are planned for Tuesday

Dignitaries of Nearly 100 Lands Converge on Capital to Pay Tribute to Kennedy

JOHNSON TO MEET MANY TOMORROW

City Is Tense—High Visitors Put Strains on Security and Protocol Officials

Continued From Page 1, Col. 7

times. Officials who had worked hard to discourage such a gathering finally worked even harder to accommodate it. They accepted it as a demonstration of respect from friends and adversaries alike, as a symbolic measure of Mr. Kennedy's far-flung activities and of the responsibilities that await his successor.

President de Gaulle of France, the proud ally whose search for independence greatly troubled Mr. Kennedy in the last year, was among the first to arrive here this evening.

Among the last tomorrow morning will be Anastas I. Mikoyan, a First Deputy Premier of the Soviet Union, whose last mission here was to close out the Cuba-missile crisis and to set the stage for a year-long effort to reach a Soviet-American accommodation.

Also coming back to Washington were Emperor Haile Selassie of Ethiopia, King Baudouin I of Belgium, Queen Frederika of Greece and nineteen other chiefs of state or government.

With Prince Philip from Britain came Sir Alec Douglas-Home, the Prime Minister. With President Heinrich Lübeke of West Germany came Ludwig Erhard, the Chancellor. Like the United States, these two major allies have new governments and must prepare for difficult elections and possibly further changes in the next two years.

Half Hour Intervals

Leaders who by themselves could have stirred this capital to pomp and excitement in ordinary days poured in at half-hour intervals at different airports around the capital.

For the most part, they remarked on the sadness of the occasion and declined any statement. They chatted only briefly with the official greeters—Secretary of State Dean Rusk or his deputies, Under Secretaries George W. Ball and W. Averell Harriman, the Assistant Secretaries of State and protocol officers.

Nearly all wished to pay their respects to Mrs. John F. Kennedy. It was finally decided tonight that she would receive the foreign dignitaries at the White House after the funeral tomorrow afternoon.

President Johnson will meet with the visitors from abroad at the State Department between 5:30 and 7 P.M. tomorrow. The new President may meet separately with some of the chiefs of government on Tuesday, but the confused schedules of all made it impossible to arrange fixed appointments.

Mr. Johnson may wish to issue vague invitations to some of the visitors, like President de Gaulle, to return to Washington in the near future, but no major policy discussions are expected.

By this evening, 84 nations had assigned special delegations to the funeral; 30 others had still to indicate how they would be represented. Only a few heeded the early appeals of the State Department that representation by the ambassadors to Washington would be perfectly appropriate.

Among the announced visitors will be at least 12 of royal title, 18 republican chiefs of state or government, at least 34 foreign ministers, six vice premiers or vice presidents, and two former presidents of other nations.

In magnitude, the assemblage will surpass even the gathering of 21 chiefs of state or government at the United Nations in 1960, though it will not include the colorful figures of Premier Khrushchev, Premier Fidel Castro and Prime Minister Jawaharlal Nehru. It will certainly be the greatest assembly of mourners since the funeral of King Edward VII in London 50 years ago.

Security Problems

For both the State Department and police authorities, the gathering poses the greatest security and protocol problems ever encountered in this capital. And it comes at a moment of enormous strain, when officials are already overburdened with the demands of a new leadership and with nervousness about the safety of the new President.

Most of the high-ranking visitors will live at their embassies here. They do not have the status of official guests and thus are responsible for their own lodging and arrangements.

But each will have the security guard of a regular visit—plainclothesmen at his side and residence and motorcycle escorts on trips through the capital.

From the planning standpoint, the State Department had an even more difficult time with protocol arrangements. It worked through the night from its operations center, normally employed for foreign crises, charting the movements of dignitaries and making provisions for them.

It was especially difficult to work out an official order of precedence in which the foreign mourners will march from the White House to St. Matthew's Roman Catholic Cathedral and the order in which they will sit for the services.

The rivalries of international politics were clearly subdued by the world community for the gathering here.

There was no representation, of course, from nations with which the United States has no diplomatic relations — Communist China, Cuba, East Germany, North Korea, North Vietnam and Albania. The governments of South Africa, Haiti, Portugal and some others with which Mr. Kennedy's Administration had strained relations did not send their highest ranking representatives.

But there was no discernible distinction in the delegations of many Communist and non-Communist nations, or in those from Israel and from Arab nations. The representatives of Morocco and Algeria, whose border war Mr. Kennedy tried so hard to end, arrived aboard the same plane.

The countries without special delegations will be represented by their ambassadors to Washington or to the United Nations, so that 110 sovereignties in all will participate in the rites for Mr. Kennedy.

In addition, special representatives will be present from the Vatican, the European Economic Community, or Common Market; from Euratom, the Western European Atomic Energy Association; the European Coal and Steel Community and the United Nations and its subsidiary agencies.

WELCOMES BRITONS: Secretary of State Rusk with Prince Philip, right, husband of Queen Elizabeth, and Sir Alec Douglas-Home, Prime Minister, at the airport last night.

Associated Press

FRENCH LEADER WELCOMED: President de Gaulle with Secretary of State Rusk last night at Dulles International Airport, near Washington. He will attend the funeral.

Airport Shields Arrivals

By MARTIN GANSBERG

Extra security measures were taken to guard European and Middle Eastern leaders who arrived yesterday at Idlewild Airport on their way to Washington for President Kennedy's funeral.

With 16 flights bringing in dignitaries on regularly scheduled planes, the police decided at 2 P. M. to close down both outdoor observation decks at the International Arrivals Building. It was the first time in the history of the airport that both decks had been closed at the same time.

Albert J. Vavrick, supervisor of the Port of New York Authority force that polices the building, ordered additional men on duty from 4 P. M. to midnight, the period when most of the planes arrived.

Besides the normal police complement at the airport, additional forces from the city Police Department were assigned to this shift.

Speed Reduces Danger

The speed with which arriving dignitaries were moved to private quarters until they could get on planes for Washington reduced the danger. State Department and United Nations representatives greeted them aboard the commercial planes, whisked them through customs to airline lounges and kept them occupied until their planes to Washington were ready.

There were few interruptions in the forward movement of the arrivals. Customs regulations were waived and aides filled out necessary forms. Baggage was left to be placed on the relay plane.

The first to arrive, at 1:40 P. M., was Prince George of Denmark, who came on a plane from London. Prince Stanislas Radziwill, brother-in-law of Mrs. Kennedy, arrived on a plane from London at 2:20 P.M. Both waited in airline lounges, hidden from the press and public, until their flights to Washington were ready.

As he boarded the plane to the capital, Prince Radziwill was told about the slaying of Lee H. Oswald, President Kennedy's assassin.

"It's terrible," he said. "It's terrible!"

After Crown Princess Beatrix of the Netherlands arrived with her party of five, including Foreign Minister Joseph M. A. H. Luns, officials at Idlewild placed a flag at half-staff in the center of the main reception hall. The flag was mounted on a small platform that was covered with black crepe paper. The area was roped off.

Among other notables arriving later at the airport on their way to Washington were President de Gaulle, President Eamon de Valera of Ireland and Mayor Willy Brandt of Berlin.

With President de Valera were his two sons Major Vivian and Dr. Brian de Valera and an honor guard of 24 cadets from the Irish Military College. The cadets were flown over at the request of Mrs. Kennedy.

Idlewild officials said that the crowds were "somewhat lighter than usual" for Sunday. Yet the open area on the first floor of the building was crowded with onlookers as each dignitary came through the reception hall to go to private quarters while awaiting his transfer plane.

Persons barred from the observation decks asked a guard there for an explanation.

"It's too windy to be out there," he said. "It's just too windy."

List of Dignitaries Expected at Kennedy's Funeral

Special to The New York Times

WASHINGTON, Nov. 24—Following is the latest available list of dignitaries expected to attend President Kennedy's funeral.

International Organizations

UNITED NATIONS

U Thant, Secretary General.
Dr. Ralph J. Bunche, Under Secretary for Political Affairs.
Paul G. Hoffman, managing director, United Nations Special Fund.
Maurice Pate, executive director, United Nations Children's fund.
David B. Vaughn, director of general services.
Carlos Sosa Rodriguez, President of the General Assembly, and his wife.
Sir Patrick Dean, President of the Security Council.
Dr. Louis Alvarado, International Labor Organization.
David Blanchard, International Labor Organization.

EUROPEAN COAL AND STEEL COMMUNITY

Albert Coppe, Vice President.
Jean Monnet, former President.

EUROPEAN ECONOMIC COMMUNITY

Jean Rey, member.

EURATOM

E. M. J. A. Sassen, member of the Council.

Europe

AUSTRIA

Alfons Gorbach, Chancellor.

BELGIUM

Baudouin I, King of the Belgians.
Paul-Henri Spaak, Foreign Minister.

BULGARIA

Miliko Tarabanov, Deputy Foreign Minister.

CZECHOSLOVAKIA

Dr. Jiri Hajek, permanent representative at the United Nations.

DENMARK

Crown Prince George.
Jens Krag, Premier.

FINLAND

Vali Merikoski, Foreign Minister.

FRANCE

President de Gaulle.
Maurice Couve de Murville, Foreign Minister.
Gen. Charles Ailleret, Chairman, Joint Chiefs of Staff.
Etienne Burin Des Roziers, Secretary General of the Presidency.

WEST GERMANY

Dr. Heinrich Lübke, President.
Dr. Ludwig Erhard, Chancellor.
Dr. Gerhard Schröder, Foreign Minister.
Kai-Uwe von Hassel, Defense Minister.
Willy Brandt, Mayor of West Berlin.

BRITAIN

Prince Philip, Duke of Edinburgh.
Sir Alec Douglas-Home, Prime Minister, and Lady Home.
Harold Wilson, Labor party leader.
Jo Grimond, Liberal party leader.

GREECE

Frederika, Queen of the Hellenes.
Sophocles Venizelos, Deputy Premier and Foreign Minister.

HUNGARY

Peter Mou, First Deputy Foreign Minister.

ICELAND

Gudmundur I. Gudmundson, Foreign Minister, and his wife.

IRELAND

Dr. Eamon de Valera, President.
Frank Aiken, Minister for External Affairs.
Maj. Vivian de Valera.

ITALY

Attilio Piccioni, Foreign Minister.
Piero Vinci, Foreign Ministry Chef de Cabinet.
Guerino Roberti, assistant chief of protocol.
Gen. Emiliano Scotti, military counselor to the President.

LUXEMBOURG

Prince Jean, hereditary Grand Duke.
Eugene Schaus, Foreign Minister.

THE NETHERLANDS

Prince Bernhard, husband of the Queen.
Crown Princess Beatrix.
J. M. A. H. Luns, Foreign Minister.

NORWAY

Crown Prince Harald.
Einer Gerhardsen, Premier.

POLAND

Prof. Stanislaw Kulczynski, deputy chairman of the Council of State.
Piotr Jaroszewicz, Deputy Premier.

PORTUGAL

Luis Supico Pinto, President of the Corporate Chamber.

RUMANIA

M. Milita, Deputy Foreign Minister.

SPAIN

Gen. Augustin Muñoz Grandes, Vice Premier.

SWEDEN

Prince Bertil.
Tage Erlander, Premier.
Olaf Palme, Minister Without Portfolio.

SWITZERLAND

Dr. Friedrich T. Wahlen, chief of the Federal Political Department.
Pierre Micheli, Secretary General of the Federal Political Department.

TURKEY

Ismet Inonu, Premier.
Feridun Cemal Erkin, Foreign Minister.

U.S.S.R.

Anastas I. Mikoyan, First Deputy Premier.

YUGOSLAVIA

Koca Popovic, Foreign Minister.
Petar Stambolic, president of the Federal Executive Council.

THE VATICAN

The Most Rev. Egidio Vagnozzi, Archbishop of Myra, Apostolic Delegate.

Africa

ALGERIA

Abdelkadir Chanderli, representative at the United Nations.
Haj Ben Alla, President of the National Assembly.
Amai Ouzegane, Minister of State.
Cherif Guellal, Ambassador to the United States.
Abdelazziz Bouteflika, Foreign Minister.

CAMEROON

Benoit Balla-Ondoux, Foreign Minister.

CONGO (BRAZZAVILLE)

E. D. Dadet, Ambassador to the United States.

CONGO (LEOPOLDVILLE)

Jacques Masangu, Deputy Premier.

ETHIOPIA

Haile Selassie I, Emperor of Ethiopia.
Ras Andare Atchew Massai.
Commander Iskander Desta.
Tefara-Woro Kidane-Wold.
Lij Kassa Wolde-Mariam.

GHANA

Miguel A. Ribeiro, Ambassador to the United States.
K. Armah, High Commissioner in London.
Alex Quaison-Sackey, representative at the United Nations.

GUINEA

Saifonlaye Diallo, Minister of State.
Leon Maka, President of the National Assembly.
Alessane Dioh, Minister of Communications.

IVORY COAST

Phillipe Yace, President of the National Assembly.
Camille Alliali, Minister Delegate for Foreign Affairs.

LIBERIA

William A. Tolbert, Vice President.
J. Rudolph Grimes, Secretary of State.

LIBYA

Dr. Wahbi Elbouri, representative at the United Nations.

MALAGASY REPUBLIC

Louis Rakotomalela, Ambassador to the United States.

MOROCCO

Prince Moulay Abdullah.
Ahmed Reda Guedira, Foreign Minister.
Abdelkadar Benjelloun, Minister of Justice.
Ali Benjelloun, Ambassador to the United States.
Ahmed Taibi Benhima, representative at the United Nations.
Badir Din Senoussi, attaché to the royal cabinet.
Mohammaed Ziani, attaché to the cabinet of the Foreign Minister.
Gen. Mohammed Ameziane, Inspector General of the royal armed forces.
Col. Moulay Hafid, director general of royal protocol.

SIERRA LEONE

Dr. John Karefa-Smart, Minister of External Affairs.

SOMALIA

Mohammed Ali Daar, Under Secretary for Foreign Affairs.

TANGANYIKA

Chief Erasto A. M. Mangyenya, representative at the United Nations.

TUNISIA

Bahi Ladgham, Secretary of State for the Presidency.
Mongi Slim, Foreign Minister.
Taieb Slim, representative at the United Nations.
Habib Bourguiba Jr.
Hachmi Quanes.

UGANDA

Apollo K. Kironde, representative at the United Nations.

UNITED ARAB REPUBLIC

Mahmond Fawsi, Foreign Minister.

Asia

CAMBODIA

Prince Norodom Kantol, President of the Council of Ministers.

CHINA

Tingfu F. Tsiang, Ambassador to the United States.

INDIA

Mrs. Vijaya Lakshmi Pandit, delegate to the United Nations.

INDONESIA

Gen. Abdul Haris Nasution, Minister for Defense and Security Affairs.
Dr. Subjarwo Tjondronegoro, Deputy Foreign Minister.

IRAN

Shaphur Gholam Reza.
Abbas Aram, Foreign Minister.

ISRAEL

Zalman Shazar, President.
Mrs. Golda Meir, Foreign Minister.

JAPAN

Hayato Ikeda, Premier.
Masayoshi Ohira, Foreign Minister.

JORDAN

Antone Atallah, Foreign Minister.

LEBANON

Ibrahim Ahdab, Ambassador to the United States.
George Hakim, representative at the United Nations.

KOREA

Chung Hee Park, President.

LAOS

Tiao Khampan, Ambassador to the United States.
Sisouk Na Champassak, Ambassador to India.

PAKISTAN

Zulfiqar Ali Bhutto, Foreign Minister.

THE PHILIPPINES

Diosdado Macapagal, President, and his wife.

SAUDI ARABIA

Rashad Pharaon, Ambassador to France.
Abdullah Hababi, chargé d'affaires in Washington.

THAILAND

Thanat Khouman, Foreign Minister.

VIETNAM

Tran Chanh Thanh, Ambassador-designate.

AUSTRALIA

Sir Alexander McMullin, President of the Senate.

Western Hemisphere

ARGENTINA

Carlos Humberto Perette, Vice President.
Dr. Miguel Angel Zavala Ortiz, Foreign Minister.
Brig. Ignacio Avalos, Secretary of War.

BAHAMAS

Sir Roland Symonette, Premier-designate.

BOLIVIA

Enrique Sanchez Delozada, Ambassador to the United States.

BRAZIL

Senator Auro Moura Andrade, President of the Senate.
João Augusto De Araujo Castro, Foreign Minister.
Roberto de Oliveira Campos, Ambassador to the United States.
Senator Zitorino Freire, majority leader.
Senator Antonio Carlos Konder Reis, minority leader.

CANADA

Lester B. Pearson, Prime Minister.
Paul Martin, External Affairs Minister.

CHILE

Carlos Martinez, representative at the United Nations.

COLOMBIA

Alberto Lleras Camargo, former President.

COSTA RICA

José Figueres, former President.

ECUADOR

Dr. Neftali Ponce Miranda, Foreign Minister.

EL SALVADOR

Dr. Hector Escobar Serrano, Foreign Minister.

GUATEMALA

Alberto Herrarte Gonzalez, Foreign Minister.
José de Dios Aguilar, private secretary to the Government.

JAMAICA

Sir Alexander Bustamante, Prime Minister.
Brig. Paul Cook, Chief of Staff.
James Lloyd, Permanent Secretary, External Affairs Ministry.
Noël Croswell, Commissioner of Police.

MEXICO

Manuel Tello, Foreign Minister.

NICARAGUA

Luis Somoza de Bayle, Senator and former President.
Dr. Alfonso Ortega Urbina, Foreign Minister.

PANAMA

Galileo Solis, Foreign Minister.
Arturo Morgan Morales, of Foreign Ministry.

PERU

Dr. Victor Andres Belaunde, representative at the United Nations.

URUGUAY

Juan Felipe Yriart, Ambassador to the United States.

VENEZUELA

Ronaldo Leandro Mora, Acting Foreign Minister.
Gen. Antonio Briceño Linares, Defense Minister.

BRITONS SEE HOPE OF LEADING WEST

Lord Avon Says Home Has Experience 'to Play Part'

By SYDNEY GRUSON

Special to The New York Times

LONDON, Nov. 24—A suggestion that President Johnson's relative inexperience with foreign affairs provides a new opportunity for British leadership has begun to appear in some London assessments of the future.

The idea was broached in articles in three Sunday newspapers. Two of the articles were by well-known Britons.

One outcome of the death of President Kennedy "seems inevitable—the responsibilities of this country will be increased," wrote the Earl of Avon, the former Sir Anthony Eden, who was Foreign Secretary and later Prime Minister.

"Fortunately," he added, "our new Prime Minister, Sir Alec Douglas-Home, is well-equipped by his years in the Foreign Office to play the part which the new circumstances and the cause of peace will now demand."

The idea of Britain's taking up some special task was also broached by Richard Crossman, a Labor party leader. His main difference with Lord Avon appeared to be in his suggestion that the task was one for a Labor Government, not for Sir Alec's Conservatives.

Mr. Crossman conceded that the leadershhip of the West must remain with the United States. But President Kennedy' "special contribution" to world peace, he added, must either be lost forever or assumed "by another member of the Western alliance."

Mr. Crossman asked "By whom?" and said: "One has only to ask the question to see the answer. Britain is the only country which could fill the gap—under the right leadership."

An unsigned editorial-page column in The People suggested that Sir Alec might become a "go-between" between the United States, Britain and France and "might even for a time be its [the Western alliance's] spokesman with Russia."

British officials, as distinct from politicians, belittle the idea that Britain, with her strained economic resources and relatively meager military strength is in a position to speak for the Western world.

But the idea's arising so swiftly after President Kennedy's death seems to reflect two things about Britain.

One is that being a secondary power still frustrates many Britons and leaves them dissatisfied.

The other is that the longing for past greatness is never far below any surface acceptance of Britain's present place in the world.

Indian Tribe Mourns Loss

BROWNING, Mont., Nov. 24 (AP)—The death of President Kennedy, named Chief High Eagle by Blackfeet Indians of Montana, was mourned as the loss of a personal friend today by Walter Wetzel, who is serving a second term as president of the National Congress of American Indians. He is chairman of the Blackfeet Tribal Business Council.

LEADERS TO WALK IN TRIBUTE TODAY

Continued From Page 1, Col. 6

lay in state today. Marching units of all services, military bands and veterans' organizations, interspersed by color guards, Government leaders and representative delegations of clergy, will take part in the funeral procession.

On the journey from the Capitol Mrs. Kennedy will sit in the lead limousine, accompanied by her brother-in-law, Attorney General Robert F. Kennedy, and by President Johnson.

At the White House, where the procession will pause before proceeding to the cathedral, Mrs. Kennedy will get out of the limousine to be joined on the walk to the cathedral by the greatest assemblage of world and United States dignitaries that this city has ever seen.

The distance is a little more than half a mile.

The assemblage is comparable in a way, to that attending the funeral of King Edward VII of Britain May 20, 1910. As Barbara Tuchman pointed out in her book, "Guns of August," which the President read and recommended to others, the assemblage of crowned heads and others representing 70 nations on that occasion marked the end of an era.

Mr. Kennedy's funeral will be attended by representatives of nearly 100 nations. They will represent every political, ideological and geographical quarter of the globe with the exception of China.

Led by Mrs. Kennedy, they will walk in slow march from the White House for five blocks to the cathedral where Richard Cardinal Cushing of Boston will celebrate a pontifical requiem mass.

This is different from the ordinary requiem low mass in that a Bishop says it. A low mass is one that is said not sung. A high mass is sung.

Services Represented

The formal lying-in-state of Mr. Kennedy in the Great Rotunda of the Capitol is scheduled to end at 9 A.M.

Servicemen then will lift the coffin off the black-draped catafalque, the same that bore the body of President Lincoln nearly 100 years ago, and carry it to the caisson in the Capitol Plaza.

At 10:30 A.M. the funeral procession will form behind a police escort. With Maj. Gen. Philip C. Wehle, commanding general of the Military District, in the vanguard, marching units composed of officers from each of the five military services—the Army, Navy, Marine Corps, Air Force and Coast Guard — will lead the funeral parade.

Military bands and full companies of servicemen and servicewomen, cadets and midshipmen from the military academies, units of the National Guard and other service forces also will take part.

The route of march will take the coffin west along Constitution Avenue to Pennsylvania Avenue and the White House.

Aircraft of the Navy and Air Force will fly over the main funeral procession, but in keeping with tradition one plane will be noticeably missing from the usual reverse-V formation.

Cordons will be posted along the route of the march. Army, Navy, Air Force and Marine Corps personnel will stand 10 feet apart on both sides of the processional route from the Capitol to Arlington.

With the exception of the Justices and Congressional leaders, who will also join in the walk from the White House, the remainder of the procession will continue to St. Matthew's.

At the White House the cortege will be re-formed. In slow cadence, to a drumbeat calling for 100 steps a minute, Mrs. Kennedy and the members of her family will lead the walkers behind the cortege as it leaves the White House grounds.

Special Honor Guard

The cortege will consist of a special honor guard representing the three services, followed by color bearers holding American flags. Clergymen will follow. A Navy seaman, in commemoration of the President's wartime Navy service, will walk alone as he carries Mr. Kennedy's personal flag, unfurled, on a staff.

Behind the limousine occupied by Mrs. Kennedy, her brother-in-law and President Johnson in the first stage of the procession from the Capitol to the White House, other limousines will follow with United States leaders in this order:

Chief Justice Earl Warren and Associate Justices of the Supreme Court, Cabinet members including the Secretaries of the military departments, members of Congress, and other mourners close to the Kennedy family.

The lead marching units will pass the White House without pausing and continue up 17th Street and Connecticut Avenue to St. Matthew's Cathedral. The funeral cortege with the horse-drawn caisson, followed by Mrs. Kennedy, the President and other leaders, will turn into the northeast gate of the White House.

The caisson will be drawn up opposite the columned North Portico.

Following Mrs. Kennedy will be, in this order, the President, chiefs of state, heads of government and chiefs of special delegations; the Chief Justice, former President Dwight D. Eisenhower and Harry S. Truman, Associate Justices of the Supreme Court, members of the Cabinet, leaders of Congress, the members of the Joint Chiefs of Staff, personal assistants to Mr. Kennedy and close friends.

Schedule for Funeral

Special to The New York Times

WASHINGTON, Nov. 24—Following is the unofficial schedule of the approximate timing of the events tomorrow:

9 A.M.—Lying in state at Capitol Rotunda ends.

10:15 A.M.—Mrs. Kennedy arrives at Capitol.

10:30 A.M.—Funeral procession from Capitol to St. Matthew's Roman Catholic Cathedral begins.

11 A.M.—Procession pauses at White House, where Mrs. Kennedy and dignitaries begin following caisson on foot.

Noon—Pontifical requiem mass begins, said by Richard Cardinal Cushing of Boston.

1 P.M.—Funeral procession starts to Arlington National Cemetery.

2 P.M.—Burial service.

3:30 P.M.—Mrs. Kennedy receives heads of state in the White House.

5:30 P.M.—Reception at the State Department for all visiting dignitaries.

President's Assassin Is Shot to Death in Corridor of Jail by a Citizen of Dallas

KENNEDY ADMIRER FIRES ONE BULLET

Operator of 2 Night Clubs Lunges at Oswald From a Cluster of Newsmen

Continued From Page 1, Col. 8

sciousness very quickly after the shooting. Whether he was at any point able to speak, if he wanted to, was not known.

The politically eccentric warehouse clerk was taken in a police ambulance to the Parkland Hospital, where President Kennedy died Friday. He died in surgery at 1:07 P.M., less than two hours after the shooting. The exact time Oswald was shot was not definitely established.

Four plainclothes men, from a detail of about 50 police officers carrying out the transfer, pounced on Ruby as he fired the shot and overpowered him.

Ruby, who came to Dallas from Chicago 15 years ago, had a police record here listing six allegations of minor offenses. The disposition of five was not noted. A charge of liquor law violation was dismissed. Two of the entries, in July, 1953, and May, 1954, involved carrying concealed weapons.

The city police, working with the Secret Service and the Federal Bureau of Investigation, said last night that they had the case against Oswald "cinched."

After some 30 hours of intermittent interrogations and confrontations with scores of witnesses, Oswald was ordered transferred to the custody of the Dallas County sheriff.

This was preliminary to the planned presentation of the case, next Wednesday or the following Monday, to the county grand jury by District Attorney Wade.

The transfer involved a trip of about a mile from the uptown municipal building, where the Police Department and jail are. The route went down Main Street to the county jail, overlooking the spot where President Kennedy was killed and Gov. John B. Connally was wounded by shots from the book warehouse where Oswald worked.

A Change in Plans

The original plan had been for the sheriff to assume custody of Oswald at the city jail and handle the transfer. Late last night, for unspecified reasons, it was decided that the city police would move the prisoner.

Police Chief Jesse Curry declined to comment on suggestions that he had scheduled the transfer of Oswald at an unpropitious time because of pressure from news media.

Chief Curry announced about 9 o'clock last night that the investigation had reached a point where Oswald's presence was no longer needed. He said that Oswald would be turned over to the county sheriff today.

Asked when this would take place, the chief said: "If you fellows are here by 10 A.M., you'll be early enough."

When newsmen assembled at the police administrative offices at 10 o'clock, Chief Curry commented: "We could have done this earlier if I hadn't given you fellows that 10 o'clock time."

Armored Van Used

This was generally construed as meaning that preparations for the transfer had been in readiness for some hours, rather than implying a complaint from the chief that the press had had any part in setting the time.

Chief Curry disclosed this morning that to thwart an attempt against Oswald, the trip was to be made in an armored van of the kind used to transfer money.

"We're not going to take any chances," he said. "Our squad cars are not bullet-proof. If somebody's going to try to do something, they wouldn't stop him."

A ramp dips through the basement garage of the municipal building, running from Main Street to Commerce Street. Patrol wagons drive down this ramp and discharge prisoners at a basement booking office. The garage ceiling was too low for the armored car, so the van was backed up in the Commerce Street portal of the ramp.

The plan was to lead Oswald out the doorway in the center of the basement and about 75 feet up the ramp to the back of the armored car.

Prisoner on Fourth Floor

At about 11 o'clock, Chief Curry left his third-floor office, followed by plainclothes detectives and newsmen, to go to the basement. Oswald was still in a fourth-floor jail cell.

As the group with the chief walked through a short corridor past the basement booking office and out the door onto the guarded ramp, uniformed policemen checked the reporters' credentials. But they passed familiar faces, such as those of policemen and collaborating Secret Service and F.B.I. agents.

Ruby's face was familiar to many policemen who had encountered him at his two night clubs and in his frequent visits to the municipal building.

Inconspicuous in Group

Neatly dressed in a dark suit and wearing a fedora, he was inconspicuous in a group of perhaps 50 men who for the next 20 minutes waited in a 12-foot-wide vestibule and adjacent portions of the ramp.

1963, The Dallas Morning News

THE SUDDEN ATTACK: Jack Ruby closes in on Lee Harvey Oswald, in custody at jail in Dallas. Ruby put the muzzle of the pistol against the assassin, and then fired.

Television cameras, facing the vestibule, were set up against a metal railing separating the 15-foot-wide ramp from the rest of the garage. Some newsmen clustered along this railing.

Across Commerce Street, in front of a row of bail bondsmen's offices, a crowd of several hundred persons was held back by a police line.

Soon Oswald was taken in an elevator to the basement. He was led through the booking office to the open vestibule between two lines of detectives.

Walks Behind Captain

Captain Fritz, chief of the police homicide division, walked just ahead of him. Oswald was handcuffed, with a detective holding each arm and another following. On Oswald's right, in a light suit, was J. R. Leavelle and on his left, in a dark suit, L. C. Graves.

As they turned right from the vestibule to start up the ramp, Ruby jumped forward from against the railing. There was a sudden loud noise that sounded like the explosion of a photographer's flashbulb. It was Ruby's revolver firing.

A momentary furor set in as Ruby was seized and hustled into the building. Policemen ran up the ramp in both directions to the street, followed by others with orders to seal off the building.

About five minutes elapsed before an ambulance could be rolled down the ramp to Oswald.

The ambulance, its siren sounding, was followed by police and press cars on the four-mile drive to the hospital.

The hospital's emergency department had been on the alert for possible injuries arising out of the projected transfer.

Oswald was moved almost immediately into an operating room, at the other end of the building from the one where President Kennedy was treated.

The bullet had entered Oswald's body just below his heart and had torn into most of the vital organs.

Dr. Tom Shires, the hospital's chief of surgery, who operated on Governor Connally Friday, took over the case. The gamut of emergency procedures — blood transfusion, fluid transfusion, breathing tub and chest drainage tube—was instituted immediately.

But Dr. Shires quickly reported through a hospital official that Oswald was in "extremely critical condition" and that surgery would take several hours.

Family Put in Custody

Oswald's brother, George, a factory worker from Denton, Tex., got to the hospital before the assassin died.

The police took Oswald's mother, wife and two infant daughters into protective custody. They were escorted to the hospital to view the body, then were taken to an undisclosed lodging place in Dallas.

Governor Connally is still a patient at the Parkland Hospital. The excitement of the Oswald case swirled around the temporary office the Governor had set up there.

Back at the jail, Ruby was taken to the same fourth-floor cellblock where his victim had been the focus of attention the last two days.

Reports that filtered out about his preliminary remarks said that he had been impelled to kill President Kennedy's assassin by sympathy for Mrs. Kennedy. It was reported he did not want her to go through the ordeal of returning to Dallas for the trial of Oswald.

District Attorney Wade said yesterday he was sure the prosecution of Oswald could be carried out without the personal involvement of any members of the Kennedy family.

A half-dozen lawyers who have worked for Ruby converged on police headquarters in the next hour or two. They said they had been directed there by relatives and friends of Ruby and had not been called by Ruby himself.

One lawyer said that he had arranged for a hearing before a justice of the peace tomorrow morning to ask for Ruby's release on bail.

"He's a respectable citizen who's been here for years and certainly is entitled to bail," the lawyer said. "We'll make any amount of bail."

"He is a great admirer of President Kennedy," the lawyer said, "and police officers."

The last remark was an allusion to the fact that Oswald was accused of fatally shooting the Dallas patrolman after the President's assassination.

Ruby, the lawyer said, "is a very emotional man."

Chief Curry called the second formal news conference of the last three days in the police headquarters basement assembly room at 1:30 P.M.

His face drawn, he said in a husky voice:

"My statement will be very brief. Oswald expired at 1:07 P.M.

"We have arrested the man. He will be charged with murder. The suspect is Jack Rubenstein. He also goes by the name of Jack Ruby. That's all I have to say."

Sheriff Bill Decker commented that the police "did everything humanly possible" to protect Oswald, as he said they had in the case of President Kennedy.

"I don't think it would have made a bit of difference if Oswald had been transferred at night," he said. "If someone is determined to commit murder, it's almost impossible to stop him."

Ironically, it appeared that Ruby might have had a number of far easier opportunities for killing Oswald than the method he finally used.

He was reported to have circulated repeatedly the last two days among the throng of people that was constantly in the third-floor corridor near the homicied bureau. Oswald was led along this corridor a number of times as he was taken down from the fourth-floor jail for interrogation.

DALLAS IS GROPING FOR A REASON WHY

Some Say 'Crackpots' Have Touched Off Violence

By JOHN HERBERS
Special to The New York Times

DALLAS, Nov. 24 — "We think it's this Western tradition," a minister's wife said. "They are used to shooting at everything they don't like."

This was one explanation for a series of impulsive acts of violence that has occurred in Dallas—the abuse of President Johnson in a hotel lobby during the campaign in 1960; the attack on Adlai E. Stevenson, chief delegate to the United Nations, a few weeks ago; the assassination of President Kennedy, and the slaying today of the President's assassin.

Dallas does have a Western tradition, but it is not predominant. The city is really neither Western nor Southern. A civic leader who has been concerned about the rise of right-wing extremism here explained it like this:

"Dallas has a lot of professional people who are responsibly conservative and individualistic. It has some leaders who are interested in making money under the free and open Texas tradition. These people have attracted a lot of crackpots and the crackpots have inflamed the weak-minded and emotionally unstable."

Attracted by the West

Jack Ruby, the night-club operator who shot Lee H. Oswald, was described as a Chicagoan who was attracted by the Western tradition in Dallas.

His club in the heart of Dallas is decorated in Western decor, with the picture of a steer's head on a street sign.

A friend of Ruby's said he was an efficient bouncer. "He was tough all right, but you can't run a night club here and be a sissy," he said.

One block from Ruby's club is a similar night club called "The Horseshoe." It is decorated with pictures of scantily clad women, some of them wearing pistols on their hips.

Both night clubs are in the shadow of a partly completed, 50-story office building. Dallas has several skyscrapers going up. A taxi driver was asked if the city needed that much office space. He replied:

"I don't know about that, but you see that new building there. It was built by a bank. Another bank is building that tall structure. They couldn't stand to let the first bank get ahead of them."

'Like a Cancer'

"Something has happened here," Dr. Thomas A. Fry, pastor of the First Presbyterian Church, told his congregation today in a memorial service for President Kennedy. He continued:

"We are proud of our heritage and our image. But something has happened like a cancer you cannot quite put your finger on.

"We have allowed the apostles of religious bigotry and the purveyors of political pornography to stir up the weak-minded.

"These events should cause us to see to it that never again will we allow persons to brand a President a Communist unless he can back up his charges in court with facts, to call a person an adulterer with nothing more than a picture of a man in front of the house to prove it."

Dr. Fry was referring to literature distributed in the city by extremists.

Oswald's slaying today added to the feeling of defensiveness, confusion and hurt that has been evidenced here since the President was killed.

People on the street have felt throughout that there was some kind of conspiracy involved in the President's death.

Hundreds of persons gathered under clear skies today at the spot where President Kennedy was shot. They placed scores of floral wreaths in the small park that adjoins the street. Many of them stood in small groups discussing Oswald's death.

"I said all along that there was something else behind this," a woman said. "This shooting proves it. He won't be able to talk now."

A waitress said, "I just don't believe Oswald was acting on his own."

These people said they found it difficult to believe that the President's assassination was the act of a single demented person.

Extremists here have contended that any left-wing activity was part of a worldwide conspiracy. Oswald has been a defector to the Soviet Union and was a self-proclaimed Marxist.

There was anger against Ruby for shooting Oswald before he could be brought to trial.

"This makes it worse than ever for Dallas," a businessman said "It seems like the police would have had enough sense to keep out people like that; it will be hard to convince the nation that Dallas people aren't wild-eyed gunmen."

Some residents expressed doubt that the authorities had enough evidence against Oswald to convict him. "I don't believe he did it," a woman said.

Dallas also has a strong Southern tradition, even though most residents claim Western ties first. It is a city of many churches and their members turned out in great numbers today, obviously deeply grieved and disturbed over what had happened.

A minister said "I think it is significant that the President received a warm and genuine reception by thousands of its residents before he was shot by a single emotionally disturbed man. Dallas cannot be explained in a few words. It is a lot of things."

The New York Times — Nov. 25, 1963

SITE OF SLAYING: Kennedy's assassin was fatally shot in municipal building jail (1) as he was to be shifted to the county jail (2). He died at Parkland Hospital (3). President Kennedy was shot on the street (4) in car.

A British Program Honoring Kennedy Shown Over N.B.C.

A taped British television program entitled "A Tribute to John F. Kennedy" was shown over the National Broadcasting Company television network last night.

The program was a special presentation of the show "That Was the Week That Was," which usually is a humorous and biting program of political satire seen in England on Saturday nights.

The 19-minute show seen here last night contained no politics and no satire. It was made up of seven young persons prominent in British arts, giving short tributes to President Kennedy.

Dame Sybil Thorndike, one of Britain's most famous actresses, also read a short poem dedicated to Mrs. Kennedy. It was entitled, "Dear Jackie."

The British commentator Richard Dimbleby, who is in the United States to broadcast President Kennedy's funeral on the British Broadcasting Corporation, said the regular program had been scrapped when the news of President Kennedy's assassination reached England Friday evening.

Mr. Dimbleby said the program was a good expression of the emotion and the sorrow felt by the British people.

Irish Cousin of Kennedy Is Asked to Attend Rites

DUBLIN, Nov. 24 (AP)—Mary Ann Ryan an Irish cousin of President Kennedy, began tonight a journey to attend his funeral.

A request for Miss Ryan, 22-years-old, to be present at the funeral came from the Kennedy family through the United States embassy in Dublin.

A special police escort sped from Dublin to Dunganstown, County Wexford, where Miss Ryan, a nurse, was spending a weekend at home

MILLIONS WATCH OSWALD SLAYING

Continued From Page 1, Col. 6

Tokyo. Tape recordings of this were played back on Japanese TV stations ten minutes later.

The Dallas shooting, easily the most extraordinary moments of TV that a set-owner ever watched, came with such breath-taking suddenness as to beggar description.

It had been a quiet and subdued morning on TV, with emphasis on religious services and plans for the funeral of President Kennedy today. N.B.C had just done a "remote" from Hyannis Port, Mass., on the condition of the late President's father, Joseph P. Kennedy. C.B.S. was giving a news report from its studio after having carried a sermon in which violence was decried.

Under stand-by arrangements for instant switching to Dallas, the two networks took their audiences to the now familiar overcrowded corridor in the Dallas Police Department. And once again there appeared in view the figure of Oswald with a plainsclothes man at each side.

On the home screen all three appeared to be looking toward the left side of the screen. Out of the lower right corner came the back of a man. A shot rang out, and Oswald could be heard gasping as he started to fall.

Tom Pettit, N.B.C. correspondent, said quickly:

"He's been shot! He's been shot! Lee Oswald has been shot. There is absolute panic. Pandemonium has broken out."

Robert Huffaker, staff newsman for television station KRLD, the Dallas affiliate of the Columbia network, happened to be at the C.B.S. microphone.

"He's been shot!" Mr. Huffaker exclaimed. "Oswald's been shot!"

On the faces of the police officers there was shock, and then a viewer could see the officers swarming over the back of the assailant, Jack Ruby, a night-club operator.

Hundreds on Duty

The television coverage showed Ruby being whisked away and Oswald being sped in an ambulance to Parkland Hospital.

The TV sequence was over almost as soon as it started, and the viewer could not help but respect the composure of the commentators and the cameramen.

The ability of television to cope with the Oswald murder reflected the extent of network preparations since the President's assassination. Hundreds of persons in the networks' news staffs have been on duty almost around the clock, organizing and presenting programs throughout the day and night.

All networks concurred yesterday in a decision not to resume regular commercial programing until tomorrow morning.

One official estimated that the expenses for the special four-day news coverage would run from $2 million to $3 million for each network.

But a larger economic consideration pertains to advertising revenue that will not be realized. If both the networks and the hundreds of individual stations are considered, it was said, the total industry loss could amount to $100 million. The three networks together realize a total of about $14 million a night from the sale of prime time. To this must be added the loss of individual station income from the sale of spot announcements.

In today's coverage of the funeral and burial services for President Kennedy, beginning at 7 A.M. and continuing until late afternoon, the networks will pool their picture resources while carrying the commentary of their own reporters.

The same arrangement was followed for the inauguration of President Kennedy.

Airlines in Capital Expect Rush of Outbound Traffic

Special to The New York Times

WASHINGTON, Nov. 24 — Domestic airlines said today that they expected a rush of outbound patrons at midweek as Thanksgiving travel coincides with the demand for seats from those going home after President Kennedy's funeral.

Most carriers reported they were able to handle the influx of dignitaries over the weekend. But officials at both United Air Lines and Trans World Airlines, for example, said they expected trouble meeting the outbound demand later this week.

Leading Washington hotels said their occupancy rates had risen to 75 to 80 per cent.

TV Coverage in Capital Starts at 7 A.M. Today

Live television coverage in Washington in connection with President Kennedy's funeral will be provided by the three networks beginning at about 7 A.M. today. An approximate schedule follows:

7-9 A.M.—Scenes from key points in Washington.

9-10:30—The Rotunda of the Capitol, where the President's body lies in state.

10:30-Noon — Funeral procession to St. Matthew's Cathedral.

Noon-1:30—Requiem mass.

1:30-2:30 — Procession to Arlington Cemetery.

2:30-4 —Burial services.

From 4 P.M. until sign-off, programs will consist of broadcasts related to the assassination of President Kennedy. Radio schedules will be substantially in accord with those of television.

Friend Offers to Take Oswald's Family Into Her Home Again

By DONALD JANSON
Special to The New York Times

IRVING, Tex., Nov. 24—"I would be very pleased to have her again if she wants to live with me."

Mrs. Michael R. Paine was speaking today of Mrs. Lee Oswald. She had just heard the news of the shooting of her friend's husband.

Mrs. Oswald and her two baby daughters had lived with Mrs. Paine in this small town near Dallas while Oswald sought to earn enough money to get an apartment.

After President Kennedy was assassinated the police told Mrs. Paine they were bringing Mrs. Oswald and the children back to her two-bedroom home in this quiet residential neighborhood.

Subsequently, policemen were stationed in the home to insure the protection of the Oswald family.

Then Mrs. Oswald called from Dallas, where she and her children and mother-in-law had spent the night at the Executive Inn in rooms rented by Life magazine. She said the police had decided to keep them in protective custody elsewhere in Dallas.

Speaking in Russian, Mrs. Oswald, who has learned little English during her year and a half in the United States, asked Mrs. Paine to send her things she needed.

Responding in Russian, Mrs. Paine agreed. She also sent toys.

She said Mrs. Oswald did not seem distraught.

Her husband died shortly afterward.

Mrs. Paine said Oswald had called her three times yesterday. He asked to speak to his wife and requested Mrs. Paine to try to get John Abt of New York, an attorney, to defend him against charges of assassinating Mr. Kennedy.

Mrs. Paine was not able to reach Mr. Abt, but had planned to try again today.

Mrs. Paine, a tall young brunette, was born in New York. She became Marina Oswald's best friend through her interest in the Russian language.

Associated Press Wirephoto

Lee H. Oswald's Russian-born wife, Marina, arriving yesterday at the hospital in Dallas where her husband died.

A Quaker, she worked with the Young Friends Committee of North America in Philadelphia before moving here with her husband four years ago.

She said the object of her work was to improve international relations, and that knowledge of the Russian language would be useful. Last summer she taught Russian at St. Mark's, an Episcopal school in Dallas.

Mrs. Paine, who wants to do more teaching, said she had met the Oswalds at a small party in the home of a friend in Dallas last February.

At the party, she said, Oswald told of his three-year stay in the Soviet Union and of his preference for Marxism over capitalism.

He said he had met Marina, a pharmacist, in Minsk and married her a month and a half later. Their first child, now 22 months old, was born there. The other child is one month old.

Mrs. Paine said she had never engaged in political or philosophical discussions with Oswald because she did not enjoy argument.

"He had very fixed ideas," she said.

Mrs. Paine's husband, an engineer at Bell Helicopter Company, sometimes debated with him, but also found him inflexibly pro-Marxist.

Mr. Paine, although not living with his family, visits often. Neither Mr. nor Mrs. Paine realized until Friday that the luggage they had helped Oswald to put in their garage had included a rifle.

The police say the rifle had been used to assassinate President Kennedy.

"As a Quaker and a pacifist I would not have allowed them to keep it here," Mrs. Paine said today.

Mrs. Oswald has stayed with Mrs. Paine twice, for two weeks last May and from Sept. 24 until yesterday. Each time it was because Oswald had lost a job and could not support his family.

His last job was as a $50-a-week stock clerk at the Texas School Book Depository Building in Dallas, where the assassination was carried out.

Mrs. William Randall, a neighbor, told Mrs. Paine of the opening while having coffee with her and Mrs. Oswald.

She said the first time she had felt any sympathy for Oswald was when he had looked "very bleak" in bidding good-by to his family in New Orleans Sept. 23.

Mrs. Paine had gone there to bring Mrs. Oswald and the baby back here after Oswald had lost a job. Oswald came to the Dallas area a short time later, but never lived full-time with his family again.

Oswald Liked Children

While visiting his wife, Mrs. Paine said, Oswald seemed to be a loving father and husband. He liked to play with his babies and Mrs. Paine's children, who are a little older.

Oswald was handy around the house, Mrs. Paine said. He had planed doors to make them fit better and had moved furniture and done other chores. He liked to watch football and late shows on television.

But he never made any friends, she said. Even the party he and his wife had been invited to last February had included them because the group was interested in Russia, and Marina was Russian.

He was never close to his mother, of Fort Worth, or his older brother, of Denton, Tex. He was a loner.

His 22-year-old wife is different, Mrs. Paine said. She says the slight young woman is likeable and "quite intelligent."

Mrs. Oswald is learning English so she can work as a pharmacist. Mrs. Paine said Mrs. Oswald liked the United States "very much."

Of her husband's death, Mrs. Paine said that it was probably better for Mrs. Oswald because "it will mean less total strain."

"All the News That's Fit to Print"

The New York Times.

LATE CITY EDITION
U.S. Weather Bureau Report (Page 95) forecasts: Snow, chance of sleet or rain today, tonight, then clearing tomorrow.
Temp. Range: 37—28; yesterday: 36—23.

SECTION ONE

NEWS SUMMARY AND INDEX, PAGE 95

VOL. CXIII . No. 38,704. | NEW YORK, SUNDAY, JANUARY 12, 1964. | THIRTY CENTS

40c beyond 50-mile zone from New York City, except on Long Island. 50c beyond 200-mile zone from New York City, higher in air delivery cities.

CIGARETTES PERIL HEALTH, U. S. REPORT CONCLUDES; 'REMEDIAL ACTION' URGED

CANCER LINK CITED

Smoking Is Also Found 'Important' Cause of Chronic Bronchitis

Committee's summary of its findings, Pages 64 and 65.

By WALTER SULLIVAN
Special to The New York Times

WASHINGTON, Jan. 11—The long-awaited Federal report on the effects of smoking found today that the use of cigarettes contributed so substantially to the American death rate that "appropriate remedial action" was called for.

The committee that made the report gave no specific recommendations for action. But health officials said that possible steps might include educational campaigns, the requirement that cigarette packages carry warnings and control of advertising.

The report dealt a severe blow to the rear-guard action fought in recent years by the tobacco industry. It dismissed, one by one, the arguments raised to question the validity of earlier studies.

Role of Smoking in Cancer

Combining the results of many surveys, the study panel found no doubt about the role of cigarette smoking in causing cancer of the lungs.

In men who smoke cigarettes, the death rate from that disease is almost 1,000 per cent higher than in nonsmokers, it said. Lung cancer has become the most frequent form of cancer in men.

Such smoking was also found to be "the most important" cause of chronic bronchitis, increasing the risk of death from that disease and from emphysema, a swelling of the lungs due to the presence of air in the connective tissues. Emphysema is a disease of increasing incidence.

As to coronary artery disease, a frequent cause of heart failure and the leading cause of death in this country, mortality is 70 per cent higher for cigarette smokers than for nonsmokers, the report said.

Relationship Assumed

The role of smoking as a cause of the disease, it said, "is not proved." However, it said, the study committee considers it "prudent" from the public health viewpoint to assume such a cause-and-effect relationship rather than wait until such a relationship has been established beyond doubt.

[The Tobacco Institute rejected the report, saying it was not the last word on smoking and health. The three major broadcasting networks said they would review their policies on tobacco advertising in the light of the report.]

The report was prepared on the initiative of President Kennedy to help the Government decide what to do about the smoking question. The committee was formed by Dr. Luther L.

Continued on Page 65, Column 6

Associated Press Wirephoto

DISCUSSES SMOKING REPORT: Dr. Luther Terry, the Surgeon General, at news conference held in Washington.

Johnson Chides the G.O.P. For Opposing His Budget

By WARREN WEAVER JR.
Special to The New York Times

WASHINGTON, Jan. 11—President Johnson made his first frankly partisan speech tonight to the first purely political group he has invited to the White House. Standing under a picture of Abraham Lincoln in the State Dining Room, the President grinned as he told members of the Democratic National Committee he could not understand why his budget had not gotten a warmer Republican reception.

"I always thought there could be nothing more satisfying to economy-minded Republicans than the reduction of the budget," he declared.

Then he quoted critical budget comments by such Republicans as Senator Thruston B. Morton of Kentucky, Governor Rockefeller of New York, Representative Charles A. Halleck of Indiana and Senator Everett McKinley Dirksen of Illinois.

Notes Arends Remark

He recalled that Representative Leslie C. Arends of Illinois had accused him of providing "something for everyone."

"He sounds kind of sorry, doesn't he?" Mr. Johnson asked, and his guests laughed.

The President quoted Senator Barry Goldwater as saying that the Johnson budget "out-Roosevelts Roosevelt, out-Kennedys Kennedy and makes Truman look like a piker."

"What finer compliment could anyone have?" Mr. Johnson inquired, and the Democratic leaders cheered.

These critical Republicans,

Continued on Page 55, Column 3

ATLANTA HOTELS DROP COLOR LINE

14 Leading Establishments Agree to Admit Negroes in Bid to Avert Protests

Special to The New York Times

ATLANTA, Jan. 11—Fourteen major Atlanta hotels and motels have publicly pledged to accept reservations regardless of race "in accordance with usual hotel practices."

Antisegregation demonstrations have appeared imminent in Atlanta. The hotels' announcement, made from the office of Mayor Ivan Allen Jr., was seen as an effort to forestall the protests.

The establishments in the agreement represent most of the city's main downtown hostelries and several on the fringes of the city. Six have been regarded as desegregated for some time. Others have been pledged to operate under the "Dallas plan," accepting some Negroes for conventions, but recently there had been word that they were quietly honoring Negro reservations.

The practices of most Atlanta hotels have been vague since last fall. The announcement today, listing the 14 participants, seemed to pin down their commitments more clearly and represented a liberalizing of policy for most.

A group of civil rights leaders, meanwhile, voted today to organize massive demonstrations against segregation in Atlanta. Immediately after the

Continued on Page 62, Column 5

City Democrats to Restore Clubs As Job Centers for Minorities

By LEONARD INGALLS

The Democratic party in New York County is moving on a broad scale to restore to its neighborhood clubhouses some of their functions of the past in helping people find jobs and better housing.

Edward N. Costikyan, the Democratic county leader, has proposed that the county organization embark on such a program that also would include a special effort to improve public education in Harlem.

He has recommended to the county executive committee, made up of district leaders, that the party's 300,000 enrolled members and 35 district clubs in Manhattan be enlisted in an intensive effort to obtain pledges of nondiscrimination and to help members of minority groups find work.

He proposed that every Democratic district club solicit every Democrat and local businesses, labor unions and institutions like hospitals to obtain pledges that they would hire any person who met the qualifications for a job.

They also would be asked to agree to advise the Democratic county organization of vacancies and job qualifications. A full-time employment expert would be kept at Democratic county headquarters in the Chatham Hotel, 33 East 48th Street.

In submitting his proposals recently, Mr. Costikyan noted that many enrolled Democrats in Manhattan owned their own businesses and that others played key roles in labor unions. The committee is scheduled to

Continued on Page 32, Column 4

SIX-PHASE INQUIRY ON ASSASSINATION CHARTED BY PANEL

Aides Chosen for Detailed Study of Kennedy Slaying and Security Agencies

By ANTHONY LEWIS
Special to The New York Times

WASHINGTON, Jan. 11—The staff of the commission investigating President Kennedy's assassination has divided its job into six broad areas of inquiry.

One covers every detail of Lee Oswald's activities on the day of the assassination, Nov. 22. Oswald was charged with the crime.

A second topic is the life and background of Oswald—an attempt to reconstruct his associations and ideas and psychology.

Oswald's career in the Marine Corps and his stay in the Soviet Union will be handled separately as a third.

His murder in the Dallas police station will be the fourth subject, including all the controversial questions of how it was allowed to happen.

Fifth will be the story of Jack Ruby, the nightclub operator who slipped into the police station and shot Oswald. This will be a particularly delicate subject because of possible conflict with Ruby's trial.

Study of Agencies

Finally, the staff will inquire exhaustively into the procedures used to protect President Kennedy. This will involve a scrutiny of the performances of the Secret Service, the Federal Bureau of Investigation and the Dallas police, as well as the influence, if any, of hate movements in the Dallas community.

The commission's counsel, J. Lee Rankin, outlined the plan in an interview.

He said it was clear to him now that the job could not be done in a matter of weeks, but he still hoped the inquiry could be finished three to six months from now. He recognized the importance of not letting it drag on.

"The commission realizes that the country wants to be sure of the facts," Mr. Rankin said. "The first thing is to do the job right. The second is to do it as quickly as possible."

New Name to Be Added

A senior lawyer assisted by a younger man will handle each of the six inquiry subjects. Mr. Rankin himself will have charge of one topic, and a group of distinguished lawyers from around the country has been gathered for the other senior posts.

The commission announced four of these senior appointments today, and a fifth is expected to follow shortly. The four named today, all men in active practice, are:

Francis W. H. Adams of New York, 59 years old. He was Police Commissioner in New York City in 1954-55.

Joseph A. Ball of Los Angeles, 61 years old, a leading criminal lawyer, a member of the Supreme Court's Advisory Committee on the Federal Rules

Continued on Page 46, Column 3

MORRISON BEATEN IN LOUISIANA VOTE

Former Diplomat Loses to McKeithen in Democratic Gubernatorial Primary

By CLAUDE SITTON
Special to The New York Times

NEW ORLEANS, Jan. 11—John J. McKeithen, a militant segregationist, today won the Democratic gubernatorial nomination in Louisiana and almost certain election by upsetting deLesseps S. Morrison.

Unofficial returns from 2,187 of the state's 2,219 precincts showed these totals:

McKeithen 484,179
Morrison 437,994

The victory of the rural northern Louisiana lawyer may spell trouble in this state for the Democratic Presidential nominee in the November election, even if, as expected, it is President Johnson. Mr. McKeithen has refused to commit himself to support the party's choice.

Scattered rains that cut the turnout of voters in the populous southern section, a Morrison stronghold, helped to account for the margin for Mr. McKeithen, 45-year-old State Public Service Commissioner.

Far more important, however,

Continued on Page 59, Column 3

U.S. AND PANAMA AGREE TO CLEAR BORDERS IN STEP TO EASE TENSION; PLEDGE ON FLAG ISSUE IS OFFERED

Associated Press Wirephoto

FUNERAL PROCESSION IN PANAMA CITY: Thousands following the coffin yesterday bearing the body of a Panamanian student killed in Thursday's rioting near Canal Zone.

TROOPS CURB RIOTS

Chiari's Regime Finds Reds Infiltrating—Arms Search On

By HENRY RAYMONT
Special to The New York Times

PANAMA, Sunday, Jan. 12—The United States and Panama have agreed to take practical steps to ease the tensions along the borders of the Canal Zone.

After consultations with Assistant Secretary of State Thomas C. Mann and Secretary of the Army Cyrus R. Vance, the Canal Zone authorities agreed last night to remove troops that had been stationed along the border since the outbreak of violence Thursday.

For its part, the Panamanian National Guard undertook to clear its side of the border of snipers and those suspected of planning to provoke incidents.

In addition, the United States, in a conciliatory gesture, promised to make sure that the flags of both nations would henceforth fly side by side in the Canal Zone.

Link to Castro Alleged

The Government of President Roberto F. Chiari charged that the demonstrations had been infiltrated by Communists and supporters of Premier Fidel Castro of Cuba. It was stressed, however, that the majority of the demonstrators were engaged in a "purely civic movement."

During the night, cars in the city were being stopped and searched for arms.

Late last night, fighting between jeering Panamanians and United States soldiers with fixed bayonets erupted again on the Canal Zone border. Rioters stormed the barricade at the Tivoli guest house, and were forced back by the soldiers.

Bands Roam City

Bands of youth roamed the city, screaming anti-American slogans and hurling bottles and other missiles toward the border. One group praised President Chiari in the same slogans used by Castro sympathizers.

The pledges to ease the tensions were made at all-day meetings among Panamanian officials, the high-level United States mission, and the Inter-American Peace Committee, representing the Organization of American States.

The three-way talks began yesterday morning after the O.A.S. group arrived from Washington and moved to conciliate the deepening United States-Panamanian crisis.

The United States and Panama each named a permanent

Continued on Page 25, Column 1

Long Panama Negotiation Expected by Washington

By TAD SZULC
Special to The New York Times

WASHINGTON, Jan. 11—The United States searched today for steps that it hoped could lead to a mutually acceptable political solution of the Panama crisis. But the Administration was aware that, in the highly charged emotional atmosphere of Panama, it might be difficult for the Government of President Roberto F. Chiari to enter immediately into what is considered here a reasonable basis for negotiations on the fundamental issues.

The United States, therefore, was preparing for what may be a prolonged and complicated negotiating process that may have to be conducted in part without formal diplomatic relations. Diplomatic ties were broken by Panama yesterday.

Mann Reports to Johnson

President Johnson received a written report from Thomas C. Mann, Assistant Secretary of State for Inter-American Affairs, who flew to Panama yesterday at the head of a high-level United States mission to try to resolve the crisis.

The crisis developed Thursday night in a battle between Panamanian and United States forces on the border of the Canal Zone, culminating a dispute over the flying of the Panamanian flag.

The report covered mainly Mr. Mann's 90-minute meeting last night with President Chiari. It is understood that Mr. Mann limited himself for the most part to listening to the Panamanian President's exposition of the situation.

The White House said later that, on the basis of the first report and of a telephone con-

Continued on Page 25, Column 3

SENATORS SCORE BALL'S AID PLAN

2 Democratic Chiefs Oppose State Department Control Urged by Rusk Aide

By FELIX BELAIR Jr.
Special to The New York Times

WASHINGTON, Jan. 11—Senate Democratic leaders rejected today a proposal that the State Department take over direction and control of the foreign aid program in place of the Agency for International Development.

The proposal, submitted by Under Secretary of State George W. Ball, was sharply criticized by the Senate majority leader, Mike Mansfield of Montana, and the assistant majority leader, Hubert H. Humphrey of Minnesota.

They said that President Johnson's interdepartmental committee now studying the aid program was "wasting its time" if it was seriously considering turning over A.I.D. to the State Department or scattering its functions among six or seven other departments and agencies.

"I can think of nothing that would foul up the foreign aid program more completely and effectively than to turn it over to a bunch of Foreign Service officers," Senator Humphrey declared.

'Scramble and Hide'

"And the 'scatteration' scheme," he continued, "is nothing more than a transparent attempt to scramble and hide the aid appropriation by breaking it down into its components and assigning a part of it to various agency budgets. It would only mean that the Senate and House Appropriations Committees would have to unscramble the items and put them back together in a single money bill again."

President Johnson has given the study group, which is headed by Mr. Ball, until next Wednesday to make recommendations for overhauling the aid program.

In his instructions to the eight-member panel, the President stressed the criterion of Congressional acceptance. For this reason, the position of the Senate Democratic leadership was viewed as spiking any

Continued on Page 31, Column 3

West Berlin Offered Emergency Passes

By United Press International

BERLIN, Jan. 11—East Germany has offered to permit West Berliners through the Communist-built wall to visit relatives in East Berlin in certain hardship cases, it was disclosed today.

The offer was made public as the East German Communist leader, Walter Ulbricht, returned from a two-day visit to Moscow and meetings with Premier Khrushchev.

West Berlin officials said that they were convinced that Mr. Ulbricht and Mr. Khrushchev had conferred on plans to revive the system of passes through the wall as a wedge to gain recognition for East Germany.

Under the terms of the hardship plan, passes would be issued to West Berliners in the event of the death or sickness

Continued on Page 9, Column 3

Mrs. Johnson Cheered in 'Poverty Pocket' Coal Towns

United Press International Telephoto

Mrs. Lyndon B. Johnson greets youngster who turned out to welcome her to Wilkes-Barre

By NAN ROBERTSON
Special to The New York Times

WILKES-BARRE, Pa., Jan. 11—Mrs. Lyndon B. Johnson visited today one of the "pockets of poverty" that President Johnson has declared war on—the Wilkes-Barre and Scranton area of Pennsylvania. It is part of that impoverished 10-state strip known as Appalachia. Here, in the anthracite mine area, the jobless rate is nearly double the nation's average. On the way from Washington, Mrs. Johnson was briefed on the region, its problems and some of the solutions that have been found by two Pennsylvania Representatives. They were Daniel

Continued on Page 42, Column 4

Today's Sections

*Included in all copies in the New York metropolitan area and adjacent territory.

Index to Subjects

Study Indicates Use of Cigarettes Is Major Cause of Lung Cancer Among Men

Continued From Preceding Page

phagus, larynx and lung, and for stomach and duodenal ulcers. These ratios are, however, based on a small number of deaths.

Cancer by Site

Lung Cancer

Cigarette smoking is casually related to lung cancer in men; the magnitude of the effect of cigarette smoking far outweighs all other factors. The data for women, though less extensive, points in the same direction.

The risk of developing lung cancer increases with duration of smoking and the number of cigarettes smoked per day, and is diminished by discontinuing smoking.

The risk of developing cancer of the lung for the combined group of pipe smokers, cigar smokers, and pipe and cigar smokers, is greater than for nonsmokers, but much less than for cigarette smokers. The data are insufficient to warrant a conclusion for each group individually.

Oral Cancer

The causal relationship of the smokin gof pipes to the development of cancer of the lip appears to be established.

Although there are suggestions of relationships between cancer of other specific site of the oral cavity and the several forms of tobacco use, their causal implications cannot at present be stated.

Cancer of the Larynx

Evaluation of the evidence leads to the judgment that cigarette smoking is a significant factor in the causation of laryngeal cancer in the male.

Cancer of the Esophagus

The evidence on the tobacco-Esophageal cancer relationship supports the belief that an association exists. However, the data are not adequate to decide whether the relationship is causal.

Cancer of the Urinary Bladder

Available data suggest an association between cigarette smoking and urinary bladder cancer in the male but are not sufficient to support a judgment on the causal significance of the association.

Stomach Cancer

No relationship has been established between tobacco use and stomach cancer.

Non-Neoplastic Respiratory Diseases, Particularly Chronic Bronchitis and Pulmonary Emphysema

Cigarette smoking is the most important of the causes of chronic bronchitis in the United States, and increases the risk of dying from chronic bronchitis.

A relationship exists between pulmonary emphysema and cigarette smoking but it has not been established that the relationship is casual. The smoking of cigarettes is associated with an increased risk of dying from pulmonary emphysema.

For the bulk of the population of the United States, the importance of cigarette smoking as a cause of chronic bronchopulmonary disease is much greater than that of atmospheric pollution or occupational exposures.

Cough, sputum production, or the two combined are consistently more frequent among cigarette smokers than among nonsmokers.

Cigarette smoking is associated with a reduction in ventilatory function. Among males, cigarette smokers have a greater prevalence of breathlessness than nonsmokers.

Cigarette smoking does not appear to cause asthma.

Although death certification shows that cigarette smokers have a moderately increased risk of death from influenza and pneumonia, an association of cigarette smoking and infectious diseases is not otherwise substantiated.

Cardiovascular Disease

Smoking and nicotine administration cause acute cardiovascular effects similar to those induced by stimulation of the autonomic nervous system, but these effects do not account well for the observed association between cigarette smoking and coronary disease. It is established that male cigarette smokers have a higher death rate from coronary disease than nonsmoking males. The association of smoking with other cariovascular disorders is less well established. If cigarette smoking actually caused the higher death rate from coronary disease, it would on this account be responsible for many deaths of middle-aged and elderly males in the United States. Other factors such as high blood pressure, high serum cholesterol, and excessive obesity are also known to be associated with an unusually high death rate from coronary disease. The causative role of these factors in coronary disease, though not proven, is suspected strongly enough to be a major reason for taking countermeasures against them. It is also more prudent to assume that the established association between cigarette smoking and coronary disease has causative meaning than to suspend judgment until no uncertainty remains.

Male cigarette smokers have a higher death rate from coronary artery disease than nonsmoking males, but it is not clear that the association has causal significance.

Other Conditions

Peptic Ulcer

Epidemiological studies indicate an association between cigarette smoking and peptic ulcer which is greater for gastric than for duodenal ulcer.

Tobacco Amblyopia

Tobacco amblyopia (dimness of vision unexplained by an organic lesion) has been related to pipe and cigar smoking by clinical impressions. The association has not been substantiated by epidemiological or experimental studies.

Cirrhosis of the Liver

Increased mortality of smokers from cirrhosis of the liver has been shown in the prospective studies. The data are not sufficient to support a direct or causal association.

Maternal Smoking and Infant Birth Weight

Women who smoke cigarettes during pregnancy tend to have babies of lower birth weight.

Information is lacking on the mechanism by which the decrease in birth weight is produced.

It is not known whether this decrease in birth weight has any influence on the biological fitness of the new born.

Smoking and Accidents

Smoking is associated with accidental deaths from fires in the home.

No conclusive information is available on the effects of smoking on traffic accidents.

Morphological Constitution of Smokers

The available evidence suggests the existence of some morphological differences between smokers and nonsmokers, but is too meager to permit a conclusion.

Psycho-Social Aspects of Smoking

A clear-cut smoker's personality has not emerged from the results so far published. While smokers differ from nonsmokers in a variety of characteristics, none of the studies has shown a single variable which is found solely in one group and is completely absent in another. Nor has any single variable been verified in a sufficiently large proportion of smokers and in sufficiently few nonsmokers to consider it an "essential" aspect of smoking.

The overwhelming evidence points to the conclusion that smoking—its beginning, habituation, and occasional discontinuation—is to a large extent psychologically and socially determined. This does not rule out physiological factors, especially in respect to habituation, nor the existence of predisposing constitutional or hereditary factors.

Head of Cancer Society Asks Follow-Up Action

WASHINGTON, Jan. 11 (UPI)—The President of the American Cancer Society urged today a program of follow-up action to the Government's report on smoking.

Dr. Wendell C. Scott said in a statement that the report "is a remarkably effective analysis of the evidence that cigarettes are a major health hazard."

He proposed acceptance by the medical profession of responsibility for advising the public about the hazards.

He urged increased research on helping adults who wish to stop smoking, as well as more research to pinpoint cancer-causing substances in cigarette smoke.

Dr. Scott proposed also consideration of discontinuing advertising aimed at getting young people to smoke; a study by economists, Government officials and the tobacco industry on ways of cushioning the economic impact of a reduction of cigarette consumption, and effective dissemination of the data in the report

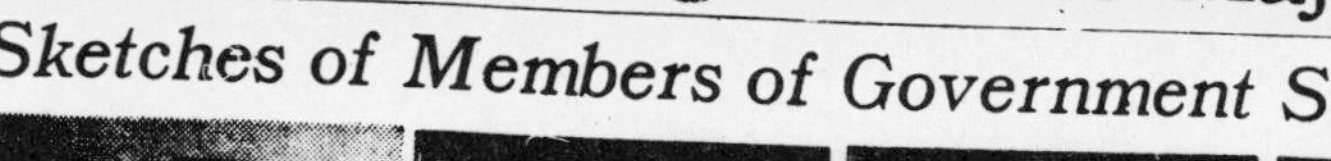

Sketches of Members of Government Study Panel

Dr. Eugene H. Guthrie

Dr. Stanhope Bayne-Jones

Dr. Walter J. Burdette

William G. Cochran

DR. EUGENE HARDING GUTHRIE . . . The panel's staff director . . . A 12-year United States Public Health Service career officer . . . Educated at Haverford College, Duke University and the University of North Carolina . . . Earned his M.D. degree at George Washington University in 1951, a Master of Public Health degree from the University of Michigan in 1955 . . . Public Health Service position is head of the Division of Chronic Diseases, Bureau of State Services . . . Head of Neurological and Sensory Disease Service since 1962 . . . Born April 9, 1924 . . . Married, has six children, quit smoking 13 years ago.

DR. STANHOPE BAYNE-JONES . . . One of America's most honored men of medicine . . . Currently a member of the Army Advisory Scientific Panel and Advisory Scientific Board of Walter Reed Army Institute of Research . . . Born in New Orleans, Nov. 6, 1888 . . . Earned bachelor's degree at Yale 22 years later, M.D. degree from Johns Hopkins University in 1914 . . . Since then has received eight honorary degrees from as many institutions . . . Most important work in bacteriology, immunology and preventative medicine . . . published some 75 scientific papers . . . Does not smoke.

DR. WALTER JAMES BURDETTE . . . Head of the department of surgery at the University of Utah . . . A graduate of the University of Texas, Baylor University and Yale University, from which he received his M.D. degree . . . Has done research in genetics and cancer, the biochemistry of the heart muscle, the cause and treatment of blood cancer . . . Heads the Research Advisory Council of the American Cancer Society and the U.S. National Committee of the International Union Against Cancer . . . Born on Feb. 5, 1915, in Hillsboro, Tex., he is the father of a 9-year-old girl and a 19-month boy. He does not smoke.

WILLIAM GEMMELL COCHRAN . . . A professor of statistics at Harvard University, he is the only committee member without a doctor's degree . . . Highly regarded for work in fields ranging from application of mathematical statistics in biology to labor and economic statistics . . . Born July 15, 1909, in Rutherglen, Scotland, now a United States citizen . . . Earned master's degree at Glasgow University and Cambridge University before coming to Iowa State College in 1939 as a professor of statistics . . . Served on several governmental committees . . . A consultant to the American Leprosy Foundation . . . Smokes cigarettes.

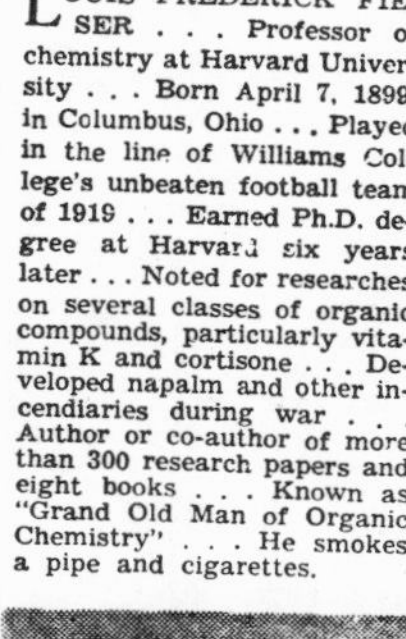

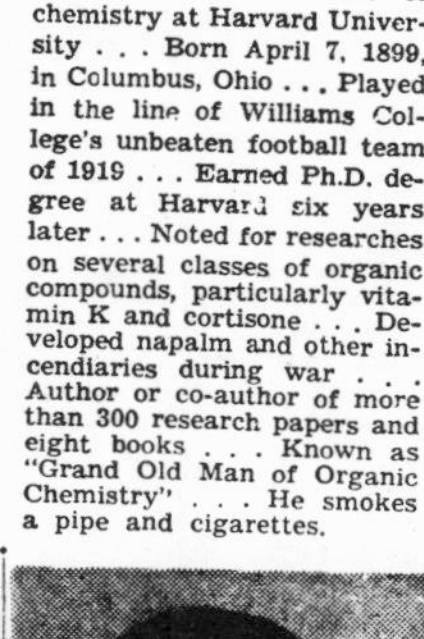

Dr. Emmanuel Farber

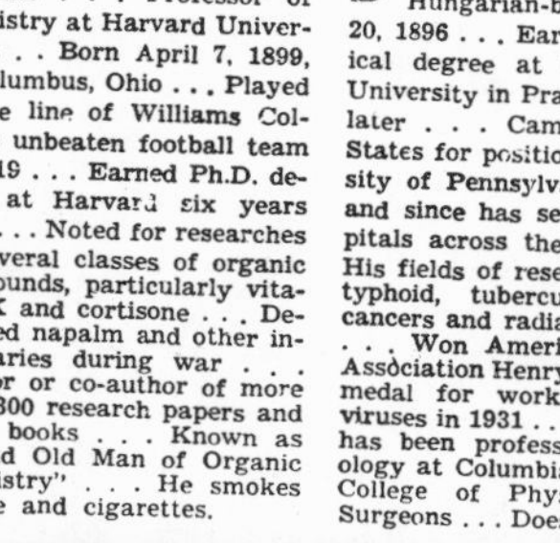

Louis F. Fieser

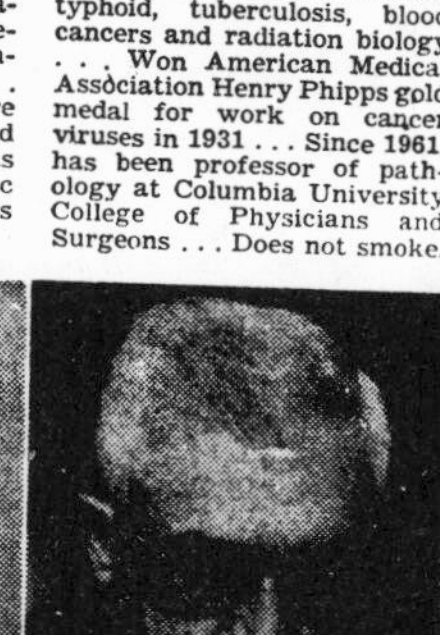

Dr. Jacob Furth

Dr. John B. Hickam

DR. EMMANUEL FARBER . . . Born in Toronto, Ont., on Oct. 19, 1918, and became United States citizen in 1956 . . . Earned M. D. degree from University of Toronto in 1942, Ph.D. degree in biochemistry at University of California in 1949 . . . Specialty is in chemical pathology and the chemistry of tissue enzymes . . . Now heads Department of Pathology at the University of Pittsburgh Medical School . . . Worked as a fellow in cancer research of the American Cancer Society at the Hektoen Institute for Medical Research of Cook County Hospital in Chicago . . . Married and a father, he does not smoke.

LOUIS FREDERICK FIESER . . . Professor of chemistry at Harvard University . . . Born April 7, 1899, in Columbus, Ohio . . . Played in the line of Williams College's unbeaten football team of 1919 . . . Earned Ph.D. degree at Harvard six years later . . . Noted for researches on several classes of organic compounds, particularly vitamin K and cortisone . . . Developed napalm and other incendiaries during war . . . Author or co-author of more than 300 research papers and eight books . . . Known as "Grand Old Man of Organic Chemistry" . . . He smokes a pipe and cigarettes.

DR. JACOB FURTH . . . Hungarian-born on Sept. 20, 1896 . . . Earned his medical degree at the German University in Prague 25 years later . . . Came to United States for position at University of Pennsylvania in 1924 and since has served in hospitals across the nation . . . His fields of research include typhoid, tuberculosis, blood cancers and radiation biology . . . Won American Medical Association Henry Phipps gold medal for work on cancer viruses in 1931 . . . Since 1961, has been professor of pathology at Columbia University College of Physicians and Surgeons . . . Does not smoke.

DR. JOHN BAMBER HICKAM . . . Head of the medical department at Indiana University . . . Born in Manila, Aug. 10, 1914 . . . Earned Bachelor of Arts degree, summa cum laude, and M.D. degree, cum laude, at Harvard University in 1936 and 1940, respectively . . . Has served at Peter Bent Brigham Hospital in Boston, Emory University and Duke University . . . Has been author or co-author of 64 scientific articles and other published works . . . Specialty is cardio pulmonary disease . . . Developed means for sampling blood going to and coming from various organs by inserting tube through elbow vein . . . Does not smoke.

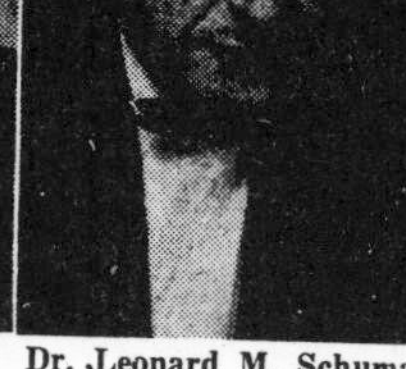

Dr. Charles A. LeMaistre

Dr. Leonard M. Schuman

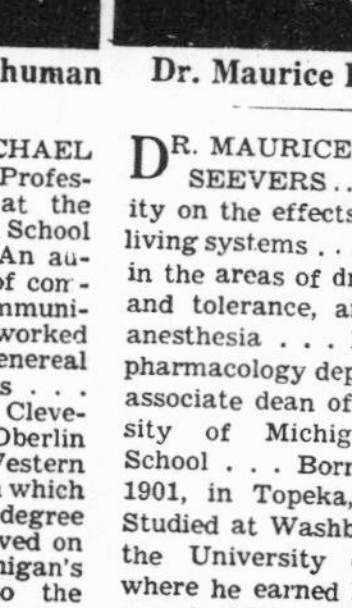

Dr. Maurice H. Seevers

DR. CHARLES AUBREY LeMAISTRE . . . The youngest member of the panel, born Feb. 10, 1924, in Lockhart, Ala. . . . Rose to current position as professor of internal medicine at the University of Texas Southwestern Medical School through work on tuberculosis and other diseases of the lungs and chest . . . Took bachelor degree at University of Alabama, M.D. at Cornell University Medical College in 1947 . . . Is author or co-author of 22 articles, books and other published works . . . Has worked at several hospitals and universities in New York and throughout the South . . . Smokes cigars and a pipe.

DR. LEONARD MICHAEL SCHUMAN . . . Professor of epidemiology at the University of Minnesota School of Public Health . . . An authority on the spread of communicable and non-communicable diseases . . . Has worked in many areas, from venereal disease to poliomyelitis . . . Born March 4, 1913, in Cleveland . . . A graduate of Oberlin College in 1934 and Western Reserve University from which he received his M.D. degree six years later . . . Served on the University of Michigan's advisory committee to the Salk vaccine evaluation center, which tested the effectiveness of the vaccine . . . Now consultant to the Public Service's Communicable Disease Center . . . Smokes cigarettes.

DR. MAURICE HARRISON SEEVERS . . . An authority on the effects of drugs on living systems . . . Has worked in the areas of drug addiction and tolerance, analgesia and anesthesia . . . Head of the pharmacology department and associate dean of the University of Michigan Medical School . . . Born on Oct. 3, 1901, in Topeka, Kan. . . . Studied at Washburn College, the University of Chicago, where he earned his M.D. degree in 1932, and the University of Wisconsin General Hospital, where he interned . . . A member of National Research Council's Committee on Drug Addiction and Narcotics . . . A cigar smoker.

U.S. REPORT CALLS CIGARETTES PERIL

Continued From Page 1, Col. 1

Terry, Surgeon General of the Public Health Service. Its work began in the summer of 1962 and consisted of evaluating and reprocessing earlier studies. No original research was done.

At a press conference in the State Department Auditorium, where the report was released, Dr. Terry said he did not anticipate any "foot dragging" by the Government in taking the "remedial action" called for in the report. He said the problem was one of "national concern."

Dr. Terry told the committee that the Public Health Service would move "promptly" to determine what steps should be taken. He said that his recommendations would be made to Anthony J. Celebrezze, Secretary of Health, Education and Welfare, after consultation with the Public Health Service staff.

F.T.C. Studies Report

"I am sure that other departments and agencies of the Federal Government, along with non-Federal agencies, will also take the report under consideration promptly," he said. Shortly after the meeting, the Federal Trade Commission said it was studying the report to see what action was necessary.

The committee could find no evidence that nicotine played an important role in causing disease. Rather, it pointed an accusing finger at the components of tobacco smoke that had been found to produce cancer in animals. These are a series of compounds known as polycyclic aromatic hydrocarbons.

These compounds are complex molecules composed of hydrogen and carbon atoms, the latter arranged in a series of rings.

A spokesman for the committee told the press conference there was no valid evidence that filters helped reduce the harmful effects. The report also said that nicotine substitutes, such as lobeline, used in so-called "withdrawal pills," seemed ineffective in breaking the smoking habit.

The committee said that smoking was a "psychological crutch" for a large part of the 70 million Americans who were smokers in 1963. This posed the question: What would happen if this prop were suddenly pulled out from under them?

'Intangible' Factors

The report said that such factors were "so intangible and elusive, so intricately woven into the whole fabric of human behavior, so subject to moral interpretation and censure, so difficult of medical evaluation and so controversial" that they could not be assessed.

It said that, from time immemorial, men have leaned on props, some harmless, such as the ginseng root of China, some lethal, like opium. So powerful is this human drive, it said, that man has always been willing to risk and accept the most unpleasant symptoms and signs.

Among these it cited hallucinations, paralysis, convulsions, poverty, malnutrition and even death. If, then, man is bound to continue his dependence on such substances, in the interests of public health this should be done "with substances which carry minimal hazard," it said.

Smoking, the report said, is a habit, rather than a form of addiction. Withdrawal does not produce a characteristic illness, as it does with addicts, and is best accomplished by psychologically replacing the prop, the committee said. However, it added, this invokes "the difficulties attendant upon extinction of any conditioned reflex"—that is, in breaking any habit.

Those who questioned the validity of earlier studies argued that no one had shown how smoking could, for example, cause lung cancer or heart disease. It was said that the statistics were confused by other factors, such as air pollution in large cities, stress and heredity.

Not a Simple Question

The report released today said that no simple cause-and-effect relationship probably existed between a complex product like tobacco smoke and any single disease in so variable an organism as the human body. It also acknowledged that it often seemed to be a combination of factors, rather than any one, that precipitated an illness.

Nevertheless, it said, cigarette smoking was clearly the most important factor in some diseases to which it was linked. For example, in chronic diseases of the lungs and bronchial tubes, it was found that the relative importance of cigarette smoking as a causative factor was "much greater" than air pollution or occupational exposure.

"Cigarette smoking is a health hazard of sufficient importance in the United States to warrant appropriate remedial action," said the report, entitled "Smoking and Health."

The conclusions of the committee rested heavily on seven "prospective" studies carried out since 1951, involving 1,123,000 men. A prospective study is one in which individuals are picked at random and observed, usually until death. In these studies, the deaths of 37,391 participants had been recorded and analyzed.

Number and Age Factors

The committee combined the results of these seven studies and found that for cigarette smokers the death rate per thousand, from all causes, was 68 per cent higher than for nonsmokers.

As in earlier studies, the death rates were strongly affected by such factors as the number of cigarettes smoked daily and the age at which smoking began. Likewise, as others have found, the use of cigars and pipes was far less a factor than cigarette smoking.

The death rates for those who smoke fewer than five cigars a day were found to be almost the same as for nonsmokers. For those smoking five or more cigars, the rate was only "slightly" higher. Even those pipe smokers who smoke 10 or more pipefuls a day and have been smoking more than 30 years did not show a substantially higher death rate.

Inhalation Rates Lower

The reason for lower rates among cigar and pipe smokers is not clear, although some attribute it to less inhalation. The report cited surveys in which 94 per cent of the cigarette smokers said they inhaled. A survey of cigar smokers has shown an inhalation rate of 19 per cent. An American study of pipe smokers has indicated 28 per cent inhalation and the figure in a Canadian study was 18 per cent.

The report said that, in men, cigarette smoking "far outweighs all other factors" as a cause of lung cancer. The incidence of this disease has risen dramatically during the years that cigarettes have replaced other forms of smoking.

"While the data for women are less extensive, the report said, they "point in the same direction."

Those who questioned such conclusions in the past argued, for example, that in earlier times deaths from lung cancer were incorrectly diagnosed. They said the increase in recorded cases was in part a reflection of better diagnostic procedures. The committee agreed but said that this effect was minor alongside that of smoking.

In the combined results from seven surveys, 1,833 of the deaths among smokers were diagnosed as resulting from lung cancer. Using the rate among nonsmokers as a guide, only 170.3 of those men would have died had they not smoked, the report said.

Thus the rate among smokers was almost 10 times as high.

In coronary artery disease, the deaths among smokers were 11,177, compared with an expected figure of about 6,430, based on the rate among nonsmokers. For smokers, therefore, the rate was less than double that in nonsmokers, but the total number of deaths was far larger.

A "puzzling" discovery in animal studies, the report said, is that all the tarry substances from cigarette smoke, when used together, are far more potent in producing cancer than one would expect from tests with the various constituents. The latter include the seven polycyclic hydrocarbons that have shown varying degrees of potency as causers of cancer.

It seems, therefore, the report said, that "the whole is greater than the sum of the known parts."

It has been found in various areas of cancer research that the disease may be caused by a combination of "insults" to the body cells, none of which is harmful by itself.

Another factor, as noted in the report, is that smoking seems to impair the function of the cilia, or tiny hairs, whose constant motion cleanses the lungs by sweeping mucous upward into the throat.

The committee found that, as long suspected, pipe smoking is a cause of lip cancer. Cigarette smoking was called a "significant factor" in cancer of the larynx. There was some evidence of a link between smoking and cancer of the food pipe (esophagus) and bladder, the report said, but this has not been proved.

It said that no relationship had been shown between tobacco use and stomach cancer. The same is true, it said, with a dimness of vision commonly attributed to cigar and pipe smoking and known as tobacco amblyopia.

It said smoking during pregnancy seemed to produce smaller babies, but asserted that it was not known whether real damage was done to the child.

Studies have not substantiated the common notion that children take up smoking as a gesture of defiance to authority, the report said.

The change in smoking habits since the turn of the century was charted as follows: In 1900 the average consumption of chewing tobacco, per person each year, was about 4 pounds, and in 1962 it was half a pound. The use of pipe tobacco, 2½ pounds per person in 1910, likewise had dropped to half a pound by 1962. In 1920 the average number of cigars smoked for every man, woman and child, was 117, but this fell to 55 in 1962.

Rise in Cigarette Smoking

By contrast, the figure for cigarettes at the start of the century was fewer than 50. In 1961 it hit its peak of 3,986 per person per year.

The sequence of events that led to establishing the committee began with a letter sent to President Kennedy on June 1, 1961, by the heads of the American Cancer Society, the American Public Health Association, the American Heart Association and the National Tuberculosis Association.

They urged the formation of a Presidential commission to study the "widespread implications of the tobacco problem." The next January they met with Dr. Terry, who proposed to the Secretary of Health, Education and Welfare the formation of a committee of outstanding experts to assess the available knowledge and make recommendations.

Further discussions included representatives of the Tobacco Institute, maintained by the industry, and of various Government agencies. It was agreed that the job should be done in two phases. The first was to be "an objective assessment of the nature and magnitude of the health hazard." This was the report submitted to Dr. Terry today.

The second phase is to include recommendations for action. It was agreed that such proposals should not be a part of the first phase and that they should not be considered until the first report was in.

As stated in today's document, "It was recognized that different competencies would be needed in the second phase and that many possible recommendations for action would extend beyond the health field and into the purview and competence of other Federal agencies."

It was stated at the press conference that the views of the committee were unanimous.

Dr. Terry was listed as chairman of the committee and Dr. James M. Hundley, Assistant Surgeon General, as vice chairman, in addition to the 10 appointed members. The director of the committee's staff was Dr. Eugene H. Guthrie, chief of the Division of Chronic Diseases in the Public Health Service.

Pending Smoking Bills

Special to The New York Times

WASHINGTON, Jan. 11—*There are four bills dealing with cigarettes and other smoking products now pending in Congress. These bills, all introduced last year, follow:*

Provisions	Disposition
Makes the Food, Drug and Cosmetics Act applicable to all smoking products and provides adulteration and misbranding provisions for such products.	Referred to appropriate House and Senate committees. No hearings scheduled.
Requires that packages of cigarettes shipped in interstate commerce bear warning that they may be dangerous to health.	Referred to House Committee on Interstate and Foreign Commerce. No hearings scheduled.
Requires label disclosures of the effectiveness of filters on cigarettes distributed in commerce.	Referred to House Committee on Interstate and Foreign Commerce. No hearings scheduled.
Provides that cigarettes sold in interstate commerce be packaged and marked so as to show the nicotine content and tar content of the cigarettes in each package.	Referred to House Committee on Interstate and Foreign Commerce. No hearings scheduled.

Smoking Report Poses Issue of Public Policy

The Government report on smoking dramatizes a human and social issue.

The report says that an $8 billion a year industry, which provides jobs and incomes for thousands of people, is based on a product damaging to human health.

This industry pays $3.3 billion a year in taxes.

But this industry is also costing American families perhaps $10 billion a year because so many men, so many wage-earners die too soon because of cigarette smoking, a statistician estimates.

The statistician, Dr. Louis I. Dublin, retired vice president of the Metropolitan Life Insurance Company, suggests that both the public injuries and public benefits of any industry be taken into account in judging future public policy.

"From the public-interest point of view, the tobacco industry is far from a glorious asset," Dr. Dublin declares. "In balance, when liabilities are placed side by side the assets, the evidence is good that from the public-interest point of view, the industry is bankrupt."

Report Not Convincing To a Scientist at Yale

NEW HAVEN, Conn., Jan. 11 (AP)—Dr. Harry S. Greene of Yale University is one scientist who is not convinced there is an association between smoking and lung cancer.

The Government has only statistics, the chairman of Yale's department of pathology said tonight, "and a statistical association has to be interpreted."

"It might show cause and effect or it might show happenstance," he said.

"But the results must be subjected to a laboratory test. They've been doing that for 15 years and have come up with absolutely nothing."

"All the News That's Fit to Print"

The New York Times.

LATE CITY EDITION
U. S. Weather Bureau Report (Page 59 forecasts:
Mostly sunny today; fair tonight.
Partly cloudy, milder tomorrow.
Temp. Range: 40—25; yesterday: 36—27.

VOL. CXIII .. No. 38,740. NEW YORK, MONDAY, FEBRUARY 17, 1964. TEN CENTS

CONGRESS EXPECTS ACCORD THIS WEEK ON TAX CUT BILL

Conferees Will Meet Today to Tackle the Remaining Conflicts Over Measure

HOUSING HEARING OPENS

Weaver to Explain Program to House Panel—College Proposal Up Thursday

By JOHN D. MORRIS
Special to The New York Times

WASHINGTON, Feb. 16—Quick agreement on the final version of the Administration's tax-reduction bill is expected this week as Congress resumes work after a six-day pause for Lincoln's Birthday.

Other major scheduled business includes the opening of hearings on housing and college student aid—programs that were submitted by President Johnson for action this session.

In addition, advocates of a strong manned-bomber force will again carry their fight to the House floor in debate on a $16.9 billion military procurement and research bill.

The tax bill, as passed by the Senate Feb. 7, provides $11.6 billion in annual tax relief for individuals and corporations through rate reductions coupled with structural revisions of the Revenue Code.

Conference Meets Today

The version passed by the House last September called for a net cut of slightly less than $11.1 billion.

A Senate-House conference committee meets tomorrow with the expectation of settling all differences in two or three days. Additional time will be required for staff work, however, and it is uncertain whether the final text will be ready for House and Senate approval before next week.

In any event the bill almost certainly will reach Mr. Johnson's desk for his prompt signature within 10 days or two weeks.

A lower income-tax withholding rate under such a schedule would go into effect early in March. The conference committee has already agreed on a provision for reduction of the 18 per cent withholding rate to 14 per cent, effective a week after the President signs the bill.

Two major issues face the conferees as they resume negotiations.

One involves a House-approved section, deleted by the Senate, for a $260 million cut in capital-gains taxes. Present indications are that the House

Continued on Page 11, Column 1

Roy Cohn Says U.S. Intercepts Mail

INDEFINITE – UNTIL CANCELED

POST OFFICE DEPARTMENT
ORDERS TO BOX SECTION OR OTHER SPECIAL ORDERS

DATE OF ORDER	NAME OF PERSON OR FIRM	OLD ADDRESS (or present street address)	NEW POST OFFICE BOX ADDRESS OR SPECIAL INSTRUCTIONS
3-29-63	THOMAS & MARIE BOLAN	238-07 121 AVE	CONFIDENTIAL SUBMIT ALL FIRST CLASS MAIL TO SUPERVISOR. DO NOT REVEAL THIS TO ADDRESSEE OR OTHER UNAUTHORIZED PERSON

POD Form 3986

Exhibit that was attached to papers submitted to Federal Court last week by Roy M. Cohn

By EDWARD RANZAL

Roy M. Cohn has asked for dismissal of a perjury indictment against him on the ground that the Government has been intercepting his mail and that of his lawyer for almost a year.

A copy of a purported special Post Office Department order for the interception of mail addressed to the home of Thomas A. Bolan, Mr. Cohn's lawyer, was attached to papers submitted to Federal Judge Archie O. Dawson last week in connection with the dismissal request.

Mr. Bolan, who is a member of Mr. Cohn's law firm of Saxe, Bacon & O'Shea, lives in Cambria Heights, Queens.

Judge Dawson ordered the Government to show cause on Feb. 28 why the indictment should not be dismissed. The court order also directs the Government to show cause why any evidence obtained as a result of the alleged interception should not be suppressed, and directs that any interceptions cease immediately.

Judge Dawson, who is in charge of all aspects of the perjury case, has scheduled the trial for March 16.

Mr. Cohn, former chief counsel to the Senate committee under the late Senator Joseph R. McCarthy, and another lawyer, Murray E. Gottesman, have been charged with lying before a grand jury investigating the United Dye and Chemical Corporation stock swindle.

The defendants also are charged with conspiring to obstruct justice by attempting to prevent indictments in the case against four men.

On the purported Post Office Department order is the heading, "Orders to Box Section or Other Special Orders." Printed in pen or pencil are the words "indefinite—until canceled."

The document pertaining to Mr. Bolan is dated March 29, 1963, and states:

"Confidential: Submit all first-class mail to supervisor. Do not reveal this to addressee

Continued on Page 10, Column 6

PANAMA INQUIRY SAID TO DISPUTE U.S. CONTENTIONS

Reported to Find Excessive Shooting During Rioting and Little Red Influence

Special to The New York Times

WASHINGTON, Feb. 16—An investigating committee of the Organization of American States was reported today to have found that Communist influence in last month's anti-United States riots in Panama was minimal.

It also found, after a week-long inquiry, that the firepower used by United States troops to keep Panamanian mobs from penetrating the Canal Zone was "disproportionate" to the threat posed to the security of the United States-occupied territory.

The five-nation committee also decided that the action of the United States forces, even if deemed excessive, did not justify Panama's charges of aggression.

Committee in Panama

The committee, still in Panama, was appointed by the Council of the inter-American organization to look into Panama's charges and to seek conciliation in the dispute.

[The head of the fact-finding group said in Panama that a formula for peace in the dispute would probably be presented to both sides Monday.]

A confidential account of the committee's investigation was received by Latin-American diplomats here over the weekend.

It conflicted on two basic points with the position taken by the United States. These were that "Castro Communist" agents trained in Cuba played a preponderant role in inciting the riots and that United States troops had acted with great discipline and restraint during the riots of Jan. 9 and 10. The disorders stemmed from a dispute over the flying of United States and Panamanian flags in the Canal Zone.

Sanctions Ruled Out

These differences were not considered, however, as giving validity to Panama's charges that the United States had turned the incidents into a "deliberate armed aggression."

It is understood, therefore, that the committee in its final report to the Council will declare that there is no ground to invoke any of the sanctions provided by the Rio de Janeiro Treaty of Reciprocal Assistance, under which the inquiry is being carried out.

Instead the investigating team will now concentrate on finding some formula acceptable to the two sides so that they can resume normal diplomatic relations and seek to remove the irritants that led to the trouble.

In reviewing the causes of the clashes, which left 24 persons dead and several hundred wounded, the committee will

Continued on Page 9, Column 1

Papandreou Party Wins in Greece

United Press International Radiophoto

George Papandreou, leader of Center Union party, as he voted yesterday in Athens during Greek national election.

By DAVID BINDER
Special to The New York Times

ATHENS, Monday, Feb. 17—George Papandreou's Center Union party won an overwhelming victory in the national election yesterday. With about 90 per cent of the ballots counted, the Center Union had 2,260,052 votes against 1,415,884 for the conservative party, the National Radical Union. The pro-Communist United Democratic Left party, which backed the Center Union in 24 of 55 districts, had 499,611. Panayotis Canellopoulos, National Radical Union leader, said in a statement conceding defeat that his

Continued on Page 4, Column 4

U. S. AND BRITAIN DRAFT NEW PLANS FOR CYPRUS PEACE

Ball and Officials in London Agree to Isolate Makarios With Diplomatic Effort

RESOLUTION PREPARED

U.N. Will Be Asked to Back International Patrol Force and Neutral Mediator

By LAWRENCE FELLOWS
Special to The New York Times

LONDON, Feb. 16 — The lines of a two-pronged approach to the Cyprus problem by London and Washington emerged today from talks between British officials and the American Under Secretary of State, George W. Ball.

First, according to diplomatic sources, there will be an effort to achieve, as completely as possible, the diplomatic isolation of Archbishop Makarios, the Cypriote President.

The second objective, taking shape on the horizon, is an attempt to end the island's communal fighting by administrative partition between the Greek and Turkish Cypriote factions, these sources said.

Britain Drafts Resolution

The first diplomatic step was taken last night when Britain, with the support of the United States, called for an early meeting of the United Nations Security Council "to consider the urgent problems raised by the deterioration of security in Cyprus."

Tonight final touches were put on a resolution that Britain plans to introduce in the Security Council tomorrow. It calls for a mandate to establish a peace-keeping force in Cyprus, and for the appointment of a neutral mediator to settle the quarrel between the communities.

[In Nicosia, President Makarios addressed Cyprus by radio for the first time since the fighting erupted Christmas week. He said internal anarchy and foreign intervention posed grave threats.]

Ball Voices Gratitude

Mr. Ball left for New York today after conferring with Foreign Secretary R. A. Butler. On his departure, he stressed that Washington and London were in complete accord on the Cyprus question.

The Under Secretary also praised the British troops who have been guarding the tenuous peace in Cyprus.

As he spoke, the Ministry of Defense prepared to establish intermediate military headquarters in several parts of Cyprus to permit quicker responses to local outbreaks of violence.

A further squadron of Life Guards prepared to leave for Cyprus to build up the force trained and equipped to use armored patrol cars.

In planning the Security Council action, London aimed to block an attempt by Archbishop Makarios to bring about a vote on a resolution of his own, which the United States and Britain regard as dangerous on several counts.

Within a few days Washington and London hope to move toward persuading the Greek and Turkish Governments to support a compromise solution

Continued on Page 3, Column 1

Alabama Compiling Files On Civil Rights Advocates

By CLAUDE SITTON
Special to The New York Times

MONTGOMERY, Ala., Feb. 14—An intelligence network of state agencies and officials is amassing information on civil rights advocates and others at the direction of Gov. George C. Wallace. Its components, which generally have only informal ties with one another, sometimes work openly.

Far more frequently however, their activities and the results are secret.

Their interest extends beyond Alabamians. They have given considerable attention to Negro leaders, Justice Department officials, newsmen and others who have come into the state during racial crises.

Intimidation Seen

In this racial aspect the operation is similar to those found in Mississippi and Louisiana. But in terms of over-all scope and amount of activity the intelligence network seems to be unparalleled in this country.

State officials say that the information being obtained will not be misused to bring pressure, political or otherwise, on anyone.

Nevertheless, the investigations alone have served as a means of intimidation in some cases. And after one such inquiry a Negro student was expelled from the University of Alabama after having won admission under a Federal court order.

Governor Wallace controls all the agencies involved, either di-

Continued on Page 16, Column 1

GOLDWATER SAYS HE HAS 450 VOTES

Finds 125 More 'Practically Sure'—655 Are Needed for G.O.P. Nomination

Special to The New York Times

CHICAGO, Feb. 16—Senator Barry Goldwater today claimed 450 "sure" votes for the Presidential nomination at the Republican National Convention in July, plus 125 more "practically sure" votes.

The total, he said, does not include votes he hopes to win in primary elections in California, New Hampshire and Oregon.

To win the nomination, 655 votes are needed.

Mr. Goldwater also said that he did not believe any candidate could be nominated without winning the California primary, which will be held on June 2. It is the last primary in the nation and the largest, with its prize of 86 convention votes.

This is the first time Mr. Goldwater has said his nomination would be impossible if he lost in California. His only opponent there is Governor Rockefeller of New York.

The Senator declared that he also planned to fight for delegates in New York. He is known to feel privately that he has a chance to pick up as many as 22 of the state's 92 votes if he challenges Mr. Rockefeller there, an estimate considered very high by most observers.

Mr. Goldwater did not docu-

Continued on Page 19, Column 3

MARCH IS PLANNED BY PUERTO RICANS

50 Leaders Schedule Protest for March 1 at City Hall to Seek Equal Schools

Puerto Rican organizations agreed yesterday to stage a silent march on City Hall on March 1 to dramatize their demands for equal educational opportunities in all of the city's schools.

A spokesman for the organizations said that the plan was for the marchers to assemble at 3 P.M. the day of the march in the vicinity of Varick and Canal Streets.

He said that invitations would be extended not only to Puerto Ricans but also to all Spanish-speaking residents of New York City.

The organizations made plans for the march at a meeting held at the La Ronda Cafe, 2689 Broadway, near 103d Street. About 50 leaders of the major Puerto Rican organizations here attended.

Gilberto Valentin, executive secretary for the National Association for Puerto Rican Civil Rights, was named president of the parade committee. He said that the proposed second school boycott was not discussed at the meeting.

"We went along with the first boycott because we felt it was a good method of highlighting the discrimination," he said. "We haven't decided on the second."

The Puerto Rican leaders said

Continued on Page 22, Column 1

SEA UNIONS RESIST U.S. ON WHEAT BAN

Will Cease Loading Soviet Grain Today, Despite Pleas

By DAMON STETSON
Special to The New York Times

BAL HARBOUR, Fla., Feb. 16—The International Longshoremen's Association went ahead today with plans to stop loading wheat for shipment to the Soviet Union tomorrow despite urgent appeals from Washington.

There were indications that the longshoremen might be willing to relax their prohibition if given assurances that at least 50 per cent of the wheat shipments would be carried in United States vessels.

However, neither Thomas Gleason, president of the I.L.A., nor Paul Hall, head of the Maritime Trades Department of the American Federation of Labor and Congress of Industrial Organizations, seemed to be in a mood to accept such assurances without iron-clad guarantees that they would be enforced.

Mr. Gleason said the longshoremen had opposed the wheat deal in the first place and had agreed last fall to load ships only at the urging of President Kennedy.

But he contended that the Administration had "reneged" on an agreement to ship half of the grain in vessels of the Unit-

Continued on Page 52, Column 7

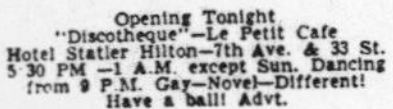

4 Beatles and How They Grew

Publicitywise

By McCANDLISH PHILLIPS

The Beatles will fly back to England late this week, having accomplished exactly what they set out to do: stir up such a whirlwind in America as to heap tinder on the enormous bonfire they have lit in Britain.

The small British cultural expedition is now resting at Miami Beach, limp from adulation.

The Beatles are undisputed titans of American popular music, a high-yield, low-security occupation. Their fame has swept two continents, and they may yet become the vocal scourge of the whole Western world.

They and their attendant frenzy, Beatlemania, did not just happen. They were brought to their present pre-eminence in latter-day vaudeville by artful contrivance.

That is not the whole explanation. The world is full of promotional wizards who would do as well, if they could. However, if an act can be manipulated to a certain vogue, all the engines of publicity can then rush to its disposal.

That is what happened here.

The Beatles could not have done what they did in America had they not done what they first did in Britain. There are so many acts here in the Rock

Continued on Page 20, Column 3

Moneywise

By MARTIN ARNOLD

Beatleggers are trying to grab a large share of the Beatle merchandising boom.

Paul G. Marshall, the group's American lawyer, said yesterday that he was investigating at least 60 cases of the use of the Beatle name without Beatle approval. Such Beatleware as shirts, hats, slacks, pajamas and wigs are involved.

Mr. Marshall said that on Saturday he obtained a State Supreme Court preliminary injunction stopping a Brooklyn company from manufacturing shirts with the name Beetles—in bugs—stamped on front.

He also said that he was asking the New York District Attorney to investigate at least two cases of the criminal piracy of the Beatle name. Similar investigations are under way in California, Pennsylvania and Rhode Island, he said.

Nicky Byrne, president of Seltaeb (Beatles spelled backward), Inc., the Beatles' licensing agent, has predicted that Americans will spend about $50 million on Beatle products in 1964. He said yesterday that he hoped to have a Beatle motor-scooter, manufactured in Europe, on the market in the United States soon.

A Beatlemobile (for adults)

Continued on Page 20, Column 3

Peoplewise

By JOHN A. OSMUNDSEN

Even before they return as promised to their native England, they have set minds across the United States to wondering what the uproar was all about.

They—the Beatles, of course—were seen and heard by, and conquered, millions of Americans.

How, people are asking, could four mop-headed, neo-Edwardian-attired, Liverpudlian-accented, guitar-playing, drum-beating, "little boys" from across the ocean come here and attract the immense amount of attention they did by stomping and hollering out songs in a musical idiom that is distinctly American?

Ask a typical Beatle fan—female, in her early teens—and she will say it is because:

"They're so keee-ooot."

Or because:

"They're different! They're just so different!"

Adults, some but not all of whom view the Beatles somewhat cynically, are likely to say that the craze sprang from the high-powered promotion that the performers received before their arrival and throughout their stay.

Social scientists agree with both the adult and teen-age views but note that, no matter

Continued on Page 20, Column 7

3 Americans Die in Blast At Saigon Movie Theater

By PETER GROSE
Special to The New York Times

SAIGON, South Vietnam, Monday, Feb. 17—A terrorist bomb exploded in the lobby of a movie theater of the American community here last night. Three Americans were killed and at least 50 were injured.

Confusion and indignation spread among American residents of the capital as investigators studied the bold attack, the second bombing in a week apparently directed against American servicemen and dependents.

A week ago tonight a bomb exploded under the grandstand at an American softball park, killing two servicemen and injuring 23 other Americans.

Added Protection Sought

The United States chargé d'affaires, David Ness, scheduled an urgent meeting with the South Vietnamese Premier, Maj. Gen. Nguyen Khanh, later today. They will "discuss the security measures to be taken to offer the American community maximum protection," the United States Embassy said.

One of the dead in the theater blast was unidentified. The two others, one a marine captain and the other a military policeman, had been standing in the lobby.

A spokesman said there was some evidence that the policeman had died of a shot in the neck. Some witnesses reported that he was shot as the bomb was planted, but witnesses' versions were confused and could not be officially confirmed.

An unspecified number of women and children were injured, the embassy said. Most were treated at a hospital for superficial wounds and released. Seven persons, six

Continued on Page 5, Column 1

ETHIOPIA CHARGES TRUCE IS BROKEN

Says Somali Troops Attack Three Points at Frontier—Addis Ababa Accused

Special to The New York Times

ADDIS ABABA, Ethiopia, Feb. 16 — Ethiopia charged tonight that troops from Somalia attacked the Ethiopian border towns of Dolo and Yet two hours after a cease-fire became effective at noon today.

[Somalia charged that Ethiopian troops had penetrated Somali territory at 12 places, The Associated Press reported from Mogadiscio.]

The Ethiopian report said Somali attempts to occupy Dolo had been repulsed. Later another Ethiopian town, Ferfer, was shelled, it was reported.

Foreign Minister Ato Ketema Yifru described the attacks as a deliberate and serious breach of the cease-fire agreement. Ethiopia is informing the Organization of African Unity and U Thant, Secretary General of the United Nations.

The truce was called for by the Council of Ministers of the African group on Friday. Acceptance by both Somalia and Ethiopia was announced yesterday.

Artillery Fire Reported

ADDIS ABABA, Feb. 16 (AP)—The Ethiopian Information Ministry said today that Somali troops had attacked the towns of Dolo and Yet under cover of artillery fire.

A Somali attack yesterday, before the cease-fire went into effect, was repulsed with heavy losses, a ministry spokesman asserted.

The Somali radio in a countercharge said that Ethiopian shelling had killed three Somali civilians and destroyed half the village.

"The Ethiopians went all-out to wreak the maximum damage

Continued on Page 8, Column 5

Churchmen Uphold Right to Be Atheist

By HENRY TANNER
Special to The New York Times

MOSCOW, Feb. 16 — The Executive Committee of the World Council of Churches, meeting in Odessa, has approved the principle that every man must have a legal right either to believe in religion or to be an atheist.

The Rev. Dr. O. Frederic Nolde of New York announced the committee's view at a news conference he held jointly here tonight with other members of the Executive Committee. Dr. Nolde is chairman of the Council's International Affairs Commission.

The Rev. Dr. W. A. Visser 't Hooft of the Netherlands, secretary general of the Council, and Dr. Franklin Clark Fry,

Continued on Page 2, Column 4

17 Gershwin Songs Are to Be Released

By MURRAY SCHUMACH
Special to The New York Times

HOLLYWOOD, Feb. 16—Seventeen unpublished compositions by George Gershwin, who died in 1937, are to be made public by his brother, Ira.

Perhaps more important than the Gershwin music that is now being made available is the fact that there is a much larger storehouse of Gershwin compositions in the composer's notebooks, which date back to 1920.

Portions of the pieces have been sent to George Balanchine by André Kostelanetz, the conductor, with the permission of the composer's brother, who wrote the lyrics for most of the Gershwin songs in Hollywood and on Broadway. Three others will be used in a film.

Mr. Kostelanetz has asked the

Continued on Page 26, Column 4

Soviet Family Law To Protect Children

By THEODORE SHABAD
Special to The New York Times

MOSCOW, Feb. 16—A Soviet law being drafted on marriage and the family will make an unmarried father responsible for his children.

The new legislation, to be published shortly, will also simplify present complicated and expensive divorce proceedings without returning to the "postcard" divorces of the early Soviet period—so called because either spouse could divorce the other simply by mailing a notice to the Bureau of Vital Statistics.

Details of a reform of the family law, long in preparation, were disclosed today by Olga P. Kolchina, a member of the Bills Committee of the

Continued on Page 2, Column 3

NEWS INDEX

HOW THEY GREW, PUBLICITYWISE

Continued From Page 1, Col. 3

'n' Roll idiom that it is difficult for one act to resolve itself out of the mass and stand forth in bold relief.

But having become a phenomenon in the newer and far less glutted British market, the Beatles could come to this country at the level to which they had lately become accustomed. They simply followed their fame across the Atlantic.

At their present peak, the Beatles face an awful prospect of demise. They are a craze. Anyone at the center of a craze finds that everything he touches turns to money. But since a craze is a form of inflation, it may precede a crash.

Everything that makes a craze—novelty, popularity, excitement, publicity, talk, satiric attack—must be constantly renewed. Fresh sensations, new exploits must be contrived.

If the Beatles had fizzled here their celebrity might have been undermined in Britain. But by show business reckoning they have scored a huge success, and the British have been entertained with gaudy accounts of the act's conquest of the Yankee branch of the English-speaking peoples.

In nine days in this country, the Beatles have made a deep impression on the American subculture.

Night and Day

They can look with gratification at the dominance of "the Liverpool sound" on those American radio stations consecrated, day and night, to rock 'n' roll, at staggering and skyrocketing sales of their records, at a thriving trade in costume wigs and at a public whose appetite for their wares has been aroused but, presumably, not sated.

The Beatles barely touched the American market. They could have barnstormed the nation, doing one-night stands at major sports arenas and concert halls in 20 or 30 cities.

They might have made several million dollars. But they are due back in Britain to do a motion picture about themselves.

The quartet expects to return in August for a tour that will more nearly realize the potential of their vogue, presuming it will last.

And they are still to reap a bonanza of publicity in this country: before the end of the month, three of the biggest national magazines will display them on their covers, with long supporting stories inside.

This morning, when those in the music trade scan the weekly charts of record sales and demand, they will see that the Beatles stand No. 1 across the board—in Billboard, Cash Box, Music Vendor, Music Reporter, Variety.

Enter Royalty

A year ago, Beatle records were on the American market but they bombed—they made an impressive record of non-sales. But that was before they had the attention of the Queen Mother and Princess Margaret (for whom they did a Royal Variety Show in November), the Prime Minister (his plane once could not take off because of the Beatle-greeters that thronged London Airport) and all Britain.

The Beatles' top record, "I Want to Hold Your Hand," released by Capitol Records in late December, has sold almost 2.6 million copies, and is expected to reach 3.5 million.

What brought the Beatles to their present station in Britain, and how was it transferred here whole?

Brian Epstein, the pink-faced young man who discovered and remade and who now manages the act, sunk his shoes into the deep pile of light tan broadloom in a lavish 12th-floor suite of the Plaza Hotel the other day, seated himself in an ivory-toned settee and discoursed upon the Rise of the Beatles.

As the operator of a family concern of record stores, he said, he wanted to build its pop record business. He found the Beatles—the name was not his creation—in October, 1961, about 100 yards from his Liverpool office in a dingy private basement that had been made into a sort of teen-age hangout. They had been working in amateur shows and music dens for about two years.

"I saw four boys with very little stage presentation. They had scrubby haircuts and scrubby clothes—black jackets and jeans. But I recognized the appeal of their beat and I rather liked their humor. Through it all came a quality of personal presence and of personality that seemed to me to be full of possibilities. I got friendly with them and became their manager."

Telephone Calls Come

"Just a sec," Mr. Epstein said seizing the telephone. Calls, calls, calls came during the interview, three of them in one 70-second stretch. Mr. Epstein conducts his telephone business in decisive monosyllables—"Yes," "No," "Quite," "Soon," "Can't"—with "No" predominating.

He picked up the thread of his narrative:

He booked the act in "tiny clubs, cabarets, church halls, youth centers, then to some of the better ballrooms and bigger ballrooms and then to theaters and finally to the concert stage."

"One did everything. One worked very hard. One shouted from the rooftops about this group when there was no enthusiasm for groups. People thought you were mad, but you went on shouting."

Until the Beatles played the London Palladium last October, he said, they had been just an increasingly important group in the entertainment realm. "The press and everybody began to come round," he said, "and it was at the Palladium that they became national." The Royal performance soon followed.

Ed Sullivan, a dealer in momentary sensations, was in Britain with his wife when the British teen public was beginning to wax apoplectic over the act. He saw a crowd of thousands squealing at London Airport.

"I made up my mind that this was the same sort of mass hit hysteria that had characterized the Elvis Presley days," Mr. Sullivan said in a telephone interview from Miami Beach.

Mr. Sullivan, who had given Mr. Presley a three-time exposure on his television program, negotiated with Mr. Epstein for some time and finally signed the Beatles for his Sunday evening show. He did not pay them a record amount.

At the Plaza, Mr. Epstein said that the most important thing to him was top billing and that he had dickered with Mr. Sullivan for two days on that score.

Just about everyone who has had anything to do with the Beatles' American adventure agrees that the signal that touched off the Beatle race in this country was their signing for three appearances on the Sullivan show. Three consecutive appearances on that show is to come on with a very loud bang in American show business.

Jack Paar was also in England when the Beatles made it big there, and he brought back a video tape that he put on his television show on Jan. 3 — well ahead of the live appearance on the Sullivan show five weeks later.

Word Reaches the U. S.

Word of the Beatles' British successes began to reach the American public. On Dec. 1, The New York Times magazine ran a piece from London under the title "Britons Succomb to 'Beatlemania.'" Later, those who had a stake in promoting the Beatles made lavish mention of that account.

In rapid succession, news magazines, trade publications, wire services, network television news shows and newspapers ran colorful Beatle stories. Variety reported that Beatle disks were "the U. K.'s hottest ever on the pop disc charts"— a report that made record makers act.

On Jan. 31, Life Magazine did an eight-page, 17-picture lead story titled "Four Screaming Mopheads Break Up England: Here Come Those Beatles;" this was accompanied by a story written in what is known as the "Gee Whiz!" idiom of American journalism.

The nation's rock 'n' roll disk jockeys went to incredible lengths to lay their lives, their fortunes and their sacred honor at the Beatles' feet. This was the most important factor in whipping up the young female population to demonstrative enthusiasm.

Capitol Aide Speaks

A north-looking picture window high in the Sperry Rand Building on the Avenue of the Americas at 52d Street forms one entire wall of the office of Brown Meggs, a handsome, sharp-featured young executive who is director of eastern operations for Capitol Records.

It was after-hours when he spoke of his involvement with the Beatles.

"I've been on full-time Beatle duty since—the date is indelibly imprinted on my mind—Jan. 6, when I returned from vacation," he said. "All this came at once, everything happened in a tremendously concentrated period.

"I'm awfully tired, but Beatles only come along once in a decade, if that."

He said that Capitol had rushed its Beatles releases to the trade well ahead of schedule because of a rising demand spurred by news accounts. To increase the demand, the company sent a million copies of a four-page tabloid full of publicity on the Beatles to disk jockeys, buyers and the press.

Capitol also supplied a seven-inch long-playing record to disk jockeys at hundreds of independent stations. The disk featured three Beatles songs and an "open-end interview with the Beatles."

The interview—a prolonged introductory plug to the quartet's "I Want to Hold Your Hand" recording—allowed every important disk jockey in the country to give the impression he was interviewing the Beatles himself.

A question-and-answer was provided so the interviewer could ask questions to fit the answers the Beatles had recorded in England.

"What sells records is radio," Mr. Meggs declared. "The Beatles got unbelievable radio play. There wasn't a single market in the country in which the air play wasn't simply stupendous."

Stations Promote Group

In New York, the hard-core rock 'n' roll stations—WINS, WABC and WMCA—did whatever they could to link their names to the Beatles.

In their genial conspiracy to promote the Beatles, so that Beatlemania would in turn promote them, the disk jockeys made it abundantly clear where young people could go to greet the group.

About 3,000 young fans met the Beatles at Kennedy Airport, the heaviest turnout anyone there could remember.

There were reports that Beatle crowds had been encouraged by the distribution of money. The principal of a girls' high school in the Bronx said that a man from a record company called the school last Tuesday and offered $75 to the student aid fund if any girl could give the four Beatles' real names within five minutes.

One girl said that several friends had been offered tickets to see the Beatles and $5 each to go in and "make like you're crazy."

When the man who headed the corps of 18 press agents that handled the quartet's appearances here was told this, he exploded.

"That's an outright lie," he said. "It's patently absurd. In these circumstances it would be inane. That is phony baloney."

But he scribbled notes on the details with the angry air of a man who was going to look into it.

Mr. Epstein had been determined to give his overworked act a chance for a brief vacation by doing only the three Sullivan shows. He rebuffed agents who sought other appearances.

But Sidney Bernstein, then an agent for the General Artists Corporation, broke Mr. Epstein's resistance by trans-Atlantic phone and got him to agree to try an Evening With the Beatles at Carnegie Hall. The Beatles got $10,500 for two back-to-back appearances at Carnegie Hall.

The producers, Mr. Bernstein, Walter Heiman, a textile manufacturer, and Hank Baron, a syrup manufacturer, also tried to get Mr. Epstein to put the Beatles in Madison Square Garden.

They offered $20,000 for one performance plus a $5,000 contribution to the British Cancer Fund. But Mr. Epstein stood in the middle of the empty arena, looking up at tier on tier of empty seats and said quietly:

"Let's do it when we get back to the United States."

Notable Event: Arrival of the Beatles in the U.S.

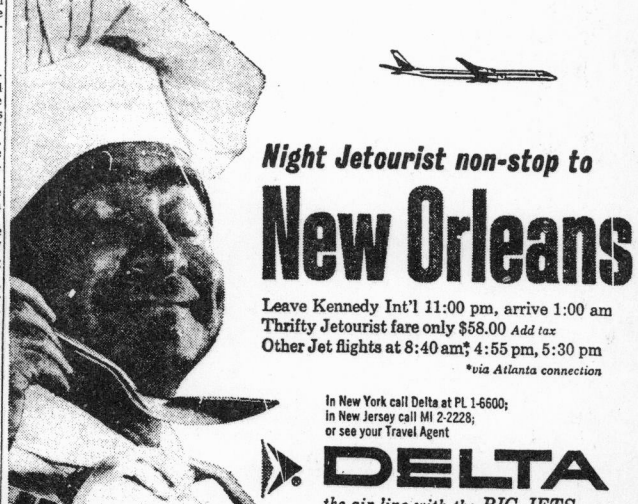

Young people striving to get past police line when the Beatles arrived at Kennedy Airport

The New York Times

The Beatles, from left: Paul McCartney, 21 years old, Ringo Starr, 23, George Harrison, 21, and John Lennon, 23.

Peoplewise, the Beatles Provide New Study for the Sociologists

Continued From Page 1, Col. 5

how effective the promotion of the Beatles may have been, the public response to them was real and deserves a deeper probe for its origins within the needs and attitudes of the Beatlemaniac himself.

Practically every standard explanation in the book has been offered by psychologists and psychiatrists for Beatlemania. The Beatles, these analyses say, serve as symbols of:

¶Adolescent revolt against parental authority.

¶Status that comes from belonging to a group, in this case, of other Beatlemaniacs.

¶Sex, both from the supposed erotic nature of the Beatles' music and the way they perform it and from the appeal they seem to have to the "mother instinct."

¶Success by persons who are seen as fellow teen-agers (although none of the Beatles are under 21) and as underdogs who came from the wrong side of the tracks and have made good.

¶The frenetically felt urgency for having a good time and living life fast in an uncertain world plagued with mortal dangers.

Deeper Reason Seen

Any or all of those explanations of Beatlemania may be more or less correct, in the opinion of a young Barnard College sociologist whose shoulder-length brown hair tends to flop Veronica Lake-fashion over one eye and who remembers attending a "Hit Parade" broadcast in the midst of girls her own age who shrieked and swooned into their bobby socks over Frank Sinatra.

But she thinks the most important answers to the Beatlemania question run much deeper than sex and status. She believes, moreover, that the phenomenon could serve as an ideal subject for a sociological study of the dynamics of fads and crazes and of social stratification.

The sociologist's name is Renee Claire Fox. She is an assistant professor of sociology at Barnard, but her researches have taken her as far away in the last two years as Belgium, where she studied the conduct of medical research and the scientists who do it, and the Congo.

Although those experiences do not qualify her as an expert on such matters as Beatlemania, her general sociological training has given her insight into the kinds of questions that could be asked about such a phenomenon.

In fact, she has developed a theory to explain Beatlemania and last week even explored ways of testing it as an exercise for students in the course on sociological research that she teaches.

Dr. Fox's theory is essentially this: The wide range of the Beatles' appeal stems from their personification of many forms of duality that exist in our society.

The Beatles, she says, constitute a treasure trove of such dualities.

For example, she explains, they are male and yet have many feminine characteristics, especially their floppy hairdos. They also play the dual roles of both adults and children. And they appear to be good boys who nevertheless dress and pose as bad ones—London's Teddy-boys.

Their fancy, Edwardian clothes suggest a sort of sophistication that, Dr. Fox believes, contrasts further with their "homespun" style of performance.

Poor Boys Make Good

Much has been made of their poor, lower-class backgrounds in Northern England. Yet they are accepted by the upper crust, having attracted the auspicious attention of the Queen Mother, Princess Margaret, Mrs. Nelson A. Rockefeller and President Johnson, the latter through a statement by White House Press Secretary Pierre Salinger.

Nor is this all. The Beatles, in their personal appearances, sing and play but seldom can be heard above the shrieks of the audience, and so they almost play the role of mimes. In addition, Dr. Fox observes, the four are both an audience for their own antics and for those of their cavorting, screaming audience, acting, as it were, a play within a play.

"There is a Chaplinesque quality to their style," Dr. Fox said. "They convey the image of absurd little men in an absurd, big world, bewildered but bemused by it at the same time."

Adults Are Fans, Too

The Barnard social scientist observes that here, as in England, the appeal of the Beatles is not confined to girls in their teens and younger, but spreads to boys and to many adults of both sexes.

She says she thinks that at least part of the attraction for adults lies in the Beatles's realistic attitudes toward their own success and their eventual eclipse.

In the Beatles, Dr. Fox believes, people see four basically nice young boys who project some of the same contradictions that exist in many Americans, who are having a wonderful time at the acceptable expense of both themselves and their audiences, who have expressed their gratitude for this fling and who have promised a graceful adjustment to the time when the party will be over.

It would seem, to paraphrase W. C. Fields, that someone who possesses all those qualities can't be all bad, no matter what some parents have been driven to think.

Beatleggers Trying to Capture A Share of Success, Moneywise

Continued From Page 1, Col. 4

is under consideration, he added.

But the field in which Beatlegging has become greatest is in the sale of Beatle clothing.

The only American company licensed to manufacture Beatleware is the Reliance Manufacturing Company, which heretofore has turned out such conservative items as Marlboro shirts for men.

Miles Rubin, Reliance president, said that the company already had sold in the United States Beatle merchandise valued at $1.4 milion wholesale, or more than $2.5 million retail.

"We had almost a tongue-in-cheek attitude when we first got into this," Mr. Rubin said, "but it turned out to be the biggest promotion in our 60 years in business."

He added that Reliance factories were "smoking night and day to meet the Beatle demand."

Included in this are 2,000 dozen Beatle hats, selling for $22.50 a dozen wholesale. Since Feb. 11, Mr. Rubin said, 3,200 dozen Beatle items have been sold to outlets in Canada for $100,000, wholesale.

The cheapest Beatleware sold by Reliance is a Beatle T-shirt, which retails for $2.98.

"We are now readying Beatle beach shirts for the better shops," Mr. Rubin said. "These will sell at $29.95, retail."

Range Is Wide

Between the T-shirts and the beach shirts are a wide range of pajamas, tight-fitting Beatle pants, sweatshirts and three-button tennis shirts.

The tennis shirts are perhaps the nattiest of all Beatle items. They are pale blue with white piping and, like all Beatleware, are embossed with pictures of the Beatles and their signatures.

Mr. Rubin said that all this business had burgeoned in the last two weeks, since his company signed the contracts with Seltaeb.

Mr. Rubin said he had uncovered 17 cases of Beatlegging in the city, "but some of them may overlap because they involve manufacturers and stores and what we now think is three cases, for example, may end up one case."

He said his lawyers planned to move this week against several textile printers in New York. These companies, he said, actually print the Beatles' pictures on shirts.

"All our Beatle sales have been by telephone order so far, directly to the New York office," Mr. Rubin said.

Salesmen Check Stores

Reliance and its subsidiary companies have 200 salesmen throughout the country, and not one has written up a Beatle order, Mr. Rubin said.

"But," he added, "we use them for policing. Each day each salesman has to compile lists of stores in his area selling Beatle items."

These lists are then phoned to New York, where they are checked against a master list.

"If we find a store that is not on our master list selling Beatle items we notify our attorney and he takes action," Mr. Rubin said.

The suddenness of the Beatle merchandising boom can best be illustrated by the rise of Seltaeb: it was formed in New York three weeks ago and has opened, or plans to open, offices in France, South Africa, Australia and Japan. Seltaeb, in turn, was licensed by Nems Enterprises, Ltd., of London, which controls all Beatle sales throughout the world.

Beatle wigs are made legally in the United States only by the Lowell Toy Company, which has been turning them out at the rate of 15,000 a day.

Beatle dolls, soon to be on the American market, are being manufactured by Remco Industries, Inc.

No one involved would say yesterday just what cut of the profits the Beatles themselves got, but everyone concerned reports that the Beatles are happy with the boom.

Girls in Miami Shriek Welcome to the Beatles

MIAMI BEACH, Fla., Feb. 16 (AP)—Shrieking teen-age girls welcomed the Beatles tonight, but the situation remained in hand.

The youngsters were outnumbered by middle-aged people watching the quartet as it appeared on the Ed Sullivan Show, televised from the Napoleon Room of the Deauville Hotel.

Policemen and the hotel's security force were everywhere in the big room but there were no incidents, in contrast to the quartet's arrival at Miami International Airport last Thursday, when windows were broken, automobiles damaged and youngsters cut by flying glass.

About 3,200 were in the audience. Hundreds were turned away because the seating capacity was reduced to accommodate television equipment. Traffic was congested for blocks surrounding the oceanfront hotel.

The Beatles originally planned to return to New York tomorrow, but Brian Summerville, their spokesman, said: "We like it here and the people seem to like us and we're staying on until Friday."

He said the group would return to New York that day, and depart for London at 8 P.M.

"All the News That's Fit to Print"

The New York Times.

LATE CITY EDITION
U. S. Weather Bureau Report (Page 52) forecasts: Fair and hot today and tomorrow. Chance of late showers each day.
Temp. Range: 91—71; yesterday: 80—65.
Temp.-Hum. Index: 80 to 85; yesterday: 74.

VOL. CXIII..No. 38,864. | NEW YORK, SATURDAY, JUNE 20, 1964. | TEN CENTS

CIVIL RIGHTS BILL PASSED, 73-27; JOHNSON URGES ALL TO COMPLY; DIRKSEN BERATES GOLDWATER

U.S. STRESSING IT WOULD FIGHT TO DEFEND ASIA

WARNING TO REDS

Commitment to Laos and South Vietnam Called Unlimited

By MAX FRANKEL
Special to The New York Times

WASHINGTON, June 19—The Administration is saying more emphatically each day that North Vietnam and its closest ally, Communist China, must leave their neighbors alone or face a war with the United States.

In the minds of officials here the United States commitment to the security of Southeast Asia is now unlimited and comparable with the commitment to West Berlin.

In diplomatic terms this means the officials find themselves unable to negotiate with anything except the threat of force to persuade the Asian Communists to stop the efforts to "liberate" South Vietnam and Laos.

Thus far, the Administration is not sure that the Asian Communists have accurately interpreted the warning signals from Washington. It is not sure that its allies in Europe appreciate the gravity of the United States commitment. And it is not sure that the American people understand the reasons for it.

Decision Publicized

Accordingly, the word is being passed with increasing vigor to the Congress, to the Washington press corps and to the Western allies.

These official assertions suggest that the decision to deny Southeast Asia to Communism was, in effect, taken a long time ago through circumstance and a cumulative series of lesser decisions.

The view that Laos can somehow be handled separately from South Vietnam has been abandoned. The earlier emphasis on limited involvement in South Vietnam's guerrilla war has been replaced by unlimited pledges of support for the whole region.

The hope here is that Hanoi and Peking are alert to this hardening of attitudes and that they have been properly forewarned by the less direct as well as public utterances of Administration leaders and, particularly, by the recent involvement of United States military planes in Laos.

Compromise Doubted

The subtleties of the situation have made the Administration reticent to discuss future military moves beyond hints that every violation of past agreements in Southeast Asia and every change in the forms of contest will draw a firm response.

All the comments here stress that the choice between war and peace lies in the hands of the Asian Communists because Washington sees no way of negotiating a compromise. It will not sit down with Peking and Hanoi until recent violations of past agreements for Laos are redressed because it could have no confidence in any new agreement.

To some extent, the Adminis-

Continued on Page 7, Column 1

JOHNSON IS FIRM

Vows in California to Oppose Violators of Freedom in World

By TOM WICKER
Special to The New York Times

SAN FRANCISCO, June 19—President Johnson promised tonight to open an "offensive in the pursuit of peace" based on an overwhelming military power that "makes it possible to seek agreement without fearing loss of liberty."

The President, addressing an audience of nearly 2,500 at a Democratic party fund-raising dinner, also pledged stern American opposition to "those who believe they can violate their neighbor's borders and steal their neighbor's freedom."

At the end of a day in California during which he gave several indications that he expected to be President for at least four more years, Mr. Johnson said he wanted to double the size of the Peace Corps, pursue what he called the "great society" with "the vision and valor of pioneers" and achieve "full equality for all our people."

Earlier in the day, after an enthusiastic welcome from more than 300,000 San Franciscans who lined Market Street to see his motorcade, the President came as near as he ever has to predicting his election in November.

Predicts the Good Life

"A Government which can get things done and knows where it is going," he said, is "the kind of Government you have had for the past four years—and that is the kind of Government you are going to get for the next four years."

Mr. Johnson's remarks were made at the dedication of a new Federal office building in downtown San Francisco. Before coming here, he also spoke at Edwards Air Force Base in the Mojave Desert and broke ground for a new Oakland Bay area rapid transit system at ceremonies in Concord.

It was not until tonight, when he attended the $100-a-plate fund-raising dinner, that Mr. Johnson played an openly political role.

At every stop he voiced his prophecies of the good life for every American, promising Californians the lion's share.

At the party dinner, he shifted his emphasis somewhat, detailing the increases since 1960 in American military might. He declared:

"We have used that strength not to intimidate others, but to

Continued on Page 6, Column 4

SENATOR KENNEDY HURT IN AIR CRASH; BAYH INJURED, TOO

Both Are in Fair Condition in Massachusetts Hospital —Pilot of Plane Killed

By The Associated Press

SOUTHAMPTON, Mass., Saturday, June 20—Senator Edward M. Kennedy, younger brother of President Kennedy, and Senator Birch Bayh were injured in the crash of a private plane last night while on the way to the Massachusetts Democratic Convention.

The pilot was killed and two other persons were injured. Mr. Kennedy was semiconscious.

Both Senators were reported in fair condition at Cooley Dickinson Hospital in nearby Northampton.

Also injured were Mrs. Bayh, reported in good condition, and Edward Moss of Andover, administrative aide to Mr. Kennedy, who was reported in critical condition.

Associated Press
Senator Edward M. Kennedy

The pilot was identified as Edwin J. Zimny, 48 years old, of Lawrence, a last-minute substitute for the regular Kennedy pilot.

Senator Kennedy, Democrat of Massachusetts, was treated in an emergency room for back and chest injuries. His wife, Joan, visited him after he was transferred to an intensive-care unit.

Senator Bayh, Democrat of Indiana, suffered a hip injury. Mrs. Bayh was reported suffering from shock.

Mr. Kennedy's parents, Mr. and Mrs. Joseph P. Kennedy, who were vacationing at their summer home in Hyannis Port, were not told of the plane crash.

Attorney General Robert F. Kennedy, brother of the Senator, boarded the family plane with an aide and was reported on the way to Boston.

Two Civil Aeronautics Board investigators were sent from

Continued on Page 54, Column 1

PRESIDENT'S PLEA

He Declares the Task Now Is to Change Law Into Custom

Special to The New York Times

SAN FRANCISCO, June 19—President Johnson called the Senate passage of his civil rights bill today a "challenge to men of good will in every part of the country to transform the commands of our law into the customs of our land."

Mr. Johnson said it was now the nation's task "to reach beyond the content of the bill to conquer the barriers of poor education, poverty, and squalid housing which are an inheritance of past injustice and an impediment to future advance."

He said that he did not "underestimate the depth of the passions involved in the struggle for racial equality."

But he also spoke of "a large reservoir of goodwill and compassion, of decency and fair play which seeks a vision of justice without violence in the streets."

Johnson Statement

If these forces, the President said, "do not desert the field, if they can be brought to the battle, then the years of trial will be a prelude to the final triumph of a land 'with liberty and justice for all.'"

The President issued his statement on the rights bill here, while he was beginning a two-day tour of California. The full text of the statement follows:

"Senate passage of the civil rights bill is a major step toward equal opportunities for all Americans. I congratulate Senators of both parties who worked to make passage possible.

"I look forward to the day, which will not be long forthcoming, when the bill becomes law. That will be a milestone in America's progress toward full justice for all her citizens.

"No single act of Congress can, by itself, eliminate discrimination and prejudice, hatred and injustice.

Broad National Consensus

"But this bill goes further to invest the rights of man with the protection of law than any legislation in this century.

"First, it will provide a carefully designed code to test and enforce the right of every American to go to school, to get a job, to vote, and to pursue his life unhampered by the barriers of racial discrimination.

"Second, it will, in itself, help educate all Americans to their responsibility to give equal treatment to their fellow citizens.

"Third, it will enlist one of the most powerful moral forces of American society on the side of civil rights—the moral obligation to respect and obey the law of the land.

"Fourth, and perhaps most important, this bill is a renewal and a re-enforcement, a symbol and a strengthening of that abiding commitment to human dignity and the equality of man which has been the guid-

Continued on Page 11, Column 8

United Press International Telephoto
ON HAND FOR THE VOTE: Visitors waiting outside the Capitol yesterday for admittance to the Senate Chamber, before the vote on the civil rights bill was registered.

ACTION BY SENATE

Revised Measure Now Goes Back to House for Concurrence

By E. W. KENWORTHY
Special to The New York Times

WASHINGTON, June 19 — The Senate passed the civil rights bill today by a vote of 73 to 27.

The final roll-call came at 7:40 P.M. on the 83d day of debate, nine days after closure was invoked.

Voting for the bill were 46 Democrats and 27 Republicans. Voting against it were 21 Democrats and six Republicans.

Except for Senator Robert C. Byrd of West Virginia, all the Democratic votes against the bill came from Southerners.

Senator Barry Goldwater of Arizona voted against the bill, as he said yesterday he would. The five other Republicans opposing it all support Mr. Goldwater's candidacy for the Republican Presidential nomination.

They were Bourke B. Hickenlooper of Iowa, chairman of the Senate Republican Policy Committee; Norris Cotton of New Hampshire, Edwin L. Mechem of New Mexico, Milward L. Simpson of Wyoming and John G. Tower of Texas.

2 Pledge Acceptance

The bill will now go back to the House for concurrence in the changes that the Senate made in the measure the House passed last Feb. 10 by a vote of 290 to 130.

Tonight, Representatives Emanuel Celler, Democrat of New York, and William M. McCulloch, Republican of Ohio, who are the chairman and ranking minority member of the House Judiciary Committee, said that they would accept the Senate version of the bill.

"We believe that the House membership will take the same position," they said.

With the support of these two men, who were responsible for the House bill, acceptance of the Senate bill in the House is assured.

President Johnson hopes to have the bill on his desk by July 3 at the latest so that he can sign it on the Fourth of July.

Powers of the Bill

The bill passed by the Senate outlaws discrimination in places of public accommodation, publicly owned facilities, employment and union membership and Federally aided programs. It gives the Attorney General new powers to speed school desegregation and enforce the Negro's right to vote.

The Senate bill differs from the House measure chiefly in giving states and local communities more scope and time to deal with complaints of discrimination in hiring and public accommodations. It allows the Attorney General to initiate suits in these areas where he finds a "pattern" of discrimination, but does not permit him, as did the House bill, to file suits on behalf of individuals.

After the roll-call, several thousand people gathered in the plaza before the floodlit Capitol to applaud the Senate Democratic leader, Mike Mansfield of Montana, and the Republican leader, Everett McKinley Dirksen of Illinois. Mr. Dirksen was instrumental in shaping the compromise that the Senate passed.

Burke Marshall, the Justice Department's civil rights chief, said after the bill was passed tonight that the department would move promptly to enforce the measure.

"I think there is going to be compliance with this bill," Mr. Marshall said. "That's the first thing."

"But where there is a pattern

Continued on Page 10, Column 1

ARIZONAN TARGET OF G.O.P. LEADER

Illinoisan, in Speech on the Senate Floor, Scores View Bill Is Unconstitutional

By ANTHONY LEWIS
Special to The New York Times

WASHINGTON, June 19 — The Republican leader in the Senate, Everett McKinley Dirksen of Illinois, closed the civil rights debate tonight with a biting attack on his party's leading Presidential prospect, Senator Barry Goldwater.

Senator Goldwater's announced opposition to the bill brought on the attack. He said yesterday that he could not "in good conscience" vote for the bill because he thought it was "unconstitutional" and would lead to a "police state."

Earlier, it was reported that former President Dwight D. Eisenhower had indicated to Mr Goldwater that the general would not hold a negative vote on the bill against the Arizonan.

On the floor of the Senate, Mr. Dirksen ridiculed the Goldwater constitutional argument and moral position.

Looking often at Senator Goldwater, though never mentioning him by name, Mr. Dirksen in effect challenged the likely nominee of his party on what may be the chief issue at the Republican National Convention next month.

Dirksen Cites Legislation

First, Senator Dirksen mentioned many past pieces of legislation that had first been denounced as "unconstitutional." He listed the child labor prohibition, the Pure Food and Drug Act, the Minimum Wage Law and Social Security.

"It required no constitutional amendment," Senator Dirksen said, "to bring about all these forward thrusts in the interests of the people.

"It leads me to one conclusion: in the history of mankind, there is an inexorable moral force that moves us forward.

"No matter the resistance of people who do not fully understand, it will not be denied."

At this point, Senator Dirksen turned and looked directly at Senator Goldwater, who sat at his desk at the side of the chamber Thrusting his right arm in Senator Goldwater's direction, he said:

"Utter all the extreme opin-

Continued on Page 11, Column 6

Rights Bill Roll-Call Vote

By The Associated Press

WASHINGTON, June 19—Following is the 73-27 vote by which the Senate passed the civil rights bill tonight:

FOR PASSAGE—73

Democrats—46

Anderson (N.M.)	Hayden (Ariz.)	Monroney (Okla.)
Bartlett (Alaska)	Humphrey (Minn.)	Morse (Ore.)
Bayh (Ind.)	Inouye (Hawaii)	Moss (Utah)
Brewster (Md.)	Jackson (Wash.)	Muskie (Me.)
Bible (Nev.)	Kennedy (Mass.)	Nelson (Wis.)
Burdick (N.D.)	Lausche (Ohio)	Neuberger (Ore.)
Cannon (Nev.)	Long (Mo.)	Pastore (R. I.)
Church (Idaho)	Magnuson (Wash.)	Pell (R. I.)
Clark (Pa.)	Mansfield (Mont.)	Proxmire (Wis.)
Dodd (Conn.)	McCarthy (Minn.)	Randolph (W. Va.)
Douglas (Ill.)	McGee (Wyo.)	Ribicoff (Conn.)
Edmondson (Okla.)	McGovern (S. D.)	Symington (Mo.)
Engle (Calif.)	McIntyre (N.H.)	Williams (N. J.)
Gruening (Alaska)	McNamara (Mich.)	Yarborough (Tex.)
Hart (Mich.)	Metcalf (Mont.)	Young (Ohio)
Hartke (Ind.)		

Republicans—27

Aiken (Vt.)	Dirksen (Ill.)	Morton (Ky.)
Allott (Colo.)	Dominick (Colo.)	Mundt (S. D.)
Beall (Md.)	Fong (Hawaii)	Pearson (Kan.)
Bennett (Utah)	Hruska (Neb.)	Prouty (Vt.)
Boggs (Del.)	Javits (N. Y.)	Saltonstall (Mass.)
Carlson (Kan.)	Jordan (Idaho)	Scott (Pa.)
Case (N. J.)	Keating (N. Y.)	Smith (Me.)
Cooper (Ky.)	Kuchel (Calif.)	Williams (Del.)
Curtis (Neb.)	Miller (Iowa)	Young (N. D.)

AGAINST PASSAGE—27

Democrats—21

Byrd (Va.)	Hill (Ala.)	Russell (Ga.)
Byrd (W. Va.)	Holland (Fla.)	Smathers (Fla.)
Eastland (Miss.)	Johnston (S. C.)	Sparkman (Ala.)
Ellender (La.)	Jordan (N. C.)	Stennis (Miss.)
Ervin (N. C.)	Long (La.)	Talmadge (Ga.)
Fulbright (Ark.)	McClellan (Ark.)	Thurmond (S. C.)
Gore (Tenn.)	Robertson (Va.)	Walters (Tenn.)

Republicans—6

Cotton (N. H.)	Hickenlooper (Iowa)	Simpson (Wyo.)
Goldwater (Ariz.)	Mechem (N. M.)	Tower (Tex.)

Negro Leaders Hail Passage; Some Southerners Voice Anger

CORE Plans Tests

By MARTIN ARNOLD

Leaders of national civil rights groups last night hailed the Senate passage of the civil rights bill, and vowed that the measure would be quickly tested.

There was little indication that the Senate's action would reduce the number of demonstrations in the immediate future.

James L. Farmer, national director of the Congress of Racial Equality, said that CORE would press for implementation and enforcement of the bill's provisions.

"There will be no breathing spell on demonstrations," Mr. Farmer said. "We breathe easiest when the pressure is on."

"The passage of the civil rights bill may well be the single most important act of our Congress in several decades," Mr. Farmer said. "It gives hope to Negroes that the American people and Government mean to redeem the promise of the Declaration of Independence and the Emancipation Proclamation."

Mr. Farmer also saw the bill

Continued on Page 16, Column 4

Region's Reaction Varied

By United Press International

ATLANTA, June 19 — Deep South politicians and businessmen lashed out angrily at passage of the civil rights bill today and an elderly Negro said, "I'll believe it when I see it."

Gov. George C. Wallace of Alabama declared that "this is a sad day for individual freedom and liberty," but a Chattanooga housewife said, "I firmly believe in it."

Reaction differed sharply between stanchly segregationist areas and areas where there has been desegregation.

Many Negroes approached on the streets in the South had little, if any, comment.

"I just don't know much about it. I'm afraid to say," said a Negro in Nashville.

"It is good. I am glad," said George Thomson, a 40-year-old Negro cab driver in Montgomery, Ala.

Jefferson Johnson, an elderly Negro selling ice cream on a street in Birmingham, Ala., said:

"I'll believe it when I see it. I hope it'll do good, but—well,

Continued on Page 12, Column 6

North Katanga City Is Seized By Rebels, the Congo Reports

Europeans Flee Albertville, Crossing Lake Tanganyika to Nearby Burundi

By J. ANTHONY LUKAS
Special to The New York Times

LEOPOLDVILLE, the Congo, June 19—Albertville, the capital of North Katanga Province, was reported today to have fallen to anti-Government rebels.

According to messages reaching here, rebels striking south along the shore of Lake Tanganyika entered the city about midday. It is not known here whether there was any resistance from Congolese soldiers there.

Many of the city's Europeans have fled in steamers across the lake. At least 150 women and children left on two steamers last night for Bujumbura, the capital of Burundi.

Another steamer, with 350 persons aboard, was scheduled to leave early this afternoon, but it was not known whether it got away.

Meanwhile, the United States Embassy here said that two American civilian pilots who had been flying combat missions for the Congolese Army had voluntarily decided to cease the flights. An embassy official said the pilots made their decision after they learned that they might be subject to penalties under United States law.

The New York Times June 20, 1964
Rebels were said to have seized Albertville (cross).

The embassy spokesman adhered to the official United States position that the two men were "individual Americans on contract to the Congolese Government."

He said the United States Government had neither authorized their contract nor directed their activities here.

The Americans, Ed Dearborn and Don Coney, also insisted in an interview here, as they had previously, that they were civilians under contract to the Congolese Government.

Mr. Dearborn said he had hepatitis and planned to return to the United States soon. However, he and Mr. Coney would answer no other questions.

Continued on Page 4, Column 3

Erhard Bars Visit To the Soviet Union

Special to The New York Times

BONN, June 19 — Chancellor Ludwig Erhard turned down today an unofficial but urgent Soviet invitation to go to Moscow for an attempt at improving Soviet-West German relations.

He suggested instead that the Soviet Premier ask for an official invitation to Bonn if he thought the trip would be worthwhile.

At his first news conference here in six months, Dr. Erhard carefully held open the door for an eventual encounter with Premier Khrushchev while dashing cold water on the prospects of settling soon any of the fundamental questions that divide Bonn and Moscow.

As he spoke, Bonn's Western allies were putting the final

Continued on Page 2, Column 4

Yanks Woo Cabbies With 20,000 Tickets

By ROBERT LIPSYTE

The New York Yankees, long lordly and aloof atop baseball's corporate standings, have gone down to the street to wage promotional warfare.

They have given away more than 10,000 reserved tickets worth $25,000 to more than 5,000 city cab drivers on the sidewalk along Broadway between 60th and 61st Streets in the last two days. Today, they expect to give away 10,000 more.

The Yankees' first mass giveaway program is the latest in a series of gimmicks to raise lagging attendance and combat the Mets at the box office.

"The idea," said Robert O. Fishel, the Yankees' public relations director, "is to make

Continued on Page 18, Column 2

NEWS INDEX

Senate Passes Civil Rights Bill by 73-27 Roll-Call Vote After 83 Days of Debate

REVISED MEASURE RETURNS TO HOUSE

President Hopes to Be Able to Sign the Legislation on Fourth of July

Continued From Page 1, Col. 8

of noncompliance, we will move as expeditiously as possible in the courts."

It was a year ago today, a few weeks after the riots in Birmingham, Ala., that President Kennedy sent a draft civil rights bill to Congress. He concluded his message with these words:

"I ask you to look into your hearts — not in search of charity, for the Negro neither wants nor needs condescension — but for the one plain, proud and priceless quality that united us all as Americans: A sense of justice.

"In this year of the emancipation centennial, justice requires us to insure the blessings of liberty for all Americans and their posterity — not merely for reasons of economic efficiency, world diplomacy and domestic tranquillity — but, above all, because it is right."

Tonight the first sign that a vote on the bill was imminent came about 7 o'clock when Senator Mansfield rose and paid tribute to Senator Dirksen, who framed the substitute bill.

"This is his finest hour," Mr. Mansfield said. "The Senate and the whole country are in debt to the Senator from Illinois."

Mr. Mansfield then paid tribute to the "great service" rendered by Senator Hubert H. Humphrey of Minnesota, the Democratic floor manager of the bill, and Senator Thomas H. Kuchel of California, the Republican floor manager.

'No Sense of Triumph'

Mr. Mansfield said that there was "no room for unwarranted sentiments of victory," and that there should be "no sense of triumph but a profound humility" upon the part of those who had labored and voted for the bill.

Then Mr. Dirksen got up, thanked Mr. Mansfield for his "patience and tolerance" and then went into what will probably be remembered as one of the finest speeches of his career.

The Illinois Republican proceeded to answer Mr. Goldwater's implied rebuke of yesterday when the Arizonan called the rights measure an "unconstitutional" bill.

Mr. Dirksen recalled that on June 5 last year the Republican Conference of the Senate urged the Administration to produce a program to guarantee the rights and privileges of all citizens.

He then addressed himself to Mr. Goldwater's argument that the sections of the bill dealing with public accommodations and employment were an unwarranted extension of the commerce clause of the Constitution.

Social Legislation Cited

Mr. Dirksen tolled a long list of social and economic legislation that had been similarly called unconstitutional when first proposed.

"Today they are accepted," he said, "because they were a forward thrust in the whole effort of mankind."

"There is latitude enough in the Constitution to embrace within its four corners these advances," he said.

All day long today the galleries were crowded. But the drama lay in the historic achievement and not in the expectation of another breath-holding vote like that on June 10, when the Senate for the first time in history shut off a Southern filibuster against a civil rights bill, 71 to 29. Eleven times before, civil rights forces tried and failed to get the two-thirds vote needed for closure of debate.

Passage of the bill was a foregone conclusion, but it was not an anticlimax. The spectators waited to see who among the Republican supporters of Senator Goldwater would follow the Arizonan's example and vote against the bill, and who would vote for it.

After closure was imposed, each Senator had one hour to speak.

On Wednesday night, by a vote of 76 to 18, a revised bill sponsored by Senator Dirksen was accepted as an amendment in the form of a substitute for the original House measure. Since then, Senators have used their remaining time to speak their valedictories on one of the Senate's longest battles.

Yesterday Senator Richard B. Russell, Democrat of Georgia, leader of the Southern opposition, angrily denounced the forces — the press, clergy, unions — that had exerted pressure on Congress to pass what he called an "unconstitutional" bill. He said the bill was destructive of the system of divided powers and states' rights, and was directed solely at the South.

Today Senator Humphrey sought to allay this bitterness, if possible; to bind up the wounds and to look to the great unfinished work before men of goodwill and reason can the nation.

Mr. Humphrey said the civil rights bill of 1964 was "the greatest piece of social legislation of our generation."

The framers of the bill, he went on, endeavored to "fashion a bill which is just, reasonable and fair." They established a framework of law "wherein men of good will and reason can seek to resolve these difficult and emotional issues of human rights," he said.

The burden has been laid primarily on the states and communities, he said, and Federal action is reserved for those occasions when local government is unable or refuses to meet its responsibilities.

Senator Humphrey said that Congress and the nation must now expect governors and mayors "to do their public duty and to carry out the law with the sense of justice and equity which is so vital to a democratic community."

Then he turned to the South and made this appeal:

"Those of us who are privileged to bear some of the burdens of this struggle must demonstrate by example that we can fight without rancor, win without pride, and, on occasion, lose without bitterness. Surely it would be one of the ironies of history if equality were purchased at the expense of the community. We must solemnly pledge that this will never come to pass.

"What we are involved in, as Lincoln once said in an earlier conflict, is too vast for bitterness. We are engaged in the age-old struggle within all men —a struggle to overcome irrational legacies, a struggle to escape the bondage of ignorance and poverty, a struggle to create a new and better community where 'justice rolls down like waters and righteouness is a mighty stream.' "

Senator Byrd explained his vote against the bill by saying that the measure "goes beyond" equal justice and provided "special treatment" for some people. In doing so, it "does violence to long-established constitutional principles," he said.

Senator Mechem said he would vote against the bill he would vote against the bill because the sections on fair employment and public accommodations "could assure the greatest assult on property ownership and private enterprise this country has known."

Senator George A. Smathers, Democrat of Florida, disagreed with Senator Russell's position that the Senate substitute was "more obnoxious" than the House bill. By their 75 days of debate prior to closure, he said, the Southerners forced Mr. Dirksen to bring in a bill "which considerably softens the harshest paragraphs of the House-passed bill."

Nevertheless, he said that the substitute had been rewritten so that "we find all of the force of the Federal Government directed at the South."

He predicted that if a dictator ever appeared in this country, "that man will ride to power on the influence and power he will get under Titles VI and VII."

These sections of the bill provide for a Federal cutoff of funds to programs administered in a discriminatory way, and for a fair-employment commission.

An Unusual Move

Before the speech-making began this morning, Senator Albert Gore, Democrat of Tennesee, made unusual use of a parliamentary device in a last-ditch effort to achieve a change in the bill.

Amendments cannot be offered after closure, and amendments already read once cannot be called up after the third reading. The bill was given its third reading two days ago.

Yesterday, however, Mr. Gore obtained unanimous consent to have an amendment qualify. It stated that the cutoff of Federal funds would not be applied to educational programs or the school lunch program in any school district "unless such school district shall have failed to comply" with a court desegregation order.

The understanding was that Mr. Gore would move to send the bill to the Judiciary Committee with instructions to report it back immediately with this amendment added. He so moved this morning.

He argued that without this provision a school district that was complying with a desegregation order but was not yet fully desegregated could lose its school lunch and milk funds.

The Gore motion to commit was defeated, 74 to 25.

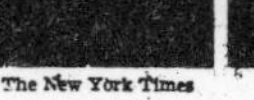

The New York Times — Associated Press

WELCOME PASSAGE OF RIGHTS BILL: Roy C. Wilkins, left, executive secretary of N.A.A.C.P.; James L. Farmer, center, national director of CORE, and the Rev. Dr. Martin Luther King Jr., the head of the Southern Christian Leadership Conference.

RIGHTS LEADERS PRAISE PASSAGE

Continued From Page 1, Col. 6

as an "act of goodwill and reconciliation" between Negroes and the white community. He said: "We in CORE pledge that we will accept it as such."

He declared, however, that Negroes wanted "the reality of equality." He added, "We will continue to demonstrate and to use our body and our spirit to secure that reality."

Roy C. Wilkins, executive secretary of the National Association for the Advancement of Colored People, hailed the bill as "a giant step forward, not only for the Negro citizens but for our country."

Mr. Wilkins, in answer to a question, said he believed the bill "may reduce the number of demonstrations, but I cannot predict that it will eliminate them."

He said that civil rights demonstrations "grow out of local irritations and problems, and if local officials refuse to discuss and plan and negotiate for change, then demonstrations will be the only recourse."

As for the bill itself, Mr. Wilkins said that "at last the legislative branch of government has caught up with the executive and judicial branches, which have recognized and attempted to protect Negro rights for many years."

The bill will give America's 20 million Negroes "a psychological lift by bringing them under the umbrella of the Constitution by an act of Congress," he said.

"There will undoubtedly be resistance to compliance," Mr. Wilkins said, "because we all know that some people are still trying to repeal the income tax law passed in 1913."

But he said he expected, because "we are a law-abiding people," that "the trend will be to uphold law."

The Rev. Dr. Martin Luther King Jr., head of the Southern Christian Leadership Conference, which is now demonstrating in St. Augustine, Fla., said that the bill's testing grounds would be St. Augustine, Albany, Ga., and Montgomery, Birmingham, Tuscaloosa, Gadsden and Selma, Ala.

He said that his group intended to test the bill soon, but he indicated that the tests would not come until after the measure was signed by President Johnson.

"The civil rights bill will bring a cool and serene breeze to an already hot summer," Dr. King said.

At Oxford, Ohio, where he is helping to train northern youths for this summer's "Mississippi Project," James Foreman of the Student Nonviolent Coordinating Committee said that he was worried about enforcement.

"There is no evidence Mississippi officials are going to comply. One may as well get ready for massive defiance. One has to be honest."

Mr. Foreman was critical of President Johnson, who, he said, seemed unconcerned about the possibility of violence in Mississippi this summer.

"Maybe after this bill passes, he will speak out about Mississippi," Mr. Foreman said.

Whitney M. Young Jr., executive director of the National Urban League, said the bill was "the greatest single triumph for human rights in our country since the Emancipation Proclamation of Abraham Lincoln."

He sent a telegram to President Johnson in which he praised the President "for the strong and impressive leadership you have given in the dramatic fight for legal weapons to abolish racial segregation and discrimination."

Mr. Young urged President Johnson to "exercise continued leadership to assure the firm and effective enforcement of the bill."

The only entirely pessimistic outlook was expressed by Malcolm X, the Black Nationalist leader.

"You can't legislate goodwill, and therefore the only thing that will eliminate discrimination and segregation is education, not legislation," he said.

"The passage of this bill," he said, "will do nothing but build up the Negro for a big letdown by promising that which cannot be delivered."

He predicted that after two or three weeks of calm "it will be worse — much more violence" because the bill would increase Negro "frustration, disillusionment and hostility."

Rockefeller Charges Goldwater 'Abandoned' G.O.P. With Vote

Governor Rockefeller, commenting last night on Senator Barry Goldwater's opposition to the civil rights bill, said that it was "inconceivable" to him that the Arizona Senator could be his party's standard bearer.

Asserting that the Arizona Senator had "effectively abandoned the Republican party on the most fundamental issue of our time," the Governor said:

"His nomination for the Presidency would create grave problems for every Republican candidate adhering to the basic spiritual concept of the worth and dignity of every individual and to the traditional Republican position of fighting to make equality of opportunity an actual reality for all."

According to the Governor, the votes on civil rights in the Senate and House reflected "the deep division within the Democratic party on the issue of human rights."

'Cites' Party's Heritage

The votes "also make crystal clear the fact that the mainstream of Republican thought and action today remains true to our party's heritage and faithful to its deep conviction of the worth and dignity of each individual," Mr. Rockefeller said.

In Washington, five clergymen, representing different faiths, declared in a joint statement their "deep gratification" over passage of the civil rights act.

The clergymen, representing the Interreligious Committee on Race Relations, were the Right Rev. Patrick A. O'Boyle, Roman Catholic Archbishop of Washington; the Right Rev. William F. Creighton, Protestant Episcopal Bishop of Washington; Bishop John Wesley Lord of the Methodist Church; Bishop Smallwood E. Williams of the Bibleway Church, and Rabbi Samuel Soolnic, president of the Washington Board of Rabbis.

They extended congratulations to "the leaders and members of our two great political parties on having achieved this important milestone in our national history."

Attorney General Robert F. Kennedy said that the vote "must hearten and encourage President Johnson and all Americans."

"I know how President Kennedy felt a year ago and I know how pleased he would be now," the brother of the late President said.

"This legislation enhances the basic concept that free people, given the opportunity, will face their problems and deal with them," the Attorney General declared.

Former President Harry S. Truman said of the passage of the bill: "I think it's a good thing. They did what was right."

Hailed by Stevenson

At the United Nations, the chief United States delegate, Adlai E. Stevenson, said that the Senate "took an historic stride forward in redeeming Lincoln's pledge that all of our citizens would be 'forever free'."

Gov. Endicott Peabody of Massachusetts, a Republican, whose mother was arrested recently in St. Augustine, Fla., while participating in an integration demonstration said:

"Equality is now reality under the law. The action of my mother in St. Augustine, Fla., now is protected by the law of the land."

In Boston, Richard Cardinal Cushing said that "a shadow that has stretched across our American life for 100 years is removed and the bright light of freedom falls on all citizens equally."

Nebraskan Comments

Gov. Frank Morrison of Nebraska, a Democrat, said:

"If this legislation is really to be effective, white people, colored people and all races are going to have to accept the responsibility of citinzenship to go along with these rights."

Gov. Matthew E. Welsh of Indiana, also a Democrat, expressing gratification for the Senate passage of the bill, said:

"This, of course, does not mean we can expect all tensions to relax and demonstrations to cease."

HISTORY OF BILL: A YEAR OF WORDS

HR 7152 Offered Casually in the House by Celler

By MARJORIE HUNTER

Special to The New York Times

WASHINGTON, June 19 — No one said a word, scarcely anyone even noticed, when HR 7152, the civil rights bill, began its long legislative journey a year ago tomorrow.

The House was busy with other things that day. It was suspending duties on metal scrap and chicory; extending a law on placement of foster children; talking about the Civil War centennial at Gettysburg and the 100th birthday party that West Virginia had given the day before.

Sometime during the 47-minute session, Representative Emanuel Celler, Democrat of Brooklyn, strolled to the front of the House and casually dropped HR 7152 into a small box on the side of the Speaker's desk. The "HR" stands for House Resolution, the number indicates that the bill was the 7,152d introduced in the House since the start of its current session.

That was the legislative beginning.

The fact that HR 7152 made a largely unheralded entry into history was not because of any complacency about civil rights. It was the most talked-about topic of the year.

Other Bills Also Offered

Congress was flooded with civil rights bills by the time HR 7152 put in an appearance. The Judiciary Committee alone had 172 civil rights bills, many of them introduced by Republicans. The Senate Judiciary Committee had 20. And there were other civil rights bills scattered among other House and Senate committees.

HR 7152, bearing the Kennedy Administration's stamp of approval, attracted little attention because, just the day before, an identical bill had been introduced in the Senate by Senator Mike Mansfield, Democrat of Montana.

Both the Mansfield and Celler bills were drafted at the Justice Department, a half-mile down Pennsylvania Avenue from the Capitol.

Some sections of the identical bills were shaped in the Civil Rights Division office, headed by Assistant Attorney General Burke Marshall. Other sections were drafted in the office of the legal counsel, Assistant Attorney General Norbert A. Schlei.

Then, the bills were given a final going-over by Attorney General Robert F. Kennedy and Deputy Attorney General Nicholas DeB. Katzenbach, and, after conferences with President Kennedy, the bills were sent to Capitol Hill for introduction in the Senate and House.

The Mansfield bill, S 1731, got the headlines, but it was HR 7152 that was to make the full legislative circuit.

It is paradoxical that HR 7152 was born in silence, for it was destined to generate millions of words in the halls and committee rooms of Congress.

The volume of time and words devoted to HR 7152 and allied civil rights bills is staggering:

¶Six Congressional committees, sitting for 81 days, heard 269 witnesses. Printed transcripts of those hearings cover 5,791 pages of eight volumes, weighing 13¼ pounds.

¶The House filled 477 pages of The Congressional Record with civil rights debate lasting 73 hours 41 minutes over nine days, Jan. 31 to Feb. 10.

¶The Senate, up to today, filled 2,890 pages of The Congressional Record with civil rights debate. The debate lasted 736 hours 10 minutes over 83 days, March 9 through today.

Debate Was Exhausting

The cost to the Government and to individuals or private organizations in getting the legislation through Congress is impossible to compute.

Telephones were constantly busy with long-distance calls. The hearing witnesses, most of them traveling at their own expense, invested many thousands of dollars on transportation. Mountains of supplies were used.

Taking the Government Printing Office estimates of $16 a page for printed transcripts of hearings and $90 a page for The Congressional Record, the printing cost alone, up today, was $352,756.

The physical toll on those who took part in debate would be difficult to estimate, too. House members suffered little, since debate lasted only nine days. But the Senate debate, the longest in its history, was physically exhausting to many of the Senators.

Only Six Senators Split Rights and Closure Votes

Special to The New York Times

WASHINGTON, June 19— Only six of the 100 Senators voted differently tonight on the passage of the civil rights bill from the way they had voted last week on closure.

Voting last week against shutting off the long debate but voting tonight for passage of the bill were Wallace F. Bennett, Republican of Utah; Alan Bible, Democrat of Nevada; Carl Hayden, Democrat of Arizona, and Milton R. Young, Republican of South Dakota.

Voting last week for closure but voting tonight against the bill were Norris Cotton, Republican of New Hampshire and Bourke B. Hickenlooper, Republican of Iowa.

Passage of Rights Bill Intact Surprises Congress

Measure Somewhat Broader Than Proposals Presented by President Last Year

Special to The New York Times

WASHINGTON, June 19 — Leaders of the civil rights forces on both sides of the aisle in both chambers of Congress were still somewhat unbelieving today over what had happened, but especially over what had not happened, during the rights bill's long journey.

Not only had the bill been passed essentially intact, but in some ways it was a broader and stronger bill than the draft sent to Congress by President Kennedy a year ago.

The original Administration bill made no provision for a Fair Employment Opportunities Commission. The President and his brother, Attorney General Robert F. Kennedy, were reluctant to include a fair-employment section, because they feared that, even if it were approved by the House, it might imperil the whole bill in the Senate.

Kennedy Had Reservations

Furthermore, although the Administration draft included a section authorizing a cutoff of funds from federally aided programs administered in a discriminatory manner, it was known that President Kennedy had reservations about this section because a cutoff could hurt innocent recipients of the aid.

In the House Judiciary Committee, a fair-employment title was added to the bill, and the Administration felt constrained to go along for political reasons. It could not offend liberal Democrats and it needed the support of liberal Republicans.

Moreover, many House Republicans developed strong feelings about the Federal funds cutoff. They believed that racial discrimination in programs financed by undiscriminating tax levies could not be justified.

Nevertheless, when the bill came to the Senate last February, it was assumed that the fair-employment and cutoff titles were the most vulnerable. In fact, they were widely regarded as sections that could be sacrificed to save three parts of the bill that the Justice Department regarded as crucial if the Negro was to secure his constitutional rights.

What Three Titles Will Do

These three titles banned discrimination in public accommodations; required voting registrars to apply the same standards to whites and Negroes on literacy tests and voter-applications forms, and gave the Attorney General new authority to initiate school-desegregation suits.

The feeling that the titles on fair employment and the cutoff of Federal funds might be sacrificed was based on the known aversion of many Middle Western Republican Senators to both of them, but particularly to the employment title as an unwarranted interference with private business.

Yet these titles not only survived but also came through largely unscathed as a result of the reworking given them by Senator Everett McKinley Dirksen of Illinois, the minority leader, and the Justice Department in the course of preparing the substitute to the House bill. Mr. Dirksen and Senator Mike Mansfield of Montana, the majority leader, sponsored the substitute, along with Senator Hubert H. Humphrey of Minnesota and Thomas H. Kuchel of California, the bill's majority and minority floor managers.

Accommodations Title Intact

The public - accommodations title, banning discrimination in motels, hotels, restaurants, theaters, sports arenas and gas stations, also came through intact.

The substitute, on Mr. Dirksen's insistence, made it mandatory that states with fair-employment and public-accommodations laws should have the first chance to handle a complaint. It also extended the time allowed for local action and for persuasion by the Federal Equal Employment Opportunities Commission and the Community Relations Service.

The second major change was in enforcement powers. The Dirksen substitute allowed the Attorney General to intervene in suits filed by individuals seeking relief from discrimination in jobs or public accommodations. But, unlike the House bill, it did not permit him to initiate such suits.

On the other hand, Mr. Dirksen acceded to the Justice Department's argument that the Attorney General should have the right to initiate suits where he found a "pattern" or "practice" of discrimination.

A third important Dirksen amendment specified that any cutoff of Federal funds must be limited to the locality and the program where the discrimination occurred. This was to insure that there would be no statewide cutoff.

Senate Cut Parts of Bill

While it is true that one or two anomalies got into the bill during its nine days on the House floor — such as the amendment permitting an employer to refuse to hire an atheist — these were taken out by the Senate.

In the same way, it is contended that the Senate substitute improved and refined the

As a matter of fact, these changes merely made explicit what had been the intention of the Justice Department. But officials conceded that Mr. Dirksen improved the bill by clarifying it. And his changes helped to win the critical Republican votes for the closure invoked last week by a vote of 71 to 29.

Although the Southerners introduced 483 amendments and called up more than 100 of them for roll-call votes, they were able to make only one significant change in the bill. That was an amendment guaranteeing that defendants in criminal-contempt proceedings arising out of violations of any title except that on voting should have a jury trial.

For contempt in voting-right suits, the Civil Rights Act of 1957 still governs. This states that the judge has discretion to give a jury trial, but the defendant must have a second trial with jury if the judge in a nonjury trial imposes a penalty of more than 45 days in jail or a fine of more than $300.

Some Senators think Senator Richard B. Russell, Democrat of Georgia, the Southern leader, might have been able to kill, or at least temper, the fair-employment and Federal cutoff titles. They believe he might have done this if he had not set his face against the whole bill and refused to concede that there was a moral issue, that southern Negroes had a real grievance, and that they had, in many areas, been denied equal protection of the laws.

If Mr. Russell and his followers had been willing to cooperate in solving the problem, some members believe, he would have found a sympathetic response, especially from Republicans who were concerned about the bill's extension of Federal power.

But when he declined to do this, when virtually all the Southern amendments were directed at evading the problem and allowing the Southern states to continue the practices that had brought the issue to crisis point, then the hand of the civil rights forces was strengthened.

Many See Vindication

Most members of Congress, the Southerners excepted, believe the civil rights bill, as it finally emerged, is a notable vindication of the legislative process that has been so much under attack in the last few years.

They concede that matters got a little out of hand last fall when a House Judiciary subcommittee sent to the full committee a bill the Justice Department regarded as bad law and dangerous, because it gave the Attorney General powers he did not want and believed he should not have.

But what matters, the defenders of Congress emphasize, is that sounder counsel prevailed, and that, in the end, the bill that emerged from the committee and passed the House was a better bill than the Administration had sent up.

This was achieved, members of both parties agree, through bipartisan cooperation of a kind normally found only on measures affecting the national security.

Obviously Mr. Dirksen has been widely praised. But there has also been recognition of the role played by Senator Humphrey, who conducted himself at all times so as to keep passions in check.

But the outstanding role of peacemaker was played by Senator Mansfield, who decided at the outset that he must remain above the battle so as to keep the lines open to powerful Southerners whose help would be later needed on other vital legislation that they are in a position to forward or obstruct. For this reason, Mr. Mansfield turned over to Mr. Humphrey the job of chief negotiator and floor captain.

And it is not forgotten by the Administration how effectively William M. McCulloch, ranking Republican member of the House Judiciary Committee, worked with the chairman, Emanuel Cellar, Democrat of Brooklyn. Sharing the Administration's gratitude are John V. Lindsay of Manhattan and Charles M. Mathias of Maryland, younger members of the House Judiciary Committee.

Digest of Civil Rights Bill's Provisions

Special to The New York Times

WASHINGTON, June 19— Following is a summary of the principal provisions of the civil rights bill passed by the Senate today:

Title I—Voting

Prohibits registrars from applying different standards to white and Negro voting applicants and from disqualifying applicants because of inconsequential errors on their forms. Requires that literacy tests be in writing, except under special arrangements for blind persons, and that any applicant desiring one be given a copy of the questions and his answers. Makes a sixth-grade education a rebuttable presumption of literacy. Allows the Attorney General or defendant state officials in any voting suit to request trial by a three-judge Federal Court.

Title II— Public Accommodations

Prohibits discrimination or refusal of service on account of race in hotels, motels, restaurants, gasoline stations and places of amusement if their operations affect interstate commerce or if their discrimination "is supported by state action." Permits the Attorney General to enforce the title by suit in the Federal courts if he believes that any person or group is engaging in a "pattern or practice of resistance" to the rights declared by the title. The latter language was added in the Senate, which also authorized three-judge courts for suits under this title.

Title III—Public Facilities

Requires that Negroes have equal access to, and treatment in, publicly owned or operated facilities such as parks, stadiums and swimming pools. Authorizes the Attorney General to sue for enforcement of these rights if private citizens are unable to sue effectively.

Title IV—Public Schools

Empowers the Attorney General to bring school desegregation suits under the same conditions as in Title III. Authorizes technical and financial aid to school districts to assist in desegregation. The Senate strengthened a provision in the House bill saying that the title does not cover busing of pupils or other steps to end "racial imbalance."

Title V— Civil Rights Commission

Extends the life of the Civil Rights Commission until Jan. 31, 1968.

Title VI—Federal Aid

Provides that no person shall be subjected to racial discrimination in any program receiving Federal aid. Directs Federal agencies to take steps against discrimination, including—as a last resort, and after hearings—withholding of Federal funds from state or local agencies that discriminate.

Title VII—Employment

Bans discrimination by employers or unions with 100 or more employes or members the first year the act is effective, reducing over four years to 25 or more. Establishes a commission to investigate alleged discrimination and use persuasion to end it. Authorizes the Attorney General to sue if he believes any person or group is engaged in a "pattern or practice" of resistance to the title, and to ask for trial by a three-judge court. The Senate added the "pattern-or-practice" condition and shifted the power to sue from the commission to the Attorney General.

Title VIII—Statistics

Directs the Census Bureau to compile statistics of registration and voting by race in areas of the country designated by the Civil Rights Commission. This might be used to enforce the long-forgotten provision of the 14th Amendment that states that discriminate in voting shall lose seats in the House of Representatives.

Title IX—Courts

Permits appellate review of decisions by Federal District judges to send back to the state courts criminal defendants who have attempted to remove their cases on the ground that their civil rights would be denied in state trials. Permits the Attorney General to intervene in suits filed by private persons complaining that they have been denied the equal protection of the laws.

Title X—Conciliation

Establishes a Community Relations Service in the Commerce Department to help conciliate racial disputes. The Senate removed a House ceiling of seven employes.

Title XI—Miscellaneous

Guarantees jury trials for criminal contempt under any part of the act but Title I—a provision added in the Senate. Provides that the statute shall not invalidate state laws with consistent purposes, and that it shall not impair any existing powers of Federal officials.

GOLDWATER SLATE WINS IN MONTANA

Special to The New York Times

HELENA, Mont., June 19— Montana Republicans today pledged their 14-man delegation to the party's National Convention in San Francisco to Senator Barry Goldwater for the first three ballots.

The Arizona Presidential aspirant picked up the votes with little opposition. The action came quickly after the State Convention nominated the 14 delegates and 14 alternates.

The motion to commit the delegation to Mr. Goldwater was made by Gov. Tim Babcock. The motion to limit the pledge to three ballots came from Representative James Battin of the state's Eastern District.

There had been some speculation that in keeping with state tradition Montana delegates might go to San Francisco as individual Goldwater backers but would be unpledged.

The commitment of the delegation by the State Convention came two hours after Governor Babcock drew wild applause by saying:

"An uncommitted delegation from Montana could be interpreted nationally as weakening the position of the candidate of our choice."

Dirksen Shaped Victory for Civil Rights Forces in Fight to Bring Measure to Vote

SENATORS PRAISE LEADER OF G.O.P.

Illinoisan Gets Major Credit for Framing Compromise Acceptable to His Party

By E. W. KENWORTHY
Special to The New York Times

WASHINGTON, June 19—When the roll was called on civil rights closure at 11:02 A.M. Wednesday, June 10, 27 Republicans joined 44 Democrats to answer "aye."

The Senate Republican leader, Everett McKinley Dirksen of Illinois, came through with two more votes than he needed. So did the bill's Democratic floor manager, Hubert H. Humphrey of Minnesota. Together, they gathered 71 votes, four more than needed to halt the historic filibuster.

The Democrats recognize Mr. Dirksen's as the harder task and their praise for him was unreserved. They called him "a statesman," a man of light and leading," a veritable Vandenberg. "He saved the bill," they said.

History may show he saved his party as well. Senator Hugh Scott of Pennsylvania has testified that the hitherto irresolute Gov. William W. Scranton was brought to the sticking point by Senator Barry Goldwater's vote against closure. Senator Dirksen has thus strengthened the hand of the progressives and moderates in his party.

Even if Mr. Goldwater wins the nomination, he will find it difficult to disavow or retreat from a party commitment to civil rights brought about by Mr. Dirksen in the Senate and Republican leaders in the House.

Framed Substitute Bill

What Mr. Dirksen did to win this praise was to piece together a substitute for the House-passed bill so near the original that it was acceptable to the Justice Department and the bipartisan civil rights coalition, and sufficiently different in tone and emphasis to win the few crucial Republican votes needed for closure.

In the resolution of the civil rights issue in the Senate, the views of the 68-year-old Senator from Illinois underwent several changes—changes that were crucial to the substance and the fate of the bill.

Just how and when and why those changes took place is something of a mystery. The answer probably lies beyond recall in the meditations of the Senator as he took his early morning strolls in the garden to see how his petunias, zinnias and marigolds were coming along.

There are some who believe that Mr. Dirksen knew where he was going to end up when he started out.

"Ev planned it that way," they insist. "It's the way he always works. He goes way out to the right, thus pleasing the opponents in his party, and gradually leads them into the center."

There are others, including Senators in both parties who were in his confidence, who believe that at some point Senator Dirksen underwent a conversion.

"Ev got religion," Mr. Humphrey said.

Talked of Amendment

The real story of the civil rights bill in the Senate lies hidden somewhere between March 26 and May 26. It may never be fully known since, for the ways that are dark and motives that are obscure, the mind of the man from Pekin, Ill., is peculiar. But there is a good deal to go on.

The bill sent up by President Kennedy and introduced in the Senate on June 19, 1963, went beyond anything in the field since the civil rights bill of 1875, which the Supreme Court declared unconstitutional in 1883.

At the outset, Mr. Dirksen said he did not favor Title II, banning discrimination in places of public accommodation. He thought it went too far and, when a similar bill came over from the House last February, he talked about offering an amendment to postpone the effective date for two years to provide an opportunity for voluntary compliance before resorting to Federal Court injunctions.

The House bill also had a fair employment section. Twice President Kennedy promised Mr. Dirksen there would be none in the Administration measure. He kept his word, but the House inserted the provision in its measure and for political reasons Mr. Kennedy had to acquiesce.

Mr. Dirksen said it was probably impossible to kill this section in the Senate, though he would vote to do so. In any event, he said he would propose eliminating the authority to initiate Federal suits.

The managers of the bill were apprehensive, as was the Justice Department.

On March 26, Mr. Dirksen rose, a sheaf of papers in his hand. After 16 days of Southern stalling, the Senate had voted to make the House bill its pending business. The motion now was to refer it to the inhospitable Judiciary Committee with instructions to report it back in two weeks. Mr. Dirksen supported the motion.

He began by quoting a statement once made by Senator Joseph C. O'Mahoney against the monopolists:

"'They are remaking America, and you won't like it.' The bill would remake the social pattern of this country. Let no one be fooled on that score."

The Senator then began a vivisection of the bill—its language, intent and effect.

He said not a word of the Negro's grievances. He would not be moved, he said, by all the clamor for passing the House bill intact. His office was filled every day with "preachers, rabbis, priests, social workers."

He told them, "The best you can do is to go and pray for me, and I will also pray for myself." When they advanced "the moral argument," he replied, "I am a legislator. I am thinking about today and I am thinking about tomorrow."

As for the argument that "unless you hurry there will be violence," well—

"A man is not fit to walk into this chamber as a U. S. Senator if he is to be bilked and influenced by that kind of argument to deter him from his duties under the laws and the Constitution."

That was Mr. Dirksen's cast of mind on March 26.

On May 26 Mr. Dirksen presented "an amendment in the nature of a substitute" for the House bill. It was, he said, based on changes he had proposed, which, in turn, had been reshaped "on the anvil of controversy and discussion" with leaders of the civil rights coalition, the Justice Department and his party colleagues. He said he hoped it would command enough support to make closure possible.

Thereupon Senators Mike Mansfield, Democrat of Montana; Thomas H. Kuchel, Republican of California, and Humphrey, who joined him as sponsors, heaped praises on him. Senator Richard B. Russell, Democrat of Georgia, leader of the Southern bloc, ridiculed him as "the center horse of a troika" that had produced a bill more punative than the House measure. And Senstor Jacob K. Javits, Republican of New York, said his leader had not emasculated a single section.

This was true. Mr. Dirksen won his point that states with fair employment and public accommodations laws should have "a first, exclusive chance" to deal with complaints for a limited period.

But he yielded on his proposal to deny the Attorney General power to file suits in these areas. A compromise was struck: The Attorney General could not bring suit on behalf of individual complainants at random but could initiate proceedings where he found "a pattern" of discrimination.

What had brought the Senator around? Not his mail (over 100,000 letters and cards), which was running 10 to 1 against the bill. Justice Department officials who worked closely with him over two months have their explanation.

Mr. Dirksen, they say, does not have a closed mind. He listens to rational argument. He wanted the states and communities to have as much authority as possible on voluntary methods. After reading the House bill, he had an idea that it contemplated making the Attorney General "a sort of one-man legal aid society" for the filing of thousands of suits.

Limits Are Explained

These officials say they convinced Mr. Dirksen that the department also wanted to rely as much as possible on local action. But they also described to him from their experience—and this he had not realized before—what the limits of voluntarism were against entrenched resistance.

They also explained that many businessmen who wanted to end discrimination did not dare to do so unless they had legal backing. Unless the Attorney General had the residual power to take action against a pattern of hardened discrimination, they said, the law would be "a phony."

"Senator Dirksen came to see this," these officials said.

This explains much. But something else, his colleagues believe, was also turning over in his mind.

On May 19 Mr. Dirksen went to the Senate press gallery and waited for questions.

"Senator," a reporter began, "we have all been making you the hero of this battle."

"Stop it," Mr. Dirksen said.

"No," the reporter persisted. "Why are you doing it? Do you have some deep feeling about this?"

"All right," the Senator replied, "you asked for the sermon and you're going to get it. On the night Victor Hugo died. it is said that he wrote in his diary: 'No army can withstand the strength of an idea whose time has come.'"

Civil rights, he said, was an idea whose time had come.

"Dick Russell," he wound up, "says the Attorney General has nailed up my skin on the barn door to dry. Well, nobody has hung up my conscience and my sense of history to dry. Pardon me for the sermon."

A few days later an interviewer asked Mr. Dirksen why he thought the time of the idea had come; why had it come for him?

His answer was infused with a sence of history, but it was strangely prosaic, too, and practical—the practicality of Joubert when he said: "Force and right rule the world, but force till right is ready."

Right was ready when Lincoln emancipated the slaves. But Mr. Dirksen suggested it was probably not ready for the Republican civil rights bill, or Reconstruction. "There was not much noise about equality during Reconstruction," he said, "but it kept boiling underneath."

"In 1883," he went on, "the Supreme Court said equal treatment in public accommodations was not the province of Congress. But the country has grown. We have gridded it with concrete to make this possible.

"A colored man and his family set out from Blytheville, Ark., for Jackson, Miss. He says to himself, 'Here is a highway I helped pay for through Federal and state taxes. They tax my gas. They tax my tires. They tax my car. This is really my highway. But if I go any distance and take the kids into a comfort station, I do so at my peril.'

"It has altered my thinking a little. The states and localities are entitled to have the first chance to work it out if they can. If they can't work it out, there has to be some place to go."

Last year when Mr. Dirksen spoke out for the nuclear test ban treaty, he said: "Mr. President, I am not a young man. One of my age thinks about his destiny a little."

A few days ago a reporter from a Chicago newspaper asked, "Why are you exerting yourself so? You know you can't get 1 per cent of the vote in Chicago's Second and Third [Negro] Wards."

"Sometime you have to do something for your country," Mr. Dirksen replied.

Associated Press Wirephoto

AFTER RIGHTS BILL VOTE: Senator Everett McKinley Dirksen of Illinois, minority leader, gestures to Senators Mike Mansfield, center, of Montana, and Hubert H. Humphrey of Minnesota, respectively majority leader and whip. They had key roles in bill's passage. Senator Jacob K. Javits, rear, New York Republican, also backed the bill.

SENATE IS FACING BACKLOG OF BILLS

Mansfield Outlines 'Must' Legislative Program

By CABELL PHILLIPS
Special to The New York Times

WASHINGTON, June 19 — A backlog of unfinished Senate business will keep Congress in session well past the Democratic convention in August, Mike Mansfield, the majority leader, said today.

The Montana Senator listed six major legislative items plus the regular appropriation bills, that he says the Senate must, at a minimum, act on before it can adjourn.

The six items are the poverty program; a bill to increase the Federal debt limit; relief for Appalachia; the Federal pay-rise bill; the Food Stamp Program, and the interest equalization tax on foreign securities.

The pile-up is due principally to the Senate's three month concentration on the civil rights bill. The House is much further ahead on its schedule, but it will be required to stay in session too until the Senate catches up with it.

Mr. Mansfield said he saw no prospect of avoiding recalling the Senate after its recess for the Democratic Convention, beginning Aug. 24. He would not guess how far beyond that the session might extend. Normally, serious campaigning in Presidential years begins on Labor Day, which falls Sept. 7 this year.

Committees Lagging

The schedule will continue to be clouded by civil rights. The bill passed by the Senate must be returned to the House. If not adopted as is, it would go to conference for the adjustment of differences, and this could consume a number of days, or even weeks, before the bill could become law. Another possibility would be that the House could amend the Senate bill and send it back to the Senate. This would raise the possibility of a new filibuster by the Southerners.

In addition to putting the finishing touches to civil rights, the Senate faces the necessity of acting on a wide range of other legislation under adjournment pressures. In a number of instances, its committees are just getting started on the hearings that must precede the reporting of the bills to the floor for consideration.

Mr. Mansfield was unwilling to assign priorities to individual measures within the "must" list. But one to which he is known to attach great urgency is the increase in the Federal debt limit to $324 billion. This passed the House yesterday, and hearings will begin in the Senate Finance Committee Tuesday. There is strong conservative pressure to hold the increase to a lower figure. Failure to complete this legislation by June 30 would create serious problems for the Treasury.

Money Bills Pile Up

Appropriation bills for major departments and programs of the Government in the fiscal year beginning July 1 represent a big slice of the Senate's backlog. The House has passed 11 of the 12 annual money bills, but the Senate Appropriations Committee has reported out only two of them.

Hearings are in progress on the others, and a committee source said that it would take at least two weeks to complete these hearings. Failure to enact the money bills before the end of the fiscal year creates no severe problems, because the departments can be supplied with funds temporarily under what is known as a continuing resolution.

The 12th bill, still to reach the House, covers the Administration's request for $3.5 billion to operate the foreign aid program next year. The Senate has yet to act on the first-step authorization bill. The Foreign Relations Committee, which suspended hearings on the measure with the onset of the civil rights filibuster last March resumed them yesterday with testimony from Secretary of State Dean Rusk.

Suit in Mississippi Seeks to Head Off Unpledged Electors

GREENVILLE, Miss., June 19 (UPI)—A sweeping voter suit was filed in Federal Court today charging widespread racial discrimination in the state's Democratic party and seeking to head off any unpledged electors movement in Mississippi.

The suit, filed on behalf of four former Negro candidates for office and others, also asks the court to set aside Democratic precinct elections held last week and to delay the county and state conventions.

The suit asked for a judgment declaring unconstitutional a 1963 act setting up a special Presidential primary in Mississippi in September.

It requested an injunction against all county registrars in the state from determining the qualifications of Negro voters by any procedure different from that "utilized for the registration of white citizens."

Among those named as defendants were Gov. Paul B. Johnson Jr., Attorney General Joe Patterson, Secretary of State Heber Ladner, and Bidwell Adam, Democratic party chairman.

A spokesman for the Council of Federated Organizations, which is sponsoring a massive voter registration drive in the state, called it the most far-reaching suit dealing with voter rights filed in Mississippi.

The suit charged that members of the executive and legislative branches of government had entered into a "conspiracy" to bar or greatly limit any increase in Negro participation in state politics.

The plaintiffs accused the state of passing laws designed to prevent Negroes and other voters from effectively voting for any national Presidential candidate "who might seek to support the political and civil rights of the Negro people."

EISENHOWER STAND ON BILL REPORTED

He Is Said to Have Informed Goldwater He'd Vote for It

By CHARLES MOHR
Special to The New York Times

WASHINGTON, June 19—As Senator Barry Goldwater understood their conversation yesterday, former President Dwight The Republican Senate leader, D. Eisenhower indicated that he would not hold Mr. Goldwater's vote against the civil rights bill against him.

However, General Eisenhower reportedly indicated he would have voted for the bill had he been a member of the Senate because he felt the Federal Government should express its commitment to equality by legislative action this year.

A qualified source today gave this description of the meeting that took place in Gettysburg a few hours before Mr. Goldwater announced to the Senate that he would oppose the bill.

The Arizonan is said to be well aware of the political gravity of his step but doubts it will cost him the Republican Presidential nomination.

Mr. Goldwater, it was learned, holds the following views:

Although he opposed the civil rights bill, he feels that if elected President he would enforce it strongly—more so, he contends, than President Johnson would.

¶If he is nominated and if Mr. Johnson attacks him on the civil rights issue, Mr. Goldwater feels he could make the President stick to the issue in the South, where it might help the Senator.

¶Mr. Goldwater is becoming increasingly disenchanted with Gov. William W. Scranton of Pennsylvania. In the Senator's opinion, Mr. Scranton's recent speeches show him much more liberal than the conservative Arizonan had imagined. As a possible Vice-Presidential candidate, Mr. Scranton seems less and less plausible to Mr. Goldwater.

¶Although he opposed the foresee a major battle over the Republican civil rights platform plank, Mr. Goldwater will never fight with the platform committee or attempt to dictate the platform. He will run on what the committee produces.

¶Mr. Goldwater hopes that civil rights will not be a heated campaign issue because he fears this could lead to violence. But he thinks it possible that picketing by Negroes, and even violence, might swirl about his own campaign entourage.

¶The Senator really does want to be President despite speculation in Washington that he sometimes appears refreshingly skeptical about the rewards of political ambition. Mr. Goldwater, however, has indicated that he is running primarily to take control of the Republican party from liberals who, in his opinion, were turning it into an appendage of the Democratic party. However, there have been times this year when Mr. Goldwater wished that someone would take the nomination away from him and allow him to resume his quieter Senate career.

Mr. Goldwater today replied sharply to Governor Scranton's telegram yesterday urging him to repudiate his announced opposition to the civil rights bill.

In a telegram to Mr. Scranton, the Senator said:

"You very recently said that 'Lincoln would cry out in pain if we sold out our principles.' Aren't you asking me to sell out my principles and aren't you, in effect, saying that unless I do, I will be punished by not receiving the nomination?"

Mr. Goldwater's telegram said that the sections of the bill on public accommodations and fair employment practices "run completely contrary" to the philosophies of Lincoln and Theodore Roosevelt, the oft-stated positions of General Eisenhower, and to the platforms of our party."

The Senator explained that it was his contention that the sections were an unconstitutional exercise of Federal power.

Despite the telegram's reference to General Eisenhower, Mr. Goldwater clearly understood in their conversation that the former President favored the civil rights bill, the qualified source said.

It was Mr. Goldwater's understanding that General Eisenhower would not come out in open opposition to his nomination on the basis of the civil rights bill alone.

Mr. Goldwater, it is said, believes that if General Eisenhower takes a stand against him it would have a decided effect on the outcome of the Republican National Convention which opens July 13 in San Francisco.

The Senator reportedly does not see any irreconcilable conflict between his civil rights stand and his role as a candidate or as a possible President. As President, he is said to reason, he would have to uphold the law whether he liked it or not, and he would do so wholeheartedly.

He will not campaign, directly or by implication, on a promise to work for repeal of the act, the source said.

Mr. Goldwater, it is said, thinks it would be redundant to include an endorsement of the civil rights bill in the Republican platform because it will already be law. In his view, it is no longer a major issue.

However, in Washington today, the chairman of the Platform Committee, Representative Melvin R. Laird of Wisconsin, said the platform would endorse the civil rights bill and possibly suggest it be broadened.

"I do not believe," he declared, "the Republican convention will nominate any candidate who will not carry out the pledges of the party platform."

An assistant platform chairman, Representative Charles E. Goodell of upstate New York, said Mr. Goldwater was "just going to have to accept" a strong civil rights plank.

One name Mr. Goldwater has considered for Vice President, sources said, is that of the Republican National Chairman, William E. Miller of New York.

Romney Assails Rights Vote

LANSING, Mich., June 19 (AP)—Gov. George Romney of Michigan today criticized Senator Goldwater's announced intention to vote against the civil "A 'no' vote on civil rights rights bill. Mr. Romney said: certainly indicates that Goldwater's views in this vital area are not in accord with the sentiment of the majority of the public, the majority of Republicans, the majority of the Congress, Republican platforms for some time, or our Republican heritage."

Shift to Goldwater Made

ROANOKE, Va., June 19 (AP) — Robert A Garland, chairman of Virginia Republicans for Rockefeller for President, said today he would support Senator Goldwater for the Presidential nomination.

Mr. Garland criticized "the waiting game" he said had been played by Governor Scranton before he finally entered the race.

G.O.P. Platform Officials Say Rights Plank Binds Candidate

WASHINGTON, June 19 (AP)—Senator Barry Goldwater is "just going to have to accept" a strong civil rights statement in the party platform if he is the Republican Presidential nominee, a platform official said today.

Representative Charles E. Goodell of New York, assistant platform chairman for domestic affairs, said the Arizona Senator "is not going to be able to advocate repealing things that have become ingrained in our system and I think he understands that."

The chairman of the platform committee, Representative Melvin R. Laird of Wisconsin, said in a separate interview:

"I do not believe the Republican convention will nominate any candidate who will not carry out the pledges and positions of the party platform . . . the platform comes first, before the nomination of a candidate.'"

Senator Goldwater said yesterday that he would vote against the civil rights bill in the Senate because parts of it "fly in the face of the Constitution."

Mr. Laird said the platform would not back down from any part of the civil rights bill, which was supported by a large majority of Republicans in the House and Senate.

If anything, the platform committee might advocate broadening the bill in areas such as voting rights, he said.

He said the party's 1960 civil rights statement went beyond the bill in some respects and that there would be "no retreat" from that position.

"Barry Goldwater has been going around the country making speeches that the law of the land is established by Congress, not the courts," Mr. Laird said. "As a constitutionalist, even though he might have disagreed at the time and voted against it, I don't see why he wouldn't be for implementing it once it is the law."

Mr. Laird and Mr. Goodell emphasized that as platform officials they were maintaining strict neutrality toward possible Republican nominees.

Mr. Goodell said:

"A national candidate no longer represents a state or a district. He represents the consensus of his party and he has to run on that consensus.

Problem in Connecticut
Special to The New York Times

HARTFORD, June 19—The chairman of the Goldwater for President Committee in Connecticut said today that the vote of Senator Barry Goldwater against the civil rights bill "will make our problem a little more difficult in Connecticut" if the Arizonan is nominated for the Presidency.

The chairman, Newman Marsilius, said he had sent Senator Goldwater a telegram Thursday urging him to vote for the civil rights bill "in spite of some questionable features." "I accept his decision," Mr. Marsilius said. "I admire the Senator's courage and forthrightness."

The Proceedings In Washington

YESTERDAY
(June 19, 1964)

THE PRESIDENT

Flew to California for weekend speaking trip.

THE SENATE

Passed civil rights bill, 73 to 27.

Adjourned at 8:10 P.M. until noon Monday.

Foreign Relations Committee heard Administrator Bell urge approval of the full $3.5 billion foreign aid bill.

Agriculture committee held final hearing on the President's food stamp program.

THE HOUSE

Held routine session.

Adjourned at 12:11 P.M. until noon Monday.

DEPARTMENTS & AGENCIES

State Department official said that a Polish proposal for a six-nation conference on Laos should be "carefully considered."

SCHEDULED FOR TODAY
(June 20, 1964)

President Johnson in California.

GOLDWATER FOES ASSAILED IN SPAIN

Madrid Paper Says Senator Fights 'Establishment'

By PAUL HOFMANN
Special to The New York Times

MADRID, June 19—One of the Spanish capital's daily newspapers has accused Spanish correspondents in Washington of disparaging Barry Goldwater.

In an editorial that was believed to express the views of influential quarters here, Madrid, an evening newspaper, said that Spanish journalists in the United States capital had limited themselves to reflecting the hostility of the American "establishment" to the Republican Presidential aspirant.

Madrid defined the "establishment" as those "obscure power organizations that actually direct the destinies of the great Anglo-Saxon democracies while respecting the appearances of uncontrolled liberty."

The United States "establishment" has organized a stop-Goldwater campaign on a giant scale, Madrid said, because the Republican Senator refused to play along with it. The editorial hailed what it described as Mr. Goldwater's victories over the "establishment" and suggested that the American "dictators of public opinion" would suffer a stinging defeat if Mr. Goldwater were to win the Republican nomination, or even the Presidency.

"A man of independent ideas, ready to jettison all clichés," was the way Madrid described Mr. Goldwater.

Madrid asserted that The New York Times was the foremost mouthpiece of the United States "establishment." In opposition to Mr. Goldwater, the editorial said, The Times "has broken all previous records of passion established in cases that it deemed really crucial."

Madrid asserted that The Times played an important role in fighting the late Senator Joseph McCarthy, Republican of Wisconsin; in establishing Premier Fidel Castro in Cuba, and in "liquidating a dangerous enemy of Communism in Vietnam"—President Ngo Dinh Diem.

The editorial hailed those Americans who defied the "establishment" and gave "massive votes" to Mr. Goldwater.

José Maria Massip, Washington correspondent for A.B.C. of Madrid and apparently a target of Madrid's criticism, wrote that Mr. Goldwater was not a historical phenomenon but "an accident capable of profoundly splitting the Republican party."

ARIZONAN TARGET OF G.O.P. LEADER

Continued From Page 1, Col. 5

ion that you will, it will carry forward."

Then Senator Dirksen made what many in the gallery thought was a reference to yesterday's Goldwater statement about "conscience."

"You can go and talk about conscience!" Senator Dirksen said. "It is man's conscience that speaks in every generation!"

The Minority Leader read with emphasis a telegram sent to him on June 10 by 40 of the nation's Governors gathered at Cleveland for the annual Governors' Conference. It urged prompt enactment of the pending civil rights legislation.

He then read, slowly and deliberately, the list of states whose Governors had signed the telegram. One of the states was Arizona, and Senator Dirksen pronounced that state's name with a special stress that drew murmurs from the gallery.

The Governor of Arizona is Paul Fannin, a Republican and a close friend and leading supporter of Senator Goldwater.

Senator Dirksen said members of the press had asked him why he had "become a crusader on this question."

He said he had been asked the same question many years ago when he worked for Chinese Relief, and he said he thought then of the lines of John Donne, the 17th-Century English poet: "Any man's death diminishes me, because I am involved in mankind."

The Senator continued:

"Whatever the color of a man's skin, we are all mankind.

"So every denial of freedom, of equal opportunity for a livelihood, or for an education, diminishes me. There is the moral basis for this legislation."

Senator Dirksen's half-hour, extemporaneous speech, the last in the 83 days of debate on civil rights, was over. He said:

"Mr. President, I'm prepared to vote."

The clerk began to call the roll.

At this point, Senator Goldwater walked over from his desk and shook Senator Dirksen's hand.

Despite this expression of continuing friendship, few here tonight doubted that the Dirksen speech foreshadowed a great struggle at the Republican Convention over civil rights that could vitally affect Senator Goldwater's chance for the nomination.

U.S. TO TEST ACT IN COURT QUICKLY

Public Accommodation Part Expected to Stir Questions

WASHINGTON, June 19 (UPI)—The Government plans to seek court tests of the Civil Rights Act as soon as possible after it takes effect, Assistant Attorney General Burke Marshall said today.

Mr. Marshall, who will be charged with enforcing much of the law, said that he expected a great deal of voluntary compliance with its provisions.

He said, however, that he was certain that there would be some who would resist the law and challenge various parts of it.

The chief of the Justice Department's Civil Rights Section said he expected most questions about application of the measure to originate from its provisions outlawing discrimination in places of public accommodation.

"In all cases we will seek voluntary compliance first," he said. "The bill makes the choice clear—either a person complies or we will file a suit.

"In cases where we can't obtain voluntary compliance, we will bring suits as quickly as possible."

Mr. Marshall said that he particularly expected that problems would be raised on the constitutionality of the bill. The first suits developed by the Government would be aimed at answering those legal questions. he said.

In addition to the public accommodations section, Mr. Marshall primarily will be responsible for enforcement of provisions dealing with voting, employment and schools.

The new voting rights section does not change the Government's powers. But it provides for expediting these cases in the court. Mr. Marshall said he expected to continue the enforcement program already in effect, although perhaps at an accelerated pace.

To meet the increased demands on the Civil Rights Division, the Justice Department will ask Congress for a supplemental appropriation of $1.2 million to increase its legal staff.

Other Measures Urged

Even at a level of 56 lawyers, Mr. Marshall's staff would be the smallest of any division of the Justice Department and he hopes to hire 50 to 60 more lawyers in the next fiscal year to help share the burden imposed by the law.

Mr. Marshall emphasized that the law would not solve all of the nation's civil rights problems, no matter how well it was enforced. It can "only end official discrimination, such as that practiced largely in the South, not the more subtle forms usually used in the North."

"But it creates a legal situation which hopefully makes the nation's racial problems solvable in the courts over the next two generations," he said.

"This bill is largely prohibitive in nature," he continued. "It will take more creative legislation, such as the poverty bill, to solve some of the deeper problems of the North."

PRESIDENT CALLS ACT A 'CHALLENGE'

Continued From Page 1, Col. 4

ing purpose of the American nation for almost 200 years.

"It is the product, not of any man or group of men, but of a broad national consensus that every person is entitled to justice, to equality, and to an even chance to enjoy the blessings of liberty. It is in the highest tradition of a civilization which, from the Magna Carta on, has used the fabric of law for the fulfillment of liberty.

"Lastly, this bill is a challenge. It is a challenge to men of goodwill in every part of the country, to transform the commands of our law into the customs of our land. It is a challenge to all of us, to go to work in our states and communities, in our homes and in the depths of our hearts to eliminate the final strongholds of intolerance and hatred. It is a challenge to reach beyond the content of the bill to conquer the barriers of poor education, poverty, and squalid housing which are an inheritance of past injustice and an impediment to future advance.

"Programs to improve the life of all underprivileged Americans will go far to liberate those who have suffered under the heavy weight of racial discrimination.

"I do not underestimate the depth of the passions involved in the struggle for racial equality. But I also know that throughout this country, in every section of this land, there is a large reservoir of goodwill and compassion, of decency and fair play which seeks a vision of justice without violence in the streets. If these forces do not desert the field, if they can be brought to the battle, then the years of trial will be a prelude to the final triumph of a land 'with liberty and justice for all.'"

Wirtz Names Father McGinley

BUFFALO, June 19 (UPI)—Secretary of Labor W. Willard Wirtz announced today the appointment of the Very Rev. James J. McGinley as an honorary recruitment chairman for President Johnson's Youth Opportunity Program. Father McGinley is president of Canisius College here.

Harlem Residents Greet Passage of Civil Rights Bill With a Shrug of the Shoulders

NO ELATION FOUND ON WEST 125TH ST.

Wait-and-See Attitude Is General Reaction—Effect In South Is Foreseen

By IRVING SPIEGEL

A sampling of Harlem's residents last night about Senate passage of the civil rights bill ranged from restrained satisfaction to open doubt and apathy.

The feeling of many was expressed by one middle-aged man as he was hurrying into a radio repair shop on West 125th Street:

"It's still a piece of paper. Let's wait until the letter of the law is carried out."

If there was any elation over the vote, one could not find it on West 125th Street, or from pedestrians ambling along on Seventh and Lenox Avenues.

In the offices of the New York branch of the Congress of Racial Equality at the Theresa Hotel, one member remarked:

"It's been long overdue. What is there to celebrate about? If anything, the Negro should recite a silent prayer and hope that this will be the beginning of a new era."

'No Dancing on Streets'

Standing nearby, Luther Seabrook, the chapter chairman, said:

"You'll find no dancing on the streets. It's a piece of paper that means little . . . but to the Negroes in the Deep South it will give them something to fight with. It gives them the power to vote, the right to public accommodations."

As volunteers of the branch hurried out of the offices on missions through Harlem to urge people to register for the forthcoming elections, Gladys Harrington, another official, remarked:

"The test will come when we go into the Southern communities and courts."

More outspoken was another official, George Johnson:

"There are enough laws to give equality for all. Why is this law necessary. I am an American citizen, I don't need a special piece of legislation to give me that assurance."

In restaurants and bars, the radio and television had announced the passage of the bill with little emotional response from patrons. There was interest in the televised game between the Mets and the Phillies.

On the sidewalk in front of the Theresa Hotel, Frank B. Sawyer, a public relations executive, said that he saw "no particular reason why the urban Negro, especially in New York City, should especially rejoice over the passage of the bill."

"The results," he said, "will not have that much effect on his problems. The rejoicing will take place in the South, where the shackles of discrimination will begin to come loose. The urban Negro is concerned with better jobs, better housing and building better business opportunities."

There were many on West 125th Street who simply shrugged their shoulders, made no comment and kept on walking.

The nearest to any positive declaration on the bill's passage came from a well-dressed young man, who said:

"Okay, I guess, I'll go along with it."

But a mother, flanked by her two children, said:

"Why did they wait so long? This should have been done before I was born."

Somewhat hopefully, she added, "Maybe my children will have it better."

But one, an 18-year old boy, bitterly remarked:

"I don't have a high-school diploma, the doors are still closed to me."

The woman, stopped, then said:

"When I was young there was no hope . . . perhaps now our children can have hope."

CORE Fete Is Restrained

By M. S. HANDLER

The throbbing beat of Solomon Hall, drummer with the Eddie Barfield All-Star Band, hammered unceasingly last night at the old Central Plaza Ballroom on lower Second Avenue.

The Seven Arts Chapter of CORE had planned a fund-raising dance but the Senate passage of the civil rights bill transformed the dance into something of a victory celebration.

A quiet euphoria pervaded the Negro and white theater folk who make up the membership of the Seven Arts chapter. There was no bombast, no shouting, no boasting. The guests exuded quiet satisfaction.

As Miss Frances Foster, an actress, who is chairman of the chapter, put it:

"We are happy the bill passed in the Senate but we have no illusions that everything will be all right tomorrow.

"It means a big step forward has been made, but it also means we are going to have to put our shoulders to the wheel and push even harder."

Nurses Elect President

Special to The New York Times

ATLANTIC CITY, June 19—Jo Eleanor Elliott of Boulder, Colo., was elected president of the American Nurses Association today. She succeeds Mrs. Margaret B. Dolan of Chapel Hill, N. C.

Pope to Mark Anniversary

ROME, June 19 (AP)—Pope Paul VI will celebrate his first anniversary as Pontiff on Sunday with a solemn religious ceremony in St. Peter's Basilica, the Vatican press office announced today.

Associated Press Wirephoto

BEACH SCENE IN ST. AUGUSTINE: Policeman patrols "white" beach with dog as Negro demonstrators enter surf at area maintained by city. There were no incidents.

School-Integration Plan Revised; 'Quality Education' May Be Cut

By LEONARD BUDER

The Board of Education announced yesterday a modification of its integration plan that could, school officials said, lead to cutbacks in some of the "quality education" features of the program.

The cutbacks, which were attributed to a lack of classroom space, might curtail the system's plans to establish pre-kindergarten programs, provide additional kindergartens, give first-graders an extra hour of instruction and reduce the extent of short-time instruction.

Under the modification, 30 elementary schools—not 45, as previously announced — would give up their sixth grades next fall to provide space for the expanded services. The schools are all in predominantly Negro and Puerto Rican areas.

A spokesman for the board emphasized that the cutbacks in quality programs would be averted or minimized if additional classroom space could be found outside some schools that are now filled to capacity or overcrowded.

Search for Space

He said that local school officials would make an intensive neighborhood search to see if classes could be set up in settlement houses and other buildings.

But he conceded, with considerable reluctance, that unless sufficient additional classrooms could be obtained there would be a reduction in the scope of the board's plans for the new school year, which starts in September.

The development came as thousands of white parents from all parts of the city converged on two Queens elementary schools, both largely white, to protest the scheduled pairing of the schools next fall with two schools that are predominantly Negro.

The demonstrators who were organized by parents and taxpayers groups, urged that children be allowed to go to schools in their neighborhoods and not be compelled to attend schools in other areas for integration purposes.

In disclosing the modification of its plans, the school board said that it had reduced the number of schools involved after "staff re-examination and consultation with parent and other community groups."

The board explained that it was dropping most of the 15 schools to prevent overcrowding the junior high schools to which the sixth-graders were to have been assigned.

Deleted Schools Listed

The deleted schools are Public Schools 119 and 197, Manhattan; P.S. 4, 53 and 63, Bronx; P.S. 256, Brooklyn; and P.S. 48, 50, 116, 140, 14, 19, 92, 143, 45 and 96, all in Queens.

The reduction will mean that 3,400 sixth-grade pupils, not 5,804 pupils as earlier reported, will be transferred to other schools in the fall.

It will also mean, the board spokesman said, that unless the additional classrooms are found the following will result:

¶The reduction in the number of pupils receiving short-time instruction (less than a five-hour day) will affect 12 schools, not 14 as originally planned.

¶A fifth hour of instruction daily will be provided to 1,863 first-grade pupils in 12 schools, not 2,686 in 17 schools.

¶Additional kindergartens will be set up in 12 schools, not 18.

¶Pre-kindergarten programs will be established in 12 schools, not 23.

The sixth-graders were originally scheduled to be transferred to 10 junior high schools, which, in turn, are to send ninth-grade students to 36 designated senior high schools

But as a result of an agreement between school officials and civil rights leaders earlier this week, the sixth-graders will be given an option of attending either the junior high schools, which are largely Negro and Puerto Rican, or 39 predominantly white or integrated elementary schools in other areas.

A list of these alternate elementary schools was also made public yesterday by the school system.

Also yesterday, the Public Education Association urged Mayor Wagner to support the Board of Education's request for additional funds to put a "saturation" improvement program in effect next fall at 10 schools in underprivileged areas.

The two large parents and taxpayers demonstrations in Queens were held outside P.S. 149, 34th Avenue and 93d Street in Jackson Heights, and P.S. 148, 32d Avenue and 89th Street in East Elmhurst.

The pickets, who said they came from all boroughs to protest the school-pairing feature of the integration plan, first paraded outside P.S. 149 for an hour, and then marched to the other school to resume the demonstration. Police estimated that about 3,000 persons took part in the protest.

There were also smaller parent demonstrations outside other schools.

Teachers at Junior High School 38 in the Bronx picketed the school before and after classes to protest the transfer of sixth-grade pupils to that school in September.

They charged that they would be compelled to teach "out of license"—that is, as junior high school teachers they were licensed to teach seventh through ninth grade pupils, not sixth-graders.

Optional Schools

Under the Board of Education's integration plan, which will go into effect in September, sixth-grade pupils who are now in the fifth grade at the 30 elementary schools listed in the first column will have the option of attending alternate elementary schools listed in the second column or certain previously announced junior high schools. Where more than one alternate elementary school is listed, the preference of the parents will be honored depending on available space.

From Present School	To Alternate School	Address of Alternate School
MANHATTAN TO BRONX		
68	73	1020 Anderson Ave. at W. 165 St.
90	46	279 E. 196 St.
100	73	1020 Anderson Ave. at W. 165 St.
123	46	279 E. 196 St.
133	91	Aqueduct Ave. & 182 St.
175	7	3201 Kingsbridge Av.
	86	W. 195 St. & Reservoir Ave.
194	56	207 St. & Hull Ave.
BRONX TO BRONX		
1	104	1449 Shakesp're Av.
2	26	1930 Andres Ave.
5	105	725 Brady Ave.
29	64	1425 Walton Ave.
42	94	1340 Sheridan Ave.
51	89	980 Mace Ave.
132	11	1257 Ogden Ave.
	33	1224 Jerome Ave.
140	106	2120 St. Raymond Ave.
BROOKLYN		
3	193	2515 Ave. L
29	160	5105 Ft. Hamilton Pkwy.
32	205	6701 20 Ave.
44	180	16 Ave. & 57 St.
	48	6015 18 Ave.
47	105	1031 59 Street
93	179	202 Avenue C
167	197	1599 E. 22 St.
191	192	4715 18 Ave.
243	199	1100 Elm Ave.
261	164	14 Ave. & 42 St.
289	238	1633 E. 8 St.
305	177	Ave. P & West 1 St.
	131	4305 Ft. Hamilton Pkwy.
QUEENS		
123	131	172 St. & 84 Ave., Jamaica
	153	60-02 60th Lane., Maspeth
	213	231-02 67 Ave., Bayside
155	71	62-85 Forest Ave., Ridgewood
	178	189-10 Radnor Rd., Jamaica
	87	67-54 80 St., Middle Village
160	128	69-26 65 Dr., Middle Village
	179	196-25 Peck Ave., Flushing

WHITES REPULSED IN ST. AUGUSTINE

Police Block Their Attempt to Get at Negro Marchers

By JOHN HERBERS

Special to The New York Times

ST. AUGUSTINE, Fla., June 19—A mob of whites, shouting threats and obscenities, tried to penetrate a shoulder-to-shoulder police line tonight in an attempt to get at a procession of Negroes celebrating passage of the civil rights bill.

The whites, fired up by Ku Klux Klan speakers, followed the 180 marchers through dark, narrow streets but were repulsed at every turn by state troopers and other officers.

Bricks and bottles were thrown, but there were apparently no injuries.

About 200 Negroes had met in a Baptist church and cheered the Rev. Dr. Martin Luther King Jr. when he called passage of the civil rights bill a "dawning of new hope" for the Negro.

At the same time about 500 whites were meeting several blocks away in the old Slave Market, which occupies one end of a plaza in the heart of town. They heard a speaker say that the civil rights bill would "bring on a race war."

Negroes Form March

Meanwhile the Negroes formed their marchers and headed for the Slave Market as they have done on previous evenings.

Sheriff L. O. Davis and a posse of officers headed them off and arrested two leaders, the Rev. Andrew Young and the Rev. C. T. Vivian, both members of Dr. King's staff, who were intent on marching into the plaza.

The Rev. Fred L. Shuttlesworth, a Birmingham, Ala., integration leader, who is an associate of Dr. King, then led the procession past the Slave Market down Menendez Avenue toward the old Spanish Fort.

At this point about 200 whites broke out of the plaza and rushed at the marchers.

Police Hold Firm

"Get the black apes," some of them yelled, but the police held them back as the procession was turning into a narrow street toward a white neighborhood.

The whites tried to break through the police line on several occasions but were unsuccessful.

After that the whites, chanting and cursing, ran through lawns and hedgegrows trying to find a weak spot in the line of officers. Repulsed, they finally gave up and returned to the rally.

Earlier, efforts to negotiate a settlement in the city's bitter racial strife collapsed and Dr. King said Negroes might be driven to "more drastic forms of civil disobedience."

Earlier today, 57 demonstrators went to the "white" beach maintained by the city, swam unmolested and returned to town.

Vancouver to Free 200

VICTORIA, B. C., June 19 (UPI)—Attorney General Robert Bonner of British Columbia has ordered the release of 200 inmates of Vancouver's Oakalla Prison on the ground that they had been illegally convicted of drunkenness. He said a card-filing system had been used to determine the basis for sentence, without the court being told of the circumstances of the charge.

Bomb Falls on Kansas

WASHINGTON, June 19 (AP)—An F-100 jet attack plane accidentally released a bomb today while flying about 20 miles northeast of Ft. Riley, Kan. The non-nuclear, 750-pound general purpose bomb, which did not explode, fell onto a river bank in an isolated area.

VIRGINIA CURBED ON SCHOOL PLANS

U.S. Court Bars Payment of Tuition for Whites

Special to The New York Times

RICHMOND, Va., June 19—The last rampart of Virginia's "freedom of choice" system of avoiding desegregation of the public schools was struck down here today by a Federal court.

The decision barred the payment of state tuition grants to support a segregated "private academy" hastily established by white authorities in Surry County, Va., to prevent "race mixing" in classrooms. But it is expected to have a far wider impact throughout the South.

Although the decision here today was nominally a narrow one, applying only to Surry County, its effect was to cast doubt on all such "legal methods" of perpetuating school segregation.

Six other Southern states have variations of the Virginia tuition grant system, under which state and local funds are paid to parents of students enrolled in "private, non-sectarian schools."

The other states are Alabama, Arkansas, Georgia, Louisiana, North Carolina and South Carolina. Mississippi's legislature is considering such a scheme for this fall.

In his sweeping order here, Federal Judge John D. Butzner Jr. directed that the Virginia Board of Education and the Board of Supervisors of Surry County be "enjoined and restrained from processing or approving any applications from persons residing in Surry County for state or county scholarships for use in any school that discriminates in the admission and education of pupils on the basis of race."

Board Enjoined

The order further enjoined the county board "from any action that regulates or affects on the basis of race the initial assignment, transfer, placement, admission, enrollment or education in any public school or any child's use of any facility owned and operated by or controlled by the school board for the use of other children in such schools."

The order also enjoined the board from failing to open and operate any school that it operated in the 1962-1963 school year.

This was to prevent a repetition of the county's action last fall in closing its only white public school.

When the Virginia Pupil Placement Board assigned seven Negro children to the white school last summer all 431 white students transferred to the hastily organized "private" Surry Academy.

Their parents received tuition grants of up to $275 a year toward the academy's fee of $380.

When the seven Negro students appeared for classes, the white public school was closed. The Negro children were returned to Negro schools, which remained open. They were denied admission to the Surry Academy.

Judge Butzner's order was regarded by many here as an "inevitable final blow" to the tuition grant system. The system has been increasingly questioned by Virginia legislators and others. Its critics have called it a costly failure that has been subsidizing the tuition of some well-to-do white students at integrated schools.

11,000 Benefited

More than 11,000 Virginia students benefited from tuition grants this year. The program has cost the state and local governments more than $8 million since the 1958-59 school year, when it was begun.

J. Segar Gravatt, of Blackstone, Va., attorney for Surry County and a number of others resisting Virginia school jurisdictions, said Judge Butzner's ruling would be appealed to the United States Circuit Court of Appeals for the Fourth Circuit.

"I assume we have 30 days in which to appeal," Mr. Gravatt said. "We will not wait that long."

Mr. Gravatt was expected to ask Judge Butzner for a stay of his order pending the appeal. But it was widely believed here that such a stay would be denied.

The decision in the Surry County case is expected to reinforce "massive resistance" groups in Prince Edward County, where the public schools have been closed since 1959. Another Federal court, under District Judge Oren R. Lewis, this week ordered Prince Edward County to reopen its public schools by Thursday and promised to lift a 1961 injunction that barred tuition grant payments there so long as the public schools remained closed.

The restoration of tuition grant support for Prince Edward's segregated "private academy" is considered a key factor in obtaining the compliance of white authorities there.

The Surry County decision, however, cast new doubt on the future solvency of Prince Edward's segregated academy.

Both counties are in Virginia's heavily Negro Southside, a predominantly rural region where white traditions of segregation and political conservatism are strong.

Surry County is a thinly populated tidewater farming area between Richmond and Norfolk. Its population of 6,200 is 65 per cent Negro.

A spokesman for the Virginia office of the National Association for the Advancement of Colored People, which brought the Surry County suit, predicted that "Judge Butzner's principle in this case will certainly control in Virginia."

U.S. Official Warns Mississippi-Bound Students

Tells Civil Rights Volunteers There Is No Federal Police Force to Protect Them

By CLAUDE SITTON

Special to The New York Times

OXFORD, Ohio, June 19 — A Justice Department official today told volunteers for the coming civil rights campaign in Mississippi that there was no Federal police force there to protect them.

John Doar, deputy chief of the department's civil rights division, suggested that the volunteers accept this fact "and guide your conduct accordingly."

His remarks brought angry reaction among the 200 student volunteers and 75 representatives of various civil rights organizations attending a one-week orientation course here at the Western College for Women.

The volunteers will leave tomorrow for Mississippi. They will be followed by another group, which will undergo orientation here next week. Some 800 persons, many of them white college students from outside the South, are expected to take part in the program of political action, education and cultural activities among Negroes.

This attempt to break down racial codes and customs in that state is being reinforced by legal steps. William Kunstler, a New York civil rights lawyer, announced here that a suit had been filed in the Federal District Court at Greenville, Miss., shortly after noon. It seeks to void the state's unpledged Presidential elector law and to give Negroes a voice in the selections of the state's delegation to the Democratic National Convention.

Mr. Doar, in a speech to the orientation class in Peabody Hall, praised the volunteers and members of the Student Nonviolent Coordinating Committee. It is a key organization involved in the Mississippi project, which also has the backing of the Congress of Racial Equality, the Southern Christian Leadership Conference, the National Association for the Advancement of Colored People and the Commission on Religion and Race of the National Council of Churches.

"I admire what you intend to do," said Mr. Doar. "I particularly admire the people who have been working in Mississippi among the student group.

"The real heroes in this country today are the students and particularly those students who have given their time and energy and dedication to correct the very bad and evil problems in the South with respect to the way in which American Negro citizens are treated before the law."

In the question and answer period, Mr. Doar emphasized that the Federal Bureau of Investigation was an investigative agency and not a police force and noted that the deputy Federal marshalls had been used only in a few specific instances for police work in civil rights controversies.

Federal Protection Sought

Parents of Mississippi-bound college students are forming an organization to press for Federal protection of civil rights workers this summer.

According to its founder, Mrs. Kaye Raphael of 14 East 75th Street, the Parents Emergency Committee for Federal Protection of Students in the Mississippi Summer Project hopes to "force intervention before an incident occurs."

"We are outraged," the committee said in a telegram to President Johnson, "by the threats of violence by the Mississippi Legislature and Southern racists."

PASSAGE SCORED BY SOME IN SOUTH

Continued From Page 1, Col. 7

I'll just have to wait and see."

Governor Wallace said, "It is ironical that this event occurs as we approach the celebration of Independence Day. On that day we won our freedom. On this day we have largely lost it."

"The American people will rise up in indignation when they realize the awful consequences of this legislation," he said. "They will then remove from office those responsible."

In Jackson, Miss., two Negroes found the day significant for other reasons.

Mrs. Myrlie Evers, widow of the slain integrationist leader Medgar Evers, said, "Passage of this bill has special meaning to me because it was one year ago today that my husband was buried." And the slain man's brother, Charles Evers, said:

"The passage of the bill is not the important thing. The most important thing is the implementation of it, that it is accepted by both races without too much hatred or bigotry."

David Capouano, manager of a restaurant in Montgomery, said, "I don't like it worth a damn. I feel it is the biggest mistake ever made in the history of the world."

In Roanoke, Va., Mayor Murray Stoller said, "When this becomes the law of the land it will be enforced in the city of Roanoke. There is nothing else we can do. Besides, we're already fully integrated."

In Atlanta, Mayor Ivan Allen Jr. issued a long statement praising the bill. "Now it is time to bind up all old wounds and past grievances and face the future realistically," he said. "I am certain that the citizens of this city will cooperate and will respect this law."

Roger W. Webb, mayor of Nashville, Ga., a little town in the southern part of the state, said, "Whatever the law is we will abide by it."

While many state leaders reacted sharply, Mr. Webb's reaction was relatively typical of small-town mayors, even in Mississippi and Alabama. Many were against it, but did not seem to have strong feelings.

"Personally I don't think we should make such an issue of it all," said Mayor James Ballard of Tupelo, Miss. "I hope it will work out for the best, but it will have to be proven first."

Businessmen appeared to be the most upset over passage of the bill.

"I tell you, Communism has taken over," said a furniture salesman in Thomasville, N. C. "A white man has no say-so over his property."

Nick Parker, an advertising executive in Montgomery, said, "I have no use for it. I agree with Goldwater 150 per cent."

Gov. Albertis S. Harrison Jr. of Virginia said, "My views in opposition to the civil rights bill on numerous grounds are too well known and have been too often expressed for any further comment."

In South Carolina, Gov. Donald Russell said he thought it was "unfortunate."

While most Negroes were pleased, if not overjoyed, and some seemed unaware of what it meant, others, like the Birmingham ice cream vender, seemed to doubt its effectiveness.

2 Killed in Bar Shooting

PHILADELPHIA, June 19 (AP) — Mrs. Judith Lopinson, daughter-in-law of a Pennsylvania state official, and her husband's partner, were shot and killed today reportedly by two gunmen during a robbery attempt. Mrs. Lopinson and Joseph Malito, 52 years old, co-owner of Dante's Bar and Restaurant in mid-city with the 25-year-old woman's husband, were found dead in the restaurant by the police. The husband, Jack Lopinson, 27, a Democratic City Committeeman, said he was shot in the thigh by the robbers.

New Quake Strikes Japan; No Casualties Are Reported

NIIGATA, Japan, June 19 (UPI)—Another strong earth shock jolted northern Japan today, frightening residents of this city devastated by a quake Tuesday.

There were no reports of casualties or damage today.

The quake that hit Niigata three days ago killed 25 persons. Eleven persons are missing and 377 persons were injured.

Oil-refinery fires, touched off by Tuesday's quake, continued to blaze.

The major concern was providing sufficient water for residents. Only 10 per cent of the quake-shattered water system has been restored.

"All the News That's Fit to Print"

The New York Times.

LATE CITY EDITION

U.S. Weather Bureau Report (Page 66) forecasts: Variable cloudiness today; clear tonight. Fair and cool tomorrow.

Temp. Range: 86—65; yesterday: 81—57. Temp.-Hum. Index: low 70's; yesterday: 73.

VOL. CXIII—No. 38,910.

NEW YORK, WEDNESDAY, AUGUST 5, 1964.

TEN CENTS

U.S. PLANES ATTACK NORTH VIETNAM BASES; PRESIDENT ORDERS 'LIMITED' RETALIATION AFTER COMMUNISTS' PT BOATS RENEW RAIDS

F. B. I. Finds 3 Bodies Believed to Be Rights Workers'

GRAVES AT A DAM

Discovery Is Made in New Earth Mound in Mississippi

By CLAUDE SITTON

Special to The New York Times

JACKSON, Miss., Aug. 4—Bodies believed to be those of three civil rights workers missing since June 21 were found early tonight near Philadelphia, Miss.

Federal Bureau of Investigation agents recovered the bodies from a newly erected earthen dam in a thickly wooded area about six miles southwest of Philadelphia, in east-central Mississippi.

The dam is several hundred yards off State Highway 21, near the Neshoba County fairgrounds.

Fulton Jackson, the county coroner, made a preliminary examination at the scene. The bodies were then sealed in plastic bags and brought by ambulance to the University of Mississippi Medical Center in Jackson, 70 miles to the southwest.

Pledge by Governor

Roy K. Moore, special agent in charge of the Jackson F.B.I. office, said physicians and fingerprint experts would seek to make positive identification and establish the cause of death.

[In Washington, authoritative sources said that President Johnson had telephoned Gov. Paul B. Johnson Jr. of Mississippi after having learned of the discovery of the bodies. However, this could not be confirmed immediately.]

Governor Johnson said in a statement:

"If these are the bodies of the three civil rights workers who have been missing several weeks, the investigative forces of the State of Mississippi will exert every effort to apprehend those who may have been responsible."

Area Searched Earlier

Mr. Johnson said he understood F.B.I. agents had searched the area once before and had noticed the new dam. Later, when they saw that the dam had collected no water despite heavy showers, they returned for a further investigation.

Excavation uncovered the bodies in the fill of the dam, the Governor said.

Sheriff L. A. Rainey, who had just returned from a vacation, visited the scene a short while after the discovery.

The missing men were Michael H. Schwerner, 24 years old, and Andrew Goodman, 20, both white and both from New York City, and James E. Chaney, 21, a Negro of Meridian, Miss.

All three had been taking part in the Mississippi Summer Project, a state-wide civil rights drive, which began on the week-

Continued on Page 37, Column 2

Scattered Violence Keeps Jersey City Tense 3d Night

400 Policemen Confine Most of Rioters to 2 Sections—Crowds Watch in Streets Despite Danger

By FRED POWLEDGE

Special to The New York Times

JERSEY CITY, Aug. 4—Scattered violence broke out again here tonight as roving groups of Negroes hurled crude Molotov cocktails in the streets. There was some gunfire but no injuries were reported.

About 400 city policemen contained most of the young rioters to two predominantly Negro neighborhoods. There were at least [illegible] arrests.

Text of Whelan's statement will be found on Page 36.

Although it was dangerous to be on the streets on this third night of violence, many people watched from sidewalks and front porches as police cars, their red lights flashing, sped from one pocket of violence to another.

On Ocean Avenue the police trained spotlights on the roof of a three-story block of apartments. A man had been seen on the roof, and it was feared that he was armed with a rifle, fire bombs, or both. Yet on the sidewalk below, a woman walked her dog, apparently without concern, through throngs of helmeted policemen. From a front porch across the street, a baby cried.

Since the rioting started Sunday night, more than 30 persons have been injured, two of them with gunshot wounds. None of the wounds was critical. More than three dozen persons have been arrested.

Five hundred more Jersey City policemen stood ready to

Continued on Page 36, Column 1

JOHNSON SEEKING EXTREMISM PLANK

Favors a Stand Against Far Left and Right Without Naming Any Groups

Special to The New York Times

WASHINGTON, Aug. 4 — President Johnson wants the Democratic platform to take a stand against extremism of the right and the left, without naming any particular organization.

Mr. Johnson, at the moment, plans to attend the party's national convention in Atlantic City only on Thursday night, Aug. 27, when he is scheduled to make his acceptance speech. But his wish on the platform is likely to be enough to make his views effective.

As yet, however, he has had no detailed discussions with the platform drafters.

The President is also planning to follow a somewhat unusual procedure in having himself placed in nomination. This is to be done by "co-nominators" — Governors Edmund G. Brown of California and John B. Connally Jr. of Texas.

These and other fairly well-advanced plans of the President have been learned from high Democratic sources.

However, on the question of most current interest, Mr. Johnson's choice for a Vice-Presidential candidate, no decision has yet been made.

Senator Hubert H. Humphrey

Continued on Page 14, Column 6

Rockefeller to Join Goldwater's Parley On Campaign Unity

Special to The New York Times

ALBANY, Aug. 4—Governor Rockefeller has accepted the invitation of Senator Goldwater to attend a meeting of Republican Governors at Hershey, Pa., on Aug. 12.

The invitation was extended by the Republican Presidential nominee in telegrams last Saturday to the 16 Republican Governors.

Mr. Rockefeller, who was a candidate for the Presidential nomination until after his defeat in the California primary, June 2, was one of Senator Goldwater's severest critics through the Republican National Convention last month in San Francisco.

Mr. Goldwater has called the Hershey gathering in an effort to promote unity within the Republican party behind his candidacy.

The prospects for success of

Continued on Page 16, Column 1

REDS DRIVEN OFF

Two Torpedo Vessels Believed Sunk in Gulf of Tonkin

By ARNOLD H. LUBASCH

Special to The New York Times

WASHINGTON, Aug. 4—The Defense Department announced tonight that North Vietnamese PT boats made a "deliberate attack" today on two United States destroyers patrolling international waters in the Gulf of Tonkin off North Vietnam.

The attack came two days after North Vietnamese torpedo boats attacked the Maddox, one of the destroyers in today's incident.

The destroyers and covering carrier-based aircraft fired on the vessels in today's attack, drove them off and apparently sank at least two of them, according to the announcement. The Pentagon said there were no United States casualties or damage.

The attack was made by an "undetermined number of North Vietnamese PT boats" during darkness about 65 miles from the nearest land, the Pentagon reported. It said the attack came at 10:30 P. M., North Vietnamese time, or 10:30 A. M., Washington time.

'Fabrication,' Reds Say

[The North Vietnamese regime said Wednesday that the report of another attack on United States ships was a "fabrication."]

The second attack was described in Washington as much fiercer than the first one, which was said to have lasted half an hour. The second battle was understood to have lasted about three hours in rough sea, with bad weather and low visibility.

"We are in a very serious situation," a Government official said.

The attack came shortly before the State Department made public a stern protest about the North Vietnamese attack Sunday on the Maddox, which was then patrolling about 30 miles off North Vietnam, also in international waters in the Gulf of Tonkin.

The protest over the first incident was announced shortly after noon here, when the

Continued on Page 3, Column 1

2 CARRIERS USED

McNamara Reports on Aerial Strikes and Reinforcements

By JACK RAYMOND

Special to The New York Times

WASHINGTON, Wednesday, Aug. 5 — Secretary of Defense Robert S. McNamara said at a postmidnight news conference that the United States planes that attacked North Vietnam yesterday and today had come from the carriers Constellation and Ticonderoga in the Gulf of Tonkin.

He said that the attacks had been directed against the bases used by the North Vietnamese PT boats that attacked two United States destroyers in international waters yesterday.

The Secretary added that the naval planes, believed to have included propeller-driven as well as jet-powered craft, had also conducted strikes against "certain other targets directly supporting the operation of the PT boats."

The United States planes used conventional weapons.

Separate Targets

Mr. McNamara, who held his news conference shortly after President Johnson had addressed the nation on television, emphasized in his report that the PT boat bases and the supporting facilities in North Vietnam had been separate targets.

He offered a guess, based on incomplete reports, that in the exchange of fire between the attacking PT boats and the United States destroyers and aircraft in international waters, at least two and possibly four of the North Vietnamese Soviet-made PT boats had been sunk.

The Defense Secretary disclosed that at one point in the Vietnamese PT boat attack, the Maddox observed an unidentified aircraft on radar, but that there was no air attack and the radar image was soon lost.

The hostilities that provoked United States retaliation began Sunday with an attack by North Vietnamese PT boats on the United States destroyer Maddox in the Gulf of Tonkin.

Hanoi Not Attacked

The first United States reaction was a note of protest and warning. But, as announced by the President and the Secretary of Defense, the second PT boat attack on the destroyers Maddox and C. Turner Joy yesterday precipitated the counteraction.

The Secretary of Defense said at the news conference that the retaliatory strikes were still under way at that time.

He made clear, in response to questions, that no targets outside North Vietnam had been attacked by the United States warplanes. He specifically ex-

Continued on Page 4, Column 3

Associated Press Wirephoto

DECISION: President Johnson, in a nationwide broadcast, tells of action he ordered taken against North Vietnam.

The President's Address

Following is the text of the President's address on Vietnam last night, as recorded by The New York Times:

My fellow Americans:

As President and Commander in Chief, it is my duty to the American people to report that renewed hostile actions against United States ships on the high seas in the Gulf of Tonkin have today required me to order the military forces of the United States to take action in reply.

The initial attack on the destroyer Maddox on Aug. 2 was repeated today by a number of hostile vessels attacking two U.S. destroyers with torpedoes.

The destroyers and supporting aircraft acted at once on the orders I gave after the initial act of aggression.

We believe at least two of the attacking boats were sunk. There were no U.S. losses.

The performance of commanders and crews in this engagement is in the highest tradition of the United States Navy.

But repeated acts of violence against the armed forces of the United States must be met not only with alert defense but with positive reply.

Action 'Now in Execution'

That reply is being given, as I speak to you tonight. Air action is now in execution against gunboats and certain supporting facilities in North Vietnam which have been used in these hostile operations.

In the larger sense, this new act of aggression aimed directly at our own forces again brings home to all of us in the United States the importance of the struggle for peace and security in Southeast Asia.

Aggression by terror against the peaceful villages of South Vietnam has now been joined by open aggression on the high seas against the United States of America.

The determination of all Americans to carry out our full commitment to the people and to the Government of South Vietnam will be redoubled by this outrage. Yet our response for the present will be limited and fitting.

We Americans know—although others appear to forget—the risk of spreading conflict. We still seek no wider war. I have instructed the Secretary of State to make this position totally clear to friends and to adversaries and, indeed, to all.

I have instructed Ambassador Stevenson to raise this matter immediately and urgently before the Security Council of the United Nations.

Congressional Resolution Asked

Finally, I have today met with the leaders of both parties in the Congress of the United States and I have informed them that I shall immediately request the Congress to pass a resolution making it clear that our Government is united in its determination to take all necessary measures in support of freedom and in defense of peace in Southeast Asia.

I have been given encouraging assurance by these leaders of both parties that such a resolution will be promptly introduced, freely and expeditiously debated, and passed with overwhelming support.

And just a few minutes ago I was able to reach Senator Goldwater and I am glad to say that he has expressed his support of the statement that I am making to you tonight.

It is a solemn responsibility to have to order even limited military action by forces whose over-all strength is as vast and as awesome as those of the United States of America.

But it is my considered conviction, shared throughout your Government, that firmness in the right is indispensable today for peace.

That firmness will always be measured. Its mission is peace.

FORCES ENLARGED

Stevenson to Appeal for Action by U.N. on 'Open Aggression'

By TOM WICKER

Special to The New York Times

WASHINGTON, Aug. 4—President Johnson has ordered retaliatory action against gunboats and "certain supporting facilities in North Vietnam" after renewed attacks against American destroyers in the Gulf of Tonkin.

In a television address tonight, Mr. Johnson said air attacks on the North Vietnamese ships and facilities were taking place as he spoke, shortly after 11:30 P.M.

State Department sources said the attacks were being carried out with conventional weapons on a number of shore bases in North Vietnam, with the objective of destroying them and the 30 to 40 gunboats they served.

The aim, they explained, was to destroy North Vietnam's gunboat capability. They said more air strikes might come later, if needed. Carrier-based aircraft were used in tonight's strike.

2 Boats Believed Sunk

Administration officials also announced that substantial additional units, primarily air and sea forces, were being sent to Southeast Asia.

This "positive reply," as the President called it, followed a naval battle in which a number of North Vietnamese PT boats attacked two United States destroyers with torpedoes. Two of the boats were believed to have been sunk. The United States forces suffered no damage and no loss of lives.

Mr. Johnson termed the North Vietnamese attacks "open aggression on the high seas."

Washington's response is "limited and fitting," the President said, and his Administration seeks no general extension of the guerrilla war in South Vietnam.

Goldwater Approves

"We Americans know," he said, "although others appear to forget, the risks of spreading conflict."

Mr. Johnson said Secretary of State Dean Rusk had been instructed to make this American attitude clear to all nations. He added that Adlai E. Stevenson, chief United States delegate, would raise the matter immediately in the United Nations Security Council. [The Council was expected to meet at 10:30 A.M. Wednesday.]

The President said he had informed his Republican Presidential rival, Senator Barry Goldwater, of his action and

Continued on Page 2, Column 3

Khanh Is Fighting Threat of a Coup

By SEYMOUR TOPPING

Special to The New York Times

SAIGON, South Vietnam, Aug. 4—Premier Nguyen Khanh struggled today to strengthen the political stability of his Government as his aides privately warned of plots to drive him from office. United States officials were concerned about the political deterioration in Saigon.

The malaise in the capital was attributed more to a clash of rival political and military personalities than to pressure from the Vietcong insurgents.

United States sources said reports from provinces indicated that conditions there were generally better than in Saigon.

Once again rumors of a coup d'état were circulating in Sai-

Continued on Page 4, Column 7

Auto Collision Insurance Rates In State Increased 4.3 to 25%

By JOSEPH C. INGRAHAM

Higher auto damage insurance rates — with increases from 4.3 to 25 per cent—will go into effect today for private passenger car owners in the state.

The increases were disclosed yesterday by the National Automobile Underwriters Association, which said that sharp rises in auto thefts and in the cost of repairs had made them necessary.

The association said that although the statewide rise would be the lesser amount, the rates in most of the metropolitan areas had been increased as much as 25 per cent.

Physical damage insurance, which reimburses a car owner for loss of or damage to his own car, is optional. The rate revisions apply to collision insurance and to comprehensive coverage, which protects motorists against loss due to theft, fire, windstorm, glass breakage and other hazards.

While each of these coverages can be bought separately, the National Automobile Underwriters Association, rating organization for more than 400 companies here, lumps the vari-

Continued on Page 67, Column 2

Salinger Appointed to the Senate

United Press International Telephoto

Pierre Salinger, left, with Gov. Edmund G. Brown of California after the announcement yesterday in Sacramento.

By WALLACE TURNER

Special to The New York Times

SAN FRANCISCO, Aug. 4—Pierre Salinger was appointed to the Senate today by Gov. Edmund G. Brown of California to fill the remaining five months of the term of the late Senator Clair Engle. Mr. Salinger is scheduled to be sworn in tomorrow about noon. He will be escorted to the rostrum by Senator Thomas H. Kuchel of California, the assistant Senate Republican leader. Governor Brown is to head a party of about 160 Democratic leaders who will be present in the Senate galleries when the new Senator takes his oath. Mr. Salinger, who was White House press

Continued on Page 16, Column 2

Congolese Battling Inside Stanleyville

By J. ANTHONY LUKAS

Special to The New York Times

LEOPOLDVILLE, the Congo, Aug. 4—Rebels of the "Popular Army" and Government troops battled tonight in the streets of Stanleyville, the chief city in the northern Congo.

Messages from the United States consul there said heavy fighting was going on early this evening in front of the consulate, about half a mile from the center of the city.

At 6:15 P. M. Stanleyville time, the consul, Michael P. E. Hoyt, telegraphed that the army was "advancing across front lawn of consulate" and seemed to be "pushing rebels back."

Eight minutes later he wired that the army troops were "advancing rapidly and in numbers beyond consulate on road to Wanie Rukula." He said that

Continued on Page 3, Column 4

NEWS INDEX

U.S. Attacks North Vietnamese Bases in Reprisal

JOHNSON ASSAILS NEW RAID BY REDS

Forces Will Be Enlarged Stevenson to Urge U.N. to Act on 'Aggression'

Continued From Page 1, Col. 8

had received his endorsement.

Congressional leaders of both parties, the President went on, have assured him of speedy and overwhelming passage of a resolution "making clear that our Government is united in its determination to take all necessary measures in support of freedom and defense of peace in Southeast Asia."

Mike Mansfield of Montana, the Senate majority leader, said the Congressional resolution Mr. Johnson had requested would be introduced "sometime in the morning."

Mr. Johnson gave Mr. Goldwater the details of his statement by telephone. He reached the Senator at Newport Beach, Calif., late today, after three telephone calls failed. Mr. Goldwater spent most of his day aboard a yacht.

"I am sure," Senator Goldwater said, "that every American will subscribe to the actions outlined in the President's statement. I believe it is the only thing he can do under the circumstances. We cannot allow the American flag to be shot at anywhere on earth if we are to retain our respect and prestige."

Nixon Voices Backing

Richard M. Nixon, the 1960 Republican candidate, also backed Mr. Johnson. Mr. Nixon, in Washington, said he believed the President should have bi-partisan support in dealing with the situation.

Mr. Johnson was long delayed tonight in making his television address. Reporters were alerted several hours before he actually appeared in the Fish Room of the White House, where television cameras had been set up.

State Department sources said he had probably been waiting for word that the attacks had been carried out on the gunboats and supporting facilities.

'Hot Line' Unused

State Department sources said there had been no effort to use the "hot line" between the White House and the Kremlin, and no effort to warn Communist China through intermediaries.

The Chinese are believed here to be the instigators of the North Vietnamese attacks.

State Department sources said the United States had last sought to carry direct warnings to Peking on May 17. Mr. Rusk then consulted with the ambassadors of Southeast Asia Treaty Organization nations and suggested that those dealing with China convey to Peking the United States' concern, which was not acknowledged by Peking.

It was clear from the crisis air in the White House, from Mr. Johnson's solemn manner as he spoke and from earlier statements issued at the State Department that the action the President had ordered here was regarded as a matter of the utmost seriousness.

Before the raids on the American ships, the question of attacking North Vietnam was a bone of contention between Washington and Saigon.

The South Vietnamese Premier, Maj. Gen. Nguyen Khanh, had irritated American officials with a series of recent calls for "a push to the North." As Washington stressed its opposition to an expansion of the conflict, Premier Khanh appeared to be retreating from his position.

Mr. Johnson said the retaliatory action he had ordered had been taken against "vessels and facilities used in these hostile operations."

Thus, despite Mr. Johnson's assurances that the United States sought no "wider war," it was plain that the sitation in South Vietnam and the surrounding area had reached new gravity.

In South Vietnam, American forces have been advising and training the South Vietnamese Army in its resistance against Communist guerrillas.

American naval vessels have been patrolling the Gulf of Tonkin, both as a show of force and to offer naval support for situations that might develop in Southeast Asia.

The first North Vietnamese attack came Sunday when torpedo boats attacked the destroyer Maddox. They were driven off.

The new attacks came in spite of orders Mr. Johnson had given that United States naval forces destroy any attackers.

The State Department sources said there had been no time to consult with the SEATO nations or other allies. In addition, they said the need for surprise in the retaliation made consultations difficult.

Notification of allied nations began after the President's address.

Mr. Johnson was occupied all day with meetings and messages on the situation in the Gulf of Tonkin. He summoned 16 Congressional leaders of both parties to the White House for a meeting at 6:45 P.M.

The meeting lasted 90 minutes. When it ended, George Reedy, the White House press secretary, said Mr. Johnson would appear on television.

The following Congressional leaders wree at the White House:

Senators Mike Mansfield, the majority leader; J. William Fulbright, chairman of the Foreign Relations Committee; Richard B. Russell, chairman of the Armed Services Committee, and Carl Hayden, President Pro Tem of the Senate, Democrats.

Senators Everett McKinley Dirksen, the minority leader; Bourke B. Hickenlooper, ranking minority member of the Foreign Relations Committee, and Leverett Saltonstall, ranking minority member of the Armed Services Committee, Republicans.

Representatives John W. McCormack, the Speaker; Carl Albert, the majority leader; Thomas E. Morgan, chairman of the Foreign Affairs Committee, and Carl Vinson, chairman of the Armed Services Committee, Democrats.

Representatives Charles A. Halleck, minority leader; Frances P. Bolton, ranking minority member of the Foreign Affairs Committee, and Leslie C. Arends, ranking minority member of the Armed Services Committee, Republicans.

Cabinet Aides Attend

Also present at the meeting were Secretary of State Rusk, Secretary of Defense Robert S. McNamara, John A. McCone, Director of Central Intelligence, and Gen. Earle G. Wheeler, chairman of the Joint Chiefs of Staff.

Earlier, Mr. Johnson held his regular Tuesday luncheon with Mr. Rusk, Mr. McNamara and McGeorge Bundy, his special assistant for national-security affairs.

A regularly scheduled meeting of the National Security Council was also held at the White House.

The second attack on the destroyers was discussed at both meetings. The decision to attack the gunboats and shore facilities had been taken, with no dissent, by the time the sessions were ended.

At about 6 P.M., the National Security Council met again, this time to go over operational details and loose ends.

State Department sources said the second North Vietnamese action was considered a calculated attack that had to be dealt with promptly and decisively. Otherwise, it was feared here, the North Vietnamese might seriously miscalculate American intentions in Southeast Asia.

None of the shore facilities under attack were near population centers, officials said.

The question of whether there would be more attacks on the gunboat facilities, state department sources said, depended on the North Vietnamese response—including developments in the guerrilla warfare in South Vietnam.

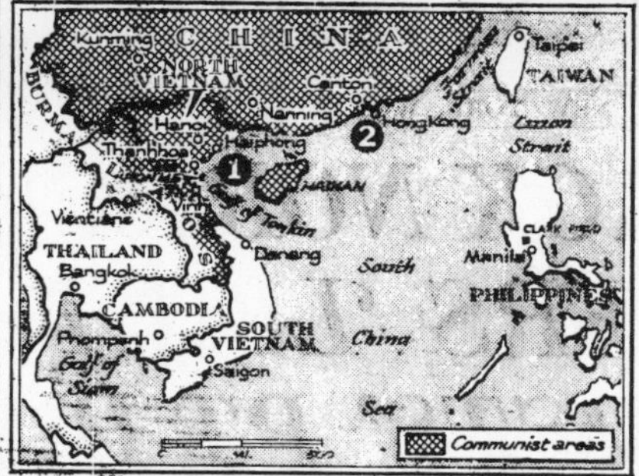

The New York Times Aug. 5, 1964

RETALIATION: American forces in the Gulf of Tonkin (1) struck at North Vietnam. The carrier Constellation, which had sailed from Honk Kong (2) joined in the action.

Johnson's Talk Recalls April TV Appearance

President Johnson's sudden appearance on television last night to discuss the Vietnam crisis recalled a similar hurried appearance in April when the railroad labor conflict was settled at the White House.

When agreement was finally reached to end the five-year dispute over work rules, the President asked the negotiators to meet in his office to announce the accord on television.

As the men filed into his office, Mr. Johnson was informed that it would take more than an hour to arrange for a live telecast from the White House. Instead, he went to a Columbia Broadcasting System studio four miles away to announce the settlement. The President's message went on the air about half an hour after he had requested time.

A message similar in its air of crisis was broadcast on Oct. 22, 1962, by President Kennedy when he announced to the nation that a naval and air "quarantine" had been imposed on the shipment of offensive military equipment

Reds Say Sunday Raid Was in 'Our Waters'

SAIGON, South Vietnam, Aug. 5 (Reuters) — The Hanoi radio said today in its first comment on Sunday's attack on the United States destroyer Maddox that the incident occurred in North Vietnamese territorial waters.

"Our boats came into action to protect our territorial waters and our people and to chase the enemy ship out of our waters," the radio said.

It accused the United States Seventh Fleet of aggressive action and said the United States was attempting to cover up its "aggression" with a story of a so-called unprovoked attack by North Vietnamese boats.

The broadcast contained a warning North Vietnam would take the necessary steps in case of what it called further American aggressive acts.

Lodge Asserts He Is Happy U.S. Met Force With Force

BEVERLY, Mass., Aug. 4 (UPI)—Henry Cabot Lodge, former United States Ambassador to South Vietnam, said tonight that he was happy the United States had met force with force when United States destroyers were attacked by North Vietnamese torpedo boats in the Gulf of Tonkin.

"The Navy has a right to be in those waters," Mr. Lodge said. He asserted the destroyers "had a right to defend themselves, and I'm glad they did."

Mr. Lodge, who resigned his diplomatic post to campaign for Gov. William W. Scranton of Pennsylvania for the Republican Presidential nomination, declined to speculate on the cause of the North Vietnamese attack.

He said he had not been in contact with President Johnson or Administration officials on the current crisis.

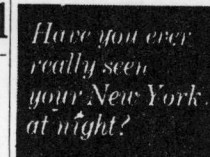

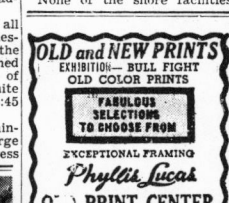

"All the News That's Fit to Print"

The New York Times

LATE CITY EDITION

Weather: Fair and warm today, tonight and tomorrow. Temp. range: today 85-63; Thurs. 85-64. Temp.-Hum. Index: today 70 to 75; Thurs. 77. Full U.S. report on Page 89.

VOL. CXVI..No. 39,948 NEW YORK, FRIDAY, JUNE 9, 1967 — 10 CENTS

EGYPT AND SYRIA AGREE TO U.N. CEASE-FIRE; ISRAEL REPORTS TROOPS REACH SUEZ CANAL; JOHNSON, KOSYGIN USED HOT LINE IN CRISIS

SENATE APPROVES A TIGHTENED RULE ON REDISTRICTING

33 States Ordered to Bring Population Variant Down to 10% by 1968 Election

By JAMES F. CLARITY
Special to The New York Times

WASHINGTON, June 8—The Senate approved today a bill requiring that by the 1968 election no state have a population variance of more than 10 cent between its largest and smallest Congressional districts.

The approval, which came in a surprise vote of 57 to 25, was a result of a fight by Senator Edward M. Kennedy, Democrat of Massachusetts, to amend a measure that would have permitted a variance of 35 per cent until the 1972 election.

The Kennedy amendment, which was soundly defeated in committee two weeks ago, is intended, according to the Senator, to make Congressional redistricting conform with the Supreme Court's one-man, one-vote ruling of 1964. The amendment also deleted language giving the states power to determine when the compactness of a district was "practicable."

An Altered Version

The measure, before it was amended today, was an altered version of a bill already passed by the House. The House bill provided for a population variance of 30 per cent, and was amended by the Senate Judiciary Committee to cover four additional states.

The version passed today, which now goes to a Senate-House conference, would apply to 33 states having variances of more than 10 per cent. Nine of these states are under Federal court orders to redistrict. The 17 states not covered by today's Senate action either elect Representatives at large or have variances lower than 10 per cent.

Mr. Kennedy's proposal was approved, first in a crucial 44-to-89 vote as an amendment, then in the final vote on the bill as amended, 57 to 25.

"We knew it would be close.

Continued on Page 28, Column 1

Arms Cost Stress Scored by Rickover

By EVERT CLARK
Special to The New York Times

WASHINGTON, June 8—Vice Adm. Hyman G. Rickover has denounced the cost-effectiveness approach to weapons development as an "ism," a "new religion" and a "fog bomb" that is keeping the nation from gaining technology that would save lives.

In Congressional testimony released today, the head of the nuclear-powered ship program attacked present management techniques in the Pentagon.

By Presidential order, many of these techniques—including the mathematical analysis of cost vs. effectiveness—are now being spread throughout the executive branch of

Continued on Page 2, Column 4

JURY FINDS LAXITY IN BUILDINGS UNIT

Graft, Shirking and Lack of Personnel Training Are Cited—Moerdler Agrees

By JACK ROTH

A New York County grand jury criticized yesterday long-standing conditions in the Buildings Department that it said had resulted in corruption among housing inspectors and landlords.

The jury also said the situation permitted some inspectors and their supervisors to quit work as early as 10:30 A.M. and go to bars and racetracks for the rest of the day.

The jury, in a presentment handed up to Supreme Court Justice Mitchell D. Schweitzer, charged that the department suffered from lack of financial and manpower resources.

It asserted that inspectors were not properly trained for their jobs, that they were unaware of their department's rules and regulations, that there was duplication in inspections, that electronic processing equipment was failing to do its job and that unauthorized persons had access to file rooms and private departmental offices.

The Buildings Commissioner,

Continued on Page 31, Column 1

ALL SINAI IS HELD

U.A.R. Loses 50 Tanks in Actions Termed Fiercest of War

By Reuters

TEL AVIV, Friday, June 9—Israeli troops have reached the bank of the Suez Canal and have taken control of the entire Sinai Peninsula, the Israeli radio reported this morning.

The radio broadcast the text of a message from the commander in the southern front, to the Chief of Staff, Gen. Yitzhak Rabin. The message said:

"Happy to inform you that our forces are stationed on the bank of the Suez Canal and the Red Sea. The Sinai Peninsula is in our hands. Greetings to you and to the whole defense forces of Israel."

Battle reports yesterday indicated that the remnants of two Egyptian armored divisions and four infantry divisions were trapped in the western part of that Sinai Desert.

50 Tanks Reported Wrecked

The news of Cairo's acceptance of the United Nations cease-fire coincided with an announcement by an Israeli spokesman that three battles in the desert yesterday had been "the fiercest in this war."

The Israelis said they had shot down eight Egyptian planes and destroyed at least 50 Egyptian tanks during the fighting.

Other tanks were wrecked and left on the road to Qantara, about 30 miles north of Ismailia, about midway along the 100-mile Suez Canal.

Among the Egyptian planes downed were a Soviet-made Ilyushin bomber and several Soviet-built Sukhoi-7's. Israeli planes also struck Soviet-made missile sites in the Suez Canal zone during daylight raids, the spokesman added.

Despite the continuation of heavy fighting, the Israeli spokesman said that all escape routes for Egyptian armored units had been closed.

He added that Israeli forces had captured oilfields at Ras Sudar, south of the port of Taufiq on the western coast of the Sinai Peninsula. Israeli soldiers said the wells were afire

Continued on Page 17, Column 6

United Press International Cablephoto

AFTER THE BATTLE: Egyptian prisoners, prone on the sand, their hands behind their heads, are guarded in a compound by Israeli troops at El Arish in the northern Sinai Peninsula. El Arish was taken by Israel Tuesday.

EGYPTIANS TOLD OF TRUCE DECISION

Cairo Broadcast Is Terse —Syrians Also Announce Approval of Cease-Fire

By ERIC PACE
Special to The New York Times

CAIRO, Friday, June 9—The Government told the Egyptian people this morning that it had conditionally accepted a cease-fire in the war with Israel.

There was no immediate popular reaction because the Cairo radio waited until early morning before announcing, more than three hours after the fact, that the United Arab Republic had told Secretary General Thant of the United Nations that it would agree to a truce if Israel did so.

[The Damascus radio announced that Syria, too, had accepted the cease-fire, Reuters reported. Page 17.]

Cairo was blacked out as protection against possible Israeli air raids when the news came, but nocturnal strollers reported that policemen were already taking down at least some of the anti-Israeli banners that have festooned the city for the last few weeks.

An early edition of a popular Cairo newspaper, Al Akhbar, put the news on the front page but made no comment. There was also no elaboration from the radio, which broadcast a military communiqué saying that the battle against Israel was continuing at all points along the Egyptian front.

The terse announcement of the cease-fire contrasted with

Continued on Page 17, Column 2

U.S. Planes Batter MIG Base in North

Special to The New York Times

SAIGON, South Vietnam, June 8 — American fighter-bombers knocked out a MIG base near Hanoi yesterday and wrecked a surface-to-air missile storage area 50 miles southwest of the capital, the United States Command reported today.

At the same time, new fighting broke out just south of the demilitarized zone at the border between North Vietnam and South Vietnam, where a fierce battle raged for control of three hills last month.

Navy carrier pilots attacked the Kep Airfield, 37 miles northeast of Hanoi, for the seventh time since April 24. A headquarters spokesman said the airfield is "closed tempo-

Continued on Page 3, Column 4

Major Mideast Developments

In the Capitals

The United Arab Republic accepted a United Nations cease-fire. Israel had previously agreed to stop hostilities if her enemies were willing to go along.

In Damascus, after a series of militant vows to fight on, the Syrians announced that they would also accept the cease-fire.

President Johnson welcomed the cease-fire agreement and urged prompt action to solve the "many more fundamental" questions in the Middle East.

An emergency declaration on oil was being considered by the Johnson Administration after major oil companies reported that a worldwide transportation problem had resulted from the war.

The hot line between Washington and Moscow was used this week for the first time during a crisis.

On the Battlefronts

Before the cease-fire went into effect, Israeli planes and torpedo boats mistakenly attacked a United States communications ship about 15 miles off Sinai. The Pentagon reported that 10 Americans had been killed and 100 wounded. Israel sent an apology.

Israel reported that her troops had reached the bank of the Suez Canal and that the entire Sinai Peninsula was under her control. Earlier Israel reported three fierce desert battles in which at least 50 Egyptian tanks had been destroyed.

The United Arab Republic announced that its air force had inflicted heavy damage on Israeli armored columns trying to advance westward from El Arish in the Sinai Peninsula.

At the Strait of Tiran, a Soviet freighter bound for the Jordanian port of Aqaba was the first ship to pass since Israel declared the waterway open to shipping on Wednesday. Two Israeli ships prepared to follow.

DONATIONS POUR IN FOR ISRAELI FUND

Many Give All They Have—Some Gifts in Millions

By M. S. HANDLER

"You have got it all now," said a brief letter containing a check for $25,000.

The message was from a professor at the Jewish Theological Seminary who said he had gladly stripped himself of his worldly goods and sent the proceeds to the United Jewish Appeal for the Israel Emergency Fund.

The owner of two gas stations arrived at the appeal's offices and turned over the deeds to the stations as his contribution to the multimillion fund drive.

Other Jews walked in with the cash-surrender values of their life insurance policies. Still others, deeply moved by the Arab-Israeli war, sold real estate and securities and sent the money to the fund's headquarters, on the Avenue of the Americas at 51st street.

These were some examples of the dramas being played out in the Jewish communities across the United States, U.J.A. officials said yesterday.

The contributions, appeal of-

Continued on Page 11, Column 1

ISRAEL, IN ERROR, ATTACKS U.S. SHIP

10 Navy Men Die, 100 Hurt in Raids North of Sinai

By WILLIAM BEECHER
Special to The New York Times

WASHINGTON, June 8—An American naval vessel was mistakenly attacked by Israeli planes and torpedo boats today in international waters about 15 miles north of the Sinai Peninsula. Reports tonight listed the toll as 10 dead and 100 wounded. Twenty of the wounded were hurt critically.

The vessel, the Liberty, was on a peaceful, though war-related mission. Pentagon sources said she had been dispatched from Spain to the war zone to provide additional communications to facilitate the evacuation of American citizens from the Middle East and North Africa.

Pentagon officials said it was too early to tell whether indemnification would be asked from Israel for the loss of life and the damage to the Navy ship.

President Johnson, in a letter to the Senate majority leader, Mike Mansfield, noted that the

Continued on Page 19, Column 1

JOHNSON PLEASED BY GAINS ON TRUCE

Looks to a Stable Peace—White House Discloses Use of the Hot Line

Texts of the Mansfield letter and Johnson reply, Page 18.

By MAX FRANKEL
Special to The New York Times

WASHINGTON, June 8—President Johnson welcomed spreading acceptance of a cease-fire agreement in the Middle East today, but urged all parties to move promptly toward the "many more fundamental questions" bearing on a stable peace.

While thus pressing for more than merely another frail armistice, the While House also disclosed that its hot-line connection with Moscow had been used for the first time this week in an international crisis.

The United States used the teletype link this morning when it heard of an attack on an American communications ship off the Sinai Peninsula. At the time, the source of the attack was not known.

The Soviet Government, whose warships have been observing the movements of the United States Sixth Fleet in the eastern Mediterranean, was advised that the carrier-based American planes were scrambling into action for the sole purpose of assisting the distressed vessel.

It was later learned that Israeli forces had attacked the American ship in error.

The announcement of quick exchanges to prevent misunder-

Continued on Page 18, Column 1

Russians Continue To Harass 6th Fleet

By NEIL SHEEHAN
Special to The New York Times

ABOARD U. S. S. AMERICA, in the Eastern Mediterranean, June 8—Two Soviet warships, a destroyer and a small, highly maneuverable patrol craft, moved into the formation of this Sixth Fleet carrier task force group this morning and began systematically harassing the American ships.

The harassment was undertaken despite a warning to another Soviet destroyer yesterday from Vice Adm. William I. Martin, the Sixth Fleet commander. Admiral Martin warned the Soviet vessel to withdraw from the area of the American formation. He said the Soviet ship, while following the carrier

Continued on Page 15, Column 1

A SHIFT BY CAIRO

Thant Notifies Council in Middle of Debate on Resolutions

Excerpts from the U.N. debate are printed on Page 16.

By DREW MIDDLETON
Special to The New York Times

UNITED NATIONS, N. Y., June 8—The United Arab Republic, the leader of the anti-Israel coalition, today accepted the Security Council's demand for a cease-fire in the Middle East provided Israel did the same.

Yesterday, the delegate of Israel said his country accepted the cease-fire provided Israel's foes agreed to it. Reports here yesterday indicated rejection by Cairo.

Syria gave notice tonight that she would also comply, informing the Secretary General after the Security Council recessed.

This afternoon, in his dry, precise voice Secretary General Thant read to the Council a brief letter from Mohamed Awad el-Kony, the Egyptian delegate, disclosing that President Gamal Abdel Nasser's Government had "decided to accept the cease-fire" called for in the two Council resolutions "on the condition that the other party ceases fire."

He Scraps Long Speech

Mr. el-Kony wrote the letter after a long telephone conversation with Cairo shortly before the Council meeting began. After the call, he scrapped a 20-page speech he had prepared and wrote the note to Mr. Thant.

The Israeli Foreign Minister, Abba Eban, hailed "the immediate prospect" of a cease-fire as "a notable step" and called on other Arab governments to follow the Egyptian lead.

Cairo's acceptance of the Council resolutions adopted unanimously on Tuesday and Wednesday raised rather than lowered the heat of the debate between the United States and the Soviet Union over the resolutions each submitted to the Council.

Arthur J. Goldberg, the United States delegate, saying he hoped for a peace "stable and just to all concerned," submitted a draft of a resolution calling for the "withdrawal and disengagement of armed personnel," the renunciation of force, "the maintenance of vital international rights" and the establishment of a durable peace in the area.

The Administration was said

Continued on Page 17, Column 1

SOVIET SHIP SAILS INTO AQABA GULF

Passage Is First Since Israel Lifted Arab Blockade

By Reuters

ELATH, Israel, June 8—A Soviet freighter bound for the Jordanian port of Aqaba passed through the Strait of Tiran today, the first ship to do so since Israel declared the passage an international waterway yesterday.

Two outgoing Israeli freighters were preparing to be the first Israeli ships to pass through the strait since the Egyptians blockaded the Gulf of Aqaba on May 23.

A report from Sharm el Sheik, which dominates the strait, dis-

Continued on Page 17, Column 7

NEWS INDEX

The New York Times — June 9, 1967

CRUSHING OFFENSIVES: Israelis thrust westward across northern Sinai (1) to the Suez Canal after sharp fighting at Bir Gifgafa and Mitla Pass, and routed Egyptians at Nakhl and Thamed in drive farther south (2). Soviet ship passed through Strait of Tiran (3), now under Israeli control. Mistaken Israeli attack on U.S. ship in Mediterranean (4) killed 10 men. Israelis hold west bank of the River Jordan as far north as Jenin (5).

United Arab Republic and Syria Tell U.N. They Accept Demand for Cease-Fire

CALL FROM CAIRO RESULTS IN SHIFT

El-Kony Move Raises Heat in the Council Debate on U.S. and Soviet Drafts

Continued From Page 1, Col. 8

to be thinking of an international guarantee of the waterways in the area, including the Strait of Tiran, leading to the Gulf of Aqaba, and the Suez Canal.

The United States also hopes that any new international arrangements in the area will deal with the status of Jerusalem and of the refugees in the area.

The purpose of the Soviet delegate, Nikolai T. Fedorenko, was to relieve the Arabs of some of the penalties of defeat and to place the onus for the war on the Israelis. The Soviet draft asked the Council to condemn Israel as the aggressor and demand that Israeli forces withdraw from the territory of the Arab states "behind the armistice lines."

The armistice agreements were concluded in 1949 among Israel and Egypt, Jordan and Syria. Israel has consistently claimed areas involved in the agreements but the three Arab states have refused to surrender the territories. The most important areas are around El Auja in the Sinai Peninsula, Jerusalem and north and east of the Sea of Galilee.

Dr. Muhammad el-Farra. Jordan's chief representative, joined Mr. Fedorenko and Milko Tarabanov, the Bulgarian delegate, in denouncing Israeli "aggressors."

Jordan is losing "villages and shrines, losing more territory and having more victims, more refugees," he said, but Israel will not "conquer our strong spirit, our faith and our determination."

The Arab states fought, Dr. el-Farra contended, because they could not compromise with aggression made possible by "generous United States help" to Israel in money and arms and by "aerial cover" during the present battle.

Most Looking Forward

The majority of Council members were looking ahead to some means of insuring that world peace is not threatened periodically by crises in the Middle East.

Lord Caradon of Britain urged the Council and the United Nations to "move on to the greater tasks of conciliation and the establishment of order and justice."

The world looks to the United Nations, he said, "not to perpetuate animosities but to heal the wounds and repair the damage" and to give the peoples of the Middle East the security they need and "a future of hope."

Foreign Minister Eban concentrated on "the completion and the effective fulfillment of the Egyptian-Israeli cease-fire which now becomes possible."

The Israeli Government will examine the United States resolution with its emphasis on a move "forward to peace" including "agreed measures of disengagement," Mr. Eban said. But the Government will reserve its comment until after detailed examination.

Mr. Eban's words appeared to be intended to establish Israel's bargaining position in the negotiations for a peace settlement. Diplomats, while conceding that Israel is in a strong position, hoped that Prime Minister Levi Eshkol's Government would not demand too much of the Arab states.

Mr. Eban saw a "patient but urgent" quest for a peace settlement as the next phase after the ceasing of fire.

The prime requirement, the Foreign Minister emphasized, is to build a new system of relations among the states of the Middle East. But Israeli thinking on this point centers on the efforts of the governments themselves and "not so much on the authority of international bodies."

Calls for Direct Contacts

He called for "direct, bilateral contacts" between governments to work out the "elements of coexistence."

The assumption is that, despite the United States draft and Lord Caradon's emphasis on the United Nations role in the Middle East, Israel is determined to make her own policy in the area. Israeli sources made clear their conviction that a durable peace can be built only by the nations of the area acting independently.

With sporadic fighting still going on in the Middle East, maximum importance is attached to a draft submitted yesterday by Canada's delegate, George Ignatieff. This requested the President of the Security Council and the Secretary General "to take all necessary measures to bring about full and effective compliance" with the resolutions demanding a cease-fire.

The Soviet Union, according to qualified sources, opposes this largely because it would give too much authority to the Secretary General. The Canadian resolution, along with those submitted today by the Soviet Union and the United States, will be considered when the Council reassembles tomorrow at 3 P.M.

Eban Leaves for Home

At Kennedy Airport, just before his departure last night for Israel, Mr. Eban spoke of the urgency of building "a new and more stable structure of relationships between Israel and the neighboring states."

In answer to a question, he said he did not think that any progress beyond the cease-fire agreements could be foreseen unless Israel and the Arab states came "face to face" in negotiations.

He also called for a resolution of "the deep divergence between us and the Soviet Union about the origins of the conflict" and expressed hope that the Soviet Union "will understand the need to achieve a more balanced relationship of its friendships in the Middle East."

Mr. Eban replied to an inquiry about Israel's plans for the territory she overran by saying, "I have no statement to make on the territorial problems. The governments concerned should hold discussions on the new structures of their relationships. The situation is not so complex that it cannot be brought to order."

El Al Resuming Flights

El Al Israel Airlines planned the resumption of its flights to Israel tomorrow, a spokesman for the line announced last night. Trans World Airlines, the only other line which has direct flights to Israel, said it did not know when operations to Israel would be resumed.

U.S. and British Envoys Ordered to Leave Iraq

BEIRUT, Lebanon, Friday, June 9 (Reuters)—The Iraqi Government has ordered the United States chargé d'affaires and the British ambassador in Baghdad to leave the country, the Baghdad radio said today.

It is said the order, transmitted last night, gave the diplomats 48 hours to leave Iraq.

The broadcast added that all buildings used by the two diplomatic missions had been closed and put under Government supervision.

Iraq severed diplomatic relations with the United States and Britain Tuesday, following arab charges that the two countries had helped Israel in her war against the Arabs.

Associated Press Radiophoto

LAST TRAIN FROM CAIRO: The wreckage of the last train to leave the capital of the United Arab Republic for the Sinai Peninsula lies next to abandoned Egyptian tank after Israeli forces swept by on their way to Suez.

Cairo's Radio Tells Nation of Cease-Fire Decision

Continued From Page 1, Col. 4

the florid commentaries on war news during the last four days. It seemed to be meant to cushion the populace against a too abrupt change from a war psychology to the prospect of a truce with the enemy.

As dawn approached there was no indication here of when the fighting might actually cease or when the Suez Canal might be reopened.

Yesterday the Egyptian Supreme Military Command announced that its air force had inflicted heavy damage on Israeli troops and armor trying to advance westward from El Arish, a strategic road center in the Sanai Peninsula.

The Cairo press also reported that Egyptian forces had shot down 25 enemy planes over the Sinai Peninsula, Sharm el Sheik and Suez.

Informed sources who declined to be identified said that the Israelis had bombed a steel plant and a factory operated by the military in Helwan, an industrial center south of Cairo. There was no word on any damage.

The Egyptian press and radio have not reported the raid, which occurred Tuesday night. A broadcast communiqué also said seven enemy planes had been downed in the Suez Canal Zone and two near Cairo.

The Supreme Command said airplanes had raided some areas in Cairo but added that there had been no damage. Civilian observers did not see the Israeli planes.

Bridges across the Nile were under heavy guard, and air-raid warnings sounded periodically through the day.

The Information Department announced that 3,500 Israeli prisoners, including 200 women, were brought to Cairo Wednesday night. The prisoners, arriving at Cairo's railroad station, were met by a shouting, hostile crowd. They were manacled and carried off in prison vans to an undisclosed place.

President Gamal Abdel Nasser received the Soviet Ambassador, Dmitri P. Pozhidayev, and former Premier Saeb Salaam of Lebanon, the Egyptian press service reported. No other details were made public about his actions. Mr. Nasser has made no public appearances since the war began. [The newspaper Al Ahram said Mr. Nasser would address the nation today, The Associated Press reported.]

All outgoing dispatches continue to be censored. Troops with riot batons remain on guard outside the United States Embassy.

Armed troops are stationed on Cairo's bridges, apparently because the authorities fear civil disorder. The troops carry rifles and submachine guns.

Brief shortages of cigarettes were reported yesterday at shops in various parts in Cairo.

No Reaction to U.S. Plan

There was no immediate comment from Egyptian officials about President Johnson's formation of a working group headed by Secretary of State Dean Rusk to "help build a new peace in the Middle East," apparently in part through foreign aid.

There was also no immediate reaction to Israel's announcement that two Israeli freighters were preparing to sail out of the Gulf of Aqaba and would thus demonstrate that the Egyptian blockade there had been broken.

The Cairo radio declared that several Israeli armored columns were "locked in between El Arish and the coast." It added that Israeli armored units had again tried to infiltrate behind El Arish, 300 miles northeast of Cairo, and to surge forward along the coastal line. The Egyptian Air Force destroyed them inside El Arish, the broadcast said.

In a broadcast communiqué, the Egyptian headquarters said: "Our planes chased the enemy, showering them with a stream of rockets and inflicting heavy damages on them."

Another military communiqué said two Israeli Mirages had been shot down in a dogfight over the Sinai Peninsula. The communiqué said one Egyptian warplane had failed to return to its base after the encounter.

The radio asserted that three United States planes had been spotted flying southward over the Suez Canal, apparently on reconnaissance. The radio repeatedly stated that yesterday would be decisive in battle.

Many Cairo residents appear to think the retreat of Egyptian troops westward on the Sinai Peninsula is a trick to trap the advancing Israelis.

The broadcast communiqué on the Sinai fighting declared: "Enemy armed forces, which attempted to infiltrate earlier behind the El Arish position, tried to surge forward on the coastal line in north Sinai, and our air force stopped their progress and destroyed then completely. Our gallant forces are still resisting with matchless courage inside El Arish itself.

"There are now a number of enemy armored columns blocked in between El Arish and the coast. At the same time that this battle was going on at 7:30 A.M., three American planes crossed over the Suez Canal, heading from north to south."

The newspaper Al Ahram asserted that 180,000 Israeli troops had been involved in the fighting and that a flight of Algerian MIG fighter planes had arrived in Egypt to reinforce the Arab forces.

Banks in Cairo remained open, as did most stores, though some had their iron shutters pulled down halfway. Construction work continued.

There was no evidence of disaffection among the people. The radio played a song with a martial chorus of "Strike, strike, strike!"

There were complaints about the bread supply. The loaves are reported to be made from flour of poor quality that is understood to have come from Eastern Europe.

Shortages of beans were also reported. The crop of beans, a staple in the Egyptian diet, was bad this year.

An independent economic analyst in Cairo said the war could have serious consequences on the Egyptian economy.

First, he said, it will reduce revenues from Suez Canal tolls, which are the Egyptians' principal source of foreign exchange. Second, he added, Cairo appears to have lost large quantities of military equipment that could be expensive to replace.

U.S. Complicity Charged

CAIRO, June 8 (Agence France-Presse) — The Cairo radio's announcement on the cease-fire included the following statement:

"The United States presented another draft resolution, proving the extent of U.S. complicity and its flagrant partiality towards Israel. At the beginning of the session, Secretary General Thant announced that he had received a communication from the U.A.R. Government announcing that Egypt accepted the cease-fire ordered by the Security Council, on condition that the others also accept it."

Damascus Announces Decision

BEIRUT, Lebanon, Friday, June 9 (Reuters)—The Damascus radio announced early today that Syria had accepted the cease-fire. The radio said Secretary General Thant had been informed of the acceptance.

Before announcing the Syrian agreement, the radio announced Cairo's acceptance.

It went on: "In view of the present situation, the Syrian Republic has informed U Thant that she has decided to accept the Security Council's call for a cease-fire, provided the other party does the same."

Libya Studies U. S. Role

WASHINGTON, June 8 (UPI)—The State Department announced today that Libya had appointed a commission to verify that Wheelus Air Force Base in Libya had not been used to send American air support to Israel. Egypt has charged that United States air cover was provided to Israel at the outbreak of war.

The State Department said it had told the Libyan Government the commission would be welcomed.

Bethlehem Area Littered With Remnants of War

Bodies and Hulks of Vehicles Line Road to Jerusalem—Villages Are Deserted

Dispatch of The Times, London

BETHLEHEM, Jordan, June 8—Bishop Pella Klavios, 60 years old, and two priests put out a fire on the roof of the Church of Nativity yesterday during a battle in Bethlehem between Israeli and Arab forces. The fire was started when an Israeli shell hit the 400-year-old English oak roof of the church's north transept.

Using buckets of water, which they carried across the roof, the three men extinguished the flames and saved the roof of the church, which otherwise suffered only minor damage.

When correspondents arrived at the church this morning, a funeral for a victim of the action yesterday was beginning and Israeli tanks and troops were stationed in the square outside.

For the Arab tourist guides, however, it was business as usual. One importuned the correspondents, saying: "Excuse me, do you want a guide for the church?"

Along the road from Jerusalem were the remnants of war. An Arab peasant woman with a small child lay dead in a ditch, only a royal blue cardigan betraying her presence. A tank had toppled over a steep embankment and lay on its back in a field.

Along the road wrecked cars had been pushed into the ditch.

White flags flew from most buildings in the deserted villages along the road, but pockmarks around some windows showed where snipers had resisted the advance.

As the correspondents left, a nun dressed in a white habit trudged along the road, carrying a suitcase. Earlier, on the road to Jericho, about 200 refugees toiled along toward Jerusalem. They pointed to their mouths, seeking food.

A small boy, apparently alone, wandered along with two coathangers in his hand. A woman carrying dead chickens on a wide tray on her head ushered her children along. An old man with a badly crippled leg leaned on a stick. A boy and girl struggled along with a treadle sewing machine. Burned out cars, wrecked tanks and trucks and expended ammunition littered the roadside.

United Press International Cablephoto

Israeli troops and tanks at the Church of the Nativity in Bethlehem, built over the site where Jesus was born.

Israelis Say Tape Shows Nasser Fabricated 'Plot'

Recording Said to Be of Phone Call to Hussein Gives Plan to Accuse U.S. and Britain

TEL AVIV, June 8 (AP)—The Israelis made public today what they said was a recording of a radio-telephone conversation in which Egypt's President, Gamal Abdel Nasser, talked with King Hussein of Jordan making charges that United States and British planes were supporting the Israelis in combat.

The Israelis said they had monitored the talk early Tuesday, after most of the Arab air forces had been disabled by Israeli attacks.

"When the extent of the military defeat was finally clear to Nasser, he began to act to save his prestige," an Israeli announcement declared.

"Nasser decided to save his prestige by claiming that Egyptian forces in the Sinai retreated not as a result of a clear and sharp military defeat in his war with Israel but because of imaginary foreign forces," it said.

Tape Recording Played

The Defense Ministry played tape recordings in Arabic, for correspondents and then issued texts in English.

The spokesman, Col. Moshe Pearlman, said the Israelis had not made the evidence public immediately because there was so much other news.

The translation provided by the Israeli authorities was under the heading: "Conversation between Cairo and Amman by radiotelephone link June 6, 0450 A.M." It went as follows:

Hello — His Majesty is ready? The President is coming.

Hello Amman, is His Majesty ready?

Hello, his honor the President is ready.

How are you? I hear His Majesty, the brother wants to know if the fighting is going on along all the front.

Yes. Shall we include also the United States? Do you know of this, shall we announce that the U.S. is cooperating with Israel?

Hello, I do not hear, the connection is the worst—the line between you and the palace of the King from which the King is speaking is bad.

Nasser: Hello, will we say the U.S. and England or just the U.S.?

Hussein: The U.S. and England.

Nasser: Does Britain have aircraft carriers?

Hussein: (Answer unintelligible).

Nasser: Good. King Hussein will make an announcement and I will make an announcement. Thank you. Do not give up. Yes. Hello, good morning brother. Never mind, be strong. Yes, I hear.

Hussein: Mr. President, if you have something or any idea at all . . . at any time.

Nasser: We are fighting with all our strength and we have battles going on on every front all night and if we had any trouble in the fighting it does not matter, we will overcome despite this. God is with us. Will His Majesty make an announcement on the participation of Americans and the British?

Hussein: (Answer not intelligible).

Nasser: By God, I say that I will make an announcement and you will make an announcement and we will see to it that the Syrians will make an announcement that American and British airplanes are taking part against us from aircraft carriers. We will issue an announcement, we will stress the matter and we will drive the point home.

Hussein: Good, all right.

Nasser: Your Majesty, do you agree?

Hussein: (Answer not clear).

Nasser: A thousand thanks. Do not give up. We are with you with all our hearts and we are flying our planes over Israel today, our planes are striking at Israel's air fields since morning.

Hussein: A thousand thanks. Be well.

Both Britain and the United States have denied the Arab charges and the Israelis have said they were fighting alone.

Later Tuesday, the Cairo radio broadcast a report that King Hussein had telephoned President Nasser that morning and had said he personally had seen on radar British planes take off from carriers.

In London, a Foreign Office spokesman said that Jordan was equipped with British-made radar that was technically incapable of detecting aircraft taking off from the British carriers, which at the time were more than 1,000 miles from Jordan.

Authenticity Is Debated

Officials at the United Nations, in Washington and London gave varying opinions when asked about the authenticity of the purported transcript of the telephone conversation between King Hussein and President Nasser published by the Israeli government.

Muhammad H. el-Farra, the representative of Jordan at the United Nations, said: "The Israelis are known to fabricate. I leave this to your judgment."

The Egyptian delegation to the United Nations declined to comment.

Western experts on the Middle East said they had no evidence to confirm or deny that such a conversation had taken place or the accuracy of the text distributed in Tel Aviv.

One expert in London said he was inclined to accept the Israeli report of the conversation. He said that the Israelis do monitor Arab radiotelephone traffic and that the Hussein-Nasser call could have been made over an ordinary radio-telephone circuit.

The expert added that he doubted that the Israelis would fake such a conversation in the delicate situation that now obtains in the Middle East.

In Washington, one expert questioned the authenticity of the text of the conversation because he felt that the reported phrases were "too noble from Nasser and sound manufactured, too pat."

An Egyptian expert on the Arabic language, after reading the Israeli-distributed English text of the purported conversation in New York, said: "It looks to me like a complete fabrication."

Beamed to Arab World

Special to The New York Times

TEL AVIV, June 8—The tapes purportedly recording the voices of the Egyptian and Jordanian rulers were played to the Arab world today by Israel's Arabic radio service.

Middle East experts here said there was no doubt that the voices were those of President Nasser and King Hussein.

Israel's radio beamed the recording to Arab countries 10 times between 4 P.M. and 6 P.M. Each time there was a commentary saying it proved that the two Arab leaders were liars.

After the Cairo radio at 6 P.M. tonight again referred to an Anglo-American-Israeli plot, the tape was broadcast again and the commentator remarked: "Apparently you've missed our earlier broadcast."

An official of the radio station said the tape would be played and over again until the Arabs dropped the charge.

Jordan Disclaimer Reported

Special to The New York Times

LONDON, June 8—According to official British sources, Jordanian military spokesmen conceded in Amman yesterday that no British or American planes had been seen in Jordan.

This was in direct conflict with earlier Jordanian claims that British and American planes had supported Israel in the fighting. These charges, branded a lie by London and Washington, have been repeated daily by Egypt.

A Foreign Office spokesman said today, without elaboration: "I can tell you that yesterday, at an official briefing at Jordan general headquarters, foreign attachés were told that the Jordanians had 'no knowledge of any British or American aircraft operating over Jordan.'"

Have Soviet Equipment

Communications authorities here said yesterday that President Nasser and King Hussein could have used a military radio circuit or facilities of the Cairo radio and Jordan's Amman radio for their conversation. One source said that Arab areas in the Middle East were supplied with Soviet communications equipment.

A message broadcast by radio can be intercepted by anyone with a receiver tuned to the frequency in use. Usually, a radio conversation between heads of state would be scrambled in transmission and thus unintelligible to an interceptor.

Some messages can be unscrambled by outsiders, however, from knowledge of the technique used to make the information unintelligible.

Israel Says Her Troops Reach Banks of Suez

Continued From Page 1, Col. 3

as a result of sabotage by the defenders.

The Israelis said that they were in complete control of the Jordanian front and that two bridges across the Jordan had been destroyed. They identified these as the Allenby Bridge, east of Jericho, and Damiya Bridge, farther north. The Hussein Bridge was heavily damaged.

Early yesterday Israel said officially that at least 250 Egyptian tanks had been destroyed, but at that stage unofficial estimates said the number was nearer 600. At least 30 tanks were knocked out in the Nakhl-Thamed sector alone.

In addition, 20 Soviet-built Stalin-3 heavy tanks were destroyed at Bir Gafgafa, 50 miles east of the Suex Canal.

In their unsuccessful escape drive, the Egyptians had tried to attack advancing Israelis in the western Sinai Desert with tanks and planes between the Mitla Pass and Bir Gafgafa.

On Israel's northern front, unofficial reports said most of the Syrian front-line forces withdrew toward Damascus and were being harassed by Israeli planes.

Communiqués said Syrian artillery had resumed shelling Israeli border villages in the Huleh Valley.

On the Jordanian front, Israeli troops cleared bodies from the streets of the Old City of Jerusalem, which was captured Tuesday, and set up occupation headquarters in the Ambassadors hotel on the west bank of the Jordan.

The Israelis control the entire west bank, from Jenin southward to the Hills of Hebron.

'The Moment They Stop'

Special to The New York Times

TEL AVIV, June 8 — A spokesman for the Israeli Foreign Ministry, commenting on Egypt's acceptance of the United Nations call for a cease-fire, said tonight, "The moment they stop, we will."

"At the moment there are conditions approximating a cease-fire in the Sinai," he said. The lull came at nightfall. "Anyway we've broken their back," he added.

'Total Destruction'

TEL AVIV, June 8 (UPI)—Maj. Gen. Itzhak Rabin, the Israeli Chief of Staff, said at a news conference tonight: "Today we actually are witnessing the total destruction of the Egyptian forces in the Sinai."

The newest Israeli claims brought to 444 the number of Arab planes destroyed in the war.

General Rabin asserted that Egypt had picked the fight. He said Egyptian armor had attacked "in force" in the hope of breaking out of Israeli lines laid down in a three-day drive.

Syrian Assertions Denied

TEL AVIV, June 8 (Agence France-Presse)—Israeli spokesmen today denied Syrian assertions that a Syrian column had entered Galilee and was advancing on Nazareth.

Syrian troops have failed to take a single yard of Israeli territory at any point in the fighting since Monday, spokesmen insister. All Syrian attacks have been repelled, they said.

The Israeli force that seized the Old City of Jerusalem yesterday captured five Arab consuls representing the United Arab Republic, Syria and Iraq. The diplomats enjoy the status of privileged prisoners, the Israeli radio said.

Mideast Phone Calls Back Up

The American Telephone and Telegraph Company reported yesterday that it had a backlog of more than 25,000 telephone calls to Israel, and that calls placed now would be delayed amost three weeks. There were aso large backlogs of calls to Arab nations, A.T. & T. said.

SOVIET SHIP SAILS INTO AQABA GULF

Continued From Page 1, Col. 8

closed that Israeli sailors took the fort yesterday.

Israeli paratroopers landed at the fort—already abandoned by its Egyptian garrison—some time later, the report said.

Diverted Tanker at Capetown

CAPETOWN, June 8 (Reuters) — A 34,000-ton tanker loaded with oil for Israel arrived here today, the first in an armada of merchantmen and tankers diverted from the Middle East.

The ships have been forced to take the long way around the southern tip of South Africa since the Egyptians closed the Suez Canal two days ago.

The first arrival here, the Liberian tanker Leon, was bound for Elath.

At least two dozen other ships are known to have changed course from the Suez route and are heading for Capetown.

All of South Africa's ports—Durban, the biggest, Capetown, East London and Port Elizabeth—are geared for a maritime traffic jam.

Mining Was Reported

The announcement from Cairo on May 23 that the United Arab Republic was blockading the Gulf of Aqaba to Israeli shipping was followed by a few hours by unofficial reports that the narrow mouth of the gulf was being mined.

The authoritative Egyptian newspaper Al Ahram reported the next day that a part of the four-mile-wide channel beneath the fortress of Sharm el Sheik had been mined. The open channel, it was reported, could easily be patrolled by Egyptian ships.

No ship, the article said, could run the risk of steaming through the minefield without the guidance of patrol boats.

Some doubt as to whether the passageway into the gulf from the Red Sea had actually been mined was raised by the Israelis, who, with the aid of binoculars, observed several freighters arriving at the Jordanian port of Aqaba, just across the border from Elath, Israel's sole outlet to the Red Sea.

The Strait of Tiran is commanded by Sharm el Sheik, whose guns can reach any vessel proceeding in or out of the 100-mile-long Gulf of Aqaba. For most of its length it separates the eastern shore of the Sinai Peninsula from Saudi Arabia and at its northern end are Elath and Aqaba.

Israel was said to have had limited countermining and minesweeping capabilities. She is reported to have four submarines and two ships in the destroyer class, while Egypt has nine of the former and six of the latter. Both nations have a number of smaller craft, such as torpedo boats and patrol vessels.

"All the News That's Fit to Print"

The New York Times

LATE CITY EDITION

Weather: Sunny and windy today; clear tonight. Milder tomorrow. Temp. range: today 42-35; Sunday 51-42. Full U.S. report on Page 93.

VOL. CXVII ... No. 40,126 | NEW YORK, MONDAY, DECEMBER 4, 1967 | 10 CENTS

Thousands Mourn Spellman at St. Patrick's

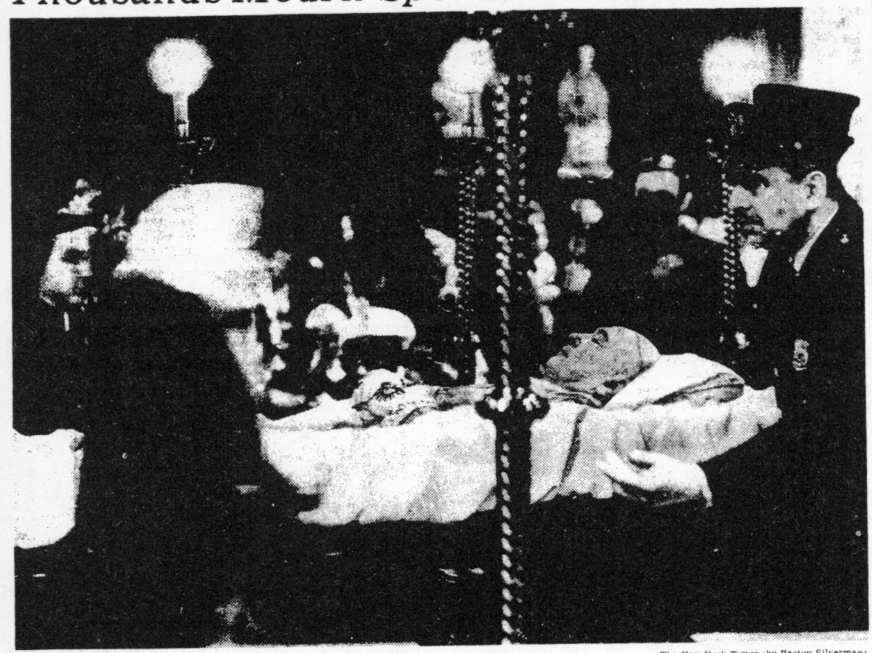

The New York Times (by Barton Silverman)

The bier of Cardinal Spellman at St. Patrick's Cathedral. Patrolman gestures to mourner to proceed past coffin.

By PAUL HOFMANN

In a somber rite, the body of Cardinal Spellman was taken to St. Patrick's Cathedral last night and placed on a catafalque in the center aisle for the first of a five-day series of requiem masses.

The Cardinal, who died Saturday morning at the age of 78, will be buried in a crypt of St. Patrick's on Thursday after a service that is expected to be attended by all seven American Cardinals.

The bronze-lined coffin of African mahogany arrived at the Fifth Avenue entrance of St. Patrick's at 6:15 P.M.

The coffin was taken into the cathedral under crossed swords held by 12 Knights of Columbus wearing white-plumed hats. The Most Rev. John J. Maguire, who is temporarily administering the archdiocese, met the open coffin inside the church and opened the ceremonies by sprinkling the Cardinal's body with holy water and blessing it.

A procession formed, with clergymen in purple and black mourning vestments preceding the coffin and volunteer members of the city's Police and Fire Departments in an honor guard following it on its way down the cathedral's 186-foot long nave. A group of 60 relatives and friends of the Cardinal walked behind the coffin and then took seats in front pews.

Votive candles lighted by hundreds of mourners flickered along the church's walls. The cathedral was filled to capacity.

Cardinal Spellman's body was clad in white liturgical vestments and a scarlet skullcap. A golden cross lay on his chest and a bishop's ring was on his right hand.

The coffin was placed on a black-draped catafalque, surrounded by six tall candles, in the center aisle in front of the main altar.

At 6:30 P.M. the cathedral's bells tolled and eight bishops and ten other prelates gathered around the altar to concelebrate a requiem mass during which a choir chanted the responses.

Concelebration is a form of offering mass jointly by more than one priest. It is believed to have been common in early Christianity and has been revived in the recent reforms of Roman Catholic liturgy.

The main celebrant was Archbishop Maguire, who as newly named Administrator of the Archdiocese is its head until a successor, to be named by Pope Paul VI, takes over.

The 17 other celebrants were members of the Board of Consultors, a body appointed by Cardinal Spellman that conferred on Archbishop Maguire on Saturday the task of administering the archdiocese during the see's vacancy.

Outside the church, hundreds of persons were waiting in triple line behind police barricades along East 51st Street from Fifth Avenue to Madison Avenue. Rain that had fallen earlier in the day had stopped by now. After the end of the concelebrated mass, around

Continued on Page 51, Column 1

TAXICAB INDUSTRY SEEKS SHARP RISE IN FARE SCHEDULE

Cost of Long Trips Would Be Increased Most—$1 Ride to Go to $1.70 Under Plan

By PETER MILLONES

The taxi industry will ask the city today for a fare increase that would raise a ride that now costs 45 cents to 60 cents, a 60-cent ride to 90 cents and a $1 trip to $1.70.

The increases would be greater for passengers taking long-distance trips than for those who ride short distances.

Under the proposal, meters would be readjusted so that a rider watching the fare would see the meter click a dime at a time instead of a nickel.

The Metropolitan Taxicab Board of Trade, which represents all but three of the 74 taxi fleets here with 6,800 cabs, says in a letter to the city:

"A larger increase is requested on the longer rides to provide incentive to the driver to take such trips and enter outlying areas which have been trips where driver resistance has occurrred up to now."

Problems of Return Trip

According to regulations of the Hack Bureau, drivers are not supposed to choose their customers but accept all orderly persons who want to go anywhere in the city. In fact, they spurn long-distance trips from Manhattan to Queens and Brooklyn, for example, because they often fail to get a passenger back to their normal area of operation.

The industry's remedy would, for example, increase the fare for a trip that now covers just over five miles to $2.90 from $1.60.

Whether these proposed increases will be acceptable to the City Council, the Mayor and the Board of Estimate was unclear yesterday. Both the Democratic-led City Council and Mayor Lindsay, a Republican, have stated their willingness to approve an adjustment in fares to help pay the costs of a new contract that gave cab drivers an increase in pay.

But whether they will approve increases of the size desired by the industry remains to be seen. The Lindsay administration is studying the finances of the $200-million-a-year industry now.

Getting Specific Proposals

It is understood that the Council prefers to wait for specific legislative proposals from the administration before holding public hearings on an increase.

The whole question of a fare increase is complicated because the new three-year contract between the industry and Local 3036 of the New York City Taxi Drivers Union is based on the assumption that the industry's requested increase will be approved.

Thus, if the increase proposed is not approved, the labor contract, arrived at after wildcat strikes by the 29,000

Continued on Page 54, Column 3

Associated Press Cablephoto

AFTER MEETING: President Makarios of Cyprus and Cyrus R. Vance, U.S. envoy, after talks in Nicosia yesterday.

3 NATIONS REPLY TO THANT APPEAL IN CYPRUS CRISIS

Greek Response Is Clearly Affirmative—Makarios Will Give Full Answer Today

TURKS RAISE U.N. ISSUE

U.S. and Britain Favor Plan to Increase Functions of International Force

By DREW MIDDLETON

Special to The New York Times

UNITED NATIONS, N. Y., Dec. 3—Greece, Turkey and Cyprus sent separate replies today to Secretary General Thant's appeal for peace on Cyprus.

All the replies could be considered as accepting his appeal for peace in the sense that they did not reject it.

This was considered a gain by Mr. Thant, the United States and Britain, which have interested themselves in trying to end the crisis from the United Nations.

The reply of Archbishop Makarios, President of Cyprus, relayed by Zenon Rossides, the Cypriote representative at the United Nations, was the least communicative of the three. President Makarios said only that he welcomed the constructive suggestion made by Mr Thant and that his full reply would be sent in 12 hours.

Proposal Is Welcomed

Greece welcomed Mr. Thant's proposal and told the Secretary General that she would be willing to carry it out.

Premier Suleyman Demeril of Turkey, however, raised a more important point. He accepted Mr. Thant's appeal, but he gave his Government's support to that point in Mr. Thant's message that emphasized that an expansion of the United Nations forces on Cyprus might be necessary to oversee demilitarization of the island and to end communal fighting there.

Ambassador Arthur J. Goldberg and Lord Caradon of Britain had urged a favorable response upon the three Governments in messages issued shortly after Mr. Thant's appeal.

Mr. Thant's key paragraph, from the Cypriote standpoint, discusses enlarging the mandate of the 4,500-man United Nations force in Cyprus to give it "broader functions in regard

Continued on Page 3, Column 1

Enemy Shells Allied Posts; Vietcong Attack Repulsed

Special to The New York Times

SAIGON, South Vietnam, Dec. 3—The Vietcong unleashed a series of mortar and ground attacks against United States and South Vietnamese positions today. In one attack, against the Binhson government subsector headquarters 12 miles north of Quangngai City and 330 miles northeast of Saigon, 35 enemy soldiers were reported to have been killed.

A South Vietnamese spokesman said that the attack started at 1:30 A.M. with a heavy mortar barrage, followed by a charge by some 600 enemy troops, who fought until allied reinforcements arrived at 5 A.M.

[The Vietcong attacked the United States military headquarters base at Longbinh with small arms and mortars Monday. The raid touched off a fire in a storage area of the base. Page 5.]

U.S. and Korean Aid

A United States spokesman said that a cavalry troop from the American Division and South Korean marines near the Binhson post were rushed to help the headquarters compound. Army helicopters and AC-47 Dragonships fired at the enemy.

The Government spokesman said that an American military adviser and a South Korean adviser in the headquarters were killed and that six United States advisers were wounded. South Vietnamese casualties were described as moderate, which means that the defending force of some 200 troops was badly hurt.

Elsewhere, the Vietcong fired 40 mortar shells at a company of the United States First Infantry Division at Budop, which is near the Cambodian border and 88 miles north of Saigon. A United States spokesman said that two American soldiers

Continued on Page 5, Column 3

TREASURY FEARS BIG INTEREST RISE

Lasting Harm to Economy Held Possible if Congress Delays on a Tax Increase

By EDWIN L. DALE Jr.

Special to The New York Times

WASHINGTON, Dec. 3 — There is a sense of quiet, but genuine, alarm in the Treasury over what might happen to interest rates in the coming weeks if Congress shows no movement on a tax increase before it adjourns.

No one is talking of financial collapse or panic. But at the top levels of the Treasury there is a deep fear that interest rates could rise so steeply as to do lasting damage—damage that could not be wholly repaired even if Congress did move on a tax increase next year.

"The markets still have some hope of action," said one high official. "If that hope goes, there is no telling how high rates will go."

Rates fell markedly on the news two weeks ago that the House Ways and Means Committee would resume consideration of the tax bill. They rose again last Thursday and Friday on the news that the committee chairman, Representative Wilbur D. Mills, Democrat of Arkansas, had still made no decision to act.

These interest rates are the

Continued on Page 38, Column 4

GROUP IN HARLEM ASKS MORE POLICE

Many Residents Say Crime Has Risen Sharply—Fear Keeps Some Off Streets

By EARL CALDWELL

A group of Harlem residents met last night to voice their concern about rising crime in their neighborhood and to seek methods of obtaining more police protection.

The residents, who live in the Lenox Terrace Apartments, a large, luxury complex in the area of 135th Street and Fifth Avenue, decided to petition the city for more police and to seek meetings with Mayor Lindsay, Borough President Percy E. Sutton and Police Commissioner Howard R. Leary.

"We've got to take some action," said Mrs. Virginia Bell of 45 West 132d Street, a resident of the six-building complex that houses more than 1,700 families.

Mrs. Bell was one of more than 100 Lenox Terrace residents to attend the meeting during the evening. The meeting was held in the apartment of Mr. and Mrs. John Meade of 2186 Fifth Avenue.

While residents of Lenox Terrace were meeting in the Meades' apartment, a group called Petitions for Protection circulated petitions for more policemen in the area from 110th to 116th Street in lower Harlem.

These Harlem residents, too, were concerned about a crime problem that has emptied the neighborhood's tenement-lined side streets at night, forced merchants to close their shops early and brought armed civilian patrols into the streets.

Residents and shopkeepers have no statistics to cite, but there is a widespread feeling that crime in the streets has risen sharply.

Many residents refuse to leave their homes at night. Some merchants close their

Continued on Page 61, Column 2

Heart Transplant Keeps Man Alive in South Africa

By The Associated Press

CAPETOWN, Dec. 3 — The world's first successful human heart transplant was announced today.

In a five-hour operation that began at 1 A.M., surgeons at the Groote Schuur Hospital removed the heart of a young woman who died after an automobile crash and placed it in the chest of a 55-year-old man dying because his own heart was damaged, the announcement said.

When the transplanted heart was in place, it was started beating by an electric shock.

Dr. Jan H. Louw, the hospital's chief surgeon, said:

"It was like turning the ignition switch of a car."

The hospital said that the man was in satisfactory condition but that the next few days would be a critical period.

The heart was removed from the body of Denise Ann Darvall, 24, an accounting machine operator, and transferred to Louis Washkansky, a businessman, the hospital said.

Mr. Washkansky was reported fully conscious, with blood pressure normal.

Doctors around the world hailed the transplant achievement but said the crucial question would be whether the man's body would accept the alien heart.

In the first stage of the operation, Mr. Washkansky and the body of Miss Darvall were put on heart-lung machines, each manned by a team of technicians.

In the second stage, the donor's heart was removed and kept going by a pump.

The third stage was the re-

Continued on Page 56, Column 1

Public's Misuse of Ambulances Is Found to Cause Delays Here

By MARTIN TOLCHIN

Public abuses of the city's emergency ambulance services have led to excessive delays, including many of more than an hour, in transporting critically ill patients to hospitals, according to an analysis made public yesterday.

The report found that nearly 4,000 of 41,632 calls took more than 60 minutes, and included a significant number of patients who might have benefited from quicker action.

"A lot of people die," David C. Dimendberg, the author of the report and former director of the Emergency Ambulance Service, said in an interview.

The desirable time it should take to complete a call, he said, is about 30 minutes.

He noted that lengthy delays had been found in transportation of cardiac cases, asthmatics, unconscious persons and victims of traffic accidents.

The delays were caused neither by a shortage of ambulances nor heavy automobile traffic, but by false alarms, the use of ambulances by persons who could take other transportation, and other abuses that diverted the vehicles from their proper function, he said.

The study found that 37 per cent of those who called an emergency ambulance walked into it.

"If you can walk, usually you don't need two men to come with a stretcher," Mr. Dimendberg said. "In certain cities, if a patient is well enough to walk to an ambulance, the ambulance won't take them."

Of those with illnesses who called ambulances, only one in four were urgent cases, a group that included cardiacs, asthmatics and those found unconscious. The remainder had vague body aches, colds, fevers

Continued on Page 58, Column 3

$9-BILLION BUDGET FOR CITY FORECAST

Chamber, Looking to 1975, Urges Stricter Control —Cites Recent Gains

By RICHARD E. MOONEY

The New York Chamber of Commerce predicted yesterday that by 1975 the city's expense budget would have risen from the present $5.2-billion to $9-billion or more if current spending trends continued.

In an annual review of budget developments the chamber cited "substantial improvement" in the city's fiscal behavior, specifically the discontinuation of borrowing to pay for day-to-day operating costs in the last two years.

But it said that "the city must exercise more effective control over expenditures in the future if it is to achieve real fiscal stability."

The review showed that the city expense budget had doubled in 10 years. This does not include spending for long-range, capital projects. Spending for education and hospitals has almost tripled during the decade, and outlays for welfare have quadrupled.

"These increases are clear manifestations of the urban crisis," said G. G. Tegnell, the chamber's executive vice president. "The problems that have caused them are not easily solved, but we must strike a balance of needs and supportable local taxation."

Publication of the review coincided with the conclusion of

Continued on Page 22, Column 4

NEWS INDEX

Rail Buses to Link Midtown to Kennedy Airport

45-Minute Runs Are Planned Next Year From East Side Over L.I.R.R. Tracks

The New York Times Dec. 4, 1967

By MARTIN GANSBERG

Buses that can travel on railroad tracks as well as highways will be put into service "sometime in 1968" to speed trips between mid-Manhattan and Kennedy International Airport.

They will run partly on roads and partly on tracks of the Long Island Rail Road.

The move, which will begin with 15 buses, is expected to reduce the traveling time from the East Side Airlines Terminal to the airport by at least half an hour, Austin J. Tobin, executive director of the Port of New York Authority, said yesterday.

"Despite severe traffic tie-ups," he said, "this will make it possible to get to the airport in 45 minutes." The same trip now takes as much as an hour and a half.

Mr. Tobin also predicted in announcing the new service that the cost of the trip would remain at the present $2. He said the buses would be able to carry 45 passengers.

He said that he and Dr. William J. Ronan, head of the Metropolitan Commuter Transportation Authority, would go to Kansas City this week to watch final tests of buses there developed by the W. T. Cox Company of Camdenton, Mo.

At a demonstration of such a bus last July in Floral Park L. I., Dr. Ronan was one of the

Continued on Page 94, Column 4

8 CHILDREN KILLED IN 2 BLAZES HERE

5 in Brooklyn Left Alone—3 Die on Lower East Side

Eight children, ranging in age from 4 months to 6 years, died yesterday in two fires, in Brooklyn and Manhattan.

Five of the children, left alone by their mothers, were asphyxiated in a bedroom of the Brooklyn apartment they shared. Desperate efforts by firemen — including mouth-to-mouth resuscitation and cardiac massage—failed to revive them.

In the other fire, earlier in the day on the Lower East Side, three children who had apparently been playing with matches were killed in their apartment at 620 East Sixth Street. Their crippled parents, Charles and Regina Scheibel, and two other children were injured.

The victims of the Brooklyn fire were the three children of Mrs. Louise Faulk—Angie, 3 years old; Keith, 2; and Kenneth, 4 months; and the two children of her sister Annie—John, 5; and Elizabeth, 4.

All were found unconscious in the smoke-filled bedroom of their mothers' three-room apartment. The families shared an apartment on the second floor of a three-story frame building at 1038 Broadway in the Bushwick section.

The alarm was turned in at 2:04 P.M. Firemen from three

Continued on Page 16, Column 4

Heart Transplanted From a Dead Woman and Started by Shock Is Keeping Man Alive in South Africa

Continued From Page 1, Col. 3

moval of Mr. Washkansky's heart.

The fourth and most intricate stage was the placing of the donor's heart in Mr. Washkansky's body. When the transplant was completed, electrodes were placed against the heart walls, and a high current was switched on for a fraction of a second.

The heart started beating immediately, Dr. Louw said.

Hospital sources said that the transplant almost took place last Wednesday with another donor but was canceled at the last moment because the donor died too soon.

Miss Darvall's kidneys were also removed and taken to the Karl Bremer Hospital for a successful kidney transplant to Jonathan Van Wyk, 10.

The announcement of the transplant to Mr. Washkansky came from Dr. Jacobus G. Burger, medical supervisor of the Groote Schuur Hospital.

"The operation was his only chance," Dr. Burger said. "Washkansky was dying and wouldn't have lived longer than a few days otherwise."

Dr. Burger said the next two or three days would be the critical postoperative period.

"The longer Washkansky goes on, the better," he said, "although that does not mean the heart will not be rejected later. The body could decide in five or 10 years' time that it doesn't want this heart."

Mr. Washkansky has a tracheotomy—a tube inserted in his throat through which he is breathing — and is unable to speak, Dr. Burger said. He is being kept absolutely quiet in a special room.

"Even the nurses don't speak to him," Dr. Burger said. "They are doing everything for him and keeping him dead quiet."

Louis Washkansky, who received transplanted heart.

Associated Press

Denise Ann Darvall, whose death made heart available.

Dr. Burger said that apart from the body's natural tendency to reject the heart, the main danger could come from blood clotting and resultant heart failure.

Mr. Washkansky is being fed anticlotting drugs to counter this.

"We are also using steroids to prevent the heart being thrown out rejected," Dr. Burger said.

He said that Mr. Washkansky had been kept alive by using pumps to assist his heart, but this could not have gone on indefinitely.

"The heart muscle was fibrosed, which means that all the muscle was gone and there was only fibrous tissue there," the doctor said. "It wouldn't pump the blood any more, and his condition was deteriorating.

"We thought he was dying a week ago, and he would have died immediately if we had taken the pumps away.

"Washkansky knew what he was going into, but it was his only chance."

Heading the team of five cardiac surgeons was Prof. Chris Barnard.

Dr. Louw assisted with arrangements and advised the surgeons, although he was not operating.

Professor Barnard is in Professor Louw's department.

In addition to the cardiac surgeons, there were two neurosurgeons and two anesthetists. Altogether there were about 20 in the theater, including five or six theater nurses, Dr. Burger said. All the surgeons were South Africans.

The woman donor was injured yesterday afternoon. Neurosurgeons, with an electroencephalogram to measure her brain waves, alerted the cardiac surgeons the instant she died, shortly before 1 A.M.

The consent to use her heart was obtained earlier from her father.

"The operation had to begin within half an hour of he death," Dr. Burger said.

The woman's mother was killed instantly in the same auto accident.

Dr. Burger said the heart transplant experiments on cats and dogs had been carried out over the last 10 years at Groote Schuur, which in Afrikaans means big barn.

Mrs. Washkansky said that before the transplant her husband's life was "hanging by a thread." She said he was approached three weeks ago by doctors who told him "in great detail what it would entail."

"I was petrified but my husband had such confidence in medical men he inspired me as well," she said.

She said he had had heart trouble for seven years and in the last two years his condition became progressively worse. She said she and her husband had emigrated from Lithuania as children and married in Capetown in 1946.

The donor's father, Edward George Darvall, said:

"I gave the doctors permission to remove my daughter's heart and kidneys and donate them to other persons if it could have their lives. It was shortly before midnight after I was informed she was dying."

"Professor Barnard has two registrars — young doctors studying for postgraduate degrees—continually experimenting in his animal laboratory," Dr. Burger said. "I know he has successfully transplanted hearts of dogs, but I don't know how long the animal lived afterwards."

United States surgeons at the Stanford Medical Center in California have performed 200 heart transplants in dogs, with a 60-to-70 per cent survival rate.

Surgeons at the center have been reported by The Journal of the American Medical Association to be ready for a heart transplant whenever the ideal donor and ideal recipient appeared at the same time.

Patient's Courage Hailed

CAPETOWN, Dec. 3 (UPI)—Professor Barnard, head of the thoracic surgery department of Capetown University, said today that Mr. Washkansky deserved credit for the operation's apparent success.

"If it had not been for this man's courage and will to live the operation would never have succeeded," he said.

The moment of decision came last night. The doctors told Mr. Washkansky that a heart with blood group and tissue compatible with his own was available. They gave him two days to make up his mind.

"He made up his mind in two minutes," Mrs. Washkansky said.

The surgeons marked one of the high points of their careers when Miss Darvall's heart was set beating anew in Mr. Washkansky's body.

"It's going to work," Professor Barnard was quoted as having said. "I need a cup of tea."

Another doctor said:

"It was the most exciting experience I have ever had. It was like watching a bullfight. Certain classical maneuvers had to be done before the grand finale."

In Chicago, a spokesman for the American Medical Association said that the surgery was "not surprising."

"South African doctors have a fine reputation and there is no reason to suspect they could not be capable of doing such an operation," the spokesman, Frank Chappell, said.

In Houston, Dr. Michael E. De Bakey, a pioneer in surgery implanting artificial heart pumps, called the operation "a great achievement."

Feat Praised in U. S.

STANFORD, Calif., Dec. 3 (AP) — The Stanford Medical Center surgeon who announced plans 13 days ago for transplanting a human heart said today that the world's first heart transplant operation at Capetown was "pretty exciting."

"The thing is it anticipated the artificial heart by possibly three to five years," said the surgeon, Dr. Norman E. Shumway, head of Stanford's division of cardiovascular surgery.

Dr. Shumway said he worked with Prof. Chris Barnard, head of the Capetown surgery team, at the University of Minnesota about 10 years ago.

"We have had numerous reunions since, the most recent in May," Dr. Shumway said. "He is a good man, a well-known, well-respected cardiac surgeon."

He predicted that the heart transplant would become as frequent as the kidney transplant within 10 years.

The surgical team must have the consent of the patient, Dr. Shumway explained.

"It has to be an extreme case, a terminal case, because legally uor are killing the person when you take this heart out and throw it away," he said.

"At the moment he goes into the operating room, he's alive. You have to assume he would be dead without the transplant in a few weeks or a few months."

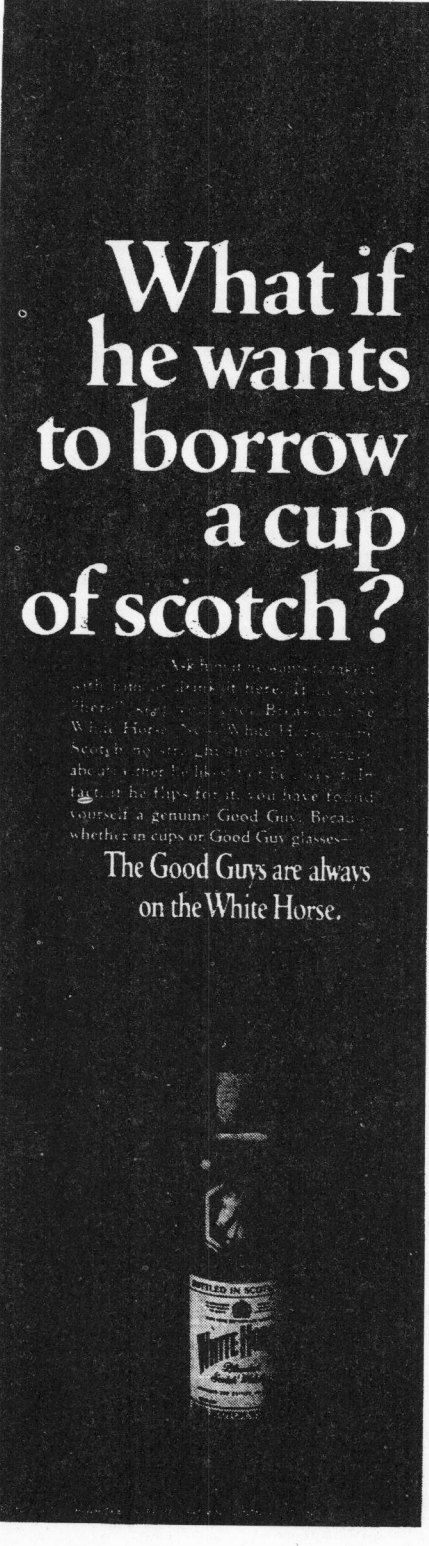

"All the News That's Fit to Print"

The New York Times

LATE CITY EDITION

Weather: Clearing today, turning cold tonight. Fair, cool tomorrow. Temp. range: today 62-44; Thurs. 73-52. Full U.S. report on Page 92.

VOL. CXVII .. No. 40,249

NEW YORK, FRIDAY, APRIL 5, 1968

10 CENTS

MARTIN LUTHER KING IS SLAIN IN MEMPHIS; A WHITE IS SUSPECTED; JOHNSON URGES CALM

JOHNSON DELAYS TRIP TO HAWAII; MAY LEAVE TODAY

President Spends a Hectic Day Here and in Capital —Sees Thant at the U.N.

By MAX FRANKEL

Special to The New York Times

WASHINGTON, April 4 — President Johnson postponed his trip to Hawaii at least until tomorrow after he heard of the death of the Rev. Dr. Martin Luther King Jr. tonight.

The news, which visibly shocked the President, came at the end of one of the most extraordinary days in perhaps the most extraordinary week of his Administration.

Mr. Johnson was to have flown from Washington at about midnight for a weekend of strategy conferences with his military and diplomatic leaders stationed in South Vietnam. On the way, he had planned a breakfast meeting in California with former President Dwight D. Eisenhower.

Instead, the President telephoned Mrs. King in Atlanta, made a brief appeal for calm on television and went to his office to follow the reports of unrest and disturbance given him periodically by Attorney General Ramsey Clark.

Cancels Dinner Appearance

Mr. Johnson also canceled an appearance before a Democratic party fund-raising dinner here —the final event of a hectic schedule that became ever more hectic as the day unfolded.

The President began the day by making final arrangements for the Hawaii meeting. It had been tentatively planned before his order Sunday to curtail the bombing of North Vietnam and the news yesterday that Hanoi was interested in establishing direct contact.

[The new United States peace moves are producing a quiet but bitter reaction in the South Vietnamese Government that is causing increasing concern among United States officials in Saigon. Page 14.]

But the diplomatic development, though not the principal subject of the Honolulu meetings, added special weight to his conversations with Gen. Wiliam C. Westmoreland, the American commander in South Vietnam, and other officials.

Mr. Johnson was careful not to arouse false hopes of peace, but he appeared encouraged and in buoyant spirt as he decided before noon to fly first to New York to attend the investiture of the Most Rev. Terence J. Cooke as Archbishop of New York.

Then, while in New York,

Continued on Page 12, Column 1

Hanoi Charges U.S. Raid Far North of 20th Parallel

By EVERT CLARK

Special to The New York Times

WASHINGTON, April 4 — North Vietnam charged in a broadcast today that United States planes had bombed a "populated area" in northwestern Vietnam far north of the 20th parallel. The Defense Department said it knew of no such raid but was investigating.

President Johnson has ordered that there be no attacks on North Vietnam north of the 20th Parallel as a step toward de-escalating the war.

[In South Vietnam, United States marines beat off an attack by about 400 North Vietnamese soldiers charging up a hill near Khesanh, killing 93, The Associated Press reported. Meanwhile, an American relief column was nearing the besieged base. Page 15.]

The Hanoi radio, in a broadcast monitored and translated here, said three waves of United States planes dropped more than 50 bombs on a "populated area" about 30 miles west of Laichau, capital of Laichau Province, this morning.

The New York Times April 5, 1968

Hanoi said that area near Laichau (cross) was target.

The nearest village to that

Continued on Page 15, Column 1

HUMPHREY HINTS HE'LL ENTER RACE

Tells Unionists in Pittsburgh He Will Act Soon—Abel and Wirtz Back Him

By ROY REED

Special to The New York Times

PITTSBURGH, April 4—Two thousand labor representatives, including the head of the United Steel Workers union, clamorously urged Vice President Humphrey today to run for President.

The Vice President left little doubt that he would oblige them, but he indicated that he would wait until President Johnson returned from his Hawaii conference before making an announcement.

"I know what your request is, and I know what your thoughts are," he told the delegates to the Pennsylvania A.F.L.-C.I.O. convention. "I am most grateful. I am not one to walk away from a decision, and a decision will come in due time."

But nothing he does should interfere with President Johnson's peace mission, he said.

Several other political leaders urged Mr. Humphrey today to enter the race for the Democratic Presidential nomination. The most prominent among them was Secretary of Labor W. Willard Wirtz, who was addressing a union convention at Miami Beach.

I. W. Abel, president of the steelworkers Union, rose as Mr.

Continued on Page 32, Column 1

Johnson Shuns Role Of '68 'Lame Duck,' Kennedy Was Told

By JOHN HERBERS

Special to The New York Times

WASHINGTON, April 4—In his meeting with Senator Robert F. Kennedy yesterday President Johnson said he would remain out of the political fight this year because he did not believe it was appropriate for a "lame duck" President to try to pick his successor.

This and other details of the Johnson-Kennedy meeting were learned today from knowledgeable sources.

The meeting, which Senator Kennedy had requested in the interest of "national unity," was described as an extraordinarily friendly one, with both the Senator and the President speaking in a conciliatory manner.

President Johnson was pictured as the "elder statesman" of the party who had decided to remain aloof from this year's scramble for the Presidency in an effort to keep the party as strong as possible and retain his own dignity and effectiveness as President.

At one point, it was reported, the President said he did not want to make a spectacle of himself as a lame duck President attempting to dictate to the party who should be nominated at the national convention.

In this rega. 1, he pointed out that in 1956 former President Harry S. Truman went to the

Continued on Page 31, Column 4

DISMAY IN NATION

Negroes Urge Others to Carry on Spirit of Nonviolence

By LAWRENCE VAN GELDER

Dismay, shame, anger and foreboding marked the nation's reaction last night to the Rev. Dr. Martin Luther King Jr.'s murder.

From the high offices of state to the man in the street, news of the moderate civil rights leader's violent death in Memphis yesterday drew, for the most part, stunned and sober statements.

Most major Negro organizations and Negro leaders, lamenting Dr. King's death, expressed hope that it serve as a spur to others to carry on in his spirit of nonviolence. But some Negro militants responded with bitterness and anger.

Roy Wilkins, executive director of the National Association for the Advancement of Colored People, said his organization was "shocked and deeply grieved by the dastardly murder of Dr. Martin Luther King."

"His murderer or murderers must be promptly apprehended and brought to justice," Mr. Wilkins said.

'A Man of Peace'

"Dr. King was a symbol of the nonviolent civil rights protest movement. He was a man of peace, of dedication, of great courage. His senseless assassination solves nothing. It will not stay the civil rights movement; it will instead spur it to greater activity."

Whitney M. Young Jr., executive director of the National Urban League, said:

"We are unspeakably shocked by the murder of Martin Luther King, one of the greatest leaders of our time. This is a bitter reflection on America. We fear for our country.

"The only possible answer now is for the nation to act immediately on what Dr. King has been fighting for—passage of the civil rights and anti-poverty bills and a true and just equality for all men. Those of us who have remained loyal to his concept of nonviolence have been dealt a mortal blow."

Mayor Richard G. Hatcher of Gary, Ind., a Negro, termed the death of Dr. King "every man's loss."

"Men who care for humankind and struggle for its salvation through reason and faith have lost a leader of monumental stature," he said. "A man of his magnitude will not soon pass this way again."

At his home in Stamford, Conn., the former baseball star Jackie Robinson called the

Continued on Page 26, Column 1

PRESIDENT'S PLEA

On TV, He Deplores 'Brutal' Murder of Negro Leader

Statements by Johnson and Humphrey are on Page 24.

Special to The New York Times

WASHINGTON, April 4— President Johnson deplored tonight in a brief television address to the nation the "brutal slaying" of the Rev. Dr. Martin Luther King Jr.

He asked "every citizen to reject the blind violence that has struck Dr. King, who lived by nonviolence."

Mr. Johnson said he was postponing his scheduled departure tonight for a Honolulu conference on Vietnam and that instead he would leave tomorrow.

The President spoke from the White House. At the Washington Hilton Hotel, where Democratic members of Congress had gathered to honor the President and the Vice President, Mr. Humphrey, his voice strained with emotion, said:

"Martin Luther King stands with our other American martyrs in the cause of freedom and justice. His death is a terrible tragedy."

The dinner was canceled 10 to 15 minutes after the Vice President spoke. Mr. Johnson, who was scheduled to appear at the dinner, canceled his plans to attend.

F.B.I. Inquiry Ordered

Attorney General Ramsey Clark ordered an immediate inquiry by the Federal Bureau of Investigation into the shooting of Dr. King in Memphis.

He said the purpose of the investigation would be to determine whether any Federal law had been violated.

One provision of the law that could be invoked makes it a crime to engage in a conspiracy to deprive a person of his civil rights.

In addition to F.B.I. agents, Department of Justice civil rights representatives were on the scene in Memphis and were in touch with the Attorney General.

Military sources said that no National Guard units had yet been Federalized and no Regular Army troops had been alerted yet for possible movement to cities where violence had broken out.

National Guard troops, such as the 4,000 men who have been called into Memphis, remain under state control until the responsible Governor requests help and the President

Continued on Page 24, Column 7

Associated Press

THE REV. DR. MARTIN LUTHER KING Jr.

Scattered Violence Occurs In Harlem and Brooklyn

12 Are Arrested Here

By THOMAS A. JOHNSON

Sporadic violence erupted in Harlem and Brooklyn's Bedford-Stuyvesant section last night after news of Dr. Martin Luther King's assassination spread in the two predominantly Negro communities.

Mayor Lindsay, who went to Harlem in an effort to quiet the outbreaks, was caught in the midst of an unruly crowd and had to be hustled into a limousine by bodyguards.

Police reinforcements, including elements of the riot-trained Tactical Patrol Force, were rushed into both communities.

Two arrests were reported in Brooklyn and 10 in Harlem. A television crewman was said to have been injured by flying glass.

There were numerous instances of rock-throwing, looting and arson reported both in Brooklyn and in Harlem, starting around 11 P.M. and continuing early today.

Gangs of youth in both areas were reported roaming through the streets, now and then taunting policemen and firemen on duty.

The police fired several volleys of shots in the air to disperse crowds along Brooklyn's Fulton Street and Harlem's

Continued on Page 26, Column 2

Widespread Disorders

Disorders broke out in scattered parts of the nation last night after the slaying of the Rev. Dr. Martin Luther King Jr. The National Guard was called out or alerted in several cities.

In Washington, scattered but persistent looting and vandalism erupted, led for a time by Stokely Carmichael, former head of the Student Nonviolent Coordinating Commitee. All available policemen were being called to duty.

About 4,000 Tennessee National Guardsmen were ordered to duty in Nashville because of disorders.

In North Carolina, Gov. Dan K. Moore alerted the Guard in Greensboro at the request of Mayor Carson Bain. State Highway patrolmen were dispatched to Raleigh.

There were riotous outbursts

Continued on Page 28, Column 8

NEWS INDEX

GUARD CALLED OUT

Curfew Is Ordered in Memphis, but Fires and Looting Erupt

By EARL CALDWELL

Special to The New York Times

MEMPHIS, Friday, April 5— The Rev. Dr. Martin Luther King Jr., who preached nonviolence and racial brotherhood, was fatally shot here last night by a distant gunman who then raced away and escaped.

Four thousand National Guard troops were ordered into Memphis by Gov. Buford Ellington after the 39-year-old Nobel Prize-winning civil rights leader died.

A curfew was imposed on the shocked city of 550,000 inhabitants, 40 per cent of whom are Negro.

But the police said the tragedy had been followed by incidents that included sporadic shooting, fires, bricks and bottles thrown at policemen, and looting that started in Negro districts and then spread over the city.

White Car Sought

Police Director Frank Holloman said the assassin might have been a white man who was "50 to 100 yards away in a flophouse."

Chief of Detectives W. P. Huston said a late model white Mustang was believed to have been the killer's getaway car. Its occupant was described as a bareheaded white man in his 30's, wearing a black suit and black tie.

The detective chief said the police had chased two cars near the motel where Dr. King was shot and had halted one that had two out-of-town men as occupants. The men were questioned but seemed to have nothing to do with the killing, he said.

Rifle Found Nearby

A high-powered 30.06-caliber rifle was found about a block from the scene of the shooting, on South Main Street. "We think it's the gun," Chief Huston said, reporting it would be turned over to the Federal Bureau of Investigation.

Dr. King was shot while he leaned over a second-floor railing outside his room at the Lorraine Motel. He was chatting with two friends just before starting for dinner.

One of the friends was a musician, and Dr. King had just asked him to play a Negro spiritual, "Precious Lord, Take My Hand," at a rally that was to have been held two hours later in support of striking Memphis sanitationmen.

Paul Hess, assistant adminis-

Continued on Page 24, Column 1

Archbishop Cooke Installed; President Looks On

By EDWARD B. FISKE

The Most Rev. Terence J. Cooke was installed as the seventh Roman Catholic Archbishop of New York yesterday in a historic pageant attended by the President of the United States and highlighted by prayers for the success of his peace efforts in Vietnam.

"Let us pray with all our hearts that God will inspire our President," the 47-year-old Archbishop said in his homily at St. Patrick's Cathedral.

"In the last few days, we have all admired his heroic efforts in the search for peace in Vietnam. We ask God to bless his efforts with success. May God inspire not only our President, but also other leaders and the leaders of all nations of the world to find a way to peace."

Then the Archbishop, speaking from a white marble pulpit and surrounded by a blaze of purple, gold and scarlet robes, addressed himself directly to Mr. Johnson, who sat below him in a front pew.

The President, sitting with his hands clasped and his legs crossed, listened with obvious intensity to the Archbishop's words.

"Mr. President," he said, "our hearts, our hopes, our continued prayers go with you."

Mr. Johnson, accompanied by his daughter, Mrs. Patrick J. Nugent, led a festive congregation of about 5,000 cardinals, bishops, priests, laymen, nuns, civic leaders

Continued on Page 38, Column 1

The New York Times (by Neal Boenzi)

President Johnson and his daughter, Mrs. Patrick J. Nugent, right, listening during yesterday's ceremonies. At left are Mrs. John F. Kennedy and Lieut. Gov. Malcolm Wilson. Security personnel are in the row between them.

Archbishop Luigi Raimondi, Apostolic Delegate to the U.S., speaking after Archbishop Terence J. Cooke was enthroned

Martin Luther King Is Shot to Death in Memphis; White Suspect Is Hunted

4,000 GUARDSMEN ARE ORDERED OUT

Curfew Is Imposed on City, but Windows Are Broken and Policemen Stoned

Continued From Page 1, Col. 8

trator at St. Joseph's Hospital, where Dr. King died despite emergency surgery, said the minister had "received a gunshot wound on the right side of the neck, at the root of the neck, a gaping wound."

"He was pronounced dead at 7:05 P.M. Central standard time (8:05 P.M. New York time) by staff doctors," Mr. Hess said. "They did everything humanly possible."

Dr. King's mourning associates sought to calm the people they met by recalling his messages of peace, but there was widespread concern by law enforcement officers here and elsewhere over potential reactions.

In a television broadcast after the curfew was ordered here, Mr. Holloman said, "rioting has broken out in parts of the city" and "looting is rampant."

Dr. King had come back to Memphis Wednesday morning to organize support once again for 1,300 sanitation workers who have been striking since Lincoln's Birthday. Just a week ago yesterday he led a march in the strikers' cause that ended in violence. A 16-year-old Negros was killed, 62 persons were injured and 200 were arrested.

Yesterday Dr. King had been in his second-floor room—Number 306—throughout the day. Just about 6 P.M. he emerged, wearing a silkish-looking black suit and white shirt.

Solomon Jones Jr., his driver, had been waiting to take him by car to the home of the Rev. Samuel Kyles of Memphis for dinner. Mr. Jones said later he had observed, "It's cold outside, put your topcoat on," and Dr. King had replied, "O. K., I will."

Two Men in Courtyard

Dr. King, an open-faced, genial man, leaned over a green iron railing to chat with an associate, Jesse Jackson, standing just below him in a courtyard parking lot.

"Do you know Ben?" Mr. Jackson asked, introducing Ben Branch of Chicago, a musician who was to play at the night's rally.

"Yes, that's my man!" Dr. King glowed.

The two men recalled Dr. King's asking for the playing of the spiritual. "I really want you to play that tonight," Dr. King said, enthusiastically.

The Rev. Ralph W. Abernathy, perhaps Dr. King's closest friend, was just about to come out of the motel room when the sudden loud noise burst out.

Dr. King toppled to the concrete second-floor walkway. Blood gushed from the right jaw and neck area. His necktie had been ripped off by the blast.

"He had just bent over," Mr. Jackson recalled later. "If he had been standing up, he wouldn't have been hit in the face."

Policemen 'All Over'

"When I turned around," Mr. Jackson went on, bitterly, "I saw police coming from everywhere. They said, 'where did it come from?' And I said, 'behind you.' The police were coming from where the shot came."

Mr. Branch asserted that the shot had come from "the hill on the other side of the street."

"When I looked up, the police and the sheriff's deputies were running all around," Mr. Branch declared.

"We didn't need to call the police," Mr. Jackson said. "They were here all over the place."

Mr. Kyles said Dr. King had stood in the open "about three minutes."

Mr. Jones, the driver, said that a squad car with four policemen in it drove down the street only moments before the gunshot. The police had been circulating throughout the motel area on precautionary patrols.

After the shot, Mr. Jones said, he saw a man "with something white on his face" creep away from a thicket across the street.

Someone rushed up with a towel to stem the flow of Dr. King's blood. Mr. Kyles said he put a blanket over Dr. King, but "I knew he was gone." He ran down the stairs and tried to telephone from the motel office for an ambulance.

Mr. Abernathy hurried up with a second larger towel.

Police With Helmets

Policemen were pouring into the motel area, carrying rifles and shotguns and wearing riot helmets.

But the King aides said it seemed to be 10 or 15 minutes before a Fire Department ambulance arrived.

Dr. King was apparently still living when he reached the St. Joseph's Hospital operating room for emergency surgery. He was borne in on a stretcher, the bloody towel over his head.

It was the same emergency room to which James H. Meredith, first Negro enrolled at the University of Mississippi, was taken after he was ambushed and shot in June, 1965, at Hernando, Miss., a few miles south of Memphis. Mr. Meredith was not seriously hurt.

Associated Press

WHERE IT HAPPENED: Memphis police standing on the balcony of the Lorraine Hotel in Memphis, where the Rev. Dr. Martin Luther King Jr. was fatally shot last night.

Outside the emergency room some of Dr. King's aides waited in forlorn hope. One was Chauncey Eskridge, his legal adviser. He broke into sobs when Dr. King's death was announced.

"A man full of life, full of love and he was shot," Mr. Eskridge said. "He had always lived with that expectation—but nobody ever expected it to happen."

But the Rev. Andrew Young, executive director of Dr. King's Southern Christian Leadership Conference, recalled there had been some talk Wednesday night about possible harm to Dr. King in Memphis.

Mr. Young recalled: "He said he had reached the pinnacle of fulfillment with his nonviolent movement, and these reports did not bother him."

Mr. Young believed that the fatal shot might have been fired from a passing car. "It sounded like a firecracker," he said.

In a nearby building, a newsman who had been watching a television program thought, however, that "it was a tremendous blast that sounded like a bomb."

There were perhaps 15 persons in the motel courtyard area when Dr. King was shot, all believed to be Negroes and Dr. King's associates.

Past the courtyard is a small empty swimming pool. Then comes Mulberry Street, a short street only three blocks away from storied Beale Street on the fringe of downtown Memphis.

Fire Station Nearby

On the other side of the street is a six-foot brick restraining wall, with bushes and grass atop it and a hillside going on to a patch of trees. Behind the trees is a rusty wire fence enclosing backyards of two-story brick and frame houses.

At the corner at Butler Street is a newish-looking white brick fire station.

Police were reported to have chased a late-model blue or white car through Memphis and north to Millington. A civilian in another car that had a citizens band radio was also reported to have pursued the fleeing car and to have opened fire on it.

The police first cordoned off an area of about five blocks around the Lorraine Motel, chosen by Dr. King for his stay here because it is Negro-owned. The two-story motel is in addition to a small two-story hotel in a largely Negro area.

Mayor Henry Loeb had ordered a curfew here after last week's disorder, and National Guard units had been on duty for five days until they were deactivated Wednesday.

Last night the Mayor reinstated the curfew at 6:35 and declared:

"After the tragedy which has happened in Memphis tonight, for the protection of all our citizens, we are putting the curfew back in effect. All movement is restricted except for health or emergency reasons."

Governor Ellington, calling out the National Guard and pledging all necessary action by the state to prevent disorder, announced:

"For the second time in recent days, I most earnestly ask the people of Memphis and Shelby County to remain calm. I do so aagin tonight in the face of this most regrettable incident.

"Every possible action is being taken to apprehend the person or persons responsible for committing this act.

"We are also taking precautionary steps to prevent any acts of disorder. I can fully appreciate the feelings and emotions which this crime has aroused, but for the benefit of everyone, all of our citizens must exercise restraint, caution and good judgment."

National Guard planes flew over the state to bring in contingents of riot-trained highway patrolmen. Units of the Arkansas State Patrol were deputized and brought into Memphis.

Assistant Chief Bartholomew early this morning said that unidentified persons had shot from rooftops and windows at policemen eight or 10 times. He said bullets had shattered one police car's windshield, wounding two policemen with flying glass. They were treated at the same hospital where Dr. King died.

Sixty arrests were made for looting, burglary and disorderly conduct, chief Bartholomew said.

Numerous minor injuries were reported in four hours of clashes between civilians and law enforcement officers. But any serious disorders were under control by 11:15 P.M., Chief Bartholomew said. Early this morning streets were virtually empty except for patrol cars riding without headlights on.

Once Stabbed in Harlem

In his career Dr. King had suffered beatings and blows. Once—on Sept. 20, 1958—he was stabbed in a Harlem department store in New York by a Negro woman later adjudged insane.

That time he underwent a four-hour operation to remove a steel letter opener that had been plunged into his upper left chest. For a time he was on the critical list, but he told his wife, while in the hospital, "I don't hold any bitterness toward this woman."

In Memphis, Dr. King's chief associates met in his room after he died. They included Mr. Young, Mr. Abernathy, Mr. Jackson, the Rev. James Bevel and Hosea Williams.

They had to step across a drying pool of Dr. King's blood to enter. Someone had thrown a crumpled pack of cigarettes into the blood.

After 15 minutes they emerged. Mr. Jackson looked at the blood. He embraced Mr. Abernathy.

"Stand tall!" somebody exhorted.

"Murder! Murder!" Mr. Bevel groaned. "Doc said that's not the way."

"Doc" was what they often called Dr. King.

Then the murdered leader's aides said they would go on to the hall where tonight's rally was to have been held. They wanted to urge calm upon the mourners.

Some policemen sought to dissuade them.

But eventually the group did start out, with a police escort.

At the Federal Bureau of Investigation office here, Robert Jensen, special agent in charge said the F. B. I. had entered the murder investigation at the request of Attorney General Ramsey Clark.

Last night Dr. King's body was taken to the Shelby County morgue, according to the police. They said it would be up to Dr. Derry Francisco, county medical examiner, to order further disposition.

The New York Times April 5, 1968

AREA OF THE MURDER: (1) Motel where the shooting occurred; (2) hospital where Dr. King died, and (3) famed Beale Street, scene of demonstrations.

Flip Schulke—Black Star

LED MARCH ON WASHINGTON: Dr. King speaking to the marchers from steps of Lincoln Memorial on Aug. 28, 1963.

Aide to Dr. King Asserts March Of Poor in Capital Will Be Held

WASHINGTON, April 4 (UPI)—A top lieutenant of the Rev. Dr. Martin Luther King Jr. said tonight that the "poor people's crusade" in the nation's capital planned for later this month by Dr. King definitely would be held.

"The march is going on," said Bernard Lafayette, coordinator of the King campaign in Washington. "If there ever was a March—this one will be held."

Mr. Lafayette spoke following the slaying in Memphis of Dr. King, who had planned to bring more than 3,000 of the nation's poorest to build a shantytown among the city's monuments to try to get Government help for the needy.

At the same time, Lestor McKinne, head of the Washington chapter of the Student Nonviolent Coordinating Committee, called on the city's Negroes to stage a strike tomorrow.

"While staying home, blacks should begin to analyze what the white racist Government is doing to black people," Mr. McKinne said. "We don't know what will happen to blacks in the United States if the Government allows King to be killed."

Mr. Lafayette said he did not know now who would lead the poor crusade, but that it might be the Rev. Ralph P. Abernathy.

Dr. King had said the poor people from around the nation would stay in the capital until the Government did something to help the poor. He had planned to bring the vanguard of the demonstration here by April 22 and have it reach full strength of at least 3,000 by mid-May.

Slaying Recalls Series of Deaths That Have Marked Rights Fight

By SETH S. KING

In Albany, Ga., in 1962, the Rev. Dr. Martin Luther King Jr. was preaching in a small church after shots were fired into nearby houses.

"It may get me crucified," he said. "I may even die. But I want it said even if I die in the struggle that 'He died to make me free.'"

Dr. King's death at the hands of a gunman in Memphis yesterday recalled those words. His death also recalled the series of racial slayings and shootings that began soon afterward and have recurred every year since then.

The first came a year later, in April, 1963. William L. Moore, a white mailman from Baltimore, was making a one-man march through the South to protest racial segregation. He was shot to death at close range as he walked one evening near the northeastern Alabama town of Attalla.

Two months later, Medgar W. Evers, Mississippi Field Secretary of the National Association for the Advancement of Colored People, was shot to death as he stepped out of his automobile in the driveway of his home in Jackson, Miss.

In the summer of 1964 hundreds of young civil rights workers from cities in the East and North converged on Mississippi to lead a drive to register Negroes to vote.

The nation was shocked in August by the disappearance of two young men from New York and their Negro companion. After an intensive search that lasted two weeks, the bullet-riddled bodies of Andrew Goodman, a student at Queens College; Michael H. Schwerner, a New York social worker, and James E. Chaney, a Negro civil rights worker from Meridian, were found in a shallow grave near that Mississippi town.

Early in 1965 the racial tensions that had been building burst forth in a bizarre direction.

Malcolm X, the fiery former supporter of Elijah Muhammed, the Black Muslim leader, was speaking in the Audubon Ballroom on Broadway in Harlem when three Negroes charged down the aisle.

A blast from a sawed-off shotgun hit the black militant, who died soon afterward.

At that time, Dr. King said: "I have learned to face threats on my life philosophically and have prepared myself for anything that might come."

A month later he was at the head of his now famous march in Selma, Ala. Within a week three persons who had participated in it were dead from violence.

Jimmie Lee Jackson, a young Negro marcher, was the first. He was shot down in a cafe in nearby Marion.

Then the Rev. James L. Reeb, a Protestant minister from Boston, was beaten by a mob of white men in a Selma street and died a few days later.

Before the march ended the nation was again appalled when Mrs. Viola Gregg Liuzzo, a Detroit housewife who had left her husband and five children to help in the march, was shot to death while driving her car between Selma and Montgomery.

The summer of 1965 marked the death and critical wounding in Alabama of two more white men who went South to participate in civil right work.

On Aug. 21, Jonathan Myrick Danials, a 26-year-old Episcopal seminarian from Keene, N.H., died from the blast of a shotgun as he walked to a grocery store with two Negro girls in Haynesville.

A Roman Catholic priest, the Rev. Richard F. Morrisroe of Chicago, was critically wounded by the same blast.

The summer of 1966 saw the wounding of James H. Meredith, the first Negro to attend the University of Mississippi.

He was injured by a blast fired from ambush along a country road near Hernando as he walked across the state to prove that a Negro civil rights leader could do so.

Early last year, as he was driving his truck home from work, Wharlest Jackson, treasurer of the N.A.A.C.P. branch in Natchez, Miss., was killed by a bomb thrown into the vehicle.

Washington Is Shaken; Leaders Call for Calm

WASHINGTON, April 4 (UPI)—Not since John F. Kennedy was assassinated on Nov. 22, 1963, has the capital been so shaken by a murder. Washington was plunged into gloom and feared the repercussions of the slaying of the Rev. Dr. Martin Luther King Jr.

Leaders called for calm. Some in Congress said open housing legislation should now be passed as a memorial to the man who marched for it.

Dr. King, said Speaker of the House, John McCormack, "was a martyr to a cause—and that cause will be strengthened if the House concurs in the Senate civil rights bill."

The bill would outlaw discrimination in the sale or rental of 68 per cent of the nation's housing.

Mrs. King Is Planning to Fly to Memphis Today

Hears About Husband's Death While at Atlanta Airport

Mayor Drives Her to Home After Breaking the News

By WALTER RUGABER

Special to The New York Times

ATLANTA, April 4 — Mrs. Martin Luther King Jr., who called off a trip to Memphis tonight after her husband's wounds were reported fatal, planned to fly there later to claim his body tomorrow.

Mrs. King, informed that her husband had been wounded, was rushed to the Atlanta Airport by Mayor Ivan Allen Jr. for Eastern Airlines Flight 399, scheduled to depart for Memphis at 8:25 P.M. A heavy rain delayed the flight, however.

She waited briefly in a private room at the airport with two eldest children, Yolanda Denise and Martin Luther 3d, until Mayor Allen learned of her husband's death. He broke the news to her at the airport.

Mr. Allen drove Mrs. King back to the King residence, a modest home about two miles northeast of the downtown business district. There she received a few visits and telephone calls from friends.

Breaks Into Tears

Mrs. King broke into tears occasionally, they reported, but otherwise she appeared outwardly composed. For a time, she watched a television recounting of her husband's career as a civil rights leader.

Several whites went to the home to offer their sympathy.

United Press International

Mrs. Martin Luther King Jr. in Atlanta last night after she learned that her husband had been assassinated.

Among them was Herbert T. Jenkins, the Atlanta chief of police, who was a member of the National Advisory Commission on Civil Disorders, and Sam Caldwell, the state Labor Commissioner.

About 15 men were posted around the King home by the police. The detail was headed by Capt. Howard Baugh, a 44-year-old Negro officer who recalled that he had lived next-door to Dr. King when they were boys.

Dr. King's father, the Rev. Martin Luther King Sr., was sequestered at his home in another section of the city. Captain Baugh, who said he had talked to the elder Mr. King tonight, said he sounded as though he was bearing up "quite well."

The father was pastor and Dr. King was co-pastor of the Ebenezer Baptist Church. A brief prayer service was held there soon after the shooting, and several other Negro churches opened their doors also.

The time of Mrs. King's trip to Memphis tomorrow was not immediately known.

Recuperating From Surgery

ATLANTA, Ga., April 4 (AP)—Mrs. King, who has been recuperating from major surgery, had lived with the threat of death for her husband.

After he won the Nobel Peace Prize in 1964, she said, "I have lived with the threat of death always present."

Mrs. King, a former voice instructor, has sung at concerts for numerous civil rights organizations and sometimes has accompanied her husband on his trips in the fight for civil rights.

KING CITED THREAT DAY BEFORE DEATH

Told 2,000 Supporters He Had Seen Promised Land

MEMPHIS, April 4 (AP)—"It really doesn't matter what happens now. I've been to the mountaintop."

The speaker was the Rev. Dr. Martin Luther King Jr. His audience was a cheering crowd of some 2,000 supporters. It was last night.

Dr. King said last night that he was aware that threats had been made on his life. But he said he had seen the fulfillment of his goals of nonviolence, and did not worry about the future.

He said that his flight to Memphis from Atlanta Tuesday had been delayed because of a baggage search that airlines officials had said resulted from threats to him.

'Difficult Days Ahead'

"And there have been some threats around here," he said. "We've got some difficult days ahead, but it really doesn't matter now," Dr. King said. "Because I've been to the mountain top."

And the Rev. Andrew W. Young, the executive vice president of Dr. King's Southern Christian Leadership Conference, said after the slaying that he had heard Dr. King make similar remarks only once before—at Demopolis, Ala., during his 1965 Selma march.

"I don't know whether it was premonition or not," Mr. Young said as he stood in the door of the emergency room where Dr. King had been taken after he was felled by the bullet.

Supreme Test Planned

The supreme test of the theory of nonviolence was to have come next Monday, when Dr. King planned to lead a massive march down the path where violence broke out last week.

That was the first time in Dr. King's long history of civil rights activity that one of his drives had erupted into violence.

He was clearly disturbed.

Mr. Young, testifying at a Federal Court hearing six hours before Dr. King was shot, was asked by United States District Judge Bailey Brown what effect violence in the upcoming march would have on Dr. King.

"I would say that Dr. King would consider it a repudiation of his philosophy and his whole way of life," Mr. Young replied. "I don't know when I've seen him as discouraged and depressed."

"Let us stand with greater determination," Mr. Young said. "Let us move on in these days of challenge to make America what it ought to be."

DR. KING'S STATEMENT

I left Atlanta this morning, and as we got started on the plane—there were six of us—the pilot said over the public address system: "We're sorry for the delay, but we have Dr. Martin Luther King on the plane. And to be sure that all of the bags were checked. And to be sure that nothing would be wrong on the plane we had to check out everything carefully. And we've had the plane protected and guarded all night."

And then I got into Memphis. And some began to say the threats—or talk about the threats that were out. Or what would happen to me from some of our sick white brothers.

Well, I don't know what will happen now. We've got some difficult days ahead. But it really doesn't matter with me now. Because I've been to the mountain top. I won't mind.

Like anybody, I would like to live a long life. Longevity has its place. But I'm not concerned about that now. I just want to do God's will. And He's allowed me to go up to the mountain. And I've looked over, and I've seen the promised land.

I may not get there with you, but I want you to know tonight that we as a people will get to the promised land.

So I'm happy tonight. I'm not worried about anything. I'm not fearing any man. Mine eyes have seen the glory of the coming of the Lord.

Statements in the Capital

Special to The New York Times

WASHINGTON, April 4—Following are the texts of statements tonight by President Johnson and Vice President Humphrey on the slaying of the Rev. Dr. Martin Luther King Jr.:

President Johnson

America is shocked and saddened by the brutal slaying tonight of Dr. Martin Luther King.

I ask every citizen to reject the blind violence that has struck Dr. King, who lived by nonviolence.

I pray that his family can find comfort in the memory of all he tried to do for the land he loved so well. I have just conveyed the sympathy of Mrs. Johnson and myself to his widow, Mrs. King.

I know that every American of goodwill joins me in mourning the death of this outstanding leader and in praying for peace and understanding throughout this land.

We can achieve nothing by lawlessness and divisiveness among the American people. It's only by joining together, and only by working together, can we continue to move toward equality and fulfillment for all of our people.

I hope that all Americans tonight will search their hearts as they ponder this most tragic incident.

I have canceled my plans for the evening. I am postponing my trip to Hawaii until tomorrow.

Thank you.

Vice President Humphrey

Martin Luther King stands with our other American martyrs in the cause of freedom and justice. His death is a terrible tragedy and a sorrow to his family, to our nation, to our conscience. The criminal act that took his life brings shame to our country.

The apostle of nonviolence has been the victim of violence. The cause for which he marched and worked I am sure will find a new strength.

The plight of discrimination, poverty and neglect must be erased from America, and an America of full freedom, full and equal opportunity, is the living memorial he deserves, and it shall be his living memorial.

Johnson, in TV Talk, Deplores 'Brutal' Killing of Negro Leader

Continued From Page 1, Col. 5

decides to assume responsibility for restoring order.

David E. McGiffert, Under Secretary of the Army, Gen. Harold K. Johnson, the Army Chief of Staff, and the general counsel of the Army, Robert Jordan, went to the Army Operations Center at the Pentagon tonight.

The XVIII Airborne Corps at Fort Bragg, N. C., also opened its emergency operations headquarters tonight. The XVIII Airborne Corps controls the 82d Airborne Division, whose remaining two brigades are the only elite Army troops capable of swift movement to a riot-torn city.

The division headquarters was alerted by the corps tonight, but none of the troop units have yet been placed on the alert.

The shock of Dr. King's death, which hit this capital with numbing suddenness, was reflected in the President's face as he spoke to the nation.

In his message, delivered shortly after 9 P.M. Eastern standard time from a doorway of the west wing of the White House, the President said:

"America is shocked and saddened by the brutal slaying tonight of Dr. Martin Luther King. I ask every citizen to reject the blind violence that has struck Dr. King, who lived by nonviolence."

Mr. Johnson said he and Mrs. Johnson had conveyed their sympathy to Mrs. King.

"I know," he added, "that every American of goodwill joins me in mourning the death of this outstanding leader in praying for peace and understanding throughout this land."

The President said that nothing could be achieved by lawlessness and divisiveness among Americans. Only by working together, he asserted, can America move toward full equality and fulfillment for everyone.

"I hope," Mr. Johnson declared solemnly, "that all Americans tonight will search their hearts as they ponder this most tragic incident."

The President and Dr. King developed a close working relationship during Mr. Johnson's first two years in the White House, but it began to cool when the Negro leader became critical of the Administration's Vietnam policies as a costly diversion of resources from pressing domestic needs.

They cooperated in Mr. Johnson's 1964 campaign against Barry Goldwater and in the development of Great Society programs, including civil rights and voting rights measures. As far as is known, they had no contact in the last year.

The Vice President announced Dr. King's death to the 2,500 persons attending the Congressional dinner. Mr. Humphrey, who was seated at the head table on a raised platform, rose, and in a solemn, heavy voice said:

"This is a very unusual and special and very difficult time. A great tragedy has taken place in America tonight. One of our renowned and active leaders in the cause of civil rights has been stricken down by an assassin's bullet. Martin Luther King has been shot and is dead."

The Vice President then read a prepared statement: "The criminal act that took his life brings shame to our country," he said. "The apostle of nonviolence has been the victim of violence. The cause for which he marched and worked, I am sure, will find new strength."

Mr. Humphrey added: "An America of full freedom, full and equal opportunity, is the living memorial he deserves, and it shall be his living memorial."

Martin Luther King Jr.: Leader of Millions in Nonviolent Drive for Racial Justice

CAREER A SYMBOL OF INTEGRATION

Nobel Winner Was Attacked by Both Negro Militants and White Extremists

By MURRAY SCHUMACH

To many millions of American Negroes, the Rev. Dr. Martin Luther King Jr. was the prophet of their crusade for racial equality. He was their voice of anguish, their eloquence in humiliation, their battle cry for human dignity. He forged for them the weapons of nonviolence that withstood and blunted the ferocity of segregation.

And to many millions of American whites, he was one of a group of Negroes who preserved the bridge of communication between races when racial warfare threatened the United States in the nineteen-sixties, as Negroes sought the full emancipation pledged to them a century before by Abraham Lincoln.

To the world Dr. King had the stature that accrued to a winner of the Nobel Peace Prize; a man with access to the White House and the Vatican; a veritable hero in the African states that were just emerging from colonialism.

Associated Press

ALABAMA—1956: Dr. King, seated behind the Rev. Ralph D. Abernathy, rides a forward seat in a Montgomery bus after the Supreme Court's desegregation order. Next to him is the Rev. Glenn Smiley of New York; woman next to Dr. Abernathy was not identified.

Between Extremes

In his dedication to nonviolence, Dr. King was caught between white and Negro extremists as racial tensions erupted into arson, gunfire and looting in many of the nation's cities during the summer of 1967.

Militant Negroes, with the cry of, "burn, baby burn," argued that only by violence and segregation could the Negro attain self-respect, dignity and real equality in the United States.

Floyd B. McKissick, when director of the Congress of Racial Equality, declared in August of that year that it was a "foolish assumption to try to sell nonviolence to the ghettos."

And white extremists, not bothering to make distinctions between degrees of Negro militancy, looked upon Dr. King as one of their chief enemies.

At times in recent months, efforts by Dr. King to utilize nonviolent methods exploded into violence.

Violence in Memphis

Last week, when he led a protest march through downtown Memphis, Tenn., in support of the city's striking sanitation workers, a group of Negro youths suddenly began breaking store windows and looting, and one Negro was shot to death.

Two days later, however, Dr. King said he would stage another demonstration and attributed the violence to his own "miscalculation."

At the time he was assassinated in Memphis, Dr. King was involved in one of his greatest plans to dramatize the plight of the poor and stir Congress to help Negroes.

He called this venture the "Poor People's Campaign." It was to be a huge "camp-in" either in Washington or in Chicago during the Democratic National Convention.

In one of his last public pronouncements before the shooting, Dr. King told an audience in a Harlem church on March 26:

"We need an alternative to riots and to timid supplication. Nonviolence is our most potent weapon."

His strong beliefs in civil rights and nonviolence made him one of the leading opponents of American participation in the war in Vietnam. To him the war was unjust, diverting vast sums away from programs to alleviate the condition of the Negro poor in this country. He called the conflict "one of history's most cruel and senseless wars." Last January he said:

"We need to make clear in this political year, to Congressmen on both sides of the aisle and to the President of the United States that we will no longer vote for men who continue to see the killing of Vietnamese and Americans as the best way of advancing the goals of freedom and self-determination in Southeast Asia."

Object of Many Attacks

Inevitably, as a symbol of integration, he became the object of unrelenting attacks and vilification. His home was bombed. He was spat upon and mocked. He was struck and kicked. He was stabbed, almost fatally, by a deranged Negro woman. He was frequently thrown into jail. Threats became so commonplace that his wife could ignore burning crosses on the lawn and ominous phone calls. Through it all he adhered to the creed of passive disobedience that infuriated segregationists.

The adulation that was heaped upon him eventually irritated even some Negroes in the civil rights movement who worked hard, but in relative obscurity. They pointed out—and Dr. King admitted — that he was a poor administrator. Sometimes, with sarcasm, they referred to him, privately, as "De Lawd." They noted that Dr. King's successes were built on the labors of many who had gone before him, the noncoms and privates of the civil rights army who fought without benefit of headlines and television cameras.

The Negro extremists he criticized were contemptuous of Dr. King. They dismissed his passion for nonviolence as another form of servility to white people. They called him an "Uncle Tom," and charged that he was hindering the Negro struggle for equality.

Dr. King's belief in nonviolence was subjected to intense pressure in 1966, when some Negro groups adopted the slogan "black power" in the aftermath of civil rights marches into Mississippi and race riots in Northern cities. He rejected the idea, saying:

"The Negro needs the white man to free him from his fears. The white man needs the Negro to free him from his guilt. A doctrine of black supremacy is as evil as a doctrine of white supremacy."

The doctrine of "black power" threatened to split the Negro civil rights movement and antagonize white liberals who had been supporting Negro causes, and Dr. King suggested "militant nonviolence" as a formula for progress with peace.

At the root of his civil rights convictions was an even more profound faith in the basic goodness of man and the great potential of American democracy. These beliefs gave to his speeches a fervor that could not be stilled by criticism.

Scores of millions of Americans — white as well as Negro — who sat before television sets in the summer of 1963 to watch the awesome march of some 200,000 Negroes on Washington were deeply stirred when Dr. King, in the shadow of the Lincoln Memorial, said:

"Even though we face the difficulties of today and tomorrow, I still have a dream. I have a dream that one day this nation will rise up and live out the true meaning of its creed: 'We hold these truths to be self-evident, that all men are created equal.'"

And all over the world, men were moved as they read his words of Dec. 10, 1964, when he became the third member of his race to receive the Nobel Peace Prize.

Insistent on Man's Destiny

"I refuse to accept the idea that man is mere flotsam and jetsam in the river of life which surrounds him," he said. "I refuse to accept the view that mankind is so tragically bound to the starless midnight of racism and war that the bright daybreak of peace and brotherhood can never become a reality.

"I refuse to accept the cynical notion that nation after nation must spiral down a militaristic stairway into the hell of thermonuclear destruction. I believe that unarmed truth and unconditional love will have the final word in reality. This is why right, temporarily defeated, is stronger than evil triumphant."

For the poor and unlettered of his own race, Dr. King spoke differently. There he embraced the rhythm and passion of the revivalist and evangelist. Some observers of Dr. King's technique said that others in the movement were more effective in this respect. But Dr. King had the touch, as he illustrated in a church in Albany, Ga., in 1962:

"So listen to me, children: Put on your marching shoes; don'cha get weary; though the path ahead may be dark and dreary; we're walking for freedom, children."

Or there was the meeting in Gadsden, Ala., late in 1963, when he displayed another side of his ability before an audience of poor Negroes. It went as follows:

King: I hear they are beating you.

Audience: Yes, yes.

King: I hear they are cursing you.

Audience: Yes, yes.

King: I hear they are going into your homes and doing nasty things and beating you.

Audience: Yes, yes.

King: Some of you have knives, and I ask you to put them up. Some of you have arms, and I ask you to put them up. Get the weapon of nonviolence, the breastplate of righteousness, the armor of truth, and just keep marching."

It was said that so devoted was his vast following that even among illiterates he could, by calm discussion of Platonic dogma, evoke deep cries of "Amen."

Dr. King also had a way of reducing complex issues to terms that anyone could understand. Thus, in the summer of 1965, when there was widespread discontent among Negroes about their struggle for equality of employment, he declared:

"What good does it do to be able to eat at a lunch counter if you can't buy a hamburger."

The enormous impact of Dr. King's words was one of the reasons he was in the President's Room in the Capitol on Aug. 6, 1965, when President Johnson signed the Voting Rights Act that struck down literacy tests, provided Federal registrars to assure the ballot to unregistered Negroes and marked the growth of the Negro as a political force in the South.

Backed by Organization

Dr. King's effectiveness was enhanced and given continuity by the fact that he had an organization behind him. Formed in 1960, with headquarters in Atlanta, it was called the Southern Christian Leadership Conference, familiarly known as SLICK. Allied with it was another organization formed under Dr. King's sponsorship, the Student Nonviolent Coordinating Committee, often referred to as SNICK.

These two organizations reached the country, though their basic strength was in the South. They brought together Negro clergymen, businessmen, professional men and students. They raised the money and planned the sit-ins, the campaigns for Negro vote registration, the demonstrations by which Negroes hacked away at segregationist resistance, lowering the barriers against Negroes in the political, economic and social life of the nation.

This minister, who became the most famous spokesman for Negro rights since Booker T. Washington, was not particularly impressive in appearance. About 5 feet 8 inches tall, he had an oval face with almond-shaped eyes that looked almost dreamy when he was off the platform. His neck and shoulders were heavily muscled, but his hands were almost delicate.

Speaker of Few Gestures

There was little of the rabblerouser in his oratory. He was not prone to extravagant gestures or loud peroration. His baritone voice, though vibrant, was not that of a spellbinder. Occasionally, after a particularly telling sentence, he would tilt his head a bit and fall silent as though waiting for the echoes of his thought to spread through the hall, church or street.

In private gatherings, Dr. King lacked the laughing gregariousness that often makes for popularity. Some thought he was without a sense of humor. He was not a gifted raconteur. He did not have the flamboyance of a Representative Adam Clayton Powell Jr. or the cool strategic brilliance of Roy Wilkins, head of the National Association for the Advancement of Colored People.

What Dr. King did have was an instinct for the right moment to make his moves. Some critics looked upon this as pure opportunism. Nevertheless, it was this sense of timing that raised him in 1955, from a newly arrived minister in Montgomery, Ala., with his first church, to a figure of national prominence.

Bus Boycott in Progress

Negroes in that city had begun a boycott of buses to win the right to sit where they pleased instead of being forced to move to the rear of buses, in Southern tradition or to surrunder seats to white people when a bus was crowded.

Negroes in that city had begun a boycott of buses to win the right to sit where they pleased instead of being forced to move to the rear f buses, in Southern tradition or to surrunder seats to white people when a bus was crowded.

The 381-day boycott by Negroes was already under way when the young pastor was placed in charge of the campaign. It has been said that one of the reasons he got the job was because he was so new in the area he had not antagonized any of the Negro factions. Even while the boycott was under way, a board of directors handled the bulk of administrative work.

However, it was Dr. King who dramatized the boycott with his decision to make it the testing ground, before the eyes of the nation, of his belief in the civil disobedience teachings of Thoreau and Gandhi. When he was arrested during the Montgomery boycott, he said:

"If we are arrested every day, if we are exploited every day, if we are trampled over every day, don't ever let anyone pull you so low as to hate them. We must use the weapon of love. We must have compassion and understanding for those who hate us. We must realize so many people are taught to hate us that they are not totally responsible for their hate. But we stand in life at midnight; we are always on the threshold of a new dawn."

Home Bombed in Absence

Even more dramatic, in some ways, was his reaction to the bombing of his home during the boycott. He was away at the time and rushed back fearful for his wife and children. They were not injured. But when he reached the modest house, more than a thousand Negroes had already gathered and were in an ugly mood, seeking revenge against the white people. The police were jittery. Quickly, Dr. King pacified the crowd and there was no trouble.

Dr. King was even more impressive during the "big push" in Birmingham, which began in April, 1963. With the minister in the limelight, Negroes there began a campaign of sit-ins at lunch counters, picketing and protest marches. Hundreds of children, used in the campaign, were jailed.

The entire world was stirred when the police turned dogs on the demonstrators. Dr. King was jailed for five days. While he was in prison he issued a 9,000-word letter that created considerable controversy among white people, alienating some sympathizers who thought Dr. King was being too aggressive.

Moderates Called Obstacles

In the letter he wrote:

"I have almost reached the regrettable conclusion that the Negro's great stumbling block in the stride toward freedom is not the White Citizens Counciler or the Ku Klux Klanner, but the white moderate who is more devoted to order than to justice; who prefers a negative peace, which is the absence of tension, to a positive peace, which is the presence of justice."

Some critics of Dr. King said that one reason for this letter was to answer Negro intellectuals, such as the writer James Baldwin, who were impatient with Dr. King's belief in brotherhood. Whatever the reasons, the role of Dr. King in Birmingham added to his stature and showed that his enormous following was deeply devoted to him.

He demonstrated this in a threatening situation in Albany, Ga., after four Negro girls were killed in the bombing of a church. Dr. King said at the funeral:

"In spite of the darkness of this hour, we must not despair. We must not lose faith in our white brothers."

As Dr. King's words grew more potent and he was invited to the White House by Presidents Kennedy and Johnson, some critics — Negroes as well as white — noted that sometimes, despite all the publicity he attracted, he left campaigns unfinished or else failed to attain his goals.

Dr. King was aware of this. But he pointed out, in 1964, in St. Augustine, Fla., one of the toughest civil rights battlegrounds, that there were important intangibles.

"Even if we do not get all we should," he said, "movements such as this tend more and more to give a Negro the sense of self-respect that he needs. It tends to generate courage in Negroes outside the movement. It brings intangible results outside the community where it is carried out. There is a hardening of attitudes in situations like this. But other cities see and say: "We don't want to be another Albany or Birmingham,' and they make changes. Some communities, like this one, had to bear the cross."

It was in this city that Negroes marched into the fists of the mob singing: "We love everybody."

Conscious of Leading Role

There was no false modesty in Dr. King's self-appraisal of his role in the civil rights movement.

"History," he said, "has thrust me into this position. It would be both immoral and a sign of ingratitude if I did not face my moral responsibility to do what I can in this struggle."

Another time he compared himself to Socrates as one of "the creative gadflies of society."

At times he addressed himself deliberately to the white people of the nation. Once, he said:

"We will match your capacity to inflict suffering with our capacity to endure suffering. We will meet your physical force with soul force. We will not hate you, but we cannot in all good conscience obey your unjust laws . . . We will soon wear you down by our capacity to suffer. And in winning our freedom we will so appeal to your heart and conscience that we will win you in the process."

The enormous influence of Dr. King's voice in the turbulent racial conflict reached into New York in 1964. In the summer of that year racial rioting exploded in New York and in other Northern cities with large Negro populations. There was widespread fear that the disorders, particularly in Harlem, might set off unprecedented racial violence.

At this point Dr. King became one of the major intermediaries in restoring order. He conferred with Mayor Robert F. Wagner and with Negro leaders. A statement was issued, of which he was one of the signers, calling for "a broad curtailment if not total moratorium on mass demonstrations until after Presidential elections."

The following year, Dr. King was once more in the headlines and on television — this time leading a drive for Negro voter registration in Selma, Ala. Negroes were arrested by the hundreds. Dr. King was punched and kicked by a white man when, during this period of protest, he became the first Negro to register at a century-old hotel in Selma.

Martin Luther King Jr. was born Jan. 15, 1929, in Atlanta on Auburn Avenue. As a child his name was Michael Luther King and so was his father's. His father changed both their names legally to Martin Luther King in honor of the Protestant reformer.

Auburn Avenue is one of the nation's most widely known Negro sections. Many successful Negro business or professional men have lived there. The Rev. Martin Luther King Sr. was pastor of the Ebenezer Baptist Church at Jackson Street and Auburn Avenue.

Young Martin went to Atlanta's Morehouse College, a Negro institution whose students acquired what was sometimes called the "Morehouse swank." The president of Morehouse, Dr. B. E. Mays, took a special interest in Martin, who had decided, in his junior year, to be a clergyman.

He was ordained a minister in his father's church in 1947. It was in this church he was to say, some years later:

"America, you've strayed away. You've trampled over 19 million of your brethren. All men are created equal. Not some men. Not white men. All men. America, rise up and come home."

Before Dr. King had his own church he pursued his studies in the integrated Crozier Theological Seminary, in Chester, Pa. He was one of six Negroes in a student body of about a hundred. He became the first Negro class president. He was named the outstanding student and won a fellowship to study for a doctorate at the school of his choice. The young man enrolled at Boston College in 1951.

For his doctoral thesis he sought to resolve the differences between the Harvard theologian Paul Tillich and the neonaturalist philosopher Henry Nelson Wieman. During this period he took courses at Harvard, as well.

While he was working on his doctorate he met Coretta Scott, a graduate of Antioch College, who was doing graduate work in music. He married the singer in 1953. They had four children, Yolanda, Martin Luther King 3d, Dexter Scott and Bernice.

In 1954, Dr. King became pastor of the Dexter Avenue Baptist Church in Montgomery, Ala. At that time few of Montgomery's white residents saw any reason for a major dispute with the city's 50,000 Negroes. They did not seem to realize how deeply the Negroes resented segregated seating on buses, for instance.

Revolt Begun by Woman

On Dec. 1, 1955, they learned, almost by accident. Mrs. Rosa Parks, a Negro seamstress, refused to comply with a bus driver's order to give up her seat to a white passenger. She was tired, she said. Her feet hurt from a day of shopping.

Mrs. Parks had been a local secretary for the National Association for the Advancement of Colored People. She was arrested, convicted of refusing to obey the bus conductor and fined $10 and costs, a total of $14. Almost as spontaneous as Mrs. Parks's act was the rallying of many Negro leaders in the city to help her.

From a protest begun over a Negro woman's tired feet Dr. King began his public career.

In 1959 Dr. King and his family moved back to Atlanta, where he became a co-pastor, with his father, of the Ebenezer Baptist Church.

As his fame increased, public interest in his beliefs led him to write books. It was while he was autographing one of these books, "Stride Toward Freedom," in a Harlem department store that he was stabbed by a Negro woman.

It was in these books that he summarized, in detail, his beliefs as well as his career. Thus, in "Why We Can't Wait," he wrote:

"The Negro knows he is right. He has not organized for conquest or to gain spoils or to enslave those who have injured him. His goal is not to capture that which belongs to someone else. He merely wants, and will have, what is honorably his."

The posibility that he might someday be assassinated was considered by Dr. King on June 5, 1964, when he reported, in St. Augustine, Fla., that his life had been threatened. He said:

"Well, if physical death is the price that I must pay to free my white brothers and sisters from a permanent death of the spirit, then nothing can be more redemptive."

United Press International

ARRESTED IN ALABAMA: In his cell at the Jefferson County courthouse in Birmingham, Nov. 3, 1967. He and other civil rights workers served a five-day sentence for contempt of court arising from a 1963 demonstration.

Dr. King 3d Negro to Get Nobel Prize

The Rev. Dr. Martin Luther King Jr. was the 14th American, the 3d Negro, and the youngest man to win the Nobel Peace Prize.

When he accepted the prize in Oslo, Norway, on Dec. 10, 1964, on behalf of the civil rights movement he said he was doing so for "all men who love peace and brotherhood."

At the presentation ceremony at Oslo University, Dr. King, then 35 years old, said that the award had come "at a moment when 22 million Negroes of the United States are engaged in a creative battle to end the long night of racial injustice."

Dr. Alfred B. Nobel, the Swedish inventor of dynamite, who established the prizes, stipulated in his will that one of the prizes to be awarded annually in his name should go to:

"The person who shall have done most to promote the fraternity of nations and the abolition or diminution of standing armies and the formation or increase of peace congresses."

However, the Nobel Peace Prize has taken on a broader interpretation of "peace" since the first one was awarded in 1901.

Emphasis in recent years has been placed upon brotherhood.

Was Deeply Moved

When it was announced on Oct. 14, 1964, in Oslo that Dr. King would be awarded the prize, the civil rights leader said in Atlanta that he was deeply moved by the honor. He also said then that "every penny" of the prize money, about $54,000, would be given to the civil rights movement.

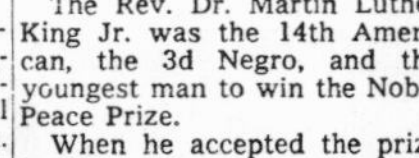

Associated Press

Dr. King being congratulated by King Olav V of Norway after the presentation of the peace prize in Oslo, 1964.

Among those who were present at the presentation ceremony three months later were King Olav V of Norway, Government and diplomatic leaders, members of Dr. King's family and his associates in the civil rights movement. The ceremony was televised throughout Europe.

Dr. King was hailed at the time by Dr. Gunnar Jahn, the chairman of the Norwegian Parliament's Nobel Committee, as an "undaunted champion of peace" and the "first person in the Western world to have shown us that a struggle can be waged without violence."

The two Negroes to previously receive the award were Dr. Ralph J. Bunche, who was awarded the prize in 1950 for his work as Under Secretary of the United Nations, and Zulu Chief Albert J. Luthuli of South Africa, who in 1960 received the award for advocating nonviolence in the solution of apartheid, South Africa's policy of racial segregation.

NONVIOLENT VIEW VOICED BY S.C.L.C.

Dr. King's Group Prepared Drive in Capital for Poor

BY STEVEN V. ROBERTS

The Rev. Dr. Martin Luther King Jr. was killed as his organization, the Southern Christian Leadership Conference, was preparing its largest demonstration for Negro rights—the Poor People's Campaign scheduled to begin in Washington on April 22.

Dr. King and his aides were planning to have 3,000 Negroes from throughout the South camp out in the capital and put pressure on Congress to provide decent jobs or adequate income for the black poor.

The Poor People's Campaign exemplified the drastic changes in the civil rights movement since 1955, when Dr. King, then a 27-year-old minister in his first parish, led a boycott of the Montgomery bus system.

In the early days the movement concentrated on legal rights, such as the right to vote, or use public accommodations. The new emphasis is on substantive improvements in the lives of Negroes—better education, more jobs and decent housing.

Clergy in Chief Roles

In addition, the campaign for increased public spending for the poor has been linked to issue of the Vietnam war and the distortion of national priorities the rights leaders say it has created.

At the same time, the strategy of Dr. King and the conference has varied little, no matter what the issue. They have steadily espoused the ideal of nonviolence and depended more on moral than political influence to win their battles. And they have used the tactic of public demonstrations to present starkly their moral case to the nation.

In some ways Dr. King was the Southern Christian Leadership Conference, an organization composed mainly of Southern Negro ministers and other professional people he helped organize at the end of the Montgomery boycott in early 1957.

The several years prior to the start of the Poor People's Campaign were difficult ones for the leadership conference. The slogan of "black power" was adopted by militant young black leaders and led to widening splits between them and the established civil rights organizations.

Financial Difficulties

Dr. King refused to decline help from the white community, but his group suffered from the financial squeeze that afflicted all civil rights groups in the wake of urban riots and increasingly angry statements by such young Negroes as H. Rap Brown and Stokely Carmichael.

In 1966, Dr. King announced a massive campaign against slum conditions in Chicago that never made much headway and was quietly abandoned.

The campaign was just one more bit of evidence that the optimism of the beginning of the civil rights movement had underestimated the problem of improving the economic and social condition of Negroes.

Perhaps the culmination of the campaign for legal rights came in March, 1965, when the leadership conference organized a drive to register voters in Selma, Ala. The drive ended with a march of 25,000 people from Selma to Montgomery, where Dr. King addressed the crowd from the steps of the state Capitol.

Pushed Voter Drives

In the years before the Selma march, Dr. King and his aides worked on voter registration and desegregation drives throughout the South. He led a five-week campaign in Birmingham in 1963 in which four little girls were killed when a church was bombed. Meanwhile, pictures of snarling police dogs were spread across the pages of the nation's newspapers.

The leadership conference also used the economic boycott and started a project called Operation Breadbasket in a number of cities, designed to encourage companies, through negotiations, to hire Negro workmen.

In 1961 the conference helped organize the freedom rides in which integrated teams tested the integration of Southern buses.

Many of these activities were managed by Dr. King's aides, such as the Rev. Ralph Abernathy and the Rev. Wyatt Tee Walker, who formed the backbone of the leadership conference while Dr. King was busy with other projects.

In 1957, Mr. Abernathy's house and church were bombed in Montgomery while he and Dr. King were in Atlanta at a meeting Southern Negro leaders they had called. The two ministers returned to Montgomery at the news and then flew back to Atlanta on the last day of the meeting.

The bombings, coming at the end of the Montgomery boycott, so inflamed the Negro leaders that they formed the Southern Leadership Conference before they dispersed and named Dr. King as its head.

He held the post until his death.

City College Closes Today for Dr. King

Dr. Buell G. Gallagher, president of the City College of New York, announced last night that the college would be closed all day today "in observance of Dr. King's memory."

Both the college's uptown campus and Baruch School will be closed, Mr. Gallagher's statement said.

He also announced that memorial services for Dr. King would be held at noon Monday in the college's Great Hall, on the uptown campus.

Dismay, Anger and Foreboding Are Voiced by Leaders Across U.S. After Slaying

NEGROES SUPPORT AIMS OF DR. KING

Bid Others Carry Out Spirit of Nonviolence—But Some Respond With Bitterness

Continued From Page 1, Col. 4

shooting "the most disturbing and distressing thing we've had to face in a long time."

Dr. Kenneth B. Clark, a Negro who is a psychologist and head of the Metropolitan Applied Research Center, said in a faltering voice: "You have to cry out in anguish for this country . . . weep for this country."

In Los Angeles, Negro leaders quickly expressed hope that community sentiment would be keyed to the nonviolence for which Dr. King crusaded rather than to the harsh circumstances of his death.

"I hope the people of the United States and especially of Los Angeles will keep a cool head and a calm spirit and let tahe law take its course," said Gilbert Lindsay, one of three Negroes on the 15-member City Council."

Sen. Edward W. Brooke, Republican of Massachusetts, a Negro declared:

"In our anguish and bitterness of this awful event, we must not lose sight of the meaning of this great man's life. The vindication of Dr. King's historic endeavors can only come through our renewed dedication to the human goals of brotherly love and equal justice which he so nobly advanced.

William Booth, chairman of New York City's Commission on Human Rights, said: "I would hope that no one would use Dr. King's death as an excuse for further violence."

Another call for restraint came from James Farmer, former national director of the Congress of Racial Equality, who said:

"Every racist in the country has killed Dr. King. Evil societies always destroy their consciences. The only fitting memorial to this martyred leader is a monumental commitment—now, not a day later—to eliminate racism. Dr. King hated bloodshed. His own blood must not now trigger more bloodshed."

Angry Response

An angry reaction came in Washington from Julius Hobson, a Negro who heads a militant but nonviolent civil rights group called ACT. Mr. Hobson said:

"The next black man who comes into the black community preaching nonviolence should be violently dealt with by the black people who hear him. The Martin Luther King concept of nonviolence died with him. It was a foreign ideology anyway—as foreign to this violent country as speaking Russian."

Another bitter reaction came from Lincoln O. Lynch, the former associate national director of CORE and chairman of the United Black Front. He said:

"The assassination of Martin Luther King, in my opinion, will begin to wake up black people to the fact that it is imperative to abandon the unconditional nonviolent concept expounded by Dr. King and adopt a position that for every Martin Luther King who falls, 10 white racists will go down with him. There is no other way. White America understands no other language."

The Most Rev. Terence J. Cooke, who was installed yesterday as the Roman Catholic Archbishop of New York, knelt in prayer with Archbishop Iakovos, the Greek Orthodox primate of North and South America, at a reception at the Greek Orthodox headquarters at 10 East 97th Street.

Side by side, kneeling on a red-carpeted stair before the Byzantine altar, the two prelates said the Lord's Prayer, and then Archbishop Cooke delivered a prayer for himself and Archbishop Iakovos:

"Dear Lord," he said, "we ask you to receive the soul of Martin Luther King, who in his days did so much to give leadership, to justice for all. We pray the ideals he struggled for, the ideals he gave his life for, will be realized, so that soon America will be one, at peace, where liberty is given to all."

Senator Jacob K. Javits said Dr. King's death "demands of all of us restraint and understanding and a renewed dedication to carry on the work of justice and decency among men of all races—the cause for which Dr. Martin Luther King gave his life. His doctrine of nonviolence will overcome, as he planned it should."

Former Vice President Richard M. Nixon called upon all Americans "to try in a new spirit of reconciliation to redeem this terrible act."

Mr. Nixon told newsmen he was canceling scheduled campaign appearances today and tomorrow in Minnesota because of Dr. King's death.

Telegrams of sympathy were sent to Mrs. King by Ambassador to the United Nations Arthur J. Goldberg and by Dr. Ralph J. Bunche, Under Secretary for Special Political Affairs of the United Nations.

Dr. Bunche, who is a Negro, said the assault on Dr. King "inevitably will be a most grievous blow to the cause of racial harmony throughout this country."

In Texas, Gov. John B. Connally Jr., who was wounded by a sniper when President Kennedy was assassinated, said Dr. King had "contributed much to the chaos and turbulence in this country, but he did not deserve this fate."

He said the murder was an act "which tends to crumble away our society."

Wallace's View

George C. Wallace, former Governor of Alabama, a segregationist candidate for President, called the assassination of Dr. King a "senseless, regrettable act."

Statements of grief at the death of Dr. King were issued by Rabbi Philip Rudin, president of the Synagogue Council of America; the Right Rev. Horace W. B. Donegan, Episcopal Bishop of New York, and Rabbi Arthur J. Lelyveld, president of the American Jewish Congress.

Expressions of grief came also from Morris B. Abram, president of the American Jewish Committee; the Right Rev. John E. Hines, Presiding Bishop of the Episcopal Church; Dr. Sterling W. Brown, president of the National Conference of Christians and Jews; the Rev. Dr. Dan M. Potter, executive secretary of the Protestant Council of the City of New York, and Dr. R. H. Edwin Espy, general secretary of the National Council of Churches.

In Milwaukee, the Rev. James Groppi, the white Roman Catholic priest who has led the city's open housing marches, said: "This is certainly not going to be conducive to peaceful racial relations."

In Brisbane, Australia, the evangelist Billy Graham said the slaying indicated that "tens of thousands of Americans are mentally deranged."

"It indicates the sickness of the American society and is going to further inflame passions and hates," he said.

IN HARLEM: Firemen fighting a blaze in a 125th Street furniture store that was looted and set afire after news of the slaying of Dr. King spread through the area last night. Associated Press

Sporadic Violence Erupts in Harlem

Continued From Page 1, Col. 6

125th Street at about 12:30 this morning.

Mayor Lindsay learned of the assassination while attending the opening of the play "The Education of H*Y*M*A*N K*A*P*L*A*N" at the Alvin Theater on West 52d Street. He was informed of the slaying at the end of the first act and immediately left the theater to return to Gracie Mansion.

From there he went to Harlem at about 10:30 P.M., where he expressed his sorrow to crowds of Negroes gathered at Eighth Avenue and 125th Street.

Mr. Lindsay then attended a meeting of Harlem leaders at 312 West 125th Street.

At about 11 P.M., Mr. Lindsay left the meeting accompanied by a group of Harlem residents and began walking along 125th Street toward Seventh Avenue.

At 126th Street and Seventh Avenue the crowd, growing more hostile began pushing and shoving.

Several Negro officials, including City Human Rights Commissioner William Booth and Deputy Chief Inspector Eldridge Waith, tried to keep the crowd orderly.

Several Negroes, shouting angrily, prevented Mr. Lindsay from speaking. Police and citizens tussled on the sidewalk.

Then a limousine, belonging to Manhattan Borough President Percy Sutton, rushed to the scene and Mr. Lindsay was pushed into the car by his bodyguards. The car sped away.

The Mayor returned to Harlem about 1 A.M. today by car. He criss-crossed the community and returned to Gracie Mansion an hour later.

Two Negro men were arrested early this morning on charges of breaking store windows in midtown Manhattan. William James, 28, a cook who gave his address as 44 West 83d Street, was charged with throwing a bottle through a window of the Wales Casual Clothes, 257 West 42d Street.

Ike Hayes, 29, of 113 West 123d Street, was charged with throwing a iitter basket through the plate-glass window of the London Character Shoe Store at Broadway and 43d Street. As he was led away by the police, some Negro youths in a midtown crowd were heard to cry: "Brothers, Unite!"

Tehre were several incidents reported of Negroes and whites engaged in pushing and shoving matches in the midtown area.

In contrast to these disturbances, a group of about 50 persons, most of them youths, began a silent march and vigil on the west side of the Allied Chemical Tower, shortly after midnight tribute to Dr. King.

"It was organized spontaneously," said one of the marchers, Harold S. York of 412 West 115th Street. 'One friend called another," he said.

The first incidents of violence were reported in the Brooklyn area where windows were broken in a branch of the Manufacturers Hanover Trust Bank and the Coronet Bar, both on Fulton Street near Bedford Avenue. No looting occurred.

Within moments, youths broke into Alvey's, a clothing store nearby and started carrying away armfuls of clothing.

Police reinforcements arrived within minutes. They were met by a barrage of rocks and bottles.

Harlem residents at an area on 125th Street, wearing Congress of Racial Equality armbands, were urging youths to "go home."

Two blocks away, scores of Negroes gathered at the corner of Seventh Avenue and 125th Street, where street-corner rallies are held daily; to protest the slaying.

Almost immediately, a fire broke out in John's Bargain Store, a few doors away. A Negro man tried to fight the blaze before firemen arrived but the youths hustled him away. Firemen extinguished the blaze within minutes.

Fulton Street—Bedford-Stuyvesant's main shopping area, where the Brooklyn riots of 1964 began—was described by one eyewitness as "pure pandemonium" for a few minutes.

"People were running wildly up and down the street," he said. "Kids were drinking whisky from bottles, playing music loudly from transistor radios, and older people stood on the sidewalk, just watching and shaking their heads. Fire engines and police cars kept running up and down the street."

At 11:30 P.M., outbreaks of rock-throwing, looting and arson were reported in three Brooklyn precincts. These were the 79th Precinct at 627 Gates Avenue; the 80th Precinct at 653 Grand Avenue and the 81st at 16 Ralph Avenue.

Several fires raged in Harlem early this morning. Firemen fought blazes at 3 A. M. along Eighth Avenue near 130th and at 136th Streets and along Lenox Avenue between 127th and 131st Streets.

Deputy Fire Chief George Fridell, who said his unit had fought five separate blazes since late yesterday, said: "If they want to burn up their neighborhood, it's their business."

Outbreak in Newark

Special to The New York Times

NEWARK, April 4—Bottles and rocks were thrown in two parts of this city's Central Ward last night, but the police said they had quieted the disturbances quickly. There were no arrests or injuries.

Looters in Hartford

HARTFORD, April 4 (AP)—Window-breaking and looting broke out in this city's North End late tonight, apparently in reaction to news of the slaying of Dr. Martin Luther King. The police said five or six blocks of North Main Street had been closed to traffic.

Greenburgh Incidents

Special to The New York Times

GREENBURGH, N. Y., April 4—More than 200 Negro youths roamed the streets of this Westchester community tonight after Dr. King's death was announced. The town police reported that some store windows were broken and said there was some looting. However, they said the incidents were minor. No injuries or arrests were reported.

McKissick Says Nonviolence Has Become Dead Philosophy

Special to The New York Times

CLEVELAND, April 4—Floyd B. McKissick, national director of the Congress of Racial Equality, said tonight that the death of the Rev. Dr. Martin Luther King Jr. meant the end of the nonviolent philosophy.

"Dr. Martin Luther King was the last prince of nonviolence," Mr. McKissick said at a news conference at the Sheraton Cleveland Hotel. "He was a symbol of nonviolence, the epitome of nonviolence.

"Nonviolence is a dead philosophy and it was not the black people that killed it. It was the white people that killed nonviolence and white racists at that." Mr. McKissick called the assassination "a horror."

"It's a horror for us, for all Americans that the apostle of nonviolence should be gunned down on an American street," he said.

Mr. McKissick is in Cleveland to promote a CORE plan to build black-owned businesses and industries in slum areas.

But leaders of the organization from around the country are coming in to meet with him here to discuss strategy as a result of the assassination.

Mr. McKissick said he would make no predictions about what would happen in the country because of the assassination.

But he said that CORE was "preparing to issue a publication on what black people have to do to survive." He indicated that the publication would tell Negroes that they had the right to own weapons, should prepare first aid kits and not be provoked.

Hosea Williams Appeals

ATLANTA, April 4 (AP)—Hosea Williams, one of Dr. King's top aides who was standing beneath the balcony on which Dr. King was shot to death, called immediately for continued nonviolence.

"Let's not burn America down," he said.

Mr. Williams, an executive in the Southern Christian Leadership Conference, telephoned his plea to The Atlanta Constitution from Memphis, where Dr. King died.

"We must—we must—maintain and advocate and promote the philosophy of nonviolence," he said.

Mr. Williams, considered one of the most militant of Dr. King's aides, told The Constitution. "We—those of us with him during his last moments on this earth—are concerned that this country might go into a turmoil that would cause great bloodshed."

He said that Dr. King had spent part of his last discussion in the motel room with his lieutenants reiterating the validity of nonviolence.

Philosophy Recalled

CINCINNATI, April 4 (UPI)—The Rev. Fred Shuttlesworth, who with Dr. King was an early organizer of the Southern Christian Leadership Conference, said tonight that one of Dr. King's philosophies was that "not one hair on the head of one white man shall be harmed by us."

"We dedicated ourselves and hoped Americans would accept the nonviolence as a way of life," Mr. Shuttlesworth said.

Fire in Houston

HOUSTON, April 4 (AP)—A furniture store in a predominantly Negro area was damaged heavily tonight by a fire that the police said had been ignited by Molotov cocktails.

RACIAL CLASHES IN SEVERAL CITIES

Continued From Page 1, Col. 7

and brief clashes with the police in Winston-Salem, New Bern, Durham and Charlotte, N. C., and in Jackson, Miss., Boston, Hartford, New York City and Memphis, when Dr. King was killed.

Looting in Washington

Special to The New York Times

WASHINGTON, Friday, April 5—Scattered but persistent looting and vandalism, led for a time by Stokely Carmichael, erupted in the nation's capital last night an hour after the death of the Rev. Dr. Martin Luther King Jr.

The looting, the work of roving groups of Negro youths racing on foot from the Negro slum area into Washington's fashionable downtown shopping district, began at about 8:30 and caused a citywide police alert.

As it began, Carmichael advised Negroes to "go home and get your guns."

Policemen were dispatched to several of more than a dozen fires to protect firemen, who came under barrages of gravel, bottles and rocks. The police said the fires appeared to have been set.

At one point, the looting reached to within six blocks of the White House. The display window of a men's store at 10th Street and Pennsylvania Avenue, N.W., on a stretch of the national boulevard that is familiar to Washington tourist, was stripped of suits before the police, heavily committed in the Negro commercial section a mile to the north, could respond.

'Mopping Up' Drive Starts

At 1 A.M. today, Police Chief John B. Layton said a "mopping up operation" was underway. The chief said there had been "some isolated window breaking." There were seven reported arrests.

But there was still a steady stream of fire alarms and calls for police to disperse looters and roving gangs of youths.

Mayor Walter E. Washington, a Negro, and Public Safety Director Patrick V. Murphy were among the top Government officials cruising the streets in the effort to restore order.

After several hours of deliberately holding the police tactical squad in reserve, away from the disturbance, cordons of helmeted officers, some of them wearing gas masks, began dispersing the crowds.

Deputy Police Chief John S. Hughes said that every member of the 2,900-man force "we can get our hands on is on duty."

"We are trying to maintain a visible presence in the troubled area," he said.

Chief Hughes told newsmen that troops of the District of Columbia National Guard were on stand-by "but we have not called for them yet."

The police said riot squad officers used tear gas once tonight to open a path through a hostile crowd for fire equipment responding to an alarm.

The area of looting and disturbances was half a mile wide and about three miles long, from Seventh to Fourteen Street N.W. and from Pennsylvania Avenue north to Randolph Street.

NASHVILLE, April 4 (AP)—About 4,000 Tennessee National Guardsmen were ordered to duty in Nashville tonight as scattered violence occurred.

The order was issued after groups of Negroes began throwing rocks at motorists in North Nashville. The police said vandalism reports were flooding into their headquarters.

The police said Negroes began gathering after two persons, one a 13-year-old boy, were wounded in a battle with police officers.

Carolina Governor Acts

RALEIGH, N. C., April 4 (AP)—National Guardsmen were alerted in Greensboro tonight as city officials sought to control Negroes.

Gov. Dan K. Moore authorized deployment of the troops at the request of Mayor Carson Bain. The Greensboro police said the troops were alerted only as a precaution and only minor incidents of violence had been reported.

The police in Raleigh, meanwhile, encircled the campus of predominantly Negro Shaw University after a march toward the Capitol turned into a window-smashing, rock-throwing spree. Rocks and bricks continued to be thrown at passing automobiles.

At least three arrests were made during the downtown clash between helmeted Raleigh policemen and some 50 Negroes. One demonstrator reportedly was injured.

Peaceful marches by crowds of Negroes were reported in Winston-Salem and Charlotte.

Disorder in Jackson

JACKSON, Miss., April 4 (AP)—Milling groups of young Negroes smashed auto windows and set a newsman's car on fire tonight.

The police broke up the demonstrations, using tear gas at one place. No injuries were reported.

While the Negro leader Charles Evers addressed a hastily called rally at the Negro Masonic Temple and urged nonviolence in respect for Dr. King's beliefs, groups outside the building hurled bricks and bottles.

Mr. Evers later walked through the area, pleading with Negroes to clear the streets. A squad of 35 policemen carrying riot guns followed him through the area.

Tampa Disturbance

TAMPA, Fla., April 4 (AP)—Two squads of policemen rushed into a Negro area tonight after 250 persons gathered following the killing of Dr. King.

Officers cordoned off a 14-block area from 26th Avenue to Buffalo Avenue after the crowd scattered.

The street was littered with glass, tin cans and rocks.

Arkansas Guard Unit Alerted

LITTLE ROCK, Ark., April 4, (AP)—An aide to Gov. Winthrop Rockefeller said tonight that the Governor had placed the 175-man National Guard at West Memphis on alert, following the slaying of Dr. King.

Rocks Hurled in Texas

TYLER, Tex., April 4 (AP)—Rocks and bottles were thrown at two police cars tonight as they answered a disturbance call in a Negro neighborhood.

Police Chief L. B. Odom said rocks were hurled from a crowd of 40 or 50 Negroes. He said the situation was under control in 20 minutes. No one was injured.

Florida A. and M. Outbreak

TALLAHASSEE, Fla., April 4 (AP)—Rock-throwing broke out tonight on the Florida A. and M. University campus.

The police said that several motorists had reported damaged cars and that two house trailers were burned in a mobile home display area near the campus.

FAMILY PORTRAIT: The young Martin Luther King Jr., right, with his parents, his grandmother, right rear, his sister, Christine, and his brother, Alfred, now a Baptist minister. Ben J. Fernandez

Court in Memphis Is Told of Gun Sales

MEMPHIS, April 4 (AP)—A Federal judge was told today that the Negro community was so worked up that another mass demonstration here next week could "be worse than Watts or worse than Detroit."

Police Director Frank Holloman said he had received reports that "Negroes are buying guns from wholesale houses in our neighboring state of Arkansas." He also said that Negro youths "have been supplied for several weeks with specific instructions on how to make Molotov cocktails and firebombs."

Mr. Holloman told United States District Judge Bailey Brown that he was convinced that the march could not be controlled.

He made his remarks in the morning.

Mr. Holloman was arguing in support of a temporary restraining order granted by the judge yesterday that forbade the march the Rev. Dr. Martin Luther King Jr. had planned in support of striking sanitation workers. Dr. King, who had been seeking to have the order set aside, had indicated he would not heed it in any case.

The march was scheduled Monday.

Mr. Holloman said he had also received information from a member of the Ku Klux Klan that a march by the white supremacy organization also "will be scheduled and carried out" on Monday.

In seeking the injunction, city officials said they feared a recurrence of the brief spurt of rioting set off by a march led by Dr. King a week earlier.

March Still Scheduled

A march in Memphis in support of that city's striking sanitation workers will take place on Monday as scheduled, despite the fatal shooting of the march's leader and chief organizer, the Rev. Martin Luther King Jr.

Labor leaders in New York said here last night that aides of Dr. King had informed them that plans for the march had not been canceled.

"We plan to go ahead with our contingent," said Victor Gotbaum, executive director of the American Federation of State, County and Municipal Employes.

"In fact," he added, "our response now is going to be greater than before. We will march as a dedication to a great American leader."

Mr. Gotbaum and John J. DeLury, president of the Uniformed Sanitationmen's Association, said they would march in Memphis despite a restraining order prohibiting the demonstration.

Mr. DeLury, who served a term in jail for contempt of court during the sanitation worker's strike here in February, said:

"We are unionists. We are going there to march—period."

About 1,000 trade unionists, including sanitation and transit employes, teachers and auto workers, are expected to leave New York for Memphis over the weekend. Three chartered planes are scheduled to leave Kennedy Airport at 8 A.M. Monday carrying a contingent of 500. Others are expected to travel by train, bus and automobile.

Mr. Gotbaum and Mr. DeLury said that, where possible, the unionists would be going on their regular days off or on vacation time. But they said that some might have to give up a day's pay.

They reported that Harry Van Arsdale Jr., president of the Central Labor Council, and Paul Hall, president of the Seafarer's International Union, had pledged their support.

The demonstration in Memphis was planned by Dr. King in support of 1,300 sanitation workers who walked off their jobs on Feb. 12 in a dispute over wages, union recognition and a dues check-off arrangement.

About 90 per cent of the Memphis sanitation workers are Negroes and the strike has sharply divided the city of 550,000 along racial lines. About 40 per cent of the population is Negro.

"All the News That's Fit to Print"

The New York Times

LATE CITY EDITION

Weather: Sunny and mild today; fair tonight. Sunny, mild tomorrow. Temp. range: today 50-35. Friday 62-46. Full U. S. report on Page 78.

VOL. CXVII..No. 40,250 | © 1968 The New York Times Company. | NEW YORK, SATURDAY, APRIL 6, 1968 | 10 CENTS

ARMY TROOPS IN CAPITAL AS NEGROES RIOT; GUARD SENT INTO CHICAGO, DETROIT, BOSTON; JOHNSON ASKS A JOINT SESSION OF CONGRESS

SIEGE OF KHESANH DECLARED LIFTED; TROOPS HUNT FOE

Relief Column, Within Mile of Base, Presses Search —Helicopters Kill 50

By The Associated Press

KHESANH, South Vietnam, Saturday, April 6—The 76-day North Vietnamese siege of the Marine base at Khesanh was officially declared lifted yesterday.

United States marines and helicopter-borne Army troops today pushed toward what was described as North Vietnamese regimental headquarters south of the base.

The 20,000-man relief column reached the base and then fanned out on three sides in search of the vanishing enemy soldiers. Army helicopter units entered the base.

The sweep could take the Americans all the way to the Laotian border, less than 10 miles away, in the effort to root out the 7,000 men said to remain in an enemy force once estimated at 20,000. North Vietnam uses Laos as a staging area for attacks along South Vietnam's borders.

Gunships Attack Near Town

The United States command said that helicopter gunships of the First Cavalry Division (Airmobile), crisscrossing the skies ahead of the ground troops, killed 50 North Vietnamese late yesterday near the town of Khesanh, which is two miles south of the base.

Earlier, United States troops fought about 150 enemy soldiers four miles east of the town. Nine enemy soldiers and one American were reported killed.

The town was made an enemy command post after South Vietnamese troops and a small unit of United States marines abandoned it in January under a heavy siege.

Ten thousand civilians, mostly montagnard tribesmen, fled the town when fighting broke out. Many are in refugee camps in the coastal lowlands.

The relief column made no immediate attempt to enter the Khesanh base. Enemy gunners zeroed in on the outpost with 110 rounds of artillery and mortar fire.

Before the pressure on the

Continued on Page 2, Column 4

Hanoi Voices Doubt Over U.S. Sincerity

By Agence France-Presse

HANOI, North Vietnam, April 5—Hanoi protested today against what it called "savage bombings" of North Vietnam and "intensification of the war in South Vietnam" since President Johnson's announcement Sunday of restriction on attacks on the North.

Under the signature "Commentator," a pseudonym customarily indicating official authorship, an editorial in the party newspaper, Nhan Dan, questioned the sincerity of Mr. Johnson's avowed desire for peace.

[Despite the tone of the Hanoi editorial, Administration officials saw no indication that North Vietnam was backing away from talks with the United States. Page 5.]

The Nhan Dan editorial said: "The decision of the United

Continued on Page 3, Column 1

SOVIET ENDORSES ASSENT BY HANOI

Moscow Mentioned as Site of Talks With U.S.—China Urges Continued War

By RAYMOND H. ANDERSON

Special to The New York Times

MOSCOW, April 5 — The Soviet Government today endorsed the agreement by North Vietnam to start discussions with the United States toward a complete halt of bombing to open the door to full-scale negotiations.

The statement came amid speculation that Moscow might be the site for a meeting between United States and North Vietnamese representatives.

Premier Aleksei N. Kosygin is cutting short his trip to Iran and will return to Moscow Sunday, one day early.

[Communist China, however, termed President Johnson's peace overture a smokescreen and urged the North Vietnamese and the Vietcong to continue fighting.]

The United States Embassy denied that it had any knowledge of arrangements for a meeting here. The United States, it was understood,

Continued on Page 4, Column 3

PRESIDENT GRAVE

Sets Day of Mourning for Dr. King—Meets Rights Leaders

President's statement and his proclamation, Page 23.

By MAX FRANKEL

Special to The New York Times

WASHINGTON, April 5 — President Johnson asked today to address a joint session of Congress no later than Monday evening so that he could propose "constructive action instead of destructive action in this hour of national need."

Gravely imploring Americans to "stand their ground to deny violence its victory" in the reaction to the slaying of the Rev. Dr. Martin Luther King Jr., the President set out to arouse the nation's conscience and to win quick action on the long-stalled major items in his domestic program.

He proclaimed Sunday a national day of mourning for Dr. King, who was shot yesterday in Memphis and died later in a hospital.

Meanwhile, Congressional leaders said that Dr. King's murder could assure passage next week of a landmark civil rights bill.

Conference Canceled

To deal with the divisiveness that he said was "tearing this nation apart," Mr. Johnson canceled the already delayed conference he had planned for this weekend in Hawaii with American military and diplomatic officials stationed in South Vietnam.

Gen. William C. Westmoreland, the American commander in the war zone, was flying to Washington instead and will probably see Mr. Johnson tomorrow morning.

The President spent almost the entire day working "to avoid catastrophe." He met with moderate Negro leaders and members of Congress and of his Administration to find ways of containing the violence, arson and looting that threatened many big cities and that spread here to within a few blocks of the White House.

He also conferred all day with officials of the District of Columbia and gave them Federal troops this evening to help restore order.

Mr. Johnson's demeanor all

Continued on Page 23, Column 1

Associated Press

ON DUTY IN WASHINGTON: A soldier with a machine gun and another with a rifle, left, stand guard on the steps outside the Senate chamber. Flag was lowered to half-staff in tribute to the Rev. Dr. Martin Luther King Jr.

MANY FIRES SET

White House Guarded by G.I.'s—14 Dead in U.S. Outbreaks

Text of proclamation and Executive order, Page 22.

By BEN A. FRANKLIN

Special to The New York Times

WASHINGTON, April 5—President Johnson ordered 4,000 regular Army and National Guard troops into the nation's capital tonight to try to end riotous looting, burglarizing and burning by roving bands of Negro youths. The arson and looting began yesterday after the murder of the Rev. Dr. Martin Luther King Jr. in Memphis.

The White House announced at 5 P.M. that because the President had determined that "a condition of domestic violence and disorder" existed, he had issued a proclamation and an executive order mobilizing combat-equipped troops in Washington. Some of the troops were sent to guard the Capitol and the White House.

Reinforcements numbering 2,500 riot-trained soldiers — a brigade of the 82d Airborne Division from Ft. Bragg, N. C.— were airlifted to nearby Andrews Air Force Base, to be held in reserve this weekend.

Guard Called In Other Cities

The National Guard also was called out in a half-dozen other cities in an effort to stem disorders or guard against them—Chicago, Detroit, Boston, Jackson, Miss., Raleigh, N. C., and Tallahassee, Fla.

The death toll from the violence stemming from Dr. King's assassination stood at a total of 14 tonight. Besides five deaths in Washington, they included seven in Chicago, one in Detroit and one in Tallahassee.

Mayor Walter E. Washington, who is a Negro, declared a 13-hour curfew, from 5:30 P.M. to 6:30 A.M. The Mayor's emergency order halted the sale of liquor and forbade the sale, transportation or possession of firearms, explosives or flammable liquids.

At midnight, the police reported five dead, all but one of them Negroes, in 28 hours of disorders in this city of about 800,000, 63 per cent of them Negroes. Four Negroes were killed today, including two suspected looters, one of them 14 years old, who were shot to death by policemen in separate isolated encounters across the Anacostia River, far from the areas of general disorders. The two other Negro deaths today were described as apparently the result of accidents.

The white man, George Fletcher, 28, of suburban Wood-

Continued on Page 22, Column 1

New York Volatile As Anger and Fear Set a Tense Mood

By MICHAEL STERN

A volatile mood of deep sorrow, fist-shaking anger and undefined fear settled on the city yesterday as it absorbed the impact of the death of the Rev. Dr. Martin Luther King Jr.

Many schools, colleges, offices and shops closed early partly out of respect for the memory of the slain civil rights leader, and partly because of reports that new outbreaks of violence would erupt.

The city's bustling waterfront grew still at noon as seamen and longshoremen stopped work as a tribute to Dr. King. The stoppage was announced by the International Longshoremen's Association and the National Maritime Union.

Seven thousand to eight thousand high school and college students released from classes assembled at a memorial rally for Dr. King at the

Continued on Page 26, Column 5

OUTBREAKS HERE RELATIVELY MILD

Negro Areas Are Quiet, but Bands of Young Vandals Roam Midtown Streets

By SYLVAN FOX

The streets of Harlem and Bedford-Stuyvesant were generally calm last night after a burst of violence and looting early yesterday in the wake of the assassination of the Rev. Dr. Martin Luther King Jr. in Memphis.

Mayor Lindsay, appearing on television at 11:30 P.M., praised New Yorkers for keeping the peace and said: "We can work together again for progress and for peace in this city and in this nation."

Earlier in the evening, bands of youths—mostly Negro teenagers—swarmed into mid-Manhattan, engaged in scattered violence and some looting and were dispersed by a massive show of police force.

The police arrested 27 adults in the Times Square area, most on minor charges, and nine youths were charged with juvenile delinquency. Two persons were reported seized at Columbus Circle, where seven shop windows were smashed and

Continued on Page 27, Column 1

7 Die as Fires and Looting Spread in Chicago Rioting

By DONALD JANSON

Special to The New York Times

CHICAGO, Saturday, April 6—Six thousand National Guard troops were called up yesterday as rioters pillaged stores along a two-mile stretch of Madison Street in the Negro West Side. Seven Negroes were killed and about 350 arrested, the police reported, as the violence and ransacking tapered off late last night.

Half of the armed guardsmen, in fatigues and riot helmets, began patrolling glass-littered West Side streets about 10 P.M. The rest stood by in armories.

About 100 city buses were damaged by bricks and rocks. Drivers, passengers, policemen, firemen, motorists and pedestrians were among at least 75 persons injured.

Mother Beaten

Mrs. Bernadine Laskow, mother of three children, was pulled from her car by Negro youths and beaten. Some white pedestrians who were in the Negro slum suffered the same treatment.

Dozens of automobiles that entered the 12-square-mile riot zone emerged with smashed windows and dented hoods. In some blocks all store windows were boarded or broken.

Cab drivers refused to enter

Continued on Page 23, Column 8

EUROPE DISMAYED; FEARFUL FOR U.S.

Murder of Dr. King Evokes Doubts Over Stability of the American Society

By ANTHONY LEWIS

Special to The New York Times

LONDON, April 5—The murder of the Rev. Dr. Martin Luther King Jr. evoked in Europe today a reaction of intense horror at the deed and of fear for the stability of American society.

In governments, in the press and among the public, there were expressions of sympathy that went beyond formalities. Dr. King was deeply admired in Europe and held up as a symbol of hope for America.

'A Common, Tragic Link'

All the concerns about the United States and its leadership that have grown here in recent years—concerns especially about the war in Vietnam and the violence in America—were fed by the killing of the civil rights leader in Memphis last night.

Everywhere in Europe, people linked Dr. King's death with the assassination of President Kennedy in 1963. That two men so admired here could so similarly be killed intensified doubts about the character of America today.

"From John Fitzgerald Kennedy to Martin Luther King,"

Continued on Page 28, Column 3

Clark Is Sure Killer Will Soon Be Seized

By MARTIN WALDRON

Special to The New York Times

MEMPHIS, Tenn., April 5—Attorney General Ramsey Clark said today that he was "confident" of a quick solution to the assassination here yesterday of the Rev. Dr. Martin Luther King Jr.

A source close to the intensive manhunt said that agents of the Federal Bureau of Investigation were close to making an arrest.

The Attorney General, who flew here this morning at the order of President Johnson with other top officials of the Justice Department, told a news conference that the F.B.I. was searching for the killer in several states.

He said that the killer, who was believed to have escaped in a white Mustang automobile,

Continued on Page 24, Column 1

Negroes Strive to Ease Tensions; False Rumors Raise City's Fears

Militants Join Effort

By THOMAS A. JOHNSON

At the height of the violence in Harlem early yesterday morning, about 30 young Negro militants fanned out from Jay's Bar and Grill on 125th Street near Eighth Avenue and tried to persuade other Negroes to stop breaking windows, looting and setting fires.

This particular group was made up of members of Harlem CORE, and they were only a part of the many hundreds of Negroes living in the violence-torn areas of Harlem and Brooklyn who worked actively to stop the disorders.

The volunteer peace-keepers tried to end the violence by a variety of methods and for a variety of reasons.

Some are church groups,

Continued on Page 26, Column 1

Racial Unrest Exaggerated

By MURRAY SCHUMACH

The city was flooded yesterday with wild and unfounded rumors that exceeded the amount of violence and heightened widespread fears of racial riots.

In some instances, the reports became so persistent that corporations allowed employes, particularly women, to leave for home early in the afternoon.

The untrue reports included subway disruptions, bombings, mass assaults and imposition of a citywide curfew. Almost any kind of holdup, apparently, was associated in the minds of some rumor-mongers with racial disturbances and was then exaggerated.

Barry H. Gottehrer, the head

Continued on Page 26, Column 6

NEWS INDEX

The New York Times (by Barton Silverman)

MARCHING DOWN BROADWAY: Demonstrators protesting the slaying of the Rev. Dr. Martin Luther King Jr. crossing 23d Street on the way to City Hall yesterday. The march began after a memorial ceremony in Central Park.

Johnson Orders Troops Into the Capital as Looting and Arson by Negroes Spread

Associated Press

BURNING BUILDINGS IN WASHINGTON send smoke over northeast section, obscuring the Capitol at top right

GUARD CALLED UP IN 6 OTHER CITIES

G.I.'s Protect White House —Toll From Violence in U.S. Stands at 14

Continued From Page 1, Col. 8

bridge, Va., died this morning from injuries he received when a gang of Negro youths attacked him and three white companions in a Washington filling station at 2 A.M.

More than 350 persons were treated at hospitals including seven policemen and six firemen. More than 800 persons were arrested.

The police said reports of fires and lootings were diminishing apparently in part due to a sudden drop in the temperature. After a sultry day, the night air was a brisk 40 degrees.

The violence in Washington affected four areas of the city. For hours this afternoon and early evening, disorderly youths roamed most of the downtown shopping district, between 15th and Seventh Streets and F and H Streets N.W.

The three other areas were all Negro sections. There was no precise count of the number of fires or looted stores, but they ran well into the hundreds.

George Christian, the White House press secretary, said the President had acted on the recommendation of Mayor Washington, the Mayor's public safety director, Patrick V. Murphy, and the police chief, John B. Layton.

The 2,800-man District of Columbia police force, after a night of looting and arson set off yesterday by the assassination, lacked the manpower to respond to mounting calls to detain looters and protect motorists and firemen.

The looting and fires continued tonight. The police dispersed crowds as they gathered but made little or no effort to stop scattered looting by individuals and groups of two and three.

The city was abandoned tonight. Buses stopped running at dusk after a midafternoon rush of Government employes to flee the city. The Government workers and other civilians were advised by the police and Federal authorities to go home at about 2:30 P.M., a decision that caused a massive traffic jam and aided the looters. Police and fire vehicles were caught in the jam.

Tourists Affected

Also caught up in the unexpected disturbances were Washington's spring crush of thousands of tourists. Events scheduled for today and the weekend in connection with the Washington Cherry Blossom Festival — a major money-making attraction in this city, where tourism is the biggest industry — were canceled.

The opening game of the baseball season, the American League debut between the Washington Senators and the Minnesota Twins at D. C. Stadium, was postponed from Monday to Tuesday as a gesture of respect to Dr. King.

Both the outbreak of trouble last night and today's renewal of arson and looting followed angry public outbursts on Dr. King's death by Stokely Carmichael, the militant former chairman of the Student Nonviolent Coordinating Committee. He has been active as a committee field representative in Washington since his return from an around-the-world trip last January.

The looting last night followed a protest march led by Carmichael down 14th Street N.W., the center of a principal Negro commercial and shopping area. He demanded that businesses close for the night as a gesture of mourning for Dr. King. Then he urged Negroes to "go home and get your guns."

A Breathing Spell

By dawn 14th Street was a shambles of shattered glass and scattered merchandise. But sunlight brought a breathing spell. Sanitation workers began shoveling up the shards of glass.

At 10 A.M. Carmichael called a news conference at the 14th Street headquarters of the New School for Afro-American Thought. Before television cameras he declared that "white America has declared war on black America" with the murder of Dr. King.

There is "no alternative to retribution," he said.

"Black people have to survive, and the only way they will survive is by getting guns," he said.

Less than an hour after the 30-minute news conference ended, Carmichael was in the street with a following of 50 Negroes. Both newsmen and the police lost track of him as the day progressed.

The police either could not or would not interfere with the looting, and much of it was done brazenly, under the gaze of outnumbered police officers. Loot was hauled away in automobiles and trucks. During most of the afternoon the police dealt only with large groups of looters and a seemingly endless series of fires.

In the downtown shopping area of large department and specialty stores, the windows of such stores as Hecht's and Woodward and Lothrop's were smashed and looted. There were fires at both stores. The police appeared to concentrate their protective maneuvers along F Street, giving the other areas less priority.

In the second area hit, along Seventh Street N.W. from K to P. Streets, looting and fires—the major fires of the day were concentrated there — gradually drained off the scattered police manpower.

In a third area, looters and firebombers struck along 14th Street from downtown F Street as far north as Park Road N.W., nearly halfway to the Maryland line at Silver Spring.

Another less well defined area of looting and arson was across the Anacostia River, in heavily Negro Southeast Washington. Two of today's deaths occurred there.

North and West of the city, the two contiguous suburban jurisdictions in Maryland, Montgomery and Prince Georges Counties, both declared local emergencies during the day, invoking most of the special powers, with the exception of a curfew, authorized in the city. More than 50 pieces of fire equipment from volunteer companies in suburban counties were rushed into the city during the afternoon to aid the overtaxed district fire department.

A rash of major fires broke out in the fourth area hit, along H Street N.E., a section of block-square department store and food warehouses just east of Union Station.

It was the opening of this new front that appeared to convince reluctant city officials that the police could not continue the battle alone. Despite extended tours of duty that had kept some officers on their feet for nearly 24 hours, no more than about 1,000 patrolmen were available to cope with the spreading disorder.

Openly, on the police radio, precinct commanders and other police officials expressed their exasperation.

Once the decision was made to summon Army troops, the deployment came rapidly. Mr. Johnson signed the orders at 4:02 P.M., similar to those he signed in sending Army troops to Detroit last summer during rioting. By the time the White House announced the arrival of military reinforcements an hour later, helmeted combat troops carrying rifles with sheathed bayonets were in position to protect the White House and the Capitol.

A company of trained riot troops was billeted in the White House itself. Outside, other troops took station at the southeast gate.

Troops ringed the Capitol and set up a light machinegun post on the Capitol's west steps, overlooking the Mall.

The precautions were more than routine in the case of the White House. Looting and fires reached within two blocks of it at about the time the troops began to arrive.

Within hours, Army troops and federalized Guardsmen began establishing "a visible presence"—merely standing at parade rest — along 14th Street. As the soldiers arrived, the looting and arson advanced ahead of them into areas nominally still under police jurisdiction.

Tonight, as Guardsmen moved to occupy the upper reaches of 14th Street, as far north as Randolph Street, N.W., besieged residents of apartment buildings — most of them Negroes—cheered from their windows.

The troops fired a rolling barrage of tear gas before them. As they advanced, they passed a small shopping area—a dry cleaning establishment, delicatessen, bar and liquor store—all in flames. There was no fire fighting equipment on the scene.

The troops included 2,000 men of the Army and Air Force National Guard of the District of Columbia, under regular Army command. There were two companies from the Third Infantry Regiment, the Capital's crack ceremonial unit at nearby Fort Myers, Va., and a squadron of the Sixth Cavalry Regiment from Fort Meade, Md., the Third Army headquarters halfway between Washington and Baltimore.

The troops also included elements of the 91st Engineering Battalion from nearby Fort Belvoir, Va.

It was the first time regular Army troops had been ordered into Washington for a civil disturbance since 1932, when cavalry under the late Gen. Douglas MacArthur drove hundreds of protesting bonus marchers from a squatters' encampment on the Anacostia River.

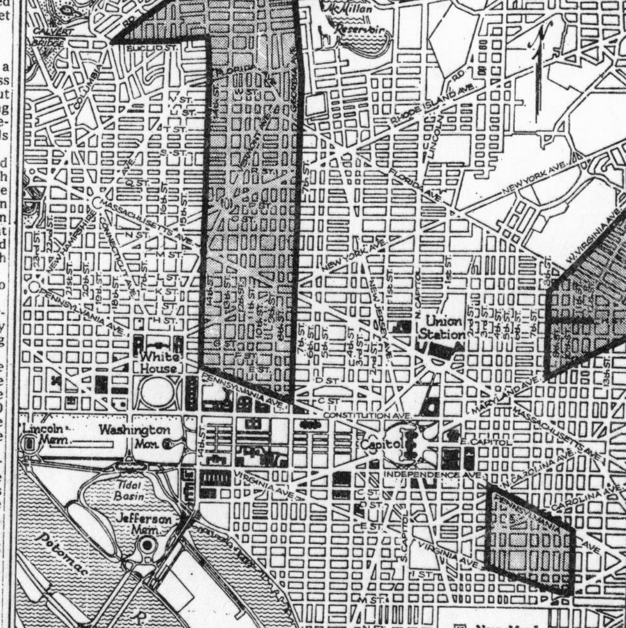

The New York Times April 6, 1968

VIOLENCE IN WASHINGTON: Dark lines enclose the major areas of disorder in the city

President's Proclamation and Executive Order

Special to The New York Times

WASHINGTON, April 5—Following are the texts of President Johnson's proclamation and executive order on the disorders in Washington:

By the President of the United States of America

A Proclamation

WHEREAS I have been informed that conditions of domestic violence and disorder exist in the District of Columbia and threaten the Washington metropolitan area, endangering life and property and obstructing execution of the laws, and the local police forces are unable to bring about the prompt cessation of such acts of violence and restoration of law and order; and

WHEREAS I have been requested to use such units of the National Guard and of the armed forces of the United States as may be necessary for these purposes; and

WHEREAS in such circumstances it is also my duty as Chief Executive to take care that the property, personnel and functions of the Federal Government, of embassies of foreign governments, and of international organizations in the Washington metropolitan area are protected against violence or other interference:

NOW, THEREFORE, I, Lyndon B. Johnson, President of the United States of America, by virtue of the authority vested in me by the Constitution and laws of the United States, do command all persons engaged in such acts of violence to desist therefrom and to disperse and retire peaceably forthwith.

IN WITNESS THEREOF, I have hereunto set my hand this fifth day of April, in the year of Our Lord nineteen hundred and sixty-eight, and of the independence of the United States of America the one hundred and ninety-second.

LYNDON B. JOHNSON.

Executive Order

Providing for the restoration of law and order in the Washington metropolitan area.

WHEREAS, I have today issued Proclamation 3840, calling upon persons engaged in acts of violence and disorder in the Washington metropolitan area to cease and desist therefrom and to disperse and retire peaceably forthwith and,

WHEREAS, the conditions of domestic violence and disorder described therein continue, and the persons engaging in such acts of violence have not dispersed:

NOW, THEREFORE, by virtue of the authority vested in me as President of the United States and Commander in Chief of the armed forces under the Constitution and laws of the United States, including Chapter 15 of Title 10 of the United States Code and Section 301 of Title 3 of the United States Code, and by virtue of the authority vested in me as Commander in Chief of the militia of the District of Columbia by the Act of March 1, 1889, as amended (D.C. Code, Title 39), is hereby ordered as follows:

Section 1. The Secretary of Defense is authorized and directed to take all appropriate steps to disperse all persons engaged in the acts of violence described in the Proclamation, to restore law and order, and to see that the property, personnel and functions of the Federal Government, of embassies of foreign governments, and of international organizations in the Washington metropolitan area are protected against violence or other interference.

Section 2. In carrying out the provisions of Section 1, the Secretary of Defense is authorized to use such of the armed forces of the United States as he may deem necessary.

Section 3. (A) The Secretary of Defense is hereby authorized and directed to call into the active military service of the United States, as he may deem appropriate to carry out the purposes of this order, units or members of the Army National Guard and of the Air National Guard to serve in the active military service of the United States for an indefinite period and until relieved by appropriate orders. Units or members may be relieved subject to recall at the discretion of the Secretary of Defense. In carrying out the provisions of Section 1, the Secretary of Defense is authorized to use units and members called or recalled into active military service of the United States pursuant to this section.

(B) In addition, in carrying out the provisions of Sections 1, the Secretary of Defense is authorized to exercise any of the powers vested in me by law as Commander in Chief of the militia of the District of Columbia, during such times as any units or members of the Army National Guard or Air National Guard of the district shall not have been called into the active military service of the United States.

Section 4. The Secretary of Defense is authorized to delegate to one or more of the secretaries of the military departments any of the authority conferred upon him by this order.

LYNDON B. JOHNSON.
The White House
April 5, 1968

Capital Traffic Jammed As Police Curb Looting

Special to The New York Times

WASHINGTON, April 5—Washington traffic was at a standstill early this afternoon at many downtown intersections as the police concentrated on areas of disorder and looting elsewhere while Federal employes, dismissed early, tried to drive home.

At a number of intersections, however, civilian volunteers took over as traffic directors, broke jams and sped the flow of drivers headed home.

The volunteers included Paul Levy, a 25-year-old law student at Georgetown University, and Edward Huffcut, 28, employed at a nearby office of the Matson Navigation Company.

Although both said they had had no previous experience in traffic directing, they managed to break numerous jams and keep traffic moving fairly smoothly.

Alert in Boston

By JOHN H. FENTON

Special to The New York Times

Boston, April 5—Lieut. Gov. Francis W. Sargent placed several units of the Massachusetts National Guard on stand-by alert tonight as a precaution against possible rioting following the assassination of the Rev. Dr. Martin Luther King Jr.

Mr. Sargent, acting in the absence of Gov. John A. Volpe, who is on a State Department trip to Japan, said the troops would be assembled in their armories and not patrol the streets.

He conferred by telephone with Mr. Volpe and in person with Maj. Gen. Joseph S. Ambrose, commander of the National Guard.

More than 15,000 persons gathered in Post Office Square today to express their grief and outrage at the slaying of Dr. King.

The throng swelled during a march that started at Northeastern University in the Back Bay district and went three miles, through Boston Common and past the Massachusetts State House. Most of the marchers were white.

The group was joined downtown by young people from the Roxbury district, the heart of the Negro slum. The demonstration, aside from tying up traffic, was orderly.

Speakers warned of "bloody violence" if white racism did not soon end. The demonstration, chiefly arranged through telephone calls during the night and morning, was called by the Congress of Racial Equality, People Against Racism and New England Resistance, an antidraft organization.

The Roxbury and North Dorchester Districts were quiet but tense today, after a night of sporadic stone-throwing at windows and cars.

Mayor Kevin H. White stayed at City Hall through most of the night, conferring with Negro leaders about avoiding destructive demonstrations.

Philadelphia Bars Closed

By MAURICE CARROLL

Special to The New York Times

PHILADELPHIA, April 5—A limited state of emergency, providing for the closing of all bars and liquor stores and a ban on outdoor gatherings of more than 12 persons, was declared here tonight.

There was only scattered disorder in Negro neighborhoods in reaction to the slaying of the Rev. Dr. Martin Luther King Jr. However, Mayor James H. J. Tate said that, "based on intelligence given us," there was a threat that the violence that struck other cities could erupt here.

So, at 9:02 P.M. Police Commissioner Frank L. Rizzo signed a sheet proclaiming a "limited state of emergency in the city of Philadelphia."

At the same time, the city's red painted police squad cars began visiting the 3,900 tap rooms, ordering them to close.

The proclamation, which also prohibits possession of dangerous weapons in public, will run until 6 A.M. Wednesday.

So far, said Mr. Rizzo, "Philadelphia has done a real fine job."

There has been no looting, he said, but some 75 windows had been broken since midnight, a couple of dozen persons had been beaten and there were some instances in which cars stopped for traffic lights had been rocked back and forth by bands of youngsters.

Earlier in the day, the 7,000-member police force was put on 12-hour shifts and all leaves were canceled. At key points through the city about 17 buses —50 policemen in each—were stationed to rush to any potential trouble spot.

State police and the National Guard had been alerted to stand by, Mr. Rizzo said.

But the city weathered without major trouble an incident that had held considerable potential for violence, a memorial rally for Dr. King in Independence Square. It spilled into a march by some 5,000 persons toward City Hall, almost a mile away. "Black, black black," chanted some of the marchers, led by a man who called himself "Freedom Smitty."

But after more oratory the march petered out without major disorder.

About one-third of Philadelphia's two million residents are Negro.

Vandalism in Pittsburgh

PITTSBURGH, April (UPI)—Widespread vandalism broke out in the predominantly Negro Hill district tonight and spilled over into several other areas of the city.

Up to 20 persons were arrested. A white man was shot and wounded seriously. Detectives said the shooting was connected with the disorders.

The city's 1,400-man police force was placed on 12-hour shifts. All days off and leaves were canceled.

Matthew Moore, an officer of the United Negro Protest Committee, said all windows in a 10-block area of the Hill district had been smashed. About 200 policemen were operating in the district. Others investigated window smashings and break ins in the adjacent Hazelwood, Uptown, fringe areas of Oakland, East Liberty and downtown Pittsburgh.

At least two liquor stores in the Hill district were broken into and some looting was reported.

Gangs of 50 to 100 persons roamed the Hill chanting "Dr. Martin Luther King" and smashing windows on white-owned stores on Fifth and Centre Avenues.

Emergency in Detroit

Special to The New York Times

DETROIT, April 5—A state of emergency was declared in Detroit this afternoon because of scattered violence, and 3,000 National Guardsmen were ordered into the streets. One looter was killed in a scuffle with policemen.

The city was placed under an 8 P.M. to 5 A.M. curfew.

By 6:30 this evening, the police said 24 adults and as many juveniles had been arrested. Two Negroes were shot, one by the police and one by persons unknown, the police said. Both were shot in the 12th Street area, the scene of last summer's riots, but neither was seriously injured, the police said.

The police also said there were only two fires that they could connect with the disorders.

A looter was killed "accidentally" by the police, Gov. George Romney said, in Highland Park, a separate city that is an enclave of Detroit.

There are 650,000 Negroes in Detroit, which has a population of 1.65 million.

Governor Romney joined Mayor Jerome P. Cavanagh at police headquarters this afternoon, the main command post for police operations in the city.

A tour of the city tonight showed the curfew completely effective. Police cruised through the areas and guardsmen were visible at marshaling points.

There were incidents all afternoon. Gangs of Negro youths marched in the streets, broke windows and looted a few stores. One cab driver was pulled from his taxi and beaten in the 12th Street area.

Mayor Cavanagh, who proclaimed the state of emergency, said, "It is better to overreact than underreact."

He went on radio and television and urged parents to keep their children home.

The Mayor ordered gasoline stations and liquor and gun stores closed this afternoon.

In Negro areas of the city people lined up in front of grocery stores to buy food, and a few Negroes painted "Soul" on their storefronts. From midafternoon on, freeways leading out of the city were jammed with workers or shoppers going home early.

Gov. George Romney ordered 9,000 National Guardsmen alerted. State policemen were also alerted for riot duty, and 400 joined the 4,500 Detroit policemen.

In the 12th Street area, crowds of young Negroes threw rocks at cars, but squads of policemen, in three-car convoys, cruised the streets dispersing the crowds.

The police wore steel Army helmets and carried shotguns.

Curfew Imposed in Toledo

TOLEDO, Ohio, April 5 (UPI)—Mayor William Ensign imposed a curfew on this city today in the wake of a disturbance involving about 2,000 Negro high school students.

Mayor Ensign said the curfew would forbid persons under 22 years of age from being on city streets and in public places during the hours it is in effect—from 8 P.M. tonight until 6 A.M. tomorrow.

The students had earlier refused to attend classes at predominantly Negro Scott High School in reaction to the slaying of the Rev. Dr. Martin Luther King Jr. The police said the students roamed a square-mile area of the West Side, throwing rocks at windows and passing cars.

Outbreak In Missouri

JEFFERSON CITY, Mo., April 5 (AP)—Some 200 Negro students from Lincoln University marched into downtown Jefferson City today, broke several store windows and, the police said, "stole at least five rifles from a sporting goods store."

The window-breaking took place after the students had gone to a newspaper office and protested an editorial that had criticized the Rev. Dr. Martin Luther King Jr. the day before his assassination. The editorial was published in The Post-Tribune and Capital-News.

The students demanded a retraction, but the newspaper declined.

Five Hurt in Greensboro

GREENSBORO, N. C., April 5 (AP)—Five policemen and National Guardsmen were injured tonight in an exchange of gunfire with snipers near the campus of predominantly Negro North Carolina A. & T. State University at Greensboro.

Two of the policemen were shot. One suffered apparently minor injuries from shotgun pellets. Another policeman and a guardsman were hit by bricks.

About 900 guardsmen and an undetermined number of police were in the university neighborhood. Guardsmen split into two groups and moved toward Hodgin Hall, a dormitory, but were pinned down. Police said sniper fire was coming from a corner of the building.

Police reports said the shooting started when someone passing in a station wagon fired into a crowd of Negroes, but missed hitting anyone. Two white men later were arrested.

Col. Guy Langston, who is commanding the guardsmen in Greensboro, sent his men to the area with orders for selected sharpshooters to return the fire.

Mississippi Guard Alerted

JACKSON, Miss., April 5 (AP)—"The entire National Guard is either on alert or stand-by," Gov. John Bell Williams told a statewide television audience today. He said "troublemakers are fanning the flames of hatred and giving encouragement to lawlessness, anarchy and violence."

Calling the assassination of Dr. King "a senseless atrocity," Mr. Williams said he had given the State Adjutant General authority to call as many National Guardsmen as needed to quell any violence.

Over 1,400 guardsmen were already on active duty, the Governor told a news conference held after his television apearance. The full force of more than 10,000 could be mobilized within minutes, he added.

Three Hurt in Savannah

SAVANNAH, Ga. April 5 (AP)—Three persons, including a fireman, were injured early today as a result of sporadic incidents of violence that broke out in the coastal city, apparently in reaction to news of the slaying of Dr. King.

The police said one white-owned department store in a predominantly Negro section was destroyed after a firebomb was thrown through a glass window of the store.

Kirk Mobilizes Guard

TALLAHASSEE, Fla., April 5 (UPI)—Gov. Claude R. Kirk Jr. mobilized 50 National Guardsmen tonight and alerted 200 others in an attempt to prevent a second night of violence near the Florida A. and M. University campus.

A spokesman for Mr. Kirk's office said that the helmeted guardsmen were being deployed by local law enforcement officials.

Roadblocks were set up in the area and nobody was allowed in or out of the area. Florida A. and M. was closed for a week. One person died last night, five were injured and 14 arrested.

San Francisco Looting

SAN FRANCISCO, April 5 (Reuters) — Gangs of Negro youths began looting stores in San Francisco and the neighboring cities of Oakland and Berkeley today, but the police said that they were "pretty well contained."

Bands of about 50 in number moved through streets here breaking store windows and taking merchandise from a five-and-dime after an open air memorial service for the Rev. Dr. Martin Luther King Jr. attended by 7,000 persons.

All members of the police force were on duty or standing by here and in Oakland, where Negroes make up almost half the population of 367,000.

Evers Decides to Pass Up Another Try for Congress

Special to The New York Times

JACKSON Miss., April 5 — Charles Evers, Negro leader, decided today to pass up another race for Congress this year because of the assassination of the Rev. Dr. Martin Luther King Jr. and his own work with the National Association for the Advancement of Colored People in Mississippi.

Mr. Evers, who lost in a runoff special election last month to Charles Griffin, a white middle-of-the-roader, had considered running as an independent candidate against Mr. Griffin in November for the full term in the Third Congressional District seat. The qualifying deadline passed this afternoon.

Memphis Strikers Aided

ATLANTA, April 5 (AP) — A Southern Presbyterian group voted today to send $5,000 to striking sanitation workers in Memphis for hunger relief so "that Martin Luther King will not have died in vain." Members of the denomination's Board of National Ministries executive committee also wired President Johnson in support of pending civil rights legislation.

"All the News That's Fit to Print"

The New York Times

LATE CITY EDITION

Weather: Sunny, warm today; fair, continued warm tonight, tomorrow. Temp. range: today 88-62; Wed. 83-59. Temp.-Hum. Index 75; Wed. 74. Full U.S. report on Page 94.

VOL. CXVII..No. 40,311 — NEW YORK, THURSDAY, JUNE 6, 1968 — 10 CENTS

KENNEDY IS DEAD, VICTIM OF ASSASSIN; SUSPECT, ARAB IMMIGRANT, ARRAIGNED; JOHNSON APPOINTS PANEL ON VIOLENCE

MARCUS TESTIFIES DE SAPIO HAD ROLE IN A CON ED DEAL

Says Itkin Sought Delay of Permit to Aid Own Scheme With Ex-Tammany Head

By BARNARD L. COLLIER

Former Water Commissioner James L. Marcus testified yesterday that he had been asked to delay approval of a permit to Consolidated Edison while the former Tammany Hall leader, Carmine G. De Sapio, was trying to make a deal with the utility company.

Marcus testified that the request came last September from his business partner, Herbert Itkin, who was in turn trying to negotiate a deal with Mr. De Sapio.

The testimony was elicited from Marcus under cross-examination on the third day of a Federal bribery conspiracy trial that has been marked by the mention in Marcus's testimony of several prominent members of both the Republican and Democratic parties.

Marcus was asked if there was a time when he, as Commissioner of Water Supply, Gas and Electricity, had "done business" with Con Edison. His answer was yes.

Says Itkin Asked Delay

"Itkin came to me," he said, "and said that Con Ed wanted a permit to increase the voltage on one of their power lines for 20 miles." He added that his approval as Commissioner was needed.

"Itkin said I should hold up for a while because he was negotiating with Carmine De Sapio, who was negotiating with Con Ed."

Marcus said that Mr. Itkin asked him to delay the approval for "a few weeks."

At that point in the trial, which came at about 4:40 P.M., Herman Zoloto, a lawyer representing Henry Fried, a contractor, and Mr. Fried's company, S. T. Grand, Inc., shouted:

"You're way ahead of your story, Mr. Marcus!"

Judge Edward Weinfeld broke in and scolded Mr. Zoloto for "a highly improper re-

Continued on Page 41, Column 1

TRANSIT PACKAGE SUBMITTED TO CITY

M.T.A. Seeks Approval of 8 New Subway Routes

By EMANUEL PERLMUTTER

A $1.27-billion package of subway and commuter railroad additions and improvements was submitted to the Board of Estimate and Mayor Lindsay yesterday.

The program was presented by the Metropolitan Transportation Authority and the New York City Transit Authority with a request for speedy city agreement on the new routes and engineering designs.

The over-all plan, which would take 10 years to complete, consists of eight new subway routes, including a Second Avenue subway, and Long Island Rail Road connections to the East Side of Manhattan and to Kennedy International Airport.

City approval of the routes and designs is a first step before application can be made for $60-million set aside by the Legislature for the engineering design of the mass transportation program presented by the Metropolitan Transportation

Continued on Page 55, Column 1

France Will Meet Tariff Deadline; Strikes Dwindling

By HENRY TANNER

Special to The New York Times

PARIS, June 5 — Maurice Couve de Murville told France's partners in the Common Market today that despite the nationwide strike now coming to a close, the Government would honor the July 1 deadline for the abolition of remaining tariffs in the European trade bloc.

Today workers in the nationalized railroad company, the Paris transit system, the post and telegraph offices and other public administrations voted to go back to work. Trains are expected to start running tomorrow on several major national lines and the Paris subways.

By the end of the week, it is expected, the nationwide strike, now in its 18th day, will be all but ended.

Mr. Couve de Murville, who is the new Minister of Economy and Finance, also reassured his countrymen

Continued on Page 15, Column 1

JERUSALEM POLICE CLASH WITH ARABS

Israelis Halt Procession on Anniversary of War—U.N. Council Meets on Fighting

Special to The New York Times

JERUSALEM, June 5—A silent Arab procession commemorating the first anniversary of the Arab-Israeli war erupted into a violent clash today when Israeli policemen intercepted the marchers at the edge of the walled Old City of Jerusalem.

The clash was the most violent aspect of a widespread protest in which Arabs shuttered shops and other businesses here and elsewhere on the west bank of the Jordan and in the occupied Gaza Strip. It came after a day-long battle yesterday across the Jordan between the Israelis and Jordanians, in which aircraft and artillery were used.

[The United Nations Security Council met Wednesday at the urgent request of Israel and Jordan to consider recurrent hostilities along their cease-fire line. It postponed debate, probably until Thursday. Page 3.]

In the west-bank towns of Nablus, Jenin and Tulkarm, all centers of Arab nationalism, the general strike was 100 per cent effective. All stores, cafes and offices were closed, public transportation ceased and the streets were virtually devoid of traffic and pedestrians.

Schools throughout the west bank and Gaza Strip had no

Continued on Page 2, Column 4

Italy's Cabinet Quits As Parliament Opens

By ROBERT C. DOTY

Special to The New York Times

ROME, June 5—Premier Aldo Moro and his center-left coalition Government, which has ruled Italy for four and a half years, resigned tonight with the convening of the new parliament, the fifth since World War II.

President Giuseppe Saragat asked Mr. Moro and his ministers to remain in office as a caretaker government while the search for a new government, which may be arduous, goes on.

Resignation of the government with the convening of a new parliament is automatic. But any hope that the Moro

Continued on Page 14, Column 3

6 IN RACE GUARDED

Secret Service Given Campaign Security Task by President

Text of the Johnson speech is printed on Page 23.

By MAX FRANKEL

Special to The New York Times

WASHINGTON, June 5—For the second time in five years, Lyndon B. Johnson undertook today, amid national shock and outrage, to offer protection, prayer, comfort and assistance to his political rivals in the Kennedy family and then to try to heal the country's political and psychological wounds.

The President's first reaction to the shooting of Senator Robert F. Kennedy this morning was that "there are no words equal to the horror of this tragedy."

But tonight, in an emotional and at times even angry statement on television, he pleaded with all Americans to end the violence in their midst once and for all, to tolerate neither hatred nor the preaching of violence and to resolve to live under the law.

A Guard for Candidates

Mr. Johnson said he was appointing a commission of distinguished citizens to investigate both the circumstances and the causes of physical violence of all kinds in the United States, in the hope that the nation can learn "how we can stop it".

Earlier he had moved swiftly to provide protective Secret Service details to the six announced Presidential candidates of major parties, other than Vice President Humphrey, who already has his protection because of his office.

Meanwhile, in the House of Representatives, a vote of 317 to 60 cleared the way for the House to accept the Senate version of an anticrime bill, including controls over the interstate sale of hand guns. The vote rejected a move to send the legislation to a Senate-House conference.

Members of Commission

To the commission Mr. Johnson named Milton Eisenhower, former president of Johns Hopkins University; Archbishop Terence J. Cooke of New York; Albert Jenner, Chicago lawyer who worked for the commission that investigated the assassination of President Kennedy; former Ambassador Patricia Harris; Eric Hoffer, the longshoreman-turned-philosopher; Senators Philip Hart, Democrat of Michigan, and Roman L. Hruska, Republican of Nebraska; Representative Hale Boggs, Democrat of Louisiana, majority whip in the House; Representative William M. McCulioch, Republican of Ohio, and Federal Judge Leon Higginbotham of Philadelphia.

The President described himself as shocked, dismayed and deeply disturbed, as he knew all Americans were, by the shooting, which he described as the "latest spectacular example" of lawlessness and violence.

"So let us, for God's sake, re-

Continued on Page 23, Column 1

NEWS INDEX

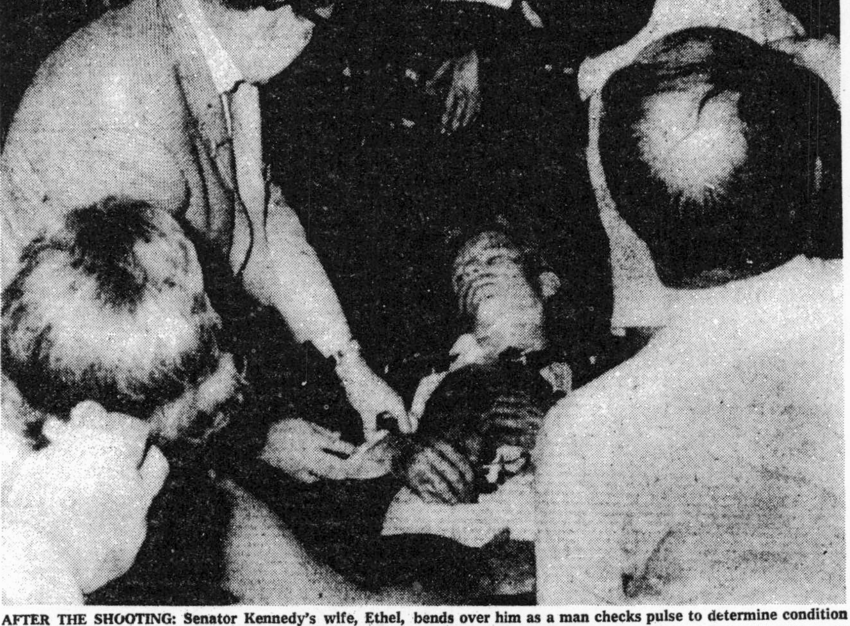

AFTER THE SHOOTING: Senator Kennedy's wife, Ethel, bends over him as a man checks pulse to determine condition

HANOI INSISTS U.S. HALT ITS BOMBING

Aides Call Talks Response to Johnson—Suspicion Voiced of a Plot Against Kennedy

By HEDRICK SMITH

Special to The New York Times

PARIS, June 5—North Vietnamese negotiators contended today that Hanoi had responded to President Johnson's restriction of American air attacks on the north by entering official talks here. They asserted that the next move, a total halt in bombing, was up to the United States.

The North Vietnamese argument, put forward in the seventh negotiating session between the two sides since May 13, produced one of the sharpest exchanges since the Vietnam talks began here.

The North Vietnamese made no direct comment on the shooting of Senator Robert F. Kennedy, but circles close to the delegation voiced suspicions in private, asking if the attack was not part of a conspiracy by the Johnson Administration. [Page 33.]

Near the end of today's session at the former Majestic Hotel, Hanoi's chief representative Xuan Thuy, leaned across the negotiating table and asked the American delegates bluntly:

"When will the United States unconditionally cease the bombing and all other acts of war against the Democratic Republic of Vietnam so that other questions can be discussed?"

In response, W. Averell Har-

Continued on Page 8, Column 4

Big Board Weighs 4 Special Closings

By VARTANIG G. VARTAN

A securities industry panel recommended yesterday that the New York Stock Exchange, the American Stock Exchange and the over-the-counter market close down for four days over the next month to cope with the deluge of paperwork in brokerage offices.

The panel proposed closing the securities markets for three Wednesdays—June 12, 19 and 26—as well as Friday, July 5.

The board of governors of the New York Stock Exchange will meet this afternoon to consider the proposal. Wall Street sources said that in view of the critical situation the governors are expected to accept the pro-

Continued on Page 73, Column 1

The New York Times (by George Tames)

ROBERT F. KENNEDY

A Pall Over Politics

Murder Raises Grave Questions for Presidency Races Now and in Future

By TOM WICKER

Special to The New York Times

News Analysis

WASHINGTON, Thursday, June 6—The murder of Robert F. Kennedy shattered the 1968 Presidential campaign and lowered a pall of uncertainty over American politics now and in the years to come. For the immediate future, it may well have assured the nominations by the Democrats and Republicans of the present front-running candidates — Vice President Humphrey and Richard Nixon. It raised grave questions, however, about the personal dangers of political campaigning in the United States.

It added a tragic new dimension to the near-martyrdom of the Kennedy family, which has now lost two sons to assassins' bullets.

It removed forever one of the most promising young political leaders in recent American history, one with particular appeal for the poor, the downtrodden and the alienated inhabitants of the Negro slums. That appeal had been proved in all of Robert Kennedy's primary victories this year.

These elements of society also revered the Senator's brother, President Kennedy, who was assassinated on Nov. 22, 1963. How they would react to Robert Kennedy's murder—both in the immediate future and for the long political pull—was a crucial question.

The murder added sorrowful emphasis to one of Robert Kennedy's major political themes—the necessity for orderly and just redress of grievances, in place of violent action.

Ultimately, Mr. Kennedy's death—the first assassination of an American Presidential candidate—might lead to changes in campaigning practices, even to the fundamental manner in which the nation chooses its President.

The most immediate effect, however, was that for the third—and most harrowing—time a shock wave of unexpected events had completely altered the shape of the 1968 campaign.

The first came on March 12 when Senator Eugene J. McCarthy of Minnesota won 42 per cent of the Democratic vote in the New Hampshire primary and Mr. Kennedy immediately thereafter became an active candidate.

The second transformation

Continued on Page 25, Column 6

SURGERY IN VAIN

President Calls Death Tragedy, Proclaims a Day of Mourning

Texts of the medical reports appear on Page 22.

By GLADWIN HILL

Special to The New York Times

LOS ANGELES, Thursday, June 6—Senator Robert F. Kennedy, the brother of a murdered President, died at 1:44 A.M. today of an assassin's shots.

The New York Senator was wounded more than 20 hours earlier, moments after he had made his victory statement in the California primary.

At his side when he died today in Good Samaritan Hospital were his wife, Ethel; his sisters, Mrs. Stephen Smith and Mrs. Patricia Lawford; his brother-in-law, Stephen Smith; and his sister-in-law, Mrs. John F. Kennedy, whose husband was assassinated 4½ years ago in Dallas.

In Washington, President Johnson issued a statement calling the death a tragedy. He proclaimed next Sunday a national day of mourning.

The Final Report

Hopes had risen slightly when more than eight hours went by without a new medical bulletin on the stricken Senator, but the grimness of the final announcement was signaled when Frank Mankiewicz, Mr. Kennedy's press secretary, walked slowly down the street in front of the hospital toward the littered gymnasium that served as press headquarters.

Mr. Mankiewicz bit his lip. His shoulders slumped.

He stepped to a lectern in front of a green-tinted chalkboard and bowed his head for a moment while the television lights snapped on.

Then, at one minute before 2 A.M., he told of the death of Mr. Kennedy.

Following is the text of the statement from Mr. Mankiewicz:

"I have a short announcement to read which I will read at this time. Senator Robert Francis Kennedy died at 1:44 A.M. today, June 6, 1968. With

Continued on Page 20, Column 1

NOTES ON KENNEDY IN SUSPECT'S HOME

Cite 'Necessity' to Murder Senator Before June 5, Anniversary of War

By PETER KIHSS

A notebook found in the Pasadena home of Sirhan Bishara Sirhan had "a direct reference to the necessity to assassinate Senator Kennedy before June 5, 1968," Mayor Samuel W. Yorty of Los Angeles said last night.

The date was the first anniversary of the six-day war, in which Israeli forces smashed those of the United Arab Republic, Syria and Jordan.

Sirhan, a 24-year-old Christian Arab, who has described himself as a Jerusalem-born Jordanian, is being held in the shooting of the New York Senator.

Justice Department records indicated that Sirhan came to the United States with his family in January of 1957 as immigrants, less than three months after the Suez war in 1956. Sirhan was 12 at the time.

The family quickly broke up in discord, the father staying in New York to work as a plumber and then going back to their former Palestine home, the mother taking five children to California, where a sixth child immigrated later.

Sirhan was described yesterday by Police Chief Thomas Reddin of Los Angeles as "very cool, very calm, very stable and quite lucid."

He was quoted as having said,

Continued on Page 21, Column 6

Father of Suspect 'Sickened' by News

By TERENCE SMITH

Special to The New York Times

ET TAIYIBA, Israeli-Occupied Jordan, Thursday, June 6—Bishara Sirhan's hands trembled as he talked about his son Sirhan Bishara Sirhan, the accused assailant of Senator Robert F. Kennedy.

Mr. Sirhan dwelled on the tragedy of the shooting. He became angry as he talked, and finally said: "This news made me sick when I heard it. If my son has done this dirty thing, then let them hang him."

Mr. Sirhan's memories of his five sons are those of 10 years ago, when he last saw them and their mother. After years of fierce family quarrels, Bishara

Continued on Page 21, Column 4

KUCHEL UNSEATED AS RAFFERTY WINS

Conservative Beats Senator in California's Primary

By LAWRENCE E. DAVIES

Special to The New York Times

LOS ANGELES, June 5—Dr. Max Rafferty, State Superintendent of Public Instruction, defeated Senator Thomas H. Kuchel in the Republican Senatorial primary in California yesterday, cutting short Mr. Kuchel's 15-year career in the Senate.

Returns from 20,714 of 21,301 precincts gave:

Rafferty	1,056,038	50%
Kuchel	985,097	47%

As the vote count continued today, it became apparent that the conservative Republicanism of Southern California had carried Dr. Rafferty to victory over the heretofore unbeatable Republican whip in the Senate.

Mr. Kuchel, an outspoken liberal-moderate who had made political extremists such as John Birch Society members his targets in recent years, was beaten by the voters in Los Angeles, San Diego and Orange Counties, after having led Dr. Rafferty last night and early Jay.

Dr. Rafferty, who has become

Continued on Page 28, Column 3

Kennedy Dies, Victim of Assassin, After Doctors Perform 3-Hour Brain Operation

ARAB ARRAIGNED; $250,000 BAIL SET

Revolver Traced to Suspect —Senator, 42, Failed to Regain Consciousness

Continued From Page 1, Col. 8

Senator Kennedy at the time of his death was his wife, Ethel; his sisters, Mrs. Patricia Lawford and Mrs. Stephen Smith; his brother-in-law, Stephen Smith, and his sister-in-law, Mrs. John F. Kennedy.

"He was 42 years old."

Senator Kennedy's body will be taken to New York this morning and then to Washington.

The man accused of shooting Mr. Kennedy early yesterday in a pantry of the Ambassador Hotel was identified as Sirhan Bishara Sirhan, 24 years old, who was born in Palestinian Jerusalem of Arab parentage and had lived in the Los Angeles area since 1957. Sirhan had been a clerk.

$250,000 Bail

Yesterday, he was hurried through an early-morning court arraignment and held in lieu of $250,000 bail.

Sirhan was charged with six counts of assault with intent to murder, an offense involving a prison term of 1 to 14 years.

Five other persons in addition to the 42-year-old Senator were wounded by the eight bullets from a .22-caliber revolver fired at almost point-blank range into a throng of Democratic rally celebrants surging between ballrooms in the hotel. The shots came moments after Senator Kennedy had made a speech celebrating his victory in yesterday's Democratic Presidential primary in California.

The defendant, seized moments after the shooting, refused to give the police any information about himself. He was arraigned as "John Doe."

Three hours later, Mayor Samuel W. Yorty announced at a news conference at police headquarters that the defendant had been identified as Sirhan. He said the identity had been confirmed by Sirhan's brother and a second individual.

Senator Kennedy, accompanied by his wife, Ethel, was wheeled into the Good Samaritan Hospital shortly after 1 A.M. yesterday after a brief stop at the Central Receiving Hospital. A score of the Senator's campaign aides swarmed around the scene.

Grim Reminder

Less than five years back many of them had experienced the similar tragedy that ended the life of President John F. Kennedy.

At 2:22 A.M., Senator Kennedy's campaign press secretary, Frank Mankiewicz, came out of the hospital into a throng of hundreds of news people to announce that the Senator would be taken into surgery "in five or ten minutes" for an operation of "45 minutes or an hour."

One bullet had gone into the Senator's brain past the mastoid bone back of the right ear, with some fragments going near the brain stem. Another bullet lodged in the back of the neck. A third and minor wound was an abrasion on the forehead.

It was after 7 A.M. when Mr. Mankiewicz reported that more than three hours of surgery had been completed, and all but one fragment of the upper bullet had been removed. The neck bullet was not removed but "is not regarded as a major problem," Mr. Mankiewicz said.

He also reported that the Senator's vital signs remained about as they had been, except that he was now breathing on his own, which he had not been doing before the surgery. Then Mr. Mankiewicz said:

"There may have been an impairment of the blood supply to the mid-brain, which the doctors explained as governing certain of the vital signs—heart, eye track, level of consciousness—although not directly the thinking process."

Senator Kennedy was taken from surgery to an intensive-care unit

At 2:15 P.M. Mr. Mankiewicz announced that Senator Kennedy had not regained consciousness and that a series of medical tests had been "inconclusive and don't show measurable improvement in Senator Kennedy's condition."

"His condition as of 1:30 P.M. remains extremely critical," the spokesman continued. "His life forces — pulse, temperature, blood pressure and heart—remain good, and he continues to show the ability to breathe on his own, although he is being assisted by a resuscitator."

The tests included X-rays and electroencephalograms.

Mrs. Kennedy remained at the hospital.

Mrs. John F. Kennedy arrived at the hospital at 7:30 P.M. yesterday, after a chartered plane flight from New York.

A team of surgeons treating Senator Kennedy included Dr. James Poppen, head of neurosurgery at the Lahey Clinic in Boston. He was rushed to Los Angeles in an Air Force plane on instructions from Vice President Humphrey.

Mr. Humphrey and Senator Eugene J. McCarthy of Minnesota have been Senator Kennedy's rivals in the Democratic Presidential competition.

Mayor Yorty said the defendant's identification had come through a brother, Adel Sirhan, after the police had traced the ownership of the .22-caliber revolver involved in the shooting to a third brother, Munir Bishari Salameh Sirhan, also known as Joe Sirhan.

The weapon was traced through three owners, one in suburban Alhambra, the next in Marin County, adjacent to San Francisco, and back to an 18-year-old youth in suburban Pasadena. The youth said he had sold it to "a bushy-haired guy named Joe" whom he knew only as an employe of a Pasadena department store.

Detectives identified the bushy haired man as Munir Sirhan. From him, the trail led to the two other brothers, who have been living together in Pasadena.

The snubnosed .22-caliber Iver Johnson Cadet model revolver seized after the shooting was described as having been picked out of a list of 2.5 million weapons registered in California in "just seconds" after the disclosure of its serial number. This was done by a new computer used by the State Bureau of Criminal Investigation and Identification in Sacramento, according to State Attorney General Thomas Lynch.

The defendant was arraigned at 7 A.M., unusually early, before Municipal Judge Joan Dempsey Klein, on a complaint issued by District Attorney Evelle Younger after all-night consultation with the police. Deputy District Attorney William Ritzi said the case would be presented to the county grand jury on Friday.

The other victims of the shooting were Paul Schrade, 43 years old, a regional director of the United Automobile and Aerospace Workers Union, a prominent Kennedy campaigner; William Weisel, 30, a unit manager for the American Broadcasting Company; Ira Goldstein, 19, an employe of Continental News Service at nearby Sherman Oaks; Mrs. Elizabeth Evans, 43, of Sangus, in Los Angeles County, and Irwin Stroll, 17.

Mr. Schrade, the most seriously wounded of the five, underwent an apparently successful operation at the Kaiser Foundation Hospital today to remove a bullet from his skull.

Mr. Weisel was reported in good condition after removal of a bullet from his abdomen.

The court complaint against Sirhan charged that "on or about the fifth day of June, 1968, at and in the county of Los Angeles a felony was committed by John Doe, who at the time and place aforesaid, did willfully, unlawfully and feloniously commit an assault with a deadly weapon upon Robert Francis Kennedy, a human being, with the intent then and there wilfully, unlawfully, feloniously and with malice aforethought to kill and murder the said Robert Francis Kennedy."

Sirhan was represented at the arraignment by the chief public defender, Richard S. Buckley. He asked Mr. Buckley to get in touch with the American Civil Liberties Union about getting private counsel for him.

Special to The New York Times

WASHINGTON, Thursday, June 6—President Johnson issued the following statement:

"This is a time of tragedy and loss. Senator Robert F. Kennedy is dead.

"Robert Kennedy affirmed this country—affirmed the essential decency of its people, their longing for peace, their desire to improve conditions of life for all.

"During his life, he knew far more than his share of personal tragedy. Yet he never abandoned his faith in America. He never lost his confidence in the spiritual strength of ordinary men and women.

"He believed in the capacity of the young for excellence and in the right of the old and poor to a life of dignity.

"Our public life is diminished by his loss.

"Mrs. Johnson and I extend our deepest sympathy to Mrs. Kennedy and his family.

"I have issued a proclamation calling upon our nation to observe a day of mourning for Robert Kennedy."

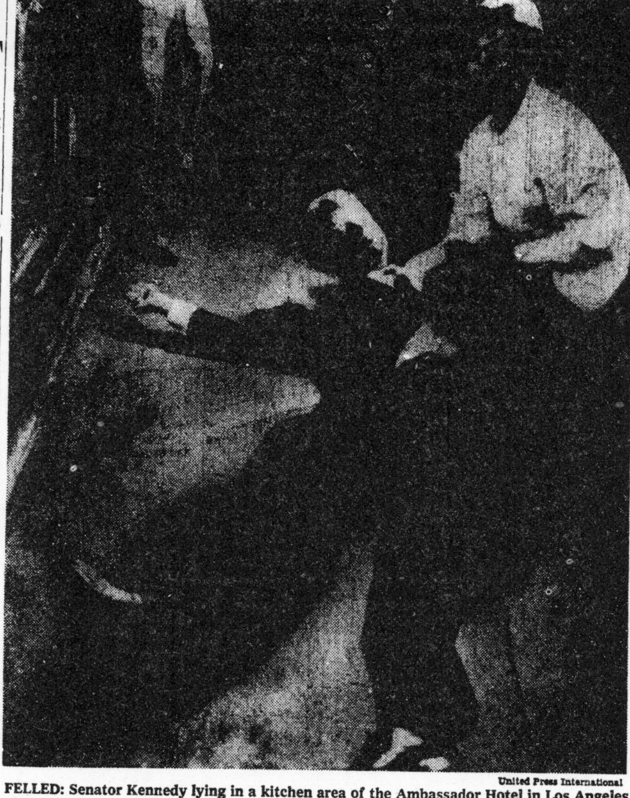

United Press International

FELLED: Senator Kennedy lying in a kitchen area of the Ambassador Hotel in Los Angeles after being wounded fatally by assassin. A hotel worker tries to give assistance.

Associated Press

ASKS FOR BREATHING ROOM: Mrs. Kennedy pleading with bystanders to stand back seconds after the shooting.

Ambulance Aide Tells of Drive To Hospital After the Shooting

By GEORGE GENT

Mrs. Robert F. Kennedy tried to prevent hospital attendants from administering emergency aid to her wounded husband, the Columbia Broadcasting System reported yesterday.

The report was by Jim Brown, a correspondent for television station KNXT, the C.B.S.-owned outlet in Los Angeles. In his report, carried by both the C.B.S. television and radio networks, Mr. Brown said that Mrs. Kennedy's behavior "undoubtedly was due to the fact that [she] was distraught and upset at this time."

The report quoted Max Behrman, the ambulance attendant who arrived at the Ambassador Hotel shortly after the shooting. He drove with the wounded Senator and his wife to the Central Receiving Hospital in Los Angeles.

"Max Behrman told me that when they reached the second floor of the Ambassador Hotel and prepared to lift Senator Kennedy onto the stretcher, the Senator said to him, 'Don't life me, don't lift me,'" Mr. Brown reported. "Those were the only words that he recalled hearing from the Senator in the entire time, from the time they arrived at the Ambassador through the trip to Central Receiving."

Mr. Behrman also said, according to Mr. Brown, that Mrs. Kennedy had indicated she did not want any assistance and that she had tried to prevent hospital attendants from administering aid of some kind to the Senator.

"This continued even in the ambulance en route to Central Receiving," Mr. Brown reported, "Mrs. Kennedy still, according to Behrman, physically tried to prevent this administering of aid to Senator Kennedy."

Despite Mrs. Kennedy's objections, Mr. Brown reported, ambulance attendants were able to place a pack under Senator Kennedy's head.

The C.B.S. report said that, upon arrival at Central Receiving, Dr. Vasilius Bazilauskas, the attending physician thought at first glance that the Senator was dead.

"However, as he began his examination and medical treatment," Mr. Brown reported, "he said he realized that there was still life, that he slapped the Senator several times in the face saying, 'Bob, Bob, Bob,' as he did so.

"He did determine," Mr. Brown went on, "there was a heartbeat, and when he did find a heartbeat of Senator Kennedy, he took the stethescope and put it to Mrs. Kennedy's ear—she was in the room at the time—so that she could hear the heartbeat."

Following the heart massage and other emergency treatment, the report concluded, Senator Kennedy was taken to Good Samaritan Hospital.

World Morality Crisis

Kennedy New Victim of Lawlessness Threatening Modern Public Order

By JAMES RESTON

News Analysis

Robert F. Kennedy is only the latest victim of a modern world that has turned loose greater forces than it can control. The struggles between the nations, between the races, between the rich and the poor, between the individual and bewildering change have produced a plague of lawlessness and violence that is now sweeping the globe. The pressures of all this are too much for weak and demented minds. The assassins of President Kennedy, the Rev. Dr. Martin Luther King Jr. and Lee Harvey Oswald and the attacker of Senator Kennedy may merely be deranged demons, tormented by frustrations and intoxicated by fear or revenge. But there is something more to it than that.

This is not merely rejection of the view that life is essentially decent, rational and peaceful, nor is it even a decline into individual moral insanity.

There is something in the air of the modern world: a defiance of authority, a contagious irresponsibility, a kind of moral delinquency, no longer restrained by religious or ethical faith. And these attitudes are now threatening not only personal serenity but also public order in many parts of the world.

Evidence of the use of force to achieve personal, group, or national ends is all around us: in the war in Vietnam, in the Arab-Israeli war of last year, in the student revolts in the United States, France and Italy, in the massacres of Indonesia, and in the political and racial assassinations of the last few years.

In America itself, the combination of poverty, in the midst of great luxury, plus the old American frontier tradition of violence as a part of life and even as an achievement, impress thoughtful students of modern psychiatry as contributing to the decline in public order.

Rejection of traditional rules of personal and institutional conduct is now common. But this is not unprecedented, and spectacular generalizations about this are not very helpful.

"At what point shall we expect the approach of danger?" Mr. Lincoln asked in 1837, speaking of this type of problem. "I answer, if it ever reach us, it must spring up amongst us."

He continued: "I hope I am not over-wary; but if I am not, there is, even now, something of ill-omen amongst us. I mean the increasing disregard for law which pervades the country; the growing disposition to substitute the wild and furious passions.

"This disposition is awfully fearful in any community; and that it now exists in ours, though grating to our feelings to admit, it would be a violation of truth and an insult to our intelligence to deny."

He added later that the American people were "destitute of faith and terrified of skepticism." Thus the contemporary analysis of our present predicament is not new. The record of violence, plain as it is, still does not match the convulsive era of 1914-1945.

Labor violence, for one thing, has visibly declined. Also, we are now in our 23d year since the last World War, which is already longer than the period of comparative peace between the two World Wars.

Nevertheless, the climate of violence in civil life in America is alarming and the death toll in Vietnam is still running at over 400 Americans a week.

The direction of verbal violence toward Robert Kennedy in this campaign has been conspicuous. His passionate defense of the Negro and the young, and his outspoken criticism of the war evoked intense and bitter feelings against himself.

Nobody who was in California during the campaign and listened to the radio harangues against him and his policies, particularly out of Oakland, could regard this as normal political criticism.

Some of it was directed against his economic views, much of it was racist in character, and a great deal of it was personal and vindictive over his campaign expenses and his appeals for peace.

Beyond this, the fantasy violence of American literature, television and the movies provide a contemporary gallery of dark and ghastly crime, which undoubtedly adds to the atmosphere in which weak and deranged minds flourish.

Fortunately, it cannot be said of this campaign that the other candidates strayed beyond the bounds of legitimate political debate. Senator Eugene J. McCarthy was mild almost to the point of boredom in his recent television debate with Senator Kennedy.

Old-Fashioned Forms

Nevertheless, the modern American political campaign goes on, as Senator McCarthy pointed out yesterday, as if this were still a lightly populated agrarian country, where old-fashioned political rallies could be carried on with safety.

Senator Kennedy himself inspired great emotion, particularly among the young, and the vast crowds that he drew in the great cities were not only a barrier to thoughtful discussion but also a menace to his person.

The need, therefore, for more restraint and security in these urban political rallies is fairly obvious. The feeling against President Johnson before he withdrew from the race was so intense that he was hopping from one military base to another on unannounced tours most of the time.

Thus, the politics of the last few months and years have been influenced and sometimes influenced decisively by a minority of militants. The attack on Senator Kennedy is likely to have almost as much of an effect on the future of American politics as the assassination of his brother did in 1963.

Campaign Prospects

It may be Senator Kennedy's brother Edward, 36 years old, who will now be a factor in the race, probably as a Vice-Presidential nominee.

Failing this, the revulsion of the nation against the crime in Los Angeles may very well add to the sentiment for a wholly new beginning with the Republicans or with Senator McCarthy, who started the political revolt against the Administration.

The outlook now is for a much more orderly and somber campaign, conducted much more on national television and much less in the streets.

This more solemn attitude is likely, moreover, to work against the continued violence of the war and thus help Senator McCarthy in his campaign for peace and the White House.

Agony and Determination Marked Kennedy Drive

By JOHN HERBERS

Special to The New York Times

LOS ANGELES, June 5—It was late Monday night when Senator Robert F. Kennedy made his last campaign appearance in the California Presidential primary.

He became ill midway in his speech to several hundred persons at El Cortez Hotel in San Diego, left the speaker's stand and was seized by a stomach upset. A few minutes later the candidate, insisting that he had recovered, returned and completed the address.

The incident was indicative of the agony coupled with fierce determination that permeated the Kennedy campaign before the Senator was shot and wounded in the Ambassador Hotel early this morning.

In 11 weeks of what was probably the most hectic primary campaign conducted by a Presidential candidate, Senator Kennedy's mood changed from seeming optimism and self-assurance to one of weariness and pessimism.

Some of his final speeches contained foreboding phrases.

'What Happens to Me'

"My fate is in your hands," he said Monday, "but it is less important what happens to me as to what happens to the cause I have tried to present."

On the eve of the Oregon primary, which he lost to Senator McCarthy, he spoke as if he had lost his chance for the Presidential nomination, telling his supporters in Portland that his cause had at least served to bring debate and discussion of the issues to the Democratic party. Observers who had seen him begin his campaign with a rousing speech, before 10,000 students at the University of Kansas on March 18, noted the decided change.

He had said in that first speech: "Give me your help, give me your hand and we will build a new America." He received a thunderous ovation.

Then followed a barnstorming tour, which was carried out with relentless drive and seemingly endless energy. The purpose was to start a people's movement that the leaders of the Democratic party could not stop.

Optimism Continued

The optimism continued through the Indiana and Nebraska primaries, even though delegates to the Democratic National Convention were lining up behind Vice President Humphrey faster than Senator Kennedy could win them in the primaries.

Some of these delegates won by Mr. Humphrey were personal friends of Mr. Kennedy whom the Senator had expected to help him win the Presidency. Associates of the Senator said he was hurt by their leaving his cause even before the primaries were over.

The Senator's friends said he also felt injured by what he considered an antagonistic press and by the bitter opposition that was evident among a number of voters in every state he visited.

"When I ride in a motorcade, you know what I hear most?" he said once. "It's people who shout, 'Get a haircut!' Well, I got a haircut, but it doesn't seem to help."

His purpose was to restore a sense of destiny and unity to the country and to check the trend toward increased violence, but he seemed to have trouble communicating this to affluent whites. His constituency was the poor and they cheered him even before they heard what he had to say.

Nevertheless, he seemed to gain solace from the huge crowds of admirers. He would go forth daily to be pulled and mauled, and he liked it.

There were virtually no security precautions, only his trusted bodyguard, Bill Barry, whose chief job was to bull a path through the crowds and keep him from being pulled from the car.

It was in the cool green valleys of Oregon that some of the spirit went out of the campaign. The crowds fell off. Everywhere Senator Kennedy went he was confronted by an increasing number of McCarthy signs carried by bright-eyed students whom Senator Kennedy would like to have led.

Trouble Apparent

Even before the vote, it was apparent that Senator Kennedy was in trouble in Oregon, and in his fatalistic fashion he stated publicly that if he lost he would no longer be a "viable candidate."

After he lost in Oregon, he promised to abandon the race if he failed to carry California.

By this time, Senator Kennedy seemed tired and drawn most of the time, his nerves raw. The marathon campaigning continued, but it was not the same. His speeches frequently were ragged and sometimes he stumbled over his words.

It was not the first agony for Robert Kennedy. After John Kennedy was assassinated in 1963, he went into a deep state of depression that lasted for months.

There was renewed agony for him when he had to decide late in 1967 and early this year whether to run for President. There was agony when he took the advice of his older advisers and rejected that of the younger ones and decided in late January not to challenge President Johnson. There was more agony when he decided, after the New Hampshire primary and after many of the young had gone over to Eugene McCarthy, to enter the race after all.

Always there were painful moments. In a small town in Oregon he was confronted by signs opposing his stand on gun control legislation, opening anew the wound of 1963.

But the outcome in California was a little better than the Kennedy supporters had expected. Although the Senator was still weary and brooding as the returns came in, the vote offered new hope that perhaps with some kind of accommodation with Senator McCarthy, Vice President Humphrey could be stopped.

Then, with this new hope only a couple of hours old, there were the shots in the kitchen of the Ambassador.

Police Chief Says Kennedy Turned Down Security Aid

LOS ANGELES, June 5 (UPI)—Police Chief Thomas Reddin said today that Senator Robert F. Kennedy had been offered security help several times during his visit here, but had refused it.

"We were asked to leave the party alone," the chief told a news conference at the central police building in downtown Los Angeles.

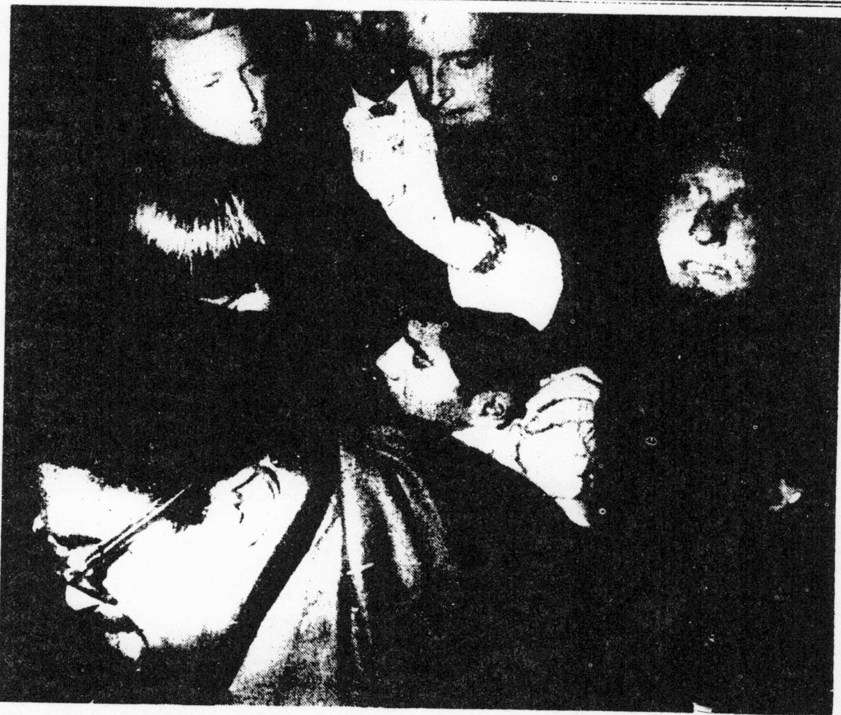

THE INSTANT AFTER: Roosevelt Grier, left, Kennedy aide, and others struggling with suspect, center, after shooting. Mr. Grier, professional football player, and Rafer Johnson, former Olympic champion, helped disarm [illegible]

The Shooting: A Victory Celebration That Ended With Shots, Screams and Curses

SUSPECT IS SEIZED WITH GUN IN HAND

Men Wrestle Him to Table as Kennedy, Bleeding, Lies in a Corridor

By WALLACE TURNER

Special to The New York Times

LOS ANGELES, June 5—A thin, intense man stood on the platform in the glare of television lights. He had come to share victory with those who had helped him win it.

Those who knew him recognized the strain in his 5-foot-nine-inch, 150-pound figure, and in his speech and manners, too.

The microphones didn't work; then the lights for the television cameras were too hot. It was annoying to Senator Robert F. Kennedy.

The crowd was noisy, and the candidate for President was eager to finish thanking those who helped him. He wanted to go to a nearby room for a news conference, and then escape to The Factory, a discothèque, for a celebration party with his friends.

He had spent the day at Malibu in the home of John Frankenheimer, the film director, where he fretted to be away and to have over and done with the agonizing wait for the vote count. Then he had returned to suite 512 in the Ambassador Hotel on Wilshire Boulevard.

Politicians and Reporters

About 50 people were there. Among them was Theodore H. White, who became a famous chronicler of elections by reporting carefully the 1960 election of the brother whose campaign the candidate himself had managed.

When that brother had been assassinated, Teddy White had written a famous interview with the widow that had caused the present campaign to be called an attempt to return to Camelot.

There was also Charles Evers, a Negro leader, whose brother was shot down in the night by someone who opposed his campaigns for equal rights for blacks in Mississippi.

There were politicians, such as Jesse M. Unruh, the Speaker of the California Assembly, who helped to persuade the Senator to offer his candidacy for President. There were also newspapermen, magazine reporters and the entourage that follows Presidential candidates.

Mr. Unruh left the suite first to prepare the crowd for the Senator's arrival. Then the Senator was led to the meeting hall through a kitchen passageway to avoid the crowd.

Kennedy Gives Thanks

Once on the platform, Senator Kennedy named some for whose help he was grateful. One was Cesar Chavez, the farm union organizer. Another was Rafer Johnson, an Olympic decathlon champion.

Senator Kennedy spoke, too, of Roosevelt Grier, the huge black man who plays defense for the Los Angeles Rams professional football team. The Senator said:

"Rosey Grier said he'd take care of anybody who didn't vote for me."

He also thanked Paul Schrade, an official of the United Automobile Workers' Union, and he thanked his wife, Ethel.

Then he turned to a statement of his campaign aims:

"I think we can end the divisions in the United States. What I think is quite clear is that we can work together in the last analysis.

"And that is what has been going on within the United States over a period of the last three years—the division, the violence, the disenchantment with our society, the division, whether it's between blacks and whites, between the poor and the more affluent, between age groups, or in the war on Vietnam—that we can start to work together.

"We are a great country, an unselfish country and a compassionate country. And I intend to make that my basis for running . . ."

The sentence was swallowed into the applause of a crowd that was hearing what it came to hear.

He said, "We want to deal with our own problems in our country and we want peace in Vietnam."

Then, as he was ready to turn away from the microphones, he said:

"So my thanks to all of you and it's on to Chicago and let's win there."

He moved slowly down the three steps of a portable stairway to his left and through two doors leading to the kitchen passageway. It was 12:13 A.M. Pacific daylight time.

He intended to go through the passageway to the smaller Colonial Room, which was in use as a press room.

Lisa Urso, an 18-year-old senior at Crawford High School in San Diego, had maneuvered herself ahead of the Senator. She was pushed to one side by the crowd and found herself behind two men. Senator Kennedy was in front of her, reaching across a table to shake hands with a waiter.

The hands never met.

The second man in front of Miss Urso reached out a hand. Miss Urso heard three shots. Senator Kennedy flinched as if reaching for his head, and fell to the floor. Miss Urso saw Mrs. Kennedy bending over her husband.

In the press room, reporters waited for Mr. Kennedy.

"I saw his head bobbing in the crowd about 25 or 30 feet away" said Robert Healy of The Boston Globe.

"Then there was gunfire. No question. The flashes lighted up the corridor."

Men ran for the double doors leading to the corridor. Women screamed and cried.

It was about 12:16 A.M.

At the other end of the corridor stood Karl Uecker, an assistant maitre d'hotel:

"I was bowing Senator Kennedy and his wife out of the room. I'm right in front of him. I have my hand on his arm. I have my other hand leading Mrs. Kennedy."

Mr. Uecker thought he heard three shots. (The police said later there were eight.)

"I recognized the danger," he said in his German accent. "I grab him by the neck."

"He was standing there by the corner and he looked like a houseman," by which Mr. Uecker meant the gunman looked like a hotel employe.

Mr. Uecker was aware that Senator Kennedy had fallen to the floor behind him, but he was busy wrestling for the gun.

The Senator was 30 steps from the platform where he had spoken and 15 steps from the press room.

Mr. Healy ran down the passage. He was unable to make his way to Senator Kennedy. He jumped to the top of a stainless steel serving counter and looked down at the Senator.

Paul Houston of The Los Angeles Times burst into the corridor.

"I could see the floodlights on Kennedy as he sank to the floor," he said. "His head was bloody, and his eyes were open, but they looked very dazed."

Mr. Unruh stood on a table in the passage. "Where is the doctor? For God's sake! Get a doctor!" he yelled.

Senator Kennedy lay on his back on the concrete floor, his knees slightly elevated. Someone put what looked to be an icepack on the wound at his right ear.

Special officers tried to block off the corridor. Mrs. Kennedy knelt beside her husband, calling out again and again that the space round Senator Kennedy must not be blocked, that he must be given room to breathe.

Members of Senator Kennedy's staff thrust themselves through a row of waiters and kitchen workers who sought to hold back the crowd.

Someone removed Senator Kennedy's coat and opened his shirt. His face was ashen. His right eye was open and his left eye partially opened. Some persons thought he was aware; others thought he was not.

A rosary was on his chest and he clutched the beads. Mrs. Kennedy knelt by his side, as did Fred Dutton, a campaign aide.

Women screamed and screamed. Men cursed. Beyond Senator Kennedy, Paul Schrade of the U.A.W. lay with a wound in his head. Bill Weisel, an assistant producer for American Broadcasting Company news, was wounded in the abdomen.

He said, "I looked up and there was a body on the floor, and the next thing I knew I was falling."

Three doctors came into the passage and began to prepare Senator Kennedy for an ambulance. It was 12:22 A.M.

A fierce struggle developed at the other end of the stainless steel serving table. A knot of men, with Rosie Grier's bulk dominating it, worried at a figure stretched on the table.

The figure was a man, and he had a gun in his hand. Mr. Grier pounded the hand repeatedly against the table top, and the gun flew to the floor. Rafer Johnson and William Barry, a Kennedy bodyguard, pounced on it.

The waiters, wearing their black dinner jackets, and kitchen workers, in white coats, pounded and pummeled their prisoner.

One jerked the prisoner's hair. Hands could be seen trying to encircle his throat.

Rosie Grier having dislodged the gun, began dislodging those who wanted to do more than hold the prisoner. He shouted that he must not be hurt, and with his huge hands he pushed men away.

Yet the prisoner, a slight man, twisted and squirmed so that about eight men were required to hold him. Nothing that he might have said could be heard.

At 12:30 A.M. a squad of Los Angeles policemen, some with shotguns, arrived.

They picked up the prisoner by arms and legs and carried him out, down the corridor through the crowd, past the registration desk of the hotel down the curved stairs, and out to the parking lot.

Speaker Unruh followed the police, shouting, "He must not be hurt."

An ambulance arrived, and Senator Kennedy was moved out a side door on a stretcher.

Dick Tuck, a political publicist and Kennedy campaign worker, helped to put the Senator on the stretcher.

"When I picked up his legs, he said, 'No, don't!' as if it gave him pain," Mr. Tuck said. "I doubt that he said anything else."

The crowd poured out of the hotel to the parking lot, threatening to immobilize the ambulance and its police escort.

Mr. Tuck, his cheeks wet with tears, begged people to stay back, then climbed in the police car that led the ambulance out of the parking lot. It was 12:43 A.M.

Associated Press

TRIUMPH, THEN TRAGEDY: Senator Kennedy and his wife, Ethel, at victory celebration at the Ambassador Hotel in Los Angeles minutes before he was shot. To the right of the Senator is Jesse M. Unruh, California Assembly Speaker.

Kennedy Firm on the U.S. Commitment to Aid Israel

By LAWRENCE VAN GELDER

For Robert F. Kennedy, Israel was a nation to be aided and admired.

As recently as last Saturday, in his televised debate with Senator Eugene J. McCarthy, Senator Kennedy was expressing—as he had many times in the past—his views on the subject.

Although he has looked with disfavor on the idea that the United States "be the policeman of the world," he stated that he did recognize some commitments around the globe, and promptly declared:

"I think we have a commitment to Israel, for instance, that has to be kept."

Last June, at a commencement address to graduate students at Fordham University, he spoke with admiration of Israel as "a tiny outpost of Western culture and ideals."

Looking back over 20 years to the beginning of Israeli statehood, he observed that its "arms and courage have allowed this tiny nation with less than the population of Queens, to defeat the armies of nations with total populations of millions."

He said: "This gallant democracy, this nation of survivors from history's greatest example of man's capacity for senseless cruelty to his fellow men cannot be allowed to succumb to the threats and assaults of her neighbors."

As he had said before and was to say again, he declared: "Our commitment to Israel is clear and must be clear."

During his recent campaigns in Oregon and California, he called for military assistance to Israel and to a negotiated settlement of differences between Israel and her neighbors that would include unequivocal recognition of Israel by the Arab states.

In Portland, he donned a yarmulka, or skullcap, to appear before Congregation Neveh Shalom, a Conservative body, and declared: "The Soviets have sent supersonic fighters to the Arabs. Soviet planes and pilots they have trained are on Arab soil. Forty Soviet warships are in the Mediterranean, and their advisers are in Arab nations."

He said the United States could not permit such an imbalance and should without delay sell Israel "the 50 Phantom jets she has so long been promised."

He went on to say: "We all desire an end to the arms race, but it cannot be unilateral — for such a course promises only more aggression and the threat of yet another bloody conflict."

On May 20, at Temple Isaiah in Los Angeles, he said that the first essential criterion for establishing an enduring peace in the Middle East was universal recognition of the state of Israel.

Calling for negotiations, he said: "This negotiation must start with a clear recognition of Israel's existence by the Arab states—an absolute commitment to respect her territorial integrity—and full guarantees of all international rights of passage."

Although he spoke strongly in behalf of Israel, he recognized the plight of the Arab nations, as when he told an audience of some 300 persons from New York City in the Senate Caucus Room last June: "Let us also hold out our hand of friendship to the Arab peoples, so long living in poverty and disease and misery, so long the tools of irresponsible propaganda, so long the greatest losers from the military adventures of their leaders."

NOTES ON KENNEDY IN SUSPECT'S HOME

Continued From Page 1, Col. 7

"I prefer to remain incommunicado," when questioned about the shooting.

Mayor Yorty said that the suspect had a schedule of Senator Kennedy's speaking engagements for this month, a clipping of a columnist's criticism of the New York Democrat—and four $100 bills.

Mayor Yorty's office said that the clipping was a Pasadena newspaper's publication of a suggestion by the Washington columnist David Lawrence that Senator Kennedy, while a dove in regard to Vietnam, was a hawk in regard to Arab-Israeli hostilities.

"All I know is he is a nice kid," Said Sirhan, identifying himself as a brother, declared in a telephone interview from Los Angeles reported by WCBS radio here.

John Weidner, owner of the Organic Health Food Store in Pasadena, said he had employed Sirhan Sirhan as a $2-an-hour stock clerk and deliveryman from last Sept. 24 until March 7, when the man left "because he didn't like what I said about his work."

"He was a man with principles," Mr. Weidner said. "He didn't smoke. He didn't drink. He always said he wouldn't lie. But he was emotional. He would resent authority. He didn't like to take orders.

"When he was very young, he saw members of his family and friends killed by Israelis. My personal opinion is that I think he did something to Kennedy because he [Kennedy] said he would help Israel."

$250,000 Bail

Mayor Yorty and Chief Reddin said that the prisoner, held in $250,000 bail on six counts of assault with intent to commit murder, had been identified through two brothers.

The brothers were identified as Munir, also known as Joe, and Adel, who had been located by the tracing of a .22-caliber pistol said to have been used in the shooting.

Chief Reddin said that the identification had been confirmed through a set of fingerprints on file in Sacramento in connection with an application by Sirhan Sirhan for a job as an exercise boy for horses at the Hollywood Park Race Track.

The application was made some time ago while Sirhan Sirhan was a student at John Muir High School in Pasadena.

In Washington, the Department of Justice said that Sirhan Sirhan was an alien on permanent resident status, on which he arrived in New York City Jan. 12, 1957.

Records of the Immigration and Naturalization Service gave his birth date as March 19, 1944, in Jordan. Jerusalem was then part of Palestine, and the end of the British Palestine mandate in 1948 until Israel took over after the war last June.

The Justice Department said that he had entered the United States with his father, identified as Bishara Salameh Ghattas Sirhan, and his mother, Mary Bishara Sirhan. Also arriving at the same time were three brothers, listed as Adel, Sharif and Munir, and a sister, Ayda. Another brother, listed as Saidallah, arrived in June, 1960.

Status Explained

The Jordan Embassy in Washington said in a statement: "We deeply regret that the suspect appears to be someone of Jordanian origin who is a permanent resident of the United States.

"The Jordanian Government strongly condemns this criminal act committed against an outstanding American leader and public servant. King Hussein has already conveyed his sense of shock and genuine sentiments to the Kennedy family."

Federal officials said that an alien on permanent resident status is one who has applied for permission to live in the United States permanently while remaining a citizen of his country of origin. Such permission is most commonly granted when the applicant already has relatives living here or has a desired skill.

In New York, a 39-year-old former Arab News Agency representative in Jerusalem, who came here in 1958 and is now working for a publishing company, said that Sirhan Sirhan's parents separated "right away after they came here." He asked not to be identified.

"The father, the journalist said, went back to Jordan, and has a house in Jerusalem as well as a new home he built recently in the village of Et Taiyiba.

Sirhan Sirhan is 5 feet 5 inches and weighs about 120 pounds. His hair is dark and curly. His complexion is swarthy. He speaks English with a slight accent that Chief Reddin reported seemed "Jamaican or Cuban."

He has been living with the brother who goes by the name of Joe at 696 East Howard Street in Pasadena, according to Mayor Yorty. The Mayor said it was Joe who owned the gun held to have been used in the shooting, and the brother told police officers he had no idea how Sirhan Sirhan got the weapon.

Mrs. Mary Sirhan, the suspect's mother, collapsed after hearing of her son's arrest.

Mayor Yorty said that notebooks found in the prisoner's home dwelled at length on the Middle East conflict.

In a copyrighted Los Angeles interview by Radio News International, Mayor Yorty said that one notebook "appeared to have been written by Sirhan Sirhan."

"There's much scribbling, repeated phrases, many references to Senator Robert Kennedy, even some references to Arthur Goldberg," the Mayor was quoted has having said.

"They're not very clear, but there's a direct reference to the necessity to assassinate Senator Kennedy before June 5, 1968. I don't know why.

"He does a lot of writing pro-Communist and anti-capitalist, anti-United States. Evidently he was quite pro-Arab in the Arab-Israeli matter. He has 'Long Live Nasser' written in there.

"And he said he favors Communism of all types, whether Russian, Chinese and so forth.

"It's very difficult to tell from that why he'd want to pick on Senator Kennedy as the one that he made reference to had to be sacrificed for all these grievances."

Chief Reddin said:

"He almost appeared to be the calmest man in the room. I spoke with him for about 15 minutes, and he sounds well-educated, speaks good English and is a good conversationalist.

"We talked about many things. He was very relaxed and wanted to talk about just about everything except the events last night.

"If I were to judge him strictly on the basis of our conversation, and that were the only basis, I would say he was a gentleman."

In a news conference later, Chief Reddin said there was a "subversive file" on Sirhan Sirhan, which, he indicated, grew out of Arab nationalist activities.

Dr. M. T. Mehdi, secretary-general of the Action Committee on American-Arab Relations, said:

"Of course we condemn his act, but his behavior reflects the frustration of many Arabs with American politicians who have sold the Arab people of Palestine to the Zionist Jewish voters."

John M. Lawrence, chairman of "a pro-Arab radical left action group," Federated Americans against Israeli Racism, 57 West 10th Street, said his organization would offer financial support to Sirhan Sirhan.

"We're for him, although we wish he hadn't used the assassination technique," Mr. Lawrence, a law researcher, said.

He declared that "there are no tears in us for Robert Kennedy," whom he called "the advocate sending American jet bombers to Israel so Jews may kill more Arabs."

Father of Suspect 'Sickened,' Says 'Let Them Hang Him'

Continued From Page 1, Col. 7

and Mary Sirhan separated in 1957 and have not seen each other since. Mrs. Sirhan moved to the United States and remained there with the boys.

Mr. Sirhan, who lives alone in a two-story stone house in this hillside village on the west bank of the Jordan River, heard the news of the attack on Senator Kennedy yesterday over the radio. But it was not until a reporter came to his house at 1:30 this morning that he learned that his son had been arrested for the shooting.

At first, he just shook his head at the news. Then he said in a soft voice: "I'm deeply sorry for both of them, for my son and for Mr. Kennedy. I admire the Kennedy family very much. I prayed that Robert Kennedy would be elected President so he could do many of the good things for the world that his brother did."

Sirhan Bishara Sirhan "was an excellent student," his father said. "We have five boys, and he was the best of all of them at school. He was such an intelligent boy I had no worries with him. I was sure he would do well."

An Excellent Student

Sirhan was the fourth of the sons born to the Sirhans in Jerusalem, where the father was for 22 years the senior Arab officer in charge of the city water supply under the British mandate rule. When their fourth son was born, the Sirhans were living in a small house in the Armenian quarter of the Old City. Though they were Greek Orthodox, they rented their house from the neighboring Armenian convent.

Sirhan, along with his brothers, studied in a small school run by the Lutheran Church of the Savior, like everyone else in Jerusalem, their lives were interrupted by the Arab-Israeli war of 1948, and they moved repeatedly after that though always within the Arab sector of Jerusalem.

After the British left Palestine, Mr. Sirhan took a job as a plumber for the Jordanian authorities, who assumed control the eastern part of Jerusalem. He held this job until 1957, when, in his words, "there was trouble between me and my wife."

"She took the children and went to America," he said. "I haven't seen them since, and for years she would not let them write to me. Only two or three months ago I got some letters from my second son, Sandallah, asking me how I was after the war.

"He asked about me in the letters," Mr. Sirhan said, "but when I asked about him and his brothers and what their situation was, he stopped writing. I know nothing about them. I dont even know if they have gone to college or served in the army or gotten married or what."

Mr. Sirhan, a wisp of a man barely 5 feet tall, looks his 52 years. His suntanned face is deeply lined, and his curly gray hair has receded at the temples.

He received his visitor in a living room furnished with two hard sofas and several straight-backed wooded chairs. The only literature in sight was some religious pamphlets.

Mr. Sirhan said that he first visited the United States in 1957 with his wife and sons and a daughter, who he said died four years ago. He has since made two visits to the United States for periods up to 18 months. He worked in New York for part of that time, he said, but he did not see his sons or wife after the initial trip.

'I Pray He Lives'

Three years ago, he built his house in Et Taiyiba, the village of his birth, about seven miles northeast of Ramallah.

Mr. Sirhan stalked about his sons for several minutes and then suddenly interrupted himself to ask: "How is Robert Kennedy? Will he survive? I pray that he lives. I feel sorrier for him and his family than I do for my son and my family.

"Please tell the Kennedy family that I am very, very sorry. I only wish it could be someone other than them and someone other than my son.

"I don't know how he could have done such a thing," he said. "Ours is a deeply religious family. Neither my father nor I ever harmed anyone or did such a thing. We hate this sort of thing, this violence and death. It is not our way."

Asked if he intended to go to the United States, Mr. Sirhan said: "What good would it do? Whatever my son has done, he has done. There is nothing I ca ndo to change that now."

Arabs in Jerusalem Refuse To Believe Attacker Is Arab

Special to The New York Times

TEL AVIV, June 5—Stunned Arabs in Jerusalem refused to believe the attacker of Senator Robert F. Kennedy was their former neighbor. Arabs who said they did not know Sirhan Bishara Sirhan recalled the doubts about Lee Harvey Oswald's role in the assassination of President John F. Kennedy and speculated that Sirhan might be the victim of a conspiracy.

"For Israel," The Jerusalem Post says in an editorial to be published tomorrow, "the sense of shock turned into disbelief with the news that the assailant was a Jordanian who, according to eye witnesses, reportedly shouted" that he shot "the Presidential candidate for 'his country.'"

Premier Levi Eshkol sent messages of sympathy to President Johnson and to the family of Senator Kennedy.

Associated Press

Sirhan Bishara Sirhan

Articulate Police Chief

Thomas Reddin

THOMAS REDDIN, the police chief of Los Angeles, looks a bit like Hubert Humphrey and is as articulate as most politicians. The 6-foot-4-inch policeman, whose calm, measured words were the nation's main link with the facts yesterday as the shooting of Senator Kennedy unfolded, was born in New York City 51 years ago and grew up in Denver. He ran a gas station and served four years as a seaman in the Navy before becoming a policeman in Los Angeles in 1941.

Man in the News

While working his way up on the Los Angeles force, he studied law at Los Angeles universities and represents what might be called the "new breed of cop" in urban America. One of his first moves, he said when he became chief last year, would be to reorganize the department so that it could apply current scientific and technological knowledge to police work.

Chief Reddin, a beaming, 210-pound giant of a man, moved into one of the world's toughest law-enforcement jobs after the death last July of William H. Parker, the 64-year-old police chief whose policy of holding his men at a distance from Los Angeles's blacks was blamed for precipitating the race riots in Watts in 1965.

Not Easy Flappable

As he demonstrated for a nationwide audience while he was being questioned by newsmen after the assassination attempt, Chief Reddin is not easily flappable. A round-faced man with dark eyes, he breaks into a wide, thin smile every few minutes, under normal circumstances. Even while replying to confused questions about the shooting, he did not lose his composure.

The chief, the son of a New York millionaire who lost his fortune while drilling for oil in Oklahoma, was forced to drop out of the University of Colorado during the Depression, in 1933.

He married the former Betty Jane Parson, a Denver girl, 30 years ago, and they have three children—2 sons, 29 and 25, and a daughter, 24.

Charges of police brutality and highhandedness have not been eliminated in Los Angeles under the Reddin regime. Last September the American Civil Liberties Union filed a suit against the department charging that the police deprived antiwar demonstrators of their constitutional rights during President Johnson's visit to the city in June, 1967. Beating of several demonstrators "with billy clubs" was also alleged.

Last July, 100 of Chief Reddin's men stormed a Black Muslim mosque to search for a reported arsenal. They did not find one, and the chief joined Mayor Samuel W. Yorty at a news conference during which they admitted, "We were misled. We made a mistake."

However, Chief Reddin's tack has generally been conciliatory. Although he proclaims that "crime in the streets" is his first priority, he has called for improved relations with slum dwellers, whom he refers to as "our first defense against riots." At the same time, keeping an eye on all contingencies, he can express interest in buying for the force a 20-ton armored vehicle costing $35,000. Designed as a barricade crusher, it carries 20 men.

Because of its sprawling vastness, Los Angeles presents special problems, and Chief Reddin's $28,000-a-year job is regarded as one of the most difficult in the nation. New York, with three times as many people as Los Angeles, last year had five times as many policemen. As a result, almost all patrols in Los Angeles are made in prowl cars, which not only cuts down the efficiency of the police but severely limits the policeman's opportunity to know the people under his protection.

The police in Los Angeles, however, have the highest pay scale in the nation, starting at $641 a month, compared with New York's $586. But the pay scale has proved inadequate to lure enough good men into the force, and Chief Reddin began pushing for across-the-board increases and overtime pay as soon as he took charge. He deplores what he calls the poor image that policemen have in the United States.

"Actually, it's exciting, stimulating, gratifying, well-paid work, and we've got to get this across. We've got to change our own attitudes," said the man with 27 years of police experience.

Associated Press

Not easily flappable
(Chief Reddin yesterday)

Risk, Kennedy Said, Is 'Part of Man's Life'

During "The Next President," a political special seen last Sunday night on Channel 5, Senator Kennedy was asked by David Frost, the moderator, if he enjoyed "physical risk."

Mr. Kennedy replied that it was "part of a man's life."

He recalled a quotation from an Edith Hamilton essay on Aeschylus: "Men are not made for safe havens."

Johnson Names a Panel on Violence and Orders a Guard for Presidential Candidates

HE VOICES HORROR ON THE SHOOTING

Pleads, in Television Talk, for 'End to Violence and Preaching of Violence'

Continued From Page 1, Col. 3

solve," he said, "to live under the law! Let us put an end to violence and to the preaching of violence."

He paid high tribute to Senator Kennedy, whose policies and tactics he has often criticized, commenting on the brutal interruption of a "brilliant career" and citing the New York Democrat's energy, dedication and voice that "touched millions."

The President said he prayed to God that Mr. Kennedy's life would be spared and that he would be restored to full health and vigor, both for his own sake and for the nation's and for the sake of his family, which Mr. Johnson said had suffered "sorrow enough."

The entire nation is not to blame, Mr. Johnson said, because 200 million Americans did not strike down Senator Kennedy any more than they did the slain President Kennedy or the Rev. Dr. Martin Luther King Jr., who was assassinated last April 4.

Yet, the President said, it is "wrong to ignore" the connection between such crimes and the general climate of lawlessness, hatred and unreason in the country, of which the nation has now had "ample warning."

A nation that tolerates violence in any form, Mr. Johnson said, cannot expect to confine it to relatively minor incidents.

There was "never any justification for violence," Mr. Johnson continued as he pleaded for "moderation with our tongues" and for an end to hostility in the hearts of the people.

Just as after the slaying of President Kennedy in Dallas in 1963, which made Mr. Johnson President, Mr. Johnson reacted to the shooting in Los Angeles swiftly to add to the protection of the fabric of Government and to offer support to the victim's family and staff.

But there was also a sense of helplessness at the White House as violence and hatred, which Mr. Johnson has bemoaned frequently, once again marred the reputation of the country and his years as its leader. On March 31 he had blamed divisions in the country for inspiring his own withdrawal from politics.

Senator Kennedy's entry into the Presidential race also had something to do with that decision. Yet the bitterness and policy differences that had hurt relations between the President and the Senator were wholly forgotten at the White House when Mr. Johnson was roused from sleep at 3:31 A.M. today, 16 minutes after the first news bulletins of the shooting reached the situation room in the executive offices.

Watch officers in the basement communications cente called the Justice Departmen and Secret Service to obtain confirmation and, as in the case of a foreign crisis, called the home of Walt W. Rostow, special assistant to the Presiden for national security.

When he had some details Mr. Rostow called the President, who in turn awakened Mrs. Johnson. The President flicked on a triple-screen color television console and began what was to be eight hours of telephoning and planning from his second-floor bedroom.

Before dawn Mr. Rostow called back with a longer report, and Mr. Johnson called Attorney General Ramsey Clark to ask whether the President had any legal authority to order prompt protection for political candidates. He had none, he was told.

The Secret Service and Mr. Johnson himself had long ago sensed the danger to the President during trips through a divided country. In March Mr. Johnson began to tell members of Congress of his concern about other political figures, specifically the Presidential candidates. Congressional hearings were arranged three weeks ago, with Secret Service testimony, to see what protection might be offered. A bill was said to be in preparation.

The matter was kept secret, to avoid any public suggestion that leading political figures were moving about defenseless.

This morning Mr. Johnson decided on his own authority that he would no longer wait for legislative action.

He ordered James J. Rowley, head of the Secret Service, to offer protective details to the six candidates for President and members of their immediate families.

Within four hours, all but former Gov. George C. Wallace of Alabama had been reached, and by noon the details were said to be attached to all six.

The candidates, in addition to Senator Kennedy and Mr. Wallace, candidate of the American Independent party, are Senator Eugene J. McCarthy of Minnesota, Democrat, and Governor Rockefeller of New York, Richard M. Nixon and Harold E. Stassen, Republicans.

Mr. Johnson then again called Attorney General Clark, as well as the F.B.I. director, J. Edgar Hoover, and Defense Secretary Clark M. Clifford, urging them to give the Secret Service all possible logistical support and manpower if needed.

The President was in touch with his press secretary, George Christian, and conferred again with Mr. Roley, and he enlisted Congressional support for legislative authority by calling Senator A. S. Mike Monroney, Democrat of Oklahoma, who was handling the Secret Service question on behalf of the Appropriations Committee.

Eventually, Mr. Johnson's efforts to reach the Kennedy party in Los Angeles brought him into touch with Theodore C. Sorensen, who had served as an aide to President Kennedy and then to Mr. Johnson; Senator Edward M. Kennedy, the victim's brother, and Stephen Smith, a brother-in-law. The President asked that his prayers and good wishes be conveyed to the family and that all requests for help be rushed to him.

Simultaneously, White House aides offered assistance to Senator Kennedy's Washington staff.

Protection Accepted

By FELIX BELAIR Jr.
Special to The New York Times

WASHINGTON, June 5—President Johnson placed six announced Presidential candidates and their immediate families today under the full-time protection of Federal law enforcement agencies.

While there appeared to be no intention of inflicting protection on candidates unwilling to have it, all of the avowed candidates had accepted it at the time of the White House announcement, at least for the immediate future.

The possibility that some candidates might later find that the security screen cramped their campaigning styles and might dispense with it is anticipated in the new authorizing legislation that was approved by the Senate Appropriations group soon after the White House announcement.

Figures on the number of agents assigned to each of the candidates was a closely held secret. But observers suggested that an eight-man detail working in eight-hour shifts would not be excessive.

Minutes after the Presidential order, Secret Service agents began to take up positions in hotel corridors and, with the local uniformed and plainclothes police, cordoned off areas where candidates were quarted.

Other details were rushed from Secret Service field offices to state capitals or outlying areas, wherever candidates were housed for the night.

Only after ordering these emergency precautions did the President take the steps necessary to make his action legal. The Secret Service has no legal authority to protect any persons except the President and Vice President and their families, or former Presidents, their widows and families on request.

The Senate Democratic leader, Mike Mansfield of Montana, met with the President at 7:15 A.M. The President also talked by telephone with the Senate Republican leader, Everett McKinley Dirksen of Illinois; Senator A. S. Mike Monroney, Democrat of Oklahoma, and Representative Tom Steed, Democrat of Oklahoma.

The Oklahomans were there as chairmen of the Senate and House Appropriations subcommittees that handle funds for the Secret Service and other Treasury agencies.

A few hours after the White House meeting, the full Senate Appropriations Committee approved $2-million more for the Secret Service.

Senators Mansfield and Monroney predicted quick Senate passage of the total appropriation tomorrow. The House is expected to vote its approval and send the measure to the White House before the end of the week.

United Press International

RETURNS TO WASHINGTON: Vice President Humphrey boarding a plane in Colorado Springs, where he had been scheduled to speak at the Air Force Academy. He canceled the speech after learning of shooting of Senator Kennedy.

Associated Press

AT THE HOSPITAL: Senator Eugene J. McCarthy, who was defeated by Senator Kennedy in the California primary, leaves Good Samaritan Hospital after a brief visit. Senator Kennedy was in the intensive care unit at the hospital.

Candidates Halt Drives; Voice Shock and Sympathy

By ROY REED
Special to The New York Times

WASHINGTON, June 5—The major Presidential candidates of both parties canceled their campaign activity today after the shooting of Senator Robert F. Kennedy.

Thus, for the second time in two months, the United States' efforts to select a new President were interrupted by an assassin. In the days after April 4, the candidates paused to mourn the slaying of the Rev. Dr. Martin Luther King Jr., who was shot in Memphis.

Today, Senator Eugene J. McCarthy, who lost to Senator Kennedy in the California Democratic primary yesterday, suspended political activity and announced that he would return to Washington to begin a "vigil" for his fallen rival.

"All of us must keep vigil with the nation in prayer and hope that Senator Kennedy will recover," Mr. McCarthy said in Beverly Hills.

'Burden of Guilt'

"It is not enough, in my judgment, to say that this is the act of one deranged man, if that is the case," he said. "The nation, I think, bears too great a burden of guilt, really, for the kind of neglect which has allowed disposition of violence to grow here in our land."

Mr. McCarthy called this violence a "reflection of violence which we have visited upon the rest of the world, or at least on a part of the world."

He said he intended to talk with Senator Kennedy's spokesmen and with President Johnson and Vice President Humphrey before resuming any political activity.

Vice President Humphrey was in Colorado Springs when Senator Kennedy was shot. He had been in bed 10 minutes when an aide woke him with the news.

He spent most of the remainder of the night watching television and talking with members of his own and Senator Kennedy's staff.

Then he canceled an address here at the Air Force Academy commencement and returned to Washington.

He canceled a series of political meetings scheduled for today and tomorrow in Albuquerque, N. M., Cincinnati, Buffalo and Rochester.

Richard M. Nixon and Governor Rockefeller, the Republican candidates, canceled all campaign activity until further notice.

Mr. Nixon remained in his New York apartment and ordered his New York and Washington campaign offices to close.

The former Vice President called off a background briefing session with newsmen that had been scheduled for 11 A.M. today at his apartment. He also canceled a speech to the Michigan Republican delegation Friday.

Rockefeller Informed

Mr. Rockefeller arrived here from Portland, Ore., last night. He was spending the night in his home on Foxhall Road when Leslie Slote, his press secretary, woke him as 3:30 A.M. and told him of the shooting.

The New York Governor immediately canceled plans for a breakfast with Republican Congressional leaders, a speech before the National Press Club and all campaigning "until further notice."

Mr. Rockefeller spoke this morning with President Johnson, with Theodore C. Sorensen, a Kennedy adviser, and others. At 10:30 A.M. he flew to Albany, where he spent the afternoon signing bills and handling other state matters.

At Albany he issued this statement:

"The attack on Senator Robert Kennedy is shocking and shameful. All Americans of goodwill are stunned and appalled. What strikes any one of us strikes all of us. We are all gravely wounded.

"I am filled with sorrow for the Senator and his family, and this sorrow extends to all our nation. For such an assault on one man is an assault on our whole national life.

"Our prayers are with the Senator for his full recovery and his continued service to our country."

Mr. McCarthy, in his first public appearance after the shooting, said in Los Angeles: "We've got to give more rational attention, rational control to the problems of America. We proceed as though we were still a pioneer country. We're not. We've become a rather complicated, sophisticated civilization."

He went to Good Samaritan Hospital in Los Angeles shortly before noon. He was met in the lobby by Pierre Salinger, one of Mr. Kennedy's press aides. He stayed about 20 minutes and did not talk to newsmen on entering or leaving.

In Washington, after the Vice President's return, a Humphrey aide said that "all" campaign activity, including the behind-the-scenes work of rounding up delegates to the Democratic National Convention, had come to a standstill.

Mr. Humphrey appeared to be badly shaken by the Kennedy shooting. He had recently spoken a number of times in private of his personally cordial relationship with the Kennedy family.

He issued a statement about an hour after the shooting, calling it "a shocking and terrible thing."

When he decided against speaking at the commencement, he drafted a message to the graduates to be read by Air Force Secretary Harold Brown. It said, in part:

"Our sorrow is for the man and for his family, which has already known too much tragedy. Our grief is that this dreadful act should follow on other dreadful acts of violence which have taken place in the recent history of this country.

"We cannot explain. We can only determine as a free people that such madness shall not reoccur."

Mr. Nixon, who had been awakened by his daughter Julie with news of the shooting, said he was "shocked and appalled."

"My deepest sympathies go to the Senator's family, which already has known more than its share of tragedy," he said.

Wallace Calls Off Trip

MONTGOMERY, Ala., June 5 (AP)—Former Gov. George C. Wallace called off a Presidential campaign trip into New England and Maryland today because of the shooting of Senator Kennedy.

Experts Link Attack on Kennedy To a Strain of Violence in U.S.

By MARTIN ARNOLD

A strain of violence in the American psychological makeup, going back even earlier than frontier days, was suggested yesterday by some experts as the cause of increased crime, rioting in the streets and acts of individual violence such as the shooting of Senator Robert F. Kennedy.

Dr. David Abrahamsen, a psychiatrist and a governor of the Lemberg Center for the Study of Violence at Brandeis University, Waltham, Mass., said here that Americans condone violence.

"We love it," he said. "We love to fight. The frontier days made the gun maniy.

"We feel we can have anything we want. We have a unique society — so affluent. No other society has such buried frustrations," Dr. Abrahamsen said. "In France, they can riot for three weeks and only two people are killed. Can you imagine how many would have been killed here?

New Era of Violence

"President Kennedy's assassination just started a new era of violence, but we've always had violence in our blood," he said. This comes in part, he said from the fact that Americans are seduced by "our rich physical environment" into thinking "that we can have what we want."

"The frustration and the violence comes when we find we cannot," he added.

At Brandeis, Dr. John P. Spiegel, director of the Lemberg Center and a professor of social psychiatry, took a somewhat different view.

He said that he believed the intensity of collective violence — riots, for example — was lower in the United States than in other countries, but that in cases of individual violence "the chances are that we are high."

'Addiction to Guns'

"The population as a whole is conditioned to expect violence," Dr. Spiegel said. "Behind this is America's gun fetish and the notion that a gun can be used to solve conflict. There is an emotional addiction, as strong as any other addiction, such as drugs, to guns."

He said, for example, that children often have toy guns among their first playthings. "They see violence produced through the [news] media and movies."

The war in Vietnam also contributes to acts of violence, he said. "We know from historical studies that acts of violence increase in time of war. When the war ends, we can pay more attention to the underlying social problems. With the war on, violence is accepted and causes an additional social stress."

Dr. Abrahamsen and Dr. Spiegel agreed that in our society not only the minority groups, such as the Negroes, but other, older immigrant groups had not been able to become integrated.

"We're not a melting pot," Dr. Abrahamsen said. "We're a damned pressure cooker. Our society is not built on the restraints of family or class; it's built on success. If you don't have it you're frustrated. Frustration. The wet nurse of violence."

Dr. Abrahamsen believes that "public figures are symbols of what America stands for," and because they are "authority figures, as such, they have to be killed by those who feel frustrated by authority."

Dr. Thaddeus Kostrubala of Chicago, a member of the American Psychiatric Association's Task Force on Aggression and Violence, also sees violence as part of our national origin, commonplace not only on the frontier of the Old West, but also among the immigrants from Europe. "Every TV western has its murder," he said.

Dr. Kenneth Kenniston, psychologist at Yale Medical Center, commented on the question whether an individual act of violence could be attributed to society.

Violence Highly Publicized

"I've spent my whole life thinking about this," he said, "but I still don't know the answer. My view is that we do live in an era of highly publicized violence. The basic impulse to violence does not originate in the media, but given an individual with that impulse, the widespread publicity provides a channel through which psychotic impulses are expressed."

Regarding the complex question of tolerance to deviant behavior in general, Dr. Kenniston said that he saw no evidence that "we are more tolerant of psychotic deviant behavior" now than we were a decade or two ago. I think they tend to get picked up earlier now," he said.

However, at Bellevue Hospital a psychiatrist, who did not wish to be identified, said that society today "has some greater tolerance to deviant behavior."

"The recent behavior of the students at Columbia is an example," he said. "The tolerance by the Columbia administration would not have been the same 10 or 15 or 30 years ago."

GUN CONTROL BILL SPEEDED BY HOUSE

Passage Scheduled Today for Anticrime Measure

By JOHN W. FINNEY
Special to The New York Times

WASHINGTON, June 5—The House, spurred by the shooting of Senator Robert F. Kennedy, moved quickly today toward adoption of broad anticrime legislation, including controls over interstate sales of handguns.

By a 317-to-60 vote, the House rejected a move to send the crime control legislation, passed last month by the Senate, to a Senate-House conference. The vote cleared the way for the House to accept the Senate version tomorrow and send the legislation to the White House.

In lonely opposition, Representative Emanuel Celler, Brooklyn Democrat, who is chairman of the House Judiciary Committee, vainly protested before a hushed but emoional House that the Senate bill was a "cruel hoax" and "bursting at the seams with unconstitutional provisions."

But in the hour-long debate it became evident that for the majority of the House the Kennedy shooting was but the final confirmation that legislative steps should be taken to curb violence.

'No Further Quibbling'

"Surely there can be no further quibbling about the urgent need for tougher law enforcement legislation," the House Republican leader, Gerald R. Ford of Michigan, observed at one point in a statement that seemed to reflect the mood of the House.

The House last year passed the Administration's crime control bill providing for Federal grants to states and local communities to improve and strengthen law enforcement agencies. But to the House bill the Senate added three controversial provisions not considered by the House and opposed to some degree by the Administration.

One of the Senate provisions would overturn recent Supreme Court decisions establishing the constitutional rights of criminal suspects. A second would authorize court-supervised wiretapping and electronic eavesdropping against a broad variety of crimes. The third would restrict interstate sales of handguns.

A staff member of the Senate Juvenile Delinquency subcommittee said the .22-caliber Iver Johnson revolver, identified by the Los Angeles police as the one used in the shooting, was a "pot metal" weapon particularly made for the cut-rate mail order trade.

The gun is made by Iver Johnson's Arms and Cycle Works, Inc., of Fitchburg, Mass., a wholesale gun manufacturer. The weapon, according to the subcommittee aide, costs $15 to $18 when sold retail through the mail.

Senator Kennedy had supported the Senate gun control provision, although, like the Administration, he had contended it should go further and include rifles and shotguns. In his position, he ran into heckling opposition in his campaigning through the Pacific Northwest, the center of much of the opposition to gun control legislation.

Kennedy Asked Local Law

In testimony before the New York City Council on Aug. 25, 1967, Senator Kennedy made an urgent plea for the passage of legislation to curb gun violence.

The Senator said:

"With the passage of these bills and the enactment of Federal legislation we will begin to meet our responsibilities. If we act now we can save hundreds of lives in this country and spare thousands of families all across this land the grief and the heartbreak that may come from the loss of a husband, a son, a brother or a friend.

"It is past time that we wipe the stain of violence from this land."

ATTACK ON KENNEDY LEADS TO TV SHIFTS

The American Broadcasting Company made two changes in its programming last ngiht, because it was felt that the original choices would have been in questionable taste, following the shooting of Senator Robert F. Kennedy.

The network ordered a switch in the story line of its British-produced adventure series, "The Avengers," and postponed a rebroadcast of "Laura," the mystery drama starring Princess Stanislas Radziwill, sister of Mrs. John F. Kennedy.

The drama scheduled for last night's "The Avengers" was titled "You Have Just Been Murdered." A less gory episode "Dead Man's Treasure," was substituted.

"Laura" was replaced by "To Catch a Thief," a film starring Cary Grant and Grace Kelly.

The Columbia Broadcasting System and the National Broadcasting Company said they had not felt called upon to change any programs.

Sammy Davis, in London, Stops Show to Ask Prayers

Special to The New York Times

LONDON, June 5 — Sammy Davis Jr., a friend of Senator Robert F. Kennedy, stopped in the middle of his performance in "Golden Boy" here tonight and told the audience he could not continue.

Mr. Davis asked the audience to pray for the recovery of the Senator, who was shot in Los Angeles early today, because he was the "only man who can bridge the gulf between black and white in America."

The start of the show had already been delayed by 20 minutes because of doubts by Mr. Davis and his co-star, Gloria de Haven, whether they could go on. Mr. Davis decided to try and perform until the intermission. Miss de Haven, who said "I just fell apart," sat in the audience from the start, leaving her role to her understudy, Marilyne Mason.

Transcript of Johnson Speech Naming Panel on U.S. Violence

Following is the transcript of President Johnson's speech last night to a national television-radio audience on the shooting of Senator Robert F. Kennedy, as recorded by The New York Times.

My fellow citizens, I speak to you this evening not only as your President, but as a fellow American that's shocked and dismayed as you are by the attempt on Senator Kennedy's life, deeply disturbed, as I know you are, by lawlessness and violence in our country, of which this tragedy is the latest spectacular example.

We do not know the reasons that inspired the attack on Senator Kennedy. We know only that a brilliant career of public service has been brutally interrupted, that a young leader of uncommon energy and dedication who has served his country tirelessly and well and whose voice and example has touched millions throughout the entire world has been senselessly and horribly stricken.

At this moment the outcome is still in the balance. We pray to God that he will spare Robert Kennedy and will restore him to full health and vigor. We pray this for the nation's sake, for the sake of his wife and his children, his father and his mother, and in memory of his brother, our beloved late President.

The Kennedy family has endured sorrow enough and we pray that this family may be spared more anguish.

Lawlessness Cited

Tonight, this nation faces once again the consequences of lawlessness, hatred and unreason in its midst. It would be wrong, it would be self-deceptive, to ignore the connection between lawlessness and hatred and this act of violence.

It would be just as wrong and just as self-deceptive to conclude from this act that our country itself is sick, that it's lost its balance, that it's lost its sense of direction, even its common decency.

Two hundred million Americans did not strike down Robert Kennedy last night, any more than they struck down President John F. Kennedy in 1963, or Dr. Martin Luther King in April of this year.

But those awful events give us ample warning that in a climate of extremism, of disrespect for law, of contempt for the rights of others, violence may bring down the very best among us. And a nation that tolerates violence any form cannot expect to be able to confine it to just minor outbursts.

My fellow citizens, we cannot, we just must not, tolerate the sway of violent men among us. We must not permit men that are filled with hatred and carelessness—and careless of innocent lives to dominate our streets and fill our homes with fear.

Violence Assailed

We cannot sanction the appeal to violence—no matter what its cause, no matter what the grievance from which it brings.

There is never—and I say never—any justification for the violence that tears at the fabric of our national life; that inspires such fear in peaceful citizens that they arm themselves with deadly weapons; that sets citizen against citizen, or group against group.

A great nation can guarantee freedom for its people and the hope of progressive change only under the rule of law.

So let us, for God's sake, resolve to live under the law!

Let us put an end to violence and to the preaching of violence.

Let the Congress pass laws to bring the insane traffic in guns to a halt as I have appealed to them time and time again to do. That will not in itself end the violence, but reason and experience tell us that it will slow it down, that it will spare many innocent lives.

Let us purge the hostility from our hearts, and let us practice moderation with our tongues.

Let us begin in the aftermath of this great tragedy to find a way to reverance life, to protect it, to extend its promise to all of our people, this nation and the people who have suffered grievously from violence and assassination.

For this reason I am appointing with the recommendation of the leadership of the Congress with whom I have talked this evening—a commission of most distinguished Americans to immediately examine this tragic phenomenon.

Commission Named

They are Dr. Milton Eisenhower, the former distinguished president of Johns Hopkins University; Archbishop Terence Cooke of New York; Albert Jenner of Illinois; Ambassador Patrick Harris; Mr. Eric Hoffer; Senator Philip Hart; Senator Roman Hruska; Congressman Hale Boggs; Congressman William McCullough and Judge Leon Higginbotham.

The commission will look into the causes, the occurrence and the control of physical violence across this nation, from assassination that is motivated by prejudice and by ideology, and by politics and by insanity; to violence in our city streets and even in our homes.

What in the nature of our people and the environment of our society makes possible such murder and such violence?

How does it happen? What can be done to prevent assassination? What can be done to further protect public figures? What can be done to eliminate the basic causes of these aberrations?

Supported by the suggestions and recommendations of criminologists, sociologists and psychologists, all of our nation's medical and social sciences, we hope to learn why we inflict such suffering on ourselves.

And I hope and pray that we can learn how to stop it.

This is a sober time for our great democracy, but we are a strong and we are a resilient people who can, I hope, learn from our misfortunes, who can heal our wounds, who can build and find progress in public order.

We can. We must. So I appeal to every American citizen tonight — let us begin tonight.

TROOPS ACROSS U.S. ARE PUT ON ALERT

Special to The New York Times

WASHINGTON, June 5 — Several thousand Army and Marine troops across the nation were placed on shortened alert early this morning should the shooting of Senator Robert F. Kennedy result in rioting that could not be handled by local and state authorities.

Pentagon sources said that the response time of some units had been cut in half.

In addition, the Air Force placed some troop transports on stand-by and checked the schedules of scores of other planes in case a large-scale airlift became necessary.

Officials were particularly watching Los Angeles, where the shooting occurred, and Washington, where thousands of people taking part in the Poor People's March were thought to be in an unpredictable mood.

In the capital, Mayor Walter Washington canceled all leave and days off for District of Columbia policemen for 24 hours and extended tours of duty for . 3,100-man police force.

"All the News That's Fit to Print"

The New York Times

LATE CITY EDITION

Weather: Sunny, warm today; fair, seasonable tonight and tomorrow. Temp. range: today 89-73; Tuesday 91-72. Temp.-Hum. Index yesterday 81. Complete U.S. report on Page 90.

VOL. CXVII No. 40,387 NEW YORK, WEDNESDAY, AUGUST 21, 1968 10 CENTS

CZECHOSLOVAKIA INVADED BY RUSSIANS AND FOUR OTHER WARSAW PACT FORCES; THEY OPEN FIRE ON CROWDS IN PRAGUE

13 INDICTED HERE IN RIGGING OF BIDS ON UTILITY WORK

Contracts Worth 49-Million Involved—14 Construction Companies Also Named

By MARTIN TOLCHIN

Fourteen major construction companies, 12 top corporate executives and one employe were indicted here yesterday on charges of rigging bids on utilities contracts totaling $49.8-million.

The defendants were accused of deciding among themselves who would be low bidder in the contracts with Consolidated Edison, the Brooklyn Union Gas Company, and the Empire City Subway Company—the latter a subsidiary of the New York Telephone Company.

The indictments charge that the defendants then accommodated the selected low bidder by submitting higher bids.

The companies included such important contractors as Lipsett, Inc., a leading demolition company that razed Pennsylvania Station, the Savoy Plaza Hotel and the Third Avenue El; the Slattery Contracting Company, which held the general contract for excavating the site of United Nations Headquarters and built subway spurs and the Lincoln Center reflecting pool, and the Thomas Crimmins Contracting Company, which did the excavation for numerous skyscrapers.

1959 Activities Covered

The companies received contracts to dig trenches for electrical conduits and gas mains and for paving work. The contracts totaled $49,788,165.

The four indictments, with a total of 28 counts, were an outgrowth of the investigation of James L. Marcus, former City Water Commissioner, who pleaded guilty in Federal court to receiving a $40,000 kickback on a city reservoir cleaning contract.

"Our interest in Marcus and [Herbert] Itkin led us to the inquiry that led to these indictments," Frank S. Hogan, New York County District Attorney, said.

He noted that the indictments alleged activities that began in 1959, "before the community at large was aware of Marcus and Itkin," and

Continued on Page 35, Column 3

Democrats Debate Position on the War in Vietnam

The New York Times

Secretary of State Rusk defended the Administration's policies at the hearing.

Associated Press

Senator George S. McGovern of South Dakota was critical of the Administration.

The New York Times (by George Tames)

Kenneth P. O'Donnell, left, who was an aide to President Kennedy, talks with Senator J. W. Fulbright, standing right, at the platform hearing. The Senator spoke against the war.

SOVIET EXPLAINS

Says Its Troops Moved at the Request of Czechoslovaks

By RAYMOND H. ANDERSON

Special to The New York Times

MOSCOW, Wednesday, Aug. 21 — Moscow announced this morning that troops from the Soviet Union and four other Communist countries had invaded Czechoslovakia at the request of the "party and Government leaders of the Czechoslovak Socialist Republic."

The announcement followed unofficial information here that Alexander Dubcek, the reform leader of the Czechoslovak party Presidium, had been overthrown.

In a statement authorized by the Soviet Government, the official press agency, Tass, declared at 7:30 A.M. Moscow time (12:30 A.M., New York time) that Czechoslovakia had come under a threat from "counterrevolutionary forces" involved in a collusion with foreign forces hostile to socialism.

Friendship Stressed

Tass said that troops from Bulgaria, East Germany, Hungary, Poland and the Soviet Union, acting from motivations of "inseverable friendship and cooperation," entered Czechoslovakia early this morning.

The troops will be withdrawn as soon as the threat to Czechoslovakia and neighboring Communist countries has been eliminated, according to Tass.

"The actions that are being taken are not directed against any state and in no measure infringe state interests of anybody," the statement said. "They serve the purpose of peace and have been prompted by concern for its consolidation."

"The fraternal countries firmly and resolutely counterpose their unbreakable solidarity to any threat from outside," the Soviet explanation continued. "Nobody will ever be allowed to wrest a single link from the community of Socialist states."

Polemics Resumed

The handwriting was on the wall for the Czechoslovak reform regime last Friday when the Soviet press abruptly resumed its bitter polemics against the country.

Czechoslovakia's seven-month-old experiment with democracy under Communist rule was explicitly doomed yesterday when the Soviet Communist party warned in an editorial that imperial intrigues must be "nipped in the bud."

Rumors swept Moscow yesterday that the Soviet party's Central Committee had met in secret session, presumably to endorse intervention. Official sources insisted, however, that

Continued on Page 14, Column 6

FIVE-POWER INVASION: Soviet planes carried troops into Prague (cross). Ground forces of bloc crossed Czechoslovak borders that are indicated by heavy line.

TANKS ENTER CITY

Deaths Are Reported —Troops Surround Offices of Party

By TAD SZULC

Special to The New York Times

PRAGUE, Wednesday, Aug. 21—Czechoslovakia was occupied early today by troops of the Soviet Union and four of its Warsaw Pact allies in a series of swift land and air movements.

Airborne Soviet troops and paratroopers surrounded the building of the Communist party Central Committee, along with five tanks. At least 25 tanks were seen in the city.

Several persons were reported killed early this morning. Unconfirmed reports said that two Czechoslovak soldiers and a woman were killed by Bulgarian tank fire in front of the Prague radio building shortly before the station was captured and went off the air.

[Soviet troops began shooting at Czechoslovak demonstrators outside the Prague radio building at 7:25 A.M., Reuters reported. C.T.K., the Czechoslovak press agency, was quoted by United Press International as having said that citizens were throwing themselves in front of the tanks in an attempt to block the seizure of the city.]

Move a Surprise

The Soviet move caught Czechoslovaks by surprise, although all day yesterday there were indications of new tensions.

Confusion was caused in the capital by leaflets dropped from unidentified aircraft asserting that Antonin Novotny, the President of Czechoslovakia who was deposed in March by the Communist liberals, had been pushed out by a "clique." The leaflets said that Mr. Novotny remained the country's legal President.

At 5 A.M. the Prague radio, still in the hands of adherents of the Communist liberals, broadcast a dramatic appeal to the population in the name of Alexander Dubcek, the party

Continued on Page 14, Column 1

Versions of the Two Sides

Following are the texts of the Prague radio announcement of the Soviet-bloc invasion of Czechoslovakia, as monitored in Washington, and of a Soviet statement distributed in New York by Tass, the Soviet press agency.

Czechoslovak Radio Broadcast

To the entire people of the Czechoslovak Socialist Republic: Yesterday, on 20 August, around 2300 [11 P.M.], troops of the Soviet Union, Polish People's Republic, the G.D.R. [East Germany], the Hungarian People's Republic and the Bulgarian People's Republic crossed the frontiers of the Czechoslovak Socialist Republic.

This happened without the knowledge of the President of the Republic, the Chairman of the National Assembly, the Premier, or the First Secretary of the Czechoslovak Communist party Central Committee.

In the evening hours the Presidium of the Czechoslovak Communist party Central Committee [had] held a session and discussed preparations for the 14th Czechoslovak Communist party congress.

The Czechoslovak Communist party Central Committee Presidium appeals to all citizens of our republic to maintain calm and not to offer resistance to the troops on the march. Our army, security corps and people's militia have not received the command to defend the country.

The Czechoslovak Communist party Central Committee Presidium regard this act as contrary not only to the fundamental principles of relations between Socialist states but also as contrary to the principles of international law.

All leading functionaries of the state, the Communist party and the National Front: Remain in your functions as representatives of the state, elected to the laws of the Czechoslovak Socialist Republic.

Constitutional functionaries are immediately convening a session of the National Assembly of our republic, and the Presidium is at the same time convening a plenum of the Central Committee to discuss the situation that has arisen.

PRESIDIUM OF THE CZECHOSLOVAK COMMUNIST PARTY CENTRAL COMMITTEE.

Announcement by Moscow

Tass is authorized to state that party and Government leaders of the Czechoslovak Socialist Republic have asked the Soviet Union and other allied states to render the fraternal Czechoslovak people urgent assistance, including assistance with armed forces. This request was brought about by the threat which has arisen to the Socialist system existing in Czechoslovakia and to the statehood established by the Con-

Continued on Page 14, Column 2

NIXON INCREASES GALLUP POLL LEAD

Tops Humphrey, 45% to 29, and Maintains His Margin Over McCarthy, 42 to 37

Special to The New York Times

PRINCETON, N. J., Aug. 20—Richard M. Nixon stretched a slim mid-July edge over Vice President Humphrey to a 45-to-29 per cent lead in voter preference immediately following the Republican National Convention, according to the latest Gallup Poll.

Against Senator Eugene J. McCarthy—Mr. Humphrey's chief rival for the Democratic Presidential nomination—Mr. Nixon held a 42-to-37 per cent lead, almost the same margin he had in the previous test in mid-July.

Mr. Nixon's improved advantage over the Vice President was caused more by Mr. Humphrey's losses than by gains by Mr. Nixon. The Republican nominee was 5 percentage points higher than the pre-convention survey, while Mr. Humphrey was 9 points lower.

Support for the independent candidacy of George A. Wallace of Alabama held up. He polled 18 per cent in the Nixon-Humphrey-Wallace test and 16 per cent in the Nixon-McCarthy-Wallace post-convention survey.

In interviewing between Aug. 8 and 11, the following question was asked of a representative sample of 1,526 adults in over 320 localities:

"Suppose the Presidential election were being held today. If Hubert Humphrey were the Democratic candidate, running against Richard Nixon, the Republican candidate, and George Wallace of Alabama were the candidate of a third party, which would you like to see

Continued on Page 34, Column 2

Guard Is Called Up To Protect Chicago During Convention

By DONALD JANSON

Special to The New York Times

CHICAGO, Aug. 20—Gov. Samuel H. Shapiro called up the National Guard today to keep order in the city during the Democratic National Convention.

At the request of Mayor Richard J. Daley, the Governor ordered 5,649 Illinois National Guardsmen to round-the-clock duty in Chicago beginning Friday to head off threats of "tumult, riot or mob disorder."

Meanwhile, an Army spokesman in Washington confirmed in a telephone interview that about 6,000 regular Army troops received rigorous riot-control training at Fort Hood, Tex., last week as a precautionary measure.

That exercise, he said, was called Operation Jackson Park, after the park in Chicago

Continued on Page 32, Column 2

Democrats to Seat Mississippi Rebels

By MAX FRANKEL

Special to The New York Times

CHICAGO, Aug. 20—Mississippi's regular delegation to the Democratic National Convention was barred from its seats tonight by an overwhelming vote of the Credentials Committee on the ground that it had failed to meet national standards to assure the full participation of Negroes in the political process.

A biracial delegation including many members who have fought many years for this moment will be seated in place of the regulars.

At the same time, the Credentials Committee rejected by various votes the delegate

Continued on Page 32, Column 6

KENNEDY BACKERS OFFER WAR PLANK

But McCarthy Group Balks at Compromise—Rusk Is for General Statement

Text of plank and excerpts from statement, Page 33.

By JOHN W. FINNEY

Special to The New York Times

WASHINGTON, Aug. 20—Supporters of the late Senator Robert F. Kennedy circulated in the Democratic platform committee today a compromise dovish plan on Vietnam calling for a halt in the bombing of North Vietnam, a cease-fire and negotiations between the Saigon Government and the National Liberation Front, the political arm of the Vietcong.

In the bitter fight developing within the platform committee, the proposed plank is designed to provide a common front for supporters of Senator Eugene J. McCarthy, Senator George S. McGovern and Senator Kennedy.

For the moment, however, some difficulty was being encountered in winning the approval of some McCarthy partisans, who were holding out for a plank that would be more critical of the Administration.

As the doves began to mount a concerted attack on the Administration's Vietnam policy, Secretary of State Dean Rusk was called in to defend the Administration position. Mr. Rusk,

Continued on Page 33, Column 2

NEWS INDEX

13 Points in Delta Are Shelled by Foe

By JOSEPH B. TREASTER

Special to The New York Times

SAIGON, South Vietnam, Wednesday, Aug. 21 — The Vietcong shelled 13 cities and military installations in the Mekong Delta this morning, extending their latest wave of attacks into South Vietnam's southern-most region.

Seven of the shellings were followed by ground attacks.

Initial reports were sketchy, but a United States military spokesman said that allied casualties and damage in all of the attacks appeared to be light.

To the north, allied troops are making an increasing number of forays into the southern

Continued on Page 4, Column 3

OUTLOOK GUARDED FOR EISENHOWER

His Condition Still Critical Despite 'Favorable Trend'

By FELIX BELAIR Jr.

Special to The New York Times

WASHINGTON, Aug. 20 — Former President Dwight D. Eisenhower clung resolutely to life today, but with a fragile grip that his doctors acknowledged could loosen at any time.

The condition of the 77-year-old General of the Army still was listed as "critical" and the outlook for his survival as "guarded." His doctors have used this term to mean uncertain or unpredictable.

A bulletin issued at Walter Reed Army Medical Center about 11 A.M. mentioned the development of a "favorable trend" in the pattern of abnormal heart rhythm.

The episodes of rapid irregularity in the heartbeat persisted, the doctors reported, but they were isolated and did not involve the sustained fibrillating, or fluttering, reported prior to last night.

At the time of the morning

Continued on Page 13, Column 1

Soviet Turns Back Clock

By JAMES RESTON

The Soviet invasion of Czechoslovakia has transformed world and American politics.

It occurred in the middle of the American Presidential election of 1968, as the Soviet invasion of Hungary took place during the Eisenhower-Stevenson Presidential election of 1956. The Soviet Union moved on Prague while the United States was preoccupied in Vietnam, as they moved on Budapest in 1956 while the British and French were preoccupied with the invasion of Suez. The latest move by Moscow startled Washington just as officials there were convening on new moves to reach an understanding with the Soviet Union on Vietnam.

News Analysis

Washington was prepared for a dramatic move by the Soviet Union against the new liberal regime in Prague, but not for anything quite so bold as an invasion by the Red Army.

It had been observing closely the increasingly violent attacks on the Czechoslovak Government in the Soviet press, and Under Secretary of State Charles E. Bohlen, former United States Ambassador to the Soviet Union and France, had warned of the possibility of a coup d'état, followed by Soviet military intervention in Czechoslovakia. But a direct invasion at this time was discounted.

In fact, the Johnson Administration, under attack on its Vietnam policy just before the Democratic Presidential nominating convention next week in Chicago, was discussing new moves to enlist the help of the Soviet Union for a compromise in Vietnam when the Red Army moved.

The first impression of the crisis was that this Soviet intervention in Czechoslovakia, like the first one at the end of World War II, would increase

Continued on Page 15, Column 1

JOHNSON SUMMONS SECURITY COUNCIL

Calls Emergency Session After Seeing Soviet Envoy

By B. DRUMMOND AYRES JR.

Special to The New York Times

WASHINGTON, Aug. 20—President Johnson met with the National Security Council in an emergency session tonight to discuss developments in Czechoslovakia after he received a visit from the Soviet Ambassador.

The Council meeting, which was held in the Cabinet Room in the West Wing of the White House, began at 10:15 P.M. and lasted for 55 minutes.

It was followed by a 15-minute meeting at the State Department between the Soviet Ambassador, Anatoly F. Dobrynen, and Secretary of State Dean Rusk.

There was no indication after either of the meetings of what course the United States would take in the crisis which clearly came as a stunning surprise here.

During the recent weeks of tension around Czechoslovakia, the Administration has insistently maintained a hands-off attitude, arguing that any gestures of support from Washington would only complicate the Prague regime's status in the Communist camp. Any move to exploit the Soviet di-

Continued on Page 15, Column 1

Czechoslovakia Invaded by the Russians and Four Other Warsaw Pact Forces

RED TROOPS FIRE ON PRAGUE CROWD

Tanks Surround the Party Office in Capital—Radic Appeals for Calm

Continued From Page 1, Col. 8

First Secretary, to go to work as usual this morning.

The radio station said: "These may be the last reports you will hear because the technical facilities in our hands are insufficient."

The announcer said that Czechoslovaks must heed the orders of ina Presidium of the Central Committee, "which is in continuing session even though the building is surrounded by foreign units."

The radio said that it remained loyal to President Ludvik Svoboda and Mr. Dubcek.

While earlier this morning the radio appealed to the population not to resist invading troops from the Soviet Union, Poland, East Germany, Hungary and Bulgaria, small-arms fire was heard shortly after 5 A.M. in the Maala Strana district of Prague.

At 2:45 A.M., as part of this dispatch was being filed by telex, the city appeared calm, though the roar of aircraft and the broadcast, heard by many, had awakened the population.

Starting shortly after midnight veritable airlift of Soviet and other Warsaw Pact aircraft flew troops into Prague. Ruzine Airport had been secured earlier by Czechoslovak troops though it was not known under whose command they were operating.

At 5:15 A.M. aircraft were still heard landing and taking off.

Despite the Prague radio broadcasts, the whereabouts of Mr. Dubcek, Mr. Svoboda and their associates was not known.

In any event, the invasion that began at 11 o'clock last night when the Czechoslovak border was crossed from several sides evidently put an end to the Dubcek experiment in democracy under Communism that was initiated in January.

The expectation was that the occupying forces would sponsor the establishment of a new regime that would be more amenable to orthodox Communist views of Moscow and its partners.

There are about 5,000 United States citizens in Czechoslovakia at this time, of whom about 1,500 are tourists and 400 are delegates to an international geological congress.

Shirley Temple Black, the former actress, is among the Americans at the Hotel Alcron here.

The news broadcast early today said that Soviet troops had sealed all border exits to Austria. Trains were not running and airline operations were halted.

After 3 A.M., all city lights went out.

Appeal to Public

A broadcast at 1:30 A.M. had appealed to the population not to resist the advance and for officials to remain at their jobs.

Yesterday, as the tension mounted, the Czechoslovak leadership was reported to have been seriously concerned over renewed Soviet press attacks on Mr. Dubcek's liberalization program.

Last night the party Presidium met unexpectedly under Mr. Dubcek's chairmanship, presumably to discuss the new tensions.

At a confidential meeting Saturday with five progressive members of the Presidium, Czechoslovak editors were told that a successful party congress next month was the most urgent priority in the country and that, therefore, their cooperation was needed.

Internal Battle Continues

Internally, however, the political tug of war between the progressives and the conservatives continued.

Rude Pravo, the party's official organ, whose editor, Oldrich Svestka, is regarded as a leading conservative, published three articles today critical of the progressives' policies.

Another example of mounting political sensitiveness was an announcement by the Foreign Ministry, published in Rude Pravo and later distributed by the official press agency, that Henry Kamm, a correspondent of The New York Times, "will not be allowed to return to Czechoslovakia."

Mr. Kamm, who left Prague for the United States and a vacation Saturday, was charged by Rude Pravo with "slanderous information" and "fabrications" concerning its editorial staff.

Dispatches by Mr. Kamm published in The Times on Aug. 14 and 15 described a continuing struggle between Mr. Svestka and the progressive members of the staff. One dispatch said that Mr. Svestka, who is a member of the party's Presidium, had curtailed coverage of the visit here earlier this month by President Tito of Yugoslavia, who is a backer of the Dubcek faction.

The newspaped said yesterday that "the management of Rude Pravo resolutely opposes this shameless provocation, which has bocome the pretext for a slanderous press compaign against Rude Pravo abroad," and that "it is indubitable that its aim is the unconcealed effort to interfere with our internal affairs."

Mr. Svestka, however, came under attack himself in the liberal weekly Reporter, which in its current issue reported that he had played down the Tito visit. The magazine said that Mr. Svestka "has set up a sort of internal police which watches over everything that goes into print."

A Rude Pravo's counterattack yesterday included a front-page article signed by Mr. Svestka, in effect defending the conservative position. He wrote that unless the Communist party regained its "antibureaucratic" character and returned to the aims of the workers, the new "demagogic slogans" could turn against the party itself.

In an allusion to the progressives' efforts to oust conservatives from key jobs, Mr. Svestka wrote that democracy was not served "by making life miserable for the honest officials and members who have not discredited themselves, by turning them away from political activity."

A second article took to tasks a television commentator, Jiri Kanturek, for what it said were attempts to discredit Mr. Svestka.

A third article charged that a "secret committee" had been established to attack the people's militia, a paramilitary organization widely considered to be controlled by the conservatives. The article referred critically to the signing of petitions in Prague last week for the abolition of the militia.

Shooting Reported in Prague

PRAGUE, Czechoslovakia, Wednesday, Aug. 21, (Reuters)—Soviet troops began shooting at Czechoslovak demonstrators outside radio Prague building at 7:25 A.M. local time (2:25 EDT) today.

Machine gun fire broke out near the Hotel Esplanade about 800 yards from Prague radio shortly after 7:30 A.M. People in the street dived into the hotel doorway for shelter.

The machine gun fire broke out only a few hours after Russian troops and tanks invaded Czechoslovakia.

Czechs Block Tanks

PRAGUE, Wednesday, Aug. 21 (UPI)—Prague citizens are throwing themselves in front of Soviet tanks in an attempt to block the Russian seizure of their city, the Czechoslovak News Agency said today.

Special to The New York Times

VIENNA, Wednesday, Aug. 21 — The Czechoslovak news agency, which apparently has still not been occupied by the Soviet military, reported in a message at 8:30 A.M. Greenwich time that there was shooting from automatic rifles in Prague's biggest square, Vaclavski Namesti.

Later the agency reported there was also shooting from cannons in Prague.

Troop Withdrawal Demanded

BELGRADE, Yugoslavia, Wednesday, Aug. 21 (Reuters)—The Belgrade radio reported today that the Czechoslovak party Central Committee and Presidium had demanded the withdrawal of Warsaw Pact troops from Czechoslovak territory.

The Belgrade radio said that so far none of the leading representatives of the Czechoslovak party had appeared on the radio and that they were not able to do so because the radio building was surrounded by Soviet troops.

Associated Press

PRAGUE—1939: Silent Czechoslovaks watching invading German troops as they entered the city on March 15

The Crisis in Prague Recalls Anxious Days in 1930's

By RICHARD D. LYONS

"Our state is the key to the whole postwar structure of Central Europe. If it is touched either internally or internationally, the whole fabric of Central Europe is menaced, and the peace of Europe seriously infringed. It would not be long before all Europe would be grievously conscious of the fact."

These were the words of a Czechoslovak leader—but they were not uttered yesterday—they were said a generation ago in the ominous years when the freedom of the little nation also was threatened.

Eduard Benes was the speaker and the time was November, 1935, one month before Mr. Benes was to take over the presidency of the small republic, which had been carved out of Central Europe with United States help.

While the cast of countries involved in the carving up of Czechoslovakia in the late nineteen thirties was almost the same, those friendly to the Czechoslovaks then are not necessarily those today.

Hitler Gave Secret Orders

The key then was Germany, which plays a role today also. Hitler was determined to smash the Czechoslovaks for their defiance of his aims at expanding into Central Europe.

Within two years, Hitler had secretely issued orders to his military chiefs for the occupation, by force or peace treaty, of both Austria and Czechoslovakia.

After Austria's turn on March 12, 1938, the pressure was put on Czechoslovakia and President Benes ordered a partial mobilization two months later.

The crisis escalated and war seemed inevitable, with the Westernpowers and the Soviet Union coming to Czechoslovakia's aid. But having failed to bluff the Czechoslovaks into surrender, Hitler turned the pressure from Prague to London and Paris.

While Prime Minister Neville Chamberlain of Britain was addressing the House of Commons on Sept. 28, 1938, he received from Hitler a telegraphed invitation to meet with Hitler, Mussolini and Premier Edouard Daladier of France the following day in Munich.

This was at a time when France, Yugoslavia, Rumania and the Soviet Union were reiterating their support for Czechoslovakia.

Without consulting Prague or Moscow, which had a military-assistance pact with the Czechoslovak, the British, French, Italians and Germans signed an agreement at Munich on Sept. 30 under which the Czechoslovakia would cede to Germany large chunks of territory.

The Poles and Hungarians then put in their bids for Czechoslovak territory and within five weeks Czechoslovakia lost about one-third of her population to the three nations.

President Benes resigned on Oct. 3, 1938, and fled the country. By the following March the Germans held sway over the remainder of the country and Hitler appeared in Prague to accept the take-over of Czechoslovakia.

Sixe months later Poland was invaded and the real war, which many had hoped to avert at the sacrifice of Czechoslovak independence, started. It was to be five more years before the Germans would start being ousted by the Russians.

Versions of the Two Sides

Continued From Page 1, Col. 7

stitution—the threat emanating from the counterrevolutionary forces which have entered into a collusion with foreign forces hostile to Socialism.

The events in Czechoslovakia and around her were repeatedly the subject of exchanges of views between leaders of fraternal Socialist countries, including the leaders of Czechoslovakia. These countries are unanimous in that the support, consolidation and defense of the peoples' Socialist gains is a common internationalist duty of all the Socialist states. This common stand of theirs was solemnly proclaimed in the Bratislava statement.

The further aggravation of the situation in Czechoslovakia affects the vital interests of the Soviet Union and other Socialist states, the interests of the security of the states of the Socialist community. The threat to the Socialist system in Czechoslovakia constitutes at the same time a threat to the mainstays of European peace.

The Soviet Government and the Governments of the allied countries—the People's Republic of Bulgaria, the Hungarian People's Republic, the German Democratic Republic, the Polish People's Republic—proceeding from the principles of inseverable friendship and cooperation and in accordance with the existing contractual commitments, have decided to meet the above-mentioned request for rendering necessary help to the fraternal Czechoslovak people.

'In Line With Vital Interests'

This decision is fully in accord with the right of states to individual and collective self-defense envisaged in treaties of alliance concluded between the fraternal socialist countries. This decision is also in line with vital interests of our countries in safeguarding European peace against forces of militarism, aggression and revanche which have more than once plunged the peoples of Europe into wars.

Soviet armed units, together with armed units of the above-mentioned allied countries, entered the territory of Czechoslovakia on August 21. They will be immediately withdrawn from the Czechoslovak Socialist Republic as soon as the obtaining threat to the gains of socialism in Czechoslovakia, the threat to the security of the socialist countries, is eliminated and the lawful authorities find that further presence of these armed units there is no longer necessary.

The actions which are being taken are not directed against any state an din no measure infringe state interests of anybody. They serve the purpose of peace and have been prompted by concern for its consolidation.

The fraternal countries firmly and resolutely counterpose their unbreakable solidarity to any threat from outside. Nobody will be ever allowed to wrest a single link from the community of socialist states.

POLES GET NEWS OF THE INVASION

Radio Says Nation's Troops Joined Allies in Move

By JONATHAN RANDAL
Special to The New York Times

WARSAW, Wednesday, Aug. 21—The state-controlled radio informed Poles this morning that Polish troops had participated in the invasion of Czechoslovakia alongside troops of the Soviet Union and other Warsaw pact countries.

An official declaration, apparently couched in terms identical to those in the Soviet statement, was broadcast at 5 A.M. and again half an hour later.

Morning newspaper deliveries were held up, an indication that the news of the invasion was received too late for the usual press run.

A large number of military transport planes droned over the Polish capital and headed south in the direction of Czechoslovakia shortly after 4 A.M. By 6:30 A.M. long lines of Poles were waiting patiently outside stores. They said they were waiting to buy staples when the stores opened.

Initial reaction to the invasion varied, but many Poles appeared shocked. "Will it mean war?" an old man asked.

Another man on his way to work said that "Hitler was nothing compared to this system" and walked off. But a taxi driver, reflecting both the Polish party line and the Poles' traditional animosity toward Czechoslovaks, said:

"With the Czechs you can never be sure. It must have been Western meddling — especially West German meddling —that was behind it all.

Informed sources noted that Soviet armored units stationed near the Czechoslovak-Polish border city of Cieszyn had not been in evidence since last Friday. At least two regiments of armored troops had been stationed in clear view of passersby for the last month.

Soviet Legal Expert Favors Wider 'Direct Democracy'

MOSCOW, Aug. 20 (Reuters)—A legal specialist proposed today thata major reform be made in Soviet democracy on the ground that the present system was subject to "bureaucracy."

In a 2,000-word article in the Government newspaper, Izvestia, Dr. V. F. Kotov urged that electors be legally empowered to give obligatory orders to their representatives, in what he termed "direct democracy."

Shirley Temple Caught In Prague by Invasion

Special to The New York Times

ATHERTON, Calif., Aug. 20—Charles A. Black, the husband of former child star Shirley Temple, said tonight that she was in Prague when Czechoslovakia was invaded by the Soviet Union. He said, however that he was not concerned.

"I never worry about her," said Mr. Black, an investor, "but I would be derclict if I did not attempt to wake her to tell her the news." He said that he assumed that she was asleep in her suite at the Hotel Alcron in Prague.

Mrs. Black, who is 41 years old, left her home here Aug. 13 and spent three days in Vienna en route to Prague. In the Czech capital, she attended a meeting of the International Federation of Multiple Sclerosis Societies, of which she is a co-founder and vice president.

Mr. Black said that she was to have left Prague Wednesday for Paris and San Francisco.

A History of Pressure: Moscow and Prague

Czechoslovaks Appeared to Have Won Acceptance of Their Program

By ROBERT M. SMITH

The dispute between the Soviet Union and Czechoslovakia has been marked by alternating pressure and reconciliation.

Czechoslovaks found themselves wondering most recently, after an apparent backdown by the Soviet Union, whether Moscow would pay the price for a strategy that staked Soviet prestige on bringing Czechoslovakia to heel and failed.

The Czechoslovak analysts believed the Soviet strategy was based on the assumptions that Prague would wilt under pressure. It did not.

On July 19, Moscow summoned the Presidium of the Czechoslovak party to the Soviet Union to explain its liberalization program. Normally, such invitations are not made public until their acceptance. Prague felt that Moscow had issued it as a means of pressure.

Prague Was Steadfast

The Czechoslovak leaders, nervous but steadfast, refused. Three days later the Soviet Union took what seemed the first step in a retreat, agreeing to come to Czechoslovakia.

For three days the Russians tried to bring the Czechoslovaks into line. They began with bluster, then became more reasonable. On the fourth day, with the Czechoslovaks still unyielding, the Russians appeared to give in.

On Aug. 3, the Czechoslovak stand was ratified in Bratislava. An empty document proclaiming unity of purpose was signed. Even a token Soviet effort to save face by including in the declaration some of its earlier position was eliminated.

The Czechoslovaks were cheered further when the last of 16,000 Soviet troops who had lingered for more than a month after the completion of Warsaw Pact exercises left their country.

On Aug. 9, the most famous Communist dissident, President Tito of Yugoslavia, who had broken from Moscow in 1948, came to visit the new leaders of Czechoslovakia.

Tito Cheered in the Rain

Ignoring a summer downpour, thousands of Czechoslovaks poured onto the runway at Prague Airport waving Yugoslav flags and shouting: "Long live Tito!"

One Czechoslovak interpretation of the apparent Soviet backdown was that the Russians knew the problems of the Czechoslovak economy. They believed that their opponents hoped that the economic condition of the country would get worse and that the Czechoslovak Communists would oust the liberals.

Another factor seemed the reliance of heavy industry on the Soviet Union for raw materials and crude oil.

The question of how the ideologically conservative Russians, East Germans and Poles would react was uppermost in the minds of the Czechoslovaks after January, when the new Communist party leadership under Alexander Dubcek began its "democratization process."

At one point last winter, the old-guard ideologist in the Soviet leadership, Mikhail A. Suslov, apparently demanded military intervention to "save socialism"—meaning dogmatic party rule—in Czechoslovakia. But, it appears, Mr. Suslov was overruled by more cautious men around the party chief, Leonid I. Brezhnev.

According to Zdenek Mlynar, a member of the new Czechoslovak party secretariat, the only Soviet action was the temporary cutoff of wheat deliveries, which normally crossed the border at Cierna Nad Tisou at a rate of 5,500 tons a day.

Mr. Mlynar attributed the stoppage to "nervousness" in Moscow over the developments in Czechoslovakia. However, on April 1 wheat shipments were resumed at an even higher rate, reaching almost 8,000 tons a day toward the end of the month.

Moscow Offered a Loan

In addition, Moscow discreetly offered Prague a $400-million loan in hard currency to be paid back with goods Moscow normally buys in the West.

The Czechoslovaks desperately need hard currency to bolster their economy, which had deteriorated under 20 years of central direction in the regime of President Antonin Novotny, who lost power this year.

In September, 1967, President Novotny called for a hardening of Czechoslovak Communist discipline and warned liberal elements that the party would not tolerate political compromise.

In June of that year Czechoslovakia followed the Soviet Union's example and severed diplomatic relations with Israel during the war with the Arabs.

In February, at the end of an unpublicized visit of Mr. Brezhnev to Czechoslovakia, an official communiqué said that the talks he held with Czechoslovak leaders showed "complete identity of views" of the two sides on "problems of the international situation and on the necessity to strengthen the cohesion of the socialist community and the unity of the international Communist movement."

In September, 1966, the Soviet Union and Czechoslovakia signed an agreement in Moscow under which the Czechoslovaks agreed to provide more than $550-million in credits for the development of the Soviet oil industry in western Siberia.

In exchange, the Soviet Union agreed to deliver oil above the quantity called for in an existing long-term trade agreement.

At the beginning of June, 1966, during the 13th Congress of the Czechoslovak Communist party in Prague, President Novotny called for unity within the Warsaw Pact and said the Soviet armed forces remained "the core of the defense of the entire Socialist camp."

In October, 1964, when Tass, the Soviet press agency, reported that Nikita S. Khrushchev had been relieved as Premier and party secretary, the presidium of the Czechoslovak Communist party issued a statement expressing "surprise and emotion" at the news of Mr. Khrushchev's ouster and affirming appreciation of "the activities of Comrade Khrushchev both with regard to the struggle to accomplish a policy of peaceful coexistence and the disclosure of the erroneous methods in the period of the cult of personality."

The "period of the cult of personality" referred to the Stalin era.

In April, 1964, Mr. Novotny supported a Soviet proposal to convene a world conference of Communist parties to defend the international Communist movement "against Chinese factional activities."

Mr. Novotny had succeeded President Antonin Zapotocky, who died Nov. 13, 1957. Mr. Novotny retained, however, his position of First Secretary of the Communist party.

Mr. Zapatocky's stewardship, beginning on March 14, 1953, saw Czechoslovakia following Soviet foreign policy just as faithfully as under his predecessor, Klement Gottwald, who came to power in the Communist takeover in 1948.

Soviet troops had remained in Czechoslovakia after the war. More were massed to the North, in East Germany. To the south were Hungarian troops, committed to Soviet policy. To the northeast were Poland's armies.

The Czechs had no choice but to accept Communist rule.

Liberation in May, 1945

On May 11, 1945, Soviet troops marched through Prague as liberators. A few American soldiers were in Prague on that day, but the main body of United States troops had been held at Pilsen, 50 miles to the east.

In April of this year the Czechoslovak Communist Party newspaper, Rude Pravo, suggested for the first time that Soviet agents might have been responsible for the death of the Czechoslovak Foreign Minister, Jan Masaryk, in 1948.

In what had become a series of increasingly sharp press comments about the Soviet Union and other Eastern European neighbors of Czechoslovakia, Rude Pravo gave official, if hedged, support to the theory that it might have been the Soviet secret police that had murdered Dr. Masaryk.

Mr. Masaryk was a non-Communist member of the Government of Mr. Gottwald, which had taken power a month before plunged to his death from an upper floor of the foreign ministry.

Other Czechoslovak newspapers have recently published articles disclosing Soviet police intervention in the Czechoslovak purge trials of the early nineteen-fifties.

MOSCOW EXPLAINS WHY IT TOOK STEP

Continued From Page 1, Col. 5

most of the members of the Central Commitee were out of Moscow on vacation.

Earlier Decision Indicated

It appears that the Soviet Union decided several months ago on armed intervention to rescue Czechoslovakia from what it considered to be the perils of "counterrevolution." The action was postponed during negotiations between the Soviet Politburo and the Czechoslovak Presidium, but was never canceled.

It was noted here last week that Marshal Andrei A. Grechko, the Soviet Defense Minister, was inspecting troops in East Germany and Poland and that maneuvers had been undertaken in Hungary as well, preparatory to striking Czechoslovakia from three sides.

Soviet maneuvers of support troops in western border regions last month were clearly aimed at preparing the way for an invasion of Czechoslovakia.

The stealth of Soviet tactics in occupying Czechoslovakia recalled the events in Hungary in 1956, when Soviet troops gave an impression of being ready to withdraw from the country but acutally were regrouping to destroy the anti-Communist rebels.

The decision to invade Czechoslovakia was not an easy one for Moscow. The action is certain to provoke an outcry not only from non-Communists but also from Communists around the world. It appears to ruin any chanaces for carrying out as scheduled a world conference of Communist parties in Moscow this November.

The Soviet Union has demonstrated before that when the issue is one of Soviet security, international Communist objectives take second place.

The march of Czechoslovakia to "counterrevolution" was feared by Moscow as a serious blow to the Soviet land shield against the West.

Equally frightening to the Kremlin leaders in Czechoslovakia's efforts to humanize Communist rule with democratic reforms was the subversive influence such a program has on the people in neighboring Communist countries. The Soviet leadership clearly decided that it could not tolerate the risk.

A repeated theme in the propaganda buildup was an allegation in the Soviet press over the weekend that Czechoslovakia was in a condition of near anarchy, with anti-communists free to terrorize loyal party members, and that the Czechoslovak Presidium, headed by Alaxander Dubcek, the First Secretary, was unable or unwilling to bring the situation under control.

Yesterday, the Soviet party's official organ, Pravda, emphasized in an editorial that Communist parties had a right and a duty to intervene in other countries to support and protect Communist party rule.

"Marxists-Leninists are not and can never be indifferent to the fate of socialist construction in other countries and the general cause of socialism and Communism on earth," the paper said.

Agitation Over Manifesto

An intense build-up of attacks on the Czechoslovak reformers in July stemmed from Soviet agitation over a manifesto, "The Two Thousand Words," circulated in Prague by ultraliberals and calling for strikes, demonstrations and boycotts to force foes of the democratization program from positions of influence.

The manifesto was interpreted by Moscow as an open call for "counterrevolution."

The revived polemics have focused mainly on accusations that pro-Soviet workers in Czechoslovakia were being subjected to persecution and that Prague newspapers continued to slander neighboring Communist parties in violation of "the spirit of Bratislava."

The Pravda editorial today, apparently aimed at the Czechoslovak reformers, charged that "apologists of the bourgeois system" dressed themselves in "pseudosocialist attire" with the purpose of subverting Communist rule from within. Their objective, Pravda asserted, is a restoration of capitalism.

The Communist parties are alert to their duties to rebuff bourgeois schemes, Pravda warned and added:

"They declare, and this was confirmed at the Bratislava conference, that no one will ever be allowed to drive a wedge between the socialist states or undermine the foundation of the socialist structure. The fraternal parties consider it their obligation to insure that imperialist intrigues are nipped in the bud and to strenghten the unity of socialist commonwealth and all revolutionary forces."

In a dispatch from Prague by Viktor Mayevsky and Vasily Zhurovsky, political commentators, Pravda asserted that Czechoslovakia was under increasing danger from West Germany, especially from Sudeten Germans expelled from Czechoslovakia after World War II.

In a continuing campaign to depict West Germany as the major menace to Communist rule in Czechoslovakia, Pravda asserted a week ago that Bonn had drafted plans for blitzkreig operations to seize East Germany and Czechoslovakia.

The allegation was made by Ernst Henry, a Soviet commentator on international affairs, who described the alleged Bonn plan as follows:

"One assault army of the Bundeswehr, made up of specially trained troops, sabotage teams and small landing parties, invades East Germany swiftly, seizes Berlin and other key points and severs East Germany from Poland.

"Another supermobile army forces Czechoslovakia 'to her knees' in another impetuous and surprise blow and cuts the country off from East Germany and its other allies. The operation is intended to be finished in a day or two, confronting the Warsaw Pact with a fait accompli.

"According to this plan, United States diplomacy then appears on the scene, backed by the North Atlantic Treaty Organization, to put pressure on the socialist countries. Negotiations then begin to stop the 'limited war,' with the Bundeswehr in possession of all that it wanted."

Loan Association Robbed

A gunman wearing a Consolidated Edison Company uniform held up the Bankers Federal Savings and Loan Association office at 187-16 Union Turnpike, Queens, and got away with more than $10,000 in cash. However, the robbery was photographed by hidden cameras.

"All the News That's Fit to Print"

The New York Times

LATE CITY EDITION

Weather: Sunny, mild today; fair and milder tonight and tomorrow. Temp. range: today 77-56; Wed. 75-57. Temp.-Hum. Index yesterday 69. Complete U.S. report on Page 70.

VOL. CXVII..No. 40,395 NEW YORK, THURSDAY, AUGUST 29, 1968 10 CENTS

HUMPHREY NOMINATED ON THE FIRST BALLOT AFTER HIS PLANK ON VIETNAM IS APPROVED; POLICE BATTLE DEMONSTRATORS IN STREETS

SOVIET TO LEAVE 2 BLOC DIVISIONS ON CZECHS' SOIL

Svoboda Tells the Cabinet Other Forces Will Depart in 'Several Months'

By TAD SZULC
Special to The New York Times

PRAGUE, Aug. 28—President Ludvik Svoboda told his Cabinet today that the withdrawal of the Soviet-led occupation troops from Czechoslovakia would take "several months and stages" and that at least two divisions would remain permanently stationed on the West German border.

Authoritative sources that provided the account of the Cabinet meeting at Hradcany Castle quoted the President as having informed the ministers that no exact date had been set to begin the withdrawal of the forces of the Soviet Union and the four other Warsaw Pact countries that invaded Czechoslovakia a week ago.

The National Assembly adopted an eight-point resolution asking that a firm date be set forthwith for removal of the occupying forces and declaring that the Czechoslovak Army of 200,000 men was capable of guarding its own frontiers.

Prague Back at Work

Meanwhile, Prague was back at work, but a curfew was maintained and Soviet armored scout cars and motorized infantry trucks with machine guns mounted on their cabs continued to cruise through the city's crowded streets.

In a speech to the nation tonight, Premier Oldrich Cernik announced that today's Cabinet session had drafted a proposal to the Soviet Union, Poland, Hungary, Bulgaria and East Germany to begin "soon" the actual negotiations for the departure of their armies.

He said that within two weeks economic talks with the Soviet Union were to begin "during which compensation for damages" caused by the invasion would be discussed among other topics.

Czechoslovakia has long been

Continued on Page 3, Column 1

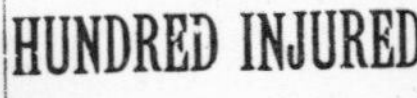

Associated Press
John Gordon Mein

U.S. ENVOY SLAIN IN GUATEMALA

Terrorists Shoot Mein After Ambushing Car—Johnson and Rusk Ask Inquiry

By Reuters

GUATEMALA, Aug. 28—The United States Ambassador, John Gordon Mein, was slain here this afternoon by unidentified youths who had ambushed his limousine.

The 54-year-old career Foreign Service officer tried to put up a fight, but fell under a hail of pistol and machine-gun fire, dying instantly. At least nine bullets struck his body.

As the Ambassador was driving along Avenida Reforma to the embassy, several youths leaped out of two small Japanese-made cars and opened the limousine's rear door to force him out. He resisted and they opened fire.

[In Washington, President Johnson and Secretary of State Dean Rusk expressed shock and grief and called on Guatemala to investigate the assassination.]

Campaign of Terror

Mr. Mein is believed to be the first United States Ambassador assassinated at his post.

The kidnapping of prominent people has been an element of the terror campaign that has been waged by extremist political elements in this uneasy Central American country, which has a population of more than 4.6 million.

The shooting occurred three blocks from the Biltmore Hotel, where Mr. Mein had attended a luncheon given by the Foreign Minister, Emilo Arenales Catalán. The scene was about 10 blocks from the embassy.

The Ambassador's chauffeur,

Continued on Page 16, Column 3

HUNDRED INJURED

178 Are Arrested as Guardsmen Join in Using Tear Gas

By J. ANTHONY LUKAS
Special to The New York Times

CHICAGO, Thursday, Aug. 29—The police and National Guardsmen battled young protesters in downtown Chicago last night as the week-long demonstrations against the Democratic National Convention reached a violent and tumultuous climax.

About 100 persons, including 25 policemen, were injured and at least 178 were arrested as the security forces chased down the demonstrators. The protesting young people had broken out of Grant Park on the shore of Lake Michigan in an attempt to reach the International Amphitheatre where the Democrats were meeting, four miles away.

The police and Guardsmen used clubs, rifle butts, tear gas and Chemical Mace on virtually anything moving along Michigan Avenue and the narrow streets of the Loop area.

Uneasy Calm

Shortly after midnight, an uneasy calm ruled the city. However, 1,000 National Guardsmen were moved back in front of the Conrad Hilton Hotel to guard it against more than 5,000 demonstrators who had drifted back into Grant Park.

The crowd in front of the hotel was growing, booing vociferously every time new votes for Vice President Humphrey were broadcast from the convention hall.

The events in the streets stirred anger among some delegates at the convention. In a nominating speech Senator Abraham A. Ribicoff of Connecticut told the delegates that if Senator George S. McGovern were President, "we would not have these Gestapo tactics in the streets of Chicago."

When Mayor Richard J. Daley of Chicago and other Illinois delegates rose shouting angrily, Mr. Ribicoff said, "How hard it is to accept the truth."

Crushed Against Windows

Even elderly bystanders were caught in the police onslaught. At one point, the police turned on several dozen persons standing quietly behind police barriers in front of the Conrad Hilton Hotel watching the demonstrators across the street.

For no reason that could be immediately determined, the blue-helmeted policemen charged the barriers, crushing the spectators against the windows of the Haymarket Inn, a restaurant in the hotel. Finally the window gave way, sending screaming middle-aged women and children backward through the broken shards of glass.

The police then ran into the restaurant and beat some of the

Continued on Page 23, Column 1

The New York Times (by Neal Boenzi)
AT CONVENTION: Cheering in the amphitheatre after Vice President Humphrey's name was placed in nomination

United Press International
IN STREETS: Police attempting to clear demonstrators on Michigan Avenue outside Conrad Hilton Hotel last night

VICTOR GETS 1,761

Vote Taken Amid Boos For Chicago Police Tactics in Street

Excerpts from the nominating speeches are on Page 22.

By TOM WICKER
Special to The New York Times

CHICAGO, Thursday Aug. 29 — While a pitched battle between the police and thousands of young antiwar demonstrators raged in the streets of Chicago, the Democratic National Convention nominated Hubert H. Humphrey for President last night, on a platform reflecting his and President Johnson's views on the war in Vietnam.

Mr. Humphrey, after a day of bandwagon shifts to his candidacy, and a night of turmoil in the convention hall, won nomination on the first ballot over challenges by Senator Eugene J. McCarthy of Minnesota and George S. McGovern of South Dakota.

The count at the end of the first ballot was:

Humphrey	1,761¾
McCarthy	601
McGovern	146½
Phillips	67½
Others	32¾

Violence Draws Attention

There was never a moment's suspense in the balloting, and throughout a turbulent evening, the delegates and spectators paid less attention to the proceedings than to television and radio reports of widespread violence in the streets of Chicago, and to stringent security measures within the International Amphitheatre.

Repeated denunciations of Mayor Richard J. Daley from convention speakers and repeated efforts to get an adjournment or recess were ignored by convention officials and Mr. Daley.

He sat through it all, usually grinning and always guarded by plainclothes security men, until just before the roll call. Then he left the hall. A few miles away, the young demonstrators were being clubbed, kicked and gassed by the Chicago police, who turned back a march on the convention hall.

Watched From Hotels

Most of the violence took place across Michigan Avenue from the convention headquarters hotel, the Conrad Hilton, in full view of delegates' wives and other watching from its windows.

From the convention rostrum, Senator Abraham A. Ribicoff of Connecticut, denounced "Gestapo tactics in the streets of Chicago."

Julian Bond, the Negro insurgent leader from Georgia, in announcing his delegation's

Continued on Page 20, Column 1

PRAGUE'S LEADERS WARNED BY SOVIET

It Says It Will Be Vigilant—Hints Doubt on Outcome

By RAYMOND H. ANDERSON
Special to The New York Times

MOSCOW, Aug. 28—The Soviet Union warned today that the reform leaders of Czechoslovakia, although allowed to return to Prague and to retain their positions after the negotiations here, were on a short leash and under the vigilant eyes of the Kremlin.

Soviet commentators asserted that a counterrevolutionary threat continued to exist in Czechoslovakia, and they indicated that Moscow had doubts that the Prague leadership could or would [illegible] with the dangers adequately.

[In Bonn, the West German Government called for a complete restoration of Czechoslovakia's sovereignty and a pullback of all Soviet invasion forces. Page 6.]

Pravda, the Communist party organ, expressed indignation that underground radio stations in Czechoslovakia had broadcast criticism of the agreement worked out in Moscow between the Soviet leadership and a Czechoslovak delegation headed by President Ludvik Svoboda.

Yuri Zhukov, the political

Continued on Page 4, Column 3

Dubcek Was Put in Handcuffs: An Account of Confrontation

The following chronological account of the confrontation of Soviet and Czechoslovak leaders after the invasion of Czechoslovakia was written by Vincent Buist of Reuters.

PRAGUE, Aug. 28—Alexander Dubcek, the Czechoslovak Communist leader, was hustled out of his party headquarters last Wednesday, handcuffed and flown to a secret destination in Slovakia in a Soviet military aircraft.

All the way he sat on the plane's metal deck.

This was disclosed in an account of Mr. Dubcek's arrest and of the Moscow negotiations given to me today by an official of the Czechoslovak Communist party's Central Committee.

The official said Mr. Dubcek was in his private room speaking on the telephone when the Central Committee building was surrounded by Soviet paratroopers with light tracked vehicles last Wednesday morning.

The party leader was trying to find out details of the extent of the invasion as a Soviet security officer and two soldiers armed with light machine guns burst into the room.

They tore the telephone out of Mr. Dubcek's hands and ripped the wire out of the wall, the official said.

The party leader was taken away and locked in a room in

Continued on Page 2, Column 5

FIGHTING INTENSE IN SAIGON REGION

G.I.'s Battle Through Night With Foe on Infiltration Routes Near Capital

Special to The New York Times

SAIGON, South Vietnam, Thursday, Aug. 29—Sharp fighting flared around Saigon last night and this morning as United States infantrymen battled a sizable enemy force on flatland infiltration routes northwest of the capital.

The United States command said this morning that fighting had continued through the night with a company-size enemy unit 32 miles northwest of Saigon and 4 miles north of Trangbang.

So far, a total of 86 enemy soldiers have been killed in the fighting, American spokesmen said. Reports from the scene were sketchy, but United States spokesmen termed American casualties light.

101st Division Involved

According to the spokesman, the fighting began Tuesday after soldiers of the 101st Air Cavalry Division set up a cordon around an area and began moving in.

Fighting tapered in the evening, but by noon yesterday units of the division, trudging through muddy fields, came under sharp fire. Fighting continued into the morning.

Farther north, near another key infiltration route into Saigon, soldiers of the United States 25th Infantry Division fought two enemy companies seven miles southeast of Tayninh. During the four-hour bat-

Continued on Page 10, Column 1

Defeat for Doves Reflects Deep Division in the Party

By JOHN W. FINNEY
Special to The New York Times

CHICAGO, Aug. 28 — A deeply divided Democratic National Convention, after a climactic floor clash between the Administration's supporters and its critics, adopted today a White House-dictated plank supporting President Johnson's policy in Vietnam. The whole platform was then approved.

By a vote of 1,567¾ to 1,041¼, the convention rejected a plank advanced by Democratic doves calling for an unconditional halt in the bombing of North Vietnam. Instead, it adopted a plank that called for a bombing halt but only on conditional terms.

Excerpts from the debate on platform, Page 22.

The vote reflected the deep, emotional division within the party over the Vietnam issue. The division manifested itself in nearly three hours of increasingly acrimonious debate, conducted against a backdrop of sporadic chants of "Stop the war!" from the galleries and the New York and California delegations.

It was a division that Vice President Humphrey, in his bid for the Presidential nomination, had hoped to avoid. But he could not avoid it when Mr. Johnson intervened behind the scenes to toughen the language of the plank so that it would correspond to Administration policy.

In the wake of the policy confrontation, the major question was whether Mr. Hum-

Continued on Page 25, Column 1

The Party and the Police

By JAMES RESTON
Special to The New York Times

News Analysis

CHICAGO, Aug. 28 — The Democratic party was deeply hurt politically here tonight by the vicious clashes between demonstrators and the police in the streets of Chicago. Though the party itself had no direct responsibility for the incidents, it held its convention here knowing of the dangers of violence and counted on Mayor Daley and his police to handle the situation without embarrassment to the party. This gamble failed, despite all the barbed wire barricades, the police, secret agents and National Guardsmen. It was not only that Mayor Daley was condemned from the rostrum and stood in the aisles mocking Senator Abraham Ribicoff, who had condemned the police action, but tens of millions watched the incidents on television to the obvious detriment of the Democratic party.

By the end of the night Daley had become a symbol in the convention of the opposition within the party to the turbulent conditions of American life. So strong was the feeling against Mayor Daley and his police that even the name of Illinois was loudly booed when the roll of the states was called for nominations for the Presidency.

Thus the convention pre-

Continued on Page 20, Column 3

HUMPHREY AIDES LIST 4 FOR TICKET

Say Muskie, Harris, Alioto and Shriver Are Leading for the No. 2 Spot

By STEVEN V. ROBERTS
Special to The New York Times

CHICAGO, Aug. 28—Aides of Vice President Humphrey advanced four names today as leading candidates for the Vice-Presidential nomination: Senators Edmund S. Muskie of Maine and Fred R. Harris of Oklahoma, Mayor Joseph L. Alioto of San Francisco and Sargent Shriver, the Ambassador to France.

The list contained no surprises. All four men have figured in recent speculation.

However, Mr. Humphrey met in his hotel suite today with key political figures, including Mayor Richard J. Daley of Chicago, and aides said the Vice-Presidency was one topic of discussion. It was generally believed that the final decision would not be made until tomorrow.

It was considered a remote possibility that Mr. Humphrey would try to heal the deep breach in the party over the Vietnam war by choosing a prominent war critic. Senators Eugene J. McCarthy of Minnesota, George S. McGovern of South Dakota and Edward M.

Continued on Page 22, Column 2

NEWS INDEX

Gruening Defeated In Alaska Primary

By LAWRENCE E. DAVIES
Special to The New York Times

ANCHORAGE, Alaska, Aug. 28 — A dramatic, unexpected victory by a dark, good-looking, 38-year-old challenger has terminated the long political career of Senator Ernest Gruening, an 81-year-old warhorse known to his admirers as "Mr. Alaska."

Mike Gravel, a real estate developer from Anchorage and former Speaker of the state's House of Representatives, won the Democratic nomination for the Senate over Mr. Gruening in yesterday's primary election in Alaska.

Unofficial returns to Secretary of State Keith Miller in

Continued on Page 26, Column 5

Humphrey Nominated on First Ballot After Convention Adopts His Vietnam Plank

The New York Times (by George Tames)

THE MAN WHO: Vice President Humphrey, in his hotel, watches Mayor Joseph L. Alioto put his name in nomination

KENNEDY'S ENDING OF DRAFT DECISIVE

Bandwagon Switches Set Off for Vice President After Disavowal By Senator

Continued From Page 1, Col. 8

votes, spoke of "atrocities" in the city.

Wire services reported that Mr. Humphrey had chosen Senator Edmund S. Muskie of Maine for Vice President. Mr. Humphrey's staff denied that a decision had been made, although they would not rule out Mr. Muskie, 54 years old, a Roman Catholic of Polish extraction.

Even the roll-call of the states that nominated Mr. Humphrey could begin only over the protests of New Hampshire, Wisconsin and Mr. Conyers, all of whom moved for a recess or adjournment because of the surrounding violence and the pandemonium in the hall.

Vote Begins Amid Boos

Representative Carl Albert of Oklahoma, the chairman, ignored all the motions and ordered the roll-call to begin amid a huge chorus of boos.

When Illinois's turn came to vote, the huge old amphitheater rocked with the sounds of boos and jeers, and the recording secretary had to ask for a restatement of its vote—112 votes for Mr. Humphrey.

Early in the evening, even Mr. Humphrey got a whiff of tear gas when it was wafted through his window at the Hilton, from the street fighting below.

Mr. McCarthy saw some of the violence from his window and called it "very bad." Later, it was reported at the convention hall, he visited a hospital where some of his young supporters, wounded in the streets, were being treated.

At one point, the police broke into the McCarthy suite at the Hilton, searching for someone throwing objects out of the hotel windows.

Mr. McGovern described the fighting as a "blood bath" that "made me sick to my stomach." He said he had "seen nothing like it since the films of Nazi Germany."

Pennsylvania Does It

Nevertheless, when Pennsylvania cast the votes that put Mr. Humphrey in nomination, the convention hall broke into a demonstration on his behalf that was loud and apparently happy. Mrs. Humphrey, watching from a box with her family, received congratulations with a gracious smile.

The day's events, moving swiftly toward Mr. Humphrey's nomination, began this morning with Edward M. Kennedy's disavowal of a draft movement in his behalf.

In an emotional afternoon debate, the delegates sealed the grip of Mr. Humphrey and Mr. Johnson on this convention by adopting a Vietnam plank drawn to the President's specifications.

They defeated by a comfortable margin a substitute proposal critical of much of the President's policy and supported by backers of Mr. McGovern, Mr. McCarthy and the "draft Ted" movement.

McCarthy's Stand in Doubt

How united this would leave the party for the fall campaign remained to be seen. Mr. McCarthy has not yet pledged his support to the ticket, the platform fight left many antiwar Democrats disappointed and bitter, and there is a pervasive fear here, based on national polls, that Mr. Humphrey cannot win against Richard M. Nixon, the Republican nominee.

The delegations of New York and California, the two biggest states, voted largely against the Humphrey-Johnson forces on all issues here, including the platform plank and the Presidential nomination.

Humphrey sources said that the nomination of a Vice-Presidential candidate would probably not be made until Thursday night, although it had been planned for tonight. Mr. Humphrey conferred with advisers this afternoon and tonight on the choice of a running mate, and numerous names were bruited about among the delegates.

Two decisive breaks clinched the nomination, as well as the platform fight, for the Vice President. One was Mr. Kennedy's Sherman-like refusal to be drafted; the other was the announcement by Mayor Daley that Illinois was casting all but six of its 118 votes for Mr. Humphrey.

Of almost equal importance was Gov. Richard J. Hughes's decision to drop his favorite-son's role; that let 61 of New Jersey's votes go to Mr. Humphrey.

By mid-day Lawrence F. O'Brien, a Humphrey manager, was claiming 1,654 delegates, without any help from the Illinois delegation then in caucus.

All the Southern states, except North Carolina, abandoned favorite-son candidacies, with most Southern votes lining K. Moore of North Carolina was expected to switch to the Vice President immediately after the first ballot.

The Southern shift to Mr. Humphrey which had been generally expected from the start of the campaign, caused Gov. Lester G. Maddox of Georgia to abandon the Presidential candidacy he had announced in the late days of the campaign. He withdrew before today's sessions.

Negro delegates here put forward a black candidate, the Rev. Channing Phillips, who had been the leader of the Kennedy slate of delegates from the District of Columbia.

Mayor Joseph L. Alioto of San Francisco was chosen to place Mr. Humphrey in nomination. Selected as seconders were former Gov. Terry Sanford of North Carolina and Mayor Carl Stokes of Cleveland.

Whether these selections had any Vice-Presidential significance could not be ascertained. Both Mr. Alioto, a Roman Catholic of Italian descent, and Mr. Sanford, a Southern progressive, have figured prominently in speculation here.

Humphrey Backers Applaud

Mr. Alioto, avoiding mention of the Vietnam war, pounded out a thumping political speech that roused Mr. Humphrey's supporters to repeated roars of enthusiasm and the biggest and noisiest demonstration of the convention.

Citing the Vice President's 20 years of leadership in liberal causes, Mr. Alioto worked in the effective refrain "but he did it" after describing each of Mr. Humphrey's various achievements in terms of overcoming the impossible.

In fact, he said, in "a lifetime of courage," Mr. Humphrey had become an expert practitioner of "the art of the impossible."

The Vice President, he said, is "a leader who can be impatient" at the slow pace of progress, and he cautioned those who were calling for "new options" that they were more likely to get them from a proved man of action than from mere talkers.

Mr. Ribicoff described Mr. McGovern as "a good man without guile" and a "whole man with peace in his soul," who could bring these qualities to a nation that needed them sorely.

"He brings out of the prairies of South Dakota a new wind," Mr. Ribicoff said, "a wind that will be able to lift the smog of uncertainty from this land of ours."

His voice rising in indignation, the Connecticut Senator then declared:

"With George McGovern as President, we would not have to have such Gestapo tactics in the streets of Chicago."

This set off a tremendous roar of approval and when it subsided briefly, Mr. Ribicoff added:

"With George McGovern, we would not have to have the national guard.

That renewed the applause but it also brought the Illinois delegates up in anger. Mayor Daley joined them in waving, catcalling and motioning for Mr. Ribicoff to sit down.

"How hard it is to accept the truth," Mr. Ribicoff replied—in a moment reminiscent of the booing of Governor Rockefeller of New York at the Republican National Convention of 1964.

Gov. Harold E. Hughes of Iowa, who was chosen to nominate Mr. McCarthy, said that "the people found Gene McCarthy for us They found him; they follow him; he is more accurately the people's candidate than any other man in recent history."

The Governor, who seconded Lyndon B. Johnson at Atlantic City in 1964, called Mr. McCarthy "a leader who can arrest the polarization of our society—the alienation of the blacks from the whites, of the haves from the have-nots, and the old from the young."

The convention adjourned at 12:06 A.M., Chicago daylight time today. The final session is scheduled to convene at 7 o'clock tonight, Chicago daylight time (8 P.M. E.D.T.).

The session will choose its Vice-Presidential nominee and head acceptance speeches from him and Mr. Humphrey.

Party and the Police: Symbol of Split

Continued From Page 1, Col. 6

sented to the vast nation-wide audience a picture of division, of old-fashioned city bossism, of clashes between the young and old, of events out of control and of a party unable even to govern itself or maintain order.

This, of course, has been precisely the atmosphere the Democrats feared the most. They have been under attack by the political opposition for the decline in law and order—indeed Richard Nixon is making this his main issue against them. They also have been condemned for the turmoil of the cities — and tonight's violence merely dramatized the party's plight.

Even before this, the Democratic party was in trouble over the war in Vietnam, and opposition not only in the cities but on the farms.

Accordingly, the Democrats' main hope for victory in November seemed to be a cease-fire in Vietnam in the next two months or some other major development that would change the present atmosphere.

Even a cease-fire in the war might not close the wide divisions in the party, but it would at least give the Democrats a chance in the Presidential race against Richard M. Nixon.

Ironically, President Johnson still holds one of the two keys to this puzzle. Hubert H. Humphrey is not free of the President's influence yet. Even if the Vice President were to change his own views and come out for another bombing pause in all of North Vietnam, Mr. Johnson will still be in charge of the Paris Vietnam talks throughout the election campaign.

The North Vietnamese and the National Liberation Front hold the other key. They must now make their judgment whether Humphrey or Nixon in the White House would follow an interventionist role in Southeast Asia, and if they thought Nixon would be more aggressive in that part of the world than Humphrey, it is just possible that they might agree to a cease-fire before November in the hope of helping Humphrey.

Otherwise, there is very little Humphrey can do to heal his party. He is being strongly urged by some of his advisers here in Chicago to break with the President on the war. Only by doing so, these aides argue, can he avoid carrying the burden of the anti-Johnson and anti-war voters into the campaign. But even a break with Johnson would probably mean exchanging one large bloc of disenchanted Democrats for another.

For the present, the Vice President has many McCarthy and McGovern supporters against him, but any concessions to them would only risk the loss of the Johnson regulars, who would then accuse him of winning the nomination on one policy and repudiating it for another in the campaign.

Mr. Humphrey might have eased this problem by allowing his delegates in the convention to vote their own convictions on the Vietnam war plank in the Democratic platform. This might have put over the plank the McCarthy and McGovern forces wanted and opened the way for the nomination of a Humphrey-McGovern ticket, but Humphrey refused to take this course.

As a matter of fact he has in some ways hardened his position on Vietnam since coming to Chicago. He did not agree to precisely the platform President Johnson wanted, but he was particularly sharp and vigorous in backing the present war policy during his appearance on the "Meet the Press" television show last Sunday, and the Johnson-Humphrey victory in the Vietnam platform fight has clearly embittered the McCarthy and McGovern forces.

McGovern is a close personal friend of the Vice President's. They were nextdoor neighbors in a suburb of Washington for many years. But while McGovern will support Humphrey, he let it be known today that he was not available to run with Mr. Humphrey on the present Democratic war platform.

Senator McCarthy is even less forgiving than McGovern. A distinct note of bitterness is now creeping into his private and even public remarks about his long fight for the nomination. He has said he will not back the nominee of a party following the present Vietnam policy, and he confirmed today that he offered to withdraw from the race last night if Senator Edward M. Kennedy of Massachusetts agreed to try for the nomination.

In all this there are curious ironies. Vietnam has been the dividing instrument between all these principal Democratic leaders, yet the dice might easily have rolled a different way. Robert Kennedy, for example, once offered to go to Vietnam as Mr. Johnson's Ambassador. Senator McCarthy wanted to be Mr. Johnson's Vice-Presidential running mate in 1964. Either way, Kennedy or McCarthy might easily have found themselves trapped in the Johnson policy as Humphrey now is.

For Humphrey, fate has been particularly capricious. He never expected to be nominated for the Presidency until President Johnson withdrew from the race last March 31. More than almost any other man in the Senate, he has been an advocate over the years of arms reduction and arms control. Yet he now finds himself condemned by old friends as a warmonger and nominated with the aid of conservatives he fought throughout the forties and fifties.

Still, he is known to the Communists as a man who wants arms control, while Nixon is regarded in the Kremlin as a hard anti-Communist who based much of his political career on cold war policies. This could also be a factor in whether the Kremlin will urge Hanoi to agree to a cease-fire in Vietnam in order to help Humphrey.

What is clear at the beginning of the Humphrey-Nixon campaign is that the country is more divided over foreign and domestic policy than it has been for years, and is faced with radical problems that will require radical and controversial solutions.

In this situation, the outlook for the period beyond next Jan. 20 is even gloomier than the outlook for the next few months. For the overriding question for the nation is whether either of these men will be able to bring about enough reconciliation or get a large enough majority in the Congress to govern effectively.

In short, the delegates will leave here even more unhappy with their work than the Republicans left Miami Beach behind Mr. Nixon and Governor Agnew of Maryland. If the Democrats have any consolation, it is that they at least argued out their differences in public, but this isn't quite enough to make up for disagreements on Humphrey and his Vietnam policy.

How the Delegates Voted

Special to The New York Times

CHICAGO, Aug. 28—Following is the roll-call vote for the Democratic Presidential nomination tonight:

STATE	VOTES	HUMPHREY	McCARTHY	McGOVERN	OTHERS*
Alabama	32	23	..	..	6
Alaska	22	17	2	3	..
Arizona	19	14½	2½	2	..
Arkansas	33	30	2	..	..
California	174	14	91	51	17
Canal Zone	5	4	..	1	..
Colorado	35	16½	10	5½	3
Connecticut	44	35	8	..	1
Delaware	22	21	..	..	..
Dist. of Columbia	23	2	..	..	21
Florida	63	58	5	..	..
Georgia	43	19½	13½	1	6
Guam	5	5	..	..	..
Hawaii	26	26	..	..	..
Idaho	25	21	3½	½	..
Illinois	118	112	3	3	..
Indiana	63	49	11	2	1
Iowa	46	18½	19½	5	3
Kansas	38	34	1	3	..
Kentucky	46	41	5	..	..
Louisiana	36	35	..	..	..
Maine	27	23	4	..	..
Maryland	49	45	2	2	..
Massachusetts	72	2	70	..	..
Michigan	96	72½	9½	7½	6½
Minnesota	52	38	11½	..	2½
Mississippi	24	9½	6½	4	2
Missouri	60	56	3½	..	½
Montana	26	23½	2½	..	..
Nebraska	30	15	6	9	..
Nevada	22	18½	2½	1	..
New Hampshire	26	6	20	..	..
New Jersey	82	62	19	..	1
New Mexico	26	15	11	..	..
New York	190	96½	87	1½	5
North Carolina	59	44½	2	½	12
North Dakota	25	18	7	..	..
Ohio	115	94	18	2	1
Oklahoma	41	37½	2½	½	½
Oregon	35	..	35	..	..
Pennsylvania	130	103¾	21½	2½	2¼
Puerto Rico	8	8	..	..	..
Rhode Island	27	23½	2½	..	..
South Carolina	28	28	..	..	..
South Dakota	26	2	..	24	..
Tennessee	51	49½	½	1	..
Texas	104	100½	2½	..	1
Utah	26	23	2	..	1
Vermont	22	9	6	7	..
Virginia	54	42½	5½	..	5
Virgin Islands	5	5	..	..	..
Washington	47	32½	8½	6	..
West Virginia	38	34	3	..	1
Wisconsin	59	8	49	1	1
Wyoming	22	18½	3½	..	..
Total	2,622	1,761¾	601	146½	100¼

*Others—Channing Phillips 67½ (California 17; Colorado 3; Connecticut 1; District of Columbia 21; loyal Georgia Democrats 3; Michigan 6½; Minnesota 2½, Mississippi 2; Missouri ½; New Jersey 1; New York 2; Oklahoma ½; Pennsylvania 1½; Texas 1; Utah 1; Virginia 2; Wisconsin 1; Indiana 1); Dan Moore 17½ (Georgia regulars 2; North Carolina 12; Virginia 3; Alabama ½); Edward Kennedy 12¾ (loyal Georgia Democrats ½; Iowa 3; New York 3; Alabama 3½; Ohio 1; Pennsylvania ¾; West Virginia 1); James H. Gray ½ (Georgia regulars ½); Paul E. Bryant 1½ (Alabama 1½); George C. Wallace ½ (Alabama ½).

Democrats' Energetic Leader

Hubert Horatio Humphrey

Special to The New York Times

Man in the News

CHICAGO, Thursday, Aug. 29—Three months ago the men around Hubert Horatio Humphrey looked at 1968 with satisfying perspective.

"He is a man whose time has come," they told each other with nods of approval. Today, at the age of 57, he is at last his party's nominee for President, and it seems that indeed his time has come. But behind the bright smiles in the news pictures there is, in the Humphrey entourage, a tone of soberness that approaches resignation. It is not just that he faces the greatest odds in 20 years against retaining the White House for his party, thanks to circumstances at home and abroad.

Beyond the harshness of the political landscape is an air of portent that is largely personal. It springs from the person of the candidate, from a knowledge, painfully acquired, that the world does not end when Hubert Humphrey loses.

He expressed this knowledge briefly one night last spring, a few days before he announced, on April 27, that he would enter the race for the nomination.

He was in airplane somewhere over the upper South. He had been talking brightly of the political year. Of the joy of being once more in the arena, of how he and Mrs. Humphrey had made up their minds to have one final try for the top prize.

"She knew she would never really have any more private life," he said.

Mrs. Humphrey sat sewing a few feet away.

But there are other compensations," he went on.

He turned from his wife to look for a moment out the darkened window. Then he turned back to the interviewer and smiled and said, "I had the feeling that if I did run and didn't get the nomination, there was still time for a lot of good fun."

A Calmer Man Now

Hubert Humphrey is a calmer man than he once was. He still has energy and hope, and he still wants very much to be President.

But he has also constructed a protective shell around whatever vital part it is that makes a man care to the point of recklessness and then plunges him into agony when he fails.

Now that an accident of history has placed him in striking distance of the Presidency, he must decide how much of his harnessed hope he can set free, how much of his ego he can afford to commit to the rigors of so hurtful a process as an American Presidential election.

Hope was probably the main part of the Humphrey political philosophy when he came out of the remote Midwest 20 years ago.

"Who could have guessed," he asks his friends sometimes, "that the son of a small-town druggist from the plains would end up as Vice President of the United States?"

The Protestant ethic was fully in charge where he came from, teaching that with hard work and a little luck anybody could make it.

That must have seemed reasonable to the son of Hubert Horatio Humphrey Sr. and Christine Sannes. The Humphreys had four children. Hubert was born May 27, 1911, in an apartment over his father's drugstore in Wallace, S. D.

Young Hubert grew up in nearby Doland, S. D., and there the Humphreys were "somebody."

Harsh Early Life

Mr. Humphrey likes to talk now of the harshness of his early life during the Depression years. Without quite saying it, he suggests that he rose out of poverty.

It is true the family suffered reverses during the Depression. But probably the essential fact of his early years is that he grew up on the right side of the tracks, with all the self-respect that comes of knowing that one's standing is secure. His father was one of the half-dozen men in Doland who made the town's important decisions.

And through the teachings of his parents and the simple act of coming to adulthood in a small, Protestant town in middle America, he came to the notion that with hard work and luck, everything around a man could be made better.

Mr. Humphrey continues to believe devoutly in the improvability, if not the perfectibility of life. He has a compulsion for order. It reveals itself in large ways and small.

He has been known to spend all day in the Government trying to arrange the affairs of mankind. Then go home at night and scrub the kitchen walls. At his home in Waverly, Minn., he can be found frequently cleaning the garage.

The same quality appears in his public life. He used to be accused quite regularly of being a socialist, or of being soft on Communism. But it is not Marxism that drives him but a compulsion to set things straight.

The New York Times (by George Tames)

Hope is a part of his political philosophy
(Mr. Humphrey with Orville L. Freemat at moment of victory)

Actually he appears to have been frightened of Marxism most of his life. One of his earliest political battles in Minneapolis, where he was elected Mayor in 1945 at the age of 34, was over Communist influence in his political party.

Mr. Humphrey's early rise in Minneapolis politics had been helped along by a variety of radicals. But when he and his friends put together a merger of the Democratic and the Farmer-Labor parties in 1944, they began to fear that Communists were about to take control.

They systematically purged the Communists from the party, along with an undetermined number of othdr radicals who were suspected of being sympathetic to the Communists.

Mr. Humphrey first moved to Minnesota to attend the University of Minnesota, after graduating from Doland High School. The Depression forced him out, and he returned to his father's drugstore—then in Huron, S.D.—and married Muriel Fay Buck.

He returned to the university six years later and, while both he and his wife worked, he earned his bachelor's degree. The first of their four children was born in Minneapolis during this period.

After taking a master's degree in political science at Louisiana State University—where he met, among others, Russell B. Long, son of Huey—he returned to Minnesota and shortly afterward entered politics.

His Mark on Legislation

His friends around the university tended to be liberal, New Deal Democrats. He led a group of them to the 1948 Democratic National Convention in Philadelphia and there made a speech so strongly urging an effective civil rights plank that he became nationally famous. He was elected to the Senate that year.

Most of his Senate career is well known. With his New Deal impulse for reforming some of the nation's more decrepit institutions and making them work, he eventually put his brand on legislation for urban renewal, Federal aid to education, the Peace Corps, Food for Peace, the nuclear test ban treaty, the Arms Control and Disarmament Agency and almost every civil rights act passed during his 16 years in the Senate.

He also continued to be a hard-line anti-Communist, as is reflected in his sponsorship in 1954 of legislation outlawing the Communist party and in his support of the cold war policy of containing Communism abroad.

A Bid From Johnson

In 1964 Lyndon B. Johnson asked him to be his running mate.

Mr. Johnson had made it clear that he wanted a Vice President who would be an "instrument" of the executive branch.

Mr. Humphrey not only has trained himself to become President if the need should arise—for example, by sitting as a member of the National Security Council—but he also has acted as Mr. Johnson's agent.

He has worked with Mayors on urban problems and with civil rights leaders on racial problems.

He has been the Administration's traveling salesman trying to explain the Vietnam war to the people.

He has made more than 525 speeches outside the capital. He has visited 240 cities in all 50 states and has traveled to 35 countries in Europe, Asia and Africa.

He will travel on anything: a Boeing 727 jet, his own rebuilt Model T Ford, a horse at the LBJ Ranch or a limousine careering through the freeways of Los Angeles.

Immersing himself in the work of President Johnson has not helped Mr. Humphrey's reputation in many quarters.

Some believe that four years in the Johnson shadow has impaired Mr. Humphrey's effectiveness as a politician and has even damaged his personality.

Many of his friends insist he will assert his own person once again, now that he is the standard-bearer of his party and owes a larger obligation to his own position than to Mr. Johnson's. Others say he will continue in the Johnson shadow, because he will not be able to do otherwise.

It may be that Mr. Humphrey has changed during the last four years, as his critics say. But some qualities have remained constant.

He is still a sentimentalist. Tears come easily (not always caused by emotion; his eyes sometimes water from a sensitivity to bright lights).

He seems to cry as readily out of joy as sadness. One night recently in Washington he wept as he thanked 2,500 contributors to his Presidential campaign. They had given more than $1-million.

He laughs as easily as he cries. He is the only one of the three major Democratic candidates who has a reputation for happiness.

However, he is not all smile and bubble. He is capable of anger. There are many stories [illegible] explosions directed at his staff that make him sound almost Johnsonian in temper.

The Issue of Gabbiness

Mr. Humphrey's gabbiness may become a full-fledged campaign issue this year. Among people who dislike him, one often hears the criticism "He talks too much."

He does not pretend to be a reflective man. He gets his ideas not from books or contemplation but from conversation, from the endless shaping of thoughts bounced off other people.

Mr. Humphrey's speeches tend to run especially long when he is tired or when he is speaking to an indifferent audience. He is reluctant to turn an audience loose without turning it on.

In Akron a few months ago he told an aide before he got up to speak that he was tired and would probably talk too long. He did. He spoke for more than an hour, and as he walked away from the yawning audience he said to the aide that he had known he was talking too long but could not find a way to stop.

But when he is good, he is very, very good. He so inspired an audience in Minneapolis recently that it gave him a ringing round of applause for reciting the Golden Rule. When he ended the speech with the last line of the Pledge of Allegiance to the Flag, it gave him a standing ovation.

Mr. Humphrey's critics on the left—the young, the Negro militants, the poor, the discontented whom he championed so long and fruitfully—contend he became a voice as well as an instrument for President Johnson and ruined himself by trying to justify the Administration's war policy.

His problem is to establish, or re-establish, contact with the disaffected minority that seems somehow to have passed him in time.

This minority would say that Mr. Humphrey's time has come, all right—but too late.

Whether that is so is the question that he will puzzle out in the glare of the nation's vision between now and the election in November.

"All the News That's Fit to Print"

The New York Times

LATE CITY EDITION

Weather: Rain, warm today; clear tonight. Sunny, pleasant tomorrow. Temp. range: today 80-66; Sunday 71-66. Temp.-Hum. Index yesterday 69. Complete U.S. report on P. 50.

VOL. CXVIII . No. 40,721

NEW YORK, MONDAY, JULY 21, 1969

10 CENTS

MEN WALK ON MOON

ASTRONAUTS LAND ON PLAIN; COLLECT ROCKS, PLANT FLAG

Voice From Moon: 'Eagle Has Landed'

EAGLE (the lunar module): Houston, Tranquility Base here. The Eagle has landed.

HOUSTON: Roger, Tranquility, we copy you on the ground. You've got a bunch of guys about to turn blue. We're breathing again. Thanks a lot.

TRANQUILITY BASE: Thank you.

HOUSTON: You're looking good here.

TRANQUILITY BASE: A very smooth touchdown.

HOUSTON: Eagle, you are stay for T1. [The first step in the lunar operation.] Over.

TRANQUILITY BASE: Roger. Stay for T1.

HOUSTON: Roger and we see you venting the ox.

TRANQUILITY BASE: Roger.

COLUMBIA (the command and service module): How do you read me?

HOUSTON: Columbia, he has landed Tranquility Base. Eagle is at Tranquility. I read you five by. Over.

COLUMBIA: Yes, I heard the whole thing.

HOUSTON: Well, it's a good show.

COLUMBIA: Fantastic.

TRANQUILITY BASE: I'll second that.

APOLLO CONTROL: The next major stay-no stay will be for the T2 event. That is at 21 minutes 26 seconds after initiation of power descent.

COLUMBIA: Up telemetry command reset to reacquire on high gain.

HOUSTON: Copy. Out.

APOLLO CONTROL: We have an unofficial time for that touchdown of 102 hours, 45 minutes, 42 seconds and we will update that.

HOUSTON: Eagle, you loaded R2 wrong. We want 10254.

TRANQUILITY BASE: Roger. Do you want the horizontal 55 15.2?

HOUSTON: That's affirmative.

APOLLO CONTROL: We're now less than four minutes from our next stay-no stay. It will be for one complete revolution of the command module.

One of the first things that Armstrong and Aldrin will do after getting their next stay-no stay will be to remove their helmets and gloves.

HOUSTON: Eagle, you are stay for T2. Over.

Continued on Page 4, Col. 1

VOYAGE TO THE MOON

By Archibald MacLeish

Presence among us,
wanderer in our skies,
dazzle of silver in our leaves and on our waters silver,
O
silver evasion in our farthest thought—
"the visiting moon" . . . "the glimpses of the moon" . . .

and we have touched you!

From the first of time,
before the first of time, before the
first men tasted time, we thought of you.
You were a wonder to us, unattainable,
a longing past the reach of longing,
a light beyond our light, our lives—perhaps
a meaning to us . . .

Now
our hands have touched you in your depth of night.

Three days and three nights we journeyed,
steered by farthest stars, climbed outward,
crossed the invisible tide-rip where the floating dust
falls one way or the other in the void between,
followed that other down, encountered
cold, faced death—unfathomable emptiness . . .

Then, the fourth day evening, we descended,
made fast, set foot at dawn upon your beaches,
sifted between our fingers your cold sand.

We stand here in the dusk, the cold, the silence . . .

and here, as at the first of time, we lift our heads.
Over us, more beautiful than the moon, a
moon, a wonder to us, unattainable,
a longing past the reach of longing,
a light beyond our light, our lives—perhaps
a meaning to us . . .

O, a meaning!

over us on these silent beaches the bright
earth,
presence among us

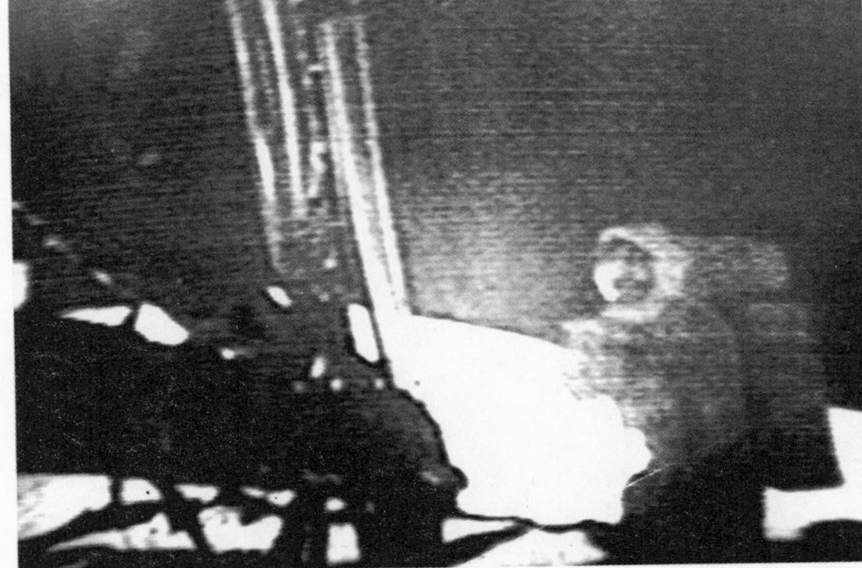

Neil A. Armstrong moves away from the leg of the landing craft after taking the first step on the surface of the moon

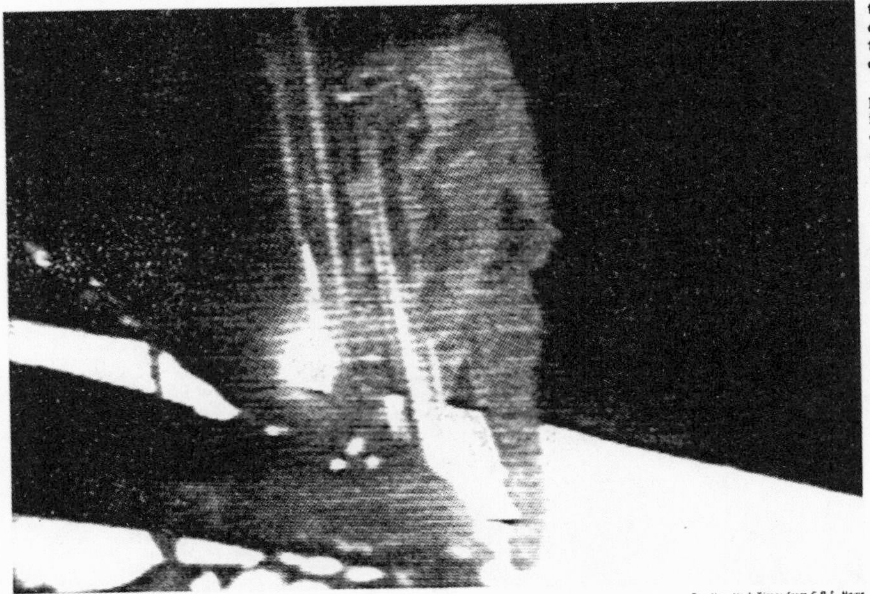

The New York Times from C.B.S. News

Col. Edwin E. Aldrin Jr. climbing down the ladder. The television camera was attached to a side of the lunar module.

Associated Press

Mr. Armstrong, right, and Colonel Aldrin raise the U.S. flag. A metal rod at right angles to the mast keeps flag unfurled.

A Powdery Surface Is Closely Explored

By JOHN NOBLE WILFORD

Special to The New York Times

HOUSTON, Monday, July 21—Men have landed and walked on the moon.

Two Americans, astronauts of Apollo 11, steered their fragile four-legged lunar module safely and smoothly to the historic landing yesterday at 4:17:40 P.M., Eastern daylight time.

Neil A. Armstrong, the 38-year-old civilian commander, radioed to earth and the mission control room here:

"Houston, Tranquility Base here. The Eagle has landed."

The first men to reach the moon—Mr. Armstrong and his co-pilot, Col. Edwin E. Aldrin Jr. of the Air Force—brought their ship to rest on a level, rock-strewn plain near the southwestern shore of the arid Sea of Tranquility.

About six and a half hours later, Mr. Armstrong opened the landing craft's hatch, stepped slowly down the ladder and declared as he planted the first human footprint on the lunar crust:

"That's one small step for man, one giant leap for mankind."

His first step on the moon came at 10:56:20 P.M., as a television camera outside the craft transmitted his every move to an awed and excited audience of hundreds of millions of people on earth.

Tentative Steps Test Soil

Mr. Armstrong's initial steps were tentative tests of the lunar soil's firmness and of his ability to move about easily in his bulky white spacesuit and backpacks and under the influence of lunar gravity, which is one-sixth that of the earth.

"The surface is fine and powdery," the astronaut reported. "I can pick it up loosely with my toe. It does adhere in fine layers like powdered charcoal to the sole and sides of my boots. I only go in a small fraction of an inch, maybe an eighth of an inch. But I can see the footprints of my boots in the treads in the fine sandy particles.

After 19 minutes of Mr. Armstrong's testing, Colonel Aldrin joined him outside the craft.

The two men got busy setting up another television camera out from the lunar module, planting an American flag into the ground, scooping up soil and rock samples, deploying scientific experiments and hopping and loping about in a demonstration of their lunar agility.

They found walking and working on the moon less taxing than had been forecast. Mr. Armstrong once reported he was "very comfortable."

And people back on earth found the black-and-white television pictures of the bug-shaped lunar module and the men tramping about it so sharp and clear as to seem unreal, more like a toy and toy-like figures than human beings on the most daring and far-reaching expedition thus far undertaken.

Nixon Telephones Congratulations

During one break in the astronauts' work, President Nixon congratulated them from the White House in what, he said, "certainly has to be the most historic telephone call ever made."

"Because of what you have done," the President told the astronauts, "the heavens have become a part of man's world. And as you talk to us from the Sea of Tranquility it requires us to redouble our efforts to bring peace and tranquility to earth.

"For one priceless moment in the whole history of man all the people on this earth are truly one—one in their pride in what you have done and one in our prayers that you will return safely to earth."

Mr. Armstrong replied:

"Thank you Mr. President. It's a great honor and privilege for us to be here representing not only the United States but men of peace of all nations, men with interests and a curiosity and men with a vision for the future."

Mr. Armstrong and Colonel Aldrin returned to their landing craft and closed the hatch at 1:12 A.M., 2 hours 21 minutes after opening the hatch on the moon. While the third member of the crew, Lieut. Col. Michael Collins of the Air Force, kept his orbital vigil overhead in the command ship, the two moon explorers settled down to sleep.

Outside their vehicle the astronauts had found a bleak

Continued on Pages 2, Col. 1

Today's 4-Part Issue of The Times

This morning's issue of The New York Times is divided into four parts. The first part is devoted to news of Apollo 11. and includes Editorials and letters to the Editor (Page 16). Poems on the landing on the moon appear on Page 17.

General news begins on the first page of the second part. The News Summary and Index is on the first page of the third part, which includes sports news, obituaries (Page 51) and transportation news and weather reports (Pages 50 and 52).

Financial and business news begins on the first page of the fourth part.

Following is the News Index for today's issue:

News Summary and Index, Page 35

Published Daily. Second-Class Postage Paid at New York, N. Y., and at additional mailing offices.

Astronauts Land Module on Lunar Plain; Collect Rocks and Plant American Flag

Powdery Moon Surface Explored Around Craft

Continued From Page 1, Col. 8

world. It was just before dawn, with the sun low over the eastern horizon behind them and the chill of the long lunar nights still clinging to the boulders, small craters and hills before them.

Colonel Aldrin said that he could see "literally thousands of small craters" and a low hill out in the distance. But most of all he was impressed initially by the "variety of shapes, angularities, granularities" of the rocks and soil where the landing craft, code-named Eagle had set down.

The landing was made four miles west of the aiming point, but well within the designated area. An apparent error in some data fed into the craft's guidance computer from the earth was said to have accounted for the discrepancy.

Suddenly the astronauts were startled to see that the computer was guiding them toward a possibly disastrous touchdown in a boulder-filled crater about the size of a football field.

Mr. Armstrong grabbed manual control of the vehicle and guided it safely over the crater to a smoother spot, the rocket engine stirring a cloud of moon dust during the final seconds of descent.

Soon after the landing, upon checking and finding the spacecraft in good condition, Mr. Armstrong and Colonel Aldrin made their decision to open the hatch and get out earlier than originally scheduled. The flight plan had called for the moon walk to begin at 2:12 A.M.

Flight controllers here said that the early moon walk would not mean that the astronauts would also leave the moon earlier. The lift-off is scheduled to come at about 1:55 P.M. today.

Their departure from the landing craft out onto the surface was delayed for a time when they had trouble depressurizing the cabin so that they could open the hatch. All the oxygen in the cabin had to be vented.

Once the pressure gauge finally dropped to zero, they opened the hatch and Mr. Armstrong stepped out on the small porch at the top of the nine-step ladder.

"O.K., Houston, I'm on the porch," he reported, as he descended.

On the second step from the top, he pulled a lanyard that released a fold-down equipment compartment on the side of the lunar module. This deployed the television camera that transmitted the dramatic pictures of man's first steps on the moon.

Ancient Dream Fulfilled

It was man's first landing on another world, the realization of centuries of dreams, the fulfillment of a decade of striving, a triumph of modern technology and personal courage, the most dramatic demonstration of what man can do if he applies his mind and resources with single-minded determination.

The moon, long the symbol of the impossible and the inaccessible, was now within man's reach, the first port of call in this new age of spacefaring.

Immediately after the landing, Dr. Thomas O. Paine, administrator of the National Aeronautics and Space Administration, telephoned President Nixon in Washington to report:

"Mr. President, it is my honor on behalf of the entire NASA team to report to you that the Eagle has landed on the Sea of Tranquility and our astronauts are safe and looking forward to starting the exploration of the moon."

The landing craft from the Apollo 11 spaceship was scheduled to remain on the moon about 22 hours, while Colonel Collins of the Air Force, the third member of the Apollo 11 crew, piloted the command ship, Columbia, in orbit overhead.

"You're looking good in every respect," Mission Control told the two men of Eagle after examining data indicating that the module should be able to remain on the moon the full 22 hours.

Mr. Armstrong and Colonel Aldrin planned to sleep after the moon walk and then make their preparations for the lift-off for the return to a rendezvous with Colonel Collins in the command ship.

Apollo 11's journey into history began last Wednesday from launching pad 39-A at Cape Kennedy, Fla. After an almost flawless three-day flight, the joined command ship and lunar module swept into an orbit of the moon yesterday afternoon.

The three men were awake for their big day at 7 A.M. when their spacecraft emerged from behind the moon on its 10th revolution, moving from east to west across the face of the moon along its equator.

Their orbit was 73.6 miles by 64 miles in altitude, their speed 3,660 miles an hour. At that altitude and speed, it took about two hours to complete a full orbit of the moon.

The sun was rising over their landing site on the Sea of Tranquility.

"We can pick out almost all of the features we've identified previously," Mr. Armstrong reported.

After breakfast, on their 11th revolution, Colonel Aldrin and then Mr. Armstrong, both dressed in their white pressurized suits, crawled through the connecting tunnel into the lunar module.

They turned on the electrical power, checked all the switch settings on the cockpit panel and checked communications with the command ship and the ground controllers. Everything was "nominal," as the spacemen say.

LM Ready for Descent

The lunar module was ready. Its four legs with yard-wide footpads were extended so that the height of the 16½-ton vehicle now measured 22 feet and 11 inches and its width 31 feet.

Mr. Armstrong stood at the left side of the cockpit, and Colonel Aldrin at the right. Both were loosely restrained by harnesses. They had closed the hatch to the connecting tunnel.

The walls of their craft were finely milled aluminum foil. If anything happened so that it could not return to the command ship, the lunar module would be too delicate to withstand a plunge through earth's atmosphere, even if it had the rocket power.

Nearly three-fourths of the vehicle's weight was in propellants for the descent and ascent rockets—Aerozine 50 and nitrogen oxide, which substituted for the oxygen, making combustion possible.

It was an ungainly craft that creaked and groaned in flight. But years of development and testing had determined that it was the lightest and most practical way to get two men to the moon's surface.

Before Apollo 11 disappeared behind the moon near the end of its 12th orbit, mission control gave the astronauts their "go" for undocking—the separation of Eagle from Columbia.

Colonel Collins had already released 12 of the latches holding the two ships together at the connecting tunnel. He did this when he closed the hatch at the command ship's nose. While behind the moon, he was to flip a switch on the control panel to release the three remaining latches by a spring action.

At 1:50 P.M., when communications signals were reacquired, Mission Control asked: "How does it look?"

"Eagle has wings," Mr. Armstrong replied.

The two ships were then only a few feet apart. But at 2:12 P.M., Colonel Collins fired the command ship's maneuvering rockets to move about two miles away and in a slightly different orbit from the lunar module.

"It looks like you've got a fine-looking flying machine there, Eagle, despite the fact you're upside down," Colonel Collins commented, watching the spidery lunar module receding in the distance.

"Somebody's upside down," Mr. Armstrong replied.

What is "up" and what is "down" is never quite clear in the absence of landmarks and the sensation of gravity's pull.

As Mr. Armstrong and Colonel Aldrin rode the lunar module back around to the moon's far side, the rocket engine in the vehicle's lower stage was pointed toward the line of flight. The two pilots were leaning toward the cockpit controls, riding backwards and facing downward.

"Everything is 'go'," they were assured by Mission Control.

Their on-board guidance and navigation computer was instructed to trigger a 29.8-second firing of the descent rocket, the 9,870-pound-thrust throttable engine that would slow down the lunar module and send it toward the moon on a long, curving trajectory.

The firing was set to take place at 3:08 P.M., when the craft would be behind the moon and once again out of touch with the ground.

Suspense built up in the control room here. Flight controllers stood silently at their consoles. Among those waiting for word of the rocket firing were Dr. Thomas O. Paine, the space agency's administrator, most of the Apollo project officials and several astronauts.

At 3:46 P.M., contact was established with the command ship.

Colonel Collins reported, "Listen, baby, things are going just swimmingly, just beautiful."

There was still no word from the lunar module for two minutes. Then came a weak signal, some static and whistling, and finally the calm voice of Mr. Armstrong.

"The burn was on time," the Apollo 11 commander declared.

When he read out data on the beginning of the descent, Mission Control concluded that it "look great." The lunar module had already descended from an altitude of 65.5 miles to 21 miles and was coasting steadily downward.

Eugene F. Kranz, the flight director, turned to his associates and said, "We're off to a good start. Play it cool."

Colonel Aldrin reported some oscillations in the vehicle's antenna, but nothing serious. Several times the astronauts were told to turn the vehicle slightly to move the antenna into a better position for communications over the 230,000 miles.

"You're 'go' for PDI," radioed Mission Control, referring to the powered descent initiation—the beginning of the nearly 13-minute final blast of the rocket to the soft touchdown.

When the two men reached an altitude of 50,000 feet, which was approximately the lowest point reached by Apollo 10 in May, green lights on the computer display keyboard in the cockpit blinked the number 99.

This signaled Mr. Armstrong that he had five seconds to decide whether to go ahead for the landing or continue on its orbital path back to the command ship. He pressed the "proceed" button.

The throttleable engine built up thrust gradually, firing continuously as the lunar module descended along the steadily steepening trajectory to the landing site about 250 miles away.

"Looking good," Mission Control radioed the men.

Four minutes after the firing the lunar module was down to 40,000 feet. After five and a half minutes, it was 33,500 feet. At six minutes, 27,000 feet.

"Better than the simulator," said Colonel Aldrin, referring to their practice landings at the spacecraft center.

Seven minutes after the firing, the men were 21,000 feet above the surface and still moving forward toward the landing site. The guidance computer was driving the rocket engine.

The lunar module was slowing down. At an altitude of about 7,200 feet, with the landing site still about five miles ahead, the computer commanded control jets to fire and tilt the bug-shaped craft almost upright so that its triangular windows pointed forward.

Mr. Armstrong and Colonel Aldrin then got their first close-up view of the plain they were aiming for. It was then about three and a half minutes to touchdown.

The brownish-gray panorama rushed below them—the myriad craters, hills and ridges, deep cracks and ancient rubble on the moon, which Dr. Robert Jastrow, the space agency scientist, called the "Rosetta Stone of life."

"You're 'go' for landing," Mission Control informed the two men.

The Eagle closed in, dropping about 20 feet a second, until it was hovering almost directly over the landing area at an altitude of 500 feet.

Its floor was littered with boulders.

It was when the craft reached an altitude of 300 feet that Mr. Armstrong took over semimanual control for the rest of the way. The computer continued to have control of the rocket firing, but the astronaut could adjust the craft's hovering position.

He was expected to take over such control anyway, but the sight of a crater looming ahead at the touchdown point made it imperative.

As Mr. Armstrong said later, "The auto-targeting was taking us right into a football field-sized crater, with a large number of big boulders and rocks."

For about 90 seconds, he peered through the window in search of a clear touchdown point. Using the lever at his right hand, he tilted the vehicle forward to redirect the firing of the maneuvering jets and thus shift its hovering position.

Finally, Mr. Armstrong found the spot he liked, and the blue light on the cockpit flashed to indicate that five-foot-long probes, like curb feelers, on three of the four legs had touched the surface.

"Contact light," Mr. Armstrong radioed.

He pressed a button marked "Stop" and reported, "okay, engine stop."

There were a few more cryptic messages of functions performed.

Then Maj. Charles M. Duke, the capsule communicator in the control room, radioed to the two astronauts:

"We copy you down, Eagle."

"Houston, Tranquility Base here. The Eagle has landed."

"Roger, Tranquility," Major Duke replied. "We copy you on the ground. You got a bunch of guys about to turn blue. We are breathing again. Thanks a lot."

Colonel Aldrin assured Mission Control it was a "very smooth touchdown."

The Eagle came to rest at an angle of only about four and a half degrees. The angle could have been more than 30 degrees without threatening to tip the vehicle over.

The landing site, about 120 miles southwest of the crater Maskelyne, is on the right side of the moon as seen from earth. The position: Lat. 0.799 degrees N., Long. 23.46 degrees E.

Although Mr. Armstrong is known as a man of few words, his heartbeats told of his excitement upon leading man's first landing on the moon.

At the time of the descent rocket ignition, his heartbeat rate registered 110 a minute—77 is normal for him—and it shot up to 156 at touchdown.

At the time of the landing, Colonel Collins was riding the command ship Columbia about 65 miles overhead.

Mission control informed the colonel, "Eagle is at Tranquility."

"Yea, I heard the whole thing," Colonel Collins, the man who went so far but not all the way, replied. "Fantastic."

When the Apollo astronauts landed on the Sea of Tranquility, the temperature at their touchdown site was about zero degrees Fahrenheit in the sunlight, even colder in the shade.

During a lunar night, which lasts 14 earth days, temperatures plunge as low as 280 degrees below zero. Unlike earth, the moon, having no atmosphere to act as a blanket, is unable to retain any of the day's warmth during the night.

During the equally long lunar day, temperatures rise as high as 280 degrees. By the time of Eagle's departure from the moon, with the sun higher in the sky, the temperatures there will have risen to about 90 degrees.

This particular landing site was one of five selected by Apollo project officials after analysis of pictures returned by the five Lunar Orbiter unmanned spacecraft.

All five sites are situated across the lunar equator on the side of the moon always facing earth. Being on the equator reduces the maneuvering for the astronauts to get there. Being on the near side of the moon, of course, makes it possible to communicate with the explorers.

CONGRATULATIONS: President Nixon talking with Neil A. Armstrong and Colonel Edwin E. Aldrin Jr. on the moon

The New York Times

Nixon Makes 'Most Historic Telephone Call Ever'

By WALTER RUGABER
Special to The New York Times

WASHINGTON, July 20—President Nixon told the Apollo 11 astronauts tonight that their arrival on the moon would inspire man to work harder for a solution of the troubles on his own planet.

He spoke to the moon explorers during a two-minute radio hookup that he said "certainly has to be the most historic telephone call ever made."

"Because of what you have done," he said, "the heavens have become part of man's world. And as you talk to us from the Sea of Tranquility, it inspires us to redouble our efforts to bring peace and tranquillity to earth.

"For one priceless moment in the whole history of man, all the people of this earth are one—one in their pride in what you have done and one in our prayers that you will return safely to earth."

Mr. Nixon spoke to the two astronauts—Neil A. Armstrong, a civilian, and Col. Edwin E. Aldrin Jr. of the Air Force—after he followed their landing and first steps on the lunar surface on television.

The conversation was televised from both ends. The President spoke from his oval office in the West Wing of the White House, and the spacemen stood in front of a small camera planted on the moon.

The voice signal went from the White House switchboard to the Goddard Space Flight Center in Maryland, over a radio link to the Space Center in Houston and through the Goldstone antenna in California.

"For every American this has to be the proudest day of our lives," the President said. "And for people all over the world I'm sure they, too, join with Americans in recognizing what an immense feat this is."

Mr. Armstrong, commander of the Apollo mission, thanked the President and said it was "a great honor and privilege for us to be here representing not only the United States but men of peace of all nations."

The President signed off by saying that he—and "all of us"—would look forward to seeing the astronauts on the Hornet. Mr. Nixon will greet the three men on that aircraft carrier after their splashdown.

Like hundreds of millions of others around the world, the President spent much of the afternoon "glued to his TV set." He returned to the West Wing just before 8 P.M.

Col. Frank Borman, the astronaut, joined Mr. Nixon in the small den just off the oval office and explained the preparations for the first step on the moon. When Mr. Armstrong made it, Colonel Borman quoted the President as saying:

"It's an unbelievable thing. It's fantastic . . . isn't that wonderful?"

Mr. Nixon told Colonel Borman the moon landing had "a significance beyond the scientific value."

A special panel is working on American space goals beyond the moon. Their recommendations are due by Sept. 1 and Donald L. Ziegler, the White House press secretary, said that the President would decide on new objectives after receiving them.

TRANSCRIPT OF TALK

PRESIDENT NIXON: Hello, Neil and Buzz. I'm talking to you by telephone from the Oval Room at the White House, and this certainly has to be the most historic telephone call ever made.

I just can't tell you how proud we all are of what you've done. For every American this has to be the proudest day of our lives. And for people all over the world I am sure they, too, join with Americans in recognizing what an immense feat this is.

Because of what you have done, the heavens have become a part of man's world. And as you talk to us from the Sea of Tranquility, it inspires us to redouble our efforts to bring peace and tranquillity to earth.

For one priceless moment in the whole history of man all the people on this earth are truly one—one in their pride in what you have done and one in our prayers that you will return safely to earth.

ARMSTRONG: Thank you, Mr. President. It's a great honor and privilege for us to be here representing not only the United States but men of peace of all nations, men with interest and a curiosity and men with a vision for the future.

It's an honor for us to be able to participate here today.

NIXON: Thank you very much, and I look forward—all of us look forward—to seeing you on the Hornet on Thursday.

ARMSTRONG: Thank you. I look forward to that very much, sir.

Two Men Quickly Adjust To Conditions on Moon

By HAROLD M. SCHMECK Jr.
Special to The New York Times

HOUSTON, Monday, July 21—Two American astronauts proved last night that man can see, walk and work on the surface of the moon.

Moving very cautiously at first, they soon found they could walk across the lunar surface easily in bounding, almost floating steps.

They seemed to have a little difficulty in adjusting their vision to the deep shadows of the airless moon, but their depth perception appeared not to suffer at all, nor did their appreciation of the scene.

"Magnificent desolation," was the phrase Col. Edwin E. Aldrin Jr. used to describe the view when he joined Neil A. Armstrong on the lunar surface.

Shortly after he emerged, slowly and with great caution, from the lunar module, Mr. Armstrong said that he was having no difficulty in moving around and that it seemed perhaps easier than the simulations in which he had trained on earth.

Soon after that he was bounding across the surface in easy kangaroo hops. His heavy spacesuit and life-support pack, that weigh 183 pounds on earth, impeded his movements very little.

"You do have to be rather careful to keep track of where your center of mass is," Mr. Armstrong said after loping across the surface for several yards.

He and Colonel Aldrin picked up samples, set out an American flag and scientific instruments all with evident ease.

Although their steps made no sounds at all on the airless surface of the moon, their running conversation with each other and with the earth more than 200,000 miles away seemed to keep them from feeling isolation.

They spoke of light and dark grays as the principal, but not the only, colors. They said they found a purple rock.

The television pictures showed deep black shadows and glaring sunlight.

Because there is no air at all on the moon there is nothing to soften the light or to diminish the sun's fierce light and ultraviolet radiation.

Mr. Armstrong said he had some trouble adjusting his vision to the deep shadow when he walked to the dark side of the lunar module.

The surface temperature was estimated at 40 to 50 degrees Fahrenheit when the astronauts first stepped outside. In the shadows it was 150 degrees below zero.

Even though the astronauts are protected by their water-cooled spacesuits they said they could feel a difference when they went from shadow to sunlight or the reverse.

At lunar midday, long after the astronauts have left the moon, the temperature in sunlight will go as high as 243 degrees above zero. In the depths of the lunar night the surface temperature sinks to about 279 degrees below zero.

The scene the astronauts showed when they moved their television camera toward the horizon was just what had been expected — an almost flat crater-pocked, undulating surface. No lunar mountain or ridges could be seen in the pictures.

The American flag, held outspread by a wire supporting its top, hung completely motionless in the harsh sunlight.

Moving easily through their brightly lit and unearthly surroundings, the first two men to make their footprints on the moon acted as though they were comfortable and very much at home.

Lunar Tests May Give Answers to Old Riddles

By WALTER SULLIVAN
Special to The New York Times

HOUSTON, Monday, July 21—After centuries of speculation as to the nature of earth's silvery satellite, men dug into the moon's surface last night, collecting specimens that should help answer a wide range of long-standing riddles.

Moving with almost gay agility, the astronauts carried a miniature seismic station to what was hopefully a safe distance and implanted it to transmit data on moonquakes after their departure.

They also set up a reflector to bounce laser beams back to earth. By means of this device, physicists hope to resolve a debate concerning the constancy of gravity. One theory says it is slowly weakening.

Almost immediately after he descended to the surface of the moon, Neil A. Armstrong set up a banner of aluminum foil facing the sun. The purpose was to capture the nuclei of atoms blowing out from the sun in the so-called solar wind. The foil is to be analyzed by a Swiss laboratory, looking in particular for nuclei of the "noble gases" such as neon, argon and krypton.

Firmness a Surprise

Perhaps the greatest surprise was the hardness of the lunar surface. It was covered with a very fine powder, but the four foot pads of the lunar module, or LM, penetrated only a few inches.

The surface powder was dark and almost carbon-like in appearance. The rocks were coated with it, making them slippery in the deep vacuum that exits on the lunar surface.

This made it more difficult to pick them up with the special tongs provided for the purpose. Millions of watchers on earth were able to witness thie first celestial geoogic prospecting. The long-handled tools—tongs and scoop—could clearly be seen as Lieut. Col. Edwin E. Aldrin Jr. made his selections.

Some of the rocks were described as vesicular, that is, full of small cavities. This is characteristic of certain forms of lava, but does not definitely establish the rock as a lava fragment.

Another rock was said to resemble biotite, a dark green or black form of mica that is characteristic of continental rocks on earth. Its presence on the moon could indicate that the history of the moon had features in cmmon with that of the earth. However, definite identification, as the astronauts pointed out, must await their return.

The samples were placed in two airtight boxes to be hauled aboard for transport home. They will be isolated from exposure to oxygen in the spacecraft or air on arrival on earth.

One of the last acts of the Apollo team was to drive coring tubes into the lunar surface, to capture material deep enough to be free of any exposure to exhaust gases from the rocket that lowered the LM to the surface. These core samples should also show any subtle layering of material near the surface.

Colonel Aldrin pointed out to the onlookers how hard he had to work to drive the tube into the resistant surface.

Although the discovery that they were coming down in the middle of a boulder-filled moon crater may have given the two Apollo astronauts a few anxious moments yesterday, it will likely prove to result in scientific boons.

They managed to delay touchdown until they had skimmed across the crater, large as a football field, and beyond its rim, but they came down in an area that was strewn with boulders of many sizes and varieties.

Some were presumably blown out of the lunar depths when the crater was formed probably by the explosive impact of a large meteorite. These boulders represent rock buried perhaps 100 feet or more below the surface—far beyond the reach of the two men's sampling tools.

Other rocks probably were thrown from over the horizon by more massive impact and thus are specimens from other regions of the moon. Since the moon has virtually no air and its gravity is only one-sixth as strong as earth's gravity, explosive impacts sometimes blow debris halfway around the moon.

The laser experiments are of major scientific interest because they could solve a number of puzzles. The reflectors should make it possible to detect variations in earth-moon distances as small as six inches. This, in turn, could provide the most sensitive tests to date of Einstein's general theory of relativity.

That theory concerns the behavior of gravity. It accounts for a slight departure of the orbit of the planet Mercury from the timetable predicted by the classical gravity laws of Sir Isaac Newton. However, another relativity theory has been devised by Drs. Robert H. Dicke and Carl H. Brans.

Continental Changes

That theory, too, accounts for the behavior of the Mercury orbit. It also predicts that, as the universe expands, gravity weakens and the moon therefore moves farther from the earth at about one inch a year.

The top priority assigned to the astronauts was the collection of moon samples. After years of inconclusive debate about the origin of the moon, it has become apparent that only with a representative collection of lunar rocks and soil samples can the correct answer be determined.

If the moon was torn from the earth, that should be evident in the composition of its rocks. If it is, in effect, a giant meteorite it should contain such formations as the chondrules (tiny, rounded inclusions that often look like rice grains scattered through the rocks).

Chondrules are not found in any rocks native to the earth.

If the moon was once molten inside, allowing the iron and other heavy materials to sink to its core, as occurred on earth, the lighter material would have risen to the surface, like scum, to form lighter rocks, like those on our continent. This will be evident if any granites are found

From the Lunar Surface, a Message to Mission Control: 'The Eagle Has Landed'

Continued From Page 1, Col. 2

TRANQUILITY BASE: Roger. Stay for T2. We thank you.

HOUSTON: Roger, sir.

APOLLO CONTROL: That's stay for another two minutes plus. The next stay-no stay will be for one revolution.

TRANQUILITY BASE: Houston, that may have seemed like a very long final phase but the auto targeting was taking us right into a football field-sized crater with a large number of big boulders and rocks for about one or two crater diameters around it. And it required us to fly manually over the rock field to find a reasonably good area.

HOUSTON: Roger. We copy. It was beautiful from here, Tranquility. Over.

TRANQUILITY BASE: We'll get to the details of what's around here but it looks like a collection of just about every variety of shape, angularity, granularity, about every variety of rock you could find. The colors vary pretty much depending on how you are looking relative to the zero phase length. There doesn't appear to be too much of a general color at all. However, it looks as though some of the rocks and boulders, of which there are quite a few in the near area—it looks as though they're going to have some interesting colors to them. Over.

HOUSTON: Roger. Copy. Sounds good to us, Tranquility. We'll let you press on through the simulated countdown and we'll talk to you later. Over.

TRANQUILITY BASE: Okay, this one-sixth G is just like an airplane.

HOUSTON: Roger, Tranquility. Be advised there are lots of smiling faces in this room and all over the world. Over.

TRANQUILITY BASE: There are two of them up here.

HOUSTON: Roger. It was a beautiful job, you guys.

COLUMBIA: And don't forget one in the command module.

TRANQUILITY BASE: Roger.

Remark by Collins

APOLLO CONTROL: That last remark from Mike Collins at an altitude of 60 miles. The comments on the landing, on the manual take-over came from Neil Armstrong. Buzz Aldrin followed that with a description of the lunar surface and the rocks and boulders that they are able to see out the window of the LM.

COLUMBIA: Thanks for putting me on relay, Houston. I was missing all the action.

HOUSTON: Roger. We'll enable relay.

COLUMBIA (4:30 P.M.): I just got it, I think.

HOUSTON: Roger, Columbia. This is Houston. Say something; they ought to be able to hear you. Over.

COLUMBIA: Roger. Tranquility Base. It sure sounded great from up here. You guys did a fantastic job.

TRANQUILITY BASE: Thank you. Just keep that orbiting base ready for us up there, now.

COLUMBIA: Will do.

APOLLO CONTROL: That request from Neil Armstrong.

APOLLO CONTROL: We've just gotten a report from the telcom here in mission control that LM systems look good after that landing. We're about 26 minutes now from loss of signal from the command module.

HOUSTON: Tranquility Base, Houston. All your consumables are solid. You're looking good in every respect. We copy the DPS venting. Everything is copacetic. Over.

TRANQUILITY BASE: Thank you, Houston. Houston, the guys that bet that we wouldn't be able to tell precisely where we are are the winners today. We were a little busy worrying about program alarms and things like that in the part of the descent where we would normally be picking out our landing spot; and aside from a good look at several of the craters we came over in the final descent, I haven't been able to pick out the things on the horizon as a reference as yet.

HOUSTON: Rog, Tranquility. No sweat. We'll figure out—we'll figure it out. Over.

TRANQUILITY BASE: You might be interested to know that I don't think we noticed any difficulty at all in adapting to one-sixth G. It seems immediately natural to live in this environment.

HOUSTON: Roger, Tranquility. We copy. Over.

APOLLO CONTROL: Neil Armstrong reporting there is no difficulty adapting to the one-sixth gravity of the moon.

TRANQUILITY BASE: [Unintelligible] . . . window, with relatively level plain cratered with fairly a large number of craters of the 5- to 50-foot variety. And some ridges, small, 20 to 30 feet high, I would guess. And literally thousands of little one- and two-foot craters around the area. We see some angular blocks out several hundred feet in front of us that are probably two feet in size and have angular edges. There is a hill in view just about on the ground track ahead of us. Difficult to estimate, but might be a half a mile or a mile.

HOUSTON: Roger, Tranquility. We copy. Over.

COLUMBIA: Sounds like it looks a lot better than it did yesterday. At that very low sun angle, it looked rough as a cob then.

TRANQUILITY BASE: It really was rough, Mike, over the targeted landing area. It was extremely rough, cratered and large numbers of rocks that were probably some many larger than 5 or 10 feet in size.

COLUMBIA: When in doubt, land long.

TRANQUILITY BASE: Well, we did.

Question on Landing

COLUMBIA: Do you have any idea whether they landed left or right of center line—just a little bit long. Is that all we know?

HOUSTON: Apparently that's about all we can tell. Over.

COLUMBIA: Okay, thank you.

TRANQUILITY BASE: Okay. I'd say the color of the local surface is very comparable to that we observed from orbit at this sun angle—about 10 degrees sun angle or that nature. It's pretty much without color. It's gray and it's very white as you look into the zero phase line. And it's considerably darker gray, more like an ashen gray, as you look out 90 degrees to the sun. Some of the surface rocks in close here that have been fractured or disturbed by the rocket engine plume are coated with this light gray on the outside. But where they've been broken, they display a dark, very dark, gray interior and it looks like it could be country basalt.

HOUSTON: Tranquility, Houston. Please vent fuel and ox again. Over. It's building back up.

TRANQUILITY BASE: Okay, ox going now.

HOUSTON: Tranquility, Houston. You can open both fuel and ox vent now. Over.

TRANQUILITY BASE: Houston, Tranquility. Standing by for go AGS to the line and lunar line. Over.

HOUSTON: Stand by.

HOUSTON: Tranquility, Houston. You're go for the AGS the line and the lunar line. Over.

TRANQUILITY BASE: Roger.

HOUSTON: Tranquility, Houston. Please vent the fuel. It's increasing rapidly. Over.

TRANQUILITY BASE: We show 30 psi in the fuel and 30 on the oxydizer.

HOUSTON: Roger, we're reading somewhat different than that. Stand by.

TRANQUILITY BASE: The fuel temperature is reading 64 in the descent two and the oxydizer off scale low. Descent one is showing 61 in the fuel and 65 in the oxydizer.

HOUSTON: Roger, stand by.

HOUSTON: Tranquility, Houston. Please take the fuel vent switch and hold it open. Over.

TRANQUILITY BASE: Okay. We're holding it open, indicating about 24 psi on board.

HOUSTON: Roger.

TRANQUILITY BASE: Now indicating 20 psi in fuel.

HOUSTON: Roger.

TRANQUILITY BASE: And 22 in the ox.

HOUSTON: Roger.

TRANQUILITY BASE: Now indicating 15 psi in both tanks.

HOUSTON: Roger.

HOUSTON: Tranquility, Houston. If you haven't

Associated Press from NASA

CONCENTRATION: Alan L. Bean, an astronaut who will be on the Apollo 12 flight, watching a tracking board at the Manned Space Center record the lunar module landing.

done so, you can release the fuel vent switch. Over.

TRANQUILITY BASE: Roger.

HOUSTON: Tranquility, Houston. We have indication that we've frozen up the descent fuel helium heat exchanger and with some fuel trapped in the line between air and the valves and the pressure we're looking at is increasing there. Over.

TRANQUILITY BASE. Roger. Understand.

HOUSTON: Tranquility Base, Houston. If you have not done so, please close both fuel and ox vents now.

TRANQUILITY BASE: They're closed.

HOUSTON: Thank you, sir.

TRANQUILITY BASE: From the surface we could not see any stars out the window, but on my overhead patch I'm looking at the earth. It's big and bright, beautiful. Buzz is going to give a try at seeing some stars through the optics.

HOUSTON: Roger, Tranquility. We understand must be a beautiful sight. Over.

APOLLO CONTROL: We would like to point out that the fuel pressure problem that has been called to the attention of the crew is in the descent system. It is apparently downstream of the tanks where a small amount of fluid has been trapped in a line and we don't expect it to cause any problem. The line should be able to take far more pressure than the fluid would exert. In the event that there was an overpressurization, we would expect that the line would spring a small leak, the pressure would drop rapidly. Again I would point out that we do not see this as a significant problem.

'Going Over the Hill'

HOUSTON: Columbia, Houston. Two minutes to LOS [loss of signal]. You're looking great. Going over the hill. Over.

COLUMBIA: Okay. Thank you. Glad to hear it's looking good. Do you have a suggested attitude for me? This one here seems all right.

HOUSTON: Stand by.

COLUMBIA: Let me know when it's lunch time, will ya?

HOUSTON: Say again?

HOUSTON: Columbia, Houston. You got a good attitude right there.

APOLLO CONTROL: This is Apollo Control. We've had loss of signal now from the command module. Of course, we'll maintain constant communication with the lunar module on the lunar surface. We have some heart rates for Neil Armstrong during that powered descent to lunar surface. At the time the burn was initiated, Armstrong's heart rate was 110. At touchdown on the lunar surface, he had a heart rate of 156 beats per minute, and the flight surgeon reports that his heart rate is now in the 90's. We do not have biomedical data on Buzz Aldrin.

APOLLO CONTROL (5:04 P.M.): We have an update on that touchdown time on the lunar surface. This still is not the final official time, which we'll get from readout of data. But the refined time is 102 hours, 45 minutes, 40 seconds, which would have been 12 minutes, 36 seconds after initiating the powered descent. That was 102 hours, 45 minutes, 40 seconds for touchdown and a total time of powered descent 12 minutes, 36 seconds. And we would expect those numbers to change perhaps a little bit when we get final data readout.

HOUSTON: Tranquility Base, Houston. If you want me to, I can give you a hack on the mission time every 30 minutes. Over.

HOUSTON: Tranquility, Houston. I'm counting down to T3 time. If you'd like to give me a hack, we can set up an event timer. Over.

TRANQUILITY BASE: Okay. How about counting up.

HOUSTON: Roger, you want it counting up? Stand by.

HOUSTON: Tranquility, Houston. On my mark 6230. Mark 6230 from pass TDI.

TRANQUILITY BASE: What we're looking for, Charlie, is time counting up to T2 that will be equal to 60 minutes or T3 equal to 60 minutes—T3.

HOUSTON: Roger. We'll have it for you.

HOUSTON: Tranquility Base, Houston. Reset the event timer to 0 and on my mark at 103 3941. Will give you a hack and it will be in one hour. Over.

TRANQUILITY BASE: Roger.

HOUSTON: And we got about almost 3 minutes to go, Neil. Over.

TRANQUILITY BASE: Okay.

HOUSTON: Tranquility Base, stand by on the event timer.

HOUSTON: Tranquility Base, on my mark start your event timer, 5, 4, 3, 2, 1, Mark.

TRANQUILITY BASE: Roger. We got it. Thank you.

HOUSTON: Rog, Neil.

Statement by Paine

APOLLO CONTROL (5:17 P.M.): There will be a brief statement from Dr. Thomas Paine, NASA administrator, in the Building 1 auditorium at 4:30 [Houston time]. We also have updated information on the landing point. It appears that the spacecraft Eagle touched down at .799 degrees north or just about on the lunar equator and 23.46 degrees east longitude, which would have put it about four miles from the targeted landing point downrange. We're now 54 minutes—or rather 27 minutes from reacquisition of the command module and of course we're in constant contact with the lunar module on the surface.

At this point all LM systems continue to look very good.

APOLLO CONTROL (5:29 P.M.): We will be taking the release line down briefly for a statement from Dr. Thomas Paine, NASA administrator. We will be recording any further conversations with the spacecraft and will play those back following the statement.

APOLLO CONTROL (5:42 P.M.): We understand there's been a brief delay in the statement from NASA administrator Thomas Paine. We will catch up with the tape-recorded conversation that we've had with Eagle on the lunar surface at this time.

TRANQUILITY BASE: Down 86 plus 0538 plus all zeros and the last one was 0012 and what's the sign of that, please?

HOUSTON: Tranquility, Houston. The delta VY is minus all zeros. The delta VZ is plus 0012. Over.

TRANQUILITY BASE: Roger plus 0012.

HOUSTON: Good readback.

TRANQUILITY BASE: Houston, Tranquility Base. The diskeys yours and up data link to data.

HOUSTON: Roger, thank you, Tranquility. Hello, Tranquility Base, Houston. On my mark it will be 37 minutes to T3. Over.

TRANQUILITY BASE: Okay.

HOUSTON: Stand by. Mark 37 minutes till T3.

TRANQUILITY BASE. Okay. Thank you.

HOUSTON: Tranquility, this is Houston. It's your computer. We've got the load in. You can start your P57.

TRANQUILITY BASE: Roger, thank you. Houston, Tranquility Base. Did somebody down there have a mike buskeyed. Over.

HOUSTON: Stand by, we'll check.

TRANQUILITY BASE: Houston, Tranquility Base. Does somebody down there have a life button keyed? Over.

HOUSTON: Stand by. We'll check. Tranquility, Houston. Do you still hear it now? Over.

TRANQUILITY BASE: No, I still hear it. Sounds like somebody is banging some chairs around in the back room.

HOUSTON: Roger, that's a VOGA you hear for the CSM to keep the noise down on the loop. Maybe we got a missed relay or something. Stand by.

APOLLO CONTROL: Ladies and gentlemen, I'd like to at this time introduce the administrator of the National Aeronautics and Space Administration, Dr. Thomas O. Paine. I have a short statement then we'll be glad to accept questions. Dr. Paine.

Report to the President

DR. PAINE: Immediately after the lunar touchdown I called the White House from Mission Control and gave the following report to the President:

Mr. President, it is my honor on behalf of the entire NASA team to report to you that the Eagle has landed on the Sea of Tranquility and our astronauts are safe and looking forward to starting the exploration of the moon. We then discussed the gripping excitement and wonder that has been present in the White House and in Mission Control during the final minutes of this historic touchdown. I emphasized to the President the fact that we still had many difficult steps ahead of us in the Apollo 11 mission, but that at the same time a giant step had been made with our successful landing.

President Nixon asked me to convey to all of the NASA team and its associated industrial and university associates his personal congratulations on the success of the initial lunar landing and gave us his good wishes for the continuing success of this mission.

APOLLO CONTROL (6:01 P.M.): During the news conference with the NASA Administrator, Dr. Thomas Paine, we had conversation with both Eagle and Columbia and we'll play that tape for you now:

HOUSTON: Tranquility Base, on my mark 25 minutes until T3. Stand by. Mark 25 minutes until T3.

TRANQUILITY BASE: Roger. Thank you, Charlie.

COLUMBIA: Houston, how do you read me?

HOUSTON: Columbia, we read you about 3 by. You might be advised we have an update for you on the P22 for the LM. We estimate he landed about four miles downrange. Your T1 times are updated and the T2 if you are ready to copy it. Over.

HOUSTON: Hello, Tranquility Base. We copy the now 93. You can torque him. Over.

COLUMBIA: Is that four miles?

HOUSTON: Stand by, we'll have a map location.

TRANQUILITY BASE: Houston, do you have an updated LM wait for us? Over.

HOUSTON: Affirmative. Stand by on the data.

HOUSTON: LM weight 10,906.

HOUSTON: Columbia with a latitude and longitude over 2 update for LM position. Over.

COLUMBIA: Go ahead.

HOUSTON: Roger, Columbia. It's plus .799 for the lat plus 11.730 for the longitude over 2 over.

COLUMBIA: Thank you.

HOUSTON: Hello Tranquility Base. You are stay for T3. We have some surface block data if you're ready to copy. Over.

TRANQUILITY BASE: Roger. Understand we're stay for T3. Stand by. Okay, Houston, go ahead with your block data.

HOUSTON: Roger. Hello Columbia, Houston. Columbia we don't want you to transmit, Mike. We just want you in that position in case you want to talk to Tranquility.

HOUSTON: Tranquility, Houston, say again. Over.

TRANQUILITY BASE: Roger. I have a fairly good-sized difference between battery volts on five and six. Six is reading 33.5 and five is reading 36.5. Is that what you expect? Over.

HOUSTON: Tranquility. They are both coming up in voltage. No problem. We're still go. Over.

Praise Is Returned

HOUSTON: Hello Tranquility Base, Houston. You can start your power down now. Over.

TRANQUILITY BASE: Roger.

HOUSTON: Tranquility Base, the white team is going off now and the maroon team take over. We appreciate the great show; it was a beautiful job, you guys.

TRANQUILITY BASE: Roger. Couldn't ask for better treatment from all the way back there.

TRANQUILITY BASE: Houston, our recommendation at this point is planning an EVA [Extra Vehicular Activity] with your concurrence starting at about 8 o'clock this evening, Houston time. That is about three hours from now.

HOUSTON: Stand by.

TRANQUILITY BASE: We will give you some time to think about that.

HOUSTON: Tranquility Base, Houston. We thought about it. We will support it. We'll go at that time.

TRANQUILITY BASE: Roger.

HOUSTON: You guys are getting prime time on TV there.

TRANQUILITY BASE: I hope that little TV set works. We'll see.

Highlights of Apollo Plan

Following are highlights of the remainder of the Apollo 11 flight plan. The timetable is subject to change at any time during the mission. Times are Eastern daylight.

TODAY

1:55 P.M.—The lunar module's ascent engine fires, lifting module's ascent stage off the moon and leaving the descent stage on the lunar surface.

5:32 P.M.—Lunar module and command ship dock. Neil A. Armstrong and Col. Edwin E. Aldrin Jr. crawl through tunnel to rejoin Lieut. Col. Michael Collins.

9:25 P.M.—The lunar module is jettisoned.

TOMORROW

12:57 A.M.—While behind the moon, the astronauts fire Apollo's main engine, boosting the craft out of lunar orbit and putting it on course back to earth.

3:57 P.M.—Midcourse correction.

9:02 P.M.—Live television show from space.

WEDNESDAY, JULY 23

7:02 P.M.—Final television show.

9:37 P.M.—Midcourse correction, if necessary.

THURSDAY, JULY 24

12:22 P.M.—Command module and service module separate in preparation for return to earth.

12:37 P.M.—Command module re-enters earth's atmosphere.

12:51 P.M.—Craft splashes down in the Pacific Ocean about 1,200 miles southwest of Hawaii.

HOUSTON: Roger. Was your 8 o'clock Houston time in reference to opening the hatch or starting the prep for EVA at that time. Over.

TRANQUILITY BASE: At the hatch, it will be.

HOUSTON: That's what we thought. Thank you, much.

TRANQUILITY BASE (6:02 P.M.): It might be a little later than that. But—in other words, start the prep in about an hour or so.

HOUSTON: Tranquility Base, Houston. That's fine. We're ready to support you any time, Neil. Over.

TRANQUILITY BASE: Right.

HOUSTON: Right. Columbia, we see the noun 49. Stand by.

HOUSTON: Columbia, Houston. We got the data. We'd like a verb 34. Over.

COLUMBIA: Roger, Stand-by one, Charlie, for . . .

HOUSTON: Roger, Columbia. How did Tranquility look down there to you? Over.

COLUMBIA (6:03 P.M.): Well the area looked smooth. But I was unable to see him. I just picked out a distinguishable crater nearby and marked on it.

HOUSTON: Roger.

COLUMBIA: Looks like a nice area, though.

HOUSTON: Hello Columbia, Houston. I understand you could not see Tranquility. What were you marking on? Over.

COLUMBIA: Houston, Columbia. I say again. I could not see him. Auto optics pointed at a spot very close to the coordinates which you gave me. So I picked out a tiny crater in that area and marked on it so that I'll be able to have repeatable data. But I was unable to see him.

HOUSTON: Roger. Copy.

APOLLO CONTROL: You heard that last exchange and there is a very strong indication we might have an early EVA, with the hatch open perhaps at 8 o'clock, Houston time. One other item of significance: The pressure rise in descent propellant line downstage of the tanks has relieved. All aspects of the mission looking very good at this time.

HOUSTON (6:05 P.M.): Hello Tranquility Base, Houston. On our dips venting and that fuel problem, our heat exchangers, it's cleared up. It appears that the ice has melted and we're in good shape now. Out.

APOLLO CONTROL (6:31 P.M.): We expect Capsule Communicator Owen Garrett to pass along data to spacecraft Columbia momentarily. We are standing by for that. Meanwhile I think we should discuss a little further the projected EVA. Our current plan is to have crew members aboard the Eagle eat and relax for a little while prior to starting EVA prep. We won't know with certainty or have a reasonable time hack until about an hour before the scheduled event. Right now it looks like it could occur at 8 o'clock, Houston time. We have conversation going now with the spacecraft and we'll pick that up.

Following is replay of tape of astronaut conversations recorded during the news briefing and press conference.

APOLLO CONTROL: At 105 hours, 30 minutes now into the mission Apollo 11. The spacecraft Columbia now out of range with Mission Control Center Houston, passing over the far side of the moon. As it passed out of sight we read an apolune of 63 nautical miles, a perilune of 56 nautical miles, a velocity of 5,367 feet per second. We've had conversation both with Tranquility Base and Columbia during this span of time. Also, as will come up in the course of that conversation, Lunar Module pilot Buzz Aldrin delivers a message to people everywhere listening. We'll play those tapes for you now.

'They'll Need Some Lunch'

HOUSTON: Columbia, we will have a stat vector update for you a little later. We're not prepared with it right now. And on another subject. From Tranquility Base they are prepared to begin the EVA early. They expect to begin depress operations in about three hours.

COLUMBIA: I guess they'll need some lunch before they go.

HOUSTON: We'd like your PRD readouts when possible and we've checked over your EM data and it's all okay.

COLUMBIA: Columbia's on the high-gain.

HOUSTON: Roger, Columbia. You're sounding much better now. Request accept and will uplink another stat vector. Over.

COLUMBIA: Roger. Accept.

HOUSTON: Suggest you put bat A on your bat relay buss. Over.

HOUSTON: Columbia, we're through with your computer. You can go to block.

COLUMBIA: Roger. Block.

HOUSTON: Tranquility Base. Over.

TRANQUILITY BASE: Go ahead, Houston.

HOUSTON: We've reviewed the checklist. About the only change in order to advance EVA that we've found is that you'll want to delay your hydroxide change and go after the EVA rather than before. Over.

TRANQUILITY BASE: Roger. We'd just as soon make the change and jettison the old one. Over.

HOUSTON: We would like to delay that LIOH change until after the EVA. There is a possibility you could jettison the canister when you jettison your pliss. Over.

TRANQUILITY BASE: All right. We'll plan it that way.

HOUSTON: Roger, Tranquility.

HOUSTON: Columbia. Over.

COLUMBIA: This is Columbia.

HOUSTON: We show your evap out temperature running low. Request you go to manual temperature control and bring it up. You can check the procedures in ECS Manual 17. Over.

COLUMBIA: Roger.

TRANQUILITY BASE: This is the LM pilot. I'd like to take this opportunity to ask every person listening in, whoever, wherever they may be, to pause for a moment and contemplate the events of the past few hours and to give thanks in his or her own way. Over.

HOUSTON: Roger, Tranquility Base.

APOLLO CONTROL (7:15 P.M.): You heard that statement in our taped transmission from lunar module pilot Buzz Aldrin. Our projected time for Extra Vehicular Activity at this point is still very preliminary. I repeat, it could come as soon as 8 P.M., Houston time. We won't know for sure about the time with reasonable certainty until about an hour before the event. Meanwhile, we'll soon be progressing toward man's first step on the lunar surface. We have an interesting phenomena here in the Mission Control Center, Houston, something that we've never seen before. Our visual of the lunar module—our visual display now standing still, our velocity digitals for our Tranquility Base now reading zero. Reverting, if we could, to the terminology of an earlier form of transportation—the railroad—what we're witnessing now is man's very first trip into space with a station-stop along the route.

HOUSTON: Tranquility Base, Houston. We'd like some estimate of how far along you are with your eating and when you may be ready to start your EVA prep.

TRANQUILITY BASE: I think that we'll be ready to start EVA prep in about a half hour or so.

TRANQUILITY BASE: We are beginning our EVA prep.

HOUSTON: Tranquility Base, this is Houston. Roger copy your beginning EVA prep. Break. Break. Columbia. Columbia. This is Houston, reading you loud and clear. Over.

COLUMBIA: You're loud and clear. The waste water dump is down to 10 per cent. I have a question on the B 22. Do you want me to do another B 22, or was all that information just for my own use in tracking the LM for photographic purposes?

HOUSTON: Columbia, this is Houston. We request that you perform another B 22. We'd like you to let the auto optics take care of the tracking and devote your energies to trying to pick out the LM on the lunar surface. If you can find the LM, of course, we're looking for marks on it. Tracking of geographical features doesn't do us at all that much good. Over.

COLUMBIA: Okay.

COLUMBIA (7:45 P.M.): Okay, I'll do it. And on the ECS system the—whatever the problem was seems to have gone away without any changing of J52 sensors, or anything like that. My evaporator outlet temp is up about 50 now and it's quite comfortable in the cockpit. So we'll talk more about that one later.

HOUSTON: Roger, Columbia. Did you shift into manual control, or did the problem resolve itself under auto control? Over.

COLUMBIA: The problem went away under auto.

Continued on Page 5

After Years of Anticipation, an Astronaut Tells About His Walk on the Moon

Continued From Page 4

HOUSTON: Roger. It's the best type. Out.

COLUMBIA: I did cycle out of auto into manual back into auto.

HOUSTON (7:55 P.M.): Tranquility Base. Tranquility Base. This is Houston. Over.

TRANQUILITY BASE: Go ahead, Houston.

HOUSTON: Tranquility, this is Houston. We need a second set of PRD ratings so that we may establish a rate. Over.

COLUMBIA (8:09 P.M.): Houston, Columbia. I'm coming up from . . . Do you have any topographical cues that might help me out here. I'm tracking between two craters. One of them is . . . that would be long at 11 o'clock. The other would be short and behind him at 5 o'clock. These are great big old craters, depressions.

HOUSTON: Columbia, this is Houston. The best we can do on topo features is to advise you to look to the west of the irregularly shaped crater and then work on down to the southwest of it. Over.

HOUSTON: Columbia, Houston. Another possibility is the southern rim of the southern of the two old-looking craters. Over.

COLUMBIA: Houston, Columbia. I kept my eyes glued to the . . . that time, hoping I'd get a flash of vector light off the LM but I was unable see in my scan areas that you suggested.

HOUSTON: Roger. On that southern of the old craters there is a small bright crater on the southern rim. One plot would put him slightly to the west of that small bright crater about 500 to 1,000 feet. Do you see anything down there? Over.

COLUMBIA: It's gone past now, Bruce. But I scanned that area that you're talking about very closely and, no, I did not see anything.

HOUSTON: Roger. Out.

HOUSTON: Columbia, this is Houston. Over.

COLUMBIA: Here I am.

HOUSTON: Columbia, this is Houston. On your LAM 2 map, we'd like to confirm the topographical area in which you were looking on this last period of sightings. As we understand you, you were looking in the vicinity of Papa 7 to November 8. Is that correct?

COLUMBIA: Stand by.

HOUSTON: Roger.

HOUSTON (8:17 P.M.): Columbia, go ahead.

COLUMBIA: One of the craters I was talking about is located exactly at 56.7.

HOUSTON: Roger, we found that one.

COLUMBIA: The other one's located at 7.2 two-thirds of the way from . . .

HOUSTON: Roger, we believe you were looking a little too far to the west and south.

COLUMBIA: Roger, I was looking where . . . was tracking on the average and I understand it should have been more to the north and more to the west; actually, a tiny bit outside the circle.

HOUSTON: More to the north and a little more to the east. The feature that I was describing to you, the small bright crater on the rim of the large fairly old crater, would be about Mike .8 and 8.2.

HOUSTON: Tranquility Base, this is Houston. Can you give us some idea where you are in the surface checklist at the present time.

TRANQUILITY BASE: They were at the top of page 27.

COLUMBIA: Roger. Finally got you back on. I've been unsuccessfully trying to get you on the high gain and I've got command to reset the process. How do you read me now?

HOUSTON: Roger. I hear you loud with background noise.

COLUMBIA: Omni Delta and you were cut out and I never got your coordinance or estimated LM position.

HOUSTON: Estimated LM position is latitude plus .799, longitude over 2 plus 11.730.

COLUMBIA: What I'm interested is in direct coordinance on that map reading.

COLUMBIA: Could you enable the S-band relay at least one way from Eagle to Columbia, so I can hear what's going on?

HOUSTON: Roger. There's not much going on at the present time, Columbia. I'll see what I can do about the relay. . . .

HOUSTON: Columbia, this is Houston. Are you aware that Eagle plans the EVA about four hours early?

COLUMBIA: Affirmative. I haven't had any word from those guys and I thought I'd be hearing them through your S-band relay.

APOLLO CONTROL (8:48 P.M.): We'll still have acquisition of Columbia for another eight minutes. All systems in Eagle still looking good. Cabin pressure 4.86 pounds, showing a temperature of 63 degrees in the Eagle's cabin.

COLUMBIA: During the next pass I'd appreciate the S-band relay mode.

HOUSTON: We're working on that. There haven't been any transmissions from Tranquility Base since we last talked to you.

APOLLO CONTROL: We've had loss of signal on Columbia. The clock here at Control Center counting down to depressurization time on Eagle shows we're 36 minutes, 39 seconds away from that event. We believe the crew is pretty well on the time line in the EVA preparation.

APOLLO CONTROL (9:36 P.M.): This latest report

Neil A. Armstrong

Col. Edwin E. Aldrin Jr.

Associated Press

Lieut. Col. Michael Collins

the crew is—they're getting the electrical checkout—indicates they are about 40 minutes behind the time line. We will acquire Columbia in six minutes.

TRANQUILITY BASE: How do you read now?

HOUSTON: Okay. I think that's going to better.

HOUSTON: We have acquisition of Columbia.

HOUSTON: Roger, Columbia. Reading you loud and clear on the high gain. We have enabled the one-way Nixon relay that you requested. The crew of Tranquility Base is currently donning PLSSes [portable life support systems]. Com checks out.

COLUMBIA: Sounds okay.

TRANQUILITY BASE (9:45 P.M.): Houston, Tranquility. You'll find that the area around the ladder is in a complete dark shadow, so we're going to have some problem with TV. But I'm sure you'll see the—you'll get a picture from the lighted horizon.

HOUSTON: Neil, Neil, this is Houston. I can hear you trying to transmit. However, your transmission is beaking up.

TRANQUILITY BASE: Neil's got his antenna up now. Let's see if he comes through any better now.

TRANQUILITY BASE. Okay, Houston, this is Neil. How do you read?

HOUSTON: Neil, this is Houston, reading you beautifully.

TRANQUILITY BASE: My antenna's scratching the roof. Do we have a go for cabin depress?

COLUMBIA: They hear everything but that.

TRANQUILITY BASE: Houston, this is Tranquility. We're standing by for go for cabin depress.

HOUSTON: You are go for cabin depressurization. Go for cabin depressurization.

COLUMBIA (10 P.M.): I don't know if you guys can read me on VHF, but you sure sound good down there.

TRANQUILITY BASE: Okay, the vent window is clear. I remove lever from the engine cover.

HOUSTON: Buzz, you're coming through loud and clear, and Mike passes on the word that he's receiving you and following your progress with interest.

TRANQUILITY BASE: Lock system, decks, exit check, blue locks are checked, lock locks, red locks, perch locks, and on this side the perch locks and lock locks—both sides, body locks, and the calm.

HOUSTON (10:17 P.M.): Columbia, this is Houston. Do you read?

COLUMBIA: Read you loud and clear.

HOUSTON: Were you successful in spotting the LM on that pass?

COLUMBIA: Negative. I checked both locations and it's no dice.

APOLLO CONTROL (10:25 P.M.): In the control center a clock has been set up to record the operating time on Neil Armstrong's total life support system. EVA will be counted from that time.

TRANQUILITY BASE: Cabin repress closed. Now comes the gymnastics. Air pressure going toward zero. Standby LM suit circuit 36 to 43. That's verified. FIT GA pressure about 4.5, 4.75 and coming down. We'll open the hatch when we get to zero. Do you want to bring down one of your visors now or leave them up? We can put them down if we need them. We have visor down.

APOLLO CONTROL (10:33 P.M.): Coming up on five minutes of operation of Neil Amstrong's portable life support system now.

HOUSTON (10:37): Neil, this is Houston, what's your status on hatch opening?

TRANQUILITY BASE: Everything is go here. We're just waiting for the cabin pressure to bleed to a low enough pressure to open the hatch. It's about .1 on our gauge now. (Aldrin) I'd hate to tug on that thing. Alternative would be to open that one too.

HOUSTON: We're seeing a relatively static pressure on your cabin. Do you think you can open the hatch at this pressure?

TRANQUILITY BASE: We're going to try it. The hatch is coming open. (Aldrin): Hold it from going closed and I'll get the valve turner. I'd better get up first.

ALDRIN: Your window cleared yet?

ARMSTRONG: It was, yeah.

ALDRIN: Mine hasn't cleared yet.

(Following Is Conversation Between Armstrong and Aldrin): Okay. Bical pump secondary circuit breaker open. Back to lean—this way. Radar circuit breakers open. Well, I'm looking head-on at it. I'll get it. Okay. My antenna's out. Right. Okay, now we're ready to hook up the LEC. Okay. Now we need to hook this. Your visor. Yep. Your back is up against the perch. Now you're clear. Over toward me. Straight down, to your left a little bit. Plenty of room. You're lined up nicely.

Toward me a little bit. Down. Okay. Now you're clear. You're catching the first hinge. The what hinge? All right, move. Roll to the left. Okay now you're clear. You're lined up on the platform. Put your left foot to the right a little bit. Okay that's good. More left. Good.

'I'm on the Porch'

ARMSTRONG: Okay, Houston, I'm on the porch.

HOUSTON: Roger, Neil.

HOUSTON: Columbia, Columbia, This is Houston. One minute, 30 seconds LOS, all systems go. Over.

ALDRIN: Halt where you are a minute, Neil.

ARMSTRONG AND ALDRIN: Okay. Everything's nice and straight in here. Okay, can you pull the door open a little more? Right.

HOUSTON: We're getting a picture on the TV.

ALDRIN: You've got a good picture, huh?

HOUSTON: There's a great deal of contrast in it and currently it's upside down on monitor. But we can make out a fair amount of detail.

ARMSTRONG: Okay, will you verify the position, the opening I ought to have on the camera.

HOUSTON: The what? We can see you coming down the ladder now.

ARMSTRONG: Okay. I just checked getting back up to that first step. It didn't collapse too far. But it's adequate to get back up. It's a pretty good little jump.

ARMSTRONG: I'm at the foot of the ladder. The LM foot beds are only depressed in the surface about one or two inches, although the surface appears to be very, very fine-grained as you get close to it. It's almost like a powder. It's very fine. I'm going to step off the LM now.

That's one small step for man, one giant leap for mankind.

The surface is fine and powdery. I can pick it up loosely with my toe. It does adhere in fine layers like powdered charcoal to the sole and the sides of my boots. I only go in a small fraction of an inch, maybe an eighth of an inch but I can see the footprints of my boots and the treads in the fine sandy particles.

There seems to be no difficulty in moving around this and we suspect that it's even perhaps easier than the simulations of 1/6 G that we performed in various simulations on the ground. Actually no trouble to walk around.

No Crater from Descent

The descent engine did not leave a crater of any size. It has about one foot clearance on the ground. We're essentially on a very level place here. I can see some evidence of rays emananting from the descent. engine, but a very insignificant amount.

Okay, Buzz, are we ready to bring down the camera?

ALDRIN: I'm all ready. I think it's squared away and in good shape. But you'll have to pay out all the LEC. Looks like it's coming out nice and evenly.

It's quite dark here in the shadow and a little hard for me to see if I have good footing. I'll work my way over into the sunlight here without looking directly into the sun.

ARMSTRONG: Looking up at the LM, I'm standing directly in the shadow now looking up at . . . in the windows and I can see everything quite clearly. The light is sufficiently bright backlighted into the front of the LM that everything is clearly visible.

I'll step out and take some of my first pictures here.

ALDRIN: Are you going to get the contingency sample? Okay. That's good.

ARMSTRONG: The contingency sample is down and it's up. Like it's a little difficult to dig through the crust. It's very interesting. It's a very soft surface but here and there where I plug with the contingency sample collector I run into very hard surface but it appears to be very cohesive material of the same sort. I'll try to get a rock in here.

HOUSTON: Oh, that looks beautiful from here, Neil.

ARMSTRONG: It has a stark beauty all its own. It's like much of the high desert of the United States. It's different but it's very pretty out here. Be advised that a lot of the rock samples out here, the hard rock samples have what appears to be vesicles in the surface.

ARMSTRONG: This has been about six or eight inches into the surface. It's easy to push on it. I'm sure I could push it in farther but it's hard for me to bend down farther than that.

ALDRIN: Ready for me to come out?

ARMSTRONG: Yeah. Just stand by a second, I'll move this over the handrail.

ALDRIN: Okay?

ARMSTRONG: All right, that's got it. Are you ready?

ALDRIN: All set.

ARMSTRONG: Okay. You saw what difficulties I was having. I'll try to watch your PLSS from underneath here. The toes are about to come over the sill. Now drop your PLSS down. There you go, you're clear. And laterally you're good. About an inch clearance on top of your PLSS. You need a little bit of arching of the back to come down.

ALDRIN: How far are my feet from the . . .

ARMSTRONG: You're right at the edge of the porch.

ALDRIN: Small little foot movement. Porch. Arching of the back . . . without any trouble at all.

ALDRIN: Now I want to back up and partially close the hatch—making sure not to lock it on my way out.

ARMSTRONG: Good thought.

ALDRIN: That's our home for the next couple of hours; we want to take care of it. I'm on the top step. It's a very simple matter tohop down from one step to the next.

ARMSTRONG: Yes, I found that to be very comfortable, and walking is also very comfortable, Houston. You've got three more steps and then a long one.

ALDRIN: I'm going to leave that one foot up there and both hands down to about the fourth rung up.

ARMSTRONG: A little more. About another inch. there you got it. That's a good step.

ALDRIN: About a three footer. Beautiful view.

ARMSTRONG: Ain't that somethin'?

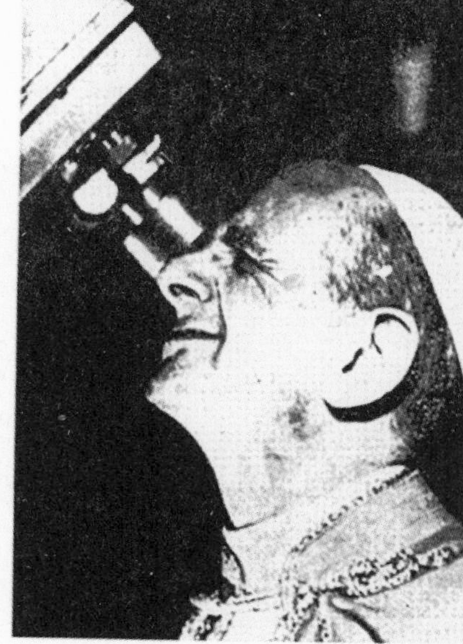

Associated Press

VIEWS LANDING ZONE: Pope Paul VI using a telescope to examine the area where the Apollo lunar module touched down. The Pope, at his summer residence at Castel Gandolfo, Italy, watched the landing on television.

A Fete in Central Park Celebrates the Landing

By McCANDLISH PHILLIPS

At dusk last night a few hundred moon-bedazzled citizens gathered in Central Park on the planet earth to celebrate man's first footsteps on another sphere.

A heavy downpour that began at 7:30 P.M. and lasted more than an hour nearly turned the moon watch into a washout. The police were ready to handle a crowd of tens of thousands.

There are no rules on how to celebrate an occasion of this kind, but the city had decided to provide a way for the people "to share the moment together" in the Sheep Meadow. The event was a cross between a carnival and a vigil.

By the time the television pictures from the moon were flashed onto three large screens grouped near the center of the meadow—one screen each for the National Broadcasting Company, the Columbia Broadcasting System and the American Broadcasting Company — the crowd had swelled to over 5,000 and the meadow had become a marsh.

Earlier in the day, in churches over the nation, prayers were said for the safety of the Apollo 11 astronauts. Everywhere, in baseball parks, in homes, on beaches, in bars, the moon landing impinged on other pursuits.

At the Yankee stadium, where the Washington Senators played the New York Yankees, the landing of the Eagle was flashed on the scoreboard with the words: "They're on the moon."

The game was halted for a moment of silent prayer and the singing of "America the Beautiful."

In the Nashville criminal court, Judge Allen R. Cornelius ordered a color TV set brought into the courtroom so a murder jury of 10 men and two women could watch the moon landing.

In a little luncheonette off Times Square a man spoke of the celebrations that would occur after the feat, and another man said, "Why not? It only happens once every several thousand years, doesn't it?"

No one knew how many Americans held their breath at once as the lunar module settled gently to the moon's surface without hint of mishap.

At Sing Sing Prison in Ossining, N.Y., there was disappointment when the warden ruled that inmates could watch television only during the normal viewing hours, which excluded most of the moon events. An exception was made for the one man on Death Row. He was allowed to watch as long as he liked.

At the Cathedral Church of St. John the Divine, Amsterdam Avenue at 110th Street, the Intercessions at the 4 P.M. Evensong were dedicated to the Apollo flight and to the astronauts.

In Spark's Pub, on Second Avenue near 79th Street, Larry Klau, a 27-year-old stockbroker from Brooklyn, and his date, Carol Kramer, a 22-year-old waitress from Manhattan, gazed raptly at the television screen as Mr. Armstrong planted his first shoeprint in moondust.

"This is our first date and I told her she'll never forget it," Mr. Klau said.

The Radio City Music Hall switched briefly from showing the film "True Grit' to congratulations for the astronauts.

A great gasp of appreciation rose from the crowd at the Time-Life Exhibition Center, Avenue of the Americas at 50th Street, when Mr. Armstrong did his kangaroo hop across the rumpled surface of the moon.

In Central Park, the sky was as bleak as the face of the moon in the early evening and the ground was soft and damp from afternoon showers, and those who came early sat mostly on outcroppings of rock that were hard but dry.

When the rain suddenly descended, spectators streamed across the broad field and into the 140-foot-long tent pitched at the west side of the meadow opposite West 66th Street, but about 125 people stood fast in front of the television screens through 68 minutes of heavy rain.

Hippies careened wildly across the meadow in what some took to be a rain dance, and Vice President Agnew's face on one big screen changed from shades of pink to red to pale green.

Young people did some jeering while simulated moon landing pictures appeared on television, but when the image of the American on the moon showed on the screens a great cheer rose from the crowd, which had grown to 8,000 people.

In commemoration of an earlier attempt to rise into space, a balloon with a man in the basket under it went up to treetop level in an enclosure in the meadow, while men held it fast by ropes.

It was a modest ascent, for at 6:50 P. M., Mrs. Doris Freedman, Director of the Department of Cultural Affairs, which staged the big show, had received a telegram from the Federal Aviation Administration permitting the balloon to go up to 150 feet.

"Anything that goes up in the air within a 5-mile radius of a major airport has to have F.A.A clearance," Mrs. Freedman explained.

Mayor Lindsay stepped out on the stage of a big Showmobile van parked near the tent and said, "This is an extraordinary evening for all New Yorkers."

The rain had held off through the moon coverage on television, but it came again just as Mr. Lindsay finished and he jumped off the stage as several thousand people left the park, having seen what men had never seen, except in dreams, before.

The New York Times (by Donal F. Holway)

CENTRAL PARK SHEEP MEADOW: Spectators watching the landing of the astronauts on three giant television screens

Apollo Doctors Pleased At Astronauts' Reactions

By RICHARD D. LYONS

Special to The New York Times

HOUSTON, July 20—Within seconds of the lunar landing today the physical condition of Neil A. Armstrong and Col. Edwin E. Aldrin Jr. told the world that man could indeed live on an extraterrestial body.

Their breath came short and their pulses raced, but they were within those limits that had been predicted and considered safe. The astronauts quickly found that the lunar heat could be withstood and that they were not disoriented by the moon's abnormal gravity.

Although they were fatigued by more than four days of space flight and 30 excruciating minutes of anxiety during the touchdown, the astronauts — both nearing 40 years of age—withstood the most demanding physical challenge of their lives.

"They're in excellent physiological condition," Apollo program doctors said three hours after the touchdown.

The fears of aerospace surgeons that men might not be able to tolerate the totally different conditions of the moon had been dispelled.

"We have entered a new era," Dr. Thomas O. Paine, the space agency's administrator, said later. "Mankind is going to establish abodes beyond the earth."

Shortly after touchdown, the steady stream of chatter from the astronauts indicated to the Mission Control Center here that the men were standing up well to the physical ordeal of landing despite having been weightless for more than 100 hours.

"I don't think we noticed any difficulty at all adapting to one-sixth G," Mr. Armstrong radioed in a somewhat surprised voice from Tranquility Base to the Manned Spacecraft Center here.

At Mission Control, Dr. Charles A. Berry, the astronauts' chief flight surgeon, nodded agreement as he anxiously monitored the 10 oscilloscopes and dials that told him that a quarter of a million miles away the two most important patients of his career were all right.

Dr. Berry was even happier when he heard Colonel Aldrin say:

"One-sixth G is just like an airplane." The term "one-sixth G" refers to the fact that the moon has only that fraction of the earth's gravity, or G.

Flight surgeons have been particularly concerned about the effect of lunar gravity because it could be simulated on earth for only five seconds at a time — in airplanes — which was almost useless for drawing serious conclusions about its effect.

After reading the scopes and dials on the console before him after touchdown, Dr. Berry signaled Maj. Charles M. Duke Jr., the capsule communicator, who then relayed to the lunar party the medical opinion, that "Everything is copacetic."

Assessing these matters received the highest priority on the check-list of things to do before permission was granted allowing them to walk on the moon.

"All the News That's Fit to Print"

The New York Times

LATE CITY EDITION

Weather: Cloudy but clearing today. Fair tonight. Cloudy, mild tomorrow. Temp. range: today 51-43; Tuesday 48-42. Full U.S. report on Page 85.

VOL. CXIX..No. 40,989 — NEW YORK, WEDNESDAY, APRIL 15, 1970 — 10 CENTS

CREW OF CRIPPLED APOLLO 13 STARTS BACK AFTER ROUNDING MOON AND FIRING ROCKET; MEN APPEAR CALM DESPITE LOW RESERVES

① LAUNCHING 2:15 P.M., Apr. 11.

② 4:48 P.M., Apr. 11 third stage of Saturn 5 fires, translunar injection begins.

③ 5:19 P.M., Apr. 11, third stage of Saturn 5 separates.

④ 6:32 P.M., Apr. 11, third stage thrusts toward moon.

⑤ 10:08 P.M., Apr. 13, oxygen tank in Apollo service module ruptures.

⑥ 3:43 A.M., Apr. 14, LM engine fires to enable Apollo to loop around moon and return to earth.

⑦ 9:41 P.M., Apr. 14, LM engine fires again so Apollo will land in Pacific Ocean.

⑧ About 12:00 P.M., Apr. 17, service and lunar modules due to be jettisoned.

⑨ 12:41 P.M., Apr. 17, command module due to enter earth's atmosphere.

⑩ 12:55 P.M., Apr. 17, expected splashdown.

TRANSLUNAR COAST

TRANSEARTH COAST

Schematic drawing.

All times are Eastern Standard

The New York Times — April 15, 1970

VOYAGE OF A STRICKEN SPACESHIP: Apollo 13, its hopes for America's third lunar landing dashed by a ruptured oxygen tank, arced around the moon last night on a course that would bring it back to earth on Friday.

TARGET IS PACIFIC

Chance of Safe Return Deemed 'Excellent' Despite the Risks

Excerpts from conversations with spacecraft, Page 28.

By JOHN NOBLE WILFORD

Special to The New York Times

HOUSTON, Wednesday, April 15—With the lives of its three astronauts hanging in the balance, the crippled spaceship Apollo 13 swung around the moon last night and rocketed toward an emergency splashdown in the Pacific Ocean Friday.

After the craft looped the moon, a crucial four-minute and 24-second rocket firing sent the astronauts on a fast and more accurate course — a drastic change of plans caused by Monday night's massive power failure aboard the moon-bound spacecraft.

The rocket blast started at 9:41 P.M. Eastern standard time as the astronauts, depending on their attached lunar landing craft as a back-up return craft, pulled away about 6,000 miles from the right side of the moon.

"That was a good burn," Mission Control radioed after the lunar module's descent rocket shut down on schedule.

Though its success sent the first ripple of relief through Mission Control in 24 hours, Capt. James A. Lovell Jr. of the Navy and Fred W. Haise Jr. and John L. Swigert Jr., both civilians, were still a long way from home and not yet out of trouble.

A Race With Time

The three astronauts were calm, despite the fact that they were racing time, trying to reach the earth before their severely limited reserves of oxygen, electricity and water ran out.

Grim-faced flight directors here called it "the most critical situation" in the history of the American space program. But, barring any further trouble, they said the chances of the astronauts' safe return were "excellent."

A rising carbon-dioxide level in the spacecraft stirred new concern late last night for the astronauts' safety. The amount rose to the point where it triggered an alarm light, but Mission Control said it was prepared to have it go to twice that level to conserve the lithium hydroxide chemical used to cleanse the cabin atmosphere.

Laboratory tests have shown that triple the present level can be tolerated without signs of organic damage, space agency doctors said.

NASA scientists were de-

Continued on Page 28, Column 3

NIXON IS BRIEFED ON APOLLO CRISIS

Meets With Space Experts During Unannounced Visit to Center in Maryland

By RICHARD D. LYONS

Special to The New York Times

GREENBELT, Md., April 14—President Nixon, looking taut and tired, met with technical experts of the space agency here for 45 minutes this afternoon and was briefed about the past and future problems of the Apollo 13 mission.

Dr. John F. Clark, director of the National Aeronautics and Space Administration's Goddard Space Flight Center here, said that the President was deeply concerned and that he asked "many knowledgeable questions" about the mission's problems and "the contingencies that have been planned."

This center is the eyes, ears and touch of Apollo 13. It is here that all the information transmitted by the spaceship is collected from 17 tracking stations around the world and sent on to the Manned Spacecraft Center in Houston for analysis.

Unannounced Visit

Hatless and dressed in a tan raincoat, dark blue suit and blue striped tie, Mr. Nixon made an unannounced visit to the center, driving from the White House, 13 miles away, through a heavy rainstorm.

The President had been briefed by his aides three times during the night and early this morning about the sudden power loss in the Apollo 13 spaceship as it was heading toward the moon. According to Ronald L. Ziegler, the White House press secretary, Mr. Nixon was informed about 4 A.M. today that the corrective firing of the lunar module's engine would bring the space craft on a free return to earth.

"The President will be receiving reports throughout the day

Continued on Page 29, Column 7

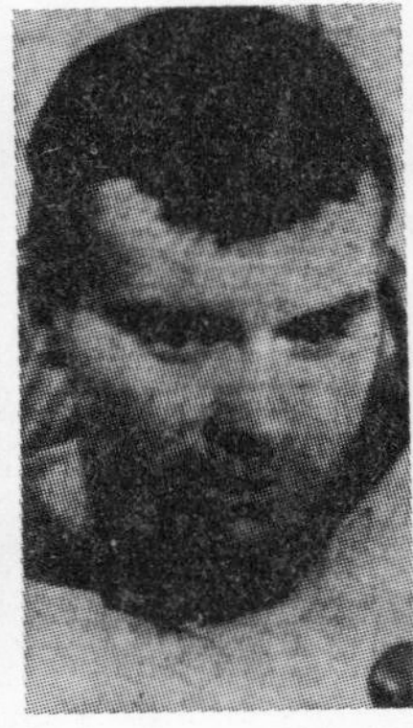

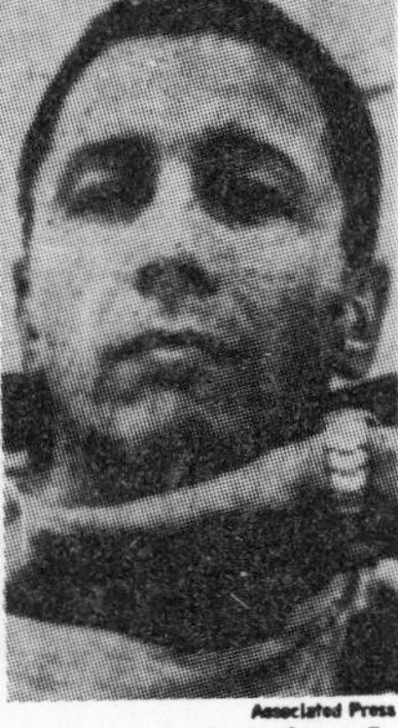

Associated Press

BEFORE FLIGHT: Capt. James A. Lovell Jr., Fred W. Haise Jr. and John L. Swigert Jr.

Plight of 3 Crewmen Stirs World Interest and Prayer

By MARTIN ARNOLD

Suddenly, in the moment it takes an oxygen tank to spring a leak, the flight of Apollo 13 was no longer something everybody took for granted and was even slightly bored with.

For all around the world yesterday, during the Apollo 13 emergency, there was a surge of interest in the flight and there were prayers, and anguish also, for the three men who were fighting to get their crippled spaceship home.

The world-wide shift in interest in Apollo 13 was best summed up in two printed lines—one in an Italian newspaper, the other in a French paper.

Before the bad news broke, Milan's Il Giorno commented in a headline: "Too Perfect; the Public Is Getting Bored."

Yesterday morning, in Paris, Le Monde said: "The whole human race is participating with them in the agony of their return."

In the United States there was an outpouring of prayer, and here and there some expression of bitterness, too, that man was reaching toward space without having first solved the problems on earth.

Both the Senate and House passed resolutions yesterday asking all Americans to pray, at 9 o'clock Eastern standard time last night, for the safe return of their countrymen. And they urged businesses and communications media to pause briefly, if they could, for the prayers at that hour.

Special services and masses were called for in thousands of churches and synagogues around the country — at St. Patrick's Cathedral and St. Thomas Episcopal Church and Temple Emanu-El in New York City, for example.

Rabbi Abraham Gross, president of the Rabbinical Alliance of America, called on all clergymen to pray for the safe return of Apollo 13, and, in Baltimore, Frank Gunter Jr., Maryland chairman of the National Conference of Christians and Jews, asked all residents of the state to observe a minute of silent prayer at 4 P.M. yesterday.

In Montgomery, Ala., T.R. Hennessey, a retired Air Force

Continued on Page 29, Column 4

Judge Blackmun of Minnesota Is Named To Supreme Court Seat by the President

Nominee, 61, Is Regarded as a Scholarly Jurist

By ROBERT B. SEMPLE Jr.

Special to The New York Times

United Press International

Judge Harry A. Blackmun in St. Louis yesterday.

WASHINGTON, April 14—President Nixon today nominated Harry Andrew Blackmun of Minnesota to the Supreme Court.

Judge Blackmun, a member of the United States Court of Appeals for the Eighth Circuit, is regarded in the legal profession as a scholarly and mildly conservative judge.

Mr. Nixon's third choice for the vacancy created by the resignation of Abe Fortas was announced by Ronald L. Ziegler, the White House press secretary, late this afternoon. The President did not appear and did not issue a statement.

Mr. Ziegler made the announcement while standing on the same small platform in the new White House press headquarters where Mr. Nixon last Thursday accused the Senate of hypocrisy and regional bias for refusing to approve his first two nominees for the vacancy.

The two men, both Southerners, were Clement F. Haynsworth Jr. and G. Harrold Carswell. The Senate rejected Judge Haynsworth last November and Judge Carswell last Wednesday.

A Prolonged Examination by Senate Panel Seen

Judge Blackmun will also require Senate confirmation, but early reaction to his nomination on Capitol Hill was inconclusive. On the basis of the Senate's recent performance, however, it seemed likely that Judge Blackmun would be subjected to prolonged and searching examination by the Senate Judiciary Committee. Until that time, there may be a reluctance on the part of many Senators to commit themselves.

Senator Sam J. Ervin Jr., Democrat of North Carolina and a senior member of the Judiciary Committee, refused to

Continued on Page 34, Column 3

RISE OF 30% URGED IN CITY REALTY TAX

G.O.P. Leaders in Albany Call On Mayor to Accept $440-Million Package

By RICHARD PHALON

Special to The New York Times

ALBANY, April 14 — Mayor Lindsay arrived here tonight for talks with Republican legislators on the city's financial problems facing the possibility that he might have to adopt a $440-million package of real estate tax increases.

The package, which some Republican leaders are urging as a part-answer to the $630-million the Mayor says he needs to balance the budget next fiscal year, would raise the real estate tax rate from $5.52 per $100 to around $7 per $100 of assessed valuation —an increase of almost 30 per cent.

City budget officials said about $200-million of the package would go into effect next year anyway through normal growth of assessed valuations and an expected increase in the equalization rate designed to iron out variations in assessment practices throughout the city.

The Mayor's mission here tonight is to persuade the Republican leaders that the city is entitled to more state aid on the basis of the tax effort it is already making and on the basis of the additional "do it yourself" revenue measures he has had introduced here in the closing days of the session.

Continued on Page 36, Column 4

Brezhnev Says Soviet Aim Is 'Reasonable' Arms Pact

By BERNARD GWERTZMAN

Special to The New York Times

MOSCOW, April 14—Leonid I. Brezhnev, the Soviet Communist party leader, said today that the Soviet Union would welcome "a reasonable agreement" with the United States on limiting strategic arms when the second round of Soviet-American talks begins in Vienna on Thursday.

But Mr. Brezhnev, making his second televised speech in two days from the Ukrainian city

Excerpts from Brezhnev talk are printed on Page 17.

of Kharkov, indicated doubt that the United States Government was sincere in wanting an accord.

Apparently alluding to Washington's decision to go ahead with new offensive and defensive missile systems, Mr. Brezhnev shook his fist and said that if anyone tried to gain military superiority over the Soviet Union "we will reply with the necessary increase in military might that guarantees our defense."

After loud and prolonged applause, Mr. Brezhnev added: "We cannot act otherwise."

His wide-ranging foreign policy speech covered the Middle East, Vietnam and Europe, in which he broke no new ground, and relations with China, which he said were being harmed by what he called continuing anti-Soviet war hysteria in Peking.

Last night's speech was devoted entirely to economic problems and reflected his view that the Soviet Union must adopt technological advances and rally the people to overcome its mediocre economic showing of recent years.

His critical words on how the

Continued on Page 17, Column 1

U.S. Arrests Russian Skipper In Alaska Gulf for Spilling Oil

By ROBERT M. SMITH

Special to The New York Times

WASHINGTON, April 14—A Coast Guard cutter sent a boarding party aboard a Soviet tanker in the Gulf of Alaska last night and arrested the ship's master on charges of spilling a mile-long oil slick near Kodiak Island.

The master of the Soviet vessel, V. C. Sherstobitov, has been flown to Anchorage where he is awaiting arraignment under the Refuse Act of 1899. His ship, the 345-foot motor vessel Mozyr, is still standing by near Kodiak Island.

In response to questions about an unconfirmed report that became available here, the State Department said the Soviet captain had been arrested.

According to information obtained by telephone from the scene, the American boarding party—consisting of a young operations officer, a representative of the Bureau of Fisheries and a seaman-photographer—encountered no resistance

The Americans spent several hours on board the Soviet vessel while Captain Sherstobitov waited for his fleet commander in Vladivostok to tell him whether he should go with the Americans.

Comdr. John H. Byrd Jr. of New London, Conn., was the captain of the Coast Guard cutter involved, the Storis. Commander Byrd was reached today by telephone on Kodiak Island—about 300 miles southwest of Anchorage—and provided this account:

"We were commencing patrol, and Coast Guard aviation units were also carrying out patrol, and they located a Soviet tanker refueling Soviet fishing vessels in U.S. territory

Continued on Page 74, Column 3

Adm. Moorer Named To Head Joint Chiefs

Special to The New York Times

WASHINGTON, April 14 — President Nixon today named Adm. Thomas H. Moorer, Chief of Naval Operations, to succeed Gen. Earle G. Wheeler as chairman of the Joint Chiefs of Staff, the nation's highest ranking military officer.

If confirmed by the Senate—and no obstacles to confirmation are foreseen here—Admiral Moorer will be the second Navy man to hold the post. Adm. Arthur W. Radford was chairman from 1953 to 1957, in the Eisenhower Administration.

Mr. Nixon also disclosed his intention to nominate Vice Adm. Elmo R. Zumwalt Jr., commander of naval forces in Vietnam and chief of the Naval Advisory Group, United States Military Assistance Command

Continued on Page 14, Column 4

SENATE APPROVES TV CAMPAIGN CURB

Limit in Spending on Races for Federal Offices Voted Over G.O.P. Opposition

By JOHN W. FINNEY

Special to The New York Times

WASHINGTON, April 14 — Over Republican opposition, the Senate approved today campaign reform legislation designed to limit and perhaps reduce the mounting spending on political broadcasts over television and radio.

The legislation would place a ceiling on how much a candidate for Federal office could spend on television and radio broadcasts. In addition, it would reduce the rates at which broadcasting stations sell air time to political candidates.

The spending limitations were incorporated in legislation repealing the so-called "equal time" provision in the communications act, thus permitting the television and radio networks to provide free broadcast time for the Presidential and Vice-Presidential candidates in the 1972 elections without giving comparable time to every minor candidate. Whether or not this free time is to be used for debates, as it was in the 1960 Presidential elections, or for some other format is to be worked out by the candidates and the networks.

The campaign reform legislation, first proposed two years ago, passed the Senate with unexpected ease after only one day of debate. It now goes to the House, where, as in the Senate, the Democratic majority is expected to prevail over Republican opposition.

The legislation is designed to

Continued on Page 88, Column 4

Cambodia Appeals To World for Arms

By HENRY KAMM

Special to The New York Times

PNOMPENH, Cambodia, April 14—Premier Lon Nol issued an urgent appeal tonight for arms from any country that wanted to provide them.

[The State Department said the United States had received no request. Other sources expected one and predicted that it would be granted.]

In a broadcast statement in French and Cambodian, the Premier declared:

"The Salvation Government has the duty to inform the nation that in view of the gravity of the present situation, it finds it necessary to accept all unconditional foreign aid, wherever it may come from, for the salvation of the nation."

The Premier underlined the

Continued on Page 3, Column 1

NEWS INDEX

The New York Times (by Edward Hausner)

PRAY FOR ASTRONAUTS: Worshipers at a special mass at St. Patrick's Cathedral for the crew of Apollo 13

Apollo Craft's Water Shortage Will Limit Astronauts' Use of Guidance System

Crew Must Coast Home Without Instrument Aid

By WALTER SULLIVAN
Special to The New York Times

HOUSTON, April 14—So low is the Apollo 13 spacecraft on water to cool its electronic equipment that the three astronauts will have to coast home without their inertial "sense of direction."

They will, however, activate and orient it in midjourney for guidance when making their final course correction, designed to bring them into the atmosphere at the narrowly defined angle necessary for a safe return.

They will then shut it down again until shortly before re-entering the earth's atmosphere, when the command module guidance and control systems, now completely shut down, are brought back into operation for the critical final maneuvers of the abortive mission.

A "sense of direction" is provided aboard both the command module and the lunar module, by a so-called inertial platform. This is a device whose orientation in space is kept steady, despite twists and turns of the spacecraft, by a system of gyros.

Alignment Preserved

The proper orientation of the platform is essential for controlling the direction of thrust in any space maneuver. Only through cool-headed improvisations did the astronauts and their advisers at the manned spacecraft center here preserve the alignment of their platform during the crisis early today.

When an explosion or other violent event ruptured an oxygen tank in the service module, or spacecraft "engine room," resulting in the rapid loss of electric power the gyros that steady the platform were about to shut down.

This could have been critical in view of two impending maneuvers—one designed to insure the return of the spacecraft to earth after circling the moon and the other this evening's rocket firing to speed the return and bring the astronauts down into the ocean.

Once lost, the realignment of the platform would have been difficult because the spacecraft is traveling in its own cloud.

But for prompt action the gyros would have stopped and the alignment of the inertial platform would have been lost. This could have been critical because the spacecraft is traveling in its own cloud of smog and debris—a cloud that became far denser following the rupture and venting of an oxygen tank in the accident.

2 Platforms on Board

This has made it virtually impossible for the astronauts to sight on stars in order to realign one of the two inertial platforms on board. One is in the main guidance and navigation system of the command module; the other is in the lunar module that is now serving as the astronauts' "lifeboat."

Sunlight shining on the smog, the debris and parts of the spacecraft blanks out the stars. During the critical minutes this evening when the spacecraft was in the moon's shadow, it was hoped that some star sightings could be obtained. During the long coast back to earth it may also be possible to obtain fixes on terrestrial and lunar landmarks, enabling computers on earth to refine estimates of the vehicle's trajectory.

The guidance alignment was preserved by two hurried stratagems. One, as described this morning by Glynn S. Lunney, who was flight director at the control center here during much of the crisis, was performed as the last fuel cell supplying power to the command module had just about breathed its last oxygen.

The rupture of the oxygen tank had cut off the supply of that gas to the fuel cells. Hurriedly on the advice from the control center, the astronauts began feeding power from one of the command module reserve batteries into the system. Upon this power will depend the proper control of the vehicle during the crucial re-entry phase.

However, the maintenance of platform alignment was considered important enough to risk using up some of this power. This gave the astronauts time to carry out the second step, which was to activate the lunar module systems, including its own inertial platform.

Power Turned Off

Once this was done, it was possible to coach the lunar module platform to its proper orientation by reference to the command module platform. All this was done in about 20 minutes, whereupon the command module battery power was quickly turned off.

Before reaching the vicinity of the moon, the astronauts were able to take some sights on the sun, which showed their lunar module platform to be properly aligned to within one degree. When they reactivate the system for their midway course correction, it is hoped that observations of the earth and sun will cut this error margin in half.

The reason for the halo of smog and debris around the spacecraft is that every particle of dumped water, every atom of escaped gas has the same momentum as the vehicle and stays with it. When the spacecraft rocket fires to change its course and speed, it may shake off this cloud of space pollution, but promptly begins to manufacture a new one.

Entry into the atmosphere must be made at an angle no greater than 7.3 degrees and no less than 5.8 degrees. If the entry is too shallow, the craft may skip out of the atmosphere and go into a wide orbit around the earth. If it is too steep, the vehicle overheats and is subjected to deceleration beyond its designed limits.

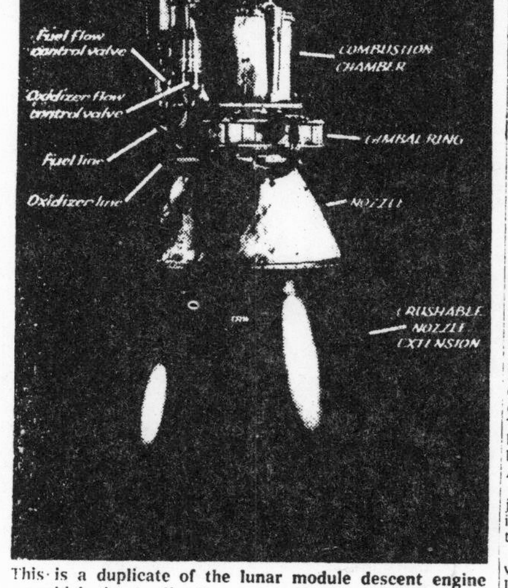

This is a duplicate of the lunar module descent engine on which the Apollo 13 crewmen depended in adjusting their course last night so as to land in the Pacific. It is seven feet one inch high and weighs 360 pounds.

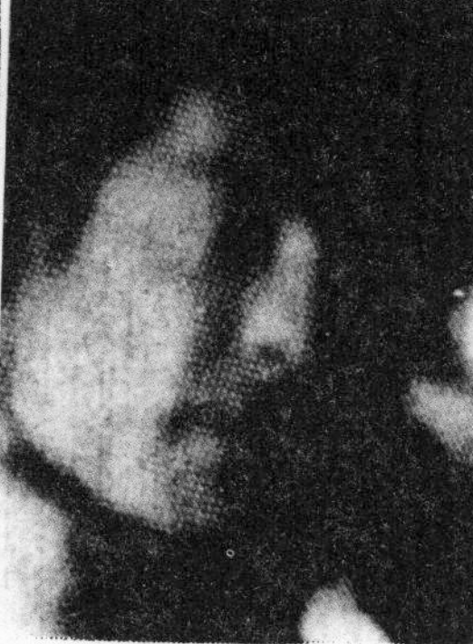

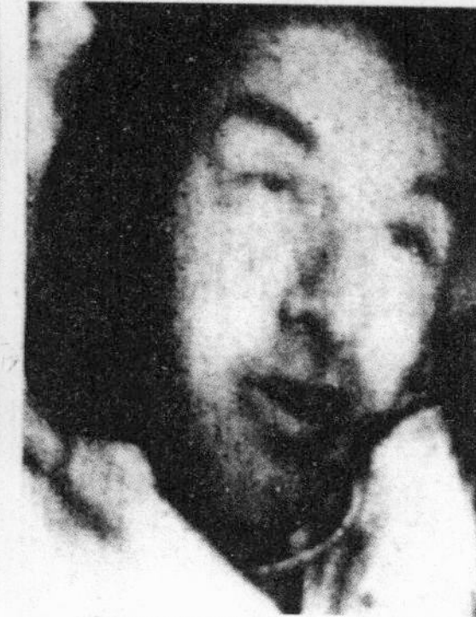

N.B.C. News and C.B.S. News via Associated Press

BEFORE TROUBLE STARTED: John L. Swigert Jr., left, and Fred W. Haise Jr., center, during a telecast from Apollo 13 Sunday night. At right, Capt. James A. Lovell Jr. in a telecast Monday just before power failure occurred on craft.

Crippled Apollo Starts Back After Rounding Moon

Continued From Page 1, Col. 8

vising alternate plans to rid the spaceship of excess amounts of the gas. One method would use the hoses of the astronauts' spacesuits to transfer lithium hydroxide from the lunar module to the command module. Another called for dumping excess carbon dioxide overboard.

Space officials seemed confident that both methods would work.

Dr. Thomas O. Paine, head of the National Aeronautics and Space Administration, said at a news conference that the exploration of the moon would continue despite the Apollo 13 crisis.

President Nixon, at the White House, kept in close touch with Dr. Paine and the Mission Control room here. The French Government offered the services of its Navy, should it be needed to help recover the astronauts after splashdown.

Under the present plan Apollo 13 should splash down in the mid-Pacific at 12:13 P.M. Eastern standard time on Friday. The U.S.S. Iwo Jima, the primary recovery ship, is steaming toward the site about 600 miles southeast of American Samoa.

A tropical storm named Helen near the New Hebrides about 1,700 miles away was being watched closely by Navy weather experts. It was not expected to interfere with the planned recovery.

Shortly before their rocket firing, the astronauts were informed that the spent third stage of the Saturn 5 booster had crashed into the moon's Ocean of Storms with the force equivalent to 11 tons of TNT. The impact touched off reverberations that were monitored by the seismometer left by Apollo 12 last November.

"It looks like your booster just hit the moon and is rocking it a little bit," Mission Control told Apollo 13.

"Well, at least something worked on this flight," Captain Lovell replied.

The three astronauts appeared calm, though a little weary, as they turned their backs on the moon and their chances for making the nation's third manned landing there. The original mission plan was for Captain Lovell and Mr. Haise to land on the moon tonight.

What would have been their landing craft, the lunar module, was now their "lifeboat." Still attached to the command ship, it was providing their oxygen, electricity and propulsion for getting home.

The astronauts were following what Mission Control decided, after hours of intensive study and computer calculations, was the least risky strategy for their returning to the earth.

Three possible courses of action were ruled out by flight directors.

They rejected a "free-return trajectory" because it would make the return trip 10 hours longer and would take the spacecraft to a splashdown in the Indian Ocean, far from any recovery forces.

Such a return was considered only as an insurance policy in case the lunar module rocket failed to put Apollo 13 on a course for the Pacific Ocean.

An initial firing of the rocket early yesterday morning steered the spacecraft on such a trajectory, which meant that without any major propulsion the vehicle would have swung around the moon and used the pull of lunar gravity to send it back toward the earth.

A "super-fast" return was ruled out as being too risky. It would have brought Apollo 13 back to the Pacific 24 hours earlier, but it would have meant firing the lunar module engine almost to depletion, leaving little fuel for possible mid-course correction.

In addition, to make the fast return it would have been necessary to jettison the command module's rear compartment, known as the service module. This would have exposed the command ship's re-entry heat shield to the possibly damaging ultraviolet rays of outer space.

A third strategy calling for a splashdown in the Atlantic Ocean off South America would have shortened the return by 10 hours. But no primary recovery ships were available in that area.

The plan chose by Mission Control calls for the astronauts to keep the lunar module attached to the command module until they come within an hour or so of the earth's atmosphere. Then they are to crawl back into the command module, shut the hatch and jettison the lunar module.

Only the cone-shaped command module is shielded for the fiery plunge through atmosphere. The return speed at that time reaches more than 25,000 miles an hour.

Although the command module's primary electric power system failed, the vehicle has enough battery power to run the guidance and communications systems during re-entry. It also has a reserve bottle of oxygen.

On an ordinary return from the moon, the lunar module is left in the vicinity of the moon—the descent stage on the surface and the ascent stage either in lunar orbit or smashed on the surface as a test of lunar seismic waves.

The astronauts ride their command module, with the service module compartment attached, until about 15 minutes before re-entry. Then the surface module, which houses the primary life-support systems, is jettisoned by the firing of explosive bolts that literally slice it off.

Under the present circumstances, the jettisoning of the service module should come about in the same way.

The lunar module's attachment to the command module is also such that the pilots can trigger explosive bolts to cast it away.

For the rest of the mission, at least one astronaut will maintain a vigil at all times in the lunar module to watch for any change in its condition. Thus far, the vehicle is said to be in smooth working order.

But astronauts cannot afford to be careless.

To conserve electricity, being supplied by lunar module batteries, they will be "powering down"—running with the guidance system off except for mid-course corrections, using the radio for only periodic status reports and turning off nearly all other systems.

It is estimated, that with such care, the astronauts should have a margin of about 22 per cent of lunar module battery power left by the time they reach the separation-for-re-entry phase.

If so, the remaining battery power in the lunar module will be used to recharge one of the command module batteries that is running slightly below full strength.

One of the most critical "consumables" is water, the flight controller said at a news conference. Water is essential for cooling the electronics systems in the vehicles' guidance and navigation and telecommunications systems.

Even so, the latest estimates were that the lunar module's water supply was sufficient to allow for "powering up" the electronics for two mid-course correction maneuvers and still have about 12 to 13 hours of water left.

Oxygen from the lunar module was being used for the atmosphere in both vehicles. The astronauts were using the larger cabin of the command module for sleeping.

The lunar module's 50 pounds of oxygen was reported to be sufficient for supporting the astronauts for 23 hours longer than the current mission time.

The decision on how to bring Apollo 13 back to the earth quickly and safely was made after more than 12 hours of intensive and often agonizing conferences involving flight controllers, spacecraft engineers and space agency officials.

It was the space program's "Longest night." Glynn S. Lunney, the weary flight director, said afterward.

While the capsule communicator near the center of the mission control room kept up an almost continuous chatter with the Apollo 13 crew, seeking information and imparting instructions, teams of engineers ran computer calculations in the back rooms on the following questions: How long a rocket firing? When should it come? How much fuel would it use? How long could the life-support system keep going?

Comdr. Eugene A. Cernan of the Navy, who was an Apollo 10 astronaut, spent much of the night in a simulator conducting all manner of alternate mission maneuvers.

Lieut. Comdr. Thomas K. Mattingly 2d of the Navy, who was pulled off the Apollo 13 crew because of exposure to German measles, also lent a hand in the simulations.

In a briefing for newsmen, Mr. Lunney reconstructed the sequence of events and decision-making that followed the sudden oxygen tank trouble at 10:11 o'clock last night—slightly less that 56 hours after Apollo 13 was launched from Cape Kennedy, Fla.

"My team," Mr. Lunney said, "has been primarily concerned with not what happened back there [in the service module] but what it is we were going to do about it."

The situation was almost immediately recognized as serious, Mr. Lunney recalled.

The crew reported a "bang," followed by a sudden and complete drop of pressure in one of the two liquid oxygen tanks in the service module. Captain Lovell could see gases venting out into space and the spacecraft began to roll.

Engineers were reported to be still mystified by what ruptured the tank. They doubt that a meteroid impact was to blame, noting that the odds are far greater for its being some internal explosion.

The two tanks containing super-cold liquid oxygen are housed in the command ship's service module, a 24-foot-long cylinder bearing the major electrical power, life-support, telecommunications and propulsion systems for the command module.

The tank that ruptured was situated behind the commander's seat on the left side of the cockpit.

When the tank failed, so did one of the three fuel cells in the service module. These are the spacecraft's power plants for generating electricity by means of a chemical reaction between liquid oxygen and liquid hydrogen. The byproduct is water for cooling spacecraft electronics and for drinking.

At first, flight controllers struggled to "stabilize the condition," hoping to keep at least one oxygen from the other tank. But pressure in that tank was also plunging.

For three hours they were able to keep only one fuel cell in operation. This gave the astronauts time to recharge the storage batteries for the re-entry maneuver, store up water and generate enough electricity to run the guidance system for a while.

When they were forced to cut off the remaining fuel cell, in a "last-ditch attempt to isolate the leak," two of the three astronauts retreated through the connecting tunnel into the attached lunar module. The third man, Mr. Haise, remained in the dark and crippled command ship, feeling his way around with the aid of a flashlight.

Experts Ponder Cause Of Spacecraft's Mishap

By RICHARD WITKIN

Excessive pressure of super-cooled oxygen may have blown up a spherical oxygen tank and produced the emergency that enveloped the Apollo 13 moon flight Monday night.

For the moment, that was the most widely held thesis among space experts trying to reconstruct what had turned an uneventful mission into a perilous race to get the three astronauts back to earth before an exhaustion of the supplied needed to keep them alive.

There was some speculation that the oxygen tank, situated in the service module below the three-man command ship, had been blown up by a micrometeoroid. But this was a minority view—a view depreciated by Glynn S. Lunney, who came on duty for his regular shift as flight director about an hour after the emergency began.

Lunney Queried

Asked at a news conference this morning whether the spacecraft might have been struck by a particle speeding through space, Mr. Lunney said:

"I don't know. I guess it's conceivable. But based on the fact that the cryo [a reference to the supercooled oxygen] pressure started to go up, reached what pressure it should have been relieved at, and then went down to zero—my personal opinion is that that probably has not occurred. But that again really remains to be seen."

United Press International quoted Dr. Harvey Nininger of Sedona, Ariz., an expert in the field, as having said that the spacecraft might well have been hit by a meteoroid.

"In my opinion, that's what happened," he said.

In either case, the loss of oxygen pressure meant a rapid loss of the spacecraft's main source of electrical power. This power was produced by the reaction of the oxygen with supercooled hydrogen in the command module's three fuel cells.

Widely Held View

Most qualified observers emphasized that any number of explanations for the accident were possible. But Mr. Lunney's tentative view drew the most initial support, particularly since it was taken to reflect the best momentary thinking in the space agency.

What he was saying was that there was hard evidence, presumably in data radioed to the ground, that the pressure not only had risen but also had gone right up to the point where relief valves should have opened to relieve it.

Then came the rapid pressure drop to zero, just about the time Capt. James A. Lovell Jr. and his crew heard the bang that indicated serious trouble.

Work got under way immediately to try to find a surer explanation for the Apollo 13 setback. The main emphasis, will be on trying to duplicate what happened by setting up comparable conditions with duplicate equipment in ground laboratories.

Engineers also began to pore over detailed records of critical pieces of service module equipment to see if the actual pieces of hardware in the Apollo 13 module had had even minor problems during the manufacturing and test processes.

However, the detective work was given a second priority at this time so as not to lessen concentration on the main job at hand—getting the three astronauts safely back to earth.

Officials Thankful

Space agency officials were thankful that the accident had taken place when it did, rather than a time when the two-man lunar landing craft might not have been immediately available to serve as a lifeboat for the stricken command ship.

The service module where the trouble erupted is a cylindrically shaped vehicle attached to the base of the cone-shaped command module. It is more than twice as long (22 feet 7 inches) and four times as heavy (52,800 pounds) as the command ship.

It is the only one of the three spacecraft modules that has no accommodations for astronauts. It contains the main spacecraft propulsion system—the powerful engine designed, under normal conditions, to curve the spacecraft into a lunar orbit and later, after the lunar landing, to start it on the long return to earth.

It also supplies most of the consumable items (oxygen, water, propellant) required by the crew and their command ship. The service module is supposed to remain attached to the command module until just before re-entry, when it is cut loose, to be destroyed by the heat of friction as it re-enters the atmosphere.

Each of the two oxygen tanks supplying the power-producing fuel cells with semi-gaseous, semi-liquid oxygen is a sphere 26 inches in diameter. They are made of a tough nickel alloy known as Inconel. Their operating temperatures range from minus 300 degrees Fahrenheit to 80 degrees above zero. To remain liquid, oxygen must be maintained at minus 297 or below.

Each tank has a heater to supply the heat needed to maintain pressure, and a fan to circulate the fluid over the elements of the heater.

There are relief valves rigged to open and relieve pressure if it gets too high.

Did something go awry with a heater and produce too much heat and pressure too fast? Did a relief valve stick for some unknown reason?

Engineers close to the program think there is a good chance they will eventually be able to pinpoint the source of the trouble, even though the best evidence will be consumed as the service module burns up on re-entry.

But it is expected to take considerable time — enough perhaps to put off the next Apollo flight, planned for fall, for a year or more.

Conversation With Apollo

Following are excerpts from conversations between the Apollo 13 astronauts and Mission Control in Houston, as recorded by The New York Times, during a rocket firing maneuver after the spacecraft rounded the moon:

APOLLO CONTROL: We're go for the burn. Apollo 13 now 5,039 nautical miles away from the moon, traveling at speed of 4,616 feet per second.

HOUSTON: Jim, you are go for the burn. Go for the burn.

APOLLO: I got it, Gene, go for the burn.

HOUSTON: One minute away now from scheduled time of ignition.

APOLLO: Roger.

HOUSTON: Apollo 13 now 5,426 nautical miles out from the moon traveling at a speed of 4,552 feet per second. Less than 30 seconds away. Engine is on standing by. Ground confirms ignition.

APOLLO: All burning 40 per cent.

HOUSTON: Houston copies. Attitude looks good at this point.

APOLLO: Roger.

HOUSTON: Aquarius, Houston, you're looking good.

APOLLO: Roger.

HOUSTON: One minute now into the burn. IPS is looking good. Two minutes into the burn. Aquarius, you are looking good at two minutes. Still looking good.

APOLLO: Two minutes. Roger.

HOUSTON: Velocity building up. Our Diskey shows we've gained 451 feet per second at this time. Reports to flight director Gene Kranz indicate all systems are looking good. Coming up on three minutes into the burn. Aquarius, you're go at three minutes.

APOLLO: Aquarius, Roger.

HOUSTON: The on-board display shows less than a minute to go in the burn now. Coming up on four minutes into the burn. Don't forget descent rate went off 10 seconds to go.

APOLLO: Shut down.

HOUSTON: Roger, shut down.

APOLLO CONTROL: That was Commander Jim Lovell reporting shut down. The engine is off. We're at 79 hours 32 minutes into the flight.

HOUSTON: Apollo control. 79 hours 33 minutes 5,707 nautical miles out from the moon at this time. I say that was a good burn.

APOLLO: Roger. Now we want to power down as soon as possible.

HOUSTON: Rog. Understand.

APOLLO: Suggest maybe that you just read off the circuit-breakers you wanted to power down as you did yesterday for us.

HOUSTON: O.K. We have a procedure ready to send up to you here in about two minutes. Let us know when you're all ready to take it.

APOLLO: O.K. Houston. Be better to write this on a blank page, Vance, or can we use some portion of the power down list there in the contingency book that already exists?

HOUSTON: Stand by. Slight delay here, Jim. It'll be a couple of minutes before we read that up to you and we're looking at the contingency check list power down and that's on Page 5. You might be getting that out while we get all ready to give it to you.

HOUSTON: 79 hours 37 minutes into the flight. O.K., make that power five in the contingency check list, Fred. And let's see, in the middle part of the page it starts emergency power down and we'll mark that up. We're 79 hours 37 minutes into the flight. Guidance reported that the flight on the duration was literally right on the money.

Apollo: Power five, emergency power down.

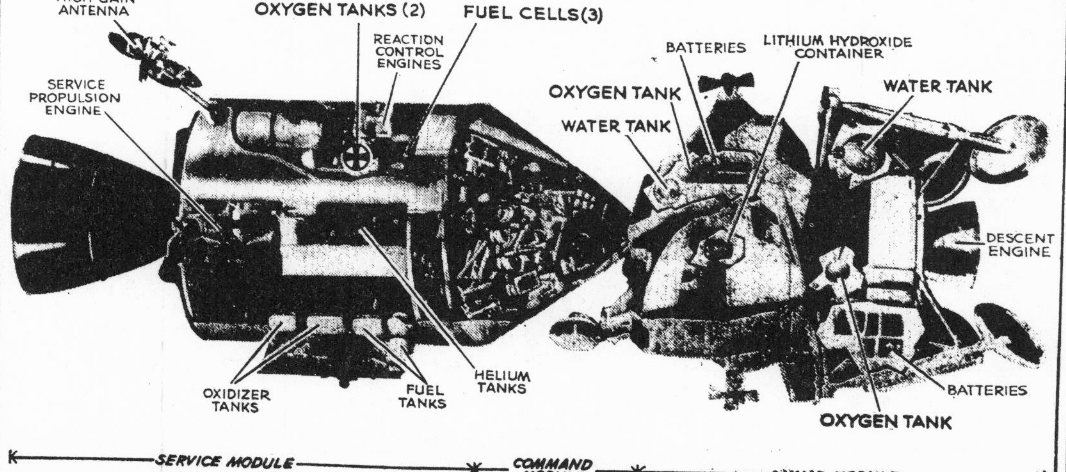

The New York Times April 15, 1970

The troubles of Apollo 13 began in its service module with the rupture of one of two oxygen tanks (cross) that nourished fuel cells. The cells produced electrical power for the command module and the service propulsion engine (SPS), and gave off cooling and drinking water as a by-product. After the mishap, astronauts closed off all connections to the service module and relied on the lunar module's batteries, water and oxygen tanks (cutaway areas) to maintain their lives and operate the spacecraft. Small reserves in command module were expected to sustain crew during re-entry into earth's atmosphere on Friday. Descent engine of lunar module (LM) replaced the SPS as Apollo's primary means of propulsion. Crew raided command module's more plentiful supply of lithium hydroxide canisters to remove carbon dioxide from atmosphere of LM.

"All the News That's Fit to Print"

The New York Times

LATE CITY EDITION

Weather: Rain ending early today; clearing tonight. Fair tomorrow. Temp. range: today 66-49; Monday 62-53. Full U.S. report on Page 90.

VOL. CXIX.. No. 41,009 NEW YORK, TUESDAY, MAY 5, 1970 — 10 CENTS

HIGH COURT BACKS CHURCHES' RIGHT TO TAX EXEMPTION

Holds, 7 to 1, That Law Does Not Violate Ban on State Support of Religion

DOUGLAS CASTS DISSENT

Majority Rejects Plea of a Bronx Lawyer Over His Plot on Staten Island

By FRED P. GRAHAM
Special to The New York Times

WASHINGTON, May 4 — The Supreme Court ruled 7 to 1 today that laws that exempt church property from taxation do not violate the Constitution's prohibition against state support of religion.

The opinion was written by Chief Justice Warren E. Burger and was disputed only by Justice William O. Douglas. In it the Court upheld the constitutionality of New York State's exemption from real estate taxes of church property used solely for religious purposes.

The law had been challenged by Frederick Walz, a lawyer from the Bronx who purchased a 22-by-29-foot, weed-choked plot on Staten Island in 1967 and promptly sued the City Tax Commission over his $5.24 tax bill for a year.

'Establishment' Is Seen

Mr. Walz, who described himself as a "religious person, not a member of any religious organization," said that tax exemptions granted to church property raised his own tax bill and forced him to contribute to religious groups against his will.

He asserted that the result was an indirect state subsidy to churches, in violation of the First Amendment's prohibition against any "establishment of religion" by the Government.

The Supreme Court rejected that argument today, partly on the ground that no particular religion is singled out for favorable treatment and partly on the historical ground that church tax exemptions have been accepted almost without challenge in all states for most of the nation's history.

Chief Justice Burger's opinion conceded that the church exemption "necessarily operates to afford an indirect economic benefit." But he reasoned that the state might be less neutral toward churches if it taxed them and that it was faced with the delicate matter of deciding on each church's proper assessment.

Surprise and Concern

He concluded that some contact between churches and the state was inevitable and that it would be unfair to deny tax exemptions to religious groups while granting exemptions to nonsectarian charities that do similar good works.

The Supreme Court's decision to review Mr. Walz's appeal prompted widespread puzzlement in legal circles and concern among churchmen. The constitutionality of church tax exemptions was considered so well settled that the New York courts brushed off the challenge with brief orders declaring that it had no merit.

The American Civil Liberties Union backed Mr. Walz, and

Continued on Page 40, Column 5

4 Kent State Students Killed by Troops

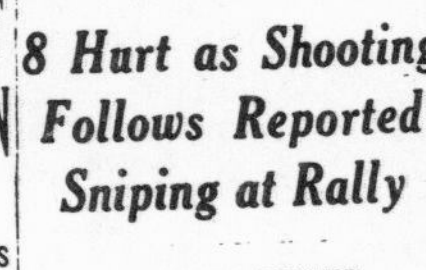

8 Hurt as Shooting Follows Reported Sniping at Rally

By JOHN KIFNER
Special to The New York Times

KENT, Ohio, May 4—Four students at Kent State University, two of them women, were shot to death this afternoon by a volley of National Guard gunfire. At least 8 other students were wounded.

The burst of gunfire came about 20 minutes after the guardsmen broke up a noon rally on the Commons, a grassy campus gathering spot, by lobbing tear gas at a crowd of about 1,000 young people.

In Washington, President Nixon deplored the deaths of the four students in the following statement:

"This should remind us all once again that when dissent turns to violence it invites tragedy. It is my hope that this tragic and unfortunate incident will strengthen the determination of all the nation's campuses, administrators, faculty and students alike to stand firmly for the right which exists in this country of peaceful dissent and just as strongly against the resort to violence as a means of such expression."

In Columbus, Sylvester Del Corso, Adjutant General of the Ohio National Guard, said in a statement that the guardsmen had been forced to shoot after a sniper opened fire against the troops from a nearby rooftop and the crowd began to move to encircle the guardsmen.

Frederick P. Wenger, the Assistant Adjutant General, said the troops had opened fire after they were shot at by a sniper.

"They were under standing orders to take cover and return any fire," he said.

This reporter, who was with the group of students, did not see any indication of sniper fire, nor was the sound of any gunfire audible before the Guard volley. Students, conceding that rocks had been thrown, heatedly denied that there was any sniper.

Gov. James A. Rhodes called on J. Edgar Hoover, director of the Federal Bureau of Investigation, to aid in looking into the campus violence. A Justice Department spokesman said no decision had been made to investigate.

At 2:10 this afternoon, after the shootings, the university president, Robert I. White, ordered the university closed for an indefinite time, and officials were making plans to evacuate the dormitories and bus out-of-state students to nearby cities.

Robinson Memorial Hospital identified the dead students as Allison Krause, 19 years old, of

Continued on Page 17, Column 1

Tarentum Valley Daily News via Associated Press

A girl screams as fellow student lies dead after National Guardsmen opened fire at Kent State

Associated Press

Ohio National Guardsmen advancing over the campus of Kent State University yesterday behind a screen of tear gas

37 COLLEGE CHIEFS URGE NIXON MOVE FOR PROMPT PEACE

Warn Invasion of Cambodia Poses New Alienation Peril —Student Strikes Begin

By ROBERT D. McFADDEN

The presidents of 37 colleges and universities urged President Nixon yesterday to "demonstrate unequivocally your determination" to end promptly the United States military involvement in Southeast Asia.

In a letter to Mr. Nixon, the presidents said that "the American invasion of Cambodia" and the weekend bombing of North Vietnam had generated "severe and widespread apprehensions on our campuses."

"We share these apprehensions," the presidents said, adding:

"We implore you to consider the incalculable dangers of an unprecedented alienation of America's youth and to take immediate action to demonstrate unequivocally your determination to end the war quickly."

The signers, representing many of the nation's leading academic institutions, "urgently" requested a meeting with Mr. Nixon.

The letter was drafted by Dr. James M. Hester, the president of New York University, and bore the signatures, among others, of the presidents of Princeton University, Columbia University, the University of Notre Dame, Dartmouth College, the University of Pennsylvania and Johns Hopkins University.

Nationwide Strike Urged

In Washington, the leaders of the National Student Association and the former Vietnam Moratorium Committee called for a nationwide university strike of indefinite duration, starting today, to protest the war and to mobilize public opinion for a withdrawal of United States forces from Indochina. It would involve students, faculty members and administrators.

Antiwar groups at dozens of colleges and universities across the nation, meanwhile, began demonstrations and rallies to protest the Administration's policies.

There were strike pledges from at least 100 colleges and universities, and at some schools the strike began yesterday. Support for the strike was expressed in the editorials of many campus newspapers, along with a condemnation of what some called President Nixon's "illegitimate" decision to send troops into Cambodia.

At many schools, the strike was officially approved by college administrations. Most of

Continued on Page 18, Column 6

President Assailed By Fulbright Panel

By JOHN W. FINNEY
Special to The New York Times

WASHINGTON, May 4—The Senate Foreign Relations Committee complained today that the Nixon Administration, by sending American troops into Cambodia "without the consent or knowledge of Congress," was usurping the war-making powers of Congress.

The committee, which is headed by Senator J. W. Fulbright, also charged that over the years the executive branch had been "conducting a constitutionally unauthorized, Presidential war in Indochina." The charge was promptly rejected by the White House, which contended that President Nixon was relying upon his constitutional powers as Commander in Chief.

"The action which the

Continued on Page 4, Column 4

U.S. SAYS BIG RAIDS IN NORTH ARE OVER

Officials Stress That There May Be Smaller Strikes if Flights Are Periled

By WILLIAM BEECHER
Special to The New York Times

WASHINGTON, May 4—The Defense Department announced today it had "terminated" large-scale air raids mounted in recent days against three areas of North Vietnam.

But Pentagon officials stressed that smaller air strikes might be conducted in the future if American reconnaissance flights over North Vietnam were attacked.

For the first time, the Pentagon acknowledged that the raids north of the demilitarized zone over the weekend had been larger in scope than any since the bombing halt in November, 1968, and that so-called "logistics support" facilities for air defense had been struck in addition to antiaircraft gun and missile sites.

3 Areas Attacked

The Defense Department said that from 50 to more than 100 planes had been employed in each of the strikes near Barthelemy Pass, Bankarai Pass and in another area immediately north of the demilitarized zone. Barthelemy Pass, about 240 miles north of the demilitarized zone, is believed to be the farthest point north raided by American aircraft since November, 1968.

All three areas, officials said, are key conduits for the flow of men and matériel to enemy military units throughout Indo-

Continued on Page 15, Column 1

KOSYGIN ATTACKS NIXON FOR MOVING G.I.'S TO CAMBODIA

He Tells News Conference Action Raises Doubts on Bids for Negotiations

WARNS ON ARMS PARLEY

China Pledges Support to Indochinese People — U.S. in New Drive

Excerpts from Kosygin's text and Q. and A., Page 2.

By BERNARD GWERTZMAN
Special to The New York Times

MOSCOW, May 4—Premier Aleksei N. Kosygin today assailed President Nixon for having sent American forces into Cambodia. He warned that the action might lead to a "further complication" in the international scene and a worsening of Soviet-American relations.

[Communist China also denounced the United States on Cambodia and pledged support to the people of Indochina in their "patriotic struggle" against American forces. Page 3.]

[The Associated Press reported that thousands of American and South Vietnamese troops launched a new offensive into northeast Cambodia Tuesday, according to an announcement by the United States command The command said the attack was launched from a base 50 miles west of Pleiku, in the Central Highlands, near the Laotian border.]

Reading from a statement at the start of his first news conference in the Soviet Union in more than five years in office, Mr. Kosygin said the Cambodia intervention raised doubts about Mr. Nixon's sincerity in seeking an "era of negotiation."

He Sees Contradictions

"Is it possible to speak seriously," Mr. Kosygin said, "about the desire of the United States President for fruitful negotiations to solve pressing international problems while the United States is grossly flouting the Geneva Agreements of 1954 and 1962 to which it is a party, and undertaking one new act after another undermining the foundations of international security?

"What is the value of international agreements which the United States is or intends to be a party to if it so unceremoniously violates its obligations? It is impossible not to give serious thoughts to the fact that President Nixon's practical steps in the field of foreign policy are fundamentally at variance with those declarations and assurances that he repeatedly made both before assuming the Presidency and when he was already in the White House."

Attack Shocks Envoys

Western diplomats, who had expected a Soviet Government statement against the Cambodian action, were surprised that it was delivered by Mr. Kosygin in person, and were shocked by the personal attack on Mr. Nixon. Although Mr. Kosygin spoke in calm tones, the diplomats were taken aback by his characterization of President Nixon as a man whose words could not be trusted.

This seemed to indicate to the diplomats that a violent campaign would be started to enlist world opinion against Mr. Nixon.

Although the news conference was called to discuss Cambodia, in answer to a question on the Middle East, Mr. Kosygin said that Soviet military advisers were attached to the armed forces of the United Arab Republic to combat Israeli "aggression" and had certain

Continued on Page 3, Column 1

WAR AND ECONOMY SPUR STOCK DROPS

Administration Economist Voices Apprehension as Market Falls 19.07

By TERRY ROBARDS

Uneasiness over the United States involvement in Cambodia and the bombing of North Vietnam, plus continuing uncertainty about the nation's business outlook, created a mood of deep pessimism on Wall Street yesterday and sent the securities markets into a tailspin.

Stock and bond prices fell sharply in response to selling by discouraged investors. The Dow-Jones industrial average, a gauge of price action on the New York Stock Exchange, plunged 19.07 points in its worst decline since the loss of 21.16 points Nov. 22, 1963, the day President Kennedy was assassinated.

In Washington, a leading Nixon Administration economist expressed apprehension about the situation. "The Administration is obviously concerned," said, declining to be publicly identified.

"An emotional reaction triggered by the stock market decline may mislead people concerning the basic strength of the economy and its favorable prospects," he asserted, adding that "the facts in the economic sense are pretty good."

His statements represented the first clear indication of anxiety by the Nixon Administration with respect to the stock market's behavior. They were issued before the close of trading and before it was clear that yesterday's nosedive would be

Continued on Page 69, Column 2

Report of Songmy Incident Wins a Pulitzer for Hersh

By PETER KIHSS

A report on the alleged Songmy massacre of Vietnamese civilians by United States soldiers won the 1970 Pulitzer prize in international reporting yesterday for Seymour Hersh, a free-lance reporter whose article was circulated through the Dispatch News Service.

A black playwright, Charles Gordone, won the drama prize for an Off Broadway play, "No Place to Be Somebody"—the first Off Broadway production so honored.

A musical composition on an electronic synthesizer won the music prize for the first time, the award going to "Time's Encomium," by Charles Wuorinen.

Ada Louise Huxtable, architecture critic of The New York Times, became the winner of the first Pulitzer prize for distinguished criticism. This was a new category, set up for criticism or commentary, and was divided in the judging, with Marquis W. Childs of The St. Louis Post-Dispatch taking the award for distinguished commentary.

The gold medal for meritorious public service went to Newsday of Garden City, L. I., for a three-year investigation and exposé of secret land deals and zoning manipulations by public and political party officeholders.

With 17 individuals named Pulitzer prize-winners in the 54th year of the awards, the laurels for history were carried off by former Secretary of

Continued on Page 48, Column 1

ISRAELIS REPORT KILLING 21 ARABS

Toll in Guerrilla Battle at Jordan River Is Termed Largest Since '67 War

By RICHARD EDER
Special to The New York Times

JERUSALEM, May 4—Israeli military authorities announced today that an Israeli patrol surprised and killed 21 armed Palestinian infiltrators shortly after they crossed the Jordan River into Israeli-controlled territory last night.

At the same time the Israelis reported some tentative signs that intensive air strikes on Egyptian artillery positions west of the Suez Canal were beginning to ease the recent pressure on Israeli troops on the east bank.

Last night's encounter with the guerrillas involved the largest death toll reported by Israeli forces since the start of the struggle with Arabs infiltrating into territories occupied by Israel after the 1967 war.

According to the account provided by Israeli military authorities, the infiltrators, members of Al Fatah guerrilla organization, were pinned down by fire from the Israeli patrol just before midnight, not far from the banks of the Jordan River.

The infiltrators tried to take shelter in scrub and thornbushes, the account continued. Apart from firing one bazooka shot, it went on, they made no move to answer the Israeli fire, which went on heavily but intermittently all night and which, by sunup, had killed all but six of them.

When it began to grow light,

Continued on Page 8, Column 4

U.S. Officials in Saigon Reduce Their Hopes in Cambodia Drive

Red Leaders Elude Sweep

By TERENCE SMITH
Special to The New York Times

SAIGON, South Vietnam, May 4—Senior United States military and civilian officials here are beginning to scale down their definitions of success for the four-day-old American-South Vietnamese sweep into the Fishhook area of Cambodia.

One of their preliminary conclusions is that the success or failure of the sweep will have to be measured in terms of supplies captured and facilities destroyed, since the top enemy command and the vast majority of the 7,000 Communist soldiers who were believed to have been in the area appear to have fled.

Another preliminary conclusion is that additional forays into other parts of eastern Cambodia are virtually inevitable if lasting damage is to be inflicted on the North Vietnamese supply system. Strikes into eastern Laos, the officials say, are not to be ruled out.

The officials consider that substantial withdrawals of United States combat troops from Vietnam will almost certainly have to be deferred to

Continued on Page 16, Column 3

Big Base Area Discovered

Special to The New York Times

LANDING ZONE NORTH ONE, Cambodia, May 4—Soldiers from this northernmost American outpost in the drive against enemy sanctuaries in Cambodia today reached the site of what is believed to be the largest North Vietnamese base area discovered in the operation, which began last Friday.

The base area, referred to on tactical maps as "The City," is situated in rolling hills and jungles near the northwestern tip of Binhlong Province of South Vietnam. The area is about two miles south of this outpost, which was hastily set up yesterday as a blocking position 20 miles north of where American tanks first plunged into Cambodia along the southern edge of the Fishhook area.

[As the American soldiers advanced, North Vietnamese and Vietcong troops increased their pressure against Pnompenh by cutting the Pnompenh-Saigon highway 29 miles from the Cambodian capital. Page 16.]

A company of soldiers from this base camp was waiting tonight for reinforcements and

Continued on Page 16, Column 3

3 in Bombing Plot Plead Guilty Here

By ARNOLD H. LUBASCH

Samuel J. Melville, Jane L. Alpert and John D. Hughey 3d pleaded guilty yesterday as the self-styled revolutionaries were about to stand trial on charges of conspiring to bomb Federal buildings here last fall.

After the case was convened amid stringent security measures in Federal Court, Judge Milton Pollack asked the bearded 34-year-old Melville why he wanted to plead guilty to three charges against him.

"I plead guilty to count one because I did conspire with others to destroy Federal property," Melville replied as he stood erectly in blue jeans and

Continued on Page 34, Column 1

Study of LSD Spurs Suspicions Of Drug's Link to Birth Defects

By SANDRA BLAKESLEE

The first extensive, long-term study comparing the incidence of birth defects with parental use of LSD has concluded that the drug "must be seriously considered as a possible mutagen"—an agent that produces genetic changes in cells.

"Although we cannot rush in and say we have unequivocal evidence at this time that LSD use causes birth defects, we are on firmer ground, more suspicious, than ever before," said Dr. Cheston M. Berlin, a principal investigator in the study.

Dr. Berlin, a pediatrician at George Washington University School of Medicine, where the study was conducted, presented his findings at two recent scientific meetings. He elaborated on the results in an interview yesterday.

The issue of whether LSD (shorthand for lysergic acid diethylamide) is a mutagenic agent has not yet been resolved, Dr. Berlin said.

Such agents, or changers, act in some way to alter the normal configuration of the genetic material within the cells of an organism, often causing the organism to reproduce itself abnormally, producing birth defects.

If LSD is a mutagenic agent, Dr. Berlin said, evidence of its cellular interference might turn

Continued on Page 23, Column 1

NEWS INDEX

United Press International

MOMENTS BEFORE TRAGEDY: Students at Kent State University campus retreating yesterday before tear-gas barrage from National Guardsmen

4 Kent State Students, 2 of Them Girls, Killed by Guardsmen

Continued From Page 1, Col. 5

Pittsburgh; Sandra Lee Scheuer, 20, of Youngstown, Ohio, both coeds; Jeffrey Glenn Miller, 20, of 22 Diamond Drive, Plainview, L. I., and William K. Schroeder, 19, of Lorain, Ohio.

At 10:30 P.M. the hospital said that six students had been treated for gunshot wounds. Three were reported in critical condition and three in fair condition. Two others with superficial wounds were treated and released.

Students here, angered by the expansion of the war into Cambodia, have held demonstrations for the last three nights. On Saturday night, the Army Reserve OOfficers Training Corps building was burned to the ground and the Guard was called in and martial law was declared.

Today's rally, called after a night in which the police and guardsmen drove students into their dormitories and made 69 arrests, began as students rang the iron Victory Bell on the commons, normally used to herald football victories.

A National Guard jeep drove onto the Commons and an officer ordered the crowd to disperse. Then several canisters of tear gas were fired, and the students straggled up a hill that borders the area and retreated into buildings.

A platoon of guardsmen, armed—as they have been since they arrived here with loaded M-1 rifles and gas equipment—moved across the green and over the crest of the hill, chasing the main body of protesters.

The youths split into two groups, one heading farther downhill toward a dormitory complex, the other eddying around a parking lot and girls' dormitory just below Taylor Hall, the architecture building.

The guardsmen moved into a grassy area just below the parking lot and fired several canisters of tear gas from their short, stubby launchers.

Three or four youths ran to the smoking canisters and hurled them back. Most fell far short, but one landed near the troops and a cheer went up from the crowd, which was chanting "Pigs off campus" and cursing the war.

A few youths in the front of the crowd ran into the parking lot and hurled stones or small chunks of pavement in the direction of the guardsmen. Then the troops began moving back up the hill in the direction of the college.

Students Cheer

The students in the parking lot area, numbering about 500, began to move toward the rear of the troops, cheering. Again, a few in front picked up stones from the edge of the parking lot and threw them at the guardsmen. Another group of several hundred students had gathered around the sides of Taylor Hall watching.

As the guardsmen, moving up the hill in single file, reached the crest, they suddenly turned, forming a skirmish line and opening fire.

The crackle of the rifle volley cut the suddenly still air. It appeared to go on, as a solid volley, for perhaps a full minute or a little longer.

Some of the students dived to the ground, crawling on the grass in terror. Others stood shocked or half crouched, apparently believing the troops were firing into the air. Some of the rifle barrels were pointed upward.

Near the top of the hill at the corner of Taylor Hall, a student crumpled over, spun sideways and fell to the ground, shot in the head.

When the firing stopped, a slim girl, wearing a cowboy shirt and faded jeans, was lying face down on the road at the edge of the parking lot, blood pouring out onto the macadam, about 10 feet from this reporter.

Too Shocked to React

The youths stood stunned, many of them clustered in small groups staring at the bodies. A young man cradled one of the bleeding forms in his arms. Several girls began to cry. But many of the students who rushed to the scene seemed almost too shocked to react. Several gathered around an abstract steel sculpture in front of the building and looked at a .30-caliber bullet hole drilled through one of the plates.

The hospital said that six young people were being treated for gunshot wounds, some in the intensive care unit. Three of the students who were killed were dead on arrival at the hospital.

One guardsman was treated and released at the hospital and another was admitted with heat prostration.

In early afternoon, students attempted to gather at various area of the Commons but were ordered away by guardsman and the Ohio Highway Patrol, which moved in as reinforcements.

There were no further clashes, as faculty members, graduate assistants and students leaders urged the crowd to go back to the dormitories.

But a bizarre atmosphere hung over the campus as a Guard helicopter hovered overhead, grim-faced officers maneuvered their men to safeguard the normally pastoral campus and students, dazed, fearful and angry, struggled to comprehend what had happened and to find something to do about it.

Students carrying suitcases and duffel bags began leaving the campus this afternoon. Early tonight the entire campus was sealed off and a court injunction was issued ordering all students to leave.

A 5 P.M. curfew was declared in Kent, and road blocks were set up around the town to prevent anyone from entering. A state of emergency was also declared in the nearby towns of Stow and Ravenna.

Statement by General

KENT, Ohio, May 4 (UPI)—Brig. Gen. Robert Canterbury, the commander of Guard troops on the Kent State campus, said today that no warning had been given to the students that the troops would shoot.

General Canterbury, at a campus news conference, said in reply to questioning that no official order had been given to open fire.

"The situation did not allow it," he said. "The emotional atmosphere was such that anything could have happened. It was over in two to three seconds."

He said a guardsman "always has the option to fire if his life is in danger."

"A crowd of about 600 students had surrounded a unit of about 100 guardsmen on three sides and were throwing rocks at the troops," he said. "Some of the rocks were the size of baseballs. The troops had run out of tear gas."

Governor Rhodes, who had ordered the National Guardsmen onto the campus Saturday after students began looting stores and breaking windows in the downtown area, said "a complete investigation" would be made into the shootings.

Dr. White, the university president, said:

"Everyone without exception is horror-struck by the tragedy of the last few hours. Unfortunately, no one is able yet to say with certainty what the facts of the situation are.

"There are many unconfirmed reports of gunfire from various sources," he went on. "We are asking for every possible appropriate investigation, which we shall undertake to pursue to the limit."

Father Is Printer

One of the dead victims at Kent State, Jeffrey Glenn Miller, was the son of Bernard Miller, a linotype operator who works in the composing room of The New York Times.

United Press International

GUNS ON CAMPUS: Policeman, backed by National Guardsman, taking gun from youth at Kent State campus yesterday.

60 Years of Quiet at Kent State Are Shattered in Era of Protest

By ANDREW H. MALCOLM

Political demonstrations, such as the one that resulted in the deaths of four students yesterday, are a relatively new phenomenon on Kent State University's attractive 790-acre campus.

On the tree-lined grounds—on Main Street in Kent, Ohio, about 10 miles northeast of Akron—such protests gained strength only in the late 1960's. Students began denouncing the Vietnam war, police recruiting and, more recently, the Air Force and Army units of the Reserve Officers Training Corps.

Previously, such large student gatherings were confined to Memorial Stadium—where crowds watched the school's Golden Flashes lose most of their football games—and to The Cove, JB's and other nearby bars that served as student haunts, particularly on Friday nights.

Until recently the school's most serious demonstration was a 1958 panty raid on two women's dormitories the last day of the school year. The Administration promptly dismissed 29 students who were involved.

Since then, except for some rowdy Friday nights, the students, mostly middle class and about 85 per cent of them from Ohio, maintained peace with local residents and, in fact, had a distinct reputation for apathy.

Just last week, for instance, an all-university dance was canceled when only seven tickets were sold. And until Thursday night, when President Nixon announced the use of American troops in Cambodia, antiwar rallies had been drawing only 200 or 300 students.

The school was founded in 1910 as Kent Normal. In 1914 it became Kent State Normal College and in 1935, after some rough Depression years, became Kent State University.

Since World War II enrollment has climbed steadily and the administration has placed [illegible] emphasis on long-range b[illegible]g programs. In addition to the 21,000-student Kent campus, the school serves 8,000 students at nine branch campuses in northeastern Ohio.

The town of Kent, like other area villages, was founded in 1807 by New England settlers. Once a rural farming town, Kent (population 29,000) has attracted some manufacturers of air compressors, electric motors, automotive parts and locks.

The school employs several hundred townspeople, including 905 full-time faculty members. Its diverse activities include the operation of an airport and an 18-hole golf course.

As part of the eight-member state university system, the school gets state financing and is under the jurisdiction of a board of nine trustees appointed by the Governor and confirmed by the State Senate. Tuition is $642 a year.

Nixon Says Violence Invites Tragedy

By ROBERT B. SEMPLE Jr.

Special to The New York Times

WASHINGTON, May 4 — President Nixon today deplored the deaths of four students at Kent State University and said they "should remind us all once again that when dissent turns to violence it invites tragedy."

"It is my hope," he said, "that this tragic and unfortunate incident will strengthen the determination of all the nation's campuses, administrators, faculty and students alike to stand firmly for the right which exists in this country of peaceful dissent and just as strongly against the resort to violence as a means of such expression."

The President's remarks came in a statement issued by his press secretary, Ronald L. Ziegler.

A Justice Department spokesman, meanwhile, said the Department had received a request from Governor James A. Rhodes of Ohio for a Federal investigation of the incident. The spokesman said no decision had been made.

When one newsman suggested that some of the demonstrations might have been inspired by the President's decision to send troops into Cambodia, Mr. Ziegler replied:

"The president made clear in his speech Thursday that the objective of the action along the Cambodia-South Vietnamese border is to bring a peaceful conclusion to the conflict in South Vietnam."

Mr. Ziegler said, "I think I've expressed the President's point of view." He would say no more when another questioner suggested that the violence might have arisen from the conviction among some students that the Administration had turned a deaf ear to their grievances and had branded them as "bums." Mr. Nixon used that word to describe student demonstrators in off-the-cuff remarks at the Pentagon last Friday.

Vice President Agnew took a similarly tough line toward campus demonstrators and those who encourage them in a speech prepared for delivery here tonight to a meeting of the American Retail Federation.

The Vice President departed from his prepared speech, which was written before today's incident at Kent State, and declared that the ordeal there was "predictable and avoidable."

"In several recent speeches," Mr. Agnew said, "I have called attention to the grave dangers which accompany the new politics of violence and confrontation and which have found so much favor on our college campuses."

The events at Kent State, he said, "make the truth of these remarks self-evident and underscore the need that they be said."

The main part of the speech dealt with those who, in the Vice President's words, have engaged in a "calculated, consistent and well publicized barrage of cynicism against the principles of this nation."

He said he was not referring to "those tomentose exhibitionists who provoke more derision than fear." The word tomentose means "covered with thickly matted hair." Instead, he said, he referred to well-educated teachers, editors, Government leaders and professional people who "scorn" the "traditions of civility" and "pander to the ignorance and the fears of those who are all too willing to believe that the criminal who throws a bomb at a bank is a hero and the policeman who gets killed trying to stop him is a pig."

Mr. Agnew singled out New York's Mayor Lindsay for particular scorn. He quoted Mr. Lindsay as having criticized those in Government who cannot "respect dissent," or "cope with turmoil," and "who believe that the people of America are ready to support repression as long as it is done with a quiet voice and a business suit."

"We have seen all too clearly," the Vice President said, "that there are men — now in power in this country — who do not represent authority, who cannot cope with tradition, and who believe that the people of America are ready to support revolution as long as it is done with a cultured voice and a handsome profile."

Investigation Request

Special to The New York Times

COLUMBUS, Ohio, May 4—Gov. James A. Rhodes tonight sent a telegram to J. Edgar Hoover, director of the Federal Bureau of Investigation, that said:

"At Kent State University today four persons were killed and others injured in a confrontation between Ohio National Guard troops and a mob of unidentified persons. I shall appreciate the assistance of the Federal Bureau of Investigation in making a complete investigation of all the facts."

In a later statement, Gov. Rhodes said:

"Today is the saddest day I have known as Governor.

"Let us hope that today's events will lead all Americans to soberly consider the direction in which our society is headed.

"It is my prayer tonight that those who have counselled our young people into the violent action that sparked today's incident will give second thought to what they are doing—to the youth of America and to the nation."

Grim Parents Recall Daughter's Comment

Special to The New York Times

PITTSBURGH, May 4—Less than an hour after learning that their 19-year-old daughter had been shot to death by National Guardsmen at Kent State University, Arthur and Doris Krause and their 15-year-old daughter, Laurie, emerged from their home in outlying Churchill Borough this afternoon.

Mr. Krause's face was grim and drawn. Tears streamed down the cheeks of his wife and daughter. They were on their way to Kent State, 125 miles west of here, to bring back the body of their slain daughter, Allison, who had been a freshman.

Mrs. Krause said Allison called at 12:30 A.M. today and had said student disorders were "a terrible way to destroy property." Mrs. Krause also quoted her daughter as having said, "This is the boys' way of telling President Nixon they don't want to go to Cambodia."

The mother added, "I don't blame 18-year-olds for not wanting to go to Cambodia. Look, I had a daughter, and now she's dead."

"All the News That's Fit to Print"

The New York Times

LATE CITY EDITION

Weather: Chance of showers today, tonight. Partly sunny tomorrow. Temp. range: today 74-94; Wed. 72-91. Temp. Hum. Index yesterday 82. Full U.S. report on Page 94.

VOL. CXX . . . No. 41,431

NEW YORK, THURSDAY, JULY 1, 1971

15 CENTS

SUPREME COURT, 6-3, UPHOLDS NEWSPAPERS ON PUBLICATION OF THE PENTAGON REPORT; TIMES RESUMES ITS SERIES, HALTED 15 DAYS

Nixon Says Turks Agree To Ban the Opium Poppy

By JOHN HERBERS

Special to The New York Times

WASHINGTON, June 30—President Nixon announced today that Turkey had agreed to eliminate within a year her production of opium poppies, which account for about two-thirds of the illegal heroin reaching the United States.

Mr. Nixon, in a brief announcement delivered in the White House press room, said that as a result of negotiations between the United States and Turkish Governments, Premier Nihat Erim had agreed to ban altogether the cultivation of opium poppies by June, 1972.

He said the joint announcement, made simultaneously in Washington and Ankara, "represents by far the most significant breakthrough that has been achieved in stopping the source of supply of heroin in our worldwide offensive against dangerous drugs."

Two weeks ago, Mr. Nixon sent a message to William J. Handley, the United States Ambassador in Turkey, saying that the time for talk had passed and the United States must have action by the Turkish Government in ending poppy cultivation.

Today, the President praised Premier Erim for "courageous, statesmanlike action" and said the United States would provide money and technical assistance in helping Turkish farmers shift to other crops.

Officials would not say how much American money would be involved, but the United States has made a $3-million commitment to Turkey on the heroin problem.

Secretary of State William P. Rogers, who helped work

Continued on Page 22, Column 1

PRESIDENT CALLS STEEL AND LABOR TO WHITE HOUSE

He Asks Both Sides to Meet With Him Tuesday Before Contract Talks Start

By PHILIP SHABECOFF

Special to The New York Times

WASHINGTON, June 30 — President Nixon has called negotiators of the steel companies and steelworkers union to meet with him next Tuesday before they sit down to begin contract negotiations, a White House spokesman announced today.

It will be the first time that the President will have met with labor and management in any industry prior to nationwide contract negotiations, according to Ronald L. Ziegler, the White House press secretary.

Discussion Issues Listed

Mr. Ziegler said that the President had called the meeting to discuss general economic developments and trends in the world steel markets.

Earlier today, the chairman of the Federal Reserve Board, Arthur F. Burns, told a Congressional committee that the "first priority" should be given to a new Government move to try to moderate price and wage increases and expressed his concern over the spread of "inflationary psychology" in this country.

The Administration has repeatedly warned that excessive increases in steel wages and prices would severely retard efforts to control inflation. Hints have been dropped that import quotas that protect domestic steel from foreign competition will be eased or lifted if prices go too high.

President Nixon has been in-

Continued on Page 38, Column 1

Pentagon Papers: Study Reports Kennedy Made 'Gamble' Into a 'Broad Commitment'

By HEDRICK SMITH

The Pentagon's study of the Vietnam war concludes that President John F. Kennedy transformed the "limited-risk gamble" of the Eisenhower Administration into a "broad commitment" to prevent Communist domination of South Vietnam.

Although Mr. Kennedy resisted pressures for putting American ground-combat units into South Vietnam, the Pentagon analysts say, he took a series of actions that significantly expanded the American military and political involvement in Vietnam but nonetheless left President Lyndon B. Johnson with as bad a situation as Mr. Kennedy inherited.

"The dilemma of the U.S. involvement dating from the Kennedy era," the Pentagon study observes, was to use "only limited means to achieve excessive ends."

Moreover, according to the study, prepared in 1967-68 by Government analysts, the Kennedy tactics deepened the American involvement in Vietnam piecemeal, with each step minimizing public recognition that the American role was growing.

The expansion of that role, over three decades, is traced in the 3,000 pages of the Pentagon's study, which is accompanied by 4,000 pages of documents on the Vietnam era. Previous articles in The Times's presentation of this material have recounted President Johnson's movement to war in 1964 and 1965.

President Kennedy made his first fresh commitments to Vietnam secretly. The Pentagon study discloses that in the spring of 1961 the President ordered 400

The Times today resumes its series of articles on the Pentagon's secret study of the Vietnam war. The study was obtained through the investigative reporting of Neil Sheehan, and the articles were researched and written over three months by Mr. Sheehan and other staff members. The fourth and fifth articles, both by Hedrick Smith, are published today and form an account of decisions in the Kennedy Administration.

Three pages of documentary material covering the Kennedy policy begin on Page 3, and documents on the 1963 coup begin on Page 9. A summary of the three earlier articles, covering the Johnson Administration, appears on Page 15.

Special Forces troops and 100 other American military advisers sent to South Vietnam. No publicity was given to either move.

Small as the numbers seem in retrospect, the Pentagon study comments that even the first such expansion "signaled a willingness to go beyond the 685-man limit on the size of the U.S. [military] mission in Saigon, which, if it were done openly, would be the first formal breach of the Geneva agreement." Under the interpretation of that agreement in effect since 1956, the United States was limited to 685 military advisers in Vietnam. Washington, while it did not sign the accord, pledged not to undermine it.

On May 11, 1961, the day on which President Kennedy decided to send the Special Forces, he also ordered the start of a campaign of clandestine warfare against North Vietnam, to be conducted by South Vietnamese agents directed and trained by the Central Intelligence Agency and some American Special Forces troops. [See text, action memorandum, May 11, 1961, Page 3.]

The President's instructions, as quoted in the documents, were, "In North Vietnam . . . [to] form networks of resistance, covert bases and teams for

Continued on Page 6, Column 1

BURGER DISSENTS

First Amendment Rule Held to Block Most Prior Restraints

Decision, concurring opinions, dissents start on Page 17.

By FRED P. GRAHAM

Special to The New York Times

WASHINGTON, June 30 — The Supreme Court freed The New York Times and The Washington Post today to resume immediate publication of articles based on the secret Pentagon papers on the origins of the Vietnam war.

By a vote of 6 to 3 the Court held that any attempt by the Government to block news articles prior to publication bears "a heavy burden of presumption against its constitutionality."

In a historic test of that principle — the first effort by the Government to enjoin publication on the ground of national security — the Court declared that "the Government has not met that burden."

The brief judgment was read to a hushed courtroom by Chief Justice Warren E. Burger at 2:30 P.M. at a special session called three hours before.

Old Tradition Observed

The Chief Justice was one of the dissenters, along with Associate Justices Harry A. Blackmun and John M. Harlan, but because the decision was rendered in an unsigned opinion, the Chief Justice read it in court in accordance with long-standing custom.

In New York Arthur Ochs Sulzberger, president and publisher of The Times, said at a news conference that he had "never really doubted that this day would come and that we'd win." His reaction, he said, was "complete joy and delight."

The case had been expected to produce a landmark ruling on the circumstances under which prior restraint could be imposed upon the press, but because no opinion by a single Justice commanded the support of a majority, only the unsigned decision will serve as precedent.

Uncertainty Over Outcome

Because it came on the 15th day after The Times had been restrained from publishing further articles in its series mined from the 7,000 pages of material—the first such restraint in the name of "national security" in the history of the United States—there was some uncertainty whether the press had scored a strong victory or whether a precedent for some degree of restraint had been set.

Alexander M. Bickel, the Yale law professor who had argued for The Times in the case, said in a telephone interview that the ruling placed the press in a "stronger position." He maintained that no Federal District Judge would henceforth temporarily restrain a newspaper on the Justice Department's complaint that "this is what they have printed and we don't like it" and that a direct threat of irreparable harm would have to be alleged.

However, the United States Solicitor General, Erwin N. Griswold, turned to another lawyer shortly after the Justices filed from the courtroom and remarked: "Maybe the newspapers will show a little

Continued on Page 15, Column 1

Soviet Starts an Inquiry Into 3 Astronauts' Deaths

By BERNARD GWERTZMAN

Special to The New York Times

MOSCOW, June 30—The Soviet authorities appointed a special commission tonight to investigate the deaths of the three astronauts who perished this morning when their Soyuz 11 craft was returning to earth after the longest manned space flight in history.

News of the astronauts' deaths shocked many Soviet people. And Western specialists predicted that their deaths would retard development of the Salyut space station program. The three astronauts had spent more than three weeks working and exercising aboard the Salyut craft, described as the world's first space laboratory.

[In the United States, American officials said the Soviet space disaster had probably been caused by a failure in the oxygen supply. They also said the accident should not delay United States space flights. Articles on Page 30.]

Tonight, the Soviet people seemed caught up in the human aspects of the disaster and the mystery of what caused the deaths of Lieut. Col. Georgi T. Dobrovolsky, the flight commander; Vladislav N. Volkov, the flight engineer, and Viktor I. Patsayev, the test engineer.

Were their deaths caused by the weakened state of their bodies after nearly 24 days of weightlessness? Were they

Continued on Page 30, Column 3

U.S. and Diem's Overthrow: Step by Step

The Pentagon's secret study of the Vietnam war discloses that President Kennedy knew and approved of plans for the military coup d'état that overthrew President Ngo Dinh Diem in 1963.

"Our complicity in his overthrow heightened our responsibilities and our commitment" in Vietnam, the study finds.

In August and October of 1963, the narrative recounts, the United States gave its support to a cabal of army generals bent on removing the controversial leader, whose rise to power Mr. Kennedy had backed in speeches in the middle nineteen-fifties and who had been the anchor of American policy in Vietnam for nine years.

The coup, one of the most dramatic episodes in the history of the American involvement in Vietnam, was a watershed. As the Pentagon study observes, it was a time when Washington—with the Diem regime gone—could have reconsidered its entire commitment to South Vietnam and decided to disengage.

At least two Administration officials advocated disengagement but, according to the Pentagon study, it "was never seriously considered a policy alternative because of the assumption that an independent, non-Communist SVN was too important a strategic interest to abandon."

The effect, according to this account, was that the United States, discovering after the coup that the war against the Vietcong had been going much worse than officials previously thought, felt compelled to do more—rather than less—for Saigon. By supporting the anti-Diem coup, the analyst asserts, "the U.S. inadvertently deepened its involvement. The inadvertence is the key factor."

According to the Pentagon account of the 1963 events in Saigon, Washington did not originate the anti-Diem coup, nor did American forces intervene in any way, even to try to prevent the assassinations of Mr. Diem and his brother Ngo Dinh Nhu, who, as the chief Diem political adviser, had accumulated immense power. Popular discontent with the Diem regime focused on Mr. Nhu and his wife.

But for weeks—and with the White House informed every step of the way—the American mission in Saigon maintained secret contacts with the plotting generals through one of the Central Intelligence Agency's most experienced and versatile operatives, an Indochina veteran, Lieut. Col. Lucien Conein. The colonel, who is now in retirement, first landed in Vietnam in 1944 by parachute for the Office of Strategic Services, the wartime forerunner of the C.I.A.

So trusted by the Vietnamese generals was Colonel Conein that he was in their midst at Vietnamese General Staff headquarters as they launched the coup. Indeed, on Oct. 25, a week earlier, in a cable to McGeorge Bundy, the President's special assistant for national security, Ambassador Lodge had occasion to describe Colonel Conein of the C.I.A.—referring to the agency, in code terminology, as C.A.S.—as the indispensable man:

"C.A.S. has been punctilious in carrying out my instructions. I have personally approved each meeting between General Don [one of three main plotters] and Conein who has carried out my

Continued on Page 12, Column 1

CHOU TIES U.N. SEAT TO TAIPEI'S OUSTER

Also Says Peking Must Have Permanent Council Post if It Is to Be Member

By TAKASHI OKA

Special to The New York Times

TOKYO, June 30 — Premier Chou En-lai of China said in an interview published here today that for his country to join the United Nations it was necessary not only that all membership rights be "restored," including a permanent seat on the Security Council, but that the Nationalists be ousted from the United Nations.

Mr. Chou made the comment in a meeting with Yoshikatsu Takeiri, chairman of Komeito, the Clean Government party, who is visiting Peking with eight of his followers. The Premier's comments were published today in the party newspaper Komei Shimbun as well as in other major Japanese newspapers.

'What Steps Are Necessary'

Mr. Chou's comments, which are consistent with the line Peking has taken on prospective United Nations membership, apparently weakened attempts by the United States, Japan and other interested members of the United Nations to safeguard at least a General Assembly seat for the Nationalists while admitting the Chinese Communists to the Security Council as well as the Assembly.

"What steps do you think are necessary in order to get China back into the United Nations?" Mr. Chou was asked,

Continued on Page 32, Column 4

Jim Garrison Is Arrested; U.S. Says He Took Bribes

By ROY REED

Special to The New York Times

NEW ORLEANS, June 30—District Attorney Jim Garrison was arrested by Federal agents today and charged with taking bribes to protect illegal pinball gambling in New Orleans.

The Justice Department said that the last payment, $1,000, was delivered to Mr. Garrison at his home last night in marked $50 bills. The payment, the department said, was handed to him by a once-trusted confidant who had secretly gone to work for the Government's agents.

Mr. Garrison, 50 years old, who attempted to prove a conspiracy in the 1963 assassination of President Kennedy, was taken into custody at his home. He was fingerprinted and placed under $5,000 bond by a Federal magistrate.

The Justice Department said that Mr. Garrison had taken up to $1,500 a month in bribes.

According to the Government, Mr. Garrison had received the bribes from pinball operators since 1962.

"I've never accepted a dollar in my life," the District Attorney told reporters as he walked into the French Quarter Courthouse to face the magistrate.

Mr. Garrison was one of 10 men arrested. The others in-

Continued on Page 55, Column 3

Cousin Asserts Jerome Johnson Told of Job With Italian League

By BARBARA CAMPBELL

A cousin of Jerome A. Johnson, who was shot to death at the site of a rally in Columbus Circle after allegedly firing three bullets into Joseph A. Colombo Sr., said yesterday that Johnson told him "several months ago" he was working for the Italian-American Civil Rights League as a photographer.

This was corroborated by a close friend of Johnson's, who said the 24-year-old slain man had also told him on a May 15 visit to California that he was working for the league.

About three months before the shooting, Johnson gave his cousin a telephone number where he could be reached and a check by The New York Times disclosed yesterday that the number had been recently changed. The operator said the number had been switched to a new number, that of the Italian-American League.

This latest development raised a series of questions for investigators. If Johnson was working for the league, was he known there? Was he an employe or a hanger-on, perhaps a temporary called in on occasions?

Chief of Detectives Albert A. Seedman said last night only that the telephone-number switch, if true, "certainly poses

Continued on Page 53, Column 1

THE STATES RATIFY FULL VOTE AT 18

Ohio Becomes 38th to Back the 26th Amendment

By R. W. APPLE Jr.

Special to The New York Times

WASHINGTON, June 30—The 26th Amendment to the Constitution, lowering to 18 years the minimum voting age in local and state as well as Federal elections, was ratified tonight.

Ohio became the 38th state to approve the Amendment when the state's House of Representatives, meeting in extraordinary evening session, gave its assent, 81 to 9. The Ohio Senate had approved the measure yesterday, 30 to 2.

The ratification of at least 38 states, or three-quarters of the total, is required for constitutional amendments.

An atmosphere of near-panic attended Ohio's climactic vote. The Republican Speaker of the House, Charles F. Kurfess, had planned to let a number of members, both Republicans and Democrats, speak on the issue before calling for a vote.

But after only three short speeches, the Republican floor leader, Robert E. Leavitt, interrupted to warn:

"I've just been informed that the Legislature of Oklahoma

Continued on Page 43, Column 1

Conferees Cut Military Pay Rise As Authority to Draft Runs Out

By DAVID E. ROSENBAUM

Special to The New York Times

WASHINGTON, June 30 — The Nixon Administration won a major budgetary victory today in the House-Senate conference on the draft extension bill.

The conference agreement also appeared to represent a setback for supporters of an all-volunteer Army, who had sought larger pay increases than those cleared by the conferees.

The conferees accepted a figure for military pay and allowances that was more than $900-million below what the Senate and House had approved. The raises voted by the conferees would cost about $1.8-billion in the fiscal year starting tomorrow and would go into effect Oct. 1.

The figure approved by the conference was still $800-million above what President Nixon sought in his budget, but the House and Senate had passed increases of about $1.7-billion over the budget.

The Nixon Administration had argued that so large an increase would force severe and possibly dangerous reductions in other parts of the defense budget.

The Government's basic authority to draft men into the military expires at midnight tonight.

The conferees completed action on all provisions of the draft bill today except the Senate-passed amendment that calls for the withdrawal of United States troops from Indochina within nine months if prisoners of war are first

Continued on Page 29, Column 1

False Advertising Laid to H&R Block

By JOHN D. MORRIS

Special to The New York Times

WASHINGTON, June 30 — H & R Block, Inc., which says it prepares income tax returns for eight million American annually, was accused by the Federal Trade Commission today of false advertising and illegally using confidential information supplied by customers.

The commission published similar but separate citations against H & R Block and the Beneficial Corporation, which offers income tax services on a smaller scale through a subsidiary, the Beneficial Management Corporation. In radio and television advertisements, the name

Continued on Page 57, Column 2

ACTION BY GRAVEL VEXES SENATORS

But No Disciplinary Action Against Him Is Expected

By JOHN W. FINNEY

Special to The New York Times

WASHINGTON, June 30—Many Senators privately expressed dismay, shock and chagrin today at Senator Mike Gravel's release of parts of the Pentagon's secret study of the Vietnam war. But it appeared that no disciplinary action would be taken against the Alaska Democrat.

Last night Senator Gravel tried to read the documents to the Senate in an all-night speech and, when he was blocked for lack of a quorum, proceeded to call an impromptu meeting of his Senate Public Works subcommittee. He read from the study for three and one-half hours, with his voice sometimes breaking into sobs, and tears occasionally rolling down his face.

His action incurred the displeasure of many of his colleagues, who felt that it reflected on the dignity and composure of the Senate. But in the clublike atmosphere of the Senate, there was a widespread reluctance, extending down from the leadership, to take any formal disciplinary

Continued on Page 16, Column 2

NEWS INDEX

Supreme Court, 6-3, Upholds Newspapers on Publication of the Pentagon Papers

Burger Is a Dissenter In Historic Press Case

Continued From Page 1, Col. 8

restraint in the future." All nine Justices wrote opinions, in a judicial outpouring that was described by Supreme Court scholars as without precedent. They divided roughly into groups of three each.

The first group, composed of Hugo L. Black, William O. Douglas and Thurgood Marshall, took what is known as the absolutist view that the courts lack the power to suppress any press publication, no matter how grave a threat to security it might pose.

Justices Black and Douglas restated their long-held belief that the First Amendment's guarantee of a free press forbids any judicial restraint. Justice Marshall insisted that because Congress had twice considered and rejected such power for the courts, the Supreme Court would be "enacting" law if it imposed restraint.

The second group, which included William J. Brennan Jr., Potter Stewart and Byron R. White, said that the press could not be muzzled except to prevent direct, immediate and irreparable damage to the nation. They agreed that this material did not pose such a threat.

The Dissenters' Views

The third bloc, composed of the three dissenters, declared that the courts should not refuse to enforce the executive branch's conclusion that material should be kept confidential — so long as a Cabinet-level officer had decided that it should—on a matter affecting foreign relations.

They felt that the "frenzied train of events" in the cases before them had not given the courts enough time to determine those questions, so they concluded that the restaints upon publication should have been retained while both cases were sent back to the trial judges for more hearings.

The New York Times's series drawn from the secret Pentagon study was accompanied by supporting documents. Articles were published on June 13, 14 and 15 before they were halted by court order. A similar restraining order was imposed on June 19 against The Washington Post after it began to print articles based on the study.

Justice Black's opinion stated that just such publications as those were intended to be protected by the First Amendment's declaration that "Congress shall make no law . . . abridging the freedom of the press."

Paramount among the responsibilities of a free press, he said, "is the duty to prevent any part of the Government from deceiving the people and sending them off to distant lands to die of foreign fevers and foreign shot and shell.

"In my view, far from deserving condemnation for their courageous reporting, The New York Times, The Washington Post and other newspapers should be commended for serving the purpose that the Founding Fathers saw so clearly," he said. "In revealing the workings of government that led to the Vietnam war, the newspapers nobly did precisely that which the founders hoped and trusted they would do."

Justice Douglas joined the opinion by Justice Black and was joined by him in another opinion. The First Amendment's purpose, Justice Douglas argued, is to prohibit "governmental suppression of embarrassing information." He asserted that the temporary restraints in these cases "constitute a flouting of the principles of the First Amendment."

Justice Marshall's position was based primarily upon the separation-of-powers argument that Congress had never authorized prior restraints and that it refused to do so when bills were introduced in 1917 and 1957.

He concluded that the courts were without power to restrain publications. Justices Brennan, Stewart and White, who also based their conclusions on the separation-of-powers principle, assumed that under extreme circumstances the courts would act without such powers.

Justice Brennan focused on the temporary restraints, which had been issued to freeze the situation so that the material would not be made public before the courts could decide if it should be enjoined. He continued that no restraints should have been imposed because the Government alleged only in general terms that security breaches might occur.

Justices Stewart and White, who also joined each other's opinions, said that though they had read the documents they felt that publication would not be in the national interest.

But Justice Stewart, a former chairman of The Yale Daily News, insisted that "it is the duty of the executive" to protect state secrets through its own security measures and not the duty of the courts to do it by banning news articles.

He implied that if publication of the material woul cause "direct, immediate, and irreparable damage to our nation or its people," he would uphold prior restraint, but because that situation was not present here, he said that the papers must be free to publish.

Justice White added that Congress had enacted criminal laws, including the espionage laws, that might apply to these papers. "The newspapers are presumably now on full notice," he said, that the Justice Department may bring prosecutions if the publications violate those laws. He added that he "would have no difficulty in sustaining convictions" under the laws, even if the breaches of security were not sufficient to justify prior restraint.

The Chief Justice and Justices Stewart and Blackmun echoed this caveat in their opinions — meaning that one less than a majority had lent their weight to the warning.

Chief Justice Burger blamed The Times "in large part" for the "frenetic haste" with which the case was handled. He said that The Times had studied the Pentagon archives for three or four months before beginning its series, yet it had breached "the duty of an honorable press" by not asking the Government if any security violations were involved before it began publication.

He said he found it "hardly believable" that The Times would do this, and he concluded that it would not be harmed if the case were sent back for more testimony.

Justice Blackmun, also focusing his criticism on The Times, said there had been inadequate time to determine if the publications could result in "the death of soldiers, the destruction of alliances, the greatly increased difficulty of negotiation with our enemies, the inability of our diplomats to negotiate." He concluded that if the war was prolonged and a delay in the return of United States prisoners result from publication, "then the nation's people will know where the responsibility for these sad consequences rests."

In his own dissenting opinion, Justice Harlan said: "The judiciary must review the initial executive determination to the point of satisfying itself that the subject matter of the dispute does lie within the proper compass of the President's foreign policy relations power.

"The judiciary," he went on, "may properly insist that the determination that disclosure of that subject matter would irreparably impair the national security be made by the head of the executive department concerned—here the Secretary of State or the Secretary of Defense—after actual personal consideration.

"But in my judgment, the judiciary may not properly go beyond these two inquiries and redetermine for itself the probable impact of disclosure on the national security."

The Justice Department initially sought an injunction against The Times on June 15 from Federal District Judge Murray I. Gurfein in New York.

Judge Gurfein, who had issued the original temporary restraining order that was stayed until today, ruled that the material was basically historical matter that might be embarrassing to the Government but did not pose a threat to national security. Federal District Judge Gerhard A. Gesell of the District of Columbia came to the same conclusion in the Government's suit against The Washington Post.

The United States Court of Appeals for the Second Circuit, voting 5 to 3, ordered more secret hearings before Judge Gurfein and The Times appealed. The United States Court of Appeals for the District of Columbia upheld Judge Gesell, 7 to 2, holding that no injunction should be imposed. Today the Supreme Court affirmed the Appeals Court here and reversed the Second Circuit.

The Supreme Court also issued a brief order disposing of a few other cases and adjourned until Oct. 4, as it had been scheduled to do Monday.

Associated Press

'DELIGHTED' WITH COURT RULING: Arthur Ochs Sulzberger, president and publisher of The New York Times, at conference on Vietnam papers with A. M. Rosenthal, left, managing editor; James C. Goodale, right, general counsel.

Sulzberger Expresses 'Complete Joy' at Ruling

Arthur Ochs Sulzberger, president and publisher of The New York Times, said yesterday that his reaction to the Supreme Court's decision was "one of complete joy and delight."

Mr. Sulzberger held a news conference with A. M. Rosenthal, managing editor of The Times, and James C. Goodale, the newspaper's general counsel, about 20 minutes after the decision was announced.

The publisher said that he had "never really doubted that this day would come and that we'd win," adding that "sometimes it seems like it was going to be a little longer waiting than I had hoped." The Times had been under court orders to suspend publication of its series on the Pentagon papers since June 15.

When asked, "Knowing what you know about what happened, would you do this again if someone came to you with what you considered to be an equally important discovery?" Mr. Sulzberger replied that he would.

'A Joyous Day . . .'

Mr. Rosenthal, asked for his reaction, said: "Well, I think it's a joyous day for the press and for American society. And I thought this was the way it would turn out. I prayed it would."

He said also that "there will be no changes in the presentation of the articles" as a result of the Government's action and the delay. "We will present them exactly as we planned." He added:

"Obviously, I'm not filled with joy that other newspapers have had pieces of this story, but I really do not think it dilutes it. Quite the contrary—I think that an enormous amount of interest has been built up in these papers, and I think that the job we intend to do will demonstrate that they are a matter of enormous historical interest."

Mr. Rosenthal was asked if he felt the decision would "open up channels of information to the news media that may heretofore have been closed?"

"Yes, I do, really," he replied. "I think this whole case will have done that. I think that people in the press, people in government and people in the public will see as the result of this whole case that a great deal of information is classified for no real national security interest and I think the move will be in the direction of more information rather than less."

Press Freedom 'Upheld'

He said also that he thought the Court, in its decision, "upheld the freedom of the press, and that is a matter for great joy."

A great deal of the material, Mr. Rosenthal said, had been "a rather profound surprise" to him. "Not individual decisions . . . but the rationale or lack of rationale, the government planning or lack of government planning," he said.

Mr. Goodale, asked if he thought there was "a new kind of antagonism between First Amendment rights and the Nixon Administration," said: "I don't really know if that's the case. I sometimes suspect it to be the case. But . . . I can't really answer that, I don't know."

Mr. Rosenthal, asked the same question, said that he felt there was "a tendency to . . . try to take legal action that is more pronounced in this Administration than in others." And in reply to the succeeding question, as to whether such antagonism between the press and government might not be "a sign of good health in both parties," he said:

"To a great extent I think it is. I don't think we'll ever see the day, nor should we see the day, when we're in bed together."

Toward the end of the 30-minute news conference, the questioning returned to Mr. Sulzberger, who was asked if he felt the motto of The Times — "All the News That's Fit to Print" — had been upheld.

"Yes, sir," Mr. Sulzberger said. "I think it was very much upheld."

The Earlier Articles: From Covert War to Bombing of North to Ground Troops

Before The New York Times was restrained by Federal court order from continuing with its series on the Pentagon study of the Vietnam war, it had published the first three parts. They dealt with the first years of the Administration of President Lyndon B. Johnson. Here is a summary of those three articles and a recapitulation of some of the key documents published with them on June 13, 14 and 15.

Covert Warfare Sponsored by U.S. in '64

President Lyndon B. Johnson's Administration, amid his hesitation and reluctance to take final decisions, was sponsoring covert South Vietnamese warfare against North Vietnam starting in February, 1964, and drawing up plans that spring for overt war.

These activities—long before the Aug. 4, 1964, Tonkin Gulf destroyer incident that led to a Congressional vote authorizing "all necessary steps" to aid Southeast Asian countries—were described in the first installment.

The series was based on a Defense Department study, commissioned in 1967 by Secretary Robert S. McNamara to learn how American involvement in Southeast Asia developed. The study ranged from World War II until the start of peace talks in Paris in May, 1968.

There are gaps in the Pentagon study — the researchers lacked access to Presidential files — and that part of it obtained by The Times lacks the chapter on diplomatic initiatives, some of which are continuing.

A Report by McNamara

The first of 13 documents published in the initial installment was a report on Dec. 21, 1963, by Secretary McNamara to President Johnson. This said "plans for covert action into North Vietnam were prepared as we had requested."

"They present," he went on, "a variety of sabotage and psychological operations against North Vietnam from which I believe we should aim to select those that provide maximum pressure with minimum risk."

The "covert military operations," drawn up by the Central Intelligence Agency station and the military command in Saigon, were begun Feb. 1, 1964, as Operation Plan 34A. President Johnson's hope was that they might eventually induce North Vietnam to halt the Vietcong and Pathet Lao insurrections.

Through 1964, they included flights over North Vietnam by U-2 spy planes, the kidnapping of North Vietnamese citizens for intelligence information, commando raids from the sea to blow up rail and highway bridges and the bombardment of coastal installations by PT boats.

'Hired Personnel' Used

They differed from relatively low-level and unsuccessful intelligence and sabotage efforts the C.I.A. had carried out earlier in North Vietnam. The 34A attacks were under the control of Gen. Paul D. Harkins, chief of the United States Military Assistance Command in Saigon, with raids performed by the South Vietnamese or their "hired personnel."

The covert war had a second major segment—air operations in Laos by 25 to 40 propeller-driven T-28 fighter-bombers. These bore Laotian Air Force markings, but were manned in part by pilots of Air America, a C.I.A.-controlled line, and in part by Thai pilots under the control of Ambassador Leonard Unger.

Regular United States Air Force and Navy jet planes, code-named Yankee Team, gathered photographic intelligence for the T-28 bombing raids. The reconnaissance moved from high-altitude flights at the start of 1964 to low-altitude sorties in May; in June armed escort jets were added, bombing and strafing when the reconnaissance planes were fired on.

A third element in the covert military pressure was the patrolling by American destroyers in the Gulf of Tonkin. Code-named De Soto patrols, the ships collected intelligence on warning radars and coastal defenses.

In a memorandum on Jan. 22, 1964, Gen. Maxwell D. Taylor, Chairman of the Joint Chiefs of Staff, contended that "the United States must be prepared to put aside many of the self-imposed restrictions" and to "undertake bolder actions," even to "commit U.S. forces as necessary in direct actions against North Vietnam."

Difference of Opinion

The Johnson Administration was convinced from radio interceptions that North Vietnam was directing the Vietcong despite intelligence analyses that argued "the primary sources of Communist strength in South Vietnam are indigenous" arising from social and nationalist aims.

On March 16, 1964, describing a worsening situation, Secretary McNamara urged new plans up to "graduated overt military pressure," ready on 30 days' notice for strikes against North Vietnam by the South Vietnamese Air Force and an American air commando squadron, code-named Farmgate, that operated with South Vietnamese markings.

President Johnson approved the McNamara recommendations at a National Security Council meeting March 17, 1964. On March 20, President Johnson cabled Ambassador Henry Cabot Lodge in Saigon:

". . . our planning for action against the North is on a contingency basis at present, and immediate problem in this area is to develop the strongest military and political base for possible later action."

On April 17, the Joint Chiefs approved a so-called scenario, Operation Plan 37-64, including escalation steps against North Vietnam up to air attacks and mining of ports, initially by South Vietnamese but possibly using United States aircraft.

Military action was not to begin until after a joint Congressional resolution.

On May 4, South Vietnam's head of government, Gen. Nguyen Khan, told Ambassador Lodge he wanted the United States to start bombing and to send in 10,000 troops.

The Pentagon study reported that at a Honolulu meeting on June 1 and 2, 1964, Secretary McNamara said "it might be necessary as the action unfolded . . . to deploy as many as seven divisions" of American troops.

One effort to apportion American aims in South Vietnam was attributed to a memorandum by John T. McNaughton, Assistant Secretary of Defense, as follows:

"70 pct.—To avoid a humiliating U.S. defeat (to our reputation as a guarantor).

"20 pct.—To keep SVN (and then adjacent) territory from Chinese hands.

"10 pct.—To permit the people of SVN to enjoy a better, freer way of life."

One move at United States request had J. Blair Seaborn, Canadian member of the International Control Commission, pass on a warning June 18 to North Vietnam's Premier, Pham Van Dong, that escalating the warfare could bring "the greatest devastation" to North Vietnam.

Separate from the Defense Department study, which was prepared in 1967 and 1968, was a 1965 Defense Department command and control study of the Tonkin Gulf incident.

In a 34A operation, South Vietnamese naval commandos raided two North Vietnamese islands in the gulf at midnight July 30. On Aug. 2, a De Soto intelligence-gathering patrol by the destroyer Maddox wound up in a clash with North Vietnamese PT boats, which the study said apparently mistook the Maddox for a South Vietnamese escort vessel.

On Aug. 3, President Johnson ordered the destroyer C. Turner Joy to reinforce the Maddox in the gulf. That night, two clandestine 34A bombardments were staged by South Vietnamese PT boats.

On the night of Aug. 4, Tonkin Gulf time, the two American destroyers were attacked by North Vietnamese torpedo boats, according to the Pentagon account.

At a national Security Council meeting on the afternoon of Aug. 4, Washington time, President Johnson ordered American reprisal air strikes, chosen by the Joint Chiefs from a 94-target list drawn up at the end of May. He also decided to seek the Congressional resolution of full military support for South Vietnam.

'Consensus' on Bombing Reached Before the Election

Leaders of the Johnson Administration reached a "consensus" at a White House strategy meeting on Sept. 7, 1964, the Pentagon study of the war says, that sustained air attacks against North Vietnam would probably have to be launched, and indicated a start for early 1965.

In the second installment, The Times reported that the analysis had added that "what prevented action for the time being was a set of tactical considerations."

First among these, the analysis went on, was that "the President was in the midst of an election campaign in which he was presenting himself as the candidate of reason and restraint as opposed to the quixotic Barry Goldwater," who was publicly advocating full-scale bombing of North Vietnam.

Before that "consensus," there had been an Aug. 18 cablegram from Ambassador Maxwell Taylor—one of 16 texts published with the installment—declaring that "the present in-country pacification plan is not enough." The Ambassador urged "deliberate escalation of pressure against North Vietnam, using Jan. 1, 1965, as a target D-Day" to start bombing military facilities.

Marines for Danang

The bombing plan, Ambassador Taylor added, would entail sending Army Hawk antiaircraft missile units to protect airfields at Saigon and Danang and a force of Marines to Danang.

On Aug. 26, a memorandum by the Joint Chiefs of Staff termed "accelerated" actions against North Vietnam "essential to prevent a complete collapse of the U.S. position in Southeast Asia."

On Sept. 3, a memorandum by Assistant Secretary of Defense McNaughton said "the situation in South Vietnam is deteriorating." He proposed actions to cause "increasing apprehension" in North Vietnam and "likely at some point to provoke a military D.R.V. [North Vietnam] response" so that "the provoked response should be likely to provide good grounds for us to escalate if we wished."

The Sept. 7 "consensus" meeting was attended by President Johnson, Secretary of State Dean Rusk, Secretary of Defense McNamara, Gen. Earle G. Wheeler, Chairman of the Joint Chiefs; Ambassador Taylor, and John A. McCone, Director of Central Intelligence.

A Sept. 8 memorandum by Assistant Secretary of State William P. Bundy described "the consensus reached in discussions . . . for review and decision by the President."

Patrols to Resume

It was followed by a Sept. 10 memorandum by McGeorge Bundy, adviser to the President on national security. This reported Mr. Johnson's approval of resumption of American naval patrols in the Gulf of Tonkin and resumption of South Vietnamese coastal raids against North Vietnam. The raids had been covert, but were to be admitted now.

The patrols resumed Sept. 12, and the raids in October. A covert step-up in air operations in Laos ordered by the President began Oct. 14.

On Nov. 1, a Vietcong mortar barrage struck American planes and facilities at Bienhoa airfield. President Johnson, at a White House meeting, held off on reprisals and expressed concern over possible counter-retaliation by North Vietnam or Communist China against American bases and civilian dependents.

On Nov. 24, a select committee of the National Security Council heard General Wheeler, speaking for the Joint Chiefs, argue for a hard, fast bombing campaign—as entailing "less risk of a major conflict before achieving success" than the option of gradually rising air strikes, favored by Assistant Secretaries McNaughton and Bundy.

'A Losing Game'

On Nov. 27, Ambassador Taylor, in a briefing, urged gradually increasing air strikes —"we are playing a losing game in South Vietnam."

On Nov. 29, there was a "draft position paper" by an interagency working group on Vietnam headed by William Bundy. It set out "first-phase actions" over 30 days to intensify South Vietnamese maritime, Laotian air and United States reconnaissance operations already under way.

Reprisal air strikes against North Vietnam by South Vietnamese forces, "supplemented as necessary by U. S. forces," were proposed to take place preferably within 24 hours of "any VC provocation."

The next phase would be "progresssively more serious air strikes," as well as possible aerial mining of ports and a naval blockade.

The Pentagon study says President Johnson became "cautious and equivocal." In a White House meeting on Dec. 1, he said he wanted "new, dramatic, effective" aid from allied countries.

Air Strikes Begin

Nevertheless, on Dec. 14, Operation Barrel Roll began the 30 days of Phase I—air strikes by United States Air Force and Navy jets against infiltration routes and facilities in the Laotian panhandle.

On Jan. 6, 1965, William Bundy, in a memorandum, suggested "an early occasion for reprisal action" against North Vietnam and "possibly beginning low-level reconnaissance" at once.

"Introduction of limited U. S. ground forces into the northern area of South Vietnam," Mr. Bundy added, "still has great appeal to many of us, concurrently with the first air attacks into the D.R.V."

The Pentagon study reported that a Jan. 27 memorandum by Mr. McNaughton, agreed to by Secretary McNamara, favored initiating air strikes against North Vietnam.

On Feb. 6, nine Americans were killed and 76 wounded in Vietcong attacks on a military advisers' compound and a helicopter base. The study said this "triggered a swift, though long-contemplated Presidential decision to give an 'appropriate and fitting' response."

Within 14 hours, 49 Navy jets raided Donghoi in North Vietnam. Next, the enemy attacked an American barracks; the President on Feb. 11 launched a heavier reprisal raid. On Feb. 13, he decided to begin Operation Rolling Thunder—the sustained air war against North Vietnam.

Use of U.S. Troops Decided in April '65

President Johnson decided on April 1, 1965, to use American ground troops for offensive action in South Vietnam because the Administration quickly found that sustained bombing of North Vietnam—begun on March 2—was not going to stave off collapse in South Vietnam.

The President's decision was described in the third installment.

One of 16 documents published with that installment was National Security Action Memorandum 328, dated April 6, 1965. This reported that the President had "approved an 18-20,000 man increase in U. S. military support forces to fill out existing units and supply needed logistic personnel."

Further, he approved sending ashore two Marine battalions that Gen. William C. Westmoreland, the commander in Vietnam, had asked for on March 17, adding to two Marine battalions with 3,500 men that had landed March 8 as defenders of Danang airfield.

A Change of Mission

Mr. Johnson also approved deployment of a Marine air squadron and "a change of mission for all Marine battalions . . . . to permit their more active use. . . " He approved "urgent" efforts to get South Korean, Australian and New Zealand troops.

And he desired that "premature publicity be avoided," and the actions "should minimize any appearance of sudden changes in policy."

There was a comment in an April 2 memorandum by Mr. McCone of the Central Intelligence Agency that bombings "have not caused a change in the North Vietnamese policy of directing Vietcong insurgency, infiltrating cadres and supplying material" and "if anything, the strikes to date have hardened their attitude."

Mr. McCone warned of becoming "mired down in combat in the jungle in a military effort that we cannot win."

The March 8 landings had brought the United States force in South Vietnam to 27-000 men. In mid-March, Gen. Harold K. Johnson, the Army Chief of Staff, made two recommendations relating to a possible ground war.

One was to send a division of American troops to South Vietnam to hold coastal enclaves or to defend the Central Highlands, freeing Saigon Government forces for offensive action against the Vietcong.

The other was to establish a four-division force of American and Southeast Asia Treaty Organization troops to interdict infiltration by patrolling the demilitarized zone on the border between North and South Vietnam and the Laotian border region.

Before N.S.C. Meeting

In preparation for April 1-2 National Security Council meetings, Assistant Secretary of Defense McNaughton wrote in a memorandum:

"Can the situation inside SVN be bottomed out (a) without extreme measures against the D.R.V. and/or (b) without deployment of large numbers of U.S. (and other) combat troops inside SVN? The answer is perhaps, but probably no."

General Westmoreland, in a report completed March 26 for the same strategy meeting, contended that South Vietnamese troops could not hold the line against growing Vietcong strength long enough for the bombing to become effective.

General Westmoreland asked for the equivalent of two American divisions to arrive by June, to bring strength in Vietnam up to about 70,000.

He proposed to send an Army division to "defeat" the Vietcong in the Central Highlands, and indicated that more troops might be required if bombing failed to achieve results.

On March 20, the Joint Chiefs of Staff had proposed sending two American divisions and one South Korean division for offensive combat operations.

The Joint Chiefs, the Pentagon study said, "had the qualified support" of Secretary McNamara.

A 'Mobile Role' Sought

On April 4, Ambassador Taylor proposed "the use of Marines in a mobile counterinsurgency role in the vicinity of Danang for the improved protection of that base and also in a strike role as a reserve in support of [South Vietnamese Army] operations anywhere within 50 miles of the base." This was described as an enclave strategy.

On April 20, Secretary McNamara met General Westmoreland and other officials in Honolulu. The Pentagon study said there were 33,500 American troops then in Vietnam.

The conferees agreed that United States ground forces should be increased from 4 to 13 maneuver battalions involving 82,000 men, with 4 battalions involving 7,250 men also to be sought from Australia and South Korea.

A series of major military victories by the Vietcong in May and June led General Westmoreland to ask on June 7 for still more help—for a total of 44 battalions.

The study said that on June 13, he proposed a "search-and-destroy strategy for U.S. and third-country forces," with the "primary focus" for South Vietnamese forces to be pacification.

Authority for Westmoreland

On June 26, the study reported, General Westmoreland was given authority to commit United States forces whenever he decided they were needed "to strengthen the relative position" of Government forces.

The first major ground action by United States forces took place June 27-30, with the 173d Airborne Brigade, an Australian battalion and South Vietnamese in "a search-and-destroy operation into Vietcong base areas."

On July 17, Deputy Secretary of Defense Cyrus R. Vance said in a cablegram that President Johnson had decided to go ahead with a plan to deploy 34 battalions. On July 30, the Joint Chiefs backed deployment of 44 battalions, involving 193,887 United States soldiers.

The search-and-destroy strategy, the study commented, "left the U. S. commitment to Vietnam open-ended." As to President Johnson and Secretary McNamara, it added, "there are manifold indications that they were prepared for a long war."

"All the News That's Fit to Print"

The New York Times

LATE CITY EDITION

Weather: Cloudy today and tonight. Partly sunny and milder tomorrow. Temp. range: today 60-67; Monday 58-62. Full U.S. report on Page 82.

VOL. CXXI . . No. 41,548 — NEW YORK, TUESDAY, OCTOBER 26, 1971 — 15 CENTS

U.N. SEATS PEKING AND EXPELS TAIPEI; NATIONALISTS WALK OUT BEFORE VOTE; U.S. DEFEATED ON TWO KEY QUESTIONS

United Press International

Tanzanian and Albanian delegations applaud defeat of "important question" resolution

United Press International

Liu Chieh, right, Nationalists' chief U.N. delegate, and delegation walk out of the hall

WASHINGTON CALM

Officials Uncertain of Effect of Defeat on Future Relations

Special to The New York Times

WASHINGTON, Oct. 25—Official Washington reacted with outward calm tonight to the crushing American defeat in the United Nations on the China issue. But there was uncertainty as to the effect the historic vote would have on future United States relations with Taiwan, the United Nations and the Peking Government.

Although the defeat was a distinct public setback for the Administration, most knowledgeable officials here had concluded in the last 48 hours that the weeks of arm twisting and private pressure in foreign capitals would fail to save Taiwan's seat and were therefore not surprised by the outcome.

At the time the vote was being held on the "important question," many prominent Administration and Congressional figures were unaware that it was taking place. On this Veterans Day holiday, most people here had assumed that the crucial voting would not take place until tomorrow. And with a heavy rain falling all day in Washington, many officials had retired early.

No television station in Washington carried the initial phases of the debate live tonight, contributing to the lack of awareness. Washington's public television station, WETA, carried the later parts of the debate, after the crucial vote.

U.S. Withholds Comment

Even James C. H. Shen, the Ambassador of Nationalist China, was caught by surprise by the vote tonight. He was in New Haven for a speaking engagement at Yale and had gone to sleep without knowing of the events at the United Nations. When awakened by a reporter's call, he said he would have no comment.

Both the State Department and the White House said there would be no immediate official comment, but privately some officials wondered aloud about the significance of what they called the most important defeat ever suffered by the United States in the world organization.

Senator James L. Buckley, Conservative-Republican of New York, reacted sharply. He said he had asked his staff to prepare legislation for "a major reduction" in the American financial contribution to the United Nations, which runs about one-third of the annual $200-million budget.

"The action taken by the General Assembly tonight," he said, "may well be recorded as the beginning of the end of the United Nations, as marking

Continued on Page 10, Column 6

SESSION IS TENSE

Washington Loses Its Battle for Taipei by 76 to 35

By HENRY TANNER

Special to The New York Times

UNITED NATIONS, N. Y, Tuesday, Oct. 26—In a tense and emotion-filled meeting of more than eight hours, the General Assembly voted overwhelmingly last night to admit Communist China and to expel the Chinese Nationalist Government.

Moments before the vote, Liu Chieh, the Chinese Nationalist representative, announced from the rostrum that his Government would take no further part in the proceedings of the Assembly. He received friendly applause from most delegations, and then led his delegation out of the hall.

Texts of U.N. resolutions will be found on Page 10.

The vote, which brought delegates to their feet in wild applause, was 76 in favor, 35 opposed, and 17 abstentions. The vote was on a resolution sponsored by Albania and 20 other nations, calling for the seating of Peking as the only legitimate representative of China and the expulsion of "the representatives of Chiang Kai-shek."

Voting Is Sudden

Thus, the United States lost—in the 22d year—its battle to keep Nationalist China in the United Nations. This development, which came with dramatic suddenness, was denounced by the chief American delegate as a "moment of infamy."

The key decision that signaled the United States defeat came an hour and a half earlier, when the Assembly voted, 59 to 55 with 15 absentees, to reject the American draft resolution that would have declared the expulsion of the Nationalists an "important question" requiring a two-thirds majority for approval.

The United States had successfully used such a resolution since 1961 to keep the Chinese Communists out and the Chinese Nationalists in. Before that time, a simple majority would have admitted Peking, but no majority could be mustered.

Pandemonium Breaks Out

Last night as the electrical tally boards flashed the news that the "important question" proposal had failed, pandemonium broke out on the Assembly floor. Delegates jumped up and applauded.

The American delegation, also in the front row, sat in total dejection. George Bush, the United States delegate, who had

Continued on Page 10, Column 2

LINDSAY DEFENDS KNAPP HEARINGS

Tells P.B.A. Head the Inquiry is in 'The Best Interest' of Everyone' on Force

By DAVID BURNHAM

Mayor Lindsay said yesterday that while the Knapp Commission hearings meant "discomfort and shock" for many policemen and citizens, dealing decisively with police corruption was in "the best interest of every member of the police force."

Mr. Lindsay made the statement in a letter to Edward J. Kiernan, president of the Patrolmen's Benevolent Association.

The Mayor also said he intended to use the recommendations of the Knapp Commission, expected in a written report by the end of the year, "as the basis for a major campaign to build public confidence in the Police Department and the integrity of our law enforcement processes."

The Mayor's letter was in response to charges made last week by Mr. Kiernan that the Knapp Commission's hearings

Continued on Page 31, Column 5

Pakistanis Report 501 of Foe Killed In Eastern Area

By MALCOLM W. BROWNE

Special to The New York Times

KARACHI, Pakistan, Oct. 25—The Government reported tonight that its forces had killed 501 "enemy troops"—defined as "Indians and Indian agents"—in heavy fighting in East Pakistan.

The Government, here in Pakistan's western wing, uses the term "Indian agents" to refer to all of its adversaries in East Pakistan, including the Pakistanis there who have been battling for Bengali independence since March with Indian support.

U.N. Observers Suggested

Today the Government said some of the bodies bore identification tags of the Indian Army. If the casualties are indeed Indians and if the toll even approaches the figures given, that would indicate that the fighting had reached its greatest intensity since the brief Indian-Pakistani conflict in 1965.

[In New Delhi, Defense Minister Jagjivan Ram reiterated that India would not pull her troops back from her borders "as long as the Pakistani threat continues." Page 17.]

Meanwhile, the Government announced that President Agha Mohammad Yahya Khan had asked for the intercession of Secretary General Thant of the United Nations in the dispute.

According to the Pakistani radio, President Yahya Khan proposed that United Nations observers be posted on both sides of the border between East Pakistan and India to supervise a mutual withdrawal

Continued on Page 17, Column 1

BREZHNEV IN PARIS, BACKED ON TALKS

Pompidou Agrees to a Quick Start on Preparations for Europe Security Parley

By HENRY GINIGER

Special to The New York Times

PARIS, Oct. 25—President Pompidou and Leonid I. Brezhnev, leader of the Soviet Communist party, agreed quickly today to begin active preparation for a European security conference.

The agreement was made known at a state dinner in Versailles that marked the end of the first day of a six-day visit by Mr. Brezhnev. The Soviet leader was received this afternoon with the honors of a chief of state, and only a few discordant notes marred the friendly atmosphere of Mr. Brezhnev's first visit to a Western country since he became party leader in 1964.

[In Washington it was reported that Mr. Brezhnev had signaled Western leaders that he had officially assumed over-all responsibility for Moscow's relations with the United States and Western Europe. Page 5.]

In toasts this evening, Mr. Pompidou and Mr. Brezhnev spoke in similar terms of the need to end hostility between blocs.

Mr. Brezhnev said that France and the Soviet Union were close "on a fundamental problem—that of ending the division of the world into political-military blocs." Mr. Pompidou declared such blocs carried within them "the certainty of

Continued on Page 6, Column 4

CHOW SAYS PEKING WILL SUBVERT U.N.

Nationalist Minister Sees Change to 'Maoist Front' As Result of Defeat

By SAM POPE BREWER

Special to The New York Times

UNITED NATIONS, N.Y., Oct. 25—Nationalist China's Foreign Minister, Chow Shu-kai, walked with his delegation out of the United Nations tonight and declared bitterly that Communist China, in his nation's place, would subvert the world organization.

"Once it has been seated both in the General Assembly and in the Security Council," Mr. Chow said of Peking, "it will surely transform the United Nations into a Maoist front and a battlefield for international subversion."

Mr. Chow, grave but unflinching in the glare of batteries of television lights, stood with Taiwan's delegate, Liu Chieh, at his side in a hallway outside the General Assembly Hall, where the overwhelming defeat for his Government had been voted. He declared:

"There are those who think that participation of the Communist regime will enhance the prospect of peace. The idea is to subject the aggressive regime to the discipline of international public opinion. This is dangerous nonsense—it is like tying a tiger with a straw rope."

Asked if he had had a foreboding of defeat when he wrote the document, Mr. Chow said, quietly: "When you are fighting a war, you prepare for

Continued on Page 11, Column 1

U.N. Roll-Calls on China

Special to The New York Times

UNITED NATIONS, N. Y., Oct. 25—Following are two roll-call votes taken in the General Assembly tonight on seating Communist China and expelling Nationalist China.

On Two-Thirds Requirement

Resolution declaring the expulsion of Nationalist China an "important matter" and thus requiring a two-thirds vote rather than a simple majority for passage.

IN FAVOR—55		
Argentina	Ghana	New Zealand
Australia	Greece	Nicaragua
Bahrain	Guatemala	Niger
Barbados	Haiti	Panama
Bolivia	Honduras	Paraguay
Brazil	Indonesia	Philippines
Cambodia	Israel	Portugal
Cent. Afr. Rep.	Ivory Coast	Rwanda
Chad	Jamaica	Saudi Arabia
China	Japan	South Africa
Colombia	Jordan	Spain
Congo (Kinsh.)	Lebanon	Swaziland
Costa Rica	Lesotho	Thailand
Dahomey	Liberia	United States
Dominican Rep.	Luxembourg	Upper Volta
El Salvador	Madagascar	Uruguay
Fiji	Malawi	Venezuela
Gabon	Mauritius	
Gambia	Mexico	

OPPOSED—59		
Afghanistan	Ethiopia	Norway
Albania	Finland	Pakistan
Algeria	France	Peru
Bhutan	Guinea	Poland
Britain	Guyana	Rumania
Bulgaria	Hungary	Sierra Leone
Burma	Iceland	Singapore
Burundi	India	Somalia
Byelorussia	Iraq	So. Yemen
Cameroon	Ireland	Soviet Union
Canada	Kenya	Sudan
Ceylon	Kuwait	Sweden
Chile	Libya	Syria
Congo (Brazza)	Malaysia	Tanzania
Cuba	Mali	Trinidad-Tobago
Czechoslovakia	Mauritania	Uganda
Denmark	Mongolia	Ukraine
Ecuador	Nepal	Yemen
Egypt	Nigeria	Yugoslavia
Eq. Guinea		Zambia

ABSTENTIONS—15		
Austria	Italy	Qatar
Belgium	Laos	Senegal
Botswana	Malta	Togo
Cyprus	Morocco	Tunisia
Iran	Netherlands	Turkey

Absent—Maldives, Oman.

On Seating Peking

Resolution to seat Communist China and expel Nationalist China.

IN FAVOR—76		
Afghanistan	Guyana	Portugal
Albania	Hungary	Rumania
Algeria	Iceland	Rwanda
Australia	India	Senegal
Belgium	Iran	Sierra Leone
Bhutan	Iraq	Singapore
Botswana	Ireland	Somalia
Britain	Israel	So. Yemen
Bulgaria	Italy	Soviet Union
Burma	Kenya	Sudan
Burundi	Kuwait	Sweden
Byelorussia	Laos	Syria
Cameroon	Libya	Tanzania
Canada	Malaysia	Togo
Ceylon	Mali	Trinidad-Tobago
Chile	Mauritania	Tunisia
Cuba	Mexico	Turkey
Czechoslovakia	Mongolia	Uganda
Denmark	Morocco	Ukraine
Ecuador	Nepal	Yemen
Egypt	Netherlands	Yugoslavia
Eq. Guinea	Nigeria	Zambia
Ethiopia	Norway	
Finland	Pakistan	
France	Congo (Brazza)	
Ghana	Peru	
Guinea	Poland	

OPPOSED—35		
Australia	Gambia	Nicaragua
Bolivia	Guatemala	Niger
Brazil	Haiti	Paraguay
Cambodia	Honduras	Philippines
Cent. Afr. Rep.	Ivory Coast	Saudi Arabia
Chad	Japan	South Africa
Congo (Kinsh.)	Lesotho	Swaziland
Costa Rica	Liberia	United States
Dahomey	Madagascar	Upper Volta
Dominican Rep.	Malawi	Uruguay
El Salvador	Malta	Venezuela
Gabon	New Zealand	

ABSTENTIONS—17		
Argentina	Greece	Mauritius
Bahrain	Indonesia	Panama
Barbados	Jamaica	Qatar
Colombia	Jordan	Spain
Cyprus	Lebanon	Thailand
Fiji	Luxembourg	

Absent—China, Maldives, Oman.

End of China's Isolation

Peking Victory Held Likely to Speed Series of International Realignments

By MAX FRANKEL

Special to The New York Times

WASHINGTON, Oct. 25—With the vote at the United Nations tonight, China burst fully and finally from the isolation first imposed on her by the United States a generation ago and periodically preferred by her own Communist Government.

News Analysis

Though Washington was calm or simply asleep at the symbolic moment, its rear-guard effort to save Taiwan in the world organization only heightened the drama of Peking's entry onto the world stage and deepened some of the resentments in conservative circles here.

President Nixon will undoubtedly show some sympathy for those resentments. He considers his projected journey to China as far more significant than most actions of the United Nations, and he sincerely hoped that his gesture would win a more gentle handling for the Chinese Nationalists.

But there was obviously a pent-up desire among many nations to make whole and unambiguous this final reversal of American policy. This will complicate the President's task in defending his new China policy and the irritations are bound to be reflected in Washington's relations with the United Nations.

There is universal agreement here, however, that whatever the consequences inside the world organization, tonight's voting and walkout by the Nationalists will further accelerate a whole series of realignments and shifts on the international scene.

Several important trends had already combined to determine

Continued on Page 10, Column 7

Powell Is Seeking To Avoid Clashes Over Court Seat

By JAMES M. NAUGHTON

Special to The New York Times

WASHINGTON, Oct. 25—Lewis F. Powell Jr., the third Southern conservative nominated to the Supreme Court by President Nixon, is attempting to avoid the collisions over ethics and racial attitudes that contributed to the Senate's rejection of his two predecessors.

Mr. Powell, aware that his life, professional record and judicial philosophy are about to undergo rigorous examination, discussed his background with unusual candor in an interview at his Richmond law office this weekend.

He pledged to do "whatever is necessary and proper" to separate himself from corporate directorships and financial holdings that might constitute potential conflicts of interest.

Mr. Powell sought to place in what he regards as the proper context the comparatively minor chinks that have appeared in his image as a racial moderate—membership in two segregated clubs in Richmond and authorship of a brief filed by

Continued on Page 22, Column 4

By Lyndon B. Johnson: First Steps Toward Peace

INSTALLMENT X

Following is the 10th of 11 installments of excerpts from Lyndon Baines Johnson's memoirs of his Presidential years, which will be published by Holt, Rinehart & Winston on Nov. 1 under the title "The Vantage Point: Perspectives of the Presidency, 1963-1969":

Wednesday, April 3, 1968, began like most days in the White House. I was up early and read through the morning papers over breakfast. I listened to the radio news and glanced again at the front pages. One item, which I had heard broadcast the previous afternoon, was receiving considerable attention. In a speech on Tuesday Senator J. William Fulbright had told the Senate that the partial bombing halt I had ordered three nights before added up to only "a very limited change in existing policy." He forecast that the halt would not move Hanoi in the direction of peace talks.

I was surprised by Fulbright's reasoning and by his timing. We had stopped bombing over more than three-fourths of North Vietnam, an area where 9 out of every 10 North Vietnamese lived. That was much more than a "limited change" in our actions. Moreover, I believed Hanoi was perfectly able to judge the significance of our move without advice from Americans.

In the Senate discussion following Senator Fulbright's speech, Majority Leader Mike Mansfield and other Senators spoke up strongly in defense of our action and disputed Fulbright's charges. Senator Mansfield recalled the long talk he and I had had on the evening of March 27 and he disclosed that I had informed him on that occasion that we were going to stop bombing north of the 20th parallel.

To my mind, the principal issue was not where the precise line marking the no-bombing area was drawn but rather how Hanoi would react to our self-imposed restriction. The key question in the Senate discussion, I believed, was raised by Senator Frank Lausche of Ohio: "How can Ho Chi Minh give any affirmative action when the Senator from Arkansas and others attack the Government before Ho can respond?"

While Fulbright's allegations dominated the news stories and headlines, Lausche's pertinent question received scant attention. I saw it mentioned only once, in The New York Times on April 3, and then only in the 30th and last paragraph on Page 14.

These reflections put me in a bad mood as I prepared to leave for the

Continued on Page 34, Column 1

Peking's Backers Jubliant Over Vote

By TAD SZULC

Special to The New York Times

UNITED NATIONS, N. Y., Oct. 25—Salim Ahmed Salim, the young chief delegate from Tanzania, jumped to his feet tonight and led his colleagues in a victory jig in front of the Tanzanian seats in the front row of the General Assembly hall.

At the opposite end of the hall, where the United States delegation occupies a front-row seat, George Bush, the American chief delegate, slumped dejectedly in his chair.

It was exactly 9:47 P.M. and the United Nations General Assembly had just finished its roll-

Continued on Page 10, Column 2

NEWS INDEX

Pro-Peking Forces Acted Early, Creating Aura of Confidence in Their Success

TACTICS LEFT U.S. ON THE DEFENSIVE

Drive Was Helped by Many Countries Seeking Ties With Communist China

By KATHLEEN TELTSCH

Special to The New York Times

UNITED NATIONS, N. Y., Oct. 25—The pro-Peking countries here made their opening moves of 1971 early, and they created an aura of confidence in their own success that left the United States defensively protesting about a bandwagon.

But more significant than tactics in this year's China debate were events far from the United Nations halls.

These were the clearly increasing efforts to establish diplomatic ties with Peking by capitalist and anti-Communist countries such at Italy and Turkey, both allies of the United States in the North Atlantic Treaty Organization.

But the most important single element was probably President Nixon's July announcement that he was going to Peking seeking normalization of relations, a fact that wavering countries saw as a good reason to look out for their own future relations with mainland China.

The first formal move to bring mainland China into the United Nations in 1971 created a mere ripple—no diplomatic waves—when Albania and a group of 16 pro-Peking countries submitted their request to the General Assembly.

Their joint resolution followed closely the pattern of other resolutions submitted in the past.

The major surprise was that the group did not wait as usual until close to the Assembly opening in September but acted on July 15. The early move was made, sponsors explained, to eliminate any doubts that Peking would insist on the expulsion of the Taiwan-based Nationalists as a condition for joining the world organization.

Stress on Expulsion

From that day until the dramatic Assembly vote tonight, the sponsors have concentrated on convincing the majority that expulsion was an absolute necessity, sometimes with complicated juridical arguments, sometimes with political attacks on the Chiang Kai-shek Government, but most often by the argument that this was the only basis acceptable to Peking.

The July move, by coincidence, was made on the same day that President Nixon announced that he would go to Peking seeking the normalization of relations between the United States and China. This was followed by Washington's announcement that, reversing a 20-year policy, it would support the seating of mainland China—but would continue to fight against the expulsion of the Chinese Nationalists.

Saving a place for the Nationalists became the focal point of the American-led campaign this year. To push its objective, the United States evolved its policy of "dual representation," which would have given the prized Security Council seat to Peking while preserving membership for the Nationalists.

Resolution Submitted

The policy was crystalized in the submission on Sept. 22 of a resolution providing for Peking and Taipei both to be members. With it the United States submitted a procedural resolution that would have required any expulsion proposal to win a two-thirds majority—the device used effectively to defeat the Albanian resolution in previous years.

The United States resolution on "dual representation," on which the Assembly voted tonight, was co-sponsored by 21 countries. Apart from Australia, Japan and New Zealand, these were drawn mainly from the ranks of small countries.

Moreover, the United States experienced considerable difficulties in obtaining co-sponsors from the outset. The willingness of important countries to put their names and prestige behind a resolution carries considerable impact, particularly on wavering states who want to be on the winning side.

Obtaining Japan's full support posed another problem. Obviously chagrined over not having been informed of President Nixon's plan to visit Peking and angered by a toughening United States policy on trade, Japan was not fully involved in lining up support and sharing the burden of tactical planning with the American initiators until September.

Australia and New Zealand agreed to become co-sponsors only after the United States agreed to put in a specific assertion that Peking would get the Security Council seat. Without it, they reasoned, the American text would have no chance of getting wide support .

By contrast, the Albanian group was able to attract an ever-increasing and impressive list of countries willing to say openly that they would support expulsion if it was the only means of getting Peking into the United Nations—Britain, Canada, the Scandinavian countries and others that usually have sided with the United States in Assembly debates.

DURING 'IMPORTANT QUESTION' DEBATE: Secretary General Thant, left, Constantin A. Stavropoulos of the Secretariat, and Adam Malik, General Assembly, president, right.

Photographs for The New York Times by MICHAEL EVANS

AS DISCUSSIONS WENT ON: Jamil Baroody, Saudi-Arabian representative, pauses to chat with Indian delegate.

Peking's Backers Jubilant Over Vote; Bush Slumps in Dejection

Continued From Page 1, Col. 8

call vote on the American resolution intended to prevent the expulsion of Nationalist China from membership.

Numbers showing the results of the vote flashed on the two large scoreboards overhead. They said that 59 delegations had voted against the United States, 54 in favor and 15 had abstained.

The first vote was the linchpin of the whole effort to replace the Nationalist regime in the United Nations with the Peking delegates. Thus, when the Assembly confirmed the admission of Peking 90 minutes later with a separate vote, it was a bit of an anticlimax.

Nationalist China's permanent delegate, Liu Chieh, and his colleagues sat ashen-faced throughout the proceedings. They were motionless when the first defeat struck the Americans and them.

When the final vote was taken, expelling the Nationalists from the United Nations, Mr. Liu and his three advisers rose quietly from their seat halfway down the hall's right-hand aisle and walked away and out.

To Mr. Salim and the delegations from 58 other countries who had voted against the Nationalists—and in full support of Peking—the tally meant a great victory for Communist China, for the "Third World" countries and the idea that superpowers can be beaten.

Albanians Embrace

Therefore, Mr. Salim, with a black tunic buttoned up at the neck, apparently felt that it was perfectly natural to rise in a victory dance—something that has never been seen before in the United Nations.

Albanian delegates, who were the floor managers for the anti-Nationalist effort, were more self-controlled than their Tanzanian co-sponsors. They smiled, laughed, applauded and exchanged embraces. So did the Algerians, who served as co-managers in the Albanian effort.

For long minutes, the packed hall rang with applause and cheers for the winners. There was rhythmic clapping. The Soviet Union's delegate, Yakov A. Malik, who voted against the United States—though Moscow is less than enthusiastic about Peking these days—applauded discreetly and smiled benignly.

A central personage in tonight's drama was Saudi Arabia's delegate, Jamil M. Baroody, who was the author of the motion of postpone the voting on China until tomorrow. He also drafted a lengthy resolution intended to take the place of the Albanian and American proposals.

There was a quality of comic relief about Mr. Baroody—an impression he did not seek to dispel—and the delegates often burst out in appreciative laughter when he began one of his slow and deliberate strolls to the rostrum. Before addressing the Assembly, Mr. Baroody never failed to halt and deliver a ceremonial bow to the chairman.

For Mr. Bush, the vote, which came suddenly and cruelly, marked the collapse of one of the most ambitious and complex diplomatic campaigns undertaken by the United States in recent years.

Not only had the United States lost the crucial "important question" test, thus opening the door to the expulsion of Nationalist China, but the margin of the American defeat was greater than the analysts at the United States Mission here and at the State Department had ever considered possible.

In fact, the five-vote margin was much more than the Albanians and their friends had expected earlier today when they suddenly set in motion a parliamentary bandwagon that led to the vote tonight over desperate United States opposition.

Ninety minutes later, the Assembly overwhelmingly approved the Albanian resolution in another roll-call vote, held admid a burst of applause for "yes" votes as they were being cast. This formalized the expulsion of the Nationalist Government on Taiwan from the United Nations and the full seating of Peking.

A loud cheer went up when Israel voted "yes" for the Albanian proposal. Another loud cheer went up when Portugal surprised the Assembly by also voting "yes" as the bandwagon accelerated.

The Assembly had, by then, been in session for over eight straight hours.

The Americans had assumed that the vote would be taken tomorrow and the United States Mission was confident that this one more day of diplomatic effort would bring the needed votes.

Albanians Spread Word

But as soon as the Assembly convened this afternoon for the concluding speeches of the debate, the Albanians quietly but deliberatly let out the word that they would push for a vote tonight.

The word, as planned, reached the Americans. A delegation friendly to the United States moved to postpone all votes until tomorrow, just as the Albanians had planned. And, just as planned, the pro-Americans failed by a handful of votes, setting in motion the psychological bandwagon that so suddenly resolved the China issue.

When the Assembly adjourned at 11:20 P.M., the Americans quietly vanished in the East River fog on First Avenue. The grim Chinese Nationalists held a news conference. The winners cheered and toasted their victory in the delegates lounge.

India, in 1950, Opened The Longest U.N. Debate

By LINDA CHARLTON

The longest debate in the history of the United Nations, one that for many years seemed incapable of resolution, simmered to a close last night.

The "China debate" has been a predictable event of autumn at the United Nations for more than 20 years. The seating of the Chinese Communists was first proposed by India in 1950, a year after they came to power on the mainland.

And adherence by succeeding administrations in Washington to the doctrine that allowing Peking to take its place with other world powers, such as Mauritius, would be tantamount to treason was, until very recently, unquestionable. Perhaps only so confirmed an anti-Communist as Richard M. Nixon could have tampered with the basis of this near-sacred tenet of American foreign policy to make the turnabout even marginally acceptable to millions of Americans who looked upon their country's intransigence as gospel.

It was India that retained the role of China's sponsor during the next decade. Just as firm, during those first years of perennial tirades at Turtle Bay, was the role of the United States, a determined opposition that kept the question from even being placed on the agenda of the General Assembly.

But, following her border troubles with Communist China, India withdrew from the leadership role, which was assumed for the next three years by the Soviet Union despite the growing quarrel between the Communist superpowers.

'Important Question' Is Born

In 1961, United States strategy changed. The United States, agreeing to allow a vote on the matter, insisted, however, on the designation of "an important question," which meant that a two-thirds majority was required for approval, rather than a simple majority. The requirement, the first time it was voted on, passed by 61-34, with 7 nations abstaining.

By last year the vote on this same resolution had shifted to 66-52, again with 7 absentions. The resolution to seat Communist China saw 51 nations voting in favor of Peking being seated, 49 voting against it and 25 abstaining. Albania, Communist China's small but dogged European champion, proposed the seating resolution in 1963 and every year since then but 1964, when no vote was taken.

In 1965, the Albanian resolution got as far as a tied vote. And there was an admission from Arthur J. Goldberg, then the chief United States delegate to the United Nations, that the question of Peking's admission was the subject of "innumerable conferences" here and abroad.

In October, 1967, Mr. Nixon wrote in the quarterly Foreign Affairs: "We simply cannot afford to leave China forever outside the family of nations."

In February, 1970, President Nixon said that the 750 million mainland Chinese "should not remain isolated from the international community," adding that the United States would "maintain its treaty commitment" to Taiwan, thereby defining the "two-China policy" for which the United States fought vainly last night.

The announcement by Secretary of State William P. Rogers last Aug. 2 that the United States, "seeking to accommodate our role to the realities of the world today," would "support action in the General Assembly this fall calling for seating the People's Republic of China" came 18 days after a far more startling announcement.

The end of more than 20 years of militant United States policy seemed almost anticlimactic in the wake of the announcement that President Nixon was planning to visit Peking.

Mr. Rogers stressed that the United States was in no way softening its opposition to the expulsion of Nationalist China from the United Nations and would insist that any move toward expulsion be considered "an important question," with its requirement of a two-thirds majority.

Mr. Rogers said that during the preceding months, the attitude of Communist China to the United Nations had changed: "And we think that they are now interested in becoming a member of the United Nations."

He did not point out that one point from which Peking had never wavered was its absolute refusal to participate in a United Nations whose members included a Nationalist Chinese delegation. But that was a problem that last night's vote resolved, too.

Peking Envoy in Ottawa Watches Voting on TV

Special to The New York Times

UNITED NATIONS, N.Y., Tuesday, Oct. 26—A spokesman for the Chinese Embassy in Ottawa said early today that no instructions have yet been received from Peking as to whether any of the diplomats in the Canadian capital should proceed to the United Nations.

The spokesman said in a telephone interview that Ambassador Huang Hua and his staff were aware of the United Nations vote admitting Peking and ousting the Nationalists. He said they had watched the proceedings on television.

Ambassador Huang is widely considered a likely appointment as Peking's first representative to the United Nations. He has served as Ambassador to Ottawa since early August.

U.N. Votes 76-35 to Seat Peking and Expel Taipei

Continued From Page 1, Col. 8

been leading the fight for Nationalist China with considerable energy, half turned away from the rostrum, looking silently at the turbulent scene.

An analysis of the voting showed that the abstention of eight nations that had been thought almost to the last to be leaning toward the United States position had been fatal to the American cause. Had they voted with the United States, the American "important question" resolution would have been adopted, 63 to 59.

The eight nations were Belgium, Cyprus, Laos, Qatar, Senegal, Togo, Trinidad and Tobago, and Tunisia.

However, the 76 members who voted for the Albanian resolution to admit Peking and expel the Nationalists constituted a two-thirds majority of those voting. While this majority would have permitted the admission of mainland China even if the American "important question" motion had won, many observers expressed the opinion that the final vote had been swelled by the pattern of the earlier voting.

Meeting with newsmen shortly before midnight at the United States Mission across the street from the United Nations, Mr. Bush said he hoped the world organization would "not relive this moment of infamy."

"The United Nations crossed a very dangerous bridge tonight," he said. Expressing surprise at the vote, he added: "I thought we would win and it would be very, very close."

Mr. Bush said that he expected a very bad reaction from the American public.

When he was asked when he thought Peking's delegates would be arriving, he said: "It's hard to believe that a few hours ago we didn't think we had anything to worry about."

But Mr. Bush said the United States would "cross that bridge when we get to it" as he replied to a question as to how the United States would act regarding Peking's Security Council seat.

During last night's meeting, Adam Malik of Indonesia, who presides as this year's Assembly President, announced that he would notify the Peking Government immediately of its admission. Communist China had said repeatedly that it would accept a seat in the United Nations only if the Chinese Nationalists were expelled.

The suddenness of the voting came as a surprise to all. As late as the afternoon, as the long China debate was in its final phase, it had been expected that the vote would come sometime in the next day.

Time, many here believed, might have worked in favor of the American position. As late as the morning, it was reported, the 131-member assembly was close to being evenly divided. Therefore, the Albanian delegation, which for years has sponsored the resolution that would admit Communist China and expel the Nationalists, made it known that it would try to force a quick decision.

This precipitated an attempt by the supporters of Nationalist China to delay the proceedings. Jamil M. Baroody of Saudi Arabia proposed that all voting be postponed for one day, but his proposal lost, 53 to 56, with 19 abstentions.

In the parliamentary maneuvering that ensued, the United States experienced a short-lived victory. By a vote of 61 to 53, with 15 abstentions, the Assembly adopted an American proposal that priority be given to the "important-question" resolution.

Earlier in the day, both Saudi Arabia and Tunisia had put forward compromise proposals for settling the China issue. The Saudi proposal included a call for a plebiscite on self-determination for the people on Taiwan.

Mr. Baroody, who made many trips to the rostrum during the eight-hour session, made his proposal for a delay in the voting so as to give time for the Assembly to study the American, the Albanian, the Tunisian and the Saudi Arabian resolutions.

The overwhelming vote for the Albanian resolution to seat Communist China and unseat the Nationalists contrasted with last year's bare majority —51 to 49. That was the first majority that advocates of admitting the Communists had obtained since the China item was first taken up by the Assembly in 1950.

WASHINGTON CALM AFTER LOSS IN U.N.

Continued From Page 1, Col. 4

that clear moment when a majority of the member nations decided to abandon principle in order to curry favor with a Government which still remains branded by the United Nations as an aggressor; a Government which by precept and action repudiates provisions of the United Nations Charter," he said.

Earlier, President Nixon, seeking to obtain last-minute votes, had encouraged optimistic public forecasts at the State Department, the White House and at the United Nations, even though the Administration had private indications that it would lose.

Secretary of State William P. Rogers had met with some key aides to discuss the predicted vote count and their conclusions were pessimistic, although they thought the vote on the "important question" would be closer than the 59 to 55 against the United States.

The Administration's immediate problems, one official source said, were to prevent an anti-United Nations feeling from developing in the Congress and the country, and to reassure Taipei that the setback in the United Nations would not mean an end to American support.

Twenty-one Senators and 35 Representatives had threatened earlier to seek major cutbacks in the American contribution to the United Nations if Taipei were expelled.

Tonight one of those Senators, William E. Brock 3d, Republican of Tennessee, said he was not only discouraged but bitterly disappointeed.

"If in fact Taiwan is expelled, then I personally would feel the United Nations would have lost its claim for leadership, and I would urge a reduction of United States support for that organization."

Senator Mike Mansfield of Montana, the Majority Leader, said that he thought the Senate would defeat any effort to amend the foreign aid bill.

He said the China issue was a matter for the United Nations, which should make up its own mind.

The United Nations vote presumably should make the Administration's efforts to establish relations with the Peking regime more straightforward.

Henry A. Kissinger, the President's adviser on national security affairs, was scheduled to return to Washington tomorrow after nearly a week in Peking, where he was making final arrangements with Chinese officials for Mr. Nixon's scheduled trip to mainland China within the next few months.

End of China's Isolation

Continued From Page 1, Col. 7

the outcome at the United Nations:

¶President Nixon's dramatic shift of American policy from hostility toward Peking to a search for accommodation there.

¶China's almost equally abrupt emergence from a convulsive Cultural Revolution, during which she remained aloof or wholly cut off from virtually every other society.

¶The slow but gradual erosion of American influence over other non-Communist nations and allies, most of whom used to be either willing to follow Washington's lead or were forced to do so in exchange for vital military protection and economic aid.

¶The slow but gradual recognition of China as a renascent great power, already armed with a primitive nuclear arsenal and destined to share power and influence with such giants as the United States, the Soviet Union and Japan.

The rapid adjustments of position that were visible on the final roll-call tonight—even by such allies as Israel and Portugal when the outcome was no longer in doubt—were only a hint of the more rapid accommodations expected from many nations.

As Washington, Moscow and Peking settle into a new and complicated pattern of triangular maneuvers, other nations will seek safety or advantage in new relationships. India's search for security in a new intimacy with the Soviet Union is only one example. Pakistan edged nearer to China several years ago. The votes of Africa and Latin America were split tonight, and their policies from now on will be, too.

Japan, which dutifully but painfully went down to defeat at the side of the United States tonight, will be tempted now to rush ahead in seeking her own new ties to mainland China. The principal American allies in Western Europe refused to stick with Washington even on the final procedural gambits in what was clearly an effort to signal a new era of independence from — and commercial rivalry with—the United States.

The shift at the United Nations will not, of course, automatically force the President to evacuate American troops from Taiwan or to leave the Nationalists there defenseless against mainland China. Peking does not possess any significant naval power and there has never been much fear—or evidence—that she would attempt to seize the island by force.

Now that the world organization has, in effect, ratified China's legal claims to Taiwan, Mr. Nixon may actually have gained more time and a better atmosphere in which to work for a peaceful reunification between the rival Chinese regimes.

Charges of Betrayal

But the President has been deeply troubled by the charges, both at home and in some foreign quarters, that he felt no compunctions about betraying the cause of a small and dependent client state on Taiwan just as soon as larger American interests dictated an accommodation with Peking.

The sanctity of United States "commitments," after all, is what the costly war in Vietnam was all about. And there is a real fear here that withdrawal from Indochina, at a moment of wider readjustment, will cause many other friendly nations to doubt the resolve and support of Washington.

That is why Secretary of State William P. Rogers and Ambassador George Bush wriggled so hard at the end, even at the known propaganda risk of making their defeat even more spectacular. That is why Mr. Nixon is expected to show some of his irritation about the United Nations vote and why he will probably make some effort, at least in private, to shore up morale on Taiwan.

But his journey to Peking was not in jeopardy throughout the jousting at the United Nations and he will protect it above all else. If there is a Tuesday-morning post-mortem at the State Department tomorrow, it will surely be said that the Administration could hardly have expected to deny full honors to Peking, where the President's most influential personal aide was visiting at the very moment for the second time in less than four mon

Texts of U.N. Resolutions on China Issue

Special to The New York Times

UNITED NATIONS, N. Y., Oct. 25—Following are the texts of the resolutions on the question of China's representation in the United Nations.

On Seating Peking

Sponsored by Australia, Chad, Costa Rica, Dominican Republic, Fiji, Gambia, Haiti, Honduras, Japan, Lesotho, Liberia, New Zealand, Philippines, Swaziland, Thailand, United States and Uruguay.

The General Assembly,

Noting that since the founding of the United Nations fundamental changes have occurred in China,

Having regard for the existing factual situation,

Noting that the Republic of China has been continuously represented as a member of the United Nations since 1945,

Believing that the People's Republic of China should be represented in the United Nations,

Recalling that Article 1 Paragraph 4 of the Charter of the United Nations establishes the United Nations as a center for harmonizing the actions of nations,

Believing that an equitable resolution of this problem should be sought in the light of the above-mentioned considerations and without prejudice to the eventual settlement of the conflicting claims involved,

Hereby affirms the right of representation of the People's Republic of China and recommends that it be seated as one of the five permanent members of the Security Council;

Affirms the continued right of representation of the Republic of China;

Recommends that all United Nations bodies and the specialized agencies take into account the provisions of this resolution in deciding the question of Chinese representation.

On Expelling Taipei

Sponsored by Albania, Algeria, Ceylon, Congo [Brazzaville] Cuba, Equatorial Guinea, Guinea, Iraq, Mali, Mauritania, Nepal, Pakistan, Rumania, Somalia, Southern Yemen, Syria, Sudan, Tanzania, Yemen, Yugoslavia and Zambia.

The General Assembly,

Recalling the principles of the Charter of the United Nations,

Considering that the restoration of the lawful rights of the People's Republic of China is essential both for the protection of the Charter of the United Nations and for the cause that the United Nations must serve under the Charter,

Recognizing that the representatives of the Government of the People's Republic of China are the only lawful representatives of China to the United Nations and that the People's Republic of China is one of the five permanent members of the Security Council,

Decides to restore all its rights to the People's Republic of China and to recognize the representatives of its Government as the only legitimate representatives of China to the United Nations, and to expel forthwith the representatives of Chiang Kai-shek from the place which they unlawfully occupy at the United Nations and in all the organizations affiliated to it.

On Two-Thirds Vote

Sponsored by Australia, Bolivia, Colombia, Costa Rica, Dominican Republic, El Salvador, Fiji, Honduras, Japan, Lesotho, Liberia, New Zealand, Mauritius, Nicaragua, Philippines, Swaziland, Thailand, United States and Uraguay.

The General Assembly,

Recalling the provisions of the Charter of the United Nations,

Decides that any proposal in the General Assembly which would result in depriving the Republic of China of representation in the United Nations is an important question under Article 18 of the Charter.

Voting Since '50 On China Question

Special to The New York Times

UNITED NATIONS, N. Y., Oct. 25—Following are the votes on questions relating to China representation since they first came before the United Nations in 1950.

The votes from 1950 to 1960 inclusive were on United States motion to keep the question off the agenda. The votes in 1961 and 1962 were on a Soviet motion to seat Peking; the votes since 1963 have been on Albanian motions to seat Peking. For uniformity, the numbers in the "yes" column indicate the vote in favor of Peking, the "no" indicates the vote against Peking.

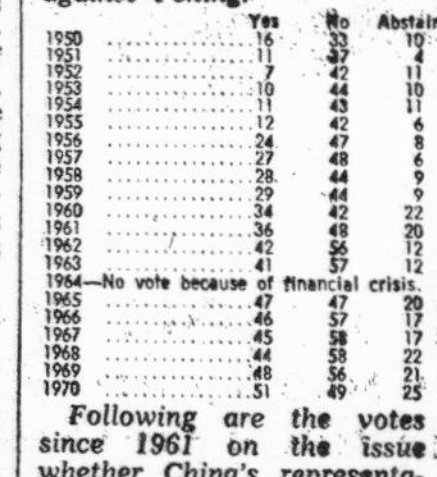

	Yes	No	Abstain
1950	16	33	10
1951	11	37	4
1952	7	42	11
1953	10	44	10
1954	11	43	11
1955	12	42	6
1956	24	47	8
1957	27	48	6
1958	28	44	9
1959	29	44	9
1960	34	42	22
1961	36	48	20
1962	42	56	12
1963	41	57	12
1964—No vote because of financial crisis.			
1965	47	47	20
1966	46	57	17
1967	45	58	17
1968	44	58	22
1969	48	56	21
1970	51	49	25

Following are the votes since 1961 on the issue whether China's representation is an "important question" requiring a two-thirds majority. A "yes" vote, advocated each year by the United States, prevented the seating of Peking even when it obtained a simple majority.

Year	For	Against	Abstaining	Absent
1961	61	34	7	2
1962				
1963				
1964 No voting.				
1965	56	49	11	*0
1966	66	48	7	0
1967	69	48	4	1
1968	73	47	5	1
1969	71	48	4	3
1970	66	52	7	*1

*In addition, one member announced that it was not participating in the vote.

"All the News That's Fit to Print"

The New York Times

LATE CITY EDITION

Weather: Cloudy, mild with chance of showers today, tonight, tomorrow. Temp. range: today 59-73; Monday 57-74. Full U.S. report on Page 86.

VOL. CXXI . No. 41,751 | NEW YORK, TUESDAY, MAY 16, 1972 | 15 CENTS

WALLACE IS SHOT; CONDITION SERIOUS; A SUSPECT SEIZED AT MARYLAND RALLY

Associated Press

AFTER SPEECH: Gov. George C. Wallace takes off jacket and goes to shake hands. At front is Secret Service agent.

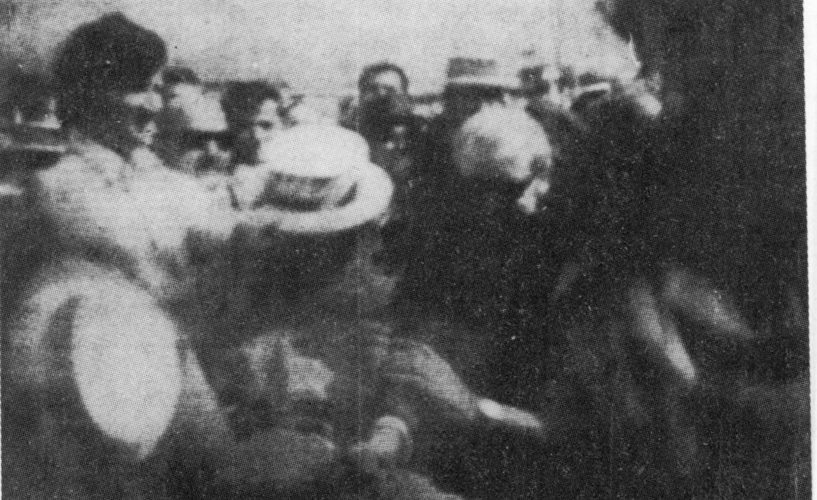

C.B.S. News via United Press International

DURING SHOOTING: Man at right with light hair and sun glasses holds gun as person in crowd tries to shake his arm

C.B.S. News via Associated Press

KNEELING OVER HUSBAND: Mrs. Cornelia Wallace bending over the Governor after he was shot at close range

3 MORE WOUNDED

Legs of Governor Are Paralyzed but Hope Is Voiced by Doctor

By R. W. APPLE Jr.
Special to The New York Times

LAUREL, Md., Tuesday, May 16—Gov. George C. Wallace of Alabama, seemingly on the verge of his greatest electoral triumphs, was shot and gravely wounded yesterday afternoon as he campaigned for President at a shopping center in this suburb of Washington.

Late last night, after the 52-year-old Governor emerged from almost five hours of emergency surgery at the Holy Cross Hospital in nearby Silver Spring, Md., one of his surgeons said that he expected Mr. Wallace "to make a full recovery."

The surgeon, Dr. Joseph Schanno, said that Mr Wallace had suffered at least four wounds and the doctors had removed one bullet. He said that another bullet was lodged near the spine and that the Governor's legs were paralyzed as a result.

Will Continue Campaign

The Governor's wife, Cornelia, said she was "very happy that he's alive and has a sound heart and a sound brain." Billy Joe Camp, his press secretary, reported this morning, after Mrs. Wallace had talked with the Governor, that he would continue his Presidential campaign and "will be at the Democratic convention as a strong, viable candidate."

The state and local police arrested a suspect, who was identified by the Justice Department as Arthur Herman Bremer, a 21-year-old white man from Milwaukee. The department said that the Secret Service had taken custody of a .38-caliber, snub-nosed, five-shot revolver allegedly used by Mr. Bremer in the shooting. Later, Federal and state charges were filed against him.

Held in $200,000 Bond

Mr. Bremer was taken before United States Magistrate Clarence Goetz in Baltimore last night and was ordered held under $200,000 bond.

Three persons who were with Governor Wallace as he plunged into the crowd at the Laurel Shopping Center were also hit by the four or five bullets fired by the attacker.

The shooting occurred after the Governor, having finished a speech here, shed his coat and stepped from behind the protection of his bullet-proof speaking stand.

A young man wearing sungasses and a red, white and blue shirt bedecked with Wallace buttons thrust his right hand between two other people

Continued on Page 34, Column 1

GUNMAN'S ATTACK CLOUDS CAMPAIGN

Uncertainty Created Both by Wallace's Status and Impact of Shooting

By MAX FRANKEL
Special to The New York Times

WASHINGTON, May 15—The bullets that felled George C. Wallace on the eve of his greatest achievements in national politics will also upset both the conduct and the calculations of the 1972 Presidential campaign.

If he could recover in time to resume some form of campaigning, and his press secretary says he will, the Alabama Governor may find an even more aroused constituency rallying to his cause. And some degree of sympathy vote may further swell his expected victories tomorrow in the Democratic primaries of Michigan and Maryland.

The Governor had 210 delegate votes of the 1,509 needed for nomination when he was struck down.

If he is forced out of the campaign, there is no one now in sight to pick up the banner of populism, tinged with an overtone of segregation, that brought the Governor 9.9 million votes, or 13.5 per cent of the total cast for President, in 1968 and seemed to promise him an equally strong following this year.

No one has ever quite

Continued on Page 34, Column 7

Shooting Suspect Shouted: 'Hey, George! Over Here!'

By WARREN WEAVER Jr.
Special to The New York Times

LAUREL, Md., May 15 — George C. Wallace was shot while standing at the new crossroads of middle America today, between the drive-in bank and variety store of a suburban shopping center.

The suspected assailant, a young white man, called the Alabama Governor over to him after Mr. Wallace had stepped from behind his bullet-proof speaking stand and came down to shake hands with the crowd of about 1,000.

"Hey, George! Hey, George! Come over here! Come over here!" the man shouted insistently, according to several witnesses. The man had been standing against the ropes that cleared a space for security guards and reporters between the crowd and the small parking lot speaking stand.

Mr. Wallace heard the shouts and veered to his left, working his way down the line of admirers. He came first to Mrs. Brigitte Howkins of Hyattsville, a plump matron, who reached over a man, took Mr. Wallace's hand and said: "Good luck, Governor Wallace."

"He smiled at me," Mrs. Howkins recalled later, "dropped my hand and reached out for another when the man who had been standing on my right lifted his right arm and suddenly there were shots."

Mr. Wallace fell to the asphalt parking surface and lay on his back in the brilliant sunshine. Witnesses said he was bleeding from the chest and appeared also to have been struck in the right arm.

Val Hymes, a columnist for several Maryland newspapers, saw the Governor sprawled on the pavement, a large red splotch spreading across his shirt front. "I thought at first he was dead," she said.

Mrs. Wallace ran to his side,

Continued on Page 34, Column 4

Kennedy Guarded By Secret Service

By BEN A. FRANKLIN
Special to The New York Times

WASHINGTON, May 15—Shortly after Gov. George C. Wallace of Alabama was shot today, President Nixon ordered Secret Service protection for Senator Edward M. Kennedy of Massachusetts, Representative Shirley Chisholm of Brooklyn and Representative Wilbur D. Mills of Arkansas.

Senator Kennedy, who has declared repeatedly that he is not a candidate for President, accepted the offer, and an unspecified number of agents were guarding his home tonight in nearby McLean, Va. Agents joined Mrs. Chisholm in Detroit, where she was stay-

Continued on Page 35, Column 1

MILWAUKEE MAN HELD AS SUSPECT

Seized on Weapons Charge Last October in Wisconsin —Many Paradoxes Seen

By JAMES T. WOOTEN
Special to The New York Times

WASHINGTON, May 15—The young white man arrested as a suspect today in the shooting of Gov. George C. Wallace is a 21-year-old resident of Milwaukee who pasted Wallace bumper stickers on his car and his apartment door and was exuberantly cheering the Democratic Presidential candidate only moments before the shots rang out.

Those apparent contradictions are but a small part of the paradoxical picture now being sketched of Arthur Herman Bremer, the man accused by Federal authorities today of having tried to kill the Alabama Governor at a shopping center in Laurel, Md.

It was reported that he was arrested on a charge of carrying a concealed weapon last Oct. 18 and was subsequently convicted of disorderly conduct.

A Justice Department spokesman said that the .38-caliber snub-nosed revolver allegedly used at Laurel had been purchased in Milwaukee Jan. 13 and fired five times today.

From descriptions supplied

Continued on Page 34, Column 3

Saigon's Forces Reoccupy Bastogne Base Near Hue

By MALCOLM W. BROWNE
Special to The New York Times

SAIGON, South Vietnam, Tuesday, May 16 — South Vietnamese troops, led by a platoon of 30 soldiers flown in by helicopters, reoccupied Fire Base Bastogne yesterday on the southwesterly approaches to Hue.

The five helicopters carrying the soldiers reportedly encountered no enemy fire as they landed at the base, which the South Vietnamese abandoned April 28 under heavy attack. The base had fallen after the North Vietnamese who had besieged it for more than three weeks sent commandos storming in to penetrate the barbed-wire defenses.

But after routing the defenders at the end of April, the North Vietnamese did not move their long-range 130-mm. artillery into Bastogne to shell Hue, the former imperial capital of Vietnam on the coast 15 miles away.

[The United States command announced the arrival of the carrier Saratoga off the Vietnamese coast Monday, bringing to six the number of attack carriers there. United Press International reported. The United States Seventh Fleet was now said to have 60 ships in the area.]

[In Washington, Secretary of State William P. Rogers angrily defended the mining of North Vietnam's harbors and said that if the Johnson Administration had taken the step earlier, the war might have ended long ago. Page 14.]

Allied officers in the Hue area said that if the re-entry into Fire Base Bastogne appeared to have been easy, this was only because it had capped more than a week of slow, hard fighting and several more days of heavy air and artillery bombardment.

South Vietnamese spokes-

Continued on Page 14, Column 3

PRESSURE GROUPS ANGER ROCKEFELLER

He Asserts Judges Blocked Court Reform and Lawyers Stymied 'No-Fault' Bill

By JAMES F. CLARITY
Special to The New York Times

ALBANY, May 15—Governor Rockefeller charged today that "inordinate pressures" placed on legislators by judges and lawyers had blocked two of his "vital programs"—court reform and no-fault insurance—in the 1972 Legislature.

Mr. Rockefeller, commenting on the action of the Legislature three days after it had adjourned for the year, said the

The no-fault insurance bill was defeated through the lobbying efforts of one small group of men—the New York State Trial Lawyers Association. Article on Page 31.

judges had stymied most of his court-reform program. The lawyers, Mr. Rockefeller said, had blocked the no-fault automobile accident insurance bill he had supported.

The Governor pledged to continue to fight for passage of the two programs next year. He said undue pressure had also been exerted on the legislators to repeal the state's liberalized abortion law. The Governor vetoed the repeal measure Saturday.

"My pledge is to make an all-out fight for no-fault automobile insurance and court reform in 1973," Mr. Rockefeller said at a news conference in the Red Room of the Capitol. "Some headlines have interpreted the failure of the Legislature to enact these two vital programs as a setback for me. The truth is that they marked a setback for the people of New York State.

"At no time," the Governor

Continued on Page 30, Column 3

Court Exempts the Amish From Going to High School

By FRED P. GRAHAM
Special to The New York Times

WASHINGTON, May 15—The Supreme Court ruled 7 to 0 today that the Amish religious sect is exempt from state compulsory education laws that require children to attend school beyond the eighth grade.

The Amish—the rural "plain people" who cling to a horse-and-buggy way of life—believe that education beyond the eighth grade teaches worldly values at odds with the simple life required by their creed.

With this in mind, the Court held that state laws requiring children to attend school until they are 16 years of age violate the constitutional rights of the Amish to free exercise of religion.

The decision specifically applied to Wisconsin, but it was written in terms broad enough to apply to all states that require attendance in public or private schools beyond the eighth grade. Mississippi and South Carolina are the only states that do not have compulsory school attendance laws.

The opinion, written by Chief Justice Warren E. Burger, was the first by the Court holding a religious group immune from compulsory attendance requirements.

The Court stressed the 300-year resistance of the Amish to modern influences and served notice that faddish new sects or communes that reject formal education would probably not be granted similar exemptions.

"It cannot be overemphasized," Justice Burger wrote, "that we are not dealing with a way of life and mode of education by a group claiming to have recently discovered some 'progressive' or more en-

Continued on Page 28, Column 1

Hogan Drops Jay Kriegel Case; Reports He Can't Prove Perjury

By DAVID BURNHAM

The question of whether one of Mayor Lindsay's closest aides, Jay L. Kriegel, committed perjury during his testimony before the Knapp Commission will not be presented to a grand jury, District Attorney Frank S. Hogan announced yesterday.

Mr. Hogan said his office was dropping the case because "the people would not be able to establish beyond a reasonable doubt that there was a willful, irreconcilable inconsistency" between Mr. Kriegel's testimony before the Knapp Commission on June 17, 1971, and Dec. 20, 1971.

The commission was created by Mayor Lindsay—on the recommendation of a special committee that included Mr. Hogan—to investigate allegations of widespread police corruption and of failure by officials in the Lindsay administration to follow up on information about cases of corruption brought to their attention.

Mr. Hogan, in a two-and-a-half-page statement, said another reason for not proceeding with the case was that "there is substantial doubt concerning the authority of the Knapp commission to administer the oath" at the December hearings.

Whitman Knapp, the chairman of the commission, said in

Continued on Page 28, Column 3

NEWS INDEX

Wallace in Serious Condition After He Is Shot at Political Rally in Maryland Suburb

Assault Comes on the Eve Of Primary Vote in State

Continued From Page 1, Col. 8

as Gov. Wallace began mingling with the crowd. In the young man's hand was a pistol. His arm was struck by the Governor's security detail, but he managed to get off several quick shots at point-blank range.

Governor Wallace toppled backward. As he lay on the pavement of the shopping center's parking lot, and as the security men seized the suspect, blood began to seep through Mr. Wallace's blue shirt.

Almost at once, the Governor's wife of 16 months knelt over him. Her yellow suit was stained by the blood from the wound.

Unpredictable Outlook

Dr. James Galbraith, head of the neurological department at the University of Alabama, said that the outlook for recovery from the paralysis was unpredictable "but not favorable." The Governor's personal physician, Dr. Hamilton Hutchinson, said, "He's hanging on and he's tough and a lot of people from Roosevelt on down have survived this much paralysis."

Representative William Nichols, Democrat of Alabama, a visitor at the hospital, said that surgery was halted about 9 P.M. so that doctors could confer with Mrs. Wallace.

Mr. Camp had said a bit earlier that all the vital signs are strong and that internal bleeding had been brought under control.

Mr. Bremer, the suspect, was roughed up as he was taken

The New York Times/May 16, 1972

Governor Wallace was shot in Laurel (1) and taken to Silver Spring (2).

into custody, but examination showed him to be suffering only cuts.

Arthur A. Marshall Jr., State's Attorney for Prince George's County, of which Laurel is a part, said after talking to Mr. Bremer, "I have no idea what motivated him."

A Justice Department spokesman said that the gun allegedly used in the shooting was purchased in Milwaukee last Jan. 13 and was fired five times yesterday.

Last night, United States Attorney George Beall filed in Baltimore charges of assault on a federal officer and violation of the Civil Rights Act of 1968 against Mr. Bremer. Mr. Marshall, the State's Attorney said that the suspect had been charged with four separate counts of assault with intent to murder.

The three others wounded were the Governor's long-time bodyguard, Capt. E. C. Dothard, and Mrs. Dora Thompson of Hyattsville, a volunteer in the Wallace Maryland campaign, both of whom were treated for minor wounds and were released, and a Secret Service agent, Nicholas Zorvas. Thomas S. Smith, superintendent of the Maryland state police, said that Mr. Zorvas was in serious condition after surgery to close a throat wound.

Seen at Earlier Rally

William W. Gullett, Executive of Prince Georges County, said that Mr. Bremer was arrested in Wisconsin on Oct. 18, 1971, and subsequently convicted of disorderly conduct. But the Milwaukee police said they had no arrest record on Mr. Bremer.

Ray Martin, who has been traveling with Mr. Wallace to sell campaign paraphernalia, said that he remembered seeing Mr. Bremer at an earlier Wallace rally in Maryland, dressed as he was yesterday, in red, white and blue with rows and rows of Wallace buttons.

Mr. Wallace was shot as he reached the climax of his insurgent, neo-Populist campaign for the Democratic Presidential nomination, which had stunned the party professionals by its success. He was considered the favorite in the primaries scheduled for today in Maryland and Michigan.

The shooting was expected to have only a limited impact on the voting in those two states, although it might prompt a sympathy vote.

In contrast to the smooth flow of his campaign in other states, Governor Wallace's Maryland effort has been marked by a series of incidents, beginning last week in Hagerstown, where several black youths were arrested. Eggs were thrown at Mr. Wallace as he left a rally, but none hit him.

In Frederick on Friday night, stones were thrown through the windows of the National Guard Armory where he was speaking. Then, as he entered his car a stone struck him in the head. He was not hurt. Finally, as he sped away, a brick or bottle struck the left side of the limousine.

The Laurel Shopping Center, where the incident yesterday occurred, is just outside Laurel, a community 20 miles from Washington that is perhaps best known for its horse-racing track. The center's buildings form an enormous U, covering four square blocks, and the stand from which Mr. Wallace spoke was in the middle.

It was hot, almost sultry, as Governor Wallace delivered his standard speech to an audience of about 1,000 people. When he finished, he stepped from behind his 600-pound bulletproof stand and went into the crowd, something he had begun to do only relatively recently at such rallies.

Witnesses variously likened the reports from the gun to "popping balloons" or "firecrackers" or "a series of auto backfires."

Laurens Pierce, a cameraman for the Columbia Broadcasting System, who was standing directly behind the Governor, said, "At about the third shot I could see the arm and a gun about two feet, three feet from Wallace's chest."

"It was pandemonium for a very short time," Mr. Pierce reported. "The moment the shots rang out there was total confusion. Immediately he [the assailant] was just covered with security people."

"There was a mess of bodies on this man while he was still firing," he went on. "All I could see was an arm and bodies massed on top of him, trying to smother him, but one arm came up out and continued to fire."

Another witness said that the assailant repeatedly called out to Mr. Wallace, "Hey, George! Hey, George!"

Harry Stine, public relations man for the 88-store Laurel complex, said that the Governor's wife was inside the one-story, white brick Equitable Trust Bank just before the shots were fired.

Appeals to Crowd

"She said something like, 'Oh, my God!' and ran and fell on top of him, threw herself on him," Mr. Stine said. "She kept crying 'Honey, Honey.' They had to pull her off."

The state, county police and local police, Secret Service men and bodyguards—some in gray uniforms, some in tan uniforms with stetsons, some in plainclothes — swarmed about the fallen Governor. George Mangum, the burly Baptist preacher who warms up Wallace crowds, shouted into the public-address system, urging the crowd not to press in too close.

The members of the medical team were identified as Dr. Schanno, a vascular surgeon, or specialist in the circulatory system; Dr. Joseph Peabody, a chest and vascular surgeon; Dr. John Haverlin, a general surgeon; Dr. Balthazar Perez, a neurosurgeon, and Dr. Herman Maganzini, an internal medicine specialist.

Lawyer Is Rejected

BALTIMORE, May 15 (AP)—Mr. Bremer declined a court-appointed attorney at his hearing. He said that he wished to be represented by the American Civil Liberties Union.

Mr. Goetz said that Dan Lipsitz, the Baltimore attorney he appointed for the hearing, would represent Mr. Bremer until other arrangements were made.

Mr. Bremer grinned slightly before the proceedings began, but later adopted a more serious appearance when questioned by the magistrate.

He answered, "Yes I do," in a firm, strong voice when asked if he understood the nature of the charges.

Throughout the appearance, Mr Bremer volunteered no statements, replying only with terse answers when questioned.

When Mr. Goetz asked if he was able to afford an attorney, Mr. Bremer replied, "No, I'm not, and I would not favor a court-appointed attorney."

Mr. Lipsitz then said that Mr. Bremer wanted the A.C.L.U. to represent him.

Mr. Goetz questioned Mr. Bremer to establish that he was unable to afford counsel.

"My worth is less than $200 dollars," Mr. Bremer replied, saying that the only property he owned was a motor vehicle.

C.B.S. News

SUSPECT SEIZED: Arthur Herman Bremer, facing camera, is surrounded by policemen after shooting in Laurel, Md.

MILWAUKEE MAN HELD AS SUSPECT

Continued From Page 1, Col. 7

by neighbors, associates, policemen and witnesses to the shooting, he emerges as a quiet, withdrawn person who had difficulty getting along with his father, S. F. Bremer, a Milwaukee truck driver.

An examination of his three-room apartment on the Near West Side of that city indicated that his interests in politics were eclectic, ranging from Governor Wallace to birth control to the Black Panthers.

That examination also turned up a gun catalogue, a box of cartridges and a pornographic comic book as well as a variety of his own writings, and a Confederate battle flag on the beige-carpeted floor.

The accused assailant moved into the $137-a-month apartment last November. He is reported to be a student at a Milwaukee area technical college and until last February he worked as a dishwasher and bus boy at the Milwaukee Athletic Club.

William Heely, the maitre d'hotel at the club, said today that Mr. Bremer first worked part-time, then full-time and then part-time again but simply did not show up for work one day and had not returned or called to explain.

'Reliable and Honest'

"He was always very reliable and honest," Mr. Heely said. As far as he could remember, he added, Mr. Bremer never talked politics. He was timid and had to be drawn out on any subject before he would give his views and opinions, Mr. Heely added.

Stephen Wasche, a 17-year-old high school student whose brother is the manager of the apartment where Mr. Bremer lived, said he tried to engage in conversation with him but was unsuccessful.

The suspect shaved his head completely bald about four months ago, the youth added. "He did it for effect, I think," he said.

On one occasion, according to Mr. Wasche, the suspect wrote an obscenity on the back of a questionnaire mailed to him by Representative Henry S. Reuss, the Milwaukee Democrat. Mr. Wasche believes Mr. Bremer wanted to draw attention to himself and to reach out to others but was unable to do so.

Mr. Bremer's father conducted an impromptu news conference in the kitchen of his home late today. His oldest son, Theodore, 34, was also present. The Bremers have two other sons, Roger, 18, and William, 32.

Dressed in a gray work-shirt and overalls and standing amid a clutter of the dinner dishes, Mr. Bremer shook his head sadly and said he couldn't believe it was his son who shot Governor Wallace.

"We had no idea he was even in Maryland," he said. "He had never mentioned Wallace. The last election he was just like me—for Humphrey."

Mr. Bremer said his son wanted to have his own apartment and moved out of the family home last October. The father said he had not seen him since, but had made one attempt on a day when he was not at home.

Mr. Wasche, the high school student, said a woman he assumed to be the suspect's mother came to the apartment not long ago.

"She asked if he was home and I said yes. But when she went up and knocked on the door he didn't answer," he said. "It was weird, really weird, just like when I tried to talk to him. He always just sort of walked away."

According to Jerry Babcock, who lives in the suspect's old neighborhood near his parents, the younger Mr. Bremer's departure from the family residence came after an altercation with his father.

The suspect's father is a truck driver for the Korhn Cartage Company in Milwaukee. His mother, Mrs. Sylvia Bremer, who is 57, was not present at the news conference. Her husband, 58, said she was "taking it very hard."

"If he is accused of this, he must have become pretty sick. I can't believe it happened," the father said.

At South Division High School, where he graduated, he went out for football, his father said, but was removed from the team after his mother wrote a letter saying he was ill.

The father said his son was not active in politics but did belong to the war unit of the Democratic party in Milwaukee. His son was "more concerned with studying," he said, and wanted to become a commercial photographer.

After his graduation from high school, he took a course in photography at the technical school and then took on a series of odd jobs, including one as a panitor for the Milwaukee Athletic Club.

The father said his son never owned a gun as long as he lived at the family home.

William W. Gullett, the chief executive of Prince Georges County, Md., where Governor Wallace was shot, said the suspect was arrested on Oct. 18, in Milwaukee and charged with carrying a concealed weapon. He was later convicted on a lesser charge, disorderly conduct, Mr. Gullet said.

Mr. Bremer's father said his son did not talk about girls.

The elder Mr. Bremer, who has worked for the same trucking company for the last three decades, spoke in the past tense of his son during the conference.

At the apartment late today, agents of the Federal Bureau of Investigation and later reporters and other residents of the building found an unkempt living room and bedroom cluttered with papers and books.

A Confederate battle flag was on the floor, along with a copy of a Black Panther newspaper and several newspaper clippings, including one from a 1968 copy of The Milwaukee Journal that said, "Meet Nixon at the Sheraton-Schroeder."

There were also many notebooks in the apartment. It seemed apparent that the suspect wrote a great deal. In one spiral notebook were the scrawled words: "In America, here one lived a pig named Arthur Herman. Arthur Herman lived in some . . ." The writing became an unintelligible scrawl at that juncture.

The agents also found a copy of a pornographic book called "Sex Comics" on the floor.

According to United Press International, a notebook found in the apartment contained such passages as:

"Happiness is hearing George Wallace singing the National Anthem or having him arrested for a hit-and-run traffic accident."

"My country, tiz of thee, sweet land of bigotry."

"Just call me canoe, my mother liked to paddle me a lot."

"Nixon uses a night light."

Associated Press

GOVERNOR'S WIFE: Mrs. George C. Wallace rushed to Holy Cross Hospital.

Gunman Called Out, 'Hey, George . . .'

Continued From Page 1, Col. 6

according to Mrs. Hymes, clasping his body in her arms and sobbing.

"The Secret Service pulled her from him and dragged her away in a scene reminiscent of Jackie Kennedy being pulled away from the dying body of President Kennedy," Mrs. Hymes said.

Mrs. Wallace managed to pull away from the men and ran back to her husband. There was blood smeared on her yellow print dress. Someone spread a coat under Mr. Wallace's head and someone else pulled his shirt up, placing a large white gauze patch on the wound. Then he was put on a stretcher and lifted temporarily into a station wagon.

Crowd Hovers

Karen Yengich, a 25-year old reporter for The Laurel News Leader, said when she heard the shots "I thought it was tear gas for demonstrators or something like that. Then suddenly the crowd was surging toward me and people were shouting 'He's been shot, he's been shot.' I got scared, my legs got weak—I thought I'd get stomped to death. It was my first day on the job here."

Miss Yengich said that when she got to the wounded candidate the crowd was hovering over him and blood trickled down his arm.

"His wife was crying, she had this grief-stricken look, and she had blood on the top of her suit. It seemed to me a long time before the ambulance came, but I looked at the clock and it was only five minutes."

Bulletproof Stand

Miss Yengich added, "I never thought I would see anything like this, especially in Laurel. It's a small community. It's probably Wallace country. I mean, it's middle America."

The afternoon Wallace rally, which was almost over when the shooting occurred, had taken place in sparkling midsummer weather in a setting that could have been any suburban shopping center in the country.

A small speakers' stand of red, white and blue, with a sign "Laurel Shopping Center" across the top, had been set up just behind the Equitable Trust Company, a white brick building in the center of the parking area.

An hour after the shooting, the bulletproof speaking stand that Mr. Wallace customarily carries to every rally he addresses, was still standing on the platform, with a large vase of red roses in front of it.

Before he came down from the platform, Governor Wallace had delivered the same well-tested political speech that has featured his 1972 primary campaign: a charge that other Democrats had stolen his program, along with an attack on tax evaders and "welfare loafers."

About an hour after the shooting, the police and agents of the Federal Bureau of Investigation circled a dusty blue coupe, an American Motors Rebel, pasted paper over its Wisconsin license plates and shooed reporters away.

After the Governor had been rushed to the hospital by ambulance, the shopping center crowd was full of eyewitnesses, many of them young people anxious to talk to reporters.

One of these, Gary Mills, a tall teen-ager with long blond hair, said he had seen blood on the right arm of Governor Wallace immediately after the shooting. He described how the police had pounced on the alleged assailant and dragged him out of the crowd, amid shouts of "Get him!" and "Get that bastard!"

Onlookers said the crowd seemed stunned and nearly silent after the shooting. The only other outbreak came, according to Mrs. Hymes, when a group of about 10 Wallace supporters turned on four young black men. The blacks, frightened, backed away saying, "No, no, we didn't do it," Mrs. Hymes said.

The onlookers who had seen the assailant described him as of medium height and with very light, almost white, short hair. One witness said "he was the kind of guy you would call whitey."

Versions Differ

Immediately after the shots were fired Walter Houkins, the husband of the woman who had just shaken Mr. Wallace's hand, dove at the gunman and grabbed him by the leg. Almost immediately, four or five members of the Prince Georges County police department leaped upon the alleged assailant and some pummeling ensued.

At a news conference about two hours after the shooting, Capt. James Ross of the Prince Georges County Police Department told reporters, "We removed the agitator."

According to the police version, the gunman fired five bullets at very close range before he was wrestled to the ground. "We wanted to get him out of there as fast as we could because the crowd was menacing," Captain Ross said. "He was removed for his own protection."

Seconds after the gunman was seized and Governor Wallace fell to the pavement, a revolver was found lying on the ground between the two men.

Shortly after the shooting, the clear Maryland skies began to cloud over darkly, and in less than two hours a torrential thunderstorm descended suddenly on the shopping center, washing discarded bumper-stickers and buttons into the gutters and dampening multicolored pennants that had hung over the parking space all afternoon.

Associated Press

AFTER ARRAIGNMENT: Arthur Herman Bremer, left, and federal agent in car at U.S. court in Baltimore.

Attack on Governor Stirs Uncertainty on Campaign

Continued From Page 1, Col. 4

agreed on whether the building Wallace candidacy this year was a bigger threat to Republicans or Democrats. President Nixon has figured that he would run better in the South without an independent Wallace challenge. The Democratic National Committee had all but decided that it could fare much better in the big industrial states of the North without a third-party Wallace challenge.

But mathematically, at least, Mr. Wallace had an even better chance this year to win 70 or 80 electoral votes and deny his major party rivals the absolute majority that is needed for a clear election by the Electoral College. All the available signs suggested that he coveted such a result and was preparing to revive his American Independent party, in many if not all states.

Regardless of the Governor's chances of recovery, his shooting has undone four years of effort and brave self-exposure by President Nixon and all those who coveted his job. From the President down, politicians had tried to pretend that the passions and the madness that struck down two Kennedys and Martin Luther King belonged to a remote and unhappy past, that the country was recovering its balance and that controversy could again be argued out in a civilized manner.

Now, yet another huge constituency of American voters has been made to feel that it cannot, after all, safely present controversial views and electric personalities to the electorate. That his how the New Frontiersmen felt when President John F. Kennedy and later his brother, Robert, were gunned down by assassins at the peak of their political promise. That is also how vast numbers of black citizens felt when Dr. King, the militant but nonviolent leader, was slain.

Candidates Take Chance

President Nixon, Senators Hubert H. Humphrey, George McGovern and Edmund S. Muskie and all the other candidates this year, like Mr. Wallace himself, had taken enormous chances since then to expose themselves once more to the crowds at airports and in shopping centers to help the country regain its pride and confidence in orderly political competition. They were heavily protected, but they knew that there really was no protection against the enraged act of a suicidal assailant.

President Nixon's first instinct, to revive security protection for Senator Edward M. Kennedy, symbolized the first reaction everywhere in Washington that the violence of the nineteen-sixties was not over. It also dramatized the fear of Senator Kennedy and many members of his family that whatever other calculations he might make, he ought not to tempt fate by exposing himself to a national campaign.

It was thought here that Mr. Kennedy would almost certainly be confirmed in his decision not to seek the Presidency this year, no matter how great the pressures that were building up.

Mr. Wallace was widely expected to win strong pluralities in the primary contests tomorrow for 132 convention delegates in Michigan and 53 delegates in Maryland. But his indicated success—in a Northern industrial state where school busing has been a particularly intense issue, and in a border state that gave him 42 per cent of the Democratic vote eight years ago—also promised to be the peak of his showing inside the party.

In all, he had won 210 delegates to the Democratic convention and stood to gain fewer than 100 more. Since even some of the delegates required to vote for the Governor have been eager to bolt to another candidate, it seemed impossible that he would even come near to the 1,509 votes needed for nomination and increasingly likely that he would organize a third-party challenge.

In the race for the nomination, the delegates formally pledged to Mr. Wallace, if released, were expected to move in almost equal numbers to Mr. Humphrey and Mr. McGovern.

In the general election, Mr. Wallace appeared to have a dual power: first, to gather the electoral votes of six or seven Southern states with which to bargain in case neither President Nixon nor his Democratic rival obtained a majority in the Electoral College; and second, to draw enough votes from the Republicans in such states as Texas or Florida or from the Democrats in such states as New Jersey and Michigan to confound the results.

Gun Foe Defeated

A further consequence of today's shooting is bound to be yet another effort to write stringent Federal laws against the indiscriminate sale of guns. Many of the voters who passionately resisted such legislation were in Mr. Wallace's constituency and President Nixon, fearful of those votes, has long resisted the pressure for gun registration and limitation from urban communities.

Paradoxically, Governor Wallace was struck in a state that only two years ago defeated the re-election bid of Senator Joseph D. Tydings, a Democrat who had aroused the ire of the groups opposing gun control.

The Johnson Administration tried to write tough gun controls after the King and Robert Kennedy assassinations in 1968, but the final version left huge loopholes leading to vastly increased imports of foreign gun components. Mr. Nixon has favored tougher penalties for criminals toting firearms, but he has been sympathetic to the demand that law-abiding citizens be spared from all restrictions or inconveniences in the acquisition of weapons and ammunition.

How the Secret Service and the Federal Bureau of Investigation will react to the shooting was not yet evident tonight, but they will almost certainly reimpose severe limitations on the conduct of the President and his challengers in uncontrollable environments. Mr. Nixon had gone so far as to defy unruly crowds in 1970 by exposing himself to their taunts to demonstrate that politicians were free to face their people people again.

Bodyguard, a Wallace Volunteer And U.S. Secret Agent Also Shot

By PHILIP SHABECOFF

Special to The New York Times

WASHINGTON, May 15 — Three other persons were injured by the bullets aimed at Gov. George C. Wallace today.

The victims included Governor Wallace's long-time personal security officer, a United States Secret Service agent assigned to protect the Alabama Governor and a young woman serving as a volunteer "Wallace girl" during the Maryland primary campaign.

The personal bodyguard was identified as Capt. E. C. Dothard of the Alabama State Highway Patrol. He was said to have been shot in the chest and was reported in "fair to satisfactory condition."

Thomas S. Smith, superintendent of the Maryland State Police, identified the Secret Service agent as Nicholas Zorvas. He said that Mr. Zorvas had been shot in the throat and was "evidently in serious condition."

However, while Mr. Zorvas was undergoing an operation to remove the bullet, which had lodged in his jaw, Dr. Ronald F. Wilkinson, general surgeon at Leland Hospital, reported that "he is expected to be O.K."

The young campaign worker was said to be Mrs. Dora Thompson of Hyattsville, Md., not far from the shopping center where today's shooting took place.

Policemen in Hyattsville said that she had been treated for a wound in the knee and then released. "She is just fine," a spokesman for police headquarters said.

Captain Dothard was said by Wallace campaign headquarters to have served as the Governor's personal security officer for many years. He was described as being married and in his mid-40's and was a familiar figure on all Wallace campaign trips.

Captain Dothard was described as being closer to Governor Wallace than any other member of the campaign entourage. Reporters who traveled with the Wallace party described the police captain as "the most popular cop" on the campaign trail and said he had a laconic, droll wit.

Mr. Zorvas was said to be a young, well-dressed agent based in Atlanta. He was second in command of the security detail assigned to protect Governor Wallace. Along with the chief of the detail, James Kelly, he was responsible for administering all security techniques for the Wallace campaign as well as for accompanying the candidate personally at all times.

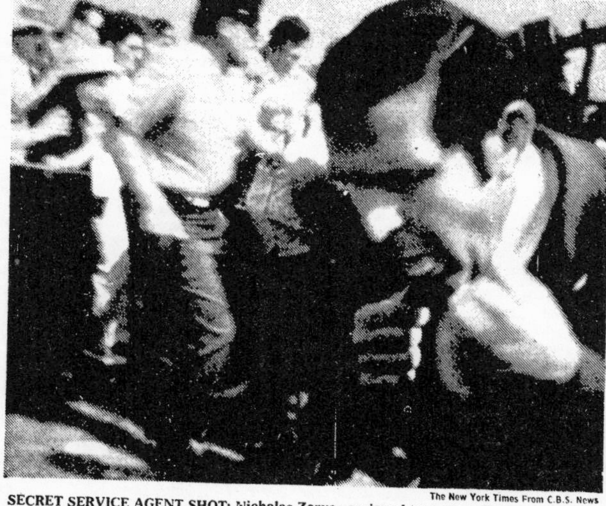

The New York Times From C.B.S. News

SECRET SERVICE AGENT SHOT: Nicholas Zorvas assigned to protect Governor Wallace clutches his throat after being hit by shot fired during rally yesterday in Laurel, Md.

"All the News That's Fit to Print"

The New York Times

LATE CITY EDITION

Weather: Rain today; showers likely tonight. Fair and milder tomorrow. Temp. range: today 68-74; Thursday 66-76. Temp.-Hum. Index yesterday 71. Full U.S. report on Page 70.

VOL. CXXI . No. 41,796 — © 1972 The New York Times Company — NEW YORK, FRIDAY, JUNE 30, 1972 — 15 CENTS

SUPREME COURT, 5-4, BARS DEATH PENALTY AS IT IS IMPOSED UNDER PRESENT STATUTES

Party Panel Strips McGovern of 151 California Delegates

SENATOR SET BACK

He Deplores Move by Coalition of Rivals—State Law Ignored

By WARREN WEAVER Jr.

Special to The New York Times

WASHINGTON, June 29—The Democratic National Convention's Credentials Committee stripped Senator George McGovern today of 151 delegates he thought he had won in the California primary, disregarding state law in a display of political power.

Accomplished by a coalition of his rivals for the Presidential nomination, the move abruptly slowed the momentum of the South Dakotan's campaign and heavily clouded his prospects for tying up the nomination before the convention meets July 10.

The committee ended nearly four hours of debate by voting 72 to 66, to divide the 271-member California delegation among all the Presidential candidates who competed in the June 6 primary, instead of following the California statute, which allots all the delegates to whoever gets the most votes.

Move Called 'Outrageous'

In an unusually bitter news conference at the Capitol, Senator McGovern called the committee decision "an incredible, cynical, rotten political steal" and "an outrageous way to treat the American people."

Informed at a National Press Club luncheon about the committee action, Senator Hubert H. Humphrey said that his chances for the nomination had been "markedly improved."

"I'm not going to say any more—I've got the votes," the Minnesotan said.

Authoritative sources said, meanwhile, that Senator McGovern, if he ultimately won the nomination, viewed Senator Edward M. Kennedy of Massachusetts as his first choice for a running mate. [Details on Page 20.]

Appeals Is Planned

The Credentials Committee decision will be appealed to the convention when it opens in Miami Beach, but it may prove difficult for the McGovern forces to reverse because the 151 delegates at issue—or perhaps the entire 271 from California—will not be able to vote on their own case.

This dramatic reversal for Senator McGovern was achieved by a tight, well-disciplined coalition of committee members who were either uncommitted or favored Senator Humphrey, Senator Edmund S. Muskie of Maine, Senator Henry M. Jackson of Washington or Gov. George C. Wallace of Alabama.

The development provoked angry protests from Mr. McGovern's supporters, who main-

Continued on Page 28, Column 3

Press Loses Plea to Keep Data From Grand Juries

Special to The New York Times

WASHINGTON, June 29—The Supreme Court held 5 to 4 today that journalists have no First Amendment right to refuse to tell grand juries the names of confidential sources and information given to them in confidence.

The decision overturned a lower Federal court ruling on behalf of Earl Caldwell, a reporter for The New York Times

Excerpts from Supreme Court action are on Page 15.

in San Francisco, who had refused to enter a Federal grand jury room to be questioned on information given him by the Black Panther party.

In two related cases, the Court held that Paul M. Branzburg, an investigative reporter for The Louisville Courier-Journal at the time his case arose, and Paul Pappas, a television newsman in New Bedford, Mass., must tell state grand juries names and other information given them in confidence or face imprisonment for contempt.

The sweeping decision by Justice Byron R. White, supported by President Nixon's four appointees, contained a firm rejection of the theory that the First Amendment shields newsmen under certain circumstances from having to testify when the result would be to cut off news sources and deprive the public of news.

This theory has never been considered before today by the Supreme Court. But in recent years, as a wave of subpoenas issued from grand juries for newsmen's notes, radio stations' tapes and television companies' films, some lower courts began to construe the First Amendment as giving journalists some protection against being compelled to disclose confidences.

The courts usually reasoned that if forcing a newsman to testify would cut off future information, he should be excused unless the Government could show a compelling need for his testimony.

"We cannot accept the argu-

Continued on Page 15, Column 4

NIXON DISCLOSES VIETNAM PARLEY RESUMES JULY 13

He Says U.S. Is Returning on Assumption Hanoi Will Negotiate Constructively

By ROBERT B. SEMPLE Jr.

Special to The New York Times

WASHINGTON, June 29 — President Nixon disclosed tonight that the United States and North Vietnam would resume the Paris peace talks on the Vietnam war on July 13.

In a nationally televised news conference—his first in more

Transcript of Nixon news conference is on Page 2.

than a year—Mr. Nixon said the United States was returning to the negotiating table "on the assumption that the North Vietnamese are prepared to negotiate in a constructive and serious way."

He said that if both sides were prepared to engage in serious talks the war could be ended by next year. He also left open the opposite possibility—that the North Vietnamese might not proceed "on that basis," in which case he vowed to continue American bombing and other forms of military pressure. [Question 1, Page 2.]

Talks 'Without Conditions'

Though Mr. Nixon seemed pleased to anounce the resumption of the talks, which were suspended by the United States on May 4, he gave no hint in his remarks that his intense diplomacy in Moscow and Peking in recent weeks had produced assurances that Hanoi was now prepared to move closer to the American position. The most he could or would say was that both sides had agreed to resume negotiating "without conditions."

The President also used the news conference to offer an unusually strong defense of his bombing policy and to give that policy an expanded rationale. In previous statements he has described the bombing as an essentially military tactic designed to protect the shrinking American ground forces in Vietnam and to compensate for the North Vietnamese attacks launched at the end of March.

Tonight he emphasized that

Continued on Page 3, Column 5

Associated Press

SPARED: Elmer Branch, 19, sentenced to die for nonfatal assault, in Huntsville, Tex., jail. He was one of condemned men whose sentences were upset by Supreme Court.

COURT SPARES 600

4 Justices Named by Nixon All Dissent in Historic Decision

By FRED P. GRAHAM

Special to The New York Times

WASHINGTON, June 29—The Supreme Court ruled today that capital punishment, as now administered in the United States, is unconstitutional "cruel and unusual" punishment.

The historic decision, came on a vote of 5 to 4.

Although the five Justices in the majority issued separate opinions and did not agree on

Excerpts from Court decision on death penalty, Page 14.

a single reason for their action, the effect of the decision appeared to be to rule out executions under any capital punishment laws now in effect in this country.

The decision will also save from execution 600 condemned men and women now on death rows in the United States, although it did not overturn their convictions. Most will be held in prison for the rest of their lives, but under some states' procedures some of the prisoners may eventually gain their freedom.

Eighth Amendment Cited

The decision pitted the five holdovers of the more liberal Warren Court against the four appointees of President Nixon, who dissented. The ruling came as the Supreme Court handed down its final decisions of the year and recessed until Oct. 2.

Three Justices in the majority, William O. Douglas, William J. Brennan Jr. and Thurgood Marshall, concluded that executions in modern-day America necessarily violate the Eighth Amendment's prohibition against "cruel and unusual punishments."

The other two in the majority, the two "swing men" of the Court, Justices Potter Stewart and Byron R. White, reasoned that the present legal system operates in a cruel and unusual way, because it gives judges and juries the discretion to decree life or death and they impose it erratically.

As Justice Stewart put it, the death penalty is "so wantonly and so freakishly imposed" that those who are sentenced to death receive excessively harsh treatment.

View of Chief Justice

"These death sentences are cruel and unusual in the same way that being struck by lightning is cruel and unusual," he said.

As the dissenters pointed out, this alignment means that no death sentence can pass muster before the present Supreme Court unless it satisfies the objections voiced by Justices Stewart and White.

Chief Justice Warren E. Burger suggested that legislatures could attempt to do this in two ways. One is to state in statute books in detail the conditions under which a judge or jury can impose the death penalty—such as rape accompanied by a vicious assault, or a convict's murder of a prison guard.

The second would be to revert to the practice of more than a century ago, and impose mandatory death sentences for

Continued on Page 14, Column 4

Gravel Is Denied Immunity In Case of Pentagon Papers

By ROBERT M. SMITH

Special to The New York Times

WASHINGTON, June 29—The Supreme Court ruled today, by a 5-to-4 vote, that Congressional immunity did not prevent a grand jury from asking Senator Mike Gravel or his aides certain questions about his version of the Pentagon papers—including the question where had he obtained the papers.

In a second case that turned on the same constitutional issue, the Court held, 6 to 3, that legislative privilege did not shield Daniel B. Brewster, a former Democratic Senator from Maryland, from prosecution on bribery charges.

Both decisions were handed down, with several others, on the last day of the Court's current term. The Gravel decision was written by Justice Byron R. White, who was joined by the four men President Nixon named to the Court—Chief Justice Warren E. Burger and Associate Justices Harry A. Blackmun, Lewis F. Powell Jr. and William H. Rehnquist.

Senator Gravel, Democrat of Alaska, reacted by issuing a

Continued on Page 16, Column 4

FUND MISUSE LAID TO 4 L.I. UNIONISTS

U.S. Says They Used Money in Labor-Industry Pool to Pay Ball Team's Debt

By DAVID K. SHIPLER

Four officials of a Long Island construction union were charged yesterday with using employer funds to pay off a union debt of $11,245.

The charges, filed by the Federal Organized Crime Strike Force in Brooklyn, came just hours after city officials discharged a veteran inspector in the Buildings Department who was accused of taking a $100 bribe from the owner of a Park Avenue cooperative apartment.

The two cases, while unrelated, continued to focus attention on the widespread corruption in the construction industry described early in the week by a New York Times report. According to the articles in The Times, based on a six-week investigation, builders pay at least $25-million a year here in bribes to inspectors, policemen, union

Continued on Page 28, Column 1

PRESIDENT WIDENS FOOD PRICE CURBS

Applies Controls to Produce After It Leaves the Farm —Seafood Also Covered

Special to The New York Times

WASHINGTON, June 29—President Nixon extended controls today to the retail and wholesale prices of such unprocessed food products as eggs, fresh vegetables, fresh fruits and all raw seafood products.

But he stopped short of the far more drastic step of placing direct controls on the prices farmers receive for these products.

The action was the President's second effort this week to impose some restraint on rising food prices, which could be a crucial issue next fall in the Presidential campaign. His reluctance to act directly on farm prices, however, appeared to reflect his concern about antagonizing the farm vote in an election year, as well as fears among some officials that direct controls might be difficult to enforce and might result in shortages.

Officials conceded at a White House briefing that the action might have little immediate effect on prices. But they expressed hope that it would exert pressure on mark-ups and profit margins at each stage of the food distribution chain that, in time, could stem the

Continued on Page 10, Column 2

Nixon Backs Death Penalty For Kidnapping, Hijacking

By WILLIAM ROBBINS

Special to The New York Times

WASHINGTON, June 29—President Nixon said tonight he hoped that the Supreme Court's decision restricting the death penalty "does not go so far as to rule out capital punishment for kidnapping and hijacking."

Asked about the Court's 5-to-4 decision, issued today, Mr. Nixon said that "any punishment is cruel and inhuman which takes the life of man or woman." He added that the death penalty had actually saved lives by deterring such major crimes as kidnapping. [Question 15, Page 2.]

The President acknowledged, however, that he had not had time to study all nine opinions. He said that he had read only the opinion of Chief Justice Warren E. Burger, which was a dissent from the majority ruling.

The words of the Chief Justice as well as those of another dissenter, Justice Powell, clearly bar capital punishment under both Federal and state laws as presently written.

"Not only does it [the ruling] invalidate hundreds of state and Federal laws," Justice Powell wrote in his dissenting opinion, "it deprives those jurisdictions of the power to legislate with respect to capital punishment in the future, except in a matter consistent with the cloudily outlined views of those Justices who do not purport to undertake total abolition."

And Chief Justice Burger himself said: "It is clear that if state legislatures and the Congress wish to maintain the availability of capital punishment, significant statutory changes will have to be made."

On other domestic questions, the President did the following:

¶He declined to say whether Vice President Agnew would be his choice as a running-mate in the next election.

¶He voiced support for legislation specifically restricting the possession of handguns.

¶He said former Secretary of

Continued on Page 14, Column 5

U.S. Copters Ferry 1,000 To Quangtri Battleground

By MALCOLM W. BROWNE

Special to The New York Times

SAIGON, South Vietnam, Friday, June 30—About 1,000 South Vietnamese marines were flown by United States helicopters yesterday into an area between the city of Quangtri and the South China Sea to join in the drive to retake the Communist-held province.

With the South Vietnamese offensive in the northernmost part of the country broadened, heavy fighting was reported from the area today. The thrust was begun Wednesday by a task force of more than 10,000 South Vietnamese marines and paratroopers.

During the night, South Vietnamese troops reported that they killed 225 enemy soldiers in various enemy sectors. Two enemy tanks were reported destroyed by artillery fire near Hailang, in the southern part of Quangtri province, where the bulk of the South Vietnamese tank force was fighting.

The helicopter-borne assault yesterday brought two battalions of South Vietnamese marines into two landing zones in a region east of the city of Quangtri. That city was abandoned to Communist forces on May 1 and the present drive is intended to oust the North Vietnamese from the whole province within three months.

The main South Vietnamese force, which began a northward drive Wednesday from positions along the Mychanh river line, northwest of the city of Hue, consists of elements of South Vietnamese marine and airborne divisions.

A United States Navy spokesman said that American marine helicopters took four hours to complete the landings. While a South Vietnamese spokesman said there had been no enemy opposition, another American spokesman said enemy ground fire had been encountered in both of the landing zones east of the city.

After heavy naval bombard-

Continued on Page 3, Column 4

$502,000 Hijacking Laid to Jobless Man

By JERRY M. FLINT

Special to The New York Times

DETROIT, June 29—Martin Joseph McNally, 28 years old, was arrested last night in front of his home in Wyandotte, Mich., outside Detroit, by agents of the Federal Bureau of Investigation and charged with air piracy in connection with an airline hijacking in the Midwest last week in which $502,000 ransom was paid. He was held today in $100,000 bond.

The hijacker bailed out over Peru, Ind., but dropped the money, which was later recovered.

Government attorneys said Mr. McNally; an unemployed

Continued on Page 9, Column 2

Senate Votes Antipoverty Bill, Including Plan for Legal Aid

By The Associated Press

WASHINGTON, June 29—The Senate passed a $9.6-billion antipoverty bill today that included a provision to put the Legal Services program for the poor under an independent corporation.

The bill, passed by a vote of 74 to 16 after a week of debate, authorizes funds for two additional years for programs designed to help 26 million Americans officially defined as poor.

The Senate vote sent the legislation back to the House, which passed a somewhat different version last February.

The conference to try to settle the differences between the two measures will be held after Congress returns July 17 from its recess for the Democratic National Convention.

The bill authorizes sums well beyond President Nixon's recommendations for many programs of the Office of Economic Opportunity, the antipoverty agency. And the bill does not give the President the completely free hand he sought in handling or transferring the programs.

In addition, Administration officials indicated that they still found unacceptable the form of the Legal Services Corporation set out in the bill.

For these reasons, there is reason to believe that Mr. Nixon

Continued on Page 10, Column 4

Parole in Capital Offenses Less Likely, Officials Say

By MARTIN ARNOLD

Governors and high state officials said yesterday that the Supreme Court's ruling that capital punishment was unconstitutional could profoundly change the structure of criminal penalties in the country.

Officials in many areas said it might become much more difficult, if not impossible, to get parole in cases that were until yesterday capital offenses. Thus, when a person is sentenced to life in prison, it may mean just that, they said.

Gov. Preston Smith of Texas said that the state legislature would be called upon to pass mandatory life prison sentences for certain crimes, barring any parole.

Gov. Jimmy Carter of Georgia said:

"This decision clears the way for us to re-examine all our laws in Georgia. I still don't think seven years is long enough for a man to serve in prison who has committed premeditated murder and is given a life sentence."

Gov. Ronald Reagan of California said he believed that the ruling would allow his state to reinstate the death penalty in certain cases — "cold-blooded, premeditated, planned murder" —if the voters approved a death penalty referendum that will be on the ballot in November.

Brendan Ryan, St. Louis Circuit Attorney, said: "We will have to re-examine our statutes and perhaps make a life sentence really mean life. Perhaps we should now redefine our homicide laws so as to make some eligible for parole after a given time, but others only parolable through executive clemency, if at all."

Prof. Yale Kamisar of the University of Michigan Law School, considered one of the nation's leading constitutional authorities, expressed surprise and delight with the ruling, but was fearful that there would be a reaction against it.

"There will be increased attention given life sentencing,"

Continued on Page 15, Column 1

NEWS INDEX

Campaign Against Capital Punishment Has Gained in West in the Last 200 Years

PENALTY LIMITED BY 37 COUNTRIES

Drive Has Reduced Grounds for Death Sentence and Kinds of Execution

By PAUL L. MONTGOMERY

The decision of the Supreme Court yesterday declaring capital punishment unconstitutional was the latest milestone in a battle against execution that has been going on in Western civilization for at least 200 years.

The history of the abolition movement has been one of a gradual narrowing of the grounds on which people can be sentenced to death, and the method of executing the sentence.

Beginning with the tiny principality of Liechtenstein in 1798, a few countries decided that there were no crimes serious enough to warrant killing its citizens.

There are now 37 countries in which capital punishment in peacetime has been abolished or abandoned. In Western Europe, only France and Spain retain the death penalty, and France is in the midst of a concerted campaign for abolition.

Trend Toward Abolition

In the Western Hemisphere, 14 countries had followed Europe's lead before the Supreme Court's decision. The areas of greatest resistance to abolition are the Middle East, Asia, Africa and the Communist bloc.

Retaliatory murder is as old as human society, but it was only with the codification of law and the concept of a neutral justice that execution acquired its trappings. In Roman law it was called the summum supplicium—the ultimate punishment.

In the medieval and early modern periods, executions were widespread, frequent and merciless, often being attended by such tortures as slow strangulation, burial alive or burning at the stake. The range of capital crimes was broad, including most crimes against property, religious offenses such as blasphemy or idolatry, and miscellaneous acts such as usury and sodomy.

Rise of Democracy

With the rise of democracy and the power of the industrial working class came a movement for reform. It proceeded on three fronts: reduction of capital crimes, adoption of swift and merciful methods of execution, and imprisonment as the alternative to death. One of the most influential works in the reform movement was Cesare Beccaria's "Essay on Crimes and Punishments," published in 1764.

Most Western countries followed England's lead in reducing the number of crimes punishable by death. There were 223 such crimes in England in 1805, reduced to 15 in 1834 and to four by 1861.

A number of countries, however, retain the death penalty to serve what are essentially political or economic ends.

Penalty for Economic Crimes

The Soviet Union, for example, abolished the death penalty in 1947 but reinstated it in 1950. Most executions are for economic crimes such as taking bribes or profiteering.

In Yugoslavia, capital crimes include "failure by a responsible person to keep public transport facilities in order." Iran reported recently that she had executed more than 100 smugglers in its effort to destroy the opium trade.

In the United States the movement for limiting capital punishment made gains largely in the North. Among the significant changes were the reduction by Pennsylvania in 1794 of crimes punishable by death to one—first-degree murder, New York's abolition of public executions in 1835, and Michigan's abolition of capital punishment except for treason in 1847.

Opposing Forces

The debate in America about capital punishment has generally been subject to opposing forces.

On the one hand, controversial executions—Sacco and Vanzetti in 1927, the Rosenbergs in 1953, Caryl Chessman in 1960—have raised outcries against the death penalty.

On the other hand, notorious crimes—the Lindbergh baby's kidnapping, the assassination of President Kennedy, the outbreak of plane hijackings—has caused adoption of laws to add these offenses to capital crimes.

Debates on the death penalty generally center on two points: whether it prevents crime, and whether it falls with equal weight on the rich and the poor.

The question of whether abolition of capital punishment encourages murder is much contested, and statistics are quoted on both sides.

Debate in Britain

In Britain in 1969, for example, there was a debate about whether abolition, adopted temporarily in 1965, should be made permanent.

Opponents pointed out that in the four years before abolition, 78 murders were committed in Britain in the course of robberies, compared with 177 in the four years after abolition. Supporters of the measure said that the figures were misleading, and that the total number of murders had stayed about the same—135 in 1957, for example, and 148 in 1968.

Most American studies have been inconclusive or have shown that crimes in states that abolished the death penalty have remained about the same in equal circumstances. Opponents, however, point to New York, where capital punishment for most murder offenses was abolished in 1965. In 1964, there were 637 murders in New York City; last year, there were 1,466.

Discrimination Charged

Proponents of abolition argue that the death penalty as applied in the United States has been clearly discriminatory against the poor, particularly against blacks and other minorities.

Of 3,859 executions for all crimes in the United States since 1930, 54.6 per cent of those executed have been blacks or members of other racial minorities, though blacks make up only 12 per cent of the population.

The New York Times/Winston Townsend, Gainesville Sun

DEATH ROW SCENE IN FLORIDA: Leslie Horton, convicted of rape, with family at prison in Raiford after Supreme Court ruling. Sisters, Janetta Davis and Kay, are at left and right, respectively; mother, Louise, is in white and brother Louie is in front.

Ruling Cheered on Florida Death Row

By MARTIN WALDRON

Special to The New York Times

RAIFORD, Fla., June 29—Hollering, hooting and the exuberant rattling of cell doors echoed through the halls this morning as the 97 inmates under death sentence at the Florida State Prison Farm got word that the Supreme Court had ruled the death penalty unconstitutional.

The condemned in Florida are by far the largest number facing the death sentence in any state. Eighty of them went to the movie "Dirty Harry" this morning, and they returned to their cells just in time to hear the news on the 11:15 A.M. radio broadcast.

"Some said things like 'Right on, Mr. Justices,'" said one inmate, Calvin Campbell. "It was such a happy occasion that I cried." And some, Campbell said, made obscene remarks about President Nixon.

Only 86 of the Florida convicts under death sentences have been kept on death row. Ten have been allowed to go back into the general prison population, and one, Marie Arrington, is kept in the prison hospital. Under sentence for murder, she is the only woman awaiting execution in Florida. Six of those on death row were not allowed to attend the movie because they were being punished.

Killed a Policeman

Campbell has been on death row for six years. He was sentenced to die in the electric chair for having killed a policeman in a robbery attempt. He is 32 years old and giggles a lot. But he was very intense as he talked about how the prison psychiatrist had helped him with his "mental problem."

"Killing that policeman was an accident," he said this afternoon.

Campbell, who worked as an embalmer for a funeral home until he had to give it up because his "empathy made me weep with the families," was one of a dozen convicts brought from death row to be interviewed this afternoon.

The interviews took place in the maximum security building, which is guarded by savage dogs as well as by armed men, at the huge state prison farm 60 miles southwest of Jacksonville.

The interview room was on the floor above "Old Sparky," as the inmates refer to the electric chair. It is of sturdy oak, stained with the sweat from 195 men put to death in it between 1924 and May 12, 1964, the date of the state's last execution.

One inmate under death sentence received the news of the Court's action while in a booth with his family. Leslie Horton, sentenced to death for rape, received a visit from his family this morning and was in the office of a prison captain talking to them when a guard entered and said, "Can you stand some more good news today? The Supreme Court has just abolished the death penalty."

One of the prisoners interviewed was Dennis Whitney, 29, who killed seven persons when he was 16 years old. He has been awaiting execution for 12 years.

"Sure, I hope to hit the streets on parole some day," he said, "or I wouldn't be trying to stay alive."

But getting parole may be difficult. In January, the Florida legislature adopted a law providing that if the Supreme Court should overturn the death penalty no one under a death sentence could ever be paroled.

In Tallahassee, the state capital, this afternoon, L. L. Wainwright, the director of the Florida division of corrections, said that he planned to ask the Florida parole commission to consider paroles for all the death row inmates before the new law took effect Oct. 1.

He said that this law, combined with the court's decision, could produce a type of prisoner, who, having nothing to lose, might not hesitate to murder guards and other prisoners.

William Craig, 43, a Negro under the death sentence for having raped a white woman, said that society has no right to condemn a man to death.

"The death penalty is the most cruel thing on the face of the earth," he said, especially for rape."

Nor, he added, is it a deterrent. The thought that he might be sentenced to death never crossed his mind while he was stalking his victim, he said.

Of the 97 persons under death sentence, 71 were convicted for murder, 26 for rape. Sixty-five of the convicts are blacks, including the woman, and 32 are white.

One Negro under death sentence for rape, Robert Shuler, 32, said that the death penalty "has no place in our everyday society."

He said he has studied law for seven of his almost 12 years in prison and that if he ever won his freedom he would try to help others get out.

Shuler said that religion had been no solace to him and said he doubted that others found any comfort in it.

Both Shuler and Whitney were within hours of being executed on two separate occasions before being granted stays of execution.

Listing of the Nations Without Death Penalty

The following 37 countries have abolished or abandoned capital punishment, or have retained it only for exceptional crimes or wartime or martial law situations. The date of abolition, de facto or de jure, is given.

Argentina, 1922; Australia (Queensland, 1922; Federal Territory, 1945; New South Wales, 1955; Tasmania, 1968); Austria, 1968; Belgium, 1863 (a); Bolivia, 1961; Brazil, 1946 (b); Britain, 1965.

Canada, 1967 (b); Colombia, 1910; Costa Rica, 1880; Denmark, 1930 (b); Dominican Republic, 1924; Ecuador, 1897; Finland, 1949 (b).

West Germany, 1949; Honduras, 1957; Iceland, 1940; India (Travancore state, 1944); Israel, 1954 (b); Italy, 1944; Liechtenstein, 1798 (c); Luxembourg, 1821 (d).

Mexico (except 3 of 32 states), 1931-70; Manaco, 1962; Nepal, 1950; Netherlands, 1886 (Netherlands Antilles, 1957; Surinam, 1927); New Zealand, 1961; Nicaragua, 1892; Norway, 1905 (b).

Panama, 1915; Portugal, 1867; San Marino, 1848; Sweden, 1921 (b); Switzerland, 1942; Uruguay, 1907; Vatican City State, 1969; Venezuela, 1863.

a-Except for one soldier executed in 1918.

b-Except for wartime crimes, or exceptional crimes such as treason or collaboration with the Nazis.

c-De facto abolition; date is of last execution.

d-De facto abolition; there was one murderer executed in 1948 for war crimes.

Excerpts From Opinions on Death Penalty

Special to The New York Times

WASHINGTON, June 29—Following are excerpts from the opinions of the nine Supreme Court Justices in the 5-to-4 decision today outlawing the death penalty:

Concurring Opinions

By Mr. Justice White

I begin with what I consider a near truism: that the death penalty could so seldom be imposed that it would cease to be a credible deterrent or measurably to contribute to any other end of punishment in the criminal justice system.

It is perhaps true that no matter how infrequently those convicted of rape or murder are executed, the penalty so imposed is not disproportionate to the crime and those executed may deserve exactly what they received. It would also be clear that executed defendants are finally and completely incapacitated from again committing rape or murder or any other crime.

But when imposition of the penalty reaches a certain degree of infrequency, it would be very doubtful that any existing general need for retribution would be measurably satisfied. Nor could it be said with confidence that society's need for specific deterrence justifies death for so few when for so many in like circumstances life imprisonment or shorter prison terms are judged sufficient, or that community values are measurably reenforced by authorizing a penalty so rarely invoked.

Most important, a major goal of the criminal law—to deter others by punishing the convicted criminal — would not be substantially served where the penalty is so seldom invoked that it ceases to be the credible threat essential to influence the conduct of others.

By Mr. Justice Stewart

The death sentences now before us are the product of a legal system that brings them, I believe, within the very core of the Eighth Amendment's guarantee against cruel and unusual punishments, a guarantee applicable against the states through the 14th Amendment. Robinson v. California, 370 U.S. 660.

In the first place, it is clear that these sentences are "cruel" in the sense that they excessively go beyond, not in degree but in kind, the punishments that the state legislatures have determined to be necessary. Weems v. United States, 217 U.S. 349.

In the second place, it is equally clear that these sentences are "unusual" in the sense that the penalty of death is infrequently imposed for murder, and that its imposition for rape is extraordinarily rare. But I do not rest my conclusion upon these two propositions alone.

These sentences are cruel and unusual in the same way that being struck by lightning is cruel and unusual. For, of all the people convicted of rapes and murders in 1967 and 1968, many just as reprehensible as these, the petitioners are among a capriciously selected random handful upon whom the sentence of death has in fact been imposed.

I simply conclude that the Eighth and Fourteenth Amendments cannot tolerate the infliction of a sentence of death under legal systems that permit this unique penalty to be so wantonly and so freakishly imposed.

By Mr. Justice Douglas

In a nation committed to equal protection of the laws there is no permissible "caste" aspect of law enforcement. Yet we know that the discretion of judges and juries in imposing the death penalty enables the penalty to be selectively applied, feeding prejudices against the accused if he is poor and despised, poor and lacking political clout, or if he is a member of a suspect or unpopular minority, and saving those who by social position may be in a more protected position.

In ancient Hindu law a Brahmin was exempt from capital punishment. And in those days, "generally, in the law books, punishment increased in severity as social status diminished." We have, I fear, taken in practice the same position, partially as a result of making the death penalty discretionary and partially as a result of the ability of the rich to purchase the services of the most respected and most resourceful legal talent in the nation.

The high service rendered by the "cruel and unusual" punishment clause of the Eighth Amendment is to require legislatures to write penal laws that are evenhanded, nonselective, and nonarbitrary, and to require judges to see to it that general laws are not applied sparsely, selectively, and spottily to unpopular groups.

By Mr. Justice Marshall

At a time in our history when the streets of the nation's cities inspire fear and despair, rather than pride and hope, it is difficult to maintain objectivity and concern for our fellow citizens. But, the measure of a country's greatness is its ability to retain compassion in time of crisis.

No nation in the recorded history of man has a greater tradition of revering justice and fair treatment for all its citizens in times of turmoil, confusion and tension than ours. This is a country which stands tallest in troubled times, a country that clings to fundamental principles, cherishes its constitutional heritage, and rejects simple solutions that compromise the values which lie at the roots of our democratic system.

In striking down capital punishment, this Court does not malign our system of government. On the contrary, it pays homage to it. Only in a free society could right triumph in difficult times, and could civilization record its magnificent advancement.

In recognizing the humanity of our fellow beings, we pay ourselves the highest tribute. We achieve a major milestone in the long road up from barbarism and join the approximately 70 other jurisdictions in the world which celebrate their regard for civilization and humanity by shunning capital punishment.

By Mr. Justice Brennan

In sum, the punishment of death is inconsistent with . . . four principles: Death is an unusually severe and degrading punishment; there is a strong probability that it is inflicted arbitrarily; its rejection by contemporary society is virtually total, and there is no reason to believe that it serves any penal purpose more effectively than the less severe punishment of imprisonment. The function of these principles is to enable a court to determine whether a punishment comports with human dignity. Death, quite simply, does not.

Dissenting Opinions

By Mr. Chief Justice Burger, with whom Mr. Justice Blackmun, Mr. Justice Powell and Mr. Justice Rehnquist join.

Today the Court has not ruled that capital punishment is per se violative of the Eighth Amendment; nor has it ruled that the punishment is barred for any particular class or classes of crimes. The substantially similar concurring opinions of Mr. Justice Stewart and Mr. Justice White, which are necessary to support the judgment setting aside petitioners' sentences, stop short of reaching the ultimate question.

The actual scope of the Court's ruling, which I take to be embodied in these concurring opinions, is not entirely clear. This much, however, seems apparent: If the legislatures are to continue to authorize capital punishment for some crime, juries and judges can no longer be permitted to make the sentencing determination in the same manner they have in the past.

While I would not undertake to make a definitive statement as to the parameters of the Court's ruling, it is clear that if state legislatures and the Congress wish to maintain the availability of capital punishment, significant statutory changes will have to be made.

Since the two pivotal concurring opinions turn on the assumption that the punishment of death is now meted out in a random and unpredictable manner, legislative bodies may seek to bring their laws into compliance with the Court's ruling by providing standards for juries and judges to follow in determining the sentence in capital cases or by more narrowly defining the crimes for which the penalty is to be imposed. If such standards can be devised or the crimes more meticulously defined, the result cannot be detrimental.

Real change could clearly be brought about if legislatures provide mandatory death sentences in such a way as to deny juries the opportunity to bring in a verdict on a lesser charge; under such a system, the death sentence could only be avoided by a verdict of acquittal. If this is the only alternative that the legislatures can safely pursue under today's ruling, I would have preferred that the court opt for total abolition.

Since there is no majority of the Court on the ultimate issue presented in these cases, the future of capital punishment in this country has been left in an uncertain limbo.

By Mr. Justice Blackmun

Cases such as these provided for me an excruciating agony of the spirit. I yield to no one in the depth of my distaste, antipathy, and, indeed, abhorrence, for the death penalty, with all its aspects of physical distress and fear and of moral judgment exercised by finite minds. That distaste is buttressed by a belief that capital punishment serves no useful purpose that can be demonstrated.

Were I a legislator, I would vote against the death penalty for the policy reasons argued by counsel for the respective petitioners and expressed and adopted in the several opinions filed by the Justices who vote to reverse these convictions.

My problem, however, as I have indicated, is the suddenness of the Court's perception of progress in the human attitude since decisions of only a short while ago.

To reverse the judgments in these cases is, of course, the easy choice. It is easier to strike the balance in favor of life and against death. . . .

This, for me, is good argument, and it makes some sense. But it is good argument and it makes sense only in a legislative and executive way and not as a judicial expedient.

By Mr. Justice Rehnquist, with whom the Chief Justice, Mr. Justice Blackmun, and Mr. Justice Powell join.

The Court's judgment today strikes down a penalty that our nation's legislators have thought necessary since our country was founded. Whatever its precise rationale, today's holding necessarily brings into sharp relief the fundamental question of the role of judicial review in a democratic society. How can government by the elected representatives of the people co-exist with the power of the Federal judiciary, whose members are constitutionally insulated from responsiveness to the popular will, to declare invalid laws duly enacted by the popular branches of government?

By Mr. Justice Powell, with whom the Chief Justice, Mr. Justice Blackmun, and Mr. Justice Powell join.

It is important to keep in focus the enormity of the step undertaken by the Court today. Not only does it invalidate hundreds of state and Federal laws, it deprives those jurisdictions of the power to legislate with respect to capital punishment in the future, except in a manner consistent with the cloudily outlined views of those Justices who do not purport to undertake total abolition.

Nothing short of an amendment to the United States Constitution can reverse the Court's judgment. Meanwhile, all flexibility is foreclosed. The normal democratic process, as well as the opportunities for the several states to respond to the will of their people expressed through ballot referenda (as in Massachusetts, Illinois, and Colorado), is now shut off.

The sobering disadvantage of constitutional adjudication of this magnitude is the universality and performance of the judgment. The enduring merit of legislative action is its responsiveness to the democratic process, and to revision and change: mistaken judgments may be corrected and refinements perfected.

Supreme Court Bars Death Penalty as Now Imposed

Continued From Page 1, Col. 8

those convicted of certain crimes.

In any event, Chief Justice Burger said, Congress and the state legislatures will be required to "make a thorough reevaluation of the entire subject of capital punishment," including a serious inquiry into whether it serves as a deterrent.

All four dissenters also filed separate opinions, in a judicial outpouring that required 243 pages to express the view of all nine Justices.

The gist of the dissenters' position was that the Eighth Amendment has been in effect for 191 years and has not, until today, been held to rule out executions. They charged that the majority had usurped the prerogative of the legislatures in the decision today.

Justice Lewis F. Powell Jr. said the action would have a "shattering effect" upon the rule that prior decisions should be followed, as well as on the principles of "Federalism, judicial restraint, and — most importantly — separation of powers."

Decision in California

Justice Harry A. Blackmun implied strongly that the majority had been "propelled toward its result" to stroke down capital punishment by the recent decision of the Supreme Court of California, which outlawed executions under the state constitution's prohibition against "cruel or unusual" punishments.

Justice Blackmun added an unusually personal insight by saying that while he had an "abhorrence" of capital punishment he felt only the legislatures could abolish it.

Justice William H. Rehnquist's dissent said the decision had underscored a fundamental question about the Supreme Court's role in reviewing the nation's laws. While overreaching legislatures may encroach upon individual rights, he said, an overreaching Supreme Court can "sacrifice the equally important right of the people to govern themselves."

The decision today culminated a campaign initiated by the N.A.A.C.P. Legal Defense and Educational Fund, Inc., five years ago, when the liberal coloration of the Warren Court made success appear much more likely than it had been presumed to be before the present Court.

Although the Supreme Court had never directly ruled that the death penalty was not cruel and unusual punishment, this was because it had been assumed throughout most of the country's history that it was not. The Court had said so, in passing, without actually making a ruling to that effect.

In his 50-page concurring opinion today, Justice William J. Brennan Jr. traced the evolution of the "cruel and unusual" punishment concept, and pointed out that the Supreme Court has traditionally considered it a growing concept, which develops with the changing mores of the times.

Therefore, even though the framers of the Bill of Rights did not intend to outlaw executions when they adopted the Eighth Amendment, Justice Brennan asserted that present conditions bring the death penalty within the prohibition.

His reasoning was that the penalty was unusually severe and degrading, it appeared to be arbitrarily imposed. It was widely condemned by contemporary society, and it might be no better a deterrent than prison.

Justice Thurgood Marshall expressed similar arguments, adding that the penalty was "morally unacceptable," if for no other reason than that it most frequently fell upon blacks, "the poor, the ignorant, and the underprivileged members of society."

Justice Douglas asserted that it is "implicit" in the ban on cruel and unusual punishment that executions cannot be imposed indiscriminately. Because it is the poor and minority groups that most ofen are executed, he concluded, capital punishment violates the 14th Amendment's guarantee of equal protection of the laws, as well as the Eighth Amendment.

Prior to today's decision, 11 state legislatures had abolished capital punishment completely, or with such narrow exceptions as the murder of a prison guard by a life convict. Thirty-nine states, the District of Columbia and the Federal Government had laws that authorized executions for various crimes.

The defendants before the Court today were William Henry Furman, sentenced to death for a robbery-murder in Georgia and Lucius Jackson Jr. of Georgia, and Elmer Branch of Texas, both condemned to death for rape.

Anthony G. Amsterdam, a professor of law at Stanford University, and Jack Greenberg of New York argued the cases for the legal defense fund. Melvyn C. Bruder of Dallas also argued against the death penalty.

The prosecutors who argued the other side were Mrs. Dorothy T. Beasley, Assistant Attorney General of Georgia, and Prof. Charles Alan Wright of the University of Texas.

In another decision the Court held, 8 to 1, that a parolee who has been returned to prison for violation of parole must be given a prompt hearing, with notice of the reasons for the revocation and an opportunity to cross-examine witnesses against him.

Justice Douglas dissented, saying that a parolee should not be returned to prison until after his hearing. He also gave his answer to a point that the Court left open, saying he believes a parolee should have counsel furnished by the state, if necessary, at such a hearing.

Illinois Slate Led by Daley Is Upheld by Circuit Court

CHICAGO, June 29 (AP)—A Circuit Court judge ruled today that challengers to Mayor Richard J. Daley and 58 other uncommitted delegates to the Democratic National Convention could not be seated in place of the Daley group.

Judge Donald J. O'Brien issued a temporary restraining order that will be in effect until next Wednesday.

The Democratic party's Credentials Committee is scheduled to rule tomorrow in Washington on the challenge brought by independent Democrats.

Nixon Backs Death for Kidnappers, Hijackers

Continued From Page 1, Col. 7

the Treasury John B. Connally had done a "fine job" and would be given other temporary missions in the future, but he declined to say what they might be.

¶He expressed optimism on the economy, although he was still dissatisfied with the current level of unemployment, and he said his Administrattion was examining new steps that might be taken.

On the question of the Vice President, the President offered only answers that left his listeners more uncertain than before.

At one point he said that, although Vice President Agnew had done a good job, he would not announce his own choice of a running-mate in the near future. Instead, he promised an announcement before the Republican National Convention, which begins Aug. 21.

Yet at another point he recalled that he had told an interveiwer that he "did not believe breaking up a winning team was a good idea."

And at another point, referring to Mr. Connally, he said, "I almost said Vice President Connally."

On the pressures for legislation restricting the possession of handguns as well as legislation now in Congress, he said he had "always thought" there should be a Federal law defining limitations.

But he said the problem was to write legislation that would define those limitations clearly enough to rule out only specific firearms. Citing the cheap, snubnosed "Saturday night specials," he said that if Congress could pass a law specifically outlawing those handguns, he would sign it.

On the economic front, Mr. Nixon said that the country was now making good strides, citing increases in the number of jobs and improvements in real spendable income.

"On the other hand," he said, "I'm not a bit satisfied with the fact that unemployment is at 5.9 per cent, and we're continuing to explore other means of trying to bring it down faster."

Majority Verdicts Backed

STATELINE, Nev., June 29 (UPI)—A gathering of the nation's attorneys general ended yesterday with a call for states to repeal laws that require mandatory unanimous verdicts in noncapital criminal cases.

"All the News That's Fit to Print"

The New York Times

LATE CITY EDITION

Weather: Sunny and milder today; fair and mild tonight, tomorrow. Temp. range: today 58-77; Tuesday 57-74. Temp.-Hum. Index yesterday 67. Full U.S. report on Page 90.

VOL. CXXI . . . No. 41,864 | NEW YORK, WEDNESDAY, SEPTEMBER 6, 1972 | 15 CENTS

9 ISRAELIS ON OLYMPIC TEAM KILLED WITH 4 ARAB CAPTORS AS POLICE FIGHT BAND THAT DISRUPTED MUNICH GAMES

United Press International

A copter making a test run before picking up Arabs involved in the attack on Israelis. At rear is the Olympic Tower. Sign in German says, "Olympic Village, Gate 6."

A 23-HOUR DRAMA

2 Others Are Slain in Their Quarters in Guerrilla Raid

By DAVID BINDER

Special to The New York Times

MUNICH, West Germany, Wednesday, Sept. 6—Eleven members of Israel's Olympic team and four Arab terrorists were killed yesterday in a 23-hour drama that began with an invasion of the Olympic Village by the Arabs. It ended in a shootout at a military airport some 15 miles away as the Arabs were preparing to fly to Cairo with their Israeli hostages.

The first two Israelis were killed early yesterday morning when Arab commandos, armed with automatic rifles, broke into the quarters of the Israeli team and seized nine others as hostages. The hostages were killed in the airport shootout between the Arabs and German policemen and soldiers.

The bloodshed brought the suspension of the Olympic Games and there was doubt if they would be resumed. Willi Daume, president of the West German Organizing Committee, announced early today that he would ask the International Olympic Committee to meet tomorrow to decide whether they should continue.

Policeman Killed

In addition to the slain Israelis and Arabs, a German policeman was killed and a helicopter pilot was critically wounded. Three Arabs were wounded.

There were some reports that two of the hostages said to have been killed might still be alive. "It is a dim hope," said Dr. Bruno Merk, the Interior Minister of Bavaria, "but I am skeptical on this point."

The bloodbath at the airport that ended at 1 A.M. today, came after long hours of negotiation between German and Arabs at the Israeli quarters in the Olympic Village where the Arabs demanded the release of 200 Arab commandos imprisoned in Israel.

Finally the West German armed forces supplied three helicopters to transport the Arabs and their Israeli hostages to the airport at Fürstenfeldbruck. From there all were to be flown to Cairo.

A Boeing-707 provided by the Lufthansa German Airlines was waiting.

Two of the terrorists, carrying their automatic rifles, walked about 170 yards from the helicopters to the plane. And then they started back to pick up the other Arabs and the hostages.

Positions Cited

As the Arabs were returning, German sharpshooters reportedly opened fire from the darkness beyond the pools of light at the airport. The Arabs returned fire.

The torment of the entire event was heightened by confusion created in the public mind by contradictory reports from German and Olympic officials after the gunfire erupted at the airport.

Dr. Merk, in a press conference at 3 o'clock this morning said:

"In this situation our task and goal to free the hostages was made more difficult by the lack of agreement from Israel to free prisoners or to get guarantees from the Arabs not to take action against the hos-

Continued on Page 18, Column 1

MRS. MEIR SPEAKS

A Hushed Parliament Hears Her Assail 'Lunatic Acts'

By TERENCE SMITH

Special to The New York Times

JERUSALEM, Sept. 5—Her voice heavy and trembling with emotion, Premier Golda Meir today denounced "these lunatic acts of terrorism, abduction and blackmail, which tear asunder the web of international life."

Speaking to a hushed and somber parliament before the fate of the Israeli hostages held captive in Munich was known, she said, "It is inconceivable that the Olympic events should continue as long as our citizens are under the threat of being murdered in the Olympic Village."

She called on all the nations participating in the Olympics to do "whatever is necessary" to rescue the nine Israelis taken hostage by Arab guerrillas in an early-morning attack in which two other Israelis were killed.

[Official sources in Jerusalem said early Wednesday that the Cabinet would meet later in the morning and that there would be no statement on the deaths of the hostages until then.]

Cabinet Still Firm

Although she was not explicit, Mrs. Meir left the impression that Israel would continue to refuse the guerrillas' demands for the release of 200 Palestinian commandos held in this country. Cabinet sources said the Government remained committed to its hard-line policy of neither dealing with nor making concessions to the guerrillas.

Most Israelis seemed stunned by the news of the bizarre attack on the Israeli athletes, which was first reported here on a radio broadcast at 9 A.M. (3 A.M. Tuesday, New York time). Although Israeli citizens traveling abroad have been attacked by Palestinian guerrillas before, the Olympics seemed to many an unlikely setting.

"The games were going so well," one Jerusalem news dealer said, "and now this."

In parliament, where the members had gathered in an extraordinary session to confirm the Justice Minister, the attack was the sole topic of conversation.

Cabinet Ministers and members of parliament sat in the building's modern, sun-washed dining room waiting for additional news from Munich. Each hour on the hour, the large room grew silent and the ministers gathered four deep around a radio as the Israeli radio summarized the developments.

The tension was greatest at

Continued on Page 20, Column 2

West German policemen talking with a spokesman, right, for Arabs who invaded Israeli quarters at Olympic Village

Associated Press

A West German Army ambulance passing through the heavily guarded gate at the military airfield in Fürstenfeldbruck, near Munich, after the commandos and the hostages landed in three helicopters.

752 Air-Conditioned Cars Ordered for City Subways

By EDWARD RANZAL

Mayor Lindsay announced yesterday that 752 new air-conditioned subway cars had been ordered for $210.5-million. He said the contract was the largest ever signed in the country for the purchase of passenger railroad cars.

The first group of cars, which will be manufactured by the Pullman - Standard Company, are to be delivered by 1973.

The cars will provide a quieter ride than present equipment, according to Dr. William J. Ronan, chairman of the Metropolitan Transportation Authority.

The new equipment, which will be used on the IND and BMT lines, will enable the authority to phase out more than 1,200 pre-World War II cars, which are smaller than the new ones. A study is being made, Dr. Ronan said, to produce an air-conditioned unit that can be used in cars in the smaller tunnels of the IRT system.

20% of Fleet by '75

Each car will cost more than $273,000. The city will provide one-third of the total funds—the money has been provided in the city's 1972-73 capital budget—and the Federal Urban Mass Transportation Administration will supply the rest.

By 1975 more than 20 per cent of the city's fleet of nearly 7,000 subway cars will consist of new air-conditioned cars.

The first order under the contract will be for 454 cars at a cost of $127.4-million. Some of them will be delivered in

Continued on Page 91, Column 2

Berrigan and a Nun Get Prison Terms In Letter Smuggling

By JOHN KIFNER

Special to The New York Times

HARRISBURG, Pa., Sept. 5—The Rev. Philip F. Berrigan—cleared of charges that he led a plot to kidnap President Nixon's adviser on national security affairs, Henry A. Kissinger—was sentenced in Federal District Court here today to four concurrent two-year terms for smuggling letters out of the Lewisburg Penitentiary.

Sister Elizabeth McAlister, also cleared of the plot charges, was sentenced to one year in jail and three years' probation for smuggling letters.

Moments after the sentences were announced, Government attorneys moved to dismiss the first three substantive counts of their indictment, confirming that the Justice Department would not seek a retrial of the controversial "Harrisburg Seven" case.

The Government charged Father Berrigan, Sister Elizabeth, two other Roman Catholic priests, a former priest, a former nun and a Pakistani scholar with conspiracy to kidnap Mr. Kissinger as ransom to force a halt to the bombing in Viet-

Continued on Page 16, Column 1

PARLEY REJECTS HIJACKING TREATY

U.S.-Canadian Project for Penalizing Nations Aiding Air Pirates Rebuffed

By ROBERT LINDSEY

Special to The New York Times

WASHINGTON, Sept. 5—Delegates to a 17-nation conference here rejected today United States-Canadian efforts to negotiate an international antihijacking treaty based on a draft proposed by the two nations.

The move for nonacceptance was led by France and Britain and supported by the Soviet Union and Egypt.

Faced with what appeared to be certain defeat of the proposed treaty if it came to a vote, the two North American nations acquiesced in a French proposal to start writing a new treaty from scratch, after debates on what "principles" should be included.

The delegates have eight working days left before the conference is scheduled to end.

Today's rejection was a significant setback for the United

Continued on Page 91, Column 2

Nixon Tightens Security In U.S. Against 'Outlaws'

By TAD SZULC

Special to The New York Times

WASHINGTON, Sept. 5—President Nixon said today that "extra security measures" would be taken in the United States to protect American citizens as well as visiting Israelis from possible attacks by Palestinian guerrillas.

Mr. Nixon, speaking to newsmen in San Francisco, left it unclear, however, whether he meant that this new protection would cover prominent American Jews or only those whom he described as "Americans of Israeli background, American citizens."

Speaking before the gunfight at a military airport in Munich, in which the Israeli hostages were killed, Mr. Nixon discussed the capture of Israeli Olympic team members by Palestinian guerrillas and the slaying of two Israelis. He said:

"Since we are dealing with international outlaws who are unpredictable, we have to take extra security measures to protect those who might be the targets of this kind of activity in the future. That might include Americans of Israeli background, American citizens."

Late tonight, after word was received in Washington of the death of the Israeli hostages and West German policemen, Secretary of State William P. Rogers issued this statement on behalf of the Administration:

"There are no words which can fully express our reaction to today's tragedy at the Olympic Games. I know I speak for all Americans in extending the deepest sympathies of the

Continued on Page 18, Column 4

Reports First Said Israelis Were Safe

Contradictory reports last night about the fate of the Israeli hostages seized by Arab terrorists in the Olympic Village threw the public into confusion all over the world.

Throughout the day, as the tragedy in Munich unfolded, millions of viewers throughout the world watched on live television, which employed circuits that had been intended for the Games. But in the evening, when the events reached their climax, viewers could get no definitive word for hours on how the hostages fared.

At first the West German Government's official spokesman, Conrad Ahlers, announced

Continued on Page 20, Column 1

GAMES SUSPENDED; RITES IN ARENA SET

Halt Is the First Since 1896, When the Classic Resumed —Egypt Team in Forfeit

By NEIL AMDUR

Special to The New York Times

MUNICH, West Germany, Wednesday, Sept. 6 — The Olympic Games were suspended yesterday for the first time since competition in the modern era began in 1896.

Late-afternoon and evening events were called off in the wake of an attack staged by Arab guerrillas before dawn on the Olympic Village in which two Israelis were killed and nine others taken hostage. The hostages were later killed.

After the attack, Mark Spitz, the American swimmer who won seven gold medals at the Munich Olympics and who is Jewish, flew hurriedly to London on his way back to the United States. There were fears before his departure that he too might become a victim. [Page 20.]

The announcement of the suspension, made by the International Olympic Committee, also said that a memorial service would be held for the victims

Continued on Page 18, Column 7

Elizabeth City Hall Under Investigation

By RONALD SULLIVAN

Special to The New York Times

TRENTON, Sept. 5—Law enforcement authorities reported here today that the administration of Mayor Thomas J. Dunn of Elizabeth was the target of a Union County grand jury investigation of alleged municipal corruption.

Mayor Dunn, a Democrat running for a third term, said in an interview that he had "no knowledge of any investigation involving me or my administration." But he said he volunteered last spring to go before a Union County grand jury.

According to official sources, the grand jury is investigating charges of payoffs and kickbacks involving city officials, contracts and businessmen. City license officials have already been subpoenaed, as have a number of city records and contracts.

Karl Asch, the county prosecutor, refused to comment on the nature of the reported investigation. He did say his staff had been instructed to seek indictments before the Nov. 7 elections.

Last week two of Mr. Dunn's three mayoral opponents were indicted in separate matters by a Union County grand jury.

Matthew J. Nilsen, a Republican freeholder in the county, was indicted on charges of atrocious assault in August in a case involving an alleged extortion.

In the other indictment, Michael J. DeMartino, a Democratic City Councilman in Elizabeth, was charged with misconduct in office in a case involving a $3,000 bribe in 1968.

Mayor Dunn recently endorsed President Nixon for reelection. Political observers in Union County noted that the indictments of two of his opponents were sought by a Republican prosecutor, and were seen as aiding the Mayor's re-election chances.

However, Mr. Asch, who has obtained indictments against prominent Union County political figures in recent months, contended today that his anticorruption drive was "absolutely nonpolitical" and that the investigation of the Dunn

Continued on Page 40, Column 6

NEWS INDEX

9 Israelis on Olympic Team Slain With 4 Arabs as German Police Fight Raiders

2 Other Athletes Killed In Rooms During Attack

Continued From Page 1, Col. 8

tages."

He said the Federal Minister of the Interior, Hans-Dietrich Genscher, had offered to substitute himself and other German officials for the Israeli hostages. This, and money, was rejected by the Arabs.

How the hostages were killed was still in doubt. One theory was that an Arab threw a grenade into a helicopter in which some or all of the hostages were bound hand and foot.

Partial explanation of how the Arabs knew so much about the Israeli compound in the Olympic Village came from Dr. Merk. He said that at least one of the terrorists was an official employe in the village and that there was reason to believe some of his confederates had also obtain accreditation.

The idea of trying to liberate the hostages at the Olympic Village was rejected, Dr. Merk said, because it could have "involved athletes from other nations" living nearby.

Hostages Agreed to Flight

He said that though the hostages had acquiesced to the Arab insistence on flying to Cairo "we felt that would have been a certain death sentence for the hostages."

Before the bloody end, tense negotiations had gone on all day yesterday between Germans and the commandos. The games were halted and the German police, wearing bullet-proof vests beneath track suits, had closed in on the Olympic Village building invaded by the Arabs.

Egyptian athletes forfeited a basketball game in protest against the commando action, which was denounced by the United Nations Secretary General, Kurt Waldheim, by President Nixon and by his Democratic Presidential rival, Senator George McGovern.

Shortly before the negotiations broke off at the Olympic Village, the police began clearing a path around the area and the commandos and their hostages left by bus. The bus halted at the main exit and one Arab left it to inspect the helicopters.

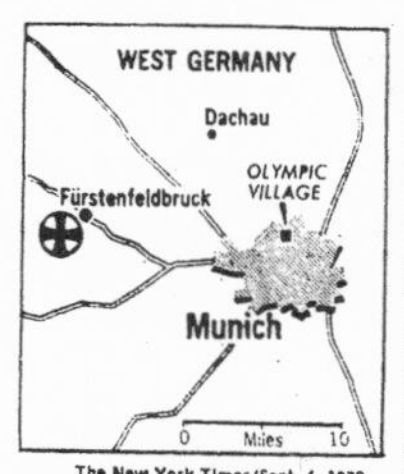

Hostages were taken to a military airfield at Fürstenfeldbruck (cross).

The bloody interlude in the Olympic games, international symbol of peace and sportsmanship, began about 4 A.M. yesterday when the Arabs climbed a fence into the lightly guarded compound that is housing more than 10,000 athletes.

About an hour later, according to witnesses, the commandos broke into the three-story structure where 26 Israelis were staying.

As they tried to rush the Israelis, they were halted at the door by a coach. He held the door against them, shouting to other athletes to flee.

There was confusion later about which of the two slain Israelis had sounded the alarm. One was identified as Joseph Romano, a weight-lifting coach. The other was Moshe Weinberg, a wrestling coach, and former wrestling champion of Israel.

But there was no doubt about what the man had done. Recalling the episode later, Tuvia Sokolsky, a weight-lifting coach, said, with traces of fear in his eyes and voice:

"I heard this shout: 'Boys get out!' I jumped to my feet and locked the door. My room is opposite the apartment entrance and I saw a strange picture—one of the men on the team trying to keep the door shut.

"The door was already open and he was using all his strength to keep the door closed. He kept shouting to us to get out and I think he saved my life. Because of the warning, I was able to escape from the room."

One of the men who escaped, Gud Psabari, a wrestler, dashed out in a hail of bullets, dodging behind pillars and around corners. Mr. Psabari said later "I think I ran faster than Valery Borzov. I think I broke the record for the dash."

Negotiations Begin

The Israeli dormitory, at 31 Connolly Street, is peculiarly inaccessible, tucked inside a "V" of larger buidings. While the commandos standing on the white-paneled balconies of the slate-gray building were exposed to police sharpshooters posted on the roof, the police still would have difficulty getting at the building rapidly in large numbers.

Chancellor Willy Brandt expressed his country's profound shock and outrage over the incident, as did hosts of other German politicians. There had been a feeling of helplessness among those who stood near the Israeli dormitory under a cloudless sky all day.

But the Israelis inside, either unable to escape, or determined to fight, grabbed up knives and fought against the guns of their assailants.

Debate Over Suspension

Once the fighting had ended, the commandos made known their demands and the bargaining began with the West Germans. Participating in the negotiations was an Olympic Games stewardess who is fluent in Arabic. However, the leader of the commandos knew German, according to officials.

Repeated efforts to gain the release of the hostages were rejected by the Arabs.

One effort at mediation by a representative of the Arab League who flew in from Bonn was coldly rebuffed by the raiders.

Before the games were ordered suspended, the feeling in the Olympic Village about whether they should be halted was sharply divided. Many Germans, Italians and French said they should be stopped altogether. But some Israelis said this would be giving in to blackmail and that the program should go on.

Shortly after 9 P.M. yesterday a West German negotiating team succeeded in persuading the terrorists to move out of the Israeli dormitory with their hostages. Security authorities cleared a path under the large dormitory housing Canadians and Hungarians, on through the Square of Nations and beyond the block where Americans are quartered to a field where helicopters were waiting.

The transfer was invisible to most of the people waiting to see what was happening — through underground passageways and along paths blocked from view by guards. It took place at about 10 P.M., roughly 17 hours after the attack had started.

The convoy, in which the Israeli hostages were held with their hands bound under guard by the Arabs, went to a helicopter pad set up for the move. The Arabs and their hostages then were flown to the airport.

Hans-Dietrich Genscher, second from left, West Germany's Interior Minister, negotiating with an Arab who gestures to one of his confederates in the window, upper right. Offers, including ransom, were rejected.

The small apartment block at center is the one in which the Arabs attacked Israelis in Olympic Village

United Press International

Games Are Suspended; Service in Arena Is Set

Continued From Page 1, Col. 7

at 10 o'clock this morning in the 80,000-seat Olympic Stadium.

Early today it was announced that the games would resume after the memorial service. But that announcement came before it was learned that all nine hostages had died. [Informed of the death toll, Maurice Herzog, one of the French members of the International Olympic Committee, said, as quoted by Agence France-Presse, "It puts doubt on the resumption of the games."]

Before the suspension went into effect yesterday, competition had gone on in 11 of the 22 sports on the Olympic program, as Avery Brundage, the retiring president of the International Olympic Committee, had first announced that the games would be held despite the shootings. Athletes competed in the morning and part of the afternoon even as the hostages were being held in the Israeli quarters by the guerrillas.

The attack drew expressions of shock, dismay and anger from many athletes, officials and visitors around the Olympic Village.

"As a human being and a Jew, I am shocked and saddened by the outrageous act," Mark Spitz said at a news conference.

"The Olympic peace was broken by a murderous attack by criminal terrorists," the International Olympic Committee said in a statement made public during the afternoon by Mr. Brundage and Willi Daume, president of the West German Olympic Organizing Committee. "The entire civilized world condemns this barbaric act with disgust."

The statement continued:

"The International Olympic Committee and the [West German] Olympic Committee will participate, together with the Olympic participants, in a memorial service for the victims tomorrow, Wednesday, at 10 o'clock in the Olympic Stadium. This service should make clear the Olympic idea is stronger than terror and violence."

Egyptian Team ir Forfeit

Reacting to the attack before the suspension was announced, the Egyptian basketball team forfeited a game it had been scheduled to play, and there were reports that the entire Egyptian delegation had decided to return home.

"They were afraid for their lives," said Dr. R. William Jones, secretary general of the Federation of International Basketball Associations.

[Later, the head of the Egyptian delegation denied any intention of pulling out of the Olympics, Agence France-Presse reported, and it was announced that the delegation would attend the memorial ceremony tomorrow.]

Sentiment appeared divided on whether the committee should have suspended competition. Many athletes and officials, with the memory of the recent Rhodesian dispute still fresh in their minds, felt that the committee should not have buckled to protest-politics.

The committee had reversed its decision to admit the Rhodesian team before the start of the games, after a bloc of black African nations had threatened to withdraw if the Rhodesians were allowed to compete.

"Keeping the games going is about the only thing that can beat something like this," said Don Wise of Levittown, Pa., a member of the American delegation.

Werner Dittmer, a cameraman from Cologne, disagreed and said that the games should be stopped as a symbol of concern to the world.

"I don't think it's a gesture of giving in," added Mr. Dittmer. "It's a demonstration to the world, just as the Arabs have demonstrated today with their terrorism."

Germans Concerned

Mr. Dittmer, along with many German athletes and officials, expressed concern that the shootings would bring more cries of condemnation against their country, just when Germany seemed to have made significant strides in living down her past before the world.

One local radio station canceled scheduled melodies to play the theme music from the movie "Exodus," along with other Israeli songs.

By coincidence, the commando attack occurred on one of the lighter days of sports activity during the two-week international competition, although thousands of curiosity-seekers still lined the grassy areas outside the fence-enclosed Olympic Village for a glimpse of the mood among the 10,000 athletes or of the building where the guerrillas were holed up during the day with their hostages.

"The feeling is very tense in the village," said Steve Evanoff, chief official for the United States wrestling team. "A lot of Americans realize how closely allied they are with the Israelis, and how it could have just as easily been them."

Mr. Evanoff termed the terrorism "a disgrace." "Now everybody's using the games as a political means to an end," he added.

Several groups of spectators carried signs protesting the violence. One read: "Arab terrorists: You can only lose by killing."

Today's memorial service will be the second attended recently by many members of the Israeli team. Before the games began, they had gone to Dachau, 20 miles from here and site of a World War II Nazi concentration camp, for a service.

"It's so terrible, just horrible," said Heinz Gürtler, a spectator who came from Hamburg to watch today's boxing matches and several other events that were suspended. "I think the Olympic freedom is crushed. First, we had Rhodesia, now the second big issue. This is so, so sad for the Olympics, for the athletes, for Germany."

Nixon Tightens Security in U.S. Against 'International Outlaws'

Continued From Page 1, Col. 6

United States to the families of those, Israelis and Germans alike, who have died because of this appalling, senseless deed."

This morning, before leaving the Western White House at San Clemente, Calif., for San Francisco, President Nixon telephoned Premier Golda Meir of Israel in Jerusalem to assure her of "all possible assistance" by the United States in seeking to obtain the release of the Israeli-team members who had been taken hostage.

'Shock and Horror'

His call was made during the tense hours when the Israeli hostages were held by the Palestinians at the Olympic Village in Munich, before the airport shoot-out.

During the seven-minute telephone conversation, the President conveyed to Mrs. Meir "my shock and horror at the news of the murderous act at the Olympic Village this morning."

He said that he had instructed Secretary Rogers and the United States Embassy in Bonn to "lend all possible assistance" to prevent "further loss of life" and obtain "the release of the hostages."

The President also told Mrs. Meir that the United States would take special measures to protect Israelis traveling in this country.

He said that the United States Government "would try to do everything we could with regard to groups of Israeli citizens traveling in the United States to see that, where there is any information at all with regard to a possible attempt of this sort, that adequate security measures are taken."

Officials here, however, were unable to say immediately what those measures would be and how the Administration proposed to guard the large numbers of Israeli citizens who come to the United States.

At the State Department, Secretary Rogers telephoned the Israeli Ambassador, Itzhak Rabin, who was traveling in California, to convey the concern of the United States Government.

During the day, according to State Department officials, United States ambassadors in the Arab countries with which the United States maintains diplomatic relations and in other friendly capitals were instructed to seek support for the release of the Israeli hostages.

The Administration also communicated to the International Olympic Committee its view that, as requested by Israel, the Munich games should not be resumed until the hostages were freed.

President Nixon, in his San Francisco conversation with newsmen, said that while guerrilla attacks were "more likely to be directed against Israeli citizens — because what they want to do is to get leverage with the Israeli Government with regard to people held by the Israeli Government—we are not taking any chances in doing everything we can to protect our own citizens."

In New York, Mayor Lindsay said police security had been increased at Israeli and Arab consulates in the city. [Page 19.]

White House sources in Washington could not immediately clarify the meaning of the President's remarks on security measures because Mr. Nixon boarded his aircraft for the return flight to Washington shortly after talking with the newsmen.

The President reached Washington late tonight. His plane landed at Andrews Air Force base and he was taken by helicopter immediately to the White House.

At the State Department, Charles W. Bray 3d, the department spokesman, urged those who had supported Palestinian guerrillas in the past to repudiate them and to see to it that the aid "they may receive be dried up," so that the commandos "come to understand that they are outlaws, brigands, murderers and an intolerable affront to human society."

The Munich incident had immediate repercussions in Congress, where speeches condemning the guerrillas were made both in the Senate and the House of Representatives, and among candidates on the campaign trail.

Senator George McGovern, the Democratic Presidential candidate, said in a statement in Portland, Ore.: "I am horrified, as I think all Americans are, by this senseless act of terrorism."

"Deliberate destruction of innocent noncombatants is an outrage by any standard of decency for humanity," he said. "The Arab terrorists have compounded the tragedy by choosing the Olympic Games as the site of their crime."

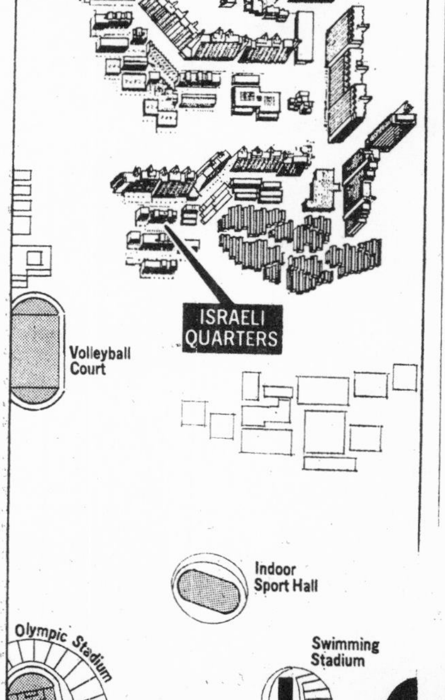

The New York Times/Sept. 6, 1972

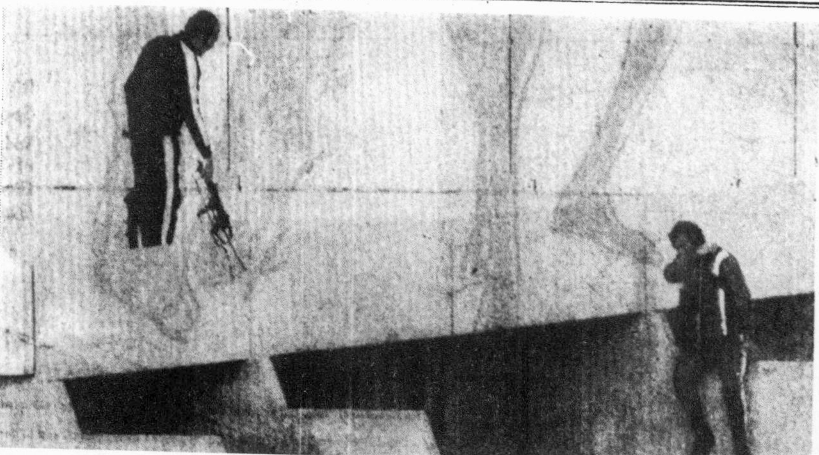

United Press International

Munich policemen, wearing athletic attire and armed with automatic weapons, taking up positions outside the apartments where the Israelis were held. They stayed during part of the negotiations between officials and Arabs.

Associated Press

One of the Arabs in the attack, in a ski mask, leans from the balcony of the building housing the Israelis.

"All the News That's Fit to Print"

The New York Times

LATE CITY EDITION

Weather: Partly sunny, mild today; fair tonight. Sunny, mild tomorrow. Temp. range: today 45-59; Monday 35-54. Full U.S. report on Page 76.

VOL. CXXII . No. 42,003

NEW YORK, TUESDAY, JANUARY 23, 1973

15 CENTS

LYNDON JOHNSON, 36TH PRESIDENT, IS DEAD; WAS ARCHITECT OF 'GREAT SOCIETY' PROGRAM

High Court Rules Abortions Legal the First 3 Months

State Bans Ruled Out Until Last 10 Weeks

National Guidelines Set by 7-to-2 Vote

By WARREN WEAVER Jr.

Special to The New York Times

WASHINGTON, Jan. 22 — The Supreme Court overruled today all state laws that prohibit or restrict a woman's right to obtain an abortion during her first three months of pregnancy. The vote was 7 to 2.

In a historic resolution of a fiercely controversial issue, the Court drafted a new set of

Excerpts from opinion and dissent are on Page 20.

national guidelines that will result in broadly liberalized anti-abortion laws in 46 states but will not abolish restrictions altogether.

Establishing an unusually detailed timetable for the relative legal rights of pregnant women and the states that would control their acts, the majority specified the following:

¶For the first three months of pregnancy the decision to have an abortion lies with the woman and her doctor, and the state's interest in her welfare is not "compelling" enough to warrant any interference.

¶For the next six months of pregnancy a state may "regulate the abortion procedure in ways that are reasonably related to maternal health," such as licensing and regulating the persons and facilities involved.

¶For the last 10 weeks of pregnancy, the period during which the fetus is judged to be capable of surviving if born, any state may prohibit

Continued on Page 20, Column 5

Cardinals Shocked —Reaction Mixed

By LAWRENCE VAN GELDER

Reaction to the Supreme Court decision on abortion fragmented yesterday along predictable lines, as leaders of the Roman Catholic Church assailed the ruling while birth control and women's rights activists praised it.

In the forefront of Catholic reaction were Cardinal Cooke of New York and Cardinal Krol of Philadelphia, who is also

Statements by Cooke and Krol appear on Page 20.

the president of the National Conference of Catholic Bishops.

Cardinal Cooke issued a statement calling the Court's action yesterday "shocking" and "horrifying." Cardinal Krol called the decision "an unspeakable tragedy for this nation."

But William Baird, a crusader for birth control and abortion, called the decision "a triumph" that culminated a long struggle.

"I'm delighted to see that our position—that women have the right to control their own bodies—has been vindicated," he said.

Dr. Alan F. Guttmacher, president of the Planned Parenthood Federation of America, called the decision "a wise and courageous stroke for the right to privacy, and for the protection of a woman's physical and emotional health."

"By this act," he said, "hundreds of thousands of American women every year will be

Continued on Page 20, Column 1

Ruling Seems to Forestall Abortion Debate in Albany

By WILLIAM E. FARRELL

Special to The New York Times

ALBANY, Jan. 22—The United States Supreme Court's abortion decision today appeared to quash the hopes of Right to Life and other anti-abortion groups for a full-scale debate in the Legislature again this year on repealing the state's liberalized abortion law.

"No way," replied Assemblyman Constance E. Cook, a Republican of Ithaca and a sponsor of the liberalized abortion law, when asked if the issue of restoring the old state statute would be seriously discussed again.

The liberalized state law permits a woman to have an abortion on demand until the 24th week of pregnancy. The old law permitted abortions only when a woman's life was in jeopardy.

Rendered 'Useless'

The Supreme Court's 7-to-2 ruling, Mrs. Cook said, rendered efforts by antiabortion lobbyists to force it to the floors of the Senate and Assembly "a useless show of strength."

Similarly, Assembly Speaker Perry B. Duryea, Republican of Montauk, said he felt it would be "futile" to bring repeal legislation up for debate again.

Well-organized opponents of the liberalized abortion law succeeded in having it repealed in both houses last year despite a pledge by Governor Rockefeller that he would veto a repeal measure. The Governor kept his promise.

Mr. Rockefeller, who did not comment on the court decision today pending a review of it by his legal staff, reaffirmed that he would again veto a repeal measure this year, but the antiabortion groups were undaunted.

Today, the comments of abortion opponents contained some of the emotional comments that the issue has always elicited here.

From his newly opened lobbying office near the Capitol, Edward J. Golden, chairman of the New York State Right to Life Committee, said, "virtually all protection under law has

Continued on Page 22, Column 1

3.7 MILLION CARS RECALLED BY G.M. TO CORRECT FLAW

Shields Will Be Installed to Prevent Entry of Gravel Into Steering System

By JERRY M. FLINT

Special to The New York Times

DETROIT, Jan. 22 — The General Motors Corporation recalled today 3.7 million 1971 and 1972 cars, its full-size Chevrolet, Pontiac, Buick and Oldsmobile models.

G.M. said it would install a shield at the bottom of the car to keep gravel from bouncing into the steering mechanism, which could jam the steering.

The automaker insisted that the trouble was rare, and rejected the idea of a recall on this problem last year. But at the same time the company said it had received reports of 96 incidents allegedly tied to the trouble, with 23 turned into accidents in which 12 injuries were reported.

Criticism by Nader

The recall is one of the largest but does not match the recall for correction of safety defects of 6.7 million G.M. cars in 1971 or 4.4 million Fords last June.

Ralph Nader, the auto industry's major critic, has criticized G.M. for its failure to recall cars to correct this problem, and last August the Government's safety agency issued a consumer warning bulletin on the problem.

At that time, General Motors said that it did not believe the safety hazard was serious but offered to repair the cars without charge. Reports of the trouble kept appearing and the company has changed its position.

Steering May Jam

The condition, General Motors said, can become a problem only if a car "is driven over loose gravel, on extremely rutted roads at speeds which caused the car to pitch excessively." If the front frame cross-member, a cross bar similar to a step on a ladder, dips so low to the ground that it scoops up loose stones or gravel "it then is possible that stones of a certain size and shape may lodge between the steering coupling and the frame." The stones fall out of the car if turned to the right, G.M. said, but the steering may

Continued on Page 78, Column 2

KISSINGER IN PARIS; CEREMONIAL SITE CHOSEN FOR TALKS

Use of Conference Center Indicates Both Sides View Truce Round as Vital

By FLORA LEWIS

Special to The New York Times

PARIS, Jan. 22 — Henry A. Kissinger arrived here tonight, and it was announced that his talks tomorrow with Le Duc Tho of North Vietnam would be moved to the ceremonial setting of the International Conference Center.

Hanoi and Washington announced jointly last week that this next round of negotiations would complete a cease-fire agreement for Vietnam. Today there was still no official word on how long that task would take, but the choice of location — after months of meetings in secluded private quarters — suggested that the two sides considered tomorrow's session important.

The announcement that the talks would be moved to the center was made by the North Vietnamese here tonight, then confirmed by the American delegation.

The conference center is the old Hotel Majestic, on the Avenue Kléber, site of the formal four-sided Paris peace conference for over four years.

At the airport Mr. Kissinger said nothing more than "I am glad to be here." He went directly to the residence of the South Vietnamese Forign Minister, Tran Van Lam, though it was nearly midnight and he had left Washington early in the morning.

That was apparently a proto-

Continued on Page 6, Column 4

NATION IS SHOCKED

Citizens Join Leaders in Voicing Sorrow and Paying Tribute

By ROBERT D. McFADDEN

Shock, sorrow and the sense of a historic leader lost were the mourning themes of public officials and private citizens across the nation last night as word spread that Lyndon Baines Johnson was dead.

From the White House and the halls of Congress where he had served, and in cities and towns across the land where he had campaigned and made his policies felt, there was an outpouring of tribute to the former President, Senator and Representative from Texas.

Statement by Nixon

Many recalled Mr. Johnson's efforts to promote racial equality, to fight poverty and to improve education; others said that his deep commitment to the war in Indochina had prevented him from achieving all his domestic goals.

President Nixon, in a statement, declared: "To President Johnson, the 'American Dream' was not a catch phrase—it was a reality of his own life. He believed in America, in what America could mean to all its citizens and what America could mean to the world. In the service of that faith, he gave himself completely."

Mr. Nixon noted that in more than three decades of public life, Mr. Johnson "knew times of triumph and times of despair—he knew controversy and adulation. Yet, no matter what the mood of the moment, at the center of his public life—and at the center of his spirit—was an unshakeable convic-

Continued on Page 25, Column 1

The New York Times/George Tames

LYNDON BAINES JOHNSON, 1908—1973

STRICKEN AT HOME

Apparent Heart Attack Comes as Country Mourns Truman

Special to The New York Times

SAN ANTONIO, Tex., Jan. 22 —Lyndon Baines Johnson, 36th President of the United States, died today of an apparent heart attack suffered at his ranch in Johnson City, Tex.

The 64-year-old Mr. Johnson, whose history of heart illness began in 1955, was pronounced dead on arrival at 4:33 P.M. central time at San Antonio International Airport, where he

An obituary article appears on Pages 26 through 29; an appraisal, Page 25.

had been flown in a family plane on the way to Brooke Army Medical Center here.

A spokesman at Austin said that Mr. Johnson's funeral would probably be held Thursday at the National City Christian Church in Washington. He said the body would lie in state at the Johnson Library in Austin from noon tomorrow until 8 A.M. Wednesday, with an honor guard, and then would be taken to Washington, where it will lie in state at the Capitol rotunda until the funeral. Mr. Johnson will be buried at the L.B.J. Ranch.

Death came to the nation's only surviving former President as the nation observed a period of mourning proclaimed less than a month ago for former President Harry S. Truman.

A Legacy of Progress

Although his vision of a Great Society dissolved in the morass of war in Vietnam, Mr. Johnson left to the nation a legacy of progress and innovation in civil rights, Social Security, education, housing and other programs attesting to his fundamental affection for his fellow Americans.

At Fort Sam Houston, where Brooke Army Medical Center is situated, flags were hoisted to full staff and then immediately lowered again in respect for the Texan who was thrust into the Presidency on Nov. 22, 1963, when an assassin's bullet took the life of President Kennedy in Dallas.

Ironically, Mr. Johnson died in what appeared to be the waning days of the Vietnam war. The man who won election in 1964 to a full term as President with the greatest voting majority ever accorded a candidate was transformed by that war into the leader of a divided nation.

Amid rising personal unpopularity, in the face of the lingering war and racial strife at home, Mr. Johnson surprised the nation on March 31, 1968, with a television speech in which he announced, "I shall not seek and I will not accept the nomination of my party as your President."

Stage Set for Defeat

He thus renounced an opportunity to cap with a second full term a career in public life that began in 1937 with his election to Congress as an ardent New Dealer and led to the majority leadership of the Senate and to the Vice-Presidency and the Presidency. His renunciation set the stage for Democratic defeat at the polls in 1968.

Two days before Mr. Johnson's death, Richard M. Nixon, the Republican who was elected in 1968, took the oath of office for his second term as President. Mr. Nixon telephoned Mrs. Johnson today at the hospital here to express his sympathy.

At a news briefing tonight in Austin at KTBC, the Johnson family's television and ra-

Continued on Page 25, Column 5

Foreman Stops Frazier In 2d Round, Wins Title

By RED SMITH

Special to The New York Times

KINGSTON, Jamaica, Jan. 22 —Under Caribbean skies that had never witnessed anything remotely like it, big George Foreman smashed Joe Frazier to the floor six times tonight and won the heavyweight championship of the world in 4 minutes 35 seconds.

Arthur Mercante, the referee from New York, stopped the uneven match with Frazier on his feet but hardly in the contest.

A crowd of 36,000 paying $412,000, substantially more than had been expected, saw one of the most startling upsets in two and a half centuries of heavyweight title matches. Frazier, in his 10th defense of the title New York State conferred on him in 1968 and his third since he whipped the former champion, Muhammad Ali, in 1971, had been favored at 1 to 3 in the betting shops here.

Foreman, unbeaten in 37 fights and author of 34 knockouts since he won the Olympic heavyweight title in 1968, had been recognized as Joe's most formidable opponent since Ali but most boxing men doubted that he could stand up under the ceaseless pressure of a characteristic Frazier attack.

They'll never know now whether they were right or wrong, for Joe never got a chance to apply pressure. Looking rather thick in the middle at 214 pounds, the champion tried to "come out smoking" but Foreman used his greater size and longer reach to smother the fire. At 6 feet 3 inches, the challenger had three and a half inches in height and a five-inch advantage in reach.

Reaching out with both hands, he fended off Frazier's early rushes, turning the challenge aside. Then he sank a hook deep into Joe's body, and the crowd had the first hint of what was in store. In a moment Foreman was moving forward, using both hands with authority. Even so, there was an instant of shocked silence when an uppercut sent Joe sprawling.

The champion got to his feet immediately and resumed his jigging style, both hands high,

Continued on Page 33, Column 6

Black Muslims Accused By Rival Sect in 7 Killings

Leader of Hanafis Calls for Muhammad Ouster

By PAUL DELANEY

Special to The New York Times

WASHINGTON, Jan. 22 — The leader of the Hanafi community of Moslems here today blamed the Black Muslims for the slaying last Thursday of seven of his followers, including three of his children, and he, in effect, declared war on the Black Muslims.

The leader, Hamaas Abdul Khaalis, called on other Moslem groups in this country and abroad to assist in deposing the Black Muslims and their leader, Elijah Muhammad.

The slayings and Mr. Hamaas's statement at a news conference evoked apprehension among law enforcement authorities and Islamic experts that more bloodshed would come.

Meanwhile, a team of Washington detectives went to New York today to investigate the possibility of a connection between the Moslem feud and the attempted robbery of a Brooklyn gun store that resulted in a 47-hour siege over the weekend. The belief is that the aborted robbery, which came one day after the mass killings here, was an attempt to obtain arms for the pending battle.

The slayings occurred at the headquarters of the Hanafi, a three-story stone mansion in the interracial "Gold Coast" section, where many of the city's black middle-class citizens reside. The seven victims included five children, four of whom were drowned, ranging in age from 9 days to 10 years old.

Mr. Hamaas revealed some

Continued on Page 77, Column 2

Four Held for Murder in Brooklyn Siege

By PETER KIHSS

The four men seized in the 47-hour weekend siege and shootout at a Brooklyn sporting goods store were held without bail yesterday on charges of murdering a policeman—which could lead to a death penalty—and of kidnapping 10 hostages.

Three were arraigned in Kings County Criminal Court with the proceedings virtually walled off by a tight guard of a dozen uniformed court officers ranged in front of the court railing.

The fourth was arraigned in Kings County Hospital, where he had undergone surgery for a bullet wound in the stomach.

District Attorney Eugene Gold told Judge Robert M. Haft that two of the defendants each had a previous arrest — one in 1964 and one in 1966. Both apparently were then about 16 years old, and Gerald Lefcourt, a defense lawyer, said the men told him the charges had been dismissed.

Outside of court, Robert M. McKiernan, president of the Patrolmen's Benevolent Association, demanded prosecution that could lead to electrocution for the fatal shooting of Patrol-

Continued on Page 77, Column 3

NEWS INDEX

Pilgrims' Jet Crashes in Nigeria; 180 Are Feared Dead, a Record

By THOMAS A. JOHNSON

Special to The New York Times

LAGOS, Nigeria, Jan. 22 — A chartered jetliner carrying Nigerian Moslems home from a pilgrimage to Mecca crashed and burned today while landing in fog in northern Nigeria, and it was feared that 180 people had been killed.

Twenty-two of the 202 aboard survived, among them the pilot and several other crew members, according to reports from the airport at Kano, 525 miles north of here.

A death toll of 180 would make the crash the worst air disaster in history. Previously, the crash of a Soviet airliner near Moscow on Oct. 13, in which 176 people died, had been listed as the worst. The chartered jet, a Boeing 707 that belonged to Royal Jordanian Airways, was one of many planes involved in transporting Nigerian Moslems, as about

Continued on Page 10, Column 4

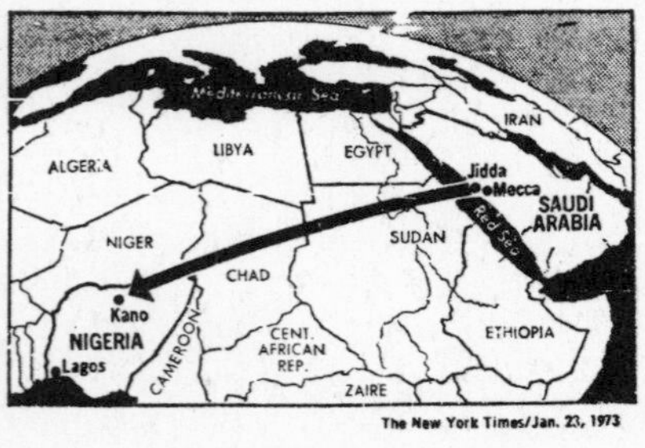
Mediterranean Sea
IRAN
LIBYA
EGYPT
ALGERIA
Jidda
Mecca
SAUDI ARABIA
Red Sea
NIGER
SUDAN
CHAD
Kano
NIGERIA
Lagos
CAMEROON
CENT. AFRICAN REP.
ETHIOPIA
ZAIRE

The New York Times/Jan. 23, 1973

Iceland Evacuates 7,000 on Isle After an Ancient Volcano Erupts

By The Associated Press

REYKJAVIK, Iceland, Tuesday, Jan. 23—Seven thousand people were being evacuated from an offshore Icelandic island early today as a volcano that had been quiet for more than a thousand years erupted.

Police authorities on the tiny island of Heimaey, one of a group off the south coast of Iceland, said boats and planes were being used to get the inhabitants of the town of Vestmannaeyjar to safety on the mainland.

But, they said, a hail of ash from the belching volcano of Helgafell was making operations from the Island's airstrip difficult. They said a stream of molten lava also threatened to seal off the harbor, trapping boats.

Telephoned reports to Reykjavik—70 miles northwest of Heimaey—said a fissure 2,000 to 3,000 yards long opened and was spewing out lava and ash.

Fiery explosions were hurtling molten debris more than 1,500 feet into the air.

One side of Vestmannaeyjar

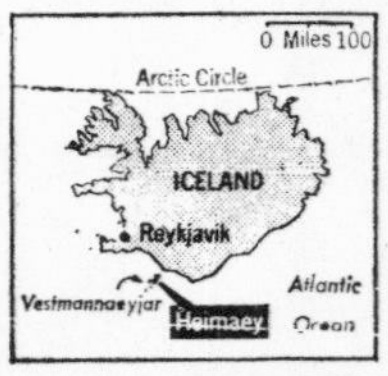
0 Miles 100
Arctic Circle
ICELAND
Reykjavik
Atlantic Ocean
Vestmannaeyjar
Heimaey

The New York Times/Jan. 23, 1973

is only 150 yards from Helgafell.

The police said the lava was flowing away from the town and into the Atlantic, but they said this could change at any time.

Women and children were being evacuated by air along with patients from the town's hospitals.

Others were boarding boats in the harbor. Iceland's big fishing fleet, Coast Guard vessels and other merchant ships were ordered to the island, the police said.

The United States Air Force base at Keflavik promised to

Continued on Page 10, Column 3

Excerpts From Abortion Case

Special to The New York Times

WASHINGTON, Jan. 22—Following are excerpts from the majority opinion, written by Justice Harry A. Blackmun, in Jane Roe v. Henry Wade, the Texas abortion case, and from the dissent written by Justice Byron R. White:

Majority Opinion

The Texas statutes under attack here are typical of those that have been in effect in many states for approximately a century. These make it a crime to "procure an abortion," as therein defined, or to attempt one, except with respect to "an abortion procured or attempted by medical advice for the purpose of saving the life of the mother." Similar statutes are in existence in a majority of the states.

It perhaps is not generally appreciated that the restrictive criminal abortion laws in effect in a majority of states are of relatively recent vintage. Instead, they derive from statutory changes effected, for the most part, in the latter half of the 19th century.

When most criminal abortion laws were first enacted, the procedure was a hazardous one for the woman.

Privacy Rights Unclear

The Constitution does not explicitly mention any right of privacy. In a line of decisions, however, the Court has recognized that a right of personal privacy, or a guarantee of certain areas or zones of privacy, does exist under the Constitution.

This right of privacy, whether it be founded in the 14th Amendment's concept of personal liberty and restrictions upon state action, as we feel it is, or, as the District Court determined, in the Ninth Amendment's reservation of rights to the people, is broad enough to encompass a woman's decision whether or not to terminate her pregnancy.

The detriment that the state would impose upon the pregnant woman by denying this choice altogether is apparent. Specific and direct harm medically diagnosable even in early pregnancy may be involved. Maternity, or additional offspring, may force upon the woman a distressful life and future. Psychological harm may be imminent. Mental and physical wealth may be taxed by child care.

There is also the distress, for all concerned, associated with the unwanted child, and there is the problem of bringing a child into a family already unable, psychologically and otherwise, to care for it.

On the basis of elements such as these, appellants and some amici argue that the woman's right is absolute and that she is entitled to terminate her pregnancy at whatever time, in whatever way, and for whatever reason she alone chooses. With this we do not agree.

The Court's decision recognizing a right of privacy also acknowleges that some state regulation in areas protected by that right is appropriate. A state may properly assert important interests in safeguarding health, in maintaining medical standards and in protecting potential life.

At the same point in pregnancy, these respective interests become sufficiently compelling to sustain regulation of the factors that govern the abortion decision.

The appellee and certain amici argue that the fetus is a "person" within the language and meaning of the 14th Amendment. In support of this they outline at length and in detail the well-known facts of fetal development. If this suggestion of parenthood is established, the appellant's case, of course, collapses, for the fetus' right to life is then guaranteed specifically by the amendment.

The Constitution does not define "person" in so many words. The use of the word is such that it has application only postnatally.

All this, together with our observation that throughout the major portion of the 19th century prevailing legal abortion practices were far freer than they are today, persuades us that the word "person," as used in the 14th Amendment, does not include the unborn.

Texas urges that, apart from the 14th Amendment, life begins at conception and is present throughout pregnancy, and that, therefore, the state has a compelling interest in protecting that life from and after conception.

We need not resolve the difficult question of when life begins. When those trained in the respective disciplines of medicine, philosophy and theology are unable to arrive at any consensus, the judiciary, at this point in the development of man's knowledge, is not in a position to speculate as to the answer.

The unborn have never been recognized in the law as persons in the whole sense.

With respect to the state's important and legitimate interest in the health of the mother, the "compelling" point, in the light of present medical knowledge, is at approximately the end of the first trimester. This is so because of the now established medical fact that until the end of the first trimester mortality in abortion is less than mortality in normal childbirth.

It follows that, from and after this point, a state may regulate the abortion procedure to the extent that the regulation reasonably relates to the preservation and protection of maternal health.

With respect to the state's important and legitimate interest in potential life, the "compelling" point is at viability. This is so because the fetus then presumably has the capability of meaningful life outside the mother's womb. If the state is interested in protecting fetal life after viability, it may go so far as to proscribe abortion during that period except when it is necessary to preserve the life or health of the mother.

Dissenting Opinion

At the heart of the controversy in these cases are those recurring pregnancies that pose no danger whatsoever to the life or health of the mother but are nevertheless unwanted for any one or more of a variety of reasons—convenience, family planning, economics, dislike of children, the embarrassment of illegitimacy, etc.

The common claim before us is that for any one of such reasons, or for no reason at all, and without asserting or claiming any threat to life or health, any woman is entitled to an abortion at her request if she is able to find a medical adviser willing to undertake the procedure.

The Court for the most part sustains this position: during the period prior to the time the fetus becomes viable, the Constitution of the United States values the convenience, whim or caprice of the putative mother more than life or potential life of the fetus.

The upshot is that the people and the legislatures of the 50 states are constitutionally disentitled to weigh the relative importance of the continued existence and development of the fetus on the one hand against a spectrum

United Press International

Justice Harry A. Blackmun

of possible impacts on the mother on the other hand.

As an exercise of raw judicial power, the Court perhaps has authority to do what it does today; but in my view its judgment is an improvident and extravagant exercise of the power of judicial review which the constitution extends to this court.

I find no constitutional warrant for imposing such an order of priorities on the people and legislatures of the states. In a sensitive area such as this, involving as it does issues over which reasonable men may easily and heatedly differ, I cannot accept the Court's exercise of its clear power of choice by interposing a constitutional barrier to state efforts to protect human life and by investing mothers and doctors with the constitutionally protected right to exterminate it. This issue, for the most part, should be left with the people and to the political processes the people have devised to govern their affairs.

Statements by 2 Cardinals

Following are statements issued by Cardinal Cooke and John Cardinal Krol, Archbishop of Philadelphia and president of the National Conference of Catholic Bishops, in reaction to the Supreme Court decision on abortions:

The New York Times

Cardinal Cooke

Cardinal Cooke

How many millions of children prior to their birth will never live to see the light of day because of the shocking action of the majority of the United States Supreme Court today?

Whatever their legal rationale, seven men have made a tragic utilitarian judgment regarding who shall live and who shall die. They have made themselves a "super legislature," They have gone against the will of those American people who spoke their minds in favor of life as recently as last November in referendums in Michigan and North Dakota. They have usurped the powers and responsibilities of the legislatures of 50 states to protect human life.

I remind all Americans, however, that judicial decisions are not necessarily sound moral decisions.

In spite of this horrifying decision, the American people must rededicate themselves to the protection of the sacredness of all human life. I hope and pray that our citizens will do all in their power to reverse this injustice to the rights of the unborn child.

Cardinal Krol

The Supreme Court's decision today is an unspeakable tragedy for this nation. It is hard to think of any decision in the 200 years of our history which has had more disastrous implications for our stability as a civilized society. The ruling drastically diminishes the constitutional guaranty of the right to life and in doing so sets in motion developments which are terrifying to contemplate.

The ruling represents bad logic and bad law. There is no rational justification for allowing unrestricted abortion up to the third month of pregnancy. The development of life before and after birth is a continuous process and in making the three-month point the cutoff for unrestricted abortion, the Court seems more impressed by magic than by scientific evidence regarding fetal development. The child in the womb has the right to life, to the life he already possesses, and this is a right no court has the authority to deny.

Apparently the Court was trying to straddle the fence and give something to everybody—abortion on demand before three months for those who want that, somewhat more restrictive abortion regulations after three months for those who want that. But in its straddling act, the Court has done a monstrous injustice to the thousands of unborn children whose lives may be destroyed as a result of this decision.

No court and no legislature in the land can make something evil become something good. Abortion at any stage of pregnancy is evil. This is not a question of sectarian morality but instead concerns the law of God and the basis of civilized society. One trusts in the decency and good sense of the American people not to let an illogical court decision dictate to them on the subject of morality and human life.

High Court Backs Abortions in First Three Months

Continued From Page 1, Col. 1

abortions, if it wishes, except where they may be necessary to preserve the life or health of the mother.

Today's action will not affect existing laws in New York, Alaska, Hawaii and Washington, where abortions are now legally available in the early months of pregnancy. But it will require rewriting of statutes in every other state.

The basic Texas case decided by the Court today will invalidate strict anti-abortion laws in 31 states; a second decision involving Georgia will require considerable rewriting of more liberal statutes in 15 others.

Justice Harry A. Blackmun wrote the majority opinion in which Chief Justice Warren E. Burger and Justices William O. Douglas, William J. Brennan Jr., Potter Stewart, Thurgood Marshall and Lewis F. Powell Jr. joined.

Dissenting were Justices Byron R. White and William H. Rehnquist.

Justice White, calling the decision "an exercise of raw judicial power," wrote that "the Court apparently values the convenience of the pregnant mother more than the continued existence and development of the life or potential life which she carries."

The Court's decision was at odds with the expressed views of President Nixon. Last May, in a letter to Cardinal Cooke, he opposed "liberalized abortion policies" and spoke out for "the right to life of literally hundreds of thousands of unborn children."

But three of the four Justices Mr. Nixon has appointed to the Supreme Court voted with the majority, with only Mr. Rehnquist dissenting.

The majority rejected the idea that a fetus becomes a "person" upon conception and is thus entitled to the due process and equal protection guarantees of the Constitution. This view was pressed by opponents of liberalized abortion, including the Roman Catholic Church.

Justice Blackmun concluded that "the word 'person,' as used in the 14th Amendment, does not include the unborn," although states may acquire, "at some point in time" of pregnancy, an interest in the "potential human life" that the fetus represents, to permit regulation.

It is that interest, the Court said, that permits states to prohibit abortion during the last 10 weeks of pregnancy, after the fetus has developed the capacity to survive.

In both cases decided today, the plaintiffs had based their protest on an assertion that state laws limiting the availability of abortion had circumscribed rights and freedoms guaranteed them by the Constitution: due process of law, equal protection of the laws, freedom of action and a particular privacy involving a personal and family matter.

In its decision on the challenge to the Georgia abortion law, the high court majority struck down several requirements that a woman seeking to terminate her pregnancy in that state would have to meet.

Decision for Doctors

Among them were a flat prohibition on abortions for out-of-state residents and requirements that hospitals be accredited by a private agency, that applicants be screened by a hospital committee and that two independent doctors certify the potential danger to the applicant's health.

The Georgia law permitted abortions when a doctor found in "his best clinical judgment" that continued pregnancy would threaten the woman's life or health, that the fetus would be likely to be born defective or that the pregnancy was the result of rape.

The same Supreme Court majority, with Justice Blackmun writing the opinion again, emphasized that this medical judgment should cover all relevant factors—"physical, emotional, psychological familial and the woman's age."

In some of the 15 states with laws similar to Georgia's, doctors have tended to take a relatively narrow view of what constituted a woman's health in deciding whether an abortion was legally justified.

The Texas law that the Court invalidated entirely was typical of the criminal statutes passed in the last half of the 19th century prohibiting all abortions except those to save a mother's life. The Georgia law, approved in 1972 and altered by the Court today, was patterned after the model penal code of the American Law Institute.

In the Texas case, Justice Blackmun wrote that the constitutional right of privacy, developed by the Court in a long series of decisions, was "broad enough to encompass a woman's decision whether or not to terminate her pregnancy."

He rejected, however, the argument of women's rights groups that this right was absolute "and she is entitled to terminate her pregnancy at whatever time, in whatever way and for whatever reason she alone chooses."

"With this we do not agree," the Justice declared.

"A state may properly assert important interests in safeguarding health in maintaining medical standards and in protecting potential life." Mr. Blackmun observed. "At some point in pregnancy, these respective interests become sufficiently compelling to sustain regulation of the factors that govern the abortion decision."

The majority concluded that this "compelling" state interest arose at the end of the first three months of pregnancy because of the "now established medical fact" that until then, fewer women die from abortions than from normal childbirth.

During this three-month period, the Court said, a doctor can recommend an abortion to his patient "without regulation by the state" and the resulting operations can be conducted "free of interference by the state."

The "compelling state interest" in the fetus does not arise, however, until the time of "viability," Justice Blackmun wrote, when it has "the capability of meaningful life outside the mother's womb." This occurs about 10 weeks before delivery.

In reading an abbreviated version of his two opinions to the Court this morning, Justice Blackmun noted that most state legislatures were in session now and would thus be able to rewrite their states' abortion laws to conform to the Court's decision.

Both of today's cases wound up with anonymous parties winning victories over state officials. In the Texas case, "Jane Roe," an unmarried pregnant woman who was allowed to bring the case without further identity, was the only plaintiff after the Supreme Court disqualified a doctor and a childless couple who said that the wife's health would be endangered by pregnancy.

In the Georgia case, the surviving plaintiff was "Mary Doe," who, when she brought the action, was a 22-year-old married woman 11 weeks pregnant with her fourth child.

2 Cardinals Denounce Decision; Other Leaders' Reactions Mixed

Continued From Page 1, Col. 2

spared the medical risks and emotional horrors of back-street and self-induced abortions. And as a nation, we shall be a step further toward assuring the birthright of every child to be welcomed by its parents at the time of its birth."

The decision was also welcomed by the Rev. Dr. Howard E. Spragg, executive vice president of the Board for Homeland Ministries of the United Church of Christ, who said, "The decision is historic not only in terms of women's individual rights but also in terms of the relationships of church and state."

'Neutrality of State'

Dr. Spragg said: "Although religious principles often form the basis of secular law, we hold that where religious beliefs vary, American law traditionally establishes the neutrality of the state. The doctrine of one religious group is not imposed by legal fiat or enforced by criminal sanction on the rest of American society."

Women lawyers from the Center for Constitutional Rights praised the Court's action as a victory for the women's liberation movement and a "tribute to the coordinated efforts of women's organizations, women lawyers and all women throughout this country."

But Barbara Meara, president of the Bronx chapter of Right to Life, an anti-abortion organization, said, "It is ironic that at a time when this country is trying to improve the lot of so many people and is so opposed to violence the Court should sanction the destruction of life."

The American Civil Liberties Union described the Court's decision as "an important step in the right direction."

"We trust that this is the beginning of the end for state efforts to interfere with the rights of women to secure medical abortions."

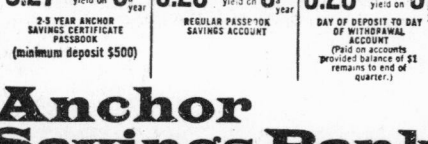

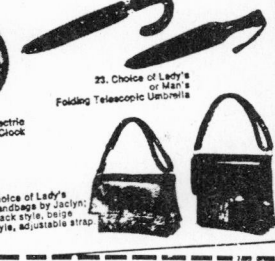

REMEMBER THE NEEDIEST!

Effect of Ruling On States' Laws

Special to The New York Times

WASHINGTON, Jan. 22—Following is a table showing how each state is affected by the Supreme Court's decision today on abortion.

States with legalized abortion laws not affected by today's decision:

Alaska	New York
Hawaii	Washington

States with relatively modern abortion laws that will require considerable rewriting to conform:

Alabama	Maryland
Arkansas	Mississippi
California	New Mexico
Colorado	North Carolina
Delaware	Oregon
Florida	South Carolina
Georgia	Virginia
Kansas	

States with older anti-abortion laws that have been entirely invalidated and that must write new laws:

Arizona	Nevada
Connecticut	New Hampshire
Idaho	New Jersey
Illinois	North Dakota
Indiana	Ohio
Iowa	Oklahoma
Kentucky	Pennsylvania
Louisiana	Rhode Island
Maine	South Dakota
Massachusetts	Tennessee
Michigan	Texas
Minnesota	Utah
Missouri	Vermont
Montana	West Virginia
Nebraska	Wisconsin
	Wyoming

"All the News That's Fit to Print"

The New York Times

LATE CITY EDITION
Weather: Rain late today, tonight becoming light snow early tomorrow. Temp. range: today 40-45; Saturday 40-44. Full U.S. report on Page 59

SECTION ONE

VOL. CXXII . . No. 42,008 NEW YORK, SUNDAY, JANUARY 28, 1973 — 75¢ beyond 50-mile zone from New York City, except Long Island. Higher in air delivery cities. — 50 CENTS

VIETNAM PEACE PACTS SIGNED; AMERICA'S LONGEST WAR HALTS

Nation Ends Draft, Turns to Volunteers

Change Is Ordered Six Months Early—Youths Must Still Register

By DAVID E. ROSENBAUM
Special to The New York Times

WASHINGTON, Jan. 27—Defense Secretary Melvin R. Laird announced today that the military draft had ended.

As a result of the announcement, men born in 1953 and afterward will not be subject to conscription, and men born before 1953 but not yet drafted will have no further liability to the draft.

These men will be the first in two generations to have no prospect of being drafted. Except for a brief hiatus in 1947 and 1948, men have been conscripted regularly since 1940.

President Nixon's authority to conscript troops into the military expires June 30. Since no one has been drafted since December, the President achieved his goal of turning the military into an all-volunteer force six months ahead of the deadline.

The President and Mr. Laird had promised repeatedly that the June 30 deadline would be met. But Mr. Laird had held out the possibility that as many as 5,000 men would be drafted this year from March through June.

Message From Laird

But, in a message to senior defense officials that was made public today, Mr. Laird said:

"With the signing of the peace agreement in Paris today, and, after receiving a report from the Secretary of the Army that he foresees no need for further inductions, I wish to inform you that the armed forces henceforth will depend exclusively on volunteer soldiers, sailors, airmen and marines.

"The use of the draft has ended."

Although no one will be drafted, the Selective Service machinery will most likely remain on the books for standby use in an emergency. Men will continue to have to register for the draft when they turn 18, and young men will still be assigned lottery numbers based on their birthdays.

Congress has mandated, however, that the Government call up Reserves and National Guardsmen before it turns to a reinstatement of the draft to meet future emergencies.

A spokesman for the Selective Service System said that men who had refused to report for induction would still be subject to criminal prosecution. But, he said, men with induction postponements that were due to expire before June 30 will not be drafted.

"We will draft nobody," the spokesman said.

Hopes Senate Will Act

Mr. Laird's single qualification about ending the draft applied to doctors and dentists. The Nixon Administration has asked Congress to approve sizable bonuses for doctors and dentists in an effort to attract enough volunteers in those professions.

The House of Representatives passed such legislation last year, and Mr. Laird said in his message today:

"I am particularly hopeful that the Senate will promptly follow the lead of the House and enact legislation giving added incentives for service from members of the health professions, so that the requirements for health services personnel can also be put on a volunteer basis."

The House is almost certainly willing to pass the bill again this year, but Representative F. Edward Hébert, chairman of the House Armed Services Committee, has said that his committee will not act until the Senate passes the legislation.

Mr. Laird also urged Congress to approve bonuses to attract men to the National Guard and

Continued on Page 28, Column 1

In the morning ceremony at the Hotel Majestic in Paris were, from the left, the Vietcong, North Vietnamese, South Vietnamese and U.S. delegations

Associated Press, United Press International and C.B.S. News

Signing, from left, William P. Rogers for U.S., Nguyen Duy Trinh for Hanoi, Mrs. Nguyen Thi Binh for the Vietcong, Tran Van Lam for Saigon

CEREMONIES COOL

Two Sessions in Paris Formally Conclude the Agreement

By FLORA LEWIS
Special to The New York Times

PARIS, Jan. 27—The Vietnam cease-fire agreement was signed here today in eerie silence, without a word or a gesture to express the world's relief that the years of war were officially ending.

The accord was effective at 7 P.M. Eastern standard time.

Secretary of State William P. Rogers wrote his name 62 times on the documents providing—after 12 years—a settlement of the longest, most divisive foreign war in America's history.

The official title of the text was "Agreement on Ending the War and Restoring Peace in Vietnam." But the cold, almost gloomy atmosphere at two separate signing ceremonies reflected the uncertainties of whether peace is now assured.

The conflict, which has raged in one way or another for over a quarter of a century, had been inconclusive, without clear victory or defeat for either side.

Involvement Gradually Grew

After a gradually increasing involvement that began even before France left Indochina in 1954, the United States entered into a full-scale combat role in 1965. The United States considers Jan. 1, 1961, as the war's starting date and casualties are counted from then.

By 1968, when the build-up was stopped and then reversed, there were 529,000 Americans fighting in Vietnam. United States dead passed 45,000 by the end of the war.

The peace agreements were as ambiguous as the conflict, which many of America's friends first saw as generous aid to a weak and threatened ally, but which many came to consider an exercise of brute power against a tiny nation.

Built on Compromises

The peace agreements signed today were built of compromises that permit the two Vietnamese sides to give them contradictory meanings and, they clearly hope, to continue their unfinished struggle in the political arena without continuing the slaughter.

The signing took place in two ceremonies. In the morning, the participants were the United States, North Vietnam, South Vietnam and the Vietcong. Because the Saigon Government does not wish to imply recognition of the Vietcong's Provisional Revolutionary Government, all references to that government were confined to a second set of documents. That set was signed in the afternoon,

Continued on Page 24, Column 7

Hanoi Lists of P.O.W.'s Are Made Public by U.S.

By BERNARD GWERTZMAN
Special to The New York Times

WASHINGTON, Jan. 27—The State Department tonight released the list of American civilians acknowledged by North Vietnam as having been captured in South Vietnam during the Vietnam war. The list left about half the 51 American civilians believed missing or captured unaccounted for.

The list that the North Vietnamese turned over to American officials in Paris today named 27 American civilians as prisoners of the Vietcong, and listed seven other Americans as having died in captivity.

At the same time, the Defense Department began releasing, in batches, the names of the military prisoners in Communist hands who were on the list turned over in Paris along with the civilians.

2 Diplomats Listed

The United States, in Paris, provided a list of 26,000 Communist prisoners held by South Vietnam in exchange. The lists were turned over following the formal signing of the Vietnam cease-fire agreement.

Frank A. Sieverts, the State Department official charged with prisoner affairs, said that Hanoi apparently did not in-

Continued on Page 26, Column 1

The Toll: 12 Years of War

Military

United States—45,933 killed, 303,616 wounded, 587 captured, 1,335 missing (up to Jan. 13, 1973).
South Vietnam—183,528 killed and 499,026 wounded.
North Vietnam and Vietcong—924,048 (an estimate by Saigon; figures on wounded not available.)

Civilian

415,000 South Vietnamese killed and 935,000 wounded in combat (1965 through 1972).
31,463 South Vietnamese killed and 49,000 abducted as result of Vietcong actions against civilians.
20,587 killed by Saigon actions against civilian Vietcong.
North Vietnamese—Casualties not known.

BATTLES CONTINUE AFTER CEASE-FIRE

U.S. Copter Sent to Pick Up Vietcong Officers Said to Have Been Shot Down

By FOX BUTTERFIELD
Special to The New York Times

SAIGON, South Vietnam, Sunday, Jan. 28—A cease-fire officially went into effect throughout Vietnam at 8 A.M. today, but widespread fighting continued and there were reports that an unarmed American helicopter sent to pick up a Vietcong delegation and bring it to Saigon had been shot down over Tay Nin Ninh Province.

The helicopter, which was painted white and which is normally used for medical evacuation flight, was to bring the Vietcong's delegation to the four-power Joint Military Commission that will oversee the cease-fire. There was no immediate word on the fate of the crew.

[North Vietnam issued a statement Sunday informing its people of the cease-fire, saying, "Today, the 28th of January, war completely ends in both zones of our country," Reuters reported from Hong Kong.]

334 Incidents Reported

The South Vietnamese command reported this morning that in the 24 hours ending at dawn, North Vietnamese and Vietcong troops initiated 334 incidents throughout the country. According to Government officers, that is the highest number since they began keeping a record. However, more Communist troops were probably involved during the 1968 Tet offensive, they said.

Only an hour and a half before the cease-fire began, Communist gunners struck Tan Son Nhut airport on the outskirts

Continued on Page 18, Column 1

A Reluctant G.I.'s Life and Death

By JON NORDHEIMER
Special to The New York Times

ST. JOSEPH, Mo.—The house on Penn Street where Charley Stockbauer used to live sits near a historic crossroads of America.

It was from St. Joseph that the pioneers who won the West a century ago set out across the prairie in rough wagons drawn by mules and oxen and gritty conviction.

They came here by railroad and steamboat in the waning days of winter and huddled in muddy encampments on the gray bluffs above the Missouri River, waiting with mounting excitement for the floodwaters to recede from the Kansas plain.

As with most American school children, the seeds of patriotism were planted deep in Charley Stockbauer, and he grew to manhood in St. Joseph surrounded by the ghosts of 19th-century heroes and the legends of the days when men strode boldly toward an uncertain horizon, enduring hardship and fear on the impulse of duty or national destiny.

Values Questioned

These values are still enshrined, but they have been questioned as never before by Charley Stockbauer's generation during the turbulent years when the vagaries of the war in Vietnam challenged traditional American attitudes about sacred abstractions such as patriotism.

Charley Stockbauer was a confused and reluctant warrior in a conflict that almost nobody fully understands, and that confusion and reluctance are mirrored here in the town that was his home before he died in Vietnam. Patriotism has not died in St. Joseph, but here, as elsewhere across the country in these days when the war has at last come to an end, there is a reticence about it all, a nervous hesitance about parading the flag.

The myths and the legends persist. Buffalo Bill and Wild Bill Hickok were raw-boned riders from the Overland Pony Express, and the mail they carried westward started out from a brick building that still stands on Penn Street. Indian fighters purchased, with leather pouches

Continued on Page 24, Column 2

Today's Sections

Index to Subjects

*Included in all copies distributed in New York City and the suburban area.

Nation Celebrates Peace In Prayer and Muted Joy

By MICHAEL KNIGHT

President Nixon, like millions of other Americans, watched the signing of the Vietnam cease-fire agreement on television yesterday and then, like many others, took part in a modest and somber celebration of the end of a tragic war.

The President, relaxing in his home at Key Biscayne, Fla. had proclaimed 7 P.M. yesterday as a "national moment of prayer and thanksgiving" and the 24-hour period thereafter as a day of prayer.

Throughout the country, in cities and in hamlets, church bells tolled, fire companies sounded their horns, and small, quiet gatherings were held in homes and in public places.

Some Voice Caution

Some of those who celebrated the end of the American war did so cautiously. The executive secretary of the Washington, D. C., Council of Churches said, "The reason many of us are not throwing our hats in the air is that we are just so stunned and ashamed because the war went on so long, so needlessly."

In Elmira, N. Y., Mrs. Lucielle Cesari did not turn on the lights of a Christmas tree in her yard, lights she had lit every night for five years in a "vigil" remembering the war.

In Longmeadow, Mass., a bell forged by Paul Revere, the silversmith and patriot, was sounded in its steeple at the First Church of Christ. The bell was first sounded to signal the end of the War of 1812.

In Key Biscayne, the President attended a special service at the Key Biscayne Presbyterian Church about a mile from his home.

The minister, the Rev. John A. Huffman, Jr., borrowed from a song by two antiwar activists,

Continued on Page 20, Column 3

United Press International

President and Mrs. Nixon and their daughter, Mrs. David Eisenhower, attending a memorial service in Key Biscayne Presbyterian Church, near the Florida White House.

Other News About Accords

CAMBODIA—The exiled Cambodian head of state said in Peking that his guerrilla forces would fight on despite the cease-fire in Vietnam. Cambodia announced a suspension of offensive activities tomorrow. [Page 26.]

TRUCE OBSERVERS—Teams of officers from Poland and Canada left for Vietnam to join with others expected from Hungary and Indonesia. [Page 24.]

INTERNATIONAL CONFERENCE—The United States proposed Feb. 26 as the date for 12-nation meeting on guaranteeing peace. [Page 16.]

LAOS—The head of the pro-Communist negotiating team returned from Hanoi and gave no indication that a cease-fire could be arranged quickly in Laos. [Page 21.]

Truce Supervisors From Poland, Hungary and Canada Leave for South Vietnam

Trudeau Says Good-By; 75 Fly From Warsaw

By JAMES FERON

Special to The New York Times

WARSAW, Jan. 27—A contingent of 75 Polish military officers and civilians left here tonight to join Hungarian, Canadian and Indonesian units in supervising the Vietnam cease-fire.

Brig. Gen. Marian Ryba, the ranking officer, said the rest of the Polish force would be leaving soon. "According to the agreement we have to be there within 48 hours of the signing," he said.

Each nation is expected to provide about 290 men for the 1,160-member International Commission of Control and Supervision. The first Hungarian unit numbering about 100 men left Budapest last night.

'We Will Rotate Them'

General Ryba, asked about provisions for rotation, said, "If this group can't maintain order we will rotate them."

He could not foresee how long the Polish forces would remain in South Vietnam. "Certain questions are prescribed in the agreement," he said, "such as the withdrawal of American troops, but other questions are not, such as when elections will be held."

The group leaving tonight appeared to be made up largely of army majors and colonels, with a smaller number of air force and navy officers. There were about two dozen civilians.

Strict airport restrictions were lifted for families to join the contingent in the departure lounge. The unit left in a turboprop Ilyushin-18 aircraft for a 30-hour trip by way of Tashkent, Teheran, Karachi, Vientiane and Hanoi to Saigon.

General Ryba was not sure when the entire Polish force would arrive in Saigon. "We're flying in winter," he said, "so it's in the hands of God."

The leader of the Polish contingent, Bogdan Wasilewski, has already arrived in Saigon, according to the Polish press agency. Mr. Wasilewski, 50 years old, is a former Polish ambassador to North Vietnam.

The Hungarian contingent similarly is headed by a career diplomat, Ferenc Esztergalyos. He is a former Ambassador to Sweden. Mr. Esztergalyos will be assisted by Imre Uranovicz, a former member of the Hungarian delegation to the United Nations, and by Brig. Gen. Ferenc Szuecs.

Mr. Wasilewski's deputies are General Ryba and Stanislaw Stawiarski, identified here only as Minister Plenipotentiary.

Poles on Earlier Body

Units of the control commission are expected to be in position by Monday morning. Poland and Canada have served on the previous control commission in Indochina.

It could not be learned whether any of the Polish officers who left tonight had been members of the earlier unit, but it was assumed that at least some of them had previous experience.

Hungarian and Polish spokesmen have stated their sympathy for the North Vietnamese in recent days. In a farewell speech to his troops in Budapest last night, Hungary's Deputy Premier, Lajos Feher, said peace had been achieved as a result of the "persistent, just fight of South Vietnamese patriots."

There were no such farewell speeches as the Polish contingent left here tonight. But Glos Pracy, the trade union newspaper, said: "We are at one with our Vietnamese brothers at this great hour for them. As always, they can count on our solidarity and support."

Canadian Group Leaves

Special to The New York Times

MONTREAL, Jan. 27—A team of tailors stayed up past midnight sewing on special Maple Leaf shoulder patches, a barber rushed over in a taxi to give last-minute military haircuts, and Prime Minister Pierre Elliott Trudeau arrived in a helicopter to say good-by.

At the center of the flurry of activity were the 290 Canadians going to Vietnam to join the international team of observers of the cease-fire. The first planeload left for Saigon this afternoon.

"We're all still a bit dazed, but hopeful that our being there will make a difference," said Maj. Clive G. Loader, a pilot who arrived at the central dispatching depot in Montreal from his home in Nova Scotia less than 48 hours after President Nixon's announcement Tuesday night.

Canada's members of the four-nation observation team had known for a couple of months that they would probably be going to Vietnam as soon as there was a cease-fire, but as Major Loader put it, "It sort of caught us by surprise, after the long negotiations."

"Most of us want to go, I guess" said the major, a 40-year-old father of four, who has a quiet voice and a soldier's bearing. "It'll be a great experience, and probably good for our careers. But there's the difficulty of leaving families behind for what might be a dangerous situation over there."

The Canadian Government has offered its men for only 60 days, reserving the right to review the situation after that, but Major Loader thinks they will be there at least several months or longer, and some of the others on the peace team seemed to agree, as they waited around a shabby supply depot here for the word to go.

The men spent the time before departure being briefed on what the world expects them to do in Vietnam, trying on their green tropical uniform shorts and knee socks, filling in forms, studying maps and photographs of beaches near Saigon, and discussing their new role, sometimes with a bit of anxiety.

More than half the men, who are led by Maj. Gen. Duncan A. McAlphine, are officers, drawn from many specialties in several parts of the country.

"The idea is that an infantryman, for example, can see things on the ground that maybe an Air Force chap might miss," explained a spokesman. "The selection of these men tried to draw on all the different talents and areas of experience."

The spokesman said that the men would take no arms with them on the 27-hour flight to Saigon, but that several hundred pistols were being sent there separately.

Questioned on that point in the House of Commons in Ottawa, National Defense Minister James A. Richardson said that the men would definitely not be armed with combat weapons, but that they might sometimes carry pistols for self-protection.

Appearing here Friday night with the Prime Minister, Mr. Richardson also assured the men that the Government had contingency plans for their swift evacuation if new hazards arose in Vietnam.

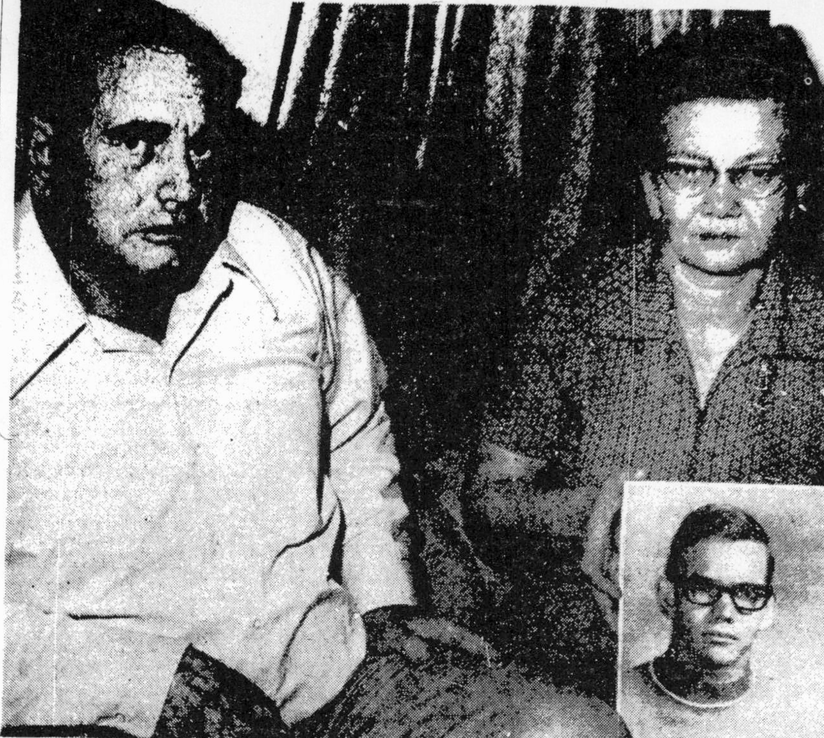
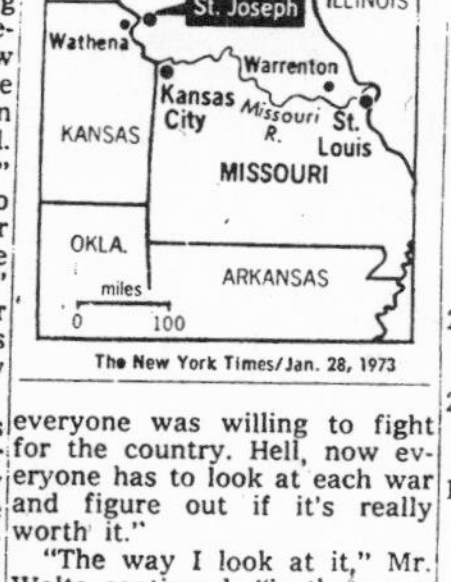

Associated Press

THE PARENTS OF ONE OF THE LAST AMERICANS KILLED IN THE WAR: Mr. and Mrs. John E. Rucker at their home in Linden, Tex., with a 1969 photo of their son, John O'Neal. The Air Force sergeant was killed in his sleep by a rocket attack on Da Nang Air Base in South Vietnam early Saturday, a little more than 24 hours before the cease-fire went into effect. The 21-year-old, next to the youngest in a family of four brothers and sisters, had been at home for Christmas. Mrs. Margie Manning, a sister, said he wanted to make the Air Force a career.

A Reluctant Soldier's Life in a Midwest Town and Death in Vietnam

Continued From Page 1, Col. 3

of gold, guns and knives from St. Joseph merchants, and Jesse James was shot dead in a weather-stained dwelling about half a mile from Charley Stockbauer's home.

But had he lived, Charley Stockbauer might have had trouble defining patriotism for anyone who asked.

By most standards of his community, Charley Stockbauer was a patriot. The President said so, in a letter of consolation to the Stockbauer family. So did the Secretary of the Army, the Army Chief of Staff, and a half dozen other generals.

But the Stockbauers do not think of Charley as a patriot in the usual sense, and they certainly do not believe that he sacrificed his life for his country and its ideals.

Specialist 4 Charles T. Stockbauer was killed in action three years ago when he was 23 years old, one of 26 young men from St. Joseph to die in the Vietnam war—one of America's 46,000 dead.

Letter on Kitchen Table

What makes Charley Stockbauer's story more illuminating than the others in an 18-page letter he wrote on lined notebook paper the night before he was scheduled for induction in the Army. In it he expressed his concepts of freedom, patriotism and love of country, and left it on the kitchen table so his family would see it after he had gone. But instead of heading for the induction center, Charley Stockbauer fled his country that day and crossed the border into Canada.

"I heard the door close in the middle of the night," his mother recalls. "I didn't know what it was. In the morning I found the letter, and only then did I realize the agony he was suffering. I prayed he'd realize his mistake and come home and do his duty."

Charley did return from Canada, five days later, saying that his conviction that Vietnam was an immoral war remained unchanged. Yet it was abhorrent for him to bring grief and shame down on the house on Penn Street. He reported for induction and one year later he was dead in a Vietnam jungle.

That was three years ago, and if time has not silenced the grief of the Stockbauer family, it has at least muted it. Charley's memory is now likely to produce fond smiles instead of hot tears. And the only time his mother has been moved to anguish is when a politician or a general has called for victory in Vietnam so that the sacrifice of Charley Stockbauer and the other dead Americans will not have been in vain.

In the entrance of Central High School is a world War I marble plaque that reads: "In Memory of Our Boys Who Gave Their Lives for Humanity." Farther down the hall, across from the principal's office, is a bronze plaque dedicated to the memory of students who died in the Second World War: "He Does Not Die Who Can Bequeath Some Influence to the Land He Knows."

There is no memorial for the Vietnam dead. If one is eventually put up no one seems to know what should be inscribed upon it. "What do you say about nothing?" said a girl in blue jeans in response to a visitor's question.

Mrs. Carol Pittman, a teacher of Latin who was a student at Central High at the outbreak of American involvement in Vietnam, can remember the fear that touched the boys in her graduating class when it began to penetrate their consciousness that they might be asked to go to fight in an obscure place called Vietnam.

"Sure," added James Rosenburger, a math teacher in his thirties, "the kids were downright scared in 1966 because most of them were going straight to Vietnam and they knew it.

"Only I wasn't too sympathetic," said Mr. Rosenburger, a baldish man with glasses who sipped coffee in a faculty lounge, "because I had just done two years' time in the Army and I figured it was everyone's patriotic duty to serve."

He put down his cup and looked at the other teachers. "If the President says it's your duty to go, you go. Even if it's a mistake. A blunder. You go. You don't stand around asking questions."

"Hell, when we marched off to the South Pacific in the Second World War," injected Frank Baker, the principal of Central High, "there was a highly patriotic feeling among us soldiers. It was like a football game and we felt we were fielding the best team. 'Let's get at 'em! Let's rack 'em up!' That sort of thing. It was a game of matching our equipment and the know-how against the gooks. It was that good old American competitive spirit."

Mrs. Pittman, who had listened silently to the men, said attitudes among the young were changing rapidly and she did not know if the Vietnam experience had fostered the changes or if there was a more fundamental cause.

"Take the other day in the student Senate," she remarked. "Some kids made a motion to abolish the morning flag-raising ceremony." The motion was defeated, she went on, but now three boys in her room refuse to stand for the ceremony, an act of defiance that is tolerated.

"When I was in high school," she said, "we wouldn't dare do something like that. As a matter of fact, the idea wouldn't have entered our heads. And that," she said, looking at the older men, "was only seven years ago when hardly anyone knew where Vietnam was."

"Dearest Mother," Charles Stockbauer wrote in his letter when he fled to Canada, "By now you realize what I have done and you are probably upset. Well, I can't console you. This was not a decision I made with little thought. I have hardly thought about anything else. . . . I've thought over the matter and I'm sorry that by this I'll be hurting you. But it has to be. I can't justify any other action. War is only a word to soothe our conscience. But it doesn't work. War is still nothing more than murder. And murder is wrong no matter who says it can be justified.

"I realize that war will possibly never cease as long as we live in this world, as long as there are flags, there will be war. . . . The trouble in America is that because freedom is written down we think we have it. But to quote Goethe, 'None are more helplessly enslaved than those who falsely believe we are free.'"

Talk in a Tavern

Young people from St. Joseph drive across the Missouri River bridge to Wathena, a farm community in Kansas where it is legal for 18-year-olds to drink 3.2 beer. On Fridays and Saturdays, the taverns fill up with teen-agers with long hair, beards and ragged denims—the new dress style only recently approved by the police, educators and blue-collar fathers in America's heartland.

"These kids just don't have respect for anything any more," muttered Paul Walts, the lean and leathery 62-year-old owner of The Keg. "Nothing means much to them any more. The war has a lot to do with it, sure, but there's a real dope problem now and the kids have all moved away from religion."

His son, Gary, who works the noisy bar on weekend nights, said that even he, at 28, felt alienated from the younger crowd. "For example," he said, "the war has made a negative attitude about serving in the Army. When I was their age everyone was willing to fight for the country. Hell, now everyone has to look at each war and figure out if it's really worth it."

IOWA
ILLINOIS
St. Joseph
Wathena
Warrenton
Kansas City
Missouri R.
St. Louis
KANSAS
MISSOURI
OKLA.
ARKANSAS
miles
0
100

The New York Times/Jan. 28, 1973

"The way I look at it," Mr. Walts continued, "is that anybody that would run off to Canada is what I'd call a great big coward. We've had some come in here who'd done that, gone off to Canada. It's all wrong."

His wife nodded in agreement. "That's the way our generation was raised," she said. "We were a patriotic people. I can remember back as a little girl in Grant City in Missouri how the American Legion always had their parades, with all those flags flying. My what a pretty sight it was!"

The Waltses were uncertain if there were any flag-snapping parades still held in St. Joseph. If there are, they do not watch them, and neither do the young people unless they are in a school band and obliged to participate.

About the only time anyone hears the national anthem these days is when a television station signs off for the night and distant jets barrel-roll across the flickering screen.

Attended Seminary

Charles Stockbauer, son of a stockyard worker, went off to a Roman Catholic seminary near Warrenton, Mo., at the age of 13, eager but scared, taking the first step toward a childhood ambition to become a priest. He went on to Jesuit College near Louisville but returned home in 1965 filled with doubts about the priesthood.

His older brother, Joe, was away in the Navy at the time, a volunteer, and the young seminarian was the focus of attention of his parents and four sisters in the frame house on Penn Street.

"He was such a bright boy he spent all of his money on books on history and architecture," said Mrs. Stockbauer, a registered nurse who worked at St. Joseph's State Hospital, a mental institution. "He even went out and bought a piano for the house and at night he'd play for the family." She paused for a moment and ran her fingers over the kitchen table where the letter written by a son had once been placed, and a furtive recollection made her smile. "The house was filled with his music. He was the source of a heck of a lot of joy for all of us."

He went to the local community college, but by 1967 he didn't have the money to continue his education. His deferment ended, and he was drafted. After his brief flight to Canada, he entered the Army and became a medical corpsman attached to the 101st Airborne Division. He wrote home that if he had backtracked on the convictions that sent him to Canada, at least as a corpsman he would not have to hurt anyone. Perhaps, he wrote, he might even help humanity. He began to keep a diary:

1 January. New Year's Day—It's good to be in 1969. It's going to be my year—I hope. Boy, am I looking forward to '70.

17 January. Again I find myself intrigued with T. S. Eliot. He begins: "Time present and time past/And both perhaps present in time future/And time future contained in time past." I don't understand why he says "perhaps" . . . why perhaps?

20 January. Convoy went smoothly. I see more beauty each day in the road we take.

25 February. Good day so far. Ulysses not moving as well as hoped.

14 March. Ambush last night—again a failure. Finished "Anna Karenina"—a great delight in reading. A beautiful portrayal of the main issues in a seemingly impossible existence. Spec/4 as of March 10. A little more money. I won't complain.

19 March. St. Joseph's Day. Many thoughts today but all seem to turn me to St. Joe. Oh! I really can't see living anywhere else.

29 April. Isn't life beautiful/Isn't life gay/Isn't life the perfect thing/To pass the time away?

2 May. Another ambush. One day less. Oh God, please help me.

19 June. Ambush tonight. What will it bring?

25 June. Not so hot last night. Nice headache. Sending in for "Selected Plays of Eugene O'Neill."

28 June. "Narcissus and Goldmund" [by Herman Hesse]. Ends beautifully. "But how will you die when your time comes, Narcissus, since you have no mother? Without a mother, one cannot love. Without a mother, one cannot die."

8 July. August 23 [R and R leave] and away we go—must write home. Glad to hear that St. Joseph is showing some signs of progress.

He was killed on July 10 by enemy fire when his unit was in a night defense position near a town called Bou Aie Ha. He went to the aid of three wounded soldiers, treated them and was shot as he searched in the dark for more wounded.

"We were just leaving for church—it was a beautiful July morning and we thought we would have a picnic afterwards," Mrs. Stockbauer remembers. "A station wagon pulled up and an Army officer got out and I suddenly felt like running away and never stop running. I turned to my husband and I said, 'God I know what that is. Oh, God, I know he's here to tell us our Charley is dead.'"

A flood of official condolences from the White House, the Army, and from Missouri politicians streamed into the house on Penn Street, all standard form letters sent to the next of kin of dead soldiers, extolling Specialist 4 Stockbauer's courage and military conduct. Some samples:

"In Vietnam today brave Americans are defending the rights of men to choose their own destiny and to live in dignity and freedom. You can cherish the thought that for his sacrifice your son is forever noble."—Gen. William C. Westmoreland.

"Charles was indeed a fine soldier who fought with courage and determination for his country and his ideals. He was brave in battle. He inspired confidence in all his associates by his dedication and strength of character."—Maj. Gen. John M. Wright Jr., commanding officer of the 101st Airborne.

"I pray for the day when this war can be ended, and peace restored. I wish that your son could have lived to see that day. His courage, his devotion and his sacrifice have brought it closer."—President Richard M. Nixon.

The words were bitter to the Stockbauers and they wrote back: "He lived what he believed and he died for it. By applying the principles he had been taught all his life he found himself at odds with his country and its policies on war. Our reaction when he applied these beliefs show how little we actually believe what we teach our children."

After Charley's death the women of the Stockbauer family joined the Fellowship of Reconciliation, a peace group, and on Wednesday afternoons they marched in small weekly antiwar protests on the steps of the downtown Post Office, like Greek women mourning their dead.

"He died and it's up to us to make his life worth while," says Janice, the oldest of the sisters. "People tell me I shouldn't think about it any more, that it's been three years and it's not healthy for me to still grieve.

"They say he died for his country and that's enough—that's something to be proud of—he was a patriot."

And there was no more music in the house on Penn Street.

Charley Stockbauer, posthumous winner of the Bronze Star, was buried in Mount Olivet Cemetery in St. Joseph. The women visit the grave on these gray winter days, with the biting wind out of Kansas whipping their coats, and drop to the hard ground in prayer before a simple marker.

The single word PEACE is inscribed in its cold granite face and below that is the peace symbol, the only tribute to the patriot lying in the ground above the bluffs where a young America once massed in excitement and hope.

Photo from the Stockbauers' family album of Charley with his Vietnam combat unit

Charley Stockbauer as a Catholic seminarian.

Vietnam Accords Signed; Longest U.S. War Ends

Continued From Page 1, Col. 8

and by only the United States and North Vietnam.

At the last moment, it was found that two copies in English of the texts, which were to have been signed by Mr. Rogers and North Vietnam's Foreign Minister, Nguyen Duy Trinh, in the afternoon ceremony, were missing.

The plan had been to give a signed copy in each language to each of the four delegations. The United States prepared the English documents and had given the two copies to the South Vietnamese to inspect. They were not returned, leaving a total of six instead of eight sets of documents to be signed by the United States and North Vietnam.

These texts began by saying that North Vietnam "with the concurrence of the Provisional Revolutionary Government of the Republic of South Vietnam" and the United States "with the concurrence of the Government of the Republic of Vietnam" had reached agreement.

South Vietnam's foreign minister, Tran Van Lam, indicated that he did not want to accept signed copies of this text, because Saigon objects to mention of the revolutionary government by that name.

Asked whether the South Vietnamese action might weaken or undermine the degree of Saigon's "concurrence," American officials said, "No, no. They have concurred."

Each of the other delegations wound up with four sets of signed agreements. Saigon took only two, the English and Vietnamese versions mentioning only "parties" to the conference.

In the morning ceremony, all four parties signed identical agreements, except for one protocol, or annexed document, in which the United States agreed to remove the mines it had planted in the waters of North Vietnam.

The preamble on the four-party documents mentioned no government by name and referred only to the "parties participating in the Paris conference on Vietnam."

That was the formula that had broken the final deadlock.

Almost immediately after the morning session involving four foreign ministers, military delegations of the Vietcong and the North Vietnamese flew off on their way to Saigon.

They, with American and South Vietnamese officers, will form a joint military commission that is to carry out the cease-fire. Their departure for the South Vietnamese capital gave a touch of reality to the strangely emotionless way in which the rite of peace was performed in Paris.

After the morning ceremony, which lasted 18 minutes, the four foreign ministers, their aides and guests filed wordlessly through separate doors into a curtained foyer.

Toast 'Peace and Friendship'

There, participants said, they clinked champagne glasses, toasted "peace and friendship" and shook hands all around. But such amiability was concealed from observers and above all from the cameras that might have recorded a scene of the Vietnamese enemies in social contact.

A similar 15 minutes of cordiality followed the 11-minute afternoon ceremony, attended only by the American and North Vietnamese delegations.

The agreement was signed at the gigantic round table, covered with a prairie of green baize, where the four parties to the Paris conference have been speechifying at each other, and often vilifying each other, almost weekly for four years.

The great ballroom of the former Hotel Majestic, where the table stands, is crammed with crystal and gilt chandeliers, lush tapestries and ornate gilt moldings. But the scene was as glum as the drizzly, gray Paris sky outside. The men all wore dark suits.

The touches of human color were few. Mrs. Nguyen Thi Binh, Foreign Minister of the Vietcong Provisional Revolutionary Government, wore an amber ao dai with embroidery on the bodice, an unusual ornament for her.

Mrs. Rogers wore a dress with a red top and navy skirt. In the afternoon, when there were only two delegations and thus more room for guests, all the American secretaries who had been involved were brought in and they brightened the room.

Colored-Leather Bindings

The texts of the agreements were bound in different colored leather—red for the North Vietnamese, blue for the United States, brown for South Vietnam and green for the Vietcong. French ushers solemnly passed them around on each signature. Mrs. Binh overlooked one place to sign and had to be given an album back for completion.

Mr. Rogers and Mr. Trinh used a large number of the black pens and then handed them to delegation members as souvenirs. William J. Porter, the new Deputy Under Secretary of State who had been the United States delegate to the semi-public talks until this month, flew to Paris with Mr. Rogers and sat at the table with him.

Heywood Isham, acting head of the United States delegation, Marshall Green, Assistant Secretary of State for East Asian and Pacific Affairs, and William H. Sullivan, Mr. Green's deputy, who has been leading technical talks with the North Vietnamese here, completed the American group at the table.

Two rectangular tables, carefully placed alongside the main table to symbolize the separation of the four delegations into two warring sides at the start of the conference in 1969, were reserved for the ambassadors of Canada, Hungary, Indonesia and Poland.

Their countries are contributing troops to an international commission that is to supervise the cease-fire.

Mr. Rogers and his Washington-based aides flew home immediately after the ceremony. Unexpectedly, Mr. Lam went with them.

Mr. Sullivan remained in Paris to receive the list of American prisoners from Hanoi and to hold further technical meetings on the many unsettled details of how arrangements are to be carried out.

At the airport before leaving, Mr. Rogers made his only comments on the event so long awaited with spurts of hope and bitter despair.

"It's a great day," he said.

He said President Nixon had devoted himself to building a structure of peace and continued: "The events in Paris today are a milestone in achieving that peace."

"I hope there'll be a cease-fire soon in all of Indochina," he added.

"All the News That's Fit to Print"

The New York Times

LATE CITY EDITION

Weather: Partly sunny today; fair tonight. Chance of rain tomorrow. Temp. range: today 50-64; Monday 45-68. Full U.S. report on Page 86.

VOL. CXXII ... No. 42,101 NEW YORK, TUESDAY, MAY 1, 1973 — 15 CENTS

NIXON ACCEPTS ONUS FOR WATERGATE, BUT SAYS HE DIDN'T KNOW ABOUT PLOT; HALDEMAN, EHRLICHMAN, DEAN RESIGN; RICHARDSON PUT IN KLEINDIENST POST

Biaggi Testimony to Jury Ordered Released in Full

U.S. Judge Criticizes Candidate's Petition —Delays Disclosure Pending Appeal —Troy Out as Campaign Chief

By JOHN CORRY

A Federal judge yesterday ordered the release of Mario Biaggi's testimony before a grand jury but held up the order when the mayoral candidate's lawyer said he would appeal to block disclosure.

In issuing the order, Judge Edmund L. Palmieri denied a motion by the Bronx Congressman for a panel of three judges to look over his testimony and state whether he had taken the Fifth Amendment "solely" on questions about his personal finances.

In the past, Mr. Biaggi had told leaders of the Conserva-

Excerpts from court testimony appear on Page 35.

tive party that he had answered all the questions put to him by the grand jury.

"Upon reflection," said Judge Palmieri in explaining why he ordered the minutes disclosed, "this court can only conclude that this blatantly unsanctioned petition [by Mr. Biaggi] was made with an expectation of its denial by the court, and for the purpose of publicly exploiting the court's denial of the motion."

Judge Palmieri said that he agreed with United States Attorney Whitney North Seymour Jr., who had asked for full disclosure of the testimony, that Mr. Biaggi's motion constituted an abuse of the court.

"What we have here is tantamount to a manipulation of legal procedures so that the truth can either be successfully concealed or at the very least made to appear different from the underlying facts," the judge said.

Appeal Set for Today

Mr. Biaggi's lawyer, Arthur H. Christy, said he would appeal the decision today to the United States Circuit Court of Appeals. Court sources reported that an appeal would probably be heard later this week or early next week.

Asked outside the court if Mr. Biaggi had told him to appeal, Mr. Christy said, "I follow the instructions of my client."

The political impact to the decision came quickly. Mr. Biaggi dismissed City Councilman Matthew J. Troy Jr. as his mayoral campaign manager. Mr. Troy said he had been preparing to quit anyway.

Simultaneously, leaders of the Conservative party, which has endorsed Mr. Biaggi for Mayor, were thrown into an argument.

Some of the leaders said they

Continued on Page 34, Column 5

ROGERS DEFENDS CAMBODIA RAIDS

Facing Fulbright Committee, He Says the Constitution Justifies the Bombing

By BERNARD GWERTZMAN
Special to The New York Times

WASHINGTON, April 30 — Secretary of State William P. Rogers said today that the continued American bombing in Cambodia was legally justified by the Constitution and was "a meaningful interim action" to force the Communist-backed insurgents there to agree to a cease-fire.

Mr. Rogers, testifying before the Senate Foreign Relations

Text of Rogers memorandum will be found on Page 10.

Committee, presented the Administration's long-awaited legal justification for the Cambodian bombing, an issue that has aroused considerable criticism from members of the committee, including its chairman, Senator J. W. Fulbright.

They have argued that President Nixon has no legal basis for the bombing, now that all American troops have been withdrawn from South Vietnam.

Though the committee members generally accorded Mr. Rogers friendly treatment, his arguments, both in his comments to the committee and in a 13-page legal memorandum, failed to sway the most vocal critics such as Senators Ful-

Continued on Page 11, Column 1

Egyptian Air Bases Reported Equipped For Libyan Planes

Special to The New York Times

BEIRUT, Lebanon, April 30—Diplomatic sources report that ground equipment has been installed at some Egyptian air bases for French-built fighter-bombers from Libya and British-built planes from other Arab countries, and that it has been tested by the aircraft during brief visits.

Israel has been charging that French-built Mirage jets from Libya and British-built Hunter interceptors from Iraq have been transferred to Egyptian bases, but there has been no comment in Cairo. A French Government spokesman said last week that French inquiries about the charges had brought denials from Libya and Egypt.

According to informed diplomats here, however, several embassies are known to have reported to their governments that ground equipment for Mirages was installed several weeks ago. These embassies are said to believe that the

Continued on Page 6, Column 1

Elliot L. Richardson, named Attorney General, yesterday

United Press International

President Nixon in White House press room after address

CONTROLS VOTED FOR ANOTHER YEAR

President Reluctantly Signs Compromise Bill Extending Wage and Price Curbs

By EDWARD COWAN
Special to The New York Times

WASHINGTON, April 30—With the reluctant support of the Administration, both houses of Congress approved today, and President Nixon signed, a compromise bill extending for another year the President's authority to regulate wages and prices.

Mr. Nixon signed the bill tonight, just after making a nationwide television and radio speech. The existing law, called the Economic Stabilization Act, was scheduled to expire at midnight.

The vote in the House was 267 to 115, a larger margin for passage than appeared likely before the Easter recess. The voice vote in the Senate was unrecorded.

Voting for the bill were 153 Democrats and 114 Republicans; opposed were 58 Democrats and 57 Republicans.

Meanwhile, the Department of Agriculture reported that prices received by farmers fell by 1.5 per cent in April, the first decline in a year. [Page 55.]

Mr. Nixon had sought a simple one-year extension of the act. But with the public frus-

Continued on Page 17, Column 1

Ellsberg Judge Demands Affidavits on Bugging Tie

By MARTIN ARNOLD
Special to The New York Times

LOS ANGELES, April 30 — The judge in the Pentagon papers trial today ordered four figures connected to the Watergate affair to produce affidavits concerning any link between that break-in and the trial here.

Federal District Judge William Matthew Byrne Jr. said that he was not foreclosing the possibility of summoning the four men here to testify, although he denied, for now, a defense request for an immediate hearing.

The affidavit order was directed to John W. Dean 3d, former special counsel to President Nixon; L. Patrick Gray 3d, former acting director of the F.B.I., and G. Gordon Liddy and E. Howard Hunt Jr., conspirators in the Watergate bugging.

Judge Byrne indicated that he also would probably require affidavits and perhaps testimony from former Attorney General John N. Mitchell, Richard G. Kleindienst, the present Attorney General; John D. Ehrlichman, until today the President's chief for domestic affairs; H. R. Haldeman, Mr. Nixon's chief of staff who also resigned today; Charles W. Colson, former Presidential special counsel, and Robert C. Mardian, former Assistant Attorney General.

Today's court session began with the judge announcing from the bench that about a month ago he met with Mr. Ehrlichman and President Nixon, "for approximately one minute or less," at Mr. Ehrlichman's suggestion.

At that time, he said, he was offered a new Government position, but he said he told Mr. Ehrlichman that he could not consider it "until this case is concluded." He did not say what the position was, but his name has been mentioned as a possible director of the Federal Bureau of Investigation.

Then, in response to demands from two defense lawyers,

Continued on Page 33, Column 6

SHAKE-UP LAUDED BY CONGRESSMEN

But Many Warn That Step Is Not Enough to Restore Faith in Administration

By JAMES M. NAUGHTON
Special to The New York Times

WASHINGTON, April 30 — Members of Congress joined in widespread, bipartisan praise today for President Nixon's shake-up of his Administration's high command.

But many Senators and Representatives coupled their commendations with warnings that a housecleaning of the White House staff would not be sufficient to restore faith in the Nixon Administration or the Government as a whole.

Furthermore, Representative John E. Moss of California urged House Democratic leaders to open a formal inquiry into the possible impeachment of President Nixon.

The suggestion by the longtime Democratic Congressman—which key leaders of both parties in the House described as "premature"—was the most severe reaction on Capitol Hill to the latest developments in the Watergate conspiracy case.

At Huron, Ohio, the nation's Democratic Governors joined in the call for appointment of a special prosecutor in the Watergate case.

Mark O. Hatfield, Republican

Continued on Page 33, Column 6

2 AIDES PRAISED

Counsel Forced Out —Leonard Garment Takes Over Job

By R. W. APPLE Jr.
Special to The New York Times

WASHINGTON, April 30 — Four top Nixon Administration officials resigned today as a consequence of the Watergate case, one of the most widespread scandals in American Presidential history.

H. R. Haldeman, the austere and secretive White House

Texts of Nixon announcement and resignations, Page 30.

chief of staff, and John D. Ehrlichman, the President's chief adviser on domestic affairs, maintained their innocence in letters submitting their resignations. Both said their ability to carry out their daily duties had been undermined.

The President chose Elliot L. Richardson, the Secretary of Defense, to succeed Richard G. Kleindienst as Attorney General and placed Mr. Richardson in charge of the Watergate investigation.

Mr. Kleindienst said he had quit because close friends had become Watergate suspects and "impartial enforcement of the law" ruled out such 'intimate relationships.'

Dean's Departure Asked

Mr. Nixon also announced that he had "requested and accepted" the resignation of John W. Dean 3d, the White House counsel, who had threatened to implicate superiors. Leonard Garment, a special Presidential consultant, was named to replace Mr. Dean temporarily.

No replacements for the two key aides were named, and the President gave no hint as to whom he might choose.

In a related development, the United States Information Agency announced tonight that Gordon Strachan had resigned as general counsel "after learning that persons with whom he had worked closely at the White House had submitted their resignations today." The statement said Mr. Strachan "stressed that he had no complicity in the Democratic National Committee break-in or in any alleged attempt to cover it up."

Mr. Haldeman's and Mr. Ehrlichman's departures strip the White House of its central operating mechanism at a time when far-reaching decisions must be made on inflation, Indochina policy and American relations with Europe.

The actions were announced

Continued on Page 30, Column 1

NEW DATA CITED

President Tells How He Changed Mind About Charges

By JOHN HERBERS
Special to The New York Times

WASHINGTON, April 30 — President Nixon told the nation tonight that he accepted the responsibility for what happened in the Watergate case even though he had had no knowledge of political espionage or attempts to cover it up.

The President went on na-

The text of Nixon's speech is printed on Page 31.

tionwide television and radio to discuss the case after he received the resignations of three top staff members who have been implicated—H. R. Haldeman, John D. Ehrlichman and John W. Dean 3d. He also accepted the resignation of Attorney General Richard G. Kleindienst.

Wrongdoing Alleged

While the President accepted the responsibility and pledged every effort to achieve justice in the case, he alleged wrongdoing or cover-up attempts on the part of those he had delegated to run his 1972 Presidential campaign and those he appointed to investigate the matter during the campaign.

And he implied that his own election officials, in the Watergate espionage, were attempting to stop wrongdoing by the Democrats.

Mr. Nixon also said that hereafter the investigation of the Watergate matters would be delegated to his new Attorney General, Elliot L. Richardson, while he, the President, turned his attention to grave foreign and domestic matters. He added that he would leave it up to Mr. Richardson whether to appoint a special prosecutor.

Weeks of Tension

The speech, which came after weeks of growing tension at the White House as developments in the Watergate scandal implicated Administration figures, was an emotional appeal to save the integrity of the Presidency for the 1,361 days, by Mr. Nixon's count, that remain in his term. This was the 100th day of his second term.

"Tonight I ask for your prayers to help me in everything that I do," Mr. Nixon said at the end. "God bless America, and God bless each and every one of you."

He accepted responsibility for Watergate with these words: "In any organization the man

Continued on Page 31, Column 5

Kissinger Is Going to Moscow For Talks on Brezhnev's Visit

Special to The New York Times

WASHINGTON, April 30 — Henry A. Kissinger will fly to Moscow this week for talks with Leonid I. Brezhnev, the Soviet Communist party leader, on plans for Mr. Brezhnev's expected visit to the United States late in June.

While in Moscow with his top staff aides, Mr. Kissinger will also discuss Vietnam, arms control negotiations, trade questions and other matters with Mr. Brezhnev and other top officials, a senior Administration official said.

The White House, in making the announcement, limited itself to saying that Mr. Kissinger would leave Thursday for four to five days in Moscow "for an exchange of views on a wide range of bilateral problems and matters of mutual interest."

But a senior Administration official said that the primary mission of the President's adviser for national security would be to discuss the details and likely agenda for Mr. Brezhnev's visit to the United States, which will return Mr. Nixon's visit to the Soviet Union last spring.

No date for Mr. Brezhnev's trip has been announced, but an Administration official said that both sides were planning on late June—around June 20.

It will be Mr. Brezhnev's first journey to the United States and the first by a top Soviet

Continued on Page 4, Column 4

Nixon Asks Tax Law Shift To Ease Filing on Income

By EILEEN SHANAHAN
Special to The New York Times

WASHINGTON, April 30 — The Nixon Administration proposed today changes in the tax laws and tax forms that would make it easier for millions of individuals to figure out their Federal income taxes.

The Administration's proposals contained little, however,

Summary of proposed changes is printed on Page 34.

that appeared likely to satisfy the demands of those who have been calling for reform of the tax laws.

All the basic provisions of the laws that reduce taxes for those who invest in business or property — the provisions relating to capital gains, depreciation, the depletion allowance and so on — would remain untouched under the Administration's plan.

The Administration did, however, recommend enactment of two new provisions that would limit the ability of wealthy individuals to combine different preferential sections of the tax laws in ways that permit them to escape all or most Federal income tax.

The proposals were submitted to the House Ways and Means Committee by the Secretary of the Treasury, George P. Shultz, in the form of a 175-page booklet called "Proposals for Tax Change."

The committee chairman, Wilbur D. Mills, Democrat of Arkansas, said he thought the proposals did not go far enough and criticized particularly the lack of any proposed changes in the taxation of capital gains and in the estate and gift taxes.

The plan for simplifying the

Continued on Page 35, Column 7

NEWS INDEX

End of Era in Nixon Presidency

By ROBERT B. SEMPLE Jr.
Special to The New York Times

News Analysis

WASHINGTON, April 30 — The resignations of H. R. Haldeman and John D. Ehrlichman from President Nixon's senior staff clearly mark the end of one era of the Nixon Presidency and the beginning of another. Things simply will not be the same. The question is how much different they will be.

The few men who remain in the President's suddenly shrunken entourage do not believe that the scandals of the moment will have much impact on Mr. Nixon's own personality. His habits are well entrenched, and any future White House operation will reflect the style of its master.

But there are some here now, in the White House and on Capitol Hill, who hope that Mr. Nixon will seize what they sense to be a rare opening to redesign his relationships with Congress, the bureaucracy, and even the press.

They hope to increase his access to others and theirs to him, to replace the closed corporation that the White House had become with the "open Presidency" to which he once aspired, and to return to his own first principles by decentralizing some of the power that has steadily flowed from the Government agencies to a few decision-makers in the White House.

Mr. Haldeman and Mr. Ehrlichman helped design that system, ran the system and, in time, came to symbolize the system. Their Teutonic names and mutual zeal for efficient execution gave rise to many jokes. Their enemies called them Hans and Fritz; their friends simply teased them.

In Mr. Ehrlichman's office on the second floor of the White House is a copy of Daniel P. Moynihan's "Understanding Poverty," which carries this inscription: "For John Ehrlichman. Achtung! D.P.M."

But their power was no joke. They were men with long ties and easy access to the President, men of loyalty, men who transmitted Mr. Nixon's orders to the bureaucracy and to whom, with few exceptions, Mr. Nixon's Cabinet members were forced to report before winning humble access to the Oval Office.

In all areas other than for-

Continued on Page 33, Column 4

Transcript of President's Broadcast Address to the Nation on the Watergate Affair

Following is a transcript of President Nixon's broadcast address in Washington last night, as recorded by The New York Times:

Good evening. I want to talk to you tonight from my heart on a subject of deep concern to every American.

In recent months members of my Administration and officials of the Committee for the Re-election of the President—including some of my closest friends and most trusted aides—have been charged with involvement in what has come to be known as the Watergate affair.

These include charges of illegal activity during and preceding the 1972 Presidential election and charges that responsible officials participated in efforts to cover up that illegal activity.

The inevitable result of these charges has been to raise serious questions about the integrity of the White House itself. Tonight I wish to address those questions.

Last June 17 while I was in Florida trying to get a few days' rest after my visit to Moscow, I first learned from news reports of the Watergate break-in. I was appalled at this senseless, illegal action, and I was shocked to learn that employes of the re-election committee were apparently among those guilty. I immediately ordered an investigation by appropriate Government authorities.

Seven Indicted in Case

On Sept. 15, as you will recall, indictments were brought against seven defendants in the case.

As the investigation went forward, I repeatedly asked those conducting the investigation whether there was any reason to believe that members of my Administration were in any way involved. I received repeated assurances that there were not. Because of these continuing reassurances, because I believed the reports I was getting, because I had faith in the persons from whom I was getting them, I discounted the stories in the press that appeared to implicate members of my Administration or other officials of the campaign committee.

Until March of this year, I remained convinced that the denials were true and that the charges of involvement by members of the White House staff were false.

The comments I made during this period, the comments made by my press secretary in my behalf, were based on the information provided to us at the time we made those comments.

New Data Received

However, new information then came to me which persuaded me that there was a real possibility that some of these charges were true and suggesting further that there had been an effort to conceal the facts both from the public—from you—and from me.

As a result, on March 21 I personally assumed the responsibility for coordinating intensive new inquiries into the matter and I personally ordered those conducting the investigations to get all the facts and to report them directly to me right here in this office.

I again ordered that all persons in the Government or at the re-election committee should cooperate fully with the F.B.I., the prosecutors and the grand jury.

I also ordered that anyone who refused to cooperate in telling the truth would be asked to resign from Government service.

And with ground rules adopted that would preserve the basic constitutional separation of powers between the Congress and the Presidency, I directed that members of the White House staff should appear and testify voluntarily under oath before the Senate committee which was investigating Watergate.

Full Truth Sought

I was determined that we should get to the bottom of the matter, and that the truth should be fully brought out no matter who was involved.

At the same time, I was determined not to take precipitive action and to avoid if at all possible any action that would appear to reflect on innocent people.

I wanted to be fair, but I knew that in the final analysis the integrity of this office — public faith in the integrity of this office — would have to take priority over all personal considerations.

Today, in one of the most difficult decisions of my Presidency, I accepted the resignations of two of my closest associates in the White House — Bob Haldeman, John Ehrlichman—two of the finest public servants it has been my privilege to know.

I want to stress that in accepting these resignations I mean to leave no implication whatever of personal wrongdoing on their part, and I leave no implication tonight of implication on the part of others who have been charged in this matter.

But in matters as sensitive as guarding the integrity of our democratic process, it is essential not only that rigorous legal and ethical standards be observed, but also that the public, you, have total confidence that they are both being observed and enforced by those in authority, and particularly by the President of the United States.

Move Held Necessary

They agreed with me that this move was necessary in order to restore that confidence, because Attorney General Kleindienst—though a distinguished public servant, my personal friend for 20 years, with no personal involvement whatever in this matter—has been a close personal and professional associate of some of those who are involved in this case, he and I both felt that it was also necessary to name a new Attorney General.

The counsel to the President, John Dean, has also resigned.

As the new Attorney General, I have today named Elliot Richardson, a man of unimpeachable integrity and rigorously high principle. I have directed him to do everything necessary to insure that the Department of Justice has the confidence and the trust of every law-abiding person in this country. I have given him absolute authority to make all decisions bearing upon the prosecution of the Watergate case and related matters. I have instructed him that if he should consider it appropriate he has the authority to name a special supervising prosecutor for matters arising out of the case.

Pursuit of Justice Promised

Whatever may appear to have been the case before, whatever improper activities may yet be discovered in connection with this whole sordid affair, I want the American people, I want you, to know beyond the shadow of a doubt that during my term as President justice will be pursued fairly, fully and impartially, no matter who is involved.

This office is a sacred trust, and I am determined to be worthy of that trust!

Looking back at the history of this case, two questions arise:

How could it have happened—who is to blame?

Political commentators have correctly observed that during my 27 years in politics, I've always previously insisted on running my own campaigns for office.

In both domestic and foreign policy, 1972 was a year of crucially important decisions, of intense negotiations, of vital new directions, particularly in working toward the goal which has been my overriding concern throughout my political career—the goal of bringing peace to America, peace to the world.

And that is why I decided as the 1972 campaign approached that the Presidency should come first and politics second. To the maximum extent possible, therefore, I sought to delegate campaign operations, to remove the day-to-day campaign decisions from the President's office and from the White House.

Accepts Responsibility

I also, as you recall, severely limited the number of my own campaign appearances.

Who then is to blame for what happened in this case?

For specific criminal actions by specific individuals those who committed those actions must of course bear the liability and pay the penalty. For the fact that alleged improper actions took place within the White House or within my campaign organization, the easiest course would be for me to blame those to whom I delegated the responsibility to run the campaign. But that would be a cowardly thing to do.

I will not place the blame on subordinates, on people whose zeal exceeded their judgment and who may have done wrong in a cause they deeply believed to be right. In any organization the man at the top must bear the responsibility.

That responsibility, therefore, belongs here in this office. I accept it.

And I pledge to you tonight from this office that I will do everything in my power to insure that the guilty are brought to justice and that such abuses are purged from our political processes in the years to come long after I have left this office.

Some people, quite properly appalled at the abuses that occurred, will say that Watergate demonstrates the bankruptcy of the American political system. I believe precisely the opposite is true.

Watergate represented a series of illegal acts and bad judgments by a number of individuals. It was the system that has brought the facts to light and that will bring those guilty to justice.

A system that in this case has included a determined grand jury, honest prosecutors, a courageous judge—John Sirica—and a vigorous free press.

It is essential now that we place our faith in that system, and especially in the judicial system.

It is essential that we let the judicial process go forward, respecting those safeguards that are established to protect the innocent as well as to convict the guilty.

It is essential that in reacting to the excesses of others, we not fall into excesses ourselves.

It is also essential that we not be so distracted by events such as this that we neglect the vital work before us, before this nation, before America at a time of critical impcıtance to America and the world.

Turning to Larger Duties

Since March, when I first learned that the Watergate affair might in fact be far more serious than I had been led to believe, it has claimed far too much of my time and my attention. Whatever may now transpire in the case, whatever the actions of the grand jury, whatever the outcome of any eventual trials, I must now turn my full attention—and I shall do so—once again to the larger duties of this office.

I owe it to this great office that I hold, and I owe it to you, to my country.

I know that, as Attorney General, Elliot Richardson will be both fair and he will be fearless in pursuing this case wherever it leads. I am confident that with him in charge justice will be done.

There is vital work to be done toward our goal of a lasting structure of peace in the world — work that cannot wait, work that I must do.

Tomorrow, for example, Chancellor Brandt of West Germany will visit the White House for talks that are a vital element of the Year of Europe, as 1973 has been called.

We are already preparing for the next Soviet-American summit meeting later this year.

This is also a year in which we are seeking to negotiate a mutual and balanced reduction of armed forces in Europe which will reduce our defense budget and allow us to have funds for other purposes at home so desperately needed.

It is the year when the United States and Soviet negotiators will seek to work out the second and even more important round of our talks on limiting nuclear arms, and of reducing the danger of a nuclear war that would destroy civilization as we know it.

It is a year in which we confront the difficult tasks of maintaining peace in Southeast Asia and in the potentially explosive Middle East.

There's also vital work to be done right here in America to insure prosperity—and that means a good job for everyone who wants to work; to control inflation that I know worries every housewife, everyone who tries to balance the family budget in America, to set in motion new and better ways of insuring progress toward a better life for all Americans.

When I think of this office, of what it means, I think of all the things that I want to accomplish for this nation, of all the things I want to accomplish for you.

Wrote Out Some Goals

On Christmas Eve, during my terrible personal ordeal of the renewed bombing of North Vietnam which, after 12 years of war, finally helped to bring America peace with honor, I sat down just before midnight. I wrote out some of my goals for my second term as President. Let me read them to you.

To make this country be more than ever a land of opportunity—of equal opportunity, full opportunity— for every American; to provide jobs for all who can work and generous help for those who cannot; to establish a climate of decency and civility in which each person respects the feelings and the dignity in the God-given rights of his neighbor; to make this a land in which each person can dare to dream, can live his dreams not in fear but in hope, proud of his community, proud of his country, proud of what America has meant to himself, and to the world.

These are great goals. I believe we can, we must work for them, we can achieve them.

But we cannot achieve these goals unless we dedicate ourselves to another goal. We must maintain the integrity of the White House.

And that integrity must be real, not transparent.

There can be no whitewash at the White House.

We must reform our political process, ridding it not only of the violations of the law but also of the ugly mob violence and other inexcusable campaign tactics that have been too often practiced and too readily accepted in the past including those that may have been a response by one side to the excesses or expected excesses of the other side.

Two wrongs do not make a right.

I've been in public life for more than a quarter of a century. Like any other calling, politics has good people and bad people and let me tell you the great majority in politics, in the Congress, in the Federal Government, in the state government are good people.

I know that it can be very easy under the intensive pressures of a campaign for even well-intentioned people to fall into shady tactics, to rationalize this on the grounds that what is at stake is of such importance to the nation that the end justifies the means.

And both of our great parties have been guilty of such tactics.

In recent years, however, the campaign excesses that have occurred on all sides have provided a sobering demonstration of how far this false doctrine can take us.

Warns on Falling in Trap

The lesson is clear. America in its political campaigns must not again fall into the trap of letting the end, however great that end is, justify the means.

I urge the leaders of both political parties, I urge citizens — all of you everywhere—to join in working toward a new set of standards, new rules and procedures to insure that future elections will be as nearly free of such abuses as they possibly can be made. This is my goal. I ask you to join in making it America's goal.

When I was inaugurated for a second term this past January 20, I gave each member of my Cabinet and each member of my senior White House staff a special four-year calendar with each day marked to show the number of days remaining to the Administration.

In the inscription on each calendar I wrote these words:

"The Presidential term which begins today consists of 1,461 days, no more, no less. Each can be a day of strengthening and renewal for America. Each can add depth and dimension to the American experience.

"If we strive together, if we make the most of the challenge and the opportunity that these days offer us, they can stand out as great days for America and great moments in the history of the world."

I looked at my own calendar this morning up at Camp David as I was working on this speech. It showed exactly 1,361 days remaining in my term.

I want these to be the best days in America's history because I love America. I deeply believe that America is the hope of the world, and I know that in the quality and wisdom of the leadership America gives lies the only hope for millions of people all over the world that they can live their lives in peace and freedom.

We must be worthy of that hope in every sense of the word.

Tonight, I ask for your prayers to help me in everything that I do throughout the days of my Presidency to be worthy of their hopes and of yours.

God bless America. And God bless each and every one of you.

Richardson Draft Surprises Pentagon

By JOHN W. FINNEY

Special to The New York Times

WASHINGTON, April 30—President Nixon's draft of Defense Secretary Elliot L. Richardson to be Attorney General, while sending a shock wave of surprise through the top ranks of the Pentagon, was not expected to disrupt the management of a defense program that has a momentum of its own.

At least momentarily the direction of the Pentagon will fall to William P. Clements Jr., a Texas oilman who has served under Mr. Richardson as Deputy Secretary af Defense. On defense policy. Mr. Clements is regarded as being considerably more conservative than Mr. Richardson.

Mr. Clements figured in the immediate speculation as a possible successor to Mr. Richardson, although it was understood he would be willing to remain as the No. 2 man in the Pentagon if the President should choose another person to be Secretary of Defense.

For the moment, the President was not tipping his hand on his plans for the Pentagon, and ultimately his choice may depend on whether he wants a business manager, such as Mr. Clements, to run the Pentagon, or a man more skilled in the political ways of Washington, such as Mr. Richardson, who could guide the defense budget over the Congressional hurdles.

The departure of Mr. Richardson, after only three months in the Pentagon, was the first direct impact of the Watergate scandal upon the business of the Defense Department. While some of Mr. Richardson's appointments of top officials had been delayed, basically the business of the Pentagon had gone on normally.

Mr. Richardson is leaving the Pentagon before he could have any direct impact on the defense program and at a time when the first grumblings of criticism about him were beginning to rise in the liberal ranks in Congress.

In a political irony that has not escaped him, Mr. Richardson's one major act as Secretary of Defense was to close some 40 military bases, including the Boston Naval Shipyard—an action that beclouded his political future in his home state of Massachusetts though perhaps not nationally.

As they have watched Mr. Richardson move from one job to another within the Nixon Administration and willingly accept policy laid down by the White House, some of his long-time friends have come to the conclusion that he is guided by a political ambition aimed at the Presidency.

Posture on the Military

In his brief stay at the Pentagon, Mr. Richardson found himself in the position of defending a defense policy he inherited while he tried to develop his own.

To win the confidence of the military and the Congressional armed services committees, who viewed with some skepticism the appointment of a Harvard-educated Bostonian to be Defense Secretary, he deliberately emphasized from the outset that he was an advocate of a "strong national defense" posture.

But in the process, he engendered growing uneasiness among Congressional critics of the defense budget, who were beginning to wonder whether he could or would chart any new directions in defense policy.

In the opinion of their subordinates, both Mr. Richardson and Mr. Clements, after an inevitable period of education, were just beginning to get their hands around the job of managing the Pentagon.

In the working relationship that was evolving between the two, Mr. Richardson concentrated on over-all policy and relations with Congress, while Mr. Clements specialized in weapons procurement programs as well as representing the Defense Department in subcommittee meetings of the National Security Council.

Like Mr. Richardson, Mr. Clements, in his caretaker role at the Pentagon, inherits a defense policy already set by the Administration, with the basic force structure, budget and weapons programs all determined.

As one official summed up the task facing Mr. Clements, "Our biggest difficulty now is not starting new programs or policies but getting the existing ones through Congress."

Mr. Richardson was playing tennis yesterday with a newspaper editor when he received a telephone call instructing him that he was to get on a helicopter and fly to Camp David, Md., to meet with the President. According to associates, Mr. Richardson's first hint that he was to shift from the Defense Department to the Justice Department had come Saturday, when the President talked with him by telephone.

Mr. Richardson told a surprised staff meeting at the Pentagon this morning that he would be leaving the Defense Department "soon" to go to the Justice Department.

"Everyone at the meeting was dumfounded," one participant in the meeting said. "He was just getting hold of the job, and it never occurred to any of us that he would leave."

Later Mr. Richardson issued a brief statement saying he had "accepted the President's nomination to be Attorney General because I believe I have an overriding duty to do so."

Officially, Mr. Richardson will remain as Secretary of Defense until his nomination as Attorney General is approved by the Senate. But unofficially, Mr. Richardson was expected to start concentrating immediately on the investigation of the Watergate case and the problems of the Justice Department.

Today, for example, he spent considerable time talking to Justice Department officials as well as individual Senators, trying, as he explained to reporters, "to develop some familiarity with the situations confronting the department."

United Press International

William P. Clements Jr., acting chief at Pentagon.

MITCHELL CAUTIOUS IN COMMENT ON CASE

Leaving his office at 20 Broad Street in lower Manhattan yesterday, former Attorney General John N. Mitchell was asked to comment on developments in the Watergate case and on the resignation of four of President Nixon's top White House aides.

"I don't know any more than you do," Mr. Mitchell said. "I'll have to wait until I hear what the President has to say."

Asked again, Mr. Mitchell said, "I have no knowledge other than what Mr. Ziegler said today." Ronald L. Ziegler is the White House press secretary.

Graham Asks Nation To Kneel in Repentence

The Rev. Billy Graham, the evangelist, who is a close friend of President Nixon, said yesterday that the Watergate scandal was a symptom of the "permissiveness, corruption and crime" permeating much of American life.

"What the country needs to do is get down on its knees in repentence before the Lord," he said, according to the Associated Press.

Mr. Graham said the entire situation "certainly must be clarified, the truth brought out," adding, "We Americans cannot accept corruption as a way of life. Democracy is based on trust and confidence."

After hearing Mr. Nixon's address last night, Mr. Graham observed:

"The President demonstrated a commendable humility. He accepted the responsibility. He promised an appropriate course of action. He asked for our prayers, and he has mine."

Fri, Ruckelshaus Deputy, Named Acting Administrator of E.P.A.

WASHINGTON, April 30 (AP) — Robert W. Fri took office today as acting administrator of the Environmental Protection Agency upon the departure of William D. Ruckelshaus to head the Federal Bureau of Investigation.

"The policies and objectives of E.P.A. have not changed and will not change under my guidance," Mr. Fri told newsmen.

Mr. Fri said that he would head the agency until a successor was named and then return to the management consulting concern he left two years ago when he was named deputy administrator of the environmental agency.

He said that he knew of no candidates for the agency post.

John R. Quarles Jr., general counsel, moves up to become Mr. Fri's deputy administrator and was replaced in turn by his former deputy, Alan Kirk.

Mr. Fri said that the agency would maintain continuity in both staff and policy, and would complete decisons and actions now pending without unusual delay.

Mr. Fri said that the major task facing the agency was the administrative job of developing and issuing tens of thousands of permits for air and water pollution emissions under national antipollution standards.

He said that he would make the decisions required of an administrator.

Mr. Fri, 37 years old, a native of Kansas City, Kan., holds degrees in physics from Rice University and in business administration from Harvard University.

The new administrator, who was a Navy officer from 1959 to 1962, joined McKinsey & Co., Inc., a management consulting concern, in 1963 and became a partner in 1968.

He was named deputy administrator of the environmental agency on June 15, 1971, when it was about seven months old.

Nixon Accepts Responsibility for Watergate Case

Continued From Page 1, Col. 8

at the top must bear the responsibility. That responsibility, therefore, belongs here in this office. I accept it."

Tonight Mr. Nixon was tense and grave. At the start of the speech he stumbled several times as he shuffled the pages from which he read. Afterward, technicians in the room said, the President brushed tears from his eyes and said, "It wasn't easy."

He gave the country the explanation that Republican leaders had been urging him to do for months.

First, he sought to establish his own innocence. For the first time in his long political career last year, he said, he had not run his own campaign. He said he had delegated that responsibility because he, as a candidate for re-election, had more important duties — the running of his office and the seeking of peace in Vietnam.

Last June, when he heard of the burglary and bugging of the Democratic National Committee he was appalled, he said, and appointed officials to look into it for any wrongdoing. Until March this year, he believed no one in the White House was involved. Since learning that members of his staff were implicated, Mr. Nixon said, he has spent much of his time attempting to get to learn the truth.

Bars Cowardly Way

"For specific criminal actions by specific individuals who committed those actions, those who committed those actions must of course bear the liability and pay the penalty," he said. "For the fact that alleged improper actions took place within the White House or within my campaign organization, the easiest course would be for me to blame those whom I delegated the responsibility to run the campaign. But that would be the cowardly thing to do."

"I will not place the blame on subordinates," he continued, his voice breaking slightly, "on people whose zeal exceeded their judgment and who may have done wrong in a cause they deeply believed to be right." He then said that he would assume the responsibility.

The President did not specify in what way he would accept the responsibility. But he made it clear that the guilty should be punished and he would not stand in the way.

"There can be no whitewash at the White House," he said.

Mr. Nixon suggested that his own investigators had lied to him. He said there had been "an effort to conceal the facts both from the public—from you—and from me."

The President's highly emotional appeal was characteristic of Nixon speeches of the past in which he has sought to defend himself from attacks. While accepting the blame, he said there had been "campaigning excesses" in both major parties and he left the implication that, in the Watergate case, one side, the Republicans, may have been trying to prevent the excesses of the other, the Democrats.

"Two wrongs do not make a right," Mr. Nixon said.

After accepting the responsibility, Mr. Nixon sought to elevate himself above the Watergate issue in order to better conduct his office. He said the prosecution of the case would be delegated to Mr. Richardson.

"I know that, as Attorney General, Elliot Richardson will be both fair and he will be fearless in pursuing this case wherever it leads," he said. "There is vital work to be done toward our goal of a lasting structure of peace in the world, work that cannot wait—work that I must do."

The President, having accepted the resignation of some top assistants, thus became faced with having to reshape the White House staff and find a way for the Administration to maintain its credibility.

The President was urged by Republican leaders around the country to name a chief of staff who has been in no way implicated in the allegations of political sabotage and who has an impeccable record for public service.

Mr. Nixon's decision to accept the resignations of his two aides was made over the weekend in the isolation of his mountaintop retreat at Camp David, Md., as both his friends and foes waited and wondered what he would do.

It was a typical performance for the 60-year-old President, who has prided himself on his handling of many crises in his long political career. There was evidence that this one was filled with as much personal trauma as any in the past.

Mr. Nixon began his retreat Friday evening after the Watergate disclosures rocked the White House all week, culminating in the resignation of L. Patrick Gray 3d as acting director of the Federal Bureau of Investigation and the President's hurried appointment of William D. Ruckelshaus as a temporary replacement.

Key Aides Left Behind

The President went by helicopter with his usual security force and his Irish setter, King Timahoe. Among those left behind were his close confidants of his four and a half years in the Presidency—Mr. Haldeman and Mr. Ehrlichman, men he characterized today as "two of my closest friends and most trusted assistants."

All week there had been indications that Mr. Nixon hoped to ride out the scandals of political espionage with Mr. Haldeman and Mr. Ehrlichman in place. They accompanied him on a trip to Mississippi on Friday, and several White House sources said that the two men had been attempting to hold their jobs.

But the pressures from Republican leaders around the country for dismissal of all major officials who had been mentioned in the Watergate case or were responsible for White House involvement had become great.

For much of the weekend, the President was reported to be in seclusion at the wooded retreat in the Catoctin Mountains, 70 miles from the White House, with only King Timahoe for company.

Then, on Saturday evening, things began to happen. The President called for his personal secretary, Rose Mary Woods, an indication that he might be preparing a statement in the Watergate case.

Yesterday, the helicopter traffic was heavy between the White House and Camp David. First, Mr. Haldeman and Mr. Ehrlichman flew up and conferred with the President. So did Mr. Kleindienst, who had not been implicated in the scandals but who had personal and professional relations with some who were. Mr. Richardson, who had been Secretary of Defense, was called off a Washington tennis court and whisked to the mountaintop.

Then this morning, shortly before noon, Ronald L. Ziegler, the White House press secretary, appearing harried and shaken, announced that the President had accepted the resignations of Mr. Haldeman, Mr. Ehrlichman, Mr. Kleindienst and Mr. Dean, the White House counsel; that he had appointed Mr. Richardson as Attorney General; and that the President was going on radio and television to discuss the matter.

The White House left the impression that, while Mr. Dean had been dismissed outright, Mr. Haldeman and Mr. Ehrlichman had agreed in their meeting with the President to resign with Mr Nixon's good wishes. It was understood, however, that Mr. Ehrlichman was more agreeable to leaving than was Mr. Haldeman, the man who had directed the White House staff with stern efficiency and had wielded more influence there than any other aide.

Nixon Asks Press for 'Hell' When Wrong

Special to The New York Times

WASHINGTON, April 30—Moments after President Nixon completed his television speech tonight, he walked into the room where the White House press briefings are held each morning.

With no Secret Service agents or staff aides accompanying him, he stepped behind the podium where Ronald L. Ziegler, his press secretary, usually answers reporters' questions. The lights in that part of the room were out. He stood in the shadows.

The President then looked out at a group of about 15 reporters and photographers who were standing there chatting. His voice was low; he appeared shaken.

"Ladies and gentlemen of the press," Mr. Nixon said, "we have had our differences in the past, and I hope you give me hell every time you think I'm wrong. I hope I'm worthy of your trust."

Then he turned and walked back toward the Presidential living quarters upstairs.

The President, according to an aide who had entered the Oval Office immediately after his address, began to say a few words to the television technicians, as is his custom, but tears welled in his eyes and his voice cracked noticeably.

The aide then reminded Mr. Nixon that he had to sign an extension of the Economic Stabilization Act before midnight. While the aide held a box of papers as a makeshift desk, the President scrawled his name.

It was immediately after this that the President went to the briefing room and talked to newsmen.

Mr. Nixon—often a bitter antagonist of the press since his days in Congress in the nineteen-fifties—paid tribute in his TV speech to the grand jury in the Watergate case, to the prosecutors, to Federal Judge John J. Sirica and finally to "a vigorous free press."

The White House held to a decision, announced earlier today, not to permit the taking of photographs of Mr. Nixon behind his desk in the Oval Office, which is customary when he makes major addresses. However, photographers snapped some quick pictures during his appearance in the briefing room.

Several news organizations protested the decision not to allow the taking of still photographs before, during or after the President's television address.

Protests were made by United Press International, The Associated Press, The New York Daily News, The Chicago Tribune and The Chicago Sun-Times.

"All the News That's Fit to Print"

The New York Times

LATE CITY EDITION

Weather: Chance of showers later today, tonight. Milder tomorrow. Temp. range: today 36-46; Friday 43-49. Additional details on Page 62.

VOL.CXXIII...No.42,406

NEW YORK, SATURDAY, MARCH 2, 1974

20c beyond 50-mile radius of New York City, except Long Island. Higher in air delivery cities.

15 CENTS

FEDERAL GRAND JURY INDICTS 7 NIXON AIDES ON CHARGES OF CONSPIRACY ON WATERGATE; HALDEMAN, EHRLICHMAN, MITCHELL ON LIST

John N. Mitchell
Former Attorney General

H. R. Haldeman
Headed White House staff

John D. Ehrlichman
Was Presidential adviser

Charles W. Colson
Former White House lawyer

Robert C. Mardian
1972 campaign coordinator

Kenneth W. Parkinson
Lawyer for campaign unit

Gordon C. Strachan
Assisted Mr. Haldeman

COLSON IS NAMED

A Question of Veracity of the President Is Indirectly Raised

By ANTHONY RIPLEY
Special to The New York Times

WASHINGTON, March 1—A Federal grand jury today indicted seven men, all former officials of President Nixon's Administration or of his 1972 re-election campaign, on charges of covering up the Watergate scandal.

Never before have so many close and trusted advisers of an American President faced criminal accusations in a single indictment.

All were charged with conspiracy — a conspiracy, the grand jury said, that continued

Five pages of Watergate material with indictment text begin on Page 14.

"up to and including" today; six were charged additionally with obstruction of justice; two with perjury and three with false statements to the Federal Bureau of Investigation, the grand jury or both.

The indictment accused one defendant, H. R. Haldeman, the former White House chief of staff, of lying when he quoted the President as saying "it would be wrong" to raise hush money for the perpetrators of the original Watergate burglary—a break-in June 17, 1972, at the Democratic National Committee headquarters.

Endorsed Statement

This indirectly raised a question about Mr. Nixon's veracity because he endorsed Mr. Haldeman's statement at a news conference last Aug. 22. The President recalled a meeting at the White House at which clemency for the Watergate defendants and financial support for their families was discussed. Mr. Nixon said he had told his White House counsel, John W. Dean 3d, "John it, is wrong, it won't work."

With the indictment, the grand jury handed to Chief Judge John J. Sirica of the Federal District Court here a sealed report, accompanied by a bulky briefcase reportedly containing information about Mr. Nixon's role in the Watergate affair.

This information was presumably intended for the House Judiciary Committee, which is considering a motion to impeach the President and put him on trial before the Senate.

The defendants and the charges against them are as follows:

John N. Mitchell, former Attorney General and director of Mr. Nixon's 1968 and 1972 Presidential campaigns—conspiracy, obstruction of justice, false statements to the F.B.I., false statements to the grand jury and perjury.

Mr. Haldeman—conspiracy, obstruction of justice and perjury.

John D. Ehrlichman, former assistant to the President for domestic affairs—conspiracy, obstruction of justice, false statements to the F.B.I. and false statements to the grand jury.

Charles W. Colson, former special counsel to the President—conspiracy and obstruction of justice.

Robert C. Mardian, former aide to Mr. Mitchell in the 1972 campaign—conspiracy.

Kenneth W. Parkinson, attorney for the Committee for the Re-election of the President—conspiracy and obstruction of justice.

Gordon C. Strachan, former aide to Mr. Haldeman—conspiracy, obstruction of justice and false statements to the grand jury.

The , key conspiracy count

Continued on Page 16, Column 1

Heath, Trailing Labor Party In Britain, Declines to Resign

Special to The New York Times

LONDON, March 1—Prime Minister Heath, deprived of his majority in Parliament by Britain's voters, declined to resign tonight. His action raised the prospect that Mr. Heath's Conservatives, outnumbered by the Labor party in the House of Commons, would try to remain in power.

Thus Britain faced one of the gravest crises in her modern political history. The last time when neither main party won an over-all majority was in 1929.

There was no official word. But sources close to Mr. Heath said that he had told Queen Elizabeth tonight that he wanted to stay in office despite his party's failure to win an over-all majority in the general election yesterday.

Wilson Prepared to Govern

A few hours earlier, Harold Wilson, the leader of the Labor party, said that he was prepared to form a new Cabinet. Labor also failed to win a majority, but it holds five more seats than the Conservatives.

With the virtual stalemate between the two big parties, the balance of power in the new House would be held by smaller ones, including the Liberals, Scottish and Welsh Nationalists and the Members from Northern Ireland.

If Mr. Heath carries on with a minority government, despite his campaign bid for a "fresh mandate" and a "strong" majority, the question is for how long. He could go down to defeat quickly in the new House of Commons if a majority voted "no confidence" on some issue that arose for debate.

If that occurred, it is expected that he would ask the Queen to call for Mr. Wilson to form a new Government. Any call for a new election is regarded as unlikely until sometime later after the party leaders have a chance to try to win support in the House.

It was Mr. Heath, on Feb. 7, who used his power as Prime Minister to order Parliament dissolved and to call yesterday's election.

His goal was a mandate to settle a strike in the Government-owned coal mines that had crippled the country's production and forced it onto a three-day work week. Yesterday, that mandate from the voters eluded him.

Tonight this was the standing of the parties in the new House of Commons, compared with their standings in the old one:

	New	Old
Labor	301	287
Conservative	296	322
Liberal	14	11
Others	23	10
Undecided	1	..

Mr. Heath, after a day of meetings with his advisers at 10 Downing Street, emerged shortly after 7:30 P.M. local time (3:30 P.M., New York time) for his meeting with the Queen, who had interrupted a visit to Australia to return here.

Statement Is Issued

A statement from 10 Downing Street said:

"The Queen has granted the Prime Minister's request to her to grant him an audience at 7:45 P.M. so that he can report on the current political situation."

If Mr. Health had submitted his resignation, the announcement would have come quickly. But it was clear that he had

Continued on Page 10, Column 1

British Pound Plunges

The value of the British pound fell 1.85 cents and prices of stocks went down 24 points in hectic trading in London yesterday in reaction to the setback for Britain's Conservative Government. Details on Page 41.

MITCHELL JUDGE HALTS TRIAL HERE

Weighs Motion for Mistrial Over 'Apparent Excesses' in Prosecutor's Speech

By RALPH BLUMENTHAL

Federal Judge Lee P. Gagliardi abruptly suspended yesterday the conspiracy-perjury trial of John N. Mitchell and Maurice H. Stans for what he called "apparent excesses" by the chief Government prosecutor in his opening statement.

Judge Gagliardi said that he would rule Monday on demands by defense attorneys for a mistrial. He ordered the prosecutor, Assistant United States Attorney James W. Rayhill, to submit a "documented response" with his "excuses."

While neither side would comment on the surprising development, some observers in the court believed it unlikely that the judge would decide to discharge the newly picked jury, which had been carefully isolated from news of yesterday's Watergate indictments naming Mr. Mitchell along with six others.

Conspiracy Charged

The historic trial was interrupted just after the Government had told the jury that it would prove that the defendants had conspired to quash a Federal investigation of Robert L. Vesco, the fugitive financier, in exchange for his secret $200,000 cash contribution to President Nixon's re-election campaign, that the defendants covered up the scheme and lied, about it when questioned under oath.

At the close of his hour and 50 minutes presentation in the fifth-floor courtroom in the

Continued on Page 18, Column 6

Nixon Urges Quick Trials, Cautions on Prejudgment

By JOHN HERBERS
Special to The New York Times

WASHINGTON, March 1 — President Nixon expressed the hope today that trials arising out of the new Watergate indictments "will move quickly to a just conclusion." He also cautioned the nation to remember that the accused are presumed innocent unless proved guilty.

"The indictments indicate the judicial process is finally moving toward resolution of the matter," Gerald L. Warren, the White House deputy press secretary, said in a statement approved by Mr. Nixon. The statement, read to newsmen, added:

"It is the President's hope that the trials will move quickly to a just conclusion. The President is confident that all Americans will join him in recognizing that those indicted are presumed innocent unless proof of guilt is established in the courts."

The statement also declared that the President had "always maintained that the judicial system is the proper forum for the resolution of the questions concerning Watergate."

Two of the seven men accused in today's indictment, Charles W. Colson and Kenneth W. Parkinson, issued personal statements of innocence and predicted their eventual exoneration on the charges. The other five relied on their attorneys to issue brief statements of innocence. [Details, Page 16.]

Word of the Watergate indictments reached the Oval Office today via the news tickers, and the President—busy with policy meetings, ceremony and entertaining of Congressmen—reacted with his brief formal statement a short time later.

Gen. Alexander M. Haig Jr. and Ronald L. Ziegler, the President's chief assistants, informed Mr. Nixon of the charges against his former high associates just as the President was ending a meeting with his economic and energy advisers and was preparing to welcome the Mayor of Meridian, Miss., Tom Stuart, who had gotten 20,000 names on a petition in

Continued on Page 17, Column 3

SIRICA SAID TO GET FINDINGS ON NIXON

Grand Jury Reported to Ask Him to Give Evidence on Watergate to House

By JAMES M. NAUGHTON
Special to The New York Times

WASHINGTON, March 1—The Watergate grand jury reportedly asked Chief Judge John J. Sirica of the United States District Court today to give the House impeachment inquiry evidence relating to President Nixon's role in the Watergate case.

The grand jury issued a sealed "report" to the judge, and investigative sources said that they understood the document contained a description of the grand jury's findings about Mr. Nixon's possible involvement in the Watergate cover-up.

Moments later, the special Watergate prosecutor's office gave Judge Sirica a large briefcase said to contain a mass of documents and other evidence sought by the House Judiciary Committee for its investigation of the President's conduct in

Continued on Page 17, Column 1

The Scene in Sirica's Court: A Historic 13 Minutes

By LINDA CHARLTON
Special to The New York Times

WASHINGTON, March 1—At 10 A.M. today, Judge John J. Sirica was sitting in his chambers, reminiscing about his 16 years on the bench, whiling away the time until he could put a black robe over his gray suit and walk into Courtroom 2 to preside over history.

He arrived to be greeted with the shuffle of a crowd rising to its feet as a court functionary intoned ceremonial phrases, ending with the prayer for the country and for "this honorable court." Some 13 minutes and surprisingly few words later, it was over.

The small, wood-paneled courtroom, with a checkerboard cork floor, an American flag and seal and two maroon ceramic water pitchers as the only decorations, was filled—with lawyers, Watergate task force staff members and reporters. The long line of would-be spectators that had started forming two hours before the 11 A.M. hearing was exiled to the corridor.

The prosecution's table was crowded with lawyers and papers. At the defense table, on the right side of the courtroom, sat a lone figure, Paul Murphy of the law firm of Hundley & Gacheris, representing John N. Mitchell.

The focus of attention was a group of 21 distributed

Continued on Page 18, Column 3

The New York Times/Marilyn Church

Assistant U.S. Attorney James W. Rayhill, standing, making his opening statement to the jury in the trial of John N. Mitchell, seated foreground, and Maurice H. Stans. Judge Lee P. Gagliardi is at upper left.

RED CROSS VISITS 65 ISRAELI P.O.W.'S

Sees Prisoners in Syria—Kissinger Confers With Assad in Damascus

By BERNARD GWERTZMAN
Special to The New York Times

DAMASCUS, Syria, March 1—Israeli prisoners held by Syria, long the focus of a dispute that prevented troop-pullback negotiations, received their first visit from Red Cross inspectors today.

The visit was arranged as part of the latest round of Middle East diplomacy, which carried Secretary of State Kissinger today from Egypt to Israel and then to Syria. He immediately began talks here with President Hafez al-Assad to convey ideas on troop disengagements that he had just received from Premier Golda Meir and other top Israeli officials.

At the end of the session between President Assad and the Secretary of State, both American and Syrian spokesmen indicated that talks on the separation of forces would continue after Mr. Kissinger left here tomorrow on his way to return to the United States. There was no announcement that any firm agreement had been reached on how negotiations between Israel and Syria would take place.

The Syrian spokesman said that Mr. Assad had not accepted the Israeli ideas presented to him by Mr. Kissinger and had offered one in return, which Mr. Kissinger "will study

Continued on Page 4, Column 3

Two-Way Radios in Taxis To Help City Fight Crime

By WILL LISSNER

The city officially began a program yesterday to put on the streets thousands of cruising taxicab drivers trained in the observation and reporting of crime and who are in radio communication with the police.

The new auxiliary arm of the police is the Civilian Radio Motor Patrol, which, Mayor Beame said, already has 500 crime watchers at work — 350 in the Bedford Park section of the Bronx and 150 in communities in Brooklyn operating from a Sheepshead Bay base.

Many taxicabs are dispatched by radio, the dispatcher having the transmitter and the cab the receiver. These one-way systems cannot be used in this program. The patrol system in use links the dispatcher and the driver by a two-way radio.

Under the system, telephone lines link the dispatcher to the switchboard operator in the police station. When necessary, the desk sergeant can then talk directly to the taxicab driver.

Two similar networks are to be opened soon in Queens, one in Long Island City and one in Richmond Hill, according to Stanley Bakalar, president of the Associated Radio Metered Taxi Owners Council.

"Eventually Manhattan and Staten Island will be covered, too," he added.

"This is another example of how we can use the city's greatest asset—its citizens—in attacking its number one problem, crime," Mayor Beame said. He and Police Commissioner Michael J. Codd and a group of Bronx officials joined in inaugurating the system at a ceremony at the Bedford Park station in the Bronx.

The program costs the city only the services of the coordinator, Lieut. John Higgins, and the training officers. In the Bronx the cost of installing the tie-lines between the taxi dispatchers and the police was paid for by the First National City Bank and the $12 monthly service charge for the tie-line phones is paid by the taxi cooperatives—the All City Radio Taxi Association and the Bronx Two-Way Radio Metered Taxi Company. Each taxi will display a yellow and black decal announcing its participation in "Civilian Radio Patrol, Community Service."

The city's police have a number of programs in operation using civilians to supplement the department's professional manpower. A primary one is the Auxillary Police, whose members patrol the streets and perform other police functions under the supervision of police officers.

Another is the Blockwatcher Program, in which civilians act as the eyes of the police on their own block.

NEWS INDEX

Federal Grand Jury Indicts 7 Nixon Aides for Conspiracy in the Watergate Case

List Includes Haldeman, Ehrlichman and Mitchell

Continued From Page 1, Col. 8

against all seven defendants charged that they "and other persons to the grand jury known and unknown, unlawfully, willfully and knowingly did combine, conspire, confederate and agree together and with each other" to commit several Federal offenses.

It cited two statutes that prohibit the making of false statements and declarations to Federal agencies and a third prohibiting efforts to prevent Federal agencies from transacting their official business "honestly and impartially."

It specifically named the Central Intelligence Agency, the Federal Bureau of Investigation and the Justice Department as agencies the defendants allegedly attempted to prevent from carrying out their duties.

The 24 separate counts in the indictment allege destruction of evidence in the case, making false statements to the Federal agencies and before the Senate Watergate committee, gathering up cash and making payments to the defendants in the original Watergate burglary trial, and giving assurances of executive clemency to the seven men accused in the break-in.

Arraignment March 9

Judge Sirica set arraignment for March 9 and, later in the day, announced that he had assigned himself to try the case.

Leon Jaworski, the special Watergate prosecutor, is expected to seek further indictments in the next few weeks.

The grand jury, which was originally sworn in June 5, 1972, before the burglary, was told it would have further work.

In all, three grand juries are sitting in the Watergate case. The one that acted today could return further indictments, although there is no assurance that it will.

Mr. Jaworski told the judge that the case could take "three or four months to try" and called it "undoubtedly long and protracted."

The judge then read an order advising all concerned to refrain from making statements outside the court "concerning any aspect of this case that is likely to interfere with the rights of the accused or the public to a fair trial by an impartial jury."

In some of the 31 Watergate-related cases that have gone before the courts, defense lawyers have contended that excessive pretrial publicity hurt their clients' chances for a fair trial.

The indictment today had been delayed by the selection of a jury in New York City in the trial of Mr. Mitchell and former Commerce Secretary Maurice H. Stans in connection with an illegal $200,000 cash gift to the re-election campaign from Robert L. Vesco, the fugitive financier. The indictment here was released after the New York jury was sequestered.

If convicted of the charges issued today, the accused face the following penalties:

Mr. Haldeman, a maximum of 25 years in prison and $16,000 in fines.

Mr. Ehrlichman, a maximum of 25 years in prison and $40,000 in fines.

Mr. Colson and Mr. Parkinson, a maximum of 10 years in prison and $10,000 in fines.

Mr. Mitchell, a maximum of 30 years in prison and $42,000 in fines.

Mr. Strachan, a maximum of 15 years in prison and $20,000 in fines.

Mr. Mardian, a maximum of five years in prison and $5,000 in fines.

The indictment listed five counts against Mr. Halderman. One count stated that Mr. Haldeman lied under oath before the Senate Watergate committee when he quoted the President as saying it would be no trouble to raise $1-million to pay in hush money to the original seven Watergate conspirators "but it would be wrong."

Ehrlichman Charges

Mr. Haldeman stated to the committee that he had listened to a tape recording of that day's meeting and that it confirmed his recollection.

"I am absolutely positive," he told the committee.

That remark was underscored by the special prosecutor's office as perjury.

The other counts against Mr. Haldeman included a general conspiracy count that all seven faced. It charged they conspired to obstruct justice, make false statements, defraud the Government and deprive the Government of its right to have its officials transact business "honestly and impartially, free from corruption, fraud, improper and undue influence, dishonesty, unlawful impairment and obstruction."

These actions, the indictment said, included attempting to persuade the Central Intelligence Agency to provide financial assistance to the original seven men convicted in the Watergate burglary, to obtain their release from jail, to remove and destroy documents, to plan deceptive and false testimony, to secretly raise and distribute money and to make offers of "leniency, executive clemency and other benefits."

Mr. Ehrlichman was named in five counts. In addition to the over-all conspiracy charge, he was accused of obstruction of justice, making a false statement to the Federal Bureau of Investigation, and making, on two occasions, false statements to the grand jury.

The grand jury said, for instance, that Mr. Ehrlichman lied when he testified before it in May, 1973, that he did not remember telling Herbert W. Kalmbach, Mr. Nixon's personal attorney, that raising money for the original Watergate defendants should be kept secret.

Also, the indictment contended, Mr. Ehrlichman lied to the F.B.I. when "he stated that he had neither received nor was he in possession of any information relative to the break-in other than what he had read in the way of newspaper accounts of that incident."

One overt act in the conspiracy charged to Mr. Colson was a telephone conversation in which he and E. Howard Hunt Jr., one of the convicted Watergate conspirators, discussed "the need to make additional payments" to the original Watergate defendants.

Mr. Mitchell faces six counts of conspiracy, obstruction of justice, false declaration to a grand jury and making a false statement to the F.B.I.

It is alleged, for example, that on Sept. 14, 1972, when he appeared before the grand jury and was asked if he knew of any plans to spy on the Democrats, he falsely answered: "Certainly not, because, if there had been, I would have shut it off as being entirely nonproductive at that particular time of the campaign."

Many of Mr. Mitchell's allegedly false statements were hedged with phrases such as "No, I don't recall that, No" and "I have no such recollection."

Mr. Parkinson, who faces two counts, was named in the conspiracy count as meeting in mid-July, 1972, with Mr. Mitchell and John W. Dean 3d. Mr. Dean is a key witness for the special prosecutor and was Mr. Nixon's counsel at the White House.

The indictment states that Mr. Parkinson met with the two other men at the headquarters of the Committee for the Re-election of the President and "Mitchell advised Dean to obtain F.B.I. reports of the investigation into the Watergate break-in for Parkinson and others."

Cash for Defendants

Mr. Strachan faces two counts, one in the conspiracy and the other for making a false declaration before the grand jury concerning the $350,000 in cash kept by Mr. Haldeman in a safe and ultimately allegedly used to pay the original seven defendants for their cooperation.

The indictment states that he lied in telling how the money had been handled.

Mr. Mardian was charged solely with participation in the conspiracy. Among the overt acts in which he was said to have been involved was a June 24, 1927, meeting at which he and Mr. Mitchell "suggested to Dean that the C.I.A. be requested to provide covert funds for the assistance" of the original Watergate defendants.

At least two figures who appeared at the Senate hearings have said they are connected with events mentioned in the indictment today but were not charged. They are L. Patrick Gray 3d, former director of the F.B.I., who admitted burning evidence with his Christmas trash, and Anthony Ulasewicz, a former New York City policeman who said he handled money that went to the original defendants.

UNITED STATES DISTRICT COURT
FOR THE DISTRICT OF COLUMBIA

UNITED STATES OF AMERICA v. JOHN N. MITCHELL, HARRY R. HALDEMAN, JOHN D. EHRLICHMAN, CHARLES W. COLSON, ROBERT C. MARDIAN, KENNETH W. PARKINSON, and GORDON STRACHAN, Defendants.	)	Criminal No. Violation of 18 U.S.C. §§ 371, 1001, 1503, 1621, and 1623 (conspiracy, false statements to a government agency, obstruction of justice, perjury and false declarations.)

INDICTMENT

The Grand Jury charges:

Introduction

1\. On or about June 17, 1972, Bernard L. Barker, Virgilio R. Gonzalez, Eugenio R. Martinez, James W. McCord, Jr. and Frank L. Sturgis were arrested in the offices of the Democratic National Committee, located in the Watergate office building, Washington, D. C., while attempting to photograph documents and repair a surreptitious elec-

Part of the first page of the indictment handed up yesterday in Washington

Charges of Nixon Misconduct Inferred By Lawyers Analyzing Action of Jury

By WARREN WEAVER Jr.
Special to The New York Times

WASHINGTON, March 1 — Federal grand juries issue reports rather than indictments so rarely that today's action by the Watergate grand jury prompted widespread discussion among lawyers and politicians of its potential meaning for President Nixon.

Unlike grand juries operating under the supervision of state courts, Federal grand juries generally observe the broad stricture to "indict or shut up" and thus do not issue the general statements on deplorable conditions that are technically known as presentments.

As a result, legal authorities concluded today that the Watergate report probably contained specific charges of misconduct that might constitute crime but were not handed up in the form of indictments for one of two legal reasons.

First, if the report includes charges against the President that might ordinarily form the basis for one or more indictments, the grand jurors may have chosen this mechanism because of their belief that the President is immune from prosecution for crime while in office.

Agreement on Law

Virtually all criminal law authorities agree that the President is not subject to legal process while in office, cannot be compelled to appear in court and is for all practical purposes not triable. Thus any attempt to indict him would be doomed from the start.

Second, if the report contains charges that would not ordinarily support a criminal indictment, the grand jury may have used the document as a vehicle to convey the information to the investigating body empowered to consider this kind of accusation, the House Judiciary Committee.

A pitched debate is under way as to whether the House committee can properly recommend impeachment of the President on the basis of information that would not support a criminal indictment in court.

The White House maintains that only accusations of crime are valid grounds while the committee staff and a majority of its members argue that impeachment can be voted on the basis of serious misconduct in office that does not necessarily constitute a crime.

The Department of Justice, in a report issued earlier this week, held that it was an open question, not clearly resolved by statue or precedent.

Some legal authorities questioned today whether a regular grand jury, such as the Watergate panel, had authority to issue a report. The Federal Criminal Code gives such power to special grand juries, empaneled with the approval of the Justice Department, but is silent as to regular grand juries.

Other lawyers, however, said that grand jury reports, while relatively rare, were issued before the 1970 statute creating special grand juries was passed, and that there were thus a number of precedents for today's action.

Judge John J. Sirica has a number of alternate courses in dealing with the grand jury report. In the first place, he may strike all or part of it from the record if he finds some charges unsubstantiated or scandalously unfair. Such portions would be automatically and permanently sealed.

Under the Federal Criminal Code, the judge must compare the report with the grand jury minutes. If he concludes that the subject matter was within the grand jury's jurisdiction and the conclusions are supported by the "preponderance of the evidence," he issues an order accepting the report.

He must also first be assured that anyone named by the grand jury in the report has been given the opportunity to testify on his own behalf. This perhaps was the reason President Nixon was requested to appear by the grand jury a month ago. He refused, as he reported in his news conference this week.

It is possible that the House Judiciary Committee could claim to be such an agency with respect to the President. In the light of its current impeachment study, the law, in the absence of specific statute or precedent, is unclear.

The criminal code also provides that any person named in a report has the right to submit an answer, stating his defense to the charges, which then becomes an appendix to the report and is made public with it.

The presentment, another name for a grand jury report, goes back to the reign of William the Conqueror (1066 to 1087), who charged a grand jury with determining who owned what land in England after the Norman invasion and then used its report to displace property owners in favor of his lords.

Historically thereafter, the presentment was the grand jury's record of its accusations written in Anglo-Saxon, which the prosecutor then translated into Latin, whereupon it became an indictment.

Later the term presentment was restricted to reports by grand juries that stopped short of accusing any individual of a crime.

Additional Funds Voted For Ervin's Committee

WASHINGTON, March 1 (Reuters)—The Senate voted today to give its Watergate committee an additional $300,000 to complete its investigations and prepare a report.

The committee, which is headed by Senator Sam J. Ervin Jr., Democrat of North Carolina, is scheduled to issue a report on its months of hearings by May 28.

The Senate had previously given the committee $1.5-million for its inquiry, which included hearings that were televised last year.

REACTION LIMITED IN THE CONGRESS

But Democratic Leaders at Meeting in Capital Cheer News of Indictments

By RICHARD L. MADDEN
Special to The New York Times

WASHINGTON, March 1 — With many members of Congress out of town, initial reaction today to the new indictments in the Watergate case was limited and mostly restrained.

But the reaction was less restrained at a meeting of the Democratic National Committee when Robert S. Strauss, the party's national chairman, interrupted the proceedings to read the names of the seven indicted men.

The audience reacted with applause and a few hoots, and Mr. Strauss said, "I believe all of us are pleased that justice might finally work its will."

The Senate minority leader, Hugh Scott, of Pennsylvania, told reporters that he thought the American people "will withhold judgment pending a fair trial."

"Nothing should be said that would interfere with the conduct of a fair trial," he added.

Quick Trial Hoped For

Mr. Scott said that he hoped the trial would be completed quickly and before the November elections, because "it ought to be kept out of the political arena."

Mike Mansfield of Montana, the Senate majority leader, said: "The Constitution, legal and judicial processes are all functioning. They are not guilty until proven, as the President said."

In Phoenix, Vice President Ford opened a news conference by saying:

"We must keep in mind that under our system of justice that anyone accused of a crime is presumed innocent until proven guilty. I trust that all the defendants in the Watergate case will get a prompt and fair trial."

Senator Jacob K. Javits, Republican of New York, said that the indictments "reflect once again that the appropriate and ordinary processes of our criminal justice system are working, and that they are working without discrimination or favor with regard to the high positions of influence and power formerly occupied by those who have been indicted."

Senator George McGovern of South Dakota, the 1972 Democratic Presidential nominee, told reporters, "It is fair to say the outcome [of the election] would have been different if we knew then what we know now." However, he declined to say that he might have won the election.

Earlier, Mr. McGovern delivered a prepared speech on the Senate floor saying that Mr. Nixon's "soiled Administration is now the chief threat to the Presidency." He said that impeachment was "the one clear constitutional remedy for the illness that is now destroying our nation."

"It can drive away the clouds of doubt, suspicion and fear and let the sun shine on America again," he said.

Representative Peter W. Rodino Jr., Democrat of New Jersey and chairman of the House Judiciary Committee, which is considering the possible impeachment of Mr. Nixon, declined to comment on the indictment. So did Representative Edward Hutchinson of Michigan, the committee's senior Republican.

Ruling by Sirica Imposes Silence on All Concerned

By BILL KOVACH
Special to The New York Times

WASHINGTON, March 1—Restricted by a carefully worded gag rule issued by Federal District Judge John J. Sirica, the seven men accused in today's indictments and their attorneys issued only terse statements of innocence of the charges.

Two of those accused in the indictment charging conspiracy to obstruct justice, Charles W. Colson and Kenneth W. Parkinson, issued a personal statement of innocence and predicted their eventual exoneration on the charges.

The five others named—John D. Ehrlichman, H. R. Haldeman, Robert C. Mardian, John N. Mitchell and Gordon C. Strachan—relied on their attorneys to issue brief statements of innocence.

When the indictments were reported this morning they were accompanied by an order of Judge Sirica that enjoined all parties from any statements on the matter outside the court.

None of the seven, some of whom at one time were among the most powerful men in Government and those closest to President Nixon, were present in the courtroom when the indictments were handed up by the grand jury.

The First to Respond

Mr. Colson, the first to respond to the charges, called a news conference when he was notified that the indictment would name him. Speaking in the offices of the law firm from which he has taken a leave of absence, Mr. Colson said:

"My conscience is clear. Regardless of how rough the road ahead may be, I know that in the end my innocence will be established because I put complete faith in God and I believe deeply in my country."

Mr. Colson had reportedly originally planned to issue a five-page statement detailing claims of his innocence but was dissuaded by his attorneys because of the judge's order against out-of-court comment.

Mr. Parkinson, who served in 1972 as an attorney for the Finance Committee to Re-Elect the President and the Committee for the Re-election of the President, also issued a brief statement, saying, "During the past months my friends at the bar have expressed confidence in me and I thank them and promise when all circumstances are brought to light my innocence will be clearly demonstrated."

The only other one of the accused to speak publicly, H. R. Haldeman, the former White House chief of staff, told newsmen in Los Angeles: "I have no comment and will have none for the time being. When the time does come that I have something, I will let you know."

'Nothing to Say'

John J. Wilson, Washington attorney who represents Mr. Haldeman and John D. Ehrlichman, the former domestic affairs adviser to the President, said his clients had neither read the charges nor had a chance to confer with him "and we have nothing to say."

William G. Hundley, Washington attorney for former Attorney General John N. Mitchell who is now on trial on conspiracy charges in New York City, also had little to say.

"We are going to fight this all the way," Mr. Hundley said, "and expect to be vindicated in the courts."

Referring to the judge's gag rule as a limiting force, Robert C. Marian, former Assistant Attorney General in Charge of Internal Security, spoke through his attorney, Thomas Green, who said: "Given this order, all we can say is we deny the charges, otherwise we risk a problem."

Neither Gordon C. Strachan, former assistant to Mr. Haldeman, nor his attorney could be reached for comment.

At least some of the reluctance of those accused and their attorneys to discuss the charges publicly apparently stems from the fact that one of the defense strategies being considered by some of them is based on prejudicial pre-trial publicity.

Challenge Considered

Other attorneys are privately chafing under the order and had briefly considered a legal challenge to the order as a violation of the First Amendment to the Constitution. Attorneys familiar with the legal situation, however, point out that a similar gag rule was challenged and upheld at the district level in Federal courts.

The order issued by Judge Sirica is directed to all those in the office of the Watergate special prosecutor, all defendants, their attorneys and all those identified as witnesses in the case. It enjoins them from making any "extrajudicial statements concerning any aspect of this case . . ." and further defines "extrajudicial statements" as "any statement which is not made during the course of judicial proceedings in this case."

Most attorneys who are connected with the case agreed that the order restricted them to little beyond statements of innocence.

Mr. Colson's statement, the most extensive issued today, defended not only himself, but President Nixon.

"Above all [I am] proud," he said, "to have served a man whom I believe history will record as one of the greatest and most courageous of our Presidents. Like most human beings, I have made my share of mistakes but during the time I served, I have always done my duty as I saw it."

Associated Press

Leon Jaworski, special Watergate prosecutor.

Sketches of the Seven Nixon Aides Indicted by the Watergate Grand Jury

John Newton Mitchell

The champion of law and order in the Nixon Administration when he was Attorney General . . . In addition to his indictment today, he is on trial in New York City, charged with trying to impede a Federal investigation in return for a secret $200,000 campaign contribution to Mr. Nixon from the fugitive financier Robert L. Vesco . . . In March, 1972, the amply-built pipe smoker left Justice to mastermind the President's re-election campaign . . . Three months later, two weeks after the break-in at the Watergate, he resigned, saying his wife, Martha, had persuaded him to leave . . . Now separated from his wife . . . Has secluded himself in a Manhattan apartment . . . Born in Detroit on Sept. 5, 1913 . . . Worked his way through Fordham University and law school to wealth and prominence on Wall Street with national recognition as a specialist in municipal and state financing . . . He learned politics, a friend said, "in the back rooms of statehouses arranging bond issues" . . . Met Richard Nixon only a year or so before their law firms merged in 1967 . . . Became Mr. Nixon's right-hand man . . . Ran Mr. Nixon's Presidential campaign in 1968 . . . At the beginning of his Administration, the President called his Attorney General "my closest adviser, as you know, on all legal matters and on many other matters as well."

Harry Robbins Haldeman

Known as the "Prussian" . . . Political philosophy falls somewhat to the right of the President . . . As the White House chief of staff, he was in the strategic position of determining who should and should not be admitted to the Oval Office . . . All the papers that wound up on the President's desk were first organized by him . . . Credited with building a "Berlin wall" around the President . . . For more than 20 years, his life moved back and forth between advertising and Nixonian politics . . . First encounter with Mr. Nixon was when he volunteered to work for the Vice-Presidential candidate in 1952 . . . Has been in every Nixon campaign since, gradually assuming a larger role . . . As advertising executive for J. Walter Thompson, he supervised the accounts for Walt Disney, 7-Up and Black Flag insect spray . . . Born Oct. 27, 1926, in Los Angeles . . . Earned degree in business administration from the University of California, Los Angeles, where he met his wife, Joanne, and his future colleague John D. Ehrlichman . . . At the White House he looked like a Marine Corps drill instructor, crew-cut, thin lips and rigid jaw, but now he has let his hair grow . . . Famous for taking home movies on his history-making trips with the President . . . Prefers an evening at home with his wife and four children . . . Has been living in Los Angeles since he resigned and is not working.

John Daniel Ehrlichman

Among the accomplishments he listed in "Who's Who" is the Distinguished Eagle Award from the Boy Scouts of America . . . Formerly Mr. Nixon's top domestic adviser . . . Now awaits trial in Los Angeles on charges he directed the White House "plumbers" unit to burglarize the office of Dr. Daniel Ellsberg's former psychiatrist . . . Born in Tacoma, Wash., March 20, 1925 . . . College chum of H. R. Haldeman at University of California, Los Angeles, where he also met his wife, Jeanne . . . They have five children . . . Graduated from Stanford Law School in 1951 . . . Practiced law in Seattle with firm of Hullin, Ehrlichman, Roberts & Hodge . . . Mr. Haldeman lured him into Mr. Nixon's campaign for President in 1960 . . . Returned to Seattle law practice . . . Worked briefly in Mr. Nixon's 1962 campaign for Governor . . . Was "tour director" of 1968 campaign . . . Reputation for hard-nosed efficiency is legendary . . . Combines an arch sense of humor with severe sense of duty . . . A Christian Scientist who neither drinks nor smokes . . . Became known as cool executor of Presidential wishes . . . "He leaves no more blood on the floor than he has to," says one colleague . . . Since the powerful White House official resigned, he has been living in Seattle . . . Formed an organization called Land Use Group, which specializes in giving businessmen advice on environmental laws.

Charles Wendell Colson

Dubbed one of the "original back room boys—the operators and breakers, the guys who fix things when they break down and do the dirty work when necessary" . . . Served as special assistant to the President in charge and liaison with outside groups, and counsel to the President for four and a half years before he formed his own Washington law firm, Colson & Shapiro . . . Frequently under attack in the press before Watergate for his tactics in the White House . . . Examples: Feeding damaging information on Senator Joseph Tydings of Maryland to a Life reporter and orchestrating an Administration attack on George Meany . . . Long experience in politics . . . Served in nineteen-fifties in Navy Department . . . Was administrative assistant to Senator Leverett Saltonstall, Republican of Massachusetts . . . Left to joint the law firm of Gadsby & Hannah in Boston, but maintained ties with the Republican hierarchy . . . Graduated from Brown University and George Washington University Law School . . . Recently reported religious conversion, saying he had found "a great inner serenity, really a new life" through Christ . . . Said to be the author of the White House "enemies list" . . . Charged with conspiracy yesterday by the Watergate Grand Jury for allegedly trying to cover up evidence in the Watergate burglary.

Robert Charles Mardian

Labeled a zealous conservative by many, a reactionary by some . . . The son of an Armenian immigrant, born Oct. 23, 1923 . . . Now a millionaire through the family's construction firm in Phoenix, Ariz . . . Practiced law until 1963, when he became a vice president of a savings and loan association . . . Developed his political appetite in Barry Goldwater's Presidential campaign . . . Also worked to seat Ronald Reagan in the California Governor's office . . . Through his friend and fellow Arizonan, Richard G. Kleindienst, he arrived in Mr. Nixon's 1968 Presidential campaign . . . Coordinated Republican efforts in Western States . . . First Administration job was general counsel for the Department of Health, Education and Welfare . . . Was the persistent apostle of Mr. Mitchell's "Southern strategy," trying to ease the pace of school integration . . . Later as Assistant Attorney General, in charge of the Internal Security Division, he pressed the Justice Department's fight against the antiwar Left . . . Followed Mr. Mitchell to the campaign committee . . . Was assigned to investigate the Watergate break-in for the re-election committee . . . Charged with conspiracy yesterday by the Watergate grand jury . . . He and John Mitchell suggested to John Dean, former White House counsel, that the C.I.A. be asked to provide covert funds for the original Watergate conspirators . . . Now living with wife in Phoenix . . . They have three children.

Kenneth Wells Parkinson

Washington lawyer . . . An equestrian . . . Selected by the Committee for the Re-election to the President to represent it after the Watergate break-in . . . He "debriefed" people who had been before the grand jury, according to Hugh Sloan, a former campaign aide who described the lawyer's duties at the committee . . . Indicted yesterday on a charge of conspiracy for allegedly operating as a conduit for hush money offers to the original Watergate conspirators from top White House officials . . . Member of the Jackson, Gray & Laskey law firm here, which does a great deal of work for insurance companies . . . He handles a number of small personal injury defense cases . . . Tall, thin, with curly blond hair . . . Native Washingtonian, born Sept. 13, 1927 . . . Graduated from George Washington University with undergraduate and law degrees . . . Law clerk to Judge David A. Pine of the United States District Court for the District of Columbia . . . Active in local bar association, on its board of directors . . . Member of bar association's admissions committee, which is being sued by local black lawyers for discrimination . . . Also served as vice president of the Legal Aid Society and on the board of the Neighborhood Legal Service Project here . . . Some colleagues observe that "he lacks street sense" but that he is an average solid lawyer.

Gordon Creighton Strachan

Called "Haldeman's go-fer" by White House colleagues . . . During President Nixon's 1972 campaign his job was liaison between the White House and the campaign organization . . . Was responsible for keeping Mr. Haldeman informed on the over-all work of the campaign committee . . . Indicted yesterday for obstructing justice . . . Destroyed documents on the instructions of H. R. Haldeman . . . Handled hush money for the original Watergate conspirators . . . Born in Berkeley, Calif., on July 24, 1943 . . . Attended University of Southern California, where he met future White House colleagues Ronald L. Ziegler and Dwight Chapin . . . Fraternity brother of Donald H. Segretti, who is now in jail for sabotaging Democratic Presidential campaigns in 1972 . . . Graduated from law school at Bolt Hall, University of California . . . Joined President's old law firm, Mudge Rose, Guthrie & Alexander . . . Worked on estates and trusts . . . Did some advance work for the President's 1970 campaign . . . Joined staff of former White House communications director, Herbert G. Klein, but his staff work for Mr. Haldeman's staff . . . Under cloud of Watergate, he left White House to become general counsel at the United States Information Agency, but quit a few months later . . . Tall, blond, commonly respected for his wry sense of humor . . . Now unemployed . . . His wife, a law professor at the University of Utah, is the breadwinner.

"All the News That's Fit to Print"

The New York Times

LATE CITY EDITION

Weather: Partly cloudy today; cool tonight. Fair, pleasant tomorrow. Temp. range: today 65-78; Thursday 64-85. Highest Temp.-Hum. Index yesterday: 75. Details on Page 66.

VOL. CXXIII..No. 42,566

NEW YORK, FRIDAY, AUGUST 9, 1974

20¢ beyond 50-mile radius of New York City except Long Island. Higher in air delivery cities

15 CENTS

NIXON RESIGNS

HE URGES A TIME OF 'HEALING'; FORD WILL TAKE OFFICE TODAY

'Sacrifice' Is Praised; Kissinger to Remain

By ANTHONY RIPLEY

Special to The New York Times

WASHINGTON, Aug. 8—Vice President Ford praised President Nixon tonight for "one of the greatest personal sacrifices for the country and one of the finest personal decisions on behalf of all of us as Americans."

Mr. Ford, who will take office as the 38th President at noon tomorrow, vowed to continue Mr. Nixon's foreign policy and announced that Secretary of State Kissinger had agreed to stay on in the new Administration.

"I pledge to you tonight, as I will pledge to you tomorrow and in the future, my best efforts in cooperation, leadership and dedication to what's good for America and good for the world," he said.

The Vice President, who never sought the nation's highest office and disclaimed any intention of seeking it after Mr. Nixon's term, will take the oath of office in a private ceremony at the White House.

Thus will he become the first man to serve as President without being chosen by the American people in an election. Tomorrow night he will address the nation on radio and television. It is expected that he will speak at 6 P.M.

All day today the signs of the historic change were in the air, sensed by the crowds that gathered along Pennsylvania Avenue near the White House. Applause rang out from the crowds when Mr. Ford appeared briefly.

Text of Mr. Ford's remarks appears on Page 2.

After watching Mr. Nixon on television tonight with his family, the Vice President stepped outside into a slight drizzle at his suburban split-level home in nearby Alexandria, Va., to face television cameras and photographers assembled in the street and about 100 cheering neighbors.

Speaks Outside Home

Speaking without notes or a prepared text, Mr. Ford pledged to continue the Nixon foreign policy and called the Secretary of State "a very great man" whom he has known for many years.

On domestic policy, he said that he had been "very fortunate in my lifetime" to have adversaries in Congress but said that he did not think he had "a single enemy" there.

President Nixon had cited in his resignation address his lack of support in Congress as one of the major reasons for his resignation.

Mr. Ford said, "The net result is that I think tomorrow I can start out working with Democrats and with Republi-

Continued on Page 4, Column 3

The New York Times/William E. Sauro

Vice President Ford meeting with newsmen last night

United Press International

President Nixon on TV as he announced his resignation

The 37th President Is First to Quit Post

By JOHN HERBERS

Special to The New York Times

WASHINGTON, Aug. 8—Richard Milhous Nixon, the 37th President of the United States, announced tonight that he had given up his long and arduous fight to remain in office and would resign, effective at noon tomorrow.

At that hour, Gerald Rudolph Ford, whom Mr. Nixon nominated for Vice President last Oct. 12, will be sworn in as the 38th President, to serve out the 895 days remaining in Mr. Nixon's second term.

Less that two years after his landslide re-election victory, Mr. Nixon, in a conciliatory address on national

Text of the address will be found on Page 2.

television, said that he was leaving not with a sense of bitterness but with a hope that his departure would start a "process of healing that is so desperately needed in America."

He spoke of regret for any "injuries" done "in the course of the events that led to this decision." He acknowledged that some of his judgments had been wrong.

The 61-year-old Mr. Nixon, appearing calm and resigned to his fate as a victim of the Watergate scandal, became the first President in the history of the Republic to resign from office. Only 10 months earlier Spiro Agnew resigned the Vice-Presidency.

Speaks of Pain at Yielding Post

Mr. Nixon, speaking from the Oval Office, where his successor will be sworn in tomorrow, may well have delivered his most effective speech since the Watergate scandals began to swamp his Administration in early 1973.

In tone and content, the 15-minute address was in sharp contrast to his frequently combative language of the past, especially his first "farewell" appearance—that of 1962, when he announced he was retiring from politics after losing the California governorship race and declared that the news media would not have "Nixon to kick around" anymore.

Yet he spoke tonight of how painful it was for him to give up the office.

"I would have preferred to carry through to the finish whatever the personal agony it would have involved, and my family unanimously urged me to do so," he said.

Puts 'Interests of America First'

"I have never been a quitter," he said. "To leave office before my term is completed is opposed to every instinct in my body." But he said that he had decided to put "the interests of America first."

Conceding that he did not have the votes in Congress to escape impeachment in the House and conviction in the Senate, Mr. Nixon said, "To continue to fight through the months ahead for my personal vindication would almost totally absorb the time and attention of the President and the Congress in a period when our entire focus should be on the great issues of peace abroad and prosperity without inflation at home."

"Therefore," he continued, "I shall resign the Presidency effective at noon tomorrow. Vice President Ford will be

Continued on Page 3, Column 1

SPECULATION RIFE ON VICE PRESIDENT

Some Ford Associates Say Selecting a Successor Could Take Weeks

By CHRISTOPHER LYDON

Special to The New York Times

WASHINGTON, Aug. 8 — Potentially the most revealing and most important decision of Gerald R. Ford's Presidential debut — his choice of a successor in the Vice Presidency — was a much-discussed mystery here today.

Close friends of Mr. Ford continued to feed speculation about more than a dozen possible candidates. But none of the friends claimed to have discussed the Vice-Presidential question with Mr. Ford or to be speaking for him on it. A number of Ford associates thought he might hold off the decision for days or even weeks.

"Everybody's on tenterhooks up here," a Senator remarked this afternoon in a telephone interview from the Republican cloakroom, "but I think they're wasting their time. It's going to be a week or two. So far I'd say he's a loner on this issue."

Former Defense Secretary Melvin R. Laird, a Ford counselor in the House for more than a decade, was being quoted again today as saying he believes that Nelson A. Rocke-

Continued on Page 4, Column 1

POLITICAL SCENE SHARPLY ALTERED

G.O.P. Prospects Improved, Ford in Good Spot for '76 and Watergate Fades

By R. W. APPLE Jr.

Special to The New York Times

WASHINGTON, Aug. 8—President Nixon's resignation drastically altered the American political landscape.

It improved Republican prospects for the Congressional elections in November, thrust Vice President Ford into the favorite's role for the 1976 Presidential election, ended the Watergate agony that has served to bind together the heterogeneous Democratic party and removed from the political stage the man who was the dominant Republican for the last 15 years.

In a larger sense, it seemed to presage an era of more open government, of more cooperation and less antagonism between Capitol Hill and the White House and of decline of the White House staff as an independent power center.

Lives Are Altered

A kind of "honeymoon" between the executive and legislative branches was widely predicted by Congressional leaders today. Congressmen who knew Mr. Ford for years as a Capitol Hill colleague said that they expected to work closely with him.

At least in the beginning, pragmatic conservatism is expected to remain the dominant ideological tone in the executive branch.

How that will be translated into policies, and how those policies will shape the political dialogue, will not be clear for weeks. But experts in the two fields forecast an essentially unchanged foreign policy and a similar, but more carefully and consistently applied, economic policy.

By his decision, Mr. Nixon

Continued on Page 6, Column 4

Rise and Fall

Appraisal of Nixon Career

By ROBERT B. SEMPLE Jr.

The central question is how a man who won so much could have lost so much. How could a public figure who so well perceived the instincts of the majority of his countrymen have misused the powers and duties those same countrymen so eagerly ceded him?

The historians will be kept busy on these questions, but for those who spent their time observing Mr. Nixon for the last six years the answer may well be found in a phrase he often applied to himself. "At bottom," he used to say, "I am a political man."

By his own description, he was a man of action rather than contemplation, a tactician rather than a theologian, a student of technique who seemed always impatient with substance, a figure whose exceptional antennae seemed to dwarf and even hide what lay at the core.

To his enemies, he was both manipulative and synthetic; to his friends, a pragmatist unencumbered by inflexible principles; to those who watched him, a man who learned to run before he had learned to walk and who, on reaching his destination, was not always certain what to do when he got there—except, perhaps, to keep going.

That image has only been reinforced and deepened by the transcripts of three conversations with H. R. Haldeman on June 23, 1972, six days after the Watergate break-in, which were released on Aug. 5, and the edited transcripts of White House conversations published April 30. Whatever history's judgment of those tapes, this much was clear: Faced with mounting evidence of deception and wrongdoing in his own official family, he sought not to confront the issue but to manipulate it until he himself became part of the deception.

Mr. Nixon used the words "I am a political man" proudly, as if to challenge the moralists, but in the end they became his epitaph—a possible explanation for both his success and failure.

For if the words implied the presence of a talent for finding opportunities for political prof-

Continued on Page 11, Column 1

JAWORSKI ASSERTS NO DEAL WAS MADE

Says Nixon Did Not Ask for and Was Not Given a Way to Avoid Prosecution

By RICHARD D. LYONS

Special to The New York Times

WASHINGTON, Aug. 8—Leon Jaworski, the special Watergate prosecutor, said tonight after President Nixon's resignation speech that no deals had been either made or offered that would have given Mr. Nixon immunity from prosecution on any charges that might stem from the Watergate scandal.

"There has been no agreement or understanding of any sort between the President or his representatives and the special prosecutor relating in any way to the President's resignation," Mr. Jaworski said in a statement issued by his office.

Mr. Jaworski's words, plus the fact that the President made no mention of the immunity issue in his address to the nation, left open the possibility, at least for the moment, that Mr. Nixon might be charged and stand trial.

No Immunity Sought

Mr. Nixon did not ask for any immunity assurances from Mr. Jaworski before the resignation speech, the prosecutor said, adding that none had been offered.

As Mr. Jaworski put it, "The special prosecutor's office was not asked for any such agreement or understanding and offered none."

"Although I was informed of the President's decision this afternoon, my office did not participate in any way in the President's decision to resign," the statement concluded.

Mr. Jaworski met earlier today with Gen. Alexander M. Haig Jr., the White House chief of staff, but that meeting was said to have been only for the purpose of informing the special prosecutor of what the President would say later in the evening.

The meeting did not take place in the White House, presumably because Mr. Jaworski would have been recognized there, and his visit would have excited speculation.

Earlier today, there were moves in both houses of Congress to grant Mr. Nixon immunity from prosecution, but

Continued on Page 2, Column 4

The Other Major News

Wholesale Prices Up

A new upward surge of farm prices joined a big jump in industrial prices to produce the year's largest monthly increase in the wholesale price index. The rise for July was 3.7 per cent, seasonally adjusted, and 3.9 per cent before adjustment. Page 45.

Election Bill Voted

The House approved by a vote of 355 to 48 a broad campaign-finance reform bill. The measure would set limits on political contributions, restrict candidate spending and provide subsidies for Presidential primaries, conventions and elections. The bill now goes to a House-Senate conference committee. Page 36.

Cyprus Talks Open

The foreign ministers of Greece, Turkey and Britain met in Geneva to try to work out an effective cease-fire on Cyprus and to tackle the political problems behind the fighting there. Page 16.

On Cyprus, acting President Glafkos Clerides named a moderate Cabinet stripped of any militant proponents of union with Greece.

Mr. Clerides, who will occupy the key posts of Foreign Affairs and Interior, left for Athens on his way to Geneva for the talks on a political settlement. Page 16.

10 Police Accused

Ten New York City police sergeants were arrested for allegedly participating in a "club" that collected more than $250,000 over a decade from legitimate businesses and illegal rackets operations in Queens. Page 68.

Meskill Named Judge

Gov. Thomas J. Meskill of Connecticut was nominated by President Nixon to a seat on the Federal bench. Mr. Meskill, a Republican, stunned the state Republican party earlier this year by declining to run for a second term amid reports that he had been offered a judgeship. Page 38.

NEWS INDEX

A Tiny G.O.P. Bastion Feels Loss and Relief

By PRANAY GUPTE

Special to The New York Times

SHELTER ISLAND, L.I., Aug. 8—Six years after he put it on his car, Evans K. Griffing sadly stripped off his bold, red-lettered bumper sticker today — the one that said "NIXON."

Mr. Griffing felt a sense of loss. So did hundreds of people in this conservative community 100 miles east of New York City.

In 1968 and 1972, Suffolk County gave Richard M. Nixon the largest single election plurality of any county in the United States. Today all that had changed on Shelter Island.

As the hour of the President's resignation announcement approached, many islanders expressed both a feeling of hurt at having been "betrayed" by Mr. Nixon and relief that he was leaving office.

"We tried to stay by him till the very end," said Thomas L. Jernick, the Town Supervisor. "But when he disclosed on Monday that he had covered up his role in Watergate, we couldn't support him any more. He lied to us, and for a President of the United States to lie is inexcusable."

"We really believed in Mr. Nixon" was a phrase used again and again by dozens of islanders today.

At the same time they spoke hopefully of the Ford Administration and of moving urgently to tasks long neglected—ending the nation's political turmoil and easing its economic distress.

Shelter Island has 1,800 year-round residents, most of whom are registered Republicans.

Only last June interviews with islanders indicated that whatever else Watergate had done, it apparently had not diluted Shelter Island's faith in Mr. Nixon. People said at the time that they felt the President was being vilified by the media

Continued on Page 7, Column 6

Only Nixon Is Serene At Sad White House

By PHILIP SHABECOFF

Special to The New York Times

WASHINGTON, Aug. 8—On his 2,027th and penultimate day as President of the United States, with his staff and family unable to conceal their anguish, Richard M. Nixon went composedly through the schedule of a busy President.

He met with his Vice President and the bipartisan leadership of Congress. He appointed Federal judges, accepted resignations from executive agencies and signed several laws.

He vetoed as inflationary an appropriation bill for the Department of Agriculture and the Environmental Protection Agency.

He also announced, over national television, that tomorrow he would resign his high office.

Mr. Nixon did not loosen his self control even when he talked of his "regret" and his "sadness" at leaving the Presidency. His delivery, with its familiar half-smiles, did not reflect the momentous message he had for his audience: that at noon tomorrow he would become the first healthy, living American President to leave office before his term expired.

At 12:30 this afternoon, the White House press secretary, Ronald L. Ziegler, announced that the President would address the nation at 9 P.M.

Mr. Ziegler did not say what the speech would be about. He did not have to. He choked on his words several times and was struggling visibly to keep himself under control as he left the rostrum of the packed but hushed briefing room at the White House.

The young women who work in the press office went through the motions of their jobs while tears streamed down their faces.

But the President himself, according to his appointments

Continued on Page 3, Column 8

THE NEW YORK TIMES, FRIDAY, AUGUST 9, 1974

Transcript of President Nixon's Address to the Nation Announcing His Resignation

Following is a transcript of President Nixon's address last night as recorded by The New York Times:

Good evening.

This is the 37th time I have spoken to you from this office in which so many decisions have been made that shape the history of this nation.

Each time I have done so to discuss with you some matters that I believe affected the national interest. And all the decisions I have made in my public life I have always tried to do what was best for the nation.

Throughout the long and difficult period of Watergate, I have felt it was my duty to persevere; to make every possible effort to complete the term of office to which you elected me.

In the past few days, however, it has become evident to me that I no longer have a strong enough political base in the Congress to justify continuing that effort.

Deliberately Difficult

As long as there was such a base, I felt strongly that it was necessary to see the constitutional process through to its conclusion: that to do otherwise would be unfaithful to the spirit of that deliberately difficult process, and a dangerously destabilizing precedent for the future.

But with the disappearance of that base, I now believe that the constitutional purpose has been served. And there is no longer a need for the process to be prolonged

I would have preferred to carry through to the finish whatever the personal agony it would have involved, and my family unanimously urged me to do so.

But the interests of the nation must always come before any personal considerations. From the discussions I have had with Congressional and other leaders I have concluded that because of the Watergate matter I might not have the support of the Congress that I would consider necessary to back the very difficult decisions and carry out the duties of this office in the way the interests of the nation will require.

I have never been a quitter.

To leave office before my term is completed is opposed to every instinct in my body. But as President I must put the interests of America first.

Full-Time President

America needs a full-time President and a full-time Congress, particularly at this time with problems we face at home and abroad.

To continue to fight through the months ahead for my personal vindication would almost totally absorb the time and attention of both the President and the Congress in a period when our entire focus should be on the great issues of peace abroad and prosperity without inflation at home.

Therefore, I shall resign the Presidency effective at noon tomorrow.

Vice President Ford will be sworn in as President at that hour in this office.

As I recall the high hopes for America with which we began this second term, I feel a great sadness that I will not be here in this office working on your behalf to achieve those hopes in the next two and a half years.

But in turning over direction of the Government to Vice President Ford I know, as I told the nation when I nominated him for that office 10 months ago, that the leadership of America will be in good hands.

In passing this office to the Vice President I also do so with the profound sense of the weight of responsibility that will fall on his shoulders tomorrow, and therefore of the understanding, the patience, the cooperation he will need from all Americans.

As he assumes that responsibility he will deserve the help and the support of all of us. As we look to the future, the first essential is to begin healing the wounds of this nation. To put the bitterness and divisions of the recent past behind us and to rediscover those shared ideals that lie at the heart of our strength and unity as a great and as a free people.

By taking this action, I hope that I will have hastened the start of that process of healing which is so desperately needed in America.

'The Best Interests'

I regret deeply any injuries that may have been done in the course of the events that led to this decision. I would say only that if some of my judgments were wrong—and some were wrong—they were made in what I believed at the time to be the best interests of the nation.

To those who have stood with me during these past difficult months, to my family, my friends, the many others who've joined in supporting my cause because they believed it was right, I will be eternally grateful for your support.

And to those who have not felt able to give me your support, let me say I leave with no bitterness toward those who have opposed me, because all of us in the final analysis have been concerned with the good of the country however our judgments might differ.

So let us all now join together in affirming that common commitment and in helping our new President succeed for the benefit of all Americans.

The New York Times/Don Hogan Charles

A crowd gathering at dusk outside the White House yesterday

I shall leave this office with regret at not completing my term but with gratitude for the privilege of serving as your President for the past five and a half years.

These years have been a momentous time in the history of our nation and the world. They have been a time of achievement in which we can all be proud—achievements that represent the shared efforts of the administration, the Congress and the people. But the challenges ahead are equally great.

And they, too, will require the support and the efforts of a Congress and the people, working in cooperation with the new Administration.

We have ended America's longest war. But in the work of securing a lasting peace in the world, the goals ahead are even more far-reaching and more difficult. We must complete a structure of peace, so that it will be said of this generation—our generation of Americans—by the people of all nations, not only that we ended one war but that we prevented future wars.

We have unlocked the doors that for a quarter of a century stood between the United States and the People's Republic of China. We must now insure that the one-quarter of the world's people who live in the People's Republic of China will be and remain, not our enemies, but our friends.

Breakthroughs With Russia

In the Middle East, 100 million people in the Arab countries, many of whom have considered us their enemies for nearly 20 years, now look on us as their friends. We must continue to build on that friendship so that peace can settle at last over the Middle East and so that the cradle of civilization will not become its grave.

Together with the Soviet Union we have made the crucial breakthroughs that have begun the process of limiting nuclear arms. But we must set as our goal not just limiting but reducing and finally destroying these terrible weapons so that they cannot destroy civilization.

And so that the threat of nuclear war will no longer hang over the world and the people, we have opened a new relation with the Soviet Union. We must continue to develop and expand that new relationship so that the two strongest nations of the world will live together in cooperation rather than confrontation.

Around the world—in Asia, in Africa, in Latin America, in the Middle East—there are millions of people who live in terrible poverty, even starvation. We must keep as our goal turning away from production for war and expanding production for peace so that people everywhere on this earth can at last look farward, in their children's time if not in our time to having the necessities for a decent life.

Here in America we are fortunate that most of our people have not only the blessings of liberty but also the means to live full and good, and by the world's standards, even abundant lives.

We must press on, however, toward a goal not only of more and better jobs but of full opportunity for every man, and of what we are striving so hard right now to achieve—prosperity without inflation.

For more than a quarter of a century in public life, I have shared in the turbulent history of this evening.

I have fought for what I believe in. I have tried, to the best of my ability, to discharge those duties and meet those responsibilities that were entrusted to me.

Sometimes I have succeeded. And sometimes I have failed. But always I have taken heart from what Theodore Roosevelt said about the man in the arena whose face is married by dust and sweat and blood, who strives valiantly, who errs and comes short again and again because there is not effort without error and shortcoming, but who does actually strive to do the deed, who knows the great enthusiasm, the great devotion, who spends himself in a worthy cause, who at the best knows in the end the triumphs of high achievements and with the worst if he fails, at least fails while daring greatly.

Dedication Pledged

I pledge to you tonight that as long as I have a breath of life in my body I shall continue in that spirit. I shall continue to work for the great causes to which I have been dedicated throughout my years as a Congressman, a Senator, Vice President and President, the cause of peace—not just for America but among all nations—prosperity, justice and opportunity for all of our people.

There is one cause above all to which I have been devoted and to which I shall always be devoted for as long as I live.

When I first took the oath of office as President five and a half years ago, I made this sacred commitment: to consecrate my office, my energies and all the wisdom I can summon to the cause of peace among nations.

I've done my very best in all the days since to be true to that pledge.

As a result of these efforts, I am confident that the world is a safer place today, not only for the people of America but for the people of all nations, and that all of our children have a better chance than before of living in peace rather than dying in war.

This, more than anything, is what I hoped to achieve when I sought the Presidency. This, more than anything, is what I hope will be my legacy to you, to our country, as I leave the Presidency.

To have served in this office is to have felt a very personal sense of kinship with each and every American. In leaving it, I do so with this prayer: May God's grace be with you in all the days ahead.

A Transcript of Remarks Made by Vice President Ford

Following is a transcript of remarks last night by Vice President Ford as recorded by The New York Times:

This is one of the most difficult and very saddest periods and one of the very saddest incidents I've ever witnessed.

Let me say that I think the President of the United States has made one of the greatest personal sacrifices for the country and one of the finest personal decisions on behalf of all of us as Americans by his decision to resign as President of the United States.

It has been my opportunity to watch over a period of nearly 25 years a foreign policy in the last five years that has been most successful in the achievement of peace for all of us here and hopefully the rest of the world.

It has been a policy that I think can continue peace in the months and years ahead. Let me say without any hesitation or reservation that the policy that has achieved peace and built the blocks for future peace will be continued as far as I'm concerned as President of the United States.

We've been fortunate in the last five years to have a very great man in Henry Kissinger who has had to build the blocks of peace under President Nixon. I think those policies should be continued.

And those policies of peace will be continued. I have asked Henry Kissinger, as Secretary of State, to stay on, and to be the Secretary of State under the new Administration.

I've known Henry Kissinger for a great many years. I knew him before he came with the Nixon Administration. I want him to be my Secretary of State and I'm glad to announce that he will be the Secretary of State.

Which means that he and I will be working together in the pursuit of peace in the future as we have achieved it in the past.

We have many other problems.

We have problems at home which must be resolved.

And they can be resolved and will be resolved by the cooperation of the Congress with the President and those that work with him.

I've been very fortunate in my lifetime and public office to have a good many adversaries in the political arena in the Congress.

But I don't think I have a single enemy in the Congress.

And the net result is that I think tomorrow I can start out working with Democrats and with Republicans in the House as well as in the Senate to work on the problems—serious ones—which we have at home.

And the spirit of cooperation which I believe will be exhibited with the Congress and the new President and the problems overseas and the problems at home will be beneficial not only to 211 million fine Americans but to the world as a whole.

And I pledge to you tonight, as I will pledge tomorrow and in the future, my best efforts in cooperation, leadership and dedication to what's good for America and good for the world.

Thank you very much.

Legal Questions Underlie the Debate Over Proposal of Immunity for Nixon

By LESLEY OELSNER
Special to The New York Times

WASHINGTON, Aug. 8—In Congress and elsewhere in Washington today, there was growing debate over whether President Nixon should be given immunity from criminal prosecution upon his resignation.

Underlying the debate were a number of legal questions, some narrow and technical, some broad and constitutional, as well as a number of competing legal interests.

Mr. Nixon could be given immunity under an arrangement with the special Watergate prosecution, with whose lawyers his own lawyers met yesterday. Or, he could be pardoned by Vice President Ford after Mr. Ford assumes the presidency.

Neither Leon Jaworski, the special Watergate prosecutor, nor Mr. Ford is expected to take such a step without having a consensus of Congress to back it up.

Proposal From Brooke

Senator Edward W. Brooke, Republican of Massachusetts, submitted to the Senate today a proposed resolution expressing the "sense" of Congress that the President not be prosecuted when he leaves office. Although this resolution, if passed, would not be binding, it would provide either Mr. Ford or Mr. Jaworski with the "consensus" each would want.

The law provides no guide as to which route would be the better way. And on the question of whether Mr. Nixon should be given immunity it provides only hints, not answers.

A major question is whether Mr. Nixon should be given immunity from prosecution for Watergate crimes when numerous Nixon subordinates have either been convicted already or are facing prosecution for alleged roles in the same crimes.

The traditional practice for prosecutors faced with evidence implicating both subordinates and their superiors in a crime is to concentrate on prosecuting the superiors. If anyone gets immunity, it is a subordinate whose testimony is needed to make the prosecutor's case against the superior.

This is, however, only practice, not a legal requirement.

The law provides at least an outside standard: Under the Constitution, people are entitled to due process and "equal protection of the laws."

There is a legal theory that "selective prosecution" violates the equal protection guarantee—that if only one conspirator is prosecuted, say, and his five co-conspirators are not, the first one can contest his prosecution on the grounds that he is being denied equal protection.

But as one Washington lawyer, Daniel A. Rezneck, noted today, this theory is rarely applied. To prove that a prosecution is unconstitutionally "selective," a defendant would have to show that there was absolutely no basis for distinguishing between the various potential defendants.

Mr. Rezneck said that there were obviously some legitimate reasons for viewing a President somewhat differently from an ordinary citizen. There are considerations, for example, such as the great penalty that the President is already receiving in leaving his office in disgrace.

At the same time, there is also the legal principle that everyone, including the President, is subject to the rule of law.

There is also the importance of what is generally called the "appearance of justice." And there is the provision in the Constitution that says that an official convicted by the Senate in an impeachment proceeding "shall nevertheless be liable and subject to indictment, trial, judgment and punishment, according to law."

There is no precise statute setting out exactly how any of these three principles or rules are to be applied. But they must obviously be considered in weighing the advantages and the disadvantages of giving Mr. Nixon immunity.

Aim of the Framers

To some lawyers, moreover, the constitutional provision is proof that the men who drafted the Constitution intended that a President who commits a crime be prosecuted for it.

The discussion of impeachment during the Constitutional Convention in 1787 was almost exclusively a discussion of impeaching Presidents, not the other officials such as judges who were subsequently placed within the impeachment clauses.

So, as Daniel Davidson, another Washington lawyer, put it today, "the Constitution was written for this situation."

Mr. Davidson rejects the rationale that Mr. Nixon has already suffered massive disgrace and that the loss of office is penalty enough. The drafters of the Constitution knew that a President who committed a crime "would be disgraced," he said, and they included the provision for prosecution nevertheless.

There has been some suggestion, in pro-Nixon circles, that Mr. Nixon should be given not only immunity from prosecution but also immunity from being called as a witness.

The suggestion raises additional legal problems, for it affects other interests as well—the interest of the special Watergate prosecution in making its case in the Watergate cover-up trial, and perhaps other trials, too, and the interests of defendants in those cases in getting fair trials.

Here, the law is clearer.

For one thing, the Sixth Amendment guarantees that a defendant may "have compulsory process for obtaining witnesses in his favor." It is possible that Mr. Nixon could provide testimony helpful to one or more defendants in the Watergate cover-up case. Also, if the defendant was barred from obtaining Mr. Nixon's testimony, the case against him might have to be dismissed.

The prosecution probably does not need Mr. Nixon's testimony in the cover-up case, for it already has abundant evidence. Indeed, it might not want him as a witness either.

3 Networks to Cover White House Farewell

All three television networks plan special coverage of President Nixon's departure from the White House set for 9:30 A.M. today and the swearing-in of Gerald R. Ford. scheduled for noon.

NBC-TV said its Presidential coverage would begin with the "Today" show that will stay on the air at least until 10:30. The network said it would start its coverage of the swearing-in at least a half an hour before the ceremony. A special hour program on the week's events is scheduled for 10 P.M.

ABC-TV said its coverage would being at 9 A.M., with tentative plans for continuous coverage through the inauguration.

CBS-TV said it planned brief interruptions of regular programing at 9:25 A.M. and 11:45 A.M. for coverage of President's Nixon's departure and Mr. Ford's swearing-in.

All three networks emphasized last night that their plans were subject to last-minute change.

United Press International

Ronald L. Ziegler as he spoke to newsmen last night

Ziegler's Final White House Briefing

Special to The New York Times

WASHINGTON, Aug. 8—Ronald L. Ziegler, President Nixon's press secretary for the last 5½ years, held a final briefing for White House reporters tonight, acknowledging the often abrasive nature of his relations with the press but saying he had "a deep sense of respect" for the nation's press.

Mr. Ziegler appeared at the press room podium shortly after 11 P.M. His eyes were red-rimmed, and several times during his brief remarks he appeared close to tears.

He began by outlining President Nixon's schedule for tomorrow, which starts at a 9:30 A.M. farewell to Cabinet members and staff and ends with his departure, by helicopter, from the South Lawn for Andrews Air Force Base. From there, Mr. Nixon will fly to California.

Mr. Ziegler noted that the official letter of resignation would be delivered to Secretary of State Kissinger "by noon," the time when Mr. Nixon will become a former President.

"This has been a difficult day," he said, adding that "the strength of the President during this period . . . I think has sustained the members of the staff . . . All, I know, have respect for the President and the cause which he had represented."

He recapitulated the events of Mr. Nixon's last full day in office, starting with his early rising, through his meetings with Alexander M. Haig Jr., his chief of staff, with members of his staff, and, after spending most of the afternoon working on his speech of resignation, seeing the Congressional leadership.

White House TV

Mrs. Nixon and their two daughters and sons-in-law, Julie and David Eisenhower and Tricia and Edward F. Cox, watched Mr. Nixon's address on a television set in the White House. "Following the speech," Mr. Ziegler said "the President left the Oval Office and walked with Secretary of State Kissinger to the residence."

Then Mr. Ziegler said, "I'd like to take a minute myself to say goodbye . . . This is the last time we will be meeting in these circumstances . . . I've been proud to be President Nixon's press secretary over the past 5½ years."

He told the reporters, photographers and TV technicians jammed into the small, stuffy room, "I hope I have never underestimated the difficulty of your jobs . . . We've been through many difficult times together and many historical times . . ."

"Whatever our differences," he said, he believed there were no simple answers to the complex issues that had concerned them all.

In ending, Mr. Ziegler said he had developed "a deep sense of respect for the diversity and strength of this country's freedom of expression, our free press . . ." then he added, "It's been an honor to be here."

Outside, a crowd estimated by the police at more than 3,000 persons swarmed across the sidewalk in front of the White House into Pennsylvania Avenue itself—which the police closed to vehicles between 15th and 17th Streets—and into Lafayette Park, facing the illuminated mansion, whose water fountain still swirled in the floodlights.

It was, as one police officer remarked, a good-natured crowd, rather like New Year's Eve revelers. And, he said "It is rather historic." Some were waving sparklers, others chanting "Jail to the Chief," still others passing out "No Amnesty for Nixon" bumper stickers.

Mr. Kissinger's limousine pulled out of the White House gate about half an hour after Mr. Nixon's speech, he was recognized and cheered.

One young woman, walking through the park, stopped a stranger to say, "I don't know much about Ford, but at least I feel better." A little group clustered across the avenue chanted: "Nixon's resignation won't stop inflation" in front of a scrawled sign hanging tipsily on the iron fence that surrounds the White House: "Ding-Dong the witch is dead."

There were signs reading "Throw the Bum Out" and "Impeach the System." Some people were holding candles. Many of the crowd were young people, but there were also Washingtonians out walking their dogs and tourists with their wide-eyed children by the hand.

Jaworski Says No Deal Has Been Made

Continued From Page 1, Col. 6

they failed for lack of support.

Senator Edward W. Brooke, Republican of Massachusetts, and Representative John Buchanan, Republican of Alabama, introduced companion resolutions that would have had Congress express the "sense" that the President should not be subject to prosecution when he leaves office tomorrow.

The type of resolution expressing the sense of Congress is not binding by law; it merely expresses the feelings of the members.

Many members took the position that, after his resignation, Mr. Nixon should be liable for prosecution just as any other citizen is, and leave it to the courts to decide the legal issues.

There was the additional sentiment of, as it was phrased by one Democratic Senator, "How can I reconcile all those other guys in the Bastille and the chief sitting on the bench?"

Starting at noon tomorrow, when Mr. Nixon becomes a private citizen, he would be liable to indictment should a grand jury indict him. The Watergate grand jury will continue to consider details of the scandal for four more months.

The jury already has named Mr. Nixon as an unindicted co-conspirator in the cover-up of the Watergate case, for which six former White House aides are scheduled to go on trial a month from now.

It also is possible that, now that the impeachment-resignation issue has been settled, Mr. Nixon might appear as a witness in that trial, as well as in other Watergate-related cases.

The events of the day also left unresolved other questions relating to the Watergate case. Mr. Jaworski was appointed by Mr. Nixon, and could be removed by Vice President Ford when he becomes President, but only with the consent of the Congressional leadership.

Thus, it might be difficult for Mr. Ford to order Mr. Jaworski to offer immunity to Mr. Nixon if the special prosecutor chose not to do so. According to a member of Mr. Jaworski's staff, the special prosecutor did not consult with Congressional leaders when he decided not to offer immunity to Mr. Nixon.

In his speech tonight, Mr. Nixon gave no hint of his views on the immunity issue. In referring to Watergate, he said, "If some of my judgments were wrong—and some were wrong—they were made in what I believed at the time to be the best interest of the nation."

Mr. Nixon has potential legal problems in at the following areas:

¶Conspiracy to obstruct justice in the Watergate affair and its cover-up, for which the six aides are pending trial.

¶His attempted use of the Internal Revenue Service against his political enemies, which would be a violation of Section 7212 of the Internal Revenue Code. This section makes it a felony for anyone "corruptly" to attempt to "obstruct or impede" its administration.

¶Potential charges of tax evasion stemming from the personal tax returns Mr. Nixon filed while serving as President.

In addition, Mr. Nixon might face the possibility of being charged with crimes resulting from the activities of the "plumbers" unit, possibly in the area of civil rights violations.

All problems of potential criminal liability would become moot, however, if Mr. Ford were to pardon Mr. Nixon after the Vice President assumes the Presidency tomorrow. On taking office, Mr. Ford has the power to grant pardons for any crime that has been committed, whether or not the person performing the deed has been formally charged.

But Mr. Ford could not pardon Mr. Nixon for civil, as opposed to criminal, actions.

The promise of Congressional immunity was laid to rest even before it was formally introduced today. Representative John J. Rhodes of Arizona, the House minority leader, said two days ago that "I have never felt Congress had the constitutional authority to grant immunity to anybody for anything."

Mr. Rhodes added tonight that he did not believe that members of Congress would be "vindictive" toward Mr. Nixon.

And Representative Donald W. Riegle, Democrat of Michigan, remarked that "no one has a desire to see the President hounded when he leaves office."

A Normal Alert Status Is Set for U.S. Forces

WASHINGTON, Aug. 8 Reuters)—The Defense Department indicated today that American military forces around the world would remain on a normal alert status during the change in the Presidency.

"The activity of the armed forces continues as normal. There is no reason to change," a spokesman said when asked what the military status would be during the transfer of power from President Nixon to Vice President Ford.

KORFF SAYS NIXON AVOIDS STALEMATE

WASHINGTON, Aug. 8 (UPI)—Rabbi Baruch M. Korff, one of Richard M. Nixon's chief defenders in recent weeks, said today the President was resigning to spare the nation "months of anguished stalemate."

In a statement he said, "Wrongfully accused of great evils, harassed for his admitted errors, President Nixon today submitted to the judgment of history."

Rabbi Korff, chairman of the National Citizen's Committee for Fairness to the Presidency, added, "We have seen what can happen to a President when the citizenry's access to information is controlled by unchecked media giants and manipulated by vested interest groups."

Nixon Resigns the Presidency Effective at Noon Today; Urges a Time of 'Healing'

Continued From Page 1, Col. 8

sworn in as President at that hour in this office."

Then he turned again to his sorrow at leaving. Although he did not mention it in his speech, Mr. Nixon had looked forward to being President when the United States celebrates its 200th anniversary in 1976.

"I feel a great sadness," he said.

Mr. Nixon expressed confidence in Mr. Ford to assume the office, "to put the bitterness and divisions of the recent past behind us."

"By taking this action, I hope that I will have hastened the start of that process of healing which is so desperately needed in America," he said. "I regret deeply any injuries that may have been done in the course of the events that led to this decision. I would say only that if some of my judgments were wrong — and some were wrong — they were made in what I believed at the time to be the best interests of the nation."

Further, he said he was leaving "with no bitterness" toward those who had opposed him.

"So let us all now join together in affirming that common commitment and in helping our new President succeed for the benefit of all Americans," he said.

As he has many times in the past, Mr. Nixon listed what he considered his most notable accomplishments of his five and half years in office—his initiatives in foreign policy, which he said had gone a long way toward establishing a basis for world peace.

Theodore Roosevelt Is Quoted

And, at the end, he expressed his own philosophy — that to succeed is to be involved in struggle. In this he quoted Theodore Roosevelt about the value of being "the man in the arena whose face is marred by dust and sweat and blood" and who "spends himself in a worthy cause."

After spending himself in a long political career, Mr. Nixon is scheduled to fly to his home in San Clemente, Calif., and retirement tomorrow while Mr. Ford is being sworn in in the Oval Office.

A White House spokesman said tonight that Mr. and Mrs. Nixon and their family would bid farewell to Cabinet members and staff personnel at 9:30 A.M. tomorrow in the East Room. Then they will board a helicopter at 10 A.M. for the short trip to Andrews Air Force Base, where they will emplane on the Spirit of '76, a jet aircraft, for their flight to San Clemente.

Ronald L. Ziegler, the Presidential adviser and press secretary, also said that Mr. Nixon's letter of resignation would be delivered to the office of Secretary of State, Kissinger in th Excutive Office Building adjacent to the White House by noon tomorrow.

Mr. Nixon's announcement came only two days after he told his Cabinet that he would not resign but would let the constitutional impeachment process run its course, even though it was evident he would be removed from office after a trial by the Senate.

In the next 48 hours the pressures for him to resign and turn the reins of the Government over to Mr. Ford became overwhelming.

His chances of being acquitted were almost hopeless. Senator Barry Goldwater, the Arizona conservative who was the Republican Presidential candidate in 1964, told him that he had no more than 15 votes in the Senate, far short of the 34 he needed to be sure of escaping conviction. Members of his own staff, including Gen. Alexander M. Haig Jr., the White House chief of staff, strongly recommended that he step down in the national interest.

In the end only a small minority of his former supporters were urging him to stay and pledging to give him their support. It was his friends, not his legions of enemies, that brought the crucial pressures for resignation.

Seventeen months of almost constant disclosures of Watergate and related scandals brought a steady attrition of support, in the country and in Congress, for what many authorities believed was the most powerful Presidency in the history of the nation.

White House Photograph via United Press International

President Nixon and Vice President Ford, whom he named last Oct. 12, conferring at the White House yesterday

However, a Presidential statement of last Monday and three transcripts of Presidential conversations that Mr. Nixon chose to make public ultimately precipitated the crush of events of the last week.

In that statement, Mr. Nixon admitted, as the transcript showed, that on June 23, 1972, he ordered a halt to the investigation of the break-in at the Democratic headquarters in the Watergate complex here six days earlier by persons in the employ of agents of Mr. Nixon's re-election campaign. He also admitted that he had kept the evidence from both his attorneys and the House Judiciary Committee, which had recommended that the House impeach him on three general charges.

Then came the avalanche. Republicans, Southern Democrats and others who had defended Mr. Nixon said that these actions constituted the evidence needed to support the article of impeachment approved by the House Judiciary Committee charging obstruction of justice. And it gave new support to other charges that Mr. Nixon had widely abused his office by bringing undue Presidential pressures to bear on sensitive Government agencies.

As the pressures mounted and Mr. Nixon held publicly to his resolve not to resign, the capital was thrown into a turmoil. A number of Senators anxious for a resignation began publicly predicting one.

At the White House yesterday, Mr. Nixon met in his White House offices with Mrs. Nixon and his two daughters, Mrs. David Eisenhower and Mrs. Edward F. Cox, and with his close aides. Members of his staff, acting independently of the Congressmen, sent him memorandums he had requested as to their recommendations. Most called for resignation rather than taking the country through a painful impeachment debate and vote in the House and a trial in the Senate.

Last night, Raymond K. Price and other speech writers were ordered to prepare a resignation statement for use tonight. Secretary of State Kissinger met with the President late in the evening and Mr. Nixon told him that he would resign in the national interest.

At 11 A.M. today, as crowds for the third day gathered along Pennsylvania Avenue outside the White House, President Nixon summoned Mr. Ford to his Oval Office and officially informed him that he would submit his resignation tomorrow to the Secretary of State, as provided by Federal law, and that Mr. Ford would become President.

Shortly after noon, Mr. Ziegler, the President's confidant and press secretary, his face saddened and weary, appeared in the crowded White House press room and announced that the President would go on national radio and television tonight to address the American people. As with most previous such announcements, he did not say what the President would talk about.

But by that time, other Presidential aides were confirming that Mr. Nixon planned to resign, and the tensions that had been building for days subsided.

At 7:30 P.M. Mr. Nixon met in his office in the Executive Office Building with a bipartisan Congressional leadership group—James O. Eastland, Democrat of Mississippi, President pro tem of the Senate; Mike Mansfield, Democrat of Montana, the Senate majority leader; Hugh Scott, Republican of Pennsylvania, the Senate minority floor leader; Carl Albert, Democrat of Oklahoma, the Speaker of the House, and John J. Rhodes, Republican of Arizona, the minority leader. The meeting was to give them formal notice of his resignation.

Among the White House staff today there was a sadness but there were no tears, according to those there. Mr. Nixon, who was described as wretched and gray yesterday while wrestling with his decision, was described today as relaxed. To some, he appeared relieved.

He ordered Mr. Price to begin drafting the resignation speech yesterday, even before he made his decision to resign, aides said. Five drafts of it were written before it was turned over to Mr. Nixon to make his own changes.

It was exactly six years ago last night that Mr. Nixon was nominated on the first ballot at the Republican National Convention to be the party's nominee for President, a note of irony that did not escape members of the President's staff.

That evening marked the beginning of an ascension to power that was to put the Nixon mark on an important segment of history. After a first term marked by innovations in foreign policy and a return of resources to the state and local governments in domestic policy, Mr. Nixon in 1972 won re-election with 60.7 per cent of the vote.

In early 1973, as he ended American military involvement in the Vietnam war and as he moved to strengthen the powers of his office in a multitude of ways, his popularity rating in the Gallup Poll registered 68 per cent. But as the Watergate disclosures broke his rating dropped quickly and was below 30 per cent before the end of the year.

Mr. Nixon made a number of counterattacks to win back his lost popularity. He campaigned from time to time across the country as if he was running for office. He disclosed information about his taxes and property. He hired a succession of lawyers to defend him in the courts and in Congress.

He made television and radio appearances. He ordered his subordinates to step up their activities to show that the Government's business was moving ahead. He made foreign trips to show he was still a world leader.

Cheered in Tour of Middle East

In the Middle East in June he was cheered by vast throngs, and he held a summit meeting with Soviet leader, Leonid I. Brezhnev, in Moscow.

Yet, when he returned to the United States, the Gallup Poll showed his rating at 24 per cent and the Watergate charges broke anew as the House Judiciary Committee stepped up its impeachment inquiry. His Administration was tottering when he made his remarkable statement last Monday, apparently in an effort to put his own interpretation on information that was expected to have been made public at the Watergate trials as a result of a Supreme Court decision upholding a court order for the information.

When the decision to resign came, Mr. Nixon moved to achieve an orderly transition of power to Mr. Ford. General Haig, who has had broad delegated authority in recent months, met frequently with the Vice President to brief him on policy, as did other Administration officials.

Mr. Kissinger gave a number of assurances that the nation's "bipartisan foreign policy" would remain firmly in place. The Defense Department announced that American military forces around the world would continue under normal status. And across this city thousands of Federal employes performed their chores as if nothing was happening

A Sense of National Reconciliation

Capital Looks Ahead Instead of Back, Glad to Forget

By JAMES RESTON

Special to The New York Times

News Analysis

WASHINGTON, Aug. 8—The capital took the news with remarkable serenity, almost as if it had lost a President but found itself. And President Nixon, in his noble farewell, contributed to this sense of national reconciliation. Washington is looking forward gladly now, having looked back for so long, and Mr. Nixon joined in forgetting—almost insisted on forgetting—the facts of the past.

Indeed, he ignored all the crimes and lies that had forced his resignation, and talked generously about the future, as if the whole Watergate thing was sort of an awkward misunderstanding, which had somehow destroyed his authority and should be forgotten.

Capital Seeks to Forget

Washington has a somewhat different view of these past tragic years, but it is willing, and almost eager to forget.

In the last 11 years, it has seen one President murdered, another choose, under attack, not to run again, and a third driven from office, so it was vaguely sad, but at the same time it was almost unanimously relieved that the dark riddle of the Nixon Administration had finally passed.

The relief was tangible in the private comments even of the President's Cabinet and most loyal supporters in Congress, and in the faces of the people who gathered quietly outside the iron palings around the White House.

The fears of an uncertain result, of division, bitterness and recrimination, and of a long trial of a paralyzed President, so menacing only a few short days ago, had been avoided. And the nation's political institutions, so long under skeptical attack, had held together and come out with a clear decision and a fairly united people.

In the end, Mr. Nixon did, as he had done so many times before, what he said he would not do. As he had switched on China, the Soviet Union, on economic policy, executive privilege, and many others things, he abandoned his threat to fight both impeachment and conviction.

"Leaders should guide as far as they can, and then vanish," H. G. Wells once wrote. "Their ashes should not choke the fires they have lit." Almost all Mr. Nixon's friends gave him this advice, and finally he took it.

What has been the effect of all this on the nation, its people, its political parties and other institutions, and its relations with the rest of the world? These were the questions that were being asked here even before Mr. Nixon resigned.

The practical and personal questions of leadership are unprecedented in the history of the Republic. There are 896 days to go before the end of the term Mr. Nixon was elected to fulfill by the largest popular majority in the history of American Presidential elections—two years and five and a half months.

The nation will be led in this period, including the 200th anniversary of the Declaration of Independence on July 4, 1976, by President Gerald Ford, and a Vice President yet to be chosen, neither of whom will have been elected by the people of the United States—a situation that was not foreseen, and probably would have startled the Founding Fathers.

Had Planned to Retire

Nevertheless, the outlook is that Mr. Ford will have the greatest support and sympathy, even if not elected by popular ballot, of any President since Lyndon Johnson took over the White House after the assassination of President Kennedy.

In Washington, there is already a marked change. Mr. Nixon was a secretive, furtive and fundamentally intricate man, who regarded Congress and the press as his enemies. Mr. Ford is just the opposite: open, uncomplicated and modest. He is conservative and partisan, but he has spent most of his mature life in the give-and-take of the House, and regards the majority Democratic leaders not only as powers that have to be dealt with, but also as his personal friends.

At 61 years old, he has got beyond all ambition, in fact has achieved far beyond his dreams. He was planning to retire to private life, on a promise to his wife, even before Mr. Nixon picked him as Vice President.

In the nation, the spirit of the people may very well be going with Mr. Ford—at least for the time being. It has gone through a long period of division over Vietnam and Watergate, and is tired of contention, and is longing for a little peace and quiet.

There is a strong feeling here that Mr. Ford could be an ideal President in such a time. Just as Calvin Coolidge took over after the scandals of the Harding Administration, and quietly calmed things down and created an atmosphere that kept the Republicans in power for another nine years, Mr. Ford has a chance to revive the fortunes of the Republicans in 1974 and 1976.

Meanwhile, Watergate has had its effects on the country as a whole, and Mr. Ford, with his simple moral approach to the Presidency, may be very much in touch with the mood of the country.

Though he is a party man, he is likely to support reform in campaign financing, preservation of personal privacy, and strict control over the integrity of the Internal Revenue Service, the Federal Bureau of Investigation, and the Central Intelligence Agency.

He will be cautious about change, and will probably keep most of the Nixon Cabinet for a while, particularly at the Department of State, Defense and the Treasury, but he is not overly enthusiastic about Attorney General William B. Saxbe so there will be no political control of Justice soon, and like President Truman, he is likely to change most of his Cabinet before the end of the year.

One of the interesting things about Mr. Ford, though he is no intellectual, is that, unlike Presidents Johnson and Nixon, he does not feel uncomfortable or threatened by exceptional talent. In this, he is more like President Truman, who could trust the sophisticated minds of Dean Acheson and Robert A. Lovett and bring into the Cabinet strong men such as Gen. George C. Marshall.

Rockefeller Appears in Lead

This is really the main question in Washington now: How will Mr. Ford approach his new responsibilities? It is clear that he will keep Secretary Kissinger at State, but who will be his Vice President, and his chief of staff in the White House? These are the questions now being asked in the capital.

The front-runner for Vice President, with the backing of Melvin Laird, is former New York Governor, Nelson Rockefeller, but there is a lot of support for George Bush, the chairman of the Republican National Committee, who is young and attractive and could be a candidate for the Presidency in 1976, if given a chance at the Vice-Presidency now.

All this, however, is speculative. The main thing is that even the thought of a Ford Presidency has changed the mood here, and increased the hope for a more open, candid and cooperative Presidency.

White House Photograph via United Press International

President Nixon and his younger daughter, Julie Eisenhower, embracing Wednesday after he decided to resign.

Impeachment Trial Urged By Nixon's 1950 Opponent

FAIRLEE, Vt., Aug. 8 (UPI) — Helen Gahagan Douglas, whose political career was cut short by Richard Nixon in 1950, said today that she was sorry the impeachment process had not proceeded to its logical conclusion in the Senate.

Mrs. Douglas, the wife of Melvyn Douglas, the actor, lost the 1950 Senate race in California to Mr. Nixon, who was chosen two years later by General of the Army Dwight D. Eisensower as his running mate. The Nixon-Douglas campaign was one of the most bitter in California history, with Mr. Nixon attempting to link his Democratic opponent to Communist causes.

Mrs. Douglas said an impeachment trial in the Senate, "would have educated us as to what a President can do and cannot do; what a Congress must do and must not give up; if we are to retain our freedom."

Only Nixon Is Serene at Sad White House

Continued From Page 1, Col. 8

secretary, Steven Bull, was "unbelievably serene."

"I've seen him like this after a tough decision has been made," said Mr. Bull, who works in close proximity to the President. "Yesterday I saw a degree of anguish. Today there is an acceptance of whatever it is he is going to do."

Mr. Bull said that the President was "calm, in control, content with himself."

"I would have to describe it as an inner peace." He added, using a term employed in the past by Mr. Nixon to describe his emotional state.

Another White House aide close to the President said that Mr. Nixon underwent "a very emotional and draining" experience yesterday while arriving at the decision to resign.

"It has been a very tough time for him," but now he is responding in a "soldierly" fashion, the aide said.

"Having faced the necessity of his decision, he has been try- spent a good part of the day ing to go about it in as decent and statesmanlike a way as he can," the official said.

While the President was working in the Oval Office and later in the old Executive Office Building, his family—his wife Pat, his daughters Julie and Tricia and their husbands David Eisenhower and Edward F. Cox—stayed together in the East Wing of the White House.

When asked what the family did today, Mrs. Nixon's assistant press secretary, Patty Matson, said she did not know because the press office had not disturbed the family over the last few days.

"This is a very private time for them," she said.

She responded angrily when asked what the mood of the family was, snapping, "How can you ask such a ridiculous question at a time like this?"

Then she said, "I'm sorry—I know you're just doing your job," and burst in tears.

Mr. Nixon and his family will fly to their home at San Clemente, Calif., tomorrow morning before Gerald R. Ford takes the oath of office and succeeds him as President. According to Mr. Bull, the Nixons will fly aboard Air Force One, the jet craft Mr. Nixon has called "the Spirit of '76."

His aides said that Mr. Nixon working on his speech. One official said that while speech writers were helping the President, he was doing much of the writing himself.

"He wants this to be his speech," the aide said.

The President also met with his chief of staff, Gen. Alexander M. Haig Jr., and Mr. Ziegler, his two closest associates since the departure of H. R. Haldeman and John D. Ehrlichman on April 30, 1973.

Shortly before 7:30 P.M. Mr. Nixon, wearing a blue suit and red tie, walked alone from the White House to the Executive Office Building to meet the Congressional leaders.

He spent several minutes with his family before going to face the members of Congress. At his request, no Secret Service agent accompanied him on the short walk. But while he was between the two buildings, newsmen were locked inside the briefing room without being told the reason.

Meeting him were Senators James O. Eastland, president pro tem of the Senate; Mike Mansfield, the Senate majority leader; Hugh Scott, the minority leader; Representative Carl Albert, the Speaker of the House, and Representative John J. Rhodes, the House minority leader.

Tomorrow, Mr. Nixon will return to private life. He faces a multitude of problems, including the need to raise mortgage payments for his property. He has not before today discussed what he intends to do. He is by formal training a lawyer, but most of his adult life has been devoted unreservedly to politics and public service.

Outside the White House, the weather was hot with a sky obscured by dirty gray clouds that occasionally dropped brief showers on the city. It was fairly typical August weather in Washington and was somehow suited to the mood of this grim but historic day.

In his speech of April 30 1973, in which he pledged to see that justice was done in the Watergate case, Mr. Nixon noted that there were "exactly 1,361 days remaining in my term. I want these to be the best days in America's history because I love America."

Tomorrow, Richard Nixon will leave office 895 days before the second term of his Presidency was to have expired.

Graham Says Nixon Deserves Prayers and Expresses Sorrow

By EDWARD B. FISKE

The Rev. Billy Graham, the evangelist who is a close personal friend of President Nixon, said last night that the President deserved the prayers "even of those who feel betrayed and let down."

"I feel sorry for President Nixon and his family," he said in an interview. "I will always consider him a friend. His personal suffering must be almost unbearable."

Mr. Graham was one of many religious leaders across the country, including several who have served Mr. Nixon as a pastor, who responded to the announcement of his resignation with appeals for understanding and prayer and for a renewal of commitment to morality in public life.

In his remarks, Mr. Graham, who was reached at a New York hotel, expressed the hope that Americans would "put the tragedy of Watergate behind us once and for all." He urged them to "unite behind our new President" and "turn to God in a fresh way."

The Rev. T. Eugene Coffin, pastor of the East Whittier Friends Church in East Whittier, Calif., where Mr. Nixon is a member, called him "one of America's great Presidents."

He said that the President was "the victim of the questionable though accepted practice in political circles of acting on the basis of political expediency," and emphasized that he and his congregation would stand by Mr. Nixon during this period of difficulty.

The Rev. John Huffman, the former pastor of the Key Biscayne Presbyterian Church which Mr. Nixon frequently attended when he was at his home in Key Biscayne, Fla. termed the resignation "the very best thing for the nation."

"Here is a case in which a law and order President has for over two years consistently lied to the American people," he said in an interview. "He lied to me personally. When I went to him with my concerns on Watergate personally over a year and a half ago, he told me he was doing everything within his power to get to the very heart of the matter."

Many religious leaders urged the country to respond to the change in leadership with renewed concern for morality in public life. The Right Rev. Paul Moore Jr., Episcopal Bishop of New York, for instance, declared: "We now have before us the greatest opportunity of our lifetime to complete the purification of our political process [and] to insist on complete integrity in public office."

Kissinger Will Remain Secretary of State; Ford Likely to Keep Other Aides Also

Both Old and New Faces Sought to Ease the Change

By MARJORIE HUNTER
Special to The New York Times

WASHINGTON, Aug. 8—Vice President Ford announced tonight that Henry A. Kissinger would continue as Secretary of State in the new Administration.

The appointment, the first by the man who will become President tomorrow, was announced by Mr. Ford as he stood in front of his home in Alexandria, Va., shortly after Mr. Nixon's resignation speech.

Mr. Ford said he had asked Mr. Kissinger to stay on and that the Secretary of State had agreed.

"He and I will be working together in the pursuit of peace as we have worked to achieve it in the past," Mr. Ford said.

Mr. Ford is also expected to ask other Cabinet members and some top White House aides to remain, at least intially, but he is believed sure to move members of his own staff and certain old political friends into key spots in his Administration.

Such a team of both old faces and new faces, Mr. Ford apparently feels, will enable him to achieve a relatively smooth transition from the Nixon Presidency while at the same time helping him to bind up the wounds of a badly battered nation.

Defense Secretary

It is understood that Secretary of Defense James R. Schlesinger is prepared to stay on, and there is reason to believe that Mr. Ford, who once expressed some misgivings about Mr. Schlesinger's ability to work with Congress, now regards him highly.

While the new President will ask other Cabinet officers to remain, he is likely to replace at least some of them later with persons more attuned to his own thinking and style, close friends of Mr. Ford said today.

Among those White House aides who almost certainly will be asked to stay on are William E. Timmons, assistant to the President for legislative affairs and others on the legislative liaison staff.

It is uncertain whether Mr. Ford will ask Gen. Alexander M. Haig Jr., Mr. Nixon's chief of staff, to remain, or whether General Haig would agree to.

Mr. Ford expressed high regard for General Haig some months ago and strongly indicated he would like to retain him in the event Mr. Nixon left office. However, at least some of Mr. Ford's close friends have expressed misgivings about keeping a staff member who was so close to Mr. Nixon.

New Faces

Those close to Mr. Ford say that one person who will not be welcome in the new Administration is Ronald L. Ziegler, press secretary to Mr. Nixon.

It was learned tonight that J. F. terHorst, Washington bureau chief of The Detroit News, had been recruited to coordinate press operations during the transition. It is not known, however, if Mr. terHorst will become a permanent member of the White House staff.

It is uncertain what role Melvin R. Laird, one of Mr. Forl's oldest political advisers, will play in the new Administration.

Mr. Laird has reportedly told friends that he would be reluctant to return to the Government, but that he would be willing to serve as an unofficial adviser. Mr. Laird was Mr. Nixon's first Secretary of Defense and later served as a White House adviser.

While there will be holdovers from the Nixon Administration — Cabinet members and some White House aides—the Ford Government will introduce many persons largely unknown to the public generally.

These are the members of Mr. Ford's own staff, and they largely reflect the man they serve. It is a staff that is predominantly middle-aged, conservative. Midwestern and very much oriented to Capitol Hill, where many of them once worked.

Some of those who are certain to follow Mr. Ford into the White House are the following:

Robert T. Hartmann, 57 years old, is the politically shrewd former head of the Washington bureau of The Los Angeles Times. He has been Vice President Ford's chief of staff and is slated for a top White House post, although perhaps not with the title he has held.

John O. Marsh, 47, is a former Demoratic member of the House who served later as an Assistant Secretary of Defense for legislative affairs in the Nixon Administration. He is now assistant to the Vice President for defense affairs.

Richard T. Burress, 52, had long experience on Capitol Hill, serving on the minority staff of the House Education and Labor Committee, later as counsel to the House Republican Policy Committee, and also on the Nixon congressional liaison team. He is an assistant to the Vice President for legislation and domestic affairs.

William Seidman, 53, a millionaire business man who, like Mr. Ford, is from Grand Rapids, Mich., is a former aide to George Romney and was active in Mr. Romney's effort in 1968 to win the Presidential nomination over Mr. Nixon. He is an assistant to the Vice President for administration.

Walter L. Moie, 50, served on Senate staffs for many years and was the principal holdover from Spiro T. Agnew's Vice-Presidential staff. He has been in charge of Mr. Ford's Vice-Presidential office on Capitol Hill.

William E. Casselman 2d, 32, also worked on Capitol Hill before becoming General Counsel of the General Services Administration. He is the Vice President's counsel.

Paul A. Miltich, 54, is a former Michigan newspaperman who joined Mr. Ford as press secretary in 1966. He is still Mr. Ford's press secretary.

Allies in Congress

Mr. Ford also is close to, and perhaps may seek to bring into his Administration, such old Congressional friends and advisers as Representative Albert H. Quie, Republican of Minnesota; Senator Robert Griffin, Republican of Michigan; Charles Goodell, a former Senator from New York, and John W. Byrnes, a former Representative from Wisconsin.

Some close to Mr. Ford believe that he will seek to recruit some Democrats for his Administration. While Mr. Ford is a strongly partisan Republican, he has many close friends in the other party.

Those who know Mr. Ford best predict that his Administration will be very much oriented to Congress and that his White House will be far more open and candid than that of the Nixon years.

Among his recent reading has been "The Twilight of the Presidency," by George Reedy, who was President Johnson's press secretary. Mr. Ford was so impressed with the book—which details the growing tendency of recent Presidents to assume kinglike roles—that he made it required reading for his staff.

"Presidents develop this aura of infallibility," Mr. Ford said recently. "I'm simply saying that I think Presidents and their staffs have to have a somewhat different attitude to the Congress and to the job."

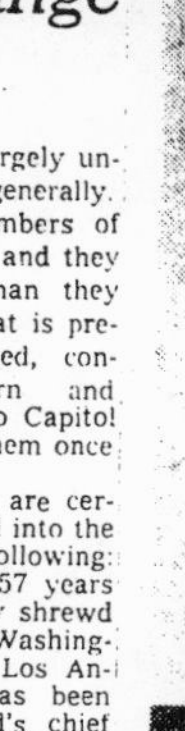

United Press International

Vice President Ford with Secretary of State Kissinger, who visited him yesterday at his suite in the Executive Office Building. Mr. Ford said later that he had asked Mr. Kissinger to remain in his post.

FORD WILL TAKE THE OATH TODAY

Continued From Page 1, Col. 2

cans in the House as well as in the Senate to work on the problems—serious ones—which we have at home."

Mr. Ford expressed his feelings of regret at the events that had brought on the first Presidential resignation.

"This is one of the most difficult and very saddest periods and one of the very saddest incidents I've ever witnessed," Mr. Ford said.

"Let me say that I think the President of the United States has made one of the greatest personal sacrifices for the country and one of the finest personal decisions on behalf of all of us as Americans by his decision to resign as President of the United States."

Agnew Resignation

Mr. Ford was selected for the Vice-Presidential post last fall after the resignation of Spiro T. Agnew, under terms of the 25th Amendment of the Constitution. Mr. Agnew resigned last Oct. 10 after pleading no contest to income tax charges growing out of the tangled web of Maryland politics.

On Oct. 26, a reporter returning with Mr. Ford from Ohio by plane—when his nomination was still under consideration before Congress—asked him:

"Would you like to be President?"

"I really would not like to be," Mr. Ford replied. "I wasn't even anxious to be the Vice-Presidential nominee. I simply had indicated to the White House that if the President wanted me to be the Vice President, I would certainly accept it and do my best."

Mr. Ford arrived at his office in the Executive Office Building shortly after 8 A.M. He met with President Nixon for an hour this morning.

He had been scheduled to begin a 12-day speechmaking tour on the West Coast and in Chicago, beginning today, but canceled it.

There were no details announced after Mr. Ford's meeting with Mr. Nixon, and later Mr. Ford went across Pennsylvania Avenue to Blair House, the Presidential guest house, where he awarded the Congressional Medal of Honor posthumously, to the families of seven Vietnam servicemen. It is a task usually performed by the President.

Ford Promises That He and Kissinger Will Continue Nixon's Foreign Policy

By BERNARD GWERTZMAN
Special to The New York Times

WASHINGTON, Aug. 8—Vice President Ford said tonight that he would continue "without any hesitation or reservation" the foreign policy of the Nixon Administration.

Speaking to newsmen on the lawn of his home in Alexandria, Va., after President Nixon had announced his resignation, Mr. Ford pledged that he and Secretary of State Kissinger would work together to promote the foreign policies of the last five and a half years.

Mr. Kissinger told Mr. Ford today that he would continue to serve as the chief foreign policy official in the Administration.

Earlier in the day, the Vice President met with Mr. Kissinger for an hour and 40 minutes. Afterward, Mr. Ford said in a statement that he believed the Nixon Administation's foreign policy, carried out by Mr. Kissinger, was "in the best interests of the United States."

"After the meeting, the Vice President noted that he has enjoyed working with Dr. Kissinger and has supported the foreign policy carried out by the Secretary," the brief statement said. "He said he believed that policy is in the best interests of the United States."

Need for Reassurance

During their far-reaching conversation, Mr. Kissinger reportedly advised Mr. Ford of the need to reassure the Russians and Chinese of Washington's intention to continue the policy of seeking improved relations.

America's friends and allies will also be advised, aides said, that Mr. Ford intends to maintain American commitments, such as those in Europe and Indochina. The nations of the Middle East will also be told of the continuing interest of the new Administration to seek a peace settlement in that area without jeopardizing Israel's security.

After Mr. Ford is sworn in tomorrow at noon, the new President and Mr. Kissinger are to receive foreign ambassadors, some individually and some in groups, to stress the continuity of American foreign policy.

Mr. Ford, who has long publicly praised Mr. Kissinger, symbolized the importance he was attaching to the Secretary's remaining in the Administration by telephoning him shortly after Mr. Nixon told him this morning of his impending resignation.

The State Department spokesman, Robert Anderson, said that during the 10-minute phone conversation, Mr. Ford invited Mr. Kissinger to a 3 P.M. meeting at his suite in the Executive Office Building, adjacent to the White House.

Photographers were invited to record the meeting, Mr. Ford's first with a prospective Cabinet officer in his administration since Mr. Nixon's intention to resign became known.

Mr. Kissinger had expressed serious concern privately in recent days about the possible danger to the United States if the impeachment crisis continued with the President's prestige undermined.

Yesterday, the Secretary went to the White House twice, the second time from 10 P.M. to shortly after midnight. During that second meeting, he conferred with Mr. Nixon in the President's living quarters.

The details of that meeting have not been made known, but Mr. Kissinger was reported to have concurred with Mr. Nixon that the national interest would best be served by an end to the impeachment crisis—that is, by the President's resignation.

Mr. Nixon informed him then that he was going to quit, and Mr. Kissinger in the early morning ordered some of his key staff members to begin the paper work necessary for a transition.

Some Key Issues

Messages will be sent to all Presidental appointees in the Foreign Service—ambassadors and high-level officials in Washington—informing them of their obligation to submit resignations to the new President, a routine action when the Presidency changes.

Drafts were being prepared for Presidential declarations to various heads of government reaffirming American policy commitments.

Among the key issues awaiting Mr. Ford's attention in the foreign policy field are the following:

¶He will come into office while efforts are under way to keep up momentum toward a settlement in the Middle East. Mr. Ford's first official visitor will probably be King Hussein of Jordan, who is scheduled to arrive in Washington late next week.

¶Talks with the Russians are due to resume in Geneva next month on limitation of strategic arms, a key issue that has eluded a solution this year. Mr. Kissinger has spoken of disagreements within the Administration on what the American negotiating stand should be, and Mr. Ford may have to make some difficult decisions in this area.

¶Relations with the Chinese have been a source of concern in Washington because of the internal problems in Peking as well as China's apparent worry that Mr. Nixon's resignation might lead to a different American attitude on better relations. Mr. Ford, who visited China while he was minority leader in the House, will probably have to assure China of the continuity of his policies.

¶The ties of the United States with its European allies have improved significantly in recent months, and the change in leadership, without a change in Mr. Kissinger's status, will probably not raise any new problems. But Mr. Ford will probably have to become acquainted with most of the key leaders, either by inviting them here or visiting them in Europe.

¶The Administration had embarked on a "new dialogue" with Latin America, but Mr. Nixon's refusal to ease the embargo on trade and relations with Cuba had caused some problems. Mr. Ford may formulate a more flexible policy toward Cuba, if encouraged to do so by Mr. Kissinger.

¶The situation in Indochina has not improved much, and Congress has cut the Administration's $3-billion aid request for Indochina. Mr. Ford will be under some pressure to try to restore the amounts cut by Congress.

Ford's Economic Policy To Differ From Nixon's

By EILEEN SHANAHAN
Special to The New York Times

WASHINGTON, Aug. 8 — People who have long known both Gerald R. Ford and Richard M. Nixon believe that Mr. Ford's posture will be subtly but significantly different from his predecessor's in the area that is of most concern to the nation today — economic policy.

Like Mr. Nixon, Mr. Ford is a conservative who believes that maintaining tight control over Government spending is essential if any inroads are to be made against inflation.

The differences between the two men that are seen by economists who know them both are less philosophical than they are personal. But these differences of personality could bring policy differences over a period of time, it is suggested.

For example, Paul W. McCracken, an old friend of Mr. Ford's, who also served as Mr. Nixon's chairman of the Council of Economic Advisers, said he felt that Mr. Nixon had "a tendency to go for the 50-yard pass, with interludes in between without much activity." He cited the wage-price freeze of August, 1971, as an example of a 50-yard pass in economic policy—a risky attempt to turn the tide toward victory.

Hayes's Strategy

In Mr. McCracken's view, Mr. Ford, on the other hand, understands the strategy of Woody Hayes, the highly successful Ohio State football coach, that "four yards and a cloud of dust gets the ball over the line more often than the opposition."

Thus, Mr. McCracken believes that, while Mr. Ford will adhere to the broad outlines of Mr. Nixon's anti-inflation policy of budgetry and monetary restraint, he will also "work more, day by day, on specific problems that need attention if the totality of things is to work better."

Specifically, Mr. McCracken expects Mr. Ford to pay closer attention to union contract negotiations in such basic industries as coal mining, and to such problems as the way the Government's own regulatory policies may be adding to inflation.

A Different View

A view of the two men that was somewhat different from Mr. McCracken's, but not inconsistent with it, was expressed by Murray Weidenbaum, who was Assistant Secretary of the Treasury for economic policy in the first three years of the Nixon Administration.

It is in Mr. Nixon's nature, he said, "to lurch to extremes." He added:

"When one policy seemed not to work, he [Mr. Nixon] tried another. And each new policy, in turn, was rigidly described as the one true religion, with extravagant claims made for its healing powers."

Mr. Ford, Mr. Weidenbaum continued, is more relaxed, and does not approach economic policy, or perhaps any other policy area, with "theological preconceptions."

Mr. Weidenbaum expects that economic policy changes under Mr. Ford will be less abrupt and drastic than, for example, Mr. Nixon's swings from budgetary restraint to budgetary stimulus in 1972, or his vacillations on wage and price controls. But milder changes, when a policy seemed inadequate, might be made by Mr. Ford with less anguish and strain, Mr. Weidenbaum indicated.

Thus, he feels that "in a curious way, Mr. Ford's economic policies may be simultaneously more flexible and steadier than Mr. Nixon's."

That Mr. Ford is committed to the battle against inflation is doubted by no one."

In dozens of speeches throughout the country since he became Vice President, he has referred to inflation as "public enemy No. 1." And, over and over, he has expressed his belief that there is no "easy road" to ending inflation, that no "quick fixes" are available, and that the only possible cure lies in keeping Government expenditures at noninflationary levels.

Yet, there are those who think that Mr. Ford might be quicker than Mr. Nixon to accept — even to advocate — a much-enlarged program of putting the unemployed on the Federal payroll in public service jobs.

The day before yesterday, for example, Mr. Ford put the following paragraph into a speech:

"It serves no purpose to lecture the harassed public, especially the low and middle-income people who have been the main losers from inflation. We are mindful that some people are suffering more than others. Certain groups—older Americans, persons on fixed incomes, the unemployed—may require special help, within budgetary limitations. Their plight must be heeded."

More Activism Hinted

Mr. Ford hinted in the same speech (which was delivered by someone else when he had to cancel his appearance) that he might take a more activist position than Mr. Nixon on other economic policy problems. Among these are the extreme difficulties that are facing different groups, ranging from would-be home-buyers to giant utility companies, in their attempts to borrow money.

"Certain industries, such as the public utilities, housing, financial institutions and others, have been especially hard hit" by policies of credit restraint that are also aimed at controlling inflation, Mr. Ford said.

"There are suggested solutions that have merit and deserve prompt consideration," he continued. "The time has come for action, not doom-saying and hand-wringing."

Mr. Ford did not specify which, among a number of new proposals for alleviating the credit shortage, he might support. But Mr. Nixon had not indicated any possibility of support for any of them.

Exercising Restraint

Many people — economic experts and nonexperts alike—have expressed the view that Mr. Ford might be able to take advantage of a mood of harmony and reconciliation that could sweep the country after Mr. Nixon's resignation to persuade business and labor to exercise restraint in the interests of curbing inflation.

Mr. Ford met on Tuesday with a group of five freshmen Senators from both parties who propounded to him their idea of an "economic summit meeting," including representatives of business, labor, consumer interests, farmers and others.

Mr. Ford said after the meeting that he thought there was "merit" in the plan, which presumably includes appeals for restraint in price and wage increases, as well as attempts to discover whether there were any economic policies that had a broad base of support among these groups.

Which of Mr. Nixon's top economic-policy advisers Mr. Ford might keep and which he might let go, at least over the long run, was not known. He reportedly had not spoken to any of these men, as the hour of President Nixon's speech to the nation neared, but he had scheduled a meeting with them for tomorrow afternoon.

A Peculiar Position

Alan Greenspan, the New York economist who was nominated by Mr. Nixon to be the new chairman of the Council of Economic Advisers, was in a particularly peculiar position. His nomination has yet to be confirmed by the Senate.

He said today that he would take over the job, as scheduled, if Mr. Ford asked him to, or bow out, if that was Mr. Ford's wish.

An economist who knows both Mr. Ford and Mr. Greenspan said he thought that Mr. Greenspan was definitely more conservative than Mr. Ford. But he added:

"That may not be especially significant. What a President wants most from the Council of Economic Advisers is good analysis, and Alan can certainly provide that."

No economist who knows Mr. Ford is arguing that he is deeply knowledgable about economics.

Mr. McCracken said, for example, that Mr. Ford's career "has been preoccupied with the craftsmanship of the legislative process rather than the substance of policy issues."

But he, like many others, rated Mr. Ford as a good listener when economic briefings were held.

Speculation Is Rife on Choice by Ford

Continued From Page 1, Col. 1

feller, the former New York Governor, would be the best choice to reassure foreign nations, heal the Republican party and attract fresh talent to the depleted Federal establishment.

Yet many other Republicans were observing that a Rockefeller Vice-Presidency, as Mr. Laird pictures it, might overwhelm Mr. Ford and his staff. And Mr. Laird's open effort to broker the Rockefeller selection was the subject of wide second-guessing, even among Mr. Rockefeller's senior staff.

"Laird could be throwing up a signal; he may have been expressing his personal choice," said one seasoned Republican politician who is close to both Mr. Laird and Mr. Ford. He added that Mr. Laird himself was a "definite contender" for the Vice Presidency, "and he ought to be."

Mr. Rockefeller, on vacation at Seal Harbor, Me., made no comment on the transition in Washington today and, according to a spokesman with him, heard "not a word from Mr. Ford or the President."

"He hasn't really talked to anyone," said Joseph Canzeri, a member of Mr. Rockefeller's personal staff. "I think the Governor's concerned about the country. He's saddened by events, as all Americans are. It's a sad day."

George Bush, the chairman of the Republican National Committee, met with Mr. Ford this afternoon, a Bush spokesman announced, in "a private talk looking to the future of the party and the country."

Party Appeal

Friends of Mr. Bush, a Texan, believe that he would have political appeal among the party faithful, particularly in the South and West, and they thought today that he might well have expressed an interest in the Vice-Presidency. Mr. Bush had flown back from California today after the cancellation of a Republican fund-raising telethon in Los Angeles; he was not responding to press injuiries himself.

An aide to Elliot L. Richardson remarked that the former Attorney General could bring as much brains and "class" as Mr. Rockefeller could to a Ford Administration, and that he had the advantage of being a "team player" while Mr. Rockefeller had always been a star in his own right.

A spokesman for Senator Barry Goldwater of Arizona observed that angry passions of the Goldwater-Rockefeller fight for the Republican Presidential nomination in 1964 had virtually died in the intervening decade. Accordingly, Mr. Goldwater's aide volunteered, the Arizona conservative would have no objection to a choice of the New York fiberal. In turn, he suggested, the Rockefeller Republicans should have no objection to a choice of Senator Goldwater, who declared yesterday that he would accept the Vice-Presidency if Mr. Ford offered it.

Other Republicans being mentioned in the guessing today were Senator Howard H. Baker Jr. of Tennessee, Representative John B. Anderson of Illinois and Governor Ronald Reagan of California. But there was speculation, too, from the Vice President's confidants that Mr. Ford might reach outside the ranks of active politicians—to the Supreme Court, for example, or to a retired Republican leader like William W. Scranton, the former Governor of Pennsylvania.

ROCKEFELLER DENIES GETTING FORD OFFER

SEAL HARBOR, Me., Aug. 8 (AP)—Nelson A. Rockefeller has not been offered the Vice-Presidency, a source close to the former New York Governor said today.

Mr. Rockefeller said in a statement today that a news conference he called for tomorrow had "nothing to do with recent events and should not be so interpreted."

He is said to be among candidates for Vice President being considered by Gerald R. Ford.

Joe Canzeri, a personal aide to Mr. Rockefeller, said the statement was issued to prevent "further misinterpretation" following televised remarks indicating that Mr. Rockefeller's news conference was related to President Nixon's resignation.

"I've not called a press conference," Mr. Rockefeller said in a statement. "I agreed last May 20 to address a Republican fund-raising dinner in Bangor, Me., on Friday, Aug. 9, and at that time agreed to meet with the press while I was there."

Mrs. Ford Sees Dress Designer Instead of Her Doctor

Special to The New York Times

WASHINGTON, Aug. 8—At 3 P.M. today the Secret Service ordered a roadblock placed on Crown View Drive, a quiet suburban street in Alexandria, Va., where Vice President Ford lives.

But Mrs. Ford's secretary, Nancy Howe, who was beckoned out of the Fords' modest brick home into the rain several times today by reporters standing on the sidewalk, insisted that "it's just a normal day" in the home of Gerald R. Ford.

Late this afternoon, Mrs. Ford, sheltered by a black umbrella held by the family chauffeur, strolled out onto her front sidewalk to wave to the cameras. She had little to say.

"How do you feel about being First Lady?" a reporter asked prematurely.

Mrs. Ford, looking startled, ignored the question by smiling and saying, "Really good to see you."

The day was obviously not as ordinary as Mrs. Howe said it was. Mrs. Ford, insteady of keeping an appointment with a foot doctor, invited a local designer, Frankie Welch, to her home.

Mrs. Welch said Mrs. Ford had not chosen a dress for a swearing-in ceremony.

Mrs. Ford returned home from a church activity in time to watch the President's speech with her husband and their daughter, Susan, 17 years old.

The New York Times/George Tames

Mrs. Gerald R. Ford, escorted by the family's chauffeur, outside her home in Alexandria, Va., yesterday.

"All the News That's Fit to Print"

The New York Times

LATE CITY EDITION

Weather: Partly sunny today; cool tonight. Partly sunny tomorrow. Temp. range: today 65-78; Friday 68-84. Highest Temp.-Hum. Index yesterday: 78. Details on Page 58.

VOL. CXXIII ... No. 42,567

NEW YORK, SATURDAY, AUGUST 10, 1974

20c beyond 50-mile radius of New York City, except Long Island. Higher in air delivery cities.

15 CENTS

FORD SWORN IN AS PRESIDENT; ASSERTS 'NIGHTMARE IS OVER'

Nixon Bids an Emotional Farewell to Washington

TEARS AT PARTING

Ex-President Warns Against Bitterness and Revenge

By JAMES T. WOOTEN

Special to The New York Times

WASHINGTON, Aug. 9 — Richard M. Nixon, his face wet with tears, bade an emotional farewell to the remnants of his broken Administration today, urging its members to be proud of their record in government and warning them against bitterness, self-pity and revenge.

"Always remember, others may hate you," he told members of his Cabinet and staff in a final gathering at the White House, "but those who hate you don't win unless you hate them—and then you destroy yourself."

The text of Nixon's speech is printed on Page 4.

Shortly thereafter, for the last time as President of the United States, he strode up the ramp of the plane that had taken him to the capitals of the world and was flown home to California, where his career in American politics began nearly thirty years ago.

It was 11:35 A.M. here when President Nixon's letter of resignation was delivered to the office of Secretary of State Kissinger. This is what it said:

"Dear Mr. Secretary: I hereby resign the office of President of the United States. Sincerely, Richard Nixon."

Greeted by 5,000

Soon after his departure, while the giant jet was soaring high above the heartland of the country, Gerald R. Ford was sworn in here as the nation's President.

Despite that new status, 5,000 people greeted his arrival in his native state at El Toro Marine Base. They cheered and applauded when, with his wife, Pat, standing nearby, Mr. Nixon stepped to a waiting microphone, squinted into the brilliant midday heat and said, "We're home."

After a few more remarks, a helicopter whisked the former President, Mrs. Nixon, their daughter Tricia and her husband Edward F. Cox, to La Casa Pacifica, the sprawling seaside villa near San Clemente.

Mr. Nixon's day began in the mist and rain of a humid Washington morning, when Manolo Sanchez, his long-time valet, laid out the clothes he would wear during the final hours of

Continued on Page 4, Column 1

Gerald R. Ford takes the Presidential oath, administered by Chief Justice Warren E. Burger. Mrs. Ford attends the White House ceremony. Associated Press

A Plea to Bind Up Watergate Wounds

By MARJORIE HUNTER

Special to The New York Times

WASHINGTON, Aug. 9—Gerald Rudolph Ford became the 38th President of the United States today, declaring that "our long national nightmare is over."

Calling upon the nation to "bind up the internal wounds of Watergate," he said, "Our Constitution works. Our great Republic is a government of laws and not of men. Here the people rule."

And then, his voice filled with emotion, he urged the nation to pray for his predecessor and friend of a quarter century, Richard Milhous Nixon.

The text of Ford's address will be found on Page 3.

"May our former President, who brought peace to millions, find it for himself," he said.

Mr. Ford assumed the powers of the Presidency at 11:35 A.M., the moment that Mr. Nixon's letter of resignation was handed to Secretary of State Kissinger.

Then, at 12:03 P.M., he was administered the oath of office in the historic East Room of the White House by Chief Justice Warren E. Burger before an overflow crowd of friends, the Cabinet and former Congressional colleagues from both parties.

Wife Holds Bible

It was in that same room, scarcely two hours earlier, that Mr. Nixon said an emotional good-by to his Cabinet and top aides.

Raising his right hand, Mr. Ford rested his left hand on a Bible held by his wife and opened to one of his favorite passages, the fifth and sixth verses of the third chapter of Proverbs: "Trust in the Lord with all thine heart; and lean not unto thine own understanding. In all thy ways acknowledge Him, and He shall direct thy paths."

Then, in a firm voice, he took the oath of office: "I, Gerald R. Ford, do solemnly swear that I will faithfully execute the office of President of the United States and will to the best of my ability preserve, protect and defend the Constitution of the United States."

As the heavy applause ended, the 61-year-old President began perhaps the most moving speech of his career. Speaking in his flat, Middle Western tone, but with what appeared to be a new sense of self-assurance, he said that he was assuming the Presidency under circumstances never before experienced by Americans.

Minds Are Troubled

"This is an hour of history that troubles our minds and hurts our hearts," he said.

"Therefore," he continued, "I feel it is my first duty to make an unprecedented compact with my countrymen. Not an inaugural address, not a fireside chat, not a campaign speech. Just a little straight talk among friends. I intend it to be the first of many."

As the first American to assume the office after the resignation of a President, Mr. Ford said that he was "acutely aware that you have not elected me as your President by your ballots."

"So I ask you to confirm me as your President with your prayers," he added.

He declared that he had not gained office by secret promises, that he had not campaigned either for the Presidency or the Vice-Presidency.

"I have not subscribed to any partisan platform," he said. "I am indebted to no man and only to one woman, my dear wife."

This was reminiscent of his earlier "I am my own man," a declaration that he repeated frequently in recent months as he sought to remain loyal to Mr. Nixon and at the same time hold himself above the spreading taint of the Watergate affair.

He said that while he had not sought the responsibility, he would not shirk it. He said that those who nominated him and confirmed him just eight months ago as Vice President were his friends from both parties.

"It is only fitting then that I

Continued on Page 3, Column 1

G.M. to Raise Prices 9.5% On 1975 Cars and Trucks

Special to The New York Times

DETROIT, Aug. 9—The General Motors Corporation announced today that it would raise prices of 1975 model cars and trucks by an average of $480 or 9.5 per cent.

The price increase will include about $130, or 2.5 per cent for government-required pollution control equipment—catalytic converters, while $350, or 7 per cent, will be to cover added labor and material costs, the corporation said.

Mack W. Worden, G.M. vice president, made the announcement in a letter sent to dealers Thursday and released publicly today. G.M. is traditionally the price pace-setter for the auto industry. The increases it sets are expected to be matched by its competitors.

Ford Sending Notices

The Ford Motor Company has already told its dealers it is sending them advanced billing notices of an average 8 per cent increase above the 1974 prices, which is calculated to mean an increase ranging from about $225 to $800, depending on the model.

Chrysler Corporation officials have indicated their price increases will be in the same area.

A Chrysler spokesman said today that next week "we are going to begin mailing tentative price bulletins on 1975 trucks. They will be in the same ball park as the G.M. and Ford increases. But that is as much as we are going to say at the present time."

Mr. Worden, in charge of the G.M. marketing staff, said that "based on past practice we would expect the Bureau of Labor Statistics will recognize "the catalytic converter's added value and not consider it a price increase in their published data."

Mr. Worden told the dealers G.M recognized the increases were "substantial" but said the corporation had "no alternative in light of rapidly rising labor and material costs over which we have only limited control and the necessity of complying with 1975 emission standards, which have been mandated by the Government."

As for the other auto com-

Continued on Page 36, Column 4

Friedmann Case Ends

The third and last person charged with the 1972 murder of Wolfgang Friedmann, Columbia University law professor, pleaded guilty to robbery last night. The others had earlier pleaded guilty to robbery. As a result, none of those who have admitted robbing the professor will be convicted of murdering him. Page 33.

PAPERS AND TAPES ISSUES IN CAPITAL

Impoundment of Nixon Data in White House Is Urged by Some in Congress

By RICHARD D. LYONS

Special to The New York Times

WASHINGTON, Aug. 9—On the heels of Richard M. Nixon's resignation, some members of Congress were urging impoundment of Presidential documents still in the White House. A few even demanded that the Watergate investigations be continued.

But Representative Peter W. Rodino Jr. said after a morning discussion of whether his House Judiciary Committee should make another attempt to obtain the 147 subpoenaed Presidential tape recordings that "we're not an investigative body."

"Our inquiry is at an end," the New Jersey Democrat said in expressing what seemed to be the feeling of the majority of the membership of both houses of Congress.

Yet the disposition and even ownership of the vast amount of Presidential records, some of which could be used as evidence in forthcoming trials, was a recurring question that remained unresolved.

As Representative Jonathan

Continued on Page 7, Column 6

Aide Doubtful That Ford Would Give Nixon Pardon

By LESLEY OELSNER

Special to The New York Times

WASHINGTON, Aug. 9—The new White House press secretary, J. F. terHorst, suggested today that President Ford was not likely to grant a pardon to former President Nixon. The press secretary was asked at a briefing this afternoon about the prospects of a pardon.

He replied that he had not spoken to Mr. Ford about the question directly, but that the President had apparently stated his position on the matter last fall, during the Senate confirmation hearings into his nomination as Vice President.

"I do not think the public would stand for it," Mr. Ford said then.

Mr. Nixon's prospects for avoiding criminal prosecution thus remained in doubt, with the office of the special Watergate prosecutor saying only that a decision on whether to prosecute had not been made.

Mr. Nixon lost whatever immunity from prosecution that he may have had when he resigned today. According to Mr. terHorst, Mr. Nixon did not try to pardon himself before leaving office, nor did he grant pardons to anyone else.

Some Republican members of Congress urged today that Mr. Nixon not be prosecuted, saying that he had already suffered enough. But even among Republicans, the sentiment was not unanimous.

Senator Edward W. Brooke, Republican of Massachusetts, submitted a resolution to the Senate yesterday expressing the "sense" of the Congress

Continued on Page 5, Column 3

4 NAMED TO HELP FORD'S TRANSITION

All on New Panel Served in House—President Vows Open Administration

By JOHN HERBERS

Special to The New York Times

WASHINGTON, Aug. 9—Immediately after he was sworn in today as the nation's 38th President, Gerald R. Ford took control of the Presidency and moved to give it a character and shape different from that of his predecessor, Richard M. Nixon.

After declaring in his inaugural speech that "here the people rule", President Ford named a four-member committee composed of former elected officials to oversee the transition and make recommendations for staff changes.

The four are William W. Scranton, former Governor of Pennsylvania; Donald M. Rumsfeld, Ambassador to the North Atlantic Treaty Organization and a former Republican member of Congress from Illinois; Rogers C. B. Morton, Secretary of the Interior and a former

Continued on Page 5, Column 3

President and Kissinger Confer With the Envoys of 60 Nations

By BERNARD GWERTZMAN

Special to The New York Times

WASHINGTON, Aug. 9 — President Ford undertook to convince foreign governments today that he would pursue the same foreign policy objectives that brought wide respect to Richard M. Nixon.

Two hours after taking the oath as President, Mr. Ford, assisted by Secretary of State Kissinger, who will retain his office, began meeting with about 60 envoys—some in groups and some individually—in brief sessions that lasted into the early evening.

The substance of what was said was, in general, a reaffirmation of well-known American policy positions. But Mr. Ford and Mr. Kissinger believed the exercise to be necessary to emphasize that there would be no significant change during the transition period in which Mr. Ford, who is less experienced in foreign affairs than his predecessor, makes his leadership felt.

Priority was given to a group meeting in the Roosevelt Room of the White House with members of the North Atlantic Treaty Organization. In a pattern followed in the other sessions, Mr. Kissinger and members of his staff met with 13 envoys for about 20 minutes

Continued on Page 6, Column 6

Gains of Watergate

Positive and Hopeful Results Found As the Transition Is Made Smoothly

By CLIFTON DANIEL

Special to The New York Times

WASHINGTON, Aug. 9—Watergate has now joined Teapot Dome, Credit Mobilier and the Whisky Ring in the lexicon of political infamy. Yet, in millions of minds it also symbolizes the finest hour of American democracy. A President has been deposed, but the Republic endures. Its institutions have survived, and some are saying they have been strengthened as well. Even the Presidency, which Richard M. Nixon professed to be so anxious to protect, shows no signs of debility. The man in the White House is as powerful today as he was yesterday, although his name has changed from Nixon to Ford.

News Analysis

He is just as powerful, although, as the new President said today, he is "acutely aware" that he was not elected by the votes of the people, whereas his predecessor had the largest popular majority in history.

Under the United States Constitution, removal of the President requires drastic surgery, not just a shift in the political balance, as it does in the parliamentary democracies.

However, the surgery performed on the American Government this week, while agonizing and painful, has done a minimum of visible damage to the body politic.

Mr. Nixon himself has said that one way to judge a country is to see how it effects a transfer of power. Today's transfer was effected without missing a heartbeat.

"Our Constitution works," President Ford proclaimed, after taking the oath of office. "Here the people rule."

"All in all," William P.

Continued on Page 7, Column 3

NEWS INDEX

President Nixon at ceremony where he bade his Cabinet and staff good-by. At left is his daughter Julie Eisenhower. The New York Times/George Tames

Ford Is Sworn In as President; He Asserts 'Our Long National Nightmare Is Over'

Plea Is Made to Bind Up 'Wounds of Watergate'

Continued From Page 1, Col. 8

should pledge to them and to you that I will be the President of all the people," he said.

He said that he would address a joint session of Congress Monday night "to share with my former colleagues and with you, the American people, my views on the priority business of the nation and to solicit your views and theirs."

The joint session, it was disclosed later, will begin at 9 P.M. Monday.

Search for Peace

Seeking to reassure the nation and the world that the United States had not been permanently damaged by the events of recent days, the new President pledged an uninterrupted and sincere search for peace.

"America will remain strong and united," he said, "but its strength will remain dedicated to the safety and sanity of the entire family of man as well as to our own precious freedom."

Repeating words that he first used in his confimation hearings for Vice President last fall, Mr. Ford said:

"I believe that truth is the glue that holds governments together, not only our Government, but civilization itself. That bond, though strained, is unbroken at home and abroad."

He pledged candor in all his public and private acts as President and then, with simple eloquence, spoke the words that Americans had once despaired of ever hearing:

"My fellow Americans, our long national nightmare is over."

In his only direct reference to Watergate, the new President said:

"As we bind up the internal wounds of Watergate, more painful and more poisonous than those of foreign wars, let us restore the Golden Rule to our political process, and let brotherly love purge our hearts of suspicion and hate."

Asking for the nation's prayers for the Nixon family, he spoke feelingly of Mr. Nixon's wife and daughters "whose love and loyalty will forever be a shining legacy to all who bear the lonely burdens of the White House."

"I can only guess at those burdens," he continued, "although I have witnessed at close hand the tragedies that befell three Presidents and the lesser trials of others."

As he spoke his final words—"God helping me, I will not let you down" —the several hundred persons present gave him a standing ovation.

Plans for the simple inauguration were coordinated by Gen. Alexander M. Haig Jr., who was Mr. Nixon's chief of staff.

General Haig, accompanied by Mr. Nixon's longtime personal secretary, Rose Mary Woods, sat with members of Mr. Ford's Vice-Presidential staff during the ceremony.

The guest list, compiled largely by Mr. and Mrs. Ford, reflected the new President's popularity among Democrats as well as members of his own party.

It was predominantly a Congressional assembly, a gathering of those to whom Mr. Ford felt closest during his long years in the House.

Former Speaker John W. McCormack, a Democrat, came down from Boston and was warmly greeted upon his entrance into the room by two friendly adversaries, Melvin R. Laird and John W. Byrnes, both former Republican members of the House.

House Speaker Carl Albert of Oklahoma, a Democrat, arrived with a newly acquired Secret Service escort: Again, as he did 10 months ago after Spiro T. Agnew resigned as Vice President, Mr. Albert stands next in line to the Presidency until Mr. Ford selects and Congress confirms a new Vice President.

Rises About Dawn

Among others in the gathering were several who have been mentioned as possible Vice-Presidential choices. They included George Bush, chairman of the Republican National Committee, and Representative John B Anderson of Illinois, the third-ranking Republican leader in the House.

Mr. Ford showed little of the strain of the last few days as he arrived for his inauguration. He wore a navy blue suit and a red, white and blue necktie.

He rose about dawn today, after only a few hours' sleep, and, wearing a robe, retrieved the morning newspaper—emblazed with black headlines, "Nixon Resigns"—from his front steps.

While the rest of the family slept, he prepared breakfast for himself and his youngest son, 18-year-old Steve, then conferred for nearly an hour at home with two of his close advisers, Mr. Byrnes and Philip W. Buchen of Grand Rapids, his former law partner.

Later, on the White House lawn, he bade an emotional farewell to his old friend, Mr. Nixon. The two men embraced just before Mr. Nixon stepped aboard a waiting helicopter.

Aides to the President said late today that it would be at least several days before the Fords moved into the White House.

The New York Times

J. F. terHorst as he was introduced in the White House Press Room by President Ford as new press secretary.

United Press International

Members of President Ford's family at the inauguration. From the left: John, 22; Steven, 18; Michael, 24, and his wife, Gayle; Susan, 17, and Gardner Britt, her boyfriend. They did not return home to eat lunch until 3 o'clock.

The New York Times

President and Mrs. Ford in the East Room of the White House. Mrs. Ford wore a blue knit dress.

Transcript of Address by New President

Following is a transcript of President Gerald R. Ford's Inaugural address yesterday in Washington, as recorded by The New York Times.

Mr. Chief Justice, my dear friends, my fellow Americans. The oath that I have taken is the same oath that was taken by George Washington and by every President under the Constitution.

But I assume the Presidency under extraordinary circumstances never before experienced by Americans. This is an hour of history that troubles our minds and hurts our hearts.

Therefore, I feel it is my first duty to make an unprecedented compact with my countrymen. Not an inaugural address, not a fireside chat, not a campaign speech, just a little straight talk among friends. And I intend it to be the first of many.

I am acutely aware that you have not elected me as your President by your ballots. So I ask you to confirm me as your President with your prayers. And I hope that such prayers will also be the first of many.

No 'Secret Promises'

If you have not chosen me by secret ballot, neither have I gained office by any secret promises. I have not campaigned either for the Presidency or the Vice Presidency. I have not subscribed to any partisan platform. I am indebted to no man and only to one woman, my dear wife.

As I begin this very difficult job, I have not sought this enormous responsibility, but I will not shirk it. Those who nominated and confirmed me as Vice President were my friends and are my friends. They were of both parties, elected by all the people and acting under the Constitution in their name.

It is only fitting then that I should pledge to them and to you that I will be the President of all the people.

Thomas Jefferson said the people are the only sure reliance for the preservation of our liberty. And down the years, Abraham Lincoln renewed this American article of faith asking is there any better way for equal hopes in the world.

I intend on next Monday next to request of the Speaker of the House of Representatives and the President pro tempore of the Senate the privilege of appearing before the Congress to share with my former colleagues and with you, the American people, my views on the priority business of the nation and to solicit your views and their views.

And may I say to the Speaker and the others, if I could meet with you right after this—these remarks I would appreciate it.

A Search for Peace

Even though this is late in an election year there is no way we can go forward except together and no way anybody can win except by serving the people's urgent needs.

We cannot stand still or slip backward. We must go forward now together.

To the peoples and the governments of all friendly nations and I hope that could encompass the whole world, I pledge an uninterrupted and sincere search for peace. America will remain strong and united.

But its strength will remain dedicated to the safety and sanity of the entire family of man as well as to our own precious freedom.

I believe that truth is the glue that holds governments together, not only our Government but civilization itself. That bond, though stained, is unbroken at home and abroad.

In all my public and private acts as your President, I expect to follow my instincts of openness and candor with full confidence that honesty is always the best policy in the end.

My fellow Americans, our long national nightmare is over. Our Constitution works. Our great republic is a government of laws and not of men. Here, the people rule.

But there is a higher power, by whatever name we honor him, who ordains not only righteousness but love, not only justice but mercy.

As we bind up the internal wounds of Watergate, more painful and more poisonous than those of foreign wars, let us restore the Golden Rule to our political process. And let brotherly love purge our hearts of suspicion and of hate.

In the beginning, I asked you to pray for me. Before closing, I ask again your prayers for Richard Nixon and for his family. May our former President who brought peace to millions find it for himself.

May God bless and comfort his wonderful wife and daughters whose love and loyalty will forever be a shining legacy to all who bear the lonely burdens of the White House.

I can only guess at those burdens although I witnessed at close hand the tragedies that befell three Presidents and the lesser trials of others.

With all the strength and all the good sense I have gained from life, with all the confidence of my family, my friends and dedicated staff impart to me and with the goodwill of countless Americans I have encountered in recent visits to 40 states, I now solemnly reaffirm my promise I made to you last Dec. 6 to uphold the Constitution, to do what is right as God gives me to see the right and to do the very best I can for America.

God helping me, I will not let you down.

Thank you.

Ford Asserts He Will Name A Vice President in 10 Days

By CHRISTOPHER LYDON
Special to The New York Times

WASHINGTON, Aug. 9—President Ford told Congressional leaders today that he would nominate his successor in the Vice-Presidency within 10 days.

Awaiting his decision, Republican politicians pictured the Vice-Presidential question as a key to the larger puzzle about the new President's plans and turned it into a lively game of party infighting.

Senator Hugh Scott of Pennsylvania, the Republican leader in the Senate, added his endorsement to others given to Nelson A. Rockefeller, the former Governor of New York. Senator Jesse A. Helms of North Carolina indicated that a score of conservative Republicans in the House and Senate would resist a Rockefeller selection in favor of Senator Barry Goldwater of Arizona.

No Suggestions Sought

The American Conservative Union, which has no formal connection with the Republican party, said in a press release, "Mr. Rockefeller would not be acceptable to a majority of conservative Republicans."

Mr. Ford's thinking on the matter remained a mystery to some of his closest associates. Melvin R. Laird, a long-time adviser who started the Rockefeller speculation earlier this week, said that he was convinced that the President "hasn't made up his mind."

Several others who have spoken with Mr. Ford in the last 24 hours said that he had not yet begun to ask for suggestions. George Bush, the chairman of the Republican National Committee who has been mentioned as a Vice-Presidential possibility by some former colleagues in the House, met with Mr. Ford yesterday and again briefly today. He said this afternoon:

"There has been no discussion of any kind that would give any indication that [the Vice-Presidency] has been under official consideration."

And thus the guesswork about names gave way today to guesswork about the specifications that Mr. Ford would set for the job and about his broader political plans. But there were few guideposts there, either.

Bryce Harlow, for example, a counselor in the Nixon White House until early this year and a friend of Mr. Ford's for 20 years, said that he had "no idea" whom Mr. Ford might choose or what standards he would apply in choosing.

"Does he want a running mate in 1976 or a fellow who will run for President in 1976?" Mr. Harlow asked rhetorically. "Or a fellow who can't possibly run again? Does he want an in-house co-worker or a spokesman? Does he want a team player or a guy who's chock-a-block full of ideas?"

None of those questions have been studied yet, Mr. Harlow and others suggested.

Advice Is Quoted

Mr. Laird's advice, quoted repeatedly this week in favor of a Rockefeller Vice-Presidency and abrupt changes in the Cabinet, became a focus of the Republican discussions today about the directions that President Ford wanted to chart and about whom he was listening to.

Mr. Laird has helped to picture himself as instrumental in Mr. Ford's accession with reports that, as President Nixon's counselor last fall, he talked Mr. Nixon out of his first choice for the vacant Vice-Pdesidency, John B. Connally of Texas, in favor of Mr. Ford.

Yet other Republican leaders recalled this week that one of the ways that Mr. Laird undermined Mr. Connally was by telling Congressional friends that Mr. Nixon favored him—putting Mr. Connally in the vulnerable front-runner's position where other opposition could rally against him.

A number of Republicans suggested today that Mr. Laird had not helped Mr. Rockefeller's chances by floating his name early and, inadvertently or not, reviving some of the old Republican controversies about the former Governor.

Lists Are Advanced

Yet few of his old friends professed to understand Mr. Laird's maneuvering. "Mel has a lot of fun with things like this," said a respected Republican power broker. "I don't know what he's been doing."

Meanwhile, Republicans on Capitol Hill continued to advance lists of names for consideration. Senator Scott said, "Governor Rockefeller has been my No. 1 choice for just about everything for a long time. He has grace and strength and tenacity."

However, he added a long list of runners-up, including almost a dozen colleagues in Congress, Gov. William G. Milliken of Michigan and former Gov. Linwood Holton of Virginia.

Senator Mark O. Hatfield of Oregon urged Mr. Ford to consider three Republican colleagues in Congress: Senator Edward W. Brooke of Massachusetts, Senator Charles H. Percy of Illinois and Representative John B. Anderson of Illinois.

Big Raise for Ford

WASHINGTON, Aug. 9 (UPI)—Gerald Ford got more than a promotion today. He also got a big raise, from $62,500 a year to $200,000 plus a $50,000 expense account.

Many Across the Country Call Inflation Biggest Problem Facing New President

By LAWRENCE VAN GELDER

Once again, as they have so often in the last 11 years, Americans pondered yesterday the future of the country in the aftermath of national trauma.

Thoughts focused on the Presidency of Gerald R. Ford, and in interviews conducted in many parts of the country, people talked of their expectations about the conduct of the nation's highest office by a man none had elected to it.

In response to questions, they assessed his principal problems, weighed the question of his successor as Vice President, looked to the conduct of foreign affairs and spoke of the possibility of Mr. Ford's election to a full term in office in 1976.

Far more frequently than any other problem, "inflation" and "the economy" were listed by those interviewed as the issue most demanding of Mr. Ford's immediate attention.

Most people expressed satisfaction with the idea of continuance of foreign policy as conducted during the Nixon Administration by Secretary of State Kissinger.

Choices for Mr. Ford's successor as Vice President ranged from Nelson A. Rockefeller, the former Governor of New York, to Representative Barbara C. Jordan, Democrat of Texas, with no individual commanding substantial support.

And although Mr. Ford has disclaimed any intention of seeking the Presidency after completing Mr. Nixon's term, many people said they felt he could win election to a full term in 1976 if he did a good job between now and then.

Doing a good job, it was made clear by many, meant making serious inroads against inflation.

"Ford's biggest problem is inflation," declared 23-year-old Dave Buchman, shirtless, hard-hatted, wearing boots and jeans as he tamped spikes at the Kennecott copper mine in Bingham, Utah. "It hits guys like me hard. I'm trying to work my way through college but everything is up. All the guys here feel the same."

And in Bethesda, Md., Eddie Wayne George, 24, the manager of a dry cleaning concern said: "Ford better start right away straightening out the messes Nixon made. The worst one is prices. They're outrageous, and he'd better cut back on them."

In Miami, John Willis, 53, a postman, said: "The main problem of the country is the economy now that we've got rid of Nixon. President Ford has to think about the little man like myself and not about fat cats and big corporations."

Although the economy emerged most often as the principal issue, people spoke frequently of the necessity of getting the country together again, winning the cooperation of Congress, uniting the people, restoring the confidence and winning the trust of the people and restoring the dignity of the Presidency.

In New Orleans, Clifton James 31, an architect, observed: "Basically people feel government is really not for them, it's for people who have money and power. This is the way I look at the whole Nixon Administration, and it's the problem that Ford is going to have to overcome."

Despite the widespread feeling that new initiatives were called for in dealing with economic problems, most people seemed to find no need for any alteration of foreign policy.

"Among all the things the Nixon Administration has done," said Gary M. Talesnik, 32, a Federal Government cost accountant from Olney, Md., "foreign policy has been the high point. Why change it?"

In Philadelphia, Miriam L. Gafni, a lawyer, said: "What Nixon did was good for business, to open markets in Russia and China. He did it in the interest of Republican businessmen. Ford is not going to change that. He's a social conservative."

Despite the lessons of recent history about the importance of the Vice Presidency, some individuals showed no interest in the matter, and one expressed disdain for the apparent possibilities to succeed Mr. Ford.

In North Bend, Wash., east of Seattle, R. E. (Shortie) Seitz, a hard-hat, said, "For Vice President, Mickey Mouse is as good as any of the rest of the bunch they've got."

Among the possibilities for Vice President, Mr. Rockefeller was mentioned several times. So were Elliot L. Richardson, the former Attorney General, and Ronald Reagan, Governor of California. Also mentioned were Senator Howard H. Baker Jr. of Tennessee; Melvin R. Laird, former Secretary of Defense; Senator Charles H. Percy of Illinois; Senator Edward W. Brooke of Massachusetts; Gov. George C. Wallace of Alabama and Representative Shirley A. Chisholm of Brooklyn.

In Miami, Manuel Barceni, 35, a carpenter, said, "Ford should choose an honest man as Vice President, and I don't care who that man is going to be as long as he's honest."

In Charlottesville, Va., Dr. Charles Frankel, 65, said he would like to see "a man who is from Congress who has proven to be honest. That's a pretty difficult assignment."

Despite the links between Watergate and the Republican party, many people said they saw no reason why Mr. Ford could not run successfully for the Presidency in 1976, if he did well until then.

Dr. Frankel said he thought Mr. Ford could win because "the Democrats aren't bound to do anything. They've got to prove their ability to do anything besides capitalize on Watergate."

Some people said Mr. Ford could not win in 1976, but in suburban Washington, John F. Freeman, an assistat principal, observed: "Although I'm a Democrat, I represent a large segment of the voting population who would look at Ford in view of his contributions to the country. If he proves worthy, he'll get elected in 1976."

And in a New Orleans suburb, Cisco Cortez, 30, serving a line of customers in front of Cisco's "Dynamite" tamale stand, said: "I don't think party will have anything to do with who's elected in '76. People just want an honest man. They want to hear the truth, no matter how bad it is."

Schlesinger Notifies Forces of New Chief

WASHINGTON, Aug. 9 (AP)—Secretary of Defense James R. Schlesinger officially notified the armed forces today that they have a new Commander in Chief.

In a message to all commanders worldwide, Mr. Schlesinger said that, as President and Commander in Chief, Gerald R. Ford "will have the fullest support, dedication and loyalty of all members of the Department of Defense."

Rockefeller Is Silent on Rumors He's in Line for Vice-Presidency

Special to The New York Times

BANGOR, Me., Aug. 9—Former Gov. Nelson A. Rockefeller of New York departed from prepared remarks at a Republican fund raising dinner tonight to praise President Ford as a man of "integrity, dedication and abiding faith in America."

Mr. Rockefeller made no mention of persistent rumors that he might be President Ford's choice as Vice President.

"The tragedy of the past two years has ended," Mr. Rockefeller said, "a tragedy that overshadowed the positive achievements of the Nixon Administration, particularly those achievements in pursuit of world peace, which undeniably attained greatness."

"Out of the traumatic experience of these past two years," Mr. Rockefeller said, "has emerged an awareness of the extraordinary strength and stability of the American people and the renewed awareness of the wisdom of the Founding Fathers and the unique constitutional system they created."

Originally, Mr. Rockefeller had scheduled a news conference this evening preceding the dinner of the Maine State Republican Committee. The news conference was canceled early this morning. Aides to the former Governor said the conference had been called off because it had been so widely misrepresented as a response to Mr. Nixon's resignation and the concurrent rumors about Mr. Rockefeller's Vice-Presidential appointment.

Rockefeller aides said that both the dinner speech and the news conference had been planned three months ago.

Earlier in the day, outside his summer home at Seal Harbor, about 55 miles southeast of here, Mr. Rockefeller met briefly with reporters but declined to answer questions on a possible Vice-Presidential appointment.

Asked why he was one of the few top Republicans who had so far not commented on the Nixon resignation, Mr. Rockefeller said:

"We don't want to thrust ourselves into the scene. The action is all in Washington. This is Jerry Ford's show."

Mr. Rockefeller will spend tomorrow resting at his Seal Harbor home. On Sunday he is scheduled to fly to Chicago to address a Republican Governors Association seminar for governorship candidates.

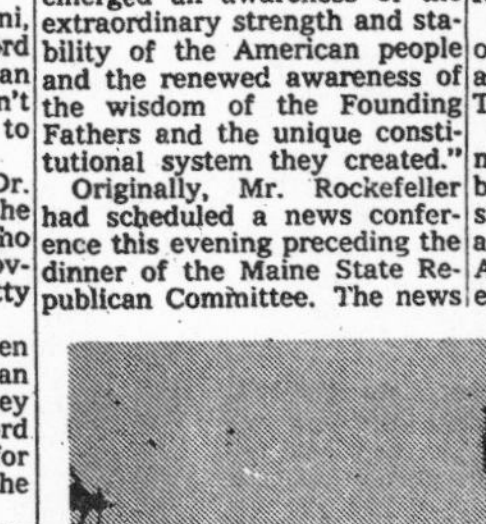

The New York Times/Arthur Grace

Nelson A. Rockefeller at his summer home in Seal Harbor, Me. He was endorsed yesterday for the Vice-Presidency by Hugh Scott, Senate minority leader.

Inauguration Guest List

Special to The New York Times

WASHINGTON, Aug. 9—Following is the official guest list for the inauguration of President Ford today:

Senator and Mrs. John G. Tower
Senator and Mrs. Bill Brock
Senator and Mrs. Norris Cotton
Senator and Mrs. John L. McClellan
Senator and Mrs. Milton R. Young
Mr. and Mrs. Charles Goodell
Senator and Mrs. Howard W. Cannon
Senator and Mrs. Marlow W. Cook
Mr. and Mrs. Jack Mills
Mr. and Mrs. William Cramer
Representative and Mrs. Albert H. Quie
John McCormack
Mr. and Mrs. John L. Monnahan
Eddie McCormick
Dorothy Cavanaugh
Scott Cavanaugh
Mr. and Mrs. David Downton
Mr. and Mrs. Charles Kilmer
Ann Kametra
Mr. and Mrs. Carl Messersmith
Mr. David Milanowski
Marba Perrott
Gail Raiman
George terHorst
Mr. Gordon Vanderlill
Mr. and Mrs. Charlene Von Pawel
Mr. and Mrs. George Willis
Joann Wilson
Josephine Wilson
Mr. and Mrs. Richard Frazier
Clara Powell
Mr. and Mrs. Robert Hartmann
Rob Hartman
Mr. and Mrs. John Marsh
Mr. and Mrs. William Seidman
Mr. and Mrs. Richard Burress
Mildred Leonard
Mr. and Mrs. Paul Miltich
Mr. and Mrs. William Casselman
Mr. and Mrs. Walter Mote
Mr. and Mrs. James Howe
Gwen Anderson
Mr. and Mrs. Milton Hoffman
Mr. and Mrs. Max Friedersdorf
Representative and Mrs. Charles E. Bennett
Representative and Mrs. Richard Bolling
Representative and Mrs. H. R. Gross
Representative and Mrs. Carl D. Perkins
Representative and Mrs. Peter W. Rodino Jr.
Representative and Mrs. Harley O. Staggers
Representative and Mrs. Tom Steed
Representative and Mrs. William B. Widnall
Representative and Mrs. Clement J. Zablocki
Representative and Mrs. John J. Rhodes
Representative and Mrs. Leslie C. Arends
Representative and Mrs. John B. Anderson
Representative and Mrs. Samuel L. Devine
Representative and Mrs. Barber B. Conable Jr.
Representative and Mrs Robert H. Michel
Representative and Mrs. Louis Frey Jr.
Representative and Mrs. Jack Edwards
Representative and Mrs. David Martin
Secretary and Mrs. Henry A. Kissinger
Secretary and Mrs. William E. Simon
Secretary and Mrs. James R. Schlesinger
Attorney General William B. Saxbe
Secretary and Mrs. Rogers C. B. Morton
Secretary and Mrs. Earl L. Butz
Secretary and Mrs. Frederick B. Dent
Secretary and Mrs. Peter J Brennan
Secretary and Mrs. Caspar W. Weinberger
Secretary and Mrs. James T. Lynn
Secretary and Mrs Claude S. Brinegar
Senator Philip A. Hart
Senator Robert P. Griffin
Representative John Conyers Jr.
Representative Marvin Esch
Representative Garry Brown
Representative Edward Hutchinson
Representative Richard F. Vander Veen
Representative Charles E. Chamberlain
Representative Donald W. Riegle Jr.
Representative Robert Traxler
Representative Guy Vander Jagt
Representative Philip E. Ruppe
Representative James C. O'Hara
Representative Charles C. Diggs Jr.
Representative Lucien N. Nedzi
Representative William D Ford
Representative John D. Dingell
Representative Martha W. Griffiths
Representative Robert J. Huber
Representative William S. Broomfield
General and Mrs. George S. Brown
General and Mrs. Fred C. Weyand
General and Mrs. David C. Jones
General and Mrs. Robert E. Cushman Jr.
Admiral and Mrs. James L. Holloway
Admiral and Mrs. Owen W. Siler
Secretary and Mrs. Howard H. Callaway
Secretary and Mrs John L. McLucas
Secretary and Mrs. William P. Clements
Secretary and Mrs. Jack L. Bowers
Representative and Mrs. Carl Albert
Representative and Mrs. Thomas P. O'Neill Sr.
Representative and Mrs. John D. McFall
Senator and Mrs. Mike Mansfield
Senator and Mrs. Robert C. Byrd
Senator and Mrs. Hugh Scott
Senator and Mrs. James O. Eastland
Chief Justice and Mrs. Warren E. Burger
Mr. Wade A. Burger
Mr. Mark Cannon
Mr. and Mrs. Dean Burch
Mr. and Mrs. Kenneth Rush
Ambassador and Mrs. George Bush
Ambassador and Mrs. John Scali
Mr. and Mrs. Roy L. Ash Jr.
Gen. and Mrs. Alexander M. Haig Jr.
Mr. and Mrs. Max Fisher
Maj. Gen. and Mrs. Brent Scowcroft
Mr. and Mrs. Clarence M. Kelley
Mary Dobbins
Anne Armstrong
Dr. and Mrs. Arthur Burns
Mr. and Mrs. Kenneth Cole
Representative Corinne C. Boggs
Adm. and Mrs. Arleigh Burke
Governor and Mrs. William G. Milliken
Mr. and Mrs. William E. Timmons
Mr. and Mrs. Tom C. Korologos
Mr. and Mrs. Bill Cramer
Representative George H. Mahon
Representative James Harvey
Representative Glen R. Davis
Mr. and Mrs. Bryce Harlow
Mr. and Mrs. Phil Buchen
Mr. and Mrs. Bill Whyte
Mr. and Mrs. Bill Scranton
Mr. and Mrs. George Shultz
Mr. and Mrs. William Baroody Jr.
Mr. and Mrs. Gerald L. Warren
Rose Mary Woods
Mr. and Mrs. Stan Scott
Mr. and Mrs. John Nidecker
Mr. and Mrs. Joe Bartlett
Mr. and Mrs. Tommy Winebrenner
Mr. and Mrs. James Brown
Mr. and Mrs. John Byrnes
Mr. and Mrs. Melvin Laird
Mr. and Mrs. Leon Parma
Mr. and Mrs. Trammel Crow
Mr. and Mrs. Robert Collier
Mr. and Mrs. Frank Welsh
Ambassador S. Edward Peal
Gardiner Britt
Mr. and Mrs. Lou Deschler
Representative and Mrs. Elford Cederberg
Mr. and Mrs. Thomas Ford
Mr. and Mrs. Richard Ford
Mr. and Mrs. James Ford

"All the News That's Fit to Print"

The New York Times

LATE CITY EDITION

Weather: Warm, partly sunny today; partly cloudy tonight, tomorrow. Temp. range: today 62-78; Sunday 58-77. Highest Temp.-Hum. Index yesterday: 72. Details on Page 66.

VOL. CXXIII . . No. 42,597 | © 1974 The New York Times Company | NEW YORK, MONDAY, SEPTEMBER 9, 1974 | Higher in air delivery cities. | 20 CENTS

FORD GIVES PARDON TO NIXON, WHO REGRETS 'MY MISTAKES'

U.S.-Bound Plane With 88 Crashes in Sea Off Greece

All on T.W.A. Flight From Tel Aviv Are Believed Dead—Wreckage Is Sighted

By The Associated Press

ATHENS, Sept. 8 — A Trans World Airlines jet bound for the United States with 88 persons aboard crashed today in the stormy Ionian Sea off Greece. The Greek Civil Aviation Authority said there appeared to be no survivors.

T.W.A. said that the Boeing 707 fell from an overcast sky after the pilot reported that an engine had failed.

Flight 841 originated in Tel Aviv, stopped in Athens and was scheduled to make stops in Rome and New York.

The airline's Tel Aviv office said 49 passengers boarded the plane there for Rome and the United States. They included 17 Americans, including a baby, 13 Japanese, four Italians, four French, three Indians, two Iranians, two Israelis, two Sri Lankans, an Australian and a Canadian.

The nationalities of 30 other passengers and the nine crew members were not immediately known. [Reuters reported a total of 37 Americans aboard.]

[In Beirut, it was reported that a Palestinian youth organization said it had placed a guerrilla aboard the plane with a bomb. In New York, however, a spokesman for T.W.A. said sabotage was "highly unlikely."]

"All that can be seen by our overflying planes are remnants of the wreckage and bodies floating on the surface," said a Greek aviation official. "The stormy sea in the area is making it difficult for our ships to approach.

"Only when our ships can get nearer will we be able to

Continued on Page 6, Column 1

The New York Times/Sept. 9, 1974

'PAIN' EXPRESSED

Ex-President Cites His Sorrow at the Way He Handled Watergate

By EVERETT R. HOLLES
Special to The New York Times

SAN CLEMENTE, Calif., Sept. 8—President Ford's pardon for Richard M. Nixon evoked today from the former President an expression of "regret and pain at the anguish my mistakes over Watergate have caused the nation and the Presidency."

Within 10 minutes after the Presidential pardon was announced in Washington, Mr. Nixon's statement was released at his Casa Pacifica estate, citing his sorrow in allowing Watergate to become "a national tragedy."

"That the way I tried to deal with Watergate was the wrong way is the burden I shall bear for every day of the life that is left in me," he said.

Hopes Burden Is Lifted

In a subsequent statement, given in response to reporters' questions, an aide quoted Mr. Nixon as saying that, in grate fully accepting the Presidential pardon, he hoped Mr. Ford's "compassionate act would contribute to lifting the burdens of Watergate from our country."

When the Nixon statement was released by his adviser and former White House press secretary, Ronald L. Ziegler, Mr. and Mrs. Nixon were already on the way to a new haven of seclusion away from the heavily guarded Casa Pacifica.

They left at 7 A.M., Pacific Coast time, in a large black limousine accompanied by Secret Service agents and Mr. Nixon's military aide, Lieut. Col. Jack Brennan, reportedly for the Palm Desert estate of Walter H. Annenberg, Ambassador to Britain.

A close friend of the Nixons said the former President planned to play golf on the Annenberg private 18-hole course.

[In New York, Mr. Nixon's daughter, Julie Nixon Eisenhower, said that her father had gone to the Annenberg estate "for a rest," The Associated Press reported.]

Mr. Ziegler and Mr. Nixon's appointments secretary, Stephen

Continued on Page 24, Column 1

Richard M. Nixon in a photo made earlier this year

Associated Press

President Ford speaking at the White House yesterday

The Statement by Nixon

I have been informed that President Ford has granted me a full and absolute pardon for any charges which may be brought against me for actions taken during the time I was the President of the United States. In accepting this pardon, I hope that his compassionate act will contribute to lifting the burden of Watergate from our country.

Here in California, my perspective on Watergate is quite different than it was while I was embattled in the midst of the controversy while I was still subject to the unrelenting daily demand of the Presidency itself.

Looking back on what is still in my mind a complex and confusing maze of events, decisions, pressures, and personalities, one thing I can see clearly now is that I was wrong in not acting more decisively and more forthrightly in dealing with Watergate, particularly when it reached the stage of judicial proceedings and grew from a political scandal into a national tragedy.

No words can describe the depths of my regret and pain at the anguish my mistakes over Watergate have caused the nation and the Presidency, a nation I so deeply love and an institution I so greatly respect.

I know that many fair-minded people believe that my motivation and actions in the Watergate affair were intentionally self-serving and illegal. I now understand how my own mistakes and misjudgments have contributed to that belief and seemed to support it. This burden is the heaviest one of all to bear.

That the way I tried to deal with Watergate was the wrong way is a burden I shall bear for every day of the life that is left to me.

Proclamation of Pardon

Richard Nixon became the thirty-seventh President of the United States on January 20, 1969, and was re-elected in 1972 for a second term by the electors of forty-nine of the fifty states. His term in office continued until his resignation on August 9, 1974.

Pursuant to resolutions of the House of Representatives, its Committee on the Judiciary conducted an inquiry and investigation on the impeachment of the President extending over more than eight months. The hearings of the committee and its deliberations, which received wide national publicity over television, radio, and in printed media, resulted in votes adverse to Richard Nixon on recommended Articles of Impeachment.

As a result of certain acts or omissions occurring before his resignation from the office of President, Richard Nixon has become liable to possible indictment and trial for offenses against the United States. Whether or not he shall be so prosecuted depends on findings of the appropriate grand jury and on the discretion of the authorized prosecutor. Should an indictment ensue, the accused shall then be entitled to a fair trial by an impartial jury, as guaranteed to every individual by the Constitution.

It is believed that a trial of Richard Nixon, if it became necessary, could not fairly begin until a year or more has elapsed. In the meantime, the tranquility to which this nation has been restored by the events of recent weeks could be irreparably lost by the prospects of bringing to trial a former President of the United States. The prospects of such trial will cause prolonged and divisive debate over the propriety of exposing to further punishment and degradation a man who has already paid the unprecedented penalty of relinquishing the highest elective office in the United States.

NOW, THEREFORE, I, Gerald R. Ford, President of the United States, pursuant to the pardon power conferred upon me by Article II, Section 2, of the Constitution, have granted and by these presents do grant a full, free, and absolute pardon unto Richard Nixon for all offenses against the United States which he, Richard Nixon, has committed or may have committed or taken part in during the period from January 20, 1969, through August 9, 1974.

IN WITNESS WHEREOF, I have hereunto set my hand this 8th day of September in the year of our Lord nineteen hundred seventy-four, and of the independence of the United States of America the 199th.

NO CONDITIONS SET

Action Taken to Spare Nation and Ex-Chief, President Asserts

By JOHN HERBERS
Special to The New York Times

WASHINGTON, Sept. 8—President Ford granted former President Richard M. Nixon an unconditional pardon today for all Federal crimes that he "committed or may have committed or taken part in" while in office, an act Mr. Ford said was intended to spare Mr. Nixon and the nation further punishment in the Watergate scandals.

Mr. Nixon, in San Clemente, Calif., accepted the pardon, which exempts him from indictment and trial for, among

Text of the Ford statement is printed on Page 24.

other things, his role in the cover-up of the Watergate burglary. He issued a statement saying that he could now see he was "wrong in not acting more decisively and more forthrightly in dealing with Watergate."

'Act of Mercy'

Philip W. Buchen, the White House counsel, who advised Mr. Ford on the legal aspects of the pardon, said the "act of mercy" on the President's part was done without making any demands on Mr. Nixon and without asking the advice of the Watergate special prosecutor, Leon Jaworski, who had the legal responsibility to prosecute the case.

Reaction to the pardon was sharply divided, but not entirely along party lines. Most Democrats who commented voiced varying degrees of disapproval and dismay, while most Republican comment backed President Ford.

However, Senators Edward W. Brooke of Massachusetts and Jacob K. Javits of New York disagreed with the action. [Page 25.]

Dangers Seen in Delay

Mr. Buchen said that, at the President's request, he had asked Mr. Jaworski how long it would be, in the event Mr. Nixon was indicted, before he could be brought to trial and that Mr. Jaworski had replied it would be at least nine months or more, because of the enormous amount of publicity the charges against Mr. Nixon had received when the House Judiciary Committee recommended impeachment.

This was one reason Mr. Ford cited for granting the pardon, saying he had concluded that "many months and perhaps more years will have to pass before Richard Nixon could obtain a fair trial by jury in any jurisdiction of the United States under governing decisions of the Supreme Court."

"During this long period of delay and potential litigation, ugly passions would again be aroused, our people would

Continued on Page 24, Column 4

State Panel Charges City Fails to Pursue Fugitives

By SELWYN RAAB

The State Commission of Investigation disclosed yesterday that the backlog of missing bail jumpers and probation violators in the city had risen during the last three years from 82,000 to 130,000.

After sifting through voluminous police and court records, the commission largely blamed the Police Department's warrant division for the 50 per cent increase since 1971 in unexecuted warrants for criminal defendants who fail to appear in court. The police division is primarily responsible for capturing such fugitives.

Sharply criticizing the performance of the division over the last three years, the investigation commission said in a report that it had found that warrant officers rarely worked at night or on weekends and that a typical attempt to track down a fugitive consisted of no more than one or two visits to an often fictitious home address given by the suspect.

The commission described the problem of fugitives here as "critical to the public safety" and called for a major reorganization of the warrant division.

"At the present time the people of New York City are unnecessarily subjected to the risk of grave harm from known criminals because of ineffective warrant enforcement," the commission declared in its report.

In response to the findings, Police Commissioner Michael J. Codd said he was "concerned" by the growing backlog, and he hinted there might be a reorganization of the warrant division.

He also announced the assignment of First Deputy Com-

Continued on Page 21, Column 1

Jaworski Won't Challenge Pardon, Spokesman Says

By JOHN M. CREWDSON
Special to The New York Times

WASHINGTON, Sept. 8 — Leon Jaworski, the Watergate special prosecutor, apparently has no plans to challenge the validity of the unconditional pardon that President Ford bestowed today on Richard M. Nixon, according to a spokesman for Mr. Jaworski.

The special prosecutor "accepts the decision," said John Barker, the spokesman. "He thinks it's within the President's power to do it. His feeling is that the President is exercising his lawful power, and he accepts it."

Mr. Barker added that Mr. Jaworski had not been consulted in advance on the decision by either Mr. Ford or White House lawyers, and learned of the President's position less than an hour before it was announced.

Some lawyers, including Senator Edmund S. Muskie, Democrat of Maine, questioned the legal and constitutional validity of a Presidential pardon conferred before an indictment had been brought or a conviction obtained.

"It could be challenged," declared Mr. Muskie, adding "there are those who say that it ought to be challenged, lest the precedent be established in an undesirable way."

But the remarks by Mr. Barker and by other lawyers familiar with the Watergate prosecutions indicated strongly that Mr. Jaworski was little inclined to test the pardon by seeking to indict Mr. Nixon, which one authority described as "the way to do it."

The principal Watergate grand jury voted earlier this

Continued on Page 25, Column 6

Nixon Tapes Must Be Kept 3 Years for Use in Court

By R. W. APPLE Jr.
Special to The New York Times

WASHINGTON, Sept. 8 — Richard M. Nixon and the Ford Administration have reached an agreement under which the former President will ultimately be permitted to destroy the White House tape recordings that led to his downfall.

The agreement, announced today by the White House, also provides that all of Mr. Nixon's Presidential papers and tapes will be preserved for three years for possible use in court cases arising out of the Watergate scandals.

Mr. Nixon signed the agreement in San Clemente, Calif., on Friday; it was countersigned yesterday by Arthur F. Sampson, head of the General Services Administration.

Philip W. Buchen, counsel for President Ford, said at a White House briefing this afternoon that Mr. Ford instructed him about 10 days ago to resolve the controversy over the White House files so the Administration would not find itself "enmeshed for a long time" in jurisdictional disputes.

Although Mr. Buchen denied

Continued on Page 28, Column 1

CANDIDATES SKIRT LAWS ON FINANCING

Evidence Shows Big Money Played a Major Role—Voting Is Tomorrow

By FRANK LYNN

Big money—from family fortunes and large contributors—played a major role in the Democratic primary campaigns despite new state and Federal

Ballot and candidate list appear on Page 28.

campaign-finance laws that were supposed to have reduced its influence.

The question of how much money was spent and where it came from was being discussed as the primary campaigns drew to a close. The polls will be open tomorrow in the city from 6 A.M. to 9 P.M. and in the rest of the state from noon to 9 P.M.

Interviews with campaign aides and campaign financial reports show that there was considerable evidence of circumventing of the new laws in fact and in spirit, possible unrecorded cash contributions and spending and even "laundering" of campaign contribu-

Continued on Page 28, Column 1

Knievel Safe as Rocket Falls Into Snake Canyon

By JON NORDHEIMER
Special to The New York Times

TWIN FALLS, Idaho, Sept. 8 —Evel Knievel failed today in an attempt to rocket 1,600 feet across the Snake River Canyon when a tail parachute deployed prematurely on the take-off of his vehicle.

The vehicle, which Mr. Knievel calls the Sky-Cycle X-2, went streaking to about 1,000 feet above the river before floating into the canyon to make a nose-down crash landing on a rocky bank at the river's edge.

Mr. Knievel was pulled from the craft several minutes later by a rescue team. He had superficial cuts and scrapes of the face and legs.

The flight aborted almost as soon as steam exploded from a rear nozzle of the 13-foot-long craft and propelled it along a 108-foot launching track aimed at the cloudless sky.

A drogue parachute designed to slow the rocket at an altitude of 2,800 feet deployed while the vehicle was still on the ramp, whipping in a blast of steam.

Once the vehicle lifted off the ramp, it turned belly up and the main chute, attached to the drogue, was automatically deployed at about 1,000 feet.

A large crowd along the canyon's south rim gasped as a 15-mile-an-hour wind blew the vehicle back toward them, rocking gently in the air nose-down like a red, white and blue Christmas ornament.

For several seconds, it appeared that Mr. Knievel, who could be seen struggling inside the open cockpit, might crash into the crowd on the rim of the canyon.

But the vehicle dropped onto a boulder-strewn ledge, bounced twice on its bottom and came to rest about 20 feet from the water's edge.

The vehicle was obscured from sight from the plateau 540 feet above, and some cries of anguish were heard in the crowd when several minutes went by and there was no sign of the stuntman.

But a helicopter picked him

Continued on Page 50, Column 5

Chris Evert Beaten

Evonne Goolagong of Australia defeated Chris Evert in the semifinals of the United States Open tennis at Forest Hills, Queens, yesterday, 6-0, 6-7, 6-3, and will meet Billie Jean King in the final today. Details, Page 45.

Some Mixed Reactions in Foley Square

By PAUL L. MONTGOMERY

A few hours after President Ford's pardon of his predecessor was announced yesterday, Mr. and Mrs. Wilson Wainwright of Olean, N.Y., were strolling in Foley Square in lower Manhattan, looking at the public buildings.

"It's going to make a lot of people mad, but I can see why he did it," Mr. Wainwright said. "It wouldn't look right to the rest of the world to have a President of the United States in jail."

Mr. Wainwright, here on a late-summer vacation, was asked if he had any doubts about former President Richard M. Nixon's guilt.

"None that I can see," his wife, Judy, replied. "I guess some people would say it would have been better to pardon him after the courts decided."

Nearby, at 100 Centre Street, the afternoon session of the arraignment part of Criminal Court was about to begin. In the dingy, crowded room, lawyers and policemen, and defendants and their families lounged on the oak benches, waiting for the judge to return from lunch.

Hal Mayerson and Peter Davis of the Legal Aid Society, which represents indigent defendants, had been discussing the pardon during the break.

"It's a bit unseemly to pardon someone before they're prosecuted," Mr. Davis said. "It doesn't do much for the concept of equal justice under law."

"How about all the young men who refused to serve in an illegal, immoral and vicious war?" Mr. Mayerson asked. "Is he going to pardon them, too? It's like Peter was saying, maybe they should give Nixon a pardon if he does 18 months of alternate service."

Mr. Mayerson looked around the room.

"Seriously, though, it's outrageous," he continued. "You get a lady here who's going to jail for stealing a blouse, or some guy in on assault because he got tired of living with the rats and hit somebody. And here's one of the biggest plun-

Continued on Page 25, Column 6

terHorst Quits Post To Protest Pardon

Special to The New York Times

WASHINGTON, Sept. 8—J. F. terHorst, whose appointment as White House press secretary was the first in President Ford's new Administration, resigned tonight in what he said was a protest over the granting of an unconditional pardon to former President Nixon.

In a statement released by the White House tonight, Mr. Ford said that he deeply regretted Mr. terHorst's decision.

"I understand his position," the statement said. "I appreciate the fact that good people will differ with me on this very difficult decision. However, it is my judgment that it is in

Continued on Page 25, Column 1

NEWS INDEX

News Summary and Index, Page 37

Statement by the President in Connection With His Proclamation Pardoning Nixon

WASHINGTON, Sept. 8 (AP)—Following is President Ford's statement in which he pardoned former President Richard M. Nixon:

Ladies and gentlemen, I have come to a decision which I felt I should tell you, and all my fellow citizens, as soon as I was certain in my own mind and conscience that it is the right thing to do.

I have learned already in this office that only the difficult decisions come to this desk. I must admit that many of them do not look at all the same as the hypothetical questions that I have answered freely and perhaps too fast on previous occasions, My customary policy is to try and get all the facts and to consider the opinions of my countrymen and to take counsel with my most valued friends. But these seldom agree, and in the end the decision is mine.

To procrastinate, to agonize, to wait for a more favorable turn of events that may never come, or more compelling external pressures that may as well be wrong as right, is itself a decision of sorts and a weak and potentially dangerous course for a President to follow.

I have promised to uphold the Constitution, to do what is right as God gives me to see the right, and to do the very best I can for America. I have asked your help and your prayers, not only when I became President, but many times since.

The Supreme Law

The Constitution is the supreme law of our land and it governs our actions as citizens. Only the laws of God, which govern our consciences, are superior to it. As we are a nation under God, so I am sworn to uphold our laws with the help of God. And I have sought such guidance and searched my own conscience with special diligence to determine the right thing for me to do with respect to my predecessor in this place, Richard Nixon, and his loyal wife and family.

Theirs is an American tragedy in which we all have played a part. It can go on and on, or someone must write "The End" to it.

I have concluded that only I can do that. And if I can, I must.

There are no historic or legal precedents to which I can turn in this matter, none that precisely fit the circumstances of a private citizen who has resigned the Presidency of the United States. But it is common knowledge that serious allegations and accusations hang like a sword over our former president's head and threaten his health as he tries to reshape his life, a great part of which was spent in the service of this country and by the mandate of its people.

Equal Justice

After years of bitter controversy and divisive national debate, I have been advised and am compelled to conclude that many months and perhaps more years will have to pass before Richard Nixon could hope to obtain a fair trial by jury in any jurisdiction of the United States under governing decisions of the Supreme Court.

I deeply believe in equal justice, for all Americans, whatever their station or former station. The law, whether human or divine, is no respecter of persons but the law is a respecter of reality. The facts as I see them are that a former President of the United States, instead of enjoying equal treatment with any other citizen accused of violating the law, would be cruelly and excessively penalized either in preserving the presumption of his innocence or in obtaining a speedy determination of his guilt in order to repay a legal debt to society.

During this long period of delay and potential litigation, ugly passions would again be aroused, our people would again be polarized in their opinions, and the credibility of our free institutions of government would again be challenged at home and abroad. In the end, the courts might well hold that Richard Nixon had been denied due process and the verdict of history would be even more inconclusive with respect to those charges arising out of the period of his Presidency of which I am presently aware.

But it is not the ultimate fate of Richard Nixon that most concerns me—though surely it deeply troubles every decent and compassionate person—but the immediate future of this great country. In this I dare not depend upon my personal sympathy as a long-time friend of the former President nor my professional judgment as a lawyer. And I do not.

As President, my primary concern must always be the greatest good of all the people of the United States, whose servant I am.

As a man, my first consideration will always be to be true to my own convictions and my own conscience.

My conscience tells me clearly and certainly that I cannot prolong the bad dreams that continue to reopen a chapter that is closed. My conscience tells me that only I, as President, have the constitutional power to firmly shut and seal this book. My conscience says it is my duty, not merely to proclaim domestic tranquility, but to use every means I have to ensure it.

Buck Stops Here

I do believe that the buck stops here and that I cannot rely upon public opinion polls to tell me what is right. I do believe that right makes might, and that if I am wrong 10 angels swearing I was right would make no difference. I do believe with all my heart and mind and spirit that I, not as President, but as a humble servant of God, will receive justice without mercy if I fail to show mercy.

Finally, I feel that Richard Nixon and his loved ones have suffered enough, and will continue to suffer no matter what I do, no matter what we as a great and good nation can do together to make his goal of peace come true.

Now, therefore, I, Gerald R. Ford, President of the United States, pursuant to the pardon power conferred upon me by Article II, Section 2, of the Constitution, have granted and by these presents do grant a full, free, and absolute pardon unto Richard Nixon for all offenses against the United States which he, Richard Nixon, has committed or may have committed or taken part in during the period from January 20, 1969, through August, 9, 1974.

In witness whereof, I have hereunto set my hand this 8th day of September in the year of our Lord nineteen hundred seventy-four, and of the independence of the United States of America the 199th.

Associated Press

President Ford as he talked to newsmen yesterday in the Oval Office before announcing his pardon for Richard M. Nixon

Ford Grants Nixon Pardon for Any Crimes in Office

Continued From Page 1, Col. 8

again be polarized in their opinions, and the credibility of our free institutions of government would again be challenged at home and abroad," Mr. Ford said in a 10-minute statement that he read this morning in the Oval Office upon signing the pardon.

Mr. Ford's decision was not unexpected, in light of his previous statements that he thought the former President had suffered enough by being forced from office. Yet the unconditional nature of the pardon, taken without the recommendation of Mr. Jaworski, was more generous to Mr. Nixon than many had expected.

Mr. Buchen, the President's soft-spoken, white-haired lawyer, said, in response to questions, that no effort had been made to obtain acknowledgment of wrongdoing. When Viçe President Agnew resigned last October he pleaded no contest to a charge of tax evasion and agreed to a bill of particulars that described in detail a number of other serious charges against him.

Before Mr. Ford finally decided to grant the pardon, the White House lawyers obtained from Mr. Nixon a letter in which he agreed to make available to the courts any subpoenaed records and tape recordings. But the agreement is also favorable to Mr. Nixon in that the documents are judged to be his personal property and the many tape recordings not yet made public are to be destroyed.

An Adverse Aspect

The only adverse aspect of today's action from Mr. Nixon's point of view is that he can now be more easily forced to testify in the forthcoming trial of several of his former aides accused of obstruction of justice in the Watergate case. The defendants have already subpoenaed the former President for the trial scheduled to open Sept. 30, and Mr. Nixon, having been pardoned, cannot decline to testify under the Fifth Amendment, which protects citizens against self-incrimination.

Mr. Ford's action today was a sharp reversal from the position his aides conveyed as he ascended to the Presidency on Aug. 9.

What would be done about prosecuting the former President was even then a major question, because Mr. Nixon admitted in a statement of Aug. 5 that he had ordered a halt to the investigation of the Watergate burglary, for political as well as national security reasons. Tape recordings released at the same time documented this.

J.F. terHorst, Mr. Ford's press secretary, when asked Aug. 9 whether Mr. Ford would grant a pardon, pointed out that the new President had addressed that question in his confirmation hearings for Vice President before the Senate Rules Committee late last year.

Mr. Ford was asked then whether, if a President resigned, his successor would have the power to prevent a criminal investigation or prosecution of the former President.

However, since taking office, there have been several changes. Mr. Nixon, in seclusion in San Clemente, has been reported by his friends to be deeply depressed and some have said that the legal troubles he faced were causing him so much anguish that his health was in jeopardy.

At the same time, high Republican officials, including Nelson A. Rockefeller, Mr. Ford's selection for Vice President, put out statements saying that the former President had suffered enough, and Mr. Ford agreed.

The way for a Presidential pardon was further prepared when Mr. Ford came out for conditional amnesty for Vietnam draft evaders and deserters as an act of mercy and as a means of uniting the nation.

The most surprising aspect of Mr. Ford's action was that it came on Sunday morning when the Government buildings were almost empty and no one was expecting any dramatic Presidential action. Mr. Ford attended early morning communion at St. John's Episcopal Church, then returned to the White House to make the announcement. He had chosen the Sabbath, it was learned later, to emphasize that the pardon was an act of mercy, not justice.

At 11:04 Mr. Ford walked into his Oval Office, where a small group of reporters and photographers was waiting, and sat at his desk. His face was grave.

An American Tragedy

He then opened a manila folder and began reading his decision, looking occasionally into the cameras, which were filming the event for later showing. He spokes of the difficulty of the decision.

"To procrastinate, to agonize and to wait for a more favorable turn of events that may never come," he said, "or more compelling external pressures that may as well be wrong as right, is itself a decision of sorts and a weak and potentially dangerous course for a President to follow."

Of President Nixon and his family, Mr. Ford said: "Theirs is an American tragedy in which we all have played a part. It could go on and on and on, or someone must write 'The End' to it. I have concluded that only I can do that."

He pointed out that there was no historical or legal precedent for him to follow. Never before had a president resigned from office and never before had a former President been faced with criminal prosecution.

"But," Mr. Ford said, "it is common knowledge that serious allegations and accusations hang like a sword over our former President's head, threatening his health, as he tries to reshape his life, a great part of which was spent in the service of this country and by the mandate of its people."

The words, "threatening his health," were not in Mr. Ford's prepared remarks, and his assistants said later that he had added them because of the reports that Mr. Nixon "is not well."

He then spoke of the un- Mr. Nixon and said that Mr. Nixon, instead of enjoying equal treatment under the law, "would be cruelly and excessively penalized in preserving the presumption of his innocence or in obtaining a speedy determination of his guilt in avoidable delay in any trial of order to repay a legal debt to society."

In the end, he added, the courts might well hold that Mr. Nixon had been denied due process and "the verdict of history would even be more inconclusive with respect to those charges arising out of the period of his Presidency."

But he said that his decision had been based first on the public good and "my conscience tells me clearly and certainly that I cannot prolong the bad dreams that continue to reopen a chapter that is closed."

"Finally," Mr. Ford said, "I feel that Richard Nixon and his loved ones have suffered enough, and will continue to suffer no matter what I do, no matter what we as a great and good nation can do together to make his goal of peace come true."

At that, Mr. Ford took a blue silver felt-tip pen and signed the proclamation granting the pardon, reading the key paragraph:

"Now, therefore, I Gerald R. Ford, President of the United States, pursuant to the pardon power conferred upon me by Article II, Section 2, of the Constitution, have granted and by these presents do grant a full, free and absolute pardon unto Richard Nixon for all offenses against the United States which he, Richard Nixon, has committed or taken part in during the period from Jan. 20, 1969, through Aug. 9 1974."

Mr. Buchen later briefed reporters on the events leading up to today's action. Sitting before the podium of the briefing room, Mr. Buchen, making his first public appearance as White House counsel, said Mr Ford approached him about the pardon about a week ago and asked him to make a study of the matter.

Mr. Buchen said that he had first consulted Mr. Jaworski about what a trial of Richard Nixon would involve and got, in writing, a statement that it would be "unprecedented."

Mr. Jaworski told him, he said, that the events leading up to Mr. Nixon's resignation—the House Judiciary Committee's rcommendation for impeachment, the release of the tapes showing Mr. Nixon ordered a halt to the Watergate investigation six days after the burglary at the Democratic national offices here, on June 17, 1972, the decision of Republicans who had been supporting Mr. Nixon in Congress to vote for his impeachment or conviction on the basis of the new evidence—would necessitate a long delay because is would involve much "prejudicial, pretrial material" that the courts would have to dispose of.

Mr. Jaworski advised Mr. Buchen, the President's counsel said, that the case against Mr. Nixon was "readily distinguishable" from that against the Watergate defendants whose trial is set for Sept. 30, because they had not been tried before a Congressional body in the way, Mr. Nixon had in the impeachment proceedings.

Mr. Buchen said that he had picked a Washington lawyer, Benton L. Becker, to negotiate with Mr. Nixon and his lawyers. Mr. Becker, a friend of both the President and Mr. Buchen, went to San Clemente last week and advised Mr. Nixon that he probably would receive a pardon. Mr. Nixon told Mr. Becker, either personally or through an aide, that in such an event he intended to issue a statement similar to the one he put out today a few minutes after Mr. Ford's announcement.

Mr. Ford, after announcing the decision, went to the Burning Tree Country Club and played a round of golf. At the White House, switchboard operators said, "angry calls, heavy and constant," began jamming their boards soon after Mr. Ford's announcement.

WIFE ASSERTS FORD ACTED IN GOOD FAITH

WASHINGTON, Sept. 8 (UPI)—Betty Ford said today that the President had acted in "good faith" in granting an absolute pardon to former President Richard M. Nixon. She reported that her husband went to church and received communion before making the announcement.

The First Lady learned of the pardon only when Mr. Ford announced it to the country, her press secretary, Helen McCain Smith, said.

She quoted Mrs. Ford as saying that her husband "gave a great deal of thought" to the matter of a pardon and was "well aware of the problems involved."

Mrs. Ford also feels that Mrs. Nixon and her two daughters "must be greatly relieved and she is happy for them," Mrs. Smith said.

The First Lady also "wishes the country would stress the great things that Nixon has done for the country," Mrs. Smith said, adding that the President's wife agreed with the thought that Mr. Nixon had "suffered enough."

Nixon Regrets Watergate 'Mistakes'

Continued From Page 1, Col. 3

Bull, who worked throughout most of today at the Nixon offices here, avoided reporters, and no direct information was forthcoming from the Casa Pacifica as to when the former President was informed of Mr. Ford's decision.

A close friend of Mr. Nixon, who has seen him several times since his arrival here on Aug. 9, said, however, that his statement was written last night after he and Mr. Ford held a long telephone conversation.

The informant said Mr. Ford and his predecessor had had at least three telephone conversations over the last four days.

In the month that he has been here Mr. Nixon has left the seclusion of his villa only twice before, once to go to the Camp Pendleton private beach club two miles south to swim, and another time to Ventura for a beach picnic with a small group of friends.

When the announcement of the Presidential pardon was made in Washington, followed by the statement released by Mr. Ziegler, Mr. and Mrs. Nixon had been gone more than an hour from the Casa Pacifica.

Even before the announcement in Washington, word of the forthcoming action by Mr. Ford had leaked through the guarded gates of the Nixon ocean-bluff residence and to the nearby San Clemente Inn, which, during the Nixon Presidency, served as a residence for staff members and visitors.

Paul Presley, a long-time friend of Mr. Nixon who is active in Orange County Republican politics, operates the inn. Last night, he had dinner with Mr. Bull and Colonel Brennan but said there had been no discussion of the impending pardon.

Mr. Presley last saw Mr. Nixon at the Casa Pacifica five days ago and said "he seemed much more relaxed and in far better humor" than at any time since his arrival on Aug. 9.

"He complained good-naturedly to me about the amount of work that confronted him here but said he was going in swimming at every opportunity," he said.

Mr. Presley, like most residents of this preponderantly Republican oceanside resort of 20,000 residents, expressed pleasure at the President's decision to protect Mr. Nixon against criminal prosecution.

"He suffered enough and so has Pat Nixon and the whole family," said Mr. Presley.

Laura Martin, a waitress at a diner a short distance north on El Camino Real, said she was happy that "they aren't going to try and pick the carcass."

However, Jerome Appleton, waiting in his car at the Texaco service station, said he had "lost some of my respect for Mr. Ford."

"I never knew that being an ex-President driven from office in disgrace provided protection from prosecution for a man's crimes," Mr. Appleton, a construction subcontractor from nearby San Juan Capistrano, said.

Most residents of San Clemente seemed as unexcited about the Presidential pardon as they have been all along about the presence here of the Nixon home and Western White House, since he acquired the estate in 1969 soon after taking office.

On this sun-blazing Sunday, a large-scale Marine Corps invasion exercise two miles southward along the coast from the Nixon home, with thousands of Marines coming ashore in landing craft from a dozen warships, seemed to be the area's most exciting event.

However, scores of motorists on Interstate 5, close by the Nixon compound, after hearing the news of the pardon on their car radios turned off onto the Via Presidente and drove up to the Coast Guard post at the entrance to the Nixon property. They were turned back after a brief glimpse of the Casa Pacifica's red-tiled roofs over the treetops.

A prominent San Clemente supporter of Mr. Nixon since he went to Congress in 1946, who asked not to be identified said he had heard that the Lincoln Club of Orange County, made up largely of wealthy industrialists who contributed millions of dollars to Republican campaign coffers, including Mr. Nixon's, had invited the former President to become a member of the select and influential group.

"You won't find Mr. Nixon living the life of a recluse," the Republican informant said. "Now that he is clear of any criminal prosecution, don't be surprised if he comes back into California politics. I think he should. I'd like to see him run for Senator John V. Tunney's Democratic seat in 1976."

Generally, the suggestion that Mr. Nixon run for the Senate appeared to have scant support among Orange County Republicans.

Recent published reports that Mr. Nixon, since his resignation, has been "terribly depressed and gloomy" and seemed to wander in conversation were heatedly denied by Mr. Presley and another San Clemente businessman who has visited the Casa Pacifica.

"He's been a saddened man, of course, but to say that what has happened has sunk him into a fit of depression is pure rot," Mr. Presley said.

Six Papers in Ivy League Disapprove the Pardon

PRINCETON, N. J., Sept. 8 (AP)—A spokesman for the Princeton University student newspaper said today that the editorial boards of six Ivy League papers disapproved of the pardon granted former President Nixon.

"President Ford's decision Sunday to grant Richard Nixon a pre-emptive and blanket pardon for all crimes he may have committed while in office as President represents a flagrant violation of the principle of equal justice under law," a joint statement said.

The newspapers that endorsed the statement were the Brown Daily Herald, Columbia Spectator, Cornell Daily Sun, Daily Pnnsylvanian, Daily Princetonian and the Yale Daily News. The spokesman said the papers at Colgate, Dartmouth and Harvard were not yet staffed for the year.

Watergate Burglars Hope for Clemency

MIAMI, Monday, Sept. 9 (UPI)—President Ford's granting of a pardon to former President Nixon has raised the hopes for clemency of two Watergate burglars.

Bernard Barker said: "I believe it was the only decent thing that a man could do. I'm very happy that this action was taken, whether it means we will be helped or not."

Mr. Barker also said he hoped the Nixon pardon might influence the outcome of appeals filed by his attorneys and attorneys for fellow Watergate burglar, Eugenio R. Martinez.

The two received suspended sentences for their part in the Watergate burglary on June 17, 1972, but are appealing their convictions. Mr. Barker said yesterday he considered a pardon a last resort.

Mr. Martinez asked, "If they can do that for the President, why can't they do it for the four Cubans, who were selected through the White House and put in the place where we are today?"

Mr. Martinez apparently referred to himself, Mr. Barker, Frank L. Sturgis and Virgilio Gonzalez.

The four were recruited by former White House consultant, E. Howard Hunt Jr., to perform the bugging of the Democratic National Committee offices in the Watergate complex.

Mr. Barker, Mr. Martinez and Felipe de Diego, another Cuban exile, were indicted in connection with the break-in in September, 1971, at the Los Angeles office of Dr. Louis J. Fielding, a psychiatrist. Dr. Fielding had treated Dr. Daniel Ellsberg, who says he leaked the Pentagon papers to the press.

Mr. Martinez said of the Nixon pardon: "I hope that something good comes out of that for us. Maybe in the future peolple will look at the people no one cares about - and I'm talking about the four Cubans who went to jail - who supported the whole thing, and not for their benefit, but who believe they were serving the best interests of the nation."

Article II of Constitution Gives Power to Pardon

WASHINGTON, Sept. 8 (AP)—The Presidential power to grant pardons is expressed in the Constitution in Article II, Section 2.

The provision says:

"He shall have power to grant reprieves and pardons for offenses against the United States, except in cases of impeachment."

Article II delineates the power of the President, and includes both the oath to "faithfully execute the Office" and the admonition that "he shall take care that the laws be faithfully executed."

Lawyer, 36, Is Liaison for 2 Presidents

By PHILIP SHABECOFF

Special to The New York Times

WASHINGTON, Sept. 8—Benton L. Becker, the young lawyer who acted as intermediary between President Ford and former President Richard M. Nixon in the negotiations that led to today's pardon announcement, was described by a former colleague in the Justice Department as "a real wheeler-dealer."

The White House counsel, Philip W. Buchen, who along with Mr. Ford sent Mr. Becker to San Clemente with an offer of pardon for Mr. Nixon, described him as "a very savvy guy whose loyalty belongs to the Oval Office."

But most of Mr. Becker's professional associates reached today expressed surprise that this relatively obscure lawyer, who has come into public notice recently as an attorney connected with a couple of fraud cases in the Washington area, should emerge as a participant in a historical moment.

Mr. Becker said in a telephone interview that he had found it "a humbling experience to be on the East Coast talking to one President and 12 hours later be on the West Coast talking to another."

Mr. Becker, a 36-year-old Washington lawyer, is well connected within the White House. He is a close friend of Mr. Ford, having known him for the last five years.

The two men became acquainted when Mr. Ford was minority leader of the House and Mr. Becker was on the staff of the House Judiciary Committee, helping to prepare what proved to be an abortive impeachment case against Associate Supreme Court Justice William O. Douglas.

On Transition Staff

When Mr. Ford was nominated by President Nixon to be Vice President last winter, Mr. Becker helped Mr. Ford prepare for his confirmation hearings. More recently, he has been working on the White House transition staff.

Mr. Becker is also a law partner of William Cramer, a former Congressman who has been close to Mr. Ford since their days in the House.

It turns out that Mr. Becker is also well connected to Mr. Nixon's lawyer, Herbert J. Miller. Both represented defendants in a case involving a Washington company that was found guilty of defrauding impoverished slum dwellers.

Mr. Becker said today that both he and Mr. Miller had since been working hard administering a fund to repay the inner city dwellers the losses they suffered from dealings with the Monarch Company, the concern involved.

Associated Press

Benton L. Becker

Mr. Buchen, who is also a long-time friend of Mr. Becker, asked him to help on the research that led to the drafting of the pardon for Mr. Nixon. After meeting with Mr. Ford, Mr. Becker flew last Thursday to the West Coast, with the proposed pardon in his briefcase.

Pardon in His Briefcase

"As you know," he explained today, "a pardon has to be accepted after it is offered."

In San Clemente he met with Mr. Miller and Ronald L. Ziegler, the former White House press secretary and Mr. Nixon's close confidant.

After presenting the pardon offer to Mr. Nixon, Mr. Becker said he came away feeling the former President "was a man who might get some peace out of this act. He seemed to me to be a man in need of peace."

Mr. Becker said he was proud of his role in this transaction and quoted Alexander Hamilton: "A timely offer of pardon can offer tranquility to the Commonwealth."

Mr. Becker, while serving in the Justice Department as an Assistant Attorney General, worked on a criminal case against the late Adam Clayton Powell.

Mr. Becker, in private practice, represented Joel Kline and Eric Baer, defendants in a recent stock manipulation case. Both men were convicted. Mr. Baer, who changed lawyers, accused Mr. Becker of advising him to give false testimony.

Later, Mr. Kline asserted that he had given false evidence about his own financial records as a witness in another trial, and that Mr. Becker had known about it. The other trial involved extortion charges against Baltimore County Executive Dale N. Anderson, who succeeded former Vice President Spiro T. Agnew as the county executive.

Mr. Becker has denied the allegations of both Mr. Baer and Mr. Kline. He said today that he had taken eight lie detector tests he said proved he was truthful.

He also said that the tests disproved another assertion by Mr. Kline that the two men had discussed a county judgeship for Mr. Becker in return for a payment of money. Mr. Becker said today that he had discussed a judgeship with Mr. Kline but added that there was no talk of any payment.

Federal authorities are still allegedly investigating a charge made by Mr. Kline that Mr. Becker participated in a illegal tax maneuver, Government officials indicated tonight. The investigation involves Mr. Kline's statement that he allegedly gave Mr. Becker $10,000 to be used as prepaid interest for the purchase of stocks valued as much as $1 million, according to some accounts.

Mr. Becker said tonight that he thought that the investigation had been ended. He said, "there is absolutely no merit whatever to the allegations made by Mr. Kline". Mr. Becker contended that he "had taken every step to demonstrate" that the allegation was untrue.

Buchen 'Satisfied'

In another telephone interview, Mr. Buchen said that Mr. Becker had informed him of these events and that he was satisfied Mr. Becker was in the right.

"Becker is just as straight as he can be," Mr. Buchen said, adding that "somehow he gets involved in those things."

He added that Mr. Becker, who had served as a volunteer without pay in his tasks for Mr. Ford, would not be joining the White House staff.

"He's just starting in a good law practice and we have a mutual understanding that he would stay there," said Mr. Buchen.

Mr. Becker, described as about 6 feet tall, fairly heavyset and blond, is married and has three children. He grew up in the Washington area, attend the University of Maryland, American University Law School and lives in Potomac, Md.

Ford Plans Speech Today

PITTSBURGH, Sept. 8 (UPI)—President Ford will be the principal speaker tomorrow at the opening of the three-day annual conference on transportation at which the problems of urban areas in moving people rapidly and efficiently will be explored. There was no advance word on Mr. Ford's topic, but convention planners were hopeful that he would outline his Administration's policy on urban transit.

"All the News That's Fit to Print"

The New York Times

LATE CITY EDITION

Weather: Continued mostly cloudy, cool today, tonight and tomorrow. Temperature range: today 46-58; Tuesday 45-53. Details on Page 81.

VOL. CXXIV... No. 42,830 © 1975 The New York Times Company NEW YORK, WEDNESDAY, APRIL 30, 1975 Price higher in air delivery cities. 20 CENTS

MINH SURRENDERS, VIETCONG IN SAIGON; 1,000 AMERICANS AND 5,500 VIETNAMESE EVACUATED BY COPTER TO U.S. CARRIERS

U.S., GREECE AGREE TO END HOME PORT FOR THE 6TH FLEET

Air Base of Americans at Athens Is Also Closed, but Some Facilities Remain

By United Press International

ATHENS, April 29—United States and Greek officials announced today the termination of the home-port arrangement for Sixth Fleet ships at the port of Eleusis near Athens and the closing of the American air base at Athens airport.

The announcement came in a joint statement at the end of a second round of talks on the status of United States military facilities in Greece.

The Greek Government threatened to close all United States bases and it withdrew from the North Atlantic Treaty Organization's military command after the invasion of Cyprus by Turkey last July.

"Certain United States facilities which contribute to Greek defense needs will continue to operate on the Greek Air Force base at Hellenikon," today's statement said.

The statement said that the second phase of the talks, held April 7 to 29 by the two delegations under the United States Embassy Minister, Monteagle Stearns, and Ambassador Petros Kalogeras of Greece also discussed the status of other facilities.

"Agreement is also expected on the elimination, reduction and conservation of other United States facilities in Greece," it said.

The two delegations said that they made progress on the review of the privileges, immunities and exemptions of American personnel in Greece.

The two Governments said

Continued on Page 4, Column 4

G.M.'s Profits Fall

First-quarter profits of General Motors declined 50.8 per cent from the depressed 1974 quarter. Page 53.

HEAVY USERS FACE CON ED INCREASE

P.S.C. Also Orders Cuts for Smaller Consumers

By WILL LISSNER

The state's Public Service Commission ordered the Consolidated Edison Company yesterday to raise its rates for those customers who accounted for the heaviest summer power demands and to cut the rates for customers whose usage did not create excess power demand.

The change — technically a revision of the rate structure approved last November to give the utility $338.7-million more a year — will not mean any extra revenue for the company. Nor will it affect the rates for the great majority of customers, the 2.5 million small residential and commercial users.

Instead, yesterday's order makes revisions in bills that will take less than $20-million from some customers and give it to others, a relatively small amount compared with its total annual billings for electricity of $2.10-billion. It affected less than 500,000 of its 2.9 million customers in New York City, Westchester County and part of Nassau County.

But the order was significant because it introduced into energy ratemaking the philosophy that the customers who are responsible for excess costs should be required to bear more

Continued on Page 34, Column 5

United Press International

A crewman from an American helicopter helping evacuees to the top of a building in Saigon for flight to a U.S. carrier

Abram Offers Bills To Curtail Abuses Of Nursing Homes

By ALFONSO A. NARVAEZ

Special to The New York Times

ALBANY, April 29—Morris B. Abram proposed today a series of changes in the laws governing nursing homes to "deal with the most serious immediate problems" uncovered during his month-long investigation.

The proposals were contained in a package of 11 bills submitted to Governor Carey and legislative leaders by Mr. Abram, head of the Moreland Act Commission investigating the nursing-home industry.

Among other things, they would authorize nursing-home residents to file class-action suits for deprivation of their rights and would entitle them to receive a minimum of 25 per cent of the daily reimbursement rate paid by government regulations for each day of a violation.

[In Washington, Senator Frank Moss, Democrat of Utah and chairman of the long-term care subcommittee of the Special Committee on Aging, introduced a package of 36 bills for nursing home reform. Among them were measures to make long-term care more readily available to all older Americans, improve inspection and enforcement procedures and provide training for nursing-home physicians, nurses,

Continued on Page 81, Column 3

CAMBODIA ORDERS FOREIGNERS OUT

Planned 250-Mile Road Trip to Border Is Protested by Paris as Debilitating

By FLORA LEWIS

Special to The New York Times

PARIS, April 29—The French Government said today that the people who have been isolated in its Phnom Penh embassy since the Cambodian Communists took over two weeks ago had been ordered expelled "in the worst possible conditions."

There are 610 refugees in the embassy. They are to be sent out by truck to the town of Poipet on the Thailand border, beginning tomorrow.

Foreign Minister Jean Sauvagnargues told newsmen after having conferred with President Valéry Giscard d'Estaing:

"We fear these extremely precarious evacuation conditions will be beyond the strength of some whose health is poor."

"We continue to insist that the plane that we have held in Vientiane for evacuation of the ill be allowed to land in Phnom Penh."

However, a Foreign Ministry spokesman said that so far there has been no response to

Continued on Page 17, Column 6

74 Saigon Planes Fly 2,000 to Thailand

By DAVID A. ANDELMAN

Special to The New York Times

BANGKOK, Thailand, April 29—At least 74 South Vietnamese Air Force planes fleeing the country streamed into U Taphao air base in southern Thailand without warning this afternoon.

The pilots and passengers—2,000 people—requested asylum, American and Thai Foreign Ministry officials said.

About 30 of the planes were F-5 jet fighters and there were reports that at least one had crashed on a highway near the base as it was making its approach.

The planes began arriving at the huge naval and air base on the Gulf of Siam at about the time that the American evacuation of South Vietnam was ending and the planes were still landing as night fell.

The aircraft were said to include C-47 transports and the C-130 cargo planes that the American military has been using to ferry refugees from South Vietnam to Guam and the Philippines. However, all the aircraft were understood to be Vietnam Air Force planes, originally supplied by the United States.

A Thai Foreign Ministry spokesman said that American authorities at U Taphao had been asked to turn over the aircraft to the Thai Government, which would return them to "the new South Vietnamese government." The pilots and passengers, the Thai spokesman said, "must leave Thailand."

"They just landed first and asked permission afterwards," said an astounded Thai Foreign Ministry official. Other Government sources said that apparently no efforts were made to prevent the planes from landing and no aircraft went up to intercept the fighters as they roared in.

American Embassy officials in Bangkok declined to comment on the Thai request that the planes be returned and their status was unclear. An unresolved question here appeared to be whether the planes were still American property or belonged to whatever government continued in Saigon. The planes could be worth $200-million, one official said.

No details were available on the status of the refugees or

Continued on Page 16, Column 6

2d Key Met Museum Aide Quits In Dispute Over Hoving Methods

By GRACE GLUECK

With an attack on Thomas P. F. Hoving's administration at the Metropolitan Museum of Art alleging its inability to function "in any way that creates or preserves trust, confidence and decency," Anthony M. Clark, chairman of the museum's department of European paintings, has resigned.

Mr. Clark's resignation, one of several that have occurred among senior curatorial personnel at the museum in recent years, represents the first open challenge to Mr. Hoving's administration.

The resignation, effective June 30, follows that of John Walsh, the vice chairman and curator of this key department a month ago. Mr. Clark would not speak for Mr. Walsh, who is abroad, but it is understood that their basic grievances are similar.

"I can't work with or for the present administration at the Met," said Mr. Clark, who had been director of the Minneapolis Institute of Arts for 10 years before his appointment to the Metropolitan in 1973. "I believe that its relation to art has become incidental, wrong and even risky. It's also hell on professionals."

In a statement last night, Mr. Hoving said that he was

Continued on Page 24, Column 1

NEWS INDEX

United Press International

President Ford and Secretary of State Kissinger returning to White House to resume talks on Vietnam. They had just said good-by to King Hussein of Jordan after visit.

FORD UNITY PLEA

President Says That Departure 'Closes a Chapter' for U.S.

By JOHN W. FINNEY

Special to The New York Times

WASHINGTON, April 29—The United States ended two decades of military involvement in Vietnam today with the evacuation of about 1,000 Americans from Saigon as well as more than 5,500 South Vietnamese.

The emergency helicopter evacuation was ordered last night by President Ford after the Saigon airport was closed because of Communist rocket and artillery fire. The 1,000 Americans were the last contingent of a force that once numbered more than 500,000.

Ford statement and excerpts from Kissinger's, Page 17.

They were carried by a fleet of 81 American helicopters to carriers in the South China Sea. The helicopters removed the 5,500 South Vietnamese citizens because their lives were presumed to be in danger with a Communist take-over of South Vietnam. Over the last two weeks, a total of about 55,000 South Vietnamese have been removed. Most of them will come to the United States. The helicopter flights ended the United States evacuation of South Vietnamese.

Last Marines Evacuated

The final withdrawal of Americans was completed at 7:52 P.M., about two hours after the White House had announced the evacuation was completed, when 11 marines were taken by helicopter from the roof of the American Embassy in Saigon. Officials said that the marines, the last of a security guard sent in to protect the evacuation, were safely removed although small-arms fire had broken out around the deserted embassy.

President Ford, in a statement issued by the White House, said the evacuation "closes a chapter in the American experience." In a plea for national unity in the post-Vietnam period, the President said:

"I ask all Americans to close ranks, to avoid recrimination about the past, to look ahead to the many goals we share and to work together on the great tasks that remain to be accomplished."

Appeal by Kissinger

At a news conference, Secretary of State Kissinger appealed to North Vietnam not to storm Saigon by force because the United States believed the new South Vietnamese Govern-

Continued on Page 17, Column 1

DEFENSE ENDS

General Tells His Troops to Turn in Their Weapons

By The Associated Press

SAIGON, South Vietnam, Wednesday, April 30—President Duong Van Minh announced today the unconditional surrender of the Saigon Government and its military forces to the Vietcong.

Columns of South Vietnamese troops pulled out of their defensive positions in the capital and marched to central points to turn in their weapons.

Within two hours, Communist forces began moving into Saigon. A jeep flying the Vietcong flag and carrying eight cheering men in civilian clothes armed with an assortment of weapons drove along the street a block from the United States Embassy compound.

This action followed by hours the ending of the American involvement in Vietnam through the evacuation of most of the approximately 1,000 Americans still here.

[In Washington, the White House said that President Ford had "no comment" on the surrender of Saigon, but a White House spokesman said the surrender was considered 'inevitable.' Page 16]

3 Decades of Fighting

The surrender announcement, made in a broadcast to the nation, signaled the end of three decades of fighting. It came 21 years after the 1954 Geneva accords divided Vietnam into North and South and a little more than two years after the Vietnam cease-fire agreement was signed in Paris on Jan. 27, 1973. The last American troops left the country in March of that year.

The text of President Minh's statement is on Page 16.

President Minh, who took office on Monday to lead South Vietnam into peace negotiations, said in his brief radio address:

"I believe firmly in reconciliation among Vietnamese to avoid unnecessary shedding of the blood of Vietnamese. For this reason, I ask the soldiers of the Republic of Vietnam to cease hostilities in calm and to stay where they are."

The President also asked the "brother soldiers" of the Vietcong to cease hostilities and added:

"We wait here to meet the Provisional Revolutionary Government of South Vietnam to discuss together a ceremony of orderly transfer of power so as to avoid any unnecessary

Continued on Page 16, Column 1

Saigon Copter Lands on Another In Stampede to U.S. Ship's Deck

By The Associated Press

ABOARD U.S.S. BLUE RIDGE, in South China Sea, April 29—Scores of South Vietnamese helicopters filled with military men and civilians fled Saigon today and headed out to sea to search for the carriers of the United States Seventh Fleet.

Seven of the helicopters arrived unexpectedly above this vessel carrying Americans and Vietnamese evacuated from South Vietnam. The seven copters made a dash for the helipad at the rear of the ship.

One pilot dropped his helicopter on the blades of another that had just landed and chunks of metal ripped through the air. The top helicopter, with its load of women and children, nearly toppled into the sea, but they were rescued and there were no injuries.

United States sailors heaved the two damaged choppers overboard to clear the landing pad. For the Vietnamese it was a last-ditch chance to survive.

As other Vietnamese helicopters landed their passengers were pulled free. American sailors ripped the doors off the craft to make them sink and the pilots then jettisoned them in the sea to make room for other arrivals circling overhead. Two small craft rescued the swimming pilots.

The American evacuation was reported orderly, although it was delayed several times because of weather and pilot fatigue.

The Blue Ridge is the command and communications vessel of the 40-ship Seventh Fleet armada waiting off the coast of South Vietnam to evacuate Americans and other foreigners

Continued on Page 17, Colum

General Minh Announces South Vietnam's Unconditional Surrender to Vietcong

ARMY IS ORDERED TO STOP SHOOTING

President, in Radio Speech, Says Move Is Being Made to Avoid Bloodshed

Continued From Page 1, Col. 8

agreement was signed in Paris on Jan. 27, 1973. The last American troops left the country in March of that year.

President Minh, who took office on Monday to lead South Vietnam into peace negotiations, said in his brief radio address:

"I believe firmly in reconciliation among Vietnamese to avoid unnecessary shedding of the blood of Vietnamese. For this reason, I ask the soldiers of the Republic of Vietnam to cease hostilities in calm and to stay where they are."

The President also asked the "brother soldiers" of the Vietcong to cease hostilities and added:

"We wait here to meet the Provisional Revolutionary Government of South Vietnam to discuss together a ceremony of orderly transfer of power so as to avoid any unnecessary bloodshed in the population."

There was no mention in his address of North Vietnam or of the North Vietnamese armies that had provided the bulk of the military force that defeated South Vietnam.

Gen. Nguyen Vuu Hanh, deputy chief of staff, then went on the air to order all South Vietnamese troops to carry out the orders of General Minh, who is known to foreigners as Big Minh.

"The military command," he said, "is ready to enter into contact with the military command of the army of the Provisional Revolutionary Government of South Vietnam in order to effect a cease-fire without bloodshed."

With the surrender announcement, made by President Minh at 10:24 A.M. (10:24 P.M. Tuesday, New York time), shellfire subsided along the northern rim of the city where the Vietcong had been bombarding the airport.

In the hours before the surrender statement, Communist troops had been pressing closer to Saigon. The Vietcong announced the fall of the Government's huge air base at Bien Hoa, 15 miles northeast of the capital, and there were reports that Vung Tau, the port city to the southeast, had also been captured during the day.

The end came as more than a dozen Communist divisions were ringing the city, which reportedly was defended by less than one division of demoralized troops. Some South Vietnamese officers complained that the evacuation of the Americans had caused panic in the miiltary with many top army officers and most of the air force fleeing.

For two years after the 1973 cease-fire accords, both Government and Communist forces attacked each other without any major change in territory. The South Vietnamese then suffered their first major setback on Jan. 9 with the fall of Phuoc Binh, capital of Phuoc Long Province, due north of Saigon.

On March 13, Ban Me Thuot, capital of Darlac Province in the Central Highlands, was captured, and this reverse prompted Nguyen Van Thieu, then President, to decide on a withdrawal from the Central Highlands cities of Pleiku and Kontum as well.

Pressure on Thieu

A precipitous rout followed, with South Vietnamese forces withdrawing from Hue, the country's cultural heart, from Da Nang, the nation's second largest city, and then swiftly from coastal regions all the way to the approaches of Saigon.

Saigon's forces turned to fight at Xuan Loc, capital of Long Khanh Province, which was invaded by North Vietnamese troops on April 9. For two weeks the opposing sides battled there, turning the city into rubble. It was abandoned April 22.

As most of the country fell into Communist hands, demands were voiced in Saigon —by political figures, religious leaders and others—for the resignation of President Thieu. The Government said two coup attempts had been uncovered and foiled.

Mr. Thieu went on radio and television April 21 to make an emotional announcement that he was resigning. He blamed the United States cuts in aid for the debacle of his forces.

Mr. Thieu's Vice President, Tran Van Huong, took over and on Monday, with the concurrence of the National Assembly, named General Minh to become the president to end the war.

In an address on taking office, General Minh appealed to "our friends of the other side, the Provisional Revolutionary Government of South Vietnam," to join in a cease-fire and in negotiations for a solution to the long conflict.

Yesterday, the Minh Government renewed the appeal as it sought ways to enter into talks with the Vietcong.

The calls for a truce were made on radio and television by Vice President Nguyen Van Huyen. He said later in an interview that a Government delegation met twice during the day with a Vietcong delegation at Tan Son Nhut air base, at the edge of Saigon. But the Vietcong representatives there, he said, pronounced themselves as not qualified to make political decisions.

The Vice President noted that one of the Vietcong demands—that all Americans leave South Vietnam—was already being met. He added that additional Vietcong demands for the dissolution of the Saigon Government and its army were being considered.

The Vietcong delegation with which the Government representatives met during the day has been at Tan Son Nhut since the first days after the Paris accords were signed.

As the Vietcong flags were raised over Saigon, no Government soldiers were to be seen on the streets. The people, however, appeared to be moving about normally.

At the Defense Ministry building, about a dozen North Vietnamese soldiers talked with a South Vietnamese army colonel and several junior officers.

There was not interference with Western newsmen taking pictures. North Vietnamese machine gunners sitting in two trucks outside the Defense Ministry posed and smiled proudly.

One man riding in a jeep flying a Vietcong flag beckoned to an American reporter and said in English:

"Go home. Go home."

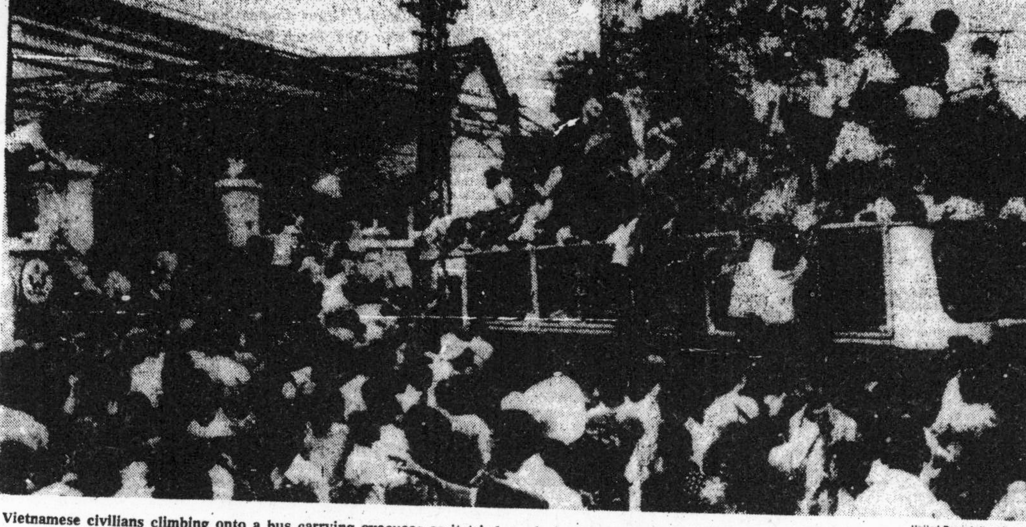

Vietnamese civilians climbing onto a bus carrying evacuees as it tried to make its way into the U.S. Embassy compound in Saigon yesterday | during the final evacuation of Americans. Others, at left, tried to scale the walls of the complex in a desperate effort to be taken along.

United Press International

Saigon's Surrender Texts

SAIGON, South Vietnam, Wednesday, April 30 (Agence France-Presse)—Following are the texts, in unofficial translation, of President Duong Van Minh's address on the surrender of South Vietnam and of the General Staff's order to South Vietnamese forces:

Minh Statement

The policy line we back is reconciliation.

I believe firmly in reconciliation among Vietnamese to avoid unnecessary shedding of the blood of Vietnamese.

For this reason, I ask the soldiers of the Republic of Vietnam to cease hostilities in calm and to stay where they are.

I ask the brother soldiers of the Provisional Revolutionary Government of South Vietnam to cease hostilities. We wait here to meet the Provisional Revolutionary Government of South Vietnam to discuss together a ceremony of orderly transfer of power so as to avoid any unnecessary bloodshed in the population.

General Staff's Order

Soldiers, regimental commanders, unit commanders, Regional Forces, People's Forces, Self-Defense Forces, I, General Nguyen Huu Hanh, Deputy Chief of General Staff, in the absence of General Vinh Loc, Chief of General Staff, ask you, generals and soldiers of all ranks, to follow strictly the order of the President of the Republic of Vietnam concerning the cease-fire.

The military command is ready to enter into contact with the military command of the army of the Provisional Revolutionary Government of South Vietnam in order to effect a cease-fire without bloodshed.

Call for Pullout, Then a Night's Vigil at White House

By JAMES M. NAUGHTON

Special to The New York Times

WASHINGTON, April 29 — The United States exit from South Vietnam, like so much that preceded it, was dictated by events in Saigon that outpaced hopes in Washington.

President Ford ordered the evacuation of the last remnants of the American presence—the United States Embassy in Saigon and the defense attaché's compound at nearby Tan Son Nhut airport—after Ambassador Graham A. Martin reluctantly recommended, at 10:41 o'clock last night, "We should go with Option 4."

Option 4 was the plan for the immediate evacuation by helicopter of all remaining American citizens and as many South Vietnamese as possible.

Mr. Ford assented to the recommendation, ordered the withdrawal of the last Americans and received a briefing on how the evacuation would be conducted.

Officials in the White House said today that there had been no emotion and no dramatics as President Ford yielded to the reality of imminent danger to the remaining Americans in Saigon.

Based on accounts by Ford Administration officials, here is how the President decided on the action that he said "closes a chapter in the American experience."

It was early yesterday evening. The President's economic and energy advisers sat around him in the Cabinet Room of the White House, discussing continued high unemployment and Mr. Ford's concern about whether Congress might soon enact a comprehensive energy program. An aide handed Mr. Ford a note.

The note described the situation in Saigon. A short time earlier, Communist rocket and artillery fire had struck Tan Son Nhut airport, killing two United States marines and destroying one of the large C-130 military transports that had been used to fly Americans and "high-risk" South Vietnamese to haven.

The new President of South Vietnam, Duong Van Minh, had called publicly for the removal of the last of the Americans as one of the conditions for a possible negotiated settlement with the Communists ringing the capital.

Top Advisers Summoned

Mr. Ford whispered to the messenger that the National Security Council should be assembled at 7 P.M.

At 7:23, Mr. Ford walked from the Cabinet Room to the Roosevelt Room to join his senior security advisers: Secretary of State Kissinger, Secretary of Defense James R. Schlesinger, William E. Colby, director of Central Intelligence, and the Chairman of the Joint Chiefs of Staff, Gen. George S. Brown.

Mr. Kissinger said today that the upshot of the 45-minute meeting was a decision by the President to wait until dawn, fast approaching in Saigon, in hopes the Communist shelling of the Saigon airport would end and the gradual evacuation by fixed-wing aircraft could resume. If so, Mr. Ford ordered, the 900 or so remaining Americans should be reduced to a substantially smaller number.

'Somber and Determined'

Mr. Ford went from the National Security Council meeting to the family quarters of the White House. At 8:30 P.M., Mr. Kissinger joined him there. Evidently they learned about that time that the shelling of Tan Son Nhut had ended.

The President and his wife, Betty, sat down to a quiet dinner, expecting the C-130 flights to resume.

Shortly before 10 P.M., two of the large American planes circled Tan Son Nhut, preparing to land. But the runways, Mr. Kissinger said tonight, were crowded with South Vietnamese seeking to be evacuated and the situation was "out of control."

At the airport, Maj. Gen. Homer Smith, the defense attaché, concluded that the planes could not land. He telephoned Adm. Noel A.M. Gayler, the Pacific commander, in Honolulu, and Admiral Gayler relayed the information to Secretary Schlesinger at the Pentagon.

At nearly the same time, Mr. Kissinger was conferring by telephone with Ambassador Martin. From the embassy in downtown Saigon, the Ambassador recommended that Option 4, the last of four evacuation options — the removal of Americans by helicopter — be put in effect.

Mr. Kissinger, in the Situation Room in the basement of the West Wing of the White House, telephoned the President to convey Ambassador Martin's recommendation. Just before 11 P.M., Mr. Ford ordered the last exit.

About 25 minutes later, Mr. Ford walked from his residence to the Situation Room. Mr. Kissinger showed the President, on a large map of Saigon, the two escape hatches still open—the defense attaché's ringed compound at the airport and the two open spots at the embassy grounds — a parking lot and the flat roof of the building.

Mr. Ford was "somber and determined," according to the Secretary of State. He listened to the description of the evacuation plans. At midnight, the President walked back toward his residence.

Phil Jones, a White House correspondent for CBS, spotted Mr. Ford and commented to him that he was working rather late.

"With good cause," Mr. Ford replied tersely.

The President went back to the residence. He got ready for bed. At 12:43 A.M., two minutes before the first of 81 helicopters lifted off from the Hancock, about 100 miles from Saigon, Mr. Kissinger telephoned the President to advise that the evacuation would soon get under way.

Exactly 30 minutes later, Mr. Kissinger telephoned Mr. Ford once more. The evacuation was on.

The President went to bed.

At 5:27 A.M., he arose as usual and picked up the phone to ask the White House switchboard if there were any messages for him.

There were none.

Mr. Ford read the morning newspapers, breakfasted and, amid periodic briefings from Mr. Kissinger on the slow pace of the evacuation, went through what might otherwise have passed for a normal day.

He met, as planned, with King Hussein of Jordan. He conferred with leaders of two dozen civic and service organizations. He formally accepted the credentials of new envoys from Peru, Haiti, Chile and Colombia.

In between those more routine meetings, Mr. Ford briefed his Cabinet and then the leaders of Congress on the reasons for the evacuation and its progress.

Throughout the day, however, there were reports of problems. The first helicopters to head for Saigon unaccountably received orders to turn back and as a result were an hour behind schedule. Rain hampered the evacuation. Exhausted pilots had to rest. Americans trying to reach the withdrawal rendezvous points had difficulty getting past anxious South Vietnamese.

The planned announcement of the end of the evacuation slipped past noon, then past 1 P.M. and was put off for 30-minute and 60-minute periods.

Shortly after 5 P.M. — 18 hours after President Ford ordered Saigon abandoned by Americans—the White House announced that Ambassador Martin had boarded the last helicopter and had flown out to sea.

The United States was out of Vietnam.

Evacuation From Saigon Tumultuous at the End

By GEORGE ESPER

The Associated Press

SAIGON, South Vietnam, Wednesday, April 30—With American fighter planes flying cover and marines standing guard on the ground, Americans left Saigon yesterday by helicopter after fighting off throngs of Vietnamese civilians who tried to go along.

Eighty-one helicopters from carriers in the South China Sea landed at Tan Son Nhut airport and on roofs at the United States Embassy compound to pick up most of the approximately 1,000 remaining Americans and several thousand Vietnamese.

But large groups of other Vietnamese clawed their way up the 10-foot wall of the embassy compound in desperate attempts to escape approaching Communist troops. United States marines and civilians used pistol and rifle butts to dislodge them.

At the airport, angry Vietnamese guards fired in the air and in the direction of evacuees on buses, shouting, "We want to go too."

The final stage of the evacuation, which stretched over 19 hours, brought to an end an American involvement in Vietnam that cost more than 50,000 lives and $150-billion. Four marines died during the final evacuation—two early yesterday as a result of a bombardment of Tan Son Nhut airport, two later when their helicopter plunged into the South China Sea.

While most Americans were pulling out, some newsmen and missionaries chose to remain.

Communist forces, meanwhile, pressed closer to Saigon. The Vietcong said they had captured the large Bien Hoa air base, 15 miles northeast of the capital. [A broadcast from Peking monitored in Tokyo said the Communists had also seized Vung Tau, a port city southeast of Saigon.].

Earlier, fighting had been reported less than 10 miles west of Saigon along Route 1.

As the American airlift came to an end at 7:52 A.M. [7:52 P.M., Tuesday, New York Time], Vietcong gunners sent rockets hurtling into Tan Son Nhut air base. The last Americans to be flown out of Saigon were 11 of the 800 marines who had guarded the evacuation operation.

The 11, who served as the rear guard, fired a red smoke grenade to guide the CH-46 helicopted in. As it touched down on the roof of the Embassy, they scrambled aboard and were airbound within four minutes.

One of the last civilians to leave was Ambassador Graham Martin, who boarded the final regular lift of 19 helicopters that had flown out about two hours earlier.

After the last marines had left, hundreds of civilians swarmed into the compound and onto the roof. On the roof of a nearby building that had also served as an emergency helipad, several hundred civilians huddled together, hoping there would be more helicopters to carry them away.

Despite a 24-hour curfew, there was moderate traffic in the city's streets early today. there were also abandoned United States Embassy behicles that had been taken over by Vietnamese and driven around until they ran out of gasoline.

The American involvement ended in tumultuous scenes at both airport and embassy. Marines in battle gear pushed all the people they could reach off the wall, but the crush of people was so great that scores got over.

Some tried to jump the wall and landed on barbed wire strung along the top. A middle-aged man and a woman were lying on the wire, bleeding. People held up their children, asking Americans to take them over the fence.

During the airport evacuation, two Vietcong rockets whistled overhead and exploded behind the United States defense attaché's compound, sending marines and evacuees diving for the pavement. The two marine guards had been killed at the compound by an earlier attack.

Across the street from the embassy, soldiers, police and youths stripped and stole scores of abandoned embassy cars. Thousands of other Vietnamese stripped apartment buildings in which Americans had lived, collecting bathroom fixtures, books, furniture and food. They sat on sidewalks with their booty, waiting for friends in cars to pick them up.

American newsmen who had been taken to Tan Son Nhut airport earlier in buses could not be evacuated from there because Vietnamese guards would not let the buses into the air base.

The buses returned to the embassy, and the newsmen climbed over the wall themselves, beating off Vietnamese who tried to cling to them.

Among the newsmen remaining in Saigon were Peter Arnett, Matt Franjola and this correspondent, of The Associated Press.

Among the missionaries was Max Ediser, 28 years old, of Turpin Okla., who works with the Mennonite Central Committee.

"We have talked about this for years," he said. "We could never come up with a definite answer. Now we realize that having talked of love to our Vietnamese people, and told them not to yield to fear or ignorance, we cannot leave them in this hour of need. So we are staying."

Others remaining with Mr. Ediser included James Klassen, from Kansas, and Luke Marin, from Pennsylvania, both Mennonites, and Claudia Krich and her husband, Keith Brinton, of the American Friends Service Committee.

The final evacuation followed the heavy shelling of Tan Son Nhut airbase yesterday morning and an order by President Duong Van Minh for the American defense attaché and his staff to leave. The general issued his order as he and his Government sought ways to open peace talks with the Vietcong.

As word of the evacuation spread, some Government officials telephoned the office of The Associated Press and asked if they could also be taken out.

Many South Vietnamese officers and officials were reported fleeing as rumors spread that Communist-led forces would soon march on the city.

Four buses drove around Saigon picking up American, European and Vietnamese evacuees. As the first bus arrived at the gates of Tan Son Nhut air base, Vietnamese guards fired at it.

Hundreds of South Vietnamese soldiers carrying weapons converged on the base, also seeking to leave the country.

Armed United States marines pushed and struck Vietnamese trying to get inside the United States defense attaché's compound where those being airlifted waited for helicopters coming from carriers offshore.

U.S. Planes in Action

SINGAPORE, Wednesday, April 30 (Reuters) — United States Navy fighter planes went into action over South Vietnam yesterday to protect fleeing refugees from marauding helicopters, according to military and civilian communications reports monitored here.

The fighters were said to have been called in when two boats on the Mekong River carrying the American consul general from the delta city of Can Tho reported that two helicopters with South Vietnamese markings were firing at his party. This consisted of 100 Vietnamese, six United States marines and 16 other Americans, according to the messages.

Later, the consul general was said to be stranded somewhere in the South China Sea.

Early in the day, United States naval authorities aboard ships about 40 miles offshore from Vung Tau, southeast of Saigon, could be heard promising air support for another group of refugees coming down the Saigon River from the South Vietnamese capital.

The messages monitored here indicated that 50,000 people fled through Vung Tau during the day. This evacuation was said to have occurred under intense shell fire.

The port's cable station, which handles much of South Vietnam's communications with the outside world, asked for United States air support early in the day when it was struck by mortar fire.

Tan Son Nhut and U.S. Embassy were evacuation sites

The New York Times/April 30, 1975

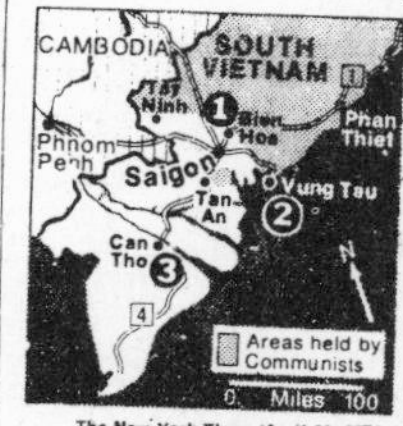

The New York Times/April 30, 1975

Fall of Bien Hoa (1) and Vung Tau (2) was reported. U.S. planes covered flight of Americans from Can Tho (3).

White House Considered The Surrender 'Inevitable'

BY BERNARD GWERTZMAN

Special to The New York Times

WASHINGTON, April 29 — A White House spokesman said tonight that President Ford had "no comment" on the surrender of the South Vietnamese Government to the Vietcong, but officials said that they had viewed the developments as "inevitable."

Earlier Secretary of State Kissinger had appealed to North Vietnam not to storm Saigon by force as the United States believed that the new South Vietnamese Government of President Duong Van Minh was prepared to capitulate.

In a lengthy news conference, Mr. Kissinger had said a bloody take-over by the Communists was now "unnecessary" since General Minh's government was "ready to draw the conclusions from the existing situation and in fact was formed to correspond to the demands of the Communist side."

Tonight, asked if the White House had anticipated that President Minh would take such action, a spokesman said that "that is implicit in the statement that it was 'inevitable.'"

He said that he was not in a position to know whether President Ford or Secretary Kissinger knew beforehand that President Minh would surrender to the Vietcong once the evacuation of Americans and South Vietnamese from Saigon was completed.

He added that he did not know whether President Minh had told American officials, including Ambassador Graham A. Martin, of his intentions before the Americans withdrew.

The President and Secretary Kissinger were at a dinner for King Hussein of Jordan when word was received of President Minh's action.

At his news conference earlier, Mr. Kissinger, who was somber and grim throughout the session at the executive office building, next door to the White House, conveyed the disappointment of the Ford Administration with the decision by the Communists yesterday to step up military activity.

He was pressed for details on the extensive American efforts in recent weeks to bring about a negotiated cease-fire and settlement—an effort that had only limited results at best.

Mr. Kissinger said the endeavor was not a "failure" because "at least some of the efforts, especially those related to evacuation" were carried out "through intermediaries" that had contacts with both Hanoi and the Vietcong.

Strongly suggesting that there was at least an understanding with the Communists to let the evacuation proceed without opposition, Mr. Kissinger said that through different third parties "we were in a position to put our views and receive responses."

The dynamics of the situation, he said, and the "impatience" of North Vietnam to "seize power" accelerated events in the last day and a half.

He also noted that as the military situation improved for them, the Communists stepped up their demands, at first asking only for the resignation of President Nguyen Van Thieu, and then the ouster of his successors, and the dismantling of the South Vietnam military and government administration.

Mr. Kissinger said "I think it is too early to make a final assessment" of the Vietnam debacle, but at the same time he said that there was no point in not admitting that the defeat in Indochina would have serious repercussions.

"There is no question that the outcome in Indochina will have consequences not only in Asia but in many other parts of the world," he said. "To deny these consequences is to miss the possibility of dealing with them.

"We are determined to manage and to progress along the road toward a permanent peace we have sought, even though there is no question there will be consequences."

Mr. Kissinger said he was opposed to any aid to North Vietnam. He said that the United States would have to wait and see what happens in South Vietnam "and whether there is going to be a South Vietnam" before deciding on aid or diplomatic ties.

He said that the United States hoped "to crystallize an Asian policy that is suited to present circumstances," reaffirming the American treaty commitments to South Korea, Japan and the Philippines, the countries most concerned about an American withdrawal from the area.

He was decidedly cool toward both the Soviet Union and China, the chief supporters of North Vietnam, but he refused to condemn them both when offered the chance by a questioner. He said the Soviet had provided "some help" in the evacuation effort.

Asked about the American commitment to countries like Israel, Mr. Kissinger said the United States must scrupulously honor its pledges.

74 South Vietnamese Planes Fly 2,000 Seeking Thailand Asylum

Continued From Page 1, Col. 6

how the planes, pilots and passengers had made their escape from South Vietnam. But all those arriving were taken to the Evacuation Reception Center at U Taphao, which is already packed with more than 1,000 Cambodian refugees.

The unexpected arrival of these planes and new refugees scattered in other border areas of Thailand, were an embarrassment to the Thai Government, which has in recent days been avoiding direct links with the Americans, with the former pro-American governments in Indochina and with the refugees themselves.

"You have lost," a Thai Foreign Ministry official told an American, with embarrassment. "Within 48 hours it will all be over for you. Yet we will still be here."

The Thais have been trying to mend fences with some of their Communist neighbors and develop a militantly neutralist foreign policy as have most of the other non-Communist countries in the area, notably the Philippines—the other major American military stronghold in Southeast Asia.

Last Friday, for instance, the Thai Foreign Minister, Chatichai Choonhavan, met with Edward E. Masters, the acting United States chief of mission here, to discuss further American troop withdrawals from Thailand.

"All the News That's Fit to Print"

The New York Times

LATE CITY EDITION

Weather: Partly cloudy and less humid today through tomorrow. Temperature range: today 64-80; Sunday 63-82. Details on page 30.

VOL. CXXV . . . No. 43,262

NEW YORK, MONDAY, JULY 5, 1976

25 cents beyond 50-mile zone from New York City, except Long Island. Higher in air delivery cities.

20 CENTS

Nation and Millions in City Joyously Hail Bicentennial

ISRAELIS RETURN WITH 103 RESCUED IN UGANDA RAID

Toll Is Put at 3 Hostages, 7 Hijackers, Army Officer and 20 of Amin's Men

FORD LAUDS OPERATION

Freed Captives Are Received Joyously at Airport After Their 7-Day Ordeal

By TERENCE SMITH
Special to The New York Times

JERUSALEM, July 4—An Israeli commando unit that last night conducted a daring raid on the Entebbe airport in Uganda flew home today with the hostages it released.

Military officials said that 103 hostages had been flown to Israel. They said that four Israelis, seven of the 10 hijackers and about 20 Uganda soldiers had been killed.

Text of the Rabin address will be found on page 2.

Some of the hostages arrived exhausted, some exuberant, to a noisy, joyous reunion here with family and friends. A majority of those freed last night were Israelis.

[President Ford sent a message of congratulation to Prime Minister Yitzhak Rabin, voicing "great satisfaction" that the passengers of the hijacked plane had been saved and "a senseless act of terrorism thwarted." Page 2. President Idi Amin of Uganda condemned the Israeli action.]

Back at Same Airport

A week to the day after they set off on an Air France airbus, the Israeli passengers and French crew members were back at the same airport where they had originally started their trip. They were weeping, laughing and literally falling into each other's arms with relief.

Their return here brought to an end seven days of terror that culminated in the spectacular rescue operation, in which Israeli airborne troops traveled 2,500 miles to pluck the hostages from the gunpoints of their captors at the Entebbe airport.

Rabin Addresses Parliament

The success of the operation, which surprised most Israelis, electrified the country. Flags were brought out, people rejoiced openly in the streets, and in the sky over Jerusalem, a skywriter wrote in Hebrew: "Kol hakavod zahal," or "All honor to the army."

Addressing a specially convened session of the Israeli Parliament, Prime Minister Yitzhak Rabin declared: "This operation will become a legend. It is Israel's contribution to

Continued on Page 3, Column 4

The New York Times/Edward Hausner

Preceded by a fireboat, the Coast Guard training ship Eagle leads the armada of ships past the Battery up the Hudson for the naval review

PRESIDENT TALKS

Philadelphia Throngs Told U.S. Is Leader—Liberty Bell Rings

By JAMES T. WOOTEN
Special to The New York Times

PHILADELPHIA, July 4 — With its famous bells ringing, bands blaring, choirs singing and fireworks exploding, this city today staged a joyous, cacophonous commemoration of that day two centuries ago when the representatives of the 13 English colonies met here to renounce their allegiance to the British Crown.

At least one million people were in Philadelphia for the centerpiece of the Bicentennial observances.

President Ford came here from Valley Forge to recall that first Fourth of July as "the beginning of a continuing adventure," unfinished, unfulfilled, but still unchallenged as a model of social and political achievement.

"The world is ever conscious of what Americans are doing, for better or for worse," he said at Independence Hall, "because the United States remains today the most successful realization of humanity's universal hope.

Says Nation Leads

"The world may or may not follow, but we lead because our whole history says we must."

Then, after he left for New York City, the Liberty Bell, that faulted but venerated symbol, was softly sounded with a rubber mallet as millions across the nation watched on television. In clamorous response, hundreds of other bells rang out in Philadelphia's steeples and towers.

Meanwhile, several miles from the official observances, more than 30,000 other Americans, most of them members of two radical coalitions, staged their own peaceful Bicentennial celebration. Mayor Frank L. Rizzo had warned of potential disorders, but there were none.

At the main celebration, blue-shirted policemen cordially gave

Continued on Page 18, Column 5

PANOPLY OF SAILS

Harbor Armada Led by Tall Ships in Salute to Fourth

By RICHARD F. SHEPARD

Buoyed by panoramic spectacles that included a unique armada of tall-masted ships, a massive fireworks display and a series of festivals that took over downtown Manhattan, millions of New Yorkers and visitors in a happy mood observed the nation's Bicentennial yesterday.

It was a day of mammoth presentations.

Uncounted crowds lining the waterfront of the magnificent but underused harbor saw a virtually unbroken bridge of small craft that reached from the shores of Brooklyn to the coast of New Jersey.

More than 225 sailing ships under 31 flags paraded up the Hudson, a river that foretold their doom in 1807 when Robert Fulton's smoky little Clermont started steamboat service on it.

International Review

A 22-nation fleet of 53 naval units gray and grim—even ships festooned with pennants—lined the upper Bay and the Hudson for the International Naval Review, which had Vice President Rockefeller as the chief United States official present.

President Ford flew onto the hulking 79,000-ton aircraft carrier Forrestal, the host ship of the review, and later went by helicopter to the U.S.S. Nashville, anchored in mid-Hudson. He watched the sailing ships and was stranded for 40 minutes by a sudden squall before taking off again, headed for Washington, without having set foot ashore in the city.

As night fell, hundreds of thousands jammed onto the shore of lower Manhattan—some dangling from trees like so many Christmas decorations—to watch the dazzling fireworks explode over the harbor and the Statue of Liberty. When it was over, the tide of the departing throngs sometimes swept people out of con-

Continued on Page 20, Column 3

French Officials See Signs Amin, Hijackers Colluded

Special to The New York Times

PARIS, July 4 — Officials and released hostages said here today that they had substantial evidence that President Idi Amin had been in collusion with the hijackers of an Air France airbus in the seizure of the plane as well as after it landed in Uganda.

Although the officials refused to be quoted publicly, one said that negotiations got "much tougher" last night after President Amin returned to Uganda from a meeting of the Organization of African Unity in Mauritius.

A highly placed French source said that President Amin had refused to allow Pierre Renard, the French Ambassador to Uganda, or a special French envoy to deal with the hijackers directly.

While President Amin was out of the country, messages from Israel had to be passed by French Government representatives through the Somalian Ambassador, Hashi Abdullah Farah, to the hijackers. Messages back to the Israelis followed the same route.

Uganda Guards

When Gen. Amin returned from Mauritius yesterday, he resumed the role of mediator. He told the French Ambassador that demands for the release of 53 pro-Palestinian prisoners in Israel, Kenya and Europe must be met by early today or all the hostages would be killed.

Officials here pointed out that on the list of prisoners were five Ugandans held in Kenya on charges of attempting to assassinate President Jomo Kenyatta.

They also noted that during the first 24 hours after the aircraft reached Entebbe, the hijackers withdrew to rest and Ugandans guarded the hostages.

Other evidence pointing to the Uganda President's involvement with the terrorists was included in comments by French diplomats and the reports of hostages freed earlier by the terrorists. At the time of the Israeli rescue operation nearly all of the hijackers' captives were Israelis or dual nationals.

Among the passengers released last week were Michel Cojot and his 12-year-old son, Olivier. Mr. Cojot, a French management consultant, served as interpreter for the hostages, and negotiated on their behalf for small conveniences during the ordeal.

'Not Shadow of Doubt'

Mr. Cojot said that he had "not a shadow of a doubt" that the Uganda President knew of the hijack plan in advance and had prepared for the action.

He said that the airbus, a new European-built plane with a normal four-hour flying capacity, flew non-stop to Entebbe after a refueling stop in Benghazi, Libya — a six-hour flight. "We couldn't possibly have made any other airport by then," he said. "The hijackers were obviously certain they

Continued on Page 4, Column 2

CARTER TO BEGIN TALKS ON TICKET

Will See Muskie Today and Other Possible Running Mates Soon After

By CHARLES MOHR
Special to The New York Times

PLAINS, Ga., July 4—Jimmy Carter has asked Senator Edmund S. Muskie to visit him here tomorrow and discuss the Maine Senator's qualification to serve as Mr. Carter's running mate on the 1976 Democratic ticket.

Mr. Carter told reporters gathered at the driveway of his home in this small Georgia town this morning that he expected to talk to at least four other persons about the Vice-Presidential nomination between now and the Democratic National Convention, which convenes July 12.

The former Georgia Governor, who is assured of the Presidential nomination, said that it would be wrong to assume that there was any special significance in the fact that Senator Muskie was the first to be invited to meet with him. And, indeed, few political observers seem to feel that Mr. Muskie is a front-runner for the job. He was the Vice-Presidential nominee in 1968 and an unsuccessful candidate for the Democratic Presidential nomination in 1972.

A highly knowledgeable source said that the three men

Continued on Page 16, Column 4

A Day of Picnics, Pomp, Pageantry and Protest

By JOHN L. HESS

The nation celebrated its 200th birthday yesterday with pageantry and prayer, with games and parades, with picnics and fireworks, with the peal of bells and the chant of protests.

It began with a flag-raising atop Mars Hill Mountain in Maine, where dawn reached the continent, and moved on to Fort McHenry, in Baltimore Harbor, where it was greeted by the rocket's red glare of the national anthem. The activities were to end nearly a day later with an indigenous festival in American Samoa.

At 2 P.M., Eastern daylight time, descendants of the Revolutionaries laid hands symbolically on the Liberty Bell in Philadelphia, and bells rang in the 50 states and in American communities overseas. At Independence Hall, President Ford read the day's keynote address.

This being an American festival, many new records were claimed: the largest cherry pie (60 square feet), at George, Wash.; the largest cake (69,000 pounds), at Baltimore; the largest fireworks display, in Washington, D.C.; the largest gathering of sailing ships, in New York Harbor.

Yet many sponsors of celebrations were disappointed at the turnouts. The Philadelphia parade, planned for 70,000 marchers, drew about half that

Continued on Page 18, Column 1

The New York Times/Teresa Zabala

President Ford waves to the crowd at Valley Forge, Pa., where he signed a bill making it a national historical site. He stands on a covered wagon that represented Michigan, his home state, in the Bicentennial wagon train.

Ethnic Diversity Adds Spice to the Holiday

The New York Times/Roger W. Strong

City Hall is the scene of street dancing and music in July 4th in Old New York Festival

By FRED FERRETTI

New Yorkers and their friends poured into lower Manhattan yesterday and compressed 200 years of their history and varied ethnic heritages into a day-long birthday party crammed with prayer, martial music, high spirits and good fellowship.

It was the tall ships and the warships that drew them there, but it was Dr. Quackenbush's Traveling Medicine Show, Delancy's Loyalist Red Coat Brigade, Fraunces Tavern, Oscar Brand, falafel and pizza and egg rolls, and John Philip Sousa that kept them there.

Not even a succession of torrential downpours late in the afternoon could drive them away. They watched George III beheaded at Federal Hall National Memorial, listened to Terence Cardinal Cooke pray at Castle Clinton, watched the Turks take over Wall Street for

Continued on Page 22, Column 4

O, Say, It Was a Glorious Patchwork-Quilt of a Fourth

By McCANDLISH PHILLIPS

The Fourth of July celebration in New York City yesterday was as American as a patchwork quilt—full of a joyous order-in-disarray and a series of brilliantly improbable juxtapositions.

It was an exercise in percussion, procession, demonstration, declamation, detonation, commemoration, vociferation, trivialization, solemnization and, for some, indigestion.

The free and independent citizens of New York City got themselves into a good many unusual postures as they scrambled for perspective on events, sometimes at the price of mild peril.

In parks and on piers, on fences, balconies, ramps, rooftops, chimneys, ledges, abutments and the ladders of water storage tanks, they sat, stooped, stood and clung, chiefly to watch great ships come sailing out of the distant past and go up the hazy Hudson like a vision.

It was a great day for family portraits to be taken with the most senior member of the American family. The process began early in the day in front of the Federal Hall National Memorial on Wall Street, on the site where George Washington took the oath as President on April 30, 1789.

Washington's statue dominates the steps leading up to the eight columns of the hall, and the base of the pedestal is a stage large enough for at least half a dozen persons to stand on.

As soon as one group posed and left, the next moved up to be photographed with the unblinkingly obliging founding father.

Seven small children in bright summer colors nearly ringed the great figure, standing under his outstretched right hand their heads reaching to half the height of the pedestal. They looked very serious for the moment or so they stood there.

Though few noticed it, Christopher Columbus was in town. Not the old boy him-

Continued on Page 20, Column 5

NEWS INDEX

The Forrestal's Bell Tolls 13 Times for 13 Colonies

President Does the Honors on Carrier in the Harbor as 3,000 Dignitaries From 70 Nations Crowd Aboard

By FRANK J. PRIAL

It was only one of tens of thousands of Fourth of July parties today, but it was the one to be at.

While most New Yorkers elbowed for room along the Hudson's shoreline, President Ford and the nation's leaders and their friends, and officials of some 70 other nations and their friends, consumed free fried chicken, free hot dogs, free doughnuts and coffee and watched Operation Sail from one of the best vantage points in the harbor.

It took the 90-foot-high flight deck of the 80,000-ton, 1,039-foot-long aircraft carrier Forrestal to have this bash, set against a dramatic background of hundreds of sails, the spray of fireboats and the distant shore of Brooklyn packed with people.

Mr. Ford arrived aboard the Forrestal just after 1:45 P.M. and, precisely at 2, began ringing the huge golden bell of the carrier, which had been specially mounted on the flight deck. He rang the bell 13 times to herald the birthday of the United States.

"This is the greatest day the city ever had," Mayor Beame said. "It's been a fantastic crowd—warm and proud. It's been wonderful for New York."

Music by the Navy

The government leaders, public officials and officials of foreign nations who had been invited aboard were entertained by Navy musicians and singers, protected by Secret Service agents and transported from and to Manhattan at Government expense.

All of the 3,000 very important guests were ferried out from shore by boat. The very, very important guests, at least most of them, arrived by helicopter. Among them, the President himself, Vice President Rockefeller, the Secretary of the Navy, the Secretary of State, the Secretary of Defense, high Navy officials, Mayor Beame and City Council President Paul O'Dwyer, who hitched a ride with the Mayor.

"The Vice President of the United States has just arrived," the announcer told the crowd. "With him is his family." The guests craned their necks to see. They saw Secretary of State Henry A. Kissinger. The Vice President's helicopter had not yet arrived.

'Special Grace and Beauty'

In brief remarks about the bell-ringing, Mr. Ford expressed his gratitude "to everyone who had had a part in making Operation Sail successful," and he called the tall ships "an escort of special grace and beauty." He said the day's celebration had been a fitting way to end the Bicentennial as "we begin our unchartered voyage to the future, to the sea of tomorrow."

"I spent a lot of time on aircraft carriers," he told a delighted group of young sailors. During World War II, the President spent 42 months on active duty in the Navy, about half of it on carriers, according to an aide.

Representative Bella S. Abzug, Democrat of Manhattan and one of the guests, said the day's events showed that "we still have a lot of kick left in us in New York." Mrs. Abzug said she had spent much of the day sitting with Princess Grace of Monaco. "She had a bigger hat on than I do," Mrs. Abzug said.

The first guests came on board just before 8 A.M. and grabbed seats under the bunting erected over the bleachers yesterday by members of the Forrestal crew. The guests were prepared to remain there until 3 P.M. or later, depending on when the review of the tall ships ended. By 9 A.M. most of the bleacher seats were filled or were marked off as taken by guests, who were wandering around the decks looking at the displays of fighter aircraft, Navy recruitment literature and Forrestal souvenirs being sold at a brisk rate.

'A Good Host'

Actually, preparations for the party began days in advance. The bleachers were erected on the flight deck before the Forrestal left Norfolk last Wednesday. Painting and polishing has been going on even longer. "We're old hands at this," said Vice Adm. John J. Shanahan, commander of the Navy's Second Fleet and tactical commander of the International Naval Review. "The Navy knows how to be a good host."

Lesser lights were not so sanguine. "We've had as many as 12,000 visitors in one day," a helicopter pilot said, "but 3,000 all at one time, expecting to be entertained for nine hours or more — that's something else."

Shortly after the President rang the bell, he left the carrier, and there was a great milling around of politicians on deck and a good deal of palaver. Navy officers and South American generals shook hands with Mayor Beame.

Where the food was being served on the hangar deck, one deck below, many who had rushed to see the President lined up again to get their lunch. Within an hour or so, most had boarded the Circle Line boats that were being used as ferries for the trip back to Manhattan.

The New York Times/Carl T. Gossett

Vice President Rockefeller turns photographer on the aircraft carrier Forrestal. Happy, his wife, is next to him.

An Armada of Ships in Hudson Highlights City Events

Continued From Page 1, Col. 8

trol on the narrow Battery streets. There were cries of anger, and some people collapsed and some fainted, and the ambulances could only inch through the masses. It was one of the few untoward moments of the day.

But the miracle was that everything went off pretty much on schedule; the disasters so many had feared did not take place. There was congestion ashore and afloat, but obliging spirits and helping hands turned the most glorious Fourth in 100 years into a happy holiday.

James S. O'Doherty, a spokesman for the organizers of the canvas-powered portion of the extravaganza, said that the performance was "magnificent."

"I never expected it to go this well," he said. "Somehow, you really believe that Murphy's law is going to go into effect. But Murphy left town this weekend."

As for the smaller spectator boats, he said, they showed "remarkable courtesy and care."

According to Murphy's law, everything that can go wrong, will go wrong. It didn't yesterday.

There were accidents.

An outboard-motor boat, carrying four passengers, sank in the upper East River, near North Brother Island. Amalia Tsikis, 37, of Montreal, was drowned. The other three persons in the boat were rescued.

Earlier in the day, two women passengers aboard a 46-foot houseboat in the East River were injured when they were struck by a cinderblock apparently thrown from the Queensboro Bridge. Ina Marlow, 47, of Madison, Wis., was listed in serious but stable condition at Bellevue Hospital. Leona Davis, 51, of Belvedere, Calif., was listed in fair condition, with an injured arm.

There were other mishaps. A spent bullet, fired from a pistol, possibly from Staten Island, grazed the leg of a petty officer aboard the Forrestal. A boy fell out of a tree in Battery Park, where he had climbed to glimpse Operation Sail, suffering a slight injury to a finger.

The Coast Guard estimated that there were 10,000 small craft in the Lower Bay alone while the parade ships shaped up. Most of these went north with the vanguard of the parade, although they were kept efficiently to one side of the route by Coast Guard and police boats that constantly nipped at them, like sheep dogs guarding their flock.

Millions of Viewers

The police estimated that there were six million people who viewed Operation Sail from the New York shores, and there were large numbers who also viewed it from New Jersey.

New Yorkers demonstrated their traditional ingenuity and disdain of planning by appearing in spots from which they were specifically excluded. Some managed to find ways to get on the elevated portions of the West Side Highway below 72d Street. Others perched on cranes, tractor trailers and tugs tied up at piers.

At a Department of Sanitation pier in the West 30's, an elderly woman sat under an umbrella and knitted as the greatest fleet of sail ever to touch at New York passed before her eyes.

E. Virgil Conway, chairman of the Committee for July 4th in Old New York and therefore a man with a vested interest in the occasion, nevertheless spoke for many New Yorkers.

"I do not believe the Fourth of July could happen anywhere else in quite the same way," he said. "New York City is what America is supposed to be."

Although the great events were the formal centerpiece of the day, it was the vast numbers of spectators who almost stole the show. At 57th Street, Howard Goldberg, who had come to look on with friends, used a megaphone to narrate, calling out the names of ships. The crowd cheered.

At 82d Street and Riverside Drive, as the Russian ship Tovarishch, northbound, went past the American ship, Eagle, bound south under full sail, Alan Scott, who had come down from Larchmont, N.Y., for the day with his wife and teen-age son, said:

"I'm so glad we came. We almost didn't come because we listened to all the talk about traffic, but we had no trouble getting here and we've enjoyed every minute of it. It's the most wonderful way to spend the Bicentennial Fourth."

The day dawned cool and bright, in the high 60's and low 70's. Below the Verrazano-Narrows Bridge, the hundreds of sailing ships somehow formed into parade column. It was a question of sorting out the participants from the floating nonparticipants.

There was an amazing variety of onlooker craft along the route: family yawls, pleasure runabouts, enormous steamships and the ferryboat John J. Kennedy. Laden on one side with passengers eager not to miss anything: the ferryboat developed a list that would have caused concern on a normal day, but did not draw undue notice under the circumstances.

2 on a Raft

In the middle of the bay, a rubber raft with an outboard motor confounded veteran boaters who admired the courage and sneered at the foolhardiness of its two-man crew, who frequently dipped out of sight in a choppy sea compounded by wind and thousands of wakes.

At exactly 11 A.M., the Coast Guard's three-masted bark Eagle, moved under the great bridge between Brooklyn and Staten Island. Her jibsails, staysails and spanker rose high above her trim white hull. On the yardarms, crewmen stood, leaning into the wind.

Next came the Danmark, her cadets lining the yardarms with their feet balanced precariously —or so it seemed to onlooking landlubbers—on ropes below the spars.

The procession sailed past the Forrestal, whose flight deck was occupied by a grandstand for 3,000 distinguished guests, among them Mr. Rockefeller, who flew off by helicopter shortly afterward to board the cruiser Wainwright near the George Washington Bridge and sail down river for the International Naval Review.

A Bewildering Variety

As each sailing ship crossed the bow of the Forrestal, crews dressed ship, on the port side. They were deployed in a bewildering variety of designs. On the Amerigo Vespucci, the elegant Italian full-rigged ship, they stood like beads up the ratlines to the masts and along the long bowsprit.

The Nippon Maru, Japan's four-masted bark, provided perhaps the livliest salute. Her crew cheered simultaneously, on cue, and waved their yellow caps. It was a roar that could be heard, but not understood, across the water.

One of the proudest ships in procession was also one of the largest, the Soviet Union's 378-foot-long, four-masted bark, Kruzenshtern. Built as a German sailing ship in 1926, she was known as the Padua and is the last of the cargo-carrying Cape Horners still in service. She carried grain from Australia and nitrates from Chile in record-making runs to Europe.

Aboard the Sagres II, Portugal's three-masted bark, the cadets stood like silhouettes in a cut-out doily pattern, arms stretched out, man almost touching man, along the bare masts. They waved their hats in unison as they went past the Forrestal.

Similarly, aboard Spain's Juan Sebastian de Elcano, the crew was spaced, not bunched, along the yardarms and bowsprit, etched against the sky in impressive formation.

All of the 16 tall ships were built after the age of sail. The oldest and smallest, the Gazela Primeiro, was built in 1883 and was, until recently, a working Grand Banks Portuguese fisherman; she now belongs to a Philadelphia museum and is the only one with a wooden hull. The Dar Pomorza, a Polish vessel, was launched in 1909. One ship present was born in [illegible] eight in the 1930's and the remaining four in the 19[illegible] and 1960's.

There were ships of character among the other sailing vessels in the show: the Sir Winston Churchill, with her all-woman crew; the towering four-masted sloop Club Mediterraneo, which can be handled by one man; the Chinese junk Mon Lei, the oldest ship afloat in the harbor, built in Fukien in 1855.

Sudden Change of Plan

By 1:30 the Eagle was under the George Washington Bridge. Instead of continuing to Spuyten Duyvil on Manhattan's northern tip, she put about early, to the consternation of thousands of northern spectators in Fort Washington and Inwood and their opposite points in New Jersey. Other ships proceeded according to plan.

About that time, the cruiser Wainwright weighed anchor with Mr. Rockefeller, Secretary of State Henry A. Kissinger and Defense Secretary Donald H. Rumsfeld aboard. The review consisted of her journey past the other anchored military shipping to the Forrestal.

The 8,500-ton Wainwright, a guided-missile cruiser, created a stir in traffic as she sailed south, opposite the uptown-bound fleet. She just managed to miss hitting an anchored catamaran and, at one point, moved to the center of the river to give more room to the sailing ships on her New Jersey beam.

Capt. Eugene B. Ackerman, the Wainwright's skipper, relaxed his naval reserve to discuss the traffic: "It was a terrifying experience, but we got through it all right. These small ships are more maneuverable than we are, and most of them got out of the way fine."

There was almost a tangible bond between ships and shore. People waved and applauded, knowing that they might not be seen or heard. There were banners and painted greetings, from large, professional welcomes to small red, white and blue salutations.

From the moment the parade formed in the Narrows, spearheaded by 16, or perhaps 20, or perhaps more tugs and preceded by a fireboat that lofted finger-like pillars of spray, the crowd was enthusiastic. It was a spirit that lasted the day, rain or shine.

At night, a brilliant effusion of pyrotechnics illuminated the harbor. The ships were at their berths and the people started home after a long day. It had been a grand Fourth, a respite from worries about municipal bankruptcy, crime in the streets and the daily realities.

Bonnie Rhodes, a 22-year-old Californian who arrived here three days ago, was selling official New York Bicentennial shirts on West 79th Street. She said what older New Yorkers would rarely dare confess:

"New York must be the most wonderful city in the world. I've never seen anything quite like it."

Norway's Crew Salutes 2 Important Birthdays

By TONY KORNHEISER

At 11:29 yesterday morning, 17-year-old Erik Blom, a cadet on board the full-rigged Norweigan tall ship, the Christian Radich, took his trumpet to his lips — from 130 feet up in the rigging above the deck — and played one chorus of "Happy Birthday."

He played it just as the the United States aircraft carrier Forrestal. He played it to Norway's Crown Princess, Sonja, who was standing on the deck of the Forrestal with her husband, Crown Prince Harald, because she was 39 years old yesterday and celebrating a birthday.

And Cadet Blom played it to the millions of United States citizens who were in the metropolitan area, in honor of their nation, which was 200 years old yesterday and celebrating its Bicentennial.

And later, Mr. Blom admitted that he had been "just a little bit nervous."

There had never been anything like this maritime salute before, and the young cadets of the Christian Radich who had attempted at first to be blasé about the event—the 15- and 16- and 17-year-old boys who make up the ship's 87-man crew—were finally swept away in the tide of the spectacle.

In the early morning hours Saturday, the crew of the Radish—the name given the ship by American tourists in Newport, R. I.—were professing equanimity toward the Bicentennial. No emotion. Just another day at the office.

"What is there to get excited about?" asked Olav Midttun, 17. "We are used to all the boats from our stay in Newport. Maybe if I were American, I'd be more excited."

'Only Sailors Understand'

"I am sorry," said Johan Meyer, 17. "I am very happy to be in America and help you celebrate your birthday. But it is your birthday. I am Norwegian, and I can't jump and scream."

It was a studied cool, a learned calm. But it did not convince the officers, and it did not last long.

"I think they are just pretending to be calm," said Hendrik Wrede, the ship's second mate. "Otherwise, they are crazy. This is an event for your whole life. I think sailors should feel it most because 99 percent of the other people will think it is a circus, and only sailors will understand it."

The Christian Radich was third in line in the parade Saturday, behind the Eagle and the Danmark. There was a picnic atmosphere aboard the ship, with 36 visiting dignitaries in the official Norwegian party, sipping drinks and eating cheese and stew as the ship sailed.

A haze shrouded the approach to New York Harbor underneath the Verrazano-Narrows Bridge, casting a surreal mood over the miles-long line of tall ships.

At the sides of the tall ships, Coast Guard boats acted like pulling guards on a football field, leading the ships through an uncluttered path, stripping all interference. Underneath the bridge the various warships and carriers and destroyers formed a path to usher them on to this greater audience.

By 11:15 A.M., the Radich was under the bridge, honking her great foghorn at the other ships in salute as she passed by. By 12:15 in the afternoon, she had opened up most of her sails for visual effects (the wind was in the wrong direction) but she was still traveling under engine power, cruising the line at a steady speed of two knots.

All Cool Vanishes

Around the Radich was spread a scene reminiscent of a Dino De Laurentiis extravaganza film. There were all the people, many stuffed into the ferryboats and day cruisers until the boats listed, swelled and bulged at the sides. There were helicopters flying by, and blimps circling lazily in the air. There were gun salutes near the Statue of Liberty and great fountains of water shooting out from fireboats.

And about that time, all cool vanished from the young men of the Radich.

Young Mr. Midttun grabbed his camera and began shooting pictures. So did Mr. Meyer. So did most of the rest of the crew, appearing on deck with all sorts of photographic equipment. And, of course, the officers—the sailing men who knew all along what a spectacle this would be—joined in taking pictures.

"I want to take these pictures to fix this adventure in my mind," said Mr. Meyer. "So I can remember it always. I was wrong about not caring. It seems I care very much."

Later, at 4 P.M., when the Christian Radich was docked at the South Street Seaport, her parade into history completed, the captain tried to put the event into perspective. Kjell Thorsen is a student of history, a man of the sea and, perhaps, very wise in both. He said:

"I think it might take years for the boys to understand and appreciate what happened here. They cannot have a wide view yet since they are so young. But some day they will know that this was history.

"Never before have so many ships gathered like this in peace and friendship. . . . I am a navy man, a fighting man. But it is time to stop fighting. This is a chance to get together for peace. It will not happen again, I shouldn't think. I hope this time it will work."

Fireworks Emblazon Sky Around Statue of Liberty

By MURRAY SCHUMACH

New York Harbor became more brilliant than Broadway last night as the biggest and most colorful fireworks display in the city's history exploded for half an hour in celebration of the nation's Bicentennial.

Never had so many people watched a fireworks show. Hundreds of thousands packed along the shoreline and river front of the city and New Jersey to marvel at the streaking rockets and the thudding guns, and to listen to quotations from great Americans and to patriotic music. In addition, many millions more watched on screens at home, as television networks broadcast the spectacle in color throughout the country.

At times this "choreographed" exhibition, operated by push-button electronics, made the night skies sheets of gold or silver, visible for more than 15 miles.

The huge crowds formed a human carpet across the tip of Manhattan, covering the parks, the sidewalks, the curbs. Spectators were perched on window ledges and on automobile roofs and hoods.

In the crush, scores of people suffered injuries. However, they were mostly minor ones. Beekman-Downtown Hospital said shortly after midnight that it still had three ambulances out on call after treating nearly 100 people for everything from bruises and exhaustion to fractures and heart attacks.

The crowds applauded and whistled as the chrysanthemums and fingers of color exploded and became brilliant drops in the sky.

But many standing well back from the waterfront expressed disappointment during a five-minute period early in the show when the display seemed geared more for the television viewers than for the spectators at the harbor. But as the fireworks approached their climax of noise and color, everyone was enthusiastic.

National Anthem Sung

But the climax of the display of fireworks—which were fired from Liberty Island, Ellis Island, Governors Island and three barges in the harbor—was not an explosion of color. It was the short period in which the masses of spectators turned toward the Statue of Liberty and joined in singing "The Star-Spangled Banner," while a helicopter, towing a flag of red, white and blue lights, 60 by 100 feet, flew over the harbor.

The fireworks display, produced by Macy's with technical help from the Disney organization, took months of preparation and the cooperation of the Navy, the Army Corps of Engineers, the Coast Guard, the Marines, the Police and Fire Departments, the New York Telephone Company, the Council of Churches, the Federal Communications Commission and the Federal Aviation Administration.

Thousands who watched the fireworks had picked their spots hours before the display began, at 9 P.M. Many people, having heard that the show would combine music and commentary with the fireworks, had brought radios and tuned them to WNYC-FM or to WNBC-AM to hear the words of Washington, Lincoln, John Adams, Grant, Dwight D. Eisenhower, Emma Goldman, John F. Kennedy and the Rev. Dr. Martin Luther King, Jr.

Gettysburg Address

From Lincoln's Gettysburg address, they heard:

"That this nation, under God, shall have a new birth of freedom; and that government of the people, by the people and for the people shall not perish from the earth."

From the speech President Kennedy had planned to deliver in Dallas in 1963:

"We in this country, in this generation are—by destiny rather than choice—the watchmen of the walls of world freedom."

"From Dr. King's speech that same year on the steps of the Lincoln Memorial:

"When we let freedom ring from every tenement and every hamlet, from every state and every city, we will be able to speed up that day when all of God's children—black men and white men, Jews and gentiles, Protestants and Catholics—will be able to join hands and sing the words of the old spiritual: 'Free at last! Free at last! Thank God Almighty, we are free at last.' "

O, Say, What a Patchwork-Quilt of a Fourth

Continued From Page 1, Col. 8

self, of course, but the closest living approximation that genes and genealogy will allow—in the person of Lieut. Cristóbal Colón de Carvajal y Gorosábel of the Spanish navy.

He crossed the great Atlantic—how else?—by commercial jetliner from Madrid, which is not the way his illustrious forebear did it, but then he is not a slavish imitator, declining as he did to get into a Christopher Columbus suit during yesterday's pageant on the water.

He was in the New World on his honeymoon with his bride—Isabel de Maudaluniz y Castelo, daughter of the Marquis of Taurisano, a captain of the fleet in the Spanish Navy—whom he wed on June 22. His intention is to trace the present status of things along the eastern ridge of his family's discovery, with stops in Atlantic City, Philadelphia and Disney World in Florida.

With no fanfare, Christopher Columbus, the 17th in a direct line of succession, stepped onto a launch off Bethune Street in Greenwich Village and went out to board the rough model of the Santa Maria that later sailed at the head of the Class C vessels. Now and then, Lieutenant Columbus took the wheel.

The couple had come at the invitation of Lowell Lytle, president of Young American Showcase, which built the imitation vessel.

"Why did you decide to come?" the guest was asked in a shoreside interview.

"Because I am aware of the heritage of my name and because it would be very representative to be here, as a humble person carrying this name, for the American holiday," he said. "There is no bettter time for us to come in our happy circumstances of discovering a new world with our new lives."

It was a perfect little speech, perfectly suited to his perfect manner. He is a flashingly handsome officer, and his wife is a finely featured young woman who could be cast in the role of a princess at a glance.

"Has there been a strong naval tradition through the generations in your family?" he was asked.

"No," he said. "There have been a few—one in about the 1600's, about four—with me, five."

"What an enormous coincidence that your name is Isabel," someone interjected, addressing his wife with almost immeasurable enthusiasm, and Mrs. Christopher Columbus smiled a very small smile.

●

The scene at the In Old New York celebration in lower Manhattan was a medley of many things verging successfully on a mishmash.

Artists and artisans, some of them people of truly dreadful talent, set up little stalls showing leather goods, wrought metal objects, wax candles, ceramics, straw goods, dried floral bouquets and a good many other things.

They were no match for the hawkers who thronged the financial district.

From No. 1 Broadway to No. 7, there were 13 of them selling sandwiches, hats, sun glasses, Op Sail programs, American flags, shirts, model ships, flag buttons, names formed in wire, posters, T shirts, field glasses and pretzels. Half of them were shouting.

The malefactors of small change were present in so high a per-capita ratio to the pedestrian population that they did not do much business.

"It's dead," one sidewalk merchant said. Then he lifted his voice: "Remember, there's only one Bicentennial. This is it."

●

On the theory that great truths can be gleaned better from small particulars than from sweeping generalities, and out of curiosity about where the spectators had come from, a census was taken of two dozen consecutive people sitting on the middle divider on the West Side Highway, which had been turned into a pocked and pitted pedestrian promenade for the day.

The result: Boston; Westchester County; Manhattan; Fitchburg, Mass.; Manhattan; Morristown, N.J.; Manhattan; Manhattan; Hilton Head Islands, N.C.; Westchester; Miami; Manhattan; Yonkers; Wilmington, Del.; Brooklyn; Huntington, L.I.; Queens; Westchester; Bolivia; Lansing, Mich.; Queens; Queens; Queens, and Manhattan.

●

At the out-of-town newsstand in Times Square, Brian Carey was asked if tourists had been clamoring for hometown newspapers in unusual numbers. The stand carries 130 papers, and Mr. Carey can snatch them on the second syllable of a request.

"No, not much call for hometown papers," he said. "It's mostly for New York papers with specials on the Bicentennial, and we're getting a lot of calls for Philadelphia and Washington papers, where they know the things are going on."

●

On almost any weekday, the dark-tinted Merrill Lynch brokerage tower at 1 Liberty Plaza has 6,000 to 7,000 occupants. Yesterday there were just about that number, too. But they were there to take semi-reserved window spaces on the upper 34 stories of the 54-story structure above the Hudson.

Eighteen floors had been opened for this purpose, but no one got in without a pass, carefully distributed in advance to employees and friends.

Those holding passes moved through a system of velvet ropes set up in the lobby to weed out eager interlopers.

Many of the city's tallest buildings used similar arrangements, and uncounted thousands saw the stately spectacle in this way.

●

Twenty-two stories above Riverside Drive at 103d Street, Vicent di Liberto walked out his back door and held a family reunion in his "backyard."

His relatives dwell in suburban-like settings and usually they think the advantage is theirs, but yesterday they flocked with one accord to share his idyllic Manhattan perch well above surrounding rooftops and commanding a great sweep of the Hudson River. At least once every 200 years, they conceded, the advantage is his.

●

Jerry Dundon, who is now 46, began working the harbor as a deckhand at 14 years of age, so he has been going at it for 32 years.

William Duncan went to work a little later, at 18, but he has lived a little longer, so he's had 38 years on the job. Now, at 56, he is a man of bulky proportions with a large and weathered, pleasant face.

Both men are exacting and skillful specialists of the harbor, working as ship docking pilots. When ships come into the harbor and there is work to do, they do it. Yesterday they were on the job for the McAllister Brothers towing concern by 7 A.M., and they were still at it after midnight.

"You've heard how it is with two porcupines who fall in love—they approach each other very carefully?" Mr. Dundon said. "Well, that's how it is when tugboats work with ships like these."

●

Many waterside spectators were of the landbound sort who cannot tell a schooner from a lobster bisque until they see the prices. Some had sketches identifying a dozen or more of the major classes of ships passing by, and, glancing from ship to paper to ship again, they managed to sound quite knowledgeable.

Yet few were prepared for the engaging flotilla of nine old leeboard Dutch sloops that came upriver in a V formation, escorting the schooner Eendracht. The crews were got up in 17th-century costumes.

Among the sloops were the Bolle Beertje, a 40-foot Vollenhovense Bolout of Woubrugge; the Dankbaarheid, a 50-foot Zeeuse Poon out of Muiden; De Hop, a 39-foot Harderwijkse Paat out of Vinkeveen; Schumer, a 30-foot Schokker out of Woudrichem, and Sevija, a 37-foot Lemsteraak out of Huizen.

Just saying them left a [illegible]-year-old Manhattanite out of breath.

"All the News That's Fit to Print"

The New York Times

LATE CITY EDITION

Weather: Chance of rain late today, tonight. Partly sunny tomorrow. Temperature range: today 72-86; Tuesday 66-90. Details on page 65.

VOL. CXXV . . No. 43,278

NEW YORK, WEDNESDAY, JULY 21, 1976

25 cents beyond 50-mile zone from New York City, except Long Island. Higher in air delivery cities.

20 CENTS

VIKING ROBOT SETS DOWN SAFELY ON MARS AND SENDS BACK PICTURES OF ROCKY PLAIN

Associated Press

A composite photo showing a 300-degree panorama of the surface of Mars, made by a camera on the Viking 1 landing craft just after touchdown on the planet yesterday morning. Parts of the craft are visible in foreground.

Associated Press

Foot pad of the Viking 1 resting on Mars. Center of this picture is five feet from camera and the rock at center is approximately four inches across.

3¼-HOUR DESCENT

Scientists Are Jubilant as News Is Flashed, Taking 19 Minutes

By JOHN NOBLE WILFORD

Special to The New York Times

PASADENA, Calif., July 20—An explorer from Earth, the robot craft Viking 1, made the first successful landing on Mars today and transmitted spectacular photographs of a rocky, wind-scoured desert plain, the site for the first direct search for life on another world.

The squat, three-legged Viking landing craft came to rest, upright and intact, on the Chryse Plain of Mars at 7:53 A.M. Eastern daylight time after a voyage of 11 months and nearly half a billion miles. The final and most suspenseful step, the craft's descent to the surface from its mother ship in Mars orbit, took 3 hours 13 minutes.

Then, Touchdown

Responding to automatic computer commands, the lander's rockets fired, its parachute unfurled, protective shielding broke away, more rockets were fired—and then, touchdown. It was 19 minutes, because of the great distance between Mars and Earth, now more than 212 million miles, before confirmation of the safe landing reached the control rooms here at the Jet Propulsion Laboratory.

"Touchdown!" announced Richard Bender, one of the flight controllers. "We have touchdown. We have several indications of touchdown."

It was an emotional moment for the scientists and engineers of the $1 billion Viking project, many of whom had spent eight years preparing for this day.

Applause and Amazement

There was applause in the control room and throughout the laboratory. There were broad smiles and moist eyes. There were soft expressions of numbed amazement at what they had wrought.

With the Viking landing begins the first surface exploration of Mars (two Soviet landings failed to produce usable data). The planet has fascinated man for centuries and been the object of legend and endless scientific speculation.

In eight days, if all continues to go according to plan, a mechanical arm on the lander is to reach out and scoop up soil samples for chemical and biological analysis by onboard instruments. This will mark the beginning of the mission's search for signs of possible life on Mars.

Though Mars is no longer seriously thought of as an

Continued on Page 12, Column 1

Nitrogen, Key to Life, Is Found

By WALTER SULLIVAN

Special to The New York Times

PASADENA, Calif., July 20—The first definitive analysis of the Martian atmosphere has disclosed the presence of a small component of nitrogen. Until now the absence of any evidence of that gas stood as a major obstacle to speculation that life might exist on the planet.

The analysis has also provided long-sought clues to the history of Mars, including the possibility that enough water is hidden beneath its surface to cover the planet one mile deep.

The chief surprise has been Viking's discovery that argon, an inert gas, constitutes far less of the Martian atmosphere than scientists previously believed. Whereas estimates of the argon level on Mars had been as high as 30 percent, data from Viking indicate that it is only about 3 percent, compared with about 1 percent in the Earth's atmosphere.

The analysis also put the level of nitrogen at about 3 percent.

This and other detailed determinations should bear on such questions as the history of the Earth's known atmosphere, including the proposal that the atmosphere of both Earth and Mars were formed in eruptions very early in each planet's history.

Such an early formation of the atmosphere would mean, as well, the early appearance of oceans or smaller water bodies suitable for the evolution of life.

Higher Ratio Suggested

When the Soviet Union's Mars 6 plunged into the Mars atmosphere in its unsuccessful landing attempt in 1974 it was thought that perplexing features of its data transmissions could be explained if 30 percent of the Martian air consisted of argon. The possibility of so large a percentage also offered an explanation for observations made near one of the Martian poles a few days ago by the Viking mother ship that cast loose the lander today.

Today's measurement, which is considered definitive, put the argon level at about 3 percent.

The lower abundance of argon is good news for those experimenters hoping to learn the composition of Mars's surface materials. Their instrument aboard the lander will determine such compositions with a gas chromatograph mass spectrometer that could have been rendered useless by an atmosphere rich in argon.

The project's scientists believe that today's measurements will help clarify whether, as some of them believe, there is still enough water hidden beneath the surface of Mars to cover that planet to a depth of one mile.

The abundance of argon in the air of Mars today is a critical index of the atmosphere's history. If volcanic eruptions and other processes generated the same atmospheric constituents as those produced by such activity on Earth the present abundance of argon could, it was argued, have been as high as reported by the Russians.

The reasoning is that since

Continued on Page 12, Column 4

United Press International

Dr. James Fletcher, left, and James S. Martin, on phones, being congratulated by President Ford as other officials watched a television set for first Mars photographs.

Ford Gains 10 Delegates And Needs Only 18 More

By JAMES M. NAUGHTON

Special to The New York Times

WASHINGTON, July 20—President Ford gained substantial delegate strength today to pull within 18 votes of the total needed to gain a first-ballot nomination at the Republican National Convention.

Amid conflicting claims from the rival Republican camps, The New York Times determined from the best available information and a canvass of the delegates involved that Mr. Ford had a net gain of 10 delegates while Ronald Reagan had a net increase of one.

The new tally by The Times listed 1,112 delegates for Mr. Ford—18 short of the 1,130 needed for nomination — and 1,064 for Mr. Reagan, with 83 still uncommitted. Thirteen of the 83 said they were leaning to Mr. Ford and three to Mr. Reagan.

James A. Baker, a deputy chairman of the President Ford Committee, claimed the conversion of several delegates and proposed to certify the President's strength by making public the identities of all Ford delegates once they constitute a convention majority.

The proposal to list the delegates by name and address was the latest move in a war of nerves between supporters of the President and of Mr. Reagan.

Mr. Baker dismissed as "blowing smoke" the largely unsubstantiated claim yesterday by John P. Sears, the Reagan campaign manager, to 1,140 delegates for the former California Governor—10 more than needed for nomination.

Mr. Sears retaliated later to-

Continued on Page 22, Column 1

U.S. AGENCY FINDS DRUG TESTING LAX

Says F.D.A., Makers and Others Expose the Public to Needless Risks

By RICHARD HALLORAN

Special to The New York Times

WASHINGTON, July 20—Congressional investigators have issued a blistering indictment of the Food and Drug Administration, pharmaceutical makers, doctors and research scientists, charging them with exposing humans to unnecessary risks in testing new drugs.

The General Accounting Office also reported that the testing procedures could result in F.D.A. approval of a new drug for public use based on "inaccurate and unreliable data."

The Congressional investigating unit disclosed instances of "alarming adverse reactions" to new drugs that went unreported and the death of eight soldiers in an Army test of a drug intended to prevent malaria.

Despite continued controversy over many aspects of the regulation of prescription drugs in recent years, the general ac-

Continued on Page 8, Column 1

South African Black Is Reported Killed In Renewed Rioting

By JOHN F. BURNS

Special to The New York Times

JOHANNESBURG, July 20—At least one black man was reported killed tonight when police reinforcements were rushed to the coal-mining center of Witbank, 75 miles east of here, which was in the grip of the most serious rioting since the widespread anti-Government upheavals last month.

Reports from the scene said that about 3,000 black youths had poured out of black townships and attacked people and buildings in areas occupied by Indians and people of mixed descent, who are called colored here.

Few details were available, and it was unclear how the reported death had occurred. However, the riot policemen, armed with automatic rifles, were acting under standing Government orders to suppress fresh outbreaks of violence with all necessary force.

The possibility of a chain reaction was raised by a police report of at least one outbreak elsewhere. At midnight, rioters were said to have set fire to several buildings in Khutsong, a black township near Carletonville, a mining town southwest of Johannesburg.

The death would be the first since the end of the rioting

Continued on Page 4, Column 7

GOLD PLUNGES 12% IN WEEK TO $107.75

Slump Hurts South Africa —Heavy Soviet Selling Is Seen as Part of Cause

By PETER T. KILBORN

Special to The New York Times

LONDON, July 20 — The turmoil that has been swirling through many nations' currencies has now swept into gold, long a major component, along with the dollar, of the world's monetary reserves.

In only five business days, the price of gold has tumbled nearly 12 percent, from $122 an ounce last Wednesday to $107.75 at its close today in London. Today alone it fell nearly $6.

The drop has been so abrupt, gold experts here said, that South Africa, the world's leading producer of gold, now faces political as well as economical consequences unless the price recovers quickly.

"If you take the gold out of South Africa," said Richard Lockwood, a mining expert for a brokerage firm in London, "you've got one of the worst economies in the world."

Experts also expected difficulties for the Soviet Union, another major producer. Ironically, they said, the Russians helped bring on the decline in

Continued on Page 47, Column 5

Rao Indictments Obtained By Nadjari Are Reinstated

By MAX H. SEIGEL

The Appellate Division in Brooklyn yesterday reinstated perjury indictments obtained by Maurice H. Nadjari against Judge Paul P. Rao Sr. of United States Customs Court; his son, Paul Jr., and another lawyer, Salvatore Nigrone.

The indictments had been dismissed last Dec. 2 by the late Justice John M. Murtagh of State Supreme Court on the ground that undercover agents had made statements to the grand jury that "were highly prejudicial to the defendants." Justice Murtagh also had questioned whether the evidence before the grand jury was legally sufficient to establish the offense charged.

Several weeks after the dismissal of the indictments, which involved a manufactured "robbery" case, Governor Carey cited the Rao reversal—and others that had occurred less than a month earlier—in announcing his intention to dismiss Mr. Nadjari as the special state prosecutor looking into the criminal-justice system in New York City.

In its 4-to-1 decision reinstating the indictments, the Appellate Division majority said that it acted "on the law" without going into the actual merits of the case.

The majority found that Justice Murtagh had said improperly that he was dismissing the indictments "in the interests of justice" while he had actually ordered the dismissal

Continued on Page 67, Column 1

Long Offers 2d Vote In Tax-Aid Dispute

By EILEEN SHANAHAN

Special to The New York Times

WASHINGTON, July 20—Russell B. Long, chairman of the Senate Finance Committee, promised today to give the panel a new opportunity to vote for or against each of 73 provisions of the pending tax bill, most of which benefit just one company or industry.

Senator Long made the commitment after an unusually heated session of the committee during which Senator Edward M. Kennedy was, in effect, called a demagogue by one Republican member and accused of not knowing what he was talking about by another.

Mr. Kennedy, Democrat of Massachusetts, has emerged as a leading foe of the kind of narrow-interest tax legislation

Continued on Page 42, Column 4

Attica Is Termed as Bad As Before 1971 Rebellion

By FRED FERRETTI

Special to The New York Times

ATTICA, N.Y., July 20 — The chief of a State Commission of Correction team sent into the Attica prison last week following the most recent outbreak of violence there described conditions within the facility today as "just as bad, perhaps worse" than in September 1971, just before an inmate rebellion that resulted in the deaths of 43 persons.

"What we have is a combat situation," said Scott Christianson, director of the Correction Commission's State Prison Unit, following five days of investigation and interrogation of inmates and guards. "The environment is so physical, so potentially dangerous, the power of both the inmates and the guards is so awesome, that it can go off at any time. Both sides have the power of death in their hands."

The superintendent of the prison, Harold J. Smith, conceded in an interview that an inmate rebellion could happen again. "Yes, it could," he said, "I'd be a damn fool to say otherwise."

The Correction Commission has reported formally to Governor Carey that a set of parallels exists between the situation here today and what it was in Attica just before Sept. 9, 1971, when the prisoners revolted. The prison was subsequently recaptured by state troopers who stormed it.

The new report urged the

Continued on Page 65, Column 1

NEWS INDEX

Viking Robot Sets Down Safely on Mars and Transmits Pictures of Rocky Plain

Scientists Jubilant as 11-Month Trip Ends and the Search for Life Begins

Continued From Page 1, Col. 8

abode of "supercivilizations," as it was as recently as the early 20th century, scientists generally believe that it, of all the planets in the solar system, could be the most hospitable to some forms of life.

But in addition to its life-detection laboratory, the Viking lander has instruments to study Martian soil chemistry, weather and atmosphere, seismic activity and geology. As such, it is the most sophisticated vehicle ever dispatched to a neighboring world.

At a news conference after the landing and the transmission of two clear black-and-white photographs of the spacecraft and its surroundings, James S. Martin Jr., the project manager, said:

"This has got to be the happiest time of my life. It's incredible to me that it all worked so perfectly."

Of the Viking's first two pictures, Dr. Thomas A. Mutch of Brown University, the geologist in charge of the imaging team, spoke with unabashed excitement, "It just couldn't be better."

The photographs disclosed that the 1,300-pound lander had settled on a plain strewn with rocks. Some were dark, others light. Many of them had sharp edges as if they had undergone very little erosion, but others were more rounded. The geologists on the Viking team refrained from giving more detailed interpretations of what they were seeing.

Sand and Craters

In a 300-degree panorama of Viking's strange new surroundings there could be seen what appeared to be sand dunes, a depression that might be an eroded crater, bright patches of sand, rocks partly buried by drifting sand, some low ridges and, out on the horizon about two miles away, a ridge that scientists said could be the rim of a large impact crater.

Dr. Carl Sagan o. Cornell University, an astronomer on the imaging team, remarked, "Even in a place chosen for its blandness, for safety reasons, Mars is an extraordinarily interesting place."

To Alan B. Binder of Science Applications, Inc., another member of the team, the landing region seemed "very reminiscent of fairly heavily eroded lava fields one sees in Arizona and northern Mexico."

Other scientists tended to agree, after a hurried examination of the pictures, that the primary material in the area was most likely volcanic in origin, but that it had been modified by meteoric impacts, the winds of the thin Martian atmosphere and possibly water erosion.

A Bright Sky

Project scientists were surprised by the brightness of the sky. It was late afternoon on a midsummer day at the landing site. (The Martian day is 24 hours 37 minutes long, and the Martian year lasts 25 months.) A shadow in one picture suggested that a cloud, formed by the small amounts of water vapor known to be in the Martian atmosphere might have passed over the lander. In the distant sky there were several horizontal layers of wispy clouds.

The photographs were taken by one of the lander's two identical cameras, beginning within a minute after the touchdown. They were transmitted in the form of electronic data to the orbiting vehicle, more than 12,000 miles above the Martian surface, and then relayed to a tracking antenna on Earth.

The first picture began taking shape on television screens in the control center at 8:54 A.M. It took 22 minutes for the picture to be completed, line by vertical scan line. The photograph covered a 50-degree-wide area, as close as two feet from the spacecraft at the bottom and six feet away at the top of the screen.

Selecting Site

Between now and the time when the mechanican arm on the lander scoops up soil samples, Viking is to transmit several more pictures, including some in color and others in stereoscopic form. These will be used by scientists in selecting a promising place for the scoop to collect its samples.

The first photograph also showed that the lander's foot pad had made little or no penetration in the firm soil. Other data indicated that it had set down gently at a velocity of 5.5 miles an hour, as planned, and that all systems aboard appeared to be functioning normally.

The exact location of the landing site has yet to be determined. But A. Thomas Young, the mission director, said that, since all steps in the descent sequence appear to have gone precisely according to plan, it is assumed that the vehicle put down close to the center of its target area, an ellipse 62 miles wide and 130 miles long. It is on the western slopes of Chryse Planitia, the "gold plain" of Mars, at 22.4 degrees north latitude and 47.5 degrees west longitude.

The Viking I spacecraft—the combined orbiter and lander vehicles—had gone into orbit of the planet on June 19 and spent the last four weeks photographing the surface in search of a relatively flat and safe place to land.

As soon as transmission of the first picture ended, the screen cleared and the vertical lines of the second and more impressive picture began to form.

It took 36 minutes to complete the panoramic view, a nearly complete circumference of the landing area. Often the view reduced Dr. Mutch to such unscientific expressions as "just lovely, just lovely," and "ths is just an incredible scene." At the sight of one field of boulders, he said with a grin, "As we sophisticated geologists say, those are dark rocks."

Pictures Are Analyzed

A more detailed analysis of the photographs is already under way by geologists, physicists, meteorologists, biologists and astronomers. The quality of the pictures is also being enhanced by computer processing of the returned electronic signals.

During the transmission, President Ford telephoned from the White House to congratulate the Viking team. He spoke to Dr. James C. Fletcher, the administrator of the National Aeronautics and Space Administration and Mr. Martin, both of whom were in the control room.

Calling it "a job well done" Mr. Ford reminded them that their success came on the seventh anniversary of the Apollo 11 landing on the moon, the first time men set foot on another world. The President had declared July 20, 1976, Space Exploration Day.

As soon as the President hung up, Dr. Mutch continued his first-impression commentary on the incoming photographs. He noted that shadows cast by rocks on Mars were softer than those on the moon, which he attributed to the diffusion of sunlight by the thin Martian atmosphere; the moon is airless.

At one point, his excitement rising, Dr. Mutch remarked, "You just wish you could be standing there, walking across that terrain."

Several other scientists said that the first pictures were much sharper and clearer than they had expected. They had also feared that they would lose radio contact with the lander before the completion of the panorama.

But the orbiting vehicle remained in range of Earth just long enough to complete the transmission before passing behind Mars.

The next picture transmission from Viking is scheduled to begin just before noon tomorrow. It is to be a color photograph.

At a news conference later, project scientists said that they had seen nothing in the photographs suggesting the presence of any forms of life, but they had not really expected any visible signs. Nor did they see any readily identifiable evidence of water, on or below the surface, having once eroded the area.

Orbital photographs of the regions nearby strongly suggested that floods of water once caused deep channels in the surface and left islands shaped like teardrops. The landing site was thought to be an area where sediment from those ancient floods could have been deposited. And instruments on the orbiting craft had detected significant amounts of water vapor in the atmosphere over the low-lying Chryse region.

The principal constituent of the Martian atmosphere, which is only 1 percent as dense as the Earth's, is carbon dioxide. Small amounts of argon, a rare inert gas, were detected in the atmosphere during the lander's descent. More substantial amounts of argon had been predicted by earlier Soviet findings and by Viking orbital observations.

The presence of sharp-edged rocks raised some scientific eyebrows, for it indicated that erosional forces (either wind or water) may not be very recent or strong. Dr. Sagan suggested three possible interpretations—either the rocks were recently fractured by some catastrophic event, or they were formed long ago but buried early and recently exhumed, or the erosional processes "are relatively feeble in this area."

Winds of more than 200 miles an hour have been observed on Mars, creating global dust storms. But with the rarefied atmosphere, a 200-mile wind on Mars would be comparable to a 20-mile wind on earth.

In many ways, Dr. Mutch reflected, the most interesting object in the photographs was the lander itself, bristling with booms and antennas, its three legs solidly planted on the plain.

"When you go to an unknown place you look around for a friend," he commented, "and the lander is a good friend, a very good friend."

Its descent to the surface began when it separated from the orbiting vehicle at 4:40 A.M. The "go" command for separation had been radioed to the spacecraft computer a couple of hours before hand. The command was a single coded word KVUGNG.

From then on, the spacecraft was on its own, operated by commands that had been programmed in its commuter over the weekend.

Pyrotechnic devices were fired to release the lander from the orbiter. Three sets of springs gently pushed it away at a rate of one foot a second. The firing of eight small rockets on the edge of the lander's aeroshell, its dome-shaped protective covering, oriented the vehicle and braked it so that Martian gravity could pull it downward out of orbit and toward the surface.

Facing Heat Shield

After a long coasting period and until just before reaching the upper fringes of the Martian atmosphere, the lander was reoriented so that its heat shield faced the angle of attack. The shield's corklike coating material was designed to protect against entry heat of up to 2,700 degrees Fahrenheit.

Atmospheric drag and lift further slowed down the craft's descent and kept it from plunging in too fast or too steeply. At an altitude of 19,400 feet, a 53-foot-wide parachute deployed, braking the descent to about 100 miles an hour. At 4,600 feet, the lander's three throttable rockets fired to ease the vehicle to a soft landing.

For the first 12 seconds it was on the surface the lander radioed engineering instructions —"how-am-I" data, as the flight controllers call it—to report on its condition. There were no anomalies, Mr. Young, the mission director, reported.

Soviet Failures

Three attempts by Soviet spacecraft to land on Mars had not been so fortunate. One crashed on landing, another ceased communication after only 20 seconds on the surface, and the third failed during the descent.

Viking 2, identical to Viking 1 in every way, is scheduled to enter Mars orbit on Aug. 7 and go for a second landing, possibly as early as Sept. 4. It may be aimed to land in the more rugged and scientifically intriguing northern latitudes below the Martian polar cap.

But for the moment all attention here at control center was on Viking 1 and the first pictures from the surface of Mars.

Dr. Noel W. Hinners, NASA's associate administrator for space science, admitted: "I had tears in my eyes for the first time since — well, I guess, since I got married. It's fantastic."

The rocky, wind-scoured desert plain where the Viking 1 made its landing. Scientists feel that material in this area is mostly volcanic in origin.

NBC News

Viking Lands 7 Years After Moon Landing

HOUSTON, July 20 (AP)—America's Viking 1 space robot landed on Mars today seven years to the day after two Apollo astronauts stepped from their spacecraft and put man's footprints on the moon.

With millions of people throughout the world watching on television on July 20, 1969, Neil A. Armstrong reported from 250,000 miles away: "Houston, the Eagle has landed."

That feat capped a $25.5 billion program that started second best to the Russians' 12 years earlier.

Mr. Armstrong, a civilian astronaut, hovered in the Apollo 11 lunar lander called Eagle near the surface, kicking up dust while trying to find a flat place to land.

Flight Offers Clue to Mars Air; Argon Level Close to Earth's

Continued From Page 1, Col. 7

too heavy to diffuse away from argon is chemically inert and either the earth or Mars, all of it orginally in both atmospheres should still be there. On Earth it constitutes only 1 percent of the air, which is 78 percent nitrogen.

If, however, the original atmosphere of Mars resembled the initial atmosphere of the earth and then was robbed of its nitrogen and oxygen, it was argued, the Martian argon would be relatively abundant.

This morning's observation was a direct measurement made as the lander plunged from 180 to 60 miles above the surface and should be definitive. The analysis was by mass spectrometer, which not only discriminate between various elements but between the various forms or isotopes of each element. The latter differ only in slight variations in weight.

The spectrometer bombarded the Martian air with an electron beam knocking electrons from the atoms so that they became electrically charged. They could then be sorted out by weight in terms of their response to a magnetic field.

The present atmosphere of Mars is very thin and cold with only one-thousandth the amount of water vapor in the earth's air. Its primary constituent is carbon dioxide. For many years it was assumed that the Martian air is dry because the planet has lost almost all its water through diffusion into space.

In this process, sunlight splits the water molecules into oxygen and hydrogen atoms that, through solar heating, move fast enough to escape the gravity of Mars. That force at the surface of Mars is only 36 percent as strong as the Earth's gravity. The rate of the hydrogen loss was measured by Mariner 9 in 1971 and the oxygen loss rate has also been estimated.

It turns out that assuming rates have remained steady and other factors such as the head of the sun have not changed greatly, the process throughout the 4.6 billion year history of Mars could have removed only enough water to cover the planet to a depth of about 300 feet.

Yet if Mars, presumably formed from about the same mix of materials as the earth's, produced proportionately as much water, there still should be enough to cover it at least one mile deep.

The earth's water—in the air, ground, oceans and lakes—is sufficient to cover the globe to a uniform depth of two miles. The surface tends to become dry because at so low an atmospheric pressure, water evaporates rapidly. While the Mariner 9 pictures showed evidence of snaking riverbeds and other water action, the new and far more detailed Viking orbter pictures show a landscape widely scoured by what are assumed to have been great floods.

The number of craters dug by occasional meteorites into these presumably water-formed features is sufficient to indicate that the flooding occurred many millions of years ago. Where, then, has the water gone?

Dr. Michael B. McElroy of Harvard University, a member of the team responsible for measurements during atmospheric entry, noted in an interview that observations from earth at infrared wavelengths have shown that water in abundance is chemically bound into the surface minerals.

He considers that even an argon level of from 1 to 3 percent is high enough to imply that Mars should have enough remaining water to form a substantial underground reservoir. He also shares with others the view that water, chemically bound or as ice, may represent 1 percent of material below the Martian surface to a depth of one mile.

Dr. McElroy, a specialist in upper atmosphere chemistry, and a colleague, Dr. Yuk Ling Yung, believe they can explain what has happened to the nitrogen of the Mars atmosphere. They doubt proposals that it has been incorporated into the surface material as nitrates, formed either by living or nonliving processes.

Instead, Dr. McElroy pointed out today, when nitrogen molecules in the upper air are split by a series of reactions initiated by ultraviolet rays from the sun, they fly apart at more than four miles a second. While this is not enough for such atoms to escape the earth, only three miles a second is needed for them to free themselves from Martian gravity.

In this way, not only the Martian nitrogen but also most of its atmospheric oxygen has escaped, Dr. McElroy believes.

The amount of residual nitrogen detected by the lander bears, he said, on whether most of the Mars atmosphere was erupted in an early, catastrophic phase, or emerged from the interior at a steady rate.

In the former case, far less than 1 percent would remain (although such depletion could also be explained by life forms that incorporated the nitrogen into their tissue). But if there is more nitrogen, that means it has emerged steadily and has been better able to keep pace with the loss rate.

The idea of early, catastrophic atmospheric formation on both the earth and Mars is shared by Dr. Robert B. Hargraves of Princeton University, another member of the Viking team, and by Dr. F. P. Fanale of the Jet Propulsion Laboratory, which is operating the Viking mission from here. Dr. Hargraves noted in an interview that such early formation of the atmosphere would mean that on earth oceans existed far longer than previously supposed and that life, consequently, may also have originated much earlier.

Dr. Fanale's concept differs from that of Dr. McElroy in that he believes not only water but other atmospheric components including nitrogen are hidden in the planet's upper rubble layer, or regolith.

'Apathetic' Reaction Disgusts a Scientist

LOUISVILLE, Ky., July 20 (AP)—"It's downright disgusting," scientist J. Richard Keefe said after Viking 1 began sending back vivid photographs from the planet Mars. "I'm rather steamed about it."

Dr. Keefe, a University of Louisville scientist who has been involved in America's space program for years, was not talking about the landing of the spacecraft.

"I can picture seven years ago today, when the first men walked on the moon. Everyone was watching. It was all on television," he said.

But when Viking touched down yesterday morning, "the only things on television were an old movie, a morning show and a game show," Dr. Keefe said, shaking his head.

"Talk about being blasé about space exploration, this was just incredible," he said. "To think it took over a year to get there. There's no question, this is a major scientific accomplishment, to pinpoint accurately your landing spot, to come down with a soft landing. And I think the population has become apathetic about the whole space program. It's kind of sad, I think."

Spokesmen for each of the television networks said that they had provided from 20 to 25 minutes of coverage in several segments yesterday morning, showing the two pictures available from the Jet Propulsion Laboratory in Pasadena, Calif., where the transmission from Mars was received.

The first picture was a tight shot showing the area immediately around the craft, and the second was a panoramic view.

NBC said its New York City switchboard had received about 30 calls asking for more, ABC said it got 25 such calls and CBS reported getting eight or 10.

The ABC spokesman said that for the time of day—around 9 A.M.—it was a significant number of callers.

"What they may not have understood was that we showed whatever we had, that was it," he said.

Dr. Keefe, the scientist, headed an experiment involving fish eggs that were carried aboard the Apollo spacecraft that linked up with a Russian space ship more than a year ago. The eggs were placed on board so that scientists could study their development when the spacecraft returned to earth.

Viking Cameras Light in Weight, Use Little Power, Work Slowly

By VICTOR K. McELHENY

Special to The New York Times

PASADENA, CALIF., July 20—When President Ford telephoned today to congratulate the Viking flight team, just as the Viking I landing craft was transmitting its first panoramic view of the landscape at Chryse, he asked the Project Manager, James Martin, what type of camera had sent back the first photographs from the surface of Mars.

The camera, Mr. Martin said, was designed to collect its images of the desert-like plain "one line at a time."

"Thats' why it takes so long to take a picture," he added.

The ceremonial conversation left no more time for explaining the complexities of a photographic system that was designed to be lightweight, use little power and take its pictures slowly enough so the information could be radioed at once across 200 million miles to Earth.

The facsimile system chosen six years ago by project managers and scientists works differently from the way a conventional still-picture camera and a television tube do. The system is like the one used on two Soviet craft that radioed back the first pictures from the surface of the planet Venus.

The two cameras on the Viking lander are able to take pictures of the sky, sun and soil in black and white, visible color and infrared light. They started their work today with a high resolution close-up of a Viking footpad and nearby soil and a low-resolution panorama of a landscape stretching out toward a horizon nearly two miles away.

Because black-and-white pictures can be transmitted in one-third the time required to transmit color signals, scientists eager to assure immediate return of information from the Chryse site postponed taking the first color picture until tomorrow.

The first color image, according to the leader of the imaging team, Dr. Thomas Mutch, a geologist at Brown University in Providence, R.I., is "potentially the most important of the entire mission." It will give the first full color view of soil and rocks and sky, he said, and will guide all the future sampling.

The image is expected to be displayed on television screens at the Jet Propulsion Laboratory here shortly before noon, Eastern daylight time.

Unlike a still-picture camera, the two identical cameras aboard the Viking lander are designed to use a movable mirror to take their pictures of Mars dot by dot and line by line.

The light intensities of each dot are recorded by one of 12 silicone semiconductor devices called diodes, each designed to be sensitive to different wave lengths of visible or infrared light. A number are placed to focus accurately at fixed distances of 6 to 43 feet from the lander.

Because all the light goes to a preselected diode, some measurements with such facsimile cameras are several times more accurate than those of a television image-recording tube, with many light-sensing dots over its surface that are exposed to light in sequence.

According to Friedrich Huck, an engineer at the Langley Research Center, who was credited today with the basic design of the lander camera system, manufacturing of dots on a television tube inevitably produces variations in the dots' ability to record light intensity.

Because of this, a television camera could not have been used for infrared radiometry studies of the Martian atmosphere, Mr. Huck said. Two engineers of Itek Corporation of Lexington, Mass., which manufactured the Viking cameras, agreed. They are Charles Ross, Itek project manager for Viking, and Robert Penninger, the technical director.

A television camera able to scan across a 360-degree panoramic view, Mr. Huck said, would need a movable mirror that would add weight to an already heavy camera.

The 15-pound camera assemblies on Viking, he said, are only half as heavy as television cameras on the Surveyor craft that landed on the moon. Also, their demand for a maximum of 35-watts of power is only a fraction of the demand of Surveyor's camera, he said.

Although the $20-million imaging system, like other Viking systems, was supposed to use existing technology to insure reliability, Mr. Huck said, the components had never been put together before in this way.

Also, they had to withstand 40-hours of heating to beyond the boiling point of water to kill any terrestrial organisms that might contaminate Mars or spoil the results of Viking's life-search experiments.

As engineers and workers of Itek made six units capable of flying to Mars, they encountered "1,001 problems," Mr. Huck said yesterday in an interview.

One difficulty, according to Mr. Ross and Mr. Penninger, was the exact placement of high-resolution diodes in the focal plane of the camera to accomplish precise photographic focus through electronic means, rather than by moving lenses back and forth.

The Viking lander cameras do their work slowly by comparison with a television camera, which typically takes 30 pictures each second, each with 90,000 or more picture-element dots.

Each second, the Viking cameras can take a total of five vertical line-scans across the scene, each with a total of 512 picture elements. A total of 9,150 such lines makes up a typical 300-degree panorama.

To make a vertical scan the camera's movable mirror must be able to turn upward in 512 precisely controlled, even steps per line. The mirror must then stop, swing down to the bottom of its path and aim slightly to one side to begin scanning upward along the adjacent path.

The light reflected off the Martian scene is bounced by the mirror through a set of lenses to the semiconductor light detectors. These convert the signals into electronic impulses that are encoded into the binary digit code used in computers.

The information can be transmitted directly to earth or tape recorded for later direct broadcast or transmission via the Viking orbiter.

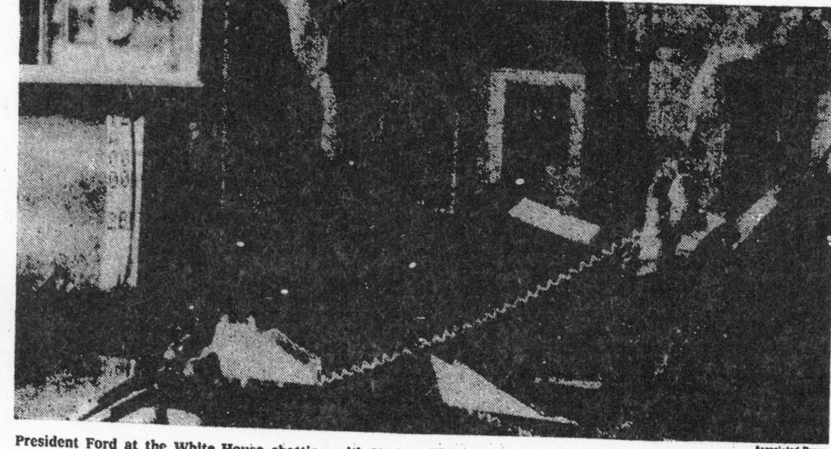

Associated Press

President Ford at the White House chatting with NASA officials as he watched photos taken after landing on Mars

"All the News That's Fit to Print"

The New York Times

LATE CITY EDITION

Weather: Rain, windy today, tonight; partly sunny and milder tomorrow. Temperature range: today 47-55; yesterday 40-62. Details, page B6.

VOL. CXXVII....No. 43,915 — NEW YORK, WEDNESDAY, APRIL 19, 1978 — 20 CENTS

25 cents beyond 50-mile zone from New York City. Higher in air delivery cities.

SENATE VOTES TO GIVE UP PANAMA CANAL; CARTER FORESEES 'BEGINNING OF A NEW ERA'

ITALIANS FAIL TO FIND MORO'S BODY IN AREA CITED BY ABDUCTORS

Searchers Sent to Mountain Lake Report Unbroken Ice Cover and No Tracks in the Snow

By HENRY TANNER

Special to The New York Times

ROME, April 18—Italian security forces on skis and in helicopters today staged a vain search for the body of Aldo Moro, the political leader, after his kidnappers had said in a statement that he was dead and that his body had been thrown into a mountain lake about 75 miles northeast of here.

The searchers at Lake Duchessa, 5,000 feet high in the Abruzzi Mountains, found the lake covered with a blanket of ice and no human tracks on the steep snow-covered slopes around it.

Toward evening, officials of Mr. Moro's Christian Democratic Party said they had reached the tentative conclusion that the terrorists' statement was a diversionary maneuver, perhaps to make it easier to move Mr. Moro from one hiding place to another.

Statement Found in Garbage Can

There was little doubt about the authenticity of the statement in which the Red Brigades, the terrorist group, announced Mr. Moro's execution by means of suicide. The statement was found in a garbage can in the center of Rome by a staff member of the newspaper Il Messaggero after it had received an anonymous phone call. Contrary to earlier messages from the Red Brigades, this one was not simultaneously distributed in Milan, Turin and Genoa.

Today marked the 30th anniversary of Christian Democratic government in Italy. The party's first Cabinet was formed on April 18, 1948, by Alcide de Gasperi. A spectacular move by the publicity-conscious kidnappers had therefore been expected.

The terrorists' statement, titled "The Trial of Aldo Moro," took note of the

Continued on Page A10, Column 4

High Court Bars Networks' Right To Nixon Tapes

Indicates U.S. Agency Could Allow Release

By WARREN WEAVER Jr.

Special to The New York Times

WASHINGTON, April 18—The Supreme Court today refused to give broadcasters and recording companies the right to copy, broadcast and sell excerpts from the White House tapes that led to the resignation of President Nixon and the criminal conviction of four of his aides.

Dividing 7 to 2, the Justices concluded that the networks had no constitutional right that was enforceable in the courts to reproduce and circulate the taped material because Congress had established a system for access to the tapes.

Texts of the taped material were printed in full at the time of the Watergate trial. The Court majority indicated today that anyone seeking sound reproductions of the tapes could apply to the General Services Administrator for permission under the Presidential Recordings Act of 1974.

No Guidelines for Access

The decision involved only the 30 tapes, covering about 22 hours of White House conversations, that were played at the Watergate trial. Eventually, as a result of the procedures that could be adopted under the recordings act, the tapes may become available for copying and broadcast. But uncertainty as to the procedure to be used, which will require further lower court consideration, makes any action in the near future unlikely.

The Court declined to give the administrator any guidelines for regulating public access to the tapes in the interests of privacy or executive privilege, saying the case before it did not require such a ruling.

In separate dissenting opinions, Associate Justices Thurgood Marshall and John Paul Stevens said that they believed Congress had intended that the tapes be made fully available to the public, includ-

Continued on Page A20, Column 3

Associated Press

President Carter shaking hands with Gabriel Lewis, Panama's Ambassador to the U.S., after Senate vote

NARROW 68-32 VICTORY

Two-Thirds Majority Gained With One Vote to Spare, as in Earlier Success

By ADAM CLYMER

Special to The New York Times

WASHINGTON, April 18—The Senate voted today to turn over the Panama Canal to Panama on Dec. 31, 1999, moving to establish a new spirit of relations with Latin America and saving President Carter from a grave political defeat.

With one vote to spare, the Senate voted to approve a treaty giving up a

Text of Senate reservation, page A16.

symbol of American power and engineering that gripped the minds of so many of their constituents..

The vote of 68 to 32, one more than the two-thirds majority required by the Constitution, was identical to one by which the Senate approved a treaty on March 16 that guarantees the neutrality of the canal. The outcome was in doubt until just before the historic roll-call at 6 P.M.

New Battle Looms

Today's vote settles an issue that has existed since Panama seceded from Colombia in 1903 and entered into a treaty with the United States. It also effectively ended a 13-year negotiating process, although some financial details remain to be resolved by both Houses of Congress, probably next year.

That is expected to be the next battle ground. Under an amendment agreed to last night formal ratification will be delayed until the implementing legislation is approved or until March 31, 1979, whichever comes earlier. Six months after the formal ratification, the United States will surrender large parts of the Canal Zone and a gradual Panamanian takeover will begin.

In television remarks after the vote, President Carter said, "This is a day of which Americans can always feel proud; for now we have reminded the world and ourselves of the things that we stand for as a nation."

'Mutual Respect and Partnership'

"These treaties can mark the beginning of a new era in our relations not only with Panama but with all the rest of the world," he said. "They symbolize our determination to deal with the developing nations of the world, the small nations of the world, on the basis of mutual respect and partnership."

Mr. Carter said Panama's Ambassador, Gabriel Lewis Galindo, had informed him that the country's leader, Brig. Gen. Omar Torrijos Herrera, would accept the treaties with the Senate's changes. He added that he had been invited to visit Panama and "I would like very much to accept."

The victory was critical for President Carter, who had repeatedly told wavering senators that his ability to conduct foreign affairs hung in the balance. But the

Continued on Page A16, Column 1

New Chancellor Would Reward Schools That Improved Reading

By MARCIA CHAMBERS

Frank J. Macchiarola, the New York City public-school system's next Chancellor, said yesterday that he hoped to find a way to give extra money to schools that improved pupils' reading scores.

At the same time, he was critical of the state and Federal systems that first funnel compensatory funds to poverty areas where pupils often read below grade level and then may cut off the school districts if the areas improve economically or scholastically. A school may improve, Mr. Macchiarola said, but there is often a dangerous regression once the funds are removed.

At his first news conference and in an interview following his designation Monday as Chancellor, Mr. Macchiarola drew the broad outlines of his educational and fiscal philosophy and the direction he hopes the nation's largest school system will take during his tenure.

Dr. Macchiarola, the 37-year-old vice president for institutional advancement at the Graduate School of the City University, and the man who won Mayor Koch's endorsement for Chancellor, said his first priority would be to get everyone in the schools to understand "that we can do the job."

In an interview, he said excellence had to be rewarded not only to stress achievement, but, also to demonstate that many public schools were working well. Then, he said, middle-class parents will want to send their children to the city's schools.

"I think when somebody does a job you've got to pat that person on the back, and say well done," Mr. Macchiarola said. "The scale of excellence and the scale of failure is a very minuscule portion of our focus. I want to broaden that scale so that the category of excellence is one that we focus on. If you try to hit that level, inevitably others aspire to it."

Cites Success in Brooklyn

He said that an incentive system that gives financial rewards to schools that improve their reading scores had been success in District 22, in Brooklyn, where, until his taking office as Chancellor, he serves as president of the school board.

The reward was based on the ranking a school achieved on the annual citywide reading examination. Mr. Macchiarola agreed with some parents' criticism that the citywide test was given too much importance in pupil evaluation, but he said it was one measure "and not the only measure" for helping him "determine who is doing the job and who is not doing the job."

In the interview, Mr. Macchiarola said

Continued on Page B5, Column 3

PANAMANIAN LEADER ACCEPTS CANAL PACTS

Torrijos Says Approval by Senate Is Great Triumph for Nation

By ALAN RIDING

Special to The New York Times

PANAMA, April 18—Panama's leader, Brig. Gen. Omar Torrijos Herrera, accepted the new canal treaties as amended by the United States Senate tonight and declared their approval to be "one of the greatest and most awaited triumphs" in this country's history.

As firecrackers exploded and sirens wailed across Panama City, General Torrijos told a nationwide radio and television audience moments after the Senate vote, "I feel proud that I have fulfilled my mission."

Clearly seeking to stir up enthusiasm after weeks of mounting opposition to the treaties, the Government urged the people to celebrate the victory in the streets, and excited crowds gathered in the May 5 Plaza close to the United States-controlled Canal Zone.

The 48-year-old general, who has ruled Panama since 1968, declared tomorrow a national holiday and announced that some 100 political exiles could immediately return to Panama and that banned political parties might soon be legalized.

The new treaties, the result of 13 years of negotiations, recognize Panama's jurisdiction over the 553-square-mile Canal Zone and provide for the handing over of the canal itself on Dec. 31, 1999. Pana-

Continued on Page A16, Column 4

Basic Provisions of Treaties

WASHINGTON, April 18—Following are the basic provisions of the two treaties that provide for turning over control of the Panama Canal to Panama by the year 2000 and for the permanent neutrality of the canal thereafter.

Panama Canal Treaty

THE CANAL: Panama will assume "full responsibility for the management, operation and maintenance of the canal" on the termination of the treaty at noon Dec. 31, 1999. Until then the canal will be operated by a new United States agency, Canal Commission, whose board will include five Americans and four Panamanians.

THE CANAL ZONE: Panama will assume jurisdiction of the 533-square-mile zone when the treaty comes into force, but the zone will be integrated into Panama over 30 months.

DEFENSE: The United States will continue to have primary responsibility for the defense of the canal until expiration of the treaty in 1999, but will establish with Panama a combined board of officers for consultation and cooperation on defense matters.

SEA LEVEL CANAL: Under the treaty, the United States will agree to negotiate only with Panama for construction of a sea-level canal across Central America, and Panama will agree not to undertake such a project except with the United States.

RESERVATIONS: The Senate adopted a measure yesterday allowing the United States to use its forces unilaterally if necessary. But another reservation specifies that any intervention would be only to keep the canal open, not to interfere in Panama's internal affairs. Another measure adopted by the Senate would nullify the mutually exclusive commitment on a new canal.

Neutrality Treaty

DEFENSE: After the treaty comes into effect on Dec. 31, 1999, the United States and Panama will each have the right to defend the canal against threats to its neutrality or to the peaceful transit of ships.

TRANSIT: Panama pledges to keep the canal open to "peaceful transit" by all nations, including warships.

RESERVATIONS: A measure adopted by the Senate last month in effect gives the United States the right to take "such steps as it deems necessary," including the use of force to reopen the canal or restore its operations, should this become necessary. Another measure adopted by the Senate keeps the possibility of maintaining United States troops or bases in Panama after 1999 if Panama and the United States decided it was necessary.

AMENDMENT: Interprets the treaty to mean that Panamanian and American vessels, in an emergency, could "go the head of the line."

United Press International

Italian security forces preparing to fly to Lake Duchessa from Valle del Salto in search for Aldo Moro

Ex-Diplomat to Head Met Museum

By GRACE GLUECK

After more than a year's search, the trustees of the Metropolitan Museum of Art have elected the museum's first full-time salaried president. He is William B. Macomber Jr., a 57-year-old retired diplomat whose last post was Ambassador to Turkey from 1973 to 1977.

The choice of Mr. Macomber, by unanimous vote of the board, surprised the museum world, because he is not known in the art field nor had his name been among the many reported to be in contention.

Under a reorganization of the museum's administrative structure voted by the board last March, Mr. Macomber as president will be in charge of management and finances while a subordinate director will be in charge of curatorial and artistic matters. The director, who will succeed Thomas Hoving, has not yet been chosen.

Mr. Macomber, whose salary was not disclosed, succeeds Douglas Dillon, who had served as unsalaried president since 1969 and now becomes board chairman.

Yesterday Mr. Dillon said that Mr. Macomber's extensive Washington background, which includes a stint as chief administrative officer of the State Department from 1969-1973 and as Assistant Secretary of State for Congressional Relations from 1957 to 1962 and from 1967 to 1969, would be "very useful in dealing with political figures in the city, in Albany and in Washington."

And he termed Mr. Macomber's lack of experience in the art world "a plus factor rather than a minus," adding, "We didn't want someone who'd second-guess or dominate the director and

Continued on Page C22, Column 3

INSIDE

Stocks Drop; Dow Off 6.85

The stock market declined moderately after three sessions of soaring prices and hectic trading as traders cashed in gains. The Dow was off 6.85. Page D1.

Setbacks for Carter Tax Plan

President Carter's income tax plan suffered setbacks when a House panel rebuffed proposals on medical expenses and charitable deductions. Page D1.

Yanks Deny Abuses On Stadium's Lease

Al Rosen, president of the New York Yankees, said yesterday that a "thorough review" by the club's fiscal experts had shown "no evidence of impropriety" in its financial dealings with New York City, which rebuilt and owns Yankee Stadium.

He said that officers of the club remained "willing to meet with any responsible official who claims to have tangible evidence that there has been a violation of our lease."

The comments, in a statement and interview at the Stadium, came a month after Comptroller Harrison J. Goldin opened an investigation into "maintenance costs" at the Stadium. Under the terms of the lease, the Yankees were able to reduce the rent due to the city by more than $1.5 million the team said it paid in maintenance costs.

Yankee front-office executives conceded that the allegation by Comptroller Goldin that $65 of the cost of a commercial by Catfish Hunter, Yankee pitcher, in 1976, had been mistakenly charged to the city as a maintenance cost. But they added that this had been corrected when

Continued on Page D16, Column 1

Canal a Source of Friction Since 1903

By GRAHAM HOVEY

Special to The New York Times

WASHINGTON, April 18—Senate approval of the basic Panama Canal treaty culminates negotiations that began formally in 1964 but have actually gone on intermittently ever since the signing of the 1903 pact under which the canal was constructed.

After United States and Panamanian negotiators reached agreement last September on the basic treaty providing for transfer of the canal to Panama on the last day of 1999, and on the sister pact providing for the permanent neutrality of the waterway, it was clear that the most difficult task remaining would be to win the required two-thirds majority in the Senate.

Now the only remaining hurdle—not regarded as insurmountable—is acceptance by the Panamanian Government of the treaties as they have been amended and with the reservations attached to them by the Senate in the long debate that began Feb. 8.

Panamanians call the 1903 accord "the treaty no Panamanian ever signed." They mean that the treaty was negotiated in haste and signed for the 15-day-old Republic of Panama by a Frenchman, Philippe Bunau-Varilla, whose authority to take such action was questionable, to say the least.

Panama's first Government, which ratified the treaty only under heavy pressure from Washington, bitterly protested the clauses that granted the United States "in perpetuity" the right to act as "if it were the sovereign" over a 10-mile-wide Canal Zone that bisected Panama.

Provisions Considered Humiliating

Most of Panama's many governments since then have demanded the elimination of those passages, which they regarded as humiliating. The 74-year history of relations between the United States and the country it helped establish by backing the Panamanian revolt against Colombia thus has often been marred by crisis.

President Franklin D. Roosevelt agreed in 1936 to a treaty that removed some irritants to the Panamanians. It ended the rights of the United States to intervene to maintain order in Colón and Panama City and to take over additional territory without Panama's consent. It also ended Panama's status as a protectorate of the United States and increased the annual annuity to Panama from $250,000 to $430,000.

In 1955, President Eisenhower agreed to a new treaty that raised Panama's annuity to $1.9 million, granted other economic concessions and handed back some land the United States had controlled outside the Canal Zone. No concessions were made on American control of the canal and the zone, however.

It was only after riots, led by students who had entered the Canal Zone, brought death to 20 Panamanians and four Americans in 1964 that President Johnson agreed to negotiations in which for the first time the eventual transfer of the canal to Panama was seriously examined.

Talks Held Under 4 Administrations

With long interruptions and changes in the principal negotiators, those negotiations continued under four Washington administrations—two Democratic, two Republican—until the successful conclusion of the basic pact and the neutrality treaty last year.

In 1967, the negotiators produced drafts of three linked treaties that were initialed by both sides but never signed by Mr. Johnson or Marco A. Robles, then the President of Panama. One would have given Panama a share in running the canal and provided for the gradual integration of the Canal Zone into the rest of Panama.

Another would have given the United States the option to build a sea-level canal across Panama and the possibility of controlling the new waterway until the year 2067. The United States would have retained the right to defend the canals indefinitely.

Panama formally rejected the 1967 treaties in 1970, after its National Guard had overthrown an elected government in 1968 and installed Brig. Gen. Omar Torrijos Herrera as Chief of Government. But negotiations were eventually resumed, and were given a major impetus with an agreement reached in 1974 between Secretary of State Henry A. Kissinger and Panama's Foreign Minister, Juan Antonio Tack.

Eight Principles Agreed On

They agreed on eight principles to guide the negotiators toward "a just and equitable treaty eliminating, once and for all, the causes of conflict between the two countries." The second of the principles was elimination of "the concept of perpetuity," against which Panamanians had protested for 70 years.

The Canal Zone would be returned to Panamanian jurisdiction, and Panama would participate in the administration of the canal and would take over "total responsibility" for its operation on termination of the basic treaty.

Even before Mr. Kissinger and Mr. Tack signed their statement in Panama on Feb. 7, 1974, President Richard M. Nixon had selected a venerable diplomatic troubleshooter, Ellsworth Bunker, to take charge of a fresh round of negotiations with the Panamanians.

The negotiations were put on the shelf in 1976, when Ronald Reagan unexpectedly uncovered what appeared to be an effective Presidential campaign issue by accusing President Ford of being willing to give away the Panama Canal. But by then Mr. Bunker had been able to work out agreements with the Panamanians on many major points of a new treaty.

During the 1976 election campaign, Jimmy Carter said he would "never give up complete control or practical control over the Panama Canal Zone." But once elected, both he and his choice for Secretary of State, Cyrus R. Vance, listed a new Panama Canal treaty as the highest priority for the Administration's policy in Latin America.

Mr. Carter retained Ambassador Bunker, strengthened his team with Sol M. Linowitz, an experienced lawyer and diplomat, as co-negotiator, and ordered a resumption of the negotiations in February 1977.

The last series of negotiations was inevitably the most difficult and the talks were sometimes acrimonious, but they were never actually broken off.

Defense Guarantee Necessary

If the treaties were to have any chance of approval by the Senate, Mr. Bunker and Mr. Linowitz had to insist on language that would allow the United States to defend the waterway, should that ever be necessary, after the transfer of the canal to Panama in 1999.

The language designed to accomplish this with the least offense to Panamanian sensibilities about "Yankee intervention" was prepared in the Pentagon and approved by the Joint Chiefs of Staff. It satisfied Panama but not the Senate, which attached a reservation spelling out the right of United States intervention.

Another crisis came over the amount of the compensation to be given Panama during the 22-year life of the basic treaty. The Panamanians started out demanding a down payment of $1 billion and an annuity of $500 million a year. They settled for an annual payment ranging from $50 to $70 million that will come entirely from canal revenues.

Panamanian officals said later that President Carter plunged the talks into a final crisis last Aug. 5 with a proposal for the option to build a sea-level canal that they found unacceptable. But the United States backed off the following day, they said, and the negotiations were brought to a successful conclusion five days later in Panama City.

The treaties were signed by President Carter and General Torrijos in a gala ceremony attended by most Latin American heads of government at the Pan American Union in Washington on Sept. 7.

In an effort to reassure Americans and head off unacceptable Senate amendments, the President and General Torrijos subsequently met again in Washington Oct. 14 to issue a Statement of Understanding. This said in effect that both the United States and Panama had the right indefinitely to defend the canal against any threat and that in an emergency American ships could go to "the head of the line" for transit of the canal.

That action formally concluded more than 13 years of negotiations and passed the issue to the Senate.

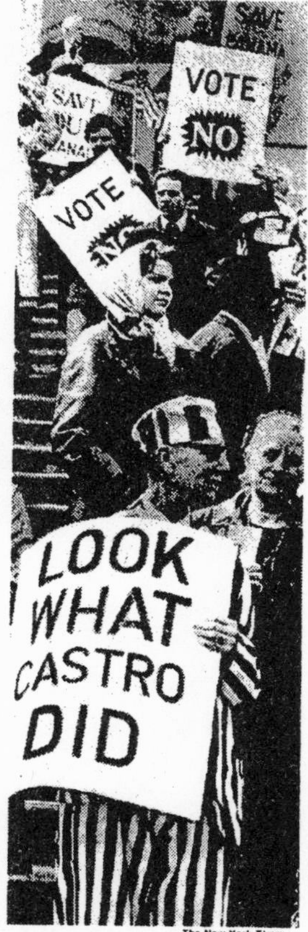

The New York Times

Demonstrators at the Capitol protesting the Panama Canal treaties.

United Press International

Panama's leader, Brig. Gen. Omar Torrijos Herrera, center, at news conference in Panama City after the Senate approved treaty. Flanking him were Aristides Royo, left, and Romulo Escobar Bethancourt, treaty negotiators.

Panama's Leader Accepts Canal Pacts as Amended

Continued From Page A1

"The armed forces had decided not to resume negotiations if the treaties had been rejected or an unacceptable amendment had been attached," he told reporters. "If we had been rejected by the United States Senate, Panama would have begun the struggle for liberation and possibly by tomorrow the canal would no longer be functioning." [In Washington, the Whitde House said the United States had not ben warned of any such action.]

The new treaties, the result of 13 years of negotiations, recognize Panama's jurisdiction over the 553-square-mile Canal Zone and provide for the handing over of the canal itself on Dec. 31, 1999. Panamanian voters ratified the treaties, which are expected to go into effect late next year, by a 2-to-1 margin on Oct. 23.

Many Still Oppose Treaties

Many Panamanians are still unhappy with the treaties because of a reservation attached to the pact guaranteeing the canal's neutrality, which was approved by the Senate last month. The reservation asserts the right of the United States to intervene militarily here to keep open the canal after its operation has been taken over by Panama. Several hundred opponents of the treaties demonstrated this morning and again this evening.

General Torrijos said tonight "that on several occasions we were about to reject the treaties because I would not accept a crude interventionist reservation."

But after the Senate today attached a reservation to the basic treaty, under which control of the canal will pass to Panama on Dec. 31, 1999, renouncing any American "right of intervention in the internal affairs of Panama," the General said the pacts had been "perfectly modified to the extreme that I can say that nothing in them legally justifies intervention."

'Massive Pressures' Noted

He said at a news conference that should the United States intervene in or invade Panama after the year 2000, "they would find the canal destroyed by the time they got here."

"Those who can best defend the canal are we Panamanians," he said. "The person who can destroy it but does not is defending it. And that capacity to destroy should never be renounced by the National Guard or by future generations."

Noting that "we have been subject to massive pressures" during the Senate treaty debate, the General complained that "never in our republic's life has a Panamanian been more insulted than me, never has a country been subject to so much disrespect as Panama, no people has ever seen crude power so closely as we saw it through the conservatives who are a dishonor to a nation of such dignity as the United States."

During the Senate debate, opponents of the treaties frequently referred to General Torrijos as "a tinhorn dictator" and cast doubt on Panama's ability to operate the canal after the year 2000.

But the Panamanian ruler called the treaties tonight "a new pact of mutual respect that places a fixed date on the end of the colonialism that we have known throughout our independent life." The 1903 treaty, which granted the United States control of the canal and Canal Zone "in perpetuity," was signed by a Frenchman just weeks after Panama proclaimed its independence from Colombia.

General Torrijos ncted that many Canal Zone facilities would soon be in Panamanian hands and he described the treaties as posing a challenge to "restructure the country" and bring more schools, welfare and jobs to the population.

There is speculation that President Carter will fly here soon to exchange the instruments of ratification with General Torrijos.

Ratification to Be Delayed

The treaties, however, may not go into effect until late next year. A reservation attached to the treaties by the Senate yesterday will delay formal ratification until legislation to carry them out is passed by Congress or until March 31, 1979, whichever is earlier.

After the ratification instruments have been formally exchanged, there will be a six-month interval before the treaties go into effect. During this period the United States and Panama will prepare for the takeover by Panama of such Canal Zone services as the railroad, the ports at each end of the canal, the fire brigade, the post office, the local movie theater and restaurant.

There will be a further 30-month transition period at the end of which Panama's National Guard will assume all police functions in the 64 percent of the Canal Zone that will come under Panama's control.

The rest of the Canal Zone will remain in the hands of either the new canal commission, which will administer the waterway until the year 2000, or of the United States armed forces, which will be able to retain as many troops in Panama as they consider necessary for the defense of the canal until the year 2000.

The treaties also contemplate that Panamanians will gradually assume greater responsibility for both the administration and defense of the canal during the life of the treaty. Additionally, Panama, which in recent years has been receiving a $2.3 million annuity, should soon begin receiving revenues from the canal of $65 million to $70 million. Economists believe that this revenue should help reactivate the country's depressed economy.

Politically, the treaties should strengthen the position of General Torrijos, whose popularity has been eroded by the economic situation and by the long delay in reaching agreement over the canal with the United States.

Text of Reservation To Treaty on Canal

Special to The New York Times

WASHINGTON, April 18—Following is the text of the Senate leadership's reservation to the second Panama Canal treaty approved today by a vote of 73 to 27. The texts of the two treaties were pubished in The New York Times on Sept. 7, 1977.

Before the period at the end of the resolution of ratification, insert a comma and the following:

"Subject to the reservation that: pursuant to its adherence to the principle of nonintervention, any action taken by the United States of America in the exercise of its rights to assure that the Panama Canal shall remain open, neutral, secure, and accessible, pursuant to the provisions of this treaty and the Neutrality Treaty and the resolutions of advice and consent thereto, shall be only for the purpose of assuring that the canal shall remain open, neutral, secure, and accessible, and shall not have as its purpose nor be interpreted as a right of intervention in the internal affairs of the Republic of Panama or interference with its political independence or sovereign integrity."

Senate Votes to Give Up Canal; Carter Sees Beginning of 'New Era'

Continued From Page A1

tight margin and the repeated difficulties the Administration met in dealing with the Senate robbed the victory of much of the political impact it might have had if it had come more smoothly.

The success was important too to Senator Robert C. Byrd of West Virginia, the majority leader, who was facing his biggest test in the Senate, and to Senator Howard H. Baker Jr. of Tennessee, the minority leader. Mr. Baker risked his Presidential ambitions and the wrath of conservatives in his party by backing the treaties if they could be changed to explain United States rights more clearly.

Mr. Carter, who followed the vote in his secretary's office with his assistant, Hamilton Jordan, his press secretary, Jody Powell, and his national security adviser, Zbigniew Brzezinski, called Mr. Byrd immediately after the roll-call and told him, "You're a great man—it was a beautiful vote."

In the end it was Mr. Byrd who did the key maneuvering, telling the Administration to stay out of the way while he negotiated a Senate assertion that provisions allowing the use of troops to keep the canal open were not a retreat from the policy of nonintervention, as angry Panamanians had charged in threatening to reject the pacts.

And Mr. Byrd moved to draw the political heat on himself, passing when his name was first called in the tally and then casting the decisive 67th vote.

The historic debate—beamed to the nation and to Panama by radio—was cut short at the very end. A planned hour of culminating argument was scrapped when unexpected roll-calls on the last of the 79 amendments the Senate had acted on since debate began Feb. 8 took up more time than expected.

Mr. Byrd tried to get unanimous consent for a final reprise of the arguments, but Senator William L. Scott, Republican of Virginia, objected.

Pacts Called 'a Dangerous Step'

Senator Robert P. Griffin, Republican of Michigan, asserted that the treaty was "a dangerous step, a gamble for the United States and the security of the United States.

But Senator Frank Church, Democrat of Idaho, and the key floor manager for the treaty, argued that the rules established in the expansionist days of 1903 were long outdated. He said that the new treaties would secure not only better relations with Panama but also with Latin America generally and would protect United States interests in the canal. Opponents, he asserted, were on a "sentimental journey back to the era of Teddy Roosevelt, the big stick, and the Great White Fleet."

Voting for the treaty were 52 Democrats and 16 Republicans. Voting against it were 10 Democrats and 22 Republicans. Before victory could be achieved, three senators who had voted for the first treaty but who had wavered publicly on the second had to be brought back into the fold. When they were, the roll-call matched exactly the March 16 vote on the neutrality treaty.

Vote 'Just as Anticipated'

One of the waverers, Senator James Abourezk, Democrat of South Dakota, told the Senate that he had been reassured that decisions in the conference committee on energy legislation would be made more openly.

Another, Senator Howard W. Cannon, Democrat of Nevada, won approval of an amendment he felt strongly about. The amendment requires the approval of both houses of Congress before the current $20 million in annual loan payments from the canal company to the Treasury can be dropped.

A third Senator who had threatened to vote against the treaty, S. I. Hayakawa, Republican of California, decided to support it after he had met with the President and Senate leaders at the White House today. They told him that he would have more influence on foreign affairs by voting "yes" and the Senator agreed. "If I was a total outsider to their thinking obviously my input wouldn't be taken seriously," he said.

After the vote Mr. Byrd said the outcome had been "just as we anticipated." He said that the result showed that Americans dealt from a position of strength and were not afraid to live up to their principles.

Paul Laxalt, the Nevada Republican who led the opposition to the treaties, said he feared the consequences "will be unpleasant." But he paid tribute to his foes, saying the result was achieved "entirely by the effectiveness of the Senate leadership."

Today's action followed an almost equally tense 68-to-32 vote March 16 on the treaty guaranteeing the neutrality of the canal. That treaty was approved only after the Carter Administration agreed to a reservation offered by Senator Dennis DeConcini, Democrat of Arizona, asserting the right of the United States to send troops into Panama to keep the canal open.

Cornerstone of U.S. Policy

Today the Senate adopted by 73 votes to 27 a reservation disavowing any United States intention of interfering in Panama's internal affairs. The new reservation, designed to soothe angry Panamanians, was laboriously drafted so that Mr. DeConcini and one or two followers would not feel affronted by it and desert the second treaty.

It was adopted after Mr. Byrd had said that it "reaffirms the principle of nonintervention, a principle which is and will remain a cornerstone of United States foreign policy."

The new reservation proclaimed that any action the United States might take under the DeConcini reservation or under any other provision of either treaty "shall not have as its purpose nor be interpreted as a right of intervention in the internal affairs of the Republic of Panama or interference with its political independence or sovereign integrity."

While other senators, such as Jacob K. Javits, Republican of New York, and Frank Church, said that the Panamanians had good reason to be alarmed at the earlier reservation, Mr. DeConcini himself called the controversy "amazing" before supporting Mr. Byrd's proposal.

Foes of the treaty accused the leadership of trying to have it both ways. They demanded to know whether Mr. Byrd's move limited the effect of the earlier DeConcini reservation and unsuccessfully offered amendments to it.

Just before the final burst of argument that ended what Mr. Byrd said was the longest treaty debate since the Senate pondered the Treaty of Versailles in 1919 and 1920, the Senate rejected an attempt by Senator Griffin, to have the Senate advise Mr. Carter that it would not consent to ratification.

The effect would have been to tell the President to have the treaties renegotiated. Mr. Griffin argued that was necessary because differences of interpretation showed that the two pacts were badly drafted. As the treaties were written now, he said, they were a "dangerous gamble."

How Senators Voted On 2d Canal Treaty

WASHINGTON, April 18 (AP)—Following is the 68-to-32 roll call vote by the Senate approving the second Panama Canal Treaty:

FOR THE TREATY—68

Democrats—52

Abourezk, S.D.
Anderson, Minn.
Bayh, Ind.
Bentsen, Tex.
Biden, Del.
Bumpers, Ark.
Byrd, W.Va.
Cannon, Nev.
Chiles, Fla.
Church, Idaho
Clark, Iowa
Cranston, Calif.
Culver, Iowa
DeConcini, Ariz.
Durkin, N.H.
Eagleton, Mo.
Glenn, Ohio
Gravel, Alaska
Hart, Colo.
Haskell, Colo.
Hatfield, Mont.
Hathaway, Maine
Hodges, Ark.
Hollings, S.C.
Huddleston, Ky.
Humphrey, Minn.
Inouye, Hawaii
Jackson, Wash.
Kennedy, Mass.
Leahy, Vt.
Long, La.
Magnuson, Wash.
Matsunaga, Hawaii
McGovern, S.D.
McIntyre, N.H.
Metzenbaum, Ohio
Morgan, N.C.
Moynihan, N.Y.
Muskie, Maine
Nelson, Wis.
Nunn, Ga.
Pell, R.I.
Proxmire, Wis.
Ribicoff, Conn.
Riegle, Mich.
Sarbanes, Md.
Sasser, Tenn.
Sparkman, Ala.
Stevenson, Ill.
Stone, Fla.
Talmadge, Ga.
Williams, N.J.

Republicans—16

Baker, Tenn.
Bellmon, Okla.
Brooke, Mass.
Case, N.J.
Chafee, R.I.
Danforth, Mo.
Hatfield, Ore.
Hayakawa, Calif.
Heinz, Pa.
Javits, N.Y.
Mathias, Md.
Packwood, Ore.
Pearson, Kan.
Percy, Ill.
Stafford, Vt.
Weicker, Conn.

AGAINST THE TREATY—32

Democrats—10

Allen, Ala.
Burdick, N.D.
Byrd, Va.
Eastland, Miss.
Ford, Ky.
Johnston, La.
Melcher, Mont.
Randolph, W.Va.
Stennis, Miss.
Zorinsky, Neb.

Republicans—22

Bartlett, Okla.
Curtis, Neb.
Dole, Kan.
Domenici, N.M.
Garn, Utah
Goldwater, Ariz.
Griffin, Mich.
Hansen, Wyo.
Hatch, Utah
Helms, N.C.
Laxalt, Nev.
Lugar, Ind.
McClure, Idaho
Roth, Del.
Schmitt, N.M.
Schweiker, Pa.
Scott, Va.
Stevens, Alaska
Thurmond, S.C.
Tower, Tex.
Wallop, Wyo.
Young, N.D.

The New York Times/April 19, 1978

The New York Times/George Tames

Carried away by his exuberance, Robert C. Byrd, the Senate majority leader, applied a vise-like handshake to Frank B. Moore, the White House liaison official with the Congress, after approval of the treaty.

Reagan Says: 'I Am Disappointed'

TOKYO, Wednesday, April 19 (AP)—Ronald Reagan, a leader of the fight against the Panama Canal treaties, said today, "naturally, I am disappointed" at the Senate's approval of them.

The former California Governor and Republican Presidential candidate, in Japan on a private visit, said: "It is no secret I feel those treaties are flawed and they have now been ratified by the Senate. I feel this is a very extreme case of ignoring the sentiment of the people of our country. They were overwhelming in their disapproval of the treaties."

"I hope my misgivings will not be realized," he continued, "bue I cannot help but be disappointed by what has happened. I feel it is a loss to the people of the United States and perhaps the people of all the world.

"The manner in which the Administration went to the Senate with this, saying because of the Administration's prestige they should vote for the treaties, was a failure to recognize that it is the function of ehe Senate to ratify treaties on the basis of whether they are good for the country.

"If it is only to enhance the prestige of the President, the Senate had better give up its power of ratification."

Griffin Hopes Carter Is Right

WASHINGTON, April 18 (AP)—Senator Robert P. Griffin, Republican of Michigan, reacting to Senate approval of the Panama Canal treaties, said today: "I hope history will prove President Carter right. I have been very concerned that history is going to prove the advocates of this treaty wrong."

"All the News That's Fit to Print"

The New York Times

LATE CITY EDITION

Weather: Sunny, warm today; fair tonight. Sunny, warm tomorrow. Temperature range: today 69-84; yesterday 75-90. Details, page B17.

VOL. CXXVII....No. 43,986

NEW YORK, THURSDAY, JUNE 29, 1978

25 cents beyond 50-mile zone from New York City. Higher in air delivery cities

20 CENTS

HIGH COURT BACKS SOME AFFIRMATIVE ACTION BY COLLEGES, BUT ORDERS BAKKE ADMITTED

GUIDANCE IS PROVIDED

Medical School Racial Quota Voided, but Advantage for Minorities Is Allowed

By WARREN WEAVER Jr.

Special to The New York Times

WASHINGTON, June 28—The Supreme Court by 5-to-4 vote affirmed today the constitutionality of college admission programs that give special advantage to blacks and other minorities to help remedy past discrimination against them.

But the Justices also ruled that Allan P. Bakke must be admitted to the University of California Medical College at

Excerpts from opinions, Pages A20, A21.

Davis, determining that the college's affirmative action program was invalid because it was inflexibly and unjustifiably biased against white applicants like him.

In today's opinion, the Court provided some guidance for educators trying to insure that their programs will pass judicial muster, and future cases will almost certainly shed some more light on what constitutes permissible affirmative action.

Most Significant Since '54

Both decisions involved 5-to-4 votes, with Associate Justice Lewis F. Powell Jr. joining four other Justices to force the admission of Mr. Bakke, then shifting to join the four remaining Justices in support of the constitutionality of carefully tailored flexible affirmative action plans.

Although the two-sided ruling aroused some confusion and controversy, it was generally regarded as the most significant civil rights pronouncement the high court had made since it outlawed public school segregation in 1954.

It was not initially clear whether the Bakke decision would affect future Supreme Court rulings on affirmative action in employment. Such hiring plans tend to incorporate fixed arbitrary formulas for blacks, women and others, somewhat akin to the Davis admissions program that was invalidated today, but the high court has generally approved them in the past.

Two Groups in Voting

Generally, however, civil rights advocates felt they had won a major victory by preserving the constitutionality of admissions plans to professional schools that favor minority group members, who had been all but barred from such education until recent years.

One group of Justices—William J. Brennan Jr., Byron R. White, Thurgood Marshall and Harry A. Blackmun—maintained that the special Davis admissions program was permissible because the Government could use racial classifications as long as it has the benign purpose of remedying past discrimination. They voted, as a result, to deny Mr. Bakke entrance.

A second group of four—Chief Justice Warren E. Burger and Associate Justices Potter Stewart, William H. Rehnquist and

Continued on Page A22, Column 1

Associated Press

Allan P. Bakke returning to home in Los Altos, Calif., after work yesterday

BELL HAILS DECISION

Calls Ruling a 'Great Gain'—Plaintiff Is 'Pleased' and Others Express Relief

By LINDA GREENHOUSE

Special to The New York Times

WASHINGTON, June 28—Among the entire spectrum of people and groups with a stake in the Bakke decision, there were degrees of satisfaction and relief today.

From Allan P. Bakke himself, who will enter medical school next September at the age of 38, to the civil rights organizations that opposed his challenge to the special minority-admissions program, people drew from the 154 pages of Supreme Court language the conclusions they most wanted to find. Mr. Bakke said he was "pleased" with the decision.

Attorney General Griffin B. Bell told reporters at the White House that he and President Carter regarded the decision as "a great gain for affirmative action."

"This is what we thought the law was," the Attorney General said.

Benjamin L. Hooks, executive director of the National Association for the Advancement of Colored People, called the decision a "clear-cut victory for voluntary affirmative action," not only in education but also in other areas.

'Quotas Are Flatly Illegal'

Arnold Forster, general counsel of the Anti-Defamation League of B'nai B'rith, said his organization was "comforted that, once and for all, the United States Supreme Court has held that racial quotas are flatly illegal."

Among educators, the reaction was almost one of relief that their worst fears had not come to pass and that most existing college admissions policies could continue unchanged. [Page A23.]

Whether the decisions in Regents of the University of California v. Bakke will go down in history as "an act of judicial statesmanship," in the words of Prof. Alan Dershowitz of Harvard Law School, the nine Justices in their six opinions did seem to be offering something for everyone in a case that has been scrutinized as closely and argued as bitterly as any to reach the Court in recent decades.

The Court both ordered Mr. Bakke's admission to medical school and upheld the use of race as a factor in university admissions programs.

Black Leader Sees Threat

At a news conference of black leaders in New York City, Jesse Jackson, chairman of Operation PUSH, warned that the part of the decision striking down the minority-admissions program at the medical school of the University of California at Davis might be received by other universities as a signal to cut back on even those affirmative action programs that quite clearly have the approval of a majority of the Supreme Court.

But other civil rights leaders chose to focus on the part of the opinion establish-

Continued on Page A23, Column 6

A Plateau for Minorities

Most College Programs Expected to Continue, But Ruling Is Seen as Brake on Rights Efforts

By JOHN HERBERS

Special to The New York Times

News Analysis

WASHINGTON, June 28—The United States Supreme Court's split decision in the Allan P. Bakke case means, according to the consensus on both sides, that the great majority of affirmative action programs, public and private, will continue, as will the debate and lawsuits over what constitutes a proper racial balance.

For that, the leaders of the nation's minorities expressed pleasure and relief today at the 5-to-4 decision, which said that race may be considered in deciding who is admitted to colleges.

The rigid affirmative action program of the medical school of the University of California at Davis, which the Court struck down, was considered extreme in that it set aside 16 of 100 places for members of minority groups. Many other programs for enrolling minorities are more flexible and seem to fall within the boundaries set in today's decision.

A Retreat Is Seen

However, as Julian Bond, the Georgia civil rights leader and state legislator, said, affirmative action efforts reached a plateau today, and there was some fear that the decision would cause a decline in attempts to broaden educational and employment opportunities for blacks and other minorities.

Associate Justice Thurgood Marshall expressed the opinion, widely held among minority leaders, that the nation has been retreating from a commitment to racial justice made in the 1960's, in a parallel to what happened in the 19th century after the Reconstruction period.

"I fear that we have come full circle," he wrote, pointing out that "several affirmative action programs" were voided in that period by the Supreme Court. He cited the decision in Plessy v. Ferguson, which upheld segregation in public education, and said, "Now we have this Court again stepping in, this time to stop affirmative action programs of the type used by the University of California."

Although the majority decision appeared to please a broad spectrum of people on both sides of the issue. Justice Marshall put his finger on a deep division remaining in this country between blacks and whites.

The division concerns whether the nation should give special preference to a people who in a unique way were subjected to a basic denial of human rights, beginning with slavery.

"It must be remembered," he wrote, "that during most of the past 200 years, the Constitution as interpreted by this Court did not prohibit the most ingenious and pervasive forms of discrimination against the Negro. No, when a state acts to remedy the effects of the legacy of discrimination, I cannot believe that this same Constitution stands as a barrier."

Associate Justice Lewis F. Powell Jr., who wrote the main opinion, made it clear that special preference for blacks was not what the majority had in mind when it said race could be considered in an admissions policy. He spoke of the need for diversity, for Asians, Mexican-Americans, people from rural as well as urban areas.

"The file of a particular black applicant may be examined for his potential contribution to diversity without the factor of race being decisive when compared, for example, with that of an applicant identified as an Italian-American if the latter

Continued on Page A22, Column 3

PRESIDENT TO ISSUE ORDER TO LIBERALIZE RULE ON SECRET DATA

Change in Procedure on Classified Documents Designed to Exhibit Interest in Open Government

By MARTIN TOLCHIN

Special to The New York Times

WASHINGTON, June 28 — President Carter plans a sweeping liberalization of the procedures governing the classification of Government documents.

He intends shortly to issue an executive order that will sharply limit the extent and duration of classifications, such as "confidential," "secret" and "top secret," and reduce the number of agencies that have classification authority.

The executive order will also provide that declassification procedures consider "whether the public interest in disclosure outweighs the damage to national security that might be reasonably expected from disclosure," according to the document, a copy of which was obtained by The New York Times.

The White House intends to present the executive order as a demonstration of the President's commitment to open government. Although civil liberty groups praised the new procedure, they said they did not believe the new policy would offset what they regarded as the Administration's commitment to secrecy in other areas.

Three Cases Cited

They cited the cases against Frank Snepp, a former agent of the Central Intelligence Agency who wrote a book critical of the agency, and the prosecutions of David Truong and Ronald Humphrey for theft.

"Nothing that they could do in the executive order could outweigh the harm to free debate on national security issues brought about by the Snepp and Truong cases," said Morton Halperin, director of the Center for National Security Studies, who helped to formulate the new procedures.

Mark Lynch, a staff attorney for the American Civil Liberties Union who specializes in government secrecy, said that the new procedures "could be very useful" because "they'll have to think harder about what they're doing."

He agreed with Mr. Halperin, however,

Continued on Page A16, Column 3

Associated Press

Gerard C. Smith

South Africans Reported Ready For Nuclear Ban

JOHN F. BURNS

Special to The New York Times

JOHANNESBURG, June 28—American efforts to persuade South Africa to sign the treaty banning the spread of nuclear weapons reportedly reached an advanced stage today as high-level officials of the two Governments ended talks in Pretoria on the nuclear issue.

Sources close to the talks disclosed tonight that Gerard C. Smith, President Carter's ambassador at large in charge of efforts to prevent the spread of nuclear weapons, had been in the South African capital of Pretoria since Sunday for discussions with Foreign Minister Roelof F. Botha and other senior officials, including Abraham J. Roux, chairman of the South African Atomic Energy Board.

[Reports from Washington indicated, meanwhile, that South Africa was considering signing the treaty and was prepared to accept stricter international controls to prevent its atomic energy program from being used to develop weapons.]

Details Not Disclosed

Neither side in the Pretoria talks would divulge any details of what went on or say whether an agreement was in prospect. However, it is known that Mr. Smith, a 68-year-old veteran of arms-limitation talks, arrived here with the aim of gaining South African accession to the nuclear treaty in return for a pledge of continued cooperation between the two Governments in the peaceful applications of nuclear energy.

The talks in the South African capital are the culmination of secret negotiations that began last year, after a diplomatic flurry over fears that South Africa was preparing to test a nuclear explosive. The

Continued on Page A6, Column 3

2 U.S. NEWSMEN GET SOVIET LIBEL CHARGE

TV Agency Files Suit Stemming From Dispatches About Dissident

By DAVID K. SHIPLER

Special to The New York Times

MOSCOW, June 28—Two American reporters were formally accused in a Moscow court today of having libeled Soviet state television by writing articles about an imprisoned dissident's televised "confession" that his friends and relatives believed had been fabricated.

It was the first time that Western diplomats and correspondents could remember the Soviet Government's taking legal action against foreign journalists for their dispatches.

The two reporters, Craig R. Whitney of The New York Times and Harold D. Piper of The Baltimore Sun, appeared in court in answer to a summons and were presented with copies of the claim against them by Lev Y. Almazov, chairman of the Moscow City Court.

Written Response Is Due Tomorrow

Judge Almazov set noon Friday as a deadline for a written response to the charge, and July 5 as a trial date. A guilty finding, according to Article 7 of the Civil Code, may result in a court order to publish a retraction and, failing that, a fine.

The claim, brought by the Soviet Government's broadcasting agency, asked that the two reporters "be held answerable for publishing in the foreign press slanderous information denigrating the honor and dignity of the members of the staff of the State Committee for Television and Radio of the U.S.S.R. and that they be caused to publish a retraction in the press."

It was not explained how a Soviet court could claim jurisdiction over newspapers

Continued on Page A13, Column 1

United Press International

WED IN MONACO: Princess Caroline and Philippe Junot during civil marriage ceremony at palace in Monaco. They exchanged vows in same room where Prince Rainier and Grace Kelly were wed in 1956. Page C10.

INSIDE

Blackout Cost Tallied

New York City's blackout last July cost at least $310 million, a study by the Library of Congress research service found. Page B9.

Levitt Disputes Vouchers

Arthur Levitt charged that the Port Authority let directors accused of falsifying expense vouchers alter them retroactively. Page B6.

News Summary and Index, Page B1

Boy, 15, Who Killed 2 and Tried To Kill a Third Is Given 5 Years

By CHARLES KAISER

A 15-year-old Harlem youth who admitted killing two subway passengers and attempting to kill a subway motorman in one eight-day period last March has been sentenced to a maximum of five years in prison.

Under the terms of the sentence, imposed by Judge Edith Miller in Family Court—it was the maximum she could impose under state law—the youth will be required to spend at least 18 months in a "secure facility." After that he could be moved to a "residential facility" or kept in the secure facility, at the option of the state's Division for Youth.

Robert H. Silberling, head of the District Attorney's juvenile offense bureau, said that the state could, at its discretion, choose to keep the youth confined beyond the court-imposed five-year sentence. But when he reached the age of 21, Mr. Silberling said, he would have to be released.

Morgenthau Comments

"We've urged longer sentences," said District Attorney Robert M. Morgenthau of Manhattan, who cited the case yesterday in renewing a call for revision of the state's juvenile-offender laws. "I don't think the present law provides for adequate sentences for violent offenders. There has to be a provision for longer sentences for unusual cases like this one."

According to police and court officials, what makes the case unusual is the violent nature of the slightly built youth who they say has threatened to kill the detectives who arrested him, the prosecutors assigned to the case and Judge Miller herself. The police said he had also stabbed a fellow inmate at the Spofford Juvenile Center in the neck with a fork, saying: "I'll kill you if you sit down next to me."

"He's a kid who showed no remorse whatsoever," said Detective Sgt. Thomas Brady, who helped supervise the investigation that led to the youth's arrest.

Special Units Formed

Crimes by youthful repeat offenders, especially against the elderly, have generated controversy over what have been called lenient sentences sometimes handed out by judges. A highly publicized series of such crimes two years ago led to the formation in November 1976 by the Police Department of senior-citizen robbery units in all five boroughs.

Last year Mayor Koch's advocacy of the death penalty for heinous crimes was a major issue in the mayoralty campaign. Some people believe that Mr. Koch's support for the death penalty provided his margin of victory over Mario M. Cuomo

Continued on Page B7, Column 1

High Court, by 5 to 4, Backs Some Affirmative Action In College Admissions, but Orders Bakke Enrolled

Continued From Page A1

John Paul Stevens—held that the Civil Rights Act of 1964 barred the program. The act prohibits discrimination based on race at any educational institution receiving Federal support. These Justices said that Mr. Bakke should be admitted.

Justice Powell agreed with the second group on the issue of the Davis plan and Mr. Bakke's admission but voted with the Brennan bloc on the issue of the constitutionality of affirmative action in general, thus creating a narrow majority for each issue.

The Bakke case had been one of the most closely followed and controversial before the high court in many years. More than 60 briefs, a record, were submitted for and against the would-be medical student, and feeling ran high between adherents of pure "merit selection" and liberals anxious to atone for past discrimination.

Five Summaries Read

For more than an hour this morning, before a hushed but uncrowded courtroom, the Justices read summaries of five of the six opinions the case produced. Relatives of the Justices and some court personnel knew the ruling was coming, but most of the spectators had not anticipated hearing a page from history.

In the unusual judicial voting, the opinion written by Justice Powell became the judgment of the Court—its official statement of the law of the case—even though most of it represented his personal views, with relatively little support from any of his eight colleagues.

"It is evident," Mr. Powell wrote, "that the Davis special admission program involves the use of an explicit racial classification never before countenanced by this Court. It tells applicants who are not Negro, Asian or Chicano that they are totally excluded from a specific percentage of the seats in an entering class." He continued:

Proof of State Interest

"No matter how strong their qualifications, quantitative and extracurricular, including their own potential for contribution to educational diversity, they are never afforded the chance to compete with applicants from the preferred groups for the special admission seats. At the same time, the preferred applicants have the opportunity to compete for every seat in the class."

"When a state's distribution of benefits or imposition of burdens hinges on the color of a person's skin or ancestry, that individual is entitled to a demonstration that the challenged classification is necessary to promote a substantial state interest." Justice Powell continued. Referring to the California Board of Regents, he said, "Petitioner has failed to carry this burden."

But, Mr. Powell contended, the California courts erred in enjoining the state from ever considering race in choosing between professional school applicants.

He said that the state could legitimately employ "a properly devised admissions program involving the competitive consideration of race and ethnic origin," such as that employed by Harvard, in which race is only one factor.

Justice Powell listed as other possible admissions considerations "exceptional personal talents, unique work or service experience, leadership potential, maturity, demonstrated compassion, a history of overcoming disadvantage, ability to communicate with the poor"—all qualifications that could promote diversity in a student body.

Applicant Rejected Twice

Today's case (Regents of the University of California v. Bakke, No. 76-811) arose when Mr. Bakke, a white engineer, was denied entry to the Davis Medical School in 1973 and 1974. In those years, the school set aside 16 of its 100 openings for minority applicants—blacks, Chicanos and Asians—and some of those admitted under this special program had lower scores than Mr. Bakke.

He went into state court, charging that his constitutional rights were being violated because he was being discriminated against on the basis of his race. The trial court found the program an impermissible racial quota but held that Mr. Bakke had not proved he would have been admitted if there had been no such program.

The California Supreme Court found in favor of Mr. Bakke and ordered the medical school to admit him. The state then appealed to the United States Supreme Court, which had never ruled on such "reverse discrimination" charges until today.

Justice Powell indicated in his opinion that the Court was more likely to sustain racial classifications when they resulted from an official finding of a governmental body of past discrimination. In the case of the Davis Medical School, which was only established in 1968, there had been no such finding.

"The purpose of helping certain groups whom the faculty of the Davis Medical School perceived as victims of 'societal discrimination' does not justify a classification that imposes disadvantages upon persons like respondent, who bear no responsibility for whatever harm the beneficiaries of the special admissions program are thought to have suffered," Mr. Powell declared.

Shift by Nixon Nominees

The Bakke decision demonstrated dramatically the increasing tendency of the four Justices named to the Court by President Nixon to divide on key issues, where they formerly voted together much of the time.

On the critical question of the constitutionality of affirmative action programs, Justices Powell and Blackmun were on one side and Chief Justice Burger and Justice Rehnquist on the other.

Writing for the four Justices who supported Mr. Bakke in full, Mr. Stevens insisted that the broad question of race as an element in college admission policy had not even been before the Court for resolution. He said it was "perfectly clear that the question whether race can ever be used as a factor in an admissions decision is not an issue in this case and that the discussion of that issue is inappropriate."

The Stevens bloc said it was unnecessary for them to engage in any constitutional interpretation because they found that the Davis admissions program violated Title VI of the Civil Rights Act on its face and that fact alone justified ordering Mr. Bakke's admission.

Hint of a Majority Draft

In a long opinion that looked as though it might have been a majority draft at an earlier stage of the Court's secret deliberations, Justice Brennan identified as "the central meaning of today's decisions" the view that "Government may take race into account when it acts, not to demean or insult any racial group but to remedy disadvantages cast on minorities by past racial prejudice, at least when appropriate findings have been made by judicial, legislative or administrative bodies with competence to act in this area."

In a footnote, Justice Stevens said, "It is hardly necessary to state that only a majority can speak for the Court or determine what is the 'central meaning' of any judgment of the Court."

Justice Brennan struck a glancing blow at the Harvard multifactor admissions system, saying, "There is no basis for preferring a particular preference program simply because in achieving the same goals that the Davis Medical School is pursuing it proceeds in a manner that is not immediately apparent to the public."

Mistreatment of Blacks

Justice Marshall concluded a historicali outline of black mistreatment, from slavery through discrimination, by accusing the Court of "stepping in to stop affirmative action programs of the type used by the University of California."

Justice White questioned in a separate opinion whether Mr. Bakke had any right to sue as a private citizen, invoking Title VI to defend himself against alleged discrimination. Of his eight colleagues, four apparently believed the plaintiff had such a right and the four others assumed it for the purposes of the case.

In his opinion, Justice Blackmun said he thought it would be impossible to draft a successful affirmative action program "in a racially neutral way."

"To ask this be so," he said, "is to demand the impossible. In order to get beyond racism, we must first take account of race. There is no other way."

Chronology of Admissions Dispute

WASHINGTON, June 28 (AP)—Following is a chronology of the case of the Regents of the University of California v. Bakke; which was decided today by the Supreme Court:

With his application to the University of California at Davis Medical School twice rejected, Mr. Bakke sued in the Yolo County Superior Court in June 1974. He charged that the medical school's special admissions policy unconstitutionally set aside 16 of 100 positions for racial minorities and that he was better qualified for admission than some of the students admitted under the special program.

In an opinion on Nov. 25, 1974, Judge F. Leslie Manker ruled that the university's program was invalid on the ground that it discriminated against Mr. Bakke because of his race. But Judge Manker refused to order the school to admit Mr. Bakke, ruling only that Mr. Bakke was entitled to have his application reconsidered without regard to race.

Both the university and Mr. Bakke appealed the ruling. In an unusual move, the California Supreme Court agreed to hear the case without waiting for a state appeals court to hear and decide it.

After hearing arguments, the California Supreme Court on Sept. 16, 1976, ruled that the university's affirmative action program was unconstitutional because it violated the equal-protection rights of whites. The court ordered the university to admit Mr. Bakke as a medical school student in the fall of 1977.

On Nov. 15, 1976 the university secured Supreme Court permission to keep its admissions policy in effect until it could appeal the state court's ruling.

Despite pleas from numerous civil rights groups that it not pursue the case further, the university on Dec. 14, 1976 sought a review by the United States Supreme Court.

That review was granted on Feb. 22, 1977.

The Justices heard almost two hours of arguments in the case on Oct. 12, 1977. A San Francisco lawyer, Reynold Colvin, represented Mr. Bakke. Archibald Cox, a former Solicitor General and former Watergate special prosecutor, represented the university. Solicitor General Wade McCree argued for the Government as a friend of the court.

Five days later, the Justices asked each side and the Government to submit new briefs in the case centering on how a portion of the Civil Rights Act of 1964 affects the Bakke case. The portion of the law makes it illegal for any institution receiving Government funds, as do most state schools, to discriminate against anyone because of race.

The New York Times/Terence McCarthy

THE SCHOOL IN QUESTION: Medical students on the University of California's Davis campus yesterday. Allan Bakke sued the university after his application for admission was rejected in 1973 and 1974.

The New York Times/Gordon Clark

Allan P. Bakke leaving his home for work at NASA's Ames Research Center, left, near San Francisco. Below: the Bakke family's home in Los Altos, Calif.

Focus of Historic Battle in Civil Rights Law

Allan Paul Bakke

By ROBERT LINDSEY

Special to The New York Times

LOS ANGELES, June 28—As he began the long wait for the United States Supreme Court to rule on his application for medical school last year, Allan Paul Bakke wrote a letter to a friend that concluded with this remark:

Man in the News

"If this takes much longer and we prevail, I may be the first person to retire from engineering to study medicine."

Mr. Bakke won his fight today. His attorney, Reynold H. Colvin of San Francisco, said Mr. Bakke would enter the University of California at Davis School of Medicine in September at the age of 38.

Mr. Bakke is a husky, baldish father of two who became the focus of a historic battle in civil rights law because of a personal obsession to become a physician that developed relatively late in life and because of what one of his friends called "an almost religious zeal" to fight a system that he felt was unfair, which treated whites less equitably than members of minority groups.

"Bakke was a man who felt as strongly as anyone I've ever known about his potential as a healer of the sick and as a benefactor of his community," recalled Peter C. Storandt, an admissions officer at Davis during Mr. Bakke's fight to enter medical school.

Mr. Bakke (the name is pronounced BAH-key) was born on Feb. 4, 1940, in Minneapolis of parents of Norwegian ancestry, and this heritage is apparent in Mr. Bakke's fair skin and blond hair. His father was a mailman, his mother a teacher.

From Minnesota to Florida

When he was a child his family moved to Florida, and he was graduated from Coral Gables High Schol. Returning to his home state, he majored in engineering at the University of Minnesota and graduated in 1952 with a grade-point average of 3.51 on a scale of 4—almost straight A's.

To help meet his expenses in college, he had enrolled in the Naval Reserve Officers Training Corps. This left him with a debt of military service, and he later served four years in the Marine Corps, including seven months in Vietnam. He left the Marines in 1967 as a captain.

Then he took an engineering job with the National Aeronautics and Space Administration's Ames Research Center south of San Francisco, where he still works. When he was in Vietnam, he said later, he became fascinated with the work of doctors, and he decided that he wanted to become a physician.

Attended Night Classes

While continuing to work for NASA Mr. Bakke attended night classes at local colleges and completed requirements for a pre-med degree. He also became a volunteer at El Camino Hospital in Mountainview, Calif.

Mr. Bakke applied to 11 medical schools, among them the University of California at Davis, which is near Sacramento, in the fall of 1972. He was then 32, old for a medical school applicant, but he asked for consideration, noting the four years taken up in military service.

Records at the Davis campus indicate that, if there had not been illness in Mr. Bakke's family, he might have been accepted in 1972, and the "Bakke case" might never have reached the Supreme Court.

Late in 1972, his mother-in-law, who lived in Iowa, became ill with lung cancer, and Mr. Bakke and his wife, Judy, were required to spend considerable time with her before her death. Because of his absence, Mr. Bakke did not complete all the paperwork for consideration as an applicant until Jan. 9, 1973.

Admission and Lower Scores

Other would-be medical students at Davis completed their applications earlier, and some were admitted to the school with lower scores than Mr. Bakke's. By the time his file was ready for consideration in the spring of 1973, there were relatively few slots remaining in the next freshman class and he was rejected—as he had been at the 10 other schools to which he applied the previous fall.

In a letter after the rejection, Mr. Bakke, referring to the allocation of 16 positions in the freshman medical class to minority members, objected that all applicants to the school were not considered equally and assailed "quotas, open or covert, for racial minorities." He added that he felt "compelled to pursue a different course of action."

The letter was answered by Mr. Storandt, who was then the manager of medical school admissions at Davis and is now an admissions officer at Yale University. Mr. Storandt sympathized with Mr. Bakke and tacitly encouraged him to challenge the minority preference program in court.

When Mr. Bakke again submitted an application at Davis in the summer of 1973, it was rejected again, and there is evidence in the files of the university that his complaints were considered in this decision at least as much as his grades and test scores.

Legal Fight Begins

After the second rejection, Mr. Bakke retained a lawyer who filed suit against the university, challenging the setting aside of 16 positions in the medical school's freshman class as a violation of the Constitution's 14th Amendment, which guarantees equal protection. This began the legal fight that ended with today's Supreme Court decision.

Although neither Mr. Bakke nor his attorneys will discuss it, it appears that the case has not been a financial burden to Mr. Bakke. He lives in Los Altos, Calif., a suburb where most houses sell for upward of $100,000. He and his wife have two young children and make frequent camping trips. Mr. Bakke, who is almost six feet tall, jogs daily.

He has refused to discuss his case with reporters and has taken great efforts to dodge photographers, Friends say that he is dedicated to his family, is not overly friendly with fellow workers and avoids discussion of his case at work.

Mr. Storandt described him this way:

"He struck me as a character out of a Bergman film—somewhat humorless, perfectly straightforward, zealous in his approach—an extremely impressive man" with a determination to become a physician.

Mr. Storandt said that he recently saw Mr. Bakke again and concluded that he had changed since the legal battle began. "When I used to think of him, I thought of words like 'calculating, cold and driven,'" he said. "I think this experience has mellowed him a little. I found him a more reflective man. He's been sobered by it all—maybe be because he's gotten older and he has children."

In the past, he said, Mr. Bakke's determination to become a doctor was a central feature of his character. "Now," he said, "I'm not so certain. He's mellowed. He didn't seem so absolutely certain about it than he was before."

A Plateau for Minorities

Continued From Page A1

is thought to exhibit qualities more likely to promote beneficial educational pluralism," Mr. Powell wrote.

Mr. Powell's arguments seemed to be directed more to a belief that has become prevalent among many people since the civil rights movement overturned laws and policies directed at keeping blacks in an inferior position—that the larger difficulty in America now may be one of class rather than race, as based on economic factors.

"The diversity that furthers a compelling state interest encompasses a far broader array of qualifications and characteristics of which racial or ethnic origin is but a single though important element," Mr. Powell wrote. He said that Davis's "special admissions program, focused solely on ethnic diversity, would hinder rather than further attainment of genuine diversity."

Although today's decision seemed in some ways equivocal, some civil rights lawyers who have represented black plaintiffs over the years saw in it the seeds of further progress for blacks and other minorities.

"The Supreme Court's decision that race is a proper factor in admissions decisions is the legal concrete on which further affirmative action programs can be made," said Joseph L. Rauh Jr., a Washington lawyer long active in civil rights. "The Supreme Court struck a blow for remedying past wrongs and providing a more equal society."

Part of this optimism was based on the fact that the Court may have been more split on procedure than on substance. Four justices refused to go to the constitutional questions involved, saying that the case should be decided on the basis of Title VI of the 1964 Civil Rights Act, which prohibits discrimination on account of race in any federally assisted program.

The legislative history of Title VI speaks to the removal of legal barriers only, a position that its sponsors took in order to get it through Congress. Some lawyers believe that affirmative action, and today's decision, would be easier to sustain on constitutional grounds and that future decisions will not be so marginal.

In any event, the decision did not remove from the nation the burden of struggling with what constitutes justice in admitting students to institutions of higher learning where there are many more applicants than places available.

"The decision will go down in history not for what it did but for what it didn't do," said Alan M. Derschowitz, professor of law at Harvard University. "It neither legitimized racial quotas nor put down affirmative action programs. The decision will make the job of admissions offices a lot harder. It will make them look at people as persons, not as members of a group and not as computerized ciphers."

Associated Press

Reynold Colvin, Allan P. Bakke's lawyer, taking a congratulatory call in San Francisco yesterday.

A Reaction of Disappointment on the Davis Campus

Special to The New York Times

DAVIS, Calif., June 28—There were not many people on campus here today. But those attending summer school or working at the University of California at Davis generally opposed the United States Supreme Court decision striking down quotas for minorities entering the medical school here.

"It almost brought tears to my eyes when I first heard it," Martha Stiles, an employee in the university personnel office, said of the decision in the Allan P. Bakke case.

"They say it won't affect affirmative action, but I can't see how it won't," she said. "And then there goes all the progress, everything that's happened in the past 10 years."

David Lee, a premedical student who will graduate after summer school, was also "kind of upset" about the decision. But he was more angered that the Justices had taken "so long" to announce their decision and remarked, "School is out and the students can't express their feelings, can't organize to show their opposition."

Only 1,500 students are on campus now, most of them graduate students. In the regular school year, more than 30,000 people attend classes on the tree-lined, grassy campus 12 miles south of Sacramento.

"The decision doesn't affect me since I'm Chinese-American and we aren't considered a minority in the admission plans," said Mr. Lee. "But I don't think it's right. And I don't know how Bakke will make it here since some feel he shouldn't be allowed to stay or study in peace."

'Ambivalent' About Decision

Lynn Lynch, a summer curator at the university museum, said she was "ambivalent" about the decision.

"I think the Third World must be given entrance to the establishment and someone must pay for it," she said. "I guess this generation has to pay, but I'm concerned that advancing minorities has to hurt others."

Byron Froman, a junior science major who is considering medical school, said he was "definite for affirmative action."

"I believe the cycle, the vicious cycle minorities are put in, has to be broken up," he said. "We have to right past injustices, and this decision seems like a step backwards to before the '60's.

"Yet, a lot of people in my department were for Bakke," he added. "The whites were saying they were fed up with the programs for blacks, like they were in a little revolt."

Miss Stiles said that many of her friends, especially the women, were worried that today's Supreme Court ruling would also affect affirmative action programs for women.

"Everybody's been waiting to see what today's ruling would be," she said. "Now they have to wait and find out what it means for women. The program here was a bad one, some of my friends tell me, but I hope that this does not mean the end of affirmative action for minorities and for women."

"All the News That's Fit to Print"

The New York Times

LATE CITY EDITION

Weather: Hazy, storms by evening; clearing tonight. Sunny tomorrow. Temperature range: today 87-67; yesterday 77-64. Details on page D15.

VOL.CXXVII . . . No.44,014

NEW YORK, THURSDAY, JULY 27, 1978

25 cents beyond 50-mile zone from New York City. Higher in air delivery cities.

20 CENTS

161 INSPECTORS HIRED BY KOCH TO COMBAT AGENCY CORRUPTION

INCOMPETENCE ALSO A TARGET

City's Employees Told They Must Report Any Malfeasance — Gotbaum Attacks Plan

By EDWARD RANZAL

Mayor Koch hired 161 new inspectors yesterday for an "overseer" program meant to root out corruption and incompetence in 30 New York City agencies.

In an executive order, he also strengthened employee guidelines for standards and discipline and made it obligatory for the agencies' 225,000 employees to inform superiors of corruption, criminal activity or conflicts of interest among fellow workers.

An employee who knows of criminal activity by another city employee, or people doing business with the city, but fails to report it, could be dismissed, said Stanley Lupkin, the Investigation Commissioner.

Gotbaum Is Critical

"While the overwhelming majority of city employees, who are honest and perform their duties competently, have nothing to fear from this program," the Mayor said, "I want to serve notice on the small number of employees who violate the public trust that they have no place in this administration."

Victor Gotbaum, head of District Council 37, the largest municipal union, promptly criticized the program as "destructive."

"Show and tell," he said of the informer requirement.

Lindsay Also Named Inspectors

The program is not new to the city. Former Mayor John V. Lindsay appointed inspectors general to monitor the conduct of city employees in major mayoral agencies. In 12 years the program has grown to cover 11 agencies.

Under Mayor Koch's program, 25 inspectors general, 17 deputies and 280 confidential inspectors will seek to end corrupt practices, misconduct and incompetence in the 30 agencies.

The Mayor announced his program at a news conference in the City Council Chamber after he swore in new inspectors general and their deputies.

After the announcement, Mr. Gotbaum called the Mayor's action "kind of sad," saying it was not going to "make for job satisfaction among employees."

During his election campaign Mr. Koch spoke out about ineptitude and dishonesty among municipal workers. In his first days in office he promised to adopt the program he put into action officially yesterday. Since then relations between Mr. Koch and some city labor leaders have been edgy.

Besides the conflicts that have been

Continued on Page D16, Column 6

Associated Press

Dr. Robert Edwards, left, and Dr. Patrick Steptoe at news conference yesterday in Manchester, England

Scientists Praise British Birth as Triumph

Early Insertion of Embryo Into Womb Is Linked to Successful Gestation

By ROY REED

Special to The New York Times

LONDON, July 26 — Scientists applauded, English churchmen nodded a qualified approval and the British press turned somersaults today to welcome the world's first baby born from an egg fertilized in a laboratory.

The 5-pound-12-ounce baby, a girl born slightly prematurely, was delivered by Caesarean section last night at the Oldham General Hospital in Lancashire. Dr. Patrick C. Steptoe was in charge of the delivery. A hospital spokesman said the baby was "quite normal."

At a news conference today, Dr. Robert G. Edwards, a Cambridge University specialist in reproductive physiology, who was one of the two physicians involved in the birth, said that the embryo was placed in the womb of Mrs. Brown two and a half days after fertilization. This was in contrast to the four and a half days that had elapsed before the embryo was placed inside the womb in earlier attempts, he said. When the embryo was placed in Mrs. Brown's womb, he added, it had only reached the eight-cell stage.

Supported Earlier Speculation

This supported earlier speculation that such early insertion, which was previously thought to endanger the embryo, had contributed to the procedure's success.

The baby was gestated in the normal manner, with placenta and umbilical cord linking it to the mother's blood supply. However, where unusual birth conditions are anticipated, Caesarean deliveries have become the practice to minimize the risk of harm to the baby.

The doctors had known the sex of the child for some time, but Mrs. Brown had insisted that she not be told. "After waiting for years for this wonderful thing to happen, I do not want to be cheated of the final thrill," she said.

Church leaders both here and in other countries generally welcomed the achievement, but with qualifications, especially from Roman Catholic leaders. [Page A16.]

Leo Abse, a Labor Party Member of Parliament, urged the regulation of

Continued on Page A16, Column 2

Doctors' Success in Conception in the Laboratory Intensifies the Debate Over Reproductive Control

By WALTER SULLIVAN

Special to The New York Times

LONDON, July 26 — The first authenticated birth of a baby conceived in a laboratory, an event that comes on the heels of other developments in reproductive control, has intensified debate among scientists that touches such issues as the sanctity of life.

Early in this decade, when the work of the two men responsible for the birth, Dr. Robert G. Edwards and Dr. Patrick C. Steptoe, first became widely known, it was denounced by a number of scientists, theologians and others. In Britain a winner of the Nobel Prize in chemistry termed the research a "stunt" and proposed that "the whole nation should decide whether or not these experiments should continue."

Some of the most vehement critics, warning of dire social consequences, have contended that procreation is sacred and that the performance of its most critical step in a laboratory degrades humanity.

Other critics have said that, in a world suffering from overpopulation, scientists should concentrate on how to prevent births rather than encourage them.

This is the last of three articles on the implanting of human embryos and its implications.

Questions about the medical procedures and the possibility of birth defects have been raised also. And there is considerable controversy involving the destruction of embryos that attempts at implantation could entail.

What Dr. Steptoe and Dr. Edwards did was enable Lesley Brown to become pregnant despite a defect in her oviducts. Mrs. Brown gave birth last night in Oldham, England, to a healthy girl that the Browns named Louise today. The pregnancy was reportedly achieved by

Continued on Page A16, Column 5

Doctors Isolate a Human Gene, Allowing Birth-Defect Detection

By United Press International

BOSTON, July 26 — For the first time, doctors have been able to identify a single gene among the millions in a human cell and can now see whether an unborn baby is missing certain parts of its genetic blueprint, a team of researchers reported today.

The report, in The New England Journal of Medicine, is the first example of applying some of the tools of gene-cutting, part of what is called recombinant DNA technology, to finding and understanding hereditary birth defects while a child is unborn.

Achievement Is Praised

Dr. Arthur W. Nienhuis of the National Heart, Lung and Blood Institute, who wrote an editorial in the journal on the implications of the achievement, said: "This is the first direct examination of the gene. The power of the technique is extraordinary, but the actual execution of it once mastered is not terribly difficult."

While the technique so far has allowed detection of only a rare group of genetic diseases, researchers predicted that within a few years they will have the genetic knowledge enabling them to detect more common ones, perhaps even cystic fibrosis.

Scientists estimate that there are three million to four million genes in each human cell. The team of researchers from Harvard and Yale Universities and the Haceteppe University in Turkey reported being able to produce an image of the gene that directs production of hemoglobin, which carries oxygen in the blood.

Thus, the team said, doctors can now detect certain debilitating and sometimes fatal forms of anemia, caused by

Continued on Page A16, Column 3

Egyptians Order Israel's Mission To Leave Today

By WILLIAM E. FARRELL

Special to The New York Times

JERUSALEM, July 26 — Prime Minister Menachem Begin said tonight that Israel had been ordered by Egypt to withdraw, by tomorrow, its military mission based in Egypt since January.

The negotiation support group went to Egypt when talks opened on peace issues, after President Anwar el-Sadat's visit to Jerusalem. It remained in Egypt even though the peace talks quickly became stalemated.

The order for the withdrawal of the 10 middle-rank military technicians and communications specialists was made after a meeting of the National Security Council in Cairo.

[Egyptian War Ministry officials confirmed in Cairo that the Israeli mission had been ordered to leave the country. They said the action reflected a Cairo decision to avoid further direct contacts until Israel adopted a new position on peace talks.]

'We Shall Do So,' Begin Says

Mr. Begin, appearing on television, seemed unruffled by the Egyptian order, implying that it was part of a new war of nerves by Cairo in the strained peace maneuvering. He urged Israelis to be patient, saying: "I don't minimize anything. I advise all Israelis to have strong nerves."

Mr. Begin said he received the order for the recall of the Israeli group a few hours earlier. "We shall do so," Mr. Begin added.

"Welcome home," he said in reference to the small Israeli mission, whose members spent much of their time at a military base near Alexandria playing volleyball and cards. The mission had been a lingering symbol of direct Egyptian-Israeli contact in the uncertain period that

Continued on Page A3, Column 1

Justice Dept. Supports Detroit Police Quotas

By STEVEN V. ROBERTS

Special to The New York Times

WASHINGTON, July 26 — In its first official interpretation of the Supreme Court's Bakke decision, the Justice Department has urged approval of an affirmative action program that sets strict numerical quotas for the promotion of blacks in the Detroit police department.

The Court's decision last month did not require public agencies to be "color-blind," the department argued, and did not disturb previous rulings that required such agencies to take positive steps to remedy the effects of past discrimination.

The Justice Department's comments came in a brief as a friend of the court filed today with the United States Court of Appeals for the Sixth Circuit in a case called Detroit Police Officers Association v. Coleman A. Young. In that case, white police officers challenged an affirmative action plan that mandated the police department to promote one black to the rank of sergeant for every white promoted. Last February, the plan was ruled unconstitutional by Judge Fred W. Kaess of Federal District Court.

The department's brief had political as well as legal implications. Supporters of

Continued on Page B18, Column 1

CURBS ON RHODESIA UPHELD BY SENATE, BUT CONDITIONALLY

CARTER COULD LIFT SANCTIONS

He Must Determine Free Vote Has Occurred and New Regime Is Intent on Negotiations

By GRAHAM HOVEY

Special to The New York Times

WASHINGTON, July 26 — The Senate rejected a move to repeal economic sanctions against Rhodesia today, but then decisively adopted a compromise measure setting conditions under which the President could be required to lift the sanctions in the future.

The sponsors of the compromise amendment to the International Security Assistance Bill insisted that it was designed to keep the United States on a

Roll-call vote on Rhodesia, page A6.

"moderate middle course" between the current Rhodesian Government, led by Prime Minister Ian D. Smith, and the Patriotic Front, the nationalist group that is waging guerrilla war to bring down that Government. Tonight, the Senate passed the full aid bill, 73 to 13.

Despite the "moderate" nature of the amendment on Rhodesian sanctions, Administration officials fear that its language would make it appear that the United States is siding with Mr. Smith and the three black members of his transitional Government, who are committed to establishing majority rule after free elections planned for December.

Good Faith an Issue

In effect, the amendment would require President Carter to lift the sanctions, but only after he had determined that a Rhodesian government had been established through free elections under impartial international observation, and that it had committed itself to negotiate in good faith with the guerrilla leaders.

The sanctions, voted by the United Nations Security Council in 1966 and 1968, have the force of American law. They ban all trade with Rhodesia.

The sponsors of today's amendment, Senator Clifford P. Case of New Jersey and Jacob K. Javits of New York, both Republicans, argued that their proposal would eliminate fears in this country and in Africa that the United States was siding with the Patriotic Front guerrilla leaders, Joshua Nkomo and Robert Mugabe.

Reluctant to Negotiate

The transitional Government has equal numbers of white and black ministers and has promised to hold elections based on universal suffrage in December, but thus far have been unwilling to negotiate with the guerrillas.

The Case-Javits amendment was adopted today by 59 to 36, but the most critical test came on an earlier movement to table it, which the Senate defeated, 57 to 39. Its adoption sidetracked the amendment of Senator Jesse Helms, Republican of North Carolina, who proposed an immediate end of sanctions.

Senator Helms withdrew his amendment after a substitute proposal by Senator John C. Danforth, Republican of Missouri, had been defeated, 54 to 42, in the closest roll-call vote of the day.

Mr. Danforth had proposed that the

Continued on Page A6. Column 1

Associated Press

ACTIVIST FREED: Mariya Slepak in Moscow after she received a suspended sentence. Page A3.

INSIDE

Trade Deficit Cut in June

The Commerce Department said the nation's trade deficit had been halved in June but had worsened sharply in the first half of the year. Page D1.

Water Supply Board Abolished

Governor Carey signed a bill abolishing the New York City Board of Water Supply, long criticized as a useless bastion of political patronage. Page B2.

News Summary and Index, Page B1

New York City Announces Moves To Halt Illegal Conversion of Lofts

By JOSEPH P. FRIED

New York City officials announced plans yesterday to prevent further illegal conversions of factory buildings to residential use and to bring "into compliance with fire, health and safety codes" the 1,000 structures that have already been illegally converted.

Under plans disclosed by Mayor Koch and City Councilman Thomas J. Manton of Queens, head of the Council's Housing and Buildings Committee, the city will not seek to evict people already living in lofts or other illegally converted space — except in a certain situation.

The exception is where city inspectors find "hazardous conditions," such as a "nonsprinklered building with an open, unenclosed stairway and without a second means of egress directly accessible by each dwelling unit." In such cases, an "immediate vacate order" will be issued.

In all the other cases, however, the city will use a combination of legal efforts and consulting aid to owners to remove whatever deficiencies prevent the structures from meeting health and safety standards, the Mayor and Mr. Manton said.

These and other steps to deal with problems stemming from the increasing number of conversions of lofts to residential use were outlined in an "action plan" on the issue that was drawn up by a Koch administration task force that was formed in March. Subsequently, the City Council urged the administration to act on the problems.

In an attempt to deal with a second problem stemming from the growing number of conversions — the reported displacement of manufacturing tenants to make way for residential tenants who pay higher rents — the plan envisions a program of relocation payments for manufacturing concerns displaced in legal conversions under the so-called J-51 tax-incentive program.

In addition to these local steps, the task-force report cited two bills passed by

Continued on Page D16, Column 4

The New York Times / Teresa Zabala

GOLDBERG GETS FREEDOM AWARD: Arthur J. Goldberg speaking at White House yesterday after President Carter awarded him the Medal of Freedom, nation's highest civilian award. Also present were Mrs. Goldberg; his daughter, Barbara Goldberg Cramer; her three sons, and Secretary of State Cyrus R. Vance. Page C2.

RELIGIOUS LEADERS DIFFER ON IMPLANT

Catholics Critical of Conception Outside the Body, but Many Other Groups Endorse It

By GEORGE VECSEY

Roman Catholic leaders criticized all forms of artificial insemination yesterday, but many Jewish, Moslem and Protestant figures endorsed a laboratory-induced conception so long as both husband and wife were the parents of the child.

The religious leaders and theologians were responding to the birth in England Tuesday night of the first baby known to have been conceived outside the body.

All the religious authorities interviewed expressed concern, however, about any possible broader uses of the technique for genetic engineering, and most expressed the fear that laboratory insemination could lead to women bearing other women's children. Others were concerned that more abortions might result from laboratory inseminations.

"I was quite touched by the passion of this woman to have a baby at a time when many women are choosing not to have children," said Blu Greenberg, an Orthodox Jewish writer, who is an advocate of women's rights.

A Reminder of Hannah

"In her determination, she reminded me of the Biblical heroine Hannah, mother of Samuel, who cried at the temple gates until God promised her she would have a child in the next year," Mrs. Greenberg, a mother of five, said.

The response from the Vatican, the headquarters of the world's 540 million Roman Catholics, was based on the same reasoning that the church has used to oppose artificial contraception.

The Rev. Pierfranco Pastore, a Vatican spokesman who noted that he was speaking personally, said, "Fecundation must be carried out according to nature and through reciprocal and responsible love between a man and a woman."

In the United States, Bishop Thomas C. Kelly, the general secretary of the National Council of Catholic Bishops, issued a statement that said in part:

"The Christian morality has insisted on the importance of protecting the process by which human life is transmitted. The fact that science now has the ability to alter this process significantly does not mean that, morally speaking, it has the right to do so."

A Somewhat Different View

A somewhat different view was taken by the Rev. Richard A. McCormick, a professor of Christian ethics at the Kennedy Institute of Georgetown University.

"If someone were to approach me about artificial insemination in which the husband were the donor, I would not have the certainty to say it's wrong," Professor McCormick said.

He noted that Pope Pius XII made four separate statements against artificial insemination from 1949 to 1958, but he added, "Since that time, there has been a long second look, a rethinking that it can be justified."

Father McCormick said that the issue would be raised in September at a meeting of the Federal Ethics Advisory Board, of which he is a member. He said he expected that the board's view would be used when research groups in the United States pursued grants to duplicate the British medical success.

'Remarkable Scientific Achievement'

Dr. C. Everett Koop, surgeon-in-chief at Children's Hospital in Philadelphia, who is a Presbyterian elder and an author on bioethics, praised the "remarkable scientific achievement." But he added, "Since I believe that life begins at conception, I must ask what happens if somebody wants to cancel the experiment and he dumps it down the sink?"

Dr. Koop said that he was concerned about "the next step, when Mrs. Jones decides she wants a child from that tall, blond gene pool down the block." He also said that he feared genetic manipulation to produce a "super race."

Dr. Haddon W. Robinson, chairman of the Department of Pastoral Missions at Dallas Theological Seminary, said that there was "no theological problem" with the English baby, but he said that he was afraid laboratory-fertilized eggs could be placed in "surrogate mothers," and that that would raise questions about "what it actually means to mother a child."

Giles Eccleston, secretary of the Church of England's Board for Social Responsibility, called the birth "an advance in meeting the problem of childlessness facing some married couples." But he said that he questioned the use of scarce medical resources for this when other needs, such as problems of the aged and the mentally handicapped, might be more pressing.

Cautious Catholic Reaction

Reaction from Roman Catholic authorities in England was also cautious. A statement by the Social Welfare Commission for the Church in England and Wales commended the birth as "a pro-life expression of love," but it added that different cases posed a variety of problems.

Gordon Cardinal Gray, Archbishop of St. Andrews and Edinburgh, who is president of the Scottish Catholic Bishops, said that he had "grave misgivings about the methods and the possible implications and consequences for the future."

Ayatullah Milani, a Moslem Shiite leader in Iran, told an Iranian radio audience that a baby born under circumstances similar to those of the birth in England "is quite legitimate and legal" according to Moslem law "as long as the father and mother are husband and wife."

Rabbi Israel Klavan, an official of the Rabbinical Council of America, the major Orthodox group, said that Orthodoxy would accept a birth so long as no third-party donor was involved.

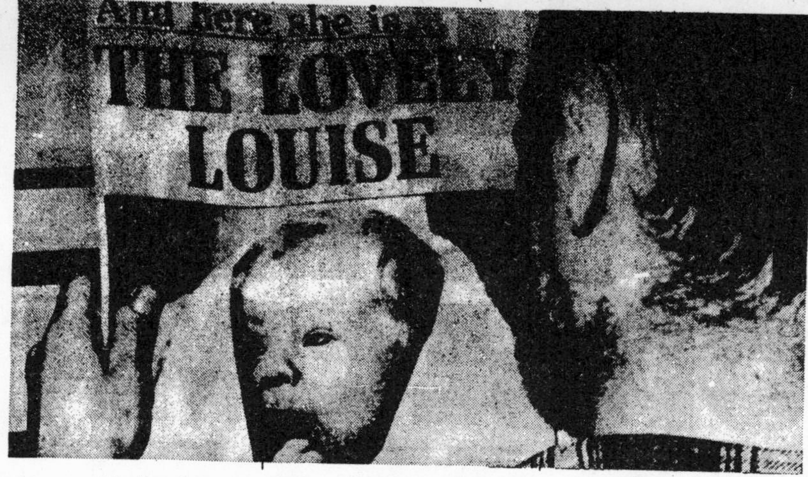

A Londoner looking at a photo of newly born Louise Brown on the front page of The Daily Mail

Associated Press

Succcessful Laboratory Conception Intensifies Debate Over Procedures

Continued From Page A1

removing an almost mature egg cell from her ovaries, exposing it to sperm from her husband, allowing it to grow briefly in the laboratory, and then implanting it in her uterus.

A similar procedure was used at Columbia Presbyterian Medical Center in New York City in an attempt to enable a Florida woman to have a child. While still in the laboratory, the day-old embryo was destroyed, however. The couple, John and Doris Del Zio, sued the medical center, which replied that the experiment was clandestine and contrary to its regulations. A decision is pending in Federal District Court in Manhattan.

Dr. Edwards, in response to his critics, has questioned why anyone should object to "giving these couples their own children" — a view reinforced by the exultant reaction of Lesley Brown and her husband, John.

Mr. Brown has been quoted by The Daily Mail, in a copyrighted article, as saying: "For a person who's been told he and his wife can never have children," the pregnancy was "like a miracle."

"I felt 12 feet high," he said.

Most Similar Cases

Most cases that Dr. Edwards and Dr. Steptoe have treated in a dozen years of attempts have been those of women like Mrs. Brown and Mrs. Del Zio, whose oviducts were inoperative because of blockage or another defect. It is in the oviducts, which carry mature egg cells from the ovaries to the uterus, that fertilization takes place.

One criticism of the Steptoe-Edwards treatment is that a surgical approach is preferable in cases of blocked or otherwise defective oviducts, which is believed to be the problem in 20 percent to 45 percent of infertile women. Dr. Edwards estimates, however, that surgery alleviates only about 17 percent of the cases.

The most controversial ethical problem associated with the Steptoe-Edwards method is the destruction of embryos that it may entail, although there are indications that in Mrs. Brown's case only one egg cell was extracted and thus only one embryo produced.

In some cases that Dr. Steptoe and Dr. Edwards have described, they used hormones to induce the prospective mother to produce a number of egg cells at the end of her monthly cycle.

Cultured in Laboratory

Several of these eggs were removed, exposed to sperm and then cultured in the laboratory until microscopic examination showed some of them subdividing as developing embryos.

One embryo that appeared normal was then injected into the woman's uterus through her cervix. The others, as one critic has put it, were "washed down the sink." It is this that has forced scientists to face the problem of when meaningful life begins.

One argument used in support of the method is that the laboratory procedure only mimics what nature does inside the reproductive system. It is estimated that a large percentage of embryos — some specialists say more than half — are shed by the body in the earliest stages of development.

A defective embryo, for example, may fail to transmit the chemical signal needed to stop monthly menstruation and create the conditions of pregnancy. Menstruation follows and the embryo is swept out.

Intrauterine devices, which are believed to prevent implantation in the uterine wall, has a similar effect. Some contraceptive pills are also said to cause contractions of the uterus that expel the embryo.

Challenged Critics' View

In the Quarterly Review of Biology, published at the State University of New York at Stony Brook, Dr. Edwards has sought to deal with his critics. In doing so he has challenged the view that human life begins at a single, sharply defined moment — that of fertilization.

In his article, entitled "Fertilization of Human Eggs in Vitro: Morals, Ethics and the Law," he contended that this step is but one in a continuing process. The thread of life, he proposed, runs unbroken from generation to generation. It is carried in the germ cells of a newborn infant girl, some of which will be fertilized to pass the germ plasm on to another generation.

'Demands Arbitrary Decisions'

"The assumption of full human rights at a single moment in a continuous developmental sequence," he wrote, "demands making arbitrary decisions that are unjustified biologically."

Some biologists contend that, in view of the process known as cloning, every cell of the body with a nucleus is a potential individual. When, for example, the nucleus is taken from the skin cell of a frog and placed in the egg of another frog whose nucleus has been removed, that egg can develop into a twin of the skin cell donor. In his article, however, Dr. Edwards said he saw little prospect for the use of cloning except in agriculture.

In response to those who said his work was opening the way for socially undesirable manipulations, he said that halting such research would be comparable to forgoing the development of airplanes because they made bombings and hijackings possible.

In addition to their attempts at implanting embryos conceived in the laboratory, Dr. Steptoe and Dr. Edwards have been studying the possibility of freezing and storing embryos, which, they say, could provide a "whole family" from a single egg-harvesting procedure. Other researchers, working with animals, have been experimenting with different methods of embryo implantation and genetic screening that could ultimately have an effect on research on humans.

Dr. Edwards did caution against other reproductive manipulations, although he said that donated semen was now "widely used." He said he envisioned, as well, the donation of egg cells for women unable to produce their own, but he noted the disputes and divided loyalties that can arise when a child's parentage is in doubt.

Another concern of the experimenters, and of others, is whether their technique selects inferior sperm and egg cells. Only a few sperm normally penetrate the reproductive system far enough to compete for fertilization, whereas in artificial insemination there is no such screening.

Those sperm that reach the goal naturally are "a highly selected sample," Dr. Edwards noted, "relatively free of genetic defects." Likewise, the egg cells that ripen under hormonal stimulation may not be those that would mature normally. Such subtle effects, if they exist, may not be evident until babies born by the Steptoe-Edwards method reach maturity.

Birth Defects Considered

If the Steptoe-Edwards procedure becomes commonplace, Dr. Edwards wrote, the situation "seems bound to arise" in which a child is born with defects not evident in the parents. He cited a landmark case in which a deformed child and its parents sued a physician for allowing the child to be born.

Because birth defects occur even under the best of circumstances, he said, it would be hard to prove that the procedure was to blame. In transplants of animal embryos the birth defect rates have been no higher than normal.

At least one other British gynecologist is apparently trying to repeat the Steptoe-Edwards procedure. He is Ian Ferguson, an acquaintance of Dr. Steptoe associated with St. Thomas's Hospital in London. Press reports today told of his efforts to implant an embryo in a patient there.

Although many scientists in the United States reportedly are eager to begin similar experiments, they have been blocked from doing so until the National Ethics Advisory Board, formed in January to rule on human experimentation, takes action. The board has control over such research in any institution receiving Federal funding for any of its activities.

Doctors to a Baby Who Made Medical History

Patrick Christopher Steptoe and Robert Geoffrey Edwards

Special to The New York Times

LONDON, July 26 — The two men whose skill and ingenuity have achieved the first known birth of a baby conceived outside the body of a woman are acknowledged pioneers in their highly specialized fields.

Men in the News

Patrick Christopher Steptoe, 65 years old, has developed the technique whereby maturing egg cells can be removed from a woman's ovary without major surgery so they can then be fertilized in glassware by sperm from the prospective father.

Robert Geoffrey Edwards, 52, has learned enough about the extremely complex chemical messages that control the successive steps of reproduction to bring about normal development of an embryo even though fertilization was "in vitro" — in a glass vessel — and the resulting embryo was artificially inserted into the prospective mother.

Once Virtually Ostracized

While many in the medical community today were hailing the achievement, the work of the two men over a dozen years of collaboration had not always received so warm a reception. For a decade and a half, Dr. Edwards, in particular, fought rear-guard actions against cancellation of grants and against criticism from many quarters.

According to colleagues he was for a long time virtually ostracized by many of his peers and for more than a year dropped his research to explore its ethical and social implications.

The personalities of the two men are said to be very different. Dr. Edwards is pictured by co-workers as ebullient; Dr. Steptoe as more reserved and somewhat avuncular. Yet his career has had its share of high adventure. His ship was reportedly shot out from under him in World War II, and he became a prisoner in Italy.

Dr. Edwards, who was born Sept. 27, 1925, comes of a farming family and retains a love of the soil that has reportedly led him to acquire land near Cambridge for small-scale farming. His interests also include politics. He has long served as a Laborite member of the Cambridge Town Council and for a time as chairman of its finance committee.

After studies at the University of Wales in Bangor, where he earned a doctorate in science, he obtained a Doctor of Philosophy degree at the University of Edinburgh and began to make a name for himself as a specialist in the physiology of reproduction.

From 1957 to 1958, he worked with the late Dr. Albert Tyler at the California Institute of Technology in Pasadena, then returned to the Institute of Animal Genetics in Edinburgh.

It was in the early 1960's that his troubles began. By then he was at the National Institute for Medical Research at Mill Hill, London, trying with hormones to induce ovaries newly removed from women to produce mature egg cells. The ovaries had been excised for a variety of medical reasons. The institute apparently saw his research as too controversial, and he departed for Cambridge, where he has worked ever since.

Ford Fund Aided Work

Beginning in 1963, the Ford Foundation became a prime supporter of reproduction research at Cambridge University's Marshall Laboratory, headed by Dr. Colin R. Austin. The foundation was particularly interested in research applicable to population control and contributed almost $1 million to the Cambridge effort.

It was Ford funds that enabled Cambridge to take on Dr. Edwards and provided his salary. However, in 1974 the foundation decided to discontinue direct support of his research. The reason given was that his work did not seem to be contributing much to knowledge that could limit fertility.

A group of specialists sent to the university by the foundation to assess the program did not, however, agree with an evaluation by Britain's Medical Research Council, which had cut off its support. The American visitors felt, on the contrary, that Dr. Edwards's work met ethical standards for human experimentation.

His wife, Dr. Ruth Fowler, also at Cambridge, is a well known specialist in hormonal control of ovary function. They have five daughters.

Received 'Conjoint' Degree

Dr. Steptoe did his training at St. George's Hospital Medical School, one of 12 such schools operated by the University of London. In 1939, he won a "conjoint diploma." He became a member of the Royal College of Surgeons and was licensed by the Royal College of Physicians.

Almost immediately he was called to active duty in the Royal Navy Volunteer Reserve, and it was not until 1948, after his release from prison camp, that he was able to complete his postgraduate work and become a member of the Royal College of Obstetricians and Gynecologists. He is married and has a grown daughter and son and two grandchildren.

It is for his development of the technique for removing egg cells that he is known on both sides of the Atlantic. With this technique, called laparoscopy, a doctor inserts through a small abdominal incision near the navel a tubular device through which the entire operation can be performed.

The abdominal cavity is inflated with an inert gas to provide working room. Hairlike optical fibers threaded through the tube, or laparoscope, carry light to illuminate the ovary. Through additional fibers, the surgeon is able to observe that organ and select a sac, or "follicle," that contains a nearly mature egg. The follicle is then aspirated (withdrawn by suction) and the egg extracted.

INFANT IN BRITAIN REPORTED 'NORMAL'

Continued From Page A1

genetic engineering before a dictatorship tried to create a "master race."

The birth was not only a scientific breakthrough but also the high, or low, point of a headline race that tested the imagination of Britain's mass-circulation tabloid newspapers.

"It's a Girl," The Daily Mail announced above a picture of Mr. and Mrs. Brown in nightclothes. The Daily Mail is the leader of Associated Newspapers, the group that bought exclusive rights to the parents' story for a reported £300,000, which is about $575,000.

The rival Evening Standard trumpeted its own "test tube baby" this afternoon, reporting that another medical team had started trying to fertilize an egg from a London woman.

In a nation where paying news sources for the exclusive rights to a story is a common practice, the "test tube baby" story cost the winning newspaper group more than half a million dollars. It also touched off an angry debate over the practice, known as "checkbook journalism."

Some of the more conservative run papers have deplored it. The editors of the popular papers have accused the more conservative papers of self-righteousness.

The dispute intensified shortly after Associated Newspapers signed a contract with the Browns early this month. The Mail placed two guards at the door of Mrs. Brown's hospital room to keep out rival reporters. The hospital referred all news inquiries to Associated Newspapers in London.

Guards Were Withdrawn

But other news organizations protested so vehemently that the guards were withdrawn and the hospital authorities resumed answering questions.

Buying the story failed to guarantee exclusivity for The Mail and its sister publications, which include London's Evening News. Several rival papers have beaten them on secret details.

A United States newspaper, The National Enquirer, was among those outbid by Associated Newspapers. Another loser was the international chain headed by Rupert Murdoch, who publishes The New York Post and The Sun of London, among others.

Doctor Doubts Ethics In Case of British Baby

The attempt to conceive a child outside the body, as in the recent British experiment that yielded a live birth two days ago, was probably unethical, a leading authority on the ethics of biomedical research said yesterday. But, he added, now that it has been demonstrated that an apparently healthy child can be produced that way, further attempts would appear to be ethical.

"The history of medicine is full of instances where things were done unethically but led to benefits for people," said Dr. Daniel Callahan, director of the Institute of Society, Ethics and the Life Sciences, based in Hastings-on-Hudson, N.Y.

Dr. Callahan, who conceded that his opinions were "not straightforward and simple," said that he based his view on the fact that the experiment was undertaken to benefit the prospective parents but that the risk of damage was borne by the child.

"Now that it has been done and it appears that it can be done safely, it appears to be justifiable," Dr. Callahan said.

The New York Times/Marilyn Church

Dr. Landrum B. Shettles being questioned by Michael Dennis, the lawyer for the plaintiff, at Federal District Court in Manhattan yesterday.

SCIENTISTS ISOLATE GENE IN HUMAN CELL

Continued From Page A1

an inadequate supply of hemoglobin.

Dr. Stuart Orkin of Harvard said the image the team produced showed a row of fuzzy-looking black bands. If one or more bands was missing, that meant that part or all of the gene was missing.

Until now, he said, the only way to tell if a fetus had anemia was to take a sample of its blood and look for the hemoglobin itself, a risky procedure. The new technique allows doctors to take cells from the fluid around the fetus and look for the hemoglobin gene.

Dr. Orkin cautioned that while the method allowed detection of two types of anemia, alpha-thalassemia and beta-delta-thalassemia, it could not show the most common form of the disease in this country — beta-thalassemia, or Cooley's anemia.

Alpha-thalassemia is fatal at birth. The other two forms are milder but often require regular blood transfusions to make up for the hemoglobin lack.

British Test-Tube Baby 'Unrelated' to Del Zio Case

By JUDITH CUMMINGS

Noting the birth in Britain yesterday of the first confirmed human "test-tube baby," a judge in Federal District Court in Manhattan cautioned the jury hearing Doris Del Zio's $1.5 million damage suit that the event had no bearing on her case.

News of the birth coincided yesterday with the first appearance as a witness of Dr. Landrum B. Shettles, a pioneer in test-tube fertilization and a central figure in the Del Zio case, as the trial continued into its eighth day.

A jury comprising four women and two men was told by Judge Charles E. Stewart Jr. of Federal District Court that Tuesday's successful delivery of a baby girl to a British woman, Lesley Brown, was "an unrelated event, which you may not consider in any way" in deciding on Doris and John Del Zio's complaint. The Del Zios charged that Columbia-Presbyterian Hospital and its chief gynecologist in 1973 had acted maliciously in destroying, without the consent of the Del Zios, a test-tube culture that the Del Zios contend might have become the first test-tube baby.

"I feel very happy about Mrs. Brown's baby's being born," Mrs. Del Zio said, "and about its being a very healthy, normal, baby girl, as we all knew it would be." Her comment on the infant's reportedly normal condition was an apparent allusion to efforts by the defense in the Del Zio case to establish that a test-tube conception carries with it a substantial risk of producing an abnormal baby, as well as endangering the life of the mother.

'Like Evel Knievel'

Dr. Raymond L. Vande Wiele, the chief of gynecology at Columbia Presbyterian, who halted the Del Zio's fertilization attempt as an unsanctioned human experiment, rejected any suggestion that the success of the British medical team's efforts lent strength to the position of the Del Zios and their doctors that their own attempt would have succeeded.

"Nineteen seventy-three was a stunt, like Evel Knievel," he said, "Nineteen seventy-eight was a scientific achievement."

Dr. Shettles, who taught obstetrics and gynecology at the Columbia College of Physicians and Surgeons until leaving there in the controversy that followed his work with Mrs. Del Zio, took the witness stand in the afternoon to have a list of his qualifications and credentials read into the record by Michael Dennis, the plaintiffs' lawyer.

Mr. Dennis made a point of reading excerpts from a book review of "Ovum Humanum," Dr. Shettle's 1960 work on the development of the human ovum, written by Dr. John Rock, a gynecologist who is credited with developing the first effective oral contraceptive. Dr. Rock called the book "a towering tribute to the dedicated ardor of a careful, resourceful, scholarly workman."

Jet Turns Back After Takeoff

SAN FRANCISCO, July 26 (AP) — A Pan American World Airways jumbo jet carrying 333 passengers to London lost power in an engine on takeoff and had to dump about 100,000 pounds of jet fuel before it turned around and landed safely at San Francisco International Airport. No passengers were hurt, officials said.

Oil Spilled After Barge Collision Endangers Wildlife in Louisiana

FORKED ISLAND, La., July 26 (UPI) — Two barges filled with oil and carbon black collided today on the Intracoastal Waterway, closing a seven-mile section of the much-traveled canal and posing a pollution threat to nearby wildlife refuges.

Both barges were torn open by the collision and at least 100 barrels of carbon black were spilled into the southwest Louisiana marshes. The second barge was leaking toxic fumes.

The Coast Guard dispatched a pollution control team based in Bay St. Louis, Miss., with booms and special cleanup equipment to be used on the spill.

Fumes from a leak in one barge overcame several crewmen, who were not seriously injured, the Coast Guard said

"All the News That's Fit to Print"

The New York Times

LATE CITY EDITION

Weather: Mostly cloudy, chilly today; cloudy, damp tonight and tomorrow. Temperature range: today 27-38; yesterday 39-49. Details on page B10.

VOL.CXXVIII . . No.44,043 NEW YORK, TUESDAY, NOVEMBER 21, 1978 — 25 cents beyond 50-mile zone from New York City. Higher in air delivery cities. — 20 CENTS

400 ARE FOUND DEAD IN MASS SUICIDE BY CULT; HUNDREDS MORE MISSING FROM GUYANA CAMP

United Press International

Chairman Hua Kuo-feng

2 Peking Wall Posters Raise New Questions On the Status of Hua

By FOX BUTTERFIELD

Special to The New York Times

HONG KONG, Nov. 20 — Two wall posters calling for a full public investigation into the suppression and cover-up of the major anti-Government demonstration in Peking in 1976 appeared in the Chinese capital today, raising questions about the status of Hua Kuo-feng, Chairman of the Chinese Communist Party.

The posters said an inquiry was necessary so that "those responsible for the suppression and cover-up could be brought to justice." According to diplomats in Peking, the posters demanded that the committee of investigation be made up of all major organs of the party and state.

Mr. Hua's present standing is closely linked to the incident, which took place in Tien An Men Square in central Peking on April 5, 1976 and was ostensibly in memory of the recently deceased Prime Minister Chou En-lai. At the time, Teng Hsiao-ping was blamed.

Two days later, "on the proposal of Mao Tse-tung, Mr. Teng was purged and Mr. Hua was named party Chairman and Prime Minister. Mr. Teng, now again a Deputy Prime Minister, was reinstated in 1977 after the death of Mao and the arrest of his radical followers.

Yesterday, another poster put up in

Continued on Page A5, Column 1

SHORTAGES GROWING IN NO-LEAD GASOLINE OF HIGHER OCTANES

Although Overall Supply Appears Adequate, Some Companies Lag on Premium Grades

By ANTHONY J. PARISI

Shortages of premium unleaded gasoline are cropping up around the country, arousing fears among motorists of a general shortage of fuel for their automobiles.

Although supplies of gasoline appear adequate over all, some companies have been unable to keep up with the keen demand for high-octane unleaded gasoline, which provides superior performance for some automobiles. Some service stations have begun to turn away customers, who then find themselves waiting on longer and longer lines at stations that still have sufficient supplies on hand.

The Shell Oil Company, which has had to shut down two of its key refineries, was the first to report such shortages. Now Mobil stations are having problems, too, and other companies say their supplies are getting tighter by the day.

Some Rationing at Stations

To spread limited supplies among as many customers as possible, some stations have even begun to ration premium unleaded fuel — the first widespread example of gasoline rationing since the Arab oil embargo of 1973-74. The Bronxville Service Station in suburban Westchester County, for example, has been limiting purchases of Mobil Super unleaded to 10 gallons at a time — when it can get supplies. Yesterday it had no premium gasoline of any kind.

The shortages have appeared just as the Department of Energy is preparing to remove controls from gasoline prices. Yesterday, the department's Economic Regulatory Administration published an environmental impact statement on gasoline decontrol, recommending that the Government proceed with the plan despite concerns that the price of unleaded gasoline may skyrocket as a result.

One reason for the shortage is that motorists whose cars require unleaded gas have grown impatient with how their cars perform using regular grades of lead-free fuel. Almost a third of all the

Continued on Page D5, Column 4

Associated Press

Bodies lie strewn about vat containing drink laced with cyanide at the Jonestown headquarters of the People's Temple

LEADER OF SECT DIES

Parents Reported to Give Children Poison Before Dying Beside Them

By JON NORDHEIMER

Special to The New York Times

GEORGETOWN, Guyana, Nov. 20 — In a scene that dashed the senses, Guyanese forces today picked their way through an open-air pavilion choked with the bodies of 405 men, women and children in an American cult group who apparently commited suicide on the orders of their leader.

Wearing gaily colored clothes, the bodies were clustered in family groups, side-by-side in deathly embrace, all but three dead from drinking a concoction made of Kool-Aid and cyanide.

The setting was the jungle church of the People's Temple, the group that has been blamed for the slaying of Congressman Leo J. Ryan and four other Americans on Saturday.

Survivor Describes Scene

A surviving cult member gave the first newsmen to reach the scene today an account that was as incredible as it was filled with horror, a story of death plots and madness, of parents spooning a poisonous punch into the mouths of their babies before drinking it themselves.

And on the altar of the pavilion, surrounded in death by his followers as he had been surrounded by them in life, was the body of James Warren Jones, also known as the Rev. Jim Jones, the charismatic leader of the People's Temple, who had promised his racially integrated flock a utopia in the South American wilds. Instead, he gave them death.

"The time has come to meet in another place," he was said to have told the cultists he had assembled around him shortly after learning of the failure of a plan to kill the entire group of newsmen and parents of cultists who had flown deep into a lonely jungle airport with Congressman Ryan, according to the survivor, Odell Rhodes, 36 years old, from Detroit.

400 Are Still Missing

And then, according to the survivor's account, cyanide was dumped into a huge soup kettle, and the liquid was fed first to the babies, then to the children old enough to drink it themselves, and finally swallowed by the adults, many of whom were older people who had turned their Social Security checks and their lives over to the custody of Mr. Jones.

The leader, who at different times had described himself as the reincarnation of Christ and Lenin, died of a bullet wound in the head, according to the Guyanese police.

Nothing is known about the whereabouts of the remaining 400 or more cultists, who either fled into the jungle to escape death, or have elected to die deeper inside the canopied rain forest, where flesh-eating piranha and electric eels move in the murky jungle streams and insects swarm in the midday heat.

Cult Was Drilled in Suicide

It was learned that the cult was routinely drilled in suicide by Mr. Jones, who had a vision of a need to destroy the community if it was ever attacked.

Apparently, Mr. Ryan, who had been asked to investigate claims by his California constituents that members of the cult were being held in virtual bondage on the commune, and the party that accompanied him last Saturday, were seen as a grave danger.

Mr. Jones had decided to kill Mr. Ryan and the two dozen or so people who ac-

Continued on Page A17, Column 1

Defectors From Sect Depict Its Rehearsals for Suicide

By ROBERT LINDSEY

Special to The New York Times

LOS ANGELES, Nov. 20 — "He has mass suicide drills, where he tells all the people, hundreds of people, to drink a certain drink, and he says, 'That's fatal, you're all going to die in 45 minutes, I want to see how you feel about dying for socialism.'"

And, said Timothy Stoen, a San Francisco lawyer and former aide to the Rev. Jim Jones, the founder of the People's Temple, when Mr. Jones ordered his followers in his Guyana commune to drink the liquid, "everybody drank."

"It was like he wanted to believe he was God," said Anna Mobley, a member for four years. "He would get you so tired it would make you lose your mind."

"He had something they called the 'blue-eyed monster,' a thing they did to children," another former member said. "They took children into a dark room and attached electrodes to them and then shocked them and told them never not to smile at Jim Jones."

"He sent spies to our home and said that if we didn't sell all our property, we would die," said Wade Medlock, the owner of a Los Angeles maintenance company, who turned over two of his homes to the cult under threats.

The remarks were made at a meeting of a group called the Human Freedom Foundation, which was set up here last summer by two psychics, Maria Papapetros and Jenita Cargile, after former cult members had sought them out for counseling on how to "deprogram" themselves. A recording of the meeting was made available to The New York Times.

According to former members, the cult was run as a police state by Mr. Jones, who was said to have enforced discipline by beatings and death threats; pursued bizarre sexual activities, and indoctrinated members in his personal brand of agrarian socialism.

According to Mr. Stoen, Mr. Jones first enticed members with a doctrine of selflessness and a simple Christian faith of social equality that found support among blacks and upper middle-class whites who had become alienated in the 1960's.

Once he got "control of their minds, he would accept no dissent and told members that a defector had no right to live," Mr. Stoen said. He is a former deputy district attorney in Mendocino County who had been attracted by Mr. Jones's views in the late 1960's and became one of his lieutenants as the cult spread to San Francisco and Los Angeles and ultimately to the settlement in Guyana.

He said that as a sect official he had transferred more than $5 million to foreign bank accounts and said he believed the church's assets probably totaled much more.

Mr. Stoen said "people who disagreed would get phone calls at 3 A.M. with heavy breathing" or cult officials would find a drunk and pay him to read a script containing threats over the telephone. The children of parents who decided to leave the sect were often seized and kept in Guyana under guard.

Mr. Jones, he continued, had a "relationships committee" that had to approve

Continued on Page A16, Column 4

© 1978, The San Francisco Examiner

CULT LEADER: Jim Jones in Jonestown before shootings. Guyana revealed references from prominent Americans. Page A16.

© 1978, The San Francisco Examiner

Bodies of five Americans lie at ambush site in Port Kaituma, Guyana. From left, in foreground: Representative Leo J. Ryan; Don Harris, reporter for NBC: Gregory Robinson, photographer for The San Francisco Examiner, and Patricia Parks, believed to be a member of the commune. At rear is Robert Brown, an NBC cameraman.

Bally Corp. Plan to Build Casino On Historic Site Backed by Jersey

By DONALD JANSON

Special to The New York Times

ATLANTIC CITY, Nov. 20 — New Jersey officials indicated today that they would permit the Bally Manufacturing Corporation, the world's leading manufacturer of slot machines, to demolish the historic Blenheim Hotel rotunda on the Boardwalk to make way for a casino.

The "preliminary" finding by the State Department of Environmental Protection is the latest step in changing the face of Atlantic City, with the classic resort hotels of the city's heyday yielding to a new line of modern casino hotels. Keeping the Moorish rotunda of the Blenheim intact — the main wing has been demolished — is the focal point of a determined drive by preservationists.

Last May 26 Resorts International opened the city's first casino in the old Haddon Hall Hotel after radically altering the structure and renaming it the Resorts International Hotel.

Since then 32 companies, including most of the major concerns operating casinos in Nevada, have either acquired potential casino sites in Atlantic City or announced plans to do so.

One company, Caesars World, operator of Caesars Palace in Las Vegas, has acquired two Boardwalk sites and has a casino under construction on one of them. Steel girders are up on the site of the Howard Johnson Regency Hotel, which will be incorporated into the new casino hotel.

Caesars hopes to open the city's second casino by next Memorial Day. It has also acquired, for possible construction of another casino, the site of the Traymore Hotel, a Boardwalk landmark that was demolished six years ago.

Bally hopes to be third to open an Atlantic City casino. Its target date is July. It acquired three adjacent, historic hotels and wants to demolish all three eventually.

Last month Bally did demolish the Marlborough, a Queen Anne 1902 wooden structure that was one of first in the city to provide a private bath with every room.

In addition Bally is ripping out the interior of the Dennis, built in 1900 in the French Chateau style, and renovating it. The Dennis is the oldest hotel name on the beachfront today.

Last week 326 pounds of dynamite top-

Continued on Page B7, Column 2

INSIDE

Carter Aides Named in Inquiry

A grand jury is studying charges that White House aides considered dropping the Vesco extradition case in return for $10 million in stock. Page B11.

Trucking Restriction Dropped

The Interstate Commerce Commission dropped a 40-year-old rule that barred companies that truck their own goods from hauling goods of others. Page D1.

News Summary and Index, Page B1

Guyanese Report Finding 405 Bodies in Commune

Continued From Page A1

companied him, according to Mr. Rhodes. The plan was to send one of his loyal lieutenants with the Ryan party as a feigned defector. When the plane was airborne, the accomplice was to kill the pilot and cause a crash in the dense jungle.

The plan was nearly carried out. But the imposter boarded the smaller of the two chartered planes at the small airstrip at Port Kaituma, and for some unexplained reason began shooting while both planes were still on the ground. At this time a tractor emerged from the jungle carrying several men who opened fire on the confused, scrambling Americans, killing Mr. Ryan, two members of a National Broadcasting Company crew, a photographer for the San Francisco Examiner and one of the defecting cultists. Eight others were wounded.

Mr. Rhodes said that an assembly of the People's Temple was called by Mr. Jones before the results of what was transpiring at the airport, six miles away, were known. He told them of his plot to kill Mr. Ryan's entourage and protect the cult from further intrusions.

Members Died in Family Groups

When word came back that the plan had been botched and survivors had escaped on one of the aircraft, Mr. Jones announced that he was invoking his ultimate plan.

Armed guards ringed the assembly as a physician, Lawrence Schact, prepared the cyanide punch, but they were not needed to coerce the true believers, according to Mr. Rhodes. They lined up in family groups, he said, took their drinks, put their arms around each other, had convulsions and died within five minutes.

Mr. Jones's legal wife and son died with him on the altar. His mistress, Maria Katsaris, whose mother was one of those wounded in the airport shooting, apparently shot herself in the head in a nearby cabin after apparently feeding cyanide to the two small boys she and Mr. Jones treated like sons. Eighty-two children in all died that day.

40 Weapons and $500,000 Found

A search of the settlement turned up nearly 40 weapons, including some automatic rifles and "hundreds of thousands of rounds of ammunition," according to Guyanese police investigators.

In addition, there was approximately $500,000 in United States currency and many United States Treasury checks. A former cult member who had worked as financial secretary for People's Temple had indicated several months ago that Mr. Jones received $65,000 a month in Social Security checks turned over to him by his older followers. More than 800 American passports were found at the settlement, and the authorities are not certain if that is the number of Americans who lived there. Earlier estimates had placed the number closer to 1,200.

Six individuals who had been on the plane at the airstrip Saturday when the shooting broke out and who had fled into the jungle turned up yesterday. One, Jim Cobb was a Californian who had flown into the jungle with Mr. Ryan. The other five, ages 5 to 20 years old, were being taken out of the settlement at the time of the incident. Two of the chidren were wounded slightly. In addition, the authorities located two adult cult members who said they had not been involved in any of the deaths. They were identified as Michael Prokes, a former television newsman in California, and Tim Carter. The authorities also hold the man suspected of starting the shooting at the airstrip, Larry Layton. All were being held for questioning.

Bodies Flown to U.S.

Two lawyers who had represented the group, Mark Lane, the author, and Charles Garry, a San Francisco lawyer, escaped from the group's village of Jonestown on Saturday night when the killings began and were picked up in the jungle by Government forces yesterday They did not see the killings.

The bodies of Mr. Ryan and the four others killed with him were flown back to the United States today after a post mortem in Georgetown, the capital city.

Tomorrow, 50 American mortuary experts are scheduled to be flown to the interior to begin identifying the 405 dead cult members whose bodies have been exposed to the tropical heat for more than two days. In addition, the United States is expected to provide the Guyanese with military helicopters to airlift the bodies to Georgetown.

Congressman Ryan had met with Mr. Jones on Saturday at the commune, called Jonestown, to negotiate for the release of cult members whose parents in California had claimed were being held in virtual bondage.

Besides Mr. Ryan, who was 53 years old, those killed Saturday were Don Harris, 42, a television reporter for NBC News, and Robert Brown, 36, an NBC cameraman, both of Los Angeles; Gregory Robinson, 27, a photographer for The San Francisco Examiner, and Patricia Parks, a cult member. Guyanese officials said she was 18 years old.

In addition, it was reported today that a People's Temple leader, Sharon Amos, and her three daughters had been found with their throats slit in the cult's headquarters in Georgetown.

The Guyanese Minister of Information, Shirley Field-Ridley, today expressed her Government's sympathy to the relatives of the dead Americans, saying her South American country had never experienced anything like the "very terrible happenings" of the weekend.

Warnings About Violence

Former members of the cult had warned that it was capable of violence. Last June, one former member, Deborah Layton Blakey, said in a deposition in a Guyana custody case involving a child in the Jonestown commune: "The Rev. Jones labeled any person who left the commune a 'traitor' and 'fair game.' He steadfastly and convincingly maintained that the punishment for defection was death."

"There was constant talk of death," said Mrs. Blakey, who was raised in an affluent family in Berkeley, Calif. "In Jonestown, the concept of mass suicide for socialism arose. Because our lives were so wretched anyway, and because we were so afraid to contradict Rev. Jones, the concept was not challenged."

Night Meetings Described

According to her account, states of emergency called "white nights" were declared about once a week and followed this routine:

Sirens woke everyone and about 50 guards with rifles rushed around the settlement corralling everyone to a mass meeting. The members were told that some enemy, like mercenaries controlled by the Central Intelligence Agency, was in the jungle and would overrun the camp and that death was imminent.

"During a 'white night' we were informed that our situation was hopeless and that the only course of action open to us was a mass suicide for the glory of socialism," she said. "We were told everyone would be tortured by the mercenaries if we were taken alive. Everyone, including the children, were told to line up. As we passed through the line we were given a small glass of red liquid to drink. We were told the liquid contained poison and we would die within 45 minutes. We all did as we were told."

When no one fell ill or died, Mr. Jones explained that what they had drunk was not poison; he was just putting them through a "loyalty test."

"He warned us that the time was not far off when it would become necessary for us to die by our own hands."

Associated Press pool photo by Frank Johnston

Hundreds of bodies lying where they fell in camp of People's Temple at Jonestown, Guyana. All but three died after drinking a poisonous concoction.

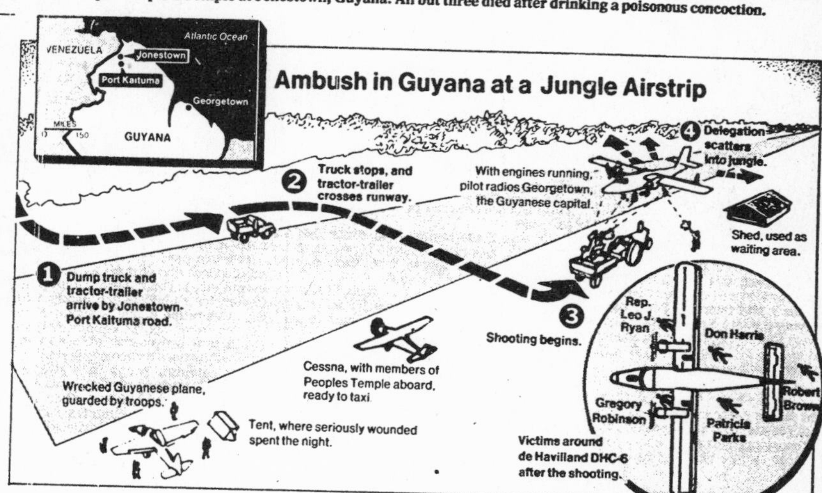

From The San Francisco Examiner, © 1978

The ambush took place Saturday night as Congressman Leo J. Ryan was about to leave for home with his investigating group from a dirt airstrip eight miles south of Jonestown.

Sect Leader's Lawyers Relish Radical Images But Have Differences

By PRANAY GUPTE

Each man has been involved for many years in some of the most sensational controversies in the United States. Each has been called a radical, and relished the reputation, but each has also been called a publicity hound, even an opportunist.

But they are different men by temperament, Mark Lane and Charles R. Garry, separated in age by almost a generation, one a feisty New Yorker, the other a reserved San Franciscan.

Now, because of what happened in a jungle clearing thousands of miles from their homes, the two men have been thrown into possibly the most sensational controversy of their lives.

For Mr. Lane and Mr. Garry, both lawyers, the trip to Jonestown started when Representative Leo J. Ryan of California insisted on investigating conditions at the jungle commune of a religious sect called the People's Temple.

From correspondence between the Congressman and Mr. Lane that was made available yesterday, it is clear that neither lawyer looked forward to the trip, but the two lawyers, who said they represented the cult's leader, the Rev. Jim Jones, helped make the arrangements.

Each man's record suggests resistance to "the establishment." Just over two decades ago, Mr. Garry, now 69 years old, was ordered to appear before the House Committee on Un-American Activities, invoked the Fifth Amendment and refused to say whether he had ever been a member of the Communist Party. He now says he never was.

"I am more than a liberal," Mr. Garry, a husky man of medium height, once said. "I am a radical."

This self-characterization is borne out in the cases he has handled. His most publicized clients have been Bobby Seale, Huey Newton and Eldridge Cleaver, leaders of the Black Panthers.

Charles Garry, born Charles Garabedian, says: "I had to fight my way home from school every night through the anti-Armenian children of Fresno. I guess one of the things that makes me so incensed about what's happening to black people is because I relate it to my early life and the discrimination that I received by just being an ethnic Armenian."

The 51-year-old Mr. Lane has been a leading proponent of the theory that the death of John F. Kennedy involved a conspiracy. His book, "Rush to Judgment," was a best-seller.

A book Mr. Lane wrote about veterans of the Vietnam War, "Conversations with Americans," was characterized by several reviewers as irresponsible. That charge was also leveled at him when, as a state Assemblyman from Manhattan's West Side in the early 1960's, Mr. Lane questioned the ethics of a former Speaker.

More recently, Mr. Lane had acted as a lawyer for James Earl Ray, convicted for the murder of Martin Luther King Jr. Mr. Lane last year furnished the House Select Committee on Assassinations with "leads" — which eventually proved fruitless — on new information suggesting that Dr. King's death was also a conspiracy.

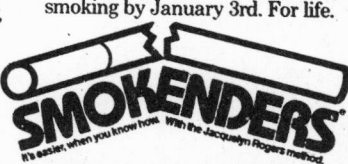

"All the News That's Fit to Print"

The New York Times

CITY EDITION

Metropolitan area weather: Mild today; colder tonight, tomorrow. Temperature range: today 51-30; yesterday 45-30. Details on page 39.

VOL.CXXVIII.... No.44,068

— NEW YORK, SATURDAY, DECEMBER 16, 1978 —

25 cents beyond 50-mile zone from New York City. Higher in air delivery cities.

20 CENTS

U.S. AND CHINA OPENING FULL RELATIONS; TENG WILL VISIT WASHINGTON ON JAN. 29

LINK TO TAIWAN ENDS

Carter, in TV Speech, Says 'We Recognize Reality' After 30-Year Rift

By TERENCE SMITH

Special to The New York Times

WASHINGTON, Dec. 15 — President Carter announced tonight that the United States and China would establish diplomatic relations on Jan. 1.

The President also said that Teng Hsiao-ping, the powerful Deputy Prime

Text of Carter statement, page 8.

Minister, would visit this country later in January. In a press briefing, reporters were told that Mr. Teng will visit the United States Jan. 29. It will be the first such visit by a high-level Chinese official since the Communists took power on the mainland in 1949.

In a dramatic, nationally televised speech, Mr. Carter also announced that the United States would terminate diplomatic relations with Taiwan as well as the mutual defense treaty with the Chinese Nationalists. In four months, the United States will also withdraw its remaining military personnel from Taiwan, the President said, but in remarks addressed especially to the people of the island, he pledged that the United States would remain interested in the peaceful resolution of the issue.

'Recognizing Simple Reality'

"We do not undertake this important step for transient, tactical reasons," Mr. Carter said. "In recognizing that the Government of the People's Republic of China is the single Government of China, we are recognizing simple reality."

"Normalization — and the expanded commercial and cultural relations it will bring with it — will contribute to the well-being of our own nation and will enhance stability in Asia," the President said.

In reassuring the people of Taiwan, Mr. Carter said he had taken care in reaching the agreement to make sure that the normalization of relations with the mainland "will not jeopardize the well-being of the people of Taiwan.

Certain Ties to Be Maintained

"We will continue to have an interest in the peaceful resolution of the Taiwan issue," Mr. Carter said. He added that the United States would maintain "our current commercial, cultural and other relations with Taiwan through nongovernmental means."

Mr. Teng's visit, Mr. Carter said, "will give our Governments the opportunity to consult with each other on global issues and to begin working together to enhance the cause of world peace."

The two countries will exchange ambassadors and establish embassies on March 1.

The President made special mention of the "long, serious negotiations" with China carried on before him by Presidents Richard M. Nixon and Gerald R. Ford. The results, he said, "bear witness to the steady, determined, bipartisan effort of our own country to build a world in which peace will be the goal and the responsibility of all countries."

Earlier in the evening, Administration officials confirmed that Treasury Secre-

Continued on Page 8, Column 1

Associated Press

President Carter making announcement last night

United Press International

Deputy Prime Minister Teng Hsaio-ping

Israel Rejects New Peace Proposal; U.S., Irritated, Charges Distortion

Cabinet Backs Begin Stand

By PAUL HOFMANN

Special to The New York Times

JERUSALEM, Dec. 15 — The Israeli Cabinet decided today to reject the latest proposals by Egypt for a peace treaty as well as the "attitude and interpretation" of the United States regarding the proposals.

At the end of a special four-hour meeting, Prime Minister Menachem Begin,

Text of Israeli decision, page 3.

looking grim, said to reporters:

"The consultations, the negotiations will resume — we cannot say when."

[An official in the Egyptian Foreign Ministry denied Israeli charges that Cairo had made new demands during Secretary of State Vance's trip. Page 4.]

No Hope for Treaty by Deadline

The endorsement by the Cabinet of Prime Minister Begin's stand in talks with Secretary of State Cyrus R. Vance here Wednesday and yesterday quashed any remaining hope that the proposed Egyptian-Israeli peace treaty might be signed by this Sunday, the original deadline.

Foreign Minister Moshe Dayan warned in an interview broadcast tonight that there was a possibility the draft peace treaty might not be signed at all, and that negotiations between Israel and Egypt would have to start all over again.

The Cabinet's refusal to go along with the United States Government's view

Continued on Page 5, Column 1

Vance Reports to President

By BERNARD GWERTZMAN

Special to The New York Times

WASHINGTON, Dec. 15 — The Carter Administration accused Israel today of deliberately distorting the nature of new peace proposals taken to Jerusalem this week by Secretary of State Cyrus R. Vance in his effort to complete an Egyptian-Israeli treaty.

Obviously irritated by the Israeli Cabinet's decision to reject the proposals, announced today by Prime Minister Menachem Begin, officials accompanying Mr. Vance on his Air Force plane from Cairo to Washington, gave reporters a highly detailed briefing intended to rebut Mr. Begin's statements.

Vance Goes to White House

Mr. Vance, who arrived at Andrews Air Force Base late this afternoon, went by helicopter directly to the White House to report to President Carter on the trip to Cairo and Jerusalem.

There was no official statement by the White House after the Vance-Carter meeting. But the State Department was instructed to draft a "white paper" to put on record the complaints against the Israelis.

Relations between Washington and Jerusalem were again under severe strain, and Mr. Vance was described as "saddened" and annoyed by the Israeli Cabinet's decision, which left little room for any early progress.

The immediate reaction of American officials in the Vance party was that a

Continued on Page 3, Column 1

CLEVELAND RACING DEFAULT DEADLINE

Bankers Grant Brief Extension — City Bond Credit Rating Cut

By REGINALD STUART

Special to The New York Times

CLEVELAND, Dec. 15 — City officials scheduled a meeting for 11 o'clock tonight to decide whether to accept Mayor Dennis J. Kucinich's sweeping fiscal rehabilitation plan for the city or find some other means of avoiding default on $15.5 million in loans that were due today.

At the same time, banker-creditors, whom the city had contracted with to repay the short-term loans, extended their hours until midnight to see if the city would either pay the debts or come up with a plan that would persuade them to renew the loans.

Mayor Assails Bank and Council

Meanwhile, Moody's Investors Service, the municipal bond credit-rating company, lowered the city's bond rating today to Caa. That was the lowest rating reached three years ago by New York City during its financial crisis. A Caa classification defines such bonds as being in default or having "present elements of danger with respect to principal or interest."

The chances for success of the Mayor's plan, which has drawn strong opposition from City Council leaders and at least two of the six lenders, were further diminished tonight when the Mayor ac-

Continued on Page 11, Column 1

China Tie Reflects Carter's Feeling That Country Was Ready for Move

By HEDRICK SMITH

Special to The New York Times

WASHINGTON, Dec. 15 — President Carter's dramatic announcement that he was taking this country into a new era of diplomatic relations with China reflects the confident political calculation that the country-at-large is now ready for this step and the hopeful diplomatic calculation that it will not jeopardize the imminent new strategic-arms agreement with the Soviet Union.

High Administration officials revealed that the breakthrough had come quicker than expected and had been pushed by the Chinese. Although the White House found the timing awkward, because of the delicate stage of negotiations with Moscow on an arms accord, Washington felt that the Chinese initiative could not be turned down.

In another way, however, the breakthrough could not have come at a more opportune moment for an Administration frustrated by the latest impasse in the Middle East talks and beset by the political upheaval in Iran and the potential tremors elsewhere in the Near East.

The move appeals to the historic American fascination with the Orient since the days when clipper ships carried missionaries and merchants to distant China from the salty harbors of Massachusetts. In the modern calculus of global power politics, the tie with China offers new leverage in the triangular relationship with the Soviet Union, as well as a counter to recent Soviet gains in Afghanistan and the Horn of Africa.

As rumors swept the city tonight before

Continued on Page 8, Column 5

China: The Long Wait

By FOX BUTTERFIELD

Special to The New York Times

News Analysis

HONG KONG, Saturday, Dec. 16 — President Carter's announcement last night that the United States and China are finally normalizing diplomatic relations comes nearly seven years after Richard M. Nixon pledged in the Shanghai Communiqué of February 1972 to work toward that goal.

The major obstacle to progress on restoring relations has been America's long-time military and diplomatic commitment to the Chinese Nationalist regime on Taiwan, a problem compounded by the continued strong support for Taiwan among many in the United States.

After the initial euphoria that accompanied Mr. Nixon's epochal trip to China, relations between the two nations seemed to languish for several years as events gave Taiwan a series of reprieves. First, Mr. Nixon's plans to improve ties were hampered by the Watergate scandal. Then President Gerald R. Ford was caught by the debacle of Vietnam's collapse. And more recently Mr. Carter himself was sidetracked by the Panama Canal negotiations, the Middle East problems and talks to limit the spread of nuclear weapons. Fears were raised that Washington was frittering away a critical opportunity to strengthen America's interests in Asia.

Recent Improvement in Relations

But in recent months, largely at China's initiative, relations began to improve rapidly. Since the summer, in fact, the two countries have been drawing together in a process that looked like normalizing without the final actual step.

Two factors impelled this change: China's increased fears of being encircled by the new alliance between the Soviet Union and Vietnam, and its desire for expanded trade and technology to

Continued on Page 8, Column 5

Koch Gets 3 Billion School Budget; Smaller Classes Among Objectives

By MARCIA CHAMBERS

The New York City School Chancellor, Frank J. Macchiarola, submitted a $3 billion expense budget to Mayor Koch yesterday that calls for smaller classes, intensified remedial instruction and additional personnel to combat truancy, vandalism and internal mismanagement.

To finance these additional programs, the Chancellor said he had to find $130 million in the budget from sources not yet committed to the public school system's anticipated revenues. The system's costs are roughly a third of the city's overall expense budget. He said that following the Mayor's lead he intended to try to get the necessary funds from the state and Federal Governments.

The Chancellor plans to have an all-day meeting on Monday with Federal officials in an attempt to obtain changes in Federal law that would give the school system more say in how and where remedial funds can be spent. Then, Mr. Macchiarola said, he intends to talk to Albany lawmakers, who are under a court ruling to revise the state-aid allocation formula for the financing of public schools.

If the city school district — the biggest in the country, with nearly a million students — "gets its fair share of state funding," he said, "we would get triple the

The Mayor's consultant on the City University has endorsed $160 million in priority construction projects. Page 25.

amount we get now." He said that would be more than enough for the new programs.

In an obvious criticism of his predecessor, Irving Anker, Mr. Macchiarola said in his budget message to the Board of Education that "additional funds will be required in order to begin the programing that has been neglected — not without severe effect — in recent years." Mr. Macchiarola's proposed 1979-80 budget is virtually the same as the Anker budget proposal last year. The Board of Education will hold a public hearing on the

Continued on Page 28, Column 1

United Press International

Mayor Dennis J. Kucinich of Cleveland, foreground, was accused at City Council debate of not acting to prevent default

INSIDE

Saudis Moderate on Oil Prices

On the eve of a meeting of oil-exporting countries, Saudi Arabia's delegate called for moderation in determining an increased price of oil. Page 29.

Cults' Funds Reported Gone

A U.S. official said a Zurich bank had told the Justice Department that as much as $8 million in People's Temple funds had been removed. Page 12.

Taiwan Leaders Confer Hurriedly After Learning of U.S.-China Step

Special to The New York Times

TAIPEI, Taiwan, Saturday, Dec. 16 — Leaders of the Chinese Nationalist Government were abruptly summoned into emergency meetings here early today, a few hours before the announcement in Washington that the United States was establishing diplomatic relations with Peking.

The United States, it appeared, gave only a few hours' notice to Taiwan that it was withdrawing its recognition of the Government of President Chiang Ching-kuo.

U.S. Decision a Heavy Blow

President Chiang first called several Cabinet ministers to his office to brief them on the developments. Then, official sources said, an emergency meeting of the central committee of the Kuomintang, the governing party, was scheduled to consider the most serious blow it has suffered in the three decades since Chiang Kai-shek led his defeated followers here from the mainland.

More than 50 countries have broken relations with Taiwan since the Chinese Nationalists were replaced at the United Nations in 1971 by the Communist regime. But the American decision comes as a particularly heavy blow since the United States, the last world power to recognize the Nationalists, has supported them since 1954 with a mutual-defense treaty.

Since President Richard M. Nixon's visit to China in 1972, the Nationalists have expected that the United States would eventually break relations. The timing, however, was apparently a surprise.

It comes during a heated parliamentary election campaign on Taiwan, when some rightist candidates have been warning that it faces a possible "betrayal" by the United States. Others, however, have campaigned on the slogan that the fate of Taiwan should be decided by the island's 16 million people.

One candidate said: "We should not repeat the history in Vietnam. Taiwan's fu-

Continued on Page 8, Column 1

President Announces That U.S. and China Will Establish Diplomatic Relations

Continued From Page 1

chairman, accused the President of "callous disregard for a fine friend and a loyal ally."

Briefing reporters after the speech, senior Administration officials conceded that they had not obtained an explicit pledge from China not to use force to retake Taiwan.

But the officials maintained that it was implicit in the Chinese acceptance of the American statement, issued unilaterally to coincide with the speech that expresses the continued interest of the United States in the peaceful resolution of the Taiwan issue.

They also felt that recent public statements by Chinese leaders indicating that the Taiwanese situation could be peacefully resolved were an indication of their true intentions.

The officials also pointed out that the United States would retain the right to maintain a full range of cultural and economic ties, including the supply of defensive arms, after the formal termination of the mutual defense treaty at the end of 1979.

They also cited as a Chinese concession the agreement to exchange ambassadors in March, before the formal termination of the United States-Taiwan defense treaty. Previously, the Chinese had said they would never do this.

No Use of Force

The major United States concession in the agreement, however, was the willingness to sign without an explicit guarantee that force would not be used to retake Taiwan.

In his speech, Mr. Carter made special mention of the key roles played in the "long, serious negotiations" with the Chinese by his predecessors, Presidents Gerald R. Ford and Richard M. Nixon.

Earlier in the evening, Administration officials confirmed that Treasury Secretary W. Michael Blumenthal would go to China soon for a broad discussion of financial and trade matters. Among the subjects on his agenda will be the complex problem of the Chinese and American assets that have been frozen in the two countries since 1950. These would have to be freed as part of the normalization process.

The United States holds that some $200 million worth of American assets in China were seized at the end of the civil war. China is seeking some $80 million in blocked assets.

The President's speech followed a day of mounting suspense and curiosity in the capital. Rumors of an impending important announcement began to circulate in midmorning, but the President's foreign policy aides were giving out no information.

The regularly scheduled White House briefing was postponed from 2:30 P.M. to 3:30 P.M., when Mr. Carter's press secretary, Jody Powell, emerged to announce that Mr. Carter would make a televised speech "on a matter of national and international importance." Mr. Powell declined to specify even the subject of the address, except to say that "we are not talking about anything that would involve military action or things of that nature."

When reporters asked if a national crisis was involved, Mr. Powell said with a smile: "I don't think there will be any need to start evacuating large cities or anything like that."

Soviet Envoy at White House

Speculation intensified when the Soviet Ambassador, Anatoly F. Dobrynin, arrived at the White House shortly after 3 P.M. The envoy smiled and waved at reporters as he entered the office of Zbigniew Brzezinski, the President's adviser on national security.

Moments later, Energy Secretary James R. Schlesinger arrived and joined the meeting. Neither man would comment after conferring with Mr. Brzezinski for 15 minutes.

Mr. Schlesinger's presence at the White House earlier in the day to confer with Mr. Powell and Hamilton Jordan, the President's top political aide led many reporters to conclude that Mr. Carter's announcement would concern China. The Energy Secretary recently returned from a visit to China where he discussed cooperation in oil exploration and other energy matters.

Later, members of the Democratic and Republican Congressional leadership and key members of the Senate and House foreign relations committees were summoned to a 6:15 P.M. special White House briefing. Several said before they went in that they had no hint of what would be discussed.

Indication Came in Jerusalem

The first indication that an important foreign policy announcement was to be made came on Wednesday in Jerusalem, where Secretary of State Cyrus R. Vance was conferrring with Israeli leaders over the proposed language of an Israeli-Egyptian peace treaty.

At the conclusion of a meeting with the Israeli Prime Minister, Menachem Begin, Mr. Vance was told that the President wanted to speak to him on the telephone The Secretary drove to the mansion that houses the offices and residence of the United States Consul General and spoke with Mr. Carter for 15 minutes. Mr. Vance emerged and told reporters later that it was imperative he be back in Washington by Friday night, regardless of how the Middle East talks were progressing.

The Secretary refused to tell the reporters accompanying him on his Middle East mission any more, except to assure them that it would all be clear by Friday night.

The impression that the speech would deal with China mounted as the day wore on. ABC television reported in the afternoon that the President would announce a meeting with Chinese leaders on United States soil sometime in the near future.

Last night, Mr. Carter discussed relations with China in an interview with Barbara Walters. Citing the "great improvements in our relationship with China in recent months," the President said that the United States was pursuing the normalization of relations with China according to the terms of the Shanghai Communiqué.

"Whenever the Chinese are ready to move, we are," Mr. Carter said.

The President added, however, that since President Nixon and President Gerald R. Ford had both gone to China without a reciprocal visit by the Chinese, "I don't intend to go to China until after the Chinese leaders come here."

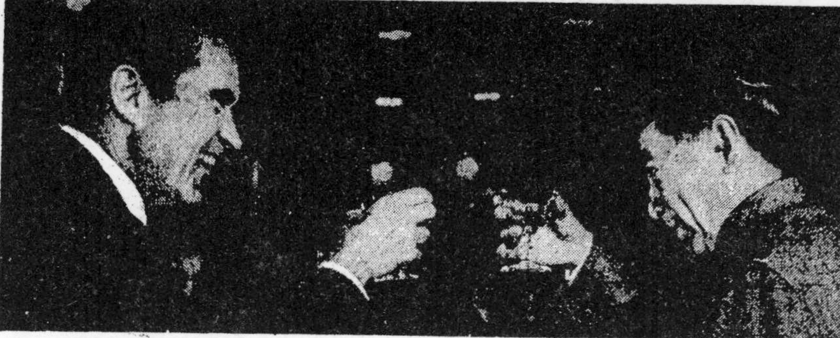

United Press International

Richard M. Nixon, first American President to visit China, toasting Prime Minister Chou En-lai, Feb. 25, 1972

The New York Times / Dec. 16, 1978

China Move Reflects Carter's Aim To Protect Arms Pact and Taiwan

Continued From Page 1

vital interest in the "peaceful resolution" of the dispute between Taiwan and Peking and that the Chinese leadership "did not take exception to that."

This was as close as Peking could come without losing face, one high official said, to renouncing any intention to invade Taiwan in order to force its incorporation into a unified China. That had long been Washington's prime condition for reopening full diplomatic relations with Peking, and Administration officials gave ample indication tonight that China had satisfied them. "We got it on our terms," one satisfied Administration official declared.

Administration officials expressed confidence that early political doubts would be eased and said they intended to seek legislation from Congress protecting American cultural and commercial relations with Taiwan, including the right, as one official put it, "to give Taiwan access to [American] arms of a defensive nature, on a restricted basis," even after 1979.

The sudden breakthrough came, officials revealed, after the Chinese shifted their position 10 days ago to accommodate some of the American demands for normalizing diplomatic relations. Although the timing was awkward for Washington because of the delicate stage of the arms negotiations with the Soviet Union, officials said President Carter felt that it was an opening that Washington could not reject.

Carter Confident on Arms Talks

Appearing in the White House press room after his speech to the nation, Mr. Carter told reporters that he did not believe the arms negotiations, the most important indicator of the state of Soviet-American relations, would be influenced by the new American opening to China.

Many thought the breakthrough could hardly have come at a more opportune moment, with the Administration frustrated by the latest impasse in the Middle East talks that President Carter has so vigorously promoted, and beset by the political upheavals in Iran with its potential ramifications elsewhere in the region.

As rumors swept the city tonight before the President spoke, critics worried that he might be trading away an old ally on Taiwan for the sake of broader interests. But high in the Administration, officials could barely contain their satisfaction with the turn of events.

In the six years since former President Richard M. Nixon's dramatic visit to Peking, three American administrations have yearned for a normalization of relations, but were held in check by their concern for the future of Taiwan and their worry about the domestic political repercussions of appearing to abandon a long-time ally.

As the years wore on, American public and political opinion appeared to gradually shift toward broadening ties with Peking. A survey by Louis Harris about a year ago showed that Americans wanted diplomatic recognition of the Peking regime by a 62 to 17 percent margin, though an equally lopsided margin favored retaining ties to the Nationalist Chinese Government on Taiwan.

After Mr. Nixon and President Gerald R. Ford edged toward normalization and then pulled back, stymied by the Taiwan issue, the Carter Administration made its first move with a visit to Peking by Zbigniew Brzezinski, the President's national security adviser, in May. A string of other high-level American visits followed, each bearing the promise of broader cooperation.

Frank Press, the Presidential science adviser, went to China in July to set up educational and scientific exchanges. Energy Secretary James R. Schlesinger went in October to talk about oil deals, and Bob Bergland, the Secretary of Agriculture, went there in November to discuss farm sales. Trade was rising from last year's $374 million to an expected $1 billion this year, and the Administration thought it sensed the domestic political climate changing in favor of full ties.

Rush of Events in China

The sudden rush of events in China — the diplomatic overtures to the West generally and the pragmatic shift toward economic progress and modernization — helped bring the promise of full diplomatic ties and closer relations with Washington to reality.

In the statements of Teng Hsiao-ping, the remarkably resilient and resourceful deputy Prime Minister, Washington began to detect hints that he wanted to strike a deal that might resolve the American worries about Taiwan.

On a visit to Japan in late October, Mr. Teng told a news conference that the Americans and Chinese were "talking about normalization," adding that he thought "this will follow in the general course of events."

In an interview with Robert Novak, the syndicated columnist, in late November, he startled and delighted American officials by asserting that even after reunification with mainland China, Taiwan could retain its economic and social system.

Reassurances About Taiwan

Mr. Teng sent a third signal in another interview, printed in The New York Times on Dec. 3, indicating that the United States "can keep its economic interests in Taiwan."

"It can continue its investments," he said. "China has no intention of bringing down Taiwan living standards."

But the Administration had difficulty finding the one guarantee that would quiet domestic critics — the pledge that Peking would not use force to reunify Taiwan with mainland China. That is what the President needed most to pacify the conservatives in Congress who were most likely to oppose full diplomatic relations with Peking.

But these same conservatives, Administration officials argued, were attracted to the idea of closer relations with Peking because Chinese rivalry with the Soviet Union could strengthen the American hand against Moscow, especially in the third world.

Soviet's Public and Private Views

At each stage of the broadening relations between the Carter Administration and the new Chinese leadership, the Soviet Union voiced its pique at what it called the American inclination "to play the China card." But in Washinton's view, the private reaction of the Kremlin was more realistic, as the Americans went to great pains to assert that full diplomatic relations between China and the United States should be seen as normal and routine, not aimed at Moscow.

Eastfoto

Teng Hsiao-ping and Leonid I. Brezhnev were foreign observers at the Rumanian Communist Party congress in 1965, when they met in Rumania.

Teng, a Deputy Premier, Is Strongest Leader

Twice purged as a "capitalist-roader," Deputy Prime Minister Teng Hsiao-ping has become China's most forceful leader since he surfaced from exile once again early last year.

It was he rather than Hua Kuo-feng, the Communist Party Chairman, who seemed to be behind the initiatives this year to reverse priorities set under Mao Tse-tung, Mr. Hua's predecessor.

Where others fought over ideology, Mr. Teng has been a pragmatist much closer to the example set by Chou En-lai, who was Prime Minister under Mao. In that spirit, he reversed China's unsuccessful policy of self-reliance and isolation.

Foreign observers see Mr. Teng's hand in the booming trade and industrial agreements with foreign companies, new wage structures to reward worker efforts, stress on technical and scientific education and the interest being shown in the "Yugoslav model" of grass-roots worker democracy in the factories. The question remains whether Mr. Teng, who is 74 years old, will have the time and tenure to make such turnabouts permanent.

Mr. Teng, a veteran of the Communists' Long March in 1934-35, is believed to have been born in the southwestern province of Szechwan into a family of landlords. As a student in Paris, he fell in with other radical Chinese, including Mr. Chou.

After the Communists seized power in 1949, Mr. Teng quickly proved himself an invaluable administrator, and by 1956 he had reached the top echelon as Deputy Prime Minister and General Secretary of the Party.

During the Cultural Revolution, Red Guards paraded effigies of him wearing a dunce cap. After he was dropped from power, he reappeared suddenly in 1973 to work closely with Mr. Hua and Mr. Chou. At the time of Mr. Chou's death in 1976 he was in effect China's chief administrator. Mr. Teng was considered Mr. Chou's logical successor as Prime Minister. Instead, he was exiled again.

The arrest of the radicals labeled the "Gang of Four" in 1976 opened the way for his second rehabilitation.

Text of President's Statement on Ties With China

Following is the transcript of President Carter's statement in Washington on normalizing relations with China, as recorded by The New York Times through the facilities of ABC News:

Good evening. I would like to read a joint communiqué which is being simultaneously issued in Peking at this very moment by the leaders of the People's Republic of China:

"A Joint Communiqué on the Establishment of Diplomatic Relations Between the United States of America and the People's Republic of China, Jan. 1, 1979.

"The United States of America and the People's Republic of China have agreed to recognize each other and to establish diplomatic relations as of Jan. 1, 1979.

"The United States recognizes the Government of the People's Republic of China as the sole legal Government of China. Within this context the people of the United States will maintain cultural, commercial and other unofficial relations with the people of Taiwan.

"The United States of America and the People's Republic of China reaffirm the principles agreed on by the two sides in the Shanghai Communiqué of 1972 and emphasize once again that both sides wish to reduce the danger of international military conflict. Neither should seek hegemony — that is the dominance of one nation over others — in the Asia-Pacific region or in any other region of the world and each is opposed to efforts by any other country or group of countries to establish such hegemony.

"Neither is prepared to negotiate on behalf of any other third party or to enter into agreements or understandings with the other directed at other states.

"The Government of the United States of America acknowledges the Chinese position that there is but one China and Taiwan is part of China.

"Both believe that normalization of Sino-American relations is not only in the interest of the Chinese and American people but also contributes to the cause of peace in Asia and in the world.

"The United States of America and the People's Republic of China will exchange ambassadors and establish embassies on March 1, 1979."

Yesterday, our country and the People's Republic of China reached this final historic agreement. On Jan. 1, 1979, a little more than two weeks from now, our two Governments will implement full normalization of diplomatic relations.

As a nation of gifted people who comprise about one-fourth of the total population of the Earth, China plays, already, an important role in world affairs — a role that can only grow more important in the years ahead.

We do not undertake this important step for transient tactical or expedient reasons. In recognizing the People's Republic of China — that it is a single Government of China, we're recognizing simple reality. But far more is involved in this decision than just the recognition of a fact.

'Long History of Friendship'

Before the estrangement of recent decades, the American and the Chinese people had a long history of friendship. We've already begun to rebuild some of the previous ties.

Now our rapidly expanding relationship requires a kind of structure that only full diplomatic relations will make possible.

The change that I'm announcing tonight will be of great long-term benefit to the peoples of both our country and China and I believe for all the peoples of the world.

Normalization and expanded commercial and cultural relations that it will bring will contribute to the well-being of our nation to our own national interest. And it will also enhance the stability of Asia.

These more positive relations with China can beneficially affect the world in which we live and the world in which our children will live.

Special Message to Taiwan

We have already begun to inform our allies and other nations and the members of the Congress of the details of our intended action, but I wish also tonight to convey a special message to the people of Taiwan.

I have already communicated with the leaders in Taiwan, with whom the American people have had, and will have, extensive, close and friendly relations. This is important between our two peoples. As the United States asserted in the Shanghai Communiqué of 1972, issued on President Nixon's historic visit, we will continue to have an interest in the peaceful resolution of the Taiwan issue.

I have paid special attention to insuring that normalization of relations between our country and the People's Republic will not jeopardize the well-being of the people of Taiwan.

Broad Ties With Taiwan Pledged

The people of our country will maintain our current commercial, cultural, trade and other relations with Taiwan througn nongovernmental means. Many other countries of the world are already successfully doing this.

These decisions and these actions open a new and important chapter in our country's history and also in world affairs. To strengthen and to expedite the benefits of this new relationship between China and the United States, I am pleased to announce that Vice Premier Teng has accepted my invitation and will visit Washington at the end of January. His visit will give our Governments the opportunity to consult with each other on global issues and to begin working together to enhance the cause of world peace.

Negotiations Begun by Nixon

These events are the final result of long and serious negotiations begun by President Nixon in 1972 and continued under the leadership of President Ford. The results bear witness to the steady, determined, bipartisan effort of our own country to build a world in which peace will be the goal and the responsibility of all nations,

The normalization of relations between the United States and China has no other purpose than the advancement of peace. It is in this spirit, at this season of peace, that I take special pride in sharing this good news with you tonight.

Thank you very much.

Taiwan's Leaders Meet Hurriedly

Continued From Page 1

assured the Nationalists during the past few years that it would maintain diplomatic relations with Taiwan and honor its treaty commitments, he went on:

"Now that it has broken the assurances and abrogated the treaty, the United States Government cannot be expected to have the confidence of any free nation in the future."

Shortly after receiving Ambassador Unger, the Chinese Nationalist President summoned several Cabinet ministers to his office. He called a meeting of the central committee of the Kuomintang, the governing party, to consider the most serious blow it had received in three decades since Chiang Kai-shek led his defeated followers here from the mainland.

More than 50 countries have broken relations with Taiwan since the Chinese Nationalists were replaced at the United Nations in 1971 by the Communists. Fewer than 24 countries still maintain ties.

The American decision came as a particularly heavy blow since the United States, the last world power to recognize the Nationalists, has supported them since 1954 with a mutual defense treatv.

The American Chamber of Commerce in Taipei called the United States decision as a mistake. It said in a statement, however, that American businessmen planned to stay in Taiwan.

Teng Hsiao-ping, the Deputy Prime Minister of China who has assumed control of that nation, said in a recent interview in Peking that American businessmen could continue in Taiwan after the normalization of Chinese-American relations. Acknowledging that Taiwan's economic conditions were than those on the mainland, Mr. Teng said that Peking did not want to lower the standard of living on the island.

The election that was called off was for 104 seats, or fewer than 10 percent of the total in the legislature. The legislators do not play any powerful role in Taiwan's affairs, but they do express public opinion.

The campaign to date has been particularly heated, with rightists warning of possible "betrayal" by the United States. Others, however, have campaigned on the slogan that the fate of Taiwan should be decided by the island's 17 million people.

Even before the Government put off the election, there had been fears that disturbances might erupt as the election date approached.

In his Peking interview, Mr. Teng had suggested that the United States could reach an arrangement with Taiwan similar to that established by Japan when it normalized relations with Peking.

Life Magazine © Time Inc.

Chiang Kai-shek, left, with Mao Tse-tung in Chungking in August of 1945 at a meeting arranged by the United States in an effort to reconcile them.

Text of Shanghai Accord

Following is an excerpt from the communiqué issued in Shanghai on Feb. 27, 1972, at the conclusion of meetings between President Richard M. Nixon and Prime Minister Chou En-lai.

The sides reviewed the longstanding serious disputes between China and the United States.

The Chinese side reaffirmed its position: The Taiwan question is the crucial question obstructing the normalization of relations between China and the United States; the Government of the People's Republic of China is the sole legal government of China; Taiwan is a province of China which has long been returned to the motherland; the liberation of Taiwan is China's internal affair in which no other country has the right to interfere; and all U.S. forces and military installations must be withdrawn from Taiwan. The Chinese Government firmly opposes any activities which aim at the creation of "one China, one Taiwan," "one China, two governments," "two Chinas" and "independent Taiwan" or advocate that "the status of Taiwan remains to be determined."

The U.S. side declared: The United States acknowledges that all Chinese on either side of the Taiwan Strait maintain there is but one China and that Taiwan is a part of China. The United States Government does not challenge that position. It reaffirms its interest in a peaceful settlement of the Taiwan question by the Chinese themselves. With this prospect in mind, it affirms the ultimate objective of the withdrawal of all U.S. forces and military installations from Taiwan. In the meantime, it will progressively reduce its forces and military installations on Taiwan as the tension in the area diminishes.

The two sides agreed that it is desirable to broaden the understanding between the two peoples. To this end, they discussed specific areas in such fields as science, technology, culture, sports and journalism, in which people-to-people contacts and exchanges would be mutually beneficial. Each side undertakes to facilitate the further development of such contacts and exchanges.

Both sides view bilateral trade as another area from which mutual benefits can be derived, and agree that economic relations based on equality and mutual benefit are in the interest of the peoples of the two countries. They agree to facilitate the progressive development of trade between their two countries.

The two sides agree that they will stay in contact through various channels, including the sending of a senior U.S. representative to Peking from time to time for concrete consultations to further the normalization of relations between the two countries and continue to exchange views on issues of common interest.

The two sides expressed the hope that the gains achieved during this visit would open up new prospects for the relations between the two countries. They believe that the normalization of relations between the two countries is not only in the interest of the Chinese and American peoples but also contributes to the relaxation of tension in Asia and the world.

"All the News That's Fit to Print"

The New York Times

LATE CITY EDITION

Weather: Snow likely and cold today; snow changing to sleet or rain tonight. Temperature range: today 28-35; yesterday 25-41. Details on page B9.

VOL.CXXVIII No.44,100

NEW YORK, WEDNESDAY, JANUARY 17, 1979

25 cents beyond 50-mile zone from New York City. Higher in air delivery cities.

20 CENTS

SHAH LEAVES IRAN FOR INDEFINITE STAY; CROWDS EXULT, MANY EXPECT LONG EXILE

New York City Gets Passing Grade On $100 Million Notes It Will Sell

By ANNA QUINDLEN

The city prepared to go ahead this month with its proposed $100 million note sale after the notes received a passing, but not superior, grade yesterday. The note sale will be the city's first foray into the public borrowing market in nearly four years.

The fiscal rating is expected to be one piece of evidence of economic recovery Mayor Koch takes with him when he testifies before the Senate Banking Committee. The committee's chairman, William Proxmire, announced yesterday that he would hold hearings Feb. 7 on the city's financial condition.

The MIG-3 rating given to the notes by Moody's Investor Service yesterday was lower than city officials had hoped for, but it was still an improvement over its last investment grade, the lowest ranked MIG-4. That rating quashed a scheduled note sale in November 1977. Moody's noted in a statement that while repayment of the short-term notes seemed secure, the "chronic financial weakness" of the city made a higher rating impossible at this time.

Moody's defines MIG-3 as an investment of "favorable quality, but lacking the undeniable strength" of the two higher classifications. The letters MIG stand for Moody's Investment Grade.

'A Climate of Uncertainty'

"Reliability of pledged revenues in the quality of the mechanism to assure payment of notes provides basic security," Moody's said in issuing its grade.

"The chronic financial weakness of the issuer (continual budget balancing efforts, persistent revenue shortages, magnitude of fixed costs) still creates an overall climate of uncertainty. The balancing of this year's budget indicates financial progress."

"I'm obviously pleased that our credit rating is better," said Mayor Koch when the rating was announced, a day after the unveiling of his own plan to close the city's budget gap. "If credit rating is better it means more people have faith in you."

Mr. Koch and Deputy Mayor Philip L. Toia said they expected the city to go ahead with the sale, although neither would speculate on how high a rate of interest the city might have to pay in the current market on such notes. The notes will be offered by a consortium of underwriters to the public in $10,000 and $25,000 denominations.

Deficit Dispute Blamed

However, Jackson Phillips of Moody's said he did not think the city would proceed with a sale if the interest rate on the notes went above the 9.5 per cent it currently pays on loans from banks. "I hear

Continued on Page B4, Column 5

New York State to Try New Negotiation Plan

By RICHARD J. MEISLIN

Special to The New York Times

ALBANY, Jan. 16 — Governor Carey's administration and New York's largest public-employees union agreed today to adopt an experimental bargaining method in which each side would negotiate to its "last, best offer" and an impartial arbitration panel would be forced to choose one proposal or the other.

The union, the Civil Service Employees Association, guaranteed as part of the agreement that its members would not strike and agreed to require the arbitration panel to give "substantial weight" to the "ability of the state to pay the cost of any economic benefit without requiring an increase in present taxes." The agreement covers 107,000 state workers, whose contracts expire March 31.

It will be the first use of binding arbitration to resolve impasses in negotiations between the state and its workers, which in the past have been subject to the state's Taylor Law requirements for state mediation and fact-finding and for legislative resolution.

If the new method, known as "last-offer

Continued on Page B5, Column 1

Battle Intensifies Over Authority Of President to Control Agencies

By MARTIN TOLCHIN

Special to The New York Times

WASHINGTON, Jan. 16 — President Carter's fight to control inflation is intensifying a constitutional conflict between his authority to develop national policies and Congress's power to mandate the independence of Government regulators.

In a direct challenge to the President's authority several environmentalist groups have brought a Federal court action asking that White House economic advisers be prohibited from interfering with the Interior Department's formulation of strip-mining regulations. The enforcement of the regulations was delayed for six months last week after the economic advisers expressed fears that they might be inflationary.

In recent years, Congress, suspicious of past Presidential abuses, has given no fewer than 60 agencies in the executive branch the authority to issue regulations on specific and distinct areas without reference to broader concerns. The mandates include authority to clean up the air and water, protect consumers and improve workplace health and safety, all of which affect Presidential concerns such as inflation, the energy gap and economic growth.

The White House View

The powers of such long-time regulatory agencies as the Interstate Commerce Commission and the Federal Communications Commission, whose independence from Presidential intervention is well established, are not in dispute.

But the White House does challenge the theory that executive branch agencies should perform their new regulatory functions without Presidential direction. It contends that the President's power to appoint and dismiss Cabinet officers carries an implicit authority to direct the agencies' actions.

Critics, mainly single-interest groups that have fought to get regulations through Congress, maintain that Congress intended that these Cabinet officers

Continued on Page D17, Column 1

West German Retailer Seeks 42% of A.& P. In a $75 Million Deal

By BARBARA ETTORRE

A major West German food retailer announced plans yesterday to acquire 42 percent of the Great Atlantic and Pacific Tea Company, the supermarket giant whose initials have long been a household term in American retailing.

The Tengelmann Group, a privately owned company, said that it planned to buy some A.& P. shares from the John A. Hartford Foundation, which has held a major interest in the chain for many years, and from several other major shareholders.

The 42 percent interest would mean effective control of A.& P. for the German company and would represent an investment of more than $75 million. Trading of A.& P. stock on the New York Stock Exchange was halted yesterday afternoon at 6⅞, up ⅛. The plan would involve a purchase of approximately 10 million of the 25 million A.& P. shares outstanding.

Jonathan L. Scott, chairman and chief executive officer of A.& P., said in a statement that the company "welcomes this expression of investment confidence." He continued, "We at A.& P. look

Continued on Page D4, Column 1

INSIDE

Vietnam Troops Lose Port

In their first reverse in Cambodia, Vietnamese troops were driven out of Kompong Som, a key port, according to Western analysts. Page A3.

52 Convicts Get Clemency

Freedom or parole eligibility was granted by Tennessee's governor while hearings on the alleged sale of clemency continued. Page A14.

United Press International

Shah Mohammed Riza Pahlevi and his wife, Empress Farah, as they prepared to leave Teheran yesterday

On Streets: Cheers, Roses and a Mink Coat

One Man in Crowd Hailing Shah's Departure Asks, 'Am I Dreaming?'

By ERIC PACE

Special to The New York Times

TEHERAN, Iran, Jan. 16 — "Shah raft! Shah raft!" The joyful shout announced: "The Shah is gone!"

As soon as the news broke on the Teheran radio, the cry began sounding along Vesel-e-Shirazi Street. Cheering crowds formed and happy women tossed candy and rosewater at them. Farokh Marvasti, an electrical engineer, had a dazed smile. "Am I dreaming?" he said. "What I have always hoped for has come true: The whole system of monarchy is collapsing here after 2,500 years."

"Salute to the mother of martyrs!" the throng of black-veiled women chanted at a rally in the Dehkade Vanek section of this sprouting, traffic-clogged city of five million. They waved their fists toward Zahra Rezai, who is revered by Islamic militants as the mother of four Islamic anti-Government "guerrillas" who died at the hands of the Shah's Government, one in prison and three in shootouts. "I never thought the Shah would leave so soon," Mrs. Rezai said, weeping. "I am glad the lives of my children were not wasted and now our country will have peace."

For the throng of hundreds of thousands that surged through the boulevard it was a day of reveling and roses, roses that marchers tossed in the air as they chanted: "O the anti-Islamic Shah!" "His return is impossible!" "The Shah has become a fugitive!"

Some demonstrators tried and eventually succeeded in pulling the equestrian statue of Riza Shah, the present Shah's father, from its pedestal on Sepah Square; it took a lot of pulling. On Pahlavi Avenue others toppled a statue of his son from its pedestal.

"May God help you," the militant Islamic clergyman known as Mullah Doost Mohammed said as he tried to comfort a strong-jawed woman, Nemati Roshan, who was weeping uncontrollably after the rally in Dehkade Vanek.

"Damn the Shah!" Mrs. Roshan had yelled when the rally was at its peak. Now she was sobbing as she told the

Continued on Page A8, Column 5

United Press International

Statue of the Shah's father, Riza Shah, being toppled shortly after Shah left

Iran, a Country Adrift

By R.W. APPLE Jr.

Special to The New York Times

News Analysis

TEHERAN, Iran, Jan. 16 — The din of triumph that echoed through Teheran today expressed the spirit of the moment. But the spirit of the future may have been more truly expressed by a phrase uttered at the same time near Paris by a resolute 78-year-old man who has made a revolution. The depature of Shah Mohammed Riza Pahlevi, said Ayatollah Ruhollah Khomeini, was "only a first step" toward his goals.

In the sense that little could be accomplished while the Shah remained here, his flight to Egypt and, later, to the United States removed a great obstacle to the resolution of Iran's yearlong political crisis. It also removed the man by whom and around whom the country's life has been organized since the start of World War II.

No one is really in charge here now — a situation symbolized by banknotes, held aloft by celebrants, from which the Shah's portrait had been excised. With what is probably the permanent departure of the Shah, the heir to Iran's proud 2,500-year imperial history, Ayatollah Khomeini has become the cardinal political figure. He has not yet established full control, but he more than anyone else commands the affection of the masses.

The central question tonight was this: Having brought down the Shah, with whom he has feuded for 15 years, will he demand that the struggle continue until an Islamic republic can be established with him as the strongman, or will he mute his militancy and compromise with the struggling social democratic Government of Prime Minister Shahpur Bakhtiar?

From the answer to that question will flow the answers to many others, both do-

Continued on Page A8, Column 3

RULER GOES TO EGYPT

He Voices Hope Bakhtiar's Government Can Make Amends for Past

By NICHOLAS GAGE

Special to The New York Times

TEHERAN, Iran, Jan. 16 — Shah Mohammed Riza Pahlevi left Iran today, driven from the country he has ruled for 37 years by a popular upheaval that gathered force until it undermined his throne.

A year of demonstrations and crippling strikes culminated in a brief farewell ceremony near the imperial pavilion at Mahrabad Airport, before the Shah's departure for Aswan, Egypt, where he was to be a guest of President Anwar el-Sadat. Tears appeared to be welling in the ruler's eyes.

"I hope the Government will be able to make amends for the past and also succeed in laying the foundation for the future," he said.

Changes Aroused Resentment

The Shah had laid ambitious plans to carry his country from feudalism to the front ranks of the industrial states within a generation. But his ambitions aroused resentment at various levels of the society.

The demonstrators who took to the streets to bring down the Shah complained most loudly about the arbitary manner in which he pressed his programs, the corruption in ruling circles and the harsh measures used to suppress opposition from the religious community and liberal political groups.

In the end, the 59-year-old Shah had accumulated so much hostility from so many quarters that his throne could be saved neither by his lavishly equipped armed forces nor by the United States, which had regarded him as a key ally.

Long Exile Thought Likely

He described his departure today as an extended vacation, but it was believed by his opponents in Iran and by government officials here and in other countries that the trip marked the beginning of a long and perhaps permanent exile.

It was at 1:24 P.M. that the royal jet, a silver-and-blue Boeing 707 named Shahin (Falcon), took off from the airport for Egypt.

[The Shah took the controls himself, The Associated Press reported, and flew the plan over Teheran and on to Egypt.]

As the jet flew over the capital, its citizens were unaware that the year of riots, which are believed to have caused the loss of more than 2,000 lives, had finally succeeded in driving out the Shah.

But within 15 minutes the news had spread throughout Teheran and hundreds of thousands of people poured out of their homes shouting "Shah raft!" — "The Shah is gone!"

The streets, nearly empty during recent days of strikes and gasoline shortages, were quickly clogged with automobiles that added the sound of their horns to the din, as people embraced, wept and

Continued on Page A8, Column 1

Other Iran News

Arriving in Aswan, Egypt, Shah Mohammed Riza Pahlevi was escorted by President Anwar el-Sadat to a secluded hotel on an island in the Nile. Page A8.

In Paris, Ayatollah Ruhollah Khomeini, the exiled leader of the Shah's religious opposition, congratulated the Iranian people for forcing the Shah's departure through their increasingly violent demonstrations over the last year. Page A8.

In Washington, the Carter Administration made no formal comment on the Shah's departure, which it had encouraged, but officials said privately that the Government of Prime Minister Shahpur Bakhtiar probably had no better than a 50-50 chance of survival. Page A10.

Also in Washington, the Iranian envoy and friend of the Shah, Ardeshir Zahedi, declared himself the "Ambassador of the Shah" and said he would continue as an attempt by six employees to bar him from his embassy failed for lack of support. Page A10.

At the United Nations, Iranian diplomats closed their mission all day in what they described as solidarity with the Iranian people on the occasion of the Shah's departure. Page A10.

In Lubbock, Tex., Crown Prince Riza Pahlevi welcomed his brother and two sisters, who arrived a few hours before their father left Teheran. Page A10.

On Beekman Place in New York, neighbors of Princess Ashraf Pahlevi, the Shah's twin sister, said they thought a visit by the Shah was likely. Page B3.

Associated Press

In Aswan, Egypt, President Sadat took Shah on canopied ferry to hotel on Nile

Shah Lands in Upper Egypt, Looking Gaunt and Weary

By CHRISTOPHER S. WREN
Special to The New York Times

ASWAN, Egypt, Jan. 16 — The Shah of Iran, looking gaunt and weary, arrived here today aboard his private jet and was escorted by President Anwar el-Sadat to the seclusion of a hotel on an island in the Nile.

Neither Shah Mohammed Riza Pahlevi nor Mr. Sadat made any statements when the Iranian stepped off his striped blue and white Boeing 707 jetliner at the small desert airport of this Upper Egypt resort town.

But the Shah looked tired in the late afternoon sunlight as he acknowledged the full protocol accorded him, including a 21-gun salute, the fanfare of a military band and an honor guard in smart new forest green uniforms.

His wife, Empress Farah, seemed composed. The royal couple were accompanied down the red carpet on the airport tarmac by Mr. Sadat and his wife, Jihan, and were introduced to waiting Cabinet officials and other Egyptian dignitaries.

The Autocrat and the Republican

There seemed to be an irony in the scene of an imperial autocrat who once reigned so securely over his wealthy country turning to a republican President of poor village origins for solace and support. It remained unclear why the Shah had chosen Egypt as his first stop on a purported vacation and why Mr. Sadat had agreed so abruptly to accommodate him.

A senior official at the airport informally explained that "it is an act of charity between friends. It's when we are in trouble that we need our friends. Egypt is not taking sides in the Iranian dispute."

The Shah has supported Mr. Sadat's efforts to negotiate a peace settlement with Israel and the two leaders share a concern about the dangers of Soviet expansionism in the Middle East. They also seemed to get along well together when the Shah visited Mr. Sadat in Aswan just over a year ago.

Some Egyptians have speculated that Saudi Arabia or the United States had encouraged Mr. Sadat to make the Shah welcome at a time when he is losing friends. Although he was said to be on holiday, his arrival here was followed within minutes by an Iranian Air Force Boeing cargo jet carrying his baggage.

Hotel Given Short Notice

Aswan, which is popular in winter for its constant sunshine and warm, dry climate, had little time to prepare for his arrival. Mr. Sadat, on the other hand, has been here nearly two weeks visiting projects in the region.

The deluxe Aswan Oberoi Hotel, which is situated on Elephantine, an island in the Nile, was informed of the visit only yesterday afternoon and had to turn out more than 300 guests last night. They had to find other accommodations in this invariably overbooked resort.

According to the hotel staff, the Shah's party is occupying 32 rooms, including three suites on the fourth floor. The Shah is staying in the presidential suite, which was stocked with flowers, fruit and chocolates.

Mr. Sadat has moved into the second floor to be with his guest, who is expected to stay in Aswan for at least two days. It now appears that they may be joined later this week by former President Gerald R. Ford, who is coming on a previously scheduled visit.

Crowds Are Not Large

When the Shah's jetliner put down just before 4 P.M. local time (9 A.M. New York time), a commercial airliner that had arrived from Cairo earlier was shunted off to one end of the runway for an hour so the welcoming ceremony would not be interrupted.

There were a half-dozen Iranian flags along the road into town and some old portraits of the Shah that seemed to have been resurrected from last year's visit. The streets were sporadically lined with soldiers, farmers, townspeople and tourists, but the spectators seemed to number a few thousand at most although Aswan's population is more than 200,000.

The Shah and Mr. Sadat seemed to be engaged in earnest conversation when they were ferried across the Nile to the island in a canvas-roofed excursion boat. As they prepred to climb into another car for the short drive to the hotel, the Iranian paused as if he might to respond to waiting reporters' questions. But Mr. Sadat waved the reporters away and shouted "No."

No program was announced for the Shah, who is expected to spend his time resting and talking with Mr. Sadat. There are unconfirmed reports that he may also stop in Morocco before going on to the United States.

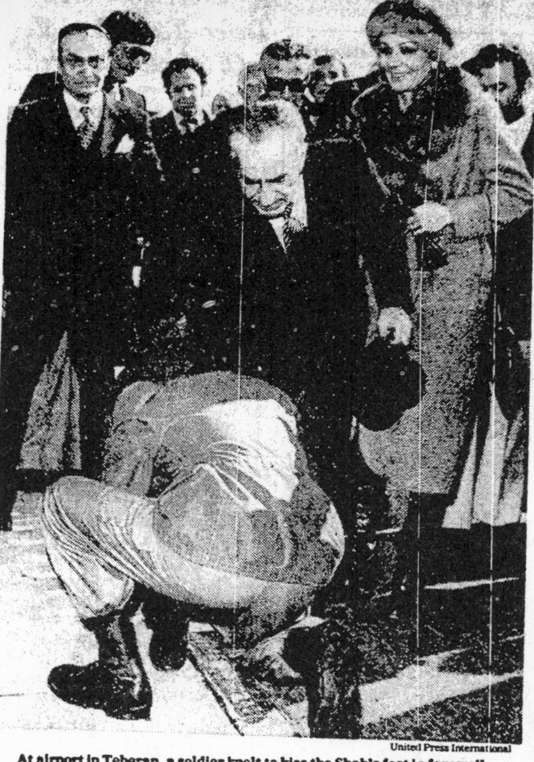

United Press International

At airport in Teheran, a soldier knelt to kiss the Shah's feet in farewell

Shah's Departure Hailed In Message by Ayatollah

By PAUL LEWIS
Special to The New York Times

NEAUPHLE-LE-CHATEAU, France, Jan. 16 — Ayatollah Ruhollah Khomeini, the leading religious opponent of the Shah of Iran, sent congratulations to the Iranian people today on having forcing the Shah to leave the country and called his departure "the first step" toward ending the 57-year reign of the Pahlevi dynasty.

"It is not a final victory, but the preface to our victory," he said at his headquarters in this small French village about 20 miles from Paris.

The 78-year-old leader of Iran's Shiite Moslems, who comprise 90 percent of the population, made clear that his next goal was to overthrow the Government of Prime Minister Shahpur Bakhtiar and the Regency Council to which the Shah has entrusted his constitutional powers during his absence.

This morning, in a statement that aides said would be distributed throughout Iran, the Ayatollah again called on the Government, Parliament and the Regency Council to resign. He ordered his followers to demonstrate against them in the streets on Friday and to continue the general strike that has brought the country to a standstill.

Ayatollah Calls for Unity

At the same time, the Ayatollah stressed the need for national unity to "rebuild the country destroyed by the Shah and foreigners" and warned that continued internal disagreements in Iran could provide a pretext for "outside intervention" — an apparent allusion to his freqently voiced fears of a military coup.

Talking to reporters from the steps of one of the two modest houses his followers rent here, Ayatollah Khomeini announced that he will "very soon" set up an alternative "provisional government" charged with organizing elections and creating a nonaligned Islamic republic in this strategically situated, Middle Eastern oil-exporting nation.

"Congratulations to the heroic people of Iran," the Ayatollah said. "I will introduce very soon a provisional government to set up a popularly elected constituent assembly for the ratification of a new constitution."

The Ayatollah said the members of this still-secret provisional government, which is also called the Islamic Revolutionary Council, are all in Iran and will shortly reveal themselves. Although he himself will have no official position in this government, he said, he will continue to guide it.

Return to Iran Not Specified

The Ayatollah again refused to say when he will return to Iran, although aides hinted that he may remain in exile. In this morning's declaration, the Ayatollah said only that he will return to Iran "at the first proper time."

Although stressing the need for national solidarity, the Ayatollah — whose statements here are recorded and distributed very quickly throughout Iran — told his followers that they have a "national and religious obligation" to participate in the marches planned throughout the country on Friday against the Bakhtari Government.

The Ayatollah made these other points in his declaration:

¶The Iranian armed forces should resist American attempts "to dismantle and destroy sophisticated military equipment bought by Iran."

¶The future Islamic government in Iran will take "legal action" to recover money transferred abroad by the Shah and his family.

¶Classes should resume at Iranian universities, although students should "continue to protest against the illegal Government and dismiss collaborators."

¶There may be "an artifical wheat shortage" unless village elders insure supplies are distributed fairly and farmers plant new crops and get credit from banks.

A large crowd of Iranians, including many religious figures in turbans and robes, gathered outside the Ayatollah's house this morning and responded enthusiastically to the news of the Shah's departure. When the Ayatollah emerged to give his statement and answer questions from the press, the crowd cheered louder and shouted "Long Live Khomeini!" and "Long Live the Islamic Republic of Iran!"

After meeting with the hundred or so reporters in the garden of his house, the Ayatollah, grim-faced but looking suprisingly strong for his years, led some of his followers in prayers in a small blue tent on the lawn.

United Press International

Ayatollah Ruhollah Khomeini commenting on the Shah's departure at his residence near Paris.

Shah Quits Iran for Indefinite Stay as Crowds Exult

Continued From Page A1

cacophony of celebration continued all afternoon and well into the evening.

The Shah's departure from the capital began about 12:30 P.M. when the ruler, grim-faced and wearing a dark suit and overcoat, with Queen Farah at his side, led his retinue out of the white marble Niavaran Palace in the north of Teheran toward a fleet of four khaki-colored helicopters, part of a $500 million military purchase from the United States.

The New York Times / Jan. 17, 1979

Shah flew from Teheran to Aswan

Ten minutes later the helicopters approached Mehrabad Airport and landed beside the imperial pavilion, a gray brick structure several hundred yards from the main building.

There a brief and poignant farewell ceremony took place as the Shah said goodbye to a small group that included Prime Minister Shahpur Bakhtiar, Minister of Court Ali Gholi Ardalan, senior Government officials, several military officers, members of the imperial guard and some palace retainers.

The Shah expressed hope that the new administration of Mr. Bakhtiar would be able to restore peace and progress to the strife-torn country, adding:

"Our economy must start rolling again and the people must resume their normal lives."

Return Depends on Health, He Says

Asked when he would return to Iran, he said: "It depends on the status of my health and I cannot define the time."

As he finished speaking, two of his imperial guards knelt to kiss his shoes, and when the Shah moved to stop them and lift them up, there were tears in his eyes.

The Queen, trying to keep her emotions under control, said: "I'm sure that the independence and national unity of our country will be preserved. I have faith in the Iranian people and in the culture of Iran. May God bless and preserve the Iranian nation."

Then the royal couple kissed a Koran held by a follower and walked under it as is the Moslem custom for one taking a long journey. It was reported that the Shah took with him a bag of Iranian earth as his father did when he was exiled in 1941, but this could not be confirmed.

Before his departure, the Shah said he would stay with President Sadat in Egypt for "a few days," but gave no further details of his travel plans. According to some of his aides, he will go to a European country for a brief stop before heading for the United States, where, the aide said, he will spend most of the time that he is away.

Lower House Endorses Bakhtiar

Shortly before his departure, the lower house of Parliament gave the new Government he has left behind to run the country an overwhelming vote of confidence, 149 to 34, with 13 abstentions.

The vote, which followed even stronger approval from the Senate yesterday, gave full legal status to the Government and enabled Prime Minister Bakhtiar to take his place in the nine-member regency council that has been set up to fill the role of the Shah in his absence.

The frenzy accompanying the Shah's departure in Iran has raised fears here that new violence may be touiched off. Ayatollah Telaghani, a follower of Ayatollah Ruhollah Khomeini, the exiled Shiite Moslem leader, has urged Iranians to celebrate "this spectacular event" in an orderly manner, and the Military Governor of Teheran, Gen. Mehdi Rahimi, has cautioned them not to allow "disruptive elements" to provoke clashes between the people and the armed forces.

Mr. Bakhtiar said in a radio broadcast that he had ordered troops to arrest anyone taking advantage of the situation.

Confusion on Departure Plans

In the 24 hours preceding the Shah's departure, palace spokesmen made confusing comments about when he was leaving, evidently to stave off advance publicity. One spokesman denied that the Shah was leaving today and said he would hold a news conference at the palace this morning to reveal his plans.

A chartered bus arrived at the Inter-Continental Hotel, where most of the foreign correspondents here are staying, and when it was filled to capacity scores of other reporters hailed taxis and instructed them to follow the bus.

The procession then headed not toward the palace but toward the airport and stopped at the well-guarded gates of the royal pavilion, confirming reporters' suspicions that the Shah's departure was imminent. But then the reporters were told that both the news conference and the Shah's departure had been rescheduled for tomorrow. All but a few reboarded the bus and the taxis and returned to the hotel.

A half-hour later the few who had stayed behind saw the four royal helicopters from Niavaran Palace appear out of the sky and watched the Shah and the Queen debark for the first step of their journey into exile.

The Shah's departure offers the ruler the only chance he has to rebuild his shattered support within Iran by removing himself as the main object of blame for whatever goes wrong in the country.

He is reported to be extremely bitter at the refusal of Iranians to recognize how much their living conditions improved under his rule. But, according to a close aide, he also feels that in his absence the majority of the people will come to see the contributions he made, will recognize the risks the country faces without him, and will ultimately join a movement to bring him back.

"He is still hoping for a miracle," the aide said.

Shah Invited to Stay in California

PALM SPRINGS, Calif., Jan. 16 (UPI) — The Shah of Iran and his family have been invited to take sanctuary at the desert estate of multimillionaire Walter Annenberg and may arrive this week, informed sources say.

Iran, a Country Adrift

Continued From Page A1

mestic and foreign: Will Dr. Bakhtiar survive? Will the army, however tenuous the loyalty of its conscripts, attempt a coup? What will the Russians do? The United States? Who will control Iran's oil and its strategic position on the Persian Gulf, through which so much of the Western world's indispensible supply of petroleum moves each day?

If Ayatollah Khomeini remains hostile to Dr. Bakhtiar's Government, virtually all politicians here believe, it will expire within a month. Without at least tacit support from the exiled Moslem leader, the Government will not be able to end either civil strife or economically punishing strikes.

And if Dr. Bakhtiar fails there is no Shah to cobble together another interim civilian government. The next one presumably would be imposed by those strong enough to impose it — either the religious leadership or, though it is considered less likely, the army.

Demonstrators in Teheran celebrate the departure of the Shah; one holds a newspaper with the headline "The Shah's Gone," others display pictures of Ayatollah Ruhollah Khomeini, the Moslem leader living in exile in France.

United Press International

The overt indications from Paris were not promising for Dr. Bakhtiar's partisans. A description of the departure of the Shah as "a first step" does not seem to reflect the view of a man ready for compromise. In a statement published here, moreover, the Ayatollah demanded things Dr. Bakhtiar cannot possibly deliver: the removal of all members of Parliament and of the regency council formed as a stand-in for the Shah, for example, and the cessation of arms purchases from the United States. Ayatollah Khomeini also seems determined to proceed with the formation of an alternative government in the days ahead.

Beneath the surface there are small signs that an explosion may not yet be inevitable. Evidence is accumulating that Ayatollah Khomeini does not intend to return immediately to Iran, which may give Dr. Bakhtiar valuable breathing space, and several other important religious leaders, including Ayatollah Shareatmadary of the holy city of Qum, are inclined to give the civilian Government a few weeks' grace.

That is also the reported private attitude of Mehdi Bazargan, a civil-rights activist with close ties to Ayatollah Khomeini who has been helping Dr. Bakhtiar ease the domestic gasoline and kerosene shortage. Mr. Bazargan and another important independent opposition figure, Ali Amini, who is a former Prime Minister, are planning to visit Paris in an effort to find some common ground.

There can be no quick judgments, then, about Ayatollah Khomeini's intentions and their likely consequences.

Dr. Bakhtiar's most pressing concern is how to capitalize on the wave of euphoria sweeping the country. The temper of the crowds today, with their cries of "Death to the Shah!" suggested that the Government might find it expedient to abandon its moderate stance and begin dismantling the remaining apparatus of the monarchy as well as ruthlessly prosecuting those held liable for national policy under the Shah.

An Extraordinary Occasion

The fraternization of the army and the demonstrators during the last 72 hours, with red carnations stuck into the muzzles of automatic rifles and soldiers pelted with candy, indicates that Dr. Bakhtiar need not fear an early attempt at a coup. The harshest of the remaining hard-liners in the army, Gen. Manuchehr Khosrowdad, told a friend yesterday that given the "unreliability" of the men in the ranks, a coup now would probably fail.

No one here was much more certain of the future than General Khosrowdad on this extraordinary day that will soon take its place in a national legend stretching back to Darius and Cyrus the Great. "It is a fantastic day for us," a gray-haired man told an American in the midst of one crowd of revelers. No doubt there will soon be 16th of January Squares and boulevards all across Iran.

For the Shah, who mounted the Peacock Throne when he was only 21 years old and who had dreamed of making Iran one of the great powers, it was the climax of a Sophoclean tragedy. Perhaps he had failed to understand, as one ambassador suggested, that for 50 years the Iranians were trying to say that they had no desire to become second-rate Europeans.

On Teheran's Crowded Streets, Cheers, Roses, Falling Statues

Continued From Page A1

mullah that her daughter, another Islamic guerrilla, was killed in a shootout with the Shah's security forces years ago.

The talk turned to the Shah's departure and Mrs. Roshan said: "Now I feel safe. Now I feel at last I will take off my mourning clothes. There is a green dress that I have had in the closet for years. I will put it on."

•

The sign at the entrance to the elegant Imperial Country Club at the northern end of the city had been taken down, apparently to avoid angering militant Moslems who hate Western-style frivolity. The grounds were deserted and the clubhouse restaurant was almost empty — many of Teheran's rich have left the country as the political and economic crisis has worn on — but in the bar there was the sound of women's voices. One woman nursed her midday highball and flopped her fur jacket around her shoulders.

"I'm not happy that the Shah is going," she said. "He was a good man. It was only that there were bad people around him. Now what will happen to us? I'm afraid the Communists will come, but we're not going to leave Iran. This is our country." Then she looked down at the child in the chair beside her and her manner softened. "I'm worried about my daughter," she said "What kind of future will she have?"

•

Whatever the attitude in the country club, many more middle-class people were in the streets today than in other demonstrations in recent months. One, a young woman in a full-length mink coat, went striding down the center strip of Elizabeth II Boulevard carrying a placard with a portrait of the chief opposition leader, Ayatollah Ruhollah Khomeini.

•

The demonstrations had a particularly strong anti-American tone. One new slogan that echoed down the boulevards was: "The Shah is gone. The Americans are next!"

•

An army second lieutenant was in command of a detail guarding a filling station. The mission was to prevent disruption among the scores of drivers waiting to buy gasoline, which is scarce because oil production has been disrupted by a strike. "Now there will be a week-long celebration," the lieutenant said. "The army and the people can relax."

But his eyes shifted nervously as he watched the unruly crowd of drivers. "For a while things may get worse — there may be more trouble," he said, cradling his steel helmet under his arm. "And then maybe the army will stage a coup d'état."

He sighed and a muscle flickered under his unshaven cheek. "Thank God my enlistment is finished in 70 days," he said.

•

The Amir Mosque, a small brick structure that has 200 regular worshipers, mostly working-class people, was slathered with posters of Ayatollah Khomeini. In the forecourt of the mosque the caretaker, Mohammed Hajibeki, was chipping away at packed snow, using an old pickax.

"No one has ever bothered me and I have never bothered anyone," Mr. Hajibeki told a visitor. "I'm in here all day and I don't know what is going on outside. I cannot read or write and I have never seen the Shah. Now he is going away. Perhaps he will come back" — he coninued chipping — "and what will happen only God can know."

•

As night fell, Niavaran Palace, the Shah's principal residence in the capital, on the northern outskirts, was dead quiet. A United States-made armored personnel carrier still stood guard at the ornate entrance gates and the imperial standard still flew, but the sentry boxes were empty.

Text of a Statement By Shah on Leaving

TEHERAN, Iran, Jan. 16 (AP) — Following is the text of the statement made by Shah Mohammed Riza Pahlevi to the official Pars News Agency on his departure from Iran today, translated by The Associated Press:

As I have said before, I am going on vacation because I am feeling tired. First I will go to Aswan, Egypt.

With the vote of confidence, given in Parliament today, I hope the Government will be able to make amends for the past and also succeed in laying the foundation for the future. This work needs a long period of cooperation and patriotism in its utmost meaning.

Our economy must start rolling again. We must have better planning for the future.

I have no other words to say but: preservation of the present system and performance of duties based on patriotism.

"All the News That's Fit to Print"

The New York Times

LATE CITY EDITION

Weather: Mostly sunny, cool today; clear, cold tonight. Sunny tomorrow. Temperature range: today 32-48; yesterday 37-49. Details on page C12.

VOL.CXXVIII No.44,169

NEW YORK, TUESDAY, MARCH 27, 1979

25 cents beyond 50-mile zone from New York City. Higher in air delivery cities.

20 CENTS

EGYPT AND ISRAEL SIGN FORMAL TREATY, ENDING A STATE OF WAR AFTER 30 YEARS; SADAT AND BEGIN PRAISE CARTER'S ROLE

OPEC PARLEY WEIGHS NEW OIL PRICE RISES AND CUTS IN OUTPUT

Saudis Say They Will Try to Resist Big Increases — Carter Puts Off Decisions on Energy

By PAUL LEWIS

Special to The New York Times

GENEVA, March 26 — Pressure for another large increase in world oil prices built up today at the opening of a meeting of oil ministers of the 13 member nations of the Organization of Petroleum Exporting Countries.

The advocates of a sharp new oil price rise, of anywhere from 20 to 35 percent from current levels on April 1, also urged other oil producers to reduce output. The aim would be to keep world markets tight as Iran resumes exports to insure that the new price levels stick.

But Saudi Arabia, the world's largest oil exporter, resisted pressure for price jumps, pointing out that they could do severe damage to the economies of both the developing and the industrialized world. "There is worry particularly about the effects of price changes on developing countries," OPEC's secretary general, René Ortise, said.

Effort to Reduce Increases

Sheik Ahmed Zaki Yamani, Saudi Arabia's oil minister, interviewed after tonight's session, said the ministers faced a "deadlock," with the Saudis feeling that the increases demanded by Iran and Libya were "too steep." Observers here interpreted his stance as an effort to cut probable increases to more moderate levels.

The ministers have not yet voted themselves the power to take any pricing action at the current two-day session but are expected to do so tomorrow. A simple majority vote would grant the meeting such authority.

On the question of possible punitive cutbacks in supplies, reflecting displeasure with some consuming nations' positions on the Palestinian question, Iraqi representatives said such moves were possible, particularly against Egypt. But they carefully noted that no such moves were planned by OPEC, although the "oil weapon" could re-emerge if conditions returned to the situation of 1973.

Carter Decisions Deferred

In Washington, meanwhile, Administration officials said that President Carter's decisions on various energy proposals, expected Thursday, would be deferred, apparently because key White House officials had not been able to devote enough time to the controversial plans. [Page D12.]

When Sheik Yamani entered the OPEC

Continued on Page D12, Column 3

United Press International

Leaders join hands after signing pact. President Anwar el-Sadat signed first, followed by Prime Minister Menachem Begin. President Carter was witness.

CEREMONY IS FESTIVE

Accord on Sinai Oil Opens Way to the First Peace in Mideast Dispute

By BERNARD GWERTZMAN

Special to The New York Times

WASHINGTON, March 26 — After confronting each other for nearly 31 years as hostile neighbors, Egypt and Israel signed a formal treaty at the White House today to establish peace and "normal and friendly relations."

On this chilly early spring day, about 1,500 invited guests and millions more watching television saw President Anwar el-Sadat of Egypt and Prime Minister

Transcripts of statements at signing are on page A11. Texts of treaty and Camp David accords are on pages A12, A13 and A14.

Menachem Begin of Israel put their signatures on the Arabic, Hebrew and English versions of the first peace treaty between Israel and an Arab country.

President Carter, who was credited by both leaders for having made the agreement possible, signed, as a witness, for the United States. In a somber speech he said, "Peace has come."

'The First Step of Peace'

"We have won, at last, the first step of peace — a first step on a long and difficult road," he added.

All three leaders offered prayers that the treaty would bring true peace to the Middle East and end the enmity that has erupted into war four times since Israel declared its independence on May 14, 1948.

By coincidence, they all referred to the words of the Prophet Isaiah.

"Let us work together until the day comes when they beat their swords into plowshares and their spears into pruning hooks," Mr. Sadat said in his paraphrase of the biblical text.

Mr. Begin, who gave the longest and most emotional of the addresses, exclaimed: "No more war, no more bloodshed, no more bereavement, peace unto you, shalom, saalam, forever."

"Shalom" and "salaam" are the Hebrew and Arabic words for "peace."

A Touch of Humor by Begin

The Israeli leader, noted for oratorical skill, provided a dash of humor when in the course of his speech he seconded Mr. Sadat's remark that Mr. Carter was "the unknown soldier of the peacemaking effort." Mr. Begin said, pausing, "I agree, but as usual with an amendment" — that Mr. Carter was not completely unknown and that his peace effort would "be remembered and recorded by generations to come."

Since Mr. Begin was known through the

Continued on Page A10, Column 1

Mood of Peace Seems Somber And Uncertain

By BERNARD WEINRAUB

Special to The New York Times

WASHINGTON, March 26 — Shortly after 6 A.M. today, President Anwar el-Sadat arose in the residence of the Egyptian Ambassador and began wandering around the five-bedroom house.

He scanned the morning newspapers, pedaled a stationary exercise bicycle, nibbled a slice of unbuttered toast, sipped a glass of orange juice and, by 7 A.M. turned on the television to watch the morning news.

Less than one mile away, in a guarded ninth-floor suite at the Washington Hilton Hotel, Prime Minister Menachem Begin of Israel peered out the windows at the traffic moving along Connecticut Avenue.

He turned away and, carrying a cup of tea, walked to a writing desk and began working on the emotional speech that he would deliver in mid-afternoon at the White House ceremony ending 30 years of war between Israel and Egypt.

It was the start of a day marked by paradox — a triumphal day of peace that seemed curiously somber, a day of celebration blurred by protests in the heart of Washington, a bright day shadowed by uncertainty.

"There is, you know, a sense of trepi-

Continued on Page A9, Column 1

Photographs for The New York Times by TERESA ZABALA

Treaty Impact Still Unknown

'Hopes and Dreams' but 'No Illusions' for Carter

By HEDRICK SMITH

Special to The New York Times

WASHINGTON, March 26 — The elusive, unprecedented peace treaty that Egypt and Israel signed today has enormous symbolic importance and the potential for fundamentally transforming the map and history of an entire region, but the agreement faces an uncertain future.

News Analysis

Israel has now won what it has sought since 1948 — formal recognition and acceptance from the most powerful Arab state and the ultimate prospect of exchanging ambassadors and entering into a full range of normal relations.

For all the violent denunciations that this historic breakthrough aroused in the Arab world, the best diplomatic estimate here is that the treaty has markedly reduced the risk of a major war in the Middle East for a considerable time by removing Egyptian strength from the active Arab arsenal.

And it has demonstrated American capacity to influence events in the Middle East despite the setbacks Washington has suffered since the overthrow of the

Continued on Page A10, Column 5

Judge Bars Hydrogen Bomb Article After Magazine Rejects Mediation

By DOUGLAS E. KNEELAND

Special to The New York Times

MILWAUKEE, March 26 — A Federal District Court judge here, acting only after his suggestion for an attempt at out-of-court settlement was turned down, granted the Government's motion for a preliminary injunction today to keep The Progressive magazine from publishing an article about the hydrogen bomb.

In so doing, Judge Robert W. Warren became the first Federal judge ever to issue an injunction imposing prior restraint on the press in a national security case.

The magazine's attorneys said they would file an appeal shortly with the United States Court of Appeals for the Seventh Circuit in Chicago.

Court's 'Awesome Responsibility'

Before announcing his decision this afternoon, Judge Warren, a former Wisconsin Attorney General, acknowledged that he considered it an "awesome responsibility."

"Stripped to its essence, then," he said, "the question before the court is a basic confrontation between the First Amendment right to freedom of the press and national security."

The judge said "a mistake in ruling against The Progressive will seriously infringe cherished First Amendment rights." However, he added, "a mistake

Continued on Page B12, Column 3

INSIDE

Michigan State Wins

Michigan State became the National Collegiate basketball champion by defeating Indiana State, 75-64, at Salt Lake City. Page C13.

H.R.A. Administrator Quits

Blanche Bernstein, the Human Resources Administrator, resigned rather than accept Mayor Koch's offer to stay in the job without power. Page B1.

Palestinians, Reacting to the Pact, Go on Strike and Denounce Egypt

Special to The New York Times

BEIRUT, Lebanon, March 26 — Vowing revenge, staging strikes and protest marches and calling for punitive measures against Egypt, Palestinians and other Arabs reacted angrily today against the signing of the Egyptian-Israeli peace treaty in Washington.

Yasir Arafat, chairman of the Palestine Liberation Organization, vowed to chase Americans out of the Middle East and to "chop off the hands" of President Carter, President Anwar el-Sadat of Egypt and Prime Minister Menachem Begin of Israel. He spoke to a group of guerrilla recruits at the Sabra Palestinian camp here as effigies of the three signers were burned.

The inhabitants of Lebanon's 15 Palestinian camps protested the signing today by refusing to work, as did many Lebanese Moslems. Similar protests were staged in the occupied West Bank of the Jordan River and the Gaza Strip, and in the Arab Old City of Jerusalem a grenade exploded tonight, wounding five tourists.

Iran Government Condemns Pact

In Teheran, the Iranian Government condemned the treaty, and 30 Arab students took over the Egyptian Embassy there. Protesters also stormed the Egyptian Embassy in Kuwait, where 250,000 Palestinians live, forming the largest foreign community in that small country. In Damascus, Syria, demonstrators occupied the offices of the Egyptian airline, Egyptair.

Meanwhile, foreign and finance ministers of Arab League countries gathered today in Baghdad, Iraq, for a meeting tomorrow on possible economic and political measures against Egypt. The countries had vowed last November to hold such a meeting if the Egyptian-Israeli peace treaty was signed, but Saudi Arabia, Egypt's principal foreign backer, has been trying to exercise a moderating influence.

King Hussein of Jordan flew to Damascus and Baghdad during the day in what was believed to be an effort to coordinate the positions of hard-liners and moderates at tomorrow's Arab meeting.

Gromyko Comments on Treaty

In Damascus, Foreign Minister Andrei A. Gromyko of the Soviet Union ended a three-day visit to Syria today by joining with President Hafez al-Assad in denouncing the peace treaty, saying it appeared bound to increase tension in the Middle East. A joint Soviet-Syrian communiqué said the treaty was aimed at perpetuating the Israeli occupation of Arab lands, the annexation of Arab East-

Continued on Page A10, Column 5

Peace Treaty Signed By Egypt and Israel

Continued From Page A1

remembered and recorded by generations to come."

Since Mr. Begin was known through the negotiations as a stickler for details, much to the American side's annoyance, Mr. Carter seemed to explode with laughter at Mr. Begin's reference to "an amendment."

Minutes later, Mr. Begin was deeply somber as he put on the Jewish skull cap and quoted in Hebrew from Psalm 126.

The signing was followed by an outdoor dinner on the South Lawn at the White House for 1,300 guests.

The treaty was the result of months of grueling, often frustrating negotiations that finally were concluded early this morning when a final compromise was reached on the last remaining issue — a timetable for Israel to give up Sinai oilfields.

Under the treaty, Israel will withdraw its military forces and civilians from the Sinai Peninsula in stages over three years. Two-thirds of the area will be returned within nine months, after formal ratification documents are exchanged. The ratification process is expected to begin in about two weeks.

In return for Israel's withdrawal, Egypt has agreed to end the state of war and to establish peace. After the initial nine-month withdrawal is completed, Egypt and Israel will establish "normal and friendly relations" in many fields, including diplomatic, cultural and economic relations.

Breakthough at Camp David

The outline for the peace treaty was achieved in September when Mr. Carter, Mr. Sadat and Mr. Begin met at Camp David, Md., for 13 days. In addition to the treaty, they also agreed on the framework for an accord to provide self-rule to the more than one million Palestinians living in the Israeli-occupied areas of the West Bank of the Jordan and the Gaza Strip.

The Camp David accords were opposed by most countries in the Arab world for two reasons. The Arabs regarded the decision by Mr. Sadat to sign a peace treaty with Israel as a betrayal of the Arab cause, since it suggested that Egypt would no longer be willing to go to war against Israel to help Syria, Jordan, and the Palestinians regain territory.

Arabs also viewed the self-rule agreement for Palestinians as insufficient because it did not guarantee the creation of a Palestinian state.

As a result of that opposition, today's signing was greeted by criticism throughout the Arab world. Echoes of that were heard in Washington, where about a thousand Arabs demonstrated in Lafayette Park, several hundred yards from the signing ceremony. Their anti-Sadat chants could be heard at the White House.

"We must not minimize the obstacles that still lie ahead," Mr. Carter said. "Differences still separate the signatories to this treaty from each other and also from some of their neighbors who fear what they have just done.

"To overcome these differences, to dispel those fears, we must rededicate ourselves to the goal of a broader peace with justice for all who have lived in a state of conflict in the Middle East.

"We have no illusions — we have hopes, dreams, prayers, yes — but no illusions."

Mr. Carter read out a long passage that turned on a metaphor of peace being waged like war. It was later disclosed by the White House that the section was quoted from an essay written by the Rev. Walker L. Knight in the House Missions Magazine of the Southern Baptist Convention.

At the end of the ceremony Mr. Carter, Mr. Sadat and Mr. Begin grasped each other in a three-way handclasp. Despite the show of cordiality, there were signs that differences between Egypt and Israel were far from over.

In his speech, Mr. Sadat never referred to Mr. Begin, whom he reportedly does not like personally. By contrast, Mr. Sadat praised Mr. Carter as "the man who performed the miracle."

"Without any exaggeration, what he did constitutes one of the greatest achievements of our time," President Sadat said.

In the printed text of his speech, Mr. Sadat made a strong appeal to Mr. Carter to lend "support and backing" to the Palestinians and reassure them that they would be able "to take the first step on the road to self-determination and statehood."

Sadat Cites 'a Grave Injustice'

The following was in the text of Mr. Sadat's address, but he did not read it publicly;

"No one is more entitled to your support and backing than the Palestinian people. A grave injustice was inflicted upon them in the past. They need a reassurance that they will be able to take the first step on the road to self-determination and statehood.

"A dialogue between the United States and the representatives of the Palestinian people will be a very helpful development. On the other hand, we must be certain that the provisions of the Camp David framework on the establishments of a self-governing authority with full autonomy are carried out. There must be a genuine transfer of authority to the Palestinians in their land. Without that, the problem will remain unsolved."

The remarks about the Palestinians would have been provocative to Mr. Begin, who has declared he will never permit a Palestinian state to be established. He has called the Palestine Liberation Organization the most "barbaric" group since the Nazis.

Later, Mohammed Hakki, the Egyptian Embassy's spokesman, said that the section on the Palestinians, which was on page seven of the printed text, had been "inadvertently" omitted because Mr. Sadat had turned two pages, instead of one, and accidently skipped that portion.

Mr. Begin's speech seemed highly charged with personal emotions, especially in two separate allusions to Jerusalem. These amounted to a reassertion of the Israeli stand on Jerusalem, in a context that was likely to prove embarrassing to Mr. Sadat.

The Israeli Prime Minister said that it was "the third greatest day in my life." The first, he said, was the day of Israel's independence, May 14, 1948, and the second "was when Jerusalem became one city and our brave, perhaps most hardened soldiers, the parachutists, embraced with tears and kissed the ancient stones of the remnants of the wall destined to protect the chosen place of God's glory."

This was a reference to Israel's capture of East Jerusalem from Jordan in the 1967 war and Israel's subsequent annexation of that part of the city to become part of Israeli Jerusalem.

A major point of difference between Israel and the Arabs is the future of Jerusalem, with the Arabs, including Egypt, insisting that Israel must relinquish control over the eastern sector, and Israel's declarations that it will never yield it.

Last night, Mr. Sadat underscored the continuing problem when, in the course of a 90-minute meeting with Mr. Begin, he invited the Israeli Prime Minister to make a one-day trip to Cairo next Monday but declined an invitation to visit Jerusalem.

Mr. Sadat visited Jersualem in November 1977, and it was that dramatic trip that started the process leading to today's treaty signing.

Egyptians officials said that Mr. Sadat wanted to put off another trip to Israel until progress was achieved on the Palestinian negotiations, which are to start in about six weeks.

The peace treaty negotiations went through a series of ups and downs and surprises.

They began in October in Washington with expectations of an early conclusion. Although the basic treaty text was approved by both Egypt and Israel by early December, three months more were needed to obtain agreement on differing interpretations of the treaty — the subject of a separate document of "agreed minutes" — and over issues such as when ambassadors would be exchanged and target dates for beginning and concluding the Palestinian self-rule negotiations.

Mr. Carter finally resolved most of the questions during a weeklong trip to the Middle East earlier this month.

Even though both Governments approved the treaty, it was not completed until late last night when Mr. Begin and Mr. Sadat agreed that the Sinai oilfield would be returned to Egypt seven months after the treaty was ratified, instead of the nine months Israel had preferred and the six months Egypt had earlier asked.

In addition, Mr. Begin agreed to turn over the El Arish area within two months instead of three months originally proposed by Israel.

An arrangement was also made to insure Israel a right to buy oil from the fields without interruption.

Even this morning, in the final drafting, differences arose over whether to call a body of water the Gulf of Aqaba or the Gulf of Eilat. The Arabic and English texts refer to it as "Aqaba," the name of the Jordanian port by that name. The Hebrew version calls it Eilat, after the Israeli port adjacent to Aqaba.

The White House made public the texts of all the documents included in the peace treaty package. These include the actual preamble, nine articles, three annexes and one appendix that comprise the actual treaty text. In addition, there is a document of "agreed minutes" covering differing interpretations of the treaty.

A letter signed by Mr. Begin and Mr. Sadat and covering the controversial "linkage" question of when negotiations on the Palestinian self-rule questions would begin — one month after ratification of the treaty — and when the negotiations would conclude — about a year afterwards — was also released, as were certain clarification letters from Mr. Carter and maps.

The New York Times / William E. Sauro

Pro-Palestinian demonstrators at Lafayette Park in Washington during the treaty-signing ceremony. Their shouts could be heard at the White House.

The New York Times / Teresa Zabala

President Sadat embracing Henry A. Kissinger, former U.S. Secretary of State, after ceremony at the White House. They developed a cordial personal relationship during negotiations that followed the 1973 war.

Impact of the Accord Remains Uncertain

Continued From Page A1

Shah of Iran. Yet by leaving unresolved the Palestinian issue and the fate of the West Bank of the Jordan and the Gaza Strip, these accords may contain the seeds of their own undoing.

As President Carter observed, with greater realism than he showed during the euphoric aftermath of Camp David six months ago, "we have hopes and dreams and prayers, but no illusions" about the difficulties of achieving a broader, lasting peace between Israel and the Arabs.

Ultimately, to grasp the full chalice of peace, the Israelis want genuine, normal relations with the Egyptians in all fields, and the Egyptians insist that the price will be progress toward Palestinian self-rule on the West Bank and in the Gaza Strip. Even the cordiality of today's celebrations did not temper the touchy discord between Mr. Sadat and Mr. Begin on these points.

In the prepared text of his speech, the Egyptian leader called for action "without delay or procrastination" on Palestinian autonomy to set the Palestinians "on the road to self-determination and statehood." These are objectives the Israeli leader has sworn to oppose. And Mr. Begin, with President Sadat sitting in stony, uncomfortable silence nearby, warmly recalled the day when Israeli troops took over East Jerusalem and vowed not to give it up despite Arab demands.

Nonetheless, the signing, conducted on the White House lawn with the brass-band festivity of a political rally, represents a stunning diplomatic triumph for President Carter, a historic accomplishment for Mr. Begin, whose predecessors were unable to get this far, and a calculated gamble for President Sadat, who now faces nearly solid opposition in the Arab world.

Furor Among Arabs Was Expected

The furor among the other Arabs was expected. Even as President Carter flew about in the Middle East earlier this month to stitch together the final crucial compromises, Egyptian officials conceded that they were in for a few months of emotional animosity from radical Arab states and possible ostracism from the Arab League.

Privately, President Sadat has appealed to Saudi Arabia, among other Arab moderates, for a neutral public reaction and continued economic subsidies to give him a chance to make headway on the Palestinian issue and thereby blunt the radicals' charge that Cairo was selling out the Palestinians for the sake of a separate peace and the return of the Sinai peninsula. So far the Saudis have been accommodating.

Egyptians acknowledge that Mr. Sadat is gambling on two things. The first is historical momentum — the hope that once the peace process takes hold, Israeli fears of Palestinaian home rule will relax. The second, as Mr. Sadat emphasized today, is the hope that President Carter will remain deeply involved in future negotiations, prodding the Israelis to go beyond today's peace treaty toward genuine Palestinian self-rule — the keystone toward a comprehensive peace settlement with other Arab states.

Less Difficult Task for Begin

In Israel, Mr. Begin faces a less difficult political situation over the short run because he has already outmaneuvered the opposition in the Cabinet and Parliament to the deal he struck today. But even some of those who went along with the treaty warned that his proposal for Palestinian autonomy was "a time bomb" that could eventually blow up the entire agreement.

For Washington, the conclusion of the peace treaty means more, not less, American involvement in the region. Over the next three years, American economic and military aid to both Egypt and Israel is expected to jump by about $5 billion. In return, the Carter Administration is counting on the peace acord to provide stability and give more backbone to moderate forces in the Middle East, stemming the recent tide of reversals.

Carter's Key Accomplishment

Yet for all these potential difficulties, President Carter himself said on the eve of the signing that in 50 or 100 years, historians would look back on the treaty as the prime accomplishment of his Presidency.

He and his aides regard its achievement as a vindication of his personal tenacity and his capacity as a mediator and as an effective rebuttal to foreign-policy critics who had been accusing him of weak and vacillating leadership.

As if responding to them directly, the President today defended his style of diplomacy. "Peace is active," he said, quoting a passage from a Baptist homily, "not passive; peace is doing, not waiting, peace is aggressive — attacking."

Politically, too, some of the President's entourage see the treaty as a potential turning point after a bad run of events for Mr. Carter. They are hopeful that it will help the White House mend fences with the largely alienated and politically influential American Jewish community. And to capitalize on the occasion, the White House invited 1,300 influential people to its celebration dinner tonight.

But for a President beset by a new round of inflation and dogged by the nation's energy problems, the political dividends of the peace treaty, however significant the accord may be in itself, may be modest if the public's primary concern is the economy.

Moreover, much depends on what is actually happening in the Middle East a year from now as the American primary season gets under way. If in early 1980 the Egyptians and Israelis have fallen to squabbling and negotiations have broken down, the political impact of today's treaty may be minimal. But if an Egyptian ambassador takes up residence in Israel, as the agreements envisage, it could prove extremely helpful for a beleaguered President.

Arabs React With Anger To Signing of the Treaty

Continued From Page 1

Jerusalem and suppression of the rights of Palestinians.

According to the state-controlled Syrian press agency, Mr. Gromyko said he had reached agreement with President Assad and the P.L.O. on dealing with the situation in the Middle East arising from the treaty. Mr. Gromyko had also conferred in Damascus with Mr. Arafat.

Last night Mr. Arafat's second in command, Saleh Khalef, who goes by the nom de guerre of Abu Iyad, called for an Arab-Soviet alliance as the best response to what he termed the triangular alliance between the United States, Egypt and Israel.

Speaking at a rally in Tyre marking Israel's invasion of southern Lebanon on March 14, 1978, Mr. Khalef proposed that the P.L.O., Syria, Algeria, Libya and Iraq join the Soviet Union in the alliance. The guerrilla official hinted that the Black September terrorist organization might be reactivated, referring to what he called a question raised in the Western press about whether the organization might make a new appearance. Mr. Khalef was once reputed to have been the head of the Black September group, which carried out a series of terrorist operations between 1971 and 1974.

"We shall fight the Americans, British and West Germans everywhere," he said, attacking Britain and West Germany for their support of the Egyptian-Israeli treaty. "We shall not tolerate West European attitudes against our Palestinian people."

Mr. Arafat, who spoke a few hours before the signing in Washington, drew loud applause when he declared, "I shall finish off American interests in the Middle East."

Arafat Notes Begin's Statement

He spoke with scorn of a statement made a few days ago by Prime Minister Begin, in which the Israeli leader warned that the P.L.O. chairman would get his fingers burned if he tried to undermine the treaty. Mr. Arafat also said he had received a warning from the United States that the Palestinians would bring trouble on themselves if they caused a disturbance over the peace move.

"They say that I will be burning my fingers," Mr. Arafat said. "But let me tell them that I shall not burn my fingers but instead I shall chop off their hands."

Noting that there was talk of vast American military aid to Egypt and Israel, Mr. Arafat declared: "This is a joke. I ask Carter what happened to all his tanks and planes in Iran."

Associated Press

Yasir Arafat denouncing the treaty at news conference he held in Beirut, Lebanon, yesterday.

Officials at U.N. Foresee Grave Political Risks in Role Under Pact

By KATHLEEN TELTSCH

Special to The New York Times

UNITED NATIONS, N.Y., March 26 — The prospect that the United Nations will have a role in carrying out the terms of the Egyptian-Israeli peace treaty is causing more anxiety than enthusiasm here.

Officials see grave political risks for the United Nations if it becomes involved in helping to carry out the treaty, ignoring the opposition of the Soviet Union and the large group of Arab nations opposed to the agreement, which was reached between Egypt and Israel with the aid of the United States.

There is no concern about the ability of the world organization to undertake the duties assigned to it under the treaty because the experienced United Nations peacekeeping force of 4,200 men in Sinai has been stationed there for six years, serving as a buffer between Egypt and Israel.

Under the pact, it would carry out similiar duties but over a much larger area as the Israelis withdraw from the occupied territory over the next three years. After that, the treaty envisages a continuing supervisory role.

Cost Is One of Main Problems

The use of the United Nations troops would raise a number of problems that are not even touched on by the treaty. One is the cost, but the major obstacle is clearly the opposition of the Soviet Union and of the Arabs who have taken a militant stand against the treaty.

Secretary General Kurt Waldheim has told United States authorities that, contrary to their opinion, he would not be able to order the redeployment of the Sinai force unless the Security Council agreed. It is the general view of many diplomats here that Moscow is prepared to veto the use of United Nations troops in carrying out the pact.

'A Question of Prudence'

Consequently, United Nations officials have been urging the Carter Administration to try to reach an understanding with the Soviet Union privately before the matter of how to carry out the treaty provisions arises. Mr. Waldheim reportedly underscored this point during talks here last week with Secretary of State Cyrus R. Vance.

United Nations officials have also advised the Egyptians and the Israelis not to rush matters by requesting the United Nations' assistance as provided under the treaty.

"It is not a matter of whether the Secretary General has a legal right to act," one senior official observed. "Rather it is a question of prudence." The official said he feared that the world organization could be "torn apart" by precipitous action if it should move to redeploy the Sinai troops without at least the tacit consent of the Soviet Union.

A number of Mr. Waldheim's worried aides cite the experience of the United Nations in the early 1960's when the Soviet Union objected to the way in which the peacekeeping operation in the former Belgian Congo, now known as Zaire, was conducted by the late Dag Hammarskjold and refused thereafter to recognize him as Secretary General.

American officials say that they understand these concerns and that they have been conferring with Soviet representatives. They seem reasonably confident that Moscow could be persuaded that it is in the Soviet Union's broader interests not to try to wreck the Middle East undertaking.

Any move to undermine the treaty provisions by Moscow might have an impact on Soviet hopes of obtaining an agreement for a treaty on limitation of strategic arms with Washington, although Americans here contend that they are not linking the two matters in making their case.

Peace Force Formed in 1973

The peace force in Sinai was formed at the end of the 1973 Middle East war and approved with the full concurrance of the Soviet Union. The Russians, who served with the Americans as co-chairmen of the Geneva Peace Conference on the Middle East, also went along with the establishment of the military committees that arranged the Sinai disengagement that was carried out in 1974 with the help of United Nations troops.

A year and a half later, Secretary of State Henry A. Kissinger's "shuttle diplomacy" led to a further Egyptian-Israeli disengagement in Sinai that required further redeployment of the United Nations force, but the Soviet Union, which was not involved in negotiating the agreements, reflected its objections by refusing to pay the increased costs.

The mandate of the present seven-nation force comes up for renewal on July 24.

The prospect that the Soviet Union might use its veto to prevent redeployment of the Sinai force was presaged last October, a month after Israel and Egypt reached their initial agreement at Camp David. Moscow then refused to to go along with Mr. Waldheim's recommendation for a one-year extension of the force's mandate and succeeded in a bid to limit the mandate to nine months.

More significant, the Russians challenged a United States assertion that the Secretary General had discretionary power to order some redeployment and need not return to the Security Council for specific approval each time he wants to take such action. Disagreeing, the Russians served notice they would not let the force be "dragged in" to help carry out a separate Egyptian-Israeli treaty, saying such deals were hatched at the expense of broader Arab interests.

The Iraqis, who represent the Arab groups most hostile to the treaty, have already initiated the campaign to prevent United Nations involvement by sending a letter to the Secretary General attacking the pact and saying he should "exert every effort to prevent its implementation."

The treaty terms do not provide alternatives for peacekeeping arrangements but the United States has assured the parties involved that it is prepared to act if the United Nations should be paralyzed.

One possibility would be to enlist the aid of friendly governments to perform the monitoring and buffer function now contemplated for the United Nations.

Bomb Explosion Hurts 19 in an Israeli Town

TEL AVIV, Israel, Tuesday, March 27 (AP) — A bomb explosion injured 19 persons today in the outdoor market at Lod, 15 miles east of Tel Aviv, a police spokesman announced. Two of the injured were in serious condition, the police said.

The first police report of the explosion said three persons were killed and four injured, but a later announcement corrected this.

"All the News That's Fit to Print"

The New York Times

LATE CITY EDITION

Weather: Cloudy and hazy today; showers likely today, tomorrow. Temperature range: today 53-73; yesterday 52-75. Details on page 10.

VOL. CXXVIII . No. 44,173

NEW YORK, SATURDAY, MARCH 31, 1979

25 cents beyond 50 mile zone from New York City. Higher in air delivery cities.

20 CENTS

U.S. AIDES SEE A RISK OF MELTDOWN AT PENNSYLVANIA NUCLEAR PLANT; MORE RADIOACTIVE GAS IS RELEASED

The New York Times / Teresa Zabala

Elementary-school children arriving at the West Shore School in Dillsburg, Pa., after they were evacuated from Middletown, site of nuclear plant

Teamster Talks Recess, and Gap Is Called Sizable

Mediator, Differing With Optimistic Report, Sees 'Tense, Difficult Spot'

By PHILIP SHABECOFF

Special to The New York Times

ARLINGTON, Va., Saturday, March 31 — Negotiations between the Teamsters and the trucking industry recessed early this morning with "substantial differences still separating the parties," according to Wayne L. Horvitz, the director of the Federal Mediation and Conciliation Service.

"We are at a tense and difficult spot right now," Mr. Horvitz said in announcing that talks would resume tomorrow morning. He added that "reports we are awfully close to a settlement are not true."

Earlier, sources close to the negotiations reported that the two sides had tentatively agreed to a wage increase of $1.50 an hour over three years plus increases in benefits totaling $30 a week over the same period.

Problems Still Unsolved

Mr. Horvitz said that there were problems still to be resolved in both economic and noneconomic areas.

Government officials said earlier in the day that they were optimistic about the prospects for a peaceful conclusion to the negotiations with a settlement that would within President Carter's wage guidelines.

In theory, the guideline would limit annual wage increases to 7 percent. However, to remove what it called inequities and to pave the way for a settlement, the Administration adjusted the guideline so that increases well over 7 percent would be technically in compliance.

26 to 30 Percent Increase

In fact, sources close to the negotiations said that they expected a total wage and benefit package providing an increase of from 26 to 30 percent over the three-year contract. A 7 percent wage guideline, when compounded, would permit a wage and benefit increase of 22.5 percent over three years.

The average wage paid to the 300,000 truckdrivers and other workers covered by the master freight agreement is estimated at about $9.50 an hour. Adminis-

Continued on Page 45, Column 1

BRITISH TORY IS SLAIN IN PARLIAMENT YARD, APPARENTLY BY I.R.A.

Bomb in Car Kills a Close Adviser to Mrs. Thatcher — 2 Groups Claiming Responsibility

By WILLIAM BORDERS

Special to The New York Times

LONDON, March 30 — A leading Member of Parliament was killed this afternoon when a bomb apparently set by Irish terrorists exploded in his car as he was driving out of the Parliament grounds.

The blast, which brought other members rushing from the House of Commons, occurred on an underground ramp in the main courtyard of the building, less than 50 yards from the clock tower. Its victim, Airey M.S. Neave, who was one of the closest advisers to Margaret Thatcher, the Conservative Party leader, died at a nearby hospital 40 minutes later without regaining consciousness.

His murder, for which two separate factions of the Irish Republican Army claimed responsibility tonight, cast a pall over the election campaign that has just begun in Britain, and it deeply shocked a nation unaccustomed to violence against its elected leaders.

'This Terrible Outrage'

Prime Minister James Callaghan, saying he was "appalled at this abhorrent act," promised that "no effort will be spared to rid the United Kingdom of the scourge of terrorism." All over London this evening, homebound workers stopped to read newspaper headlines about Mr. Neave's murder, shaking their heads and murmuring about what one of them called "this terrible outrage."

The bombing came just eight days after Britain's Ambassador to the Netherlands, Sir Richard Sykes, was shot to death in The Hague. Anonymous callers said later that the Provisional wing of the I.R.A. was responsible for his murder.

Mr. Neave, a much-decorated hero of World War II who had been in Parliament for 25 years, was the member of Mrs. Thatcher's shadow Cabinet responsible for the affairs of Northern Ireland. He knew, according to his friends, that the job made him a natural target for the terrorists who are trying to drive the British out of that province.

He was, nevertheless, outspoken on the

Continued on Page 4, Column 3

CHILDREN EVACUATED

But Governor Says Later Further Pullouts Are Not Thought Likely

By RICHARD D. LYONS

Special to The New York Times

MIDDLETOWN, Pa., March 30 — Gov. Dick Thornburgh advised pregnant women and small children today to stay at least five miles away from the crippled Three Mile Island nuclear power plant as radioactivity continued to leak and another burst of contaminated steam had to be released for safety reasons.

Tonight, at a Harrisburg news conference, Government nuclear experts said there was no immediate threat to public health, but Governor Thornburgh said his suggestion for the women and children "remains in force until tomorrow."

Earlier in the day several thousand schoolchildren were evacuated from the plant area, 10 miles southeast of Harrisburg, and other people began leaving on the Governor's advice. More than 150 pregnant women and young children were at a shelter in Hershey, for example.

No Evacuation Order

As for others in the area, the Governor said tonight: "No evacuation order is necessary. My earlier advice that people try to remain indoors expires at midnight."

The highest levels of radioactive material yet vented were let go from the facility today, and one official of the Nuclear Regulatory Commission, Dennis Crutchfield, said that up to one-fourth of the fuel rods, or 9,000 of the 36,000 fuel elements, may have been damaged since Wednesday.

Further, Government and nuclear

Continued on Page 8, Column 3

The New York Times / March 31, 1979

Gov. Dick Thornburgh of Pennsylvania urged young children and pregnant women to avoid the area within five miles of the Three Mile Island plant until sometime today. His request to those within 10 miles to stay indoors expired at midnight. Earlier, residents of Lancaster, Adams, Cumberland and Dauphin counties were alerted to possible evacuation, an alert that was canceled.

CONGRESS IS BRIEFED

Carter Aide at Scene Says Danger to the Public Is Believed Remote

By DAVID BURNHAM

Special to The New York Times

WASHINGTON, March 30 — The Nuclear Regulatory Commission told Congress today that the risk of a reactor core meltdown had arisen at the crippled Three Mile Island atomic power plant at Middletown, Pa., an event that could necessitate a general evacuation of the surrounding area.

A core meltdown — a melting of the reactor's stainless steel fuel rods or the enriched uranium pellets within them — is second only to an explosion in terms of seriousness of a nuclear accident.

At a televised news conference in Middletown tonight, Gov. Dick Thornburgh said that no general evacuation was deemed necessary, and Harold Benton, an N.R.C. official sent to the scene as President Carter's representative, said, "There is no imminent danger to the public." He called the possibility of a core meltdown "very remote."

Bubble of Hydrogen Forms

Earlier, officials said that a large pressurized hydrogen bubble had formed in the top of the reactor's sealed core vessel, which is supposed to be full of water for cooling the fuel rods. They said that unless the bubble was removed carefully, it could expand and leave the top of the fuel rods out of the cooling water, allowing them to overheat, melt and release large amounts of radioactivity.

While calling the situation stable for the moment, they noted that both methods under discussion for removing the bubble — letting it sink to the bottom of the vessel by drawing off water, or trying to break it up with steam — involved risks of further exposure of the fuel rods and a possible meltdown.

At the request of Gov. Thornburgh, young children and pregnant women began evacuating an area within five miles of the plant today. In addition, 23 schools were closed, and 15 mass-care centers were established as a precaution in counties surrounding the Middletown area.

Evacuation Plan Developed

In Washington and elsewhere, concern mounted over what has become the nation's most serious commercial nuclear reactor accident.

At the White House, President Carter was briefed by the National Security Council, and Jody Powell, the President's Press Secretary, said that a contingency

Continued on Page 8, Column 1

Delay on U.S. Debt Ceiling Hurts Treasury and Financial Markets

By JOHN H. ALLAN

The delay by Congress in raising the legal ceiling on the national debt is disrupting financial markets across the country.

Although most observers are confident that the fiscal drama will be settled by Congressional action on Monday, the Treasury had to scramble yesterday to make sure it had enough money to last until then.

To keep its debt under the ceiling and to gather in all its tax payments being held by banks, the Treasury announced a comprehensive program.

It postponed plans to borrow $6 billion on Monday, and it also suspended sales of Government savings bonds. Banks were called on for any tax receipts they are holding, and the Treasury arranged to borrow $3 billion from the Federal Reserve. It also asked the Federal Reserve to make its monthly Government payment from earnings — about $700 million — on Monday instead of Tuesday.

In addition, the Treasury said that, starting Monday, it would not make interest payments on its trust funds for Social Security and Civil Service. If Congress raises the debt ceiling on Monday, however, the payments would be resumed quickly.

The temporary ceiling on the debt, now $798 billion, will revert at 12:01 A.M. tomorrow to its "permanent" level of $400 billion. The reversion does not invalidate the $398 billion difference, but it prevents the Treasury from borrowing more and it means the Government must pay off its debt as it matures.

The debt ceiling limits the amount of money the Government can borrow at

Continued on Page 30, Column 4

Within Sight of Stricken Plant, A Town's Main Street Is Empty

By B. DRUMMOND AYRES Jr.

Special to The New York Times

GOLDSBORO, Pa., March 30 — At 5:15 P.M. today on Main Street here, the only living thing in sight was a brown-and-white dog, wandering aimlessly, oblivious to the radiation that was leaking from the crippled nuclear power plant just across the muddy Susquehanna.

"Almost everybody's gone," Annette Baker said, emerging from Reeser's grocery and casting a wary eye toward the plant's huge cooling towers, looming ominously above Goldsboro less than half a mile away. "Normally at this time of day, the people are around, coming home. I don't mean this place is a traffic jam or anything like that. We've only got 600 or so people. But this . . ."

'You Just Don't Know When'

She gestured toward the empty town square and the surrounding houses and stores, every window and door tightly shut despite an unseasonable afternoon temperature in the 70's.

"You live with that plant over there for years and years and don't think much about it," Terry Heidler, a print shop operator, said during a quick visit to Reeser's. "But it's like living with a rattlesnake. Sooner or later it's going to bite you. You just don't know when."

The people of Goldsboro, like the 20,000 or so other Pennsylvanians living within a five-mile radius of the Three Mile Island power plant, began pulling out Wednesday within an hour or so of the malfunction that caused what appears to be America's worst nuclear accident.

Most went to the homes of relatives of friends in other counties. At first, there was only a trickle. But this morning, when the authorities advised that pre-school children and pregnant women definitely should abandon the area, the trickle became a stream, then a river.

Switchboards Tied Up

There were jammed gasoline stations. There were panicky phone calls that so cluttered up switchboards that hours went by when nothing could be heard but the buzz, buzz, buzz of a busy signal.

"This is really like '1984,'" a local radio announcer commented, searching frantically for a metaphor that would somehow put the unthinkable into perspective. He got it wrong — Big Brother wasn't really involved — but somehow the message came through.

"People have really been shaken by this," Goldsboro's Mayor, Kenneth Myers, said. "We're prepared to

Continued on Page 7, Column 4

United Grounds Jets As Union Walks Out

By RICHARD WITKIN

United Airlines, the nation's largest carrier, was grounded today by a strike of 18,600 mechanics and other ground workers after they voted down a new contract tentatively agreed to by their union officers.

The union, the International Association of Machinists and Aerospace Workers, notified the company at midday yesterday that the strike would get under way today at 12:01 A.M. And early last evening, United announced that it had canceled all of its 1,600 daily flights from today through April 8.

The airline said that flights that were under way at 12:01 this morning would continue to their first stop; the crew on each flight with more than one stop was to decide whether to continue to the final destination.

There was no indication when negotiations might be resumed. The airline's switchboards were ablaze yesterday as customers with reservations sought help

Continued on Page 26, Column 1

The New York Times / Keith Meyers

Duane and Marian Shuttlesworth leave Middletown with daughter, Rebecca

INSIDE

Arabs Deadlocked on Egypt

Despite Saudi offers of concessions, an Arab conference stayed deadlocked over what to do about Egypt's signing of the treaty with Israel. Page 2.

New Sea Creatures Found

Ten-foot-long, wormlike animals that may constitute a new phylum have been discovered on the floor of the sea in the Galapagos Islands. Page 26.

Conflicting Reports Add to Tension

By BEN A. FRANKLIN

Special to The New York Times

HARRISBURG, Pa., March 30 — When an air raid siren shrieked what turned out to be an unauthorized alert near the state Capitol here before noon today, setting off an unscheduled midday traffic jam of jittery state employees, it was only the most dramatic result of three days of conflicting and sometimes flatly contradictory statements about the nuclear emergency at the Three Mile Island atomic plant near Middletown in south-central Pennsylvania.

The alert was variously said to have been a malfunction or to have been sounded by a Civil Defense official who misinterpreted Gov. Dick Thornburgh's widely misreported early-morning decision to prepare for, but not to carry out, a mass evacuation.

Mr. Thornburgh acted after receiving reports of what he called an "uncontrolled" release of radioactivity from the nuclear plant. And again, as has happened so often since details of the accident were announced Wednesday, the public was receiving information that was at loggerheads with other reports.

While the Governor, after four hours' sleep, said he was preparing to act "in the interest of taking every precaution" against radiation injuries, the power plant's top nuclear engineer, citing radiation readings far lower than those re-

Continued on Page 8, Column 1

U.S. Aides See Risk Of Meltdown at Plant

Continued From Page 1

plan had been developed for an evacuation of the area's population in the event more serious trouble develops.

But experts consulted about the accident said that, despite the failure of some of the plant's components, the safety system as a whole had held up.

According to staff assistants of Senator Gary Hart and Representatives Morris K. Udall and John Dingell, officials of the Nuclear Regulatory Commission said that, while the situation at the damaged reactor was stable, there was a chance that a core meltdown could occur.

President Carter's spokesman, Jody Powell, said at a briefing that, although the word "meltdown" had been used in a discussion between officials of the N.R.C. and Pennsylvania, there had been "unwarranted and disproportionate amounts of speculation about this matter . . . ."

During the day, official Washington was gripped with increasing tension as word of the reactor experts' concern began to circulate to the White House, then to Capitol Hill and finally to newsmen. President Carter was said by Mr. Powell to have ordered the chairman of the N.R.C., Joseph Hendrie, to err on the side of safety, and several Senators held brief news conferences and announced future hearings.

But safety question centered on the massive reactor on an island in the Susquehanna River was unresolved.

'Not a Hazardous Condition'

Dudley Thompson, executive officer for operations and support at the Nuclear Regulatory Commission, said at a briefing to reporters late this afternoon that the current situation "is not a hazardous condition — the plant condition is stable."

Asked if he was confident that they could remove the bubble and if they had ever done before, the official said, no, it was a new problem. "We are in a situation not comparable to previous conditions," he replied.

Mr. Thompson, who used the word "meltdown" in one press briefing, later pulled back.

"The word 'meltdown' to the general public is a buzzword," he said, "and connotes a complete melting of the active inventory of nuclear fuel." He added, however, that "it is fair to say the possibility of some limited, localized melting of fuel exists."

Senators Briefed by Phone

Senator Hart, Democrat of Colorado and chairman of the subcommittee on nuclear regulation; Senator Alan K. Simpson, the senior Republican of the subcommittee, and the two senators from Pennsylvania, Richard S. Schweiker and H. John Heinz 3d, were briefed in a 40-minute telephone conference late this afternoon.

Their briefing came from Lee V. Gossick, the top staff official of the N.R.C. and Dr. Roger Matson. The situation at the Three Mile plant, as described by a staff assistant to Senator Hart, seemed more serious than the impression given reporters by Mr. Thompson.

According to the Hart aide, the Senators were told by the two officials that they were pleased with the temperature and pressure in the reactor now. They added, however, that it was "difficult to judge at this juncture" how many of the stainless steel rods that hold the uranium fuel pellets already had been damaged.

Dr. Matson was quoted as telling the Senators, "There is some risk of meltdown." He was also quoted as saying, "The situation is stable right now, but we have to deal with that hydrogen bubble."

Mr. Gossick and Dr. Matson were asked what would happen in the event of a meltdown. They replied that experts at the Brookhaven National Laboratories on Long Island had estimated that local and state officials would have from four to five hours to order an evacuation after receiving the first indications that the situation had worsened.

The officials told the Senators, the staff aide said, that Pennsylvania civil defense experts had estimated they could evacuate Harrisburg, the largest population center near the plant, with more than 62,000 residents, within two hours.

The officials were also quoted as saying that one N.R.C. study of hypothetical meltdown situations had concluded that, in about 75 percent of the cases, evacuation would involve all people living within 10 miles of a reactor.

Representative Dingell was told by commission officials that there were two possible methods of removing the troublesome hydrogen bubble, both of which posed some risk.

In one approach, the experts were quoted as saying, the bubble would be allowed to "sink to the bottom" of the containment vessel by drawing off some of the cooling water. This option, however, might expose the rods to extremely high heat and possible meltdown if the bubble did not sink fast enough.

The second option, the experts said, was to start up the reactor again and try to saturate the bubble with steam and break it up.

Timing of Attempt Unknown

Exactly when the safety experts at the scene of the damaged reactor will decide to attempt the removal of the bubble is not clear.

A staff assistant to Representative Dingell said a team of meteorologists is at the scene trying to decide when the wind will be blowing from a direction that would carry whatever radiation is released to areas with the smallest population.

White House Press Secretary Powell said President Carter had created a special task force under the National Security Council to act as a clearinghouse for information in the case. He also said that the Defense Department was providing improved communications equipment in Pennsylvania and had ordered a total review of the nation's nuclear policy.

In a related development, the General Accounting Office released a report today that concluded that evacuation plans for areas surrounding many of the nuclear plants in the United States were inadequate to protect the public in a serious accident.

The General Accounting Office, in a past report, had recommended that the Government set a policy of refusing to license new nuclear power plants unless state and local governments have adopted and tested plans to evacuate the public from the area of a possible accident.

The N.R.C., in a response prepared several months ago, opposed the G.A.O. suggestion on the grounds that the commission's safety requirments were sufficiently stringent.

The New York Times/William E. Sauro

A large steel storage tank is driven into the nuclear plant. It is possible that it will be used as container for the contaminated coolant water.

Children and Pregnant Women Near Nuclear Plant Leave

Continued From Page 1

safety experts disclosed today that the technical problems were far more difficult than first believed as they worked to shut down the nuclear facility after what has evolved into the nation's most serious civilian nuclear power reactor accident.

But Harold Denton, director of the Nuclear Regulatory Commission's office of nuclear reactor regulation, who was dispatched here as President Carter's representative, stressed at tonight's news conference that "there is no immediate danger to the public."

Growing Hydrogen Pocket

Of paramount concern to Federal safety experts and those of the utility that operates the plant, the Metropolitan Edison Company, is the growth of a large pocket of radioactive hydrogen gas at the top of the reactor containment vessel. The larger this bubble becomes the less water there is to cool the fuel rods and the hotter they get.

The worst possible case is a total meltdown of the uranium dioxide fuel elements, a rupture of the containment vessel, and the release of large amounts of extremely dangerous radioactive debris over the countryside.

Safety experts stress that this has not happened and probably will not happen but that safety measures are being planned in the event that such a series of events actually occurs.

Governor Thornburgh told a news conference at the Capitol in Harrisburg early this afternoon, "I am advising those who may be particularly susceptible to the effects of radiation — that is, pregnant women and preschool-age children — to leave the area within a five-mile radius until further notice."

That warning and the deliberate release of a large puff of radioactive gas that Metropolitan Edison officials vented from the plant this morning — without telling anyone in advance — aggravated a situation in which some people in this Susquehanna Valley area are visibly worried.

Officials Fear Meltdown

Fears for public safety rose today when officials of the Nuclear Regulatory Commission in Washington raised the possibility of a meltdown, an event that the critics of nuclear power have warned of for years and that defenders of atomic power have contended could never happen.

In discussing the question of the hydrogen bubble, Dudley Thompson, a senior official in the commission's office of inspection, said "We are faced with a decision within a few days, rather than hours," on means of cooling down the core. Some fuel rods in the core were said by officials to be registering temperatures of 700 degrees Fahrenheit while a meltdown would require heat of several thousand degrees.

"We face the ultimate risk of a meltdown," Mr. Thompson said. "If there is even a small chance of a meltdown we will recommend precautionary evacuation."

This would be an enormous task involving the transportation out of the area of at least a hundred thousand people, and perhaps many more. It was not immediately clear how state and Federal authorities could cope with a departure of such size, which would dwarf any that has taken place in this country.

Since Wednesday morning's accident, utility officials have stated repeatedly that relatively few of the 36,000 fuel rods in the core had overheated and ruptured.

John G. Herbein, the company's vice president for power generation, set the number yesterday at between "one-half and one percent" — that is, 180 to 360. This entails the overheating of uranium dioxide pellets inside the rods, and they are melting completely through the zirconium cladding of their containers.

Such melting through the cladding opens the insides of the fuel rods to the coolant water and thus allows to circulate through the water system large amounts of radioactive debris released in the fission process.

In the event of a full meltdown and rupture of the containment vessel, it is these radioactive elements, such as iodine 131, that would be released into the atmosphere.

Addressing the fuel problem, Frank Ingram, a public affairs officer with the regulatory commission in Washington, said, "There is evidence of severe damage to the nuclear fuel."

High Fuel Temperatures

"Samples of the primary coolant contain high levels of radioactive iodine, and instruments in the core indicate high fuel temperatures in some of the fuel bundles and the presence of" the hydrogen bubble, he continued.

"Because of these noncondensable gases, the possibility exists of interrupting coolant flow within the reactor when its pressure is further decreased and the contained gases expand.

"Several options to reach a final safe state for the fuel are under consideration. In the meantime, the reactor is being maintained in a stable condition."

Some of these options apparently were being exercised tonight when a 25,000-gallon steel tank arrived at the plant by truck, with another said by utility officials to be on the way. It was not immediately clear what the tanks were going to be used to contain.

The xenon gas that was released this morning was monitored aboard a plane flying over the plant as having emitted 1,200 millirems an hour. This is inert and cannot react with other elements and quickly dissipated into the air.

Detected on River Bank

Along the west bank of the Susquehanna — the plant is on an island in the middle of the river — levels of about 15 millirems an hour were detected, according to the utility. A dental X-ray contains about 20 millirems.

Utility officials were grim-faced when they held a news conference this morning in the American Legion Hall here. They insisted, as they have previously, that there was no public health threat and no need to evacuate the area.

But Mr. Herbein, an engineer who has acted as the main utility spokesman, acknowledged that the problems of cooling down the reactor were much more complicated than had at first been conceded. He twice used the word "serious" in relating problems associated with containing radioactive material.

He described the presence of the bubble, which he said had grown to 1,000 cubic feet in size, and said that the utility had yet to devise a way to siphon the gas from within the reactor. If that could be done, more liquid coolant could be circulated around the fuel rods and thus cool them down faster.

Another means of cooling the reactor would be the withdrawal of some fuel elements, but this has been stymied by the fact that Wednesday's accident melted some of them, thus deforming them and making them hard to extract.

In addition to safety experts from Washington, a dozen nuclear safety specialists arrived from the Brookhaven National Laboratory in Suffolk County, L.I. The total number was not clear, but the influx of nuclear scientists and engineers could well be as many as a hundred.

Some members of Governor Thornburgh's staff were openly speculating that the cleanup operations at the plant, even if the immediate problems are settled and no meltdown or evacuation takes place, may stretch into weeks and even months because some of the problems resulting from the accident have never been encountered in a civilian power reactor.

Schools Are Closed

In discussing the possibility of evacuation, Governor Thornburgh said: "We have also ordered the closing of any schools within this area." The district within a diameter of 10 miles has a population of roughly 20,000.

"I repeat that this and other contingency measures are based on my belief that an excess of caution is best. However, the continued presence of radioactivity in the area and the possibility of further emissions lead me to exercise the utmost of caution," he said.

Under a barrage of questions, Mr. Thornburgh conceded that there had been many conflicting versions of the events of the the last 72 hours and that "there are a number of conflicting versions of every event that seems to occur."

"I have just got to tell you that we share your frustration," he said to reporters. "It is a very difficult thing to pin these facts down."

Conflicting Reports Add To Harrisburg Tensions

Continued From Page 1

ported by Mr. Thornburgh, insisted at a news briefing that the hazards were "minuscule," "negligible" and certainly unworthy of evacuation.

John G. Herbein, vice president for power generation of the Metropolitan Edison Company, which operates the nuclear plant, at first indirectly disputed a report from the Governor's office.

Mr. Thornburgh's press aides said he had been told by other plant officials that this morning's emission of radioactive gases had brought one brief radiation reading of as high as 1,200 millirems.

Mr. Herbein said, however, that an aircraft flying over the power plant had measured only 300 to 350 millirems in a rapidly dispersing gas plume.

"We don't see any reason for emergency procedures," he said, repeating the company's contention that the level of radiation released from the plant was "less than that of a dental X-ray," and adding: "I am here today to try to ease the level of panic. No evacuation is needed."

But, when Mr. Herbein was pressed to say that his figures were right and the Governor's wrong, he said he would "not dispute" the 1,200 millirem figure, and added, "I guess there are conflicting readings — I heard 350."

The rem is a standard radiation measurement that relates the strength of radiation to the duration of exposure. The exposure from a standard diagnostic X-ray has been put at 72 millirems.

Reporters grew angry when Mr. Herbein went on to defend the company's repeated emissions of radioactive material, including 400,000 gallons of slightly radioactive water dumped into the Susquehanna at midnight yesterday, without prior announcement.

At one point he replied sharply, "I don't know why we need to tell you each and every thing we do." Nuclear power protesters who attended the briefing, which was held in the American Legion hall in Middletown, shouted in outrage at Mr. Herbein for "withholding information from the community."

Reports of Dumping Denied

Another conflict occurred last night, when state and Federal agencies were preparing to approve plans to dump the contaminated water into the river, Karl Abraham, a public relations spokesman for the Nuclear Regulatory Commission, specifically denied reports then moving on wire services that water containing low-level radioactivity would be piped into the river.

From the beginning of the radiation leak here, which Mr. Herbein said today might not be finally secured for "four or five days," there have been complaints from local officials that they had not been kept informed or have been misinformed.

Yesterday, Mr. Herbein said that the faulty reactor would be cooled and shut down by today. Today, he said there would be further radioactive emmissions through the weekend because of "problems" in shutting it down.

Governor Thornburgh also complained of receiving conflicting information, and implied at a news conference this noon that this had led him to to obtain, through President Carter, the services of Harold Denton, chief operations officer of the Nuclear Regulatory Commission.

Mr. Denton, the Governor said, would "dispel some of the multi-directional reports or facts."

"It is a very difficult thing to pin these facts down," Mr. Thornburgh told reporters. "We share your frustration. We're getting conflicting reports, too. Our responsibility is to protect the citizens of central Pennsylvania. To protect their safety we need better information."

Associated Press

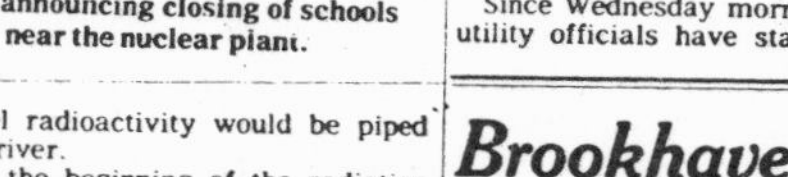

Gov. Dick Thornburgh of Pennsylvania announcing closing of schools near the nuclear plant.

The New York Times/William E. Sauro

At their home on Ann Street in Middletown, Pa., less than two miles from the site of nuclear plant, Mr. and Mrs. John Houseman and their children watched Gov. Dick Thornburgh's news conference on television last night.

Brookhaven Aide Says Safety Equipment Held Up at Pennsylvania Plant

By MALCOLM W. BROWNE

The head of the thermal reactor safety division at the Brookhaven National Laboratory said yesterday that the network of safety equipment at the Three Mile Island nuclear generating plant had held up well despite the failure of some of its components.

Dr. Melvin M. Levine, whose organization has been following the situation at the Pennsylvania plant, said in an interview that problems had resulted from some continued heating inside the reactor. But he added that this was the result of the continuing low-level decay of radioactive material in the core rather than a fission reaction.

There were reports from the Nuclear Regulatory Commission that a meltdown in the reactor had become a possibility, but Dr. Levine expressed confidence that the painstaking and expensive work of removing dangerous radioactive substances from the plant can be carried out without the extreme hazard of a meltdown.

A meltdown, Dr. Levine said, can involve either the melting of the metal rods in which pellets of enriched uranium fuel are contained, or of the pellets themselves. The metal rods are capable of melting at lower temperatures than the pellets, which are encased in ceramic material, and withstand temperatures of several thousand degrees Fahrenheit.

If the heat continued to build up, the ceramic pellets could conceivably melt. And if all of the fuel from all of the rods were to collect in a molten puddle in the bottom of the reactor, fission could resume. The resulting heat would melt the bottom of the rector vessel, and all of the radioactive material would then spill to the bottom of the building housing the reactor.

Theoretically, the building was constructed with this vastly remote possibility in mind, and it would contain the radioactive material.

Reports from the scene suggested, however, that some of the metal rods had already melted, presumably spilling their loads of fuel pellets into the core cavity of the reactor.

Furthermore, a bubble inside the reactor of hydrogen reaction products was growing, forcing cooling water down and away from the fuel rods and causing their temperature to rise still higher.

"Clearly, some way will have to be found of getting rid of that bubble," Dr. Levine said. "If the temperature rises enough, even the pellets could melt, enormously increasing the contamination problem inside the reactor.

'Molten Uranium' Held Unlikely

"However, the emergency core cooling system apparently is working, and there is still a lot of water in the cooling part of the rods. There's not going to be any pool of molten uranium in there."

He also said there was no danger that the growing pressure of the gas bubble could cause the shell of the reactor to leak or explode.

Dr. Levine said [illegible] posed serious problems, particularly in salvaging the reactor, which sustains increasing damage as fuel rods melt.

"I don't want to seem to be pooh-poohhing this situation," he added. "But at the same time, it would be a mistake to exaggerate matters."

He said the radiation leakage [illegible] occurred had apparently been the result of a leak between the primary and secondary circulation systems, possibly through a valve or through the relatively thin tubes of the two systems in the steam generator plant.

The primary circulation system is in direct contact with the nuclear fuel rods. The heat of this system is transferred through heat exchangers with the secondary system, which does not normally come into contact with any radioactive material. Both systems are sealed from contact with the environment.

"All the News That's Fit to Print"

The New York Times

LATE CITY EDITION

Weather: Mostly cloudy, mild today; showers tonight. Showers, tomorrow. Temperature range: today 52-68; yesterday 54-70. Details on page A27.

VOL.CXXVIII . . No.44,207

NEW YORK, FRIDAY, MAY 4, 1979

25 cents beyond 50 mile zone from New York City. Higher in air delivery cities.

20 CENTS

CONSERVATIVES WIN BRITISH VOTE; MARGARET THATCHER FIRST WOMAN TO HEAD A EUROPEAN GOVERNMENT

United Press International

Margaret Thatcher leaving polling station after casting her vote in London yesterday

BIG SHIFT FROM LABOR

Tory Leader Is Given Clear Mandate to Change the Country's Course

By R. W. APPLE Jr.

Special to The New York Times

LONDON, Friday, May 4 — Margaret Thatcher and the Conservative Party won a decisive victory in Britain's general election yesterday.

Mrs. Thatcher, an Oxford-educated chemist and lawyer who entered Parliament in 1959, won a substantial majority and a clear mandate to reverse the nation's course. She promised during her campaign to restrain the trade unions, to cut personal income taxes and to bolster the armed forces.

She will become Europe's first woman Prime Minister.

Voting Pattern Changes

Projections by the television networks and by the Press Association suggested that the Tories would hold a majority over all other parties of approximately 30 to 35 seats. But the voting pattern was not as uniform as in past elections, and the ultimate majority might therefore be somewhat smaller.

With results declared in 510 of 635 constituencies, the totals were as follows:

Conservatives	255
Labor	244
Liberals	7
Scottish Nationalists	2
Welsh Nationalists	2

The totals reflected a gain of 45 seats for the Conservatives, a loss of 37 for Labor and a loss of one for the Liberals. The Scottish Nationalists had lost six seats and the Welsh Nationalists had lost one.

British Analysts Baffled

For Prime Minister James Callaghan and the Labor Party, the brightest spots were in Scotland and northern England, where the Conservative tide was running far less strongly than in the London area. The irregular pattern baffled British analysts such as David Butler of Nuffield College, Oxford, who said, "The confident simplicities of past elections don't apply."

Before going to bed shortly after dawn, Mrs. Thatcher said she hoped "to announce victory about midday." The Prime Minister, still smiling despite the late hour and the adverse trend, commented, "I shall have something more to say when things are entirely clear."

The former Liberal Party leader, Jeremy Thorpe, who had represented North Devon for 20 years, was beaten by 8,000 votes. His highly publicized legal difficulties — his trial on charges of conspiracy and incitement to murder opens Tuesday — apparently proved too big an obstacle to overcome.

Although national trends suggested he would lose, Dr. David Owen, the Foreign Secretary, clung to his seat in Plymouth by 1,001 votes.

But a number of well-known Members of Parliament were swept away, including Hugh Jenkins, a former Arts Minis-

Continued on Page A10, Column 1

The New York Times/George Tames

Senator Abraham A. Ribicoff

Ribicoff Decides He Won't Seek A Fourth Term

By STEVEN R. WEISMAN

Special to The New York Times

WASHINGTON, May 3 — Senator Abraham A. Ribicoff of Connecticut announced today that he would retire from the Senate after his current term of office — his third — expires next year.

His decision startled his political colleagues, as well as his staff aides, and immediately set off a scramble to succeed him. At least three Democrats and three Republicans in Connecticut indicated their interest in running for his seat. [Page B4.]

Mr. Ribicoff, a 69-year-old Democrat, has become Connecticut's most influential elected official in modern times, and his departure from Washington would bring to a conclusion an extraordinary public career that has included service as a United States Representative, Governor, Cabinet member under President John F. Kennedy and, since 1963, United States Senator.

Today he dismissed any suggestion that he would accept either a Cabinet post or an ambassadorship after he retired.

"As Mike Mansfield said, 'There is a time to stay and a time to go,'" Mr. Ribicoff told reporters this morning, referring to the former Senate majority leader, who is now Ambassador to Japan. "I've watched them come and go," Mr.

Continued on Page B4, Column 1

PRODUCER PRICES UP BY 0.9% FOR APRIL; FOOD DOWN A LITTLE

Rises Expected to Keep Consumer Costs High and Further Harm Carter Fight on Inflation

By STEVEN RATTNER

Special to The New York Times

WASHINGTON, May 3 — Producer prices rose by nine-tenths of 1 percent in April, and, despite a slight slowing from March, signs pointed to at least another month of substantial increases, according to Labor Department figures released today.

The increase would have been greater if food prices had not fallen slightly last month. The overall increase in prices at the producer level was the smallest for any month since last November. Food prices have been rising rapidly, and Carter Administration officials were particularly relieved by last month's abatement.

The Government now computes producer prices for finished goods ready for shipment to retailers to compile a more accurate economic indicator than the former Wholesale Price Index, which has been abandoned. But producer prices are roughly equivalent to wholesale prices.

Period of Weeks or Months

Producer price increases do not directly affect consumers but gradually work their way over a period of weeks or months to the retail level. Accordingly, last month's rise in the Producer Price Index suggests that high rates of consumer price increases will continue.

The increases would, in turn, further jeopardize President Carter's anti-inflation program, which seeks to hold wage increases to 7 percent annually. Meanwhile, consumer prices rose at a 13 percent rate in the first three months of the year. The April rise in producer prices translated into a compound annual inflation rate of 11.5 percent.

The rises last month in wholesale prices were paced by sharply higher prices for fuel, plastics, cars and leather. Home-heating oil, for example, rose by 6.7 percent in the month alone. Gasoline prices increased by 4.4 percent. The increases in energy prices reflects the worldwide shortage of oil as a result of the shutdown earlier this year of Iranian oil production and the price increases imposed as a result by the Organization of Petroleum Exporting Countries.

Perhaps more worrisome was the news that the most recent increases in energy prices appeared to have begun to filter

Continued on Page D14, Column 5

Terrorists Bomb the Rome Offices Of the Christian Democratic Party

By HENRY TANNER

Special to The New York Times

ROME, May 3 — A group of urban guerrillas raided the Rome area headquarters of Italy's dominant Christian Democratic Party today, wrecked two floors with bombs, killed one policeman, wounded two others and escaped.

The attack, the largest terrorist operation since Red Brigade terrorists kidnapped former Prime Minister Aldo Moro last year, killing five bodyguards and subsequently Mr. Moro, came on the eve of a general election campaign.

The raiders spray-painted the walls of the party headquarters with the initials of the Red Brigades and with its emblem, a five-pointed star. They also left behind this inscription: "We shall transform the fraudulent elections into a class war."

Fears were expressed that there would be a wave of terrorist attacks during the campaign for the elections that are scheduled for June 3 and 4.

Shaken by the magnitude of today's attack, former President Giuseppe Saragat and other political figures called for stronger antiterrorist measures. Some suggested that martial law was needed, as they had done when Mr. Moro was abducted on March 16, 1978. His body was found nearly two months later.

"Political terrorism," Mr. Saragat said, "is turning into full-scale civil war and must be confronted not only by the police but also by the armed forces of the republic."

The Red Brigades, the most feared of Italy's terrorist groups, have as their aim the destruction of the Italian state and society as a step toward a revolutionary takeover. They accuse the Communist Party of having sold out to the bourgeoi-

Continued on Page A4, Column 3

'Genuine' Tory Taking Charge

Margaret Roberts Thatcher

By WILLIAM BORDERS

Special to The New York Times

Woman in the News

LONDON, May 3 — To Margaret Thatcher, "free choice is ultimately what life is about," and she likes to illustrate what she means in political terms with this example: "If somebody comes to me and asks, What are you going to do for us small businessmen? I say, the only thing I'm going to do for you is make you freer to do things for yourselves. If you can't do it then, I'm sorry. I'll have nothing to offer you."

Judging by what she has been saying over the years, in public and in private, that is the center of Mrs. Thatcher's political philosophy, — what she calls "a positive creed, to promote, not destroy, the uniqueness of the individual."

In the election campaign Mrs. Thatcher sketched a vision of a Britain that would be rebuilt, on the strong base of that kind of individualism, to the economic strength it used to know, "so that once again the products stream from our factories and workshops while the customers of the world scramble over each other to buy them." She also promised a government that "would stop trying to step in and take decisions for you that you should be free to take on your own."

Now, the British people, having chosen as their leader the first woman to head a modern European government, will have a chance to put to a practical test what she terms the genu-

Continued on Page A11, Column 1

CALIFANO REASSESSES RADIATION HAZARDS

He Now Says Some Cancer Deaths From Accident Are Possible

By CHARLES MOHR

Special to The New York Times

WASHINGTON, May 3 — Joseph A. Califano Jr., Secretary of Health, Education and Welfare, said today that radiation exposure from the Three Mile Island reactor accident was higher than earlier measurements had indicated. As a result, he said, statistical probability indicates that at least one cancer death caused by radiation could be expected among the two million people living within 50 miles of the Pennsylvania power plant.

He also said that the radiation could be expected to cause as many as 10 additional nonfatal cancers.

Mr. Califano, who testified a month ago that no deaths would result from the exposure, said today that subsequent measurements showed radiation levels had been nearly twice as high as earlier estimates. He also said that the estimates were expected to rise further.

His testimony, before the Subcommittee on Energy, Nuclear Proliferation and Federal Services of the Senate Government Affairs Committee, took note of the contention of some scientists that assumptions about low-level radiation as a cause of cancer might be 10 times too low. Mr. Califano quoted some experts as saying that the increase in cancer deaths from the accident could be as high as 10.

Under normal conditions, the number of cancer deaths in a population of two million would be 325,000.

Meanwhile, the Nuclear Regulatory Commission reported that the Oyster Creek Plant at Forked River, N.J., was shut down automatically yesterday during a test of the reactor's pressure-reading instruments. [Page B3.]

And the Nuclear Regulatory Commission, considering the status of a Maine reactor that was among five closed in

Continued on Page A19, Column 4

The New York Times/John Sotomayor

Bird watchers stalking their "prey" early yesterday morning in Central Park

For Central Park Bird Watchers, Thrills Take Flight Every Spring

By ROBIN HERMAN

Why don't bird watchers get "warblers' neck" in Central Park? Why does the Police Department assign a patrolman to watch the bird watchers? And have you ever seen a rock dove?

Bird watchers don't get warblers' neck from craning to see warblers in the treetops because the hills in Central Park put bird watchers at eye level with the tops of the trees. The Police Department assigns an officer to watch bird watchers because many of them carry expensive field glasses that make them likely targets for muggers. And if you think you have never seen a rock dove you probably have because they are otherwise known as pigeons and Central Park is full of them.

Fifty New Yorkers who went "birding" yesterday at 7 A.M. along the Central Park Ramble spotted nearly 40 species of birds in an hour and a half, including multitudes of rock doves bobbing and cooing on the paths and outcroppings. The real prizes, however, were the visiting warblers who stop in Manhattan this month for a drink and a bite to eat on their way to summer

Continued on Page B3, Column 2

In Her Own Words

Comments by Margaret Thatcher since taking the party leadership in 1975.

Limitation of government doesn't make for a weak government — don't make that mistake. If you've got the role of government clearly set out, then it means very strong government in that role. Very strong indeed. You weaken government if you try to spread it over so wide a range that you're not powerful where you should be because you've got into areas where you shouldn't be.

•

Overtaxation is transparently foolish. Most of us are willing to work for our families and neighbors but not for the Chancellor of the Exchequer. In a free country people will work hard if it pays them to do so. At present, taxes are so high that for many it is not worthwhile working hard, and for some it is not worthwhile working at all. The first step to recovery, therefore, is to lower taxes on earnings.

•

There are two ways of making a cabinet. One way is to have in it people who represent all the different viewpoints within the party, within the broad philosophy. The other way is to have in it only the people who want to go in the direction in which every instinct tells me we have to go. As Prime Minister I couldn't waste time having any internal arguments.

•

The power of trade unions over individual members is far too great. We shall have to stand up against those elements who are prepared to use their present freedom in society to destroy society. . . . A strong trade-union movement is an integral part of modern industrial society, but it must not ride roughshod over the rest of that society.

•

On immigration from the Commonwealth: Small minorities can be absorbed — they can be assets to the majority community — but once a minority in a neighborhood gets very large, people do feel swamped. They feel their whole way of life has been changed.

•

On male colleagues: I'm not conscious of them as men at all. Don't mistake me: I see A as taller than B; I see X as more handsome than Y. What woman wouldn't? What man wouldn't have such perceptions about women? But I don't see me and my colleagues in an "I'm a woman, you are men" relationship.

INSIDE

Giants Pick Quarterback

The Giants' first pick in the National Football League draft was Phil Simms, a quarterback from Morehead State in Kentucky. Page A21.

Islanders Tie Series

Bob Nystrom's goal in overtime gave the Islanders a 3-2 victory over the Rangers, tying their playoff series at two games apiece. Page A21.

Conservatives Win British Election by Sizable Margin

Continued From Page A1

ter, who lost a supposedly safe seat at Putney in London.

In addition, two of the foremost campaigners for women's rights were defeated — Maureen Colquhoun, a militant lesbian, and Helene Hayman, who represented a suburban London area.

Although the Liberal Party failed to achieve its aim of winning enough seats to deny either of the major parties an overall majority, it appeared to be holding most of the 14 seats it had in the last Parliament. But the Scottish Nationalists, who only two years ago were piling success upon success, saw their vote cut in half and most of their Members of Parliament heavily defeated.

Startling Result in Glasgow

Reversing a five-year trend, the major parties seemed likely to capture all but 25 of the seats at stake.

One of the most startling results came in Glasgow, where Edward Taylor, the Conservative spokesman on Scotland, was ousted by John Maxton, the nephew of Jimmy Maxton, the legendary Clydeside leftist who helped found the Labor Party.

On the island of Anglesey, off the coast of Wales, a Conservative was elected for the first time in at least 250 years. But most of the Tory gains came in seats that are always closely contested — in London, the Midlands and the belt of marginal seats north of Manchester.

However, Labor held on to the weathervane constituency of Bolton East, which for the first time since World War II failed to vote the same way as the nation as a whole.

Initial indications suggested that last winter's industrial disputes had cost the 67-year-old Mr. Callaghan the election.

United Press International

James Callaghan outside City Hall in Cardiff, Wales, last night before announcement of election results.

The swing against the Government in the area east of London surrounding the big Ford Motor Company factory at Dagenham was one of the largest anywhere.

The swing against the Prime Minister, who was expected to resign later today, was strongest in the London area, where it approached 7 percent and weakest in northern England, where it barely reached 2 percent.

In the popular vote, the Tories held a lead of about 10 percentage points, 47 to 37.

The number toward which both parties had worked during the four-week campaign was 318, a bare majority of the House of Commons. Whether either met that figure or exceeded it will not be known for certain until this afternoon, since 116 of the 635 constituencies decided not to attempt an overnight count.

Among those counting late were constituencies of considerable importance to the Liberals and the Scottish Nationalists.

Record Number of Candidates

A record number of candidates, 2,575, entered the Parliament contests, including nominees of nine parties that were represented in the last Parliament. In addition, there were nominees of serious fringe groups such as the Ecology Party, the Communist Party and the National Front, as well as candidates representing such spur-of-the-moment creations as the Dog Lovers' Party and the East London People's Front.

It was the coldest day in May on record in parts of Britain, with hail in Inverness in Scotland and snow in northeast and southwest England. Snow was falling as David Steel, the Liberal leader, walked 30 yards to the polling station near his home in the hamlet of Ettrick Bridge in the hilly Scottish border country.

Mrs. Thatcher voted in Chelsea shortly after 9 A. M. She slipped her ballot through the slot, then reached into the bag of clichés that politicians always seem to have and told reporters, "We never count our chickens before they're hatched."

The Prime Minister voted at a school in Cardiff, Wales, that he dedicated in 1964. He said that his own vote and that of his wife meant that he had two certain supporters, then told onlookers that he had ended the campaign feeling "confident, successful, relaxed, rejuvenated, reinvigorated — you name it."

Queen Not Allowed to Vote

In London, more than 300 members of the household staff at Buckingham Palace walked to Westminster School to cast their ballots. Queen Elizabeth II is constitutionally not allowed to vote.

As the balloting began, London's oddsmakers were quoting the Conservatives as odds-on favorites at 1-4. They had taken in more than $7 million in election wagers.

United Press International

In Belfast, Northern Ireland, British soldiers protected the polling places

For Mr. Callaghan, the campaign leading up to the election had been an unusually difficult one. He decided last October against an election, at a time when he seemed to have a good chance of winning, then was forced into one at an awkward moment when he lost a vote of confidence in Parliament.

After a winter of industrial trouble, the Prime Minister's political trump card, his ability to deal with the trade unions, was of limited value. Labor began the campaign as much as 20 percentage points behind in some national public-opinion polls.

Tories Were Ill-Prepared

Mrs. Thatcher had her problems as well. Her voice and her manner reminded many voters of unfondly remembered schoolmarms, and many of those who liked her policies could not bring themselves to help her become Prime Minister. In addition, her party was ill-prepared when Labor demanded to know how the Conservatives would pay for their proposed cuts in income taxes.

It was Britain's 11th postwar general election. Labor won six of the preceding 10, and held power for 12 of the last 15 years. Mr. Callaghan succeeded Sir Harold Wilson as Prime Minister in 1976, so this was his first election as party leader. It was also Mrs. Thatcher's and Mr. Steel's first such experience.

Associated Press

British Army veterans arriving at a London polling station

Russian in London Asks Asylum, Then Decides to Return to Soviet

MOSCOW, May 3 (Reuters — A Soviet journalist who flew back to Moscow yesterday just after British officials said he had been granted asylum in London may face disciplinary action by the Communist Party, Soviet sources said today.

They said the journalist, Aleksandr Istomin, 31-year-old correspondent for the feature agency Novosti, was now staying at his parents' Moscow home.

The British Home Office said yesterday that he disappeared from his London office on April 13 and later went to a police station to ask for asylum. He was subsequently granted permission to stay in Britain for 12 months.

Two Drums of Caustic Chemicals Are Found in Ontario Town Dump

TORONTO, May 3 (AP) — An official of the Ontario Environment Ministry said today that two drums of caustic chemicals had been discovered at a Fort Erie dump that is described as hazardous in ministry records.

The official, Ray Stewart, who is the ministry's district manager at Welland, west of Fort Erie, said one drum contained caustic soda and the other a chlorine derivative.

Vanessa Redgrave Loses

LONDON, Friday, May 4 (UPI) — The actress Vanessa Redgrave polled only 225 votes for her Workers Revolutionary Party in the Moss Side constituency in Manchester yesterday. The Labor incumbent, G.M. Morton, won with 17,765 votes. T.E. Murphy, a Conservative, was second with 13,234.

HELP THE FRESH AIR FUND

Uganda Refugees in Kenya Town Getting Red Cross and U.N. Aid

NAIROBI, Kenya, May 3 (Reuters) — The Red Cross and the United Nations are providing blankets, medicine and food for 2,600 displaced Ugandans now in a camp at the western Kenyan town of Karamega, Charles Rubia, president of the Kenyan Red cross, said today.

He said at a news conference that the League of Red Cross Societies and the United Nations Children's Fund had offered cooking utensils, milk powder, medicine and blankets and that the United Nations High Commissioner for Refugees in Geneva had made available $100,000 for food for a month.

Enslaving and Torture of Indians Charged by Missionary in Brazil

BRASILIA, May 3 (Reuters) — A Catholic missionary has accused some officials of virtually enslaving an Indian tribe in remote western Brazil and of torturing them, church sources said today.

They said the Rev. António Iasi Júnior had reported the abuse to the National Indian Foundation, a Government agency, and had named Senator Altevir Leal, a large property owner in Acre Territory, as one of the officials.

Father Iasi also accused the mayor of the town of Bôca do Acre of coercing one Indian to drink gasoline mixed with sand under the threat of being burned alive, the sources said.

"All the News That's Fit to Print"

The New York Times

LATE CITY EDITION

Weather: Partly sunny today; mostly cloudy and cold tonight and tomorrow. Temperature range: today 28-38; yesterday 36-43. Details on page D21.

VOL.CXXX . . . No. 44,835

NEW YORK, WEDNESDAY, JANUARY 21, 1981

30 cents beyond 50-mile zone from New York City. Higher in air delivery cities

25 CENTS

REAGAN TAKES OATH AS 40TH PRESIDENT; PROMISES AN 'ERA OF NATIONAL RENEWAL'

MINUTES LATER, 52 U.S. HOSTAGES IN IRAN FLY TO FREEDOM AFTER 444-DAY ORDEAL

'ALIVE, WELL AND FREE'

Captives Taken to Algiers and Then Germany — Final Pact Complex

By BERNARD GWERTZMAN

Special to The New York Times

WASHINGTON, Wednesday, Jan. 21 — The 52 Americans who were held hostage by Iran for 444 days were flown to freedom yesterday. Jimmy Carter, a few hours after giving up the Presidency, said that everyone "was alive, was well and free."

The flight ended the national ordeal that had frustrated Mr. Carter for most of his last 14 months in office, and it allowed Ronald Reagan to begin his term free of the burdens of the Iran crisis.

The Americans were escorted out of Iran by Algerian diplomats, aboard an Algerian airliner, underscoring Algeria's role in achieving the accord that allowed the hostages to return home.

Transferred to U.S. Custody

The Algerian plane, carrying the former hostages, stopped first in Athens to refuel. It then landed in Algiers, where custody of the 52 Americans was formally transferred by the Algerians to the representative of the United States, former Deputy Secretary of State Warren M. Christopher. He had negotiated much of the agreement freeing them.

They then boarded two United States Air Force hospital planes and flew to Frankfurt, West Germany early this morning. They will stay at an American military hospital in nearby Weisbaden, where they will be visited by Mr. Carter, as President Reagan's representative, later today. They will stay in Wiesbaden for a week or less to "decompress," as one official described it.

The 52 Americans were freed as part of a complex agreement that was not completed until early yesterday morning, when the last snags holding up their release were removed by Mr. Carter and

Continued on Page A3, Column 5

Teheran Captors Call Out Insults As the 52 Leave

By JOHN KIFNER

Special to The New York Times

TEHERAN, Iran, Jan. 20 — The 52 American hostages began to roll down the runway to freedom today minutes as President Reagan was finishing his inaugural address.

As the Algerian 727 lifted off from Mehrabad Airport, ending 444 days of captivity for the Americans, they could see, most of them probably for the last time, a full moon picking out the sharp white peaks of the Elburz Mountains to the north. The time was 8:55 P.M., 12:25 P.M. New York time.

"God is great! Death to America!" cried the young Islamic militants who kept custody of the hostages to the last minute, hustling them to the stairs of the airplane.

They Soon Are 'Former Hostages'

The American diplomats, Marine guards and the other hostages stepped one at a time from a bus, whose windows were covered with checked curtains, into a clear cold night. As they touched the tarmac, two young militants, the hoods of their parkas up against the chill, took them just above the elbows and propelled them through the shouting crowd toward the Algerian plane with its red stylized bird emblazoned on the tail.

Looking dazed, some with long hair and beards that contrasted with the neat trims of their official days before the embassy takeover Nov. 4, 1979, they stumbled into the first-class section of the plane. Now they were what a bulletin on Pars, the state press agency, would describe later as "former hostages."

"They seem stunned, as if they cannot believe they are going free," Ahmad Azizi, the Government's director of hostage affairs, remarked to an Iranian state television crew covering the departure.

At 8:20, the doors were sealed, Pars reported, and the engines began to whine. A

Continued on Page A8, Column 1

United Press International

11:57 A.M.: Ronald Reagan being sworn in as 40th President by Chief Justice Warren E. Burger. Nancy Reagan held the Bible and Senator Mark O. Hatfield witnessed the ceremony.

FREEZE SET ON HIRING

Californian Stresses Need to Restrict Government and Buoy Economy

By STEVEN R. WEISMAN

Special to The New York Times

WASHINGTON, Jan. 20 — Ronald Wilson Reagan of California, promising "an era of national renewal," became the 40th President of the United States today as 52 Americans held hostage in Iran were heading toward freedom.

The hostages, whose 14 months of captivity had been a central focus of the Presidential contest last year, took off from Teheran in two Boeing 727 airplanes at 12:25 P.M., Eastern standard time, the very moment that Mr. Reagan was concluding his solemn Inaugural Address at the United States Capitol.

The new President's speech, however, made no reference at all to the long-awaited release of the hostages, emphasizing instead the need to limit the powers of the Federal Government, and to bring an end to unemployment and inflation.

'Government Is the Problem'

Promising to begin immediately to deal with "an economic affliction of great proportions," Mr. Reagan declared: "In this present crisis, government is not the solution to our problem; government is the problem." And in keeping with this statement, the President issued orders for a hiring "freeze" as his first official act. [Page B6.]

Wearing a charcoal gray club coat, striped trousers and dove gray vest and tie, Mr. Reagan took his oath of office at 11:57 A.M. in the first inaugural ceremony ever enacted on the western front of the United States Capitol. The site was chosen to stress the symbolism of Mr. Reagan's addressing his words to the West, the region that served as his base in his three Presidential campaigns in 1968, 1976 and 1980.

Oldest to Assume Presidency

The ceremony today, filled with patriotic music, the firing of cannons and the pealing of bells, marked the transfer of the Presidency back to the Republicans after the four-year term of Jimmy Carter, a Democrat, as well as the culmination of the remarkable career of a conservative former two-term Governor of California who had started out as a baseball announcer and motion picture star.

At the age of 69, Mr. Reagan also became the oldest man to assume the Presidency, and in five months he will become the oldest man to serve in the office.

Mr. Carter, looking haggard and worn after spending two largely sleepless nights trying to resolve the hostage crisis

Continued on Page B8, Column 2

More News And Pictures

The Inauguration

The Hostages

Summary and Index, Page A2

Anxious Families and Towns Erupt Into Long-Postponed Celebrations

Black Star / John Troha for The New York Times

Anita Schaefer, wife of a hostage, embraced Mr. Carter at airport.

By JOSEPH B. TREASTER

Saying his final farewells at Andrews Air Force Base yesterday, Jimmy Carter spotted Anita Schaefer, the wife of one of the hostages, and exuberantly embraced her.

"Tom is in the air," Mr. Carter said, speaking of her husband, Col. Thomas E. Schaefer of the Air Force, who was the senior military officer at the United States Embassy in Teheran.

"Really, truly, Mr. President," she whispered.

"Really, truly — at long last," he said, "Tom is safe. I'll be with him tomorrow morning in Germany."

"Oh, thank God, Mr. President."

Then they both cried. And they embraced again.

The First Glimpse

As the hostages arrived in Algiers, relatives strained close to television screens for the first glimpse of their loved ones out of captivity in more than 14 months.

"There's Billy," cried Letezia Gallegos, as her brother, Sgt. William Gallegos of the Marines, stepped down the ramp. His mother, Theresa, broke into deep sobs.

News that the plane carrying the hostages had taken off from Teheran came to Penelope Laingen, the wife of L. Bruce Laingen, the embassy's chargé d'affaires, as she sat in a reserved seat at the inauguration of President Reagan. A military policeman shouted the word for everyone to hear.

Some had gotten the word from radio and television broadcasts, and still others, like Marjorie Moore, the wife of Bert C. Moore, the administrative consul, received phone calls from the State Department.

Most of the homes of the hostages' families, torn by doubt, fear and anger for so long, exploded with joy. They cried

Continued on Page A5, Column 1

Pars via Associated Press

12:25 P.M.: Sgt. Joseph Subic Jr. propelled by militants to waiting plane at airport in Teheran

A Hopeful Prologue, a Pledge of Action

By HEDRICK SMITH

Special to The New York Times

WASHINGTON, Jan. 20 — For a President who has promised Americans a new beginning, an era of national renewal at home and restored strength and stature abroad, the release of the American hostages in Iran was exquisitely timed.

News Analysis

The extraordinary deadline diplomacy that put the 52 captured Americans into the air over Iran minutes after the howitzers thundered a new leader into office provided a graceful exit for Jimmy Carter, a hopeful prologue for Ronald Reagan and relief for a nation weary from 14 months of humiliation and seeming impotence.

Almost unavoidably the human drama in Iran overshadowed an Inaugural Address that was less an inspirational call to national greatness than a plain-spoken charter of Mr. Reagan's conservative creed, less a sermon than a stump speech, less a rallying cry than a ringing denunciation of overgrown government and a practical pledge to get down to the business of trimming it at once.

For all the new President's vaunted reputation as one of the nation's most polished political orators, his Inaugural Address offered surprisingly few rhetorical flourishes beyond the populist tribute to ordinary Americans that "those who say that we are in a time when there are no heroes, they just don't know where to look."

Although Mr. Reagan made no direct mention of the hostages, their release was on everyone's lips. Moments before Mr. Reagan took his oath of office, word that the hostages were about to be flown out of Iran swept through the crowd stretched out before the Capitol, and though that news was premature, it provided the perfect symbolic backdrop for

Continued on Page B7, Column 1

News Summary and Index, Page A2

Hostages: The Last Day / Jubilation in America, Relief Abroad

Lights Go On, Bells Ring In Big Cities and Villages

By ANNA QUINDLEN

The nation flew its flags, rang its church bells, sounded its fire alarms, draped bunting across its main streets, put welcome signs in its windows and tied yellow ribbons everywhere to celebrate the freedom of 52 of its citizens yesterday.

From its small towns to its biggest city, jubilation and celebration swept America. After four days of watching and waiting and false alarms, the hostages flew out of the country where they had been held for 444 days, and their countrymen rejoiced.

Civil defense sirens in Albuquerque, N.M., blared in the afternoon quiet for 444 seconds, one for each day of the long captivity.

Bells at City Hall in Albany rang 52 times, once for each of the captives.

In Spokane, Wash., the 52 tattered flags that had flown for more than a year were finally removed. The last flag was raised in the small cemetery in Hermitage, Pa., where each day of captivity has seen a new flag flying. And the flag at the Massachusetts Statehouse in Boston was raised for the first time since the hostages were taken captive. "I haven't been so happy at a flag raising since Iwo," said House Speaker Thomas W. McGee, a Marine veteran.

Bells and a Subway Announcement

The massive carillon at the Cathedral of St. John the Divine rang out an hour-long "festal peal" after the White House had announced that the rescue plane was in the air, and a conductor on a West Side IRT express train rumbling through the Bronx announced on his public address system, to much applause, "The hostages are on a plane to Algeria."

And just before 2 P.M., the corner of 57th Street and Madison Avenue erupted with cheers and shouting as employees of office buildings in the area threw open their windows to tell the workmen on a construction site who had memorialized the hostages with an enormous countdown sign that day 444 would be the last. A crowd of a thousand gathered below, adding-machine confetti and toilet paper ribbons were thrown from above, and, with wild whooping, the workmen cut the yellow ribbon on a substitute sign: "Free at last! Free at last! Thank God they are free at last!" At the bottom it read, "Never again."

Later, when the aircraft carrying the hostages landed in Algiers, and the smiling, waving Americans stepped down a metal ramp into the glare of television lights, many watching at home wept openly, as the realization that the 52 hostages had left Iran began to take hold.

"Thank God! Thank God! I can't help but cry a bit," said Elizabeth Noble of New Canaan, Conn., moments after hostages stepped into view at 8:33 P.M. "I'm sitting here saying prayers. It has been a wonderful night."

Some were struck by the good spirits and health apparent among the hostages; others thought of the families of the hostages waiting at home. "What really got to me was their attitude," said Eileen Nolan, a teacher who lives in Glen Rock, N.J. "I really expected them to be bitter, but they didn't seem that way at all. They seemed very happy."

National Tree Is Lighted

As he watched the ceremony in Algiers from his perch in a Manhattan bar, Larry Cavada, said he felt great, but he added, "I'm also thinking about the eight Americans who died."

Lights that had long been dark glowed all over the country. The national Christmas tree on the ellipse near the White House was finally lighted. The floodlights on the Statue of Liberty, last turned on during the Bicentennial, crisscrossed the statue last night. The Olympic torch at the Los Angeles Memorial Coliseum, lighted in mourning for John F. Kennedy and the Rev. Dr. Martin Luther King, was illuminated for a joyous occasion for the first time since the games opened there in 1932.

But in El Paso, Tex., the lights will go out: the five-pointed electric star that has shown on that city since the hostages were first taken captive will be extinguished in a celebration tomorrow.

There were small celebrations as well. Jimmy Rosolino, who owns the Old Homestead restaurant in Oyster Bay, L.I.,, broke out champagne, and Ed Landry, the owner of Mother's in New Orleans, provided noisemakers. "People are acting like a war has ended or something," said Mr. Rosolino. "We've been packed ever since the word got out."

And at the Senior Citizens Center in White Plains, N.Y., 40 people stood to sing along with the national anthem on television. "It was really a very beautiful moment," said Peggy Pierce, director of the center.

Church Bells in Detroit

Not everyone was happy, of course, and not everyone was excited. The months of captivity and the long final hours had taken a toll. While church bells tolled in Detroit, William Hinds, a writer there, said: "I'm glad of course, but I can't get all that excited about it. It was mishandled from the start."

Mayor Koch, who has asked that New York City be designated the official host city for the hostages and who wants to give them a ticker-tape parade, nevertheless said that it was "baloney" to say that the United States had not paid ransom. Maria Di Pasquale, manager of a telephone answering service in Millburn, N.J., agreed. "It's a poor precedent paying them off," she said.

In many American cities people said, "It's about time." But in some they said sadly that it was the wrong time. Jim Toohey, who works at a bank in midtown Manhattan, said: "I'm glad for President Carter, but I'm sorry he wasn't able to announce their release. The Iranians just wanted to humiliate him one last time, I guess. That's too bad. And I voted Republican, too."

But as the Empire State Building glowed red, white and blue, and the 30-story Foshay Tower in Minneapolis was swathed in a 300-square-foot band of yellow, it seemed as though most people thought anytime was the right time.

"Everyone's thrilled, but not screaming thrilled," said Frances Borden, who works for the Waldorf-Astoria Hotel. "It's certainly not like the end of World War II, when everyone was on the streets, drinking champagne and soldiers kissing girls. People are quietly jubilant, I would say."

Relatives of 8 Who Died Are Praised in a Tribute

WASHINGTON Jan. 20 (UPI) — The families of the eight Americans who died in the attempt to rescue the hostages in Iran last April were remembered and praised today by the wife of one of the hostages.

"On behalf of the families, I'd like to offer a tribute to the families of the men who will not be coming home," said Katherine Keough, wife of William F. Keough of Waltham, Mass.

Mrs. Keough made her comments while waiting at the State Department for final confirmation of the report that the 52 American hostages were on the way to freedom after their 444-day ordeal.

"Of all the emotions that have run through us these past 15 months, perhaps the most emotional was the day I stood at Arlington Cemetery to honor the eight servicemen who died in that valiant rescue attempt," she said. "Those emotions ran through all of us."

"We looked into the eyes of those young widows and we saw national honor, national dignity and the kind of tradition that makes us proud to be Americans," said Mrs. Keough, a leader of the hostage families' organization.

Associated Press

Former hostages leaving a plane in Algiers were tentatively identified, from the top, as: Malcolm Kalp; Col. Charles W. Scott, military attaché; Clair Cortland Barnes and William E. Belk, communications officer.

52 Hostages Fly to Freedom, Ending Long Ordeal in Iran

Continued From Page A1

his aides, in the final diplomatic action of their Administration.

Under the terms of the accord, as the Algerian plane left Iranian air space, nearly $3 billion of Iranian assets that had been frozen by the United States were returned to Iran, and many more billions of dollars were made available for Iranian repayment of debts.

The 52 Americans were freed only minutes after Ronald Reagan was sworn in as the 40th President of the United States. The concurrence in timing held millions of Americans at their radios and television sets, following the pageantry of Inauguration Day and the news of the hostages' release.

Negotiations Were Intense

The negotiators, who had worked around the clock for five days in an effort to bring the crisis to an end before Mr. Carter left office, said that they had no idea whether the Iranians had deliberately dragged out the talks so as to insure that the hostages were not actually in the air until Mr. Reagan was President.

Mr. Reagan was informed that the Algerian plane carrying the hostages had left Iranian airspace as he was about to have lunch with the Congressional leadership at the Capitol after the inauguration ceremony.

"With thanks to Almighty God, I have been given a tag line, the get-off line, that everyone wants for the end of a toast or a speech, or anything else," the President said after brief remarks.

"Some 30 minutes ago, the Algerian planes bearing our prisoners left Iranian airspace and they're now free of Iran."

Ringing applause drowned out his final remarks and Mr. Reagan responded by lifting a glass of white California wine to his lips and drinking to the end of the crisis.

Drama Seized World's Attention

The end of the drama that has seized American and world attention for nearly 15 months evoked a jumble of emotions from the families of the 52, ranging from exhilaration to disbelief.

Anita Schaefer, wife of Col. Thomas E. Schaefer, who was the senior military officer in the embassy in Teheran when it was seized on Nov. 4, 1979, was told that the plane carrying the hostages had left Teheran by Mr Carter at Andrews Air Force Base, only minutes before the former President boarded his plane for the trip home to Plains, Ga.

"Tom is in the air," Mr. Carter told her as they embraced, both crying.

Mr. Carter, at Plains, said that while he was on Air Force One, "I had received word, officially, for the first time, that the aircraft carrying the 52 American hostages had cleared Iranian airspace on the first leg of the journey home and that everyone of the 52 hostages was alive, was well and free."

He had hoped to fly to West Germany Monday, his last full day in office. But at Mr. Reagan's invitation, Mr. Carter, together with other senior members of his Administration, will make the trip today.. Former Secretary of State Cyrus R. Vance had already gone to Wiesbaden to be there when the Americans arrive.

"Throughout this time of trial, we Americans have stood as one, united in our prayers, steadfast in our concern for fellow Americans in peril," Mr. Carter said. "I doubt that at any time in our history more prayers have reached heaven for any Americans than have those given to God in the last 14 months."

Carter Administration officials have been very sensitive to allegations that the arrangement amounted to "ransom." This charge has been made by some Republicans and columnists — but not by Mr. Reagan — because the United States agreed to return Iran's frozen assets, to drop claims against Iran and to help Iran seek to recover the property of the late Shah in the United States.

Yesterday afternoon, four hours after they were out of office, former Secretary of State Edmund S. Muskie and former Treasury Secretary G. William Miller, as well as several other outgoing officials, took part in a news conference at the State Department that had been permitted by the Reagan Administration.

Mr. Muskie stressed that "the assets returned are Iranian property" and that the terms of the agreement "were determined to be fair and technically feasible."

Aides to Mr. Carter have maintained that Iran was "punished" for the seizure of the hostages by having had its billions of dollars worth of assets frozen for nearly 15 months, and by being isolated politically and economically as a result of the crisis.

The hostages themselves, a virtual cross-section of this country, ranging from Ivy League Foreign Service officers to teen-age enlisted men, and including two women and one black, were described by the Swiss Ambassador in Teheran, Eric Lang, as having been very emotional at the airport there prior to departure.

"They were laughing and crying and hugging each other," he said. "Many of them could not believe they were on their way to freedom."

The Swiss have represented the United States in Teheran, but in recent weeks the most significant help given the hostages was provided by Algeria, which at the request of Iran became the intermediary in three months of protracted negotiations.

Americans Examined by Doctors

As part of the agreement, worked out through the Algerians, the American hostages were turned over to Algerian custody, and they and their belongings were flown out on two Algerian aircraft. A third, and smaller, Algerian plane carried six doctors who had examined the Americans before their release.

The Americans were taken to Algiers not only as part of the arrangement but to demonstrate the United States Government's gratitude for the Algerian efforts, State Department officials said.

The negotiations, which last month seemed on the verge of collapse when Iran demanded that the United States provide $24 billion in financial guarantees, picked up momentum in the last two weeks. The last five days were particularly active as diplomats and financial experts in Washington, Algiers, Teheran, London and New York worked around the clock to conclude the accord.

Early Monday morning, Mr. Christopher signed the formal agreement in Algiers and Behzad Nabavi, the chief Iranian negotiator, signed it in Teheran. That led to a sense of anticipation that the hostages would be freed late Monday.

But the Iranians objected to a document sent to Iran by the United States to allow the complex agreement to be put into effect. American officials said that there were several other snags in the final hours, as messages went back and forth through Algiers.

It was uncertain Monday night whether Mr. Carter would be able to bring about the hostage release during his Presidency, but at about 3 A.M. yesterday, Jody Powell, Mr. Carter's spokesman, told a crowd of reporters at the White House that a formula had been agreed upon by Washington and Teheran on removing the last obstacle to the carrying out of the accord.

Under terms of the agreement, the 12 American banks holding frozen Iranian assets funneled them to the Federal Reserve Bank of New York. At about 6 A.M. the Federal Reserve sent nearly $8 billion to the Bank of England for a special escrow account in the name of the Algerian central bank.

By 7 A.M. the Algerians were able to notify Iran that they had possession of the frozen assets and that Iran was now obligated to release the American hostages to them.

This happened in the morning hours Washington time, which is eight and a half hours behind Teheran time. The hostages were then put aboard one of the two Boeing 727's that Algeria had sent there Monday, and their belongings on the other.

Text of Reagan's Luncheon Toast

Following is a transcript of a toast by President Reagan at a luncheon with Congressional leaders in Washington yesterday, as recorded by The New York Times:

Senator Mark Hatfield, Speaker O'Neill, the others here who are hosting this very beautiful luncheon: I'm going to take the liberty of speaking for my partner George, for Barbara and Nancy in responding to this toast.

Twice this morning in the ceremony was mentioned the fact of the unusualness in this world of what has taken place here today: the orderly transfer, the continuity of government that has gone on and that I think is the envy of the world.

Now there's even more of unity represented here today: the crystalware Speaker Tip O'Neill graciously provided from the House side; the plates have come from the Senate; the wine is from California, but I didn't have a thing to do with that; it just turned out that way.

But I would like to drink to the idea that this great system that sometimes puts us in adversary relationships — and perhaps sometimes unnecessarily so, but was based on checks and balances to insure that we do what is right for the people — that that kind of cooperation will continue.

I'm delighted to be a guest here in the House of the Congress and I look forward to coming back; I look forward to you being guests with us; I look forward to working with you in behalf of the people, and that this partnership will continue.

And now to conclude the toast with thanks to Almighty God, I have been given a tagline, the get-off line that everyone wants for the end of a toast, or a speech or anything else: Some 30 minutes ago, the planes bearing our prisoners left Iranian airspace and they're now free of Iran.

So we can all drink to this one: To all of us together, doing what we all know we can do to make this country what it should be, what it can be, what it always has been. Thank you all.

Allies Move to End Sanctions Against Iran

By WERNER WISKARI

Special to The New York Times

With the release of the 52 American hostages, the Common Market countries and other Western nations have moved toward lifting the economic sanctions they imposed against Iran in support of the United States.

Publicly numerous governments around the world expressed joy and relief at the ending of the crisis that began with the occupation of the American Embassy in Iran on Nov. 4, 1979. But privately some allied officials voiced concern over the implications that they felt the episode might have on the future world role of the United States.

These reactions have been registered over the last two days, beginning soon after the announcement on Monday that Iran and the United States had signed accords that would permit the release of the 52 Americans.

Within hours, officials in Canada, West Germany, Italy, Norway and Japan announced that their Governments would move toward lifting the sanctions once the hostages were actually freed and flown out of Iran.

Ministers in Accord

Yesterday, shortly before the hostages left Teheran, the foreign ministers of the 10 Common Market countries, meeting in Brussels, agreed to remove the limited trade sanctions imposed last May. But they also specified that action would be withheld until the Americans were free.

Britain, a Common Market member, agreed to go along, but officials said normal Iranian-British diplomatic relations would not be resumed until four Britons being held in Iran on espionage charges had also been freed.

The British broke diplomatic relations with Iran last spring in support of the United States position, and the four Britons — John and Audrey Coleman, both Anglican missionaries; Jean Waddell, a former secretary to the Anglican Bishop of Iran, and Andrew Pyke, an English businessman — were seized in the summer, accused of espionage but not charged.

In imposing the sanctions, the Common Market countries had specified that they would be limited to severing trade contracts signed since Nov. 4, 1979, and to banning new ones. But Britain agreed only to ban new contracts beginning May 30. Nevertheless, Iran's President, Abolhassan Bani-Sadr complained earlier this month that the Western actions, including the cutoff of trade ordered by the United States, had hampered Iranian forces in fighting the war against Iraq.

'A Tribute to Your Skill'

With the release of the hostages delayed by Iran until minutes after Ronald Reagan had taken the oath as President, congratulatory messages were sent yesterday to both Mr. Reagan and former President Jimmy Carter.

Prime Minister Margaret Thatcher of Britain told Mr. Carter that the release was "a tribute to your skill and tenacity in handling an agonizing problem."

The French Foreign Ministry said in a statement that France paid "homage to the role played by Algeria" and that "this ordeal" demonstrated the necessity for the "most energetic measures" to avoid any similar hostage-taking incidents. President Valéry Giscard d'Estaing sent a letter to Louisa Kennedy asking her as a representative of all hostage families to transmit to them the "best wishes of all the French people."

Chancellor Helmut Schmidt of West Germany, addressing Mr. Reagan as "Mr. President," expressed his country's "joy and satisfaction" at the release and, addressing Mr. Carter as "Jimmy," praised him for his "firmness and presence of mind."

In Ottawa, Mark MacGuigan, Canada's External Affairs Minister, said his Government would move to reopen its embassy in Teheran, closed after Canadian diplomats evacuated six American diplomats from Iran last January. He congratulated the Carter Administration for its patience in handling the crisis and Algeria for what he described as its effective help.

In Warsaw, a Polish Government spokesman said both Government and public were "pleased to learn of the agreement" to free the hostages. But in Havana, the official Cuban press agency Prensa Latina described the entire hostage crisis as a "great victory" for the Iranian people.

While French and other government leaders publicly lauded the United States, French officials were quoted by Reuters as being privately critical of the American handling of the crisis. They reportedly said, however, that they felt it caused less harm to United States prestige than to the personal standing of Mr. Carter, whom they pictured as a vacillating leader.

Officials in Turkey, Washington's North Atlantic Treaty Organization ally, were quoted as having said they were relieved that United States actions generally had been restrained. But they said they felt that Washington had lost face by not resolving the crisis more quickly.

In Egypt, Washington's closest friend in the Arab world, officials reportedly commented that they viewed the hostage crisis as worrying evidence of a loss of United States prestige and confidence.

And in Algiers, some Western diplomats said they were concerned by what they described as Mr. Carter's apparent concessions to the Iranian captors. These diplomats, from Europe, said the accords appeared to them to exonerate Iran for detaining the hostages and to establish the principle that Iranian leaders had the right to set conditions for the Americans' release.

The New York Times / Chester Higgins Jr.

Members of the staff of the U.S. Mission to the United Nations reading news bulletin announcing the hostages' release

"All the News That's Fit to Print"

The New York Times

LATE CITY EDITION

Weather: Mostly sunny, mild today; fair tonight. Chance of showers tomorrow. Temperature range: today 48-72; yesterday 56-65. Details on page C9.

VOL.CXXX . No. 44,904 NEW YORK, TUESDAY, MARCH 31, 1981 — 30 cents beyond 50-mile zone from New York City. Higher in air delivery cities. — 25 CENTS

REAGAN WOUNDED IN CHEST BY GUNMAN; OUTLOOK 'GOOD' AFTER 2-HOUR SURGERY; AIDE AND 2 GUARDS SHOT; SUSPECT HELD

Bush Flies Back From Texas Set to Take Charge in Crisis

By STEVEN R. WEISMAN

Special to The New York Times

WASHINGTON, March 30 — Vice President Bush, cutting short a trip to Texas, returned to the White House this evening to take charge of the crisis in the Government and to assume the responsibilities of the Presidency if President Reagan's injuries prevented him from serving in the office.

It was unclear tonight how long Mr. Bush would remain in charge of Government functions, however. At George Washington Univerity Hospital, the dean of clinical affairs said that President Reagan was "alert" and that he "should be able to make decisions by tomorrow." But he said Mr. Reagan might have to remain in the hospital for two weeks.

"I can reassure this nation and a watching world that the American Government is functioning fully and effectively," Mr. Bush said this evening after presiding over a half-hour Cabinet meeting in the White House situation room, where participants also heard the televised news conference reporting on Mr. Reagan's condition.

'Officers Fulfilling Obligations'

"We've had full and complete communications throughout the day, and the officers of the Federal Government have been fulfilling their obligations with skill and with care," Mr. Bush continued. He added that "all our prayers" and "all our hope" were extended for the recovery of the two wounded law enforcement men and for James S. Brady, the White House press secretary.

White House spokesmen said this evening that no steps had been taken to install Mr. Bush as Acting President under the terms of the 25th Amendment to the Constitution, which provides for succession in case of Presidential disability.

Mr. Bush was scheduled to fill in for the President tomorrow, however, at a series of previously scheduled functions, including a Cabinet meeting, a session with Congressional leaders, and a lunch with the Prime Minister of the Netherlands, Andreas A. M. van Agt. He prepared to spend the night at his own official residence in northwest Washington, a few miles from the White House.

Americans were saddened and outraged by news of the shooting of the President. In the business community, activity came to a standstill; stock trading was halted. Pages A5 and D1.

Contradictory Statements

There were contradictory statements in the afternoon and evening about who was in charge of the Government.

Shortly after 4 P.M., Secretary of State Alexander M. Haig Jr., who rushed to the White House minutes after the attack, announced he was in control pending the return of the Vice President to Washington. Mr. Haig also said he was in charge because the newly created system of "crisis management" was in effect, and he suggested that it was his role to serve as crisis-management coordinator until the

Continued on Page A5, Column 2

Suspect Was Arrested Last Year In Nashville on Weapons Charge

Associated Press

John W. Hinckley Jr. in photo made Jan. 21 for his driver's license.

By PHILIP TAUBMAN

Special to The New York Times

WASHINGTON, Tuesday, March 31 — The 25-year-old son of a Denver oil executive was overpowered by police officers and Secret Service agents yesterday at the scene of an attack on President Reagan. He was charged with the attempted assassination of the President and the shooting of three other persons.

The suspect was identified as John W. Hinckley Jr., who was said to have been in psychiatric care recently. He was arrested in Nashville last Oct. 9 for possession of concealed weapons, according to Nashville police records, and was released after paying a fine of $62.50. President Carter had arrived in Nashville a few hours earlier that night to speak at Opry Land.

Yesterday, in the tumult that followed the firing of a series of shots at Mr. Reagan's party, Mr. Hinckley was grabbed and pushed against a wall outside the Washington Hilton Hotel. Secret Service agents said that a Harrington Richards .22-caliber pistol was recovered from him, and he was quickly taken away in a District of Columbia police car.

Mr. Hinckley, described as a blue-eyed, sandy-haired man about 5 feet 10 inches tall, was turned over by the police to the Federal Bureau of Investigation and was arraigned early this morning in Federal District Court here.

He was ordered held without bail by Federal Magistrate Arthur L. Burnett on a charge that he "knowingly and intentionally" attempted to kill President Reagan and assaulted a Secret Service

Continued on Page A2, Column 4

Witnesses to Shooting Recall Suspect Acting 'Fidgety' and 'Hostile'

By RICHARD D. LYONS

Special to The New York Times

WASHINGTON, March 30 — "I spotted him walking rapidly up and down outside the back door of the hotel," John M. Dodson said. "He looked fidgety — agitated — a little strange, and I said to myself 'What if he takes a shot at the President?' "

Mr. Dodson, a computer specialist, was not the only person to take note of the behavior of the blond young man outside the Washington Hilton where President Reagan was making a speech. Walter C. Rogers, a reporter for Associated Press Radio, said the young man had been hostile to the group of reporters he had penetrated. And another witness, Samuel Lafta, an iron worker from Warren, Mich., said that a police lieutenant had stared at the young man several times.

But, nothing was done until the shots that wounded the President, his press secretary and two guards rang out. Then, the young man was overwhelmed by police officers and Secret Service agents.

Mr. Dodson, who works for the Pinkerton Detective Agency was standing on the seventh floor of the Universal North

Continued on Page A4, Column 3

Other News

Polish Strike Suspended

A nationwide strike threatened for today was averted after leaders of Solidarity reached a tentative settlement with the Polish Government. Page A9.

Indonesians Storm Hijacked Jet

Four of five hijackers were slain and 55 hostages freed when commandos in Bangkok retook an Indonesian airliner held since Saturday. Page A8.

ABC News

President Reagan leaving the Washington Hilton. At right is James S. Brady. As Mr. Reagan waved to the crowd . . .

Associated Press

. . . the gunman fired, hitting the President below his left arm. In photo made over roof of Presidential car . . .

Associated Press

. . . Secret Service agents are seen pushing Mr. Reagan into the vehicle, which immediately sped to a hospital.

NBC News

Circle at right shows gun held by suspect. Legs of Timothy J. McCarthy, the wounded agent, are visible at center.

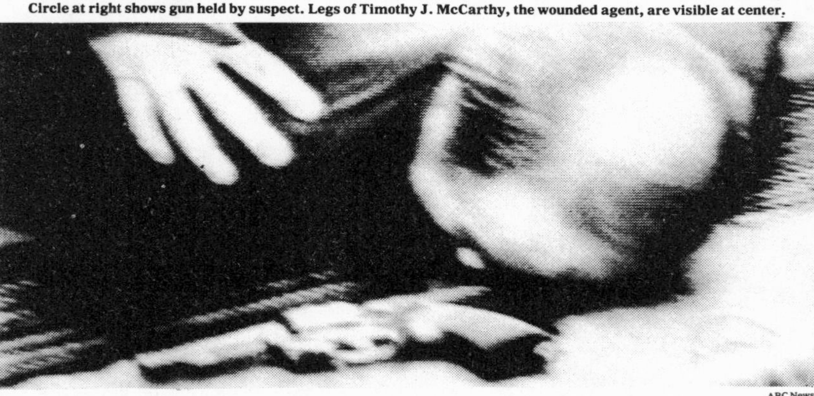

ABC News

James S. Brady lies on sidewalk. The pistol is believed to belong to a security agent, who put it down while helping.

LEFT LUNG IS PIERCED

Coloradan, 25, Arrested — Brady, Press Chief, Is Critically Injured

By HOWELL RAINES

Special to The New York Times

WASHINGTON, Tuesday, March 31 — President Reagan was shot in the chest yesterday by a gunman, apparently acting alone, as Mr. Reagan walked to his limousine after addressing a labor meeting at the Washington Hilton Hotel. The White House press secretary and two law-enforcement officers were also wounded by a burst of shots.

The President was reported in "good" and "stable" condition last night at George Washington University Hospital after undergoing two hours of surgery. "The prognosis is excellent," said Dr. Dennis S. O'Leary, dean of clinical affairs at the university. "He is alert and should be able to make decisions by tomorrow."

Statements in capital, pages A5 and A7.

The hospital spokesman said surgeons removed a .22-caliber bullet that struck Mr. Reagan's seventh rib, penetrating the left lung three inches and collapsing it.

A rapid series of five or six shots rang out about 2:30 P.M. as Mr. Reagan left the hotel. A look of stunned disbelief swept across the President's face when the shots were fired just after he raised his left arm to wave to the crowd. Nearby, his press secretary, James S. Brady, fell to the sidewalk, critically wounded.

Eyewitnesses said six shots were fired at the Presidential entourage from a distance of about 10 feet. The assailant had positioned himself among the television camera crews and reporters assembled outside a hotel exit.

The authorities arrested a 25-year-old Colorado man, John W. Hinckley Jr., at the scene of the attack. He was booked on Federal charges of attempting to assassinate the President and assault on a Federal officer, and early this morning he was ordered held without bail by Federal Magistrate Arthur L. Burnett.

According to police records, Mr. Hinckley was arrested in Nashville last fall on weapons charges on a night when President Carter was speaking there.

Scene of Turmoil

Within minutes after the attack yesterday afternoon, Americans were witnessing for the second time in a generation television pictures of a chief executive being struck by gunfire during what appeared to be a routine public appearance. For the second time in less than 20 years, too, they watched as the nation's leaders scrambled to meet one of the sternest tests of the democratic system.

Mr. Reagan, apparently at first unaware that he had been wounded, was shoved forcefully by a Secret Service agent into the Presidential limousine,

Continued on Page A3, Column 3

A Bullet Is Removed From Reagan's Lung In Emergency Surgery

By ROBERT REINHOLD

Special to The New York Times

WASHINGTON, March 30 — President Reagan was treated for a partly collapsed lung today, but the bullet that entered his left side and lodged in the tissue of his left lung did not do much further damage, according to doctors who operated on him. Surgeons removed a .22-caliber bullet from the President's lower left lung.

Neither Mr. Reagan's heart nor such vital blood vessels as the aorta were affected, Dr. Dennis S. O'Leary, dean for clinical affairs at George Washington University, said at a briefing this evening. "The bullet was never close to any vital structure," he said. He called Mr. Reagan's prognosis "excellent."

Emergency surgical procedures, which took about two hours, found no bleeding or damage in the abdominal area. Mr. Reagan received five units, or two and a half quarts, of blood in a transfusion before surgery. His vital signs were stable throughout his ordeal.

The adult body contains five to six quarts of blood. The hazard of blood loss relates to how rapidly the blood is lost and whether the volume of the blood sup-

Continued on Page A7, Column 1

Shooting of the President: The President's Press Secretary Is a Victim

Reagan's Press Secretary Has Served As a Longtime Spokesman for G.O.P.

By MAURICE CARROLL

For James S. Brady, the post of White House press secretary was the culmination of a long career as a spokesman for Republican officials.

When he was spokesman for Ronald Reagan's transition team, however, Mr. Brady had an irreverence about him that made it questionable whether he would be named White House press secretary.

He had been grounded temporarily from the Reagan campaign for joking about the candidate. "Killer trees, killer trees!" Mr. Brady had shouted in an unsubtle reference to Mr. Reagan's statement that trees were a major source of air pollution.

There were doubts, too, about just how close he would be to the President.

But Mr. Brady waited and hoped, telling self-depreciatory jokes. ("It's gotten so bad," he said of the complaints that he did not have much information, "that lunches with me as a source are no longer tax deductible.") In early January, however, he got the White House job.

Shot in the Forehead

Yesterday, walking close to the President, the 40-year-old press secretary was wounded by the bullets that were aimed at Mr. Reagan. Shot in the head, Mr. Brady fell face forward on the sidewalk and was taken to George Washington University Hospital, the same hospital where the President was treated for his wounds.

The bullet entered the side of Mr. Brady's forehead, passed through the brain and came out the other side. Dr. Dennis S. O'Leary, dean of clinical affairs at the university, said that Mr. Brady suffered some significant brain damage and underwent surgery last night.

While he has conducted his job with an amiable professionalism that seems devoid of ideology, those who know him best say Mr. Brady has strong convictions.

"He's very much in tune with the Reagan philosophy," said one of his former employers, Senator William V. Roth Jr., Republican of Delaware. "He's just a delightful guy. He's a sheer delight around the office."

It was that side that has been seen by most of those who deal with Mr. Brady.

The White House press secretary serves an exceptionally demanding group of reporters, and he works in a gossipy world. So, after serving the transition team amid rumors that this or that journalist was being sought for the press secretary's job, when he finally got it himself he laughed and said: "I got the benefit of trial by fire. I was the only one to get to audition for the job."

Plumpish, with a round, cheery face and thinnish hair, James Scott Brady was nicknamed "Pooh-bear" back home in Centralia, Ill., where he was born on Aug. 29, 1940, the only child of Harold and Dorothy Brady.

In the Presidential campaign last year, when he first served John B. Connally Jr. of Texas, then switched to the Reagan side after the Connally campaign collapsed, some of the reporters picked up the nickname. They also kidded him about his onetime role as a fill-in for Chief Illiwinek, the cheerleader dressed like an Indian who cavorts acrobatically along the sidelines during University of Illinois football games.

Mr. Brady had lost the trim figure that, as a member of the university's class of 1962, had let him fill that role. But occasionally, late of a campaign night, he has done a version of an Indian dance for reporters.

He has a serious view of his job, too. "Do you see yourself," an interviewer asked him recently, "as the President's press secretary or the press's press secretary?"

"I see myself as the press secretary for the nation," Mr. Brady replied.

Criticizes Press 'Junkies'

When some reporters complained that they were not getting the accustomed "guidance" in last week's controversy over the role of Secretary of State Alexander M. Haig Jr., Mr. Brady complained in turn that, over the years, the reporters had become "junkies," too dependent on background information on foreign policy from the White House rather than the State Department.

He did not try to limit the sources of news, but urged the senior White House staff to talk with reporters. "We don't play cop at all," he said, referring to the plug-that-leak mentality of some of his predecessors.

Mr. Brady had started inviting reporters into his office on Saturday afternoons for informal conversation, and was an amiable host.

"He loves to eat," Senator Roth recalled. "He always had popcorn in our office."

"He loves to cook," said William L. Greener, a friend with whom Mr. Brady had served in the Department of Defense, the Department of Housing and Urban Development and the White House.

"He loves to entertain," said a reporter who traveled in campaigns with him. Mr. Brady often boasted of winning a chili "cook-off" with his "Bear's Goat Gap Texas Chili," and had been a St. Patrick's Day host, sometimes serving corned beef and cabbage, sometimes Irish stew, and always green beer.

He and his wife, the former Sarah Kemp, a former director of administration for the Republican National Committee, have a son, James Jr. A daughter, Melissa, by a previous marriage that ended in divorce, studies forestry at Colorado State University.

Mr. Brady taught government for two years while working for his Ph.D. at Southern Illinois University, then went to Washington in 1961 as an aide to then Senator Everett McKinley Dirksen, Republican of Illinois.

Later, he worked in advertising and public relations, then returned to Washington in 1973 and held a series of administration jobs before going to work for Senator Roth.

Mr. Brady left the Senator's staff in mid-1979 to join the Connally campaign. For awhile, he did not have a specific title, but he persisted and other campaign aides came to depend on him.

Before Mr. Brady's appointment as White House press secretary, there were rumors that Mr. Reagan's wife, Nancy, thought Mr. Brady was not "good-looking" enough for the job, which involves frequent press briefings before television cameras.

"Nancy couldn't be more delighted," Mr. Reagan said when he made the announcement, "and she thinks he's absolutely handsome."

Associated Press

A Washington policeman leaping over James S. Brady to join other security men wrestling with the gunman. A wounded policeman, Thomas K. Delahanty, is also visible, at lower left.

Associated Press

Maureen Reagan and her fiancée, Dennis Revell, yesteray in Los Angeles after learning of the assassination attempt on her father.

'Honey, I Forgot to Duck,' Injured Reagan Tells Wife

By LYNN ROSELLINI

Special to The New York Times

WASHINGTON, March 30 — Shortly before he was wheeled into the operating room, President Reagan looked up at his wife, Nancy, and told her: "Honey, I forgot to duck."

Nancy Reagan kissed her husband and then, as he was wheeled into surgery, she turned and went into a nearby room to wait out the long afternoon.

She was pale but appeared calm.

Mrs. Reagan had just returned to the White House from a luncheon when she was told by the Secret Service at 2:35 P.M. that there had been a shooting at the Capital Hilton Hotel. But it was not until she reached George Washington University Hospital a few minutes later that she learned her husband had been shot.

Joins President in Room

As her limousine pulled up to the emergency entrance of the gray, cinderblock hospital on Washington Circle, she jumped out and sprinted through the doorway. Inside, Mrs. Reagan joined the President in his room while doctors prepared him for surgery. When it was time for Mr. Reagan to be wheeled down the hall, his wife held on to the handrail of his bed while doctors and Secret Service men accompanied them.

But when the group reached the automatic doors that lead to a suite of 10 operating rooms, Mrs. Reagan was told that she could not accompany her husband inside. She went for a time to the hospital chapel and also met with the wives of James S. Brady, the President's press secretary, and Tim McCarthy, a Secret Service agent. Both men were also wounded in the attack on the President.

Mrs. Reagan saw her husband after the operation and then went back to the White House.

Sheila Patton, the First Lady's press secretary, said tonight that she was grateful for the outpouring of support and prayers for her husband.

The President's younger son, 23-year-old Ronald Prescott Reagan, a dancer with the Joffrey II ballet, was in Lincoln, Neb., preparing to perform with the troupe this evening at Lincoln's Kimball Recital Hall when he received word of the assassination attempt.

He and his wife, Doria Palmieri, went from their hotel under heavy security to Lincoln Municipal Airport and flew to the capital to join his mother.

Maureen Reagan, 39, and Michael Reagan, 35, President Reagan's daughter and son by the actress Jane Wyman, were in California when they learned of the shooting. Mr. Reagan said he, his wife and Miss Maureen and another sister, Patti Davis, 28, would fly to Washington so that when their father "opens his eyes and comes out of sedation, we will be there."

"This mission," he said with tears streaming down his face, "is really is a mission of love — love for Ronald Reagan"

"A lot of things have been written about our family and our family's independence. One thing about us, we love Ronald Reagan and we love Nancy Reagan."

His sister Maureen urged the "the American people to get angry and propose laws" to prevent such incidents. "I've often said perhaps it's not guns we should outlaw, but ammunition," she said. "But something has to be done."

Son Is Optimistic

Her brother, speaking to reporters on the lawn of his home in the Sherman Oaks section of Los Angeles, was optimistic about the President's recovery.

"My father is a strong person and is in good shape," he said. "He'll probably come out here at the end of April, go to my sister's wedding and go to the ranch and cut some wood and put this thing behind him."

Reagan, Shot in Chest by Gunman, 'Good' After Surgery

Continued From Page A1

which sped away with the President in a sitting position in the back seat.

Behind him lay a scene of turmoil. A Secret Service agent writhed in pain on the rain-slick sidewalk. Nearby a District of Columbia policeman had fallen alongside Mr. Brady. The press secretary lay face down, blood from a severe head wound dripping into a steel grate. A pistol, apparently dropped by one of the security aides, lay near his head.

At the sixth shot, uniformed and plainclothes agents piled on a blond-haired man in a raincoat, pinning him against a stone wall. "Get him out," a gun-waving officer yelled as the President's limousine sped off. At first, it raced down Connecticut Avenue toward the White House.

Only then, according to some reports, was it discovered that Mr. Reagan was bleeding. The vehicle turned west toward the hospital.

Upon learning of the shooting, Vice President Bush returned to the capital from Austin, Tex., where he was to address the Texas Legislature. In Washington, Secretary of State Alexander M. Haig Jr. and other Cabinet officers began gathering in the White House situation room as soon as they learned of the assassination attempt.

At 4:14 P.M, Mr. Haig, in a voice shaking with emotion, told reporters that the Administration's "crisis management" plan was in effect, and citing provisions for Presidential succession, Mr. Haig asserted that he was in charge.

Mr. Reagan's wife, Nancy, and senior White House advisers rushed to the hospital and talked to Mr. Reagan before he entered surgery at about 3:24 P.M. Despite his wound, the 70-year-old President walked into the hospital and seemed determined to assure his wife and colleagues that he would survive.

"Honey, I forgot to duck," Mr. Reagan was quoted as telling his wife.

As he was wheeled down a corridor on a hospital cart, he told Senator Paul Laxalt, a political associate, "Don't worry about me. I'll make it."

According to Lyn Nofziger, the White House political director, Mr. Reagan winked at James A. Baker 3d, his chief of staff. Then, spying Edwin Meese 3d, the White House counselor, Mr. Reagan quipped, "Who's minding the store?"

'Tell Me You're Republicans'

The operating room was said to be the scene of a bit of the partisan humor favored by the chief executive. Mr. Nofziger said that Mr. Reagan, eyeing the surgeons, said, "Please tell me you're Republicans."

At this point, Mr. Reagan had apparently not been told of the grave wounds to the three men who went down in the spray of bullets aimed at him.

Mr. Brady, 40, was struck above the left eye. Doctors performed a skull operation and discovered a trauma so severe as to probably cause permanent brain damage.

Dr. O'Leary described his condition as "critical." "This is not a good injury," he said. "It causes a lot of damage."

Mr. Brady emerged from four and a half hours of surgery about 8:15 P.M., according to Mr. Nofziger, who relayed a report from Dr. Arthur Koprine, the neurosurgeon who operated on the press secretary. Mr. Nofziger said, "The prognosis is better at this moment than it was this afternoon."

He quoted the physician as saying "there may be some impairment" of Mr. Brady's mental faculties, but added, "He doesn't know how much." Mr. Nofziger said, apparently elaborating on the surgeon's report, "The brain stem apparently is functioning." Mr. Brady's condition was still listed as critical.

A Secret Service agent, Timothy J. McCarthy, 31, was shot in the right side and surgeons at the hospital removed a bullet from his liver.

The other wounded man was Thomas K. Delahanty, 45, a District of Columbia policeman, who was listed in serious condition at the Washington Hospital Center with a bullet lodged in his neck.

Noting that Mr. Reagan's lung had been reinflated, Dr. O'Leary said that the President "was never in any serious danger" since the bullet did not damage the heart. Dr. O'Leary said Mr. Reagan probably would be hospitalized for about two weeks.

Mr. Reagan regained consciousness early last night, according to a White House statement. It said: "At 8:50 this evening, the President joked with his doctors in the recovery room and, despite the tubes in his mouth, he gave them a handwritten note that said, 'All in all, I'd rather be in Philadelphia.'"

Mr. Reagan entered Operating Room 2 at the hospital at 3:24 P.M., according to an eyewitness. He was wheeled out to the recovery room over three hours later at 6:46 P.M., the witness said. The operation itself lasted about two hours. The remainder of the time was used to prepare the President for the operation and later to close and bandage the wound.

Mr. Reagan was operated upon by Dr. Benjamin Aaron and Dr. Joseph Giordano of the university's staff. Asked if it was "medically extraordinary" for Mr. Reagan to have walked into the hospital, Dr. O'Leary said, "Maybe not medically extraordinary, but just short of that."

Dr. O'Leary said the surgeons made an incision about six inches long just underneath the left nipple. Mr. Reagan received two and a half quarts of blood through transfusions during what Dr. O'Leary called a "relatively simple procedure."

The bullet was removed intact, although its shape had been distorted by striking Mr. Reagan's rib. A .22-caliber bullet is relatively small, and although capable of killing, generally does less tissue damage than the larger calibers typically used by law-enforcement officers.

'Never in Serious Danger'

Mr. Reagan, who has been in office just over two months, is the eighth American President to become an assassin's target. Abraham Lincoln, James A. Garfield, William McKinley and John F. Kennedy were killed by gunmen. Unsuccessful attempts were made on the lives of Andrew Jackson, Harry S. Truman and Gerald R. Ford. This is the third assassination attempt since President Kennedy's death in 1963. Two attempts were made on President Ford's life in September 1975.

Mr. Reagan arrived at the hotel at Connecticut Avenue and T Street, about one and a half miles from the White House, at 2 o'clock on a warm, rainy afternoon. His speech in the hotel ballroom to the Building and Construction Trades Department of the A.F.L.-C.I.O. got a subdued reception, reflecting the concern of many union members that Mr. Reagan's budget cuts will endanger their jobs.

Accompanied by Mr. Brady, Michael K. Deaver, deputy chief of staff at the White House, other aides and Secret Service agents, a smiling Mr. Reagan emerged from the hotel through a side entrance set into a steep rock wall along the T Street side of the hotel.

The President, wearing no top coat despite the light drizzle, paused to acknowledge the applause of a crowd of several hundred. He waved to the right, then turning a bit, raised his left arm in salute to the crowd. He was smiling as Mike Putzel, an Associated Press reporter standing with reporters behind the rope barricade about 20 feet away, shouted, "Mr. President —"

Just then, the first shot was fired. Tape recordings at the scene indicated that there were six shots in all, although the Secret Service later said there were five. "Reagan was stunned," Mr. Putzel said. "He just sort of stood there. Then the smile just sort of washed off his face."

The gunfire, allegedly from a Harrington and Richardson revolver held by Mr. Hinckley, came from within the small group of reporters that watches routine events such as Presidential departures on behalf of colleagues who cannot be accommodated in a restricted space.

One of the first bullets is thought to have hit Mr. Reagan. Jerry S. Parr, the special agent in charge of the Presidential Protection Division of the Secret Service, was standing behind Mr. Reagan. With a powerful shove, he bent the President forward, thrust him into the limousine and piled in behind him.

Almost in the same instant, the other three men went down, and a chaotic scene unfolded. The alleged assailant was smothered under a shouting mass of bodies.

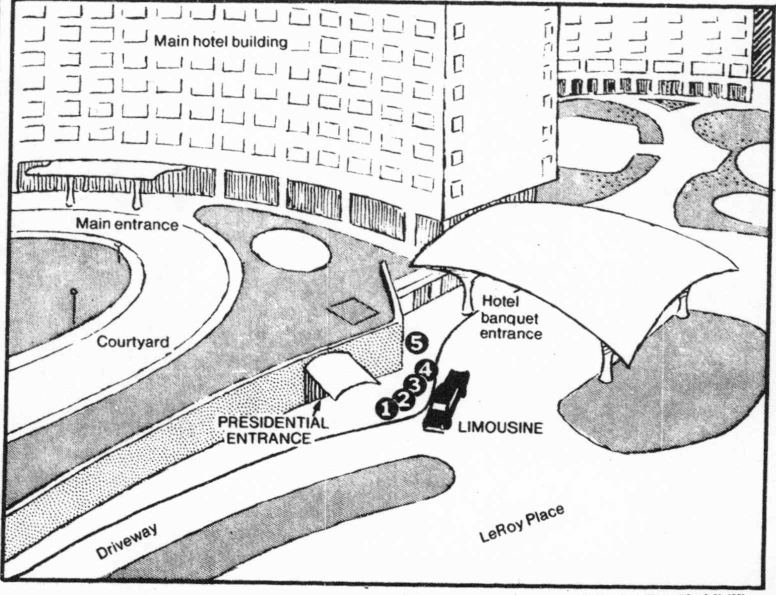

Diagram shows approximately where shootings occurred. The President was hit at (1); Timothy J. McCarthy, Secret Service agent, at (2); Thomas K. Delahanty, police officer, at (3), and James S. Brady at (4). Suspect was apprehended at (5). Mr. Reagan and Mr. Brady were taken to George Washington University Hospital.

The New York Times/March 31, 1981

"All the News That's Fit to Print"

The New York Times

LATE CITY EDITION

Weather: Mostly sunny, windy today; mostly clear tonight. Sunny tomorrow. Temperature range: today 35-50; yesterday 43-58. Details are on page B8.

VOL.CXXX . . No. 44,919 | NEW YORK, WEDNESDAY, APRIL 15, 1981 | 30 cents beyond 50-mile zone from New York City. Higher in air delivery cities. | 25 CENTS

COLUMBIA RETURNS: SHUTTLE ERA OPENS

First Re-usable Spaceship Glides to Landing in Desert; Commander Calls Flight 'Tremendous, Start to Finish'

Goal: 2d Trip in 6 Months And 100 in Ship's Lifetime

By WALTER SULLIVAN
Special to The New York Times

EDWARDS AIR FORCE BASE, Calif., April 14 — With the nearly flawless completion of the voyage of the shuttle Columbia, space agency officials began today to draw up firmer plans for the future of man in space, a future that they had always envisioned with a clarity that left their critics scoffing.

The triumph of the Columbia is expected to lead to flights with far-reaching commercial, scientific and military applications.

An agency official said at a briefing this afternoon that the Columbia would probably begin its return flight to Cape Canaveral, Fla., riding piggyback on a Boeing 747 jet in about a week.

He said that the "optimistic" estimate was that the shuttle would fly again under its own power in "less than six months" on a four-day flight from which it might be able to turn around and return to space in four months. Ultimately officials envision the shuttle being able to turn around in a matter of weeks. Each shuttle would have a life of 100 missions.

Apparently responding to the space program's critics, Christopher C. Kraft Jr., director of the Johnson Space Center in Houston, in a message relayed to the astronauts just before they left the shuttle, said: "We just became infinitely smarter."

What uncertainty remaining today centered on questions about just how quickly the spaceship could be readied for another flight. Specialists still have to determine the extent of the damage to the tiles that protect the ship from the searing heat of re-entry into the atmosphere. There was also some question about the suitability for quick re-use of the launching pad at Cape Canaveral, which was significantly damaged at liftoff on Sunday. [Page A23.]

Donald K. Slayton, orbital flight test manager and a former astronaut, said that a preliminary inspection revealed no more tiles missing than had been seen earlier on television from space. He said,

The shuttle's success is sweet vindication of American know-how, but social scientists say the psychological uplift will pass. News analysis, page A22.

"minimum work" would be required to replace them. But he added that a more detailed inspection would follow.

If close inspection of the tiles here and later when the Columbia is airlifted back to Florida reveals no fundamental problems, the "optimistic" estimate of a launching in the fall would prove true, with the third test mission in the spring and the fourth and final one later in 1982. One of the last two test missions, both of which are to last for seven days, would orbit while opened to the sky, rather than flying upside down to scan the earth.

The first operational, or nonexperimental, flight would take place by the end of that year.

The payload for that flight, as now planned, will be a TDRS or Tracking and Data Relay Satellite to be gently released into earth orbit. Among other roles, this

Continued on Page A22, Column 1

A Speck Pierces Horizon

By ROBERT LINDSEY
Special to The New York Times

EDWARDS AIR FORCE BASE, Calif., April 14 — First came the sonic boom announcing that it was near: two loud shocks that reverberated like cannon blasts across the desert floor.

Over the public address system, the voice of Mission Control read out the orbiter's speed and altitude, now rapidly declining: "Columbia, you're right on the money, right on the money,"

"Where is it, where is it?" perhaps 10,000 voices asked at once from the edge of Rogers Dry Lake.

Dropping to the Desert

Then, the sharpest eyes on the ground, squinting upward, saw it: a tiny, moving speck high over the horizon, dropping fast through a dusty, luminescent haze that rose from the surface of the parched dry lake like a cloudy mist. Suddenly, the tension broke.

"There it is!" the first voice said, and then others. The spectators, in clusters and large crowds, some who had been up all night waiting, broke into cheers as the space shuttle orbiter Columbia glided gracefully toward the hard-packed, cream-colored desert runway.

"Incredible!" shouted Joseph Lyon, who sells plywood for a living. "Can you believe it?" he asked, as he recorded the Columbia's descent with his portable home video recorder.

The Columbia, perhaps only 60 seconds after it had first been seen from the desert gallery, touched down, and the spectators continued to cheer.

The craft then rolled to a stop and seemed, from a distance, to become mired in a shimmering lake, a desert mirage that gave the illusion that the prehistoric dry lake was no longer dry.

Even before the Columbia had stopped its landing roll, a convoy of 21 service vehicles whose operators had been been training for that moment for almost three months, was moving in a phalanx toward the craft, stirring up a cloud of dust like a battalion of tanks moving over the Sahara before battle.

"It's a great day for the country," Albert Wheelon, an aerospace executive in the crowd said when he spotted a friend. "America's confidence ought to be up 100 percent."

It was a thought expressed repeatedly in the crowd of spectators, estimated by the National Aeronautics and Space Administration at more than 250,000, who had come here to watch a spaceship for

Continued on Page A23, Column 1

'Welcome Home, Columbia'

—Joseph Allen, Mission Control Communicator, 1:21 P.M.

HOUSTON: Columbia, we show you crossing the coast now.

CAPT. ROBERT L. CRIPPEN: What a way to come to California!

HOUSTON: Columbia, you're out of 130K [130,000 feet] on the tracking, 6.4 Mach, looking good.

Mach 6, 124,000 feet, range 177 miles.

JOHN W. YOUNG: John Young rolling, using manual control now.

HOUSTON: Mach 4.4, 107,000 feet, range 112.

Roll reversal complete. Control looks good.

Ejection seats can be used now, below 100,000.

You're coming right down the chute.

Rudder active now, looking good. Range 73 miles.

We now have a live television picture from the long-range optics at Dryden Flight Research Center.

Columbia, you're coming right down the track. The tracking data, map data and preplan trajectory are all one line on our plot boards here.

YOUNG: Roger, we concur.

HOUSTON: Columbia, we show you very slightly high in altitude, coming down nicely.

Mach 1 at 51,000 feet, range 28 miles.

Columbia, you're going subsonic now out at 50K, looking good.

YOUNG: Roger that.

HOUSTON: Columbia getting ready to start the big sweeping turn into the runway.

Columbia, you're really looking good, right on the money, right on the money.

25,000 feet, 1.6, range 13 miles; 22,000 feet. Control looking very smooth, speed brake at——. We have a television picture now.

You're right on the glide slope, Columbia. Right on glide slope, approaching center line, looking great.

That's TV from the chase plane. 16,000 feet.

Air speed 271 knots.

5,290.

2,500 feet.

50 feet, 40, 30, 20, 10, 5, 4, 3, 2, 1. Touchdown.

Welcome home, Columbia! Beautiful, beautiful.

More from the dialogue, page A23.

The New York Times / Jim Wilson

The Columbia, accompanied by two escort planes, descending toward a landing at Edwards Air Force Base

NBC News

The shuttle's rear wheels touch the runway on Rogers Dry Lake. Craft was traveling about 215 miles an hour.

CBS News via Associated Press

John W. Young, left, and Capt. Robert L. Crippen walking away from their craft after landing safely in the desert

FLIERS EMERGE ELATED

Crippen Says That Nation Is 'Back in the Space Business to Stay'

By JOHN NOBLE WILFORD
Special to The New York Times

EDWARDS AIR FORCE BASE, Calif., April 14 — The space shuttle Columbia rocketed out of orbit and glided to a safe landing on the desert here today to conclude the successful first demonstration of a bold new approach to extraterrestrial travel, the re-usable winged spaceship.

Heralding its triumphant return with a sharp double sonic boom, one of technology's fanfares, the 122-foot-long Columbia appeared in the clear blue sky, soared over the base, looped back and touched its wheels down in the wash of a mirage on the hard-packed clay of a dry lake bed. Touchdown came at 1:21 P.M., Eastern standard time.

"Welcome home, Columbia!" was the simple message from Joseph Allen in Mission Control.

215 Miles an Hour

Capt. Robert L. Crippen of the Navy and John W. Young brought the 80-ton gliding vehicle with its stubby delta wings to a smooth landing at a speed of 215 miles an hour, about twice the velocity of a jetliner landing.

Never before had a space vehicle returned to the earth in such a way so that it could be flown again. The Columbia and its three sister ships now under construction are each designed for as many as 100 flights to and from the space frontier.

"It was really a tremendous mission from start to finish," said Mr. Young, the commander, in a brief post-landing appearance before officials of the National Aeronautics and Space Administration.

Right on Course in Approach

Moments earlier, the Columbia had come over the California coast, and Mission Control reassured the astronauts that "we've got good data, looking good."

At 1:09, the astronauts were advised, "You've got perfect energy, perfect ground track," meaning that they were on target and slowing for the kind of landing they had practiced so many times.

"What a way to come to California!" Captain Crippen exclaimed.

The Columbia was launched Sunday morning at the Kennedy Space Center in Florida and orbited the earth 36 times over a period of 54 hours and 22 minutes. It was the first orbital test of the shuttle and the first time American astronauts had ventured into space in nearly six years.

"I think we're back in the space business to stay," Captain Crippen said.

The development of the shuttle, a hybrid spacecraft-airplane, has cost almost $10 billion since the project was initiated

Continued on Page A21, Column 1

Other News

Bloc Maneuvers Said to End

Reagan Administration officials say that unusual military activity by Warsaw Pact forces in and around Poland has virtually ended. Page A8.

Fighting Traps Beirut Premier

Artillery and mortar fire between Syrian and Lebanese Christian forces exploded around Parliament, trapping the Prime Minister inside. Page A3.

Aid Planned for Banks

Federal regulators plan to draft legislation soon to help financially troubled savings and loan associations and other institutions. Page D1.

Bradley Wins Third Term

Mayor Tom Bradley of Los Angeles was re-elected, becoming the first Mayor in the city's history to win a third term without a runoff. Page A13.

The Return of Columbia: Exhilaration Fills the Air at Edwards

Columbia Returns to the Earth, Opening a New Era of Space Flight

Continued From Page 1

in January 1972. A fleet of four and perhaps five shuttles is expected to be in operation by the mid-1980's if the Columbia's next three test flights are equally successful. The shuttles, replacing the throwaway rockets and spacecraft of the past, will be used to carry satellites, manned scientific laboratories and other payloads into space.

Declaring that the Columbia had opened the "gateway" to many opportunities for space travel, Dr. Alan M. Lovelace, acting NASA Administrator, said, "I think this epic flight of Columbia proves once again that the United States is No. 1."

After a preliminary inspection of the Columbia, Donald K. Slayton, the orbital flight test manager, reported that the condition of the spaceship appeared to be "pretty good." None of the almost 31,000 heat-shielding tiles that coated the Columbia was lost in re-entry. The delicate silica tiles gave developers some of their biggest headaches, and several were damaged in launching.

In about a week, after undergoing a post-flight inspection at NASA's Dryden Flight Research Center here, the Columbia is to be ferried atop a modified Boeing 747 jumbo jet back to the Kennedy Space Center. There it will be more thoroughly checked out and refurbished and then sent back to the launching pad for another test flight in about six months.

At Cape Canaveral, Fla., meanwhile, NASA officials said that the two solid-fuel rocket boosters used to lift the Columbia into orbit were less damaged than originally thought and were fully re-usable.

Mr. Young and Captain Crippen awoke at about 3:30 A.M. to begin preparations for their return to earth. They were in their 30th orbit, cruising upside down at 17,500 miles an hour.

The astronauts' official wakeup call from Mission Control, raucous music followed by a bugle call, came 30 minutes later.

Crippen's First Space Trip

Captain Crippen, 43 years old, was on his first space journey after years as an astronaut-in-waiting. It was the fifth trip for the Mr. Young, 50, whose last one was a journey to the moon on Apollo 16 in 1972.

Flight controllers announced early in the morning that, after a review of spacecraft and photographic data of Columbia's heat-shielding tiles, there was "no basis for altering our plans for the landing." Several tiles on the two pods housing the orbital maneuvering rockets were lost or damaged in the launching, but this had never been considered a serious problem by project officials.

Before they took out time for breakfast, the astronauts checked flight systems and realigned the guidance and navigation instruments. They tested once again the 44 reaction control thrusters they would depend on for controlling their re-entry.

Only two problems caused much comment between the crew and their flight controllers: a temporary failure of an auxiliary power unit, and a malfunction of a flight recorder. Two, or only one, of the power units would have been sufficient to power the hydraulics for the Columbia's control surfaces: the elevons, rudder and body flaps.

A few minutes after 11:50 A.M., the astronauts were given a "final go" for firing their de-orbiting rockets by Don Puddy, the flight director.

To get in position for the re-entry rocket firing, Mr. Young pushed computer buttons to fire the small thrusters and turn the ship around 180 degrees so that the aft rockets pointed forward.

The two orbiting maneuvering rockets fired on computer command at 12:22 P.M., while the Columbia was 169 miles over the Indian Ocean and out of contact with any tracking stations.

When the Yaragadee tracking station in Western Australia established contact, Mr. Young reported that the firing had been nominal, which is the space-engineering synonym for normal.

The next time the astronauts were heard from, at 12:42, in range of the Guam station, they reported that "the doors are plus." That meant the cargo bay doors, which had been open for most of the mission to allow radiators on them to cool the spaceship, were securely closed. The Columbia had also turned back around to face forward for re-entry.

Mr. Allen, an astronaut acting as the Mission Control communicator, told the crew, "Everything looks perfect going over the hill," which means out of radio contact.

Mr. Young's only reply coming through the radio noise was, "I mark."

Then, at about 12:48, over Wake Island, Columbia pitched up to an angle of 40 degrees, exposing the black tiles of its underbelly to the maximum thermal stresses, and plunged into the upper reaches of the atmosphere at an altitude of about 400,000 feet. A 16-minute communications blackout followed, the result of an expected buildup of electrified gases around the craft that blocked out all radio signals.

The spaceship glowed red hot, with some temperatures on its exterior reaching more than 2,700 degrees Fahrenheit.

After the Columbia crossed the California coast, it proceeded southeast across the coastal mountains, the San Joaquin Valley south of Bakersfield and the Tehachapi Mountains. Then it was over Edwards, down to subsonic velocity, which was when the sonic booms could be heard by the thousands of people who waited along the roads and runways.

"Right on the money, right on the money," Mr. Allen reported from Mission Control, talking the crew home.

Telescopic cameras had already detected the bright reflection of sunlight off Columbia. Mr. Young, who had been guiding the ship for several minutes, having taken over from the computers, banked Columbia after it passed over Edwards, made a U turn and approached the desert landing strip from the southwest. The Columbia was clearly visible to the unaided eye.

After it rolled to a full stop, a 21-vehicle motorized convoy raced across the desert, leaving a wake of dust, and helicopters flew in.

After more than 150 technicians moved in to secure the craft, it was about an hour before Mr. Young stepped down from the ladder. After a few handshakes, he did what every test pilot would do. He walked around the ship, examing the fuselage, and squatted to look at the landing gear. Captain Crippen came out a few minutes later and the two of them were driven in a van to a reception attended by their wives and Government officials.

When they returned to Elllington Air Force near Houston this evening, they were greeted by the cheers of almost 1,500 people. They were also met by top NASA officials and James A. Baker 3d, the White House chief of staff, who read a message from President Reagan and invited the astronauts and their families to the White House to visit Mr. Reagan "when his schedule permits."

The space shuttle Columbia as it landed yesterday at Edwards Air Force Base in California

Associated Press

Text of Message From President To Astronauts

WASHINGTON, April 14 (AP) — Following is the text of a message by President Reagan welcoming John W. Young and Capt. Robert L. Crippen, the Columbia astronauts, home today:

Your brave adventure has opened a new era in space travel.

You put new worlds within closer reach and more knowledge within our grasp.

We thank God for your safe return.

You were right, Captain Crippen, when you said the Columbia and her voyage would mean much to this country and to the world. Today the world watched us in triumph. Today our friends and adversaries are reminded that we are a free people capable of great deeds. We are a free people in search of progress for mankind, and today we found a little more.

We are grateful to you and to those who have worked with you. We are proud of you and we are proud of our country. Welcome home.

After the mission, John W. Young was joined at microphone by his wife, Susy. Capt. Robert L. Crippen is at right with his wife, Virginia

Associated Press

Old Man of the Mission Exceeds His Junior in Joy

By WOLFGANG SAXON

Having made history, the dean of the spacefarers and his rookie companion stepped onto the dust of the Mojave Desert with bounce in their steps, but it was the normally unflappable veteran of five space flights and a walk on the moon who showed the jubilation of the event as he strode about, flapping his arms, to inspect the Columbia.

John W. Young, commander of the mission, gave a thumbs-up signal to the ground crews and punched the air after leaving the craft's cockpit where he and his junior pilot, Capt. Robert L. Crippen of the Navy, had bided their time — Mr. Young with obvious impatience — for an hour after the 1:21 P.M. landing.

Mr. Young, who is 50 years old and has ridden more space missions of greater variety than any other human being, exultantly examined the life-saving thermal tiles on the Columbia's underbelly. "You can't believe what a flying machine this is!" he said. "It's really something special."

Mr. Crippen, who had remained in the cockpit a while longer, as if to allow Mr. Young his demonstration of joy at the peak of his career, then emerged, markedly calmer but bearing the same broad grin. After bouncing down the portable ramp that had been moved to the open door of the Columbia, he joined Mr. Young in being driven in an "Astrovan" to a NASA building for a quick medical check and a welcoming ceremony.

Clasping the hand of his wife, Susy, Mr. Young told an excited crowd of the space shuttle's "fantastic and remarkable capability."

"It's a really tremendous mission from start to finish," he declared, adding, "We're really not too far, the human race isn't, from going to the stars."

Mr. Crippen, 44, also held hands with his wife, Virginia, whom he introduced. "I can say that waiting 12 years to get my flight in space was well worth it," he remarked. "Now I'll go to stand in line for another 12 years, if that's what it'll take, but I don't think it will."

It was a more relaxed and joyous moment that formally closed the book on the 54 hours and 21 minutes of the first flight by a recoverable spaceship and its remarkable landing. Never before had a craft returned from space without either splashing into the ocean, American-style, or hitting the ground in the Soviet Union after parachutes had slowed the descent.

The drama built from early morning as tens of thousands of onlookers converged by car or van on Edwards Air Force Base, the sprawling site of the vast desert landing strip. Cheers went up everywhere when the Columbia made its perfect, pinpoint landing at the exact time called for in the flight plan.

And then there was another wait, seemingly interminable, as ground crews went to the spaceship to check for dangerous gases and to drain it of its remaining fuel.

The two men in the cockpit were left to fret, and Mr. Young's remarks to ground controllers grew testy despite the initial advice that about 45 minutes were needed for "safing" the craft and the area around it.

"I'm looking out the watch window," he complained by radio half an hour after bringing the craft down. "I don't see anybody out there. I can meet you in a second if you'd like me to open the hatch and jump out."

"Oh, we're just trying to keep you happy, John," a voice from mission control replied.

Although he was informed that everything was being done as quickly as possible, Mr. Young nevertheless made the kind of sardonic comment that might come from impatient airline passengers when told that a long-delayed debarkation would take still a while longer.

"If we're going to get this thing operational," he said, referring to the shuttle, "this is one of the parts we're going to have to work on, if you know what I mean. Do you realize, we could have almost orbited once in this time." It was only a slight exaggeration since the Columbia took about 90 minutes for each of its 36 orbits after the launching from Cape Canaveral, Fla., early Sunday.

Mr. Young, a former Navy fighter pilot, joined the space program nearly two decades ago. He first ventured into space in 1965 aboard the initial flight of the Project Gemini series and commanded the Apollo 16 moon mission in 1972. He later retired from the Navy as a captain but stayed with the space program to become the civilian chief of the astronaut office.

Mr. Crippen, a Navy captain, became a NASA astronaut in 1969 and was involved in the Skylab project. But until now, cutbacks had frustrated his hopes of flight into space.

At Mission Control, Even Exhilaration Came on Cue

By WILLIAM K. STEVENS

Special to The New York Times

HOUSTON, April 14 — A moment after the wheels of the space shuttle Columbia touched ground in two puffs of dust, Don Puddy, chief of the flight control team at Mission Control here, announced into the wire-thin microphone at his lips: "Room, get ready for exhilaration."

Mr. Puddy had actually cued the applause and cheers that immediately erupted, for a reason: Everyone had to get right back to work within seconds; for this flight was the first for which splashdown, or landing, did not signify mission's end. That would not come until the astronauts, John W. Young and Robert L. Crippen, were safely out of the orbiter.

Getting right back to work is the way Mission Control hopes to be operating from now on, since the nearly flawless shakedown cruise of Columbia is over.

Tension Goes With Job

Yesterday Mr. Puddy, the tall, burly man who ran Mission Control at the climax of the Columbia's triumphant flight, was asked whether, at the crucial moment, he expected to be as calm and businesslike as he invariably appeared on the job. "Anyone who isn't a little bit tense, who doesn't have a sweaty palm, doesn't understand what the whole damned thing's all about," he answered.

Today, as the space shuttle Columbia sped towards its most crucial test, its fiery plunge into the atmosphere, he was as obviously contained as ever. You couldn't tell whether his palms were sweating or not.

But behind him, the bearded face of a silver-vested Neil B. Hutchinson, whose team had been on duty earlier, was a taut mask of tension.

Suddenly the mask dissolved in a broad grin. Radar had picked up the Columbia at an altitude of 165,000 feet. The spaceship had safely come through the fires of re-entry. Mr. Puddy just sat there, a study in concentration amid the mild clutter, the empty coffee cups and stacks of paper.

The big screen in the front of the room displayed a map of the world, land in turquoise and water in black. A tiny symbol of Columbia traversed it slowly, tracing the real orbiter's movement. When the orbiter moved within range of a radio tracking station, the symbol was white; out of range, it turned green.

Flanking the screen, big digital clocks counted down the time to retrofire, the time to re-entry, the time to touchdown.

Behind a glass partition, friends and relatives of the astronauts and controllers filled the visitors' gallery to standing room only.

Eager Anticipation

The real ship's main engines fired, but aside from the changing digits on the controllers' displays, the only thing that marked the firing was the flashing-down-to-zero of the digital clock.

In the long moments when the friction of re-entry blocked radio communications from the spacecraft, both flight controllers and visitors sat quietly, watching and waiting. Finally Mr. Young's flat voice beamed down from above. The gallery broke into applause.

The controllers never blinked. They just kept their eyes glued to the numbers and displays on their console television screens. But there was a definite shift in mood, as Mr. Hutchinson's transformed face clearly testified. The spacecraft's radically new kind of heat shield had done its job, and in the place of wet-palmed tension, eager anticipation began to grow and then blossom.

Final Moments of Mission

Up front, the map of the world was gone, replaced by two other graphic displays. One, in blue, represented the descending spacecraft's desired trajectory. Another, in red, represented its actual trajectory. The red line sometimes surged above the blue one, sometimes below. On the other display, a yellow line represented the circuitous path, as if viewed from above, of the gliding orbiter as it circled to seek its landing spot slowly and thereby dissipate its speed.

Suddenly the orbiter appeared on live television in the back and on the sides of the control room and in the gallery. Heads of those not actively engaged in controlling the craft swiveled to gaze in sometimes open-mouthed wonder.

All that could be heard for a time was the voice of Joseph Allen, the capsule communicator, transmitting to the astronauts information about how fast the Columbia was losing headway.

Then touchdown was imminent. Some of the expressions in Mission Control could only be described as rapt.

"Gear locked," Mr. Puddy was told.

"Roger," he said.

And then the room was cheering, applauding, thrusting fists into the air.

Mr. Hutchinson stood with his arms folded across his chest and a look of bemused satisfaction on his face.

As the orbiter sat on the Edwards Air Force Base runway, safely home, Don Puddy remained at his console, receiving report after report that told of the flight's success and the orbiter's good condition.

"I don't know how much more good news I can take," he said. Soon he was standing up along with everybody else, relaxed, laughing at John Young's witticisms.

And then it was over. The astronauts were out of the space shuttle. The flight controllers were on their feet, giving first one crewman and then the other a standing ovation.

Mr. Hutchison lit a huge cigar.

"Mr. Knight, will you do the honors?" Mr. Puddy said to Jack Knight, one of his subordinates.

Mr. Knight climbed an aluminum ladder that had just been brought in. He placed the Columbian mission's official medallion on the wall, the latest in a gallery that has been hung there in the last two decades. But now, surely not the last of such medallions.

A Transcript Of Statements By Astronauts

Following is a transcript of the statements made by the astronauts of the spaceship Columbia at Dryden Research Center in California, as recorded by The New York Times:

JOHN W. YOUNG: This is Susy, the best thing that ever happened to me.

It was really tremendous mission from start to finish. Crippen is one of the hardest workers I know, and he carried me through that whole thing.

I think we've got a fantastic and remarkable capability here. We're really not too far, the human race isn't, from going to the stars. And Bob and I are mighty proud to have been a part of that evolution.

Thank you.

CAPT. ROBERT L. CRIPPEN: John is our speech maker. This is my wife, Ginny.

As the rookie of the group, I can say that waiting 12 years to get my flight in space was well worth it. Now I'll go stand in line for another 12 years if that's what it'll take, but I don't think it will.

I think we're back in the space business to stay. And I think myself and all of my compatriots are going to get many more opportunities to fly.

And I think that it's been said here, we are really in the space business to stay.

"All the News That's Fit to Print"

The New York Times

LATE CITY EDITION

Weather: Increasing cloudiness today; chance of showers tonight and tomorrow. Temperature range: today 54-71; yesterday 42-72. Details on page C18.

VOL.CXXX . No. 44,948 | NEW YORK, THURSDAY, MAY 14, 1981 | 30 cents beyond 50-mile zone from New York City. Higher in air delivery cities. | 25 CENTS

POPE IS SHOT IN CAR IN VATICAN SQUARE; SURGEONS TERM CONDITION 'GUARDED'; TURK, AN ESCAPED MURDERER, IS SEIZED

MADE THREAT IN '79

Alleged Assailant Wrote a Letter Saying He'd Kill John Paul on Trip

By R. W. APPLE Jr.

Special to The New York Times

ROME, Thursday, May 14 — The first reports said only that he spoke no Italian, that he was young and that he had dark hair.

But within a matter of minutes, a picture of the man accused of shooting Pope John Paul II in St. Peter's Square yesterday afternoon began to emerge, a picture of a militant Turkish terrorist, already convicted of one murder, who escaped from a maximum security prison in 1979 and then threatened in a letter to assassinate the Pope.

The Turkish Ambassador in Washington, Sukru Elekdag, said after the news of the shooting had flashed around the world, "The Turkish police have been under instruction to shoot him on sight."

Said He Was a Student

Moments after he was wrestled to the ground by pilgrims who had been standing near him, the alleged assailant told the Italian police that his name was Mehmet Ali Agca. He gave his age as 23 and said he was Turkish. He said also that he was a student at the University for Foreigners in Perugia in central Italy, but the records of the university showed that he had attended Italian-language classes there for only one day last month.

Mr. Agca was described by the police and by bystanders as a dark-haired young man, clean-shaven, with an angular face. He was wearing an open-neck white shirt under a lightweight jacket.

Mr. Agca was convicted in February 1979 of having murdered Abdi Ipekci, the editor of the independent Turkish daily newspaper Milliyet. He was jailed. But in late November, he escaped from the military prison where he was being held, and he had apparently been in hiding ever since.

When he fled from the prison, Turkish authorities say, he left behind a letter, addressed to Milliyet, threatening the life of the Pope. If the Pontiff did not cancel his visit to Turkey, which was then imminent, Mr. Agca wrote, he would shoot him in revenge for the attack by Moslem extremists on the Grand Mosque in Mecca earlier that year.

Blame Put on U.S. and Israel

The attack was considered a desecration of the Islamic holy place by Moslems, and Mr. Agca charged that the incident was of American or Israeli origin. His letter denounced the Pontiff as "the masked leader of the Crusades."

A partial text of the letter, made available by the Turkish police, reads as follows:

"Western imperialists who are afraid of Turkey's unity of political, military and economic power with the brotherly Islamic countries are sending Crusader

Continued on Page A3, Column 5

United Press International / The Vatican

Pope John Paul II, with blood on his left hand, being comforted by aides moments after being shot yesterday as he rode through St. Peter's Square at the Vatican

2 BULLETS HIT PONTIFF

Part of Intestine Removed in 5-Hour Operation— Hand Also Injured

By HENRY TANNER

Special to The New York Times

ROME, Thursday, May 14 — Pope John Paul II was shot and seriously wounded yesterday as he was standing in an open car moving slowly among more than 10,000 worshipers in St. Peter's Square.

The police arrested a gunman who was later identified as an escaped Turkish murderer who had previously threatened the Pope's life in the name of Islam.

The Pontiff, who was struck by two pistol bullets and wounded in the abdomen, right arm and left hand, underwent 5 hours and 25 minutes of surgery in which parts of his intestine were removed. A hospital bulletin at midnight said he was in "guarded" condition, but the director of surgery expressed confidence that "the Pontiff will recover soon."

By morning the Pope was reported conscious and still in guarded but stable condition.

Pope Falls Into Aides' Arms

The attack occurred as the Pope, dressed in white, was shaking hands and lifting small children in his arms while being driven around the square. Suddenly, just outside the Vatican's bronze gate, there was a burst of gunfire.

One hand rising to his face and blood staining his garments, the Pope faltered and fell into the arms of his Polish secretary, the Rev. Stanislaw Dziwisz, and his personal servant, Angelo Gugel.

The 60-year-old Pope, the spiritual leader of nearly 600 million Roman Catholics around the world, was rushed by ambulance to Gemelli Hospital, two miles north of the Vatican, for surgery.

'How Could They Do It?'

The Pope was conscious as he was taken to the operating room and seemed to speak of the attack on him as the work of more than one person.

"How could they do it?" a nurse quoted the Pope as asking.

The gunman fired four times in the attack, the police said. Two tourists, an American and a Jamaican, were wounded by two of the bullets. Ann Odre, 60, of Buffalo, was struck in the chest; she underwent surgery and was listed in critical condition. Rose Hill, 21, of Jamaica, was slightly wounded in an arm.

The gunman, who the police said was armed with a 9-millimeter Browning automatic, was set upon in the square by bystanders, who knocked the pistol out of his hand. He was then arrested, taken away and later identified as Mehmet Ali Agca, 23. Despite reports that another man had been seen fleeing from the square, the police said they were convinced that the gunman had acted alone.

The police quoted Mr. Agca as having told them, "My life is not important."

He was said to have arrived in Italy

Continued on Page A3, Column 3

Amid Prayers, World Voices Its Indignation

Prayers, shock and indignation resounded around the world yesterday after the shooting of Pope John Paul II.

President Reagan, recovering from wounds inflicted six weeks ago by a gunman, said he would pray for the Pope. In a message Mr. Reagan said, "All Americans join me in hopes and prayers for your speedy recovery."

Queen Elizabeth II said she was horrified. President-elect François Mitterrand of France spoke indignantly of "this new manifestation of destestable violence."

In Poland, the Pope's native land, television broadcasts were interrupted with news bulletins. Stanislaw Kania, head of the Communist Party, and other leaders offered "the best wishes for a speedy recovery necessary for the mission in service of humanist ideals of peace for the benefit of mankind." In Warsaw, people gathered somberly on street corners and around television sets in hotel lobbies, and wept during church services.

Americans shared in the grief at services in cathedrals, parochial schools and neighborhood churches.

In New York, more than 2,500 people, including Mayor Koch, jammed St. Patrick's for a mass led by Terence Cardinal Cooke. Protestant and Jewish leaders leaders joined in appeals for prayers.

The Connecticut Senate reversed itself and approved a bill calling for mandatory one-year jail sentences for illegal possession of a handgun.

"Regardless of what religion you are, he is a man of God," said Maria Lougee, a waitress on Ninth Avenue, who cried when she learned of the shooting. "Who could do something like that?"

For many, the shooting of President Reagan remained fresh in their minds. "When you shoot a President, you shoot a country," said the Rev. Miles Riley of the Archdiocese of San Francisco. "When you shoot a Pope, you shoot the church. We all felt shook, we all felt wounded."

The world, nation and region respond with shock. Pages A4-A6.

United Press International

Man identified as Mehmet Ali Agca, a 23-year-old Turkish citizen, is led away

A Firm Papacy For the People

Pope Strives to Deliver His Message Worldwide

By KENNETH A. BRIGGS

News Analysis

From the day that Karol Cardinal Wojtyla stepped confidently onto the balcony of St. Peter's Basilica as the newly elected Pope John Paul II, he has boldly challenged the church and the world. Striving to make Christianity a renewed force, he has taken his message from St. Peter's Square around the globe, traveling widely with little apparent regard for his personal safety.

The "Popemobile," an open vehicle such as the one he was riding in when he was shot yesterday, has become a symbol of his mobility. Before his weekly audiences in the square, he stands in the vehicle as it winds through the crowds. The act is a byproduct of his instinctive showmanship and his irrepressible desire to bring the church to the people.

Whether his efforts have been applauded or criticized, John Paul has made the world pay attention to the church. He is a subject of great contentiousness as a leader, but he has remained personally popular to all sides in disputes and has gained a reputation for bending decorum and playing to crowds.

The Pope has undertaken nine major trips in his mission of evangelization, a concept that includes not only the preaching of the Gospel as an alternative to ideologies such as Marxism but also the advocacy of the rights of the poor and oppressed. Repeatedly he has warned Roman Catholics against using violence to erase injustice. "Violence," he said during his trip to Brazil, "kills what it intends to create."

John Paul II, a laborer in Poland in his youth, has won the world's affection and respect as Pope. Page A7.

Elected to the papacy on Oct. 16, 1978, he promised "a ministry of love," and he has plunged into the world scene with a sense of fearless resolve and tireless devotion.

On his trips, he has thrived on schedules that most of his aides find exhausting. Though an intensely private man, he has a knack for stirring crowds — wandering into their midst, donning the hats worn by local people, often speaking in the local language and reaching out to touch hands.

Some of his aides have been nervous

Continued on Page A5, Column 4

Infection Is Main Risk In Pontiff's Recovery; New Surgery Required

By LAWRENCE K. ALTMAN

The medical information on the shooting of Pope John Paul II, although incomplete, showed that the most serious damage was done to the intestines.

Three sections of the bowel, or intestines, were removed in surgery, which was termed successful, at the Gemelli Hospital in Rome.

A second operation will be needed to reconnect portions of the bowel that were surgically severed in a procedure called a temporary exclusion colostomy, which allows removal of bodily wastes through an opening of the colon part of the bowel outside the body.

The Pope received about six pints of blood, the equivalent of about 60 percent of his total blood volume.

Surgical repair of the bowel is common in gunshot wounds to the abdomen, and a temporary colostomy is often necessary in such injuries. Recovery is often complete, provided complications do not develop.

"The main risk now is infection," a hospital spokesman said.

In addition to the bullet that "went through the abdominal cavity," the Pope suffered two minor gunshot wounds in his right arm and one in his left hand, ac-

Continued on Page A2, Column 5

For New York, Tearful Memories

By LESLIE BENNETTS

In the rectory basement at St. Charles Borromeo Church in Harlem, the women in the Senior Citizens Group wept quietly over the crepe paper banner they were making for a dance and recalled how the Pope leapt from his car to kiss the ground in front of their church.

At the school next door, students were wide-eyed and solemn as they chanted Hail Marys and prayed for the Pope's recovery.

And in the Bronx, where the Pope had stopped on Morris Avenue on his trip to New York in 1979, worried neighborhood residents gathered on the sidewalk to exchange rumors about his condition.

Many Remember His Visit

But for those New Yorkers with personal memories of the Pope's visit to their own school or street, the news came as a particular shock. "How could somebody shoot the Pope?" wondered Lynda Anderson, a 10-year-old student at St. Charles Borromeo, who had presented the Pope with a bouquet of roses.

Her incredulity was shared by those much older than she, many of whom had found the Pope's visit one of the great thrills of their lives. "It could not have been more wonderful," said Juanita Taylor, a retired nurse who overheard yesterday's bad news on the street and hurried to the church. "I don't think it would have been much different if Jesus Christ himself had come here. All I can do now is pray."

At the Senior Citizens' meeting, Emily Allred sighed and wiped a tear from her cheek. "He left some sort of feeling with us when he was here," she said. "It worked inwardly on us. If you could have seen him jump from his car and kiss the earth, it was one of the most fantastic things that ever happened in Harlem. He's a wonderful leader."

Many people commented on the helplessness of world leaders to defend themselves against deranged individuals. "So many people are walking around who are sick and need help," said Gwendolyn Burwell, a church volunteer. "I imagine this was a person who wanted to be seen or heard, and this was the only way he thought he could be heard."

Memories of the Pope's presence and

Continued on Page A6, Column 1

Other News

Reagan Tax Compromise Seen

President Reagan is prepared to compromise on the size of his tax cuts, an aide said, because of the financial markets' unsettled conditions. Page D1.

Social Security Plan Assailed

The Reagan Administration's plan to trim Social Security benefits aroused wide protest and the first hint of serious Congressional opposition. Page B15.

U.S. Envoy Returns to Beirut

Philip C. Habib, President Reagan's special envoy, arrived from Jerusalem with a plan for easing the crisis over Syrian missiles in Lebanon. Page A17.

U.S. Holds Soviet Cargo

Federal agents, suspecting violations, boarded a Soviet jetliner in Washington and seized gear, some of which was properly licensed for export. Page A9.

Reagan's Son Cited Ties

Michael Reagan, elder son of the President, referred to his father in letters seeking military contracts, an official of his company said. Page A24.

Plans for Battery Park Shown

Plans for the long-delayed Battery Park City commercial complex call for office buildings, plazas, restaurants, gardens and a skating rink. Page B1.

Shooting of the Pope: Joy Turns to Turmoil in St. Peter's Square

A Mellow Roman Evening Shattered By Salvo, Followed by Wail of Sirens

By PAUL HOFMANN
Special to The New York Times

ROME, May 13 — A joyful, cosmopolitan crowd of tens of thousands was filling St. Peter's Square this afternoon, cheering Pope John Paul II and holding up rosaries to be blessed by him. Suddenly a sharp salvo of what sounded like firecrackers was heard.

Those who were standing closest to the Pope, as he was being driven slowly around the square in an open, white cross-country car, saw him falter and raise a hand to his face. Then confusion broke out.

While the Pope was rushed to the ambulance that is always standing by during general audiences and other Vatican ceremonies, Italian policemen swarmed into the square and detained a suspect who was in danger of being lynched by enraged bystanders.

The public address system, which was to have relayed John Paul's address at the end of his weekly audience, announced in various languages that the Pope had been shot and wounded.

Rosary Over Loudspeakers

Preceded and followed by police cars with screaming sirens, the Vatican ambulance with the wounded Pope sped to the Gemelli Hospital, two miles from the Vatican. In St. Peter's Square, the loudspeakers started transmitting the rosary and other prayers in Latin, and thousands in the square, some kneeling on the cobblestones, repeated the ancient formulas. Many wept.

As more and more policemen arrived, many pilgrims who had come from the Italian provinces or foreign countries drifted off to their buses, parked along the broad Via Della Conciliazione, which leads from Vatican City to the Tiber. Other pilgrims and tourists remained in the square to pray and to watch the coming and going of police and Vatican officials.

Elsewhere in the Italian capital, the first sign that it was not to be just another mellow Roman evening was the sudden wail of the police sirens.

In the broad, tree-lined Via Crescenzio, 10 blocks from St. Peter's Square, an elderly news vendor shook his head when a carabinieri car, the siren full blast, careened by, followed by a truck with steel-helmeted policemen.

"Something serious has happened," the news vendor said loudly. "They must have bumped off somebody again, or maybe they kidnapped some bigwig."

Nobody needed to ask who "they" might be. Rome has for years been jumpy with murders, abductions and bombings by terrorists.

Police Helicopters Overhead

Two police helicopters appeared, flying over the Prati and Borghi districts, the densely populated neighborhoods closest to St. Peter's Square.

In the Via Crescenzio, just opposite the news vendor, a second-floor window that is usually closed even on hot days flew open, and a nun, tears streaming from her eyes, shouted down to the crowded sidewalk: "Two shots have been fired at the Holy Father." She was a Canadian, and her accent became even thicker in the emotion.

Like thousands of Romans, the nun had heard the news on the state radio, which had broken off its program to start a nonstop broadcast on the Pope.

While more police cars raced by toward Piazza Risorgimento at the approaches to St. Peter's Square, other cars stopped, their drivers getting out and asking people on the sidewalks what had happened. A white-faced man in overalls outside a garage said to passers-by: "Criminals, criminals. But the Pope should have taken better care of himself. He exposed himself to danger unnecessarily. The world is full of terrorists, murderers and nuts."

An elderly woman entered an espresso bar and said in a thin, tearful voice: "Could I have a glass of water, please. I feel faint. But I want to go to church and pray for the Holy Father."

In the Piazza Risorgimento, just outside the Vatican's old walls, an entire class of schoolchildren knelt on the sidewalk and, following the instructions of a friar, recited an invocation to the Virgin Mary to save the Pope's life.

In other parts of the city, espresso bars and cafe terraces emptied and churches filled up. It was a mild day that had started with a forecast of "unstable weather," but the sky had cleared in the afternoon and many Romans were in the streets when the news of the attack came.

Everywhere, people crowded around parked cars whose drivers had turned their radios to maximum volume and rolled down their windows so everybody could listen to the bulletins.

Hundreds of Romans, learning that Pope John Paul had been taken to the Gemelli Hospital on Mount Mario, drove to the hospital. It is operated by the local medical school of the Roman Catholic Sacred Heart University of Milan. The modern hospital, named after the university's founder, the late Father Agostino Gemelli, a Franciscan scholar, was surrounded by strong police forces. No outsider was allowed into the hospital compound.

Had Visited Hospital Before

A nurse in her early 30's who was off duty when she learned of the attack on the Pope and his transfer to the hospital pushed through the throng, pleading: "Let me in, let me in. I may be needed. I hadn't thought I would see the Holy Father here again."

On the day after his election on Oct. 16, 1978, the Pope slipped out of the Vatican, to the bafflement of the papal entourage, and with only a few aides went to the Gemelli Hospital to visit a Polish friend who was a patient there. The friend was the Most Rev. Andrzej Maria Deskur, president of the Pontifical Commission for Social Communications, in charge of news media.

After a long visit, the new Pope gave an impromptu address to hundreds of patients, nurses and doctors in a large corridor. When he was about to leave, an aide, Archbishop Giuseppe Caprio, now a Cardinal, whispered into the Pope's ear. "He reminded me I ought to bless you," the smiling Pope told the crowd. "I haven't yet learned how to perform as a Pope."

Tonight, prayer vigils for John Paul were held in the chapel of the Gemelli Hospital and in many churches throughout Rome. Some householders put lighted candles in their windows.

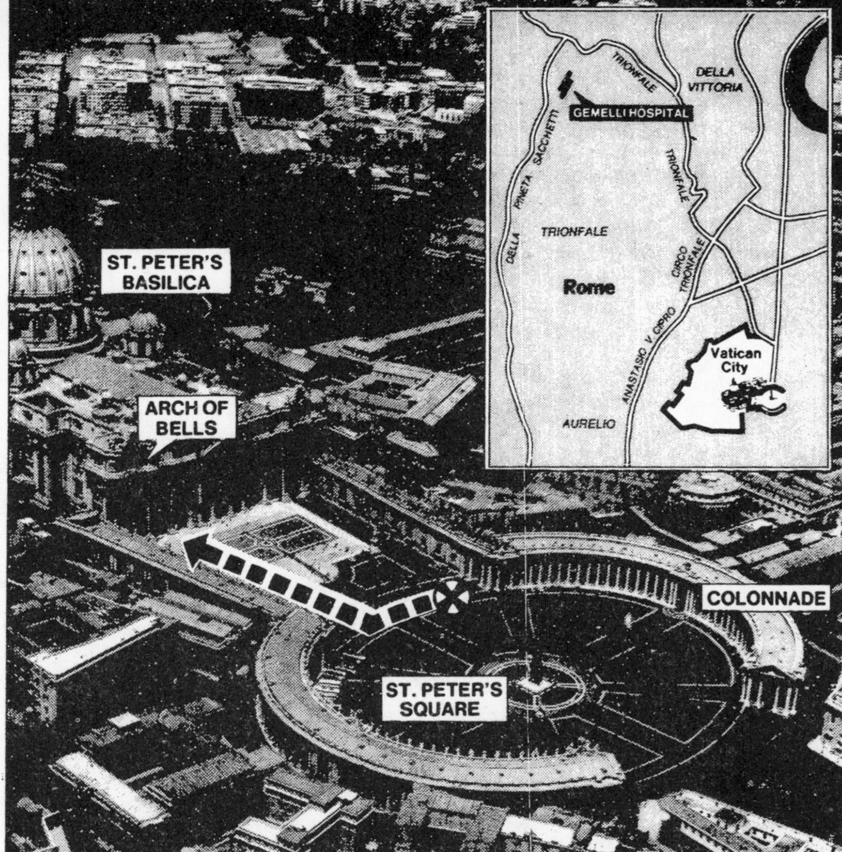

As Pope John Paul II was being driven through St. Peter's Square, a gunman fired on him just outside the bronze gate on the northern side of Bernini's colonnade. | The Pope's vehicle sped away through the Arch of the Bells. Out of sight, he was transferred to a waiting ambulance and then taken about two miles to Gemelli Hospital.

Associated Press

A woman praying for the Pope during vigil last night on St. Peter's Square

Pope Is Shot in St. Peter's Square; Condition Is 'Guarded'

Continued From Page A1

last Saturday, landing at the Milan airport, and to have come to Rome on Monday. The police said that he had in his pocket several notes in handwritten Turkish, one of them saying, "I am killing the Pope as a protest against the imperialism of the Soviet Union and the United States and against the genocide that is being carried out in El Salvador and Afghanistan."

The Turkish news agency Anatolia reported that Mr. Agca had been convicted of murdering Abdi Ipekci, the editor of the Turkish newspaper Milliyet, in February 1979 but escaped from prison later that year. Anatolia said he wrote a letter to the newspaper on Nov. 26, 1979, saying that he had fled from prison with the intention of killing the Pope, who was just then due in Ankara and Istanbul.

That threat caused a tightening of security for the Pope's Turkish visit.

Shock and Compassion

The attack yesterday drew expressions of shock and compassion from around the world. Pilgrims in St. Peter's Square fell to their knees to pray for the Pope's recovery.

The shooting occurred at 5:19 P.M., near the start of the Pope's weekly general audience. As the Pope fell into the arms of his aides, Vatican security men in plain clothes jumped on the vehicle, which then raced through an opening in the crowd to a gate where an ambulance was parked. An ambulance is always ready at general audiences and other Vatican ceremonies.

The ambulance sped through the interior of the Vatican to Porta Sant'Anna, a side gate and from there to Gemelli, the teaching hospital of the Catholic University of the Sacred Heart and one of Rome's best hospitals. Gemelli physicians were with him in the ambulance.

'Holy Father Has Been Wounded'

At the square a few minutes after the attack, a loudspeaker announced in Italian, English, French, Chinese and several other languages:

"The Holy Father has been wounded. We will now offer prayers for him, for his speedy recovery."

Many in the crowd — priests, nuns and others — burst into tears. Some of the worshipers rushed toward the spot where the shooting had occurred. Some formed into groups to offer their own prayers and sing hymns. After a few minutes a hymn in Polish could be heard over the loudspeakers, and the square slowly emptied.

The gunman was rescued from angry pilgrims by the police and taken to a police station half a block from St. Peter's. From there he was transferred to another place in Rome that was not made public.

Helicopters Circle Over Vatican

The police at first assumed that the assailant had one or more accomplices, and police cars, both marked and unmarked, raced in various directions from St. Peter's where they had gathered. Police helicopters circled over the Vatican and adjacent areas.

This activity had been prompted by reports from witnesses who said that they had seen another dark-haired, dark-skinned man with a bag fleeing from the scene as the gunman was overpowered.

The gunman is expected to be tried in Italy rather than in the independent Vatican City and, if convicted, faces life imprisonment.

In theory, the Holy See is empowered to try people for crimes committed on its territory. But as has been its practice, it is expected to give Italy the right to try the gunman for the assassination attempt.

Pope in Intensive Care

The first precise medical report on the Pope's condition was issued last evening after two hours of surgery.

Prof. Luigi Candia, the director of Gemelli Hospital, said the Pope was underoing "abdominal surgery for multiple intestinal lesions caused by a bullet that went through his intestinal cavity."

"Cardiocirculatory conditions are satisfactory," the professor said. He reported that the Pope, whose 61st birthday is next Monday, had received a transfusion of some blood of the type Rh negative.

At midnight a second report from the hospital said that after the operation the Pope had been transferred to the intensive care unit of the hospital.

Prof. Carlo Castiglione, director of surgery at the hospital, told reporters that "the prognosis remains reserved," an expression that in Italian medical parlance means that the patient is still on the critical list. He confirmed that the Pope had been hit by two bullets and said:

"We are confident the Pontiff will recover.

"The Holy Father has been fortunate, and as he has a very strong fiber we trust that he will return to normal."

"One of the bullets came very close to hitting vital organs, such as the aorta," he said, making it clear, as did other doctors, that no vital organ had actually been hit.

Another doctor at the hospital told an Italian television reporter on camera that the Pope's life had been in danger at the start of the operation because of severe loss of blood through hemorrhaging.

Transfusion of 6 Pints of Blood

The doctor, whose name was not given, said that the Pope would remain in intensive care for 12 to 24 hours. He explained that doctors had to remove parts of the intestines in three places.

The Vatican announced that the Pope was in surgery from 6 to 11:25 P.M.. It said he had suffered multiple lesions of the abdomen and a massive hemorrhage and had been given a transfusion of about six pints of blood. The Vatican also said that he had been wounded in the right forearm and the second finger of his left hand.

A surgeon at the hospital said that several parts of the Pope's bowel had to be removed and that a temporary colostomy, or opening of the colon, was made to permit the removal of wastes from the body. A second operation would eventually be needed to close the opening in the colon.

Alleged Assailant Wrote A Threat to Pope in 1979

Continued From Page A1

Commander John Paul under the mask of a religious leader. If this ill-timed and meaningless visit is not called off, I will definitely shoot the Pope. This is the only reason I escaped from prison."

His threats were taken seriously enough to warrant a tightening of the security net that surrounded the Pope during his Turkish visit. There was no assassination attempt.

Although Mr. Agca today gave a somewhat confusing account of his political and religious beliefs to the Italian authorities, the Turkish police labeled him a Moslem extremist, which appeared to fit in with his use of the phrase "brotherly Islamic countries" in the letter.

Mr. Agca also said at one point, however, that while he was a Turkish citizen, he was an ethnic Armenian. Armenians are Christians. Many of those who live in Turkey were unhappy with the Pope's visit, arguing that it was an insult to the memory of the hundreds of thousands of Armenians who were killed by the Turks in genocidal campaigns at the beginning of this century.

Since 1973, a total of 17 Turkish diplomats have been murdered by Armenian terrorist organizations in many parts of the world.

It was not clear where the accused assailant had spent his time since escaping from prison. One report said he had been in West Germany since 1979. Diplomatic sources here said that the Turkish Embassy had told the Italian Government that he had only recently left Turkey and might be in Italy.

Records Show Arrival in Milan

After interviewing police officials in several cities, Ansa, the Italian news agency, reported that Mr. Agca had arrived at Malpensa Airport in Milan last Saturday. He was aboard a charter flight from Palma, Majorca, in the Spanish Balearic Islands, which landed at 10:26 A.M. He cleared customs with the help of a forged passport in the name of "Farouk Osgun."

It was not known how he got aboard the flight, most of whose passengers were Italian tourists returning from vacations in Spain.

The police in Perugia told Ansa that the same man had appeared there on April 8, with the same passport, which gave his date of birth as 1953. Carrying a brown suitcase and wearing elegant clothes, he had arrived in Rome on an international flight three days before. He was wearing a neatly trimmed beard at the time.

"Mr. Osgun" checked into the Posta Hotel in Perugia, and on the morning of April 9 registered at the university for a single-trimester course in Italian, for which he paid about $160. He said he had been given a fellowship by his government.

The course had already begun, but "Mr. Osgun" reported for class on April 10, attending morning and afternoon sessions. That night he checked out of the hotel, paid his bill, reclaimed his passport and dropped from sight.

Photo Matched That Shown on TV

The police said that the photograph of "Mr. Osgun" in the university's records matched the picture of Mr. Agca shown on Italian television. They speculated that he had left the country sometime in April, made his way to Spain and then reentered Italy five days ago.

Mr. Agca reportedly took a room in a small hotel near the Vatican several days ago. A passport with his photograph was found there.

The assassin had in his pocket several notes in handwritten Turkish when he was seized, the police said. One of the texts, according to the police, said: "I am killing the Pope as a protest against the imperialism of the Soviet Union and the United States and against the genocide that is being carried out in Salvador and Afghanistan."

Mr. Agca, who was said to be a native of Malatya Province in southeastern Turkey, was a student at a college or university in Istanbul but dropped out after only one year. According to Interpol, the International Police Organization, he joined a neo-Nazi organization called the Gray Wolves, known also as the National Movement Party.

But that group disavowed him, and the Turkish police quoted him as having said at the time of his first arrest that he was "an individual terrorist" with no ties to any organization.

In New York, Altemur Kilic, deputy representative of Turkey at the United Nations, said Mr. Agca had escaped from Turkey to West Germany two weeks ago and had then been spotted by Turkish officials in Rome. Mr. Kilic said the Turkish police had immediately notified the Rome police of the terrorist's presence.

The diplomat described the accused assailant as being 23 years old, with a high school education, and jobless. He said that, before the assassination of the newspaper editor, Mr. Agca had been arrested for terrorist acts including bombings, shootings and bank robberies. Mr. Kilic said Turkey would seek his extradition from Italy when Italian authorities have completed his case.

United Press International

After the shooting, traffic into St. Peter's Square was halted. Armed policemen guarded the intersections.

"All the News That's Fit to Print"

The New York Times

LATE CITY EDITION

Weather: Mostly sunny today; clear tonight. Mostly sunny tomorrow. Temperature range: today 76-99; yesterday 74-94. Details on page B8.

VOL.CXXX . . . No. 45,003

NEW YORK, WEDNESDAY, JULY 8, 1981

30 cents beyond 50-mile zone from New York City. Higher in air delivery cities.

25 CENTS

REAGAN NOMINATING WOMAN, AN ARIZONA APPEALS JUDGE, TO SERVE ON SUPREME COURT

Associated Press

Judge Sandra Day O'Connor at news conference yesterday in Phoenix

REACTION IS MIXED

Senate Seems Favorable but Opposition Arises on Abortion Stands

By STEVEN R. WEISMAN

Special to The New York Times

WASHINGTON, July 7 — President Reagan announced today that he would nominate Sandra Day O'Connor, a 51-year-old judge on the Arizona Court of Appeals, to the United States Supreme Court. If confirmed, she would become the first woman to serve on the Court.

"She is truly a 'person for all seasons,'" Mr. Reagan said this morning, "possessing those unique qualities of temperament, fairness, intellectual

Remarks on Court post, page A12.

capacity and devotion to the public good which have characterized the 101 'brethren' who have preceded her."

White House and Justice Department officials expressed confidence that Judge O'Connor's views were compatible with those espoused over the years by Mr. Reagan, who has been highly critical of some past Supreme Court decisions on the rights of defendants, busing, abortion and other matters.

Some Quick Opposition

From the initial reaction in the Senate, it appeared her nomination would be approved. However, her record of favoring the proposed Federal equal rights amendment and having sided once against anti-abortion interests while she was a legislator provoked immediate opposition to her confirmation by the National Right to Life Committee, Moral Majority and other groups opposed to abortion.

At a brief news conference in Phoenix, Judge O'Connor declined to explain her views, saying that she intended to leave such matters to her confirmation hearings before the Senate Judiciary Committee. [Page A12.]

Mr. Reagan, himself an opponent of abortions, said in response to a question that he was "completely satisfied" with her position on that issue.

No Radical Shift Expected

White House officials were hopeful that Judge O'Connor's appointment could be historic not only because she is a woman but also because her presence on the Court, as a replacement for Associate Justice Potter Stewart, who was often a swing vote between ideological camps on the Court, could shift the Court's balance to the right.

However, an examination of the Court's voting patterns suggests no radical shift is likely even if she does vote with the more conservative Justices. [News analysis, page A13.]

It is the additional hope of Mr. Reagan's aides to make the Court even more conservative in the years ahead, when more vacancies are possible.

Judge O'Connor was appointed to

Continued on Page A12, Column 2

'A Reputation for Excelling'

Sandra Day O'Connor

By B. DRUMMOND AYRES Jr.

WASHINGTON, July 7 — Judge Sandra Day O'Connor's place in history is already secure, based on today's announcement that she will be President Reagan's nominee as the first woman on the United States Supreme Court.

Woman in the News

But if her past is prologue, after her Senate confirmation Judge O'Connor might well go on to leave even larger "footprints on the sands of time," as Mr. Reagan, quoting Longfellow, described the mark of United States Justices. Thus far in her 51 years, Judge O'Connor has compiled an impressive list of academic, civic, political and legal achievements.

"She's finished at the top in a lot of things," said Mary Ellen Simonson of Phoenix, who was a legislative aide when Mrs. O'Connor was majority leader of the Arizona State Senate, the first woman in the nation to hold such a leadership position.

"She has a reputation for excelling," Mrs. Simonson continued. "As a result she's been one of the state's leading role models for women. Now she's a national role model."

Judge O'Connor, who currently sits on the Arizona Court of Appeals, the state's second highest court, refused this afternoon to discuss "substantative issues" when she met with reporters in Phoenix. And, because of her short, 18-month tenure on the appeals court and its somewhat limited docket, she has faced few of the nettlesome issues routinely taken up by the United States Supreme Court. Nevertheless, her past and her acquaintances provide some insights into her mind and personality.

She is said, by friend and foe alike, to be notably bright, extremely hard-working, meticulous, deliberate, cautious and, above all, a Republican conservative.

"But she has an open mind when it comes to her conservatism," said a longtime friend, Sharon Rockefeller, wife of Gov. John D. Rockefeller IV of West Virginia. "I can't conceive of her closing off her mind to anything."

A leading Democratic politician in

Continued on Page A13, Column 5

Baker Vows Support for Nominee

By FRANCIS X. CLINES

Special to The New York Times

WASHINGTON, July 7 — Anti-abortion groups today denounced President Reagan's decision to nominate Judge Sandra Day O'Connor to the Supreme Court, but initial reaction in the Senate, which will vote on confirmation, was favorable.

"I commend the President for the courage of his decision," said Howard H. Baker Jr., the Senate Republican majority leader. "I am delighted with his choice, and I pledge my full support for her confirmation by the full Senate."

The National Right to Life Committee, an amalgam of anti-abortion lobbying groups in the 50 states, said that it would mobilize its members to "prevail upon senators to oppose this nomination." The committee said that Judge O'Connor was "pro-abortion" as a member of the Arizona State Legislature.

Dr. Carolyn Gerster, a vice president of the National Right to Life Committee, said that the nominee, as a legislator, voted in 1974 not to allow an anti-abortion resolution out of caucus, thus killing it. The resolution asked Congress to pass a Constitutional amendment protecting the fetus except when the mother's life was in danger, and allowed abortions in the case of rape.

Dr. Gerster based her statement of Judge O'Connor's record on that and other votes, which were characterized as "pro-abortion," on newspaper accounts and the recollections of other legislators, she said. Before 1975, the State Legislature kept no records of

Continued on Page A12, Column 1

Rupturing of Reservoir Pipelines Imperils Newark's Water Supply

Chain Reaction Set Off as Valve Is Opened — Vandalism Suspected

By ROBERT HANLEY

Special to The New York Times

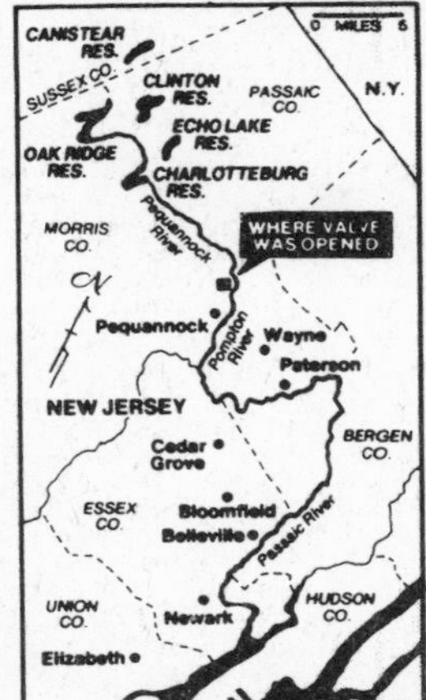

The New York Times / July 8, 1981

PEQUANNOCK TOWNSHIP, N.J., July 7 — A valve at an aqueduct was opened here today, apparently by vandals, starting a chain reaction that burst two huge pipelines and cut off Newark from its main water supply.

"It's an imminent catastrophe," said James F. Conley, the chief engineer of Newark's Division of Water Supply.

Mr. Conley said that unless the city could activate two existing pipeline interconnections with three other water supply systems and could build two new ones, parts of Newark "will be out of water" in five days.

Other Communities Affected

The pipelines that ruptured, he said, normally carry about 75 million of the 120 million gallons a day used by 600,000 people in Newark and parts of Elizabeth, Bloomfield, Belleville and Wayne.

Those four other communities, all of which purchase some of their water from Newark, began planning for alternative supplies.

Mayor Kenneth A. Gibson of Newark declared a water emergency in the early afternoon, prohibiting all nonessential uses of water, including lawn watering, car washing and opening of hydrants for any purposes other than firefighting.

Douglas Eldridge, a spokesman for the Mayor, said officials did not expect any declines in water pressure or other serious difficulties in the next day or two. He said some discolored water could come from taps because of adjustments being made on the distribution system following the huge loss of water.

But officials said that if the city could not restore a steady water source within five days, parts of Newark would run out of water. A heat wave that pushed temperatures today into the mid-90's and may see higher readings tomorrow is expected to increase water use and has heightened the officials' concern.

A 1,200-foot section of the two pipelines was torn away after they ruptured, sending tens of millions of gallons of water down a hillside here from about 4 A.M. today until the aqueduct's main supply valves at the Charlotteburg Reservoir were shut off sometime after 5 A.M., Mr. Conley said.

The cascading water, estimated at 40

Continued on Page B2, Column 4

U.S. FRAMES POLICY ON HALTING SPREAD OF NUCLEAR ARMS

American Reliability as Seller of Technology Stressed — Use Must Be Peaceful

By TERENCE SMITH

Special to The New York Times

WASHINGTON, July 7 — The Reagan Administration plans to announce shortly that while it is committed to halting the spread of nuclear weapons abroad the United States will be a "clearly reliable and credible" supplier of nuclear technology for peaceful purposes.

This policy is contained in an eight-point set of guidelines that has been prepared by the State Department and submitted to the White House. The White House is expected to issue the list before a meeting in Ottawa July 20-21 of the leaders of seven industrial nations. The spread of nuclear weapons will be one of the items on the agenda.

Although the guidelines are couched in the most general of terms, Administration officials say, they reflect a stronger commitment to halting the spread of nuclear weapons than was contained in Mr. Reagan's campaign statements last year and in a transition paper prepared by his advisers in December.

A Bigger Nuclear Umbrella

As described by Administration officials who have seen the guidelines, there are several principal points:

¶The goals of stopping the spread of nuclear weapons must be strongly reaffirmed.

¶A determined effort should be made to reduce the motivation of other countries to obtain nuclear weapons and an acknowledgement should be given that security considerations are often a basic factor in that decision. To this end, officials said, the United States would be prepared to sell conventional arms and consider extending its own nuclear umbrella.

¶The 1968 Nonproliferation Treaty, by which the nuclear powers undertook not to help others make or acquire nuclear weapons, and the 1967 Treaty of Tlatelolco, Mexico, which established a nuclear-free zone in Latin America, must be emphatically supported.

¶The International Atomic Energy Agency and its system of safeguards against the conversion of nuclear power and research facilities to weapons purposes should be strongly supported.

¶The United States should cooperate with other supplier countries to prevent the transfer of sensitive technology and material to nonnuclear countries where such transfers carry a risk of weapons production.

¶A high level of intelligence activities, including the possible upgrading of

Continued on Page A8, Column 1

New Pact Ends 7-Day Strike Of Garbage Haulers in Jersey

By ALFONSO A. NARVAEZ

Special to The New York Times

WEST PATERSON, N.J., July 7 — A seven-day strike against private garbage haulers in 108 northern and central New Jersey communities ended today when 1,400 drivers and loaders accepted a three-year contract that gives them a 50 percent pay increase.

Garbage trucks in the 12 affected counties will begin rolling early tomorrow. and Picket signs that had blocked municipal sanitation employees will come down from entrances to landfills.

The new contract was accepted after a long and confusing day in which the union members first rejected an agreement hammered out by negotiators in an 18-hour session at the Sheraton Heights Hotel in Hasbrouck Heights.

$155-a-Week Raise

When that proposal was rejected, the negotiators immediately went into new talks.

The union then approved a proposal that gives the drivers the $155-a-week raise over three years that was contained in the proposal they rejected, but adds three days of sick leave a year and guarantees that double time for work on the sixth day will go to workers with seniority. The drivers currently earn $310 a week for an average six-day, 48-hour week, and the loaders get about $50 less.

The union also won an additional paid holiday, four weeks of vacation after 15 years and $56 in increased health and welfare benefits.

The agreement provides for an immediate increase of $55 a week, then $35 a week on Jan. 1, 1982, $20 a week on July 1, 1982, and $45 more on July 1, 1983.

The cost of the package to residents and communities in the affected area has not yet been calculated. However, during the negotiations, the State Attorney General, James J. Zazzali, assured the owners — members of the New Jersey State Municipal Contractors Association and the Solid Waste Industry Association — that their requests for rate increases would be handled expeditiously.

The membership did not vote on the final package. The leaders of the union,

Continued on Page B4, Column 1

Sun-Powered Airplane Crosses Channel

Special to The New York Times

MANSTON, England, July 7 — After several earlier unsuccessful attempts, the first solar-powered airplane succeeded today in crossing the English Channel.

It took an atypically sunny English summer afternoon and a five-and-a-half-hour flight, but late this afternoon, the Solar Challenger dropped slowly onto the concrete landing strip of Manston Royal Air Force Base, on the southeastern coast of England.

Designed by Paul MacCready, who also designed the first human-powered plane to cross the Channel, the 210-pound Solar Challenger is powered by 16,000 photovoltaic cells on the wings that convert solar energy to electricity, which drives the motor.

No Battery Power

Other airplanes have flown on solar power, but only the Solar Challenger has been able to do so without the help of storage batteries. The project was paid for largely by DuPont and employed many high-strength, low-weight materials made by that company.

Starting from an airport at Cormeilles-en-Vexin, 25 miles northwest of Paris, the spidery plane, which has a wingspan of 47 feet, made the 165-mile journey at an average speed of about 30 miles per hour and a cruising altitude of 11,000 feet.

Standing in the deep grass along the main east-west runway at Cormeilles, a small crowd of about 30 persons had gathered to cheer on the tiny, transparent aircraft and its pilot. They watched the delicate plane corkscrew slowly and almost silently into the sky above the airport. The 2.7 horsepower electric motor produced only a slight buzz.

At an altitude of about 2,000 feet, Stephen Ptacek, the 28-year-old pilot from Golden, Colo., headed northwest in the direction of the Channel. In two or three minutes, he disappeared from sight.

Mr. Ptacek was greeted at the Man-

Continued on Page B4, Column 1

Associated Press

French policemen watch as Solar Challenger begins flight to England

Prelate, 52, Chosen By the Pope to Lead The Polish Church

By JOHN DARNTON

Special to The New York Times

WARSAW, July 7 — Bishop Jozef Glemp of Warmia was named today by Pope John Paul II as Archbishop of Gniezno and Warsaw and the Primate of Poland, succeeding Stefan Cardinal Wyszynski, who died on May 28.

The new head of the Church in this overwhelmingly Roman Catholic nation said he would continue the policies begun by his predecessor of dialogue and cooperation with both the Government and the Solidarity labor union.

"I am convinced I must follow the road laid out by Cardinal Wyszynski," he said in an interview. "The work of the Primate is not political. It is pastoral. But if we in the church are to do our duty, we must not remain above social issues. If the Solidarity and other social movements want to follow the truth and the light, we will give them our protection. It is in line with the proper role of the church."

Archbishop Glemp, 52 years old and a specialist in both canon and civil law, said he believed in working closely with the Conference of Bishops and would strive for collegial rule. Cardinal Wy-

Continued on Page A6, Column 1

INSIDE

9 More Executed in Iran

Iran executed nine opponents in its drive against "counterrevolutionary" elements. It also ordered Reuters to close its Teheran bureau. Page A3.

Upset in Mississippi Vote

Wayne Dowdy, a Democrat, apparently won a Congressional election in Mississippi, beating a strong supporter of President Reagan. Page A18.

Transcript of Remarks by Reagan and Nominee to High Court

Following are transcripts of President Reagan's remarks and answers to questions yesterday in announcing his selection of Judge Sandra Day O'Connor to serve on the Supreme Court, as recorded by The New York Times, and of a news conference in Phoenix by Judge O'Connor, as recorded by The Associated Press:

Reagan Remarks

As President of the United States I have the honor and privilege to make thousands of appointments to positions in the Federal Government. Each is important and deserves a great deal of care, for each individual is called upon to make his or her contribution, often at personal sacrifice, to shaping the policy of this Administration. Thus, each has an obligation to you and in varying degrees has an impact on your life.

In addition, as President I have the privilege to make a certain number of nominations which have a more lasting influence on our lives, for they are the lifetime appointments of those men and women called upon to serve on the judiciary in our Federal district courts and courts of appeals. These individuals dispense justice and provide for us those most cherished guarantees of protections of our criminal and civil laws.

But, without doubt the most awesome appointment a President can make is to the United States Supreme Court. Those who sit on the Supreme Court interpret the laws of our land and truly do leave their footprints on the sands of time, long after the policies of Presidents, Senators and Congressmen of a given era may have passed from the public memory.

After very careful review and consideration I have made a decision as to my nominee to fill the vacancy on the United States Supreme Court created by the resignation of Justice Stewart. Since I am aware of the great amount of speculation about this appointment, I want to share this very important decision with you as soon as possible.

Hints About a Woman

Needless to say, most of the speculation has centered on the question of whether I would consider a woman to fill this first vacancy. As the press has accurately pointed out, during my campaign for the Presidency I made a commitment that one of my first appointments to a Supreme Court vacancy would be the most qualified woman I could possibly find.

That is not to say I would appoint a woman merely to do so. That would not be fair to women, nor to future generations of all Americans whose lives are so deeply affected by the decisions of the court. Rather, I pledged to appoint a woman who meets the very high standards I demand of all court appointees.

I have identified such a person.

So, today, I am pleased to announce that upon completion of all necessary checks by the Federal Bureau of Investigation I will send to the Senate the nomination of Judge Sandra Day O'Connor of the Arizona Court of Appeals for confirmation as an Associate Justice of the United States Supreme Court.

She is truly a "person for all seasons," possessing those unique qualities of temperament, fairness, intellectual capacity and devotion to the public good which have characterized the 101 "brethren" who have preceded her.

I commend her to you and urge the Senate's swift bipartisan confirmation so that as soon as possible she may take her seat on the Court and her place in history.

Her Position on Abortion

Q. Do you agree with her position on abortion, Mr. President? A. I said I'm going to turn over all questions to the Attorney General here and let him answer the questions.

Q. The right-to-life people may oppose it, sir, and we just wonder if. . .? A. All of those questions the Attorney General is prepared to answer.

Q. Mr. President, your's is a pro position on that; can you give us your feelings about that pro position? A. I am completely satisfied. Q. On her right-to-life position? A. Yes. Q. And did you interview her first personally? A. Yes.

Judge O'Connor Remarks

Good morning. This is a momentous day in my life and the life of my family and I'm extremely happy and honored to have been nominated by President Reagan for a position on the United States Supreme Court. If I am confirmed in the United States Senate I will do my best to serve the Court and this nation in a manner that will bring credit to the President, to my family and to all the people of this great nation.

Q. [Unintelligible.] A. We haven't even thought about questions like that pending the confirmation hearing.

Q. When did you find out President Reagan would nominate you? A. He called me yesterday afternoon, about 4 o'clock our time and spoke with me at that time.

Q. Had you considered you were a serious contender for the post? A. I assumed that I was because I was interviewed late last week in Washington.

The New York Times/Teresa Zabala

President Reagan announcing his nominee for the Supreme Court yesterday at a briefing in the White House press room.

Q. By the President? A. Yes.

Q. What kind of questions did the President ask? A. I'm not at liberty to disclose the contents of the conversation and you can check with the White House on that. Q. How long did the conversation last? A. Not very long. I'd say no longer than 15 minutes.

Q. Did you speak with Senator Goldwater, Senator DeConcini, Congressman Rhodes? Have they had the opportunity to speak to you this morning?

A. Not yet. Senator DeConcini's office got through, but my line has been very busy this morning. I think it's been hard for people to get through.

Position of Congressmen

Q. Has our state's Congressional delegation been unanimous in endorsing your nomination?

A. As far as I know they have. I've had, of course, calls from Senator Goldwater and from Representative John Rhodes previously, indicating support.

Q. Judge O'Connor, Mr. Reagan said this morning that you would have your chance, so to speak, to leave your tracks in the sands of time. When you assume your post, assuming that you do, what kind of changes do you think you might bring about to the Supreme Court? Do you have any thoughts on that at this point?

A. I don't think that's anything [unintelligible].

Q. How do you view yourself as a legal, as far as the law's concerned? Your legal approach? A. I simply try to do as good a job as I can with each question as it arises.

A Philosophical Label

Q. Would you put a label on yourself — moderate or constructionist? A. No, I can't do that.

Q. You've been attacked by the right-to-life people for your stand on abortion. How would you characterize your position on that issue?

A. I'm sorry, I can't address myself to substantive questions pending the confirmation hearing.

Q. What were your thoughts when you first realized that you were being considered, you might be the first woman on the Supreme Court?

A. Well I was greatly honored by the suggestion but never thought it would be a reality.

Q. Do you consider lack of Federal court experience on the appeals or on the district court level a negative factor in your appointment? Is that going to be a difficulty you're going to have to overcome?

A. I can't see that. Certainly I've not had Federal experience and time will tell whether that means I have a lot more to learn than I otherwise would.

Rejection of Questions

Q. Why can you not address substantive questions? A. Pending the confirmation hearing I'm not able to do that. Q. You have been asked not to? I don't understand. Is it something you're just not allowed to do? By whom? A. Well I simply am not going to address myself to substantive issues pending the confirmation hearing.

Q. [unintelligible] because you're the first woman? A. Well, I hope not.

Q. Would you reflect on that aspect of it — being the first woman? What that means to you. What you think it means to the judicial system.

A. I don't know that I can. In approaching the work on the bench, I can only say that I will approach it with care and effort and do the best job that I possibly can do and I've always tried to do that with any position that I've held.

Q. Does your experience in the state legislature have any impact on your thinking as a judge?

A. Undoubtedly it does. All of our experiences reflect in some way in what we are and I have an appreciation for the legislative process because I have been part of that process.

Q. Your husband has a very active law practice here in Phoenix. Have you thought about how you will [unintelligible]?

A. We haven't thought about all those questions pending a confirmation hearing. Thank you.

HONORED BY POST, NOMINEE DECLARES

But Judge Declines to Answer 'Substantive Questions' at Brief News Conference

Special to The New York Times

PHOENIX, July 7 — The first woman to be nominated to the United States Supreme Court declared herself "extremely honored and happy" today but told reporters at a hastily called 15-minute news conference, "I can't address myself to substantive questions pending confirmation."

"If confirmed, I will do my best to serve the Court and this nation in a manner that will bring credit to the President, to my family and to all the people of this great nation," Judge Sandra Day O'Connor of the Airzona Court of Appeals said in a brief statement.

Judge O'Connor, who has a reputation for being calm in the most difficult courtroom situation, appeared not only very happy but also a little nervous as she spoke to reporters in the courtroom.

She said the news of her appointment made today "a momentous day in my life and the life of my family." She was flanked by her husband, John Jay O'Connor 3d, a Phoenix lawyer; her three sons, Scott, Brian and Jay, and other members of the court.

Although Judge O'Connor spoke with President Reagan for about 15 minutes last week, the news of her appointment came as something of a surprise to her.

Background Similar to Rehnquist's

As late as Saturday, she told a group of friends that she thought the chance of her appointment was remote, partly because of the similarity between her background and that of Associate Justice William H. Rehnquist, another Arizonan. Judge O'Connor was graduated third in the Stanford University Law School class in which Justice William Rehnquist was first.

But Judge O'Connor said at the news conference that the President called her about 4 P.M. yesterday and told her he would announce her appointment today.

Among the questions that Judge O'Connor declined to answer were those related to the announced opposition to her appointment from the Right to Life Organization and her position on the proposed equal rights amendment.

When a reporter asked her to reflect on the change that having a woman on the Court can make, Judge O'Connor replied: "I don't think I can. In approaching the work on the bench, I can only say I will approach it with care and effort and do the best job that I can do."

Foes of Abortion Are Upset But Senate Seems Receptive

Continued From Page A1

committee, subcommittee or caucus votes.

"We feel betrayed by the President," said Paul Brown, chairman of the Life Amendment Political Action Committee, who contended that Mr. Reagan had violated a campaign pledge to support anti-abortion positions and appointees. "We've been sold out."

In contrast, the National Organization for Women called the nomination a "victory for women's rights." Eleanor C. Smeal, president of the organization, contended that increasing political pressure from women's groups and a drop in ratings among women in public opinion polls had forced Mr. Reagan to the choice of Judge O'Connor. She rated the judge "sensitive to women's rights, a moderate on women's rights."

Any Senate opposition was thought likely to be led by Jesse Helms, Republican of North Carolina, a leader of conservative causes. The Senator was reported to have spent much of the day today at the White House, "seeking reassurances," as one anti-abortion lobbyist put it, but he offered no immediate comment.

The anti-abortion groups insisted that they would marshal Republicans and Democrats to fight the nomination in the Senate. But in some of their statements were acknowledgments that the nomination might be approved.

"I'm not sure we'll defeat her," said Peter Gemma, executive director of the National Pro-Life Political Action Committee. "But we want to send the President a clear signal at how much of an insult this is, and how his next court appointment had better be pro-life."

Senator Paul Laxalt of Nevada, a key Republican on the Judiciary Committee who is a confidant of the President, discussed the appointment with him this morning at the White House and later endorsed Judge O'Connor as "an excellent addition" to the court, emphasizing Mr. Reagan's assurances that he is "fully satisfied with Mrs. O'Connor philosophically."

This same emphasis on assurances from Mr. Reagan that Mrs. O'Connor finds abortion "personally abhorrent" was cited by Senator Orrin G. Hatch, Republican of Utah, in his endorsement of "an excellent choice."

"I'm relying on the President of the United States," Senator Hatch said in describing the opposition of anti-abortion groups as premature and perhaps misinformed. "If it turns out serious opposition develops, that's another matter."

Democrats on the Judiciary Committee offered lengthier and warmer endorsements of Judge O'Connor. Senator Edward M. Kennedy of Massachusetts said: "Every American can take pride in the President's commitment to select such a woman for this critical office." The ranking Democrat on the committee, Joseph R. Biden of Delaware, said: "From all outward appearances Sandra D. O'Connor seems to be eminently well qualified for this position, and I'm personally very glad that the President has named a woman to fill the vacancy."

As anti-abortion groups cited her legislative record to prove their contention that Judge O'Connor was "pro-abortion," Alfredo Gutierrez, a rival Democrat who succeeded her as majority leader of the State Senate in Arizona, denied this. "That's absolutely not in the record," he said. "It just isn't there. I'm surprised at the choice: she's conservative in a conventional way, but no ideologue. She's a terrific lady and they ought to put her on the court quick."

The issue of naming the first woman to the Supreme Court, while a major feminist goal in recent years, has stirred little general public interest, according to the latest New York Times/CBS News News Poll. The poll, conducted last month, showed that 72 percent of the public believed that it made no difference whether a man or a woman was appointed.

The National Women's Political Caucus celebrated the nomination as proof that "women are breaking the barriers of nearly 200 years of exclusion from decision making in our nation."

Potter Stewart, whose retirement from the Supreme Court created the vacancy, said that he was "delighted" by the choice.

United Press International

Sandra Day O'Connor with her family yesterday in Phoenix. With her was her husband, John, and their sons, from left, Jay, Brian and Scott.

Reagan Selects Woman, an Arizona Judge, for Supreme Court

Continued From Page A1

Arizona's second-highest court in 1979 by Gov. Bruce Babbitt, a Democrat, after five years as an elected Superior Court judge in Maricopa County, Ariz. Before becoming a judge, she served in the Arizona State Senate for six years.

With the selection, Mr. Reagan fulfilled a campaign promise last year to pick a woman for the Court at one of his earliest opportunities. Associate Justice Stewart announced his retirement last month after 23 years on the Court.

In a brief statement before television cameras at the White House, Mr. Reagan urged the Senate's "swift bipartisan confirmation so that, as soon as possible, she may take her seat on the Court and her place in history."

Reagan Administration officials had said earlier that Mr. Reagan placed a high priority on finding a woman with conservative views for the Court. It seemed likely, however, that Judge O'Connor's past positions on issues linked to feminists would serve as a focus for any confirmation battle.

While a member of the Arizona Senate, Judge O'Connor at first advocated passage of the equal rights proposal, and then, for reasons that are unclear, supported a different version that was regarded by some as less sweeping. She is also on record as opposing a measure that would have outlawed abortions in some state facilities.

White House officials asserted that Judge O'Connor had assured President Reagan in an Oval Office interview last Wednesday that she was personally opposed to abortions. They quoted her as saying that she opposed the anti-abortion measure only because it was not germane to the legislation to which it was attached and the Arizona Constitution forbids nongermane amendments. But those officials also said that she felt the legality of abortions was a legitimate matter for the legislative branch to decide.

Abortion foes, however, also cited votes in which, they said, Mrs. O'Connor supported a 1970 bill to legalize abortion and a 1973 bill permitting Arizona state agencies to participate in family planning.

In response, the White House said that there was no record of the 1970 vote and that, contrary to what the anti-abortion groups say, the 1973 bill was not pro-abortion and made no mention of abortion. The White House also noted that Mrs. O'Connor had sponsored a 1973 bill, which passed, giving hospitals, physicians and other medical personnel the right not to participate in abortion procedures.

Position on Rights Proposal

As for the proposed equal rights amendment, a senior White House official maintained that Judge O'Connor's onetime support had lessened and that she now had "more problems" with the proposal. He pointed out that Mr. Reagan himself had once supported the proposal before changing his position. Feminist groups characterized Judge O'Connor as a supporter of the amendment, however.

Tonight an enthusiastic Mr. Reagan said in Chicago that his appointment made it "a happy day for me and I hope for my country."

Speaking before a Republican fund-raising dinner, he praised Judge O'Connor's "long and brilliant record as a legislator and jurist" and said she had impressed him "as a thoughtful and capable woman whose judicial temperament is highly appropriate for the Court." He added that her principles adhered to those in the Repubican Party platform.

Impression on Reagan

Michael K. Deaver, the deputy White House chief of staff, told reporters in Chicago that Mr. Reagan was impressed with "her kind of moderate approach" in the sense that "she had not been an activist" on the rights amendment or abortion issue and had taken "a moderate position" on both.

The decision on Judge O'Connor came quickly because Mr. Reagan was impressed with her immediately, Mr. Deaver said, adding: "I guess that was the first one, and it's like buying a car."

The selection of Judge O'Connor brought to a conclusion a search that, according to Mr. Reagan's aides, was one of the most exhaustive conducted by the Administration. An initial list of about 25 candidates was winnowed last week to a "short list" of only a few potential nominees.

Among the names on the shorter list, a Reagan aide said, were Dallin H. Oaks, a Utah Supreme Court judge; J. Clifford Wallace, a California judge on the United States Court of Appeals for the Ninth Circuit; Robert Bork, a former Solicitor General and law professor at Yale, and Cornelia Kennedy, a Michigan judge on the United States Court of Appeals for the Sixth Circuit.

Interviews by Key Aides

Several potential choices were interviewed by Attorney General William French Smith and his aides. Judge O'Connor was interviewed June 30 by Mr. Smith and four White House officials — Fred F. Fielding, the counsel, and Mr. Reagan's three top advisers, Mr. Deaver, Edwin Meese 3d and James A. Baker 3d.

Mr. Reagan himself spoke to Judge O'Connor the next day and made the decision to choose her yesterday, according to the White House. An Administration official said she was the only person who was interviewed by Mr. Reagan or White House officials.

Fears Seen Misplaced

White House officials said a lengthy survey had been made of Judge O'Connor's views and that fears among conservatives about her record would be seen as being misplaced.

Judge O'Connor's confirmation prospects in the Senate were seen as significantly enhanced by the backing of the two conservative Senators from Arizona — Barry Goldwater, a Republican, and Dennis DeConcini, a Democrat.

Not until today did the White House ask the Federal Bureau of Investigation and the American Bar Association to conduct their examinations of Judge O'Connor. Mr. Smith said her name would be forwarded to the Senate formally, pending completion of the F.B.I. check.

He said her record on the bench was "quite satisfactory," even though it contained opinions on few, if any, major constitutional issues. He said he was confident that her philosophy was, like President Reagan's, "that it is the responsibility of elected representatives of the people to enact laws and not that of the judiciary."

One insight into the selection process was provided by an Administration official who said that Judge O'Connor had been asked several questions in her interviews with top White House aides.

Among the questions were whom she felt she was closest to on the Court philosophically; what were her opinions on the exclusionary rule, under which evidence that is obtained unconstitutionally is deemed inadmissible in court; and whether she felt that the Court should take into consideration the practical implications of its decisions.

The official said that Judge O'Connor's answers had been considered satisfactory, but he would not give details.

"All the News That's Fit to Print"

The New York Times

LATE CITY EDITION

Weather: Chance of drizzle today and tonight. Partly cloudy tomorrow. Temperature range: today 51-63; yesterday 59-68. Details, page D24.

VOL.CXXXI . . No. 45,094

NEW YORK, WEDNESDAY, OCTOBER 7, 1981

30 cents beyond 50-mile zone from New York City. Higher in air delivery cities.

25 CENTS

SADAT ASSASSINATED AT ARMY PARADE AS MEN AMID RANKS FIRE INTO STANDS; VICE PRESIDENT AFFIRMS 'ALL TREATIES'

Israel Stunned and Anxious; Few Arab Nations Mourning

Worry in Jerusalem

By DAVID K. SHIPLER

Special to The New York Times

JERUSALEM, Oct. 6 — Israel, which had such a high stake in the survival of President Anwar el-Sadat, reacted with stunned anxiety today to news of his assassination in Cairo.

A fear for the peace treaty between Egypt and Israel dominated all emotions. So thoroughly had the Egyptian leader come to personify that peace, and so deeply had Israelis distrusted the motives of other Egyptians, that his death today swept away confidence as swiftly as his historic visit to Jerusalem in 1977 had brought hope.

"The very fact that one bullet can cancel an agreement," said Geula Cohen, who heads the Tehiya Party in Parliament, "is a sign that not only the withdrawal, but all these procedures, must be stopped. There is no doubt that this incident confirms all that we have been saying; there is no stability in this region and one cannot make an agreement which is dependent on a nondemocratic regime and one man."

Question About Treaty

Even in the likelihood that Mr. Sadat's successor will adhere to the treaty's precepts, serious questions are bound to linger for some time, and the Government of Prime Minister Menachem Begin is certain to face rising political difficulties domestically in completing the return of Sinai to Egypt, scheduled for April 1982.

This afternoon, voices on the right were raised in demands that all prepa-

Continued on Page A9, Column 5

Jubilation in Beirut

By JOHN KIFNER

Special to The New York Times

BEIRUT, Lebanon, Oct. 6 — There was no mourning in most of the Arab world today for President Anwar el-Sadat of Egypt, whose separate peace with Israel had led to his isolation.

Public jubilation was reported in Syria, Iraq and Libya, and the streets of mostly Moslem, leftist-dominated West Beirut echoed with gunfire in celebration of the assassination. Most public statements attributed Mr. Sadat's death to discontent with the Egyptian-Israeli peace accord.

However, the Sudan, Egypt's closest friend in the Arab world, condemned the assassination and said it stood with the Egyptian Government against all forms of conspiracy and aggression.

Hope for Arab Unity Expressed

There was little public comment in Saudi Arabia. At the United Nations, Gaafar M. Allagany, the acting head of the Saudi mission, expressed sorrow "that this had to happen at a crucial stage." Noting Saudi opposition to Mr. Sadat's policies, he said, "We hope that our sister country will rejoin the Arab states."

An aide to Yasir Arafat, the leader of the Palestine Liberation Organization, said here on hearing of the shooting of Mr. Sadat, "We shake the hand that fired the bullets."

The aide, Saleh Khalef, better known by the code name Abu Iyad, said that "all attempts at dialogue" with Mr. Sadat had failed and that "it was inevi-

Continued on Page A9, Column 1

Associated Press

As President Sadat watched parade with Vice President Hosni Mubarak, left, and Defense Minister Abu Ghazala . . .

CBS News

. . . uniformed men, apparently part of the assassination team, approached the reviewing stand. Moments later, . . .

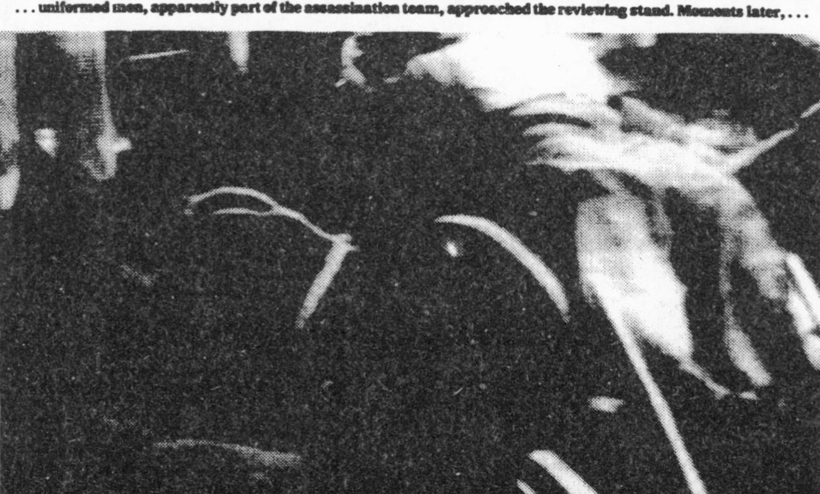

CBS News

. . . after the attack, victims lay sprawled on the floor of the stand.

AT LEAST 8 KILLED

Speaker of Parliament Is Interim President — Election in 60 Days

By WILLIAM E. FARRELL

Special to The New York Times

CAIRO, Oct. 6 — President Anwar el-Sadat of Egypt was shot and killed today by a group of men in military uniforms who hurled hand grenades and fired rifles at him as he watched a military parade commemorating the 1973 war against Israel.

Vice President Hosni Mubarak, in announcing Mr. Sadat's death, said

Mubarak speech excerpted, page A9.

Egypt's treaties and international commitments would be respected. He said the Speaker of Parliament, Sufi Abu Taleb, would serve as interim President pending an election in 60 days.

The assassins' bullets ended the life of a man who earned a reputation for making bold decisions in foreign affairs, a reputation based in large part on his decision in 1977 to journey to the camp of Egypt's foe, Israel, to make peace.

Sadat Forged His Own Regime

Regarded as an interim ruler when he came to power in 1970 on the death of Gamal Abdel Nasser, Mr. Sadat forged his own regime and ran Egypt singlehandedly. He was bent on moving this impoverished country into the late 20th century, a drive that led him to abandon an alliance with the Soviet Union and embrace the West.

That rule ended abruptly and violently today. As jet fighters roared overhead, the killers sprayed the reviewing

Of humble origin, Anwar el-Sadat became a statesman known for daring actions. Obituary, pages A8 and A9.

stand with bullets while thousands of horrified people — officials, diplomats and journalists, including this correspondent — looked on.

Killers' Identity Not Disclosed

Information gathered from a number of sources indicated that eight persons had been killed and 27 wounded in the attack. Later reports, all unconfirmed, put the toll at 11 dead and 38 wounded.

The authorities did not disclose the identity of the assassins. They were being interrogated, and there were no clear indications whether the attack was to have been part of a coup attempt.

[In Washington, American officials said an army major, a lieutenant and four enlisted men had been involved in the attack. The major and two of the soldiers were killed and the others captured, the officials said.]

The assassination followed a recent crackdown by Mr. Sadat against religious extremists and other political op-

Continued on Page A8, Column 1

Egypt After Sadat

Washington's Policies Facing New Problems

By BERNARD GWERTZMAN

Special to The New York Times

WASHINGTON, Oct. 6 — The assassination of President Anwar el-Sadat of Egypt created a new series of problems for future American policy in the Middle East at a time when the Reagan Administration was already worried about the spread of disorder in the region.

Administration officials, concerned about the chaos in Lebanon, the increased subversive activity of Libya and the Soviet inroads in Afghanistan, Southern Yemen and Ethiopia, had viewed Mr. Sadat as a solid, pro-American anchor of stability in the Middle East. With his death, there is now apprehension about the situation in Egypt as well.

At the White House, President Reagan said the United States had lost "a close friend" and "a champion of peace." But the Administration refrained from any public assessment of the possible repercussions of the assassination. [Page A12.]

The mood in Washington was one of shock and sadness at the loss of a leader who had done what would have seemed impossible a decade ago. He replaced the Prime Minister of Israel as the favorite Middle East statesman in Washington.

On virtually every Middle East, African and world issue, the Reagan Administration and Mr. Sadat saw eye to eye. With the expectation that Mr. Sadat would be in control of Egypt's policies

Continued on Page A9, Column 2

Cairo Regime's Plans Now Question Marks

The following article is by William E. Farrell, who has reported on Anwar el-Sadat's diplomacy from Jerusalem as well as Cairo.

Special to The New York Times

News Analysis

CAIRO, Oct. 6 — Anwar el-Sadat's rule in Egypt was that of one man who skillfully engineered, in his 11 years in power, the means of controlling every important facet of Egyptian life.

Although he was dismissed by many as a somewhat feckless interim leader when he became President after the death of Gamal Abdel Nasser, Mr. Sadat gradually showed that he had staying power, political skill and an ability that transformed him into a world statesman when he paid his historic visit to Jerusalem in the search for peace.

Now, with his sudden, violent death, many questions about the future of Egypt and its role in the world are beginning to be raised in this saddened capital and in many other countries.

Over the years, Mr. Sadat controlled his political party, the National Democratic Party; he supervised the Egyptian press, which lauded him; he was commander of the military, a key factor in his rule, and he had a facility for taking the pulse of Egypt's masses — about 43 million people. Some 67 percent of them are illiterate, but he was able to reach them by television and radio. He often did, in long speeches that had a pedagogical tone.

Some Egyptians opposed Mr. Sadat,

Continued on Page A8, Column 5

Other News

'Safety Net' Bill Passes

The House of Representatives approved spending $87.3 billion for social programs, despite President Reagan's threat to veto the bill. Page B10.

Ulster Prison Rule Is Eased

Britain gave inmates in Northern Ireland the right to wear their own clothing but stopped short of meeting the hunger strikers' demands. Page A3.

Runoff Due in Atlanta

Andrew Young, the former diplomat, and a State Representative, Sidney Marcus, won places in a mayoral runoff in Atlanta. Page A20.

Lindbergh Papers Unsealed

Evidence in the kidnapping-murder of the infant son of Charles A. Lindbergh 49 years ago will be opened to review by scholars and others. Page B1.

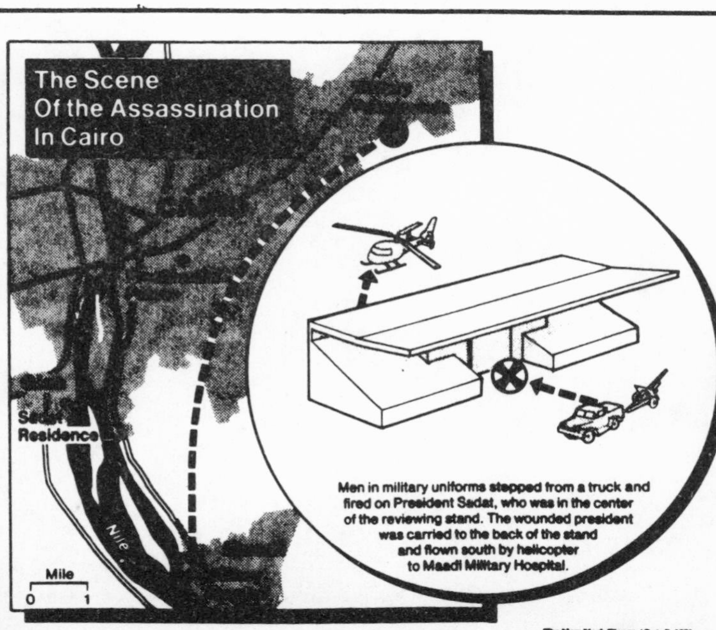

Men in military uniforms stepped from a truck and fired on President Sadat, who was in the center of the reviewing stand. The wounded president was carried to the back of the stand and flown south by helicopter to Maadi Military Hospital.

The New York Times / Oct. 7, 1981

Who Murdered President Sadat?

In the confusion swirling around the assassination of Egypt's President, Anwar el-Sadat, little information was made public in Cairo about the killers. Egyptian authorities were known to have several uniformed men in custody last night, but the Egyptians gave no details about the number or identity of the attackers or the reasons for the attack.

"Islamic fundamentalists" within the Egyptian Army was the characterization offered by Secretary of State Alexander M. Haig Jr. to a group of senators late yesterday afternoon. He also mentioned discontent among some Egyptian officers with the peace treaty that Mr. Sadat signed with Israel.

Reagan Administration officials said their information was that six uniformed men had taken part in the shooting, that three were killed and that the others were captured. They said that at least one was linked to the Takfir Wahigra Society, a radical right-wing Islamic group whose name translates as Repentance and Atonement. Its past actions include the slaying of the Egyptian Minister of Religious Affairs in 1977.

In Beirut, a handful of organizations stepped forward to claim responsibility for the killing, with representatives calling news agencies with their statements. But Reagan Administration officials said they doubted that any of them had been involved in the killing. Details are on page A12.

Assassination in Egypt: A Stunned Nation Braces for Future

U. S. Academic Experts Predict Power Struggle

By THOMAS L. FRIEDMAN

The death of President Anwar el-Sadat, at a time of internal unrest, is expected to ignite a power struggle, according to interviews with American analysts of Egyptian affairs.

Nadav Safran, professor of government at Harvard University. said:

"With the death of Sadat, power and the direction of Egypt's foreign and domestic policies are up for grabs among the generals, cabinet ministers and aides who worked closely with him."

In addition to the impact on Egyptian politics, Professor Safran said, the assassination will have ramifications for Arab-Israel relations.

"Sadat looked as though he was going to get away with it," said Mr. Safran, "He had made his separate peace with Israel, survived the Arab boycott and his regional isolation. Other Arab leaders were beginning to draw the lesson that maybe peace with Israel was politically possible. The peace plan proposed last summer by Crown Prince Fahd of Saudi Arabia was an indication of that trend. Now Sadat is dead, and that lesson is not going to be lost on other Arab leaders. You can look for Fahd to take more of a hard line the next time he makes a speech."

Speaker to be Titular Leader

There is no indication who President's Sadat's successor will be. For the next 60 days, until an election can be organized, a temporary president, Sufi Abu Taleb, the Speaker of Parliament, will be the titular leader.

Vice President Hosni Mubarak, Mr. Sadat's longtime protégé, will exercise effective authority through his control of the armed forces and key government posts and he is the apparent frontrunner in any race for the presidency, according to the analysts..

But even if Mr. Mubarak is chosen, the analysts said, it will take him several months at least to consolidate his grip on the sprawling bureaucracy, the army and the public at large.

In the meantime, rivals for power are likely to challenge his authority in the political back alleys, as they did when Mr. Sadat succeeded Gamel Abdel Nasser in 1970, and when Mr. Nasser toppled King Farouk in 1952.

Mr. Mubarak's tenuous position will not only limit his room for maneuver in domestic and foreign affairs, but could force him, or his rivals, to appeal for support to internal political groups or outside powers that have not previously been a factor in Egyptian politics.

"By their very nature," Raymond Baker of Williams College said, "power struggles in Arab politics reopen issues about foreign affairs and domestic politics that once appeared settled."

To a great degree, Professor Baker said, many of those issues were reopened in recent months. The Egyptian unrest was sparked by sectarian clashes between Moslems and Coptic Christians, but it developed into a more broadly based opposition movement. Left-wing intellectuals and right-wing Moslem extremists found common cause in decrying Mr. Sadat's rule and staged the most violent demonstrations since he came to power 11 years ago.

The severity of the demonstrations was reflected in Mr. Sadat's decision early last month to arrest 1,500 of his opponents, mostly Moslem extremists. But they also included some of the nation's best known political personalities, notably Mohammed Hassanein Heikal, a confidant of Mr. Nasser.

Results of Camp David Talks

"Sadat promised that Camp David would provide real peace and real prosperity," said Mr. Baker, referring to the accords signed with Israel in 1978.

"But the average Egyptian was beginning to realize that it brought neither. This increasing awareness was at the root of the latest disturbances. All of these issues — relations with the West, with Israel, with the surrounding Arab states, the direction of the economy — are still lying in the street, ready to be picked up by any contender for power.

"Sadat's death opens the possibility of realignment in these areas. It will be easy for Mr. Mubarak's rivals to seek popularity by pandering to these issues."

Malcolm Kerr, a political scientist of the University of California at Los Angeles, said that, even if Vice President Mubarak were able to obtain power, it was not immediately certain that he would continue Mr. Sadat's policies.

"A lot will depend on who is found to be responsible for Sadat's assassination and how Mubarak interprets the opposition that has built up in recent months," Professor Kerr said. "He may seek to make a quick accommodation with the domestic opposition to consolidate his own hold on power."

Associated Press

President Sadat watching aerobatics display moments before the shooting.

This could lead to some degree of cooling in Egypt's relations with both Israel and the United States, which in turn could set off a chain of events that might unravel the Camp David accords.

Relations with the other Arab countries, almost all of whom have severed diplomatic ties with Egypt, are also expected to undergo a major change, the analysts said.

Rapprochement with Egypt was impossible for any Arab leader as long as Mr. Sadat was in power. Now Saudi Arabia and the other conservative Persian Gulf states are expected to make it easy for Mr. Sadat's successor to return to the Arab fold, both to entice him away from Israel and to bolster the ranks of the conservative states in their competition with the more radical Arab regimes.

As for Egypt's relations with Syria, Libya or the Palestine Liberation Organization, a rapprochement will depend on how far Mr. Sadat's successor is ready to move toward their end of the political spectrum. The radical Arab regimes can be expected to use whatever means possible to influence the selection of Egypt's new president.

Policies of Cairo Regime Are Now Big Questions

Continued From Page A1

but he kept them under control. Many opponents, religious and political, were jailed when Mr. Sadat cracked down on dissenters a month ago, saying they were fomenting strife between Moslems and Coptic Christians and undermining his fragile experiment in democracy.

Egypt's democracy, judged by Western standards, does not measure up to the definition. But viewed against the tortured history of subjugation endured for thousands of years by this ancient land, Mr. Sadat's claims to have made strides are not without merit.

Mr. Sadat nevertheless did not take easily to criticism, and the powers that he sought he found in the Egyptian Constitution, a broad document that bears his imprint.

Those qualities of imposing his will brought Mr. Sadat to the world's attention — particularly in the West and most specifically in the United States. In 1972, angered by the Soviet Union's treatment of him and of Egypt, Mr. Sadat threw out 17,000 Soviet technicians in a week.

An Ally of the U.S.

He gradually resumed ties with the United States, long strained and battered in the Nasser years. The United States eventually became Mr. Sadat's principal ally, chief supplier of aid and partner in his major achievement — the peace treaty with Israel.

A question now is what the United States-Egyptian relationship will be with a new government and a new leader. More pertinent in the short run is what kind of government Egypt will have now that Mr. Sadat is gone.

For the next 60 days Sufi Abu Taleb, the Speaker of Parliament, will be Acting President and titular leader. Vice President Hosni Mubarak, a longtime associate of Mr. Sadat, will remain in his post but will take on key responsibilities such as running the military establishment.

Mr. Mubarak lived under the shadow of Mr. Sadat, not unlike the way Mr. Sadat was subsumed by Nasser.

If Mr. Mubarak is elected President about two months from now, in an election scheduled at an emergency Cabinet session tonight, what kind of President will he be? It is an unanswerable question now.

It remains to be seen what forces will begin to emerge in the days ahead. The Cabinet has already declared a yearlong state of emergency, something provided for in the Constitution but left vague.

Will there be infighting? Power struggles? Or will the legacy of Mr. Sadat be invoked and used to cloak Mr. Mubarak?

A major question is the status and the durability of the peace treaty with Israel. Mr. Sadat was scheduled to receive the last portion of the Israeli-occupied Sinai Peninsula, captured in the 1967 war, next spring. He raised the subject in all his recent speeches, and he promised Egypt a weeklong festival when the joyous moment came.

Many Egyptians of education and rank distrusted the treaty with Israel, but they muted their criticism because Mr. Sadat wielded the power and saw the accord as a major achievement, one that brought him world renown.

Egypt and Israel recently resumed their stalemated talks on autonomy for the 1.3 million Palestinian Arabs in the Israeli-occupied West Bank and Gaza Strip. More meetings are scheduled, but the assassination of Mr. Sadat may defer them.

Sadat Alienated Arab World

In signing the treaty with Israel, Mr. Sadat alienated most of the fractious Arab world, which broke relations with Egypt. Mr. Sadat had lately been sending signals to Saudi Arabia, supporting, for instance, the sale of Airborne Warning and Control System planes by the United States to the Saudis. But he continued to express his distain for Col. Muammar el-Qaddafi, the Libyan leader, a foe whom he called "evil" and "fanatic."

Another key question is what moves other Arab leaders will make to Egypt's new leader and what responses the new Egyptian leader will give. The moves and the responses will undoubtedly affect Egypt's relations with Israel, and possibly with the United States.

In his speeches Mr. Sadat always said there was no such thing as Arab unity without Egypt. He said that those who spurned him would in time woo him and that he would not make the effort, since he had not broken relations; they had.

A close aide of Mr. Sadat told a visitor recently that most of the resentment in the Arab world revolved around the fact that Mr. Sadat had made himself an outstanding world figure, one who transcended the bickering and power struggles of Arab countries. There was some fawning in the statement, but also some truth.

The New York Times/Gamal Mohieddin

The scene at the rear entrance to the reviewing stand after the shooting. The helicopter at left was used to carry President Sadat to the hospital.

Sadat Is Slain at Army Parade as Men Fire Into Stands

Continued From Page A1

ponents. There were unverifiable reports that some members of the armed forces had also been detained.

Those standing nearby at the parade today said six to eight soldiers riding in a truck towing an artillery piece had broken away from the line of march and walked purposefully toward the reviewing stand. Onlookers thought the procession was part of the pageant. Suddenly, a hand grenade exploded and bursts of rifle fire erupted while French-made Mirage jets screeched overhead.

The 62-year-old leader was rushed to Maadi Military Hospital by helicopter and died several hours later. He was said to have been struck by two bullets. A medical bulletin said he might have been hit by as many as five bullets and shrapnel fragments.

Business leaders said President Sadat's assassination underscored the volatility of the Middle East with its vital oil supplies. Page D1.

The bulletin said he had no heartbeat when he arrived at the hospital. It attributed his death, at 2:40 P.M. (8:40 A.M. New York time), to "violent nervous shock and internal bleeding in the chest cavity, where the left lung and major blood vessels below it were torn."

The death of Mr. Sadat raised serious questions about the direction the nation would now take.

At least for the time being, affairs of state are expected to be run largely by Vice President Mubarak, a longtime associate who promptly took over direction of the armed forces after the President died. Egypt's ruling National Democratic Party announced that Vice President Mubarak would be its candidate in the presidential election.

Mr. Mubarek, in his broadcast announcing Mr. Sadat's death seven hours after the assassination, indicated that Egypt would continue to respect the peace treaty with Israel.

"I hereby declare," he said, "in the name of the great soul passing away and in the name of the people, its constitutional institutions and its armed forces, that we are committed to all charters, treaties, and international obligations that Egypt has concluded."

Security police patrolled Cairo's streets, nearly empty except for some shoppers because of the holiday marking the 1973 war, and government buildings were being closely guarded.

Regular television programming was canceled after the announcement of Mr. Sadat's death and was replaced by readings from the Koran and film clips of his achievements — the 1973 war against Israel, which Mr. Sadat said restored Egyptian dignity after its defeat in 1967, the peace treaty with Israel and other milestones. No film of the attack on the reviewing stand at today's parade was shown on Egyptian television.

Reviewing Stand Awash in Blood

Within seconds of the attack, the reviewing stand was awash in blood. Bemedaled officials dived for cover. Screams and panic followed as guests tried to flee, tipping over chairs. Some were crushed under foot. Others, shocked and stunned, stood riveted.

This correspondent saw one assailant, a stocky, dark-haired man, standing in a half crouch, firing a rifle into the stand used by Mr. Sadat, who was wearing black leather boots and military attire crossed by a green sash.

Some onlookers reported a short, fierce exchange of fire between the killers and Mr. Sadat's security men. Others said the attackers had been overcome by some of the thousands of military men in the area.

While spectators sought a way out, the reviewing stand for a few seconds was nearly empty. Flanked on each side by displays of sleek missiles, the stand was a blood-soaked horror.

Mr. Sadat was promptly carried away, but others felled by bullets remained writhing on the ground. A few did not move. One man, seriously wounded, was slumped over a railing separating Mr. Sadat and his party from the parade about 20 yards away.

Among those hit was reported to be Bishop Samuel, whom Mr. Sadat had named one of five clerics to run the Coptic Christians' affairs after he deposed their Pope, Sheunda III. The bishop was later reported to have died.

Others said to have died were two presidential aides — Mohammed Rashwan, the official photographer, and Sayed Marei, a confidant. The Belgian Ambassador, Claude Ruelle, was seriously wounded, and three American military officers were hurt.

Egypt's Defense Minister, Gen. Abdel Halim Abu Ghazala, who had opened the parade with a speech, stood in the midst of the carnage. His face was bleeding, his gold-braided uniform was blood-soaked. He waved away attempts to assist him and began issuing orders.

Soldiers wearing red berets and perfectly creased uniforms promptly joined hands to cordon off the scene of the attack, widening the circle as more soldiers arrived. Some of the soliders were sobbing, a few screamed hysterically, others looked dumbfounded.

Overhead, the air show continued. Planes looped and swerved and dived and arced and sent colorful sprays of vapor over the pandemonium below. The roar of engines drowned out the screams and the clatter of chairs.

Camel Corps on Parade

The parade ground, which had witnessed a joyful procession of Egypt's most advanced arms as well as the colorful camel corps, with its turbaned soldiers, and the cavalry, with its sleek, elegant Arabian horses, was littered with little Egyptian souvenir flags dropped by panicked guests. As members of military bands scattered, the brilliant sun beamed off shiny, yellow tubas and other brass instruments.

The Egyptian military establishment has long been regarded as the ingredient needed by any leader to remain in power. Diplomatic and military analysts said that Mr. Sadat had the support of the military and that it assured the stability of his regime and permitted him to take daring steps, such as the peace overture to Israel and, finally, the peace treaty. In the absence of information, it was hard to tell whether the assassins represented a disenchantment with Mr. Sadat within the military.

Speculation abounded. Some thought the attackers, who many felt must have known that they were on a suicide mission, might be Moslem fundamentalists opposed to the alliance with Israel and to Mr. Sadat's recent crackdown.

About a month ago, he ordered the arrest of some 1,500 Coptic and Moslem extremists, along with some of his political opponents. He said they had fomented sectarian strife and endangered his efforts to bring democracy to Egypt.

A devout Moslem, Mr. Sadat was harsh toward fundamentalist groups, such as the Moslem Brotherhood and the Islamic Association. He banned both groups, calling them illegal. He said that he would not tolerate mixing religion and politics and that these groups were using mosques to denounce him.

Arrest of Some Military Rumored

The published names of those arrested in the crackdown did not include those of military personnel. But there were reports that some of those detained were in the armed forces.

After Mr. Sadat's helicopter had left the scene, diplomats rushed to their limousines. Soldiers cleared the grounds and drove away the stunned spectators. Ambulances wailed, women clutching their children raced away. And the airshow above continued.

Early in the parade, a rocketlike object had been launched. It rained down Egyptian flags and portraits of Mr. Sadat hanging from tiny parachutes that were whipped by the wind. Most of them floated over a nearby housing development called Nasser City.

As the grounds were being cleared, one of the parachuted portraits was seen hanging from a flag pole on which it had become impaled in landing. The portrait of Mr. Sadat had been torn by the sharp tip of the Egyptian flag that was fluttering from it.

Egypt's Acting Leaders

Hosni Mubarak

Special to The New York Times

CAIRO, Oct. 6 — The man most likely to succeed Anwar el-Sadat as President of Egypt is Vice President Hosni Mubarak, Mr. Sadat's protégé and closest adviser.

In the temporary Government declared tonight by Acting President Sufi Abu Taleb, Speaker of the Egyptian Parliament, Mr. Mubarak retains crucial control of the armed forces and is authorized to issue presidential decrees.

Since his appointment as Vice President by Mr. Sadat in April 1975, Mr. Mubarak has presided over the weekly Cabinet meetings, run the presidential office and attended most of Mr. Sadat's international discussions on Middle East policy. He controls the intelligence services and Egypt's rearmament program and is secretary general of the ruling National Democratic Party.

Born in 1928 in the Nile Delta province of Minufiya, where Mr. Sadat was also born, Mr. Mubarak graduated from the air force academy as a fighter pilot and continued his training in the Soviet Union.

In 1969, at the early age of 41, he was appointed Chief of Staff of the air force and in 1972 became its commander. He was largely credited with the successful performance of the Egyptian Air Force in the early days of the October 1973 war with Israel.

When President Sadat appointed Mr. Mubarak Vice President, he said: "We want a new generation to step forward to the country's leadership. We want this generation to express the spirit of Oct. 6."

Those who know Mr. Mubarak describe him as cautiously ambitious, an efficient organizer and a voracious reader. His name has been free of the rumors of corruption that often surround high officials in Egypt. He lives modestly in small vice presidential

villa in the Cairo suburb of Heliopolis and enjoys playing squash and hockey.

He is married and has two grown sons. His wife, Suzy, has a degree in anthropology from the American University in Cairo and heads a community project that helps poor families in the Cairo slum of Bulaq.

Until now, Mr. Mubarak has been the butt of popular jokes in Egypt, pictured as a smiling and silent nonentity at the right hand of the President. But his taciturnity has been viewed by some as a survival tactic in a country where overly popular military figures are often quickly shuffled off to posts away from the centers of power.

Sufi Abu Taleb

Special to The New York Times

CAIRO, Oct. 6 — Sufi Abu Taleb, who will be acting President of Egypt for the next two months, is a former president of Cairo University and was a key member of President Sadat's team that negotiated a peace treaty with Israel.

He was elected Speaker of the Egyptian Parliament in November 1978 and customarily introduced the President with warm praise before Mr. Sadat's numerous addresses to it.

Born in 1925 in Fayum in an agricultural region south of Cairo, Mr. Abu Taleb graduated from Cairo University Law School and obtained further law degrees from the Sorbonne in Paris.

He was a member of the Arab Socialist Union, President Nasser's ruling party, but after disagreeing with Nasser's policies went abroad for three years, from 1969 to 1972.

An advocate of "democratic socialism," a political ideology he says is based on Arab and Islamic theories, he helped found the ruling National Democratic Party, which Mr. Sadat created in July 1978.

Heavyset and jocular, Mr. Abu Taleb has been married since 1948 to Rafahia al-Otaibi. They have four chil-

dren. He enjoys reading historical and political works; his favorite light reading is Agatha Christie. His brother, Ahmed Abu Taleb, is chief of the Egyptian Tourist Police.

"All the News That's Fit to Print"

The New York Times

LATE CITY EDITION

Weather: Increasing cloudiness today; rain likely tonight, tomorrow. Temperature range: today 29-40; yesterday 28-38. Details, page C21.

VOL. CXXXI . . . No. 45,162

NEW YORK, MONDAY, DECEMBER 14, 1981

30 cents beyond 50-mile zone from New York City. Higher in air delivery cities.

25 CENTS

POLAND RESTRICTS CIVIL AND UNION RIGHTS; SOLIDARITY ACTIVISTS URGE GENERAL STRIKE

Judge Reduces Westway Suits To Single Issue

Landfill's Effect on Fish Still to Be Considered

By ROBIN HERMAN

A Federal judge has whittled down the longstanding legal attacks on the Westway highway project to a single issue — the fate of fish in the Hudson River — and he will set a hearing date today for arguments on that obstacle.

The judge, Thomas F. Griesa of Federal District Court in Manhattan, has dismissed all objections to the highway contained in two remaining lawsuits except for questions on the effect the landfill for the project would have on aquatic life.

John Marino, the state's Assistant Transportation Commissioner for New York City, said that the judge's action was "a very positive development" and that it reflected the Carey administration's interest in seeing the highway built.

As for environmentalists' concern about aquatic life — especially striped bass — Mr. Marino said yesterday: "When was the last time you had striped bass from the Hudson? That's our comment on it. I don't expect that in the end this will be a serious issue. The way is clear for Westway. It's a go-ahead."

Most Objections Dismissed

The judge, meeting in private on Friday with both the plaintiffs and the state and Federal defendants, dismissed altogether a suit brought in 1974 by Action for Rational Transit, an anti-Westway group, which was attempting to block the project. The suit contended chiefly that the highway would violate Federal clean-air standards.

Also, according to both sides, Judge Griesa dismissed most objections made in a 1977 suit brought by the Sierra Club and other environmental and civic groups. That suit challenged the dredge-and-fill permit for the project granted by the Army Corps of Engineers.

The suit charged that the Government had not adequately examined alternative routes, the trade-in of the Federal Westway funds for mass-transit funds or the possibility that the landfill on which the highway would be built could threaten New Jersey with flooding. It also questioned whether the river's aquatic life had been considered in the environmental impact statement. The highway's official cost is $1.7 billion, but it is expected to exceed that figure by millions of dollars.

After a hearing, possibly next month, on the aquatic-life question, Judge Griesa has said he will issue a written decision on all claims. At that time, the two groups of plaintiffs can appeal the earlier dismissals, which the judge made orally.

Albert Butzel, the lawyer representing the Sierra Club, said yesterday that,

Continued on Page B10, Column 3

HAIG WARNS SOVIET

He Says U.S. Is 'Seriously Concerned' and Backs New Warsaw Talks

By BERNARD GWERTZMAN

Special to The New York Times

BRUSSELS, Dec. 13 — Secretary of State Alexander M. Haig Jr. said today that the United States was "seriously concerned" about the imposition of martial law in Poland, and he renewed the West's warning to the Soviet Union not to interfere in the crisis.

After talking by phone with President Reagan, who was then at Camp David, Md., Mr. Haig said at a news conference here that the United States was urging

News conference excerpts, page A19.

the Polish Government to resume negotiations and to pursue a policy of compromise with the Solidarity trade union to prevent an outbreak of civil strife that could worsen the situation.

Mr. Haig said Polish authorities had assured the United States Embassy this morning that "there will be no return" to the situation that existed in Poland prior to establishment of the independent union in 1980. In addition, he said Western intelligence agencies had not detected any Soviet military moves "which would be a source of alarm."

"But we continue to watch the situation very carefully," he said.

'Very Serious' Consequences

If the Soviet Union intervened in Poland, Mr. Haig said, "the consequences would be very serious and long lasting." Western officials have previously said that, in that event, all trade with the Soviet Union would be suspended and political relations would be sharply curtailed.

President Reagan, arriving back at the White House, was asked about the danger of Soviet intervention and said that the United States had several times "made it plain how seriously we would view interference" by the Soviet Union. The Polish Ambassador and the Soviet Deputy Chief of Mission were summoned to the State Department for discussions on the situation. [Page A15.]

Mr. Haig was scheduled to leave Brussels this morning for a seven-day trip to Israel, Turkey, Pakistan, India, Egypt and Morocco. But after talking by phone with Vice President Bush and with various foreign ministers, Mr. Haig decided at the last minute to scrap his travel plans. Reporters traveling with him

Continued on Page A19, Column 4

Sipa Press / Black Star

Police in Wroclaw surround the Solidarity offices and keep crowds away. Photo was made from inside the building. Wroclaw, formerly Breslau, is an industrial city 190 miles southwest of Warsaw, near the Czechoslovak border.

WALESA NEGOTIATES

New Army Council Bans Rallies and Sets Wide Grounds for Arrests

By JOHN DARNTON

Special to The New York Times

WARSAW, Dec. 13 — Poland's new military leaders issued a decree of martial law today, drastically restricting civil rights and suspending the operations of the Solidarity union. The union's activists reacted with an appeal for an immediate general strike to protest.

A proclamation broadcast by the newly formed Martial Council for National Redemption, now the top authority in the country, also banned all kinds

Premier's address, page A16.

of public gatherings and demonstrations and ordered the internment of citizens whose loyalty to the state was under "justified suspicion."

The military rule was announced in a dramatic broadcast at dawn by Gen. Wojciech Jaruzelski, the Prime Minister and Communist Party leader, who said a strict regime was necessary to save Poland from catastrophe and civil war. Hours before, Solidarity leaders meeting in Gdansk had proposed holding a national referendum on forming a non-Communist government.

No Reports of Violence

Following a provision in the constitution, General Jaruzelski, declared a "state of war," equivalent to a state of emergency in other countries.

There were no immediate reports of any violence, but opposition to the military move seemed in the offing. Union activists, in dozens of leaflets being circulated in the streets, called for an immediate general strike.

Many Solidarity activists were in detention following coordinated police raids across the country after midnight last night. So were several former leaders of Poland's Communist Party.

Among the detained were some of the top leaders and advisers of the Solidarity union who had assembled in Gdansk to work out strategy in the latest confrontation with the Government.

Walesa Flown to Warsaw

Lech Walesa, Solidarity's chairman, who became an international figure by his role in the workers' uprising of last summer, was meeting with Government officials at a site outside Warsaw today, Jerzy Urban, a Government spokesman, said at a news conference.

Mr. Walesa was flown to Warsaw in a Government plane at 4 A.M. to begin talks with Stanislaw Ciosek, the Minister of Trade Union Affairs, according to the Interpress information agency. Mr. Urban said that Mr. Walesa had not been detained at any point.

Mr. Urban also stressed that Soli-

Continued on Page A16, Column 1

Communism and Better Life: Poles Found Wait Too Long

John Darnton, who has been chief of The New York Times bureau in Warsaw since September 1979, reports in the following article on the problems underlying the crisis in Poland.

Special to The New York Times

WARSAW — Behind the workers' revolt that began with strikes in the summer of 1980 and grew to a revolution on the shoulders of the Solidarity union, the operation of which was suspended when martial law was declared, lies a story of failure. It is the failure of Communism, in the eyes of the workers, to deliver on its promise of a better life.

The revolt sprang from an unspoken consensus among Poles that despite more than three decades of sacrifice and toil, conditions of everyday life were scarcely improving and that the Communist system had failed most dramatically in precisely those areas, in the realm of social welfare, where its ideology called for greater exertion and improvement.

Appalling dirt and safety conditions in factories, cramped and unavailiable apartments, substandard and sloppy health care, lines in front of meat shops — food shortages in general despite a stringent rationing system — these were the distingushing traits of what the Government referred to as "people's Poland." They were glossed over, ignored or denied by successive governments that pressed instead for higher production statistics in heavy industry.

They certainly did not keep pace with expectations and, compared with the West, which more and more Poles were visiting when restrictions were loosened as the cold war period came to a close, Poland was failing behind.

'My Life Doesn't Count'

"All my adult life I've been told that my life doesn't count, that I'm sacrificing myself for my children," said one well-known Polish journalist, speaking privately. "Well, now I'm 48. My son is 19. His life is no better than mine and he's being told he must sacrifice himself for his children. What's life all about, anyway?"

Satisfying the basic needs of the population was given low priority when it came to allocating investment in the national budget, but it was given lip service in public propaganda and high-

Continued on Page A18, Column 1

Army's Rule: Two Targets

General Hits at Foes In Party and Solidarity

By DAVID BINDER

Special to The New York Times

News Analysis

WASHINGTON, Dec. 13 — Poland's soldier-leader, Wojciech Jaruzelski, has struck at what he perceives as the two main roots of his country's current troubles: the radical "confrontationists" of the Solidarity labor movement and the still influential members of the Communist Party's old guard.

His martial law decree, accompanied by the detention of Solidarity leaders and former party leaders and an internal communications blackout, has eliminated the cadres and the instruments that might have been used to rally supporters against his rule.

A 56,000-Member Force

The state of emergency was long in the making, in the estimate of Administration specialists on Polish affairs, and was foreshadowed not only by large-scale maneuvers of Soviet troops on Poland's borders earlier in the year, but also by the brief mobilization of the Polish Internal Defense Forces last September.

The Internal Defense Forces are heavily equipped paramilitary security troops with 56,000 members. They are trained for riot control, and are deployed in three contingents, one in War-

Continued on Page A18, Column 1

Budget Cuts, Weak Market Hurt Gasohol

By DOUGLAS MARTIN

Special to The New York Times

DES MOINES — Interest in gasohol, which has attracted more Government encouragement in recent years than any other energy source, has been fading — the result of an oversupply of crude oil and the Administration's efforts to curb Federal spending.

Enthusiasm for gasohol, a mixture of gasoline and alcohol, was born amid farmers' anger over the restrictions on grain sales to the Soviet Union and consumers' concern about the shutdown of Iran's oil fields. The fuel seemed a way for America to cultivate its way out of the energy crisis, drawing on this nation's unrivaled agricultural strength. Most commercial gasohol is a 90-10 mixture of refined gasoline and ethanol derived from corn.

Pledge of Subsidies

The Carter Administration and Congress responded to the apparent groundswell by pledging subsidies for gasohol exceeding $30 billion by 1992, making it, gallon for gallon, by far the most heavily subsidized fuel.

But over the past few months, the White House has moved vigorously to slash funding for gasohol plants, large

Continued on Page D5, Column 5

The New York Times / Dith Pran

Demonstrators marching past the Polish Consulate on 37th Street near Madison Avenue. Similar protests against the military takeover in Poland were held in Paris, Vienna, London, Rome, Brussels and other European cities.

Biotechnology: Better Breeds and Crops

By HAROLD M. SCHMECK Jr.

The first major products from the young industry using the techniques of gene-splicing are expected to go on world markets next year, a development that some experts believe will usher in a new era in the prevention and treatment of disease.

Agriculture will probably be the first to benefit from such products, including vaccines against foot-and-mouth disease and scours, two economically serious diseases that afflict cattle.

Two important medical products now undergoing extensive clinical tests are expected to follow, probably in 1983 in the United States: human insulin and human growth hormone produced in bacteria that have been adapted for the purpose by gene-splicing techniques. Animal growth hormone produced by the same techniques is also being developed for agricultural use.

The predicted uses of gene-splicing techniques include such diverse products as industrial enzymes, food additives, medical and veterinary test chemicals and drugs, as well as improved plant species.

The long-range potential uses for the chemical, mining, energy and forest products industries, and for agriculture, dwarf all the prospective uses for medicine. Except for products related to health and food, however, the emergence of competitive major industrial

Continued on Page D13, Column 1

The New Genetics

Biology at a Turning Point

Second of three articles.

Other Developments

Warsaw mood — Every hour on the hour beginning at 6 A.M., Poles listening to their radios heard Prime Minister Wojciech Jaruzelski speak in solemn tones about having placed the country under martial law. The interludes were filled with music. More cars were on the streets than is usual for a Sunday, particularly in a period of acute gasoline shortage. All telephones had stopped functioning, presumably to keep those who might wish to resist from coordinating actions. Page A17.

Washington concern — The Reagan Administration called in the Polish Ambassador and the Soviet Deputy Chief of Mission for discussions. Several allied diplomats were also called to the State Department. President Reagan returned ahead of schedule from a weekend at Camp David to be briefed on Poland by Administation officials. Page A15.

Soviet silence — The Soviet Union made no official comment on the declaration of martial law in Poland. The Polish developments were reported in a series of brief and largely factual dispatches by the official news agency Tass. Page A19.

Papal appeal — Pope Paul John II asked his fellow Poles to pray for peace and to do everything in their power "to peacefully build a peaceful future." Page A14.

German reaction — Chancellor Helmut Schmidt of West Germany, visiting a small East German town, seemed intent on demonstrating through his presence that there was no reason for the West to dramatize the situation in Poland. Page A20.

Polish-American reaction — Tens of thousands of Polish-Americans across the nation voiced outrage and despair. In the New York metropolitan area and in Chicago, Philadelphia and other centers of Polish-American life, the outpouring was emotional but nonviolent as workers, scholars, writers, clergymen and diplomats spoke of their homeland. With a communications blackout severing their contacts with friends and relatives in Poland, there was also widespread concern over loved ones and acquaintances. Page A17.

INSIDE

U.S. Wins Davis Cup

John McEnroe defeated José-Luis Clerc in five sets to give the United States a victory over Argentina in the final of the Davis Cup. Page C1.

Sakharovs: Weak but Elated

The Soviet dissident Andrei D. Sakharov and his wife were said to be emaciated but in high spirits at the success of their hunger strike. Page A3.

Poland Curbs Civil Rights; Activists Ask General Strike

Continued From Page 1

darity had been suspended, not banned altogether.

He said the Soviet Union was aware that Poland was about to mount a military operation, stating, "It's hard to imagine that Poland's allies were not informed of such an action."

General Jaruszelski also announced that several former officials had been "interned" because they were "responsible personally for pushing the country into crisis" by their policies in the 1970's and had been guilty of "abusing their posts for personal profit." He specifically mentioned Edward Gierek, the party chief who was ousted in September 1980, Piotr Jaroszewicz, his longtime Prime Minister, Zladislaw Grudzien, a former party leader from Katowice, and Jerzy Lucasziewicz, a former Politburo member in charge of party propaganda.

Corruption Alienated Public

The abuse of power and corruption were among the reasons for the loss of public confidence in the party and Government. The announcement of the internment was seen as an attempt to gain some support for the military takeover.

The Government moves came hours after the Solidarity leaders meeting in Gdansk had proposed a nationwide referendum on setting up a non-Communist Government and defining Poland's military relationship with the Soviet Union.

The union leaders, assembled at the Lenin Shipyard where their independent labor movement was born 16 months ago, said that, unless the Government met a series of demands, the union would conduct its own national referendum asking four questions:

Are you for a vote of confidence in General Jaruzelski?

Are you for the establishment of a temporary government and free elections?

Are you for providing military guarantees to the Soviet Union in Poland?

Can the Polish Communist Party be the instrument of such guarantees in the name of the whole society?

Union Headquarters Surrounded

Political sources pointed out yesterday that the mere threat by Solidarity to hold such a referendum on its own could be unacceptable to the Government. Why it made the threat is unknown, but in recent weeks there have been signs that Mr. Walesa's control over the union membership has been weakened. There had been more frequent challenges to his leadership from more militant factions within the union.

Within hours after the meeting in Gdansk, Polish troops surrounded the union's headquarters in Warsaw.

Mr. Urban, the Government spokesman, said the events of the last 24 hours had prompted scattered transport strikes around the country but that the bus and trolley workers had returned to their jobs everywhere except in Cracow.

The situation around the country, where most internal and external communications have been severed, remained unclear. The capital was calm and the downtown area was nearly deserted by late this afternoon, as thousands of motorists left, passing through military checkpoints and past armored cars parked at strategic intersections. Soldiers patroling the streets and bridges in pairs had bayonets fixed on their rifles.

Poster Calls for a Strike

A handscrawled red and white poster reading "Strajk Generalny," or "General Strike," with today's date, hung on the front door of the five-story former school building that houses the Solidarity chapter in Warsaw. The headquarters was stormed early this morning by policemen who seized 32 people inside, according to a Solidarity worker.

The police returned later today, again in force, wearing plastic riot helmets and carrying riot sticks, to raid the headquarters again. This time they took files, documents, cash and equipment, while an angry crowd of several hundred looked on, jeering and yelling "Gestapo!" The police at one point used a fire hose to disperse the crowd, which quickly gathered again as soon as the policemen had departed.

The measures announced in the proclamation from the new Martial Council were sweeping. They were read out over television by the usual announcers newly dressed for the occasion in military uniforms. The measures grew in number as the day wore on. By nightfall, there were 61 separate points.

All Strikes and Protests Banned

All strikes, demonstrations, protests, meetings and public gatherings other than those for religious services were bannned. A curfew from 10 P.M. to 6 A.M. was imposed. The country's airspace was closed to international and domestic commercial flights, the borders were virtually sealed and Poles were told not to travel to border regions.

Western diplomats and foreign correspondents were informed that they could not travel outside Warsaw. The sale of gasoline to private motorists was prohibited. Dissemination of any publications without prior approval of the authorities was made a punishable offense.

Censorship of mail and other communications was legalized. The proclamation also granted the authorities the right to make preventive detention arrests of those "whose behavior in the past gives rise to the justified suspicion that, if left free, they would not observe the legal order or that they would engage in activity that threatens the interest, security or defense of the state."

Poles were ordered to carry their identification cards at all times.

Regional Broadcasts Suspended

In a move to control the vital centers of mass communication, all regional radio and television broadcasts were suspended, so that only programs originating from Warsaw could be aired. Over half a dozen public service sectors, ranging from transport to post offices and electric power stations, were placed directly under the military, apparently rendering the employees subject to a military-type command structure. Orders from superiors are equivalent to "military orders during a war," the radio said.

The decree also stated that "contributions" by citizens would be required. Persons between the ages of 16 and 60, it said, "may have to carry out at any time various kinds of ad hoc, unpaid work for a period up to seven days" in connection with "the needs of the state's defense."

A tape of General Jaruzelski's broadcast was played over television throughout the day. He sat stiffly, staring into the camera without his customary dark glasses, next to emblems of patriotism, a shield depicting the Polish eagle and the flag. He declared that what had been done was for the good of the nation.

Poland had reached "the limits of mental endurance," he said. Catastrophe was "not days, but hours" away. History would judge the momentous steps being undertaken to save the country from disintegration at the hands of extremists and "adventurists." Not to have acted would have been "a crime," he declared.

The general insisted that the military's assumption of power was not a military coup or installation of a military dictatorship. The constitutional organs of state will continue to function, he said, and the Martial Council "will be dissolved once the rule of law is re-established."

'Mortal Danger' to Nation Cited

The military council's proclamation, plastered along with movie posters on walls and concrete pillars lining downtown shopping arcades, insisted that the move had been undertaken to save the country from "mortal danger."

"Forces hostile to socialism" have brought the society to the brink of civil war and "anarchy, lawlessness and chaos," it said. A reactionary coup was openly being prepared, it asserted.

Bystanders who stopped beside dirty snowbanks to read such statements were sometimes handed leaflets by union men. "The attack on our union is aimed at its liquidation," said one, signed by the Solidarity chapter at the Ursus tractor factory. "Do not let them smash our Solidarity."

Public reaction, except among the crowd drawn to the union headquarters, was difficult to gauge. Many people seemed to fear that the move by the Government was a prelude to bloodshed. Monday, when the factories open, will be critical, many said.

"It won't stop here," said a grandmother pulling a young child on a sled. "Solidarity won't accept it and so there's real trouble ahead. For the first time, I'm afraid."

The union had laid plans for a huge demonstration at Victory Square in downtown Warsaw on Thursday. It was to be part of a "national day of protest" that the Warsaw chapter had called out of anger over what it denounced as the Government's confrontational policies. The protest was officially endorsed by the entire union leadership.

Travelers from Gdansk said that several union leaders had been taken by the police from their hotel rooms after the session in the Lenin Shipyard ended shortly after midnight. The only inkling that something was wrong was a statement by Mr. Walesa that communications were down. The arrests started about two hours later.

Troops were stationed on the roofs of buildings surrounding the Hotel Monopol as union members were taken away in a bus. A Government official said that altogether 17 people had been taken into custody in Gdansk.

The travelers said they had passed a column of about 55 modern T-72 tanks crossing the road at Paslek, about 40 miles south of Gdansk. The tanks were fully equipped for battle, with spare gasoline tanks at the backs.

ABC News

A Polish Army armored personnel carrier on patrol in Warsaw, where troops were positioned throughout the city.

Archbishop Bids Poles Refrain From Violence

LONDON, Dec. 13 (Reuters) — Poland's Roman Catholic Primate, Archbishop Jozef Glemp, appealed to the Polish people today not to resort to violence against what he called the current infringement of civil and human rights, according to the Warsaw radio.

Archbishop Glemp took over as primate earlier this year following the death of Stefan Cardinal Wyszynski. He has played a leading role in talks with the Government and the Solidarity union's leader, Lech Walesa, in an attempt to settle the Polish crisis.

Referring to the imposition of martial law and the suspension of a wide range of civil liberties, the Archbishop pleaded that Poles not start fighting one another. "Every pair of hands will be needed" to rebuild Poland once martial law has ended, he said.

Archbishop Glemp's remarks in a sermon at the Jesuit church in Warsaw were broadcast by the radio and were monitored in London.

Transcript of Polish Premier's Radio Address on Declaration of Martial Law

WARSAW, Dec. 13 (AP) — Following is a transcript of the radio address today by Gen. Wojciech Jaruzelski, Poland's Prime Minister and Communist Party leader, as transcribed and translated from the Polish by The Associated Press:

Citizens of the Polish People's Republic, I address you today as a soldier, as the chief of the Polish Government. I address you on the most important matters.

Our country is on the edge of the abyss. Achievements of many generations, raised from the ashes, are collapsing into ruin. State structures no longer function. New blows are struck each day at our flickering economy. Living conditions are burdening people more and more.

Through each place of work, many Polish people's homes, there is a line of painful division. The atmosphere of unending conflict, misunderstanding and hatred sows mental devastation and damages the tradition of tolerance.

Strikes, strike alerts, protest actions have become standard. Even students are dragged into it.

Last night, many public institutions were occupied. There are calls for physical debate with "Reds," with people of different opinions. There are more and more examples of terror, threats, moral lynching and direct assaults. Crimes, robberies and break-ins are spreading like a wave through the country. Fortunes of millions are being made by the sharks of the economic underground.

Chaos and demoralization have reached the level of defeat. The nation has reached the borderline of mental endurance, many people are desperate. Now, not days but hours separate us from a nationwide catastrophe. Honesty demands a question: Must it come to that?

ABC News

Gen. Wojciech Jaruzelski, the Prime Minister and Communist Party leader, seen during television broadcast explaining the decree of martial law.

What Nation's Leaders Have Done

When accepting the post of Prime Minister, I believed that we can rise up by ourselves. Have we done everything to stop the spiral of crisis? History will estimate our work. We did not avoid the blunders and we can draw conclusions from that. First of all, the past months were very busy for the Government. It was fighting with the difficulties and unfortunately the national economy was converted into an area of political fighting. The conscious torpedoing of Government efforts prevents the effects from corresponding with the effort.

With our aims, it cannot be said that we did not show good will, moderation, patience, and sometimes there was probably too much of it. It cannot be said the Government did not honor the social agreements. We even went further. The initiative of the great national understanding was backed by the millions of Poles. It created a chance, an opportunity to deepen the system of democracy, of people ruling the country, widening the reforms. Those hopes failed.

Solidarity Is Criticized

Around the negotiating table there was no leadership from Solidarity. Words said in Radom and in Gdansk showed the real aims of its leadership. These aims are confirmed by everyday practice, growing aggressiveness of the extremists, clearly aiming to take apart the Polish state system.

How long can one wait for a sobering up? How long can a hand reached for accord meet a fist? I say this with a broken heart, with bitterness. It could have been different in our country. It should have been different. But if the current state had lasted longer it would have led to a catastrophe, to absolute chaos, to powerty and starvation.

And a severe winter could multiply the losses, cause casualties especially among the weakest, whom we want to protct the most. In this situation, doing nothing would have been a crime against the nation. We have to say stop, it is enough and we have to block the path of confrontation which was openly declared by the leaders of Solidarity.

Time for Action

We have to declare today, when we know the forthcoming day of mass political demonstrations, including the ones in the center of Warsaw called in connection with the anniversary of the December events — that tragedy cannot be repeated. It must not. We cannot let these demonstrations be a spark causing a fire in the country.

The self-preservation instinct of the nation must be taken into account. We must bind the hands of adventurers before they push the country into civil war. Citizens of Poland, heavy is the burden of responsiblity which lies upon me at this very dramatic moment in Polish history. But it is my duty to take it, because it concerns the future of Poland for which my generals fought on all the fronts of the Second World War and gave the best years of their lives.

I declare that today the Martial Council for National Redemption has been constituted, and the Council of State obeying the Polish Constitution declared a state of emergency at midnight on the territory of Poland.

I want everybody to understand my motives and aims for action. We do not aim at a military takeover, a military dictatorship. The nation is strong and wise enough to develop a democratic system of socialist government. And in such a system, military forces could stay where their place is. None of Poland's problems can be solved by force.

The Martial Council for National Redemption is not a substitute for the constitutional government. Its only task is to protect law in the country, to guarantee re-establishment of order and discipline. That is the way to start coming out of the crisis, to save the country from collapsing. The committee for the country's defense nominated army military commissars on every level of state administration and in certain economic units.

They are granted a law for supervising the activity of the state administrative organs from the ministry down to the local government level. The declaration of the Martial Council for National Redemption and other decrees published today define the terms and standards of public order for the duration of the state of emergency. The military council would be disbanded when law governs the country and when the conditions for the functioning of civilian administration and representative bodies are created. As the situation stabilizes itself gradually, the limits on freedom in public life will be overrulled. But nobody can count on weakness or indecision.

In the name of national interests, a group of people threatening the safety of the country has been interned. The extremists of Solidarity are included in this group as well as other members of illegal organizations.

On the demand of the military council, several people responsible personally for pushing the country into the crisis during the 1970's and abusing the posts for personal profit have been interned. Among them are Edward Gierek, Piotr Jaroszewicz, Zdzislaw Grudzien, Jerzy Lukaszewicz, Jan Szydlak, Tadeusz Wrzaszczyk and others. The full list will be published. We will consequently clean Polish life from evil no matter where it arises.

Looking to the Country's Future

Despite all the failures and mistakes we made, the party is still the leading and creative force in the process of changes to fulfill its mission sufficiently and cooperate with the allies. To achieve this it must lean on honest, modest and brave people, on those who deserve the name of fighter for social justice in every environment. This will decide the party's authority in society.

This is its perspective. We shall clean up the everlasting sources of our ideals from deformations and deviations. We shall protect universal values of socialism, enriching it with our national elements and tradition. This way the socialist ideals will come closer to the majority of the population, nonparty members, the younger generation and the healthy workers trend in Solidarity, which will move away from the prophets of confrontation by its own strength and its own interest.

This is how we understand the idea of national accord. We sustain it as we respect differences of views. We appreciate the patriotic support of the church. There is a superior goal uniting all thinking and responsible Poles — love of their country, the necessity to secure independence gained with such difficulty, respect to one's own country. This is the strongest foundation of accord.

Citizens of Poland — as there is no turning back from socialism, there is no turning back to the false methods and practices from before August 1980. Steps being taken today serve the preservation of basic features of socialist renewal. All the reforms will be continued in the atmosphere of order, businesslike discussion and discipline. This also refers to the economic reform.

I do not want to make promises. A difficult period is ahead of us. To make tomorrow better, we must recognize the hard realities of today. We must understand the need to make sacrifices.

There is one thing I would like to achieve — peace. This is the fundamental condition from which a better future should begin. We are a sovereign country, so we must get out of this crisis by ourselves. We must remove the danger with our own hands. History would never forgive the present generation for wasting this chance.

We must stop further degradation of Poland's international position. This country, with 36 million people in the heart of Europe, cannot indefinitely be in a humiliating position as a petitioner. We cannot allow ourselves not to notice that detracting opinions about the republic "standing on disorder" are reviving again. We must do everything to put them away to the storeroom of history. At this difficult moment I turn to our socialist allies and friends. We value their confidence and constant help. The Polish-Soviet alliance is and will be the cornerstone of the Polish raison d'état and the guarantee of inviolability of our borders. Poland is and will be a firm link of the Warsaw Pact, an unfailing member of the socialist community.

I address our partners in other countries with whom we want to develop good and friendly relations. I address the whole world. We appeal for understanding of the extraordinary conditions that developed in Poland and of the extraordinary measures which proved to be necessary.

Our actions do not endanger anybody. They are aimed at one thing: the removal of internal threats and by that preventing any danger to peace and international cooperation. We are going to keep the agreements we reached. We wish the word Poland would always evoke respect and sympathy in Europe and the whole world.

Appeals to Poles of All Positions

Poles, brothers and sisters: I address all of you as a soldier who remembers well the cruelty of war. Let's not allow a drop of Polish blood to flow in this tormented country which experienced so many defeats and suffering. Let's restrain the phantom of civil war, let's not erect barricades where a bridge is needed.

I turn to you, Polish workers. For the sake of the fatherland, renounce your inalienable right to strike for such a period as will prove necessary for overcoming the most acute difficulties. We must do everything that the fruit of our hard work is not wasted.

I turn to you, brother peasants. Do not allow your fellow countrymen to starve. Take care of the Polish soil so it can feed us all.

I turn to you, citizens of the older generation. Save from oblivion the truth about the years of war, about the difficult times of reconstruction. Hand it over to your sons and grandchildren, hand them over your ardent patriotism, your readiness to make sacrifices for the benefit of the fatherland.

I turn to you, Polish mothers, wives and sisters. Make all efforts that in Polish families no more tears are shed.

I turn to young Poles. Display civil maturity and deep reflection about your own future, the future of the fatherland.

I turn to you teachers, creators of science and culture, engineers and physicians, writers. Let reason win at this dangerous turn of history over excited emotions, an intellectual interpretation of patriotism over seductive myths.

I turn to you, soldiers of the Polish Army, those on active duty and reservists. be faithful to your oath you made to your fatherland, for better or for worse. On your attitude today the fate of the fatherland depends.

I turn to you, members of the people's militia and the security service. Guard the state against the enemy and the working people against lawlessness and violence.

I turn to all citizens. The hour of hard trial has come. We must meet this challenge, prove that we are worthy of Poland.

Fellow countrymen, before the whole world I want to repeat these immortal words: Poland is not yet lost as long as we live.

"All the News That's Fit to Print"

The New York Times

LATE CITY EDITION

Weather: Windy and cold, chance of flurries today; clear, cold tonight. Temperature range: today 0-23; yesterday 22-31. Details are on page 22.

VOL.CXXXI . . . No. 45,188 | Copyright © 1982 The New York Times | NEW YORK, SATURDAY, JANUARY 9, 1982 | 30 cents beyond 50-mile zone from New York City. Higher in air delivery cities. | 25 CENTS

U.S. SETTLES PHONE SUIT, DROPS I.B.M. CASE; A.T.&T. TO SPLIT UP, TRANSFORMING INDUSTRY

NEW LAYOFFS PUSH U.S. JOBLESS RATE TO 8.9% FROM 8.4%

Impact in Heavy Industry Puts Level for Adult Males at a Post-World War II High

By SETH S. KING

Special to The New York Times

WASHINGTON, Jan. 8 — Layoffs of 460,000 workers in December pushed the nation's unemployment rate from 8.4 percent of the labor force to 8.9 percent, the second highest monthly level since the beginning of World War II. The number of unemployed Americans climbed to a nearly 9.5 million.

At the same time, the total number employed last month fell to 97,188,000, a decline of 840,000 from November, when the total fell 190,000 from the preceding month.

The Bureau of Labor Statistics reported today that the unemployment total, seasonally adjusted, was 9,462,000, an increase of half a percentage point above the November rate. The 8.9 percent rate for December was within a tenth of a percentage point of the postwar monthly high of 9 percent reached in May 1975 in the deepest recession of the postwar years.

Rate in Region Increased

The job market in New York and New Jersey showed some weakness last month, as the unemployment rate rose in both states. New York City's rate, which dropped sharply in November, moved upward again in December. [Page 13.]

The loss of jobs last month was particularly severe in basic durable goods manufacturing, where the unemployment rate rose to 11.8 percent, from 9.4 percent in November. There was further evidence of deepening recession in the jobless totals for virtually all of the bureau's statistical categories.

The unemployment rate for adult men jumped to 8 percent, a post-World War II high, from November's 7.2 percent. Labor economists consider this figure to be among the most significant in the bureau's reports because it indicates a high number of layoffs of family breadwinners in the vital goods-producing sector of the economy.

16.1% Level for Blacks

Dr. Janet L. Norwood, Commissioner of Labor Statistics, also noted that the number of people on payrolls declined by 300,000 in November. Unemployment among blacks rose to 16.1 percent, one of the highest rates on record, she said, from November's 15.5 percent.

The number of unemployed workers in December was almost two million above the level in July, when private economists say the current recession began. The jobless rate for automobile

Continued on Page 13, Column 1

U.S. Drops Rule On Tax Penalty For Racial Bias

By STUART TAYLOR Jr.

Special to The New York Times

WASHINGTON, Jan. 8 — The Reagan Administration, reversing an 11-year-old Federal policy, announced today that it would no longer deny tax-exempt status to private schools, colleges and certain other nonprofit institutions that practice racial discrimination.

The decision on the interpretation of the tax laws will apparently entitle more than 100 schools and other organizations whose tax exemptions were revoked in the last decade to receive favorable tax treatment as charitable organizations. It is also expected to open the door to tax exemptions for many other private segregated schools that have never had them.

Justice and Treasury Department officials said that the reason for the policy change was that policies against racial discrimination should be enforced by Congress, not the tax authorities.

Reversal Since September

Allowing tax exemptions to racially discriminatory institutions is the opposite of the legal position the Justice Department took in the Supreme Court last September in a case involving a university and a school that had been denied tax exemptions for racially discriminatory admissions policies.

The department argued then that the Federal tax laws required the Government to deny tax exemptions to racially discriminatory organizations.

Today the Justice Department notified the Supreme Court that the Treasury Department had moved to reinstate the tax-exempt status of one of the two institutions in the case, Bob Jones University in Greenville, S.C., whose exemption was revoked in 1970, and to grant the tax-exempt status that had been denied to the other, Goldsboro Christian Schools in Goldsboro, N.C., which denies admission to blacks.

Religious Grounds Cited

Bob Jones University used to deny admission to all blacks and now bans interracial dating or marriage among its students, some of whom are black. Both of these fundamentalist Christian schools tie their racially restrictive policies to religious beliefs.

Civil liberties lawyers who had supported the Government's previous policy said today that they were appalled by the Administration's decision to reverse it and to allow what some called an indirect subsidy for racial discrimination. But representatives of the two schools that had battled the Govern-

Continued on Page 10, Column 6

William F. Baxter, Assistant Attorney General, above left, and Charles L. Brown, chairman of the American Telephone and Telegraph Company, at a Washington news conference on the settlement.

Thomas Barr, right, chief attorney for the International Business Machines Corporation, outside Federal court in New York after the Government dropped its antitrust suit.

The New York Times / George Tames; United Press International

COURT HEARING SET

$80 Billion Divestiture Is Required — Rises in Local Rates Seen

By ERNEST HOLSENDOLPH

Special to The New York Times

WASHINGTON, Jan. 8 — The American Telephone and Telegraph Company settled the Justice Department's antitrust lawsuit today by agreeing to give up the 22 Bell System companies that provide most of the nation's local telephone service.

On a landmark antitrust day, the Justice Department also dropped its marathon case against the International Business Machines Corporation, a suit

Excerpts from decree, page 36.

that had sought to break up the company that has dominated the computer industry. The Justice Department said the suit was "without merit and should be dismissed."

The A.T.& T. agreement, if finally approved by a Federal court, would be the largest and most significant antitrust settlement in decades. It is likely to be compared with the 1911 settlement that divided the Rockefeller family's Standard Oil Company into 33 subsidiaries, some of them huge oil companies in their own right.

Two-Thirds of Total Assets

The heart of the agreement requires A.T.& T. to give up all its wholly owned local telephone subsidiaries, which are worth $80 billion, or two-thirds of the company's total assets. That would radically alter a company that has accounted for more than 80 percent of the nation's telephone service, changing the course of the industry.

But A.T.& T. would be free to enter such previously prohibited fields as data processing, communications between computers and the sale of telephone and computer terminal equipment, all rapidly growing and a profitable aspect of the telecommunications industry. And it would retain its long-distance service.

In divesting itself of local telephone subsidiaries, it would be dropping the least profitable of its operations, accounting for about a third of its $6.9 billion in net income in the last fiscal year.

Disclosed at News Conference

"A.T.& T. is getting to keep its good businesses and is getting rid of the less attractive operations," said Winston E. Himsworth, a telecommunications analyst for Lehman Brothers.

The settlement was announced by the Justice Department's Assistant Attorney General in charge of the antitrust division, William F. Baxter, and by Charles L. Brown, chairman and chief executive officer of A.T.& T., at a news conference at the National Press Club.

District Court Judge Harold Greene, who is hearing the case here, announced late today that a hearing would be held at 2 P.M. Tuesday on the motion to drop the proceedings.

Although Mr. Baxter, Mr. Brown and most analysts said the agreement presaged increased competition in the tele-

Continued on Page 34, Column 1

RISE IN LOCAL RATES MAY COME RAPIDLY

Subsidy From Long-Distance Fees to End With Breakup

By LYDIA CHAVEZ

Consumers could . . a rapid increase in local telephone rates — possibly a doubling in certain parts of the country — and a decline in long-distance charges as a result of the Government's antitrust settlement with the American Telephone and Telegraph Company.

In the past, A.T.& T.'s long-distance rates have subsidized its local service. However, as a result of the settlement, local and long-distance services will be provided by separate companies.

Under the terms of the agreement, A.T.& T.'s 22 regional companies will become independent entities that must earn a profit from their local service charges.

Loss of Subsidy

"The long-distance subsidy will be gone, and obviously the local companies will be under a lot of pressure to raise prices," said Jay Grossman, a spokesman for A.T.& T. Local rates had already started to rise, as A.T.& T. and its regional companies began to try to bring the prices closer in line with costs.

"Over the last several years, the trend has been for prices to reflect the costs of local service, and this decision will hasten that trend," said Delbert C. Staley, president of New York Telephone, one of the companies. He said that prices here would probably have doubled in five years anyway.

Mr. Staley said that in New York the basic local charge is now about $10 a month, compared with the company's cost of $20.

Paul L. Gioia, chairman of the State Public Service Commission, declined to comment on how the antitrust settlement might affect prices.

"If the local operating companies

Continued on Page 35, Column 2

End of Action on I.B.M. Follows Erosion of Its Dominant Position

By BARNABY J. FEDER

The Justice Department announced yesterday that it had decided to drop an antitrust suit that it started almost 13 years ago in an effort to dismember the International Business Machines Corporation.

The move was widely anticipated. Recently numerous court decisions in antitrust complaints filed by competitors have favored I.B.M.

Also, decisions in private suits against the American Telephone and Telegraph Company and the Eastman Kodak Company weakened the Government's legal position in the I.B.M. case. And I.B.M.'s dominance of the computer industry has undergone general erosion since the case was filed.

The suit charged I.B.M. with monopolizing the general purpose computer market, consisting of companies that sold computer equipment, programming and services. The requested relief included breaking I.B.M. up into smaller companies.

Announcements of the ending of the suit came simultaneously at a 4 P.M. news conference in Washington called by William H. Baxter, an Assistant Attorney General who had spent six months reviewing the case, and in the Manhattan courtroom of David N. Edelstein, the Federal district judge who had presided over it. The Government said the case was "without merit and should be dismissed."

Computer analysts said the decision would not have a major impact on the computer industry, where I.B.M. is facing a growing challenge from Japanese computer makers and from American companies that make equipment that can operate with I.B.M.'s programs. I.B.M. and its competitors alike were said to have expected an outcome favorable to the company.

"This case didn't have a ghost of a chance," said Calvert D. Crary, a litigation specialist with the Wall Street firm of Bear, Stearns & Company.

The stipulation for dismissal stated that both sides would pay their own costs. The Reagan Administration reportedly has estimated that the case cost the Government as much as $13.4 million. I.B.M. has refused to disclose its cost, but it is believed to be several million dollars.

At the hearing in New York, Thomas Barr, I.B.M.'s chief lawyer, said, "This case led to the filing of many private antitrust actions." Noting that I.B.M. had gained favorable rulings from 16 Federal judges in various antitrust actions, he concluded, "I.B.M. has been completely vindicated."

Minor cases against the company are

Continued on Page 37, Column 1

Warsaw Rulers Put Toll of Dead at 17, Double Earlier Total

By BARBARA CROSSETTE

Special to The New York Times

WASHINGTON, Jan. 8 — Poland's military Government announced today that 17 people have died since the imposition of martial law, according to the Warsaw radio. The figure is more than double the number of deaths previously disclosed by the Government.

The disclosure of the official death toll — eight fatalities at the Wujek coal mine and nine in Gdansk — was part of a comprehensive report on events of the last month in Poland that was presented to a parliamentary commission today by Boguslaw Stachura, the Deputy Minister for Internal Affairs.

On Dec. 29 the Polish authorities announced a total of eight deaths in disturbances and strikes. On Jan. 2 a high-ranking party source was quoted in unofficial reports reaching the West as saying two others, including a policeman, had died.

In another development, a group of Polish intellectuals and cultural figures have told Gen. Wojciech Jaruzelski, the Polish leader, that there will be further bloodshed unless martial law is lifted, according to information arriving from Poland. The appeal was said to be contained in a document being circulated in Warsaw. [Page 6.]

In Warsaw, the Communist Party's

Continued on Page 7, Column 1

Associated Press

PROMOTED: Walter J. Stoessel Jr., a career diplomat, was named Deputy Secretary of State. Page 3.

A Communications Battle Ahead

By LEONARD SILK

News Analysis

The settlements by the Justice Department of two critical antitrust suits promise to accelerate the communications revolution in American and worldwide.

At the same time, the moves to deregulate the communications industry are likely to open up a battle royal among behemoths in the marketplace. The impact promises to be highly uneven on different customers — personal and business — and on the competitors for shares of the market in communications, data processing and the manufacture of equipment.

The twin moves, announced within hours of each other, represent the most dramatic actions thus far by the Reagan Administration to carry out its philosophy that the role of the Government in the marketplace should be shrunk severely, in the belief that competition, even among giant corporations, will best serve consumer interests by increasing efficiency and stimulating innovation.

Under the agreements, American Telephone and Telegraph Company will give up its local operating companies as part of a settlement ending a seven-year-old suit. And the Justice Department decided to drop its suit against the International Business Machines Corporation. The I.B.M. case is 13 years old.

Assistant Attorney General William F. Baxter conceded yesterday that "there is a sense in which the antitrust division is backing off" from policies of earlier administrations, but he contended that the law had been pushed in directions contrary to what he regarded as its proper values and goals.

In declaring that the I.B.M. case was "flimsy," Mr. Baxter appeared to be giving voice to the Administration's view that size alone should not be a consideration in antitrust matters.

However, since the consent decree is likely to involve major reallocations of costs and services, it almost certainly will have to run a gamut of challenges in the courts and in Congress. Business competitors, consumers and public utility commissions can appeal to the courts to set aside or modify the consent decree, if it is judged to be unfair. And Congress has the power to pass legislation blocking or modifying the actions of the Administration.

Nevertheless, it appears probable that, when the dust has settled, A.T.& T. will exist as a smaller, leaner and more profitable company, including its Long Lines division, the Western Electric Company and Bell Laboratories.

It will have divested itself of the relatively low-profit local operating companies, whose growth potential has been limited and whose efforts to generate adequate earnings have been, and are likely to continue to be, severely constrained by state utility regulators.

The end of cross-subsidization by Mother Bell to the operating companies almost certainly will mean much higher telephone bills for "ordinary" local customers, whose use of the telephone is largely limited to local calls. Approximately 30 percent of the cash flow from long-distance calls currently goes to local lines; that subsidy will stop if the consent decree stands.

But the remaining elements of A.T.& T. as a na-

Continued on Page 38, Column 5

INSIDE

Steel Import Talks Collapse

The Commerce Secretary said import negotiations with Europe had broken down; steelmakers plan complaints against foreign producers. Page 31.

Rothko Dealer to Surrender

Frank Lloyd, owner of the Marlborough Gallery, indicted in connection with sales of Mark Rothko's paintings, plans to surrender Monday. Page 15.

U.A.W. Agrees to Talks

The United Automobile Workers agreed to talks with Ford and General Motors that could cut pay and benefits in return for job guarantees. Page 8.

Brink's Suspect Arrested

A suspect in the Brink's holdup in Rockland County Oct. 20 and the murder of a policeman in Queens April 16 was seized in Philadelphia. Page 29.

Antitrust Landmarks: Men Who Helped Form Policy

Justice Department's Watchdog

William Francis Baxter

By ROBERT PEAR

Special to The New York Times

WASHINGTON, Jan. 8 — William Francis Baxter, an assistant Attorney General in charge of the antitrust division of the Justice Department, was on a skiing vacation in Utah until late this week. But from out West, he followed the last-minute, secret negotiations for a settlement of the historic antitrust case against the American Telephone and Telegraph Company.

Men in the News

A Justice Department attorney served as a courier, delivering documents to him in Utah. He was in constant contact with his office by telephone to check on the status of the case against the International Business Machines Corporation, which the Justice Department dropped today.

That ability to combine diverse activities illustrates the way in which Mr. Baxter practices the "efficiency" principles that he preaches as a conservative economist.

Redirection of Policy

The 52-year-old lawyer had been a professor at Stanford University Law School in California and came to Washington to preside over a fundamental redirection of Federal antitrust policy. The new policy is expressed in the slogan, expressed by Attorney General William French Smith: "Bigness in business does not necessarily mean badness." But that simple formula requires elaboration in a multitude of specific cases, and for that task, Mr. Baxter is well prepared.

Donald F. Turner, a former Harvard University professor who served as antitrust chief in the Johnson Administration, echoed the comments of many experts when he said that Mr. Baxter "has a very, very sharp analytical mind."

Mr. Baxter also has a stronger background in economics than many of his predecessors. "He learned differential calculus so he could understand the economic literature, much of which is incomprehensible to the layman," Mr. Turner said.

Mr. Baxter has much in common with the conservative Chicago school of economic theory. He has a deep dislike for the populist political and social doctrines that, according to some historians, have been an underlying theme of Federal antitrust policy since the Sherman Act of 1890.

Proponent of Efficiency

He rejects the view that "big is bad and small is beautiful." Instead, he emphasizes again and again the way in which antitrust laws — and even business mergers and acquisitions — can promote economic efficiency and spur output.

A soft-spoken, punctilious man with curly black hair and an urbane manner, Mr. Baxter seems to relish any opportunity to expound upon his ideas in response to questions, from either journalists or members of Congress.

"The thesis that large corporate size yields overweening political power" is not even "remotely true," Mr. Baxter told Congress in 1979. "Very large companies, far from being all-powerful in our economy, have become the most politically vulnerable scapegoats for problems whose complex origins include a heavy leavening of governmental error."

Before entering the Government, Mr. Baxter had been a consultant to many companies. His financial disclosure statement, filed with the Federal Office of Government Ethics, shows that he received fees last year from Levi Strauss & Company, Visa, the credit card organization, Fairchild Industries, the Crocker National Bank and the Northrop Corporation, among others.

Maintaining Independence

Even when he was a paid witness testifying on behalf of an industry, he displayed substantial intellectual independence. Likewise, from his office on the third floor of the Justice Department, he resisted efforts by the Secretary of Defense, Caspar W. Weinberger, and other Administration officials to have the A.T.& T. case dismissed.

"I intend to litigate it to the eyeballs," Mr. Baxter declared last April, adding, however, that he was "always interested in negotiating a settlement." The terms of the consent decree outlined today are remarkably similar to the terms that Mr. Baxter said he wanted last April.

He always indicated that he was less enthusiastic about the effort to break up the International Business Machines Corporation. In that case, he said, "the Government's theory was not clearly defined before it went into court" and the Government today did indeed agree to drop that case.

Mr. Baxter was born in New York City on July 13, 1929. His family moved to California in 1939 when his father went into the gold-mining business, dredging rivers in the northern part of the state. When his father went bankrupt a few years later, the young Baxter took jobs in lumber mills and mining camps.

Working summers in a variety of blue-collar jobs, he attended Stanford University, where he received a bachelor's degree in 1951 and a law degree in 1956. From 1951 to 1954, he was a navigation officer in the Navy. He taught at Stanford for more than 20 years.

Mr. Baxter was married in the early 1950's to Barbara Metzger, and they were divorced in the early 1970's. (He said he was not certain of the years.) They had three children, William F. Baxter, 27, Marcia Bearman, 26, and Stuart C. Baxter, 23.

Mr. Baxter now lives with Carol Treanor, a statistician and computer expert from Stanford University's Center for Advanced Study in the Behavioral Sciences. Mr. Baxter said he avoided remarriage for tax reasons: "It would cost us many thousands of dollars a year."

They live in a town house at Kalorama Square, in an elegant section of downtown Washington just off Connecticut Avenue. In his free time, Mr. Baxter likes to play tennis and golf.

He is the author of several books including "People or Penguins," which explored the trade-offs between environmental improvement and other social objectives.

Associated Press

William F. Baxter

Quiet Force at A.T.&T.

Charles Lee Brown

By LESLIE WAYNE

The New York Times/Fred R. Conrad

Charles L. Brown

Charles Lee Brown, chairman of the American Telephone and Telegraph Company, is described as a quiet, determined man who, over the last three years, has moved a highly entrenched bureaucratic corporation — the largest in the world — from the protective umbrella of regulation to a new era of competition.

"A.T.& T. has been forced to shift dramatically in a short time," said Donald S. MacNaughton, a former A.T.& T. director and chairman of the Hospital Corporation of America, in an interview yesterday.

"Instead of lying back and saying 'We're No. 1,' Mr. Brown saw the future was in competition and he had to fight people in the organization," Mr. MacNaughton said. "If he had barged in, loud and brassy, he would have ruffled feathers. But he's soft-spoken and very, very firm, verging on stubborn, and he won the support of the entire organization."

Yesterday, Mr. Brown also won some measure of peace when settlement was announced of a seven-year-old antitrust suit brought against A.T.& T. by the Justice Department. The settlement essentially requires that A.T.& T. divest itself of its local telephone companies — nearly two-thirds of its assets — in exchange for the freedom to enter unregulated areas, primarily the growing computer field.

Defining Ground Rules

Earlier, Mr. Brown had said that settlement of the suit would "be a load off my mind," finally defining A.T.& T.'s operating ground rules. "They," Mr. Brown has said of the Justice Department, "seem to think we've been unlawful almost since the day Mr. Bell invented the telephone."

The 60-year-old Mr. Brown is described as an introvert with a soft professorial air, but one who is also a fighter, quietly digging in his heels. "He's extremely able, quiet and self-possessed, patient and determined," a former A.T.& T. director Archie K. Davis, said yesterday. Mr. Davis is a director and former chairman of the Wachovia Bank and Trust Company.

Mr. Brown's quiet manner stands in sharp contrast to that of his predecessor, John D. deButts, a gregarious former Washington lobbyist for A.T.& T., who relished the public eye, snapping back at shareholders at annual meetings and making television commercials for his company.

But where Mr. deButts fought to retain A.T.& T.'s monopoly over the phone industry, Mr. Brown saw that technological advancements and changing Government attitudes would eventually pierce the wall of regulations that gave A.T.& T. dominance in the telecommunications industry. As a result, Mr. Brown sought to prepare A.T.& T. for the competition ahead and move the company toward acceptance of the fact that it will no longer monopolize the phone industry.

Organizing the Breakup

"Charlie Brown inherited a major disaster," said William G. McGowan, chairman of the rival MCI Corporation. "The whole house of cards was coming down. A.T.& T. had just been ignoring Government rulings and kept getting hit with antitrust violations. He's trying to resolve a terrible situation and he's done very good."

But the days ahead, as A.T.& T. begins the breakup of its operations, will be as difficult for Mr. Brown as the days past. "They will have to face this splitting-up," Mr. McGowan said, adding that such changes would be difficult for any organization, and even more difficult for "one not accustomed to change."

Twice, Mr. Brown reorganized A.T.& T. Both were among the most sweeping reorganizations in corporate history. Before he became chairman, Mr. Brown had realigned A.T.& T.'s bureaucracy of more than a million employees into three separate organizations divided along customer needs — home, business and national. Then, in 1980, after becoming chairman, Mr. Brown restructured the company again, this time into two parts: one to handle regulated activities such as local phone service and the other to enable A.T.& T. to enter unregulated fields, primarily in computer-related businesses.

And he pushed A.T.& T. to experiment with such new technologies as mobile telephones, glass-fiber transmission lines and voice-activated computers.

A Family Affair

A.T.& T. has provided employment for more than 30 years for Mr. Brown, and earlier, provided jobs for both his parents. His mother, the former Mary McNamara, was a telephone operator before her marriage. His father, Charles Lee Brown Sr., had a 37-year career with the phone company, working as a district traffic manager in the Long Lines division. Mr. Brown has held 23 positions during his rise to the top, necessitating 15 moves.

Mr. Brown was born on Aug. 23, 1921, in Richmond. While pursuing an engineering degree at the University of Virgina, he worked during the summers for the phone company, digging ditches for cables and climbing poles to do repair work.

This training came in handy in 1967 when, as chief operating officer of Illinois Bell, Mr. Brown went out fixing phone poles during a strike by craft unions. One weekend, he startled other members of a country club to which he belonged by appearing with the repair crew after the club requested repair work.

Mr. Brown leads a quiet private life. He commutes daily by limousine from his Princeton, N.J., home, and takes an annual three- or four-week vacation, usually at a home he owns north of Palm Beach, Fla. He tries to squeeze in two tennis games, one history book and at least a round of golf every week. He is married to the former Ann Lee Saunders, his second wife. He has a son by his first marriage, Charles A. Brown, a physician in California.

I.B.M.'s Persistent Leader

John Roberts Opel

By ISADORE BARMASH

In March 1980 John Roberts Opel was named chief executive officer of the International Business Machines Corporation in addition to his title of president. I.B.M.'s decision ended brief speculation that he might be passed over in favor of someone deemed more likely to help the giant, but troubled, company improve its less-than-customary performance. In the end, it seemed, loyalty, a plan of succession and his role as a sort of alter ego won out.

Yesterday the Justice Department wearily dropped its 13-year-old antitrust suit against I.B.M., and Mr. Opel, as the company's top officer, again appeared to be a victor against great odds. Two and a half years ago his triumph was over unfounded rumor. This time it was over "big government."

The 57-year-old Mr. Opel has long trod a trail blazed by Frank T. Cary, I.B.M.'s tight-lipped, tough-minded, former chief executive officer. It was Mr. Cary who held out against legions of Government lawyers, countless court hearings, mountains of written testimony and, some say, intrigue from competitors eager to help the Government's efforts against I.B.M.

A Time for Accolades

But if steadfast support and professional and personal loyalty mean anything, the Kansas-born Mr. Opel — an I.B.M. man since 1949, when he joined the company as a salesman — would appear to deserve the accolades he received yesterday at corporate headquarters in Armonk, N.Y.

Mr. Opel was a member of the giant computer manufacturer's ruling council for a decade prior to his appointment as C.E.O. In all, he was at Mr. Cary's right hand for about 20 years. Mr. Opel is described by close associates as thoughtful, soft-spoken and, according to one of them, "not too dramatically different in behavior from Frank Cary." Mr. Opel's steady advancement through the years is evidence of his sponsor's unflagging support through some difficult times, such as when I.B.M.'s conservatism allowed upstart competitors to carve out market niches for themselves.

After joining I.B.M. as a salesman at Jefferson City, Mo., Mr. Opel traveled a wide circle from the Ozarks to the Iowa border. He served 10 years in the field, creating a record that attracted the attention of Thomas J. Watson Jr., the head of the company, who made Mr. Opel his executive assistant and two years later a corporate vice president.

Ascending the Ladder

In 1968, somewhat less than 20 years after he joined the company, Mr. Opel was appointed senior vice president and chairman of the executive committee. He had entered the inner circle of I.B.M.'s elite.

Still more recognition and responsibility lay ahead. In 1972 he was named head of the data processing division, representing the company's main marketing activity. By then, rival executives either had come under his wing or had been outpaced, and in 1974 it seemed only natural when he was named president at age 49. For some time Mr. Opel and Mr. Cary, behind their executive desks, had been physically separated by only a tiny anteroom. Mr. Opel's next move, to chief executive officer, was just as natural six years later when Mr. Cary stepped down at age 60 in line with I.B.M.'s policy.

Mr. Opel's wife is the former Julia Carole Stout, and they have two sons and three daughters. His outside interests include opera, fishing and ornithology.

Last October I.B.M. moved to simplify its product-group marketing approach in favor of allowing single sales representatives to sell a wide rantge of I.B.M. products.

Outlining I.B.M.'s Aims

Analysts considered this an effort to compete more effectively in the proliferating field of personal computers. But Mr. Opel declared in a statement that "this new marketing structure will simplify the distribution of our products and better serve our customers' needs." These twin objectives could easily have been lifted out of a business management textbook.

Like Mr. Cary, Mr. Opel holds a Master of Business Administration degree. Mr. Opel's is from the University of Chicago; Mr. Cary's is from Stanford University.

Members of I.B.M.'s top brass, perhaps savoring yesterday's glowing victory, seemed slow to leave for home late in the day. But efforts to reach Mr. Opel for comment proved unsuccessful. A corporate spokesman explained that "Mr. Opel is involved in meetings at Armonk."

What would prompt meetings so soon after yesterday's bombshell in Washington? Surely not another antitrust suit? The I.B.M. spokesman laughed. "Not for another 13 years, at least," he said.

John R. Opel

A.T.& T. and U.S. Settle Antitrust Suit; Company to Be Split

Continued From Page 1

communications industry and ultimately lower prices, there were widespread fears today that, in the short term, local phone rates might rise quickly.

William M. Ellinghaus, president of A.T.&T., said at a news conference that local rates would double in the next few years to make up for the subsidy that long-distance revenues have provided.

A.T.&T. officials added that long-distance rates would be likely to drop once the payment of local service subsidies ended. This would benefit large corporations and other big long-distance users.

Filed in Newark Court

A proposed consent decree, embodying the settlement, was filed in the Federal District Court in Newark, which in 1956 approved a settlement of an earlier Federal suit against the Bell System that confined A.T.& T. to regulated telephone service. Under the new settlement, supervision of the 1956 consent decree would be transferred from Newark to the District Court in Washington, where the seven-year-old antitrust suit was being tried.

"That earlier decree did not anticipate an evolution in modern electronics technology that would in time erase the distinction as between computers and communications," Mr. Brown said. "Yet its provisions have effectively prohibited the Bell System companies from applying the fruits of their own research and development to their own business purposes. The new decree would entirely eliminate such restrictions."

A critical aspect of the proposed settlement is that it would sever a key source of the giant company's economic and political power, namely the phone companies that blanket nearly every major metropolitan area of the nation and provide a protected market for the parent company's equipment production and facilitated the long distance service.

A number of analysts speculated that A.T.& T. agreed to the huge divestiture because the company feared that Judge Greene, who was expected to rule on the case early this summer, would find the phone company guilty of antitrust law violations and perhaps force it to give up other subsidiaries as well.

Comment by Judge Greene

When the Justice Department completed the presentation of its case earlier this year, Judge Greene had commented that the department had shown that "the Bell System has violated the antitrust laws in a number of ways over a lengthy period of time."

Asked why A.T.& T. agreed to surrender the operating companies, Mr. Brown said, "We have no stomach at all for a long appellate review."

Mr. Baxter indicated that in return for giving up the 22 operating companies, A.T.& T. would be free to go into a variety of unregulated businesses without the necessity of running these businesses through a separate subsidiary — sometimes dubbed Baby Bell — that could not be subsidized by telephone revenue.

This was specified in a Federal Communications Commission ruling in 1980 and in legislation now in Congress. Both the agency and Congress were expected to review their actions in light of today's settlement.

'Continue With Our Plan'

Nevertheless, Jay Grossman, an A.T.& T. spokesman, said that even though the consent decree would lift the ban on entering unregulated businesses, the F.C.C. decision still stood because that agency was not governed by a court decree. "We assume that we will continue with our plan for a separate subsidiary," he said, although he added that the F.C.C. might reconsider its decision because the settlement accomplished many of the agency's goals.

A.T.& T. will have six months to file a reorganization plan that specifies how the 22 operating companies — which employ 80 percent of A.T.& T.'s million employees — will be divested. It will retain the Long Lines Department, which operates the nationwide long-distance network; the Western Electric Company, the manufacturing arm, and Bell Laboratories, the research division.

In addition, the agreement will allow A.T.& T. to retain its minority interests in two regional telephone companies: 29.7 percent in Cincinnati Bell Inc. and 21.1 percent in the Southern New England Telephone Company.

Divestiture Options Available

Under the settlement hammered out in bargaining sessions between Mr. Baxter and William Trienens, general counsel of A.T.& T., the company has options available as to how it will divest itself of the operating companies — whether by selling the phone companies to A.T.& T.'s three million shareholders, by combining them into a single large operating company and selling the company as a unit or by selling the subsidiaries individually or in combinations.

Mr. Brown said that A.T.& T.'s shareholders would retain their stock and would also own "proportionate values" in the local operating companies after they were divested.

Both Mr. Baxter and Mr. Brown claimed some element of victory in their tentative agreement.

Settlement Termed Good

"I think it is a very good settlement," said Mr. Baxter, "that completely fulfills the objectives that the antitrust division had been pursuing."

Mr. Brown told some 200 reporters at the news conference that the announcement was "a historic decision" and added: "I believe we have chosen the right course, although clearly it was not the solution that we sought."

Many key people here who influence national telecommunications policy reacted cautiously to today's dramatic developments. Mark S. Fowler, chairman of the Federal Communications Commission, said: "The impact upon local and long distance, and indeed the ancillary services provided through our nation's telecommunications system, will require considerable study and we will undertake such a study as soon as we receive the complete details of the agreement."

The commission has been trying to implement its own restructuring of the telecommunications industry, mostly by keeping A.T.& T. basically intact except for requiring it to form the separate subsidiary for unregulated competitive businesses.

Senator Bob Packwood, an Oregon Republican who is chairman of the Commerce Committee, which crafted the telecommunications bill that passed the Senate last year, said he has misgivings about the settlement.

House Hearings Due Feb. 2

Representative Timothy E. Wirth, a Colorado Democrat who is chairman of the House telecommunications subcommittee, said he would hold hearings starting Feb. 2 on the bill he has drafted for House consideration as well as the settlement.

Mr. Packwood said: "Long distance used to subsidize and keep local phone rates down. I fear no such accommodation is present in this settlement, and local telephone rates are going to suffer."

In the revamping proposed today, A.T.& T. would retain ownership of its long-distance lines and even gain control of some long-distance facilities now owned by local phone companies. In retaining ownership of Western Electric, it would have a huge manufacturing arm that supplies about 65 percent of the nation's market for telephones and conventional switching devices and an even larger share of the market in switching equipment.

The phone companies that would be spun off include the following: Bell Telephone of Nevada, Illinois Bell Telephone, Indiana Bell Telephone, Michigan Bell Telephone, New England Bell Telephone and Telegraph, New Jersey Bell Telephone and New York Telephone.

Also, Northwestern Bell Telephone, Pacific Northwest Bell Telephone, South Central Bell Telephone, Southern Bell Telephone and Telegraph, Southwestern Bell Telephone and Bell Telephone of Pennsylvania.

Also, Chesapeake and Potomac Telephone, Chesapeake and Potomac Telephone of Maryland, Chesapeake and Potomac Telephone of Virginia, Chesapeake and Potomac Telephone of West Virginia, Diamond State Telephone, Mountain States Telephone and Telegraph, Ohio Bell Telephone, Pacific Northwest Bell Telephone and Wisconsin Telephone.

May Not Own Stock Again

Once A.T.& T. has disposed of its stock in the phone companies, the agreement stipulates that it may not own any such stock again.

A number of forces are thought to have led the Justice Department and A.T.& T. to the bargaining table after seven years of fierce struggle, including a year of trial. A.T.& T. says it has spent $360 million on the case and Mr. Baxter estimated that his department may have spent $15 million.

Other agencies of the Administration, especially the Defense Department and the Commerce Department, had wanted to drop the suit, fearing that Judge Greene, who has been trying the case without a jury, might well find the company liable for antitrust abuses and break up the company even more drastically than required by today's agreement.

The judge could have forced the divestiture of even Bell Laboratories and Western Electric.

The Defense Department had expressed fears openly that the breakup of the company could jeopardize national security.

The original suit, filed in 1974, had sought to break up A.T.& T. on the ground that, in the 1960's and early 1970's, it had thwarted competition in the marketing and manufacturing of phone equipment and the offering of services.

Equal Access Required

The Government held that A.T.& T. placed unwarranted restrictions on the connection of equipment provided by other companies to the Bell System. The new settlement would require the divested operating companies to grant equal access to local lines for all communications companies.

Many of the actual and potential competitors of A.T.& T. are expected to have much to say. For instance, Thomas E. Wheeler, president of the National Cable Television Association, which has always dreaded A.T.&T.'s possible entry into that business, criticized the "closed-door agreement" and said that only Congress should be allowed to restructure the industry.

While the tentative settlement had its critics, others welcomed it.

Cost Division Called Vital

William McGowan, the president of MCI Communications, one of A.T.&T.'s earliest competitors in long-distance service, said: "It sounds damned good for the business, but much depends on how they order Bell to divide up the costs between local and long-distance service for purposes of setting rates."

He said he was confident MCI could compete strongly with A.T.& T. if, as the settlement provides, it could obtain the same kind of connections to local phone exchanges that the Bell System's Long Lines unit enjoys so that its customers could dial fewer numbers and use both rotary and push-button phones.

MCI customers must now use 21 numbers to reach a long-distance customer, compared to as few as 10 dialed by the Bell System's long-distance customers.

"All the News That's Fit to Print"

The New York Times

Late Edition
Weather: Rain ending today, mostly cloudy and cool; cloudy and cooler tonight. Partly cloudy and mild tomorrow. Temperatures: today 61-66, tonight 54-56; yesterday 55-60. Details, page B10.

VOL. CXXXI . . No. 45,337 | NEW YORK, MONDAY, JUNE 7, 1982 | 30 CENTS

BIG ISRAELI FORCE INVADES SOUTH LEBANON; SHARP FIGHTING WITH GUERRILLAS REPORTED

United Press International

An armored personnel carrier, part of the Israeli invasion force, breaks through the border with southern Lebanon.

THOUSANDS ATTACK

Some Syrian Units in Area Said to Have Clashed With Raiding Force

By THOMAS L. FRIEDMAN
Special to The New York Times

BEIRUT, Lebanon, Monday, June 7 — The Israeli Army invaded southern Lebanon by land, sea and air Sunday in an attack aimed at destroying the main military bases of the Palestine Liberation Organization.

More than 250 Israeli tanks and armored personnel carriers, as well as thousands of infantrymen, rolled past the observation posts of the United Nations peacekeeping troops in southern Lebanon at 11 A.M. (5 A.M., New York time) and fanned out across the frontier, according to a United Nations spokesman in Beirut.

By late Sunday evening the Israelis had taken several P.L.O. outposts in the craggy hills of southern Lebanon and were engaged in fierce firefights with the Palestinians for control of scores of other strongholds along the 33-mile front, stretching from the port city of Tyre to the foothills of Mount Hermon, the United Nations spokesman said.

Main Targets Besieged

In the first day of the invasion the Israelis besieged all their main targets — Tyre, Beaufort Castle, Nabatiye and Kawkaba — but the Palestinians stood their ground and did not flee north. The number of casualties was not known.

Israel said this morning that Beaufort Castle, a Crusader stronghold overlooking the border that the Palestinians have used as a communications and artillery base, was captured during the night by an Israeli infantry battalion. But the Palestinians denied that the castle had fallen.

It appeared that at least a few elements of Syria's force of about 25,000 men in Lebanon had become involved in confrontations with the Israelis.

The state-run Beirut radio reported Sunday night that Syrian artillery north of Hasbeya was exchanging fire with the Israelis on the eastern route of their advance. This could not be confirmed. In Damascus, a Syrian military spokesman said Israeli forces had come into contact with Syrian troops in three places, but it was not clear whether fighting had occurred. [Page A12.]

The Israel radio broadcast a state-

Continued on Page A12, Column 1

Limited Summit Agreement Set on Trade and Currency

By RICHARD EDER
Special to The New York Times

VERSAILLES, France, June 6 — The eighth summit conference of the industrialized nations reached limited agreement today on two contentious subjects — East-West trade and the handling of currency fluctuations — and produced something of a breakthrough on North-South relations.

The agreements themselves were the subject of some disagreement: whether they bridged or merely papered over fundamental differences. Prime Minister Margaret Thatcher of Britain described the atmosphere as one of unanimity. Prime Minister Pierre Elliott Trudeau of Canada called it "difficult."

The conference was, in any case, shaded and sometimes interrupted by the fighting in the Falklands and Israel's invasion of Lebanon. Today's final hard bargaining on East-West trade was interrupted by the announcement by President François Mitterrand of France of the Israeli move, and the assembled leaders approved a statement expressing shock.

The accord fell short of American hopes and was seen as having little world impact. News analysis and economic analysis, with text of the communiqué, page D6.

Associated Press

President Reagan at economic meeting yesterday in Versailles.

The Falkland crisis, apart from producing an embarrassing flip-flop over the United States vote in the Security Council, caused Mrs. Thatcher to fly back to London tonight after the state dinner in the Versailles chateau's Hall of Mirrors.

She thus missed the musical masque and ballet and other festivities organized by France to make this the most glittering summit conference, whether or not it will have turned out to be the most productive.

The seven nations — the United States, Japan, Britain, France, West Germany, Italy and Canada — agreed to a compromise on the East-West trade issue. It fell short of American hopes for abolition of government-subsidized financing for such trade. Instead, it calls for "caution" in financial dealings with the Soviet bloc, and it says there is a need for "commercial prudence in limiting export credits."

The Reagan Administration had

Continued on Page D7, Column 1

U.N. COUNCIL ASKS ISRAELI PULLBACK

But Delegate, Hinting Refusal, Notes 'Limit of Endurance'

By BERNARD D. NOSSITER
Special to The New York Times

UNITED NATIONS, N.Y., June 6 — The Security Council unanimously demanded tonight that Israel pull its invading forces out of Lebanon. There was, however, no indication that Israel would pay any more attention to this order than to the unanimous Council demand Saturday night for a cease-fire.

Instead, Yehuda Z. Blum, the Israeli delegate, taunted the Council's 15 members for "evincing not the slightest interest" in scores of terrorist acts he attributed to the Palestine Liberation Organization. "How many Israelis have to be killed by terrorists for this Council to be persuaded that the limits of our endurance have been reached?" he asked rhetorically. "Israel cannot expect this body even to deplore P.L.O. barbarism against Israel's civilian population, let alone take any steps with a view towards curbing that barbarism."

Leaders of the major industrial democracies expressed shock at Versailles over Israel's move. Page A14.

Tonight's text, a compromise drafted by Ireland after a day of discussion behind closed doors, directed Israel to withdraw its forces "forthwith and unconditionally." The Soviet Union insisted on that last phrase.

At the demand of the United States, the resolution calls on Israel and the Palestinians to halt all military action "within Lebanon and across the Lebanese-Israeli border." That language was designed to cover P.L.O. shelling into Israel as well as Israeli strikes. The document directs both sides to report

Continued on Page A14, Column 5

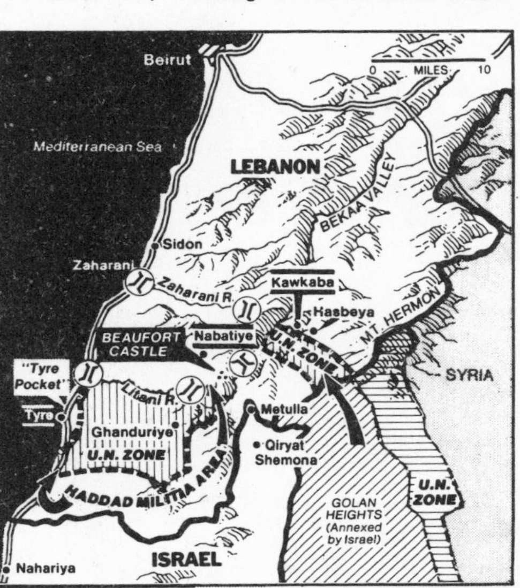

The New York Times / June 7, 1982

Israeli tanks and troops moved into Lebanon in three columns (arrows). The land assaults, together with air and sea attacks, were aimed at the main Palestinian strongholds — Tyre, Beaufort Castle, Nabatiye and Kawkaba. Warships destroyed the Qasmiye Bridge spanning the Litani River north of Tyre, cutting the main Palestinian supply line. Towns shown in northern Israel were among those shelled last week by Palestinian forces.

Britain Confirms the Landing Of 3,000 Soldiers From QE2

By R.W. APPLE Jr.
Special to The New York Times

LONDON, June 6 — British troops besieging the Argentine garrison at Stanley in the Falkland Islands have been reinforced by 3,000 fresh infantrymen from the liner Queen Elizabeth 2, the Defense Ministry announced tonight.

The arrival of the Fifth Infantry Brigade, including a battalion each of Scots and Welsh Guards and Gurkha Rifles, raises British strength on East Falkland Island to about 8,000. About 5,000 paratroops and Royal Marine commandos went ashore last month, and most are drawn up opposite the 7,000 Argentine defenders of Stanley, the Falklands capital.

In Buenos Aires today, Argentina said its planes and artillery had bombarded the British positions surrounding Stanley. Senior military officers said they expected the British to launch a major assault on the Argentine garrison at any moment. [Page A6.]

There were hints in London that the long-awaited assault on Stanley had already begun in a report from Michael Nicholson of Britain's Independent Television News.

"The British push is really on," he said in a broadcast this evening. "There are under way at this moment operations which I can only describe as extraordinarily daring which cannot be revealed until they are completed, but which, almost certainly if they are successful, will surely bring the end of this war that much closer."

Mr. Nicholson reported that the Gurkhas, composed entirely of Nepalese volunteers, were operating on their own, "crisscrossing East Falkland" in a search for Argentine units lurking in the interior, between the British base at San Carlos Bay and their forward headquarters near Mount Kent.

According to unofficial sources, the Fifth Brigade transferred from the Queen Elizabeth to the assault ships In-

Continued on Page A8, Column 3

Why Israelis Invaded Now

Heavy P.L.O. Shelling Said to Tip the Scale

The following dispatch has been subjected to military censorship.

By DAVID K. SHIPLER
Special to The New York Times

News Analysis

JERUSALEM, June 6 — Israel's invasion of Lebanon came today as the culmination of months of military and political calculation in which Prime Minister Menachem Begin repeatedly allowed the troops to be massed and the saber to be rattled, only to pull back at what seemed like the last moment.

Until today the crucial factors favoring a major assault never quite lined up, and the risks seemed greater than the potential benefits.

This time, however, Mr. Begin decided to make the military gamble and to pay the political costs that he and his advisers know exist. The crucial reason was the intensive shelling of northern Israel by forces of the Palestine Liberation Organization, which began Friday afternoon after Israeli air strikes on Palestinian bases near Beirut.

P.L.O. Has Become an Army

The Israeli command described the air raids as retaliation for the shooting Thursday of Israel's Ambassador to Britain, Shlomo Argov, who was critically wounded in London. Five suspects, all traveling on passports from Arab countries, were captured. The P.L.O. denied any responsibility for the attack.

The Palestinian shelling, with artillery and rocket launchers, was the most severe ever directed against Israeli towns and kibbutzim by the P.L.O.,

Continued on Page A13, Column 1

Begin Orders Israelis to Push Palestinians 25 Miles to North

The following dispatch has been subjected to military censorship.

Special to The New York Times

JERUSALEM, Monday, June 7 — Prime Minister Menachem Begin said Sunday that the Israeli Army had been ordered to push the Palestinian forces northward to a distance of 25 miles from the Israeli border, to place their artillery beyond the range of Israeli territory.

Mr. Begin made his statement in a letter to President Reagan, excerpts of which were reported on the Israeli radio. The Cabinet, after an emergency session, issued a statement saying Israel would not attack any Syrian forces in Lebanon or Syria unless the Syrians engaged the Israelis.

The Damascus radio said the Syrian Army was battling the Israelis near Hasbeya, 10 miles north of the border. The Israeli military spokesman said there had been no verification that any such clashes with the Syrians had occurred.

Reagan Urged Restraint

Mr. Begin's letter to President Reagan, disclosing the orders to the army to push the Palestine Liberation Organizaton 25 miles north of the border, came after the President sent a letter to the Israeli leader. That letter, delivered Sunday morning, requested Israeli restraint.

In his reply, as reported by the Israeli radio, Mr. Begin said that "the terrorists aim their weapons only at the civilian population." He went on: "The aim of the enemy is to kill Jews, men, women and children. Is there any people in the world that would accept such a situation?"

The invasion operation, called "Peace for Galilee," would not be aimed at acquiring any Lebanese territory and was not being undertaken against Lebanon, according to Mr. Begin's letter. It was begun after months of sporadic terrorist attacks on Israelis here and abroad, attacks that Israel regarded as violations of the cease-fire that had been negotiated across the Lebanese-Israeli border last July.

As Israeli armored columns swept through the lines of the United Nations peacekeeping forces, a United Nations spokesman in Jerusalem reported, several United Nations units were caught in crossfire. By Sunday evening, one

Continued on Page A12, Column 3

Floods Rampage in Connecticut; 8 Believed Dead

By ROBERT D. McFADDEN

Torrential weekend rains and overflowing rivers swamped wide areas of Connecticut yesterday with the state's worst floods in decades.

The state police said that eight persons were dead or missing in the storm. More than 1,300 others were removed from their homes as floodwaters invaded residential areas, washed out roads and earthen dams and disrupted electric and telephone service and public transportation for tens of thousands of residents.

The floods, accompanied by 5 to 8 inches of pounding rain, struck a wide swath of the state, from Westport and other Fairfield County communities on the west to Waterford and New London on the east. At least 38,000 homes were hit by power blackouts, and 6,000 telephones were knocked out.

Nearly all trains in the state, including those operated by Amtrak between New York and Boston, were halted as Conrail and Amtrak used buses to carry passengers. Commuters and long-distance travelers were expected to face further delays today. Many communities in flooded areas canceled school for today.

The rest of the New York metropolitan area was relatively unscathed. But on eastern Long Island, up to 9.79 inches of rain also triggered heavy weekend flooding. Many traffic accidents were reported, and a stretch of Long Island

Continued on Page B4, Column 1

The New York Times / Alan Decker

Matthew Giuristano clearing a storm drain yesterday in Higganum, Conn.

INSIDE

Defeat for Schmidt's Party

The Social Democrats were defeated in state elections in Hamburg in what was considered a direct blow to Chancellor Helmut Schmidt. Page A9.

'Nine,' 'Nickleby' Win Tonys

"Nine," based on "8½," won the Tony award for musicals. The Royal Shakespeare Company's "Nicholas Nickleby" won for plays. Page C11.

Invasion in Lebanon: For Damascus, Dangerous Alternatives

ISRAELI SAYS MOVE IS TO FORM BUFFER

Envoy to U.S. Says Objective Is to Push P.L.O.'s Heavy Weapons Out of Range

By CHARLES MOHR
Special to The New York Times

WASHINGTON, June 6 — Moshe Arens, the Israeli Ambassador to the United States, said today that the sole objective of Israel's invasion of Lebanon was to push Palestine Liberation Organization forces out of artillery and rocket range of northern Israeli settlements.

He added that it was clear there would be no end to "anarchy and terror" in Lebanon until "such time as the military capability of the P.L.O. gets moved out of Lebanon." This is the "clear-cut, single mission" of the Israeli forces, Mr. Arens said.

The Ambassador's remarks, on the ABC News program "This Week," gave an Israeli perspective on the more than seven-year cycle of complex, closely related acts of violence among Lebanese political and religious factions, Palestinian groups, Syrians and Israelis.

Philip C. Habib, a retired Under Secretary of State who is President Reagan's special envoy now assigned once more to the turbulent area, had helped arrange a cease-fire last July 24. That respite followed heavy Israeli air strikes on Palestinian offices in Beirut and heavy Palestinian shelling of settlements in northern Israel. However, neither Israel nor the P.L.O. would call it more than a "cessation of hostilities." No written agreement of any kind was made or signed and neither side would acknowledge that it had reached an agreement with the other party.

P.L.O. Denigrated U.S. Efforts

Instead, Israel insisted on the diplomatic fiction that Mr. Habib had used his good offices to make the agreement with the Government of Lebanon; and the P.L.O., which had dealt with Mr. Habib only in second-hand fashion through Saudi Arabia, denigrated his efforts and mainly praised the United Nations for bringing about a cessation in the fighting.

Almost immediately, beginning in August of last year, Israeli officials began complaining that the Palestinians were again moving artillery and ammunition south of the Litani River over rebuilt bridges, which Israel had bombed in July. The Litani flows westward into the Mediterranean just north of Tyre in southern Lebanon. It is the northern limit of the United Nations peacekeeping buffer zone, which was set up in 1978.

A key issue — among Israeli politicians as well as between Israel and the international community — has been the Israeli contention that the July 24 cease-fire prohibited the P.L.O. from any hostile action against Israel and not just shellfire or infiltration over the Lebanese-Israeli border.

However, the full Israeli Cabinet refused to approve an earlier plan to invade Lebanon proposed in January by Defense Minister Ariel Sharon, after an incursion by five Palestinian guerrillas from Jordan. United States diplomats believe that the April 25 schedule for the full return of Sinai to Egypt played some role in the decision to hold back.

Roots of Violence

The deepest roots of the present violence, however, go back to the 1970 ejection of the P.L.O. military forces from Jordan into Lebanon and the 1975-76 Lebanese civil war that began with clashes between Lebanese Christian armed groups and Palestinians.

Although Syrian troops entered Lebanon as a "deterrent" force, they hesitated to move into southernmost Lebanon for fear of bringing on an Israeli intervention. This permitted the Palestinians to take over most of southern Lebanon. In March 1978, Israel invaded southern Lebanon in force to drive the Palestinians back.

A United Nations force, with no real military muscle, was introduced, but the Israelis did not withdraw until June 1978, and not until encouraging Maj. Saad Haddad, a right-wing Lebanese Christian officer, to declare a semi-independent enclave in the six-mile deep United Nations area north of the Israeli border.

In early April 1981, Israeli-supported Christian militia in northern Lebanon appeared to be in jeopardy of defeat by Syrian forces, and Israeli jets shot down two Syrian helicopters. The Syrians then moved surface-to-air missiles into the Bekka Valley east of Beirut to threaten what had become routine Israeli air reconnaissance of Lebanon. Israeli hawks quickly began to discuss the destruction of those missiles.

It was to deal with that eventuality that Mr. Habib was called back from retirement as a special envoy. As he went from one Middle East capital to another, Israel first bombed an Iraqi nuclear reactor on June 7, creating serious tensions with the United States. Then, after Israeli air raids into Lebanon and Palestinian shelling of Israeli settlements, Israel bombed Palestinian offices in a crowded quarter of Beirut, killing scores and possibly hundreds of people.

It was this event that led to Mr. Habib's strenuous and ultimately successful effort to arrange a cessation of hostilities.

United Press International

The body of an Israeli pilot is taken into Saida, Lebanon, by Palestinians.

Israeli Intervention in Lebanon Poses Both Temptation and Peril for Syria

By DREW MIDDLETON
Special to The New York Times

LONDON, June 6 — Israel's main risk in the invasion of southern Lebanon is not resistance by the Palestine Liberation Organization, but the possibility that the operation will provoke a strong military response from Syria.

Military Analysis

Israeli intelligence experts agree that Syria is the Arab country best prepared militarily and psychologically for war.

British analysts believe that Syrian will react immediately if the Israeli tanks that are now thrust into Lebanon should veer toward the Bekkaa Valley. Since the end of the 1973 Arab-Israeli war, the Syrian high command has considered that valley the sector most dangerous in the event of war with Israel. Its possession would enable an Israeli force to bypass the main Syrian defenses and push north into central Syria.

Syrian forces in the area consist of 25,000 men of the Arab Deterrent Force based in Lebanon and a screening force of one brigade and seven commando units along the frontier. The major force of four armored divisions and two mechanized infantry divisions is in the Golan Heights area.

Strongest Arab Force

Israeli sources regard these divisions as the best armed and best led Arab force in the Middle East. Originally the Syrian armor was equipped mainly with Soviet-made T-62 tanks. Now, according to Western and Israeli intelligence, newer T-72 tanks have replaced the T-62's. The number of Soviet-built BMP armored personnel carriers also has been increased and there has been an appreciable expansion of the number of self-propelled field guns, anti-tank weapons and surface-to-air missiles, with SAM-8's replacing the SAM-6 missiles now in service.

Analysts here believe that the Israeli forces now pushing into Lebanon are not strong enough in armor and men to deal with a counter-offensive by forces as strong as those deployed by Syria. Initial reports from the battle zone put Israeli armored strength at about 100 tanks, the strength of an armored brigade, plus about 100 armored personnel carriers.

The Israeli advances, analysts said, appear calculated to avoid provoking Syrian reaction at the outset. One armored unit is moving up the coast road toward the Palestinian strongholds in and around Tyre. Another is pushing into central Lebanon while a third, farther east, is moving northward toward the Litani River.

Objective for Israelis

Palestinian sources here tonight said that Israeli troops had crossed the river near the town of Kakaiet.

Analysts here say that as far as Israel is concerned the P.L.O. ammunition and fuel dumps north of the river must be destroyed if the Palestinian forces to the south are to be neutralized.

The advance is being supported by Mirage fighters, which have bombed and strafed P.L.O. positions. The Israeli fighters are said to have effectively used balloon to neutralize the heat-seeking missiles fired by the P.L.O. The Mirages also carry more sophisticated electronic countermeasures for use should they encounter the newer Syrian surface-to-air missiles.

Israeli and Western sources are concerned about the possibility that since Syria and the Soviet Union signed their Treaty of Cooperation and Friendship in October 1980, Moscow has secretly agreed to provide Syria with immediate replacements of weapons and equipment in the event of war with Israel.

A diplomatic source said that such an agreement would make sense from Moscow's standpoint. Syria, he said, was the only Arab country now in a position to challenge Israeli military dominance in the Middle East and the one prepared to fight Israel on its own without allies.

A Deterrent to Syria

The absence of allies, Middle East experts here said, however, could be a strong deterrent to a major Syrian reaction to the Israeli attack.

Syria, they said, is unlikely for find support in the Arab world. Egypt, potentially the strongest Arab military power, has not yet consolidated its territorial gains under the Camp David agreement and its army and air force have not yet absorbed new American weapons. Iraq, as a result of the Iranian victories in the last three months, is virtually powerless to intervene. Jordan is in no position to fight Israeli forces superior in weapons and training until it receives the promised supplies of mobile Hawk missiles and advanced fighters from the United States.

These are all arguments against a Syrian military reaction, the analysts said.

But they said Syria knows that, despite the initial successes of the Israeli forces into Lebanon, the Israeli armed forces are not mobilized for war and that the present operation is being carried out by, at the most, 25,000 to 30,000 men supported by about 100 aircraft.

Attack on Israeli Flank

The Syrians, analysts said, might be tempted to take what is primarily an Israeli punitive operation as a cause for war and retaliate by launching its armored divisions against the Israeli flank and bombing Israeli depots and supply lines supporting the combat forces.

The Syrians, according to Israeli intelligence sources, have at their disposal a number of commando battalions, in addition to those deployed in the screening forces, which could be used to bolster the P.L.O. units now fighting the Israeli advances.

The P.L.O. forces could be more formidable than they have shown in the past. As early as October 1981 the P.L.O. exercised a full armored brigade north of the Litani River. This brigade, supported by Syrian aircraft, analysts here said, could be a major factor in an expanding conflict north of the river.

For the moment, P.L.O. resistance is the key. If the Palestinians are able to inflict serious losses on the advancing Israelis, the Syrians will be content with political protests, analysts said. But if the Israeli forces plunge forward across the Litani towards Beirut and the Bekkaa Valley, then Syrian intervention must be contemplated.

Syria Tells of Israeli Contacts

DAMASCUS, Syria, June 6 (Reuters) — The Israeli forces that invaded Lebanon today have come into contact with Syrian troops in three places, a Syrian military spokesman said. However, it was not clear from his statement whether the Syrians were actually fighting the Israelis or whether they were just holding their ground.

The Syrians had been ordered to oppose the Israelis and had been doing so since this afternoon, the spokesman said.

Some 30,000 Syrian troops are stationed in Lebanon on peacekeeping duties under a mandate given to them by the Arab League after they intervened in Lebanon in the 1975-76 civil war.

The Syrian spokesman said the advancing Israelis had come into contact with Syrians at Jarmaq, a village only three miles east of the Palestinian stronghold of Nabatiye, and further east at Berghoz and a crossroads near Hasbeya.

About 30 miles north of the places mentioned by the Syrian spokesman are Syrian antiaircraft missile batteries that were at the center of a crisis between Israel and Syria last year.

Syria moved the missiles into Lebanon at the end of April 1981 after Israeli planes shot down two Syrian helicopters in the area. Israel threatened to destroy the missiles unless Syria removed them.

Before the crisis was solved, two weeks of heavy fighting broke out between Israeli forces and Palestinian guerrillas, with Israeli air raids on Beirut and southern Lebanon and intensive artillery duels across the border.

A cease-fire was finally arranged last July by the United States special envoy, Philip C. Habib.

Southern Lebanon Invaded By a Powerful Israeli Force

Continued From Page A1

ment saying that the invasion was not aimed at the Syrians and that Israeli troops would not engage Syrian units as long as they stayed out of the fighting.

But the situation could become increasingly difficult if the Palestinians are forced to pull back into Syrian-controlled areas. Major Syrian involvement could raise the danger of a much wider conflict.

Along with the invasion of the south, Israeli jet fighters and gunboats bombarded the main street of Sidon and the surrounding hills, destroying several buildings and cutting the coastal highway leading from Beirut to the south. Israeli warplanes also bombed the main Lebanese oil refinery in the south, at Zaharani, setting fire to an oil storage tank.

The number of casualties in Sunday's fighting, which followed two days of Israeli air strikes and cross-border artillery duels with the Palestinian forces, was impossible to determine. More than 200 people were killed in clashes Friday and Saturday, and about 500 were wounded.

Heavy Shelling Precedes Push

The Israeli Army preceded its invasion with five hours of heavy shelling and aerial bombing of a string of Palestinian positions between Tyre and Beaufort Castle, sending up huge clouds of smoke across the horizon.

The hills of southern Lebanon reverberated with the thud of Israeli shells punching into the Palestinian redoubts nestled in the villages and caves just north of the United Nations peacekeeping zone. The zone was established to separate Israel and the Palestinians after an Israeli incursion into Lebanon in 1978.

According to United Nations officials in Ghanduriye and Beirut, the invasion began with armored personnel carriers sweeping past the Dutch United Nations outpost at Al Baiyada, about three miles north of the border. The armored column then moved north along the coastal highway and engaged the Palestinians dug in at Tyre.

Both the United Nations spokesman and the Palestinian press agency Wafa said an intense firefight was raging late into the night Sunday between the Israeli armored force, which had driven to the outskirts of Tyre, and the Palestinian forces inside the town's devastated buildings and Roman ruins.

Israeli warships off the southern coast have blown apart the Qasmiye Bridge spanning the Litani River north of Tyre, cutting off the Palestinians from their main supply line.

A Wafa communiqué Sunday said a joint force of Palestinians and Lebanese Moslem leftists had opened a counterattack against Israeli units ringing Tyre, killing 15 Israelis and knocking out 14 tanks. They did not disclose their own casualties. The Palestinians are armed with an array of Soviet-made 130-millimeter guns, antitank guns, T-34 tanks and Katyusha rockets of various sizes.

Today, a Wafa communiqué from the battlefront said that 36 Israeli tanks and other armored vehicles had been destroyed overnight, in addition to 42 earlier.

Wafa said Sunday night that helicopter-borne Israeli troops landed near the refugee camp of Rashidiye, just south of Tyre, apparently as part of an operation to reinforce ground troops in the area. It gave no figures for the troops involved.

Israeli planes reportedly dropped Arabic leaflets into Tyre, warning the largely Palestinian townspeople against harboring guerrillas and ordering them to put out white flags of surrender.

Wafa said Israeli naval commandos had tried to land to the north on the beach near Zaharani but had been repulsed by heavy artillery fire.

A second and larger segment of the Israeli invasion force came through the central sector of the south, between Ghanduriye and Taibe. An armored brigade, estimated by United Nations officers at more than 100 tanks and armored personnel carriers, pushed north from the border enclave controlled by the Israeli-backed Chrisitan militia of Maj. Saad Haddad toward Nabatiye and Beaufort Castle.

Fijians Slow Israelis

United Nations officers said one group of Israeli troops had tried to cross the Khardali Bridge, which straddles the Litani River just below Beaufort Castle, but had been prevented from progressing by intensive Palestinian artillery fire and by Fijian United Nations soldiers guarding the bridge.

Wafa said the Israeli armored units had finally thrown pontoon bridges across the Litani and then moved toward Beaufort Castle, one of the strongest positions of the Palestinian forces in the south.

Meanwhile, a second group of Israeli tanks and infantrymen crossed the Litani at the Kakaiet Bridge and took control of the main road leading north to Nabatiye, an old hillside market town that serves as the P.L.O's southern command center.

United Press International

A column of Israeli armored vehicles moving yesterday toward the border with Lebanon.

According to a Wafa communiqué late Sunday night, the Israelis were on the outskirts of Nabatiye and were trading heavy tank and artillery fire with the Palestinians in the town.

Israeli Skyhawk Downed

Earlier Sunday Palestinian antiaircraft fire brought down an Israeli Skyhawk jet near Nabatiye, and the guerrillas captured the pilot, who had parachuted into their territory. The Israeli, Capt. Aharon Achian, was exhibited in Beirut Sunday night at a P.L.O. news conference. He said he was being "well treated" by his captors.

The Palestinians also reported having shot down another Israeli fighter at Sarafand along the coast, as well as two helicopters used in an attempt to land Israeli troops near Tyre.

A third segment of the Israeli strike also went through the United Nations peacekeeping zone in southern Lebanon. United Nations officers said about 50 Israeli tanks and 500 men had moved north across the border toward the Palestinian guerrilla positions around Kawkaba and Hasbeya along the western slope of Mount Hermon.

The only firm report of fighting in that area came from a United Nations spokesman, who said the Israeli troops had destroyed a Palestinian position west of Kawkaba and were besieging another east of the town.

Norwegian U.N. Officer Killed

A Norwegian United Nations officer was killed at Ibl as-Saqi, just south of Kawkaba, when an artillery shell exploded near the observation post, the United Nations announced in Beirut.

The P.L.O. leader, Yasir Arafat, has not made any formal statement since the start of the invasion, but his spokesman said he had sent urgent letters to President Fidel Castro of Cuba; President Daniel arap Moi of Kenya, the current President of the Organization of African Unity; King Khalid of Saudi Arabia, and Leonid I. Brezhnev, the Soviet leader, apparently seeking their help.

Begin Orders Israelis to Push Palestinians to North

Continued From Page A1

Norwegian soldier was reported killed, a Nigerian position was being shelled by an unknown force and Nepalese troops at the Khardali bridge over the Litani River were refusing to withdraw and were being threatened by Israeli troops, the spokesman said.

The latest terrorist attack occurred last Thursday night in London, where Israel's Ambassador, Shlomo Argov, was shot in the head. He is in critical condition. Israel reacted Friday with intensive air strikes on Palestinian bases near Beirut, reportedly killing 45 people. The Palestinians responded with extensive shelling of more than 20 towns and kibbutzim in northern Israel, and Israel intensified its air attacks, killing 130 people Saturday, according to Wafa, the Palestinian press agency.

Israeli officials gave few details of the ground operation Sunday, but United Nations officials in Lebanon said that a three-pronged armored attack had been mounted and that Israeli forces were sweeping up the coast to Tyre and Sidon. Tyre is a major Palestinian communications and command base. An extensive mobilization of Israel's reserves was under way.

This morning, the Israeli Army said that Beaufort Castle, a 12th-century Crusader stronghold that the Palestinians have used as a base, was captured during the night by an Israeli infantry battalion. The Palestinians denied the report.

Sunday, the Israeli military spokesman said that two Israeli aircraft — a jet fighter and a helicopter — had been shot down, apparently by either missile or gunfire from the ground. No Syrian planes were reported to have intervened. The Palestinians are known to have Soviet-built SAM-7 missiles, which are fired from shoulder launchers, and Libyan-supplied SAM-9 missiles have also been deployed in southern Lebanon.

The jet fighter was hit over the Nabatiye area, and reporters on the Israeli side of the frontier could see it crash as the pilot ejected and parachuted to the ground. The military spokesman said that he had been captured by Palestinian guerrillas. The helicopter was lost Saturday night, the spokesman said. Both crewmen were found dead Sunday in the wreckage by advancing Israeli troops. There was no word on other casualties.

Defense Minister Sees Troops

Rocket attacks continued Sunday on Israel's western Galilee and on a Christian-controlled enclave along the Lebanese side of the border. About 50 shells fell in the region during the afternoon, according to military sources.

Defense Minister Ariel Sharon, who has been pressing for the invasion for several months, visited the troops in the north. Prime Minister Begin also made a tour of northern settlements, which were hard hit by the Palestinian shelling.

After meeting in Jerusalem, the Cabinet issued a statement announcing the operation. The communiqué said that the Cabinet instructed the military "to place all the civilian population of the Galilee beyond the range of the terrorists' fire from Lebanon where they, their bases and their headquarters are concentrated."

The Cabinet statement also said, "during the operation, the Syrian army will not be attacked unless it attacks our forces." The communiqué stated Israel's desire to sign a peace treaty "with independent Lebanon, its territorial integrity preserved."

In his letter to President Reagan, the Prime Minister cited the example of Britain fighting in the Falkland Islands, 8,000 miles from home, and said the Israeli action was pure self-defense.

"All the News That's Fit to Print"

The New York Times

Late Edition

Weather: Sunny today with light southeasterly winds; clear and mild tonight. Cloudy with a chance of rain tomorrow. Temperatures: today 81-83, tonight 63-67; yesterday 54-72. Details, page D24.

VOL.CXXXI. No. 45,345

NEW YORK, TUESDAY, JUNE 15, 1982 — 30 CENTS

BRITAIN ANNOUNCES ARGENTINE SURRENDER TO END THE 10-WEEK WAR IN THE FALKLANDS

Israelis Cut Off West Beirut, Trapping P.L.O. Leaders

ACTION IN LEBANON

Tank Units Push Through the Christian Suburbs Around the Capital

By THOMAS L. FRIEDMAN

Special to The New York Times

BEIRUT, Lebanon, June 14 — Israeli tank columns completely cut off Moslem western Beirut today, trapping the military and political leadership of the Palestine Liberation Organization.

At the same time, other Israeli armored units, greeted by rice and flowers from sympathetic Lebanese Christians, began driving still deeper into Lebanon, apparently in an effort to push Syrian troops northeast of the capital into the Bekaa Valley.

There is a concentration of Syrian troops in the Khalde junction area on the coastal highway south of Beirut near the airport, and fighting was reportedly continuing there today between Israeli forces and Palestinians and Syrians.

The Israeli radio quoted Israel's Chief of Staff, Lieut. Gen. Rafael Eytan, as saying that Israeli troops had trapped guerrilla forces in Beirut and that the troops' mission was to smash the P.L.O.'s political and military nerve center there. [Page A18.]

Lebanese Leader Forms Council

The Israeli siege of guerrilla forces in Beirut came as the Lebanese Government announced the formation of a six-member Council of National Salvation to deal with the political repercussions of the Israeli invasion.

The committee, which was to contain the leading Christian and Moslem militia commanders, was formed by President Elias Sarkis and Prime Minister Shafik al-Wazzan to determine the Government's response to Israeli conditions for withdrawal.

Israel's withdrawal terms were delivered this evening to Mr. Sarkis at the presidential palace in Baabda by the special United States envoy, Philip C. Habib. Mr. Habib arrived by car from Damascus, to which he had flown earlier today from Jerusalem.

Mr. Habib declined to make any statements to the press, but Israel's conditions are reportedly the creation of a demilitarized zone stretching 25 miles north of its border to prevent attacks by Palestinian guerrillas and the withdrawal of the 30,000 Syrian peacekeeping troops from Lebanon.

Leftist Rejects Council

A meeting of the national council to consider the conditions, scheduled for this afternoon, was canceled after one proposed member, Walid Jumblat, leader of the leftist Moslem National Movement, said he would not have anything to do with the group as presently constituted.

Mr. Jumblat, who is under virtual house arrest by Israeli invasion forces occupying his mountain village of Mukhtara south of Beirut, said through a spokesman that the board should be "more comprehensive."

The other proposed council members are Bashir Gemayel, a Chrisian Phalangist militia commander; Nabim Berri, head of Lebanon's Shiite Moslem Party; Nasri Maalouf, another leading Christian political leader; Foreign

Continued on Page A18, Column 1

Associated Press

Israeli soldier atop armored vehicle in position overlooking western Beirut.

In Lebanon, White Flags Fly Amid the Misery and Rubble

By DAVID K. SHIPLER

Special to The New York Times

SIDON, Lebanon, June 14 — Along the battered Lebanese coast, in the wake of the invasion, white flags still fly.

They flutter from the antennas of cars without windows or windshields. They hang from bamboo poles stuck into the shell-pocked roofs and verandas of concrete houses. Even some pedestrians carried torn strips of white cloth to signify their neutrality, their surrender to the storm of war.

The Israeli Army warned residents of Lebanon's picturesque coast to leave their homes before the bombing and shelling began, and many followed the instructions on leaflets dropped from planes.

Battles Silently Traced

But when the fighting was over and they returned home from the beaches and the orange groves and the banana plantations where they had camped for days without food or water, what they saw took the strength out of them.

In Tyre, a stronghold and command center of the Palestine Liberation Organization, not a single building was untouched by the flying shrapnel.

Some high-rise apartments had collapsed like houses of cards, some villas were chewed into piles of dust and rubble.

Many other buildings revealed the course of battle: pits and chips around the doors and windows as Israeli troops fired at guerrillas, then a single gaping hole in a wall where a heavier weapon finished off the resistance.

The Israeli military governor of the town, Maj. Joseph Dana, who in civilian life is a lecturer in Arabic at Haifa University, estimates that 30 percent of all buildings in the town were destroyed.

In Sidon, farther up the coast toward Beirut, the damage was less ex-

Continued on Page A18, Column 4

A MIDEAST WARNING

Soviet Conveys Concern Over Military Activity Near South Border

By JOHN F. BURNS

Special to The New York Times

MOSCOW, June 14 — The Soviet Government warned Israel today not to forget that the Middle East was close to the Soviet Union's southern borders and that developments in that area "cannot help affecting the interests of the U.S.S.R."

The warning was coupled with a demand, apparently directed at the United States, for "urgent effective measures" to halt Israel's "criminal act of genocide" against Palestinians and to bring about a withdrawal of Israeli troops from Lebanon.

Text of Soviet statement, page A20.

The statement, issued through the official press agency Tass, said in part:

"The Soviet Union takes the Arabs' side not in words but in deed and presses to get the aggressor out of Lebanon.

"The present-day Israeli policy makers should not forget that the Middle East is an area lying in close proximity to the southern borders of the Soviet Union and that developments there cannot help affecting the interests of the U.S.S.R. We warn Israel about this."

Implications of Soviet Action

The statement was evidently intended to arouse concern that American inability to arrange an early cease-fire between Israeli forces and Palestinian guerrillas could provoke direct Soviet intervention.

Theoretically, Soviet options would include an emergency airlift of arms to Palestinian guerrillas by way of Syria, which has signed a Treaty of Friendship and Cooperation with Moscow, or a new supply of weapons to the Syrian forces.

As if to underscore the Soviet warning, a Soviet general was reported to have begun talks in the Syrian capital.

Sources in Damascus identified the officer as Col. Gen. Yevgeny S. Yurasov, a first deputy commander of the air defense system. The sending of the general to Syria suggested that the

Continued on Page A20, Column 1

United Press International

Prime Minister Margaret Thatcher after addressing Parliament.

Bus-Only Lanes To Be Increased To Speed Travel

By ARI L. GOLDMAN

Mayor Koch announced yesterday the creation of a system of 10 "red zone" lanes for buses in Manhattan to help relieve traffic congestion, increase bus speeds and reduce what has long been the bane of bus travelers — bus bunching.

Along the pavement at each of the 10 thoroughfares in the program, a bright red eight-inch thermoplastic strip will remind motorists of heavy fines if they park, stand or travel in the bus lane.

"Don't Even Think of Parking Here," a sign along the routes will read. Other signs will warn that fines of at least $100 will be imposed on violators. Only cars preparing to make right turns will be permitted to travel in the lanes, and then only for short distances.

Next Tuesday, the first of the red zone lanes will go into effect, on Third Avenue from 36th to 58th Streets from 7 A.M. to 7 P.M. The others, which will be added over the course of the summer, will be in effect at various times on major thoroughfares in both midtown and lower Manhattan. Fourteen miles of city streets will be affected.

The other streets to get red zone lanes will be: Eighth Avenue from 42d to 57th Streets between 4 P.M. and 7 P.M.; Avenue of the Americas from 40th

Continued on Page B6, Column 1

TRIUMPH BY LONDON

Commander Says Enemy Troops Are Assembled 'for Repatriation'

By R. W. APPLE Jr.

Special to The New York Times

LONDON, Tuesday, June 15 — Argentine forces in the Falkland Islands have surrendered, halting the war in the South Atlantic, Prime Minister Margaret Thatcher's office announced early this morning.

A spokesman quoted Maj. Gen. Jeremy Moore, the commander of British land forces in the archipelago, as saying that enemy troops were being rounded up for eventual repatriation to Argentina. The surrender came at 1 A.M. British time, (8 P.M. Monday New York time), the official announcement said.

There was no confirmation of the surrender from Buenos Aires by early this morning, but the Argentine high command announced Monday afternoon that an unofficial cease-fire had gone into effect on the Falklands. [Page A14.]

'God Save the Queen'

General Moore radioed from his command post on Mount Kent: "Falkland Islands once more under Government desired by their inhabitants. God Save the Queen." It had taken the British three weeks and four days of fighting on the ground to retake the islands following their landings at San Carlos Bay.

The Prime Minister signaled that the end of the conflict, or at least this phase of it, was at hand in a statement to Parliament Monday night in which she said that Argentine forces in Stanley, the last major enemy stronghold in the Falklands, had begun throwing down their arms and hoisting white flags.

As the House of Commons erupted in prolonged cheers, the Prime Minister disclosed that the deputy commander of British land forces, Brig. John Waters, was negotiating surrender terms with the commander of the 6,500 Argentine defenders of the town, Brig. Gen. Mario Menéndez. The surrender terms, she added, would cover both East Falkland, the island on which Stanley is situated, and West Falkland, where two small Argentine forces are based.

Crowds Hail Victory

Within minutes of her statement to the House, crowds gathered outside Mrs. Thatcher's residence at 10 Downing Street, singing "Rule Britannia." When she returned from the House, they cheered her and she said, "What matters is that it was everyone together — we all knew what we had to do and we went out there and did it."

Although it remained possible that fighting would continue on or around

Continued on Page A15, Column 1

United Press International

Yasir Arafat, left, leader of the Palestine Liberation Organization, and an aide yesterday in Beirut.

1,600 Are Arrested In Nuclear Protests At 5 U.N. Missions

By PAUL L. MONTGOMERY

Offering daisies to policemen or chanting prayers for peace, more than 1,600 nonviolent demonstrators for disarmament were arrested in midtown Manhattan yesterday as they tried to block the entrances of the United Nations missions of five countries that have atomic weapons.

In an assembly-line operation that began at 7:30 A.M., the police carried the unresisting demonstrators to rented city buses to be booked for disorderly conduct. Some who had been arrested in the morning were back later in the day, encouraging their friends or sitting down again for another arrest.

The Police Department, which had 3,000 extra officers at the demonstration sites, said the total booked was a record for a civil disobedience campaign in the city. Patrick J. Murphy, the department's chief of operations, said, "almost everybody was very well-behaved — it was a textbook exercise."

The demonstrations, for which the participants were rehearsed and the police were briefed in advance, were a continuation of the protest that brought

Continued on Page A23, Column 1

U.S. Is Easing '68 Antitrust Guidelines on Mergers

By ROBERT D. HERSHEY Jr.

Special to The New York Times

WASHINGTON, June 14 — The Government, seeking to reduce uncertainty about the types of corporate mergers that it will allow, today published a new set of enforcement guidelines "more lenient" than previous antitrust policy.

Nevertheless, the Justice Department and the Federal Trade Commission, which share antitrust responsibility, said they did not believe that their long-awaited statements would lead to any significant increase in mergers, which have diminished recently.

Attorney General William French Smith described the new guidelines as an "evolutionary change — not a revolutionary change" from actual practices in recent years. William F. Baxter, the Assistant Attorney General in charge of the antitrust division, said that, "in general, the new guidelines would have to be regarded as more lenient." But he added that he did not expect them to encourage more corporate combinations than guidelines that have existed since 1968. Antitrust experts said the new guidelines were more than

Continued on Page D8, Column 4

INSIDE

Sports Pages

The New York Times today introduces Sports Pages, an expanded and redesigned sports section appearing Tuesday through Saturday. It will include added news as well as new columns and features. Today's section begins on page D25.

U.S. Enters Dollar Market

As the dollar reached new highs against the devalued French franc, the Administration intervened in trading to try to restore order. Page D1.

Ruling Due on Copying TV

The Supreme Court agreed to decide whether use of home video recorders to tape television broadcasts violates Federal copyright law. Page D1.

U.S. Challenged in Space

A lack of planning and foreign competition were reported to threaten United States leadership in nonmilitary space technology. Page C1.

17 Fakes at Met Museum

The Metropolitan Museum has discovered that 17 gold vessels it had been believed to be ancient Egyptian are modern fakes. Page C9.

War in the Falklands: On Downing Street, the Strains of 'Rule Britannia'

Britain Says Argentina's Forces Have Surrendered

Continued From Page A1

the islands, it appeared that Britain's campaign to reclaim its colony, which Argentine troops seized April 2, had been crowned with victory. Britain's triumph in the 10-week-old Falkland war was hailed here Monday night as a brilliant feat of arms, involving the assembly and support of a task force more than 7,000 miles from this country, hazardous amphibious landings and the crossing of a barren wasteland in arduous winter conditions.

The dramatic moves Monday and today toward an end of the war came after British troops under General Moore stormed into the outskirts — and, unofficial reports said, into the streets — of the Falkland capital. Argentine defenses were reported to have crumbled under the onslaught of artillery, naval gunfire, air attacks and the charge of as many as 7,500 foot soldiers — paratroopers, marines, Gurkhas and Guards.

Sweeping forward from their positions on the high ground just west of Stanley, which they had taken on Friday and Saturday, the British forces overran the main Argentine defensive perimeter in three places — Tumbledown Mountain, Mount William and Wireless Ridge. The Argentines broke and ran, falling back into a promontory of only about seven square miles around the capital and its strategic airstrip, it was reported.

General Moore's offensive plan had originally envisaged a pause there before the final assault, but as organized opposition collapsed he urged his men forward and they pushed to the edge of town.

It appeared that the defenders were short of food and water, and British correspondents in Chile, who have been monitoring the radio links between General Menéndez and the mainland, reported that the circuit went dead after an officer said the power was failing.

Even with the British triumph, extraordinary problems remain. The Argentine junta has vowed that it will not give up its claim to sovereignty over the Falklands, or the Malvinas, as they are called in Argentina, and most British politicians and military analysts expect Argentine forces to continue harassing actions from the mainland.

That means that Britain will have to maintain a large and costly garrison for the foreseeable future. Mrs. Thatcher has explored with the United States the possibility of American participation in a multinational peacekeeping force, but has been given little encouragement. There has also been talk of a possible administration by the United Nations.

But as the struggle for the Falklands reached its crescendo in the last 10 days, the Prime Minister has been insisting that Britain will go it alone, if necessary. Although the civil population of the islands is only 1,800, she has even begun to talk of independence.

The most difficult problem facing the Government is its commitment to self-determination for the Falklanders, who appear to have become even more unwilling to contemplate any role for the Argentines on the islands as a result of prolonged enemy occupation.

"All the News That's Fit to Print"

The New York Times

Late Edition

Weather: Mostly sunny and warm today; increasing cloudiness tonight. Mostly cloudy, chance of rain tomorrow. Temperatures: today 73-78, tonight 53-58; yesterday 62-77. Details, page B6.

VOL.CXXXII . . . No. 45,689 | NEW YORK, WEDNESDAY, MAY 25, 1983 | 60 cents beyond 75 miles from New York City, except on Long Island. | 30 CENTS

The New York Times / Dith Pran and Vic DeLucia

Part of the parade crossing the Brooklyn Bridge on the way to Manhattan. At left, fireworks exploding over the bridge last night.

An Old Bridge's Birthday Is a Hometown Carnival

By DEIRDRE CARMODY

With an unabashed outpouring of affection, New York celebrated the 100th anniversary of the Brooklyn Bridge yesterday.

It had been billed as a great day in the history of the city, and that is exactly what it turned out to be. In the morning, thousands of pedestrians, horse-drawn carriages and marching bands — filling the air with martial music — paraded across the stately bridge under summerlike skies.

Later there were street fairs, speeches, roof parties, boat rides and a harbor-craft parade. Evening fell gently over the bridge. As darkness came, a luminescent full moon filled the sky while a dramatic sound and light show was played on the bridge and recreated its history.

Then the sky simply exploded with fireworks. Red, white and blue shells, golden comets changing to silver, crackling stars in red and green, appeared to fill the entire sky, while hundreds of thousands of people gasped at the sheer dazzle of it all.

At times both towers were bathed in a golden glitter as a barrage of meteors showered down on the bridge. It was the biggest show ever put on by the Grucci family of Bellport, L.I., and included a total of 9,600 rockets, comets, aerial shell bursts and other pyrotechnics.

Many of the spectators rode a flotilla of fireboats, tugboats, military craft, private yachts and fishing boats that had moved up river under the bridge earlier in the evening. Some of the fireboats shot plumes of water into the air.

It was not the events, however, that made the day. It was the crowds. All day, it was abundantly clear that people were there by the thousands for no other reason except that they wanted to be there. They were there not so much to see as to participate. Enthusiasm and good humor burst from behind the barricades along the parade route.

The police estimated that 2.1 million people watched the evening festivities

Continued on Page B4, Column 2

High Court Bans Tax Exemptions For Schools With Racial Barriers

Burger Writes Forceful Opinion on Bob Jones and Goldsboro Cases, a Rebuff to Administration

By LINDA GREENHOUSE
Special to The New York Times

WASHINGTON, May 24 — The Supreme Court ruled today, 8 to 1, that racially discriminatory private schools are ineligible for Federal tax exemptions.

In an opinion by Chief Justice Warren E. Burger, the Court said there was no question that the Internal Revenue Service was correct when, in 1970, it stopped granting tax-exempt status to discriminatory schools.

President Reagan sought last year to revoke the 1970 policy because, he said, it had "no basis in law," in that there was no specific ban written in the revenue service code. This action came to symbolize his Administration's break with the civil rights policies of the recent past.

Excerpts from opinions, page A22.

The Court's decision today, phrased in unusually unequivocal and forceful language, was a nearly complete repudiation of the Administration's legal position. Associate Justice William H. Rehnquist cast the dissenting vote.

The White House referred questioners today to a statement by Attorney General William French Smith. Mr. Smith said the Court's ruling made it "clear that additional legislation is not needed" and that the I.R.S. should enforce the law.

"There can no longer be any doubt," Chief Justice Burger wrote, "that racial discrimination in education vio-

Continued on Page A22, Column 4

United Press International

William T. Coleman Jr., who argued position upheld by Court.

PRESIDENT'S PLAN FOR BASING OF MX APPROVED IN HOUSE

KEY VICTORY FOR REAGAN

Vote Is 239-186 for Resolution to Release $625 Million for Tests and Engineering

By STEVEN V. ROBERTS
Special to The New York Times

WASHINGTON, May 24 — The House of Representatives today approved President Reagan's plan to base 100 MX missiles in existing shelters under the plains of Wyoming and Nebraska. The vote, a major victory for the President, was 239 to 186.

The vote reversed a decision by Congress last year to block funds for the huge weapon, which could deliver 10 warheads to Soviet targets with great accuracy. The key to the switch was an intense lobbying campaign by Mr. Reagan, who played on the inclination of many lawmakers to support the President in matters of foreign policy and national security.

House roll-call, page A18.

The measure approved today would release $625 million for engineering and flight testing on the missile, funds that had been frozen by the lawmakers last year in disagreement with the Administration's plan for basing the missile in a closely spaced pattern known as "dense pack."

Senate Approval Likely

The Senate is also likely to approve the resolution when it votes on Wednesday. The measure does not need the President's signature.

The MX survived a test vote in the Senate today when the lawmakers, 59 to 35, blocked an attempt to delay consideration of the resolution.

The resolution freeing the $625 million is only the first hurdle facing the MX in coming weeks. The lawmakers must also vote on bills to authorize and appropriate $4.8 billion for the actual procurement of the weapons, a reduction from the original Administration request of $6.2 billion.

Reagan Links Vote to Arms Talks

In his lobbying efforts, the President portrayed the missile as the essential leverage in his search for an arms control agreement with the Soviet Union. In an article on the Op-Ed Page of The Washington Post this morning, Mr. Reagan described the impending vote by saying, "At stake is the future of arms reductions — balanced, verifiable arms reductions that can make the world a safer place for all the earth's people."

Critics retorted that spending billions on a vulnerable new weapon at a time of

Continued on Page A18, Column 1

Mutiny Dismissed by Arafat As a Bit of Qaddafi's Mischief

By JAMES M. MARKHAM
Special to The New York Times

MEJ EL ANJAR, Lebanon, May 24 — Yasir Arafat sat smiling tonight under a photograph of himself surrounded by equally jovial commanders of the Yarmouk brigade.

In a bantering humor, the chairman of the Palestine Liberation Organization dismissed a mutiny among a handful of his commanders down the road — in a place called Ait el Fukha — as a bit of mischief by Col. Muammar el-Qaddafi of Libya and Palestinian radicals gathered around a renegade known as Abu Nidal.

"All of them are about 150," said Mr. Arafat in his enthusiastic but imprecise English. "Now the head of this problem is Qaddafi. You can go anywhere in the Bekaa, in Tripoli. All the troubles they are exaggerating."

Since May 7, when Col. Abu Musa, a commander of the Fatah guerrilla group, tried to seize control of the elite Yarmouk brigade, Mr. Arafat has been traveling just about everywhere in the Bekaa region, rallying the 12,000 men he says he has here in eastern Lebanon and checking the contagion of rebellion.

For a group of journalists brought into the Syrian-controlled Bekaa today at dusk in the company of Mr. Arafat, Palestinian hospitality did not include a visit to Ait el Fukha, where the band of mutineers is said to have established itself behind barricades. Less than a mile, and some Syrian troops, separate the group from the Israeli lines.

'Only the Bad Ones Have Stayed'

"All the good people have left them, and only the bad ones have stayed," declared a young green-uniformed Fatah man who said he had deserted Colonel Abu Musa today. Sitting around a bright kerosene lamp, he and his comrades said that Colonel Abu Musa had some heavy guns but that the people with him were mostly gullible Palestinian teen-agers trucked in from Damascus, who had been told they were going to fight the Israelis.

The rebellion in the Bekaa has presented Mr. Arafat and his lieutenants with a problem, since it is evident that Colonel Abu Musa could not hold out

Continued on Page A8, Column 1

April Consumer Prices Up 0.6%; Jump Is Tied to Gasoline Tax Rise

By ROBERT D. HERSHEY Jr.
Special to The New York Times

WASHINGTON, May 24 — Higher prices for gasoline, housing and food helped raise the Consumer Price Index six-tenths of 1 percent in April, the biggest increase since last July, the Labor Department reported today.

However, most analysts said the rise, which was twice the average monthly advance for the period from September 1981 through March, did not signify any worrisome revival of inflation that some have feared could erupt as the economic recovery gathers strength. Rather, it was regarded as an aberration resulting in part from the 5-cent-a-gallon increase in the Federal gasoline tax on April 1.

"This figure does not provide cause for alarm and does not indicate a long-term upward shift in the inflation rate," Martin S. Feldstein, the chairman of the President's Council of Economic Advisers, said in a statement.

The rise in the New York-northeastern New Jersey area was even greater, 1.1 percent, and was the sharpest increase since last October, with higher shelter costs, airline fares and gasoline prices the main factors. [Page D6.]

The national increase in April amounted to an annual inflation rate of 7.2 percent, but Mr. Feldstein noted that, if energy were excluded, the annual rate of increase for the month would drop to 4.7 percent.

"Statistical distortions, whether on the up side or the down side, do not change the fact that, when transitory effects are excluded, the rate of inflation is now somewhere in the 4 to 5 percent range," Mr. Feldstein said.

Private analysts generally agreed. "It's a one-month blip, not anything to

Continued on Page D6, Column 3

Nash Convicted of Killing 4 in Parking Lot on Pier

The New York Times / Marilyn Church

Donald Nash listening as the verdict was read in State Supreme Court.

By SELWYN RAAB

Donald Nash, whom the prosecution described as a hired assassin, was convicted yesterday of murdering a Federal witness and three CBS employees in a Hudson River parking lot last year.

He was also found guilty of conspiracy to murder the witness and another potential witness last year. The second witness disappeared 16 months ago and is presumed by the police to have been slain.

A jury in State Supreme Court in Manhattan deliberated 13 hours over two days before returning with a verdict at 4:30 P.M. To reach the jury box, the nine men and three women had to walk in front of the 47-year-old defendant as he sat at the defense table. None of the jurors looked at him.

Then the jury foreman, Jean Shaw, announced that Mr. Nash was guilty of all charges — four counts of second-degree murder and one count of conspiracy to commit second-degree murder.

Mr. Nash, a husky, dark-haired man who wears thick tinted glasses, retained the same composure he had during the seven-week trial. After hearing the five guilty verdicts, he vigorously shook the hand of his lawyer, Lawrence Hochheiser. Later, Mr. Hochheiser said Mr. Nash had told him, "You did the best you could, don't worry."

As Mr. Nash was escorted out of the courtroom by guards, he smiled and nodded at the prosecutor, Gregory L. Waples.

Mr. Hochheiser said he would appeal.

Each murder count carries a minimum sentence of 15 years to life or a maximum sentence of 25 years to life. The conspiracy conviction provides for

Continued on Page B2, Column 1

Health Chief Calls AIDS Battle 'No. 1 Priority'

By ROBERT PEAR
Special to The New York Times

WASHINGTON, May 24 — The Government's top health official said today that the investigation of acquired immune deficiency syndrome had become "the No. 1 priority" of the United States Public Health Service.

Dr. Edward N. Brandt Jr., an Assistant Secretary of Health and Human Services, said the Government was taking steps in an effort to identify the cause and find a cure for the mysterious illness, known as AIDS, which leads to a breakdown of the body's immune system against disease. Dr. Brandt announced six new research grants for study of the ailment and the approval of a new heat treatment for blood products, through which some scientists believe the infectious agent might be transmitted.

At a news conference, Dr. Brandt also said he was urging state and local health officers to report all cases of AIDS. He said the Federal Centers for Disease Control had stepped up surveillance of the disease. Since June 1981, the centers have received reports of 1,450 AIDS cases, of which 558, or 38.5 percent, resulted in death. Among the 78 cases diagnosed at least two years ago, the fatality rate was 82 percent.

In the last three weeks medical journals have carried reports suggesting that the disease could be sexually transmitted from men to women and could

Continued on Page A19, Column 1

INSIDE

Satellite Sale Questions

The Justice Department has data that may contradict a former Administration aide on his role in a plan to sell Government satellites. Page A17.

Margiotta Clemency Drive

Nassau County Republicans are seeking Presidential clemency for Joseph M. Margiotta, whose two-year prison term is to start next week. Page B1.

U.S. Health Chief Calls AIDS Fight 'No. 1 Priority'

Continued From Page A1

be transmitted to children through "routine close contact" with adults. But Dr. Brandt said there was "no cause for fear among the general public that individuals may develop AIDS through casual contact with an AIDS patient."

He confirmed that half the AIDS cases had occurred in New York City, but he said he did not know why. "If we knew the answer why," he said, "we would really begin to understand this disease much more effectively."

While expressing "a sense of great urgency" about the disease, Dr. Brandt said: "We have seen no evidence that it is breaking out from the originally defined high-risk groups. I personally do not think there is any reason for panic among the general population."

Dr. Jeffrey P. Koplan, an assistant director of the Centers for Disease Control, said 71 percent of the AIDS cases had occurred among homosexual or bisexual men. Seventeen percent of those who contracted the disease had taken drugs such as heroin through their veins. Haitian immigrants accounted for 5 percent of the cases, and people with hemophilia accounted for 1 percent. Six percent of the cases were not in any of these groups, but Dr. Koplan said they might have fit into one of the categories if doctors had done more complete investigations.

Dr. Brandt rejected the suggestions of some critics who said the Public Health Service had neglected the disease because it occurred mainly among homosexuals.

But after he spoke, Virginia M. Apuzzo, executive director of the National Gay Task Force, a homosexual rights organization, said: "The entire agency is conducting business as usual insofar as this particular health crisis is concerned. It is inexcusable that a supplemental budget request has not been submitted to Congress."

Shellie L. Lengel, a spokesman for Dr. Brandt, said the disease had been emerging as the top priority of the Public Health Service in the last 6 to 12 months. The priority, she said, was reflected in spending, in personnel devoted to work on the disease, in the number of investigations under way and in the time and attention given to the subject by Federal officials.

Dr. Brandt said the Government expected to spend $14.5 million for work on AIDS this year. That is almost as much as the $15.9 million the Government has spent combating legionnaires' disease since the first recognized outbreak in 1976, he said.

In another indication of growing concern in Washington, aides to Senator Lowell P. Weicker Jr. reported that he would seek $12 million in additional funds for research and other activities related to the immune deficiency syndrome. The money, to be proposed as part of a supplemental appropriation bill for the current fiscal year, would increase Federal spending on the disease by 83 percent. Mr. Weicker, a Connecticut Republican, is chairman of the Appropriations subcommittee that handles money bills for the Department of Health and Human Services.

Some police officers have expressed fears that they might contract the disease through first-aid work involving mouth-to-mouth resuscitation, and some laboratory technicians have worried about being infected when they handle blood samples.

But Dr. Brandt said: "There have been no cases of suspected transmission of AIDS from a patient to a health care provider, nor have there been any cases of suspected transmission of AIDS from laboratory specimens to laboratory workers. There is no evidence to date that indicates AIDS is spread by casual contact. On the contrary, our findings indicate that AIDS is spread almost entirely though sexual contact, through the sharing of needles by drug abusers and, less commonly, through blood or blood products."

Dr. Brandt emphasized that the disease posed a high risk to homosexual men only if they had many partners. The disease has reportedly led to significant changes in the "gay life style." Miss Apuzzo of the National Gay Task Force said homosexual men "had become a lot more reflective" in their relationships, and in some cases, there was a "reduction in the number of partners."

U.S. Promises Navajos Help In Conserving Soil and Water

WASHINGTON, May 24 (UPI) — The Government agreed Monday to help the Navajo Indians with soil and water conservation programs on some reservation land.

In a memorandum signed by Agriculture Secretary John R. Block and the Shiprock Soil and Water Conservation District in Arizona, New Mexico and Utah, the department agreed to help a "broad program of assistance to land users in natural resource protection and improvement and rural development."

Shiprock is the fifth conservation district formed on the reservation.

The district includes 18,000 acres of irrigated farmland, 5,500 acres of unirrigated farmland, and forestland, the department said.

Bishops in Plea Against Smut

By CHARLES AUSTIN

Nearly 100 Roman Catholic bishops have written to President Reagan in the last month to ask that a Federal coordinator be named to monitor enforcement of obscenity laws, according to officials of Morality in Media, an interfaith organization concerned with pornography.

More than a dozen Eastern Orthodox bishops also wrote the President on the same cause, Evelyn Dee, the organization's director of information, said.

Members of Morality in Media and several conservative religious and political groups met with the President on March 28 to ask for stricter enforcement of the obscenity laws. Laws upheld by the Supreme Court enable the Customs Service, Postal Service and Justice Department to take action against those who broadcast pornography, import obscene materials or transport those materials across state lines, according to the Rev. Morton Hill, who heads Morality in Media.

But the priest said enforcement had "completely broken down" and that a Federal coordinator was needed.

Father Hill called the many letters from United States bishops "almost a miracle" because he said Catholic prelates in the past did not pay much attention to obscenity laws.

A Concerted Effort Is Rare

While Catholic organizations and some bishops have petitioned Government agencies about such laws, rarely has there been a concerted effort. "The average bishop or priest doesn't realize how serious the problem is," said Father Hill, a Jesuit who has been head of Morality in Media for 21 years.

John Cardinal Krol, Archbishop of Philadelphia, a participant in the meeting March 28, urged his fellow bishops to write the President, Father Hill said.

While Mr. Reagan made no commitment, Father Hill said the petitioners felt "very much encouraged that there would be an effort to move after this $6 billion industry."

Among the Catholic bishops writing the President were Terence Cardinal Cooke of New York; Timothy Cardinal Manning of Los Angeles; Joseph Cardinal Bernardin of Chicago; Archbishop James A. Hickey of Washington; Archbishop John F. Whealon of Hartford; Bishop James V. Casey of Denver; Bishop Gerald O'Keefe of Davenport, Iowa; Bishop Michael J. Dudick of the Byzantine Diocese of Passaic; Bishop Ernest C. Unterkoefler of Charleston, S.C.; Bishop Walter Sullivan of Richmond, and Bishop James D. Niedergeses of Nashville.

The Orthodox prelates who wrote were Archbishop Iakavos, head of the Greek Orthodox Archdiocese of North and South America, and the bishops of Atlanta, Detroit, Toronto, Boston, San Francisco and Pittsburgh. Bishops of the Rumanian, Antiochan, Serbian, Ukrainian, Albanian, Bulgarian and Russian Orthodox Churches also sent letters, according to Morality in Media officials.

Olympic Security Aide Hired

WASHINGTON, May 24 (UPI) — Col. Charles Beckwith of the Army, retired, has been hired as a special Defense Department consultant to study security for the 1984 Olympic games in Los Angeles, a White House spokesman said today. Colonel Beckwith, one of the most decorated soldiers in the Vietnam War, led an unsuccessful mission to rescue American hostages in Iran in 1980.

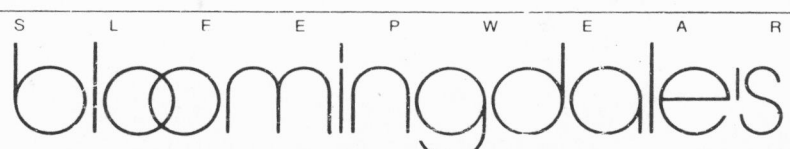

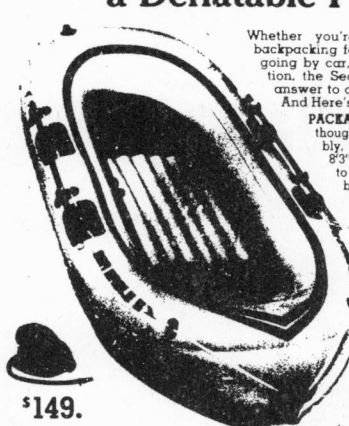

"All the News That's Fit to Print"

The New York Times

Late Edition
Weather: Mostly cloudy, humid, chance of showers today; cloudy, chance of showers tonight. Clearing tomorrow. Temperatures: today 78-83, tonight 67-73; yesterday 67-83. Details on page 33.

VOL.CXXXII . . No. 45,714 | NEW YORK, SUNDAY, JUNE 19, 1983 | $1.50 beyond 75 miles from New York City, except on Long Island. | ONE DOLLAR

Associated Press

Pope John Paul II at the Jasna Gora monastery in Czestochowa, Poland.

Pope Hails the 'Solidarity' of Poles And Gets a Tumultuous Ovation

By JOHN KIFNER
Special to The New York Times

CZESTOCHOWA, Poland, June 18 — Pope John Paul II, addressing a crowd estimated at more than a million people here, hailed the Polish people today for their acts of "solidarity" with those who were interned or dismissed from work under martial law. His remark drew a tumultuous ovation.

Although the Pope did not use the word solidarity to refer to the outlawed union of that name, his reference was unmistakable. The crowd rose in applause, with many people raising their arms in a V-for-victory sign signifying resistance, and they shook their red and white Solidarity banners.

Earlier in this increasingly politically charged visit, the Pope said on arriving here that the 1980 workers' uprising that led to the creation of Solidarity had "touched hearts and consciences" all over the world.

It was the Pope's strongest direct reference to the events surrounding the creation of the union since he arrived in his homeland Thursday on an eight-day trip.

The Pope flew to the Jasna Gora monastery here by helicopter this afternoon after visiting the monastery in Niepokalanow that was founded by the Rev. Maksymilian Kolbe, who gave his life for a fellow Pole at Auschwitz and who was elevated to sainthood last fall. [Page 12.]

Speaking soon after his arrival in Czestochowa, the Pontiff said the events of 1980 marked a time "when the Polish worker stood up for himself with the Gospel in his hand and a prayer on his lips."

The commitment of Poles to that struggle, he said, was "a testimony that amazed the whole world."

Gdansk Strikes Are Recalled

"The pictures that went around the world in 1980 touched hearts and consciences," the Pope said, referring to the August 1980 strikes that began at the Gdansk shipyard. The walkouts were settled under an agreement with the Government that permitted the creation of the first independent union in the Soviet bloc.

John Paul's first address here today was directed to members of the Baltic diocese of Szczecin. His later remarks, in which he used the word solidarity, were at a mass for Polish youths.

At that service, the Pope spoke of solidarity twice, first in reference to "historical experiences" that "tell us how much the immorality of certain periods cost the whole nation." In such circumstances, he suggested, there is a need for "love of neighbor," which he de-

Continued on Page 13, Column 1

CUBAN COMMANDER IN NICARAGUA POST

U.S. Says Intelligence Report Places Him on Duty There

By LESLIE H. GELB
Special to The New York Times

WASHINGTON, June 18 — Cuba's top military combat commander has been working in Nicaragua for about a month and has been "secretly assigned to duty" there, according to an intelligence report disclosed by a Reagan Administration official.

The commander was identified as Gen. Arnaldo Ochoa Sánchez, who as a brigade commander was said to have been instrumental in negotiating, organizing and leading the Cuban military buildup in Angola in 1976 and in Ethiopia in 1977. He is now deputy to Raúl Castro, Minister of the Armed Forces.

No Independent Confirmation

The report is based primarily on Central American military sources who, two officials said, have been reliable in their accounts of Cuban activities in Nicaragua.

These sources, according to the report, believe General Ochoa is organizing a "large-scale Cuban move into Nicaragua." One of the sources even said he would be chief of all Nicaraguan and Cuban armed forces.

Over the last few days, calm has returned to two Nicaraguan border towns where heavy fighting was reported last week between Nicaraguan forces and Honduran-based rebels. But a visit to the area turned up evidence that the insurgents caused extensive damage to farms and warehouses. [Page 10.]

Administration officials acknowledged that apart from the Central American sources, they had no independent confirmation that General

Continued on Page 10, Column 3

Shuttle Rockets to Orbit With 5 Aboard

Physicist Is First U.S. Woman in Space — Satellite Launched

By JOHN NOBLE WILFORD
Special to The New York Times

CAPE CANAVERAL, Fla., June 18 — Four men and a woman, the first American woman to go into space, rocketed into orbit today aboard the space shuttle Challenger and then launched the first of two satellites in the successful beginning of a busy six-day mission.

The winged spaceship lifted off on schedule at 7:33 A.M. after one of the smoothest countdowns of the shuttle program. It carried two communications satellites, an assortment of scientific experiments and a West German satellite that is to be released and then retrieved in a critical test of the shuttle's 50-foot mechanical arm.

Deployment of Missiles

On future missions astronauts expect to release small satellites with the mechanical arm and to rendezvous with ailing satellites to retrieve them for repairs in orbit or back on the earth.

One of the communications satellites, Canada's Anik C, was launched from Challenger's cargo bay late this afternoon and, with a boost from its own small rocket, sent spinning into the darkness of space on a course toward a 22,300-mile-high orbit. The other satellite, Indonesia's Palapa B, is set to be similarly launched Sunday morning to complete the mission's primary objectives.

But what set this flight apart from the 36 other manned American space missions over the last 22 years was not the cargo but the occupant just behind the two pilots. She was Dr. Sally K. Ride, a 32-year-old physicist who has been in astronaut training since 1978. She is the third woman to fly in space, but the first on an American mission.

2d Flight for Crippen

A crowd estimated at 250,000 stood in the bright morning sun to watch the seventh shuttle launching, and many of them wore "Ride, Sally Ride" T-shirts.

In his weekly radio address, President Reagan said that Dr. Ride's flight was "another example of the great

Continued on Page 20, Column 1

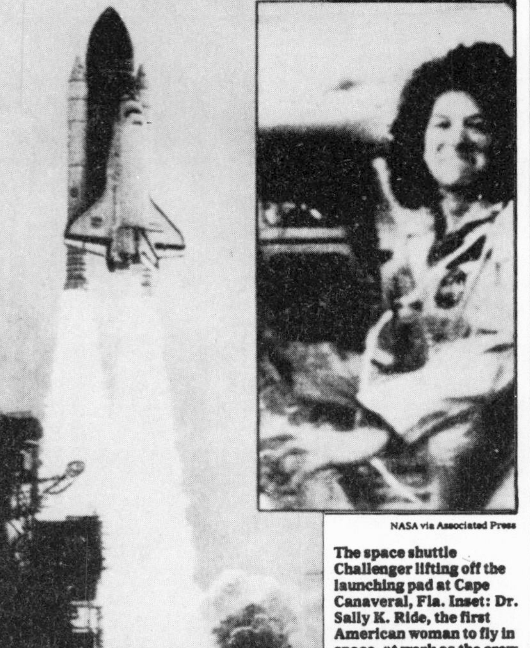

NASA via Associated Press

The space shuttle Challenger lifting off the launching pad at Cape Canaveral, Fla. Inset: Dr. Sally K. Ride, the first American woman to fly in space, at work as the crew prepared to deploy a communications satellite.

Cool, Versatile Astronaut

Sally Kristen Ride

By WILLIAM J. BROAD

The celebration over sending the first American woman into orbit has tended to overshadow the fact that Dr. Sally K. Ride is to be the first person to perform one of the most significant tasks of the space age.

Woman in the News

Reaching into the void with a 50-foot robotic arm, she plans to capture a satellite as it hurtles about the earth and, using mechanical might conferred by gears and motors, bring it safely to rest in the cargo bay of the space shuttle.

Her aerial exercise points to the not-so-distant future when it could be routine to grasp satellites, mine asteroids, build space stations — in short, to clutch and shape instead of just to pass through space as an awestruck visitor. It marks a new stage in the taming of the high frontier.

Even before liftoff, Dr. Ride had achieved world renown as the woman designated to break the all-male barrier in the American space program. There are now eight women in the astronaut corps.

Important Future Role

Dr. Ride will also play an important role in preparation for future missions. She will act as a liaison agent between the Government and private companies when clients from aerospace and military industries contract for space aboard the shuttle.

In the course of 32 years, Dr. Ride has devoted herself to the conquest of tennis, Shakespeare, physics and now the intricacies of space flight. Her diverse background, at odds with the narrow path of the speed-loving test pilots who pioneered the space program, has prepared her in an unusual way for the historic mission.

Sally Kristen Ride was born May 26, 1951, to Dale B. and Joyce Ride. Growing up in the Los Angeles neighborhood of Encino, she used to stretch

Continued on Page 20, Column 1

New China / United Press International

CHINA NAMES PRESIDENT: Li Xiannian, left, a veteran of the revolution, accepting the post in Peking. At right is Peng Zhen, new chairman of Parliament. The presidency had been vacant for years. Page 9.

Kean Orders 3d Dioxin Site Shut

By DOUGLAS C. McGILL
Special to The New York Times

CLIFTON, N.J., June 18 — Governor Kean said today that preliminary tests had discovered dangerous levels of dioxin in the soil at a chemical plant near an elementary school in a mostly residential area here.

He ordered the closing of a section of the plant, which is operated by the Givaudan Corporation, pending the results of further tests and an examination of employees who may have been exposed to the toxic chemical. The area to be closed is 160 feet long and 30 feet wide and contains 14 small buildings.

The Givaudan plant, at 125 Delawanna Avenue, is the third industrial area in New Jersey where dioxin contamination has been found. However, it is the first operating plant found to be contaminated, and the first whose daily business will be affected by a gubernatorial order.

Earlier this year, the New Jersey Department of Environmental Protection checked industrial records and identified 11 areas in the state where dioxin contamination might be found. The owners of the eight remaining areas are cooperating with the state to test for dioxin.

The two other areas, both of which were abandoned industrial plants, were in Edison and in the Ironbound section of Newark.

The Governor, at a news conference at Clifton's City Hall today, emphasized that there was "absolutely no evidence of off-site contamination" in Clifton. He added that "a number of precautionary steps have been taken to assure protection of public health."

The steps included covering contami-

Continued on Page 28, Column 1

Today's Sections

Index to Subjects

VOLCKER RENAMED BY REAGAN TO RUN FEDERAL RESERVE

WIDE SPECULATION ENDED

President's Declaration Cites Chairman's Record in Fight to Bring Down Inflation

By STEVEN R. WEISMAN
Special to The New York Times

WASHINGTON, June 18 — Ending months of speculation that has roiled the financial markets, President Reagan announced today that he would reappoint Paul A. Volcker to another four-year term as chairman of the Federal Reserve Board.

Taking time from his regular Saturday radio address for what he said was "a news flash," Mr. Reagan told listeners that he telephoned Mr. Volcker this morning and asked him to accept the reappointment.

"He's agreed to do so," the President said. "And I couldn't be more pleased. He is as dedicated as I am to continuing the fight against inflation. And with him as chairman of the Fed, I know we'll win that fight."

Credited for Cutting Inflation

Mr. Volcker's tight money policies in 1981 and 1982 were credited by most economists with helping to bring down the nation's inflation rate, and by critics with causing the recession.

The chairman issued a statement saying he was "gratified and honored by the expression of confidence by the President."

"As I have said on a number of occasions, I do believe we now have a rare opportunity to achieve sustained growth on a firm foundation of stabil-

The reappointment of Mr. Volcker appears to mean a stronger recovery this year and continuing into 1984. Economic analysis, Page 26.

ity," Mr. Volcker added. "I am sure I can speak for the entire Federal Reserve System as to our commitment to work toward that objective."

Mr. Volcker was appointed chairman by President Carter in 1979. His appointment to a new term beginning Aug. 6 is subject to approval by the Senate, but he was not expected to have much difficulty winning confirmation.

Support From Eagleton

In the regular Democratic response to Mr. Reagan's address, Senator Thomas F. Eagleton of Missouri, said, "I vigorously support President Reagan's reappointment of Paul Volcker."

Another Democratic Senator, Gary Hart of Colorado, who is seeking his party's Presidential nomination, issued a statement saying that "to the degree this represents a continuation of the policies of the past two years," the selection "could be a disaster for our economy and for the unemployed."

"But it actually matters little whom President Reagan appoints to head the Federal Reserve Board if the Reagan Administration's economic policies don't change," Mr. Hart added.

Senator John Glenn of Ohio, another

Continued on Page 26, Column 1

Debate Grows Over Adoption Of National Industrial Policy

By KAREN W. ARENSON

The ills of the American economy are obvious — high interest rates, high unemployment, low productivity, uncompetitive plants.

The cures are not so evident. In recent decades, Americans have successively taken, and then discarded, a variety of economic medicines, from Keynesianism to monetarism to supply-side economics.

Now, a new prescription — industrial policy — is sweeping intellectual and political circles. It is an idea that has been spurred by the success of the Japanese economy, and by the crucial role played by Japanese industrial policy and its centerpiece, the Ministry of International Trade and Industry.

The issue is prompting much debate. To supporters, a national industrial policy, aimed at helping particular industries, holds the key to reshaping America's economy and setting the course for future growth. To others, it is simply the latest brand of snake oil or voodoo economics.

The issue is attracting high-powered attention. In the past year, the Council on Foreign Relations, the Aspen Institute, Harvard University, Columbia Law School and the Federal Reserve Bank of Kansas City have all scheduled symposiums on the topic, with participants from politics and the academic world, unions and business.

In addition, industrial policy is expected to be an important issue in the 1984 Presidential race, provided the economy continues to have visible problems as the recovery progresses. Several Democrats have endorsed the concept, and industrial policy bills are beginning to appear in Congress.

The Republicans, on the other hand, are hoping that recovery will make the discussion moot, that the worst of the economy's troubles will disappear with the recession.

Industrial policy remains an elusive concept. It encompasses ideas, some of them contradictory, ranging from the establishment of an industrial development bank to support winning industries, to an industrial conversion agency to rehabilitate losing industries and their workers. Many proposals prescribe some type of three-way bargain-

Continued on Page 38, Column 1

INSIDE

Affirmative Action Gauged

A Labor Department study says affirmative action has raised minority employment in companies dealing with the Government. Page 16.

P.L.O. Guerrillas Clash

New fighting was reported between Palestine Liberation Organization units in Lebanon, scene of a month-old mutiny against Yasir Arafat. Page 6.

Shuttle Rockets Into Orbit; Crew Launches a Satellite

Continued From Page 1

strides women have made in our country."

Shortly after liftoff, John McLeaish, a public affairs officer at Mission Control in Houston, announced, "Space shuttle Challenger has delivered to space the largest human payload of all time — four men, one woman."

The four men are Capt. Robert L. Crippen of the Navy, who was a pilot on the first shuttle flight in 1981; Capt. Frederick H. Hauck of the Navy; Col. John M. Fabian of the Air Force, and Dr. Norman E. Thagard, a physician. A crew of four took the Challenger on its maiden flight last April.

Dr. Ride and Colonel Fabian, who holds a doctorate in engineering, are the nonpilot astronauts designated as mission specialists. They are responsible for deploying the two communications satellites and operating the mechanical arm as well as monitoring other payloads.

In his prelaunching commentary, Hugh W. Harris, another public affairs officials, noted Dr. Ride's repeated efforts to minimize the attention she has received as the first American woman to become an astronaut. "Dr. Ride emphasizes she is a mission specialist and a scientist who also happens to be a woman," he said.

Still, her presence was manifest before, during and after the launching. The last message to the crew before liftoff was, "Sally, have a ball." It was from her husband, Dr. Steven Hawley, who is also an astronaut.

'See You, Friday'

In the ascent, as the spaceship climbed toward an 184-mile-high orbit, Dr. Ride could be heard, in her role as a flight engineer, calling out checklists in a clear, businesslike voice.

Then, relaxing somewhat as the Challenger approached orbit, Dr. Ride radioed Mission Control, "See you Friday," referring to the crew's planned landing here at the Kennedy Space Center. This would be the first time a shuttle has been brought back to the three-mile runway at its launching base.

And, like any other astronaut after his or her first ascent into orbit, Dr. Ride sought to give expression to the thrill of a first flight.

"Have you ever been to Disneyland?" she asked Roy Bridges, the astronaut acting as the crew communicator at Mission Control.

"Affirmative," replied Mr. Bridges.

"This is definitely an E ticket," Dr. Ride remarked, referring to a ticket that the amusement park used to have for admission to the best rides, including the super roller coaster.

Setting Up in Orbit

Captain Crippen, more laconic, said after the craft reached orbit, "Nice flying machine." He was the pilot, with John W. Young, of the shuttle Columbia on its first flight and had now become the first astronaut to make a second shuttle flight.

The astronauts were generally quietly busy as they unstowed gear, checked out all systems and opened the doors to the Challenger's 60-foot cargo bay, in which were housed the two communications satellites, the West German satellite and another collection of scientific experiments. They transmitted television pictures showing the cargo bay and tail section had survived the vibrations of liftoff without visible damage.

Jay Greene, a flight director at the Johnson Space Center in Houston, said all the crew "seem to be in high spirits and performing well."

Observing the Payload

For the deployment of the Anik C communications satellite Dr. Ride and Colonel Fabian stood at a panel of controls at the rear of the flight deck, where they could observe through windows and television monitors the satellite at the aft section of the cargo bay. The satellite and its attached solid-fuel rocket weighed 7,400 pounds.

"It sure is fun," Dr. Ride said when she began operating the satellite deployment controls.

The satellite, built for Canada by the Hughes Aircraft Company, is a huge cylinder 22 feet high and seven feet wide when fully deployed. It will be placed in an orbit 22,300 miles over the Pacific Ocean. From there it is supposed to be able to relay the equivalent of 21,500 voice channels and is to be used initially by the GTE Satellite Corporation's direct-to-home pay television service in the United States.

The Palapa B satellite, similar in size and weight and also built by Hughes, is to provide telecommunications services for Indonesia and the Association of Southeast Asia Nations, which includes the Philippines, Thailand, Malaysia, Singapore and Papua-New Guinea.

The Challenger's Cargo

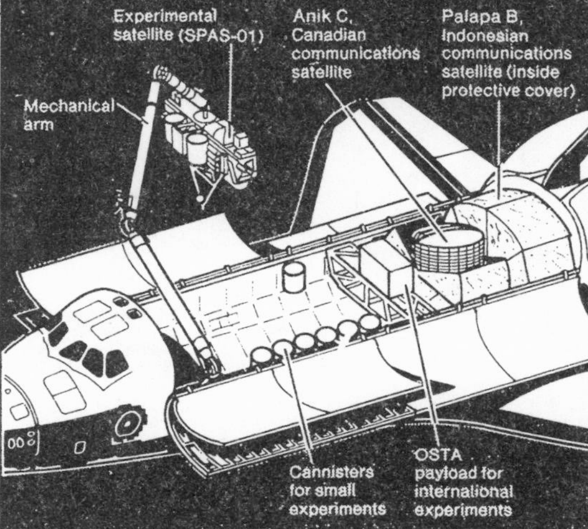

The New York Times / June 19, 1983

A chief assignment of the Challenger mission is to deploy two communications satellites, Anik C and Palapa B. Later the shuttle will test its ability to release and recover SPAS-01, the Shuttle Pallet Satellite. Other tasks include the small experiments called "Getaway Specials" and six experiments of the Office of Space and Terrestrial Applications that will be used to investigate the processing of materials in space.

United Press International

The Challenger lifting off yesterday in what Dr. Ride called "definitely an 'E' ticket." An E ticket covers the most popular rides at Disneyland.

Sketches of the Four Men of the Challenger's Crew

By BRYCE NELSON

Associated Press

Challenger crew members leaving their quarters at Cape Canaveral, Fla. In foreground are, from left, Dr. Sally K. Ride, Col. John M. Fabian of the Air Force and Capt. Robert L. Crippen of the Navy. Behind them are Dr. Norman E. Thagard, left, and Capt. Frederick H. Hauck of the Navy.

Robert Crippen

Capt. Robert L. Crippen of the Navy is the first astronaut to fly aboard an American shuttle twice. This time he got a promotion. After almost 14 years as an astronaut, the pilot of the Columbia's first flight in April 1981 has achieved his desire to command a space flight.

The flight commander is clearly overshadowed in public attention by Sally K. Ride, but when a reporter told him Texans did not think a woman could do an astronaut's job, Captain Crippen, a native Texan, bristled.

"I've found that all the women in the astronaut office have carried their share and more," he said. "We work together as a unit, but the fact that one is male and one is female, I haven't found made one bit of difference."

George Abbey, director of flight operations at the astronaut training base. said of Captain Crippen, "He's capable of some horseplay and he keeps the crew in a pretty good mood."

Captain Crippen was born 45 years ago in in a crossroads community north of Houston. He attended the University of Texas, where he received a bachelor of science degree in 1960 before entering the Navy.

He flew Navy jets from a carrier, and in 1981 he helped land the first space shuttle at Edwards Air Force Base. "What a way to come to California," he said at the time.

He is married to the former Virgina E. Hill, a Texan he met at the university. They have three daughters. On weekend mornings, he cooks waffles or onion-potato omelets.

Norman Thagard

The mission of Dr. Norman E. Thagard is to study the problem of space sickness, which has afflicted almost half the United States astronauts.

"I don't have to come up with a solution, fortunately, but there is pressure to get good data, and I feel real keen about doing that," he said. He will also be responsible for any emergency spacewalk. For amusement, he plans to listen to a tape of the rock group Devo and classical music including Gustav Holst's "The Planets."

While he was an intern, his wife, the former Rex Kirby Johnson of Atlanta, learned that NASA was looking for a mission specialist and sent in his application. He was accepted in 1978.

Norman Thagard was born in Florida 37 years ago and considers Jacksonville, where he attended high school, his hometown. He received bachelor's and master's degrees in engineering science from Florida State University before entering the Marine Corps in 1966.

He became a captain and flew 163 missions over Vietnam in 1969 and 1970. After military service he entered the University of Texas Southwestern Medical School where he completed his medical training in 1977. He has written articles on small computers' design.

John Fabian

Col. John M. Fabian of the Air Force, 6 feet 1 inch tall, feared he would never be an astronaut, but in 1977 NASA changed its height limit to 6 feet 4 inches from 5 feet 11 inches. Colonel Fabian, who was teaching at the Air Force Academy, was selected in January 1978.

He helped develop the mechanical arm that moves objects from the shuttle's cargo bay. Dr. Ride was his supervisor. Now they are to launch and retrieve a West German satellite with the arm. "Anything can put stuff into space," he said, "but only with the shuttle can you bring it home."

Of Dr. Ride, he said, "I don't think anybody in the crew feels the slightest pang of jealousy because Sally is getting all the exposure. I'm not speaking for my mother."

Colonel Fabian, 44 years old, was born in Goosecreek, Tex., the son of a Houston police officer. He received a bachelor's degree in mechanical engineering in 1962 from Washington State University and, in 1974, a doctorate in aeronautics and astronautics from the University of Washington.

As a pilot he won several medals, including the Vietnam Cross of Gallantry. He is married to the former Donna Kay Buboltz of Spokane. They have two children. He jogs, skis and collects foreign stamps.

Frederick Hauck

Capt. Frederick H. (Rick) Hauck of the Navy, the co-pilot, wanted to be a scientist much of his life. He never thought much about flying.

He took to physics at St. Alban's School in Washington, D.C., received a bachelor's degree in physics at Tufts University in 1962 and, after he joined the Navy, a master's in nuclear physics in 1966 at the Massachusetts Institute of Technology.

He is the son and grandson of Navy men, and had served two years on destroyers when he began his work for his master's. He decided nuclear physics was not really his field; the Navy then gave him a chance to fly.

Captain Hauck flew 114 missions in Vietnam and won nine Air Medals. In 1972, he was named the Navy's outstanding test pilot. He was selected for the astronaut program in January of 1978.

He is 42 years old and married to the former Dolly Bowman of Washington, D.C. They have two children. He says his pastime is to serve on the "backup crew" of a refurbished 1951 pickup truck he has given his 18-year-old son Stephen.

Women's Leaders Hail Sally Ride

By United Press International

Women who blazed trails in their own professions hailed the space mission of the astronaut Sally K. Ride yesterday as a giant leap for American women.

Elizabeth Hanford Dole and Margaret M. Heckler, members of the Cabinet; Beverly Sills, the director of the New York City Opera, and other women applauded as Dr. Ride, who is 32 years old, joined four men on a six-day mission aboard the space shuttle Challenger.

Even the feminist Gloria Steinem and Phyllis Schlafly, leader of the movement against the proposed Federal equal rights amendment, agreed.

"Neil Armstrong took one small step for man back in 1969, but Sally Ride is making a much longer step for both man and woman," said Mrs. Heckler, the Secretary of Health and Human Services.

Miss Steinem, the editor of Ms. Magazine, said it was about time the National Aeronautics and Space Administration realized that women were qualified for the space program. "Millions of little girls are going to sit by their television sets and see they can be astronauts, heroes, explorers and scientists," she added.

Mrs. Schlafly said Dr. Ride deserved a seat on the space flight but she said she did not envy the achievement. "I think it's fine, and I'm glad to give her my place; I have no desire to be an astronaut," she said. "My 18-year-old daughter doesn't want to be an astronaut either."

A Cool and Versatile Trailblazing Astronaut

Continued From Page 1

mightily in tennis tournaments to pull down a speeding ball. In her teens she was ranked 18th nationally in her age group, and Billie Jean King urged her to turn professional.

But in her junior year of high school a physiology teacher touched off a deep love of the scientific method that has dominated her adult life. The mentor was "intelligent, clear thinking and extremely logical," Dr. Ride recalled. "I had never seen logic personified before." Absorbed in science, she never forgot the art of staying cool under pressure, a trait developed through tennis that has speeded her career in the space program.

She graduated in 1968 from Westlake School for Girls and headed for Swarthmore College outside Philadelphia. Homesick for California after three semesters, she transferred to Stanford University and embarked on a program that satisfied her search for new worlds. Ever the athlete, she played rugby. And in 1973 she graduated with a B.S. in physics and a B.A. in English, having studied both equations and Shakespeare.

In graduate school at Stanford, she turned to the abstractions of X-ray astronomy and free-electron lasers. The work became quite esoteric. Whenever an electron is bent by a magnetic field it emits light, and a free-electron laser applies this principle to the generation of laser beams. She would spend hours lost in the contemplation of this process, imagining with the aid of equations how electrons would behave as they sped free through magnetic fields in the void of outer space.

Her research interested the National Aeronautics and Space Administration because the free-electron laser is considered a potentially efficient way of transmitting energy in space. It is also seen as a possible powerhouse for laser battle stations.

When her doctoral program was almost completed in 1977, she came across an advertisement in the student newspaper that changed the course of her life. NASA was looking for scientists who wanted to become astronauts. Women were urged to apply.

NASA Sought Generalists

NASA said it wanted people with eclectic backgrounds, with the flexibility to pursue excellence outside their field. The job, after all, was to be a mission specialist, which could entail such diverse tasks as studying the effects of weightlessness on a salamander, repairing a broken computer, launching a payload into space or capturing a failed satellite. Some scientists had dropped out of the program, longing for specialization.

Competing against 8,370 others, Dr. Ride easily passed entrance examinations and psychological testing. In early 1978 she was assigned to a team designing the shuttle's robotic arm, an engineering job far removed from her work in theoretical physics.

In this training she received her pilot's license. Col. John M. Fabian of the Air Force, a colleague aboard the Challenger who is a veteran of 90 combat missions in Southeast Asia, commented on her flying: "She's very cool — a very cool operator."

On the second shuttle flight Dr. Ride had the highly visible job of capsule communicator, the person on the ground who relays messages to the astronauts. Soon after that she was named mission specialist for the seventh flight of the shuttle.

Last July Dr. Ride and Steve Hawley were quietly married, making them the first astronauts to do so. He will fly aboard the 12th shuttle flight. Their house outside the Johnson Space Center in Houston is laced with mementos of the space age, including NASA posters, shuttle dishware, and a large photograph of astronauts on the moon in the master bedroom.

In her pioneering role, Dr. Ride has been subjected to a host of personal questions, such as whether she would wear a brassiere in orbit and whether she feared the flight would adversely affect her reproductive organs. Through it all she has remained unrattled, direct and concise.

"It's too bad this is such a big deal," she remarked at a NASA news conference. "It's too bad our society isn't further along."

"All the News That's Fit to Print"

The New York Times

Late Edition

Weather: Rain ending in the afternoon, cool, southeasterly winds today; remaining cloudy tonight and tomorrow. Temperatures: today 53-57, tonight 40-45; yesterday 48-59. Details, page D12.

VOL.CXXXIII . . No. 45,841 | Copyright © 1983 The New York Times | NEW YORK, MONDAY, OCTOBER 24, 1983 | 80 cents beyond 75 miles from New York City, except on Long Island | 30 CENTS

BEIRUT DEATH TOLL AT 161 AMERICANS; FRENCH CASUALTIES RISE IN BOMBINGS; REAGAN INSISTS MARINES WILL REMAIN

ATTACK IS ASSAILED

U.S. Says Terrorists Tied to Iran May Have Set Off the Lethal Blast

By FRANCIS X. CLINES

Special to The New York Times

WASHINGTON, Oct. 23 — President Reagan, voicing outrage over the "despicable" destruction of the Marine Corps headquarters in Lebanon, called on the nation today to be more determined than ever to keep a force in that country and resist "the bestial nature of those who would assume power."

The President, plunging into a day of emergency strategy meetings on the bombing, denounced the unidentified forces behind the attack and said the

Reagan statement, page A8.

nation "must be more determined than ever that they cannot take over that vital and strategic area of the earth."

Administration officials, emphasizing that there would be no change in the United States' military role in Lebanon, said there was "circumstantial evidence" that fanatic terrorists aligned with Iran may have been responsible for the truck bomb that razed the four-story Marine Corps headquarters in Beirut, leaving 161 dead and 75 wounded.

The White House spokesman, Larry Speakes, said this evening that the Administration was also "looking into" Syria's possible role in the incident, but he did not cite any evidence.

No Dramatic Moves Anticipated

Official spokesmen stressed that no dramatic countermoves by the military were anticipated.

In the aftermath of the attack, legislators from both parties said the Administration must redefine and clarify the role of its troops and their long-range mission in the Middle East. [Page A8.]

The troops, who were fired on by snipers even as they rescued the wounded at the Marine headquarters, have been drawing sniper fire from areas near their base at the Beirut airport for weeks. There have been re-

Prime Minister Pierre Mauroy of France condemned the Beirut attacks and said French forces would stay in Lebanon. Page A7.

ports that Palestinian guerrillas who have returned to the Beirut area were responsible.

The bombing put the Administration at crisis alert, with Secretary of State George P. Shultz postponing a trip Monday to Brazil and El Salvador.

"There is much that points to the direction of Iran," Secretary of Defense Caspar W. Weinberger declared after the first of two emergency briefings of the President by his national security advisers. The White House said, however, that the Administration had no conclusive findings and that the President had ordered additional intelligence investigations.

The President directed the Marine Corps commandant, Gen. P. X. Kelley, to go to Beirut to inspect the scene and

Continued on Page A8, Column 2

Associated Press

Rescuers removing a wounded marine on a stretcher from the rubble of the bombed-out building that housed a U.S. Marine battalion in Beirut.

BUILDINGS BLASTED

Truck Loaded With TNT Wrecks Headquarters of a Marine Unit

By THOMAS L. FRIEDMAN

Special to The New York Times

BEIRUT, Lebanon, Oct. 23 — A suicide terrorist driving a truck loaded with TNT blew up an American Marine headquarters at the Beirut airport today, killing at least 161 marines and sailors and wounding 75.

In an almost simultaneous attack, another bomb-laden truck slammed into a French paratroop barracks two miles away.

According to Lebanese Civil Defense authorities, at least 27 French paratroopers were killed, 12 were wounded and 53 were reported missing and believed buried in rubble. Official Defense Ministry figures issued in Paris listed 12 French soldiers dead, 13 wounded and 48 missing.

It was the highest number of American military personnel killed in a single attack since the Vietnam War.

The identity of the attackers still had not been determined tonight.

Vehicle Smashes Barriers

According to a Pentagon spokesman, a Mercedes truck filled with some 2,500 pounds of TNT broke through a series of steel fences and sandbag barricades and detonated in the heart of the Marines' administrative headquarters building shortly after dawn. The explosion collapsed all four floors of the building, turning it into a burning mound of broken cement pillars and cinder blocks.

Although a marine sentry was able to fire about five shots at the suicide driver and another marine threw himself in front of the speeding, explosive-filled truck, neither could block its entry into the headquarters building, where it exploded in a fireball that left a crater 30 feet deep and 40 feet wide.

In a haunting scene late tonight, rescue workers using blow torches, pneumatic drills and cranes worked furiously under floodlights to pry out the dead and wounded still crushed beneath the smouldering debris. Marine spokesmen said there might have been as many as 300 men sleeping in the building — which doubled as a bunk house — at the time of the blast.

'Carnage' Like That in Vietnam

"I haven't seen carnage like that since Vietnam," the Marine spokesman, Maj. Robert Jordan, said shortly after emerging from the rescue operation with his forearms smeared with blood.

Today's blast brought to 184 the number of Americans killed in Lebanon since the bombing of the American Embassy here in April.

Rescue workers were hindered in their movements by unidentified snipers who intermittently fired shots into the Marine compound from the nearby southern suburbs of Beirut. The marines occasionally returned the fire.

Less that two minutes after the attack on the Marine compound, a truck laden with explosives slammed into a building used by the French as a headquarters for one of their 110-man companies in the southern Beirut suburb of

Continued on Page A8, Column 1

MARINES' SECURITY RAISES QUESTIONS

Reagan Sends Commandant to Lebanon to Investigate

By CHARLES MOHR

Special to The New York Times

WASHINGTON, Oct, 23 — After a car bomb blew up the United States Embassy in Beirut on April 18, killing 63 people, the Marine force at the Beirut airport took steps to strengthen security measures against a similar incident, Marine Corps officers said today.

The embassy bombing, and at least seven other serious car bombings this year in Beirut, gave warning of a common tactic. But a determined terrorist overwhelmed the new airport defenses, raising questions about why the security measures were inadequate.

Larry Speakes, the chief White House spokesman, said tonight that President Reagan had ordered the Marine Commandant, Gen. P. X. Kelly, to go to Beirut to determine what security measures could be taken to improve protection for the marines in Lebanon.

'Unbelievable,' Kennedy Says

Senator Edward M. Kennedy, Democrat of Massachusetts, a member of the Armed Services Commitee, asked for an investitation by the committee into what he called the "unbelievable breakdown in security that allowed it to happen."

In testimony before the Senate Foreign Relations Committee in September, General Kelly said in answser to a question that the area of responsibility given the marines in the multinational force dictated their position and that the Marines Corps was satisfied with

Continued on Page A12, Column 3

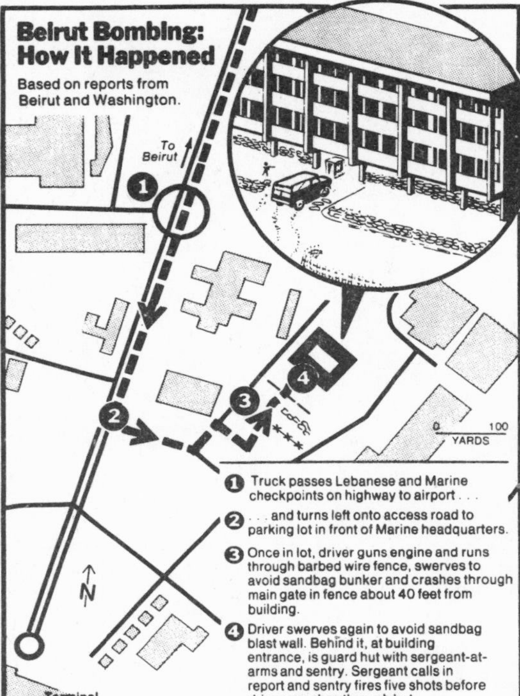

Beirut Bombing: How It Happened
Based on reports from Beirut and Washington.
To Beirut
1
2
3
4
N
Terminal
0 100 YARDS
1 Truck passes Lebanese and Marine checkpoints on highway to airport . . .
2 . . . and turns left onto access road to parking lot in front of Marine headquarters.
3 Once in lot, driver guns engine and runs through barbed wire fence, swerves to avoid sandbag bunker and crashes through main gate in fence about 40 feet from building.
4 Driver swerves again to avoid sandbag blast wall. Behind it, at building entrance, is guard hut with sergeant-at-arms and sentry. Sergeant calls in report and sentry fires five shots before driver smashes through hut.
Truck reaches central atrium and driver detonates bomb.

The New York Times / Oct. 24, 1983

'DON'T LEAVE US,' TRAPPED MEN CRY

Survivors Recount the Horror of Scene at Marine Base

Special to The New York Times

BEIRUT, Lebanon, Oct. 23 — Gunnery Sgt. Herman Lange was one of the first marines to get down to the bombed Marine headquarters from a nearby barracks.

"Bodies were lying around all over," he said. "Other people were trapped under the concrete. I could hear them screaming: 'Get us out. Don't leave us.' I just started digging, picking men out and taking them away on a jeep. It was total devastation."

The blast at the Marines' headquarters building, which housed the Battalion Landing Team and was known by the marines as the BLT, was so massive it dug a crater in the heart of the building 30 feet deep and 40 feet across. In the crater, piles of reinforced concrete, marines still in their cots, files, air conditioners, clothes and crates all intermingled.

Playing Cards and Deodorant

Classified papers were blown all over the area and the marines who survived scrambled to pick them up. The pile of rubble was peppered with personal items — a can of deodorant, a jack of hearts from someone's deck of playing cards and a United States quarter, twisted out of shape by the blast. "It felt just like an earthquake," said Staff Sgt. Alfonso Hernandez.

"I was sleeping in my rack in a tent about 200 yards away," Sergeant Hernandez said. "We were all thrown out

Continued on Page A7, Column 1

Questions on Mission

By BERNARD GWERTZMAN

Special to The New York Times

News Analysis

WASHINGTON, Oct. 23 — The devastating attack on the American marines in Lebanon today stunned the Reagan Administration and put it under new pressure to come up with a clearer explanation of why the marines are there.

Tonight the White House, seeking to justify the presence of the marines in Lebanon, said they had to remain there and not yield to "international terrorism." If they were withdrawn now, the White House said, "the civilized world" would suffer.

In the 13 months since the marines were sent to the Beirut area, the reasons for their presence there have shifted with the situation. At first they were dispatched to bolster the morale of the Lebanese people and Government and to be ready to help police areas that the United States had expected would be evacuated by the Israeli, Syrian and Palestinian forces.

But more recently, as the hopes for an early withdrawal of these forces faded, the marines, augmented by United States Navy ships, have become in effect a protector of the Lebanese Army, fighting off efforts by Syrian-backed Druse and Shiite factions to undermine the Lebanese Government. But even this role was ambiguous because the Administration would not sanction an all-out military role for the marines for fear of alienating Congress and friendly Arab nations.

Today President Reagan, clearly frustrated by the Marine casualties, vowed even before he had met with his National Security Council that the United States would not be driven out of Lebanon.

Yet after the morning meeting of the

Continued on Page A9, Column 1

United Press International

French paratrooper holding trapped comrade's hand at site of second blast.

Other News

Stirring Marathon Victory

Rod Dixon of New Zealand took the lead in the final mile to win the men's title. Grete Waitz won a fifth women's crown. SportsMonday, page C1.

Grenada Warns of Invasion

Grenada's radio issued a warning to the island's residents to expect an imminent invasion from the country's Caribbean neighbors. Page A4.

Mixed Signals for Bonn

The antimissile protests in West Germany conveyed signs of both disquiet and reassurance for Bonn and its allies. News analysis, page A3.

Augusta Suspect 'Troubled'

The suspect charged with taking hostages while President Reagan played golf was a 'troubled' man who may have been drinking. Page A14.

Food Tests Reviewed

A Louisiana laboratory's tests of chemicals for consumer use are being reviewed because a test on a coffee chemical was "sloppy." Page D12.

DeLorean Tape Shown

CBS News won a court battle and televised a videotape of the scene culminating in the arrest of John Z. DeLorean on drug charges. Page A16.

Bombings in Beirut: What Was the Motive?

Disruption of Peace Parley Is Termed Terrorists' Goal

By IHSAN A. HIJAZI
Special to The New York Times

BEIRUT, Lebanon, Oct. 23 — Some Lebanese officials asserted today that the terrorist explosions here that killed scores of United States marines and French paratroopers this morning were aimed at undermining the planned peace conference of the country's religious and political factions.

"Every time we make some headway, evil elements act to set us back by killing and destruction," Prime Minister Shafik al-Wazzan told reporters as he joined President Amin Gemayel and other officials in an emergency Cabinet session.

Others, such as former Prime Minister Saeb Salam, a key figure in the peace conference, said the attacks appeared primarily to be an effort to compel the withdrawal of the international force of United States, French, Italian and British troops.

Butros Harb, a member of Parliament and former Cabinet minister, said the deaths of the American and French soldiers had poisoned the political atmosphere and overshadowed the reconciliation process.

Political Effects Discussed

The state-controlled Beirut radio said the Cabinet in its emergency session today discussed the political implications of the bomb attacks against the marines and French troops.

While no evidence is yet available as to who may have been responsible for today's explosions, believed to have been caused by pickup trucks laden with huge quantities of explosives, accusations have been made.

The Christian Phalangist Voice of Lebanon radio said Syria and the Palestinians were to blame. The radio referred to an intensification of criticism of the United States in the state-controlled informational organs in Damascus and a declaration by an official of the Palestine Liberation Organization that preceded the violence today. The P.L.O. official said the multinational force must be withdrawn.

Today's explosions, which destroyed two buildings used by units of the multinational force, one at the Marines' headquarters at Beirut International Airport, the other at the French headquarters, came as President Gemayel was preparing for the peace conference now scheduled to begin in Switzerland at the end of this month.

Parley to Start Oct. 31

According to Lebanese press reports today and a statement in Bern by the Swiss Foreign Ministry, the Government-sponsored meeting of Lebanese Christian and Moslem delegations is to open at a Geneva hotel on Oct. 31.

An effort to open the talks last Thursday at the Beirut Airport failed after some of the principal participants objected to the site. They said they did not believe they would be safe at the airport, which is under the control of the American Marines and the Lebanese Army. The decision to hold the conference was part of the overall Lebanese cease-fire accord reached Sept. 26.

In Syria, a commentary broadcast on the Damascus radio today said that United States policy in the area was doomed to failure, but made no reference to the deaths of the French and American troops.

The radio commentary went on to say that American pressures on Syria would compel the Syrians to act to preserve their interests in the Arab world.

On Saturday, a Syrian Government newspaper, responding to President Reagan's remarks at a news conference last Wednesday, at which he accused Syria of obstructing the peace process in Lebanon, warned that Syrian troops in Lebanon had standing orders to retaliate in strength if attacked.

The article, in the newspaper Tichrin, said that Soviet-made surface-to-air missiles now in Syria's possession would not differentiate between American and Israeli jets flying over Syrian positions.

Some analysts here said the way the explosions were carried out today was similar to the manner in which the United States Embassy here was blown up last April 18. Sixteen Americans and more than 50 Lebanese were killed when a terrorist drove a car laden with high explosives into the embassy compound in West Beirut.

Druse Leader Condemns Attacks

PARIS, Oct. 23 (Reuters) — The Lebanese Druse leader, Walid Jumblat, condemned today's attacks on the international force as "tragic."

"I have nothing to do with this affair," he said in an interview in Amman, the Jordanian capital, with Radio France International. "But the military approach, from whichever side, is not the way to solve the Lebanese problem. There must be a political solution."

Mr. Jumblat said a withdrawal by the French contingent in the multinational force in Beirut could have severe effects.

"It's possible that the withdrawal of the French contingent, because it occupies certain strategic positions, especially in giving confidence to the Lebanese and Palestinian refugee population, would be disastrous," he declared.

"The presence of the Americans is another matter," he said. "But in any case I condemn these two attacks."

Swiss Announce Conference Date

BERN, Oct. 23 (AP) — The Lebanese peace talks will open Oct. 31 at the Inter-Continental Hotel in Geneva, the Swiss Foreign Ministry said today.

A spokesman, Maria Luisa Caroni, said the date for the talks among Lebanon's rival political factions had been set in coordination with Beirut authorities. Swiss officials said they would step up security at the hotel because of the bombings in Beirut today.

The meeting could not be scheduled earlier because hotel rooms were booked in Geneva by more than 10,000 people attending the World Telecommunications Exhibition this week. Swiss sources said they expected about 50 participants in the Lebanese conference, including advisers.

United Press International; Associated Press

THE FRENCH BARRACKS: A French paratrooper, above, standing guard by building that housed French troops, which collapsed after terrorist attack yesterday. Below: Rescuers carrying away a victim.

The Bombings

Following are the highlights of the stories on the bombing of Marine headquarters in Lebanon:

PAGE 1

A truck packed with explosives was driven into the United States Marine headquarters in Beirut, killing at least 161 marines and sailors and wounding 75.

President Reagan, expressing outrage, called on the nation to be more determined than ever to keep United States forces in Lebanon.

The Reagan Administration came under new pressure to provide a clearer explanation of the continued American presence in Lebanon.

The marines' defenses against penetration of their Beirut base were elaborate, officers in Washington say.

Marines at the scene recall the explosion — the fire, the screams, the bodies, the "total devastation."

PAGE A6

Derailing the peace talks was seen by Lebanese officials as the aim of the explosions.

PAGE A7

Israel offered help in rescue efforts.

France has no plans to withdraw its troops from Lebanon.

PAGE A8

New questions are raised as to what steps President Reagan can legally take in Lebanon.

Congress insisted on redefining and clarifying the role of American forces in the Middle East.

A re-examination of the military options available to the United States forces in Lebanon and offshore is under way.

PAGE A9

Americans reacted with sorrow and expressions of growing doubt about the nation's involvement in Lebanon.

The United States' participation in the mission will not be abandoned, but marines will take steps to protect themselves, Secretary of Defense Caspar W. Weinberger says.

PAGE A13

Marines should be removed from Lebanon, Mayor Koch and several officials from the New York area say.

Beirut Death Toll Put at 161 Americans; French Casualties Rise in Bombings

Continued From Page A1

Jnah, two miles north of the Marine headquarters. The explosion brought all eight floors down in a heap, like a fallen house of cards.

[A caller to the Beirut office of Agence France Presse said a group calling itself the Free Islamic Revolution Movement took responsibility, United Press International reported. The caller was quoted as saying that two youths carried out the attacks]

The two suicide missions were almost identical to the assault on the American Embassy here on April 18, when a pickup truck slammed into the front lobby and exploded, killing 63 people including 17 Americans. A collection of previously unknown pro-Iranian and pro-Palestinian organizations said they had been responsible for the embassy bombing, but the real identity of the attackers has still not been determined.

No 'Special' Precautions

According to Major Jordan, the Marine unit took no "special" precautions to guard against car-bombs after the embassy bombing, because it was constantly upgrading its security and it was felt that the combination of sandbag checkpoints and steel fence barriers was sufficient to deter any attack.

Major Jordan said the attack on the headquarters of the 1,600-man American force came at around 6:20 A.M.

A French officer who was standing near the Jnah barracks of the Third Company of the Sixth French Parachute Infantry Regiment at the time said the soldiers in that building ran to the windows to see what was happening after being jarred from their beds by the explosion at the Marine compound.

Less than two minutes later, as they peered from the windows, their own structure was blown out from under them by an almost identical attack.

A Lebanese Army explosives expert, Yousef Bitar, said the bomb that demolished the Marine headquarters consisted of roughly 2,600 pounds of TNT, while the charge that destroyed the French base consisted of about 600 pounds of the same explosive.

Bodies Thrown 50 Yards

The blast at the Marine compound was so strong it threw some bodies out of the building to distances of up to 50 yards. The force rattled windows and shook apartment buildings all over Beirut.

The marines and sailors in the barracks who escaped death or injury were quartered in other Marine installations tonight. An accounting of all the men who had been stationed in the bombed building was complicated by the fact that 30 or 40 men were on leave in Egypt when the attack occurred, and all personnel records were destroyed in the blast.

Marine replacements for today's casualties were being flown from Camp Lejeune, N.C., but it was not known how many were on the way.

The explosion at the French barracks blew the whole building off its foundations and threw it about 20 feet westward, while breaking the windows of almost every apartment house in the neighborhood. More than 20 Lebanese civilians were injured in the blast.

Grim-faced French paratroopers and Lebanese civil defense workers aided by bulldozers also worked under spotlights through the night at the French barracks, trying to pull apart the eight stories of three-foot-thick cement that had fallen on top of one another and to reach the men they could still hear screaming for help. They regularly pumped oxygen into the mountain of rubble to keep those who were still trapped below alive.

A Lebanese family lived on the ground floor of the French-occupied structure. According to neighbors, the father had just gone out to buy bread when the blast ripped through the building, trapping his wife and three children inside. The father leaned against a fence weeping with his aged mother as the rescue workers tried to extricate his family.

The explosions seemed timed to coincide with the start of Lebanon's long-awaited national reconciliation conference. Beirut newspapers said today the discussions were scheduled to begin in Geneva on Oct. 31. A statement issued in the name of President Amin Gemayel after an emergency Cabinet meeting tonight expressed deep regret for the loss of life among the multinational force and vowed that "no obstacles will affect the reconciliation process."

Heavy fighting broke out again this evening in the mountain village of Suk al Gharb, five miles southeast of Beirut, between the Lebanese Army and Druse militiamen.

Whoever carried out the attacks against the Marines and the French seemed to have had detailed knowledge of both the layout of their compounds and their mode of operation. The building occupied by the Marines had been controlled at various times in the last two years by Syrian troops, Palestinian guerrillas and the Israeli Army.

The French Defense Minister, Charles Hernu, flew into Beirut this evening to inspect the destroyed French building. After touring the blast site, he affirmed that the French troops would remain in Beirut.

One of the first American officials to tour the devastated Marine headquarters was the new United States Ambassador, Reginald Bartholomew. Mr. Bartholomew arrived here only yesterday afternoon. Today was his first full day on the job.

Conversations with some of the marines who took part in the rescue operations, as well as others who were caught up in the attack, made it possible to put together a rough reconstruction of how the terrorist bombing took place.

It is believed that at roughly 6:15 A.M. shortly after the sun rose over the mountains, a two-and-a-half-ton Mercedes truck came rumbling down the main highway leading toward the Beirut airport.

About a half mile from the airport there is a Lebanese Army checkpoint, behind which is a sandbag-surrounded bunker where a marine is normally on duty. The truck was apparently waved through the army checkpoint without a search, not unusual here, and it apparently continued on toward the airport. Marine sources could not say at this time whether a marine had been on duty at the post when the truck went through.

About 200 yards before the truck reached the airport building, it apparently turned left, crossed the highway and entered a large parking lot between the airport terminal and the Marine headquarters, situated in a structure called the Aviation Safety Building. There is no guard at the entrance to the parking lot.

Seventy-five yards long and 50 yards wide, the Aviation Safety Building was a sand-colored four-story structure with an atrium in the middle extending from the ground floor to the roof. It was the headquarters for all the Marine companies serving in the area around the airport and contained a mess hall, library, chapel, gymnasium, administrative offices holding all the medical records of the marines in Beirut, an infirmary, a supply room, an ammunition dump in the basement and cots on almost every floor.

The top of the building contained several telescopes that were used for spotting the sources of attacks on the Marines during the last two weeks. The building was known officially as the "BLT" — Battalion Landing Team headquarters — but was dubbed by the marines "The California Hilton."

It was not the overall command center, however. That building, where the officer in charge, Col. Timothy Geraghty, has his offices, is situated 200 yards farther north. Colonel Geraghty was there at the time of the blast.

According to an unidentified Marine witness quoted by Major Jordan, the Mercedes truck entered the asphalt parking lot, started to pick up speed and began heading north, straight for the headquarters building. The first barrier it apparently encountered was a simple row of barbed wire that bisected the parking lot. The truck apparently ran right over the wire without difficulty.

By now it was speeding and entered the northern half of the parking lot. This is an open area with a bunker made of sandbags situated in the middle. The bunker houses guards from the Lebanese Army and usually a Marine. Whether a Marine was on duty with the Lebanese guards is not clear. In any event, the Mercedes easily drove around the sandbagged bunker and headed straight for the six-foot-high wrought-iron fence that surrounded the headquarters.

At about this point, according to Major Jordan, the Marine sergeant-at-arms standing outside the headquarters radioed the operations room and said something like, "A large truck is barring down on me." That was all he had time to say.

Truck Bursts Through Gate

Seconds later the truck reached the main gate protecting the entry of the building, which also consists of iron grillwork, and smashed through it.

As the truck was bursting through the gate, an unidentified marine quoted by Major Jordan was taking a drink of watr from a tank off to the side of the building.

"The marine said he heard a roar as the truck burst through the fence and approached the BLT," Major Jordan said, "and then he remembers thinking, 'Oh God, a car-bomb.'"

Once the truck was through the fence gate, according to Major Jordan, the sergeant-at-arms standing at the sentry post at the front door of the building ordered his sentry to lock, load and fire his M-16 rifle. According to the witness, the sentry fired at least five rounds at the truck.

But it did no good. The truck broke down the gate and then swerved around a blast wall of sandbags about 15 feet in front of the building entry. According to the witnesses quoted by Major Jordan, another marine threw himself in front of the truck, but to no avail.

Now the truck was moving even faster, said Major Jordan, and the only thing between it and the building was the sentry box at the front door. The sentry box consisted of sandbags and glass in wood frames. The Mercedes apparently smashed right through it and drove straight into the heart of the building's lobby. There, the driver of the truck detonated the explosive.

Some Marines said that the presence of mind of the driver, who steered the truck through all the barriers, swerved around bunkers, ignored the rifle fired directed at him and then detonated the bomb not a moment too soon was nothing short of remarkable.

International Forces In Lebanon

FRANCE: 2,000 soldiers — two armored squadrons, one armored car detachment, five infantry companies, a company of engineers and a signal unit — armed with heavy machine guns, mortars light armored cars and conventional infantry weapons.

ITALY: 1,400 soldiers, armed with heavy machine guns, mortars and conventional infantry weapons.

BRITAIN: 90 soldiers in a squadron of light armored cars.

UNITED STATES: 1,600 marines, most ashore, armed with howitzers, mortars and conventional infantry weapons, the rest in reserve offshore in amphibious ships.

Four Cobra helicopters armed with Tow missiles and machine guns or cannon.

Four M-60 tanks armed with 105-mm. guns.

Three destroyers, the battleship New Jersey and one aircraft carrier, the Dwight D. Eisenhower, carrying 84 aircraft, stationed with amphibious ships offshore.

The New York Times / Oct. 24, 1983

"All the News That's Fit to Print"

The New York Times

Late Edition

Weather: Mostly cloudy and cool, brisk northeasterly winds today; remaining cloudy and cool tonight and tomorrow. Temperatures: today 49-51 tonight 41-43; yesterday 46-53. Details, page C20.

VOL.CXXXIII . No. 45,843 NEW YORK, WEDNESDAY, OCTOBER 26, 1983 — 50 cents beyond 75 miles from New York City, except on Long Island — 30 CENTS

1,900 U.S. TROOPS, WITH CARIBBEAN ALLIES, INVADE GRENADA AND FIGHT LEFTIST UNITS; MOSCOW PROTESTS; BRITISH ARE CRITICAL

Toll Climbs In Bombing In Lebanon

216 Americans Dead, 20 to 30 Missing

By THOMAS L. FRIEDMAN

Special to The New York Times

BEIRUT, Lebanon, Oct. 25 — Gen. Paul X. Kelley, the United States Marine commandant, arrived here from Washington today as the Marine contingent was placed on its highest state of alert.

Late in the day, it was announced that the number of American military personnel killed in Sunday's bombing of the Marine headquarters had risen to 216, with 20 to 30 bodies still believed buried in the rubble of the headqurters building at the Beirut airport.

The alert was ordered after an early morning intelligence warning was passed to the marines by the Lebanese Army saying that three vehicles reportedly carrying high explosives were circling the area and might strike at the Marine compound.

[Vice President Bush left Washington for Beirut, where he will meet with President Amin Gemayel and visit with the Marine force, The Associated Press reported. Mr. Bush, whose trip was announced after his departure, is expected to return Wednesday night, a White House spokesman said.]

Removal of Barrier Reported

In another development, a marine officer familiar with the bombed compound said that two long, thick pipes that had been placed as barriers in front of the entryway of the headquarters to protect against car-bomb attacks had been removed several days before Sunday's attack.

This evening, a Marine spokesman, Maj. Robert Jordan, said he could not say for certain whether the pipes, which had apparently been installed months ago, had been in their position at the time of the attack.

General Kelley came to the Lebanese capital to review security measures at the Marine compound and to meet with the members of the American contingent in the multinational force here.

Replacements Arrive

Hours before General Kelley reached Beirut, 300 more marines arrived by plane from the United States to replace their fallen comrades.

General Kelley toured the ruins of the Battalion Landing Team headquarters, while marines and Lebanese civil defense workers continued to excavate bodies from the jagged wreckage of the

Continued on Page A6, Column 1

United Press International

President Reagan, accompanied by Prime Minister Eugenia Charles of Dominica, holding a news conference on the Grenada invasion. Listening were Secretary of State George P. Shultz, Defense Secretary Caspar W. Weinberger and, behind them, David R. Gergen, the White House communications director.

Key Events in Caribbean Invasion

Puerto Rico and Barbados: 1,200-member Marine unit reportedly assembles in Panama and in Puerto Rico, while 700 Army Rangers are said to leave from Barbados; 300 soldiers are provided by Organization of Eastern Caribbean States.

FLA. BAHAMAS CUBA DOMINICAN REP. JAMAICA HAITI PUERTO RICO ANTIGUA DOMINICA ST. LUCIA BARBADOS Caribbean Sea ST. VINCENT GRENADA COLOMBIA PANAMA VENEZUELA TRINIDAD AND TOBAGO

St. George's: Invaders reportedly seize most of southern half of capital, where Cubans had been living.

PEARLS AIRPORT Grenville GRENADA

Medical School: Both campuses of school where Americans are enrolled are quickly secured.

St. George's SOUTH EAST MOUNTAIN SOVIET EMBASSY POINT SALINES

Point Salines and Pearls Airport: 700 U.S. troops land at Point Salines, where Cubans were building an international airport; 600 Americans land at Pearls. Later 300 Caribbean soldiers are flown in, and 600 U.S. marines remain in helicopter carrier offshore.

Miles 0 4

The New York Times/Oct. 26, 1983

Airports Seized, Drive on Capital Faces Stiff Fire

By MICHAEL T. KAUFMAN

Special to The New York Times

BRIDGETOWN, Barbados, Oct. 25 — An assault force spearheaded by United States troops invaded Grenada before dawn today and soon seized both of the island's airfields. But the advance of the invaders, who included contingents from seven Caribbean nations, was reportedly slowed in the afternoon by heavy fire in the capital.

According to military and intelligence sources in the Caribbean, the initial landings were made by helicopter. Fire from armed Cubans met those landing at a jet runway being completed by Cuban workers at Point Salines, four miles south of St. George's, the capital.

In the initial contact, 12 Cubans were killed and 24 captured, according to officials of the Barbados Government, one of the contributors of troops to the invading force.

Russians Reported Seized

The United States contingent consisted of marines and army rangers. At least one marine was reported here to have been killed; in Washington the Defense Department put the number of Marine dead at two.

Radio stations here reported that 30 Soviet advisers to the Grenadian Government had been seized. But officials here said they could not confirm that report.

By this afternoon, a source who had returned from Grenada reported that the invading force had established a perimeter that included the southern half of St. George's. The part of the city held by the multinational force included the deep-water harbor, the Prime Minister's residence and the Grenada Beach Hotel, the former Holi-

Continued on Page A17, Column 3

2 AMERICANS KILLED

Cubans Clash With Force — 30 Soviet Advisers Are Reported Safe

By HEDRICK SMITH

Special to The New York Times

WASHINGTON, Oct. 25 — President Reagan announced today that he had ordered a predawn invasion of Grenada by nearly 1,900 marines and Army airborne troops.

He said the invasion was intended to protect American citizens and to help restore democratic institutions on the Caribbean island.

The Defense Department said two Americans had been killed.

Four hours after the American landings began, the President said the

Reagan statement, page A16; Shultz news conference, page A18.

operation was launched in response to an urgent request from some members of the Organization of Eastern Caribbean States, some of which provided 300 troops for the operation.

'No Choice But to Act'

The United States, President Reagan told a 9 A.M. news conference, "had no choice but to act strongly and decisively" to oppose "a brutal gang of leftist thugs" that had violently seized power on Oct. 12, later executed Prime Minister Maurice Bishop and other Cabinet ministers, recently imposed a "shoot on sight" curfew and shut down the international airports this weekend when some of the 1,000 Americans on the island wanted to leave.

The President said American forces had quickly "secured" the island's two airports. This afternoon, Secretary of State George P. Shultz said American troops had identified and were assuring the safety of 30 Soviet military advisers on the island and had also taken over part of the island's medical school, where more than 500 Americans are studying.

'Pockets of Resistance'

Mr. Shultz said American forces had encountered "pockets of resistance" around the capital city of St. George's and were also fighting some of the 600 armed Cuban construction workers building an airfield near Point Salines. But he gave no details. A Cuban broadcast, quoted by The Associated Press, said that "at nightfall the heroic resistance of our constructors and collaborators continued."

Tonight, at an urgent meeting of the United Nations Security Council called to discuss the situation in Grenada, the United States clashed sharply with Latin American countries critical of the invasion. [Page A18.]

Extremely tight secrecy surrounded the invasion and only at 9 P.M. did the Pentagon release its first combat communiqué, reporting that two American troops had been killed and 23 wounded

Continued on Page A16, Column 1

U.S. WAS WARNED BY MRS. THATCHER

She Urged Caution on Reagan — London Played No Role

By BARNABY J. FEDER

Special to The New York Times

LONDON, Oct. 25 — Prime Minister Margaret Thatcher said today that the British Government had urged President Reagan to reconsider his plans to launch an invasion of Grenada after learning of them Monday, and that no British ships or forces had taken part.

The announcement in the House of Commons that Grenada, a member of

The Soviet press called the invasion an "act of undisguised banditry." Cuba said its workers in Grenada had been ordered not to give up under any circumstances. Page A17.

the Commonwealth, had been invaded by an ally despite the Government's expressed misgivings led to harsh criticism of both the British Government and President Reagan by opposition parties and some of Mrs. Thatcher's own Conservatives.

France described the invasion as "a surprising action in relation to international law" and said it had not been informed of the action. [Page A17.]

Opposition Speaks of Deception

Sir Geoffrey Howe, the Foreign Secretary, underwent 45 minutes of tumultuous questioning when called upon to explain the events that had begun to unfold hours after he assured the House on Monday that there was no reason to anticipate any military intervention in Grenada.

Denis Healey, the Labor Party's spokesman on foreign affairs, said the United States and some Commonwealth nations in the Caribbean had deceived Britain about their plans.

"None of the objectives stated by President Reagan justifies the invasion of an independent state," Mr. Healey said.

The Government, however, refused to condemn the invasion. Mrs. Thatcher said, "We understand that what weighed heavily with the United

Continued on Page A17, Column 1

Associated Press

Gen. Hudson Austin, head of Grenada's military junta.

Agony of Lebanon Is Felt in Connecticut

By SUSAN CHIRA

Special to The New York Times

NAUGATUCK, Conn., Oct. 25 — Schoolchildren passed around Dwayne Wigglesworth's picture and talked about why people were killing one another in Lebanon. Older men talked about why the young always had to die, and young boys talked about whether they would have to fight, too.

Lance Corporal Wigglesworth, 19 years old, died Sunday in Beirut, a victim of the terrorist bombing against the Marines. Today, as word of his death spread, people here thought of how they could comfort members of his family, who live in this town of nearly 30,000. Neighbors and strangers called the Wigglesworth home, offering help or bringing food.

The fighting in Beirut came home to this town Monday morning, when three marines in dress blues knocked on the door of the Wigglesworths' home to tell them what they had been praying not to hear.

"The first reaction is anger, hatred, all the frustration," said Henry Wigglesworth, Corporal Wigglesworth's father. "There are a lot of whys, a lot of questions, and we haven't had the answers yet to give anybody else."

The Wigglesworths have seven other sons and one daughter. Robyn, 21, is a marine stationed in Japan. Gary, 22, is in the Army, stationed at Fort Bragg, N.C.

Gary and Dwayne spent the last month before Corporal Wigglesworth was sent to Beirut "fishing and enjoying each other," their father said.

Today Robyn arrived home to be with his family, and Corporal Wigglesworth's death was the topic of conversation at shoe stores and stationers, at schools and at City Hall.

"It's not only people outside that we don't know getting killed," said Paul DeFranzo, 18. "It's somebody from your own hometown. It makes you think even harder."

"I feel sorry for people who have to suffer because it's in the family," said Robin Henao, a 13-year-old seventh grader at the Hillside Middle School. Her teacher passed Corporal Wigglesworth's picture around her social studies class and read them news of Lebanon from the newspaper.

Five flags surrounded the war me-

Continued on Page A7, Column 1

Days of Crisis for President: Golf, a Tragedy and Secrets

By FRANCIS X. CLINES

Special to The New York Times

WASHINGTON, Oct. 25 — At midday Saturday, as President Reagan was in the midst of a round of golf at the Augusta National Golf Course in Georgia, he had under active consideration a secret request from Caribbean nations to join in the invasion of Grenada.

The President, already a legend in the Administration for keeping his own counsel, had begun the most secretive and momentous week of his incumbency with a golf club in his hands.

One of his golfing partners, Secretary of State George P. Shultz, was receiving the latest details of Grenada plans going on back in Washington, and discussing them with the President on the golf course, according to White House officials.

At the same time, the President's national security adviser, Robert C. McFarlane, was monitoring the situation nearby as the President stroked away.

On Sunday morning, the Grenada issue was further laid out in Administration study papers as Mr. Reagan made a sudden return home and appeared standing in the rain outside the White House, grief-stricken and mourning the marines who had died in the shocking Beirut explosion a few hours earlier.

The national security meetings that followed were ostensibly devoted entirely to the Lebanon crisis, but today it became clear that they also advanced the Grenada invasion decision

Continued on Page A22, Column 3

An Invasion Prompted by Previous Debacles

By BERNARD GWERTZMAN

Special to The New York Times

News Analysis

WASHINGTON, Oct. 25 — Behind President Reagan's decision to invade Grenada today was his concern that the island not become either "another Iran," where Americans were held hostage for 444 days, or "another Beirut," where the United States was powerless on Sunday to prevent the death of more than 200 marines, Administration officials said.

But in addition to these reasons, which Secretary of State George P. Shultz insisted were the paramount ones, there was additional motivation, officials said: to rid the Caribbean of a potential outpost for Cuba and the Soviet Union and to stop what the Administration perceived as a drift toward more radicalism in the region.

Some officials said the White House could not afford "another Nicaragua," the Cuban ally in Central America, while others said a more real concern was that there not be "another Suriname," the former Dutch colony in northern South America that was taken over by leftists last year in a coup.

The move also demonstrated the determination of this Administration not to appear passive in the face of foreign crisis. A French diplomat, who derided the Grenada invasion, said the President looked as if he was "flailing around," striking at the Grenadians out of his frustration at not being able to hit Damascus, Havana or Moscow. White House officials defended the President as being suitably cautious, but unwilling to run the risk of being compared to his predecessor, Jimmy Carter, whose handling of the hostage crisis in Iran may have caused him to lose the election to Mr. Reagan.

The invasion, however, has produced a new series of international problems for the Administration, already faced with a difficult crisis in Lebanon. Launching the action without advance consultation with Congress, and without the cooperation of its key North Atlantic Treaty Organization and Latin American allies, the Administration

Continued on Page A17, Column 2

INSIDE

Civil Rights Dismissals

In an unexpected move, President Reagan removed three Democratic critics from the United States Commission on Civil Rights. Page A24

Indian Pt. Change [illegible]

A panel told the [illegible] Commission [illegible] improvements [illegible] the Indian Point [illegible] Page B2.

Invasion of Grenada: American Military Is Stretched Thin

U.S. Forces: Need Arising for More Troops, Ships and Planes

By DREW MIDDLETON

The strain on United States military resources is growing, and Defense Department officials say they believe that if it continues, as appears likely, more troops, ships and aircraft will be needed.

Military Analysis

They said present military commitments and operational plans for future contingencies had stretched available forces thin in this country and abroad. The demands responsible for the strain include the landing yesterday of about 2,000 troops in Grenada, the replacement of marines lost in Sunday's bomb attack on the Marine contingent's base in Lebanon, the probable reinforcement of that force and the deployment of Army and Navy forces in Central America.

The armed forces of the United States total 2,136,400 people.

The Marine Corps, which has been called on to plug strategic holes in the Middle East and Central America, is 194,600 strong. It is organized in three divisions from which the Marine Amphibious Units that have been used in Lebanon and Grenada are drawn.

Army personnel amounts to 780,800. There are four armored divisions, six mechanized infantry divisions, four infantry divisions, one air assault division, one airborne division, twenty brigades and three armored cavalry regiments.

Reserves the First Option

Senior officers in the Pengagon and some State Department officials said they believed that, at the moment, the military resources would suffice. But should another serious contingency arise — the Persian Gulf and a possible Soviet threat to Saudi Arabia were cited as a constant worry — they said the United States might be hard pressed to meet it.

In that case, the sources said, the Administration would have to look first to the Individual Ready Reserve, whose members have recently served in the regular forces or the Selected Reserve and have some period of obligatory service remaining.

The sources said they thought the recall of this force — a total of just under 400,000 troops for all services — should enable the regular forces to meet new global crises. If not, they said, the National Guard and the reserves might be required to fill out the regular forces.

In estimating the ability of American forces to fulfill military commitments or meet new contingencies, the Pentagon must take into account that the reservoir of forces in the United States is not large and that seven of its divisions are scheduled for reinforcement of the Seventh Army in West Germany in a crisis.

A military response to, for instance, a Communist-inspired revolution in Iran, officials said, could force the use of the Rapid Deployment Joint Task Force of one airbone, one air assault, one mechanized infantry division and one air cavalry brigade. The full use of this force, the officials said, would denude the services in the continental United States of rapid response resources unless units were taken away from those earmarked for use in West Germany in a European crisis.

Marines' Resources Stretched

The Marine Corps, a force organized and trained for rapid intervention in trouble spots and not, as some officers emphasized, for garrison duty in areas like Beirut, also finds its resources limited by the increase in global contingencies. For example, the Marine landing force with the Sixth Fleet in the Mediterranean is engaged on land and offshore in Lebanon, and the replacements for one of the Marine amphibious units assigned to Lebanon were diverted for a time to waters off Grenada.

The Army and Air Force commitment to the defense of Western Europe in West Germany is considered by operations planners as the most serious constraint on American military flexibility. Pentagon sources admitted the strategic importance of the North Atlantic commitment but said it tied up a large percentage of American forces.

Ability to Shift Is Limited

The Seventh Army amounts to more than 25 percent of the entire Army, and the percentage rises when other troops in Europe, like the Berlin Brigade, are counted. The Air Force in Europe has 700 combat aircraft and 54,000 troops.

Military sources said any administration's ability to shift these forces to trouble spots in the Middle East or the Mediterranean was limited. Any Soviet threat in Europe, they said, would cause this country's North Atlantic Treaty Organization allies to urge the Reagan Administration not to move any of its forces from the Continent.

Other important military commitments include the deployment of one of the Army's best divisions in South Korea and the stationing of an Army brigade in Panama and another in Alaska. About 420 marines are stationed at Guantánamo Bay, Cuba.

The Navy was described by one former admiral as "at full stretch" as a result of the deployment of a squadron in the Indian Ocean to meet contingencies arising in the Persian Gulf, the reinforcement of the Sixth Fleet in the Mediterranean to deal with the Lebanon crisis and the recent diversion of carrier squadrons to Central America.

Major U.S. Military Deployment Around the World

Figures listed are basic strengths and can vary with each military situation.

UNITED STATES
ARMY:
10 divisions:
1 airborne
1 air assault
2 armored
4 mechanized infantry
2 infantry
3 brigades:
1 armored
1 armored cavalry
1 infantry
1 armored car regiment
AIR FORCE:
27 wings:
18 strategic bomber
7 military airlift
2 strategic reconnaissance
58 squadrons:
6 fighter interceptor
39 tactical fighter
3 tactical reconnaissance
2 tactical air support
9 tactical airlift

ATLANTIC
MARINES: 1 division
20 squadrons:
1 attack helicopter
8 lift helicopter
6 attack
5 fighter attack
NAVY:
6 aircraft carriers
101 surface combatants
30 amphibious ships
53 attack submarines
31 ballistic missile submarines
53 squadrons:
18 attack
6 early-warning
13 fighter
8 patrol
1 fleet air reconnaissance
2 logistic support
5 antisubmarine warfare

ICELAND
AIR FORCE:
1 fighter interceptor squadron

EUROPE AND MEDITERRANEAN
NAVY: Sixth Fleet
14 squadrons:
3 attack
1 early warning
2 fighter
6 patrol
1 fleet air reconnaissance
1 fleet logistics support
1 antisubmarine warfare
ARMY: 4 divisions:
2 armored
2 mechanized infantry
4 brigades:
1 armored
1 mechanized infantry
1 cavalry
1 infantry (Berlin Brigade, outside Seventh Army)
2 armored cavalry regiments
30 air defense batteries
AIR FORCE:
750 combat aircraft
57,900 personnel

LEBANON
MARINES: 1,600 troops
NAVY:
3 destroyers
1 battleship
1 aircraft carrier

SOUTH KOREA
ARMY: 1 infantry division

ALASKA
ARMY: 1 infantry brigade
AIR FORCE:
7 squadrons:
2 tactical fighter
1 tactical air support
1 tactical airlift
1 strategic reconnaissance wing (3 squadrons)

PACIFIC
MARINES: 1 division
31 squadrons:
2 attack helicopter
13 lift helicopter
8 attack
7 fighter attack
1 photo reconnaissance
NAVY: Seventh Fleet
75 squadrons:
21 attack
10 tactical early-warning
7 early-warning
14 fighter
13 patrol
2 fleet air reconnaissance
2 fleet logistics support
6 antisubmarine warfare
AIR FORCE: 1 strategic bomber wing
1 air reinforcement wing
15 squadrons:
10 tactical fighter
2 tactical air support
1 tactical reconnaissance
2 tactical airlift
HAWAII: 1 Marine brigade
1 Army division, less a brigade
OKINAWA: 1 Marine division

CENTRAL AMERICA
Panama: 1 Army infantry brigade
El Salvador: 56 advisers
Honduras: 500 troops

GRENADA
2,000 troops drawn from Army Airborne, Marines and Rangers
1 carrier and escorts

INDIAN OCEAN, PERSIAN GULF
NAVY: Aircraft carrier battle group with Marine amphibious unit

Military definitions

Division: 18,300 men and 324 tanks (armored), 18,500 men and 216 tanks (mechanized), 16,800 men (airborne). A division is made up of three brigades.

Brigade: 4,500 men and 108 tanks (armored), 4,800 men and 54 tanks (mechanized). A brigade is made up of three battalions or regiments.

Aircraft carrier battle group: 1 aircraft carrier with cruiser and destroyer escorts.

Sources: Defense Department, International Institute for Strategic Studies

Sixth Fleet: 2 aircraft carrier battle groups and marine amphibious units

Seventh Fleet: 7 aircraft carriers, 86 surface combatants (destroyers, cruisers, etc.), 32 amphibious ships, 38 attack submarines, 2 ballistic missile submarines, Marine amphibious units.

Wing: 3 squadrons

Fighter squadrons: 18-24 aircraft

Bomber squadrons: 12-18 aircraft

The New York Times/Oct. 26, 1983

1,900 U.S. Troops, With Caribbean Allies, Invade Grenada and Battle Leftists

Continued From Page A1

in the first 10 hours of the operation. The communiqué also reported that more than 200 armed Cubans had been taken prisoner.

Both the Soviet Union and Cuba were informed of the invasion shortly after the American helicopters and parachute landings began, Administration officials said. Secretary Shultz said the Soviet Union had asked the United States to "look to the safety" of the Soviet advisers and had vigorously objected to the American action. Tass, the official Soviet press agency, termed it "an act of international banditry" to place Grenada under "neo-colonialist rule."

The American-led invasion also brought a storm of protest in the Organization of American States, which is scheduled to meet Wednesday to discuss the issue. Comments of diplomats indicated that such nations as Mexico, Colombia, Costa Rica, Panama, Perú and Venezuela opposed the attack.

Administration officials said both Canada and France had turned down requests to take part in the invasion. British Government sources said London had refused to take part in the military action and had ordered a British warship, which was standing off Grenada, to stay clear of the area of operations. Grenada was a former British colony and is now an independent member of the Commonwealth.

Coming so quickly after Sunday's bombing in Beirut, which killed 216 American servicemen, the President's decision to invade Grenada stunned many members of Congress.

The bipartisan leadership, briefed by President Reagan in the White House Monday night and again this morning, generally supported the operation. Senator Charles H. Percy of Illinois, Chairman of the Foreign Relations Committee, said "no objections were raised, only questions" during the sessions with the President.

"We weren't asked for advice," countered House Speaker Thomas P. O'Neill Jr. "We were informed what was taking place. I have no intent to get into any type of dialogue critical of my Government at this time."

But other congressional Democrats contended that the action violated the Rio Treaty of the Organization of American States, which prohibits outside intervention in member states.

"We do not have the right" to invade Grenada in spite of the coup d'état there two weeks ago, asserted Senator Daniel Patrick Moynihan of New York. "I don't know that you bring in democracy at the point of a bayonet."

Reagan Notifies Congress

Tonight, President Reagan formally notified Congress, under the provisions of the War Powers Resolution, that American troops were engaged in combat in Grenada. That resolution stipulates that the troops must be withdrawn from the battle zone within 60 days unless Congress provides permission for them to remain.

At briefings today, Administration officials said they intended to withdraw the troops within a week, but many lawmakers expressed doubt that this deadline could be met.

Administration officials said the American landings began at 5 A.M. today by marines from amphibious ships from the carrier Independence task force that had been diverted toward Grenada a week ago and by two Army Ranger battalions operating from the continental United States and the Caribbean island of Barbados.

They said that in the initial assault, about 600 marines had been flown into the northern end of the island to take over Pearls Field, the international airport that had been closed Monday blocking the departure of some Americans. By this account, about 700 Army Rangers were landed in the southern end of the island near Point Salines where Cuban teams had been building a new airfield.

About 600 American troops were kept in reserve. The American forces on the island were later joined by 300 military personnel from Jamaica, Barbados, Dominica, St. Lucia, St. Vincent, Antigua and St. Kitts-Nevis.

'Violent Uncertainty'

For a couple of years, the Reagan Administration has been concerned about the growing ties of Grenada with the Soviet Union and Cuba and especially the construction of a 10,000-foot runway at Point Salines, which American intelligence saw as a potential way-station for Soviet and Cuban arms shipments to Central America.

Secretary Shultz said the island had been thrown into an "atmosphere of violent uncertainty" since the overthrow of Prime Minister Bishop on Oct. 12 and his execution a week later by a group of military leaders led by Gen. Hudson Austin, the commander of Grenada's 1,200-man army, and Deputy Prime Minister Bernard Coard.

Other Administration officials said Washington became concerned about the safety of about 1,000 Americans on the island, especially when the airport was closed preventing their departure.

"We see no responsible government in the country," Secretary Shultz told an afternoon news conference. "We see arrests of leading figures. We see a shoot-on-sight curfew in effect. Reporters — their validity uncertain — but reports rife about arrests, deaths and so forth, and certainly random sporadic firing that one could hear."

"All of these things are part of an atmosphere of violent uncertainty that certainly caused anxiety among U.S. citizens and caused the President to be very concerned about their safety and welfare," Mr. Shultz added. "He felt that it is better under the circumstances to act before they might be hurt or be taken hostage than to take any chance."

In response to repeated questioning, Secretary Shultz said the action had not been undertaken primarily to signal Cuba, Nicaragua and other leftists in Latin America of American willingness to use force.

He said it had been undertaken primarily to protect American citizens and to respond to a request from the Organization of Eastern Caribbean States under Article 8 of their 1981 treaty to help restore peace and security in the region.

The treaty specifies that the members can take collective action against external aggression provided they act unanimously.

Text of Reagan's Announcement of Invasion

WASHINGTON, Oct. 25 (Reuters) — Following is the text of President Reagan's announcement on the landing on Grenada today by United States and Caribbean troops, as made available by the White House:

On Sunday, Oct. 23, the United States received an urgent, formal request from the five member nations of the Organization of Eastern Caribbean States to assist in a joint effort to restore order and democracy on the island of Grenada.

We acceded to the request to become part of a multinational effort with contingents from Antigua, Barbados, Dominica, Jamaica, St. Lucia, St. Vincent and the United States. I might add that two of those, Barbados and Jamaica, are not members of the organization but were first approached, as we later were, by the O.E.C.S. and asked to join in that undertaking. And then all of them joined unanimously in asking us to participate.

Early this morning, forces from six Caribbean democracies and the United States began a landing, or landings, on the island of Grenada in the eastern Caribbean.

We have taken this decisive action for three reasons:

First, of overriding importance, to protect innocent lives, including up to 1,000 Americans whose personal safety is, of course, my paramount concern.

Second, to forestall further chaos.

And third, to assist in the restoration of conditions of law and order and of governmental institutions to the island of Grenada, where a brutal group of leftist thugs violently seized power, killing the Prime Minister, three Cabinet ministers, two labor leaders and other civilians, including children.

Let there be no misunderstanding. This collective action has been forced on us by events that have no precedent in the eastern Caribbean and no place in any civilized society.

American lives are at stake, so we have been following the situation as closely as possible.

Between 800 and 1,000 Americans, including many medical students and senior citizens, make up the largest single group of foreign residents in Grenada.

From the start, we have consciously sought to calm fears. We were determined not to make an already bad situation worse and increase the risks our citizens faced.

But when I received reports that a large number of our citizens were seeking to escape the island, thereby exposing themselves to great danger, and after receiving a formal request for help, a unanimous request from our neighboring states, I concluded the United States had no choice but to act strongly and decisively.

Let me repeat: The United States objectives are clear — to protect our own citizens, to facilitate the evacuation of those who want to leave and to help in the restoration of democratic institutions in Grenada.

I unerstand that several Caribbean states are asking that the Organization of American States consider the situation in Grenada.

Our diplomatic efforts will be in close cooperation with the Organization of Eastern Caribbean States and the other countries participating in this multinational effort.

Invasion Troops Trained To Make Surprise Raids

Special to The New York Times

WASHINGTON, Oct. 25 — The United States troops who invaded Grenada early this morning consisted of marines and Army Rangers, units trained for such operations. Rangers are soldiers specially trained to fight in small groups and to undertake surprise raids in any terrain or weather.

Government officials said in press briefings today that about 700 Rangers and 1,200 marines of a Marine amphibious unit landed in the island. The officials said some of the Rangers parachuted into the Point Salines area near the southern end of the island. If so, this would be the first combat jump by United States airborne troops since the Vietnam War, when such jumps were a sparingly used tactic.

The marines were landed by helicopter in a more conventional air-mobile assault, officials said. Some Rangers were taken in by planes after the Point Salines airstrip had been secured by paratroops. About 600 marines remained in reserve on the helicoper carrier and amphibious ship Guam.

2 Ranger Battalions

There are two operational Ranger battalions in the United States Army, the First Battalion stationed at Fort Stewart, S.C., and the Second Battalion stationed at Fort Lewis, Wash. Together, the units make up the 75th Ranger Regiment, which represents all the operational Ranger troops in the Army.

Many other officers and enlisted men in the Army go through the nine-week Ranger training course and are then assigned to more conventional units. There are also mobile Ranger training teams that give special training to troops in infantry and armored divisions.

The Rangers' name is derived from Roger's Rangers, a group of expert woodsmen commanded by Maj. Robert Rogers in the French and Indian Wars. The term was subsequently applied to United States military units from time to time in the Revolutionary War and in the 19th century.

In World War II, six Ranger battalions were formed to undertake operations similar to those of the British commando units. Ranger companies were reactivated in 1950, but then for a time Ranger-trained troops were scattered throughout regular units rather than in Ranger units.

The Rangers are light infantry who carry little in the way of heavy support weapons. All are jump-qualified parachutists. Those in Ranger units or training units wear a distinctive black beret when not in combat.

The Marine amphibious unit that is fighting in Grenada had been scheduled to go to Lebanon and relieve the Marine unit in Beirut. An amphibious unit has five tanks, five 155-millimeter howitzers, eight 81-millimeter mortars and four Cobra helicopter gunships. The infantry companies are also equipped with amphibious armored personnel carriers.

"All the News That's Fit to Print"

The New York Times

Late Edition
Weather: Partly sunny today; cloudy, showers possible tonight. Partly sunny after lingering showers tomorrow. Temperatures: today 60-63, tonight 50-53; yesterday 57-72. Details, page C24.

VOL.CXXXIV. . No. 46,215 | NEW YORK, THURSDAY, NOVEMBER 1, 1984 | 60 cents beyond 75 miles from New York City, except on Long Island. | 30 CENTS

GANDHI, SLAIN, IS SUCCEEDED BY SON; KILLING LAID TO 2 SIKH BODYGUARDS; ARMY ALERTED TO BAR SECT VIOLENCE

U.N. SAYS LEBANESE AND ISRAELIS PLAN TALKS ON PULLOUT

A Meeting of Military Teams Reported Set for Monday in South Lebanon Town

By JAMES FERON
Special to The New York Times

UNITED NATIONS, N.Y., Oct. 31 — The United Nations announced today that Israeli and Lebanese military teams would begin talks Monday in southern Lebanon on the subject of Israeli withdrawal from that region.

The conference, which is to take place at Naqura, headquarters of the United Nations Interim Force in Lebanon, also will deal with the security of Israel's northern border, which Israel has long demanded as a precondition for any withdrawal.

United Nations officials declined to discuss the agreement, indicating that to do so might jeopardize any prospect of success. Syria, which also occupies part of southern Lebanon, will not take part in the talks.

Apparently a Breakthrough

But a source familiar with the negotiations that prepared the way for the conference said that "the Israelis and the Lebanese want to get on with it and the Syrians don't want to get in the way." Diplomats here said Lebanon would almost certainly not have agreed to the negotiations without having consulted Syria.

The terse announcement appeared to represent a breakthrough in efforts by both Israel and Lebanon to end an occupation that has been costly to both. The Israelis invaded Lebanon in 1982 in an operation they said was intended to secure their northern border against attacks by Palestinians.

U.N. Role Not Specified

It was understood that the Israeli and Lebanese military teams probably would include senior staff officers. Israeli newspapers said today that the talks would be conducted directly by the two sides, but there was no confirmation of that here.

The United Nations role, similarly, was not spelled out. But the organization's involvement renewed speculation here that the role of the United Nations force in Lebanon might be expanded. Such a decision would require

Continued on Page A8, Column 1

Rebel Asserts C.I.A. Pledged Help in War Against Sandinistas

By JOEL BRINKLEY
Special to The New York Times

WASHINGTON, Oct. 31 — A senior director of the largest Nicaraguan rebel force says the Central Intelligence Agency recruited him to serve as a director two years ago and told him, "We are going to help you change the Government in Managua and do it within a year."

The officer, speaking in an interview, said the C.I.A. paid his family's expenses for more than a year and coached him and other rebel leaders on what to say in public so they would not anger members of Congress, who had to approve financing for the contras, as they are called.

In interviews at his home in Key Biscayne, Fla., the officer, Edgar Chamorro, one of seven directors of the Nicaraguan Democratic Force, gave a detailed description of the relationship between the group and the C.I.A.

He said he was telling the story now, contrary to orders he and other rebel officers received from the C.I.A., partly because he now believes that the United States is not likely to renew aid to the rebels. Aid was ended last spring.

Mr. Chamorro also said: "I resent some of the things the C.I.A. did. The

Continued on Page A14, Column 1

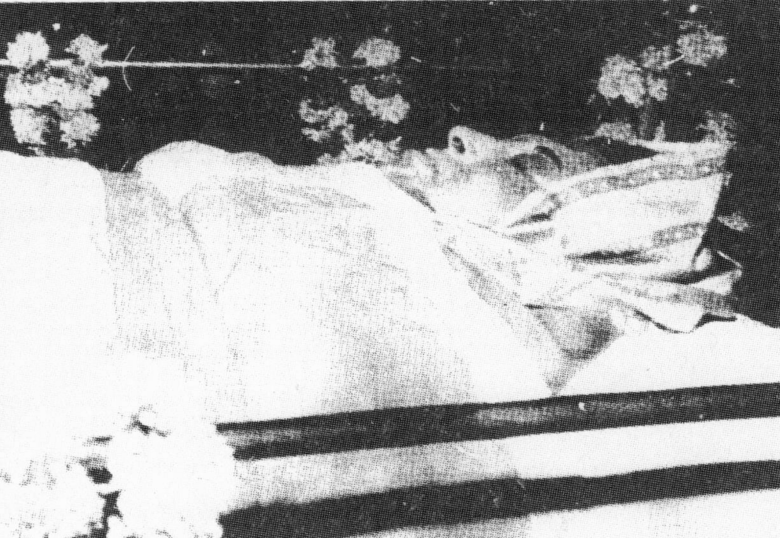

Agence France-Presse

The body of Indira Gandhi outside the All-India Institute of Medical Sciences before being taken to her residence.

Son in Charge In New Delhi

Rajiv Gandhi

By SANJOY HAZARIKA
Special to The New York Times

NEW DELHI, Oct. 31 — Rajiv Gandhi, who was chosen today to become India's new Prime Minister after the assassination of his mother, Indira, was propelled into public life after his younger, more politically ambitious brother, Sanjay, died in a stunt plane crash in 1980.

Man in the News

At the time, Sanjay was regarded as his mother's likely successor and, after Mrs. Gandhi, the most powerful politician in the country. Sanjay's death left a vacuum that Mrs. Gandhi and her followers urged Rajiv to fill.

Rajiv, who is now 40 years old, apparently reluctantly resigned his job with Indian Airlines and agreed to contest an electoral race to fill Sanjay's seat in Parliament the next year. He won the election by a large margin, promising to rid Indian politics of corruption and venality, a campaign that earned him the nickname "Mr. Clean."

Better Known as Indira's Son

Yet as a freshman Member of Parliament, Rajiv was still better known as Mrs. Gandhi's unassuming elder son. After his election he began helping his mother — screening appointments, advising her on reorganizing the affairs of her ruling but decaying Congress Party and receiving petitions. Recognizing him as a major influence on his mother, party leaders began to cultivate him.

Mrs. Gandhi, who increasingly turned to him for support and advice after Sanjay's death, is also known to

Continued on Page A24, Column 3

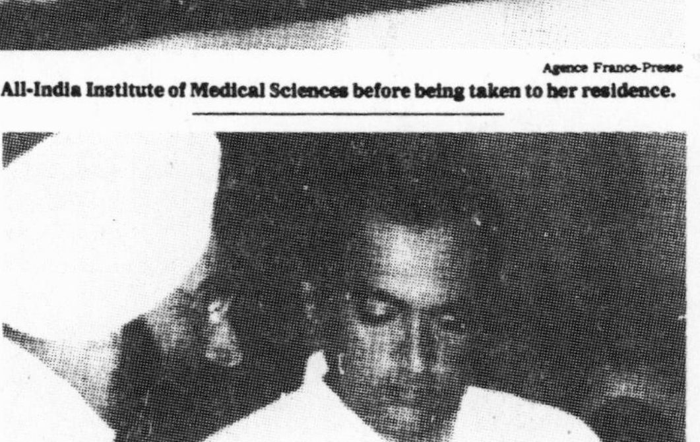

Associated Press

Rajiv Gandhi being sworn in as Prime Minister by President Zail Singh.

For India, Huge Void

Ability of Son Seen As Major Question

The writer of this dispatch, William K. Stevens, has been The Times's New Delhi correspondent since 1982.

Special to The New York Times

NEW DELHI, Oct. 31 — So thoroughly had Prime Minister Indira Gandhi dominated Indian politics over the last two decades that even some of her critics said she was what held the fractious country together.

News Analysis

Many called her Madam, Madamji, Mrs. G., Indiraji, Amma (Mother) or just "She." Not everyone thought of her in kind terms, but all knew who "She" was,

Facts and figures: a profile of India, in charts, page A22.

and her assassination leaves an incalculable void in the life of the country. Her sudden disappearance from the public scene represents a considerable challenge to the future of the Indian experiment in democracy.

Hours after her death, her 40-year-old son, Rajiv Gandhi, was sworn in as her successor. His abilities and performance are perhaps the biggest uncertainty for many people as the nation tries to adjust to the events of today.

Charan Singh, another former Prime Minister, who failed to hold an opposition Government together in 1979 and 1980, thereby paving the way for Mrs. Gandhi's return from three years out of power, expressed as much horror as anyone else when he heard the news of Mrs. Gandhi's assassination.

'Dynastic Rule' Feared

But when he heard about Rajiv Gandhi's rapid elevation, he said it confirmed his fear that "democracy is being gradually eroded in the country in order to establish a dynastic rule."

Whether that interpretation turns out to be correct, or whether Mr. Gandhi's swift installation as Prime Minister will exercise a stabilizing influence, is not clear.

What seems clearer is that Mr.

Continued on Page A19, Column 3

ATTACKS IN 8 CITIES

New Leader Tells Nation 'Maximum Restraint' Is Vital in Crisis

By WILLIAM K. STEVENS
Special to The New York Times

NEW DELHI, Thursday, Nov. 1 — Prime Minister Indira Gandhi was shot and killed at her home Wednesday by two gunmen identified by police officials as Sikh members of her personal bodyguard. Mrs. Gandhi's only surviving son, Rajiv, was sworn in Wednesday night as her successor.

Mrs. Gandhi was killed by at least eight bullets fired at close range from a submachine gun and a pistol by two men, according to police officials. One of the men was said to have been killed by other guards on the scene. The other was reported captured.

If Mrs. Gandhi was killed by Sikhs, it would be the second time since independence that an Indian leader had been the victim of a killing motivated by religious hatred. Mohandas K. Gandhi, who was not related to Mrs. Gandhi, was killed in 1947 by Hindu extremists opposed to partition.

The shooting occurred as Mrs. Gandhi, dressed in an orange-colored

The United States and the Soviet Union both assailed the assassination. Page A23.

Fierce condemnations also came from political and religious leaders in all parts of the world. Page A23.

sari, was walking from her house to her office in the same compound shortly before 9:30 A.M. (11 P.M. Tuesday, New York time). She was pronounced dead at a nearby hospital.

The assassination plunged this country, one-third the size of the United States and with more than 685 million people, into a major political crisis. As word of the assassination spread, Hindus began attacking Sikhs in the streets of the capital and in at least seven other cities. [Page A18.]

Apparently in anticipation of disorder, the army was put on alert. All military personnel on leave were called back to their posts. Approaches to New Delhi were sealed off, as were the approaches to the hospital and Mrs. Gandhi's residence.

Street violence was reported in at least six areas of New Delhi today.

Funeral Is Saturday

In his first radio broadcast to the nation as Prime Minister, Mr. Gandhi, 40 years old and previously the ranking general secretary of his mother's party, appealed for "maximum restraint" in view of the violence that was already beginning.

Mrs. Gandhi, a Hindu, had at age 66 led India for all but 3 of the last 18 years and was regarded as a major international figure. The Government announced that her funeral would be held Saturday and that she would then be cremated. Many world leaders are expected to attend the funeral.

Today, some mourners burst through barricades and surged to within 30

Continued on Page A18, Column 1

Father and Daughter: A Remembrance

By A. M. ROSENTHAL

In India's great years of hope, when Jawaharlal Nehru was Prime Minister and the people called him their beloved jewel, the young woman was almost always with him, usually not at his side, but a few steps behind.

Indira, Nehru's only child, appeared with him at receptions and meetings in New Delhi, smiling, nodding, holding her hands together gently to her forehead in greeting, murmuring a word now and then.

Boosts Up the Ladder

In villages far from New Delhi she walked behind him down dusty roads. She sat motionless on platforms while he talked to city crowds of hundreds of thousands, millions sometimes, usually scolding them for their faults, a father quite loving but quick to anger.

She was close to him and he favored her. He gave her boosts up the political ladder within his Congress Party. Then, in 1964, Jawaharlal Nehru died, and two years later, Indira Gandhi was Prime Minister.

And now she is dead herself, one more victim of the religious hatreds of India against which her father used to harangue the crowds. Now she is dead and her son Rajiv is Prime Minister. Rajiv, whom she had selected as her heir when her first choice, her younger son, Sanjay, died in a wild, senseless airplane stunt over New Delhi, almost within sight of his mother's offices.

Because of Indira Gandhi's open and obvious preparation to turn over rule to one of her sons, the theory of Indian dynasty has been growing and now will become written into history. Father to child to grandchild, just like the old Indian rajahs.

It is a neat theory, fitting comfortably into the stereotypes of India, but at best it is only half true — and it will take time to discover whether even that half holds.

For the fact is that there is no evidence that Jawaharlal Nehru ever really thought in dynasty terms, of turning over office to Indira.

There was a closeness between them, but also a certain aloofness. For years — the years he spent in fighting for Indian independence and the years in prison that were part of that struggle — he was remote, a father she knew mostly from his jail cell letters. Then her mother, the lonely, sad, often neglected Kamala, died and Indira went off to school abroad, far from home and father.

All this was in the 1920's and 30's, and

Continued on Page A19, Column 1

INSIDE

Forecast Index Rises

The index of leading indicators, used to predict economic change, rose modestly in September, after three consecutive declines. Page D1.

Charges in Priest's Death

Poland said murder charges would be filed soon against three security officers arrested in the killing of a pro-Solidarity priest. Page A15.

Suit on Loan Bias Settled

The Household Finance Corporation settled a suit charging loan discrimination against welfare recipients, women and the unmarried. Page D32.

The Inquiry Report On the Vatican Plot

Mehmet Ali Agca, the man convicted of shooting Pope John Paul II, told Italian investigators that a second gunman had instructions to carry out the assassination if Mr. Agca was unable to get off at least five shots, according to a judicial report filed yesterday in Rome.

Key sections of the report, prepared by Judge Ilario Martella, begin on page D30.

United Press International

Prime Minister Indira Gandhi with her son, Rajiv, who has succeeded her.

Assassination in India: Violence Ripples Through the Nation

Sikhs Attacked by Hindus In at Least 8 Indian Cities

Special to The New York Times

NEW DELHI, Oct. 31 — Hindus attacked Sikhs in New Delhi and at least seven other Indian cities today after the assassination of Prime Minister Indira Gandhi, who police officials said was killed by two Sikh gunmen in her own bodyguard.

Army troops were deployed in Calcutta and Agartala in eastern India to control the trouble. The authorities announced a curfew in Agartala, capital of Tripura State, and said they were transporting Sikhs there out of the town to army and paramilitary camps to protect them from mob attacks.

One person was reported killed in New Delhi, apparently in a mob assault, and another said to have been killed in police firing in Calcutta. The victims were not identified.

Attacks on Sikhs also were reported in Patna, capital of the eastern state of Bihar, in Kanpur in the north and in Madras in the south. Many Sikhs are distinguishable by their traditional long hair, beards and turbans.

Soldiers Deployed in Calcutta

Curfews were also ordered in Jubbulpore in central India and in Jammu in Kashmir State to curb trouble.

Officials in Calcutta said soldiers would patrol and take up positions in Sikh-dominated areas. In New Delhi, the local administration ordered a ban on the assembly of more than five people. The armed forces in the heavily Sikh Punjab have been placed on alert.

Sikh shrines were reportedly attacked in New Delhi, Calcutta, Madras and Kanpur.

In New Delhi, reporters saw gangs of young men dragging Sikhs off buses and beating them up. Outside the All-India Medical Institute, where Mrs. Gandhi's body lay, mobs attacked Sikhs on the road, burning their motorcycles and ripping their turbans off and setting them ablaze.

A pillar of smoke rose from a blazing scooter rickshaw, and the road was littered with pieces of cloth and rocks.

Punjab Violence Cited

A group of agitators angrily disputed a suggestion that all Sikhs should not be blamed for the assassination. "They have been all involved," one said. "Look at what was happening in the Punjab."

He was referring to terrorist killings of civilians in Punjab State over the last two years. Nearly 600 people, including both Hindus and Sikhs, were killed in this period. Mrs. Gandhi ordered army action against the terrorists in June, including a raid on the Golden Temple at Amritsar, outraging many Sikhs.

About 200 yards down the road from the burning scooter, a small group of young men set fire to a cycle. Witnesses said they had beaten and chased the cycle's Sikh owner. The group rushed down the broad avenue yelling anti-Sikh slogans.

Religious violence appeared to be spreading in different parts of the country. Sikhs make up about 2 percent of India's population of 700 million and are among its most prosperous minority groups. They are a numerical majority in their home state of Punjab, and many Sikhs have set up thriving businesses in New Delhi, Bombay, Calcutta, Madras and other important trade centers.

Hindu-Sikh violence is a new development in India's long history of strained relations between different religious and linguistic groups. Until now, clashes had revolved around disputes involving Hindus and Moslems. There are riots every year in which hundreds from either religion are slain.

Associated Press

VIOLENCE: A Sikh under attack by angry Hindus outside hospital in New Delhi where Mrs. Gandhi died.

Linguistic, economic, ethnic and religious differences combined to produce the killings in the northeastern state of Assam last year in which it is estimated that 6,000 people died, most of them Moslems.

The current antagonisms between Hindus and Sikhs have been fueled by the trouble in Punjab.

"People are boiling over with rage," said one of the group of agitators as he asked bystanders to disperse, warning them that the area was unsafe.

Some people in the crowd outside the hospital where Mrs. Gandhi had been brought after the shooting hurled stones at the bulletproof car carrying President Zail Singh, who is a Sikh. Mr. Singh, who had been driven directly to the medical institute from the New Delhi airport after returning from a state visit to Yemen, was not injured, and the car was undamaged.

Gandhi, Slain, Is Succeeded by Son and Killing Is Laid to Sikh Bodyguards

Continued From Page A1

yards of where Mrs. Gandhi lay in state in a museum that was once the palatial home of her father, Jawaharlal Nehru.

According to police officials, Mrs. Gandhi was killed by two men identified as Beant Singh, a member of the Prime Minister's special security force, and Satwant Singh of the Delhi armed police constabulary. Other security guards reportedly shot Beant Singh to death and overpowered and captured Satwant Singh as he tried to escape. He was said to be in critical condition.

The assassination took place as Mrs. Gandhi was walking from her house at 1 Safdarjang Road, a broad, leafy boulevard in one of New Delhi's most elegant areas, to her office in the same compound.

She was on her way to a film session with the actor Peter Ustinov, who was featuring her in an Italian television program called "Peter Ustinov's People."

The killing was being widely interpreted here as part of a conspiracy by Sikh terrorists who have been seeking autonomy for the predominantly Sikh state of Punjab for three years.

Mrs. Gandhi was known to wear a bullet-proof jacket at times. There was speculation, a retired intelligence officer said today, that the men who killed her knew when she wore it and when she did not and that the infiltration of the Prime Minister's security force indicated a well-organized conspiracy.

Last June Mrs. Gandhi tried to break the back of the terrorist movement by raiding the Sikhs' holiest shrine, the Golden Temple in Amritsar, Punjab. The Sikhs broke away from the Hindus around A.D. 1500 to form a separate religion based on a belief in one God and the rejection of the caste system.

When Government troops attacked the Golden Temple this spring, the shrine was being used by the Sikh terrorists to launch a campaign of violence in the Punjab and as a fortress and headquarters. At least 600 people, including the terrorist leaders, died in the temple fight on June 5 and 6.

On Wednesday, the Hindu attacks on Sikhs began as word of the assassination spread. In scenes reminiscent of earlier sectarian violence, Sikhs were stopped at random on the streets and beaten, and sometimes their beards were set afire.

There were fears that the violence would spread and worsen. Tens of thousands of angry people gathered outside the cordoned-off All-India Institute of Medical Sciences, where Mrs. Gandhi was taken after being shot, and much of the violence took place there. Later, gatherings of more than four people were banned in New Delhi.

Rajiv Gandhi, who had been almost universally regarded as heir apparent to Mrs. Gandhi, was sworn in Wednesday night as Prime Minister in the Ashoka Hall of Rashtrapati Bhavan, the domed, imperial-looking, red sandstone presidential palace that was once the palace of the British Viceroy of India.

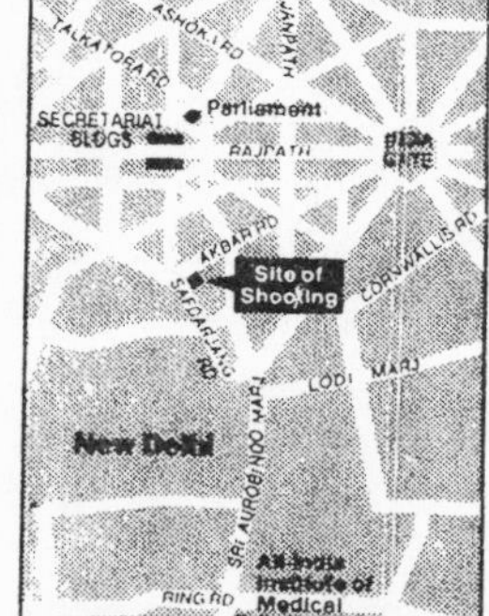

The New York Times/Nov. 1, 1984

SPOT OF ATTACK: Mrs. Gandhi was shot near her house at 1 Safdarjang Road.

India's 6th Prime Minister

Mr. Gandhi became the sixth Prime Minister of India since it became independent in 1947. His succession perpetuated the rule that began with his grandfather, Jawaharlal Nehru, the nation's first Prime Minister.

President Zail Singh, a Sikh, administered the oath. Mr. Gandhi, wearing a flowing Indian tunic, took the oath in English. He held his first meeting with his new five-member Cabinet shortly afterward.

Mr. Gandhi is a former Indian Airlines pilot who seemed reluctant when his mother drafted him into politics after the former heir apparent, his younger brother, Sanjay, was killed in a plane crash in 1980.

Mr. Gandhi flew back to New Delhi on an air force jet from Calcutta, where he had been on a political tour of the state of West Bengal. He reportedly learned of the shooting by way of a transistor radio to which one of his aides had been listening.

Mr. Gandhi's swift swearing-in came as a surprise to many. When Nehru and later his successor, Lal Bahadur Shastri, died, the Home Minister was interim Prime Minister. Mr. Gandhi, although a Member of Parliament, has held no Cabinet post. Nevertheless, the executive committee of the ruling Congress Party contingent in Parliament selected him to be head of the party and, therefore, Prime Minister.

In his radio broadcast, Mr. Gandhi said: "Nothing would hurt the soul of our beloved Indira Gandhi more than the occurrence of violence in any part of the country. It is of prime importance at this moment that every step we take is in the correct direction."

"The foremost need now is to maintain our balance," he said. "We can and must face this tragic ordeal with fortitude, courage and wisdom. We should remain calm and exercise the maximum restraint. We should not let our emotions get the better of us, because passion would cloud judgment."

Of Mrs. Gandhi, he said: "She was mother not only to me but to the whole nation. She served the Indian people to the last drop of her blood."

Effect on Election

Mr. Gandhi is to be formally elected leader of the party in Parliament after his mother's funeral and cremation on Saturday.

Mrs. Gandhi and her party had been preparing for a national election that must come, by law, before Jan. 20. Not the least of the uncertainties surrounding the assassination was that of whether and when the election would now be held.

Shocked reaction poured into New Delhi from around the world. Among the first to express sorrow was the President of Pakistan, Gen. Mohammad Zia ul-Haq. Relations between his country and India have been bad recently because of what India perceived as United States favoritism to Pakistan with military aid. India also accused the Pakistanis of abetting and encouraging the Sikh rebellion in Punjab, which borders on Pakistan.

General Zia said in a statement issued in Islamabad that he had heard the news of the shooting "with deep shock and horror."

Mrs. Gandhi, in recent campaign statements, had been playing on the theme of outside involvement — without identifying the countries — in India's internal affairs. She accused the external forces of trying to destabilize India and retard its development.

Ustinov Describes Events

Mr. Ustinov was in the compound at 1 Safdarjang Road with H. Y. Sharada Prasad, Mrs. Gandhi's press secretary, just before and during the shooting. Mr. Ustinov gave this account in an interview:

"We were in the garden at 8:30 and it was her idea to have the interview in the garden over a cup of tea. The tea had already been set up, the mike was in place and we were all ready. We told the press secretary we were ready and he went to fetch her.

"When he went off toward the house, I heard three single shots. No cries, no shouts. Just three single shots. It didn't alarm anyone, and our Indian assistants said it was probably someone bursting firecrackers.

"And immediately after it there was a long burst from a submachine gun obviously set at automatic. He probably emptied the whole magazine into her. They caught her in the little gate between the office and the residence.

"Then soldiers started running all over the garden toward the road, crouching and a lot of to-ing and froing. Sharada Prasad apparently reached in time to see her being pulled into the house.

"It all felt unreal. I mean, there was hardly any commotion. The birds were chirping, you know, it sounded normal, at least on this side of the garden. But we had a feeling that on the other side of the garden, something hideous was going on."

Mr. Ustinov said there was one more burst of gunfire, apparently from those firing at the assassins.

"The garden reminded me of the scene in 'Gandhi,' the film, where Gandhi was shot in a garden," he said.

Bad Outlook From the Start

Some reports said Mrs. Gandhi was hit by 16 bullets. At least 8 hit her in the abdomen and chest. At least one, according to a junior doctor at the hospital, pierced her heart.

The doctor, who attended the Prime Minister when she arrived, said that although physicians worked for some time to save Mrs. Gandhi, she appeared to be dead on arrival. The doctor said she had no pulse and her pupils did not react to light.

Nevertheless, Mrs. Gandhi was moved to an operating room where she was given continuous blood transfusions as doctors tried to remove the bullets and save her life.

Her body, draped in the white-saffron-and-green Indian tricolor, was taken from the hospital to her home on an army gun carriage Wednesday night.

Mrs. Gandhi's death was widely reported by 2 P.M., but officials refused to confirm it until nearly 4:30 P.M.

Then the Speaker of the lower house of Parliament, Bal Ram Jakhar, grim-faced and restraining tears, nodded a silent yes to a reporter's question.

Members of Parliament arrived weeping at the hospital. Outside in the city, life for the most part seemed to go on normally for a while. Solemn-faced people roamed through Connaught Place, the main downtown shopping area, hungrily buying up and devouring the newspaper extras being hawked on the street.

Small knots of stunned people gathered outside the building of The Hindustan Times, where a news bulletin board outside read: "Mrs. Indira Gandhi is dead."

Attacks on Sikhs Begin

As the sun was setting about 6 P.M., the reprisals by Hindus upon Sikhs began. A common scene in the street was a turbaned Sikh fleeing from a mob, being caught and being beaten. Many hid in the homes of strangers.

Satwant Singh, once of the two people said to have killed Mrs. Gandhi and perhaps the only person who can shed light on the circumstances of the crime and whether there was a conspiracy, was said to be in critical condition at Ram Manohar Lohia Hospital in New Delhi.

The entire security unit at the Prime Minister's house was taken off duty and interrogated for possible links to the assassins, the police said.

Beant Singh, who was identified as a police subinspector, had been a member of the Prime Minister's security staff for four years and had ingratiated himself with the household, according to a Press Trust of India report. Although he was on the afternoon shift, he had asked to be transferred to morning duty Wednesday, according to the report. The report, attributed to witnesses, said he shot her first with the pistol, and Satwant Singh, a constable, then fired into her with an automatic weapon.

Mrs. Gandhi was well known, even among her critics, for her physical courage. She often left herself open to danger in crowds and often disregarded the danger of being the leader of such a volatile country as India.

In a campaign speech in Orissa State the night before her death, Mrs. Gandhi said: "I don't mind if my life goes in the service of the nation. If I die today, every drop of my blood will invigorate the nation."

In a private conversation last June, the day after the raid on the Golden Temple, she said she did not want to be "a little island by myself."

She said: "I mean, what's the point of living if one must do that? And I've had a full life, honestly. I'd much rather, if something was to happen, it should happen when I'm doing something."

Hindu Funeral Traditions

The Hindu belief in reincarnation provides the basis for its funeral rituals. Though these practices differ somewhat among social and economic groups, there is a common core of tradition.

For married Hindus, men and women alike, cremation is the normal procedure for disposing of the body. There is no specific time element involved, but in most cases the rite takes place within a day of the death. Those who are unmarried may be buried.

Preparation of the body usually entails bathing, anointing with a mixture of water and sandalwood and daubing with turmeric powder and water. The body must be garbed with new cloth. Flowers, incense and rose water enhance the bier.

Priests, or Brahmans, chant ritual forms, called mantras, along with the family, and ritual offerings of rice and milk are made to the Brahmans. Soon the body is removed to the cremation grounds, usually on the banks of a river.

By custom, the eldest son presides at the cremation in the company of a priest. The ashes are collected and deposited in one of India's holy rivers. For the next 10 days, family members are considered ritually impure and normally remain in the home. By the end of that time, the soul of the deceased is believed to have acquired a new body, and the consequences of the last life, its rewards and punishments, are unfolded.

Sikh in Exile Warns Of Terror Campaign

Special to The New York Times

LONDON, Oct. 31 — The leader of the Sikh revolutionary forces warned today that the assassination of Prime Minister Indira Gandhi was the beginning of a campaign of terror against the Indian Government.

The warning from Dr. Jagjit Singh Chohan, who describes himself as the president of the Sikh government of Kalistan in exile, came in a statement issued in London. Kalistan is the revolutionaries' name for the independent state they want to create.

The statement asserted that Mrs. Gandhi had been killed because she ordered the storming of the Golden Temple in Amritsar by Indian Army troops June 5-6. The Indian Government has said about 600 people died in the attack, but other reports have put the death toll as high as 1,200.

The Scene At the Assassination

All distances and locations are approximate.

Mrs. Gandhi was shot at close range by two gunmen as she walked from her residence to her office in the same compound.

500 yards

400 yards

Gardens

Office

Residence

Gate

Police

Guard post

Police

Safdarjang Road

Security personnel in unmarked vehicles

Source: United Press International

Statements by India's Premier and President

NEW DELHI, Oct. 31 (AP) — Following are a transcript of Prime Minister Rajiv Gandhi's address after he was sworn in today, as recorded by The Associated Press, and the text of a statement by President Zail Singh:

By the Prime Minister

Indira Gandhi, India's Prime Minister, has been assassinated. She was mother not only to me but to the whole nation. She served the Indian people to the last drop of her blood.

The country knows with what tireless dedication she toiled for the development of India. You all know how dear to her heart was the dream of a united, peaceful and prosperous India, an India in which all Indians, irrespective of their religion, language or political persuasion, live together as one big family in an atmosphere free from mutual rivalries and prejudices.

By her untimely death her work remains unfinished. It is for us to complete this task.

This is a moment of profound grief. The foremost need now is to maintain our balance. We can and must face this tragic ordeal with fortitude, courage and wisdom. We should remain calm and exercise the maximum restraint. We should not let our emotions get the better of us, because passion would cloud judgment.

Nothing would hurt the soul of our beloved Indira Gandhi more than the occurrence of violence in any part of the country.

It is of prime importance at this moment that every step we take is in the correct direction.

Indira Gandhi is no more, but her soul lives. India lives. India is immortal. The spirit of India is immortal. I know that the nation will recognize its responsibilities and that we shall shoulder the burden heroically and with determination.

The nation has placed a great responsibility on me by asking me to head the Government. I shall be able to fulfill it only with your support and cooperation. I shall value your guidance in upholding the unity, integrity and honor of the country.

By the President

My dear countrymen, on this the saddest day of my life, I speak to you when I am totally overtaken by the dark cloud of cruel fate. Our beloved Mrs. Indira Gandhi is no longer with us. I have lost my dearest friend. We have all lost one of the greatest leaders our country has ever produced. And the world has lost a harbinger of peace who was undoubtedly the greatest woman leader mankind has ever produced.

My association with her family spans over four decades. Panditji's passing away was my first personal bereavement. The loss of Mrs. Gandhi is for me unbearable. In spite of her preoccupation with her official duties, we met often. For me, each such meeting was a memorable experience. She was gentle, soft-spoken, brilliant and above all an epitome of culture. She was a daughter Panditji would have been proud of.

Now all that has ended. The dastardly act of assassins, which is not only heinous but a crime against humanity itself, has put the nation to test at an extremely critical juncture of our history.

The unity and integrity of the nation is being challenged. Let our grief not cloud our good sense and maturity both as individuals and a nation. God shall grant us the strength to meet the new challenges.

Let us rally behind the ideals we have inherited from our forefathers. Let us demonstrate to the world that India's stability cannot be jeopardized by a handful of subhuman assassins.

"All the News That's Fit to Print"

The New York Times

Late Edition

Weather: Mostly sunny and cold today, westerly winds; clear and cold tonight. Partly sunny and milder tomorrow. Temperatures: today 30-35, tonight 20-25; yesterday 20-41. Details on page 46.

VOL.CXXXV. . No. 46,637 | NEW YORK, SATURDAY, DECEMBER 28, 1985 | 60 cents beyond 75 miles from New York City, except on Long Island | 30 CENTS

AIRPORT TERRORISTS KILL 13 AND WOUND 113 AT ISRAELI COUNTERS IN ROME AND VIENNA

REAGAN TO TRADE TELEVISION TALKS WITH GORBACHEV

New Year's Day Greetings Are to Be Broadcast at Same Time in Both Nations

By GERALD M. BOYD

Special to The New York Times

LOS ANGELES, Dec. 27 — President Reagan and Mikhail S. Gorbachev have agreed to exchange videotaped New Year's Day greetings that are intended for broadcast in the United States and the Soviet Union, the White House announced today.

The announcement said the exchanges would give Mr. Reagan his first chance to talk to the Soviet people directly on television and would give the Soviet leader the same chance to speak to the American people.

The announcement came as Mr. Gorbachev, in Moscow, offered a cautiously upbeat assessment of relations between the Soviet Union and the United States, saying points of "potential convergence" had emerged in arms control talks. [Page 3.]

'Barbaric Methods' Assailed

Shortly before the announcement, Mr. Reagan, who flew here today to begin a weeklong vacation, issued his latest statement condemning the Soviet intervention in Afghanistan.

The statement, noting the sixth anniversary of the intervention, accused the Russians and their surrogates of resorting "to barbaric methods of waging war" to try to crush a liberation effort in Afghanistan. Mr. Reagan said the United States stood "squarely on the side of the people of Afghanistan."

The videotape exchange will achieve a longtime Administration goal of having Mr. Reagan talk on Soviet television.

Three to Five Minutes Long

Late today, the news divisions of the American networks indicated that they all planned to broadcast both addresses.

The speeches, both of which are to be broadcast on Wednesday, are to be three to five minutes long and will contain New Year's greetings, the officials said. One White House aide said Mr.

Continued on Page 3, Column 5

Further Growth In the Economy Forecast for '86

But Inflation and Jobless Rate Worry Analysts

By ROBERT D. HERSHEY Jr.

Special to The New York Times

WASHINGTON, Dec. 27 — The United States economy seems headed for a fourth consecutive year of expansion in 1986, but its course will be marred by gradually rising inflation and stubbornly high unemployment, according to a consensus of business and academic forecasters.

The possibility of a recession, which at various times in the last year has seemed just over the horizon, has receded and is no longer regarded as an apparent threat.

One important reason is the roaring bull market in stocks and bonds. By making investors richer, it has raised both confidence and the outlook for consumer spending, which accounts for two-thirds of the economy.

'Rather Sluggish Fashion'

"The prospects for the economy in 1986 are quite good," said A. Gilbert Heebner, chief economist for the Philadelphia National Bank, in a prediction that typifies current professional thinking. "It's going to seem like more of the same, with the economy growing but in a rather sluggish fashion."

The Reagan Administration, for its part, is believed to have tentatively adopted a 4 percent growth forecast for next year, somewhat higher than that of most private analysts.

To be sure, few economists or politicians are satisfied with the current rate of American growth, less than 2.5 percent for 1985 after 6.6 percent in 1984. This year's rate has been barely enough to keep unemployment from rising and it has left industry with large amounts of idle productive capacity.

Moreover, agriculture and parts of the oil, real estate and banking industries are in disarray despite an expansion that this month reached its third anniversary. Weak farm and crude oil prices, as well as a glut of unrented office space in some cities, could cause more problems for banks in 1986.

Yet most economists predict solid growth for 1986. They cite several factors for this tempered optimism. Both

Continued on Page 31, Column 4

Reuters

VICTIMS: Bodies bearing tags affixed by police on the floor at Leonardo da Vinci Airport near Rome.

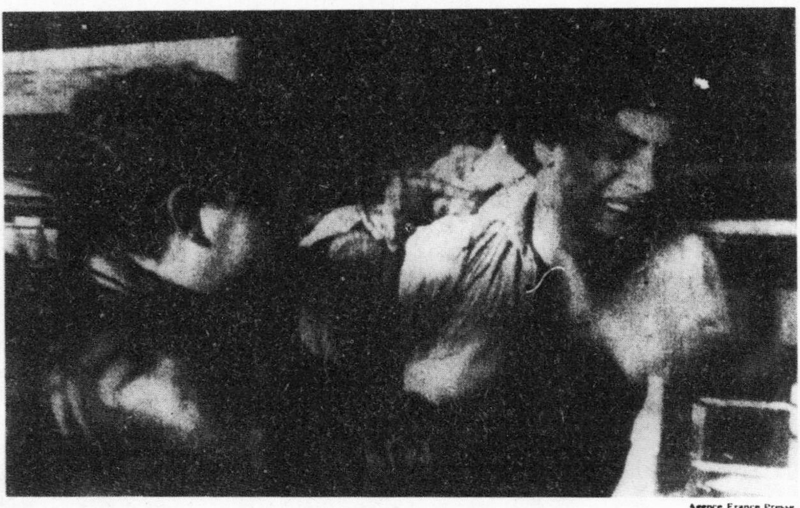

Agence France Presse

SUSPECT: A man suspected as a terrorist being taken into custody after the attack on the Rome airport.

4 ATTACKERS KILLED

Gunmen Fire Into Crowds and Throw Grenades Near Lines at El Al

By JOHN TAGLIABUE

Special to The New York Times

ROME, Dec. 27 — Terrorists hurled grenades and fired submachine guns at crowds of holiday travelers at airports in Rome and Vienna today in attacks on check-in counters of El Al Israel Airlines.

Authorities quoted by news services said the gunmen had killed at least 13 people, including 4 Americans, and wounded 113 in the two attacks. Four terrorists were killed, and three others were wounded and captured.

While El Al appeared to be a target in both attacks, the authorities said the terrorists in Rome had also thrown grenades and fired indiscriminately with Soviet-made assault rifles into crowds of New York-bound passengers checking in at Pan American World Airways and Trans World Airlines.

Terrorists Not Identified

The assailants, who were not immediately identified, left the two airline terminals strewn with bloodied and torn bodies, luggage, overturned furniture and broken glass.

Israeli Government officials asserted that the Palestine Liberation Organization might be responsible, but P.L.O. officials here and in Tunis denied any role in the apparently coordinated attacks.

Witnesses at the airport in Vienna said panic broke out as the explosions and firing began, with passengers and airport staff throwing themselves to the ground and crawling desperately for cover. [Page 4.]

Gunmen Jumped and Shrieked

Similar accounts were given in Rome, where survivors described chaos amid thundering explosions and raking bursts of gunfire unleashed by young masked men in blue jeans who jumped up and down and shrieked as their victims fell. Bystanders screamed and dived for cover.

"It was an inferno — they started throwing hand grenades and firing with submachines guns," said one witness who was wounded in Rome, Dora Silvestri. "We all threw ourselves to the ground. Blood spread over the floor. I

Washington said the attackers were "beyond the pale of civilization." Page 5. These comments were echoed worldwide. Page 6

fell on the body of a girl, and a grenade splinter hit me in the face."

As the weary and shaken travelers caught in the airport attacks returned to New York, some of them told of their minutes of terror in a series of interviews. [Page 6.]

The authorities said seven terrorists were apparently involved — four in the attack in Rome, which began shortly after at 9 A.M. (3 A.M. New York time), and three in the attack in Vienna, which started a few minutes later.

At Leonardo da Vinci Airport at Rome, three terrorists were slain and one was seized after being wounded in a gun battle with the police and plainclothes Israeli security men in the terminal. Security had been increased there after recent hijackings and official warnings that airports might be attacked during the Christmas holidays.

A total of 13 people were killed in the Rome attack, including the three terrorists, and 70 wounded.

[A wounded American man died later at a Rome hospital, The Associated Press reported from Rome.]

At Schwechat Airport in Vienna, 3 were killed, including a gunman, and 47 wounded, one of them critically.

Two of the terrorists in Vienna were seized after a wild car chase and a run-

Continued on Page 4, Column 3

Road Repairs to Snarl Traffic On Both Sides of East River

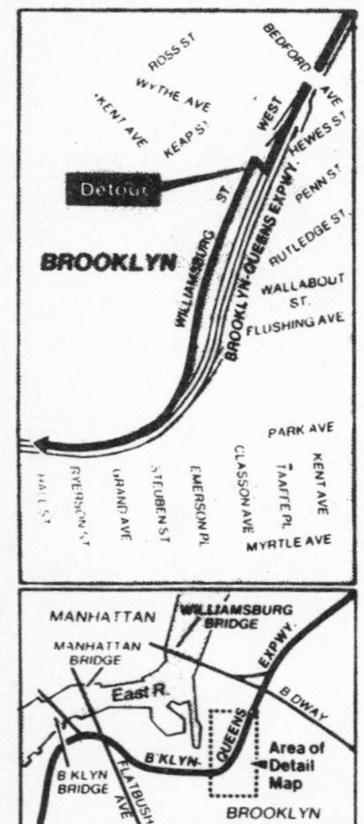

The New York Times / Dec. 28, 1985

Williamsburg Bridge will carry more Manhattan-bound traffic.

By DEIRDRE CARMODY

A section of the Brooklyn-Queens Expressway near the Williamsburg Bridge will be closed in January for reconstruction, and the work is expected to cause heavy traffic on the Brooklyn and Manhattan ends of the bridge for more than a year.

The project, beginning in mid- to late January, is part of a five-year, $2.6 billion state program to rebuild many of the city's highways. The starting date depends on the availability of construction crews, according to the City Bureau of Traffic Operations.

70,000 Vehicles a Day

Westbound traffic on the expressway, which the Traffic Bureau says is used by about 70,000 vehicles a day, will be rerouted at the Wythe Avenue exit in Brooklyn onto Williamsburg Street West for two and a half blocks. Cars will be able to get back on the expressway at the Flushing Avenue entrance.

Williamsburg Street West has been widened by a lane and a shoulder has been added. The Flushing Avenue entrance has also been widened by a lane.

"It is not an easy detour, not one we look forward to," said Traffic Commissioner Samuel I. Schwartz.

The detour is not expected to be able to carry all the traffic, but according to Abel Silver, a spokesman for the City Transportation Department, some of the vehicles that normally take the Brooklyn and Manhattan Bridges into

Continued on Page 26, Column 1

Israel, Blaming P.L.O., Issues a Warning

By THOMAS L. FRIEDMAN

Special to The New York Times

JERUSALEM, Dec. 27 — Although the Palestine Liberation Organization denied involvement in the attacks in Rome and Vienna, Israeli officials blamed the guerrilla group today and made it clear that Israel would respond at the appropriate time and place.

"Israel is shocked and outraged by these two new acts of senseless terror against innocent civilians," a Foreign Ministry statement said.

"The terrorist attacks come against a background of declarations by the head of the P.L.O., and those Arab states that support this organization, that these terrorists will cease terrorist operations outside of Israel. Israel will continue its struggle against terrorism in every place and at any time it sees fit."

Syrian Missiles in Lebanon

Meanwhile, Israeli analysts said Israel's ability to retaliate for the attacks had been limited by Syria's decision to move mobile surface-to-air missiles into Lebanon.

In the past, Israel has often retaliated for terrorist attacks abroad by bombing Palestinian guerrilla bases in Lebanon, regarding these as convenient "return addresses."

To do so now, however, Israeli jets would have to penetrate the new curtain of surface-to-air missiles Syria has drawn over the Bekaa region in Lebanon, which could lead to an all-out war with Syria, the analysts said.

Since Israel already destroyed the main P.L.O. compound in Tunisia last October, that too is no longer an option for retaliation. The analysts said new P.L.O. offices in Baghdad would not be easy to reach and were widely dispersed. This would seem to leave as the only option for retaliation a more surgical strike against specific individuals, the analysts said.

A Political Statement

To appreciate the full Israeli quandary, officials said, it must be understood that the Syrian decision to deploy the SAM-6 and SAM-8 mobile batteries a few miles inside Lebanon, for the second time in a month, was as much a political statement as a strategic military maneuver.

It was apparently designed, Israeli officials say, to send Israel and the United States clear signals about Damascus's intentions to change some of the rules in the Middle East.

To begin with, said Itamar Rabinovich, an authority on Syria at Tel Aviv University, the Syrians are apparently trying to establish a new relationship with Israel in Lebanon after the Israeli withdrawal.

While Israel wants to hold onto all of its old perquisites in Lebanon, particularly its freedom to fly reconnaissance missions over the Syrian-controlled Bekaa, the Syrians want to reverse once and for all this free Israeli access to their neighboring client state.

"By sending the missiles back, the

Continued on Page 5, Column 1

For Families of 2 Americans, Sudden Sorrow

By SARA RIMER

Natasha Simpson, the 11-year-old daughter of a foreign correspondent in Rome, was on her way to New York with her family for a three-week vacation with friends and relatives. John Buonocore 3d, a 20-year-old student, was on his way home to Wilmington, Del., after a semester in Rome, just in time for his father's 50th birthday.

Both died at Leonardo da Vinci Airport in Rome yesterday. They were among the 14 people killed there when terrorists hurled hand grenades and opened fire with submachine guns into crowds of holiday travelers. The Associated Press said two other Americans, Frederick Gage, of Madison, Wis., and Don Maland, of New Port Richey, Fla., were also killed.

Natasha Simpson was killed apparently as her father, Victor L. Simpson, a New Yorker who is the news editor for The Associated Press in Rome, tried to shield her from the bullets. Mr. Simpson, 43, was wounded in the right wrist and hand.

'Put His Arm Around Her'

"I think he put his arm around her to try and push her down and that's how he injured his finger," said his wife, Daniela Petroff Simpson, who was reached by telephone at her parents' home in Rome.

Mrs. Simpson, 40, had been outside the terminal walking the family terrier while her husband and two children — Natasha and 9-year-old Michael — checked in for their flight to Kennedy International Airport. Then she heard the exploding grenades.

"Suddenly there was a shattering noise as if something were collapsing," Mrs. Simpson, who is also a journalist, told The Associated Press in Rome. "And then there were machine-gun bursts. Two distinct machine-gun bursts. And then silence. I rushed into screams and cries and saw my husband dripping blood from his hand and my son on the floor shot in the stomach."

Mr. Simpson and his son were hospi-

Continued on Page 6, Column 3

INSIDE

3 on Miami Force Arrested

Three members of the Miami police force were charged with murder in the drownings of three men thought to have been dealing in drugs. Page 8.

West Side Rail Proposal

New York State and New York City are studying the possibility of a light rail line — perhaps a monorail — on Manhattan's West Side. Page 25.

Airport Terror: All Austria Is Stunned

In Vienna, Panic in Middle Of Shooting and Grenades

By PAUL LEWIS
Special to The New York Times

VIENNA, Dec. 27 — Panic broke out in the check-in lounge at the airport here when three gunmen stormed in, spraying the hall with submachine-gun fire and rolling grenades along the floor.

Witnesses said that as the firing began during check-in for an El Al Israel Airlines flight, passengers and Schwechat Airport staff members threw themselves to the ground and scrambled desperately for cover.

The attack in Vienna took place just minutes after 10 passengers and 3 attackers were killed in another terrorist assault at an El Al check-in counter at Leonardo da Vinci Airport outside Rome.

[The Associated Press reported from Rome that an 11th passenger died at a Rome hospital after the attack.]

In Vienna, Inspector Gottfried Maly, the first police officer on the scene, told reporters he heard one of the terrorists telling the passengers to lie down.

16 Others Hospitalized

The gunmen killed a 50-year-old Viennese man who was identified as Eckehard Kaerner. Another person, whose name was not released immediately by the authorities, died later in a hospital. The Austrian police said that 47 people were wounded, including two gunmen, and that 16 people were hospitalized. One woman, whose name was not released, was in critical condition, the police said.

It was not clear how many of the dead and wounded were passengers on the departing El Al flight, and how many were other passengers and airport staff members.

The Austrian police said three men, who they said were apparently Arabs, charged into the crowded check-in area at Schwechat Airport shortly after 9 this morning, spraying the hall with machine-gun fire and rolling grenades along the floor.

Franz Kaefer, the airport police chief, said the terrorists' target appeared to be passengers who were waiting to check in for Flight 364 on El Al, which was scheduled to leave for Tel Aviv at 10:45 A.M. The passengers were waiting at a designated El Al check-in counter among the long line of Austrian Airlines counters that forms one side of the L-shaped departure hall. Another group of passengers was waiting nearby for a charter flight to Heraklion in Greece.

Nationalities Unknown

Mr. Kaefer described the terrorists as people "appearing to be Arabs." Their nationalities were not known.

Airport officials described the departure lounge right after the attack as a chaotic mass of wounded people lying in pools of blood on a floor strewn with baggage, spent machine-gun shells and shards of broken glass. One of the wounded people fell bleeding beneath a brightly decorated Christmas tree.

About 40 armed Austrian policemen, aided by El Al security guards and Austrian plainclothesmen, counterattacked with machine guns and pistols. They fought the terrorists down a stairway leading to the road.

The gunmen seized an unattended car and drove off to the east, toward the town of Fischamend, shooting at the pursuing police cars and throwing at least one grenade.

After a mile or two, the terrorists were forced to abandon their car, which had been badly damaged by police fire.

One Gunman Killed

The gunmen then tried to force a passing motorist to hand over his car, but the police closed in. One terrorist was killed, and two others were wounded and captured.

"We emptied our magazines," one police officer involved in the chase said later.

Col. Robert Danziger of the Austrian State Police said the three gunmen had Soviet-made Kalashnikov automatic rifles. Dr. Heinz Resch of the airport security staff said three policemen were wounded in the fight, two of them seriously.

Several hours after the attack, passengers arriving at the airport found walls and illuminated signs in the departure halls pockmarked with bullet holes. Several big glass windows had been shot out, and grenades had blown chunks of concrete out of the pillars supporting the roof.

Tonight an Interior Ministry spokesman said one of the men who was captured and wounded was too seriously hurt to be questioned. The spokesman said the other captured man was refusing to answer questions put to him in English or German.

No Travel Documents

Before undergoing surgery for his wounds, this man reportedly said he was a Lebanese traveling on a Jordanian passport. The Interior Ministry spokesman said no travel documents were found on either of the captured men.

Immediately after the attack, the Palestine Liberation Organization's representative in Vienna, Daud Barakat, telephoned the Austrian news agency to condemn the assault.

He expressed concern that such an "act of terror" might damage "the excellent relations between the P.L.O. and the Austrian Government." The Austrian police said no one had taken responsibility for the attack.

Austrian leaders also condemned the attack.

At a news conference, Chancellor Fred Sinowatz said, "We condemn most forcefully and sharply this shameful and criminal act of terror that was committed in a peace-loving country, which has advocated peace in all international forums."

He also firmly rejected Israeli charges that Austria had shown flexibility in dealing with terrorism. He said the police action "was the best proof that there is no such flexibility."

Fighting Terrorism

The Austrian Deputy Chancellor, Norbert Steger, said there is no complete defense against such terrorist attacks, except for restrictions on individual freedom of movement that he called "unacceptable" for a democracy.

"It is only possible to rule out such attacks in a police state," he said.

Mr. Steger recalled that Austria has played an active role in efforts to bring peace to the Middle East.

The Mayor of Vienna, Helmut Zilk, who visited the airport after the attack, called it "an act of terror with an unsurpassed level of brutality."

"Let nobody say this is a war against Israel, because Austrians who are not involved were dragged into the fighting," he said.

Mayor Zilk also defended security measures at the Vienna airport as being as tight as a democracy can accept.

The attack today is the latest of several acts of terrorism, many of them against Israeli or Jewish targets, that have occurred in the Austrian capital.

In 1973, Arab guerrillas took hostage a train full of Jews emigrating from the Soviet Union.

In 1975, terrorists overran the Vienna-based headquarters of the Organization of Petroleum Exporting Countries. They captured several oil ministers attending a meeting there, including the Saudi Arabian Oil Minister, Sheik Ahmed Zaki Yamani. The terrorists flew the oil ministers to Algeria and Libya, where they were released.

In 1981, Heinz Nittel, the president of the Austria-Israel Society, an organization promoting friendship between the two countries, was assassinated in Vienna. Later two people were killed in a terrorist attack on a synagogue in the city.

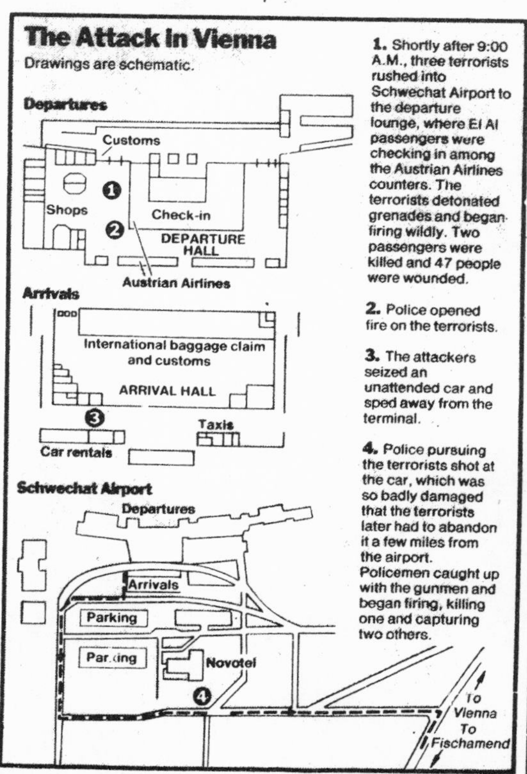

The Attack in Vienna
Drawings are schematic.
Departures
Customs
Shops
Check-in
DEPARTURE HALL
Austrian Airlines
Arrivals
International baggage claim and customs
ARRIVAL HALL
Taxis
Car rentals
Schwechat Airport
Departures
Arrivals
Parking
Parking
Novotel
To Vienna
To Fischamend
1. Shortly after 9:00 A.M., three terrorists rushed into Schwechat Airport to the departure lounge, where El Al passengers were checking in among the Austrian Airlines counters. The terrorists detonated grenades and began firing wildly. Two passengers were killed and 47 people were wounded.
2. Police opened fire on the terrorists.
3. The attackers seized an unattended car and sped away from the terminal.
4. Police pursuing the terrorists shot at the car, which was so badly damaged that the terrorists later had to abandon it a few miles from the airport. Policemen caught up with the gunmen and began firing, killing one and capturing two others.

The New York Times/Dec. 28, 1985

Agence France-Presse

PROTECTION: People in a corridor of Leonardo da Vinci Airport in Rome diving for whatever cover was available as the shooting started.

Terrorists Kill 13 in the Rome and Vienna Airports

Continued From Page 1

ning gun battle with the police that ended several miles from the airport.

Among the dead were two Americans, Natasha Simpson, the 11-year-old daughter of an Associated Press editor in Rome, and John Buonocore 3d, 20, a college student from Wilmington, Del.

[The Associated Press identified the American who died later at a Rome hospital as Don Maland, 30, of New Port Richey, Fla. The A.P. said another victim had been tentatively identified as an American, Frederick Gage Jr., of Madison, Wis.]

An Israeli security agent and a Mexican military attaché in Rome were also reported killed.

An Italian police spokesman said all four attackers in Rome were heard speaking Arabic, and the police in Vienna said the attackers appeared to be Arabs.

Italian police officials said bank and hotel receipts found on the terrorists seemed to indicate that they had entered Italy in early December and had stayed in hotels near the capital. They said the five had Moroccan passports.

The captured gunman in Rome was heard to shout, "I am a Palestinian combatant" as he was carried away by the police.

CBS News said it had learned that the authorities in Rome had found a note in Arabic on the body of one of the terrorists. CBS said the note was addressed to "Zionists" and said, "The war has begun." It was reportedly signed, "the martyrs of Palestine."

Italian officials said the attack was the worst terrorist assault at Leonardo da Vinci Airport since Palestinian guerrillas, firing into bands of Christmas travelers, left 32 people dead on Dec. 17, 1973.

Claim for Abu Nidal Group

"People were falling, screaming — it was terrible," said a witness in Rome, who saw a man near him pull out a Kalashnikov assault rifle and shoot "everything in sight." He said all the gunmen were "screaming something as they were shooting."

In a telephone call to a Spanish radio station, a caller said the attacks were the work of a group calling itself the Abu Nidal Organization of the Costa Del Sol. But a spokesman for the Israeli Embassy here said it was too early to determine whether the assertion was accurate.

In a statement, the P.L.O. office here, which holds a kind of diplomatic status, voiced "indignation at the criminal act," which it said was part of a "plot against the Palestinian cause."

Officials of the P.L.O. in Tunis condemned the killings, and they recalled that the organization's leader, Yasir Arafat, had pledged this month that armed Palestinian actions would be confined in the future to Israel and areas it occupies.

The assaults were especially awkward for the Governments here and in Vienna, since they have been particularly understanding of the Palestinian cause.

Austria's former Chancellor, Bruno Kreisky, despite bitter criticism from Israel, was one of Western Europe's earliest champions of a Palestinian voice in resolving the Middle East conflict.

String of Attacks in Italy

The Italian Government of Prime Minister Bettino Craxi has been at the forefront of a Common Market effort to assure a broader role to the Palestinians. Italy risked souring its ties with the United States by taking a conciliatory stance toward the P.L.O. after the hijacking in October of the cruise liner Achille Lauro.

In recent months, Italy has experienced a string of terrorist attacks at the hands of Palestinian activists, including bombings of the offices of the Jordanian and British airlines this summer, in which Palestinian youths killed several people. In the hijacking of the Achille Lauro by four Palestinians, an American, Leon Klinghoffer, was killed.

Those wounded here today were taken to four hospitals in the capital and at Ostia, a nearby seaside resort. At Sant'Agostino Hospital in Ostia, the chief surgeon, Dr. Giancarlo Pedace, said Natasha Simpson, the daughter of Victor L. Simpson, the Associated Press news editor here, was dead on arrival of gunshot wounds in the thorax and neck.

"There was nothing we could do," Dr. Pedace said.

Wife Was Outside Terminal

Mr. Simpson and his son Michael, 9, were both treated for wounds at Sant'Eugenio Hospital in Rome and hospitalized. His wife, Daniela, escaped injury because she was walking the family dog, Jimmy, outside the airport building when the attack began.

Mrs. Simpson later told the Italian news agency ANSA that she had heard "an explosion, then machine-gun volleys, then quiet, and again more explosions and shots."

This afternoon, the far end of the cavernous international arrival and departure building, where the attack occurred, was blocked off by 7-foot high white plywood partitions. Reporters who walked through the area saw ashtrays overturned and a sea of shattered glass in front of the Quick hamburger stand, a German-owned fast-food outlet near the El Al and T.W.A. desks.

Anna Lisa del Grand, 22, said of the terrorists, "They were jumping up and down and they were shooting in sort of a semicircle." She said she fell to the floor and, after several minutes of gunfire and explosions, saw a terrorist fall and flash a victory sign as he died.

The Rome airport was closed for nearly four hours after the attack. Additional patrols and emergency security measures were put into effect there and at other airports in Italy.

The Attack in Rome
Drawing is schematic.

1. Four terrorists rushed into Leonardo da Vinci Airport and threw hand grenades near the TWA desk shortly after 9 A.M.

2. The terrorists fired machine guns at passengers, killing 10 people and wounding at least 70. The attack lasted only a few minutes.

3. Policemen returned the gunfire. Three of the terrorists were killed and one was wounded.

Gates 31-37 · Gates 21-23 · Passport control and security · TWA · El Al · Gates 1-10 · Snack bar · Post Office · Check-in counters

The New York Times/Dec. 28, 1985

For El Al, Vigilance Against Violence

By RICHARD WITKIN

El Al Israel Airlines maintains the tightest security of any airline in the Western world, most security specialists agree.

This has minimized incidents of in-flight hijacking and sabotage, but it has not totally prevented them. And terrorists also have been able, since the late 1960's, to carry out sporadic on-the-ground attacks on El Al passengers, crew members and aircraft that have caused considerable death, injury and destruction.

A close call came in August 1972 when an explosive device went off in the baggage hold of an El Al Boeing 707 that had taken off from Rome, bound for Tel Aviv with 140 passengers and eight crew members.

Officials of the airline said the plane's baggage hold had been reinforced with armor plating. This precaution apparently limited the damage to a six-inch-wide hole in the compartment and a small crack in the rear door. The plane returned safely to Rome.

El Al officials are extremely reluctant to go into detail about their much-admired security system. So it can only be assumed that some if not all other El Al planes have been similarly reinforced to limit the effects of cargo-hold explosions. Furthermore, El Al planes are reliably reported to have devices under their wings to protect against surface-to-air missiles by altering their flight through electronic or other means. So far as is known, no ther airline uses such devices.

One Successful Hijacking

Evidently the only time an El Al plane has been successfully hijacked was in 1968, when members of the Popular Front for the Liberation of Palestine commandeered a plane and directed the crew to land in Algeria. The incident ended without injury.

Two years later, Israeli air marshals overpowered two Arabs, one a woman, who tried to take over a plane bound from Amsterdam to New York. The plane landed in London with the male hijacker dead from a bullet fired during the aerial gun battle.

The worst airport loss suffered by El Al took place in May 1972. Twenty-six passengers were killed and 76 wounded in an attack by members of the Japanese Red Army organization at Ben-Gurion International Airport outside Tel Aviv.

At least seven other attacks on El Al personnel or property between 1968 and the double assault yesterday resulted in loss of life. They included the tossing of a hand grenade into an airline office in Athens in 1969 in which a boy was killed and 14 others wounded, and a 1976 attack on a plane preparing to take off from Istanbul in which 4 died and 21 were wounded.

The consensus among security experts yesterday, after the airport attacks in Rome and Vienna, was that El Al, like any other airline, was especially vulnerable to attack where all the carriers have counter space in one sprawling building and local authorities must provide security for an area that may be filled with hundreds or even thousands of people.

"In Israel, they have total control over their airport," said the former security chief of a major American carrier. "But outside Israel, they must defer to foreign governments.

"If someone wants to come into a terminal shooting, there's nothing an individual airline can do," he said. "This is not true in Israel. But what can they do in a place like Rome? El Al is victimized there as much as anyone."

For travelers who have flown on El Al, memories of the trip usually include a baggage inspection and an interrogation that are remarkably thorough.

Questions in 'Great Detail'

Two young American women were not allowed aboard a New York-to-Tel Aviv flight early this month until the stepmother of one was called by an El Al security officer five minutes before takeoff time to verify the passengers' account of their reasons for going to Israel.

Linda Stewart, whose stepdaughter Jennifer was one of the two bluejean-clad travelers (the other was Katie Leachman), said yesterday:

"The man from security went into great detail. He wanted to know what university Jenny had gone to, the purpose of the trip, how long she had known Katie. He was very polite and ended up thanking me and adding that they were just checking. I didn't know whether to be reassured or scared out of my socks."

Two other travelers who went to and from Tel Aviv not long ago told of interrogations at the Israeli airport that lasted 45 minutes.

Baggage Depressurized

Among the questions frequently asked are: whether the passenger personally did the packing; whether anyone else had access to the luggage; whether it contained electronic devices and, if so, where they had been bought, and whether the passenger was carrying a package received from someone else.

Security experts, declining to be quoted by name, said El Al took precautions that appear to go beyond those of many if not most other carriers. They said that such precautions were understandable because El Al represents a nation that is under constant siege from guerrillas, and emphasized that they were feasible because El Al operates only a fraction of the flights of the industry's giants.

El Al passengers are routinely told they must report to the airport at least two and a half hours before scheduled departures to allow time for security procedures.

Baggage destined for the cargo hold is generally given a thorough initial search. In addition, the bags and other cargo are placed inside armored altitude chambers, from which the air is pumped out to simulate the drop in atmospheric pressure as a plane gains altitude. The purpose is to double check that the bags do not contain an explosive rigged to go off when the pressure drops.

Use of magnetometers and X-ray machines to check for weapons on a passenger's body or in carry-on luggage is conducted with great care. And the magnetometer check often is supplemented by frisking.

Separate Security at Kennedy

Seven years ago, at Kennedy International Airport, El Al began using a new check-in terminal of its own that is separated by walls from the check-in counters of other foreign carriers in the International Arrival Building. The El Al area is known to have special security features, but an official of the airline declined to discuss them except to say, "In effect we have our own security at Kennedy."

The implication was that the Kennedy set-up was far preferable to that at other airports like Rome's, where the check-in counters are not isolated from those of other airlines and are vulnerable to attack from whoever gains access to the general terminal area.

The security situation for El Al differs from airport to airport, depending partly on the degree of special assistance the airline can obtain from local authorities. In Switzerland, for instance, passengers departing on El Al flights are processed and boarded at relatively isolated areas of the terminal.

One security expert suggested that authorities consider screening passengers, as well as companions seeing them off, at checkpoints set up at the entrance to a terminal.

Arafat Is Reported Ill And in Need of Rest

TUNIS, Dec. 27 (AP) — The chairman of the Palestine Liberation Organization, Yasir Arafat, is recovering from an illness, and his doctor said he required "many days of rest," according to the Palestinian press agency Wafa.

The agency was quoting Dr. Ashraf al-Kordi. Mr. Arafat was recently reported by another P.L.O. leader, Khalil Wazir, also known as Abu Jihad, to have complained of severe pain caused by an inflammation.

"All the News That's Fit to Print"

The New York Times

Late Edition

Weather: Partly cloudy and cold today, chance of snow; chance of snow tonight. Partly cloudy, cold tomorrow. Temperatures: today 27-30, tonight 13-19; yesterday 14-23. Details, page C19

VOL.CXXXV . . . No. 46,669

NEW YORK, WEDNESDAY, JANUARY 29, 1986

50 cents beyond 75 miles from New York City, except on Long Island

30 CENTS

THE SHUTTLE EXPLODES

6 IN CREW AND HIGH-SCHOOL TEACHER ARE KILLED 74 SECONDS AFTER LIFTOFF

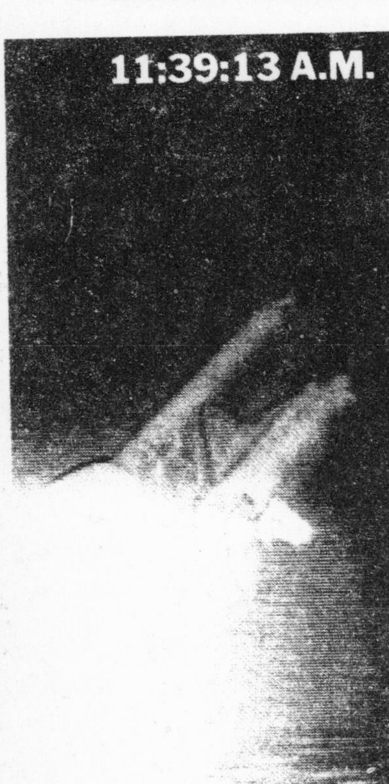

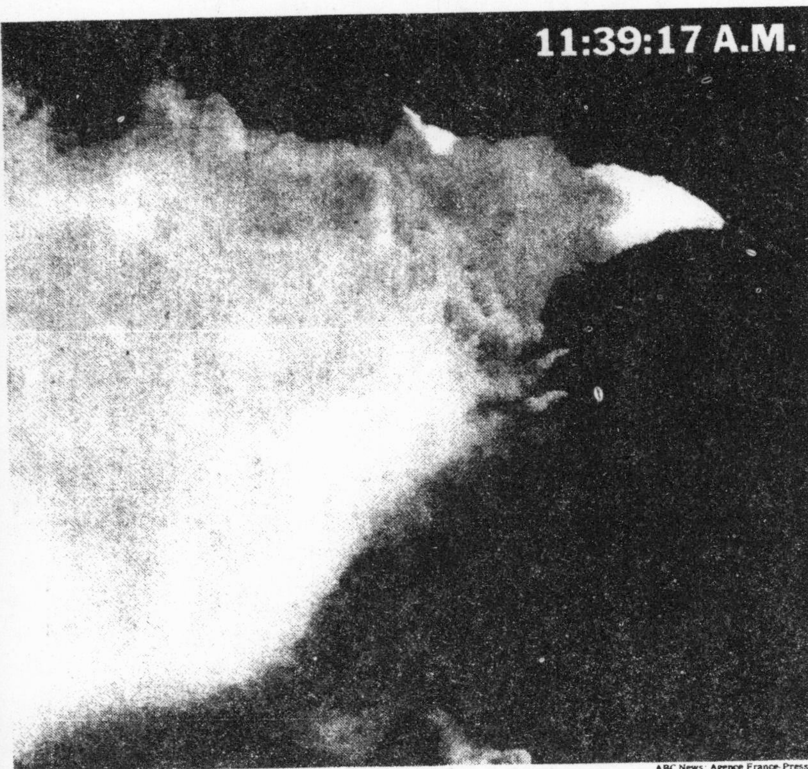

ABC News; Agence France-Presse

Thousands Watch A Rain of Debris

By WILLIAM J. BROAD

Special to The New York Times

CAPE CANAVERAL, Fla., Jan. 28 — The space shuttle Challenger exploded in a ball of fire shortly after it left the launching pad today, and all seven astronauts on board were lost.

The worst accident in the history of the American space program, it was witnessed by thousands of spectators who watched in wonder, then horror, as the ship blew apart high in the air.

Flaming debris rained down on the Atlantic Ocean for an hour after the explosion, which occurred just after 11:39 A.M. It kept rescue teams from reaching the area where the craft would have fallen into the sea, about 18 miles offshore.

It seemed impossible that anyone could have lived through the terrific explosion 10 miles in the sky, and officials said this afternoon that there was no evidence to indicate that the five men and two women aboard had survived.

No Ideas Yet as to Cause

There were no clues to the cause of the accident. The space agency offered no immediate explanations, and said it was suspending all shuttle flights indefinitely while it conducted an inquiry. Officials discounted speculation that cold weather at Cape Canaveral or an accident several days ago that slightly damaged insulation on the external fuel tank might have been a factor.

Americans who had grown used to the idea of men and women soaring into space reacted with shock to the disaster, the first time United States astronauts had died in flight. President Reagan canceled the State of the Union Message that had been scheduled for tonight, expressing sympathy for the families of the crew but vowing that the nation's exploration of space would continue.

Killed in the explosion were the mission commander, Francis R. (Dick) Scobee; the pilot, Comdr. Michael J. Smith of the Navy; Dr. Judith A. Resnik; Dr. Ronald E. McNair; Lieut. Col. Ellison S. Onizuka of the Air Force; Gregory B. Jarvis, and Christa McAuliffe.

Mrs. McAuliffe, a high-school teacher from Concord, N.H., was to have been the first ordinary citizen in space.

After a Minute, Fire and Smoke

The Challenger lifted off flawlessly this morning, after three days of delays, for what was to have been the 25th mission of the reusable shuttle fleet that was intended to make space travel commonplace. The ship rose for about a minute on a column of smoke and fire from its five engines.

Suddenly, without warning, it erupted in a ball of flame.

The shuttle was about 10 miles above the earth, in the critical seconds when the two solid-fuel rocket boosters are firing as well as the shuttle's main engines. There was some discrepancy about the exact time of the blast: The National Aeronautics and Space Administration said they lost radio contact with the craft 74 seconds into the flight, plus or minus five seconds.

Two large white streamers raced away from the blast, followed by a rain of debris that etched white contrails in the cloudless sky and then slowly

Continued on Page A5, Column 4

From the Beginning to the End

The last flight of the shuttle Challenger lasted about 74 seconds. Here is the transcript, as recorded by The New York Times, of its final moments, before and after liftoff.

PUBLIC AFFAIRS OFFICER: Coming up on the 90-second point in our countdown. Ninety seconds and counting. The 51-L Mission ready to go. . . .

T minus 10, 9, 8, 7, 6, we have main engine start, 4, 3, 2, 1. And liftoff. Liftoff of the 25th space shuttle mission and it has cleared the tower. . . .

MISSION CONTROL CENTER: Watch your roll, Challenger.

PUBLIC AFFAIRS OFFICER: Roll program confirmed. Challenger now heading down range. [Pause.] Engines beginning throttling down now at 94 percent. Normal throttle for most of flight 104 percent. Will throttle down to 65 percent shortly. Engines at 65 percent. Three engines running normally. Three good cells, three good ABU's. [Pause.] Velocity 2,257 feet per second, altitude 4.3 nautical miles, down range distance 3 nautical miles. [Pause.]

Engines throttling up, three engines now at 104 percent.

MISSION CONTROL: Challenger, go with throttle up.

FRANCIS R. SCOBEE, CHALLENGER COMMANDER: Roger, go with throttle up.

PUBLIC AFFAIRS OFFICER: One minute 15 seconds, velocity 2,900 feet per second, altitude 9 nautical miles, down range distance 7 nautical miles. [Long pause.]

Flight controllers here looking very carefully at the situation. [Pause.]

Obviously a major malfunction. We have no downlink [communications from Challenger]. [Long pause.]

We have a report from the flight dynamics officer that the vehicle has exploded.

How Could It Happen? Fuel Tank Leak Feared

By MALCOLM W. BROWNE

Debris from the explosion of the shuttle Challenger was scattered so widely over the Atlantic Ocean that investigators may never recover enough of it to pin down the cause of the disaster. But suspicions quickly focused on the craft's huge external fuel tank, a potential bomb that carried more than 385,000 gallons of liquid hydrogen and more than 140,000 gallons of liquid oxygen at liftoff.

The most logical explanation is that a large leak must have occurred either in the tank itself or in the pipeline and pumping system that carried liquid hydrogen to the orbiter's three main engines.

Barbara Schwartz, a spokesman for the Johnson Space Center, acknowledged that pure liquid or gaseous hydrogen cannot burn; only if the pure hydrogen carried in the rear section of the shuttle's tank were allowed to come into contact with air, or with the liquid oxygen in the tank's nose section, could it have burned or exploded.

Potential Dangers of Hydrogen Gas

But what might have started the leak, and what could have ignited the explosion that followed?

Parallel questions, never fully answered, were raised after the fire that destroyed the German airship Hindenburg as it was landing at Lakehurst, N.J., on May 6, 1937. The shuttle Challenger, like the Hindenburg, had been releasing hydrogen gas into the air shortly before the disaster, and some of the gas might have remained aboard the craft, mixed with air and ready to detonate if exposed to the smallest spark.

Neither NASA nor Martin Marietta Aerospace, the manufacturer of the external fuel tank, would comment yesterday on possible causes of the disaster.

But the geometry of the shuttle's external fuel tank, as described by official manuals from NASA and the Rockwell International Corporation, a major shuttle contractor, suggest one potential danger point in particular: the "intertank," or midsection of the structure, which separates the liquid oxygen tank from the liquid hydrogen tank. The bulk of the hydrogen fuel is closest to the liquid oxygen at this point, and a rupture or leak in the plumbing or walls of the intertank could have flooded the two fluids together to create a gigantic bomb.

Suggestions that the unseasonably cold weather at

Continued on Page A4, Column 1

After the Shock, a Need to Share Grief and Loss

By SARA RIMER

The nation came together yesterday in a moment of disaster and loss. Wherever Americans were when they heard the news — at work, at school or at home — they shared their grief over the death of the seven astronauts, among them one who had captured their imaginations, Christa McAuliffe, the teacher from Concord, N.H., who was to have been the first ordinary citizen to go into space.

Shortly before noon, when the first word of the explosion came, daily events seemed to stop as people awaited the details and asked the same questions: "What happened? Are there any survivors?"

In offices, restaurants and stores, people gathered in front of television sets, mesmerized by the terrible scene of the shuttle exploding, a scene that would be replayed throughout the day and night. Children who had learned about Mrs. McAuliffe were watching in classrooms across the country.

It seemed to be one of those moments, enlarged and frozen, that people would remember and recount for the rest of their lives — what they were doing and where they were when they heard that the space shuttle Challenger had exploded. The need to reach out, to speak of disbelief and pain, was everywhere. Family members telephoned one another, friends telephoned friends.

"It was like the Kennedy thing," said John Hannan, who heard the news when his sister called him at his office, a personnel recruiting concern in Philadelphia. "Everyone was numb."

'I Felt Very Close to Her'

Florine Israel, a legal secretary at the New York Civil Liberties Union, echoed the sentiments of many who spoke of Mrs. McAuliffe not as an astronaut but as a friend. "I felt very close to her," she said. "She was ordinary people. She was a mother, a working woman. I felt like I was a part of it."

The image of the shuttle exploding flashed across 100 television sets in the electronics department of Macy's, in midtown Manhattan, where a crowd of workers from nearby offices and facto-

Continued on Page A3, Column 1

Reagan Lauds 'Heroes'

President Reagan, shaken by the explosion of the space shuttle, postponed his State of the Union Message. "We mourn seven heroes," he said in a talk broadcast from the White House after the disaster. "There will be more shuttle flights and more shuttle crews and, yes, more volunteers, more civilians, more teachers in space."

He also sought to console the nation's pupils, many of whom saw telecasts of the loss of the teacher who was to have been sent into space. Article and transcript, page A9.

Francis R. Scobee
Commander

Michael J. Smith
Pilot

Judith A. Resnik
Electrical Engineer

Ellison S. Onizuka
Engineer

Ronald E. McNair
Physicist

Gregory B. Jarvis
Electrical Engineer

Christa McAuliffe
Teacher

The Shuttle Explosion: How It Happened

COMPUTER EXPERTS BAFFLED BY CRASH

Data From On-Board System Failed to Warn of Problem — Tape to Be Studied

By DAVID E. SANGER

Special to The New York Times

WASHINGTON, Jan. 28 — Computer experts were baffled today about why none of the five I.B.M. on-board computers that have aborted so many space launchings detected anything wrong with the shuttle Challenger's operation until the instant the craft exploded.

"On first glance, there were no anomalous data at all," said Steven Eames, a spokesman for the International Business Machines Corporation team at the Johnson Space Center in Houston that monitors the flow of data from the space shuttle's processors. "Nothing was unusual, and then the screen just went blank."

Until pieces of the actual wreckage can be examined, however, a stretch of magnetized computer tape, packed with thousands of instrument readings sent from the shuttle until the explosion, may prove to be the best trail available for investigators who will be studying the catastrophe.

Meanwhile, the absence of warning from the shuttle's processors and the complex network of sensors connected to them could mark a tremendous setback for the nation's computer and avionics industries.

Technology Is Cited

The combination of computer equipment and programs aboard the shuttle has long been hailed as one of American technology's greatest achievements. In recent times it has frequently been cited as evidence that enormously complex programming, like the kind that would be needed to control the Reagan Administration's proposed high-technology antimissile shield, is well within the industry's reach.

Gentry Lee, a top official of the Jet Propulsion Laboratory in Pasadena, Calif., said all that had changed. "It's the kind of thing that marks a tremendous setback for new technology of any kind," said Mr. Lee, who headed one of the first studies of the software designed for the shuttle program. "It forces the whole society to examine the margins of error we build into technology, and that will probably prove a valuable exercise."

Most confusing to experts familiar with the craft's design is that the disaster appeared to defy every computer simulation ever written for the shuttle.

"It's very, very strange," said Dr. L. John Lawrence, a NASA spokesman at the Houston space center. "In all the models, the data show a deterioration before failure. You begin to see pressures change, or temperatures, or valve failures or voltage or hydraulic changes. Things begin to happen. Here, nothing happened."

Past Problem Detected

The events also contradicted five years of experience in the space program. The only other severe failure of a Challenger component occurred in July, when a computer's response to the failure of two heat sensors led to the shutdown of engine No. 1, forcing the shuttle into a lower orbit than planned. It was the first time a manned space mission had ever lost a main engine in flight.

But in that case, as in the computer models, there was ample evidence from the sensors that something was amiss, and both the astronauts and technicians on the ground had time to respond. I.B.M. spokesmen said the entire computer system had been used in previous flights.

If the computers aboard the Challenger and its sister ships have been faulted for anything in recent years, it has been for their oversensitivity, rather than lack of precision.

Starting with the first shuttle flight in 1981, launching after launching has been delayed because one of the four primary I.B.M. AP 101 computers or a fifth backup unit failed to agree that each of thousands of components was working properly. That has triggered automatic shutdowns that sometimes proved embarrassing to NASA

Dependent on Processors

At the same time, space officials say they have little choice but to depend on the processors, because human pilots could never keep track of the thousands of bits of information that stream from the shuttle's sensors.

As a result, the computers have virtually complete control of the flight, which is why they will be a centerpiece of the disaster investigation.

In the industry's terminology, the shuttle's processors are a "redundant," or "fault tolerant," system, each programmed to do exactly the same thing at exactly the same time, like soldiers marching in formation. Thus, if they disagree, a "vote" is staged and the out-of-step machine is ignored. Much the same redundancy is used for the sensors.

"If anything, the system is overly conservative," said Algirdas Avizienis, a professor of computer science at the University of California at Los Angeles who has worked extensively on fault-tolerant systems for the space program. "False alarms are not unusual, and that has been a headache from the beginning."

Immediately after the explosion today, flight controllers in Houston played back the telemetry record. "We found nothing at all," said Dr. Lawrence.

But Mr. Eames, the I.B.M. spokesman, said a full examination of the tape would take some time. "We're talking weeks," he said, before it is all sorted out.

Most experts seemed to agree yesterday that the computers themselves would not ultimately be found at fault.

The Last Moments

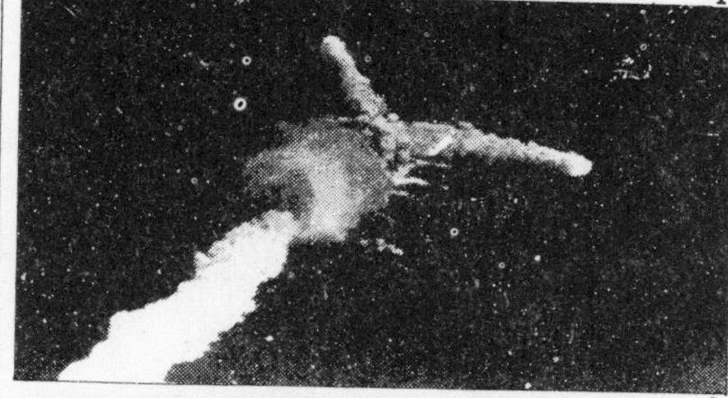

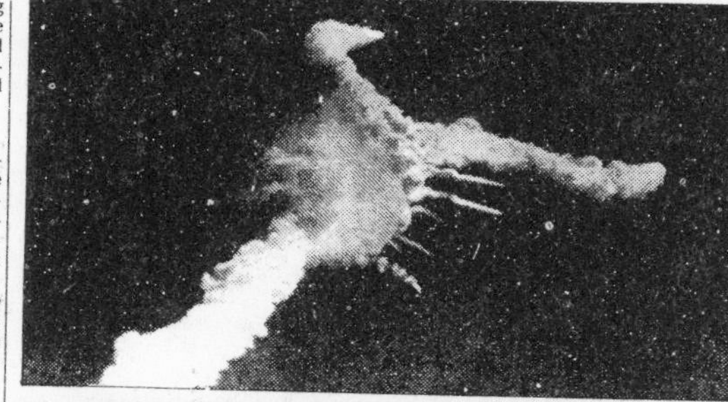

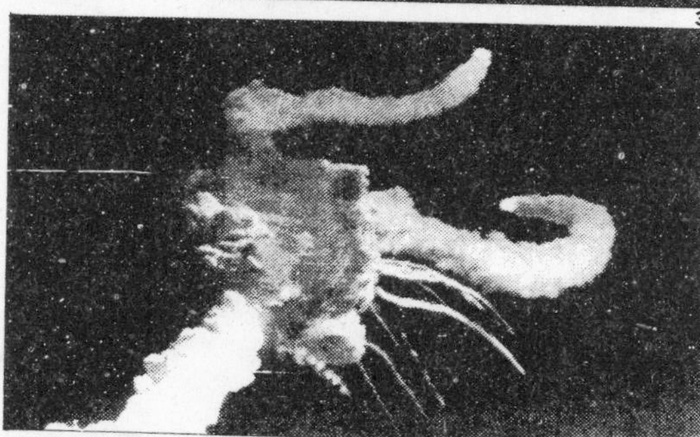

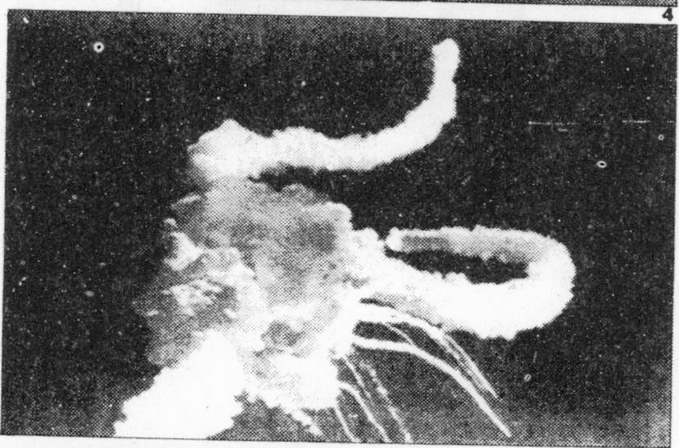

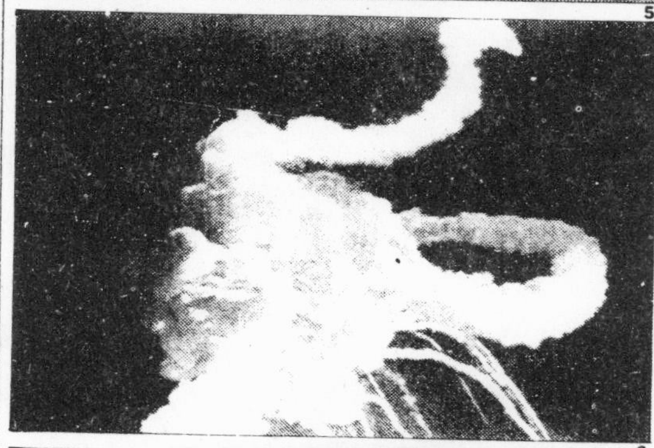

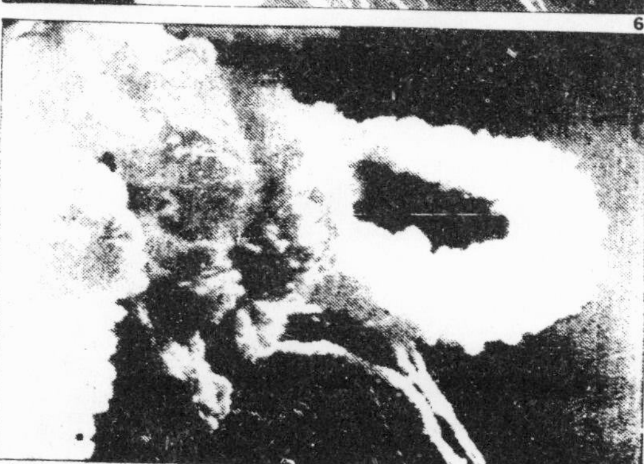

Associated Press

EXPLOSION: The story of the destruction of the Challenger told in plumes of smoke and water vapor high above Earth. The two streams starting in the upper right of the second picture from the top, and curving around in the others, are believed to be the solid fuel booster rockets, still burning, flying off on their own.

Shuttle Explodes, Killing All 7 Aboard

Continued From Page A1

headed toward the cold waters of the nearby Atlantic.

The eerie beauty of the orange fireball and billowing white trails against the blue confused many onlookers, many of whom did not at first seem aware that the aerial display was a sign that something had gone terribly wrong.

There were few sobs, moans or shouts among the thousands of tourists, reporters and space agency officials gathered on an unusually cold Florida day to celebrate the liftoff, just a stunned silence as they began to realize that the Challenger had vanished.

Among the people watching were Mrs. McAuliffe's two children, her husband and her parents and hundreds of students, teachers and friends from Concord.

"Things started flying around and spinning around and I heard some oh's and ah's, and at that moment I knew somethng was wrong," said Brian Ballard, the editor of The Crimson Review at Concord High School

"I felt sick to my stomach. I still feel sick to my stomach."

Ships Searching the Area

At an outdoor news conference held here this afternoon, Jesse W. Moore, the head of the shuttle program at NASA, said:

"I regret to report that, based on very preliminary searches of the ocean where the Challenger impacted this morning, these searches have not revealed any evidence that the crew of Challenger survived." Behind him, in the distance, the American flag waved at half-staff.

Coast Guard ships were in the area of impact tonight and planned to stay all night, with airplanes set to comb the area at first light for debris that could provide clues to the catastrophe. Some material from the shattered craft was reported to be washing ashore on Florida beaches tonight, mostly the small heat-shielding tiles that protect the shuttle as it passes through the earth's atmosphere.

Films of the explosion showed a parachute drifting toward the sea, apparently one that would have lowered one of the huge reusable booster rockets after its fuel was spent.

Pending an investigation, Mr. Moore said at the news conference this afternoon, hardware, photographs, computer tapes, ground support equipment and notes taken by members of the launching team would be impounded.

The three days of delays and a tight annual launching schedule did not force a premature launching, Mr. Moore said in answer to a reporter's question.

'Flight Safety a Top Priority'

"There was no pressure to get this particular launch up," he said. "We have always maintained that flight safety was a top priority in the program."

Several hours after the accident, Mr. Moore announced the appointment of an interim review team, assigned to preserve and identify flight data from the mission, pending the appointment of a formal investigating committee.

The members of the interim panel are Richard G. Smith, the director of the Kennedy Space Center; Arnold Aldridge, the manager of the National Space Transportation System, Johnson Space Center; William Lucas, director of the Marshall Space Flight Center; Walt Williams, a NASA consultant, and James C. Harrington, the director of Spacelab, who will serve as executive secretary.

A NASA spokesman said a formal panel could be appointed as soon as Wednesday by Dr. William R. Graham, the director of the space agency.

All American manned space launchings were stopped for more than a year and a half after the worst previous American space accident, in January 1967, when three astronauts were killed in a fire in an Apollo capsule on the launching pad.

'Hope We Go Today'

This year's schedule was to have been the most ambitious in the history of the shuttle program, with 15 flights planned. For the Challenger, the workhorse of the nation's shuttle fleet, this was to have been the 10th mission.

Today's launching had been delayed three times in three days by bad weather. The Challenger was to have launched two satellites and Mrs. McAullife was to have broadcast two lessons from space to millions of students around the coutnry.

All day long, well after the explosion, the large mission clocks scattered about the Kennedy Space Center continued to run ticking off the minutes and seconds of a flight that had long ago ended.

Long before liftoff this morning, skies over the Kennedy Space Center were clear and cold, reporters and tourists shivering in leather gloves, knit hats and down coats as temperatures hovered in the low 20's.

Icicles formed as ground equipment sprayed water on the launching pad, a precaution against fire.

At 9:07 A.M., after the astronauts were seated in the shuttle, wearing gloves because the interior was so cold, ground controllers broke into a round of applause as the shuttle's door, whose handle caused problems yesterday, which was closed.

"Good morning, Christa, hope we go today," said ground control as the New Hampshire schoolteacher settled into the spaceplane.

"Good morning," she replied. "I hope so, too." Those are her last known words.

The liftoff, originally scheduled for 9:38 A.M., was delayed two hours by problems on the ground caused first by a failed fire-protection device and then by ice on the shuttle's ground support structure.

The launching was the first from pad 39-B, which had recently undergone a $150 million overhaul. It had last been used for a manned launcing in the 1970's.

Just before liftoff, Challenger's external fuel tank held 500,000 gallons of liquid hydrogen and oxygen, which are kept separate because they are highly volatile when mixed. The fuel is used in the shuttle's three main engines.

At 11:38 A.M. the shuttle rose gracefully off the launching pad, heading into the sky. The shuttle's main engines, after being cut back slightly just after liftoff, a normal proceedure, were pushed ahead to full power as the shuttle approached maximum dynamic pressure when it broke through the sound barrier.

"Challenger, go with throttle up," said James D. Wetherbee of mission control in Houston at about 11:39 A.M.

"Roger," replied the commander, Mr. Scobee, "go with throttle up."

Those were the last words to be heard on the ground from the winged spaceplane and her crew of seven.

As the explosion occured, Stephen A. Nesbitt of Mission Control in Houston, apparently looking at his notes and not the explosion on his television monitor, noted that the shuttle's velocity was "2,900 feet per second, altitude 9 nautical miles, downrange distance 7 nautical miles." That is a speed of about 1 977 miles an hour, a height of about 10 statute miles and a distance down range of about 8 miles.

The first official word of the disaster came from Mr. Nesbitt of Mission Control, who reported "a major malfunction." He added that communications with the ship had failed 1 minute 14 seconds into the flight.

"We have no downlink," he said, referring to communications from the Challenger. "We have a report from the flight dynamics officer that the vehicle has exploded."

His voice cracked. "The flight director confirms that," he continued. "We're checking with the recovery forces to see what can be done at this point."

Tapes Showed Small Fire

In the sky above the Kennedy Space Center, the shuttle's two solid-fuel rocket boosters sailed into the distance.

The explosion, later viewed in slow-motion televised replays taken by cameras equipped with telescopic lenses, showed what appeared to be the start of a small fire at the base of the huge external fuel tank, followed by the quick separation of the solid rockets. A huge fireball then engulfed the shuttle as the external tank exploded.

At the news conference, Mr. Moore would not speculate on the cause of the disaster.

The estimated point of impact for debris was 18 to 20 miles off the Florida coast, according to space agency officials.

"The search and rescue teams were delayed getting into the area because of debris continuing to fall from very high altitudes, for almost an hour after ascent," said Mr. Nesbitt of Mission Control in Houston.

Speaking at 1 P.M. in Florida, Lieut. Col. Robert W. Nicholson Jr., a spokesman for the rescue operation, which is run by the Defense Department, said range safety radars near the Kennedy Space Center detected debris falling for nearly an hour after the explosion. "Anything that went into the area would have been endangered," he said in an interview.

In addition, the explosion of the huge fuel supply would have created a cloud of toxic vapors. NASA officials said tonight that the hazardous gases presented no danger to land, but the Coast Guard was advising boats and ships to avoid the area.

'Not a Good Ditcher'

In an interview last year, Tommy Holloway, the chief of the flight director office at the Johnson Space Center in Houston, talked about the possibility of a shuttle crash at sea.

"This airplane is not a good ditcher," he said. "It will float O.K. if it doesn't break apart, and we have hatches we can blow off the top. But the orbiter lands fast, at 190 knots. You come in and stop in 100 yards so so. You decelerate like gangbusters, and anything in the payload bay comes forward. We don't expect a very good day if if comes to that."

On board Challenger was the world's largest privately owned communication satellite, the $100 million Tracking and Data Relay Satellite, which with with its rocket boosters weighed 37,636 pounds.

This morning, water froze on the shuttle service structure, used for fire-fighting equipment and for emergency showers that technicians would use if they were exposed to fuel. The takeoff was delayed because space agency officials feared that during the first critical seconds of launching, icicles might fly off the service structure and damage the delicate heat-resistant tiles on the shuttle, which are crucial for the vehicle's re-entry though the earth's atmosphere.

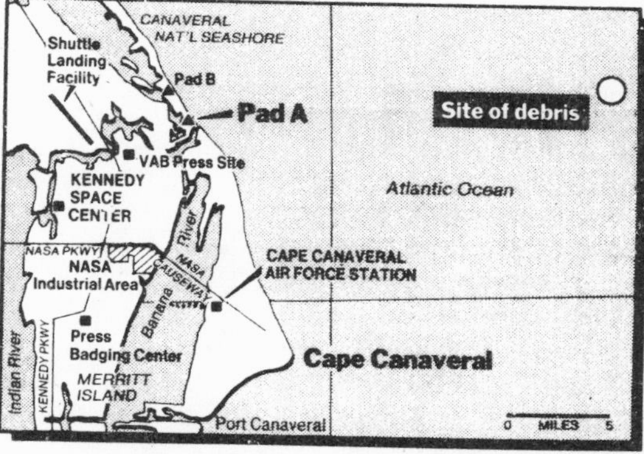

Search for survivors was centered 30 miles southeast of Cape Canaveral.

Search by Air and Sea Yields No Sign of the Shuttle Crew

By DUDLEY CLENDINEN

Special to The New York Times

CAPE CANAVERAL, Fla., Jan. 28 — As night fell along the Atlantic coast and debris began to wash up on the shore, the United States Coast Guard pulled back the 13 aircraft that had been searching today for the remains of the space shuttle Challenger and its crew of seven. They returned to base with no human effects found, and prepared to resume the search Wednesday.

"We have not recovered any," Col. John N. Shults of the Air Force, who is coordinating military resources for the search, said tonight. Jesse Moore, the NASA administrator for space flight, said at a news conference earlier in the day that the search "has not produced any evidence that the crew survived."

But beyond the doubts about the crew's survival were questions about the likelihood of their remains being found. "I don't know," Colonel Shults said. "I have no idea what we're going to find. We're still in the preliminary search."

The search by air and by a small surface fleet of seven Navy, Coast Guard and National Aeronautics and Space Administration ships could not begin until pieces of the wreckage shot into the atmosphere by the explosion stopped raining from the sky, nearly an hour after the shuttle's destruction.

Some Wreckage Found

The searchers did recover some material from the space mission in the first hours of the rescue effort today, but the amount and kind of wreckage salvaged was not made known. Mr. Moore said that all material recovered would be impounded as part of the NASA effort to determine what had ignited the explosion that destroyed Challenger.

"I know that they have brought some pieces back, but I have not heard what the dimensions are," Colonel Shults said. "I understand that it's on its way back in. We'll turn it over to NASA, and they'll lock it up."

Lieut. Col. Robert Nicholson of the Air Force, a Defense Department spokesman, said that "some tiles have been washed up on the beach."

"Some have been carried to us by citizens," he said. "We're recommending that any citizens who find anything call law enforcement."

Colonel Nicholson and others issued a plea for citizens to turn over anything they found, and to stay away from the search area offshore. "We really need every bit," he said. "There are no souvenirs. We need it for the investigation. The intention is to gather every piece and take it to one central location and lay it out."

Ships Continue Search

The Challenger, its rockets and fuel weighed 4.5 million pounds at liftoff. Tonight, the surface ships continued to search an area 60 miles wide — from the coastline of Melbourne north to New Smyrna Beach — and 120 miles out to sea.

Officials here estimated that the floor of the Atlantic in the search area lay 70 to 200 feet down. The search thus far has been conducted by sight, officials here said. Representatives from the office of the Navy Superintendent of Salvage were expected here Wednesday to help plan the underwater aspects of the search, and the aircraft were to resume sweeping the ocean surface at daylight Wednesday.

Air Museum to Mount Exhibit As Memorial to Shuttle Crew

WASHINGTON, Jan. 28 (AP) — The National Air and Space Museum plans to mount an exhibition as a memorial to the seven-member crew of the space shuttle Challenger, which exploded shortly after liftoff today.

Holly Haynes, a spokesman for the museum, which is part of the Smithsonian Institution, said the exhibition, including photographs, biographies and other information on the crew, would be opened by Wednesday afternoon.

The museum plans to continue showing its film on the shuttle program, "The Dream Is Alive," she said. Two members of today's crew, Francis R. Scobee and Judith Resnik, are in the film. A tribute to the crew is to be added to the film, Miss Haynes said.

"All the News That's Fit to Print"

The New York Times

Late Edition

Weather: Mostly sunny and cold today; cloudy, chance of snow tonight. Continued cold, chance of snow tomorrow. Temperatures: today 28-32, tonight 20/23; yesterday 21-38. Details, page D11.

VOL.CXXXV . . No. 46,697 | Copyright © 1986 The New York Times | NEW YORK, WEDNESDAY, FEBRUARY 26, 1986 | 50 cents beyond 75 miles from New York City, except on Long Island | 30 CENTS

MARCOS FLEES AND IS TAKEN TO GUAM; U.S. RECOGNIZES AQUINO AS PRESIDENT

ROCKET ENGINEERS TELL OF PRESSURE FOR A LAUNCHING

Testify NASA Forced Them to Reverse Decision-Making Role on Shuttle Safety

By PHILIP M. BOFFEY

Special to The New York Times

WASHINGTON, Feb. 25 — Rocket engineers testified today that pressure from the space agency to launch the space shuttle Challenger forced them to reverse their normal role — that instead of having to prove that the shuttle was ready to go, it was up to them to show that a launching would be unsafe.

The engineers from Morton Thiokol Inc., which manufactured the shuttle's booster rockets, described a series of tense meetings and telephone conferences on Jan. 27, the day before the launching that resulted in an explosion that killed seven astronauts. They said that in those discussions they felt pres-

Key hearing testimony, page B6.

sure from NASA officials to allow the launching to proceed unless they could prove beyond doubt that disaster would result.

Meanwhile today, James M. Beggs resigned as Administrator of the National Aeronautics and Space Administration. He had been on leave while facing fraud charges resulting from his tenure as an executive of the General Dynamics Corporation. [Page B7.]

The Thiokol engineers' testimony came at a hearing of the Presidential commission that is investigating the Challenger accident. "I felt pressure," said one of them, Brian Russell. "I felt we were in the position of having to

Continued on Page B7, Column 1

The New York Times/Marilynn K. Yee

Allan J. McDonald, engineer for Morton Thiokol, as he testified.

Gorbachev Says U.S. Arms Note Is Not Adequate

Also Tells Party Change In Economy Is Urgent

By SERGE SCHMEMANN

Special to The New York Times

MOSCOW, Feb. 25 — Addressing a landmark meeting of the Soviet Communist Party, Mikhail S. Gorbachev today criticized President Reagan's recent response on arms reduction and said the timing of the next summit meeting could hinge on progress in arms control.

The Soviet leader's comments were included in a speech of five and a half hours on the state of the Soviet Union in

Excerpts from speech, page A11.

the opening session of the 27th congress of the ruling party.

Addressing 5,000 delegates and 152 foreign delegations, Mr. Gorbachev presented a sweeping overview of the problems facing the nation, most of which he blamed on stagnation under the 18-year rule of Leonid I. Brezhnev ending in 1982. Mr. Gorbachev said the key to the future was a qualitatively new approach to Soviet economic development.

Focus on Medium-Range Missiles

Two days ago, Mr. Reagan responded in a letter to a proposal made Jan. 15 by Mr. Gorbachev to eliminate nuclear arms by the year 2000 in a sequence of three stages. Mr. Reagan focused on the first of these stages, involving the elimination of medium-range nuclear missiles.

Mr. Gorbachev said in his speech that he presumed the timing of the response was intended to solicit his reaction at the congress.

He said that Mr. Reagan's proposal "seems to contain some reassuring opinions and theses," but that these "are swamped in various reservations, 'linkages' and 'conditions'."

"To put it in a nutshell," Mr. Gorbachev said, "it is hard to detect in the letter we have just received any serious readiness of the United States Administration to get down to solving the cardinal problems involved in eliminating the nuclear threat."

'No Sense in Empty Talks'

On the question of a summit meeting, Mr. Gorbachev essentially made any further planning contingent on progress in arms control.

"There is no sense in holding empty talks," he said.

Mr. Gorbachev and Mr. Reagan had agreed last November in Geneva that the Soviet leader would visit the United States this year, but officials in Washington have been saying that Moscow has evaded setting a date.

Mr. Gorbachev made clear that this

Continued on Page A10, Column 3

Associated Press

A looter slashing a painting of Ferdinand E. Marcos at presidential palace, which was stormed last night.

Shultz Praises 'Peaceful Transition' in Philippines

By GERALD M. BOYD

Special to The New York Times

WASHINGTON, Wednesday, Feb. 26 — The Reagan Administration moved quickly Tuesday to recognize the new Government of Corazon C. Aquino.

At the same time, the Administration praised what it called the peaceful manner in which Ferdinand E. Marcos had relinquished his 20-year rule as President of the Philippines.

The Administration had issued a statement Monday urging Mr. Marcos to resign. Tuesday, Secretary of State George P. Shultz welcomed the new Government only hours after Mr. Marcos, his family and other associates fled the presidential palace in Manila aboard United States helicopters.

Administration's Involvement

Mr. Marcos's abrupt departure capped days of close involvement by the Administration in the Philippines situation. That involvement was deepened when Senator Paul Laxalt, after conferring with President Reagan, told Mr. Marcos "the time has come" for him to surrender power. Senator Laxalt, a Republican of Nevada and a close friend of Mr. Reagan, had served as his special emissary to Manila last October.

"With the peaceful transition to a new Government of the Philippines, the United States extends recognition to this new Government headed by President Aquino," Mr. Shultz said in a statement pledging United States cooperation.

U.S. Encourages Reconciliation

Larry Speakes, the White House spokesman, said the Administration welcomed Mrs. Aquino's call for "reconciliation and nonviolence" and looked forward to working with the new Government on changes in political, military and economic areas. He said Philip C. Habib, the special Reagan envoy, was en route to Manila to discuss how the United States could help.

A senior Administration official said Mr. Reagan would telephone both Mrs. Aquino and Mr. Marcos, possibly as early as today. He said Mr. Reagan wanted to wait before contacting the new President because things were "unsettled" in the Philippines.

Mr. Shultz said the shift in power should have no effect on relations be-

Continued on Page A14, Column 1

Reuters

Supporters of Corazon C. Aquino and Salvador H. Laurel rejoicing at palace.

From a Symbol to a Leader: The Rise of Corazon Aquino

Special to The New York Times

MANILA, Wednesday, Feb. 26 — Corazon C. Aquino began to exercise presidential power even before Ferdinand E. Marcos left the country today, telling some of the country's most powerful men what they would be doing in her Cabinet, and making a key decision about the nation's top financial institution.

She did so in the same quiet-spoken manner in which, as a self-described housewife, she had hovered in the background during the political career of her husband, Benigno S. Aquino Jr.

Her manner today, however, obscured a personal transformation that has been noted both by political analysts and by members of her own family, who say they have watched her grow in strength and confidence.

In the four months since she decided to run for office, Mrs. Aquino, a genuinely reluctant candidate, has moved from being a symbol around which the nation could unite to being a leader.

"It's astonishing," says a member of her husband's family. "She was just a housewife. Her strength has astonished all of us. The transformation is amazing. It has even affected her children, who have grown as well."

Mrs. Aquino's cool and even tone, her advisers say, overshadows the stubbornness and growing self-assurance that have put her in increasing command of their inner councils. The self-assurance, they say, has been reinforced by the broad popular support that has continued to grow for the woman who has styled herself "almost the complete opposite" of Mr. Marcos.

One Aquino adviser, Teodoro Locsin, said, "By the end of the election, she realized that now she was speaking for the entire nation."

Mrs. Aquino had also come to demonstrate a greater familiarity with the issues than she had in an interview pub-

Continued on Page A13, Column 1

20-YEAR ERA ENDS

'New Life' for Philippines Seen by Successor — Nation Celebrates

By SETH MYDANS

Special to The New York Times

MANILA, Wednesday, Feb. 26 — Ferdinand E. Marcos fled the Philippines Tuesday, ending 20 years as President. Corazon C. Aquino succeeded him, saying "a new life" had begun for her country.

Mr. Marcos, facing pressure from all sides to step down, left the presidential palace shortly after 9 P.M. (8 A.M. Eastern standard time) and traveled by helicopter to Clark Air Base.

There, accompanied by his wife, Imelda, and Gen. Fabian C. Ver, a close associate and former chief of the Philippines military forces, he boarded an American Air Force plane for Guam, a United States territory in the Pacific.

[A Defense Deapartment statement said 55 people were in Mr. Marcos's party aboard two aircraft, The Associated Press reported from Agana, Guam.]

Greeted by Acting Governor

Mr. Marcos arrived at Andersen Air Force Base in Guam this morning, where he was greeted by Acting Gov. Edward D. Reyes.

In Washington, officials said the 68-year-old leader, who reportedly suffers from a kidney ailment, would receive treatment at the Naval Medical Center on Guam. One official described his hospitalization as precautionary.

According to a Defense Department spokesman in Washington, Mr. Marcos was to leave Guam this evening (between 5 A.M. and 8 A.M. E.S.T.) for an unspecified air base near Honolulu.

The departure of Mr. Marcos from Manila ended a day in which he pleaded with Washington for help in clinging to office, then went through an inaugural ceremony that was held apparently after he had decided to leave.

Aquino Too Is Inaugurated

Mrs. Aquino was also inaugurated in the morning to head what was dubbed a provisional government, and although Mr. Marcos made no public resignation when he departed, the United States immediately recognized her administration.

The news of Mr. Marcos's departure set off celebrations in the capital as hundreds of thousands of Filipinos surged into the streets, honking horns, setting off firecrackers and burning tires.

As crowds converged on the presidential palace, fighting broke out between supporters and opponents of Mr. Marcos. Stones and knives were used in the clashes, and a number of injuries were reported. Eventually, a noisy crowd surged into the palace, tearing down portraits of Mr. Marcos and his wife and helping themselves to souvenirs.

Earlier, three civilians were reported killed in Manila during a pitched battle between loyalist and rebel troops for control of a television transmitting tower.

In Washington, the Reagan Administration hailed Mrs. Aquino for "her commitment to nonviolence" while praising Mr. Marcos for a decision "characterized by the dignity and strength that have marked his many years of leadership."

Request to Stay Rejected

The official said that even after Mr. Marcos arrived at Clark Air Base, he asked if he could remain in his home province in northern Luzon, but that the Aquino side refused.

Legal questions remained to be resolved about Mrs. Aquino's mandate following the Feb. 7 election in which Mr. Marcos was proclaimed the winner

Continued on Page A12, Column 3

High Court Backs Use of Zoning To Regulate Showing of Sex Films

By STUART TAYLOR Jr.

Special to The New York Times

WASHINGTON, Feb. 25 — The Supreme Court held today that local zoning officials have broad powers to restrict the location of movie theaters showing sexually explicit films.

Extending a 1976 decision that allowed Detroit to prevent "skid row" concentrations of adult theaters by dispersing them around the city, the Court ruled that a town may limit such theaters to a small area away from homes, schools, churches and parks.

The Justices announced several other decisions today, including their ruling that states cannot require utility companies to include in their billing envelopes the messages of groups with which they disagree. [Page A20.]

Limit on Protection Reaffirmed

In the sex movie case, the seven-Justice majority rejected arguments by a theater owner that the zoning ordinance in Renton, Wash., might effectively ban adult theaters altogether by restricting them to an industrial area where no "commercially viable" sites were available.

While the First Amendment guarantees sexually explicit entertainment facilities "a reasonable opportunity to open and operate," Associate Justice William H. Rehnquist wrote for himself and five others, it does not require zoning under which they "will be able to obtain sites at bargain prices."

On Monday, in striking down an Indianapolis law that outlawed pornographic materials that "subordinate women" as a form of sex discrimina-

Continued on Page A20, Column 1

The New York Times/Larry C. Morris

NETS' STAR BANNED: Micheal Ray Richardson, who was barred from playing in the N.B.A. after a positive cocaine test. Page B11.

INSIDE

Cable TV and 3 Boroughs

Groups set up by three borough presidents have spent more than $700,000 on local programs for cable television systems still being readied. Page B1.

Consumer Prices Up 0.3%

The Consumer Price Index increased last month by the smallest amount since September. Food and energy costs were restrained. Page D1.

For Marcos, a Restless Night of Calls to U.S.

By BERNARD GWERTZMAN

Special to The New York Times

WASHINGTON, Feb. 25 — It was about 3 A.M. today in Manila and President Ferdinand E. Marcos was telephoning to find out whether the message he had received from Washington calling for "a peaceful transition" to a new government actually meant he should quit.

Senator Paul Laxalt, who received the call in Washington — where it was then 2 P.M. Monday — said later that Mr. Marcos was "a desperate man, clutching at straws," even though he would be formally sworn in for another term as President in about nine hours.

Mr. Marcos told the Nevada Republican, whom he seemed to trust as a confidant of President Reagan, that he did not want to resign. Nor did he want to come to the United States, where he might be harassed by congressional committees.

The telephone call touched off the events that led to Mr. Marcos's reluctant decision to give up his fight to remain as President only hours after his inaugural ceremony. But, according to senior Administration officials, Mr. Marcos has resisted accepting Mr. Reagan's offer of a safe haven in the United States.

Even after being taken to Clark Air Base by a United States Air Force helicopter, Mr. Marcos asked the United States Embassy to intercede with those close to Corazon C. Aquino and ask if he could be allowed to live in his home province of Ilocos Norte in northern Luzon.

According to a senior American official, the Aquino side refused on the grounds that passions were running too

Continued on Page A14, Column 4

The Fall of Marcos: Behind the Presidential Walls

After Marcos Abandons His Palace, Filipinos Shout, 'This is Ours Now!'

By FOX BUTTERFIELD

Special to The New York Times

MANILA, Wednesday, Feb. 26 — Up the marble stairs, down the red carpet, past the carved mahogany walls, lies the master bedroom of Malacanang Palace. And there, beside the king-sized bed, sits what appears to be a dialysis machine. It helped keep Ferdinand E. Marcos alive as President of the Philippines, warding off the effects of lupus, a disease characterized by skin lesions.

But Tuesday evening, after he had fled by helicopter and after a huge crowd of Filipinos had poured into the spacious park-like grounds of the palace, the machine had become a mere curiosity.

"Marcos was President for 20 years, but this is the first time I've ever been inside Malacanang," said Enrique Tobego. Mr. Tobego, who has been without a job for months, like many Filipinos, then shouted "This is truly the day of our liberation!"

On the second-floor balcony of the main office building, three young men held up a full-length portrait of Mr. Marcos, a crimson sash around his chest. The crowd outside roared as they dropped it to the ground.

Then, when the men returned a minute later with a smiling portrait of the President's wife, Imelda, the crowd booed, and a chant began: "Burn it! Burn it!"

The more indignant reaction to Mrs. Marcos, who presided over a host of high Government positions and lived in regal style, reflected a widespread feeling among Filipinos that she was the greater of two evils.

Despite the size of the crowd and the intensity of the moment, there was little looting or unruly behavior.

Several men wearing yellow headbands, the color of Corazon C. Aquino, the country's new President, pleaded with people not to break into the old, ornate Spanish-style office and presidential buildings.

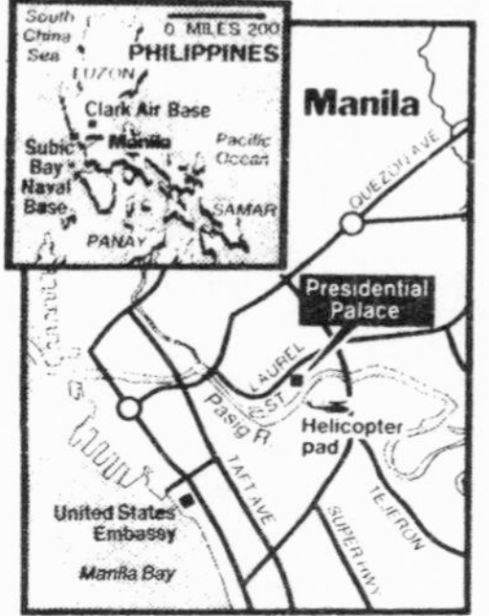

The New York Times / Feb. 26, 1986

A vast crowd poured into the grounds of the presidential palace after Ferdinand E. Marcos fled.

"This is ours now," a man said to people who pushed forward toward the glass doors. "This is for our new President. If you take things away, we will have nothing."

Gradually, the few people who managed to get inside the residence, including some reporters, left. One of the last to go was a man in his 20's who had been playing the palace piano, in the dark.

Outside, some people perched atop three tanks left behind by Mr. Marcos's palace guards. Others lay on the ground to sleep. Some had carried images of the Madonna with them.

Although the 5,000 troops guarding the palace withdrew at 8:30 P.M. Tuesday night and Mr. Marcos left shortly after 9 o'clock, the crowd did not get in for two more hours.

The path was blocked by a group of 30 to 40 men whom Filipinos have taken to calling "goons," local policemen, village captains and rowdies who helped prolong Mr. Marcos's rule. Mr. Marcos invited them to his inauguration this morning when foreign diplomats boycotted the proceedings, and they remained at the palace's outer gates tonight, his last allies.

As a throng of young men tried to advance down Laurel Street toward one of the palace's main gates, the Marcos loyalists built a barricade of burning tires and pelted the crowd with stones. The crowd then ripped up sections of pavement to use as weapons of their own and protected themselves with sheets of tin torn from the roofs of adjacent houses.

As first one side and then the other charged forward, several people were hit by stones. There were no street lights, but by the light of a full moon, the injured could be seen bleeding.

"I don't know who those guys are," said Benji Hermosa, peering toward the palace, still 300 yards away. "You could call them Marcos loyalists, I suppose, but fanatics might be a better word. I don't think Marcos is still in there."

A Peek as a President Flees

One man who did know Mr. Marcos had left was Anacleto Del Rosario, a 63-year-old management consultant who lives on a side street overlooking the back of the palace. Peeking out his rear window, Mr. Del Rosario heard the sound of a motorboat cross the Pasig River from the palace to a park on the other side, where the President's helicopter pad is situated.

Mr. Del Rosario, who was an intelligence officer in World War II, fighting against the Japanese, then saw two helicopters land in the dark. They were gone in less than five minutes.

Mr. Del Rosario had watched the guests go in for Mr. Marcos's inauguration at noon, but he said he was not surprised that Mr. Marcos left so soon after claiming he had again been legally installed as President.

"He is a smart man," Mr. Del Rosario said. "He wanted to leave as President, with his dignity."

The day's events reminded him of 1945, when the Japanese were driven out of Manila after weeks of savage house-to-house fighting. "But here, miraculously, there was no bloodshed," Mr. Del Rosario said.

The Troops Arrive

But early this morning, half an hour after midnight, a convoy of five army trucks arrived at the palace, and soldiers then slowly cleared the mass of people from the palace grounds. They had been sent to protect the palace by Gen. Fidel V. Ramos, the Chief of Staff in Mrs. Aquino's new government.

As people were pushed out, the mood of jubilation ebbed. A strange hush fell, replacing the earlier cheers for Mrs. Aquino of "Cory! Cory!"

There was a hint of menace, too. Capt. Ricardo Galios said his troops had found 15 cases of TNT in one of the administration buildings and a cluster of booby traps where the personnel records were kept.

Captain Galios said the body of a man of student age had been found, with a head wound, perhaps a victim of the earlier street battle. Where the last Marcos loyalists had gone, no one knew, but Captain Galios said he suspected they might still be hiding on the grounds.

Underfoot were hundreds of documents tossed out of an office window. Among them was an orange-colored campaign poster, with a picture of Mr. Marcos as a 27-year-old soldier in World War II. The poster read, "Marcos, tested in war and peace."

Agence France-Presse

VIOLENCE: A man with a knife standing over a victim of fighting outside the presidential palace.

Marcos Flees the Philippines and Is Taken to Guam

Continued From Page A1

by the National Assembly, which he controlled, on the basis of a vote count marred by widespread fraud and violence by his supporters.

Thirty people were taken by helicopter from the palace to the United States Embassy and 80 others were evacuated down the Pasig River and then by car convoy to the embassy, according to Mrs. Aquino's new military chief, Gen. Fidel V. Ramos.

General Ramos did not say who was evacuated besides Mr. Marcos and his family, which includes his wife, Imelda, a son, Ferdinand Jr., two daughters, Imee Manotoc and Irene Araneta, and three grandchildren.

Mrs. Aquino, wearing a yellow dress, as she did throughout her campaign, appeared on television in the early hours of the morning to tell the nation, "The long agony is over. A new life starts for our country tomorrow."

'We Are Finally Free'

For her 52-second address, which was repeated periodically, Mrs. Aquino removed her glasses, as she does for photographers when she wants to look her best.

"We are finally free, and we can be truly proud of the unprecedented way in which we achieved our freedom, with courage, with determination and most of all in peace," she said, smiling at the camera.

"A new life starts for our country tomorrow, a life filled with hope and I believe a life that will be blessed with peace and progress."

Her sentiments appeared to be reflected throughout Manila, where there was a tangible sense of elation and relief. "We are free now," cried a man who had worn a "Marcos for President" button throughout the campaign.

'Happy New Year'

Late into the night, cars traveled the streets of Manila honking their horns, as people shouted to each other, "Happy New Year!" and "Happy Birthday!"

"This was their show," said a senior American Embassy official this morning. "They deserve all the credit. We find the whole thing an engulfing human experience."

He praised Mrs. Aquino's patience and serenity throughout the pressures of the election and its aftermath, and the courage of Defense Minister Juan Ponce Enrile and General Ramos in challenging the power of Mr. Marcos.

The official also praised the democratic drive of the Filipinos against the forces of Mr. Marcos and his military.

The groundswell of support that has carried Mrs. Aquino into office appears to have left no doubts here about her mandate, despite her inability to win a formal proclamation of victory from the Marcos-controlled National Assembly, the nation's parliament.

The Power of the People

The desire of many Filipinos for change and their frustration with Mr. Marcos's long years in power were heightened over the past three weeks as he openly manipulated the forces at his command to deny Mrs. Aquino her victory.

The role of the popular will, rather than political dealings, in her victory was underscored over the past four days by the massing of hundreds of thousands of Filipinos in the streets to protect a group of breakaway military officers who challenged Mr. Marcos.

It was this final challenge by Mr. Enrile and General Ramos that helped force Mr. Marcos out of power.

The two men, who were named Tuesday morning to Mrs. Aquino's new Cabinet as her Defense Minister and military Chief of Staff, barricaded themselves in a military base. Although their forces were far inferior to those of Mr. Marcos and General Ver, the massed presence of the people around them made retaliation by the Government impossible.

Speaking on television this morning, General Ramos said that "pockets of resistance" remained but that "99.5 percent" supported the new Government.

Throughout the campaign, and as late as his final statements before leaving the country, Mr. Marcos made it plain that although he had called this special election 16 months before the end of his six-year term, he had no intention, whatever the outcome, of relinquishing office.

Legislators Will Meet

He continued to struggle with all the legal and military forces at his command for a technical victory, long after it had become clear that the national will was not with him.

In the face of his stubbornness, Mrs. Aquino's victory was seen as victory for the millions of people who protected their right to vote in the face of intimidation by Mr. Marcos's backers.

"Now he is one of the soon-to-be-forgotten exiles," said Homobono Adaza, an Assemblyman who supported Mrs. Aquino. "I never thought Marcos would go along the same classical way the others have gone, the Somozas and the Batistas."

He said legislators supporting Mrs. Aquino, who hold only one-third of the National Assembly seats, would meet today to seek an agreement with the majority to gain parliamentary proclamation for the new President.

Mrs. Aquino has said that if the legislature stands in the way of reforms she intends to institute, she will use Mr. Marcos's special decree-making powers, which she has opposed, for one last time before abolishing them.

New Charter Is a Priority

She and her supporters have also said a priority of her new Administration would be the drafting of a new constitution to replace the one Mr. Marcos fashioned under martial law.

At her inauguration Tuesday morning, Mrs. Aquino named Mr. Enrile and General Ramos to their new posts, and said her Vice President, Salvador H. Laurel, would also hold the position of Prime Minister.

She called for the resignations of high public officials and Supreme Court justices, but assured civil servants that they could keep their jobs if they had not violated the law.

On the question of the Communist insurgency, Mrs. Aquino has said she will declare a six-month cease-fire and an amnesty for insurgents who lay down their arms and renounce violence.

On the issue of Clark Air Base and the American naval base at Subic Bay, Mrs. Aquino has said she will allow the current agreement to run its course through 1991 and then seek to negotiate a full-fledged treaty rather than the current executive agreement.

In the early hours of Tuesday morning, Mr. Marcos made a number of telephone calls to both Filipinos and Americans, seeking some way to remain in office, if only as the shell of a President, giving all the real power to Mrs. Aquino.

"It's too late," Mr. Enrile said he told Mr. Marcos when he telephoned him.

'The Time Has Come'

"I said I thought that was impractical," said Senator Paul Laxalt, Republican of Nevada, who had visited Mr. Marcos as a special envoy of Mr. Reagan.

"Then he asked me the gut question, 'Senator, what should I do?' " Mr. Laxalt said. "I wasn't bound by diplomatic niceties. I said, 'Cut and cut cleanly. The time has come.'

"There was the longest pause. It seemed to last minutes. It lasted so long I asked if he was still there. He said, 'Yes,' and then he said, 'I am so very, very disappointed.' "

The conversation ended without Mr. Marcos saying what he intended to do.

Before leaving Clark Air Base for Guam, Mr. Marcos told American officials he had made a last plea to Mrs. Aquino's supporters to be allowed to retire to his home province of Ilocos Norte, in northern Luzon, a senior State Department official said.

The President was quoted as having said he was told the idea was not "practical."

Marcos True to Form

In holding an inauguration, which came at noon Tuesday, Mr. Marcos left office in much the same way he had held it, with a tenacious insistence on the forms and legalisms of government, though holding a less firm grasp of the spirit of the law.

Though his mandate has slipped away, he stood firmly and confidently on a low platform in the reception hall of the palace. Hundreds of supporters — though no foreign representatives and few of his own officials — sat on the floor and on chairs and cheered as he looked directly into a television camera and raised his right hand to take the oath.

His wife stood smiling radiantly in a white dress just behind him, and at one point kissed him on the cheek. His son, dressed in green fatigues, stood behind her. At their side, his daughters, both in white, sat on velvet chairs, smiling at their supporters and sometimes quietly joining them in calling "Mabuhay," or "Hooray."

"No man can be more proud that I am at this moment," Mr. Marcos said, as if forcing himself to proceed with the forms of the leadership he now knew he had lost.

"Whatever be the challenges, whatever be the obstacles before us, I say to you as I say to everybody else that we will overcome," he said.

His supporters cheered, and one whispered, "Just like Lincoln."

But in a final indignity, as he stood with his right hand raised, his opponents, who had been waging a pitched battle for the television station, disconnected it at the very moment he was to take the oath of office, and television screens went blank.

The battle for the television transmitter, which began at 7 A.M., was one of the few real military engagements of the change in government.

Troops Surround Tower

Forces under the command of General Ramos surrounded the 1,000-foot television tower, with an armored car with machine guns and small cannons, and exchanged fire with government troopers positioned at the station.

The thousands of people gathered in the street, part of the masses who have made "people power" the catchword of this political event, threw themselves onto the ground screaming. Three were killed.

The confrontation calmed as a priest, the Rev. Nestor Rabon, came forward to negotiate, a symbol of the decisive role the church has played in the election and its aftermath.

Television reporters said it was not the battle itself that disconnected transmission at the moment of Mr. Marcos's inauguration, but technicians who managed to cut the microwave signal from the palace at the decisive moment.

Coverage of the inauguration was replaced by a John Wayne movie.

After the Fall, Joyous Pandemonium Grips Manila

By CLYDE HABERMAN

Special to The New York Times

MANILA, Wednesday, Feb. 26 — This rumor-driven city took a hard look before deciding that it could begin its celebration.

On Monday, there had been at least three reports, each billed as authoritative, each widely believed, each claiming that Ferdinand E. Marcos had given up his presidency and fled.

The fourth rumor, Tuesday night, proved to be accurate.

Fittingly, it was carried here on the country's main television station, a Marcos microphone until insurgents took it over three days ago. The report came quietly, with a caution from announcers that it required closer study.

But after an hour, by about 10:30 P.M., there could be no doubt. The Philippine capital allowed itself to throw back its head and let forth a self-satisfied laugh over its liberation.

"Liberation" was a frequently heard word as hundreds of thousands of Filipinos surged into the streets of Manila in an uncorking of pleasure that was still reverberating this morning. What celebrants may have lacked in creativity, they more than made up for in enthusiasm.

Cars, "jeepneys" and open trucks jammed with banner-waving men roamed the streets, horns honking endlessly. They were cheered by streams of people lining the roadways, their hands raised, thumbs and forefingers forming an "L," the symbol of the party headed by the new President, Corazon C. Aquino.

Firecrackers punctuated the night. At many intersections, people set fires, which they fueled with car tires that sent billows of acrid smoke rolling through neighborhoods.

'We Are a New Generation'

On Times Street in Quezon City, cars went back and forth past Mrs. Aquino's house, but she was not there to watch. Her whereabouts were unknown, and presumably her aides had continued a recent policy of shuttling her each night to a different "safe house" as a security precaution.

Most of the celebrants were young, befitting a country where half the population is under 18 years old. "We are a new generation," said a 26-year-old man who gave his name only as Rudy. "We deserve a new President."

There were uneasy moments, notably at Malacanang, the presidential palace. Huge crowds converged there after Mr. Marcos fled the capital. Thousands of Filipinos surged through the palace gates, and although the country's new leaders had warned against looting, there were reports of shots fired and of stealing.

According to one version, people were seen carrying items such as monogrammed towels and calendars. Some accounts described this as looting, but the haul did not appear to be much different from that which many travelers take from hotels.

Aside from the palace, there were no reports of ugly incidents in Manila. For the most part, the transfer of Philippine power had been performed with ease and even gentleness. Denunciations of Mr. Marcos were few.

'People Power' and U.S. Help

Manila has grown accustomed to enormous throngs. They became a part of daily life in the waning days of the Marcos regime, as Filipinos took to the streets in support of a military rebellion that gave the President his final shove.

"People power" has turned into an instant buzzword. But some people suspected that American intervention was a big factor, and they seemed to appreciate it.

An American caught up in the street crowds this morning was asked occasionally for his nationality. Three times, after he responded, people shook his hand and said "Thank you."

Among other things, Manila on Tuesday was a city of sudden exiles, Marcos friends and aides looking for the exits.

Mrs. Aquino's armed forces Chief of Staff, Gen. Fidel V. Ramos, said he had heard that his counterpart in the Marcos regime, Gen. Fabian C. Ver, had taken an "executive jet" to "an unknown destination." Later, it turned out that General Ver had flown to Guam in the Marcos plane.

The television station now controlled by the new Government reported that Justice Minister Estelito Mendoza was stopped as he tried to board a plane for San Francisco. Others in flight were said to be Pacifico Castro, the acting Foreign Minister; Benjamin T. Romualdez, the Ambassador to the United States and the brother of Mr. Marcos's wife, Imelda; Eduardo Cojuangco, a Marcos family friend and a cousin of Mrs. Aquino, and J. V. Cruz, the Ambassador to Britain. Mr. Marcos's Labor Minister, Blas Ople, was in the United States already on an official trip.

How accurate these reports were could not be immediately determined. The day before, the same station reported the arrest of some Marcos deputies, who then turned up at Malacanang for their leader's final inauguration.

In the days leading to Mr. Marcos's exit, Manila seemed almost to be several cities. Tensions were high, spilling into violence almost every day on the streets outside the palace. Gunfights and sniper shootings occured at broadcasting stations as rival military forces battled for control.

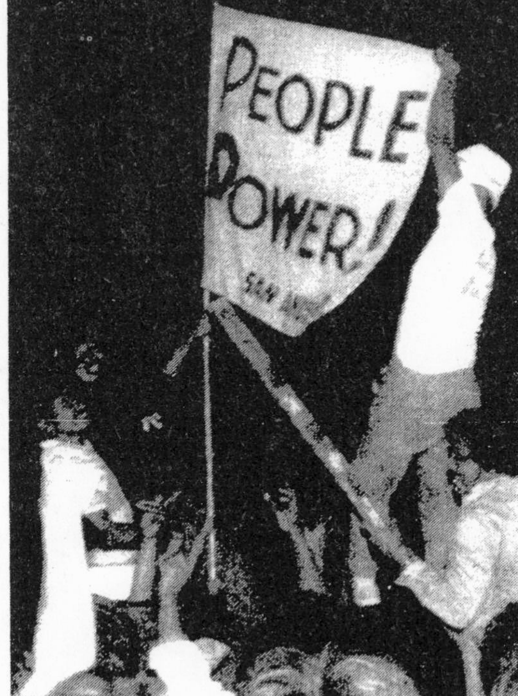

Agence France-Presse

STORMING THE GATES: Foes of the Marcos regime climbing the gates outside the presidential palace early yesterday in Manila.

But elsewhere, the crowds were calm and hopeful, filled with talk of reconciliation and hope. In a country that is overwhelmingly and devoutly Roman Catholic, spirituality figured prominently in much of the rhetoric.

A Cautious New Beginning

Still, this was an apprehensive capital. Some residents had stocked up on staples such as rice in anticipation of possible civil strife and resulting shortages. Many businesses have not opened this week. All banks were shut, but the central bank of the Philippines said it would ask them to reopen today.

In the first hours of the post-Marcos era, some people sensed that it might take a while to adjust to their new world. The Rev. William Arana, a Catholic priest, said the preferred to move tentatively.

He had joined the many thousands outside the presidential palace, a place he had visited as a student 25 years ago. This was his first time back since then, but as he watched others surge past the gates onto the Malacanang grounds, he decided against joining them.

"Maybe tomorrow," he said.

"All the News That's Fit to Print"

The New York Times

Late Edition

Weather: Mostly sunny, warm today; increasing cloudiness tonight. Mostly cloudy, chance of showers tomorrow. Temperatures: today 78-82, tonight 50-59; yesterday 52-71. Details, page A18.

VOL.CXXXV . . . No. 46,760 NEW YORK, WEDNESDAY, APRIL 30, 1986 — 50 cents beyond 75 miles from New York City, except on Long Island. — 30 CENTS

SOVIET, REPORTING ATOM PLANT 'DISASTER,' SEEKS HELP ABROAD TO FIGHT REACTOR FIRE

VIRTUAL CERTAINTY OF FAILURE SHOWN FOR SHUTTLE SEAL

New Tests Indicate That Cold and Design Flaws Doomed Challenger From Start

By DAVID E. SANGER

Special to The New York Times

WASHINGTON, April 29 — New and unpublished test results show that a failure of a safety seal on the space shuttle Challenger was virtually inevitable because of a combination of cold weather on the morning of the launching and serious design flaws.

The test results, conducted for the Presidential panel studying the accident and summarized for The New York Times, also determined that the joint would sometimes begin to fail at temperatures as high as 50 degrees Fahrenheit.

In the past, officials of the National Aeronautics and Space Administration have testified that they felt confident the shuttle could be launched at far lower temperatures without undue risk to the crew.

Failure Was Probable

The Challenger was launched Jan. 28 in 36-degree weather, but investigators estimate that the temperature of the joint that contained the failed seal was about 28 degrees, a temperature at which failure is more likely than not, the tests show.

The analysis of the accident, in which the seven crew members died, is expected to serve as the centerpiece of the Presidential commission's report, due in early June. On Monday panel members received a summary of the results, based on tests conducted in recent weeks primarily by NASA engineers and outside aerospace experts working for the commission's working group analyzing data and design.

'I Wouldn't Fly That Rocket'

"The bottom line is that temperature is the key variable, but temperature alone didn't cause it," Maj. Gen. Donald J. Kutyna, who led the working group, said in response to questions about the results. General Kutyna, a former fighter pilot, warned against a "quick fix" of the joint, saying that under the current design "even on a warm day I wouldn't fly that rocket."

The findings, when taken with testimony before the commission, strongly suggest that the middle-level NASA officials from the Marshall Space Flight Center who decided to go ahead with the launching, despite warnings about the low temperature from engineers working for the manufacturer of the booster rocket, acted with virtually no knowledge of the true performance limitations of the crucial joints and the synthetic rubber rings that were relied on to seal them.

Investigators say they are at a loss to

Continued on Page B7, Column 1

Agence France-Presse

AN IMPERIAL ANNIVERSARY: Emperor Hirohito reading a message at ceremony in Tokyo marking his 60th anniversary on the throne as well as his 85th birthday.

Indonesia Bars Two Journalists In Reagan Party

By GERALD M. BOYD

Special to The New York Times

DENPASAR, Bali, April 29 — President Reagan arrived today on this Indonesian island on the first major stop of his trip to the Far East, but the occasion was marred, White House officials said, when the Indonesian Government detained two Australian journalists in the President's party and barred them from the country.

In a separate incident, Indonesian authorities detained and expelled Barbara Crossette, a correspondent for The New York Times who was seeking to report on the Reagan visit. [Page A6].

Moments before Mr. Reagan was greeted at the island's airport by President Suharto, the Indonesian leader, and colorfully clad Balinese dancers, Indonesian authorities removed the two Australians from the White House press plane.

Ordered to Leave Country

The journalists, from the Australian Broadcasting Corporation, were ordered to leave the country in a move that White House officials said highlighted sharp differences between the United States and Indonesia over press and political freedoms.

The two correspondents, Jim Middleton and Richard D. Palfreyman, are based in Washington and had been told that they would not be allowed to enter, despite the protests of American officials, following unfavorable reports in

Continued on Page A6, Column 1

ASSESSMENT OF U.S.

Intelligence Sources Say Accident Began Days Ago and Continues

By PHILIP M. BOFFEY

Special to The New York Times

WASHINGTON, April 29 — United States intelligence sources said today that the nuclear disaster in the Soviet Union started as long as four or five days ago and was continuing to spread radioactive material into the atmosphere.

Most experts agreed that the graphite core of the Chernobyl reactor, at Pripyat in the Ukraine, had caught fire and was burning fiercely.

Details of the accident remained scarce today, the day after the Russians announced that an accident had taken place at the reactor. Without such details, experts found it difficult to speculate about the short- and long-term dangers the disaster posed to health and the environment.

Soviet Technology Faulted

But they faulted Soviet technology, which uses graphite, a form of carbon, to moderate nuclear reactions. In the United States, water is used as a moderator.

They also said the stricken reactor was not encased in a protective concrete containment dome, as is customary in the United States. The external shell could cut down on the radioactive material spewed into the atmosphere.

The experts warned that such graphite fires can be very difficult to extinguish, and that an unextinguished fire continues to release more radioactivity over the Soviet Union and other countries downwind of the reactor.

"The graphite is burning and will continue to burn for a good number of days," said Kenneth L. Adelman, the United States arms control administrator. He told Congress that, because the reactor is on a river, "there is concern over water contamination."

Europeans Are Critical

European officials and nuclear experts criticized the Soviet Union for not disclosing the accident as soon as it occurred. Some United States intelligence officials say they believe it happened Friday or possibly even Thursday. Moscow did not reveal the accident until Monday.

The Associated Press quoted a ranking information official, who was not identified, as saying that today "smoke was still billowing from the site" at the reactor.

"The roof had been blown off and large portions of the walls had caved in, and it seemed at the time that the nuclear unit just above it might still be in some danger," The A.P. said, adding that it was understood — but not officially confirmed — that much of the American intelligence information had been gathered by a KH-11 spy satellite.

Zhores Medvedev, the exiled Russian

Continued on Page A11, Column 2

Reuters

Photograph published in the February issue of Soviet Life magazine shows cooling system of a reactor at the Chernobyl nuclear power plant near Kiev.

The Nuclear Disaster

What Happened

In an unusual public admission, the Soviet state radio said a "disaster" had occurred at a nuclear power plant in the Ukraine. West German and Swedish officials said Soviet officials had asked for help in controlling a burning nuclear reactor. The nuclear accident, described by Swedish experts as potentially the worst ever at a power plant, sent a radioactive cloud across parts of the Soviet Union, Eastern Europe and Scandinavia. Moscow provided few details, but intelligence sources believe that the accident occurred last Thursday or Friday and that radiation was continuing to spew yesterday. Western experts say they believe graphite used to moderate the nuclear reaction in the plant caught fire. They disagree on whether the fire was associated with a meltdown, in which nuclear fuel rods burn out of control.

The Health Damage

The Russians reported that four nearby localities had been evacuated, two people had died and others had been treated. Western experts say they fear that a great many more, perhaps thousands, who lived near the plant may become ill or die from radiation poisoning in coming years or suffer cancers and genetic mutations later. So far, radiation levels reaching Scandinavia are not considered dangerous.

Could It Happen Here?

American commercial reactors use water rather than graphite, a flammable material, to moderate nuclear reactions. They also, unlike the Soviet reactor in the accident, have steel and concrete containment structures designed to prevent the escape of radiation. But experts say they do not have enough information to tell whether the accident holds any lessons for nuclear power safety here.

Unanswered Questions

These are among the unanswered questions: When did the accident begin? What caused the accident? How much radiation of what types has been released? How many people have been killed, injured or exposed to dangerous radiation? Have soils, crops, water and livestock in the Ukraine been dangerously contaminated?

2 DEATHS ADMITTED

Moscow, in Terse Report, Asserts the 'Radiation Situation' Is Stable

By SERGE SCHMEMANN

Special to The New York Times

MOSCOW, April 29 — The Soviet Government was reported today to have asked West Germany and Sweden for assistance in handling a fire in a nuclear reactor core.

The reports, from officials in those countries, came amid indications that a reactor accident reported Monday in the Ukraine, 70 miles north of Kiev, was a major disaster, perhaps the worst in the history of nuclear power.

[The United States formally offered humanitarian and technical assistance to the Soviet Union to help it deal with the accident. Page 6.]

'Radiation Situation' Stable

The developments came as the Soviet Government issued its second official statement on the accident in the Chernobyl nuclear power station at Pripyat, saying that the "radiation situation has now been stabilized."

The four-paragraph statement disclosed for the first time that the accident at the four-reactor plant had occurred in the No. 4 reactor, which went into service in 1983, and that the three others were in operating order, but had been shut down. Each of the four reactors had an electrical generating capacity of 1,000 megawatts.

[At one point, according to Reuters, the Moscow radio referred to the accident as "a disaster," but later dropped the word. United Press International quoted the radio as having said, "The disaster was the first one at a Soviet nuclear power plant in more than 30 years." There was a nuclear accident in the Urals in 1957 that the Soviet Government has never acknowledged.]

Four Localities Evacuated

The Soviet Government statement, which was read on the evening television news, said that two people had been killed in the accident and that the power-station settlement, an allusion to Pripyat, and three other nearby localities had been evacuated.

[Some Western officials questioned whether the death toll could be as low as two. In Washington, Kenneth L. Adelman, director of the Arms Control and Disarmament Agency, called the Soviet assertion "frankly preposterous."]

The reported Soviet request for assistance from West Germany and Sweden indicated to experts that the reactor's graphite core was burning uncontrollably, and therefore that the fuel rods in it might have melted down partly or completely. Some foreign scientists agreed that if this was the case, the accident was the worst nuclear-power disaster in history.

But the Soviet authorities provided

Continued on Page A10, Column 5

Casualties in Soviet Could Keep Rising, U.S. Experts Assert

By HAROLD M. SCHMECK Jr.

American experts said yesterday that deaths and injuries from the reactor accident in the Soviet Union may continue to mount for several weeks in the vicinity of the disaster if severe radiation has been released.

These experts on health and radiation said there appeared to be no danger for the Western Hemisphere and probably little in the Scandinavian countries, on the basis of what has been reported thus far.

When the Soviet Union announced that two people had been killed in the accident at the Chernobyl power plant in the Ukraine, there was no indication if the cause of death was radiation, fire or other nonnuclear effects.

There was an unconfirmed report from the area that many more may have died. If that report is confirmed, said Dr. Kenneth Mossman of Georgetown University Medical School, it would suggest extremely high levels of gamma radiation.

Two types of radiation exposure are likely to be involved in the damage at and near the reactor site.

The first and most immediately dangerous is external gamma radiation, which is similar to X-rays and equally penetrating. Gamma radiation can damage cells, genes and vital tissues,

Continued on Page A12, Column 1

The New York Times / Paul Hosefros

BODIES OF CHALLENGER'S CREW LEAVE FLORIDA: Coffin of Francis R. Scobee being carried from plane at Dover Air Force Base, Del. Remains of astronauts will be turned over to their families for burial. Page B7.

INSIDE

Dismissal in Secrets Case

Officials said a Pentagon aide was dismissed on the ground that he gave information about covert U.S. operations for a news article. Page A17.

Methodists' Nuclear Stand

The United Methodist Church's Council of Bishops voted to issue a pastoral letter declaring opposition to any use of nuclear weapons. Page A15.

Red Sox Pitcher Fans 20

Roger Clemens of Boston set a major league record by striking out 20 Seattle batters in the Red Sox 3-1 victory. He issued no walks. Page A27.

Nuclear Disaster: A Spreading Cloud and an Aid Appeal

U.S. Offers to Help Soviet In Dealing With Accident

Special to The New York Times

WASHINGTON, April 29 — The United States formally offered humanitarian and technical assistance to the Soviet Union today to help it deal with the nuclear accident near Kiev.

A State Department spokesman, Charles E. Redman, said the offer was extended by Rozanne L. Ridgway, Assistant Secretary of State for European and Canadian Affairs, in a meeting with Oleg M. Sokolov, the chargé d'affaires of the Soviet Embassy. Mr. Redman said she also urged the Soviet Union to make available more information about the incident.

The meeting preceded a Soviet Government statement that said two people had died and that the "radiation situation" had been "stabilized."

The White House decided overnight to set up an interagency task force headed by the Environmental Protection Agency to coordinate the American response to the disaster at the Chernobyl station.

The initial American concern was to diagnose the radioactivity being sent into the atmosphere to see if it posed any threat to the United States, an Environmental Protection Agency spokesman said. But the secondary concern, according to State Department officials, was to make the offer of help to the Russians.

Wanted to Discuss Atomic Arms

Mr. Sokolov had come to the State Department to discuss the latest Soviet arms-control offer on reducing conventional and tactical nuclear forces in Europe and apparently did not have any instructions for discussing the nuclear accident, department officials said.

Mr. Redman said Miss Ridgway "expressed on behalf of the President the United States' deep regret over the accident at the Chernobyl atomic energy station."

"We hope casualties and material damage are minimal," he said. "The United States is prepared to make available to the Soviet Union humanitarian and technical assistance in dealing with this accident."

"We hope the Soviet Union will provide information about the accident in a timely manner," he said.

State Department officials said that other Western nations had also offered help but that to the best of their knowledge Moscow had not asked for any assistance. There had been reports from Sweden and West Germany about Soviet officials' asking for help, but the State Department aides said they doubted that Moscow had officially asked for such assistance.

The task force set up under the aegis of the Environmental Protective Agency includes the National Oceanic and Atmospheric Administration, the Department of Energy, the Air Force, the Federal Aviation Administration, the Food and Drug Administration, the Nuclear Regulatory Commission, the State Department and the Central Intelligence Agency.

Administration officials said the Soviet leadership had obviously had delayed as long as possible in making public what had happened. Some officials said that they believed the incident occurred last Thursday or Friday and that the first word from Moscow on Monday came only after Scandinavian countries noted a rise in radioactivity.

American Government radio monitors noted, for instance, that the Kiev radio, which is the local Ukrainian-language station for the population near the Chernobyl reactor, had not broadcast anything except brief Soviet Government statements issued in Moscow.

Officials said they believed special troops had been sent into the area to handle the evacuation of the population, a task that may have involved thousands of people and vehicles.

The Voice of America has limited itself to broadcasting what was being carried by news agencies and other press outlets, officials said. There have been no editorials. "We are trying to avoid reporting rumors," he said.

Some State Department officials said they thought the nuclear accident would have an impact on Soviet dealings with the West, at least for the short run. They said Moscow, which has prided itself on its nuclear energy industry, now finds itself in the embarrassing center of world attention over a serious breakdown.

"The delay in saying anything about the disaster, the fragmentary information that has been issued, all are typical of the Soviets," a State Department official said. "But it contrasts with the more modern image they have been trying to portray recently."

Canada Ready to Assist

OTTAWA, April 29 (Reuters) — Canada joined other Western nations today in offering aid to the Soviet Union after the reactor accident. External Affairs Minister Joe Clark said Canada offered technical assistance to the Soviet Union while seeking more information on details of the accident and the effect on the surrounding population.

Worst-Case Scenario: Core Meltdown

Details of the accident at the Chernobyl nuclear power plant have not been released by the Soviet Union. Following is a description of the worst that could happen. The actual accident may have been less severe or may be different in some details.

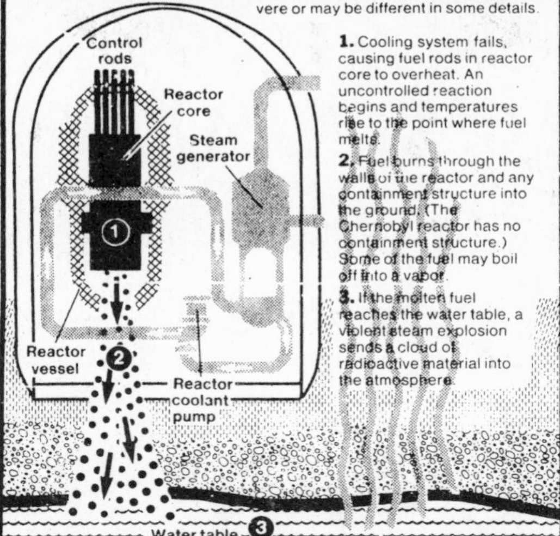
Control rods
Reactor core
Steam generator
Reactor vessel
Reactor coolant pump
Water table
1. Cooling system fails, causing fuel rods in reactor core to overheat. An uncontrolled reaction begins and temperatures rise to the point where fuel melts.
2. Fuel burns through the walls of the reactor and any containment structure into the ground. (The Chernobyl reactor has no containment structure.) Some of the fuel may boil off into a vapor.
3. If the molten fuel reaches the water table, a violent steam explosion sends a cloud of radioactive material into the atmosphere.

The New York Times/April 30 1986

Moscow Is Now Reporting A Disaster at Nuclear Plant

Continued From Page A1

no information on the extent and intensity of the spread of radioactive debris, the number of people exposed or even the date and time of the accident.

Beyond the official statement, Soviet medical, Government and ministerial officials reached in Moscow and in Kiev declined to give any information.

The Foreign Ministry placed Kiev temporarily off limits to Western reporters and diplomats living in Moscow. In normal times, the authorities require 24-hour notice to travel to Kiev, the third most visited city in the Soviet Union after Moscow and Leningrad.

The Government newspaper Izvestia was the only paper today to mention the accident, carrying the terse initial report issued by the Government on Monday after Sweden demanded an explanation for heightened radioactivity levels across Scandinavia.

Tourist Is Given Information

Residents of Kiev said radio stations there had reported the official announcement only once, though Moscow stations repeated it in broadcasts through the day.

A high school teacher from Garden City, N.Y., said in a telephone interview from Kiev that a Soviet guide had supplied additional information, saying that there had been no explosion.

The teacher, James J. Tarrou, who is in Kiev with a group of high school students, said their Intourist guide had told him that in addition to the two people killed, 17 had been injured and about a hundred hospitalized for examinations.

The guide told Mr. Tarrou that 30,000 residents of the town of Chernobyl, 10 miles southeast of the power plant, and others who lived within a 12-mile radius had been evacuated.

The Soviet Government statement's mention of the "power station settlement" suggested that it was Pripyat rather than Chernobyl that had been evacuated. The nuclear plant, though named for Chernobyl, an older town, is actually just southeast of Pripyat, a new town of 25,000 to 30,000 that was built to house the station's construction workers and operating personnel.

Alarmed Report From the U.S.

Mr. Tarrou said the Intourist guide had briefed him after one of his group had received an alarmed report from relatives in the United States, and after he had been reached by American news organizations. The details and timing of her report suggested that she had been given official guidance.

According to the teacher, the Intourist guide said that a power-generating unit had caught fire and that the heat had cracked a wall separating it from the nuclear reactor 60 yards away. Contamination seeped through, the guide said, and as a precaution, surrounding areas were evacuated.

The guide said that the power-generating unit was subsequently covered with heavy lead and that workers were now dealing with the fire, which she described as "under control."

Mr. Tarrou said life in Kiev, 70 miles from the power station, was normal. He said the city was dressed up for the May Day holiday with red banners, and bicyclists had been rehearsing for the celebrations.

The Soviet Government statement today, in addition to giving a few additional details about the accident, said a Government investigatory commission announced on Monday was led by Boris Y. Shcherbina, a Soviet Deputy Prime Minister who is a Ukrainian.

Soviet Informs Agency

Special to The New York Times

BONN, April 29 — The Soviet Union informed the International Atomic Energy Agency in Vienna on Monday of the Chernobyl nuclear accident, an agency spokesman said today.

The spokesman, James Daglish, said the information, conveyed in a telex message from the State Committee for the Utilization of Atomic Energy, simply said that an accident had occurred at the nuclear plant, without giving a date or other details.

Mr. Daglish said the Russians were not obliged to inform the agency since a convention providing for automatic notification of such accidents had not been ratified.

"They did all they were required to do, and slightly more," he said.

Mr. Daglish said that, under an agreement with its Eastern European allies within the Council for Mutual Economic Assistance, the Soviet Union was required to inform its allies of any such accident, and he said he believed the Soviet Government had done so.

But at a news conference in Warsaw, the Polish Government spokesman, Jerzy Urban, refused to answer a question on whether the Soviet Union had informed Poland. Mr. Urban said simply that the two governments had "been in touch."

U.P.I. Says Toll May Pass 2,000

United Press International, quoting a resident of Kiev, reported yesterday that the death toll at the site of the nuclear disaster in the Soviet Union north of Kiev may have surpassed 2,000.

The source of the report was as Kiev woman who has long provided accurate information, according to Sylvana Foa, the foreign editor of U.P.I. "This source has never proved to be unreliable," she said.

The unidentified Kiev resident reported by telephone yesterday morning that between 10,000 and 15,000 people had been evacuated from Pripyat, the site of the Chernobyl nuclear reactor where the nuclear accident occurred.

"Eighty people died immediately and some 2,000 people died on the way to hospitals," said the Kiev resident. "The whole October Hospital in Kiev is packed with people who suffer from radiation sickness."

U.P.I. said it could find no Soviet official to confirm the report.

The woman in Kiev said, "The people were not buried in ordinary cemeteries but in the village of Pirogovichi, where radioactive wastes are usually buried." Pirogovichi is 30 miles south of Pripyat.

Meanwhile, Anatoiy Y. Romanenko, the Ukrainian Minister of Health, who was attending a conference in Atlanta, said yesterday that reports of 2,000 killed were "just imaginary figures."

"If this was of that catastrophic proportion, I would be leaving to go home," he said, suggesting the fallout in Scandinavia — 10 times the normal amount of background radioactivity — could have come from nuclear weapons tests or "using coal, the kind for heating material, during winter."

Moscow's Silence on Disaster Assailed in Europe

By JOHN TAGLIABUE

Special to The New York Times

BONN, April 29 — European officials today bitterly denounced Soviet delays in announcing the nuclear accident and reluctance to supply information to neighboring countries.

Denmark's Prime Minister, Poul Schlueter, said at a news conference that it was "quite unacceptable that the Soviet Union did not unhesitatingly inform other countries."

Officials said they expected the accident to spur already strong opposition to the use of nuclear energy in Europe.

Appeals for Technical Help

West German and Swedish officials reported today that the Soviet Union had made urgent appeals for technical advice and assistance in handling what were said to be uncontrolled graphite fires and the meltdown of the radioactive core at the Chernobyl nuclear power station.

But officials in both countries said they were hampered by a dearth of information, and were limited in the type of assistance they could offer because of the absence in their countries of the specific type of reactor, using graphite components, involved in Chernobyl.

Officials here agreed that the accident was the worst nuclear-power disaster in history.

On Monday, the Soviet Union at first responded to urgent Swedish inquiries about the high levels of radioactivity by saying they had no explanation. Scandinavian leaders denounced the Soviet information policy.

In Britain, the Environment Secretary, Kenneth Baker, chided the Soviet Union in an address to Parliament for failing to report the accident.

"I would urge the Soviet Government to give a full account of what has happened, and the steps that have been taken to bring the incident under control," he said.

The accident, which Western diplomats said evidently occurred last weekend or earlier, sent a cloud of radioactivity, measured by Swedish experts at roughly 100 times normal levels, across Northern European countries.

The reported appeals for foreign help came as officials in the United States and European countries declared their willingness to supply aid if requested.

Experts said the reported Soviet requests seemed to reveal critical shortcomings both in safety mechanisms and the know-how needed to deal with serious reactor accidents.

West German and Swedish officials said advice and help was being sought from industry and scientific organizations, in the form of technical equipment, trained personnel, and know-how in methods of battling graphite fires and dealing with intense radioactive contamination. They said it appeared to indicate that the fire, evidently in connection with a partial or total reactor-core meltdown, continued out of control.

West German officials said they were coordinating a search for technical advice from chemical companies, like Bayer A.G. and Hoechst A.G., that are major suppliers of graphite, and for technical equipment, such as remote-control robots, and trained personnel from organizations such as Germany's Nuclear Technology Assistance Service, a kind of fire brigade maintained by the nuclear-power industry to deal with serious accidents.

West Germany and Sweden are world leaders in the manufacture and maintenance of nuclear power generating equipment. West Germany operates 20 nuclear power stations. But only one uses graphite.

Margareta Hallencreutz, an official at the Swedish Nuclear Inspection Board in Stockholm, said a Soviet Embassy third technical secretary sought "technical advice" in talks today with officials of the Swedish agency. But she said the diplomat "did not know the reason" for the fire and "did not know the extent of the damage done."

Adolf Birkhofer, director of the West German Society for Reactor Safety and a leading European expert, said the presence of elements such as cesium 134 and cesium 137 in the atmosphere appeared to indicate a partial or total meltdown, of the reactor core and its possible exposure to air.

"Evidently there was a loss of coolant, and a malfunctioning of the reserve capacity," Mr. Birkhofer said in a telephone interview.

Mr. Birkhofer described the mishap as a "design-basis accident," indicating that safety systems had evidently proven insufficient. Asked whether it could be considered the most serious such accident ever, he replied, "Yes, judging by available information."

Meeting in Bonn

Officials of the German Atom Forum in Bonn, an organization linking industries and scientific groups involved in atomic energy, said they met for two to three hours this morning with a Soviet Embassy "scientific official" to coordinate contacts with companies and organizations capable of supplying aid.

A spokesman said the organizations included the Nuclear Technology Assistance Service, the German Nuclear Energy Research Center in Jülich, west of Bonn, and the Society for Reactor Safety, in Cologne.

Wolfgang Neumann, technical director of the Nuclear Technology Assistance Service, said further detailed information about the accident was neeeded before officials could decide what form of aid was necessary. He said Soviet Embassy officials in Bonn promised to supply further information, but had not yet done so.

At the same time, the Soviet Union was reported to be seeking assistance from individual companies. In Mannheim, West Germany, officials of Brown Boveri, a subsidiary of the Swiss engineering company of the same name, said Soviet representatives had asked it for expert advice.

POLES ARE WARNED TO SHUN SOME MILK

Radioactive Fallout Is Cited in Area Bordering Soviet

By MICHAEL T. KAUFMAN

Special to The New York Times

WARSAW, April 29 — Polish television tonight warned citizens in the northeastern provinces to avoid drinking milk from grazing cows, which it said could be contaminated by particles of radioactive iodine detected here, after the nuclear accident at the Chernobyl power plant in the Ukraine.

The warning came toward the end of a day in which the Government sought to calm spreading fears that the accident, which took place 300 miles from the Polish border, might impair the health of people here.

The Government, which set up a commission to monitor air samples, made it clear that the danger of contamination was at the moment centered on the northeastern provinces around the town of Bialystok.

A Government bulletin said the sale of milk from cows grazing in the region would be banned. Only the sale of milk from cows feeding on stored fodder was being permitted, it said.

Iodine Tablets Issued

The bulletin noted "high levels of radioactive iodine" attributable to the reported meltdown at the Soviet nuclear plant. Because such particles could interfere with the function of the thyroid gland, it said, iodine tablets were being issued to infants, children and pregnant mothers in the region.

The Government also ordered people there to wash fresh vegetables carefully.

As the health advisory was being issued in Warsaw this afternoon, long lines formed at newspaper kiosks and knots of people eager for news stood around people with shortwave radios. There was no reports about the accident in this morning's Polish papers and the first word was spread by people who had heard foreign shortwave radio broadcasts.

In trolleys, buses and trains, people shared those details they had learned. On the Warsaw-Lodz train, passengers in one campartment debated the assurances given by the Government at noon that the radioactive leakages posed no immediate health problems for Poland.

"Do you remember they once told us that blue bugs found in fish were safe to eat," an old woman recalled.

The announcement that there were no immediate hazards was issued by Jerzy Urban, the Government spokesman. He told foreign reporters that a radioactive cloud had passed over northeastern Poland but had been carried by brisk winds at such a high altitude that there was no danger to health.

Mr. Urban said a Government commission had been set up, with specialists from many ministries monitoring the levels of radioactivity.

The first radio broadcast this morning dealing with the accident compared it to the nuclear leak at Three Mile Island in the United States, but gradually such references disappeared as the seriousness of the situation at Chernobyl became clear.

Winds over Poland for the last two days have come from the southeast and according to meteorologists they swept the radioactive cloud to the Baltic and Scandinavia, away from the Polish heartland. Today, however, the prevailing winds reversed themselves and there appeared to be some anxiety that the radioactive particles could be blown back.

There are two trains a day to Warsaw from Kiev, which is 70 miles from the Chernobyl plant, and railroad workers said that they had arrived on time and that the passengers had shown no signs of panic.

Still, while the Government was clearly seeking to calm fears there were indications of incipient panic.

For example, visitors to the Foreign Ministry noticed mimeographed instructions to office workers to keep the windows shut on this hot and sunny day.

Associated Press

RADIATION TESTING: A technician in Warsaw taking an air sample yesterday.

Signs Point to a Meltdown, Scientists in Sweden Assert

By STEVE LOHR

Special to The New York Times

STOCKHOLM, April 29 — Swedish scientists said today that they were convinced that the radioactive core of a Soviet power-generating reactor melted after an accident at the weekend, making it the worst nuclear power plant disaster in history.

They said their conclusion was based partly on discussions with Soviet experts, who sought advice from the Swedes today on handling the accident.

In addition, the scientists said, their own analysis of atmospheric samples from Sweden's east coast, more than 700 miles from the Chernobyl station in the Ukraine, supported the view that a meltdown had occurred at the plant.

"It is clear what happened," said Frigyes Reich, a chief engineer at Sweden's Nuclear Inspection Board, a Government agency. "The nuclear plant's reactor core has melted, in part or even completely."

One technical fact that points to a meltdown, one nuclear expert said, is that measurable amounts of cesium are contained in the radioactivity coming from the Soviet Union. In accident planning for reactors, operators typically assume that at worst about 10 percent of the radioactive core will be vaporized and that the releases from any small accident will therefore be volatile elements, such as iodine and rare gases. The presence of the less-volatile cesium, the scientist said, suggests a more serious incident.

"He wanted no material assistance, but he was interested in information on how to extinguish fires in nuclear plants," Mr. Reich said of the Soviet diplomat. He said the diplomat, a technical attaché at the Soviet Embassy here, had asked for manuals and any other available reference materials.

Scandinavia is the main region outside the Soviet Union that has absorbed the radioactive fallout from the Ukraine accident. Snow and rain that fell on parts of Sweden's east coast contained radiation counts up to 100 times the normal level.

Fallout 'Not Dangerous'

In some areas, the level of atmospheric radioactivity has been 10 times the normal reading, while for the country as a whole it is twice as high as usual.

Yet an official at Sweden's Institute for Radiation Prevention stressed that the atmosphereic contamination would have to rise much higher before it posed a danger to Scandinavian populations. Another official called the radiation fallout "disturbing but not dangerous."

However, the Government is testing the radiation content of cow's milk, which one Government scientist said could be a "concentrated carrier" of radiation.

In most Scandinavian capitals, political leaders sharply criticized the Soviet Union's handling of the incident, especially for its denial at first that there had been an accident. Moscow, after repeated questions from the Swedish authorities, conceded there had been a nuclear accident, but gave few details.

In Denmark, Prime Minister Poul Schluter said today, "The Government takes the view that it is quite unacceptable that the Soviet Union did not unhesitatingly inform other countries about the accident."

In Copenhagen, there were reports that several pharmacies quickly sold out their stocks of iodine tablets, which are thought to combat the effects of radiation. In Stockholm, there were similar reports of iodine hoarding.

"All the News That's Fit to Print"

The New York Times

Late Edition
New York: Today, increasing clouds. High 62-67. Tonight, cloudy, breezy, showers likely. Low 51-57. Tomorrow, showers ending. High 58-63. Yesterday: High 68, low 48. Details on page B6.

VOL.CXXXVII . . . No. 47,298 NEW YORK, TUESDAY, OCTOBER 20, 1987 — 50 cents beyond 75 miles from New York City, except on Long Island. 30 CENTS

STOCKS PLUNGE 508 POINTS, A DROP OF 22.6%; 604 MILLION VOLUME NEARLY DOUBLES RECORD

U.S. Ships Shell Iran Installation In Gulf Reprisal

Offshore Target Termed a Base for Gunboats

By STEVEN V. ROBERTS

Special to The New York Times

WASHINGTON, Oct. 19 — United States naval forces struck back at Iran today for attacks on American-registered vessels and other Persian Gulf shipping by shelling two connected offshore platforms that American officials said were a base for Iranian gunboats.

A few hours later, a naval commando detachment boarded a third platform five miles away and destroyed radar and communications equipment, Pentagon officials said.

No American casualties were reported in the actions, which occurred 120 miles east of Bahrain at about 2 P.M. (7 A.M., Eastern daylight time).

A 20-Minute Warning

American officials said the attacking force took pains to avoid killing Iranians, giving the crew on the first two platforms a 20-minute warning before four destroyers, stationed about three miles away, began the shelling.

At the United Nations, an Iranian delegate said "several innocent people" had been killed in the attack, but the assertion could not be confirmed.

With the bombardment, the Administration intended to send a message to Iran: The United States had shown restraint in the level of its attack this time, but might respond with greater force if Iran continued "unprovoked attacks" on gulf shipping. [Military analysis, page A10.]

'Prudent Yet Restrained'

President Reagan issued a statement describing the actions as a "prudent yet restrained response." Defense Secretary Caspar W. Weinberger warned that "stronger countermeasures" would be taken if Iranian attacks continued.

Administration officials acknowledged that today's action was unlikely to halt the cycle of violence that has ensnared American forces in the gulf since 11 Kuwaiti tankers were placed under their protection this summer. "Nobody thinks that this will end it," Vice President Bush said today.

But the actions were necessary, Mr. Bush added, because American credibility was at stake in the region after a

Continued on Page A10, Column 1

1982 1983 1984 1985 1986 1987

A Huge Blow to the Five-Year Bull Market

Dow's Record Fall
Yesterday's close was down 22.6 percent from Friday's close.

2,200 2,100 2,000 1,900 1,800 1,700

10 A.M. 11 12 1 2 3 4 P.M.

The Dow Jones industrial average, which has been marching up since August 1982, began a dramatic fall last week that continued through yesterday when it closed at 1,738.74. Shown: Weekly close of the Dow.

2,800 2,400 2,000 1,600 1,200 800

Source: Knight-Ridder Tradecenter

The New York Times/Oct. 20, 1987

Does 1987 Equal 1929?

By ERIC GELMAN

As stock prices soared this year, a chorus of pessimists warned that 1987 was looking more like 1929, when a stock market crash helped to usher in the Great Depression. Yesterday, after a plunge reminiscent of the worst days of 1929, one pressing question was whether the aftershocks would be as devastating to individuals and the nation.

News Analysis

The quick answer, many economists say, is no. The huge losses on Wall Street constitute a substantial blow to the economy at large. But there are many safeguards in place today — some instituted directly in response to the Depression — that would tend to prevent the cascading financial collapse that characterized the crash, impoverishing millions of Americans.

"A stock market crash doesn't ripple out into the economy with the same force" as it did in 1929, said Geoffrey H. Moore, director of the Center for International Business Cycle Research at Columbia University.

To be sure, there are some unsettling similarities between the current era and the pre-Depression years. Like the Roaring Twenties, the 1980's have seen an astonishing boom Wall Street. Now as then, individual and corporate debt are high, and some sectors of the economy are extremely weak. Trade relations are strained, with protectionist sentiment growing.

But today's economy is better equipped to handle financial shocks. "I don't see this decline in the stock market leading to a great breakdown in the economy," said Robert A. Kavesh, a professor of finance and economics at the New York University School of Business. "There are still many elements of strength in the economy —

Continued on Page D34, Column 5

Who Gets Hurt?

By ROBERT A. BENNETT

Unless the stock market bounces back quickly and substantially, most Americans are likely to be hurt by the dramatic decline in stock values — even those who own no stock at all.

Although it is a long jump from a record stock market plunge to a second Great Depression, it is much more likely that the plunging market may shake the economy and lead to a distinct downturn.

The biggest threat may be the spread of worry and fear. If investors feel poorer and employees begin to worry about the fortunes of their employers, consumers may draw back from spending of all kinds. They will postpone trading in the family car, do without a winter vacation and put off buying the home they wanted.

Reluctant to Build Plants

Similarly, businesses, stunned by the decline in their shares' value and facing the prospect of curtailed consumer spending, will shy away from building new plants or buying new equipment. Universities, churches, hospitals and other nonprofit institutions will likewise see their endowments shrink in value and are likely to brake their own spending.

And for all these diverse investors, the lower level of stock-market wealth will make it tougher to raise money by selling stock or borrowing against it.

"This affects even those who don't have direct investments in stocks," said Henry Kaufman, the chief economist of Salomon Brothers, a major

Continued on Page D34, Column 1

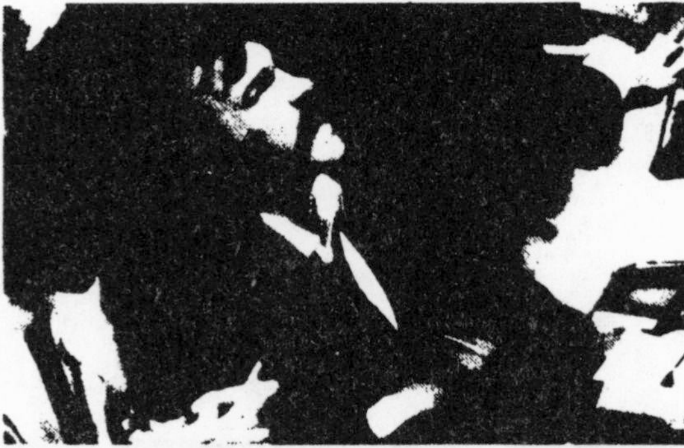

The New York Times/Marilynn K. Yee

Terrence J. McManus, a specialist with Spear, Leeds & Kellogg, on the floor of the New York Stock Exchange yesterday. Articles on Wall Street's day to remember and the sinking of investor hopes, page D1.

WORLDWIDE IMPACT

Frenzied Trading Raises Fears of Recession — Tape 2 Hours Late

By LAWRENCE J. De MARIA

Stock market prices plunged in a tumultuous wave of selling yesterday, giving Wall Street its worst day in history and raising fears of a recession.

The Dow Jones industrial average, considered a benchmark of the market's health, plummeted a record 508 points, to 1,738.74, based on preliminary calculations. That 22.6 percent decline was the worst since World War I and far greater than the 12.82 percent drop on Oct. 28, 1929, that along with the next day's 11.7 percent decline preceded the Great Depression.

Since hitting a record 2,722.42 on Aug. 25, the Dow has fallen almost 1,000 points, or 36 percent, putting the blue-chip indicator 157.5 points below the level at which it started the year. With Friday's plunge of 108.35 points, the Dow has fallen more than 26 percent in the last two sessions.

Unprecedented Trading

Yesterday's frenzied trading on the nation's stock exchanges lifted volume to unheard of levels. On the New York Stock Exchange, an estimated 604.3 million shares changed hands, almost double the previous record of 338.5 million shares set just last Friday.

With the tremendous volume, reports of brokers' trades on the New York Stock Exchange were delayed by more than two hours at one point. The New York Stock Exchange said that, as a result, it would not have definitive figures for the Dow's point decline and the exchange's volume until today.

Yesterday's big losers included International Business Machines, the bluest of the blue chips, which dropped $31, to $104. In August the stock was at $176. The other big losers among the blue chips were General Motors, which lost $13.875, to $52.125, and Exxon, which dropped $10.25, to $33.50.

More Than $1 Trillion Lost

According to Wilshire Associates, which tracks more than 5,000 stocks, the rout obliterated more than $500 billion in equity value from the nation's stock portfolios. That equity value now stands at $2.311 trillion. Since late summer, more than $1 trillion in stock values has been lost.

The losses were so great they sent shock waves to markets around the world, and many foreign exchanges posted record losses. In a sign of the continuing effect, the Tokyo Stock Exchange fell sharply today. The Nikkei Dow Jones average plummeted a record 3,395.95 yen, to 22,350.61, a drop of 13.2 percent, by late afternoon. Also, The Hong Kong exchange decided to close for the week.

In Washington yesterday, the White House spokesman, Marlin Fitzwater, issued a statement saying that President Reagan had "watched with concern" the stock market's collapse. But Mr. Reagan remained convinced that the economy was sound.

Economy Called Sound

Mr. Fitzwater said the President had directed Administration officials to contact leading financial experts. "Those consultations confirm our view that the underlying economy remains sound," he added.

Stock market analysts scrambled for explanations, which ranged from rising interest rates to the falling dollar to the possibility of war between the United States and Iran.

Indeed, the panic selling may have been bolstered by the news that the United States Navy destroyed an Iranian offshore oil platform in the central Persian Gulf yesterday, and Iran vowed retaliation.

But many experts seemed to think

Continued on Page D34, Column 1

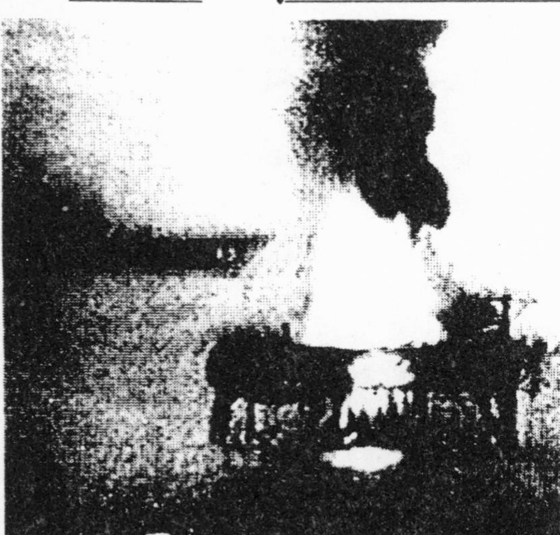

ABC News

Two connected Iranian offshore platforms on fire after being shelled by American destroyers. A U.S. warship can be seen in the background.

More About the Markets

Bonn and the United States agreed that the dollar should be stabilized near current levels. Disagreement on currency levels and interest rates had contributed to unrest in the markets. Page D1.

Small investors searched for news much of the day. Many held on to their stocks, as they tried to determine what really was happening in the stock market. Page D1.

Washington officials hesitated to offer investors immediate advice. The shouts of panic on Wall Street echoed only faintly in the corridors of the Reagan Administration. The White House maintained that the underlying economy remained sound. News analysis, page D32.

Investors bought U.S. securities in a search for a safe place to put their money. Some interest rates hovered just below 10 percent. Page D1.

Tokyo's stock market plummeted to record losses today and the Hong Kong market suspended trading for the week as Asian investors reacted in fright to the collapse on Wall Street. Page D1.

Business leaders were shaken by the collapse, which wiped out huge amounts of the market value of their companies. And they seemed to have been caught by surprise. But many leaders were confident the panic would pass. Page D32.

Overseas investors sold actively on Wall Street after years of having poured money into the bull market. Accounts of the volume of foreign selling varied widely. Page D14.

Wall Street firms are uncertain about the effect the historic drop could have on them, but some analysts fear that smaller and poorly capitalized firms may find rough going in the days ahead. Page D33.

Mutual funds sold stock shares in huge numbers, feeding the historic drop. Several mutual fund management companies said the number of phone calls from investors was about double the normal volume. Page D33.

New York City could be affected significantly because of its large number of securities industry employees. Some experts maintain that the city's economy has grown too reliant on Wall Street. Page D32.

Trading tested computers' ability to handle a volume of trading that had not been expected until the early 1990's. Page D34.

The dollar closed lower against leading currencies except the Canadian dollar. Analysts said trading was quiet as traders were preoccupied by the jarring news from the stock market. Gold was $486.50 an ounce, up $15.50 from Friday to reach its highest level in over four years. Page D26.

Democratic leaders called for talks with President Reagan on a deficit-reduction package that would include tax increases. Page D32.

In politics, two questions loomed: How badly were the Republicans' 1988 chances hurt? How were the Democrats' prospects helped? Political Memo. Page A30.

Goetz Given 6-Month Term on Gun Charge

Bernhard H. Goetz, who ignited a nationwide debate about self-defense when he shot four teen-agers on a Manhattan subway train, was sentenced yesterday to six months in jail for carrying an unlicensed concealed pistol.

Mr. Goetz, who was acquitted of charges of attempted murder and assault at his trial last June, was also sentenced to five years' probation and ordered to undergo psychiatric counseling. He could have received as much as seven years' imprisonment.

The judge, Acting Justice Stephen G. Crane, stayed the sentence pending an appeal by Mr. Goetz, who left the courtroom without making any comment to reporters.

Outside the courthouse, however, Mr. Goetz's lead lawyer, Barry I. Slotnick, said, "We think that he's being treated harsher as a result of the fact that he's Bernhard Goetz."

The case began Dec. 22, 1984, when Mr. Goetz shot the youths on a downtown IRT train with a .38-caliber revolver. From his surrender that month through his indictments, the long legal maneuvering and the trial, Mr. Goetz steadfastly insisted that he had shot the youths because they were about to rob him.

Article, page B1.

INSIDE

Turnaround on Schools
A week after adopting a year-round term, the Los Angeles Board of Education reversed itself. A new vote was set for March 1. Page A17.

Senator Stennis to Retire
John C. Stennis, Democrat of Mississippi, will leave the Senate at the end of this term, when he will have served more than 41 years. Page A16.

Martin Back With Yankees
The Yankees promoted Lou Piniella to the post of general manager and brought Billy Martin back for his fifth stint as manager. Page B7.

The Market Plunge: A Frenzied Session

Dow Drops by 508, to 1,738.74

Continued From Page A1

that a major catalyst was fears of a breakdown in accords to maintain trading and currency stability between the United States and its major trading partners.

Some others, meanwhile, blamed program traders for the debacle, and predicted that regulators would curb, and perhaps outlaw, the practice. In program trading, huge blocks of stock are traded by arbitragers seeking to profit from the difference in value between the actual cash value of the stocks and futures contracts based on those stocks.

A 'Meltdown' Monday

Discussing yesterday's collapse, John J. Phelan Jr., chairman of the Big Board, said: "It's the nearest thing to a meltdown that I ever want to see. We were fortunate this occurred when the American economy is very strong. We are not operating in an environment of weakness."

Meanwhile, Treasury Secretary James A. Baker 3d met in Frankfurt, West Germany, with top economic officials, who agreed to keep currencies "around current levels." For several days, Mr. Baker had been criticizing West Germany's recent increase in interest rates.

Some analysts said that Mr. Baker's public criticism of Bonn was taken by stock investors as a sign that recent currency accords were crumbling and the dollar was likely to weaken further. A volatile dollar discourages huge foreign investors, such as the Germans and the Japanese, because it does not allow them to make reasonable assumptions about the return on their investments in American securities.

To defend the dollar, the Federal Reserve could allow American interest rates to move higher, which would have the effect of drawing funds into Treasury securities. Foreign buying of those instruments is important, in that it helps to pay for the nation's huge budget deficit.

'Sucking in Foreign Capital'

Robert C. Holland, a former member of the board of governors of the Fed, and now president of the Committee for Economic Development, said that the United States, the world's largest debtor nation, had made itself too vulnerable to foreign financial influence because its budget and trade deficits are "sucking in foreign capital."

In a news conference, Mr. Phelan, at the Big Board, said that the exchange had been in "constant" contact with the Securities and Exchange Commission throughout the day, but had never seriously considered closing. "If the S.E.C. had asked us to do so, we would have," he added.

Mr. Phelan called the selloff "the worst market I have ever seen in my lifetime or would hope to see again."

Rumors on Closing Abound

Rumors that the commission would seek a stock trading halt swept Wall Street all afternoon. Many economists and analysts said such an unprecedented move would almost surely destroy any lingering confidence in the securities markets. The fact that it was even suggested was an indication of the completeness of Wall Street's dismay.

The Securities and Exchange Commission's chairman, David S. Ruder, said at one point: "I'm not afraid to say that there is some point, and I don't know what that point is, that I would be quite anxious to talk to the New York Stock Exchange about a temporary, and very temporary, halt of trading."

Late in the day, it was announced that the Pacific Stock Exchange would close a half-hour early, at 4 P.M. Eastern time. Ordinarily, the Pacific exchange's normal 4:30 P.M. close allows East Coast investors to transact business after the close of their own markets. Had they been able to do so, yesterday's selloff might have been even greater.

Hugh A. Johnson Jr., an economist at the First Albany Corporation, said the market collapsed because "so much damage has been done to confidence in the financial markets" by the apparent falling out of the United States, West Germany and Japan.

The current crisis, he said, "has to be dealt with quickly." Mr. Johnson said, adding that "they should call Paul Volcker back" to head up an international meeting of finance ministers and central bankers to restore confidence. Mr. Volcker is the former head of the Federal Reserve Board.

'Genuine Financial Panics'

"This is the stuff of history," he said. "We can't forget this one. Historians generally refer to these things as genuine financial panics."

The rout was of such magnitude that Wall Street's professionals were at a loss for words. Many had, in fact, not even recovered from Friday's 108.35-point decline in the Dow, which was the first time the blue-chip indicator had ever lost more than 100 points.

While many brokers and analysts were concerned that trouble was brewing over the weekend, as investors at home and abroad digested the news from the financial markets, no one conceived that the Dow, which had tripled since August 1982, could lose 500 points in one day.

Traders suspected that there might be a big increase in mutual fund redemptions and, because many people have bought stock on credit, in margin account selling as brokerages demanded more collateral for customers' accounts. And there was concern that mutual fund redemptions and margin calls would snowball even further today.

Stock prices around the world plummeted, taking their cue from Wall Street. Panic selling swamped stock exchanges in Tokyo, Hong Kong, London, Frankfurt, Amsterdam, Mexico City and other centers.

Declines Often Portended

The stock market's incredible decline, analysts said, might have repercussions far beyond the immediate ones. The stock market has often portended economic declines. What a decline such as has occurred may mean is hard to imagine.

Tens of millions of Americans are tied to the stock market, either directly, or through mutual funds, or through pension funds that invest in equities.

In addition, rumors began to spread yesterday that some financial institutions might have lost heavily in the frantic trading, and might be in trouble. Small firms may have liquidity problems, and be forced to close. Individual traders and investors have undoubtedly been wiped out. Large firms may have to cut back, and it is not inconceivable that the ripples may spread to the banking community, which has been edging into the securities business.

That could lead to layoffs, and further economic dislocations.

"One word is operative out there now," said one very shaken trader. "Fright."

Not everyone was ready to give up on stocks, however. Many made the obvious argument that stocks are now cheap and are yielding perhaps 10 percent in dividends.

Other huge stock losers included Teledyne, down $49.75, to $292.50; Digital Equipment, down $42.25, to $130; CBS down $42.125, to $152.50, and Eastman Kodak, down $27.25, to $62.875.

The blue chips were not the only stocks that were devastated. As some smaller issues lost almost 50 percent of their value, broader market gauges crumbled in record fashion.

The New York Stock Exchange composite index fell 30.51, to 128.62, and the Standard & Poor's 500-stock index dropped 57.86, to 224.84. On the Big Board, the ratio of losing stocks to gainers was at one point 100 to 1; at the close 52 stocks were up and 1,973 were down.

On the American Stock Exchange, the market index slumped 41.05, to 282.50, and in over-the-counter trading, the Nasdaq index sagged 46.12, to 360.21.

About the only issues that gained anywhere were gold and silver mining stocks, both precious metals being a traditional haven.

Investors apparently also fled into Treasury issues, as both bills and bonds rallied sharply late in the day. That raised the hope that stocks might now also rally.

Busiest Trading Days

Following are the 10 heaviest trading days on the New York Stock Exchange.

Date	Volume
Oct 19 1987	604 330 000*
Oct. 16, 1987	338,480,000
Jan. 23, 1987	302,390,000
Aug. 11, 1987	278,130,000
April 14, 1987	266,540,000
Oct. 15, 1987	263,180,000
Feb. 5, 1987	256,660,000
Jan. 15, 1987	253,120,000
Dec. 19, 1986	244,680,000
Sept. 8, 1987	242,800,000

*Estimate

Hopes of Investors Sink With Market

Continued From First Business Page

investing is gone, as is the sense of security that their equities once provided.

Before the market opened yesterday, Casper H. Bejoian Jr., a 35-year old Boston importer, was fairly confident about the safety of his $10,000 stock portfolio. "I grew up in a market that was 800 or 900 points," he said, referring to the Dow Jones industrial average. "Now it's in the mid-2,000's. I don't think it's going down drastically."

Shortly before 5 P.M., he was told that the market had plunged more than 500 points. "I am shocked," he said with a gulp before laughing, almost giddy from the blow of the news. "I am going to have to re-evaluate," he added.

For Mr. Bejoian and investors like him, there was an overwhelming sense of bewilderment, of not knowing what was behind the precipitous drop in stock prices. "You can't tell me that G.E. is not as good a company tomorrow as it was three weeks ago," said Kenneth Polosky, a retired executive who lives in Rancho Mirage, Calif. "I'm stunned and I don't understand it."

Theories and 'Greed'

Not surprisingly, theories abound. To some, the stock market plunge seems almost like divine retribution, which could perhaps have been avoided if people had not been blinded by greed.

"I was walking down the street and I was wondering whether I would see people jumping out of windows," said Harold Snedkof, who raises money for the New York Public Library. "Then you realize that nothing is different. But maybe all this will make people serious about real problems, like how to cure AIDS. Maybe it will take the excessive greed out of things for a while."

To others, yesterday's stunning market developments were a sign that modern trading methods are potentially dangerous.

"They should bar buying and selling by programming," grumbled Alexander Kopelman, an 80-year-old Florida man who said he had worked on Wall Street as a clerk at the time of the '29 crash. "They can't stop the

'In my wildest dreams, I would not have imagined this.'

selling once it gets going, it's just computers selling to computers. It became a gamble, not an investment anymore. All those guys with 65 credit cards and Porsches who think they are all genuises at 25 — now see what's happened."

There are, of course, a few very happy individuals, those who were prescient enough — or lucky enough — to pull out before the market started its disastrous slide.

Until August, Martin J. Blaser, a 38-year-old physician who is chief of the infectious disease section of a Veterans Administration hospital in Denver, had three-quarters of his family's wealth in equities. But that month, he sold half of his stocks and bought gold.

"We had made a lot of money and I didn't feel I had to sell at the top," he said. "The market was rising too high and I was concerned that the bottom could fall out. I wanted to hedge my bets."

A Few Optimists Remain

And amid the gloom, there are still optimistic investors who see the market's dismal showing as an opportunity to buy stocks at bargain prices. "I put in a buy order today," said Gregory Camin, a certified public accountant who said in Grand Central Terminal that he sees the market drop as "like walking into Crazy Eddie and they say everyting is half price."

Maybe so — but not all buyers have his unbridled optimism. "I'm looking to buy right now," said Howard Weidberg, a salesman of computer services who lives in Manhattan. But he is not totally sure he has made the right decision. "The public may never come back in," he said. "The small guys have gotten so hurt, I think they'll be scared for quite a while."

Who Gets Hurt? Many, In or Out of the Market

Continued From Page A1

Wall Street firm.

"If you're just an average citizen," he said, "you're working somewhere, and the developments in the financial markets today may influence the company you work for. It may result in cutbacks."

Those hurt most immediately, of course, are investors who sold stocks yesterday that they had purchased at higher prices while the market was surging upward during the summer.

The market plunge also put pressure on many other consumers who had put up stock as collateral for past loans. As their stock declined in value, they were forced by their banks to put up more assets as collateral to back their loans. In fact, the market's decline probably was aggravated by people forced to sell their stock to repay loans as the value of their collateral declined.

Another large group wincing from yesterday's market plunge consists of workers who are close to retirement and who had planned to cash in stocks that they held in Individual Retirement Accounts or 401(k) employee savings plans.

Some Are Poorer on Paper

People who sat tight and held their stocks or mutual funds are poorer on paper, but the decline in stock values should have no direct effect on them until they decide to sell.

Although the values of most pension funds have plunged, that should not affect pensioners. Under most plans, a retired person's company is obliged to make the promised payments, whether or not the pension's assets are earning enough to finance the payments. The drop in stock values, though, might put a squeeze on many companies that suddenly find their pension plans underfunded.

Market Profile

New York Stock Exchange
Friday, October 16, 1987

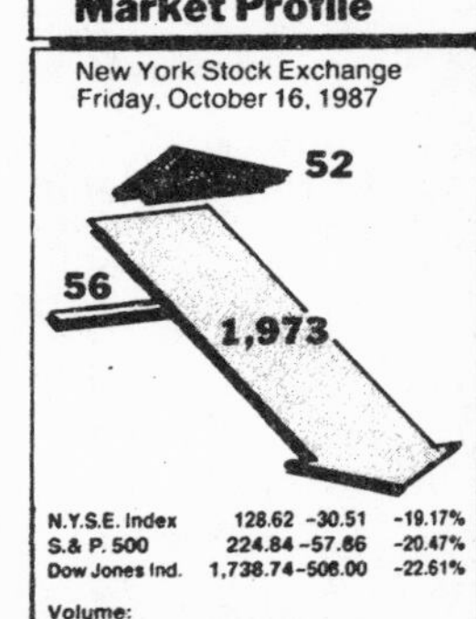

N.Y.S.E. Index	128.62	-30.51	-19.17%
S.& P. 500	224.84	-57.86	-20.47%
Dow Jones Ind.	1,738.74	-508.00	-22.61%

Volume:
N.Y.S.E. 604.3 million shares
Other Markets 51.8 million shares

As a result of the bull market, many pension funds had become "overfunded" and some companies were able to skim the excess off the top and include that amount in their profits.

Although most pension funds are guaranteed by the Federal Government, the labor movement is concerned about the drop in their values because the companies contributing to them will be less profitable.

"Overfunding gives labor bargaining room to seek more," said Henry Schechter, deputy director of the department of economic research at the American Federation of Labor and Congress of Industrial Organizations.

But the greatest fear by far is the psychological effect the stock market's plunge might exact.

"We've been expecting a trigger mechanism that was going to scare consumers into pulling in their spending horns to produce the next recession, and this could do it," said A. Gary Shilling, who heads his own New York economic consulting firm.

If stock prices remain at or below their closing levels of yesterday, "it will undoubtedly lead to a recession because it depletes confidence," said Irwin L. Kellner, chief economist for the Manufacturers Hanover Trust Company. "People who own stocks are obviously less wealthy than before."

Benjamin E. Friedman, professor of economics at Harvard University, fears that the plunge in stock values may extend to similar declines in other assets that have risen sharply in value, particularly housing.

If 'the Bubble Has Popped'

"The rise in both the stock market and house values stemmed from the same thing — the euphoric sense that the economy would continue to be wonderful," Mr. Friedman said. "If the stock market is telling us the bubble has popped, and people are taking a more realistic view of the economy's future, then that same bursting of the bubble could affect the prices of houses and other assets. And that's the level where the average citizen could be affected."

If payments on adjustable-rate mortgages were to rise and the value of homes were to fall, many people might just walk away from them, he said.

Milton Hudson, an economist at the Morgan Guaranty Trust Company, said, "No matter what your economic forecast was, you have to recognize the possibility that there will be adverse consequences that will weaken economic activity."

The major fear is that the uncertainty in the financial markets will cause both consumers and businesses to cut back on their spending, sending the economy into a recession.

A Cutback in Spending

"When people see a selloff like this, they tend to panic even if they don't own stock," said Paul Getman, director of United States financial services for the WEFA Group, an economics consulting firm in Philadelphia. "My 55-year-old mother called me twice today to ask if we're going into a depression, and she doesn't own a share."

The stock market's decline, Mr. Getman said, has reduced his mother's confidence and will cause a retrenchment in her spending. "That insures that bad times are ahead," he said.

Businesses will also cut spending because raising capital by selling new issues of stock will be more expensive, said Mr. Kellner of Manufacturers Hanover. "Production will be cut, and unemployment will rise," he said. But that will be self-correcting, he added, as interest rates fall and set the stage for a recovery.

Several economists said that often a sharp market decline can have a much greater effect on the economy than a strongly rising market. One reason is that the falling market sets off margin calls that force investors to liquidate all sorts of assets, not just stocks.

"People can't meet those calls, and they'll have to sell other assets," said Mr. Getman of the WEFA Group. "It spirals."

Most economists agreed that the degree to which people will be hurt will depend largely on how the market behaves in the future.

The Dow's Worst Days

Following are the 10 largest one-day percent declines for the Dow Jones industrial average.

Date	Point Drop	Percent Drop	Close
Dec. 12, 1914	17.42	24.4%	54.00
Oct. 19, 1987	508.00	22.6	1,738.74
Oct. 28, 1929	38.33	12.8	260.64
Oct. 29, 1929	30.57	11.7	230.07
Nov. 6, 1929	25.55	9.9	232.13
Dec. 18, 1899	5.57	8.7	58.27
Aug. 12, 1932	5.79	8.4	63.11
March 14, 1907	6.89	8.3	76.23
July 21, 1933	7.55	7.8	88.71
Oct. 18, 1937	10.57	7.8	125.74

Does 1987 Equal 1929? Economists Say No

Continued From Page A1

profits are strong, for example."

Among the important differences between today and 1929 are Federal deposit insurance, unemployment insurance and Social Security insurance and other elements of what has come to be known as the safety net. These not only guarantee against widespread destitution; their very existence should also help to prevent the kind of financial panic that fed on itself in the Depression.

"In 1929, you didn't have insurance of bank deposits, you didn't have the Securities and Exchange Commission, you had much less knowledge of how the economy worked," Professor Kavesh said.

Today the Government is much more willing to intervene to keep the economy growing. "All governments, liberal and conservative, have assumed that responsibility, which wasn't the case in 1929," said John Kenneth Galbraith, a retired professor of economics at Harvard University and author of "The Great Crash." Huge Federal budget deficits make it difficult for Washington to increase Government spending, however, which has been one response to economic slowdowns.

First Line of Defense

The Federal Reserve would be the first line of defense if the financial system began to falter. "If necessary — and I don't think it will be — the Federal Reserve could provide additional bank reserves and other support to make sure any loans that turned sour because of what's happened in the market wouldn't result in a banking crisis," said Charles L. Schultze, director of the economic studies program at the Brookings Institution.

After the crash, historians say, the Federal Reserve did precisely the wrong thing and tightened credit, putting further pressure on financial institutions that had suffered large losses.

In general, Federal regulation plays a far greater role in the financial markets. Banks, for example, were allowed to trade stocks for their customers in 1929; today they are not. In 1929, an investor could buy stock almost entirely with borrowed money; today, investors may borrow no more than half a stock's purchase price.

The Government plays another role as well, that of employer. Government employment has become a significant sector in the economy, one that is relatively immune from the gyrations of financial markets.

Broader changes in the economy tend to limit the effects of a drop in stock prices. The growth of the service sector is an example. Service industries tend to be more resistant to recession, according Mr. Moore.

Specific factors will also work to contain the damage. Federal insurance protects individual bank accounts up to $100,000; there was no such insurance in 1929. "In terms of confidence and faith, deposit insurance prevents panic," Mr. Schultze said.

Brokerage Accounts Insured

Similarly, the Securities Investors Protection Corporation insures brokerage account for up to $500,000. Thus, if a brokerage house were to fail, its clients would not be wiped out.

Today, Federal benefits would supply many individuals who lost their jobs or savings with at least some income, and those dollars in turn would provide some fuel for the economy. The sharp contraction of consumer demand was a key ingredient in the Depression.

Mr. Galbaith cautioned that at least one factor was worse today than in 1929: the large presence of foreign investors. If they should suddenly withdraw, it would not only depress the markets further but hurt the dollar as well. Fear about the decline of the dollar is one of the factors being cited in the stock market decline.

Deluge Pushes Computers to the Breaking Point

By DAVID E. SANGER

The computers and communications links that bind the nation's stock markets strained — and in some cases cracked — under a deluge of trading that computer designers did not expect until the early 1990's.

At brokerage firms across the country yesterday, some traders saw their flickering green screens covered with question marks, while others watched helplessly as their terminals fell blank or hopelessly behind as more than 600 million shares were traded on the New York Stock Exchange.

The Pacific Stock Exchange, overloaded by volume, closed early.

'It Was a Rugged Day'

The American Stock Exchange narrowly averted disaster in the last five minutes of trading, when the disk drives that record trades on the exchange's computers ran out of space for more data.

At the New York Stock Exchange, computer engineers watched in amazement while the system largely kept up with a volume of trading that it was never designed to handle.

"It was a rugged day and we were a little bruised, but we did it," said Richard E. Leyh, executive vice president of the Securities Industry Automation Corporation, which runs hundreds of computers that are the electronic backbone of the market.

What tripped up the New York Stock Exchange throughout the day was not its advanced technology but some of its oldest: the card printers that spit out buy and sell orders on the floor of the exchange. At times the printers ran more than an hour behind, and the exchange was unable to guarantee that any trade made after 3 P.M. yesterday could be executed by the time the market closed.

For a market system that has come to depend entirely on the wonders of "real-time" technology, it was a day to test the limits of the computer industry's inventions.

'Useless Garbage'

At Gruntal & Company, for example, traders were forced to ignore basically all the prices that flashed on their screens. "Useless garbage," concluded Jack A. Barbanel, the firm's director of futures trading. "The delays played havoc with us for most of the day. In a market like this, being even a minute out of date can be deadly. And we could not rely on the computers."

Other traders said that because everyone's pricing data were so far behind, they found themselves at little competitive disadvantage in executing orders. "Our quotes turned out to be pretty accurate," said Gordon Smith, the managing director of listed trading at Alex. Brown & Company in Baltimore.

At the close, Mr. Smith's screen showed the Dow Jones industrial average down 178 points. The Dow actually fell 508 points.

Those who watched the New York Stock Exchange tape, a listing of all transactions that harkens back to ticker machines, found it of little use. When the market closed at 4 P.M., the tape was more than two hours behind.

A Miracle on Wall Street

It seemed to be a miracle that the Big Board's computers kept working at all. The system is composed of about 200 Tandem "fault-tolerant" minicomputers, each of which monitors others and picks up the work of any that fails.

For the operators of the exchange's computer system, the important figure was not the number of shares traded but the number of transactions executed — it takes far more computer power to process 10 one-share transactions than one 10,000-share transaction.

The system had never executed more than about 250,000 transactions in a day; experts guessed that it handled 500,000 to one million yesterday.

Some of the "fault-tolerant" Tandem systems did drop out yesterday, leaving a few posts on the floor stranded for three to five minutes. But other computers kicked in.

The backup system also worked when the American Stock Exchange overloaded the disk drive that stores trade data, causing another five-minute pause while systems operators rushed to get backup storage without losing trading information.

If there was a measure of how backlogged the markets' computer systems were last night, it came in the stock tables that newspaper readers are accustomed to scanning. The Associated Press, which provides the tables to The New York Times and other newspapers, said it had begun transmitting the data at 9:30 P.M., or five and a half hours later than usual.

"All the News That's Fit to Print"

The New York Times

Late Edition
New York: Today, partly sunny and warmer. High 43-48. Tonight, clear and calm. Low 26-32. Tomorrow, sun then increasing clouds. High 45-50. Yesterday: High 43, low 29. Details, page C22.

VOL. CXXXVII . . No. 47,447 NEW YORK, THURSDAY, MARCH 17, 1988 — 50 cents beyond 75 miles from New York City, except on Long Island. 30 CENTS

NORTH, POINDEXTER AND 2 OTHERS INDICTED ON IRAN-CONTRA FRAUD AND THEFT CHARGES

3 Killed by Grenades at I.R.A. Funeral

Associated Press

Mourners ducking for cover as grenades exploded at a burial service in Belfast, Northern Ireland.

Gunman Terrorizes Belfast Crowd Gathered at Rites for 3 Guerrillas

By FRANCIS X. CLINES

Special to The New York Times

BELFAST, Northern Ireland, March 16 — Three people were killed and dozens wounded today as an assailant threw grenades into a screaming crowd at a funeral and then fled across the graveyard from enraged mourners.

Panic broke out and grieving families dived for cover by the mud of the open grave as four grenades exploded amid thousands of mourners gathered for the burial of three Irish Republican Army guerrillas. The guerrillas, unarmed but on a bombing mission, were slain March 6 by British undercover agents in Gibraltar.

"Kill the bastard!" came cries from the crowd as dozens of mourners ignored the gunshots fired by the retreating assailant and chased him a quarter mile to an adjacent expressway.

Crowd Is Stunned

Families, clergy members, pallbearers and grave diggers watched stunned on the cemetery hill as the wounded mourners, who had been saying the rosary moments before, staggered bleeding among the headstones.

The collective screams of shock and panic soon changed to cheers when the crowd of more than 5,000 saw the blue-coated invader finally collared and pummelled after he coolly turned and threw the last of his grenades and fired bullets at furious pursuers.

"We beat him unmercifully," said George McMurray after racing down the hill toward the gunman, who was widely suspected of being on a terrorist mission for one of the paramilitary Protestant gangs. The gunman was rescued and arrested by officers of the Royal Ulster Constabulary.

Beyond the three dead men, four mourners were listed as seriously wounded among the dozen who were hospitalized. More than 30 others were treated and released, according to the hospital.

Agence France-Presse

The gunman firing at pursuers.

The attack on the eve of St. Patrick's Day in Milltown Cemetery pushed this city toward a fresh cycle of the sectarian vendetta and street violence that has marked the last two decades of Northern Irish life. Cars were hijacked and set afire by youths as anger built at nightfall in the heavily policed ghettos

Continued on Page A6, Column 3

U.S. TO SEND FORCE TO AID HONDURAS, CITING 'INCURSION'

White House Charges a Raid by the Nicaraguan Army — 3,200 Troops to Go

By STEVEN V. ROBERTS

Special to The New York Times

WASHINGTON, March 16 — President Reagan tonight ordered the deployment of four battalions of American troops, about 3,200 men, to Honduras as a sign of support for the Government there.

In announcing the move, Marlin Fitzwater, the President's spokesman, said Honduras had suffered a "significant cross-border incursion" by 1,500 to 2,000 Sandinista troops.

That contention is disputed by President Daniel Ortega of Nicaragua, who has invited international observers to view the border region. [Page A12.]

Troops Will Be Restricted

Mr. Fitzwater called the troop movement an "emergency deployment readiness exercise," and said the soldiers would not be sent "to any area of ongoing hostilities." The troops, from Fort Bragg, N.C., and Fort Ord, Calif., are to leave Thursday morning. They are to be confined to the area surrounding the Palmerola Air Base in Honduras, about 125 miles from the Nicaraguan border.

The spokesman said the troops represented "an important signal and a deterrence, just by being in the region." The President, he added, sees the American forces as "an important show of solidarity" with Honduras.

Mr. Fitzwater insisted that President José Azcona Hoyo of Honduras had requested the military assistance tonight after consultation with Everett Briggs, the American ambassador to Honduras. "We are responding to his request," the spokesman asserted.

Military officials said, however, that

Continued on Page A12, Column 1

Indicted

The New York Times/Paul A. Souders

Lieut. Col. Oliver L. North

The New York Times

Rear Adm. John M. Poindexter

The Prosecutor

Agence France-Presse

Lawrence E. Walsh

23 COUNTS DETAILED

Arms Middlemen Named — Walsh Acts After 14-Month Inquiry

By PHILIP SHENON

Special to The New York Times

WASHINGTON, March 16 — Lieut. Col. Oliver L. North, Rear Adm. John M. Poindexter and two other key participants in the Iran-contra affair were indicted today on charges of conspiracy to defraud the United States by illegally providing the Nicaraguan rebels with profits from the sale of American weapons to Iran.

The indictment was the most sweeping criminal action against former White House officials since the Watergate scandals, and presented to President Reagan the politically delicate issue of whether he should pardon his former aides before his term ends next January.

The long-awaited indictment, following a 14-month grand jury investigation, named Colonel North, who was a member of the National Security Council staff, and Admiral Poindexter, President Reagan's former national security adviser. It also med two middlemen in the arms nsfer — Richard V. Secord, a retired Air Force major general, and Albert A. Hakim, an Iranian-American businessman.

'Exploiting for Own Purposes'

All four were accused in the 23-count indictment of stealing money belonging to the Government — proceeds from the arms sales to Iran in 1985 and 1986 — and transfering a portion of the money to rebel groups, known as the contras, battling the Sandinista Government of Nicaragua.

They also were accused of wire fraud — using telephones or other wire communications to further their scheme.

The four have repeatedly denied wrongdoing, arguing their actions in the Iran-contra affair were motivated strictly by patriotism.

Money Involved Not Specified

According to the indictment the defendants, as part of what prosecutors described as the central conspiracy, defrauded the Government by "deceitfully exploiting for their own purposes" the Iran-contra initiative, "rather than pursuing solely the specified governmental objectives of the initiative, including the release of Americans being held hostage in Lebanon." [Excerpts from indictment, page D26.]

Today's indictment did not specify how much money may have been stolen. It said the arms sales to Iran generated about $30 million, of which the United States Government was paid $12 million.

Each of the defendants faces a different set of charges, and they could all go to prison for decades under the indictment. Law-enforcement officials said it

Continued on Page D27, Column 1

CONSUMER OUTLAYS SPURRING ECONOMY

Rebound From October Crash Surprises Many Analysts

By PETER T. KILBORN

Special to The New York Times

WASHINGTON, March 16 — The latest reports on jobs, consumer debt, production and the like are convincing many economists that the economy is a lot stronger these days than they were predicting just a few weeks ago. Today's announcement of an 8.9 percent jump in home construction last month is further evidence of the economy's surprising resilience.

The reason seems to be a consumer livelier than economists expected, particularly after the October rout of the stock market. Even without the rout, however, this was to have been a period when consumer spending, which had been pulling the economy through most of the last five years, would run out of steam.

The Earlier Assumption

The assumption had been that consumers would pass the baton to industry, which would sell more of its goods abroad, thanks to the cheaper dollar, and build more factories at home. During this first-quarter transition, the economy would slow down considerably and perhaps even slip into a recession.

But after pinching pennies for a month or two after the market's plunge, consumers are stepping up their spending again. They are still a lot more restrained than they were in recent years, but with industry pulling the weight expected of it, firmer consumer spending augurs a more robust economy than most forecasts showed. There is more talk now of inflation, the price the economy sometimes pays for strong growth, than of recession.

Right after the market collapsed, about half the members of the economics community revised their forecasts for the first quarter of this year from

Continued on Page D24, Column 1

INSIDE

College Credits for Police

Two or more years of college will be required for members of the New York City force seeking promotion to sergeant, lieutenant or captain, Commissioner Benjamin Ward said. Supervisors now holding such posts will keep them, however. Page B1.

Reagan Firm on Mideast

After meeting with Prime Minister Yitzhak Shamir of Israel, President Reagan pledged to pursue his Middle East negotiating plan. Page A3.

Rogue Software Is Loose

A program that can secretly spread from computer to computer and destroy data has been found in commercial software. Page D1.

Prado Gains Collection

The Prado Museum in Madrid has been chosen to house several hundred pieces of the Thyssen-Bornemisza art collection. Page C23.

Noriega Foils Coup Attempt; Civilians Take to the Streets

By LARRY ROHTER

Special to The New York Times

PANAMA, March 16 — An attempt to overthrow Gen. Manuel Antonio Noriega failed here today, but it was followed by widespread civil disorders across Panama.

The uprising, which was marked by sharp exchanges of gunfire at military headquarters, was led by Col. Leónidas Macias, the chief of police, the Government said later.

General Noriega, the country's military leader, was apparently unhurt in the incident and later appeared on the doorstep of military headquarters to speak briefly to reporters.

No figure on the number of officers and men arrested in the coup attempt was given, and no mention was made of any casualties. But residents of the area around military headquarters said they had seen wounded soldiers being removed from the command building, which houses General Noriega's main office.

Senior United States officials in Washington said that the coup attempt demonstrated a deepening division within Panama's armed forces and police, but that they were uncertain whether it would weaken General Noriega's hold on power. [Page A6.]

The disturbances at military headquarters followed two days of demonstrations by doctors, teachers, dock workers and other Government employees protesting the Government's inability to pay them. The cash shortage stems from moves to block the Noriega Government from access to some $50 million in deposits in American banks.

A Display of Force

The United States has applied other economic sanctions as well in an effort to force the ouster of General Noriega, who is under indictment by two Federal grand juries in Florida on drug-trafficking and racketeering charges.

Rumors that the coup attempt had succeeded sent thousands of Panamanians into the streets of the capital this morning. They erected barricades, set cars, garbage dumpsters and tires on fire, brought traffic and commerce to a standstill and burned some buildings, including a military checkpoint.

But by midafternoon the military forces were back in action, firing shotguns and tear and pepper gas in a huge show of force as they sped down the palm-lined boulevards of the capital. Paramilitary squads in civilian clothes also took to the streets, firing shotguns and pistols at knots of confused civilians who had gathered on street corners to await the outcome of events.

"This morning, an attempt by some officers to seize and control the general headquarters of our institution was

Continued on Page A6, Column 4

Bush vs. Dole: Behind the Turnaround

This article was reported by Gerald M. Boyd, E. J. Dionne Jr. and Bernard Weinraub and was written by Mr. Dionne.

History is written by the victors, and that is true even of political campaigns not yet concluded. In retrospect, the winning side's decisions invariably appear brilliant, and losers almost always look foolish.

And so it is now with the battle between Vice President Bush and Senator Bob Dole for the Republican Presidential nomination. A Bush victory is now spoken of as the inevitable product of a long-term battle plan that worked out exactly as it was supposed to. All the organizing the Bush campaign did in 1986 and 1987, discounted at the time by some, is now seen as critical to his victory.

'Firewall' in the South

And after Mr. Bush's sweep of Southern primaries on March 8, nothing looks more brilliant than having set up the South as a "firewall" against possible early defeats.

Mr. Dole, once the hero of the political circuit and even at times described as the inevitable nominee, is spoken of now in almost contemptuous terms, especially as he vows to continue his quest against impossible odds. His campaign, it is now said, was marked by blunders, internal rivalries, and the unpredictable personality of a candidate who switched signals and traveling plans with abandon. Mr. Dole, the argument goes, failed to appoint a single, dominant campaign manager and allowed his organization to go on a 1987 spending binge that left the cupboard bare when it came time for television commercials on Super Tuesday.

George Bush's success in transforming himself from a loser to an almost certain winner in just 29 days is one of the remarkable stories of recent American political history. It is also the lucky consequence of facing off against a foe, Mr. Dole, who at crucial moments seemed to do everything wrong.

What follows is an account of the rise of Mr. Bush and the fall of Mr. Dole, based on interviews with top officials and former officials of both campaigns and other Republican political professionals.

Staff, Organization, Planning

Mr. Bush won in large part because he had a better staff, a keener sense of organization and a more prescient long-term plan.

But in politics, one brilliant last-minute decision can make up for months of bad ones and a key strategic miss can leave even the best organization in chaos.

Thus amid the praise that Mr. Bush's campaign manager, Lee Atwater, receives now, what is not mentioned is that Mr. Bush, according to several aides, was prepared to dismiss or demote him if Mr. Dole won the New Hampshire primary.

And Mr. Dole, in the meantime, had many opportunities in the last month to turn the race around.

In New Hampshire, many of his allies believe he could have won if he

Continued on Page B7, Column 1

News Summary, Page A2

Reagan Vetoes Bill That Would Widen Federal Rights Law

By JULIE JOHNSON

Special to The New York Times

WASHINGTON, March 16 — President Reagan disregarded warnings of a political backlash from Republican Congressional leaders today and vetoed a major civil rights bill.

The measure, which would expand the reach of Federal anti-discrimination laws that the Supreme Court had limited in 1984, was passed by both houses of Congress with more than enough votes to override a veto, and Senate leaders planned to call the bill up Thursday.

But Mr. Reagan offered an alternative that he said would "protect civil rights and at the same time preserve the independence of state and local governments, the freedom of religion and the right of America's citizens to order their lives and businesses without extensive Federal intrusion."

The President said Congress "has sent me a bill that would vastly and unjustifiably expand the power of the Federal Government over the decisions and affairs of private organizations, such as churches and synagogues, farms, businesses, and state and local governments," adding, "In the process, it would place at risk such cherished values as religious liberty."

The bill the President vetoed was intended to overturn the effects of a Supreme Court decision involving Grove City College in Pennsylvania. The

Continued on Page A14, Column 1

For Reagan, Bizarre Turn

The Options Dwindle On Central America

By JOEL BRINKLEY
Special to The New York Times

WASHINGTON, March 16 — Even with the long and tortured history of the Reagan Administration's Central American policies, no one could have anticipated the bizarre convergence of events today.

News Analysis

In the United States Capitol this afternoon, Congressional Democrats found themselves in the unusual position of blaming Republicans for letting down the Nicaraguan contra rebels.

At the same time, the special prosecutor in the Iran-contra affair issued an indictment against four people accused of illegally assisting the contras.

Then, this evening, the White House announced that it was sending 3,200 American troops to Honduras in an "emergency deployment readiness exercise" of unspecified duration.

The White House said that the troops would not be deployed "to any area of ongoing hostilities."

In a classified report to Congress almost two years ago, President Reagan warned that the use of American military force in Central America "must realistically be recognized as an eventual option in the region, if other policy alternatives fail."

Today, more than at any other time in the contra program, it seems as if all the other options are failing.

'Politics of Cynicism'

This afternoon Representative Tony Coelho, a California Democrat who is a leading opponent of renewing aid to the contras, stood on the House floor asserting that "the Republicans abandoned the contras to the politics of cynicism."

The remark set off something close to a brawl as Republicans shouted back, "Shame, shame, shame!"

Successive attempts to renew United States aid for the contras have floundered, and the prospects for coming up with a bipartisan package in the House looked bleak this evening.

At the same time today, the special prosecutor, Lawrence E. Walsh, issued a long-awaited indictment against Rear Adm. John M. Poindexter, Lieut. Col. Oliver L. North and two others involved in the Iran-contra affair — the ultimate testimonial so far to the failure of their covert and apparently illegal program to finance the contras.

All United States assistance to the contras ended two weeks ago, hobbling the rebel movement and, according to the Reagan Administration, emboldening the Sandinistas. The White House says the Nicaraguan Army has launched a major offensive against the contras, most of whom are now inside Honduras. The Sandinistas have denied entering Honduras.

Psychological Support

The purpose of sending troops American troops to Honduras is apparently to give at least psychological if not actual military support to Honduran forces trying to repel any Sandinista troops that have crossed the border. The White House said the exercise was also intended "as a signal to the governments and people of Central America of the seriousness with which the United States Government views the current situation in the region."

The convergence of these events "may be ironic," said Representative Les Aspin, chairman of the House Armed Services Committee, "but I don't think it was done with malice aforethought. I think it was coincidence."

It may be coincidence, but for years the White House has warned that the contras were the only thing restraining the Sandinistas from military adventurism and keeping United States forces out of combat.

Secretary of State George P. Shultz warned in 1985 that members of Congress who voted against financing the contras "may be hastening the day when the threat will grow, and we will be faced with an agonizing choice about the use of American combat troops."

North Sees 'Irony'

On the occasion of his indictment today, Colonel North said, "It is a sad irony that the decision to indict me should occur today, a day in which the Communists in Nicaragua have invaded a democratic neighbor."

Some in Congress said they suspected that Mr. Reagan's actions today might have been just one more theatrical attempt to win renewed contra aid.

"An incursion is another way to justify increased military assistance to the contras," said Senator Christopher J. Dodd, a Connecticut Democrat and an opponent of contra aid.

The last time the White House accused the Sandinistas of invading Honduras — in March 1986, at the height of another contra aid debate — the Administration declared an emergency and United States Army helicopters airlifted Honduran troops to the border area. It became apparent later, however, that the Nicaraguans had crossed the border several times previously, but nobody in Washington had seemed to care.

Warning From Wright

This time though, the House Speaker, Jim Wright, who leads the House opposition to renewing contra aid, said that if the reports of a Sandinista incursion were true, "that would be a very serious matter and would introduce an element of gravity that could profoundly alter the situation" and perhaps shift the balance in Congress toward renewing some form of aid to the rebels.

As President Reagan's time in office dwindles, renewed aid to the contras is far from assured, and peace negotiations in Central America drag on and on showing little apparent progress.

For years, Administration officials who have been involved with Central American policy have said they did not believe Mr. Reagan would be willing to end his Presidency leaving the Nicaragua problem unsolved.

But as the events today make clear, Mr. Reagan has few options left.

As rancor grows over contras, aid planners are indicted.

Associated Press

Lawrence E. Walsh, special prosecutor, arriving at Federal court in Washington after indictment was handed up.

Poindexter Charged With Deleting Files

By STEPHEN ENGELBERG
Special to The New York Times

WASHINGTON, March 16 — After the Iran-contra affair erupted, John M. Poindexter, the national security adviser, methodically deleted from White House computer files all messages he wrote or received, prosecutors charged in an indictment made public today.

It was the first time it has been suggested that Admiral Poindexter, who resigned as national security adviser Nov. 25, 1986, had been involved in wholesale destruction of documents between Nov. 22 and Nov. 29, 1986.

The broad conspiracy charges brought by Lawrence E. Walsh, the special prosecutor, otherwise contain little new information about the Iran-contra affair beyond the evidence amassed by the Congressional committees last year. The indictment does not allude to any actions by Vice President Bush or his staff.

The Role of the C.I.A.

People familiar with the special prosecutor's inquiry said that with the four principal figures indicted, Mr. Walsh would turn his attention to the role of present and former Central Intelligence Agency officials in possibly illegal attempts to aid the contras.

The grand jury was said to have begun examining the relationship between Lieut. Col. Oliver L. North, who was dismissed as the White House aide charged with directing the contra resupply effort, and Joe Fernandez, who was dismissed as C.I.A. station chief in Costa Rica. The prosecutors were said to have obtained thousands of pages of C.I.A. documents and to have extensively interviewed agency officials about their knowledge of the Iran and contra operations.

It was disclosed in testimony to the Congressional inquiry that Mr. Fernandez received instructions from Colonel North through portable code devices that were not part of normal Government communications. Mr. Fernandez acknowledged to Congress that he had helped the contras receive air drops of weapons and supplies during the period Congress barred such aid.

Mr. Fernandez was dismissed from his post at the C.I.A. late last year by Judge William H. Webster, the director of Central Intelligence. He has told friends that he believes his actions in Costa Rica were lawful, particularly since they were directed by a White House official who said he was speaking for President Reagan.

A Missing C.I.A. Cable

Other C.I.A. officials who are subjects of the grand jury's further investigation include Dewey Clarridge, an officer who insisted in sworn Congressional testimony that he was not aware that arms were being sent to Iran in November of 1985. The Congressional Iran-contra report said a C.I.A. official overseas had sent Mr. Clarridge a cable clearly saying weapons were being sent. Mr. Clarridge denied receiving it, but the Congressional report said the committees were "troubled" that the cable and one other were "inexplicably missing from an otherwise complete set of 78 cables."

The charges in the indictment appear to be based on the documents and computer messages that survived Colonel North's acknowledged efforts to shred evidence and on the testimony of cooperating witnesses who also appeared before Congress. It does not appear from the indictment that Mr. Walsh found either a witness or a document that was unavailable to the Congressional committees.

The committees had access to testimony by Colonel North, Admiral Poindexter, and Albert A. Hakim, an Iranian-American businessman. All three testified under grants of immunity, which meant that Mr. Walsh's staff could not use any of their testimony for a prosecution. Richard V. Secord, a retired Air Force major general who was also named in the indictment today, testified without immunity, which meant any of his sworn testimony could be used to buttress the indictments.

North's Personal Notebooks

The Walsh inquiry did not have access to Colonel North's personal notebooks, which were viewed by Congressional investigators as among the most revealing documents they obtained. Colonel North's lawyers have successfully resisted attempts by the grand jury to get this material.

Without the notebooks, the major record of the secret White House dealings appears from the indictment to be the computer notes used by White House officials.

Admiral Poindexter was a computer expert and was involved with the creation of the White House system. Early in his tenure as national security adviser, Admiral Poindexter told Colonel North to send his notes via a computer channel called Private Blank Check. This bypassed the National Security Council's main computer files and went only to the Admiral. The notes were called PROF notes.

When investigators from Mr. Walsh's staff and the Tower Commission began going over the White House computer system, they found backup tapes containing some key notes sent by Colonel North. They also found paper copies of other notes that had been shredded. But they found virtually none sent by Admiral Poindexter.

In his testimony, Admiral Poindexter said this was because he deleted from the system each note after reading it.

"As I think you've heard Colonel North testify, we frankly did not realize the old PROF notes existed. My policy was to erase them, and I apparently did it the right way, and I don't think Colonel North did it the right way."

The indictment did not specify from what source Mr. Walsh had learned of the destruction of computer records.

Drawn-Out Legal Battle Is Predicted in Iran Trial

By STUART TAYLOR Jr.
Special to The New York Times

WASHINGTON, March 16 — The 23-count indictment today against four defendants in the Iran-contra affair aims some of the standard weapons in the arsenal of Federal prosecutors at high-level officials who say they were lawfully carrying out President Reagan's national security policies.

The outcome of the case is impossible to predict, experts agreed today, but one thing is certain: defense lawyers will unload a barrage of legal challenges at the prosecution's case, delaying if not derailing the trial. Those challenges may not be resolved until the appeals from any convictions resulting from the indictment are resolved by the Supreme Court years after Mr. Reagan has left office.

The only event that would be likely to pre-empt a drawn-out legal battle would be if Mr. Reagan were to exercise his power under the Constitution to pardon the defendants and others involved in the Iran-contra affair.

Possibility of Pardons

Most experts agreed that Mr. Reagan could end the prosecution of any defendant at any time by pardoning him. The political damage of such a course to the President and to Vice President Bush could be substantial. Mr. Reagan could wait until after the Presidential election in November to issue pardons. He will not leave office until next January.

If the cases proceed, said Philip A. Lacovara, a Washington lawyer who was a member of the Watergate prosecution force, "there is going to be a lot of skirmishing on a lot of highly debatable issues that could go either way."

Mr. Lacovara and other experts, including Philip B. Heymann, a law professor at Harvard University who worked with the Watergate special prosecution force and who later headed the Justice Department's criminal division, consider the legal challenges that might be raised by the Iran-contra defendants more substantial than those that were raised by the former aides to President Nixon.

The expected challenges by defense lawyers include arguments that no criminal law was violated when the defendants diverted profits from the Iranian arms sales to the contras, and that the appointment of Lawrence E. Walsh as special prosecutor was unconstitutional.

The central charges in the indictment are conspiracy to defraud the United States by deceitfully violating Congressional restrictions on aid to the contras, committing wire fraud in the course of this conspiracy and the theft of Government property by diverting profits from Iran arms sales to the contras.

A Favorite Statute

Each defendant was separately charged with a range of other crimes.

The broadest charge in the indictment, conspiring to defraud the United States, is based on a long-established Federal statute that is a favorite weapon of prosecutors and was at the heart of the successful prosecution of Nixon aides in the Watergate case.

But in the present case this conspiracy charge also depends to some extent on accusations that the Boland amendments, which put restrictions on American aid to the contras, were violated. The applicability of the conspiracy charge here is more problematical.

It has been established for decades, in cases including the Watergate cover-up prosecution, that the crime of conspiracy to defraud the United States is not limited to schemes to take the Government's money or property. It also extends to misuse of Government office or money for a variety of improper purposes.

But defense lawyers are sure to challenge the premise of the conspiracy charge on multiple grounds.

President Reagan has argued that the Boland amendments did not apply to the National Security Council and thus were not binding on Colonel North or Rear Adm. John M. Poindexter, the President's national security adviser at the time of the affair and who was also indicted today.

Defense lawyers are sure to argue that the Boland amendments were an unconstitutional encroachment on the President's power to conduct policy.

U.S. Grand Jury Indicts North, Poindexter and Two Arms Dealers Involved in the Iran-Contra Affair

Continued From Page A1

was unlikely that any would receive the maximum penalty, especially Colonel North, Admiral Poindexter and General Secord, who have distinguished military records.

The White House had no immediate comment on the indictment, although President Reagan insisted again today that he had no knowledge of any violation of the law in the Iran-contra affair.

According to the grand jury, the conspiracy deprived the Government "of the honest and faithful services of employees free from conflicts of interest, corruption and self-dealing." Similar wording was used repeatedly in the criminal conspiracy charges brought against Nixon Administration officials in the Watergate affair.

In addition, Colonel North, who was intimately involved in both the arms sales and the contra diversion, was accused of obstructing a Presidential inquiry when he shredded stacks of classified documents as details of the Iran-contra affair became public in November 1986.

The 44-year-old colonel, whose passionate testimony during Congressional hearings last summer seemed for a brief period to have made him something of a national folk hero, was also accused of conspiracy to defraud the Internal Revenue Service and receiving an illegal gratuity, a home-security system valued at about $13,800.

More Indictments Expected

The 101-page indictment will almost certainly lead to months, if not a year or more, of what one law-enforcement official described as "pre-trial nuclear warfare" between the special prosecutor, Lawrence E. Walsh, and some of the capital's most respected lawyers.

Law-enforcement officials stressed that the criminal investigation of the Iran-contra affair, particularly of the actions of current and former officials at the Central Intelligence Agency, was not over. Additional indictments are expected this year.

During a news conference outside Federal District Court here Mr. Walsh, who is formally known as an independent counsel, said that "the grand jury is not finished."

He added, without elaboration: "The grand jury is continuing — this is simply an interim report. They will be back again Monday."

At the age of 76, Mr. Walsh, a former Federal judge, highly regarded Wall Street litigator and lifelong Republican, is capping his career with the Iran-contra investigation. It was Mr. Walsh who appeared this morning before the grand jury and, in what one aide described as a "moving" summation, asked them to return today's indictment.

Implications for Bush

The criminal charges could have important political implications, particularly for Vice President Bush, who is seeking the Republican presidential nomination, and whose actions in the Iran-contra affair have come under intense scrutiny.

Despite the criminal investigation, Mr. Bush has said on a number of occasions that he is a friend and admirer of both Colonel North and Admiral Poindexter. The Vice President was not mentioned in the indictment issued today and a campaign spokesman had no comment on the matter.

Another key figure in the Iran-contra affair, Robert C. McFarlane, who was Admiral Poindexter's predecessor at the National Security Council, pleaded guilty last week to four misdemeanor counts of withholding information from Congress about the Administration's contra supply efforts.

He agreed to serve as a prosecution witness against Colonel North, his former protégé at the White House, and the others indicted today.

Although his public statements on the Iran-contra affair have been marred by contradictions and inaccuracies, Mr. McFarlane is expected to be an important witness at trial because of his extensive involvement in the arms transfer and his repeated contacts with Colonel North.

During a news conference in his lawyer's office in Washington, Colonel North, in full Marine Corps uniform, said, "I did not commit any crime — I intend to fight allegations of wrongdoing for as long as necessary."

The New York Times/Paul A. Souders

Lieut. Col. Oliver L. North at news conference after his indictment.

With the same proud tone that he used in testimony last year before Congress, he continued, "It is a sad irony that the decision to indict me should occur today, a day in which the Communists in Nicaragua have invaded a Democratic neighbor." He was referring to reports that Sandinista troops had entered Honduras while attacking the contras.

Lawyers for General Secord and Admiral Poindexter were not immediately available for comment. Mr Hakim's lawyer, Richard N. Janis, said his client would plead not guilty.

"We believe strongly that Mr. Hakim has committed no crimes and that his indictment is unfair and unwarranted," the lawyer said in a statement.

Under the immunity granted some of the individuals who testified before the Congressional Iran-contra panels, Mr. Walsh cannot bring charges based on information in the testimony. He has ordered his staff not to read or listen to accounts of testimony from witnesses with immunity.

The Congressional committees found that the President's staff repeatedly broke the law in the Iran-contra affair.

Policy on Iran and Nicaragua was set by a few members of the President's National Security Council and carried out with the help of a secret band of private operatives, including General Secord and Mr. Hakim, the lawmakers concluded.

General Secord and Mr. Hakim acknowledged during their Congressional testimony that they helped arrange the Iran arms transfers and the transfer of some profits to the contras.

The White House would not discuss the possibility that President Reagan would issue pardons to Colonel North and Admiral Poindexter, whose actions he has repeatedly defended.

'No Knowledge,' Reagan Says

Hours before the announcement of the indictment, President Reagan was asked by reporters at the White House if he still stood by his assertion that no laws were broken in the Iran-contra affair. "I have no knowledge of anything that was broken," he said.

Asked why he felt that way, he answered, "Because from all of the investigation and everything else, we don't know where that money came from and we don't know who had it and we don't know where it went."

"All I know was that we got the purchase price we asked for," he said.

In today's indictment, all four defendants were accused jointly of conspiracy to defraud the United States, theft of Government property and wire fraud.

The conspiracy charge carries a maximum penalty of five years in prison and a $250,000 fine. Conviction of theft of Government property can result in 10 years' imprisonment and a $250,000 fine, and wire fraud is punishable by five years in prison and a $250,000 fine.

These additional counts were brought against each suspect:

¶Colonel North, 13 counts, including obstruction of Congress, obstruction of justice, making false statements, accepting a gratuity and conversion for personal use of nearly $4,300 in travelers checks drawn on Government funds.

¶Admiral Poindexter, four counts, including obstruction of Congress and making false statements.

¶General Secord, three counts, including conspiracy to pay illegal gratuities to Colonel North and offering an illegal gratuity, namely financial assistance for the colonel's children.

¶Mr. Hakim, two counts, including conspiracy to pay illegal gratuities to Colonel North.

Amendments Banned Contra Aid

A few counts apply to more than one defendant, so the total does not add up to the 23 in the indictment.

According to the indictment, the four defendants, "together with others known and unknown to the grand jury," conspired to defraud the United States by "deceitfully and without legal authorization" organizing a program to support the contras despite a Congressional ban on most aid.

The ban was contained in a series of statutes that became known collectively as the Boland amendments, named for Representative Edward P. Boland, Democrat of Massachusetts.

Prosecutors left unclear the exact role of William J. Casey, the former Director of Central Intelligence, who died last year. Law-enforcement officials have said previously that Mr. Casey, a key figure in the Iran-contra affair who had close contact with Colonel North, would almost certainly have faced criminal charges.

The indictment mentioned Mr. Casey only in passing, charging that Colonel North participated in the preparation of a false chronology of the Iran-contra affair in anticipation of Mr. Casey's testimony before Congress shortly after details of the scandal became publicly known.

"All the News That's Fit to Print"

The New York Times

Late Edition

New York: Today, clouds, fog, drizzle, afternoon sun. High, 75 inland, 64 coast. Tonight, clear. Low 46. Tomorrow, sunny. High, 78 inland, 60's coast. Yesterday: High 58, low 52. Details, page 32.

VOL.CXXXVII . . No. 47,498

NEW YORK, SATURDAY, MAY 7, 1988

50 cents beyond 75 miles from New York City, except on Long Island. 30 CENTS

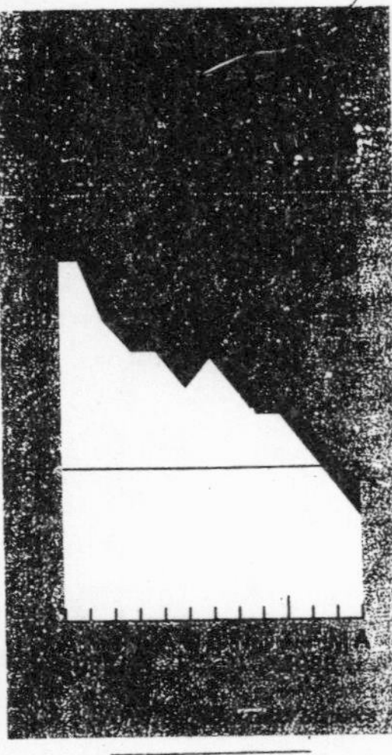

Unemployment Shows a Decline To 14-Year Low

By ROBERT D. HERSHEY Jr.

Special to The New York Times

WASHINGTON, May 6 — The nation's unemployment rate fell a tenth of a point last month to 5.4 percent, the lowest since 1974, as the proportion of the population with jobs hit a record, the Labor Department reported today.

Today's figures, the first major indication of the economy's April performance, were widely seen as reflecting continued moderate, well-balanced growth. The report was also good news for the Presidential prospects of Vice President Bush and other Republicans running for office this fall.

"The good news on the economy continues," President Reagan said at a White House briefing. "And inflation is under control."

Ranks of Employed Soar

As measured by the department's survey of households, the ranks of the employed soared by 606,000 last month. Over all, 116,445,000 held jobs in April, 114,713,000 of that total civilians and 1,732,000 members of the armed forces stationed in this country, the report showed. The number of jobless people shrank to 6,610,000. About 191,000 people who were previously unemployed found jobs, while about 416,000 jobs were filled by people entering the labor force for the first time.

In both New York State and New Jersey, the unemployment rate dropped to 3.5 percent in April. It was the lowest rate in 18 years for New York; for New Jersey, the rate approached the record low of 3.4 percent recorded in February. The improvement cut across all major groups of workers. Labor Department officials cited seasonal booms and a labor force that has been diminished by fewer young people entering the job market. [Page 8.]

Lower Than in March

Both the overall jobless rate and the civilian jobless rate, after conversion to round figures, were 5.4 percent for the month. The civilian rate was two-tenths of a point lower than in March.

At 5.4 percent, the nation's unemployment rate is now exactly half the peak postwar level of 10.8 percent, reached in the final months of 1982 when the most recent recession was ending. Last month's April rate equaled the rate in June 1974, when the nation was in a deep recession. The survey of non-farm payrolls, a figure professional economists consider even

Continued on Page 8, Column 2

BUSH IS TROUBLED BY ISSUES RAISED ON MEESE'S ETHICS

2 ADVISERS SEE A LIABILITY

Vice President Avoids Direct Criticism — Tells Press, 'Let the System Work'

By MAUREEN DOWD

Special to The New York Times

WASHINGTON, May 6 — Vice President Bush conceded publicly for the first time today that he was "troubled by some of these allegations" of ethical impropriety surrounding Attorney General Edwin Meese 3d. He said Mr. Meese's fate should depend on the findings of a special Federal prosecutor.

Mr. Bush's comments followed more critical words from two of his top advisers. Interviews in The Detroit News with Peter Teeley, the campaign's communications director, and Robert Teeter, a strategist, made it clear that they felt Mr. Meese could damage Mr. Bush's Presidential campaign.

Mr. Teeley bluntly said that Mr. Meese was "a liability" whose ethical problems diverted attention from the Bush campaign and added that the "issue will diminish" if the Attorney General resigns. Mr. Teeter said he agreed.

Laying the Groundwork

They appeared to lay the groundwork for Mr. Bush himself to distance himself from President Reagan's staunch support of the Attorney General.

For weeks his advisers and Republican Party workers have been telling the Vice President that Mr. Meese could be a problem in the fall campaign, but Mr. Bush had chosen to resist commenting directly on the Attorney General's legal troubles.

Today Mr. Bush was bombarded with questions about whether he had authorized his aides to criticize Mr. Meese. At first he professed ignorance about their remarks. But later in the day he said that the special prosecutor's report would be a proper yardstick by which to measure Mr. Meese's behavior.

Report Expected Soon

James C. McKay, the special prosecutor, is to issue a report soon on Mr. Meese's activities. Mr. McKay has said he lacks evidence at this time to bring criminal charges against the Attorney General.

When asked whether Mr. Meese should resign, Mr. Bush told reporters at a campaign stop in Billings, Mont.: "You ought to let the system work. You know that the special investigator is out there coming in with a report and we'll see what it says. It's only a matter of a few days."

"I know him," the Vice President said of Mr. Meese. "I know him well. I know him favorably. But I must say I'm troubled by some of these allegations. But I think fair play dictates that the system go forward and make the determination."

He was asked if he considered Mr. Meese "an albatross." He replied "An albatross? I don't think so."

The closest the Vice President had come to today's remarks was after two

Continued on Page 34, Column 5

The New York Times/Witold Jaroslaw Szulecki

Strikers singing about their cause near the main gate of the Lenin shipyard in Gdansk, Poland.

ISRAEL TO DEPORT AN ARAB-AMERICAN

Charges He Aided in Uprising — U.S. Registers Protest

By JOHN KIFNER

Special to The New York Times

JERUSALEM, May 6 — Prime Minister Yitzhak Shamir today ordered the deportation of a Palestinian-American who has advocated nonviolent resistance in the Israeli-occupied territories. The United States strongly objected to the move.

An Israeli Government statement accused the Palestinian-American, Mubarak E. Awad, of being "one of the main contributors to the violent disturbances" in the West Bank and the Gaza Strip. "He was a focal point for the activity of elements hostile to Israel, and he was involved in inciting media and political elements abroad to act against Israel."

Proceedings Begun in November

The United States Ambassador, Thomas R. Pickering, went to the Prime Minister's office during the day to express displeasure at the deportation order. He was received by one of Mr. Shamir's advisers.

Israel began deportation proceedings last November after refusing to extend Mr. Awad's tourist visa and canceling his residence permit. But it held off in the face of official American support for Mr. Awad, including visits by several diplomats to his Center for the Study of Nonviolence, a two-room office in East Jerusalem.

At the time, Ambassador Pickering described Mr. Awad as "a moderate

Continued on Page 5, Column 1

Young and Wary Strikers Take Solace From Walesa

By JOHN TAGLIABUE

Special to The New York Times

GDANSK, Poland, May 6 — Stubble covered his face and exhaustion was written around his eyes as Lech Walesa spoke to the shipyard workers whom a Government propagandist derides as "Walesa's teenagers."

There were about 800 of them in the yard today, from a work force of 10,000 at the Lenin shipyard, and they had the place to themselves except for a detachment of security police.

A Consoling Voice

They sat at the feet of the leader of the outlawed Solidarity movement, a man whose voice seven years ago seemed to shake the state to its foundations. Now that same voice, weary and consoling, was speaking of the despair of a worker who tried to throw himself through the plate glass of a second-story window.

The young man, a teen-ager, apparently cracked under the strain of the long vigil in the yard as the workers waited for a possible confrontation with riot police. He was badly cut but saved by his friends, who rushed him to the infirmary wrapped in a blood-stained blanket.

Mr. Walesa tried to deal with the despair of the others.

"Every one of you has a thousand problems, each different," he said. "One has a problem because he loves his wife, but has to stay here. There are ambitions, colleagues and so forth. Another guy left 500 zlotys for his wife when he left, and suddenly he realizes she has nothing to live on."

'We Have to Carry On'

"You know, Solidarity also means watching the guy standing next to you," he said. "You have to look into his eyes. If there's a strange look, you have to ask him: 'What's your problem? Can I help?' And you can come to Walesa, pull on his sleeve and say, 'Walesa, I have a problem.' We have to carry on. Especially now, when we

Continued on Page 6, Column 2

India's Nuclear Energy Policy Raises New Doubts on Arms

By STEVEN R. WEISMAN

Special to The New York Times

NEW DELHI, May 6 — Bolstered by advances in its own technology, India is proceeding with an ambitious nuclear energy program requiring the storage of tons of plutonium of potential use for nuclear weapons in installations without international safeguards, according to Indian officials.

India's program to produce plutonium, a key ingredient in nuclear weapons, has been under way since the 1960's. But only in the last three years has India been able to make large quantities from domestically built sites so that the plutonium is not subject to outside inspection.

Prime Minister Rajiv Gandhi and other Indian officials continue to insist that India has no nuclear weapons program, despite its proven ability in the field. India exploded what it called a "peaceful" nuclear device in 1974 after years of secret research.

But India also refuses to bring several domestically constructed nuclear installations under international inspection by signing the nuclear nonproliferation treaty, which outlaws the spread of nuclear weapons. India asserts that the treaty is discriminatory because it does not apply to countries that already possess nuclear bombs.

"The intent of India has been from the very beginning to concentrate on a comprehensive program of nuclear technology exclusively for our energy needs," M. R. Srinivasan, chairman of the Atomic Energy Commission, said in an interview at the commission headquarters in Bombay.

"India's political leadership over the last 40 years has been remarkably responsible in this matter," Dr. Srinivasan added. "It has not launched a weapons program in spite of the fact that the technology basis of the Indian energy program is quite comprehensive."

Indian officials also dismissed as "absurd" and "inaccurate" news reports this week that large quantities of Norwegian heavy water, a material used in nuclear reactors, was illegally diverted to India four years ago.

Indian spokesmen asserted that all

Continued on Page 4, Column 2

BISHOPS DENOUNCE WARSAW FOR USING FORCE ON STRIKERS

SPLIT IN PARTY ALSO SEEN

Raid at Nowa Huta Steel Mill Strains Church-State Ties at a Sensitive Moment

By JOHN TAGLIABUE

Special to The New York Times

GDANSK, Poland, May 6 — Poland's Roman Catholic bishops today denounced the Government's use of force to end the strike at a major steel complex near Cracow.

The statement came as serious divisions appeared to emerge in the Polish Communist leadership over the handling of recent labor trouble. Hard-line members of the Politburo, the party's ruling body, appeared to have prevailed over more liberal members.

In a statement released in Warsaw, the bishops said: "We express deep sorrow that an attempt at dialogue and social conciliation did not bring the expected results. This does not serve the welfare of society, or the country."

Particularly Bad Timing

The events seemed to cast a deep shadow over church-state ties, when Poland is drafting an agreement to become the first East bloc country to establish diplomatic relations with the Vatican.

On Wednesday, the Polish bishops appointed five prominent Catholic laymen to mediate in efforts to end strikes at the huge Lenin steel foundry at Nowa Huta, near Cracow, and at the Lenin shipyard, in Gdansk, the most serious eruptions of labor turmoil in Poland in six years. There were indications that the Government approved of the conciliation initiative.

But in a violent raid early Thursday, scores of armed riot policemen swept into the steel mill and arrested most of the strike leaders.

Details emerged today that indicated the force of the raid. The Rev. Tadeusz Zaleski, a Catholic priest who was with the striking workers, said plainclothes officers had beaten the workers with long sticks. Vestments the priest used to celebrate Mass for the workers were scattered, he said, and an altar destroyed.

Medical Help Restricted

Later that day, large numbers of police officers surrounded the sprawling Lenin shipyard in this Baltic port sealing hundreds of striking workers inside. The ring was so tight that strike leaders complained that not even doctors and nurses, as well as medical supplies for the yard infirmary, were being allowed through.

Tonight, there were frequent movements of large numbers of the Government's paramilitary riot police, known from their Polish initials as Zomos, near the shipyard.

[A worker active in the banned Solidarity trade union, Bogdan Lis, was convicted of calling an illegal strike at the Lenin shipyard and sentenced to three months in prison, The Associated Press said. And at least five other Solidarity activists were reported detained in various cities.

[Legislators also drafted a bill that would punish organizers of strikes and anti-Government protests with prison sentences of up to a year, The A.P. reported.]

The church statement said that "unfortunately, during the course of talks at Nowa Huta, the strike was liquidated

Continued on Page 6, Column 1

For Computers, the Year 2000 May Prove a Bit Traumatic

By BARNABY J. FEDER

The dawn of the new century may come as a shock to thousands of computers around the world. Programs that record years in two digits and know no time but the 1900's may be stymied by the year 2000.

As things now stand, many computers would malfunction or miscalculate because they rely on programs that fail to recognize that the day after Dec. 31, 1999, is Jan. 1, 2000.

Some computer programmers are already at work on the problem, but most experts in data processing say ample time remains to avoid trouble. Although everyone agrees that the blind spot exists, expert opinion differs widely about how pressing the problem is and how to address it.

The problem, which could affect information ranging from pension records to credit ratings, stems from the widespread practice since the 1960's of programming computers to identify the year by reading two digits and assuming 19 is in front of them. When the 1900's are over, many of today's programs will figure that the 00 or 01 in a date refers to 1900 or 1901.

One great comfort to data processing executives is that many of today's problem programs — up to 80 percent by some estimates — will have been replaced by 1999 in the normal course of business. Presumably, new software will be written with the millennium in mind.

Just as important, the changes necessary to keep a computer from getting confused by dates after 1999 are often simple. "None of the changes are fun but they also are not brain surgery," said William H. Anderson, a spokesman for Prudential-Bache Securities Inc.

Few types of data are so widely used in software as dates. Over the years programmers have used countless

Continued on Page 41, Column 5

INSIDE

Hostage Brutality Reported

A recently freed French hostage was quoted as saying that American captives in Lebanon were treated brutally after trying to escape. Page 3.

Koch Seeks Bridge Agency

Mayor Koch will ask the Legislature to create a new authority with a $2.7 billion fund to repair, maintain and replace New York City's crumbling bridges. Page 29.

D'Amato on Wedtech

The New York Senator testified that he did less for the Bronx contractor than for other New York companies that sought his help. Page 29.

Knicks and Devils Lose

The Celtics eliminated the Knicks from the N.B.A. playoffs. The Devils lost to the Bruins and trail, two games to one, in their Stanley Cup semifinal series. Page 51.

Makarova Live on TV

Television viewers will be able to watch Natalia Makarova dancing in "Romeo and Juliet" at the Met, live tonight at 8, on Channel 13. Page 54.

The New York Times/Fred R. Conrad

AIDS Babies Find Love With Foster Parents

Chelli Jackson singing to her foster child, who has AIDS. While many people hesitate to tell friends and neighbors their foster children have AIDS, some have found support for their venture. Page 29.

News Summary, Page 2

Market Indicators

CONSOLIDATED TRADING / FRIDAY, MAY 6, 1988

N.Y.S.E. Issues

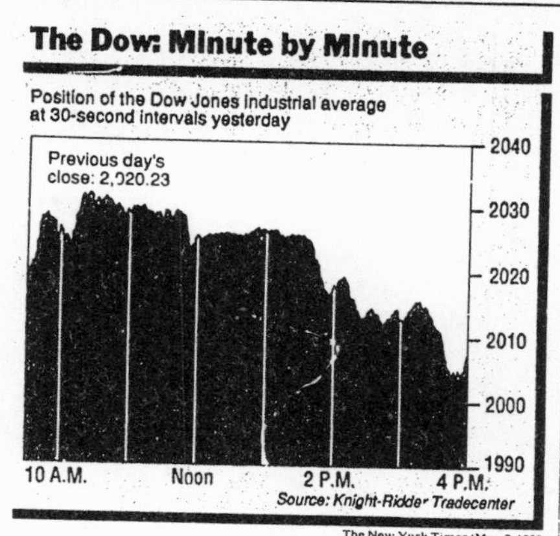

Source: Knight-Ridder Tradecenter

The New York Times/May 7, 1988

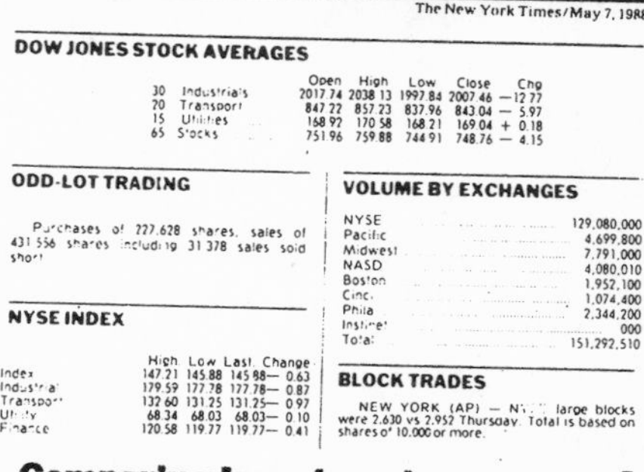

DOW JONES STOCK AVERAGES

	Open	High	Low	Close	Chg
30 Industrials	2017.74	2038.13	1997.84	2007.46	−12.77
20 Transport	847.22	857.23	837.96	843.04	− 5.97
15 Utilities	168.92	170.58	168.21	169.04	+ 0.18
65 Stocks	751.96	759.88	744.91	748.76	− 4.15

ODD-LOT TRADING

Purchases of 227,628 shares, sales of 431,556 shares including 31,378 sales sold short.

NYSE INDEX

	High	Low	Last	Change
Index	147.21	145.88	145.88	− 0.63
Industrial	179.59	177.78	177.78	− 0.87
Transport	132.60	131.25	131.25	− 0.97
Utility	68.34	68.03	68.03	− 0.10
Finance	120.58	119.77	119.77	− 0.41

VOLUME BY EXCHANGES

NYSE	129,080,000
Pacific	4,699,800
Midwest	7,791,000
NASD	4,080,010
Boston	1,952,100
Cinc.	1,074,400
Phila	2,344,200
Instinet	000
Total	151,292,510

BLOCK TRADES

NEW YORK (AP) — NYSE large blocks were 2,630 vs 2,952 Thursday. Total is based on shares of 10,000 or more.

Comparing Investments

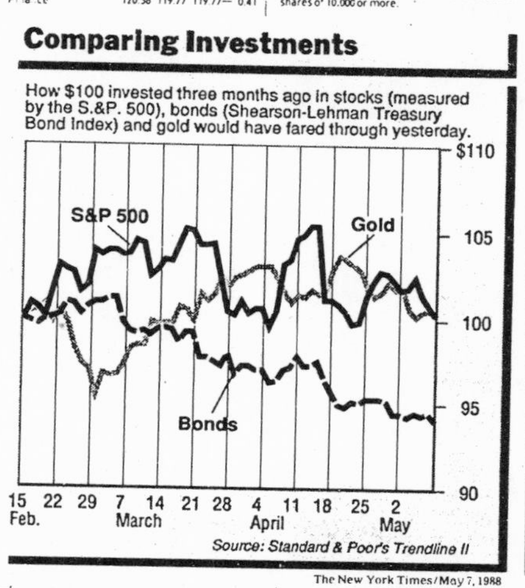

Source: Standard & Poor's Trendline II

The New York Times/May 7, 1988

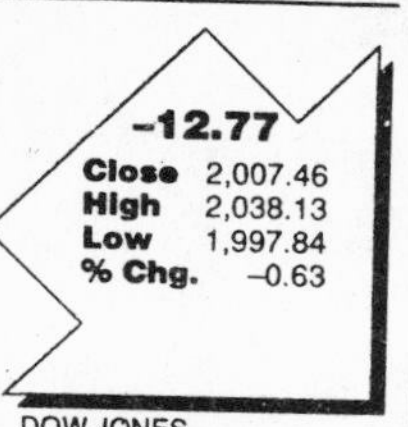

MARKET DIARY

	Friday	Prev. day
Advanced	602	559
Declined	845	925
Unchanged	545	509
Total issues	1992	1993
New highs	16	16
New lows	21	23

MOST ACTIVE: SHARE VOL.

Name	Volume	Last	Chg.
MarionLab	6,490,400	16½	+1⅛
Texaco	2,963,100	52⅛	+ ¼
Duke Pow	2,376,100	43	− ⅜
Amer T&T	2,005,500	26	− ⅛
Genetch	1,311,700	30¾	−2¾
Exxon s	1,241,000	44⅛	+ ¼
GenElct	1,208,000	39½	− ½
Aristech	1,176,600	32⅜	+ ¼
Varity	989,800	3⅛	− ⅛
LIL Co	968,900	9½	+ ¾

MOST ACTIVE: DOLLAR VOL.

Name	Tot($1000)	Sales(hds)	Last
Texaco	$153,340	29631	52⅛
Duke Pow	$102,469	23761	43
MarionLab	$101,412	64904	16½
IBM	$85,125	7669	110½
Merck	$67,744	4399	152
Exxon s	$55,069	12410	44⅛
Amer T&T	$52,143	20055	26
GenElct	$48,018	12080	39½
PhilipMor	$45,657	5340	85½
DowChem	$43,551	5177	83⅞

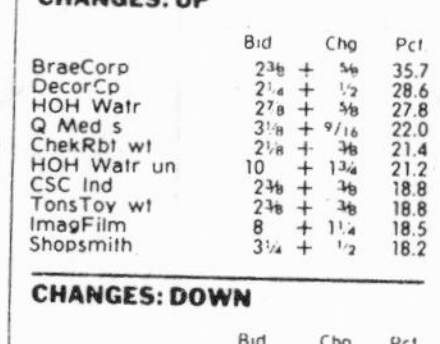

CHANGES: UP

	Last	Chg	Pct
PilgrmPrd	6	+ ⅞	17.1
ChockFON	10⅛	+ 1¼	14.1
Banner Ind	18¾	+ 2	11.9
viToddShp	2½	+ ¼	11.1
ONEOK	12⅝	+ 1¼	11.0
Quanex	10	+ ⅞	9.6
LIL Co	9½	+ ¾	8.6
MaxxamGp	12¼	+ ⅞	7.7
GrowGp	10¾	+ ¾	7.5
FtCapitHd pf	23½	+ 1⅝	7.4

CHANGES: DOWN

	Last	Chg	Pct
Coleco	2⅛	− ¼	10.5
Genetch	30¾	− 2¾	8.2
Elect Assoc	3¼	− ¼	7.1
NwAmShoe n	3⅝	− ¼	6.5
Jepson	7¾	− ½	6.1
SystemsInteg	5⅞	− ⅜	6.0
Berkey Inc	2	− ⅛	5.9
GlfSU 8.80pf	52¼	− 3¼	5.9
WiniakInc	2	− ⅛	5.9
Upjohn	27⅛	− 1⅝	5.7

VOLUME COMPARISIONS

Day's Sales	129,080,000
Thursday's Sales	171,840,000
Year Ago	215,200,200
1988 year to Date	15,258,109,506
1987 year to Date	12,859,923,193

Nasdaq Issues

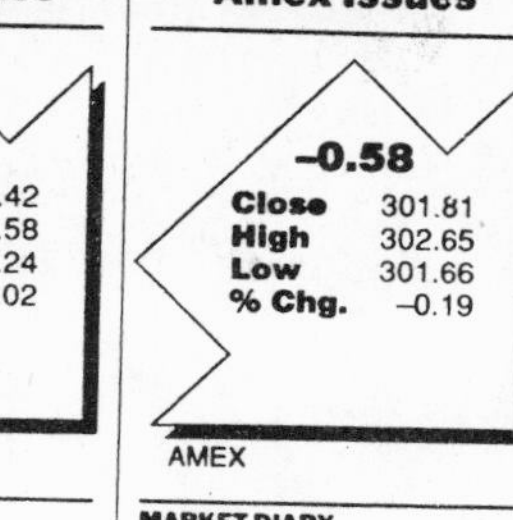

MARKET DIARY

Advanced	1,019
Declined	993
Unchanged	2,639
Total issues	4,651
New highs	108
New lows	37
Total sales	122,739,800

MOST ACTIVE: SHARE VOL.

Name	Volume	Last or Bid	Asked	Chg.
MCI	2,047,900	14⅝		+ ¼
MicrTc	1,628,700	23⅛		+1⅝
Intel s	1,518,100	32		− ¼
SlkGrn	983,000	16¼	16⅜	......
LizCla s	970,600	15		− ⅝
AppleC s	961,200	41¼		− ½
Seagate	759,200	18¼		+ ⅜
WsInPb	740,600	22		−1¼
Bombay	737,000	2 15-16		−1-16
ChrmSh	708,800	10¾		− ⅝

MOST ACTIVE: DOLLAR VOL.

Name	Tot($1000)	Sales(hds)	Last
IntelCp s	$49,338	15181	32
AppleCptr s	$39,889	9612	41¼
MicronTch	$36,340	16287	23⅛
MCI Comm	$29,438	20479	14⅝
FarmersGp s	$21,177	3486	60¾
Microsoft s	$17,522	3054	57¼
WsInPubl	$16,663	7406	22
AshtonTate	$15,335	6014	25⅝
LizClabr s	$14,801	9706	15
SeagateTc	$13,760	7592	18¼

CHANGES: UP

	Bid	Chg	Pct
BraeCorp	2⅜	+ ⅝	35.7
DecorCp	2¼	+ ½	28.6
HOH Watr	2⅞	+ ⅝	27.8
Q Med s	3⅛	+ 9/16	22.0
ChekRbt wt	2⅛	+ ⅜	21.4
HOH Watr un	10	+ 1¾	21.2
CSC Ind	2⅜	+ ⅜	18.8
TonsToy wt	2⅜	+ ⅜	18.8
ImagFilm	8	+ 1¼	18.5
Shopsmith	3¼	+ ½	18.2

CHANGES: DOWN

	Bid	Chg	Pct
CommceGrp	2	− ½	20.0
HytekMicro	2½	− ½	16.7
AmPacific	3⅛	− ½	13.8
Carver	4	− ⅝	13.5
Hauserman	10	− 1½	13.0
Balchem	4⅜	− ⅝	12.5
CousinHme	2⅝	− ⅜	12.5
Daltex un	7½	− 1	11.8
Longwood wt	2⅞	− ⅜	11.5
MillsJen	4⅞	− ⅝	11.4

INDEX

Index	Close	Chg.	Week Ago.	Month Ago.
Composite	379.42	− 0.09	379.23	381.83
Indust	391.23	− 0.46	391.16	392.06
NMS Comp	163.92	− 0.05	163.84	165.10
NMS Inds	151.21	− 0.19	151.28	151.71

Amex Issues

−0.58
Close 301.81
High 302.65
Low 301.66
% Chg. −0.19
AMEX

MARKET DIARY

	Friday	Prev. day
Advanced	228	293
Declined	334	302
Unchanged	269	264
Total issues	831	859
New highs	10	4
New lows	11	5

MOST ACTIVE: SHARE VOL.

Name	Volume	Last	Chg.
DomePtrl	1,753,800	1 1-16	......
Amdahl	550,500	44⅜	+1½
MediaGen s	533,800	46¾	+ ¼
MichaelStr	371,500	5⅜	− ⅛
WangLabB	365,900	10¾	......
BolarPh s	355,700	27½	−1¾
Atari	285,700	8⅛	− ⅜
LorimarTel	264,900	13	− ⅝
US Cellular n	263,100	15⅞	+ ¾
FtAusIPr	203,900	9⅛	......

MOST ACTIVE: DOLLAR VOL.

Name	Tot($1000)	Sales(hds)	Last
MediaGen s	$25,088	5338	46¾
Amdahl	$24,222	5505	44⅜
BolarPh s	$9,781	3557	27½
Viacom pf	$4,646	1840	25¼
ImperOil A g	$4,183	867	48½
US Cellular n	$4,078	2631	15⅞
WangLabB	$3,933	3659	10¾
LorimarTel	$3,476	2649	13
EchoBay s	$3,360	1680	19⅞
NY Times	$3,298	1178	27⅞

CHANGES: UP

	Last	Chg	Pct.
Salem Corp	9⅜	+ 1¼	15.4
UnivPat	5½	+ ½	10.0
BaldwnTch	16⅝	+ 1½	9.9
HudsonFood	9⅛	+ ¾	9.0
Synalloy	4⅜	+ ⅜	8.8
TriStMot	12⅞	+ 1	8.4
Unimar	7¼	+ ½	7.4
CaglesIn A	5⅜	+ ⅜	7.1
VermntResh	3⅞	+ ¼	6.9
MCO Holding	9⅞	+ ⅝	6.8

CHANGES: DOWN

	Last	Chg	Pct
PatientTch	2¾	− ⅜	12.0
AmCapCp	3¼	− ⅜	10.3
Ketchum	11¼	− 1⅛	9.1
AmTr-ko sc	5¼	− ½	8.7
AmTechCer	2¾	− ¼	8.3
LinPro	3⅛	− ¼	7.4
Lionel	4¾	− ⅜	7.3
ResidMtg	5⅛	− ⅜	6.8
PresidO B	5⅜	− ⅜	6.5
ManufactHme	9⅛	− ⅝	6.4

VOLUME COMPARISIONS

Day's Sales	9,556,845
Thursday's Sales	9,442,430
Year Ago	11,392,075
1988 year to Date	939,415,820
1987 year to Date	1,284,887,785

Other Measures

VALUE LINE

NEW YORK (AP) — The Value Line Geometric Index of 1,685 NYSE, American and OTC stocks was 228.13 Friday, off 0.42 points, or off 0.18 percent, from Thursday. A year ago the index was 262.99. The Arithmetic Index, created Feb. 1, 1988, was 232.35 off 0.38 points, or off 0.16 percent.

UP-DOWN SHARE VOLUME

	Shares Advanced	Shares Declined
NYSE	47,553,980	64,685,050
AMEX*	3,166,350	3,983,405
NASDAQ	38,482,499	33,461,793

WILSHIRE

SANTA MONICA, Calif. (AP) — The Wilshire Associates 5,000 Equity Index, the market value of 5,000 NYSE, American and OTC issues, was $2,578.307 billion Friday off $10.367 billion or off 0.40 percent from Thursday. A year ago the index was $2,935.914 billion.

Computers Not Ready For Change of Century

Continued From Page 1

methods of coding dates, many of them so obscure that a programmer searching a program for portions dealing with dates may have trouble locating all of them.

Unless vulnerable programs are replaced or repaired, the oddity could affect such things as insurance coverage, receipts and payments by businesses, inventories and factory production schedules.

'An Absolute Horror Show'

"It could be an absolute horror show for anyone with mainframe computers," said Anthony Graffeo, the senior vice president of information systems at the Home Group, a New York-based insurance company. "The joke in computing circles is that every data processing manager, no matter how old they are, is saying they plan to retire early in 1999."

Some computer programs assume that a new date is erroneous if it does not appear to be more recent than the one before it. They will simply grind to a halt, the data experts predict, when they see dates ending in 00 following the last entries from the 1900's, which will end in 99.

Yet another group of problem programs operate on five-digit calendars that cannot go higher than 365/99, which represents the 365th day of 1999. These built-in expiration dates may cause computer systems to freeze or wipe out valuable data.

A Diversity of Strategies

Citibank, one of the world's largest data processors, does not expect to focus on date problems until 1997 or 1998, according to Paul F. Glaser, chairman of the Corporate Technology Committee.

The Hartford Insurance Company, which has about 35,000 computer programs, expects to study the problem

> **Software experts cannot agree on how to address date problems.**

next year and will probably start making changes in 1993, said John T. Crawford, Hartford's vice president of information management.

But Libby-Owens-Ford Inc., a glass manufacturer based in Toledo, Ohio, that became a subsidiary of Britain's Pilkington P.L.C. in 1986, said it began four years ago to eliminate potential problems with the year 2000.

'A Lot of Subtle Problems'

"I suspect there will be a lot of subtle problems, even for those who have been setting aside four digits to represent years," said Edward Yourdan, a pioneer in the development of standardized methods for writing software. "Large organizations have thousands of programs with millions of lines of code. It's very difficult to track down everywhere in the program where they are doing date calculations."

Some programs, of course, already handle events that will take place after 1999 and will have no problem with the arrival of the millennium. For example, banks and other financial institutions that issue or trade long-term mortgages and bonds have programs that calculate investment yields into the 21st century. And businesses have programs managing physical assets with long lives, such as buildings and oilfields.

Programs written for the newest generation of computing equipment — work stations and personal computers — typically run off of calendars that will function well into the next century or further. The standard set by Lotus Development Corporation's popular spread-sheet programs, for instance, uses five digits to record days and disregards years. Jan. 1, 1900, is 00000. Today is 32270.

Problems for Procrastinators

Such time calculations will work until the programs reach 99999, about halfway through the 22d century. Until recently, however, few programs that run on mainframes were designed with even the next century in mind.

"Those who don't take it seriously are going to be faced with a real problem in the late 1990's," said D. Dean Mesterharm, associate deputy commissioner for operations at the Social Security Administration, the third-largest Federal software user after the Defense Department and the Census Bureau. "They are going to have to tell their bosses they can't do any new applications because they will have all their resources tied up on fixing dates. There are people who feel they can write a special routine to get around it, but I think they will find their programs use dates in ways they aren't aware of."

Nevertheless, there are strong pressures to procrastinate. Most data processing operations face large backlogs of requests for new applications. Data processing executives are more likely to receive complaints than kudos if they put new projects on hold to address the date issue any sooner than absolutely necessary. Such considerations weigh especially heavily on those who hope to be promoted out of their current jobs long before the millennium.

The programmers who work under them are even less likely to regard the date problem with a sense of urgency. Upgrading old programs is widely regarded as tedious work compared with developing new applications.

"The average programmer never thinks beyond next Tuesday," said Richard D. Harrison, director of the Federal software management support division of the Federal Government's General Services Administration.

Unknown Factors

Another concern is that there may be a far smaller pool of people with the experience to fix date problems in older software by the end of the 1990's.

In many cases, companies have little idea how their older programs work because the programmers who developed them have left and others have updated them without creating accurate records. Some experts believe that such problems and the rise of powerful networks based on personal computers is accelerating the retirement of older programs, a trend that should ease the transition to the year 2000.

The development of new programming techniques will help too. For example, isolating dates in data bases shared by many programs is becoming standard practice.

Software Design Aids

And a number of companies have computer programs that write computer programs themselves. These software design aids may help companies locate the dates they need to change. The capabilities of such programs could be strikingly increased if they focus specifically on the date problem and use a new generation of artificial intelligence analysis techniques based on studies of how the mind works.

"Our projections for the development of artificial intelligence systems suggest that by 1994 and 1995, they may be able to handle most of this relatively easily," said Harry Pontius, head of systems architecture and programs in the Information Resource Management Group at the Defense Department.

Skeptics point out that it will take almost as much effort to look for the 5 or 10 percent of problems that even the best automated search systems are likely to miss. At best, they say, companies will end up with scores of niggling problems in the first months of the new millennium.

For now, it looks like big data processors are relying heavily on computer vendors and the suppliers of software to provide leadership on standards. Mr. Harrison said that the General Services Administration may soon be encouraging such efforts at the Federal level. And nearly everyone expects a slew of entrepreneurs to emerge with software and consulting services focused on date problems as the new millennium draws closer.

"Very few people are thinking about it yet," Mr. Harrison said. "But it's about to come out of the data processing cocktail circuit and into the coding room as an issue."

Judge Trims Utility Suit

SEATTLE, May 6 (AP) — A Federal judge has dismissed the damage claims of some of the bondholders suing the Washington Public Power Supply System over the termination of two nuclear power plant projects.

Judge William Browning, at a pretrial hearing Thursday in Seattle, granted a defense request to dismiss claims from plaintiffs who bought bonds after the projects were terminated in early 1982.

Judge Browning appeared to reverse an earlier decision in which he had allowed claims from plaintiffs who had bought bonds between Jan. 22, 1983, when the projects were terminated, and June 15, 1983, when the Washington Supreme Court invalidated the agreements under which the projects were financed.

It was not clear how many of the 35,000 bondholders in the suit would be affected by the ruling.

The power system terminated the two plants in 1982, causing an eventual default on the $2.25 billion in bonds sold to finance their construction. It was the biggest default ever in the municipal bond market.

Airbus Agrees To a Shake-Up

HANOVER, West Germany, May 6 (Reuters) — The European aircraft consortium Airbus Industrie agreed this week to shake up its management structure to improve its efficiency in response to a critical report from a panel of experts.

The measures, to be carried out by the end of this year, will prepare Airbus for the European Community's abolition of internal trade barriers in 1992, said ministers from the four nations in the consortium: Britain, France, West Germany and Spain.

"This is not a minor administrative change," the British Trade Minister, Kenneth Clarke, told a news conference Thursday after a meeting in Hanover. "It's a fundamental change for Airbus Industrie."

A report commissioned by Airbus members said that unless the consortium changed its management structure, it would suffer production delays, extra costs and loss of good will among major airlines.

New York Stock Exchange Issues

CONSOLIDATED TRADING / FRIDAY, MAY 6, 1988

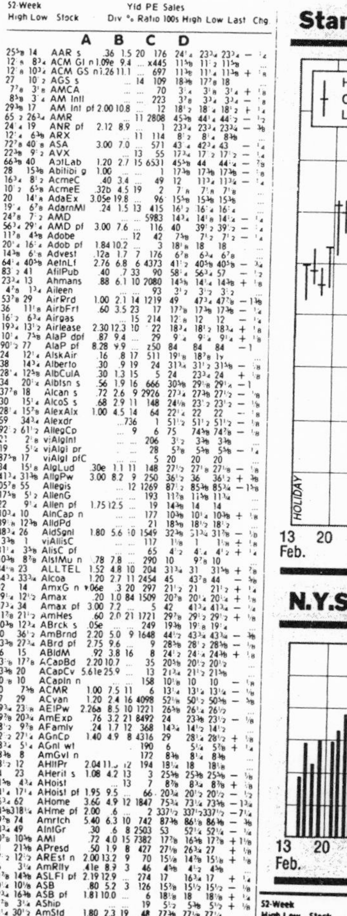

52 Week High	52 Week Low	Stock	Div	Yld %	PE Ratio	Sales 100s	High	Low	Last	Chg
A B C D										
[illegible]										

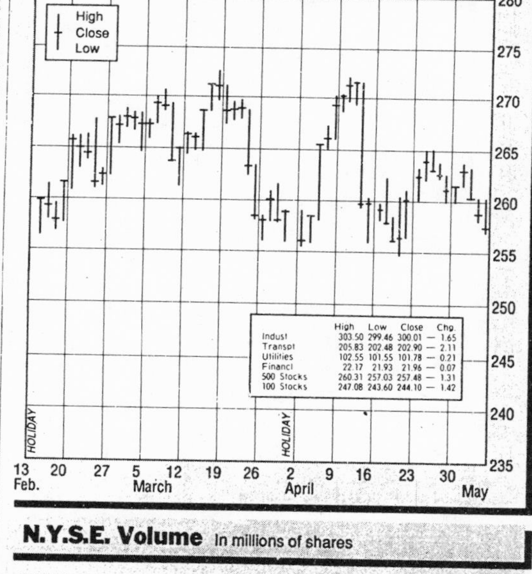

	High	Low	Close	Chg.
Indust	303.50	299.46	300.01	− 1.65
Transpt	205.83	202.48	202.90	− 2.11
Utilities	102.55	101.55	101.78	− 0.21
Financl	22.17	21.93	21.96	− 0.07
400 Stocks	260.31	257.03	257.48	− 1.31
100 Stocks	247.08	243.60	244.10	− 1.42

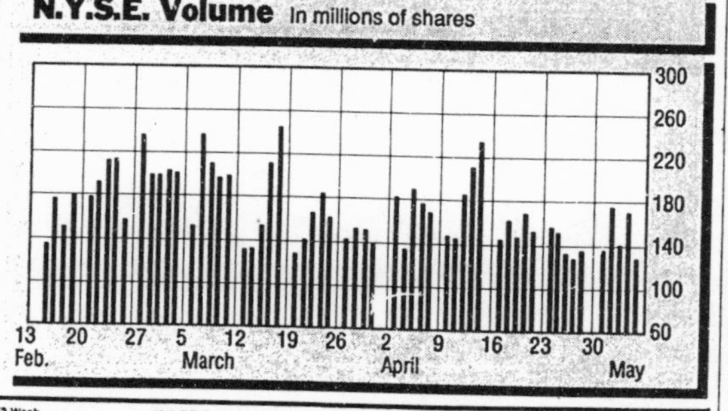

52 Week High	52 Week Low	Stock	Div	Yld %	PE Ratio	Sales 100s	High	Low	Last	Chg
[illegible]										

52 Week High	52 Week Low	Stock	Div	Yld %	PE Ratio	Sales 100s	High	Low	Last	Chg
[illegible]										

Continued on Following Page

"All the News That's Fit to Print"

The New York Times

Late Edition

New York: Today, mostly sunny, more seasonable. High 38-44. Tonight, clear, cold. Low 18-28. Tomorrow, becoming cloudy, showers. High 36-41. Yesterday: High 53, low 39. Details, page D20.

VOL.CXXXVIII . . No. 47,727 NEW YORK, THURSDAY, DECEMBER 22, 1988 35 CENTS

50 cents beyond 75 miles from New York City, except on Long Island.

DREXEL CONCEDES GUILT ON TRADING; TO PAY $650 MILLION

The New York Times

Frederick H. Joseph

Black Star

Michael R. Milken

CIVIL CASE REMAINS

Settlement Would Close 2-Year Investigation Into Boesky Deals

By STEPHEN LABATON

In the largest settlement ever of Federal securities law violations, Drexel Burnham Lambert Inc., the Wall Street powerhouse, agreed in principle yesterday to plead guilty to six felony counts and pay $650 million.

If the settlement is approved by officials in Washington, it would end an investigation lasting more than two years into Drexel's relationship with Ivan F. Boesky, the Wall Street speculator who settled insider-trading charges in 1986. He was the Government's main witness against Drexel.

Government lawyers have said the investment firm and Mr. Boesky traded on insider information and concealed the ownership of stock in more than a dozen deals from 1984 to 1986. Many were related to corporate takeovers and restructurings.

The settlement, which will include guilty pleas to charges of mail fraud, wire fraud and securities fraud, marked a stunning reversal by the firm. A day earlier, Drexel rejected a deal and seemed resolved to fight the charges.

A Dramatic Meeting

The agreement was reached after a dramatic meeting Tuesday evening between the firm's chief executive, Frederick H. Joseph, and United States Attorney Rudolph W. Giuliani, who gave the investment house until 4 P.M. yesterday to settle or be indicted. The charges would have included racketeering and obstruction of justice.

In a brief statement, Drexel said it had concluded that a settlement "is in the best interests of our firm and our employees."

Neither Mr. Giuliani nor Drexel mentioned Michael R. Milken, the central figure in the Government's two-year investigation. Mr. Milken, based in Beverly Hills, Calif., made Drexel the dominant Wall Street force in the busi-

Continued on Page D4, Column 1

More on the Drexel Case

The Decision to Settle — An indictment of the investment firm appeared imminent until late Tuesday afternoon, when U.S. Attorney Rudolph W. Giuliani placed a call to Drexel's chief executive, Frederick H. Joseph. Page D5.

A Climactic Deal — The long Government investigation of trading abuses on Wall Street, leading to the Drexel settlement, raises serious questions about Wall Street's ability to police itself and serves notice that many innovative trading and takeover practices will be closely scrutinized. News Analysis, Page D5.

The Storm Around Milken — Michael R. Milken's name was not mentioned in Drexel's agreement to plead guilty, but the financial machine he created was clearly at the center of the Federal investigation. Page D4.

AGENCY DEFENDED IN DEATH OF CHILD

Official Says Custody Is Given Even With Known Neglect

By SUZANNE DALEY

New York City's top child-welfare official said yesterday that even if his agency had been aware that a Brooklyn mother had a history of child neglect, it still would have recommended that she retain custody of a 5-year-old girl who died in her care last week.

At the time of the custody battle in 1986, neither the judge in the case nor caseworkers were aware that the mother had been charged with neglect three years earlier and had lost custody of two other children.

But the official, William J. Grinker, said that despite this lack of knowledge, caseworkers investigating the family for the court had made the right choice in favoring the mother over the father in the custody battle.

The 25-year-old mother, Abigail Cortez, and her live-in companion, who is also 25, have been charged in the beating death of the girl, Jessica. Police officials have described the child-abuse case as one of the worst they have ever seen.

"From my total review of the case file, in my judgment, knowledge of any prior activities and facts that we have on the record would not have affected our recommendation," said Mr. Grinker, the city's Human Resources Administrator and Commissioner of Social Services.

Mayor Koch, in an interview, dif-

Continued on Page B6, Column 3

Pentagon Official Accuses 8 Concerns on Secret Data

By RICHARD HALLORAN

Special to The New York Times

WASHINGTON, Dec. 21 — The director of a Defense Department investigative agency said today that eight of the nation's leading arms makers face possible criminal prosecution for illegal possession of secret Government documents.

The planning and budget documents were used to prepare bids for Government contracts, Government officials said.

The official, John F. Donnelly, said in Congressional testimony that the companies were Boeing, the Amecon division of Litton Systems, McDonnell Douglas, Northrop, TRW Inc., Sanders Associates, General Dynamics and Martin Marietta.

A Congressional staff report said the names of four companies — Boeing, General Dynamics, Martin Marietta and Sanders — had been referred to the United States Attorney in the Eastern District of Virginia for possible prosecution.

'Black Market' Seen

In the testimony today, a senior official in the Pentagon Inspector General's office, Donald Mancuso, said the trafficking in secret documents was "insidious," corrupted the procurement process, undermined public confidence and endangered national security.

Asked by Senator William Proxmire, Democrat of Wisconsin, whether the trade in such documents continues, Mr. Mancuso said, "Absolutely; it is going on today."

The accusations today were separate from the Justice Department's well-publicized inquiry into possible improprieties by consultants to arms makers in which inside information was said to have been used to gain unfair competitive advantage in weapons sales.

After a flurry of activity and publicity last summer, that case has been quiet as grand juries in New York and Virginia have been considering the evidence out of the public eye. Officials close to the case have said for several weeks that indictments were expected

Reaction From Companies

Reaction from several of the companies named by Mr. Donnelly was mixed. A spokesman for Boeing said, "We are aware of the investigation and we are fully cooperating with the Government."

But a spokesman for Litton said: "We have no knowledge of any current investigation. We have no knowledge of anyone in this company trafficking in classified information."

Similarly, a spokesman for McDonnell Douglas said, "We are not aware of any such investigation." He said several employees had been interviewed earlier but that the company believed the matter to have been closed. A spokesman for Northrop said, "We are not aware of it."

In a hearing before Senators Proxmire and Senator Charles E. Grassley, Republican of Iowa, Mr.

Continued on Page A19, Column 1

Army Technician and a Civilian Are Held as Spies for Soviet Bloc

By MICHAEL WINES

Special to The New York Times

WASHINGTON, Dec. 21 — An Army intelligence specialist and a Turkish-born civilian living in Florida were arrested today, breaking what American officials said was a major espionage operation that funneled information about the West's eavesdropping capacity to the Soviet Union and East Germany for six years.

American officials said the operation appeared to have inflicted serious damage on the United States' electronic spying efforts in Europe but added that the extent of the damage was still being assessed.

On Tuesday an agent of the Federal Bureau of Investigation, posing as a Soviet spy, met for two hours with the central figure in the case, an Army warrant officer, James W. Hall, in a Savannah, Ga., hotel.

An F.B.I. affidavit made public today said that Mr. Hall, believing the Federal agent was a Soviet contact, "described in notable detail his espionage history against the United States" and "admitted his motivation to be greed." His annual salary from the Army is about $20,000.

["He was living far above his pay grade," a Pentagon official told Reuters.]

Mr. Hall, a native of New York City who is 30 years old, was a signals intelligence and electronic warfare technician who had served in West Berlin and Frankfurt. He was arrested by Army intelligence agents early today at his home in Richmond Hill, near Savannah.

Earlier today, Federal agents in Belleair, Fla., near Tampa, took into cus-

Continued on Page D22, Column 3

JETLINER CARRYING 258 TO U.S. CRASHES IN SCOTTISH TOWN

SCOTLAND
Glasgow
Edinburgh
Prestwick
N. IRELAND
Lockerbie
BRITAIN
ENGLAND
IRELAND
WALES
London
FRANCE
English Channel
North Sea
Miles 0 100

The New York Times/Dec. 22, 1988

Houses and cars near Lockerbie were set ablaze by the crash.

ALL BELIEVED DEAD

Syracuse University Had 36 People Aboard — Cause Is Unknown

By CRAIG R. WHITNEY

Special to The New York Times

LONDON, Dec. 21 — A Pan Am Boeing 747 on a flight from London to New York with 258 people aboard crashed tonight in a southern Scottish village, British military authorities reported. The airline said it knew of no survivors.

The passengers included at least 36 Syracuse University students of a group of 38 who purchased tickets for the flight. An unknown number of American military personnel flying home for the holidays were also reported to have been aboard.

The plane was flying at 31,000 feet when it suddenly disappeared from radar and crashed into two rows of houses, setting them on fire.

There was no immediate indication of the cause of the crash. British officials would not respond to speculation by some about a structural failure or an on-board explosion in the jumbo jet.

Flight Originated in Germany

Pat Coffey, a spokesman for the British Royal Air Force, said the plane, Pan American World Airways Flight 103, left Heathrow Airport outside London after originating at Frankfurt, West Germany, and was bound for Kennedy International Airport.

Among those on board was the chief administrative officer of the United Nations' Council for Namibia, Bernt Carlsson of Sweden, who was flying to New York for the signing of an accord on Namibian independence, aides to Mr. Carlsson said. Others were believed to include two executives of Volkswagen's United States affiliate — James Fuller, a vice president, and Lou Marengo, marketing dirctor. and also executives of The Associated Press. There were also unconfirmed reports that six members of the State Department's Diplomatic Security Service were aboard.

Pan Am officials in New York said it was the worst single-plane disaster in the airline's history.

Disappears From Radar Screens

The plane left Heathrow about 25 minutes behind schedule at 6:25 P.M. (1:25 P.M., New York time). It disappeared from air controllers' radar scopes 52 minutes later, shortly before a series of explosions and fires were reported on the ground in the Scottish village of Lockerbie, according to witnesses and official accounts. [The Associated Press quoted authorities as initially saying that the plane may have hit a hillside in the hamlet of Corrie, six miles from Lockerbie, and that debris was strewn across the countryside.]

"The aircraft is reported to have hit two rows of houses, which have been

Continued on Page A16, Column 1

Armenia Opens To Show Capital Under Tight Lid

By BILL KELLER

Special to The New York Times

YEREVAN, U.S.S.R., Dec. 20 — At Yerevan University and at the Polytechnical Institute, where passions have run high during this year of Armenian self-assertion, soldiers with automatic rifles take attendance each morning.

Army tanks and armored personnel carriers straddle entrances to city squares that earlier this year teemed with tens of thousands of demonstrators. After midnight, armed soldiers stop any car not bearing a pass from the Ministry of Defense.

In the last week and a half, the authorities have methodically arrested many nationalist leaders, including a member of the Armenian legislature, and others have gone into hiding, emerging occasionally to give defiant interviews to Western reporters.

All the Markings of Martial Law

The authorities do not call it martial law, but the capital of Armenia has all the outward markings of a city under military rule.

The Soviet press briefly reported the imposition of military discipline after ethnic unrest broke out in the city last month. But the sense of occupation has been conveyed far more dramatically in the past two weeks, as Armenia has been opened to crowds of outsiders, both Soviet and foreign, in the relief effort mounted since the devastating earthquake north of here on Dec. 7.

For many of the visiting relief workers, journalists, doctors and diplomats, the emergency measures are a visible

Continued on Page A8, Column 3

Agence France-Presse

Relocation of Quake Victims Hampered by Bad Weather

In Leninakan, U.S.S.R., Armenians wait for trains to Yerevan and Moscow. Heavy snow and cold temperatures are causing difficulties in relocating survivors of the earthquake that devastated Armenia.

Homeless Addicts in Oregon Find Aid in Restoring Lives

Portraits Of the Homeless

Last of four articles.

By TIMOTHY EGAN

Special to The New York Times

PORTLAND, Ore. — When city officials here proposed putting homeless drug addicts and alcoholics under one roof with nothing but peer pressure to keep them clean, a chorus of skepticism could be heard all the way up the Willamette River.

Five years later, the program, begun
A by Mayor Bud Clark of Portland, has a
demonstrated record of success in aiding a category of homeless people often
B considered beyond hope or rehabilitation.
C A recent study by the city has found
that about a third of all residents leave
the program with a job, and 60 percent
D leave free of their chemical dependency.
E The program has attracted the attention of officials in New York and San
F Francisco, among other cities. A representative of the Port Authority of New
York and New Jersey recently visited
G Portland in search of solutions to the
problem of homeless people sleeping in bus and train stations. San Francisco, meanwhile, adopted parts of the Portland program after looking at what the city had done.

The first step in the program is offering alcoholics and drug abusers a room in a residential hotel for up to six months on one condition: that they stay off drugs and alcohol. With the housing as an anchor, the program provides intensive counseling and therapy for up to 200 people a year, many of them addicted to both alcohol and crack, the smokable form of cocaine.

Recently all 29 residents of the Everett Hotel, one of three hotels in the program, were given surprise urine tests,

Continued on Page A18, Column 1

Probable Appointee Assures Lawmakers On Abortion Views

By ROBIN TONER

Special to The New York Times

WASHINGTON, Dec. 21 — Leading Congressional opponents of abortion met with Dr. Louis W. Sullivan today and later termed him an acceptable candidate to be Secretary of Health and Human Services, a sign that President-elect Bush might be able to proceed with the selection of his first black Cabinet appointee.

In the meetings, Dr. Sullivan promised he would have "strong pro-life people" under him in the department, one of the lawmakers said.

But leaders in the anti-abortion movement appeared to be unswayed.

"There are many questions remaining," Dr. John C. Willke, president of the National Right to Life Committee, said in a statement released tonight that repeated the group's opposition to the appointment. "The most immediate one is this: Either Dr. Sullivan has been totally misquoted or he has completely changed his position in the last few days, for he now says that is pro-life."

Officials handling the transition to a Bush administration said today that

Continued on Page D22, Column 6

INSIDE

News Summary, Page A2

Labor Backs Israeli Pact

After a stormy meeting, the Labor Party gave final approval to the new Israeli coalition government led by the Likud party. Page A14.

Panamanian in U.S.

Panama's ousted President arrived in Washington as the United States sought ways to remove Gen. Manuel Antonio Noriega. Page A3.

Action on 2 Nuclear Plants

The Nuclear Regulatory Commission took steps to allow the operation of the Seabrook and Pilgrim power plants in New England. Page A18.

All 258 Are Believed Dead In Crash of Jet in Scotland

Continued From Page A1

demolished by the impact, and also to have hit vehicles on the highway," said a spokesman for the Royal Air Force's rescue and coordination center near Edinburgh. Houses and cars along the highway to Glasgow were still blazing fiercely several hours after the crash, he said. There were no survivors in these houses, about 40 in all, The Associated Press reported.

The Press Association, Britain's domestic news agency, said that 9 or 10 bodies had been recovered about two miles from the crash site.

"A rescue situation does not exist anymore," the rescue and coordination center said. "We are just recovering bodies."

'A rescue situation does not exist anymore,' the disaster center reports.

BBC television late tonight broadcast pictures of raging fires, devastated houses and cars and shreds of aircraft wreckage. Witnesses said the huge aircraft had left a deep crater where it came down, near a gasoline station.

A retired policeman, Bob Glaster, who lives near the site of the crash, said: "The plane came down 400 yards from my house. There was a ball of fire 300 feet into the air, and debris was falling from the sky. When the smoke cleared a little, I could see bodies lying on the road. At least one dozen houses were destroyed."

The spokesman at the rescue and coordination center said that the first impact of the plane was in the southwestern corner of the village, which has a population of about 4,000, and that the aircraft had bounced after hitting the ground, spreading wreckage over six areas over 10 miles. "We obviously fear many people were killed, but there are no reports of casualties yet," he said more than three hours after the crash.

The airplane had a capacity of 412 passengers. There were 243 passengers on board, and 15 crew members, Pan Am said. Jeff Kreindler, a Pan Am spokesman in New York, said the was "no sign at all" of adverse weather that might have been a factor.

Emergency blood supplies were sent to the crash site from hospitals all over Scotland. The village hall was being used as a makeshift mortuary.

Mr. Kreindler, the Pan Am spokesman, said, "There was no indication of any problems on board that aircraft or with the machine itself." Asked whether the plane's crew had received any bomb threats, he said, "There were no threats."

No Midair Collision, Either

The British Defense Ministry said there had been no midair collision with another plane, civilian or military, and Michael Vertigans, a spokesman for the Civil Aviation Authority, said there were no reports of emergency signals from the plane before it went down. An air-traffic controller at Prestwick Airport near Glasgow was reported to have spoken to the pilot of the plane a few minutes before the crash, and he reportedly gave no sign he was in difficulty.

The crash was the worst aviation accident in British history. Prime Minister Margaret Thatcher said tonight that she was "shocked by this terrible disaster" and expressed her sympathy to the United States Ambassador, Charles H. Price 2d. She sent her Secretary of State for Scotland, Malcolm Rifkind, to the scene this evening, and Britain's Transport Secretary, Paul Channon, said he would make a report on the findings Thursday morning.

Mr. Price and Mr. Rifkind flew to the scene tonight. Earlier, the United States Embassy in London said it was not known how many of the passengers were Americans.

Homes burning in Lockerbie, Scotland, after the fiery crash of a Pan American 747 jetliner last night. Reuters

Pan American's planes from Germany and Britain are often used by United States Government employees and military servicemen stationed in Europe and their families.

The rescue-center spokesman said the fire on the ground had hampered rescue attempts by teams of police and Royal Air Force doctors who flew by helicopter from military bases near the crash area. The A74 highway between Glasgow, about 70 miles northwest of the site, and the Scottish border with England, 20 miles to the south, was cut, and telephone lines to the area were also brought down by the crash.

Witness' Account

Mike Carnahan, who lives two miles south of Lockerbie, said: "I was driving past the filling station when the aircraft crashed. The whole sky lit up and the sky was actually raining fire. It was just like liquid."

Mr. Carnahan said he thought the aircraft had been trailing flames before it hit the ground, but there was no confirmation of this from authorities.

The plane that went down tonight was delivered to Pan American in February, 1970, according to Craig Martin, a spokesman for the Boeing Company, the manufacturer. He estimated that it had 72,000 hours in service and had made 16,500 landings.

Aviation authorities thought that since the jet disappeared from ground controllers' radar screens when it was at 31,000 feet, without an emergency call from the cockpit, whatever brought it down must have happened instantaneously.

What Happened to Transponder?

If the power to the electrical system operating the plane's transponder had not been suddenly cut, the transponder would have kept sending signals about the aircraft's position and altitude to radar screens on the ground, which would have shown it losing altitude as it fell.

Among the kinds of things that might have suddenly cut power would be a bomb, an explosive decompression caused by a structural weakness, or a decompression caused by a midair collision.

Mr. Kriendler said there was no indication of an explosion and that Pan Am had not received any threats.

He said that 30-mile-an-hour winds were reported at about 4,000 feet when the aircraft took off, but there was no information of how strong the winds were at 31,000 feet, the plane's cruising altitude before it apparently lost power.

The 747 was a relatively old plane, the 15th such aircraft built, and had been involved in one previous accident, according to National Transportation Safety Board records. That was in 1970, when it encountered severe turbulence near Nantucket on a flight from New York to Paris. Seven people were seriously injured.

However, Mr. Kreindler, the Pan Am spokesman, said at a news conference tonight there was no indication that the age of the plane had anything to do with the crash. He said that in 1987, it was renovated under the Civil Reserve Air Fleet Program of the United States Air Force.

Under that program, he said, commercial aircraft are specially outfitted to expand the airlift capabilities of the Air Force, including adding a large cargo door and reinforcing the floor.

Pan Am officials have said that the changes put no extra strain on the aircraft. In addition, Mr. Kreindler said, the plane underwent cyclical maintenance in San Francisco on Dec. 14 after 250 flight hours.

Town's Hall Used as Clinic, Then Morgue

LOCKERBIE, Scotland, Dec. 21 (AP) — Soon after the Pan Am Boeing 747 plowed into Lockerbie this evening, its council hall became a makeshift clinic. Within hours, it was a morgue.

Nobody knows how many of the 2,500 villagers have lost their lives, but many houses were flattened, and others caught fire and were gutted.

Mayor Frank Park stood in the street, dazed and in tears, too distraught to talk. Pleasant village lanes were littered with debris, masonry, ripped-up fences and shrubbery.

Royal Air Force rescue authorities say two rows of houses were demolished and no survivors have been found in the wreckage.

Village Center Sealed Off

Sherwood Crescent, the village center that bore the brunt of the crash, was sealed off, and traffic jams blocked the routes to Lockerbie, so that rescuers had to fly in and out by helicopter. There were fears that a gas station apparently hit by the wreckage might blow up.

Initial accounts from authorities said the jet apparently hit a hillside near the hamlet of Corrie, about six miles from here, and left debris and bodies across the countryside.

Along a country road leading to Lockerbie, rescue parties could be seen examining pieces of smoking wreckage, and there were what looked like blanket-covered bodies.

Some of the wreckage also landed on cars on the four-lane bypass around Lockerbie and they went up in flames.

'A Mighty Bang'

A former police inspector, Archie Smith, ran out of his house with his son when he heard the crash.

"I didn't know what it was at first," Mr. Smith said. "It was just a mighty bang. Where the houses were seems to be just a black hole. The fire spread quickly and my home soon caught alight and it is now destroyed as well."

Mr. Smith, who was a policeman for 30 years, said: "Never, ever have I seen anything so appalling, so horrific as this."

The flames sent up a pall of thick, choking smoke and the streets were littered with rocks and twisted pieces of metal.

Sheila McDonald was delivering Christmas presents to a friend's home on a hillside overlooking the town when she heard "a horrible droning sound."

"This V-shaped object just seemed to come flying through the air," she said, adding that "it was the wings and front section of an aircraft. She said that "another part came just behind and all around seemed to be red dots like sparks.

"It hit some houses in the town and there was a mass of flame and everything just started to shake," she said.

11 in Red Cross Quit Lebanon

LARNACA, Cyprus, Dec. 21 (AP) — Eleven Red Cross officials who were evacuated from Lebanon after they received death threats arrived in Cyprus today on their way home to Switzerland. The International Committee for the Red Cross said in Geneva on Tuesday that it was suspending its humanitarian operations in Lebanon because of the "serious threats." Later today, the two largest Muslim militias in southern Lebanon appealed to the Red Cross to return, blaming a "criminal minority" for terrorist attacks on humanitarian workers.

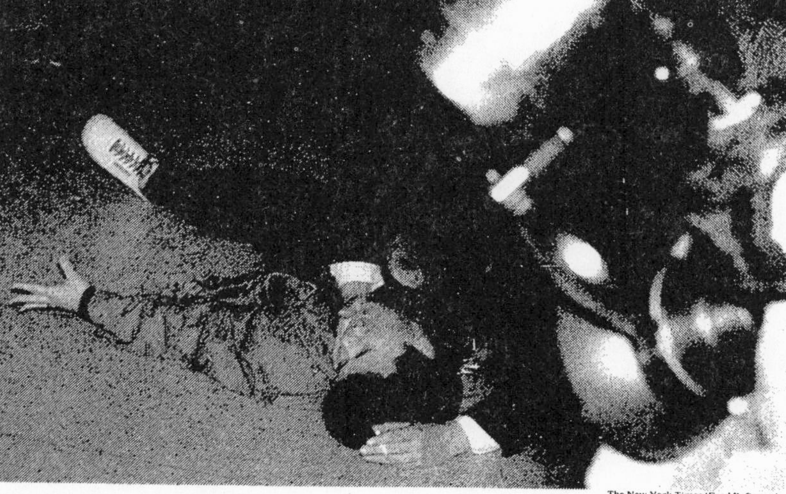

The New York Times/Fred R. Conrad

A woman being comforted by her husband at Kennedy International Airport last night after learning that her child was aboard the Pan American plane that crashed in Scotland.

Jarred by Tragedy, Syracuse Students Grieve

By ERIC SCHMITT

Special to The New York Times

SYRACUSE, Dec. 21 — The Chancellor of Syracuse University joined faculty and students here tonight in mourning the loss of at least 36 students killed in the Pan American jetliner crash in Scotland. He called the crash "the greatest tragedy in the history of Syracuse University."

Two more student may have been aboard the flight. The students were taking part in a program of studies abroad, in London and other cities, and were returning home for the holidays after their first semester.

"We have lost some of our best and brightest," the Chancellor, Dr. Melvin A. Eggers, said at a news conference tonight. "They were talented and beautiful people. It will be hard to express our sorrow."

Moment of Silence at Game

As word of the crash spread across this campus of 16,500 students, groups of students and teachers huddled around radios and televisions, staring through tears and in disbelief. "It's shocking, especially at this time of year," said Neil Wollerstein, a 19-year-old freshman from Dix Hills, L.I.

Many students here had already finished fall-semester exams and had left the campus.

A memorial service was held tonight in Hendricks Chapel. A moment of silence was observed before the Syracuse-Western Michigan basketball game at the Carrier Dome. Word of the crash had come too late to cancel the game.

Counseling sessions will be available to students and members of the university community on Thursday, university officials said.

University officials said the students killed in the crash in the southern Scottish village of Lockerbie were among 250 in the Syracuse program in London. Officials said 29 of the confirmed dead had been taken the program in London, and the seven others were believed to have been attending Syracuse programs in other European cities.

Switch to an Earlier Flight

At least one student who was scheduled to take the flight, Pan American World Airways Flight 103 from London, switched his plans at the last minute.

The student, Matthew Trento, a 22-year-old senior, said on a flight from New York to Syracuse this evening that he had taken an earlier flight instead.

Mr. Trento said that one of his roommates and two other friends from the London program had been on Flight 103.

"Just last night, three of us went out for drinks, and then were just hanging around our apartment, looking forward to Christmas," said Mr. Trento, who said he heard of the crash when his Pan Am flight landed at Kennedy International Airport.

"I just broke down and called my mom," said Mr. Trento, who was met at the airport here by his mother and sister.

Worst Air Crashes on Record

By The Associated Press

March 27, 1977 582 killed in a collision of two Boeing 747's operated by Pan American and KLM Royal Dutch Airlines at the airport at Tenerife in the Canary Islands.

Aug. 12, 1985 520 killed when a Japan Air Lines Boeing 747 crashed into a mountain on a domestic flight.

March 3, 1974 346 killed in when a Turkish DC-10 crashed 26 miles northeast of Paris.

June 23, 1985 329 killed when an Air India Boeing 747 crashed off the coast of Ireland.

Aug. 19, 1980 301 killed in a fiery emergency landing of a Saudi Arabian L-1011 jet at the airport in the Saudi capital of Riyadh.

July 3, 1988 290 killed when an Iran Air A300 Airbus is shot down over the Persian Gulf by the American warship Vincennes after being mistaken for an attacking plane.

May 25, 1979 275 killed when an American Airiines DC-10 crashed on takeoff in Chicago.

Sept. 1, 1983 269 killed when a Korean Air Lines 747 was shot down by a Soviet fighter after flying through Soviet airspace near Sakhalin Island.

Nov. 28, 1979 257 killed when an Air New Zealand DC-10 taking tourists to the South Pole struck a mountain in Antarctica.

Dec. 12, 1985 256 killed when an chartered Arrow Air DC-8 carrying members of the 101st Airborne Division crashed on takeoff at Gander, Newfoundland.

Jan. 1, 1978 213 killed when an Air India 747 en route to the Middle East sheikdom of Dubai crashed less than two minutes after taking off from Bombay.

Dec. 4, 1974 191 killed when a chartered Dutch DC-8 returning Indonesian Muslims from Saudi Arabia went down in Sri Lanka.

Aug. 3, 1975 188 killed when a chartered Moroccan Boeing 707 crashed near Agadir, Morocco.

May 9, 1987 183 killed when a Polish LOT airliner crashed near Warsaw.

Nov. 15, 1978 183 killed when a chartered Icelandic Airlines DC-8 crashed short of an airport in Colombo, Sri Lanka.

Nov. 27, 1983 183 killed when an Avianca Boeing 747 crashed near Barajas Airport in Madrid.

36 Students at Syracuse Among the Passengers

By DENNIS HEVESI

Among those reported aboard Pan Am Flight 103 when it crashed yesterday were 38 students from Syracuse University and executives from several corporations.

Pan American executives declined last night to release a passenger list, but a spokesman for the airline said "some people of note" were on board.

The spokesman, Jeff Kreindler, said: "We are currently formulating a passenger list. We have not heard of any survivors from that aircraft, though we do know there were some people of note on it. We are not able to provide any breakdown of nationalities."

A spokeswoman for Syracuse University, Diane Sloan, said: "We can confirm that 38 students were in the Syracuse party. They were on their way back after spending the semester abroad. All of them were undergrads."

Under the university's Division of International Programs Abroad, some undergraduates spend a semester or a year abroad. The spokeswoman could not say how many were now in the program.

At the university last night, students and faculty held a prayer service and a moment of silence before the start of a basketball game on campus.

Associated Press

John Mulroy, director of international communications at The Associated Press, was a passenger on the plane.

Other Passengers Identified

Also on board, according to The Associated Press, was the news service's director of international communications, John Mulroy; his son, Sean, and his daughter-in-law, Ingrid. Reuters said two top executives of Volkswagen's American operations were on board, but their identities could not be determined last night.

At the same time, relatives of Julian Benello, a 25-year-old American graduate student at Cambridge University, said there was "an awful weight of circumstantial evidence" that Mr. Benello was on the plane.

Mr. Benello's aunt, Mallen DeSantis of New York, said: "He was dropped off at Heathrow at 4:30. He was planning to take Flight 103. We don't know beyond a shadow of a doubt that he was on the plane, but if he wasn't, he would have called by now. It's an awful weight of circumstantial evidence that he was on the plane."

At Heathrow Airport in London, his cousin, Everard Whitehouse, said Mr. Benello, from Boston, had delayed his flight one day "because he wanted to see a friend who was ill."

At the Pan Am terminal at Kennedy Airport, the airline set up a receiving lounge, cordoned it off and instructed security guards to escort any relatives to the lounge. They then set lines up.

In the evening, a middle-aged woman arriving at the Pan Am terminal was told that the plane had crashed, and she fell to the floor, on her back, screaming, "Oh, my baby! Oh, my baby!" Her husband tried to hug her, helped her up, and then walked her through the more than 100 journalists.

At about 9:30 P.M., a Protestant minister, the Rev. Frank Rafter, who said he was a chaplain with the city's Emergency Medical Service, emerged from the lounge, which was closed to journalists. He said that about 25 relatives or friends of passengers were in the lounge and that airline personnel were telling them that there were no survivors.

The U.N. Today

General Assembly

Meets at 3 P.M.

Ticket information phone: 963-7113. Tours are conducted 9 A.M.-4:45 P.M.

U.N. Officer on Flight 103

Special to The New York Times

UNITED NATIONS, Dec. 21 — Bernt Carlsson, who was a passenger on the Pan Am flight that crashed over Scotland, had served as chief administrative officer of the United Nations Council for Namibia since July 1987. He was on his way here for a ceremony on Thursday, at which accords providing for Namibia's independence are to be signed by Angola, Cuba and South Africa.

The officer is, in theory, the United Nations' appointed governor for Namibia, the South African-ruled territory also known as South-West Africa. But because United Nations authority over Namibia is not recognized by South Africa, he is in practice the chief United Nations officer in charge of development programs intended to prepare Namibia for independence.

Mr. Carlsson, a 51-year-old Swedish diplomat, had been in London for a meeting with nongovernmental groups, United Nations officials said. He telephoned his office from the boarding gate at Heathrow Airport before the flight to New York.

From 1983 to 1985 Mr. Carlsson served as a Swedish Ambassador at Large to the Middle East. He was General Secretary of the Socialist International, the world federation of socialist and social democratic parties, from 1976 to 1983. From 1983 to 1985, he was an Ambassador at large and special emissary of Prime Minister Olof Palme to the Middle East and Africa.

He also served as international secretary of the Swedish Social Democratic Party and as Under Secretary of State for Nordic Affairs in the Swedish Foreign Ministry.

"All the News That's Fit to Print"

The New York Times

Late Edition
New York: Today, morning showers, thunderstorms, then clearing skies and windy. High 82. Tonight, clear. Tomorrow, chance of late showers. Yesterday: High 86, low 65. Details are on page 41.

VOL.CXXXVIII — No. 47,891 · NEW YORK, SUNDAY, JUNE 4, 1989 · $1.50 beyond 75 miles from New York City, except on Long Island. · $1.25

TROOPS ATTACK AND CRUSH BEIJING PROTEST; THOUSANDS FIGHT BACK, SCORES ARE KILLED

Khomeini, Imam of Iran And Foe of U.S., Is Dead

By The Associated Press

NICOSIA, Cyprus, Sunday June 4, — Ayatollah Ruhollah Khomeini, Iran's spiritual and political leader, died today, 12 days after he underwent surgery for bleeding in his digestive system, the official Iranian news agency reported. He was believed to be 89 years old.

"The leader of the Islamic revolution and founder of the Islamic Republic, Imam Khomeini, passed away at a Teheran Hospital," the Islamic Republic News Agency reported in an urgent dispatch.

[Reuters reported that a statement from his son, Hojatlislam Ahmad Khomeini, his chief aide, accompanied the announcement.

Associated Press, 1980

Ayatollah Ruhollah Khomeini

["The lofty spirit of the leader of Moslems and free men everywhere, His Excellency Imam Khomeini, has gone to Heaven and his heart, which was brimming with love for God and the oppressed of mankind, stopped beating," it said.]

The Ayatollah was referred to by Iranians as the imam, or spiritual leader. He led the 1979 revolution that toppled 2,500 years of monarchy and set up the Islamic Republic of Iran, turning the relatively Western-style country ruled by Shah Mohammed Riza Pahlevi into the most hard-line Islamic nation in the world.

He emerged as an implacable foe of the United States, which had supported the Shah, and it was under his direction that Iranian students overran the United States Embassy in Teheran and held many of the diplomats inside hostage for over a year, a development that was one of the chief causes of the electoral defeat of the Jimmy Carter Administration.

Reaction From Ex-Hostage

He was equally an enemy of the Soviet Union, referring to both the superpowers as "The Great Satans," and he led his country in an eight-year-war against neighboring Iraq.

A former American hostage in Iran said the Ayatollah's death ends a chapter for the former captives.

"I'm not the type to say I'm happy he's dead," said Barry Rosen, of Brooklyn, one of the 52 hostages held 444 days by radical Iranian students from 1979 to 1981. "But I do feel, to a certain degree, that that part of the

Continued on Page 39, Column 1

Associated Press

A student placing debris in front of a moving armored personnel carrier early today in Tiananmen Square.

SQUARE IS CLEARED

General Strike Is Urged as Officials Announce End of 'Rebellion'

By NICHOLAS D. KRISTOF

Special to The New York Times

BEIJING, Sunday, June 4 — Tens of thousands of Chinese troops retook the center of the capital from pro-democracy protesters early this morning, killing scores of students and workers and wounding hundreds more as they fired submachine guns at crowds of people who tried to resist.

Troops marched along the main roads surrounding central Tiananmen Square, sometimes firing in the air and sometimes firing directly at crowds who refused to move.

Early this morning, the troops finally cleared the square after first sweeping the area around it. Several thousand students who had remained on the square throughout the shooting left peacefully, still waving the banners of their universities. Several armored personnel carriers ran over their tents and destroyed the encampment.

Casualty Reports Sketchy

Reports on the number of dead were sketchy. Three Beijing hospitals reported receiving at least 68 corpses of civilians and said many others had not been picked up from the scene. Four other hospitals said they had received bodies of civilians but declined to disclose how many. Students said, however, that at least 500 people may have been killed in the crackdown.

[A report on the state-run radio put the death toll in the thousands and denounced the Government for the violence, The Associated Press reported. But the station later changed announcers and broadcast another report supporting the governing Communist Party, the A.P. said.]

Most of the dead had been shot, but some had been run over by personnel carriers that forced their way through the protesters' barricades.

Official Version

The official news programs this morning reported that the People's Liberation Army had crushed a "counter-revolutionary rebellion." They said that more than 1,000 police officers and troops had been injured and some killed, and that civilians had been killed, but did not give details.

[President Bush called for an end to the violence. "I deeply deplore the decision to use force against peaceful demonstrators," he said. Page 20.]

Changan Avenue, or the Avenue of Eternal Peace, Beijing's main east-

Continued on Page 20, Column 4

In the Streets, Anguish, Fury and Tears

Reuters

A protester injured in a clash with troops yesterday at the Great Hall of the People in Beijing.

By SHERYL WuDUNN

Special to The New York Times

BEIJING, Sunday, June 4 — As the crackle of automatic weapons filled the air today on the Avenue of Eternal Peace, tens of thousands of Beijing residents, even elderly men and women, rushed out to see what they could do to turn back the troops.

"The citizens have gone crazy," said a driver watching as a tank plowed its way down the main thoroughfare. "They throw themselves in front of the tank, and only when they see it won't stop, they scatter."

The driver himself was shaken by what he had seen: A tank had rammed into an army truck used as a barricade. As the truck turned over, it crushed a man to death. Elsewhere, he had seen three bloodied bodies lying in the street. Several soldiers still standing in their trucks were crying.

Students and workers threw beer bottles, gasoline bombs, lead pipes, whatever they could find, at the tanks and armed personnel trucks, which nevertheless continued rumbling down the avenue. One truck drove back and forth along the east side of the Changan Avenue, as the Avenue of Eternal Peace is known in Chinese, and did not stop when people stood in its path.

Amazement had already turned to fear and defiance earlier in the evening as citizens saw the military convoys entering the city. Some troops from other provinces practically paraded their AK-47 rifles as they stood in their trucks, stranded by the human blockades that had formed around the trucks.

By dark, tensions had soared throughout the city. Hundreds of thousands of people were impelled outdoors by their disbelief and anger, yet brought back to their homes by fear of the violence. The sound of tanks whizzing by and reports of open firing fanned their fears.

"You beasts! You beasts!" shouted the people at the troops.

'We Have to Obey Orders'

Around a convoy of about 45 military trucks in the eastern part of the city, people pushed and shoved their way to the troops, shouting and urging them to consider their role as fellow citizens. But the sympathy that had characterized the troops last week was gone; the soldiers seemed to have a certain resolve.

"Will you shoot at us if they order you to?" was a question asked by many of the people surrounding the truck. The soldiers gave weak assurances to the people that they would not fire, but they also admitted that

Continued on Page 20, Column 1

Soviet Emigré Mob Outgrows Brooklyn, and Fear Spreads

By RALPH BLUMENTHAL with CELESTINE BOHLEN

A criminal underworld of Soviet émigrés, some of them skilled in white-collar crime and hardened by Soviet prison and labor camps, is reaching beyond its base in Brooklyn, using extortion and violence in its own neighborhoods and engaging in multimillion-dollar racketeering schemes on an international scale.

The network of Russian-speaking criminals is small and loosely grouped compared with the hierarchies of traditional American organized crime. But camouflaged within the country's growing Soviet immigrant communities, the network is fast outstripping the ability of local and Federal agencies to curb its illegal schemes, some of which are linked to Mafia crime families, officials of the Federal Bureau of Investigation and other agencies say.

Intelligence reports trace the network to black marketeers and other professional gangsters, many of whom plied their criminal trade in the Soviet Union before winning exit visas — or being planted — in the wave of Jewish emigration.

One mob boss who was said to have spent 10 years in Soviet prisons before turning up in Brooklyn was known to enforce his threats with an electric cattle prod he kept in his car. Investigators say he once extorted $15,000 from another immigrant by threatening to kill the man's daughter on her wedding day. Another crime kingpin, convicted of credit card fraud and now facing extradition from West Germany, is reputed to have amassed a fortune of more than $600 million from bootlegged gasoline in less than a decade after he arrived from Odessa.

Greater Numbers Coming

As Soviet emigration policies loosen up, greater numbers of Jews, Armenians and ethnic Germans have been given permission to leave. Since 1975, some 150,000 have come to the United States. About 50,000 have settled in the New York area; another 15,000 are expected to settle here this year.

Law-enforcement officials say that, while the network comprises no more than a few hundred active criminals out of all those who arrived, some of these are highly skilled mob enforcers, forgers and confidence men.

Their criminal activities range from old-fashioned jewelry swindles on 47th

Continued on Page 38, Column 1

Gingrich, Pursuer of Democrats, Now Finds Himself the Pursued

By E. J. DIONNE Jr.

Special to The New York Times

WASHINGTON, June 2 — Representative Newt Gingrich's role in bringing down House Speaker Jim Wright seems to have set him up for a Wright-style roasting that could determine his future as the leader of the young and aggressive backbenchers bidding for control of their party in the House.

Obviously a target for Democratic revenge, the 45-year-old Georgia Republican is also facing some criticism as a divisive figure within his own party.

One sign of Mr. Gingrich's political difficulties, party strategists say, is that his main competitor for leadership of the young conservatives, Representative Vin Weber of Minnesota, has already begun to distance himself from Mr. Gingrich, his longtime friend.

The strategists interpret recent comments by Mr. Weber as suggesting that while the party needs Mr. Gingrich's inspirational example right now, House members might want a cooler leader for the long haul.

Some Republicans scoff at Democratic suspicions that there is an organized "stink-tank" campaign under way, saying the majority party is merely suffering trouble that it brought on itself. [Page 34]

If Mr. Gingrich has his Republican

Continued on Page 34, Column 1

The Polish Vote

The Solidarity labor union takes a step toward becoming a broad political movement today as Poles vote in the first openly contested elections in the Soviet bloc.

Some say that, four years hence, the opposition will be in control. Others predict a splintering of Solidarity's factions.

Article, page 15.

The New York Times/Dith Pran

$12.1 Million Desk

An 18th-century American desk, which sold at a price usually paid for famous paintings. Page 36.

INSIDE

U.S. in Afghan Shift
Prompted by doubts that the Afghan guerrillas can topple the Kabul Government, the Bush Administration is edging toward a new policy that emphasizes the possibility of a political solution to the conflict. Page 15.

Storm Around a Mayor
Mayor Tom Bradley of Los Angeles, long admired for his reputation of absolute integrity, now finds himself engulfed by controversy resulting from four criminal inquiries into his financial dealings. Page 24.

With the 3 R's, a C: Choice
Scores of districts and some states are allowing parents to choose public schools for their children. Page 32.

TODAY'S SECTIONS

Students in Beijing beating the driver of an armored personnel carrier after he rammed a crowd of protesters early today. The driver had been forced from the vehicle after demonstrators set fire to it.

Reuters

Demonstrators trying to pry open the hatch of an armored personnel carrier, which was later set on fire, as students attacked oncoming soldiers early today in Tiananmen Square.

Troops Smash Protests and Kill Scores

Continued From Page 1

west thoroughfare, echoed with screams this morning as young people carried the bodies of their friends away from the front lines. The dead or seriously wounded were heaped on the backs of bicycles or tricycle rickshaws and supported by friends who rushed through the crowds, sometimes sobbing as they ran.

The avenue was lit by the glow of several trucks and two armed personnel carriers that students and workers set afire, and bullets swooshed overhead or glanced off buildings. The air crackled almost constantly with gunfire and tear gas grenades.

'General Strike!'

"General strike!" people roared, in bitterness and outrage, as they ran from Tiananmen Square, which prodemocracy demonstrators had occupied for three weeks. "General Strike!"

While hundreds of thousands of people had turned out to the streets Saturday and early today to show support for the democracy movement, it was not clear if the call for a general strike would be successful. The Government had been fearful that a crackdown on the movement would lead to strikes, but its willingness to shoot students suggested that it was also capable of putting considerable pressure on workers to stay on the job.

The morning radio news program reported that it would be "very difficult" to hold a meeting of the National People's Congress standing committee as scheduled. The committee, which had been scheduled to meet June 20, has the power to revoke martial law and oversee the Government, and many members of the panel are known to be deeply upset by the crackdown.

The announcement by the Beijing news program suggested that Prime Minister Li Peng, who is backed by hard-liners in the Communist Party, was still on top in his power struggle for control of the Chinese leadership. The violent suppression of the student movement also suggested that for now, the hard-liners are firmly in control, and that those who favor conciliation, like party leader Zhao Ziyang, at least temporarily have little influence on policy.

It was too early to tell if the crackdown would be followed by arrests of student leaders, intellectuals who have been critical of the Party, or members of Mr. Zhao's faction. Blacklists have been widely rumored, and many people have been worried about the possibility of arrest.

Students and workers tried to resist the crackdown, and destroyed at least 16 trucks and 2 armored personnel carriers. Scores of students and workers ran alongside the personnel carriers, hurling concrete blocks and wooden staves into the treads until they ground to a halt. They then threw firebombs at one until it caught fire, and set the other alight after first covering it with blankets soaked in gasoline.

The drivers escaped the flames, but were beaten by students. A young American man, who could not be immediately identified, was also beaten by the crowd after he tried to intervene and protect one of the drivers.

Clutching iron pipes and stones, groups of students periodically advanced toward the soldiers. Some threw bricks and firebombs at the lines of soldiers, apparently wounding many of them.

Many of those killed were throwing bricks at the soldiers, but others were simply watching passively or standing at barricades when soldiers fired directly at them.

Two groups of young people commandeered city buses to attack the troops. About 10 people were in each bus, and they held firebombs or sticks in their hands as they drove toward lines of armored personnel carriers and troops. Teen-age boys, with scarves wrapped around their mouths to protect themselves from tear gas, were behind the steering wheels and gunned the engines as they weaved around the debris to approach the troops.

The first bus was soon stopped by machine-gun fire, and only one person — a young man who jumped out of a back window and ran away — was seen getting out. Gunfire also stopped the second bus, and it quickly caught fire, perhaps ignited by the firebomb of someone inside. No one appeared to escape.

It was also impossible to determine how many civilians had been killed or injured. Beijing Fuxing Hospital, 3.3 miles to the west of Tiananmen Square, reported more than 38 deaths and more than 100 wounded, and said that many more bodies had yet to be taken to its morgue. A doctor at the Beijing Union Medical College Hospital, two miles northeast of the square, reported 17 deaths. Beijing Tongren Hospital, one mile southeast of the square, reported 13 deaths and more than 100 critically wounded.

> 'We're doctors, but we've never seen such a tragedy.'

"As doctors, we often see deaths," said a doctor at the Tongren Hospital. "But we've never seen such a tragedy like this. Every room in the hospital is covered with blood. We are terribly short of blood, but citizens are lining up outside to give blood."

Four other hospitals also reported receiving bodies, but refused to say how many.

In addition, this reporter saw five people killed by gunfire and many more wounded on the east side of the square. Witnesses described at least six more people who had been run over by armored personnel carriers, and about 25 more who had been shot to death in the area. It was not known how many bodies remained on the square or how many people had been killed in other parts of the capital.

It was unclear whether the violence would mark the extinction of the seven-week-old democracy movement, or would prompt a new phase in the uprising, like a general strike. The violence in the capital ended a period of remarkable restraint by both sides, and seemed certain to arouse new bitterness and antagonism among both ordinary people and Communist Party officials for the Government of Prime Minister Li Peng.

'Maybe We'll Fail Today'

"Our Government is already done with," said a young worker who held a rock in his hand, as he gazed at the army forces across Tiananmen Square. "Nothing can show more clearly that it does not represent the people."

Another young man, an art student, was nearly incoherent with grief and anger as he watched the body of student being carted away, his head blown away by bullets.

"Maybe we'll fail today," he said. "Maybe we'll fail tomorrow. But someday we'll succeed. It's a historical inevitability."

On Saturday the police had used tear gas and beat dozens of demonstrators near the Communist Party headquarters in Zhongnanhai, while soldiers and workers hurled bricks at each other behind the Great Hall of the People. Dozens of people were wounded, but exact numbers could not be confirmed.

It appeared to be the first use of tear gas ever in the Chinese capital, and the violence seemed to radicalize the crowds that filled Tiananmen Square and Changan Avenue in the center of the city. The clashes also appeared to contribute to the public bitterness against the Government of Prime Minister Li.

The violence on both sides seemed to mark a milestone in the democracy movement, and the streets in the center of the city were a kaleidescope of scenes rarely if ever seen in the Chinese capital: furious crowds smashed and overturned army vehicles in front of Zhongnanhai, and then stoned the Great Hall of the People; grim-faced young soldiers clutching submachine guns tried to push their way through thick crowds of demonstrators near the Beijing train station; and the police charged a crowd near Zhongnanhai and used truncheons to beat men and women disabled by tear gas.

A Changing View of the Army

"In 1949, we welcomed the army into Beijing," said an old man on the Jianguomenwai bridge, referring to the crowds who hailed the arrival of Communist troops at the end of the Communist revolution. Then he waved toward a line of 50 army trucks that were blocked in a sea of more than 10,000 angry men and women, and added, "Now we're fighting to keep them out."

Most Chinese seemed convinced that the tanks and troops had been ordered into the city to crush the pro-democracy demonstrations once and for all. The immediate result of the first clashes was to revitalize the prodemocracy movement, which had been losing momentum over the last 10 days, and to erase the sense that life in the capital was returning to normal. But the use of tanks and guns came later,and it was not clear if they would succeed in ending the movement or would lead to such measures as a general strike.

The tension was exacerbated by an extraordinary announcement on television Saturday night, ordering citizens to "stay at home to protect your lives." In particular, the announcement ordered people to stay off the streets and away from Tiananmen Square.

"The situation in Beijing at present is very serious," the Government warned in another urgent notice read on television. "A handful of ruffians are wantonly making rumors to instigate the masses to openly insult, denounce, beat and kidnap soldiers in the People's Liberation Army, to seize arms, surround and block Zhongnanhai, attack the Great Hall of the People, and attempt to gather together various forces. More serious riots can occur at any time."

There were some reports that the Communist Party's ruling Politburo had met Friday and given the Beijing municipality the authority to clear the square and end the protests. The People's Daily and the television news on Saturday took a hard line against the unrest, and the evening news warned that "armed police and troops have the right to use all means to dispose of troublemakers who act willfully to defy the law."

> Students take buses and try to ram troops.

The clashes and enormous outpouring of support for the students were an unexpected turnaround for the democracy movement. Just a few days ago, the number of students occupying Tiananmen Square had dropped to a few thousand, and students seemed to be having difficulty mobilizing large numbers of citizens to take to the streets. The Government's strategy, of waiting for the students to become bored and go home, seemed to be leading to the possibility of a resolution to the difficulty.

Then a police van crashed into four bicyclists late Friday night, generating new outrage against the Government. One cyclist was killed instantly, and two died in the hospital Saturday, while the fourth seemed less seriously hurt.

Rumors were less meticulous about detail, and word spread early Saturday morning through the capital that four people had been killed by the police. Tens of thousands of people took to the streets to protest, and immediately found themselves confronting more than 2,000 unarmed troops who were marching toward Tiananmen Square.

The troops retreated, but that confrontation seemed to set the tone for the massive demonstrations later Saturday and early today.

Reporter's Notebook

'Please, Tell the World,' Students Beg

By NICHOLAS D. KRISTOF
Special to The New York Times

BEIJING, Sunday, June 4 — The violence against students and workers in Tiananmen Square was most obvious today, because for the most part they were the ones getting killed. But they, too, were violent against the police and army troops, although less effectively so.

Clutching iron bars and bricks, the students glared at soldiers 100 yards away on the other side of the square. It was dark, although the fire from an armed personnel carrier that students had set ablaze cast an eerie glow over part of the square, and the troops and their rows of vehicles could be dimly discerned in the haze.

From time to time, a group of them would advance on the soldiers to throw rocks and otherwise harass them. And then often, they would be shot and killed. It was an unequal competition.

Whenever the students got their chance, spotting an unarmed group of soldiers, they attacked with bricks and iron bars. However, the soldiers, most of whom had guns, tended to stick together.

Until now, students had emphasized the need for nonviolent tactics, and today some still begged their friends to put down their bricks and iron bars. But many students seemed to have crossed their personal Rubicon today, and those who previously had clutched leaflets and megaphones today picked up firebombs.

'Our Government Is Mad'

To be an American on the square this morning was to be the object of fervent hope and inarticulate pleas for help.

"We appeal to your country," a university student begged as bullets careened overhead. "Our Government is mad. We need help from abroad, especially America. There must be something that America can do."

Enraged and desperate as they saw their friends fall and crimson stains grow on their chests, students and workers rushed to any foreigner they could find to express such appeals for help. Almost nobody had any idea what the United States could do, and perhaps it was more a cry of outrage than a plea for help. But this sometimes wordless craving for an international response seemed almost universal on Tiananmen Square.

It was not that students wanted or expected foreign forces to actively intervene. Rather, it seemed to be a moral judgment that they sought, and especially the hope that the news of the bloodshed would reach the outside world and not be covered up.

Most were convinced that the Chinese authorities would never report an accurate toll of the dead and wounded, nor explain what had truly happened in the capital. The morning news programs seemed to justify their skepticism: a brief report said little more than that soldiers had successfully crushed a "counterrevolutionary rebellion."

Denied recognition at home, it became all the more important that the blood and sorrow and bitterness somehow find expression abroad. Even if it did not reverberate back home, students said, at least it could give some meaning to the sacrifices. And so they sought out foreign journalists, tugging them toward the corpses, showing them the blood on the pavement, and begging them to write about what had happened.

"You must tell the world what is happening," a long-haired university student urged, nearly incoherent with fury, "because otherwise all this counts for nothing."

Many asked that their appeals be transmitted to the United Nations, although none had a clear idea of what the United Nations could possibly do to help.

"Maybe it can discuss this situation," a student said impatiently. "Anyway, we have to do something."

Diplomats Wary

While reassurances to the rest of the world that China welcomes foreign tourists and investment presumably remain a consideration, such matters seemed to take a back seat in this morning's military crackdown.

The diplomatic quarter in Beijing was roused from slumber this morning by the almost deafening rumble of seven armed personnel carriers rolling by on the way to Tiananmen Square. Then, truckloads of soldiers arrived and, directly in front of the Jianguomenwai diplomatic compound where many diplomats live, began firing their submachine guns in the air.

In front of the Friendship Store, where tourists go to buy souvenirs, students and workers had turned over an army van and set it ablaze. In the Sanlitun diplomatic compound to the north, opponents of the Government expressed their outrage by setting a police station on fire.

In the lobby of the Beijing Hotel, undercover police officers searched photographers for film they had taken of the clashes, and one photographer was beaten when he refused to hand it over.

While there were no direct attacks on foreigners, there seemed to be a hostility in the air from the Government toward Western influences that had helped the democracy movement. Student demonstrators may appeal to Americans for help, but the Government is suggesting that Americans keep their distance.

Crackdown in Beijing

Events began Saturday afternoon; times shown are local times.

1. **2:15 P.M.** Protesters overturn and set fire to several army vehicles. Troops fire tear gas and beat dozens of protesters.
2. **4:00 P.M.** Protesters stone Great Hall of the People.
3. **6:00 P.M.** Troops in trucks are stopped by protesters. **1:00 A.M.:** Military vehicles drive through barricades, killing at least one protester.
4. **Midnight** First reports of shots fired.
5. **12:30 A.M.** Troops enter Tiananmen Square from all directions. **1:30 A.M.:** Troops fire on protesters, sending thousands fleeing.

FUCHENC RD.
FUXING RD.
LUKOUCHIAO RD.
BEIJING FUXING HOSPITAL
Beijing
Zhongnanhai Compound
CHANGAN AVE.
FORBIDDEN CITY
BEIJING UNION MEDICAL COLLEGE HOSPITAL
Tiananmen Square
BEIJING TONGREN HOSPITAL
Miles 0 2

The New York Times June 4, 1989

In the Streets, Anguish, Fury and Tears

Continued From Page 1

they had to follow orders.

"We have to obey orders because we are soldiers," said one uniformed trooper who was driving a truck. "Otherwise, we will be punished. In any case, there's no way they will order us to shoot the people."

His platoon commander was firm. "We don't fear being beaten by you people," he said as he climbed out of the truck. "We just fear that our guns will be taken and then we will have chaos." Everywhere in the vicinity of the convoy was the sound of hissing, as people let out the air from the tires of as many trucks as they could.

"Why do you have guns?" shouted one man.

"A man is not a soldier without his gun, is he?" came the reply of a soldier carrying an Ak-47 automatic rifle.

Citizens Plead With Soldiers

An old man took up the cause. "I tell you, there will be no good end for you if you follow your order loyally," he screamed as though his life depended upon it. "You have parents, you have brothers and sisters. You should not beat your fellow citizens under any circumstances."

> Some troops from other provinces practically paraded their AK-47's.

The nearly crazed citizens were climbing onto the trucks, trying to intimidate the soldier. But everywhere in the vicinity, anger was mixed with horror as the people saw how the soldiers handled their rifles and watched as several tanks pulled up.

"Is this the way Li Peng shows how martial law protects the people?" said an old man sitting on a rail.

Another young man said, "When they shoot with real bullets, it will be doomsday." Only hours later did the troops open fire.

In the afternoon, the scene near the walled-in Communist Party compound, where about 30 tear-gas bombs were released, had been the first site of violence. But now that seemed tame. A 20-minute conflict between 300 to 400 riot policemen and hundreds of citizens seemed to have galvanized the citizens. They began to believe that the Government was willing to use force — rubber bullets, broken bricks, truncheons — against the people.

Chaotic Swirl of People

"I couldn't keep my eyes open because of the dense tear gas," said Lu Baochun, a 26-year-old assistant engineer. "It was the troops that first used bricks and tiles to attack, and the citizens fought back."

Mr. Lu had rushed back out to the scene, a chaotic swirl of thousands of people darting back and forth inspecting broken bricks and glass and examining the white powder-like splotches on the street apparently from the tear gas.

"When I went into the house of a nearby citizen to wash my eyes with fresh water, I saw several children lying on their stomachs on a bed," said Mr. Lu, whose own face and neck were reddened from the gas. "They had wet towels covering their mouths, and an old woman was beside them weeping."

Reuters

Beijing residents erecting a barrier in an effort to prevent troops from marching into Tiananmen Square.

He was standing at the Communist Party headquarters shouting with rage now at the two-dozen military troops with long truncheons and green helmets, sweating in their heavy green uniforms under the pelting sun.

Some citizens gathered in small huddles around people they thought had been witnesses to the attack. Others crowded together discussing the event, many apprehensive about how far the Government would go.

"They are simply ruffians and bandits," said a young well-dressed woman who had gotten caught in the cross-fire of bricks and stones as she was on her way to the office. "They bit people just like mad dogs."

A Chinese journalist was trying to comfort her. "We are shocked," he said. "We thought that this kind of thing only happened during the reign of the corrupt Government of the Kuomintang. Yet this happened in our People's Republic. The troops and the police, they are supposed to be our brothers."

"All the News That's Fit to Print"

The New York Times

Late Edition

New York: Today, increasing clouds, windy, cool. High 54. Tonight, clearing, breezy. Low near 40. Tomorrow, mostly sunny conditions. High 57. Yesterday: High 55, low 44. Details are on page 32.

VOL.CXXXIX . . No. 48,051 · NEW YORK, SATURDAY, NOVEMBER 11, 1989 · 50 cents beyond 75 miles from New York City, except on Long Island. · 40 CENTS

JOYOUS EAST GERMANS POUR THROUGH WALL; PARTY PLEDGES FREEDOMS, AND CITY EXULTS

Agence France-Presse

East Germans pouring through a gate leading to the newly opened Berlin wall and, beyond it, West Berlin.

D'AMATO BACKED SUPPORTERS' BID FOR H.U.D. MONEY

Senator's '84 Letter Appears to Contradict Assertions He Never Urged Grants

By MICHAEL WINERIP

Senator Alfonse M. D'Amato urged the Federal Housing Secretary to approve a grant worth several million dollars for a Buffalo housing-renovation project run in part by two of the Senator's supporters, according to a newly obtained document.

In a March 15, 1984, letter written on Mr. D'Amato's Washington office stationery, the Senator asked Secretary Samuel Pierce of the Department of Housing and Urban Development to use "deliberate speed" in approving the moderate-rehabilitation grant for the 65-unit Buffalo project. Within two months the grant was approved.

The letter, marked as having been hand delivered, appears to contradict repeated assertions by the Senator that he never asked department officials to approve specific moderate-rehabilitation projects. A statement issued to The New York Times last month by the Senator's office said, "The Senator has made no contact with any officials of H.U.D. on behalf of any development or developer as it relates to mod rehab."

Links to Projects

In May 1984, when the department's Buffalo office informed local officials of the moderate-rehabilitaton grants that had won approval that year, that letter was marked "cc: Sen. Alfonse M. D'Amato." He was the only elected official designated by the department to receive a copy of its letter about the Buffalo projects.

The Buffalo matter is the most recent in a series of disclosures that have linked the Senator with department projects that benefited his family members, friends and campaign contributors and that have stretched from his hometown, Island Park, L.I., throughout New York State and to Puerto Rico. Federal prosecutors and Congressional investigators are conducting inquiries into several of these programs although Mr. D'Amato has not been identified as a subject of any inquiry.

Allegations in '85

A spokeswoman for the Senator, Zenia Mucha, said last night that the Senator "can't be expected to remember every single letter over a nine-year period." She said that when Mr. D'Amato called on behalf of projects it was "based on merit and need, and no other factors were ever considered."

The moderate-rehabilitation program, which was intended to rebuild housing for low-income people, has been a central focus of inquiries into political favoritism by the department

Continued on Page 32, Column 1

BERLIN A FESTIVAL

Communist Leadership Announces a Program of Radical Change

By SERGE SCHMEMANN

Special to The New York Times

WEST BERLIN, Nov. 10 — As hundreds of thousands of East Berliners romped through the newly porous wall in an unending celebration, West German leaders today proclaimed this the moment Germans had yearned for through 40 years of division.

At the same time, change continued unabated in East Berlin, where the Communist Party's Central Committee concluded a three-day session with the announcement of a program of radical changes. They included "free, democratic and secret elections," a "socialist planned economy oriented to market conditions," separation of party and state, parliamentary supervision of state security, freedom of assembly and a new law on the press and broadcasting.

'In the Midst of an Awakening'

"The German Democratic Republic is in the midst of an awakening," the Central Committee declared in the prologue to the newly adopted program. "A revolutionary people's movement has brought into motion a process of great change. The renewal of society is on the agenda."

Though the West Berlin police could give no estimate of the numbers of East Berliners who crossed over in the last 24 hours, the authorities said that only 1,500 so far had announced their intention to stay.

Beyond Berlin, only one of many points along the border between the two Germanys where people could cross, 55,500 East Germans crossed over the border between the two Germanys since the wall was opened on Thursday, and 3,250 remained in West Germany, the West German Interior Ministry said.

Chancellor Helmut Kohl, who interrupted a state visit to Poland to come to West Berlin, told an emotional crowd of East and West Berliners gathered outside the West Berlin city hall: "I want to call out to all in the German Democratic Republic: We're on your side, we are and remain one nation. We belong together."

Speaking on the steps of the city hall, from which President John F. Kennedy had made his "Ich bin ein Berliner" speech shortly after the wall was raised, Mr. Kohl declared: "Long live a free German fatherland! Long live a united Europe!"

Kurfürstendamm Is Packed

All through the night and through the day, East Berliners continued to flood into West Berlin in vast numbers, filling the glittering Kurfürstendamm until traffic came to a halt, forming long lines to pick up the 100-mark "welcome money" — about $55 — that West Germany has traditionally given East Germans on their first time in the West, gaping at shop windows and drinking in the heady new feeling of freedom.

A festival air seized the entire city. West Berliners lined entry points to greet East Berliners with champagne, cheers and hugs. Many restaurants offered the visitors free food. A television

Continued on Page 6, Column 1

Reuters

An East German border guard handing a flower back to West Berliners who sat atop the Berlin wall. (Detail from a scene that appears on page 7.)

Redefining Europe

As the Revelry Goes On, Politicians Ponder The Ramifications of Changes in Germany

By CRAIG R. WHITNEY

Special to The New York Times

News Analysis

WEST BERLIN, Nov. 10 — By the simple act of forcing their Communist rulers to open the Berlin wall and allow them to go wherever they wish, the people of East Germany have irrevocably changed the way Berlin, Germany and all of Europe have defined themselves for more than 40 years.

Thousands and thousands of East Berliners celebrated their triumph today by promenading up and down the elegant, tree-lined shopping boulevards of the western part of the city, which most of them had never before been allowed to see. They made the Kurfürstendamm into a street festival this evening as church bells pealed joyously into the night.

'A Different Relationship'

Willy Brandt, who was Mayor of West Berlin when the wall was built in 1961, said at a rally this evening, "The moving together of the German states is taking shape in reality in a different way than many of us expected." said . No one should act as if he knows in which concrete form the people in these two states will find a new relationship. But that they will find a relationship, that they will come together in freedom, that is the important point."

But the entire postwar European order has been based on the assumption that Germany, and Europe, would remain divided, and the countries of Eastern and Western Europe firmly anchored in their respective alliances.

In that assumption the United States, in the NATO alliance, guaranteed the security of Western Europe. And in that same assumption France, West Germany and the other major industrial countries of Western Europe began the economic and political unification of the European Community.

West German politicians, including Mr. Brandt and Chancellor Helmut Kohl, who interrupted an official visit to Poland today to fly to Berlin, all insist that West Germany's commitment to West European integration and the alliance remains.

But politicians, diplomats and business leaders all over Europe are considering new implications for both institutions now that the end of German partition is at last imaginable.

"Europe, though Europeans did not always appreciate it, has been a haven of order these past 44 years," The Economist wrote today. "For East Europeans the price of that stability has been high: a lifetime wasted under a government you loathed. For West Europeans the stability has been marvelous. They could get rich, and start to build a new unity, within a clearly defined zone which ended at the river Elbe and the Bohemian forest."

Now, a NATO diplomat in Brussels said, "The end of the wall raises questions of what's going to happen in Europe. The whole concept of the European Community now may have to change."

So would the concept of the NATO alliance, this diplomat conceded: "Our role will be to design a new role for the alliance — maintaining a balance of stability with the East while all this change is going on.

"There's a reassessment of the War-

Continued on Page 9, Column 4

U.S. ENTHUSIASTIC, BUT HAS CONCERNS

New Order in Eastern Europe Astonishes Washington

By THOMAS L. FRIEDMAN

Special to The New York Times

WASHINGTON, Nov. 10 — Like the rest of the world, Washington is scrambling to keep pace with the changes unfolding by the hour in Eastern Europe. But in contrast with the pivotal role the United States played 40 years ago in shaping the postwar European order that now seems to be coming apart, Washington finds itself more of a bystander — astonished, enthusiastic and concerned.

Twice in the last 24 hours, Secretary of State James A. Baker 3d found himself being slipped notes from aides informing him of major changes in Eastern Europe that only a week earlier no one had imagined, let alone predicted. Officials said a policy review that Mr. Baker ordered three weeks ago on how the United States should relate to changes in East Germany will have to be tossed out and begun anew.

The political changes reverberating across Europe, and the diminished threat of military conflict, also promised to stir new debate in Washington about the need for maintaining a large, expensive American military presence in Western Europe. Moving quickly to deflate such speculation, Defense Sec-

Continued on Page 8, Column 1

Bush Offers Housing Plan to Aid Poor, Homeless and New Buyers

By ANDREW ROSENTHAL

Special to The New York Times

DALLAS, Nov. 10 — President Bush today proposed a $7 billion, three-year package of housing programs and tax breaks to aid low-income families, first-time home buyers and the homeless "who live a nightmare in the midst of the American dream."

"This initiative will address the full range of housing concerns," Mr. Bush said in a speech to the National Association of Realtors here. He termed the program "a comprehensive agenda to help bring basic shelter and affordable housing within reach of millions of Americans."

The three-year program would provide mortgage assistance for low-income families and tax breaks for first-time buyers, but it does not include money for building new public and low-income housing units, which some advocates for the homeless regard as essential. Instead, it seeks to generate additional housing units through a variety of means that Republicans have been urging.

For example, a major element of the proposal involves matching grants to local authorities and nonprofit organizations for the acquisition of property and the rehabilitation of housing units.

Democratic legislators, advocates of low-income housing and spokesmen for the housing industry praised it as signaling a new interest in housing problems after years of relative inattention during the Reagan Administration. But several said the level of financing was insignificant compared to the needs of the homeless or people in substandard housing.

Jack F. Kemp, the Secretary of Housing and Urban Development, said the program was directed more toward stimulating the low-income housing industry than directly subsidizing individual purchases.

In announcing the plan, Mr. Bush

Continued on Page 13, Column 1

INSIDE

The Debate on Child Care

Deep divisions have emerged in Congress over how much money should be spent on child care and who should benefit. Page 12.

Over 30 and Unmarried

Researchers whose study saw poor marriage prospects for well-educated women over 30 omit those findings in a revised paper. Page 10.

Warnings From Koch

He didn't exactly criticize David N. Dinkins, but the Mayor made it clear that he and his successor differ on many important issues. Page 29.

Chairman to Leave Ford

Donald E. Petersen, who led the company from a financial crisis to record profits, plans to retire. Page 35.

Bulgarian Chief Quits After 35 Years of Rigid Rule

By CLYDE HABERMAN

Special to The New York Times

SOFIA, Bulgaria, Nov. 10 — Todor I. Zhivkov, Eastern Europe's longest-serving leader, resigned today as Bulgaria's President and Communist Party leader, after 35 years of guiding the country with old-line orthodoxy.

Mr. Zhivkov, 78 years old, was immediately replaced as the party's General Secretary by his longtime Foreign Minister, Petar T. Mladenov, who is viewed here as likely to take a somewhat more flexible approach toward economic and political restructuring. It will be up to the politically weak National Assembly to choose his successor as President.

Since Mr. Zhivkov and other top officials recently began to talk about the need to separate state and party roles, it seemed possible that someone other than Mr. Mladenov could be selected.

Mr. Zhivkov's resignation came as a surprise but not as a total shock to Western diplomats, who said that the Bulgarian leader had apparently fallen victim to the fast-paced changes elsewhere in Eastern Europe.

Bulgarian officials reportedly said in confidence that Mr. Zhivkov did not want to stay too long and risk being forced from power in disgrace, as were Janos Kadar of Hungary or Erich Honecker of East Germany.

There were strong rumors of more shifts to come in top party echelons, but the state press agency and television network made no announcements. The prospects for genuine change here, several diplomats said, are likely to be determined by the extent of any future shake-up.

Doubts on Rapid Change

Mr. Mladenov, who is 53 and was Foreign Minister for 18 years, wasted no time as the new leader in warning that "there is no alternative to restructuring" Bulgaria's struggling economy and tightly controlled political apparatus. The present system has "handicapped progress in our society in all spheres," he told the party Central Committee, adding: "We have to turn Bulgaria into a modern, democratic and lawful country."

Despite his words, however, many

Continued on Page 9, Column 4

Agence France-Presse

Todor I. Zhivkov

Clamor in the East: 'The Wall Is Gone!'

Thousands of Germans standing on the Berlin wall facing East German border guards near the Brandenburg Gate yesterday, the first full day of the opening of the border.

Agence France-Presse

The Border Is Open

East Germans Pour Through Frontier; Party Pledges Freedoms and Berlin Exults

Continued From Page A1

station urged West Berliners to call in with offers of theater tickets, beds, dinners or just guided tours of the "Ku'damm."

The Hertha soccer club, popular both in West and East, offered 10,000 free tickets to the game against Wattenscheid on Saturday.

Both West and East German television gave saturation coverage to the reunion, often under titles like "The End of the Wall," contributing to a widespread sense that a great moment was in the making.

In a development that gave further evidence of the figurative crumbling of the wall, East Germany announced the opening of five new crossings. One was at the Glienicke Bridge, famed as the site of past exchanges of captured spies between East and West, and another was at Potsdammer Platz, once the heart of Berlin.

The arrival of an army bulldozer at Eberswalder Strasse to drill another new opening quickly attracted a crowd on both sides and sent rumors through the city that the East German Army was breaking down the wall. When the machine finally broke through, West Berliners handed flowers to the driver and rushed to pick up pieces of the wall for souvenirs.

At the Potsdammer Platz crossing site, West Berliners mounted the wall to chip away pieces while East German workers laid paving stones in the no-man's land, watched by about 50 soldiers.

The East German authorities also announced that bus shuttles would connect East and West Berlin.

In the giddiness of the grand reunion, German reunification was in the air. "We've done it! The wall is open!" proclaimed the popular tabloid Bild in a giant headline. "This is the first step to unity."

The conservative Frankfurter Allgemeine tempered its excitement with caution: "Since Thursday evening that monstrous construction and barbed wire no longer divide the people. But with the joy over the end of the torment of German division, we must realize that faster German rapprochement needs a faster consideration of how politically to handle a situation changing by the hour."

A group of young men walked down the Kurfürstendamm with the two German flags, identical save for a Communist emblem at the center of the East German banner, sewn together.

The theme was there, too, in the emotional speeches from the steps of city hall. Willy Brandt, the former West German Chancellor who was West Berlin's Mayor in 1961 when the wall was raised, declared in a choked voice: "This is a beautiful day after a long voyage, but we are only at a way station. We are not at the end of our way."

"The moving together of the German states is taking shape in reality in a different way than many of us expected," Mr. Brandt said. "No one should act as if he knows in which concrete form the people in these two states will find a new relationship. But that they will find a relationship, that they will come together in freedom, that is the important point."

'Happiest People on Earth'

Walter Momper, the Mayor of West Berlin, raised cheers when he declared: "The whole city and all its citizens will never forget Nov. 9, 1989. For 28 years since the wall was built we have yearned for this day. We Germans are now the happiest people on earth. Yesterday was not yet the day of reunification, but it was a day of reunion."

The West German Foreign Minister, Hans-Dietrich Genscher, who returned with Mr. Kohl from Poland for the gathering, opened his address by recalling his roots in East Germany, from which he fled after the war.

"My most hearty greetings go to the people of my homeland," he said. "What we are witnessing in the streets of Berlin in these hours is that 40 years of division have not created two nations out of one. There is no capitalist and there is no socialist Germany, but only one German nation in unity and peace."

Evidently anticipating the anxieties of other countries, Mr. Genscher added: "No people on this earth, no people in Europe have to fear if the gates are opened now between East and West. No people have to fear that liberty and democracy have returned to the G.D.R."

Kohl Gets Loud Jeers

Mr. Kohl was met by loud jeers from the crowd, evidently reflecting his unpopularity among many West Berliners, as he declared this "a historic moment for Berlin and for Germany."

The Chancellor appealed to East Germans to stay in their country now that it was evidently firmly on the road to political and economic change. "We are sure that when these reforms come to pass, and if the G.D.R. goes forward on this path, our compatriots there who now think of leaving will stay in their homeland," he said.

Mr. Kohl flew from West Berlin to Bonn, where he will preside over an emergency Cabinet meeting on Saturday morning before returning to Poland to continue his official visit.

Krenz Addresses Party Rally

In East Germany, the conclusion of the Central Committee meeting was followed by a mass rally of Communist Party members that was addressed Egon Krenz, the new party leader.

"We plan a great work, a revolution on German soil that will bring us a socialism that is economically effective, politically democratic, morally clean and will turn to the people in everything," Mr. Krenz declared.

"That's why the Council of Ministers issued new travel regulations for all mature citizens in our country as an expression that we are serious in our policy of renewal and that we reach out our hands to everyone who wants to go with us," he said.

The "action program" adopted today, Mr. Krenz said, was "a program for our people to win back trust among the people."

"We want better socialism, we want free elections, we want our people to send their best representatives to Parliament," he said.

Mr. Krenz also reaffirmed his loyalty to Moscow, as he has taken care to do since he came to power. "Our close links to the Soviet Union make us strong, and give new meaning to our slogan, that to learn from the Soviet Union is to learn to win, especially in these days," he said.

3-Day Session a Turning Point

The action program outlined by the official press agency A.D.N. followed the proposals first made by Mr. Krenz on the opening day of the Central Committee meeting. The three-day meeting proved a turning point in the dramatic upheaval that has seized East Germany over the last month.

The Central Committee issued only broad directives for change. On the economic front, it called for making the planned economy sensitive to market conditions, though it did not elaborate how this would be done. With an eye to the most widespread complaints, it said the economy would concentrate on areas such as consumer goods, meat, beer and spare parts.

The proposed election law promised to be the most fateful of the new measures. The West German radio said Hans Modrow, the new Prime Minister, had discussed with Mr. Krenz the possibility of forming a coalition government with some of the small parties, including the Social Democrats and the Liberals.

Mr. Modrow said the action program of the Communist Party would not be enough without the input of the other parties, which have become more independent and vocal over the last month.

Ousted Leaders Censured

The Central Committee also strongly censured Erich Honecker, the fallen party leader, and two Politburo members ousted with him, Günter Mittag and Joachim Hermann. "The Central Committee has learned that serious mistakes of the previous General Secretary and Politburo led the party and republic into deep crisis," the final communiqué of the session said.

The committee reserved its sharpest criticism for Mr. Mittag, who had been the secretary charged with the

Thousands more cross over. 'Long live a united Europe!'

economy. "Comrade Mittag was excluded from the Central Committee because of the gravest violations of inner-party democracy, against party and state discipline and because of damaging the reputation of the party," it said.

The program also called for approval of freedom of assembly, legalization of new political organizations, a constitutional court and changes in criminal law to include independent juries. It also said the party would immediately take measures to lift privileges held by party leaders.

It declared, too, that military policy would be publicly discussed, and that military spending might be reduced.

The program is expected to come under more detailed discussion when Parliament meets on Monday.

Jubilation in Berlin

A Day for Celebrations And a Bit of Shopping

By FERDINAND PROTZMAN

Special to The New York Times

EAST BERLIN, Nov. 10 — Church bells pealed, long-separated friends and family members fell into each other's arms, people wept for joy and complete strangers pressed money into newcomers' hands or offered them rides to wherever they wanted to go.

It was a day that made an indelible imprint on Berlin's collective memory. Hundreds of thousands of East Berliners crossed into West Berlin today, according to police estimates.

"The mood is just fantastic," said a woman from East Berlin. "The West Berliners have been wonderful to us. I thank them all." The East Berliners, coming from a land where nearly all prices are kept artificially low by subsidies, were also greeted by price-tag shock.

'But Cheap It's Not'

"It's all quite lovely," said a young woman from Rostock, as she gazed at the display window of a women's clothing store on the Kurfürstendamm,

'We won't be closed again. The people will not allow that.'

West Berlin's main street and the city's toniest shopping area. "But cheap it's not."

The sky was a high, clear blue and the "Berliner Luft" — the air of Berlin, that is lauded by natives for its invigorating qualities — overcame the usual pollution and lived up to its reputation. It rang with the sounds of celebration.

The city center of West Berlin became a giant festival grounds, forcing police to ban auto traffic because of the press of pedestrians. Some restaurants gave out free food and drink. Bottles, cans and broken glass seemed to be everywhere.

'Now We Know the Way'

"The wall is gone!" Those slightly hyperbolic words were uttered countless times here in the last 24 hours, by people in both sides of the city. Although the forbidding concrete barrier still stands, it has fallen in the minds of East and West Berliners alike.

"I knew as soon as I heard the news on the radio last night what it meant," said Stani, a 19-year-old East Berliner, as he jostled for position in a West Berlin subway packed with East Germans on their way to celebrate on the Kurfürstendamm. "There is no turning back from this now. Allowing people to travel freely is a step that our Government can never retract. We won't be closed in again. The people will simply not allow that. Now we know the way here."

The celebration Stani and five of his schoolmates were going to join in grew throughout the day as more and more East Germans arrived in the West, many for the first time in their lives. What began late Thursday evening as a trickle of the curious, cautiously testing their Government's newly announced promise of free travel to the West, turned to a torrent today.

Police Stop Counting

Police officials on both sides of the increasingly porous border simply stopped counting the East Germans who were crossing into West Berlin. Their best estimate was that hundreds of thousands had done so. West Berliners did not flock to the eastern half of the city, however, preferring, perhaps, to celebrate on their home turf.

Throughout the day, people poured through the border crossing points. As factories, schools and offices in East Berlin closed in the late afternoon, masses of people began moving in one direction — the border.

By 5 P.M. the Bornholmerstrasse border crossing point in the northeast section of the city was a sea of humanity. There were no formalities. Border guards on both sides merely waved the throng through and tried to direct traffic as best they could. A stream of East Berliners of all ages, walking seven abreast and stretching about 1,000 yards from end to end, filed across the border. They passed into West Berlin through a 60-yard-long gauntlet of cheering, whistling and applauding West Berliners. Autos and motorcycles were also lined up, and they honked their horns and flashed their lights as they crossed.

A 10-year-old boy, walking across with his parents and little brother, was nonplussed. Looking up at dozens of West Berliners shouting greetings as he stepped onto West German soil, he doffed his baseball cap, threw his arms in the air and cried, "Hello, fans." The crowd burst into laughter.

Home From the Store

A few feet away, a counterflow of thousands of other East Berliners headed home, many carrying plastic bags from West Berlin supermarkets and department stores. Their purchases, often made possible by the 100 marks of "greeting money" — about $55 — provided by the West German Government, range from groceries and cosmetics to used washing machines and satellite dishes.

There were block-long lines of East Germans at banks throughout West Berlin, where the money was given out. In an unprecedented step for a place with the most rigid business hours in Western Europe, West Berlin banks will be open on both Saturday and Sunday for East Germans wishing to pick up cash.

"We went in about midnight Thursday," said a 22-year-old East Berliner, sitting with her husband in their Soviet-built Lada as they waited in a line of cars to cross back into East Berlin at Bornholmerstrasse. On the backseat was a hand-painted Japanese fan, which they had purchased today.

The couple spent the night with the woman's grandmother in West Berlin, then drove around the city shopping and just looking. While they had been allowed to visit the city twice previously to see the woman's grandmother, they said today was different.

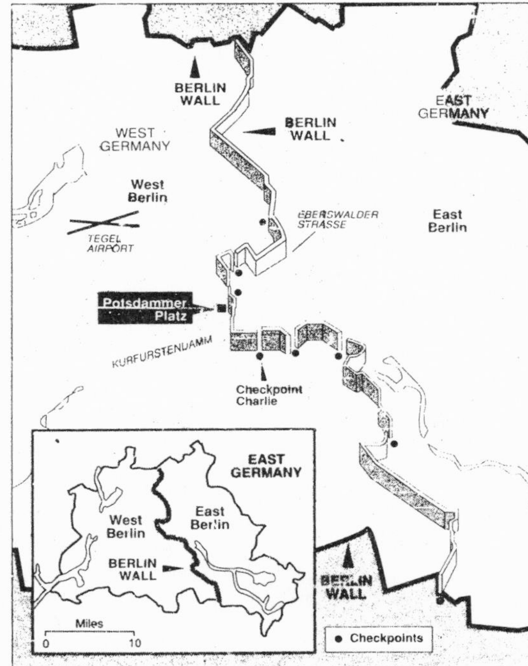

East Germany announced the opening of new crossings, including one at the Potsdammer Platz, once the heart of Berlin.

Lining Up for Visas

Where Brutality Reigned, The Police Turn Mellow

By FERDINAND PROTZMAN

Special to The New York Times

EAST BERLIN, Nov. 10 — At the Immanuel Kirchstrasse Police precinct in East Berlin's Prenzlauer Berg district, thousands of East Germans lined up today to receive visas allowing them to travel freely to the West.

By midafternoon, some 3,000 people were in front of the station. They drank from thermoses, chatted with the uniformed officers, and listened to news and music from the radios that neighborhood residents had placed on window sills for their benefit.

Exactly one month ago, a very different lineup took place in the courtyard behind the same police station. A group of East Berliners, who had been arrested at a rally calling for reforms, were brought here for interrogation. They were forced into the courtyard. Some were beaten and the protesters were then ordered to stand all night against the walls.

It is a measure of how fast, and how far, changes have come, that some of the same officers involved in that incident were stamping identity cards with exit visas Friday.

"We've been open since 8 A.M., and we will be open until all these people have gotten the exit stamp," said a captain of the People's Police, motioning to about 70 people who were still waiting late in the day. "What do I think of all this? I think it's a good thing."

When the station opened up this morning the mood was far from friendly. The police were requiring people to fill out visa application forms in meticulous and time-consuming detail. As the movement of the line slowed, the mood of those waiting grew restive and tense.

Eventually, the police commander announced that identity papers would be stamped and that no more forms would have to be filled out. Immediately anxieties vanished.

"It was taking too long," the police captain said later. "We told everyone that they could have the visa right away, without filling out the form. We like doing this. It's good to have people smile at you again. After what happened one month ago they wouldn't look at us."

"All the News That's Fit to Print"

The New York Times

Late Edition
New York: Today, light snow, becoming partly sunny. High 38. Tonight, clear, breezy late. Low 30. Tomorrow, partly cloudy, windy. High 49. Yesterday: High 48, low 32. Details, page C8.

VOL.CXXXIX . . . No. 48,144 NEW YORK, MONDAY, FEBRUARY 12, 1990 — 50 cents beyond 75 miles from New York City, except on Long Island. — 40 CENTS

MANDELA, FREED, URGES STEP-UP IN PRESSURE TO END WHITE RULE

SPEECH IS RESOLUTE

He Asks Other Nations Not to Lift Sanctions Against Pretoria

Reuters

Nelson Mandela leaving Victor Verster prison yesterday after spending 27 years in South African jails.

By CHRISTOPHER S. WREN
Special to The New York Times

CAPE TOWN, Feb. 11 — After 27 and a half years in prison, Nelson Mandela finally won his freedom today and promptly urged his supporters at home and abroad to increase their pressure against the white minority Goverment that had just released him.

"We have waited too long for our freedom," Mr. Mandela told a cheering crowd from a balcony of Cape Town's old City Hall. "We can wait no longer."

"Now is the time to intensify the struggle on all fronts," he said. "To relax our efforts now would be a mistake which generations to come will not able to forgive." [Transcript of the address, page A15.]

First Speech Since '64

Mr. Mandela's 20-minute speech, which he prepared before leaving prison today, constituted his first remarks in public since before he was sentenced in June 1964 to life imprisonment for conspiracy to overthrow the Government and engage in sabotage.

He asked the international community not to lift its sanctions against South Africa, despite the recent changes introduced by President F. W. de Klerk, which culminated in Mr. Mandela's release.

"To lift sanctions now would be to run the risk of aborting the process toward ending apartheid," he said.

An Eloquent Militancy

Mr. Mandela's voice sounded firm and his words as eloquently militant as when he defended violence as the ultimate recourse at his political trial in 1964. Though he looked all of his 71 years and was grayer than artists' renditions over the years had depicted, he walked out of Victor Verster prison erect and vigorous.

In Washington, President Bush rejoiced over the release of Mr. Mandela, spoke to him by telephone and invited the anti-apartheid leader to visit the White House. [Page A17.]

Mr. Mandela gave no evidence that his militant opposition to apartheid had been tempered by the more than 10,000 days he spent in confinement. But he also said nothing that would have surprised the Government had he said it during his years of incarceration. Indeed, there appeared to be nothing in Mr. Mandela's initial remarks after his release to give the Government much consolation or encouragement.

Although he has been viewed as a potential leader for all South Africans, he stressed time and again that his loyalty lay with the African National Congress, for which he was working under-

Continued on Page A14, Column 1

On Mandela's Walk, Hope and Violence

By JOHN F. BURNS
Special to The New York Times

PAARL, South Africa, Feb. 11 — When Nelson Mandela made his walk to freedom today, he did it with the same simplicity and command of occasion that made him a leader among millions of South African blacks when his imprisonment began more than 10,000 days ago.

At 4:14 P.M. on a sun-warmed day — 27 years, six months and one week after his arrest on Aug. 5, 1962 — Mr. Mandela stepped from the car that drove him to the last guard post at the Victor Verster prison.

From there, smiling gently, he passed under a raised barrier and flicked his right hand quickly out from his body in greeting. He then raised his right arm several times in the bolder, black nationalist salute, his left hand holding the hand of his wife, Winnie, and walked to the point where the prison entrance road abuts the highway running through the undulating wine country of the Western Cape.

It was a walk of perhaps 70 yards, through a corridor of policemen, and as he made it, Mr. Mandela said not a word, at least none that could be heard by any in the crowd of 5,000 blacks and whites chanting his name. But to those who have come to know Mr. Mandela in the only way that was possible under the total ban that the South African Government threw around the black leader in prison — through his speeches and writings of a generation ago — there was no mistaking the symbolism involved in beginning his life outside jail on foot.

About the time in 1961 when President John F. Kennedy was spending his first summer in the White House, Mr. Mandela, then about the same age as Mr. Kennedy, used a phrase that became the title of a book of Mr. Mandela's speeches and writings. The book has been passed hand to hand in dog-eared copies among South Africans, who were forbidden until today under censorship laws and statutes governing political prisoners to own any book by or about the black leader. There was, Mr. Mandela said, "no easy walk to freedom" for South African blacks after three centuries of white domination and repression.

Dignified and Resolute

The Nelson Mandela who made his own walk to freedom today, after more than 22 years in the fortress prison on Robben Island, in the gale-swept mouth of Cape Town harbor, and five more years in a series of other prisons, had hair that had turned to gray. He looked at least 30 pounds lighter than he had at his last public appearance, in June 1964 when, with the physique of the heavyweight boxer he had been in his youth, he stood in the dock at the Rivonia Trial in Johannesburg and acknowledged that he was guilty as charged of sabotage and attempting to overthrow the Government.

But in other respects, the 71-year-old

Continued on Page A14, Column 1

Agence France-Presse

A South African youth celebrating Nelson Mandela's release yesterday at an African National Congress rally in Soweto. Mr. Mandela urged supporters to increase their pressure against the white Government.

U.S. INVITES IDEAS FROM THE SOVIETS ON STRATEGIC CUTS

AN ADMINISTRATION SHIFT

Moscow's Earlier Suggestions on Reducing Nuclear Arms Have Been Spurned

By MICHAEL R. GORDON
Special to The New York Times

WASHINGTON, Feb. 11 — In a shift of position, the Bush Administration has told Moscow that it is now prepared to receive Soviet proposals about reductions in long-range nuclear arms that go beyond the emerging strategic arms treaty, Administration officials disclosed today.

Until recently, the Bush Administration has rebuffed Moscow's suggestions that the two sides open discussions on a possible second arms treaty that would make deeper reductions in long-range nuclear weapons, like ocean-spanning ballistic missiles, cruise missiles and bombers, than does the arms treaty now under negotiation.

But Secretary of State James A. Baker 3d told Soviet leaders in Moscow last week that the Administration is now ready to entertain new Soviet ideas on what sort of subsequent reductions in long-range nuclear arms should be carried out after the current Strategic Arms Reduction Talks are concluded.

Thinking of 'Next Phase'

"Up to now we have not been willing to discuss the Soviet ideas on Start-2 on the ground that we still have work to do on Start-1," said a senior Administration official. "Now we are saying you can raise your ideas if you want to. We are getting to the point where we need to think a little bit about the next phase."

The question of whether to seek further reductions in long-range nuclear weapons after an agreement is reached has been a contentious one for the Bush Administration. Some Administration officials, like the White House national security adviser, Brent Scowcroft, have argued that reductions in nuclear weapons should not be pursued for their own sake, and the Administration has yet to formulate a basic position of what additional cuts in long-range nuclear arms, if any, might be sought.

The treaty currently under negotia-

Continued on Page A11, Column 1

The Price of Peace

Movements that fought in the trenches of the cold war are flushed out as peace breaks out in Central and Eastern Europe. Page A10.

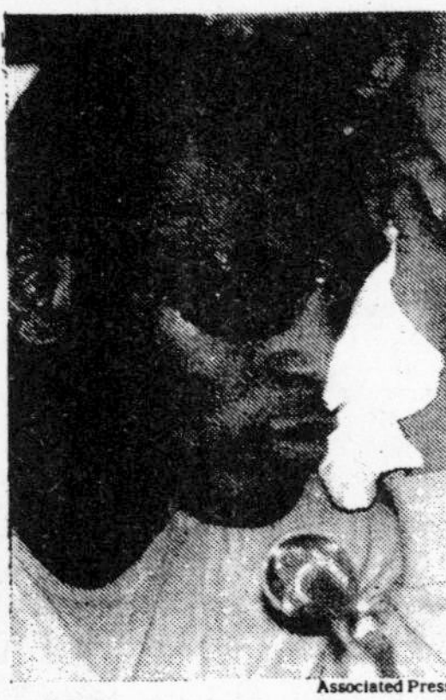

Associated Press

Mike Tyson applying a cold towel to his swollen eye during a news conference after the fight.

Boxing Officials Could Overturn Defeat of Tyson

By PHIL BERGER

James (Buster) Douglas knocked out Mike Tyson this weekend and won the world heavyweight championship in one of the greatest upsets in boxing history. But Douglas's victory in Tokyo may be undone by a rancorous dispute over a long count on Tyson's knockdown of Douglas in the eighth round.

Two of boxing's major governing bodies, the World Boxing Association and the World Boxing Council, suspended the result of the fight yesterday pending hearings into the controversy. The third major group that recognized Tyson as the champion, the International Boxing Federation, said it now considers Douglas to be the champion.

Tyson's corner had protested that Douglas received a long count, and, according to the W.B.C., a formal protest was later lodged by Japanese boxing authorities.

The result of the bout, fought Sunday in Tokyo (Saturday night in the United States), could ultimately be determined by the political and legal wrangling of the governing bodies as well as the considerable influence of Tyson's promoter, Don King.

Tunney-Dempsey Recalled

But this much is clear: By dominating the fight and knocking out the undefeated and seemingly invincible Tyson in the 10th round, Douglas, a relative unknown, shocked the sports world. And he also apparently upset the carefully laid plans for Tyson's boxing future, including a projected $22 million payday for a title defense against Evander Holyfield in June.

The knockdown in dispute, recalling the famous long count in the 1927 Gene Tunney-Jack Dempsey title fight, occurred after Tyson, battered by Douglas for most of eight rounds, connected on a right uppercut to Douglas's jaw that sent the challenger backward to the canvas.

Referee Octavio Meyran Sánchez leaped to Douglas's side and, after a pause, began counting with his fingers

Continued on Page C4, Column 5

Bush Homeless Plan: 'Godsend' or False Hope?

Federal Aid, New York Homeless

A special report.

By JASON DePARLE

On the night of Sept. 25, 1988, a previously obscure piece of Federal legislation was ushered onto political center stage before a television audience of millions.

During the season's first Presidential debate, a panelist asked George Bush what he would do for the homeless, "this voiceless segment of our society."

Mr. Bush answered without hesitation. "I want to see the McKinney Act fully funded," the Republican candidate said.

The McKinney Act?

The reference hardly resonated in the living rooms of America. Most viewers had never heard of the McKinney Act, and Mr. Bush's terse answer offered virtually no basis on which to judge it.

But Mr. Bush has kept his word. Last year, at his urging, Congress came close to fully financing most McKinney programs for the first time since the act was passed in 1987.

And the legislation remains a central provision of the Administration's plan for helping the homeless. As recently as last month, Mr. Bush pointed toward funds from the McKinney Act in telling a convention of home builders in Atlanta that "my Administration is going to do its part" in working to "solve the problems of the helpless and the homeless."

$67 Million for New York

The act itself is a quiver of 16 programs, each taking a different aim at homelessness. Some of the programs support shelters, with food or funds. Others provide services like job training, health care or treatment for alcohol or drug abuse.

The funds approved last year are likely to raise New York State's share to about $67 million, from $45 million. Because the money filters through a variety of governments and private organizations, it is impossible to determine how much of it is spent in New York City.

But despite the McKinney Act's broad aims and the recent increase in financing, many of those who provide shelter and services to the homeless say the McKinney Act falls short in at least these three respects:

¶It provides relatively little money.

¶It creates daunting bureaucratic obstacles.

¶And it provides almost no funds for low-income housing, which advocates argue must be part of a solution to homelessness.

"It's much ado about nothing," said Douglas H. Lasdon of the Legal Assistance Center for the Homeless in Manhattan. "It gives people the impression that something's being done, but it's not."

Measured in paint or plaster, protein or pajamas, the law has made a difference in the lives of dozens of New York organizations. Some money from the act, named for Representative Stewart B. McKinney, a Connecticut Republican

Continued on Page B8, Column 1

Rural Doctor's Struggle to Care for the Poorest

By PETER APPLEBOME
Special to The New York Times

TCHULA, Miss. — There aren't many doctors like Ronald Myers, a jazz-playing, Baptist-preaching family practitioner whose dream has always been to practice medicine in the kind of place most other doctors wouldn't even stop for a tank of gas.

But there are plenty of places like Tchula, a forlorn patch of Mississippi Delta poverty where it is hard to find a street that's not rutted, a sign that's not crooked, a paint job that's not peeling or a life that's not perched on the brink of economic ruin.

Dr. Myers's story — how hard it has been for him to get here and how hard it may be for him to stay — provides a dispiriting look at health care in rural America. The situation is worsening because the Government's program to provide doctors for the nation's neediest areas is being dismantled as health care needs continue to grow.

"Working in Tchula, Miss., is like working in a third world country," said Dr. Myers, who became Tchula's only doctor when he opened a clinic this month in an abandoned restaurant next to an empty liquor store. "The needs are that great. So how is it that here's a well-trained physician who wants to come to an area that's desperately poor, and I can't get any assistance? I can't get a loan. I'll take a tongue depressor if someone will give me one. There's a problem somewhere."

In poor rural areas, particularly in the South, regular medical care is seldom more than a distant dream. In areas like Tchula and nearby Belzoni, where Dr. Myers previously worked, infant mortality rates are three times the national average, most women receive little if any prenatal care and people usually see a doctor only when they have no choice.

"The health problems in this area

Continued on Page B11, Column 1

INSIDE

Not Quite Watchdogs Yet
Across Eastern Europe, the once mighty official press is in even bigger trouble than the Communist parties it has praised for so long. Some papers have fallen into oblivion. Others are hoping for independence. Page A12.

A Turn in the Drug War?
In what experts hope is a turning point, the crime rate in and around Washington, D.C., is growing more slowly, and the number of suspects testing positive for cocaine use has dropped in recent months. Page B9.

Crisis Among Counselors
As the problems they confront grow more serious than those of 20 or even 10 years ago, guidance counselors in New York schools remain heavily overloaded. Page B1.

Checking-Account Bonus
Some banks are giving customers insurance that automatically protects goods bought by check against damage or loss and extends manufacturers' warranties. Page D1.

South Africa's New Era: One Man's Walk to Freedom

Mandela, Freed, Urges Rise In Pressure on White Rule

Continued From Page A1

ground when he was jailed in August 1962 on charges of incitement and leaving the country illegally. He was serving time on that conviction when he was sentenced to life imprisonment in 1964.

Mr. Mandela told a crowd that he remained a "loyal and disciplined member" of the African National Congress and still endorsed its policies, including its use of armed struggle against the white minority Government.

He said he saluted the congress's military wing, Spear of the Nation, and its ally, the South African Communist Party, "for its steady contribution to the struggle for democracy."

But he also thanked the Black Sash, an organization of white women working to end apartheid, and the predominantly white National Union of South African Students for being "the conscience of white South Africans." And he held out an olive branch to all whites, asking them to join in shaping a new South Africa.

'A Political Home'

"The freedom movement is a political home for you, too," he said.

In his first speech after his release, Mr. Mandela may have taken an orthodox line with a mass audience sympathetic to the African National Congress and might in private discussions show greater flexibility on the question of discussions that the Government wants to have with blacks, who are 28 million of the population, compared with the 5 million whites of the ruling minority.

He said he was only making some preliminary comments following his release, and would have more to say "after I have had the opportunity to consult with my comrades." By this he meant the leaders of the African National Congress now in exile in Zambia as well as colleagues still based in South Africa.

But he appeared to discourage any leading role for himself, such as the Government has in mind, saying, "A leader of the movement is a person who has been democratically elected at a national conference."

De Klerk Offers Talks

President de Klerk has invited black leaders to join talks leading to the formulation of a new constitution that would let black South Africans take part at last in their nation's politics.

Mr. Mandela acknowledged to the crowd that he had conducted a dialogue with the Government during his last years in prison. But he added: "My talks with the Government have been aimed at normalizing the political situation in the country. We have not yet begun discussing the basic demands of our struggle."

"I wish to stress that I myself have at no time entered into negotiations about the future of our country, except to insist on a meeting between the A.N.C. and the Government," he said.

He described Mr. de Klerk, whom he has met twice since December, as "a man of integrity."

"Mr. de Klerk has gone further than any other Nationalist President in taking real steps to normalize the situation," Mr. Mandela said.

Still a 'Harsh Reality'

"But as an organization we base our policy and strategy and tactics on the harsh reality we are faced with," he said. "And this reality is that we are still suffering under the policies of the Nationalist Government."

The National Party, which Mr. de Klerk now leads, instituted apartheid after taking power in 1948.

Mr. Mandela said the Government had to take further steps before negotiations could begin.

As a prerequisite for negotiations, he reiterated two demands that he had conveyed from prison through recent visitors. These are are the lifting of the state of emergency, which was imposed in June 1986, and the release of all political prisoners, including those accused of crimes committed in the struggle against apartheid.

"Only such a normalized situation which allows for free political activity can allow us to consult our people in order to obtain a mandate," Mr. Mandela said.

He said the people had to be consulted about who would represent them in talks with the Government.

Democratic Election Urged

"Negotiations cannot take place above the heads or behind the backs of our people," he said. "It is our belief that the future of our country can only be determined by a body which is democratically elected on a nonracial basis."

Mr. Mandela appeared to allude to a formula under which a constituent assembly, in effect supplanting the existing Parliament, would draft a new constitution. Such a plan would mean the creation of an interim government in South Africa and has previously been rejected by Mr. de Klerk for the foreseeable future.

Mr. Mandela walked out of Victor Verster Prison near Paarl at 4:15 P.M., 75 minutes later than the release time announced Saturday afternoon by Mr. de Klerk. Acquaintances of the Mandela family said his departure from the prison was delayed by family discussions.

He was greeted by about 5,000 supporters lining the asphalt road outside the prison farm where he has been held since December 1988. Some waved the black, green and yellow flags of the African National Congress, from which Mr. de Klerk removed a ban on Feb. 2.

Mr. Mandela was then driven 40 miles from Paarl to Cape Town, passing several hundred people who had parked by the roadside or waited on overpasses in hope of seeing him. They held homemade signs, some of which read simply, "Welcome home."

A huge crowd, which organizers said reached 250,000 people, assembled in the square in front of the old City Hall in Cape Town to greet Mr. Mandela. Reporters covering the rally put the crowd's size at only 50,000 people at its peak. They became impatient and sometimes unruly, waiting up to six hours in the hot sun and had dwindled to about 20,000 by sunset, when Mr. Mandela finally appeared.

Blacks a Minority in Area

In the 1950's it was Government policy to prevent blacks from settling in the Western Cape, so they are not in the clear majority in Cape Town, where Mr. Mandela was released. People of mixed race, known as "coloreds," are the largest population group in Cape Town, where whites also outnumber blacks.

Blacks, who account for nearly 75 percent of the population in the country as a whole, are in the overwhelming majority in the Johannesburg region, where Mr. Mandela can expect his most tumultuous welcome.

The festive occasion was marred by violence after some youths who had been drinking on the fringes of the rally started breaking windows and looting shops in downtown Cape Town.

The police tried to disperse them by firing shotguns and tear gas, and some of the youths retaliated by throwing bottles and stones. At one point, drunken protesters invaded a Chinese restaurant, snatched up the liquor and wine and threw bottles at the police from the rooftop. One man in the crowd was also injured in a knife fight.

Two Reported Killed

The South African Press Association reported tonight that 2 people had been killed and 13 wounded in the confrontations. A physician treating casualties on the scene estimated that 100 people had been wounded, mostly by buckshot. Most suffered only light injuries, including three journalists covering the rally.

Cheryl Carolus, a spokeswoman for the United Democratic Front, which helped organize the rally, attributed the violence to outsiders who, she said, were "beyond our usual crowds, or who supported the rival Pan-Africanist Movement.'"

At times, some supporters at the rally had to scramble for cover as the police chased or fired at looters and stone-throwers. The Rev. Allan Boesak, a prominent figure in the anti-apartheid movement, pleaded for more than 45 minutes with the crowd to maintain discipline and move back.

Dullah Omar, a lawyer representing the Mandela family, said Mr. Mandela had been unaware of the violence.

Due in Johannesburg Today

This evening, Mr. Mandela failed to appear at a news conference arranged by the reception committee that is handling his schedule. A representative said Mr. Mandela would meet the press later this week in Johannesburg.

Mr. Mandela and his wife, Winnie, are expected to fly to Johannesburg on Monday and proceed to their home in the black township of Soweto.

One of the organizers, Saki Mocozoma, said security considerations precluded him from revealing where the Mandelas were spending their first night.

Mr. Mandela also paid tribute to his wife, who has lived apart from him for more than 27 years, and their children. "I am convinced that your pain and suffering was far greater than my own," he told them.

Associated Press

Nelson Mandela and his wife, Winnie, saluting supporters yesterday in Cape Town after Mr. Mandela was released.

Parliament
Cape Town City Hall
CORPORATION ST.
DARLING ST.
STRAND ST.
Grand Parade
Police Station
PARADE ST.
BUITENKANT ST.
HARRINGTON ST.
The Castle
Atlantic Ocean
VICTOR VERSTER PRISON
Paarl
ROBBEN IS. PRISON
Cape Town
Athlone
POLLSMOOR PRISON
Miles 0 10
Pretoria
SOUTH AFRICA
Cape Town

The New York Times/Feb. 12, 1990

A few hours after his release from Victor Verster Prison, outside Paarl, Nelson Mandela spoke on the steps of Cape Town City Hall.

'Power!' 'It Is Ours!'

At the start of his speech in Cape Town yesterday, Nelson Mandela led the crowd in a chant that has become a regular feature of anti-apartheid gatherings in South Africa. He led the chant in his native language, Xhosa, each time receiving a response in Xhosa from the crowd. Here is how the exchange went:

Mandela: Amandla! (Power!) pronounced ah-MAHN-dlha.

Crowd: Ngawethu! (It is ours!) pronounced ntsa-WEH-too.

Mandela: Amandla!

Crowd: Ngawethu!

Mandela: i-Afrika! (Africa!) pronounced ee-AH-free-ka.

Crowd: Mayibuye! (Let it come back!) pronounced mah-yee-BOO-yeh.

Mandela: Mayibuye!

Crowd: i-Afrika!

Mandela Steps Back Into a South Africa of Strife but of New Hope as Well

Continued From Page A1

black leader who emerged from prison today to the ecstatic salute of millions of his fellow countrymen and of much of the world seemed unchanged from the man whose closing address in his own defense in 1964 has become one of the central documents in the South African struggle.

As always before, he was erect and dignified, immaculately dressed in a dark-grey suit tailored for him in Cape Town during his closing weeks in prison. And above all, he was resolute — resolute in his opposition to any accommodation with apartheid, and just as resolute in his insistence that blacks in South Africa have always preferred a peaceful settlement with whites to one rooted in violence.

No black man in South Africa has had as wide an audience as Mr. Mandela had tonight when he stepped to the microphone on the steps of Cape Town's Victorian City Hall, watched live by tens of millions of television viewers in countries including the United States, Australia and Japan, and, in a delayed but uncensored broadcast, on South Africa's Government-owned television service. It was an occasion Mr. Mandela used to the full, beginning, in a strong, unquavering voice, with the first word he had uttered in public — "Amandla!" meaning power in the Xhosa language, the rallying cry of the black resistance — since the speech at his trial.

Need for Armed Struggle

To anybody who wondered whether Mr. Mandela had compromised during his three years of secret talks with the Government, the black leader gave a blunt answer. As in 1964, he offered no compromise on the principle of majority rule, calling for the creation of "a democratic, nonracial and unitary South Africa."

Perhaps most jarring to many whites, he said that "the factors which necessitated" the African National Congress's resort to guerrilla attacks in 1961, under his own leadership, "still exist today," so that the congress had "no option but to continue."

He also demanded what he called "a fundamental restructuring" of the economy, a phrase many whites will take to signal an intention to nationalize mines, banks and major industries.

But along with those strictures, Mr. Mandela showed the same strong preference for a peaceful solution, the same appreciation for whites who are prepared to join blacks in dismantling apartheid, and the same confidence that his cause will triumph that he showed at his trial.

Associated Press

Violence marred the Mandela celebrations in Cape Town yesterday as a group of African National Congress supporters ran through the streets breaking shop windows and clashing with the police.

Using the phrase he coined last year when he met with the former President, P. W. Botha, and later with the current President, F. W. de Klerk, Mr. Mandela said that he hoped that "a climate conducive to a negotiated settlement" would allow the African National Congress to abandon its armed struggle. He referred to Mr. de Klerk, who watched the televised replay of the speech at the presidential mansion half a mile from City Hall, as "a man of integrity," and he added: "Our march to freedom is irreversible."

But as Mr. Mandela looked out at the crowd of 50,000 people in front of the City Hall, a few blocks from Mr. de Klerk's office, and in the two and a half hours he spent conferring inside the building with black leaders who accompanied him on the 40-mile motorcade from the prison, he was confronted with dismaying evidence of the uphill struggle that lies ahead of blacks in the contest to wrest power.

For three hours, police officers along Darling Street, in front of City Hall, and across the maze of streets and pathways around the Grand Parade that lies across from the municpal building, fought running battles with black youths, including at least three who were shot dead by the police with shotguns.

What prompted most of the police action, if not all of it, were gangs of black youths smashing windows of cars and shops, and looting clothing, toys, and alcohol, an action that was followed in many cases by the tossing of full or half-full bottles of wine, spirits and beer off rooftops toward ranks of policemen.

Tear Gas and Ambulances

But the result was that Mr. Mandela, and the worldwide television audience, were exposed to the sounds that have made South Africa's image in the world for 40 years — the crack of tear-gas canisters being fired, the blast of shotguns and the whine of ambulance sirens, some of it during the black leader's 25-minute speech.

How Mr. Mandela reacted to any of that was unknown, since the black leader's aides canceled a news conference that was to have ended his day. But one remark he made, an appeal at the end of his speech for all attending the rally to disperse without doing anything that "will lead others to say that we can't control our own people," suggested his chagrin.

Earlier, aides suggested that being suddenly confronted with realities outside prison might be taxing for the anti-apartheid leader. Although he has been moved between prisons, and from the prisons to hospitals, and in and out of Cape Town for his meetings with Mr. de Klerk and Mr. Botha, most of his trips over the years have been at night.

The aides' suggestion came at the prison during a 75-minute delay in Mr. Mandela's scheduled release. Cheryl Carolus, a 33-year-old high-school teacher who is spokeswoman for the Mandela family, said that Mr. Mandela had completed the signing of official documents related to his release earlier in the day but needed an extra hour at a bungalow inside the prison grounds with his wife, two daughters and old friends from his Robben Island days, before emerging into what Ms. Carolus called "a situation that is going to be quite perplexing at the personal level."

Whites and Blacks Line Route

With many South Africans, whites as well as blacks, inclined in recent weeks to see Mr. Mandela as a colossus who can somehow resolve the nation's political problems, it was a reminder that what lies ahead would be daunting for any man, let alone one who has spent more than a quarter of a century largely cut off from the world.

Something of that may have been on Mr. Mandela's mind when he referred in Cape Town to his "long and lonely years in prison," when he said that "no individual leader" can dismantle apartheid, and when he insisted that there could be "no exception" to the rule that political leaders must be legitimized by elections among their followers.

Still, much of what the black leader did see in his first hours of freedom may have encouraged him. Everywhere — outside the prison, along the route into Cape Town, at the rally — there were large numbers of whites among the blacks, far more proportionally than he would have seen during his days as a lawyer in Johannesburg in the 1950's.

Mandela's Prison Memories

Some moments on the trip seem sure to have been emotionally charged. As six white motorcycle policemen led the Mandela motorcade into Cape Town's suburbs, the travelers had their first glimpse of the Atlantic Ocean. There, bathed in the sunshine of the late afternoon was Robben Island, the former leper colony five miles offshore where Mr. Mandela was taken first after a trial in 1962, and then held for 21 years, after his life sentence in 1964.

But the sight of the island may also have prompted feelings other than regret. Because of Mr. Mandela's efforts to educate other prisoners, the island became known among its inmates — all of them blacks, Asians or of mixed race — as "Mandela University." And the black leader ended his time there with at least one strong friend among the white warders, a warrant officer named Gregory, who said farewell to Mr. Mandela at the Victor Verster prison this morning.

Mr. Mandela got glimpses of extraordinary scenes outside the prison during the hours before his release. In an unprecedented scene, the 200 white policemen and an equal number of khaki-uniformed marshals assigned to the scene by the African National Congress — many of them young men and women who have spent months and years in detention — cooperated through long hours in the sun in their efforts to maintain crowd control. When Mr. Mandela appeared, all semblance of order collapsed, but it was not for want of efforts by the two sides.

As the police and marshals conferred in the center of the road, sometimes laughing together, conversations with blacks revealed that many of them, like Mr. Mandela, see no reason why whites and blacks cannot ultimately live together in peace.

"This is very nice, this is very right," said Rev. Vuyani Mtini, a 33-year-old minister from Mbekweni, the black township outside Paarl who wore peacock-blue shorts and a "Free Mandela" T-shirt. "I hope that Mr. Mandela will stop all these fightings and moanings among us, and take out that thing of whites and blacks not respecting each other politically."

"All the News That's Fit to Print"

The New York Times

Late Edition
New York: Today, some light rain. High 66. Tonight, patchy dense fog. Low 54. Tomorrow, clouds, then some sun by afternoon. High 72. Yesterday, high 64, low 44. Details are on page 27.

VOL.CXXXIX . . . No. 48,234 NEW YORK, SUNDAY, MAY 13, 1990 — $1.50 beyond 75 miles from New York City, except on Long Island. — $1.25

Some Computer Conversation Is Changing Human Contact

By JOHN MARKOFF

Patricia Gemmell met Brian Dear by replying to a friendly note that appeared on her computer screen one day, a message sent on a computer network linking her machine with many others. She responded with a computer quip of her own and the two, who were programmers at different campuses of the University of Maryland, struck up a friendship that went on electronically for weeks before they finally met. Two years later, they were married.

"It's a fascinating way of making friends," Mr. Dear said.

The city of Santa Monica, Calif., opened a computer network last year so that people could weigh in, without charge, from computers in their homes or offices, with comments about local council meetings. This electronic equivalent of an 18th-century town meeting has proved enormously popular. "There would be a near-revolution if we thought about taking it down," said John Jalili, the City Manager.

Changes at Work and Home

William H. Gates, chairman of the Microsoft Corporation, runs his company largely through a computer network that can be used by most of the software maker's 5,200 employees. Decisions from product plans to changes in vacation policy are debated and then announced on the network. Anyone is free to send a message to Mr. Gates, who receives and dispatches hundreds of electronic notes a day. Within the next five years or so, he predicts, "most corporations will flip over to this kind of system."

The growth of computer networks is changing the way millions of Americans work, find friends, seek entertainment and even govern themselves.

The New Printing Presses

Enthusiasts, like Ithiel de Sola Pool, the late Massachusetts Institute of Technology political scientist, have declared that "networked computers will be the printing presses of the 21st century." Robert Lucky, executive director of research at Bell Laboratories, notes that computer networks often become electronic communities that give people thousands of miles apart the feeling of being connected in a small village, with all the intimacy and ease of communication that implies.

Known as "electronic bulletin boards," "computer conferences" or "electronic mail" exchanges, these networks are made up of computers linked by telephone lines and equipped with software that allows them to send and receive messages. The programs permit a group of people to carry on an extended discussion by typing in messages that can be read by all members of the group.

The first computer networks

Continued on Page 20, Column 1

Soviet Economy: A Shattered Dream

Perestroika in Crisis: The Failing Reforms

First of two articles.

By BILL KELLER

Special to The New York Times

MOSCOW, May 12 — During last Saturday's soccer match between Spartak and Dynamo Kiev, television viewers were presented with a uniquely Soviet half-time entertainment: an interview with a presidential economic adviser, Stanislav S. Shatalin.

Mr. Shatalin is the newest addition to Mikhail S. Gorbachev's team of economic pitchmen, and his message was the very latest in Kremlin doctrine.

"The market," Mr. Shatalin urged the soccer fans, cooly proffering a concept synonymous here with cruel capitalism. No need to fear the market, he was saying. It won't hurt you.

Timetable Not Available

Mr. Gorbachev has not made clear how and how soon he wants the country to be on a market economy. But after five years of failed economic nostrums, most of them aimed at preserving the rough outlines of Communist central planning, the Kremlin is turning in desperation to the very idea that Communism was intended to replace — an economy driven by the self-interest of buyers and sellers rather than by the dictates of state planners.

What has forced the Kremlin toward a market policy is the realization that the more conventional reforms of the collapsing economy that Mr. Gorbachev inherited when he came to power in 1985 have all failed to remedy the consumer desperation that threatens the country's stability, and have all failed to remedy the technological backwardness that endangers its superpower status. Halfway measures have in some ways even made the feeble economy worse.

Grave Questions Face Nation

Whether the fascination with the market will mean a breakthrough in practice and whether Mr. Gorbachev has the nerve to let free prices and competition run riot in this backward society are perhaps the gravest questions confronting the Soviet Union in the coming months.

"Now everyone agrees that we have to introduce a market system," Mr. Shatalin, a member of Mr. Gorbachev's Cabinet, said in an interview this week. The timing and mechanics, he said, are still being debated, but "the choice is made."

The impact of the economic collapse on consumers has been a combination of insult and injury.

For the big cities, which is where planners themselves live, the shortages have meant longer lines and endless grousing.

For the provinces, which get lower priority, they have meant rationing cards for meat, milk, butter and other staples.

For the poor, the pensioners and for those who live in the neglected rural

Continued on Page 12, Column 1

Peter Marlow/Magnum

At a large textile factory near Ulyanovsk, Soviet women work with antiquated machinery under the watchful eye of Lenin.

Insulting Gorbachev: A Crime?

The Soviet Parliament moved to adopt criminal penalties, including prison terms, for public remarks insulting President Mikhail S. Gorbachev or his policies. Page 10.

U.S. SHOWS DOUBTS ABOUT GORBACHEV AND FUTURE PACTS

BAKER IS DUE IN MOSCOW

Ability of the Soviet President to Conclude Agreements on Arms Is Questioned

By THOMAS L. FRIEDMAN

Special to The New York Times

WASHINGTON, May 12 — More than at any time since President Bush took office, a deep sense of uncertainty has settled over the Administration about President Mikhail S. Gorbachev's prospects for success and his ability to conclude the broad range of Soviet-American arms-control agreements sought by Washington.

Secretary of State James A. Baker 3d leaves for Moscow on Monday for a final round of negotiations with Soviet leaders that should determine whether the May 30 summit meeting between Mr. Bush and Mr. Gorbachev will be a boon or a bust for Soviet-American relations.

Mr. Bush announced a new effort to help Eastern Europe today, saying he would try to export his "thousand points of light" through a new Citizens Democracy Corps to strengthen the emerging democracies. [Page 10.]

Prepared for the Worst

Administration officials still hope that major progress in arms control is possible, but they are prepared to come home empty-handed.

A number of factors have left Administration officials wondering how much power or inclination Mr. Gorbachev has to conclude the far-reaching nuclear, conventional and chemical disarmament agreements that Washington hoped would be largely completed by the time of the summit meeting. Those factors include recent shifts in his relationship with his military establishment, the turmoil in the Baltic republics, the weakening of the Soviet economy and the possibility of a split at a scheduled July congress of the Soviet Communist Party.

Bush Administration officials are already trying to diminish expectations, apparently seeking to cushion the negative publicity if this week's trip goes badly, and to make any breakthroughs appear that much more dramatic.

U.S. Setting a Later Scenario

"It is not the end of the world if you don't conclude these agreements now," a top Administration policy maker said. "If we don't do it at this summit, we will have plenty of other things to discuss. If these arms control agreements make sense for both sides, they will emerge at some point."

Nevertheless, American officials are complaining about Mr. Gorbachev's "foot dragging" and asking themselves whether he will sign treaties

Continued on Page 10, Column 2

Dinkins, the Volume Up

In a Speech on Race, the Mayor Responded To Complaint That He Hadn't Said Enough

By TODD S. PURDUM

New Yorkers long used to a vocal white mayor some had blamed for racial tensions were suddenly grappling last week with a quiet new black mayor some blamed for not doing more to ease the turmoil.

News Analysis

Faced with a spate of disparate racially charged incidents, Mayor David N. Dinkins was also confronting a test of the very image that helped elect him as New York's first black mayor — that of a healer who could hold together the fractious city he calls a gorgeous mosaic. He set the challenge the day after a black teen-ager was shot to death in predominantly white Bensonhurst last August, saying, "The tone and climate of this city does get set at City Hall."

Now, with two juries weighing the Bensonhurst case and blacks boycotting two Korean-American groceries in Flatbush, Mr. Dinkins has been hearing conflicting advice as well as criticism. Former Mayor Edward I. Koch, the Brooklyn judge presiding over the grocery dispute and a range of others have questioned the tone Mr. Dinkins had set, saying he should have been more vocally and visibly involved.

Implicit in much of the criticism was a suggestion that because of his reputation and his race, Mr. Dinkins should have particular power to resolve disputes like the one between a manager and a black customer that led to the boycott of the groceries.

"I think it is true that some feel that any involvement that has as one of its components African-Americans, that I'm supposed to have some especial ability to sway," he said at one point last week. "In this particular circumstance involving these particular people, my judgment at the moment is it would not assist" to go to the store and cross the picket line.

"Some people think that confrontation is superior to conciliation," he said Thursday. "I disagree."

'A Different Style'

But also implicit in the criticism was an impatience with the Mayor, a sense that he may have swung so far toward conciliation as to have created the impression of inaction. "Everybody for a long time would have been accustomed to precisely what Ed Koch said he would do," said Simon P. Gourdine, general counsel for the National Basketball Association's Players Association. "That simply would have told people where Mayor Koch stood on the

Continued on Page 24, Column 1

Bensonhurst Jury Stuck

The jury in the trial of Keith Mondello said it had decided some counts but was unable to reach agreement on other charges. The judge told the jurors to keep trying. Page 24.

New Political Realities Create Conservative Identity Crisis

By ROBIN TONER

Special to The New York Times

WASHINGTON, May 12 — After a decade of Republican Presidents, years that saw many of the most cherished conservative precepts enshrined in policy, the conservative movement itself is in the midst of an identity crisis, trying to redefine its causes and goals for the 1990's.

The leaders and many of the issues that sustained the movement for 30 years have receded. Communism seems in retreat; domestic issues long championed by liberals, like poverty and the environment, have risen on the public agenda, and the White House is no longer the charismatic voice of the conservative movement that it was in the Reagan Administration.

"There is a lot of ferment, and perhaps just as importantly there is the lack of a horse to ride," says Gary Bauer, a former domestic policy adviser to President Ronald Reagan who now heads the Family Research Council, a Washington organization that lobbies for traditional family values. "From 1960 on, there was Barry Goldwater as some future hope, and then later there was Reagan. Now, there is not one individual who is clearly seen by all elements of the movement as someone they would unite behind."

A Variety of Conservatives

There are many varieties of conservatives who think of themselves as part of "a movement" that came to power with the election of President Reagan. Some were principally motivated by the social and moral agenda of the religious right, some by the conviction that American foreign policy had weakened and foundered in the 1970's, and some by the passion to cut taxes and reduce the powers of the Federal Government.

Conservatives also have widely differing constituencies: some remain ardent foot soldiers in the trenches of advocacy groups, while others are in Congress and the Administration, trying to balance the movement with a variety of other political demands.

Some theorists on the right say the movement is struggling with the transition from being outsiders to

Continued on Page 20, Column 1

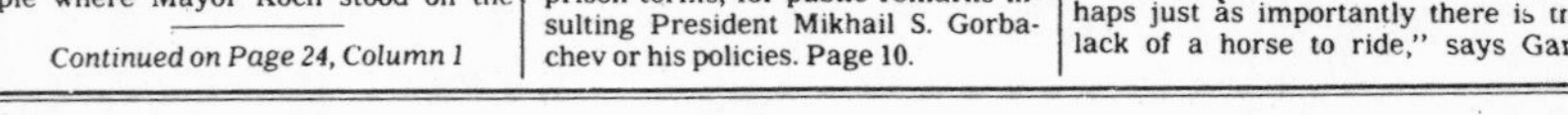

Abortion Foes' Centers Guiding Lives After Births

By MICHAEL deCOURCY HINDS

Special to The New York Times

PHOENIXVILLE, Pa., May 12 — In a day care center here, far from the abortion clinics where demonstrators march with photographs of fetuses, opponents of abortion are changing diapers, wiping toddlers' noses and leading choruses of "The more we get together, the happier we'll be."

"This is the pretty face of the right-to-life movement," said Dorothy A. Ireton, director of the nonprofit center Mom's House, which is affiliated with the Delaware Valley Pro-Life Alliance.

Even those on the other side of the fence agree that those who oppose abortion have created centers that provide unwed mothers with support, including baby clothes, career counseling, legal assistance and housing.

Afterward: Education and Jobs

Homes for unwed pregnant women have a long history in the United States, and foes of abortion have actively sponsored them. But most of the new centers go a step further, providing services for the mother long after she has given birth and offering opportunities for education and jobs. This new wave of homes is intended to help women get their lives back in order, but the way back is not just an avenue for proselytizing.

Hundreds of these organizations have arisen since the Supreme Court in 1973 established a woman's constitutional right to choose abortion. Many centers began in churches or community buildings; almost all draw on the vast reservoir of abortion foes who are willing to donate time, goods and money to their cause.

Some groups offer social services along with talking women out of having abortions, but all of them help mothers whether or not they have contemplated having an abortion.

Kate Michelman, executive director of the National Abortion Rights Action League, said: "It is very important to have programs and services that do in fact insure that women facing a crisis pregnancy have real options. If they are serving women without any ideological coercion, that is nothing but good."

Mom's House is a modest stucco building that was once a Roman Catho-

Continued on Page 22, Column 3

Mark Lyons for The New York Times

Patty R. Keating lives with her 2-year-old daughter, Kasi, at Madonna House in Newport, Ky., a support center for unwed mothers.

Chile Agrees to Pay Reparations to U.S. In Slaying of Envoy

By ROBERT PEAR

Special to The New York Times

WASHINGTON, May 12 — The new Government of Chile agreed in principle today to pay compensation for the killing of Orlando Letelier, a Chilean exile leader assassinated in Washington 14 years ago.

Chilean and American officials said the two countries had reached an agreement to create an international tribunal to determine the amount of compensation. Chile would make payments to the United States Government, which has said it would give the money to relatives of Mr. Letelier and Ronni Moffitt, a co-worker of Mr. Letelier's who was also killed when their car was bombed on Sept. 21, 1976.

Mr. Letelier served as Chile's Ambassador to Washington and as Foreign Minister when Salvador Allende Gossens, a Socialist, was President of Chile in the early 1970's. After Mr. Allende was overthrown in a coup led by Gen. Augusto Pinochet in 1973, Mr. Letelier took up residence in Washington to press for sanctions against the military Government.

Officials said the payments would be made without any admission of Chilean Government liability. The United States offered such payments to the families of the hundreds of people killed when an American warship shot down an Iranian passenger plane over

Continued on Page 9, Column 1

INSIDE

TODAY'S SECTIONS

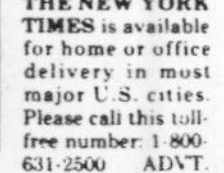

'Talking' by Computer: A New Kind of Contact

Continued From Page 1

appeared two decades ago. But their rapid growth in recent years has magnified their impact, extending far beyond the scientists, engineers and amateur computer enthusiasts who were once the main users. The broader use has been made possible by new software and the surge in personal computers in America, now estimated at 40 million, compared with fewer than a million in 1980.

Today, the many groups using computer networks are as diverse as the work forces of multinational companies like the International Business Machines Corporation, followers of the Grateful Dead rock band and Chinese students organizing protests against the Beijing Government's crackdown on the democracy movement. Indeed, thousands of specialized networks now cater to a huge variety of interests, including those of comedians, cooks, travelers, recovering alcoholics, sports fans, homosexuals, wine lovers, retirees and Go players. Over the computer they get acquainted, trade anecdotes and exchange and debate ideas.

The growth of these electronic communities is difficult to measure precisely, but by all accounts the increase has been striking in the last few years. At work or at home, there are several million Americans now

Quick and easy in ways that phones and letters are not.

using computer networks of some kind, and their numbers continue to grow rapidly, computer specialists say.

International System Emerging

There are large collections of computer networks, like the Internet, with an estimated two million members, and Usenet, with more than a million users, that now form the backbone of an emerging international system. These big groupings are partly paid for with Federal funds and fees paid by companies.

In addition, there are many commercial networks, which are typically linked to Internet and Usenet. For example, Compuserve, a nationwide electronic conference and information service, now has 550,000 members and is adding 8,000 a month. An independent network, the Prodigy Services Company, a joint venture between I.B.M. and Sears, Roebuck & Company, has grown from 160,000 subscribers last October to 381,000 today.

Besides the costs of a personal computer and telephone charges, subscribers often pay fees ranging from several dollars a month to several dollars an hour. Networks advertise in computer magazines usually, but also in some newspapers. Still, most people who join networks learn of them from friends or colleagues at work or school. Users can sign up in a variety of ways, from writing in to to calling a designated toll-free telephone number.

The sociological impact of computer networks is a matter of much debate, and the evidence so far is mainly anecdotal. Still, it seems beyond doubt that the effect of this new generation of electronic communication will be significant. Simply put, the computer network allows many people to communicate with many others who might be anywhere in the world. It provides for participation quickly and easily in a way that letters, telephones and television do not.

Yet the spread of computer networks also raises troubling possibilities. Some adolescents, for example, seem to find computer communication so easy and captivating that they spend hours a day at the keyboard, perhaps retarding the development of face-to-face social skills.

Computer networks can also pose ethical issues, especially in matters of personal privacy and access to a network. These issues surfaced recently in a political dispute in Colorado Springs, after it was learned that the mayor had been reading the electronic messages that City Council members had been sending each other.

Widening Scientific Research

Still, the benefits of the electronic networks seem to insure their continued growth. For example, the networks have allowed the creation of groups whose members would never have worked together before.

More than 200 physicists on three continents, most of whom have never met, are participating through a shared computer network in large high-energy physics experiments at the Fermi National Accelerator Laboratory in Batavia, Ill. The scientists can share the task of software development for their experiments by passing prototype programs back and forth electronically. Over the network they can also share data generated by the accelerator.

"I still remember as one of those transition moments of my life the day when the first message appeared on my screen," said Tom Nash, an experimental physicist at Fermi in Illinois, recalling a communication from a physics research laboratory in Switzerland. "I remember the feeling that my horizon had just popped to twice its former size."

More Effective Conferences

In other cases, computer networks have enhanced the work of existing groups that used to rely on newsletters and academic journals. More than a quarter of the 383,000 employees of I.B.M. around the world take part in electronic conferences on specific subjects, from product development to computer languages.

To participate, the employees simply call up the conference on the computer screen adding their own comments. For example, a conference may deal with making semiconductor chips. If a production problem surfaces in one of I.B.M.'s three chipmaking plants in Burlington, Vt., Sindelfingen, West Germany, or Yasu, Japan, scientists from all three locations discuss the difficulties and possible solutions on the computer network.

"Problems get solved in minutes that might otherwise never get solved," said Michael Connors, the director of computing systems for I.B.M. Research.

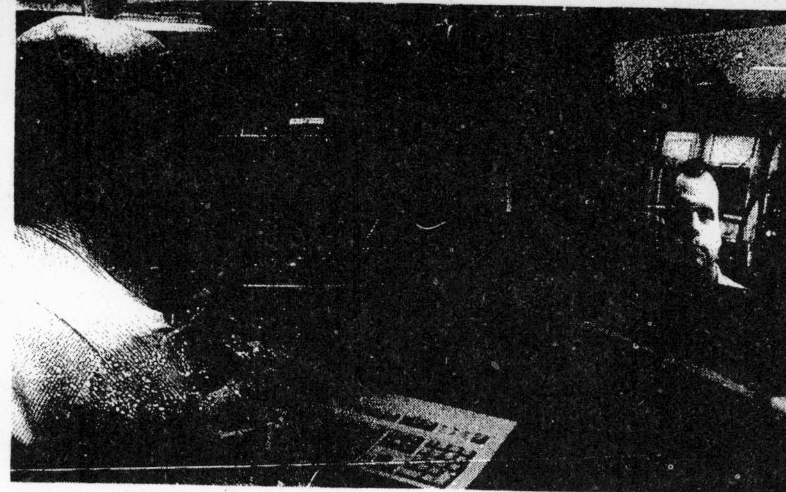

Eddie Hausner/The New York Times

The growth of computer networks is changing the way millions of Americans work, find friends and seek entertainment. Some computers, like the one being used by Dr. Robert W. Potts at the Bellcore Corporation Laboratories in Morristown, N.J., allow voice, visual and written communication.

Alan Decker for The New York Times

Brian and Patricia Dear, who met after sending messages to each other on a computer network at the University of Maryland, demonstrating a network they have developed in San Diego.

In some corporate and government organizations, computer networks have been found to improve communications. For example, a Rand Corporation study of two groups of employees at the Los Angeles Department of Water and Power found that a group that could exchange messages on a computer network worked together more closely and became better friends than a group that could only meet in person or talk on the phone.

Other studies have found that the ease with which electronic messages are sent between office computers encourages lower-level workers to contact their superiors, and vice versa — much along the lines that Mr. Gates of Microsoft described.

For entertainment, "interactive" electronic games played over computer networks may someday displace television cartoons or situation comedies, some social scientists say, by satisfying a human need to participate. "There is a general craving to make it happen, to be a part of it and not to sit back and watch it all," said Gary T. Marx, a sociologist at M.I.T.

Interactive games are already in use; hundreds of people using Commodore 64 personal computers around the country each control a different cartoon character in an animated computer game called Club Caribe, developed by Lucasfilms, the San Rafael, Calif., entertainment production company.

As if in an electronic doll house, the participants can choose among various "rooms" by pressing various keys. In one room, for example, the stage is set for a nightclub in which a participant plays a stand-up comedian and tries out jokes on others. Many experiments in advanced television systems now under way involve developing this kind of ability for home television sets.

Use for Political Ends

Computer networks are also being used for political ends. Chinese students used the Internet network to help organize protests outside China after the crackdown on protesters in Tiananmen Square in June.

"White power" and neo-Nazi extremist groups in the United States have exploited the anonymity and secrecy of inexpensive electronic bulletin boards to schedule clandestine meetings and plan activities.

For people with shared leisure interests, computer networks provide what traditional clubs cannot: the ability to participate whenever one has the time rather than at a scheduled time and the ability to join with those of like interest around the world.

"You can find exactly the people who share your passions," said Rob Fulop, president of Interactive Productions, a Foster City, Calif., software design house.

$1 MILLION IS GIVEN TO BOY WITH AIDS

Judge Rules That Negligence by Navy Surgeon Led to a Tainted Transfusion

Special to The New York Times

PROVIDENCE, R.I., May 12 — The Federal Government has been ordered to pay more than $1 million to a 12-year-old boy who contracted AIDS from blood transfusions after a tonsillectomy at a Navy hospital. His mother was awarded almost $250,000 for his medical expenses.

Federal District Judge Ernest C. Torres determined that a surgeon at the Newport Naval Hospital, Richard Busch, was negligent in his treatment of the boy after taking out the child's tonsils in 1983.

"The plaintiff is a young boy who has been deprived of the opportunity to live out most of his life," said Judge Torres in a decision handed down May 9. "The court recognizes that no amount of money could adequately compensate him for that aspect of his loss and acknowledges being deeply touched by the tragedy that has befallen this youngster."

The boy is expected to die within two years, according to testimony at the nonjury civil trial. For privacy reasons and "the stigma associated with AIDS," the boy's lawyer, R. Daniel Prentiss, and the Justice Department would not identify the child or his mother or say whether they still live in Rhode Island. He is identified only as John Doe in court papers.

Dr. Busch, who is no longer a Navy doctor, was not a defendant; the suit was filed against the Government, as his employer. Government lawyers and Mr. Prentiss said this week that the surgeon was now in private practice on the West Coast and last known to be in California.

Guidance Is Sought

The Government has 60 days to appeal the ruling. Everett Sammartino, an assistant United States attorney, said guidance was being sought from Washington.

After the tonsillectomy, the boy, then 5 years old, suffered numerous episodes of heavy bleeding and needed several transfusions at the Navy hospital and later at Children's Hospital in Boston. Judge Torres said "the facts strongly suggest" that the blood contaminated with the AIDS virus was administered to the boy at Children's Hospital. But the judge determined that if Dr. Busch had taken better care of the boy, the boy would probably not have needed transfusions.

A witness presented by the Government testified that fewer than 1 percent of all tonsillectomy patients require blood replacement.

No suit was filed against Children's Hospital because Mr. Prentiss said "the negligence was not a failure to detect contaminated blood that was administered to the boy, but the medical treatment that caused the successive transfusions."

Cause of AIDS Was Not Known

Government lawyers had argued that the Government should not be held liable because the human immunodeficiency virus was not identified as the cause of AIDS until 1984 and tests to determine its presence were not licensed until 1985.

Judge Torres awarded the boy $1,029,895 for pain and suffering and his mother $246,229. The mother's money covers unreimbursed medical bills of $63,897 as well as $182,332 for the medical treatment her son is likely to require. The boy is no longer covered by health insurance, for reasons not revealed at trial.

The boy's mother and several psychiatrists testified that he was extremely apprehensive about dying and felt guilty about the burden he had placed on his mother for his care. Judge Torres also said in the decision that the boy was very self-conscious about a prominent scar on his neck and feared that the scar might reveal the fact that he had AIDS and would cause him to be ostracized by other children.

In calculating the damages awarded the boy, Judge Torres said, "While all of us live with the knowledge of our own mortality, few of us know it to be so imminent or are reminded of it as frequently and as emphatically as the plaintiff."

Change in Political Landscape Creates Identity Crisis for Right

Continued From Page 1

being insiders, from simply opposing liberal programs to proposing conservative solutions to problems that the public wants addressed, like the environment.

"Conservatism is in the process of evolving from an opposition movement to a governing movement," said Representative Newt Gingrich, the Republican whip in the House. "We won the argument from '65 to '85 that *they're* dumb."

Bush Is Seen as Retreating

The restiveness on the right is fed by what many see as a number of retreats by President Bush from conservative doctrine, from his cautious approach to the Soviet crackdown in Lithuania to his new willingness to discuss higher taxes.

"If there's one thing that can bind the conservative movement together, if it's not the threat of the Soviet Union, it would be George Bush reneging on the one campaign pledge that everyone remembers and that really distinguished conservatives from liberals," said Stuart Butler, an analyst at the Heritage Foundation, the influential conservative research organization.

The debate in conservative circles goes beyond how to deal with the White House. For years the movement was largely defined by a fierce anti-Communism. Now, as Edwin J. Feulner Jr., president of the Heritage Foundation, recently wrote, "In an era when even many Communists have turned anti-Communist, anti-Communism is no longer enough to unify and energize conservatives."

'Missiles Are Still Aimed'

They have hardly abandoned their wariness toward the Soviet Union. Howard Phillips, chairman of the Conservative Caucus, a Washington advocacy group, is sending out fund-raising letters warning, "Soviet missiles are still aimed at our homes and families," and urging people to "stop Secretary Baker and the Washington establishment" from "sending welfare to the Communists."

But many analysts say it is time for conservatives to redirect their attention to the domestic agenda as international tensions ease. "It's clear that having won the cold war and having won the intellectual battle against collectivism, we now have to win new battles against less cosmic problems here at home," said James P. Pinkerton, deputy assistant to the President for policy planning.

A Shift in Direction

Mr. Pinkerton has been espousing "a new paradigm" for American politics, an approach to meeting social needs while abiding by the fiscally restrained, anti-big-government philosophy of the conservatives. It is an attempt to meet two of Mr. Bush's campaign promises that many Democrats say are fundamentally at odds: "a kinder, gentler nation" and "no new taxes."

Mr. Pinkerton and other conservatives emphasize increasing individual choice, like giving parents the right to choose which public school their children can attend, and decentralizing bureaucracies.

Once there was Goldwater. Then, Reagan. Now, who?

Mr. Gingrich also argues that conservatives have an array of galvanizing issues they can push in the 1990's. "Conservativism is at least five years behind the curve in defining and articulating personal security as a fundamental right," he said. "We have an obligation to define how conservatives would create a safe society where your child would not become a drug addict, your spouse would not be raped, and you would not be in danger of being shot while standing on a street corner."

Mr. Gingrich also argues that conservatives need to focus on "the collapse of the bureaucratic welfare state" and what he portrays as entrenched and inefficient Democratic bureaucracies around the country, including Congress.

Mr. Gingrich's organization, Gopac, is sponsoring a nationwide conference on May 19, with 620 workshops connected by satellite, intended "to launch the citizens' opportunities movement needed to invent common-sense alternatives to the failed programs of the bureaucratic welfare state and its permissive values." While Gopac is a political action committee dedicated to electing Republicans, organizers of the workshops say the events are intended to be nonpartisan.

"Conservatism has challenges; it has opportunities; it has things it needs to do," Mr. Gingrich said. "People are sort of walking around saying, 'Oh, gee, if we win the cold war, liberate the entire planet, then what will we do for an encore?' Well, we could then try to liberate New York City. We could bring perestroika to the New York School Board. There are all sorts of possibilities."

Senator Phil Gramm, the Texas Republican who is a leading voice of conservatism in the Senate, also argues that conservatism is simply in a state of transition after a period of extraordinary success.

A Time of Consolidation

"We've made tremendous progress," Mr. Gramm said. "We have moved the mainstream of American political thinking. And any time you do that you have to go through a period of consolidation."

Mr. Gramm has high praise for Mr. Bush as a fitting President "to consolidate our gains." He added: "Are we talking about the great visionary Ronald Reagan was? No. But we're talking about a guy who understands government and is fundamentally conservative."

But other conservatives are arguing that they need a tougher approach toward the White House. Mr. Phillips of the Conservative Caucus said, "Many of the Washington-based conservative groups which have been supping at the President's table and holding their breath waiting for the next invitation from the White House are going to discover they'll be cut off from their natural constituency unless they reflect a growing upset."

Representative Vin Weber, Republican of Minnesota, said the conservative movement of the early 1970's took shape with the premise that "conservatism cannot be left to the Republican Party." He added that members of the movement stood as watchdogs and frequent critics of the policies of the Nixon Administration.

The Bush Administration has embarked on a series of policy decisions that "are tailor-made to help revive a conservative movement outside the Republican Party," Mr. Weber said, adding that he was not advocating that approach.

Already, some elements of the anti-abortion movement, a key part of the conservative coalition of the 1980's, are worried that the party is waffling on its commitment to their cause.

Some conservatives also worry about the lack of a galvanizing, transcendent leader. Vice President Dan Quayle has sought to position himself as a voice for the right, but Kevin Phillips, an analyst with ties to the Republican Party, asserts, "It's a rare conservative power broker who sits and exalts in the position or acumen of Dan Quayle."

Behind the ferment on the right is the realization that the movement must adjust to a radically altered political landscape.

"The father figure of Ronald Reagan is gone, the issues that really moved and motivated people throughout the 1980's have changed, and the national and international political situation is operating in a different context," said Paul Weyrich, another strategist on the right. "And movements that don't recast themselves are movements that die."

While liberal Democrats are haunted by a decade in the political wilderness, conservatives worry about matching past successes.

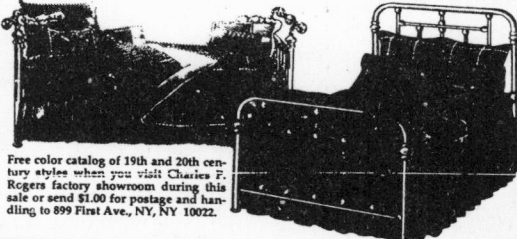

Exxon's Alaska Cleanup Plan Is Approved by Coast Guard

ANCHORAGE, May 12 (AP) — The Coast Guard has formally approved the Exxon Corporation's final plan for the cleanup of the Alaska oil spill, including use of chemical fertilizers to speed the growth of oil-eating bacteria.

The fertilizers have been opposed by the National Park Service, which says too little is known about their toxicity. But the Coast Guard manager, Rear Adm. David Ciancaglini, approved the plan on Friday, specifying that Exxon notify landowners and Federal and state agencies two weeks before using the fertilizers.

Admiral Ciancaglini said the company, whose tanker Exxon Valdez spilled nearly 11 million gallons of crude oil into Prince William Sound in March 1989, must also develop a program to protect "cultural resources" like archeological artifacts.

An Exxon spokesman, Joe Tucker, said the company was pleased with the approval and added that it was already working on plans to protect cultural and archeological resources.

"All the News That's Fit to Print"

The New York Times

Late Edition

New York: **Today**, sunny. High 89. **Tonight**, clear, not as cool. Low 70. **Tomorrow**, mostly sunny, very warm, more humid. High 91. **Yesterday**, high 89, low 65. Details are on page C22.

VOL. CXXXIX . No. 48,316 | NEW YORK, FRIDAY, AUGUST 3, 1990 | 50 cents beyond 75 miles from New York City, except on Long Island | 40 CENTS

INVADING IRAQIS SEIZE KUWAIT AND ITS OIL; U.S. CONDEMNS ATTACK, URGES UNITED ACTION

The New York Times

Representative Floyd H. Flake

INDICTMENT NAMES QUEENS LAWMAKER IN MISUSE OF FUNDS

Rep. Flake Faces 17 Federal Counts Involving Church and Housing Complex

By ARNOLD H. LUB[illegible]CH

Representative Floyd H. Flake, a powerful Queens minister who rode his popularity into Congress four years ago, has been indicted on charges of diverting tens of thousands of dollars in church funds to his own use.

The 17-count Federal indictment, which was unsealed yesterday, charges that Mr. Flake and his wife, Margarett, engaged in a two-pronged conspiracy involving his church and the housing complex for the elderly that it built in Jamaica under his stewardship. They are accused of fraudulently obtaining $66,700 from the church, embezzling $75,000 from the housing complex and evading income taxes on both amounts.

Pastor Since '76

The Representative, a Democrat whose Sixth Congressional District covers southern Queens, issued a detailed statement denying the charges. His lawyer said he still intended to run for re-election in November, and Mrs. Flake's lawyer added that the charges would fuel "a perception that minority politicians are being unfairly targeted for prosecution."

Since 1976, the 45-year-old Congressman has been pastor of the Allen A.M.E. Church in Jamaica, one of the largest and oldest black churches in New York City, with 6,000 members and a history reaching back into the 1830's. During his tenure, Mr. Flake has built up the church, and his own influence, with a network of social-services for the largely poor and largely black Jamaica neighborhood.

3d Congressman to Be Indicted

And yesterday, under the warm afternoon sun, there was a wary feeling of racism at work and an insistence that the charges against the pastor had to be false. [Page B4.]

Mr. Flake is the third New York City Congressman indicted in the last three years. The others, Mario Biaggi and Robert Garcia, both Bronx Democrats, were convicted in the Wedtech racketeering case. Mr. Garcia's conviction was overturned in June.

In announcing the unsealing of the indictment, the United States Attorney

Continued on Page B4, Column 5

Covenant Report Is Said to Find Sex Misconduct

By M. A. FARBER

An investigation ordered by the Covenant House board of directors concludes that the Rev. Bruce Ritter, the charity's founder and longtime president, engaged in sexual misconduct with young men living at Covenant House shelters for runaway youths, according to people who have read the investigation's report.

They say the four-month investigation, headed by Robert J. McGuire, a former New York City Police Commissioner, finds that had Father Ritter not resigned last February, the board would have had to dismiss him.

A Secretive Personal Fund

The report, which is to be issued today, also says the Covenant House board, controlled by Father Ritter until this year, failed to exercise proper oversight. The report notes, for example, that the board did not know that Father Ritter was receiving a salary of $98,000, the bulk of which was going into a secretive personal fund.

The fund, called the Franciscan Charitable Trust, had accumulated close to $1 million. Plans now call for it to be liquidated, with the assets going to Covenant House, as Father Ritter says he intended all along.

Father Ritter, who has vehemently denied the allegations, calling them "garbage," has declined to be interviewed for months and is said to have refused to cooperate with Mr. McGuire's investigation. The 63-year-old

Continued on Page B4, Column 2

IRAQ — SYRIA — Teheran — Baghdad — IRAQ — IRAN — JORDAN — SAUDI ARABIA — KUWAIT — Persian Gulf — Yenbu — Riyadh — Red Sea — Jidda — 0 Miles 400

0 Miles 2 — Kuwait Bay — Sief Palace — Dasman Palace — U.S. Embassy — British Embassy — Central Kuwait — Saudi Arabian Embassy — Bayan Palace — SECOND RING RD — THIRD RING RD — AIRPORT RD — SHUWAIK

Umm Qasr — Shatt al Arab — IRAN — Fao — RAUDHATAIN OILFIELD — SABRIYA OILFIELD — BUBIYAN I. — KUWAIT — PIPELINE — Kuwait Bay — FAILAKA I. — Mutla — AREA OF DETAIL — Jahra — Kuwait City — INTERNATIONAL AIRPORT — Persian Gulf — Ahmadi — Fahaheel — Sea Island (Oil loading terminal) — MINAGISH OILFIELD — PIPELINE — BURGAN OILFIELD — 0 Miles 20 — SAUDI ARABIA

Jim Perry/The New York Times

Iraqi invaders quickly moved into Kuwait City, taking control of Government buildings and the airport.

'NAKED AGGRESSION'

Bush Suggests Action by U.N. — Emir Flees to Saudi Arabia Exile

By R. W. APPLE Jr.

Special to The New York Times

WASHINGTON, Aug. 2 — Iraqi troops stormed into the desert sheikdom of Kuwait today, seizing control of its capital city and its rich oilfields, driving its ruler into exile, plunging the strategic Persian Gulf region into crisis and sending tremors of anxiety around the world.

President Bush condemned the invasion as "naked aggression" and sought to enlist world leaders in collective action against Iraq.

Faced with a dire threat from the truculent Iraqi leader, Saddam Hussein, to a region containing much of the world's oil reserves and with world financial markets in turmoil, Mr. Bush banned nearly all imports from Iraq and froze the nation's assets in the United States. At a news conference in Woody Creek, Colo., the President and Prime Minister Margaret Thatcher of Britain raised the possibility of economic or even military action by the United Nations.

Iraq Suspends Payments

In response, Iraq, which had been accusing Kuwait for weeks of stealing its oil and violating production limits set by the Organization of Petroleum Exporting Countries, suspended debt payments to the United States. Western experts asserted that Iraq had been motivated by a financial squeeze that only more oil dollars could ease and by ambitions for regional dominance.

Although oil prices rose sharply today, analysts noted that world inventories are unusually high, and they saw no immediate threat to supplies.

Witnesses in Kuwait said that hundreds of people were killed or wounded today as Iraqi ground forces, led by columns of tanks, surged into the desert emirate at the head of the gulf. Other troops came by air.

For Mr. Bush, the invasion posed manifold problems: the difficulty of direct military action despite the huge commitment of money and resources to the gulf in recent years; fear of another surge in oil prices, which could hurt economic growth and rekindle inflation; the potential disruption of the fragile budget negotiations between the White House and the Congress, in which a gasoline tax has been considered, and possible damage to the Re-

Continued on Page A8, Column 1

IRAQ'S ADVANTAGE LIMITS U.S. OPTIONS

Lack of Warning or Proximity Hinders American Action

By MICHAEL R. GORDON

Special to The New York Times

WASHINGTON, Aug. 2 — The Bush Administration faced the sobering reality today that despite a longstanding commitment to defend America's vital interests in the Persian Gulf, there was no easy military means to compel Iraq to withdraw its forces from Kuwait.

With the forces of pro-Western Arab powers like Saudi Arabia no match militarily for Iraq's powerful army, and with only a token American military presence in the area, the Administration's immediate responses included condemning the invasion, freezing Iraqi assets in the United States and calling for international sanctions.

Pentagon officials said that the United States had undertaken some military preparations as a result of the Iraqi attack. One aircraft carrier, the Independence, was under way at high speed from the Indian Ocean toward the Arabian Sea, adjacent to the Persian Gulf. It is expected to reach the area in several days.

A 2d Carrier Is Shifted

Another aircraft carrier, the Eisenhower, was being shifted to the Eastern Mediterranean Sea to put its attack planes within range of Iraq. The modest fleet of American ships in the Persian Gulf was expanded from six to eight. And some Air Force aerial refueling tankers were said to have been dispatched to the Indian Ocean region.

Defense Secretary Dick Cheney canceled plans to go with President Bush to Aspen, Colo., for Mr. Bush's speech on military issues and instead monitored the Gulf crisis from the Penta-

Continued on Page A8, Column 4

A New Gulf Alignment

Iraqis, Bargaining on Anti-U.S. Sentiment, May Profit by Intimidating the Monarchies

By YOUSSEF M. IBRAHIM

Special to The New York Times

News Analysis

PARIS, Aug. 2 — Iraq's invasion of Kuwait ushers in a new alignment in which Iraqis, Iranians and Palestinian hard-liners appear to share an interest in subduing the oil-rich monarchies of the region and challenging United States influence in the Arab world.

In ordering his forces to attack Kuwait, President Saddam Hussein of Iraq calculated that the odds were largely in his favor.

Arab diplomats and military experts said the only serious risk for Iraq was swift retaliation from the United States military forces. But that is a move that Washington may not be ready to take, given that the Iraqi armed forces are widely considered the most tested and best equipped in the Gulf region.

The Iraqis have much to gain from their invasion of Kuwait. A successful offensive could establish Baghdad as the dominant power in the Middle East, giving it a much greater say in decisions on oil production and prices.

Beyond that, the attack could become a rallying point for those in the Arab world who resent United States influence in world affairs and who feel that some Middle Eastern nations like Egypt have gone too far in accommodating Washington. Lastly, it could finally settle Iraq's longstanding border disputes with Kuwait.

The prospects for an effective counter to the attack appear slimmer in view of evidence that the Iraqis coordinated their move with Iran, which helped exert diplomatic pressure on Kuwait and the United Arab Emirates to raise prices last month at a meeting of the Organization of Petroleum Exporting Countries.

Iran officially condemned the Iraqi move late today, but the suspicion remained that it had at the very least not discouraged Baghdad's action.

Sense of Powerlessness

In the wake of the invasion, the Arab world is discovering how powerless it is in countering an Iraqi attempt to assert its dominance.

Saudi Arabia is Kuwait's closest ally in the region and the founder of the Gulf Cooperation Council, the alliance to which both Kuwait and the United Arab Emirates belong. But it has hardly lifted a finger to halt the Iraqi invasion, giving the impression that it is powerless and ever more dependent on American assistance. Although the Saudis have spent billions of dollars on

Continued on Page A10, Column 3

Reuters

Iraqi gunners yesterday on the coast near Kuwait City, where they fired on Kuwaiti naval vessels offshore.

Soviet Smokers Vow Strikes As Cigarettes, Too, Disappear

By CELESTINE BOHLEN

Special to The New York Times

MOSCOW, Aug. 2 — It happens like clockwork, all over the city. A truck pulls up to a boarded-up kiosk, unloads its wares, the sale window opens and within minutes smokers appear out of nowhere to take places in line, hopeful that for this day, anyway, their addiction can be fed.

Along with other ills, the Soviet Union is now in the throes of a nicotine fit, brought on by a painful and puzzling withdrawal of cigarettes from a nation of heavy smokers.

In many parts of the country, the cigarette shortage — caused by a series of typical economic lapses — has galvanized the patient, line-suffering Soviet consumer into action.

In the city of Perm last week, a demonstration that began in front of an empty tobacco shop spilled into downtown streets, ending in a rally outside City Hall, where 2,000 people chanted and waved banners, badgering the Communist Party for cigarettes. "Hey, you up there, your people have nothing to smoke as well as nothing to eat," one banner read. "Party, have you got a smoke?" asked another.

Aircraft Workers Threaten Strike

In Kuibyshev, smokers at an aircraft plant threatened a strike over the cigarette shortage and protesters mounted a daily vigil at a local tobacco plant that had been shut for repairs.

Warning strikes have also been reported in Ulyanovsk and Ufa, while in Voronezh and Orel, angry smokers have smashed the windows of tobacco kiosks. This month, at the height of the harvest in the Krasnador region, combine operators brought their machines to a stop with a nonnegotiable demand: "No tobacco, no work."

Such public vehemence has been absent during other shortages: when cheese, onions, lemons or sausages disappear from the stores, Soviet shoppers simply shift their queues from one

Continued on Page A4, Column 5

2 Teen-Agers Shot As Violence Persists On New York Streets

The tide of violence in New York City in the last two weeks — four children killed by stray gunfire, an advertising executive shot dead in the West Village, two cab drivers murdered, a young couple bludgeoned in Central Park — continued yesterday as officials struggled to respond to growing fears.

A 14-year-old Queens boy was shot and killed after he told another teenager to stop riding a friend's moped. In the Bronx, a 15-year-old girl standing with friends in a park was critically wounded when a youth fired a gunshot into her group. A homeless drifter was charged with Monday's fatal shooting of the ad executive at a phone booth.

And pressure grew on city officials to cope with the latest wave of violence. Mayor David N. Dinkins today will announce a crackdown on gun users. Police Commissioner Lee P. Brown, in an interview, contended that the police alone could not solve the problems of crime and violence.

Articles, pages B1 and B3.

INSIDE

Why a Bishop Quit

The recent resignation of the Roman Catholic Archbishop of Atlanta came about after evidence of his "intimate relationship" with a woman, church officials said. Page A12.

A Troubled Savings Rescue

Almost a year after the Federal bailout of the savings and loan industry, economists see problems, including a danger to banks. Page D1.

Barry Case Goes to Jury

The drug case against Washington's Mayor is now in the hands of 12 of the city's residents. Page A12.

The Iraqi Invasion: Global Reverberations

OIL PRICES Spot market prices surged, with the American benchmark crude rising to $23.11 a barrel, up $1.57. The invasion stirred fears of slower economic growth, higher inflation and OPEC domination of the world oil market. But price increases should be limited by a near-record stockpile worldwide. Page A9.

FINANCIAL MARKETS The dollar rose, gold prices jumped and most stock markets fell. Japan, dependent on imported oil, was hard hit. As of today's close in Tokyo, its stock market had fallen 4.3 percent since the invasion took place. Page D1.

THE SOVIET UNION Moscow announced a suspension in the delivery of arms and military hardware to Iraq. The move interrupted Moscow's longtime role as Baghdad's chief arms supplier. Page A10.

UNITED NATIONS With Moscow and Washington in agreement, the Security Council voted 14 to 0 to condemn the invasion and demand an Iraqi withdrawal. Page A10.

DIPLOMACY Secretary of State James A. Baker 3d cut short a visit to Mongolia and plans to issue a joint statement about the crisis in Moscow today with the Soviet Foreign Minister, Eduard A. Shevardnadze. Syria condemned the invasion and called for an emergency Arab summit conference.

ISRAEL Israeli leaders condemned the invasion, but they also appeared relieved by the move. For months, President Saddam Hussein has been sharply threatening Israel. Officials in Jerusalem were openly frustrated that the rest of the world did not seem adequately concerned. Page A10.

THE EUROPEAN ALLIES Western European countries unanimously condemned the invasion, with Britain and France joining the United States in freezing billions of dollars worth of Kuwaiti assets. Page A10.

Invading Iraqis Seize Kuwait and Its Oil

Continued From Page A1

publican Party in elections this fall.

Reuters reported that the Kuwaiti forces continued to resist tonight in at least one area of the capital, at the main military barracks. Earlier reports spoke of explosions and gunfire echoing around the steel-and-glass skyscrapers of the city center in fierce fighting at dawn. But the Iraqi Army, the most powerful in the Arab world, vastly outnumbered the Kuwaiti forces, and 12 hours after the invasion began the Iraqis were reported in control of the airport, central bank and all key government buildings.

The State Department reported that Iraqi troops had taken six American oilfield workers into custody near the Kuwait-Iraq border. Officials said their whereabouts were unknown.

The President said he could not confirm that Americans had been seized, but that if it were true, "it would affect me in a very dramatic way because I view as a fundamental responsibility of my Presidency protecting American citizens."

Mr. Bush said this morning that American military intervention was not under active consideration, but Lieut. Gen. Howard Graves of the Joint Chiefs of Staff, traveling in Mongolia with Secretary of State James A. Baker 3d, said the United States was considering "political, military or economic moves" against Iraq. And after flying west to meet Mrs. Thatcher and deliver a speech at the Aspen Institute, the President said, "We're not ruling any options in but we're not ruling any options out."

Warships Head Toward Gulf

An American naval task force, headed by the carrier Independence with 60 fighters and bombers, sailed from the Indian Ocean toward the mouth of the Persian Gulf in a show of strength. The Kuwaiti Ambassador in Washington, a close relative of the Emir, Sheik Jaber al-Ahmed al-Sabah, who is now in Saudi Arabia, pleaded for immediate American military intervention.

At the United Nations, the Security Council issued a unanimous call for an Iraqi withdrawal despite Iraqi assertions, brushed aside by virtually all nations, that Baghdad had been asked to send troops into Kuwait by rebel elements there and that Iraqi forces would be withdrawn from Kuwait within a few weeks.

Mrs. Thatcher called Mr. Hussein's behavior "intolerable" and said that "a collective and effective will of the nations belonging to the U.N." was needed.

United States and British officials referred to Chapter 7 of the United Nations Charter, which permits the Security Council to use economic sanctions or military action against any nation that threatens the peace.

Such action was always difficult to take during the cold war because it was very rare to find all five permanent members of the Security Council in agreement on any major dispute.

Soviet Shipments Suspended

But the Soviet Union, a principal arms supplier to Iraq, immediately suspended its military shipments to that country, and the United States and the Soviet Union planned a joint statement on Friday after Mr. Baker arrives in Moscow. He hurriedly changed his travel plans after receiving news of the invasion.

Baghdad swoops in and the world recoils; but what is the West to do?

Still there seemed to be little practical action that anyone could take in the days immediately ahead to reverse the Iraqi conquest. If Baghdad absorbs Kuwait or sets up a compliant government there, the oil reserves under Iraqi control will be doubled to about 195 billion barrels, making it second only to Saudi Arabia, which has 255 billion barrels.

The invasion appeared to have the potential to shift not only the economic but also the military and political balance in the region.

Moving swiftly today to endorse the President's actions against Iraq, the House voted 416 to 0 to impose trade sanctions and to cut off Export-Import Bank credits.

The Senate unanimously approved a resolution calling for multilateral actions "involving air, sea and land forces" under the United Nations charter to restore international peace and security to the region.

Senator Claiborne Pell of Rhode Island, the Democratic chairman of the Senate Foreign Relations Committee, called Mr. Hussein "the Hitler of the Middle East" and criticized Mr. Bush for not having moved earlier to forestall an invasion. Representative Lee H. Hamilton, Democrat of Indiana, an influential member of the House Foreign Affairs Committee, complained that there had been "a kind of inertia" to American policy toward Iraq in recent weeks.

Fears Over Saudi Arabia

Several lawmakers suggested that Mr. Hussein might now be emboldened to move into neighboring Saudi Arabia. Senator David Boren, Democrat of Oklahoma, who was briefed by the Central Intelligence Agency this morning, noted that the primary Saudi oilfields are only 250 miles from Kuwait, with no terrain "that would impede a rapid movement of forces" by Iraq.

"We have to understand that our national interests are very much at stake," Mr. Boren said. "I think it would be wrong to underestimate the ultimate aims of Saddam Hussein. He really hopes in the long run to put Iraq on a par with the kind of power he sees the Western powers as having."

Judith Kipper, a Middle East specialist at the Brookings Institution, described the conflict in Kuwait as "a war of resources."

"This is the first post-cold-war crisis in the economically dependent world," she said. "With the end of the East-West game, small countries can act with impunity to rearrange the neighborhood. Iraq is a superpower in its own area, but they need cash to service their debt and rebuild their oil industry. He gets cash from oil; oil prices are going up. Plus, they have historic claims to Kuwait, which Saddam Hussein has chosen to act upon."

Gary Sick, a Middle East expert in the Ford, Carter and Reagan administrations who now teaches at Columbia University, said that condemnations by nations around the world would have "no effect at all."

"Saddam Hussein obviously expected that when he did it," Mr. Sick said. "He can't be surprised by the reaction, and he obviously discounted that in advance. Some tangible steps will have to be taken if in fact Saddam Hussein is to be persuaded that this didn't work out to his benefit."

Washington Is Galvanized

The news of the invasion galvanized Washington on Wednesday night and this morning.

Mr. Bush was told of the invasion at 9 P.M. on Wednesday in the residential quarters of the White House, officials said, and was awakened from time to time during the night for briefings by his national security adviser, Brent Scowcroft. He signed his orders on Iraqi assets and trade at 5 A.M., they said.

At 8 this morning, the President met at length with his senior advisers, including the chairman of the Joint Chiefs, Gen. Colin L. Powell.

Michael J. Boskin, Mr. Bush's chief economic adviser, said that if oil prices rose 25 percent, and he seemed to consider this plausible, it would have "some deleterious effect on our economy."

Such a rise in prices would slow growth slightly, he said, but not enough to produce a recession. Growth, though meager, is still running at slightly more than 1 percent.

Later the Department of Energy said the turmoil in the Middle East posed "no immediate threat" to American supplies of petroleum products. It estimated that in January to May of this year, Iraq supplied 8 percent of United States oil imports, about 3.6 percent of total United States demand. For Kuwait, the department said, the comparable figures were much smaller — just over 1 percent and less than one-half of 1 percent.

The Energy Secretary, James D. Watkins, said that crude oil stocks in the United States stood at near-record levels and that world inventories were also unusually high at the moment. This country's Strategic Petroleum Reserve, a statement by the department said, could offset the amount of oil the United States has been importing from both Iraq and Kuwait — about 730,000 barrels a day — for more than 800 days.

Crude Oil Prices Rise

Still, crude oil prices shot up to more than $23 a barrel, and some economists said that gasoline prices would rise by at least a nickel a gallon within a week.

Recalling the Arab oil embargo of the 1970's that forced millions of Americans to wait in long lines, analysts noted that the United States is more dependent on Middle East oil now than it was then. The American Petroleum Institute, which represents United States oil companies, spoke recently of a "potentially ominous" trend that has brought oil imports to nearly half of total American consumption.

Mediation Efforts Collapse

Arab mediation efforts to head off the crisis broke down Wednesday with the collapse of talks between Iran and Kuwait in the Saudi Arabian port of Jidda on the Red Sea. Mr. Bush said tonight, after talking by phone with a number of Arab leaders, that he was hopeful of a new regional initiative, but there were no reports of concrete plans to bring the two sides together.

Only a few hours after the collapse of the talks, Iraqi armor, led by more than 350 main battle tanks, began racing across the 80-odd miles of desert that separate Kuwait City, a modern enclave on the gulf, from the frontier. It took the Iraqi forces, using weapons supplied largely by the Soviet Union, France and China, little time to overwhelm the Kuwaiti defenders.

Paul Hosefros/The New York Times

"There is no place for this sort of naked aggression in today's world," President Bush said of the Iraqi invasion of Kuwait. He was accompanied by Vice President Dan Quayle and John H. Sununu, the White House chief of staff, as he left the White House yesterday for a trip to Colorado.

The Trouble Zone | At a Glance

Iraq

VITAL STATISTICS

Population: 16,110,000 (1986).

Area: 167,924 square miles (about the size of California).

Capital: Baghdad (pop. 3,844,608).

Government: Power is held by President Saddam Hussein and an 11-member ruling council.

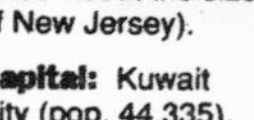

MILITARY STRENGTH

Troops 1,000,000

Combat Aircraft 513

Tanks 5,500

Ships 51

Estimated military spending: $13 billion (1988)

ECONOMY

Oil accounts for more than 98 percent of exports. Some agriculture; dates are the principal cash crop. Per capita income (1988): $6,200.

Kuwait

VITAL STATISTICS

Population: 1,872,569 (1987).

Area: 6,880 square miles About the size of New Jersey).

Capital: Kuwait City (pop. 44,335).

Government: Power is held by the Emir, Sheik Jaber al-Ahmed al-Sabah.

MILITARY STRENGTH

Troops 20,300

Combat Aircraft 36

Tanks 275

Ships 46

Estimated military spending: $1.4 billion (1988)

ECONOMY

Oil is the mainstay. Kuwait has the third-largest petroleum reserves in the world (after Saudi Arabia and Iraq) and produces 1.6 milllion barrels a day. There is virtually no other industry. Per capita income (1986): $13,890.

Sources: Europa World Yearbook; Regional Surveys of the World; World Almanac; Desk International; Associated Press

The New York Times

U.S. Weighs Its Options in Gulf Crisis

Continued From Page A1

gon. But there was no effort to dispatch Army forces or move Marine Corps supplies based on ships toward the Persian Gulf for a possible ground campaign.

In a morning news conference, Mr. Bush suggested that a military response to Iraq was not imminent, but he did not formally exclude it. Asked if the United States would intervene militarily in response to urgent Kuwaiti calls for assistance, he said, "I'm not contemplating such action, and I, again, would not discuss it if I were."

Senator Sam Nunn, the Georgia Democrat who is head of the Senate Armed Services Committee, expressed the prevailing view on Capitol Hill when he said that the proper response should be economic and political pressure and not military action.

'Intensive Diplomatic Activity'

"I don't think we have a military option at the moment, nor do we have a treaty obligation," Mr. Nunn said. "I believe that our primary recourse should be to very intensive diplomatic activity." His comments were made on the NBC News program, "Today."

Pentagon officials said that the Administration was actively considering a number of military responses but stressed that the first course of action would be to apply political and economic pressure.

Iraq warns against any foreign intervention.

The impediments to military action are the simple facts of geography and the phenomenal growth of Iraq's military power.

Pentagon officials said, for example, that it would take close to a month to deploy an Army corps of two "heavy" — armored or mechanized — divisions to the gulf, assuming that Saudi Arabia was prepared to receive it.

Smaller forces, like a Marine Expeditionary Brigade, numbering about 16,000 troops, could be dispatched more quickly. It would take about a week to move such a unit and its equipment to the gulf, a Pentagon official said. But such a unit would be no match for Iraq's large, battle tested Army.

Concerns About Americans

Further, as Thomas L. McNaugher, a military specialist at the Brookings Institution noted, Iraq's President, Saddam Hussein, is holding as virtual hostages the Kuwaiti population and the several thousand Americans living in Kuwait. The Iraqi radio, in an official statement today, warned against intervention, saying "our armed forces" would make Iraq and Kuwait "a graveyard" if such action were attempted.

For some military officials, a punitive air strike against Iraq did not appear to be an attractive option, though others said it was under consideration. Such an attack could be carried out by Air Force or Navy planes, or by Navy ships in the gulf firing conventionally armed cruise missiles.

But having endured an eight-year war with Iran, Iraq's leadership might calculate that its population would not be shaken by such a blow, some Pentagon officials say. Iraq also has surface-to-air missiles to defend its installations; this raises the prospect that American planes could be shot down and their crews killed or captured.

Beyond that, there is the possibility that Iraq could respond to an American air raid by sending its force beyond Kuwait and into Saudi Arabia. Unless the United States was ready to defend Saudi Arabia, an air raid could be risky, a military official cautioned.

"With warning time, we could move into Saudi Arabia and develop a defensive position. All of this is predicated on warning. We have lost that. What warning we had was ambiguous," a military official said, noting that many in the Administration were inclined to interpret Iraqi military moves as merely intimidation.

But one senior Administration official took exception to this analysis, saying that the United States could adequately defend Saudi Arabia.

The obstacles to an immediate American military response, as well as the failure by the Bush Administration to anticipate the Iraqi attack, have raised questions about the Administration's strategy toward Iraq.

When Iraq began making public threats toward Kuwait and the United Arab Emirates and moving forces toward the Kuwaiti border last month, the United States response was to hold a joint air and sea exercise with the United Arab Emirates.

Signal to Iraq

The exercise, while very modest in military terms, was intended as a signal to Iraq to abandon any aggressive designs on the gulf states.

But when Iraq, in effect, called the Administration's bluff with its lightning attack on Kuwait, many Administration officials were surprised.

Bush Administration officials had been well aware before the attack of the threatening deployment of large numbers of Iraqi troops on the border with Kuwait, and the Central Intelligence Agency had reportedly flagged the possibility of an attack. The force eventually reached 120,000. But many officials fundamentally misjudged the Iraqi leaders' intentions. The prevailing view in the Administration, the military official said, had been that Iraq intended to use its forces to intimidate Kuwait, or perhaps snatch a small piece of territory.

The United States is not devoid of military options, and they remain under consideration.

Mr. Bush and Prime Minister Margaret Thatcher of Britain, after meeting in Colorado, called for economic sanctions against Baghdad under the United Nations Charter, which provides for collective military action to enforce such measures. That raised the possibility that American naval vessels could be deployed to mount a blockade of Iraq, an option under discussion.

The United States could also buttress the defense of Saudi Arabia by moving military supplies and forces toward the gulf country. One option being discussed is to dispatch American tactical aircraft to Saudi Arabia. But the Saudis have not officially requested any military assistance.

The Iraqi attack might influence the debate here about the proper level of military spending and how the Pentagon should reshape its forces. Faced with a declining budget, the Navy no longer keeps an aircraft carrier continuously on station in the Indian Ocean, and no carrier was deployed there when Iraq moved troops last month toward the border with Kuwait.

In Two Arab Capitals, Gunfire and Fear, Victory and Cheers

KUWAIT, Aug. 2 (Reuters) — Iraqi troops who invaded Kuwait before dawn today swiftly gained the upper hand in the capital despite occasionally fierce resistance by outnumbered Kuwaiti defenders.

Fighting in the city was concentrated in Shuwaik, Kuwait's main military barracks. The area was covered with smoke and witnesses said Kuwaiti forces were putting up a strong resistance. Gunfire was heard from other points outside the capital.

But by nightfall pockets of resistance which had held out in parts of the country appeared to have been eliminated and about 200 Iraqi tanks clanked through the capital. Some parked along the seaside highway, their guns pointing to the Gulf.

Lloyds Intelligence reported that Iraqi troops, who quickly took control of the airport and royal palace, were moving south of the capital toward the oilfields at Mina al-Ahmadi on the Kuwaiti-Saudi border.

Even after the fighting died down, the Government of Sheik Jaber al-Ahmed al-Sabah continued to issue calls for resistance from radio transmitters in the desert.

They urged Kuwaitis to "make the aggressors taste the chalice of death."

"We shall fight them everywhere until we clean their treachery from our land," the broadcasts said. "Our Arab brothers are with us. Our Muslim brothers are with us. The entire world is with us. And above all, God is with us."

The Emir's younger brother, Prince Fahd, died defending Dasman Palace, the sheik's residence on the banks of the Persian Gulf, which was strafed by Iraqi jets in the initial assault.

Kuwait's al-Emiri Hospital, near Dasman Palace, reported 3 Kuwaiti dead and 45 wounded there alone. About 95 Iraqis had been admitted with wounds, the hospital said, adding that it knew of more casualties at other hospitals.

At dawn, explosions and gunfire echoed around the skyscrapers of the capital, Kuwait, as the vastly stronger Iraqi Army, backed by tanks and helicopters, stormed into the city and quickly took control of the palace, the international airport and the central bank.

Hundreds of Iraqi tanks, armored personnel carriers, fuel and water tankers and truckloads of troops had trundled 80 miles from the border across sand and scrub toward Kuwait in temperatures above 105 degrees.

The Iraqi-backed "Free Provisional Kuwait Government" broadcast to the nation, announcing that it had taken power and was imposing an indefinite curfew.

Iraq said it struck to support a coup by young Kuwaiti revolutionaries against the Sabah family, whom it denounced as "traitors and agents of Zionist and foreign schemes."

The invasion across the disputed border was begun at 2 A.M. (7 P.M. Wednesday, Eastern daylight time) and within several hours the first Iraqi troops were taking up positions in downtown Kuwait.

Waving Iraqi flags, jubilant soldiers in cars raced through streets and Iraqi helicopters clattered overhead.

Iraqis Exult, a Bit Warily

BAGHDAD, Iraq, Aug. 2 (Reuters) — Motorists honked their horns and flashed their lights here today to celebrate the Iraqi Army's invasion of Kuwait.

An atmosphere of war engulfed the capital. The radio and television broadcast patriotic songs and orders for mobilization of the armed forces.

A quick sampling suggested that many Iraqis considered President Saddam Hussein's offensive to be justified by his quarrel with Kuwait over oil, money and land. Some Iraqis, recalling their long and bloody war with Iran, which ended less than two years ago, worried about what would follow.

Ahmed Khalis, a college student, said, "The Kuwaiti rulers deserve what Saddam did to them."

Recalling the war from 1980 to 1988, in which Gulf Arab states gave Iraq billions of dollars' worth of aid, Mr. Khalis said: "The Kuwaitis boast of their aid to Iraq, but it was Iraq that defended their thrones and wealth with blood. We sacrificed our brothers, fathers and sons to let them enjoy life."

Mohammed Saadun, a college graduate who was recently discharged from military service, said: "I have been expecting a cross-border operation since Kuwait humiliated Iraq by refusing even to write off debts. Saddam cannot tolerate this."

"All the News
That's Fit to Print"

The New York Times

Late Edition
New York: **Today,** sunny, becoming windy. High 73. **Tonight,** breezy, mild. Low 62. **Tomorrow,** quite windy, sunny, warmer. High 77. **Yesterday,** high 69, low 56. Details are on page C7.

VOL.CXL . . No. 48,377 · NEW YORK, WEDNESDAY, OCTOBER 3, 1990 · 50 cents beyond 75 miles from New York City, except on Long Island. · 40 CENTS

TWO GERMANYS UNITE AFTER 45 YEARS WITH JUBILATION AND A VOW OF PEACE

A MILLION IN BERLIN

Flag at Reichstag Marks Start of a New Era at Center of Europe

By SERGE SCHMEMANN
Special to The New York Times

BERLIN, Wednesday, Oct. 3 — Forty-five years after it was carved up in defeat and disgrace, Germany was reunited today in a midnight celebration of pealing bells, national hymns and the jubilant blare of good old German oom-pah-pah.

At the stroke of midnight Tuesday, a copy of the American Liberty Bell, a gift from the United States at the height of the cold war, tolled from the Town Hall, and the black, red and gold banner of the Federal Republic of Germany rose slowly before the Reichstag, the scarred seat of past German Parliaments.

Then the President, Richard von Weizsäcker, drawing on the words of the West German Constitution, proclaimed from the steps of the Reichstag: "In free self-determination, we want to achieve the unity in freedom of Germany. We are aware of our responsibility for these tasks before God and the people. We want to serve peace in the world in a united Europe."

Singing of Anthem

With that, a throng estimated at one million joined in the West German national anthem, now the anthem for united Germany: "Unity and justice and freedom for the German fatherland . . ." The words are from the third stanza of the prewar anthem, whose opening verses, now banned began, "Deutschland, Deutschland über Alles."

The moment marked the return of a nation severed along the front line between East and West to the center stage of Europe, this time as an economic powerhouse vowing never again to bring grief to a continent it had so terribly ravaged in the past century.

It is the smallest unified German state to rise in the 119 years since Otto von Bismarck first gathered the Germans under the Prussian crown.

Beer and Revelry

Hundreds of German flags waved and firecrackers snapped in the chilly autumn night. Beer and sparkling wine flowed freely and the strains of divergent bands mingled in a rowdy cacophony. Soon bottles began smashing on the pavement and celebration turned to intoxication, and by early morning the center of the new capital was deep in smashed bottles and weaving revelers.

A force of about 5,000 police officers had been massed in case radicals tried

Continued on Page A17, Column 1

Associated Press

The German flag was unfurled in front of the Reichstag building in Berlin at midnight as the two Germanys were reunited.

Germany by the Numbers

In some respects, the united Germany is less than the sum of its parts. The statistical tale is told in charts and a map on page A16.

DINKINS PROPOSES RECORD EXPANSION OF POLICE FORCES

Mayor Offers New Programs for Corrections and Youth to Help Combat Crime

By RALPH BLUMENTHAL

Seeking to take command of an issue that has shaken his leadership, Mayor David N. Dinkins announced a barrage of proposals yesterday to fight crime, including a record expansion of New York City's police forces and ambitious new corrections, youth and education programs. The total cost would be $1.8 billion over the next four years.

With New York City already in financial straits, the Mayor proposed paying for the initiatives through a rise in the real-property tax, a new city payroll tax to be shared by workers and employers and a 25-cent surcharge on state lottery tickets.

The taxes, which would rise from $138 million in what remains of the first fiscal year to $644 million in the fourth year, would require approval by the City Council and the State Legislature.

'Assault on All Fronts'

"We will not wage war by degree," Mr. Dinkins said, releasing a 535-page police manpower study and a 57-page mayoral report that began a day of briefings and culminated in a news conference timed for live television coverage on the evening news. "Our strategy calls for an assault on all fronts." [Excerpts, page B2.]

The anti-crime program was hailed by many community leaders, but reaction to the tax plan was mixed. The State Senate majority leader, Ralph J. Marino, voiced strong reservations about the potentially negative effect on commuters and businesses. Gov. Mario M. Cuomo said that if it were necessary for public safety, he "could" support the payroll tax, but that he had yet to review the plan in detail.

Assembly Speaker Mel Miller also urged caution. "We're going to have to go slowly in weighing the tax package," most of which, he noted, would not take effect until the fiscal year beginning next July. The City Council Speaker, Peter F. Vallone, voiced general support for the plan but seemed taken aback that it went so far beyond the Council's own proposal to hire more officers through a lottery surcharge.

Thomas Reppetto, president of the

Continued on Page B2, Column 1

In Appeal for Support for Budget, President Calls Plan Best for Now

By DAVID E. ROSENBAUM
Special to The New York Times

WASHINGTON, Oct. 2 — Faced with a revolt in his party's Congressional ranks and wariness around the country, President Bush appealed on television tonight for public support of the budget compromise he and Congressional leaders struck last weekend. He predicted "economic chaos if we fail to reduce the deficit."

In a show of bipartisanship that verged on coalition Government, the President was followed with a broadcast by Senator George J. Mitchell of Maine, the Democratic leader. He urged support for the President "because the nation is more important than partisan differences." [Transcripts of the Bush and Mitchell speeches appear on page D28.]

Tough Task for Bush

Mr. Mitchell was preaching to the converted for the most part. Despite considerable opposition among liberals, a majority of Congressional Democrats appear to support the agreement.

But Mr. Bush has the more difficult task of swaying enough dissident Republicans to win enactment of the plan.

The President said that neither he nor anyone else was completely satisfied with the compromise, but he said it was "the best agreement that can be legislated now."

In the strongest statement he has made about economic perils that might lie ahead, Mr. Bush emphasized: "If we fail to enact this agreement, our economy will falter, markets may tumble and recession will follow."

He called on the public to "tell your Congressmen and Senators you support this deficit-reduction agreement."

A Bipartisan Appeal

The President continued: "If they are Republicans, urge them to stand with the President. If they are Democrats, urge them to stand with their Congressional leaders."

"Those who dislike one part or another may pick our agreement apart," Mr. Bush said, "but if they do, believe me, the political reality is no one can put a better one back together again."

Senator Mitchell made almost identical points. He would have preferred "a budget that asks more from the wealthy and less from the elderly," he said. But as for the compromise, he

Continued on Page D27, Column 1

Pivotal Moment for Bush

By ANDREW ROSENTHAL
Special to The New York Times

News Analysis

WASHINGTON, Oct. 2 — With his speech tonight from the Oval Office, George Bush completed a fundamental transition: The President who succeeded for so long at giving Americans only good news is now telling them to prepare for economic pain at home and the possibility of war abroad.

With remarkable speed, Mr. Bush has moved from the most protracted honeymoon in recent White House history to twin crises that could determine the success of his Presidency.

The decision to confront the Republican rebellion on Capitol Hill over the budget agreement quickly and directly in a nationally televised speech represented a judgment that any delay could allow events to spin out of control. If the emerging prospects for passage of the budget package turn into defeat, Mr. Bush would immediately lose his calculated gamble that such an agreement would be good for the economy and thus bolster his re-election campaign in 1992.

For more than a year and a half, everything seemed to be going Mr. Bush's way, especially in Europe. Then on Aug. 8, six days after the Iraqi invasion of Kuwait, Mr. Bush went on national television to announce that he was sending troops to the Persian Gulf and to prepare the country for the possibility that American soldiers and civilians could die in a far-off war.

Tonight, less than two months later, Mr. Bush again spoke from the Oval

Continued on Page D27, Column 4

More on the Budget

A SECOND LOOK Some experts say the deficit will be cut less than predicted. Page D27.

TAX BREAKS Big companies may benefit from provisions aimed at small ones. Page D29.

PLANNING AHEAD How changes in deductions will affect some taxpayers. Page D29.

Senate Confirms Souter, 90 to 9, As Supreme Court's 105th Justice

By RICHARD L. BERKE
Special to The New York Times

WASHINGTON, Oct. 2 — Ten weeks after President Bush nominated David H. Souter, a little-known New Hampshire judge, for the Supreme Court, the Senate voted overwhelmingly today to confirm him as the Court's 105th Justice.

The vote was 90 to 9, with only Democrats voting against confirmation. The balloting came after nearly four hours of speeches on the Senate floor in which supporters said they were confident Judge Souter would preserve fundamental constitutional values, while opponents said too much was not known about his positions on critical issues like abortion.

Case on Sensitive Issue

Chief Justice William H. Rehnquist will swear in Judge Souter at a relatively short ceremony at the Court on Tuesday morning, in time to sit for oral arguments later that day in the second week of the Court term.

On Wednesday, Judge Souter will be among the Justices hearing a major case on the lawfulness of corporate policies that exclude women from jobs that might endanger a developing fetus. Today the Court took up the major issue left unresolved from the era of official school segregation: what a school system that was segregated by law decades ago must do to free itself from Federal court supervision. [Education, page B8.]

With the Souter nomination behind him, Senator Joseph R. Biden Jr., the Delaware Democrat who is chairman of the Judiciary Committee, was looking to future vacancies on the Court. He said he hoped that the Administration "will not learn the wrong lesson" from the strong bipartisan support the nominee received.

"Our overwhelming approval is not a sign that the Senate intends to be lax about exercising its advise-and-consent power, or intends to use that power only to screen out extremist nominees," Mr. Biden said. "Rather, it is a sign that we take this power seriously, and that we intend to exercise it responsibly. And in doing so, Judge Souter falls within the sphere of candidates acceptable to the Senate."

Mr. Biden emphasized, however, that he and several other Democrats who supported the nomination had serious misgivings because Judge Souter

Continued on Page A24, Column 1

Top Soviet General Tells U.S. Not to Attack in Gulf

Jack Manning/The New York Times

Gen. Mikhail A. Moiseyev, left, chief of the Soviet General Staff, discussing options in the Persian Gulf crisis yesterday in New York City. With him was Gen. Colin L. Powell, the Chairman of the Joint Chiefs of Staff.

By MICHAEL R. GORDON

The head of the Soviet military said yesterday that the economic sanctions against Iraq were working and that no force should be used in the Persian Gulf unless it was approved by the United Nations.

The remarks by the Soviet general, Mikhail A. Moiseyev, Chief of the Soviet General Staff, were the most explicit comments made so far by a Soviet official on the need to have United Nations approval for the use of force by the United States and other nations that have opposed the Iraqi invasion of Kuwait.

The Soviet general's comments — in an unusual joint interview with Gen. Colin L. Powell, Chairman of the Joint Chiefs of Staff — signaled a basic disagreement with Washington about the circumstances under which military force could be used in the Persian Gulf.

"We cannot view the resolution of any crisis like this by means of using arms," said General Moiseyev, who is on a tour of the United States as a guest of General Powell. But General Powell pointedly said President Bush had not ruled out any options.

The two generals were interviewed by writers and editors of The New York Times.

Suggesting that military force was not needed to force Iraqi troops out of Kuwait, General Moiseyev said the economic embargo was beginning to hurt Iraq.

"Saddam Hussein has really understood now finally how far he has gone," General Moiseyev said. "He is finding himself in economic and political isolation, and he can't survive very long that way."

General Moiseyev asserted that protests, uprisings and desertions in Iraqi were sapping the strength of the Iraqi military and impelling President Hussein to seek a diplomatic solution.

"You can't keep an army together

Continued on Page A12, Column 1

INSIDE

Air Crash Mystery in China

Did a cockpit struggle cause a hijacked Chinese plane to crash into a parked jet at Canton's airport, killing 127 people? Chinese officials would not confirm the report. Page A3.

South African Rift Persists

The leader of the Inkatha movement spurned a meeting with the African National Congress, dampening prospects for a reconciliation between the two warring groups. Page A3.

Melee in Pakistan

A mob stormed the courtroom where former Prime Minister Benazir Bhutto is to stand trial on corruption charges. Page A6.

Women in Locker Rooms

Three recent incidents in football have reopened the issue of access to locker rooms by women covering men's sports. Page D31.

Bitter Dispute Is Threatening Program for Marrow Donors

By GINA KOLATA

A program that has the lofty goal of finding altruistic people to donate bone marrow to save the lives of dying patients has become enmeshed in a dispute that threatens its ability to function.

The conflict involves charges that a former subcontractor in the federally financed program provided misleading information to dying patients and volunteers who wanted to help them; withheld the names of thousands of potential marrow donors, and failed to account to families for large sums of money raised in their names.

The subcontractor, the Life-Savers Foundation of America, has denied the allegations and accused the National Marrow Donor Program of overcharging patients and being inefficient in matching patients and donors.

Registry of Potential Donors

The national program has amassed a file of 200,000 people who are willing to donate marrow if their tissue is compatible with that of a patient with leukemia or another disease. Without transplants, the patients will die, and the demand for donors far exceeds the supply.

But Federal officials, transplant surgeons and ethicists are worried that allegations of questionable conduct in the treatment of dying patients and their families could cause the network of volunteer donors to fall apart. They say altruism is fragile at best, and any hint of misconduct is more than enough to make people shy away from donating.

The national program has asserted in court and in a letter to Senator Al Gore, Democrat of Tennessee, that Life-Savers caused patients unnecessary anguish by raising false hopes that there was a donor.

Officials of the national program, who say they have severed all ties with the subcontractor, say some families

Continued on Page A26, Column 1

Evolution in Europe: Europe Holds Its Breath

Several Germanys Since 1871, but Today's Is 'Very Different'

By RICHARD BERNSTEIN

In 1871 when Germany was first unified under Otto von Bismarck, the way ahead was marked by his phrase "blood and iron." This time the slogan has been inappropriate.

There have been several Germanys over the 119 years since the country first became a single national unit, governed from Berlin. They have in turn stretched over widely varying territories, incorporated different peoples, erected different political systems, and, perhaps most significant, caused innumerable human tragedies.

Historians generally agree that the Germany about to come into being has never existed before, not in its precise territorial condition, not in its political makeup and not in its relation to the rest of the world.

A 'Very Different' Germany

"I think we're going to see a new Germany very different from anything that existed before 1945, but I hope quite continuous with what we have seen in West Germany since 1949," said Fritz Stern, a German historian at Columbia University. "In some ways the real test of whether the Federal Republic constitutes a historic break with the past will come now.

"If, as I hope, it can assimilate East Germany into its political culture, respecting the social and psychological needs of the East Germans but gradually winning them over to a free and democratic society, then the break with the past will be assured," Professor Stern said.

Another historian, James Sheehan of Stanford University, argues that the newness of the emerging Germany makes the word "reunification" inaccurate.

"To think of a reunification is to suppose that there is some natural entity out there called Germany that was separated and is now reunited," he said. "But this is, after all, a state that never existed in its current boundaries. And it's not only a matter of borders. My impression is that Germany never was before a Western European state and society. The eastern border has moved west, and, in a much more important and significant way, German allegiences have turned west."

Any country's relationship with its past is complicated and often troubled, but the place of the new Germany in its history has a special meaning given its colossally flawed, tragic nature. Historians, looking at two world wars and the Holocaust, have identified certain fundamental themes of the German past, all of them related to the country's historic inability to satisfy its national aspirations and, at the same time, to remain peaceful and democratic. It is in this sense that the latest unification of Germany seems a departure from previous models, and a happy departure, historians say.

"The classic account of German history talks about the struggle for unity and freedom," Professor Sheehan said. "The liberal tradition within Germany always hoped that the two would turn out to be one and the same, but, in fact, the Germans seemed continually to have been confronted by the apparent need to choose one or the other."

Four Separate Periods

In all, German history since the first unification could be divided up into four separate periods, each of them seeming to be characterized by a different Germany. Each of the German incarnations gripped the geographical center of Europe. Every version of the German nation has also been at the heart of the overall contest that continued, in one form or another, right up to the end of the cold war.

The Germany forged in war and diplomacy by Bismarck stretched in the west from Alsace and Lorraine, seized in a war with France in 1870, to the territories of East Prussia, now parts of either Poland or the Soviet Union. Bismarck's Germany had some fundamental features that have endured throughout modern history. It had the largest population in Europe, outside Russia. It had the continent's most powerful economy. It had the most advanced system of social welfare in Europe.

Unlike the present day unified Germany, however, it was a highly militaristic state. Unlike France and Britain, which both made progress, however difficult and halting, toward genuine representative democracy, Germany, despite some democratic trappings, remained autocratic, controlled by the emperor and the chancellor in league with large, conservative landowners and industrialists. It was, moreover, highly nationalistic, yearning, as the phrase had it, for its "place in the sun."

Responsibility for the outbreak of World War I is a complicated question, much disputed by historians. But German militarism and expansionism certainly played a major, very likely decisive role. Professor Stern argues that the central element of German history at the time was a deep antagonism between the deeply conservative, authoritarian ruling classes and the growing Social Democratic Party in Germany that was both reformist and patriotic. This was an antagonism that explains the tragic violence of German history, the country's long failure to make peace with itself and the outside world.

"The antagonisms that existed after 1918 were, of course, profoundly sharpened by the defeat in World War I, which the ruling classes and the military immediately tried to blame on domestic opponents — the infamous 'stab in the back' lie," Professor Stern said.

The Germany that remained after the World War I, the second of the modern Germanys, was vastly changed in its size and extent from Bismarck's era, though, internally, much remained unaltered. The last emperor, William II, abdicated and what came to be known as the Weimar Republic was formed two days before Germany surrendered. In the peace treaty imposed by the Allies, Germany gave back Alsace and Lorraine to the French. A newly reconstituted Poland got large portions of previous German territory, including a coridor to the sea and the mining territory of Upper Silesia.

Seeds of Further Conflict

The remaining antagonisms inside Germany, the belief that domestic traitors had been responsible for the defeat, the humiliation of the peace, which formally blamed Germany for the war, a crippling inflation and the impossibility of paying the huge indemnity imposed by the peace treaty all were seeds of further conflict.

The Weimar republic struggled on with a succession of Socialist-led coalition governments, but all of the conservative forces, the monarchist army officers, the large landowners, even the former police agents of old imperial Germany remained in place. There were armed bands of anti-democratic rightists and agitators, one of whom, Adolf Hitler, went to prison after staging an abortive revolt in Munich in 1923.

Hitler, who joined the newly formed National Socialist German Workers Party in 1920, came to power in 1933 in a free election, and, once again, the old German urge toward militarism and expansion was ascendent, combined with a virulent strains of racial supremacy and a vicious anti-Semitism whose final result was the destruction of six million European Jews.

Hitler's Third Reich lasted until the end of World War II, and pushed the German borders to their widest extent. Germany in 1942 stretched from its pre-1919 borders on the West to the border of the Soviet Union in the East, a state of imperial dimensions built on old Prussian power, but far larger than anything envisaged, or desired, by Bismarck. It included Austria, which Bismarck had forcibly excluded from his Prussian-controlled federation.

Borders Were Redrawn

After the German defeat in World War II, the borders were dramatically redrawn to what they will be in the newly unified Germany. The border of Poland was moved about 100 miles to the west to compensate it for Polish lands taken in the war by the Soviet Union. The former German territory of East Prussia was divided between Poland and the Soviet Union, so that old German cities like Danzig (now Gdansk) and Königsberg (now Kaliningrad), where Immanuel Kant lived, were German no longer. Germany itself, after the war, became divided into the western zones, occupied by France, Britain and the United States, and the eastern zone, occupied by the Soviet Union.

Thus, the united Germany formally constituted today, with its capital in Berlin, is only a portion of the historic Germany created first by Bismarck and expanded, briefly, by Hitler. Will it remain that way? Nobody, of course, can be sure; but historians, comparing the new Germany with past Germanys, cite important differences that suggest an end to the old German habit of autocracy and expansionism.

"The Germany that was created in 1866 did have a chance to bring together the elements of unity and freedom," said Professor Sheehan. "It failed for lots of reasons, but the most important was that it refused to accept its geopolitical limits. The disasters that Germany brought upon itself were disasters of overreaching itself.

"That underscores the important difference between now and the past," Professor Sheehan continued. "I think that the Germans have now recognized their limits and have become Europeans in a way that was never the case in the past."

Referring to the Thirty Years' War, Professor Stern said: "The 17th century for Germany was a disaster of unprecedented magnitude. That was followed by efforts at Enlightenment in the 18th century, but, since then, from 1914 to 1945 — and, for the East Germans, from 1949 to 1989 — the Germans went though devastation and hardship, which they also inflicted on others. I have to believe they will have learned from all that."

Associated Press

Berliners celebrating German unity last night at the Brandenburg Gate.

A historian wonders if a break with the past will come now.

Bush Delivers Pledge of Help

WASHINGTON, Oct. 2 (Reuters) — President Bush hailed the German unification today as the end of East-West conflict and vowed that the United States would work to help Germany meet the challenges of the future.

"Forty-five years of conflict and confrontation between East and West are now behind us," Mr. Bush said in a statement. "At long last the day has come. Germany is united. Germany is fully free.

"America is proud to count itself among the friends and allies of free Germany, now and in the future. Even as Germany celebrates this new beginning, there is no doubt that the future holds challenges, new responsibilities," the President continued.

"I'm certain that our two nations will meet these challenges, as we have in the past, united by a common love of freedom. Together, building on the values we share, we will be partners in leadership."

After 45 Years of Division, The Two Germanys Reunite

Continued From Page A1

to disrupt the festivities, and the police reported seven arrests. But what protests there were passed with no major incidents.

Unity essentially meant that the German Democratic Republic with its 16 million citizens acceded to the Federal Republic of Germany, which expanded to become a state of 78 million souls and 137,900 square miles. The accession meant that the name, anthem, Constitution and Government of the Federal Republic became those of all Germany, that Chancellor Helmut Kohl became the first Chancellor of the reunited state and Mr. von Weizsäcker the first President.

Berlin Is Capital

Berlin, a city divided by the infamous wall into a gray Communist capital and a glittering capitalist enclave, became once again the political and spiritual capital of Germany.

"Everybody should know: Germany will not go it alone, there will be no unilateral nationalism and no 'restless Reich,' " vowed Mr. Kohl in an article written for the Frankfurter Allgemeine newspaper.

It was also a moment of poignant lasts. The German Democratic Republic, founded by Soviet occupiers as the "first state of workers and peasants on German soil," expired bankrupt but not entirely unmourned.

At the final session of Parliament, Jens Reich, a leader of the citizens' movements that led demonstrations a year earlier to bring down the Communists, assailed the first and only democratic legislature of East Germany for having done nothing but surrender the state to the West. "Unity must not become a memory of a stab in the back," he said.

'Farewell Without Tears'

But a more prevalent note was struck by the East German Prime Minister, Lothar de Maizière, at the final "state act" of the East German Government in the grand Schauspielhaus concert hall, attended by the political and cultural elite of the nation.

There, the first and last democratically elected leader of East Germany committed his state to history with the words: "In a few moments the German Democratic Republic accedes to the Federal Republic of Germany. With that, we Germans achieve unity in freedom. It is an hour of great joy. It is the end of many illusions. It is a farewell without tears."

Then Kurt Mazur, the conductor from Leipzig and a hero of the peaceful revolution last fall, rose to conduct Beethoven's Ninth Symphony, with the grand "Ode to Joy" in the final movement that for Germans stands as a spiritual hymn to hope.

Address by Kohl

Mr. Kohl, capping a year of political successes, addressed the nation on television several hours before unity.

"In a few hours a dream will become reality," Mr. Kohl said, his eyes turning misty. "After 40 bitter years of division, Germany, our fatherland, will be reunited. This is one of the happiest moments of my life. From the many letters and conversations I have had, I know the great joy also felt by the vast majority of you."

Many Germans, in fact, had spent the last several weeks complaining of the cost and dislocation of unity. But at the moment of unity, Mr. Kohl seemed correct in finding that it was a moment to celebrate.

'It Is Really Moving'

The Chancellor also made a point of thanking and reassuring Germany's allies and neighbors. "In particular," he said, "we thank the United States of America and above all President George Bush." Mr. Bush was among the first world leaders to abandon reservations about German unity and endorse Mr. Kohl's efforts.

In recent weeks, the process of unity had drawn growing grumbles from both East and West as Germans came to realize the huge cost of the undertaking. But for the hundreds of thousands who had gathered from across Germany and abroad, this was a night not to moan, but simply to celebrate.

"It is really moving," said Heinz Schober, a Berlin shopkeeper who had come with his wife. "We were here when the wall went up and we were here when it came down, and now we see something children will read about in history books."

Hundreds of stands along the Unter den Linden peddled everything from bratwurst and beer to "Day of Unity" T-shirts and chunks of the Berlin wall.

Musicians ranging from rock bands to a Soviet military band to Wolf Biermann, a onetime East German dissident, blared from 16 stages set up among the beer and sausage stands, and all along the mile-long avenue the mood was festive and joyous.

At one point, revelers before the Reichstag pressed hard against the steps, where Chancellor Kohl and other political leaders were gathered, but no problems developed.

The most serious trouble was reported in Göttingen, a West German city near the former border, where about 1,000 radical youths went on a rampage, smashing windows and denouncing unity.

Year of Rapid Change

Unity came to the Germans barely a year after streams of East Germans began pouring out through newly porous borders in Hungary and Czechoslovakia, forcing the East German leader, Erich Honecker, to confront a crisis just as he prepared to preside over the celebrations of his state's 40th anniversary.

A year before unity came, on Oct. 3, 1989, a flood of East German refugees had all but overwhelmed the West German Embassy in Czechoslovakia, and the East German Government finally gave permission for the refugees to go west. It also closed its borders, touching off new discontent and disorders.

The celebration of East Germany's anniversary four days later marked the beginning of the state's undoing. The Soviet leader, Mikhail S. Gorbachev, gave the first indications that he was not prepared to prop up the East German Government, and waves of demonstrators clashed with the police in East Berlin and other cities.

The demonstrations rapidly grew, driving the Government into disarray until it took the fateful action on Nov. 9 of opening the Berlin wall a crack, touching off a rush to unity. By March 18 East Germany held its first democratic elections, and by July 1 its economy was merged into West Germany's. The pace accelerated through the summer, bringing formal unity up to Oct. 3 and setting the scene for the celebration.

The pace of events also required a rapid termination of the vestigial occupation under which both the Germanys and the Berlins existed, and the moment of unity was preceded by a flurry of final arrangements and actions to end the Allied controls.

The commanders of the Western Allied forces, the United States, Britain and France, which merged their occupation zones of the city after the war to form West Berlin and defended it against Communist encirclement in ensuing years, met for the last time and ceded authority over the city.

"I now close this final meeting of the Allied Kommandatura with a good, solid bang," said the British commander, Maj. Gen. Robert Corbert, pounding the gavel at the Allied headquarters with a solid thump.

Associated Press

Berliners crowded the streets last night as unification neared. One carried an East German flag with its insignia crossed out.

"All the News That's Fit to Print"

The New York Times

Late Edition

New York: **Today,** partly cloudy, windy. High 49. **Tonight,** clear, cold winds. Low 32. **Tomorrow,** variable clouds. High 40. **Yesterday,** high 55, low 38. Details are on page D22.

VOL.CXL . . No. 48,483 NEW YORK, THURSDAY, JANUARY 17, 1991 — 50 cents beyond 75 miles from New York City, except on Long Island. — 40 CENTS

U.S. AND ALLIES OPEN AIR WAR ON IRAQ; BOMB BAGHDAD AND KUWAITI TARGETS; 'NO CHOICE' BUT FORCE, BUSH DECLARES

A TENSE WAIT ENDS

News of Attack Sweeps the Country, Stirring Profound Feelings

By JAMES BARRON

In one long moment yesterday, word that the United States had attacked Baghdad swept the country.

In split-level suburban homes on the East Coast where dinner was in the oven, in big-c... restaurants in the Midwest where bars were jammed with the happy-hour crowd and in skyscraper offices on the West Coast where people were still at work, there was an odd mixture of apprehension, sadness and relief.

In malls, shoppers emptied out of stores and cried. In supermarkets, cashiers rushed to call relatives and share the news that after five months of waiting and wondering America was at war. In department stores, people crowded in front of television sets, with some saying they were stunned that President Bush had decided to act so soon after the United Nations deadline for Iraq to withdraw from Kuwait.

A Scene Out of World War II

Suddenly, in public places where a buzz of cacophony is the norm, there was an unusual silence, eerie rather than giddy. Grand Central Terminal in Manhattan — where even whispers can take on an echoing, high-decibel intensity — was quiet. On trains to Connecticut, passengers gathered around people who had radios with headsets. "The people with the radios would listen to the news and then relay it to the other passengers," said Dan Brucker, a spokesman for the Metro-North Commuter Railroad, "kind of like World War II radio dispatchers delivering the news."

The word that waves of air attacks were striking Iraq silenced black-tie galas in Manhattan. And in a Houston hotel, the chatter around the bar stopped when the President began his speech from the Oval Office. Only the machine making frozen margaritas kept whirring.

Some people applauded Mr. Bush's decision to order the attack. "It was direct and to the point," Lester Alexander, a New Orleans real-estate investor, said of Mr. Bush's speech. "He did

Continued on Page A19, Column 4

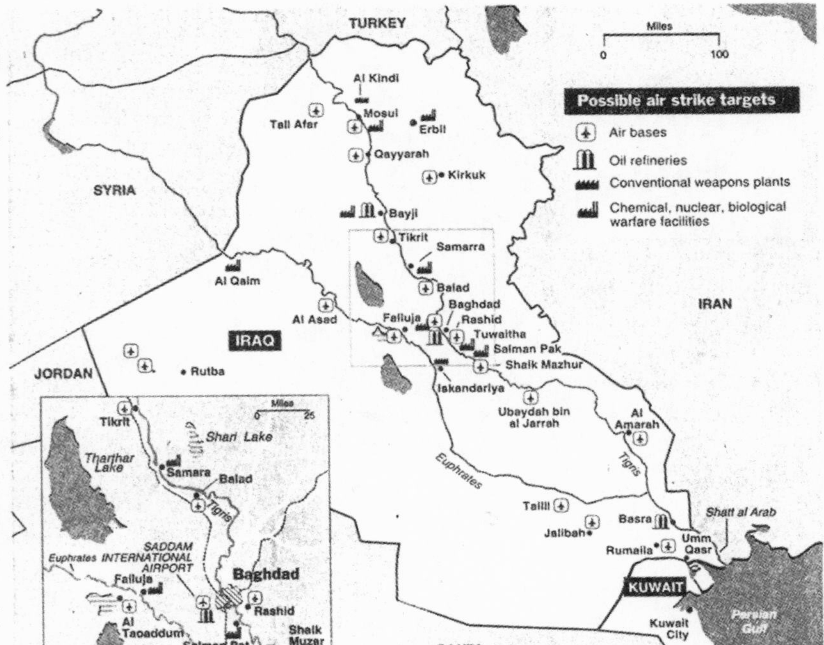

The New York Times

No Ground Fighting Yet; Call to Arms by Hussein

By ANDREW ROSENTHAL

Special to The New York Times

WASHINGTON, Thursday, Jan. 17 — The United States and allied forces Wednesday night opened the long-threatened war to drive President Saddam Hussein's army from Kuwait, striking Baghdad and other targets in Iraq and Kuwait with waves of bombers and cruise missiles launched from naval vessels.

"The liberation of Kuwait has begun," President Bush said in a three-sentence statement confirming the start of the attack that was read by his spokesman, Marlin Fitzwater, shortly after the raids began.

Later, in a televised address to the nation from the Oval Office, a somber Mr. Bush said that after months of continuous diplomatic overtures had failed to produce movement by Iraq, the United States and its allies "have no choice but to force Saddam from Kuwait by force. We will not fail." [Transcript, page A6.]

No Planes Reported Missing

United States officials said shortly after midnight Wednesday night that none of the planes that took part in the raid were reported missing.

In Baghdad, Mr. Hussein said in a speech broadcast by the Iraqi radio that "the mother of all battles has begun," according to news service reports. He called Mr. Bush a "hypocritical criminal" and vowed to crush "the satanic intentions of the White House." It was unclear when Mr. Hussein had read his remarks, whether they had been pre-recorded, or where he was at the time. [Page A18.]

Mr. Bush said his goal "is not the conquest of Iraq, it is the liberation of Kuwait." But he also said, "We are determined to knock out Saddam Hussein's nuclear bomb potential. We will also destroy his chemical weapons facilities."

3 Other Nations Take Part

Defense Secretary Dick Cheney and Gen. Colin L. Powell, the Chairman of the Joint Chiefs of Staff, told reporters at the Pentagon Wednesday night that those targets had been among those assigned to the first wave of American F-117 Stealth fighter-bombers, F-15 fighter-bombers, British Tornado attack planes and Saudi and Kuwaiti F-15's that raided Iraqi military targets at about 3 A.M. local time Thursday (7 P.M. Wednesday Eastern standard time.)

Administration officials also said United States Navy ships in the waters off the Arabian Peninsula had fired ground-hugging cruise missiles at targets that had been programmed into their guidance systems for months. The officials said the ships fired a total of 50 Tomahawk missiles in an assault on Iraqi command and communications centers.

Seeking to Avoid Civilians

Mr. Cheney said the initial targets were spread throughout Iraq and Kuwait and were chosen to "do everything possible to avoid injury to civilians." Both officials declined to say if there had been any American or allied losses, or to describe in any detail how badly they thought they had damaged Baghdad or the other Iraqi targets.

"The response of the Iraqi forces at this point has been limited," Mr. Cheney said, leading analysts to conclude that the allies may have succeeded in their goal of largely incapacitating Iraq's Air Force at the outset.

But Mr. Cheney said that the war was just beginning and that "it is likely to run for a long period of time."

Reports of New Attack

Cable News Network reported that the air raids on Baghdad resumed at about 9:30 A.M. Iraqi time.

He said the United States could not confirm reports that Iraq had fired Soviet-made Scud missiles at allied positions after the attack began. Reuters reported from Bahrain that the civil defense authorities there had detected missile launches but that the weapons fell short of their targets.

Assuring Americans that ground forces were not yet engaged in the battle, the President added: "Five months ago, Saddam Hussein started this cruel war against Kuwait. Tonight, the battle has been joined."

He said initial reports indicated that "our operations are proceeding according to plan."

"Our objectives are clear," he said. "Saddam Hussein's forces will leave Kuwait, the legitimate Government of Kuwait will be restored to its rightful place and Kuwait will once again be free."

"Some may ask, why act now? Why not wait?" the President said. "The answer is clear. The world could wait no longer."

Repeating his promises that Saudi

Continued on Page A14, Column 1

Raids, on a Huge Scale, Seek to Destroy Iraqi Missiles

ABC News

President Bush as he announced in a televised address last night that an air attack had been launched against Iraq.

By MICHAEL R. GORDON

Special to The New York Times

WASHINGTON, Thursday, Jan. 17 — The military campaign to evict Iraq from Kuwait began, as expected, with air strikes on a huge scale at targets deep in Iraq and Kuwait.

According to early reports of the operation from Pentagon officials, no American aircraft were lost and grave damage appeared to have been done to Iraqi military forces.

American officials said the onslaught against Iraqi air defenses, communications and weapons sites included the firing of Tomahawk sea-launched cruise missiles, as well as F-117 Stealth fighter-bombers, F-15E fighter-bombers and a wide variety of other Air Force and Navy planes.

British and Saudis Join In

The American aircraft were accompanied by British and Saudi Tornado fighter-bombers, Saudi F-15's and Kuwaiti combat planes.

The aims of the nighttime attack were to damage the Iraqi military establishment by destroying command and control centers, including those in Baghdad, and to establish air superiority by knocking out Iraqi air defenses and airfields.

Pentagon officials said that all Navy planes were reported to have returned safely. There were no reported Air Force losses, though the return of some of the planes to an air base near Taif, Saudi Arabia, was being delayed by bad weather there. Britain reported that all of its planes had returned safely.

Pentagon officials said that its bomb-damage assessments were still being conducted, and they disputed reports that the attacks had decimated the Republican Guards, the elite of the Iraqi Army.

Satellite Reports Awaited

Pentagon officials said the attack on Iraq appeared to be very successful because the Iraqi Air Force had not challenged the attacking planes and because the United States has no confirmed reports of launchings of Iraqi Scuds, long-range surface-to-surface missiles that are considered a threat to the allies' bases and to Israel. But they added that they were still awaiting definitive satellite and other reconnaissance reports.

Gen. Colin L. Powell, the chairman of the Joint Chiefs of Staff, said at a Pentagon news conference that "there has been no air resistance" from the Iraqis. Pentagon officials said that they hoped to destroy the Iraqi planes in their hardened shelters.

The allied air forces also attacked Scud batteries, and, as President Bush emphasized, American planes struck at Iraqi nuclear and chemical-weapons production sites. No ground forces were used in the operation, the Pentagon said.

Reassurance for Israel

In mounting the air attack, the United States is also trying to make good on assurances to the Israelis that Washington would blast the Scud missiles that threaten Israel to make it unnecessary for Israel to enter the war, the American officials said. Defense Secretary Dick Cheney said that the Pentagon had no information to confirm that Iraqi Scud missiles had struck Saudi Arabia.

The timing of the attack was designed to take advantage of the weakness of the Iraqi Air Force, which has

Continued on Page A15, Column 1

Rumble in the Sky Ends a 5-Month Wait

By PHILIP SHENON

Special to The New York Times

IN SAUDI ARABIA, Thursday, Jan. 17 — "It's absolutely awesome, I mean the ground shook and you felt it," said Col. Ray Davies, describing the takeoff of the first planes to attack Iraq from a big Saudi air base where he is chief maintenance officer.

The 44-year-old colonel said the first group of jets left at 12:50 A.M., about an hour before the first word of attack was broadcast by television reporters in Baghdad.

"We've been waiting here for five months; now we finally got to do what we were sent here to do," Colonel Davies told a group of American reporters who were brought to the base. "This is history in the making."

The F-15 fighter bombers, heavily loaded with bombs and supplemental underwing fuel tanks, thundered off in pairs into what had been a still desert night. The aircraft, which quickly became faint red dots, were also armed with cannon and air-to-air missiles to be used in their own defense.

The activity at the airfield, whose exact location cannot be identified under military reporting rules, was the first indication here that the assault was under way. All commercial traffic at the airport had been suspended a short time earlier.

Just before 4 A.M. Saudi time, hundreds of journalists and other guests at the Dhahran International Hotel, including many Filipino and Pakistani workers, were herded into the bomb shelter in the hotel basement and instructed to put on gas masks. Sirens started to wail throughout the city.

Waiting for the Signal

As the guests, primarily journalists, waited for the signal "gas clear," a hotel employee serving as warden directed guests to spread out in the area, which serves as a kitchen. The air conditioning had been turned off to prevent the spread of chemical agents in case the hotel in the eastern Saudi oil city was hit by Iraqi missiles. The room was quiet except for the sound of a radio on which a news announcer was saying that the attack had begun.

A British defense consultant who is working for the hotel, Philip Congdon,

Continued on Page A17, Column 6

MORE ON THE GULF

Bush Evokes Glory Of Past, Not Vietnam

To tell Americans that war with Iraq had started, President Bush harked back to one of the great days in American military history — D-Day, June 6, 1944. News analysis, page A16.

In Cairo, Jubilation Among Kuwaiti Exiles

Hundreds of Kuwaitis drove their cars through the Egyptian capital, honking and waving flags after hearing news of the American-led attack. "Thank God! Thank God!" was a cry heard over and over again. Page A18.

Israel on Alert

Israel declared a state of emergency minutes after word of the attack. There was no indication of an Iraqi attack on Israel. Page A18.

OTHER NEWS

Gorbachev Is Moving To Muzzle the Press

Faced with mounting condemnation of the assault by Soviet forces on demonstrators in Lithuania, President Mikhail S. Gorbachev moved to undermine a law guaranteeing freedom of the press — a hallmark of the era of openness that he himself ushered in. Page A8.

In a show of defiance in the Lithuanian capital, hundreds of thousands of mourners streamed through the streets to bury the dead. Page A8.

Dinkins Offers Budget With Layoffs and Cuts

Mayor David N. Dinkins presented a preliminary New York City budget of $29.3 billion for the next fiscal year. The announcement was met with a mix of pain and uncertainty. The plan includes thousands of layoffs and service cuts. Page B1.

Daily News Threatens To Close or Sell

The management of The Daily News threatened to close or sell the paper unless it stems heavy losses. Both sides in the 12-week-old strike agreed the move was an ultimatum to the unions to make major concessions or lose their jobs for good. Page B1.

C

The War Begins

"The liberation of Kuwait has begun. In conjunction with the forces of our coalition partners, the United States has moved under the code name Operation Desert Storm to enforce the mandates of the United Nations Security Council.

"As of 7 o'clock P.M. Operation Desert Storm forces were engaging targets in Iraq and Kuwait."

STATEMENT, PRESIDENT BUSH, 7:06 P.M.

War in the Gulf: 'The Liberation of Kuwait Has Begun'

The Overview

Gulf War Begins With U.S. Air Strikes in Iraq and Kuwait; Baghdad Is Bombed

Continued From Page A1

Arabia would not become "another Vietnam," Mr. Bush said he would bring American troops home as soon as possible.

"I'm hopeful that this fighting will not go on for long and that casualties will be held to an absolute minimum," he said. "Our troops will have the best possible support in the entire world, and they will not be asked to fight with one hand tied behind their back."

In the written statement issued earlier, Mr. Fitzwater said: "In conjunction with the forces of our coalition partners, the United States has moved under the code name Operation Desert Storm to enforce the mandates of the United Nations Security Council. As of 7 o'clock P.M., Operation Desert Storm forces were engaging targets in Iraq and Kuwait."

The current President of the United Nations Security Council, Bagbeni Adeito Nzengeya of Zaire, convened the Council late Wednesday night to discuss the outbreak of fighting.

Security Council Resolution 678, which authorized the use of force against Iraq after Jan. 15, also requires "the states concerned" to keep the Council regularly informed about any action they take under the resolution.

Skies Over Baghdad Alight

The nighttime attack was first revealed in television reports by American correspondents in Baghdad that the skies over the Iraqi capital were alight with anti-aircraft and tracer fire. Initial reports were that multiple waves of warplanes bombed central Baghdad, hitting oil refineries and the airport.

Mr. Bush notified Congressional leaders of the planned attack between 6 and 7 P.M., telephoning House Speaker Thomas S. Foley and Robert C. Byrd, the President pro tem of the Senate. In a letter and a report, he also sent the formal notification, as required under the war resolution passed by the House and Senate last week, that all efforts at diplomacy had failed and that he had made his final decision to commit America to its first all-out war since Vietnam.

"The Government of Iraq remains completely intransigent in rejecting the U.N. Security Council's demands, despite the exhaustive use by the United States and the United Nations of all appropriate diplomatic, political and economic measures to persuade or compel Iraq to comply," the report said.

Foley Urges Unity

Mr. Foley said: "We must now pray for a conflict that ends quickly, decisively and with a minimum loss of life. We must now stand united in support of our armed forces in the gulf who have embraced the duty and burden of conducting the war."

Senator Bob Dole of Kansas, the Republican Leader, said, "The cause of this war is Iraqi aggression, not American determination."

In New York, the United Nations Secretary General, Javier Pérez de Cuéllar, said, "I think it is for me to express deep sorrow."

United States officials said that the decision to go to war had been developing over several days, and that Mr. Bush had been working on at least four drafts of his speech for two or three weeks.

But he put into motion the actual order for battle only at 8 A.M. Wednesday, when Saudi officials said Secretary of State James A. Baker 3d called in the Saudi Ambassador, Prince Bandar bin Sultan, and told him that American forces would attack Iraq.

Code Word to King Fahd

The Ambassador telephoned King Fahd of Saudi Arabia, using a prearranged code word, the informants said. The King then repeated back a code word that constituted the final acknowledgement that the offensive would begin.

Mr. Bush monitored the offensive from the Oval Office, where he had watched the evening news and waited for the first signs of attack with Vice President Dan Quayle, Brent Scowcroft, the national security adviser, and John H. Sununu, the White House Chief of Staff. Mr. Scowcroft spent the night in the Situation Room in the White House basement, connected electronically to the Central Intelligence Agency, the State Department and the Pentagon, where Mr. Cheney and General Powell worked through the night as well.

Making good on his repeated warnings to Mr. Hussein, who had defied 12 United Nations resolutions and a naval blockade, Mr. Bush began the largest American military offensive since the Vietnam War about 19 hours after the expiration of the United Nations deadline for Iraq to leave Kuwait peacefully. The President said he decided to order the attack because "the world could wait no longer." He added, "Sanctions, though having some effect, showed no signs of accomplishing their objective."

Congressional Vote Cited

He said he had hoped that the Congressional vote authorizing the use of force last weekend would prompt Mr. Hussein to agree to withdraw from Kuwait. "Instead he remained intransigent, certain that time was on his side," Mr. Bush said.

"No President can easily commit our sons and daughters to war," he said.

Mr. Fitzwater's statement about the start of war was prepared Tuesday night, the President's spokesman said, but Mr. Bush could have withheld the final order to attack "if there was a massive pullout by Saddam Hussein."

"It could have been changed," Mr. Fitzwater said.

Late Wednesday night, the White House said that Mr. Bush had authorized the Energy Secretary, James Watkins, to distribute 1.12 million barrels a day from the Strategic Petroleum Reserve for the next 30 days in a measure "designed to promote stability in world markets."

The United States had spent the day formalizing a command system under which international forces are expected to fight under United Nations auspices but under the actual leadership of the United States.

Bush Calls Other Leaders

Mr. Bush called Prime Minister John Major of Britain and other leaders of the anti-Iraqi alliance Wednesday from his private study to inform them that the attack was about to begin.

The White House also sought to reassure the American people that all prospects for a peaceful solution had been exhausted, leaving Mr. Bush no choice but to begin what he has said will be an overwhelming display of air, sea and land power that will end Iraq's occupation of Kuwait swiftly and decisively.

"This military action, taken in accord with United Nations resolutions and with the consent of the United States Congress, follows months of constant and virtually endless diplomatic activity on the part of the United Nations, the United States and many, many other countries," Mr. Bush said.

Some of those who had opposed the Congressional resolution on the use of force issued statements rallying behind the President.

Senator David L. Boren, Democrat of Oklahoma and chairman of Senate Intelligence Committee, said: "Now that the war has begun, all Americans should unite behind our troops. We hope and pray that victory will come quickly and with minimum loss of life."

The House majority leader, Richard A. Gephardt, said, "My prayers and thoughts are with the soldiers and their families, and my hopes are for a swift and successful conclusion to this war."

Although initial reports from Saudi Arabia and Iraq were very sketchy, the first wave of attacks appeared, as expected, to exploit the alliance's overwhelming air power, perhaps in an attempt to bomb strategic command targets in Baghdad.

Reports from members of the news pool stationed in Saudi Arabia with American forces said two squadrons of F-15E fighter-bombers loaded with bombs and air-to-air missiles took off at 12:50 A.M. today from the largest American military base, in central Saudi Arabia.

They made the 600-mile-plus flight to Baghdad in about 90 minutes, flying into the clear night sky in pairs. "We've been waiting here for five months now," said Col. Ray Davies, the base's chief maintenance officer. "Now we finally got to do what we were sent here to do."

A steady stream of F-15E's were taking off from central and eastern Saudi Arabia, part of an international air force that includes the deadliest, fastest and most technologically advanced warplanes in the world.

The United States alone has about 1,800 warplanes in the Persian Gulf region, based at military installations in Saudi Arabia and aboard six aircraft carriers plying the gulf, the Red Sea and the Arabian Sea.

The Pentagon said Wednesday that there were now 425,000 American soldiers stationed in the region after the swiftest and largest mobilization of arms in American military history. There are an additional 265,000 troops from 27 other countries, facing what the Pentagon estimates is an Iraqi Army of 545,000 in southern Iraq and Kuwait.

From Baghdad, television broadcasts said the pounding of the city continued intermittently through the night. The city had gone black, shaking from bomb reports as the night sky was pierced by tracers from batteries of anti-aircraft weapons massed around the city. At one point, reporters in Baghdad said volleys of anti-aircraft fire, and the glow of distant explosions lit the entire night sky.

A Cable News Network correspondent said he had seen a fire near a mosque, while another reported that a refinery near the presidential palace was being fired on. Loud explosions and machine-gun fire could be heard in the background as the reporters spoke by telephone with their oprganizations in the United States.

In Saudi Arabia, news reports said that air raid sirens had been turned on at air bases and that reporters had been ordered to go inside and advised to put on their gas masks, but there were no reports of enemy attacks.

Congress had given Mr. Bush authority to use force against Iraq on Saturday after a long and emotional debate. The President also acted with the authorization of the United Nations. It had given Iraq until Tuesday to leave Kuwait, which Baghdad occupied on Aug. 2 in a lightning raid that shattered what the United States and Europe had hoped would be a time of peace following the end of the cold war.

The American response had been orchestrated over the next five months, as Mr. Bush moved virtually the entire might of the nation's non-nuclear forces to the gulf while the United Nations sought to dislodge Iraq from Kuwait through a constantly tightening chokehold of economic sanctions.

The United States had expressed growing impatience with the sanctions, however, and the planning for war was stepped up sharply after Nov. 29, when the United Nations approved the resolution authorizing the use of force if Iraq did not withdraw by Jan 15.

Associated Press

Seaman Norm Beck listening yesterday as the captain of the battleship Wisconsin announced that all ships in the gulf were put on high alert.

Iraqi television via Reuters

President Saddam Hussein touring military installations in Kuwait on Tuesday.

> President Bush orders the United States into a major conflict.

The President

Transcript of the Comments by Bush on the Air Strikes Against the Iraqis

Following is a transcript of President Bush's remarks in the Oval Office last night about the Persian Gulf action, as recorded by The New York Times:

Just two hours ago, allied air forces began an attack on military targets in Iraq and Kuwait. These attacks continue as I speak. Ground forces are not engaged.

This conflict started Aug. 2, when the dictator of Iraq invaded a small and helpless neighbor. Kuwait, a member of the Arab League and a member of the United Nations, was crushed, its people brutalized. Five months ago, Saddam Hussein started this cruel war against Kuwait; tonight, the battle has been joined.

This military action, taken in accord with United Nations resolutions and with the consent of the United States Congress, follows months of constant and virtually endless diplomatic activity on the part of the United Nations, the United States and many, many other countries.

Arab leaders sought what became known as an Arab solution, only to conclude that Saddam Hussein was unwilling to leave Kuwait. Others traveled to Baghdad in a variety of efforts to restore peace and justice. Our Secretary of State, James Baker, held an historic meeting in Geneva, only to be totally rebuffed.

This past weekend, in a last-ditch effort, the Secretary General of the United Nations weht to the Middle East with peace in his heart — his second such mission. And he came back from Baghdad with no progress at all in getting Saddam Hussein to withdraw from Kuwait.

No Choice but to Attack

Now, the 28 countries with forces in the gulf area have exhausted all reasonable efforts to reach a peaceful resolution, and have no choice but to drive Saddam from Kuwait by force. We will not fail.

As I report to you, air attacks are under way against military targets in Iraq. We are determined to knock out Saddam Hussein's nuclear bomb potential. We will also destroy his chemical weapons facilities. Much of Saddam's artillery and tanks will be destroyed. Our operations are designed to best protect the lives of all the coalition forces by targeting Saddam's vast military arsenal.

Initial reports from General Schwartzkopf are that our operations are proceeding according to plan. Our objectives are clear: Saddam Hussein's forces will leave Kuwait. The legitimate government of Kuwait will be restored to its rightful place, and Kuwait will once again be free.

Iraq will eventually comply with all relevant United Nations resolutions, and then, when peace is restored, it is our hope that Iraq will live as a peaceful and cooperative member of the family of nations, thus enhancing the security and stability of the gulf.

'Why Not Wait?'

Some may ask, why act now? Why not wait? The answer is clear. The world could wait no longer. Sanctions, though having some effect, showed no signs of accomplishing their objective. Sanctions were tried for well over five months, and we and our allies concluded that sanctions alone would not force Saddam from Kuwait.

While the world waited, Saddam Hussein systematically raped, pillaged and plundered a tiny nation no threat to his own. He subjected the people of Kuwait to unspeakable atrocities, and among those maimed and murdered, innocent children.

While the world waited, Saddam sought to add to the chemical weapons arsenal he now possesses, an infinitely more dangerous weapon of mass destruction — a nuclear weapon. And while the world waited, while the world talked peace and withdrawal, Saddam Hussein dug in and moved massive forces into Kuwait.

While the world waited, while Saddam stalled, more damage was being done to the fragile economies of the Third World, emerging democracies of Eastern Europe, to the entire world, including to our own economy.

The United States, together with the United Nations, exhausted every means at our disposal to bring this crisis to a peaceful end. However, Saddam clearly felt that by stalling and threatening and defying the United Nations, he could weaken the forces arrayed against him.

While the world waited, Saddam Hussein met every overture of peace with open contempt. While the world prayed for peace, Saddam prepared for war.

I had hoped that when the United States Congress, in historic debate, took its resolute action, Saddam would realize he could not prevail, and would move out of Kuwait in accord with the United Nations resolutions. He did not do that. Instead, he remained intransigent, certain that time was on his side.

Saddam was warned over and over again to comply with the will of the United Nations, leave Kuwait or be driven out. Saddam has arrogantly rejected all warnings. Instead he tried to make this a dispute between Iraq and the United States of America.

Well he failed. Tonight 28 nations — countries from five continents, Europe and Asia, Africa and the Arab League — have forces in the Gulf area standing shoulder to shoulder against Saddam Hussein. These countries had hoped the use of force could be avoided. Regrettably, we now believe that only force will make him leave.

Prior to ordering our forces into battle, I instructed our military commanders to take every necessary step to prevail as quickly as possible, and with the greatest degree of protection possible for American and Allied servicemen and women. I've told the American people before that this will not be another Vietnam, and I repeat this here tonight. Our troops will have the best possible support in the entire world, and they will not be asked to fight with one hand tied behind their back. I'm hopeful that this fighting will not go on for long and that casualties will be held to an absolute minimum.

'An Historic Moment'

This is an historic moment. We have in this past year made great progress in ending the long era of conflict and cold war. We have before us the opportunity to forge for ourselves and for future generations a new world order, a world where the rule of law, not the law of the jungle, governs the conduct of nations.

When we are successful, and we will be, we have a real chance at this new world order, an order in which a credible United Nations can use its peacekeeping role to fulfill the promise and vision of the U.N.'s founders. We have no argument with the people of Iraq. Indeed, for the innocents caught in this conflict, I pray for their safety.

Our goal is not the conquest of Iraq. It is the liberation of Kuwait. It is my hope that somehow the Iraqi people can, even now, convince their dictator that he must lay down his arms, leave Kuwait and let Iraq itself rejoin the family of peace loving nations.

Thomas Paine wrote many years ago: "These are the times that try men's souls." Those well-known words are so very true today. But even as planes of the multi-national forces attack Iraq, I prefer to think of peace, not war. I am convinced not only that we will prevail, but that out of the horror of combat will come the recognition that no nation can stand against a world united. No nation will be permitted to brutally assault its neighbor.

No President can easily commit our sons and daughters to war. They are the nation's finest. Ours is an all-volunteer force, magnificently trained, highly motivated. The troops know why they're there. And listen to what they say, because they've said it better than any President or Prime Minister ever could. Listen to Hollywood Huddleston, Marine lance corporal. He says: "Let's free these people so we can go home and be free again." And he's right. The terrible crimes and tortures committed by Saddam's henchmen against the innocent people of Kuwait are an affront to mankind and a challenge to the freedom of all.

'Worth Fighting For'

Listen to one of our great officers out there, Marine Lieut. Gen. Walter Boomer. He said: "There are things worth fighting for. A world in which brutality and lawlessness are allowed to go unchecked isn't the kind of world we're going to want to live in."

Listen to Master Sgt. J. P. Kendall of the 82d Airborne: "We're here for more than just the price of a gallon of gas. What we're doing is going to chart the future of the world for the next hundred years. It's better to deal with this guy now than five years from now."

And finally, we should all sit up and listen to Jackie Jones, an Army lieutenant, when she says, "If we let him get away with this, who knows what's going to be next."

I've called upon Hollywood and Walter and J. P. and Jackie and all their courageous comrades-in-arms to do what must be done. Tonight, America and the world are deeply grateful to them and to their families.

And let me say to everyone listening or watching tonight: When the troops we've sent in finish their work, I'm determined to bring them home as soon as possible. Tonight, as our forces fight, they and their families are in our prayers.

May God bless each and every one of them and the coalition forces at our side in the Gulf, and may He continue to bless our nation, the United States of America.

> **A NEW WORLD ORDER**
>
> *"We have in this past year made great progress in ending the long era of conflict and cold war. We have before us the opportunity to forge for ourselves and for future generations a new world order, a world where the rule of law, not the law of the jungle, governs the conduct of nations."*

"All the News That's Fit to Print"

The New York Times

Late Edition
New York: **Today,** partly cloudy, not as cold. High 43. **Tonight,** some clouds. Low near 40. **Tomorrow,** some sun, windy, warmer. High 58. **Yesterday,** high 36, low 26. Details, page B14.

VOL.CXL . . No. 48,525

NEW YORK, THURSDAY, FEBRUARY 28, 1991

50 cents beyond 75 miles from New York City, except on Long Island. 40 CENTS

BUSH HALTS OFFENSIVE COMBAT; KUWAIT FREED, IRAQIS CRUSHED

Associated Press

Under skies darkened by smoke from burning oil wells, Kuwaitis celebrated the recapture of Kuwait City from Iraq. The Kuwaiti flag, which had vanished from public display during Iraq's occupation, suddenly appeared everywhere. Page A6.

Associated Press

Gen. H. Norman Schwarzkopf as he discussed allied successes at a news briefing yesterday in Saudi Arabia.

MILITARY AIMS MET

Firing Ending After 100 Hours of Ground War, President Declares

By ANDREW ROSENTHAL
Special to The New York Times

WASHINGTON, Thursday, Feb. 28 — Declaring that "Kuwait is liberated" and Iraq's army defeated, President Bush ordered allied forces on Wednesday night to suspend offensive military operations against President Saddam Hussein's isolated and battered army.

Mr. Bush said the suspension, which began at midnight Eastern time, would continue as long as Iraq did not attack allied forces or launch missile attacks on any other country. In an address from the Oval Office that was televised around the world at 9 P.M. Eastern time, he called on Mr. Hussein to send his commanders to meet with allied officers in the war zone within 48 hours to settle the military terms of a permanent cease-fire.

For such a cease-fire to be approved, he said, Iraq must comply with all 12 United Nations resolutions concerning Kuwait, including measures calling for Iraq to void its annexation of the territory and agree in principle to pay reparations to Kuwait and other countries. Iraq must also free all prisoners of war and detained Kuwaiti citizens, and give the allies the location of all land and sea mines that Iraq had laid in the region, Mr. Bush said.

No Official Word From Iraq

Administration officials said they had received no authoritative response from the Iraqi Government. At the United Nations, Soviet diplomats said Iraq had submitted a letter signaling its willingness to comply with all 12 resolutions adopted by the Security Council. But the letter did not say whether Baghdad was willing to comply with the rest of Mr. Bush's demands, including the freeing of Kuwaiti civilians seized in recent days. [Text of the letter, page A10.]

Pentagon officials said this morning there were no reports of renewed Iraqi attacks on allied positions.

Speaking in a solemn voice, President Bush said: "This war is now behind us. Ahead of us is the difficult task of securing a potentially historic peace." [Transcript of his remarks, page A12.]

He seemed to invite the citizens of Iraq to overthrow the man who had defied the assembled military and political power of the international alliance. "Coalition forces fought this war only as a last resort," Mr. Bush said, "and look foward to the day when Iraq is led by people prepared to live in peace with their neighbors."

Unusually Low Casualties

Mr. Bush, who had staked his Presidency on being able to resolve a crisis that had shattered the post-cold war calm and led to the largest single American military offensive since World War II, declared an end to the war in his third nationally televised speech from the Oval Office since Iraq invaded Kuwait on Aug. 2.

To arrive at the point where he was able to declare victory last night, Mr. Bush had to command what military experts said was one of the largest combat operations ever conducted with such low casualties, counter political opposition at home and navigate the shoals of diplomacy complicated by last-minute Soviet peace ventures that plainly irritated the President and his war council.

"At midnight tonight, Eastern standard time, exactly 100 hours since ground operations commenced and six weeks since the start of Operation Desert Storm, all United States and

Continued on Page A12, Column 1

Freed Kuwaitis Tell of Iraqi Abuse Including Some Cases of Torture

By CHRIS HEDGES
Special to The New York Times

KUWAIT CITY, Feb. 27 — On the third floor of a gutted mansion, a Kuwaiti Army major slowly pushed open a door with his foot to what was once a laundry room. It had been converted by the Iraqis, he said, into a torture chamber.

In one corner were metal box springs, raised off the floor by chairs. Next to the springs was a crude brown box with bare electrical wires protruding from black cords.

"They put the prisoners on the springs, poured water over them and then applied the current," said the Kuwaiti Army officer, Maj. Jamal al-Hassan, who was a leader in the underground during the occupation. "If they were not happy with the answers, they turned up the voltage."

Accounts of Torture

Kuwaitis who were picked up by the Iraqi secret police had their own stories to tell.

"They beat me, did not let me sleep and made me sit naked on a bottle of hot sauce," said 21-year-old Faisal al-Anizi. "This went on for three days in what used to be the reform school."

Others tell of being rubbed down with sandpaper, having their heads thrust into cold water and being hung by their hands from a hook.

When an American correspondent arrived in Kuwait City on Tuesday, ahead of entering allied troops, he found Kuwaitis who were eager to tell the world that Saddam Hussein brought more to Kuwait than Iraqi license plates and innumerable portraits of himself. He had also brought the techniques of control that have kept his authoritarian Government in power.

Members of the Kuwaiti underground, acting on information provided by people who said they were tortured by the Iraqi secret police, have identified places where Kuwaitis were questioned, beaten and tortured.

A visitor is overwhelmed by reports that hundreds, perhaps thousands of young men were taken by the Iraqis, many in the final hours before the Iraqi forces left the city on Monday. Their parents and friends fear that they may not reappear.

"A lot of people have disappeared in Iraq and never been seen since," said

Continued on Page A6, Column 4

IRAQ ELITE ROUTED, U.S. SOLDIERS SAY

Officers Brace for Prisoners as Hussein's Force Retreats

By PHILIP SHENON
Special to The New York Times

WITH U.S. VII CORPS, in Iraq, Feb. 27 — American troops described a ferocious armored battle between the United States and troops of Iraq's Republican Guards that resulted, they said in interviews tonight, in devastating losses for the Iraqis and a torrent of thousands of battle-weary Iraqi prisoners of war.

In battlefield interviews with troops from three of the four Army divisions involved in the assault on the guards, American soldiers said that the tank clash raged across dozens of miles of the southern Iraqi desert. Speaking before President Bush ordered military operations suspended, the soldiers said that the Iraqi guards were offering fierce resistance despite overwhelming odds.

Tanks Are Charred Bits of Steel

During a helicopter tour today close to the front lines, the devastation wrought by allied forces on the Iraqi military in recent days and weeks was made plain.

The burned-out shells of scores of Iraqi tanks, some smoldering, some still on fire, sat in what had been extensive dug-in fortifications of sand and dirt. All that remained of several Iraqi tanks and artillery installations were charred bits of steel spread across hundreds of square yards of scrub-covered desert floor.

From the air, large bands of captured Iraqi soldiers could be seen in the custody of American soldiers.

The Americans described prisoners captured today from other, regular Iraqi units as desperate for food, water and medical attention, after a month-long allied bombing campaign cut them off from supply lines.

Some of the Iraqis said they had not been fed for days. As many as one-third

Continued on Page A7, Column 1

Allies Destroy Iraqis' Main Force; Kuwait Is Retaken After 7 Months

By R. W. APPLE Jr.
Special to The New York Times

DHAHRAN, Saudi Arabia, Thursday, Feb. 28 — Hours before President Bush announced the conditional suspension of offensive military operations in the Persian Gulf, allied armored units, which had trapped Iraq's vaunted Republican Guard, cut it to pieces in a furious tank battle that began Wednesday and raged until early this morning, American officials said.

At midday Wednesday, United States Marines captured the Kuwait International Airport after a smaller but nonetheless intense two-day fight, and later, marines and Kuwaiti and other Arab troops rode in triumph down the broad boulevards of Kuwait City, past scenes of devastation and desolation. That essentially completed the expulsion of President Saddam Hussein's forces from Kuwait, which they had overrun in a surprise assault last Aug. 2.

Casualties among coalition forces were light and Iraqi losses heavy, the allied command said.

But the honking horns, waving flags and scenes of jubilation as the capital was retaken scarcely concealed the agony generated by tales of torture, kidnapping, rape and pillage over the final days of occupation. As many as 40,000 Kuwaitis were said to have been taken hostage by the Iraqis as they fled north on Tuesday.

Gen. H. Norman Schwarzkopf, commander of the American-led coalition that has trounced Iraq in a lightning-fast ground war reminiscent of the World War II blitzkrieg, said the Iraqi leader had been stripped of the offensive weapons that made his army one of the most fearsome in the Middle East.

'Not Enough Left'

"There's not enough left for him to be a regional threat," the general said in a detailed briefing on the campaign Wednesday night, adding pointedly, "unless someone chooses to rearm them in the future." [Excerpts, page A8.]

"We've accomplished our mission," General Schwarzkopf said, hours before Mr. Bush spoke, "and when the decision-makers come to the decision that there should be a cease-fire, nobody will be happier than me."

With his army shattered and reeling after 100 hours of ground combat, Mr.

Continued on Page A9, Column 1

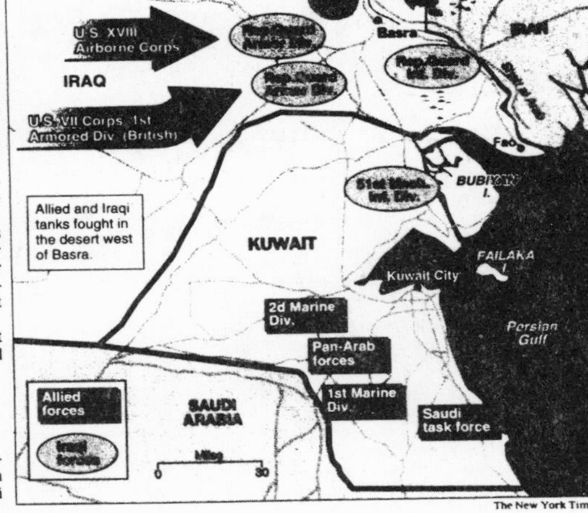

The New York Times

Ethics Unit Singles Out Cranston, Chides 4 Others in S.& L. Inquiry

By RICHARD L. BERKE
Special to The New York Times

WASHINGTON, Feb. 27 — Seeking to set standards for the way lawmakers raise money and do favors, the Senate Ethics Committee concluded today that Senator Alan Cranston engaged in "an impermissible pattern of conduct" that might warrant disciplinary action by the full Senate.

In written rebukes to four other Senators who were also investigated for their ties to Charles H. Keating Jr., a savings and loan executive and contributor to the Senators' campaigns or causes they supported, the committee asserted that their behavior reflected poor judgment at the very least.

The committee's finding on Mr. Cranston essentially clears the way for it to recommend that the full Senate reprimand him as the panel is expected to do. But the committee said the other lawmakers' actions were not significant enough to require such further action.

Aside from Mr. Cranston, a California Democrat, the findings against two other Democrats, Senators Dennis DeConcini of Arizona and Donald W. Riegle Jr. of Michigan, were the most stern. The committee said their conduct "gave the appearance of being improper and was certainly attended with insensitivity and poor judgment." The lightest rebukes went to Senators John Glenn, an Ohio Democrat, and John McCain, an Arizona Republican, who were found to have "exercised poor judgment." [Excerpts from the committee's statement, page B10.]

Today's announcement came after the committee voted unanimously on each Senator, ending a 14-month inves-

Continued on Page B10, Column 1

Women Among War Dead

At least three women were reported to be among the 28 American soldiers who were killed in an Iraqi missile attack on Tuesday. Page A13.

INSIDE

Condom Plan Approved

The New York City Board of Education narrowly approved a plan to make condoms available to the city's 250,000 high school students. Page B1.

New Rival to Phone Industry

Three cable television companies plan to build experimental networks that would allow people to use very small wireless telephones. Page D1.

Pool photo via Associated Press

Legions of bedraggled Iraqi warriors on buses, trucks and flatbed trailers voiced cheers of relief at the end of their fighting days. Page A10.

War in the Gulf: The White House View

The President

Bush Calls Off Allied Attacks; Kuwait Is Freed

Continued From Page A1

coalition forces will suspend offensive combat operations," Mr. Bush said.

Mr. Bush did not say when he would start bringing American troops home. Marlin Fitzwater, his spokesman, said late Wednesday night that there was no specific timetable, but added: "We'll measure it in days, not weeks. Clearly, the President wants to start the withdrawal as soon as possible."

Within hours after Mr. Bush spoke, the United States, Iraq and the Soviet Union each tried to gain control of the public relations of peace with messages directed at their domestic political audiences.

Baghdad Radio defiantly proclaimed Iraq's triumph over "the forces of evil" and Soviet diplomats at the United Nations said that it was Iraq's promises to heed the United Nations resolutions, delivered through Moscow's intercession, that had prompted Mr. Bush to give his speech.

Senior White House officials insisted that Mr. Bush knew nothing of the reported letter of agreement from Iraq when he went on television Wednesday night. Mr. Fitzwater said the speech was motivated in part by a desire to assure the families of military personnel that they would soon be coming home.

The President, who had brushed aside Iraq's last attempt to win a cease-fire on favorable terms earlier in the day, said: "Iraq's Army is defeated. Our military objectives are met. Kuwait is once more in the hands of Kuwaitis in control of their own destiny.

"The Kuwaiti flag once again flies above the capital of a free and sovereign nation, and the American flag flies above our embassy," Mr. Bush said.

The 100-hour ground war halts with stiff terms set for Iraq.

After seven months of holding together a disparate international coalition and rallying American public opinion with the promise that he would not allow the Persian Gulf crisis to become another Vietnam, Mr. Bush said he was sending Secretary of State James A. Baker 3d to the Middle East to "look beyond victory and war" and to "meet the challenging of securing the peace."

Mr. Bush's speech capped a six-week allied military offensive against Iraq in which fewer than 100 Americans were killed, according to the latest report today from the Pentagon, and whose swiftness astonished even the President's war council.

He spoke only a few hours after his commander in the Persian Gulf, Gen. H. Norman Schwarzkopf, described the last major battle of the war, between allied armored divisions and Iraq's Republican Guard, the last remants of what had been Mr. Hussein's huge military machine, near the southern Iraqi city of Basra.

A Balancing Position

Mr. Bush's speech, scheduled less than three hours before it was delivered, seemed to represent a balancing of the American position, that Iraq should not get off too easily, with mounting international pressures to stop the assaults on an obviously defeated army.

Reflecting those pressures, Mr. Bush said: "In the future, as before, we will consult with our coalition partners. We've already done a good deal of thinking and planning for the postwar period."

He said: "There can be and will be no solely American answer to all these challenges, but we can assist and support the countries of the region and be a catalyst for peace."

With Mr. Hussein still in power in Baghdad, the declaration of victory left major political and diplomatic issues ahead, including the question of a postwar role for Iraq in the region, the durability of Mr. Hussein himself and the inevitable pressure on the United States to take a leading role in resolving the so-far intractable Middle East problems to which the Administration is now turning its attention, including the Israeli-Palestinian dispute.

Jubilation in Washington

Mr. Bush's speech produced jubilation in Washington. Residents streamed to the gates of the White House, waving small American flags, and drivers honked their horns as they passed by along Pennsylvania Avenue.

Senator George J. Mitchell, the majority leader, said, "All Americans rejoice at the news that our servicemen and women may soon be returning home." He added, "Our hearts go out to the families who have suffered the loss of loved ones in this effort."

The Speaker of the House, Thomas S. Foley, said: "The majority in Congress voted to give the President the authority, and he has taken that authority and I think conducted this operation brilliantly. And we can all be deeply grateful that the casualties have been so low and the victory has come so fast."

Mr. Bush's declaration of victory was the climactic moment in a crisis that began in the early hours of Aug. 2, when a huge Iraqi armored column swept into sparsely-defended Kuwait. It followed the breakdown of negotiations over Mr. Hussein's demands for territorial concessions and financial payments in return for his eight-year war against Iran.

Rallied Coalition, Choked Iraq

Startling the world with the swiftness of his response, Mr. Bush began sending American soldiers to the Middle East six days later, a deployment that quickly surpassed even that of Vietnam. He rallied a coalition that revived the moribund Security Council, with the crucial help of the Soviet Union, and began choking Baghdad with a series of economic sanctions enforced by allied naval power.

As diplomacy faltered and sanctions failed to drive Iraq out of Kuwait, Mr. Bush doubled the American force in October, until there were more than a half-million allied forces in Saudi Arabia. In late November, the allies gave Mr. Hussein a final ultimatum: Get out of Kuwait by Jan. 15 or face war.

An offer for direct talks with Baghdad floundered in diplomatic brinksmanship and Mr. Bush sent allied warplanes into combat on Jan. 16. For six weeks, they poured an unequalled rain of explosives onto Iraqi communications networks and military positions until, judging that Iraq's forces were ripe for the kill, Mr. Bush unleashed the ground offensive last Saturday night.

Before Mr. Bush spoke, it had been a day for optimistic predictions of victory, tough talk against Iraq and the back-and-forth struggle of diplomacy and semantics between Washington and Baghdad. Defense Secretary Dick Cheney, speaking to the American Legion yesterday afternoon, said, "It looks like what's happened is that the mother of all battles has turned into the mother of all retreats."

In his office Wednesday night, Marlin Fitzwater, Mr. Bush's spokesman, said the President had not been strongly encouraged by a 2:30 P.M. briefing from his military advisers. "He was pretty serious and concerned," Mr. Fitzwater said. "He had just rejected the Iraqi offer complying with three of the resolutions. That didn't seem like such a good sign in spite of the fact of what was happening on the battlefield. But as it became more and more clear that the fighting was over and that the military objectives were met, the President's spirits improved considerably."

'Certainly not a time to gloat, but it is a time of pride.'

The President asked his military advisers when he could tell the American people that the shooting had stopped and that the troops were going to come home. "I'd like to do it tonight," Mr. Fitzwater quoted Mr. Bush as saying.

The President decided to speak on Wednesday night because he was assured by his advisors, Mr. Fitzwater said, "that the military backbone of Iraq was broken."

Arranging 'a Solid Peace'

"As a fighting force, it was over for them," Mr. Fitzwater said. "The President wanted to tell the American people at the earliest possible moment and to tell the families that their children, husbands and wives were out of harm's way. His advisers talked about tommorrow, and he said, 'What about tonight?' "

Gen. Colin L. Powell, the chairman of the Joint Chiefs of Staff, replied, "I think we can do that," Mr. Fitzwater said.

"The message here was we've won the war and we've now got to go through the arrangements for a solid peace," he said.

As usual, Mr. Bush had consultations with his allies, speaking to President François Mitterrand of France in the morning and Prime Minister Brian Mulroney of Canada, who has emerged as perhaps his closest confidant among foreign leaders, in the evening. He also spoke with the British Prime Minister, John Major.

Mr. Baker and Brent Scowcroft, the President's national security adviser, called other allies to tell them of the President's decision and Mr. Baker had an extensive discussion with Foreign Minister Douglas Hurd of Britain.

Mr. Fitzwater said the allies had been solidly behind the President for not accepting the Iraqis' last attempt at winning a cease-fire and had not been under pressure to call an end to the fighting.

No Calls to Gorbachev

Notably absent from Mr. Bush's round of calls was President Mikhail S. Gorbachev, who had made a failed attempt at mediating peace before the ground war began.

Wednesday began with a message to the United Nations from Baghdad in which Foreign Minister Tariq Aziz of Iraq said his Government, which had promised to heed the United Nations resolution requiring its withdrawal from Kuwait, now "agrees to abide" by two other resolutions. One would nullify Iraq's annexation of the occupied sheikdom, and the other would require Baghdad to pay war reparations.

Mr. Aziz also said iraq would release all prisoners of war "within a very short time." But he conditioned these promises on a cease-fire enforced by the United Nations and on the lifting of all economic sanctions imposed on Baghdad after the invasion of Kuwait on Aug. 2.

The alliance held out for Iraq's unconditional acceptance of all 12 United Nations resolutions, the continuation of sanctions beyond the war, and the surrender of all Iraqi tanks and other weapons. Official statements had made it clear that the coalition had political and military aims beyond driving the Iraqis out of Kuwait.

Mr. Cheney said, "Even after we've achieved our military objectives, even after we've destroyed his offensive military capability and expelled his forces from Kuwait, liberated Kuwait, the world will still be vitally interested in the future course of events with respect to the kinds of activities and policies pursued by the Government in Baghdad."

Jose R. Lopez/The New York Times

President Bush in the Oval Office after announcing suspension of offensive military operations against Iraq.

United Nations

Allies Wary of Overture By Iraqis on Cease-Fire

By PAUL LEWIS

Special to The New York Times

UNITED NATIONS, Thursday, Feb. 28 — The United States and its coalition partners resisted demands today from the Soviet Union and Iraq for a Security Council resolution calling for a permanent cease-fire to bring a formal end to the Persian Gulf war.

Diplomats from the coalition countries said a formal cease-fire was not necessary at this point because the United States had already agreed to stop offensive combat at midnight Wednesday.

Before any formal cease-fire is declared, the allies say, Iraq must improve on its 11th-hour offer to accept all Security Council resolutions related to the gulf crisis. Foreign Minister Tariq Aziz of Iraq said that Iraq had agreed to comply fully with the 12 resolutions in a letter delivered to the United Nations Wednesday evening.

The Other Conditions

But the coalition also wants Iraq to account for, and quickly return, all the prisoners of war it has captured as well as thousands of Kuwaiti and other civilians it has seized or taken hostage.

The allies also want Iraq to hand over plans of minefields it has laid in Kuwait. And they say that units of the elite Iraqi Republican Guard now surrounded by coalition forces near the border with Kuwait must agree to abandon their tanks and other heavy arms for destruction before they will be given safe passage home.

While Iraq's intentions on these points remain unclear, the allies' partners sa-id early today that they do not wish to give up the option to resume fighting. The Security Council agreed to meet later today to discuss the Iraqi letter and the Persian Gulf War.

Diplomats from countries in the allied coalition say the Soviet Union is pushing for an immediate and formal cease-fire decision because it wants to emphasize its role as a peacemaker in the conflict and strengthen its ties with Iraq and Arab countries supporting Baghdad.

Before President Bush's announcement of the suspension of fighting, the Security Council had rejected yet another Iraqi cease-fire offer that fell short of the terms the United States has set for ending the conflict. As a result, the Soviet Union said it would step up its efforts to persuade President Saddam Hussein to stop trying to bargain with the Council and agree to settle the conflict on America's terms.

After the Council met, the Soviet Union said it would strongly urge President ussein to stop trying to bargain and instead settle on the American-led coalition's terms for ending the conflict.

Before Mr. Bush's speech, many diplomats werearguing that, by repeatedly seeking concessions in the coalition's terms for a truce, President Hussein, encouraged by Soviet efforts to achieve a compromise, was merely giving the United States more time to accomplish what they assumed to be one its major undeclared war aims — the crippling of the Iraqi military.

Soviet Role in Offer

In the proposal that was defeated earlier Wednesday, Baghdad offered to renounce its claim to Kuwait and pay reparations for damage its forces have done there, as the allies insist. But Baghdad said it would do so only in exchange for a cease-fire agreement and the lifting of the trade and other economic sanctions the Security Council has imposed on it.

That was the third peace offer Baghdad had made and had seen rejected since the ground offensive against its occupation of Kuwait began last weekend.

At the private meeting of the Security Council's 15 members, only Cuba and Yemen were said to have shown any interest in Baghdad's new proposal.

The Soviet Union apparently played an important role in obtaining that offer from Iraq, Western diplomats said.

The peace offer rejected Wednesday was transmitted to New York by the Soviet Embassy in Baghdad, since Iraq no longer has effective international communications. Some Western diplomats said they suspected that Soviet officials had a hand in drafting the text, even though they would have known the United States was likely to reject it.

A letter from Iraq said it would abide by the U.N. resolutions.

Council members told Iraq at the time that they were ready to give urgent consideration to a cease-fire only after Baghdad had unambiguously accepted the 12 resolutions passed by the council calling for a withdrawal from Kuwait and imposing sanctions and conditions on Baghdad.

The Soviet Union's United Nations representative, Yuli M. Vorontsov, had said earlier Wednesday that he was hopeful that Moscow would be able to persuade President Hussein to agree to the allies' terms.

"We're hopeful we might receive that word from him soon," he said after the meeting.

'Its Made No Deals'

He said the Soviet Union was in constant contact with the Iraqi leadership, adding that it would "strongly recommend" that Baghdad give the assurances the allies are demanding.

Britain's representative, Sir David Hannay, said the Security Council was looking for "a simple, straightforward, uncluttered acceptance" of its terms for ending the war.

The American representative at the United Nations, Thomas R. Pickering, said: "The council isn't here bargaining with Iraq. Its made no deals. The council's been very clear. Tell us when you are ready to comply with the 12 resolutions, and we'll take our next steps from there."

The allies' refusal today to trade the lifting of sanctions for Baghdad's acceptance of some of their other demands was in line with their repeated refusal to accept any kind of a conditional cease-fire agreement, which they say amounts to bargaining with President Hussein.

Chester Higgins Jr./The New York Times

Abdul Amir al-Anbari, Iraq's delegate to the United Nations, on his way yesterday to deliver a letter to the Secretary General detailing an Iraqi peace offer. The offer was rejected by the Security Council.

The White House

Transcript of President's Address on the Gulf War

Following is a transcript of President Bush's address from the Oval Office last night, as recorded by The New York Times:

Kuwait is liberated. Iraq's army is defeated. Our military objectives are met. Kuwait is once more in the hands of Kuwaitis in control of their own destiny. We share in their joy, a joy tempered only by our compassion for their ordeal.

Tonight, the Kuwaiti flag once again flies above the capital of a free and sovereign nation, and the American flag flies above our embassy.

Seven months ago, America and the world drew a line in the sand. We declared that the aggression against Kuwait would not stand, and tonight America and the world have kept their word. This is not a time of euphoria, certainly not a time to gloat, but it is a time of pride, pride in our troops, pride in the friends who stood with us in the crisis, pride in our nation and the people whose strength and resolve made victory quick, decisive and just.

And soon we will open wide our arms to welcome back home to America our magnificent fighting forces. No one country can claim this victory as its own. It was not only a victory for Kuwait, but a victory for all the coalition partners. This is a victory for the United Nations, for all mankind, for the rule of law, and for what is right.

Offensive Is Suspended

After consulting with Secretary of Defense Cheney, the Chairman of the Joint Chiefs of Staff, general Powell, and our coalition partners, I am pleased to announce that at midnight tonight, Eastern standard time, exactly 100 hours since ground operations commenced and 6 weeks since the start of Operation Desert Storm, all United States and coalition forces will suspend offensive combat operations.

It is up to Iraq whether this suspension on the part of the coalition becomes a permanent cease-fire. Coalition, political and military terms for a formal cease-fire include the following requirements:

Iraq must release immediately all coalition prisoners of war, third country nationals and the remains of all who have fallen.

Iraq must release all Kuwaiti detainees.

Iraq also must inform Kuwaiti authorities of the location and nature of all land and sea mines.

Iraq must comply fully with all relevant United Nations Security Council resolutions. This includes a rescinding of Iraq's August decision to annex Kuwait and acceptance in principle of Iraq's responsibility to pay compensation for the loss, damage and injury its aggression has caused.

Meeting With Iraqis

The coalition calls upon the Iraqi Government to designate military commanders to meet within 48 hours with their coalition counterparts at a place in the theater of operations to be specified to arrange for military aspects of the cease-fire.

Further, I have asked Secretary of State Baker to request that the United Nations Security Council meet to formulate the necessary arrangement for this war to be ended.

This suspension of offensive combat operations is contingent upon Iraq's not firing upon any coalition forces and not launching Scud missiles against any other country. If Iraq violates these terms, coalition forces will be free to resume military operations.

At every opportunity I have said to the people of Iraq that our quarrel was not with them but instead with their leadership and above all with Saddam Hussein. This remains the case. You, the people of Iraq are not our enemy. We do not seek your destruction. We have treated your P.O.W.'s with kindness.

Coalition forces fought this war only as a last resort and look forward to the day when Iraq is led by people prepared to live in peace with their neighbors.

Postwar Planning

We must now begin to look beyond victory in war. We must meet the challenge of securing the peace. In the future, as before, we will consult with our coalition partners.

We've already done a good deal of thinking and planning for the postwar period and Secretary Baker has already begun to consult with our coalition partners on the region's challenges. There can be and will be no solely American answer to all these challenges, but we can assist and support the countries of the region and be a catalyst for peace.

In this spirit Secretary Baker will go to the region next week to begin a new round of consultations. This war is now behind us. Ahead of us is the difficult task of securing a potentially historic peace. Tonight though, let us be proud of what we have accomplished. Let us give thanks to those who risked their lives. Let us never forget those who gave their lives.

May God bless our valiant military forces and their families and let us all remember them in our prayers.

Good night and may God bless the United States of America.

U.N. Chief Would Disband Truce Monitors

UNITED NATIONS, Feb. 27 (Reuters) — Secretary General Javier Pérez de Cuéllar recommended today that the United Nations observer group monitoring a 1988 cease-fire between Iran and Iraq be disbanded and replaced with civilian offices in Teheran and Baghdad.

In a written report to the Security Council, the Secretary General said that the duties of the Iran-Iraq Military Observer Group had been completed and that what remained were essentially diplomatic tasks.

The group, whose mandate expires on Thursday, was charged with monitoring the withdrawal of Iraqi and Iranian troops behind recognized international boundaries, among other duties. It numbers 114 military personnel from 18 countries.

It is still operating in Iran but observers stationed in Iraq were moved to Cyprus in January when war loomed between Iraq and the coalition led by the United States seeking to end Baghdad's occupation of Kuwait.

"All the News That's Fit to Print"

The New York Times

Late Edition
New York: **Today,** cloudy, cool, early sprinkles. High near 60. **Tonight,** partial clearing. Low 46. **Tomorrow,** cloudy, late clearing. High 56. **Yesterday,** high 61, low 50. Details, page 17.

VOL.CXLI . . No. 48,751 — NEW YORK, SATURDAY, OCTOBER 12, 1991 — 50 CENTS

THOMAS ACCUSER TELLS HEARING OF OBSCENE TALK AND ADVANCES; JUDGE COMPLAINS OF 'LYNCHING'

Photographs by Jose R. Lopez/The New York Times

Professor Anita F. Hill and Judge Clarence Thomas as they were sworn in yesterday before testifying.

DRAMA IN SENATE

Court Nominee Rejects Charges Laid Out in Frank, Vivid Detail

By RICHARD L. BERKE

Special to The New York Times

WASHINGTON, Oct. 11 — Confronting a disputed nomination to the Supreme Court and a boiling political furor, the Senate Judiciary Committee heard gripping but contradictory testimony today from Judge Clarence Thomas and the woman accusing him of sexual harassment.

The proceedings in a jammed hearing room at the Russell Senate Office Building here amounted to a political drama centered on two extraordinarily composed figures, Judge Thomas and his accuser, Anita F. Hill, an Oklahoma law professor.

Judge Thomas and Professor Hill, who worked for him in two Federal agencies, both testified under oath and offered accounts of their social and professional relationships that differed so starkly that Senator Howell Heflin, an Alabama Democrat, said, "One of them is not telling the truth."

'I Had a Duty to Report'

Professor Hill complained of sexual approaches in vivid detail and said she had not volunteered to bring this issue to the Senate but was there because Senate aides had asked her if she was aware of any harassment. "I felt I had a duty to report — I have no personal vendetta against Clarence Thomas," she said.

Judge Thomas angrily denied the charge and compared his ordeal to a "lynching." [Excerpts from the hearing appear on pages 10-15.]

Testifying first in a hearing that lasted 12 hours and 35 minutes, Judge Thomas sounded by turns defiant and sorrowful in insisting to committee members that he never sexually harassed Professor Hill, depicting himself and his family as victims who were betrayed by the professor and a Senate confirmation process that had run amok.

The Process on Trial

In his opening statement in the morning, and even more strongly when he returned to the Congress tonight to testify, Judge Thomas tried to rebut the charges against him by putting the process on trial — a political process that has been widely disdained as cutthroat and out of control.

He called it "a travesty" that such "sleaze," "dirt," "gossip" and "lies," which he said were improperly disclosed by the committee, should be "displayed in prime time to an entire nation." In answer to a question, he said that he did not watch Professor Hill's testimony.

Professor Hill said that she, too, had been tormented by the issue and the intense scrutiny. Facing sometimes sharp questions from Republicans and more gentle questioning from Democrats, Professor Hill testified for near-

Continued on Page 9, Column 1

Reuters

Kiichi Miyazawa at a meeting of his party faction yesterday.

Miyazawa Gets Party Approval To Lead Japan

By DAVID E. SANGER

Special to The New York Times

TOKYO, Oct. 11 — Kiichi Miyazawa, a stalwart of Japan's governing party and one of the architects of the country's postwar economic ascent, was virtually assured election as the next Japanese prime minister today, ending a bruising weeklong scramble for the leadership.

Mr. Miyazawa, an urbane 72-year-old politician who has held virtually every key political post in Japan except prime minister, was endorsed this evening by the largest and wealthiest faction in the Liberal Democratic Party, controlled by former Prime Minister Noboru Takeshita.

At a news conference earlier in the day, Mr. Miyazawa said he expected no significant changes in Japan's relations with Washington, where he has been a well-known and influential player in Japanese-American relations for more than two decades.

'The Same Values'

"We have the same values," he said of Japan and the United States. "If we have something to complain about to each other, we should do so frankly."

It was the Takeshita faction that withdrew its support from Prime Minister Toshiki Kaifu a week ago, forcing him to abandon his hopes of seeking a second term. Political analysts said they expected Mr. Miyazawa, a far more senior member of the party and a leader of a major faction, to hold somewhat more independent sway over the conduct of the Government than did Mr. Kaifu, who was widely viewed as a weak leader entirely dependent on the good graces of Mr. Takeshita and his aging ally in the governing party, Shin Kanemaru.

For Mr. Miyazawa, known as one of the party's keenest minds and one of its most fluent English speakers, the endorsement today completes a stunning political turnaround. Less than three years ago, he was forced to step down

Continued on Page 5, Column 5

SOVIET REPUBLICS AGREE TO CREATE AN ECONOMIC UNION

10 OF 12 PLEDGE SUPPORT

Yeltsin Leads Way in Pressing for an Accord — Gorbachev Calls Plan 'Last Hope'

By FRANCIS X. CLINES

Special to The New York Times

MOSCOW, Oct. 11 — Russia and a majority of the other republics announced their commitment today to soon forming a new economic community devoted to free-market resuscitation of the fallen Soviet nation.

President Boris N. Yeltsin of the Russian federation, the centerpiece republic in the complex plan, led the way in pressing nine other republics for a formal signing of the economic compact as early as next Tuesday.

The Soviet President, Mikhail S. Gorbachev, leading a meeting of 10 republic leaders at the Kremlin, warned that the economic plan represented the people's "last hope" for decisive action toward national reconstruction after the harrowing failed coup and collapse of the central Government in August.

Yeltsin's Return

"People's patience is at a breaking point," Mr. Gorbachev cautioned, according to the press agency Tass.

The news that Mr. Yeltsin was back from vacation and recommitting Russia to the economic plan immediately bolstered proponents of the free-market community.

In his absence for the last two weeks, critics of the plan came forward in his own cabinet to warn that Russia, the nation's dominant republic, would be slighted in creating such an economic community from the dregs of the Communist Soviet Union.

'Common Economic Space'

But Mr. Yeltsin reaffirmed his view that the plan for a "common economic space" of trade, currency, banking and customs procedures was the only hope for the crippled Soviet nation to turn itself toward reform and a chance of joining the global free market.

The most Mr. Yeltsin offered to critics, according to initial reports, was the possibility of a common banking system less central in nature. That was in concession to an apparent sensitive point among the now sovereign republics still fearful of echoes of the central monolith that marked Communism's handling of the economy.

The republics, meeting together as members of the new State Council emergency Government, also followed through on earlier agreements to reshape the K.G.B. state police into sepa-

Continued on Page 4, Column 6

On Thomas: More Questions, Not Fewer

A Political Process Becomes the Focus

By R. W. APPLE Jr.

Special to The New York Times

News Analysis

WASHINGTON, Oct. 11 — The choices presented to the United States Senate by today's lurid, gut-wrenching proceedings on Capitol Hill could hardly have been much starker.

By the time Anita F. Hill had finished her testimony, filled with vivid and often excruciating sexual detail that few had anticipated, but delivered with a prim earnestness that seemed to bespeak reserve and reluctance to discuss such subjects, the Senators who must vote on Tuesday were left with only two options: Either she was telling the truth or she is a sociopath; either these horrifying events took place or she, for some reason, invented them.

By the time Judge Clarence Thomas had made his response, the Senators had been rocked even further back on their heels by a blast that have had few precedents as a statement by a senior Federal official in an official forum. Dropping his usual accommodating manner, he let the fury pour out of him, calling the current inquiry "a national disgrace" and "a high-tech lynching for uppity blacks."

He stopped only a hair short of explicity accusing the committee, composed entirely of white males, of racism.

He Said Them, Or He Didn't

What Professor Hill asserted, and what Judge Thomas said in his implacably resolute testimony, made it crystal clear that this was no case of tragic misunderstandings nor of ambiguous conversations that could be interpreted as sexual harassment or not, depending on one's frame of reference or state of mind. Either he said these wretched things to her — things that one associates with the seamiest of criminal cases or the raunchiest of locker rooms, not with the Senate or Supreme Court — or he did not. Yes or no. Up or down.

If Judge Thomas did say them, few, if any, Senators would vote to confirm, whatever the pull of partisan solidarity. So a vote to confirm the judge, in the rawest political terms, will mean the voter thinks Professor Hill fabricated (or was fed) these "ugly" incidents and phrases, to use her own word.

Such a vote will not be easy for the jury of 100 Senators, a group of professional politicians, a third of whom face re-election next year, who have already been burned by the wrath of women when they seemed willing to brush off Professor Hill's allegations earlier this week.

It will be harder because the judge's defenders struggled all day, with limited success, to suggest what kind of twisted motive she might have had for telling monstrous lies about him.

It will be hardest of all for the Democrats, and the arithmetic gives them the upper hand. If 51 of the 57 Democrats vote no on the nomination — vote, in effect, to back Professor Hill — then Judge Thomas will not make it to the Supreme Court, even if all 43 Republicans reject what she told them.

To bring about that result, only about five or six of the Democrats who had intended to support Judge Thomas before Professor Hill's allegations became public would have to change their minds. At least that many have indicated they had serious doubts by pressing to hold new hearings.

But what of Judge Thomas's testimony? Like Professor Hill a child of the civil rights movement, a success story that would have made the Rev. Dr. Martin Luther King Jr. beam with

Continued on Page 9, Column 1

In an Ugly Atmosphere, the Accusations Fly

By MAUREEN DOWD

Special to The New York Times

WASHINGTON, Oct. 11 — With a powerful invocation of racial imagery that he had not used in his public remarks before this day of testing, Clarence Thomas tried to put the Senate on trial tonight, accusing Congress of tactics that went "far beyond McCarthyism."

As his wife, Virginia, sat behind him with a trembling chin, wiping away tears, Judge Thomas delivered a forceful rebuttal to Anita F. Hill's accusations of sexual harassment with a stony face and a voice bristling with anger.

When his testimony, filled with racially charged images, collided with the counterpoint of the Oklahoma University law professor's cool, dispassionate testimony, nearly devoid of references to race, the hearing reached an emotional high point.

Furious Denunciations

Confounding those who thought he would give up after the testimony by Professor Hill, testimony that many Senators found impressive and credible, President Bush's nominee put the process on trial and offered a furious denunciation of the Judiciary Committee's handling of the case.

"You are running the country," he told the senators, accusing them of going "far beyond McCarthyism." At another point, he said that black men who did not "kowtow to an old order" would "be lynched, destroyed, caricatured by a committee of the U.S. Senate rather than hung from a tree."

In comparing his ordeal to a "high-tech lynching, for uppity blacks," Judge Thomas evoked one of the most powerful images of the civil rights movement, a movement with which he has long had an uneasy relationship.

It was during his tenure as chairman of the Equal Employment Opportunity Commission that he became an increasingly fervent spokesman against the approaches of the traditional civil rights groups. As his relations with those groups worsened, he complained in an interview with The Washington Post in 1984 that all the nation's traditional civil rights leaders do is, "bitch, bitch, bitch, moan and whine."

Offended by Justice Marshall

He said he was offended by Justice Thurgood Marshall who once complained that he did not want to celebrate the Constitution because it condoned slavery. But when he opened his testimony on Sept. 10, he was careful to give great credit to the civil rights movement for his own journey.

"So many others gave their lives, their talents. But for them, I would not be here today. Justice Marshall, whose seat I have been nominated to fill is one of those who had the courage and the intellect," he said.

Initially today, Mr. Thomas refused to rebut the individual charges, relying instead on monolithic outrage and a categorical denial. He said he had been "drawn and dragged" into a national forum to discuss allegations that "should have been discussed in a confidential way."

At first, Senator Howell Heflin

Continued on Page 8, Column 1

America Listens In On a Private Subject

In cities and towns across the country, Americans took time out from their workaday lives to tune into the riveting collision between Judge Clarence Thomas and Anita F. Hill.

The hearing capped a week in which Professor Hill's charges became the leading topic in offices and on university campuses, in restaurants and on street corners, with many women applauding public discussion of a frequently private subject and many men wondering about their own conduct.

Article, page 8.

Keith Meyers/The New York Times

Haitians in New York Rally for Ousted Leader

Tens of thousands of Haitian demonstrators spilled across the Brooklyn Bridge into lower Manhattan yesterday in a spirited display of support for Haiti's ousted President, Jean-Bertrand Aristide. Page 31.

INSIDE

Bush Vetoes Benefits Bill

Citing a need for budget discipline, the President rejected legislation that would have given additional unemployment benefits to people out of work more than six months. Page 6.

One Step Closer

The President formed a Bush-Quayle '92 Primary Committee, a move that allows him to go ahead with already scheduled fund-raising events for his re-election campaign. Page 6.

Yes, He Is. No. Maybe.

Political contributors say Gov. Mario M. Cuomo told them he was considering running for President. But later he said he had no plans. Page 31.

Twins Win and Lead Playoff

A home run by Mike Pagliarulo in the 10th inning gave Minnesota a 3-2 victory over Toronto and a 2-1 lead in the American League playoff. Page 35.

THE NEW YORK TIMES

The Thomas Nomination: A Gripping Day of Stark Details and Defiant Denials

Thomas Accuser and Nominee Offer Contradictory Testimony to Senate Panel

Continued From Page 1

ly seven hours. She told of a childhood that sounded like that of Judge Thomas's, dominated by work and poverty.

"When I was asked by a representative of this committee to report my experience," she said, "I felt that I had to tell the truth. I could not keep silent."

Judge Thomas, in his return appearance tonight, said, "I think something is dreadfully wrong with this country when any person, any person, in this country could be sujected to this."

'A National Disgrace'

"This is a circus," the judge continued, his voice brimming with outrage. "It's a national disgrace. From my standpoint as a black American, it is a high-tech lynching for uppity blacks who in any way deign to think for themselves, to do for themselves."

But this time, he said he was being lynched by a committee of the United States Senate rather than "hung from a tree."

Under questioning tonight from Senator Heflin, Judge Thomas said he did not watch Professor Hill's testimony because he could not bear to watch untruths.

"If you didn't listen," Senator Heflin said, that made it difficult "to find out what the actual facts are."

A Question of Temperament

In one of the most emotional moments of the proceedings, Senator Heflin said that Judge Thomas's attitude toward Professor Hill's testimony raised questions of "judicial temperament."

"Senator, there is a big difference between approaching a case objectively and watching yourself being lynched," Judge Thomas said in one of a series of remarks denouncing the proceedings.

At times, the nominee seemed barely able to contain his anger, even under friendly questioning from Senator Orrin G. Hatch, Republican of Utah, as he denounced "this nonsense, garbage, trash that you've siphoned out of the sewer against me" and the committee's "leaks."

"This leaked on me, and it is drowning my life, my career and my integrity," Judge Thomas said. "You have robbed me of something that can never be restored."

Five minutes after the Senate hearing adjourned for the night, Marlin Fitzwater, the White House spokesman, said: "Judge Clarence Thomas's message tonight was a powerful testament to his integrity and character. He should be confirmed to the Supreme Court. His test speaks for itself."

A 'Kafkaesque' Process

In wrenching terms in his opening statement this morning, Judge Thomas, a black man who rose from an impoverished boyhood in segregated Georgia to the United States Court of Appeals for the District of Columbia Circuit, characterized himself as someone who was never daunted until caught in what he described as a "Kafkaesque" Senate confirmation process.

"But I have not been able to overcome this process," he added. "This is worse than any obstacle or anything that I have ever faced."

Judge Thomas, at the high point of a speech that he said he had written himself, with "no handlers, no advisers," declared: "No job is worth what I've been through — no job. No horror in my life has been so debilitating. Confirm me if you want. Don't confirm me if you are so led. But let this process end. Let me and my family regain our lives."

Jose R. Lopez/The New York Times

Seated across from the Senate Judiciary Committee, Judge Clarence Thomas began his testimony in which he disputed the sexual harrassment charges leveled by Anita F. Hill.

Moments after Judge Thomas departed from the packed Senate hearing room, Professor Hill took her seat in the same leather witness chair and described Judge Thomas as a boss who repeatedly badgered her for dates and engaged in sexual conversation in the privacy of his offices at the Department of Education and later, at the Equal Employment Opportunity Commission.

Pressed for details, Professor Hill spoke calmly and willingly but in langauge seldom heard in formal hearings: "He talked about pornographic materials depicting individuals with large penises or large breasts involved in various sex acts," she said. "On several occasions Thomas told me graphically of his own sexual prowess."

Affidavit of an Acquaintance

In a surprise move intended to raise questions about Professor Hill's credibility, Senator Arlen Specter of Pennsylvania, the primary Republican questioner, introduced into evidence an affidavit of John N. Doggett 3d, a classmate of Judge Thomas at Yale Law School who described himself as an acquaintance of Professor Hill when they both lived in Washington.

Mr. Doggett said in the affidavit that Professor Hill had "fantasies about my sexual interest in her," which he attributed to her "problem with being rejected by men she was attracted to."

> **A political drama that centers on two compelling figures.**

But Professor Hill said she was puzzled by the affidavit, saying: "It's meaningless to me. I did not at any time have any fantasy about a romance with him."

In another disclosure that raised questions about Ms. Hill's account, Judge Thomas, under questioning tonight from Senator Hatch, said that when he and Professor Hill worked together he occasionally drove her home and was invited in to "have a Coke or a beer or something and continue arguing about politics for maybe 45 minutes to an hour."

News to the Lawmakers

Senator Joseph R. Biden Jr., the committee chairman, told Judge Thomas the committee still had an open mind and urged him to give the panel whatever information he could to defend himself. The Senator, a Democrat from Delaware, said the information about driving Professor Hill home was news to the lawmakers.

"It was not unusual to me," Judge Thomas said.

Louise Hilsen, a press spokeswoman for Professor Hill, said after the hearing when asked about Judge Thomas's account of meetings at Professor Hill's home that it was "inconsistent with the testimony" of the professor. "We stand by her testimony," Ms. Hilsen said.

Lawmakers said they would reconvene on Saturday with Judge Thomas completing his testimony, and, if necessary, would continue work on Sunday. It was unclear when the committee would hear the other possible witnesses, including Angela Wright, a former press secretary at the employment commission who has also made a sexual harassment allegation against Judge Thomas.

A Vastly Different Scene

The scene in the stately Senate Caucus Room today was vastly different from what it was during Judge Thomas's five days of testimony three weeks ago, when his character not only went unquestioned, but also was considered one of his strongest assets. Although they split largely on party lines over his judicial qualifications to be an Associate Justice, lawmakers on both sides had praised Judge Thomas for advancing through Yale Law School to the Federal appellate court. Today, however, it was allegations about Judge Thomas's personal conduct that threatened to undo his nomination.

The committee deadlocked, 7 to 7, on whether to recommend that Judge Thomas be confirmed. But he was widely viewed as having enough support for confirmation when the full Senate was scheduled to vote on Tuesday. After an emotional debate on and off the Senate floor that day, the Senate abruptly postponed the vote until next Tuesday after a political firestorm erupted when Professor Hill's allegations were disclosed last weekend on National Public Radio and in Newsday.

Judge Thomas said his opening statement was not read beforehand by anyone other than his wife, Virginia Lamp Thomas, and his chief defender, Senator John C. Danforth. In contrast to his his earlier appearance before the committee, Judge Thomas sat alone, without his coaches from the White House. His wife and Senator Danforth, a Missouri Republican, sat immediately behind him.

Judge Thomas told the committee that his life was permanently altered on Sept. 25, when agents of the Federal Bureau of Investigation came to his home to ask him about allegations made by Professor Hill, who worked for him from 1981 to 1983.

'Such Pain, Such Agony'

"I have never in all my life felt such hurt, such pain, such agony," he said. "My family and I have been done a grave and irreparable injustice. During the past two weeks, I lost the belief that if I did my best, all would work out.

"I called upon the strength that helped me get out of Pin Point," he said, referring to the Georgia village where he was born. "And it was all sapped out of me. It was sapped out of me because Anita Hill was a person I considered a friend, whom I admired and thought I had treated fairly and with the utmost respect."

Professor Hill was accompanied by 3 lawyers, by her parents and by many of her 12 siblings. Like Judge Thomas, the 35-year-old professor at the University of Oklahoma Law Center described the torment she had endured in the public eye.

"It is only after a great deal of agonizing consideration that I am able to talk of these unpleasant matters to anyone but my closest friends," Professor Hill said. "Telling the world is the most difficult experience of my life."

'The Easier Approach'

She went on to explain why she did not report her allegations years ago. "I was aware that he could affect my future career and did not wish to burn all my bridges," she said. "I may have used poor judgment; perhaps I should have taken angry or even militant steps, both when I was in the agency or after I left it. But I must confess to the world that the course I took seemed to me to be the better as well as the easier approach."

Moments after she had affectionately introduced members of her family to the committee, Professor Hill spoke in detail about her allegation that Judge Thomas turned office conversations to sexual matters.

"One of the oddest episodes I remember was an occasion in which Thomas was drinking a Coke in his office," she said. "He got up from the table at which we are working, went over to his desk to get the Coke, looked at the can and said, 'Who has put pubic hair on my Coke?' On other occasions he referred to the size of his own penis as being larger than normal, and he also spoke on some occasions of the pleasures he had given to women with oral sex." Another time, she said, he talked about a movie called "Long Dong Silver."

Professor Hill said she was hospitalized in February 1983, for five days for acute stomach pain, which she attributed to stress from her contacts with Judge Thomas.

She also recounted a farewell dinner with Judge Thomas, in the summer of 1983, when she was leaving the Equal Employment Opportunity Commission. "He made a comment which I vividly remember," she said. "He said that if I ever told anyone about his behavior toward me it could ruin his career. This was not an apology, nor was there any explanation. That was his last remark about the possibility of our going out or reference to his behavior."

A High-Tension Event

From the start, it was clear this would be an event of high political tension. After Judge Thomas delivered his opening statement, Senator Biden proposed to begin questioning him without reference to Professor Hill's confidential statement to the committee that had led to the renewed hearings. Senator Biden said Professor Hill wanted the document kept confidential.

That prompted Senator Hatch to angrily remind Senator Biden that it was nonsensical to ignore a statement that had already been cited in the press.

"It would be the greatest travesty I've ever seen in any court of law," Senator Hatch said, practically shouting, "let alone an open forum in the nomination process of a man for Justice of the United States Supreme Court, to allow her attorneys or her or anybody on this committee or anybody else, for that matter, to tell us what can or cannot be used now that this man's reputation has been very badly hurt."

> **The judge describes the process as 'Kafkaesque.'**

Senator Biden shot back that Professor Hill wanted to make her allegations in her own words and not have them disclosed in a committee report.

But Senator Hatch said that if the document was not made available to Judge Thomas, "then I'm going to resign from this committee today."

Use of Report Allowed

Finally, Senator Biden called a recess. When the committee reconvened, the chairman said Professor Hill would permit the use of the report, and she then began her testimony. In a prepared statement and in response to questions from Senator Biden, she detailed her allegations.

On cross-examination, Senator Specter, a former district attorney in Philadelphia, sought to portray Professor Hill as someone who was never troubled by Judge Thomas's behavior until he was nominated for the Supreme Court.

He suggested that Professor Hill was imagining things, and pressed her about why she waited years to come forward, why she did not tell the F.B.I. more details about her allegations and why she maintained contacts with Judge Thomas over the years.

Professor Hill acknowledged that while she could be faulted in her dealings with Judge Thomas, she offered explanations to all the Republicans' questions. She said she moved with Judge Thomas to the employment commission because he had stopped harassing her. She said she was afraid to speak out about him for fear that she would lose her job. She said her contacts since working with Judge Thomas were minimal and that some of her phone calls were responses to his initial calls.

On Trial: Nominee, Accuser and Political Process

Continued From Page 1

pride, Judge Thomas took the offensive against the process. He accused the Judiciary Committee of having irredeemably besmirched his reputation and he reacted with such rivetingly persuasive indignation and anger that some thought he was about to withdraw his name from nomination.

When he said that the inquiry, with its leaks and its trolling for dirt, was unfair, un-American and Kafkaesque, he struck a chord with many onlookers. Robert H. Bork, who was rejected for the Supreme Court in another such proceeding, plainly spoke for more than himself when he said, acting as a network analyst, "The process has steadily degenerated and now it's become a Roman circus."

In fact, the impression is rapidly gaining ground in Washington, among Thomas friends and foes, Republicans and Democrats, conservatives and liberals, that the whole confirmation system badly needs to be rethought and reshaped. Increasingly, people are asking what sort of person could withstand the ceaseless, intrusive examination of his or her private life to which Judge Thomas has been subjected, and what sort of potential public servant would be willing to submit to it.

A Look of Disarray

Already on the defensive, the committee contributed to the impression of disarray and partisan squabbling moments after it convened, when the ground rules of Senator Joseph R. Biden Jr. of Delaware, the Democratic chairman, were challenged by the Republicans and then abandoned after a brief, acrimonious recess.

Judge Thomas had other things going for him, too. Could John C. Danforth, the Missouri Republican who is his old friend and former employer, have really been so deceived about the kind of man Judge Thomas is? And what about the statement of John N. Doggett 3d that Professor Hill had fantasized about his sexual interest when he, in fact, had none?

Like the Army-McCarthy hearings and the Watergate hearings, today's high drama took place not only on Capitol Hill but in the larger theater of television, and the conclusions reached around the country will be fed back to the Senate. Indeed, that has already happened at one crucial juncture. It was Professor Hill's convincing demeanor in her first televised news conference, combined with what looked to many people like the Senate's indifference, that detonated the public rage that prompted today's hearings.

In so explosive a situation, all the participants were conscious of vulnerability. President Bush, for example, issued his re-endorsement of Judge Thomas, including his assertion that the judge was the victim of a "smear campaign," before Professor Hill was questioned. At least in part, this was because he did not want to appear to be attacking her directly.

Judge Thomas, criticized earlier for what seemed to some foes like programmed responses, made a point of saying his statement was not the work of White House handlers, and his chief handler, Kenneth M. Duberstein, was not visible on television. The committee members, criticized earlier for insensitivity to the sexual harassment issue, had their female aides in prominent positions in the hearing room, very visible on television.

The Senators who questioned Professor Hill did all they could to avoid appearing to bully the witness. Even the pro-Thomas forces' designated questioner of her veracity, Republican Senator Arlen Specter of Pennsylvania, a former prosecutor, made a show of solicitousness, almost apologizing when he challenged her. And he took a lot of time to demonstrate that he and his colleagues knew far less about her accusations when they decided last week that they did not need to hear her.

Senator Orrin G. Hatch, the Utah Republican, has been saying for days that neither Judge Thomas nor Professor Hill would emerge whole from this week's ordeal. The reputations of American politics, politicians and political institutions seem unlikely to fare a lot better.

What Happened Between Them: Testimony in Conflict

Anita F. Hill	Clarence Thomas
"After approximately three months of working there, he asked me to go out socially with him."	"Contrary to some press reports, I categorically denied all of the allegations, and denied that I ever attempted to date Anita Hill when first interviewed by the F.B.I. I strongly reaffirm that denial."
"After a brief discussion of work, he would turn the conversation to a discussion of sexual matters His conversations were very vivid. He spoke about acts that he had seen in pornographic films. . . . On several occasions, Thomas told me graphically of his own sexual prowess."	"I have been racking my brains and eating my insides out trying to think of what I could have said or done to Anita Hill to lead her to allege that I was interested in her in more than a professional way, and that I talked with her about pornographic or X-rated films."
"Because I was extremely uncomfortable talking about sex with him at all, and particularly in such a graphic way, I told him that I did not want to talk about this subject. I would also try to change the subject to education matters or to nonsexual personal matters, such as his background or his beliefs."	". . . Our relationship remained both cordial and professional. At no time did I become aware, either directly or indirectly, that she felt I had said or done anything to change the cordial nature of our relationship."

"All the News That's Fit to Print"

The New York Times

Late Edition

New York: **Today,** clear, mild for the season. High 44. **Tonight,** cloudy late, breezy. Low 34. **Tomorrow,** cloudy, then colder, windy. High 45. **Yesterday,** high 40, low 28. Details, page D12.

VOL.CXLI . . . No. 48,826

NEW YORK, THURSDAY, DECEMBER 26, 1991

50 CENTS

GORBACHEV, LAST SOVIET LEADER, RESIGNS; U.S. RECOGNIZES REPUBLICS' INDEPENDENCE

RETAILERS REPORT SALES FELL SHORT OF DIM FORECASTS

Last-Minute Buying Spree Fails to Carry Merchants Ahead of Last Year's Receipts

By EBEN SHAPIRO

Retailers would probably like to forget Christmas 1991. While most merchants had been prepared for a sluggish season, many said sales turned out to be even worse than expected. Even the last-minute shopping frenzy was not enough to give merchants anything to cheer about.

As recently as a month ago, many retailers had hoped to exceed last year's sales by 5 percent. But results through the close of business on Monday indicate that spending will be flat or up slightly in December. The major retail chains are scheduled to release their final monthly sales results next week.

"We are disappointed with the season," Stephen E. Watson, president of the Dayton Hudson Corporation in Minneapolis, said in a telephone interview on Tuesday.

'Too Little Too Late'

Business surged in the final days, and a number of retailers said that Monday was the busiest day of the year. But Mr. Watson said, "In our view, it's really been too little too late." Dayton Hudson, which relies on California for one-third of its business, was hit hard by the slowdown in that state's economy.

This is the third consecutive sluggish Christmas shopping season — the make or break season for retailers — and many analysts say this year's dismal results are likely to force thousands of companies into bankruptcy.

The economy received most of the

Continued on Page D8, Column 3

Associated Press

Mikhail S. Gorbachev after announcing his resignation last night as President of the Soviet Union.

Communist Flag Is Removed; Yeltsin Gets Nuclear Controls

By FRANCIS X. CLINES

Special to The New York Times

MOSCOW, Dec. 25 — Mikhail S. Gorbachev, the trailblazer of the Soviet Union's retreat from the cold war and the spark for the democratic reforms that ended 70 years of Communist tyranny, told a weary, anxious nation tonight that he was resigning as President and closing out the union.

"I hereby discontinue my activities at the post of President of the Union of Soviet Socialist Republics," declared the 60-year-old politician, the last leader of a totalitarian empire that was undone across the six years and nine months of his stewardship.

Mr. Gorbachev made no attempt in his brief, leanly worded television address to mask his bitter regret and concern at being forced from office by the creation of the new Commonwealth of Independent States, composed of 11 former republics of the collapsed Soviet empire under the informal lead of President Boris N. Yeltsin of Russia.

'A New World'

Within hours of Mr. Gorbachev's resignation, Western and other nations began recognition of Russia and the other former republics.

"We're now living in a new world," Mr. Gorbachev declared in recognizing the rich history of his tenure. "An end has been put to the cold war and to the arms race, as well as to the mad militarization of the country, which has crippled our economy, public attitudes and morals. The threat of nuclear war has been removed." [A transcript of Mr. Gorbachev's speech and excerpts from interviews with Mr. Gorbachev and Mr. Yeltsin are on pages A12 and A13.]

Mr. Gorbachev's moment of farewell was stark. Kremlin guards were preparing to lower the red union flag for the last time. In minutes, Mr. Gorbachev would sign over the nuclear missile launching codes for safeguarding to Mr. Yeltsin, his rival and successor as the dominant politician of this agonized land.

Yeltsin's Assurance on Weapons

Earlier today, Mr. Yeltsin told his Russian Parliament that "there will be only a single nuclear button, and other presidents will not possess it."

But he said that to "push it" requires the approval of himself and the leaders of Ukraine, Byelorussia and Kazakhstan, the four former republics that have strategic nuclear weapons on their soil.

"Of course, we think this button must never be used," Mr. Yeltsin said.

Out in the night beyond the walled fortress as Mr. Gorbachev spoke, a disjointed people, freed from their decades of dictated misery, faced a frightening new course of shedding collectivism for the promises of individual enterprise. It is a course that remains a mystery for most of the commonwealth's 280 million people.

"I am very much concerned as I am leaving this post," the union President told the people. "However, I also have feelings of hope and faith in you, your wisdom and force of spirit. We are the heirs of a great civilization and it now depends on all and everyone whether or not this civilization will make a comeback to a new and decent living."

Still Against Commonwealth

In departing, the Soviet leader took comfort in the world's supporting his singular achievements in nuclear disarmament. But even more, he firmly warned his people that they had not yet learned to use their newly won freedom and that it could be put at risk by the

Continued on Page A12, Column 1

The Soviet State, Born of a Dream, Dies

By SERGE SCHMEMANN

Special to The New York Times

End of an Empire

A special report.

MOSCOW, Dec. 25 — The Soviet state, marked throughout its brief but tumultuous history by great achievement and terrible suffering, died today after a long and painful decline. It was 74 years old.

Conceived in utopian promise and born in the violent upheavals of the "Great October Revolution of 1917," the union heaved its last in the dreary darkness of late December 1991, stripped of ideology, dismembered, bankrupt and hungry — but awe-inspiring even in its fall.

The end of the Soviet Union came with the resignation of Mikhail S. Gorbachev to make way for a new "Commonwealth of Independent States." At 7:32 P.M., shortly after the conclusion of his televised address, the red flag with hammer-and-sickle was lowered over the Kremlin and the white-blue-red Russian flag rose in its stead.

No Ceremony, Only Chimes

There was no ceremony, only the tolling of chimes from the Spassky Gate, cheers from a handful of surprised foreigners and an angry tirade from a lone war veteran.

Reactions to the death varied widely, according to Pravda, the former mouthpiece of the empire: "Some joyfully exclaim, 'Finita la comedia!' Others, heaping ash on their heads, raise their hands to the sky in horror and ask, what will be?"

The reaction depended somewhat on whether one listened to the ominous gunfire from Georgia, or watched spellbound the bitter if dignified surrender of power by the last leader of the Union of Soviet Socialist Republics, Mr. Gorbachev.

Most people vacillated. The taboos and chains were gone, but so was the food. The Soviet Union had given them pitifully little, but there was no guarantee that the strange-sounding "Commonwealth of Independent States" would do any better.

As for Mr. Gorbachev, public opinion polls indicated a virtually universal agreement that it was time for him to move on — not because he had failed, but because there was nothing more he could do.

It was perhaps a paradox that the ruler who presided over the collapse of the Soviet Union was the only one of its ill-starred leaders to leave office with a measure of dignity intact. It was possible that history would reach a different verdict, but among many thoughtful Russians, it was to his undying credit that he lifted the chains of totalitarian dictatorship. Whether he could also have saved the economy was another question.

"Gorbachev was unable to change the living standards of the people, but he changed the people," Komsomolskaya Pravda wrote in a sympathetic farewell that seemed to capture the dominant mood. He didn't know how to make sausage, but he did know how to give freedom. And if someone believes that the former is more impor-

Continued on Page A14, Column 1

BUSH LAUDS VISION OF SOVIET LEADER

In Farewell, President Cites Gorbachev's Historic Role

By MICHAEL WINES

Special to The New York Times

WASHINGTON, Dec. 25 — President Bush moved quickly tonight to recognize Russia and other former republics of the now-extinct Soviet Union.

After praising the former Soviet leader, Mikhail S. Gorbachev, Mr. Bush went out of his way to express support for President Boris N. Yeltsin of Russia, who has emerged as the first among equals in the new Commonwealth of Independent States and as the custodian of the old Soviet Union's nuclear arsenal.

In his brief televised speech, Mr. Bush said that the United States now recognized the independence of the 11 former Soviet republics that have banded together, as well as a 12th, Georgia, which has shunned the alliance. [Text of Mr. Bush's remarks, page A16.]

But he indicated that the equally important step of establishing diplomatic ties between Washington and all 12 parts of the old Soviet empire would be more complicated.

The President said he was satisifed with the assurances on nuclear controls that he has received from Mr. Yeltsin and from leaders of other former republics with nuclear arms on their soil. Mr. Bush said that the United States would move rapidly to establish diplomatic relations with Russia, Armenia, Ukraine, Byelorussia, Kazakhstan and Kirghizia.

Diplomatic relations with the re-

Continued on Page A16, Column 3

On Tom Harkin

Mixing pugilism and politics, the Iowa Senator is running for President with an appeal built on his combative personality.

Strategies: The Democrats and '92. Page D11.

Pineapple, After Long Affair, Jilts Hawaii for Asian Suitors

By ROBERT REINHOLD

Special to The New York Times

LANAI CITY, Hawaii — For the last 13 years Kathleen Ruaburo dressed for work in thick rubberized pants and goggles and spent her days, just as her immigrant Filipino father did, in the heat and the dust picking pineapples on the Dole plantation. Now she dons a crisp white jacket with gold buttons and sets tables for wealthy tourists at the new Manele Bay Hotel here.

Mrs. Ruaburo's transition tells the story of pineapples in Hawaii. The crop that symbolizes this state and for decades has been a mainstay of the islands' economy is almost gone. Hawaiian pineapples can no longer compete in the world market.

Over the next 18 months, crews will harvest the last planting on this island, once the largest pineapple plantation in the world. Then the fields will go to alfalfa and oats, and the pineapple crews will either have to accept jobs in two new luxury hotels or leave the island for work. It is a future that some welcome and some fear on this tiny island, where 2,144 residents still live an isolated plantation life that has scarcely changed since James Drummond Dole started growing pineapples here 69 years ago.

A big worry is that the island's economy will be just as dependent as ever on one industry. When the hotels were first proposed, pineapple cultivation was expected to continue and tourism was intended as a way to diversify the types of jobs here. But gradually, Dole managers said, it became clear that pineapples were no longer profitable enough.

Seventy-two miles away in Honolulu the Dole Packaged Foods Company on Dec. 1 began laying off about 500 workers at the big cannery near downtown that has processed the Lanai fruits for more than half a century. Its largest competitor, Del Monte, ended canning almost a decade ago. Only one canner remains in Hawaii, the Maui Land and Pineapple Company, which produces private labels for supermarkets. The Dole brand will stay on the shelves, but the pineapples will come from its plantations in Asia, as some do now.

Some Hawaiian pineapples will be grown for local consumption and to provide fresh fruit to markets on the

Continued on Page A18, Column 2

E

Lee Romero/The New York Times

Having a Home Is Not a Prerequisite for Having the Spirit of Christmas

Leroy Lewis built a Christmas tree at his sometime home under the Queensboro Bridge on First Avenue in Manhattan. Lenore Elners stopped yesterday to wish Mr. Lewis a merry Christmas.

From L.I. to Angry Illinois: A 5-Day Trash Odyssey

By SARAH LYALL

Special to The New York Times

TAYLORVILLE, Ill., Dec. 20 — The story of Ocke Ketelsen's garbage began Dec. 15, when he put it out on his curb in Westbury, L.I. It was nothing special, just things like an old milk carton and some scraps of aluminum foil, and Mr. Ketelsen didn't give it a second thought. "Garbage is garbage," he said.

Not really, not anymore.

Garbage has become a multimillion-dollar industry, a touchy environmental issue and a major headache for crowded states like New York and New Jersey. And the next day, while Mr. Ketelsen stayed home, his trash began an odyssey that took it north, south, and finally 900 miles west to the flat, open community of Taylorville, where the major industries are farming, paper and New York State refuse.

The system that got Mr. Ketelsen's garbage here is as messy as trash itself. Mr. Ketelsen now pays five times as much in waste-disposal taxes as he did 15 years ago. And as they deal with closing landfills, wildly varying environmental regulations, and a crazy-quilt pricing system that can draw garbage halfway across the country in search of a good deal, many municipalities are finding that garbage is their biggest worry and their biggest expense.

"Garbage is the most serious problem that we face," said Ernest J. Strada, as Mayor of Westbury, is responsible for removing Mr. Ketelsen's trash. "The general public talks about it in a general sense — we make garbage and it goes away. But it doesn't."

In the uneven picture of garbage in America, few places are as complicated as Long Island. The Island has dozens of overlapping jurisdictions, no

Continued on Page B4, Column 1

INSIDE

Health Care on Wheels

Home health care has emerged as a $15 billion industry with more than 12,500 companies and not-for-profit services, from simple nursing to mobile emergency rooms. Page D1.

11 Turks Die in Firebombing

Kurdish separatists threw firebombs at a department store in Istanbul, setting the seven-story building ablaze and killing 11. Page A5.

Television and radio news and listings appear today on pages D18-19.

End of the Soviet Union: Leaving the Stage

Gorbachev Resigns Post as Soviet Leader

Continued From Page A1

commonwealth, which he fought to the last.

"I am concerned about the fact that the people in this country are ceasing to become citizens of a great power and the consequences may be very difficult for all of us to deal with," he declared, implicitly arguing that his union could have remained a superpower despite the cold war's end, which he helped engineer.

"We have paid with all our history and tragic experience for these democratic achievements," Mr. Gorbachev said, assessing centuries of suffering across serfdom and revolution, "and they are not to be abandoned whatever the circumstances, and whatever the pretext. Otherwise, all our hopes for the best will be buried."

Mr. Gorbachev's stringent gaze and strong caution to the now dismembered nation were in contrast to the smiling ease displayed during this transition day by President Yeltsin, chief heir to this land's political and economic chaos.

'They Need Some Belief'

"The people here are weary of pessimism, and the share of pessimism is too much for the people to handle," Mr. Yeltsin declared in an interview with CNN. "Now they need some belief, finally."

Mr. Yeltsin made a point in the interview of sending Christmas wishes to his listeners today as the West celebrated the holiday, although the Russian Orthodox Christmas is not until Jan. 7. Mr. Yeltsin also took care in addressing the outside world to stress that commonwealth leaders had agreed to fulfill the disarmament commitments made by Mr. Gorbachev.

"I don't want the international community to be worried about it," President Yeltsin said, vowing that there would "not be a single second after Gorbachev makes his resignation" that the missile codes would go astray.

The weapons are only one item in a long list of needed precautions that the commonwealth republics must attend to if they are to establish credibility in a decidedly skeptical world that has watched the Soviet Union reverse its totalitarian course and collapse in a matter of a few years.

Agence France-Presse

The Soviet flag being lowered at the Kremlin yesterday after Mikhail S. Gorbachev resigned.

Mr. Yeltsin is first among equals in the 11-member commonwealth. This is a very loose political association resorted to by the former Soviet republics because of their disenchantment with the very notion of union and their need, nonetheless, for some common arrangement that might ease the escape from post-Communist destitution.

The commonwealth members are free to decide their individual economic and political plans. But they are pledged to a common military command for joint defense needs and to certain economic denominators as well, including the hope of a resuscitated ruble as their common currency.

Russia has already taken the lead in economics as well as defense, with the giant republic of 149 million people bracing for Mr. Yeltsin's first steps toward free-market reform next week. Sweeping price rises are to be legalized on Jan. 2 as an end comes to much of the consumer-goods subsidies that Communism maintained to make its regime minimally palatable.

Mr. Yeltsin made a point in his CNN interview of expressing some displeasure at the limited amount of aid that has been extended by the outside world.

"There has been a lot of talk, but there has been no specific assistance," he said, offering a small smile. He quickly offered an explanation that with the union collapsing for the last year, willing nations probably found no clear address to which to donate.

"Now everything is clear, and the addressees are known," he said, beaming as if in invitation. "And I think that this humanitarian aid will step up now."

A Poke at Baker

He offered the same hint of mischief in dealing with the fact that Secretary of State James A. Baker 3d waited until he headed home from an initial visit before talking quite pessimistically of the commonwealth's chances.

"Mr. Baker, when he and I had a four-and-a-half-hour meeting here in Moscow, Mr. Baker never told me that," Mr. Yeltsin said. "So those who doubt as to the success of the commonwealth should beware and not be so pessimistic," he advised. "We are sick and tired of pessimism."

In leaving, Mr. Gorbachev had no kind words in the televised speech for the commonwealth and never mentioned Mr. Yeltsin.

He reviewed his own campaign to preserve a drastically revised union. It would have accepted the sovereignty the republics gained after the hard-line Communist coup failed in August. This led to the fall of the Communist Party and, tonight, of the union's most prominent defender, Mr. Gorbachev.

"The policy prevailed of dismembering this country and disuniting the state, which is something I cannot subscribe to," Mr. Gorbachev told the nation, his jaw set forward firmly in defeat as the presidential red union flag gleamed its last behind his right shoulder.

As Mr. Yeltsin deftly acquired the Moscow remnants of the union's powers and real estate across the last few weeks, the huge red union flag atop the Kremlin's domed Council of Ministers building had waved mainly as a symbol of Mr. Gorbachev's holdout resistance to the commonwealth.

Associated Press

President Boris N. Yeltsin of Russia during an interview yesterday at the Russian Parliament in Moscow with reporters from CNN. They were, from left, Claire Shipman, and Steve Hurst.

The Flag Comes Down

The flag was lowered from its floodlit perch at 7:32 tonight. A muted moment of awe was shared by the few pedestrians crossing Red Square.

"Why are you laughing at Lenin?" a man, obviously inebriated against the winter cold, suddenly shouted in the square. He reeled near Lenin's tomb.

The mausoleum was dusky pink against the evergreen trees outside the Kremlin walls. Within, for all the sense of history wheeling in the night sky, the embalmed remains of the Communst patriarch still rested.

The drunk was instantly shushed by a passer-by who cautioned that "foreigners" were watching and he should not embarrass the reborn Russia.

"Foreigners?" laughed another Muscovite. "Who cares? They're the ones who are feeding us these days."

In the Gorbachev era there were countless moments of floodlit crisis and emergency solutions hurriedly concocted and rammed through in the Kremlin. Previously, Mr. Gorbachev prevailed and often proved brilliant in his improvising. Tonight, though, he was the executive focus for the last time and he seemed brisk and businesslike, a man containing himself against defeat.

In an interview with CNN later, when asked about his plans, he said he would not comment now on the "many proposals and offers" he had received. He said he would "have to recover a little bit, relax, take a rest."

'Respect' From Rival

"Today is a difficult day for Mikhail Gorbachev," President Yeltsin said a few hours before the Soviet President resigned, when the Russian leader was invited to describe Mr. Gorbachev's main mistakes along the difficult road of reform.

"Because I have a lot of respect for him personally and we are trying to be civilized people and we are trying to make it into a civilized state today, I don't want to focus on these mistakes," Mr. Yeltsin responded.

Gorbachev Looks Back: Few Regrets

By Reuters

Following are excerpts from a CNN interview in Moscow yesterday with former President Mikhail S. Gorbachev. His remarks were translated by CNN from the Russian.

Q. I would like to ask you first, sir, looking back on your career as President and General Secretary, can you think of a moment when you feel you might have done things differently and the outcome would have not been — would have been that you did not resign tonight?

A. As for my overall choice, I wouldn't change anything in that this society was so overloaded with problems and it was as a result of the implementation of a certain model. It was in a difficult situation. Perestroika and all that was associated with perestroika had been prepared by the entire preceding period. So far as strategy, nothing should have been done differently and I am convinced that that is so because I am basing this on the arguments of all those seven years.

As for the tactical approaches to the various problems and the political and economic reform in reforming our multi-ethnic state, also so far as the sequence of steps is concerned and particularly as regards cooperation with democratic forces and generally as regards stimulation of the processes of democracy, here I think we really had some very important breakthroughs and achievements and a great change in our society. But certain mistakes and blunders could have been avoided and that would have made this process less painful.

. . .

Yeltsin and Grudges

Q. We'd like to ask you, sir, if you are feeling a grudge towards Boris Yeltsin for the way he pushed and pushed and finally brought the situation to tonight's events?

A. I think that that would be a simplistic answer, that you know, they applied some pressure on Gorbachev once or twice. One person, Yeltsin, did it. Well, it's much more complex. This is a very complicated process — a big and important development. We had cooperation. We had confrontation, too, over the past months. There was more — there has been more cooperation. It is still there.

I have just signed the decree about the discontinuation of my functions as Commander in Chief and the transfer of the control of nuclear weapons and the command and control of the use of nuclear weapons to the President of the Russian Federation, Boris Yeltsin. This is the decree.

We will be meeting shortly and this act of the transfer of authority will take place. So we are cooperating, I think, in the interest of our states, in the interests of the commonwealth, in the interests of the world.

But I do not want to justify the way my colleagues are carrying out politics in certain episodes and in handling certain questions. I cannot share some approaches that they adhered to. I have said that I disagree with that. I think that now we have to place above all else the fact that the country is awaiting very resolute, decisive steps and cooperation between all the republics in order to move out of the crisis.

. . .

Plans for Future

Q. President Gorbachev, you mentioned that you would like to remain involved in politics in some way. Do you have specific plans for the future that you could tell us about now? And also, how would you hope to be remembered by historians?

A. Well, the second question, let me answer that first. I would like to make sure that people give their recognition to what we've been doing over these years. I think they will do it one day. Currently the hardships of life make it difficult for people to just sit down and think and talk about what happened and what is happening to us, and the kind of people that we have become.

We have become a different kind of people, a different kind of country, and therefore we can expect that there will be change, and that we will become a democratic and prosperous country.

Kremlin Roll-Call

1917-24: Vladimir I. Lenin

1924-53: Iosif V. Stalin

1953-55: Georgi M. Malenkov

1955-64: Nikita S. Khrushchev

1964-82: Leonid I. Brezhnev

1982-84: Yuri V. Andropov

1984-85: Konstantin U. Chernenko

1985-91: Mikhail S. Gorbachev

Associated Press

President Mikhail S. Gorbachev signing a decree relinquishing control of the Soviet strategic arsenal to Boris N. Yeltsin shortly before announcing his resignation as President of the defunct Soviet Union.

Gorbachev Sees Strain on Family

Special to The New York Times

MOSCOW, Dec. 25 — In leaving the Kremlin tonight, Mikhail S. Gorbachev talked briefly of the strain his family suffered during the tumultuous final months leading to his resignation.

"Things are happening to this country and to my family and this has to affect my family, a very close-knit family," he said in an interview with Cable News Network. His wife, Raisa, suffered what he has called a "very bad attack" during the coup attempt.

But he celebrated the strength of his family. "My family, I would say, does not lose heart and is in courageous spirit and solidarity with me," he said, adding that this gives him fresh energy to play a new public role.

Text of Gorbachev's Farewell Address

By Reuters

Following is a transcript of Mikhail S. Gorbachev's resignation speech in Moscow yesterday, as recorded through the facilities of CNN and translated by CNN from the Russian:

Dear fellow countrymen, compatriots. Due to the situation which has evolved as a result of the formation of the Commonwealth of Independent States, I hereby discontinue my activities at the post of President of the Union of Soviet Socialist Republics.

I am making this decision on considerations of principle. I firmly came out in favor of the independence of nations and sovereignty for the republics. At the same time, I support the preservation of the union state and the integrity of this country.

The developments took a different course. The policy prevailed of dismembering this country and disuniting the state, which is something I cannot subscribe to.

After the Alma-Ata meeting and its decisions, my position did not change as far as this issue is concerned. Besides, it is my conviction that decisions of this caliber should have been made on the basis of popular will.

However, I will do all I can to insure that the agreements that were signed there lead toward real concord in society and facilitate the exit out of this crisis and the process of reform.

This being my last opportunity to address you as President of the U.S.S.R., I find it necessary to inform you of what I think of the road that has been trodden by us since 1985.

Squandered Resources

I find it important because there have been a lot of controversial, superficial, and unbiased judgments made on this score. Destiny so ruled that when I found myself at the helm of this state it already was clear that something was wrong in this country.

We had a lot of everything — land, oil and gas, other natural resources — and there was intellect and talent in abundance. However, we were living much worse than people in the industrialized countries were living and we were increasingly lagging behind them. The reason was obvious even then. This country was suffocating in the shackles of the bureaucratic command system. Doomed to cater to ideology, and suffer and carry the onerous burden of the arms race, it found itself at the breaking point.

All the half-hearted reforms — and there have been a lot of them — fell through, one after another. This country was going nowhere and we couldn't possibly live the way we did. We had to change everything radically.

It is for this reason that I have never had any regrets — never had any regrets — that I did not use the capacity of General Secretary just to reign in this country for several years. I would have considered it an irresponsible and immoral decision. I was also aware that to embark on reform of this caliber and in a society like ours was an extremely difficult and even risky undertaking. But even now, I am convinced that the democratic reform that we launched in the spring of 1985 was historically correct.

The process of renovating this country and bringing about drastic change in the international community has proven to be much more complicated than anyone could imagine.

However, let us give its due to what has been done so far.

This society has acquired freedom. It has been freed politically and spiritually, and this is the most important achievement that we have yet fully come to grips with. And we haven't, because we haven't learned to use freedom yet.

However, an effort of historical importance has been carried out. The totalitarian system has been eliminated, which prevented this country from becoming a prosperous and well-to-do country a long time ago. A breakthrough has been effected on the road of democratic change.

Market Format Nears

Free elections have become a reality. Free press, freedom of worship, representative legislatures and a multi-party system have all become reality. Human rights are being treated as the supreme principle and top priority. Movement has been started toward a multi-tier economy and the equality of all forms of ownership is being established.

Within the framework of the land reform, peasantry began to re-emerge as a class. And there arrived farmers, and billions of hectares of land are being given to urbanites and rural residents alike. The economic freedom of the producer has been made a law, and free enterprise, the emergence of joint stock companies and privatization are gaining momentum.

> An ex-President insists that his reforms were 'historically correct.'

As the economy is being steered toward the market format, it is important to remember that the intention behind this reform is the well-being of man, and during this difficult period everything should be done to provide for social security, which particularly concerns old people and children.

We're now living in a new world. And end has been put to the cold war and to the arms race, as well as to the mad militarization of the country, which has crippled our economy, public attitudes and morals. The threat of nuclear war has been removed.

Once again, I would like to stress that during this transitional period, I did everything that needed to be done to insure that there was reliable control of nuclear weapons. We opened up ourselves to the rest of the world, abandoned the practices of interfering in others' internal affairs and using troops outside this country, and we were reciprocated with trust, solidarity, and respect.

We have become one of the key strongholds in terms of restructuring modern civilization on a peaceful democratic basis. The nations and peoples of this country have acquired the right to freely choose their format for self-determination. Their search for democratic reform of this multinational state had led us to the point where we were about to sign a new union treaty.

Popular Resentment

All this change had taken a lot of strain, and took place in the context of fierce struggle against the background of increasing resistance by the reactionary forces, both the party and state structures, and the economic elite, as well as our habits, ideological bias, the sponging attitudes.

The change ran up against our intolerance, a low level of political culture and fear of change. That is why we have wasted so much time. The old system fell apart even before the new system began to work. Crisis of society as a result aggravated even further.

I'm aware that there is popular resentment as a result of today's grave situation. I note that authority at all levels, and myself are being subject to harsh criticisms. I would like to stress once again, though, that the cardinal change in so vast a country, given its heritage, could not have been carried out without difficulties, shock and pain.

The August coup brought the overall crisis to the limit. The most dangerous thing about this crisis is the collapse of statehood. I am concerned about the fact that the people in this country are ceasing to become citizens of a great power and the consequences may be very difficult for all of us to deal with.

I consider it vitally important to preserve the democratic achievements which have been attained in the last few years. We have paid with all our history and tragic experience for these democratic achievements, and they are not to be abandoned, whatever the circumstances, and whatever the pretexts. Otherwise, all our hopes for the best will be buried, I am telling you all this honestly and straightforwardly because this is my moral duty.

I would like to express my gratitude to all people who have given their support to the policy of renovating this country and became involved in the democratic reform in this country. I am also thankful to the statements, politicians and public figures, as well as millions of ordinary people abroad who understood our intentions, gave their support and met us halfway. I thank them for their sincere cooperation with us.

Avoidable Mistakes

I am very much concerned as I am leaving this post. However, I also have feelings of hope and faith in you, your wisdom and force of spirit. We are heirs of a great civilization and it now depends on all and everyone whether or not this civilization will make a comeback to a new and decent living today. I would like, from the bottom of my heart, to thank everyone who has stood by me throughout these years, working for the righteous and good cause.

Of course, there were mistakes made that could have been avoided, and many of the things that we did could have been done better. But I am positive that sooner or later, some day our common efforts will bear fruit and our nations will live in a prosperous, democratic society.

I wish everyone all the best.

End of the Soviet Union: Explosion in Czar's Universe

Glory and Heartbreak: The 7 Raging Decades Of the Workers' State

Exclusive News Agency

BORN OF REVOLUTION

After the overthrow of Czarist rule in February 1917, ferment continued as crowds rallied for "Land, Freedom and a Democratic Republic." On Nov. 7, Lenin, as head of the Bolsheviks, seized power from the democratically minded provisional government and set out to organize the world's first Communist state, while waging a civil war that lasted until 1922. He is shown at a Red Square rally in 1919.

Tass from Sovfoto

Bettmann Archive

INDUSTRIALIZATION

Centralized planning placed stress on the construction of huge industries and extolling a proletarian culture in propaganda such as the pageantry accompanying the dedication of a steel mill in 1932.

Sovfoto

STALINISM

Terror, forced collectivization and intensifying totalitarianism characterized the rule of Stalin, which lasted from 1924 through World War II until 1953.

Camera Press

THE WAR YEARS

The German invasion of Russia, breaking the Hitler-Stalin non-aggression pact, began in June 1941. After Nazi forces were eventually slowed and halted in bitter, long and very costly battles like the victorious defense of Stalingrad in 1943, left, the Red Army moved onto the offensive to occupy lands that enabled Stalin to orchestrate the postwar divison of Europe into East and West.

Soviet State: Born of a Dream, Raised in Nightmares

Continued From Page A1

tant than the latter, he is likely never to have either."

Another man might have done things differently. But it was difficult to conceive that any of those then available — the conservative Yegor K. Ligachev, the rough-hewn Boris N. Yeltsin, the bureaucratic Nikolai I. Ryzhkov or the scholarly Eduard A. Shevardnadze — possessed just that blend of reformer and ideologue, of naïveté and ruthlessness, that enabled Mr. Gorbachev to lead the Communists to the edge of the cliff.

"Gorbachev was a true instrument of fate," declared Viktor Yerofeyev, a writer and literary critic. "He had just enough intelligence to change everything, but not enough to see that everything would be destroyed. He was bold enough to challenge his party, and cautious enough to let the party live until it lost its power. He had enough faith in Communism to be named its head, but enough doubts about it to destroy it. If he had seen everything clearly, he would not have changed Russia."

Mr. Gorbachev struggled to the end, and beyond it, to keep the union alive. But in the end, it was by letting the union die and by stepping aside that he gave a new lease on life to the great Eurasian entity, whatever its name.

The Union

Epic Achievement And Epic Failure

Measured against its own ambitions, the U.S.S.R. died a monumental failure.

It had promised no less than the creation of a "Soviet new man," imbued with selfless devotion to the common good, and it ended up all but crushing the initiative and spirit of the people, making many devoted only to vodka. It had proclaimed a new humanitarian ideology, and in its name butchered 10 million of its own. It envisioned a planned economy in which nothing was left to chance, and it created an elephantine bureaucracy that finally smothered the economy. Promising peace and freedom, it created the world's most militarized and ruthless police state.

Promising a people's culture, it created an anti-culture in which mediocrity was glorified and talent was ruthlessly persecuted. An entire department of the K.G.B. existed to wrestle with art, trying first to co-opt any rising talent "to the service of the state" and if that failed, to muzzle or exile it. The roll-call of repressed or exiled artists is a stunning indictment: Mandelstam, Malevich, Pasternak, Solzhenitsyn, Rostropovich, Brodsky, and so many more.

In the end, promising a new life, it created an unspeakably bleak society — polluted, chronically short of everything, stripped of initiative and spirituality. While the bulk of the nation stood in line or guzzled rot-gut vodka, the Communist elite raised corruption to new heights: The likes of Leonid I. Brezhnev and his cronies pinned endless medals on one another and surrounded themselves with a peasant's notion of luxury — grandiose candelabras, massive cars, vast hunting estates, armies of sycophants, secret hospitals filled with the latest Western technology.

And yet the Soviet Union was also an indisputable superpower, a state and a people that achieved epic feats in science, warfare, even culture.

Perhaps all this was achieved despite Communism, not because of it. Yet by some combination of force and inspiration, the system begun by Lenin and carried out by Stalin unleashed a potent national energy that made possible the rapid industrialization of the 1930's, the defeat of Nazi Germany in the 1940's, the launching of the first Sputnik in the 1950's, the creation of a nuclear arsenal in the 1960's and 1970's. Even now, for all the chaos in the land, two astronauts, Aleksandr A. Volkov and Sergei Krikalev, continue to circle the globe.

In culture too, both the "thaw" of Nikita S. Khrushchev in the 1960's and the "glasnost" of Mr. Gorbachev offered testimony that the enormous creativity of the nation was as tenacious as the people.

And in sport, the tangle of Olympic medals and international victories were a tacit source of national pride even among the staunchest critics of the Communist regime.

The Dream

A Utopian Illusion Survived Injustice

It is easy now, gazing over the smoldering ruins of the Soviet empire, to enumerate the fatal illusions of the Marxist system. Yet the irresistible utopian dream fired generations of reformers, revolutionaries and radicals here and abroad, helping spread Soviet influence to the far corners of the globe.

Until recently, rare was the third world leader who did not espouse some modified Marxist doctrine, who did not make a regular pilgrimage to Moscow to join in the ritual denunciations of the "imperialists."

Much of it was opportunism, of course. In the Soviet Union as in the third world, Communism offered a handy justification for stomping on democracy and keeping one party and one dictator in power.

Yet it was also a faith, one strong enough to survive all the injustices done in its name. Lev Kopelev, a prominent intellectual now living in Germany, recalled in his memoirs how prisoners emerged from the gulag after Stalin's death firmly believing that at last they could start redressing the "errors" of Stalinism and truly building Communism.

And only last March, Mr. Gorbachev would still declare in Minsk, "I am not ashamed to say that I am a Communist and adhere to the Communist idea, and with this I will leave for the other world."

The tenacity of the faith testified to the scope of the experiment. It was a monumental failure, but it had been a grand attempt, an experiment on a scale the world had never known before.

Perhaps it was the height of folly and presumption that Russia, a country then only at the dawn of industrialization and without a bourgeoisie or proletariat to speak of, would have been the one to proclaim itself the pioneer of a radically new world order.

Two Worlds

'Westernizers' Vs. 'Slavophiles

But Russians have always had a weakness for the broad gesture. The greatest czars — Ivan the Terrible, Peter the Great — were those with the grandest schemes. The greatest writers, Dostoyevsky and Tolstoy, explored ultimate themes in immense novels. The Russian Orthodox Church embroidered its churches and its liturgy in the most elaborate gilding and ceremony.

Nothing happened small in the Soviet era, either. Twenty million died in the war, 10 million more in the gulag. And the pride of place was always given to grandiose construction projects — the world's biggest hydroelectric plant at Bratsk, the world's biggest truck factory at Kamaz, the trans-Siberian railroad.

The czarist merchant wrapped in coats of gold and sable racing in his sleigh through wretched muzhiks in birch-bark shoes translated into the ham-fisted party boss tearing through Moscow in his long black limousine.

Many theories have been put foward to explain these traits. There is the sheer expanse of a country that spans 11 time zones. There is the climate, which imposed a rhythm of long, inactive winters punctuated by brief summers of intense labor. Some posited the absence of a Renaissance, which stunted the development of an individual consciousness and sustained a spirit of collectivism.

Above all it was a nation straddling two continents and two cultures, forever torn and forever fired by the creative clash at the faultline of East and West.

Russians have ever split into "Westernizers" and "Slavophiles," and the death of the Soviet Union had everything to do with the struggle between the "Westernizing" democrats and free-marketeers and the anti-Western champions of powerful statehood and strong center.

The West has always been deemed both attractive and dangerous to Russia. Peter the Great campaigned desperately to open his nation to the West, but Westerners remained suspect and isolated. Communism found nourishing soil in the Russian spirit of collectivism, but its Western materialism proved alien.

Western democracy is foundering here on

End of the Soviet Union: The Superpower Years

THE SPACE RACE

While the Soviets did not explode their first atomic bomb until five years after the United States ushered in the nuclear age, they launched the world's first earth satellite, Sputnik, in 1957, four months before the first American satellite was orbited. Four years later, the Soviets sent Yuri Gagarin on the first manned space flight.

Associated Press

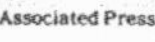

Associated Press

SUPERPOWER

On May Day, 1963, the Soviet military showed off a powerful arsenal to compete with the weapons of the United States. A year earlier, Nikita Khrushchev backed off a nuclear showdown when he responded to President Kennedy's order of a "quarantine" of Cuba by withdrawing missiles from the Caribbean nation.

Associated Press

COLD SPOT

Khrushchev showing the Supreme Soviet an aerial photograph made by Francis Gary Powers, pilot of a U.S. spy plane, who was shot down and captured in May 1960.

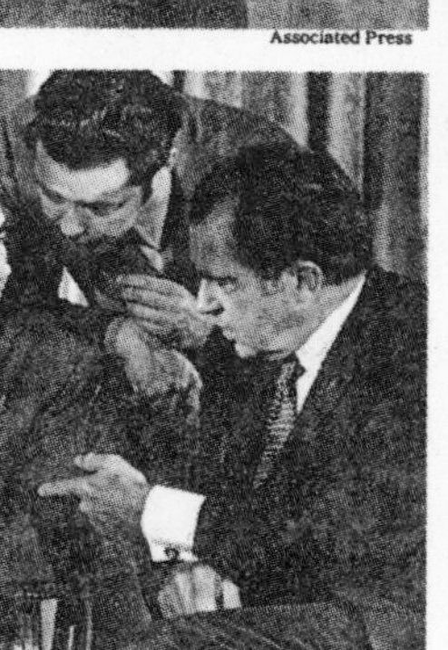

Mike Lien/The New York Times

DETENTE

Leonid I. Brezhnev and President Nixon soon after the signing of the 1972 strategic arms agreement, which paved the way for greater discussion and lessening tension.

Associated Press

THE BEGINNING OF THE END

As Mikhail S. Gorbachev was held captive by hard-line Communists in August, Boris N. Yeltsin mounted a tank in Moscow to rally resistance to the coup plotters. The coup collapsed and Mr. Gorbachev was restored, but with steadily weakening authority.

Finally, Gorbachev's Reforms: Too Little or Too Late

the same ambivalence. The Soviets plunged whole-heartedly into the plethora of new councils and parliaments inaugurated by Mr. Gorbachev. But their endless debate and inability to organize into cohesive interest groups soon diminished public attention, and at the end the parliaments readily transferred most of their powers to Mr. Gorbachev, Mr. Yeltsin and other powerful men.

"What remains after the Soviet Union is this Eurasian essense, this unique interplay of Europe and Asia, which will continue to amaze the world with its culture and totally unexpected actions," Mr. Yerofeyev said.

"What was imported in Western Marxism will vanish," he continued. "But Communism will not disappear, inasmuch as the spirit of collectivism is at the heart of this nation. The nation will always say 'we' rather than the Anglo-Saxon 'I'.

"This was Lenin's deftness, that he realized Russia was ready to accept Communism, but needed only 'class struggle' for everything to fall into place. As soon as it had an enemy, the collective consciousness became dynamic."

Contrasts

Impressive Feats, Awesome Litter

That spirit was forever captured in the revolutionary posters, with their capitalists in top hats dripping with workers' blood, or the muscular young Communists crushing bourgeois vipers.

Lenin's successors understood this equally well, that it was easier to fire Soviets to enormous feats and extraordinary sacrifice than to organize them for sustained work and steady growth.

The capacity for suffering and sacrifice, whether in the war or in the endless lines today, is something that still awes foreigners. The ability to focus enormous talent and energy on a grand project is equally impressive, and from this came the great achievements in science, weaponry and construction.

Yet the sloppiness and inefficiency of everyday life make an even stronger impression on visitors. The shoddiness of even the newest apartment block or hotel is shocking. Old houses seem to list precariously in the mud. Wreckage litters every yard. Cars come off the assembly lines half broken.

The planned economy served only to intensify the squalor. It made volume, not quality or inventiveness, the primary measure of production, and it put a premium on huge factories over flexibility or distribution.

The system also gave consumer goods the lowest possible priority, thus institutionalizing shortages and reducing ordinary people to a permanent state of dependence on the state and rude salespeople.

Icons

The Cults End In State's Dotage

Whether Lenin would have built the Soviet state this way is not certain. Three years before his death, in 1921, he replaced "War Communism" with what became known as the "New Economic Policy," but was in fact a return to a measure of old laissez-faire. The national income rose to pre-revolutionary levels, but that failed to dissuade Stalin from starting the first Five-Year Plan.

Nonetheless, it was Lenin who became the first deity of the new order. He was a convenient hero: He had died while still enormously popular, and he left behind enough writings on every topic to support whatever position his successors chose to take.

Thus his goateed visage soon became the mandatory icon in every official building or every town square, and his words became scripture. All the powers of science were summoned to preserve his remains forever, and his mausoleum became the spiritual heart of the new empire. His name became an adjective denoting orthodoxy, as in "the Leninist way." Plaques were raised at every building he stayed in, and an enormous temple was built over his childhood home.

The cult seemed only to gain strength with the passing years, as his successors denounced one another and struggled to portray themselves as the one true interpreter of Lenin. Stalin set the trend, killing most of Lenin's comrades as he perfected the machinery of repression, all the while claiming to act in the name of the great founder.

Next, Khrushchev dismantled the Stalin cult and halted the worst of the terror in the name of restoring "true Leninism," only to be overthrown himself. Before long, Brezhnev was the sole heir, and Khrushchev's "voluntarism" joined Stalin's "personality cult" among the heresies of Leninism.

With Brezhnev, the Soviet state passed visibly into dotage. As he grew bloated and incoherent, so did the state. Production fell while an uncontrolled military machine devoured ever-larger portions of the national product. Foreign policy sank into a pattern of stagnant coexistence and fierce military competition with the West, while at home the political police steadily put down the small but brave dissident movement inspired by the brief Khrushchevian thaw.

After 18 years in power, Brezhnev was succeeded by two other old and sick men, Yuri V. Andropov and Konstantin U. Chernenko, and by the time Mr. Gorbachev took the helm in 1985, it was obvious to all that the state was in radical need of help.

Mr. Gorbachev, at 54 the youngest Soviet leader since Stalin, electrified the land almost immediately with the introduction of "glasnost," or openness. Suddenly the people could talk and think freely, taboos began to crumble, East-West hostilities evaporated, and dissidents emerged from labor camps and exile. The sweet perfume of hope scented the air.

But Mr. Gorbachev's parallel attempts to reform the economy perished on the same shoals as all previous reforms — the thick and privileged Communist party apparat. The more glasnost flourished, the more it became evident that perestroika was foundering, and everything Mr. Gorbachev did seemed to be too little or too late.

Floundering in the end, he lurched first to the left, ordering a radical "500 day" reform plan in the summer of 1989, then to the right, rejecting the plan and encircling himself with party stalwarts and letting them use force, then back to the left last spring, opening negotiations with the republics on a new Union Treaty.

By then it was too late. The rejected right-wingers tried to seize power by force in the August coup, and with their defeat, the republics had no more need for or faith in Mr. Gorbachev or the remnants of his union.

On Dec. 8, the leaders of Russia, Ukraine and Byelorussia pulled the plug, proclaiming a new Commonwealth of Independent States, and after that it was only a question of time before the breathing stopped.

Afterlife

Problems Survive But Will Pride?

The union was dead. But the great Eurasian entity on which it fed remained very much alive — as Russia, as a new Commonwealth of 11 republics, as a culture and a worldview, as a formidable nuclear arsenal, as a broad range of unresolved crises.

The gunfire in Georgia, the long lines across the land, the closed airports and the myriad unanswered questions about the new Commonwealth — would it confer citizenship? would it remain a single military and economic entity? would it manage transport and communications? — made clear that the legacy of the union would long survive.

Mr. Gorbachev had given people a new freedom. But the Soviet Union had also given them something tangible — the pride of superpower. Whatever their problems and shortages, they had been one of the two arbiters of global destinies, a nation that nobody could intimidate or bully.

Now that was being taken away, too, and how the humiliation would play out, especially in conditions of hunger and poverty, was among the troubling questions for the future.

"The parting with the Union of Soviet Socialist Republics will be long and difficult," Izvestia warned. "We must acknowledge that many will not believe or agree to the end of their days with the death warrant written in Minsk and confirmed in Alma-Ata. The idea of superpower has a force equal to nationalism, and in certain conditions it is also capable of uniting millions of fanatic supporters."

"All the News That's Fit to Print"

The New York Times

Late Edition

New York: **Today,** becoming mostly sunny. High 57-62. **Tonight,** showers late. Low 47. **Tomorrow,** clouds breaking, breezy. High 72. **Yesterday,** high 62, low 42. Details are on page B16.

VOL.CXLI . . No. 48,953 | NEW YORK, FRIDAY, MAY 1, 1992 | 50 CENTS

23 DEAD AFTER 2D DAY OF LOS ANGELES RIOTS; FIRES AND LOOTING PERSIST DESPITE CURFEW

SENATORS APPROVE A BILL TO CURTAIL CAMPAIGN SPENDING

Curbs on Unrestricted Money Pass in Vote With Margin Too Thin for Override

By ADAM CLYMER
Special to The New York Times

WASHINGTON, April 30 — On a near party-line vote, the Senate today passed a campaign finance bill that would set voluntary spending limits in Congressional races and sharply reduce the role of money raised outside of existing Federal rules on contributions.

The 58-to-42 vote sent the most sweeping campaign finance legislation in 18 years to the White House, where it faces a certain veto. President Bush has said he would reject any legislation providing public money for candidates and setting spending limits, a move that he says would favor incumbents.

Neither today's margin nor the 259-to-165 tally by which the House approved the Democratic bill on April 9 is close to the two-thirds' vote required to override a veto.

A Milestone Vote

Despite that hard reality and the bill's failure to say how the Government would pay for the benefits it offers, supporters called today's vote and the agreement between House and Senate Democrats a milestone on the way to changing the current system.

The spending limits were the subject of the most heated argument as the Senate ended a three-day debate today. Senator Bob Dole of Kansas, the Republican leader, said: "Often the only way a challenger can compete with the built-in advantages of incumbency is to spend money. The bottom line is that spending limits are designed to prevent change at a time when the American people are demanding change."

Senator George J. Mitchell of Maine, the majority leader, called such arguments "nonsense." He said incumbents almost always raised more than their challengers, often three or four times as much, and therefore limits would help even the odds in those contests.

That partisan division was reflected

Continued on Page A16, Column 3

Leadership And Its Limits

Political Needs Prevail In Check-Scandal Vote

By ADAM CLYMER
Special to The New York Times

WASHINGTON, April 30 — The leaders wanted to resist. The followers didn't.

The leaders tried to look after the House as an institution. The ordinary members preferred to look after their own careers.

News Analysis

That is the quickest explanation of what happened when the House voted Wednesday night to comply with a subpoena from the Justice Department, asking for records of every check written on the now closed House bank between July 1988 and October 1991.

Indeed, dozens of members who voted to comply with the subpoena regarded it as an improper "fishing expedition" but one they could not effectively resist, and only 131 Democrats stood up and voted to challenge it in court. Perhaps 30 or 40 more had promised to do so if their votes mattered. They waited, saw it was hopeless and cast the vote that was easier to explain back home.

Spotlight on Foley

For months, some Democrats have faulted Speaker Thomas S. Foley for not anticipating the perils that the bank's tolerance of dubious checks posed for all of them. They also faulted him for being thoughtful and judicious but not political enough.

A Texan, John Bryant, took the floor four weeks ago to complain that the Speaker was not defending the House adequately. Mr. Foley is certainly not succeeding in defending the House against what he and most Democrats see as irresponsible intrusions by a zealous Justice Department. But on Tuesday night Mr. Bryant voted to surrender the records.

Yes, there are complaints about the leadership, but basically the followers have the leadership they want, leaders who plead with them but do not or cannot order them about. The demand that Mr. Foley become a stronger, firmer leader is not easily squared with the independent search for survival that marks the House today.

His circumstances were made al-

Continued on Page A24, Column 4

Associated Press

Flames engulfing a building in South-Central Los Angeles on Wednesday night as rioting spread.

900 REPORTED HURT

National Guard on Patrol — Violence Spreads to San Francisco

By SETH MYDANS
Special to The New York Times

LOS ANGELES, April 30 — Social order broke down today across a broad area of the nation's second-largest city as vandals and looters roamed the streets, carloads of young men attacked pedestrians and uncounted fires burned out of control.

Mayor Tom Bradley and the Police Chief, Daryl F. Gates, appealed for order and imposed a dusk-to-dawn curfew, saying they had been overwhelmed by the violence and rioting that broke out after Wednesday's acquittal of four white police officers on trial for beating a black motorist, Rodney G. King.

The authorities said at least 23 people had been killed, more than 900 injured and nearly 500 people arrested. Hundreds of buildings burned as the violence spread from South-Central Los Angeles into wealthier white areas, and entire inner-city blocks lay in ruins.

National Guard Arrives

As the night wore on, officials said, the violence and lawlessness increased even as National Guard troops summoned by Gov. Pete Wilson were put on the streets.

"The situation is getting worse, despite the dusk-to-dawn curfew," said Deputy Larry Mead of the Los Angeles County Sherriff's Department. "There's been an increase in looting and fires in the southern sections of the city of L.A. and L.A. County."

Near midnight there were signs that the number of new fires was decreasing, but the police were still trying to control roving bands of looters. A police spokesman, Lieut. John Dunkin, said officers had killed three people in separate incidents since nightfall.

In Washington, the Justice Department announced that it was reopening an investigation into the March 3, 1991, videotaped beating of Mr. King to prepare the ground for a possible civil rights case against the four officers who were acquitted.

Violence in Other Cities

But it was clear from the words of the rioters, as well as black elected officials and others, that their anger ran far deeper than reaction to the acquittal. There were demonstrations around the nation, gangs on the loose in Atlanta and San Francisco and fears that the violence, shown vividly on television, might spread further. [Page A20.]

Just before 7 P.M., two white men on a motorcycle were attacked by a group of about 15 black men in Long Beach, south of Los Angeles. The two motorcyclists were beaten and shot, and one was killed, according to Comdr. Anthony Batts of the Long Beach Police Department.

The violence in Los Angeles spread today as smoke from burning buildings mingled with the city's smog. The first 1,200 of 4,000 National Guard members to be deployed took up positions this afternoon alongside hundreds of police and highway patrol officers in South-Central Los Angeles, the mostly black and Hispanic section where the violence began Wednesday afternoon.

Governor Wilson this afternoon doubled the original summons of 2,000 troops as the violence spread through-

Continued on Page A20, Column 1

Surprised, Police React Slowly as Violence Spreads

By ROBERT REINHOLD
Special to The New York Times

LOS ANGELES, April 30 — The Los Angeles Police, apparently caught off guard by the violent reaction to the acquittal of four white officers in the beating of a black motorist, were slow to react, even after the scope of the anarchy sweeping the city had become apparent.

As unruly demonstrators threatened to invade police headquarters downtown early Wednesday evening, Chief of Police Daryl F. Gates was attending an event in the affluent Brentwood area, about 11 miles away, to raise money to fight a proposal on the June ballot to limit the term of the police chief. Matthew Hunt, the deputy chief in charge of the affected area, was attending a community meeting about 6 miles from the police command center.

It was hours before the police entered many of the areas in South-Central Los Angeles where stores were being looted and motorists were being dragged from their cars and beaten.

Chief Resisted National Guard

As late as 11 P.M., with at least two dozen fires blazing out of control, Chief Gates resisted Mayor Tom Bradley's call for National Guard troops, telling Gov. Pete Wilson in a conference call with the Mayor that he was not sure the police needed help handling the situation, according to someone who is close to Mayor Bradley and who spoke on the condition of anonymity.

The Mayor prevailed with the Governor, and by this morning Mr. Gates agreed that the Guard was needed. But the first contingent, about 2,400 guardsmen, including 100 military police, was not deployed on the streets until midafternoon today. The Governor traced the delay in part to a shortage of ammunition.

Fires Burned Unattended

Similarly, the Los Angeles Fire Department, had no special contingency plan apart from declaring a tactical alert, meaning engine companies moved in special teams. The department was forced to let many fires burn unattended, not because it lacked sufficient engines at first but because the police did not have enough officers to protect firefighters. There were barely enough officers on hand to prevent Parker Center, the police headquarters downtown, from being overrun.

The slow response was due in part to the fact that almost nobody, including the Mayor, anticipated such a sweeping acquittal of all four officers and

Continued on Page A22, Column 1

Reuters

Suspected looters, handcuffed and forced to lie down, in police custody.

Afghans' Battle Lines Are Drawn As One Rebel Denounces Another

By EDWARD A. GARGAN
Special to The New York Times

KABUL, Afghanistan, April 30 — Afghanistan's strongest guerrilla leader, Ahmad Shah Masood, took charge of the security of Kabul today after entering the capital overnight with a three-mile-long convoy of military vehicles and an estimated 10,000 troops.

Shortly after arriving, Mr. Masood denounced the lone guerrilla leader who has refused to take part in the coalition that proclaimed an Islamic republic in Afghanistan on Tuesday.

The holdout, Gulbuddin Hekmatyar, who heads the hard-line Islamic group Hezb-i-Islami, has marshaled his guerrillas just south of Kabul in Logar Province, from where he is continuing to mount attacks on the capital.

A barrage of rockets, presumably fired by Mr. Hekmatyar's forces, hit the airport this evening. Mr. Masood's forces did not counterattack, but the guerrilla leader's criticism of Mr. Hekmatyar left little doubt that a new round of fighting could be in store.

"Every group which is fighting the Government, which is acceptable to the majority of the people, is baghi," Mr. Masood said. The word refers to un-Islamic behavior akin to criminality.

As late as Wednesday the new Government, headed by Sibgatullah Mojadedi, was considering some way to placate Mr. Hekmatyar by giving him a role in the new administration. But today, with the continuing attacks, Mr. Hekmatyar was branded an enemy.

Full Attack Weighed

"He's out," said Assam Akram, a spokesman for Mr. Mojadedi, who is to hand over leadership of the ruling coalition in two months to the head of Mr. Masood's guerrilla group, Jamiat-i-Islami or Islamic Society. Mr. Akram accused Mr. Hekmatyar of sabotaging Kabul's electrical grid; the capital has been without power for two days.

Nurul Haq Ullumi, a general in the

Continued on Page A10, Column 4

Smell of Fear in Los Angeles

By JANE GROSS
Special to The New York Times

LOS ANGELES, April 30 — The City of Angels endured another siege of violence today with an acrid smell of smoke in its nostrils and a cold stone of fear heavy on its heart.

Hopes were dashed early that daylight would quiet the beating, looting and burning that followed Wednesday's verdict in the Rodney G. King case, and residents took to the streets warily, knowing that terrible things had happened here overnight, with more terrible things likely to come.

Throughout the sprawling metropolis, even in neighborhoods far from the epicenter of the violence, Angelenos sensed that the next car that passed might carry hooligans waving crowbars and axes, that the next store to burn or be looted could be the one on their corner. This was not a disturbance with a clear perimeter, they came to understand, and while some street corners were safer than others, there was really no place to hide.

The roadways were emptier than usual, but chaotic as a bumper-car ride as nervous motorists navigated a shifting maze of barricades and craned their heads skyward to track the newest plume of smoke rising in the heavy haze. The drivers' eyes darted from side to side, taking the measure of the stranger in the car beside them, plotting new routes as streets and highways closed and reopened, and gazing in horror at the ravaged and smoldering stores that dotted the city.

Evacuation in Koreatown

In some neighborhoods more than others, one could almost smell the fear. Four miles north from the genesis of the violence, Koreatown, for instance, was an edgy place this morning, braced for trouble because of longstanding tensions between the black and Asian communities here.

By midafternoon, the bands of looters were moving in waves toward the small strip shopping centers near Olympic Boulevard and Vermont Street, the heart of the Koreatown, but hours earlier some Korean merchants decided they were taking no

Continued on Page A21, Column 3

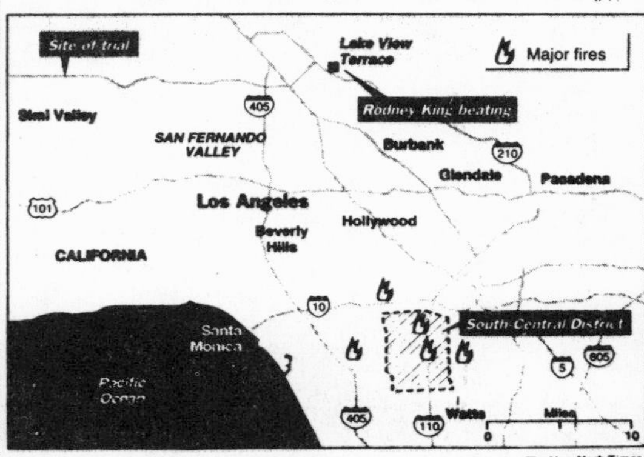

The New York Times

INSIDE

Familiar End in Mideast Talks

Israelis and Arabs ended their fifth round of talks without signs of progress on major issues or a commitment on meeting again. Page A6.

Navy Report on Sex Assaults

The Navy said many women, not just a few, were abused at an aviators' convention and said many officers would not aid the inquiry. Page A14.

An Everglades Cleanup Idea

A system of trading pollution credits could help to rid the Everglades waters of phosphorous from fertilizers, economists believe. Law, page B18.

Exxon Official Still Missing

The disappearance of the president of Exxon International remained a mystery and officials refused to discuss the investigation. Page B1.

Nets Walk the Plank

New Jersey's season of near-mutiny ended in a 98-89 loss to the Cleveland Cavaliers in the fourth game of their N.B.A. playoff series. Page B9.

MORE ON THE RIOTS

'I Know It's Not Right'

In some areas, looters said they were expressing their bitterness at the status of blacks in America. Page A21.

Clinton and Bush Spar

Gov. Bill Clinton and aides to President Bush criticized each other's response to the events. Page A22.

Public Topic No. 1

On call-in programs, at rallies and on the job, Americans voiced apprehension about race relations. Page A23.

How Lawyers See the Case

Los Angeles lawyers who have followed the case dissected the tactics of prosecution and defense. Page A20.

Riots in Los Angeles: After the Verdict, Anger Unleashed

Reuters

Rampaging youths in Atlanta attacking a passerby yesterday after a demonstration turned violent.

700 Arrested in San Francisco Violence

By KATHERINE BISHOP
Special to The New York Times

SAN FRANCISCO, April 30 — Chanting "Rodney, Rodney, Rodney," an unruly mob of a few hundred young people rampaged through the streets of downtown San Francisco tonight, breaking windows, looting stores and setting trash fires.

Mayor Frank Jordan declared a state of emergency and imposed a curfew as police officers, who were outnumbered, struggled to disperse the crowd. The Mayor ordered people off the streets from 9 P.M. to 6 A.M. Friday.

More than 700 people were arrested in tonight's outbreak of violence, The Associated Press reported. Dozens of the looters were arrested and laid out on sidewalks across the street from Macy's department store, their hands held behind them with plastic restraints.

Hours earlier, similar violence broke out in Atlanta as gangs of young people protested the acquittals of four white Los Angeles police officers in the beating of a black motorist, Rodney G. King.

Fighting between blacks and whites was reported at high schools in Maryland, Tennessee, Texas and New York City. And in Madison, Wis., the windshields of 34 police squad cars parked at a garage were shattered, and a note left at the scene said "Justice for King" and "All pigs must die."

Over a four-hour period in San Francisco, the demonstrators roved up and down Market Street between Third and Sixth Streets, gleefully looting stores and jeering at the police officers who were trying to to gather them in.

The young people erected a barricade of newspaper vending machines across Market Street and set the papers on fire, then pelted the police with empty cans. A solid wall of police officers in riot gear managed to push the group out of the area temporarily, only to have them surge back again and again to smash more store windows.

Police officers pleaded with the crowd, saying, "Please, go home, folks." Young people answered the pleas with obscenities. The crowd, made up largely of white youths in leather and black teen-agers, slapped high fives and played rap music on portable tape players, lending a party atmosphere to the evening.

Running along Market Street, they slapped stickers reading "L.A. Police Department cowards" on store fronts and bus shelters.

Guests in downtown hotels huddled in the lobbies, afraid to go out in the streets as the wail of sirens from police cars and fire trucks echoed in the night.

The looters, who had broken away from a demonstration against the verdict in the Los Angeles police case, also smashed the windows of parked cars and overturned one car atop Nob Hill.

A car was overturned in the intersection of Sacramento and Powell Streets, and the city's historic cable car system, whose lines intersect at Powell and California Streets, was shut down for the night, forcing tourists to walk from the Fisherman's Wharf area to their hotels downtown.

Macy's Broken Into

The glass door of Macy's department store was broken, and neckties lay scattered on the floor. Witnesses said that some looters had emerged with armsful of merchandise, especially men's leather jackets.

In Atlanta, what began as a peaceful protest at the predominantly black Atlanta University Center turned violent as marchers reached the downtown area. At least two dozen stores were vandalized, and young blacks attacked whites randomly in a downtown subway station, seriously injuring one bystander, the police said. State troopers in riot gear ringed the Capitol, where a car belonging to a black aide to Gov. Zell Miller was turned over and vandalized.

Overview

23 Are Dead in Rioting in Los Angeles; Troops Called Out as Looting Continues

Continued From Page A1

out the day. The deployment came nearly 24 hours after Mayor Bradley made his first request to the state.

A spokesman for the Los Angeles Police Department said the guard members were manning road blocks in the harder-hit areas, providing security for firefighters and assisting police officers in bringing specific areas under control. He said the police department put 3,000 officers on the street this evening, double the number from this afternoon.

Gunfight in Koreatown

The violence in Los Angeles jumped a boundary from the South-Central area today, bringing racial conflict for the first time into the insulated, mostly white areas of West Los Angeles and Beverly Hills. Shops were looted and burned in Hollywood and nearby Santa Monica.

A gunfight broke out this afternoon between Korean merchants and a group of black men in the Koreatown section, a sharp escalation in the tensions that have divided the groups in recent months. Tall plumes of smoke rose from burning shops in the neighborhood, just north of South-Central.

As fires, police sirens and pockets of violence spread, most of the city shut down, with offices and shops closing and public transport scaling back its operations early.

The sheriff's department said that 5 black men and 1 Hispanic man were killed Wednesday night and that the total killed had risen to 23 by late tonight.

As the guard members were taking up positions in the badly battered South-Central area, convoys of cars carrying young men headed out into affluent West Los Angeles and Beverly Hills, shouting, brandishing hatchets, crowbars and bottles, beating passers-by and looting shops.

The glittering Beverly Center mall, a mammoth shopping center on the edge of Beverly Hills, was closed this afternoon after looting began among its high-priced boutiques. Looters later raided frilly lingerie at Frederick's of Hollywood.

Like Wells of Kuwait

As night fell, what had been scattered pillars of smoke broadened to become a huge black cloud reminiscent of the burning oil wells of Kuwait during the Persian Gulf war. The fires moved north toward the Hollywood Hills to strike apartment buildings as well as businesses.

With firefighters slow to respond, some home owners tried to fight back the fires with garden hoses.

The fires brought interruptions of electrical power to parts of the city. Debra Sass, a spokeswoman for the city's Department of Water and Power, said at 10 P.M. Pacific time that about 12,700 customers, including businesses and residents, had no power.

She said that most of the problems were in South-Central Los Angeles and that repair crews had been instructed not to go into the neighborhoods and restore power unless they had a police escort. For that reason, she said, it was unclear how long the customers would be without power.

Deputy Mead said rioters had thrown rocks and bottles at National Guard members and law-enforcement officers in a number of locations, and that there were some reports of gunfire aimed at officers. But he said there were no reports of officers being injured or killed.

Although streets in most sections of the city were unusually quiet or deserted by 10 p.m., fires raged into the night in some places and the sounds of sirens and swirling helicopters filled the night.

Mayor Bradley announced the curfew on the city's 3.5 million residents at a televised news conference this morning. It allowing the police to stop and question anyone on the streets. Later, he went on television to say he had taken a helicopter tour of the devastated area and "was so touched, so hurt by what I saw, it was difficult to describe." Curfews were also put into effect in Compton, Inglewood and Santa Monica as well as the County of Los Angeles, which also banned sales of guns, ammunition and gasoline.

Saying he was "sickened by what I saw on television," Governor Wilson, who flew in from Sacramento this evening, said he had requested the doubling of the National Guard contingent because of a "real and genuine" need for reinforcements.

Agence France-Presse

About 4,000 National Guard troops dispatched by Gov. Pete Wilson began taking up positions, this one at a burning shopping center, in Los Angeles. Infantry and military police units from throughout the state were activated. Guard members receive 16 hours a year in riot training.

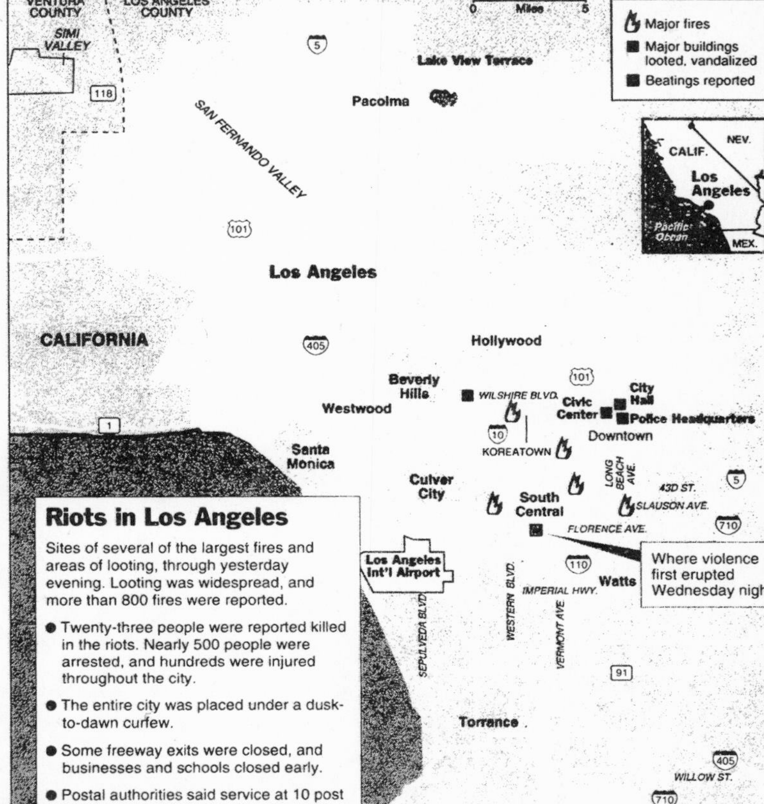

The New York Times

He said the initial deployment was slowed by a shortage of ammunition and by difficulties in organizing the command structure. He said the Guard members would fire their weapons if fired upon.

Air traffic at Los Angeles International Airport was hampered by the smoke from the fires, with some flights diverted and others delayed. Telephone calls could not be completed in some parts of the city because of a high volume of calls.

Bush Speaks of Anguish

In words that reflected Americans' reactions to both the verdict and the rioting that followed it, President Bush appealed for tolerance and order. "Yesterday's verdict in the Los Angeles police case has left us all with a deep sense of personal frustration and anguish," he said in a statement. "Yet it is important that we respect the law and the legal processes that have been brought to bear in this case."

Gov. Bill Clinton of Arkansas, his probable Democratic opponent, said before leaving Washington, "It is obvious that lurking beneath that verdict there is this huge, gaping feeling that the system is broke and unresponsive and unfair."

Those thoughts were repeated often here today among Los Angeles residents. The acquittals added fuel to anger that had flared over the suspended sentence given last year to a Korean-American grocer who had shot dead a young black customer.

Though acquitted of assaulting Mr. King, one defendant, Officer Laurence M. Powell, faces a possible retrial on a charge of using excessive force under color of authority, on which the jury failed to reach a verdict.

But the verdict itself seemed mostly forgotten in the energy of the vandalism and looting that continued throughout the day and into the night.

This morning, entire blocks of buildings were left in smoldering ruins. But some areas took on the atmosphere of a street party as black, white, Hispanic and Asian residents mingled to share in a carnival of looting.

As the greatly outnumbered police looked on, people of all ages, some carrying small children, wandered in and out of stores and supermarkets with shopping bags and armloads of shoes, liquor, radios, groceries, wigs, auto parts, gumball machines and guns.

Some stood patiently in line to take their turn. Some pulled up their cars to fill their trunks with goods. At a Bank of America branch, a group of people managed to pull an entire automated teller machine out of the wall and cart it off.

The looters paused when the police occasionally intervened, then went back to business when they left.

The Verdict

Switching Case to White Suburb May Have Decided Outcome

By DAVID MARGOLICK

Lawyers throughout the country debated yesterday why a jury in Simi Valley, Calif., acquitted four white police officers in Los Angeles of charges that they had brutalized a black motorist, Rodney G. King. But in Los Angeles, where the episode took place, the second-guessing was particularly intense and fine-tuned.

Much of the analysis focused on the performance of the prosecution. A few asserted that from the outset prosecutors were lukewarm about the case. Others accused prosecutors of tactical errors: declining to call Mr. King to the stand, failing to stress the racial animus of the defendants, losing their cool during closing arguments.

Some thought the prosecutors outmatched. While the defense lawyers in the case had built their careers defending police officers from such charges, even senior prosecutors have scant familiarity with brutality cases. Conversely, others thought the prosecutors were overconfident — convinced that even the defense's insistence that the case be moved to lily-white Ventura County could not overcome the devastating impact of the home video that all of America has seen.

In fact, however, the outcome of the case may well have been decided when Judge Stanley Weisberg of California Superior Court transferred the case from the city to Simi Valley, an overwhelmingly white, conservative enclave that is the home of the Ronald Reagan Presidential Library. Like Rockland or Nassau counties in New York, it is a place to which many members of the Los Angeles Police Department have fled.

Worshiping the Police

"The responsibility for this verdict falls on the jury," said Prof. Laurie L. Levenson of Loyola Law School in Los Angeles, one of two law schools shut down yesterday by the turmoil on the streets around it. "Frankly, the people in Simi Valley worship the police."

Courts have wide discretion to grant changes of venue in notorious cases, even where the demographics of the substituted locale are dramatically different. Still, some lawyers questioned the purpose of transferring the case, particularly since Simi Valley jurors would have been every bit as familiar with the videotape.

"Sirhan Sirhan didn't get a change in venue; Charles Manson didn't get a change of venue," said Tom Barham, a lawyer in Los Alamitos who has represented many victims of police brutality. "But the facts were so overwhelmingly in favor of conviction that the court did backflips to give this trial every appearance of fairness."

California legislators said yesterday that they were considering proposals requiring that when cases are moved they be transferred to areas of comparable ethnicity and density.

Even Veterans Are Stunned

Even hardened veterans of police brutality cases said they were stunned by the outcome. Thomas E. Beck, who has been counseling complainants in police brutality cases for 14 years, said he was "staggered" by the verdict.

One of the few lawyers who said they were not surprised by the King verdict was John C. Burton of Pasadena, co-chairman of the Police Misconduct Lawyers Referral Service in Los Angeles. He asserted that Ira Reiner, the District Attorney of Los Angeles County, was ambivalent about the case from the outset, and that the chief prosecutor, Terry White, who is black, took his cues from his boss.

"There was simply no zeal in their prosecution, and the reason is that they're part of the same state apparatus as the police," he said. "They're used to prosecuting Rodney Kings, not defending them. To them, he's just another minority young man who's been chucked onto the junk pile."

Mr. Barham disagreed. "Terry White demonstrated he had a total commitment to the case," he said. "If a jury makes up its mind it's not going to listen to the facts or apply the law to those facts, there's not much a prosecutor can do. Simi is really the word, only it should be spelled 's-e-a-m-y.'"

Three Crucial Points

Interviews by several television news organizations with jurors afterward demonstrated that defense lawyers won them over on three crucial points: that it was Mr. King, not the police, who set the agenda that night; that since Mr. King could have avoided the beating in the first place by failing to resist, he got his just deserts; and third, that if force were justified at the outset, circumstances justified whatever force followed.

Like others, Mr. Barham said the decision not to call Mr. King to testify, for fear it would shift the jury's gaze toward him and away from the four policemen, was both understandable and defensible. But, he continued, "the jurors were putting Rodney King on trial anyway, so you had nothing to lose putting him on."

Prof. Peter Arenella of the U.C.L.A. Law School agreed. "With all the attendant risks, if the prosecution had Rodney King on the stand it would have been harder for the jury to dismiss the significance of the damage that had been done to a human being," he said.

But Professor Arenella said the videotape might have been overplayed, thereby losing its impact. "By watching the tape over and over again in slow motion," he said, "the jurors might have been desensitized to the human tragedy they were witnessing."

"All the News That's Fit to Print"

The New York Times

Late Edition

New York: **Today,** partly sunny warm winds. High 75, but cooler along south shores. **Tonight,** cloudy. Low 58. **Tomorrow,** showers. High 71. **Yesterday,** high 79, low 49. Details, page B16.

VOL.CXLII . . . No. 49,307

NEW YORK, TUESDAY, APRIL 20, 1993

75 cents beyond 75 miles from New York City, except on Long Island

50 CENTS

SCORES DIE AS CULT COMPOUND IS SET AFIRE AFTER F.B.I. SENDS IN TANKS WITH TEAR GAS

Agence France-Presse

The wood-frame compound of David Koresh and his cult followers turned into an inferno of death yesterday as a standoff of 51 days was ended.

Apparent Mass Suicide Ends A 51-Day Standoff in Texas

By SAM HOWE VERHOVEK

Special to The New York Times

WACO, Tex., April 19 — Hours after Federal agents began battering holes in the walls of the Branch Davidian compound and spraying tear gas inside, David Koresh and more than 80 followers — including at least 17 children — apparently perished today when flames engulfed the sprawling wooden complex on the Texas prairie.

Officials of the Federal Bureau of Investigation said they believed that Mr. Koresh, a self-described messiah who prophesied to his followers that they would meet their end in an apocalyptic confrontation with the law, gave the order to burn the compound down in the 51st day of a standoff with Federal agents.

F.B.I. officials said smashing the walls and filling the building with tear gas was intended to increase pressure on the cult members, who had resisted all previous demands for surrender. But the officials insisted that the tear gas was not flammable and that the fire was set by cult members who poured fuel around the perimeter of the compound and lit matches.

'They All Willingly Followed'

"David Koresh, we believe, gave the order to commit suicide and they all willingly followed," said Bob A. Ricks, a senior F.B.I. agent who has been here for most of the standoff, which began seven weeks ago with a deadly shootout between cult members and agents from the Federal Bureau of Alcohol, Tobacco and Firearms who wanted to search the compound.

Mr. Ricks said only nine people were rescued from the compound today, including one woman who had sought to return to the burning building and tried to fight off a Federal agent who came to her aid. Ammunition in the cult's storehouse of weapons sporadically exploded during the afternoon, hindering rescue workers.

Mr. Ricks said that so far "several bodies" had been found in a bus buried on the compound, and only "two or three" other bodies. The authorities believed that some of these were cult members who had been killed in the original confrontation on Feb. 28, he said.

"We had hoped the women would grab their children and flee," Mr. Ricks said. "That did not occur and they bunkered down the children and allowed them to go up in flames with them." Mr. Ricks said that it was only speculation at this point but that the authorities had received reports, apparently from some of the survivors, that the children had been injected with some kind of poison to ease their pain.

F.B.I. officials said they believed that 95 people were inside the compound when the fire began, including 17 children under the age of 10, and that it only knew of the 9 survivors, 4 of whom were at hospitals this evening and 5 of

Continued on Page A20, Column 3

RENO SEES ERROR IN MOVE ON CULT

Fatigue of Agents and Failure of Talks Brought Assault

By STEPHEN LABATON

Special to The New York Times

WASHINGTON, April 19 — Attorney General Janet Reno conceded tonight that in hindsight the Government's plan to assault the heavily armed cult near Waco, Tex., had been a mistake.

"It was based on what we knew then," she said this evening on the "Larry King Live" program on CNN. "Based on what we know now, it was obviously wrong."

Earlier in the day, a shaken and somber Ms. Reno said she had worried over the weekend that the plan could bring mass suicide, but she decided that it was "highly unlikely" and approved the operation.

Taking responsibility for the assault, she acknowledged that it had in fact led to a mass suicide, as members of the Branch Davidian cult burned down their wooden compound.

She added that Federal agents had decided to move in this morning in the 51st day of the standoff because negotiations had proved fruitless, because the cult members were prepared to hold out for many months and because there was no backup team to replace weary agents. She also said that the authorities had received reports that children in the compound were being beaten.

Ms. Reno said that the gassing of the

Continued on Page A21, Column 1

Italians Support Political Reform By a Big Margin

By ALAN COWELL

Special to The New York Times

ROME, April 19 — After months of scandal, recession and Government paralysis, Italians voted overwhelmingly for political change in a referendum on Sunday and today that repudiated the country's leadership of the last 48 years, but that left the future uncertain.

Final computer projections late tonight, 10 hours after polls closed, showed 82 percent of voters endorsing a proposal to scrap the current system of pure proportional representation for most of the Senate and replace it with the majority voting used in other parts of Europe and the United States.

The magnitude of the vote is expected to put heavy pressure on legislators to enact similar changes in the lower house, or Chamber of Deputies.

The ballot had assumed the proportions of a popular judgment on Italy's postwar political system, and the result was widely interpreted as a mandate for a new government to press through broader electoral reform.

That, in turn, would set a political calendar for new elections — and thus a fresh start — after a debilitating corruption scandal that has tainted much of the political and business elite and exposed ties between some government leaders and the Mafia.

While some of Italy's traditional parties, notably the Christian Democrats and the former Communists, would probably survive the process of re-

Continued on Page A8, Column 1

Vietnam Report on Prisoners A Fake, Reputed Author Says

By PHILIP SHENON

Special to The New York Times

HANOI, Vietnam, April 19 — A Vietnamese general denied today that he had written in 1972 that Hanoi held more than twice as many American prisoners as it ultimately released. Any such report attributed to Hanoi is a forgery, he declared.

And a special envoy, sent by President Clinton to tell the Vietnamese that relations could not improve until the matter was cleared up, said he saw no reason to disbelieve the Vietnamese denial.

Nearly two weeks ago, Russian archivists turned over to the United States a Russian translation of what was said to be a secret report to Hanoi's Politburo given by Gen. Tran Van Quang, described in the document as Deputy Chief of Staff of the Vietnamese armed forces at the time. The document said Hanoi held 1,205 American prisoners of war in September 1972.

591 Released in 1973

Because Vietnam released only 591 prisoners in 1973 and has maintained repeatedly that there were no other prisoners, the Russian translation raised the recurring question of whether Hanoi had kept some prisoners back, and if so, what happened to them. An alternative explanation offered by some experts was that Hanoi might have killed hundreds of prisoners.

Hanoi immediately denied the accuracy of the Russian document, saying it was a "fabrication."

In a meeting today, General Quang told President Clinton's special envoy, Gen. John W. Vessey Jr., that he did not write the 1972 report on which the Russian translation was supposedly based. If the Vietnamese report exists, General Quang said, it is a forgery that may have been prepared by someone interested "in undermining advances in relations between Vietnam and the United States."

At a news conference today after meeting with General Vessey, General Quang said of the 1972 report: "I did not write it. I tell you, never in my life have I made such a report, because it was not in my area of responsibility."

He stressed that although he was

Continued on Page A6, Column 4

Law Firm for S.& L. Is Fined $51 Million

Jones, Day, Reavis & Pogue, one of the nation's biggest law firms, agreed to pay the Government $51 million to settle charges that it aided the financier Charles H. Keating Jr. in the fraud that brought on the costliest bankruptcy in the savings and loan debacle. The agreement came as a trial was about to begin.

The settlement, which is the largest against a law firm in the savings and loan rescue, also ends litigation against the Jones, Day partner in charge of work for Mr. Keating's Lincoln Savings and Loan Association, which collapsed in 1989 at a cost to taxpayers of $2.5 billion.

Business Day, page D1.

New Country Is Like Prison to Asenhat, 18

By DAVID GONZALEZ

Asenhat Gomez used to peer out the windows of her childhood home in the Dominican countryside and relish a landscape of willowy palm trees and verdant fields where her extended family would gather for daylong reunions.

In her new home in Brooklyn — a cramped apartment on Williamsburg's South Side — the windows frame a claustrophobic vista of brick walls, and the few relatives she has in this country are so preoccupied with making ends meet that family get-togethers seem as long gone as the father who died a dozen years ago.

It has been nearly a year since Asenhat was reunited with her mother, who six years before had left her children with their aunt and illegally entered the United States in search of the opportunities that had eluded the family in the Dominican Republic.

Longing for Home

But the immigrant journey of Asenhat Gomez is only beginning. For 18-year-old Asenhat, the joys of reunion are constantly tempered by the struggles of life in a hard new land. Hundreds of miles from all that was familiar, unable to shake her longing for home, she tentatively ventures into a future that beckons with equal measures of promise and fear.

In many ways, hers is the oldest of immigrant stories, played out time and again by wave after wave of newcomers to America's shores. But for today's immigrant children, in places like Williamsburg, that process of adjustment is made all the more difficult by the modern plagues of drugs, guns and recession.

Asenhat, a shy girl, has become even shyer since arriving last May, the strangeness and the frustrations coalescing in a sometimes overwhelming feeling that she is trapped.

'Sense of Confinement'

"Everybody talked about the sense of confinement," she said recently, recalling her first weeks in New York. "I expected that, but just not so much.

Monica Almeida/The New York Times

Children of the Shadows

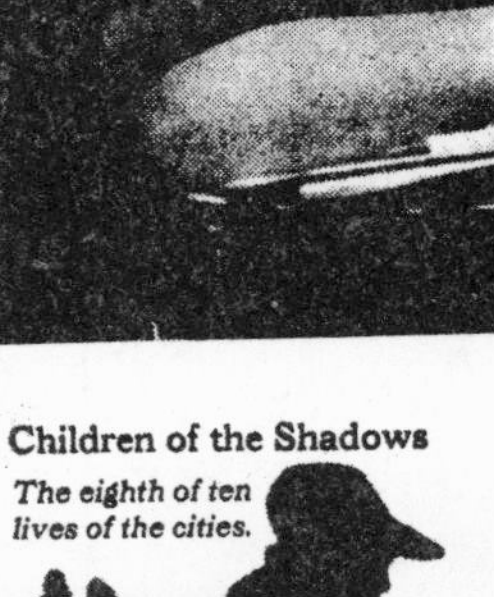

The eighth of ten lives of the cities.

"Lying in bed I would think about what I left behind. There you got accustomed to visiting people, my friends from school, since we were infants. The whole place was different; you could go out to play. I miss my school."

Williamsburg — its bumpy narrow streets lined with age-worn two-family homes and apartment buildings closed in by the shadows of hulking waterfront factories and the Williamsburg Bridge — can seem forbidding to someone used to the easy freedom of the countryside. The family's two small bedrooms are shared by six people who subsist on meager earnings.

Still, even as she bridles at her confinement, it has become her defense mechanism in a city whose ways and language are not her own. She seldom ventures beyond her neighborhood, partly from fear of getting lost on unexplored streets and subway lines and partly from fear of drug dealing and violent crime on nearby blocks.

"It makes you feel insecure," said Asenhat, a short girl whose floppy ponytail and baggy jeans give her the look of someone just entering her teen-age years. "You can be going down the street and not know what can happen."

She has few friends, feeling that she has little in common with American-born teen-agers, who she says are too "liberal" — so preoccupied with boyfriends, clothes and the latest fads that

Continued on Page B6, Column 1

John Kluge Gives Columbia $60 Million to Aid Minorities

By MARIA NEWMAN

John W. Kluge, the chairman of the Metromedia Company and a 1937 graduate of Columbia University, presented his alma mater last night with $60 million for minority scholarships. It is the largest gift the university has ever received.

In making his gift, Mr. Kluge recalled what a hardship it was for him to afford his tuition — only $500 a year at the time — when he was earning $7 a week working in the school dining hall. Fortunately for him, he said, Columbia helped by giving him a scholarship.

"Columbia made a difference really in my life and I really want to assure that it will continue to make a difference for others," Mr. Kluge said in an interview from his office in Manhattan. At 78, Mr. Kluge, who made his fortune building up a string of radio and television stations, is one of the wealthiest people in America.

By itself, the $60 million donation is believed to be the fifth largest to any university or college. When added to the $50 million Mr. Kluge already donated to Columbia in two previous gifts, it would be second only to the $125 million pledged to Louisiana State University in 1981 by Claude B. Pennington.

One of Mr. Kluge's two previous gifts of $25 million, presented in 1987, was also for minority scholarships and the other, in 1990, went to aid young scholars and junior faculty members.

The new gift comes at a critical time as Columbia battles serious fiscal problems. With its $1 billion operating budget, the university has a $15 million deficit this year and is working to cut costs to balance its budget for next year.

Luring Minority Candidates

But officials of the university said it was unclear whether the gift, because it was specifically for scholarships for undergraduates, would have any impact on the deficit.

The gift would, they said, help the university attract minority candidates who might otherwise go to other universities better able to help them with steep college costs.

Fred Knubel, a spokesman for Columbia, said last night that the gift would provide at least 300 students a year with grants of $10,000. Mr. Knubel said that the money would be used in

Continued on Page B7, Column 1

INSIDE

Arrest in Capital Shootings

The police arrested a suspect in a series of shootings that had left three people dead and terrorized Washington since Feb. 23. Page A12.

Slain South African Buried

South Africa turned the burial of a slain black Communist into the biggest political rite since Nelson Mandela's release from prison. Page A8.

New Abortion-Rights Politics

Now that abortion-rights supporters finally have an ally in the White House, they face a new set of priorities and challenges. Page A18.

Rustling Scholarly Feathers

Flightless bird or feathered dinosaur, a turkey-sized fossil from Mongolia has scientists debating the history of flying. Science Times, page C1.

Today's TV Listings

Television and radio listings and advertising appear today on pages B16-17.

Death in Waco: Drawn From the Corners of the World, Then Swept Away

The Lost Cause

Texas Cult Membership: Many Lives, Shared Fate

By MICHAEL deCOURCY HINDS
Special to The New York Times

WACO, Tex., April 19 — The 30-minute inferno that consumed the Branch Davidian compound today also swept away the lives of people drawn to Waco from as far away as Israel, Britain, Australia, New Zealand and the Philippines. The attraction: a man with a penchant for playing rock music, having an occasional beer and preaching Scripture with unwavering conviction.

That man, David Koresh, a 33-year-old high school dropout turned evangelist, apparently led those followers to their deaths today.

"David Koresh, we believe, gave the order to commit suicide, and they all followed his order," said Bob A. Ricks, a special agent with the Federal Bureau of Investigation at a news conference here today.

But Mr. Koresh's grandmother, Jean Holub of Houston, told The Associated Press today: "No, no way. He wouldn't do that to those children."

Mr. Koresh's mother, Bonnie Haldeman of Chandler, blamed the Federal authorities for the fire.

"I am scared to death," Ms. Haldeman said. "Where's our civil rights? It's just terrible. The way they handled this whole thing has been wrong."

Karen Doyle, a cult member whose father and sister were apparently inside the compound when it was destroyed, said her faith in Mr. Koresh

'Do not judge a person by his actions, but by the message.'

had not been shaken by what happened today. "I know that God will take care of them," she said of those who died. "Even in ordinary death, you know, we all put off the body."

Mr. Koresh, who is believed to be among the dead, was born Vernon Howell in 1959 to Ms. Haldeman, a single mother. He had a history of learning disabilities that gave him much trouble in school, and he ultimately dropped out of a high school in Garland, a Dallas suburb, in 1977.

But Mr. Koresh had an extraordinary ability to recite passages of the Bible at length and to cite passages that were persuasive for any argument he was making.

Mr. Koresh became extremely religious in the 1970's. "He would come home and go to the barn and pray for hours," Ms. Haldeman told The AP last month. Mr. Koresh drifted to Southern California and by the mid-1970's was recruiting for the Branch Davidian sect, an obscure splinter group of the Seventh-Day Adventist Church that interpreted the Bible literally.

In 1987, he took control of the sect's compound near Waco after a long struggle with another aspiring leader that culminated in a gun battle. Mr. Koresh and seven of his followers managed to drive off the rival, George Roden, whose family had led the cult for many years. A jury acquitted all the followers of attempted murder, and Mr. Koresh's trial ended in a hung jury.

Earlier this year, the sect had about 120 members. They were mostly white people in their 30's and 40's from Texas, but there were also blacks from Jamaica and England, Americans with diverse ethnic backgrounds and others from a half-dozen foreign countries.

"We're just ordinary people," said Paul G. Fatta, a cult member who missed the confrontation on Feb. 28 only because he left early that Sunday morning to sell guns at a flea market in Austin. "The only thing that brought us together was the Book," he said in an interview last month.

Aggressive Recruiter

The sect had a fairly stable membership from the 1930's until the 1980's, when Mr. Koresh began recruiting aggressively, often by going to night clubs with prospective members. In recent years he had taken to calling himself the Messiah. "If the Bible is true, then I'm Christ," he said on an audio tape for his followers.

Mr. Koresh is said to have dazzled his recruits with Bible lectures that could last 17 hours, and it was the certainty of his message and doomsday prophecies that attracted fundamentalist Christians.

One was Douglas Wayne Martin, a 42-year-old lawyer who was something of an anomaly among the cult members. Mr. Martin attended Harvard Law School, from which he graduated in 1977, and was a history major at the City College of New York, where he made the Dean's List.

The Cult's Income

Like most cults, this one was largely financed by its members' savings, the wages of those who had local jobs and the Social Security and pension checks of the elderly.

Some aspects of the cult's life were bizarre, even though members spent most of their days on the humdrum tasks of living and renovating the block-square compound. The women lived separately from the men, except for Mr. Koresh, who apparently took as a wife any woman he wanted.

Mr. Fatta said Mr. Koresh had presented this behavior as a way to test the faith of the men who had lost their wives.

Work fell along patterns that were traditional in years past, Mr. Fatta said. The women did the cooking and taught the children at home. The men did construction work and worked in Mr. Koresh's professional sound studio on about 150 "melodic rock" songs that conveyed his obscure messages.

Robyn Bunds, a former "wife" of Mr. Koresh who has since left the cult, said that she had never heard Mr. Koresh discuss a mass suicide but that he had often talked about his own death. "He used to prophesize that he would be murdered, and I believe he would want to make his prophesy come true," she said last month.

In an interview this month, Mrs. Holub said: "I don't really know what happened to him. He never said nothing about being Jesus, but he did say, 'Grandma, I'm a prophet.'" She said this did not perturb her because she felt everyone should study the Bible.

The F.B.I. said it did not have a complete list of the people who were in the compound during the 51-day standoff. There were reports from a variety of sources that six cult members were killed in the original confrontation on Feb. 28, although the authorities have confirmed the deaths of only two, Peter Gent and Michael Schroeder.

Peter Gent, 21, was on top of the water tower when he was shot and killed. He was an Australian citizen whose twin sister was also a member of the group. Mr. Gent's parents became involved with the Branch Davidians first, but they left after a disagreement with Mr. Koresh's teaching.

Mr. Schroeder, whose age is not known, was killed as he tried to enter the compound with two other cult members on the evening after the raid. His wife, Judy, was among the first to voluntarily leave the compound.

Other cult members who voluntarily left say these were the members who were killed on Feb. 28:

¶Winston Blake, a British citizen.

¶Peter Hipsman, 28, the son of a New York fireman. He was a mechanic who had lived and worked in California before joining the cult.

¶Jaydone Wendell, 34, daughter of a retired police officer with the Honolulu Police Department. She was apparently killed during the raid.

¶Perry Jones, in his early 60's, who was a longtime member of the group.

Mr. Ricks of the F.B.I. identified these survivors of the inferno at the compound, adding their nationalities where known: Clive Joseph Doyle, 52, an American citizen; Jaime Castillo, 24; Misty Ferguson, 16; Derek Lloyd Lovelock, 37, of Britain; David Thibodeau, 24; Renos Avraam, 29, of Britain; Ruth Ellen Ottman, 30, and Graeme Leonard Craddock, 31, a citizen of Australia. One survivor, a woman listed as unconscious and in critical condition, was not identified.

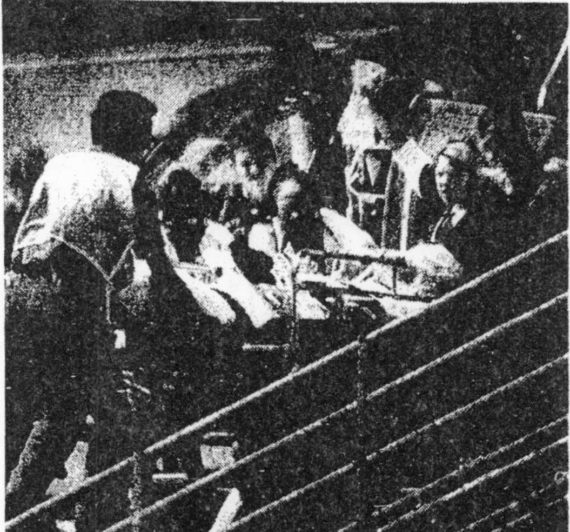

Associated Press

Emergency personnel transporting an unidentified woman, who was one of nine survivors of the fire inside the Branch Davidian compound in Waco, Tex., from a helicopter into Parkland Hospital in Dallas. She was listed in critical condition with burns over much of her body.

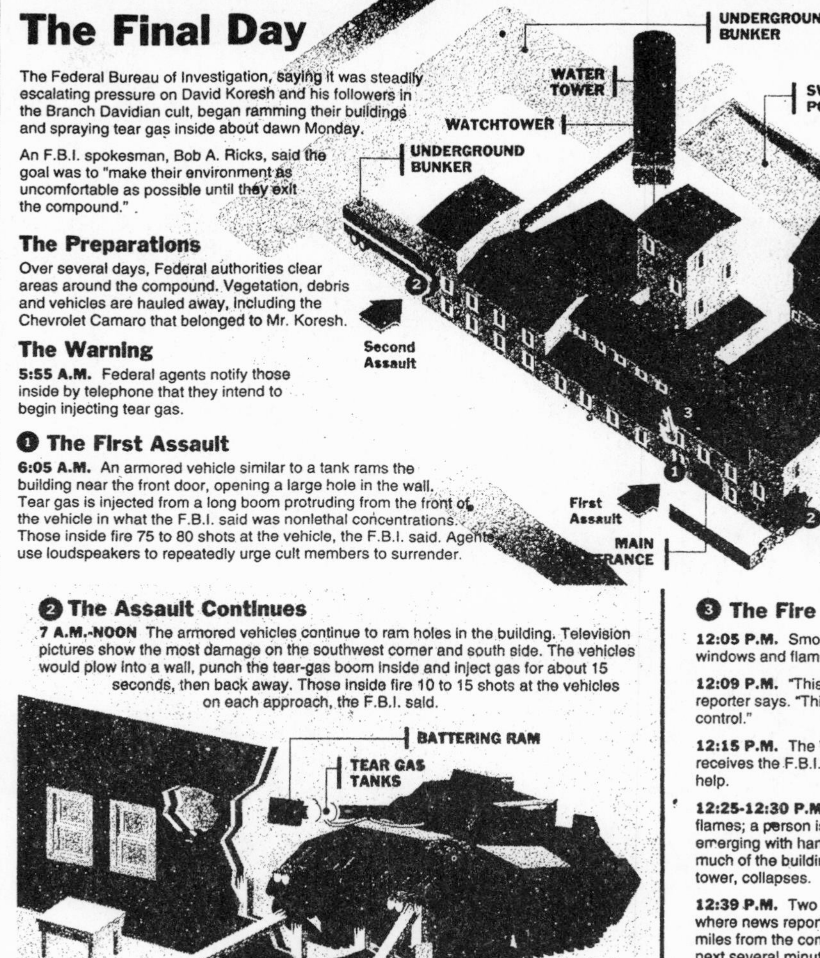

The Final Day

The Federal Bureau of Investigation, saying it was steadily escalating pressure on David Koresh and his followers in the Branch Davidian cult, began ramming their buildings and spraying tear gas inside about dawn Monday.

An F.B.I. spokesman, Bob A. Ricks, said the goal was to "make their environment as uncomfortable as possible until they exit the compound."

The Preparations

Over several days, Federal authorities clear areas around the compound. Vegetation, debris and vehicles are hauled away, including the Chevrolet Camaro that belonged to Mr. Koresh.

The Warning

5:55 A.M. Federal agents notify those inside by telephone that they intend to begin injecting tear gas.

1 The First Assault

6:05 A.M. An armored vehicle similar to a tank rams the building near the front door, opening a large hole in the wall. Tear gas is injected from a long boom protruding from the front of the vehicle in what the F.B.I. said was nonlethal concentrations. Those inside fire 75 to 80 shots at the vehicle, the F.B.I. said. Agents use loudspeakers to repeatedly urge cult members to surrender.

2 The Assault Continues

7 A.M.-NOON The armored vehicles continue to ram holes in the building. Television pictures show the most damage on the southwest corner and south side. The vehicles would plow into a wall, punch the tear-gas boom inside and inject gas for about 15 seconds, then back away. Those inside fire 10 to 15 shots at the vehicles on each approach, the F.B.I. said.

3 The Fire

12:05 P.M. Smoke billows from several windows and flames appear minutes later.

12:09 P.M. "This is a roaring fire," a CNN reporter says. "This fire is really burning out of control."

12:15 P.M. The Waco Fire Department receives the F.B.I.'s call asking for fire-fighting help.

12:25-12:30 P.M. The entire compound is in flames; a person is seen on television emerging with hands in the air. Within minutes, much of the building, including the lookout tower, collapses.

12:39 P.M. Two fire trucks pass the point where news reporters were stationed, three miles from the compound, followed over the next several minutes by a string of fire-fighting and other emergency vehicles.

Information compiled from reporters at the scene, Cable News Network, The Associated Press and the F.B.I.

David Montesino and John Papasian/The New York Times

The Overview

Scores Die as Compound Is Set Afire After F.B.I. Move

Continued From Page A1

whom were taken to the local jail. At a news conference here, Mr. Ricks announced their names and then added that he doubted there would be any more.

"It was truly an inferno of flames," he said. "It would be very surprising if any of the names not read survived."

In Washington, Attorney General Janet Reno said today that she regretted the loss of life. "Today was not meant to be D-Day," said Ms. Reno. "This was just a step forward in trying to bring about a peaceful resolution by constantly exerting further pressure to shrink the perimeter."

She said officials in charge of the operation, who had interviewed scores of former cult members and their families, simply did not believe that Mr. Koresh's reaction to the battering of the compound would be to order a mass suicide.

But tonight a shaken Ms. Reno said that in hindsight the Government's plan to assault the heavily armed compound had been a mistake.

"It was based on what we knew then," she said on the CNN program "Larry King Live." "Based on what we know now, it was obviously wrong."

Early-Morning Raid

The last, tumultuous day at the compound started around 6 A.M when armored vehicles knocked holes in the building's walls, then began shooting the gas inside. Federal officials insisted today that the doses would cause eye, nose and skin irritations but would do no long-term damage to anyone inside, including the children. Throughout the morning, the vehicles returned to attack the compound and each time were met with a hail of gunfire, the F.B.I. said.

The fire started a few minutes after noon on the second floor of the northeast wing of the wooden compound. Officials said an F.B.I. sharpshooter saw at least one cult member apparently sprinkling liquid in a room moments before it erupted in flames.

Fed by winds of up to 30 miles an hour and some type of accelerant inside, the fire spread rapidly and the entire structure was devoured in less than half an hour. One of the last things to fall on the pyre was a pole with a flag bearing the Star of David, which had flown since the third day of the standoff.

Early this evening, there was nothing left of the compound except a cinderblock structure amid the smoldering ruins that Federal agents said Mr. Koresh had intended as a bunker where he and his followers could withstand tear gas or an invasion.

Agents at the scene said there were many dead bodies inside but they could not give any exact numbers, and there were no indications that Mr. Koresh's body had been identified yet.

A Shootout, Then Tedium

The standoff began on the morning of Feb. 28, when more than 100 Federal agents arrived at the compound and tried to serve search and arrest warrants on charges that there were illegal weapons on the compound.

Associated Press

David Koresh with his wife, Rachel, and son Cyrus in a photograph taken six years ago. They are believed to have died in yesterday's fire.

A spokesman for the Bureau of Alcohol, Tobacco and Firearms, which led the initial assault on the compound, said a months-long investigation had uncovered evidence of possession and manufacture of illegal weapons inside the compound, including the illegal conversion of legally purchased semi-automatic weapons into automatics.

Some cult members have confirmed that they stockpiled weapons in preparation for what Mr. Koresh long prophesied would be an apocalyptic firefight with law-enforcement officials that could be a precursor to the end of the world. But they insist the weapons were acquired legally.

A 45-minute gun battle ensued in which four Federal agents and at least one cult member were killed. A few hours later, one cult member died in a second and much shorter gunfight.

But from that moment on, not a single shot was heard until this morning, when cult members fired on the tanks that were battering their fortress. In the interim, negotiators engaged in a tedious, see-saw set of talks with Mr. Koresh that produced the sporadic release of his followers and their children in frustratingly small groups and also led to many dead ends.

Early in the standoff, Mr. Koresh, a 33-year-old high school dropout who changed his name from Vernon Howell, demanded that his statements on the Bible be broadcast on local radio stations. More recently, he said he would leave the compound when he finished a manuscript about the Book of Revelation.

F.B.I. officials also said today that they been told by cult members that all the negotiations in recent days with two Houston lawyers representing the cult, which at one point seemed to promise an end to the standoff, had actually been a delaying tactic.

A major question today was why there was so little preparation for a fire. There appeared to be no fire engines at the scene as the fire erupted, and one was not seen entering the compound area until nearly 25 minutes after the fire began. Mayor Bob Sheehy of Waco, about 10 miles west of the compound, said that the city fire department "first got a call after the fire had already started."

Mr. Ricks said fire engines were not brought to the compound earlier because firefighters would not have been

A tactic to add pressure leads to a conflagration.

equipped to withstand the ammunition that cult members had inside their fortress. He said cult members had already fired at agents operating the combat engineering vehicles that were knocking down the compound walls.

But, he conceded, officials in charge of the operation had not expected a fire.

"We did not introduce fire to this compound, and it was not our intention that this compound be burned down," said Mr. Ricks, the only Federal official here whom reporters were allowed to question about the episode. "I can't tell you the shock and the horror that all of us felt when we saw those flames coming out of there. It was, 'Oh, my God, they're killing themselves.'"

The cult members jailed today were hurried past reporters and given no opportunity to describe their version of events. But one follower of Mr. Koresh, 34-year-old Brad Branch, who has been out of the compound for weeks, telephoned a local radio station from the McLennan County Jail and said he did not believe that Mr. Koresh had ordered his followers to commit suicide or that they had set the fire.

THE VIEW FROM THE TV SET
For television audiences, the fire in Waco ended a long-running drama that seemed to need a shocking climax. Critic's Notebook, page B16.

Mr. Ricks acknowledged that the mass suicide was contrary to what bureau officials believed the cult leader would order or endure himself. For the first time, Mr. Ricks also said that two days after the Feb. 28 gunfight, when Mr. Koresh announced he would give himself up, the cult leader planned to strap on grenades and kill himself on national television but had "chickened out" of the plan.

"We went throughout the world and interviewed former cult members, associates of cult members, the number that I last checked was 61 people," Mr. Ricks said. "The vast bulk, the substantial majority of those believed that they would not commit suicide."

Why Today?

Nonetheless, it seemed inevitable questions would arise over why the F.B.I., which last week encircled the compound with concertina wire and seemed prepared to wait for at least several more weeks, did not do so.

Mr. Ricks and Attorney General Reno insisted that the action today was not necessarily intended to bring the matter to a close, but was the next step in a weeks-long campaign to increase the pressure on Mr. Koresh. "Our desire was to get them out, use nonlethal means in a systematic manner, so that they could come before the bar and face justice," Mr. Ricks said.

At her news conference, Ms. Reno did not discuss whether any new information had prompted officials to act today. Other than phone conversations between cult leaders and F.B.I. negotiators, the only other such information available from someone inside the compound in recent days would have come from Luis A. Alaniz, a 24-year-old Houston man once described by the bureau as a "religious fanatic." He sneaked into the compound last month and left two days ago, when he was sent to McLennan County Jail.

But Ms. Reno did suggest that there was a particular urgency to the decision to move in. "We had information that babies were being beaten," she said. "I specifically asked, 'You really mean babies?' 'Yes, that he's slapping babies around.' These are concerns that we had." Cult members, in interviews from jail in recent weeks, have steadfastly denied that Mr. Koresh abused children.

During the siege, Mr. Koresh repeatedly claimed that the initial gunfight was simply a fulfillment of his vision, which seems to have included his belief that he was a messiah destined for persecution.

"If the Bible is true, then I'm Christ," he once said. "But so what? Look at 2,000 years ago. What's so great about being Christ? A man nailed to the cross. A man of sorrow acquainted with grief. You know, being Christ ain't nothing."

"All the News That's Fit to Print"

The New York Times

Late Edition

New York: Today, patchy fog, then mostly sunny. High 86. Tonight, clear. Low 72. Tomorrow, sunshine mixed with clouds, humid. High 88. Yesterday, high 84, low 65. Details, page C16.

VOL.CXLII .... No. 49,454 NEW YORK, TUESDAY, SEPTEMBER 14, 1993 — 75 cents beyond the greater New York metropolitan area. — 50 CENTS

RABIN AND ARAFAT SEAL THEIR ACCORD AS CLINTON APPLAUDS 'BRAVE GAMBLE'

Associated Press

"The children of Abraham . . . have embarked together on a bold journey." — President Clinton.

Old Warriors Now Face Task Of Building Upon Foundation

By THOMAS L. FRIEDMAN

Special to The New York Times

WASHINGTON, Sept. 13 — In a triumph of hope over history, Yitzhak Rabin, the Prime Minister of Israel, and Yasir Arafat, the chairman of the P.L.O., shook hands today on the White House lawn, sealing the first agreement between Jews and Palestinians to end their conflict and share the holy land along the River Jordan that they both call home.

At 11:43 A.M. on the sun-splashed South Lawn of the White House, Foreign Minister Shimon Peres of Israel and Mahmoud Abbas, the foreign policy aide for the Palestine Liberation Organization, signed a Declaration of Principles on Palestinian self-government in Israeli-occupied Gaza and the West Bank. Three thousand witnesses watched in amazement, including former Presidents Jimmy Carter and George Bush.

Mr. Rabin, whose face is etched with the memories of every Arab-Israeli war, captured in his remarks the exhaustion of all parties with the centuries-old conflict. "We the soldiers who have returned from the battle stained with blood," he said, "we who have fought against you, the Palestinians, we say to you today in a loud and clear voice: 'Enough of blood and tears! Enough!' "

Mr. Arafat, relishing his moment of acceptance on the White House lawn, strove to give Mr. Rabin the appropriate response, declaring in Arabic: "Our two peoples are awaiting today this historic hope, and they want to give peace a real chance."

An Awkward Moment

And President Clinton, who gracefully shepherded Mr. Arafat and Mr. Rabin through their awkward moment of public reconciliation, hailed them both for their "brave gamble that the future can be better than the past." [Transcripts of the leaders' remarks are on page A12.]

The agreement, which will eventually allow Palestinians to run their own affairs as Israeli troops pull back within months from the Gaza Strip and Jericho in a first step, was reached during secret negotiations over the past few months between Israelis and Palestinians, under the direction of Mr. Peres and Mr. Abbas, through the mediation of Norway.

The documents were signed on the same wooden table on which the Peace Treaty between Egypt and Israel was signed in 1979. That table stood today as a silent memorial to the assassinated Egyptian President, Anwar el-Sada, whose path-breaking visit to Israel in 1977 and subsequent agreements at Camp David brought him denunciations as a traitor by Mr. Arafat.

But the audience in attendance, and perhaps the millions more watching back in the Middle East, seemed less interested in the formal signing than in the visual moment that would somehow make this tentative peace real: the handshake between the two old warriors who personified the conflict between their peoples.

A Nudge, a Hand, a Smile

Moments after the documents were signed, Mr. Clinton took Mr. Arafat in his left arm and Mr. Rabin in his right arm and gently coaxed them together, needing to give Mr. Rabin just a little extra nudge in the back. Mr. Arafat reached out his hand first, and then Mr. Rabin, after a split second of hesitation and with a wan smile on his face, received Mr. Arafat's hand. The audience let out a simultaneous sigh of relief and peal of joy, as a misty-eyed Mr. Clinton beamed away.

Two hands that had written the battle orders for so many young men, two fists that had been raised in anger at one another so many times in the past, locked together for a fleeting moment of reconciliation.

But much difficult work, many more compromises, will now have to be performed by these same two men to make it a lasting moment.

That reality was underscored by the fact that both Mr. Rabin and Mr. Arafat invoked their peoples' undying attachment to Jerusalem in their respective speeches.

Meeting in White House

Before the ceremony, the Israeli and Palestinian leaders did not shake hands as they came together for the first time in the White House, officials said. They both walked to the Blue Room, where several people were already drinking coffee and orange juice, including Vice President Al Gore, Secretary of State Warren Christopher and diplomats from Russia and Norway. The Israelis clustered at the southern end of the oval room, with Mr. Arafat and Mr. Abbas gravitating to the west end, about 15 feet away.

After all the other dignitaries filed out of the Blue Room to be introduced, Mr. Clinton, Mr. Arafat and Mr. Rabin were left alone together for a minute in the Diplomatic Entrance and it was then that the two old antagonists exchanged their first words.

"You know, we have a lot of work to

Continued on Page A13, Column 1

MORE ON THE ACCORD

Arafat's Strategy: '2 Olive Branches'

Transforming one's image from guerrilla leader to statesman is not easy, but Yasir Arafat was trying hard to make it happen. Efforts in the past have had mixed results for all the countries involved. "This time," he said just an hour after making peace with Israel, "I am coming with two olive branches." Page A15.

Arabs and Jews Reflect

As many speak out about the events of recent days, there are new hopes, on both sides, but fears from years past remain. Page A16.

Divisions in Syria

Thousands marched in Syria, waving black flags in protest against Mr. Arafat, but elsewhere in the nation the response was more stunned, disbelieving, silence. Page A17.

Security Surprises

Security for the dignitaries was about what you would expect in the capital, but despite the hardware and planning, there were surprises. Page A14.

A 45-Year Struggle

Over the years since the birth of Israel in 1948, the Palestinian movement has drawn support from Palestinians inside Israel, in Israeli-occupied territories and in neighboring Arab countries while pressing for nationhood or self-rule. Page A15.

The Next Challenge for the U.S.

Peace Momentum Up to Washington

By R. W. APPLE Jr.

Special to The New York Times

News Analysis

WASHINGTON, Sept. 13 — As he himself said, this was not Bill Clinton's day. It was not he who brought together the sober old soldier and the grinning guerrilla fighter in the leafy calm of the South Lawn of the White House, far from the battlefields of the Middle East, for a paean to peace.

However deft, however sagacious, he was but the master of ceremonies. He thanked those who had labored to bring about the latest in a series of once-inconceivable changes that have remade the world in five short years. He bestowed the congratulations of the world's only superpower. And he gave Yitzhak Rabin a timely little nudge when he seemed reluctant to grasp the outstretched hand of Yasir Arafat.

Now, though, President Clinton will have to assume the central role if the momentum toward a comprehensive peace settlement is not to be lost. That is likely to be a long, messy job of diplomatic donkey work in the dark corners of history — a much less gratifying chapter than today's carefully scripted pageant of good intentions.

Israel and Jordan are poised to move forward tomorrow. But the other Arab nations whose representatives watched today's ceremony from the front rows know that only the United States can provide the impetus needed for the next round of negotiations. Mr. Arafat spoke for them, too, when he said his people "are relying on your role, Mr. President" to "usher in an age of peace."

So this President, who so longs to concentrate on problems at home, is thrust like so many of his predecessors into an international arena not of his choosing. Along with the rest of the world, the United States has a new ward, the inchoate entity called Palestine, and it has the main responsibility for fostering Israeli settlements with its other neighbors while deepening the one with the Palestinians.

It will be up to Mr. Clinton, who does not much like doing so, to butt heads between the Israelis and the Syrians, and perhaps take considerable heat from American Jews in the process, which he did not have to endure this time.

Neither Mr. Clinton nor any other American President has ever wanted to do business with Mr. Arafat and the Palestine Liberation Organization. As Mr. Rabin, the Israeli Prime Minister, said in one of his many moments of eloquence this morning, "It's not so

Continued on Page A13, Column 6

Jim Estrin/The New York Times

Palestinian women dancing with joy in Jericho, on the West Bank.

Palestinians: Glee And Flag-Waving

Special to The New York Times

JERICHO, Israeli-Occupied West Bank, Sept. 13 — Palestinians took to the streets of the West Bank and Gaza Strip today in rapturous and noisy celebrations of the Palestine Liberation Organization accord with Israel and what they said was the cornerstone of their future state.

In the sleepy city of Jericho, the seat of the future Palestinian self-governing authority, it looked as though every one of the 15,000 residents was in the streets.

Savoring a new reality few had dared to imagine just a few weeks ago, they danced all day and into the night. In the Gaza Strip they handed flowers to Israeli soldiers. In East Jerusalem they shouted "Shalom!" to Israeli well-wishers.

The accord also changed the face of the occupied territories and East Jerusalem, where Palestinian flags, which had technically been banned, flew with impunity.

Reuters

Israelis watching the signing on television on a Jerusalem street.

Israelis: Searching For New Bearings

Special to The New York Times

BEIT ZAYIT, Israel, Sept. 13 — When Yitzhak Rabin shook hands with Yasir Arafat, six Israelis watching it on television together on the western outskirts of Jerusalem might as well have been struck by lightning. They could only sigh deeply in disbelief before their thoughts and emotions unscrambled themselves.

The dominant feeling, in the room and across the country, is that there is no alternative to having Israelis and Palestinians come to terms with each other, as they are now trying to do.

Like many Israelis, Eliezer Shenhav, a surgeon who had friends into watch the ceremony, wrestled with religious convictions that taught him that God intended all of the biblical Land of Israel to be in Jewish hands.

Articles, page A17.

President's Tie Tells It All: Trumpets for a Day of Glory

By MAUREEN DOWD

Special to The New York Times

WASHINGTON, Sept. 13 — The President who loves to stay up late told his aides that he went to bed at 10 P.M. on Sunday, so he could be rested for the historic day.

They did not believe him, of course. "No way," said Dee Dee Myers, the White House press secretary. "He got the big hand and the little hand mixed up."

"It was Jerusalem time," suggested Mark Gearan, the White House communications director.

But what happened next is not in contention: The President said he woke up at 3 A.M. and could not go back to sleep. He was worrying about the speech he would make to mark what was sure to be one of the most remarkable events of his Presidency: the moment when the two men who had been bitter enemies for so long, the Israeli Prime Minister, Yitzhak Rabin, and the Chairman of the Palestine Liberation Organization, Yasir Arafat, would recognize each other's existence on the South Lawn of the White House.

With his wife and daughter still asleep, Mr. Clinton put on a blue jogging suit and went into the study in the White House residence. He picked up a Bible. He read the entire Book of Joshua, wanting to review the part about the trumpets in Jericho that toppled walls and making sure he put a reference in his speech contrasting the victory of war and the victory of peace.

In another part of the White House, a team led by Jeremy Rosner, a National Security Council speechwriter, was scrambling to fulfill the President's last request: Mr. Clinton wanted a passage from the Koran to balance his Biblical allusions. The desperate White House staff members finally called Prince Bandar bin Sultan, the Saudi ambassador, who helped them pick out an appropriately soothing passage: "If the enemy inclines toward peace, do thou also incline toward peace."

Watching for the Dawn

At some point, Mr. Clinton moved from the study to the kitchen to read and drink coffee. He wanted to sit near the window, where he could keep track of when the dawn arrived and what the sky looked like.

The White House staff had worked over three days to compile a 26-page step-by-step log choreographing every movement that the leaders would make, and yet Mr. Clinton knew as well as anyone that, with this most delicate of all diplomatic meetings, a million things could go wrong — a look, a word, a handshake, the weather.

At dawn, as he later told aides, who

Continued on Page A14, Column 5

INSIDE

Primary Candidates Work on Voter Turnout

Appearing at subway stops and centers for the elderly and monopolizing the talk shows, candidates in the Democratic primaries for New York City offices played to their surest supporters in the closing hours of the campaign. The races could hinge on voter turnout. Page B1.

POLLING PLACES will be open from 6 A.M. to 9 P.M. today in New York City, Westchester and Nassau, and from 6 A.M. to 8 P.M. in Connecticut.

Fall Air Fares Cut by 45%

The nation's airlines cut fares by up to 45 percent on domestic flights through Dec. 16, but tickets must be bought by Saturday. Page D1.

MIDEAST ACCORD: THE SIGNING

"Today we bear witness to an extraordinary act in one of history's defining dramas, a drama that began in a time of our ancestors when the word went forth from a sliver of land between the River Jordan and the Mediterranean Sea."

PRESIDENT CLINTON

The Overview

Rabin and Arafat Seal Pact With Handshake at Signing

Continued From Page A1

do," Mr. Rabin said somberly, according to a Clinton aide.

"I know and I am prepared to do my part," Mr. Arafat answered.

Once they reached the podium, the contrast in demeanor between Mr. Arafat and Mr. Rabin was striking. Mr. Arafat was relaxed and ebullient — a man who had spent a lifetime in the political wilderness suddenly finding himself at the pinnacle of power on the White House lawn. Mr. Rabin, the general-turned statesman, was nervous and palpably uncomfortable — staring down at his shoes, never applauding anyone, shifting nervously and taking his speech in and out of his pocket.

When he delivered that speech, though, Mr. Rabin was both eloquent and frank. He articulated the deep ambivalence that he and so many Israelis felt about this reconciliation with a man they have only known by the name "terrorist" for 30 years. Mr. Rabin made clear that this was a moment he came to not out of some soaring vision of peace, but out of a grudging acknowledgement of reality: that Israel could no longer go on ignoring the P.L.O., the organization that represents the Palestinian people.

"This signing of the Israeli-Palestinian declaration of principles here today, it's not so easy, neither for myself as a soldier in Israel's war, nor for the people of Israel, nor for the Jewish people in the diaspora who are watching us now with great hope mixed with apprehension," the 71-year-old Israeli Prime Minister said.

Both sides agree that a lot of work remains to be done for peace to become a reality.

"It is certainly not easy for the families of the victims of the wars, violence, terror, whose pain will never heal; for the many thousands who defended our lives in their own and have even sacrificed their lives for our own. For them, this ceremony has come too late."

Mr. Arafat's speech was delivered with a resonant timbre and in a flowing, classical Arabic, translated by the official State Department interpreter. It was less memorable for its substance than for the simple sight of Mr. Arafat, dressed in his familiar khaki uniform and black-and-white-checked Arab headdress, framed between the President of the United States and the Secretary of State.

Appeal to American Public

Mr. Arafat, whose face was painted throughout with the broad smile of a man living a dream, actually addressed himself as much to the Americans as to the Israelis, seeking to remind Washington that he will expect — and need — its continued involvement as he negotiates the details of today's peace accord with Israel.

"Mr. President, I am taking this opportunity to assure you and to assure the great American people that we share your values for freedom, justice and human rights — values for which my people have been striving," Mr. Arafat said. "We are relying on your role, Mr. President, and on the role of all the countries which believe that without peace in the Middle East, peace in the world will not be complete."

In an overture to Israelis, though, Mr. Arafat refrained from articulating his goal of creating an independent Palestinian state, and stressed that Palestinian self-determination should not come at the expense of Israeli security.

"Our people do not consider that exercising the right to self-determination could violate the rights of their neighbors or infringe on their security," he said. "Rather, putting an end to their feelings of being wronged and of having suffered a historic injustice is the strongest guarantee to achieve coexistence and openness between our two peoples and future generations.'

Mr. Arafat received warm applause from the audience, which was made up of all the members of Congress, former Secretaries of State, including Henry Kissinger and James A. Baker 3d, who organized the Madrid peace talks, the ambassadors from key countries, like Syria and Saudi Arabia, as well as hundreds of Jewish and Arab Americans, who seemed to waver between enthusiasm and expressions of disbelief.

Last-Minute Dispute

A last-minute dispute over the wording of the peace agreement between Israel and the P.L.O. resulted in a small, but crucial, alteration in the text. A White House official said that in a Blue Room reception just before the signing ceremony, the word "Palestinian" was changed to "P.L.O." in the preamble of the agreement, at the insistence of Mr. Arafat, who wanted to make sure that his organization was being acknowledged as the representative of the Palestinian people.

The Israeli-Palestinian accord in many ways grows out of the 1978 Camp David accords, with its emphasis on an interim stage of Palestinian autonomy before the two sides negotiate a final status for the West Bank and Gaza Strip. But today's agreement goes beyond Camp David by accepting the notion that Israeli troops have to actually withdraw from some territory on the West Bank, and to give Palestinians far broader control so that the agreement would have credibility with Palestinians.

It also goes beyond Camp David in its recognition that such a deal could only be struck between Israel and the Palestine Liberation Organization, not with Jordan or the Palestinians of the occupied territories, both of whom are the relevant parties of the Camp David accords.

Associated Press

President Clinton leading Prime Minister Yitzhak Rabin and Yasir Arafat to the signing ceremony.

Clinton nudges two old warriors to gesture at the White House ceremony.

The parties now must move into negotiations that will translate today's declaration of principles into an detailed, working plan for carrying them out. That will include deciding exactly where Israeli troops withdraw, not only from Gaza and Jericho, but from all Palestinian population centers in the West Bank, by the end of next summer. The parties also have to agree on such matters as how the Palestinians will establish their own police force and either elect or appoint a self-governing council.

Clinton Defines U.S. Role

The United States role, Mr. Clinton said in an interview on Saturday, will be to help the parties work out these details, while also generating financial support for the new Palestinian homelands in Gaza and Jericho.

Mr. Clinton seemed to see his role today as creating the emotional space for Mr. Arafat and Mr. Rabin to come together. With the biblical allusions of his remarks and his politician's natural instinct for conciliation, the President seemed at ease in his role — even introducing Mr. Arafat and Mr. Rabin to his daughter, Chelsea, who was seated with a group of Israeli and Palestinian schoolchildren.

"Today we bear witness to an extraordinary act in one of history's defining dramas, a drama that began in a time of our ancestors when the word went forth from a sliver of land between the River Jordan and the Mediterranean Sea," said Mr. Clinton.

After the ceremony, Mr. Clinton held a brief, unscheduled 10-minute, one-on-one meeting with Mr. Arafat in the White House map room, urging him to work quickly with Israel to implement the new peace agreement, and to remember that Israelis must feel confident of their security if this deal is to work, aides said. From there, Mr. Clinton met with a group of Jewish and Arab Americans.

"I think this is a very big deal," he told them, adding that everyone now had to work to insure that the Rabin-Arafat handshake, "instead of being a magic moment in history will truly be a turning point."

News Analysis

Challenge Is Passing To the U.S.

Continued From Page A1

easy," swallowing all this change.

But in the end even as stiff-necked a leader as Charles de Gaulle had to deal with the National Liberation Front in Algeria. Henry A. Kissinger had to deal with the Vietcong, South Africa's white leaders had to deal with Nelson Mandela and now the United States must deal with the P.L.O. If rebellions succeed, or even end in stalemate, the rebels win a place at the table.

The United States will have to do its utmost to make this accord work. That means, first and foremost, helping to persuade ordinary Israelis and Palestinians that their self-interest lies in its working, not in its failing. The naysayers among both peoples will have to be answered with accomplishments — Benjamin Netanyahu and his followers, settlers and others, in Israel, and the prophets of continuing violence both inside and outside the P.L.O.

Much will depend on building viable economies in the areas that the Palestinians are to take over. Waxing poetic, the Israeli Foreign Minister, Shimon Peres, promised to help them in "making Gaza prosper and Jericho bloom again." Arab countries will also help, and so will Japan, but some of the money will have to come from the overburdened United States Treasury.

Secretary of State Warren Christopher has suggested that at some point American troops will probably have to play a role in keeping the peace, perhaps replacing the Israelis who now man the Golan Heights overlooking Syria.

After this week, perhaps even by Wednesday or Thursday, the attention of the capital will turn back to the twin domestic issues that Mr. Clinton has put atop his agenda, the North American Free Trade Agreement and reform of the nation's health-care system. They will once again be viewed as the prime measures of the President's success over the next 12 months or so.

Clinton Accepts New Role

But to them, and not far below them, must now be added the Middle East.

Mr. Clinton accepted his new role in his speech, asserting that "the United States is committed to insuring that the people who are affected by this agreement will be made more secure by it, and to leading the world in marshaling the resources necessary to implement the difficult details."

No doubt the details are difficult. Such questions as the nature and borders of any Palestinian state, whether the Israeli settlers are to remain on the West Bank, and especially the question of Jerusalem have been put aside. Mr. Arafat continued to promise that the Palestinian flag will fly over Jerusalem in the next two years; Mr. Rabin replies curtly, "Forget it."

Ahead, a messy job of diplomatic donkey work.

Moreover, Mr. Clinton concedes that he does not know quite how to proceed. In an interview over the weekend, he said, "I'm going to develop a whole strategy; I just haven't had time to do it yet." Much will depend on whether he gets it right when he does.

For this is a part of the world where the United States has vital interests, economic as well as political.

If the United Nations operation in Somalia fails, and United States policy fails with it, that is embarrassing. The President, according to his aides, rebukes himself for the failure of the Western nations to end the suffering in Bosnia. But he is unlikely to suffer politically, even if the United States suffers strategically, for miscalculations in the Balkans or in Africa.

The Middle East is another matter. If Mr. Clinton bungles there — if he shows an unsure touch or fails to follow through — his reputation and that of his country will suffer.

Not that success will guarantee a second term. When Jimmy Carter pulled off the Camp David agreement between Egypt and Israel, one of his top aides asked another, "If this doesn't get us re-elected, what will?" It did not, of course, in large part because of trouble in another part of the Middle East.

There was plenty of euphoria at the White House today, but not that kind; the lesson of 1992, when George Bush won in the Persian Gulf but lost at the ballot box, is far too fresh.

By all accounts, a settlement between Syria and Israel, which once seemed far more likely than what was achieved in recent days, now seems the most difficult item on the agenda. A senior White House official said that a lot of low-level talking would be necessary before President Clinton could take a more direct role in talks with President Hafez al-Assad and the Israelis.

Because of the difficult road ahead, there was a concerted effort by the participants in today's drama to diminish expectations. But that was hard to do, when something everyone had considered impossible — even Mr. Kissinger, by his own account — was unfolding there on the Lawn, bigger than life.

The Accord: What Comes Next

Highlights of the agreement signed yesterday in Washington.

OCT. 13

- The Declaration of Principles on Palestinian self-rule takes force.
- Authority for education and culture, health, social welfare, direct taxation and tourism is transferred from Israel to "authorized Palestinians" in the West Bank and Gaza, but it is not clear what authority they will have in East Jerusalem.
- Palestinians start building police force based on Palestine Liberation Organization fighters from outside West Bank and Gaza.
- Joint Israeli-Palestinian Liaison Committee is formed.
- Israeli-Palestinian Economic Cooperation Committee is established to work on water, electricity, energy, finance, transport and communications including Gaza seaport, trade, industry, labor relations, training, environmental protection and the media; an internationally supported economic development program for the West Bank and Gaza and a regional economic development program.
- Jordan and Egypt invited to join Continuing Committee to decide on procedures for admission of Palestinians displaced from West Bank and Gaza in 1967 (estimated at about 800,000 people including dependents) and measures to prevent "disruption and disorder."

DEC. 13, 1993

- Israel and Palestinians sign agreement on Israeli withdrawal from Gaza Strip and Jericho area and detailed arrangements for Palestinian control of the two areas.
- Israelis begin withdrawal from Gaza and Jericho.
- Five-year interim period of Palestinian self-rule officially begins.

APRIL 13, 1994

- Latest date for Israelis to complete withdrawal from Gaza and Jericho.

JULY 13, 1994

- Latest date for elections for Palestinian Council, which is to operate under an as yet undetermined interim agreement. Palestinians from East Jerusalem will be able to vote and perhaps run in the elections.

- Israeli military forces, already withdrawn from Gaza and Jericho, would redeploy outside populated areas in the rest of the West Bank by the eve of elections at the latest. Israeli forces would remain responsible for security of Israeli settlers.
- Israeli military government withdrawn and Civil Administration dissolved.

DEC. 13, 1995

- Latest date for talks to start on permanent agreement.

DEC. 13, 1998

- Permanent agreement takes effect.

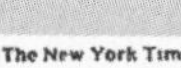

The New York Times

Paul Hosefros/The New York Times

Agence France-Presse

Moments after the documents were signed, President Clinton took Yasir Arafat in his left arm and Yitzhak Rabin in his right arm and gently coaxed them together for their historic moment, needing to give Mr. Rabin just a little extra nudge in the back.

"All the News That's Fit to Print"

The New York Times

Late Edition

New York: **Today, some clouds,** windy, becoming very cold. **High 30. Tonight,** frigid. Low 4. **Tomorrow,** partly sunny, windy. High 11. **Yesterday,** high 47, low 12. **Details, page B8.**

VOL.CXLIII . . . No. 49,580 NEW YORK, TUESDAY, JANUARY 18, 1994 — 75 cents beyond the greater New York metropolitan area — 50 CENTS

SEVERE EARTHQUAKE HITS LOS ANGELES; AT LEAST 30 KILLED; FREEWAYS COLLAPSE

Reuters

The body of a motorcycle police officer lying near the wreckage of his vehicle in the center of an overpass that collapsed onto Interstate 5. He drove off the edge and fell 25 feet.

HUNDREDS INJURED

Predawn Tremor Levels Buildings and Ignites Dozens of Fires

By SETH MYDANS

Special to The New York Times

LOS ANGELES, Jan. 17 — A violent earthquake jolted millions of people out of bed before dawn today, crumpling freeway overpasses, leveling buildings and igniting scores of fires. Hundreds of people were injured and at least 30 were reported killed, including 15 at a three-level apartment complex that was reduced to two stories.

The quake, centered in the Northridge area in the San Fernando Valley, 20 miles northwest of downtown Los Angeles, measured 6.6 on the Richter scale of ground motion and was felt for hundreds of miles, knocking out power and water service for hundreds of thousands of residents.

In a region held together by its network of freeways, three overpasses collapsed, crippling major highways for weeks and possibly months. Roads cracked and buckled across the San Fernando Valley.

State of Emergency

People lingered on the streets throughout the day as the thuds of aftershocks sent dust rising above the mountains. Others formed long lines outside hardware stores and tried to buy batteries, water, propane or plywood to repair damaged homes. And when evening came, hundreds of people whose homes were destroyed or too dangerous to re-enter camped in city parks and on tennis courts in a nervously festive atmosphere, some of them with campfires and cases of beer.

A state of emergency was declared at the local, state and Federal levels in this latest disaster to strike the city. Aerial pictures of blocks of burning buildings evoked traumatic memories of the 1992 riots and last autumn's wildfires.

"I couldn't stop screaming as I ran out of the house," said Erik Wyler, 19, still shaking an hour after the quake. "I looked up and all I could see was darkness coming toward us, and it got real windy. I thought it was the sun exploding."

Hundreds of buildings were damaged, including Anaheim Stadium, which was expected to need $3.4 million in repairs. The quake, which struck at 4:31 A.M., was not the strongest to hit the region in recent years but was by far the most destructive because it struck in a heavily populated area.

Curfew Is Imposed

The Chief of Police, Willie L. Williams addressed the city on television this evening, telling people to remain calm and to stay home from work on Tuesday if possible. He said that city offices would be open on Tuesday but that schools in the Los Angeles Unified School District would be closed.

He also announced a dusk-to-dawn curfew and issued a warning against any potential looters, with reference to the rampage that overtook the city during the 1992 riots.

"We're not going to tolerate what

Continued on Page A17, Column 1

Associated Press

An injured man being treated at an emergency unit set up outside Olive View Medical Center in Sylmar.

Airborne in Bed: A Building Collapses, Leaving 15 Dead

By ELIZABETH KOLBERT

Special to The New York Times

LOS ANGELES, Jan. 17 — Erik Pearson heard a loud explosion and felt a jolt like a bomb. Still on their bed, he and his wife then fell 12 feet through the ceiling of the apartment below.

"We were airborne," said Mr. Pearson, a 27-year-old nursing student. "I heard the glass break from the glass sliding doors. Our apartment came down and pitched diagonally." The door was jammed shut, the couple said, but they climbed down to safety off their once third-floor, now second-floor, balcony.

But at least 15 other residents of the tan stucco apartment complex, the Northridge Meadows, did not. They died as building suffered some of the worst damage of the earthquake today and its residents bore the brunt of the casualties.

The building, half a block from California State University at Northridge, housed many college students. An identical building next to it, the Northridge, buckled but did not collapse.

The Meadows, a three-story, 164-unit apartment complex near the epicenter of the quake in the San Fernando Valley, looked like a cardboard box that someone had stepped on. In several sections of the building, the first floor no longer existed; it lay crushed beneath the two other floors. Windows had popped out of their frames, balconies dangled at odd angles and entire walls buckled.

Famous From Now On

Until 4:31 A.M. today this sleepy middle-class section of Los Angeles, about 20 miles northwest of downtown, was known only for its tree-lined branch of the California State University. From now, it will be known as the epicenter of a devastating 6.6 earthquake.

Simply put, city officials said the 15 deaths made this building the site of the largest number of earthquake fatalities in the city's history.

John William, 36, a survivor who lived on the first floor, managed to slither to safety by following a small path of light to a crack in the building's foundation.

"I pushed open the crack in the wall; my fiancée and I were pressed together, and we squeezed ourselves free," said Mr. William, who had cuts on both hands and arms. "I felt like we were going to lose circulation at any minute.

"I was hearing moans and whining and banging from people pinned in the other apartments. I'm not exaggerating: the second floor is now in the dirt. There is not two inches of room in my apartment."

Residents described a scene of panic in the hours before dawn as people tried to climb from their balconies or pick their way down dark staircases that had been torn apart by the quake.

Search for Bodies

This afternoon, many residents of the complex were still milling around in front of the ruined building, at 9565 Reseda Boulevard, as firefighters, sweaty and exhausted, continued to search the debris. Eight hours after the quake, firefighters held out little hope that anyone still trapped would be found alive, but they said they were inserting electronic listening devices into the rubble that could pick up sounds as soft as human breathing. Earlier, they brought in dogs trained to find survivors in building rubble.

There was no power in the area, most of the shops were closed and, in an incongruously festive gesture, people up and down the street had taken to eating half-melted ice cream cakes from a nearby Baskin-Robbins.

The force of the tremor ripped apart homes, businesses, roads and utilities, leaving thousands of people without water, power or shelter.

Reseda Boulevard, a main thoroughfare, resembled a war zone: broken water mains flooded streets; gas permeated the air, fuel for numerous fires that were controlled by the late afternoon. Traffic lights were knocked out, and accidents occurred throughout the area.

Many of the community's 20,000

Continued on Page A19, Column 1

OTHER MAJOR NEWS

U.S.-China Pact Averts Trade Fight

China and the United States reached an 11th-hour textile agreement, averting a major clash about the $7.3 billion in Chinese textiles sold annually in the American market.

The Clinton Administration had threatened to reduce Chinese textile imports by more than $1 billion unless a new agreement could be signed to end persistent instances of cheating by Chinese companies. Page D1.

Israelis Are Hopeful But Cautious on Syria

Israel said it saw a promise of peace, but expressed caution about remarks by Syria's President that he was ready for normal relations. "Normalization was also mentioned by the Syrians in the past," Prime Minister Yitzhak Rabin said. Page A8.

Facing Down Boos, Giuliani Praises King

After days of criticism over two confrontations between blacks and the police, Mayor Giuliani faced hecklers at a tribute to Martin Luther King Jr. He told his audience, "For you to succeed, I have to succeed." Page B1.

Collapsed Freeways Cripple City Where People Live Behind Wheel

By BERNARD WEINRAUB

Special to The New York Times

LOS ANGELES, Jan. 17 — The earthquake that struck Los Angeles before dawn today crippled crucial freeways, raising the prospect that the American city most defined by its cars and interlocking highways would be gripped by traffic chaos for months.

The city's freeways and highways, mostly built since World War II, soar and wind like roller coasters, often resting atop columns as they crisscross one another. The buckling and collapse today of three heavily traveled elevated portions raised the prospect of at least partial paralysis for a city where the automobile is seen as intrinsic to the region's life.

As a result, city officials said, almost every facet of life for the nine million people in the Los Angeles area is likely to be disrupted for up to a year or more.

With nearly 3 million vehicles using 616.3 miles of freeway in Los Angeles during the evening rush hour, the city's residents are extraordinarily dependent on main highway arteries. The city has never confronted, until today, the possibility that many of these freeways would be partially unusable for long periods.

The city's new subway line, the Metro Red Line, which opened in January 1993, is expected to offer little help. It runs through just 4.4 miles of downtown Los Angeles, from Union Station to MacArthur Park.

'Not Going to Be Easy'

The area's Metrolink commuter trains will operate on Tuesday, though some stations and stretches of track that were damaged will be closed. The service will add passenger cars to trains on the line from Santa Clarita and Antelope Valley, the Associated Press reported. Freeways linking those areas to Los Angeles were severed by the quake.

"It's not going to be easy," a grim Mayor Richard J. Riordan said this afternoon as Gov. Pete Wilson stood beside him.

Patricia Reid, a spokesman at Cal

Continued on Page A18, Column 1

Lives and Nerves Shattered, but Not Civility

By JANE GROSS

Special to The New York Times

LOS ANGELES, Jan. 17 — Ventura Boulevard, the main thoroughfare through the devastated San Fernando Valley, was ghostly this morning, its shops a shambles, its sidewalks littered with broken glass, its traffic signals out and its automatic teller machines useless.

But the stillness was misleading.

Behind a shuttered Thrifty drugstore in the Studio City section, where the aisles were clogged with fallen ceiling tiles, a tangle of toys and broken cosmetic bottles, employees peddled batteries and flashlights to a stunned throng of men and women still shaking from the jolt of a lifetime, which occurred before dawn.

"I need a good flashlight! And eight D batteries! And a couple of Triple A's! And one of those heavy-duty things!" sputtered one man in line, as harried clerks dispensed these limited goods from a shopping cart and apologized that nothing else was for sale because the store was knee-deep in ruined merchandise.

Across the region — from the eastern edge of the San Fernando Valley, where buildings shuddered and fell, to the graffiti-scarred streets of downtown, to the manicured confines of Beverly Hills and Pasadena — residents were stunned and shaken, but largely composed.

Some homes were ruined. Most were without power. Some lacked telephone service. And all of their inhabitants were shaken to the core. But residents of the City of Angels, where disasters have lately been heaped one upon the other, kept their heads.

The closest thing to bedlam, as of nightfall, was the scene at Hughes Market, the only open grocery store for

Continued on Page A19, Column 6

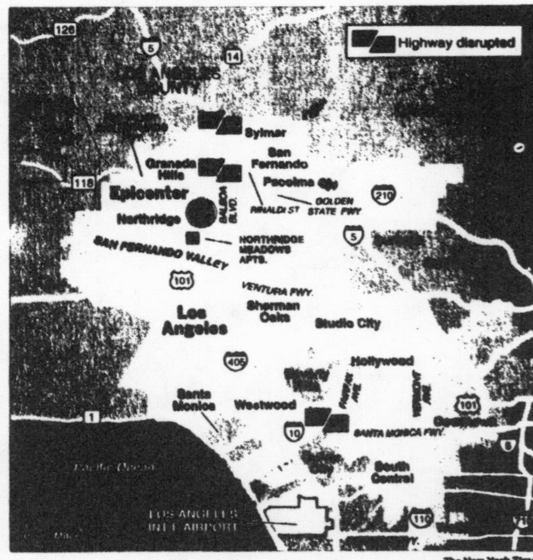

The New York Times

The earthquake severed the freeway system in three places and killed 15 people in a building near its epicenter in the Northridge section.

The Earthquake: Crumpled Freeways, Collapsed Buildings, Power Failures and Fires

The Overview

Big Quake Hits Los Angeles; 30 Die and Roads Crumple

Continued From Page A1

took place a year and a half ago," he said. Half a dozen people were arrested in downtown Los Angeles today for looting.

Late in the day, 90 percent of the city remained without power, and utility officials said electricity would be unavailable in certain areas for up to three days.

Officials urged San Fernando Valley residents to boil drinking water because power was lost to machinery that chlorinates the region's water.

As night fell, searches intensified through shattered buildings and collapsed parking garages. Federal teams threaded fiber optic sensors into the rubble to supplement their listening devices and trained dogs as they probed for life.

Neighbors sought a moment on local television broadcasts to hold up photographs of missing friends or relatives; a smiling woman with her smiling daughter; a robust young man holding a giant pizza.

Hardest hit was the Northridge section of the city near California State University, where a three-story apartment building collapsed into its bottom floor. As rescuers used hydraulic drills and diamond-blade saws to dig for survivors, shaken residents described "a rumbling, ripping noise," that seemed to tear the whole building apart.

But mixed with stories of death were tales of amazing rescues. In a shopping center, firefighters struggled to reach a street cleaner they knew only as Salvador, who was trapped in his sweeping machine in an underground garage. As tremors continued to shake

Fire and death in the most destructive tremor in years.

the building, firefighters shored up the rubble with wooden struts and fed him air and water. More than eight hours later he was pulled out alive.

The Santa Monica Freeway, or Interstate 10, which is the nation's busiest freeway, was rendered impassable. A section of the Simi Valley Freeway also collapsed. And the four-level intersection between Interstate 5, the main north-south artery on the West Coast, and Highway 14, was splintered into fragments of concrete and steel.

In a grotesque image of destruction, sections of the lacy cloverleaf of Highway 14 that soars 75 feet above I-5 lay tangled on the ground, support beams sprouting above the rubble like broken bones. When the overpass collapsed, it took with it a police officer on motorcycle who tumbled through the air to his death.

Like a Bomb

Officials said the dead also included a person who fell from a sixth-floor window at a downtown hotel; a woman who broke her neck when she slipped and hit her head on a baby crib; two people whose home in Sherman Oaks slid down a hill, and five people who died of heart attacks because of the quake.

In addition, a 92-year-old woman was killed in a trailer fire in Northridge; a man died, apparently from head injuries, after objects fell on him in his Chatsworth trailer home; a 5-year-old girl was killed when her house collapsed; a 45-year-old man was pronounced dead at Cedars-Sinai Hospital from head trauma, and a young man was electrocuted after he touched a live wire.

The earthquake struck with a shuddering jolt that some residents likened to a bomb blast and others to a ride on a roller coaster. For 30 seconds, bookcases, crockery and even refrigerators were thrown through the air, and on the streets outside, car alarms could be heard under the still-swaying trees as far as the ear could hear. Then, after a long, breathless silence, the sirens of rescue vehicles began.

In Mission Hills, Luz Becerra was in the shower when the earthquake struck. "It picked me up and knocked me over to the bed," she said. "I was crying, 'Please, God, please, God, don't let anything happen to me.'"

In West Los Angeles, Jossein Vameghi said: "Things were moving in both directions, up and down and crossways. I was terrified. I thought I was going to vomit. I ran to the door."

On the still-dark streets outside, as people asked each other what had happened, electrical transformers exploded into flames. Suddenly, some streets were engulfed in fire, blackening rows of parked cars. In some places, broken water mains turned streets into fast-rushing rivers.

In Santa Monica, Alan Hunter took refuge in his car only moments before a gas line exploded and demolished his apartment.

Other gas explosions set entire blocks aflame in the Sylmar section. At least 44 homes, some in a mobile-home park, were destroyed, and the neighborhood was reduced to rubble, resembling streets destroyed by the Southern California wildfires only two months ago.

Jump to Safety

At the apartment complex that collapsed, the Northridge Meadows, Sheila Chulick, a 34-year-old college student, jumped from her second-story balcony when the exits became blocked.

"I crawled around but all the exits were blocked," she said, describing the blackness of the smoke and strange terrain of broken walls and debris. "People were freaking out and yelling all over the streets. I was just glad to be alive. I have nothing left but my life."

A 64-car freight train derailed between the Chatsworth and Northridge sections, leaking sulfuric acid from a tanker, a Southern Pacific Railroad spokesman, Jack Martin, was quoted by The Associated Press as saying. Crews were cleaning up the spill.

At the Northridge Fashion Center mall, the Bullocks department store collapsed into a gnarled pile of concrete and steel. Windows were shattered throughout the mall, and the parking structure was flattened into a 20-foot-high pile of rubble.

One of two aqueducts that carry water from the Sierra Nevada to Los Angeles was ruptured, and water mains broke in several neighborhoods. Telephone service was lost throughout the region and power was disrupted as far away as Canada. Los Angeles International Airport was briefly closed as a precaution.

White House Response

Gov. Pete Wilson and Mayor Richard J. Riordan of Los Angeles each declared a state of emergency. California National Guard troops were sent in, and the Office of Emergency Services sent about 300 search-and-rescue teams.

In Washington, President Clinton said he was told of the earthquake at about 8 A.M. Eastern time in a phone call from Housing Secretary Henry G. Cisneros. This afternoon, he signed an official declaration of disaster, making aid available for rebuilding highways and schools, low-interest loans and emergency unemployment funds.

"I ask the American people to remember the people of Los Angeles County in their thoughts and prayers today," Mr. Clinton said.

Dee Dee Myers, the White House press secretary, said that Mr. Cisneros; the director of the Federal Emergency Management Agency, James Lee Witt, and Transportation Secretary Federico F. Peña left this afternoon for Los Angeles.

For all its damage, the quake was not the long-predicted Big One that experts fear will cause catastrophic damage someday. It was neither as powerful nor as deadly as the quake that hit the San Francisco Bay area on Oct. 17, 1989, which killed 63 people.

Seismologists at the California Institute of Technology said the earthquake hit on a previously unknown branch of a fault that is part of a network of fissures that trembles constantly underneath the Los Angeles area.

It is part of a system that is responsible for a 5.9 magnitude quake that was involved in the 1987 Whittier Narrows earthquake, said Kate Hutton of Caltech. She said it appeared to be about nine miles under the ground but did not break the surface in visible fissures.

Strong Aftershocks

Throughout the day, strong aftershocks as high as 5.5 on the Richter scale continued to jolt the area in what Ms. Hutton said was a classic pattern.

The jolts shook buildings in San Diego, 125 miles to the south, and in Las Vegas, Nev., 275 miles to the northeast, and brief power failures were reported as far north as British Columbia.

Some hospitals were overwhelmed with injuries. At Holy Cross Medical Center in Sylmar, an emergency room admissions officer, Toni Regaldo, said the injuries included heart attacks, broken bones, lacerations and "a lot of blood." At the Granada Hills Community Hospital, officials set up a makeshift emergency room in the parking lot where hundreds of people were treated. The hospital itself suffered considerable damage and was operating on a generator.

Just yards away, the Kaiser Permanente administration building was all but demolished, its midsection squashed and its walls yawning open. Several buildings at the Sepulveda Veterans Administration Hospital were also damaged, forcing evacuation of more than 300 patients.

In Anaheim, 40 miles southeast of the epicenter, Anaheim Stadium was littered with debris and the "Big A" sign and the giant replay screen leaned precariously over the upper deck. A game between Los Angeles and Sacramento was canceled.

Milder Quake Hits to North

NAPA, Calif., Jan. 17 (AP) — A mild earthquake shook the area north of San Francisco today. The United States Geological Survey said the quake, at 6:46 A.M., measured 3.5 on the Richter scale.

It was centered on the Green Valley fault north of Napa, between Lake Berryessa and Clear Lake, the agency said. There were no reports of damage.

Pat Jorgenson, a spokeswoman for the Geological Survey, said there was no apparent connection between the quake and the much larger quake in the Los Angeles area two and a quarter hours earlier.

After the earthquake struck in Southern California, Ray Hudson reacted as a friend's home went up in flames at the Oak Ridge Trailer Park in Sylmar. Mr. Hudson, who lost his home in an earthquake that hit the area in 1971, did not lose his trailer yesterday.

Reuters

A collapsed garage in the Northridge Fashion Center, where a street sweeper was pulled out alive, was reduced to a pile of concrete and steel.

California's Previous Quakes

Some of the quakes of magnitude 6.1 or greater on the Richter scale. The measurement for the 1906 San Francisco quake is an estimate, because the quake occurred before the Richter scale was developed.

	Year	Location	Magnitude
1	1906	San Francisco	8.3
2	1952	Tehachapi-Bakersfield	7.7
3	1927	Offshore San Luis Obispo	7.7
4	1992	Landers	7.4
5	1923	North Coast	7.2
6	1989	San Francisco	7.1
7	1980	Eureka	7.0
8	1992	Ferndale (three)	6.3-6.9
9	1940	Imperial Valley	6.7
10	1994	Northridge	6.6
11	1980	Mammoth Lakes	6.5
12	1992	Big Bear	6.5
13	1983	Coalinga	6.5
14	1971	San Fernando-Sylmar	6.5
15	1979	Imperial Valley	6.4
16	1968	Anza-Borrego Mountains	6.4
17	1992	Los Angeles	6.3
18	1933	Long Beach	6.3
19	1925	Santa Barbara	6.3
20	1984	Morgan Hill	6.2
21	1987	Los Angeles	6.1

CALIFORNIA
San Francisco
SAN ANDREAS FAULT
Yesterday's earthquake
Los Angeles

Source: Associated Press

The New York Times

THE EARTHQUAKE REPORT

The New York Times report on the earthquake was reported and written by Sandra Blakeslee, Bill Carter, Ashley Dunn, Jonathan Fuerbringer, Philipp M. Gollner, Jane Gross, Dirk Johnson, Elizabeth Kolbert, Seth Mydans, Jonathan Rabinovitz, Calvin Sims and Bernard Weinraub in Los Angeles; Malcolm W. Browne, Walter Goodman and Maria Newman in New York and Martin Tolchin in Washington.

Photographs were contributed by Scott Robinson, Marissa Roth, Jan Sonnenmair and Jim Wilson.

Maps and graphics were provided by Arnold Bombay, Baden Copeland, Newman Huh, Patrick Lyons, John Papasian, Rachel Powell and Julie Shaver.

"All the News That's Fit to Print"

The New York Times

Late Edition

New York: **Today,** sunny with a few high clouds. High 75. **Tonight,** breezy, mild. Low 60. **Tomorrow,** showers, windy, cooler. High 68. **Yesterday,** high 72, low 54. Details, page B14.

VOL.CXLIII . . . No. 49,693 | NEW YORK, WEDNESDAY, MAY 11, 1994 | 75 cents beyond the greater New York metropolitan area. | 50 CENTS

SOUTH AFRICANS HAIL PRESIDENT MANDELA; FIRST BLACK LEADER PLEDGES RACIAL UNITY

Giuliani's Budget Proposes Cuts For Spending and Work Force

By JAMES C. McKINLEY Jr.

Mayor Rudolph W. Giuliani proposed a $31.6 billion budget for New York City yesterday that would reduce spending slightly for the first time in 16 years and sharply cut the municipal work force in almost every major agency except the Police and Fire Departments.

Submitting his first executive budget to the City Council, Mr. Giuliani said the city "has been spending itself beyond its economy" for more than a decade, creating perennial gaps between what it spends and what its tax base can support. The Mayor said the city's overspending had drained the local economy, driving private industry from the city.

"The purpose of this budget is to redirect the economy of New York," Mr. Giuliani said. Saying the city was "hemorrhaging jobs" while the rest of the nation was recovering, Mr. Giuliani added, "We can't employ people through government alone."

In drafting his plan, Mr. Giuliani needed to close a $2.3 billion gap between projected spending and revenues for the fiscal year that begins on July 1. To do that, he has suggested about $1.2 billion in spending cuts from city agencies, mostly through cutting 15,000 workers, or 7 percent of the city-financed work force. Mr. Giuliani said those cuts could be made without serious damage to services if managers learned to run agencies more efficiently. Over all, spending would fall by $102 million.

He also proposed some modest tax cuts totaling about $35 million.

The extent of the service cuts is likely to figure in the debate over Mr. Giuliani's budget as it moves to the City Council, particularly since the budget makes no cuts in the Police or Fire Departments. Already some lawmakers are asking whether protecting those agencies is worth the pain for schools, youth programs and hospitals. [News analysis, page B5.]

Besides cutting jobs, the Mayor relied in his efforts to close the budget gap on some actions that will still require the cooperation of the State Legislature, the Federal Government

Continued on Page B4, Column 4

Closing the Gap

Principal measures the Mayor proposes in his budget for fiscal year 1995 and the **PROJECTED SAVINGS (OR COST)** in millions.

Cuts to spending in city agencies	$1,269
Increased state aid	275
Increased Federal aid	125
Union co-payments for retirees' benefits	200
Refinancing of city debt	225
Asset sales (WNYC-FM, U.N. Plaza Hotel)	110
Changes in payments on pension debt	51
Fiscal year 1994 surplus	98
Cuts in hotel tax and commercial rent tax	(35)
TOTAL SAVINGS	$2,318

Reuters

Nelson Mandela takes the oath of office as President from Chief Justice Michael Corbett in Pretoria.

Dance for Joy! Come Dance a Toyi-Toyi!

By FRANCIS X. CLINES

Special to The New York Times

PRETORIA, South Africa, May 10 — Hours before Nelson Mandela took possession of the Government, and had his air force delight an outdoor throng with a fly-over wafting rainbow-hued vapors, Elsie Njokweni was dancing her shoes off in the most fitting of places.

She was a bobbing, crooning blur aboard one of the packed commuter trains from the Soweto ghetto, traditionally a sardine-can affair for the ostracized black underclass of apartheid, but today a vessel of historic exultation.

Numerous trains clacked and boomed along the rails with the special chanted resistance songs and the foot-stomping dances known as toyi-toyi that South African blacks turned into a swarming political art form in defeating racist oppression.

"I was arrested six years ago for behaving this way," Mrs. Njokweni said, sliding into a toyi-toyi with hip-swaying grace to join her neighbors from Soweto Extension No. 1, southwest of Johannesburg.

It was soon after dawn when they all crammed and capered onto one of the ceremonial excursion trains that carried scores of thousands of ordinary people to the grand Government Lawn to witness President Mandela's inaugural triumph.

Whatever the exuberance level of the formally choreographed proceedings, most of the watching world missed the full truth of South Africans' joy, not being aboard the toyi-toyi train nor trying to keep up with Mrs. Njokweni and three generations of her neighbors.

They were leaping, scuttling and back-sliding into a pounding version of "Hold On, Boys," a work-song for barracks laborers near the breaking point, a song intended to snatch courage from intimidation.

"Your gun, Mr. Policeman, only reminds me of our hero, Oliver Tambo," the Sowetans sang and danced, in praise of a founder of the African National Congress who died a year ago.

Their noise graced the passing countryside, stirring white suburbanites to wave V-signs and fists of triumph along the three-hour ride. More often, it was blacks looking out suddenly from their track-side shanties

Continued on Page A8, Column 1

Ozier Muhammad/The New York Times

Elsie Njokweni singing on her way to inauguration ceremonies.

President Is Said to Pick Babbitt For Court Despite Senate Concern

By GWEN IFILL

Special to The New York Times

WASHINGTON, May 10 — In spite of last-minute concerns expressed by members of the Senate over the weekend, President Clinton has settled on Interior Secretary Bruce Babbitt as his nominee to the Supreme Court, officials said today.

A senior White House official said there was a "95 percent chance" that Mr. Babbitt, a former Arizona Governor and Attorney General, would be Mr. Clinton's choice to replace Justice Harry A. Blackmun, who is retiring at the end of the current term. Other advisers said Mr. Clinton was satisfied that Mr. Babbitt could face down any objections.

The President has been leaning toward Mr. Babbitt for several days, but he only disclosed his list of finalists for the Court to senators last weekend in a series of telephone conversations.

Mr. Clinton held a final one-hour meeting with his Supreme Court search team today, and aides said afterward that he was still "going through the calculus" to weigh the selection. One aide acknowledged that Mr. Babbitt could be a "political lightning rod," but said that the White House had determined it could overcome opposition led by Senator Orrin G. Hatch of Utah, the senior Republican on the Senate Judiciary Committee.

In an interview, Senator Hatch described Mr. Babbitt "as a nominee who would be pushed by the far left" and as the kind of judge "who would legislate from the bench laws that the liberal community doesn't have a tinker's chance of getting through the people's elected representatives."

Mr. Hatch suggested that Democratic and Republican senators would join his campaign to block a Babbitt nomination, but two other Western Senators who have tangled with Mr. Babbitt over environmental issues, Harry Reid of Nevada and Ben Nighthorse Campbell of Colorado, said today that they would welcome his

Continued on Page A17, Column 1

DE KLERK PRAISED

An Inauguration Tumult for 'the Old Man' and His Diverse Guests

By BILL KELLER

Special to The New York Times

PRETORIA, South Africa, May 10 — With the commanding dignity that has carried him through more than half a century of defiance, captivity and conciliation, Nelson Rolihlahla Mandela became the first black President of South Africa today.

He stood before a crowd of world leaders who shunned this capital during its decades of infamy, and in a husky, resolute voice swore the oath to become the 10th leader of South Africa since its union in 1910, but the first elected with the participation of the black majority.

Then the 75-year-old leader opened his presidency with an intimate speech of shared patriotism, speaking of South Africans' common exhilaration in the seasons and the soil, their common pain for their country's humiliation before the world and their shared relief at being readmitted to the company of civilized nations.

"Never, never, and never again shall it be that this beautiful land will again experience the oppression of one by another and suffer the indignity of being the skunk of the world," he said. [Transcript, page A8.]

As a token of renewal, Mr. Mandela promised that an amnesty would soon be announced for "various categories" of prisoners.

He lavished praise on F. W. de Klerk, the President who collaborated with him in negotiating the end of white rule and who today took the oath as one of Mr. Mandela's two Vice Presidents in a unity Government.

In a post-inaugural visit to the 50,000 ordinary citizens celebrating on the lawn far below the Government buildings, Mr. Mandela held Mr. de Klerk's hand aloft and hailed his predecessor as "one of the greatest reformers, one of the greatest sons of our soil."

For the day, at least, blacks and whites were united by the mutual strain of taking in the recently unimaginable:

There was Fidel Castro on his first visit to the country that tried to pulverize his army in Angola, the only one among the scores of dignitaries singled out by the crowd for lusty shouts of "Viva!"

And Muslim and Hindu prayers broadcast into the air of what has been the most rigidly, officially Christian of capitals.

And the Navy band in dress whites entertaining the inaugural dignitaries with a Zulu migrant labor song.

And finally President Nelson Mandela, now Commander in Chief, reviewing the defense force that was built, in large part, to prevent some-

Continued on Page A8, Column 1

Trail of Despair by a Father Leaves 4 Dead and Son Hurt

By CLIFFORD J. LEVY

After being dismissed last week from his $7.50-an-hour job at a paper factory in Brooklyn, Jose Luis Berroa grew despondent about how he would care for his 2-year-old son. He had lived on the grim streets of New York City with little Carlos before, his friends said, and he could not bear to return. So he decided to give Carlos back to the boy's mother, Awilda Enriquez.

But something snapped in Mr. Berroa when he arrived at the home of Ms. Enriquez's family in Newark, something that caused him to go on a rampage that left a trail of death yesterday, ending when he wounded the child and then killed himself after a confrontation with police officers on a stairwell in Washington Heights.

The night before in Newark, Mr. Berroa killed two of Ms. Enriquez's brothers, the police said, and shot to death a woman who had earned a reputation for kindness in the neighborhood by adopting 12 children. [Page B6.] He then fled with the boy in her car and sought refuge in Washington Heights with a woman who had helped him build a new life after he immigrated from Cuba a decade ago.

It was there that his life ended. The police said they caught up with him and, instead of surrendering, Mr. Berroa fired a bullet into his son's face before shooting himself.

He left only two small plastic bags that he lugged from place to place in recent months, his friends said. They contained Carlos's baby clothes and tiny sneakers, a broken toy motorcycle and a box that once held shells for a 9-millimeter gun, the weapon the police said Mr. Berroa had used on his victims and himself.

"He told us he was going crazy about maybe losing the baby," said Georgina Gonzalez, 26, the daughter of Emma Maria, 50, in whose Washington Heights building Mr. Berroa died. She recalled how her mother had persuaded Mr. Berroa to stay with her recently after he had spent much of the winter sleeping on park benches, huddling with the child against the cold.

The police said Mr. Berroa, 33, showed up unexpectedly about 6:30 P.M. on Monday at the home of Ms. Enriquez's family at 231 Sixth Ave-

Continued on Page B6, Column 4

INSIDE

Italian Government Formed

Italy's right-wing Prime Minister-designate formed a Government after weeks of wrangling, including five seats for neo-Fascists. Page A5.

Identifying a Real Lobbyist

The Government's new 30-page description of lobbying imposes micrometer precision on an activity that seemed kind of obvious. Page A16.

Collapse at Christie's

At an auction of Impressionist and modern art, only 38 of 76 works were sold; proceeds fell nearly $40 million below estimates. Page C18.

Associated Press

Agence France-Presse

A Rare Sight

A solar eclipse darkened skies yesterday at midday in a 150-mile-deep swath across the United States. Sunlight filtered through tree branches in Chicago, above, projected the rare annular eclipse. Page B7.

Fetal Harm Is Cited As Primary Hazard In Dioxin Exposure

By KEITH SCHNEIDER

In a report on dioxin, scientists at the Environmental Protection Agency have concluded that cancer is not the most serious health hazard at common exposure levels. Of greater concern, their report said, are subtle effects on fetal development and the immune system that may be the result of very low levels of exposure.

The scientists said that most people already have levels of dioxin in their bodies at or near the concentrations that cause such fetal and immune system problems in laboratory animals.

This new assessment of the risk of dioxin, one of a class of toxic chlorine-based compounds present everywhere in the environment, comes in a draft summary of a 2,000-page report scheduled to be made public this summer. The conclusion, that current levels of exposure may already pose human health problems, is based on new mathematical assumptions that have not been published in scientific journals.

And it has already caused a storm of dissent in Federal agencies, principally in the Food and Drug Administration and the Department of Agri-

Continued on Page A20, Column 1

NEWS SUMMARY A2

THE OVERVIEW

South Africans Hail President Mandela

Continued From Page A1

Four years after jail, Mandela takes control of a nation.

one like him from taking power.

When nine Mirage jet fighters streaked overhead as part of an aerial salute, the citizens assembled on the grass sent up a roar, it seemed, out of a new feeling of custody rather than at the thrill of high-speed machinery.

Mr. Mandela's ascent has been virtually inevitable, at least since last July when negotiators cinched the dates for the first elections open to all races.

In the elections that finished on April 29, the African National Congress won more than 62 percent of the vote, earning 252 of the 400 seats in the National Assembly that elected Mr. Mandela on Monday without opposition.

Mr. Mandela, whose Xhosa name, Rolihlahla, means "someone who brings trouble on himself," knows well enough the difficulties he has taken on in maintaining the richest economy in Africa while satisfying the promises inherent in his triumph.

Still, today was a last occasion to contemplate the distance the country has traversed before it looks ahead.

Four years and three months ago — just midway through the Bush Administration — Nelson Mandela was serving a life sentence for trying to overthrow the Government. Today he heads it.

He became President on a stage erected in the reddish sandstone crescent of the Government building that overlooks Pretoria and, beyond, the hulking monument to the great inland trek of the Afrikaner Voortrekkers.

Mr. Mandela is a President who comes to power preceded by a myth, already embodied in liberation songs that swelled spontaneously in the waiting amphitheater: "Nel-son Man-DEL-a! Nel-son Man-DEL-a!"

He arrived, an hour behind schedule, between two of his daughters, and listened to the swearing-in of his two

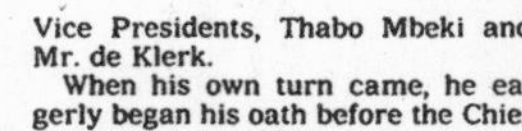

Vice Presidents, Thabo Mbeki and Mr. de Klerk.

When his own turn came, he eagerly began his oath before the Chief Justice prompted him.

Salute by Guns and Aircraft

After he spoke, the cannons thundered a 21-gun salute and buzzing formations of helicopters and aged warplanes passed overhead.

The guests arrayed in the autumnal sun included 45 heads of state, plus an American delegation headed by Vice President Al Gore and including Hillary Rodham Clinton. Prince Philip, the husband of Queen Elizabeth II of England, attended, as did Secretary General Boutros Boutros-Ghali of the United Nations.

So did James Gregory. Mr. Gregory was Mr. Mandela's warden for two decades, first at the Robben Island Prison and later at Victor Verster Prison, and they became so close that after Mr. Mandela was released the jailer retired out of boredom. "Life had become empty for me," Mr. Gregory told a Johannesburg newspaper.

Castro and Arafat Welcomed

World figures long shunned here as Communists and sponsors of guerrilla insurgency, like Mr. Castro and Yasir Arafat, chairman of the Palestine Liberation Organization, arrived today to more enthusiastic welcomes than the Americans received.

At an inaugural lunch in the residence called the Presidency, Mr. Mandela introduced the Cuban leader to Mr. de Klerk and then to the military chief of staff.

"Welcome to South Africa," Mr. de Klerk said.

"I hope you are successful," Mr. Castro replied.

It was a day for conciliatory gestures.

Joe Modise, a former guerrilla leader and now Mr. Mandela's Defense Minister-designate, noticed a delegation led by Chief Mangosuthu G. Buthelezi, of the rival Inkatha Freedom Party, and the Zulu king, Goodwill Zwelethini, languishing in the B-list seats and moved them to the front row.

Someone likewise rescued Winnie Mandela, the estranged wife of the new President, and led her from her chair behind a low sandstone wall to the covered stage where family and invited guests were seated.

A Victory in Soccer

Tonight the new President dropped in at the packed soccer stadium where the South African national team defeated Zambia in an inaugural special. He frowned when the 60,000 spectators failed to raise their voices in the two anthems of the new South Africa — the old Afrikaans poem, The Call of South Africa, and the liberation anthem, God Bless Africa.

"You have to learn the words to both anthems," he scolded the crowd. "If you don't know Afrikaans, you must learn it. If you don't know Zulu or Xhosa, you must learn those."

"It's nice that he came, but I think this is the last time we'll come together like this," said one fan, a resident of the Phola Park squatter camp who declined to give her name. Wrapped in a huge A.N.C. flag but already feeling the seep of disillusionment, she wondered, "What are we going to do now? There's nothing to protest against."

Associated Press

Thousands of South Africans at the inauguration ceremony yesterday.

Reuters

Nelson Mandela and F. W. de Klerk held their hands high as they addressed crowds in Pretoria yesterday.

Mandela's Address: 'Glory and Hope'

PRETORIA, South Africa, May 10 (AP) — Following is a transcript of Nelson Mandela's speech here today at his inauguration as President of South Africa, as recorded by The Associated Press:

Your majesties, your royal highnesses, distinguished guests, comrades and friends:

Today, all of us do, by our presence here, and by our celebrations in other parts of our country and the world, confer glory and hope to newborn liberty.

Out of the experience of an extraordinary human disaster that lasted too long must be born a society of which all humanity will be proud.

Our daily deeds as ordinary South Africans must produce an actual South African reality that will reinforce humanity's belief in justice, strengthen its confidence in the nobility of the human soul and sustain all our hopes for a glorious life for all.

A Sense of Renewal

All this we owe both to ourselves and to the peoples of the world who are so well represented here today.

To my compatriots, I have no hesitation in saying that each one of us is as intimately attached to the soil of this beautiful country as are the famous jacaranda trees of Pretoria and the mimosa trees of the bushveld.

Each time one of us touches the soil of this land, we feel a sense of personal renewal. The national mood changes as the seasons change.

We are moved by a sense of joy and exhilaration when the grass turns green and the flowers bloom.

That spiritual and physical oneness we all share with this common homeland explains the depth of the pain we all carried in our hearts as we saw our country tear itself apart in terrible conflict, and as we saw it spurned, outlawed and isolated by the peoples of the world, precisely because it has become the universal base of the pernicious ideology and practice of racism and racial oppression.

Guests Are Thanked

We, the people of South Africa, feel fulfilled that humanity has taken us back into its bosom, that we, who were outlaws not so long ago, have today been given the rare privilege to be host to the nations of the world on our own soil.

We thank all our distinguished international guests for having come to take possession with the people of our country of what is, after all, a common victory for justice, for peace, for human dignity.

We trust that you will continue to stand by us as we tackle the challenges of building peace, prosperity, nonsexism, nonracialism and democracy.

We deeply appreciate the role that the masses of our people and their democratic, religious, women, youth, business, traditional and other leaders have played to bring about this conclusion. Not least among them is my Second Deputy President, the Honorable F. W. de Klerk.

A Pledge of Liberation

We would also like to pay tribute to our security forces, in all their ranks, for the distinguished role they have played in securing our first democratic elections and the transition to democracy, from bloodthirsty forces which still refuse to see the light.

The time for the healing of the wounds has come.

The moment to bridge the chasms that divide us has come.

The time to build is upon us.

We have, at last, achieved our political emancipation. We pledge ourselves to liberate all our people from the continuing bondage of poverty, deprivation, suffering, gender and other discrimination.

We succeeded to take our last steps to freedom in conditions of relative peace. We commit ourselves to the construction of a complete, just and lasting peace.

Issue of Amnesty

We have triumphed in the effort to implant hope in the breasts of the millions of our people. We enter into a covenant that we shall build the society in which all South Africans, both black and white, will be able to walk tall, without any fear in their hearts, assured of their inalienable right to human dignity — a rainbow nation at peace with itself and the world.

As a token of its commitment to the renewal of our country, the new Interim Government of National Unity will, as a matter of urgency, address the issue of amnesty for various categories of our people who are currently serving terms of imprisonment.

We dedicate this day to all the heroes and heroines in this country and the rest of the world who sacrificed in many ways and surrendered their lives so that we could be free.

Their dreams have become reality. Freedom is their reward.

We are both humbled and elevated by the honor and privilege that you, the people of South Africa, have bestowed on us, as the first President of a united, democratic, nonracial and nonsexist South Africa, to lead our country out of the valley of darkness.

We understand it still that there is no easy road to freedom.

We know it well that none of us acting alone can achieve success.

We must therefore act together as a united people, for national reconciliation, for nation building, for the birth of a new world.

Let there be justice for all.

Let there be peace for all.

Let there be work, bread, water and salt for all.

Let each know that for each the body, the mind and the soul have been freed to fulfill themselves.

Never, never, and never again shall it be that this beautiful land will again experience the oppression of one by another and suffer the indignity of being the skunk of the world.

The sun shall never set on so glorious a human achievement!

Let freedom reign. God bless Africa!

THE CELEBRATION

Dance for Joy! On the Road From Soweto, Dance a Toyi-Toyi!

Continued From Page A1

A lilt turns songs of protest into songs of victory.

at the passing ruckus, the train sending off sparks of toyi-toyi that put some to dancing in dusty lanes.

"We resisted apartheid back then with protest songs and dance," said Mrs. Njokweni, thinking back to 1988. "And I got detained." The swaying woman savored the hand-clapping, foot-pounding, lyric-rich music of neighbors deep into a Zulu song composed when Mr. Mandela was only midway through his 27 years of political imprisonment.

"Dear Nelson Mandela," the carload of bobbing Sowetans sang in a natural harmony. "We are struggling nicely: Don't worry."

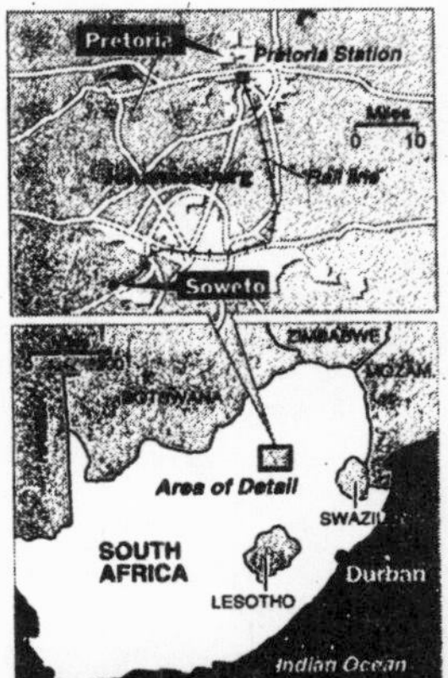

The New York Times

Supporters crowded aboard trains from Soweto to Pretoria to witness Nelson Mandela's triumph.

They were soon dancing into another old song, treating the original vow of its lyric as an accomplished fact: "We have cleansed this land."

There were added yips of emphasis to the chants and melodies washing across the rails. The memory of these great old songs of protest seemed to accentuate Mrs. Njokweni's sashay.

She said she was greatly amused that the once threatening boldness of toyi-toyi defiance had evolved, like Nelson Mandela's ascent from his cell, into a soothing outlet of joy in the new South Africa. "I will tell my great-grandchildren this is my favorite day," she said.

Nothing marred the Sowetans' commute to the side of their hero. A half dozen perfunctory police friskings along the way — President Mandela is firmly insistent there be no weapons at his rallies — only seemed to tickle the collective fancy.

Why Not Dance on the Bus?

Three hours of toyi-toyi on the train was followed by 20 minutes more as the crowd wended its way through the Pretoria station and onto buses where, yes, after a moment, many had to stand to toyi-toyi in the aisles.

There wasn't a Walkman in sight, just countless a capella chorus lines converging on "the Old Man," as they affectionately call their President.

Once at the lawn rally, the Sowetans joined a vast crowd that seemed finally exhausted from the many days of celebrations for the political victory in which the black majority was allowed to claim its share of power. People mostly lounged on the lawn, picnicking and chatting.

Ozier Muhammad/The New York Times

Elsie Njokweni singing on a train from Soweto to Nelson Mandela's inauguration in Pretoria yesterday.

But they revived and rose and cheered at hearing Mr. Mandela's Whitmanesque celebration of their "glory and hope and new-born liberty."

And they cut him off with roaring approval as he described the utter finality of apartheid. "Never, never and never again shall it be," his voice boomed across the lawn in a speech that served once more to leave the crowd looking spent.

Soon, though, the Mandela Government graphically demonstrated the peaceful revolution accomplished by the voters and their President. Waves of warplanes suddenly flew over in celebratory formations, fully harmless toward the former subjects of apartheid, wreathing them in vaporous of colors of the new national flag.

Instantly everyone on the lawn understood Mr. Mandela's new powers. They waved and shouted at the dazzling aircraft.

"Yes! Yes!" shouted Martha Mtozima, pointing upward at the blue skies and the soothing drone of empowerment. "Oh, so exciting," she shouted, plucking at her billowy Sunday-best dress and making flapping motions with her hands. "If could fly, I'd fly just like that."

In lieu of that, of course, she toyi-toyied once more across the lawn, in the direction of President Mandela.

"All the News That's Fit to Print"

The New York Times

Late Edition

New York: **Today,** sunny, mild, light winds. High 71. **Tonight,** increasing clouds. Low 50. **Tomorrow,** cloudy, cool, occasional rain. High 59. **Yesterday,** high 76, low 51. Details, page C13.

VOL.CXLIV.... No. 50,037 NEW YORK, THURSDAY, APRIL 20, 1995 — $1 beyond the greater New York metropolitan area. — 60 CENTS

AT LEAST 26 ARE DEAD, SCORES ARE MISSING AFTER CAR BOMB ATTACK IN OKLAHOMA CITY WRECKS 9-STORY FEDERAL OFFICE BUILDING

CLUES ARE LACKING

U.S. Officials Scurry for Answers — Reno to Ask Death Penalty

By DAVID JOHNSTON

WASHINGTON, April 19 — The Federal authorities opened an intensive hunt today for whoever bombed a Federal office building in Oklahoma City, and proceeded on the theory that the bombing was a terrorist attack against the Government, law-enforcement officials said.

President Clinton appeared this afternoon in the White House press room and somberly promised that the Government would hunt down the "evil cowards" responsible. "These people are killers," he said, "and must be treated like killers."

Attorney General Janet Reno, speaking to reporters at the White House in early evening, said that casualty figures from the scene were climbing and that of the 550 people who worked in the building, 300 were unaccounted for.

Ms. Reno said Federal prosecutors would seek the death penalty against the bombers. "The death penalty is available," she said, "and we will seek it."

But questions about the identity of the bombers swirled around the case. The only solid fact was the explosion itself.

Some law-enforcement officials said the bombing might be linked to the second anniversary today of the F.B.I.'s ill-fated assault on the Branch Davidian compound near Waco, Tex., an operation that ended in a fire that killed about 80 people, including many children. Among the offices housed by the Federal building in Oklahoma City was one quartering local agents of the Bureau of Alcohol, Tobacco and Firearms, the agency that Branch Davidians and their sympathizers blamed for the confrontation.

But other officials said that neither the Branch Davidians nor right-wing "militia" groups that have protested the Government's handling of the Davidians were believed to have the technical exper-

Continued on Page B8, Column 1

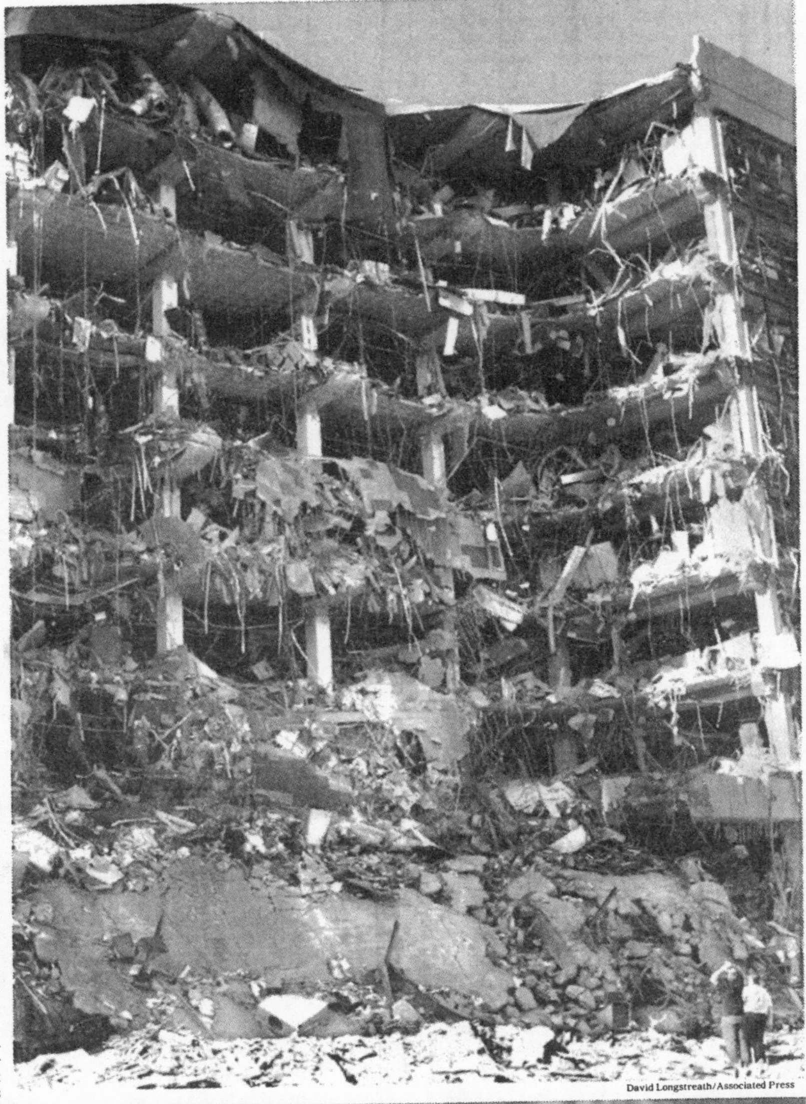

David Longstreath/Associated Press

12 Victims Were Children in 2d-Floor Day-Care Center

By JOHN KIFNER

OKLAHOMA CITY, April 19 — A car bomb went off with a thunderous explosion here this morning, ripping through a Federal office building, collapsing walls and floors, and killing at least 26 people. Many others were buried in the wreckage, and the death toll seemed certain to rise.

At least 12 children whose parents had just dropped them off at a second-floor day-care center were among those immediately known dead in the deadliest bombing in the United States in 75 years.

As dusk fell, scores of the more than 500 people who normally work in the building were still missing. John Hansen, an Assistant Oklahoma City Fire Chief, said it appeared that dead and wounded victims were underneath the piles of concrete, plaster and glass. Late tonight, rain fell from the gray clouds that had threatened for much of the day, adding hardship to horror and raising the possibility the wreckage would shift, imperiling the trapped injured and their rescuers.

The National Guard has been called in, and late tonight limited martial law was declared to keep the streets clear.

Reflecting on the early report of the death toll, Fire Chief Gary Marrs said, "We're sure that it will go up, because we've seen fatalities in the building."

At the White House, President Clinton convened an inter-agency task force to coordinate Federal assistance and called on Americans to pray for the dead and stricken. He also dispatched a small army of Federal investigators to Oklahoma and pledged a relentless hunt for the killers.

Attorney General Janet Reno, noting that the dead children ranged from 1 to 7 years old, and that some had been burned beyond recognition in the day-care center just above the curb where the bomb detonated, said the crime was a capital one and that the Government would seek the death penalty if those responsible were caught. She also said that there were 550 people working in the building and that about 300 were still unaccounted for.

By late tonight, no one had claimed responsibility for the bombing, which occurred on the second anniversary of the Federal raid on

Associated Press

The Alfred P. Murrah building in Oklahoma City before its north side, facing left, was bombed.

the Branch Davidian compound near Waco, Tex., in which David Koresh and scores of his followers perished. There was no evidence that today's bombing, which was similar in intensity to the World Trade Center bombing in New York two years ago but far more deadly, was linked to the Davidians.

Rescue teams, bringing in backhoes, bulldozers and other heavy equipment, dug in the rubble tonight in darkness, rain and a cutting wind, searching for victims in the flattened center of the nine-story Alfred P. Murrah Building.

Three survivors were pulled out of the wreckage by firemen shortly after 9:30 P.M. There were cries from a woman in the basement, firemen said, but they were having difficulty getting to her because there appeared to be bodies in the way. That vignette of horror was just one of hundreds played out all day long, from morning to dark.

Federal buildings in seven other cities were evacuated because of bomb threats, and security was tightened at government buildings from coast to coast.

Shards of glass littered the street around the Federal Building here, and much of the masonry was literally peeled away from the building, leaving a gaping nine-story hole. Federal Bureau of Investigation agents in bright yellow rain slickers,

Continued on Page B9, Column 1

OTHER NEWS

Gas Fumes Create Panic in Yokohama

In a chilling reminder of the gas attack last month in Tokyo, caustic fumes spread through Yokohama's railroad station and through a train, sending about 300 people to hospitals. No one took responsibility for release of the gas. Page A10.

Court Upholds Anonymity

In a decision threatening state election laws, the Supreme Court ruled the Constitution guarantees the right to distribute anonymous campaign literature. Page A20. Add two more lines of type in all.

Lugar Declares Candidacy

Saying he has an unblemished character, Senator Richard Lugar of Indiana announced that he would seek the Republican nomination for President in 1996. Page A16.

Mayor Wants to End Relief

A day after touting the success of new rules for a welfare program, Mayor Giuliani said he really favors abolishing the program. Page B1.

Charles H. Porter IV/Associated Press

Emergency workers remove a child injured in the explosion in downtown Oklahoma City, which occurred as employees began reporting for work yesterday. At least 26 were killed, including numerous children at a day-care center, and scores were injured or missing, some still buried in the rubble.

In Shock, Loathing, Denial: 'This Doesn't Happen Here'

By RICK BRAGG

OKLAHOMA CITY, April 19 — Before the dust and the rage had a chance to settle, a chilly rain started to fall on the blasted-out wreck of what had once been an office building, and on the shoulders of the small army of police, firefighters and medical technicians that surrounded it.

They were not used to this, if anyone is. On any other day, they would have answered calls to kitchen fires, domestic disputes, or even a cat up a tree. Oklahoma City is still, in some ways, a small town, said the people who live here.

This morning, as the blast trembled the morning coffee in cups miles away, the outside world came crashing hard onto Oklahoma City.

"I just took part in a surgery where a little boy had part of his brain hanging out of his head," said Terry Jones, a medical technician, as he searched in his pocket for a cigarette. Behind him, firefighters picked carefully through the skeleton of the building, still searching for the living and the dead.

"You tell me," he said, "how can anyone have so little respect for human life."

The shock of what the rescuers found in the rubble had long since worn off, replaced with a loathing for the people who had planted the bomb that killed their friends, neighbors and children.

One by one they said the same thing: this does not happen here. It happens in countries so far away, so different, they might as well be on the dark side of the moon. It happens in New York. It happens in Europe.

It does not happen in a place where, debarking at the airport, passengers see a woman holding a sign that welcomes them to the Lieutenant Governor's annual turkey shoot.

It does not happen in a city that has a sign just outside the city limits, "Oklahoma City, Home of Vince Gill," the country singer.

"We're just a little old cowtown," said Bill Finn, a grime-covered firefighter who propped himself wearily up against a brick wall as the rain turned the dust to mud on his face. "You can't get no more Middle America than Oklahoma City. You

Continued on Page B11, Column 1

More on the Blast

THE RESCUE When rescuers found the hundreds of cut, burned and terrified victims, it became a matter of grasping for the living while trying to ignore the dead. Page B10.

AROUND THE NATION Shocked and fearful, government officials at Federal, state and some local levels shut down offices in at least eight cities, including New York. Page B10.

THE BOMB The powerful bomb was very likely made of ingredients that are widely available from gardening centers, chemical suppliers and gasoline stations. Page B8.

TERROR IN OKLAHOMA CITY: The Blast and Its Aftermath

THE OVERVIEW

At Least 21 Dead and Scores Missing After Car Bomb Attack in Oklahoma City

Continued From Page A1

and other investigators and rescue personnel, surrounded the building, and National Guardsmen in helmets and combat camouflage began setting up a perimeter.

Mayor Ron Norick said that a car bomb had gone off on the street in front of the building, leaving a crater eight feet deep. Explosive experts on the scene estimated the size of the bomb as from 1,000 to 1,200 pounds.

Local television stations reported that the Oklahoma City police department had found a piece of a maroon mini-van that may have been used to carry the explosives. Fragments of the exploded vehicle's license plate also were found, the television reports said, and indicated that the mini-van had been leased from a National Car Rental agency. But in Washington, Federal investigators said they knew nothing to confirm these reports.

Planeloads of Oklahoma City residents who had been out of town when they heard news of the explosion, hurried home, either to wait for word about loved ones or simply to be available to help in some way.

The ordeal of Jackie Bair, who once worked alongside her sister in the Federal employees' credit union on the third floor of the building, was typical of the anxiety and grief felt throughout this city of 440,000 in west-central Oklahoma.

After seeing the devastation on television, Ms. Bair hurried back to Oklahoma City from her home in Prattville, Ala.

"Her office wasn't there anymore," she said, patting her chest and taking deep breaths. "The walls were so thin we used to hear each other talking through them. Now it's just a bunch of rocks. Lord, my heart hurts."

Late tonight, she still had received no news about her sister, Vicky Texter, 38, who has worked in the credit union for 15 years. She said her brother-in-law continued to make the rounds of trauma centers. His was the sort of agonizing search seen again and again near the wreckage, as relatives of victims and possible victims desperately sought word of their kin.

Dr. Jim G. Duckett was in the Poconos, gearing up for a bicycle trip with his daughter when he heard the news and caught the next plane home.

"I just thought I should be there in case I was needed," said Dr. Duckett, 68, who is a plastic surgeon.

The stories told and retold by horrified emergency crews — stories of people mangled and in pain and, for the time being at least, beyond the reach of rescuers — left no doubt that the surgeon's skills would be useful.

Like others on their way home, Dr. Duckett said he was afraid that this was only the beginning of a major terrorist campaign.

Assistant Fire Chief Hansen arrived at the scene finding some 100 people, cut, bruised and dazed walking outside of the Federal Building. The corpses of several adults lay among the debris from the blast, and more bodies were inside the lobby and hallway. As his firefighters entered the building, they were taken aback by the sight of toys from the day-care center, littering the street.

"It's been tough," he said. "They stopped, took a deep breath and went in."

No part of the building, he said, was left untouched by the blast, with one wall ripped away and the debris from upper floors strewn below.

"This is something you see in Bosnia and war-torn areas," he said. "It's hard to imagine this happening in the heartland."

He said it could take "a couple of days" to complete the search for survivors as heavy equipment is bought in to remove the debris. He said there were pockets throughout the building where people could be blocked off by heaps of debris. He would not say how many more dead could be inside, but their corpses would not be removed immediately.

Pat Sullivan/Associated Press

The facade of the Alfred P. Murrah Federal Building in Oklahoma City was ripped away yesterday by the explosion of a car bomb, leaving a nine-story hole and victims under the debris.

Photographs by Librado Romero/The New York Times

Families of victims of the explosion gathered yesterday at First Christian Church in Oklahoma City for counseling and help in finding the missing, and they consoled one other.

"It is our hope there are people alive in the building," he said. "We're not going to leave anything untouched."

With so much damage to the day-care center, he said, there may still be some children to be found. Perhaps allowing his hope to overcome realism for a moment, he added: "You know how kids are. Kids survive wherever people can't."

Two registered nurses, Sundra Everly and Janet Gallegly, said they were told their help was not needed anymore.

"They just think all the rest of them are dead," Ms. Gallegly said, walking past street corners where yellow tape cordoned off spots where glass had fallen to the ground.

The shock of the blast was evident along the blocks surrounding the building, where windows to stores and offices were shattered, spraying glass to the street. Workers were busy placing wooden boards over storefronts that had been blown out.

A busload of military police officers arrived early in the evening as access to the area was being limited.

As rescue workers waited their shift in the battered building, three women stood on a nearby street corner, the crumpled building visible in the searchlights, holding hands in prayer, a Bible at their feet.

V. Z. Lawton was signing papers in his eighth-floor office of the Department of Housing and Urban Development when the blast went off. He came closer to death than he at first realized. "My first thought, it was an earthquake," he said.

"I could hear things like shots going off. I think they were the electrical lines snapping," he went on, remembering how he tried to get under his desk. "When I finally did get the courage to get up, I looked north and there was no floor. I was eight feet away from the drop."

The air was thick with gypsum, dust, asbestos, even heating ducts. Through the haze, he heard a woman, a co-worker, crying: "I can't see. Help me, don't leave me."

He managed to crawl to her, and they got down a stairwell. But of the 25 people working in his area, he said tonight, 4 or 5 were still unaccounted for.

"That this could happen in Oklahoma City, Oklahoma," Mr. Lawton said in a cold fury. "It's not Jerusalem. It's not Baghdad. Its not Bolivia. It's Oklahoma.

Dr. Camisa Stewart, an emergency room doctor rushed to the building as soon as she heard the news.

"It was just debris everywhere," she said.

Of the six people she came across in the wreckage, only two were alive. A woman was trapped under so much wreckage, rescuers had to amputate her right leg on the spot.

"We all just hope after hope there may be more survivors," Dr. Stewart said. "Look, there have been earthquakes where there have been survivors found 20 hours later."

Appeals were broadcast for survivors to call a police line to report that they were all right in hopes of getting a grip on the scope of the disaster.

Frantic relatives and friends gathered tonight at the First Christian Church, which had been set up as an emergency victim identification center. But, the Medical Examiners office said it would not be able to make further identification until Thursday, leaving a fretfull night ahead for the relatives.

"Obviously, no amateur did this," Gov. Frank Keating said. "Whoever did this was an animal."

LOOKING BACK

Other Bombings in America

1978-1994 A series of mail bombings injures 10 and kills 2 in 15 separate incidents nationwide. The F.B.I. believes the cases are connected, and that a lone bomber is responsible. The investigation, code-named Unabom, continues.

FEB. 26, 1993 A bomb in a van in a parking garage under the World Trade Center in Manhattan kills 6, injures more than 1,000 and cripples the twin 110-story towers. Four men are convicted and sentenced to 240 years in prison each. A fifth man, accused as the mastermind, was captured in February and awaits trial.

NOV. 7, 1983 A bomb blows a hole in a wall just outside the Senate chamber in Washington. No one is hurt. Two people plead guilty.

MAY 16, 1981 A bomb explodes and kills a man in a bathroom at the Pan Am terminal at Kennedy Airport in New York. A group calling itself the Puerto Rican Armed Resistance claims responsibility. No arrests are made.

JAN. 24, 1975 A bomb goes off at Fraunces Tavern in Manhattan, killing four people. It was one of 49 bombings attributed to the Puerto Rican nationalist group F.A.L.N. between 1974 and 1977.

DEC. 29, 1975 A bomb hidden in a locker explodes at the T.W.A. terminal at LaGuardia Airport in New York, killing 11 people and injuring 75. Palestinian, Puerto Rican and Croatian groups are suspected, but no arrests are made.

JAN. 27, 1972 A bomb wrecks the New York City office of Sol Hurok, an impresario who had been booking Soviet artists. One person is killed; Mr. Hurok and eight others are injured. No arrests are made.

MARCH 6, 1970 Three members of the revolutionary Weather Underground accidentally blow themselves up in their town-house in Greenwich Village while making bombs.

AUG. 24, 1970 A bomb planted by anti-war extremists explodes at the University of Wisconsin in Madison, killing a researcher. Three people are convicted. A fourth suspect has not been found.

1951 TO 1956 George Metesky, a former employee of Consolidated Edison who held a grudge against the company, sets off a series of blasts at New York landmarks, including Grand Central Terminal and Radio City Music Hall. No one is killed.

Source: Associated Press

"All the News That's Fit to Print"

The New York Times

Today, cloudy, showers, more humid. High 75. **Tonight**, diminishing showers, patchy fog. Low 65. **Tomorrow**, showers. High 75. **Yesterday**, high 81, Low 60. Details are on page C10.

VOL.CXLV.... No. 50,204 NEW YORK, WEDNESDAY, OCTOBER 4, 1995 — $1 beyond the greater New York metropolitan area. + 60 CENTS

Welcoming the Pope

TODAY

3 P.M. Arrival at Newark International Airport at restricted terminal. Welcoming ceremony, address and meeting with President Clinton.

Today's Host Diocese
Archdiocese of Newark

5 P.M. Evening prayer at Sacred Heart Cathedral, Newark. Afterward, the Pope spends the night at the residence of the Vatican's representative to the United Nations on East 72d Street in Manhattan.

TRAFFIC Interstate 280 and New Jersey Turnpike closed as Pope and President pass; traffic barred from area around Sacred Heart Cathedral for much of the day. East 72d Street between Fifth and Madison Avenues closed to vehicles and passing pedestrians.

VIEWING ABC, NBC, WWOR, New York 1, FOX and CNN will provide live coverage of the arrival.

TOMORROW
Addresses the United Nations and celebrates Mass and delivers homily at Giants Stadium.

FRIDAY Celebrates Mass and delivers homily at Aqueduct Racetrack in Queens. Leads evening prayer and delivers an address at St. Joseph's Seminary in Yonkers.

SATURDAY
Celebrates Mass and delivers homily in Central Park. Recites rosary and delivers a brief address at St. Patrick's Cathedral.

The Reidys, All 11, Reflect On a Faith Proudly Lived

One Catholic Family Awaiting the Pope

By FELICIA R. LEE

To William J. Reidy, an Irish-Catholic father of nine, Pope John Paul II operates in the world in much the manner Mr. Reidy operates his large household in the affluent Riverdale section of the Bronx: offering guidelines and hoping his flock will believe.

"It's like a father," said Mr. Reidy, who was educated in Catholic schools from kindergarten through college and attends Mass every Sunday. "He talks first, makes a lot of noise, and you have guidelines." As a father, Mr. Reidy knows well that it's not at all certain how the message will be received.

"There is the presumption that the central voice is the universal voice," said the 54-year-old Mr. Reidy, adding, "but I am not sure what Catholic means."

Still, every last Reidy child — from Tim, 20, to Gavin, 3 — is a proud Catholic, and all are looking forward to the Pope's arrival today, each in his or her own way.

Ask Marcia Reidy, their mother, who spends much of her time taking care of her 10-year-old handicapped son, what Catholicism means to her, and she says: "It's an impossible question. It means to be a Christian. It means taking care of the children."

To 12-year-old Michael Reidy, an altar boy at St. Gabriel's in the Bronx, the Pope represents "the closest thing we have to God on earth." But already, his 14-year-old brother, Owen, also an altar boy, isn't so sure. "He's the Pope," he said. "I sort of find that just a name. How closer to God can he be than lay people? It's not like God is going to walk into his living room."

And then there is the Reidy's oldest, Tim. From the church, he learned that homosexual acts are sinful, but at Princeton, where he is a junior, he met openly gay people for the first time and has tried to fit them in with his idea of Catholicism.

Like so many area Catholics, the Reidys will be personally touched by the Pope's visit this week. Owen and his sisters Marcia, 16, and Anne, 17, will attend his Mass on the Great

Continued on Page B6, Column 1

A.M.A. Has Objection to Limits On Fees in G.O.P. Medicare Plan

By ROBERT PEAR

WASHINGTON, Oct. 3 — After months of public silence, the American Medical Association expressed deep concern today about Republican proposals to redesign Medicare, saying that new limits on payments would make the program unattractive to many doctors.

James H. Stacey, a spokesman for the medical association, said today that doctors in the standard Medicare program were facing not just a cut in the growth of Medicare payments, but an absolute reduction in payment for many services under the Republican plan.

"This causes real problems for the A.M.A.," Mr. Stacey said in response to a question. "It would be a major blow to the traditional fee-for-service Medicare program."

The doctors' concerns echo comments from the Clinton Administration and Democrats in Congress, who say the Republicans would cut payments to doctors so severely that many doctors would decide not to treat Medicare patients. As a result, they say, patients would be forced to obtain care through health maintenance organizations and other private health plans, even though the Republicans insist that beneficiaries will always be free to keep traditional Medicare coverage.

Until today, the American Medical Association had generally refrained from criticizing the Republican proposals on Medicare. Indeed, it has praised some of those proposals, including one that would relax antitrust laws for doctors and another that would limit payments to victims of medical malpractice.

By contrast, in the battle over President Clinton's health care plan in 1993 and 1994, the American Medical Association regularly made itself heard. It supported Mr. Clinton's goal of guaranteeing health insurance coverage for all Americans, and it initially supported his proposal that all employers be required to buy such insurance for their employees. But the association later urged Congress to consider alternatives to the "employer mandate," and many doctors said Mr. Clinton's health plan envisioned too big a role for Government.

The specific points raised today concerned the fee schedule Medicare has used since 1992 to pay doctors. Each physician service is assigned a numerical value, and this

Continued on Page A22, Column 1

INSIDE

Giuliani's Plan for Schools

Mayor Giuliani outlined for the first time a specific proposal for City Hall to gain control over the New York City school system. Page B1.

Veto With a Message

President Clinton vetoed a bill to pay Congress's administrative expenses, scolding lawmakers for slow action on other spending bills. Page A22.

Satellite Link to the Internet

AT&T is planning a global satellite network that would let computer users connect to the Internet via small satellite dish antennas. Page D1.

Heat Deaths Scrutinized

For three months, Federal researchers have been trying to figure out why a summer heat wave was so deadly in Chicago. Page A9.

Islands Off China at Peace

The decades-long dispute between China and Taiwan over the islands of Kinmen and Matsu, once a major irritant, has subsided. Page A3.

Jury Clears Simpson in Double Murder; Spellbound Nation Divides on Verdict

Pool photo by Reuters

At the words "not guilty," a tense O. J. Simpson uncoiled and breathed a sigh of relief.

Fast Conclusion for 16-Month Legal Fight

By DAVID MARGOLICK

LOS ANGELES, Oct. 3 — Orenthal James Simpson, a man who overcame the spindly legs left by a childhood case of rickets to run to fame and fortune, surmounted a very different sort of obstacle today, when a jury of 10 women and 2 men cleared him of charges that he murdered his former wife and one of her friends.

The verdict, coming 16 months after Nicole Brown Simpson and Ronald L. Goldman were slashed to death in the front yard of Mrs. Simpson's condominium and after 9 months of what often seemed like interminable testimony, sidebars and high-priced legal bickering, was reached in the end with breathtaking speed. When it was read, much of the nation, President Clinton included, stopped their work. And with the Simpson verdict, as with the Simpson case, the nation was once more divided — largely along racial lines.

In a scene that lent a certain symmetry to the entire Simpson saga, Mr. Simpson returned to the freeways of Los Angeles in a white van, and as fans waved from the street he headed to his home at 360 North Rockingham. While a dozen helicopters flew overhead, and fans festooned the fence with roses and balloons, Mr. Simpson was met by A.C. Cowlings. It was Mr. Cowlings who was in the driver's seat of the white Ford Bronco on June 17, 1994, five days after the killings.

Mr. Simpson pursed his lips, gulped a few times and wore a forced, pained grin as Deirdre Robertson, the law clerk to Judge Lance A. Ito, read the verdict. Mrs. Robertson tripped over "Orenthal," but not over what came next: "not guilty." When she uttered those words, Mr. Simpson's body instantly uncoiled. He then breathed a sigh of relief, and a faint and untroubled smile appeared.

As Mrs. Robertson's recitation continued — "... in violation of Penal Code Section 187A, a felony, upon Nicole Brown Simpson, a human being," Mr. Simpson waved at the panelists and mouthed the words "Thank you." The reading then unfolded again, with the name "Ronald L. Goldman" substituted for Mrs. Simpson. When that was through, Mr. Simpson embraced his chief lawyer, Johnnie L. Cochran Jr., and silently thanked and rethanked the jury again.

"Ladies and gentlemen of the jury, is this your verdict, so say you one, so say you all?" Mrs. Robertson then asked. "Yes," the panel members — nine black, two whites and a Hispanic man — replied matter-of-factly. Critics of the verdict maintained that the jurors were manipulated by a cynical defense team that talked more about the racism of the Los Angeles police than about guilt or innocence; Mr. Simpson's lawyers countered that prosecutors simply had not proven their case.

After they were individually polled, and the victims' families fled the premises, Judge Ito discharged his last duty in the case. "The defendant, having been acquitted of both charges, he is ordered transported to an appropriate sheriff's

Continued on Page A10, Column 1

Racial Split at the End, as at the Start

By MARTIN GOTTLIEB

The seven workers at the Pasqua Coffee Bar in lower Manhattan like to joke around with one another, to trade stories about family and regular customers, and to help one another out in jams.

But until the astonishingly abrupt culmination of the O. J. Simpson murder trial yesterday, they never seemed to get around to discussing what, for much of America, has been a prickly and divisive topic.

Then, as the voice of the court clerk intoning "not guilty" came over the restaurant's radio, Charmon Savage, a kitchen worker who is black, jumped up, punched the air with both fists, and exclaimed, "Yes! Yes! Yes!"

Geraldine Foney, the restaurant manager, who is white, lowered her head with disgust in her eyes. "I thought he should have rotted in hell," she said.

And several other women on the staff, including Debi Diaz, a counterwoman, grumbled in disbelief. "They have to retry him," she said. "It's ridiculous, you know."

The scene at the Pasqua Bar was repeated in thousands of different settings across the country yesterday, with reactions that seemed often to be shaped by race — especially by race — sometimes by the person's sex and frequently by a jaded belief that personal wealth can triumph over just about anything.

At the Texas Bar-B-Q in downtown Dallas, a black-owned restaurant, a couple of black men greeted the verdict with eruptions of elation. Several white customers quietly left shortly afterward.

At Jocks n Jills Sports Bar at the CNN Center in Atlanta, the reaction was much the same as the verdict came over a bank of wall-to-wall television sets — black customers often embraced and cheered; whites sat in stony silence.

Over the Internet, the comments were often starkly racial and polarized.

Since it first began to transfix the country in June 1994, the Simpson murder case has been a combination soap opera, passion play and national Rorschach test laden with sex, celebrity, wealth, violence and, perhaps most sensitively, race.

The reactions to the verdict parallel the dramatic racial divide in every opinion poll taken since the trial began. Separated by a constant gap of about 40 percentage points, many whites seemed to hold fast to the belief that Mr. Simpson was guilty, while blacks believed as adamantly in his innocence. Several polls indicate that behind the response of many blacks is a deep suspicion of the police and the criminal justice system.

A poll taken by CBS News immedi-

Continued on Page A12, Column 1

Carrie Boretz for The New York Times

Ozier Muhammad/The New York Times

Passers-by watched the verdict with shock through the windows of the "Today" show studios at Rockefeller Center, left; at her restaurant in Harlem, Sylvia Woods cheered as she hugged her daughter and a waitress.

The Day (10 Minutes of It) the Nation Stood Still

By N. R. KLEINFIELD

The country stopped.

Between 1 and 1:10 P.M. yesterday, people didn't work. They didn't go to math class. They didn't make phone calls. They didn't use the bathroom. They didn't walk the dog.

They listened to the O. J. Simpson verdict.

Airplane flights had to wait. At Hartsfield International Airport in Atlanta, passengers and airport workers alike were so fixedly watching the televisions at the departure gates that several Delta Air Lines flights due to leave between 1:24 and 1:32 boarded late. When a Delta agent with poor timing tried to start her boarding instructions for a Louisville flight just as the verdicts were being read, a hundred passengers shouted her down.

Finance ceased. At the Barnett Bank branch on Biscayne Boulevard in Miami, tellers stopped counting bills and the lines of impatient customers evaporated as everyone turned tantalized to the television on the wall. Seeing the envelope containing the verdict, a sales manager implored: "Open it. Open it."

It was an eerie moment of national communion, in which the routines and rituals of the country were subsumed by an unquenchable curiosity. Millions of people in millions of places seemed to spend 10 spellbinding minutes yesterday doing exactly the same thing.

The curiosity infected everyone, no matter what larger matters might be under consideration. President Clinton left the Oval Office at two minutes before 1 to catch the verdict in his secretary's office with several of his aides.

The Supreme Court was hearing arguments at the big moment. Immediately after the verdicts were announced, two messengers appeared. One went to the side, where Justice Ruth Bader Ginsburg sat and the other to the side where Justice Stephen G. Breyer sat, and they

Continued on Page A12, Column 3

MORE ON THE TRIAL

A Free Man

O. J. Simpson left court free of criminal charges but not of the side effects of the case, from possible television deals to huge legal bills. Page A10.

The Cryptic Jury

Jurors who made an art form out of being unreadable finally showed a few small signs of emotion, but only for a moment. Page A11.

The Los Angeles Factor

The trial was a national event, but the dynamics of Los Angeles, particularly the Police Department's images, were crucial. Page A13.

Opinions Everywhere

There was rejoicing at a black college in Atlanta, cynicism at a health club in Massachusetts, disbelief at a bar in Michigan. Page A13.

THE OVERVIEW

Jury Exonerates Simpson In Double-Murder Trial

Continued From Page A1

facility and released forthwith," he said.

Within an hour or so, Mr. Simpson, who faced life in prison for the double killings, traded his blue jailhouse jumpsuit and his courtroom woolens for blue jeans, checked out of the cell where he has lived for the last 474 days and began what promises to be a well-remunerated but awkward new life — a life of glamour and highly-compensated interviews, but a life, too, of bodyguards and ostracism from those passionately convinced of his guilt.

After Judge Ito told them to "expect the worst" from swarms of reporters seeking their stories, virtually all of the jurors disappeared without saying anything of substance. "I think we did the right thing — in fact, I know we did," was all that one panelist, Brenda Moran, a 44-year-old black computer technician, said outside her home. As to how jurors were able to render judgment in a few hours, Ms. Moran added simply: "We were there for nine months. We didn't need another nine months to decide."

A quick verdict ends 16 months of legal maneuvering.

The victims' families quickly went into seclusion, though Fred Goldman, the father of one of the victims, called the outcome his second biggest nightmare, exceeded only by the murder of his only son.

Mr. Simpson said nothing to the press after the decision. But in a statement read by his eldest son, Jason, he expressed relief that an "incredible nightmare" was over. He said that his first obligation was to his two youngest children, "who will be raised the way that Nicole and I had always planned." But another task, he said, was to bring to justice whoever killed their mother and Mr. Goldman 16 months ago.

"When things have settled again I want to pursue as my primary goal in life the killer or killers who slaughtered Nicole and Mr. Goldman," he stated. "They are out there somewhere. Whatever it takes to identify them and bring them in I'll provide somehow. I can only hope that some day, despite every prejudicial thing that has been said about me, people will understand and believe that I would not, could not and did not kill anyone."

When the verdict was announced, a strange mix of gasps and sobs arose from the gallery. "Oh, my God!" Mr. Simpson's eldest daughter, Arnelle, exclaimed. Jason Simpson placed his head in his hands and began to weep. Mr. Simpson's elderly mother, Eunice, smiled gently in her wheelchair. At a press conference afterward, she explained her apparent serenity.

"I knew that my son was innocent," she said. "The prayer of the righteous prevaileth much." Her daughter, Shirley Baker, was more demonstrative. "I just feel like standing on top of this table and dancing a jig," she said.

Across the aisle, Nicole Brown Simpson's parents, Louis and Juditha Brown received the verdict stoically, though two of her sisters began crying outside court. But the family of Ron Goldman broke out into paroxysms of grief and anger. Mr. Goldman's sister, Kimberly, looked down to the floor and sobbed convulsively, despite the caresses of her father. Under their breaths, the Goldmans uttered obscenities at Mr. Simpson.

The jury's decision, made after only three hours of deliberations, was one "rush to judgment" to which Mr. Cochran did not object. Defense lawyers exulted in their victory, which they attributed not to racial considerations but to their ability to shatter a tenet of the prosecution's case. No reasonable person, Mr. Cochran said, could possibly have believed that Mr. Simpson killed two people, returned home, changed clothes, cleaned up and hidden his weapon in the time that prosecutors had alloted.

"We said that if we could shatter the prosecution's timeline so that O. J. Simpson couldn't have committed this crime, that there would be a reasonable doubt," Mr. Cochran said at a press conference in Judge Ito's courtroom, where he had strutted and charmed his way around for much of the lat year. "That's even before we ever got to the socks, the glove and Fuhrman or anything." By building much of its case around former Detective Mark Fuhrman, he said, it was the prosecution, and not the defense, that had injected race into the case.

Mr. Cochran began at that news conference much as he closed his closing statement: on a religious note. "I want to thank God," he said, as a chorus of "Yeah!" arose from the Simpson family's side of the table. "He always directs our paths and He's worthy to be praised. We think this verdict bespeaks justice."

At another news conference, District Attorney Gil Garcetti, stunned by a humiliating repudiation of a case based on what he often called a "mountain of evidence," said he was "profoundly disappointed" with the verdict — and angry, too. "The evidence was there," said Mr. Garcetti, whose political future has clearly been clouded by the outcome of the case. "This was not, in our opinion, a close case. Apparently their decision was based on emotion that overcame the reason."

At the same wake-like news conference, a sombre and subdued Deputy District Attorney Marcia Clark saluted colleagues for striving to make sure "that the lives of Ron and Nicole were not thrown away." Ms. Clark also importuned law students working in her office not to lose faith in the system, based on what they had seen here. Her fellow prosecutor, Christopher A. Darden, who as a high school football player had aspired to wear Mr. Simpson's number, then said that he never anticipated having to tell the Goldmans that "he" had been acquitted.

"We came here in search of justice," Mr. Darden said. "You have to be the judges, I expect, as to whether or not any of us found it today. But I'm not bitter and I'm not angry." He then began to thank his colleagues. But as he did so, he broke down and the words abruptly stopped. Waving his hand, he left the lectern and doubled over, with Mrs. Goldman and some lawyers offering solace.

For all of the prosecutors, a whole new ordeal is about to begin: an orgy of post-mortems and second-guessing. Commentators and political opponents now will debate just what it was that turned the tide: the decision to try the case in downtown Los Angeles, where juries are more predominantly black; relying so heavily on a police officer whom they knew to be a racist; asking Mr. Simpson to put on the murderer's gloves, or the overwhelming popularity and wealth of the defendant.

"What this verdict tells you is how fame and money can by the best defense, can take a case of overwhelming incriminating physical evidence and transform it into a case riddled with reasonable doubt," said Peter Arenella, a law professor at the University of California at Los Angeles.

Mr. Arenella acknowledged that prosecutors had suffered a number of self-inflicted wounds. But even had they tried a perfect case, he said, they might not have prevailed given the haste with which even prosecutors said Mr. Simpson did his deeds and the predominantly black jury's antagonism toward the Los Angeles Police Department even before they heard of Mr. Fuhrman.

"A predominantly African-American jury was more susceptible to claims of police incompetence and corruption and more willing to impose a higher burden of proof than normally required for proof beyond a reasonable doubt," he said. "This was not a good day for the American criminal justice system unless one believes that the L.A.P.D. were not only imcompetent but criminal in their investigation of this case."

The aftershocks of the verdicts reverberated along the same racial fault lines as the rest of the Simpson case. Many blacks reacted jubilantly to the exoneration of someone whose heroic status only seemed enhanced by what they saw as the bigotry of police and prosecutors. Many whites, by contrast, were aghast, including some of Mrs. Simpson's friends.

"Nicole was right," said Faye Resnick, who wrote a book about her friendship with Mrs. Simpson. "She said he was going to kill her and get away with it."

In Washington, President Clinton left the Oval Office and walked to his secretary's television to watch the verdict. Afterwards, he scribbled out a statement, urging respect for the decision and "our thoughts and prayers" for the victims' families. His was not the only day in Washington altered by the decision; former Secretary of State James Baker's luncheon speech to the National Press Club had to be canceled.

The verdict will surely have repercussions for the legal system as well, though what those will be is not yet clear. Never again, it seems likely, will a jury be sequestered for so long a time, a brand of gilded incarceration that many people think shortened the deliberations.

The Brown family, who may now have to share custody of their two youngest grandchildren with the man they believe murdered the children's mother, vanished quickly from the courtroom. Any change in custody arrangements would have to be approved by a probate court in Orange County.

The jurors, too, quickly disappeared. As he left, one juror, a former Black Panther whom prosecutors had inexplicably left on the panel, gave Mr. Simpson a clenched fist salute with his left arm. On filing in minutes earlier, the same juror, a 44-year-old black man, winked at Mr. Simpson. That led one defense lawyer, Carl Douglas, to turn to his client and whisper, "We won! We won!"

CNN

Christopher A. Darden and Marcia Clark, prosecutors in the Simpson case, as the verdict was read.

Associated Press

O.J. Simpson, center, arriving at his home yesterday in Los Angeles, after being acquitted of murder charges and released from jail. With him were Al Cowlings, left, a friend, and an unidentified man.

THE DEALS

Publishers Lining Up A New List Of Memoirs

By DEIRDRE CARMODY

Moments after the jury in the O. J. Simpson trial delivered its verdict, telephones rang and faxes beeped at publishing houses and book agents' offices around the country.

At 1:12 P.M. a fax sent out from St. Martin's Press, which is owned by Holtzbrinck, announced plans to publish an instant book, "O. J. A to Z: The Complete Handbook to the Trial of the Century" by Clifford Linedecker. Another book contract was immediately signed by Crown Publishers, a division of Random House. The publisher bought a memoir by Mr. Simpson's first wife, Marguerite Simpson Thomas, for an undisclosed amount.

"Everyone was calling after the verdict to find out about our books," Andrew Martin at Crown Publishers said. "The fact that it was an acquittal makes it an even bigger story and everything O. J. does from now on will no doubt be watched very closely."

At least 30 books already and more are on the way.

To date, at least 30 books on the Simpson trial have been published. Many are paperbacks, instant books and spoofs, but most have made money.

Several major book projects are still outstanding, including one from Jeff Toobin, who has covered the trial for The New Yorker, and which will be published by Random House. The writers Dominick Dunne and Joe McGinniss have been signed up by Crown Publishers.

Even as many participants in the case, particularly some of the defense lawyers, were trying to sell their stories, newspapers and magazines were scrambling to capture the breaking news. Maynard Parker, editor in chief of Newsweek, said that more than a dozen people from his magazine, which is owned by The Washington Post Company, were covering the story yesterday. "Not as many as we would have for the Olympics or the conventions," he said.

Many newspapers rushed out with extra sections. After the verdict, The Los Angeles Times, which is owned by the Times Mirror Company, printed 180,000 additional copies of the morning paper, wrapped with a four-page special section on the trial. The New York Post published 70,000 extra copies of yesterday's paper with five full pages about the verdict.

And in Ocala, Fla., the Star-Banner, a 50,000 circulation paper owned by The New York Times Company,, printed 10,000 copies of a special eight-page section, with most of the staff working on it. Much of the copy was devoted to local reaction.

A headline the width of the page trumpeted, "Not Guilty." But the executive editor, Bruce Gaultney, said, "We were ready to go either way."

THE MAN

A Free Man, Simpson Walks Out of the Courtroom and Into the Lucrative Free Market

By JAMES STERNGOLD

LOS ANGELES, Oct. 3 — O.J. Simpson walked out of the courtroom today a free man for the first time in 15 months, saying he was eager to rebuild his life and move on. But it was clear from the way he was driven home to the deals his lawyers were trying to cut that the past and his notoriety are likely to be constant emotional and financial companions.

In an eerie reprise of his famous flight from the authorities last year, he rode home today in a white police van, tailed once again by reporters in cars and helicopters as bystanders waved from overpasses. Once there he was folded in a tearful embrace by Al Cowlings, the same close friend who had driven the white Ford Bronco in the bizarre televised chase that also ended in Mr. Simpson's driveway.

But it was also clear that the past that has dogged him so mercilessly could also prove a financial bonanza, potentially making Mr. Simpson far wealthier than he was before his former wife and a friend were slain on June 12, 1994.

Even before today, his agents had been discussing deals that could allow Mr. Simpson to earn as much as $50 million trading on his notoriety. The richest deal being discussed would involve an interview on pay-per-view cable television, which could bring Mr. Simpson and his advisers tens of millions of dollars.

Others involved with Mr. Simpson and the trial are likely to earn millions. Robert L. Shapiro, one of his lawyers, has reportedly hired an agent to sell a book, and several publishing executives said a book by Judge Lance A. Ito could bring him more than $5 million.

People involved in television, book publishing and films said that while it seemed certain Mr. Simpson would profit to some degree — even after paying as much as $10 million for his defense — they cautioned that many media companies were still trying to calculate how much appeal a man accused of being a killer, even one who had been acquitted, might have to a popular audience.

Advertising companies, for instance, said they doubted any major national company would risk being associated with Mr. Simpson, in part because of lingering suspicions over the killings and in part because of disclosures that he had beaten his wife. Before his arrest, Mr. Simpson had a long career as a spokesman for Hertz Corporation.

"He's poison," said Jerry Della Femina, chairman of Jerry & Ketchum Inc. in New York, referring to Mr. Simpson's prospects as a pitchman.

But others said Mr. Simpson's name recognition was so great after the media frenzy surrounding his trial that some companies would gladly try to cash in on it.

"After the brouhaha of the case dies down, I think that O.J. Simpson will find himself in a very lucrative position," said Richard Kirshenbaum, co-chairman of Kirshenbaum Bond & Partners, an advertising agency in New York. "There are many untraditional companies who will be ready to jump on the bandwagon."

Indeed, an official with one of the companies involved in selling Mr. Simpson expressed deep personal anger today over the verdict because of her view that he murdered his former wife. But then she proceeded to discuss details of one of his ventures, praising the bankability of his name.

Added an executive of a media company, "It is hard to think about these things, but it is even harder not to consider them, because of the kind of money that would be involved."

A potential for far more wealth than before his arrest.

Mr. Simpson's football, acting and promotional careers had made him a very wealthy man prior to the killing of his former wife and his imprisonment last year; his net worth during his divorce in 1992 was estimated at about $11 million and he earned close to $1 million a year at that time, much of it from his work for Hertz. The 6,000-square-foot home that Mr. Simpson bought in February, 1977, for $650,000 is now worth about $4 million, according to real estate agents.

It has been speculated that his defense expenses, which have not been disclosed, could eat up much of that fortune.

By far the most lucrative deal that his lawyers are now discussing is the pay-per-view interview, which would be broadcast on a cable television network. CNN was approached several weeks ago by Mr. Simpson's lawyers about an interview conducted by Larry King, the talk show host, according to people with knowledge of the discussions.

These people said no hard figures were discussed, and the proposal was eventually rejected by Ted Turner, the head of the network, and other top executives because of the feeling it was improper to pay for a news interview.

But the people said that such an event might bring in from $50 million to $100 million, depending on how much Mr. Simpson was willing to disclose, and that Mr. Simpson and his advisers might receive about 80 percent of that sum.

The New York Observer reported earlier that Mr. Simpson's representatives had cut a deal for such an interview, but it gave no figures and did not say with what broadcaster the agreement had been made. Officials at Palmer & Dodge, the firm reportedly representing Mr. Simpson in that deal, did not return calls today seeking comment.

This spring, Mr. Simpson's agents set up a phone line people could call for a charge and hear a message in which Mr. Simpson declared from jail, "Hi, this is O.J. Thanks for using the juice line. I'd like to thank all of my fans for your support." That venture was expected to bring in many hundreds of thousands of dollars and demonstrated to some Mr. Simpson's earning potential.

Mr. Simpson has already earned more than $1 million from his book, "I Want to Tell You," published by Little, Brown & Company. A total of 650,000 copies have been printed and 580,000 shipped so far.

A publishing executive said that a follow-up book has been discussed, with a proposed advance of about $5 million, but that no agreements had been signed.

Mr. Simpson has put together a special limited edition of his current book that will be sold through a "tele-auction" by Anmar Inc., a marketing company here. The 3,000 numbered copies are bound in blue fake leather and are contained in a similarly bound box. The books contain a leaf signed by Mr. Simpson. They will also have a certificate signed by one of his lawyers, Robert Kardashian, verifying their authenticity.

The bidding for the books begins at $250 and it is expected that offers could run as high as $5,000. Mr. Simpson is believed likely to take in several hundred thousand dollars from this sale.

Apart from the financial side, Mr. Simpson's travails could prove a liability in one critical aspect of his life, custody of the two children from his marriage with Nicole Brown Simpson. Mrs. Simpson's parents were granted legal custody of the children after Mr. Simpson was charged with murder, and the two continue to live with their grandparents in Orange County, just south of Los Angeles.

Mr. Simpson had been paying $10,000 a month to Mrs. Simpson in child support after their divorce in 1992, but after her killing and his imprisonment he unilaterally cut that to $5,000, people close to the families said.

Now he is expected to seek to gain custody. California law tends to prefer placing children with their parents, but some lawyers said that may be difficult in this instance, if Mrs. Simpson's parents choose to fight. Scott A. Altman, a professor of family law at the University of Southern California Law Center, said enough evidence of domestic violence was disclosed at the trial to permit a strong challenge.

"I think it would be very unlikely for a judge to give custody to O.J. after the preliminary hearing, given the question of murder and domestic violence," he said.

In addition, the parents of Ronald Goldman, the man slain with Mrs. Simpson, have filed a civil suit against Mr. Simpson claiming he killed their son. Their chances of winning were not helped by Mr. Simpson's acquittal, but if they do succeed they could exact a large financial penalty, putting at least one dent in his still sizable earnings potential.

"All the News That's Fit to Print"

The New York Times

Late Edition
New York: **Today,** sunny, not as windy, very cool. High 50. **Tonight,** clouds. Low 39. **Tomorrow,** becoming sunny, milder. High 59. **Yesterday,** high 55, low 38. Details, page 51.

VOL.CXLV . No. 50,236 — NEW YORK, SUNDAY, NOVEMBER 5, 1995 — $2.50

RABIN SLAIN AFTER PEACE RALLY IN TEL AVIV; ISRAELI GUNMAN HELD; SAYS HE ACTED ALONE

Associated Press

THE SPEECH Prime Minister Yitzhak Rabin addressing a peace rally yesterday in Tel Aviv before he was shot to death.

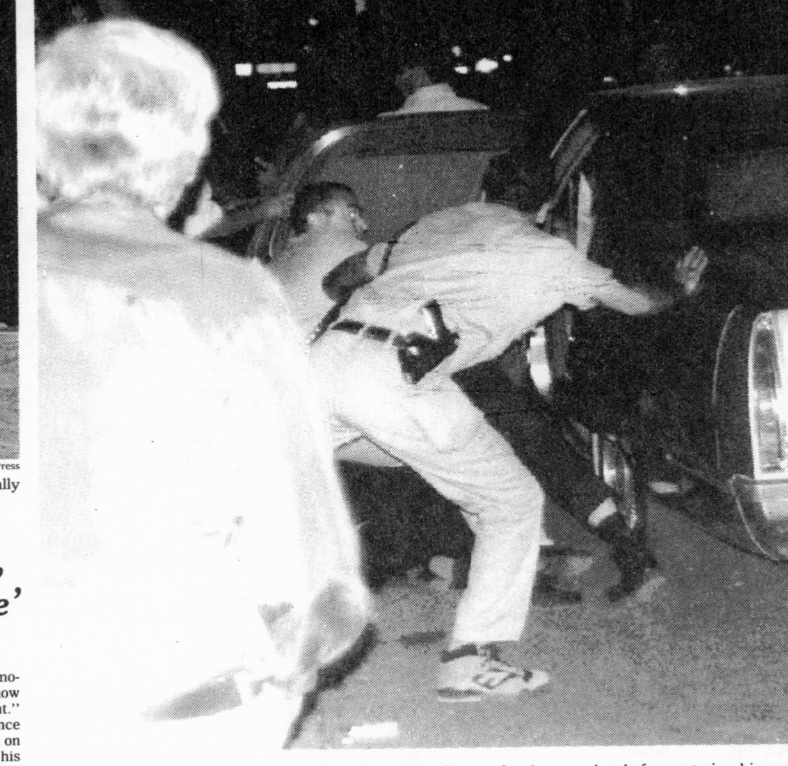

Reuters

THE ATTACK Mr. Rabin lying at the feet of security officers after he was shot before entering his car.

PERES TAKES OVER

Stunned Nation Asks if Talks With the P.L.O Are in Jeopardy

By SERGE SCHMEMANN

JERUSALEM, Nov. 4 — Prime Minister Yitzhak Rabin, who led Israel to victory in 1967 and began the march toward peace a generation later, was shot dead by a lone assassin this evening as he was leaving a vast rally in Tel Aviv.

Mr. Rabin, 73, was struck down by one or two bullets as he was entering his car. Police immediately seized a 27-year-old Israeli law student, Yigal Amir, who had been active in support of Israeli settlers but who told the police tonight that he had acted alone.

The police said Mr. Amir had also told them that he had tried twice before to attack the Prime Minister.

It was the first assassination of a prime minister in the 47-year history of the state of Israel, and it was certain to have extensive repercussions on Israeli politics and the future of the Arab-Israeli peace.

Mr. Rabin was to lead his Labor party in elections scheduled for November next year, and without him the prospects for a Labor victory, and of a continuation of his policies, were thrown into question.

In the immediate aftermath, Foreign Minister Shimon Peres, Mr. Rabin's partner in the peace negotiations, automatically became Acting Prime Minister. It was widely expected that he would be formally confirmed as Mr. Rabin's successor.

Mr. Rabin, who rose to national prominence as commander of the victorious Israeli army in the 1967 Six-Day War, became the second Middle Eastern leader, after President Anwar el-Sadat of Egypt, to be killed by extremists from his own side for seeking an Arab-Israeli peace. Mr. Sadat, the first Arab to make peace with Israel, was assassinated in 1984.

Mr. Rabin and his Labor Government have come under fierce attack from right-wing groups over the peace with the Palestinians, especially since the agreement transferring authority in the West Bank to the Palestine Liberation Organization was reached in September. Mr. Rabin has been heckled at many of his appearances in recent weeks and his security has been tight.

A gruff, chain-smoking career military man, Mr. Rabin led Israel both in its greatest military triumph and in one of its most dramatic bids for peace.

Shortly before his death, Mr. Rabin, obviously buoyed by the huge turnout of more than 100,000 supporters of the peace process, told the rally, "I have always believed that the majority of the people want peace and are ready to take a chance for peace." [Excerpts, page 16A.]

He then joined other participants in singing the "Song of Peace," a popular paean. Unfamiliar with the words, the prime minister followed from a text he tucked into his pocket.

Hours after the shooting, Mr. Peres said the blood-soaked sheet of music was found in his pocket and

Continued on Page 16A, Column 1

A Shaken Clinton Mourns Rabin, 'Martyr for His Nation's Peace'

By DAVID E. ROSENBAUM

WASHINGTON, Nov. 4 — President Clinton, who plans to leave on Sunday for the funeral of Prime Minister Yitzhak Rabin of Israel, went to the Rose Garden of the White House tonight and, his voice cracking, called Mr. Rabin "a martyr for his nation's peace."

"Peace must be and peace will be Prime Minister Rabin's lasting legacy," Mr. Clinton said.

The President and other officials here, though shocked and saddened by Mr. Rabin's assassination, said tonight that they expected the peace effort in the Middle East to continue uninterrupted.

Secretary of State Warren Christopher issued a statement in which he said, "History will record Prime Minister Rabin as one of the towering figures of this century."

As a political matter, Mr. Rabin was a crucial ally of Mr. Clinton's. The President's success in 1993 in bringing together Mr. Rabin and Yasir Arafat, the leader of the Palestine Liberation Organization, is the most important foreign policy success of the Clinton Presidency.

"Yitzhak Rabin was my partner and my friend," the President said. "I admired him, and I loved him very much."

To Israel's people, he said, "Just as America has stood by you in moments of crisis and triumph, so now we all stand by you in this moment."

The President was in his residence watching a college football game on television when Anthony Lake, his national security adviser, called about 3:20 P.M. to tell of the shooting, the White House said.

Other top officials rushed to the White House situation room to receive information from the United States Ambassador to Israel, Martin Indyk, who had gone to the hospital in Tel Aviv where Mr. Rabin died.

Around 4 P.M., Mr. Lake went to the President's office to tell him that Mr. Rabin had died.

Mr. Clinton then called Mr. Rabin's widow, Leah, and the new Acting Prime Minister, Shimon Peres, to express his sympathy.

Michael D. McCurry, the President's press secretary, said Mr. Rabin and Mr. Peres had said they had never seen Mr. Rabin happier than he was tonight, right after his speech at the peace rally in Tel Aviv and just before he was shot.

Mr. McCurry said Mr. Clinton had invited leaders of Congress of both parties to join him at the funeral.

The President issued a proclama-

Continued on Page 16B, Column 1

Suspect Says He Tried to Kill Rabin Before

Arrested Law Student Often Joined Protests Against Government

Associated Press

THE SUSPECT An Israeli police officer grabbed Yigal Amir, the suspected assassin, around the neck after the shooting.

By JOEL GREENBERG

JERUSALEM, Nov. 4 — Yigal Amir, the 27-year-old law student who was arrested for the assassination of Prime Minister Yitzhak Rabin tonight, was described by acquaintances as a militant critic of the Government who regularly joined protests against Mr. Rabin's policies.

He told interrogators that he had carried out the killing on his own.

Under questioning by the police, Mr. Amir said he had been planning the assassination for a long time and had intended to kill Mr. Rabin on two previous occasions but was thwarted by tight security measures.

After his self-appointed mission tonight, Mr. Amir, a short, dark-haired man dressed in a blue shirt and light-colored pants, was pinned to a wall by police officers and rushed to a waiting police car.

"I have no regrets," he was quoted as telling investigators. "I acted alone and on orders from God."

According to some accounts, Mr. Amir had links to a small militant anti-Arab group known as Eyal that is virulently opposed to the Government's accords with the Palestine Liberation Organization.

A leader of the group, Avishai Raviv, acknowledged tonight that he knew Mr. Amir. But he denied that the assassin belonged to Eyal or that the group had anything to do with the shooting.

After the shooting, Israeli reporters received beeper messages signed Ain, a Hebrew acronymn for the Israeli Avenging Organization, a previously unknown group. The group claimed responsibility for the killing, though it was not immediately known if it had any connection with Mr. Amir.

The assassination was the second incident of extreme violence by right-wing Jewish militants since the 1993 signing of the Israeli-Palestinian accord.

In February 1994, Baruch Goldstein, an American follower of the anti-Arab group Kach, massacred 29 Muslims at prayer at the Shrine of

Continued on Page 16A, Column 4

Teachers' Union Reaches Accord That Protects Jobs

By STEVEN LEE MYERS

Mayor Rudolph W. Giuliani and the leaders of New York City's teachers union announced a tentative agreement yesterday on a contract that would increase wages and benefits by 13 percent over five years and offer an unusual written commitment protecting union members from layoffs through 1998.

But the agreement included no significant concessions from the union's rank and file, even though the Mayor and his aides had vowed to achieve them to pay for raises. And by that measure, it fell short of the goal Mr. Giuliani set for himself: to scale back generous benefits and force employees to work harder for what they already earn.

The contract, subject to ratification by the union's 90,000 members and the Board of Education, provides no wage increases in the first two years, giving the city time, the Mayor said, to find ways to pay for raises of 3 to 4 percent in each succeeding year.

By the end of the pact in September of the year 2000, the top salary for teachers with 25 years experience would rise to $70,000, from $60,000 now. In the final year, the city would also contribute $75 per worker to the union's welfare fund. In all, the salary of a starting teacher would increase to $31,900, from $28,700.

"This contract is a historic breakthrough for the school system and for labor relations in the City of New York," the Mayor said. "It provides for much more educational value and at the same time is fiscally sound."

For Mr. Giuliani, the Republican Mayor nearing the midpoint of his term, the contract with the United Federation of Teachers was the first in the first round of bargaining conducted entirely by his administration. And it sets, he said, the general parameters for contracts with all of the city's 83 municipal unions.

Although the Mayor entered office

Continued on Page 46, Column 4

NEWS SUMMARY — 2

TODAY'S SECTIONS

Education Life
Under the Glare of the Presidency

* *In New York City and the metropolitan region. († Elsewhere, auto pages are in section 3.)*
§ *In most parts of New York City.*
¶ *In Long Island, Westchester, Connecticut and central and northern New Jersey.*

THE DEATH OF RABIN

Associated Press

A Soldier-Statesman
Yitzhak Rabin was a soldier turned peacemaker, a man who tried to end the bloodshed that had plagued his country. Obituary, page 16.

Israeli Politics Clouded
The assassination threw a question mark over Israeli politics just a year before elections that could decide the future of the Arab-Israeli peace. News analysis, page 16A.

Horror and Condolences
Leaders of American Jewish groups were horrified by the killing. The head of the Palestine Liberation Organization offered condolences, while some other Arabs celebrated the assassination. Page 16B.

ASSASSINATION IN ISRAEL: A Life of Risks

Yitzhak Rabin, 73, a Soldier Turned Prime Minister and Peacemaker

By MARILYN BERGER

Prime Minister Yitzhak Rabin of Israel, who was shot dead yesterday at age 73, was a soldier turned statesman who led his country into uncharted territory to make peace with the Palestinians and put an end to the wars, bloodshed and terrorism that had plagued his country since its founding.

It was General Rabin, the Commander in Chief of Israel's armed forces in 1967, who had led the lightning strike that captured broad swaths of Arab territories. Twenty-six years later, on Sept. 13, 1993, it was Prime Minister Rabin who reluctantly extended his hand to Yasir Arafat, leader of the Palestinian Liberation Organization, to put a symbolic seal of approval on an accord that would lead to the return of much of that territory and to Palestinian self-rule on the Israeli-occupied West Bank and the Gaza Strip.

In an extraordinary ceremony on the South Lawn of the White House, one that few had ever expected to see, Mr. Rabin came face-to-face with Mr. Arafat — the man who had been reviled for decades by Israelis as the mastermind behind one attack after another on their people, the man with whom the following year he and his Foreign Minister, Shimon Peres, would share the Nobel Peace Prize.

"The time for peace has come," Mr. Rabin declared. "We, the soldiers who have returned from battles stained with blood, we who have seen our relatives and friends killed before our eyes, . . . we who have come from a land where parents bury their children, we who have fought against you, the Palestinians — we say today in a loud and clear voice: Enough of blood and tears. Enough."

Speaking as much to his own people as to the astonished world that was watching, Mr. Rabin explained in mournful tones how painful and how necessary it was for Israel to take this step.

"It's not so easy — either for myself as a soldier in Israel's war nor for the people of Israel. . . . It is certainly not easy for the families of the victims of the war's violence, terror, whose pain will never heal, for the many thousands who defended our lives and their own and have even sacrificed their lives for our own. For them this ceremony has come too late."

But he said Israel was not seeking revenge. It was seeking peace.

The tragedy was that some of Mr. Rabin's own people were seeking revenge. As Mr. Rabin came closer to achieving his goal of peace, a wide schism opened within the Israeli populace. Much of the bitterness of those opposed to making peace with Israel's historic enemies was directed at Mr. Rabin, and he became the soldier who paid the ultimate price to make peace.

He had been unrelenting in his drive to institutionalize that peace. Only a month ago, Mr. Rabin took part in another White House ceremony to mark the beginning of another withdrawal from the West Bank. This time the handshakes with Mr. Arafat were less reluctant and the peace process was well established.

A New Generation Brings a New Vision

Mr. Rabin was the only one of Israel's eight Prime Ministers to have been born in the land of Palestine, a Sabra who had not experienced the long history of attacks on European Jewry and the horror of the Holocaust. With his election, Israel turned over its leadership from the fathers to the sons and he appealed for a new vision. On taking office in 1992 for his second term as Prime Minister, Mr. Rabin said it was time for Israel to jettison its siege mentality.

"No longer is it true that the whole world is against us," he said. He accepted his election as a mandate to make peace. One of his first steps was to put a freeze on all new construction in the occupied territories.

For their part, the Palestinians were ready to deal. With the end of the cold war and the collapse of the Soviet Union, the P.L.O. was deprived of diplomatic, financial and military support. At the same time, the P.L.O. was reeling from the loss of contributions from wealthy Arab states angered by Mr. Arafat's support of Iraq during the 1991 Persian Gulf war.

To achieve agreement with the Palestinians, Mr. Rabin followed the lead of Foreign Minister Peres, a Labor Party colleague and longtime political rival. They had fought for decades over the leadership of the party and the country, but they joined forces in the search for peace. To the opposition that branded Mr. Rabin a "traitor," the Prime Minister replied that peace must be made with enemies, not with friends.

Mr. Rabin had been at the center of the major events in his nation's history for five decades. In 1948, he fought in the siege of Jerusalem during Israel's war of independence. In 1967, as Chief of Staff of the Israeli Army for the three years before the June war, he brought to fighting strength the formidable force that rolled over three Arab armies in six days. Later, as Ambassador to the United States he helped assure Israel a steady supply of sophisticated weapons. In his first term as Prime Minister he negotiated the crucial and lasting disengagement of Israeli and Egyptian forces in the Sinai, which paved the way for the Camp David accords. And as Defense Minister, in 1986, he presided over the withdrawal of Israeli forces from Lebanon although he continued to respond with force to terrorist attacks.

Never Charismatic, But a Man to Be Trusted

As a boy growing up in Palestine, Mr. Rabin wanted to be an agronomist, and attended the Kadoorie Agricultural School in Galilee where he won the High Commissioner's Gold Medal as the best student in Palestine. But like many patriotic young people of his time he gave up his childhood ambition and joined the Palmach, the elite strike force of the Haganah underground

Camera Press

Yitzhak Rabin
1922-1995

Jewish army, saw action in World War II, and developed into a brilliant military tactician.

He also developed into a politician. Israelis trusted him for his single-minded devotion to the good of the country and he was repeatedly asked to accept high government positions. But he was the antithesis of the convivial party man. Taciturn, introspective, controlled, intensely private, he had almost no close advisers and reached decisions independently, often announcing them in an authoritarian manner that alienated the party leadership. He spoke in a deep monotone that made his public personality seem colorless, and even in private he was almost devoid of humor.

Mr. Rabin was born in Jerusalem on March 1, 1922. His father, Nehemiah, who came from a poor family in Ukraine, had escaped from Czarist Russia and gone to Palestine by way of Chicago and St. Louis. In Palestine, he became a trade union organizer in the labor movement of David Ben-Gurion. His mother, Rosa Cohen, born to a well-to-do family in Gomel, Russia, was active in politics and became the dominant influence on the young Rabin. Theirs was a home where young Yitzhak was taught that public service was a duty and where, he remembered, "It was a disgrace to speak about money."

He was 7 years old when Arabs began attacking Jewish settlements. Later, during the 1936 Arab riots and general strike, he was at the Khadouri school where he was trained in the use of arms by Yigal Allon, who was later to become his commander and his mentor. Five years later, during World War II, Moshe Dayan, then a young commander in the Haganah, invited Mr. Rabin to join the Palmach. As part of the British invasion of Greater Syria, which was in the hands of the Axis powers, Mr. Rabin was sent across the border. The youngest in his unit, it was his job to climb up telephone poles to cut the wires so the collaborationist Vichy French forces could not call up reinforcements.

In June 1945, just after the end of the war in Europe, Mr. Rabin commanded a daring raid to liberate about 200 illegal Jewish immigrants held by the British in a camp at Athlit, on the Mediterranean just south of Haifa. The exploit was said to be the prototype for a similar raid in the novel "Exodus," and Mr. Rabin the prototype for Ari Ben Canaan, the hero, played in the movie version by Paul Newman. But the shy Mr. Rabin always insisted that he was not the fictional Ari Ben Canaan.

Mr. Rabin was arrested by the British and imprisoned for six months in a camp in Gaza. Soon after he was released the British turned the problem of Palestine over to the United Nations, which, in 1947, voted for partition into a Jewish and an Arab state.

The Arabs attacked, and as hostilities intensified between the Jews and the Arabs, Mr. Allon, then the commander of the Palmach, appointed Mr. Rabin his deputy. During the 1948 Israeli war of independence, Mr. Rabin commanded the Har-El Brigade, a makeshift unit that failed to take Jerusalem for Israel but kept open the vital supply lines between Jerusalem and the sea. Later, with the rank of colonel, Mr. Rabin served on the southern front against Egyptian forces.

When Mr. Rabin disclosed in his 1979 memoir his role in forcing 50,000 Arab civilians to leave their homes at gunpoint during the war of independence, there was a furor in Israel, where officials had long denied that Arab civilians were pushed out of their lands.

In the middle of the war, on Aug. 23, 1948, Mr. Rabin married Leah Schlossberg, who had joined the Palmach and served in his battalion. They had two children, a son, Yuval and a daughter, Dalia, and three grandchildren. They all survive him.

Mr. Rabin's first venture into diplomacy came when he was sent to the island of Rhodes as part of the delegation to the Israeli-Egyptian armistice talks in 1949.

In 1953, having finally committed himself to a career in the army, Mr. Rabin went to England to study at the British Staff College at Camberley. Back home he went on to hold a series of high posts in the Israeli Army, mainly involving manpower training, and was named chief of staff in 1964.

He became Israel's top expert on military matters. Even as he rose through the ranks, he became known as the man who who knew more than the generals. Eventually, he became a general himself, a lieutenant-general.

The Army that fought the six-day war in 1967 was essentially Mr. Rabin's army. Shab'tai Teveth, professor of history at Tel Aviv University, said, "It was the army he trained, planned, built and armed in his three years as chief of staff." But, he added, "There his glory ends."

His "glory" ended when, on the eve of the fighting, Mr. Rabin suffered a nervous collapse.

The Terrible Burden Of Leadership in War

In his memoir, Mr. Rabin wrote of going to see Mr. Ben-Gurion, then in retirement. He went in search of encouragement but instead got a dressing-down. Mr. Ben-Gurion, he wrote, scolded him for mobilizing the reserves after President Gamal Abdel Nasser of Egypt closed the Straits of Tiran. "You have led the state into a grave situation," Mr. Ben-Gurion told him. "We must not go to war. We are isolated. You bear the responsibility."

Mr. Ben-Gurion's words reverberated in his ears as he worked himself into a state of physical and mental exhaustion. He recovered in time to carry out his duties during the war, but some observers thought he was not functioning normally and was only being "propped up" so that the troops and the people would not lose confidence in their leader.

Whatever the source of Mr. Rabin's difficulties, the results achieved by his army were astonishingly clear. At the end of the war Hebrew University conferred on him an honorary doctorate. In a modest, occasionally poetic speech, Mr. Rabin said he accepted the honor not for himself but as the representative of an army of civilians who had never been trained for conquest, of battle-hardened paratroopers who had leaned on the stones of the Wailing Wall and wept at the capture of the Old City of Jerusalem. He spoke about his army, but perhaps even more about himself.

"Our Sabra youth, and most certainly our soldiers," he said, "do not tend to be sentimental and they shrink from any public show of feeling. But the strain of battle, the anxiety which preceded it, and the sense of salvation and of direct confrontation with Jewish history itself cracked the shell of hardness and shyness and released wellsprings of emotion and stirrings of the spirit."

In 1968, Mr. Rabin was appointed Ambassador to the United States, where he became known as an effective advocate for Israel and a master at procuring sophisticated American weapons. In his five years as Ambassador he developed a close relationship with Henry A. Kissinger, President Richard M. Nixon's national security adviser and later his Secretary of State. Mr. Kissinger called on him for intelligence about troop movements in the Middle East and even consulted him on Vietnam.

Shortly after he returned to Israel in 1973, Mr. Rabin entered national politics for the first time. Then, on Yom Kippur, while the country was in the middle of an election campaign, Syria and Egypt launched a surprise attack. The country's leaders — Prime Minister Golda Meir and her Minister of Defense, Mr. Dayan — were held responsible for the country's lack of preparedness in that October war, but the Labor Party won enough votes to form a new Government. Mr. Rabin won in his first attempt at election and was given the post of Minister of Labor.

But within a month of forming her Cabinet, Mrs. Meir resigned and the party turned to Mr. Rabin, who had been out of power at the time of the war and was therefore untainted by the heavy casualties.

Diplomatic Departures, And a Final Legacy

In 1974, Mr. Rabin became Israel's fifth Prime Minister and, at 52, its youngest. "The time has come," he said, "for the sons of the founders of the state to take over their role."

Mr. Rabin became the first Israeli Prime Minister to make an official visit to West Germany. He also said he met secretly with King Hussein of Jordan six times in an unsuccessful effort to open peace negotiations with him. His Government weathered the Arab oil embargo and the skyrocketing prices of oil, and negotiated a second Sinai disengagement with the Egyptians, but only after incurring the wrath of Mr. Kissinger when it turned down one of his early proposals. The Secretary of State returned to Washington in March 1975 and persuaded President Ford to undertake a "reassessment" of American policy toward Israel, a move seen as a threat to withhold arms shipments. Mr. Rabin had been ready to negotiate what he called "a piece of land for a piece of peace," but he believed the plan Mr. Kissinger brought back during his shuttle trips between Cairo and Jerusalem demanded maximum Israeli territorial concessions in exchange for minimal Egyptian political concessions.

Mr. Schiff, of the newspaper Haaretz, said that Mr. Rabin had been "absolutely right to say 'no' to the Americans," and in doing so to win in the long run. "It caused a rift between the Egyptians and the Syrians. This was as important a cornerstone on the road to Camp David as the Yom Kippur War."

Five months later he accepted what he called a "risk for peace" and signed an Egyptian-Israeli disengagement agreement.

During his term as Prime Minister, Mr. Rabin faced down terrorists who hijacked an Air France plane en route from Tel Aviv to Paris. At first, he was seen as weak because he waited several days before dispatching an assault group to Entebbe, Uganda, where the plane and almost 100 Israeli citizens were being held hostage. When he finally approved a military operation and, when the daring raid succeeded, he was hailed as a hero.

But in 1977, his image was damaged when an Israeli newspaper disclosed that he and his wife had violated currency laws by maintaining bank accounts in the United States after he had returned home. At first he lied about how much money was in the accounts and, finally, he was forced to step down, opening the way for the victory of Menachem Begin and the Likud party. Mr. Rabin accepted responsibility for the bank accounts, which had been used mainly by his wife.

The Rabins paid a fine imposed by an Israeli court, but six months after Mr. Rabin resigned, the currency regulations were rescinded.

Mr. Rabin bounced back from the scandal not because he was a skilled politician, but because he was not a politician at all. He returned to government as Minister of Defense in a Labor-Likud national unity coalition that presided over the Israeli pullout from Lebanon. His was the policy of the "iron fist," promising swift retaliation for guerrilla raids against Israelis withdrawing from southern Lebanon.

Sitting in his office at the Defense Ministry one evening in 1987, he looked back at his life with satisfaction tinged with disappointment. His disappointment, he said, was in what he saw as a loss of national spirit, the failure of the creators of the state to pass on their sense of commitment. Of his most satisfying moment he had no doubt — the liberation and unification of Jerusalem in 1967.

But there was more, a legacy delivered that day in 1993 when he led the country to come to terms with the Palestinians, "to live together on the same soil in the same land."

He acknowledged the risk. But in going to Washington to endorse the agreement, he said, "We have come to try to put an end to the hostilities so that our children, our children's children, will no longer experience the painful cost of war."

1948 Rabin, then a lieutenant colonel in the Israeli Army, with his wife, Leah, during the first Arab-Israeli war.

Associated Press

1967 As Chief of Staff of the Israeli Army during the Six-Day War, Rabin was welcomed after his troops captured East Jerusalem.

Associated Press

1974 Rabin took his seat as Prime Minister after succeeding Golda Meir.

Associated Press

1993 Rabin and Yasir Arafat shook hands on the White House lawn after signing their historic peace agreement.

"All the News That's Fit to Print"

The New York Times

Late Edition

New York: **Today,** some sun, windy, a flurry. High 43. Tonight, part cloudy, chilly. Low 33. **Tomorrow,** mainly cloudy. High 46. **Yesterday,** high 54, low 43. Details are on page B16.

VOL.CXLV . . . No. 50,253 NEW YORK, WEDNESDAY, NOVEMBER 22, 1995 · $1 beyond the greater New York metropolitan area. · 60 CENTS

ACCORD REACHED TO END THE WAR IN BOSNIA; CLINTON PLEDGES U.S. TROOPS TO KEEP PEACE

Reuters

SERBIA Slobodan Milosevic President · **BOSNIA-HERZEGOVINA** Alija Izetbegovic President · **CROATIA** Franjo Tudjman President · **UNITED STATES** Warren Christopher Secretary of State

All Sides Make Concessions To End 4 Years of Conflict

By ELAINE SCIOLINO

DAYTON, Ohio, Nov. 21 — The presidents of three rival Balkan states agreed today to make peace in Bosnia, ending nearly four years of terror and ethnic bloodletting that have left a quarter of a million people dead in the worst war in Europe since World War II.

The leaders — Alija Izetbegovic of Bosnia, Franjo Tudjman of Croatia and Slobodan Milosevic of Serbia — initialed the peace agreement and 11 annexes in a hastily-arranged ceremony in the same conference room at Wright-Patterson Air Force Base where they opened their talks 21 days ago.

The agreement is to take effect when it is formally signed by the parties in Paris in mid-December.

Unlike previous peace accords that have collapsed, this one was reinforced by widespread fatigue of a war that has uprooted two million people from their homes and appalled the world with scenes of harrowing atrocities, and by the promise of enforcement by 60,000 NATO troops. President Clinton, hailing the agreement in a White House Rose Garden ceremony, reiterated his pledge that the NATO force would include 20,000 Americans.

"The agreement is a victory for all those who believe in a multi-ethnic democracy in Bosnia," said Secretary of State Warren Christopher, who spent several exhausting days brokering the final details of the accord. "It offers tangible hope that there will be no more days of dodging bullets, no more winters of freshly dug graves, no more years of isolation from the outside world."

But underneath the self-congratulation of today's ceremony was a grim awareness that the basic questions the parties failed to settle before the war remain: Can Bosnia, with its mutually suspicious populations of Muslims, Serbs and Croats, survive as a single state? What degree of self-government should be given to the Serb minority within its borders? And does Mr. Milosevic have the power to force the Serbs of Bosnia to do what he says?

Today the Bosnian Serb representatives who served in a delegation headed by Mr. Milosevic did not show up for the ceremony to initial the various annexes that affect the Serbian part of Bosnia.

The Bosnian Serbs were particularly upset by the military annexes in the agreement, which they charged essentially made NATO an occupying force, American and European negotiators said.

Under the agreement, NATO will have the right to remove or relocate specific forces and weapons from any location in the country whenever it determines that they constitute a threat to its troops.

The Bosnian Serbs were even

Continued on Page A10, Column 1

Study Finds Doctors Refuse Patients' Requests on Death

By SUSAN GILBERT

After 25 years of public outcry over the right to die with dignity, doctors are still ignoring patients' last wishes, according to a new study of terminally ill patients.

The study, reported in today's issue of The Journal of the American Medical Association, has found that doctors often misunderstand or ignore the patients' requests, with the result that large numbers of people still die alone, in pain and tethered to mechanical ventilators in intensive care units. Twenty-five years since the living will movement began, the study's authors say they have discovered that the wills, which are supposed to give terminally ill patients legal safeguards against unwanted medical treatment, offer virtually no protection.

The study also found that increasing communication between doctors and patients did not help.

"People think advance directives are solving the problem," said Dr. William Knaus, one of the researchers who directed the study. "We have very good information that they aren't, that nothing has changed — the amount of pain at the end of life, the number of people dying alone attached to machines."

The $28 million study, financed by the Robert Wood Johnson Foundation, took place at six medical centers around the country. It was divided into two parts, each one lasting two years and involving similar groups of terminally ill patients.

In the first phase, the researchers gathered base-line information, including the percentage of patients who did not want aggressive medical treatment like cardiopulmonary resuscitation and mechanical ventilation, the percentage of doctors who knew their patients' wishes, how often aggressive treatment was used and how much pain patients were in before they died.

The researchers found large gaps between what the patients wanted and what they got. Thirty-one percent of patients said they did not want cardiopulmonary resuscitation, but 80 percent of the doctors misunderstood or ignored their patients' wishes.

Forty-nine percent of the patients who wanted to avoid cardiopulmonary resuscitation by having their doctors write do-not-resuscitate orders did not get their wish.

The patients who did had to wait a long time for the doctors' orders. Depending on their medical specialty, doctors took an average of 22 to 73 days to write the orders after the patients requested them, and 46 percent of the orders were written within two days of the patient's death. Half the patients spent eight or more days in what the researchers de-

Continued on Page C7, Column 1

HIGHLIGHTS

TERRITORY Bosnia would maintain its current borders, but be divided into two entities — a Bosnian-Croat federation and a Bosnian Serb republic. A central government, with a parliament and presidency, would remain in a united Sarajevo.

WAR CRIMINALS Would not be allowed to hold office, but no requirement to arrest them was specified.

TROOPS Forces would be withdrawn to agreed positions and an international force sent in to keep the peace. NATO has outlined a plan for a 60,000 member force — one-third of it American — to act as peacekeeper.

REFUGEES Would have the right to return home; human rights would be monitored by an independent commission.

SLOVENIA · CROATIA · VOJVODINA · KRAJINA REGION · Bihac · SERBIA · Tuzla · BOSNIA AND HERZEGOVINA · Srebrenica · Sarajevo · Zepa · Gorazde · YUGOSLAVIA · MONTENEGRO · KOSOVO · MACEDONIA

ONE NATION, DIVIDED · Bosnian-Croat federation · Serb republic

The New York Times

An Imperfect Peace

By ROGER COHEN

News Analysis

DAYTON, Ohio, Nov. 21 — A cold Balkan peace was concluded today, one built over the graves of numberless victims by the very leaders who unleashed the Yugoslav wars, but still a peace that almost certainly offers the last hope for the stubborn vestiges of civilized life in Bosnia.

The American-brokered peace is necessarily imperfect and so could contain the seeds of future conflict. It divides Bosnia along ethnic lines, thus offering some endorsement to the racist politics of the Serbs who fought for secession. It offers no cast-iron guarantees that war criminals will be brought to justice. It will provide scant solace to the myriad bereaved and homeless of a long and savage conflict.

The possibility is real that the de facto division of Bosnia agreed upon today could prove permanent despite the establishment of central government institutions and the vows of the Bosnian, Croatian and Serbian presidents to work for the contrary.

For this peace remains to be defined. On paper, it is a bewildering, apparently unworkable jigsaw setting up two distinct self-governing units — a Muslim-Croat federation and a Serb republic — overseen by a rotating collective Bosnian presidency, a federal parliament, a constitutional court and other central institutions.

The Bosnian state laid out today has two armies — that of the Serbs and that of the federation. It has three administrations — that of the Serb republic, that of the federation, and that of the central Government. And it has an independent history made up entirely of a war whose legacy is one of deep mistrust and lingering anger.

Out of such confusion, it seems, a civil society could now grow; equally, a new and perhaps yet more savage conflict could erupt.

Even today, in an ominous sign, the Bosnian Serbs showed deep unhappiness with parts of the agreement, especially the establishment of a unified Sarajevo, and refused to initial all the documents.

For the Muslim-led Bosnian Government, it was another agonizing day. President Alija Izetbegovic showed no joy at the accord, shaking the hand of American officials and the Serbian and Croatian presidents in a distinctly perfunctory way. But

Continued on Page A11, Column 1

China Charges Leading Dissident With Trying to Overthrow Regime

By PATRICK E. TYLER

BEIJING, Nov. 21 — China formally charged the country's best-known dissident, Wei Jingsheng, today with trying to "overthrow the Chinese Government," a step that almost certainly will lead to conviction and a second, lengthy prison sentence for the 44-year-old democracy advocate.

Mr. Wei had been held incommunicado at an undisclosed police "guest house" without charge since April 1994, when he was seized by seven carloads of plainclothes policemen while driving into the Chinese capital from the nearby city of Tianjin.

At the time he was on parole after serving 14½ years of a 15-year prison sentence on charges of counter-revolutionary incitement and passing state secrets to foreigners for his activities during the 1978-79 Democracy Wall movement in Beijing.

Mr. Wei, an electrician turned political essayist, gained wide attention for his biting criticisms of the Communist Party leadership, particularly the Government's failure to pursue democratic reforms promised by Deng Xiaoping and other senior leaders during the years after the death of Mao in 1976.

Today's decision by the party leadership to bring criminal charges against Mr. Wei caught many of his supporters and family members by surprise and indicated a determined effort by the Government to prevent him from returning to Chinese society, where he has been a magnet for pro-democracy forces.

In one sense, the Government acted to ease the contradiction between its often-stated position that China seeks to become a nation ruled by law, and Mr. Wei's continued secret detention without charges in blatant violation of the country's own published criminal procedures.

The action against Mr. Wei went forward despite recent appeals by President Clinton and Chancellor Helmut Kohl of Germany. Mr. Kohl visited here this month seeking the release of China's political prisoners, especially Mr. Wei, who has now spent more than 16 years in detention, nearly half that time in solitary confinement.

Earlier this year, Mr. Wei's younger sister, Wei Shanshan, wrote a letter to Mr. Deng pointing out the illegality of his detention.

"No formal charges have been brought against him, nor is he being

Continued on Page A7, Column 1

Education Chief in Trenton Asks Legislature to Set School Budgets

By NEIL MacFARQUHAR

TRENTON, Nov. 21 — New Jersey officials, under court order to equalize spending between rich and poor school districts, today proposed that the State Legislature, rather than local voters, set the basic school budget for all districts.

The New Jersey Commissioner of Education, Leo F. Klagholz, presented the plan — the latest development in a 25-year legal battle — without actual dollar figures. The Commissioner said it would take weeks to determine whether following the recommendation would mean an increase in the state budget for education and what effect it might have on local property taxes.

The 77-page report released unexpectedly today was developed from suggestions put forward in 70 public hearings and meetings over the last year, Dr. Klagholz said. It now goes to the State Legislature for consideration.

Once combined with curriculum standards, which the department said it would submit by January, the government will determine what the state will pay for in every classroom, defining for the first time the minimum level of education that the state guarantees.

New Jersey is one of a dozen states that are under court orders to close the disparity in spending among school districts. Spending for students in New Jersey ranges from a low of $5,900 per pupil to a high of $11,500 per pupil in districts with kindergarten through 12th grade students. In districts with just kindergarten through eighth grade, spending runs from $4,800 to $15,900.

New Jersey joins a small group of states seeking to address such court orders to establish equity between wealthy and poor districts through the quality of the education delivered rather than the dollars spent.

Presently, each district determines its own curriculum, applying to the state for relief if it needs more money. New Jersey spends $12 billion a year on education — more per pupil than any other state — but Dr. Klagholz said the spending was not reflected in overall student achievement.

Under the new plan, the state would both establish the curriculum and outline school spending levels. It would determine everything from the number of teachers needed by an

Continued on Page B5, Column 1

Back to Square One At Columbus Circle

After more than a decade of neighborhood battles, environmental studies and court fights over the fate of the New York Coliseum, New York State and New York City have decided to turn the clock back to 1984 and look for a new buyer for the valuable Columbus Circle site.

Requests for new development proposals are to be issued before the end of the year.

Article, page B1.

INSIDE

The Dow Surges Past 5,000

The extraordinary bull market in stocks shows no sign of letting up, with the Dow Jones industrial average surging past 5,000 for the first time. Market Place, page D1.

Yesterday: 5,023.55 · Oct. '87 crash · '90-'91 Gulf conflict · 4,000 · 3,500 · 3,000 · 2,500 · 2,000 · 1,500 · 1,000 · Source: Datastream · 1987 · 1988 · 1989 · 1990 · 1991 · 1992 · 1993 · 1994 · 1995

New Cabinet for Israel

Acting Prime Minister Shimon Peres of Israel announced his Cabinet, in which he will direct the Defense Ministry as troops leave parts of the West Bank. Page A3.

Crowded Day in the Skies

Airports across the nation will be busy today, but it will not be the busiest day of the year, a distinction that goes to the Sunday after Thanksgiving. Page A12.

NEWS SUMMARY A2

Clinton's Next Task Will Be to Sell Plan To the U.S. Public

By ALISON MITCHELL

WASHINGTON, Nov. 21 — Even as he triumphantly announced the Balkan accord, President Clinton today began the difficult task of convincing a skeptical public and a hostile Congress to support sending 20,000 American troops to enforce the peace in Bosnia.

"We are at a decisive moment," the President said in a mid-morning appearance in the White House Rose Garden. "The parties have chosen peace. America must choose peace as well."

Clearly aiming his remarks at the American public, Mr. Clinton spoke of the "senseless slaughter of so many innocent people that our fellow citizens had to watch night after night for four long years on their television screens."

White House advisers were keenly aware that Mr. Clinton will have to make a major personal investment in the effort to convince Americans that their country's leadership responsibilities require that their soldiers be sent to a chaotic region to patrol a peace that could yet revert to war.

With a NATO plan to enforce a Balkans peace expected to be submitted to the President within a week — and large-scale deployment of troops possibly only weeks away — Mr. Clinton and his foreign policy team were preparing to mount a quick and extensive campaign, including a televised presidential ad-

Continued on Page A11, Column 1

BALKAN ACCORD: From Ohio, a Flowering of Hope

THE OVERVIEW

Accord Reached to End the War in Bosnia; Clinton Pledges G.I.'s to Keep the Peace

Continued From Page A1

more enraged by the map of the capital, Sarajevo, which turned Serb-held neighborhoods over to the Bosnian Government. One American negotiator said that when the Bosnian Serbs saw the map — which Mr. Milosevic refused to show them until today — they went "berserk."

"The agreement that has been reached does not meet even the minimum of our interests," said Momcilo Krajisnik, president of the self-styled Bosnian Serb parliament.

The Bosnian Serb pParliament scuttled a peace settlement in the spring of 1993, after the same three presidents signed the so-called Vance-Owen peace plan that divided Bosnia into 10 provinces along to ethnic lines.

But in the antiseptic, fiuorescent lit conference room in the Hope Conference Center, the mood was palpably upbeat, as the Balkan presidents took turns at the podium to explain — in English — why making peace was important to them.

For Mr. Milosevic, who longs to be embraced again by the West, the war in Bosnia was a merely "civil war" that "should be left to the past." What was important now, he said, was not only peace and understanding but also economic and cultural development. He portrayed himself as a conciliator, saying, "the solutions achieved here include painful concessions by all sides, however; without such concessions it would be impossible to succeed."

For Mr. Izetbegovic, who is determined to preserve Bosnia as a multiethnic democracy, the importance of the agreement is that it guarantees the sovereignty and territorial integrity of his country, he said, as well as the "development of an open society based on tolerance and freedom."

In announcing the agreement earlier in the day, President Clinton said, "The people of Bosnia finally have a chance to turn from the horrors of war to the promise of peace." He added, "Something stirred among the leaders themselves and they decided that they should not let this moment pass."

But it also means that he now will have to make good on his pledge both to the allies and to the Balkan nations to send American troops to Bosnia as part of the NATO-led force.

The agreement calls for the preservation of Bosnia as a single state. But it also divides Bosnia into two almost-equal parts, with one side controlled by a Muslim-Croat federation and the other by a Serb republic.

The plan also envisages a central government with an elected president and parliament, the return or compensation of refugees, the separation of Bosnian and Croatian troops on one side and Serbian troops on the other, and the reconstruction of the country. But it is not at all clear how a government made up of enemies who only recently have put down their arms will function.

The capital, Sarajevo, remains united — a key demand of the Bosnian Government — but some eastern suburbs, including the Bosnian Serbs' headquarters in Pale — are to remain under Serb control.

The agreement also leaves unresolved the fate of Radovan Karadzic and Gen. Ratko Mladic, the two Bosnian Serb leaders who have been indicted by an international war crimes tribunal.

Although the agreement prohibits any indicted war criminal from running for office, it does not meet the initial demand of the Bosnian Government that Mr. Milosevic turn the two men over to the United Nations-sponsored tribunal.

The agreement is to be followed by actions by the United Nations Security Council. One would suspend trade sanctions that have crippled the Serb economy in the last three-and-a-half years. Secondary sanctions, like a ban on Serbia's membership in the United Nations and access to World Bank loans, would remain until the Serbs showed compliance with the peace accord.

Another Security Council resolution would gradually lift the arms embargo on the six republics of the former Yugoslavia, beginning 90 days after the agreement is signed. The embargo is believed to have handicapped the Bosnian Government during the course of the war against the better-armed Serbs.

But while the embargo is to end, the rivals agreed today to temporarily forswear arms purchases.

Each side is to retain its own army. Throughout the talks the Serbs refused pleas by the negotiators to give up their heavy weapons, and the Bosnian Government was unable to get a side agreement with the United States pledging immediate American help in arming and training its army.

In a news conference after the ceremony, European negotiators, who will be responsible for organizing a plan to reconstruct Bosnia, stressed that success depends on how the agreement is put into effect.

"These agreements are not self-implementing," said Pauline Neville-Jones, the head of the British delegation. Even Richard C. Holbrooke, the chief American negotiator, warned that on every page of the agreement "lie challenges to both sides to set aside their differences," which he called "raw and open wounds." He added: "On paper we have peace. To make it work is our next and our greatest challenge."

Until this morning, there was no deal and the rollercoaster, marathon talks seemed doomed.

At first, the sticking point seemed to be the width of a 30-mile-long passage linking Serbia with the Serb-held territory in northwestern Bosnia, around Banja Luka. Last night the United States thought a deal was near, after the Serbs agreed to the Bosnian demand that the corridor be no wider than three miles.

At 10 P.M. Mr. Christopher went to the Bosnian delegation with a last, take-it-or-leave-it offer.

"If you can agree we have a final agreement and we can initial a peace," he told them. "If you don't, these proceedings are going to have to be suspended."

He said he needed their answer at 11:30 and went to bed. By that time, the Bosnians had no answer. Mr. Christopher called Mr. Clinton, told him he wanted to suspend the talks and went to bed.

About midnight the Bosnians issued a new demand — control over the town of Brcko in northern Bosnia, which is currently under Serbian control and is in the middle of the corridor linking the Serbs' Bosnian territories. By morning there was no accord. The defining moment came after all three presidents agreed that the issue of Brcko could be resolved by a still-undetermined method of arbitration over the next year.

The first tangible sign that the deal was complete was a gesture as the ceremony opened. On the first day, Mr. Christoher did not shake the hand of Mr. Milosevic, who is widely blamed for starting the war. Today he did — twice.

It was a personal achievement for both Mr. Christopher and Mr. Holbrooke, and the result of an extroardinarily complicated negotiating process in which the United States brought together the three Balkan presidents and their delegations and negotiators from Britain, France, Germany and Russia.

It also represented the evolution of Mr. Christopher's own thinking. Even before he was confirmed as Secretary of State, he was skeptical that diplomacy could bring peace to Bosnia. But he later came to the conclusion that the only way for the parties to make peace was if the United States seized control of the negotiations from the Europeans and pressured all the parties.

A CLOSER LOOK

The Dayton Accord: A Peace Agreement for the Balkans

The settlement is a compromise among conflicting aims. For the Muslim-dominated Government of Bosnia, it affirms the legal integrity of the country and restores the unity of the capital, Sarajevo. The Serbs get — if not the separate state they want — a semi-autonomous republic. The Croats secure their national borders and will be able to nurture ties to Croats in Bosnia.

An elaborate governmental structure is spelled out, involving a central elected presidency and parliament presiding over two entities — a Bosnian-Croat federation, and a Serb republic. Some issues, such as the fate of Bosnian Serb leaders who have been indicted as war criminals, are not fully addressed. The agreement does not take effect until it is formally signed, expected in Paris in early December.

The Final Disputes

Serbian Corridor
The Serbs wanted a wider corridor around the town of Brcko, linking the Serb-held areas of eastern Bosnia with the territory around Banja Luka. This will be decided by arbitration.

Sarajevo
The Serbs wanted some parts of the city to be part of the new Serb republic; the Bosnian Government wanted and won a unified, open city, the symbolic heart of the unified nation it seeks.

Path to Gorazde
The Bosnian Government regains control of a swath of land linking Sarajevo with the enclave of Gorazde, strengthening its presence in the east.

War criminals
People indicted by the international tribunal cannot hold elected office. The Governments pledge to cooperate with the tribunal, but are not explicitly required to arrest indicted people, who include top Bosnian Serb leaders.

Serb republic
Banja Luka
Brcko
Tuzla
Srebrenica
Zepa
Sarajevo
Bosnian-Croat federation
Gorazde
BOSNIA AND HERZEGOVINA
Proposed new boundary between regions.

The Next Steps

The United Nations will lift the arms embargo against all states of the former Yugoslavia. Trade sanctions against Serbia will be suspended, but limits remain on its participation in international organizations.

The peace agreement will be formally signed in Paris in December, after which a NATO-led force, including some 20,000 American troops, will enter Bosnia to police the settlement.

EXISTING AREAS OF CONTROL
Bosnian Government and Croatian
Serbian

The Broad Outline

TERRITORY The Bosnian-Croat Federation will control roughly 51 percent of the land, the Serb republic 49 percent. Some areas of current control are to be given up by each side.

CONSTITUTION A constitution creates a central government with a group presidency, a two-house legislature, a court and a central bank. The two sub-entities, the Bosnian-Croat Federation and the Serb republic, will each have their own presidents and legislatures. Officials at all levels are to be chosen in internationally supervised elections. How much power the central government will have, in practice is a major question.

TROOPS Parties must withdraw forces behind agreed cease-fire lines within 30 days. All heavy weapons and forces will withdraw to barracks areas within 120 days. Arms imports to all sides are temporarily halted and negotiations will begin on limits for heavy weapons and aircraft.

PEACEKEEPERS A peace-keeping force will be under NATO command, headed by an American general. The force will monitor the cease-fire and control the airspace. It will be "an active, robust force capable not only of implementing a peace agreement but also of defending itself vigorously."

REFUGEES Displaced people will have the legal right to reclaim their homes or receive compensation. A commission will investigate human rights violations.

The New York Times

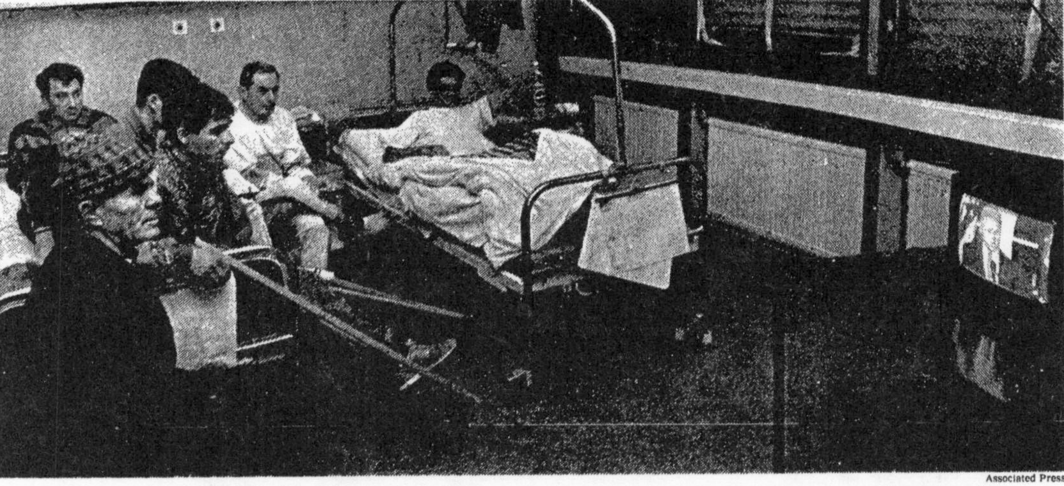
Associated Press

Sarajevo residents closely followed the peace talks. Hospital patients, refugees from an area under Serb control, watched President Clinton.

IN BELGRADE

For Milosevic, a Chance at a New Lease on Political Life

By CHRIS HEDGES

BELGRADE, Serbia, Nov. 21 — President Slobodan Milosevic of Serbia, who presides over an economy in a shambles, a state that has been internationally branded as a pariah and a populace exhausted by war, will return to Belgrade carrying the one thing he hopes will keep him in power: a signed peace agreement.

"The war is finally over in Bosnia-Herzegovina," Mr. Milosevic said in remarks broadcast from Dayton, Ohio. "It is now time for all to turn to peace, reconstruction and economic recovery."

Mr. Milosevic told Serbs that the Balkan peace agreement meant that sanctions would be lifted against the truncated Yugoslavia, opening the road to "economic development."

The Security Council is expected to consider suspending sanctions against Serbia and Montenegro and lifting the arms embargo on all former Yugoslav republics.

And some of the President's fiercest critics acknowledged his accomplishment and said they feared its success would strengthen Mr. Milosevic's grip on power.

"Milosevic's dream of restoring Communism is not over," said Vuk Draskovic, an opposition leader. "Now that this deal is signed the biggest problem we face will be how to stop Milosevic from consolidating his totalitarian state."

Despite his triumphant tone, the last four years have been devastating for Mr. Milosevic and the Serbs. He was largely responsible for the war that led to the dissolution of Yugoslavia, the death of more than a quarter of a million people and the economic sanctions. And he has serious problems with a recalcitrant Bosnian Serb leadership, on whose behalf he negotiated, and who he must now cajole into abiding by the agreement.

Defending the deal, Mr. Milosevic said talks were long, but had given the Serbs a fair share of territory. And he said the division was better for the Serbs than a previous peace plan drawn up by the major powers.

"Everyone has now forgotten that Milosevic started the war," said Dusan Jaksic, a 30-year-old engineer. "What is important is that he ended it."

The 54-year-old President could call for new elections as early as next spring, diplomats say. He faces no real opposition, and the lifting of the sanctions will prove a potent weapon in his hands.

But the decision by Mr. Milosevic to push the Bosnian Serbs into this agreement is also a gamble, especially if they defy him, as they have in the past. Mr. Milosevic could also face growing unrest from workers who called a series of strikes around Belgrade last week, if the moribund economy does not begin to improve.

The President's toughest battle when he returns will be with the Bosnian Serb leadership. Government-run news outlets in Belgrade said today that the Bosnian Serb leader, Radovan Karadzic, and the military commander, Gen. Ratko Mladic, had agreed to resign in exchange for assurances that they would not be handed over to an international war-crimes tribunal.

The President intends to force the two men out of power soon after returning to Belgrade, Western diplomats said. But the two Bosnian Serb leaders said they would remain in their posts. And the Bosnian Serbs, many of whom dislike the agreement, say they are in no mood to follow dictates from Belgrade.

"What they should do with Milosevic is hang him from the nearest tree," said Mico Kovacevic, a soldier in the Bosnian Serb army, who is in Belgrade visiting friends. "There will never be peace here. There is too much hatred on both sides."

IN SARAJEVO

In Weary Bosnian Capital, Joy, and Tears for the Dead

By KIT R. ROANE

SARAJEVO, Bosnia and Herzegovina, Nov. 21 — For 20 days, Sarajevo had been waiting for this news. And while the terms of the agreement signed today did not satisfy everyone, it at least promised an end to the years of war.

Among the burnt-out cars and shell-holes of the besieged Bosnian capital, residents wept and talked of this respite from destruction and death.

"This means a rebirth," said Almasa Mulic, 67, as she sat in her battered apartment on the front line. "I have been crying ever since I found out. I am too happy for words. I wish everyone good luck and a long life."

Mrs. Mulic sat in her kitchen, inches from the balcony where her husband was killed by a shell in 1993, and only 20 yards from the Bosnian Serb gunners who took him from her. But she expressed little bitterness.

"I am ready to live with the Serbs again," she said. "Why shouldn't I?"

"We all just want peace and to be allowed out of the house to fetch our groceries without worrying about being shot," she added. "This has to end."

Most Sarajevans felt the same yearning for a conclusion to the fighting. In the front-line neighborhoods, shots could still be heard even in the days leading up to the agreement, and children still played behind walls.

Many city residents in the town had taken on a trance-like state, tuning in their radios to the hourly news and turning on their televisions to catch a glimpse of progress in the talks. As deadlines passed for the negotiators in Ohio, people here awaited the outcome with trepidation.

Not everyone could believe the news once it came. After so many scuttled negotiations and broken agreements, it was hard to accept the possibility of an end to the war that has consumed more than 250,000 Bosnian lives.

"Thank God," said Vahidin Pilav, a 19-year-old soldier, of the news as he walked his girlfriend home through the snow of another Sarajevo winter. "This means the war is over and I can live again. No more being afraid of a bullet finding me or freezing on the front line."

He looked at his sweetheart, Nihada Sabanovic, and squeezed her hand. "And no more being afraid that I won't come back," he added.

At the Piccadilly Cafe, a bar patronized mostly by taxi drivers and wounded soldiers, patrons complained that the agreement had not addressed the underlying causes of the conflict. The war would come again, and only NATO could prevent that, they said.

"But when NATO leaves, may the Lord help us," said Suad Jabucar, a 29-year-old soldier, as he sat drinking beer with his comrades.

"That's right," said Mohamed Niksic, 44. "The evil that befell Yugoslavia will resurrect itself again. The Serbs will attempt another genocide, because that is what is in their blood. Hopefully, I will be dead by then."

Sarajevo residents also complained that places where Muslims had been massacred and a suburb around Sarajevo would apparently remain in Serbian hands. They also were not pleased that the issue of a land corridor linking Serbian-held land in eastern and western Bosnia had yet to be resolved.

"It's not fair," said Dragana Zametica, 38, a dental technician, as she worked in her second job as a cook in a neighborhood cafe. "The Serbs have been given everything they wanted and in the end we will remain divided. I don't know why so many people had to die for an agreement like this."

Mrs. Zametica, a Serb married to a Muslim, added: "We fought to live together. That is what we were taught for 40 years. But that time is over and the dream has passed."

"All the News That's Fit to Print"

The New York Times

Late Edition
New York: **Today,** sunny, less windy, colder. High 45. Tonight, clear, chilly. Low 36. **Tomorrow,** sunny to partly cloudy, breezy. High 42. **Yesterday,** high 69, low 48. Details on page 46.

VOL. CXLVI . . No. 50,712
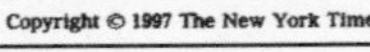

NEW YORK, SUNDAY, FEBRUARY 23, 1997

$3 beyond the greater New York metropolitan area. $2.50

DEMOCRATS SHOW SOME FLEXIBILITY ON CAPITAL GAINS

ROOM FOR COMPROMISE

Farmers and Business Owners Have Pushed for Changes — Problems Still Loom

By RICHARD W. STEVENSON

WASHINGTON, Feb. 22 — After years of deriding any cuts in the capital-gains tax as a handout to country club Republicans, Democrats in Congress have softened their opposition and, in some cases, have come to support a reduction in the tax, increasing the likelihood of a compromise this year on the often bitter partisan dispute.

Democrats said the change had been driven to some degree by the stunning rise in the stock market, which has left many small, middle-class investors sitting on big gains and interested in minimizing their tax bills if they sell shares.

But the political dynamic of the issue has been most changed by increasing complaints about the tax from farmers and the owners of small businesses, powerful constituencies. Those voters have received a far more sympathetic hearing from Democratic lawmakers than have the Wall Street securities firms and other traditional proponents of reducing the tax on profits from the sale of stocks, bonds, real estate and other property and investments.

"This issue has moved from the country clubs and the boardrooms to the barrooms of middle America," said Senator John B. Breaux of Louisiana, a leading Democratic proponent of capital-gains cuts, whose view would be disputed by his more liberal colleagues.

Important differences still hinder a compromise. Most Republicans want to slash the top capital-gains rate of 28 percent on all profits, arguing that such a reduction would unleash new investment and create jobs and economic growth. Democrats tend to favor narrower and far less costly proposals aimed specifically at small-business owners, farmers and homeowners.

Still, because a compromise will be essential to efforts by the Clinton Administration and the Republican-controlled Congress to reach agreement on balancing the Federal budget, members of both parties said that enough common ground existed on

Continued on Page 26, Column 1

A People's Liberation Army guard carries a glass coffin in a rehearsal for the cremation of Deng Xiaoping, whose funeral is scheduled for Tuesday.

Reuters

SCIENTIST REPORTS FIRST CLONING EVER OF ADULT MAMMAL

FEAT IS SHOCK TO EXPERTS

In Creating Lamb, Researcher Sees Benefits for Medicine, but Others Fear Abuse

By GINA KOLATA

In a feat that may be the one bit of genetic engineering that has been anticipated and dreaded more than any other, researchers in Britain are reporting that they have cloned an adult mammal for the first time.

The group, led by Dr. Ian Wilmut, a 52-year-old embryologist at the Roslin Institute in Edinburgh, created a lamb using DNA from an adult sheep. The achievement shocked leading researchers who had said it could not be done. The researchers had assumed that the DNA of adult cells would not act like the DNA formed when a sperm's genes first mingle with those of an egg.

In theory, researchers said, such techniques could be used to take a cell from an adult human and use the DNA to create a genetically identical human — a time-delayed twin. That prospect raises the thorniest of ethical and philosophical questions.

Dr. Wilmut's experiment was simple, in retrospect. He took a mammary cell from an adult sheep and prepared its DNA so it would be accepted by an egg from another sheep. He then removed the egg's own DNA, replacing it with the DNA from the adult sheep by fusing the egg with the adult cell. The fused cells, carrying the adult DNA, began to grow and divide, just like a perfectly normal fertilized egg, to form an embryo.

Dr. Wilmut implanted the embryo into another ewe; in July, the ewe gave birth to a lamb, named Dolly. Though Dolly seems perfectly normal, DNA tests show that she is the clone of the adult ewe that supplied her DNA.

"What this will mostly be used for is to produce more health care products," Dr. Wilmut told the Press Association of Britain early today, the Reuters news agency reported.

"It will enable us to study genetic diseases for which there is presently no cure and track down the mechanisms that are involved. The next step is to use the cells in culture in the lab and target genetic changes into that culture."

Simple though it may be, the experiment, to be reported this coming Thursday in the British journal Nature, has startled biologists and ethicists. Dr. Wilmut said in a telephone interview last week that he planned to breed Dolly next fall to determine whether she was fertile. Dr. Wilmut said he was interested in the technique primarily as a tool in animal husbandry, but other scientists said it had opened doors to the unsettling prospect that humans could be cloned as well.

Dr. Lee Silver, a biology professor at Princeton University, said last

Continued on Page 22, Column 3

China's Rulers Face Key Test: Power of Army

By PATRICK E. TYLER

BEIJING, Feb. 22 — On the seventh day after he took up the title of Commander in Chief of China's armed forces in November 1989, President Jiang Zemin went to the far western province of Xinjiang to inspect a frigid frontier post. He demanded to know why the soldiers were sleeping with only one blanket. "Aren't they cold at night?" he asked.

There in the barracks, like George Washington looking after the men of Valley Forge, he admonished the officers, "Our cadres must care for each and every soldier and be concerned with their welfare."

Every few months over the last five years, China's state-run propaganda apparatus has added a new page to the legend of Mr. Jiang's "paternal care" for China's soldiers. Once, when 1,000 sailors lined up for review on the deck of a ship in the scorching sun, Mr. Jiang was reported to have seen the sweat running down their faces and "quickened his steps" so they could stand down. And in 1995, he climbed 77 stairs — someone actually counted them — to meet sentries on the Russian border, even though it was raining and his clothes were soaked through.

For more than 47 years after the Communists came to power in 1949, China had been governed by men who had been military and political commanders. But unlike Mao and Deng Xiaoping before him, Mr. Jiang has no military background, he did not fight in the Communist revolution and he has never worn the uniform of the People's Liberation

Continued on Page 10, Column 1

Drug Ties Taint 2 Mexican Governors

By SAM DILLON and CRAIG PYES

SHADOW ON THE BORDER

A special report.

The Governor of the Mexican state that borders Arizona is collaborating with one of the world's most powerful drug traffickers, creating a haven for smugglers who transport vast quantities of narcotics into the United States, according to American officials and intelligence.

Officials said this conclusion was based on a wealth of evidence, including "highly reliable" informers' reports that the Governor, Manlio Fabio Beltrones Rivera, took part in meetings in which leading traffickers paid high-level politicians who were protecting their operations.

According to the accounts, Raúl Salinas de Gortari, the brother of the former President, received suitcases full of cash and was responsible for distributing the money to those attending.

Present and former officials said the evidence of Mr. Beltrones's role was so detailed and compelling that the United States had included his name on a confidential document provided to the transition team of President Ernesto Zedillo listing more than a dozen officials suspected of corruption. Another Mexican Governor, Jorge Carrillo Olea, was also included on the American blacklist because of reported entanglements with major drug dealers.

While Mr. Zedillo did not name either man to a federal post, both continue to wield considerable power in their states and nationally through their prominence in Mexico's governing party. Both seem to enjoy a tacit immunity from concerted criminal investigation in Mexico and the United States.

Although Mexican governors are popularly elected, presidents have the power in practice to force their removal.

Mr. Beltrones, in an interview, denied any links to drug traffickers and disputed American law enforcement officials' assertions that Amado Carrillo Fuentes, one of Mexico's most wanted drug kingpins, was operating with impunity in his state, Sonora. In addition, Mr. Carrillo Olea, who presides over Morelos, the state just south of Mexico City, disputed charges that he had cooperated with traffickers.

In a four-month investigation that draws on intelligence documents and interviews in the United States and Mexico, The New York Times examined how both Governments handled the allegations against the two Governors.

The result is a picture of official frustration on both sides of the border and, several officials asserted, a case study of why traffickers' political patrons often go unpunished.

Despite the recent disclosures about official corruption, American officials say the Clinton Administration is planning to certify later this month that Mexico is cooperating with anti-drug efforts.

Senior Administration officials say that decision reflects a belief that Mexico's leadership is doing all it can against staggering odds.

But many law enforcement officials say it also shows that the Clinton Administration considers the narcotics fight less important than fostering commerce with this country's third-largest trading partner. Thus, these officials assert, intelligence reports suggesting corruption among Mexican politicians like Mr. Beltrones receive little attention in Washington. Similarly, agents working in Mexico feel they will get little support if they scrutinize the activities of powerful Mexican officials.

President Clinton praised Mexico last week for arresting the head of its anti-narcotics program on drug charges, citing the act as evidence that corruption, even "at the highest levels," was not being tolerated.

Privately, however, American officials acknowledge that Mexican traffickers' political patrons are seldom the targets of law enforcement offi-

Continued on Page 8, Column 1

Albert Shanker, 68, Combative Leader Of Teachers, Dies

By JOSEPH BERGER

Albert Shanker, who rose from being a substitute mathematics teacher to become a tough, canny labor leader who in the 1960's transformed New York City's United Federation of Teachers into one of the nation's most powerful unions, died yesterday at Memorial Sloan-Kettering Cancer Center in Manhattan. Mr. Shanker, the longtime president of the American Federation of Teachers, the parent organization of the United Federation of Teachers, was 68 years old and lived in Mamaroneck, N.Y., and Manhattan.

He died following a three-year battle with bladder cancer, said Janet Bass, a spokeswoman for the American Federation of Teachers.

Sandra Feldman, who succeeded Mr. Shanker as president of the U.F.T. in 1986, yesterday called her predecessor a teacher's teacher who was "deeply committed to both public education and the labor movement as a means of creating a better life for all Americans."

"He could be passionate about his beliefs, yet at the same time he had the rare ability to rethink issues and come up with fresh approaches as times changed," she said.

Although he became a respected thinker on national educational issues, Mr. Shanker is best remembered for his combative role as the head of the 85,000-member U.F.T., the New York City teachers' union, during the turmoil of the city's school decentralization experiments in 1968, turmoil that resulted in the closing of most schools for 55 days during the fall term and which were so racially and religiously divisive

Continued on Page 38, Column 1

He Crossed Color Barrier, But in Another's Shadow

Left, Associated Press; right, Fred R. Conrad/The New York Times

He was all smiles for photographers on his first day in the majors, but Larry Doby recalls it now as pride mixed with humiliation.

By IRA BERKOW

Larry Doby remembers clearly his first day in the major leagues, that day 50 years ago when he broke the color barrier in the American League. It was 11 weeks after Jackie Robinson had played his first game for the Brooklyn Dodgers in the National League. Doby remembers the excitement of that day when he became only the second black player in the major leagues — he had hardly slept in four nights leading up to it — and he remembers the dismay.

Saturday, July 5, 1947, a sunny morning in Chicago: Lou Boudreau, the manager of the Cleveland Indians, took the 22-year-old second baseman into the visiting team's locker room in Comiskey Park and introduced him to the players. Each of Doby's new teammates stood at his locker and looked over the young black man who had just been purchased by the Indians' owner, Bill Veeck, from the Newark Eagles of the Negro National League. Doby and the manager went from player to player.

"Some of the players shook my hand," Doby recalled recently, "but most of them didn't. It was one of the most embarrassing moments of my life."

As Major League Baseball and the nation prepare for a season of homage to the integration of the game, virtually all of the attention is centered on Jackie Robinson, which is understandable, since he was the first. Jackie Robinson commemorative coins, a Jackie Robinson video, a Jackie Robinson seminar.

"And that's the way it should be," Doby said. "But Jack and I had very similar experiences. And I wouldn't be human if I didn't want people to remember my participation."

Doby went through much the same kind of discrimination and

Continued on Page 30, Column 1

TODAY'S SECTIONS

Fashions of The Times

Special Today: Fashions of The Times
Magazine Part 2

Arts and Leisure/Section 2
Jazz composers have long shied from the subject of slavery. In his large new work "Blood on the Fields," Wynton Marsalis takes on the subject, trying to acknowledge the particularities of race while transcending them.

Automobiles/Section 11*†

Book Review/Section 7
"Gladstone" is Roy Jenkins's biography of the four-time Prime Minister in Britain's great 19th century, an icon of towering rectitude and intellectual authority to millions and a solitary sinner to himself; reviewed by Norman Stone.

The City/Section 13§

Editorials and Op-Ed/Section 4

Magazine/Section 6
No President has been put at the center of more conspiracy theories, nor has been the object of more virulent accusations. What is it about Bill Clinton, and the nation he leads?
When Paul Marchal's daughter disappeared, Belgian police dismissed him. Now her case, and those of three others, have sent a Government to the brink.

Money and Business/Section 3
The Prudential Insurance Company of America does business with no fewer than one in five Americans. But a series of setbacks has shattered the company's rock-solid image and explains why an outsider is running the show for the first time in 120 years.
Members of the rock group Kiss have been kissing their money goodbye for much of the last two decades. But those days are ending, they say, and maybe they mean it.

Real Estate/Section 9*
In the Hamptons, Cape Cod and the Jersey Shore, rental brokers are reporting brisk business.

Regional Weeklies/Section 13¶

SportsSunday/Section 8

Television/Section 12*

Travel/Section 5
That home away from home can prove to be charming or, occasionally, disappointing, visitors to France, Britain and Switzerland discover. Also, dining in Beverly Hills, from deli to sushi bar.

Week in Review/Section 4
After Deng and his evolving Market-Leninist economy, China is poised for a new dynasty.

Employment Advertising/Section 10*

* *In New York City and the metropolitan region. († Elsewhere, auto pages are in section 3.)*
§ *In most parts of New York City.*
¶ *In Long Island, Westchester, Connecticut and central and thern New Jersey.*

INSIDE

Bomb at Atlanta Gay Club Leaves 5 People Injured
Another bombing in Atlanta injured five people at a gay nightclub, and law-enforcement officials, already investigating earlier incidents, are wondering whether a serial bomber is at work. Page 18.

Turkey's Identity Crisis
Straddling Europe and Asia, Turkey is forever asking where it belongs. Now, it feels rebuffed as it tries to enter the European Union. Page 3.

Florio Says He Won't Run
Ending months of speculation, former Gov. Jim Florio of New Jersey says he will not try to get his old job back. Page 33.

New Disney Vision: The Past
In a profound shift, the Walt Disney Company has largely given up on imagining a new future and on its founder's dream as well. Page 24.

On the Internet: www.nytimes.com

Scientist Reports First Cloning of Adult Mammal

Continued From Page 1

week that the announcement had come just in time for him to revise his forthcoming book so the first chapter will no longer state that such cloning is impossible.

"It's unbelievable," Dr. Silver said. "It basically means that there are no limits. It means all of science fiction is true. They said it could never be done and now here it is, done before the year 2000."

Dr. Neal First, a professor of reproductive biology and animal biotechnology at the University of Wisconsin, who has been trying to clone cattle, said the ability to clone dairy cattle could have a bigger impact on the industry than the introduction of artificial insemination in the 1950's, a procedure that revolutionized dairy farming. Cloning could be used to make multiple copies of animals that are especially good at producing meat or milk or wool.

Although researchers have created genetically identical animals by dividing embryos very early in their development, Dr. Silver said, no one had cloned an animal from an adult until now. Earlier experiments, with frogs, have become a stock story in high school biology, but the experiments never produced cloned adult frogs. The frogs developed only to the tadpole stage before dying.

It was even worse with mammals. Researchers could swap DNA from one fertilized egg to another, but they could go no further. "They couldn't even put nuclei from late-stage mouse embryos into early mouse embryos," Dr. Silver said. The embryos failed to develop and died.

As a result, the researchers concluded that as cells developed, the proteins coating the DNA somehow masked all the important genes for embryo development. A skin cell may have all the genetic information that was present in the fertilized egg that produced the organism, for example, but almost all that information is pasted over. Now all the skin cell can do is be a skin cell.

Researchers could not even hope to strip off the proteins from an adult cell's DNA and replace them with proteins from an embryo's DNA. The DNA would shatter if anyone tried to strip it bare, Dr. Silver said.

Last year, Dr. Wilmut showed that he could clone DNA from sheep embryo cells, but even that was not taken as proof that the animal itself could be cloned. It could just be that the embryo cells had DNA that was unusually conducive to cloning, many thought.

Dr. Wilmut, however, hit on a clever strategy. He did not bother with the proteins that coat DNA, and instead focused on getting the DNA from an adult cell into a stage in its normal cycle of replication where it could take up residence in an egg.

DNA in growing cells goes through what is known as the cell cycle: it prepares itself to divide, then replicates itself and splits in two as the cell itself divides. The problem with earlier cloning attempts, Dr. Wilmut said, was that the DNA from the donor had been out of synchrony with that of the recipient cell. The solution, he discovered, was, in effect, to put the DNA from the adult cell to sleep, making it quiescent by depriving the adult cell of nutrients. When he then fused it with an egg cell from another sheep — after removing the egg cell's DNA — the donor DNA took over as though it belonged there.

Dr. Wilmut said in the telephone interview last week that the method could work for any animal and that he hoped to use it next to clone cattle. He said that he could use many types of cells from adults for cloning but that the easiest to use would be so-called stem cells, which give rise to a variety of other cells and are present throughout the body.

In his sheep experiment, he used mammary cells because a company that sponsored his work, PPL Therapeutics, is developing sheep that can be used to produce proteins that can be used as drugs in their milk, so it had sheep mammary cells readily available.

For Dr. Wilmut, the main interest of the experiment is to advance animal research. PPL, for example, wants to clone animals that can produce pharmacologically useful proteins, like the clotting factor needed by hemophiliacs. Scientists would grow cells in the laboratory, insert the genes for production of the desired protein, select those cells that most actively churned out the protein and use those cells to make cloned females. The cloned animals would produce immense amounts of the proteins in their milk, making the animals into living drug factories.

But that is only the beginning, Dr. Wilmut said. Researchers could use the same method to make animals with human diseases, like cystic fibrosis, and then test therapies on the cloned animals. Or they could use cloning to alter the proteins on the surfaces of pig organs, like the liver or heart, making the organs more like human organs. Then they could transplant those organs into humans.

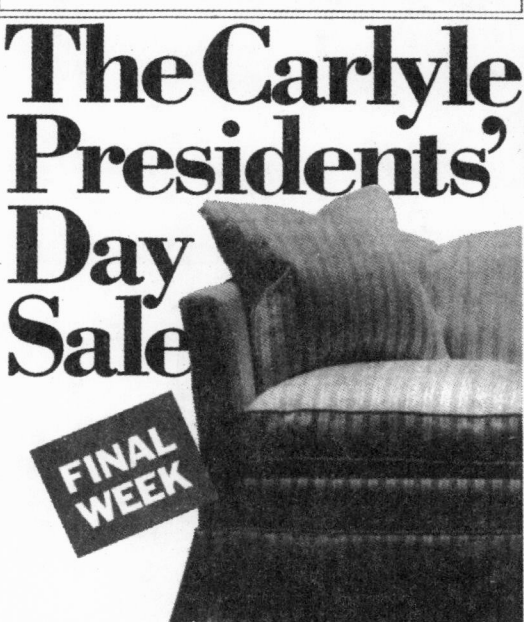

Dr. First said the "exciting and astounding" cloning result could shake the dairy industry. It could allow the cloning of cows that are superproducers of milk, making 30,000 or even 40,000 pounds of milk a year. The average cow makes about 13,000 pounds of milk a year, he said.

"I think that if — and it's a very big if — cloning were highly efficient," Dr. First said last week, "then it could be a more significant revolution to the livestock industry than even artificial insemination."

Although Dr. Wilmut said he saw no intrinsic biological reason humans, too, could not be cloned, he dismissed the idea as being ethically unacceptable. Moreover, he said, it is illegal in Britain to clone people. "I would find it offensive" to clone a human being, Dr. Wilmut said, adding that he fervently hoped that no one would try it.

But others said that it was hard to imagine enforcing a ban on cloning people when cloning got more efficient. "I could see it going on surreptitiously," said Lori Andrews, a professor at Chicago-Kent College of law who specializes in reproductive issues. For example, Professor Andrews said last week, in the early days of in vitro fertilization, Australia banned that practice. "So scientists moved to Singapore" and offered the procedure, she said. "I can imagine new crimes," she added.

People might be cloned without their knowledge or consent. After all, all that would be needed would be some cells. If there is a market for a sperm bank selling semen from Nobel laureates, how much better would it be to bear a child that would actually be a clone of a great thinker or, perhaps, a great beauty or great athlete?

"The genie is out of the bottle," said Dr. Ronald Munson, a medical ethicist at the University of Missouri in St. Louis. "This technology is not, in principle, policeable."

Dr. Munson called the possibilities incredible. For example, could researchers devise ways to add just the DNA of an adult cell, without fusing two living cells? If so, might it be possible to clone the dead?

"I had an idea for a story once," Dr. Munson said, in which a scientist obtains a spot of blood from the cross on which Jesus was crucified. He then uses it to clone a man who is Jesus Christ — or perhaps cannot be.

On a more practical note, Dr. Munson mused over the strange twist that science has taken.

"There's something ironic" about study, he said. "Here we have this incredible technical accomplishment, and what motivated it? The desire for more sheep milk of a certain type." It is, he said, "the theater of the absurd acted out by scientists."

In his interview with the Press Association, Britain's domestic news agency, Dr. Wilmut added early today: "We are aware that there is potential for misuse, and we have provided information to ethicists and the Human Embryology Authority. We believe that it is important that society decides how we want to use this technology and makes sure it prohibits what it wants to prohibit. It would be desperately sad if people started using this sort of technology with people."

Beyond the Test Tube Baby: A Cloned Lamb

An embryologist at the Roslin Institute in Edinburgh has created a lamb using DNA from a mammary cell from an adult sheep. The DNA had to be processed so that it would be accepted by an egg from another sheep. The embryo that was created then had to be transplanted into yet another sheep.

Sources: Roslin Institute; Collier's Encyclopedia

Donor sheep's mammary cell . . . Extracted and grown in a test tube.

Mammary cell

Donor sheep

. . . And another sheep's unfertilized egg whose nucleus has been removed . . .

Unfertilized egg

Nucleus

. . . Are fused together. The donor nucleus causes the egg to develop into an embryo.

Cell

Egg

The embryo is transferred into a surrogate mother sheep . . .

Surrogate mother sheep

. . . Where it divides like a normal embryo.

A lamb is then born genetically identical to the donor sheep

The New York Times

A PRIMER

Questions About Genetic Possibilities

Could people be cloned?

Theoretically, yes. Sheep and humans are both mammals and the technology used to clone one species could theoretically be applied to the other.

Who are the parents of a clone?

In genetic terms, the parents of a clone would be the man and woman whose sperm and egg formed the person who, in turn, was cloned. In some states, the woman who bears a child is its legal mother.

Could a cell from any part of the body be used to make a clone?

Researchers do not know, but they believe that a kind of cell called a stem cell would be easiest to work with. These cells, which later give rise to a variety of other cells, occur all over the body, even in hair.

Could you clone the dead?

No. You have to fuse two living cells: the egg and the cell containing the DNA you want to replicate.

Could people who died and had their bodies frozen be cloned?

No. Their cells are dead.

Could a woman bear a clone of herself?

Theoretically, yes.

How would clones produced this way differ from identical twins?

Identical twins are born when a single fertilized egg splits in two, giving rise to two separate embryos. Scientists working with animals have long been able to split early-stage embryos in the laboratory to produce multiple births of genetically identical offspring. In this case, by contrast, the clone was made from an adult animal, whose genetic material was inserted into an egg cell.

Could you put the nucleus of a human cell into a sheep egg?

No. When the genetic material inserted in the egg begins to divide, it acts on instructions it receives from proteins in the egg. If the egg and the DNA are from different species, the instructions will not match.

Is it legal to clone people?

Britain, Spain, Denmark, Germany and Australia have laws barring human cloning, but the United States does not. Laws restricting use of Federal funds on human embryo research might not apply because any cloning would be done with eggs, not embryos.

Mother Wins Health Care for Paralyzed Son in the Marines

By DANIEL J. YOVICH

CHICAGO, Feb. 22 — Joanne Bertalan won the battle her paralyzed son could not fight — a five-month struggle with Navy and Marine officials who had sought to strip her 22-year-old son of his veterans benefits.

Mrs. Bertalan was at her son's bedside at the Rehabilitation Institute of Chicago on Friday, bags under her blue eyes, her gray hair tousled by the five-hour flight from San Diego after a four-hour hearing. Months of uncertainty about the quality and cost of the care her son will receive had ended.

It is doubtful that her son, Cpl. Joseph Bertalan, understood much of what she said. He is only minimally conscious after emerging from a coma eight months ago.

"It's been an uphill battle all the way, and I was never sure how this would conclude," Mrs. Bertalan said. "But in the end, the system worked; it did what it was supposed to do. It's been incredibly hard, but things worth fighting for always are."

In a ruling last Thursday, a hearing panel of the Navy Physical Evaluation Board, meeting at the Naval Medical Center in San Diego, recommended a rare reversal of earlier findings that attributed the marine's injuries to his own misconduct. Corporal Bertalan's health costs have averaged more than $50,000 a month since his injury. He had faced the prospect of being stripped of all his veterans benefits, including his medical care.

That would have severely hurt any chances for even the most minimal improvement in his condition, said Dr. James Kelly, director of the Rehabilitation Institute's brain injury program. Corporal Bertalan now can communicate, although inconsistently, only by blinking his eyes.

On Jan. 16, 1996, four days after his 21st birthday, Corporal Bertalan and 15 other marines were traveling to sick bay for inoculations at the Navy base in Norfolk, Va., in four cars.

While trying to pass another marine's car, Corporal Bertalan lost control of his vehicle, which skidded and smashed against a tree. All four marines in his car were injured.

All except Corporal Bertalan returned to active duty. The crash damaged his brain stem and frontal brain lobe.

An investigation into the accident by Capt. William F. McCollough, an officer in Corporal Bertalan's unit, found that his injuries were the result of intentional misconduct. It found that Corporal Bertalan had been going much faster than the speed limit of 25 miles an hour.

The Navy Physical Evaluation Board's review panel recommended that no Veterans Administration benefits be paid.

Mrs. Bertalan, a 48-year-old widow from Lansing, Ill., about 25 miles south of Chicago, borrowed money from family members, took a second mortgage on her home and hired the law firm of Tomes & Dvorak, of Chicago and Kansas City, Mo. She has spent $50,000 to help build her son's case.

"All the News That's Fit to Print"

The New York Times

Late Edition

New York: Today, rain ending, then cloudy, breezy, chilly. High 59. Tonight, clearing, cool. Low 50. Tomorrow, some sun, cool. High 67. Yesterday, high 62, low 57. Details, page A20.

VOL. CXLVI . . . . No. 50,812 — NEW YORK, TUESDAY, JUNE 3, 1997 — $1 beyond the greater New York metropolitan area. — NJ — 60 CENTS

McVEIGH GUILTY ON ALL COUNTS IN THE OKLAHOMA CITY BOMBING; JURY TO WEIGH DEATH PENALTY

Angel Franco/The New York Times

Malcolm Shabazz, 12, accused of setting the fire that critically burned his grandmother, Betty Shabazz, left Family Court in Yonkers yesterday.

Now, Charges in Chaotic Life Of Malcolm X's Grandson, 12

By RACHEL L. SWARNS

When Malcolm Shabazz flew to San Antonio to rejoin his mother a few months ago, he and his family hoped it would be a new beginning for the boy, who had endured years of nomadic wanderings through cheap rooming houses, then a two-year separation from his troubled mother.

But as Malcolm, 12, the grandson of Malcolm X, was brought into Family Court in Yonkers yesterday, accused of setting a fire that left his grandmother near death, it seemed he had found not stability but chaos.

When he arrived in Texas around the beginning of the year, his mother, Qubilah Shabazz, was newly married to a man who the police said sometimes beat her and hurled her against the wall. She fell into drunken stupors, the police said, and refused to drive the boy to school.

Enraged, Malcolm attacked her in February, damaging the one-bedroom apartment they shared until the police took him to a psychiatric hospital, according to police reports and interviews with family friends.

With the promise of a new life quickly unraveling, Malcolm withdrew from school and was sent back to New York about a month ago to live with his grandmother, who had cared for him before when his mother could not. But yesterday, the boy who had once dreamed of a stable family stood accused of nearly killing the most stable figure in his life, his grandmother, the widow of Malcolm X, Betty Shabazz.

Malcolm walked into court yesterday afternoon to face charges of juvenile delinquency, mumbling and hiding his head under a red plaid blanket. As he stood in the courtroom, his grandmother clung to life, her body covered with burns from the fire that the police say Malcolm set deliberately outside her bedroom early Sunday morning.

Dr. Bruce Greenstein of Jacobi Medical Center in the Bronx said Dr. Shabazz "is in a life-threatening situation and will be for a long time." [Page B6.]

The crime was another stunning blow to a family that has suffered

Continued on Page B6

Top Art Dealers Are Subpoenaed In Possible Price-Rigging Scheme

By CAROL VOGEL

Justice Department investigators have subpoenaed truckloads of financial documents from more than a dozen prominent Manhattan art dealers and from Sotheby's and Christie's, the world's largest auction houses, in what appears to be a wide-ranging antitrust investigation.

Dealers, many of whom spoke with anxiety about the Federal investigation yesterday, said they had been served with the subpoenas over the last month.

On the basis of questions asked of them and their lawyers, they said, they believe investigators are looking for the possibility of collusion and price fixing among art dealers buying at auction.

Among the documents subpoenaed were correspondence between dealers and auction houses, travel logs, telephone bills and invoices and other records of business transactions.

It has long been rumored in the art world that some dealers try to buy on the cheap, by forming rings of dealers who agree to refrain from bidding against one other. The practice, called "bid pooling" or "bid rigging" inhibits prices from reaching their fair value at auction. Then the dealers resell the work at an exaggerated profit. Such collusive behavior is prohibited as an illegal restraint of trade under the Sherman Antitrust Act. Penalties for violations can include substantial fines and imprisonment of up to three years.

"People in specialized businesses like the art business that are far away from the mainstream of milk and cement don't necessarily think of themselves as subject to the laws that were designed to protect the public against robber barons," said Donald I. Baker, a lawyer and a former head of the antitrust division of the Justice Department. "And thus they come up surprised."

Gina Talamona, a spokeswoman for the Justice Department would only say that "the antitrust division is looking at the possibility of anti-competitive practices in the fine art auction industry."

Several of the dealers confirmed receiving subpoenas, but refused to comment further. Others did not return calls. Still others referred inquiries to the Art Dealers Association of America, which declined to

Continued on Page B7

At Troubled Base, Commander to Retire

The two-star general who commands the Army's Aberdeen Proving Ground, the troubled base in Maryland where drill sergeants have been court-martialed for sexual encounters with female recruits, has decided to retire at a lower rank. His decision follows an anonymous tip about an affair he had with a civilian while separated from his wife more than five years ago.

Article, page A12.

NEWS SUMMARY A2

On the Internet: www.nytimes.com

HEALING MUST WAIT

Still Haunted, Families See Justice in Shape of a Killer's Grave

By RICK BRAGG

OKLAHOMA CITY, June 2 — After the explosion, people learned to write left-handed, to tie just one shoe. They learned to endure the pieces of metal and glass embedded in their flesh, to smile with faces that made them want to cry, to cry with glass eyes. They learned, in homes where children had played, to stand the quiet. They learned to sleep with pills, to sleep alone.

Today, with the conviction of Timothy J. McVeigh in a Denver Federal court, with cheers and sobs of relief at the lot where a building once stood in downtown Oklahoma City, the survivors and families of the victims of the most deadly attack of domestic terrorism in United States history learned what they had suspected all along: That justice in a far-away courtroom is not satisfaction. That healing might come only at Mr. McVeigh's grave.

"I want the death penalty," said Aren Almon-Kok, whose daughter, Baylee, was killed by the bomb one day after her first birthday. Pictures of the baby, bleeding and limp in the arms of a firefighter, became a symbol of that crime, of its cruelty. "An eye for eye. You don't take lives and get to keep your own."

Mrs. Almon-Kok saw the announcement of the verdict on television at her mother's house, then went immediately to the site of her daughter's death, where she was joined by some people who had lost children in the bombing, by others who had just felt drawn there. She said how happy she was with the verdict, but her face was stricken, haunted.

"I cried, and I cheered," Mrs. Almon-Kok said. "I don't think there will ever be closure. I love her so much, and I miss her, still, a lot. Baylee meant the world to me."

In what some people here see as poetic justice, the powerful image of Baylee, taken by an amateur photographer, will be used by prosecutors in the penalty phase of the trial to try to send Mr. McVeigh to his death.

Throughout Oklahoma City and the little towns that surround it, the people who lost something in the explosion said the same thing, over and over: that the verdict is a victory on paper. It insures that Mr. McVeigh, a failed Green Beret and Persian Gulf War veteran who came to hate the Government, will pay for his crime somehow. The penalty phase of his trial, the battle for his life, is what counts here.

"Not until the day I die will I be over this," said Stan Mayer, who was shredded with shrapnel when a truck

Continued on Page A19

The Verdict

Timothy J. McVeigh was convicted of 11 counts of conspiracy and murder in the Oklahoma City bombing.

COUNT 1 Conspiracy to use a weapon of mass destruction.

COUNT 2 Use of a weapon of mass destruction.

COUNT 3 Destruction by an explosive.

COUNTS 4-11 First-degree murders of eight Federal law-enforcement agents.

What's Next

TODAY Motions from lawyers on both sides relating to the penalty phase of the trial.

TOMORROW Jurors return to begin hearing evidence from both sides about whether Mr. McVeigh should get the death penalty.

- After Mr. McVeigh is sentenced, Judge Richard P. Matsch is expected to announce when the trial of Terry L. Nichols, the other person accused in the bombing, will start.
- The District Attorney in Oklahoma City has said he intends to prosecute Mr. McVeigh for the first-degree murders of the 160 slain victims who were not Federal law-enforcement agents.

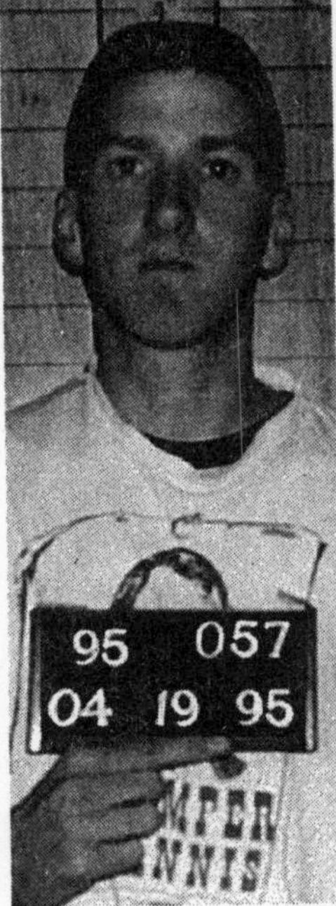

Reuters

Timothy J. McVeigh after he was arrested near Perry, Okla., shortly after the bombing.

VERDICT IS CHEERED

Affixing Blame in Worst Terrorism Attack on United States Soil

By JO THOMAS

DENVER, June 2 — As silent tears streamed down the faces of victims and their families in the packed courtroom, a Federal jury today found Timothy J. McVeigh, an angry drifter, guilty of the Oklahoma City bombing, which killed 168 people, injured hundreds more and shook the nation's sense of security within its borders.

Mr. McVeigh entered the courtroom smiling and showed no emotion as Judge Richard P. Matsch took the verdict from the foreman and read it aloud.

The jurors found Mr. McVeigh guilty on 11 counts of conspiracy and murder. They concluded that he had conspired with Terry L. Nichols, a friend he had met while they were both in the Army, and others unknown to use a truck bomb to destroy the Alfred P. Murrah Federal Building on April 19, 1995. Mr. Nichols is awaiting a Federal trial in the case.

The jury found Mr. McVeigh guilty of first-degree murder in the deaths of eight Federal law-enforcement agents who were at work in the building that day. While all the killings violated Oklahoma law, only the killings of the Federal agents fell under the Federal law that makes such murders capital offenses.

Later this week, the same jury will begin to consider whether Mr. McVeigh will be sentenced to death.

For weeks after the bombing, the worst act of terrorism on American soil, Americans were riveted by what became familiar sights: the hull of the Federal Building and scenes of tearful rescue workers pulling the dead, many of them small children, from the wreckage.

Mr. McVeigh was arrested shortly after the bombing on a routine traffic stop. After he was linked to the attack, the country learned of a right-wing netherworld where anti-Government propaganda flourishes and dark conspiracy theories of a New World Order are spread by the Internet and short-wave radio.

Today, as word raced through the courthouse that the jury was about to deliver a verdict, tension mounted among the victims and victims' families who had been waiting since Friday morning.

"I'm anxious," said Roy Sells, 63, a retired Air Force employee at Tinker Air Force Base whose wife, Leora Lee, was killed in the explosion. "I didn't get a vote."

When Joseph H. Hartzler, the lead prosecutor, entered the courtroom, he saw Mr. Sells standing in the second row. Mr. Hartzler, who uses a

Continued on Page A18

Six Weeks, One Theory

Judge Kept Tight Rein on Defense Tactics, Leaving Prosecution to Build a Solid Case

By JO THOMAS

News Analysis

DENVER, June 2 — When everything was said and done, Timothy J. McVeigh, the loner who liked to travel fast and light, was still alone. No friend, no family member, no stranger came forward to give him an alibi for the Oklahoma City bombing, and he did not take the stand in his own defense.

His lawyers — who combed the backwoods compounds and desert haunts of anti-Government groups in this country, and sent investigators to Asia, the Middle East and Europe in search of terrorist conspiracies — were never able to put before the jury their theory that the real culprit was still at large. Their every effort to introduce the specter of a wider conspiracy was thwarted by Judge Richard P. Matsch, who tightly controlled the proceedings and focused the evidence on the crime and the defendant.

As a result, defense lawyers were unable to score points with a Justice Department report that criticized the Federal Bureau of Investigation's crime laboratory, which analyzed evidence in the case.

Instead, the jurors heard damaging testimony from Mr. McVeigh's sister and his closest friends, and read letters he had written detailing his intense hatred for the Federal Government and his determination to act on this belief. The prosecutors offered a powerful case that alternated emotional testimony from survivors and rescue workers — which the defense left unchallenged — with other testimony, physical evidence and documents connecting Mr. McVeigh to preparations for the bombing.

In the end, the jurors were largely left with the prosecution's theory — that Mr. McVeigh and his co-defendant, Terry L. Nichols, conspired to bomb the Federal Building on April 19, 1995, on their own — and a plea by the defense not to believe it.

And so, after four days of jury deliberations, the Government won its conviction even though it presented no evidence of where or when the bomb was built and placed in the Ryder rental truck that carried it; no witness who saw Mr. McVeigh in that truck on the day of the bombing, and, indeed, no witness who saw Mr. McVeigh in Oklahoma City that day.

The prosecutors, who first considered calling as many as 400 witnesses, pared their list to 137, some of whom appeared for only a few minutes. They took off the list any nonessential witness who might have introduced problems for the Government. One such witness was Tom Kessinger, a mechanic at the Ryder rental office who had said he had seen two men there renting the truck and identified one as Mr. McVeigh,

Continued on Page A18

Kevin Moloney for The New York Times

Ronnie and Barbie Trent left the Federal courthouse in Denver yesterday after the verdict. Mrs. Trent's parents were killed in the blast.

INSIDE

Wary Bonn Holding Firm To Europe Currency Plan

As France's Socialist leader was asked to form a new Government, Germany insisted it was committed to a single European currency. But it issued a veiled warning to French leaders who are talking of relaxing the rules for the euro. Page A8.

A Primary Test of Strength

For New Jersey's county organization leaders, today's primary could enhance their stature or relegate them to the past. Page B1.

Africans Act to End Coup

A Nigerian-led force sent ships, airplanes and troops into action to put down an eight-day-long military coup in Sierra Leone. Page A10.

Canada's Liberals Retain a Majority For Austerity Policy

By ANTHONY DePALMA

TORONTO, June 2 — Canadian voters returned Prime Minister Jean Chrétien to power today, giving him a slim parliamentary majority and a mandate to continue with the severe fiscal austerity that has practically eliminated the country's huge federal deficit while cutting deeply into Canada's revered social programs.

Mr. Chrétien, 63, has won at least part of the gamble he took by calling the election one and a half years before his term ended, convinced that he could build on the sizable majority that his party, the Liberals, had held in Ottawa. He said he wanted a mandate for another term to complete the overhaul of Canada's economy and to prepare for a new challenge on Quebec separation expected before the year 2000.

But the election did not turn out to be the cakewalk Mr. Chrétien envisioned. The Liberals lost support throughout the campaign, as the four major opposition parties focused on the Prime Minister's record of failing to scrap unpopular taxes. The Liberals were also hammered for their austerity budgets, which reduced spending on health, welfare and higher education by $10 billion

Continued on Page A6

THE OKLAHOMA CITY BOMBING: The Verdict, the Emotions, the Strategems

THE OVERVIEW

McVeigh Guilty in Oklahoma Bombing; Jury to Weigh Death Penalty Evidence

Continued From Page A1

second row. Mr. Hartzler, who uses a wheelchair because he has multiple sclerosis, leaned out of the chair to ask Mr. Sells if he was all right.

Victims of the bombing and members of victims' families squeezed together to make room for one another on the crowded benches. One clutched a crucifix. Another held a lucky coin. One woman knelt to pray. A hush fell over the room when Mr. McVeigh walked in. "He looks like such a nice boy," one spectator murmured sadly.

Judge Matsch (pronounced MAYTCH) warned the spectators before the jurors returned that "there must be no audible or visible emotion" when the verdict was read. "Any person who violates this order will be removed from the courtroom," he said.

After the verdict was announced and the judge had polled the jurors, one by one, about whether they agreed with the verdict, Judge Matsch lifted his order sequestering the jurors and sent them home. They will return at 9 A.M. on Wednesday to begin the second phase of the trial, in which they will hear evidence on whether Mr. McVeigh should be sentenced to death.

The last American executed for a Federal crime was Victor Feuger, who was hanged in 1963 in Iowa for kidnapping.

Judge Matsch ordered Mr. McVeigh led out of the courtroom first. As the spectators left, they hugged each other and wept. Outside, as if by magic, the largest crowd since the trial began had gathered to clap and cheer for them.

Some family members raised their thumbs in a victory sign, and one woman shouted, "We got him!" But others were crying so hard that friends had to hold and console them.

Mr. Hartzler, smiling broadly, was greeted by an ovation. "We're obviously very pleased with the verdict," he said. "We always had confidence in our evidence. Now maybe everyone else will have confidence in our evidence."

As Mr. Hartzler paused to cross the street, a crowd of well-wishers surrounded him, clapping and cheering him and the prosecutors at his side: the United States Attorney from Oklahoma City, Patrick M. Ryan, wearing his usual white cowboy hat; Beth Wilkinson; Scott Mendeloff, and Larry Mackey. The cheers rolled down the street.

Mr. McVeigh's lawyer, Stephen Jones, said he could not comment on the verdict. He congratulated Mr. Hartzler and the other prosecutors and the Federal Bureau of Investigation agents for their work.

"We are ready for the second stage," Mr. Jones said. "I visited with Mr. McVeigh, and I will work with him tonight and tomorrow for the second stage."

For relatives, a victory that can never bring peace.

Jannie Coverdale, who lost her grandchildren in the bombing and has been a regular at the hearings ever since, confessed that she felt mixed emotions. "This is bittersweet," she said. "After all, this is a young man who has wasted his life. I'm glad they found him guilty, but I'm sad for him, too. I feel sorry for him. He had so much to offer his country.

"I want him to get the death penalty," she added, "but not out of revenge. It's necessary. I haven't seen any remorse from Timothy McVeigh. If he ever walked the streets, he would murder again."

Paul Douglas Ice, a special agent for the United States Customs service, was one of the eight victims named in the first-degree murder counts. His sister, Sharon Ice, was smiling as she left the courthouse. "I am ecstatic over the verdict," she said. She said that when she had seen Mr. McVeigh in the courtroom, "I saw a monster."

She will testify in the penalty phase of the trial.

In Washington, President Clinton said he could not comment on the verdict. But he said, "I say to the families of the victims, no single verdict can bring an end to your anguish. But your courage has been an inspiration to all Americans. Our prayers are with you."

At the Pendleton, N.Y., home where Mr. McVeigh grew up, his father, William, and sister, Jennifer, watched the verdict with Lou Michel, a family friend and reporter for The Buffalo News. Mr. Michel read a statement attributed to the family. "Even though the jury has found Tim guilty, we still love him very much and intend to stand by him no matter what happens," the statement said. "We would like to ask everyone to pray for Tim in this difficult time."

In Oklahoma City, near the fence at the Federal Building site, the district attorney, Bob Macy, said he would file state charges against Mr. McVeigh and Mr. Nichols to make sure that those convicted of the bombing would receive the death penalty. He said he feared that a Federal death penalty could be vacated on appeal because the Federal statute was new and untested.

Survivors and victims' families also gathered near the bombing site after the verdict, near a tree that was damaged in the blast but lived to become a symbol of rebirth.

On that April morning in 1995, the homemade 4,800-pound bomb shattered not only Oklahoma City's Federal Building and scores of lives, but also America's very notion of itself.

To some, it seemed at first as if the blast must be the work of foreign enemies, perhaps Islamic extremists like those convicted of bombing the World Trade Center in New York.

But for a routine traffic stop of Mr. McVeigh on Interstate 35 by Trooper Charles J. Hanger, a highway patrolman called "the hangman" because of his zeal, the bombing might have stayed a mystery.

The nation was stunned to discover that the chief suspect in the case was an American, a lanky former Army sergeant with a crew cut who had been decorated with the Bronze Star during the Persian Gulf war. A computer search linked Mr. McVeigh to the axle of the rented Ryder truck used in the bombing just moments before he would have been released from a tiny jail in Perry, Okla. He was seen on television in handcuffs, wearing an orange prison jumpsuit and surrounded by F.B.I. agents as a crowd screamed, "Baby killer." That image was burned into the collective consciousness.

When he was stopped, 75 minutes after the explosion, Mr. McVeigh was wearing a T-shirt inscribed with the motto: "The tree of liberty must be refreshed from time to time with the blood of patriots and tyrants." Instead of fruit, the tree above those words bore droplets of bright red blood. On the front of the shirt, President Abraham Lincoln appeared on what looked like a "wanted" poster; under it was the Latin phrase his assassin, John Wilkes Booth, is said to have shouted: "sic semper tyrannis," or, "thus always to tyrants."

Mr. McVeigh was carrying a 9-millimeter Glock semiautomatic pistol and passages from "The Turner Diaries," a venomous far-right novel that had become his bible. The passages described a bombing of F.B.I. headquarters that touched off a white "Aryan" revolt, with wholesale slaughter of blacks and Jews.

Among his belongings in the car was a slip of paper that carried a quote from Samuel Adams: "When the Government fears the people, there is liberty. When the people fear the Government, there is tyranny." Underneath, in Mr. McVeigh's handwriting, was the note, "Maybe now, there will be liberty."

For Mr. McVeigh and others involved in the far-right fringe, three events had confirmed their view of a runaway Government out to take their guns.

The first was a raid on Aug. 22, 1992, by Federal agents on a white supremacist's cabin in Ruby Ridge, Idaho. The second was another Federal raid, in Waco, Tex., on April 19, 1993, that left more than 80 Branch Davidians dead. And the third event occurred in November 1993, when Congress passed the Brady bill, which mandates a five-day waiting period for the purchase of guns.

But Mr. McVeigh was not on trial for his ideas, the prosecution emphasized, but for a crime of immense proportions. As it turned out, an ordinary citizen saw the clue that broke the case, even before most law enforcement agents reached the scene.

He was Richard Nichols, a maintenance man standing a block and a half away from the bomb's target. Just after 9 A.M. on April 19, 1995, he told the jury, as he and his wife were about to get into their car, they were spun around by the force of a vast explosion. A large shaft of metal hurtled toward them and landed on their little red car. The piece of metal, which weighed more than 250 pounds, was the rear axle of a truck.

Before noon, while rescuers dug for victims, an F.B.I. agent, James Norman, found a partial vehicle identification number on the axle and started a search for the truck's owner, which turned out to be Ryder Rental Inc. in Miami.

By 2:15 P.M. that day, while stunned Americans still suspected foreign terrorists, Ryder officials had traced the truck. "Robert Kling" had rented it on Monday, April 17, at Elliott's Body Shop in Junction City, Kan., they said.

By 4:30 P.M., less than eight hours after the blast, Agent Scott Crabtree of the F.B.I., based in Salina, Kan., was in Junction City, looking for the rental contract and for anyone who could remember "Mr. Kling."

Based on descriptions given by Tom Kessinger, a mechanic at Elliott's, an F.B.I. artist was at work before dawn on drawings of two suspects. The nation and the world came to know those suspects as John Doe No. 1 and John Doe No. 2.

Lea McGown, the owner of the Dreamland Motel in Junction City, did not hesitate a moment when she was shown the F.B.I. sketches on Thursday, April 20. John Doe No. 1 was Tom McVeigh, she said. He had checked into Room 25 on Good Friday, April 14, and stayed the weekend. She remembered that he had driven a big Ryder truck.

Mr. McVeigh gave his address as the Decker, Mich., farm of James Nichols, brother of Terry Nichols. That information led Federal agents to the Nichols brothers and, just before he was to be released from the Perry, Okla., jail, to Mr. McVeigh.

Terry Nichols, an Army friend of Mr. McVeigh who had tried farming and had drifted from place to place, never appeared at Mr. McVeigh's trial. But evidence seized from Mr. Nichols's home was critical to the case against Mr. McVeigh. In a drawer, wrapped around some coins, agents found a pink piece of paper that turned out to be a receipt for 2,000 pounds of ammonium nitrate, fertilizer that can be used to make a bomb. On that receipt, made out to "Mike Havens," were two fingerprints from Mr. McVeigh.

As the prosecutors made their case against Mr. McVeigh, they never let the jury lose sight of the horror of the bombing, beginning their presentation with the sound of the explosion. They called witness after witness who had survived the bombing to tell of their experiences and to identify the dead, most of them in photographs from happier days.

Interspersed with this were accounts from witnesses who offered a motive connecting Mr. McVeigh to the bombing. Mr. McVeigh's younger sister, Jennifer, identified his handwriting on many documents expressing hatred for the Government. She said he had told her to expect "something big." His friend Kevin Nicholas brought with him a letter, written in February 1995, in which Mr. McVeigh said he wanted to take action against the Government. And Mr. McVeigh's friends Lori and Michael J. Fortier detailed Mr. McVeigh's bombing plan.

The defense tried to undermine the credibility of the Fortiers. But the defense was unable to provide either an alibi for Mr. McVeigh or any alternative theory to the prosecution's version of events.

Kevin Moloney for The New York Times

Peggy Broxterman, whose son, Paul, was killed in the 1995 Oklahoma City bombing, reacted to a jury's finding Timothy J. McVeigh guilty yesterday in Denver on 11 counts of conspiracy and murder.

Michelle V. Agins/The New York Times

Many view this tree, which is thriving after being shredded in the blast, as a symbol of hope. Bridgett Robertson, left, 15, and her cousin Sharonda Garrett, 7, whose brother was killed, were there yesterday.

NEWS ANALYSIS

Judge Kept Tight Rein on Defense Tactics as Prosecution Built a Solid Case

Continued From Page A1

but later said he had been mistaken in his description of the other. The simplified case, which seemed interminable in the two years of pretrial proceedings, took off like a rocket.

Although the investigation that led up to the trial produced 25,000 interviews, ten of thousands of telephone records and 7,000 pounds of physical evidence, Joseph H. Hartzler, the lead prosecutor, said from the outset that he could try the case in six weeks. In fact, the verdict came in less time — just under six weeks.

In the week before opening arguments, lawyers for Mr. McVeigh asked Judge Matsch for a delay. But the judge refused. And so once the jury was seated, the defense was left with the themes it had stressed beforehand: that Federal agents botched the investigation, stopped looking for anyone else after they arrested Mr. McVeigh and Mr. Nichols, and never caught the real criminals.

In pretrial motions, Stephen Jones, the lead lawyer for Mr. McVeigh, asserted that the bombing was the product of a shadowy conspiracy of terrorists sponsored by a foreign power, operating out of the Philippines and helped by radical right-wing groups in the United States.

Mr. Jones contended that an informer had warned the Government that the bombing was imminent, and he demanded access to confidential documents from the Bureau of Alcohol, Tobacco and Firearms and national intelligence agencies.

Although he did receive some of those documents, his theory about a wider conspiracy never made its way into the courtroom. A lawyer familiar with the case said Judge Matsch denied defense requests to take testimony from several witnesses to support this theory, ruling that none could be tied directly to the crime.

And so the defense was denied the opportunity granted to lawyers who defended O. J. Simpson in his murder trial, who were allowed broad latitude by Judge Lance Ito to suggest that there were a variety of alternate theories and suspects.

In his opening statement, Mr. Jones promised the jury that he would do more than raise a reasonable doubt about his client's guilt. He said he would prove that his client was innocent. But he could not.

Instead he tried to show that the Government had not proved its case, and he suggested that a severed leg found at the scene, a leg for which no body can be found, meant that the real bomber had died in the blast. The defense presented its case in just three and a half days.

As prosecutors pointed out in court, the defense could have called witnesses discarded by the Government — like Mr. Kessinger — to present evidence that others might have taken part in the conspiracy in the months, days and hours before the bombing. But those witnesses, as one defense lawyer pointed out, presented a minefield for Mr. McVeigh. Whatever else they might have said, most were also expected to offer testimony that would incriminate Mr. McVeigh or his co-defendant.

Mr. Jones did call Daina Bradley, an unwilling witness who lost a leg and her family in the bombing, in hopes of ascribing the bombing to someone other than Mr. McVeigh. Ms. Bradley had told investigators that just before the blast she saw a short, dark man who looked nothing like Mr. McVeigh get out of the passenger seat of the Ryder truck that carried the bomb.

A three-day effort to discredit the Government case.

But on the witness stand Ms. Bradley testified instead that she had seen a second man get out of the truck. And on cross-examination by the prosecution, she said that even though she could not see him well, that second man could have been Mr. McVeigh. She also said she had a bad memory and had suffered for years from mental illness.

The defense attacked the F.B.I. laboratory, which Christopher L. Tritico, a defense lawyer, characterized as "a ship without a rudder." But Judge Matsch refused to let Mr. McVeigh's lawyers present the jury with the 517-page Department of Justice report, which was issued April 15 by its inspector general and which criticized some of the laboratory's practices.

Frederic W. Whitehurst, the whistle-blowing chemist whose complaints about these practices provoked the investigation and report, was called as a witness for the defense, but he testified that he knew of no specific instance in which evidence from the bombing case had been contaminated.

The best effort by the defense to explain away explosives residue found on Mr. McVeigh's clothing after the bombing came in their questioning of Steven G. Burmeister, an F.B.I. chemist, who said on cross-examination that residue of PETN, a chemical that is found in detonation cords, could have come from bullets Mr. McVeigh carried in his pockets.

Though the Government's case had its holes, the swiftness of the investigation helped prosecutors acquire crucial evidence before it could be destroyed and led them to witnesses who were interviewed while their memories were fresh. For example, they presented a witness who swore that it was Mr. McVeigh who had rented the Ryder truck. Friends and associates said Mr. McVeigh had made a determined effort to collect components that could be used in a bomb: blasting caps, explosives, detonation cord and racing fuel.

Prosecutors said ammonium nitrate was also used to make the bomb. Mr. McVeigh's fingerprints were found on a receipt for a ton of the chemical and his prints were found on the rental contract for a storage unit where prosecutors said he had kept the ammonium nitrate before he built the bomb. Tire tracks that could have been made by the Ryder truck were found in the wet ground in front of that storage unit after the bombing.

Although the defense team made a concerted effort to cast doubt on their accuracy, painstakingly reconstructed records from a telephone debit card obtained under the alias Daryl Bridges, and used by both Mr. McVeigh and Mr. Nichols, showed calls to racetracks, chemical companies and hobby shops that could have supplied racing fuel to intensify the explosion.

Michael J. Fortier, Mr. McVeigh's friend from their Army days, and Mr. Fortier's wife, Lori, testified that Mr. McVeigh had told them of his plans to bomb the building. Mrs. Fortier said Mr. McVeigh had used soup cans from her kitchen to demonstrate how he would "shape" the charge. Mr. Fortier said Mr. McVeigh had taken him to Oklahoma City to case the Federal Building. On the way, Mr. Fortier said, Mr. McVeigh discussed his getaway plans.

On Friday, Judge Matsch told the jury in his final instructions that the Fortiers had a motive to lie. Mrs. Fortier received immunity from prosecution for her testimony. Her husband, who pleaded guilty to four bombing-related charges, is hoping that his testimony will help reduce his time in prison. His sentencing hearing will be held after the trial of Mr. Nichols. It was Mr. Fortier who received the harshest words from Mr. Jones, who urged the jury not to believe anything he said.

Still, it was Mr. McVeigh's younger sister, Jennifer, who supplied what Larry Mackey, a prosecutor, called "perhaps the single most significant document in this entire case in terms of evaluating whether a person, any person, this person, may come to hold a hatred so deep to do something so horrible."

That document, a letter written by her brother and left on her computer, was addressed to the "tyrannical" agents of the Alcohol, Tobacco and Firearms bureau, whom he blamed for the deaths of about 80 members of the Branch Davidian sect at their compound near Waco, Tex., on April 19, 1993. In the letter, Mr. McVeigh warned that the agents "will swing in the wind one day for your treasonous actions against the Constitution and the United States." He also wrote: "Remember the Nuremberg trials, war trials — 'but, but, but I was only following orders.' Die, you spineless cowardice bastards."

In his closing arguments, Mr. Mackey told the jury: "Those are words of Tim McVeigh. They measure his intent, and they were delivered to you through a witness who would rather not."

"All the News That's Fit to Print"

The New York Times

New York: **Today,** sunshine, late clouds. High 82. **Tonight,** cloudy, a shower. Low 69. **Tomorrow,** cloudy, chance of showers. High 78. **Yesterday,** high 88, low 71. Details, page B12.

VOL. CXLVI . . . . No. 50,840 | NEW YORK, TUESDAY, JULY 1, 1997 | $1 beyond the greater New York metropolitan area. | 60 CENTS

CHINA RESUMES CONTROL OF HONG KONG, CONCLUDING 156 YEARS OF BRITISH RULE

Associated Press

Reuters

In a ceremony marked by precision and martial music, Gov. Chris Patten solemnly received the British flag that flew at Government House. Hours later, a Chinese flag was raised inside the Exhibition and Convention Center.

Clinton Outlines Tax Cut Plan, Putting Emphasis on Education

By JAMES BENNET

WASHINGTON, June 30 — President Clinton laid out his plan today for divvying up $135 billion in tax cuts over the next five years, bending to Republican demands for a broad reduction in taxes on investment gains but shifting money away from the wealthiest families and toward his cherished higher education programs.

Arriving as Congress prepares to grapple with precisely how to substantially cut Federal taxes for the first time in 16 years, the plan was less a line in the sand than a formal statement of the President's bargaining position. After this week's recess, House and Senate negotiators are to hammer out a joint version of the tax cut plans that each passed last week, trying to arrive at a bill that Mr. Clinton will sign.

The President sharply criticized the Congressional tax cut plans today.

"They do an inadequate job of opening the doors to college," he said at the White House this morning, before departing on a political fund-raising trip to Boston and New York. "They direct far too little relief to the middle class. They include time-bomb tax cuts that threaten to explode the deficit."

Unlike the Congressional plans, Mr. Clinton's proposal would mean a tiny reduction or even an increase in capital gains taxes for the richest taxpayers, while people with incomes under $100,000 would see significant savings. [A17.]

Mr. Clinton also accused Republicans of backing away from commitments in the budget agreement to provide tax incentives to revive inner cities.

But he joined in the bipartisan optimism about an eventual deal, declining to say what proposals he would rule out. "I don't want to get into veto now," he said.

Although some Congressional Republicans suggested that he was acting a bit late, party members generally strove today for a magnanimous tone, congratulating Mr. Clinton for

Continued on Page A16

Registry Laws Tar Sex-Crime Convicts With Broad Brush

By TODD S. PURDUM

LOS ANGELES, June 30 — A 63-year-old closeted gay man, arrested in the 1950's in San Diego for having oral sex in a parked car with a fellow sailor, suddenly finds his life shattered when a neighbor opens a letter meant for him from the State of California ordering him to be photographed, fingerprinted and registered as a sex offender.

A Southern California youth counselor, convicted of having consensual sex with a teen-ager, has served his sentence and is striving to make a new life with his family when the local authorities, checking up on the whereabouts of known sex offenders, arrives on his doorstep with journalists in tow and his picture appears in the local newspaper.

An 18-year-old Wisconsin man, convicted of sexual assault after impregnating his under-age 15-year-old girlfriend — whom he wants to marry — must provide a DNA sample and then register with local police every year for the next 15 years as a convicted sex offender.

As states have rushed to adopt laws requiring registration of sex

Continued on Page A19

On the Internet: www.nytimes.com

Sunset? Not Yet.

The handover of Hong Kong removes from British rule 6.3 million people, reducing Her Majesty's possessions to a scattering of outposts and islands. But it can still be said that the sun does not set on the British Empire. At every moment, at some far-flung corner of the revolving globe, it is daytime in a place where the Union Jack flies.

Those corners keep getting smaller, of course. Britain now retains nine inhabited territories, with a total population of about 200,000, and a few tinier uninhabited holdings.

The largest remaining time-zone gap is between Pitcairn Island in the eastern Pacific, and Diego Garcia, a military base in the Indian Ocean.

According to Chief Petty Officer Patrick McCarthy of the United States Naval Observatory in Washington, when the sun set yesterday at 02:02 Greenwich Mean Time in Pitcairn Island, it had already risen 40 minutes before, at 01:22, in Diego Garcia. It is winter in the Southern Hemisphere, so that is about as short a day as the Empire can expect.

HONG KONG'S PEOPLE marked the moment with festivity and anxiety — not tension. Page A9.

THE BIGGEST COLONY remaining, Bermuda, sees Britain's loss in Asia as its gain: a great business opportunity. Page A10.

Associated Press

TIANANMEN SQUARE was the scene of a tightly controlled nationalistic display. Page A10.

Benchmarks of Justice

Over the Course of Nine Notable Months, The High Court Laid Down New Standards

By LINDA GREENHOUSE

News Analysis

WASHINGTON, June 30 — It was a Supreme Court term that defied labels and made history.

Perhaps the single most important fact about the term that ended last Friday after a weeklong torrent of landmark opinions is how important it was.

In case after case, whether venturing into new areas or revisiting old disputes, the Justices established new reference points, frameworks within which not only law but, to no small degree, social and political arrangements will now evolve.

In rejecting Congress's effort to regulate speech on the Internet, the Court delivered, with essential unanimity, a broadly forward-looking charter for free speech in the world's newest medium of communication; in terms of immediate practical consequence, this may have been the term's most significant decision.

In ruling that there is no general constitutional right to doctor-assisted suicide, the Court held the door open to future legislative developments and even, somewhat surprisingly, to future legal claims on behalf of a right of terminally ill people to control the timing and the manner of their death.

In overturning a part of the Brady gun-control law on the basis of a forcefully expressed, if narrowly supported, vision of state sovereignty, the Court served notice that long-settled assumptions about the primacy of the national government within the Federal system may no longer be valid.

All this from a Court that preached judicial restraint even as it overturned four Federal laws, including the Religious Freedom Restoration

Continued on Page A18

Crime Drops, Again

Preliminary statistics obtained yesterday show that serious crime has continued to decline in New York City. Page B1.

	1995	1996	1997
Murder Down 37% (from 1995)	592	529	371
Rape Down 11%	1,513	1,494	1,341
Robbery Down 25%	28,054	25,143	20,988
Assault Down 17%	17,704	15,100	14,749
Burglary Down 28%	37,011	31,390	26,581
Grand larceny Down 14%	30,965	28,791	26,671
Auto theft Down 27%	34,922	30,818	25,491

Source: Number of crime complaints to the New York City Police Department through June 29 of each year.

The New York Times

INSIDE

North Korea Agrees to Talks

After 44 years, North Korea said it would talk with South Korea, the United States and China on formally ending the Korean War. Page A11.

Art Dealer Accused of Fraud

A former New York art dealer was charged with defrauding clients, including the actor Jack Nicholson, of more than $2.5 million. Page B3.

In Jail and in the Spotlight

As three men convicted in a 1989 sexual assault were sent to jail, Glen Ridge, N.J., found itself in an unwanted spotlight again. Page B1.

Tyson Asks Forgiveness

"I couldn't tell you why I acted exactly as I did," Mike Tyson said as he apologized for biting Evander Holyfield's ear. SportsTuesday, page B7.

Time of Uncertainty Begins: Will Beijing Honor Vows?

By EDWARD A. GARGAN

HONG KONG, Tuesday, July 1 — In the first moments after midnight, in a ceremony of solemn precision and martial music, China resumed sovereignty over Hong Kong today, ending 156 years of British colonial rule.

Seconds after British soldiers lowered the Union Jack for the last time to the strains of "God Save the Queen," China's red banner was raised, marking the transfer of this free-wheeling capitalist territory to Communist control.

It was an event awaited with trepidation as well as excitement since 1984, when Britain and China agreed on terms for the transfer of power over this territory wrested from China in the 19th century wars over the opium trade. And it ushered a time of uncertainty over whether China would honor its pledge to maintain Hong Kong's way of life largely unaltered for the next 50 years.

For many ordinary people in the streets of Hong Kong, this was a time of celebration, not necessarily over the departure of the British or the arrival of the new masters from Beijing, but for experience of witnessing a big moment in history. [Page A9.]

In the convention center where the handover of power took place, China's President, Jiang Zemin, using a Mandarin dialect as alien to Hong Kong's Cantonese-speaking people as the English of the British authorities, declared the event "a festival for the Chinese nation and a victory for the universal cause of peace and justice."

"The return of Hong Kong to the motherland after a century of vicissitudes indicates that from now on, our Hong Kong compatriots have become true masters of this Chinese land and that Hong Kong has now entered a new era of development," Mr. Jiang said.

Change came quickly as the territory's new rulers assumed control.

At the stroke of midnight, Hong Kong's elected legislature was abolished, and a Beijing-appointed body of lawmakers took its place. A range of Hong Kong's civil liberties were rolled back as new constraints were placed on the right to protest and association, and any form of speech promoting the independence of Taiwan or Tibet was banned.

Change came in small ways too. Across Hong Kong, police officers, fire fighters and all the uniformed services unpinned their colonial insignia and replaced it with the new symbols of China's Hong Kong. The British coat of arms was removed from above the main government building at midnight, and the royal emblem was pried from the Rolls-Royce that used to ferry the British Governor about and will now serve Hong Kong's new Chief Executive.

Quietly, almost forgotten, Prince Charles of Britain and the former colonial Governor, Chris Patten,

Continued on Page A8

Year of the Trojan Horse

By NICHOLAS D. KRISTOF

News Analysis

HONG KONG, Tuesday, July 1 — As dawn rises for the first time over red Chinese flags officially fluttering here in a capitalist breeze, the most fascinating question is not how China will change Hong Kong but how Hong Kong will change China — and the world beyond.

At stake is not just the fate of the 6.3 million people who live here but, more important, the 1.2 billion neighbors next door in China, plus the 20 million who live in Taiwan and the hundreds of millions more who live elsewhere in the region.

To an enormous extent, many of the critical issues of the 21st century will depend in part on how events unfold in this peculiar crossroads of scones and dim sum.

Whether the United States and China are headed for partnership or for conflict, whether Taiwan will eventually become independent or return to China's embrace, whether China will grow strong and democratic or collapse in chaos — all these will be determined in part by what happens in Hong Kong.

The central question is whether Hong Kong amounts to a colossal Trojan horse: a prize so glorious that China's Communists cannot leave it outside the gates but which, once inside, will destroy those in power.

Indeed, looking at the way Hong Kong and China have influenced each other in the last dozen years, one could easily conclude that the hand-wringing over Hong Kong's future is misplaced. No one has ever made money betting against Hong Kong, though many have tried, and perhaps it is the Chinese Communist Party leaders who should tremble about whether their style of life and leadership can long survive.

"I think the democratic struggle of people here in Hong Kong for freedom and human rights will influence China," mused Han Dongfang, a Chinese labor leader who was impris-

Continued on Page A9

THE OVERVIEW

China Resumes Control of Hong Kong, Ending 156 Years of British Rule

Continued From Page A1

were driven from the handover ceremony to the harbor front, where the royal yacht Britannia waited to bear them away from Hong Kong.

Shortly after the midnight change of sovereignty, President Jiang gave the oath of office to Beijing's choice to govern this territory, Tung Chee-hwa, a 60-year-old British-educated shipping magnate.

As dawn broke, an unbroken procession of Chinese Army armored personnel carriers, trucks and buses carrying 4,000 soldiers streamed over the border and through the streets of Hong Kong. At villages along the way, thousands of Hong Kongers waited in the rain, waving flags and bouquets of flowers and shouting welcomes to the soldiers.

British rule ended in a ceremony whose details exhausted the negotiating skills of both sides.

On a simple dais inside the just completed Exhibition and Convention Center, two pairs of flagpoles — one flying the Union Jack and the British Hong Kong flag, the other bare — stood before chairs for Mr. Jiang's party and those accompanying Prince Charles.

Prince Charles spoke briefly. "The United Kingdom," he declared, "has been proud and privileged to have had responsibility for the people of Hong Kong, to have provided a framework of opportunity in which Hong Kong has so conspicuously succeeded, and to have been part of the success which the people of Hong Kong have made of their opportunities."

"God Save the Queen" was played by a band of Scots Guards in tall, bearskin hats, and the Union Jack was brought down.

After a five-second pause, time for British cymbals to stop vibrating, the Chinese national anthem was played and the Chinese flag raised alongside the new flag of Hong Kong.

Hong Kong had returned to Chinese rule.

The transfer from British rule began at 4:30 P.M. Monday, when the doors of Government House, the home for British governors since 1855, opened and Mr. Patten, his wife, Lavender, and their three daughters walked down the steps.

Drawn up at attention in the sweeping circular drive was the police band in snow-white tunics. In a blue suit, the bags under his eyes heavier than usual, his now gray-white hair a bit disheveled, Mr. Patten mounted a small stepped dais.

The band broke into the first stanza of "God Save the Queen," and Mr. Patten, Hong Kong's 28th Governor, lowered his head, swallowing heavily in a surge of emotion, emotion that would shake the Governor repeatedly through the day.

Eight officers from the Royal Police Training School snapped through a sharply choreographed flipping of rifles, turns and slow-step marching in a salute to the last Governor.

Stepping from the dais, Mr. Patten walked slowly down a line of representatives of each of the territory's services, from the Correctional Services Department to the Auxiliary Medical Services, all in wilting white dress uniforms.

Then, as a single bugler played "Last Post," a thin drizzle brushed the courtyard, and the British flag slipped down the flagpole. The police band struck up Mr. Patten's favorite song, "Highland Cathedral," and with the folded flag on a royal blue pillow, he stepped into a Rolls-Royce.

Slowly, the long black car flying the Governor's ensign from the hood circled the courtyard before Government House three times, a Chinese ritual performed by all previous governors to signal "we shall return."

As Mr. Patten's car pulled from the gates of Government House, gates that still bore the Queen's seal, crowds waved and cheered. A small contingent of police officers in their green summer uniforms swung the iron gates closed, ending 122 years of British residence.

The drizzle turned to showers and then to a downpour that washed the harbor front in sheets of monsoon-borne rains. Still, the British farewell ceremony began sharply at 6:15 P.M. as a gray sky melted into hues of gold and rose. Two dragon dance teams rose and fell across a tarmac ground that once was the main British naval base here.

A succession of performances by choirs and orchestras, and arias sung by Dame Gwyneth Jones and Warren Mok followed.

With rain pelting down on him, Mr. Patten delivered his final speech as Governor, a short piece of oratory that remained as robustly defiant as any he has given, a declaration of his own principles as Governor and a public challenge to much of Chief Executive Tung's philosophy of governance.

"Our own nation's contribution here," he said, "was to provide the scaffolding that enabled the people of Hong Kong to ascend: the rule of law, clean and light-handed government, the values of a free society. The beginnings of representative government and democratic accountability."

"Hong Kong's values are decent values," he continued. "They are universal values. They are the values of the future in Asia as elsewhere, a future in which the happiest and the richest communities, and the most confident and the most stable too, will be those that best combine political liberty and economic freedom as we do today."

At 8:45 in the evening, just after the fireworks celebrating British rule ended, 509 officers, soldiers and sailors from the Chinese Army began moving over the border in glossy black Audis, buses and open-back trucks, in which troops stood at attention, their white gloved hands gripping the wooden side rails. Other trucks in camouflage paint, some with green canvas covers, followed slowly behind.

In Hong Kong's newly built convention center, a curving, sculpted-roofed edifice jutting into the harbor, a banquet was given by the British for 4,000 guests, including Secretary of State Madeleine K. Albright and China's Foreign Minister, Qian Qichen, who has spearheaded Beijing's arrangements for Hong Kong.

Over Scottish salmon, stuffed chicken breast and a red fruit pudding with raspberry sauce, Hong Kong's wealthiest and most powerful people, British and Chinese alike, ate their last meal under a British flag.

Neither President Jiang nor Prime Minister Li Peng, the first Communist Chinese leaders to set foot in colonial Hong Kong, attended the banquet.

With only an hour of sovereignty left, Foreign Secretary Robin Cook of Britain, relaxed with hands in his pockets, waited at the entrance of the new Hong Kong convention center, Chief Executive Tung at his side, for the arrival of President Jiang.

An honor guard of Black Watch in white jackets and kilts stood at attention.

Mr. Jiang's black bulletproof Mercedes, with both Hong Kong and Chinese license plates, arrived moments later. The Chinese President was helped from the car, and Mr. Patten shook his hand, saying simply, "Welcome to Hong Kong."

Against the surge of patriotic sentiment and the wisps of nostalgia for the departed British, there were protests from pro-democracy figures who had been expelled from the legislature with the advent of Chinese rule.

From the balcony of the Legislative Council building, Martin Lee, the leader of the pro-democracy forces in the disbanded legislature, told thousands of demonstrators that democracy would return to Hong Kong.

"We know," he told the crowd below, "that without a democratically constituted government and legislature, there is no way for our people to be insured that good laws will be passed to protect their freedoms."

"If there is no democracy, there is no rule of law," he continued. "We want Hong Kong and China to advance together and not step back together. We are proud to be Chinese, more proud than ever before. But we ask: Why is it our leaders in China will not give us more democracy? Why must they take away the modest democracy we have fought so hard to win from the British Government?"

Meanwhile, detachments of Chinese troops fanned out across Hong Kong, taking possession of military bases. At the Prince of Wales barracks, still bearing that name this morning, an honor guard stood at attention while the Chinese flag was raised. And on the radio station that had served British forces here, 107.4 FM, there was nothing but the hiss of empty static.

At Possession Point, the place where on Jan. 26, 1841, Capt. Edward Belcher first raised the British flag, there were memories, expressions of happiness, pride and worry.

On a bench in what is now Hollywood Road Park, Choy Sum Mui, 75, reflected on her long life and the future that awaits her under a new sovereign.

"I came to Hong Kong when the Japanese bombed my village," she said, speaking slowly. "I'm illiterate, so I don't know much about things unless people tell me. People say this is Possession Point, but it doesn't mean much to me. I've never seen a Communist before. I don't know what they are like. Really, I'm so old already, all this change doesn't mean much to me."

On Possession Street, a Mr. Lam, 72, said: "It's a good thing we can finally get rid of the imperialists. We're all Chinese. I feel great. This land belongs to China."

Associated Press

Governor Chris Patten left Government House in Hong Kong in his car yesterday after a ceremony in which he said goodbye to his staff and the British flag was lowered for the last time.

Words of a Prince and a President: Continuity, Change and Assurances

HONG KONG, Tuesday, July 1 (Agence France-Presse) — Following are excerpts from speeches made by the Prince of Wales and Jiang Zemin, President of China, on the formal handover of Hong Kong to Chinese rule. The official translation of President Jiang's remarks was provided by the New China News Agency.

PRINCE CHARLES

. . . This important and special ceremony marks a moment of both change and continuity in Hong Kong's history.

It marks, first of all, the restoration of Hong Kong to the People's Republic of China, under the terms of the Sino-British Joint Declaration of 1984, after more than 150 years of British administration.

This ceremony also celebrates continuity because . . . the Hong Kong Special Administrative Region will have its own government, and retain its own society, its own economy and its own way of life. . . .

I should like to pay tribute to the people of Hong Kong themselves for all that they have achieved in the last century and a half. The triumphant success of Hong Kong demands — and deserves — to be maintained.

Hong Kong has shown the world how dynamism and stability can be defining characteristics of a successful society. These have together created a great economy which is the envy of the world. . . . As a flourishing commercial and cultural crossroads, it has . . . enriched all our lives.

Thirteen years ago, . . .the United Kingdom and the People's Republic of China recognized . . . that these special elements which had created the crucial conditions for Hong Kong's success should continue.

They agreed that, in order to maintain that success, Hong Kong should have its own separate trading and financial systems, enjoy autonomy and an elected legislature, maintain its laws and liberties, and be run by the people of Hong Kong and be accountable to them.

Those special elements have served Hong Kong well over the past two decades. Hong Kong has coped with the challenges of great economic, social and political transition with almost none of the disturbance and dislocation which in other parts of the world have so often accompanied change on such a scale. . . .

In a few moments, the United Kingdom's responsibilities will pass to the People's Republic of China. Hong Kong will thereby be restored to China and, within the framework of "one country, two systems," it will continue to have a strong identity of its own. . . .

Ladies and gentlemen, China will tonight take responsibility for a place and a people which matter greatly to us all. The solemn pledges made before the world in the 1984 Joint Declaration guarantee the continuity of Hong Kong's way of life.

For its part, the United Kingdom will maintain its unwavering support for the Joint Declaration. Our commitment and our strong links to Hong Kong will continue, and will, I am confident, flourish. . . .

I should like on behalf of Her Majesty the Queen and of the entire British people, to express our thanks, admiration, affection and good wishes to all the people of Hong Kong, who have been such staunch and special friends over so many generations. We shall not forget you, and we shall watch with the closest interest as you embark on this new era of your remarkable history.

John Giannini for The New York Times

Leaving Hong Kong's convention hall yesterday after the transfer ceremony were, from left, Prime Minister Li Peng and President Jiang Zemin of China and Prince Charles and Prime Minister Tony Blair of Britain.

PRESIDENT JIANG ZEMIN

The national flag of the People's Republic of China and the regional flag of the Hong Kong Special Administrative Region of the People's Republic of China have now solemnly risen over this land.

At this moment, people of all countries in the world are casting their eyes on Hong Kong. In accordance with the Sino-British Joint Declaration . . . the two Governments have held on schedule the handover ceremony to mark China's resumption of the exercise of sovereignty over Hong Kong and the official establishment of the Hong Kong Special Administrative Region of the People's Republic of China.

This is both a festival for the Chinese nation and a victory for the universal cause of peace and justice. . . .

I wish to express thanks to all the people in both China and Britain who have contributed to the settlement of the Hong Kong question. . . . I wish to extend my cordial greetings and best wishes to the six million or more Hong Kong compatriots who have now returned to the embrace of the Motherland.

After the return of Hong Kong, the Chinese Government will unswervingly implement the basic policies of "one country, two systems," "Hong Kong people administering Hong Kong" and "a high degree of autonomy" and keep the previous socioeconomic system and way of life of Hong Kong unchanged and its laws basically unchanged. . . .

The Hong Kong Special Administrative Region shall be vested, in accordance with the Basic Law, with executive power, legislative power and independent judicial power, including that of final adjudication.

The Hong Kong residents shall enjoy various rights and freedoms according to law. The Hong Kong Special Administrative Region shall gradually develop a democratic system that suits Hong Kong's reality. . . .

Hong Kong will retain its status as a free port, continue to function as an international financial, trade and shipping center and maintain its economic and cultural ties with other countries, regions and relevant international organizations. The legitimate economic interests of all countries and regions in Hong Kong will be protected by law.

I hope that all the countries and regions that have investment and trade interests here will continue to work for the prosperity and stability of Hong Kong. . . .

I am confident that . . . the Government of the Hong Kong Special Administrative Region and Hong Kong compatriots will be able to manage Hong Kong well, build it up and maintain its long-term prosperity and stability. . . .

"All the News That's Fit to Print"

The New York Times

Late Edition
New York: Today, mostly sunny and pleasant. High 83. Tonight, tranquil. Low 69. Tomorrow, ample sun, warmer, more humid. High 88. Yesterday, high 79, low 63. Details, page 32.

VOL. CXLVI . . No. 50,901 NEW YORK, SUNDAY, AUGUST 31, 1997 — $3 beyond the greater New York metropolitan area. — $2.50

In Bronx Club, Welfare Mothers Prepare for Jobs, and Then Wait

By RACHEL L. SWARNS

Linda Bailey walked nervously into the world of work, smoothing the wrinkles in her cream pants suit, fiddling with the pearls around her neck, reading and rereading her crisp new résumé and imagining that she belonged in the crush of professional women in midtown Manhattan.

Then she swung back to reality and her brittle confidence cracked.

The suit was the only one she owned. The two dollars in her wallet had to last for two days. She had promised her sons 50-cent ice creams and the world "once Mommy has work." But Ms. Bailey has not worked in eight years. Ms. Bailey is on welfare. And on days like these, she fears she will never escape the dole.

"Sometimes I think these people got all the jobs," said Ms. Bailey, 33, dazed by the throngs of workers shoving past as she hawked her résumé from office to office. "Will there be any jobs for me?"

Librado Romero/The New York Times

Linda Bailey, 33, seeking job leads in a work-readiness program.

New York City is pushing thousands of anxious welfare mothers into the job market for the first time in years, sending them to job readiness programs to learn to dress professionally, to write résumés, to give an employer a firm, confident handshake and to believe in the prospect of financial independence and new-found self-respect.

But while the four-week programs, known as job clubs, have already sent nearly 8,000 women to pound the pavement with résumés and newly fired dreams, the vast majority of these women fail to find work, city officials say. Of the 13 women who participated in a Bronx job club with Ms. Bailey last month, 3 found jobs to push them off the welfare rolls. Ms. Bailey was not among them.

One year after the passage of the landmark Federal welfare law, the experiences of the women in the Bronx job club reflect the challenges confronting states as they struggle to move welfare recipients with little education and little work experience into jobs.

Most states offer job readiness programs for welfare recipients and some have demonstrated marked success. But until recently, New York City has focused more on placing women in six-month workfare assignments, where they work for their benefits, than on programs to place them directly in permanent jobs.

But this strategy has been criticized for simply shuttling some welfare mothers from workfare assignments to job clubs and back. And this summer, as the City Comptroller's office reported faltering job placement rates at several clubs, city officials decided to extend the contracts of the private agencies that run the programs only through December, while they consider a new plan.

"The problem was that job clubs

Continued on Page 30

U.S. Is Seeking More Influence Over Education

By PETER APPLEBOME

As vacations end and 52 million students return to school, their elders find themselves in a historic tug of war pitting the traditional local control of education against a growing national presence that is making Washington a bigger player in education now than at perhaps any other time in the nation's history.

When Congress convenes in September, President Clinton will try to win support for the first truly national performance tests in the schools, and Republicans in Congress will mobilize to kill the initiative.

In a radio address yesterday in which he promoted his testing plan, the President said he was encouraged by a report on long-term trends that showed student improvement in some subjects. [Page 18]

Republicans and a few Democrats will push for proposals to increase vouchers and school choice, a California Congressman will argue for a bill designed to upgrade teaching by linking Federal aid to improved state teaching standards, and other issues like national reading initiatives and development of a national curriculum will receive enormous attention.

Experts disagree on how much of what is happening reflects a long-term shift toward greater Federal involvement or is a result of a historical moment: a politically adroit President intensely focused on education, aging baby boomers who

Continued on Page 18

U.S.-MEXICO STUDY SEES EXAGGERATION OF MIGRATION DATA

JOINT SCRUTINY IS A FIRST

Elusive Statistic on Increase in Yearly Mexican Influx Lowered to 105,000

By SAM DILLON

MEXICO CITY, Aug. 30 — The first formal migration study to be sponsored by the American and Mexican Governments has concluded that the number of undocumented Mexican workers who have settled in the United States in this decade is far lower than some politicians have suggested, only about 105,000 a year.

Drawn from a two-year analysis of American and Mexican census and other data, the figure is the first authoritative estimate of the net annual flow of illegal Mexican workers into the United States, which has been an elusive statistic at the center of political and academic dispute on both sides of the border.

During the last Presidential campaign in the United States, some conservatives made immigration a powerful issue, with lurid portrayals of an America overrun by illegal Mexicans, a million of whom were said to pour across the border each year, taking jobs from Americans and driving up welfare costs.

The new estimate appears alongside a series of other groundbreaking conclusions in a new Binational Study on Migration. The document was commissioned by Presidents Clinton and Ernesto Zedillo in early 1995 and brought together 20 prominent demographers and scholars — 10 Mexican and 10 American — for two and a half years of research, field work and analysis.

"No controversy ever really ends, so it would be ingenuous for us to think this will resolve all the disputes over migration," said Francisco Alba Hernández, a demographer at the Colegio de México who took part in the study. "But this is our attempt to arrive at the most reasonable overview."

The study was circulated Friday to Secretary of State Madeleine K. Albright, Attorney General Janet Reno, Foreign Minister José Ángel Gurría of Mexico and other senior officials; it is to be made public Tuesday. A contributor to the study provided The New York Times with its executive summary and key chapters.

Migration is one of the most contentious issues dividing the countries, and for three decades each Government has molded policies to suit its own needs. The joint study is part of a shift toward increased cooperation, officials said.

Continued on Page 9

Diana Killed in a Car Accident in Paris

Pool photo by John Stillwell

Diana in May, at the opening of an arts center in Leicester.

In Flight From Paparazzi — Friend Dies

By CRAIG R. WHITNEY

PARIS, Sunday, Aug. 31 — Diana, the Princess of Wales, was killed shortly after midnight today in an automobile accident in a tunnel by the Seine. The accident also killed Emad Mohammed al-Fayed, the Harrods heir, and their driver, the police said.

Diana's death was announced this morning by the Interior Minister, Jean-Pierre Chévènement. She died after being hospitalized in intensive care at the Pitié-Salpétrière Hospital in southeast Paris.

A bodyguard was seriously injured, according to a police spokesman.

"The car was being chased by photographers on motorcycles, which could have caused the accident," a spokesman for the Prefecture of Police said. Several motorcyclists were detained for questioning after the crash, Reuters reported, quoting police officials.

The Princess, 36, was divorced from Prince Charles, the Prince of Wales and heir to the British throne, last year. She had vacationed with Mr. al-Fayed, 41, the son of Harrods's owner, Mohammed al-Fayed, on the French Riviera earlier this month and had been expected to return to London today to be with her two sons, the Princes William and Harry. [Obituaries of Diana and Mr. al-Fayed appear on page 31.]

French radio stations reported that a spokesman for the British royal family in London expressed anger and said the accident was predictable because photographers relentlessly pursued the Princess wherever she went.

The crash occurred 35 minutes past midnight in the Alma Tunnel, on the right bank of the Seine under the Place de l'Alma, the police said.

The driver was hired from the Ritz Hotel in Paris. The Princess and Mr. al-Fayed had been pursued from the Ritz Hotel, where they were believed to be staying after spending time together on the Riviera.

The Paris police said that the Interior Minister, Jean-Pierre Chévènement, and the Prefect of Police, Philippe Massoni, had accompanied the British Ambassador in Paris to the hospital where the Princess was treated.

The police said the car was totally wrecked. The impact was so great, the car's radiator was hurled onto the knees of the front-seat passenger. The Princess was in the back seat.

The site of the accident, in the Eighth Arrondissement, is on a high-speed road along the Seine with a divided roadway as it passes under the Place de l'Alma to the Place de la Concorde.

On Aug. 21, Diana and Mr. al-Fayed, who is of Egyptian ancestry and is commonly called Dodi, flew to the French Mediterranean resort of St. Tropez for their third holiday in each other's company in five weeks.

Mr. al-Fayed's father said in an interview with The New York Times in London last week that the two were simply "young people getting

Continued on Page 10

Limerick, Burned, Also Finds A Salve in 'Angela's Ashes'

By WARREN HOGE

LIMERICK, Ireland, Aug. 24 — This sodden city in western Ireland has been such a hard-luck town that it cannot even lay claim to the form of verse everyone assumes was named after it.

"The truth is you can go into pubs here, and you'll hear yarns and doggerel and songs and parodies," said Brendan Halligan, editor of The Limerick Leader. "But I've never heard anyone recite a limerick."

H. D. Inglis, author of an early travel guide, came here in 1834 and found Limerick "the very vilest town" he had ever visited. Heinrich Böll, the German Nobel-Prize-winning novelist, saw it for the first time in 1950 and pronounced it a "gloomy little town" with "everything submerged in sour darkness."

More recently it has been been made fun of in a popular television show as "stab city," a label — arising out of several muggings in the 1980's — that the Mayor, Frank Leddin, finds so objectionable he will not utter it. "You can mention it," he said in his office by the Shannon River, "but you won't be quoting Frank Leddin."

Long considered Ireland's most entrenched Catholic city — the author Conor Cruise O'Brien once called its bishop the "Mullah of Limerick" — it has suffered from stereotyping as "violent, intolerant, obscu-

Continued on Page 12

Economies in Asia Are Losing Some Zip

Has the Asian boom fizzled?

For years, Asian stock markets were the hottest in the world. But lately, currency and stock market turmoil is splashing throughout Asia. Just this week, Malaysia curbed the selling of stocks, setting off a convulsion that sent the Philippine market tumbling 9 percent on Thursday, and the Hong Kong index cascading 5 percent on Friday.

By now, the Thai market has plunged 70 percent from its peak in 1994, and some experts are questioning how secure the foundation might be under the Asian miracle.

Article, page 6.

Billion-Dollar Plan to Clean New York City Water at Its Source

Suzanne DeChillo/The New York Times

Scientists from New York City's Department of Environmental Protection testing for impurities at the Kensico Reservoir, near White Plains.

By ANDREW C. REVKIN

TROUBLED WATERS
A special report.

The flow of drinking water to New York City begins as far away as a damp spot under some leaves on a mountainside 120 miles north of Times Square. For 155 years, the city has maintained a complicated network of reservoirs and aqueducts to carry rain and melted snow from distant hills to bathtubs in Brooklyn and sinks on Staten Island.

Now the purity of that flow faces the gravest threats ever, from both old sewage systems and a new wave of unbridled development in the watershed. To combat those threats, a growing force of scientists, engineers, special police officers and others from the city's Department of Environmental Protection has fanned out this summer across suburbs and farmland to explain and enforce the first new pollution rules for the watershed in 44 years.

They have 10 years and a billion dollars to fix faulty sewage treatment plants, to rebuild barnyards and pastures to control the flow of manure, and to buy tens of thousands of acres of land to build a buffer zone against encroaching development. Cities across the nation are developing programs to prevent pollution of drinking water at its source, but nothing approaches the magnitude of the cleanup that has just begun in the 2,000 square miles of hills and river valleys funneling water to the nine million people who use New York City's system.

But the grand experiment has shaky underpinnings: scientists have only an embryonic understanding of the forces that keep water pure or allow pollution to accumulate. And the plan depends on a fragile political alliance between rural upstate communities and New York City that can be upset at any time.

In essence, the city's task is to control three distant, sprawling regions where, since 1911, it has had the right under New York State law to limit water pollution. But for decades the main goal of city water officials was to increase the supply of water; its purity was rarely at issue. Now, the bureaucracy is forced to reinvent itself and to put the emphasis on cleanliness.

The Federal Government has made the rules clear: if the city cannot insure purity by managing the far-flung watershed, it will have to spend billions on a filtering plant. And while all involved emphasize that there are no health problems today with the flow of what a succession of New York City mayors have called "the champagne of drinking water," the problems are mounting.

Already, 10 out of 19 reservoirs are

Continued on Page 28

INSIDE

First Ladies of the Court
The Houston Comets defeated the Liberty to win the inaugural championship of the Women's National Basketball Association. Sports, section 8.

A Boycott in Mexico
The long-dominant party in Mexico boycotted the opening of Congress, the first in more than four decades that it does not control. Page 8.

TODAY'S SECTIONS

Arts and Leisure/Section 2
Whether on Broadway, at a rock concert or at the symphony, the backstage show is different from the one on stage.

Automobiles/Section 11*†

Book Review/Section 7
Christina Vella's "Intimate Enemies" reconstructs a marital scandal of the 19th century, spanning four generations of two families, involving sums of money and provoking a man to take his life.

The City/Section 13§

Editorials and Op-Ed/Section 4

Magazine/Section 6
Rudy Crew, New York City Chancellor, is off to a strong start in turning a few model schools into a system.

Real Estate/Section 9*
For a fortunate few, luxury apartments in new buildings at bargain rents.

SportsSunday/Section 8
A look at the coming season.

Money and Business/Section 3
Fitness center, cooking school, sushi bar, shoe shop and driver's license station — the grocery store is changing.

Regional Weeklies/Section 13¶

Television/Section 12*

Travel/Section 5
Nova Scotia: a rich cultural mix.

Week in Review/Section 4
It's the economy, stupid. Again.

Employment Advertising/Section 10*

News Summary	2		
International	3-13		
Metro	25-30		
National	14-23		
Obituaries	31	TV Update	38
Radio Highlights	38	Weather	32
Styles	33	Weddings	36

* In New York City and the metropolitan region. († Elsewhere, auto pages are in section 3.)
§ In the five boroughs of New York.
¶ In Long Island, Westchester, Connecticut and central and northern New Jersey.

On the Internet: www.nytimes.com

In South, Korean Unity Appealing in Abstract Only

By NICHOLAS D. KRISTOF

KUMGOK, South Korea, Aug. 26 — Sitting cross-legged on the linoleum floor of her living room, across from a plastic basketball hoop with a picture of a beaming Michael Jordan that her son had stuck to the wall, Kim Sun Ye shrugged and wriggled in embarrassment and finally blurted out the heresy.

"For ordinary people, unification will cause a lot of problems," said Ms. Kim, a 33-year-old farm wife in this little village near the North Korean border. "I don't honestly know if it's a good thing."

Then she giggled again in horror and paused, as if to see whether Mother Korea might strike her dead with a lightning bolt.

This heresy is becomingly increasingly common, but it still makes people profoundly uncomfortable. It challenges the holy teaching that Koreans are nurtured on — that the overwhelming national goal must be to unify with North Korea as soon as possible.

All across South Korea, on city streets and in villages like this, ordinary people like Ms. Kim are beginning to voice such doubts as they think about unification in a concrete sense, as something that might actually happen any time because of the hunger and economic crisis in North Korea.

And some are finding to their shock and dismay that unification — Korea's sacred cause for half a century — is not necessarily what they want right now.

So some South Koreans are coming to regard unification the way Saint Augustine felt about virtue, in his prayer: "Please give me chastity, but not yet."

Kumgok is a little village of about 700 people, with a jutting mountain of dense forests behind it and vivid green rice paddies unfurled in front of it, about two hours' drive northwest of Seoul on winding roads flanked by periodic tank traps intended to stop any North Korean invasion. It is just one randomly chosen village, but it seems to be torn by the same ambivalence toward the North as is the rest of the country, riven by fault lines that divide neighbor from neighbor.

There are old peasants like Kim Wan Seok, who has family members in the North and yearns for unification as soon as possible so that he can visit his old home and bring his relatives to live here in Kumgok. Then there are women like Suh Myong Ok, who does not sound welcoming toward Mr. Kim's long-lost relatives, as she frets about the possibility of hordes of North Koreans descending on villages like this.

Photographs by Nicholas D. Kristof/The New York Times

Kim Wan Seok has relatives in North Korea and yearns for unification as soon as possible. He worked in his rice paddy recently in Kumgok.

"Just think about it," she muttered darkly, shaking her head. "All those people flooding down here. It'd make life very difficult for us."

Shin Jin Kyun, a carpenter who lives nearby, said he felt sorry for North Koreans but suggested that their mind-set is different.

"It's possible," he said delicately, "that they are not so honest."

The famine that is reportedly sweeping the North is now testing the traditional patriotic mantras about all Koreans being members of the same family. The most obvious saviors for the hungry North are people in the South, and some South Koreans argue fervently that they should be doing more for their "brothers and sisters" in the North. But for others, the talk about kinship is fine so long as it does not mean higher taxes.

"Why should we give them money?" said Lee Han Gwee, a 69-year-old widow who was sorting red peppers by her house to make kimchi. "They should work for their own food and money. They have plenty of land up there."

Lee C-um Lan, a 58-year-old woman, frowned and said: "We don't even have enough food for ourselves. Why should we send it to the North?"

The New York Times

Ambivalence toward North Korea divides neighbors in Kumgok.

Yet there is sympathy for the North as well as suspicion, and arguments among the villagers are common. When Shin Il Kyun, a pudgy 60-year-old with a fringe of gray around his bald pate, suggested that after unification it would be a mistake to allow North Koreans to vote, his neighbor, Park Ki Woon, looked at him in outrage.

"That would make the North Koreans our slaves!" Mr. Park declared, waving his hand, his animation perhaps fortified by the cup of clear liquor he had just drunk. "South Korea would be making North Korea a colony, just as we all used to be the slaves of Japan."

Mr. Shin shook his head sharply. If North Korea offered just one candidate for president of the unified country, he suggested ominously, that candidate might well beat the handful of candidates who would compete from the South. "So," he added fiercely, "we could be ruled by North Koreans."

Mr. Park, a lean 44-year-old, paused and reflected on that. "Well," he said mildly, "there should be a three-to-five-year transition before holding presidential elections." In that interim, he explained, it would be best for South Koreans to rule the country.

To be sure, the two Koreas are among the most nationalistic countries in the world, and eventual reunification remains a deeply felt patriotic goal. Mr. Park said he worried about the cost of reunification and the economic consequences, but he added a common mantra:

"Everybody in Korea wants unification to happen as soon as possible," he said. "That's obvious to everyone."

At least it used to be. In the last few years a growing number of Korean and Western studies began to look at the financial burden on West Germany from the absorption of East Germany in 1990 and began to calculate the cost to South Korea of unifying with the North. The estimates of the cost vary enormously, from about $130 billion up to $2 trillion, but they all suggest that the economic dislocations would be staggering for the South.

It is startling how many ordinary people in South Korea, whether on the street in Seoul or in a little village like Kumgok, can knowledgeably discuss trends in Germany's post-unification G.N.P. All this has left South Koreans torn between the patriotic yearning for unification and their reluctance to risk a surge in unemployment and taxes.

"A lot of people in private will tell me what they regard as a confession: that they want reunification, but only after they are dead," said Roy Richard Grinker, an anthropologist at George Washington University who is completing a book on South Korean attitudes toward the North. Professor Grinker added that the experience of North Korean defectors in the South underscores how difficult the North's adjustment to capitalism will be.

"Half of the 800 known North Korean defectors in the South are unemployed," he said. "They suffer from depression and emotional distress and other problems, and they are to some extent a model of how difficult it is to cross the border between the two Koreas."

Lee Han Gwee says of the North, "Why should we give them money?"

The tangle of complex feelings toward North Koreans is raising new questions about what would happen if the two nations did actually unify. The division of the two Koreas remains the greatest remaining challenge left over from the cold war, but the ambivalence in South Korea underscores that unification would be an immensely complex and painful process that could require a generation to complete.

South Korea is already torn apart by regional rivalries that go back many centuries, particularly between the southwest and the southeast, and unification would add a new overlay of provincial antagonisms. For while many people repeat the refrain that "we are all one family" or "we are all flesh and blood," they often look horrified when asked whether after reunification they would allow a son or daughter to marry a North Korean.

"I would not allow my kids to marry a North Korean," Roh Geum Hee, a housewife with permed hair and gold earrings, declared worriedly as she stood in the entrance to her house in Kumgok. "Since they are from the North, I can't trust them. I don't know what they are thinking."

She paused and added softly, "I can't just change my attitude all of a sudden and welcome them here."

Company News:
Tuesday through Saturday,
Business Day

Agence France-Presse

The wreckage of Princess Diana's car in a tunnel in Paris. She and two others died in the accident, which occurred early today.

Diana and Arab Friend Die In Automobile Crash in Paris

Continued From Page 1

to know each other."

British newspapers reported that Diana first met Mr. al-Fayed almost 10 years ago when he and Prince Charles played polo on opposing teams. Films he had produced or co-produced included the 1981 Oscar-winning "Chariots of Fire," "The World According to Garp," "F/X" and "Hook."

Reportedly a multimillionaire, Mr. al-Fayed had homes in London, New York, Los Angeles and Switzerland and a garage full of luxury cars. He was divorced after a marriage that lasted eight months in 1994.

Diana was catapulted into the public eye at age 19 in 1981 when it was announced that she was engaged to Charles, the heir to the British throne and 12 years her senior.

The couple were married on July 29 that year in London in a ceremony watched by millions and billed as a "fairy-tale wedding."

Diana soon became a mother, to Prince William in June 1982, but by the birth of her second son, Harry, in September 1984, her biographer Andrew Morton wrote in "Diana: Her True Story," she was already suffering from bulimia and had attempted suicide five times.

From 1986, the first press stories began appearing of cracks in the marriage, and Mr. Morton later wrote that Charles had resumed his relationship with a married friend, Camilla Parker Bowles, at that time.

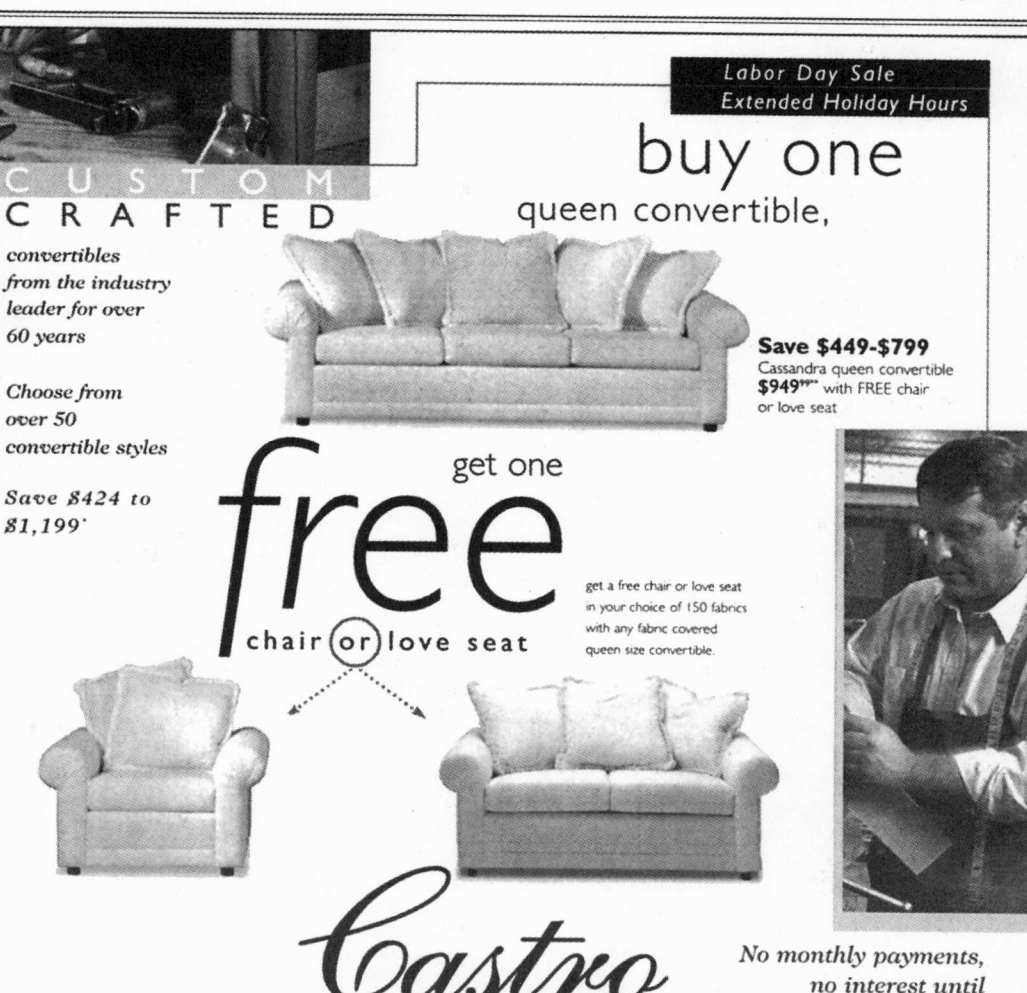

"All the News That's Fit to Print"

The New York Times

Late Edition
New York: **Today**, sunshine, light breeze. High 79. **Tonight**, clear, cloudy late. Low 60. **Tomorrow**, mix of sun and clouds, a shower. High 77. **Yesterday**, high 74, low 52. Details, page 34.

VOL. CXLVII . . . . No. 51,167 — Copyright © 1998 The New York Times — NEW YORK, SUNDAY, MAY 24, 1998 — $2 beyond the greater New York metropolitan area. — $2.50

IRISH VOTERS, NORTH AND SOUTH, GIVE RESOUNDING 'YES' TO PEACE

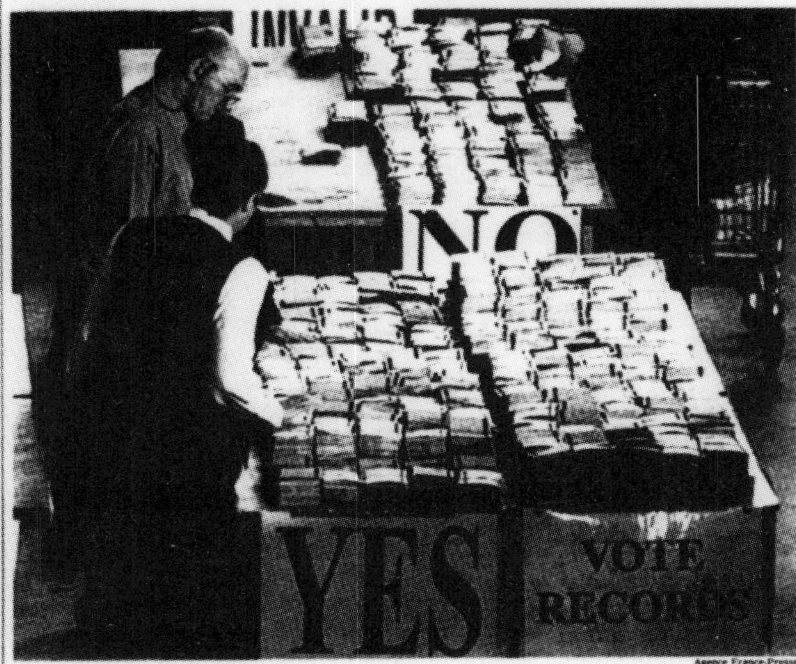

Agence France-Presse

Counting votes in Belfast yesterday. Advocates of the pact considered a large margin crucial, and they got it.

2½ TO 1 IN ULSTER

Fierce Opposition Fails to Turn Protestants Against Accord

By WARREN HOGE

BELFAST, Northern Ireland, May 23 — The voters of Northern Ireland and the Irish Republic have given overwhelming support to the peace agreement aimed at settling the sectarian conflict that has convulsed their island for centuries.

The official tally showed that voters in the North approved the accord by 71 percent to 29 percent, a margin that advocates of the agreement considered crucial to deny opponents the opportunity they vigorously sought to undermine the new institutions that will be set up.

"It is a resounding victory for the people of Northern Ireland," said Mo Mowlam, Britain's Secretary for the province, at King's Hall, where the 954,000 paper ballots were stacked and counted through the morning and early afternoon. "They have voted to take the gun out of politics north and south of the border."

Prime Minister Tony Blair of Britain called today "a day for joy" and said, "From now on, no one who turns to violence to make their case can do so other than in open defiance of the will of the people."

There were similar welcoming statements from Ireland and from the United States. [Page 6.]

The referendum on the historic compromise was the first time since 1918 that Irish throughout the island had voted at the same time on the same issue, and the ballot counting today came on the 200th anniversary of one of the island's many violent events, the first day of the Rising of 1798, in which Irish rebels tried to free their island from the British.

"It shows that the best way to resolve our problem is by spilling our sweat together and not our blood across the divide," said John Hume, a mainstream Catholic leader and longtime campaigner for a negotiated settlement of the Catholic-Protestant clash, which has cost more than 3,200 deaths in the last three decades.

The key question of how the fiercely contested Protestant vote went could not be answered conclusively because the ballots were counted in one central location, effectively disguising where they had come from, and the one exit poll, which showed a slight majority of Protestants in favor, covered only 1,750 of the voters. But election officials regarded anything above a 70 percent "yes" vote as proof that a majority of Protestants must have voted for the accord.

In the Irish Republic, where the accord caused little controversy, the "yes" vote was 94 percent. The "yes" vote for Northern Ireland and Ireland combined was 85 percent.

The voters of Northern Ireland, to whom the passionate antagonisms in their culture are so wearyingly familiar that they are known simply as

Continued on Page 6

Taxi Owners Deftly Dodge Claims of Accident Victims

By CHRISTOPHER DREW and ANDY NEWMAN

The taxi came barreling up Third Avenue late on a damp October night. As the driver tried to bear left, the cab skidded onto a traffic island, slamming into Edward Shalala, who was waiting to cross the street. He was hurled onto the pavement, his face a bloody mess and his right leg shattered, as his surgeon put it, "like cornflakes."

In five operations since the 1992 accident, doctors put Mr. Shalala, a 43-year-old artist, back together well enough that he can hobble around on crutches. And last year a jury tried to make him whole financially with a $3.2 million award for damages. But it was mostly an empty promise.

Already undone by an erratic cabby, Mr. Shalala then fell victim to the dodging and weaving

HAILING DANGER
The Liability Question

the taxi industry uses to avoid paying large claims, even in devastating accidents. Unable to collect the jury's award, Mr. Shalala settled this year with the taxi company for $132,000.

The sharp rise in taxi and livery accidents since 1990 and the recent spate of high-profile collisions have fed an image of rogue cabbies run amok. But the drivers are only the most visible players in a lucrative industry that has deftly used laws and regulations to keep its earnings safe, even as its cabs hurt more and more people.

Interviews and an examination of dozens of lawsuits show that cab companies are among the most recalcitrant businesses in paying claims to accident victims. And while the city has long ignored these practices, Mayor Rudolph W. Giuliani is now roiling the industry with a proposal to clamp down on dangerous drivers and make it easier for injured people to collect.

Most of the city's 12,000 cabs and 30,000 car-service vehicles carry minimal liability insurance, far less than most trucking and bus companies. Many taxi owners, including those with large fleets, organize their operations into subsets of much smaller companies, protecting the bulk of their assets from lawsuits.

And the biggest asset in the yellow cab industry, the taxi medallion, is the hardest to seize. As the taxi industry has boomed and the limited pool of medallions — the valuable permits to operate a cab — has soared in value to an average of $275,000 each, owners have routinely used them as security for loans. So even when the rare victim tries to seize a medallion in court, it is common to find that the owner has attached so much debt to it that there is little money left to recover.

In Mr. Shalala's case, the owners of the taxi company — two former city cabbies — borrowed $100,000 against their medallions just as a state court judge was entering the $3.2 million judgment, complicating Mr. Shalala's efforts to collect.

In another instance, a taxi owner named Natan More, who was facing two suits from accident victims, defied a judge's order by borrowing $1.6 million using his medallions as collateral. He also took off on a sailing trip in the Mediterranean, according to court papers, saying he had "no clue" when he would return.

Through such tactics, the industry has transformed the medallion — the 4-by-5-inch rectangle of aluminum bolted to the hood of every yellow taxi — into both a source of wealth and a financial

Continued on Page 32

Michelle V. Agins/The New York Times

Edward Shalala, an artist, in his Manhattan loft. He was hit by a cab in 1992, but was stymied in his efforts to collect a jury award.

In School Shooting, One Youth's 2 Sides

Kip Kinkel's parents had worried about his temper since he was a little boy. They sent him to a psychiatrist and taught him at home for a time. In recent months, they thought that their work and concern were making a difference and that Kip, at 15, was turning around.

But the teen-ager, who is accused of killing his parents and two of his schoolmates in Springfield, Ore., never made a secret of his angry heart.

The picture of him that has emerged since the shootings on Thursday at his school and his home is split: The boy with a great sense of humor, as well as that terrible temper. The teen-ager who built tree houses for his friends, and tortured squirrels and chipmunks. The polite youngster who behaved impeccably around adults and was a tough-talking mischief-maker at school.

Article, page 14.

Indonesia Struggles to Find New Reasons to Stay Intact

By NICHOLAS D. KRISTOF

SURABAYA, Indonesia, May 23 — To travel around Indonesia is to be overwhelmed by its diversity, from the tribespeople at the eastern end of the country who wear loin cloths (or even less) to the strict Muslims at the western tip, where some women could scarcely wear more.

About all those two areas have in common, in fact, is a history of secessionist movements.

So the collapse of the strongman rule of President Suharto, toppled Thursday after 32 years in power, raises basic questions about the future of an illogical chain of 17,000 islands that today are clumped together as Indonesia.

Mr. Suharto was a ruthless leader, but he forged modern Indonesia, suppressing militant Islam in a country where 90 percent of the people are Muslims and preaching harmony with the Christian, Hindu and animist minorities. Partly because of his sermons about moderation, and partly because of his readiness to use brute force, he not only held together this improbable archipelago but even expanded it by invading East Timor in 1975 and adding it to his island collection.

So when the students ousted Mr. Suharto this week, they also created profound uncertainties about what kind of a country Indonesia will be. Above all, a more democratic Indonesia will have to confront wrenching questions about religious coexistence and about whether there is anything but force that can serve as the national adhesive.

"Indonesia is not a kingdom but an empire," said an American businessman with broad experience in this country.

"Suharto was like Tito, in that he has been a very strong leader who has been able to hold a diverse country together the way Tito did in Yugoslavia.

"But now, can Indonesia stay together?"

Many experts say that Indonesia is so unpredictable in the post-Suharto era that no one knows quite how to analyze it, but the most common view appears to be that an Indonesian identity is well enough estab-

Continued on Page 8

A Top Clinton Donor Says Money Didn't Buy Approval on Satellites

By JILL ABRAMSON and DON VAN NATTA Jr.

In the six years that Bernard L. Schwartz built a friendship with President Clinton — fortified with $1.3 million in donations to the President and his party — the 72-year-old New York aerospace executive stresses that he never asked for special treatment.

"I consider him a friend, but not the kind of friend that you can call upon for favors," Mr. Schwartz said on Friday in a lengthy interview in the headquarters of his company, Loral Space & Communications, in midtown Manhattan.

But at a White House dinner on Feb. 5, there was something that Mr. Schwartz, who is Loral's chairman, desperately wanted: a quick decision approving the launching of a Loral satellite aboard a Chinese rocket later that month. Mr. Schwartz wanted to plead the case that his company could lose millions of dollars if Mr. Clinton did not act expeditiously.

Mr. Schwartz had intended to raise the issue with Samuel R. Berger, the President's national security adviser, but could not find him among those gathered in the East Room to honor Prime Minister Tony Blair of Britain, a gala whose guest list included John F. Kennedy Jr. and Barbra Streisand.

Another Loral official relayed the company's concerns in a letter to Mr. Berger. On Feb. 18, the President gave Loral permission for the launching, despite opposition from Federal prosecutors who warned that the approval would jeopardize their investigation into the satellite maker's earlier, unauthorized help to China's rocket program.

Mr. Schwartz said in the interview

Continued on Page 22

G. Paul Burnett/The New York Times

Bernard Leon Schwartz, a Presidential ally and loyal Democrat.

Mysterious Virus at Source Drives Up the Price of Pearls

By DANA CANEDY

In simpler times, only nature could make a pearl. Then mankind came up with the cultured variety, and pearls were transformed from nuggets of magic to predictable commodities.

In recent years, though, nature has struck back: a mysterious virus has teamed up with disruptive weather patterns to kill more than half the oysters in the world's busiest undersea factory.

At first, shoppers at jewelry counters were blissfully unaware of all this because dealers, alerted to the blight, kept plenty of pearls on hand. But those supplies are running short, and suddenly — just in time for prom and wedding season — pearl prices are shooting up.

Luxury chains like Tiffany & Company as well as small, family-owned jewelers like Wilson & Son in Scarsdale, N.Y., have been forced to raise prices, in some cases by as much as 25 percent, for top-quality strands. And prices are still rising.

A necklace that cost $800 to $1,200 a year ago might bring $1,500 today. A set of single-stud earrings now costs $200, up from $170 this time last year, according to the Cultured Pearl Information Center.

"This could not have come at a worse time, because pearl demand is way up," said Devin Macnow, executive director of the center, a trade group that is financed by the Japan Pearl Exporters Association.

But the surge in consumer demand for luxury items, born of the powerful economy, pales next to the death of millions of Akoya oysters in Japan's coastal waters in the last several years.

In 1996, the last year for which full figures are available, 150 million Akoya mollusks died, according to the exporters' group. Cultured pearls dominate the American market, and

Continued on Page 16

Cultured Pearl Information Center

INSIDE

Nuremberg Prosecutor Dies

Telford Taylor, a principal prosecutor of high Nazi officials at the Nuremberg war crimes trials after World War II, dies at 90. Page 37.

Bulls Hit a Bump in the Road

Chicago lost for just the second time in 11 playoff games, as Reggie Miller scored 28 points for Indiana. The Bulls lead the four-of-seven-game series, 2-1. SportsSunday, section 8.

On the Internet: www.nytimes.com

TODAY'S SECTIONS

** In New York City and the metropolitan region. († Elsewhere, auto pages are in section 3.)*
§ In the five boroughs of New York.
¶ In Long Island, Westchester, Connecticut and central and northern New Jersey.

THE IRISH VOTE: Yes From Catholics, Yes From Protestants

THE OVERVIEW

Irish Voters, in North and South, Strongly Endorse the Ulster Accord

Continued From Page 1

the Troubles, turned out to vote Friday in record numbers. The attendance figure was 81 percent, compared with 67 percent in last year's general election.

The Rev. Ian Paisley, the province's thundering orator and formidable vote-getter, had waged a belligerent "no" campaign that threatened to turn Protestants against the accord. Had he succeeded, it would have signaled his ability to elect enough members of his Democratic Unionist Party to the new Northern Ireland Assembly to have crippled it.

David Trimble, the leader of the largest Protestant party, the Ulster Unionists, was abandoned by six of the nine other members of his party in the British Parliament and seemed to be losing his case in favor of the accord with the rank and file until this past week, when Mr. Blair made two trips here to shore up the campaign. Polls showed that a large number of undecided Protestant electors moved into the "yes" camp in the last days.

In addition to the new legislature, the settlement creates a cross-border council of ministers from the Dublin and Belfast governments, something sought by the Catholic community, and a consultative council bringing together officials from England, Scotland, Wales and Northern Ireland, an innovation sought by Protestant leaders.

The agreement promises the most significant transformation of Northern Ireland since partition from the South created the province in 1922.

The accord emerged on April 10 after 26 months of negotiations involving 8 of Northern Ireland's 10 political parties and the Governments of Britain and Ireland. It was carefully patterned to give equal weight to the Catholic longing in the North to pursue eventual unity with Ireland and the Protestant desire to remain part of Britain.

The Protestants benefit from language that guarantees that Northern Ireland will remain part of the United Kingdom as long as a majority of its residents want it to, and from the settlement's provision that Ireland rid its Constitution of its territorial claims on the North.

The Catholics get more involvement of the Irish Republic's Government in the affairs of the North, a new legislature that cannot be gerrymandered in favor of Protestants the way the old Stormont parliament was and pledges addressing their demands for equality, police reform and prisoner releases.

Since 1994, cease-fires have reduced the bloodshed that has long roiled Northern Ireland. But splinter paramilitary groups opposed to the talks tried in recent months to scuttle them with killings and mortar attacks on police stations. Predictions of fresh outbreaks as the voting day approached turned out to be false, though part of the reason was greater success by the authorities in discovering and dismantling bombs and rocket launchers.

Election day itself was almost entirely peaceful throughout the province. The only incidents occurred in Londonderry and Strabane, where youths from Catholic housing projects threw paint and gas bombs at heavily armored Royal Ulster Constabulary Land Rovers that had arrived to take ballot boxes to Belfast. No one was harmed.

The dispute between the two communities has been particularly intense and violent since 1969, when Catholics opened their civil rights campaign for a better deal from the dominant Protestants.

The clashes led the British in the early 1970's to adopt a policy of internment without trial of suspected guerrillas, put troops in the streets of North Irish towns, suspend the Stormont legislature in Belfast and introduce direct rule from London.

In 1972 there were two horrific outbreaks of violence: the "Bloody Sunday" killings of Catholic marchers in Londonderry by British paratroopers and a one-day series of car bombings in Belfast by guerrillas of the Irish Republican Army, which killed 11 people.

In a protest that drew world attention in 1981, 10 I.R.A. prisoners starved themselves to death in an effort to obtain the status of prisoners of war for fellow guerrilla inmates.

The talks that produced the peace settlement began in June 1996, sponsored by the British and Irish Governments and led by a former United States Senate majority leader, George J. Mitchell. Sinn Fein, the political wing of the I.R.A., was excluded because the I.R.A. had abandoned a 17-month cease-fire in February by exploding a bomb in London, killing 2 people and injuring 100.

The talks proceeded only haltingly, with no notable progress through the last months of John Major's term as British Prime Minister. When Mr. Blair came to power last May 1, he declared his intention to get movement back into the talks. His first trip outside of London as Prime Minister was to Belfast.

He called upon the I.R.A. to resume its cease-fire as a condition for considering the entry of Sinn Fein into the negotiations. In July, the group declared an "unequivocal" truce, and six weeks later Sinn Fein was permitted to join the talks.

Reopening the talks in September, Mr. Blair set an ambitious May deadline for producing a settlement. By then 8 of the 10 Northern Ireland parties were participants, with the only hold-outs two hard-line Protestant parties, Mr. Paisley's Ulster Democrats and the U.K. Unionists of Robert McCartney.

Over the following months Mr. Blair approved a series of "confidence-building measures" to shore up the fragile talks, reducing the number of British troops in Northern Ireland, moving prisoners from British jails to Irish ones and visiting the talks in Belfast and inviting negotiators to 10 Downing Street.

The cease-fire by the Protestant paramilitary group that began in 1994 and the I.R.A. truce that began in July 1997 held firm while their political representatives stayed at the bargaining table, but splinter groups opposed to the talks committed random killings and bombings in an effort to disrupt them.

In late December, Billy Wright, the leader of one of the violent splinter groups, the Ulster Volunteer Force, was shot dead in the Maze prison by three members of a Catholic fringe group. A spate of retaliatory killings broke out, and 18 people died over the next three months.

Sinn Fein and the Protestant Ulster Democratic Party were both briefly suspended from the talks when it emerged that their guerrilla allies were involved in some of the killings.

The talks withstood these attacks, but Mr. Mitchell became concerned that growing violence might succeed in derailing them. So on March 25 he announced that he was setting an earlier deadline, April 9, for the final settlement. In a marathon session with both Prime Ministers, Bertie Ahern of Ireland and Mr. Blair, the talks continued past their midnight deadline and into the next day, Good Friday.

That afternoon, 17 hours after the deadline, Mr. Mitchell wearily announced that the parties had reached an agreement. Finding the right words to try to lay to rest decades of discord, it turned out, filled 68 pages of a settlement document. Today they became Northern Ireland's words to live by.

Associated Press

Prime Minister Tony Blair of Britain described it as a "day for joy," and Paul Shiels, 11, of Old Park in Belfast was of the same mind yesterday about the historic voting as he vaulted over a billboard stating the outcome.

A vote to 'take the gun out of politics north and south of the border.'

IN THE UNITED STATES

Clinton Leads Americans' Cheers on Irish Vote

By NEIL A. LEWIS

WASHINGTON, May 23 — An elated President Clinton today offered a warm message of congratulations to the voters in both the Irish Republic and Northern Ireland after their approval of a wide-ranging peace accord.

"It is the culmination of a springtime of peace and it must be the beginning of a long season of happiness and prosperity," Mr. Clinton said. "We are rejoicing at the news from across the Atlantic."

Mr. Clinton, who claims a bit of Irish heritage, said, "All over America, the eyes of Irish-Americans, and indeed, all our peace-loving citizens are smiling. We are very proud of you." Mr. Clinton strongly backed the accord and it was his envoy, former Senator George Mitchell, who brokered the deal.

George P. Mitchell, the former Senate leader from Maine who played a major role in negotiating the settlement, said in a telephone interview from New York, "There still will be many difficult decisions ahead, but this vote gives great momentum to the process and makes clear the people of Ireland, North and South, want this process to go forward.

"They have said they prefer mutual respect and tolerance and will not succumb to appeals to bigotry and hatred, which have been so effective in the past."

Representative Peter T. King, a Long Island Republican and co-chairman of an ad hoc Congressional committee for Irish affairs in the House, called the results "the most historical moment for Ireland in this century," which "ends horrific violence, creates real democratic institutions and provides a road map for what will be a united Ireland one day."

But Mr. King also said he expects continued resistance to the peace plan from Protestant Unionists in the north.

IN THE SOUTH

Eloquent And Elated: 'Great Day For Ireland'

By JAMES F. CLARITY

DUBLIN, May 23 — From Dublin on the Irish Sea to rocky Connemara and Galway Bay in the west, from Cork in the south to Dundalk near the border with Northern Ireland, people in the Irish Republic congratulated themselves and their northern neighbors today on their overwhelming vote for the Northern Ireland peace agreement in Friday's referendum.

"It's a great day for Ireland," words repeated over and over across this country of 3.5 million, became an instant and joyous national cliché, reflecting as well satisfaction that the agreement was convincingly approved in a separate referendum in the British province.

"There's not going to be dancing in the streets," said Lucy McKeever, an official of the Abbey Theater, after buying a head of lettuce in the Temple Bar section, the center of night-life cafés in downtown Dublin. "But it's as if everybody is of one mind for once."

She said the vote was a message to the Irish Republican Army, which for 30 years has used guerrilla warfare to try to force Britain out of the North, that "we have moved on, and violence is not the way." She noted that the voters had approved the abandonment of the Republic's constitutional claim to sovereignty in the North.

Michael Simonds, the owner of a bookstore in the suburban town of Dalkey, said of the vote: "It's fantastic. It shows that the vast majority wants peace."

The official count showed that 94 percent of the voters approved the agreement, with a turnout of 56 percent of the eligible electorate — lower than in referendums in recent years on divorce and abortion. Officials attributed the relatively low turnout to a widespread conviction that the accord would pass easily.

The pact promises the Roman Catholic minority in the North greater political power and is intended to give the overwhelmingly Catholic Irish Republic more influence in predominantly Protestant Northern Ireland.

Everyone called the results historic, and most said it promised hope for a lasting peace in the British province, where more than 3,200 people have been killed in 30 years of sectarian warfare. "It's a great day for Ireland," people repeated.

The first public official to say it, on an early morning radio program, was Mary O'Rourke, a legislator representing Longford, County Westmeath, whose family has had members in Parliament for decades. "It's also a great day for democracy," she added.

She noted that voters had agreed to abolish the constitutional claim to sovereignty in the North, which remained British when southern Ireland gained independence, after a bloody rebellion, in 1922. The abolition of the claim was the Irish Republic's greatest concession in the current settlement.

Ms. O'Rourke's party, Fianna Fail, only approved it after Prime Minister Bertie Ahern persuaded dissidents to agree. Every major party in Ireland also advocated a "yes" vote.

But she acknowledged, with other Irish officials and experts, that the vote was only a first step toward lasting peace, and that many obstacles remained.

Attention is now focused on the June 25 election for a new Northern Ireland assembly. The group will have no authority to deal with three of the major problems: the release of paramilitary prisoners; the disarmament of the I.R.A. and Protestant paramilitaries, and the reform of the Royal Ulster Constabulary, the predominantly Protestant police force in the North.

Work on these issues will be done by Mr. Ahern's Government and Britain, which sponsored the talks that led to the new peace agreement.

Fergus Finlay, a former senior official in the Irish Foreign Affairs Department who spent four years negotiating with the British Government on the North, said of the vote: "It's beyond people's wildest expectations. There's a new way of doing things. They've built a new platform."

But, he added, the first dangerous test will come at the end of June, the season for Protestant parades in the North. These marches have sparked violence in recent years.

Irish Republic voters also approved, by a smaller majority, a European Union document dealing mostly with administrative procedures. A strong campaign was waged against the document, the Amsterdam Treaty, by people who said it would lead to the end of Irish military neutrality.

But there was little popular interest in that treaty today. And many people seemed to share the shadow of doubt expressed by Mr. Simonds, the bookstore owner, who said of the peace agreement, "I hope it works."

THE POLITICS

In the End, Voters Found, a Real Chance at Peace Was Irresistible

By RICHARD L. BERKE

BELFAST, Northern Ireland, May 23 — No one was a more stubborn or obstreperous opponent of the Northern Ireland peace agreement than the Rev. Ian Paisley. So moments after its resounding passage was announced at the King's Hall here this afternoon, "yes" supporters encircled the "no" preacher, taunting, "Dinosaur!"

They thrust hastily produced placards in his face that bragged, "70% Yes." Then, encouraging Mr. Paisley to get out of the way of the new Irish politics, they broke into a lusty chant of "Cheerio, Cheerio, Cheerio!"

Such unrestrained, boastful glee is uncommon in dour, beaten-down Northern Ireland. But the peace agreement's supporters managed to do the politically unthinkable in a place where compromise has not been part of the vocabulary: They built a coalition — even more remarkable because it was so brittle — that included a majority of Catholic nationalists and a large share of Protestant Unionists. The first group wants this British province to merge with the Irish Republic; the second wants to retain union with Britain.

The 71 percent who voted "yes" in the referendum on Friday decided, as they say in Ireland, that half a loaf is better than none.

Most Catholics favored the agreement from the start, viewing it as a chance to gain more influence in a province where they are in the minority. But the commanding victory came about because supporters appeared to persuade more than half of the wavering Unionists to consider one argument above all others: like it or not, the treaty is at least an attempt at peace.

This is what John Major, the former British Prime Minister — borrowing from President Clinton — called "the politics of hope."

P. J. Mara, who ran the campaign for the agreement in the Irish Republic, explained it in an interview before he began the effort late last month. "Our focus-group research shows that the one argument that transcends others is, 'This is our best chance in a generation to get peace.' The prize of peace transcends every other argument."

While the accord was always expected to pass — and indeed registered an even more convincing majority in Ireland, backers in Northern Ireland faced a big hurdle in pulling Unionists to their side. Polls showed that a large share of the roughly one million prospective voters in the province were undecided in the closing days, and that many of the undecided were moving to the "no" camp. Their biggest objection was a provision that calls for the accelerated release of political prisoners.

But supporters managed to halt the loss of support by dispatching Britain's Prime Minister, Tony Blair, and other prominent politicians, who conceded that there were distasteful elements but repeated over and over that the accord could not be "cherry-picked." Their pitch was that, though flawed, it was the best hope for peace.

So many celebrities swarmed into Belfast seeking support that one disc jockey quipped, "Nobody would be surprised to see the Queen, the Pope and the Spice Girls at this point."

Another strategy of the supporters in the closing days was to reach out to young Protestant voters, who were viewed as perhaps less intransigent than their parents, as well as to women, who might find the peace message particularly appealing.

To win over young people, the "yes" campaign sent five-minute videotapes to 15,000 first-time voters. The tapes featured rock bands and young people's testimonials that the accord offered a chance at peace. And in its appeal to women, the campaign ran a full-page newspaper advertisement the morning of the vote with the photograph of an infant born the day before. Once again, the message was peace for the children.

"The last week was worrying for us," said Quintin Oliver, who ran the "yes" campaign in Northern Ireland. "But we turned it around."

Sydney Elliott, a senior lecturer in politics at Queens University Belfast, said the supporters ran a lackluster campaign until the end, but were helped by their opponents' inability to put forth a positive message.

Ultimately, many people chose to put aside their suspicions, fears and hatreds for the larger goal of peace. In recent interviews throughout Ireland and in this province, many said that while they were not particularly optimistic about peace, they were open to giving it a chance.

Veronica Tate, for one, was not overjoyed about having supported the accord. "I had nightmares over it," she said after voting on Friday at a West Belfast school that is riddled with bullets from years of quarrels. "What if it doesn't work out?"

Mrs. Tate, 47, a Catholic, said the referendum could backfire and trigger more violence.

So why did she take her chances and vote yes? "It's very important for the grandchildren," she said.

As for those who want Mr. Paisley to exit, stage right, the master of "no" had one thing to say: "Paisley is not going away."

Reuters

With 71 percent of voters in Northern Ireland approving the peace accord, the Alliance Party celebrated yesterday at King's Hall in Belfast where Britain's secretary for the province called it "a resounding victory."

"All the News That's Fit to Print"

The New York Times

Late Edition
New York: **Today,** hazy sun, some afternoon thunder. High 90. **Tonight,** clearing, less humid. Low 66. **Tomorrow,** sunny, breezy. High 76. **Yesterday,** high 79, low 73. Details, page C5.

VOL. CXLVII . . . No. 51,253 · *NEW YORK, TUESDAY, AUGUST 18, 1998* · $1 beyond the greater New York metropolitan area. · *60 CENTS*

CLINTON ADMITS LEWINSKY LIAISON TO JURY; TELLS NATION 'IT WAS WRONG,' BUT PRIVATE

JANUARY 26, 1998

"I want to say one thing to the American people. I want you to listen to me. I'm going to say this again: I did not have sexual relations with that woman, Miss Lewinsky."

AUGUST 17, 1998

"I did have a relationship with Miss Lewinsky that was not appropriate. In fact, it was wrong."

Reuters

Expresses Regret but Asserts It Is Now Time to Move On

By JAMES BENNET

WASHINGTON, Aug. 17 — Trying to wrest political forgiveness from profound personal embarrassment, President Clinton admitted in testimony today and in an extraordinary address tonight that he misled his wife and the public and conducted a relationship with a White House intern that was "not appropriate."

"It was wrong," he said, speaking in somber yet defiant tones from the same straight-backed chair from which, hours earlier, he carried on a far more contentious exchange with prosecutors. "It constituted a critical lapse in judgment and a personal failure on my part for which I am solely and completely responsible."

After seven months of emphatic denials of a sexual relationship with Monica S. Lewinsky, the former intern, Mr. Clinton also found himself addressing the most personally painful of matters — adultery — in the most public forum imaginable.

Speaking just after 10 P.M., he tried to turn the very freakishness of the day to his advantage, issuing a proud, almost angry demand for his privacy back.

"Now, this matter is between me, the two people I love most — my wife and our daughter — and our God," he said. "It's nobody's business but ours. Even Presidents have private lives."

To the grand jurors, Mr. Clinton declined to answer some questions from prosecutors about the details of his relationship with Ms. Lewinsky. Mr. Starr's team told the President that they might subpoena him again, and Mr. Clinton's lawyers said in return that he might fight such a subpoena. The Whitewater independent counsel, Kenneth W. Starr also left open the possibility that he would recall Mr. Clinton to testify further.

Mr. Clinton acknowledged in his testimony having had "inappropriate intimate physical contact" with Ms. Lewinsky, according to one lawyer and adviser to the President knowledgeable about his appearance.

Mr. Clinton denied that he had obstructed justice and tried to cover up his relationship with the intern, Ms. Lewinsky. "I told the grand jury today and I say to you now that at no time did I ask anyone to lie, to hide or destroy evidence or to take any other unlawful action," he said in his public address. He urged the public to put the matter behind it. "It is past time to move on," he said.

In testifying and then speaking to the public, Mr. Clinton tried the riskiest high-wire act of his career, trying to balance legal and political burdens. Two days short of his 52d birthday, he sought to protect his Presidency and elude legal jeopardy by acknowledging an intimate relationship in the White House with a subordinate less than half his age.

Mr. Clinton had been working on his speech for several days, aides said, trying to strike the right balance between disclosure and dignity, remorse and pride.

Mr. Starr is investigating whether the President lied under oath in denying an affair with Ms. Lewinsky last January in his depostion during the Paula Corbin Jones sexual misconduct suit. Beyond the nature of Mr. Clinton's relationship with Ms. Lewinsky, Mr. Starr has been investigating whether Mr. Clinton tried to obstruct justice and suborn perjury, matters that the President did not address in detail tonight.

Mr. Clinton had been working on the speech himself for days, aides said, trying to strike the right balance between disclosure and dignity, regret and pride. His address followed by less than four hours the

Continued on Page A12

RUSSIA ACTS TO FIX SINKING FINANCES

Takes Drastic Steps on Loans and on Value of the Ruble

By CELESTINE BOHLEN

MOSCOW, Aug. 17 — The Russian Government moved hastily today to avert financial collapse with a series of drastic measures, including delaying payments for 90 days on foreign debt owed mostly by banks, restructuring Government bonds and sacrificing the ruble to market forces.

Holding tonight at 6.43 rubles to the dollar, off slightly from Friday's level, the value of the Russian currency is now free to float as low as 9.5, a risky step — tantamount to devaluation — that many fear could set off a new round of inflation. It could also wipe out as much as a third of the ruble's purchasing power in an economy heavily dependent on imports.

Letting the ruble float marks a major change in strategy for President Boris N. Yeltsin's Government, which after seven years of economic reforms could point to a stable currency and low inflation as its two major achievements. But that policy has been overwhelmed by a crisis brought on by Russia's other economic realities, including the insolvency of its banking system.

The decision came over the weekend after Russian officials had once again asked foreign backers for more financial aid. Coming one month after a major drive, spearheaded by Washington, to put together a $22.6 billion package of loans and credits to Russia, the request was denied, and top Russian officials today acknowledged that further help from the West was unlikely.

At a news conference this morning, Prime Minister Sergei V. Kiriyenko said the steps had been made necessary by the near-collapse of

Continued on Page A8

Strong at Politics, Weakened by Lapses

A Career Marked by Bending Both Rules and Truth

By TODD S. PURDUM

WASHINGTON, Aug. 17 — On Jan. 20, 1997, as an ebullient Bill Clinton took the oath of office for the second term that he hoped would secure his place in history, he returned to a theme that had been at the core of his claim to be a new kind of Democrat, declaring: "Each and every one of us, in our own way, must assume personal responsibility, not only for ourselves and our families but for our neighbors and our nation."

Exactly one year later, Mr. Clinton learned that Kenneth W. Starr, the Whitewater independent counsel, was investigating accusations that the President had started a sexual relationship with a White House intern in 1995 and then tried to cover it up.

Had the man who won the Presidency by speaking out for the people who "play by the rules" once more surrendered to a lifelong compulsion to bend and break them? Tonight, in the most painfully personal public confession of his life, and perhaps in American political life, Mr. Clinton was forced to acknowledge, in tight and reluctant tones, that he had.

"I must take complete responsibility for all my actions, both public and private," the President said, adding that his relationship with Monica S. Lewinsky was wrong and "constituted a critical lapse in judgment and a personal failure on my part for which I am solely and completely responsible."

How someone of such surpassing intellect and such protean political talents could indulge in such reckless conduct at a time when he knew a special prosecutor was already scrutinizing his Administration and when his own re-election still hung in the balance remains the most puzzling question about William Jefferson Clinton. But it is not a new question, and in some ways it was entirely predictable that this President should have come to this pass, his promise once again shadowed by his shortcomings.

For Mr. Clinton has always been convinced that he could outsmart, out-talk, out-charm and outlast any adversary, and very often, enough to confirm that conviction, he has. In the darkest days of the 1992 primaries, he dared to campaign on a platform of personal responsibility, despite widespread questions about his own marital fidelity, marijuana use and draft record, and widespread doubt that his answers were candid or complete. In his first term, he shifted ground so many times that even his best friends sometimes said they did not know where he stood.

Time and again in the risky running melodrama of his public life, Mr. Clinton has treated the truth as an à la carte menu.

Last Jan. 21, as news of the accusations involving Ms. Lewinsky came out, Mr. Clinton told National Public Radio: "I don't know any more about it than I've told you, and any more about it, really, than you do."

Even tonight, Mr. Clinton insisted that when he testified under oath in January that he had not had sexual relations with Ms. Lewinsky, his answers were "legally accurate," though he added: "I did not volunteer information."

In the end, such sweeping elisions lie far beyond the ken of conventional political analysis. But professionals who have studied the arc of Mr.

Continued on Page A13

Testy Finale, Risky Gambit

A Partial Confession To Stave Off Pursuers

By JOHN M. BRODER

News Analysis

WASHINGTON, Aug. 17 — With his grand jury testimony and his brief and defiant public admission of an inappropriate relationship with Monica S. Lewinsky tonight, President Clinton is hoping, as he has so many times in the past, that the public will respond with forgiveness and not disgust.

The President, relying on polls and his own sense of the public's weariness with a sordid story of Presidential sex, took a calculated gamble that he can escape indictment by prosecutors or impeachment by lawmakers over what he declared was a private matter. In his testimony and his testy four-minute speech to the nation, he offered partial admissions but refused to answer many of questions that have swamped his Presidency since January.

And almost before he finished his grudging televised confession, he turned on his inquisitors and demanded that the investigation of his private life come to an end.

He confessed, he expressed regret and he asked for instant redemption.

"Now it is time — in fact it is past time — to move on," the President said with anger, not anguish, in his eyes, laying the blame for seven months of national trauma on his political enemies and Kenneth W. Starr, the independent counsel.

His words of apology and contrition were belied by a tone that was laced with anger and in an important way, unrepent He left no doubt that his strategy is the same as it has been for the past seven months: To give as little ground as possible.

The President sacrificed some of

Continued on Page A15

Justin Lane for The New York Times

News crews began setting up on the White House lawn at 5 A.M. yesterday for President Clinton's testimony before the Federal grand jury.

One by One, the President Told His Closest Aides the Painful Truth

By RICHARD L. BERKE and DON VAN NATTA Jr.

WASHINGTON, Aug. 17 — Before he addressed the grand jury and then the nation, President Clinton called in some of his closest aides over the weekend, associates said, and one by one, he told them that the accusation they had steadfastly denied for months was true: he had had an improper relationship with Monica S. Lewinsky.

The meetings, which took place on Saturday and Sunday, were described by close Clinton associates as informal and involving only some aides. And only in some cases, they said, did Mr. Clinton express regret for his conduct.

After seven months of public denials and private anguish over the inquiry by Kenneth W. Starr, it was those conversations that helped Mr. Clinton fully come to terms with the toll the sex scandal has wrought on his friends and on his Presidency, two people close to him said.

"It hit him hardest on Sunday," one close friend said. "This was a very, very difficult weekend for him. Nothing is more important to him than his place in history. He is worried that this investigation will eclipse everything else."

Even late last week while Mr. Clinton's associates were telling reporters that he might acknowledge having had sexual relations with Ms. Lewinsky, the friend said he was still "in denial."

"Four days ago," he said, "the President told me he never had sex with Monica."

Some who met with the President — and who had stood loyally by the President — expressed feelings of betrayal and humiliation, people close to Mr. Clinton said. One friend said that there was "a lot of disappointment" and that it was the aides' reaction that was most distressing to the President, leading him to "beat himself up."

Even if the American public forgives Mr. Clinton for bending the truth in explaining his relationship with Ms. Lewinsky, he now faces a problem closer to home: repairing relations with aides, friends and Cabinet members who for months have adamantly, and publicly, defended him. Collectively, these people face hundreds of thousands of dollars in legal bills related to the investigations that have punctuated his Presidency.

Michael D. McCurry, the White House press secretary, was unequiv-

Continue on Page A14

INSIDE

Bomb Suspect Questioned

American investigators in Kenya questioned a key suspect in the embassy bombing, and are confident he is implicated in the plot. Page A7.

5 Held in Ulster Bombing

The British police arrested five men near Omagh, Northern Ireland, in the bomb attack on Saturday that killed 28 people. Page A3.

Alaska Is Thawing

The planet's northern tier is warming, in what many call a signal that the climate is changing. Page F1.

The Writer Julian Green Dies

The novelist, playwright and candid memoirist, who became the first American elected to the Académie Française, was 97. Page B8.

More on the Testimony

A PIVOTAL ROLE Hillary Rodham Clinton helped the President write his speech and plan his strategy. Page A15.

A MOMENTOUS DAY A confrontation setting the course of a Presidency plays out without an audience. Page A13.

A SHIFT FOR STARR As questioning ends, the independent counsel will focus on grounds for impeachment. Page A14.

NEWS SUMMARY A2

On the Interne **www.nytimes.com**

TESTING OF A PRESIDENT: A Quiet Acknowledgment

IN HIS OWN WORDS

Last Night's Address

Following is the statement President Clinton made last night after testifying by closed-circuit television to a grand jury, as recorded by The New York Times:

Good evening. This afternoon in this room, from this chair, I testified before the office of independent counsel and a grand jury. I answered their questions truthfully, including questions about my private life, questions no American citizen would ever want to answer.

Still I must take complete responsibility for all my actions, both public and private. And that is why I am speaking to you tonight.

As you know, in a deposition in January, I was asked questions about my relationship with Monica Lewinsky. While my answers were legally accurate, I did not volunteer information. Indeed I did have a relationship with Miss Lewinsky that was not appropriate. In fact it was wrong.

It constituted a critical lapse in judgment and a personal failure on my part for which I am solely and completely responsible.

But I told the grand jury today, and I say to you now, that at no time did I ask anyone to lie, to hide or destroy evidence, or to take any other unlawful action.

I know that my public comments and my silence about this matter gave a false impression. I misled people. Including even my wife. I deeply regret that.

I can only tell you I was motivated by many factors. First, by a desire to protect myself from the embarrassment of my own conduct. I was also very concerned about protecting my family. The fact that these questions were being asked in a politically inspired lawsuit which has since been dismissed was a consideration too.

In addition, I had real and serious concerns about an independent counsel investigation that began with private business dealings 20 years ago — dealings, I might add, about which an independent Federal agency found no evidence of any wrongdoing by me or my wife over two years ago.

The independent counsel investigation moved on to my staff and friends. Then into my private life. And now the investigation itself is under investigation. This has gone on too long, cost too much, and hurt too many innocent people.

Associated Press

Paul Begala, adviser to the President, preparing Mr. Clinton for his address last night.

Now this matter is between me, the two people I love most, my wife and our daughter, and our God. I must put it right. And I am prepared to do whatever it takes to do so.

Nothing is more important to me personally, but it is private. And I intend to reclaim my family life for my family. It's nobody's business but ours. Even Presidents have private lives. It is time to stop the pursuit of personal destruction and the prying into private lives and get on with our national life.

Our country has been distracted by this matter for too long, and I take my responsibility for my part in all of this. That is all I can do. Now it is time, in fact it is past time, to move on. We have important work to do, real opportunities to seize, real problems to solve, real security matters to face.

And so tonight I ask you to turn away from the spectacle of the past seven months, to repair the fabric of our national discourse and to return our attention to all the challenges and all the promise of the next American century.

Thank you for watching and good night.

Previous Statements

JAN. 17 From President Clinton's deposition in the Paula Corbin Jones sexual misconduct lawsuit.

"I have never had sexual relations with Monica Lewinsky. I've never had an affair with her."

JAN. 21 "All Things Considered" (National Public Radio)

"I don't know any more about it than I've told you, and any more about it, really, than you do. But I will cooperate. The charges are not true. And I haven't asked anyone to lie."

JAN. 21 "Newshour With Jim Lehrer" (PBS)

"It means that there is not a sexual relationship, an improper sexual relationship, or any other kind of improper relationship."

JAN. 22 Remarks at a photo session at the White House with Palestinian leader Yasir Arafat

"The allegations are false, and I could never ask anybody to do anything other than tell the truth. Let's get to the big issues there — about the nature of the relationship and whether I suggested anybody not to tell the truth. That is false. Now, there are a lot of other questions that are, I think, very legitimate. You have a right to ask them; you and the American people have a right to get answers. . . . I'd like for you to have more rather than less, sooner rather than later. So we will work through it as quickly as we can and get all those questions out there to you."

JAN. 22 Roll Call

"It is not an improper relationship and I know what the word means. . . . The relationship was not sexual."

JULY 31 Remarks after delivering a statement on the domestic economy at the White House

"No one wants to get this matter behind us more than I do, except maybe all the rest of the American people. I am looking forward to the opportunity, in the next few days, of testifying. I will do so completely and truthfully. I am anxious to do it. I hope you can understand why in the interim I can and should have no further comment on these matters."

Reuters

JAN. 26 White House, education news conference

"I'm going to say this again: I did not have sexual relations with that woman, Miss Lewinsky. I never told anybody to lie, not a single time."

THE OVERVIEW

Clinton Admits Liaison to Grand Jury, Telling Nation 'It Was Wrong' but Private

Continued From Page A1

testimony having had "inappropriate intimate physical contact" with Ms. Lewinsky, one lawyer and adviser to the President knowledgeable about his appearance said. But he argued that the contact did not fit the definition of sex used by the Jones lawyers, and therefore he did not commit perjury.

In his brief speech tonight, Mr. Clinton hinted at the depth of animosity between the two sides, saying that the investigation had "gone on too long, cost too much and hurt too many innocent people."

Mr. Clinton testified today, and delivered his speech, from the White House Map Room, from which President Franklin Delano Roosevelt monitored the progress of World War II.

Beginning at 12:59 P.M., President Clinton met with prosecutors in the Map Room, on the ground floor of the White House. His testimony was videotaped and transmitted live by closed-circuit television to a grand jury at the Federal courthouse, just blocks away.

While his lawyers were also in the room, Mr. Clinton sat alone before a table, facing off against a cadre of prosecutors who, his associates say, he believes are bent on destroying him.

The details of President Clinton's testimony were not immediately disclosed. But in a brief statement his lawyer, David E. Kendall, said: "As to a very few highly intrusive questions with respect to the specifics of this contact, in order to preserve personal privacy and institutional dignity, he gave candid, but not detailed answers."

In announcing his plans to testify earlier this month, Mr. Clinton said he would speak "truthfully and completely." But some of his advisers had raised the possibility before his testimony that he might rebuff detailed questions about his sexual contact with Ms. Lewinsky.

Ms. Lewinsky testified Aug. 6 that she had had a sexual relationship with Mr. Clinton. She had previously denied such a relationship in a sworn affidavit.

Mr. Clinton took several breaks from his testimony today to confer with his lawyers in the doctor's office next door to the Map Room. At about 3:30 P.M., he took a break that lasted roughly an hour, one Clinton ally said.

The furor over the Lewinsky accusations has consumed seven months of Mr. Clinton's Presidency, his aides have acknowledged. Mr. Clinton viewed his own place in history as riding in part on his performance today and its impact on public opinion, one of his friends said.

Statement From the President's Lawyer

By The New York Times

WASHINGTON, Aug. 17 — Following is a statement by David E. Kendall, President Clinton's personal lawyer, that was released by the White House after the President's testimony by closed-circuit television to a grand jury:

For over four hours, the President responded truthfully to the questions of prosecutors from the Office of Independent Counsel. He made the painful admission that he had had inappropriate contact with Ms. Lewinsky.

As to a very few highly intrusive questions with respect to the specifics of this contact, in order to preserve personal privacy and institutional dignity, he gave candid but not detailed answers.

Some Republican Congressional leaders have said that an acknowledgment by Mr. Clinton that he had not told the truth about his relationship with Ms. Lewinsky might blunt the threat of impeachment proceedings on Capitol Hill. Erskine B. Bowles, the chief of staff, called Democrats on the Hill this evening to rally support for the President.

But even if Mr. Clinton heads off such hearings, it is far from clear whether he will put his second term back on track, or put to rest smirking speculation about his private life and new doubts, reflected in public polls, about his truthfulness. More fundamentally, it was uncertain whether the Presidency itself has been diminished by a tawdry spectacle that today drew so much attention that one television camera monitored the scene from the top of the Washington Monument.

With a grave expression and a brief wave, Mr. Starr left the White House through the Diplomatic Entrance at 6:40 this evening. Moments later, Mr. Kendall stepped through the same door and made brief remarks by the rain-slicked White House drive.

"We're hopeful that the President's testimony will finally bring closure" to the four-year inquiry into the Clintons' Whitewater real estate investment, he said, adding that it had culminated "in an investigation of the President's private life."

White House aides picked up on Mr. Kendall's call for closure, declaring that the President's statement tonight would satisfy any public interest in the long-running Lewinsky drama, and any sense of aggravation with Mr. Clinton for his role.

"The American people are not pounding on the door for details, they're pounding on the door for closure," one senior Administration official said. "He doesn't owe them details, he owes them an explanation."

The official compared Mr. Clinton's remarks tonight to his acknowledgment on national television in January 1992 of "causing pain" in his marriage. Mr. Clinton, while campaigning in New Hampshire for the Democratic nomination, had been accused of an affair with Gennifer Flowers, a singer in Little Rock, Ark.

Despite the calls for closure, Mr. Starr's investigation shows no signs of concluding immediately. On Tuesday, Dick Morris, the former Clinton adviser forced to resign in 1996 after disclosure of an affair with a prostitute, is scheduled to testify before the grand jury.

On a sweltering, rainy Washington day, White House officials today abandoned almost any pretense of the business-as-usual approach they have taken in the head-snapping swerves and reversals of the Lewinsky investigation.

At the senior staff meeting this morning, Mr. Bowles reminded the staff of the importance of sticking together. Michael D. McCurry, the White House press secretary, said that Mr. Bowles quoted his own father, saying "it's easy to be there for someone when they're up, but it's the good ones who are there when you're down."

It was a rare admission by the White House that the President's spirits had sagged. One friend said that the President avoided focusing until Sunday on the implications of his testimony. "It hit him hardest on Sunday," the friend said. "This was a very very difficult weekend for him. Nothing is more important to him than his place in history. He is worried that this investigation will eclipse everything else."

The President's wife, Hillary Rodham Clinton and his daughter, Chelsea, remained at the White House today, and were believed to have met with him after he testified. Mr. Clinton plans to leave for a vacation with his family on Martha's Vineyard at 2 P.M. on Tuesday.

Drawing a curtain over "private" family matters.

Some of the President's own advisers expressed relief today that he was finally telling his side of the story. Some, however, said they felt misled by him, because he denied an affair to them as well.

Mr. Clinton worked out this morning in the White House gymnasium, then spent about two hours preparing with his lawyers in the White House residence. At noon, he broke for a briefing on domestic and national security matters. Advisers described him as engaged and interested in his 10-minute foreign policy discussion, asking Samuel R. Berger, the national security adviser, how the Russian ruble was trading.

The White House released a photo of that meeting, the only public glimpse of the President before tonight. Then, at 12:30 P.M., Mr. Starr's blue-gray Crown Victoria sedan swept up the White House drive, and he and his team of prosecutors headed for the Map Room.

The room is named for its wall map of Europe still stuck with the colored pins that Mr. Roosevelt used to follow World War II. Mr. Clinton used the room to hold "coffees" for large donors to the Democrats during the 1996 campaign.

In his deposition on Jan. 17 in the Jones lawsuit, the President acknowledged a mere acquaintance with Ms. Lewinsky, whom he met in 1995 when she was a 21-year-old unpaid intern. Mr. Clinton said that he could not even recall ever being alone with her.

"I have never had sexual relations with Monica Lewinsky," Mr. Clinton said. "I've never had an affair with her."

Ms. Lewinsky had sworn in an affidavit that she did not have a sexual relationship with him.

Unknown to Mr. Clinton, an associate of Ms. Lewinsky, Linda R. Tripp, had secretly tape-recorded numerous conversations in which her friend described an affair with Mr. Clinton.

Mrs. Tripp provided those tapes to prosecutors, and also met with Ms. Jones' lawyers before they interviewed the President.

THE BACKGROUND

Though Strong at Politics, President Is Hurt by Lapses

Continued From Page A1

themselves," wrote Stanley A. Renshon, a political scientist and psychoanalyst at New York University in his 1996 study of Mr. Clinton, "High Hopes." "However, Bill Clinton appears to have come to believe the *best* of himself and, either to avoid or discount evidence from his own behavior, that all is not as he believes it to be. He attributes to himself the most sincere and best of motives. His errors, when acknowledged, are the result of basically correct efforts gone temporarily awry, misunderstandings that, if one knew more of what *he* knew, would disappear or be mitigated, or else are attributable to naïveté and inexperience."

Mr. Clinton may have come by his capacity for denial and compartmentalization naturally. They were among the qualities that allowed his widowed mother, Virginia Kelley, to persevere after Mr. Clinton's father died three months before he was born, and that allowed Mr. Clinton to make what most critics regarded as a splendid State of the Union address just days after the intern scandal broke.

"When bad things do happen, I brainwash myself to put them out of my mind," Mrs. Kelley wrote in her autobiography, published after her death in 1994 under the President's review. "Inside my head, I construct an airtight box. I keep inside it what I want to think about and everything else stays behind the walls. Inside is white, outside is black: The only gray I trust is the streak in my hair."

A history of outlasting any adversary.

But gray is Mr. Clinton's favorite weapon. It has been central to his successes and to his setbacks. As Governor of Arkansas and then as a Presidential candidate, he succeeded in blurring old distinctions of ideology, proclaiming himself neither liberal nor conservative but "new." As President, he at first promised both a tax cut and new spending, then raised taxes instead. Two years later, he apologized for raising taxes too much, claiming that Congress had forced him to do so, a claim at sharp variance with the facts.

This is the man who pledged not to raise taxes "to pay for my programs" (he raised them to cut the deficit), who said he had never "broken the laws of my country" (he tried marijuana as a Rhodes Scholar in England), who defended his campaign finance practices by saying he had never "changed Government policy solely because of a contribution." His reputation for shading the truth grew so encrusted that he faced semi-serious questions from reporters over trivial matters, from his golf scores to whether he really shot two ducks on a New Year's outing in Arkansas, or just carried some that were shot by others.

Many times, Mr. Clinton has accepted responsibility and forsaken blame. After his 1980 defeat after one term as Governor of Arkansas, his political consultant Dick Morris advised him to apologize for past mistakes, like raising taxes and car license fees. Mr. Clinton resisted repeated entreaties to say he was sorry, devising his own folksy formulation for a television commercial: "When I was a boy, my daddy never had to whip me twice for the same thing."

In fact, the only daddy Mr. Clinton knew was an alcoholic stepfather who sometimes beat his mother, not him. And the President has spent a great part of his life being whipped, often quite publicly, for repeating his own mistakes. In his very first run for office, in 1974, his girlfriend, Hillary Rodham, reportedly sent her father and brother to help on his Congressional campaign because she worried about the rumors of his multiple romances on the road.

In 1992, faced with accusations by Gennifer Flowers of a 12-year sexual affair, Mr. Clinton said, "That allegation is false," acknowledged causing pain in his marriage and largely put to rest an issue that had derailed the 1988 campaign of Gary Hart. But under oath in his deposition in the Paula Corbin Jones civil suit this year, Mr. Clinton acknowledged sexual contact with Ms. Flowers.

Over the years, Mr. Clinton has occasionally articulated a personal hierarchy of relative wrongdoing, once blurting out in a conversation with reporters aboard Air Force One — apropos of nothing — that it was the money-changers in the temple who really made Jesus mad, not the adulterous woman, of whom Jesus said in the Book of John: "He that is without sin among you, let him first cast a stone at her."

"All the News That's Fit to Print"

The New York Times

Late Edition
New York: **Today**, sunny with cool breezes, high 77. **Tonight**, mainly clear, low 55. **Tomorrow**, sunny with light winds, high 72. **Yesterday**, high 89, low 69. Weather map, page D10.

VOL. CXLVIII . . No. 51,294 NEW YORK, MONDAY, SEPTEMBER 28, 1998 — $1 beyond the greater New York metropolitan area. — 60 CENTS

McGwire's Grand Finale Makes It 70

Associated Press

After his second home run of the day, St. Louis's Mark McGwire rounded the bases for the 70th and final time of a historic season.

By MURRAY CHASS

ST. LOUIS, Sept. 27 — His seasonlong performance so surpassed any individual performance major league baseball has ever seen that Mark McGwire said, "I'm in awe of myself right now."

Finishing that performance with a flourish, McGwire clouted two more home runs on the last day of the regular season today, raising his record total to 70. Like a long-distance runner with an explosive finishing kick, McGwire sprinted away from the guy next to him, Sammy Sosa, by hitting five home runs in his last 11 at-bats.

Sosa, who remained at 66 home runs after hitting none today, is not finished playing. The Cubs, the team he has carried all season, will meet the San Francisco Giants in Chicago on Monday night — the Mets missed a chance to force a three-way tie by losing in Atlanta today — to determine the fourth and final team, the wild-card team, in the National League playoffs.

But Sosa will be hard-pressed to catch McGwire, the larger-than-life superstar who has imbedded himself in the hearts of St. Louis fans and captivated the rest of the country with his performance and his demeanor. A player has hit four home runs in a game only 12 times in major league history, none for five years. "Good luck," McGwire said earnestly long distance to Sosa, who has become his ally in home runs and understanding of what he has gone through the past six months. "We've been going back and forth. It's been a tremendous ride for he and I."

McGwire, who broke Roger

Continued on Page D5

A SEASON TOO ENTERTAINING TO END

METS COLLAPSE The Mets missed the wild-card playoff, losing their fifth straight game.

YANKEES ROLL INTO PLAYOFFS The Yankees won their 114th game as a rookie, Shane Spencer, hit his third grand slam in 10 days. The Yankees begin the playoffs tomorrow night against Texas.

WILLIAMS WINS BATTING TITLE The Yankees' Bernie Williams, below, won the American League batting title with an average of .339.

Vincent Laforet/Allsport

Barton Silverman/The New York Times

50 TIMES FOUR Greg Vaughn hit his 50th homer, the fourth player to hit 50 or more this year. Before 1998, no more than two players had reached 50 in a season.

ONE MORE DAY San Francisco and Chicago face off in a one-game playoff tonight for the National League wild card. The extra game will give Sammy Sosa, above, a chance to catch Mark McGwire, but Sosa will need a four-homer night.

	W	L
Chicago	89	73
San Francisco	89	73
Mets	88	74

Articles, SportsMonday

GERMAN VOTERS END AN ERA, REJECT KOHL AFTER 16 YEARS AND PICK A SOCIAL DEMOCRAT

Associated Press

Chancellor-elect Gerhard Schröder applauding his supporters in Bonn.

SCHRODER IS VICTOR

His Campaign Stressed State of the Economy and Joblessness

By ROGER COHEN

BONN, Sept. 27 — Gerhard Schröder, a Social Democrat, defeated Helmut Kohl today in the race to become Chancellor, ending an era in Germany and opening a new one in Europe where center-left governments now dominate the continent's politics.

After a hard-fought campaign, the victory was decisive, a clear expression of the weariness of Germans with Mr. Kohl's 16-year rule. Mr. Schröder swept aside the Christian Democrat Chancellor, who oversaw the peaceful unification of Germany in 1990 and personified the cold war's end in Europe.

With the defeat of Mr. Kohl, 68, the last European leader in office when the Berlin wall came down in 1989 has departed, reflecting the new priorities that confront a continent grappling with the competitive pressures of a global economy, overburdened welfare systems and high unemployment.

"The voters have chosen a change of generation," Mr. Schröder, 54, declared to a cheering crowd outside the Social Democratic Party headquarters in Bonn. He had embodied youth during the campaign, and a Germany less burdened by its past, and it was on this wave that he rode to victory.

Born into poverty, Mr. Schröder came into politics on the leftist wave of the 1960's. But his outlook evolved toward pragmatism, and he fought this campaign on an often vague platform of modernization and renewal under the slogan "the New Middle" and the inspiration of Bill Clinton and Tony Blair of Britain.

While Mr. Kohl pressed his vision of the rise from the ruins of Nazism and his view of Germany's place in Europe on his countrymen, Mr. Schröder talked about jobs. The strategy worked because a new generation of Germans is tired of history lessons and more concerned that their society is fraying than worried about their geo-strategic status.

But Mr. Schröder and his followers said many things at once, reassuring business executives with talk of lower taxes and the need to reform the welfare system, while reassuring workers with promises of better benefits and pensions. The first months in office may confront him with wrenching choices between divergent campaign promises.

"I think politics is more psychological than rational, and this result for us Germans is an injection of energy," said Henning Frase, a 20-year-old student. "It is ridiculous, in a democracy, to have a leader for as long as we had Mr. Kohl."

Like other center-left leaders in

Continued on Page A10

In Defeat, the Unifier of Germany Claims Yet Another Political First

By SERGE SCHMEMANN

It was characteristic that even when Helmut Kohl was finally ousted in Germany's national elections, he scored a first — this time as the first postwar German Chancellor to be voted out of office.

It was not a first that Mr. Kohl relished, to be sure, nor one he likely worried about. For all his extraordinary records, both political and physical — the first Chancellor of a reunited Germany, the longest-serving German Chancellor since Otto von Bismarck, and, at 6 foot 4 and somewhere around 300 pounds, indisputably the largest leader in modern Europe — Mr. Kohl has not spent much of the past 16 years pondering his place in history.

"To hell with history," he once snapped at an aide who raised the subject. His medium was politics, and it was a medium in which he was a master, even if in the end he failed to recognize when to step aside.

Throughout his career, Mr. Kohl attracted an unending stream of unflattering jokes, and was often perceived by intellectuals as something of an embarrassing provincial politico. But nobody ever questioned his total control of his own party, the Christian Democratic Union, nor his skill in guiding his nation through the Byzantine politics of post-war and post-Communist Europe.

If he disdained talk of his "place in history," Mr. Kohl bridled when his opponents accused him of lacking vision. His was as concrete as it was consistent: to unify his people in the context of a unified Europe.

"Who has a better vision here in the Federal Republic?" he declared in 1990, on the eve of German unification. "I know no better concept than the one I represent — European unification — because in 10 years we will write 2000 and not 1900, and this country and this continent will have a chance in the year 2000, and beyond, only if they are united. O. K., there is the vision."

He spoke of unity as a "compass" in his politics. "My compass also says, to an almost emotional degree, friendship with France, friendship with the United States," he said.

If his formulation lacked the elo-

Continued on Page A10

Recharged Hurricane Batters Gulf Coast With 105 M.P.H. Winds

By B. DRUMMOND AYRES Jr.

NEW ORLEANS, Sept. 27 — Hurricane Georges, rampaging again after earlier devastating islands in the Caribbean and the Florida Keys, slammed into the seaside cities and resorts of the Gulf Coast tonight with rain-packed winds of up to 105 miles per hour and a sea surge of 10 feet or more.

Recharged after a three-day wander at 10 m.p.h. across the Gulf of Mexico's tropical waters, the storm first began to move ashore early this evening with 50 m.p.h. winds at the leading edge. As the night wore on, the winds grew stronger, blowing twice as hard near the eye of the storm.

There was concern that the storm, one of the most dangerous to hit the vulnerable, low-lying gulf region in many years, might not move immediately inland if it collided with a high-pressure area to the north. In that case, disaster experts said, there was the possibility of catastrophic damage from a lingering pounding by wind, rain and surf along the coastal strip that stretches for more than 300 miles, from just east of Panama City in the Florida Panhandle to just west of New Orleans. Damage estimates were still being figured in the Caribbean islands that had been devastated earlier. [Page A12.]

Early damage reports made no mention of deaths or injuries, but cities, towns, and resort strips in the path of the storm were already suffering, with extensive power failures, large numbers of downed trees and widespread damage to windows and roofs.

Waves from the Gulf of Mexico leaped across beachfront roads along Route 90 in Mississippi, and

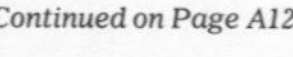

Continued on Page A12

Andrew Boyd/The Times Picayune, via Associated Press

The sky turned ominous over the Gulf of Mexico yesterday in Biloxi, Miss., as Hurricane Georges approached.

INSIDE

White House Strategy

To defend President Clinton, the White House and Congressional Democrats have agreed on an aggressive offense. Page A14.

Three-Way Mideast Meeting

The Secretary of State met with Prime Minister Benjamin Netanyahu of Israel and Yasir Arafat, the Palestinian leader. Page A6.

No Letup in Kosovo Pain

Although Serbia said, under United Nations pressure, that it had ended its offensive in Kosovo, attacks on civilian villages continued. Page A3.

Calculated Risk: U.S. and I.M.F. Lead Push for Brazil Bailout Plan

By LOUIS UCHITELLE

With the Clinton Administration and the International Monetary Fund taking the lead, a package of loans for Brazil, likely to total more than $30 billion, is gradually being put together to limit the damage to Latin America's biggest economy from the Asian crisis. But the bailout plan is a calculated risk: rather than save Brazil, it could sink the country into deep recession.

The stakes for Americans are considerable. The huge Brazilian economy dominates Latin America, which purchases nearly 20 percent of America's exports and is host to thousands of American-owned factories, whose sales and profits contribute significantly to corporate America's bottom line. A sharp cutback in the flow of all this income, coming on top of a similar blow from the Asian crisis, might reduce economic growth in the United States to a crawl.

Now that Asia and Russia have been flattened, Brazil is suddenly the new front line in the struggle to halt the spreading financial crisis, with its power to pull down markets and plunge countries into recession. If Brazil goes down, then Europe or the United States would become the next battlegrounds.

"It is very clear from the statements being made by top officials in the Clinton Administration that Brazil is fundamental to the system," said Desmond Lachman, an economist at Salomon Smith Barney, a Wall Street firm with money at risk in Brazil. "There is just no way they can allow Brazil to fail."

The whole purpose of the proposed loan package is to preserve the present value of the Brazilian currency — the real — to avoid the steep devaluations that have been so ruinous in Asia.

Because Brazil spends much more on imports than it earns from exports, it must finance overseas purchases by continually borrowing money abroad.

That is not easy, given that foreign lenders are increasingly nervous

Continued on Page A6

McGwire Shifts Focus to His Tan

By SELENA ROBERTS

ST. LOUIS, Sept. 27 — Two police officers poked their heads out of a side door to the Cardinals' clubhouse. All clear. A hulkish redhead ducked into the dank corridor beneath Busch Stadium and began to run.

With two officers at his side, the drained slugger legged out a sprint to a gray BMW, making a mad dash for a life closer to normal almost two hours after his unfathomable season came to an end with a day as thrilling and bizarre as a David Lynch plot.

Farewell, Mark McGwire. California, here he comes. "I'm white, white," McGwire said. "I don't have a tan."

Maybe at some point this week, he will dust off the sand, recline on a couch and savor the satisfaction of achieving the unthinkable: hitting 70 home runs. Maybe he will even watch the video that has been stashed away, the one marked Sept. 8, 1998.

He has never replayed the moment he broke Roger Maris's record of 61 home runs, a night forever remembered by an elation so deep that McGwire nearly forgot to touch first base on his historic trot. McGwire seemed to feel that indulging himself with his greatness would have been too distracting. For an entire season, he displayed the concentration of a man who defuses bombs for a living. The crush of pressure never cramped his swing.

He was proud of this but grateful for an end to a hot and humid day. McGwire had sent a thank-you to the fans by doing something no one had thought possible: He willed himself to hit his 69th and 70th home runs of the season.

"It blew me away," McGwire said. "I think it'll take a little time to come down from this."

Moments after 5:15 P.M., as his getaway car roared out of Busch Stadium, two crestfallen fans emerged from an office across from the clubhouse. The two, Philip Ozersky, 26, and Kerry Woodson Jr., 22, wanted desperately to meet McGwire.

An hour or so earlier, Ozersky had come up with McGwire's 70th home run ball, while Woodson had uncovered No. 69. After Woodson and his parents were hustled into a side room by the police, an officer told the parents to get out.

"He had a gun, and I had a camera," Woodson's mother, Bobbie, said in a half-serious tone. "So we left."

Inside the room, which lacked only a naked lightbulb in this surreal scene, the police stood by as a team official tried to broker a deal: a signed jersey and bat for the baseballs, plus a chance to meet McGwire. Woodson and Ozersky wanted to think about their decision and show their baseballs to their friends. Neither said he was interested in selling his baseball right now.

"There was pressure to decide what to do," Ozersky said. "It was like, 'Mr. McGwire has a flight, and he needs to know now.' It was either give it up, or Mr. McGwire was gone."

As this hourlong ordeal began for Ozersky and Woodson, McGwire was in the locker room, hugging friends before he hit the shower. He had already packed his duffel bag before the game, although there was still a cartoonish can of spinach and a stick of deodorant to tuck away.

It was a time for McGwire to laugh with his teammates and embrace Manager Tony La Russa, who, at times, has wanted a home run title for McGwire more than the player he watched sprout up from his rookie season with Oakland. As McGwire signed the bat he hit his 70th home run with, a trophy for the Hall of Fame, he was greeted by a gentleman wearing a sportcoat and a smile.

"It's been a long time since I sat down with your dad," said Rod Dedeaux, the coach who recruited McGwire at the University of Southern California. "Good to see you."

McGwire's face lit up in a day filled with hellos to old friends and goodbyes to the new ones he has made this season. He was polite and gracious until the end. Perhaps Ozersky and Woodson left disappointed, but no one else did on a day that shocked the imagination.

When he delivered his 69th and 70th home runs, an effort that seemed ripped from a page of fiction, not even McGwire believed how this final day was unfolding. Seventy home runs?

"I can't believe I did it," McGwire said. "Can you?"

No one could, near or far. Just seven blocks away, at the Trans-World Dome, the Arizona Cardinals were playing the Rams. When McGwire hit his 70th home run, the fans carrying radios relayed the action, and the dome exploded. In turn, the Rams were socked with a 5-yard penalty as a result of the excessive noise.

Who could blame the Ram fans? The ones packing Busch Stadium understood the elation.

"It's like everyone's in a trance when he comes up to hit," said Mike Bisch, a project leader for Bausch & Lomb who came up with his season tickets by luck: he won an airline promotion. "No one's in the aisle, no one moves. It's like he's hit a home run before he hits one."

Dividing Up the Long Balls

Home runs by month for Mark McGwire and Sammy Sosa this season and for the record seasons of Babe Ruth, who hit 60 in 1927, and Roger Maris, who hit 61 in 1961.

	McGWIRE	SOSA	RUTH	MARIS
MARCH	1	0	NO GAMES	NO GAMES
APRIL	10	6	4	1
MAY	16	7	12	11
JUNE	10	20 (circled)	9	15
JULY	8	9	9	13
AUGUST	10	13	9	11
SEPTEMBER	15	11*	17	9
OCTOBER	NO GAMES	NO GAMES	0	1

(20 circled) Major league record; * Sosa has one more game tonight

The whole country absorbed each blast. And the city of St. Louis took notice. McGwire's day was far from over when the game ended. A few minutes after the game, he popped out of the dugout wearing a hat with a 70 on it, a surprise that was prepared and waiting in his locker when he left the game in the ninth inning. He was ready to receive the St. Louis Award, which was described as an honor given to a man "for lifting the spirits of a community and a nation." Almost 40,000 remaining fans would not stop cheering.

McGwire was visibly moved. He swallowed, took a deep breath and let out a brief thank-you. He parted the crush of cameras that have been following him for weeks and trotted up the tunnel and into a closed-off clubhouse. His good friend, Tom Lampkin, was waiting for him.

"I'm just so happy for him," Lampkin said. "No one can understand what this has been like for him. What a way to end it!"

As the game neared its last inning, a clip rolled across the jumbo screen in center field. It was the clip McGwire's teammates say he has never glanced at. It was the video of his 62d home run, accompanied by a Green Day song, "Good Riddance (Time of Your Life)."

Farewell, Mark McGwire.

A Grand Finale Makes It 70 for McGwire

Continued From Page A1

Maris's 37-year-old record of 61 with a line drive over the left-field fence at Busch Stadium on Sept. 8, trailed Sosa only twice this season, each time for less than an hour. Sosa slugged his way into the lead last Friday night by hitting his 66th home run in Houston, but 45 minutes later, McGwire tied him, then did not look back. He socked a pair of home runs against Montreal pitchers on Saturday and connected against two Expos rookies today. He lofted a towering fly ball against Mike Thurman in the third inning that descended gracefully into the left-field stands for No. 69. Then in the seventh inning, an hour and nine minutes later, he swung at the first pitch he saw from Carl Pavano and lined it over the left-field fence for No. 70.

"I can't believe I did it; can you?" McGwire said at a post-game news conference that had become as much a part of his day as hitting home runs. "It's absolutely amazing. It blows me away."

Hitting five home runs in the span of 11 at-bats is incredible even for the hitter who finished the season with a record low ratio of 1 home run every 7.27 at-bats. McGwire had registered the previous low ratio of 8.13 in 1996, when he hit 52 home runs, surpassing Babe Ruth's record 8.48 achieved in 1920.

"I've always said hitting home runs is getting pitches to hit, keeping your stroke intact and working hard," he said, discussing his fantastic finish. "Home runs aren't easy to do. When you work as hard as I've worked the last few years to really work on my swing and get full extension, it's paid off."

In the Cardinals' first six games against the Expos, McGwire hit one home run. Then came the deluge. In his last 11 at-bats, he hit a home run, singled, struck out, struck out, hit a home run, flied out to center field, hit a home run, grounded out to third base, singled, hit a home run and (after walking) hit a home run. His last two swings of his already legendary season produced home runs.

"He's amazing," said Orlando Cabrera, the Expos' rookie shortstop. "Everything he hits goes out." Cabrera, who hit a home run of his own in the third inning, congratulated McGwire as the Cardinal slugger passed him in the seventh inning. "I'll be able to tell my kids I hit a home run the same day as McGwire hit his 70th," he said.

Neither Thurman nor Pavano, the rookie pitchers, was distraught over his contribution to baseball history.

Thurman, a 25-year-old right-hander, said he threw McGwire a breaking ball, "a bad breaking ball that most guys don't hit, up and in." He added: "Most guys take it or pop it up. He just muscled it out. That's why he's so special."

On the last day of the season, a pair of rookie pitchers join the list of victims.

Thurman said he was not particularly happy about giving up the home run. "But to be part of something that's special is a good feeling," he said. "It's something I'll look back on."

Thurman faced McGwire again in the fifth inning and walked him on four pitches, the fourth making the 6-foot-5-inch batter duck as the ball sailed over his head.

"I was completely out of gas," Thurman said. "I think everyone knows I wasn't trying to hit him. No one felt worse about it than I did, coming in with a 3-0 fastball at his head. It could have been pretty ugly. Fortunately, he got out of the way. I hope he knows I wasn't doing it on purpose." It was, McGwire said, "no big deal."

When he went to bat in the seventh inning, the game was tied, 3-3, runners were at first and second, and Pavano was pitching. Pavano, acquired from Boston last November in a trade for Pedro Martinez, was making his first relief appearance of the season after 23 starts.

"I didn't have to pitch; I could've said no," the 22-year-old right-hander said. "It was my decision. If I had said no, I'm done, they wouldn't have pitched me. But I said I could do it. I don't have any regrets doing it."

Pavano had made his last start last Tuesday in New York. He was the winning pitcher in the game that started the Mets' slide out of wild-card contention. McGwire had never faced him and decided to take a cue from J. D. Drew, who batted just ahead of him and singled to right field.

"I had no idea how his ball moves," McGwire said. "J.D. swung at the first pitch, so I might as well be aggressive."

Why would this veteran of 456 home runs, 69 this season, borrow from a rookie who became a major leaguer the night McGwire broke Maris's record?

"You have to amuse yourself sometimes when you play this game," McGwire said. "I said if he's going to be aggressive, I might as well, too."

Pavano threw a fastball up and in. "I was going right after him," Pavano said, then added, smiling, "He came after me."

McGwire said: "I hammered down and got a lot of top hand on it, and it carried just enough."

Like No. 62, it took off on a line rather than soaring high into the sky, but it traveled about 30 feet farther than No. 62, an estimated 370 feet.

Pavano knew instantly he had just given up McGwire's last home run of a record season.

"Oh yeah," the pitcher said. "I knew he didn't have any at-bats left." Then he said: "If you're going to give up a home run, you might as well give it up to him. What he's accomplished for baseball is unbelievable. I could see if he was cocky and had an attitude about it, but he's so genuine. You can't be nothing but happy for the guy."

The Cardinals' 14th consecutive sellout crowd of 46,110 roared and roared and roared some more after each home run, but especially the second. Pavano noted that McGwire had fed off the fans. He also profited financially from them.

The attendance bonus in his contract — $1 for each ticket sold over 2.8 million — provided McGwire an extra payday of $395,021. But that is one bonus the Cardinals will be happy to pay.

McGwire was asked whether he thought someone would break his record, assuming it remains the record after Sosa's bonus game.

"I think it will stand for a while," he said. "I know how grueling it is to do what I've done this year. It will be broken someday."

Might he break it?

"I don't know if I want to break my own record," McGwire said. "I think I'd rather just leave it as is."

Associated Press

Mark McGwire acknowledging cheers from the crowd during a post-game ceremony in which he received the St. Louis Award from the city.

TV SPORTS

Richard Sandomir

Go Punt, Football; Baseball Is On Throne

Somewhere on television yesterday, football existed. But it hardly mattered — no, not even on a day when New Orleans won its third straight game — on a dizzying baseball afternoon when the Mets lost and were eliminated from playoff contention, the Cubs and Giants lost but will meet tonight in a playoff and Mark McGwire slugged his 69th and 70th home runs.

And it was all there: the Mets-Braves game played in tandem on Fox Sports New York and ESPN2, which took viewers on a surfer's magical tour from Atlanta to Houston for the 11-inning Cubs-Astros game (where Sammy Sosa got two hits but no home runs beyond his current 66) and to Denver for the Giants-Rockies game.

There was also a Toronto stopover for the no-hit bid of the Blue Jays' rookie pitcher Roy Halladay, which was spoiled by a two-out, ninth-inning home run.

It meant nothing to the standing, but the Yankees, on the MSG Network, beat Tampa Bay for their 114th victory. Shane Spencer hit another grand slam and Bernie Williams won the American League batting title. Who said baseball was boring?

"This season just won't end," a delighted Gary Thorne of ESPN2 said during yet another twist in the Cubs-Astros game.

The only way you knew football existed was to see it on ESPN2's bottom-screen scores ticker. (Sure Fox and CBS combined to show three games locally, but did they matter?) The omnipresent ticker got ditsy during a replay of McGwire's 70th home run, when the slow-to-be-updated ticker read, "McGwire hits 69th home run." On a red-letter day, history beats technology.

By the end of the day, baseball itself made ESPN2 shine. The Astros had just beaten the Cubs, 4-3, when ESPN2 switched to Denver. As if fated by the cable deities, the first thing viewers saw was Colorado's Neifi Perez hitting a game-winning home run in the bottom of the ninth to make the Rockies a 9-8 victor over the Giants.

The camera stayed on Dusty Baker, the Giants' manager, long enough to see his expression change from astonishment to gloom to happiness, as he realized that his team was headed to Chicago for the playoff game despite the loss.

"Sammy gets another day," Thorne said to Joe Morgan. "Hey, maybe he'll hit four," Morgan said.

McGwire's 70th home run ended his season — and even if Sosa hits four, the friendly battle is less fun when there is only one contender — but ESPN2 offered McGwire in replays from early to late afternoon. By tape, ESPN2 carried post-game ceremonies and his news conference, where he said: "This is unheard-of for someone to hit 70 home runs. I'm in awe of myself right now."

Everything ESPN2 did is what it should do. This is what an all-sports network is capable of when it works at its technical best on a mesmerizing story. The home run chase revived baseball, which is more popular than it has been in many years. Baseball, once maligned and shunned for its miserable labor relations, looks like a hot property compared with the National Basketball Association, now shuttered by a lockout and in danger of looking as stupid as baseball during the 1994-95 strike.

Suddenly, the story in baseball is not about sinking ratings. ESPN, ESPN2 and Fox all benefited by showcasing the McGwire-Sosa home run bacchanal.

Still, a feud continues between Major League Baseball and ESPN.

Remember, baseball wrested three Sunday night games from ESPN because the network wanted to move them to ESPN2 to make way for Sunday night National Football League games. (One of those games happened to be last Sunday's, when Cal Ripken Jr. sat down.)

Baseball should be thrilled with the job ESPN2 did yesterday, even if it has only 60 million cable households, not ESPN's 74 million. You could quibble and ask why baseball wasn't on ESPN yesterday, not the NAPA Auto Care 500, a Nascar race. But that's a small complaint. What ESPN2 did was a bonus, not a contractual obligation.

Now comes the great twist in baseball's testy relationship with ESPN: The Cubs-Giants playoff game will be carried at 8 o'clock tonight, on ESPN, directly against the "Monday Night Football" Tampa Bay-Detroit game on ABC, ESPN's corporate sister in the Disney empire.

Are you ready for some baseball? Sosa vs. Sanders? Bonds vs. Dilfer?

GEORGE VECSEY/Sports of The Times

In the Year of the Home Run, McGwire and Sosa Just Kept Going

Continued From Page D1

merely reflecting the gut knowledge of the arena, the way baseball players always knew Mickey Mantle was "the man" in his league and Willie Mays was "the man" in his league, way back when. McGwire was almost expected to challenge 60, 61, 62 this season, and he did it first. Then Sosa roared right along with him.

People looking for trouble began to see some form of American benign neglect when, days after McGwire had done it, Sosa passed Ruth and Maris with somewhat less pageantry.

Asked if he detected any pattern of racism, Sosa, a dark-skinned man from the Dominican Republic, denied it, saying: "Come on, man. It's 1998." He plays in the city of Michael Jordan. He's not living a few decades in the past. His words should be the last on that subject.

Late yesterday afternoon, Mark McGwire had spoken twice with his bulging muscles and his aggressive mind and his big bat, had left a record that will last forever — or at least 11 months and change. Now the big man was packing for a vacation with his 10-year-old son, Matthew, up in St. Louis, but the baseball kept getting better and better.

In the last hours and minutes of what should have been the end of the regular season, two teams a third of a continent apart staged a pitch-by-pitch struggle just to stay alive, to try to win something called the wild card. This had been the season of the home run, the most easily marketable commodity in baseball. Big man swings bat. Ball flies over fence. Everybody gets it. Babe Ruth invented the home run. Now Mark McGwire has refined it. But always, even when the ball is flying out of some artificial dome or rickety relic or retro palace, the game is not merely about home runs, as exciting as they are.

Baseball is about old-fashioned scoreboards, like the one here, electronic instead of tin numbers fitted into slots, but with all games listed at all times, inning by inning — not some idiot message board hawking fizzy water instead of the real product, the game itself.

On this scoreboard, runs are posted in yellow numbers until the inning ends. The fans could follow the Yankees' 114th victory, the second-highest total in major league history. The fans could follow a kid named Roy Halladay with Toronto, pitching a no-hitter until two outs in the ninth. The fans could follow Mark McGwire's own yellow numbers. But the real action was in Colorado and here.

Two of the ancient franchises, the Giants and the Cubs, teams with roots back to the 19th century, were tied going into this last day. The team of John J. McGraw and Frankie Frisch, now located in San Francisco, was playing in Colorado. The team of Hack Wilson and Ernie Banks was playing here in the shabby old erstwhile Eighth Wonder of the World, a doomed dome.

They went back and forth, on their fields, on the scoreboards, on the televisions, on the radios, on the Internet, on little electronic gadgets, pitch by pitch.

Sosa was the central figure, starting the game two homers behind McGwire, soon falling four behind. His first time up, Sosa did the responsible thing and rapped a run-scoring single to center. Later he singled up the middle and stole second base.

"I've got to be patient, to help the team," Sosa said later.

His home runs and his engaging personality have obscured his old reputation for being a mediocre right fielder, at best. Maybe Babe Ruth in his early years would have caught the line drive by Carl Everett in the 11th inning; Roger Maris in his prime would have run it down. Sosa had it fall a step between him and the fence, for a triple. Two batters later, the winning run.

"Only Superman can catch that ball," Sosa said.

This warm and alert man has been a blessing in this year of the home run. Now he received a blessing in return. As he trooped up the stairs from the field, he heard a whooping in the clubhouse. A Colorado player named Neifi Perez had beaten the Giants. Mark McGwire is on vacation; Sammy Sosa has another game. The season of the home run is not quite over.

"All the News That's Fit to Print"

The New York Times

Late Edition
New York: **Today**, variable clouds, mild. High 49. **Tonight**, mostly cloudy, light rain possible. Low 42. **Tomorrow**, cloudy, limited sun. High 53. **Yesterday**, high 50, low 39. Details, page 64.

VOL. CXLVIII . . . . No. 51,377 Copyright © 1998 The New York Times NEW YORK, SUNDAY, DECEMBER 20, 1998 $3 beyond the greater New York metropolitan area. $2.50

CLINTON IMPEACHED

HE FACES SENATE TRIAL, 2D IN HISTORY; VOWS TO DO JOB TILL TERM'S 'LAST HOUR'

PRESIDENT DIGS IN

After Speaking of Vote, He Confers on Iraq — Halts the Bombing

By JAMES BENNET and DON VAN NATTA Jr.

WASHINGTON, Dec. 19 — President Clinton declared this afternoon that he intended to serve "until the last hour of the last day of my term," in an appearance outside the Oval Office with his wife at his side and two busloads of Congressional Democrats shoulder to shoulder behind him.

Mr. Clinton called for a quick, Constitutional and fair means of "resolving this matter" and vowed to "to do the work of the American people." He never used the word impeachment, which friends say he fears will now be bound forever to his name.

Then, as dusk darkened a gray, clammy day in Washington, the President grasped Hillary Rodham Clinton's hand and waded back through the Democrats to attend a meeting of his senior foreign policy advisers. He called off the air strikes against Iraq that he launched Wednesday night, on the evening before the scheduled House debate on his impeachment.

"I am confident we have achieved our mission," Mr. Clinton said this evening in a second statement to reporters, demonstrating to his supporters that he would resolutely perform his job despite all distractions — but fueling suspicions of detractors that the raid was timed for political effect.

A few of each group were clustered outside the iron gates of the White House this evening, and their distant cries of support or protest could be heard just beyond the Rose Garden, where Mr. Clinton appeared with the Democrats in a stark display of the partisanship cleaving Washington.

After announcing his decision on Iraq, Mr. Clinton donned black tie for a holiday dinner at the White House. That brought to a jarringly festive end his darkest day in an almost unimaginable sequence of events set in motion 20 years ago when he and Mrs. Clinton signed papers on a money-losing land investment along the White River in the Ozark Mountains in Arkansas.

It was while investigating that deal and related matters that Kenneth W. Starr, the independent prosecutor, learned of a possible Presidential affair and lies under oath.

And it was from the dining room off the Oval Office where he sometimes met with Monica S. Lewinsky that Mr. Clinton watched today as the House voted on articles of impeachment against him. He missed the vote on Article I, aides said, because he was meeting in the Oval Office with a spiritual adviser, the Rev. Tony Campolo.

As he watched, Mr. Clinton showed great interest in the handful of members that broke with their parties to

Continued on Page 31

Scott Applewhite/Associated Press

The President and Hillary Rodham Clinton leave the Oval Office to meet supporters after the House vote.

Livingston Urges Clinton to Follow Suit

By KATHARINE Q. SEELYE

WASHINGTON, Dec. 19 — Representative Robert L. Livingston, who rocked the House on Thursday with his revelation that he had had adulterous affairs, stunned the Capitol again today by saying that he would not serve as Speaker and would quit Congress in six months.

Republicans moved swiftly to fill the leadership vacuum and by tonight, Representative Dennis Hastert of Illinois, an affable conservative who is perceived as a pragmatist, was the all-but-acclaimed successor.

Mr. Livingston jolted his colleagues, standing in the well of the House he has served for two decades and outlining his reasons why he would vote to impeach President Clinton, when he veered unexpectedly into calling on the President to resign. This drew boos and catcalls from Democrats who shouted that he should quit instead.

He then did just that.

"I was prepared to lead our narrow majority as Speaker, and I believe I had it in me to do a fine job," he said. "But I cannot do that job or be the kind of leader that I would like to be under the current circumstances. So I must set the example that I hope President Clinton will follow. I will not stand for Speaker of the House on Jan. 6."

The move was so unexpected that it momentarily eclipsed, at least in the House, both the vote to impeach

Reuters TV

Robert L. Livingston told his colleagues that he would leave Congress.

the President, which had seemed inevitable for days, and the bombing in Iraq, which was deemed so momentous earlier this week that the House postponed its vote on impeachment until today. Members were reeling from sensory overload as they staggered off the House floor in between the four impeachment votes.

"There have been so many bombshells," said Representative Michael N. Castle, a Delaware Republican. "We have bombshells in Baghdad and we have bombshells in the House of Representatives. You can't turn your back for 10 seconds."

Members were surprised not only by Mr. Livingston's gesture but by its timing, leaving the Republicans and the House with no leader in the midst of a process that could result in the removal of the President from office. The Speaker is second in line to the Presidency after the Vice

Continued on Page 32

Speaker-Elect Is Resigning

By ALISON MITCHELL

WASHINGTON, Dec. 19 — William Jefferson Clinton was impeached on charges of perjury and obstruction of justice today by a divided House of Representatives, which recommended virtually along party lines that the Senate remove the nation's 42d President from office.

A few hours after the vote, Mr. Clinton, surrounded by Democrats, walked onto the South Lawn of the White House, his wife, Hillary, on his arm, to pre-empt calls for his resignation. The man who in better days had debated where he would stand in the pantheon of American Presidents said he would stay in office and vowed "to go on from here to rise above the rancor, to overcome the pain and division, to be a repairer of the breach." Later, Mr. Clinton called off the bombing in Iraq, declaring the mission accomplished.

Mr. Clinton became only the second President in history to be impeached, in a stunning day that also brought the resignation of the incoming Speaker of the House, Robert L. Livingston.

At 1:22 P.M., the House of Representatives approved, 228 to 206, the first article of impeachment, accusing Mr. Clinton of perjury for misleading a Federal grand jury last Aug. 17 about the nature of his relationship with a White House intern, Monica S. Lewinsky. [Roll call, page 36.]

In the noisy House chamber, a lone Republican applauded. Five Republicans crossed party lines to vote against impeachment. Five Democrats broke with their party to support it.

The margin was enough to forestall charges that the President's fate might have been different if the vote had been delayed to the 106th Congress, which will have five more Democrats.

A second article of impeachment, charging Mr. Clinton with obstruction of justice, passed on a narrower vote of 221 to 212. It accused him of inducing others to lie in order to conceal his affair with Ms. Lewinsky. This time 12 Republicans voted no, while 5 Democrats voted yes.

"The President of the United States has committed a serious transgression," said Representative Dick Armey of Texas, the House majority leader. "Among other things, he took an oath to God to tell the truth, the whole truth and nothing but the truth, and then he failed to do so, not once, but several times." To ignore this, he said, is to "undermine the rule of law." [Excerpts from the debate, pages 35-36.]

Two more charges against Mr. Clinton were defeated. An article accusing the President of perjury in the Paula Jones sexual harassment lawsuit was rejected, 229 to 205, with 28 Republicans breaking ranks.

C-Span

Representative Ray LaHood announcing vote.

And the House overwhelmingly rejected, 285 to 148, an accusation of abuse of power stemming from Mr. Clinton's legalistic answers to 81 questions put to him by the House Judiciary Committee. Eighty-one Republicans defected from their party. Only one Democrat deserted his.

The Senate would conduct only the second impeachment trial of a President in the 209-year history of the Republic. Mr. Clinton will be the only elected President put on trial. Andrew Johnson, impeached and acquitted by one vote in 1868, had been elected Vice President and succeeded to the White House on Abraham Lincoln's assassination in 1865.

Senator Trent Lott of Mississippi, the majority leader, announced just after the House vote that senators "will be prepared to fulfill their Constitutional obligations."

Mr. Lott said, "There are steps that precede the beginning of an impeachment trial. Once the Senate is organized as an impeachment

Continued on Page 30

What Next? Don't Guess

By R. W. APPLE Jr.

News Analysis

WASHINGTON, Dec. 19 — The only thing certain now is uncertainty.

The smart money shouts that President Clinton will never resign, and he vows to serve "until the last hour of the last day" of his second term. The smart money argues that the Senate will never muster the 67 votes needed to remove the wounded President from office, which would require the defection of 12 Democrats if all the Republicans stand against him. The smart money insists that someone will cut a deal soon to end all this.

Maybe so. But the smarter money whispers, "Remember."

Remember that everyone in Washington, including Representative Henry J. Hyde, the chairman of the Judiciary Committee, said the House would never, ever, vote impeachment along partisan lines. Wrong. Remember that all the pundits predicted Democratic losses in the midterm elections, and when the opposite happened, they said impeachment was dead. Twice wrong.

And remember that in the new year the nation will travel down a road it has never traveled before. One other President, Andrew Johnson of Tennessee, has been tried by the Senate, of course. But that happened in a different country — one with only 37 states, with primitive communications, with a simple economy based on agriculture, with minimal commitments abroad.

In the toxic politics of century's end in Washington, the inconceivable has become the commonplace.

The wholly unanticipated announcement this morning by Representative Robert L. Livingston, Republican of Louisiana, that he would not serve as Speaker and would resign from Congress, after his equally unanticipated disclosure on Thursday night of several extramarital affairs, only deepened the capital's profound sense of insecurity.

The deadly sweep of the scythe of neo-Puritanism appears unstoppable, at least for the moment, and Mr. Livingston's forthcoming resignation will increase the pressure on the

Continued on Page 34

U.S. and Britain End Raids on Iraq, Calling Mission a Success

By STEVEN LEE MYERS

WASHINGTON, Dec. 19 — The United States and Britain ended their attack on Iraq tonight after carrying out a fourth day of air and missile strikes as the holy month of Ramadan began in the Islamic world.

President Clinton, appearing at the White House only hours after the House voted to impeach him, called off the campaign at 6 P.M. Eastern time, or 2 A.M. Sunday in Iraq. Mr. Clinton declared the attack a success but warned that the United States and Britain would strike Iraq again if President Saddam Hussein took any steps to rebuild chemical or biological weapons or threaten his neighbors.

"I am confident we have achieved our mission," Mr. Clinton said, appearing in the Roosevelt Room with his senior national security aides. "We have inflicted significant damage on Saddam's weapons of mass destruction programs on the command structures that direct and protect that capability and on his military and security infrastructure."

Iraq, battered but unbowed, reacted with defiance. Its Vice President, Taha Yassin Ramadan, today declared an end to its cooperation with United Nations weapons inspections, imposed as part of conditions for ending the Persian Gulf war in 1991. Although not unexpected after the American and British attack, the declaration means that the United States has entered a new phase in its seven-year-old standoff with Mr. Hussein.

In the wake of the strikes, Mr. Clinton once again called for a new government in Baghdad, as did Prime Minister Tony Blair of Britain in London, though both had stopped short of making that an objective of the bombing campaign, knowing that to do so would invite failure. Still, Mr. Clinton said the United States would work to maintain Mr. Hussein's diplomatic isolation and increase support for opposition groups that might someday overthrow him.

"Over the long term, the best way to end the threat that Saddam poses to his own people and the region is for Iraq to have a different government," he said.

From the outset of the bombing on Wednesday night, Mr. Clinton and Mr. Blair said they were sensitive to carrying out strikes against an Arab country during the Muslims' month of fasting and religious study. Tonight they said the campaign had always been meant to last nearly four days, even though that had pushed it into Ramadan.

And so as night fell in Iraq today, antiaircraft fire once again burst over Baghdad, in reaction to one last day of strikes.

Today's attack included still more Tomahawk cruise missiles and American and British fighters and

Continued on Page 20

INSIDE

Jets Win Their Division For First Time Since 1969

The Jets clinched a title with a 17-10 victory over the Buffalo Bills. The last time the Jets were champions, they played in the American Football League and Joe Namath was their quarterback. SPORTSSUNDAY

On the Internet: www.nytimes.com

C-Span

About half of the 206 House Democrats walked out in protest after the Republican leadership blocked a proposal to allow censure of the President instead of impeachment.

THE SCENE

After the Vote, a Pause — Then Back-Pats and Glumness

By FRANCIS X. CLINES

WASHINGTON, Dec. 19 — When the impeachment of President Clinton became a fact of history this afternoon, the wrenching event seemed as plain and inevitable as the time spilling downward on the voting clock of the House of Representatives.

The dark moment was projected onto the very walls of the debating chamber, with the lawmakers' names and votes flickering as a running tally reflected above the members. They looked up again and again to see their verdict evolve, as if it might suggest something of their own legacy, along with that of the President.

A sense of exhaustion, as much as of history, was in the air as the lawmakers gaped at the results, a weariness born of 11 months' daily preoccupation by the nation with the President's misbehavior, and its aftermath. When the clock was done, Democratic anguish could be seen, as well as an initial Republican reserve at any temptation to exult.

But soon the first few Republican handshakes of well-done were exchanged in the post-vote buzz of excitement, anxiety and confusion welling up from the chamber. The politician's tribal back-pat started breaking out on the Republican side; the Democrats sat glum and sour-spirited. Some appeared crushed, as Republicans began seeking out their floor champions, like Henry J. Hyde of Illinois, for autographs on souvenir copies of the resolution impeaching the President.

Then, the deed done, many representatives seemed eager to be on their way. "Some members would like to leave here sooner rather than later," Mr. Hyde told the chamber.

But first came one last routine task on this most unroutine day: the appointment of House members as "managers" to officially shepherd the impeachment charges to the Senate for trial. Democrats, appalled, declined to serve, as if being invited onto a burial detail now that an armistice had followed their legislative war.

It was a woeful day for the Democrats. In

Exhaustion, as much as a sense of history, filled the air.

little more than five hours in the debating chamber, their reactions moved from combative fury to sorrowful resignation at the spectacle of their president actually being impeached.

In the morning, their passions had been raw and feisty, as when they bellowed "You resign! You resign!" at the designated Speaker, Robert L. Livingston, when he called for the President's resignation.

Shockingly, Mr. Livingston did just that.

He quit in one breathtaking utterance, as if flicking a trump card onto the heap of impeachment angst festering before his eyes in the debating chamber.

Amazed Democrats saw their fury vaporized in an instant. They stood, almost staggering to their feet, and joined the Republicans in a prolonged, emotional ovation for Mr. Livingston and his undeniable self-sacrifice.

As they clapped, the Democrats appeared to sense that Mr. Livingston had suddenly closed a trap on the President and his defenders. For, with impeachment a certainty, Mr. Livingston, whose own marital indiscretions were now obviously and miserably before the public, chose to show that the question of a political leader's resignation was very much in play.

"I must set the example that I hope President Clinton will follow," Mr. Livingston declared, flabbergasting all attending the debate and the nation as well.

He walked off the floor like the sheriff in some bullet-pocked, political "High Noon," tossing aside the leadership badge he had wrested from the outgoing Speaker, Newt Gingrich.

In the corridor just beyond, a doorman shouted to a police officer: "Livingston just resigned!"

"What? What?" came the reply from the officer, who obviously thought the momentous announcement expected would be about Mr. Clinton's impeachment, not Mr. Livingston's political self-immolation.

In closing the circle on his career, the man who wanted the Speakership in the worst way gave it up in a fashion that almost eclipsed the gravest issue before the House, the impeachment of the President, making it seem almost an anticlimax.

The Democrats, already deeply exasperated after their long fight to save the President, grasped for their bearings.

"It is a surrender to a developing sexual McCarthyism," declared Representative Jerrold Nadler of New York, a Presidential defender intent on rallying Democrats around the argument that Mr. Livingston should not resign any more than President Clinton should.

But Mr. Livingston left the floor resolved, daring the President to emulate him in resigning under fire.

"They must not succeed," David Bonior, the Democratic whip, said of the Republicans, as he grappled with the task of refocusing the day on the misdeeds of the President, not the departure of the Speaker. "We are here to debate impeachment and should not be distracted from that."

But the lawmakers were off and reeling through the day. The fateful vote on the Presidency was approaching and the notion of resignation was licking about the capital city like a flame in a forest.

THE FIRST LADY

Clinton's Top Defender Rallies Troops at Front

By MELINDA HENNEBERGER

WASHINGTON. Dec. 19 — As defiant as the day she blamed the Monica Lewinsky scandal on a "vast right-wing conspiracy," Hillary Rodham Clinton went to Capitol Hill this morning and blasted the impeachment process as unfair and politically motivated. She told House Democrats that the President would continue to fight and that they should, too.

In a closed meeting with the House Democrats, Mrs. Clinton said she was there in part as "a wife who loves and supports her husband" and charged that Republicans were impeaching her husband — "hounding him out of office," she said — because they opposed his agenda.

"She said this is as much about ending his agenda on health care and other things as about hounding him out of office," Representative Robert Menendez of New Jersey said. "She said there would be no resignation and we should not and cannot allow them to hound him out of office."

Mrs. Clinton's continued support for her husband has been seen as crucial to his popularity, cited again and again by those who say they will stick with him, too, in statements along the order of, "If Hillary doesn't mind, why should I?" or "That's between him, his God and Hillary."

She had been credited with saving his political skin at least twice before, appearing at his side on "60 Minutes" as he denied a long affair with Gennifer Flowers, and going solo on the "Today" show to complain about a "vast right-wing conspiracy" after Mr. Clinton's denial of "sexual relations with that woman, Miss Lewinsky."

And though Mrs. Clinton got generous credit for campaigning before the November elections, some Democrats had expressed a little nervousness lately, wondering, Why hadn't she offered fresh support for the President?

Her staff has insisted that she did all that she could, consulting constitutional scholars and regularly discussing the issue with the President. Friends said she had been annoyed by suggestions to the contrary: Was she supposed to issue daily statements of support? Lobby Republicans who wince at the mention of her name?

Today, though, her mission was clear. Mrs. Clinton is extrememly popular among Congressional Democrats — far more so than her husband — and she came to inoculate him against the possibility that Democrats could be persuaded that his resignation might be best for the country. Two House Democrats, Louise M. Slaughter of New York and William O. Lipinski of Illinois, had already said they would urge resignation if he were impeached.

Associated Press

Hillary Rodham Clinton visited the Capitol for a final appeal to lawmakers.

"She was determined and defiant," said Representative Jerrold Nadler of New York. "Her message was that they've been pursuing him since the day he came into office."

The President has not always enjoyed warm relations with Congressional Democrats, many of whom disagreed with him on welfare and thought at times that he worked rather too cozily with their Republican counterparts. Today, Mrs. Clinton reminded them that her husband was not the real issue.

"She said this goes beyond her husband, to the Constitution and the Presidency," said Representative Charles Rangel, who has himself been critical of the President at times. Not today, though: "Resign? We say, 'Hell, no.' "

In what several members called a pep rally, she thanked Democrats for their support and asked them to keep it coming, receiving half a dozen standing ovations. Afterward, members stood in line to give her a hug. And as they left, several House Democrats referred at least obliquely to Mrs. Clinton's own political prospects.

"She's probably the most popular person in the country with Democrats, period, and that's also true of us in the caucus," said Representative Eliot L. Engel of New York, where Mrs. Clinton has been mentioned as someone with the potential to succeed Daniel Patrick Moynihan, who is retiring from the Senate.

Her appearance today, following supportive remarks she made on Friday, did seem to end a week of speculation that Mrs. Clinton had decided to protect her political future by distancing herself from her husband in the hour of his greatest political need.

That the Clintons held hands rather less on their recent trip to Israel than on earlier trips, and that Mrs. Clinton seemed to pull away from her husband at one moment were reported on CNN, NBC and a number of newspapers as evidence that Mrs. Clinton was no longer on the team. The headline on a page 1 story in the Washington Times on Wednesday was, "Hillary shows signs of relinquishing role as the defender in chief for her husband."

But today she said she had gone to the Capitol as "a wife who loves and supports her husband," as a Judiciary Committee staff member during Watergate who knows first-hand how the process should work, and as an American who feels proud of the Democrats.

Rep. Dennis J. Kucinich of Ohio said he felt pumped up by the meeting with Mrs. Clinton.

"It's a campaign all over again," he said. "This needs to be a fight every step of the way, and we're going to wake the town and tell the people."

And he suggested that at this late date, the two-for-one Presidency has new life.

"She's so terrific," he said. "It's lucky for America we have a woman with the strength to lead the nation right now. And everybody understands she is one of the leaders of the nation right now, as much as the President."

Now, the question is whether Mrs. Clinton's pep talk will sustain Democrats in the days ahead, amid a steady succession of jaw-dropping events on Capitol Hill. Less than an hour after the meeting — after Representative Robert L. Livingston made the surprise announcement that he won't become Speaker — Representative Jane Harman of California said the meeting with the First Lady had been quite emotional, but then added, "It seems like we've lived a century since then."

IN THIS SECTION

CANDIDATE FOR LEADERSHIP The front-runner in the unexpected race for Speaker of the House is Dennis Hastert of Illinois, backed by the powerful and loyal base of support of Representative Tom DeLay of Texas, the Republican whip. Page 33.

BEYOND THE VOTES Members of the Senate are uncertain exactly what lies beyond the impeachment votes, whether it be a long trial, a deal that will drastically shorten the process or something in between. But they agree on one thing: Unless new and damaging evidence arises against the President, there will not be the two-thirds vote needed to convict Mr. Clinton and remove him from office. Page 30.

THE SPEECHES Excerpts of remarks from the final day of debate, as well as the text of the two articles of impeachment voted against the President by the House of Representatives. Pages 35 and 36.

THE HISTORY A chronology of the year's events leading to the House votes on impeachment. Pages 30 and 31.

THE REACTION

Americans Benumbed By the Crisis In the Capital

By ROBERT D. McFADDEN

Many Americans voiced anger, disgust and frustration with the proceedings. Some radiated grim satisfaction. But as President Clinton's long, painful journey from scandal to impeachment ended yesterday, most Americans were just benumbed, inoculated by the seemingly endless months of lies, legalisms and disillusionment with politics, Washington-style.

As the House cast the fateful votes to send perjury and other charges against Mr. Clinton to the Senate for trial, countless Americans paid scant attention, opting for football on television or Christmas shopping, a reflection of polls that had shown that the people overwhelmingly opposed an impeachment that was a forgone conclusion and were sick of the whole mess.

Still, there was great drama in the day — the bombs falling in Iraq, the stunning announcement that Robert L. Livingston would not serve as Speaker and would resign from the House after admitting adulterous affairs, and the realization by many that the impeachment of a President had happened only once before, 130 years ago.

And around the nation, Americans paused in homes, restaurants and shopping malls decked out for Christmas to watch the televised spectacle. Some endorsed the Republican-dominated vote to impeach, insisting that even a President was not above the law, and that impeachment was necessary for moral accountability. Others called on the President to resign and spare the nation months of agony.

But in interviews in New York, Seattle, Boston, Los Angeles, Chicago, Miami, Houston and other cities, most people, while deploring Mr. Clinton's behavior in trying to cover up his affair with Monica S. Lewinsky, said they opposed impeachment, calling it excessive punishment and perhaps harmful to the nation.

"It strikes me as dangerous," Greg Noonan, a law student at Harvard, said as the impeachment vote flashed on a television screen at the Three Aces restaurant in Cambridge, Mass. "And most infuriatingly of all, it strikes me as completely ignoring the will of the American people."

In Seattle, several people working out at the Olympic Athletic Club shook their heads in disgust as the vote unfolded on overhead screens. "I'm very, very saddened and I'm very, very angry," said Ross Carey, a doctor, who said the Republicans had "put politics ahead of what is best for the country."

For fateful votes, many pay scant attention.

Bob and Carol Wentink, a Chicago couple, said impeachment seemed excessive for what the President did. "It's a shame," Mr. Wentink, 54, an electronics designer, said. "I think there's too much interest in private lives. While he did wrong, I don't think he deserves to be impeached." His wife, a retired teacher, added: "I think it's a huge mistake. It's going to affect the way people around the world look at us."

Evan Ackerman, 28, a financial consultant in Miami, also called impeachment inappropriate. "But that doesn't necessarily mean I like Clinton," he added. "Even if he is a sleazebag, they should wait until he leaves office. He should be scolded, sued for millions of dollars, reprimanded."

Greater forgiveness was to be found at the Hair Place, a beauty salon in the New York City borough of Queens. "So he lied under oath," said Diane Barnett, 41, an office manager who lives in Roosevelt, L.I. "That's a petty issue. Everybody lies. It's like his wife said: there are so many other issues, like hunger and health care, to be concerned about."

Paul Trageser, 62, a silversmith from Cincinnati, said the impeachment had been motivated by pure politics. "It's partisan, it's unfair, it's a witch hunt," he said in Los Angeles, where he was visiting. "I'm sick of what the Republicans have done over the past few years — so squeaky clean and hypocritical. It's sad and bizarre."

Around the country, however, there were many who approved of impeachment.

"Hooray," yelled Ann Jewel, who heard the news as she wheeled a cart full of grocery bags in Chicago.

A 57-year-old receptionist for an insurance company and the mother of five children, Ms. Jewel said she had voted twice for President Clinton, but had come to believe that he betrayed the country and was not sincere in his many apologies. "He put his hand on the Bible and lied," she said. "A lot of things can be forgiven, but to be forgiven a person has to be sorry. He cannot be forgiven just because he is caught."

In Houston, Monika Miura, 48, a legal librarian, said Mr. Clinton, like any citizen, had to be called to account for lying under oath. "If anyone needs to be above reproach and needs to be an honorable individual, it should be the President," she said. "This is not an issue about sex. This is an issue about honor and truthfulness."

Gertrude Jackson, 75, a retired Chicago

Continued on Page 34

IMPEACHMENT: Looking to the Senate

The Road to Impeachment

JANUARY

JAN. 12 Linda R. Tripp provides prosecutors for the Whitewater independent counsel, Kenneth W. Starr, with taped conversations in which she and Monica S. Lewinsky discuss Lewinsky's sexual relationship with President Clinton.

JAN. 13 Wearing a hidden microphone supplied by the F.B.I., Tripp meets with Lewinsky.

JAN. 16 A panel of Federal judges secretly authorizes Starr to expand his investigation to include accusations that the President and his confidant, Vernon E. Jordan Jr., encouraged Lewinsky to lie under oath.

JAN. 17 Clinton is questioned by lawyers for Paula Corbin Jones in her sexual misconduct suit. He denies that he had a sexual relationship with Lewinsky.

JAN. 18 Clinton discusses with Betty Currie, his personal secretary, his deposition of the previous day comparing recollections of his interactions with Lewinsky.

FEBRUARY

THE SCANDAL BREAKS

JAN. 21 News accounts first appear of the alleged affair between Clinton and Lewinsky. Clinton denies the accusations publicly.

CLINTON DENIAL

JAN. 26 Clinton makes his most emphatic denial since the scandal surfaced: "I did not have sexual relations with that woman, Miss Lewinsky. I never told anybody to lie, not a single time — never."

MARCH

MARCH 5 Lewinsky's lawyer, William H. Ginsburg, argues before a Federal district judge in Washington that Starr's office had made, then retracted, a firm offer of immunity for Lewinsky in return for her full testimony. Starr denies making such a deal.

APRIL

JONES'S SUIT THROWN OUT

APR. 1 A Federal district court judge in Arkansas throws out Jones's lawsuit. Her lawyers say they will appeal.

MAY

MAY 4 A Federal district judge rules that the President is not entitled to invoke executive privilege or attorney-client privilege to stop prosecutors from questioning his closest advisers.

MAY 22 A Federal district judge rules that Secret Service agents can be compelled to testify.

JUNE

JUNE 2 Lewinsky dismisses Ginsburg and hires Jacob A. Stein and Plato Cacheris. One week later, the new lawyers discuss possible immunity for Lewinsky with independent counsel prosecutors.

THE OVERVIEW

President Is Impeached and Faces Trial In the Senate, the Second One in History

Continued From Page 1

proceeding, there will be pleadings and motions that come before the taking of evidence. That makes it difficult to determine at this time when an actual trial will begin."

The House acted on a crisp pre-Christmas Saturday when American politics seemed to be descending into the very cannibalism that Speaker Newt Gingrich had warned of when he was toppled a month ago.

Hours before Mr. Clinton was impeached for his efforts to cover up his affair with Ms. Lewinsky, Mr. Livingston, who had been chosen to succeed Mr. Gingrich, shocked the House by announcing he would leave Congress because of revelations of his own adulterous affairs.

Still, it was Mr. Livingston today who called for Mr. Clinton's resignation from the House floor. Charging that Mr. Clinton had undermined the rule of law and damaged the nation, Mr. Livingston said, "I say that you have the power to terminate that damage and heal the wounds that you have created. You, sir, may resign your post."

As some Democrats shouted back, "You resign," the Louisiana Republican said, "I was prepared to lead our narrow majority as Speaker and I believe I had it in me to do a fine job. But I cannot do that job or be the kind of leader that I would like to be under current circumstances. So I must set the example that I hope President Clinton will follow."

With a sex scandal now consuming one of their own, the House's impeachment debate turned more than ever into a discourse on sin and morality in politics.

Representative Tom DeLay of Texas, the House majority whip, who had helped make Mr. Livingston the Speaker-designate and has been one of the fiercest critics of Mr. Clinton, choked back tears as he praised Mr. Livingston. He said his friend "understood what this debate was all about."

The articles of impeachment on the desk of Gary Sisco, Secretary of the Senate.

"It was about honor and decency and integrity and the truth," Mr. DeLay said, his voice breaking, "everything that we honor in this country. It was also a debate about relativism versus absolute truth." He charged that the President's Democratic defenders would lower the standards of society.

Equally passionate, Richard A. Gephardt of Missouri, the House minority leader, said that men were imperfect, and he asked Mr. Livingston not to resign, for a moment drawing a bipartisan standing ovation.

"Our founding fathers created a system of government of men, not of angels," Mr. Gephardt said, his face reddening with emotion as he spoke. "No one standing in this House today can pass a puritanical test of purity that some are demanding that our elected leaders take. If we demand that mere mortals live up to this standard, we will see our seats of government lay empty and we will see the best, most able people unfairly cast out of public service."

When he finished he walked slowly up the Democratic side of the aisle, Democrats applauding him and hugging him as he moved along. The Republicans remained fixed in their seats.

Today's votes were the penultimate step in the most serious conflict between Congress and a President since Richard M. Nixon resigned in the face of impeachment and certain conviction on Aug. 9, 1974.

But while that case spun out from a 1972 break-in at Democratic headquarters in the Watergate complex, this began with a murky land deal in Arkansas in 1978. Through the efforts of Kenneth W. Starr, the independent counsel, under the law enacted in the wake of Watergate, the investigation spread to examine Mr. Clinton's affair with an intern.

Mr. Clinton, in a finger-wagging performance last January at the White House, told the nation he did not have sexual relations with "that woman," Ms. Lewinsky. He denied sexual relations with her in a deposition in the sexual harassement case brought against him by Paula Corbin Jones.

Only in August, after it became known that Ms. Lewinsky had preserved a blue dress that provided evidence of their affair, did Mr. Clinton tell the nation and a grand jury that he had had an "inappropriate relationship" with her.

Republicans today took great pains to distinguish Mr. Clinton's case from Mr. Livingston's revelations that "on occasion I strayed from my marriage."

Representative Henry J. Hyde, the chairman of the House Judiciary Committee, who himself saw a past affair come to light as he presided over the House's nine-week impeachment inquiry, said: "Infidelity, adultery is not a public act, it's a private act, and the Government, the Congress, has no business intruding into private acts."

But he said that Mr. Clinton had become a Commander in Chief who by lying in legal forums "trivializes, ignores, shreds, minimizes the sanctity" of his oath of office. Representative Nancy L. Johnson of Connecticut said "there can be no justice without the truth."

Photographs by Paul Hosefros/The New York Times

Henry J. Hyde, chairman of the House Judiciary Committee, giving the articles of impeachment to Gary Sisco, right, Secretary of the Senate. Thomas Mooney, the Republican staff director, is behind Mr. Hyde.

MODERATES IN QUANDARY

Moderate Republicans tried to distance themselves from the President's bitterest adversaries. Page 60.

Democrats argued back that the President's actions were wrong and deserved censure but did not rise to the level of impeachment. Representative David E. Bonior of Michigan, the House minority whip, said Republicans were trying to "hijack an election and hound the President out of office."

Moments before the impeachment votes, Democrats tried to bring to the floor their own proposal to censure Mr. Clinton. But after some debate, their motion was held to be not germane to impeachment and ruled out of order by Representative Ray LaHood, an Illinois Republican whom Speaker Gingrich named to preside over the impeachment proceedings.

The Democrats appealed the ruling, expecting to lose because such appeals are considered a challenge to the right of the majority party to run the House. Their motion failed, 230 to 204. Two Republicans, Constance A. Morella of Maryland and Peter T. King of Long Island, broke with precedent and crossed party lines to vote with the Democrats.

As their motion failed, the Democrats briefly marched out of the House chamber in protest. But they returned to vote on the four articles of impeachment.

For one year the Lewinsky scandal has preoccupied the capital despite an immense disconnection with public opinion. Since the scandal became public last January, polls have shown the public opposed impeachment and wanted the inquiry brought to an end. Even on Friday night, after a 13-hour debate, a CBS News Poll of 548 people showed only 38 percent wanted their representative to vote for impeachment; 58 percent wanted a no vote.

The conflict now enters uncharted seas. The Nixon resignation cut the matter short, and the Andrew Johnson trial occurred more than 100 years ago, in a different America, one without nuclear weapons or cable television or public opinion polls.

Despite Mr. Lott's recent assurances that he will move ahead, some wonder whether the Senate may yet flinch from a trial because of the popular will. But Republicans have steadfastly ignored the polls all year.

Representative J.C. Watts of Oklahoma, the newly elected chairman of the House Republican conference, said in debate today, "What's popular isn't always right. You say polls are against this. Polls measure changing feelings, not steadfast principle. Polls would have rejected the Ten Commandments. Polls would have embraced slavery and ridiculed women's rights.

"You say we must draw this to a close," Mr. Watts continued, "I say we must draw a line between right and wrong, not with a tiny fine line of an executive fountain pen, but with the big fat lead of a No. 2 pencil. And we must do it so every kid in America can see it. The point is not whether the President can prevail, but whether truth can prevail."

Yet, for all of the Democrats' charges of excessive partisanship today, enough Republicans did pick and choose among articles of impeachment to send only two of the four that had come out of the House Judiciary Committee on to the Senate.

A number of Republicans said they did not think a perjury charge in Ms. Jones's civil case warranted impeachment, particularly since Mr. Clinton's deposition had been held by a judge to be immaterial. Many of them also looked dimly at impeaching the President for abuse of power — a term taken from the proceedings against Mr. Nixon in 1974 — simply because his answers to 81 questions from the Judiciary Committee were legalistic and evasive.

Representative David Hobson, Republican of Ohio, said he supported impeachment of the President for lying to a grand jury but not in the Jones case. "Even if it's true, I worry whether it rises to the same threshold for impeachment," he said. "I didn't want to pile on."

ON THE WEB

Late news on impeachment, along with full texts of significant debates and statements, can be found at The New York Times on the Web:

www.nytimes.com

THE SENATE

Senators Agree on One Thing: That Conviction Seems Unlikely

By DAVID E. ROSENBAUM

WASHINGTON, Dec. 19 — As they plunge into the uncharted waters of an impeachment trial of a modern President, senators are uncertain about what lies ahead.

Some think they are in for a long ordeal on the Senate floor that could last until next summer or even longer. Others think that President Clinton and the Senate will quickly cut a deal in January and short-circuit a trial before it gets started in earnest. And still others expect something in between: a procedure short of a full trial that lasts for some weeks but that may then be shelved.

But all the senators and staff experts interviewed this week agreed on an essential point: Unless unanticipated, damaging new evidence against arises, the Senate will never muster the two-thirds majority necessary to convict the President and remove him from office.

"There is no question that there are not 67 votes against him," said Senator Phil Gramm of Texas, an ardent Republican opponent of the President's but also a senator who usually has a sure sense of where his colleagues stand.

And although it takes a two-thirds majority to remove a President from office, a trial can be stopped before it begins or at any time after it starts by a simple majority vote of the senators. The Senate will have 55 Republicans and 45 Democrats.

The fact is that no one knows what may develop. There is no reference book that spells out what an impeachment trial in 1999 would look like. There is no staff expert who has mastered all the legal and political nuances.

Most important, the Senate has been out of session for two months, so there has not been the give and take necessary to reach a political consensus.

Senator Trent Lott, the Republican leader, insists that he has made no plans for how the Senate will proceed. He has said he did not want to appear presumptuous while the matter w. . before the House.

In a statement issued by his office today, Mr. Lott said: "There are steps that precede the beginning of an impeachment trial. Once the Senate is organized as an impeachment proceeding, there will be pleadings and motions that come before the taking of evidence. That makes it difficult, at this time, to determine when an actual trial will begin. That timing will depend greatly on the President and his lawyers."

Mr. Lott hinted in an interview on CNN this week that after the trial began, the Senate might decide to pull the plug on it. "There are a number of votes on procedures that may be demanded along the way," he said, "and we'll have to work the will of the Senate."

President Clinton said today that he hoped that "there will be a constitutional and fair means of resolving this matter in a prompt manner" in the Senate.

The best guess is that on Jan. 6, when the 106th Congress convenes, the Senate will pass a resolution stating that it is prepared to receive the articles of impeachment from the House managers, appointed today, as the group of representatives selected to act as official prosecutors of the case are called.

On Jan. 7, if the schedule holds, the managers will walk across the Capitol to the Senate and read the articles on the Senate floor. That day or the next, Chief Justice William H. Rehnquist will be sworn in to preside over the trial, as the Constitution requires. The Chief Justice will then swear in the 100 senators as jurors in the trial.

Next, the Senate will vote to notify President Clinton formally that the proceedings had begun, and a schedule will be set. The President will probably get a month or more to file a written response to the impeachment charges, and the House will get time to prepare its reply.

During this hiatus, the negotiations over a deal will begin.

One possibility is that the Senate might agree to stop the trial in return for the President's acceptance of a stiff censure. A trial could also end quickly if Mr. Clinton decides not to present a defense at all.

Senator Orrin G. Hatch, Republican of Utah, is one who thinks that is the most likely outcome. He explained: "If I were the President, I would want to get this thing over with as soon as you can. He knows there are not 67 votes there. I don't know anybody who would argue there's a chance to have 67 votes at this point. But who knows what else might come up if he got into a trial?"

Senator Frank R. Lautenberg, Democrat of New Jersey, said he thought that script was unlikely. "I think it goes nine innings, meaning we have a long, drawn-out process," he said.

Taking the middle ground, Senator Robert F. Bennett, Republican of Utah, said he expected that after a time, the Senate could vote to end the trial.

> **There could be a quick deal, a long trial or something in between.**

"The Senate can't just pass a motion right up front to stop the trial," he said. "That would be a terrible slap in the face of the House institutionally. But if after a while, we can say we have sifted through the issues and have decided to suspend the trial, then there's face-saving all around."

Lawyers in the Senate believe the new House that takes office next month will have to vote to reappoint the managers who would present the case to the Senate.

Senator Patrick J. Leahy, Democrat of Vermont, said possibly the new House, with a smaller Republican majority than the current one, would end the case then. Otherwise, he said, "we are in for a long, long, long trial."

If there is a full-scale trial, it would be governed partly by arcane Senate rules that were created for the trial of President Andrew Johnson in 1368 and partly by rules of law.

In all of American history, there have been only 13 such trials and only 7 convictions, all of Federal judges. Johnson's trial was the only one of a President.

In some respects, the trial would be like one in a courtroom. There would be opening statements, presentation of witnesses and evidence by both sides, cross-examinations, rebuttals and closing arguments.

Witnesses like Monica S. Lewinsky would testify under oath, in public, no matter how distasteful and embarrassing their testimony.

But in other ways the proceedings would be quite different from a courtroom trial. The senators, sitting as jurors, would be the judges not just of facts but also of law. By majority vote, they could overrule decisions of Chief Justice Rehnquist.

The senators, who in normal circumstances think nothing of talking for hours on the most routine matters, would not be permitted to speak in public session. To question witnesses, they could pass notes to the Chief Justice, who would pose the questions.

All the senators' deliberations would be in closed session, and their time for speaking would be strictly limited — 10 minutes maximum for each senator on preliminary motions and 15 minutes on the final verdict.

The biggest difference from a courtroom trial would be that the verdict would not be based primarily on facts or law. Some senators would doubtless decide on the basis of politics, others on their judgment of what would be best for the country.

Senator Hatch, the chairman of the Judiciary Committee, said, for instance, that lying to a grand jury, the first charge against President Clinton, was an offense that could justify removal from office, but that he might not vote that way.

"It comes down to what is in the best interest of the American people," Senator Hatch said. "Should we really throw the President out of office for this kind of prevarication? I don't know. It's not an easy question to answer. It's one I'm struggling with."

IMPEACHMENT: The White House Strategy

JULY

SECRET SERVICE TESTIFIES
JULY 17 Chief Justice William H. Rehnquist rejects an 11th-hour plea by the Justice Department to block the testimony of Secret Service agents. The agents, including Larry L. Cockell, left, the chief of the President's security detail, arrive at the Federal courthouse to begin testifying. The independent counsel's office secretly issues a subpoena for Clinton to testify before the grand jury. The subpoena is later withdrawn in return for Clinton's voluntary testimony.

JULY 28 Lawyers for Lewinsky broker an immunity deal with Starr in which she promises "full and truthful testimony" in exchange for a sweeping grant of immunity.

AUGUST

LEWINSKY TESTIFIES
AUG. 6 Lewinsky arrives at the Federal courthouse to begin telling her story to the grand jury.

AUG. 17 Clinton testifies before the grand jury. In a televised speech that evening he acknowledges, "I did have a relationship with Ms. Lewinsky that was not appropriate."

SEPTEMBER

STARR REPORT RELEASED
SEPT 9 Starr notifies House leaders that he has found "substantial and credible information" that may constitute grounds for impeachment of President Clinton.

OCTOBER

OCT. 5 By a vote of 21 to 16 along party lines, the House Judiciary Committee sets the impeachment process in motion by recommending that Congress open a formal investigation into possible grounds for the impeachment of Clinton.

OCT. 8 The House votes 258 to 176 to authorize an impeachment inquiry. Republicans vote unanimously for the authorization and are joined by 31 Democrats.

NOVEMBER

ELECTION DAY
NOV. 3 Democrats pick up five House seats in the election while Republicans retain control of the House and Senate. Exit polls show that almost two-thirds of the voters do not want Clinton impeached.

NOV. 5 Henry J. Hyde, chairman of the House Judiciary Committee, sends a letter to the White House asking Clinton to admit or deny 81 selected findings gleaned from Starr's report. On Nov. 27, Clinton responds.

JONES SUIT SETTLED
NOV. 13 Clinton and Jones settle her lawsuit out of court for $800,000.

DECEMBER

JUDICIARY HEARINGS
NOV. 9, 19; DEC. 1 The Judiciary Committee holds hearings on impeachment. Starr testifies.

DEC. 3 The committee abandons a brief effort to add campaign finance issues to the impeachment inquiry.

DEC. 8-10 Judiciary Committee hearings continue, with the White House presenting its side.

DEC. 11-12 In party-line votes, the Judiciary Committee approves four articles of impeachment and rejects a Democratic resolution on censure.

The New York Times

BEYOND THE VOTE

President Maps Out a Strategy for Governing While He Stands Trial

By JAMES BENNET

WASHINGTON, Dec. 19 — Anticipating the outcome of today's vote, President Clinton has been devising a strategy to govern as no President has for 130 years, under impeachment and in the glare of Senate trial.

The White House is planning a much more aggressive defense of Mr. Clinton's conduct before the Senate than it presented to the House, alongside a blaze of campaign-style events early next year to promote his policies around the country.

This morning, the President's senior aides spent more than two hours discussing proposals for his State of the Union Message on Jan. 19, at the same time as some of them were monitoring the turbulent debate on Capitol Hill.

Mr. Clinton's strategists, who expect Republican resistance to any legislation backed by the President, are prepared to argue that the Republicans are in effect shutting down the Government for partisan reasons, once again.

"The Republicans run a risk if they pursue a strategy that puts America's interest last," warned Joe Lockhart, the White House press secretary. "The public has a certain amount of tolerance for partisan politics, and they've had just about enough."

Some wonder if the old approach will work again.

But even some of the President's loyalists wonder if this approach — versions of which he has used time and again to battle back from political reversals — will work now, in the untried, complex political environment he entered after today's vote.

"There's no way he's going to be able to get anything done," said Leon E. Panetta, the former chief of staff. "It's very tough to get anybody's attention when there's a train going by behind you. They'll see your lips moving, but they won't hear anything."

White House aides as well as outside experts argue that Mr. Clinton will probably retain a stronger hand in foreign policy, where the chief executive is always freer to act. The question, they say, is whether he can promote his ideas at home.

Mr. Clinton has been acting on a lesson he has repeated to his aides since he first confronted national scandal as a candidate in 1992: "If I make this about their life, rather than mine, we'll all be better off," as one Clinton adviser recalled it on Friday. But Republicans will try to make it about him, the White House expects, arguing that he should resign.

However, Mr. Clinton declared today that he would remain in office "until the last hour of the last day of my term."

Impeachment and the Senate trial, together with the venom coursing through Washington, could guarantee legislative stalemate well into 1999, in the view of White House aides and other political experts.

But the President will be ready. For weeks, Mr. Clinton has been meeting behind closed doors at the White House to pick budget priorities for next year and to tote up his annual laundry list for the State of the Union address. He plans to promote those ideas in a trip around the country immediately after the speech, with Vice President Al Gore.

Topping that list is a plan, which the White House is still formulating, to fix Social Security. For years, Mr. Clinton has counted on entitlement reform as a lasting accomplishment.

The White House is also planning to push for more spending for school construction, tax cuts for scientific research and regulation of managed care plans. The President also wants to present a plan to cut smoking among children, and to revive a call to tighten the campaign finance system.

In foreign affairs, Mr. Clinton can also expect challenges to his authority, which began even before he ordered strikes on Iraq this week. But the United States — and the executive branch — still wields so much clout abroad that Mr. Clinton is likely to keep more room to maneuver there.

Over and over, Mr. Clinton's aides have recalled the battles over the last six years, when they were counted out: The health care debacle of 1994; the budget shutdowns of 1995; and even 1998, when Mr. Clinton managed to achieve many of his budget priorities despite the furor over his relationship with Monica S. Lewinsky.

Rahm Emanuel, a former adviser who is close to Mr. Clinton, had a preview of the likely White House line of attack: "One way or another, they've determined to have another lockdown of the Government, and you can't allow that kind of political carelessness to govern."

But the argument that the Republicans are obstructionist may not work now that the House has branded Mr. Clinton unfit for office.

The argument might work "if Clinton were a Franklin Roosevelt," said William E. Leuchtenburg, a professor of history at the University of North Carolina at Chapel Hill. But, he said, "There's not a lot of Clinton program to rally around." Republicans, with new leadership in the House, may try to push their own proposals through, rather than block the President's program, to capitalize on and underscore his weaker status. But a larger House Democratic minority in the next Congress and an infuriated White House are likely to block any such move.

If Mr. Clinton's strategy works, and he survives the Senate trial, his urge to score some legislative achievements may cause dissension within the Democratic Party. Congressional Democrats will be more interested in storing up frustrated goals to run on in 2000 than in passing legislation.

"You could see a very delicate situation between the President and the Democrats," Mr. Panetta said.

While Mr. Clinton is pushing his policy proposals, an expanded team of Presidential defenders will be fighting conviction by the Senate. White House aides said the model would be the two days of defense before the House. Unlike in the House proceeding, in a Senate trial the President's defenders will have a role every day.

"We're going to fight it aggressively," said Douglas Sosnik, Mr. Clinton's senior adviser. "Our people are motivated; they know the President was not treated fairly. This was not about facts or the law, it was about politics and trying to get the President."

While the White House had only weak links to the House Democrats, four of Mr. Clinton's senior aides have strong ties to the Senate, including to such prominent Republicans as Orrin G. Hatch, the chairman of the Judiciary Committee. John Podesta, the chief of staff; Gregory B. Craig, the special counsel; Steve Ricchetti, the deputy chief of staff, and Mr. Sosnik have all worked as Senate aides.

Mr. Clinton is also trying to recruit George Mitchell, the former Senate majority leader, to help with his defense.

And James Carville, the longtime Clinton strategist, said he would form a political organization — perhaps a political action committee — to hold Republicans accountable for their impeachment votes.

"They're going to get the blame for doing this," Mr. Carville said. "They've put something into motion, and they're going to have to live with the consequences of it."

Keith Meyers/The New York Times

President Clinton with Congressional Democrats in the Rose Garden yesterday after declaring that he would finish his term despite impeachment.

Text of the President's Address After Impeachment

Following is the text of President Clinton's address yesterday at the White House after the House of Representatives voted two articles of impeachment against him, as recorded by The New York Times:

Let me begin by expressing my profound and heartfelt thanks to Congressman Gephardt and the leadership and all the members of the Democratic caucus for what they did today. I thank the few brave Republicans who withstood enormous pressure to stand with them for the plain meaning of the Constitution and for the proposition that we need to pull together, to move beyond partisanship, to get on with the business of our country.

I thank the millions upon millions of American citizens who have expressed their support and their friendship to Hillary, to me, to our family and to our Administration during these last several weeks.

The words of the members here with me and others who were a part of their endeavor in defense of our Constitution were powerful and moving, and I will never forget them.

The question is, What are we going to do now? I have accepted responsibility for what I did wrong in my personal life, and I have invited members of Congress to work with us to find a reasonable, bipartisan and proportionate response. That approach was rejected today by Republicans in the House. But I hope it will be embraced by the Senate. I hope there will be a constitutional and fair means of resolving this matter in a prompt manner.

Meanwhile, I will continue to do the work of the American people. We still, after all, have to save Social Security and Medicare for the 21st century. We have to give all our children world-class schools. We have to pass a patients' bill of rights. We have to make sure the economic turbulence around the world does not curb our economic opportunity here at home. We have to keep America the world's strongest force for peace and freedom. In short, we have a lot to do before we enter the 21st century.

And we still have to keep working to build that elusive one America I have talked so much about. For six years now I have done everything I could to bring our country together across the lines that divide us, including bringing Washington together across party lines.

Out in the country, people are pulling together. But just as America is coming together, it must look, from the country's point of view, like Washington is coming apart.

I want to echo something Mr. Gephardt said. It is something I have felt strongly all my life. We must stop the politics of personal destruction. We must get rid of the poisonous venom of excessive partisanship, obsessive animosity and uncontrolled anger. That is not what America deserves. That is not what America is about.

We are doing well now. We are a good and decent country. But we have significant challenges we have to face. In order to do it right we have to have some atmosphere of decency and civility, some presumption of good faith, some sense of proportionality and balance in bringing judgment against those who are in different parties. We have important work to do. We need a constructive debate that has all the different voices in this country heard in the halls of Congress.

I want the American people to know today that I am still committed to working with people of good faith and good will of both parties to do what's best for our country, to bring our nation together, to lift our people up, to move us all forward together. It's what I've tried to do for six years. It's what I intend to do for two more until the last hour of the last day of my term.

So with profound gratitude for the defense of the Constitution and the best in America that was raised today by the members here and those who joined them, I ask the American people to move with me, to go on from here, to rise above the rancor, to overcome the pain and division, to be a repairer of the breach — all of us — to make this country as one America what it can and must be for our children in the new century about to dawn.

Thank you very much.

THE PRESIDENT

Clinton Digs In, Vowing to Serve 'Until Last Hour'; Confers on Iraq and Halts Bombing

Continued From Page 1

support or oppose impeachment, advisers said. Vice President Al Gore entered the room during the fourth vote and said, "It's not fair, what they've done to you," an aide who was present said.

Different friends and advisers of Mr. Clinton sensed different emotions in him over the last 24 hours. Some detected deep anger where others felt a wash of remorse. To many of his aides, nervously searching for signs of distraction or weakness, Mr. Clinton presented only the confident, upbeat face he has maintained through years of personal and political crisis.

One aide found Mr. Clinton to be "like a Calvin Klein ad: he's somewhere between obsession and denial."

Uniformly, Mr. Clinton's friends and advisers said that he is confident the Senate will not convict him, and that he will not resign. And uniformly, they said he is sick at heart about the "politics of personal destruction," which he denounced from the White House lawn this afternoon.

"We are a good and decent country," Mr. Clinton said in his five-minute remarks. "But we have significant challenges we have to face. In order to do it right, we have to have some atmosphere of decency and civility, some presumption of good faith, some sense of proportionality and balance in bringing judgment against those who are in different parties. We have important work to do."

Though he had expected impeachment and had braced himself for it today, the President was still in for a shock this morning, when he was told that Robert L. Livingston had stepped aside as Speaker after acknowledging extramarital affairs.

"What is happening?" President Clinton asked in astonishment of an old friend, Terence McAuliffe, moments after learning the news. "This is terrible for the country."

In describing the telephone conversation later, Mr. McAuliffe said, "The unfairness that the President has been subjected to, he doesn't want to see it happen to anybody else." Indeed, Mr. Clinton dispatched Joe Lockhart, his press secretary, to tell reporters that he wished Mr. Livingston would reconsider.

But Mr. Lockhart said that Mr. Clinton had no intention of accepting Mr. Livingston's challenge from the House floor that he follow his example. He presented Mr. Clinton's decision as a matter of principle. "He believes it would be wrong to give in to the politics of personal destruction," Mr. Lockhart said.

Mr. Clinton's friends insist that he is deeply remorseful about his behavior. "He has had a knot in his gut for months," Mr. McAuliffe said. "He is in agony over this."

But he maintained his normal routine, giving his weekly radio address in the morning, about Iraq, and shaking hands with some 80 family members of aides who sat in.

The President made only a glancing reference to any heartfelt contrition this afternoon. "I have accepted responsibility for what I did wrong in my personal life," he said, as Mrs. Clinton nodded. "And I have invited members of Congress to work with us to find a reasonable bipartisan and proportionate response.".

By car and bus, the Democrats came to the White House today after losing their battle to fend off the impeachment of their party's leader. They attended a brief, private rally with Mr. Clinton in the East Room, before strolling in clumps of two and three under the colonnade and past the Rose Garden, where a few white roses were in bloom, to wait for the President in front of a bare, spreading saucer Magnolia tree.

They jostled one another and some joked, until Representative John Lewis of Georgia, standing with hands folded and brow furrowed in the front row, shushed them.

Mr. Clinton emerged moments later from the Oval Office, brushing his cheeks before Mrs. Clinton slipped her right hand into the crook of his left arm and, smiling, they descended a curving path to join the members of Congress.

Mr. Clinton appeared to choke up when Vice President Gore introduced him, declaring: "I know his heart and his will."

Then the President stepped to the blue lectern affixed with the golden Presidential seal, to thank the members for their defense of the Constitution and the best in America."

"All the News
That's Fit to Print"

The New York Times

Late Edition
New York: **Today**, sunshine with cold breezes, high 31. **Tonight**, clear and quite cold, low 16. **Tomorrow**, cloudy and cold, high 29. **Yesterday**, high 25, low 17. Weather map is on page B8.

VOL. CXLVIII . . . No. 51,389 *NEW YORK, FRIDAY, JANUARY 1, 1999* $1 beyond the greater New York metropolitan area. *60 CENTS*

New Wave of Evangelists Vying for National Pulpit

By GUSTAV NIEBUHR and LAURIE GOODSTEIN

One is an Argentine-born preacher who appeals to both Hispanic and Anglo audiences. Another is a young megachurch pastor in Southern California who peppers his sermons with quotations from Hollywood stars and sports idols. A third is an African-American equally beloved by convicts and unhappy homemakers. And then there are two of the Rev. Billy Graham's children.

Ever since the Colonial era, America has had a pre-eminent preacher who played an unofficial role as national evangelist, preaching a simple message of repentance and salvation and drawing vast crowds in the process. For the last 50 years, that role has been filled by the Rev. Billy Graham. But at the turn of the century, with Mr. Graham now 80, the question arises, Who, if anyone, can take his place.

Mr. Graham revolutionized revival evangelism, using every available technology from lapel microphones to television and radio to satellite links. He preached a straightforward Gospel message that appealed to Christians of every denomination. When other evangelists sullied their names in scandal, Mr. Graham's stayed clean. While others joined political wars, he ministered to every President from Eisenhower to Clinton.

Many scholars and observers of American evangelism predict that no single preacher now on the scene has the universal appeal of Mr. Graham, who rose to prominence when a stadium crusade was like Barnum & Bailey's coming to town. Today, stadium evangelists compete for attention with televangelists, with self-help advocates and motivational speakers who blend religion and psychology, and with powerful pastors who draw thousands to weekly services in their megachurches.

"Billy Graham is not an official position in the Christian church that must be filled — it's not an office," said William Martin, a professor of sociology at Rice University and author of "A Prophet With Honor" (William Morrow, 1991), a biography of Mr. Graham.

But others survey the field and conclude that it may be only a matter of time before one candidate, through charisma, organization and ability to capture the popular imagination, catapults to prominence.

"In every generation there is somebody who emerges as what I call the point man," said Stephen F. Olford, a British evangelist whose fervent speaking style inspired Mr. Graham 53 years ago,

THE PREACHERS
A special report.

and who now trains new preachers at the Stephen Olford Center for Biblical Preaching in Memphis.

Keith J. Hardman, a professor of religion and philosophy at Ursinus College in Collegeville, Pa., said, "It's very true that Christians generally seem to have room for one extremely prominent person at a time."

In more than a dozen interviews with scholars, theologians, religious historians and evangelical leaders, a handful of evangelists were consistently mentioned as possible successors to Mr. Graham. The five most frequently mentioned evangelists who are drawing large crowds are Luis Palau, Franklin Graham, Anne Graham Lotz, Greg Laurie and Bishop T. D. Jakes. Like Billy Graham, all five travel widely preaching the Bible to large crowds in stadiums and conference centers. Two have their own churches, the others are itinerant

Continued on Page A14

Chang W. Lee/The New York Times

Punctual as Always, Father Time Joins the Party

A giant puppet of Father Time accompanied New Year's Eve revelers last night in Times Square to celebrate the passing of 1998 and the arrival of 1999. The crowd, bundled against the cold and chaperoned by 5,000 police officers, watched the aluminum ball make its last trip down the big pole. Page B1.

11 COUNTRIES TIE EUROPE TOGETHER IN ONE CURRENCY

OFFICIAL RATES ARE FIXED

Champagne Flows, but Role of New Central Bank Is Still a Hot Political Issue

By EDMUND L. ANDREWS

BRUSSELS, Dec. 31 — Finance ministers from 11 countries celebrated New Year's Eve today by launching the euro as Europe's new single currency, the culmination of an effort first conceived in the 1950's as a means of unifying Europe and thus preventing another world war.

After years of preparation, the 11 countries locked in the exchange rates of their currencies to the euro, and thereby set the value at which euros will begin trading when financial markets open around the world on Monday. Based on these rates, the euro will be worth about $1.17.

In technical terms, today's action was perfunctory — nothing more than plugging numbers into a formula. But in political and economic terms, it was far broader.

"We stand at the dawn of a new era in the integration of Europe," said Rudolf Edlinger, Austria's Finance Minister and chairman of today's meeting. "Forty years of inexorable striving toward integration has been crowned by the realization of economic and monetary union."

Today's fixing of exchange rates also kicked off a frenzied scramble by banks, stock exchanges and securities traders across Europe to adapt their computer systems between now and Monday morning.

And despite the celebrations, there were clear signs of continuing divisions over both economic policy and the levers of power. German officials demanded that the new European Central Bank, roughly the equivalent of the United States Federal Reserve Board, use monetary policy to help increase employment and not focus simply on fighting inflation — a demand that has already created deep animosity among other countries' central bankers.

Euro notes and coins will not circulate until Jan. 1, 2002, but banks and stock exchanges must now carry out all non-cash transactions in euros.

In London's financial center, more than 30,000 people will work through the weekend to reprogram computers and trading systems on the basis of the currency values agreed upon today, though the pound is not part of the euro system. Across Europe, banks are converting their systems to offer euro-denominated bank accounts immediately for any customers who want them.

Though national currencies like the German mark and the French franc will remain in circulation until July 1, 2002, they will trade in lockstep to the euro until they phase out.

Today's action was necessary to set the relative values of participating countries' currencies. But the values have been more or less established since members of the new currency union yoked their monetary policies last spring, and exchange rates have varied little.

"In the end, it turned out to be almost a formality, different from

Continued on Page A10

Opposition Emerges to Plan To Avert Full Trial of Clinton

By LIZETTE ALVAREZ and ERIC SCHMITT

WASHINGTON, Dec. 31 — In the first signs of serious discord among Senate Republicans over impeachment, several senators, both conservative and moderate, said today that they opposed a proposal that would permit a preliminary vote on articles of impeachment without a full trial.

"That's a whitewash and a shirking of our responsibility the Constitution gives us," Senator James M. Inhofe, a conservative Oklahoman, said in a telephone interview. "We have to have witnesses and have a full trial. How can someone vote without hearing from witnesses and without hearing all the evidence?"

Senator Fred Thompson of Tennessee, who served as a lawyer for Republicans on the Senate Watergate committee, echoed Mr. Inhofe's concerns and said the Senate must guard against moving too hastily as it prepared to sit in judgment of President Clinton.

"It's beginning to appear that there's an effort to cut this down to a very short period of time at all costs," Mr. Thompson said. "It's important that we not try to jury-rig some kind of process that will solve our short-term political problems but might not do justice to our obligations."

The proposal being floated by Senators Trent Lott of Mississippi, the majority leader, and Tom Daschle of South Dakota, the minority leader, was prepared amid doubt that there would ever be the necessary two-thirds vote in the Senate for Mr. Clinton's removal, particularly since the public is strongly opposed to it.

Under the plan, the House and the White House would take no more than two weeks, and as little as a few days, to make their cases to the Senate. No witnesses would be called, although Chief Justice William H. Rehnquist would preside.

At the conclusion of the proceeding, the Senate would vote on whether the charges were serious enough, and the evidence behind them strong enough, to warrant a full trial that could lead to Mr. Clinton's removal from office. In order to measure eventual support for Mr. Clinton's removal, the plan calls for a vote of 67 senators to have a full proceeding,

Continued on Page A17

Bell Atlantic In Talks to Buy Cellular Giant

By LAURA M. HOLSON and DAVID J. MORROW

The Bell Atlantic Corporation, the nation's largest local telephone company, is in talks to buy Airtouch Communications Inc., the largest wireless phone company for $45 billion in stock, executives close to the companies said last night.

The deal, which could be announced as early as Monday, would bring New York-based Bell Atlantic, which already has 5.7 million cellular customers in services blanketing the East Coast, one step closer to creating a nationwide and even international wireless network.

Airtouch, which has 7.8 million customers in the United States and more than 11 million worldwide, serves the entire West Coast and has a number of partnerships in Europe and Asia that would expand Bell Atlantic's network considerably on those continents. Among those is a partnership with Mannesmann Mobilfunk of Germany that makes Airtouch one of the biggest providers of cellular services in Europe. In all, international wireless services make up 57 percent of Airtouch's operating income, according to Deutsche Bank Research.

As with any deal not yet sealed, talks could fall apart at any time.

But if announced, the purchase price would be about a 10 percent premium over Airtouch's closing

Continued on Page C4

Two Khmer Rouge Leaders Spend Beach Holiday in Shadow of Past

By SETH MYDANS

SIHANOUKVILLE, Cambodia, Dec. 31 — Liberated at last from a life of revolution, two Khmer Rouge leaders came to the beach today with their families, their leisure wear and their sunglasses.

But their holiday was a drab one, spent mostly behind the dirty brown curtains of their tiny hotel rooms, trapped inside by their fear of a small group of reporters.

"Right now, His Excellency wants to relax," an aide, Long Norin, said, explaining the strange behavior of the former Khmer Rouge head of state, Khieu Samphan, 67.

Even the teen-age daughter and two teen-age granddaughters of Nuon Chea, 71, the chief ideologue of the Khmer Rouge revolution, spent the sunny afternoon in their darkened room watching a Thai television station.

"Right now, His Excellency wants to relax," an aide, Long Norin, said, explaining the strange behavior of the former Khmer Rouge head of state, Khieu Samphan, 67, who came here with Nuon Chea, 71, the chief ideologue of the Khmer Rouge revolution.

Even the men's two grown daughters and one teen-age granddaughter spent the sunny afternoon in their darkened room watching a Thai television station.

After about six hours of this — during which a waiter brought seafood lunches to the two leaders' rooms — and after reporters assured an aide that they would be polite, the two men emerged, said a few innocuous words and took a brief tour of the city.

"I'm fine; I just need to rest a little bit," Mr. Khieu Samphan said as he walked past a plastic Santa Claus pasted to the hotel's glass door. "I have already said what I have to say."

At a rowdy news conference on Tuesday, the two men had pleaded to "let bygones be bygones" but were overwhelmed by aggressive questions about their roles as leaders of a brutal Government that caused more than a million deaths from 1975 to 1979.

"They're going to start a riot!" Mr. Nuon Chea exclaimed as security men bundled him past reporters

Continued on Page A4

On Campus, Tripping the Light Fantastic

By ETHAN BRONNER

STATE COLLEGE, Pa. — The E-mail messages arrived first in a trickle, then in a flood.

Students at Pennsylvania State University were contacting their president, Graham B. Spanier, with a desperate plea in the fall semester: Create more classes in ballroom dancing. Nearly 1,500 undergraduates were languishing on dance class waiting lists; on Friday nights, the ballroom dance club was overwhelmed trying to teach hundreds how to cha-cha and fox trot.

After an emergency meeting in November, Dr. Spanier announced that in January, the number of ballroom dance classes at Penn State would rise to 48 from 8, increasing the number of slots to 1,440 from 240.

"We are in a society that is increasingly impersonal and there is a need for a way to meet one another, to touch without immediate sex," said Dr. Spanier, a sociologist with a scholarly interest in interpersonal relations, in explaining why he moved with such speed. "Ballroom dancing offers that."

Across the country, at Yale and Arizona State Universities, at the University of Wisconsin and San Diego State University, partner dancing, both traditional ballroom and swing, is sweeping campuses.

Kay A. Teague, vice president of the youth college network of the United States Amateur Ballroom Dancers Association, said the rise was so sudden and so fierce that it was not yet possible to know the exact numbers.

"Put it this way," Ms. Teague said, "five years ago there were dozens of schools with hundreds of students doing ballroom dance. Today there are hundreds of schools with thousands and thousands of dancers. In the Washington, D.C., area alone we have gone from 1 school, Catholic University, with 20 to 30 dancers to 5 schools with 2,000 dancers."

And while fads, fed by trendsetters on the two coasts and popular movies, are nothing new on campuses, scholars say that in the era of AIDS, this is a phenomenon worthy of a close look.

"We may be moving back to the medieval notion of romance, love that is unrequited," offered Geoffrey Godbey, professor of leisure studies at Penn State. "These dances provide sensuality and imagination. But, like Web pornography or phone sex, they are safe."

It is the structured nature of the male-female relationship in ballroom dancing, the courting rituals and prescribed steps that have drawn the attention of analysts. They also note other aspects: the strenuousness of the dances for a generation that knows the impor-

Continued on Page A16

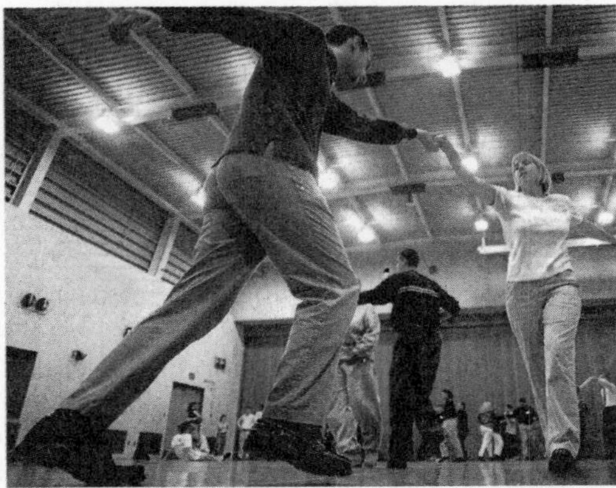

Librado Romero/The New York Times

At Penn State, where classes in ballroom dancing have expanded, Shawn Bonham and Aimee Feist gave the jitterbug a whirl.

A Turbulent but Profitable Year

Investors who stuck with United States stocks in 1998 were rewarded, defying expectations by many Wall Street professionals that the market would falter on the uncertainty of economic turbulence abroad. The Nasdaq market rose nearly 40 percent on the strength of Internet and technology stocks. The Standard & Poor's index rose more than 20 percent for a record fourth consecutive year. Business Day, page C1.

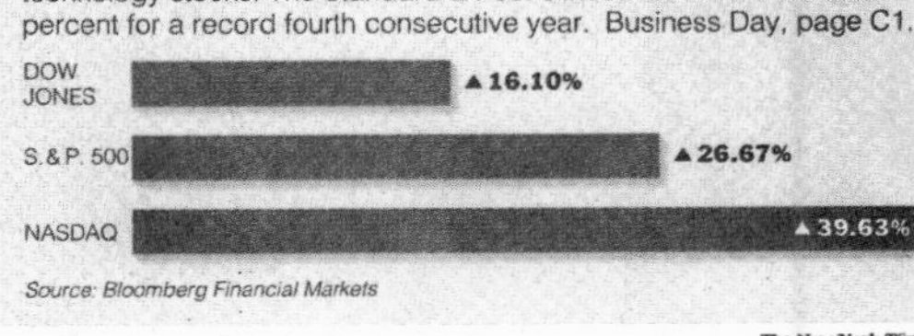

Source: Bloomberg Financial Markets

The New York Times

On the Internet: www.nytimes.com

INSIDE

Gore Taking a First Step

Aides to Vice President Gore say papers to form an organization for the 2000 election will be sent so fund raising can begin. Page A17.

Voice From a Wanted Poster

Filiberto Ojeda-Ríos's often speaks out on important issues in Puerto Rico, even though he is a fugitive in an armed robbery in 1983. Page A12.

U.S. Shuts Embassy in Israel

The United States Embassy in Tel Aviv was closed after a "direct and credible" threat of attack. Page A8.

Gay Party Is Cancelled

Concerns about drugs and unsafe sex have led organizers to cancel a gay party on Fire Island. Page B1.

Its 3 Fathers Are Proud of Baby Euro, and Certain It Will Grow Up Strong

By CRAIG R. WHITNEY

HAMBURG, Germany — Twenty years ago, when he was Chancellor of West Germany, Helmut Schmidt thought there would be a single European currency by the early 1980's. Instead, he is still carrying around six different kinds of money in his briefcase.

"I always have the German mark, English pounds, French francs, Swiss francs and Italian lire, plus American dollars, but I always end up just using credit cards," laughed Mr. Schmidt, who travels frequently as a publisher of the weekly newspaper Die Zeit.

But starting in January, he can write checks in euros, the common currency that 11 countries in the European Union are introducing, almost two decades later than he and other European leaders had planned. And three years from now, he will finally be able to put euro notes in his briefcase.

The euro's launching is a particular point of pride for Mr. Schmidt and two other prominent European leaders, Valéry Giscard d'Estaing, once President of France, and Sir Edward Heath, the former Prime Minister of Britain. The three men took some of the earliest steps toward a single currency, in the 1970's, and kept promoting the idea even when it lost its luster.

"It should have happened a lot earlier," said Mr. Schmidt, who turned 80 on Dec. 23.

Indeed, it could have, agreed Sir Edward, 82, who negotiated the 1972 treaty that took Britain into the European Economic Community when he was Prime Minister. Later that year, he and other European leaders endorsed a plan devised by Pierre Werner, then the Prime Minister of Luxembourg, for a common European currency to combat the monetary instability caused by the collapse of the Bretton Woods system, which had been based on the dollar.

"We hoped then to have it done by 1980," he said, but the sharp rise in oil prices in 1973 derailed the project.

Mr. Giscard d'Estaing, now 72, and Mr. Schmidt, friends from the days when both served as finance ministers, tried to get monetary union back on the rails over drinks in Mr. Schmidt's lakeside cottage north of here in 1978.

They persuaded fellow European leaders to establish something called the European Currency Unit, expecting it to become coin of the European realm by the early 1980's, but it failed to speed the process.

"The delay was unnecessarily long," Mr. Giscard d'Estaing said in an interview in Parliament, "and without wanting to be too severe, I think it was caused by indifference and to some extent lack of financial literacy on the part of the European leaders of the early 1980's. They did not ascribe the same importance to it as we did, and maybe they were hesitant to get into the technical details, so the system went into a kind of hibernation from 1981 to 1988."

Then, with the collapse of Communism in 1989, President François Mitterrand of France and Chancellor Helmut Kohl of Germany pushed harder for the common currency again, partly to bind a reunited Germany more firmly into a new single European market.

But even then, Prime Minister Margaret Thatcher and her successor, John Major, kept Britain out. And, Mr. Schmidt said, "the central bank officials in the other countries did not want to lose their power so they invented a thousand conditions, but in the end the idea finally prevailed."

"If they'd only listened to us" was the common refrain in separate interviews recently with these fathers of the euro as they fretted impatiently for the long-awaited birth.

To listen to them now, a common currency, strengthening the unified market that came into its own in 1993 when the last customs and tariff barriers fell in the European Union, will finally give Europe the opportunity to become a global power.

Sir Edward harrumphed all reservations aside in an interview in his London pied-à-terre, near Eaton Square. "There's no single market in the world without a single currency, not in Japan and certainly not in the United States," he said. "Imagine what the United States would be now if each of the 50 states had its own currency!"

With new confidence in the stability of the economic and monetary policy of Europe, according to the these most enthusiastic of the euro's cheerleaders, dynamic growth could finally cure the Continent's chronic unemployment problem. And investors around the world, they say, may welcome a strong new currency that can diversify portfolios.

That could weaken the dollar and force up interest rates in the United States, they concede, but they shrug that off almost as easily as most Presidents since Richard M. Nixon have shrugged off the effects of American monetary policy on smaller currencies.

"America and Europe will continue to need each other into the 21st century," Mr. Schmidt said, "but it remains to be seen whether the euro is good for the United States. Some governments will shift dollar-denominated assets into euro-denominated ones, which means the U.S. Treasury might have to pay higher interest rates to attract investors."

Mr. Giscard d'Estaing, though, wishes the euro were not quite so strong at the start. "The dollar at the moment is a little too weak," he said. "I have the feeling the American economy is slowing down a bit, and that the American authorities accept that. There will be a dynamic between the euro's spontaneous tendency to strengthen, and a monetary policy for the euro that will try to contain that tendency."

The difference in views reflects long-standing divergence in German and French attitudes toward money. For Germany, a strong mark was a symbol a defeated nation could take pride in after the war, a fact Mr. Giscard d'Estaing said he had felt obliged to take into account when he and Mr. Schmidt devised their 1978 plan.

"For the Germans, the idea of abandoning the Deutsche mark, losing it, and entrusting it to a bank controlled by governments they did not feel as much confidence in as in their own independent central bank, was impossible," Mr. Giscard d'Estaing said. "So independence for the European central bank was an essential core idea.

Christian Irrgang for The New York Times

Helmut Schmidt
Chancellor of West Germany, 1974-82
"America and Europe will continue to need each other into the 21st century, but it remains to be seen whether the euro is good for the United States."

Jonathan Player for The New York Times

Sir Edward Heath
Prime Minister of Britain, 1970-74
"There's no single market in the world without a single currency, not in Japan and certainly not in the United States. Imagine what the United States would be now if each of the 50 states had its own currency!"

Thomas Haley for The New York Times

Valéry Giscard d'Estaing
President of France, 1974-81
"The ease with which the Germans have accepted the end of the mark surprised me, and I think it surprised them, too. The strict criteria, the requirement to cut budget deficits, the independence of the central bank in the plan, all had the merit of reassuring the Germans."

THE NEW EUROPE
Founding Fathers

"The ease with which the Germans have accepted the end of the mark surprised me, and I think it surprised them, too. The strict criteria, the requirement to cut budget deficits, the independence of the central bank in the plan, all had the merit of reassuring the Germans."

The idea of a strong central bank found its way into the treaty that spelled out the final plan for the euro more than a decade later, though not quite the way Sir Edward would have preferred. Britain, alas, will not use the euro, at least at the start.

"Under our original plan, the City of London would have been the center of the whole deal," he said. Instead, he added, "it all went to Frankfurt," where the new European Central Bank is located.

All three leaders, with vivid memories of what World War II did to their countries, said they hoped monetary union would force the members of the European Union still closer, encouraging them to share sovereignty in foreign, military and domestic policies, not just economics.

Mr. Schmidt, a junior officer in the Wehrmacht during the war, looked out of his corner office high over prosperous Hamburg, a city rebuilt on postwar trade with Britain and France, and remembered seeing it as a vast expanse of rubble and flames strewn with bodies after a huge raid by British and American bombers in July 1943. "I'll never forget it," he said.

He and Mr. Giscard d'Estaing, who joined the French Resistance as a boy, were on opposite sides then, and both said French reconciliation with Germany is at the heart of modern Europe.

"I want the euro to be an instrument in the federative approach to Europe," Mr. Giscard d'Estaing said. "The word 'federative' is a French 18th-century word Montesquieu used. It means sharing power or competence."

That is not the same at all, he added, as the English word "federal," as in the "federal European superstate" so dreaded by Lady Thatcher.

Mr. Schmidt said it was nonsense to think that a common currency would fail without a federal European state. "Before 1914 Europeans had one currency: gold," he said. "Parities were fixed and did not change, and all countries followed the constraints that the system entailed."

Sir Edward, who fought Germans as a British artillery officer during the war, thinks his country's reserve is a historical mistake. "I was the only one bold enough to do it," he huffed.

British markets, like the Continent's, will start dealing in euros in January, even though Prime Minister Tony Blair's Labor Government, like its Conservative predecessor, wants to see how the euro works before Britain decides whether to give up the pound. Mr. Giscard d'Estaing said he thought the British attitude was entirely reasonable, but Sir Edward disagreed.

"Ever since the 1950's, Britain has stood aside while all the European arrangements were made, so we had no influence on them, and then we decided to come in later," Sir Edward lamented.

Britain first started negotiations for European membership in 1961, but France's autocratic President, Charles de Gaulle, vetoed it two years later. His successor, Georges Pompidou, relented in 1972.

"Now we're back on the old path," Sir Edward said.

A previous engagement, he said, would keep him from coming to Hamburg on Jan. 6 for a delayed celebration of Mr. Schmidt's 80th birthday. But Mr. Giscard d'Estaing said he would be there. "We'll celebrate the arrival of the euro together," he said.

ON THE WEB

Additional information, including past coverage, about the transition to a common European currency can be found at The New York Times on the Web:

www.nytimes.com/international

11 Members of European Union Tie Their Currencies to Euro

Continued From Page A1

what many of us expected just a year ago," remarked Wim Duisenberg of the Netherlands, the president of the European Central Bank.

To liven things up a bit, European officials capped off their formal action by launching hundreds of balloons with blue and yellow euro markings. Finance ministers also posed for pictures unpopping the ritual bottles of champagne, though some bottles proved so balky that several ministers turned red in the face as they wrestled with the corks.

Champagne aside, most of those here today focused on the great distance they had come, and predicted a Europe that would be bigger, stronger, more prosperous and peaceful when it used a single currency.

"Europe will now have the wherewithal to direct its own future," said Jacques Santer, president of the European Commission. "The euro is not an end in itself. It is an instrument for economic development, social development. And now it is up to us to use this instrument."

Dominique Strauss-Kahn, the French Finance Minister, said: "Today is clearly a historic day for the European enterprise. Europe will be strong, stronger than in the past, because it will speak with a single monetary voice."

But even today, there were signs of potential battles.

One hint came from Mr. Duisenberg, who was named president of the European Central Bank only after a bitter political fight last May between France and Germany. Mr. Duisenberg was favored by Helmut Kohl, then Chancellor of Germany. But President Jacques Chirac of France insisted on the head of the Bank of France, Jean-Claude Trichet.

Germany and French eventually made a deal under which Mr. Duisenberg would become president of the European bank, then "voluntarily" step down well before the end of his eight-year term. But in an interview published Wednesday in the French newspaper Le Monde, Mr. Duisenberg indicated he might not quit after all. He would not elaborate today.

Mr. Duisenberg's apparent new stance comes as many political leaders are pressing the European bank to focus more on stimulating growth. Under the Maastricht Treaty, which set the ground rules for the euro, the bank is supposed to focus exclusively on combating inflation.

Mr. Duisenberg has been an outspoken defender of that mandate, putting him on a collision course with Germany's new center-left Government and its Finance Minister, Oskar Lafontaine.

Mr. Lafontaine did not take part in today's ceremonies, pleading long-standing vacation plans. But his stand-in, Economics Minister Werner Müller, appealed for coordinated action among European countries to increase jobs — with help from the new central bank.

"We must now score tangible successes in the areas of employment and growth," Mr. Müller said. "The European Central Bank facilitates this not only by fulfilling its responsibilities for stability. It can also, within the framework of its resources, target itself toward the support of growth and employment."

Mr. Müller also called for "coordinated" wage policies that "have a goal of greater employment success." That echoed Mr. Lafontaine's calls for European countries to avoid undercutting each other on labor costs.

Unity on economic policy will be difficult. In Britain, which is staying outside the currency union for at least the next year or two, some newspapers have demonized Mr. Lafontaine as a man who would force Britain to abandon its comparatively laissez-faire policies.

But Mr. Strauss-Kahn of France captured the thoughts of many here today, saying European countries would gain self-determination by having more strength in the face of global economic turbulence.

"My profound conviction," he said, "is that we will gain in sovereignty rather than losing it by sharing it with others."

BY THE NUMBERS

For What It's Worth . . .

The conversion rates involving the 11 countries participating in the euro were set today. The worth of the euro as of today:

13.76	Austrian schillings
40.34	Belgian francs
2.20	Dutch guilders
5.95	Finnish markkas
6.56	French francs
1.96	German marks
0.79	Irish punts
1,936.27	Italian lire
40.34	Luxembourg francs
200.48	Portuguese escudos
166.39	Spanish pesetas

The euro is expected to start trading on Monday at $1.17.

Euro exchange rates are listed in the foreign exchange tables in Business Day.

European Union countries adopting the euro

European Union countries not adopting the euro

The New York Times

Happy Birth Day!

PARIS, Dec. 31 (Agence France-Presse) — Each baby born in France on Jan. 1 will receive 100 euros to mark the birth of the new currency, the Finance Ministry said today. Around 1,500 babies are expected on New Year's Day, when the euro is formally launched in 11 European Union countries. (Non-euro-adept parents will probably still think of the babies' savings accounts as 656 francs.)

"All the News That's Fit to Print"

The New York Times

Late Edition
New York: **Today**, sunny, windy and cool, high 42. **Tonight**, clear, low 24. **Tomorrow**, sunny, chilly and less breezy, high 35. **Yesterday**, high 61, low 46. Weather map, page A17.

VOL. CXLVIII . . . No. 51,432 NEW YORK, SATURDAY, FEBRUARY 13, 1999 — $1 beyond the greater New York metropolitan area. — 60 CENTS

CLINTON ACQUITTED DECISIVELY: NO MAJORITY FOR EITHER CHARGE

President Says He Is Sorry And Seeks Reconciliation

By JAMES BENNET and JOHN M. BRODER

WASHINGTON, Feb. 12 — Teetering between remorse and anticipation, President Clinton said today that he felt humbled and "profoundly sorry," as he pledged to make the most of his latest second chance.

Bill Clinton has survived, again. After the Senate found him not guilty on two articles of impeachment, he tried today to contend with two inescapable questions: At what cost, and for what purpose?

"I want to say again to the American people how profoundly sorry I am for what I said and did to trigger these events and the great burden they have imposed on the Congress and on the American people," Mr. Clinton said. But, he said, the outcome of his trial presented an opportunity: "This can be and this must be a time of reconciliation and renewal for America."

Hoping to betray no hint of smugness, the President spent part of Thursday evening in the White House residence working on his five-sentence statement, barely longer than a sound bite. His aides said he revised it this morning in the residence, where he remained until early afternoon.

As a strong southerly wind rustled the magnolia trees and puffed into the microphone, Mr. Clinton walked alone from the Oval Office two hours after the Senate finished voting. Speaking slowly and shaking his head for emphasis, he kept his statement short and bittersweet; its essential elements reflected those in a statement of regret he made on Dec. 11, before the House impeached him.

Mr. Clinton took one shouted question, pausing to consider it after he had started walking away: Could he forgive and forget?

He smiled slightly after he turned back to the crowd of reporters, jostling on a springlike day that would later turn stormy and cold. "I believe any person who asks for forgiveness has to be prepared to give it," he said. Then he left.

Hoping to mold history's judgment, Mr. Clinton is bent on remaking his protean Presidency once again, his friends and advisers say. As of today, it had become something no one could have imagined at his second inaugural two years ago, when he laid his hand on a biblical passage declaring, "Thou shalt be called the repairer of the breach."

Over 13 months of investigations, revelations and political venom, the President has put his family through misery, taxed the loyalty of his Cabinet and his aides, and admitted outright lies to the nation about his affair with Monica S. Lewinsky. The political breach in Washington is gaping.

But for all the personal damage done, Mr. Clinton has prospered politically and his Republican foes have suffered. The President remains firmly in office and resoundingly popular, while Speaker Newt Gingrich and the man who was to succeed him, Robert L. Livingston, are departing for private life.

Besides apologizing again to the country, Mr. Clinton expressed remorse and gratitude today to his staff. Not a single member of Mr. Clinton's Cabinet or staff resigned to protest his behavior.

Via electronic mail, the Presi-

Continued on Page A9

The Fallout Of the Trial

Assessing Breakdown In Codes of Behavior

By R. W. APPLE Jr.

WASHINGTON, Feb. 12 — There are those who think it will end up as Much Ado About Nothing, at least as far as the country, its political culture and its institutions of government are concerned.

News Analysis

"I don't think the whole impeachment drama will have much long-term impact on anybody or anything except President Clinton," said Howard H. Baker Jr., the former Republican Senator from Tennessee, who made his name during the Watergate hearings. "And even the impact on him is questionable."

But Arthur M. Schlesinger Jr., the historian and passionate Clinton defender, begs to differ. A Democrat who served John F. Kennedy as a White House adviser, Mr. Schlesinger sees the travail of President Clinton as an event of considerable moment.

"The failed impeachment of Andrew Johnson left a wounded, weakened Presidency, one that lasted for many years," he said, "and I think the failed impeachment of Bill Clinton will do the same thing."

If it was imprudent to predict many months ago how the drama would end, as it finally did today, to the relief of almost everyone, it might be considered downright foolhardy to guess at its consequences. But that does not stop Washington or Washington-watchers elsewhere from trying.

Few people doubt that the events of the last year have coarsened the national political discourse. It is as if Mr. Clinton's own habit of pushing the limits — "indulging all choices and accepting no consequences," as Representative James E. Rogan of California, one of the House managers, put it last week — infected the behavior of all the major players.

The capital has witnessed the breakdown of long-standing codes of behavior on every side. Senior Democrats on the House Judiciary Committee accused their Republican counterparts of staging a coup d'état; Trent Lott, the leader of the

Continued on Page A10

Anger and Outrage At Rite for African Killed by the Police

By SUSAN SACHS

Held aloft by strangers and clutched at by a chanting crowd, the plain pine coffin holding the body of Amadou Diallo became the centerpiece of both an emotion-fraught memorial service yesterday and a furious demonstration against racism and Mayor Rudolph W. Giuliani, who was heckled when he made a brief appearance to pay his respects.

Mr. Diallo, 22, a West African street vendor, was killed on Feb. 4 by four plainclothes police officers as he stood, unarmed, in the entrance to his Bronx apartment building.

In life, his friends said, he was a quiet, sweet-tempered young man with big ambitions. But in death, Mr. Diallo has become a rallying point for critics of the Giuliani administration, who turned the religious service at the Islamic Cultural Center on the Upper East Side into a sometimes unruly political rally.

At the end of the service, hundreds of men gathered at the foot of the red-carpeted platform where the Muslim imam, or prayer leader, had just finished his sermon on what he said was Islam's message of justice and equality.

Despite the entreaties of the imam, Mohamed M. Gemeaha, for order and calm, the crowd cheered when one speaker called Mr. Diallo a martyr. There were shouts of "We want justice" as many people pushed and shoved to get out the mosque's door. The mood outside was just as tumultuous. When Mr. Diallo's coffin was carried out of the mosque, people in the crowd surged toward it, calling "Allahu akbar" — God is great — and "Justice, justice." Many threw themselves at the coffin,

Continued on Page B7

COMING ON SUNDAY

STEVEN THE GOOD

Unfailingly patriotic and populist, Steven Spielberg has become the most successful filmmaker of all time. But his need to please may have denied him a certain kind of genius. *A report by Stephen J. Dubner, in The Times Magazine.*

Stephen Crowley/The New York Times

Two hours after the Senate voted yesterday, President Clinton spoke in the Rose Garden of the White House.

'Senators, How Say You?'

Article 1		GUILTY	NOT GUILTY
PERJURY	Republicans	45	10
	Democrats	0	45
	TOTAL	**45**	**55**

Article 2		GUILTY	NOT GUILTY
OBSTRUCTION OF JUSTICE	Republicans	50	5
	Democrats	0	45
	TOTAL	**50**	**50**

A Dispirited Hyde Opposes Indicting Clinton

By LIZETTE ALVAREZ

WASHINGTON, Feb. 12 — The lead prosecutor of the impeachment trial, Representative Henry J. Hyde, said today that Kenneth W. Starr should not indict President Clinton, now that the Senate has acquitted him.

With two articles of impeachment lying in a heap at his feet, Mr. Hyde said Mr. Starr, the independent counsel, should "put to bed" the case against the President.

"I don't think indicting and criminally trying him, after what we have all been through, is going to be helpful to the country," Mr. Hyde said. "I think we should try to find areas we can agree on and get some legislation passed."

Other House Republicans also expressed a need to move on, while affirming the legitimacy of their decision to impeach the President.

Speaker Dennis Hastert said in a statement, "Republicans in the Congress can be proud that they stood by the principles that have made this nation strong: a respect for the rule of law and an abiding faith in the strength of our Constitution."

"The American people expect us to move this nation forward, and that is exactly what we plan to do in the 106th Congress," he added.

In a post-mortem on the impeachment case on the eve of the vote today, Mr. Hyde, the Illinois Republican who heads the House Judiciary Committee, reflected more broadly on his stewardship of the prosecution and the decisions made by his team of prosecutors since the very first days in September when Mr. Starr referred the case to the House and the Judiciary Committee.

The 74-year-old lawmaker entered the fray to accolades from Republicans and Democrats as a judicious, fair-minded leader, only to see his standing in the country plummet. There is a trace of bitterness about the way he has been treated, and also a sense of astonishment at his own rose-colored expectations.

"We felt if the story were told coherently, chronologically, that maybe the public would focus on it and move from its total indifference to concern," Mr. Hyde said today. "That hope was unrequited."

Mr. Hyde said perhaps his most serious mistake was not insisting on questioning witnesses in his own committee, when he, and not the Sen-

Continued on Page A11

Carol T. Powers for The New York Times

Representative Henry J. Hyde, lead prosecutor of President Clinton, sitting at the end of a news conference yesterday after the Senate voted to acquit. "There was nothing noble or high" in the process, he said.

CENSURE IS BARRED

But Rebuke From Both Sides of Aisle Dilutes President's Victory

By ALISON MITCHELL

WASHINGTON, Feb. 12 — The Senate today acquitted President Clinton on two articles of impeachment, falling short of even a majority vote on either of the charges against him: perjury and obstruction of justice.

After a harrowing year of scandal and investigation, the five-week-long Senate trial of the President — only the second in the 210-year history of the Republic — culminated shortly after noon when the roll calls began that would determine Mr. Clinton's fate.

"Is respondent William Jefferson Clinton guilty or not guilty?" asked Chief Justice William H. Rehnquist, in his gold-striped black robe. In a hushed chamber, with senators standing one by one to pronounce Mr. Clinton "guilty" or "not guilty," the Senate rejected the charge of perjury, 55 to 45, with 10 Republicans voting against conviction.

It then split 50-50 on a second article accusing Mr. Clinton of obstruction of justice in concealing his affair with Monica S. Lewinsky. Five Republicans broke ranks on the obstruction-of-justice charge. No Democrats voted to convict on either charge, and it would have taken a dozen of them, and all 55 Republicans, to reach the two-thirds majority of 67 senators required for conviction.

Chief Justice Rehnquist announced the acquittal of the nation's no President at 12:39 P.M. "It is therefore ordered and adjudged that the said William Jefferson Clinton be, and he hereby is, acquitted of the charges in the said articles," he said. Almost immediately, the mood in the Senate lightened.

As required by the Senate's impeachment rules, Secretary of State Madeleine K. Albright was formally notified of the Senate's judgment.

Mr. Clinton responded by once again declaring himself "profoundly sorry" for his actions and words that had thrown the nation into a 13-month ordeal. "Now I ask all Americans, and I hope all Americans here in Washington and throughout our land, will re-dedicate ourselves to the work of serving our nation and building our future together," he said in a brief appearance in the White House Rose Garden.

Yet for all the hopes of healing, the bitterness and turmoil of the past months were underscored when the Senate side of the Capitol had to be cleared for more than an hour because of a bomb scare shortly after the trial had ended, just as senators had begun a series of news conferences. [Excerpts, pages A13-14.]

Just before the bomb scare, the Senate, by a 56-to-43 vote, rebuffed an effort by Senator Dianne Feinstein, a California Democrat, to force a vote today on a censure measure that would rebuke Mr. Clinton for "shameful, reckless and indefensible" behavior.

Even many of those who chose to acquit Mr. Clinton today delivered

Continued on Page A9

AFTER THE VERDICT

Harsh Words From Lott

Senator Trent Lott denounced the President in an interview that called into question the ability of the two leaders to work together. Page A11.

Maneuver Kills Censure

A Democratic proposal to censure Mr. Clinton died after a Republican parliamentary maneuver doomed its chance of being considered. Page A8.

On the Internet: www.nytimes.com

INSIDE

No Reprieve at Airline

American Airlines again scrapped half its flights because of a pilots' sickout, causing chaos for holiday weekend travelers. Page C1.

Ruling on Steel Dumping

The Government ruled that Japanese and Brazilian exporters sold steel at large discounts. It plans to impose big penalty tariffs. Page C1.

U.S. Troops for Kosovo

President Clinton is expected to announce that he is prepared to send troops as part of a peacekeeping force for Kosovo. Page A4.

THE PRESIDENT'S ACQUITTAL: Humble at Victory

THE OVERVIEW

Clinton Acquitted Decisively as Senate Fails to Muster Majority for Either Charge

Continued From Page A1

stinging judgments of him while concluding that his evasions and attempts to conceal a sexual relationship with a former White House intern did not constitute the kind of high crimes the nation's founders had contemplated when they wrote the impeachment clause of the Constitution.

"In voting to acquit the President, I do so with grave misgivings for I do not mean in any way to exonerate this man," Senator Susan Collins of Maine, one of the Republicans to break with her party, said in a statement.

"He lied under oath," she said. "He sought to interfere with the evidence; he tried to influence the testimony of key witnesses. And while it may not be a crime, he exploited a very young star-struck employee whom he then proceeded to smear in an attempt to destroy her credibility, her reputation, her life."

Some of the Democrats who had stayed so staunchly at Mr. Clinton's side throughout the impeachment saga warned that he should not see his acquittal as political vindication. "This has been a long, tortured trial," said Senator Byron L. Dorgan of North Dakota. "There are no winners. The President should take no solace from this."

Almost immediately after two votes, the mood in the Senate lightened.

The Republicans who wanted to remove him from office were far harsher, raising questions of how Mr. Clinton and the Congressional majority that pursued his impeachment will ever reconcile over the remaining two years of Mr. Clinton's term.

Senator Robert F. Bennett, Republican of Utah, called Mr. Clinton a man "with a capacity to lie about anything." And Senator Trent Lott of Mississippi, the majority leader, quoted the words of the novelist William Faulkner to make clear his profound distrust of Mr. Clinton. "One of the sayings that's always guided my life is, 'I will witness your advent and judge of your sincerity,'" he told reporters. "I guess you could say, in a little bit more of a Reagan way, 'trust and verify.'"

Until now the only impeachment trial of a President had taken place in 1868 when Andrew Johnson escaped conviction by a single vote. That trial left in its wake a weakened Presidency and came to be viewed over time as a partisan vendetta, a term many Democrats applied to this case, too.

It will now be up to historians to judge what happened in this impeachment, the first one to be conducted under the independent counsel law enacted after Watergate. For now the impeachment drive has left the Republican Party at record lows in public opinion polls, while Mr. Clinton has retained some of the highest job approval ratings of his Presidency. But many in both parties believe that public opinion could shift with the passage of time, once Mr. Clinton is out of danger of removal.

Far from ending the national ordeal, today's verdict is likely to propel forward a new cultural and political debate in the 2000 elections over morality and the right to privacy, creating sharp lines of demarcation between the political parties, which have seen so many of their policy differences diluted in the Clinton years.

Some of the signs of the emerging debate were visible today as all sides tried to assess the meaning of a vote that saw both articles fall short of even majority support.

Democrats and some Republicans argued that the votes signaled that the House had erred in sending forth impeachment articles against the will of the public and on a partisan vote in December.

But Randy Tate, the executive director of the Christian Coalition, said the House prosecution, in defiance of public opinion, "will be seen by history as an example of true American greatness."

Mr. Tate deplored Mr. Clinton's acquittal, saying, "Children now have the lesson that lying, cheating and breaking the law are permissible on the pathway to success."

The failure to reach a majority, said Senator Edward M. Kennedy, Democrat of Massachusetts, "reflected quite clearly the weakness of the House managers' case." He added, "These articles should never have been brought in the first place."

Senator John F. Kerry, another Massachusetts Democrat, who is weighing a Presidential bid, asked whether the many senators who were once prosecutors were "not deeply disturbed by an independent counsel grilling a sitting President of the United States about his personal sex life, based on information from illegal phone recordings."

The seeds of the impeachment saga were planted five years ago when Kenneth W. Starr was named independent counsel to investigate a real estate deal known as Whitewater. In January 1998, the investigation took a new tack with allegations that Mr. Clinton had had an affair with an intern and had induced her to submit a false affidavit in the sexual harassment suit brought against him by Paula Corbin Jones.

In a deposition in the Paula Jones case taken on Jan. 17, 1998, Mr. Clinton laid the groundwork for the impeachment case by denying that he had ever had sexual relations with Ms. Lewinsky and by sitting silently as his lawyer brandished her false affidavit to support him.

In a finger-wagging televised appearance, Mr. Clinton denied to the nation that he had ever had sexual relations with "that woman, Ms. Lewinsky." And for almost eight months, he steadfastly deceived aides and the country about his relationship with the intern. One aide told a grand jury that the President had called Ms. Lewinsky a "stalker."

Only in August, after it became known that Ms. Lewinsky had saved a stained blue dress that provided irrefutable evidence of their affair, did he tell a grand jury and the American public that he had had an "inappropriate relationship" with the young woman.

His belated and grudging confession did not stay the prosecutors. On Sept. 9, catching lawmakers off-guard, Mr. Starr delivered to Congress 36 boxes containing a report and supporting evidence of what he called "substantial and credible information" that Mr. Clinton had committed impeachable offenses.

Bitterness and turmoil are underscored by a bomb scare.

The House vote to begin an investigation that would lead to the first impeachment proceedings since Watergate was 363 to 63, bipartisan and overwhelming. But the House Judiciary Committee, one of the most polarized panels in the House, split almost immediately along party lines as the committee released the entire Starr report. Soon all the lurid details of Mr. Clinton's affair were available on the Internet, and the public could see the videotape of Mr. Clinton's grand jury appearance.

The disputes were heightened as each side looked toward the midterm elections. Republicans lost five House seats in a repudiation thought to be partly a result of their focus on investigation and scandal.

Stunned by the election and determined to get the case over with rapidly, the committee returned in a lame-duck session and approved four articles of impeachment along party lines, accepting Mr. Starr's case without ever calling witnesses.

In December, after a bitter debate, the House narrowly approved two of the articles in near party-line votes.

From the start of the trial on Jan. 7, the Senate tried assiduously to avoid the partisan bitterness of the House. Fearful of public backlash, Senate Republicans forced the House prosecutors to scale back their witness list to only three and allowed only depositions to be taken. Democrats and many Republicans recoiled from the idea of Ms. Lewinsky testifying in the well of the Senate.

The Republicans also insisted on keeping the Senate's final deliberations behind closed doors. And for three days this week, the senators debated in private.

When the doors opened again today at noon, the exhausted senators were openly longing to return to legislation.

In the hushed chamber, senators stood one after another to pronounce Mr. Clinton guilty or not guilty. Some barely whispered their verdict. Others shouted it out with emphasis.

There was barely a stir at the moment when Senator Patrick J. Leahy, Democrat of Vermont, cast the 34th vote of not guilty that guaranteed Mr. Clinton's acquittal on the first count of perjury, or when Senator Carl Levin, a Michigan Democrat, cast the vote that assured his acquittal on the second count. But a low murmur broke out toward the end of the first roll call when the declaration of "not guilty" by Senator John W. Warner, Republican of Virginia, brought to 10 the number of Republicans who broke with their party on the charge of perjury.

As the trial ended, and Mr. Lott bid farewell to Chief Justice Rehnquist, the relief was palpable. "I would like to close with our traditional Mississippi parting: Y'all come back soon," the majority leader told the Chief Justice. He quickly added, as laughter broke out, "But I hope that's not taken the wrong way. And not for an occasion like this one."

U.S. Senate

Chief Justice William H. Rehnquist, left, presided in the Senate chamber yesterday as President Clinton was acquitted on articles of impeachment.

Clinton Statement

By The New York Times

WASHINGTON, Feb. 12 — Following is President Clinton's statement to reporters after his acquittal in the Senate impeachment trial, as transcribed by the Federal News Service, a private transcription service.

Now that the Senate has fulfilled its constitutional responsibility, bringing this process to a conclusion, I want to say again to the American people how profoundly sorry I am for what I said and did to trigger these events and the great burden they have imposed on the Congress and on the American people.

I also am humbled and very grateful for the support and the prayers I have received from millions of Americans over this past year.

Now I ask all Americans, and I hope all Americans here in Washington and throughout our land, will rededicate ourselves to the work of serving our nation and building our future together. This can be and this must be a time of reconciliation and renewal for America.

Thank you very much.

Q. In your heart, sir, can you forgive and forget?

PRESIDENT CLINTON. I believe any person who asks for forgiveness has to be prepared to give it.

THE WHITE HOUSE

The President Says He Feels Humbled and Is 'Profoundly Sorry'

Continued From Page A1

dent's chief of staff, John Podesta, forwarded to the White House staff an apology from Mr. Clinton, who for all his praise of information technology does not use a computer.

"Your dedication and loyalty have meant more to me than you can ever know," the message read, in part. "The best way I can repay you is to redouble my own efforts on behalf of the ideals we share, and to make the most of every day we are here."

After leaving the Rose Garden, Mr. Clinton telephoned several Democratic Senators to thank them. Then, in a display of the business-as-usual briskness that carried him through his yearlong crisis, he met with his foreign policy team to begin preparing for an overnight trip to Mexico on Sunday.

Later, Mr. Clinton met in the Oval Office with his public and private lawyers to thank them, and then received a visit from the Rev. Jesse L. Jackson, who has counseled him and supported him politically during his ordeal.

As he told House Democrats at a retreat this week, Mr. Clinton wants to score legislative gains on Social Security, health care and education — even as he fights to win back Congress for the Democrats in 2000.

He wants to work with the Republicans who voted to eject him from office, while he tries to eject some of them from office.

Some of his allies think that Mr. Clinton has gained the upper hand and will be able to do both. "This thing has empowered him," said James Carville, the President's former campaign manager and informal adviser. "His own party is unified, and the opposition party desperately needs him to get some things done before the election. He's become stronger and his opponents have become weaker."

Other Clinton advisers worry that his approval ratings may slide once a public urge to rally around him subsides. They fret that today's unity might crumble, if House Democrats prove less interested in agreement than in fighting Republicans on issues like raising the minimum wage.

Mr. Clinton's history — as college politician, Arkansas Governor, Presidential campaigner and President — is a stuttering series of reversals and political fresh starts. Some of his aides divide his Presidential terms into as many as five distinct periods of governance and politics, since the Clintons arrived here as bright-eyed outsiders promising intelligence, integrity and compassion. That was only six years ago.

First came a burst of energy and innovation, culminating in the Clintons' politically disastrous health care proposal and the first Republican Congress in 40 years. There followed a period of drift and despondency, some officials recalled, as Mr. Clinton publicly insisted on his relevance and privately wondered what to do.

By appearing firm and compassionate after the Oklahoma City bombing and then standing up to the Republicans during the Government shutdown, Mr. Clinton regained his political footing. Under the influence of his sometime adviser, Dick Morris, he took the initiative again, this time with smaller proposals tested to insure their popularity.

Those ideas carried him to re-election in 1996, but the Administration seemed to run out of gas after his second inaugural. Then, as he began to regain his bearings, the disclosures about Ms. Lewinsky swamped him.

Mr. Clinton's advisers say there is no mystery about what comes next. Mr. Clinton unrolled his policy wish list in his State of the Union message, and he is hoping that success in shoring up Social Security will counterbalance the weight of impeachment.

Some of his aides suspect that the Republicans who tried to remove him will be more scarred by their votes than he is.

"Their votes on impeachment will be in the first paragraph of their obituaries," said one senior White House official. Mr. Clinton, he said, "will try to get impeachment erased from the first paragraph of his — or at least make it a very, very long paragraph."

Mr. Clinton did not watch the Senate vote today, his aides said. Instead, Mr. Podesta telephoned him after each ballot to report the outcome. A group of senior aides had gathered in the chief of staff's office, confident of acquittal but worried that the second charge, obstruction of justice, might draw a majority. "There was a good bit of suspense," said one who was present.

But, cautioned by Mr. Podesta at the senior staff meeting this morning, Mr. Clinton's aides avoided any celebration. Only his legal team permitted themselves public grins, as they strolled from the White House to an Indian restaurant for lunch.

"I think, given the circumstances of this matter that's gone on for this long, we can be relieved it's over," said Joe Lockhart, the White House press secretary. "But there's really nothing to celebrate."

Stephen Crowley/The New York Times

President Clinton at the Rose Garden yesterday after acquittal.

THE INVESTIGATION: Starr's Inquiry Finds Grounds for Impeachment

JANUARY 1998	FEBRUARY	MARCH	APRIL	MAY	JUNE	JULY	AUGUST	SEPTEMBER
58% 56% 72%	66% 73% 68% 64%		67%	64% 62%	60%	64% 61%	67% 71% 65%	62% 67%

JAN. 7 Lewinsky signs affidavit denying any sexual relationship, but does not file it immediately.

JAN. 12 Tripp gives tapes to prosecutors for the independent counsel, Kenneth W. Starr.

LEWINSKY QUESTIONED

JAN. 16 Starr is authorized to investigate the Lewinsky matter. Starr's deputies have Tripp meet Lewinsky at a hotel, then intercept and question Lewinsky for several hours. Her lawyer files a motion to quash her subpoena and attaches the signed affidavit.

JAN. 17 Clinton questioned by Jones's lawyers. He denies a sexual relationship with Lewinsky.

JAN. 21 News accounts of the affair first appear. Clinton denies the accusations.

JAN. 26 Clinton makes his most emphatic denial: "I did not have sexual relations with that woman, Miss Lewinsky. I never told anybody to lie, not a single time — never. These allegations are false."

JONES'S SUIT THROWN OUT

APRIL 1 A Federal district court judge in Arkansas throws out Jones's sexual harassment lawsuit.

JULY 17 The independent counsel's office secretly issues a subpoena for Clinton to testify before the grand jury investigating the Lewinsky matter.

JULY 28 Lawyers for Lewinsky broker an immunity deal with Starr in which she promises "full and truthful testimony."

JULY 29 Clinton agrees to submit voluntarily to questioning at the White House by Federal prosecutors after Starr withdraws the subpoena to compel his testimony.

JULY 31 Jones's lawyers ask to reinstate her suit.

AUG. 6 Lewinsky begins grand jury testimony.

AUG. 17 Clinton testifies before the grand jury. That evening he acknowledges, "I did have a relationship with Ms. Lewinsky that was not appropriate."

STARR REPORT RELEASED

SEPT. 9 Starr notifies House leaders that he has found information that may constitute grounds for impeachment.

The New York Times

"All the News That's Fit to Print"

The New York Times

Late Edition
New York: **Today,** sunny and breezy, high 48. **Tonight,** mainly clear and chilly, low 32. **Tomorrow,** sunny and cool, high 47. **Yesterday,** high 58, low 45. Weather map is on page D8.

VOL. CXLVIII . . . No. 51,472 NEW YORK, THURSDAY, MARCH 25, 1999 — $1 beyond the greater New York metropolitan area. — 60 CENTS

NATO OPENS BROAD BARRAGE AGAINST SERBS AS CLINTON DENOUNCES YUGOSLAV PRESIDENT

Early Attacks Focus on Web Of Air Defense

By STEVEN LEE MYERS

WASHINGTON, March 24 — Waves of NATO strikes today opened what officials said would be a protracted assault on the Yugoslav military, but one that would do little immediately to end the deadly crackdown in Kosovo.

The first barrage of several dozen cruise missiles started falling on air defenses across Yugoslavia, Pentagon and NATO officials said. They were fired from six B-52 bombers and four American ships, two American submarines and a British submarine.

After a brief lull, American warships fired another burst of cruise missiles at a target, not long before dawn in Yugoslavia. That strike — involving only a handful of missiles — was not part of the original plan but rather came after NATO commanders saw an opportunity to hit Yugoslav aircraft that had returned to one of their bases, Pentagon officials said.

NATO warplanes also pressed new attacks, the officials said, describing rolling waves of strikes. "It's a fairly continuous attack," one official said.

The offensive entailed scores of fighter jets and bombers from the United States and seven other NATO members, including Britain, Germany and the Netherlands, the officials said, speaking on condition of anonymity.

Today's strikes were not aimed at the Serbian troops and tanks that have been systematically destroying village after village in Kosovo with renewed fury since peace talks collapsed last week. The battering focused largely, though not entirely, on the air defenses and command network that pose the greatest threat to allied pilots crisscrossing Yugoslavia.

"You need a few days of this," a NATO official said, "before you can put in a larger number of the aircraft you need to go after the forces involved in the repression."

The attacks today included strikes by F-117 stealth fighters, as well as the combat debut of the B-2 stealth bomber, which at $2.1 billion apiece is the most expensive warplane ever built. Two of the B-2 bombers, flying from Whiteman Air Force Base in Missouri, each dropped 16 one-ton bombs.

As expected, Yugoslavia mounted a fierce defense, though not precisely the one expected. American and NATO officials said. The Yugoslav

Continued on Page A13

Some of the sites attacked — According to Serbian officials; Army bases; Yugoslav troops in Kosovo; Antiaircraft sites and air bases

Source: Periscope — The New York Times

Missiles Rock Kosovo Capital, Belgrade and Other Sites

By FRANCIS X. CLINES

WASHINGTON, March 24 — The forces of NATO opened an assault on Serbia with cruise missiles and bombs today as President Clinton denounced the Yugoslav President, Slobodan Milosevic, for feeding the "flames of ethnic and religious division" in Kosovo and endangering neighboring countries.

The missiles began striking Serbian targets within minutes of Mr. Clinton's midday announcement that the long-threatened attack was under way. It was expected to be a broad, sustained barrage intended to stun the Yugoslav leader and punish the military for its yearlong onslaught against the ethnic Albanian separatists of Kosovo.

"Ending this tragedy is a moral imperative," Mr. Clinton declared in an address to the nation tonight from the Oval Office. "It is also important to America's national interests." [Text, page A15.]

He spoke several hours after the first explosions of incoming missiles erupted in the night skies of Pristina, Kosovo's capital. The Yugoslav news agency Tanjug said the city's main commercial and military airport had been hit.

[At 5:24 A.M. Thursday (11:24 P.M. Wednesday, Eastern time), all-clear sirens sounded in Belgrade, indicating the end of the raids, Agence France-Presse reported.]

The biggest allied military assault in Europe since World War II occurred after a day in which Serbian forces maintained their military pressure against the ethnic Albanian majority in Kosovo. Steady streams of alarmed residents fled toward Kosovo's borders.

Sirens sounded, and the flash and thunder of explosions cut through the night sky of Belgrade and other scattered targets, including Novi Sad, in northern Serbia, and the main airport in the Yugoslav coastal republic of Montenegro. One explosion was reported near Batajnica, the main Serbian airport and military base near Belgrade.

As he explained the NATO attack — an attempt to solve a problem that Serbia considers purely internal — Mr. Clinton sought to reassure the United States against a commitment to any large-scale ground war.

"I don't intend to put our troops in Kosovo to fight a war," he emphasized. He denounced Mr. Milosevic as a dictator "who has done nothing since the cold war ended but start new wars and pour gasoline on the flames of ethnic and religious division."

"We act to prevent a wider war, to defuse a powder keg at the heart of Europe that has exploded twice before in this century with catastrophic results," the President said gravely of the military attack by the 19-member NATO alliance.

In his afternoon announcement of the military attack, Mr. Clinton said, "President Milosevic, who over the past decade started the terrible wars against Croatia and Bosnia, has again chosen aggression over peace."

A defiant Mr. Milosevic called for defense of his nation "by all means possible," terming Kosovo "only the door intended to allow foreign troops to come in and steal away our freedom." [Page A14.]

The Belgrade Government, in denouncing what it called neo-Nazism,

Continued on Page A12

Paul Hosefros/The New York Times

President Clinton after his television talk on Serbia last night.

Before Explosions, a Rush for Safety and Supplies

By CARLOTTA GALL

PRISTINA, Serbia, March 24 — Two enormous flashes filled the sky shortly after 8 P.M. Seconds later came the sound of the explosions as the first NATO missiles struck somewhere south of the city, possibly the airport, or one of the military bases.

Minutes later the electricity went off, pitching the city into blackness.

Under a bright moon, tracer fire from an antiaircraft gun tore upward into the sky.

A few lone cars roared through the streets, mostly deserted long before darkness fell. An hour later, ripples of powerful explosions resounded far off in the distance. Otherwise, Pristina, the Kosovo capital, lay dark and quiet.

The air raid sirens first sounded just after 1 P.M. over the city, as a test apparently, but raised tensions as people piled into buses to escape the province. Many of those who stayed behind prepared for a time of crisis.

Shoppers cleaned out the stores of basic supplies of sugar, flour and candles. Long lines of cars formed at gas stations. Buses pulled out of town, packed full with passengers and belongings, heading for Macedonia and Turkey.

Still other people were out walking the streets, soaking up the warm sunny weather.

Even before the bombing began today, the war being fought here — in villages, from the hills, and along the roads — was continuing in full swing.

With air strikes imminent, army and police units seemed to be pressing their offensive against the guerrillas in all parts of Kosovo and stepped up police activity in the city.

Heavy explosions sounded across the northern part of Kosovo as Serbian forces continued to shell positions held by ethnic Albanian rebels on either side of the Cicavica mountain range.

In southern Kosovo, near the main border crossing, the military was out in force and the village of Gajre, taken by Serbian forces almost two weeks ago, was on fire, reporters said.

Here, police officers and army sol-

Continued on Page A14

U.S. Navy via Agence France-Presse

Srdjan Ilic/Associated Press

THE ATTACKERS, AND THEIR TARGETS A Tomahawk missile being launched yesterday from the U.S. Navy cruiser the Philippine Sea, in the Adriatic. Near Pristina, the capital of Kosovo, a Yugoslav Army barracks burned.

A Fresh Set Of U.S. Goals

By R. W. APPLE Jr.

WASHINGTON, March 24 — For half a century, the United States and other countries have pursued political goals through air power, bombing their adversaries in an effort to persuade them — force them, if possible — to change their policies.

News Analysis

It has seldom if ever worked, unless combined with resolute action on the ground.

That may be one reason why the Clinton Administration's explanation of its policies underwent a subtle shift today.

In the hours just before missiles began striking targets in Kosovo, there were vehement denials at the State Department and at the White House that NATO was trying to bomb Serbia back to the bargaining table and force President Slobodan Milosevic of Yugoslavia to sign a peace agreement.

"The threat of force was there to help him come to the conclusion that a peaceful solution was the best solution," said James P. Rubin, the State Department spokesman. But the use of force, as opposed to the threat of force, was completely different, he said.

What NATO was now trying to do, President Clinton said this afternoon, was "to stop the brutal repression" by the Serbs.

"Our strikes have three objectives," he said — to "demonstrate the seriousness of NATO's opposition to aggression," to deter President Milosevic "from continuing and escalating his attacks" in Kosovo, and to damage Serbia's capacity to wage war in the future.

A top Pentagon planner conceded, "We have no great expectations that Milosevic is going to back down and agree to a satisfactory peace settle-

Continued on Page A12

Mayor, Under Fire, Opens Door Wider To Black Officials

By DAN BARRY

After an hourlong meeting with C. Virginia Fields, the Manhattan Borough President, whom he had shunned for more than a year, Mayor Rudolph W. Giuliani said last night that he would meet again with her and with other leading black officials at a time when the aftershocks of the Amadou Diallo shooting continue to rumble through the city.

The Mayor's office also announced that he would finally meet with the state's highest-ranking black elected official, State Comptroller H. Carl McCall. The two men last met in November 1994; since then, the Mayor has refused several requests from Mr. McCall for another meeting.

The sudden decision to open his door marked a stark turnaround for the Mayor, who had previously dismissed Ms. Fields and Mr. McCall as being more interested in publicity than in substantive discussion.

But the Mayor has come under increasing pressure to appear more conciliatory, as the outcry continues over the death of Mr. Diallo, an unarmed black man killed in a hail of 41 bullets fired by four white officers.

The Mayor also said yesterday that he expected Police Commissioner Howard Safir to keep his job, though he declined to comment on whether it was appropriate for Mr. Safir to have accepted a free trip to Los Angeles for the Academy Awards ceremony from a cosmetics executive. Mr. Safir has been under fire for the trip and for the Diallo case. [Page B12.]

Yesterday, Police Headquarters in lower Manhattan drew the largest

Continued on Page B12

INSIDE

737 Rudder Action Advised

Changes should be made in Boeing 737's to bolster their rudder control, the National Transportation Safety Board said. Page A28.

Microsoft Offers to Settle

Microsoft has sent the Justice Department a proposal to settle its antitrust case, but it apparently falls short of expectations. Page C1.

Ruling on Pinochet

England's top court ruled that Gen. Augusto Pinochet could face extradition to Spain, but him narrowed the charges against him. Page A6.

Updated news: www.nytimes.com

Russian Anger at U.S. Tempered by Need for Cash

By MICHAEL R. GORDON

MOSCOW, March 24 — Stung by NATO's decision to carry out air strikes against Yugoslavia, Russia tonight suspended cooperation with the Western alliance and denounced the attack as an act of brazen aggression.

Behind the words, however, was a tempering factor: Russia still needs billions of dollars in Western loans.

That need was underscored by Russia's announcement tonight that Michel Camdessus, the managing director of the International Monetary Fund, would arrive in Moscow this weekend for more talks. A senior American official said today that the visit was occurring with the encouragement of the United States.

Caught between the imperatives of its pro-Serbian policy and its pressing economic needs, Russia did its best today to head off a NATO attack. In a telephone conversation, President Boris N. Yeltsin urged President Clinton not to go through with the air strikes and made an impassioned television address carrying the same message.

"I am appealing to the whole world," Mr. Yeltsin said. "I am appealing to people who survived the war, to those who experienced the bombings, their children, to all political figures. As long as there remain some minutes, let's persuade Bill Clinton not to take this tragic, dramatic step."

Prime Minister Yevgeny M. Primakov, for his part, telephoned the Yugoslav President, Slobodan Milosevic, to encourage him to reach an accommodation on the Kosovo issue.

Washington's and Belgrade's rebuffs to the Kremlin appeals were taken here as a powerful blow to

Continued on Page A13

MORE ON THE BOMBINGS

Clinton Explains Decision

The President said he decided to use force because of moral revulsion at the killings in Kosovo and to serve American interests. Page A15.

Serbs Turn Back to Loyalty

Even the Serbs most bitterly opposed to President Slobodan Milosevic feel a surge of nationalism at a threat from the West. Page A14.

CONFLICT IN THE BALKANS: 'To Stop the Brutal Repression'

Associated Press

Flames lit up the Belgrade skyline yesterday after NATO missiles and planes punished Yugoslavia for not signing a peace agreement for Kosovo.

THE OVERVIEW

NATO Opens a Broad Barrage Against the Serbs Over Kosovo

Continued From Page A1

called upon the United Nations Security Council to condemn "NATO's criminal, terrorist, underhanded and cowardly attack."

American defense officials said their targets included missile batteries, radar installations and military communication sites in Kosovo, Belgrade and other key areas. Some air-to-air combat was reported by Pentagon officials, who said all NATO planes had returned safely.

President Boris N. Yeltsin of Russia, which has longstanding ties to the Serbs, angrily denounced the American-led raids as "open aggression." Mr. Clinton had tried to justify the military action today in a 35-minute phone call with Mr. Yeltsin. But the Russian leader recalled his chief military envoy to NATO.

After months of threats, NATO finally resorted to military action as Mr. Milosevic, far from heeding peace overtures, stepped up his latest offensive against ethnic Albanian villages and rebels of the Kosovo Liberation Army.

Since violence began intensifying a year ago, more than 400,000 ethnic Albanians have fled their homes as Serbian forces have torched and bombarded villages, massacring civilians in some raids. In recent decades ethnic Albanians have come to outnumber Serbs by 9-to-1 in Kosovo, which Serbs long have revered as the birthplace of Serbian nationhood.

The ultimate fear about the mounting violence in Kosovo, the southernmost province of Serbia, is that it might reignite the ethnic and religious wars in the Balkans that NATO earlier worked to resolve in Bosnia with the commitment of troops.

Critics who until now accused the Administration of equivocating in facing Mr. Milosevic's assault fear that Albania and Macedonia could be drawn into a larger war or even break up if the Serbs are not prevented from an "ethnic cleansing" of the Albanian majority in Kosovo. Even beyond that, it is feared that Turkey and Greece, two NATO members, might take opposite sides.

Trent Lott, the Senate majority leader, voiced qualified support for the NATO attack. "Whatever reservations about the President's actions in the Balkans," the Mississippi Republican said, "let no one doubt that the Congress and the American people stand united behind our men and women who are bravely heeding the call of duty."

The attack was the first uninvited offensive against a sovereign nation by NATO, the alliance founded 50 years ago as the European bulwark against the cold war military power of the Soviet Union. NATO's 17 days of air strikes against Serbian forces in Bosnia in 1995 were conducted at the request of the embattled Bosnian Government against military targets of the Bosnian Serbs.

No detailed casualty reports were immediately available. But scores of Serbian military bases and depots, aircraft and munitions factories were expected to be hit by NATO forces equipped with more than 400 bomber aircraft from European bases, and missile weaponry aboard a half dozen warships in the Adriatic region. The operation marked the first combat use of the B-2 "stealth" bomber designed to elude radar, according to Pentagon officials who said two B-2's had journeyed from Whiteman Air Force Base in Missouri on a mission to drop dropped satellite-guided bombs.

"Clear responsibility for the air strikes lies with President Milosevic, who has refused to stop his violent action in Kosovo and has refused to negotiate in good faith," said NATO's Secretary General, Javier Solana.

The attack began after Mr. Milosevic rebuffed a final peace plea from the United States intended to restore the autonomy that Mr. Milosevic had stripped from Kosovo and its ethnic Albanian majority 10 years ago. Under diplomatic prodding, he signed a peace agreement in October but then reneged. The proposed peace plan would include the deployment of thousands of NATO peacekeeping troops in Kosovo.

Denouncing Mr. Milosevic for ethnic violence and atrocity, Mr. Clinton conceded that NATO forces risked casualties against Mr. Milosevic's modernized military. But he warned: "The dangers of acting now are clearly outweighed by the risks of failing to act: the risks that many more innocent people will die or be driven from their homes by the tens of thousands; the risks that the conflict will involve and destabilize neighboring nations."

Months of threats end as the Yugoslav offensive persists.

The NATO attack was authorized after Mr. Clinton's envoy, Richard C. Holbrooke, paid an 11th-hour visit to Mr. Milosevic and failed to persuade him to join the peace proposal accepted by the ethnic Albanians. The military task then was placed in the hands of NATO's Supreme Commander, Gen. Wesley K. Clark of the United States, with orders to deal with Mr. Milosevic's authoritarian assault on the Kosovo majority.

"It's the right decision, and we have to see it through all the way," said Prime Minister Tony Blair of Britain.

Mr. Clinton said the action had three objectives: "to demonstrate the seriousness of NATO's opposition to aggression," to deter Mr. Milosevic from "continuing and escalating his attacks on helpless civilians by imposing a price for those attacks" and "if necessary, to damage Serbia's capacity to wage war against Kosovo in the future by seriously diminishing its military capabilities."

While Congressional Republican leaders' support of the NATO attack was qualified, Senator John H. Chafee, a Rhode Island Republican, declared, "The danger of inaction in Kosovo — of doing nothing — greatly exceeds the dangers of the action begun today."

Representative John P. Murtha, a ranking Democrat and ex-Marine from Pennsylvania with close ties to the Pentagon's senior commanders, predicted a prolonged air war against dug-in Serbian forces. "I think it could go on for a month," he said.

Elizabeth Dole, former American Red Cross president and Republican Presidential aspirant, endorsed the NATO attack. "Because I believe this action can be instrumental in forging a peaceful solution to a dangerous, escalating military conflict, I support it," she said. "The atrocities carried out by Serbian nationalists must be halted."

Commenting on alternatives if the air strikes fail, Senator Mitch McConnell, Republican of Kentucky, said, "Arming the Kosovars would be a lot cheaper, less dangerous to American troops and wouldn't put us in the middle of a civil war."

Mr. Clinton, however, maintained that the stakes were far higher than a Yugoslav civil war.

"At the end of the 20th century, after two world wars and a cold war," he said, "we and our allies have a chance to leave our children a Europe that is free, peaceful and stable. But we must, we must, act now to do that, because if the Balkans once again become a place of brutal killing and massive refugee flights, it will be impossible to achieve."

NEWS ANALYSIS

With Decision to Attack, A New Set of U.S. Goals

Continued From Page A1

ment because of one bombing raid or 10."

In his televised speech tonight, Mr. Clinton left no easy way out for Mr. Milosevic, insisting that he would have to agree to allied terms to end the bombing. On the other hand, the President let the Serbian leader know that he need not fear an American invasion.

"I do not intend to put our troops in Kosovo to fight a war," Mr. Clinton said, apparently seeking to reassure the American public but at the same time giving Mr. Milosevic an incentive to hang on.

But neither Mr. Clinton nor other senior American officials would address the questions that troubled many in this and other NATO capitals tonight: What would constitute success for the NATO effort? If the ultimate goal is peace in Kosovo, who is to maintain it once the bombs have stopped falling? Is the plan to keep bombing more or less indefinitely? If so, how will that help Kosovo?

"These bombs are not going to do the job," said Senator John McCain of Arizona, a Republican who was a naval pilot in the Vietnam War. "It's almost pathetic. You're just going to solidify the determination of the Serbs to resist a peace agreement.

"You'd have to drop the bridges and turn off the lights in Belgrade to have even a remote chance of changing Milosevic's mind," he said. "What you'll get is all the old Vietnam stuff, bombing pauses, escalation, negotiations, trouble."

Mr. McCain, who is expected to announce his candidacy for President next month, said the Administration was caught with unpalatable alternatives — bombing, which he said "has never worked without ground forces," and the use of ground forces, which he said had little support on Capitol Hill or in the nation as a whole.

Clearly irritated by the President's critics, Mr. Rubin said that "in their opposition to the use of air power, they have offered no alternative other than the appeasement of President Milosevic's policies, which is something unacceptable to this Administration."

But in fact some of the critics offered more.

David Owen, the former British Foreign Secretary, said in a telephone interview that he sympathized with Mr. Clinton's wish to make a stand in Kosovo. But it was "completely useless," he added, to resort to air power while letting it be known that there was no intention of using or threatening to use ground forces.

"NATO seems to think it can have half a war," said Lord Owen, who worked as a high-level mediator in the Bosnian crisis. "They should have built up ground forces in Macedonia — not a token force, a big one, say 60,000 troops or more. The only thing that will get Milosevic's attention is the real prospect that you're going to sweep his troops out of Kosovo and stay there to keep them out."

An allied force of 25,000 in Kosovo was the goal, of course, of the peace treaty that Mr. Milosevic spurned after talks near Paris. But invading in order to install such a force might require as many as 100,000 men, and they would have to impose peace, not keep it.

Once before, Mr. Milosevic yielded to the force of bombing. But that was during the Bosnian crisis. Bosnia was an independent country, and the problem concerned Serbs who lived there, not Serbs who live in a province (Kosovo) that is Serbian. And the bombing of 1995 was backed by a Croatian ground offensive.

Otherwise, bombing has worked only when followed up. More often, it has failed.

Hitler pulverized the East End of London, to say nothing of industrial cities like Coventry, without weakening the Churchill Government or the British people's will to resist. The United States never broke the spirit of Ho Chi Minh or the North Vietnamese with its ceaseless raids on Hanoi and Haiphong. Quite the opposite.

Without ground troops, what can bombing achieve?

More recently, Iraq offers a relevant case in point.

The weeks of bombing that preceded the all-out American ground attack in the Persian Gulf war in 1991 reduced the efficacy of such fighting units as the Republican Guard. But as Washington admitted at the time, it was not enough. Tanks and infantrymen were also needed.

In the years since then, there have been many more air attacks, each intended to "teach Saddam Hussein a lesson" or to "maintain our credibility" or to "reduce his war-making capacity." None achieved much.

The stakes this time are much higher. A botched operation could seriously damage the effort to formulate a new peacekeeping and crisis-management role for NATO, which Mr. Clinton had hoped to unveil at NATO's 50th anniversary summit here next month. Even a successful operation could seriously damage American relations with Russia.

Quite apart from the broader implications, the bombing campaign, which is the first offensive action ever undertaken against a sovereign nation by NATO, constitutes a leap in the dark. No one really knows how Mr. Milosevic will react or, for that matter, how the Kosovo Albanians will react. Protected by alliance bombers, they may feel less inclined than before to accept the peace agreement, which includes an interim autonomy deal that would defer independence for at least three years.

IN BELGRADE

Televised Defiance Lost Amid Sirens, Blasts and Fireballs

By STEVEN ERLANGER

BELGRADE, Serbia, March 24 — As NATO bombs and cruise missiles brought the Balkan wars he initiated to his doorstep tonight, the Yugoslav President, Slobodan Milosevic, called on his people to defend their country "by all possible means."

Then, about 8 P.M., four hours after the Serbian leader had addressed the nation on television, the first cruise missiles hit Kosovo. Air-raid sirens sounded here in the capital. Flashes of antiaircraft fire dotted the night sky and, over the next few hours, three large orange fireballs could be seen on the city's outskirts, one to the northwest in the direction of a large air force base, and two to the south, one of which seemed to be near Zarkovo, where there is an aircraft plant.

State television broke into its programming to announce the air strikes, urging people to remain calm. "The criminals of NATO can inflict a lot of damage," one news anchor said. "But they can never win, and they can never defeat us."

Local newspaper and magazine editors said that the Yugoslav Information Minister, Aleksandar Vucic, had called them in and given them a list of regulations, which included the requirement to call NATO "criminal," and injunctions not to demoralize the population with detailed descriptions of "targets."

Serbian authorities also moved to cut off incoming transmissions of television pictures from Western networks, in particular those from NATO-member countries.

On state television, there was much martial music and old footage of Yugoslav Army soldiers handling sophisticated weaponry. The first two state television channels showed an old movie, "Battle on Kozara," about the victory of Yugoslav partisans over the Nazis. Keeping to the theme, the Foreign Ministry issued a statement saying: "From this moment, neo-Nazi America suspends international law."

IN FINANCIAL CHAOS, AN UGLY SECURITY

The Yugoslav economy has been so battered by years of international sanctions that air strikes are not likely to make things worse. *Page C4.*

A statement from the military chief of staff said that 20 installations had been attacked by NATO forces, including the civilian and military airfield near Pristina, the Kosovo capital, and the air base northwest of here at Batajnica. A Serb who spoke to his mother there by telephone said that a large explosion had blown out the windows of houses, including hers, about a mile from the air base.

The sky over a blacked-out Pristina was full of explosions and light, and there were reports of blasts in other cities, including Krusumlija, Pancevo, Novi Sad, Golubovac, Danilovgrad and the air base near Podgorica, the capital of Montenegro, the other republic of Yugoslavia. But there was no way to tell how accurate the strikes were, and there were no specific reports of casualties.

In his television appearance, Mr. Milosevic, defiant, said the decision not to allow foreign troops into the southern Serbian province of Kosovo was to protect Yugoslavia's sovereignty. He hinted darkly that NATO wanted to occupy all of Yugoslavia, and said: "What is at stake here is the freedom of the entire country, and Kosovo was only the door intended to allow foreign troops to come in and steal away our freedom."

Mr. Milosevic said that he still wanted to solve the Kosovo problem peacefully, with equal guarantees for all the people of the province. But he vowed: "We will defend the country if it is attacked."

Earlier in the day, at Batajnica, where the air base is, Mr. Milosevic's citizens were scarcely gung-ho. They were depressed, anxious, slightly hostile and still disbelieving.

"I don't believe they'll bomb us; something will happen," said Sadi Dragan, staring up at the sunny sky outside his auto-parts shop.

In the last few days, Mr. Milosevic has tried to insure that people have access only to state media. Early this morning, the police shut down the independent radio station B-92, which has been an important dissident voice, and detained its editor, Veran Matic. He was released eight hours later, around 11 A.M., but the radio's transmitters were sealed.

This afternoon, in Belgrade, police also shut down a satellite transmitter of the European Broadcasting Union used by Western television networks, who were forced to transmit from Government centers. Later, those broadcasts were restricted.

Vuk Obradovic, a former general in the Yugoslav Army who leads an opposition party called Social Democracy, also criticized NATO's decision to use military force.

"There is no doubt that Milosevic is most guilty in bringing the country to war," Mr. Obradovic said in an interview today. "But NATO will also be losers, and the ones who will lose the most are ordinary civilians, in Serbia and especially in Kosovo. As a general, I tell you, even in the most modern war, civilians are the main casualties."

Mr. Obradovic, 51, a career officer who quit in 1992 out of disgust with Mr. Milosevic's Balkan ambitions, said that the Yugoslav Army "will defend Kosovo, and they do not joke when they say they will defend it in every possible way."

Some in the army would prefer a different policy, Mr. Obradovic said. "Mr. Milosevic not only brings us into a war with the whole world, but he pushes us into a war with one another," he said. "That is the whole organizing principle of his politics, if he has one."

And he said that the West miscalculated the difficulty of any Serb accepting foreign troops and a loss of control over Kosovo. "It may sound like only a phrase, but it is really true that Kosovo is something special to the Serbs," Mr. Obradovic said. "And it is also true that the person who signs a document giving up Kosovo will have the stamp of a traitor on himself and his children forever."

Mr. Milosevic would rather lose Kosovo, said an official considered close to him, than be accused of surrendering it. "If it is lost, we keep the right to reconquer it, even 100 years from now," he said. "If we give it away, it is lost forever."

In Kosovo itself, where the Yugoslav military has driven thousands of ethnic Albanians out of their homes during its pursuit of the Kosovo Liberation Army, military and police officers began to dispatch their heavy equipment in preparation for NATO attacks, officials said.

In Batajnica, near a monument to the town's World War II dead, one man spoke about Yugoslavia's decline under Mr. Milosevic and the need to work two jobs to make a living.

He has two sons, ages 6 and 4, he said. "If I thought that my sons' lives will be better in 20 years, I would go lie on the tarmac of the Batajnica air base and wait for the bombs, throwing a party for my friends," he said.

"But I don't think this attack will make their lives or this country any better. Quite the contrary."

The Breakup of Yugoslavia

SLOVENIA
JUNE 1991 Declares independence.

CROATIA
JUNE 1991 Declares independence.

BOSNIA AND HERZEGOVINA
APRIL 1992 War erupts after Muslims and Croats vote for independence. Peace agreement was reached in Dayton, Ohio, in November 1995.

MACEDONIA
JANUARY 1992 Declares independence, without bloodshed.

SERBIA AND MONTENEGRO
APRIL 1992 Proclaim a new Federal Republic of Yugoslavia. In March 1998, war breaks out in Kosovo, a province of Serbia.

The Ethnic Mix

Where Yugoslavia's ethnic populations resided in 1991, prior to internal conflicts.

Source: Central Intelligence Agency

The New York Times

"All the News That's Fit to Print"

The New York Times

Late Edition
New York: **Today,** early sprinkles, then clearing, high 66. **Tonight,** patchy fog, low 57. **Tomorrow,** clouds with afternoon showers, high 71. **Yesterday,** high 60, low 47. Details, page D8

VOL. CXLVIII . . No. 51,500 NEW YORK, THURSDAY, APRIL 22, 1999 $1 beyond the greater New York metropolitan area. 60 CENTS

15 Bodies Are Removed From School in Colorado

Kevin Moloney for The New York Times

Students, relatives and friends of the victims of Tuesday's violence at Columbine High School after attending a memorial service yesterday.

Portrait of Outcasts Seeking to Stand Out

By DIRK JOHNSON and JAMES BROOKE

LITTLETON, Colo., April 21 — Eric Harris and Dylan Klebold, students at Columbine High School, worked last Friday making pizzas. On Monday, they went bowling. And on Tuesday, it seems, they committed mass murder.

Nobody had taken the two youths seriously.

They wore long black coats and hung out with a clique of middle-class suburban teen-agers that called itself the trench coat mafia. They lived with the familiar trappings of suburban comfort in a town with glorious views of the Rocky Mountain foothills.

They struck sullen, brooding poses. They talked about Hitler and wore clothes with German insignia. In February they completed a "diversion program" for first-time juvenile offenders, after their arrest for breaking into a van and stealing electronic equipment, the Jefferson County District Attorney said.

The other students, who came to know Mr. Harris and Mr. Klebold from mingling in the hallways and the commons, said the two youths had wanted to portray themselves as rebels or villains. But they were mostly viewed as losers.

"They were just a little weird," said Dara Ferguson, a 17-year-old junior and a cheerleader. "They wanted to be different."

Late Tuesday night, after the mass shooting at the high school, agents of the Bureau of Alcohol, Tobacco and Firearms, acting on a warrant, searched the house where Mr. Harris lived at the end of a cul-de-sac in Columbine Knolls. It is an 11-year-old subdivision the family moved to two years ago when Mr. Harris's father retired from the military and took a civilian job.

The agents carted away computers, computer printouts, gas cans, boxes of matches, videocassettes and bags of books, including one titled "Doom," after the computer game. Reporters did not see any weapons removed from the house.

On Monday, the Harrises' next-door neighbor, Bill Konen, was in his yard when he heard Mr. Klebold drive up and ask Eric Harris, "Do you have a metal baseball bat?"

"For the next 15 minutes, they were breaking bottles in a sack," Mr. Konen said, standing in his driveway, near a neighborhood watch association sign. "Apparently, they were making shrapnel. I would never have figured in a million years that bombmaking activities were going on, or any suspicious activities."

Some classmates said Eric Harris was good with computers and apparently maintained a Web site on America Online. Files on the Web site, discovered after the shootings, depicted him as an avid player of Doom and Quake, two popular computer games in which players stalk their opponents through dungeonlike environments and try to kill them with high-powered weapons.

The files on Mr. Harris's Doom and Quake exploits contained programs he had written to work with the games, as well as his commentary on them. But despite coming in the context of computer games famous for their realistic violence, these files, scattered with enthusiastic observations and exclamation points, provided a glimpse at a teenager who seemed less angry and morbid than in the other postings attributed to him.

"It took me about 10 hours to finish this level, so send some comments to me once in awhile!" Mr. Harris

Continued on Page A28

MORE ON THE MASSACRE

A CHANGED TOWN In Littleton, Colo., residents are mourning not only the loss of lives, but the area's old-fashioned sense of safety. Page A26.

CLASS DISTINCTIONS Columbine High School is like a lot of other suburban high schools, with its sports teams, clubs and parties. It is also separated into cliques and classes and ins and outs, as complicated a place as the society beyond. Page A27.

SEEKING ANSWERS Finding common symptoms and patterns to school shootings may be the easy part. The more troubling question, perhaps, is why the problems of adolescence sometimes seem to be resolved violently. News analysis, page A27.

LESSONS AROUND THE NATION With prayers, poems and special assemblies, schools around the country turned inward with an intensity inspired by no previous school mayhem, as students sought solace and answers. Page A28.

Eric Harris had his own Web site, other students said.

Photographs by Associated Press

Dylan Klebold disdained athletes and was said to feel "ostracized."

2 Are Suspects; Delay Caused By Explosives

By SAM HOWE VERHOVEK

LITTLETON, Colo., April 21 — After a long day of agony for victims' parents and anxiety for police officers searching for explosives, the authorities this evening removed the bodies of 15 people killed in a massacre at Columbine High School on Tuesday.

Among the dead were the two students who are believed to have unleashed the carnage before turning their guns on themselves. They were found shot in the head.

Twelve of the dead, including both suspected gunmen, were found in the school library, said the Jefferson County Sheriff, John Stone. Sheriff Stone said there were so many weapons and explosive devices — including 30 bombs, a semi-automatic rifle and pistol and two shotguns — that investigators were still unsure how the gunmen got it all inside the school.

They may have hidden it during several trips or they may have had help, Sheriff Stone said.

David J. Thomas, the district attorney, at a press conference at the school this afternoon, said that investigators were looking at 8 to 10 people who might have knowledge of the case through familiarity with a Web site connected to one of the presumed gunmen.

"I think there is evidence to suggest that other people were at least aware of what was going on," Mr. Thomas said. "There were a lot of devices. They took a long time to

Continued on Page A28

Behind Every Door, Different Tales of Terror

By JODI WILGOREN

LITTLETON, Colo., April 21 — They will never forget where they were when the alarm went off.

Josh Casey had just opened a bag of potato chips in the lunchroom. Steve Broden was taking a test on the digestive system in sophomore biology. Stephanie Bresee was waiting for her gym classmates to finish changing so they could head out to the baseball diamond.

They are teen-agers, and this is high school, after all, so they groaned and dropped their stuff and started to line up for yet another fire drill. But this was no false alarm.

As gunshots and explosions rocked the campus of Columbine High School, rocked their very world, the students descended into their own private nightmares. For some, it lasted only a few minutes, as they sprinted through hallways and climbed over cars to the safety of a nearby park and library. For others, it was an hours-long siege behind locked doors and in cramped closets, clueless about the craziness outside and unsure when help would come.

Michelle Alsom could not hear the alarm. She was miles away at the Cherry Creek Mall, running an errand. She is a 26-year-old paramedic, long since graduated from fire drills. But soon the buzzer went off on the pager on her hip, and she, too, will never forget the moment.

"It's my job and I'm proud to be doing it," Ms. Alsom said, trembling and sobbing as she told her story to a priest in the park adjacent to Columbine this afternoon. Ms. Alsom does not live anywhere near Littleton, but she came back, she said, because "I needed some closure."

The authorities say they still do not have many details about the architecture of the rampage that left 15 dead, including the two presumed gunmen, who apparently killed themselves, and more than 20 injured at Columbine on Tuesday. They do not know when the two died, or how many rounds they fired, or who they shot at first or last.

An officer assigned to the school, Neil Gardner of the Jefferson County Sheriff's Department, heard an explosion about 11:30 A.M. and went to an area near the cafeteria, said Steve Davis, a sheriff's spokesman. Mr. Gardner "saw one of the gunmen firing," Mr. Davis said, and "laid down some fire." Then, two other deputies fired at the gunmen, though all the shots apparently missed.

Law-enforcement officers did not encounter the suspected gunmen again, Mr. Davis said, until their bodies turned up in the library about 4 P.M. The rest of the time, he said, hundreds of officers from two dozen agencies "very slowly, quietly and methodically swept through the building."

In the hours before the police se-

Continued on Page A26

354613

2 ALLIES PRESS U.S. TO WEIGH THE USE OF GROUND FORCES

White House, Wary, Agrees Only to NATO Review of Options

By MICHAEL R. GORDON and CRAIG R. WHITNEY

BRUSSELS, April 21 — On the eve of the NATO summit meeting in Washington, Britain and France are pressing the United States to start thinking seriously about sending ground forces into Kosovo without a peace settlement.

With the meeting, commemorating NATO's 50th anniversary, opening on Friday, there is still no consensus about using a powerful ground force to drive Serbian troops and paramilitary police units out of Kosovo. The differences are so pronounced that the issue has been left off the formal agenda.

So far, the Clinton Administration has been wary of any suggestions involving ground troops in a combat role, and American officials have generally tried to avoid public discussion of the matter.

But tonight Washington signaled some flexibility, agreeing to a broad review of the options that NATO developed last summer on the use of ground troops in Kosovo. That review will now proceed, Javier Solana, the NATO Secretary General, said tonight.

The behind-the-scenes debate over ground forces broke out into the open this week in a coordinated series of statements by the British Prime Minister, Defense Minister and Foreign Minister.

With four weeks of bombing attacks already behind them, they argued that more weeks, if not months, of sustained bombing might so weaken the Serbian military that a NATO land force could move into Kosovo without a formal peace agreement and establish order there with minimal casualties. The scenario has been discussed so much in the corridors of NATO headquarters here that it even has a name: "a semipermissive environment."

The British proposal would be a major shift from the NATO's current plan, which is to send in a peacekeeping force of 28,000 troops, but only if the Yugoslav President, Slobodan Milosevic, agrees, withdraws his forces and accepts a peace settlement that allows the hundreds of thousands of exiled Kosovo Albanians to return to their shattered homes.

As Britain's Foreign Minister, Robin Cook, put it Tuesday in an address to Parliament, it is possible to "conceive of circumstances in which it may be feasible to commit ground troops."

The main condition would be that NATO's forces were not facing "organized armed resistance." As British officials tell it, Mr. Milosevic would not be given a veto over the introduction of allied ground troops.

The British are not the only ones urging consideration of a ground mission. President Jacques Chirac of France said in a televised speech tonight that the alliance should apply "additional means" besides stepping up the current air campaign to stop "massacres, rapes, burned villages, families separated and thrown onto the roads."

French officials said that Mr. Chirac's statement was an allusion to ground forces and that France's plan

Continued on Page A14

Michel Euler/Associated Press

APACHE COPTERS ARRIVE Flying over an antiaircraft launcher, a helicopter gunship arrived yesterday at Rina Airport in Tirana, Albania. Officials said the Apaches might be used in Kosovo in a week or so. Page A14.

NATO Confronts a New Role: Regional Policeman

By JANE PERLEZ

WASHINGTON, April 21 — As heads of NATO countries began arriving here today for the 50th anniversary of the alliance, they were embarking on a summit meeting transformed from a celebration of triumph to a war council on the Balkans.

The future of the alliance — which successfully stood up to the Soviet Union and its Communist allies in the Warsaw Pact but which has been grappling for a new role since the collapse of the Soviet bloc — has unexpectedly come to hinge, NATO leaders say, on the outcome of the battle against President Slobodan Milosevic of Yugoslavia.

Simply put, Senator Joseph R. Biden Jr. said in remarks at the Senate Foreign Relations Committee this week, "if we do not achieve our goals in Kosovo, NATO is finished as an alliance."

Administration officials say the allied leaders are hoping that the talks here will demonstrate the utility of NATO and show that the alliance, rather than being an obsolete ornament striving for a new mission, is alive and acting.

"Our message is that the NATO of the future is as good as the NATO of the past," said Ronald D. Asmus, Deputy Assistant Secretary of State for European Affairs.

For the alliance to be meaningful, he said, it must be able to deal with crises outside its member states, and Kosovo underscored the fact that NATO had come together on such a mission. Thus the war against Mr. Milosevic has become the first example of NATO as a regional policeman rather than a body of collective defense, as intended 50 years ago.

But this new position is one to which the alliance is totally unaccustomed, officials and analysts said.

In contrast to its sudden war against a Balkan dictator, NATO spent its first 40 years as an alliance bound by a mutual defense treaty, and did not fire a shot.

After its enemy evaporated with the fading of Communism, the alliance methodically expanded by selecting three former satellites of the Soviet Union — Hungary, the Czech Republic and Poland — as new members. It also extended its mission to include peacekeeping operations outside its membership, as happened in Bosnia.

There were other programs planned in the past year that were intended to bring the alliance into a more forward-looking mode.

Before Kosovo came onto the horizon, for example, the Administration was pushing NATO to address the spread of chemical, biological and nuclear weapons. This was a way, the Administration argued, for the alliance to become a modern, post-Soviet organization.

Secretary of Defense William S.

Continued on Page A16

INSIDE

Smallpox Wins Reprieve

President Clinton has defied international pleas and decided to retain America's sample of smallpox virus, officials said, on military and scientific grounds. Page A12.

Fetal Cell Experimentation

In the first Government-financed study using tissue from aborted fetuses, researchers said they had relieved symptoms of Parkinson's disease in some patients. Page A29.

Knicks Dismiss Grunfeld

In danger of missing the playoffs, the Knicks dismissed Ernie Grunfeld as team president and general manager. SportsThursday, Page D1.

Updated news: www.nytimes.com

TERROR IN LITTLETON: A Day of Reliving

THE MEMORIES

Behind Every School Door, a Tale of Terror

Continued From Page A1

cured the building, a different drama unfolded behind every door.

•

What people everywhere else heard, those in the cafeteria saw. A student in a black trench coat raced by the windows, firing all the time. A bomb went off in someone's trunk in the adjacent senior parking lot.

"I looked up and looked out the window and saw two people laying on the ground," recalled Bo Baribeau, a 15-year-old freshman. Wondering if there had been a fight, he went outside to see what was happening. "Once we got close," he said, "we saw the blood."

From the lunchroom, students saw the gunman racing down the hallway. A janitor ordered them to duck under the table. Then the janitor exhorted them to escape. Bo raced through the foreign language hall in what became a stampede. "About 100 kids, bam, just hit the streets, and went and jumped over the cars and, bam, went into the park," he said, almost breathless again.

But Josh Casey, also 15, could not get to the door. He was one of about 30 students who crammed, instead, into an elevator, seeking safety upstairs in the library. When they got there, though, the smoke from the bombs and the mist from the fire sprinkler system was blinding. They went down again — avoiding, unknowingly, the death trap the library was to become.

Back on the first floor, two teachers locked the students in the cafeteria and everyone sat underneath a chair, Josh said. Then the janitor returned, once again telling the crowd to flee. So they ran.

"I just kept hearing all the gunshots and the pipe bombs," Josh said today. "I didn't care to look back."

•

Upstairs in the science wing, there was no place to run.

Steve Broden and his classmates were chewing on pencils, searching for answers about the digestive system, when William David Sanders, a business teacher and coach, burst through the door. "He came in with two shots in his back," Steve said of the teacher, who died. "He just came in and fell on his face and busted a bunch of teeth."

The students quickly knocked over the tables and crouched behind them, as four or five other teachers brought their classes in to the room. One female teacher spent hours on a cell phone getting advice for how to care for Mr. Sanders, Steve said, and many students took their shirts off to help mop up the blood.

Orders to stay quiet lasted for about an hour, Steve said, but then emotion overcame them. Girls screamed. Boys cried. People with cell phones were frantically making calls. "We were just talking about our families," he said, "trying to keep ourselves happy."

It was about 3 P.M., Steve recalled, when the teacher on the cell phone said SWAT teams were about to rescue them. Another 30 minutes passed, and she said it again. Still nothing.

Next door, another biology class was crammed into a supply closet, first laying down on top of one another under sinks and scientific paraphernalia, then sitting so close they felt each other's breath.

"Gunshots kept going off forever it seemed," said Jessica Cave, a 16-year-old sophomore, who spoke with her mother's arms wrapped tightly around her sinewy figure. "I was just hoping I'd see my mother again."

Jessica said the students at times got noisy.

"It was just like a war zone for, like, two and a half hours," said Jason Baer, who was also in the closet. "I was wondering where the cops were."

Jason said that the teacher asked him, at one point, to peek out the closet window. He saw SWAT officers. "They clapped their hands and all of a sudden rifles were pointed at me," he recalled. "I dropped back down."

Shortly, the students in the closet heard SWAT officers talking about ramming down the door. They called out. They were rescued.

"We ran down the stairs, and there was blood everywhere," Jason said. "We had to jump over dead bodies to get out."

•

Mr. Davis, the sheriff's department spokesman, said the first officers arrived on the scene just three minutes after the initial call to 911. A makeshift SWAT team entered the building 20 minutes later, he said.

Sgt. George Hinkle and his SWAT crew from the Lakewood Police Department moved in at 1:02 P.M. Students had said, via cell phone, that the gunmen were exchanging clothes with the hostages, so every student leaving the building had to be searched, Sergeant Hinkle said. "It was chaos outside," he said, "It was a different sort of chaos inside."

Ms. Alsom, the paramedic, had shared a turkey sandwich on a park bench with her mother, a stockbroker, and then gone into the mall to exchange something that was the wrong size. Moments later, she was speeding toward Littleton, lights blazing, sirens wailing.

"I was being briefed via my pager and on my cell phone and on my radio," said Ms. Alsom, who has been a paramedic for nine years and said was the only one from her department, North Metro, to respond. "The word was multiple gunshots, possible bombing."

The first victim was a young woman "who we thought was probably the worst, at the time," Ms. Alsom explained. She had been shot several times in the abdomen. But they kept coming.

Ms. Alsom was one of the first emergency workers to arrive at about 11:40 A.M. There were three triage centers set up, and the students came through in waves. First, groups of critical patients who had been shot. Then scores of escapees with cuts and scrapes and sprains. Then a lull. Then hundreds more students, some struggling to breathe after hours in hiding.

"We had neighbors coming out with blankets, with Band-aids, four by four gauze," she said. "They were bringing kids into their homes, giving them beverages." It was 6 P.M. before Ms. Alsom left the scene.

"I'm just worried about these kids," she said. "I worked in Chicago when I was in college and I witnessed the same thing, and I still have nightmares."

Tuesday night, she said, she did not dare sleep.

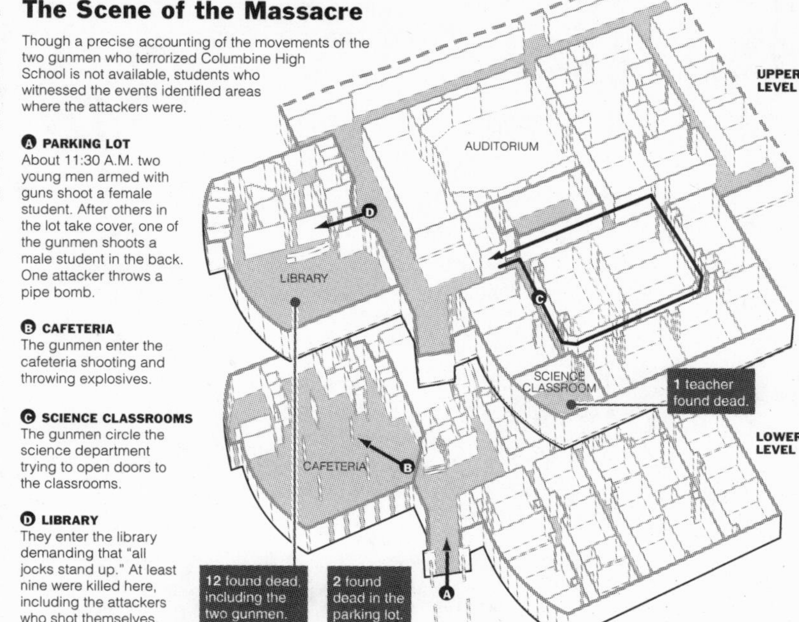

The Scene of the Massacre
Though a precise accounting of the movements of the two gunmen who terrorized Columbine High School is not available, students who witnessed the events identified areas where the attackers were.
A PARKING LOT
About 11:30 A.M. two young men armed with guns shoot a female student. After others in the lot take cover, one of the gunmen shoots a male student in the back. One attacker throws a pipe bomb.
B CAFETERIA
The gunmen enter the cafeteria shooting and throwing explosives.
C SCIENCE CLASSROOMS
The gunmen circle the science department trying to open doors to the classrooms.
D LIBRARY
They enter the library demanding that "all jocks stand up." At least nine were killed here, including the attackers who shot themselves.
UPPER LEVEL
AUDITORIUM
LIBRARY
SCIENCE CLASSROOM
1 teacher found dead.
LOWER LEVEL
CAFETERIA
12 found dead, including the two gunmen.
2 found dead in the parking lot.

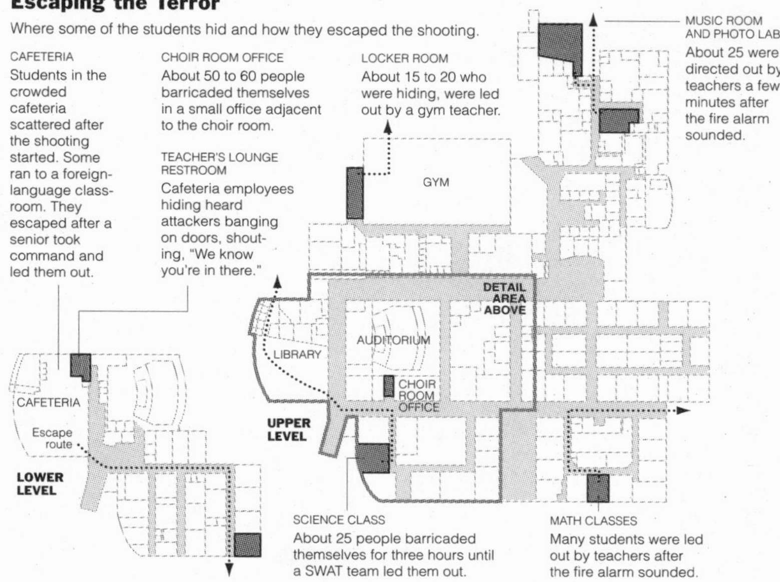

Escaping the Terror
Where some of the students hid and how they escaped the shooting.
CAFETERIA
Students in the crowded cafeteria scattered after the shooting started. Some ran to a foreign-language class-room. They escaped after a senior took command and led them out.
CHOIR ROOM OFFICE
About 50 to 60 people barricaded themselves in a small office adjacent to the choir room.
LOCKER ROOM
About 15 to 20 who were hiding, were led out by a gym teacher.
TEACHER'S LOUNGE RESTROOM
Cafeteria employees hiding heard attackers banging on doors, shouting, "We know you're in there."
MUSIC ROOM AND PHOTO LAB
About 25 were directed out by teachers a few minutes after the fire alarm sounded.
GYM
DETAIL AREA ABOVE
LIBRARY
AUDITORIUM
CHOIR ROOM OFFICE
CAFETERIA
Escape route
UPPER LEVEL
LOWER LEVEL
SCIENCE CLASS
About 25 people barricaded themselves for three hours until a SWAT team led them out.
MATH CLASSES
Many students were led out by teachers after the fire alarm sounded.

John Papasian, Archie Tse and Tom Zeller/The New York Times

THE OVERVIEW

15 Bodies Found as Police Search Colorado School

Continued From Page A1

site," Mr. Thomas said.

Sheriff John P. Stone said that a computer had been seized at a suspect's house, and that they were tracing the E-mails.

An unfathomable set of questions surrounded the motivations of the two presumed gunmen, 18-year-old Eric David Harris and Dylan Bennett Klebold, 17, who were described by many students today as members of a self-styled group of loners and outcasts who called themselves the trench coat mafia after the long black coats they wore and shared a fascination with popular violent video games and an antipathy toward the more popular students that they referred to as "jocks."

Both Mr. Harris and Mr. Klebold were arrested last year for breaking into a car, and parents of another student at the school said that they had complained to the authorities last year about death threats made by Mr. Harris against their son. Nonetheless, school authorities and many students insisted today that they never seriously considered either young man to be inclined toward the horrific violence let loose here on Tuesday.

The incident set off a national bout of soul-searching and debates over whether the killings were spurred by easy access to guns or by the violent images on television and in video games to which American children are routinely exposed. President Clinton said in Washington that "all of us are struggling to understand exactly what happened and why."

The shootings had immediate political reverberations as well: in Colorado and at least two other states, sponsors of legislation expanding the rights to carry guns or insulating gunmakers from lawsuits withdrew those measures today.

The authorities were still so concerned about the possibility of more danger that most of the bodies were removed from the school only this evening. Some were so unrecognizable that parents were asked to bring dental records of their missing children to the school.

It is unclear whether the death toll, which represents the largest school massacre in the country's history but was also a downward revision from the possible 25 deaths that the authorities had considered possible on Tuesday, will rise again as the search inside the school continues. Eleven of the dead are male, including at least one teacher and one black student whom the killers shot in the head.

Sixteen people were still hospitalized, 11 of them in serious or critical condition, a spokesman for the sheriff's office said. A total of about two dozen people were injured.

All day long, under sunny skies that turned slate gray with an approaching storm this afternoon, students gathered near the high school for any news about friends still officially listed as missing. Many were crying or clutching flowers that they brought to a makeshift memorial.

"I can't even imagine walking into that school right now," said 17-year-old Dara Ferguson, a junior, who had three friends whom she feared were dead. "I don't think I ever want to set foot in there again."

Officials with the Jefferson County School District said that the high school building, with hundreds of bullet holes and several inches of water that came from sprinklers that went off after the bombs did, would remain closed for the rest of the school year.

In Alabama and Florida, the school shooting led lawmakers to postpone consideration of bills that would prohibit cities and counties from suing gun makers for the cost of gun violence. The bills, similar to others passed around the country, were introduced at the behest of the National Rifle Association to protect the firearms industry from liability suits.

But at least some politicians said that the violence might have been averted if someone else had been armed at the school.

"Had there been someone who was armed, in this particular situation, in my opinion, it may have stabilized," said Gov. Jesse Ventura of Minnesota, who supports loosening restrictions on concealed handguns. "I believe it supports conceal-and-carry because of the fact that what happens when a group of unarmed individuals are confronted with people with weapons like this, you have no defense."

And Charlton Heston, president of the National Rifle Association, said the incident showed that there should be armed guards in the nation's schools.

"If there had been even one armed guard in the school, he could have saved a lot of lives and perhaps ended the whole thing instantly," Mr. Heston said in Los Angeles today. There was, in fact, an armed guard at the school and he exchanged fire with one of the suspects.

Here in Littleton, a Denver suburb where spiffy housing developments and shopping malls are rising out of farmland that backs up to the foothills of the Rocky Mountains and where many parents say they moved to enroll their students in good and safe public schools, grief and shock were pervasive.

The names of the dead began to filter out this evening, though the authorities said they were not prepared to release an official list. The

After a hail of bullets, a stream of questions.

families of Rachel Scott, 15, and Isaiah Shoels, 18, said that their children had died in the shooting and a teacher, William David Sanders, was widely identified as the faculty member who had died.

Mr. Shoels, who was black, was apparently singled out for killing, said some of the students who survived the library rampage.

"They seemed to seek him out," said Joshua Lapp, a senior at the school who dove for cover with other students in the library. "They went past a row of desks and one of them said, 'Look, there's that little nigger.' Then there were three shots and one of them said, 'Is he dead?' and the other one said, 'Yes, he's dead all right.' "

Crystal Woodman, a junior who was also in the library at the time, told the ABC program "Good Morning America" that the two were laughing as they went about their killing binge.

"They were just, like, they thought it was funny," Miss Woodman said. "They were just, like, 'We've waited to do this our whole lives.' And every time they'd shoot someone, they'd holler, like it was, like, exciting."

In the killers' arsenal, found today at several places in the school, were 30 bombs, including several constructed from propane gas cylinders, a 9-.mm semiautomatic rifle, two pistol-grip shotguns, one handgun and at least 100 rounds of ammunition, said Sheriff Stone. Two or three cars in the parking lot had bombs in them, the authorities said.

"We're not sure two people could carry all that in," he said. "The other scenario could be that maybe that stuff was hidden in the school" over a period of time.

THE TOWN

Day of Violence Threatens Residents' Sense of Safety and Faith in the Future

By DON TERRY

LITTLETON, Col., April 21 — The good life is gobbling up the old life in every direction around here. Where not too long ago there was prairie and small-town America in the shadow of the foothills, now there are new and expensive houses, lush golf courses, shopping malls, multiplex movie theaters and modern walled communities with bygone names like Country Farms and Grant Ranch.

But today, 24 hours after two teen-age boys turned nearby Columbine High School into a killing field, many people here are mourning not just the sons and daughters who were cut down but also the area's old-fashioned sense of safety and maybe even its old-fashioned faith in the future.

"This used to be one of the quietest places in the state," said Kay Chambers, the box officer manager of the Town Hall Arts Center. "Now, it just feels like the world is out of control, that it is a much more violent and dangerous place. When I look at what's going on in Kosovo and Africa and now here, it breaks my heart."

Still, people here say they leave their doors unlocked and most said they had no plans to lock them — yet. There are dozens of homeowner associations, ball fields, tennis courts, a new nature path and three or four forests worth of new houses going up.

Downtown Denver is about 10 miles away and it seems as though every one of those miles is filled with strip malls, fast-food restaurants and commuters.

"There's been so much growth, we can't even get across the street any more," said Marion Nygren, who has lived here for 40 years.

And every summer, this middle- to upper-middle-class city of 40,000 residents holds its Western Welcome Week with hand-cart races, a firemen's tug-of-war and square dancing in the streets.

"It was a great place to grow up," said Jared Smith, 18, after he left flowers outside the high school to remember the dead and wounded. "This is the last community you'd think something like this would happen."

Littleton was founded in 1890, and its early residents were mostly farmers and gold prospectors. The first industry in town was the Rough and Ready grain mill on the South Platte River, where baptisms were sometimes performed.

After World War II, ranching and farming

Some find the good life has become a world out of control.

gave way to electronics and the aerospace industry, still a factor today, and Littleton's population began to skyrocket, making long-time residents like Marty Garcia a little worried that perhaps Littleton was moving too fast.

"It's still nice, but it used to be a whole lot nicer," said Mr. Garcia, the owner of a barber shop in the older downtown section of Littleton. "Today, people are moving so fast that they just don't seem to take the time to pass the time of day with their neighbors. Maybe if we did, maybe if we looked out more for each other, we could prevent some of these tragedies."

Columbine High's mailing address is in Littleton, but the school is actually in unincorporated Jefferson County. The school accepts students from around the area, and almost everyone refers to its location as Littleton. Today here and in Denver almost everyone was in mourning as school sessions were canceled, sporting events rescheduled and flags lowered to half staff.

"We will get through this," said Rich Couris, who has lived in Littleton for just a few years after his employer transferred him here from Southern California. His daughter, Kristin, is on the Columbine lacrosse team.

"It's a real hodge podge of incomes, talents, education," Mr. Couris said of Littleton. "It's a great mix and we love it."

There is little racial diversity. The area is overwhelmingly white and heavily Republican, said Bill Babcock, the director of the Town Hall center, who grew up in Denver and has lived here since last July. "It's a very conservative area," Mr. Babcock said. "I used to think that I was the only Democrat in town."

Tony Amaro, who is Hispanic, moved to the area from California in 1992 after being transferred by the Union Pacific Railroad. Although Mr. Amaro said there had been a few times when he felt hostile stares from white residents, by and large, he said he and his family had not encountered racism here.

That is why he was a little surprised at some reports — still not confirmed — that the teen-age gunmen wanted to shoot the few black and Hispanic students who attend Columbine High.

"This whole thing is mind boggling," Mr. Amaro said. "I can't believe that somebody didn't see this coming, that somebody didn't see that these kids were so troubled."

Mr. Amaro came back to the school today with his daughter, Crystal, 17, who attends Columbine and saw a friend get shot.

"She was helping a girl who was shot," he said. "When she got home, she found blood on her boots, her pants. We just tossed everything in the garbage. We're going to take her to counseling in a few minutes. She just wanted to come by for another look. None of us can believe this happened."

The police were still collecting evidence at Columbine today. But once the school reopens, Andrea Grimm, 17, a senior, said she would be one of the first in line to go back to class. Miss Grimm was also there when the killing spree began and watched in horror as one victim staggered and then fell bleeding on the floor.

"I'm going back to graduate," she said. "That's my main goal."

"All the News That's Fit to Print"

The New York Times

Late Edition
New York: **Today,** mostly sunny and windy, high 58. **Tonight,** clear and cold, low 37. **Tomorrow,** abundant sunshine, high 52. **Yesterday,** high 64, low 44. Weather map is on Page C16.

VOL. CXLIX . . No. 51,698 | Copyright © 1999 The New York Times | NEW YORK, SATURDAY, NOVEMBER 6, 1999 | $1 beyond the greater New York metropolitan area. | 75 CENTS

U.S. JUDGE DECLARES MICROSOFT IS A MARKET-STIFLING MONOPOLY; GATES RETAINS DEFIANT STANCE

Help Wanted, Meaning Help Can Be Fussy

Workers Hop From Job to Slightly Better Job

By PETER T. KILBORN

ROANOKE, Va. — Not so long ago, most people were wary of leaving a job. Whatever its faults, they had too much at risk, like their seniority, security and benefits. But these times of prosperity and low unemployment have changed all that. Now, for the most part, people do not lose jobs. Jobs lose them.

For three and a half years, Joya Patsel, who is 19, worked for a Hardee's restaurant here. "They kept me at $5.50 the whole time," she said. "I quit." Now, she said, "I've been at McDonald's about five weeks. They started me at $6.25 and worked me up to $6.75."

Scott Marshall, 22, earns $11 an hour, or about $22,000 a year, installing heating and air-conditioning systems. He wants a higher wage, a shorter drive to work and a more empathetic boss. In late October, he called four companies like his own, and all were encouraging. "They all said just come in and fill out an application," he said.

Businesses are desperate for workers, and workers know it. Emboldened by that knowledge, they often bolt for nothing more than a shorter drive, more flexible hours, a marginal increase in pay or an employer's latest lure: the sign-on bonus. At the Roanoke office of the Virginia Employment Commission, for example, counselors originally trained to help the unemployed are busiest now helping fully employed

Continued on Page A11

COMING ON SUNDAY

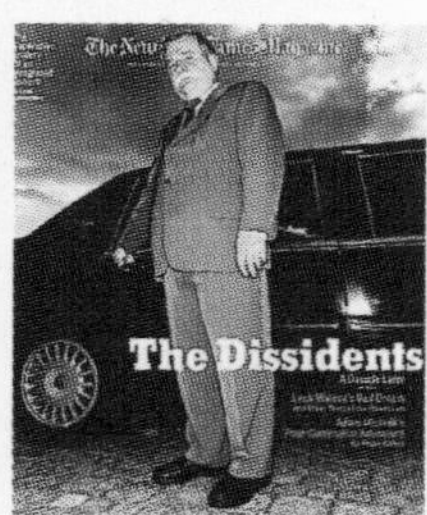

A DECADE LATER

Ten years after the revolution, Solidarity's main strategist is friends with his old enemies and enemies with his old friends. No one said post-Communism was going to be easy. *A report by Roger Cohen in The Times Magazine.*

Plus: Lech Walesa, Jerzy Urban and others on life after the collapse of Europe's wall.

Daily News Error: $100,000 Dreams Turn to Nightmare

By ROBERT D. McFADDEN

Mary Ann Ronga's heart began to pound as she rubbed the boxes on The Daily News "Scratch 'N' Match" game yesterday. One, two, then three boxes matched, indicating that the Staten Island housewife had won $100,000. "I sat there looking at it for 25 minutes," she recalled. "I couldn't believe my eyes."

Beverly Lasoff, a secretary at 1199 of the health and hospital workers union in Manhattan, also scratched off the game boxes and discovered she had won $100,000. Visions of that mink coat danced in her brain. "I had people in the office look at it to make sure I wasn't hallucinating," she said.

Joe Winegrad, a retired telephone worker, scratched off the boxes at home in Brooklyn. He stared at them, flabbergasted, and he recalled: "I said to my wife, 'Maybe I'm not looking at this right. You read the numbers.' It was incredible. We had won $100,000! She began talking about getting the downstairs finished."

Like thousands of other dreamers yesterday, Mrs. Ronga, Ms. Lasoff and Mr. Winegrad called the game's "hot line" to validate their winnings

Continued on Page B2

MOST 8TH GRADERS IN NEW YORK CITY FAIL STATE TESTS

FEARS ON PROMOTIONS

Questions Raised on Quality and Curriculum Statewide in the Middle Schools

By ANEMONA HARTOCOLLIS

A large majority of New York City eighth graders have failed to meet tough new state standards on tests in mathematics and English, raising questions about the quality and content of the curriculum in middle schools.

A 77 percent failure rate in mathematics, combined with a 65 percent failure rate in English, both announced by state officials yesterday, cast doubt on whether many students in years to come will be able to earn a high school diploma under equally rigorous statewide Regents tests required for graduation, educators said.

Forty-eight percent of New York City eighth graders scored in the bottom of the four categories in math, meaning that they had barely moved beyond elementary addition and subtraction.

The new tests caused dismay even in the state's affluent suburbs and rural areas, where 54 percent of eighth graders failed to meet state standards in mathematics and 46 percent failed to do so in reading.

From Kentucky to Massachusetts, more and more states are in the middle of a drive to set and enforce standards that are based on more rigorous and objective tests of hard knowledge. New York is being closely watched as a laboratory for the most demanding approaches.

In future years, New York City will use the new state tests to determine whether students are promoted to the next grade, but city officials said they will also weigh other factors like classroom work and attendance.

The tests whose results were announced yesterday were intended exclusively for New York and the scores were based not on a comparison to how a national average of students perform — the way New York City's own reading and math tests have been — but on a judgment about what children should know, such as elementary algebra, the Pythagorean theorem, finding means and medians and calculating proba-

Continued on Page B7

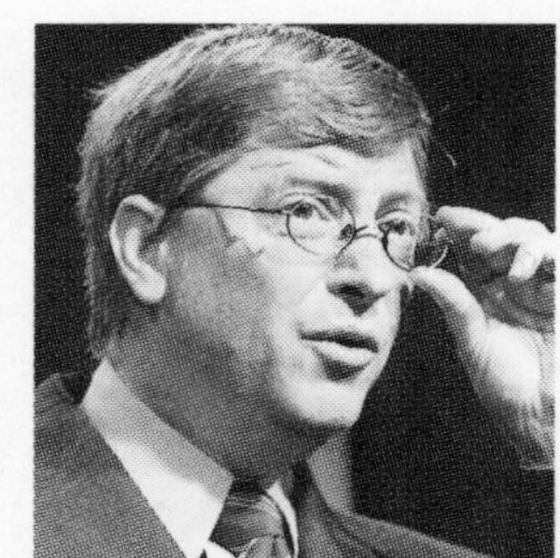
Larry Davis for The New York Times

William H. Gates

Shana Raab for The New York Times

Judge Thomas Penfield Jackson
Man in the news, Page C1

The Court's Findings

MONOPOLY

Microsoft enjoys so much monopoly power that "it could charge a price for Windows substantially above that which could be charged in a competitive market."

UNNECESSARILY LINKING PRODUCTS

"The preferences of consumers and the responsive behavior of software firms demonstrate that Web browsers and operating systems are separate products."

ANTICOMPETITIVE PRACTICES

"Through its conduct toward Netscape, I.B.M., Compaq, Intel and others, Microsoft has demonstrated that it will use its prodigious market power and immense profits to harm any firm" that challenges it.

CONSUMER IMPACT

"The ultimate result is that some innovations that would truly benefit consumers never occur for the sole reason that they do not coincide with Microsoft's self-interest."

NOT A FINAL RULING

Court Says Arguments Offered by Company Are 'Specious'

By JOEL BRINKLEY

WASHINGTON, Nov. 5 — The judge in the government's antitrust trial against the Microsoft Corporation issued a broad denunciation of the software giant this evening as the first part of his verdict in the landmark case.

The judge, Thomas Penfield Jackson of Federal District Court, said the company had used its monopoly power to stifle innovation, reduce competition and hurt consumers.

"Most harmful of all is the message that Microsoft's actions have conveyed to every enterprise with the potential to innovate in the computer industry," Judge Jackson wrote in his 207-page findings of fact.

"Through its conduct," he added, "Microsoft has demonstrated that it will use its prodigious market power and immense profits to harm any firm that insists on pursuing initiatives that could intensify competition against one of Microsoft's core products."

Judge Jackson's findings of fact clearly show that he found the government's case against Microsoft credible and rejected as "specious," as he stated in one part, virtually all the arguments Microsoft put up in its defense.

The findings are the judge's conclusions about who presented the most compelling and believable case during the yearlong trial that opened in his United States district courtroom on Oct. 19, 1998. As such, they clearly signal how he will rule in his final verdict — the determination of whether the facts as he sees them amount to violations of antitrust law.

Microsoft and the government both reacted quickly after receiving the much-anticipated findings this evening.

The Justice Department was jubilant. "This is a great day for American consumers," Attorney General Janet Reno said. "This case is about the protection of innovation, competition and the consumers' right to choose the products they want."

But Microsoft's chairman, William H. Gates, said: "We respectfully disagree with the court's findings. Microsoft competes vigorously and fairly. Microsoft is committed to resolving this case in a fair and equitable manner." He added that his com-

Continued on Page C4

Clear Finding in Blunt Language

Chances to Settle Might Be Limited

By STEVE LOHR

With a 207-page legal document, Judge Thomas Penfield Jackson has fashioned a club and wielded it against the Microsoft Corporation.

News Analysis

In findings of fact that echo almost every one of the Government's accusations in its sweeping antitrust suit against the big software maker, Judge Jackson has concluded that Microsoft is a monopolist that time and again bullied other companies in the computer industry, harming consumers and hindering innovation.

"It's a bad day for Microsoft," observed William Kovacic, a professor at the George Washington University law school. "The judge relentlessly accepted the Government's story of what happened."

At times, Judge Jackson used carefully calibrated legal prose, but at the end of his findings he shifted to uncommonly blunt language.

Microsoft's actions, he said, conveyed the message that the company would use "its prodigious market power and immense profits to harm any firm" that chooses to compete with the company's mainstay products — especially its corporate crown jewel, the Windows operating system, which acts as the equivalent of the central nervous system in more than 85 percent of personal computers sold today.

Before the findings of fact were released yesterday evening, legal experts had expected that Judge Jackson would generally favor the Government but also nod on occasion in Microsoft's direction. He had suggested in the past that he would prefer to broker an out-of-court settlement between Microsoft and the Government. Such an outcome would relieve the Federal courts of the burden of having to make fine-tuned decisions about products and business practices in the Internet economy.

A settlement is still a possibility — but only, it seems, if William H. Gates, the company chairman, and his top lieutenants decide that Judge Jackson has done what no industry competitor ever accomplished: brought Microsoft to its knees.

Yet with these findings, antitrust experts say it is more likely that Microsoft will persevere, hoping that Judge Jackson's final ruling is not such a one-sided rout as yesterday's document might seem to portend. The company's next step might then be to appeal his decision to a federal appeals court and then perhaps the Supreme Court.

"If the judge's goal was settlement, he would have to leave enough

Continued on Page C4

Trying to Heal Old Hatred in Ruins on Danube

By DONALD G. McNEIL Jr.

ESZTERGOM, Hungary — The road north from Budapest ends abruptly at a pale green fence here in Esztergom, on the banks of the Danube. And a good thing, too: the bridge is out. Spans of pale green steel reach to the first pilings in the river from both the Hungarian and Slovak sides, but the three middle supports stand alone. It has been thus for 54 years, since the bridge was blown up by retreating Nazis.

In Novi Sad, Yugoslavia, three more Danube bridges lie in ruins. All were bombed by NATO in the spring to cut Belgrade's links with its northern provinces. A hastily erected orange pontoon bridge has restored land traffic, but the ruins in the river are causing a crisis, cutting off barge traffic and threatening to flood the lowlands if an ice dam forms on the wreckage this winter.

In Lom, Bulgaria, there are some far older ruins; they are all that are left of a bridge built by Rome to link its provinces of Thracia and Dacia, the present-day Bulgaria and Romania. And in the "Iron Gate" between Romania and Serbia, only a plaque marks the spot where the troops of the Roman emperor Trajan built a bridge.

These collections of rubble — twisted snares of steel or algae-covered green stones — are metaphors for the shifting fates of the jigsaw puzzle of countries that make up Eastern Europe a decade after the fall of Communism, and for their tangled relations with one another.

Here in Esztergom, the ruined bridge is a harbinger of a new spirit of amity: Hungary and the Slovak Republic, both eager to earn entry to the European Union by showing that they can embrace their neighbors, have decided to put aside centuries of ethnic animosity and rebuild the bridge by 2001.

The Novi Sad bridges, and the stubborn demands made by those preventing the rubble from being cleared, are part of the shreds left by ethnic hatred in the former Yugoslavia, and the animosity between the Serbs and the outside world.

The long, cranky negotiations between Bulgaria and Romania over where to build one more bridge on their 600-mile river border show how difficult it is for the old order to give way to the new. The Bulgarians want a bridge on the west end of the border to zip trucks quickly from Asia Minor to Western Europe; the Romanians are happy with the old bridge at Giurgiu on the road to Moscow, its former No. 1 ally, because they collect bigger road-use fees by forcing trucks to detour several hundred miles east.

The Danube, the longest river in continental Europe, is a crucial link between the eastern and western forces pulling at mid-Continent. Beyond inspiring Viennese waltzes, it has served as a frontier, separating

Continued on Page A6

Associated Press

A full ferry crossing the Danube past one of the bridges destroyed by NATO air strikes last spring in the Serbian town of Novi Sad.

ONE EUROPE, 10 YEARS
Rebuilding Bridges

Conceding Nothing, Gates Sees Finding As Only One Step

By SAM HOWE VERHOVEK

REDMOND, Wash., Nov. 5 — Smiling stiffly, conceding no predatory behavior whatsoever and insisting that Microsoft's actions had in fact "brought tremendous benefits to millions of consumers," William H. Gates defiantly took issue this evening with a federal judge's finding that the company had engaged in monopolistic behavior.

With the company he co-founded in 1975 under siege from the government, Mr. Gates appeared at a news conference at Microsoft headquarters here barely an hour after Judge Thomas Penfield Jackson issued his finding.

While repeating assertions that Microsoft has always "wanted nothing more than to resolve this case," Mr. Gates, the chairman of the company, yielded no apparent ground on which a settlement might be reached.

"Microsoft competes vigorously and fairly," Mr. Gates said. "Americans should wish that every business was as competitive as the personal computer business."

There was little attempt to put a good face on the judge's findings, which Justice Department officials in Washington were hailing as a smashing victory for their side and for consumers across the country and even around the world.

Instead, the word throughout Microsoft was that this was simply a step in a process that is far from

Continued on Page C5

INSIDE

New School Job for Cortines
The Los Angeles superintendent agreed to resign. Ramon C. Cortines Jr., the former New York City superintendent, will replace him. **PAGE A9**

U.S. Pursues Missile System
The administration said it might go ahead with a missile defense system, even if it meant withdrawing from the 1972 ABM treaty. **PAGE A8**

Moseley-Braun Testifies
Carol Moseley-Braun appeared before a Senate committee as she sought confirmation as ambassador to New Zealand. **PAGE A10**

Updated news: www.nytimes.com

354613

U.S. VERSUS MICROSOFT: Setting the Stage for a Judgment

THE OVERVIEW

U.S. Judge Declares Microsoft a Monopoly That Stifles Industry

Continued From Page A1

pany "operates within the laws and operates in a way that is great for the people we develop software for."

Mr. Gates's comments followed a company statement suggesting that Microsoft was already formulating an appeal.

"While we disagree with many of the findings," the statement said, "we are still confident that the law supports us on these points and that the American legal system will ultimately rule that Microsoft's actions were fair, legal and good for consumers."

Neither Microsoft's statements nor those of the Justice Department offered much likelihood of settling the case. Joel I. Klein, head of the Justice Department's antitrust division, said the government would consider a settlement, but only one that "fully and properly addresses" the issues raised in the judge's findings.

"From the very beginning Microsoft has wanted nothing more than to resolve this case," Mr. Gates said. "Getting this behind us would be a very good thing."

The judge, who in years past wrote his decisions longhand, transmitted the document to both sides by e-mail this afternoon. It was made public at 6:30 p.m., after the stock markets had closed.

In after-hours trading, Microsoft closed down more than $4, at $87, compared with its closing price of $91.5625 during the regular session on the Nasdaq.

Microsoft is expected to seek grounds for appeal, should Judge Jackson eventually rule against the company. But Microsoft's lawyers will have to find grounds in law or precedent because the judge's findings of fact are virtually impervious to appeal. Under federal court rules, appeals courts must give great weight to the conclusions the trial judge draws from hearing the testimony and studying the witnesses as they offer their accounts.

As a result, appeals courts are allowed to challenge findings of fact only if they are "clearly erroneous." And if the judge's verdict is largely based on which witnesses he believed, the verdict stands a better chance of withstanding appeal.

At the outset of his findings, the judge declared that Microsoft "enjoys monopoly power in the relevant market." This is a key assertion because under antitrust laws monopolies cannot engage in practices that would be legal for other companies. The government's charges rested on the assumption that Microsoft has a monopoly in the operating systems market with it Windows operating systems. In a key test for monopoly power, Judge Jackson concluded that Microsoft could charge almost any price for Windows without fear that price increases would reduce demand.

Microsoft expended considerable energy in court arguing that it was not a monopoly. It asserted that a host of small competitors — from the Be operating system to Palm Pilot personal organizers — were long-term threats. But Judge Jackson dismissed those arguments, saying that competition from those competitors was, at the very least, a long way off.

"That day has not arrived, nor does it seem imminent," he wrote of one such claim.

"Microsoft's monopoly power," he concluded, "is also evidenced by the fact that, over the course of several years, Microsoft took actions that only could have been advantageous if they operated to reinforce monopoly power."

From there, the judge ran through each of the charges raised by the Justice Department and the 19 state attorneys general who joined in the suit. In each case, he endorsed the government's charge while rejecting Microsoft's rebuttals.

He found that Microsoft had tried to divide the market for Internet browsing software with the Netscape Communications Corporation in 1995 — a key charge in the government's case and a clearly illegal activity under antitrust law. He wrote that other companies had had similar encounters with Microsoft, and "these interactions demonstrate that it is Microsoft's corporate practice to pressure other firms to halt software development" that threatens Microsoft's dominance "or competes directly with Microsoft's most cherished software products."

He found that Microsoft's decision to bundle its Web browser with Windows and give it away free was not, as Microsoft asserted in court, simply an effort to add a desirable feature to Windows.

"Senior executives at Microsoft decided Microsoft needed to give its browser away in furtherance of the larger strategic goal of gaining market share," he wrote. Microsoft, he added, "viewed browser market share as the key to preserving its dominance."

And in one of his most damning findings, Judge Jackson concluded that "Web browsers and operating systems are separate products." Microsoft's key argument was that its browser was simply a feature of Windows, not a separate product.

He turned that argument around on Microsoft by finding that the company had actually harmed consumers by bundling the two products. Consumer harm is a key test in antitrust cases. Bundling the browser with Windows "unjustifiably jeopardized the stability and security of the operating system." With this he meant that including the browser had made the operating system more likely to crash and more vulnerable to break-ins by intruders. "There is no technical justification for Microsoft's refusal to meet consumer demand for a browserless version of Windows 98," he added.

He wrote that Microsoft had threatened and bullied Apple Computer, Intel, America Online and other companies that Microsoft perceived as competitors. In the case of the International Business Machines Corporation, he wrote, "when I.B.M. refused to abate the promotion of those of its own products that competed with Windows and Office," Microsoft's suite of business productivity software, "Microsoft punished the I.B.M. PC Company with higher prices, a late license for Windows 95 and the withholding of technical and marketing support."

"Microsoft's past success in hurting such companies and stifling innovation deters investment in technologies and businesses that exhibit the potential to threaten Microsoft," the judge concluded. "The ultimate result is that some innovations that would truly benefit consumers never occur for the sole reason that they do not coincide with Microsoft's self interest."

Judge Jackson's final verdict is expected in late December or early January, after which he may hold hearings on possible remedies, if the verdict goes against Microsoft. Proposed remedies could range from relatively minor adjustments in the company's contracts and business practices to more drastic measures like breaking Microsoft's operating system and applications divisions into separate companies.

Antitrust lawyers say they cannot recall another instance in which findings of fact in an antitrust case have been issued ahead of the actual verdict. "I've been at this for 40 years, and I've never heard of anything like this," said Stephen Axinn, an antitrust litigator at Axinn, Veltrop & Harkrider in New York.

Usually the findings are packaged with the conclusions of law — the legal precedents justifying a ruling — and the verdict. But Judge Jackson's decision to separate the findings offers at last two benefits.

"It's potentially a very clever thing to do," said Robert Litan, a former senior official in the Justice Department's antitrust division, now with the Brookings Institution.

For one thing, it will allow Judge Jackson to modify his final ruling if written responses from the litigants suggest to him that he might be standing on weak ground.

Publishing the findings ahead of the verdict also "prompts the parties to try to settle," said Andrew Gavil, a professor at Howard University.

Judge Jackson has repeatedly urged Microsoft and the government to settle the case. Though the two sides have held fitful discussions during the trial, they remain far apart, and most lawyers and analysts watching the case are not hopeful that they will settle, even with today's strong findings in favor of the Government.

Shana Raab for The New York Times

Janet Reno listens as Joel I. Klein of her antitrust division answers a question. To Mr. Klein's left are Richard Blumenthal, attorney general of Connecticut; David Boies, the lead trial lawyer; Phillip R. Malone, another trial lawyer, and A. Douglas Melamed, Mr. Klein's deputy.

THE FUTURE

Filings, Hearings and Decisions: Next Phase of the Case

The publication of Judge Thomas Penfield Jackson's findings of fact yesterday began a rolling series of filings, hearings and decisions that could bring the case to a close by early next year.

Next, Judge Jackson will ask **Microsoft** and the Justice Department to file conclusions of law. These are the legal arguments and precedents that give the ruling its legal basis. Assuming Microsoft and the government do not settle the case in the meantime, these filings will probably be due by early December.

By publishing his findings of fact ahead of the two sides' conclusions of law — the reverse of the normal schedule — Judge Jackson may find that he is given documents that are more useful for his purposes.

That is because the filings are likely to be aimed directly at the conclusions in Judge Jackson's findings of fact. Normally, the litigant's conclusions of law are simply legal elaborations of the cases they have advocated in court.

Soon after Judge Jackson receives these filings, he will issue his final verdict, probably in January. It will include his own conclusions of law and his decision on whether Microsoft is guilty — or "liable," in antitrust terms — on some or all of the counts in the government's suit.

If Microsoft is found liable, proceedings will be scheduled to establish the penalty, or "remedy," perhaps as soon as February.

Judge Jackson is expected to request briefs and hold a hearing. At the hearing, the Government will advocate its proposed remedy, and Microsoft will counter with its own proposal.

The judge has not said whether the two sides will be allowed to call witnesses. But in the end he will decide the remedy, and he is not bound by the proposals the litigants offer him.

In this circumstance, Microsoft is almost certain to appeal to the United States Court of Appeals and the Supreme Court — a process that could take two years.

NEW ANALYSIS

A Clear Finding In Blunt Language

Continued From Page A1

at the end of his findings he shifted to uncommonly blunt language.

Microsoft's actions, he said, conveyed the message that the company would use "its prodigious market power and immense profits to harm any firm" that chooses to compete with the company's mainstay products — especially its corporate crown jewel, the Windows operating system, which acts as the equivalent of the central nervous system in more than 85 percent of personal computers sold today.

The judge's findings of fact are preliminary step and not a final ruling. But they form the all-but-unshakable foundation and framework for the outcome of the case — either a legal judgment or a settlement. A court's legal judgment can be routinely overruled by a higher court on appeal. But findings of fact can be overturned only in the rare instance when the higher court finds a "blatant contradiction" between the written record of the case and a judge's finding.

"Judge Jackson has poured a lot of concrete here," said Mr. Kovacic of George Washington University.

The scope of the defeat that Microsoft suffered yesterday is illustrated by the way Judge Jackson dealt with one of the Government's main allegations: that Microsoft had tied its Web-browser software to its industry-standard Windows operating system merely to thwart the challenge posed by Internet software makers, especially the Netscape Communications Corporation, the commercial pioneer in software used for browsing the World Wide Web.

Microsoft had replied that it simply made a product-design decision to include browsing software in Windows, rather than make it a separate product. The company noted that it

'It's a bad day for Microsoft,' says a legal scholar.

had added new features to Windows over the years, a strategy that it said had helped consumers by making computers easier to use.

Indeed, this product-tying claim by the Justice Department and 19 states who jointly sued Microsoft had appeared to suffer a sharp setback shortly after the suit was filed in May 1998. A month later, a federal appeals court ruled in a related case that Microsoft should be free to blend its browser into Windows as long as it can make a "plausible claim" of business efficiency or consumer benefit from doing so.

Despite the very high hurdle the appeals court had put in the way of a product-tying claim, Judge Jackson proceeded to find one. "In conclusion," he wrote on that subject, "the preferences of consumers and the responsive behavior of software firms demonstrate that Web browsers and operating systems are separate products." After reviewing Microsoft internal E-mail and licensing deals, he concluded that Microsoft had decided to "bind" its browser to Windows and give it away free mainly to hobble its rival Netscape "rather than for any pro-competitive purpose."

As his product-tying finding showed, Judge Jackson has accepted not only the Government's version of events but also its theory of the case. The Justice Department had consistently argued that while Microsoft operated in the high-technology economy, it was an old-fashioned monopolist. The practices at issue, the Government charged, are similar to those used since the turn-of-the-century days of smoke-filled railroad cars — threats and restrictive business contracts forced on other companies.

Microsoft argued that the Government was launching an assault on the company's right to make its own product decisions, protect its own intellectual property and innovate as it saw fit. And the Government, Microsoft insisted, simply did not understand how the fast-paced software business worked.

But Judge Jackson agreed with the Government, and found Microsoft to be an old-fashioned monopolist.

THE LITIGATORS

Government Lawyers Say Facts, Not Strategy, Proved Case

By DAVID STOUT

WASHINGTON, Nov. 5 — Justice Department lawyers savored a resounding victory this evening in their case against **Microsoft**, a victory that one official attributed not to any brilliant strategy but to the simple truth.

"This is a great day for American consumers," Attorney General Janet Reno said, declaring herself pleased that the court had agreed with the government. "This case is about the protection of innovation, competition and the consumers' right to choose the products they want."

Joel Klein, head of the antitrust division, exulting in a 207-page decision that found for the government on virtually every important point, said, "Facts are stubborn things."

Asked if he thought Microsoft had made any strategic errors during the trial, Mr. Klein said: "Theatrics are always interesting, and there were some fun moments in this trial. I think this case was about the evidence."

Mr. Klein's comments notwithstanding, the Justice Department's lead lawyer in the Microsoft case, David Boies, is one of the most highly regarded litigators in the country. At first, Mr. Boies shied away from the microphone. "I had my shot in the courtroom," Mr. Boies said, smiling broadly.

But Richard Blumenthal, the attorney general of Connecticut, who worked closely with the Justice Department, encouraged Mr. Boies to say something. "You're the man," Mr. Blumenthal said. "Go ahead."

Then Mr. Boies indicated that he, too, thought the outcome had less to do with strategy and more to do with facts. "In some senses, this is not a surprise," he said. "In a lot of ways, this is exactly what the evidence showed."

Pronouncing himself "enormously pleased" with the decision, Mr. Klein said it showed that "in America, no person and no company is above the law."

Mr. Blumenthal had some of the harshest words for Microsoft, asserting that the opinion by Federal Judge Thomas Penfield Jackson had portrayed "a predator that has misused its monopolistic power."

Some of the most damning evidence against Microsoft was furnished by Microsoft itself, Mr. Blumenthal said, in its internal e-mail and other records that he said proved the company is a monopoly determined to remain a monopoly.

Mr. Blumenthal recalled that, early on, he had likened the suit to D-Day in its complexity and far-reaching implications. "Today, we have established a solid beachhead," he said.

Like Mr. Klein, Mr. Blumenthal said he would not rule out any remedy to break up Microsoft's hold on the software industry. But Mr. Klein deflected a question to compare the case against Microsoft to another landmark antitrust case, the one that reconfigured the nationwide telephone system.

"Each market and each case presents its own facts," Mr. Klein said. While he did not say so, the case against the telephone system was played out about two decades ago, when personal computers were a novelty and virtually no one had heard of the Internet.

Pressed on what kind of remedies the government might now pursue, and whether it might go so far as to break up Microsoft, Mr. Klein said it was far too early to dismiss any. Whatever they are, he said, he hopes today's finding will deter other monopoly-minded companies.

Several state attorneys general whose offices assisted in the case expressed elation at the ruling. "The opinion is really a clean sweep for the perspective we presented at trial," said Attorney General Eliot L. Spitzer of New York State.

Attorney General Tom Miller of Iowa said he was glad the judge had zeroed in on what he called Microsoft's ruthless discouraging of innovation in the computer industry.

Mr. Blumenthal of Connecticut called antitrust law "the Magna Carta of consumer protection." He added, "I would wager that these findings of fact will be used in law school classes around the country to demonstrate what happens when the antitrust laws are flagrantly violated."

Mr. Klein saw another reason to hold up the Microsoft case as an example. Only about a year and a half elapsed from the start of the case to today's finding — lightning speed for such a complex case, by the usual standards of the law.

The attorney general of California, Bill Lockyer, said he expected the decision to "unleash powerful engines of innovation and consumer benefit."

"California is so impacted by the colossus of Microsoft, and so many businesses were impacted and felt that their competitive opportunities were smothered," Mr. Lockyer said. "Silicon Valley is cautiously cheering."

There was good reason for his use of "cautiously." Appeals lie ahead. Microsoft is a powerful adversary with deep pockets — not as deep as the government's, but deep enough to wage a long fight, if it chooses.

And Microsoft did not get to be Microsoft by shrinking from the battlefield.

Text Tomorrow

Key sections of the judge's findings of fact will appear in The Times tomorrow. The text is available on The New York Times on the Web, at www.nytimes.com.

"All the News That's Fit to Print"

The New York Times

Late Edition
New York: **Today,** sunny, high 50. **Tonight,** increasing clouds, low 41. **Tomorrow,** sprinkles then partial sun, high 56. **Yesterday,** high 43, low 34. Weather map appears on Page C16.

VOL. CXLIX . . No. 51,254 NEW YORK, SATURDAY, JANUARY 1, 2000 — $1 beyond the greater New York metropolitan area. — 75 CENTS

1/1/00

Yeltsin Resigns; Putin Takes Over; Elections in March

President Boris N. Yeltsin stunned his nation with a New Year's Eve resignation, concluding a tempestuous political career on the same note of surprise and high drama that accompanied his entire path from an early convert to perestroika to the erratic master of a free but foundering Russia.

Mr. Yeltsin, 68, said he was vacating the presidency to clear the way for "smart, strong and energetic people."

That meant Vladimir V. Putin, 47, the most popular of a string of prime ministers Mr. Yeltsin had named in hopes of finding a malleable and viable successor. A former KGB official who has won great popularity for waging the war in Chechnya, Mr. Putin was named acting president with the blessing of the Russian Orthodox Church.

One of Mr. Putin's first presidential decrees was to grant Mr. Yeltsin immunity from any future prosecution — a critical action, given the charges of high corruption swirling around the Kremlin.

Beset in recent years by heart problems and purported drinking and assailed for the corruption and the sad state of the Russian economy, Mr. Yeltsin is also certain to be remembered as the man who faced down the Communists from atop a tank.

In elections now set for March 26, Mr. Putin is, for now at least, the undisputed front-runner.

8-Day Hijacking Ends And Hostages Are Safe

The hijackers of an Indian Airlines plane won the release of three prominent militants jailed in India. All of them sped away from the airport in Afghanistan, trying to get out of the country. The names and nationalities of the hijackers are still unknown. With the release, more than 150 haggard passengers, kept on board for eight days, were freed unharmed. They flew to New Delhi, for family reunions, both wrenching and joyous.

The Top World News, Page A11

Chang W. Lee/The New York Times

TIMES SQUARE Up to two million people packed midtown Manhattan for a 26-hour marathon of music, fireworks and confetti. Events around the world, Pages A2-10.

Computers Prevail in First Hours of '00

By STEVE LOHR

Despite a few sputters and glitches, the world's computers appear to have survived the year 2000 rollover without major problems — and with humanity's faith in technology intact, at least for another day.

As clocks passed midnight around the world, there were a flurry of reports of apparently minor problems: a timing device at a electric plant in Wisconsin jumped ahead 35 days, but it was quickly reset; a monitoring system at a Japanese nuclear plant malfunctioned, but it did not affect the operation of the reactor; in Australia, ticketing machines on some buses jammed.

The technology failures with greater impact were a result of crowding — circuits jammed when too many people tried to make cellular phone calls in Japan, New Zealand and elsewhere — instead of computer software that could not fathom the year 2000.

Yet the day arrived without the kind of catastrophic problems once feared, of widespread power failures or planes crashing. The computers of the United States power grid and air-traffic control system rolled over to the New Year just past 7 p.m. Eastern time, which is midnight Greenwich Mean Time, and things went without a hitch.

"I've never felt there was any significant chance the United States would have any problem in its infrastructure," said John A. Koskinen, chairman of the President's Council on Year 2000 Conversion. But he cautioned against complacency in the United States and around the world. "There are likely to be some glitches along the way," he said.

The real test, experts say, will come in the days and weeks ahead as people return to work, as factories, offices and stores begin normal oper-

Continued on Page A10

Associated Press

BALI Romance blossoms in bubbles at a disco.

Past, Present and Future in One Stroke

An Essay on 'Millennium,' a Defiant and Elusive Notion

By RICHARD EDER

"But where are the snows of yesteryear?" the poet François Villon asked in the 15th century, not even halfway through the millennium we are making a fuss about leaving. Nothing new under the sun, though in his case it was not an early global-warming alert but a lament for departed loveliness. Nothing new there either.

Maybe the past is prologue, but here at the changing of the hundred-and thousand-year guard, prologue is chiefly the past. The flood of writing on the subject, including this additional teacupful, looks back more than forward. "Millennium" has a great gong sound, but is it the gong announcing the end of an era or summoning the one to come? The first is bronze, the second is tin.

If the past is another country where things are done differently, as L. P. Hartley put it, at least it *is* a country, with features, memories good and bad and maybe lessons to be drawn. The future is no country at all. At best it is a reservation made through a fly-by-night travel agency that may send us quite otherwise than we'd planned, or go out of business overnight and no refunds.

History, we are told, is the use the present makes of the past for the sake of the future. This millennial looking-ahead is the use the present makes of the future for the sake of the past — to salute or at least to confirm it. Hey, we call out ahead to the year 3000 while stuffing a time

Continued on Page A5

Associated Press

MOSCOW A lighted sky over a changing Kremlin.

SPECIAL TODAY

The Millennium

Envisioning the future of politics, people, cities and machines — even the front page of The Times — and reflecting on the past. **SECTION E**

INSIDE

Dow 3 Million, or Bust?
The stock market: where it's been, and might be going. **PAGE C1**

Correction, 102 Years Later
The issue number on this page was wrong until yesterday. So was an article in 1995 about No. 50,000. The Times regrets its math. **PAGE A22**

Elliot Richardson Dies
The official who would not fire a Watergate prosecutor for President Richard M. Nixon was 79. **PAGE B7**

Associated Press

PARIS An explosion of colors at the Eiffel Tower.

A Glittering Party For Times Square

Gleeful Embrace of a New Year Links the Globe's Midnights

By ROBERT D. McFADDEN

Two thousand years after Christ's obscure birth in a dusty town in Judea, the world's six billion people — most of them non-Christian and many of them preoccupied with terrorism, computers, diets, bank accounts, politics and the perils of the future — rode their turning blue planet across time's invisible line today and, by common consent, looked into the dawn of a new millennium.

What they saw first was a party. It was garish, glittering and global, and millions, setting religious considerations and personal concerns aside, joined in the festivities to celebrate the conjunction of a new year, a new century and a new thousand-year cycle of history. They also put aside the inconvenient fact that the millennium, technically, is still a year off.

It hardly mattered. In Times Square and across the United States, in Europe, Asia, Africa and Australia, in cities and towns all over the world, bells pealed, crowds shrieked and surged, skyrockets soared into the night, fireworks burst into supernovas, "Auld Lang Syne" rang out, lights pulsed, loved ones and friends embraced, and the music and Champagne flowed.

On a rainbow day whose moods ran the spectrum from tensions and prayers to euphoria and irresistible hyperbole, what most were calling Christianity's Third Millennium arrived in 24 stages as the earth revolved through the time zones and midnight elapsed again and again in an around-the-clock, around-the-world series of golden moments that began at the international date line in the Pacific and raced westward across Asia, Africa, Europe and the Americas.

In New York, a vast crowd of revelers — the guesses ran as high as an improbable two million — packed Times Square and much of Midtown Manhattan for the biggest public event ever held in the city — a 26-hour, $7 million marathon of music, fireworks, confetti and deafening voices as a 1,070-pound crystal ball descended at midnight and the crowds roared berserkly, while the police sweated out an enormous potential for trouble.

And there were lavish celebrations in Washington, London, Paris, Rome, Berlin, Jerusalem, Moscow, Cape Town, New Delhi, Shanghai, Beijing, Tokyo, Mexico City, Rio de Janeiro, Buenos Aires and hundreds of other cities. There were parties, concerts, dances, torchlight parades and televised extravaganzas that brought the worldwide show to billions more at home, and back to the crowds in Times Square over giant video screens — a case of celebrators watching celebrators.

To a Martian Earthwatcher (tuning in with delicate ear and Cyclopean eye), it might have appeared that the inhabitants of the third world from the Sun had suddenly lost their

Continued on Page A6

1/1/00

FROM BALI TO BROADWAY

A Glittering Party for Times Square as Midnight Ticks Across Globe

Continued From Page A1

Edward Keating/The New York Times

BIG NUMBERS, SQUARED Estimates of the crowd in Times Square ran to an improbable two million. Regardless, a huge mass of people greeted 2000.

Nicole Bengiveno/The New York Times

ONCE IN A LIFETIME At the stroke of midnight, there were fireworks, brilliant lights and cacophony. There was also a big celebration in Times Square.

senses or gone to war again. But it was only humanity on the threshold of a new age, exercising its primal urge to celebrate.

There had been an avalanche of happy millennial overkill in recent days — claims of the last-game, last-meal, first-baby kind — and yesterday it was the turn of world leaders in government, religion, science and other fields, who spoke of the millennium's meaning in more serious tones.

"Today, we celebrate more than the changing of the calendar," President Clinton, extending millennium greetings to the world, said in an address to diplomats and children from 100 nations. "We celebrate the opportunity we have to make this a true changing of the times, a gateway to greater peace and freedom, to prosperity and harmony."

In Moscow, Boris Yeltsin, who has been plagued with heart and other problems for most of his eight years as Russia's president, unexpectedly announced his resignation. "Russia must enter the next millennium with new politicians, with new personalities and with new smart, strong and energetic people," he said. "And we who have been in power for many years must go."

At the Vatican, Pope John Paul II, fulfilling his dream to lead the Roman Catholic Church across the threshold of 2000, gave his blessing to a vast crowd in St. Peter's Square, reiterated his calls for an end to war and poverty, and thanked God for "the events of this year, this century and this millennium."

There were millions around the world who had no reason to be festive, people like Tom Nganga, 40, who lives in Kangemi, a vast slum of Nairobi, Kenya. "We as Kenyans and people of Kangemi are very, very angry as we celebrate this millennium," he said. "People are very poor. People have nothing to eat. We have nothing to celebrate."

While the millennium celebrations drew millions, there were relatively few casualties. In the Philippines, two people were killed by stray gunfire and a 5-year-old boy died after a firecracker exploded in his face. At least 200 other Filipinos were injured by fireworks. In Paris, 70 people were hurt in crowds.

After years of concern over Y2K computer problems that had cost billions of dollars to fix, there were no immediate reports of computer-related disasters anywhere in the world, no plane crashes, major power failures, nuclear plant shutdowns or collapses of banking, business, government or health care systems.

But elevators, intercity trains and subways in many American cities and in other countries as well were halted briefly over the witching hour, and some airlines canceled flights for the day, just to be safe. Many airports were all but deserted, with wary travelers staying put. Experts said it might take days for some computer problems to develop, in part because many businesses and government agencies were closed for the holiday weekend.

There had also been fears that terrorists, publicity seekers or the insane might set off explosions or mount chemical or biological attacks as millions gathered to celebrate, while vast audiences watched on television. No specific threats had been reported, although some suspects had been seized recently. Still, there were no immediate reports of trouble, and law enforcement authorities seemed ready for almost anything.

The millennium, an idea with overtones ranging from Biblical to commercial, had swelled recently into a coercive miniculture as the countdown ticked away and a flood of books, articles, television specials and studied commentaries by academic, political and religious leaders reflected upon the last thousand years of human achievements and missteps, and speculated on the next thousand.

Purists still insist that the millennium will not start until Jan. 1, 2001, and they have a point. Centuries and millennia have always ended with the last day of the "zeros" year. But it is all a muddle, because the calendar, at best, is arbitrary. There were problems from ancient times based on inaccuracies in measuring the year's duration and its uneven division into days, weeks and months. By 1582, the spring equinox was 10 days early, and the days were dropped when the Gregorian calendar replaced the old Julian version. While Pope Gregory's calendar uses the birth of Christ in 1 B.C. as a starting date, many scholars now suggest that the year was probably closer to 4 B.C.

In any case, as Voltaire noted, history is the lie that historians agree upon, and the tide of popular opinion — always impatient for early results — swept nearly everyone along in recent months. And with the climax of the celebrations, and especially when the nines rolled into zeros at midnight and humanity went ballistic, purists' talk of technicalities was the last thing anyone wanted to hear.

For doomsayers who had prophecied conflagrations, earthquakes, volcanic eruptions and other end-of-the-world scenarios (and kept a weather eye out for U.F.O. rescue ships), the new millennium was something of a nonevent, although the anxiety prompted by all the wild predictions of chaos was real enough.

The Book of Revelations, Chapter 20, speaks of a resurrection of the dead and a Judgment Day, of sinners cast into a lake of fire and Christ reigning for a thousand years. But if it was not the Second Coming of Jesus as foretold in the Bible, there was still a year to go, or this was the wrong millennium.

And if, as some said, even the idea of a Third Christian Millennium was a Western conceit in a world where Christians are a minority, and one that overlooked other calendars calling this 1420 (Muslim) or 5760 (Jewish), it was also true that the world had long ago come by economic and social necessity to agree upon the Western calendar for trade, travel and other common purposes.

The millennium, if nothing else, was a celebration of history, marking human survival after a deadly century of wars, genocide and revolution that saw the end of colonialism, fascism and communism, as well as the achievements of the past thousand years — printing and widespread literacy; the exploration of the last frontiers on earth; the first ventures into outer space, the inner mind and the microscopic universe, and the flowering of democratic government, and of art, literature, science, technology and communications into undreamed eminences.

The world on this Millennium Day was still beset with terrible problems — with grinding poverty that afflicted a third of its 6 billion inhabitants, with ethnic and national strife, with the continuing curse of racial and religious bigotries, and with the exclusion of millions from adequate health care, education, jobs and even such basic needs as shelter and clean water, not to mention freedoms of speech and political association.

But with a few exceptions — notably threats of terrorism and limited wars in the Balkans, Chechnya and other regions — it was a world largely at peace, with the apocalyptic threat of nuclear annihilation receding and new understandings growing between old enemies in the Middle East, Ireland, South Africa and other long-troubled areas.

And it was a world on the threshold of a new era — one that offered visions of astounding strides in science and technology and seemed to hold out anew the ancient promises of universal peace and prosperity, although the only certainty seemed to be that the world a thousand years from now would be unrecognizable.

As Dec. 31, 1999 gave way to Jan. 1, 2000, in each time zone at midnight, with atomic clocks marking it to a millisecond, celebrators went ecstatic. It began in Fiji and the Kiribati and Marshall Islands in the Western Pacific (it was 7 a.m. E.S.T. yesterday) and moved westward, hour by hour, as the earth turned and 23 more midnights fell across Australia, Asia, Europe, Africa, the Americas and back across the Pacific, ending in Samoa at 6 a.m. E.S.T. today.

Islanders in Kiribati welcomed the millennium with the mournful sounds of a conch shell and with traditional chants and dancing on the beach of a normally uninhabited coral atoll, dubbed Millennium Island.

In Japan, which has absorbed many of the trappings of the Western world while preserving its own cultural and religious traditions, bells tolled in a Buddhist ritual to dispel evils as thousands flocked to temples and shrines. In Tokyo, people went to parties and crowds swarmed to bayside events, including rock concerts and lavish fireworks.

In China, torchbearers in Imperial-era costumes lighted signal fires on the watchtowers of the Great Wall, which snakes 3,000 miles from the Gobi Desert to the North China Sea, and President Jiang Zemin lighted an eternal flame to greet the new millennium and pledged a "great rejuvenation" by reuniting with Taiwan. Over Hong Kong Harbor there were brilliant fireworks displays, and parties abounded, a prelude to the Chinese New Year, the Year of the Dragon, which starts Feb. 5.

The festivities for most of India's one billion people were muted by comparison with those in wealthier nations, but hundreds of thousands danced, drank and ate at open-air stalls in New Delhi and partygoers were out in force in other cities, celebrating the peaceful end of an eight-day hostage crisis on an Indian Airlines jet hours before midnight.

Iran and its Persian Gulf neighbors largely ignored the new millennium, which fell during the Islamic holy month of Ramadan, a time for prayer and reflection.

In Israel, where religious tension is high at the best of times, security was heavy as three religions and some doomsday cultists marked the occasion, each in its own way. It was especially tight on Jerusalem's Mount of Olives, where Christian fundamentalists had camped to witness the end of the world, and at the Old City's Temple Mount, with sites sacred to Muslims and Jews.

On the last New Year's Eve of the Christian millennium, observant Jews ushered in the Sabbath, as they do every Friday, and many went to pray at the Western Wall, Judaism's holiest site, while 400,000 Muslims flocked to Al Aksa Mosque on the Temple Mount to mark the last Friday of prayer and fasting in the holy month of Ramadan.

With religious bans on celebrations that might desecrate holy days, the celebrations in Israel were relatively subdued. In Palestinian-governed Bethlehem, the town revered by Christians as the birthplace of Jesus, 2,000 doves were released at midnight on Manger Square, and in secular Tel Aviv, thousands just went to the beach to watch the sun set over the Mediterranean.

In Paris, with new lighting on buildings, boulevards and bridges over the Seine twinkling like the bonfires of a great medieval encampment, people packed the Champs-Élysées from the Tuileries to the Arc de Triomphe as a digital clock at the Eiffel Tower counted down — overcoming an old-fashioned glitch that shut it down five hours before midnight — and announced the millennium in a burst of 20,000 electronic flashes.

In London, two million people lined the Thames for a spectacular fireworks show, while Queen Elizabeth, Prime Minister Tony Blair and other dignitaries gathered under the 20-acre Millennium Dome, a flying-saucer-like colossus at Longitude Zero in Greenwich, to mark the transition while the bells of St. Paul's and Westminster and churches across Britain pealed. Huge street parties were held in hundreds of Britain's cities.

In Egypt, floodlights, lasers and fireworks illuminated the ancient pyramids at Giza and electronic music reverberated over the desert as 50,000 people wined and dined in luxurious tents and watched a sparkling millennium show under the watchful eyes of police officers on camels.

Elsewhere, there were torchlight parades in the streets of Stockholm; fireworks and singing by massed choirs in Reykjavik, Iceland, and Helsinki, Finland; concerts and a ball at the opera house in Tallinn, Estonia; enormous street parties in Edinburgh, Scotland, and a Millennium Ball at the Catherine Palace in St. Petersburg, Russia.

In the United States, huge festivities were held on the Washington Mall, and in New Orleans, Chicago, Miami, Los Angeles, Boston, San Francisco and other cities.

In New York, it was a day to remember. The centerpiece was the spectacle billed as "Times Square 2000: the Global Celebration at the Crossroads of the World." Worried authorities had closed 50 blocks of Midtown to traffic, banned alcohol in open containers and flooded the area with 8,000 officers just in case. All vehicles were towed away as a precaution against car bombs.

Throughout the city, 37,000 of New York's police officers were on duty, and there was plenty for them to survey. The Times Square celebration was only one of 329 public events in the city, the biggest of the others at Grand Army Plaza in Brooklyn, at Flushing Meadows-Corona Park in Queens, at the Bronx Zoo and in Central Park and Bryant Park in Manhattan.

The celebration in Times Square went off as planned with all-day, all-night pulsing music and cacophonous entertainments by 1,000 musicians, actors, dancers, puppeteers and other performers working from a stage on Seventh Avenue between 45th and 46th Streets.

Broadway, curving like a dancer's leg, was packed from 42nd Street to Central Park, along with most of the side streets between the Avenue of the Americas and Eighth Avenue. The old wickedness of Times Square was missing, but for most in the crowd it was an adventure just to be caught, shoulder to shoulder, jostling for happiness at the intersection of past and future.

The show ran all day and all night, from 6 a.m. yesterday to 8 a.m. today, and thousands showed up early to stake claims near ground zero. By the time the sun went down, the crowds were already gigantic. They came in shoals from the suburbs, from across the nation and from countless places abroad, and they swept into the vast clogged carnival, determined to experience the exotic and illusory evening.

They were in a euphoric mood, capped and scarved and padded like armadillos against the cold. They watched twilight print the sky with darkness, and the blue night city come to life, glittering like a tiara. By midevening, much of Midtown was seized up in human gridlock. Laser lights slid up the skyscrapers and washed over the writhing mass of Lilliputian figures below.

The crowds were squeezed into police-barrier pens to create lanes for emergency vehicles, and many had to watch events on giant video screens. The closer to 1 Times Square, where the ball descended, the more bleary the crowd looked, many having stood their ground for a day and a half. A stench arose from a layer of garbage underfoot that included pizza and other less identifiable things.

The tradition of celebrators' watching others celebrate was continued on a global scale. Live video from festivities around the world were pumped into Times Square, and the scenes there were beamed by 45 networks out to a worldwide audience of a billion people.

It was all perfect for television — the images clear and colorful, reducing everything, even the millennium, to entertainment. There were no distracting speeches by dignitaries striking the just-right crystal phrases; indeed, the program — including an international pageant that, hour by hour, reflected the countries where midnight was then occurring — was deliberately languageless.

That, too, was perfect for this crowd, which seemed preoccupied with itself: people taking pictures of each other, fussing with food, gawking at the neon forest, looking for Peter Jennings and paying little attention to the pageant of Japanese yogi-bushi umbrellas, Sri Lankan monk chants, Russian ballerinas, Kenyan war dancers, Argentine rain forest butterfly puppets and Lakota Sioux in face paint.

But the crowd got into the spirit of things, screaming numbers as the final seconds of the failing millennium were counted down. The tensions that had been building for weeks reached a climax, and there was an inescapable sense of a great public moment at hand, one that most generations could never experience.

On center stage, the buckram face of Mayor Rudolph W. Giuliani, proud as a drum major, stood at the controls of the descending ball with Dr. Mary Ann Hopkins, 36, who was being honored for her work in war-torn countries as a volunteer in Doctors Without Borders.

And when midnight struck, the roar was deafening: a din of horns, amplified music and countless voices shrieking at the edge of madness. In the chaos, lasers zoomed, flashbulbs sparkled, a blizzard of confetti and streamers and balloons filled the air, and in the distance a blinding dazzle of fireworks exploded.

They sang, "Auld Lang Syne," and the joyous screams and congratulatory embraces went on and on. The fireworks, too, went on and on — over the East River off South Street Seaport, in Central Park, in Brooklyn's Prospect Park — the biggest pyrotechnic display in history — a booming, sparkling, scintillating barrage of rockets and sunbursts that bathed the awed faces in eerie light and echoed off the facades of a city that seemed to exist only in the imagination.

THE NEW YORK TIMES
229 West 43rd Street New York, N.Y. 10036-3959
Home Delivery Information:
1-800-NYTIMES (1-800-698-4637)

The New York Times (ISSN 0362-4331) is published daily. Periodicals postage paid at New York, N.Y., and at additional mailing offices. *Postmaster:* Send address changes to The New York Times, P.O. Box 3009, South Hackensack, N.J. 07606-1009.

Mail Subscription Rates*	1 Yr.	6 Mos.
Weekdays and Sundays	$452.40	$226.20
Weekdays	265.20	132.60
Sundays	234.00	117.00
Times Book Review	54.60	
Large Type Weekly	78.00	

Higher rates, available on request, for mailing outside the U.S., or for New York edition outside the Northeast: 1-800-631-2580. *Not including state or local tax.

"All the News That's Fit to Print"

The New York Times

EARLY EDITION

Sunday: Mostly cloudy, high 57. Decreasing cloudiness at night, low 47. Monday, partly sunny, high 62. Weather map, Page 37.

VOL. CLXIX .... No. 51,367 NEW YORK, SUNDAY, APRIL 23, 2000 $3 beyond the greater New York metropolitan area. $2.50

CUBAN BOY SEIZED BY U.S. AGENTS AND REUNITED WITH HIS FATHER

Drug Firms Reap Profits On Tax-Backed Research

By JEFF GERTH and SHERYL GAY STOLBERG

MEDICINE MERCHANTS

Birth of a Blockbuster

On Jan. 7, 1982, in a laboratory at Columbia University, a little-known science professor, Laszlo Z. Bito, finished a nine-month experiment on the eyes of cats. In his handwritten data, carefully charted in gray hardcover notebooks, lay the origins of what every pharmaceutical company longs for: a blockbuster drug.

The drug is Xalatan, a best-selling eyedrop for glaucoma. With $507 million in sales last year — and the potential for billions more, most of it pure profit — the four-year-old medicine is the equivalent of liquid gold for its manufacturer, the Pharmacia Corporation. The eyedrop earned Columbia University about $20 million in royalties last year, and it has made a millionaire of Dr. Bito as well.

Yet there are other, unseen, partners in the creation of Xalatan: the American taxpayers, who backed Dr. Bito's work with $4 million from the National Institutes of Health. The taxpayers have reaped no financial return on their investment; their reward, government officials say, is the eyedrop itself.

Xalatan costs patients $45 to $50 for a tiny bottle that lasts six weeks. That price — about $1 a day for a drug that staves off blindness — may not seem excessive. But the key ingredient in that daily dose costs Pharmacia only pennies to make, and Americans, who live in the only industrialized nation that lacks government restraints on drug prices, pay more than twice what European patients pay for the drug.

That puts Xalatan out of reach for patients like Albert Russell, a retired optician and part-time blues singer from Prince George's County, Md. Mr. Russell, whose glaucoma has left him nearly blind, lives on an $832-a-month Social Security check. He is among the one-third of elderly Americans who lack prescription drug coverage, and when he talks about Xalatan, he uses the word "outrageous" to describe its price.

To officials at Pharmacia, the price is fair. "We are bringing forth innovation," said Dr. Anders Harfstrand, the company's vice president for ophthalmology, "and innovation always brings a premium."

In this election year, the cost of prescription medicines is at the center of the political debate. With the biomedical revolution yielding a flood of new therapies, drugs are now the fastest-growing component of the nation's trillion-dollar-a-year medical bill. As Congress contemplates expanding Medicare to include prescription drug coverage, and some states move to bring drug prices more in line with those in foreign countries, the industry is struggling to fend off federal regulation that might limit its ability to set prices.

This drug to fight glaucoma, developed with government help, is not cheaper because of it.

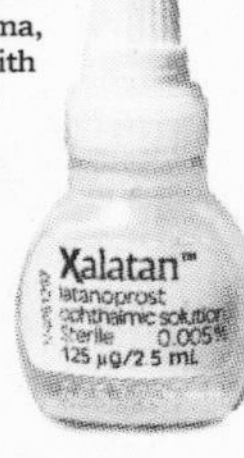

Continued on Page 26

Federal Welfare Overhaul Allows Albany to Shift Money Elsewhere

By RAYMOND HERNANDEZ

ALBANY, April 22 — In the four years since the overhaul of the nation's welfare laws, New York has taken at least $1 billion given to it by the federal government for new antipoverty programs and used it instead to indirectly finance huge tax cuts and other programs that appeal to middle-class voters, according to government and private estimates.

The budgetary switch has been employed by other states, prompting Congress to open an investigation to determine the scope of the practice nationwide. But New York, with the nation's second-largest welfare population, appears to be among the most aggressive states in using its federal welfare dollars to help pay for other programs it would otherwise find difficult to afford.

To date, New York has taken in roughly $6.1 billion in federal welfare funds and earmarked about $5 billion of it — there is some disagreement as to the exact figure — to finance traditional programs for the poor, like public-assistance grants. But it has spent very little of the remaining money to create programs intended to help welfare recipients make the transition to permanent employment, as proponents of the new federal welfare law had intended.

Instead, the state used that money, as much as $1.3 billion by some estimates, for welfare programs that the state and local governments once financed themselves. That has freed up an unprecedented amount of state money that has been used to help pay for politically popular programs, from a host of new tax cuts to fiscal relief for cash-strapped local governments.

The situation represents a missed opportunity, say advocates for the poor, who have been urging the state to invest its welfare money in the kinds of innovative antipoverty programs envisioned by proponents of the welfare overhaul, including in-

Continued on Page 30

INSIDE

Updated news: www.nytimes.com

Courtesy of Juan Miguel González via Associated Press

Juan Miguel González held his son Elián yesterday at Andrews Air Force Base, near Washington, in a photo released by the family's lawyer. Mr. González's wife, Nersy Carmenate Castillo, held their 6-month-old son.

OUTRAGE IN MIAMI

Youth Is Reported Calm After Tense Moments in Little Havana

By RICK BRAGG

MIAMI, April 22 — Armed United States immigration agents smashed their way into the Little Havana home of Elián González's Miami relatives before dawn today, took the sobbing 6-year-old boy from a bedroom closet and flew him to a reunion with his father outside Washington.

As demonstrators wept in rage and coughed from pepper spray and tear gas, the agents wrapped the child in a blanket and carried him to an airport to fly him to Washington. The action touched off a fury in the streets outside the Miami home where Cuban exiles have kept a vigil since November.

"What's happening? What's happening?" Elián said in Spanish as he was taken away. "Help me. Help me."

The agents, wearing shirts with the words "INS FEDERAL AGENT" in bold yellow letters, ended a bitter standoff between Miami's exile community and a federal government that stopped fruitless negotiations with the child's defiant great-uncle and a community that saw Elián as a symbol of freedom and a precious victory, now perhaps lost, over President Fidel Castro of Cuba.

"God, how could you have performed only half a miracle," said a frantic, weeping Marisleysis González, a 21-year-old cousin who had been the boy's closest companion since he was rescued at sea on Nov. 25 on a failed crossing from Cuba that drowned his mother.

The United States Justice Department said this morning that Elián was taken safely from the home at about 5:10 a.m. and was flown to Andrews Air Force Base near Washington, where his father, Juan Miguel González, waited.

Later in the morning, Mr. González was seen carrying Elián from a car at the base.

"They are together," said Myron Marlin, a Justice Department spokesman. Photographs released by Mr. González's lawyer showed a beaming Elián, joined by his father, stepmother and infant half-brother. The family was taken to an undisclosed location in Maryland, where they could be assured of privacy, officials said.

Elián, one Justice Department spokesman said, was subdued and calm on the flight from Miami, as federal agents gently explained what was happening.

As pockets of unhappy Cuban-American demonstrators clashed with the police here this afternoon, the distraught Miami relatives, claiming they wanted to assure themselves that the boy was happy and safe, boarded a plane from Miami to Washington, seeking a meeting with Mr. González, who had not yet decided whether to grant one.

Attorney General Janet Reno told reporters this morning that she had tried until the final moment of the standoff to try to find some other way that father and son could be reunited, but no agreement could be

Continued on Page 16

90 Miles Away

Castro's revolution has divided many Cuban families, but none as publicly as Elián González's feuding clan. MAGAZINE

For Reno, a Difficult Call in the Last Minutes

By DAVID JOHNSTON

WASHINGTON, April 22 — Their self-imposed deadline was 5 a.m., and as the minutes ticked away before federal law-enforcement officials had to decide whether to seize Elián González at gunpoint, Attorney General Janet Reno was on the phone to the boy's Miami relatives, appealing to them one last time to end the impasse.

"You are running out of time," an aide to the attorney general recalled Ms. Reno as having said, describing her voice as emphatic but laced with emotion and fatigue after all-night negotiations. "You've got to decide now," Ms. Reno said. "That's all the time you have."

With that, as Ms. Reno held the phone in her office at the Justice Department, a team of eight agents, some of them armed and wearing body armor and jumpsuits, swarmed into the house of Elián's great-uncle, Lázaro González. It was just the kind of raid, armed and confrontational and carried out under darkness, that the officials had said for weeks was the situation they wanted to avoid. In fact the image of an armed federal agent flushing the boy from a closet was displayed on television through the day.

Within three minutes the agents were gone, taking the child to a waiting minivan, ending a five-month-long custody battle that had haunted Ms. Reno, who had tried, and repeatedly failed, to conclude the case without the use of force.

This morning after the raid, President Clinton said Ms. Reno had made the right decision and that he supported her. "The law has been upheld," he said, "and that was the right thing to do."

"She made the decision," Mr. Clinton said. "She managed this. But I fully support what she did. And it was clear to me from our long conversations that we were in agreement about this." He added, "I think she did the right thing and I'm very pleased with the way she handled it."

Federal law-enforcement officials, who had scheduled the operation for today, had said that they had to begin the operation no later than 6 a.m., when traffic lights in the area would change from flashing amber to the normal red and green and when crowds were expected to gather. Operational commanders had informed Ms. Reno that the order to go ahead had to be given no later than 5 a.m. in order to carry it out today. At about 4 a.m., she warned representatives of the relatives that time had all but run out. "At one point she said, 'Don't make us do what we don't want to do,' " an aide said. " 'We're going to take a law-enforcement action and we don't want to do it.' "

The plan, which agents had rehearsed for nearly two weeks, hinged on their ability to carry out a lightning raid, with little warning to local authorities, who federal authorities

Continued on Page 17

Wilfredo Lee/Associated Press

Elián González, as he was carried out of the home of his Miami relatives yesterday by agents of the Immigration and Naturalization Service.

In Japan, Start-Up and Risk Are New Business Watchwords

By STEPHANIE STROM

TOKYO, April 22 — Starting this week, music fans across Japan will be stepping up to a gadget that resembles a souped up, stand-alone automated teller, plugging in a blank minidisk, dropping in some coins and, 30 to 40 seconds later, walking away with their favorite recordings. And they will not be limited to just a few selections; thanks to a super-fast, high-capacity digital connection to a central computer, thousands upon thousands of popular songs will be potentially available at the touch of a few buttons.

No more long waits. No more illicit downloading of MP3 files. Just music fast, simple and cheap.

It's called a Music POD, and while it may seem like just another plaything for Japanese teenagers, it is in fact a powerful representation of the tectonic shifts taking place in the economy here.

What the Music POD embodies is the entrepreneurial vision of a 30-year-old college dropout and the business skills of a 40-something former salary man, founders of a young company called V-Sync. They are the sorts of men who five years ago would have toiled anonymously inside a major corporation, climbing the ladder of seniority and keeping their dreams tightly locked up in their heads.

But today changes in the relationship between employer and employee, the liberalization of the financial markets and the explosion of new business models in the freewheeling arenas of the Internet and information technology are spawning a whole new breed of entrepreneurs who care little for the conventions that have dominated Japan Inc. for decades.

"I don't want to be a gear turning the wheels of a big company," said Katsuma Fujii, V-Sync's chairman and the younger of its co-founders. "It's difficult for a lowly gear to get his bosses to listen to, let alone accept, his out-of-this-world ideas in a traditional Japanese corporation. I want to do what I want to do."

While the number of start-ups that can be counted is still low in comparison with the United States, venture capitalists say they began detecting a significant increase in activity last year that is continuing today despite the weak economy. The number of initial public offerings was up for the first time last year since the peak in 1995, and the percentage of those companies that were less than 10 years old was the highest it had ever been, according to Jafco, Japan's largest venture capital company.

Japan, of course, has always been a nation with many small businesses, despite its image as the land of corporate leviathans manned by regiments of salary men. And what gets forgotten is that some of those leviathans — Honda, Kyocera and Sony, to name a few — were spawned by visionary entrepreneurs.

But the economic structure that evolved after World War II, with its heavy emphasis on government-directed bank lending, its punitive tax

Continued on Page 6

THE ELIÁN GONZÁLEZ CASE: Time Runs Out

THE OVERVIEW

Cuban Boy Seized by Agents And Reunited With Father

Continued From Page 1

reached.

Ms. Reno also defended the decision to use force, and armed agents, saying there were reports that people in the crowd or the neighborhood had weapons.

She had no other choice, she said, but to order the raid on the home of Lázaro González. "Elián is safe and no one is seriously hurt," she said.

This does not mean Elián is on his way back to Cuba. Under an order by a three-judge panel of the United States Court of Appeals for the 11th Circuit, in Atlanta, Elián's father cannot take the boy home before a decision in a hearing on Elián's application, filed by his relatives, for political asylum. The hearing is scheduled for May 11.

But at the two-bedroom house in Little Havana, where Elián has lived under the constant watch of television cameras and eyes of demonstrators who have turned him into an almost saintlike presence as well as a prize in the 41-year-old cold war with Mr. Castro, people wailed, sank to the ground and cursed the United States government for what it had done.

"They're animals," screeched Marisleysis González to the swelling crowd this morning.

While exiles here have kept vigil in anticipation of such a raid for months, the timing — the morning after Good Friday and the day before Easter in a heavily Roman Catholic community — and the violent, sudden nature of it, left them in as much disbelief as rage.

A crowd of demonstrators had slowly dwindled overnight from hundreds to about 50 people, some sleeping behind police barricades, when three white, unmarked vans sped down the dark street and stopped in front of the house.

"They're here! They're here!" demonstrators shouted.

About 20 agents of the Immigration and Naturalization Service leaped from the vans, tore through a chain link gate, broke through the front door and, with brandished automatic weapons, stormed through the tiny house in search of Elián. The Justice Department said that eight immigration agents actually went into the house to retrieve the boy.

Cesar Camejo, a cousin of Lázaro González, was in the house with the family watching television as they agents burst in. "They held Marisleysis down and told her not to move in Spanish," said Mr. Camejo. The agents shouted at the others not to move or interfere, as Marisleysis pleaded: "Don't take the boy. Don't take the boy."

ANGRY MARCHERS, ANGRY MAYOR

Demonstrators marched in Union City, N.J., to protest the removal of Elián González, which was also denounced by Mayor Rudolph W. Giuliani. The Metro Section, Page 32.

The boy was hiding in a closet in the arms of Donato Dalrymple, one of the two fishermen who rescued Elián from the Atlantic Ocean and has been constant presence at the house.

An agent in helmet and body armor, holding an automatic rifle, pulled the boy from Mr. Dalrymple's arms. The agent, Mr. Dalrymple said, pointed the rifle at him as Elián cried "No! No!. No!"

An Associated Press photograph, sent around the world, showed the gun close to Elián's face, but Ms. Reno said the barrel was never pointed at the boy, and the agent's finger was not on the trigger, and the photograph bears out that description.

The boy was handed to a female agent who cradled him in her arms and, with help from another agent, raced out into the din and confusion of the street outside and quickly into the side doors of a van.

A few protesters tried to form a human chain to block the front of the house and keep the agents from taking the boy. Ramon Saul Sanchez, an exile in Miami who has become the leader in the demonstration, said he was struck by an agent's gun butt. He bled from an ear as a young man held him upright.

Moments after Elián was taken from the bedroom closet, he was aboard a plane and headed for Washington and his father. A female United States immigration agent comforted him.

"This may seem very scary," the agent said in Spanish. "It will soon be better."

Within minutes of being reunited with his father, Elián was "totally at ease," and laughing withhis father, Juan Miguel's second wife and their infant son, said Gregory Craig, the lawyer for Mr. González.

Ms. Reno called for giving father and son privacy to become reacquainted. They were to stay for a time at Andrews Air Force Base and then move to an undisclosed location in the Washington area.

"Let us give him and his father the space, the calm, the moral support they need to reconnect and reaffirm their bond between father and son," Ms. Reno said.

Agents had whisked Elián to nearby Watson Island, where they boarded a helicopter to Homestead Air Force Base in southern Miami-Dade County.

A doctor examined him there, and ensured that the boy had not been injured in the transfer.

Continuing an extraordinary voyage for a boy who was shipwrecked off Florida and had never flown before, Elián was then put on a United States Marshals Service plane for Washington.

Once aboard, the female immigration agent comforted Elián, the officials said. She was joined by a psychiatrist, a flight surgeon and the Immigration and Naturalization Service agent who had led the rescue operation.

"All of our reports so far are that the child has been very calm, has not been anxious, has not been thrashing, has not been crying," said Doris Meissner, Immigration and Naturalization Service commissioner. "And the basic feedback that we have from a series of people now, who have been directly with him, is that he is a real terrific, tough kid."

Elián was offered a few toys: some Play-Doh, an airplane, a map and a watch, an administration official said.

Few details had been ignored.

The female I.N.S. agent at Elián's side, whose name was not released for security reasons, soothed him with prearranged words cleared by psychologists. He was offered food and drink. Experts had recommended the Play-Doh as the "best thing that you can do for a child who might be experiencing stress," Mrs. Meissner said.

Juan Miguel González rushed to Andrews in a convoy of vans to await Elián's arrival. Juan Miguel had been staying at the residence in Bethesda, Md., of Cuba's top diplomat in the United States.

"They need more space," Mrs. Meissner said. "And they need more privacy."

Mr. Craig, the attorney, reiterated Juan Miguel González's pledge to remain in the United States while the boy's Miami relatives seek a political asylum hearing on his behalf.

Mr. Craig said that he had merely to witness the warmth of the father-and-son reunion to conclude that "something terrible was done" by keeping them apart for nearly five months.

It apparently came as a shock to the family in Miami. The family had thought that negotiations would continue, said family members and their lawyers, but Ms. Reno said that it was obvious that the family was not going to budge.

President Bill Clinton said this morning that "the law has been upheld."

"When all efforts failed," Mr. Clinton said, "there was no alternative but to enforce the decision by the I.N.S. and federal court that Juan Miguel González have custody of his son.

"I think that it was the right thing to do," Mr. Clinton said. "I am very pleased with the way she handled it."

But in Miami, people compared the raid to communist Cuba and swore that the United States government would regret its actions.

"We never expected the federal government to come in like they did, like thieves in the night," said Carlos Brito, a demonstrator who has been outside the house almost every night for months. "I've always been proud of being an American but this morning I wish I were a citizen of any other country. I've always defended this country, but to take this boy in the middle of the night? Today, the federal government has betrayed me."

Rosa de la Cruz, 58, said she was knocked to the ground by an armed man, near a gardenia bush in front of the house. "I was praying," Ms. Cruz said.

"Janet Reno was lying the whole time," she said.

Outside the house, in the minutes after the raid, three young men held each other and sobbed. One woman sat in a ditch, crying, and holding her face in her hands. People rushed back and forth yelling, but not sure who to vent their anger on. An American flag was flown upside down in disrespect.

In the city, protests gradually swelled as groups for blocks around the house burned tires in intersections and snarled traffic by standing or marching in the road. Protesters punched and kicked at spit at the police and hurled bus benches into streets, which soon clogged with backed-up traffic, ambulances and fire trucks.

Protesters blocked the access roads to the Miami International Airport, and traffic backed up for miles. An apparently abandoned house burned near the downtown.

The police made several arrests as of noon, but earlier in the morning as the raid was being conducted, they appeared to have no uniform presence at the house. Miami police had stood watch at the house for months, but as the federal agents moved in, there seemed to be no uniformed officers there to aid with the operation, though one Miami officer was reportedly in one of the vans. That could not be confirmed.

Only several minutes later, after the federal agents had left, did Miami police move in.

Miami Mayor Joe Carollo said he had not been told about the raid, but that was not a surprise. Mr. Carollo has made it clear that he sides with the exile community in this fight.

The exile community in Miami, Mr. Carollo said, is "destroyed, emotionally destroyed."

Miami-Dade Mayor Alex Penelas, who had also sided with the exile community here, said he had not heard about the raid until after it was over, also. Mr. Penelas had pledged that his officers would not aid the federal government in any attempt to take Elian.

But later in the day, as smoke drifted over Miami, police from both Miami and Miami Dade responded to try and keep the peace.

Al Diaz/Associated Press

Attorney General Janet Reno, responding to accusations that an agent held a gun to Elián González's head, said a photograph showed that the agent "pointed to the side, and that the finger was not on the trigger."

Inside the House

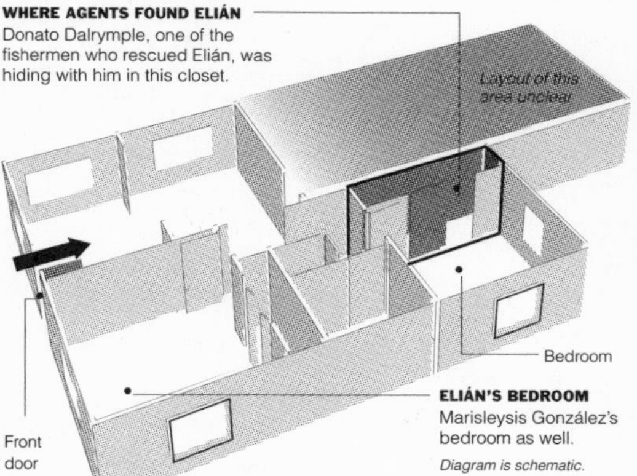

The New York Times

Ending a bitter standoff between Cuban-Americans and Washington.

Associated Press

Elián González, at the center of this television image, was carried yesterday to a building on Andrews Air Force Base, near Washington.

THE CUBANS

Havana Outwardly Calm but Privately Gleeful After 'Rescue' of a Native Son

By RANDAL C. ARCHIBOLD

HAVANA, April 22 — They are calling it the rescue of Elián.

"Through a police operation, Elián González was rescued from his kidnappers in Miami," was how the excited commentator on Cuban state radio described it 90 minutes after the raid, an unusually swift delivery of news.

But as this city awoke to the news that United States agents had taken Elián from the Miami home where he has stayed with relatives opposed to President Fidel Castro, the streets appeared calm and normal. The government here had broadcast warnings not to celebrate because "that could negatively affect the outcome of the case."

Later this morning, the government issued a statement saying: "The fight for Elián González has not ended. But the reunion with his father is a favorable step."

Cuban radio reported jubilation in the neighborhood of Juan Miguel González, Elián's father, who has spent two weeks in the United States seeking the return of his son.

Cuban radio carried a telephone interview from Cárdenas, the seaside city two hours east of Havana that is Elián's hometown, with a man the station identified as Juan Miguel's father, Juan González. He said Juan Miguel woke him around 6 a.m. to tell him that Elián had been taken from the Miami home and was on his way to a reunion.

"There is tremendous happiness here — a great deal of emotion we are feeling here," Juan González said. He said Juan Miguel told him he was "very happy and a little nervous" about his first encounter with Elián after five months.

A neighbor said people gathered in the streets to share the news but were now "calmly waiting for what is going to happen next."

There were no spontaneous celebrations in Havana. Such displays are rare in a country that has no law guaranteeing freedom of assembly. But markets, bus stops, parks and other gathering places, nevertheless, were abuzz with the news though many wondered just when Elián would return to Cuba.

"They took him out!" a friend passing on a bike called to Abdul Hernández, as he waved back from his perch on a park bench.

"Yes, my friend, this news makes us very happy," Mr. Hernández said turning to a visitor. "After how many months? Five. The United States is the most powerful country in the world and they could not do this sooner."

Neither he nor other residents seem fazed by the forceful manner in which Elián was removed, a source of boiling anger in Miami.

There even seemed a bit of glee, as Cuba's two television stations, which are state-run, broadcast CNN footage of Marisleysis and Lázaro González, Elián's cousin and great-uncle in Miami, weeping.

"We just saw the face of betrayal and defeat of Lázaro González," said the commentator in front of a large poster of Elián's face behind a fence, with the caption: "Return our boy!"

Cuban television by midmorning began broadcasting footage of the raid, the demonstrations in Miami, Attorney General Janet Reno's news conference translated into Spanish, and by late morning, the news that the boy and father had been reunited.

The newly built José Martí grandstand, which sits next to the United States Interests Section, the de facto American embassy, stood vacant this morning guarded as always by a couple of police officers.

Nearby, however, people talked. "Elián now is with his father and soon he will be in Cuba," said a woman sweeping her walk, who seemed unaware that a court order prevents the boy from leaving the country until a court rules on whether he deserves an asylum hearing. "I imagine he will readjust quickly and be a Cuban again." Another woman said she did not look forward to endless displays that she figured are inevitable when the boy returns.

"Now we are going to see what happens when he comes back here," she said. "Poor thing, he loses his mother and then he almost drowns in the sea and then he does not see his father, and now he has to come back here to who knows what, really."

Cuban officials have said Elián will not be paraded, and will live with classmates, relatives and doctors in a government-owned Havana house for a few months as a transition.

CRITIC'S NOTEBOOK

Pictures Tell 2 Versions Of the Story, As Planned

By CARYN JAMES

It was unintentional that a still photograph became an instant icon of the television-driven saga of Elián González. The photograph of a federal agent in riot gear, a gun pointed in the direction of the little boy in the arms of the man who had rescued him from the sea, was shown and discussed all day, rarely mentioned without the words "searing" or "chilling" attached. And though the photograph demonstrates the power of a single dramatic image, the González family intended for the taking of Elián to be televised live.

"We got Maced, we got kicked, we got roughed up" by federal agents, Tony Zumbado, an NBC camera man, told his colleagues on the air yesterday afternoon, explaining why his pictures never materialized. Mr. Zumbado and an NBC sound person, who were providing the pool coverage to be shared by all the networks and cable channels, entered the house alongside the Associated Press photographer who took the central image.

Over the previous 10 days, the family had flip-flopped about whether to invite a camera inside if federal officials arrived. Late Friday afternoon, they consented. As Mr. Zumbado described the events, he and the Associated Press photographer essentially raced the federal agents to the door. A family member was pulling him into the house while a federal agent was pulling him out, he said. When he got inside he was kicked in the stomach and landed on the floor; by the time he recovered, he said, the three-minute raid was over.

That is the most ironic twist in what continues to be a battle of television imagery, with the networks on the air from minutes after the dawn raid through most of the morning, and the cable news channels continuing all day. That battle calls for television anchors to put events in the context of media manipulation, and yesterday Dan Rather on CBS provided the most cogent analysis of the public relations war. He reminded viewers that the circumstances behind the volatile picture needed to be seen from two sides. And he called attention to the fact that Marisleysis González went outside to give an emotional response to the cameras while Attorney General Janet Reno was holding a news conference, pulling coverage away from the attorney general. The timing was surely not coincidental, he said, commenting that Ms. González had "trumped" Ms. Reno in that media skirmish.

The government's position was explained by Ms. Reno, who said that the gun was not pointed at the child and that the agent's hand was not on the trigger. The opposite view was presented soon after in a live tour of the González house, one more bit of imagery proving how the family has learned to play a hungry media. In the tour, conducted by an NBC pool reporter and carried by everyone, Donato Dalrymple, the man holding the boy, said they had not been hiding in the closet, but standing in front of the open closet door. Then he and Ms. González emotionally, angrily attacked the government.

The day's most tilted coverage may have come from Brian Williams on MSNBC, who said that "it is feared this photograph will have an incendiary effect," and that "the excuse given by the federal government for the armaments" was that they had information that guns may have been in the house. The word "excuse" may have been careless rather than deliberate, but it was characteristic of a tone that undercut any attempt at balance.

"One of the beauties of television is that it shows exactly what the facts are," Ms. Reno said, but of course imagery is always more complicated than that. CNN, early in the day, had shown a version of the photograph that zoomed in to eliminate Mr. Donato, making the gun seem aimed at Elián. But live images can be frozen and manipulated too.

The second-most-seen image of the day was video of the federal marshal carrying Elián as they raced from the house to the waiting van. Often, that image was frozen, giving greater impact to the image of the crying, terrified-looking boy. When Gregory Craig, the lawyer for the Juan Miguel González, the boy's father, announced that he and his son had been happily reunited, Andrea Mitchell reported that on MSNBC, adding, in an objective tone, "despite those devastating images."

Mr. González, who has criticized his relatives for putting Elián on display for the media, has waged a milder media campaign. And soon Mr. Craig released the inevitable counterimages, a happy family photograph of a smiling Elián in his father's arms, along with Mr. González's wife and their infant son. There was a second still of Elián with his half-brother. The networks broke into their afternoon programming to show these new images, the latest weapons in the media war.

"All the News That's Fit to Print"

The New York Times

Late Edition
New York: **Today**, partly to mostly sunny, warmer, high 83. **Tonight**, mild, low 69. **Tomorrow**, hazy sun, hot, humid, high 93. **Yesterday**, high 73, low 49. Weather map is on Page B15.

VOL. CXLIX . . . . No. 51,413 NEW YORK, THURSDAY, JUNE 8, 2000 — $1 beyond the greater New York metropolitan area. — 75 CENTS

MICROSOFT BREAKUP IS ORDERED FOR ANTITRUST LAW VIOLATIONS

After a Rout, Still Fighting

Appeal Tries Chipping Away at Tough Ruling

By STEVE LOHR

With his final order yesterday in the Microsoft antitrust case, Judge Thomas Penfield Jackson said yes to the government one more time. He has agreed with the government, almost without qualification, on the facts of the case, on the law and now on the harsh remedy of splitting the company in two.

News Analysis

In Judge Jackson's Federal District Court, the result has been not just a defeat for Microsoft but a rout, not a closely fought legal contest but a judicial ratification of the government's case.

Yet the two-year-old case is far from over. And with a year or two of appeals ahead, the chances of Microsoft's ever being broken up are uncertain. Microsoft will try to reverse every element in Judge Jackson's ruling that the company is a monopoly that has repeatedly violated the nation's antitrust laws, stifling software competition and innovation.

The odds against Microsoft's winning outright on appeal are extremely high, according to antitrust experts. But they say that there are legally vulnerable points in the judge's ruling that if reversed on appeal might well enable the company to avoid the drastic sanction Judge Jackson has now endorsed.

"Microsoft is going to try to whittle away at the judge's ruling on appeal," said Andrew I. Gavil, professor at the Howard University law school. "And once you get an incremental erosion of the case, you erode the power of the argument for a breakup as well."

In his order yesterday, Judge Jackson acknowledged that the federal appeals court or the Supreme Court, or both, might disagree with

Continued on Page C10

"Microsoft has shown no disposition to voluntarily alter its business protocol in any significant respect."

JUDGE THOMAS PENFIELD JACKSON

Photograph by Paul Hosefros/The New York Times

HOW IT MIGHT SPLIT

Based on estimated revenues for fiscal 2000, ending June 30.

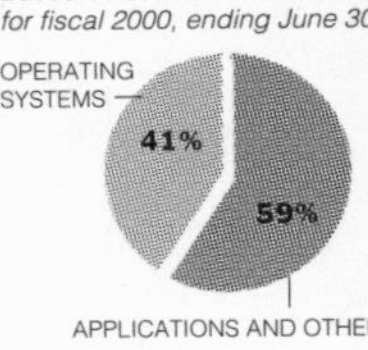

MORE ON THE DECISION

OLD RULES IN NEW ECONOMY The legal principles that led to the breakup of Standard Oil in 1911 and AT&T in 1984 are not obsolete. PAGE C1

WALL ST. VIEW Investors face the question of how Microsoft will perform now that a breakup has been ordered. MARKET PLACE, PAGE C1

CURBS ON CONDUCT

Split Is Stayed Pending Appeal — Gates Calls Ruling Unjustified

By JOEL BRINKLEY

WASHINGTON, June 7 — A federal judge ordered the breakup of the Microsoft Corporation today, saying the severe remedy was necessary because Microsoft "has proved untrustworthy in the past" and did not appear to have accepted his ruling that it had broadly violated the nation's antitrust laws.

"There is credible evidence in the record to suggest that Microsoft, convinced of its innocence, continues to do business as it has in the past and may yet do to other markets what it has already done" to dominate operating systems and Internet software, Judge Thomas Penfield Jackson said in his final ruling in the long-running trial. [Text, Page C12.]

Under his order, Microsoft would be broken into separate and competing companies, one for its Windows operating system and one for its other computer programs and Internet businesses. It would also be forced to comply with a long list of restrictions on its conduct lasting three years if the breakup order withstands appeal, and 10 years if it does not.

Microsoft said it would appeal the case to the Court of Appeals, filing the papers within a few days, while the government said this evening that it would try to bypass that court and ask immediate review by the Supreme Court.

While an appeal proceeds, Judge Jackson's order stays the breakup plan, but not the restrictions on the company's conduct. Microsoft intends, however, to ask that the entire order be stayed.

The government charged, and the judge agreed, that Microsoft had used its monopoly in operating systems to put competitors at a disadvantage and stifle innovation.

In surprisingly assertive language, Judge Jackson accepted the government's remedy proposal in its entirety, attaching it to his ruling — utterly rejecting Microsoft's repeated assertions that the breakup plan was "Draconian," "unwarranted" and "bad for consumers, the high-tech industry and our economy."

William H. Gates, the chairman of Microsoft, called the judge's ruling "an unwarranted and unjustified intrusion into the software marketplace, a marketplace that has been an engine of economic growth for America."

"The idea that someone would say that a breakup is a reasonable thing comes as quite a surprise to us," Mr. Gates added. "We have a very strong case on appeal, and we look forward to resolving these issues through the appeals process and putting this case behind us once and for all."

Mr. Gates was in Washington on

Continued on Page C10

Yielding to Embarrassed F.C.C., AT&T Delays Its Rate Increase

By STEPHEN LABATON

WASHINGTON, June 7 — AT&T gave into pressure from embarrassed federal regulators and outraged consumer groups today and said that it would put off a planned rate increase that would have raised telephone bills for tens of millions of customers.

The announcement came after a flurry of calls between senior AT&T executives and the chairman of the Federal Communications Commission, William E. Kennard, who said that the company, the nation's largest long-distance provider, had broken a promise to reduce overall phone charges under an agreement reached last week.

Mr. Kennard and AT&T had promoted that agreement, under which the F.C.C. reduced the fees paid by long-distance carriers to local phone companies, as a "historic" rate cut. But at the same time, AT&T filed documents with the commission that said the company would actually be raising most of the per-minute charges on the basic accounts of millions of customers who make few calls.

"AT&T promised to pass on savings to all consumers," Mr. Kennard said in a statement issued after his conversations with AT&T executives, including its chairman, C. Michael Armstrong. "Their new rate plan does not do that."

"It is in our order and I am going to enforce it," he said. "AT&T promised to tell their consumers which plan would be most cost-effective for them. This was not done. I will also hold AT&T to this commitment."

Gloria Tristani, another F.C.C. commissioner, issued a blistering six-word statement. "I was totally misled by AT&T," she said.

Their statements were curious in light of comments on Tuesday from other officials at the commission who said that they knew all along that AT&T had intended to raise certain rates and that they were not particularly troubled by the knowledge because the company had agreed to send a letter to customers informing them of lower-cost plans.

AT&T, which handles 60 percent of the nation's residential long-distance calls, said it had decided to defer the rate increases in light of the F.C.C.'s

Continued on Page C16

Turmoil in Israel

Prime Minister Ehud Barak's government was thrown into tumult when Parliament approved a preliminary bill to disperse and head toward new elections. The bill requires three more hearings to become law. But it could break up the ruling coalition and create a chaotic interlude at a diplomatically inopportune moment.

Article, Page A8.

G.O.P. Senate Candidate Offers Regular-Joe Image

By IVER PETERSON

SPRINGFIELD, N.J., June 7 — If a moment can have a message, Robert D. Franks was sending one by beginning his race as the Republican nominee for the United States Senate at the Lido Diner here.

"The Lido Diner, that's as middle-class New Jersey as you can get," Raymond Bateman, an experienced Republican leader in the state, said with a laugh. "That's Bob Franks."

For most of the spring, Mr. Franks, who is in his fourth term in Congress, and the other three Republican candidates were eclipsed by the civil war within the Democratic Party between Jon S. Corzine and Jim Florio.

Now that Mr. Franks is the presumed Republican nominee, he will step out into the limelight alone to face Mr. Corzine in the general election. The face he is most likely to present is of a typical New Jerseyan, a successful suburban lawyer with a wife and a little daughter, stepping out of the Lido Diner after breakfast.

With 99 percent of the vote counted, Mr. Franks had 95,801 votes, 35.4 percent, and State Senator William L. Gormley had 92,454, 34.2 percent. But with absentee ballots uncounted, Mr. Gormley refused to concede this morning, saying in a statement that the vote had to be certified first.

The image Mr. Franks presented at the Lido is one he evidently expects New Jerseyans to be comfortable with, and one he hopes to contrast with Mr. Corzine's self-financed $35 million scorched-earth campaign against Mr. Florio. Mr. Franks has said that Mr. Corzine is out of touch with average New Jerseyans, and in his victory speech early this morning he challenged Mr. Corzine to meet him at the Lido for the first debate.

As it happened, Mr. Corzine was up just as early, thanking voters at Journal Square in Jersey City. So Mr. Franks stood alone in front of the diner and took a poke at his rival.

"Jon is going to have to answer the voters' questions," Mr. Franks said in the early light of a sparkling day. "He can no longer hide behind the multimillion-dollar ad campaigns and the focus groups. He is going to have to come out here to these diners and answer the tough questions."

One of the sharpest contrasts

Continued on Page B6

Keith Meyers/The New York Times

Robert D. Franks began his campaign yesterday at a diner.

Reading Scores Improve Citywide; Still, Only 41% Meet Standards

By ABBY GOODNOUGH

Bolstering the encouraging results of recent state tests, the Board of Education reported yesterday that students in New York City performed significantly better this year on a citywide reading test. Still, only 40.8 percent met the rigorous new curriculum standards on which they were being tested, compared with 35.7 percent last year.

The increase of 5.1 percentage points for third, fifth, sixth and seventh graders, who took their test in April, came less than a week after state education officials reported that fourth graders across the state had shown a remarkable improvement of 11 percentage points in the second year of a new fourth-grade reading test. The scores of New York City's fourth graders increased by nine percentage points.

Board of Education officials said yesterday that the combined improvements on the state and city scores showed that their efforts to improve literacy rates among elementary school students over the last five years were finally taking hold throughout the long-troubled school system.

Indeed, all of the city's 32 community school districts improved their scores. Even the chancellor's district — a new district comprising the worst schools in the city — had 11.8 percent fewer students score at the lowest of the four performance levels used in grading the tests.

The citywide test scores, along with the state scores released last week, will help determine which of the city's 1.1 million schoolchildren will be required to attend summer school this year. Classroom performance and attendance rates are the other two factors. Schools will decide by tomorrow which students they will require to attend the summer program, which will be the largest in the city's history.

Comments by education experts interviewed yesterday were notable for their absence of skepticism, with most saying that this second round of tests affirms the efforts by Richard P. Mills, the state's education commissioner, and Rudy Crew, New York City's former chancellor, to impose more uniform standards for what students should learn in each grade and to demand that those standards be heeded.

"I am surprised," said Norman

Continued on Page B7

INSIDE

Obstacle for Abortion Pill

Efforts to bring the French abortion pill to the United States face a new hurdle: a suggestion the government may tightly restrict its distribution and prescription. PAGE A21

Drought Torments Afghans

A drought is adding to the misery in Afghanistan, where the economy is in ruins after years of war and foreign aid is hard to come by. Page A12

Athlete Sent Back to Cuba

Andy Morales, a prominent Cuban baseball player, was returned home by the Coast Guard after failing to win political asylum. PAGE A14

Herb Suspected in Cancer

Doctors are reporting that a Chinese herb, Aristolochia fangchi, already linked to kidney failure, may cause cancer as well. PAGE A24

Apocalyptic Potboiler Is Publisher's Dream

By DINITIA SMITH

WHEATON, Ill., June 4 — The latest thriller in a hugely popular Christian fundamentalist series about the Apocalypse will enter the New York Times fiction best-seller list at No. 1 on Sunday, an unparalleled achievement for an evangelical novel.

The book, "The Indwelling: The Beast Takes Possession," by Tim F. LaHaye, a retired evangelical minister, and Jerry B. Jenkins, a professional writer, is the seventh installment in the "Left Behind" series, which in the last five years has sold some 17 million copies in the United States, about three million less than the Harry Potter series. In April, before its official publication, it reached No. 1 on the Amazon.com best-seller list, based on advance orders.

On the Times fiction best-seller list, it is displacing "Easy Prey," a detective novel by John Sandford.

The authors of "The Indwelling," who say they have so far made $10 million each from the series, are on a 10-city tour, and their stop in this college town this weekend had all the panoply of a revival meeting. They attracted 900 people who paid $12 to $25 each to hear them talk about the book in a Wheaton College auditorium.

Mr. LaHaye and Mr. Jenkins were accompanied by a retinue of 17, including a blind singer, Ginny Owens, and a singer-guitarist, Wayne Watson, who played with a throbbing rock sound as the authors sat on thronelike black leather chairs bathed in cyclamen-colored lights. Two huge candelabra lent the scene a "Phantom of the Opera" ambience as they took questions from a rapt audience.

The latest book combines traditional elements of science fiction with the authors' unorthodox interpretation of the Book of Revelation to create a Rambo-style potboiler with a strong conservative ethos and noticeably contemporary characters who drive Range Rovers, use the Internet and have everyday worries.

The star of the series is Rayford Steele, a married commercial airline pilot who in an early scene in the first book flirts with a stewardess and minutes later discovers that more than 100 of his passengers have disappeared in midflight. As it turns out, his devout wife and son have vanished, too. All of them have, in evangelical parlance, "accepted Christ" and have been summoned by Jesus to the Rapture, a precursor to the Apocalypse.

In "The Indwelling," Steele is suspected by the authorities of assassinating Nicolae Carpathia, the Antichrist, a former secretary general of the United Nations.

But the false god is resurrected, battle rages between Heaven and Earth, and the Beast takes control

Continued on Page C13

Todd Buchanan for The New York Times

Tim F. LaHaye, left, and Jerry B. Jenkins, right, interviewed by Mike Trout on an elaborate tour to promote their apocalyptic novels.

G.O.P. Says It Seeks to Avoid Partisan Vitriol at Convention

By FRANK BRUNI and ALISON MITCHELL

AUSTIN, Tex., June 7 — Hoping to preserve and perpetuate an upbeat tone that has served them well over the last several months, advisers to Gov. George W. Bush say they are fashioning a party convention that will emphasize policy over partisan vitriol and perhaps abandon the frequent practice of devoting one night to an attack on the opposition.

They say they want the second of the four nights, which has often been reserved for such sniping, to adhere to a mostly positive, sustained focus on exalting Governor Bush rather than eviscerating Vice President Al Gore. They want every night to underline a different set or area of Mr. Bush's substantive proposals.

And, on a less atmospheric note, they want Gen. Colin L. Powell and Senator John McCain front and center, in prominent speaking roles on different nights, so that each of them serves as a separate lure for the fickle and finite attentions of the major television networks.

These sorts of issues will be a primary focus at a retreat Mr. Bush and his aides are taking starting this weekend at his parents' compound in Kennebunkport, Me., as the campaign increasingly turns its attention to the convention, which begins in Philadelphia at the end of July.

And what is most striking about their plans, at least as they were described in interviews with several of Mr. Bush's advisers over the last few days, is the campaign's stated desire to avoid harsh attacks and to try to make the intrinsically partisan proceedings seem less so.

"We expect it to be a somewhat different convention," Karen P. Hughes, the Bush campaigns direc-

Continued on Page A22

NEWS SUMMARY A2

Updated news: www.nytimes.com

THE OVERVIEW

Breakup of Software Giant Ordered in Antitrust Case

Continued From Page A1

Tuesday, planning to meet with lawmakers today. Anticipating the ruling, though, he canceled the meetings and hurriedly flew back to Seattle overnight.

Attorney General Janet Reno, smiling broadly, said this afternoon that the ruling "will have a profound impact, not only by promoting competition in the software industry, but also by reaffirming the importance of antitrust law enforcement in the 21st century." And Joel I. Klein, head of the department's antitrust division, said, "Microsoft itself is responsible for where things stand today."

If the judge's order withstands appeal and Microsoft is eventually broken up, it would join a handful of major national monopolies that have been taken apart over the last 90 years as a result of antitrust violations, including Standard Oil, American Tobacco and the Aluminum Company of America.

Tom Miller, the attorney general of Iowa, speaking on behalf of the 19 states that are partners with the Justice Department in the Microsoft case, said the ruling "sends a strong message that no company is above the law." (Two of the 19 states, Illinois and Ohio, declined to support the breakup plan.)

Adding to the legacy of antitrust law enforcement.

If Microsoft's request for a stay of Judge Jackson's order is rejected, the company must begin complying with the conduct restrictions by Sept. 7 and submit a detailed plan for dividing the company by Oct. 7.

With Judge Jackson's encouragement, the Justice Department announced that it would take the case directly to the Supreme Court, under a 1974 revision to the federal antitrust laws allowing fast-track consideration of significant antitrust cases.

Microsoft opposes the direct appeal to the Supreme Court, preferring to take its case first to the Court of Appeals, which ruled in its favor in a related lawsuit two years ago and reversed a decision by Judge Jackson.

Whether the Supreme Court would even take the case is at best uncertain. Microsoft argued this evening that the suit filed by the states would not be eligible for expedited appeal because the states have no similar law. In that case, the states' appeal would be taken to the Court of Appeals. But state and federal officials said that because the cases were joined for trial, it would make no sense to separate them for differing legal appeals.

The officials acknowledged that the point of law was ambiguous. But Richard Blumenthal, attorney general of Connecticut, said, "Today's victory vindicates and soundly validates our decisions as state law enforcement officers to join this historic action."

If the conduct restrictions are allowed to take effect, computer manufacturers will be allowed to offer customized versions of Windows on their computers in ways they never could before. And future versions of Windows will be offered in a form that allows buyers to accept certain new software features Microsoft chooses to offer — or to decide they do not want them and use a competing product.

It was Microsoft's decision four years ago to tie a Web browser to Windows that prompted the investigation and lawsuits that led to the breakup order today.

Years from now, if the government's remedy plan works as intended, consumers might also begin to see alternate operating systems on sale that are competitive with Windows. If that occurs, the broad compatibility among personal computers that exists today might begin to erode.

Judge Jackson issued his ruling at 4:30 this afternoon, just after the stock markets had closed. His decision had been widely expected, and investors appeared to have already taken the breakup plan into account. Microsoft stock was up 87.5 cents today, to close at $70.50.

Asked at a news conference today if he had any regrets, Mr. Gates said: "If I look back at anything, I think, perhaps I should have taken the opportunity to go in person and talk about this industry."

Whether Mr. Gates might be called as a witness was a continuing question during the antitrust trial. His halting, obdurate performance in a videotaped deposition proved to be a powerful tool for the government in court.

Though Judge Jackson accepted the remedy plan put together by the federal and state governments, his endorsement was not unequivocal.

He noted that the plan was the collective work of senior state and federal officials "in conjunction with multiple consultants." And, he said, the remedy "appears to the court to address the principal objectives of relief in such cases, namely to terminate the unlawful conduct, to prevent its repetition in the future and to revive competition in the relevant markets."

But even though several experts provided "some insight as to how the provisions" of the remedy might work, "for the most part they are merely the predictions of purportedly knowledgeable people as to effects which may or may not ensue if the proposed final judgment is entered," he added. "In its experience, the court has found testimonial predictions of future events generally less reliable even than testimony as to historical fact."

Microsoft severely criticized the judge this evening for his decision to hold no substantive hearings on the government's remedy proposal. Microsoft said it had been surprised by the scope of the plan and had been unable to respond to it adequately in

Associated Press

Outside of federal court in Washington yesterday, reporters scanned copies of Judge Thomas Penfield Jackson's ruling against Microsoft.

the six weeks since it was offered.

But in his order today, Judge Jackson retorted: "Microsoft's profession of surprise is not credible. From the inception of this case Microsoft knew, from well-established Supreme Court precedents dating from the beginning of the last century, that a mandated divestiture was a possibility, if not a probability, in the event of an adverse result at trial."

In fact, the government first made plain to Microsoft during settlement negotiations a year ago that it planned to ask for a so-called structural remedy. That was repeated during mediation efforts by a federal judge early this year, though the government offered terms short of a breakup after Microsoft said it would not discuss structural remedies.

The judge also explained why he moved through the remedy phase so quickly, saying that he wanted to pass the case to a higher court as soon as possible for validation, revision or rejection of his decision, "to abort any remedial measures before they become irreversible as a practical matter."

If necessary, the judge said he could hold hearings later or "modify the judgment as necessary in accordance with instructions from an appellate court."

Judge Jackson noted, with some apparent irritation, that after he ruled on April 3 that Microsoft was in wide violation of the nation's antitrust laws, Microsoft's leaders continued to assert that "the company has done 'nothing wrong' and that it will be vindicated on appeal."

"The court is well aware," he added, "that there is a substantial body of public opinion, some of it rational, that holds a similar view. If true, then an appellate tribunal should be given an opportunity to confirm it as promptly as possible."

Microsoft's continued assertions of innocence were one reason for his ruling, he said. Another was that "Microsoft has shown no disposition to voluntarily alter its business protocols in any significant respect."

A third reason, he said, was that Microsoft "has proved untrustworthy in the past." As an example, he referred to the precedent case he tried in late 1997, after the government accused Microsoft of illegally tying a Web browser to Windows.

In December 1997, Judge Jackson issued a preliminary injunction ordering Microsoft to separate the two products. That was the ruling later overturned by the Court of Appeals.

But "Microsoft's purported compliance while it was on appeal," the judge said today, "was illusory and its explanation disingenuous."

THE INDUSTRY

In Silicon Valley, Ruling Won't Change Culture

By MATT RICHTEL

SAN FRANCISCO, June 7 — Even if Judge Thomas Penfield Jackson's order to break up Microsoft survives appeal unscathed, potential competitors will not feel the impact of the antitrust trial for at least a year, industry executives said today.

In part, they say, the culture in the software industry will take time to change. For example, they said it might take a year or more before investors like venture capitalists begin to finance potential competitors to Microsoft.

"Within a year, you'll see some clever ideas coming out; within two years, you'll see some options" for consumers, said James Barksdale, former president and chief executive of **Netscape** who is now a private investor in Silicon Valley.

Mr. Barksdale said he believed that venture capitalists had just begun to finance competitors to Microsoft, but that they would greatly increase that once Microsoft's appeal of Judge Jackson's breakup ruling is rejected.

"It's going to be at least a year before people believe it's going to take hold," he said.

But there are deep divisions in Silicon Valley about when the court decision will have an impact on competitors.

Some say the shift is already under way, a shift driven by the market, not the courts. Heidi Roizen, a former Microsoft consultant and longtime friend of William H. Gates who is now a venture capitalist, said that the attitude toward funding potential Microsoft competitors changed a long time ago.

For the last four or five years, one of the first questions a venture capitalist has asked was whether an entrepreneur was entering a business that belonged to Microsoft or that it could easily enter, but that is no longer the case, she said.

"I've been a venture capitalist for a year and Microsoft has come up only once in a meeting," she said. "Because of the Internet and the movement of people's attention from the O.S. wars (operating system wars) to the Internet, attention for Microsoft has diminished."

She described today as a sad day but said that, given the appeals process, "it's going to be a long time before we know what's going to happen."

T. Paul Thomas, the president and chief executive of TurboLinux, which makes a version of the **Linux** operating system that competes with Microsoft's Windows, agreed some change is already under way because Linux "still is the fastest growing operating system." And, he said, it seems that Microsoft has already modified its business practices in light of the scrutiny by the government and Judge Jackson. "They're more conscious of what they do," he said.

But he said he believes more fundamental change in business practices by Microsoft — and innovations from competitors — could be two or more years away because he expects the litigation to drag on and he believes that Microsoft is a formidable competitor.

Associated Press

James Barksdale, former chief of Netscape, said it would take at least a year before consumers see a shift in the software industry.

Wounded in court, the giant remains a formidable opponent.

"Nothing is going to change at Microsoft today, nor is there going to be any change in the near term," he said.

Executives at several of the top technology companies, including **Novell**, **3Com** and **Adobe Systems**, declined comment on the outcome of the antitrust trial. Throughout the trial, executives from many top technology companies have been silent about the proceedings.

One exception has been **Sun Microsystems** Inc. Michael H. Morris, vice president and general counsel, said today that the company felt the verdict was "justified."

He said Microsoft has engaged in a public relations effort to make it appear the technology market is moving so quickly that it is unnecessary to split it up. But Mr. Morris said Microsoft continues to "have monopoly power today and the absolute ability to wield it ruthlessly."

He said he has not met one person who makes a credible argument that market forces will alone mitigate Microsoft's behavior.

Mr. Barksdale said he feels vindicated by the court's decision, but he said it may have come too late for the Netscape Navigator, a Windows competitor. "I regret it didn't happen a few years sooner," he said. "Navigator would've been a bigger option for people."

The decision also inspired continued criticism of the government from some in Silicon Valley. Alan M. Cooper, the founder and president of **Cooper Interaction Design** in Palo Alto, Calif., a software consulting company with 55 employees, said he believes some of Microsoft's behavior has been inappropriate, but he does not believe the government should act so drastically.

Specifically, he said the government action will not have the desired impact, in part because he still does not believe that venture capitalists and other investors will want to fund companies to compete against the major Microsoft businesses, even if those businesses are owned by two companies.

"I don't think there is going to be a rush to jump into Microsoft's markets," he said.

THE APPEAL

Trying to Chip Away at a Tough Ruling

Continued From Page A1

some of his work. Two weeks ago, he surprised both sides in the case and most legal experts when he abruptly ended the court proceedings without a further round of hearings on the government's plan to split Microsoft in two and require a series of curbs on its business conduct.

In his order, Judge Jackson explained that he had moved quickly because, if his findings or legal conclusions are overruled, a higher court might decide on its own remedies or send the case back to him.

After noting that Microsoft contends it will be vindicated on appeal, he wrote: "The court is well aware that there is a substantial body of public opinion, some of it rational, that holds to a similar view. It is time to put that assertion to the test."

So Judge Jackson chose this approach as a way to speed along a case of national economic importance. The alternative, he decided, would be to risk going through two time-consuming sets of hearings on remedies — one based on his legal ruling and one based on a case perhaps scaled back on appeal.

Still, some antitrust experts say that simply accepting the remedies plan from the Justice Department and states suing Microsoft could prove to be a mistake.

"If he's assuming that this case is probably coming back to him anyway, I think that is a safe assumption," said William Kovacic, a professor at the George Washington University law school. "But the danger of his approach is that it increases the chances it will come back to him."

Microsoft's prime target on appeal, antitrust experts say, will be the judge's ruling that it illegally tied its Internet browser to its monopoly product, the Windows operating system, which handles the basic operations on 85 percent of all PC's.

To Microsoft, the tying charge is the heart of the case. If that ruling is upheld on appeal, Microsoft sees a threat to its corporate way of life — its ability to add new software features to its operating system, as it has repeatedly over the years.

In several rounds of settlement talks with the government, Microsoft was willing to change some of its practices, but it stood firm on not allowing any tampering with Windows or letting personal computer makers pick and choose from an àla carte menu of Windows features.

To Microsoft, this stance is not arrogance or hubris — or an antitrust violation, for that matter — but a stand of principle.

"This case, in our view, is about whether we are free to improve our products and whether we can protect the integrity of our most important product, Windows," said William Neukom, senior vice president and general counsel of Microsoft.

Microsoft has argued that Web browsing software should not be considered as a separate product but as a feature in the ever-evolving Windows operating system.

The government contended, and Judge Jackson ruled, that Microsoft had illegally tied its Internet browser, a separate product, to Windows to thwart competition and illegally protect its monopoly. To accept Microsoft's argument, the government said, would amount to granting the dominant software maker an exemption from broad swaths of the nation's antitrust laws.

But antitrust experts note that product-tying charges are tricky, especially when dealing with software, in which the products are rendered in the 1's and 0's of programming code and product boundaries often blur. And a federal appeals court in June 1998 sided with Microsoft in a separate but related case. That court said Microsoft had the right to fold a browser into its operating system as long as it could make a "plausible claim" of consumer benefit.

In addition to the tying charge, Microsoft, antitrust experts say, stands a good chance of getting a reversal on the court's finding that Microsoft made an illegal offer to Netscape Communications to divide the browser market between them. The collusion offer, Judge Jackson ruled, was made during a meeting between executives of Microsoft and Netscape, the commercial pioneer in Internet browsers, in June 1995.

The legal hurdle in attempted collusion cases, antitrust experts say, is fairly high. The crucial case, they say, occurred in 1984 and involved airline executives talking about jointly raising fares in a conversation that was tape-recorded. Whether the meeting notes, e-mail messages and conflicting witness testimony about the Microsoft-Netscape meeting are evidence that reaches the standard of "clearly unequivocal," established in the 1984 case, is open to question, experts say.

Microsoft is also expected to argue that much of the rest of the case — mainly contracts and practices that the court found to be a "pattern of anticompetitive behavior" — is merely evidence of a company competing aggressively in a dynamic industry, not of an economic outlaw.

"We think this ruling is very vulnerable on appeal," Mr. Neukom said. "We're in the middle innings of a contest that won't be over for another year or two. And the most critical innings are yet to come."

Yet antitrust experts say that the steepest uphill climb for Microsoft on appeal will be to overturn Judge Jackson's determination that the company engaged in an array of illegal acts to protect its monopoly, wielding its market power like a club to bully industry partners and rivals.

"It's the whole gestalt that is a real problem for Microsoft — the court's finding that these are bad guys, who repeatedly acted to stifle competition and not for any efficiency reasons," said Richard Steuer, an antitrust specialist and a partner at Kaye Scholer Fierman Hays & Handler. "That is a lot harder for an appeals court to overturn."

Where the Case Goes Next

In his ruling against Microsoft yesterday, Judge Thomas Penfield Jackson stayed his order to break up the company, but not his restrictions on its business practices. Microsoft will seek a stay of the entire ruling while it appeals the overall case.

U.S. DISTRICT COURT FOR THE DISTRICT OF COLUMBIA

The Justice Department, with Judge Jackson's encouragement, intends to take the case directly to the Supreme Court for review.

Microsoft wants the matter to go to the Court of Appeals, which ruled in its favor in a related case two years ago.

U.S. SUPREME COURT

If the court takes the case, it is likely to rule by June of next year, the end of its next term.

The Supreme Court may decide not to take the case, sending it to a three-judge panel of the Court of Appeals.

U.S. COURT OF APPEALS FOR THE DISTRICT OF COLUMBIA

The first question is whether the court will stay Judge Jackson's ruling. If it does, it would be likely to do so quickly.

The full appeal could last as long as two years. The court could uphold the verdict, or overturn it in full or in part. Whatever the court decides is likely to be appealed to the Supreme Court.

In any event, the case will return to Judge Jackson, either to oversee implementation of the remedy or to amend it according to the higher court's findings.

IF THE JUDGE'S RULING IS NOT STAYED A long and detailed list of restrictions on the company's conduct will take effect on Sept. 7. Microsoft will also have to file a detailed plan for breaking up the company by Oct. 7.

IF APPEAL FAILS Microsoft must complete the breakup and begin life as two separate and competing companies within one year of the date of the appeals ruling.

Allen to Sell Some Of Microsoft Stock

WASHINGTON, June 7 (Reuters) — Paul Allen, a co-founder of the **Microsoft** Corporation, has filed with the Securities and Exchange Commission to sell two million common shares of the company, valued at more than $128 million.

Mr. Allen, who held a stake of 4.1 percent in Microsoft as of May 23, made the filing last Thursday.

According to Mr. Allen's filing, Microsoft has 5.103 billion shares outstanding.

The filing was released today by the S.E.C.

A spokeswoman for Mr. Allen did not immediately return a telephone call seeking comment. But in the past she has said Mr. Allen has routinely sold Microsoft stock to diversify his portfolio.

The S.E.C. filing also showed he sold 28,585,000 shares between March 1 and May 30 for more than $2.5 billion. The biggest one-day sale in that period came on March 6 when he sold 6.46 million shares for more than $594 million.

"All the News That's Fit to Print"

The New York Times

Late Edition
New York: **Today**, decreasing clouds, high 81. **Tonight**, scattered showers and thunderstorms, low 71. **Tomorrow**, warmer, high 91. **Yesterday**, high 61, low 53. Weather map, Page D7.

VOL. CXLIX . . . . No. 51,420 NEW YORK, THURSDAY, JUNE 15, 2000 — $1 beyond the greater New York metropolitan area. — 75 CENTS

KOREAS REACH ACCORD SEEKING RECONCILIATION AFTER 50 YEARS

Pool photo via Associated Press

Kim Dae Jung, left, and Kim Jong Il yesterday before they signed a pact aimed at easing 50 years of conflict.

UNITY CALLED GOAL

A Deal on Family Visits and Talks in Seoul — Language Is Vague

By HOWARD W. FRENCH

SEOUL, South Korea, Thursday, June 15 — With surprising speed and warmth, the presidents of North and South Korea reached a broad agreement on Wednesday to work for peace and unity on their bitterly divided peninsula, the biggest step by either side to ease tensions in 50 years.

The agreement, which came after more than three hours of talks in the North Korea capital, Pyongyang, on the second day of their first summit meeting, was signed and toasted by President Kim Dae Jung of South Korea and President Kim Jong Il of the North, who were shown on South Korean television clinking champagne glasses, shaking hands vigorously and smiling broadly.

The agreement, while deliberately vague, had clearly left both men buoyant. If carried through, the accord would reduce the precarious isolation of the North and address many basic points that have long been seen as keys to ending the cold war on the heavily fortified peninsula, where the United States still maintains 37,000 troops.

The general points agreed on included the need for reconciliation and unification; the establishment of peace; the commencement in August of exchange visits by members of divided families; and more cultural exchanges. [Text, Page A14.]

In addition, it was agreed that Kim Jong Il would visit Seoul "at the earliest appropriate moment." The two sides also discussed the creation of offices in each other's capitals, and establishing a hot line between their leaders.

"At this very hour, the attention of the 70 million Korean people is drawn to Pyongyang, and the eyes of the entire world are riveted to this place," the South Korean president said in a banquet prior to the signing. "For the first time, the Korean people can see a bright future as a dawn of hope for reconciliation, cooperation and unification is breaking."

While the agreement provides no road map for the future and did not address pressing security issues, it left many people here hopeful that a decisive turn was shaping up in relations between two governments that have vilified each other for decades.

In addition, the emergence of the reclusive North Korean leader in the role of a jovial statesman was certain to challenge the image of North Korea as a "rogue state" so dangerous that Washington is proposing to spend billions of dollars on an antimissile system to defend against it.

"It is important to remember the symbolic importance of this meet-

Continued on Page A14

U.S. Says It Will Soon Drop Its Sanctions on North Korea

By DAVID E. SANGER

WASHINGTON, June 14 — Clinton administration officials, trying to build on the progress of the Korean summit meeting, said tonight that they would announce within a week the lifting of a broad set of economic sanctions that have been in place against North Korea since it invaded the South 50 years ago this month.

The end of these sanctions would allow North Korea, which is economically desperate, to export raw materials and goods to the United States and would open air and shipping routes between the two countries. American companies would be allowed to invest in agriculture, mining, roads, ports, travel and tourism in the North, though it is likely that far more Japanese and South Korean companies would try to do so.

The Clinton administration's decision to end sanctions — a carrot that President Clinton dangled in front of the North last fall as part of a strategy formulated by former Secretary of Defense William J. Perry — has limits. Prohibitions on the sale of high technology and "dual-use goods" — those that could be used for both civilian and military purposes — will remain in place as long as North Korea is still classified a terrorist state by the State Department, officials said. The United States is also required by law to oppose financing to terrorist countries from the World Bank and the International Monetary Fund.

But administration officials said today that they hoped the North might, in coming months, make concessions that would get it off the terrorist list.

Today, Mr. Clinton cautiously referred to the agreement on the Korean peninsula as "just the first step," but added, "It's clearly a move in the right direction, and everyone else in the world should be encouraged."

Perhaps as striking as the imminent lifting of the sanctions is the administration's sudden change of tone about the North's mysterious leader, Kim Jong Il. Until recently, Mr. Kim was usually described by American officials as paranoid, a recluse, a kidnapper and a patron of European prostitutes. But this evening, one senior administration official went to some lengths to praise Mr. Kim and compare him to his South Korean counterpart, Kim Dae Jung.

"We knew that Kim Dae Jung was courageous and a visionary," the official said. "Kim Jong Il clearly has some of those qualities, and is displaying some vision himself."

That new approach to the North marks a big risk for the Clinton

Continued on Page A14

Deal Reached On Fire Safety For Cigarettes

Pataki Backs Bill With Curbs on Bootlegging

By RICHARD PÉREZ-PEÑA

ALBANY, June 14 — The Legislature approved a bill today making New York the first state to impose fire-safety standards on cigarettes, striking a deal with Gov. George E. Pataki three weeks after he vetoed a similar bill.

The Senate and the Assembly also passed a bill strengthening criminal penalties for cigarette bootlegging, and restricting cigarette sales on the Internet, a measure Mr. Pataki had demanded in return for signing the fire-safety bill. State officials are concerned that bootlegging and the Internet are increasingly being used to avoid paying the state's cigarette tax of $1.11 a pack, the highest in the country.

The new fire-safety bill, which the governor pledged to sign, requires that all cigarettes sold in New York meet flammability standards by mid-2003. The goal is to have cigarettes, the leading cause of accidental fires, go out after a short time if they are not being puffed, rather than burning continually.

Cigarettes are the leading cause of fatal fires in New York, resulting in 48 fire deaths statewide in 1997, the most recent year for which detailed figures are available, according to the State Office of Fire Prevention and Control.

"This is the first time tobacco products have ever been regulated in any significant way, anywhere in the United States," said Russell Sciandra, director of the Center for a Tobacco-Free New York, drawing a distinction between regulation of sales and of content. "This now sets a huge precedent. Finally, cigarettes are being treated as a consumer product like anything else."

New York's actions have been closely watched by antismoking

Continued on Page B5

Citing Own Cancer, Giuliani Offers Plan On Health Coverage

By ELISABETH BUMILLER

Mayor Rudolph W. Giuliani announced a health initiative yesterday aimed at aggressively enrolling nearly one million uninsured New York City children and adults in Medicaid and other government health care programs. He said his ambitions for the plan came about partly because of his change in attitude toward illness after he learned he had prostate cancer.

"If we can do this, it becomes a model for the rest of the country," Mr. Giuliani said as he presided over a news conference and a long slide presentation in the city's public hearing chamber. He added that "this is a big goal that has eluded New York City and most of America in the past."

As the mayor explained it, the plan, called Health Stat, is an expansion of a more modest program that his administration began working on six months ago. The new plan will divide the city into eight regions, each administered by a manager. Within each region, schools, hospitals, food stamp offices, job centers, police precinct headquarters and others will either help enroll or give information to the more than 900,000 people eligible for state and federal health insurance who are not now covered.

Mr. Giuliani described them as "people who literally could have health insurance today if they knew about it, we knew about them, and we made the proper connection and got them to fill out the correct forms and

Continued on Page B14

CLINTON LAWYERS GIVE A GO-AHEAD TO MISSILE SHIELD

LOOPHOLE SEEN IN TREATY

Russia Is Likely to Disagree — Opinion Would Let U.S. Stall on Final Decision

By ERIC SCHMITT and STEVEN LEE MYERS

WASHINGTON, June 14 — Administration lawyers have advised President Clinton that, in their view, he can begin building the first piece of a national missile defense without violating a 1972 arms control treaty with Russia, senior officials said.

The lawyers' interpretations, which were drafted at the White House's request, are likely to be rejected by Russia, and the president has not made a decision on them. But they offer Mr. Clinton a way to announce that the United States would go ahead with missile defenses while letting the next administration decide whether to break the Antiballistic Missile Treaty.

The prospect of withdrawing from the treaty has already threatened to undermine relations with Russia, as well as with European allies who view the pact as a foundation of nuclear arms control. But a delay in construction of a missile defense could leave Mr. Clinton, and especially Vice President Al Gore, vulnerable to Republican criticism in the middle of the presidential campaign.

The lawyers' findings could allow work on a defense system to begin while giving Mr. Clinton and his successor another year to decide whether to abrogate the treaty. The findings could also give the United States more time to test its nascent antimissile system and to negotiate with Moscow and with Washington's allies in hopes of averting a crisis in arms control.

"Basically the administration is working hard to free up as much wiggle room as it can before it has to make a decision," one administration official said. "And that makes sense. There's still a long way to go to come to an arrangement with the Russians."

The advice overturns a legal understanding dating from the Reagan administration that even the most minimal steps to construct parts of a missile defense — laying concrete or raising walls, for example — would breach the treaty.

The advice amounts to a unilateral interpretation of the treaty, and, if the president embraces it, the Rus-

Continued on Page A5

U.S. Says Mobsters Joined Stock Fraud

Prosecutors have charged dozens of people with using stock manipulation, fraud and violence to steal from thousands of investors nationwide in a scheme that federal authorities are calling one of organized crime's most aggressive forays into the stock market.

Prosecutors said their investigation swept up one high-ranking member and several lower-level members of New York's organized-crime families, as well as brokers, stock promoters and a retired police officer who served as treasurer of the union that represents New York City detectives.

At the center of the investigation is a Manhattan investment firm, DMN Capital Investments, which prosecutors said was infiltrated by mob associates.

Federal agents charged that the defendants used a range of schemes to defraud investors, from running traditional high-pressure boiler-rooms sales operations to bribing brokers and creating phony stock trades. Such tactics would artificially inflate the price of stocks, which could then be sold at an illicit profit.

Business Day, Page C1.

The Silent Senior Partner in Bush's Campaign

By FRANK BRUNI

WASHINGTON, June 14 — By most outward signs, former President George Bush has maintained a cautious distance from Gov. George W. Bush's quest for the White House, seldom making joint appearances with his son and rarely commenting on the election.

But behind the scenes, Mr. Bush is anything but remote. On several occasions between December and May, Karl Rove, the chief strategist for his son's campaign, traveled from Austin, Tex., to Houston, where the former president spends the winter, to give him private briefings.

His friends say that Mr. Bush regularly exchanges calls or e-mail messages with about a half-dozen senior officials in the Texas governor's campaign and that his chief of staff, Jean Becker, is on the phone with Mr. Rove almost every day.

And neither father nor son is shy about reaching out to the other. One close family friend said they usually chatted within 15 to 30 minutes after the end of each of the debates in the Republican primaries.

"George and I do talk often," former President Bush said this week in written responses to questions that were electronically mailed to Ms. Becker. (Mr. Bush had declined through Ms. Becker to be interviewed on the telephone or in person for this article.) "When he asks for advice," the former president added, "I give it. He knows I will never breach a confidence or tell anyone."

Their closeness was suggested by the fact that the Texas governor, who arrived at the family compound in Kennebunkport, Me., late Friday for a weekend celebration of Barbara Bush's 75th birthday, extended his stay until today, and punctuated meetings of his campaign's senior staff with plenty of time with Dad. They golfed together twice, Ms. Becker said, and fished every day.

In recent interviews with nearly a

Continued on Page A24

Associated Press

The George Bushes teamed up for a big catch off Maine on Tuesday.

Violence Dogs Rural Candidates In Crucial Election in Zimbabwe

By RACHEL L. SWARNS

MUTASA, Zimbabwe, June 10 — After night falls and yawning villages like this one finally settle into sleep, Evelyn Masaiti, an opposition candidate, and three of her volunteers creep into a battered 1981 Peugeot. Through a crack in the car window, they send hundreds of campaign flyers fluttering among the thatched houses as their gray jalopy sputters along the dark, winding roads.

Even by Mrs. Masaiti's calculations, this is a strategy of desperation, not efficiency. With less than two weeks to go before Zimbabwe's parliamentary elections, her chief opponent, Mandi Chimene, a government official from the ruling party, is holding daily rallies in dusty shopping centers, plastering her portrait on tree trunks and wooing the local chiefs.

But Mrs. Masaiti, a 35-year-old science teacher, cannot hold rallies or wear political party T-shirts or even hang party posters during the day without risk. Last month, angry thugs killed a man because they believed he supported her, the police said. And two weeks ago, a mob torched the houses of dozens of opposition party members in broad daylight, leaving about 90 people homeless, including Mrs. Masaiti's in-laws.

On the television screens in the capital, Harare, this country's first heated race for Parliament is depicted mostly as a contest between two men, President Robert Mugabe and his chief rival, Morgan Tsvangirai, the opposition party leader.

But the real battle is fought far from the cameras, in rural hamlets like this one, where little-known opposition candidates are struggling to spread their message in a campaign characterized by intimidation and political violence.

Since March, at least 26 people have been killed and 150 have been injured, most of them black supporters of Mr. Tsvangirai's new party, the Movement for Democratic Change. And this week, Amnesty International, a human rights group, accused the government of either instigating or condoning the attacks, echoing some Western observers who have warned that the climate of fear has made free and fair elections unlikely.

Government officials deny that

Continued on Page A4

NEWS SUMMARY — A2

Updated news: www.nytimes.com

INSIDE

Coke Settles Bias Case

Coca-Cola said that it had reached a tentative settlement with black employees who sued the company contending they were denied promotions and other opportunities because of the color of their skin. PAGE C1

Ex-Army Worker Held as Spy

A former civilian employee of the Army was charged with providing the Soviet Union with classified documents for at least 25 years. PAGE A16

Devils Party, Jersey Style

Devils' fans celebrate the Stanley Cup with a family-style party on acres of asphalt, but it's a setting they know and love. PAGES B1, D1

THE KOREAN BREAKTHROUGH: Glasses Clink, Smiles Are Broad, a Pact Is Signed

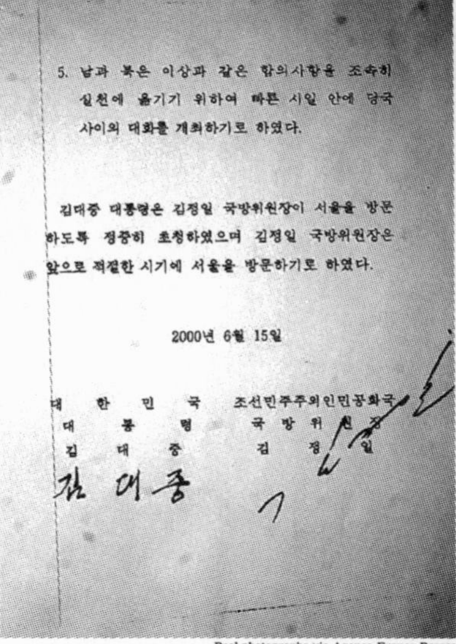

5. 남과 북은 이상과 같은 합의사항을 조속히 실천에 옮기기 위하여 빠른 시일 안에 당국 사이의 대화를 개최하기로 하였다.

김대중 대통령은 김정일 국방위원장이 서울을 방문하도록 정중히 초청하였으며 김정일 국방위원장은 앞으로 적절한 시기에 서울을 방문하기로 하였다.

2000년 6월 15일

대 한 민 국	조선민주주의인민공화국
대 통 령	국 방 위 원 장
김 대 중	김 정 일

Pool photographs via Agence France-Presse

The agreement that was signed by both Korean leaders yesterday. Kim Jong Il of North Korea, left, and Kim Dae Jung, browse through South Korean newspapers that are covering their summit meeting.

THE OVERVIEW

Koreas Reach Accord Seeking Reconciliation After 50 Years of Bitterness

Continued From Page A1

ing," said a diplomat. "Hopefully, things will continue to proceed from here, but this has already been an unexpected success."

If the agreements lacked the kind of fine detail that is often carefully worked out in important negotiations like these, they may have more than compensated for that by the strongly personal imprimatur placed on them by leaders whose repeated performances before the cameras left no doubts about their enthusiasm.

"In societies as hierarchical as Korea, that counts for a lot," said Leon V. Sigal, a North Korea expert at Columbia University. "In the North, having Kim Jong Il sign his name to a communiqué like this makes it the equivalent of dogma."

Perhaps the brightest moment of the day came at the toast shared by the two leaders at the signing ceremony, which took place at 11:20 p.m. on Wednesday and was broadcast in South Korea an hour later.

While the 75-year-old South Korean president paused between draughts as he tried to empty his glass, the younger Kim Jong Il, who has been characterized in the South as a heavy drinker, tilted his head back and finished his champagne in one go.

One of the meeting's most significant achievements was to help fill in a sketchy portrait of the 58-year-old Kim Jong Il, who has been caricatured outside his country as a crackpot and a playboy.

He was frequently on view again on Wednesday, for the second consecutive day, as he was shown talking with his southern counterpart in a relaxed and self-confident manner. He himself joked about his reputation as a recluse.

"Westerners seem to have been very anxious about why I live like a hermit," he said in an informal chat with Kim Dae Jung, moments before the two leaders went into a two-hour and 20-minute meeting. "And now, with your visit, they've got the answer."

Seeking to dispel this image, the North Korean leader said he had traveled overseas many times, naming two countries he had visited, China and Indonesia, but said that he had done so secretly.

Kim Dae Jung, who had smiled politely throughout this impromptu banter, set off laughter among the aides in the room from both sides when, referring to the reports about the North Korean leader, he replied, "You seem to know everything."

South Koreans, who paused from work throughout the day to watch the events on television, and were riveted to the their screens for the dramatic late night conclusion, expressed surprise about the warm and apparently relaxed atmosphere surrounding the talks, which began with the unexpected greeting of Kim Dae Jung by the northern president upon his arrival at the airport.

Many people said they were impressed by how normal and personable the mysterious northern leader was, after years of denigrating propaganda in the south.

"This will change the relationship between the two countries," said Park Han Sung, a clerk at an eyeglass shop in downtown Seoul.

"Maybe nothing dramatic will happen right away," he added, "but most people would agree that a surprising amount of progress and understanding has been achieved already."

In his reply to the South Korean leader's banquet toast, the second-ranking figure in North Korea, Kim Young Nam, said: "History gives us opportunities only once. Reunification is not for the future but for the present."

Western journalists, who were not invited to the North for the summit meeting, covered it via a special television link in Seoul and were told to expect a streamlined, four-point agreement. But the final text appeared to have hastily added other items, like language about a search for reconciliation and respect for each country's political system, both of which appeared to be included to appease the prickly North.

For Pyongyang, there was also little doubt that mention of increased exchanges in fact meant a boost in aid and investment from the South that northern leaders hope will prop up their failing economy. Famine in the North has claimed the lives of as many as two million people, according to the estimates of aid workers and outside experts.

The southern delegation rushed to leave little doubt of its willingness to help, on Wednesday offering to speed delivery of 200,000 tons of fertilizer, and also reportedly offering to provide $450 million in economic assistance.

For the South Korean leader, progress on reunion was a vital gauge of the success of the meeting. Seven million of his compatriots have relatives in the North.

"Many of the family members are passing away due to their advanced age," Mr. Kim said in a speech intended to give a clear sense of urgency to their agenda. "We have to attend to their life-long wishes."

While both sides clearly have di-

A deliberately vague agreement inspires great hope among many Koreans.

rect interests in reconciliation and reaching a peace agreement to finally end the state of war that formally persists between them, those interests are also keenly shared by the United States, China, Japan and other countries.

Japan has only recently renewed diplomatic contacts with North Korea, after a breech caused by Pyongyang's test-firing of a ballistic missile over Japan in 1998.

Washington has long been engaged in painstaking negotiations with North Korea seeking an end to the country's missile program, as well as a commitment not to develop or deploy nuclear weapons. For American defense planners, the divided peninsula remains one the most dangerous spots on the planet and the North's weapons programs have been seen as so potentially threatening that Washington is considering spending billions of dollars on a missile defense system to counter them.

How events of this summit meeting will shape those perceptions remains to be seen, but the North Korean leader has cleverly succeeded in changing an image that has alternated from flake to a modern-day Dr. Strangelove.

By showing himself far more publicly than ever before in meetings with the country's historic arch-enemy, whose peace initiatives he accepted with little of the North's usual intractability, he may have powerfully affected the dynamics surrounding American proposals to build an expensive antimissile shield.

North Korea's missile program has been the leading justification in Washington for the unproven shield. But Pyongyang has already suspended testing of missiles for over a year at Washington's request, and Mr. Kim's détente with the South, if upheld, with further chip away at the regime's image as being dangerous and unpredictable.

Despite the good feeling of the last two days, leaders in Seoul and elsewhere are likely to remain wary of the North's promises.

"I think it's very important that they've met, it's very important that they've signed this agreement," Joe Lockhart, the White House spokesman, said in Washington. "But I think it's also very important that a process comes out of this summit that allows them to implement the important work they have agreed to in the last two days."

The South Korean president took a moment out to bluntly advise his North Korean counterpart, "It is important to improve your relations with the United States and Japan."

Over the last 20 years, the North and the South have held innumerable rounds of lower-level talks on issues like the reunion of families, and twice before such agreements have later come apart.

Most recently, in 1991, talks led to an agreement promoting peace and eventual reunification, but it was never put into practice, partly because of a dispute over the North's suspected development of nuclear weapons. And in the 1970's, Red Cross officials of both sides began talks that lasted 14 years on the reunification of families, bearing only meager results.

President Kim Dae Jung, who is expected to fly home later today around a border that separates over a million men under arms, often spoke with passion to his host in their second day of meetings.

In one statement he told his younger counterpart that, in the age of the Internet, competition between nations now rests on brain power and economic strength, and no longer so much on the weapons of old.

"To survive the fierce international competition, the North and South must be one," he said. "I would like to quote an old proverb: 'United, strength and mind wins over heaven.' When all Korean people join forces, there is nothing we cannot achieve."

In Words of the Pact: 'To Work Together'

SEOUL, South Korea, June 14 (AP) — Following is the text of the accord signed by the leaders of North Korea and South Korea in Pyongyang, North Korea:

Upholding the lofty wishes of the Korean people yearning for peaceful reunification of the fatherland, President Kim Dae Jung of the Republic of Korea and Kim Jong Il, chairman of the National Defense Commission of the Democratic Peoples' Republic of Korea, held a historic meeting and summit talks on June 13-15, 2000.

Noting that the meeting and talks held for the first time in the divided Korean history carry grave significance in promoting mutual understanding and developing South-North relations and achieving peaceful, national reunification, the top leaders of South and North Korea declared as follows:

(1) The South and North, as masters of national unification, will join hands in efforts to resolve the issue of national unification independently.

(2) Acknowledging that the different formulas that the North and South favor for reunification have common factors, they will strive to work together to achieve this goal.

(3) The South and North will exchange groups of dispersed family members and their relatives around Aug. 15 and resolve as soon as possible humanitarian issues, including the repatriation of Communist prisoners who have completed their terms in jail.

(4) The South and North will pursue a balanced development of their national economies and build mutual trust by accelerating exchange in the social, cultural, sports, health and environmental sectors.

(5) In order to put these agreements into practice, the South and North will hold a dialogue between government authorities at an early date. President Kim Dae Jung cordially invited National Defense Commission chairman Kim Jong Il to visit Seoul, and he agreed to do that at an appropriate time.

WASHINGTON

U.S. Prepares To Remove Its Sanctions On the North

Continued From Page A1

administration, especially if the accords reached today dissolve in bickering over the details.

There is reason to worry about that: some of the concessions announced today, such as cultural exchanges and visits across the demilitarized zone by Koreans who have not seen family members for half a century, were the centerpieces of a 1991 agreement between the two nations that was never put into action.

But the agreement today, officials noted, bears the imprimatur of both nation's leaders. And Kim Jong Il, they said, made a public about-face, inviting North Koreans to line the streets as he welcomed a South Korean leader that the North has regularly characterized as an evil lackey of the Americans.

If the change in the North's attitude proves real, however, it creates a whole new set of questions for the United States. Would the United States be willing, over time, to withdraw some of the 37,000 American troops based in South Korea? Is it ready to resume diplomatic relations with the North, as it did five years ago with Vietnam?

And how could the United States justify spending $60 billion on a missile defense system predicated partly on the threat of a nuclear attack from North Korea, if it believed the North was changing course?

While the administration has gone to extraordinary lengths in the past two years to coax the North out of its shell, it is unready and unable to answer those questions.

"The sticking point is the North's nuclear weapons and their missiles," said Donald Gregg, the former Central Intelligence Agency station chief and then American ambassador to Seoul. "As soon as we raise those, they are going to raise the question of why we still have troops on the Korean peninsula. And no one is ready to deal with that."

He added, "Kim Dae Jung very wisely went to Pyongyang with an agenda that deals with those issues that are within the control of South Korea and North Korea." Diplomats familiar with Kim Dae Jung's talking points say he went determined to raise the security issues, but only in an oblique way. South Korean officials say that Kim Dae Jung planned to tell Kim Jong Il that those issues needed to be resolved, but not to press specific ideas.

"That may be the subject of the return visit to Seoul," one senior South Korean official said.

North Korea watchers here — from intelligence officials to State Department diplomats — say that even if a new era of cooperation is dawning, there is little reason to believe that the agreement reached today heralds any imminent unification of the Korean peninsula.

Neither side really wants that any time soon. The North's leaders have long been focused on survival — keeping their regime together at any cost. Kim Jong Il appears to have concluded that his best chances of survival lie in milking South Korea and Japan for the aid and trade he needs to achieve that goal.

And South Korea, for all its talk about the ultimate goal of reunifying the nation, knows that true reunification would cost a fortune. The billions spent propping up the country could endanger the South's recovery from the Asian economic crisis that threatened to ruin it two years ago. And it would dramatically change the country's social dynamics.

"Unification is a national goal," one senior South Korean diplomat said earlier this year, "and it should stay that way for a good while."

THE SCENE

For the South, a TV Stunner; in the North, Fanfare Is Lacking

By HOWARD W. FRENCH

SEOUL, South Korea, Thursday, June 15 — All day long and late into the night, the remarkable scenes from their president's visit to the mysterious brother-land to the north kept South Koreans locked to their television sets.

There was the visiting first lady, Lee Hee Ho, being entertained at an elementary school, watching impeccably dressed children perform dance and musical recitals with icy precision. She also met a former teacher, Kim Ji Han, in their first encounter in more than 60 years.

There was the strangely birdlike traffic police officer, swiveling 180 degrees with astonishing crispness as she repeatedly reversed direction and executed elaborate hand signals on a broad boulevard visibly empty of vehicles, or even pedestrians.

Perhaps most intriguing, there was the sight of the relaxed presidents of two Korean states long bitterly divided, Kim Dae Jung of the South and Kim Jong Il of the North, exchanging quips. The North Korean leader spoke of having slipped overseas secretly and dismissed his reputation in the West as an enigmatic recluse.

The old and familiar rules are invoked by Pyongyang's leaders.

The scenes and import were captured in the banner headline of The Korea Times this morning that read, "Two Koreas Sign Accord to Promote Peace." Like the rest of the South Korean media, it relied on joint reports filed by a pack of South Korean reporters who traveled to Pyongyang.

But the people of the North, a totalitarian society, did not even see this breath of "Truman Show"-like glimpses of history in the making. The remarkable scene of the arrival of the president from Seoul on Tuesday and his surprise airport greeting and ride to town with Kim Jong Il were shown on Northern television.

But beyond that, coverage of the summit meeting has been sparse and carefully edited. None of Kim Dae Jung's stirring words about unity, or about overcoming differences, have been broadcast on North Korean media. Indeed, as of Wednesday night's historic banquet, South Korean monitors said Pyongyang's official press had not once quoted the visiting head of state.

The North Korean media have made no special broadcasts, and it has acted without fanfare.

Instead, each time the two leaders met under the glare of South Korean video cameras, there has been an audible whir of Soviet-era cameras capturing the event on film for broadcast to the nation later. That allows editing intended to maintain the prestige and dignity of the Northern leader.

North Korean leaders watched closely, and probably with disquiet, the experience of their remaining ally in the world, China, as it has gradually relaxed political controls. And for Pyongyang, a lesson of the Tiananmen Square uprising in 1989, when student demonstrators invoked the name of the reformist Soviet leader, Mikhail Gorbachev, seems to be that the people must not be allowed to have competing heroes.

"If nothing else, the North Koreans have been attentive to history," a former high ranking South Korean official said. "Their priority remains controlling the messages that their people are allowed to hear."

South Korean experts said the North seemed to be treating this event according to old and familiar rules. Accordingly, those who engage with the Dear Leader, as Mr. Kim is officially known, must be seen by the public as supplicants.

According to this view, even the historic car ride from the airport shared by the two leaders was an act of supreme manipulation. The unexpected scene produced tears in the eyes of many South Koreans.

Seen another way, however, whisking the visitor into a waiting limousine deprived Kim Dae Jung of a chance to read an arrival speech, depriving him of a chance to address the North in a setting that would have been difficult to edit out.

"Everything about the way this has been covered has been controlled by the North Korean authorities," Kwan Okie, a former South Korean newspaper editor, said. "In the Western sense, there has been no coverage at all. Sure, the ride together was history. But looked at another way, it was almost a hostage taking."

Pool photo via Associated Press

Lee Hee Ho, South Korea's first lady, left, embraced Kim Ji Han, 85, her former math teacher, in Pyongyang yesterday.

"All the News That's Fit to Print"

The New York Times

Late Edition
New York: **Today,** afternoon thunderstorms, high 88. **Tonight,** showers end, low 67. **Tomorrow,** partly cloudy with showers late, high 81. **Yesterday,** high 88, low 74. Weather map, Page D8.

VOL. CXLIX . . . No. 51,432 | NEW YORK, TUESDAY, JUNE 27, 2000 | 75 CENTS

$1 beyond the greater New York metropolitan area.

Genetic Code of Human Life Is Cracked by Scientists

JUSTICES REAFFIRM MIRANDA RULE, 7-2; A PART OF 'CULTURE'

By LINDA GREENHOUSE

WASHINGTON, June 26 — The Supreme Court reaffirmed the Miranda decision today by a 7-to-2 vote that erased a shadow over one of the most famous rulings of modern times and acknowledged that the Miranda warnings "have become part of our national culture."

The court said in an opinion by Chief Justice William H. Rehnquist that because the 1966 Miranda decision "announced a constitutional rule," a statute by which Congress had sought to overrule the decision was itself unconstitutional.

Miranda had appeared to be in jeopardy, both because of that long-ignored but recently rediscovered law, by which Congress had tried to overrule Miranda 32 years ago, and because of the court's perceived hostility to the original decision.

The chief justice said, though, that the 1968 law, which replaced the Miranda warnings with a case-by-case test of whether a confession was voluntary, could be upheld only if the Supreme Court decided to overturn Miranda. But with Miranda having "become embedded in routine police practice" without causing any measurable difficulty for prosecutors, there was no justification for doing so, he said. [Excerpts, Page A18.]

Justices Antonin Scalia and Clarence Thomas cast the dissenting votes.

The decision overturned a ruling last year by the federal appeals court in Richmond, Va., which held that Congress was entitled to the last word because Miranda's presumption that a confession was not voluntary unless preceded by the warnings was not required by the Constitution.

The decision today — only 14 pages long, in Chief Justice Rehnquist's typically spare style — brought an abrupt end to one of the odder episodes in the court's recent history, an intense and strangely delayed refighting of a previous generation's battle over the rights of criminal suspects. Miranda v. Arizona was a hallmark of the Warren Court, and Chief Justice Rehnquist, despite his record as an early and tenacious critic of the decision, evidently did not want its repudiation to be an imprint of his own tenure.

There was considerable drama in the courtroom today as the chief justice announced that he would deliver the decision in the case, Dickerson v. United States, No. 99-5525. The announcement meant that he was the majority opinion's author. Given his statements over more than 25 years about Miranda's lack of constitutional foundation, there was the distinct possibility that he was about to announce that Miranda had been overruled.

The way Chief Justice Rehnquist chose to begin his announcement did little to clarify matters. "You have the right to remain silent," he intoned in a firm voice, moving on to the other familiar warnings without further introduction. Some in the courtroom audience wondered whether they might be hearing these phrases as the official words of the court for the last time.

By the time the chief justice fin-

Continued on Page A18

Multiple-Party Ballot Rejected in Primaries

The Supreme Court invalidated California's blanket primary, in which voters can cast ballots for candidates of any party. The 7-to-2 decision also cast serious doubt on the more common open primary, which allows voters in more than half the states to request a particular party's ballot.

Article, Page A19.

Clinton Raises Estimate of Surplus And the Stakes on How to Use It

By RICHARD W. STEVENSON

WASHINGTON, June 26 — President Clinton raised his projection of the federal budget surplus today by nearly $1.3 trillion for the next decade, putting a breathtaking sum of new money on the table as the two parties and their presidential candidates battle over tax cuts, spending and how to prepare for the nation's long-term challenges.

"How we use these surpluses in this moment of prosperity will determine America's future for decades to come," Mr. Clinton told reporters in the Rose Garden.

The new estimate put up for political grabs an amount of money two and a half times greater than what the White House had projected less than five months ago. The robust forecast is the latest result of a strong economy that is rewriting the budget outlook on an almost continuous basis by recasting projections for years to come, even though events could easily undermine those projections. And those assumptions are promoting an economy that has shown tentative signs of slowing in recent months.

The new estimate brought the total surplus projection to slightly less than $4.2 trillion for 2001 through 2010. Of that, $2.3 trillion is projected to come from the Social Security system and is considered by both parties to be off limits for tax cuts or spending programs.

The rest — almost $1.9 trillion, up from $746 billion under the White House's last estimate in February — is projected to come from general tax receipts, and is the pot of money that Democrats and Republicans are fighting over.

Seeking to frame the debate over how the money should be used, Mr. Clinton immediately proposed a deal to divide part of the windfall with the Republican majority in Congress.

Mr. Clinton said he would agree to

Continued on Page A20

Updated news: www.nytimes.com

354613

The Book of Life

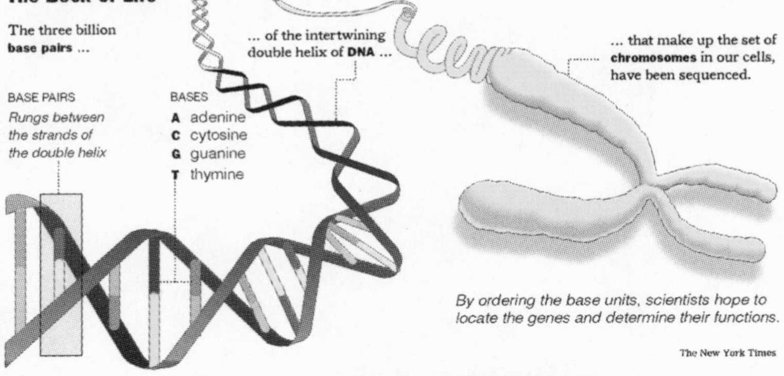

By ordering the base units, scientists hope to locate the genes and determine their functions.

The New York Times

Science Times
A special issue

- Putting the genome to work.
- Some information has already paid research dividends.
- Two research methods, two results.
- From Mendel to helix to genome.
- More articles, charts and photos of the genome effort.

Section F

Francis S. Collins, head of the Human Genome Project, left, with J. Craig Venter, head of Celera Genomics, after the announcement yesterday that they had finished the first survey of the human genome.

Paul Hosefros/The New York Times

A Pearl and a Hodgepodge: Human DNA

By NATALIE ANGIER

The human genome, the sum of all genetic material encased in nearly every cell of the human body, is very, very long — at least three billion chemical letters long, as many letters as you would find in a thousand copies of an entire Sunday issue of The New York Times.

The human genome is pithy. The English alphabet has 26 letters; the Russian, 33 letters; and the Japanese, 1,850 symbols. Yet, with just four distinct characters at its disposal, four nucleic acid bases, the human genome has given rise to the creators of every language uttered, every ballad sung, every Pokémon card traded.

The human genome is a pigsty, bulging with nongenes, ex-genes, freeloader genes, viral detritus, pocket lint and chewing gum. All but a few percent of it appears to be doing nothing at all.

The human genome is a pearl, a model of high performance and reliability. Millions of times a year, egg genome meets sperm genome, and the result is a human baby, its parts all in place, its brain a universe of love and meaning.

In short, the human genome exults in contradictions.

And scientists, with their announcement that they have completed a so-called working draft of the entire sequence of the human genome, must traffic in a few contradictions of their own. They rightly regard the sequencing of the genome as a major scientific landmark.

"This is a milestone in biology unlike any other," said Francis S. Collins, director of the National Human Genome Research Institute. "We only have to do this once, reading out the sequence of our own instruction book, and here we are on brink of it."

At the same time, scientists know that the bulk of their work in deciphering that sequence has yet to be done. "Complexity is the word on everybody's lips these days when they see what the genome really looks like," said David Baltimore, the molecular biologist and Nobel laureate who is president of the California Institute of Technology. "We've got another century of work ahead of us, to figure out how all these things relate to each other."

Though scientists underscore the importance of their accomplishment by calling the genome a "portrait of who we are," they quickly append that: people are not, and never will be, mere products of their genes.

"One of my concerns is that, as we begin to glimpse some of the biological contributions to certain personality traits, in people's minds those contributions will loom larger than they should," Dr. Collins said, "and the notion of genetic determinism will gather further momentum that it doesn't deserve."

Even in the case of a seemingly familial disease like schizophrenia,

Continued on Page A21

Sharansky in Eyes of Israelis: A Hero or Betrayer of Peace?

By DEBORAH SONTAG

JERUSALEM, June 26 — It has been 14 years since Interior Minister Natan Sharansky began making the transition from icon to man when he emigrated to Israel. It has been four since he morphed further from man to politician.

But his experience as a prisoner of conscience in the former Soviet Union not only stamped him forever; it also shaped others' expectations of him in unyielding ways.

To Israelis and to Jews worldwide, Mr. Sharansky is somewhat frozen in time behind the bars where he sat for nine years while they invested in him as a hero and fought for his freedom. And everything that he does is judged as a return on that investment, which means some amount of disappointment for everyone, left and right, secular and religious.

"Everybody marched for me," Mr. Sharansky, 52, said in an interview today. "And everybody feels I owe them."

Right now, Mr. Sharansky is fighting an uphill battle to persuade Prime Minister Ehud Barak to join hands with the rightist Likud Party to form a national unity government. He portrays this, too, as an outgrowth of his days as a Soviet dissident. In his old punishment cell, he says, he did not distinguish between different kinds of Jews, and ever since meeting the divided reality of the Jewish nation, he has sought to forge a consensus.

Some lionize him for this, and contend that Mr. Sharansky would be an ideal national leader, much as he would break the mold with his thickly accented Hebrew and a military record that consists of three weeks in

Continued on Page A10

Buildings' Savior Now a Troubled Landlord

By AMY WALDMAN

This spring, the grievances at 1084-1086 Home Street in the South Bronx piled up like the garbage in the courtyard: sporadic heat and hot water, unpaid light bills, water-cracked walls, rats swaggering through like neighborhood bullies. Hallway graffiti cursed the landlord, who had not bothered to paint over it.

The building's state was not the handiwork of a profiteering landlord. Rather, the overseer of 1084-1086 Home Street is the Banana Kelly Community Improvement Association, a Bronx nonprofit community development corporation once praised as a national model for residents who want to restore failing housing and reclaim lost neighborhoods.

Today, its own properties are increasingly troubled, whether by periods without heat or by unrealized plans, as with a former synagogue, empty and encrusted with scaffolding, on Fox Street.

For a group that got its start rehabilitating abandoned buildings, there may be no symbol more dispiriting than 866 Beck Street, a Banana Kelly building that deteriorated so much that it was emptied of tenants and boarded up.

"Our savior has become a slumlord," said Marta Rivera, the chairwoman of the local community board and a tenant at 1084 Home Street since 1987.

The criticism, if harsh, is understandable, given what Banana Kelly, which drew its memorable name from the curve of the Bronx street where it was born, once meant in the South Bronx.

Two decades ago, foundations, reporters and government officials flocked to the Hunts Point-Longwood neighborhoods to see how Banana Kelly had transformed drug-infested, derelict tenements into livable spaces, and had created low-income housing co-ops that proved the salvation of

Continued on Page B8

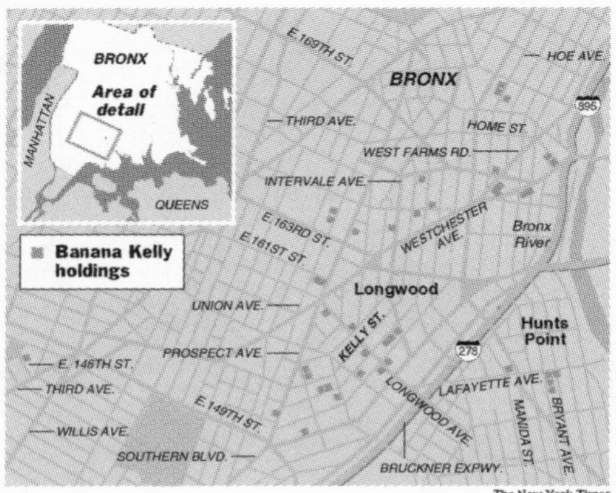

[Map: BRONX, Area of detail, MANHATTAN, QUEENS; Banana Kelly holdings; E. 169th St., Third Ave., Home St., West Farms Rd., Intervale Ave., E. 163rd St., Westchester Ave., Bronx River, E. 161st St., Longwood, Union Ave., Kelly St., Hunts Point, Prospect Ave., E. 146th St., Longwood Ave., Lafayette Ave., E. 149th St., Willis Ave., Southern Blvd., Manida St., Bryant Ave., Bruckner Expwy. — The New York Times]

A DREAM FORECLOSED
A special report.

A SHARED SUCCESS

2 Rivals' Announcement Marks New Medical Era, Risks and All

By NICHOLAS WADE

WASHINGTON, June 26 — In an achievement that represents a pinnacle of human self-knowledge, two rival groups of scientists said today that they had deciphered the hereditary script, the set of instructions that defines the human organism.

"Today we are learning the language in which God created life," President Clinton said at a White House ceremony attended by members of the two teams, Dr. James D. Watson, co-discoverer of the structure of DNA, and, via satellite, Prime Minister Tony Blair of Britain. [Excerpts, Page F8.]

The teams' leaders, Dr. J. Craig Venter, president of Celera Genomics, and Dr. Francis S. Collins, director of the National Human Genome Research Institute, praised each other's contributions and signaled a spirit of cooperation from now on, even though the two efforts will remain firmly independent.

The human genome, the ancient script that has now been deciphered, consists of two sets of 23 giant DNA molecules, or chromosomes, with each set — one inherited from each parent — containing more than three billion chemical units.

The successful deciphering of this vast genetic archive attests to the extraordinary pace of biology's advance since 1953, when the structure of DNA was first discovered and presages an era of even brisker progress.

Understanding the human genome is expected to revolutionize the practice of medicine. Biologists expect in time to develop an array of diagnostics and treatments based on it and tailored to individual patients, some of which will exploit the body's own mechanisms of self-repair.

The knowledge in the genome could also be used in harmful ways, particularly in revealing patients' disposition to disease if their privacy is not safeguarded, and in causing discrimination.

The joint announcement is something of a shotgun marriage because neither side's version of the human genome is complete, nor do they agree on the genome's size. Neither has sequenced — meaning to determine the order of the chemical subunits — the DNA of certain short structural regions of the genome, which cannot yet be analyzed.

With the rest of the genome, which contains the human genes and much else, both sides' versions have many small gaps, although these are thought to contain few or no genes. Today's versions are effectively

Continued on Page A21

Vote in Zimbabwe Shows Opposition Making Big Gains

By RACHEL L. SWARNS

HARARE, Zimbabwe, Tuesday, June 27 — Supporters of the opposition party cheered and danced on Monday as election results from the weekend's parliamentary elections showed their fledgling party making unprecedented gains on the governing party that has dominated Zimbabwe for 20 years.

The final result was unclear, but with more than three quarters of the vote in today from counting stations across the country, tallies quickly established that the nine-month-old party had become a powerful opposition force in Zimbabwe — a feat considered unimaginable just a year ago.

For years, President Robert Mugabe's governing party has controlled all but three seats in Parliament. But the new opposition party, the Movement for Democratic Change, easily surpassed that figure, winning 48 seats and claiming lopsided victories in urban districts, where voters have been squeezed by skyrocketing inflation and deepening unemployment.

Based on the early returns, it appeared that the governing party would likely maintain its majority as it carried 51 mostly rural districts, where the party's support has traditionally been strongest. Mr. Mugabe was also guaranteed 20 appointed

Continued on Page A6

INSIDE

Chechnya Assault to Resume

The day after a top commander announced a halt to Russian attacks in Chechnya, the Kremlin said that the attacks would continue. PAGE A9

A Move Ahead for Ulster

Two envoys have inspected a number of Irish Republican Army arms caches, a step in advancing Northern Ireland's peace pact. PAGE A3

Miami Relatives File Appeal

The Miami relatives of 6-year-old Elián González asked the Supreme Court to block his return to Cuba pending a formal appeal. PAGE A14

Fed Unlikely to Raise Rates

The Federal Reserve is expected to leave interest rates unchanged when it completes its two-day meeting tomorrow. BUSINESS DAY, PAGE C1

READING THE BOOK OF LIFE: A Historic Quest

THE OVERVIEW

Scientists Crack Genetic Code of Humans

Continued From Page A1

complete representations of the genome but leave much more work to be done.

The two groups even differ on the size of the gene-coding part of the genome. Celera says it is 3.12 billion letters of DNA; the public consortium that it is 3.15 billion units, a letter difference of 30 million. Neither side can yet describe the genome's full size or determine the number of human genes.

The public consortium has also fallen somewhat behind in its goal of attaining a working draft in which 90 percent of the gene-containing part of the genome was sequenced. Its version today has reached only 85 percent, suggesting it was marching to Celera's timetable.

Today's announcement heralded an unexpected truce between the two groups of scientists who have been racing to finish the genome. Veering away from the prospect of asserting rival claims of victory, the two chose to report simultaneously their attainment of different milestones in their quest.

Celera, a unit of the PE Corporation, has obtained its 3.12 billion letters of the genome in the form of long continuous sequences, mostly about 2 million letters each, but with many small gaps.

A less complete version has been reported by the Human Genome Project, a consortium of academic centers supported largely by the National Institutes of Health and the Wellcome Trust, a medical philanthropy in London. Dr. Collins, the consortium's leader, said its scientists had sequenced 85 percent of the genome in a "working draft," meaning its accuracy will be upgraded later.

READING THE BOOK OF LIFE

A special issue explores the efforts and consequences of deciphering the chemical structure of life, Science Times, Section F.

Both versions of the human genome meet the important goal of allowing scientists to search them for desired genes, the genetic instructions encoded in the DNA. The consortium's genome data is freely available now. Celera has said it will make a version of its genome sequence freely available at a later date.

In their remarks at the White House, Dr. Collins and Dr. Venter both sought to capture the wider meaning of their work in identifying the eye-glazing stream of A's, G's, C's and T's, the letters in the genome's four-letter code.

"We have caught the first glimpses of our instruction book, previously known only to God," Dr. Collins said. Dr. Venter spoke of his conviction from seeing people die in Vietnam, where he served as a medic, that the human spirit transcended the physiology that is controlled by the genome.

The two genome versions were obtained through prodigious efforts by each side, involving skilled management of teams of scientists working around the clock on a novel technological frontier.

Spurring their efforts was the glittering lure of the genome as a scientific prize, and a rivalry fueled by personal differences and conflicting agendas.

Dr. Venter, a genomics pioneer whose innovative methods have at times been scorned by experts in the consortium's camp, has often cast himself, not without reason, as an outsider battling a hostile establishment.

The consortium scientists were halfway through a successful 15-year program to complete the human genome by 2005, when Dr. Venter announced in May 1998 that as head of a new company, later called Celera, he would beat them to their goal by 5 years.

His bombshell entry turned an academic pursuit into a fierce race. Dr. Collins responded by moving his completion date forward to 2003 and setting this month as the target for a 90 percent draft.

"These folks have pulled out all the stops," he said of his staff in an interview last week. "They have achieved a ramp-up that is beyond anything one would have imagined possible."

The 15-year cost of the Human Genome Project, which began in 1990, has been estimated at $3 billion, but includes many incidental expenses. The consortium has spent only $300 million on sequencing the human genome since January 1999, when its all-out production phase began. Celera has not released its costs, but Dr. Venter said a year ago that he expected Celera's human genome to cost $200 million to $250 million.

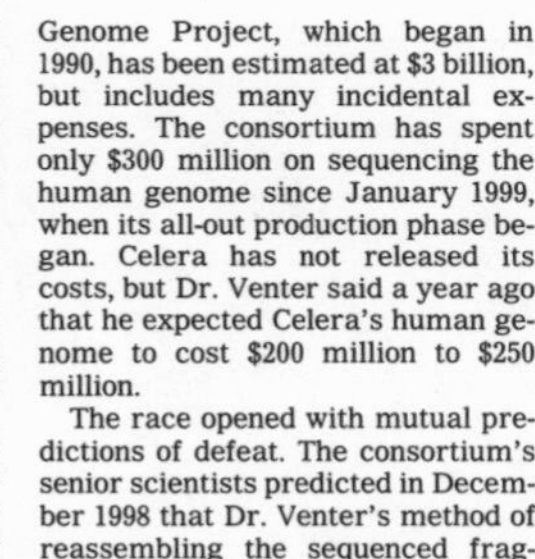
The Sequence of the Human Genome
Two efforts to determine the order of all the units, or bases, in the human genetic code have reached a milestone.
CELLS Each has a nucleus containing pairs of 23 chromosomes, one from each parent, that together contain the human genome.
Nucleus
CHROMOSOMES Each chromosome is made of long chains of deoxyribonucleic acid, or DNA, wrapped around proteins.
DNA A molecule with intertwined strands, or double helix shape. Rungs between the strands are bases: adenine (A), thymine (T), guanine (G) and cytosine (C).
G
A
T
C
GENES These sections of DNA instruct the cell to make proteins, which perform all the body's essential tasks, like digestion, and determine physical features, like eye color.
THE SEQUENCE A private company says it has ordered all the bases, with some small gaps, and a public effort has roughly 90 percent of the bases in order, in small batches that remain to be assembled.
T
G
A
C
Source: "Genome," by Matt Ridley

Steve Duenes/The New York Times

The race opened with mutual predictions of defeat. The consortium's senior scientists predicted in December 1998 that Dr. Venter's method of reassembling the sequenced fragments of genomic DNA was bound to fail. In May 1999, Dr. Venter, confident of Celera's impending success, observed that the National Institutes of Health and the Wellcome Trust were "putting good money after bad."

The groups were divided by political as well as technical agendas. The consortium's two principal scientists, Dr. John E. Sulston of the Sanger Center in England and Dr. Robert Waterston of Washington University in St. Louis, insisted that the genome data should be published nightly, an unusually generous policy because scientists generally harvest new data for their own discoveries before sharing it.

Both of the consortium's administrative leaders, Dr. James D. Watson, and his successor, Dr. Collins, made a point of seeking out international partners so that the rest of the world would not feel excluded from the genome triumph. Thus even though centers in the United States and Britain have done most of the heavy lifting, important contributions to the consortium's genome draft have been made by centers in Germany, France, Japan and China.

Academic scientists have felt some chagrin that an altruistic, open and technically successful venture like the Human Genome Project should be upstaged by a commercial rival financed by the company that made the consortium's DNA sequencing machines.

But though Celera seeks to profit by operating a genomic database, Dr. Venter also believed that he could make the genome and its benefits available a lot sooner. He has succeeded in doing so, and in spurring the consortium to move faster.

Today's truce between the two teams offers several advantages. For Celera to claim victory over the consortium would risk alienating customers in the academic community. For the consortium, the surety of opting into a draw now may have seemed better than the risks of claiming victory with a complete genome much later.

Reaching a pinnacle of human self-knowledge, full of promise and risk.

Celera's version of the genome depends on the consortium's data. And the many small gaps in Celera's sequence will probably be filled by the consortium's scientists, adding further to their claim on credit for the final product.

The present truce between the sides is limited to today's announcement and an agreement to publish their reports in the same journal, although the details remain to be worked out. A joint workshop will be held to discuss the genome versions.

The versions of the human genome produced by the two teams are in different states of completion because of the different methods each used to determine the order of DNA units in the genome.

The consortium chose first to break the genome down into large chunks, called BAC's, which are about 150,000 DNA letters long, and to sequence each BAC separately. This BAC by BAC strategy also required "mapping" the genome, or defining short sequences of milestone DNA that would help show where each BAC belonged on its parent chromosome, the giant DNA molecules of which the genome is composed.

BAC's are assembled from thousands of snippets of DNA, each about 500 DNA letters in length. This is the longest run of DNA letters that the DNA sequencing machines can analyze. A computer pieces together the snippets by looking for matches in the DNA sequence where one snippet overlaps another.

But the BAC's do not assemble cleanly from their component snippets. One reason is that human DNA is full of repetitive sequences — the same run of letters repeated over and over again — and these repetitions baffle the computer algorithms set to assemble the pieces.

The stage the consortium has now reached is that all its BAC's are mapped, making the whole genome available in a nested set of smaller jigsaw puzzles. But the BAC's are in varying stages of completion. The BAC's covering the two smallest human chromosomes, numbers 21 and 22, are essentially complete. But many other BAC's are in less immaculate states of assembly. Many consist of assembled pieces no more than 10,000 units long, and the order of these pieces within each BAC is not known.

The sum of the assembled pieces in each BAC now covers 85 percent of the genome. This working draft, as the consortium calls it, is maybe not a thing of beauty but is of great value to researchers looking for genes and represents a major accomplishment.

Celera's genome has been assembled by a different method, called a whole genome shotgun strategy. Following a scheme proposed by Dr. Eugene Myers and Dr. J. L. Weber, Celera skips the time-consuming mapping stage and breaks the whole genome down into a set of fragments that are 2,000, 10,000 and 50,000 letters long. These fragments are analyzed separately and then assembled in a single mammoth computer run, with a handful of clever tricks to step across the repetitive sequence regions in the DNA.

The approach ideally required sequencing 30 billions units of DNA — 10 times that in a single genome. Dr. Venter seems to have taken a considerable risk by starting his assembly at the end of March this year when he possessed only a threefold coverage of the genome. He has since raised his total to 4.6-fold coverage.

The decision may have been influenced by Celera's rate of capital expenditure — the company's electric bill alone is $100,000 a month — and by the need to sequence the mouse genome as well so as to offer database clients a two-genome package. The mouse genome is expected to be invaluable for interpreting the human genome, and Dr. Venter said today that Celera would finish sequencing it by the end of the year.

Because of having relatively little of its own data, Celera made use of the consortium's publicly available sequence data and, indirectly, of the positional information contained in the consortium's mapped set of BAC's. The consortium can justifiably share in the credit for Celera's version of the genome, another cogent factor in the logic of today's truce.

Biotech Shares Rise and Fall

Stocks of biotechnology companies rose early yesterday after a White House announcement that the first survey of the human genome had been completed, but investors cashed in some of their profits before trading ended, causing several issues to fall.

Biotechnology shares peaked in March in a speculative frenzy, before backsliding sharply. In recent weeks, they again posted significant increases in anticipation of the genome announcement.

The Celera Genomics unit of the PE Corporation, which participated in the mapping project and has been one of the highest fliers, dropped $12.25, to $113 yesterday. The stock of the company, based in Rockville, Md., hit a record high of $252 a share on Feb. 25. Although well off its high, Celera shares are still up 1,400 percent from this time last year.

Humanity

Paul Hosefros/The New York Times

Dr. J. Craig Venter, right, president of Celera Genomics, and Dr. Francis S. Collins, director of the National Human Genome Research Institute, joined President Clinton at the White House yesterday.

THE CONTEXT

A Pearl and a Hodgepodge: Genome Is Rife With Contradictions

Continued From Page A1

for example, unknown environmental factors still loom large, which is why if one identical twin comes down with the disorder, the other twin has only a 50 percent chance of suffering the same fate — despite being genetic clones.

Researchers want to talk about the medical miracles they expect to come from a better knowledge of the human genome. They don't want to promise any cure or palliative too soon. Yet they feel inspired to let their imaginations go, in loftiness and gravitas, as they fantasize about what the sequence may reveal, and what it may forever conceal.

For some, the emerging details of the genome sequence are most fascinating for what they say about the fraternity between the human species and all other creatures on earth.

"Looking at the genome, and taking it as a kind of image of who we are, places us squarely with the rest of nature," said Jon Seger, an evolutionary biologist and geneticist at the University of Utah in Salt Lake City.

"You can see the same genes in flies, worms, monkeys, mice and people. It's evolution laid out for all to see. There's nothing peculiar or distinctive about us."

Except, perhaps, for the species-wide homogeneity of humans.

Some scientists emphasize the genetic fraternity of humanity. Humans may be genomically similar to mice and monkeys, but it turns out that people are extraordinarily similar to each other: there are far fewer genetic differences, or polymorphisms, among different peoples, and populations of peoples, than are observed in individual members of other species, including ape relatives.

This discovery, scientists say, has profound implications for understanding the various human "races."

Kelly Owens and Mary-Claire King, geneticists at the University of Washington in Seattle, argued last year in the journal Science that whatever genetic differences existed between, say, Africans and Europeans, or Asians and aborigines, they were likely to be literally skin-deep.

The researchers described how the recent analysis of the so-called melanocortin-stimulating hormone receptor gene, which is involved in melanin production, indicated that small discrepancies in this receptor gene appeared to account for most of the variations observed in human skin and hair color and texture. If true, they wrote, then variation at a single, tiny genetic locus in charge of "superficial traits" had been "the cause of enormous suffering."

"Of course, prejudice does not require a rational basis, let alone an evolutionary one," they said in the article. "But the myth of major genetic differences across 'races' is nonetheless worth dismissing with genetic evidence."

Scientists are also falling over each other for the prize for the most apt analogy. What is the genome really? Is it the Book of Life, the Booklet of Life, a blueprint for a human being, an atlas, a master parts list? Martha Stewart's "How to Replicate?"

"There's a metaphor contest going on," said Harold Varmus, the former director of the National Institutes of Health and now president of Memorial Sloan-Kettering Cancer Center in Manhattan. "I've used quite a few of them myself."

The human genome's structure is 'evolution laid out for all to see.'

These days, he said, "I've decided we've got to get away from the idea of this as a blueprint. That doesn't convey what we have. Because we don't just have the linear sequence, we have the physical parts, too."

In other words, he said, computer databases may hold the sequence information, the lineup of billions of A's, T's, G's and C's. But the segments of the genome also exist in physical form, in the bellies of bacterial and yeast cells, which can be manipulated. "The important thing is having pieces of DNA in your hand, and being able to figure out how they work by modifying and mutating them," he said. "That's where the game is now."

Which is why his favorite metaphor is a kid with a clock. "You can take the clock apart, lay the pieces out in front of you, and then try to understand what makes it tick by putting it back together again," he said.

Yet, as any would-be Edison soon discovers, it's easier to deconstruct than reconstruct. And scientists are having a difficult time making sense of even the most basic springs and gears of the genome. They don't yet know how many genes the three billion chemical letters hold, for example, with estimates ranging from a low of 25,000 to a high of 150,000.

"The fashionable arguing over gene number," said David Page of the Whitehead Institute in Cambridge, Mass., who is studying the sequences of the human sex chromosomes, "reveals just how difficult it is to deliver anything concrete with the current state of sequence analysis."

Biologists also disagree vehemently on the meaning of the vast stretches of non-gene material in the genome, the estimated 2.5 billion to 2.8 billion chemical letters that do not appear to take part in the synthesis of proteins, which are the body's worker bees, the molecules that comprise the body and keep it alive.

"More than 95 percent of our DNA is just there, and it's described as not functional," said C. Robert Cloninger, who studying personality and genomics at Washington University in St. Louis. "But I don't know of anything in nature that's just laying around and is not functional."

But "functional" from whose perspective? The human body may not recruit the sequences for protein duty, but if the sequences do us no harm, natural selection may not have bothered to get rid of them. Just as microscopic mites live on our cheek cells and eyelashes, so our genomes may carry a plethora of nucleic squatters.

"We can identify almost 50 percent of the genome as being so-called repetitive elements, or transposable elements, which are like little viruses that have taken advantage of the cell's machinery to replicate themselves," said Phil Green, a genomics researcher at the University of Washington. "And the real number may be more like 95 percent of the genome, although a lot of these transposable elements are so ancient that they're hard to identify."

In Dr. Green's view, the notion of the human genome as a haven for transposable elements is humbling.

"Not only aren't we the center of the universe," he said, "we're not even the center of our own genome. We only have a small part of our own genome that's really us."

As he sees it, the human genome, compared to the genomes of fast-breeding organisms like bacteria, is "distinctly suboptimal. A bacterial genome is densely packed with genes, and there's almost no junk — bacteria just can't afford the baggage." But because humans live long and reproduce slowly, and historically have existed in small numbers, their genomes have not been under competitive pressure to streamline themselves to Swiss-watch efficiency.

"Even the genes that are there may be suboptimal," he said. "Many genes may have picked up mutations that cause their protein products to work not quite as well as they could, but there hasn't been selective pressure to weed out all mutations."

Another insight that emerges from a meditation on the human genome: not only is no man or woman an island, no gene is, either. Genes work in groups, and the performance and specific architecture of each intimately affects the performance of the others.

"Nothing is simple, and everything depends on everything else," said Dr. Cloninger. He and his colleagues have been working on genome scans to link personality traits with specific genes and genetic patterns. The more they look, the more tangled the human portrait becomes. From studies of twins and similar research, scientists had estimated that, as with schizophrenia, about half of the observed variations in many personality traits were environmental in origin, and half were genetic.

But comprehending the genetic half is now complicated by the fact that it is not enough to tally up the impact on a trait of this, that and the other gene, said Dr. Cloninger. "You must consider the complex and nonadditive interactions between the different genes," he said. For example, he and his colleagues have studied the trait called novelty seeking — the thirst for new experiences — and found it to be influenced by three genes: one involved in the brain's use of the neurochemical dopamine, another in the neurochemical serotonin, and a third in catecholamine production, part of the body's fight-or-flight response.

If two siblings share identical forms of all three genes, they turn out to correlate in their degree of novelty-seeking behavior by about 40 percent. But if just one of the three genes differs in form between the siblings, the correlation drops, not to 20 percent or 30 percent, as one might expect, but to 10 percent or less. The three genes work as a tightly knit team, together with other tightly knit teams that have yet to be discovered.

"We tend to like to think in terms of separate things operating causally in linear sequence," said Dr. Cloninger. "But that's not an accurate picture of the way biology works."

So maybe another metaphor for the human genome is a human dream: rich with significance, personal yet universal, stuffed with nonsense, all out of order yet infused with its own mad logic.

"All the News That's Fit to Print"

The New York Times

Late Edition
New York: **Today,** mostly sunny and seasonable, high 71. **Tonight,** remaining clear, low 59. **Tomorrow,** sunny and warm, high 74. **Yesterday,** high 65, low 48. Weather map is on Page 41.

VOL. CL . . . No. 51,528 NEW YORK, SUNDAY, OCTOBER 1, 2000 — $3 beyond the greater New York metropolitan area. — $2.50

BASIC DIFFERENCES IN RIVAL PROPOSALS ON DRUG COVERAGE

COMPARISON IS DIFFICULT

In Philosophical Divide, Gore Promises Higher Subsidy as Bush Focuses on Choice

By ROBIN TONER

WASHINGTON, Sept. 30 — The campaign debate over prescription drugs for the elderly has become a confusing muddle of partisan charges and countercharges, with both sides invoking the standard bogymen of health care debates, from "big government" to "H.M.O. bureaucrats."

But a few things are clear, health analysts say.

It is very difficult for the average Medicare beneficiary to sit down with the Bush and Gore plans and compare how much she would pay in premiums and co-payments and how much she would receive in benefits. That is because the approaches of the two candidates are so different, and there are so many unknowns about Gov. George W. Bush's plan.

Given what is known, many analysts and consumer advocates consider Vice President Al Gore's plan to be more generous; he would devote much more money to it, they note, and he promises a higher federal subsidy for premiums. Mr. Bush's health care advisers counter that his plan offers more flexibility and more choices for older Americans.

For all the promises, experts say none of the drug benefits being proposed for Medicare are as generous as what many working people routinely receive. But critics of entitlement programs are already complaining about expanding benefits in a program with long-term financial problems.

This often arcane policy discussion is occurring in a white-hot political environment. Few would have predicted it two years ago, but the cost of prescription drugs — and the lack of Medicare coverage for them — has remained at the top of the political agenda in this campaign. In the most recent New York Times/CBS News Poll, 65 percent of those surveyed, including 71 percent of the women, said reducing the costs of prescription drugs for the elderly mattered "a lot" to them.

Health care and Medicare combined overshadowed most other is-

Continued on Page 22

Debate Stakes Seen as Critical By Candidates

Both Camps Emphasize Tightness of the Race

By RICHARD L. BERKE

WASHINGTON, Sept. 30 — When Gov. George W. Bush and Vice President Al Gore appear side by side in Boston on Tuesday before the largest single television audience of the presidential campaign, officials in both camps say, the stakes will be far greater than they had anticipated because the contest is so excruciatingly tight.

The debate has emerged as so consequential, in fact, that operatives for Mr. Gore and Mr. Bush said they had suspended many important strategic decisions, at least until Wednesday, so they could gauge whether the fundamental dynamics of the contest have been shifted. Those decisions include where to buy advertising and where, precisely, the candidates should be deployed in the final weeks of the campaign.

Karl Rove, Mr. Bush's chief strategist, played down the debates a few weeks back, saying they tended only to reinforce voters' support of one candidate or another.

Now, given that the race has no front-runner, Mr. Rove argues that the 90-minute debates — the one is Boston is followed a week later with a debate in Winston-Salem, N.C., then one in St. Louis a week after that — may be pivotal. Not since Richard M. Nixon and John F. Kennedy squared off in 1960, he said, have debates been so significant in a presidential contest.

"With the polls so close," Mr. Rove said, "an impact of three or four or five percentage points could easily have a significant impact on the race."

Mark Fabiani, a strategist for Mr. Gore, put it this way: "No question it's a huge event. It's a really, really important event. It's a time when people really tune in to who you are and what you've done."

The campaigns have been so preoccupied with the debates that negotiators on both sides devoted more than six days of closed talks to the details before they emerged on Friday with a detailed agreement that spells out everything from the height of the lecterns to the number of aides each candidate can have backstage. Negotiators discussed such seemingly trivial matters as the temperature in the hall (65 degrees) and whether to allow props (no).

Officials involved in the negotiations said that they had not been particularly contentious, but that the

Continued on Page 26

France 2 via Associated Press

A Palestinian and his 12-year-old son cowered behind a cement block from crossfire between Palestinians and Israeli troops in Gaza. Moments later the son was dead and the father wounded. The scene, including the boy's cries as he was shot, was filmed by a foreign television crew and broadcast in Israel.

Strike Fears Grip Hollywood As Unions Flex New Muscle

By BERNARD WEINRAUB

HOLLYWOOD, Sept. 30 — For decades Hollywood was a town run by a few moguls. Films were churned out like autos on an assembly line. Labor negotiations in the 1930's and 1940's were often resolved through the strong-arm tactics of dynastic studios. By the 1960's, with the power of studios ebbing, the unions and film studios as well as television networks placed labor negotiations in the hands of the town's top broker, Lew R. Wasserman, then the chairman of MCA Inc.

The town has changed. Mr. Wasserman is 87 and frail, and Hollywood's power structure is a complex amalgam of competing corporate interests. The unions, once weak and divided, are emboldened. And, most important, Hollywood is now beset by issues that go beyond simple wage increases for actors and others. The growth of foreign markets for films and television series, the expansion of the video and DVD industries and, more recently, the Internet explosion have left writers, actors and directors with deep grievances about their pay and status.

Now Hollywood is in a panic mode. For the first time, unions are confronting networks and studios about how writers and actors should be paid when films and television shows are shown on the Internet and on the growing number of cable outlets. And they are threatening strikes that union officials and television and film executives all expect to define the issues that will shape the entertainment industry's labor relations for decades.

The impact of the strike threats is already rippling across the entertainment business and is affecting what viewers around the world will see in movies and television next year. Although the job actions are not scheduled until mid-2001, studios and networks are consumed with making films and television series in advance of the possible walkouts.

Television networks are already planning more reality and news shows, which would not be affected by an actors' strike. In the rush to make movies now, executives ac-

Continued on Page 28

Low-Wage Jobs Leading Gains In Employment

By STEVEN GREENHOUSE

New York City's rebounding economy has produced a record number of jobs, but a new study shows that the number of low-wage jobs, those paying less than $25,000 a year, is growing much faster than the number of middle- or high-wage jobs.

The study, to be released tomorrow, found that while the city had added thousands of high-paying Wall Street and Silicon Alley jobs in recent years, the fastest job growth had been among low-wage service employees, like restaurant workers, security guards, day care workers and home attendants for the elderly.

Since 1993, when job growth in New York City began rebounding after the national recession of 1991-92, the number of jobs paying less than $25,000 a year has climbed 22 percent, nearly four times as much as jobs paying $25,000 to $75,000, according to the study. And the number of low-wage jobs has risen twice as much as jobs paying more than $75,000.

The study, conducted by the Working Group on the New York City Low Wage Labor Market, a team of economists from government agencies and nonprofit groups, focuses on some largely overlooked cracks in the city's economic boom. It notes, for instance, that many jobs created in the last decade do not pay enough to support a family. It also found that for the city's low-wage workers, the median wage dropped by 2 percent from 1989 to 1999, after taking inflation into account.

"Despite the strong pace of private-sector job growth," the study

Continued on Page 36

MIDEAST VIOLENCE CONTINUES TO RAGE; DEATH TOLL RISES

A THREAT TO PEACE TALKS

Hundreds of Palestinians Hurt — Gaza Protests Aimed at Both Sharon and Arafat

By WILLIAM A. ORME Jr.

JERUSALEM, Sept. 30 — Violent clashes between Palestinians and Israeli troops left at least 12 Palestinians dead and hundreds wounded in the third day of fierce fighting set off by the defiant visit on Thursday of a right-wing Israeli leader, Ariel Sharon, to the steps of the ancient mosques atop Jerusalem's Old City.

The fighting today, on the first day of the Jewish New Year, an Israeli national holiday that is commemorated as a time for quiet reflection and prayer, was among the bloodiest confrontations between Israelis and Palestinians in recent years.

The violence, which began in Jerusalem, spread today from the northern edge of the West Bank to the end of Gaza Strip, escalating in two places into gun battles between Palestinians and Israeli security forces. Palestinian youths burned tires and bombarded Israeli soldiers and the police with rocks and firebombs; Israeli troops responded variously with tear gas, rubber bullets and live ammunition.

The Israeli military said tonight that seven soldiers had been "lightly wounded" by rocks in the disturbances today. At least 16 Palestinians have been killed and hundreds injured in the last three days.

Prime Minister Ehud Barak said in a statement that he spoke with the Palestinian leader, Yasir Arafat, tonight "and stressed the importance of Arafat's immediate personal involvement to stop the violence." They agreed that "senior security officials from both sides will be in constant contact for the purpose of restoring calm," the statement said.

Still, with the death toll rising, there were fears that the violence may quash hopes for a quick resumption of the peace talks between Israel and the Palestinians. Negotiators returned from Washington on Thursday after parallel talks with State Department officials that both sides called inconclusive.

"We will have funerals tomorrow, and the situation is still tense and explosive," Nabil Aburdaineh, a senior adviser to Mr. Arafat, said tonight. "This tension will negatively affect the peace process."

Palestinian and Israeli security forces engaged in a fierce gun battle for more than an hour at the entrance to Netzarim, one of several Jewish settlements in the Gaza Strip. A Palestinian policeman was killed in the crossfire, witnesses and officials in Gaza said.

An ambulance driver and a 12-year-old boy were also killed.

The boy was filmed by a foreign television crew as he cowered behind a cement block with his father, who shouted at the Israeli soldiers to hold their fire. The ambulance driver was

Continued on Page 10

Chang W. Lee/The New York Times

Sunset for Sydney's Olympics

When the sun went down, Kronos Hill above the Olympic Village in Sydney was a favorite place to watch from. The XXVII Olympiad closes today.

Israel Seeks to Uncover Fate Of 11 Jews Lost Fleeing Iran

By DEBORAH SONTAG

BAT YAM, Israel, Sept. 27 — In her immaculate apartment here, Farahnaz Rabizade, an Iranian immigrant, was tempted to set an extra place at the Rosh Hashana table for her missing husband. But she did not let herself be that maudlin, she said, because she did not want to upset her children, who have been waiting four years for their father to show up in Israel for the Jewish New Year.

Mrs. Rabizade's husband is one of 11 Iranian Jews who disappeared while emigrating. The men set off from Iran at different times — three groups in 1994 and Mr. Rabizade's group in 1997. Lacking travel documents, they all chose to leave illegally, presumably by hiring smugglers to help them across the perilous Iranian border, where many travelers disappear in kidnappings. None of the Jews have been heard from since.

"My father sacrificed himself for us," Dahlia Rabizade wrote in a 10th-grade essay at her new Israeli school. "He was like a candle that lights the way while he himself is the wax that melts."

The 11 missing men came to the attention of human rights and American Jewish groups only in the last month. Until then, Iranian Jews, who prefer to handle sensitive issues with the Iranian government very quietly, had used back channels to search for the men.

Recently, Israeli officials, frustrated by the lack of response, decided to push for an international campaign on behalf of the 11 men. Given Iranian governmental hostility toward Israel, some Jewish groups and experts on Iran did not think that this was wise.

One expert here said that he was personally told by a Jewish member of the Iranian Parliament that the government was working hard to locate the men.

"I think they might get some good results," the expert said, "and maybe the Israeli authorities should be a little more patient."

But the Israeli officials believe that, on the heels of the recent convictions of 10 Iranian Jews on espionage charges, which the American government and others condemned as unjust, the time was ripe to develop international sympathy for the

Continued on Page 10

INSIDE

Dream Team Wins Gold; Jones Adds Two Medals

The United States men's basketball team came through with the gold medal it was expected to win and Marion Jones finished the Sydney Olympics with five medals by winning her third gold and second bronze. SPORTSSUNDAY

Standoff in Serbia

As the Serbian opposition continued trying to convince President Slobodan Milosevic that he lost last week's elections, Russia offered to send its foreign minister to mediate. PAGE 12

Fujimori's Eroding Power

The buttresses of power for Peru's president appear to be cracking, even with his surprise visit to Washington. NEWS ANALYSIS, PAGE 16

Schools Try Reward System

At schools in North Carolina, teachers are offered bonuses and students are offered rewards like discounts on pizza, all in an effort to raise standardized test scores. PAGE 20

The Cheneys' Family Affair

The hardest working family in this presidential campaign may be Dick Cheney's. His wife gives speeches to warm up audiences, and his daughters are trusted aides. PAGE 24

The Call of Ports

Fall and Winter Cruises: A flotilla of new ships bring fares down, and send cruise lines scrambling for new destinations. But when creditors seize a fleet, stranded passengers get a lesson in claiming refunds. Also: A low roller's guide to Las Vegas. TRAVEL

Only Connecting

In "The Talmud and the Internet," Jonathan Rosen explores the surprising affinities between two all-embracing information systems; reviewed by Frank Kermode. BOOK REVIEW

19 Hours of 'Jazz'

The filmmaker Ken Burns shifts his focus to jazz, and Louis Armstrong, in a 10-night PBS documentary. ARTS & LEISURE

L.A.P.D. Confidential

The arrest of one corrupt policeman has led to the Los Angeles Police Department's being brought under federal supervision. MAGAZINE

Talking Points

What to watch for in the first presidential debate. WEEK IN REVIEW

Employment Advertising/Section 10
In New York City and the metropolitan region.

Updated news: www.nytimes.com

12 More Arabs Are Killed in Confrontations With Israelis

Continued From Page 1

killed as he tried to rescue the boy.

The excruciating scene, including boy's screams as he was hit by the fatal gunfire and the father's cries of horror, was broadcast on Israeli and Palestinian television tonight.

"This is a killing in cold blood, an attack on an innocent child without any excuse," Mr. Aburdaineh said. "This cannot be forgiven."

There was little reaction from Israelis, many of whom spent the day strolling to synagogues and family gatherings on the Rosh Hashana holiday that represents a conscious break from the usual national preoccupation with hourly news reports.

Eight Palestinians, including two policemen, were killed in a chaotic confrontation with Israeli troops outside Nablus, on the West Bank, Palestinian officials said. Hundreds of protesters there attacked an Israeli army checkpoint with rocks and homemade firebombs, Israeli army officials said. The officials said the troops fired live ammunition only after being hit by rifle fire from Palestinian policemen.

More than 200 Palestinians were reported wounded in the bloody Gaza clash, which erupted from demonstrations protesting Mr. Sharon's visit to the mosques on Thursday morning and the storming of the Muslim religious site on Friday afternoon by heavily armed Israeli troops.

The Gaza protesters, many of them sympathizers of the radical fundamentalist Hamas movement, directed their fury not just at Mr. Sharon, but also at Mr. Arafat, ripping up posters of the Palestinian leader.

In East Jerusalem, Palestinian protesters fought sporadically with Israeli troops throughout the day, and a teen-age boy was killed during a clash with Israeli forces near Ramallah.

Mr. Barak told Mr. Arafat that Israel "will not allow the violence to serve as a negotiating tool," the statement from his office said.

The prime minister also spoke today by telephone with President Hosni Mubarak of Egypt, who was meeting in Cairo with Mr. Arafat, Mr. Barak's office said. Mr. Mubarak had lashed out Friday at what he called "provocative Israeli actions" at Jerusalem's Islamic holy sites. The Egyptian foreign minister, Amr Moussa, said tonight that Israel and the Palestinians are now "at a very critical stage of the peace process, and we hope it will make progress, but with these actions it will never advance."

In Washington, P. J. Crowley, a White House spokesman, said American officials were talking to both sides at the highest levels and asking them to end the violence. "Issues have to be resolved at the negotiating table and not in the streets," he said.

Israel's army chief, Shaul Mofaz, said in a statement that he had spoken with two Palestinian security chiefs, Mohammed Dahalan and Jibril Rajoub, and "we agreed that the Palestinians will cease fire in the West Bank and the Gaza Strip."

Photographs by France 2 TV via Associated Press

In images from television, at top, a Palestinian man, Jamal Aldura, and his 12-year-old son, Rami, sheltered from Israeli-Palestinian crossfire yesterday behind a cement block in Gaza City. In center photo, Mr. Aldura tried to signal his position to stop the firing, yelling "The child! The child!" Then both were hit, and the boy lay dead and his father unconscious. Mr. Aldura was hospitalized and is expected to live.

Osama al-Ali, a senior Palestinian security official, said the Israelis and Palestinians had agreed mutually to "exert maximum effort to stop the fire."

The Israeli army today ordered the evacuation of Jewish worshippers from the Western Wall, the site of rock-throwing attacks by Palestinian youths yesterday. Army helicopters criss-crossed the skies and troops blocked Israeli access to what are normally heavily traveled crossing points into the West Bank.

In Arab East Jerusalem, and in Palestinian-ruled cities in Gaza and the West Bank, Palestinians called a general strike today to protest the Israeli incursion on Friday into the Old City plaza that Jews call the Temple Mount and Muslims call the Noble Sanctuary.

The New York Times

The three days of Israeli-Palestinian clashes began in Jerusalem.

The fighting between Palestinians and Israeli security forces since Thursday is the worst sustained violence the area has seen since riots erupted in 1996 after Israel opened an ancient tunnel deep beneath the plaza. The Western Wall, the most sacred place of worship to Jews because of its proximity to where the last Jewish temple is believed to have stood two millennia ago, is part of the foundation of the great raised courtyard, now dominated by the seventh-century mosque the Dome of the Rock.

Though Israel asserts sovereignty over the site, its security forces normally stay on the plaza's walled perimeter. Internal policing is handled by Palestinian Authority officials and by the Islamic clerics who exercise religious control over the mosques and surrounding courtyard.

Mr. Sharon, who obtained Israeli police permission to lead a delegation from his rightist opposition Likud party to the plaza, has vociferously objected to suggestions that a peace pact might give an independent Palestine state whole or partial sovereignty over the site.

His visit infuriated Palestinians, who continue to associate Mr. Sharon with the massacres of Palestinian refugees in Lebanon two decades ago, and who are united in demanding control over what is considered the third most sacred site in Islam.

On Israeli television tonight, Mr. Sharon denied that it was his visit that had touched off violence. "It was not my visit that lit the fire, but Palestinian incitement," he said.

Mr. Barak did not comment on Thursday about Mr. Sharon's action, nor did he on this holiday, when domestic politics is traditionally given a rest. And neither he nor his associates publicly linked the violence to the Likud leader's Temple Mount visit.

The scenes of heavily armed Israeli riot troops storming the plaza as it was packed with worshippers, shown on Palestinian television on Friday night and in Palestinian newspapers this morning, enraged many in the West Bank and Gaza.

In Gaza City, protesters marched this morning from a local university, converging on a heavily fortified Israeli army outpost outside the Netzarim Jewish settlement. As Israeli troops hidden behind their protective barricades opened fire on bands of rock-throwing student demonstrators, the sirens of the ambulances that began converging on the scene attracted even larger crowds, witnesses said.

Agence France-Presse

Israeli policemen ran through the Old City of Jerusalem yesterday during a third day of clashes with Palestinian protesters that have left at least 16 Palestinians dead and several hundred people wounded.

Israeli army spokesmen said the troops came under live fire from the Palestinian police. But television footage of the incident, including the shooting of the 12-year-old boy, and the absence of any serious Israeli casualties, served to reinforce the Palestinians' belief that the Israelis were responding with disproportionate force.

Miguel Angel Moratinos, the European Union envoy to the Middle East, condemned the violence in Gaza and the West Bank after a meeting in Cairo today with Mr. Arafat, and expressed his condolences to the families of those killed.

"This is a sad day for everyone who is working to achieve peace," he said. "We are shocked by these violent actions."

Israel Seeking Fate of 11 Who Vanished in Fleeing Iran

Continued From Page 1

men. Iran might be more receptive than imagined, the officials added, having become more sensitive about its image and eager to portray itself as tolerant of minorities.

"The original assumption was that it would be easier for the Iranians to respond positively when they were approached discreetly," said Sallai Meridor, chairman of the Jewish Agency. "But this assumption has not been proven correct. And we don't think the families should have to wait any longer. It's time for answers."

Whether the men were arrested and imprisoned by the authorities or fell prey to the violence of the no man's land that exists in Iran's border zones is unclear. The frontier with Pakistan, in particular, is treacherous territory for a stranger, with tourists and others — including many Bahais from Iran — disappearing in kidnappings.

But Israeli officials and Iranian Jewish leaders outside Israel say they have reason to believe that at least some of the men are alive and in prison; there have been recent reports of sightings by other prisoners, they said.

If they were behind bars, the men would be in the company of thousands of Muslims and other Iranians who have also been apprehended while fleeing the country. A senior Clinton administration official told an American Jewish leader that the case of the 11 men should be treated as part of a broader human rights problem.

Emigration from Iran is restricted in general and, an Amnesty International official noted, record numbers of Iranians are seeking political asylum elsewhere, even in this time of peace and relative openness in Iran.

But world Jewish leaders say the issue of emigration is particularly resonant for Jews because of a history of flights from peril.

"The idea of Jews in this day and age seeking safety and being intercepted is a horror story and even worse," said a senior official at an American Jewish organization, who requested anonymity because he has not decided that going public with the case is a good idea.

Mrs. Rabizade, 37, has taken a Hebrew first name, Urit, a job as a nanny, and an apartment in this immigrant-filled town near Tel Aviv. Her children have assimilated very rapidly. But the whole idea of coming to Israel was her husband's dream, not hers. So, she said, she cannot help but feel displaced in her new life, especially when her old one, in the southern Iranian city of Shiraz, was quite nice.

Her husband owned a clothing shop, and she was a sales clerk, she said. Their Jewish life was open and free, she said, with plenty of kosher food available and a lovely old synagogue in walking distance from their home.

Jews are a protected minority in Iran; although they do suffer official discrimination, the case of the 13 convicted of spying for Israel on what many believe were trumped-up charges was an anomaly in their history.

Still, Mrs. Rabizade's husband, who is 18 years older than she is, set his sights on a life in Israel after several trips here, and she, too, believed it was "our land."

Generally, the Iranian government did not permit all members of a Jewish family to travel abroad at once. But in late 1996 the Rabizades decided to try.

After their farewell parties, they packed a few suitcases and, with four children ranging in age from 7 to 15, presented themselves to the immigration authorities at the airport. Mr. Rabizade's passport was seized.

Her husband told her to "go, go," that he would follow the family as soon he could arrange it, she said. Mrs. Rabizade said that she felt, psychologically, that she could not turn around; she had already left Iran. To this day, she said, she regrets what she now calls that wrongheaded feeling.

Within days, Mrs. Rabizade and her children, having presented themselves to Israeli consular officials in Turkey, had landed in an immigrant absorption center in Mevasseret Zion, outside Jerusalem. Several months later, her husband told her by telephone that he had arranged passage through the Iranian-Pakistani border town of Zahedan, a difficult and dangerous route that traverses desert and drug-trafficking terrain.

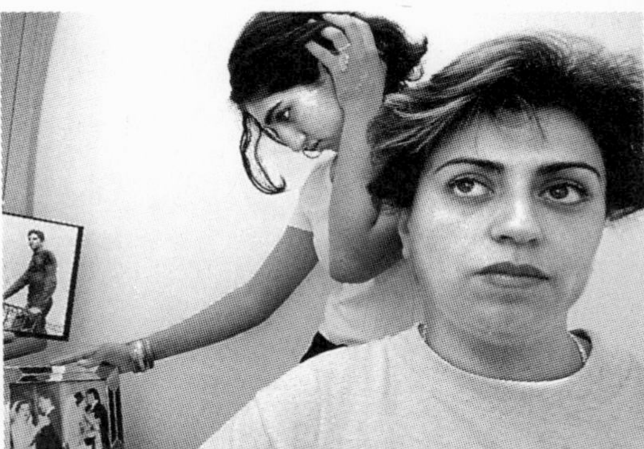

Rina Castelnuovo for The New York Times

Another Rosh Hashana has come without Farahnaz Rabizade learning the fate of her husband, Nouralla, who vanished in emigrating illegally from Iran in 1997. Their daughter Dina adjusted pictures of her father.

He would leave on Feb. 15, 1997; later she learned that he left with two other Iranian Jews, brothers, Syrous and Ibrahim Ghahremani.

After two weeks, when she had not heard from her husband, Mrs. Rabizade said, she was certain that something had befallen him. "Maybe the police caught him," she said, "but until this day, they haven't said word one about him."

Alone with her children in a new country, she did not know where to turn. Eventually, she went to an Iranian community group, and, she said, "they made a tremendous effort," but she acknowledges that she does not really know what they did.

The wife of one of the brothers who traveled with her husband did not handle the disappearance as well as she did, said Azriel Nevo, a retired general who is serving as the Jewish Agency's point man on the case of the missing 11 men.

That woman remains in the immigrant absorption center four years later, not ready to take the step into Israel itself without her husband.

In contrast, Mrs. Rabizade, presiding over an elegant display of pastries and soda pop, looks very composed. But she said she was sleepwalking through her days, "limbo days," as she called them.

At night, she dreams of her husband and does not feel as lonely, she said. In the dreams, he is behind bars, and she is pleading with the guards to release him, telling them that she needs him and that he does not deserve a heavy punishment "for being an innocent, just a Jew who wanted to come to Israel."

"That's why I say to myself that he's alive," she said. "Because I dream so much about him."

"All the News That's Fit to Print"

The New York Times

Late Edition
New York: **Today,** turning brighter by afternoon, high 73. **Tonight,** partly cloudy, low 53. **Tomorrow,** cloudy and cooler, high 59. **Yesterday,** high 65, low 56. Weather map is on Page A25.

VOL. CL . . . . No. 51,533 NEW YORK, FRIDAY, OCTOBER 6, 2000 — $1 beyond the greater New York metropolitan area. — 75 CENTS

Yugoslavs Claim Belgrade for a New Leader

Zeljko Safar/Associated Press

The police, who chose in the end not to take serious action in Belgrade against protesters, fired tear gas yesterday in an early effort to disperse crowds in front of the Parliament building.

POLICE JOIN CROWD

Milosevic Whereabouts Uncertain — State TV Is 'Liberated'

By STEVEN ERLANGER

BELGRADE, Serbia, Oct. 5 — As the federal Parliament burned and tear gas wafted through chaotic streets, vast throngs of Serbs wrested their capital and key levers of power away from Slobodan Milosevic today, bringing his 13-year reign to the edge of collapse.

Vojislav Kostunica, the opposition leader who claimed victory in the presidential election on Sept. 24, moved through an ecstatic crowd of several hundred thousand and proclaimed, "Good evening, dear liberated Serbia!"

The crowd shouted his name, and he shouted back: "Big, beautiful Serbia has risen up just so one man, Slobodan Milosevic, will leave."

Behind the crowds, smoke from the burning Parliament building mingled with the blacker smoke from the burning state television and radio center — bombed by NATO during last year's war over Kosovo — and tear gas, all set loose as hundreds of thousands of Serbs roamed through the city to demand the exit of a leader who had brought them years of ethnic conflict, isolation and international contempt.

The whereabouts of Mr. Milosevic and his family were unknown, though he was believed to be in Serbia. Two main pillars of his regime, the state news media and many of his police, were gone. But though the army stayed out of the fray, the chiefs of the security forces had yet to formally shift their allegiance to Mr. Kostunica, and Mr. Milosevic had not relinquished power.

While the Belgrade police did not take serious action against the protesters and many joined them, Mr. Milosevic's interior minister, Vlajko Stoiljkovic, refused to meet Mr. Kostunica's representatives, instead asking them, "What have you done to Belgrade?"

Opposition leaders, including Momcilo Perisic, the chief of staff whom Mr. Milosevic fired in October 1998, were reportedly talking to the army to persuade them to recognize Mr. Kostunica as president.

For the time being, there were no contacts between Mr. Milosevic and Mr. Kostunica. The opposition leader told the crowd not to march on Mr. Milosevic's home and office in Dedinje, a suburb, saying: "Answer their violence with nonviolence. Answer their lies with the truth."

As Mr. Kostunica tried to call the new federal Parliament and city government into session, the mood was boisterous, ecstatic and proud. "All of us have simply had enough," said Petr Radosavljevic, a mechanical engineer. "All we want is a normal country, where there is a future for young people."

Damir Strahinjic, 25, waving his arm over the crowd, said: "This should be enough to see the end of him. But you never know in this country, with this guy." His fears

Continued on Page A14

Reuters

Vojislav Kostunica, the opposition leader, waving to crowd last night.

In Quiet Tone, Cheney and Lieberman Debate Taxes, Education and Military

By RICHARD PÉREZ-PEÑA

DANVILLE, Ky., Oct. 5 — Dick Cheney and Senator Joseph I. Lieberman faced off tonight over tax policy, education and national security, in a vice-presidential debate that stood in gentlemanly contrast to Tuesday's combative presidential debate.

Mr. Cheney, a former defense secretary, came out on the offensive in what will be the only debate between the two men, arguing repeatedly that the Clinton-Gore years had been ones of wasted opportunity. Painting Vice President Al Gore as a throwback to an intrusive, big-government form of liberalism, Mr. Cheney promised "a new course, a new era."

"One of the difficulties we have, frankly, is that for the last eight years we've ignored a lot of these problems," Mr. Cheney said. "We haven't moved aggressively on Social Security; we haven't moved, for example, on Medicare." On education, he said, test scores have stagnated.

Mr. Lieberman, in turn, returned to Mr. Gore's favored line of attack, saying the Republican ticket would spend so much on tax cuts that favor the rich that the government would end up $1.1 trillion in debt over 10 years and there would be no money left for programs like Medicare and education.

"We're taking $300 billion off the top to put in a reserve fund," Mr. Lieberman said. "We're saving money to invest in education. You cannot reform education and improve it in this country without spending some money."

Based on a coin flip, the first question, on projected budget surpluses, was addressed to Mr. Lieberman, who used nearly all of his allotted two minutes to thank and welcome people and tell a story about his mother. This left the field at first to Mr. Cheney. [Excerpts, Page A28.]

Both men began by promising not to make personal attacks, two days after a highly aggressive encounter on Tuesday between Mr. Gore and Gov. George W. Bush, the first of three scheduled debates between the presidential candidates. Unlike the more formal presidential debate, in which the candidates stood at lecterns, Mr. Lieberman and Mr. Cheney sat with the moderator, Bernard Shaw of CNN, around a table, as if in a boardroom. They made no grand entrance; the broadcast began with them already seated.

When the questioning turned to military affairs and the Middle East, the candidates traded barbs and efforts to take credit, some subtle, some overt.

Mr. Cheney contended, as he has for months, that President Clinton had allowed military readiness to suffer, saying, "We're running now off the build-up and the investment made in the Reagan years."

Mr. Lieberman countered that "we are ready to meet any contingency that might arise."

The debate dwelt at considerable length on the Middle East, an area where both men showed — and claimed — a level of comfort, Mr. Cheney based in his years as defense secretary during the Persian Gulf war, and Mr. Lieberman based on his interest in Israel.

Here the candidates' differences were more subtle, as each spoke in favor of the Israeli-Palestinian peace process and containment of Saddam Hussein. Mr. Cheney said credit for progress toward Middle East peace belonged to former President George Bush and Yitzhak Rabin, while Mr. Lieberman implied that the efforts of Mr. Clinton had been

Continued on Page A27

Swaying Voters in St. Louis

The presidential debate moved some undecided voters in Missouri. Women said they were now leaning toward Al Gore, men toward George W. Bush. Page A26.

Nebojsa Parausic/Associated Press

Protesters waving a Yugoslav flag yesterday outside the Parliament.

Serbia's Reluctant Revolutionary Calmly Looks Beyond the Chaos

By STEVEN ERLANGER

BELGRADE, Serbia, Oct. 5 — Vojislav Kostunica had just made a rousing speech from the balcony of City Hall to several hundred thousand roaring supporters, who had just made him a revolution, and as he slouched in a leather chair, as aides and politicians rushed about, he had trouble believing that it was really his own life that was being transformed.

"I could never have imagined this for myself," he said quietly in an interview, as those below shouted his name. "First, to be in party politics and then suddenly elected to the highest position in the land, and also," he stopped, then laughed, "to be in a way a very mild revolutionary."

Then he hardened a bit, leaning forward. "I didn't want it this way. But there was no other way to defend democratic institutions and the people's will. There was no other possibility; we tried in every other way to get Slobodan Milosevic to recognize his defeat."

The smell of the burned and looted federal Parliament hung in the air across the park. "At one moment, I feel sorry seeing all that is happening," he said. "And on the other hand, we are coming closer to the end of our suffering."

Mr. Kostunica (pronounced kosh-TOON-eet-zah), in his trademark gray suit, rumpled white shirt and simple tie, is 56 years old, a constitutional lawyer who spent much of his career in academic institutes.

He was chosen by a fragile coalition of 18 opposition parties to run against Mr. Milosevic because of his polling figures: he is perceived by Serbs as one of their own — a Serb from the heart of Serbia, unlike Mr. Milosevic, whose father hailed from Montenegro — and he seems honest, uncorrupted and has an abiding and even mystical sense of Serbian nationhood.

As important, he had never served in a Milosevic government or — unlike other leaders of the Serbian opposition — even talked with him.

But Mr. Kostunica, who was reluctant until the very last moment to accept the opposition's nomination for the presidential elections on Sept. 24, has developed an extraordinary serenity and sense of mission over these past weeks of campaigning and quiet, but determined struggle.

"What makes me calm," he said tonight, "is that the people here trust in me, and those on the other side, in

Continued on Page A14

Barak and Arafat Order Their Forces to Pull Back

By WILLIAM A. ORME Jr. with JANE PERLEZ

JERUSALEM, Oct. 5 — Deadly clashes in Israel and the Palestinian territories slowed but did not stop today, even as the Palestinian and Israeli leaders issued orders to curb the violence and both sides continued talks on how to end the rioting that has spilled over the region for a week.

After a stormy meeting in Paris with Secretary of State Madeleine K. Albright failed to reach a cease-fire agreement early today, Prime Minister Ehud Barak of Israel and Yasir Arafat, the Palestinian leader, promised to order their commanders to pull back and restore calm to flash points under their control.

"Both sides actually gave instructions simultaneously to commanders back in the field," said the chief American negotiator, Dennis B. Ross, who resumed talks today with Israeli and Palestinian officials at the Red Sea resort town of Sharm el

TEENAGERS AT WAR

"You want to express your anger," said the Arab stone-thrower, 17. "I see a lot of hate," said the 19-year-old Israeli corporal nearby. Page A8.

Sheik, in Egypt.

But in an unusual public assessment en route to Egypt from Paris this morning, Mr. Ross expressed caution over whether the pledges would immediately quell the violence, which officials on both sides feared could yet surge with the Muslim holy day on Friday. "Obviously this has to be translated on the ground," he said.

As part of the effort to end the fighting, Dr. Albright flew to Egypt to meet with President Hosni Mubarak, who was host for a negotiating session with the secretary and Mr. Arafat. After initially indicating that he would join the talks, Mr. Barak stayed home, apparently to watch over events in Israel and the Palestinian territories.

By midday, Israeli tanks had begun pulling away from checkpoints outside Nablus, Bethlehem, Ramallah and other West Bank cities under Palestinian control where some of the worst clashes took place this week. And despite three more Palestinian deaths reported today, the atmosphere in the Palestinian territories and Israel's Arab neighborhoods seemed notably less volatile.

Israeli field commanders met with their Palestinian counterparts, and there were few reported uses of live ammunition by either Israeli soldiers or the Palestinian police.

At a Gaza Strip crossroads where stone-hurling protesters have battled daily with Israeli soldiers, the Israeli Army at first withheld fire as rioters massed for a new round of fighting.

Continued on Page A8

INSIDE

Cardinals Dominate Braves

With its 7-2 victory, St. Louis put Atlanta, the National League champion, on the brink of playoff elimination. SPORTSFRIDAY, PAGE D1

Priceline Affiliate Closed

A Priceline.com affiliate that let people bid for groceries and gas was abandoned because it could not raise enough cash. PAGE C1

A Church's Trust Shattered

An investigation into money missing from a Queens parish has sparked a painful reassessment of the legacy of a long-revered pastor. PAGE B1

NEWS SUMMARY A2

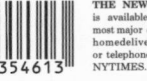

Updated news: www.nytimes.com

SHOWDOWN IN YUGOSLAVIA: 'Believe Us, It's Over'

THE OVERVIEW

Yugoslavs Claim Belgrade for New Leader as Police Step Aside

Continued From Page A1

were echoed by a senior member of Mr. Kostunica's staff tonight, who said: "I'm thinking Milosevic has one more trick up his sleeve."

Earlier, Mr. Milosevic's ruling Socialist Party attacked the opposition for causing unrest and violence and vowed to fight back with "all means to secure peaceful life." But faced with an uprising that has spread throughout much of Serbia, Mr. Milosevic may have run out of moves. Party members were talking to opposition leaders and even human rights lawyers.

The United States and European governments threw their support behind Mr. Kostunica. In Washington, President Clinton declared: "The people of Serbia have made their opinion clear. They did it when they voted peacefully and quietly, and now they're doing it in the streets."

With the massive outpouring in the streets, major bastions of state power defected to Mr. Kostunica. The state news agency Tanjug began referring to him as "the elected president of Yugoslavia" in a report signed, "Journalists of Liberated Tanjug." The state newspaper Politika, founded in 1904 and deeply degraded under the Milosevic regime, went over to the opposition. And on state television, a new slide appeared: "This is the new Radio Television Serbia broadcasting."

At 11:30 tonight, Mr. Kostunica appeared on the "liberated" state television, urging reconciliation on a nation used to a steady diet of government propaganda.

Speaking of the burning buildings and clashes, Mr. Kostunica said: "We hope that these sad incidents are behind us. My first hours started with pleasure, that a vision of Serbia I had all these years has started to be fulfilled." He promised that state television would remain "open to all views and all voices," including those of the coalition that has run this country.

He called for the lifting of international sanctions against Yugoslavia, which he said the European Union tonight promised him it would do as early as Monday. While he said "we cannot forget what some countries did to us last year during the NATO bombing, we can't live against the grain," and he promised normal relations with the world.

As thousands of people pressed into Belgrade from opposition strongholds, some were spoiling for a fight. They pushed aside police barricades on the roads to Belgrade, and some stripped police officers of their shields and weapons. Some were equipped with sticks and rocks, and they led the taking of the federal Parliament building, which was heavily guarded by police.

The building was soon on fire, its windows broken, and some demonstrators began to loot it for souvenirs, including chairs, hatracks and leather briefcases used by Parliament members. Portraits of Mr. Milosevic and ballot papers for the Sept. 24 elections were dumped from the second floor, all of them already circled to vote for Mr. Milosevic.

The police were lavish with their use of tear gas, which filled downtown Belgrade, but they did not charge the crowd. They used batons and stun grenades, but those who did were overwhelmed by the crowd, and some young men marched happily with their trophies: plastic police riot shields and helmets.

When crowds approached the back entrance of Radio Television Serbia, the police started to come out with their hands raised. The crowd greeted them with "plavi, plavi," or blue, the color of their uniforms, and gave them opposition badges.

As people entered the building, some workers came out the side, including television anchors and personalities like Staka Novakovic, Simo Gajin and Tanja Lenard, who is a senior member of the Yugoslav United Left party of Mr. Milosevic's wife. The crowd began to spit on them, and Ms. Lenard found refuge behind some garbage containers.

The crowd then looted the building.

There was a similar scene at a police station in nearby Majke Jevrosime Street. When the police left the building, some in the crowd gave them civilian clothes. But the building was then looted — with weapons taken — and was set afire with gasoline bombs.

In the skirmishing, at least one person died and 100 were injured today, according to independent radio B2-92, which also returned to its old frequency in Belgrade when its own headquarters were taken. The station had been seized by the government twice, and had been broadcasting by satellite. Belgrade Studio B television was also taken back from political control, and private stations affiliated with the Milosevic regime, like TV Palma and TV Pink, stopped broadcasting and put up slides that read: "This program is canceled because of the current situation in the country."

The day's vast uprising was the culmination of a campaign to defend Mr. Kostunica's victory in the presidential elections that Mr. Milosevic called in an effort to restore his own tattered legitimacy. It was a tactical mistake of the first order, because Serbs took the election as a referendum on Mr. Milosevic's 13 years of rule and misrule.

According to the opposition, Mr. Kostunica won at least 51.33 percent of the vote against four other candidates, an outright victory. But with electoral fraud, the Federal Election Commission reduced his percentage to just under 50 percent and called a runoff.

Mr. Kostunica called it theft and vowed that he would not accept a runoff for an election he had won. Strikes and protests on his behalf began to spread through Serbia this week.

The key moment may have come on Wednesday, when Mr. Milosevic's police failed to break a strike at a key coal mine in Kolubara. The workers, who had struck Friday to support Mr. Kostunica, refused to leave and called for help. Some 20,000 relatives and ordinary citizens from surrounding towns came to their aid, and the police let them go through, refusing to attack. Tonight, the police withdrew entirely from the mine.

Later that night, Tanjug reported that the highest court had ruled that the presidential election was invalid because of irregularities. But the court's judgment, supposed to be published today, did not come, and Mr. Kostunica made it clear tonight that it was simply too late to think about any compromise over the election with the authorities.

Kamenko Pujic for The New York Times

Against a backdrop of smoke from the Parliament building mingling with smoke from the TV and radio center in Belgrade, thousands of Serbs demanded that Slobodan Milosevic leave power. With the outpouring in the streets, important bastions of state power defected to the opposition.

Associated Press

A member of Yugoslavia's secret police saluted opposition demonstrators yesterday as security forces turned against Slobodan Milosevic.

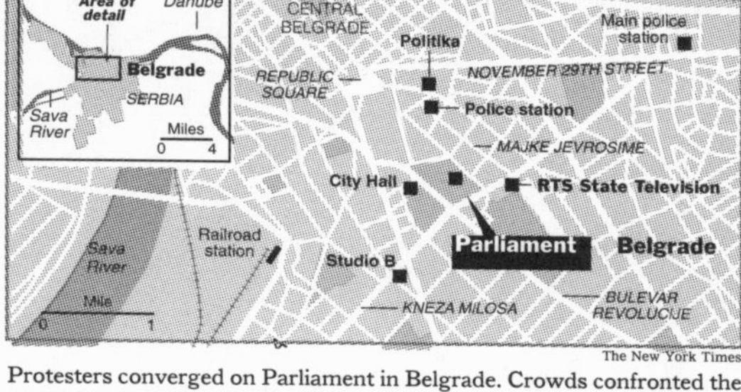

The New York Times

Protesters converged on Parliament in Belgrade. Crowds confronted the government at sites like the TV center and a nearby police station.

THE NEW FACE

Kostunica Steps Forth As Nation's Calm Savior

Continued From Page A1

the Socialist Party, know I'm the safest option for them."

Mr. Kostunica has pledged no revenge against those who served the old regime. He said tonight that he had no intention of arresting Mr. Milosevic, who was indicted for war crimes last year over the action of his security forces in Kosovo. When some in the crowd shouted, "to Dedinje!" the Belgrade suburb where Mr. Milosevic lives, he told them: "No one is marching to Dedinje."

Mr. Kostunica expected Mr. Milosevic to take one of the legal opportunities the opposition provided him to concede the momentous election held 11 days ago — the first ballot in which Mr. Milosevic had stood for direct election since 1992.

Despite some private wavering among his staff, Mr. Kostunica stuck to his principles, and refused to let Mr. Milosevic require a second-round runoff through vote stealing. But Mr. Kostunica also shied away from street confrontations, feeling grave responsibility for sending people against the police, said Zarko Korac, another opposition leader.

But Mr. Korac, a psychologist, insisted in a private meeting with opposition leaders this week that the responsibility would rest with Mr. Milosevic for his election fraud, not with Mr. Kostunica. Still, Mr. Kostunica said, he did not expect today to turn into a revolt.

Asked if today was a revolution, the man now broadly hailed as president of Yugoslavia hesitated. "It's a democratic revolution," he finally said. "When I always thought of what would be the revolution in this country, it was Tocqueville and his democratic revolution. That's what I had in mind. But I suppose this is a revolutionary way of defending the will of the people."

He said that he had made many efforts to establish contact with Mr. Milosevic, without success. But with the rage of the people today, the silence of the regime, its manipulation of the courts to annul the election result and the burning of the Parliament, legal compromise ran out of time, he said. "Now too many steps have been taken to retreat, that's for sure," he said.

"Milosevic tried his old tactics from 1996," when he delayed as protests built for three months, then finally gave in to the opposition's victory in local elections, saving his power. "But now it's too late," Mr. Kostunica said, a touch wearily. "He doesn't command matters here anymore."

His aides were beckoning. Other political leaders were waiting. He rose up, listening to whispers. He was told that the state media, television and the newspaper Politika, long a mouthpiece for Mr. Milosevic, now belonged to the opposition. He made arrangements to go to state television, to speak to the nation.

Then he said, "Politika is very important to us — so go prepare the next edition of Politika." Aides dispersed, carrying out his orders. Only he seemed surprised.

THE ULTRANATIONALIST

After the Lost Wars and the Ruined Economy, 'the Greater Slobo' Falls Silent

By ROGER COHEN

BUDAPEST, Oct 5 — The Serbian nationalist hysteria that swept Slobodan Milosevic to power in the late 1980's evaporated long ago, leaving him an isolated figure ruling over a shrinking land. But with resilience, ruse and ruthlessness, he outmaneuvered his enemies, until at last the enemy became his own people.

News Analysis

Always, Mr. Milosevic believed he could outlast his foes. But the hundreds of thousands of Serbs storming the Parliament in Belgrade today and seizing the television network that has long sustained him with its propaganda made clear that the tide of history had escaped him.

Of the Kosovo Albanians, his first enemies, Mr. Milosevic could say that they were intent on a "demographic genocide" against the Serbs — a reference to their high birthrate. Of the Croats, that they were reincarnated fascists — a reference to their World War II past as a Nazi puppet state. Of the Bosnian Muslims, that they were the Ottoman Turks of old bent on destroying the Serbs. Of NATO, that it represented evil American imperialism.

But of his own people, seemingly undivided at last, intent on ending their European isolation, enraged by one maneuver too many that seemed to rob them of their vote in the recent presidential election, Mr. Milosevic could find nothing to say today. He could summon no specter or myth that might divert or divide or cow.

His whereabouts were unknown, but the possibility that even so cunning a man might recover authority seemed remote.

From Western capitals — Washington, London, Berlin — the calls to Mr. Milosevic were unambiguous, reflecting a conviction that the man who stirred and sustained the wars of Yugoslavia's long unraveling had at last run out of options: Go, go now, accept your people's verdict and go before more damage is done or blood is spilled.

On the evidence, Mr. Milosevic's time should have been up long ago: his years of rule have seen a succession of lost wars, hundreds of thousands of Serbs uprooted, an economy ruined, wages slashed and an area that was among the most prosperous in the Communist bloc turned into a conspicuous center of poverty.

But it was easy to underestimate him. It was not until the Kosovo war last year that Western governments, including the United States, turned against him equivocally.

At the Dayton conference in 1995 that ended the war in Bosnia, he was still central to American diplomatic efforts, winning friends with his focus on the big picture and his evocative language: details, to Mr. Milosevic, were mere "technology."

In diplomacy, as at home, the Serbian strongman long succeeded in convincing others that he could not be circumvented.

His methods for conveying and retaining this authority were multiple. In the late 1980's, he saw the power of crude nationalism in a Serbian society whose binding ideology — Communism — was disintegrating. The motto of his Communist-turned-socialist party was straightforward: "Serbia does not kneel."

Such slogans earned him at first a mob appeal. His posters were everywhere in the early 1990's as Yugoslavia descended into violence. But kneel Serbia ultimately did in a succession of wars — in Croatia, then in Bosnia.

Mr. Milosevic always portrayed these conflicts as defensive attempts to allow Serbs to "remain in Yugoslavia" even as he did more than anyone else to precipitate the conflicts through his hate-filled propaganda against all his neighbors.

Most Serbs believed him: the deaths of thousands of Muslims in the Serbian concentration camps in Bosnia in 1992 and at Srebrenica in 1995 were often dismissed in Belgrade as "Muslim propaganda." In fact, they were a demonstration of Mr. Milosevic's readiness to resort to force — against the Albanians of Kosovo in the 1980's as he suppressed their autonomy, against demonstrators on the streets of Belgrade in 1991, against the Muslims of Bosnia in the violent rampage of 1992, and against the Albanians again in the late 1990's.

No Stalin, no Hitler, Mr. Milosevic, 59, nonetheless proved himself over the past 13 years to be the most violent ruler Europe has seen in many years. Over 200,000 people have died in the wars of Yugoslavia's destruction. His inability to use force today showed how his strength has evaporated.

His instinct for survival had long proved remarkable. As the wars turned in 1995 and the vision of "Greater Serbia" receded, to be replaced by a vision of "Greater Slobo," many expected Mr. Milosevic to fall. The streets of Belgrade were filled with demonstrators for three months as 1996 turned to 1997. But he deployed a succession of other tactics to replace the galvanizing frenzy of military conflict.

One constant ploy was "divide and rule" — a highly effective tactic in a society disoriented by the propaganda of Serbian television and used to subjugation. One old Serbian joke had a farmer saying that he would "vote for the opposition when it is in power"; the unfunny thing was that many people long thought that way.

Even as Serbia's resources dwindled, Mr. Milosevic used what money there was to buy loyalty from the secret police he armed and from a coterie of business and political associates who dominated the trafficking in the country's increasingly closed and corrupt economy. Behind this loyal entourage, he hid himself.

The reality of Serbia was increasingly grim, a country poor and isolated, a far cry from the exalted vision that Mr. Milsovic started by offering the Serbs, most memorably, at Kosovo Field in 1989, on the 600th anniversary of the Serbs' losing battle to the Ottoman Turks.

Then he declared that the Serbs "never conquered or exploited others" and were imbued with a "historical being that throughout history was a liberating one." But a "vassal mentality" among Serbian politicians had too long allowed "the humiliation of Serbia." He concluded, "Here we are today on the field of Kosovo to say that it is not so any longer."

For much of his rule, Mr. Milosevic succeeded in sustaining his rule through such myths: that a Balkan enemy, or the outside world, or NATO, was intent on humiliating Serbia and the only way to resist was to stick together.

But the purpose of doing so seemed increasingly elusive. Survival seemed to become Mr. Milosevic's only political intent. As the Serbs of Croatia lost their homes in 1995, and large chunks of Bosnia slipped from his grasp, and finally Kosovo too was lost in an avoidable war with NATO in 1999, he persisted.

The son of parents who both committed suicide, he seemed intent on dragging his people toward the sort of collective death that Serbian myth tends to portray as a form of redemption. Even Serbian myths exhaust themselves, however. Last year, Mr. Milosevic was indicted by the war crimes tribunal in The Hague. As the country suffered, the police and army became estranged.

Vojislav Kostunica, the man who appears on the verge of taking power, faces overwhelming problems, not least the fact that the disintegration of Yugoslavia may not be over. Both Montenegro and Kosovo seek independence that he, like Mr. Milosevic, opposes.

But Mr. Kostunica understands his most effective weapons. He talks unceasingly about the lifting of economic sanctions, the need for dialogue and his desire to turn Serbia once more into a "normal" country.

"All the News That's Fit to Print"

The New York Times

Late Edition
New York: Today, increasing clouds, high 63. Tonight, mostly cloudy, low 53. Tomorrow, mostly cloudy with late rain, high 65. Yesterday, high 56, low 40. Weather map is on Page D15.

VOL. CL . . . No. 51,566 | NEW YORK, WEDNESDAY, NOVEMBER 8, 2000 | $1 beyond the greater New York metropolitan area. | 75 CENTS

BUSH AND GORE VIE FOR AN EDGE WITH NARROW ELECTORAL SPLIT; HILLARY CLINTON GOES TO SENATE

Big Victory for First Lady in Contest With Lazio

By ADAM NAGOURNEY

Hillary Rodham Clinton was elected senator from New York last night, ending a 16-month spectacle of a campaign and ensuring that a Clinton will remain in Washington after her husband, the president, leaves the White House on Jan. 20.

It was the first time in the nation's history that a first lady was elected to public office. Mrs. Clinton soundly defeated Rick A. Lazio, a 42-year-old four-term congressman from Long Island, who had rushed to enter the race in May after Mayor Rudolph W. Giuliani of New York stepped aside, citing health reasons. Late returns signaled that after a race that had seemed so close for so long, the first lady defeated her opponent by a double-digit margin.

Mr. Lazio called Mrs. Clinton at her hotel suite about 10:40 p.m. to concede and offer her congratulations, according to aides to both candidates. With her husband wiping tears from his eyes as he stood silently behind her on the stage, Mrs. Clinton declared victory at 11:06 p.m., not even waiting for Mr. Lazio to finish conceding as she took the stage in time for the 11 p.m. news.

"I just want to say from the bottom of my heart: Thank you, New York," the senator-elect said. "Thank you for opening your minds and your heart, for seeing the possibility of what we could do together for our children and for our future here in this state and in our nation. I am profoundly grateful to all of you for giving me the chance to serve you."

"I promise you tonight that I will reach across party lines to bring progress for all New York families," she said. "Today we voted as Republicans and Democrats. Tomorrow we begin again as New Yorkers."

Just blocks away, in another ballroom at the Roosevelt Hotel, Mr. Lazio grinned and repeatedly sought to hush his own crowd as it erupted in boos and catcalls at the news that Mr. Lazio had conceded the campaign to the first lady.

"I feel like the Mets: We came in second," said Mr. Lazio, adding: "It's time to hold our heads up high and to unify our state and to stand together. It's time for us to stand as New Yorkers together. She has won this race, and it's time for us to march together forward."

With 98 percent of the votes counted at 1 a.m. today, Mrs. Clinton had 3,401,168 votes, or 55 percent, compared with 2,659,158 votes, or 43 percent, for Mr. Lazio. The remaining 2 percent went to other minority candidates.

With her victory tonight, Mrs. Clinton, 53, ended 24 years of being known as a politician's wife, albeit a politician who was elected president of the United States, to become an elected public figure in her own right. She is the first woman to have been elected senator from New York, the latest turn in an improbable if

Continued on Page B12

G.O.P. IN POSITION TO RETAIN SENATE

Democrats' Bid to Win Control of House Is Also Faltering

By ADAM CLYMER and ERIC SCHMITT

Republicans scored an important victory yesterday when former Gov. George F. Allen defeated Senator Charles S. Robb in Virginia, a turnover that led Democratic leaders to say they would not regain control of the United States Senate.

Even with final results yet to come in a few states that Democrats hoped to win, Senator Thomas A. Daschle of South Dakota, the minority leader, said that at best "We could be at 50-50 in the Senate."

But that would still leave the Senate in Republican hands. One of those seats was won by Senator Joseph I. Lieberman of Connecticut. If he is also elected vice president, Gov. John G. Rowland would appoint a Republican to succeed him. If Dick Cheney is elected vice president, he would preside and cast tie-breaking votes for the Republicans.

The Democrats did win four Republican Senate seats, defeating Senators William V. Roth Jr. of Delaware, the five-term incumbent who heads the Finance Committee, Rod Grams, a Minnesota freshman, and John Ashcroft of Missouri, as well as taking the seat vacated in Florida by the retiring Senator Connie Mack.

Incomplete returns for the House of Representatives suggested that a Democratic bid to capture control there was also faltering. Republicans held on to two sharply contested Kentucky seats, those of Representatives Anne Northup in Louisville and Ernie Fletcher in the Lexington-Frankfort area.

Those results presaged a series of victories by incumbents of both parties who had seemed in danger this fall. But Samuel Gejdenson, a 20-

Continued on Page B5

Dead Man Wins Race in Missouri

Republicans in Missouri conceded late last night that Gov. Mel Carnahan, the Democrat who was killed in a plane crash on Oct. 16, had defeated Senator John Ashcroft, the Republican incumbent, at the polls.

Mr. Carnahan's name stayed on the ballot after his death, and the interim governor, Roger Wilson, said he would appoint Mr. Carnahan's widow, Jean, to the seat. But Republicans said they planned to challenge the result in court.

Richard Perry/The New York Times | Associated Press

After more than 30 hours of nonstop campaigning, Vice President Al Gore voted yesterday at Forks River Elementary School at Nashville. Gov. George W. Bush expressed optimism after voting in Austin, Tex.

Voters Remain Divided, to the Very End

By R. W. APPLE Jr.

News Analysis

After all the dollars and debates, after all the ads and adjectives, the country still found it immensely difficult to make up its mind.

And so the race for the presidency, which had seemed to teeter on a knife edge for the last few weeks of the campaign, teetered a bit more as the polls closed across the country.

The lead in the popular vote switched back and forth throughout the night, with Gov. George W. Bush holding a narrow lead over Vice President Al Gore as the count went into its final hours. The all-important battle for supremacy in the Electoral Ccollege came down to Florida, and early this morning, Gov. Jeb Bush seemed to have delivered a hair's-breadth victory to his brother in that fast-growing state, putting him over the top.

But Mr. Bush's margin dwindled and dwindled until only a handful of votes separated the two candidates, throwing the picture into confusion.

No overarching national themes emerged from the voting, but a few things were clear as the last ballots were tabulated, including these:

¶Neither of the candidates, for all their exertions, ever closed his deal with the American public. Each candidate won overwhelming majorities among voters in their own parties, but independent voters — the crucial quarter of the electorate that decides so many elections — split evenly.

¶In the final stages of the race, Mr. Bush faded. Among those who made up their minds in the last week, the surveys showed, slightly more than half went to Mr. Gore; among those who decided earlier, a bare majority ended up favoring Mr. Bush.

¶Mr. Bush, who announced early on that he was a compassionate conservative, did a good job of rubbing the rough edges off his ideology, a better job than his rival. Voters were more likely to see Mr. Gore's positions as too liberal than to see Mr. Bush's views as too far to the right.

¶To a degree difficult to quantify, President Clinton appeared to have been a drag on Mr. Gore's candidacy. Fully 60 percent of the voters interviewed from coast to coast, a startling figure, said they disliked Mr. Clinton as a person, whatever they thought of his policies. They said they will remember the president more for the scandals that plagued him than for anything else, and some of that seemed to brush off on Mr. Gore, whom voters found less honest and trustworthy than Mr. Bush.

Almost one voter in five said their

Continued on Page B2

James Estrin/The New York Times

Hillary Rodham Clinton celebrated at a victory rally in Manhattan last night after winning the United States Senate race in New York. She was accompanied by President Clinton and their daughter, Chelsea.

Corzine Wins Costly Bid for Senate in New Jersey

By DAVID M. HALBFINGER

Jon S. Corzine, a liberal Democrat who made a fortune as a Wall Street executive and spent about $60 million of it on his first campaign for public office, won election to New Jersey's open seat in the United States Senate yesterday after shattering the national spending record for a statewide race.

Mr. Corzine fended off a determined but poorly financed challenge from Representative Bob Franks by outspending him 10 to 1, unleashing a nine-week barrage of television advertisements and an army of political foot soldiers who searched out votes in inner-city housing complexes and sprawling subdivisions across the state.

In selecting Mr. Corzine, 53, the former co-chairman of Goldman, Sachs & Company, to succeed the retiring Frank R. Lautenberg, New Jersey voters chose the Democratic candidate's vision of ambitious but costly new government programs in health care and education over Mr. Franks's more frugal but cautious approach to solving social problems.

With 89 percent of precincts reporting, Mr. Corzine had received 50 percent of the popular vote, compared with 47 percent for Mr. Franks.

Mr. Corzine, who roughly doubled the previous spending record for a Senate race set by the Republican Michael Huffington in a losing bid in California in 1994, greeted jubilant supporters at his East Brunswick hotel at 11:40 p.m.

"Good evening, New Jersey!" he shouted after being introduced by his wife, Joanne. "This is absolutely one of the greatest thrills of my life."

Mr. Corzine called his campaign a

Continued on Page B15

Today's Sections

Section B is devoted to election news today. The Metro Section begins on Page D1 and SportsWednesday on Page D9.

MORE ON THE VOTE

A Tossup to the End
Surveys of voters leaving the polls showed how brutally competitive the presidential race had become, with the candidates fighting each other to a standstill among crucial segments of the electorate. PAGE B1

The Nader Factor
Ralph Nader fell short of his goal of 5 percent of the vote, which would have qualified his Green Party for millions of federal campaign dollars in 2004. But he may have played a spoiler's role in key states. PAGE B5

On Further Review . . .
"Oh, waiter," said Jeff Greenfield, the CNN analyst, "one order of crow." Blaming data from a polling organization, the networks retracted an early projection that the vice president had won Florida. PAGE B1

Governors Hang On
Democrats won at least 7 of the 11 races for governor, picking up a statehouse in West Virginia. PAGE B4

More Than a Campaign
The two-year campaign of a first lady against two dizzyingly different men — the famous, irascible mayor of New York and a little-known congressman from Long Island — broke all the normal rules. PAGE B1

FLORIDA IS PIVOTAL

Long Night of Seesawing Tallies for Governor and Vice President

By RICHARD L. BERKE

The outcome of the presidential race between Gov. George W. Bush and Vice President Al Gore balanced early this morning on no more than a few thousand votes in the closely contested state of Florida.

Shortly after 2 a.m., Mr. Bush appeared to have won Florida, and several news organizations, including The New York Times, declared that he had captured the White House. Aides to Mr. Gore said he was preparing his concession speech, while Mr. Bush expected to announce his victory.

But later in the morning, as the count in Florida neared an end, the narrow margin that Mr. Bush had achieved unexpectedly evaporated, and state officials said they might have to count the overseas absentee ballots before they could be certain of the result.

By 4 this morning, the candidates were separated by only the barest of margins in the popular and electoral votes as the electorate seemed agonizingly split between Mr. Gore and Mr. Bush.

Mr. Bush was able to claim much of the South, while Mr. Gore captured the largest states on both coasts. But the two divided a patchwork of Midwestern states that are crucial for victory.

Mr. Bush, the governor of Texas who presented himself as an antidote to the scandals of the Clinton years and pledged to reach across the partisan divide and restore dignity to the White House, swept the south and won a patchwork of states in the Middle West. Mr. Gore claimed the largest states on the two coasts but fell just short of victory.

It appeared to be the narrowest electoral margin since 1916, when Woodrow Wilson drew 277 votes from the Electoral College and Charles E. Hughes won 254. When the final tally is in, it may even turn out to be the closest race since 1876, when Rutherford B. Hayes beat Samuel J. Tilden by a single electoral vote.

The closest margin in more recent times was in 1976, when Jimmy Carter won the presidency with 297 electoral votes, and President Gerald Ford captured 240.

All night long, there were signs of hope — and despair — for each candidate.

At one point, surveys of voters leaving their polling places projected that Mr. Bush was one percentage point ahead in the popular vote; at another point, they had him one point behind. At still another point, all the major networks called Florida, a critical battleground, for Mr. Gore. But in a rare reversal, they declared two hours later that the state was too close to call.

The electoral map seemed to have been turned on its head, as were many of the assumptions about which states were safely in one camp or another.

Mr. Gore was defeated in Tennessee, for example, becoming the first presidential contender to lose in his home state since George McGovern

Continued on Page B2

NEWS SUMMARY A2

Updated news: www.nytimes.com

THE OVERVIEW

Bush and Gore in an Extremely Close Race as the Vote Tallies Seesaw

Continued From Page A1

lost in South Dakota in 1972. The results in many states were so close that it was possible that Mr. Gore would contest the outcome in some of them.

By late last night Mr. Gore had won in California, New York, New Jersey, Illinois, Pennsylvania, Connecticut, New Mexico, Maine, Maryland, Rhode Island, Vermont, Delaware, Massachusetts and the District of Columbia. Mr. Bush prevailed in Florida, Texas, Ohio, Tennessee, Utah, West Virginia, Georgia, Indiana, Kansas, Kentucky, Virginia, Mississippi, Nebraska, North Carolina, North Dakota, Oklahoma, Alabama, South Carolina, Wyoming, Arizona, Colorado, Louisiana and South Dakota. Even hours after polls closed in most states, officials in both camps seemed neither confident nor pessimistic — just downright jittery. Mr. Gore was so unsure that he made calls throughout the early evening to radio stations in critical states, moving through Arkansas and then westward as polls closed in the East. The campaign also enlisted President Clinton to make last-minute telephone calls to radio stations in battleground states.

"Our focus is on the fact that this is one of the closest elections in a generation," said Douglas Hattaway, a campaign spokesman. "For the first time in three decades, people who live on the West Coast will decide who will be the next president of the United States."

Around 7 p.m. in Texas, less than an hour after Mr. Bush and his family, including his parents, arrived at an Austin restaurant for dinner, they aborted their plan to watch the returns from a suite in the adjacent Four Seasons hotel and retreated to the governor's mansion. The decision came about the time that the networks were declaring Mr. Gore the winner in Michigan and Florida.

Soon after, Mr. Bush told reporters that he questioned early projections that he had lost Florida, where his brother Jeb is governor, and Pennsylvania, where one of his staunchest backers, Tom Ridge, is governor. "The networks are calling this thing awfully early," Mr. Bush said. "The people counting the votes are coming in with a different perspective."

In an interview on CNN, Karl Rove, Mr. Bush's chief strategist, chastised the network for its initial call of Florida, telling the anchor, Bernard Shaw, "I do think that is one criteria you might want to think about changing because you called the state before the polls have closed in a considerable part of the state."

The voter surveys found that Ralph Nader, the Green Party nominee, had won roughly three percent of the popular vote. He did not seem to have done the damage to Mr. Gore's candidacy that many Democrats feared, particularly in states like Minnesota and Washington. Still, in Florida, Wisconsin, Iowa and Oregon, the margins between Mr. Gore and Mr. Bush were less than Mr. Nader's projected vote.

The only state where Mr. Nader appeared to pose an outright threat to the prospects of Mr. Gore was Wisconsin. He would need more than five percent of the popular vote to qualify his party for millions of dollars in federal campaign matching money in the next presidential race.

"Today is the takeoff day for this new era," Mr. Nader said at a rally last night in Washington. "The end of the beginning of an honorable, exemplary eight-month campaign and the beginning of a political movement to establish clean money, clean elections, toward a responsive, clean government."

Patrick J. Buchanan, the Reform Party candidate, was drawing less than one percent.

By early this morning, it still appeared possible — though unlikely — that one candidate could win the Electoral College vote, and therefore the White House, but place second in the popular vote. The last time that happened was 1888, when Benjamin Harrison was elected over Grover Cleveland, who won the popular vote. Some strategists also said it was possible that Mr. Bush and Mr. Gore could tie in electoral votes, and in that case the election would be decided by Congress.

The surveys of voters leaving their polling places found no significant shifts in the bases of support for the two candidates. Men were largely backing Mr. Bush; women were siding more with Mr. Gore. Independents were breaking evenly. Voters who once considered themselves supporters of Senator John McCain of Arizona, who drew powerful support from independents in the Republican primaries, gave about a third of their votes to Mr. Gore and about two-thirds to Mr. Bush.

And Mr. Bush drew the votes of more than half the people who say they voted for Ross Perot in 1996, while Mr. Gore drew about a quarter.

Mr. Gore prevailed in the battle over the vaunted undecided voters, an estimated 10 percent of the electorate who had seemed to waver between the major-party contenders.

Mr. Bush enjoyed the wide support of people who identify themselves as religious conservatives. But perhaps because Mr. Bush presented himself as a "compassionate conservative" who would reach out to Democrats, his conservative views on abortion did not stop substantial numbers of people who disagreed with him on that issue selecting him anyway.

Mr. Bush had no trouble winning the most partisan core of his party, and neither did Mr. Gore; his support among union households was overwhelming.

This presidential race capped an extraordinary campaign in which both candidates frequently traded the front-runner position.

Even as the candidates tangled over their remedies for prescription drugs, reforming Social Security and cutting taxes, no galvanizing issue seemed to emerge in this campaign, and much of the contest seemed to revolve around more personal factors. A fundamental question was whether voters would side with Mr. Bush, whom they found more appealing personally, or Mr. Gore, who was more compatible on the issues, most people felt, and had much deeper seasoning in government, with eight years in the House, eight in the Senate and eight in the vice presidency.

But Mr. Bush, 54, sought to overcome concerns of many voters that he was not adequately prepared for the presidency. Mr. Bush is a one-time oilman and part owner of a baseball franchise. But he was known mostly as the son of a former president when he was elected governor of Texas only six years ago — his first successful race for public office — in an upset victory over the popular incumbent, Ann Richards. Even his mother had implored him not to take on Ms. Richards.

Yet some Bush family friends viewed this election as a way to settle the score only eight years after his father was ousted by the governor of Arkansas, Bill Clinton.

Mr. Gore's father, a onetime senator from Tennessee, had groomed him for the White House from childhood. But he devoted much of the campaign to trying to put to rest enduring doubts about his candidacy. Many voters did not warm personally to Mr. Gore, and he often seemed haunted by President Clinton, not quite knowing how closely to embrace a president who presided over the longest economic expansion in American history, but who was also tainted by scandal.

Voters said they liked the way things were going in the country and did not want big changes, and that their level of contentment rose in the Clinton years. Even so, they said they did not particularly like Mr. Clinton. Asked what they thought of him as a person, 6 in 10 voters said they had an unfavorable opinion and 3 in 10 had a favorable one. And asked whether history would remember Mr. Clinton more for his leadership or his scandals, nearly 7 in 10 said scandals.

The surveys taken throughout the country as voters left their polling places found that honesty in a president was a more critical consideration than a candidate's experience or grasp of complex issues.

While both Mr. Gore and Mr. Bush were viewed as honest, Mr. Bush was seen as more of a straight talker, more direct than the vice president and more likely to speak his mind.

Voters who favored Mr. Bush said they were drawn by his personality, his denunciation of Mr. Clinton and some of his positions on issues, like his proposal for a huge tax cut. Mr. Gore's support was based largely on his experience, his understanding of the issues, his promise of health care reform and his less ambitious plan for cutting taxes.

The surveys found that Mr. Bush was never able to shed the image of not being as well prepared as Mr. Gore for the enormous responsibilities of the presidency. He still managed to win the support of one in 10 of the people who said he was ill-equipped. Six in 10 voters said it was more important that a president be a good manager of the government than an exemplary moral leader.

Even after voting, people registered lingering doubts about the two candidates. Four in 10 voters said they cast their votes with reservations. And about half the voters said they would be concerned, if not downright scared, about the prospect of a President Bush or a President Gore.

In their final hours of stumping, Mr. Gore seemed far less confident of the outcome than Mr. Bush. The vice president did not sleep at all on Monday night, his aides said, and for more than 33 hours dropped in at battleground states, particularly focusing on Florida. At 4 a.m. yesterday, for instance, Mr. Gore, 52, was sitting at a table with eight nurses at a cancer center in Tampa.

Mr. Bush had a much calmer schedule, saying he slept — in his own bed in Austin — four or five hours on Monday night. Asked yesterday how she felt, Mr. Bush's wife, Laura, put her hand on her stomach, as if indicating a churning there. She looked nervous. But then she said: "I feel good. We got a lot of sleep in our own bed, with our own animals."

As he watched the returns with his parents last night, Mr. Bush said he did not feel he had his entire future on the line. "Actually, my whole future isn't on the line," he said. "I'm not worried about me getting through it."

RESULTS

The Race for President

WASH. ORE. MONT. N.D. MINN. IDAHO S.D. WIS. WYO. MICH. N.Y. NEB. IOWA PA NEV. UTAH ILL. IND. OHIO COLO. KAN. MO. W.VA. VA. KY. N.C. CALIF. TENN. S.C. ARIZ. N.M. OKLA. ARK. MISS. ALA. GA. LA. TEX. FLA. ALASKA HAWAII N.H. VT. ME. MASS. R.I. CONN. N.J. DEL. MD.

Bush — Gore — Incomplete results

Popular vote, in millions: 45 / 45

Electoral votes (270 needed): 256 / 238 — 54 not assigned

Results as of 4:02 a.m.	Pct. of districts reporting	George W. Bush REPUBLICAN	Al Gore DEMOCRAT	Patrick J. Buchanan REFORM	Ralph Nader GREEN	Electoral votes: Bush	Gore	Not assigned
States won by Bush								
Texas	97%	3,702,754 (59%)	2,369,247 (38%)	12,039 (0%)	134,452 (2%)	32	0	0
Ohio	99%	2,276,211 (50%)	2,107,030 (46%)	25,905 (1%)	113,830 (3%)	21	0	0
North Carolina	99%	1,545,949 (56%)	1,186,442 (43%)	8,475 (0%)	0 (0%)	14	0	0
Georgia	92%	1,269,490 (57%)	934,232 (42%)	9,803 (0%)	105 (0%)	13	0	0
Virginia	99%	1,405,315 (52%)	1,197,786 (45%)	5,497 (0%)	57,393 (2%)	13	0	0
Indiana	98%	1,205,547 (57%)	869,747 (41%)	16,559 (1%)	0 (0%)	12	0	0
Tennessee	99%	1,014,884 (51%)	953,274 (48%)	4,057 (0%)	19,059 (1%)	11	0	0
Missouri	92%	1,149,505 (51%)	1,054,457 (47%)	9,367 (0%)	36,707 (2%)	11	0	0
Alabama	96%	883,784 (57%)	644,372 (41%)	6,189 (0%)	17,237 (1%)	9	0	0
Louisiana	99%	924,840 (53%)	789,821 (45%)	14,479 (1%)	20,821 (1%)	9	0	0
Kentucky	99%	862,699 (57%)	631,353 (41%)	4,226 (0%)	22,756 (1%)	8	0	0
Oklahoma	99%	727,127 (60%)	466,252 (39%)	8,868 (1%)	0 (0%)	8	0	0
South Carolina	98%	751,604 (55%)	540,770 (40%)	10,451 (1%)	26,420 (2%)	8	0	0
Arizona	92%	639,253 (50%)	574,333 (45%)	10,279 (1%)	37,869 (3%)	8	0	0
Colorado	87%	738,031 (51%)	608,379 (42%)	8,806 (1%)	73,508 (5%)	8	0	0
Mississippi	96%	518,474 (57%)	371,345 (41%)	2,117 (0%)	7,397 (1%)	7	0	0
Kansas	96%	591,974 (57%)	400,758 (39%)	6,993 (1%)	34,122 (3%)	6	0	0
Arkansas	90%	413,321 (50%)	380,986 (46%)	10,220 (1%)	11,809 (1%)	6	0	0
Nebraska	88%	381,107 (63%)	195,968 (32%)	3,150 (1%)	20,911 (3%)	5	0	0
Utah	73%	358,049 (68%)	132,009 (25%)	6,371 (1%)	22,450 (4%)	5	0	0
West Virginia	97%	313,332 (52%)	279,047 (46%)	3,004 (0%)	9,898 (2%)	5	0	0
New Hampshire	99%	273,026 (48%)	265,807 (47%)	2,602 (0%)	22,151 (4%)	4	0	0
Idaho	76%	239,882 (69%)	92,096 (27%)	5,674 (2%)	4,015 (1%)	4	0	0
Nevada	99%	291,622 (49%)	272,544 (46%)	4,468 (1%)	14,421 (2%)	4	0	0
Alaska	62%	123,892 (60%)	55,981 (27%)	3,767 (2%)	21,055 (10%)	3	0	0
North Dakota	89%	157,840 (61%)	86,656 (33%)	6,487 (2%)	8,637 (3%)	3	0	0
South Dakota	97%	183,274 (61%)	112,548 (37%)	3,155 (1%)	0 (0%)	3	0	0
Montana	81%	195,876 (58%)	111,281 (33%)	4,512 (1%)	20,968 (6%)	3	0	0
Wyoming	99%	147,453 (69%)	60,420 (28%)	2,718 (1%)	0 (0%)	3	0	0
States won by Gore								
California	69%	2,796,287 (43%)	3,450,391 (53%)	26,829 (0%)	254,272 (4%)	0	54	0
New York	99%	2,210,142 (35%)	3,736,036 (60%)	33,297 (1%)	221,953 (4%)	0	33	0
Pennsylvania	99%	2,254,079 (46%)	2,450,285 (51%)	15,907 (0%)	102,114 (2%)	0	23	0
Illinois	99%	1,976,090 (43%)	2,538,550 (55%)	15,838 (0%)	101,733 (2%)	0	22	0
Michigan	80%	1,575,775 (47%)	1,712,682 (51%)	0 (0%)	66,424 (2%)	0	18	0
New Jersey	99%	1,244,793 (40%)	1,722,841 (56%)	6,857 (0%)	92,308 (3%)	0	15	0
Massachusetts	87%	796,493 (33%)	1,417,866 (59%)	9,930 (0%)	148,164 (6%)	0	12	0
Maryland	100%	770,904 (40%)	1,093,344 (57%)	4,067 (0%)	51,078 (3%)	0	10	0
Minnesota	81%	918,948 (45%)	992,901 (48%)	18,623 (1%)	108,425 (5%)	0	10	0
Connecticut	93%	501,273 (39%)	726,797 (56%)	5,148 (0%)	56,538 (4%)	0	8	0
Iowa	99%	624,669 (48%)	630,106 (49%)	6,765 (1%)	27,458 (2%)	0	7	0
New Mexico	99%	256,384 (47%)	260,003 (48%)	1,265 (0%)	19,707 (4%)	0	5	0
Maine	82%	229,021 (43%)	261,358 (50%)	3,464 (1%)	30,952 (6%)	0	4	0
Hawaii	18%	31,261 (34%)	55,604 (60%)	281 (0%)	5,192 (6%)	0	4	0
Rhode Island	100%	132,212 (32%)	252,844 (61%)	2,250 (1%)	24,115 (6%)	0	4	0
D.C.	100%	17,020 (9%)	162,004 (85%)	0 (0%)	9,925 (5%)	0	3	0
Vermont	97%	114,282 (41%)	141,203 (51%)	2,082 (1%)	19,230 (7%)	0	3	0
Delaware	100%	137,081 (42%)	180,638 (55%)	775 (0%)	8,288 (3%)	0	3	0
States with incomplete results								
Florida	99%	2,886,311 (49%)	2,875,282 (49%)	21,390 (0%)	95,031 (2%)	0	0	25
Washington	78%	632,818 (44%)	724,024 (51%)	3,941 (0%)	54,857 (4%)	0	0	11
Wisconsin	94%	1,17 9,311 (48%)	1,181,425 (48%)	10,621 (0%)	88,682 (4%)	0	0	11
Oregon	82%	478,224 (48%)	454,785 (46%)	4,653 (0%)	41,545 (4%)	0	0	7
TOTAL		**45,049,493 (48%)**	**44,765,910 (48%)**	**414,221 (0%)**	**2,385,982 (3%)**	**256**	**238**	**54**

Ruth Fremson/The New York Times

Supporters of Vice President Al Gore waited for festivities last night in Nashville's War Memorial Plaza. Mr. Gore returned to the city yesterday after a 33-hour campaign swing.

Monica Almeida/The New York Times

In Austin, Tex., supporters of Gov. George W. Bush celebrated early this morning after the networks announced that Mr. Bush had won a narrow victory over Vice President Al Gore.

NEWS ANALYSIS

Electorate Divided, Even After Polls Closed

Continued From Page A1

vote had been cast to register opposition to Mr. Clinton.

Mr. Bush gained valuable support from the pivotal border states, running a strong campaign in Missouri, Kentucky and West Virginia. Mr. Gore put on a powerful showing in the hard-fought Great Lakes States.

Suburbanites, so avidly pursued by both nominees, split 50-50. The suburbs cast well over 40 percent of the total vote in yesterday's election.

Without the backing of labor Mr. Gore would have been in deep trouble. Mr. Bush took 60 percent of the vote in nonunion households nationwide. On the other hand, Mr. Bush was heavily dependent on the white religious right, gaining the votes of three of four people who so identified themselves.

A number of important questions remained unanswered last night, quite apart from the victor's identity.

¶With neither nominee within reach of a big popular majority, and the polls suggesting a close electoral contest as well, how would the winner lead? As John F. Kennedy showed after winning in a squeaker in 1960, leaders can lead whatever their majorities, but it is hard for those who win narrowly to push broad legislative programs. Many Kennedy administration ideas came to fruition only after Lyndon B. Johnson's landslide victory in 1964.

¶Is American politics entering a nonideological or an anti-ideological phase? Only six years ago, the Republicans swept into control of the House on a radical right-wing program. But they were able to enact relatively little of it, and in this election, Congressional and presidential candidates alike did their best to skitter toward the center.

¶What does the country want? The candidates enunciated different views of government, with Mr. Gore espousing a more activist philosophy. When voters were asked which candidate shared their view of government, about a third said Mr. Gore, about a third said Mr. Bush, and the rest said both or neither. Yet in response to other questions, as they left the polls, voters said that they wanted less government and that they preferred economic growth to protecting the environment, another small-government view.

Questions about how the winner will lead.

Mr. Bush received the votes of most people who disliked Mr. Clinton, who made their decisions on the basis of personality and who wanted across-the-board tax cuts. No surprises there. Mr. Gore won his backing among those who put the greatest emphasis on experience, grasp of the issues, targeted tax cuts and promises of health care reform. Mr. Bush had hoped that his promise of a radical overhaul of Medicare would prove popular.

Signs of confusion flowed through the voters' responses. In the surveys, almost two-thirds of the respondents said the country was on the right track as opposed to headed in the wrong direction. But in moral terms, close to 60 percent said the country was on the wrong track.

The political map and political convention were knocked askew by the results. Mr. Bush won in Florida, where his brother is governor, and Mr. Gore lost Mr. Clinton's home state, Arkansas, but his own, Tennessee. In Tennessee two-thirds of those polled said it made no difference in their voting decision that Mr. Gore was from their state.

No president has been elected without carrying his home state since Woodrow Wilson, a former governor of New Jersey, lost that state in the 1916 election.

Changing patterns of opinion formation were reflected in the survey. More than 60 percent of those questioned said they used the Internet on a regular basis, and almost 30 percent said they sought political information when they did so.

A slim majority of those who said they used the Internet cast their votes for Mr. Bush.

One big winner was the political polling trade. For weeks, as surveys disagreed with one another and showed large swings in some states, their methodology was questioned. But most of the final surveys, completed in many cases Sunday and Monday, came remarkably close to the actual votes, state by state.

The final CBS News survey, released on Election Day morning, showed Mr. Gore with a lead of one percentage point in the popular vote.

"All the News That's Fit to Print"

The New York Times

Late Edition

New York: **Today,** cloudy, high 61. **Tonight,** rain arriving, low 53. **Tomorrow,** rain early, drier in the afternoon, high 58. **Yesterday,** high 59, low 43. Weather map appears on Page D15.

VOL. CL . . No. 51,567 NEW YORK, THURSDAY, NOVEMBER 9, 2000 — $1 beyond the greater New York metropolitan area. — 75 CENTS

BUSH BARELY AHEAD OF GORE IN FLORIDA AS RECOUNT HOLDS KEY TO THE ELECTION

CONGRESS IS CLOSE

G.O.P. Retains Control, but Democrats Gain in Both Chambers

By ADAM CLYMER

Democratic gains in the House and Senate on Tuesday fell short of control but produced the most narrowly divided Congress in almost half a century. Democrats gained at least three Senate seats and one or two in the House.

With one Senate race undecided, Republicans had 50 seats and Democrats 49. In the House, Republicans won an apparent majority of 221 to 211, with 2 independents and one seat undecided, with the Democratic candidate leading. But Republicans asserted that recounts or absentee ballots would give them two or three of the seats where Democrats now had more votes, and Democrats predicted that a recount would get them one Republican seat.

The last time both houses were so closely divided was at the end of the 83rd Congress of 1953-55, when Republicans ended with a 49-to-46 Senate edge (with 1 independent) and the House had 219 Republicans, 215 Democrats and 1 independent.

But that was an entirely different era, when lawmakers drank and golfed together and when blunt partisanship as seen in today's attack advertisements was almost unheard of.

A widely recalled saying of the time has a senior Democrat correcting a freshman who called House Republicans the "enemy."

The elder Democrat explained: "The Republicans are the opposition. The Senate is the enemy."

There were some bows to the older spirit yesterday. Senator John Ashcroft of Missouri, the Republican who was narrowly beaten by the late Mel Carnahan after his widow agreed to accept appointment if he won, rejected any legal challenge to the result, saying, "I believe that the will of the people has been expressed with compassion and the will of the people should be respected."

But more typical was the sort of call for bipartisanship made by Senator Robert G. Torricelli of New Jersey, head of the Democrats' Senate campaign committee. Republicans must recognize, Mr. Torricelli said, that "there is no constituency in this country for stopping progress on prescription drugs or hiring new teachers or defeating the building of new schools."

Senator Mitch McConnell of Kentucky, who heads the Senate Republican Campaign Committee, brushed off Mr. Torricelli's call for new campaign finance legislation, saying Democrats "would love to cripple the parties because they have allies in the A.F.L.-C.I.O. and the Sierra

Continued on Page B10

Rhona Wise/Agence France-Presse

Workers at the Miami-Dade election headquarters began recounting ballots yesterday. George W. Bush led Al Gore by 1,784 votes in Florida.

State of the Presidential Race

With 99% of precincts reporting.

	POPULAR	ELECTORAL
AL GORE	48,707,413	255
GEORGE W. BUSH	48,609,640	246
THE DIFFERENCE	97,773	270 NEEDED
REPRESENTING ...	0.1% of votes cast	37 UNDECIDED (Fla., N.M., Ore.)

The New Party Balance

How the parties fared in Tuesday's elections, with the outcome of two races still unclear.

D R I Seats ...
Held over
Defended or no contest
Gained

HALF

	DEMOCRATS		REPUBLICANS
U.S. House	211 (was 209)		221 (was 222)
U.S. Senate	49 (was 46)		50 (was 54)
Governorships	19 (was 18)		29 (was 30)

The New York Times

Recipe for a Stalemate

By R. W. APPLE Jr.

News Analysis

"Now we learn," said the political scientist Thomas Mann, one of the leading authorities on Congress, "who the grown-ups are around here." Like the rest of the nation, Mr. Mann, who is based at the Brookings Institution, a Washington research group, awoke to a situation unprecedented in modern American history, shaped by a once-in-a-lifetime series of electoral events that holds the potential for stalemate and instability.

For the first time this century, if not the first time ever, the United States must simultaneously deal with the following realities:

¶A president elected by a narrow electoral majority — and, if Gov. George W. Bush of Texas is the ultimate winner in Florida and the nation, elected although his main rival, Vice President Al Gore, prevailed in the popular vote. Accusations of ballot irregularities in Palm Beach County raised the possibility, furthermore, of doubts about the legitimacy of the Florida result.

¶A Senate closely and perhaps evenly divided along party lines, with the incoming vice president casting the decisive vote, and a House of Representatives more nearly balanced than the outgoing House, making the passage of any far-reaching policy measures extremely unlikely.

¶All of this taking place in a fierce new political world where the collapse of party discipline has made it extraordinarily hard for officials on Capitol Hill, let alone for a president, whether of their party or not, to lead.

The first order of business will be the profoundly serious question of legitimacy. Suppose, for example, that the final count in Florida, where the preliminary totals show Mr. Bush ahead, confirms him as the winner. Suppose, also, that careful scrutiny suggests, as seems at least possible, that flawed ballots in Palm Beach County caused some Gore supporters mistakenly to register votes for Patrick J. Buchanan, the Reform Party candidate. Suppose, finally, that the number of misdirected votes exceeds Mr. Bush's margin.

Suppose, in short, that Mr. Gore in a sense actually won Florida but Mr. Bush is credited with its electoral votes, which give him victory.

In that situation, Mr. Mann asked, would Mr. Gore and Mr. Bush engage in a series of recriminations or even lawsuits, or would they decide, separately or together, to accept the verdict, however flawed, and move forward?

Comparisons to 1960 are inevitable. In that year, John F. Kennedy carried Illinois over his rival, Vice President Richard M. Nixon, by only 8,858 votes out of 4.8 million cast and Texas by 46,233 votes out of 2.3 million cast. There were suspicions that Mayor Richard J. Daley of Chicago, the father of Mr. Gore's campaign manager, William M. Daley, and Senator Lyndon B. Johnson of Texas, Mr. Kennedy's running mate, might have manipulated the votes.

In his book, "RN, the Memoirs of Richard Nixon," published 18 years later, Mr. Nixon wrote, "There is no doubt that there was substantial vote fraud in the 1960 election. Texas and Illinois produced the most damaging as well as the most flagrant examples." But he quickly accepted the verdict.

Why? "A presidential recount

Continued on Page B9

How Gore Stopped Short On His Way to Concede

By KEVIN SACK and FRANK BRUNI

When his limousine arrived at the War Memorial Plaza in Nashville, where a few thousand despondent, rain-soaked supporters awaited the concession, Vice President Al Gore assumed he had lost the election.

He had called Gov. George W. Bush at the Governor's Mansion in Austin, Tex., and extended his congratulations. He had written a short and gracious speech about moving the country forward and cooperating with the victor.

But several vans back in the motorcade, an aide's Skytel pager vibrated with a message to call Michael Whouley, a top Gore strategist who was monitoring Florida results at Gore headquarters. What Mr. Whouley had to say, the aide, Michael B. Feldman, recalled, was that the Florida secretary of state's Web page had winnowed Mr. Bush's advantage of 50,000 votes to 6,000, with precincts still to tally.

That changed everything.

About a half-hour later, at 2:30 a.m. Central time, Mr. Gore placed his second call of the evening to Mr. Bush.

From a holding room beneath the plaza, where he had gone to concede, Mr. Gore told his Republican rival that circumstances had changed in the last 45 minutes. The race, Mr. Gore said, was now too close to call, and there would be an automatic recount in Florida. He was going to wait it out.

"You mean to tell me, Mr. Vice President, you're retracting your concession?" Mr. Bush asked, his tone incredulous, one aide said. The Texas governor had already begun preparing his victory remarks.

"You don't have to be snippy about it," Mr. Gore responded, according to several of those who heard Mr. Gore's side of the conversation.

Mr. Bush told Mr. Gore that his brother Jeb, the governor of Florida, had just assured him that Florida was his, Gore aides said.

"Let me explain something," Mr. Gore said. "Your younger brother is not the ultimate authority on this."

The conversation drew quickly to a close. The election did not.

After two sleepless days of campaigning, after a gut-wrenching night in which they had been convinced that they had won and then devastated that they had not, Mr. Gore and his aides were back in the game.

"I don't think there's ever been a night like this one," William M. Daley, the Gore campaign chairman, told the crowd at the plaza around 3:05 a.m.

No one in the Bush campaign would disagree with that assessment. Less than two hours earlier, around 1:15 a.m., when the television networks had called the election for

Continued on Page B9

Richard Perry/The New York Times

Stephen Crowley/The New York Times

Al Gore, in Nashville, and George W. Bush, in Austin, Tex., made brief statements yesterday as they awaited news from Florida.

Florida Democrats Say Ballot's Design Hurt Gore

By DON VAN NATTA Jr. and DANA CANEDY

WEST PALM BEACH, Fla., Nov. 8 — Senior Democratic officials seized on disputed votes cast in Palm Beach County to challenge Gov. George W. Bush's slim lead for the state's 25 electoral votes, vowing to fight beyond Thursday's vote recount if the Texas Republican prevails.

The dispute centers on the peculiar layout of a presidential ballot in Palm Beach County that some Democratic voters say caused them to become confused and mistakenly vote for Patrick J. Buchanan when they had intended to vote for Vice President Al Gore.

After the final tally, with Mr. Gore trailing Mr. Bush by just 1,784 votes in Florida, several senior Democratic officials said if the ballot had not flummoxed their supporters, Mr. Gore would have won enough votes to win Florida and the presidency.

Even though he never made even one campaign stop in Palm Beach County, Mr. Buchanan, the Reform Party candidate, finished with 3,704 votes in the staunchly Democratic county — nearly 2,700 more than Mr. Buchanan received in any of Florida's other 66 counties. A lawsuit was filed in West Palm Beach challenging the county's election and seeking a repeat of the vote two weeks from now.

"Leading Democrats have become increasingly concerned about the ballot in Palm Beach County," said a senior Democratic Party official. "This issue threatens to become a focal point for us even after the recount."

More than 29,000 ballots in Palm Beach County were thrown out because they included votes for more than one presidential candidate or had no names punched, according to records released today by the county's Supervisor of Elections.

Democratic aides and lawyers said the 29,000 ballots that were thrown out — about 4 percent of the votes cast in the county — were compelling evidence that the ballot was too confusing and possibly illegal.

Late today, three angry Palm Beach County residents, who said they mistakenly voted for Mr. Buchanan when they intended to vote for Vice President Gore, filed a lawsuit in state circuit court in West Palm Beach challenging the validity of the Palm Beach County vote. Other lawsuits were also planned, Democratic officials here said.

The legal challenges will most likely complicate and could delay the tense fight for Florida's all-impor-

Continued on Page B6

TALLY DUE TODAY

Vice President Clings to Slim Edge in Popular Vote Nationwide

By RICHARD L. BERKE

For the first time in more than a century, the winner of a presidential election remained unknown a full day after the polls closed, as Gov. George W. Bush of Texas and Vice President Al Gore dispatched teams of lawyers to Florida yesterday to wrangle over the handful of votes upon which their White House dreams now rest.

The fate of the two rivals appeared to ride on the verdict in Florida, where an incomplete vote count had Mr. Bush leading Mr. Gore by 1,784 votes, an extraordinarily narrow margin in a nationwide race in which more than 96 million people voted. His lead in Florida was three one-hundredths of 1 percent of the votes cast.

The Florida secretary of state said she would probably declare a winner by the close of business today after a recount of nearly six million votes and the tallying of absentee ballots. But it was far from certain that the matter would be resolved swiftly.

Even if Florida's 25 electoral votes are delivered to Mr. Bush, Democrats suggested that they would pursue complaints about voting irregularities. Some Democrats in Palm Beach called for a new election in the county, saying the punch-card ballot was so perplexing that people mistakenly voted for Patrick J. Buchanan, the Reform Party candidate, instead of Mr. Gore. In addition, election officials in other states with close outcomes, like Iowa and Wisconsin, said they were bracing for challenges.

With Mr. Gore clinging to the slimmest popular vote margin in modern times, and Mr. Bush grasping for a bare majority of electoral votes to pull him over the top, both candidates were no doubt wondering if, had they done things a bit differently, they might now be mulling over choices for their Cabinet, not mulling over their job prospects.

Still dazed by the events since Tuesday, an official at the Gore headquarters in Nashville proclaimed breathlessly last night, "We have just reached the twilight zone of American politics."

Officials in both campaigns described the extraordinary series of events since the election as nothing short of surreal. It thrust the American political system into a limbo of sorts, with Mr. Bush and Mr. Gore not knowing whether they should disband their campaigns, prepare to govern or retreat behind closed doors.

Mr. Bush and his running mate, Dick Cheney, stepped out of the gov-

Continued on Page B4

MORE ON THE VOTE

Hillary Clinton's New Role As a Political Powerhouse

After decades as a political spouse, Hillary Rodham Clinton will become a senator and one of the nation's most important Democrats. As she is acquiring her power, her husband will be relinquishing his. PAGE B1

Media Take a 3rd Look

Some network news executives, conceding they had twice been premature in calling the presidential race in Florida, said they were examining how such critical errors could have taken place. PAGE B1

A Disappointment for Gore

If Vice President Al Gore had carried his home state of Tennessee, with its 11 electoral votes on Tuesday, Florida would not be playing a decisive role in the 2000 presidential election. PAGE B1

Anger at Nader

Some staunch Democrats and their liberal allies angrily threatened retribution against Ralph Nader and his Green Party allies if Vice President Al Gore wound up losing by a hairbreadth. PAGE B3

Electoral College Debate

A long-running academic debate came alive with election results showing George W. Bush nearing a majority of Electoral College votes while falling short of Al Gore in the popular vote. PAGE B8

INSIDE

Attacking Runway Gridlock

The Federal Aviation Administration plans to ration flights at La Guardia Airport in a move to restructure airline fees and discourage gridlock during peak flying times at airports nationwide. PAGE D1

New President at Brown

Brown University is expected to name Ruth J. Simmons, who is currently the president of Smith College. She would be the first black head of an Ivy League institution. PAGE A18

Today's Sections

Section B is devoted to election news today. The Metro Section begins on Page D1 and SportsThursday on Page D9.

Updated news: www.nytimes.com

THE 2000 ELECTIONS

PRESIDENT

Photographs by Nicole Bengiveno/The New York Times

At Michigan State University, Clay Conklin, Brian Pincik, Levi Zdunic and Nick Wieber, left to right, discussed the election and lamented the delay. Terry Bulson, getting his hair cut by Dale Rathbum in Lansing, opined, "I think I'm going to end up feeling robbed," and he was not speaking of his hair.

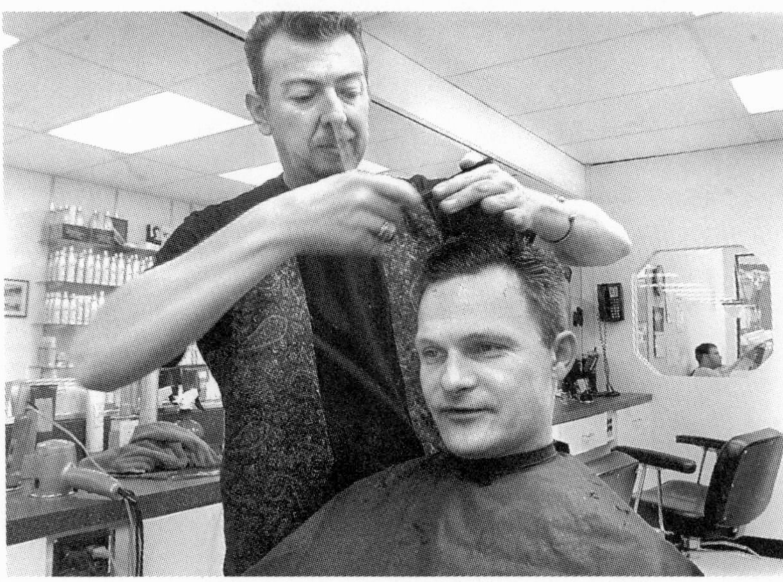

DEAD CENTER

Eternal Spotlight Yields to Infernal Wait

By JODI WILGOREN

LANSING, Mich., Nov. 8 — For so long, the people of this tossup city in this swing district in this battleground state had waited for it all to be over. Instead, they awoke to the election that refused to end.

The celebrities had stopped stalking the university campus, and the candidates were gone from the front stoop. Even the ubiquitous red, white and blue lawn signs had begun to disappear. But on television, the barrage of advertisements that had caused a communal headache for months had only been replaced with a migraine-inducing monologue by the talking heads.

On the morning after here, as in the rest of the country, it was a political hangover.

"I just want some closure right now," said Megan Thomas, 23, a piano teacher at Michigan State University who scurried to the student union between lessons today for news updates.

"It's like ripping the Band-Aid off little by little," added Ms. Thomas, who stayed up until 4 a.m. watching returns, then checked the television soon after the alarm went off — to no avail. "I just want to rip it off in one fell swoop."

Finally, the eyes of the world had moved away from Michigan and this capital city that had been designated ground zero repeatedly by the national media. Now they were in Florida, where the votes were being double-checked, the presidency hanging in the balance. But while Vice President Al Gore was a decisive victor here in Michigan, the results of the fiercely fought, expensive races for the United States Senate and the House of Representatives were unclear until morning. There is even some talk of a recount.

In an odd microcosm of the bizarre seesaw that played out on national television in the wee hours, Dianne Byrum, the Democratic candidate for the Eighth Congressional District, declared victory at 12:15 a.m., only to take it back around breakfast. Supporters had chanted "By-rum, By-rum" and "Congress-woman, Congress-woman," crying tears of joy; less than 12 hours later, the campaign manager, Tom Russell, said simply, "I've had better days."

Associated Press

Dianne Byrum declared victory in her House race just after midnight but had retreated by breakfast.

Ms. Byrum's campaign says she will seek a recount in her 524-vote loss to Mike Rogers, a state senator. A victory by Mr. Rogers helps the Republicans maintain control of the House, since he is replacing a Democrat, Debbie Stabenow. Ms. Stabenow came back from a deficit of 17 percentage points in some polls in her United States Senate race to oust the incumbent, Spencer Abraham.

Bill Hollister, a Republican candidate for the Michigan State Legislature who ended up losing by 14 percentage points, said he wished he had followed Ms. Byrum's lead, rather than disbanding his victory party at 12:30 a.m., before the results were in.

"Everybody would have had a great time if I'd said we won," Mr. Hollister said with a laugh. "They wouldn't have known."

Nothing seemed certain as voters here tried to sort out the results today, debating the relative merits of the Electoral College and the popular vote, mail-in balloting versus the punch-card method, and the probable politics of a bunch of anonymous enlisted soldiers overseas.

Democrats were positing conspiracy theories, raising nepotism questions about irregularities that just happened to occur in a state whose governor is the brother of the Republican presidential nominee. Republicans seemed happy to wait it out, preparing to gloat. And everyone had a sense that they were witnessing history in the making.

"This will never happen in our lifetimes again," said Jay Rising, a lawyer from Williamston who was having lunch at Dimitri's, a diner near the Capitol. Mr. Rising's friend Chris Dembowski said his 15-year-old son had been teaching him things about the last time a candidate had won the popular vote and lost the election, in 1888.

"It's really been kind of an opportune education for the kids, they've seen kind of the nitty-gritty," Mr. Rising said. "I woke my kids up this morning — they went to bed at 11 o'clock — and they said, 'Who won?' I said, 'Guess what, it's not over yet.' "

For Terry Bulson, who was getting a haircut this afternoon at Roberta's Hair Company, the downtown salon where Ms. Stabenow gets coiffed, the lesson is that the Electoral College has outlived its usefulness.

"I think I'm going to end up feeling robbed, the people's will is not going to be fulfilled," Mr. Bulson said, adding, "I'm a little biased. I'm a Democrat."

Sure enough, the five employees of the Republican caucus in the Legislature who were capping their election all-nighter with lunch at Dimitri's said the Constitution must not be changed.

"If you don't want to follow the rules, don't play the game," said Ralph Fiebig, 39, a computer analyst who lives in nearby Mason. "What if it was decided by one vote, would they go recount every single state, every single precinct?" Mr. Fiebig wondered. "In this case, they're just counting one state, and it's not mine, so I don't have to worry about it."

But even as the eye of the political storm moved south, folks here could not escape the election hoopla that had dominated local news and gossip for months.

David Rohde, a political scientist at Michigan State, gave his 330th interview of the year this morning. Everywhere, it seemed, televisions blared with the frustrating headline "Too Close to Call."

"What's taking so long?" demanded Levi Zdunic, 19, a freshman bowling with his buddies at Spartan Lanes, in the basement of the Michigan State student union.

"It's just getting pretty annoying," agreed Nick Wieber, 18. "I was hoping it'd be over," Mr. Wieber said. "I'm just sick of the wait."

THE OVERVIEW

Bush Barely Ahead of Gore in Florida, Where a Recount Holds the Key to the Election

Continued From Page B1

ernor's mansion in Austin, Tex., yesterday afternoon to reassure their supporters, and the nation.

In brief remarks, Mr. Bush said he expected the recount in Florida to confirm his victory there. He announced that he had called upon James A. Baker III, the secretary of state in his father's administration, to travel to Tallahassee, Fla., to look after his interests.

In what had the ring of a truncated version of an acceptance speech, Mr. Bush thanked Mr. Gore's supporters and said, "Secretary Cheney and I will do everything in our power to unite the nation, to call upon the best, to bring people together after one of the most exciting elections in our nation's history."

He said he hoped the matter was "finalized as quickly as possible and in a calm and thoughtful manner."

Later in the afternoon, Mr. Gore and his running mate, Senator Joseph I. Lieberman of Connecticut, appeared before a backdrop of American flags in Nashville, where the vice president said the outcome should not be hastily determined.

"Because of what is at stake," Mr. Gore said, "this matter must be resolved expeditiously, but deliberately and without any rush to judgment." He added, "No matter what the outcome, America will make the transition to a new administration with dignity, with full respect for the freely expressed will of the people, and with pride in the democracy we are privileged to share."

While Mr. Bush sent Mr. Baker, Mr. Gore said he had asked another former secretary of state, Warren Christopher, to join the team of lawyers representing him in Florida.

Yet for all the words about cooperation, prominent Democrats made clear in private conservations that they had no intention of standing by if Mr. Bush claimed the White House on the slimmest of margins. Noting that Mr. Gore can be a scrappy street fighter, an official who is close to the campaign said, "The sense is we're going to play hardball."

The situation ensured that the election of 2000 would be one for the history books. The popular vote margin was the closest since John F. Kennedy defeated Richard M. Nixon in 1960 by about 100,000 votes. And the electoral vote margin appeared to be the tightest since 1876, when Rutherford B. Hayes beat Samuel J. Tilden by a single electoral vote.

How the Voters Turned Out . . .

While the voting age population grows, so does the amount of people voting. But the percentage who vote is declining.

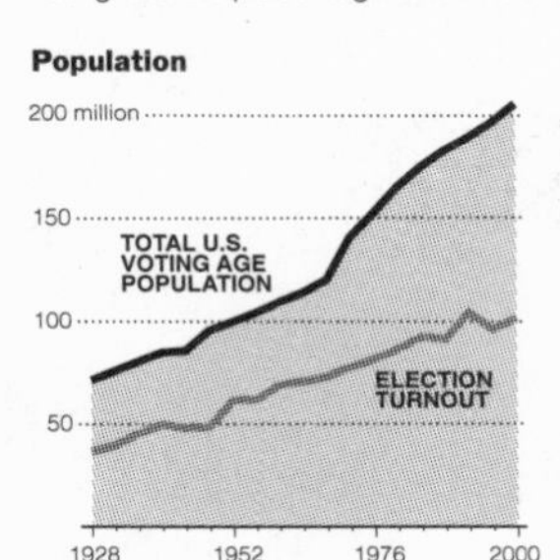

Source: Committee for the Study of the American Electorate

. . . And What They Decided

States won by the two candidates.

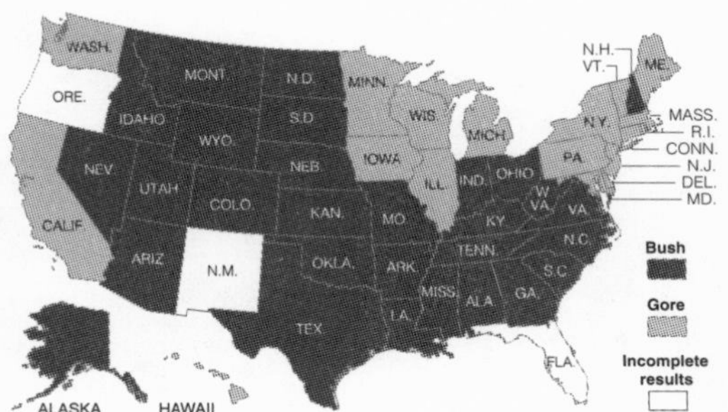

The New York Times

The tally set off rounds of second guessing in each campaign. For instance, if Mr. Gore had won his home state, Tennessee, which slipped from his grasp by only a small margin, he would have enough electoral votes to be president.

A day in the 'twilight zone of American politics.'

If a confident Mr. Bush had not taken last Sunday off, while Mr. Gore was barnstorming the nation, the outcome might have been more decisive for him.

Many Gore advisers said they were furious at Ralph Nader, the Green Party candidate, arguing that he drained enough votes from the vice president to potentially cost him Florida. As President Clinton celebrated his wife's victory in the New York Senate race on Tuesday night, he was overheard angrily denouncing Mr. Nader, who did not capture the 5 percent of the vote needed for him to claim federal matching funds in the next election.

The outcome suggested that voters were truly agonizing between the two major party nominees. Mr. Gore and Mr. Bush split the vote evenly, with Mr. Gore relying on larger states like California and New York, and Mr. Bush building his support on a larger sum of smaller states, including a swatch from North Dakota straight down to his home state of Texas. In addition to Florida, Oregon and New Mexico were too close to confidently call last night.

No matter whether Mr. Bush or Mr. Gore ultimately prevails, the 43rd president will be forced to lead with a tenuous mandate at best.

If Mr. Bush wins, he would have the benefit of being the first Republican since the Eisenhower era to have a Republican House and Senate as well.

But because Mr. Gore surpassed him in the popular vote — and the partisan margins in Congress will be the tightest in years — Mr. Bush will have to aggressively work with the other party. But if he becomes president, Mr. Gore will have to deal with a Congress that is controlled by his political foes.

In what felt like the most interminable election night ever, both campaigns endured perhaps as many highs and lows after the polls closed on Tuesday as they had over months of stumping around the country. First, the networks declared that Mr. Gore won Florida. Then they rescinded that projection. Then they called the state for Mr. Bush. Then they declared Mr. Bush the next president. Then they changed their mind.

No one was more tormented than the contenders themselves. Mr. Gore telephoned Mr. Bush early yesterday morning to congratulate him on his triumph. But barely an hour later, he called his rival to take back what he said.

"He was just incredulous," one Bush aide said of the governor's reaction to Mr. Gore's second call.

The initial news about a Bush victory left Mark McKinnon, Mr. Bush's media adviser, practically dancing in the streets, only to be chastened moments later. And it left Edward G. Rendell, the Democratic National Committee's general chairman, in the embarrassing position of telling CNN that Mr. Gore had forfeited the election by making wrong-headed decisions about advertising and not sufficiently turning to Mr. Clinton to stump for the ticket. By yesterday, Mr. Rendell seemed to be staying clear of the cameras.

There were other ways in which the outcome was unpredictable. Many strategists predicted that no matter who won the electoral college, Mr. Bush would prevail in the popular vote because his support in many states was by larger margins than Mr. Gore's. The opposite turned out to be true.

For weeks, Gore officials played down the importance of the popular vote. But yesterday, Mark Fabiani, a senior Gore official, said the vice president's popular vote victory was "by any measure, important — all this would be different if he had loss the popular vote."

There were also some unforgettable scenes. William M. Daley, Mr. Gore's campaign chairman, met with reporters early yesterday morning to call for a clean recount in Florida. His late father, Mayor Richard J. Daley of Chicago, had been accused of helping steal votes for John F. Kennedy 40 years ago.

"There is one state left to be decided," Mr. Daley said at another news conference yesterday, "and we believe when those votes are counted and that process is complete, totally complete, Al Gore will have won the electoral college and the popular vote, and therefore will be the next president."

And there was the tableau yesterday of Mr. Bush's younger brother Jeb, the governor of Florida, who was assuring the public that he would make sure the recount was conducted smoothly. He stood at a news conference with, of all people, Bob Butterworth, Mr. Gore's Florida chairman, who also happens to be the state attorney general.

"The attorney general and I sit next to each other in cabinet meetings, and we have discussed how close and how hard fought it's been all the way from the very beginning to the end, and we thought it would be close," Jeb Bush said. "Never in my wildest dreams did I ever imagine it would be this close."

A night when both campaigns endured a number of highs and lows.

Officials in both campaigns were trying to figure how the outcome in Florida might be affected by absentee ballots from residents who are abroad. To be counted, those ballots must have been postmarked by Election Day and must arrive by Nov. 17. There is no record of how many were requested, but four years ago, roughly 2,300 were cast.

Republicans contended that most of those ballots would come from military personnel, who typically vote Republican. But Democrats countered that many in the military are minorities who would support Mr. Gore.

The voting even led a bemused President Clinton to appear before reporters at the South Lawn of the White House to reassure the nation — and friends and foes abroad — that the muddied verdict did not amount to a national crisis. "No American will ever be able to seriously say again, 'My vote doesn't count,' " he said.

After congratulating Mr. Gore and Mr. Bush "on a vigorous, hard-fought, truly remarkable campaign," Mr. Clinton told reporters: "I was just like you last night. I was a fascinated observer."

Mr. Christopher, speaking at a news conference after Mr. Gore, tried to reassure the public of the Democrats' intentions. "Last night was an extraordinary night," Mr. Christopher said. "None of us have ever seen anything quite like it. But I don't have any reason to think we're on the edge of a constitutional crisis. And we don't intend to try to provoke a constitutional crisis."

Yet those very words suggested that there were deep and consequential implications in the aftermath of the election for both the government — and for the American political system.

"All the News That's Fit to Print"

The New York Times

Late Edition

New York: **Today**, bright start, then cloudy, high 31. **Tonight**, snow arriving, low 28. **Tomorrow**, snow changing to rain, high 35. **Yesterday**, high 52, low 37. Weather map is on Page D8.

VOL. CL . . No. 51,601 NEW YORK, WEDNESDAY, DECEMBER 13, 2000 — $1 beyond the greater New York metropolitan area. — 75 CENTS

BUSH PREVAILS

BY SINGLE VOTE, JUSTICES END RECOUNT, BLOCKING GORE AFTER 5-WEEK STRUGGLE

An Awareness of Hazards

By LINDA GREENHOUSE

WASHINGTON, Dec. 12 — The Supreme Court effectively handed the presidential election to George W. Bush tonight, overturning the Florida Supreme Court and ruling by a vote of 5 to 4 that there could be no further counting of Florida's disputed presidential votes.

The ruling came after a long and tense day of waiting at 10 p.m., just two hours before the Dec. 12 "safe harbor" for immunizing a state's electors from challenge in Congress was to come to an end. The unsigned majority opinion said it was the immediacy of this deadline that made it impossible to come up with a way of counting the votes that could both meet "minimal constitutional standards" and be accomplished within the deadline.

The five members of the majority were Chief Justice William H. Rehnquist and Justices Sandra Day O'Connor, Antonin Scalia, Anthony M. Kennedy and Clarence Thomas.

Among the four dissenters, two justices, Stephen G. Breyer and David H. Souter, agreed with the majority that the varying standards in different Florida counties for counting the punch-card ballots presented problems of both due process and equal protection. But unlike the majority, these justices said the answer should be not to shut the recount down, but to extend it until the Dec. 18 date for the meeting of the Electoral College.

Justice Souter said that such a recount would be a "tall order" but that "there is no justification for denying the state the opportunity to try to count all the disputed ballots now." [Text, Page A27.]

The six separate opinions, totaling 65 pages, were filled with evidence that the justices were acutely aware of the controversy the court had entered by accepting Governor Bush's appeal of last Friday's Florida Supreme Court ruling and by granting him a stay of the recount on Saturday afternoon, just hours after the vote counting had begun.

"None are more conscious of the vital limits on judicial authority than are the members of this court," the majority opinion said, referring to "our unsought responsibility to resolve the federal and constitutional issues the judicial system has been forced to confront."

The dissenters said nearly all the objections raised by Mr. Bush were insubstantial. The court should not have reviewed either this case or the one it decided last week, they said.

Justice John Paul Stevens said the court's action "can only lend credence to the most cynical appraisal of the work of judges throughout the land."

His dissenting opinion, also signed by Justices Breyer and Ruth Bader Ginsburg, added: "It is confidence in the men and women who administer the judicial system that is the true backbone of the rule of law. Time will one day heal the wound to that confidence that will be inflicted by today's decision. One thing, however, is certain. Although we may never know with complete certainty the identity of the winner of this year's Presidential election, the identity of the loser is perfectly clear. It is the nation's confidence in the judge as an impartial guardian of the rule of law."

What the court's day and a half of deliberations yielded tonight was a messy product that bore the earmarks of a failed attempt at a compromise solution that would have permitted the vote counting to continue.

It appeared that Justices Souter and Breyer, by taking seriously the equal protection concerns that Justices Kennedy and O'Connor had raised at the argument, had tried to persuade them that those concerns could be addressed in a remedy that would permit the disputed votes to be counted.

Justices O'Connor and Kennedy were the only justices whose names did not appear separately on any

Continued on Page A26

Associated Press

Thirty-five days after Election Day, the Supreme Court effectively handed George W. Bush the presidency.

G.O.P. IS CAUTIOUS

Camps Choose to Digest Ruling and Refuse to End Their Battle

By RICHARD L. BERKE

WASHINGTON, Dec. 12 — Exactly five weeks after one of the most unsettled presidential elections in American history, George Walker Bush appeared tonight to have swept away any lingering legal obstacles, gaining the right, at long last, to consider himself president-elect.

While the campaigns of Mr. Bush and Vice President Al Gore were still reading and digesting the Supreme Court's tangled and elaborate ruling as midnight approached, officials in both camps said it was now virtually impossible for Mr. Gore to reach the White House.

The post-election tumult overshadowed a spectacular political rise for Mr. Bush only eight years after his father was turned out of the White House.

In perhaps a fitting coda to a turbulent election night that never seemed to end, the court's verdict was not issued until about 10 p.m., and — as campaign officials pored over the ruling page by page — Gore aides said there would be no concession speech tonight.

Just the same, the Bush campaign proceeded with extreme caution, mindful that it appear presumptuous — or unduly triumphant. In a terse statement he read to reporters in Tallahassee, Fla., late tonight, James A. Baker III, the former secretary of state and Mr. Bush's top adviser in the case, said Mr. Bush and his running mate, Dick Cheney, were "very pleased and gratified" that the court agreed that "there were constitutional problems with the recount ordered by the Florida Supreme Court."

Careful not to declare victory, Mr. Baker added, "This has been a long and arduous process for everyone on both sides."

Mr. Bush's advisers said they wanted to give Mr. Gore room to concede before the governor, who was cloistered in the Governor's Mansion in Austin, Tex., publicly proclaimed victory.

Mr. Gore himself, who collected more popular votes than Mr. Bush, and who insisted that a full and accurate recount would show him to be the winner in Florida, remained in his home in Washington with his family.

His campaign chairman, William M. Daley, issued a statement describing the complicated ruling and not leaving any hint of a concession that other Gore aides said would be forthcoming.

"The decision is both complex and lengthy," Mr. Daley said. "It will take time to completely analyze this decision."

Mr. Daley said the Gore camp would comment further on Wednes-

Continued on Page A30

A Shaky Platform on Which to Build

By R. W. APPLE Jr.

News Analysis

WASHINGTON, Dec. 12 — Whatever else it did tonight, the Supreme Court failed to speak with the kind of clarion political voice about the vexed 2000 presidential election that much of the nation had hoped for.

If, as seems sure, Gov. George W. Bush has won, he has won a narrow victory — narrow in Florida, narrow in the Electoral College and narrow in the Supreme Court. He will have only a shaky platform from which to begin his presidency in January, and it will require immense skill to remove the questions about his legitimacy that were left hanging by tonight's decision.

The court provided no clear, unanimous validation of the electoral process. Its extraordinarily complex ruling led to widespread confusion in the first few minutes after it was issued, and it may well provide ammunition in the months ahead for embittered supporters of Vice President Al Gore, whose chances seemed to have been sorely and in all probability fatally damaged.

Nor was there any certainty that the Democrats would refrain from further challenges, either in the courts or in the halls of Congress. One possible line of attack is the Florida Legislature's actions to choose electors. But there was no clear avenue for further legal maneuvering by the Gore team.

"I had hoped that the court would bring the country together," said Senator Dianne Feinstein, Democrat of California. "I had hoped that it would send a clear message, but that does not appear to have happened."

One of Mr. Gore's confidants described the court's opinion as "confusing but devastating." Some backers, including Edward G. Rendell, the general chairman of the Democratic party, and Laurence H. Tribe, one of Mr. Gore's top lawyers, said it was time for the vice president to concede, but some others disagreed.

James A. Baker III, Mr. Bush's chief spokesman in the Florida fight, confined himself to a statement of pleasure, without appearing triumphant and without putting any pressure on Mr. Gore to quit the contest.

In reversing the order of the Florida Supreme Court, the court came down on the side of Governor Bush. With less than a week remaining until the Electoral College is to cast its votes, the justices in the core ruling that the Florida court was wrong to order a recount found a way to speak with one voice, avoiding a contentious split, but no sooner had they done so than they started bickering again among themselves.

Still, beneath the welter of verbiage, the same five justices who had voted on Saturday to halt a partial recount ordered by the Florida Supreme Court remained convinced that the court's recount plan was unconstitutional.

As a formality, Washington

Continued on Page A24

The Tally

ELECTORAL VOTES	(270 NEEDED)
GEORGE W. BUSH	271
AL GORE	267
NATIONAL POPULAR VOTE	
AL GORE	50,158,094
GEORGE W. BUSH	49,820,518

Source: Associated Press

Once Again, the TV Mystery Prevails as Late-Night Fare

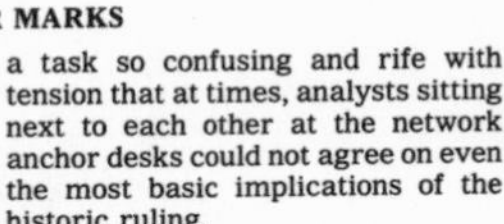

By PETER MARKS

Was the election over, or did Vice President Al Gore still have a chance? Had the United States Supreme Court sent the case back to Florida, or settled the matter once and for all? Was the vote 5 to 4, or 7 to 2? And what exactly had the justices voted on, anyway?

For the better part of an hour last night, correspondents, commentators and legal experts frantically tried to make sense on live television of a ruling that seemed about as easy to reduce to simple language as the assembly manual for the space station.

Viewers across the channels were given the opportunity to watch as anchors and reporters struggled mightily to digest and summarize a complex, voluminous decision. It was a task so confusing and rife with tension that at times, analysts sitting next to each other at the network anchor desks could not agree on even the most basic implications of the historic ruling.

Some were quick to declare it the definitive victory for Gov. George W. Bush; others thought it still held out some sliver of hope for Mr. Gore. But talking heads on every channel seemed to agree that the job of parsing it on the air was monumental.

"It may take an army of lawyers to translate this thing," Dan Rather said on CBS at 10:18 p.m., Eastern Standard Time, about 20 minutes after the opinion was released. To which his colleague Bob Schieffer, searching for the appropriate adjective, added, " 'Complicated' is the understatement of the year."

A long day of network calm over the court's deliberations was broken just before 10 p.m., when the first word reached the anchors on cable that the opinion was about to be issued. MSNBC trained a camera on Bob Kur, an NBC correspondent who was posted on the Supreme Court steps like a member of a relay team, waiting for the baton to be passed.

"Tell me if you see any movement

Continued on Page A25

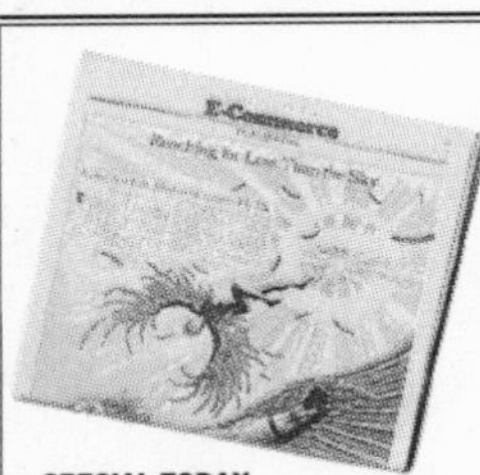

SPECIAL TODAY

E-Commerce

After a year in which the boldest Internet entrepreneurs soared and plunged, Saul Hansell finds that the Web has changed business in modest but still substantial ways. **SECTION H**

354613

NEWS SUMMARY

Updated news: www.nytimes.com

Part of Drug Battle: Keeping It in Stores

Critics of the Food and Drug Administration have argued that the agency has been allowing drugs to be rushed into use since a 1992 law enabled speedier reviews. A case in point is that of Odell Buggs, a 28-year-old counselor who suffered a stroke that her doctors attributed to an ingredient in her over-the-counter decongestant, Tavist-D. She sued the manufacturer, the pharmaceutical giant Novartis A.G., saying its cold pills had left her with brain damage. Novartis, based in Switzerland, had a strong defense: the ingredient, phenylpropanolamine, or PPA, was in dozens of cold remedies, as well as appetite suppressants, and had been taken in billions of doses with no ill effects. The Buggs case offers a glimpse into how companies marketing PPA worked aggressively to assuage concerns about the safety of a drug that for six decades was a staple in American medicine cabinets.

Article, page A31.

With a Victory Apparently His, Bush Plays the Strong, Silent Role

By DAVID E. SANGER

AUSTIN, Tex., Dec. 12 — For 35 days Gov. George W. Bush has insisted that he won Florida and with it the presidency. But when the Supreme Court appeared to seal his victory late this evening, there was silence from the Governor's Mansion here and Mr. Bush's aides quite deliberately avoided any claim of victory.

All day Mr. Bush had stayed out of sight, never venturing from his house. But just before 11:30 p.m., Mr. Bush's chief legal strategist, former Secretary of State James A. Baker III, said he had spoken with the Texas governor and Dick Cheney, his running mate, and described them as "very pleased and gratified" by the court's ruling, and he thanked the Bush legal team as well as the hundreds of volunteers in Florida for their efforts.

But Mr. Baker left it open to Vice President Al Gore to make the next move. Aides said they would wait to see whether Mr. Gore would make a concession announcement, but made it clear that under their reading of the court's opinion, that that was now inevitable.

The Gore camp was even more subdued, with no official announcement by the vice president or his staff. But aides and supporters were clearly downcast and in some cases stunned. "It makes you want to call 911 and report a burglary," said Greg Simon, a longtime Gore adviser who has been working in Florida on the recount.

Before Mr. Baker's brief comment, Mr. Bush's aides here were poring through faxes of the opinion and the lengthy dissents, trying to figure out whether their victory was, in fact, in hand. "We're just reading it like everyone else," said one top aide, speaking in the busy but surprisingly subdued campaign headquarters about eight blocks from Mr. Bush's residence. The governor is not expected to say anything in public until Wednesday, and even then, the aide said, may wait for Mr. Gore to act first.

Mindy Tucker, a Bush spokeswoman, said, "We are heartened it does mean the Florida Supreme Court has been reversed, and the recount they called for will not happen."

Tonight's decision appeared to mark the end of one of the most bizarre periods in American political history. Twice in that period, first on election night and then last Friday afternoon, Mr. Bush and his aides thought that the presidency would be his within moments. Twice those moments disappeared, only to come back tonight for the third — and it appeared the final — time.

The first time Mr. Bush thought he had been elected president was in the early morning hours of Nov. 8, as the networks put Florida's votes in his column. Mr. Bush received a congratulatory call from Mr. Gore, who told him he was about to go before his supporters in Tennessee and concede the election.

So the governor prepared to speak before a victory rally here, in front of the Capitol. He waited to see Mr. Gore's public concession, and waited

Continued on Page A25

INSIDE

Fatal Crash Grounds Osprey

The Marine Corps grounded its V-22 Ospreys after another of the problem-prone aircraft crashed, killing four marines. PAGE A33

Clinton's Pledge to Ireland

President Clinton, on his third trip to Ireland, said he would keep working for reconciliation in Ulster even after leaving the White House. PAGE A8

Pressure to Free Pollard

A new push is being mounted to persuade President Clinton to free the convicted spy Jonathan Jay Pollard before leaving office. PAGE A14

McVeigh Drops Appeal

Timothy J. McVeigh, sentenced to die for the 1995 Oklahoma City bombing, has asked to be executed within four months. PAGE A18

Putin Nurturing Old Friends

President Vladimir V. Putin of Russia visits Cuba this week, part of an attempt to rebuild ties with client states of the Soviet era. PAGE A8

CONTESTING THE VOTE: Examining the Court's Decision

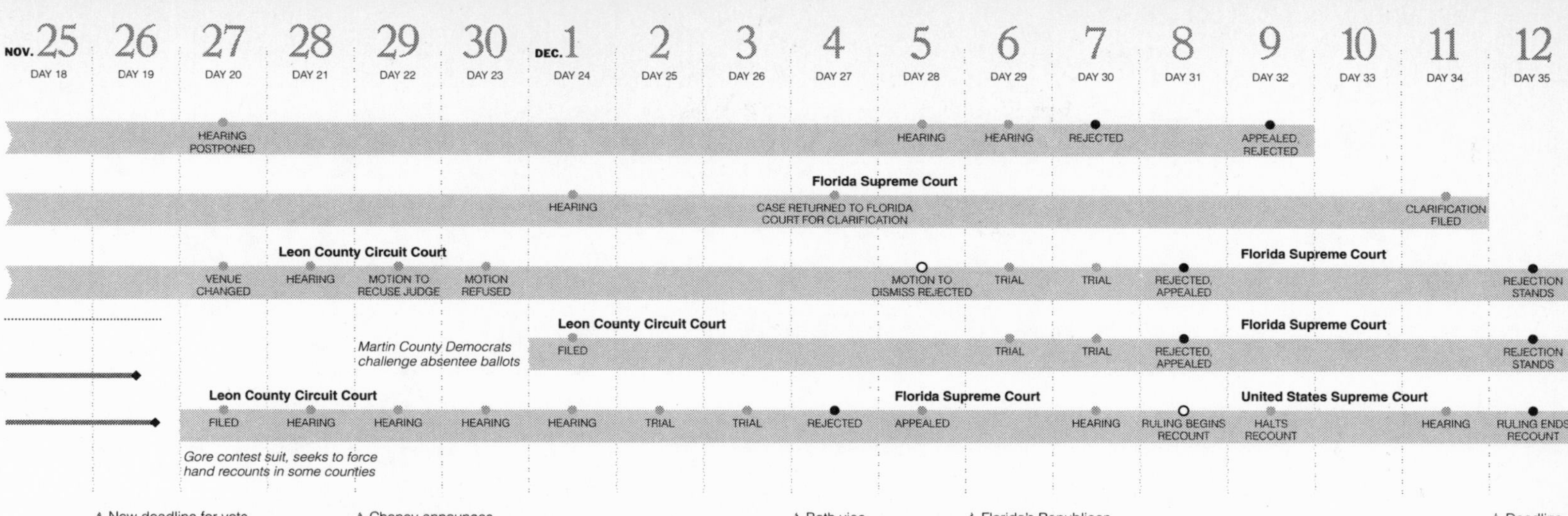

Andrew Phillips/The New York Times

THE MEDIA

The Mystery Prevails As Late-Night TV Fare

Continued From Page A1

yet," Brian Williams, the MSNBC anchor, said to Mr. Kur on the air, as the correspondent peered right and left for the first sighting of the network employee who was to deliver the opinion to him.

"Here comes our runner!" Mr. Kur announced, and as Mr. Williams offered bits of encouragement, the reporter began flipping anxiously through the document. "Hang on, Brian!" Mr. Kur said, struggling to find a page that offered some encapsulation of the decision. "Looking for the summary."

When at last he found something, Mr. Kur began reading aloud, but the legalese was almost impossible to make sense of. The mandate placed on television for instant clarity and coherence proved elusive.

The struggle was shared by all the networks, which had assembled their A-list teams of court reporters and commentators for what appeared to be one of the toughest assignments of the election. Having been criticized by politicians and academics for the missed projections on the presidential race in Florida on election night, and for imprecision in describing the previous Supreme Court ruling in the election deadlock, the networks appeared to be taking special pains to avoid overstating the new decision.

On ABC, for instance, George Stephanopoulos declared in the first moments after the decision's release that it meant "effectively, George Bush wins, 271 to 267" in the electoral vote count. But after listening to others on the ABC team analyze the decision, Peter Jennings, the anchor, told Mr. Stephanopoulos that at first blush that might be a stretch.

One problem for the networks was extracting a clear narrative from the many people they had reading the document simultaneously. On the steps of the Supreme Court, ABC had three staff members: the on-the-air reporters, Jeffrey Toobin and Jackie Judd, and the off-the-air reporter assigned to the court, Ellen Davis. Terry Moran, another correspondent with extensive experience in covering courts, was outside Mr. Gore's home in Washington, while Jack Ford, like Mr. Moran a Court TV veteran, was seated next to Mr. Stephanopoulos on the ABC set. A constitutional expert from Florida, Steven Gey, was enlisted, too.

On the steps, Ms. Judd effectively contradicted Mr. Stephanopoulos's analysis, saying the justices had "left open the door a little bit" by sending the case back to the Florida Supreme Court, a train of thought picked up by Mr. Ford in the studio. "I think if we were looking for finality from this decision, we haven't captured it," he said about 10:22 p.m.

Trying to get all the nuances, Mr. Jennings asked for clarification from Mr. Gey, who offered this ambivalent take: "You've got a legal answer and a political answer."

When Ms. Judd apologized for the attenuated effort at getting the gist of the opinion, Mr. Jennings stopped her. "Nobody," he said, "should be embarrassed about working through a Supreme Court decision" before a national audience.

The moment-by-moment evolution in the networks' absorbing of the meaning was reflected in the explanatory banners they ran at the bottom of the screen. In the initial minutes, the networks chose carefully inconclusive headlines, like CBS's "Reverses and Remands Case to Florida Supreme Court."

As the reporters got a chance to read through the majority opinion and the dissents, the banners became more definitive. "United States Supreme Court Bars New Recount in Florida," NBC flashed on screen just before 10:30.

With a consensus gathering that the opinion had indeed made it impossible for Mr. Gore to obtain a recount, the network commentators grew more confident that the court had identified a real winner and a real loser. Even the actual vote by the justices had been clarified. "No question," Pete Williams said on NBC, "it is a 5-to-4 vote."

By 11 p.m., the general chairman of the Democratic National Committee, Edward G. Rendell, appearing on MSNBC, had called for Mr. Gore to concede, and the networks were coalescing around the conclusion that Mr. Bush had won Florida's 25 electoral votes.

"Thirty-five days after the official election date," Tom Brokaw said on NBC, "it does appear that this election came to an end as a result of an intervention by the United States Supreme Court."

Photographs by Paul Hosefros/The New York Times

Bob Kur of NBC News, right, received the court ruling last night from an assistant and immediately began trying to sort it out. On CBS, Deirdre Hester and Bob Schieffer went through a similar procedure.

CONGRESS

Joy and Bitterness, Along Party Lines

By ERIC SCHMITT and IRVIN MOLOTSKY

WASHINGTON, Dec. 12 — Members of Congress reacted tonight with the same mix of confusion and hesitation to the United States Supreme Court ruling as most Americans watching or listening to the news unfold.

But as it became apparent that the court's complex, divided ruling had in effect ended the nation's longest election night in favor of Gov. George W. Bush, Republicans wearily rejoiced and Democrats voiced bitter disappointments.

"It looks to me that this should make Bush president," said Representative Christopher B. Cannon, a Republican of Utah. "I hope Al Gore concedes soon. There's been a lot of talk about Democrats getting even that I don't think is appropriate. I hope we can get that all behind us and get on with the business of America."

Senator John W. Warner, Republican of Virginia, said: "Al Gore will do the right thing at the right time. The rule of law has prevailed."

At the same time, Democrats expressed frustration, with some condemning the justices' ruling.

Representative Earl F. Hilliard, Democrat of Alabama, reprised some of the vituperative language hurled at the court following its stay of the recount of contested ballots in Florida on Saturday.

"They have been extremely political," Mr. Hilliard said in a telephone interview. "The total effect has been to deliver the election to Bush."

"The total conspiracy of the Republican Party has put the credibility of Bush on the line," Mr. Hilliard said. "With half of the American people, he will have no credibility. With half of the members of Congress, he will have no credibility.

"The Supreme Court of the United States has supported a mockery of our democracy."

Other Democrats, equally disappointed in the outcome, offered words of resignation rather than resentment.

"It looks like the end of the road for Al Gore," said Representative John M. Spratt Jr., Democrat of South Carolina. "In the end, we have to put this behind us and do the country's business."

House and Senate leaders from both parties declined to comment tonight, with their aides insisting that their bosses needed time to study the court's 65-page ruling and various opinions.

"This was a night for the lawyers," said Michele Davis, a spokeswoman for Representative Dick Armey of Texas, the majority leader.

Ranit Schmelzer, a spokeswoman for Senator Tom Daschle of South Dakota, the Democratic leader, said the situation was too "murky" for a definitive comment.

For weeks, Republicans have said that if Mr. Bush and his running mate, Dick Cheney, were elected, they would usher in a new era of bipartisanship to official Washington, including Capitol Hill.

Tonight, Mr. Spratt, the ranking Democrat on the House Budget Committee, said Mr. Bush would soon face the first test of that pledge, in the budget process.

Hours before the court's ruling tonight, several Democrats said that if the Supreme Court held against Mr. Gore, the decision should be considered final, and that there would be no appetite to challenge the electors of the Electoral College when they are officially approved by Congress in January.

"The overwhelming consensus has been behind Gore to go through the judicial process, but to call it a day once the judicial process is exhausted," said Senator Charles E. Schumer, Democrat of New York. "There would be worry among people in our party that it would hurt our party to go further."

Senator Byron L. Dorgan, Democrat of North Dakota, agreed, saying, "If the Supreme Court rules against Mr. Gore, I think it's been game, set, match."

Mr. Dorgan added, "If the Supreme Court rules that the counts ordered by the Florida Supreme Court shall not happen, I think it's pretty much the end of the line."

Senator Robert G. Torricelli, Democrat of New Jersey, said tonight, "It was both a controversial and a close judgment of the Supreme Court but it was also a final decision, and I hope the people will accept the finality of the judgment.

"I think George Bush comes to the presidency in very difficult circumstances, and it is incumbent on all of us to put the bitterness behind us and help him to succeed."

Mr. Torricelli headed the Democrats' successful campaign to pick up seats in the Senate, and he said he regretted Mr. Gore's defeat.

Calls from both sides to get on with the business of America.

"We've all learned something about our government and Constitution," Mr. Torricelli said. "They are more fragile than we might have imagined."

Representative Charles B. Rangel, Democrat of New York, said: "This court has found that politics is better than the Constitution. This is terribly disappointing. The respect for the court has been seriously diminished."

While Mr. Rangel was harshly critical of the Supreme Court and the decision, he said that the American people had to rally around Mr. Bush for the good of the country.

He recalled that Harry Truman was regarded by many as not bright enough to succeed Franklin Delano Roosevelt when Roosevelt died in office, but that Truman proved to be a successful president.

"I remember when John F. Kennedy was assassinated," Mr. Rangel said, "and I remember the image of Lyndon Johnson as someone who was put on the ticket just to win the election, and he turned out to be a great president.

"I was a member of the impeachment committee when President Nixon was forced to reign, and Gerald Ford held this country together. Bush will have to work hard to bring the country together."

THE TEXAS GOVERNOR

Bush Aides Confront Possibility That Public Opinion May Shift

Continued From Page A1

some more.

After 45 minutes, Mr. Gore called back and in a tense exchange with his Republican rival said that the numbers in Florida had narrowed, and that he would not be conceding after all.

"You mean to tell me, Mr. Vice President, you're retracting your concession?" Mr. Bush asked, his tone incredulous.

"You don't have to be snippy about it," Mr. Gore responded, according to several of those who heard Mr. Gore's side of the conversation. That was the last time the two men have spoken.

What followed was a machine recount of the Florida vote, then demands from the Gore campaign for hand recounts of certain counties. Mr. Bush and his aides, in a strategy that for a while looked very risky, did not seek any recounts of their own, even in heavily Republican counties. They knew that recounts only rarely reverse an initial count. And their strategy was to hold on to the lead that the networks announced election night, even as it dwindled in size through various recounts and a Florida Supreme Court order.

When a decision appears to seal Bush's victory, he is silent.

Once the Republican secretary of state of Florida had certified the result of the election in Mr. Bush's favor, his strategy was to hold on to that declaration for dear life and hope that time would run out on Mr. Gore's efforts.

That strategy nearly paid off last Friday. Two local Florida courts declined to throw out ballots that had been submitted by absentee voters, cases in which Democrats challenged the validity of applications for those ballots. Mr. Bush's legal advisers thought he would win a third case that day, before the Florida Supreme Court. Had the court refused to order any recounts, Mr. Bush would have won that day.

On Saturday morning, his aides truly sweated: A recount was under way, and Mr. Bush's lead appeared to have narrowed to just 100 votes. Then the Supreme Court halted the recount. And tonight, the Bush strategy finally appeared to pay off.

In the end he appeared to have won the presidency in a way no one could have predicted: Because the United States Supreme Court said Florida's counties were all judging the intent of voters in a different way, and that there was no time left to apply a uniform standard.

"What a roller coaster this has been," one of Mr. Bush's top advisers, Tucker Eskew, said the other day. "We've been up, we've been down. Sometime it has to end."

But now the pressure is on Mr. Bush to perform well in public, after a rocky several weeks. He has said little, and seemed flustered and distracted at different times. When his vice presidential running mate, Mr. Cheney, suffered a mild heart attack, Mr. Bush was not informed, and acted as if it was only a scare. But two hours before he spoke, doctors had conducted emergency surgery on Mr. Cheney. It is unclear whether Mr. Bush knew that.

At various times, Mr. Bush has tried to act as a president-elect, inviting photographers in as he was being briefed by his national security expert, Condoleezza Rice, or his economic adviser, Larry Lindsey. Those sessions were conducted in a room with a fireplace and flags that closely resembled such scenes in the Oval Office, creating the effect of a government-in-waiting. But in recent days Mr. Bush has suspended those photo opportunities, and waited to announce both his staff and his cabinet members until victory was assured.

Now he will likely go ahead, after delivering a speech that advisers say is full of conciliatory language about healing the nation and achieving bipartisanship.

Company News: Tuesday through Saturday, Business Day

"All the News That's Fit to Print"

The New York Times

Late Edition
New York: **Today,** morning rain, then cloudy, high 39. **Tonight,** becoming partly cloudy, low 32. **Tomorrow,** partial sunshine, high 40. **Yesterday,** high 31, low 20. Weather map, Page B13.

VOL. CL . . . No. 51,602 NEW YORK, THURSDAY, DECEMBER 14, 2000 — $1 beyond the greater New York metropolitan area. — 75 CENTS

BUSH PLEDGES TO BE PRESIDENT FOR 'ONE NATION,' NOT ONE PARTY; GORE, CONCEDING, URGES UNITY

AN END TO A QUEST

Vice President Offers to Aid Bush but Admits Disappointment

By RICHARD L. BERKE and KATHARINE Q. SEELYE

WASHINGTON, Dec. 13 — Vice President Al Gore reluctantly surrendered his quest for the presidency tonight, telling the American public that while he was deeply disappointed and sharply disagreed with the Supreme Court verdict that ended his campaign, "partisan rancor must now be put aside."

In a gracious eight-minute televised speech from his ceremonial office next to the White House, Mr. Gore said he had telephoned Gov. George W. Bush to offer his congratulations. He promised to stand behind Mr. Bush, honoring him, for the first time, with the title of "president-elect."

"Now the United States Supreme Court has spoken," he said. "Let there be no doubt. While I strongly disagree with the court's decision, I accept it. I accept the finality of the outcome, which will be ratified next Monday in the Electoral College. And tonight, for the sake of our unity as a people and the strength of our democracy, I offer my concession."

The speech was an emotional and political crest for Mr. Gore, 52, who had such qualms about giving up his race for the White House, a lifelong goal, that aides said he was on the telephone with them at least until 1:30 this morning, asking about possible legal avenues that the Supreme Court's decision might have left open. He told his advisers that he wanted to sleep on it before making a final decision.

Many politicians said Mr. Gore's address was as important as the one by Governor Bush that followed. By submerging any bitter feelings and sounding a conciliatory tone, they said, Mr. Gore could help reduce the festering tensions between Republicans and Democrats who cling to the belief that their candidate should rightfully claim the White House.

Mr. Gore declared that he would "honor the new president-elect and do everything possible to help him bring Americans together."

For all his outreach to Mr. Bush, Mr. Gore dropped several not-so-veiled hints that this might not be his last try. Making clear that he is not about to fade away — or stop fighting — Mr. Gore said, "I do have one regret, that I didn't get the chance to stay and fight for the American people over the next four years, especially for those who feel their voices have not been heard. I heard you and I will not forget."

He added: "I've seen America in

Continued on Page A26

Stephen Crowley/The New York Times

"I know America wants reconciliation and unity," said George W. Bush. "I know Americans want progress."

The 43rd President

George Walker Bush

By ALISON MITCHELL

AUSTIN, Tex., Dec. 13 — Gov. George W. Bush cast his quest for the presidency as a stand against poisonous Washington — its gridlock, its scandals, its bruising partisanship — and in the very last week of his campaign he was barnstorming under bright banners that promised, "Bringing America Together."

Man in the News

But as Mr. Bush was finally able to claim a belated and minuscule victory over Vice President Al Gore, after a debilitating month of bare-knuckled court fighting, it was as if he had somehow crossed through the looking glass.

In the contested aftermath of Election Day, the man who presented himself as a Texas outsider turned to the ultimate Washington insiders to secure his victory. James A. Baker III, Dick Cheney and Andrew H. Card, all from Mr. Bush's father's administration, became the faces of the Bush presidency in waiting, and Theodore B. Olson, the capital's reigning conservative litigator, argued the case at the Supreme Court.

Far from calming the flames of partisanship, Mr. Bush's struggle for victory against Mr. Gore fanned them to an intensity not seen since President Clinton's impeachment. And suddenly Mr. Bush seemed lassoed to the Congressional leaders whom he had once kept so carefully at a distance, as they thundered on his behalf against the "unelected judges" of Florida who were rendering verdicts about the vote.

Now George Walker Bush, 54, comes into office as only the fourth man in history — and the first in more than a century — to assume the presidency without winning the popular vote. Like the only other son of a president to win the office himself, John Quincy Adams in 1824 (who had fewer popular votes than Andrew Jackson), Mr. Bush lost the popular vote in a disputed election to a Tennessean. Indeed, Mr. Bush won office with 271 electoral votes, just one more than the minimum.

Mr. Bush is not facing personal scandal, as President Clinton did. But his situation may be just as searing politically, for Mr. Bush ultimately won through a bruising legal battle over the 25 electoral votes in a state run by his brother, Gov. Jeb Bush of Florida. It was a fight that was finally decided by nine Supreme Court justices, who split bitterly over the issue.

With his speech tonight from the Texas House of Representatives, Mr. Bush began trying to pull the nation together after this grueling ordeal, choosing the House because it is a chamber where the Democrats have a majority. He quoted the words of Thomas Jefferson who won the presidency in 1800 only after 36 ballots in the House of Representatives.

And he said that the rancor and strange circumstances of his election could lead to healing and help him bring the warring Congressional leaders together.

"I am optimistic that we can change the tone in Washington, D.C.," Mr. Bush said. "I believe things happen for a reason, and I hope the long wait of the last five weeks will heighten a desire to move beyond the bitterness and partisanship of the past."

Republicans say Mr. Bush's quick instincts about people and his years of reaching across the aisle in Texas

Continued on Page A25

Theme of Reconciliation After Five-Week Wait

By DAVID E. SANGER

AUSTIN, Tex., Dec. 13 — George W. Bush spoke to the nation for the first time as president-elect tonight, declaring that the "nation must rise above a house divided" after one of the closest and most disputed presidential elections in United States history.

Speaking from the podium of the Texas House of Representatives, precisely 24 hours after the United State Supreme Court ended a five-week-long dispute by halting a recount of Florida's disputed votes, and thus preserving Mr. Bush's razor-thin lead, the 54-year-old governor devoted his entire speech to themes of reconciliation.

"I was not elected to serve one party, but to serve one nation," Mr. Bush said.

"Whether you voted for me or not, I will do my best to serve your interests," he said, "and I will work to earn your respect."

A little more than an hour before, Vice President Al Gore called Mr. Bush to say he was withdrawing from the 17-month-long presidential race, and congratulated the Texas governor, who was first elected to office here only six years ago, on being elected the 43rd president of the United States.

Minutes later, in his own speech from his ceremonial office next door to the White House, Mr. Gore said that while he disagreed with the court's ruling "I offer my concession."

Mr. Bush appeared by turns relaxed and slightly nervous, licking his upper lip as he looked around the large chamber, dominated by a huge Christmas tree and filled with his supporters and staff. "I have a lot to be thankful for," he said in a speech that emphasized only common ground between Democrats and Republicans, and made only glancing references to the disputes that punctuated the campaign and its often bitter aftermath. "I am thankful for America, and thankful that we are able to resolve our electoral differences in a peaceful way."

The choice of locale for his speech underscored the theme: The Texas House is under Democratic control. Mr. Bush used the moment to reiterate some of his campaign themes, talking of making "all our public schools excellent," strengthening Medicare and creating a prescription drug benefit for "all of our seniors." He talked of a "broad, fair and fiscally responsible tax relief" a phrase so vague that it could embrace many varieties of tax cuts — and like Mr. Gore an hour before him, talked of "common ground."

"During the fall campaign, we differed about details of these proposals but there was remarkable consensus about the important issues before us." He spoke of serving "every race and every background," aware that minorities voted overwhelmingly against him in last month's election.

It was not the kind of speech Mr. Bush would have delivered had he won the large victory his aides were predicting on election night. He offered nothing to the conservative

Continued on Page A24

Another Kind Of Bitter Split

When Jurisprudence Is Pulled Into Politics

By LINDA GREENHOUSE

WASHINGTON, Dec. 13 — The Supreme Court justices who drove off into the night on Tuesday left behind more than a split decision that ended a disputed presidential election.

News Analysis

They also left behind an institution that many students of the court said appeared diminished, if not actually tarnished, by its extraordinary foray into presidential politics.

They point to the contradiction between the majority's action in this case and those justices' usual insistence on deference to the states.

The members of the majority appeared at pains to refute any suggestion that the court had intervened unduly by stopping the Florida recount on Saturday or by ruling Tuesday that it could not resume. It was "our unsought responsibility to resolve the federal and constitutional issues" in the case, the majority said in its unsigned opinion.

And Justice Clarence Thomas, a member of the 5-to-4 majority, told a group of high school students at the court today that "I have yet to hear any discussion, in nine years, of partisan politics" among the justices.

"I plead with you that, whatever you do, don't try to apply the rules of the political world to this institution; they do not apply," Justice Thomas said, adding, "The last political act we engage in is confirmation."

Be that as it may, the events of the last few days were jarring even for people who pride themselves on being realists rather than romantics about how the court works.

One federal judge, a Republican appointee who was a Supreme Court law clerk decades ago, said today that he had long since become accustomed to watching the justices

Continued on Page A32

Now, Lifting the Clouds

By R. W. APPLE Jr.

WASHINGTON, Dec. 13 — The victor and the vanquished turned this evening to the arduous task of mending a body politic riven by the painful presidential election of 2000.

News Analysis

As the two nominees — first Vice President Al Gore and then Gov. George W. Bush of Texas, now the president-elect — appeared on television to appeal to the nation for a measure of unity, they spoke in the context of a Supreme Court decision that had sown the seeds of potential disunity. The court's muddled, if decisive, ruling on Tuesday night gave Mr. Bush his long-sought victory, yet denied him clear, unclouded title to the Oval Office.

Mr. Gore did his best to remedy that by buttressing confidence in the rule of law. Without a trace of rancor, in a speech that seemed both less stiff and more personal than many of his stump speeches, the vice president said, "I accept finality," and pledged to put himself at Mr. Bush's disposal.

"What remains of partisan rancor must now be put aside, and may God bless his stewardship," he said.

The Bush camp could not have hoped for more. And when the president-elect's turn to speak came, he saluted his defeated rival, promising to change the tone of Washington by emphasizing consensus, not confrontation.

"Our nation must rise above a house divided," Mr. Bush declared. "Republicans want the best for our nation, and so do Democrats. We must seize the moment and deliver."

Mr. Bush must live with the knowledge that he won Florida by just 537 votes out of 6 million cast, with a manual recount abandoned, thousands of ballots short of completion, at the order of a court split 5 to 4. Many people noted today that he would take office as the 43rd president by a margin of a single judicial vote, and some people, politicians as well as journalists, vowed to complete the recount on their own.

If such a recount showed Mr. Gore the "winner," it could destabilize the

Continued on Page A28

The 36th Day

The nation's closest presidential race in more than a century is over. Looking back at a five-week battle. Looking ahead to the transition. Articles, addresses, and the text of the ruling that ended it all.

THE 43RD PRESIDENT PAGES A23-36

NEWS SUMMARY A2

Updated news: www.nytimes.com

354613

THE NEW YORK TIMES is available for delivery in most major cities. On the Web: homedelivery.nytimes.com, or telephone, toll-free: 1-800-NYTIMES. ADVT.

CNN

"I say to President-elect Bush that what remains of partisan rancor must now be put aside," Vice President Al Gore said last night in his speech.

INSIDE

Judge Upholds Use of Race In University's Admissions

A federal judge upheld the University of Michigan's use of affirmative action in its admissions, ruling that diversity is a critical component of higher education. PAGE A16

Clinton in Ulster Debate

President Clinton found himself in a debate with a group of hard-line lawmakers who oppose a peace accord that he helped forge. PAGE A10

Plant's Genes Are Mapped

Scientists have determined the complete genetic sequence of a plant, a finding that should provide ways to genetically alter crops. PAGE C4

THE TEXAS GOVERNOR

Bush, Newly Victorious, Pledges to Be the President of 'One Nation,' Not One Party

Continued From Page A1

fered nothing to the conservative wing of his party, and evoked none of the cultural issues that often divide the two parties.

Mr. Bush is expected to travel to Washington next Tuesday, aides said, and meet both President Clinton and Vice President Gore. But his transition is already under way, and with tonight's concession by Mr. Gore, Mr. Bush will now have use of the $5 million transition budget and a large office blocks from the White House. Within days, he is expected to start naming his senior staff and cabinet members, probably starting with Gen. Colin L. Powell as secretary of state.

Though he briefly invoked the words of Abraham Lincoln at the opening of his speech, Mr. Bush referred directly to only one of his predecessors, Thomas Jefferson, who took office in a disputed election in 1800.

"I will be guided by President Jefferson's sense of purpose," he said, "to stand for principle, to be reasonable in manner, and, above all, to do great good for the cause of freedom and harmony."

"The presidency is more than an honor. It is more than an office," he concluded.

"It is a charge to keep." The last phrase was also the title of a book he published at the beginning of the campaign to introduce himself to the American people.

Mr. Bush's speech to the nation tonight was no ordinary victory address. After weeks of legal maneuvering and two rapid-fire decisions by the Supreme Court which effectively ended Mr. Gore's hopes for a recount on Tuesday night, Mr. Bush had much more to accomplish tonight than declaring himself the victor on a typical Election Day.

A man who is at his most uncomfortable with formal addresses in formal settings was called on to give one that he knew would set the tone of his first term. It was a night for perfect pitch and appropriate symbolism, "chiefly the olive branch," one aide said.

Stephen Crowley/The New York Times

President-elect George W. Bush was joined last night by his wife, Laura, and Speaker Pete Laney of the Texas House for his victory speech.

His words were simple, his rhetoric not as lofty as the speech Mr. Gore gave an hour before. In discussions leading up to the drafting of the speech, aides said he had to be humble, while making it clear that other nations and his political opponents at home should not question his command of the office. It is unclear whether he accomplished that goal; his only reference to America's role in the world was a call for bipartisan foreign policy and "a military equal to every challenge, and superior to every adversary."

He had to appeal to those who, despite a nearly year-and-a-half-long campaign and a five-week recount, still question whether he comes to the job adequately prepared, or risks becoming captive to a talented set of advisers.

The Bush camp is acutely aware that the Republican majority in the House of Representatives is so small as to be virtually useless. That creates a far larger challenge than Mr. Clinton had in 1993, when he enjoyed a substantial Democratic majority — before losing it, for the rest of his presidency, in the 1994 midterm elections. Moreover, the Senate is now divided 50-50, though the vice president elect, Dick Cheney, will cast the deciding vote if there is a tie.

So it was no surprise that Mr. Bush chose his setting with bipartisan care: he was introduced by the Democratic speaker of the Texas House, Pete Laney, who praised Mr. Bush effusively as a leader and a partner. Though the Legislature is not in session, many of its members attended.

But even such a show of bipartisan comity could not overcome some of the bitterness of today's events. The Rev. Jesse Jackson, angry at the Supreme Court's decision, declared that while Mr. Bush would legally serve as president, he had no "moral authority." Perhaps that is why Mr. Bush chose to paraphrase Lincoln.

"There were also questions about Lincoln's legitimacy," David Donald, a Lincoln biographer, noted recently. "Those dissipated, and I hope these questions will dissipate too."

Nonetheless, Mr. Bush is the first president to take office in an election that was for all practical purposes settled by Supreme Court. And not since 1888, when Benjamin Harrison won the presidential election, has anyone assumed the presidency after losing the popular vote but winning the electoral vote.

Mr. Bush also shares that dubious electoral distinction with two others: Rutherford B. Hayes in 1876 and John Quincy Adams in 1824. Mr. Adams was also the only other son of a president to win the presidency.

Under very different circumstances, other presidents have faced tasks similar to Mr. Bush's tonight. Another politician who learned his political skills in the chamber where Mr. Bush spoke tonight, Lyndon B. Johnson, faced a similar challenge of unifying the nation after he was thrust into the presidency by the assassination of his predecessor, John F. Kennedy. But the tragic circumstances of his ascendancy created a well of sympathy that Mr. Bush does not enjoy.

Gerald R. Ford had a more analogous job of reunifying the nation after a bitter and partisan division, and hours after President Richard M. Nixon resigned he declared that "our long national nightmare is over."

"Both Johnson and Ford were far more successful in sending out unifying messages than anyone thought at the time they could be," said Michael Beschloss, a historian who has focused on Mr. Johnson's term.

But both men, he noted, were thrown into the Oval Office by fate; Mr. Bush must overcome suspicions among many of his political opponents that he took office by obstructing a reliable recount of the Florida vote. And both Mr. Johnson and Mr. Ford were creatures of Congress and understood how it operated; Mr. Bush, like Mr. Clinton before him, must learn that territory on the job.

Tonight Mr. Bush also had to take firm command of a national agenda, when many suggest that the manner of his election may impose limitations on his powers. He did not refer to that problem, though Mr. Gore, in his speech, addressed the question head-on. He said that while many believed Mr. Bush would be hampered, "I do not believe it need be so." In some ways, Mr. Gore's speech was a more passionate call for the nation to rally around the new president than Mr. Bush's was.

Many of Mr. Bush's advisers say that in the next few months, he must focus on common ground with his Democratic opponents, and win bipartisan passage of some major piece of legislation to show that he is willing to come to the middle. But there is still debate within the Bush camp about what that piece of legislation should be.

He also faces an array of immediate challenges, at home and abroad, that will not wait for Senate confirmations or the selection of roughly 800 senior White House staff.

The economy is clearly slowing, and while Mr. Cheney has warned of an impending recession born in the Clinton administration, it will be up to a Bush administration to keep it from happening. Privately some of his advisers worry that Mr. Bush's economic bench is not as deep as his national security bench.

His chief economic adviser, Lawrence B. Lindsey, is a respected former member of the Federal Reserve Board, but the search for a treasury secretary has focused on Wall Street.

Whoever gets the job will have to help decide whether to pursue the kind of deep tax cuts that Mr. Bush talked about as a candidate. Many Republicans believe that Mr. Bush's plans will have to be dramatically scaled back given the composition of Congress, though most believe some reductions in estate taxes and the elimination of the marriage penalty could prove low-hanging fruit for Mr. Bush's first few months in office.

A man who has traveled abroad only three times, with the exception of many trips to Mexico, must now handle an increasingly assertive Russia, a Middle East in crisis, and enormous division in his own party about how to deal with China.

He also faces increasing suspicion of America's economic, military and cultural power, and the resentments it has engendered. None of these issues were discussed tonight, but they cannot be avoided in coming days.

"That will be a key test for him," said Joseph S. Nye, the dean of the John F. Kennedy School of Government at Harvard and an official in the C.I.A. and the Defense Department in Mr. Clinton's first term. "He has said he will not tolerate isolationism. What isn't clear is what his position is on unilateralism."

THE LEGAL ISSUES

Concession on 'Deadline' Helped Seal Gore's Defeat

By WILLIAM GLABERSON

Back on Nov. 20, during what would be the first of a series of historic oral arguments, the chief justice of the Florida Supreme Court turned to David Boies, the chief lawyer for Vice President Al Gore, and asked a question.

In that exchange, Mr. Boies made a pivotal concession that, in retrospect, helped bring the vice president's defeat in the legal war for White House.

The chief justice, Charles T. Wells, mentioned the date Dec. 12. He wondered whether battles over the Florida vote "have to be finally determined by that date," and asked, "Do you agree with that?"

Mr. Boies looked up. "I do your honor," he said.

That concession began a chain of legal events that ended with the conclusion by a majority of the justices of the United States Supreme Court on Tuesday — Dec. 12 — that time had simply run out. Florida recounts could not go on after that date, the justices said, even if they could be conducted constitutionally.

Yesterday, legal experts of differ-

A chain of events may have turned a nondeadline into the end of the line.

ing political persuasions said the skirmish over what came to be called "the deadline" proved decisive. But some of them said that under federal law, at least, it was not a deadline, but merely advice by Congress to states about how to assure that their voters' choice for president would be honored.

"It is a promise by Congress that if you do three things a state's electors will be conclusive in Congress" should some other slate claim to be the real one, said John C. Yoo, a conservative constitutional law professor at the University of California at Berkeley.

To win what has been called the Dec. 12 "safe harbor," states must name electors; must do so under rules enacted before Election Day, and must resolve any contests over who the electors are by six days before the meeting of the Electoral College, which is to meet on Dec. 18.

The United States Supreme Court's majority opinion on Tuesday did not say Dec. 12 was a federal deadline. Instead, the majority said that was what Florida law provided.

There is no provision of Florida law specifying a Dec. 12 deadline. But the majority of the justices in Washington said the Florida Supreme Court had held that the State Legislature meant to gain the "safe harbor" protection for Florida's electors.

The four justices in the minority suggested that Florida law provided no such thing. And yesterday, legal experts said that central conclusion of the majority was a debatable legal point.

"The problem with that is it is not clear that's what the Florida Supreme Court would say the law of Florida is," said Philip P. Frickey, a constitutional law expert at the University of California at Berkeley.

For the Florida Supreme Court to reach that conclusion in the presidential battle, Professor Frickey said, it would have to decide that Florida law said it was more important to obtain the "safe harbor" protection than it was to complete a recount to see which candidate had won.

But some experts said it was reasonable for the justices to conclude the Florida Supreme Court had decided the Legislature meant to get all election contests completed in time to assure that Florida's electoral votes would be counted.

"The way they read the Florida Supreme Court decisions is not inevitable, but it is quite justifiable," said Daniel H. Lowenstein, an election law expert at the University of California at Los Angeles.

The evidence for that view of Florida law can be traced back to Mr. Boies's concession about the "deadline" back on Nov. 20.

For a while after that argument, the idea of a Dec. 12 deadline slipped from notice. That may have been because Chief Justice Wells, apparently its primary proponent on the Florida court, agreed to go along with a unanimous ruling that ordered recounts in three heavily Democratic counties be included in Florida's tally.

But by Dec. 8, when the Florida court made its next major decision, the court had been bruised by a reversal from the justices in Washington. The justices in Washington had taken notice of the "safe harbor" law and seemed to, in their words, "counsel against" taking any action that would result in Florida losing any benefit the Legislature might have intended from an early completion of election contests.

On Dec. 8, the Florida justices split bitterly, with Chief Justice Wells filing his own angry dissent. By then,

Pool photograph by Chris O'Meara

David Boies, the chief Gore lawyer, at the pivotal Nov. 20 session of the Florida Supreme Court.

the dissenting Florida justices suggested they were concerned about the "safe harbor" issue.

But Mr. Boies's agreement that there was a deadline meant even the justices who did not think there was a true deadline were undercut by one of the chief adversaries in the case.

In the Dec. 8 ruling, the four-justice majority fended off the issue. The majority opinion said the four were "cognizant" of it. In a footnote, they said they were doing their best in light of the "looming deadlines."

It is apparently those references that convinced the majority in Washington this week that "the Supreme Court of Florida has said that the Legislature intended" to establish a Dec. 12 deadline.

But after Mr. Boies's exchange with Chief Justice Wells on Nov. 20, the Florida Supreme Court seemed, simply, confused about the deadline issue, said L. Kinvin Wroth, dean of Vermont Law School, who wrote a law review article about the "safe harbor" law's operation in the 1960 presidential election.

The footnote reference to the "looming deadline" may have reflected that confusion. If so, Mr. Wroth said, the majority of the Washington justices may have been wrong when they concluded that Florida law required that counting could not continue past Tuesday.

"The presidency," Mr. Wroth said, "is being decided on the basis of a confused situation in which the Florida court, almost inadvertently, spoke as though the Florida Legislature had intended to have any contest proceeding complete by Dec. 12."

The majority of the Washington justices, Mr. Wroth said, "played 'gotcha' with that."

Bush's Remarks on End of the Race

Following is a transcript of President-elect George W. Bush's address last night in Austin, Tex., as recorded by The New York Times:

Thank you very much. Good evening, my fellow Americans. I appreciate so very much the opportunity to speak with you tonight.

Mr. Speaker, Lieutenant Governor, friends, distinguished guests, our country has been through a long and trying period, with the outcome of the presidential election not finalized for longer than any of us could ever imagine. Vice President Gore and I put our hearts and hopes into our campaigns; we both gave it our all. We shared similar emotions.

So I understand how difficult this moment must be for Vice President Gore and his family. He has a distinguished record of service to our country as a congressman, a senator and a vice president.

This evening I received a gracious call from the vice president. We agreed to meet early next week in Washington, and we agreed to do our best to heal our country after this hard-fought contest.

Tonight, I want to thank all the thousands of volunteers and campaign workers who worked so hard on my behalf. I also salute the vice president and his supporters for waging a spirited campaign, and I thank him for a call that I know was difficult to make. Laura and I wish the vice president and Senator Lieberman and their families the very best.

I have a lot to be thankful for tonight. I am thankful for America and thankful that we are able to resolve our electoral differences in a peaceful way. I'm thankful to the American people for the great privilege of being able to serve as your next president. I want to thank my wife and our daughters for their love. Laura's active involvement as first lady has made Texas a better place, and she will be a wonderful first lady of America.

I am proud to have Dick Cheney by my side, and America will be proud to have him as our next vice president.

Tonight, I chose to speak from the chamber of the Texas House of Representatives because it has been a home to bipartisan cooperation. Here, in a place where Democrats have the majority, Republicans and Democrats have worked together to do what is right for the people we represent.

We've had spirited disagreements, and in the end, we found constructive consensus. It is an experience I will always carry with me, an example I will always follow.

I want to thank my friend, House Speaker Pete Laney, a Democrat, who introduced me today. I want to thank the legislators from both political parties with whom I've worked. Across the hall in our Texas Capitol is the State Senate, and I cannot help but think of our mutual friend, the former Democrat lieutenant governor, Bob Bullock. His love for Texas and his ability to work in a bipartisan way continue to be a model for all of us.

The spirit of cooperation I have seen in this hall is what is needed in Washington, D.C. It is the challenge of our moment. After a difficult election, we must put politics behind us and work together to make the promise of America available for every one of our citizens.

I am optimistic that we can change the tone in Washington, D.C. I believe things happen for a reason, and I hope the long wait of the last five weeks will heighten a desire to move beyond the bitterness and partisanship of the recent past.

Our nation must rise above a house divided. Americans share hopes and goals and values far more important than any political disagreements. Republicans want the best for our nation. And so do Democrats. Our votes may differ, but not our hopes.

I know America wants reconciliation and unity. I know Americans want progress. And we must seize this moment and deliver. Together, guided by a spirit of common sense, common courtesy and common goals, we can unite and inspire the American citizens.

Together, we will work to make all our public schools excellent, teaching every student of every background and every accent, so that no child is left behind.

Together, we will save Social Security and renew its promise of a secure retirement for generations to come.

Together, we will strengthen Medicare and offer prescription drug coverage to all of our seniors.

Together, we will give Americans the broad, fair and fiscally responsible tax relief they deserve.

Together, we'll have a bipartisan foreign policy true to our values and true to our friends. And we will have a military equal to every challenge, and superior to every adversary.

Together, we will address some of society's deepest problems, one person at a time, by encouraging and empowering the good hearts and good works of the American people. This is the essence of compassionate conservatism, and it will be a foundation of my administration.

These priorities are not merely Republican concerns or Democratic concerns; they are American responsibilities.

During the fall campaign, we differed about the details of these proposals, but there was remarkable consensus about the important issues before us: excellent schools, retirement and health security, tax relief, a strong military, a more civil society. We have discussed our differences. Now it is time to find common ground and build consensus to make America a beacon of opportunity in the 21st century.

I'm optimistic this can happen. Our future demands it, and our history proves it. Two hundred years ago, in the election of 1800, America faced another close presidential election. A tie in the Electoral College put the outcome into the hands of Congress. After six days of voting, and 36 ballots, the House of Representatives elected Thomas Jefferson the third president of the United States. That election brought the first transfer of power from one party to another in our new democracy. Shortly after the election, Jefferson, in a letter titled "Reconciliation and Reform," wrote this: "The steady character of our countrymen is a rock to which we may safely moor. Unequivocal in principle, reasonable in manner, we shall be able to hope to do a great deal of good to the cause of freedom and harmony."

Two hundred years have only strengthened the steady character of America. And so as we begin the work of healing our nation, tonight I call upon that character: respect for each other, respect for our differences, generosity of spirit and a willingness to work hard and work together to solve any problem.

I have something else to ask you, to ask every American. I ask for you to pray for this great nation. I ask your prayers for leaders from both parties. I thank you for your prayers for me and my family, and I ask you to pray for Vice President Gore and his family.

I have faith that with God's help we as a nation will move forward together, as one nation, indivisible. And together we will create an America that is open, so every citizen has access to the American dream; an America that is educated, so every child has the keys to realize that dream; and an America that is united in our diversity and our shared American values that are larger than race or party.

I was not elected to serve one party, but to serve one nation. The president of the United States is the president of every single American, of every race and every background. Whether you voted for me or not, I will do my best to serve your interests, and I will work to earn your respect.

I will be guided by President Jefferson's sense of purpose, to stand for principle, to be reasonable in manner, and, above all, to do great good for the cause of freedom and harmony.

The presidency is more than an honor. It is more than an office. It is a charge to keep, and I will give it my all.

Thank you very much, and God bless America.